THE
ENCYCLOPEDIA
OF
WORLD
METHODISM

Sponsored by The World Methodist Council
and The Commission on Archives and
History of The United Methodist Church

NOLAN B. HARMON

Bishop of The United Methodist Church, General Editor

ALBEA GODBOLD
LOUISE L. QUEEN

Assistants to the General Editor

VOLUME II

Prepared and edited under the supervision
of The World Methodist Council and The
Commission on Archives and History

Published by
The United Methodist Publishing House

Copyright © 1974 by The United Methodist Publishing House

ISBN 0-687-11784-4

SET UP, PRINTED, AND BOUND BY THE PARTHENON PRESS AT
NASHVILLE, TENNESSEE, UNITED STATES OF AMERICA

HOW TO USE THE ENCYCLOPEDIA

The names of persons, places, and most institutions treated in this volume will be found listed alphabetically through these pages. However, institutions such as local churches, hospitals, chapels, and the like will usually be found under the name of the city or town where they are located. Exceptions are those unusual institutions whose names are perhaps even better known than the cities in which they are located.

Bibliographical references in most cases have been placed below each article, pointing the reader to further information. The more important of these works appear in abbreviated form with the article, but are gathered together in the appendix, where the alphabetical Bibliography should be consulted for fuller publishing data. Where there is no such entry in the general bibliography,

these details are given in the reference at the end of the individual article, except in a few instances where full information was not available.

In addition to the main alphabetical bibliography, we have included in the appendix a subject bibliography listing standard works in many areas of study. In this subject bibliography, as usually in the articles in the main encyclopedia, works are listed only by their short titles.

A feature of presentation in the *Encyclopedia* is the use of capital letters to indicate that the name so treated is to be found elsewhere in the work as a separate item of its own. This obviates the prolific use of *q.v.* ("which see"). Exceptions in such capitalization appear when a name reoccurs in any one item.

ABBREVIATIONS

Ala.—Alabama
AME—African Methodist Episcopal
AMEZ—African Methodist Episcopal Zion
Ariz.—Arizona
Ark.—Arkansas
Aug.—August

B.A.—Bachelor of Arts
B.C.E.—Bachelor of Civil Engineering
B.D.—Bachelor of Divinity
B.Mus.—Bachelor of Music
B.R.E.—Bachelor of Religious Education
B.S.—Bachelor of Science
B.W.I.—British West Indies

Calif.—California
C.B.E.—Commander of (the Order of) the British Empire
CME—Christian Methodist Episcopal
Co.—County
Colo.—Colorado
Conn.—Connecticut

D.C.—District of Columbia
D.D.—Doctor of Divinity
Dec.—December
Del.—Delaware
Dip.Ed.—Diploma in Education
D.R.E.—Doctor of Religious Education
D.S.—District Superintendent

E.—East; Eastern
E.C.—Evangelical Church

Ed.D.—Doctor of Education
E.E.—Electrical Engineer
EUB—Evangelical United Brethren

F.B.A.—Fellow of the British Academy
Feb.—February
Fla.—Florida
FMC—Free Methodist Church

Ga.—Georgia

Ida.—Idaho
Ill.—Illinois
Ind.—Indiana

Jan.—January

Kan.—Kansas
Ky.—Kentucky

La.—Louisiana
L.H.D.—Doctor of Humane Letters
Lit.D.—Doctor of Literature
Litt.D.—Doctor of Letters
LL.D.—Doctor of Laws

M.A.—Master of Arts
Mass.—Massachusetts
MC—The Methodist Church (United Kingdom); see TMC for The Methodist Church (U.S.A.)
M.D.—Doctor of Medicine
Md.—Maryland
ME—Methodist Episcopal
Me.—Maine
MES—Methodist Episcopal, South

M.H.A.—Master of Hospital Administration
Mich.—Michigan
Minn.—Minnesota
Miss.—Mississippi
Miss. Soc.—Missionary Society
M.L.S—Master of Library Science
Mo.—Missouri
Mont.—Montana
MP—Methodist Protestant
M.Th.—Master of Theology
MYF—Methodist Youth Fellowship

N.—North; northern
N.C.—North Carolina
N.D.—North Dakota
N.E.—Northeast
Neb.—Nebraska
Nev.—Nevada
N.H.—New Hampshire
N.J.—New Jersey
N.M.—New Mexico
Nov.—November
N.S.—Nova Scotia
N.S.W.—New South Wales
N.W.—Northwest
N.Y.—New York
N.Y.C.—New York City
N.Z.—New Zealand

Oct.—October
Okla.—Oklahoma
Ont.—Ontario
Ore.—Oregon

p.—page
Pa.—Pennsylvania

P.E.—Presiding Elder
Ph.D.—Doctor of Philosophy
P.I.—Philippine Islands
PMC—Primitive Methodist Church in Great Britain
P.R.—Puerto Rico
Prov.—Provisional

ret.—Retired
R.I.—Rhode Island

S.—South; southern
Sask.—Saskatchewan
S.C.—South Carolina
Scand.—Scandinavia
S.D.—South Dakota
S.E.—Southeast
Sept.—September
S.T.B.—Bachelor of Sacred Theology
S.T.D.—Doctor of Sacred Theology
supt.—Superintendent
S.W.—Southwest
Switz.—Switzerland
S.W.A.—Southwest Africa

Tenn.—Tennessee
Th.B.—Bachelor of Theology
Th.D.—Doctor of Theology
Th.M—Master of Theology
Theo.—Theological
TMC—The Methodist Church (U.S.A.); see MC for The Methodist Church (United Kingdom)

U.—University
U.B.—United Brethren in Christ
U.E.—United Evangelical Church
U.K.—United Kingdom
UMC—United Methodist Church (U.S.A.)
UMC(UK)—United Methodist Church (Great Britain)
UMFC—United Methodist Free Churches (Great Britain)
U.S.A.—United States of America
USSR—Union of Soviet Socialist Republics

Va.—Virginia
Ver.—Vermont
V.I—Virgin Islands

W.—West; western
Wash.—Washington
W.I.—West Indies
Wisc.—Wisconsin
WFMS—Women's Foreign Missionary Society
WHMS—Woman's Home Missionary Society
WMC—Wesleyan Methodist Church (Great Britain)
WMMS—Wesleyan Methodist Missionary Society
WMS—Women's Missionary Society
WSCS—Women's Society of Christian Service
WSWS—Women's Society of World Service
W.Va.—West Virginia
Wyo.—Wyoming

L

LACE, JOHN JAMES (1861-1947), was born in Glen Auldin, Ramsey, Isle of Man, May 17, 1861, son of William and Anna Lace, Wesleyan Methodists. Licensed to preach in 1880, he was educated in the schools of the Isle of Man, graduated from the Conference Course of Study in 1889, having been ordained deacon in 1888, and elder in 1891. He received his A.B. degree from the old Chaddock College in Quincy, Ill., U.S.A., in 1896, later attending NORTHWESTERN UNIVERSITY and GARRETT BIBLICAL INSTITUTE at Evanston, Ill.

He served pastorates in MISSOURI and IOWA until 1902 when, for health reasons, he transferred to the COLORADO CONFERENCE where he served as pastor and district superintendent until 1916, when he was appointed superintendent of the UTAH Mission where he served until 1925. Then, returning to the Colorado Conference, he was again a district superintendent for two terms, and in 1932 took the retired relation, making his home in DENVER, Colo., where he passed away April 12, 1947, survived by his wife and four children. His body rests in the cemetery at Fort Collins, Colorado.

John J. Lace was a cultured and fervent preacher, a wise and successful administrator, and a leader of keen insight and ability.

Journals of the Utah Mission and the Colorado Conference. H. M. Merkel, *Utah.* 1938.   WARREN S. BAINBRIDGE

LACKINGTON, JAMES (1746-1815), was an eccentric bookseller, who was born at Wellington, Somersetshire, and became a Methodist about 1760. Self-educated but penniless, he was befriended by the London Methodists, and was given £5 from a benevolent fund to set himself up in business. His business prospered and became the largest of its kind in London. With prosperity he turned from the Christian faith altogether, and wrote books which were regarded as being of a light nature, in which he poured scorn on Methodism. He returned to the faith some years later and, in 1804, renounced his infidel views in his *Confessions.* In reparation for his infidelity he built chapels at Taunton and Budleigh Salterton. He had an erratic and unpleasing personality.

Confessions of J. Lackington. London, 1804.
J. G. Hayman, *Methodism in North Devon.* London, 1871.
Memoirs of the First Forty-Five Years . . . of James Lackington. London, 1791.   THOMAS SHAW

LACY, GEORGE CARLETON (1888-1951), bishop of the Methodist Church, was born in Foochow, Fukien, China, on Dec. 28, 1888, and was educated in Foochow and Shanghai mission schools. His father, WILLIAM H. LACY, directed the Foochow Mission Press and, after 1903, the Methodist Publishing House in Shanghai. His grandmother, Mary Clarke Nind, helped to organize the WOMAN'S FOREIGN MISSIONARY SOCIETY (MEC) in the

GEORGE C. LACY

North Central states, and in the 1890's embarked on an unprecedented world tour of Methodist mission stations.

Carleton Lacy was graduated from OHIO WESLEYAN UNIVERSITY in 1911 and entered GARRETT BIBLICAL INSTITUTE, to receive his bachelor of divinity degree in 1913, and master of arts from NORTHWESTERN UNIVERSITY the following year. During student days he filled pastorates in Detroit, Mich., U.S.A., in Bloomington, Ill., U.S.A., and Somers, Wisc., U.S.A. He was received on trial in the WISCONSIN Annual CONFERENCE in September 1912, was transferred two years later to North China Annual Conference, then in rapid succession to Foochow and Kiangsi Conferences.

After studying at Nanking Language School, he served as an itinerant missionary and district superintendent in Kiangsi Province, later as principal of William Nast Academy in Kiukiang.

In 1918, he married Harriet Lang Boutelle, who had gone to Canton, China, as a Y.W.C.A. secretary. They had two children, Creighton Boutelle and Eleanor Maie. From 1921 until 1941, Lacy was lent by the Methodist Board of Missions to the AMERICAN BIBLE SOCIETY, as secretary of its China agency, and then to the China Bible House formed with the BRITISH AND FOREIGN BIBLE SOCIETY. For many years he wrote as China correspondent for *Zion's Herald, The Christian Century* and other church periodicals. In 1928-29 he studied at Union Theological Seminary and Columbia University, receiving a second master's degree. He was also awarded honorary doctorates of divinity by Ohio Wesleyan and Garrett. He was a delegate to the GENERAL CONFERENCE of 1932.

He was appointed in 1935 as a member of the Joint

Commission on Unity of the M. E. Church and the M. E. Church, South, in China. He was elected bishop by the China Central Conference of 1941 and assigned to the Foochow Area.

During the Second World War, when part of his Episcopal Area was occupied by Japanese troups, Bishop Lacy travelled extensively through remote regions, several times from West China to INDIA and thence to America and back. During the earlier years of Japanese occupation he wrote two monographs on *The Great Migration and the Church in West China* and *The Great Migration and the Church Behind the Lines.* He also published in Chinese a series of Bible studies, *The Book of Revelation* and the *Messages of the Old Testament Prophets.*

Under "term episcopacy" in China, Bishop Lacy's tenure was to end in 1949, but the advent of Communist Government made it impossible to hold a Central Conference with new elections. With tightening pressures on the Church and on American personnel after the Korean War began, he officially resigned and turned his authority over to Bishop W. Y. CHEN. Communist police, however, refused to grant an exit permit when other missionaries left, and kept him under increasing surveillance, restriction, and eventual house arrest until his death of a heart attack in December 1951. His body was buried in the city of his birth, in the little mission cemetery beside his parents, attended—and this was at Communist orders—only by his faithful cook.

W. N. Lacy, *China.* 1948.
F. D. Leete, *Methodist Bishops.* 1948.
Who's Who in America, 1950-51.   CREIGHTON B. LACY

LACY, HENRY ANKENNY (1917-   ), is Executive Secretary for India and Nepal, Board of Missions of The United Methodist Church. He was born in Foochow, CHINA, where his parents, grandparents and great-grandmother, and a number of uncles and aunts were Methodist missionaries. He was graduated from Whittier College in 1940 and married his classmate, Elizabeth Day Pickett. After training in social work at George Williams College in Chicago, Ill., U.S.A., he went to INDIA in 1941, arriving just before the Japanese attack on Honolulu. He served as manager of the Parker High School and the Nathaniel Jordan Hostel in Moradabad. His first term was interrupted by a call to serve in the Office of Strategic Services in CHINA, and he spent a year there.

Returning to America eager to take more additional training than a furlough would allow, he accepted an appointment with the Methodist Children's Home Society of Detroit and studied at Wayne University, earning his Master's Degree in social work. When he went back to India, he was appointed principal of the Ingraham Institute, Ghaziabad.

In 1961, the Division of World Missions asked him to become the first lay missionary chosen to serve as one of its executive secretaries. His field was India, NEPAL, and PAKISTAN. When the board was reorganized in 1964, and unified administration of the work of the Woman's Division and the World Division was accomplished, he and CHANDA CHRISTDAS of India were appointed executive secretaries for India and Nepal with coordinate responsibility.

He represented the laymen of the Delhi Annual Conference in the GENERAL CONFERENCE of 1956.

J. WASKOM PICKETT

LACY, WILLIAM H. (1858-1925), an American missionary who spent thirty-seven years as such in Foochow and Shanghai, CHINA, most of that period in the publishing of Christian literature in various Chinese dialects. He was born in Milwaukee, Wisc., on Jan. 8, 1858, graduated from NORTHWESTERN UNIVERSITY in 1881; and later received the A.M. and D.D. degrees from that University, and the B.D. from GARRETT. He joined the WISCONSIN CONFERENCE in 1882, and the following year married Emma Nind. In 1887 they sailed for China as missionaries. He was manager of the Methodist Press in Foochow until 1903, when he moved to Shanghai and together with YOUNG J. ALLEN organized the Methodist Publishing House, probably the first official collaboration of the two branches of the Methodist Church which had been separated since 1844. For a period he was secretary of the All-China Finance Committee.

Lacy's wife, affectionately known as "Mother Lacy," died in Kuling a month before her husband's death in Shanghai, Sept. 3, 1925. All five of the Lacy children became missionaries: Walter (author of *A Hundred Years of China Methodism*) in Foochow, 1908-27; Henry, in Foochow and Singapore, 1912-52; CARLETON; Irving for one term in Yenping; and Alice, 1917-21, in Foochow, where she died. And a grandson, HENRY, JR. is a Mission Board executive secretary for India and Nepal.

FRANCIS P. JONES
W. W. REID

LADE, FRANK M. A. (1868-1948), Australian minister and educator, was the foundation principal of Wesley Theological College in the South Australian Conference. After training at Queen's College, MELBOURNE, and eighteen years circuit experience in the Victoria and Tasmania Conference he was transferred to South Australia in 1911. He was a circuit minister for eleven years, then in charge of the Brighton College for training ministers from 1922 until its reconstitution and relocation in 1927 as Wesley College. He was Principal of this institution until his retirement in 1937.

Lade became a well-known public figure through his relentless opposition to the gambling and liquor interests. For two years he led a campaign on behalf of the Prohibition League and for a time edited the temperance paper, *The Patriot.*

He was widely recognized as an expository preacher of exceptional quality and a much-respected teacher by successive generations of theological students. Lade was twice President of the South Australian Conference (1916 and 1936), and was Secretary-General from 1920-1929 and President-General of the Methodist Church of Australasia from 1929-1932.

AUSTRALIAN EDITORIAL COMMITTEE

LADIES' AID SOCIETIES. Activities and organizations which might have been called Ladies' Aid Societies existed from the beginning in American Methodist local churches. In JOHN STREET CHURCH (built in 1768), New York City, "the women provided a house for the preacher and furnished it."

However, the women's organizations which furnished PARSONAGES and promoted social activities were slow to gain official recognition. Ladies' Aid Societies are not mentioned in the *Discipline* of the M. E. Church until 1904. The M. E. Church, South and the Methodist Protestant Church never officially recognized the Ladies' Aid Society as such, though in 1890 the former provided for a "Woman's Parsonage and Home Mission Society," the purpose of which was to "procure homes for itinerant preachers and otherwise aid the cause of Christ." Four years later the name was changed to "Woman's Home Mission Society" while its purpose remained the same. In 1910 the Southern Church voted that its General Board of Missions should include a Woman's Missionary Council with Home and Foreign Departments. But regardless of the nomenclature used, there were in effect Ladies' Aid Societies in the Methodist denominations.

In 1911 the Methodist Book Concern published *The Ladies' Aid Manual* which gave pointed suggestions on how to organize and conduct a Ladies' Aid Society. Opposing questionable means of raising money, the book suggested plans and activities which it said would "contribute to the social, intellectual, and financial development of the church without incurring any just criticism."

Pastors and others believed that the Ladies' Aid Society and similar organizations were helpful to the churches. DAN B. BRUMMITT, editor of one of the editions of the M. E. Church *Christian Advocate*, praised the Ladies' Aid Society as "an organization that never suspends, dies, nor takes a leave of absence. It is many things in one: a pastoral reinforcement, a financial treasure chest, a woman's exchange, a recreation center, a cookery school, a needlework guild, a relief society, a school of salesmanship, a clearing house for domestic and church problems, a prayer meeting—each in turn plays many parts."

In 1939 The Methodist Church effectively combined the work of the women in the WOMAN'S SOCIETY OF CHRISTIAN SERVICE. Since that time there has been no real dichotomy in the work of the women in Methodism, though a few small churches may maintain Ladies' Aid Societies in name or in fact while some women's circles in larger churches may emphasize local church and social activities more than the total program of the Women's Society of Christian Service.

Discipline, ME, MES, and MP.
R. E. Smith, *The Ladies' Aid Manual.* New York: Methodist Book Concern, 1911.

JESSE A. EARL
ALBEA GODBOLD

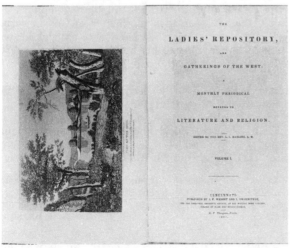

LADIES REPOSITORY

LADIES REPOSITORY, THE. A journal established by the GENERAL CONFERENCE of the M. E. Church in 1841,

designed especially for women. The OHIO CONFERENCE in 1840 memorialized the General Conference to establish such a publication, and that Conference directed the BOOK AGENTS at CINCINNATI to issue such as soon as proper arrangements could be made. In January 1841, the first number of *The Ladies Repository* came from the press as a monthly magazine under the editorial care of L. L. Hamline (later bishop), who had been elected assistant editor of *The Western Christian Advocate*. What were described as "sprightly and classical editorials" gave character to the publication, and its circulation rapidly increased. On the election of Hamline to the bishopric in 1844, he was succeeded by EDWARD THOMSON, who had been principal of Norwalk Seminary, and under whose editorship the *Repository* continued to prosper. Thomson, however, became president of OHIO WESLEYAN UNIVERSITY in 1848, to be succeeded as editor by Benjamin F. Tefft, then professor of the Greek Language and Literature in the Indiana Asbury University. Under his care, the *Repository* obtained a still wider circulation. When Tefft in turn accepted the position of president of the Genesee College, then at Lima, N. Y., WILLIAM C. LARRABEE, who had been in the chair of Mathematics in the Indiana Asbury University, was elected his successor. Succeeding him, when he became state Superintendent of Education in Indiana, the Book Committee of the M. E. Church elected DAVIS W. CLARK in his place, who was re-elected editor by the General Conferences of 1856 and 1860. Clark, however, was also elected bishop in 1864 and was succeeded by ISAAC W. WILEY, who served two quadrennia but likewise was elected bishop in 1868. Erastus Wentworth became editor then in 1872. Four years later the General Conference of 1876 elected DANIEL CURRY as editor and authorized the appointment of a committee who should have power to change the name and style of publication of the journal. The committee on consultation resolved that the title should be changed to that of *National Repository*, and under that name it continued to be issued after January 1877. The *National Repository* was a monthly magazine devoted to general and religious literature. In time it changed its scope from the pattern which had been followed by the old *Ladies Repository* to a more general type of issue. The journal was illustrated and adapted to the wants of the general reader. Daniel Curry continued to be editor for some time until the General Conference of 1880 discontinued the publication of the magazine.

M. Simpson, *Cyclopaedia*. 1881.

N. B. H.

LAFAYETTE, INDIANA, U.S.A. **Trinity Church** began about 1824 in what was then a small log cabin settlement known as Star City on the banks of the Wabash River. An itinerant Methodist preacher named Hackalieh Vreedenburg came to the settlement, and John Huntsinger, whose cabin was then in what is "downtown Lafayette," welcomed the preacher, told him several Methodists lived in the settlement, called them together and that night a Methodist service—the first church service of any kind held in Lafayette—was held in the John Huntsinger home. Hackalieh Vreedenburg is recorded in 1825 as being the preacher of a circuit in which Lafayette was one appointment on the Crawfordsville work. Services continued to be held in the Huntsinger home.

After a time Henry Buell, the second pastor to be assigned to the circuit, came to Lafayette, but he was disturbed by firing of guns and yelling outside the courthouse and seems to have left the ministry after that. He was followed by Eli Pearce Farmer who organized the first church in Lafayette at the courthouse there, and in 1828 Stephen R. Boggs was sent from the ILLINOIS CONFERENCE to the Crawfordsville Circuit. The next year came James Armstrong who held the first Methodist Quarterly Conference in the town in the Eli Huntsinger wheelwright shop.

The first house of worship in the city was erected by Boyd Phelps in 1831. It was a 30 x 40 foot frame structure located on Sixth Street on the second lot south of Main Street facing the east. The building cost $1,500. In 1836, the lot on the northwest corner of Fifth and Perry Streets was purchased for $400 and the building moved there. This building was dedicated in 1845 and was rented weekdays as a schoolhouse at $5 per month. Thus early, the Methodist Church was linked with educational possibilities and forces of the day.

In 1850 the congregation was divided in order to start a new congregation at Ninth and Brown Streets. The cemetery for the church was where St. Boniface Church now stands. It is believed that the body of John Huntsinger still rests beneath St. Boniface.

In 1868, the lot now occupied by Trinity Methodist Church was purchased by Henry Taylor and John W. Heath at a cost of $7,000, and presented to Trinity Church as a suitable place of worship. The present Trinity Church building was constructed in 1869 on the lot at a cost of $90,000. The building is yet looked after and kept in repair, and was the scene of a centennial celebration in 1969. The old parsonage one day gave way to a new modern education building. This is astir seven days a week with church activity. A new $42,000 parsonage was built in Vinton Woods, one of Lafayette's exclusive residential areas.

Trinity Methodist Church early attained great stature and prestige in the NORTHWEST INDIANA CONFERENCE, indeed throughout the entire state, especially during the unprecedented twenty-nine year pastorate of Thomas Frederick Williams (1919-1948). It has always been a downtown church—a church at the heart of the city.

Trinity is the mother Church of all Methodism in the entire area. Its people believe that the history of its influence for good in countless ways through more than a hundred years can never be adequately told.

M. Simpson, *Cyclopaedia*. 1878.   BERNICE HARNESS EZRA

LAFETRA, ADELAIDE WHITEFIELD, founder of Santiago College, SANTIAGO, Chile, was born and educated in New York State. She was preceptress of MOUNT ALLISON Seminary, Sackville, New Brunswick, when in 1878 WILLIAM TAYLOR invited her to go to Santiago to develop a school. There she met and in 1882 married IRA HAYNES LAFETRA, and they worked together in a school with sections for boys and girls. The school later developed into Santiago College, now an outstanding school for young women. She worked in Chile for twenty-five years.

G. F. Arms, *Missions in South America*. 1921.
W. C. Barclay, *History of Methodist Missions*. 1957.
          EDWIN H. MAYNARD

LAFETRA, IRA HAYNES (1851-1917), missionary to South America, was known as "builder of the Chile Mission." On completion of studies at BOSTON UNIVERSITY SCHOOL OF THEOLOGY he was invited to go to CHILE by WILLIAM TAYLOR (later bishop), arriving at Valparaiso in 1878 and ministering first to seamen in that port city. The next year LaFetra moved to SANTIAGO, where he reorganized the English-language Union Church and founded a school. There he met and married ADELAIDE WHITEFIELD (LAFETRA), and their labors, with those of others, resulted in SANTIAGO COLLEGE, one of the leading educational institutions of Chile. In 1880 he was elected as the first president of the conference of missionaries set up to administer the self-supporting missions that had been established by Taylor on the West Coast of South America. Ill health forced his retirement in 1906.

G. F. Arms. *Missions in South America*. 1921.
W. C. Barclay, *History of Methodist Missions*. 1957.
          EDWIN H. MAYNARD

LAFFERTY, JOHN JAMES (1837-1909), colorful American editor and the fifth editor of what is now the *Virginia Methodist Advocate*, was the only child of George and Elizabeth Lightfoot Lafferty. His father was educated in IRELAND, and later served with an engineer who surveyed a railroad connecting VIRGINIA and NORTH CAROLINA. His mother was of the historic Virginia family of the Lightfoots. When the son was eleven months of age, his father was drowned at a James River ferry during a windstorm.

Young Lafferty made an excellent record at EMORY AND HENRY COLLEGE in Virginia. He was graduated next to the head of his class.

He served as chaplain of a cavalry regiment in the War Between the States. After a year he was stricken with a "severe malady," but recuperated sufficiently to accept the post of major of cavalry offered him by the Confederate States War Department. He served in this capacity until the war was over.

Immediately following the war, pastoral appointments were scarce, so Lafferty took his family to Lexington, Va., and engaged in several business enterprises. These proved quite successful financially.

In 1874 he was offered a connection with the *Richmond Christian Advocate*, predecessor of the *Virginia Methodist Advocate*. The financial plight of the *Advocate* was not encouraging from the standpoint of support. The successful businessman took the matter to God in earnest prayer. The outcome was his decision to cast his lot with the church paper. Due to his business ability, the *Advocate* prospered financially. He served as its editor for twenty-seven years.

Editor Lafferty quickly became known as the best editor in the M. E. Church, South. This deeply spiritual man was "a master of sarcasm" when the occasion demanded it. He was widely known throughout the Southland not only as editor, but as a college and chautauqua lecturer. He died on July 23, 1909.

J. J. Lafferty, *Sketches of Virginia Conference*. 1890-1901.
Minutes of the Virginia Conference, 1909.
Richmond Christian Advocate, May 26, 1932, and various other numbers.   GEORGE S. REAMEY

LA GRANGE, ILLINOIS, U.S.A. **First Church** is one of the larger suburban churches west of CHICAGO. This church had its beginning in 1872 in the home of Isaac P. Poinier, one block from the site of the present church. Later in the same year a "Methodist Society" was organized. Upon completion of a two-story school building on the site of the present church, services were held in the school building. Poinier, whose home was only one block away, served as Sunday school superintendent, organist and janitor. He often carried coal from his own home to heat the building. The first resident pastor was William H. Holmes, who served from 1875 to 1877. The Society grew in zeal and numbers, due largely to the consecrated efforts and diligent work of the LADIES AID SOCIETY.

After a time land was donated for a new church building, stone was purchased and a contractor engaged, but as work was about to begin, the project was discontinued because Poinier and several other influential members moved away. For a time, members of the Methodist Society joined persons of other denominations in services held in the railroad station, with the Rev. Mr. Metcalf, the station agent and a Baptist preacher, in charge.

By 1884, the Methodists had become stronger, and in October 1884, the First M. E. Church of La Grange was organized by Luke Hitchcock, presiding elder of the Chicago District. A pastor was appointed and services were held in the Masonic Hall. The year ended with nine members. Financial expenditures for the year were: $216 for the pastor; $52 for the rent of the hall; and $10 given to missions.

In 1885 and 1886, services were continued in the Masonic Hall and later were held in a skating rink. Additional families were added to the membership of the church. A Board of Trustees was elected and incorporation papers were completed on July 21, 1886. The frame school building which had been used by the church in its beginning was purchased by the trustees at a cost of $2,000. The building was remodeled to make it an acceptable place of worship and was dedicated on Nov. 28, 1886. Electric lights were installed in 1892 at a cost of $75.

Plans for a new church building began to develop in 1890. In May 1893, construction was started and by Nov. 5, 1893, one section of the new building was completed. In 1894 a parsonage was built. Work on the main part of the church building was continued and the sanctuary was dedicated on Jan. 6, 1895. A pipe organ was installed in 1907, and in 1908 the building was enlarged. As the church continued to grow in membership, need was seen for more adequate church school facilities, and a two-story educational building was added and dedicated in 1917.

By 1947, the church had 1,179 resident members. The building which had served the congregation well for fifty-two years was becoming inadequate. So in 1951, a new sanctuary and fellowship hall were completed and in 1962 there had been added a new educational building, chapel and offices, bringing the total value of the church building to $1,250,000.

This church has been served by a succession of twenty-nine ministers. The parish boundaries now encompass an area ten miles long and two miles wide. Within this parish are the villages of La Grange and La Grange Park, having a total population of more than 30,000. With a membership now of 2,100, the First United Methodist Church of La Grange will celebrate its centennial in 1972.

EUGENE E. STAUFFER

LAGRANGE COLLEGE, LaGrange, Georgia, U.S.A., was chartered as LaGrange Female Academy in 1831 and has had the longest history among non-tax-supported institutions of higher education in Georgia. It was purchased by the NORTH GEORGIA CONFERENCE of the M. E. Church, South in 1856, and on Jan. 29, 1857, began operation as a Methodist institution. In 1934 its name was changed to LaGrange College, and in 1953 it became a coeducational college. It offers the B.A. degree. The governing board is made up of thirty-four members nominated by the board and confirmed by the North Georgia Conference.

JOHN O. GROSS

LAHORE (population 1,297,000) is the capital of West PAKISTAN. Pakistan's federal capital is 200 miles to the northwest, near the city of Rawalpindi. Lahore is eighteen miles west of the Indo-Pakistan border. It is headquarters for the West Pakistan Railways and for Punjab University, which includes many colleges and high schools in Lahore, and other colleges and high schools throughout the Punjab. Many factories and business and government offices make Lahore an important business center.

Lucie Harrison Girl's High School was the first Methodist Primary School organized in the beginning of Methodist work in the Punjab. It became a high school in 1953. The school includes all classes, kindergarten through high school. The present principal, Mrs. Priscilla P. Peters is a well qualified and capable Pakistani, with an efficient teaching staff.

United Christian Hospital, an institution in which Methodists cooperate, was organized in 1947 when the throes of partition, including an influx of Moslem refugees from India, and departing Hindu and Sikh fugitives bound for India, created great medical, health and sanitation problems. The various denominations combined, rented an empty Forman College Hostel for a temporary hospital center, and later moved into a fine permanent new hospital set-up in a Lahore outskirt, Gulberg (sometimes spelled Gulbarg), in 1965. The United Christian Hospital has established a fine reputation with its skilled Pakistani and missionary doctors, nurses, supervisors and technicians. Its managing committee represents all major denominations and those provide missionary doctors and nurses, pay their salaries, and finance the budget so as to add to the income from hospital fees, and thus provide adequate salaries for Pakistani members of the staff.

Kinnaird College for Women is an Anglican Institution. Methodists and Presbyterians cooperate by providing missionary members of the staff and supply additional funds to help in providing for expenses of Pakistani staff members and other college expenses. The enrollment is limited to 300 girls. Christian girls who wish to go to college seek admission to Kinnaird. Miss P. Mangat Rai, a competent and well known Pakistani, is principal.

Kinnaird Teacher Training Center trains Christian women to become teachers in primary schools, or in primary and junior high classes in recognized high schools. Candidates for such training must have a government certificate, as high school passed. Many who have completed two years of college work also come here for training.

Forman Christian College is an old institution of far-reaching fame. It is staffed and supported jointly by the Presbyterians and the Methodists. Forman celebrated its centenary anniversary in 1965. The present principal is E. J. Sinclair, a well qualified senior Pakistani staff mem-

CHAPEL, FORMAN CHRISTIAN COLLEGE, LAHORE, PAKISTAN

ber, well trained, with a fine reputation and recognized administrative ability. The enrollment of Forman before Partition was almost one thousand; in late 1947, only 150 students remained. Enrollment however is again near the one thousand mark. The College enjoys an admirable standing and reputation, and many Pakistani leaders in government are graduates of the college.

CLEMENT ROCKEY

LAITY, GENERAL BOARD OF. (See LAY MOVEMENT IN AMERICAN METHODISM.)

LAKE BLUFF, ILLINOIS, U.S.A. **Lake Bluff Children's Home,** founded in 1894 by Methodist deaconesses, is a church-related child care agency under the control of a regularly constituted Board of Trustees. Chartered and licensed by the State of ILLINOIS to serve as an Illinois Corporation, not for profit, it is a member agency of the Child Welfare League of America and the Welfare Council of Metropolitan Chicago. It is affiliated with the ROCK RIVER CONFERENCE of The United Methodist Church, and with the National Association, as well as the BOARD OF HEALTH AND WELFARE MINISTRIES of The United Methodist Church. The home is also approved and endorsed by the Chicago Association of Commerce and Industry, the Subscription Investigating Committee, and by the Community Fund of Chicago.

Care is provided for children whose own homes have been disrupted by illness, death, divorce, and other social and emotional problems; who are within the normal range of physical and mental health; who have Protestant backgrounds; whose residence is within the area served by the Rock River Conference.

Services to children from their infancy for as long a time as care is needed include group living at the Home for boys and girls of grade school age; adoption of infants and older children; care in Group Homes in nearby communities for high school boys and girls; foster Boarding Homes within the area for boys and girls of all ages;

casework services to all children under care and to their families; counseling services to minor unwed mothers; and remedial "school" care for some types of emotionally disturbed children.

ERSKINE M. JEFFORDS

LAKE FARM. The home of JAMES THORNE, the Bible Christian leader. (See BIBLE CHRISTIANS.)

LAKE JUNALUSKA ASSEMBLY, INC., an American Methodist assembly ground, owned and operated by the Southeastern Jurisdiction of The United Methodist Church, is located at Lake Junaluska, N. C., U.S.A., on Highway 19, twenty-six miles west of ASHEVILLE, and three miles north of Waynesville. Its doors were first opened on June 25, 1913. About thirteen years prior to this occasion the idea had been expressed that there was a need of a "Chautauqua type" of Southern Assembly. JAMES ATKINS (later bishop), visited Chautauqua, N. Y., and conversed with Bishop VINCENT, then Sunday School Editor of the M. E. Church. Later Atkins became Sunday School Editor of the M. E. Church, South, and invited members of the Sunday School Board to be his guests in Waynesville for their meeting. There he proposed the idea of a "Southern Assembly."

In 1908 during the Second Laymen's Missionary Conference, the statement was made that "we need a place where ministers and laymen, together with their families, can meet on the common level of Worship, Inspiration, Instruction and Wholesome Recreation." The response was gratifying and a committee was appointed. Headed by Atkins, the committee members, some of whom had visited Waynesville, settled upon Tuscola in Haywood County, N. C., now Junaluska—a location universally described as "beautiful for situation." The Blue Ridge and the Great Smoky Mountains surrounding the lovely Richland Valley, are rich in beauty and majesty. Among the men most responsible for the establishment of this noted religious center, which soon became known as the "Sum-

LAKE JUNALUSKA, NORTH CAROLINA

mer Capital of Southern Methodism," were: JOHN R. PEPPER, John P. Pettijohn, General JULIAN S. CARR, B. M. olds, S. C. Satterthwaite, B. J. Sloan, Hugh Sloan, Riley Burgher, R. B. Schoolfield, L. B. Davenport, A. D. Reyn- M. Ferguson, GEORGE R. STUART, Alden Howell and S. C. Welch.

JAMES CANNON (later bishop), was elected first Super- intendent; W. F. TILLETT became Superintendent of Gen- eral Program and Evangelistic Work. The first permanent officers, with Atkins as Chairman and leader, were elected in 1910. From 1911 to 1913 a dam was built, to form the 250-acre lake; the auditorium was erected, a few streets were opened and thirteen private cottages were built. On June 25, 1913, W. F. QUILLIAN, SR. turned the light switch and a great conference of laymen opened with singing, under the leadership of J. Dale Stentz. The Mis- sionary address was by Robert E. Speer. Four thousand people attended, $152,000 was raised for Missionary work, and seven young people were consecrated for Missionary work in Africa with Bishop WALTER LAMBUTH.

Four years after the opening of the Southern Assembly, the Sunday School Board of the M. E. Church, South held a demonstration Leadership School for the training of volunteer teachers at Junaluska. This was a fore-runner of a new type of Leadership training. In 1922 the Sunday School Board built an Education Building (now known as Shackford Hall), as well as lodges and a cafeteria on the southwest shores of the Lake. The system of Leadership Training Schools conducted by the International Council of Religious Education had its beginning at Lake Juna- luska.

The Board of Missions of the M. E. Church, South in time purchased the "Junaluska Inn" and used it for Mis- sionary training Conferences. Following a disastrous fire, a new Mission Building was erected, later to be known as Lambuth Inn. This popular center is used regularly by the Missionary Groups and the Women's Society of Christian Service. Junaluska is the site for Candler Camp Meeting and the Annual Schools of Evangelism for the Southeastern Jurisdiction. It was at Junaluska that the

Board of Lay Activities of the M. E. Church, South was organized, with GEORGE L. MORELOCK as its first Secretary.

During the late twenties and early thirties the owner- ship of the Assembly was still vested in a Board of Com- missioners. The war, the panic and the depression made its operation very difficult financially, and it was forced into receivership. Under the leadership of the bishops and of W. A. Lambeth, funds were raised and all assets were purchased by the Methodist Church, South. A new Board of Trustees was elected and a new charter and certificate of incorporation were secured. The name was changed from The Southern Assembly to The Lake Juna- luska Methodist Assembly.

Following World War II, EDWIN L. JONES of Charlotte, N. C., was elected President of the Board of Trustees, which was then composed of the bishops and one lay and one clerical member from each annual conference in the Jurisdiction. In 1948 the GENERAL CONFERENCE of The Methodist Church, in session at Boston, Mass., accepted ownership of the Assembly, and then transferred it to the Southeastern Jurisdiction, where it was accepted at the session in Columbia, S. C., the same year.

The Southeastern Jurisdictional Conference elects trus- tees, who in turn set up the administration and super- vise the management of the Assembly's business and op- eration. The properties, formerly owned by the Board of Missions, the Sunday School Board and the Commission- ers, have all been transferred to the Lake Junaluska Assembly, Inc.

In the course of a summer's season, thousands of people come to attend the conferences, workshops, training schools, platform hours, and engage in wholesome recrea- tional activities. The George R. Stuart Auditorium, with a seating capacity of three thousand, has provided the platform for world renowned leaders in religion, govern- ment, education and science. The Memorial Chapel, with its Room of Memory, is the spiritual center of the Assem- bly. Bounded by the mountains, lake and landscape, fami- lies have here established homes; hotels and lodges have been erected, and all the comforts and conveniences of modern civilization have been installed.

The WORLD METHODIST COUNCIL built its headquarters for the American Section at Junaluska. A handsome building of native stone was erected on the site formerly occupied by the Cherokee Hotel. ELMER T. CLARK, Executive Secretary, gave his collection of Wesleyana to the Council, and this notable collection, with supplements, is housed in the museum there. The offices and library of the Association of Methodist Historical Societies (now COMMISSION ON ARCHIVES & HISTORY) are in the building, also. Thousands of visitors annually come to this building, including many scholars and students of Methodist history.

The WESTERN NORTH CAROLINA ANNUAL CONFERENCE and the quadrennial sessions of the Southeastern Jurisdictional Conference usually meet at Junaluska. In 1956 the WORLD METHODIST CONFERENCE was held there.

Speakers of national and international prominence who have appeared on the platform throughout the years include Mrs. Eleanor Roosevelt, Vice President (then) Richard Nixon, commentator Lowell Thomas, United Nations Representative Dr. Frank Graham, World Evangelist Dr. Billy Graham, and Lord Caradon, Representative of The United Kingdom to the United Nations.

Mason Crum, *The Story of Junaluska.* Greensboro, N. C.: Piedmont Press, 1950.
Elmer T. Clark, *Junaluska Jubilee.* Nashville: the Assembly, 1963.
Maud M. Turpin, *The Junaluska Story.* Published by the Greater Junaluska Development Campaign, 1946.

JAMES W. FOWLER, JR.

LAKELAND, FLORIDA, U.S.A. **First Church** is the largest church in the headquarters city of Florida Methodism, where the Episcopal Residence, FLORIDA SOUTHERN COLLEGE, and the conference offices are located. First Church Lakeland is noted for its large church school and for its commitment to missions. It stands high among the denomination's larger churches in the proportion of its total income devoted to benevolences. It is located on an exceptionally beautiful site, with spacious lawns sloping down to Lake Morton. Membership in 1970 was 2,768.

ROBERT CAXTON DOGGETT

LAKESIDE, OHIO, U.S.A., is a religious center and encampment on the shores of Lake Erie. The old-time CAMP MEETING that flourished over a century ago and was a mark of early Methodism is said to have been the genesis of the Lakeside of today.

As early as 1842, camp meetings and "Sunday outings" were being held on the rocky shores of Lake Erie near Port Clinton. Many families were influenced at these meetings and converted under the powerful preaching of the pioneer ministers. Following the suggestion of Richard P. Duvall, a movement began to establish Lakeside as a Christian meeting and vacation center.

A few houses, gingerbread in style, rose on the cleared lots overlooking Lake Erie. But for many years wooden tents were the prevalent structures. In reality simply shanties, these tents were used only for sleeping—with piles of straw covered with quilts serving for beds. Cooking was done outdoors, with the earliest risers responsible for starting the morning coffee.

As more and more people visited Lakeside, the need for a hotel grew. In 1875 the first unit of Hotel Lakeside

was built. With the first regular "season" in 1890, Lakeside began its tradition of combining in its program, religion, education, culture, and recreation.

Almost all of the great Chautauqua lecturers and performers came to Lakeside. In those early summers the throngs arrived at "the Summer City on the Lake" by excursion boats, special trains, private buggies, and eventually cars.

The Lakeside Methodist Church was dedicated in 1900, and a pavilion was built in 1909. Hugh Hoover Auditorium was consecrated in 1929 "to the highest uses of worship and the noblest interests of mankind."

A Lakeside Crusade was launched by Ohio Methodists in 1959. By 1964 over $750,000 had been raised and Lakeside given an entirely new look.

Wesley Lodge, a winterized multipurpose building of natural stone, became the focal point of the Youth Center. The administration building and Auditorium Hotel were modernized and winterized and became the Fountain Inn. With these fine facilities, groups now come to Lakeside throughout the year.

The new pavilion, with spacious sun decks; the Schunk Memorial Carillon Tower and aluminum cross are new landmarks on the Lake Erie Shore. A trailer park offers completely modern facilities for trailers and for camping.

Over the years countless thousands of men, women, children, and youth, have been strengthened in faith and purpose because of the guidance and inspiration they found at Lakeside. This is the Lakeside which truly has its place in history, and which will continue to serve through the years as "the vacation place with a purpose."

LAKEVIEW METHODIST ASSEMBLY, Palestine, Texas, U.S.A. This assembly, owned and operated by the TEXAS CONFERENCE (UMC), is located twelve miles southwest of Palestine on state route 294. The board of trustees, elected by the conference, is composed of ministers and laymen. Established in 1947 on 452 acres of land donated by Anderson County and Palestine, it has since grown to 1,400 acres. There are two lakes and two olympic-sized swimming pools on the grounds. With two cafeterias, twelve brick cabins, and twenty-four air-conditioned camp units, the Assembly can accommodate 1,400 people at one time. Four buildings provide space for offices, assembly rooms, class rooms, a book store, a gift shop, as well as quarters for the Texas Conference Historical Center with its valuable archives. A beautiful stone chapel was given by the J. R. Peace family, East Bernard, Texas. A big tabernacle is used for large assemblies. There are homes on the grounds for the permanent staff of four, as well as housing for a number of summer staff workers. The assembly is open the year round for use by conference and church agencies. Youth assemblies for each of the eleven districts of the conference are held at Lakeview each summer. The assembly registers some 30,000 persons per year for meetings and activities. The property is valued at $2,250,000. The Texas Conference contributes about $100,000 per year for its operation and maintenance.

NACE B. CRAWFORD

LAKEWOOD, COLORADO, U.S.A. **Lakewood Church** is the third largest Methodist church in metropolitan DENVER. The church began in 1881, when a small group of Christian men and women met for worship, first in private homes and then in a school house, in the sparsely settled farming community of Lakewood. To reach the little school house, worshipers had to cross fields and open a wire gate which crossed a road that is now a six-lane highway.

In 1902, Miss Hannah Robb of Lakewood gave one-half acre of ground with the stipulation that a Methodist church be built on it within five years or the property would revert to the owner. Accordingly, in 1904, the men of the church built a one-room frame chapel. Its simple furnishings consisted of pulpit, thirty wooden chairs, an organ and a kitchen range.

The presiding elder's report of September 1904 states, "Last Spring a new church was built in Lakewood and Sunday, August 28th, Brother Wood and I dedicated it free of debt, with enough money to buy a new organ and $97.00 to spare."

The church became known as the Lakewood M. E. Church, and was the only place of worship in the community until 1930. In March 1921, the women organized the "Willing Workers." In those early years, they literally held the church together through their efforts. They helped pay the pastor's salary, assisted a hospital and sponsored a nurse's training there, and met conference demands by holding bazaars and suppers. This was no easy task as food was prepared by kerosene lamplight and water had to be carried from across the street.

During the early years, student ministers from the ILIFF SCHOOL OF THEOLOGY served the church. Then in 1941 H. Preston Childress became the first full-time minister. At that time the membership was 165, but babies and children must have been counted; for on that first Sunday he preached, there were only thirty-five present, four of whom were men. H. P. Childress served the church for eleven years; he saw it through the depression, the growing pains of the war years, and the throes of a building campaign, when the need for a larger church became evident.

The new Lakewood Methodist Church, of early American design, opened its doors for worship March 1950, at 1390 Brentwood Ave. Much of the interior furnishing was done by the men of the church: pews to seat 250, chancel furniture, paneling and kitchen cabinets.

In 1953, church membership jumped to 917, with 596 enrolled in Sunday School. A full-time secretary was hired, and a newspaper, "The Church Visitor," was started. The church again experienced an almost phenomenal growth and construction was started September 1955 on the present sanctuary which seats approximately 500. September 1961 the new educational wing was consecrated to serve the ever increasing enrollment of the Sunday school. A Moller pipe organ was installed in 1964. A church staff of eleven, of whom three are full-time ministers, now serves the membership of over 2,000.

AVERY WHITE GIBBS

LAKEWOOD, OHIO, U.S.A. **Lakewood Church** of 1968 is the third structure erected on its site at the corner of Detroit and Summit Avenues. The first church, a small one-room building, was built in 1876, near the center of the church lot at a cost of $5,005, including the lot. Its membership was twenty. The eighteen charter members mortgaged their homes as security to cover the cost of the first church.

The initial subscription for the second building was made in January 1902. The cornerstone was laid in June 1904. The new Lakewood M. E. Church was dedicated on March 26, 1905; 185 names were then on the rolls. Its cost was $13,000. The new church stood as a monument to the faithful and harmonious effort of the entire membership.

Today the church worships in a third structure, a beautiful stone church of Gothic design. The original part of the present edifice was constructed in 1913, at a cost of $50,000. A week of special dedicatory services was arranged and a bishop from Washington, D. C. came to deliver the sermon for the dedication services on Sunday, Sept. 21, 1913.

1914 saw the opening of the east wing, used then for the Sunday school. 1951 was the year of a ground-breaking ceremony for the new education building which was added to the north of the main part of the church, at a cost of approximately $500,000.

While Methodist heritage is the glass through which is seen not only the various deeds of past years but the history of the church's spiritual nature, there is one tangible, material link to the past—the church bell. During the construction of the first church (in 1876), a member contracted for a bell to be cast and shipped from the Fulton Company of Pittsburgh, Pa. The bell has been used in all three churches and yet summons people to church Sunday morning. Its heartwarming peal is caused by the bell itself swinging and allowing the clapper, hanging inside, to strike against its sides.

1968 started another phase in the life of the church, with the sanctuary refurbished and refurnished. Lakewood United Methodist Church has grown to a present membership of approximately 4,000. It continues to be a church dedicated to the Glory of God.

MRS. WALTER M. LUTSCH

A. J. LAMAR

LAMAR, ANDREW JACKSON (1847-1933), an American minister, long-time secretary of the ALABAMA CONFERENCE (1909-1929), and Publishing Agent of the M. E. Church, South, in its closing years, and a man of great influence in his connection, was born in Walton County,

Ga., on May 29, 1847. He was the son of Andrew Jackson and Mary Athena (Jackson) Lamar. His grandfather was an officer in the Continental Army and a governor of GEORGIA. He was educated at the high school in Athens, Ga., and was a sophomore at the University of Georgia until the Fall of 1863 when he, with his fellow students, went into the Confederate States Army. He served through the war in VIRGINIA in Cabell's battery of Artillery. "I was a powder monkey," he told B. A. WHITMORE, his fellow Publishing Agent, years later. At the end of the war he went to ALABAMA where he had an opportunity to attend again the University of Georgia, where he graduated in law in 1873.

He was converted in 1874 under the preaching of the unique and colorful Simon Peter Richardson, his presiding elder, and joined the Alabama Conference. Thereafter he served Alabama pastorates "from some of the least to some of the highest"—Union Springs; Greenville; Auburn; Mobile; Montgomery; Salina were among them, and he was made the presiding elder of the Mobile and then the Montgomery districts later on in life. He was elected Publishing Agent of the M. E. Church, South, in 1903, and moving to NASHVILLE where the Publishing House was located, served in this position for thirty years.

A small man in size but with keen gray eyes, Lamar brought to his work great sagacity and understanding, both of business and of the church which he served and loved. His Conference elected him to all the GENERAL CONFERENCES of the M. E. Church, South, from 1890 to and including that of 1930. He became a man of marked influence at all sessions of this great body, and exerted enormous influence over his church. Together with B. A. Whitmore, the Publishing Agent, he helped the Publishing House of the Church develop into a great and successful institution as the years went by.

He married Martha Elsworth of Mobile on Jan. 8, 1878; and after her death married Mary U. Urquhart of Selma, Ala., on June 9, 1897. A daughter, Mrs. William M. Teague, survived her parents.

Lamar was a decided opponent of Unification that finally came about in 1939 and spoke accordingly. He continued active in the management of the Publishing House until 1932 when he formally retired. He died in Nashville, Tenn., March 27, 1933, and was buried in Montgomery, Ala. Bishop WARREN A. CANDLER wrote his memoir for the Alabama Conference and said of him, "He was an intimate and beloved friend. I do not recall that I ever heard words fall from his lips that were amiss, or deeds done by his hands that were unworthy."

Journal of the Alabama Conference, MES, 1933.
C. F. Price, *Who's Who in American Methodism*. 1916.
N. B. H.

LAMAR, LUCIUS QUINTUS CINCINNATUS (1825-1893), American senator, Supreme Court Justice, and strong Methodist layman, was born in Eatonton, Putnam County, Ga., on Sept. 1, 1825. He graduated from Emory College (Oxford, Ga.) in 1845 with the highest honors. He married the daughter of A. B. LONGSTREET, the president of Emory, and to them were born one son, L. Q. C. Jr., and three daughters. Having studied law at Macon, Ga., he was admitted to the bar in 1847, moved in 1849 to Oxford, Miss., and continued further studies as well as teaching mathematics at the University of Mississippi. The distinguished ALBERT T. BLEDSOE, then teaching

philosophy at the University, later said, "I taught Lucius to think." Justice Lamar long afterward commented that there was "something in" what his old teacher said.

Lamar was elected to Congress in 1856 from MISSISSIPPI and was a member of that body at the time the Civil War broke, resigning his seat after Mississippi passed her ordinance of secession. During the War he served as a Lieutenant-Colonel in the Confederate States Army for a time and was sent by the Confederate states on a European mission. In 1872 he was again elected to Congress from Mississippi and in 1876 to the Senate. His speech in the Senate on the death of Charles Sumner was acclaimed over the nation, as it proved one of the first moves toward establishing again the brotherhood which had been broken by the terrible years of war. For if ever there was a northern champion it was Charles Sumner of Massachusetts, and if ever there was a southerner it was L. Q. C. Lamar of Mississippi. Seconding the motion to adjourn when the death of Sumner was announced in the Senate, Lamar delivered a deeply moving address which he closed by saying, "If we knew each other better, we would love each other more." For this President John F. Kennedy gave Lamar a chapter in his book *Profiles in Courage*.

He was put in the Cabinet in 1885 by President Cleveland, and then appointed to the Supreme Court in 1888. A constant churchman he was ever loyal to Methodism. He was one southern layman of prominence whom Bishop SIMPSON put in his *Cyclopaedia*.

The Justice died Jan. 23, 1893 and was buried in Macon, Ga.

Wirt A. Cate, *Lucius Q. C. Lamar, Secession and Reunion*. Chapel Hill, N. C., 1935.
Dictionary of American Biography.
John F. Kennedy, *Profiles in Courage*. New York: Harper & Row, 1964.
M. Simpson, *Cyclopaedia*. 1878.
N. B. H.

LAMB, ELKANAH J. (1832-1915), American United Brethren missionary to Colorado and colorful Western preacher, was born Jan. 1, 1832, in Wayne County, Ind., son of Esau and Elizabeth Moon Lamb. He received a common schooling, was a cooper by trade. Lamb became acquainted with Chief Black Hawk and leaders and warriors of other Indian tribes and was wounded in border warfare in KANSAS in 1864. He was noted as a mountain climber and supervised various Rocky Mountain rescue operations. E. J. Lamb was licensed by Kansas Conference, Church of the United Brethren in Christ, in 1864 and ordained by the same Conference in 1870. He married Mrs. J. J. Morger and was father to seven children.

Lamb was appointed by the mission board to COLORADO in 1871, where he helped build the first United Brethren Church in Colorado, along the Platte River about twelve miles from DENVER. In 1872 he surveyed NEBRASKA in preparation for organizing a Nebraska Conference. He served as presiding elder in Colorado Conference several years. Lamb died at Estes Park, Apr. 7, 1915. A daughter had been murdered in a log cabin several years previously.

Religious Telescope, April 21, 1915. ROBERT R. MACCANON

LAMBERT, JEREMIAH (?-1786), was the first American Methodist itinerant appointed to serve beyond the Alleghenies, and the first Methodist preacher to be stationed in TENNESSEE. Sixty members were already in

Tennessee at the time of Lambert's appointment in 1783, but nothing is known of their origin. One theory is that JOHN KING, JOHN DICKINS and Lee Roy Cole, who had labored in NORTH CAROLINA in 1777, may have also preached in Tennessee. This has not been proved, although if it were, it would not alter the fact that Lambert was the first man officially appointed to serve beyond the Alleghenies. His circuit was enormous, comprising all the settlements on the Watauga, Nolichuckey and Holston Rivers. Living conditions were exceedingly primitive and the danger from the Indians was very real. Lambert's work was fruitful although not astounding, and at the next Annual Conference he reported seventy-six members, a gain of sixteen.

He served various appointments including Old ST. GEORGE'S in PHILADELPHIA, and in 1785 ASBURY appointed him to serve as a missionary to ANTIGUA. It is not known whether he actually reached Antigua in the West Indies, since his health broke shortly after his appointment, and he died the following year, 1786.

Lambert was a native of NEW JERSEY although the date of his birth is not known. That he was an outstanding preacher is attested by THOMAS WARE, another early Methodist itinerant, who writes, "He had in four years . . . without the parade of classical learning, or any theological training, actually attained to an eminence in the pulpit which no ordinary man could reach by the aid of any human means whatsoever . . . The graces with which he was eminently adorned were intelligence, innocence and love. . . ."

In the Conference *Minutes* he is spoken of as "an Elder; six years in the work; a man of sound judgment, clear understanding, good gifts, genuine piety, and very useful, humble and holy; diligent in life, and resigned in death."

A. W. Cliffe, *Our Methodist Heritage.* 1957.
A. Stevens, *History of the M. E. Church.* 1867.

FREDERICK E. MASER

LAMBETH, WILLIAM ARNOLD (1879-1952), American clergyman, was born at Thomasville, N. C., on Oct. 5, 1879. He received degrees from DUKE, Yale, and Harvard Universities, did graduate work at VANDERBILT UNIVERSITY, and honorary degrees were conferred on him by three institutions.

He entered the ministry of the M. E. Church, South in 1905 and was pastor in SALISBURY, GREENSBORO, Walkertown, WINSTON-SALEM, Reidsville, HIGH POINT, and GASTONIA, all in the WESTERN NORTH CAROLINA CONFERENCE. From 1924 to 1930 he was pastor of Mount Vernon Place Church in WASHINGTON, D. C. He then returned to his native state and served churches in DURHAM, ASHEVILLE, and High Point, and was superintendent of the Winston-Salem District.

Lambeth was a member of the UNITING CONFERENCE at Kansas City in 1939, and of all the GENERAL and JURISDICTIONAL CONFERENCES between 1938 and 1948. In 1936 the COLLEGE OF BISHOPS of the M. E. Church, South asked him to conduct a campaign to pay the indebtedness of $100,000 on the LAKE JUNALUSKA ASSEMBLY. This he did, and the Assembly was accepted by the General Conference in 1938 as an institution of the church. Lambeth then became its president, superintendent, and treasurer (without salary), a position which he held until 1944. He then became superintendent of the

Greensboro District, where he served until he retired in 1949. He died at Morehead City, N. C., on Nov. 20, 1952.

Mason Crum, *The Story of Junaluska.* Greensboro: Piedmont Press, 1950.
Who's Who in America.   ELMER T. CLARK

LAMBUTH, JAMES WILLIAM (1830-1892), American missionary and father of the more famous Bishop WALTER R. LAMBUTH, was born in Louisiana on March 2, 1830, but was reared in Madison County, Miss. His grandfather, William Lambuth, was born in Hanover County, Va., and was sent by BISHOP ASBURY in 1800 as a missionary to the Indians in TENNESSEE; he died at Fountain Head in that state in 1837. His son, John Russell Lambuth, was born at Fountain Head in 1800 and volunteered as a missionary to the Indians in LOUISIANA.

The family moved early to Louisiana. James graduated from the University of Mississippi in 1851 and began to preach among the Negroes. In 1854 he was sent to CHINA to aid in establishing the mission of the M. E. Church, South, in Shanghai. At the outbreak of the Civil War, he returned to MISSISSIPPI but went back to China in 1864. In 1886 he and his son, Walter, went to JAPAN and formed the Southern Methodist mission there. He died at Kobe, Japan, on April 28, 1892.

J. Cannon, *Southern Methodist Missions.* 1926.
Dictionary of National Biography.
William Washington Pinson, *Walter Russell Lambuth, Prophet and Pioneer.* Nashville: Cokesbury Press, 1924.

ELMER T. CLARK

WALTER R. LAMBUTH

LAMBUTH, WALTER RUSSELL (1854-1921), American missionary and bishop of the M. E. Church, South, was born in Shanghai, China, on Nov. 10, 1854, the son of missionary parents, JAMES WILLIAM and Mary Isabella (McClellan) LAMBUTH. In 1859 he was sent to his relatives in TENNESSEE and MISSISSIPPI for his early education. His parents returned during the Civil War, and the son went back to CHINA with them in 1864 and remained five years.

He graduated from EMORY AND HENRY COLLEGE in

1875, studied theology and medicine at VANDERBILT UNIVERSITY and received a medical degree. In 1877 he was ordained an elder in the TENNESSEE CONFERENCE and was sent to China, where he worked in Shanghai and adjacent areas. He returned on furlough in 1881 and studied at Bellevue Hospital Medical College in New York and received a second degree of Doctor of Medicine.

He returned to China in 1882 and organized medical and hospital service at Soochow and Peking. In 1885 with his father he founded the JAPAN Mission of his Church and established the notable Kwansei Gakuin and the Hiroshima Girls' School.

In 1891 he was assigned to field service in the United States and editor of the *Methodist Review of Missions*, and in 1894 he was elected General Secretary of the Board of Missions with headquarters at Nashville, Tenn. In this capacity he helped in uniting Methodism in Canada and forming the autonomous Japan Methodist Church, a union of all Methodist bodies working in that field.

Lambuth was elected bishop by the M. E. Church, South in 1910 and was assigned to BRAZIL. In the same year the Board of Missions projected a mission in Africa and in 1911 Lambuth, accompanied by JOHN W. GILBERT of PAINE COLLEGE and a leader in the C.M.E. Church, went to that continent; they travelled 2,600 miles by boat and rail and 1,500 miles on foot through the jungles to the village of WEMBO NYAMA in the Belgian Congo, where their cordial reception by Chief Wembo Nyama convinced Lambuth that he had been providentially led to the Batetela tribe, and he proceeded to arrange for a mission. He was away from home a year or more and on his return he recruited a group of missionaries which he took to the CONGO in 1913. For his travels through Africa he was made a Fellow of the Royal Geographic Society at London.

During World War I he went to Europe and visited the front and made arrangements for establishing Southern Methodism in BELGIUM, POLAND, and CZECHOSLOVAKIA. In 1921 he took a party of missionaries to Siberia and founded a mission there, but it met opposition and was of short duration. He served briefly on the Pacific Coast and for a period resided at Oakdale, Calif.

Bishop Lambuth participated in the ECUMENICAL METHODIST CONFERENCES, the WORLD MISSIONARY CONFERENCE, and other movements involving the cooperation of the churches. He was the author of three books on medical missions, the Orient, and the missionary movement. He died at Yokohama, Japan, on Sept. 26, 1921, and his ashes were buried by the side of his mother in Shanghai. He is rightly considered to be one of the great missionary leaders of Methodism.

Dictionary of American Biography.
J. Cannon, *Southern Methodist Missions.* 1926.
General Conference *Journal*, 1922. MES.
William W. Pinson, *Walter Russell Lambuth: Prophet and Pioneer.* Nashville: Cokesbury Press, 1925.
Who's Who in America.   ELMER T. CLARK

LAMBUTH COLLEGE, Jackson, Tennessee, is a continuation and expansion of Memphis Conference Female Institute which was established in 1843. It became a coeducational school in 1923, when its name was changed to Lambuth College honoring Bishop WALTER RUSSELL LAMBUTH, whose death had occurred two years before.

In 1939, at the time of Union, it lacked accreditation and its total properties were valued at $225,100. Today the buildings and grounds are valued at almost $7,000,-000. The college is in a period of academic growth and enrichment. It offers the B.A. and B.S. degrees. The governing board has twenty-eight members elected by the MEMPHIS ANNUAL CONFERENCE.

JOHN O. GROSS

LA MESA, CALIFORNIA, U.S.A. **First Church** was organized in 1895 at a small resort called La Mesa Springs. This is Spanish for "the table," inasmuch as it was upon the tableland of the little town of SAN DIEGO. The church gives witness of having the greatest mission outreach of the entire SOUTHERN CALIFORNIA-ARIZONA CONFERENCE. In the current budget of the church, over forty percent of all funds received are designated for various mission concerns.

The church grew slowly, but since the influx of the huge population movement to the southwest part of the nation, the whole community has increased remarkably. The church grew toward 1,000 members during World War II, with the tremendous number of service personnel, particularly from the United States Navy, living in the area. By 1950 its membership had passed the thousand mark, and eight years later had doubled. It reached 2,500 in 1962. The growth toward a truly significant church was accelerated in 1956, when a Spanish styled sanctuary was built, of the classic style appropriate to the history and culture of the region. This sanctuary greatly appealed to the community, and the church rapidly enlarged all areas of its life.

The mission emphasis for which the church is noted, had its origin in the needs of the Mexican people in the town of Tijuana, some thirty-five miles distant across the border to the south. Responding to the recognition of the need, there was organized in the '50's a Settlement House called Casa de Todas (House for All), with First Church the motivating factor. By 1961, Casa de Todas had grown into a group of buildings: chapel, hospital, clinic, a social welfare center and school. A "person to person" type of Christian fellowship has developed, with over 120 families "adopting" families south of the border, and sharing friendship and concern with them.

This international mission concern has expressed itself in other Tijuana projects: Casa de Esperanza (House of Hope), an orphanage for double orphans which has found its chief support from the La Mesa Church; Project Amigos (Friends), a social welfare center of which the Church is a major supporter, including the support of the Laubach Literacy Director for Baja California (State of Lower California); and Bethel Methodist Church in Tijuana, La Mesa again being a major supporter. The Mission outreach is not limited to "south of the border." The Church is supporting missionaries in PERU, where it also built a high school building, in ARGENTINA and Africa, with a deep involvement in Ludhiana Medical School in INDIA, where a building was given.

In 1952 La Mesa Methodist Church, mindful of its own community needs, commissioned nearly ten percent of its active worshiping members to become charter members of the new adjacent San Carlos Methodist Church, and gave a $71,000 gift of land to the new congregation. The church currently has a staff of three full-time ministers and a membership of 2,308.

HERSCHEL H. HEDGPETH

LAZARUS LAMILAMI

LAMILAMI, LAZARUS, the first ordained Australian Aboriginal minister. He was one of the earlier Aboriginal converts after the establishment of a mission in Arnhem Land by the Methodist Church of Australasia. With headquarters in Darwin, the North Australia district included five mission stations, at Milingimbi, Yirrkala, Elcho Island, Croker Island and Goulburn Island.

It was at Goulburn Island's small but picturesque church in November 1966, that Lazarus Lamilami was ordained as the first Australian Aboriginal minister. He thus serves his own people who have known only European, Fijian, Tongan, Chinese and Rotuman missionaries as their spiritual leaders in the past.

For the past twenty years Lazarus has worked and preached among his fellows and has travelled widely throughout Australia on missionary deputation, making a great impact on his audiences. He became the first Aboriginal Christian pastor and submitted himself to special study and intense preparation to ready himself for the unique and historic day of his ordination.

AUSTRALIAN EDITORIAL COMMITTEE

LAMPARD, JOHN (1859-1935), a one-time associate of General WILLIAM BOOTH in the Salvation Army, founded an independent mission among the Gonds in a village in the Satpura Hills of Balaghat, Central Provinces, INDIA. He began his work as a bachelor. He wore the simplest of village-style clothes and lived for four years in a two-room mud hut with a grass roof.

In a famine in 1897, many orphans came to the mission. Seven other European missionaries joined him and his wife. In 1906, the missionaries decided that the interests of the work required integration in a church. They asked the Methodist Church to take over from them. The Rev. and Mrs. John Lampard and the Rev. and Mrs. Thomas Williams joined the Methodist Church and became missionaries of the Board of Missions. The small school of the independent mission has developed into a coeducational middle school and has produced many leaders of the church and servants of the people.

Lampard later rendered distinguished service in Baroda State, where he became a friend of the Gaekwar (Ruler) and influenced state policy on questions related to the civil rights of Christians and the responsibilities of the state to promote the welfare of its citizens.

J. WASKOM PICKETT

LAMPE, JOHN FREDERICK (1703-1751), was a musician and a friend of Handel. Lampe was born in Saxony, GERMANY, but settled in England in 1726 and was associated with Handel at Covent Garden, London, as a bassoonist and composer. Lampe came under the influence of the Wesleys on Nov. 29, 1745, and was converted from Deism. In 1746 his tunes for CHARLES WESLEY's hymns were published in *Hymns on the Great Festivals and Other Occasions.* From 1748-51 he was in DUBLIN, and there produced *A Collection of Hymns* and *Sacred Poems* (1749). He died in Edinburgh, SCOTLAND. The Wesleys thought highly of his music, and Charles Wesley wrote an ode in memory of him. Two of Lampe's tunes are still in the British Methodist hymnbook.

J. T. Lightwood, *Music of the Methodist Hymn-book.* 1935.
Wesley Historical Soc. *Proceedings.* H. MORLEY RATTENBURY

LAMPLOUGH, EDMUND SYKES (1860-1940), a British Methodist layman, was an underwriter at Lloyd's. He was born on April 6, 1860, at Islington, London, and made his career at Lloyd's, of which he became deputy chairman. For thirty-three years he was a member of the committee of the Wesleyan METHODIST MISSIONARY SOCIETY, and became its treasurer and then president of the Laymen's Missionary Movement. With JOHN H. RITSON he was treasurer of the Theological Institution. President of the WESLEY HISTORICAL SOCIETY from 1937-40, Lamplough discovered 162 original letters of JOHN WESLEY, preserved many Wesley relics and buildings, and established Wesleyan memorials. A keen musician, he served on the committee for the Methodist hymnbook. He was vice-president of the BRITISH AND FOREIGN BIBLE SOCIETY, and vice-president of the Methodist Conference in 1935. He died on Oct. 20, 1940.

J. T. Lightwood, *Music of the Methodist Hymn-book.* 1935.
Wesley Historical Soc. *Proceedings.* H. MORLEY RATTENBURY

LAMPTON, EDWARD WILKINSON (1857-1910), an American bishop of the A.M.E. Church, was born in Hopkinsville, Ky., on Oct. 21, 1857. His education was self-acquired. He was admitted to the North Mississippi Annual Conference in 1886, ordained deacon in 1886 and elder in 1888. He held pastorates in KENTUCKY and MISSISSIPPI. He was presiding elder in Mississippi. He served as a General Officer (Financial Secretary) from 1902-1908, and was elected bishop in 1908 and died in 1910. He was the author of two books: *Analysis of Baptism* and *Digest of Decisions of the Bishops of the A.M.E. Church.*

R. R. Wright, *The Bishops.* 1963.   GRANT S. SHOCKLEY

LAMSON, BYRON S. (1901-   ), an American Free Methodist minister and ordained elder of the Central Illinois Conference and editor of *The Free Methodist,* was born at Boone, Iowa. His degrees are: A.B., GREENVILLE COLLEGE, Ill.; M.A., University of Southern Calif.; graduate studies, University of Rochester; NORTHWESTERN UNIVERSITY; GARRETT BIBLICAL INSTITUTE, D.D., SEATTLE PACIFIC; Litt.D., Los Angeles Pacific. He served as pastor of churches in California and Illinois, and was Dean, 1927-30, and President, 1930-39, of Los Angeles Pacific College. He was General Missionary Secretary, 1944-64, and became editor of *The Free Methodist* in 1964.

While pastor of the college church, Greenville, Ill., Lamson was elected General Missionary Secretary. He served in this capacity for twenty years, has visited the overseas churches in Asia, Africa, and Latin America. The mission church membership increased from less than 9,000 to over 50,000 during this time, and many mission fields became regular conferences. General Conferences were established in EGYPT and JAPAN. The Free Methodist World Fellowship was organized under Dr. Lamson's leadership.

After serving as editor of *The Free Methodist* since 1964 and becoming eligible for retirement in June 1969, the denomination's Board of Administration requested him to continue as editor until June 30, 1970, with the title of "Acting Editor." Under his editorship, *The Free Methodist* (circulation 100,000) celebrated in 1967 its one hundred years of service with a special anniversary issue. Included were special greetings from the President, the Prime Minister of Canada, editors of church publications and many denominational leaders.

Dr. Lamson has written *Holiness Teachings of Jesus; Modern Prayer Miracles; Venture; To Catch the Tide.* He serves as chairman of the Committee on Research for Church Growth. He is the editor of the FREE METHODIST CHURCH material in this *Encyclopedia of World Methodism.* Dr. and Mrs. Lamson reside at Winona Lake, Ind.

N. B. H.

LANAHAN, JOHN (1815-1903), an American minister and BOOK AGENT of the BOOK CONCERN of the M. E. Church, was born at Harrisonburg, Va., in 1815. His parents were Roman Catholic, but of liberal tendencies, and they allowed their children to attend Protestant churches. He was converted at eighteen years of age and received on trial of the BALTIMORE CONFERENCE in 1838. He served prominent appointments, including the district superintendency and proved popular as a man and as a preacher. He is said to have been of commanding presence and always enlisted the undivided attention of his Conference when he rose to speak.

When the Civil War came, Lanahan continued to adhere to the section of the Baltimore Conference which remained with the M. E. Church, although most of his brethren adhered to the M. E. Church, South, they eventually becoming the "Old Baltimore." Lanahan supported Bishop SIMPSON in his bringing pressure on President Lincoln to appoint more Methodists into the offices of government. He was elected in 1860 to the GENERAL CONFERENCE of that year as an alternate, but took the place of Thomas Sewell who was not present. At the General Conference of 1868, he was elected as one of the Agents of the New York Book Concern and acted in

that capacity for four years. He continued to be elected by his Annual Conference to the General Conference of his Church, serving in every one from 1868 to 1900. He died on Dec. 8, 1903, in Baltimore, Md.

J. E. Armstrong, *Old Baltimore Conference.* 1907.
M. Simpson, *Cyclopaedia.* 1878.   N. B. H.

LANCASTER, JAMES PRESTON (1877-1963), missionary to CUBA and MEXICO, was born on March 1, 1877, in Troup County, Ga., U.S.A. He attended Lafayette College, in Lafayette, Ala., and later enrolled in Roanoke Normal College in Roanoke, Ala.

In May 1900, he received his first license to preach from the NORTH ALABAMA CONFERENCE. In November 1901 he joined the North Alabama Conference of the M. E. Church, South, and was assigned to the Millerville Circuit which included seven churches.

In 1904 he was appointed by the BOARD OF MISSIONS (MECS) to La Gloria, Cuba, where he was to take charge of the English work. In 1908 he was appointed by Bishop Candler as Director of the school Colegio Ingles in Camaguey, Cuba. He married Elsie Whipple in 1908 in Camaguey and five children were born of this union.

In 1910 his health broke in Cuba and he and his family returned to the United States and went to COLORADO. At the Denver Conference (1910), he was appointed to Trinidad, Colo. In 1912, Bishop HENDRIX appointed him to the English work at Torreon, Mexico and he became a member of the Mexican Conference.

In 1914, due to political unrest in Mexico, Bishop CANDLER again appointed him to the church in La Gloria, Cuba. In 1918 he was allocated by the Mission Board to the Women's Council to work as Director of Palmore College, Chihuahua, Mexico.

In 1921 he accepted the leadership of the Mexican work in TEXAS and NEW MEXICO and in 1927 he left the Spanish work and became a member of the NEW MEXICO CONFERENCE, where his membership remained until his retirement in 1949.

In 1952 he became pastor of the Chadbourn Spanish Gospel Mission in Colorado Springs, Colo., a pastorate he held until his death in October 1963. His name was included in the memorial service of the New Mexico Conference Annual Meeting in 1964.

Minutes of the New Mexico Conference, 1964.

MARY JO BENNETT

LANCASTER, OHIO, U.S.A. **First Church** owes its origin to a group of Methodists who met in a log cabin, the home of Edward Teal, to hear JAMES QUINN preach in 1799. Bishop FRANCIS ASBURY is said to have been a personal friend of Edward Teal, and visited there many times previous to the forming of the permanent organization which took place in 1812. The Methodist Society (not yet an organized church) was one of the first religious groups to hold meetings in this area, and had been meeting for nearly three years before the town of Lancaster came into being in 1801. However, the records indicate that the group had met in various cabins, and in the open, until 1812, when they organized themselves into a Methodist church, and built the first log cabin church.

The present church building is the third constructed by this congregation. It is located about two city blocks from the original first church location. It was built in 1905-07, and extensively remodeled and expanded into a much larger structure in 1950-51. The church membership had grown to 3,000 members by the year of its Sesquicentennial Celebration in 1962. The present buildings, grounds and parking areas cover about one-fourth of a city block and are located just one block from the center of the city. The congregation numbered 3,111 in 1970.

GEORGE W. HERD

LANCASTER, PENNSYLVANIA, U.S.A. **First Church** is one of the leading churches of the PHILADELPHIA CONFERENCE, and, through the years, has been one of the most influential Methodist churches in and about Lancaster. Its early preachers extended Methodism as far as POTTSVILLE in the anthracite area.

The first Methodist sermon was probably preached in Lancaster by JOSEPH PILMORE in the Old Court House in Center Square on June 2, 1772. Later a class was formed, but it eventually died out and for some years there was no Methodist preaching in Lancaster. MATTHEW SIMPSON says that HENRY BOEHM conducted a Methodist service in Lancaster in 1803, preaching in the market-house from a butcher's block.

In 1807, WILLIAM HUNTER and Henry Boehm were assigned as missionaries to that part of PENNSYLVANIA lying between the Delaware and Schuylkill Rivers, and FRANCIS ASBURY requested Boehm to translate the *Discipline* into German for the large German population in this area. On one occasion when Boehm was proof-reading the German *Discipline,* he was forced to remain in Lancaster overnight because of a heavy rain. He called upon a Philip Benedict whom he had heard about from a Methodist woman in Lancaster who felt Benedict was desirous of becoming a Methodist. Boehm had a satisfactory interview with Benedict and his wife, and on Oct. 14, 1807, when Boehm next came to the city, he formed a class of six members consisting of Benedict, his wife and four others. The home of the Benedicts on 125 or 129 Duke Street then became a regular Methodist preaching place.

The class grew, larger quarters were needed, and a property was secured and a building erected on Walnut and Christian Streets. It was dedicated Dec. 17, 1809. Growth for a time was slow. Originally on the Lancaster Circuit, the church was made a single station in 1811 with THOMAS WARE as pastor; but it was again placed on a circuit the following year, not becoming a separate station permanently until 1828.

In 1842 a new building was erected on Duke Street below Walnut, and it was dedicated Sept. 4 of that year. Although now heavily in debt, the church assisted in the building of another Methodist Church in Lancaster, St. Paul's on Queen Street. By 1855 First Church had grown to such proportions that a session of the Philadelphia Annual Conference was held there with Bishop BEVERLY WAUGH presiding.

The church gave increased impetus to the expansion of Methodism in Lancaster, building a mission which later became Western Church. In a real sense First Church became the mother church of Lancaster city, and the Lancaster area, either directly or indirectly assisting in the founding and growth of many of the Methodist churches. As the church continued to grow, larger quarters became increasingly necessary, and in 1889 the present Church edifice was begun. It was completed at a cost of $87,000 and was dedicated by Bishop CHARLES H. FOWLER June

12, 1892. In subsequent years renovating and expansion programs added to the practicality and beauty of this mother church of Lancaster.

In 1970 First Church reported 1,307 members, property valued at $1,550,715, and $132,834 raised for all purposes.

Centennial Jubilee Souvenir Program, First Methodist Episcopal Church, Lancaster, Pennsylvania, edited by a Committee. Lancaster, 1907.

M. Simpson, *Cyclopaedia.* 1878.   FREDERICK E. MASER

LANCE, JOSEPH R. (1925-   ), pastor, chaplain, Indian bishop, was born on Oct. 15, 1925, at Meerut, U.P., India. His father, Rockwell Lance of Rajasthan India, served in the former Delhi Conference and retired as district superintendent of the Roorkee. Educated at the Ingraham Institute in Ghaziabad and at Parker High School, Moradabad, Joseph Lance studied at LUCKNOW CHRISTIAN COLLEGE, India, (A.B., 1948); GARRETT THEOLOGICAL SEMINARY (Crusade Scholar), A.M., B.D., 1956. Ordained deacon in 1944, he began his ministry as chaplain of the Madar Union Sanatorium near Ajmer, India. While here he married Sushila Sentu, a post-graduate nurse, the daughter of a United Presbyterian minister. After studying in America, 1953-56, he returned to Madar in 1956. Then he moved to Delhi as pastor of Christ Methodist Church (1,200 members), 1957-66. In 1966 he was appointed executive secretary of the Council of Christian Social Concerns covering the whole of The Methodist Church in India. An effective preacher in English and Hindustani, he was a delegate to the General Conference (TMC) in 1964; attended the Asia Consultation at Port Dickson, Malaya; and the Assembly of the East Asia Conference at Singapore. He went to the United States as a member of the Mission to America team in 1966, and toured widely for five months, speaking in various churches. In September 1968, Lance and the Council on Social Concerns sponsored a major conference of ministers and laymen in New Delhi dealing with the place of the foreign missionary in India. From the conference came a recommendation that there be more "Indianization" of church personnel, and that invitations to new foreign missionaries be based "on local needs for specialists and experts." At forty-four years of age, Joseph R. Lance was elected bishop on the second ballot on Jan. 2, 1969, at the Southern Asia Central Conference, Bangalore, India. He was assigned to the Lucknow Area.

Daily Indian Witness, Bangalore, India, January 2, 1969, Vol. XIV, No. 4, p. 58.

Garrett *Alumni News,* February, 1969.   JESSE A. EARL

LANDER, JOHN McPHERSON (1858-1924), an American preacher, educator, and missionary to BRAZIL, was born in Lincolnton, N. C., on Dec. 17, 1858. He was the son and grandson of Methodist preachers. He graduated from WOFFORD COLLEGE in 1879. Desirous of becoming a missionary to CHINA (as China was in those early days the "dramatic" and desirable mission field), he went to VANDERBILT where he spent two years studying in the medical and theological departments. On Jan. 14, 1886, he married Thompson Hall.

He taught two years at Williamston Female College in SOUTH CAROLINA, and while there was approached by Bishop J. C. GRANBERY, who was trying to find an educator to start a school for boys in JUIZ DE FORA, Brazil.

Lander accepted the call, and with his wife and first child, Laura, sailed for Brazil in June 1889. The voyage was dangerous because of a fire on board and consumed thirty-three days. They arrived, however, in time for Lander to be received into the annual conference on July 7, 1889. He was appointed at once to found the school; and since he did not know the language, J. W. Wolling was sent as his associate. Total equipment seems to have been a blackboard and box of chalk. Lander remained some twelve years at Granbery (now called INSTITUTO GRANBERY) and established it on a sound basis. He also served as pastor of several churches, presiding elder, editor of the official church paper *Expositor Cristão* and agent of the publishing house. In all his work, expecially at Granbery, Mrs. Lander was a devoted helper, teaching most of the time. In 1903, Lander received a D.D. degree from Wofford College.

Illness beset the last years of his life, and he died in the Palmyra Sanatorium, Minas Gerais, on March 20, 1924.

World Outlook, January 1940.　　　EULA K. LONG

LANDER, SAMUEL (1833-1904), American clergyman-educator, was born in Lincolnton, N. C., on Jan. 30, 1833. A graduate of RANDOLPH-MACON COLLEGE, Va., he taught in various schools, served as president of DAVENPORT FEMALE COLLEGE in NORTH CAROLINA, and in 1861 was licensed to preach. In 1864 he was admitted on trial into the SOUTH CAROLINA CONFERENCE, M. E. Church, South.

As pastor of the Williamston, S. C., circuit, 1872, he was led to establish the Williamston Female College, and remained the head of the institution until his death, July 14, 1904. Previously that year the college had moved to Greenwood, S. C. It was renamed for its founder, Lander College, and from 1906 to 1948 was owned and operated by the Methodist Conference (MES and subsequently The Methodist Church, SEJ). Lander College now, through offer of the Conference in 1948, is owned and operated by the community of Greenwood.

Lander was a delegate to the GENERAL CONFERENCES of 1890 and 1894.

Samuel Lander was married to Laura A. McPherson on Dec. 20, 1853. They were the parents of eleven children, nine of whom lived to useful adulthood, namely: Martha (Mrs. George E. Prince), John, William Tertius, Angus, Neil, Kathleen (Mrs. John O. Willson), Malcolm, Frank, and Ernest. Tertius and Frank became physicians in Williamston; Kathleen became the wife of the Rev. John O. Willson, D.D., who succeeded Lander as president of Lander College. John became a missionary to BRAZIL and founder of Granbery College there.

J. MARVIN RAST

LANDER COLLEGE, Greenwood, South Carolina, for more than seventy-five years a Methodist college, was founded by SAMUEL LANDER (1833-1904) at Williamston, S. C., on Feb. 12, 1872, as Williamston Female College. In 1904 it was moved to Greenwood and named Lander, honoring its founder.

The college was offered to the SOUTH CAROLINA CONFERENCE of the M. E. Church, South, in 1898 as a part of its educational system, and in 1906 it came under the jurisdiction of the conference. It continued this relationship until 1948, when the South Carolina Conference voted to deed the college to the Greenwood County

Education Commission in order to concentrate support on COLUMBIA and WOFFORD COLLEGES.

Serving as president of the college during its church-related period were: Samuel Lander (1872-1904); John O. Willson (1904-23); Robert O. Lawton, acting president (1923); B. Rhett Turnipseed (1923-27); R. H. Bennett (1927-32); John W. Speake (1932-41); JOHN MARVIN RAST (1941-48).

JOHN O. GROSS

LANDON, ALFRED MOSSMAN (1887-　　), American layman, governor, and presidential candidate, was born at West Middlesex, Pa., on Sept. 9, 1887. He was educated at Marietta Academy in Ohio, and graduated in law from the University of Kansas in 1908. He received the honorary LL.D. degree from Washburn and Marietta Colleges and BOSTON UNIVERSITY and the L.H.D. from Kansas State University.

Removing to KANSAS in young manhood, he was employed in a bank at Independence until 1912, after which he was an oil producer and operator of radio broadcasting stations. He was an officer in the Chemical Warfare Service of the U.S. Army during World War I.

Mr. Landon was chairman of the Republican State Central Committee in Kansas and in 1932 he was elected governor of the state and served two terms. In 1936 he was the Republican nominee for President of the United States, losing to Franklin D. Roosevelt.

Long active in Methodist affairs, he was a member of the KANSAS CONFERENCE delegation of the M. E. Church at the Uniting Conference of 1939. He was elected chairman of the important committee on Publishing Interests of that Conference and helped formulate the legislation which correlated the publishing work of the three Methodist Churches then merging into The Methodist Church. He resides in Topeka, Kansas.

Who's Who in America, Vol. 34.　　　ELMER T. CLARK

LANDSDALE, PENNSYLVANIA, U.S.A. **Bethel Hill Church,** located on Skippack Pike and Bethel Road, is the successor church to and is erected very near the site of the first chapel used by the Methodists in PENNSYLVANIA outside of PHILADELPHIA. JOSEPH PILMORE in various places in his *Journal* wrote of preaching at Metchin (now Bethel Hill). On Oct. 13, 1770 he wrote, "Mr. Edward Evans and I set out in the morning for Metchin—a place about 20 miles from the city, to open a new Chapel which had been built by a few persons who loved the Redeemer, and wished to advance His Kingdom in the World." The ground on which the chapel was built was the gift of Hance Supplee who donated also an adjoining lot for a cemetery.

During the Revolutionary War Washington's Army was twice encamped in the general region of the church, and in October 1777, several of Washington's officers were quartered with Abraham Supplee, a local preacher and son of Hance Supplee. Following the Battle of Germantown the chapel was used as a temporary hospital for the wounded, and about thirty Revolutionary War Veterans are buried in the cemetery.

The chapel at first was not under the care of any particular denomination. In the year 1782, however, it was regularly organized under the Methodists. In January of that year the ground and buildings upon it were deeded by David Wagener and his wife to John Tyson, Andrew Supplee, Samuel Castner, Christopher Zimmerman, Abraham Supplee and Benjamin Tyson for the sum of five shillings. The deed further states it was for them or their heirs ". . . or any that shall hereafter become members of that Society forever for the Special use of that Society called the Methodist for a worship house and Burying place for the only use of that Society or such whom they of that Society (sic) or belonging to that meeting or that may at any time become members of that Society shall tolerate to preach or allow to hold worship in . . . ."

The church was used until 1845 when the present building of stone and brick was erected on ground given by Samuel Supplee adjacent to the original church. A new front was added to the church in 1904 and two years later the original building was torn down.

For many years the size of the church and congregation remained static, but recently, with the movement of many persons to the suburbs, the church has been slowly growing. The church building has been renovated, and an educational unit and a new parsonage have been added. The present Bethel Hill Church is in possession of the original deed quoted above.

J. Lednum, *Rise of Methodism*. 1859.
Maser and Maag, *Journal of Joseph Pilmore*. 1969.

FREDERICK E. MASER

LANE, GEORGE (1842-1904), Australian minister and conference president, was born at Hitchin, England, on July 31, 1842. He was the son of a Baptist minister and with his parents came to New South Wales, AUSTRALIA when twelve years of age. While still young he was led, under the ministry of JOHN WATSFORD, to dedicate his life to Christ. He offered himself as a candidate for the Methodist ministry in 1864, and was accepted.

His gifts as preacher and administrator soon attracted the attention of the Conference, and in 1883 he was appointed Secretary of the Home Mission Society—a position he held for six years. He subsequently administered the property affairs of the Church for several years, and his business acumen and abundant energy won for him the confidence of all who were associated with him. He was twice elected President of the General Conference and throughout the whole of his career he was held in the highest esteem by the Methodist people in general.

He took a prominent part in uniting the Wesleyan, the PRIMITIVE METHODIST and the UNITED FREE METHODIST CHURCHES at the beginning of the century, and in all he did he exhibited a fraternal and humble spirit. Every gift he possessed he placed at the disposal of the Master whom he served with unflagging zeal, and great efficiency to the end.

Toward the close of his life the University of Victoria in Canada conferred on him the D.D. degree.

AUSTRALIAN EDITORIAL COMMITTEE

LANE, ISAAC (1834-1937), American bishop of the C.M.E. Church, was born a slave on March 3, 1834, five miles north of Jackson, Tenn. He joined the M. E. Church, South on Oct. 21, 1854. Licensed to exhort in November of 1856, he received a license to preach shortly thereafter. In 1866, he was ordained deacon and elder by the newly formed Tennessee, North Alabama, and North Mississippi Annual Conference. At the same meeting of the Conference, he was appointed presiding elder of the Jackson

ISAAC LANE

District and served in that capacity until 1870. Then, he was appointed minister of Liberty Church in JACKSON, Tenn., the "Mother Church" of his denomination, and elected as a delegate to the first General Conference of the C.M.E. Church. At the General Conference of 1873, he was elected to the office of bishop.

Deprived of a formal education himself, he received what he had by his own hard work. He had a great interest in the education of his race and founded LANE COLLEGE in Jackson, Tenn., which bears his name. As a bishop, he was a leader in church expansion and promoted the taking of the church to his people as they moved into the north and west.

Bishop Lane served until 1914 when he was granted release from administrative duties upon his request. He died on Dec. 5, 1937.

Harris and Patterson, *C.M.E. Church*. 1965.
I. Lane, *Autobiography*. 1916.

RALPH G. GAY

LANE COLLEGE, JACKSON, Tennessee, an institution of the C.M.E. CHURCH, was founded in 1882 by Bishop ISAAC LANE. The name Lane Institute was adopted in 1883, but the present name of Lane College was adopted in 1895, when the institution offered its first instructional program at the college level. The college has a four-year undergraduate program in the liberal arts, and offers B.A. and B.S. degrees.

The governing board is made up of eighteen members elected by the board upon nomination by sponsoring conferences of the C.M.E. Church. Each member serves a three-year term.

Lane College statistics are as follows: library, 40,989 volumes; total enrollment, 1,034; number of foreign students, nine; total faculty, forty-nine; campus acreage, forty-two; number of buildings, seventeen; value of physical plant, $2,985,242; endowment, book value, $378,487; market value, $3,600,000; current income, $2,004,314; current expenditures, $1,880,958.

LANGDALE, JOHN WILLIAM (1874-1940), American minister and BOOK EDITOR of the M. E. Church, was born in Newcastle, England, on Aug. 14, 1874, of American and English parentage. He was naturalized by his father's citizenship, being the son of John Wilkenson and Annie (Walton) Langdale, and was brought to the United States in his infancy. He received the B.A. degree from WESLEYAN UNIVERSITY, Conn. 1903, its D.D. in 1914, and also studied at the BOSTON UNIVERSITY SCHOOL OF THEOLOGY and at Harvard. His wife was Alice Belle Barnatt of Crafton, Pa., whom he married on Jan. 10, 1905.

In 1905, he entered the Methodist ministry and became pastor of Meyersdale, Pa., 1905-08; Beaver, Pa., 1908-12; Avondale Church, Cincinnati, Ohio, 1912-16; New York Avenue Church, Brooklyn, N. Y., 1916-25; at which time he became the superintendent of the Brooklyn South District. He served as district superintendent 1925-28, when he was elected Book Editor of the M. E. Church, and in this office exercised great influence and gave decided general leadership to his Church in many ways. He was a member of the executive committee of the Board of Foreign Missions, a director of the Brooklyn Federation of Churches, and chairman of the committee on policy of the FEDERAL COUNCIL OF CHURCHES, the chairman of the Commission on the Revision of the *Ritual,* which revision he presented to the GENERAL CONFERENCE of 1932. He served on the Joint Hymnal Commission of 1930-34, as its secretary, and took a place of acknowledged leadership in the revision of the *Hymnal,* as well as in that of the Responsive Readings in the *Hymnal* which were reworked at that time.

A large genial man with a passion for details and with an avid interest in all Church-wide moves and affairs, Langdale enjoyed great popularity and the abiding affection of his brethren. He was the founder and first editor of *Religion in Life.* This Journal was begun by him with an interdenominational outreach designed to take the place of the old *Quarterly Review* which had gone out of existence. It has since been continued as an official publication of the Church.

His health became greatly impaired after a time and shortly after the reorganization of the METHODIST PUBLISHING interests at Church union, he died in the BROOKLYN METHODIST HOSPITAL on Dec. 10, 1940. His funeral was conducted by Bishop FRANCIS J. McCONNELL in the New York Avenue Church in Brooklyn, and a large representation of ministers from the entire New York area was present to do him honor.

Journal of the New York East Conference, 1941.   N. B. H.

LANIUS, JACOB (1814-1851), American minister and leader in MISSOURI Methodism, was born at Fincastle, Va., Jan. 9, 1814. His parents moved to Potosi, Washington County, Mo., when he was a child. The elder Lanius was a saddlemaker and the boy learned the trade. At fourteen Jacob joined the Methodist Church in Potosi, and soon felt called to preach. He was licensed to preach Aug. 20, 1831, and was admitted to the MISSOURI CONFERENCE on trial that fall at Jackson. He was ordained DEACON by Bishop JOSHUA SOULE in 1833, and elder by Bishop ROBERT R. ROBERTS in 1835. His appointments were as follows: 1831, Bowling Green Circuit, junior preacher; 1832, St. Charles Circuit, junior preacher; 1833, Paris Circuit; 1834, Richmond Circuit; 1835, Meramec Circuit; 1836-1837, Belleview Circuit; 1838, Springfield District; 1839-1840, Cape Girardeau District; 1841-1842,

JACOB LANIUS

Palmyra Station; 1843, Hannibal Station; 1844-1845, Bowling Green Station; 1846-1849, Hannibal District; 1850-1851, Columbia District.

In 1833, Lanius started keeping a journal on loose sheets of paper, and apparently continued it the rest of his life. The journal shows that as a young preacher Lanius was dedicated, devout, popular, humble, studious, and successful. There are constant references to books which he was reading. At twenty he wrote, "I am convinced . . . that . . . education is too much neglected by the ministry." He refers frequently to "flattery" and prays that his head will not be turned by the words of commendation which he hears. He was a good revival preacher, and rejoiced when the saints shouted and the sinners came to the mourners' bench. He expected the church to be built up under his ministry, and if there were no conversions and no additions to the church, he felt that he had failed. Because he did not win a convert or a new member during his first year at Palmyra, he insisted in all seriousness that he ought to move. But the people asked for his return and the bishop reappointed him for a second year.

Lanius' health became impaired when he was about twenty-five, and on occasion he was incapacitated for weeks at a time. Notwithstanding physical weakness, he persevered with diligence and zeal, and his reputation as a preacher and a leader in the conference grew. He was a delegate to the GENERAL CONFERENCE (MES) of 1850.

In the 1830's Lanius sensed the growing tension in Methodism over slavery. In 1837 he noted in his journal that the Methodist preachers of the north and the south had apparently come to think of themselves as members of different ecclesiastical bodies. He deplored the situation and said he favored sending southern preachers north and northern preachers south; he believed "this would prevent local interest and selfish feelings from entering the ministry." He felt that the preservation of "ministerial peace and harmony" was essential for the cause of Christ. As early as 1834 Lanius resolved "to pay more attention to the slave population than I have hitherto done," though he said he knew that would not be popular with the white people. When the division of the church came in 1844, Lanius adhered to the south.

Lanius died in 1851 at thirty-seven years of age, leaving a wife and several children. For decades afterward his memory was green in Missouri Methodism. D. R. Mc-Anally, Editor of the St. Louis *Christian Advocate*, said in 1881 that Lanius "became eminent among the eminent in the Missouri work." W. S. Woodard in *Annals of Missouri Methodism* said in 1893, "Missouri has produced many faithful heralds of the cross, but probably no one who was more deeply consecrated to his work nor successful in it than Jacob Lanius. . . . He was one of the most successful preachers that ever traveled in Missouri."

Jacob Lanius, Journal, original manuscript in Historical Depository of Missouri East Conference, Centenary Church, St. Louis.
Andrew Monroe, Recollections, manuscript in Commission on Archives and History, Lake Junaluska, N. C. ALBEA GODBOLD

L'ANSE, MICHIGAN, U.S.A., is situated on the south shore of Keweenaw Bay, which is formed by the Keweenaw Peninsula, a strip of land jutting sixty-five to seventy miles in a northeasterly direction into Lake Superior. This area receives its name from the Indian word "Ke-wa-we-non" which means "carrying place or portage."

Into this area in the year 1834 came the young Daniel M. Chandler from NEW YORK State, who had received and responded to a call to minister to the Chippewa Indians of the Upper Peninsula of the MICHIGAN Territory. The way had been prepared for him by Elder John Sunday, a Chippewa evangelist who had come into this region two years before from the missions of upper CANADA. A log cabin was purchased from a trader of the American Fur Company and it served D. M. Chandler as a dwelling house, school and church. Soon the young missionary was teaching thirteen or more Indian children in the kitchen.

Thus begins the history of the Methodist Church at L'Anse. Chandler was a beloved missionary who found an early grave due to overexertion and exposure. Others followed his pattern of devotion. The experiences of JOHN PITEZEL, who came to this mission in 1844, are written very interestingly in his book, *Lights and Shades of Missionary Life*. Peter Marksman, one of the early preachers, a Chippewa convert, is among the names to be remembered. He is buried in the local cemetery. Kewawenon was a flourishing Indian mission for many years; in 1844 it reported sixty-five members.

In 1873 a Methodist church was built at L'Anse. This building is still standing but is no longer being used for worship. In 1879 a Methodist Society was founded at Pequaming, ten miles away, the same year that the village was organized. The Ke-wa-we-non mission was coupled with this congregation. This became the site of the Indian CAMP MEETINGS where services were held for two weeks each year for many years. Later the camp meetings were transferred to grounds closer to L'Anse. A church was built at Pequaming which was later to become the building for worship at L'Anse.

Soon after the Ford Motor Company moved out of Pequaming the town was abandoned and is now a ghost town. The church building was moved to L'Anse, it was covered with native stone and an addition was built on. This is the building where the L'Anse congregation now worships. In 1964 a small educational wing was added. After the Pequaming congregation merged with the L'Anse congregation, the Baraga Methodist Church, located on the west side of Keweenaw Bay, was added to the charge. The present charge includes L'Anse and Baraga Methodist Churches and the Zeba (Ke-wa-we-non) Mission.

KONSTANTIN WIPP

LANSING, MICHIGAN, U.S.A., was named by settlers from Lansing, New York, who built the first house in Lansing, Mich., in 1843. The settlement was located at the confluence of Grand and Red Cedar Rivers, and was chartered as a city in 1859. It is now the capital of MICHIGAN.

Lewis Coburn preached the first Methodist sermon there in the log house of Joab Page, a Justice of the Peace who lived in "Lower Town," now North Lansing. Page became the first leader. The first meeting was held in 1845, and the first society was organized in 1846. F. A. Blade was pastor from 1847 to 1848, and preached on April 7, 1847 to sixty people when Lansing had less than thirty in population. Lansing first appeared in the M. E. Church records in 1848, with R. R. Richards as pastor for six months, and seventy members were then reported. That year a horse barn was purchased and used by the Methodists until 1865.

A class was organized in the winter of 1849-50 in "Middle Town," meeting principally in the State Capitol legislative halls. This was the beginning of **Central Church**. Resin Sapp, pastor 1849-50, also acted as chaplain of the Michigan Legislature. In 1850 a lot was deeded to First Church by the State of Michigan. Subsequently this lot was deeded to Central Church, which in 1859 started a subscription list to erect a new building. A brick structure was begun in 1862, at a cost of $10,000, and was dedicated by Bishop SIMPSON on Aug. 4, 1863.

The present Ionia sandstone building was dedicated on April 20, 1890 by Bishop JOYCE. A revolving lighted cross, the gift of Mr. and Mrs. Joseph Burton, was dedicated Dec. 31, 1922. D. STANLEY COORS, a native of Michigan, was appointed pastor of Central Church in 1938, remaining until 1952, when he was elected bishop.

With the help of Central Church, three other Methodist churches were organized in Lansing: Asbury Church, Mt. Hope Avenue, and Potter Park. In 1868 First Church bought a site and erected a wooden structure in North Lansing in 1870. Methodism prospered, and in 1876 Lansing had three Methodist churches: Central with 313 members; First with 138 members, and the German Church, with 133 members.

In 1970 Lansing, including East Lansing, had 8,046 members. Central Church had 2,129 members and property valued at $2,150,844; Mt. Hope Avenue had 969 members; and First Church had 722 members. The city itself lists twelve United Methodist churches, one A.M.E. church, one Wesleyan, and one Free Methodist.

General Minutes.
E. O. Izant, *History of Central Methodist Church.* 1950.
M. Simpson, *Cyclopaedia.* 1878. JESSE A. EARL

LA PAZ, Bolivia, is the largest city in that land with 347,394 people. Because of its accessibility, it is the seat of government in BOLIVIA, though Sucre is the legal capital. La Paz lies in the heart of a gigantic canyon about three miles wide, ten miles long, and 1,500 feet deep, at an altitude of about 11,800 feet, and is framed with high Andean peaks. The city is served by several airlines and has the Pacific terminus of the only railroad that crosses the continent.

In La Paz there is the Church of the Reformation; the Central Church, with a fine modern building at a strategic intersection in the downtown city; the Church of the Redeemer, the principal Aymara Indian church, with the largest Methodist congregation in Bolivia. Its program includes social service in the poorer section of the town, the section in which it is located. The Church of the Resurrection is in Obrajes, adjoining the American Clinic, and is a church which ministers to that community as well as the hospital community; the Church of the Messiah is a new church in Tembladerani, organized in 1958, and at last reporting was the church most rapidly growing in La Paz. This church, as well as the Church of the Resurrection, has Bolivians as pastors. Other institutions in La Paz are the American Clinic, the Colegio Evangelico Metodista, and the Methodist School of Nursing.

CHAPEL, AMERICAN INSTITUTE, LA PAZ, BOLIVIA

American Clinic (Pfeiffer Memorial Hospital) is a Methodist hospital in La Paz. In 1920 plans were made to begin a hospital on land adjoining the American Institute, as COLEGIO EVANGELICO METODISTA was then called, in La Paz. A retired American army doctor, Dr. Warren, and a Methodist missionary nurse, La Rose Driver, came to La Paz to open this hospital, but Warren was unable to secure a general license to practice medicine in Bolivia, so this medical work was postponed.

By 1930 FRANK S. BECK had returned to Bolivia, and he opened the American Clinic in the location where it was originally planned. Although the Methodist BOARD OF MISSIONS did not have funds to maintain medical work in Bolivia, it affirmed the project with the hope that paying patients could help support the work with the poor. The clinic was started with three beds, a pressure cooker for a sterilizer, and a kit of instruments bought as war surplus from the First World War. The first patient treated was a woman in labor suffering from eclampsia, and Beck saved both mother and child. As more income became available, better equipment was obtained, and a new wing was added for an operating room and patient rooms.

The clinic had grown to fifteen beds by 1935, but this was insufficient. While home on furlough Beck told the needs to Mrs. HENRY PFEIFFER of New York. She offered $30,000 toward a new building and equipment. Land was purchased in Obrajes, a suburb of La Paz about a thousand feet lower than the main city, an altitude in which it was felt patients would recover more quickly. As construction began on the large clinic and the nurses' home,

contributions came in from individuals and business firms in Bolivia and the United States. Mrs. Pfeiffer donated another $25,000 and left $50,000 more in an endowment fund. The building was finished in 1940. Other groups and persons from the United States and from the American and British communities in La Paz donated equipment. The clinic was named Pfeiffer Memorial Hospital in gratitude to the Pfeiffers, but locally continues to be known as the American Clinic.

Bill Jack Marshall, who came to Bolivia in 1955, succeeded Beck as director. Pablo Monti, a missionary from ARGENTINA, and Enrique Cicchetti, an Argentine church worker and pastor, both worked at the clinic. Louis Tatom III, a missionary surgeon, had been there for almost two years when he and MURRAY DICKSON were both killed in an automobile accident. Director since 1966 is Thoburn Thompson.

The American Clinic continues to serve all levels of Bolivian society—from the country's Aymara Indian to the foreign community. In 1965 there were 3,050 outpatients, 1,780 bed patients, 545 operations performed, and 514 babies delivered. Plans for the near future call for adding a service wing, and later a pediatrics and preferential unit.

Methodist School of Nursing, the first nursing school in Bolivia, is related to the American Clinic. The school has had a great influence on changing the status of nursing in Bolivia from a menial job into a respected profession. Although the school was started unofficially earlier, it was organized formally in 1939 by Miriam Beck, daughter of Dr. and Mrs. FRANK S. BECK, and was recognized by the government a year later. Miss Beck was director for many years, then returned to work after her marriage to Robert Knowles in 1946.

High school graduation is required for admission. Nurses who have been trained at the school have made a great contribution to the welfare of the Bolivian people through their work as instructors and supervisors of nursing at the clinic and in other hospitals or clinics, in the mines, and in public health work. Students receive practice at the American Clinic and other hospitals and clinics of La Paz.

The school has graduated 170 nurses from its beginning to 1966. In 1962 the program was changed from three years to four, placing more emphasis upon subjects such as public health and anthropology.

The enrollment in 1966 was fifty girls. There are five Bolivian instructors, plus the Bolivian director, Señorita Eunice Zambrana, daughter of one of the first Methodist pastors. Several doctors from the clinic and city teach at the school, some without remuneration.

In 1963 a section was built onto the original building for offices, classrooms, laboratories, and dormitories, and the unit named "Residencia Bessie de Beck" in honor of Mrs. Frank S. Beck.

Barbara H. Lewis, *Methodist Overseas Missions, Gazetteer and Statistics.* New York: Board of Missions, 1960.

NATALIE BARBER

LA PORTE, INDIANA, U.S.A. Historically the First Methodist Church in La Porte was one of the first Protestant churches in the northern part of the state. It was the first Protestant organization in La Porte County.

In 1832 the La Porte Mission was organized. In 1836 the first church building was built in what is now the city of La Porte. In 1919 the First Methodist Church and the German M. E. Church united. This united congregation has grown to be one of the two largest Methodist Churches in the NORTHWEST INDIANA CONFERENCE.

The La Porte Church has a history of unique programming to meet the needs of its community. As early as 1896 a church school and worship service was organized to minister to mute and deaf people in northern INDIANA. Today it continues to lead in creative church programming under its four ministers: a senior pastor, minister of evangelism, minister of education, minister to senior adults. Each minister is responsible for his particular area of the church program.

In 1970 First Church reported a membership of 1,926, property valued at $1,165,725, and $67,743 raised for all purposes.

LARGE, RICHARD WHITFIELD (1873-1920), Canadian medical missionary, was born Feb. 8, 1873, at Kincardine, Ontario, where his father Richard was the Methodist minister. Educated in various primary and secondary schools, he studied medicine at Trinity Medical College, Toronto, from which he graduated in 1897.

Large came to British Columbia in 1898 under the auspices of the Methodist Church, and for a period was superintendent of a hospital built by the Japanese in Steveston, at the mouth of the Fraser, to serve a fishing community of between five and six thousand people. After special ordination by the Methodist Conference, he moved to the Indian village of Bella Bella where his skill as physician and surgeon quickly became known. He soon saw that without a hospital his work could not succeed. With the help of the church, government and the villagers, a twelve-bed unit was opened in October 1902. He also rebuilt the hospital at Rivers Inlet, some seventy miles distant.

He then undertook to train the Indians in preventive medicine. With the extensive use of charts and lantern slides, he initiated a campaign of education on such subjects as ventilation, sanitation, cleanliness, and nutrition, as well as on the effects of alcohol. "No Spitting" signs throughout the village gave warning of a fine to those who might be guilty of this method of spreading tuberculosis.

In 1910, Large was asked to take over the medical work at Port Simpson, a large Indian village thirty miles north of Prince Rupert. Adjoining it was a white community which offered educational opportunities for his three sons, all of whom became physicians. Here at Port Simpson, as at Bella Bella, Large was not only medical superintendent but also health officer, coroner, and justice of the peace. His hobby was music. Gifted with an outstanding baritone voice, he was much in demand on the concert platform as well as at church gatherings.

As with many pioneer ministers, he was a victim of the hardships and overwork of frontier communities. Doubtless these contributed to his death on Aug. 25, 1920, at the early age of forty-seven. The hospital at Bella Bella, now known as the "R. W. Large Memorial Hospital," stands as a tribute to the dedicated life of this man of God.

R. G. Large, *The Skeena: River of Destiny*. Vancouver: Mitchell, 1958.
Mrs. F. C. Stephenson, *Canadian Methodist Missions*. 1925.
W. P. BUNT

LARGE MINUTES are summaries of several conferences held with his preachers by JOHN WESLEY, beginning in 1744. Their origin lies in a pamphlet, entitled *Minutes of Some Late Conversations between the Revd. Mr. Wesley and Others,* published by Wesley in 1749. This pamphlet was concerned with the organization and polity of the Methodist movement, and it came to be known as the "Disciplinary Minutes," to contrast it with a second such pamphlet which dealt with the doctrinal position of the Methodists. The Disciplinary Minutes were revised and edited by Wesley in 1753 to form a code of regulations to which the preachers were asked to subscribe if they wished to remain in connection with Wesley. This code of regulations of 1753, entitled simply *Minutes of Several Conversations*, came to be called the Large Minutes. The adjective "large" referred to the fact that these minutes were a distillation of Wesley's several conferences with his preachers, and not to the actual bulk of the document itself, which was not great.

The edition of 1753 underwent revisions and additions in editions which appeared in 1763, 1770, 1772, 1780, and 1789. Preachers in the Methodist connection were asked to signify their loyalty to the Large Minutes by signing their names to them. When they had done so, they were presented with copies bearing an inscription of the fly-leaf signed by Wesley: "As long as you freely consent to and earnestly endeavor to walk by these rules we shall rejoice to acknowledge you as a fellow laborer."

In the light of problems which developed after Wesley's death in 1791, the Wesleyan Methodist conference of 1797 decided to accept a revision and rearrangement of the Large Minutes which had been drawn up by JOHN PAWSON. This edition of 1797 became the basic ecclesiastical document of nineteenth century British Methodism, having the same role in Britain as the *Discipline* in America. (Original copies of the document bear the incorrect date 1779 on the title page, due to a printer's error.) After reading and subscribing to the Large Minutes, each British ordinand was presented with a copy bearing Wesley's inscription on the fly-leaf, signed by the President and the Secretary of the Conference.

The edition of 1797 does reflect the Arminian and evangelical quality of early Methodist theology, but its main concern is with the practical on-going life of the Methodist Church. There is an abundance of advice on pastoral visitation, the religious instruction of children, a preacher's use of his time, and other such matters. The Large Minutes also deal with such questions of polity as property deeds, the means of removing men remiss in their duties from pastoral office, the administration of the Preachers' Fund, and the support of the KINGSWOOD SCHOOL for the children of preachers. In 1831 David Thomson, the Secretary of the conference, published a definitive edition of the edition of 1797 to assure its being standard throughout British Methodism.

The Large Minutes exercised a crucial influence on American Methodism. The 1773 conference at ST. GEORGE'S CHURCH, Philadelphia, affirmed its loyalty to "the doctrine and discipline of the Methodists, as contained in the Large Minutes" and declared that "if any preachers deviate from the Minutes, we can have no fellowship with them till they change their conduct." American conferences after 1773 continued to accept the Large Minutes as their guide, though they came increasingly to amend and adapt them to American conditions.

The *Discipline* adopted by the Christmas Conference at Baltimore in 1784 was based upon the 1780 edition of the Large Minutes. Since the 1784 *Discipline* became the basis for all further editions of the American *Discipline*, the Large Minutes thus exerted an important influence upon American as well as British Methodism in the nineteenth century. This was true in the Canadian and other Methodist churches which developed in this period as well.

R. Emory, *History of the Discipline.* 1856.
M. Simpson, *Cyclopaedia.* 1878.   Thomas Tredway

LARRABEE, WILLIAM CLARKE (1802-1859), American pioneer educator and minister, was born at Cape Elizabeth, Maine, Dec. 23, 1802. His father, a sea captain, died soon after he was born. From his seventh year he lived with his grandparents and uncle, working on the farm and attending school. At sixteen William went to work in the house of John L. Blake, to whom he was bound for five years.

Converted in a Methodist meeting, he was licensed to preach in June 1821. He joined the Oneida Conference in 1832 but never took a pastoral appointment. Larrabee was graduated at Bowdoin, Brunswick, Maine, A.B., 1828. He married Harriet Dunn on Sept. 28, 1828, and was the father of four children. He named his home "Rosabower" in memory of his daughter Emma, who died in infancy and who is buried on the campus of DePauw University.

Larrabee taught in and later was principal of the Wesleyan Seminary at Kent's Hill, Maine; principal of the Academy at Alfred, Maine; tutor in the preparatory school at Middleton, Conn., which was the forerunner of Wesleyan University; and was principal of Oneida Conference Seminary, Cazenovia, N. Y., 1831-35. In 1840 he was sent as a delegate to the General Conference.

Bishop Matthew Simpson persuaded Larrabee to go to DePauw, where he was professor of mathematics and natural science, 1840-52, acting as president for one year during that time.

He was the first state superintendent of public instruction in Indiana, 1852-54, and in a sense was the founder of the public school system of that state. From 1854 to 1856 he was superintendent of the Indiana Institute for the Blind at Indianapolis.

In 1856 he was made superintendent of public instruction again and kept that office until the year of his death. He wrote *Lectures on the Scientific Evidences of Natural and Revealed Religion; Wesley and His Coadjutors* (2 vols.); *Asbury and His Coadjutors* (2 vols.); and *Essays, Rosabower*.

Larrabee gained in a rare degree the confidence and affection of his students. Retiring in January 1859, he died May 4 of that year at Greencastle, Ind.

Dictionary of American Biography.
National Cyclopedia of American Biography.
M. Simpson, *Cyclopaedia.* 1878.   Jesse A. Earl

LARSEN, CARL J. (1849-1934), American minister and Scandinavian Conference organizer, was born in America, settling at Chicago, where the family became Methodists. Upon his marriage in 1878, he and his bride moved to Oakland, Calif. There, as a wood carver by trade, he became foreman in one of the largest carving and designing factories on the Pacific Coast.

He accepted a call to the ministry and began to preach to the Scandinavian people in Oakland. In 1880 he led in the erection of the first Scandinavian church on the Coast and entered the California Conference on trial. His missionary zeal in 1881 led him to visit Oregon and Washington where he found many persons from the Scandinavian countries who welcomed the Christian gospel. In 1882 he was transferred to the Oregon Conference and organized a Norwegian-Danish congregation in Portland.

In 1884 he became a charter member of the Puget Sound Annual Conference and was appointed to Tacoma. There he organized a congregation of his fellow-countrymen in 1885. Later he organized churches in Seattle; Spokane; Moscow, Idaho; Montana, and did pioneer mission work in Alaska.

When the Norwegian-Danish work in the Northwest was organized into a Missionary Conference in 1888, Larsen became superintendent. His field covered Idaho, Oregon, and Washington.

C. J. Larsen is credited with organizing churches in San Francisco, Calif.; Tacoma, Seattle, and Spokane, Wash.; Portland, Ore.; and Blaine, Idaho. He presided over the first Quarterly Conference at Fair Haven, Bellingham, Wash., in 1890, and delivered the sermon at the opening of the church at Butte, Mont., in 1895. He died at Portland, Ore. in 1934 and was buried there.

Martin Larson, ed., *Memorial Journal of Western Norwegian-Danish Methodism.* (A brief history of Western Norwegian-Danish Methodism.) Privately printed in 1944 by Melvin L. Olson, M. K. Skarbo, David C. Hassel, and Martin T. Larson.
Erle Howell

LARSON, HILDA (1864-1901), was the first foreign missionary of the Swedish Methodist Church (U.S.A.), born in Nettraby, a suburb of Karlskrona, Sweden, on Dec. 24, 1864. She was brought to the United States as a small child and she and her parents were charter members of the Swedish Methodist Church in Evanston, Ill. She was converted at the Des Plaines Camp Meeting and at once wished to go into Christian service. She was trained as a Deaconess at the Lexington Avenue Methodist Church in New York until she sailed for Africa with John Oman and his wife and daughter, on Aug. 24, 1895. She was stationed at Vivi, Congo, until after John Oman's untimely death. Bishop Hartzell then in charge of work there appointed her to Quessua, Angola, which she reached on Sept. 13, 1897, after two months of traveling. At the Conference at Quhongua which opened on June 1, 1899, she was appointed Teacher-in-Charge of the school at Quessua. She was very ill the last few months in Africa but became a great deal better on a long voyage home and arrived in New York on Aug. 30, 1900. She spoke in many of the Swedish Methodist Churches and influenced many for Christian service. She died on Nov. 21, 1901, and is buried in the family plot at Rosehill Cemetery, Chicago, Ill.

Central Northwest Conference *Minutes,* 1942.
Sändebudet, Dec. 4, 1901.
Vinter-Rosor, 1903. A series of Christmas annuals published by the Swedish M. E. Book Concern, Chicago.
Beulah Swan Blomberg

LARTEY, S. DORME (1900-1969), the first native African bishop to be elected in the A.M.E. Zion Church, was born and educated in GHANA, later moving to LIBERIA. In 1933 he entered the ministry of the Presbyterian Church and in 1939 joined the A.M.E. Zion Church under the late Bishop J. W. Brown. The following year he was appointed a presiding elder by Bishop Brown. Under Bishop Cameron C. Alleyne he was again appointed to this position as well as to the superintendency of the Mount Coffee Mission.

Under the late Bishops Edgar B. Watson and Hampton T. Medford (1946-1952) he served as Bishops' Deputy. He was married to the former Alicia Smith, daughter of the late Vice President James S. Smith of Liberia.

S. Dorme Lartey was elevated to the episcopacy of the Church in May 1960. At the time he listed his birth date as Sept. 10, 1900. He died suddenly Aug. 2, 1969.

DAVID H. BRADLEY

LARWOOD, SAMUEL (? -1755), a British Methodist, was a traveling preacher. He was at Conference in BRISTOL in 1745, LONDON in 1748, Leeds in 1753, and at the Irish Conference at Limerick in 1752. He became an Assistant in 1747 and was in IRELAND during 1748-52.

He had a dispute with JOSEPH COWNLEY in DUBLIN in 1748, because Cownley considered Larwood autocratic in admitting and expelling members. In August 1749 the Grand Jury "presented" CHARLES WESLEY, John (sic) Larwood, and seven others to be of ill fame, vagabonds and disturbers of the peace, and fit to be deported. Larwood became involved in the breach of 1754, and took and repaired the Presbyterian Meeting House in Zoar Street, Southwark, and settled there as an Independent minister. He died of fever in November, 1755, and Wesley buried him, commenting that he was "deeply convinced of unfaithfulness and yet hoping to find mercy."

V. E. VINE

LAS CRUCES, NEW MEXICO, U.S.A., St. Paul's United Methodist Church. The city of Las Cruces was founded in 1840 on the lower Rio Grande River, near El Paso, Texas, but Methodism here, according to a local historian, dates back to 1873 "when itinerant preachers rode into the dusty little town and preached to the few Anglo inhabitants." THOMAS HARWOOD, superintendent of the New Mexico Mission, recorded the date as "in October, about the 20th."

Hendrix M. E. Church, South, was built about 1880 by a twenty-family congregation under leadership of a layman, Judge R. L. Young. This building at times also served Presbyterians, Christians, Disciples, Baptists, and Episcopalians, some of whom joined the Methodists for Sunday school, with an average attendance of thirty-five.

In the early days the irrigated valley lands brought in settlers to produce cotton, fruits, and livestock with consequent prosperity for the church. Old Hendrix was razed in 1912 and replaced by St. Paul's, which served till 1965, when offices, church school rooms, fellowship hall, and kitchen were added as well as a new sanctuary which, with supplementary facilities, can seat more than 1,000. A great narthex window, thirty-five feet high and sixteen feet wide, depicts sword and Bible with the inscription, *Spiritus Gladius*. Other art windows illustrate the lives of St. Paul and John Wesley, and the development of Methodism.

In 1950 St. Paul's donated land and supplied a membership nucleus for the University Church. Its parish is associated with the New Mexico State University of Agriculture, Engineering, and Science.

St. Paul's has been served by thirty-three pastors since 1888 (James W. Weems), to the present (Robert M. Templeton, Jr., 1967). Membership reported in 1970 was 1,688.

LELAND D. CASE

LAS VEGAS, NEVADA, U.S.A. Methodism is strongly established in the internationally publicized city of Las Vegas, whose population exceeded 124,000 in 1970. Renowned for its desert climate, legalized gaming resorts, and nearby atomic experiments, Las Vegas is also an important center for air travel, national defense, conventions, education (Southern Nevada University), and natural wonders, being a gateway to Grand Canyon, Bryce Canyon, Zion Park, Hoover Dam, Lake Mead, Colorado River, Death Valley and ghost towns of a bygone mining era.

When the railroad came through in 1905, the first organization completed in the fledgling community was the Methodist Church, begun in a tent before the town was chartered. Official minutes of the Nevada Mission of the M. E. Church, Sept. 3, 1905, said, "This is a great country. We have entered it. We will stay." The first appointed pastor was J. W. Bain. Later Las Vegas and Clark County were assigned to the SOUTHERN CALIFORNIA-ARIZONA CONFERENCE with headquarters in LOS ANGELES.

Las Vegas Methodism celebrated its fiftieth anniversary with unusual community response in 1955, the historical statement being prepared by Fred J. Wilson. At that time a church sanctuary was erected for the newly formed Griffith Church, a memorial to E. W. Griffith, pioneer merchant and the first Las Vegas Sunday school superintendent. Ten years later, his son Robert Griffith was cited by Bishop GERALD KENNEDY as Conference Layman of 1965 and presented the Distinguished Layman's Award. As part of the sixtieth anniversary celebration, the Methodist Foundation of Southern Nevada was begun to aid in church extension. In 1970 there were five United Methodist churches in Las Vegas with a combined membership of 3,505.

DONALD R. O'CONNOR

LASKEY, VIRGINIA MARIE DAVIS (1900-   ), American missionary executive and president of the Woman's Division of the BOARD OF MISSIONS of The United Methodist Church, was born in Columbia County near Magnolia, Ark., on Jan. 12, 1900. She was the daughter of Virgil Montrey and Marie (Ansley) Davis. She studied at Newcomb College, New Orleans, La., 1917-21, received a B.A. degree from SOUTHERN METHODIST UNIVERSITY in 1922, and took post-graduate at Columbia University, 1922-23. On March 19, 1925, she married Glenn Eugene Laskey, a petroleum geologist, and their daughter is Ann Marie (Mrs. Howard Cecil Kilpatrick, Jr.). For a time Mrs. Laskey taught in the Ruston (Louisiana) High School. She joined the M. E. Church, South in 1915 and became president of the WOMAN'S SOCIETY OF CHRISTIAN SERVICE of the LOUISIANA CONFERENCE, 1945-53; and was the recording secretary of the South Central Jurisdiction of W.S.C.S., 1953-56. She has been a member of the Board of Missions of The Methodist

Church since 1956, and in 1964 became president of the Woman's Division of the Board of Missions. Mrs. Laskey has also served as a member of the executive committee of the American Section of the WORLD METHODIST COUNCIL, 1965. She was a delegate to the GENERAL CONFERENCE of 1948 and '52, and to the WORLD METHODIST CONFERENCE, Oslo, Norway, 1961. She served upon the Board of Directors of the Lincoln Parish, Louisiana Foundation, 1950-60; is a trustee of SUE BENNETT COLLEGE; CENTENARY COLLEGE, where she was awarded the degree of L.H.D. in 1967; the ST. PAUL SCHOOL OF THEOLOGY; SCARRITT COLLEGE; and PFEIFFER COLLEGE. Her home is in Ruston, La. In May 1968 the library at Scarritt College was named in her honor, the Virginia Davis Laskey Library.

Who's Who in America, Vol. 34.
Who's Who in The Methodist Church, 1966.   N. B.H.

LATCH, EDWARD GARDINER (1901-   ), American pastor and chaplain in the Congress of the United States, was born in Philadelphia, Pa., Jan. 14, 1901, the son of William J. and Caroline (Lockhart) Latch. He was educated at DICKINSON COLLEGE (A.B., 1921; A.M., 1925; D.D., 1944); DREW UNIVERSITY, (B.D., 1924); AMERICAN UNIVERSITY (L.H.D.).

On March 1, 1926, he married Maria Vandervies, and they had one daughter and one son.

Joining the BALTIMORE CONFERENCE of the M. E. Church in 1922, his appointments were: Vienna, Oakton, Va., 1925-28; Arlington, Va., 1928-32; Chevy Chase, Md., 1932-41; Metropolitan Memorial, WASHINGTON, D. C., 1941-67. He was appointed Chaplain of the U. S. House of Representatives in 1966, and was elected Chaplain in 1967.

Dr. Latch was a delegate to the WORLD METHODIST CONFERENCE in 1951, 1956, and 1961. He has been a trustee of Dickinson College, American University, WESLEY THEOLOGICAL SEMINARY, Sibley Memorial Hospital, and Ocean Grove Camp Meeting Association.

Under his guidance the Metropolitan Church grew from 624 members to more than 3,100, making it today the largest Methodist church in Washington, D. C.

In retirement Dr. Latch continues to live in Washington.

Who's Who in The Methodist Church, 1966.   JESSE A. EARL

LATHAM, FREER HELEN ROBERTSON (1907-   ), international woman leader of AUSTRALIA, was born in Mullumbimby, New South Wales, on July 4, 1907, the daughter of John Francis and Florence (Norris) Robertson. She was educated at Sydney Teachers Training College, SYDNEY, Australia. She was married to Raymond John Latham on March 24, 1932, and their children are John Granville and Helen (Mrs. Fenton George Sharpe).

Mrs. Latham was President of the WORLD FEDERATION OF METHODIST WOMEN, 1961-66; President Emeritus and member of the Executive Committee of the World Federation of Methodist Women, 1966-71; Area Vice-President for Australasia of the World Federation of Methodist Women, 1956-1961; and Vice-President of the WORLD METHODIST COUNCIL, 1961-1966. She is on the Executive Committee of the Australasian Federation of Methodist Women; Vice-President and secretary of New South Wales Federation of Methodist Women; Vice-President of New South Wales Executive of Women's Auxiliary to Over-

seas Missions; Secretary of Five Dock Branch of Women's Auxiliary to Overseas Missions. She has been a representative to the National Council of Women; Pan-Pacific and South-East Asian Association; and the United Nations Organization.

LEE F. TUTTLE

LATHBURY, MARY ARTHEMISIA (1841-1913), American hymn writer, whose hymn "Day is Dying in the West" was rated by W. Garrett Horder, the English hymnologist, as "one of the finest and most distinctive hymns of modern times. It deserves to rank with 'Lead, kindly Light,' of Cardinal Newman, for its picturesqueness and allusionness, and above all else for this, that devout souls, no matter what their distinctive beliefs, can through it voice their deepest feelings and aspirations."

Miss Lathbury was born at Manchester, N. Y., on Aug. 10, 1841. She was the daughter of a local Methodist preacher and had two brothers who were ministers of that church. She contributed to periodicals for children and young people, and was one of the editors of the Methodist Sunday School Union of which JOHN H. VINCENT (later bishop) was the secretary. Through him she became associated with the Chautauqua movement—which Bishop Vincent founded—and she became known as the "Laureate of Chautauqua." She founded what she called the "Look Up Legion," based on Edward Everett Hale's four rules of good conduct: "Look up, not down; Look forward, not back; Look out, and not in; And lend a hand." The music for her famous hymn—named "Chautauqua"—was written by W. F. Sherwin in 1877 especially for Miss Lathbury's verses. The hymn has not been especially popular in England, but the tune is deeply fixed in American church life so that, as Robert G. McCutchan put it, " 'Day is dying in the west' and the tune *Chautauqua* have become synonymous in the American mind."

Since this hymn contains only two stanzas, or divisons, other writers have attempted to lengthen it by adding other verses. However, one of the brothers of Miss Lathbury, who held the copyright after his sister's death, refused to allow the hymn to be used in the *Methodist Hymnal* of 1930-34 unless the exact words Miss Lathbury wrote and them only should be printed. Miss Lathbury, who never married, died in East Orange, N. J., on Oct. 20, 1913.

R. G. McCutchan, *Our Hymnody*. 1937.   N. B. H.

LATHERN, JOHN (1831-1905), Canadian minister, was born at New Shield House, Cumberland, England, July 13, 1831. Educated at Alston Grammar School and as a mining engineer, he volunteered in 1855 to become a Wesleyan missionary. He was received on probation by the Conference of Eastern British America and stationed in Fredericton. Ordained in 1859, he served on various circuits for twenty-seven years.

In 1886 he was appointed editor of *The Wesleyan*, and in 1895 he returned to circuit work in Dartmouth. In 1899 he became a supernumerary and lived in Halifax until his death.

Honored with a D.D. by MOUNT ALLISON UNIVERSITY in 1884, he held many eminent positions in the church. He was elected president of the Nova Scotia Conference in 1881; and was a delegate to many General Conferences. He was a regent of Mount Allison University from 1891 until his death.

He published a number of books and pamphlets, among which are *A Macedonian Cry; Baptisma, Exegetical and Controversial;* and the *Institute Lectures—Cromwell, Havelock, Cobden, and English Reformers.*

D. W. Johnson says of him: "As a preacher he stood in the front rank. His intellectual powers were of an high order, and whilst a devoted Methodist, he belonged to all the churches and was a most ardent advocate of Christian unity."

D. W. Johnson, *Eastern British America.* 1924.
T. W. Smith, *Eastern British America.* 1890.   E. A. BETTS

LATIN AMERICA CENTRAL CONFERENCE was a Central Conference of The United Methodist Church composed of the annual conferences of that church in Central and South America. It met quadrennially to govern its affairs and elect bishops. The conference was proposed in a memorial from CHILE to the GENERAL CONFERENCE of the M. E. Church of 1920 and was authorized by that General Conference in 1924. This Central Conference was a development from the old South America Annual Conference.

The Latin America Central Conference was organized at a session in Panama City, April 3-13, 1924. It included work of the M. E. Church in ARGENTINA, BOLIVIA, CHILE, COSTA RICA, PANAMA, PERU, URUGUAY, and at that time MEXICO. Twenty-two ministers, seven laymen, and four laywomen were members. The second session, also held in Panama, took place April 9-14, 1928. This session asked the General Conference for power to elect and consecrate its own bishops and proposed that the bishops should be national ministers, two in number in order to better administer its vast territory. By the third session, held in Santiago de Chile, Feb. 6-14, 1932, the request had been granted. The conference, however, asked for the return of the beloved North American bishop, GEORGE A. MILLER. It then elected as the first national bishop, JUAN E. GATTINONI, pastor of Central Church, BUENOS AIRES.

The tenure of national bishops was established as a term episcopacy of four years. A bishop could be re-elected, but no one could be elected bishop if more than sixty-five years of age. Bishops elected in 1932 and 1936 were consecrated at M. E. General Conferences in the United States the same years. Since 1940 bishops were consecrated at the sessions of the Central Conference itself.

After the second session, Mexico withdrew from the Central Conference in order to organize in 1930 the autonomous church of Mexico, made up of former work of the M. E. Church and M. E. Church, South. The South American annual and provisional annual conferences thereupon formed two areas. The River Plate Area consisted of Argentina, Uruguay, and Bolivia; the Pacific Area consisted of Chile, Peru, Panama, and Costa Rica.

The Latin America Central Conference continued to meet every four years in the principal cities of both areas: Buenos Aires, MONTEVIDEO, LIMA, COCHABAMBA, and SANTIAGO de Chile. In 1966 it reported a membership of thirty-five ministers and thirty-five laymen, all of whom were, of course, elected by their respective annual conferences.

The Latin America Central Conference came to an end as it held its last meeting in Santiago, Chile, Jan. 27—Feb. 6, 1969. Its delegates and the conference itself had decided to disband as a Central Conference of The United Methodist Church, since its component annual conferences were granted permission by the U.M.C. to go into, and become autonomous churches, if and as they could. They did decide to do this at the 1965 meeting, adopting measures permitting the separate conferences in the different countries to become autonomous churches; and at the same time, organizing themselves together with Mexico and CUBA into the Council of Latin American Evangelical Methodist Churches, (Consejo de Iglesias Evangelicas Metodistas de America Latina) commonly referred to as CIEMAL. This Central Conference of 1969 saw the retirement of Bishop SANTE U. BARBIERI and Bishop PEDRO ZOTTELE. In their places it elected FEDERICO PAGURA and RAIMONDO A. VALENZUELA, each for a four-year term.

The Chile Conference, being ready for autonomy, organized itself into an autonomous Methodist Church in the Santiago meetings and elected as its superintendent Bishop Valenzuela. The Central Conference itself assigned Bishop Pagura to Panama and Costa Rica, and requested that the bishops of The United Methodist Church provide episcopal supervision for the other Latin American countries involved which had not as yet been able to organize as autonomous churches.

E. S. Bucke, *History of American Methodism.* 1964.
                                        ADAM F. SOSA

LATIN AMERICA, COMMITTEE ON COOPERATION IN, was an agency for coordination of mission work conducted in Latin America by boards of missions based in North America. It lasted from 1913 until 1965, when its work was assigned to the Division of Overseas Missions of the NATIONAL COUNCIL OF CHURCHES, U.S.A.

Latin America was excluded from the agenda of the Edinburgh Missionary Conference of 1910 on the ground that Latin America, at least nominally, was already Christian. However, the secretaries of boards having work there held two meetings during the Edinburgh conference and agreed to hold a conference to do for Latin America what Edinburgh had done for the rest of the world. A committee was appointed, including Samuel Guy Inman, later to become secretary of the Committee on Cooperation in Latin America; and H. C. TUCKER, Methodist missionary to BRAZIL.

In 1913 a committee of the Foreign Missions Conference of North America convened a Conference on Latin America in New York, and at its conclusion a continuation committee was set up, called the Committee on Cooperation in Latin America. Members were from five United States denominations, including the M. E. Church and M. E. Church, South. Later the committee was expanded, and in 1914 it was decided to hold the Congress on Christian Work in Latin America. This took place in PANAMA in 1916 and is commonly known as the Panama Congress.

The congress was the first great meeting of Evangelicals to be held in that area, and it gave impetus to the development of Protestant missions in Latin America. It also served to arouse interest of churches in the United States. At the close of the congress, the Committee on Cooperation in Latin America was made permanent, and headquarters were established in New York.

The committee dealt with some of the major issues raised by the congress, including adequate occupation of territory, comity agreements, Christian literature, and education.

In 1919 the committee established a Spanish language magazine, *La Nueva Democracia,* which continues to the present. In the same year the committee stimulated the broadening of Colegio Ward in BUENOS AIRES, Argentina, from a Methodist institution into a joint work with the Disciples of Christ. The Evangelical Union Seminary of Puerto Rico (Seminario Evangelico de Puerto Rico) was founded in 1919 with six mission boards cooperating. The committee fostered the International Faculty of Theology and Social Sciences in Buenos Aires, which later developed into the Union Theological Seminary (FACULTAD EVANGELICA DE TEOLOGIA).

Prior to formation of the CCLA, there was not a single union paper, school, or coordinating agency in any country of Latin America. The CCLA fostered national committees on cooperation, many of which later developed into National Christian Councils.

Methodist leadership in the CCLA during its early years incuded Tucker, FRANK MASON NORTH, Harry Farmer, RALPH E. DIFFENDORFER, and THOMAS S. DONOHUGH. WADE CRAWFORD BARCLAY led a project to create and publish a church-school curriculum known as *Curso Hispano-Americano,* and under Barclay a Conference on Christian Literature—the first of its kind—was held in Mexico City in 1941. GONZALO BAEZ-CAMARGO, Methodist of Mexico, served as secretary of the CCLA's Committee on Christian Literature and organized a curriculum conference at MONTEVIDEO in 1949.

Subsequent to the Panama Congress, the committee sponsored missionary conferences at Montevideo, Uruguay, in 1925, and at Havana, CUBA, in 1929.

Throughout its life the CCLA conducted many surveys, of which two are noteworthy here: One requested in 1919 in the West Indies, led to formation of the Board for Christian Work in Santo Domingo by the Methodist, Presbyterian, and United Brethren Churches; a study of ECUADOR in 1943 led to formation in 1945 of the United Andean Indian Mission, with the Evangelical United Brethren as one of four participants.

In its later years the committee gave up many of its functions to the churches and Evangelical Councils of Latin America. With the formation of the National Council of Churches of Christ in the U.S.A. in 1950, the CCLA became a part of the Council's Division of Foreign Missions. It retained its identity within the Council until re-structure in 1965, when the CCLA was discontinued and its responsibilities assigned to the Division of Overseas Ministries.

W. Stanley Rycroft, "The Committee on Cooperation in Latin America" (unpublished ms., translated from article in Spanish in *El Predicador Evangelico,* located in office of the National Council of Churches, New York).   EDWIN H. MAYNARD

LATIN AMERICAN EVANGELICAL BOARD OF MISSIONS

is a missionary-sending board organized first by Methodists of Central and South America, and now representing both Methodists and Waldensians.

In 1960, prior to the GENERAL CONFERENCE of The Methodist Church, several delegates from the Latin American countries met with Bishop SANTE UBERTO BARBIERI to discuss the idea of forming a Latin American Board of Missions. The idea was carried back to their home churches, and in October of that year, on the occasion of the LATIN AMERICAN CENTRAL CONFERENCE (with delegates also attending from the autonomous Methodist churches of MEXICO and BRAZIL, and also from CUBA), the board was officially constituted.

The board engaged in some exploratory investigation and decided to begin work in ECUADOR. It was felt that the witness to the Gospel was weakest in this nation. It is true that work was being carried on by several denominations or independent missionary boards, but that such work was limited by the origin and nature of these groups —mostly representing "nonhistorical" or "conservative evangelical" groups—as well as by the fact that the emphasis was primarily on work among the Indians. It was felt that there was a deep need for a strong evangelical witness among other sectors of the society, particularly those who, by reason of their relatively advantaged social position, constituted the leadership groups with influence and authority in society.

Further exploration and consultation were carried on by the board in Ecuador. It was decided not to start a Methodist Church there, but rather to work through the denominations already present, wherever cooperation should prove to be possible. A relationship was established with the United Evangelical Church of Ecuador, which was emerging as the result of consultations between the United Andean Indian Mission, the mission of the Church of the Brethren, and the Evangelical Covenant Church (though the last-named dropped out before the united church was formed).

In 1964 Bishop ALEJANDRO RUIZ of Mexico undertook responsibility for finding a couple to initiate this cooperative work, and in 1965 Dr. and Mrs. ULISES HERNANDEZ arrived in Ecuador to represent the Latin American Board of Missions. This couple, joining forces with the United Evangelical Church, has devoted its time to the training of the ministry, strengthening the Christian education program, and evangelism. The board in 1967 was considering sending another couple.

In 1962 the Waldensian Church showed interest in forming a part of the Latin American Methodist Board of Missions. Therefore the word "Evangelical" was substituted for "Methodist" in the name.

CARLOS T. GATTINONI

LATIN AMERICAN EVANGELICAL CHRISTIAN EDUCATION COMMISSION (CELADEC: Comision Evangelica Latino Americana de Educacion Cristiana) is an interdenominational body that serves Methodist churches of Latin America, and to which Methodists have contributed financial support and leadership.

The commission states as its purpose to serve Protestant churches in all of the Americas except in the United States and CANADA, and "to help the churches of Latin America in the fulfillment of their mission of proclaiming the Gospel through Christian education."

CELADEC was founded in October 1962, by the action of councils of federations of churches and, where they do not exist, by individual denominations. Membership is on the same basis for all, and the Methodist churches of all Spanish- and Portuguese-speaking countries of Central and South America are related to CELADEC.

In turn, CELADEC serves as a regional grouping in affiliation with the World Council of Christian Education and Sunday School Association, which gives technical and financial aid to some of its projects. It also enjoys the sponsorship and financial assistance of the Latin America Department of the Division of Overseas Ministries of the

NATIONAL COUNCIL OF the CHURCHES of Christ in the U.S.A.

A triennial Assembly, made up of delegates from member bodies, governs CELADEC. An executive committee, elected by the Assembly, meets once a year. Gerson A. Meyer of Brazil has been general secretary since the organization of CELADEC. First chairman of the executive committee and presiding officer was RAIMUNDO VALENZUELA of CHILE, who was succeeded in January 1967, by FEDERICO PAGURA of ARGENTINA. The territory that CELADEC serves is divided into five regions, each with a secretary.

Specific tasks undertaken may be divided roughly into two categories: (1) the development of curriculum and occasional teaching materials, and (2) the training of leaders for Christian education. Reasoning that traditional materials, which presume a high level of education, cannot reach some eighty percent of the population, CELADEC makes extensive use of audiovisuals and drama.

CELADEC sponsors a series of regional study seminars and held a continental curriculum conference in 1968.

In the area of leadership training, CELADEC sponsored a conference in Alajuela, COSTA RICA, in 1964 to celebrate the centennial of Christian education in Latin America. Seventeen countries were represented.

In 1966 ninety percent of CELADEC's budget was contributed by churches in the United States through the National Council of Churches, with The Methodist Church a major contributor. The churches of Latin America are expected to increase their portion of the support in due time.

RAYMOND A. VALENZUELA

LATIN AMERICAN EVANGELICAL METHODIST CHURCHES, COUNCIL OF (Consejo de Iglesias Evangelicas Metodistas de America Latina), known briefly as CIEMAL, is an organization formed at SANTIAGO, Chile, Jan. 27-Feb. 6, 1969. The formation of this new regional body is considered an epochal step in South American Methodism, and also in that of MEXICO and CUBA since the autonomous churches of these lands joined with CHILE, ARGENTINA, URUGUAY, BOLIVIA, PERU, PANAMA, COSTA RICA, and BRAZIL to form CIEMAL.

This organization move was made pursuant to the authorization given to the former members of the Latin America Central Conference to become autonomous churches. The Chile Conference took advantage of this to organize itself into the Methodist Church of Chile (Iglesia Metodista de Chile) during this series of meetings.

This was the first of seven autonomous churches scheduled to come into being if this should prove possible and expedient during the 1968-72 quadrennium. Although the churches in these seven countries would no longer be organically related to The United Methodist Church in the United States, they will have a close relationship with fraternal and other ties just as does the church in Brazil, Mexico and Cuba.

This organizational meeting in Santiago immediately followed and was based upon the last meeting of the Latin America Central Conference. That conference among its last actions recognized the formal retirement of Bishop SANTE U. BARBIERI, who had served the BUENOS AIRES Area for twenty years; and that of Bishop PEDRO ZOTTELE of the Santiago Area who had been elected in 1962. Taking the places of these were two new bishops elected by the Latin America Central Conference, FEDERICO PAGURA, 45, who had been professor of pastoral counseling and chaplain at the Union Theological Seminary in Buenos Aires (who was assigned to head the Methodist work in Panama and Costa Rica); and RAIMONDO A. VALENZUELA, 53, a Christian education executive and United States missionary to Cuba, who following his election was assigned to head the new Methodist Church of Chile.

CIEMAL marks a positive and definite linkage of the Methodists in these ten Latin American countries in a single body. In setting up CIEMAL, the constituting assembly specified that it would be a non-legislative, non-executive body, reserving the functions of legislation and administration to the several Churches comprising it. The purposes, as defined by the organizing leaders, are on co-ordinated planning, strategy, and programming; mutual support, and depth of relationships. As one delegate put it, "We seek to preserve the autonomy of each church, but to have a strong nexus for interdependence and mutual support."

The policy and work of CIEMAL will be determined by its General Assembly, which will meet every five years. Between Assemblies, the work will be in the hands of an eleven-member Directive Committee, comprising one representative from each country, and the president of the Latin American College of General Superintendents (all bishops, presidents, and other heads of churches). The president of the College in 1969 was Bishop ALEJANDRO RUIZ of the Methodist Church of Mexico.

The Directive Committee for the next five years, elected by the constituting assembly, it is noted, have laymen as all three of its officers. The chairman is EDUARDO GATTINONI, publisher from Buenos Aires; the vice-chairman, Mrs. Celia Hernandez, Women's Society leader from Mexico; and the secretary, Gerson Rodrigues, educator from Bauru, Brazil.

The constituting assembly drafted a "Message to the Methodist Churches of Latin America" which emphasized hope, the need for change, ecumenism and the place of youth.

At this writing it appears that the membership of CIEMAL will be expanded to include the METHODIST CHURCH IN THE CARIBBEAN AND THE AMERICAS. This comprises British Methodist-related churches in Jamaica, Haiti, and other Caribbean islands, Central America and Guiana. The constituting assembly invited the Church of the Caribbean and the Americas to join in its organization, and that Church's president, HUGH SHERLOCK of ANTIGUA, attending the assembly, expressed the view that the invitation would be accepted.

CIEMAL has set up a JUDICIAL COUNCIL along the lines of that of The United Methodist Church, and laid out broad guidelines for common planning and action in education, social action, mission, evangelism and other program areas. The nine-member Judicial Council is representative of all Latin America and will have authority to adjudicate not only actions of CIEMAL but also to handle judicial matters of the churches themselves where this is desired and so enacted. The Methodist Church of Chile delegated such authority to the Judicial Council at its organizing conference.

N. B. H.

LATIN AMERICAN METHODIST WOMEN, CONFEDERATION OF, is an organization representing women in the countries of Latin America. The confederation was founded in 1938 under leadership of Lena Knapp (now Mrs. John Haynes) and Mrs. CARLOS GATTINONI. The purpose is to unite the Latin American Methodist women to do together things they could not do so effectively in each country alone. This has included the support of missionaries, publication of study books, missionary texts and bulletins, and the exchange of ideas.

The confederation has held a Congress every four years: 1942 in BUENOS AIRES, ARGENTINA; 1946 in SANTIAGO, CHILE; 1950 in MONTEVIDEO, URUGUAY; 1955 in LIMA, PERU; 1959 in RIO DE JANEIRO, BRAZIL; and 1963 in MEXICO City; the seventh in COCHABAMBA, BOLIVIA, in January, 1967.

The presidents have been Maria Aguirre of Chile, Mrs. Juanita R. Balloch (wife of Bishop BALLOCH), Mrs. Bessie Archer Smith (Mrs. EARL M. SMITH) of Uruguay, Mrs. Esther Moore Saenz of Argentina, and Mrs. Teresa P. Araneta of Peru.

The confederation began supporting missionaries in 1942, after its first Congress, when Adelina Gattinoni became the first missionary. The number was increased to two and, in October 1955, to three. They were serving in 1966 in Chile, Bolivia, and Peru. Missionaries who have served have been Margarita Caminos, an Argentine to Bolivia; Dorcas Courvoesier, an Argentine to Bolivia; Berta Garcia, a Bolivian to Bolivia; Rosa Sherlian, an Argentine to Bolivia; Teresa Silvera, a Uruguayan to Bolivia; Maria Glicinia Fernandez, a Brazilian to Peru; Francisca Cariqueo, a Chilean to Chile.

From 1951 to 1966 the confederation published eight study books. The group has also published mission study texts each year since 1953, translating the books published in the United States by Friendship Press of New York. The work has been done with the backing of the COMMITTEE ON COOPERATION IN LATIN AMERICA, and is used in eight countries. This is the only translation of Friendship Press texts into other languages.

Since 1955 the *Confederation Bulletin* has served women's work in all the Latin American countries where there is Methodist work, functioning as a channel for interchange of ideas. Editors have been Mrs. Evodia C. Silva of Mexico, Mrs. Sylvia P. Huaroto of Peru, and Mrs. Rubi Rodriguez Etchagoyen of Argentina.

Pamphlets are issued on subjects such as prayer and Family Week. Prayer calendars have been published at times by the Spiritual Life Department.

The confederation has enjoyed the support and cooperation of the Woman's Division of the BOARD OF MISSIONS of The Methodist Church in the U.S.A.

BESSIE ARCHER SMITH

LATIN MISSION, located in south FLORIDA, was organized by the M. E. Church, South in 1930. It grew out of work among Cuban refugees and Italian immigrants who resided mostly in Key West, Miami, and Tampa. H. B. Someillan, a young preacher in the Florida Conference, vowed to devote his life to a ministry among the Cubans. His special service began in 1894 in Ybor City, a Latin quarter in Tampa. Someillan had some help from the Woman's Missionary Council of the denomination.

In time some seven churches were organized in the three cities mentioned. Someillan's work laid the foundations for a Latin District which the FLORIDA CONFERENCE formed in 1913. In 1917, the district reported six churches, 481 church members, and 1,212 Sunday school pupils.

In 1930, the Latin District was elevated to the status of a mission. At that time the number of churches still stood at six, but the total church membership had fallen to 320. Gradually the number of members increased. When the Latin Mission was absorbed by the Florida Conference in 1943, there were five churches and 622 members.

General Minutes, MES, TMC.
E. S. Bucke, *History of American Methodism.* 1964.
ALBEA GODBOLD

LA TROBE, BENJAMIN (1725-1786), British Moravian, was born in DUBLIN on April 19, 1725. A Baptist of Huguenot stock, he was influenced by JOHN CENNICK when a student in Dublin. La Trobe became a Moravian minister and did much to make Moravianism understood by members of other churches. Friendly with CHARLES WESLEY, he took part in the abortive negotiations for union of MORAVIANS and Methodists in 1785-86. He greatly influenced Samuel Johnson and visited him on his death bed. With AUGUST SPANGENBERG he compiled an authoritative survey of Moravian doctrine. La Trobe became president of the Brethren's Society for the Furtherance of the Gospel, and warmly supported Count ZINZENDORF's ecumenical ideas. He died in London on November 29, 1786.

W. C. Addison, *The Renewed Church of the United Brethren.* London, 1932.
E. Langton, *History of the Moravian Church.* 1956.
C. W. Towlson, *Moravian and Methodist.* 1957.
C. W. TOWLSON

LATVIA. (See BALTIC STATES.)

LAVINGTON, GEORGE (1684-1762), British critic of Methodism and Moravianism, was born at Mildenhall, Wiltshire, Jan. 8, 1684, and was educated at Winchester and Oxford. He was appointed chaplain to George I and, in 1746, Bishop of Exeter. A faked pastoral charge, representing him as a friend of Methodism, provoked his *Enthusiasm of the Methodists and Papists Compar'd* (Parts I-III, 1749-51). To this catalog of Methodist extravagance, which ignored or misunderstood the good results of the revival, replies were published by GEORGE WHITEFIELD and VINCENT PERRONET (1749) and by JOHN WESLEY (Feb. 1, 1750; Dec. 1751). Lavington's most interesting argument was that Methodist conversion experiences could be explained in physical and psychological terms; he rejected Wesley's claim that they were the work of the Holy Spirit. Later Wesley records a visit to Exeter Cathedral on Aug. 29, 1762, when he was "pleased to partake of the Lord's Supper with my old opponent, Bishop Lavington." Lavington died soon after, on Sept. 13, 1762.

R. Polwhele, ed., *The Enthusiasm of Methodists and Papists Compared* (reprint, including life of Lavington; London: Whitaker, 1820, 1833).
J. Wesley, *Letters,* iii, 259-71, 295-331.
Frank Baker, "Bishop Lavington and the Methodists," *Proc. Wes. Hist. Soc.,* xxxiv, 37-42.
HENRY RACK

LAW, WILLIAM (1686-1761), British Nonjuror and mystic, was born at King's Cliffe, Northamptonshire, and was educated at Cambridge. He refused the oath of allegiance to the Hanoverian King George I, and resigned his fellowship at Emmanuel (1716). After some years in the household of Edward Gibbon (grandfather of the historian) at Putney, Law retired to King's Cliffe (1740) and died there, April 9, 1761.

JOHN WESLEY read Law's *Practical Treatise upon Christian Perfection* (1726) and *A Serious Call* (1728) at Oxford, and began to pursue "inward holiness" by self-discipline as Law recommended. By 1738 he had adopted the Moravians' views of salvation by faith, and attacked Law for failing to teach this. From the 1740's Law developed a mystical theology based on the writings of Jakob Böhme (d. 1624). Wesley attacked Law (1756) for departing from Scripture by teaching unconditional salvation for all, based on a divine spark in every man; for his weak doctrine of the atonement; and for his disparagement of the means of grace. Although Law opposed eighteenth-century rationalism, Wesley believed that his system, by contradicting the "Scriptural" scheme of salvation, destroyed the Christian case against Deism.

E. W. Baker, *A Herald of the Evangelical Revival*. 1948.
J. B. Green, *John Wesley and William Law*. 1948.
Law, *Collected Works*. 9 vols.; ed., Richardson, 1792; G. Moreton, 1893.
J. H. Overton, *William Law: Non-Juror and Mystic*. 1881.
C. Walton, *Notes and Materials for an Adequate Biography of William Law*. 1854.   HENRY RACK

LAW, METHODIST (U.S.A.). The ruling law of The United Methodist Church is found in the *Book of Discipline* of that and the other respective Methodist Churches. The *Discipline* contains and sets forth first the constitutional law of the church. Also certain JUDICIAL COUNCIL decisions interpreting the Constitution may be referred to in the published decisions of that body.

Constitutional law may only be changed by constitutional processes. This calls for the joint action of the GENERAL CONFERENCE and of the members of all the annual conferences who must agree to any constitutional change by a two-thirds majority of those "present and voting" both in the General Conference and in the several annual conferences. In the event an ARTICLE OF RELIGION or a standard of belief is to be changed, it requires a three-fourths vote of the electorate in the annual conferences following a two-thirds General Conference vote recommending the change.

Constitutional law is interpreted by the Judicial Council according to processes outlined in the Constitution, and by the rules of procedure developed by the Judicial Council itself.

The larger part of the *Book of Discipline* is in the form of statutory law which may be written, revised, amended or changed at the instance of any General Conference acting within its normal powers. A majority vote in most instances suffices to alter or write statutory law for The United Methodist Church.

Statutory law itself may be divided into *administrative law* dealing with the processes and procedures of the organizational work of the church in all its departments; and *trial law* or the procedures which are to be followed when a church member—whether a bishop, elder, local preacher, supply preacher, deaconess or regular church member—is to be tried for a violation of some phase of Methodist discipline. Offenses against the moral law are, of course, the most heinous, and when a person is found

guilty, such person may be expelled from the membership of the church. Disciplinary infractions for maladministration on the part of certain church officers may be tried according to the processes outlined in the *Book of Discipline*, if these offenses are such as to warrant a trial. All matters relating to trial law are carefully prescribed and when followed out according to the law of the church, there is no recourse in the civil law by the person found guilty. Civil authorities in the United States have long taken the position that a church member is bound by the law of his own church, which law he subscribed to upon his admission to that church; if therefore the church follows its own announced procedures in dealing with those who offend against its laws, the civil power refuses to take jurisdiction over the result of such ecclesiastical proceedings.

The *Book of Discipline* containing Methodist law is often held up before judicatory bodies as the "book of law" of The United Methodist Church and referred to in all matters which have to do with its life, teachings, and processes. When any matter touching Methodist rules, regulations, or law is brought before a civil court and the court does take jurisdiction over such matter, the *Book of Discipline* is usually formally presented to the court as authoritative Methodist law.

Parliamentary law also governs Methodist bodies when they meet in session, in order that proceedings may move smoothly but formally in line with accustomed processes which prevail in such bodies. The General Conference has a Committee on Rules which prescribes all such matters, and many annual conferences likewise formally adopt rules for their own procedures. Quite often the rules of the General Conference in so far as they apply are adopted for the governing of annual conferences and of other formal church gatherings. The authoritative Roberts' *Rules of Order* which has established itself as the arbiter in this entire field in America, is usually the basic guide and director in all matters of rule and parliamentary governance in American Methodist bodies.

N. B. H.

LAW AND GOSPEL. The relation of the religion of the Law to the gospel of God's grace is a matter which is important for the understanding of the gospel, and for its spiritually balanced and healthful proclamation. This was a subject of constant controversy in Wesley's time, and there are numerous references in Wesley's work to teachers whom he felt were in error, and replies to attacks made upon his understanding of the gospel. This controversy still goes on today, though stated in somewhat different terms. A note on this matter is therefore necessary for the understanding of Wesley's doctrine, and for its application today.

Historical background. The preparation for the Christian gospel and the Christian Church was the religion of the Old Covenant, the religion of the Law of Moses. The foundation of this Covenant was in the grace of God, in that He had freely set His love upon the Hebrew people, the descendents of Abraham, and chosen them to be His Covenant people (Genesis xii 1-3, xvii 1-8, etc., Deuteronomy iv 32-9, vii 7-9). However, the basis on man's side for the continuance of this Covenant was obedience to God's revealed Law (Exodus xxiv, 3-8, etc). Nevertheless, the idea of faith, and of loving trust in God, was always there as well (Genesis xv 6, Deuteronomy vi 3-7, Habbakuk ii 4). Thus the normal pious Jew loved the Law, regarded the possession of it as the privilege of his nation, and obeyed it gladly (Psalm cxix, etc). In this no formal difference was made between liturgical and ceremonial commandments, such as the law of the Temple, worship, and of unclean meats, and the moral and social commandments, such as justice, truthfulness, humanity, and charity. All these things were the Law of God alike. Thus in the Decalogue some commandments, like those forbidding idolatry and enjoining the Sabbath, are ceremonial; others, like the prohibition of theft and adultery, are moral; whereas the commandment regarding the taking of the name of God in vain is both. It is not possible to draw a sharp distinction between inward and outward commandments, because a sincere worshipper sees an inward meaning symbolized in a religious ceremony. Nevertheless, the more thoughtful and spiritually minded among the Hebrews always contrived to emphasize that God is more concerned with the inward spirit of moral obedience than with the mere performance of customary ritual, no matter how venerable and significant (Psalm xl 6-8, Amos v 21-4, Micah vi 6-8).

Our Lord came as the fitting climax of this tradition. He reverenced and confirmed the religious institutions of Israel as an expression of the will of God (Matthew v 17-19, xxii 2-3, Luke iv 16, John ii 17). He sternly denounced externalism and hypocrisy (Mark vii 5-16, Luke xi 37-42), and He taught that a stricter standard of inward obedience was required in the new age (Matthew v 27-8, Mark x 2-12). The rest of the New Testament substantially answers to this principle. Thus in particular, though St. Paul under controversial pressure to vindicate the proposition that the Gentile Christians do not need to be circumcised, and to adopt the whole religion of the Mosaic Law, can on occasion make rather extreme statements of the antithesis between Law and Gospel (Galatians v 1-4), yet he does assent to the master-proposition that the Law is of divine origin, and good (Romans iii 1-2, vii 12), and it is the due preparation for the Gospel (Galatians iii 23-4). The great essay upon this theme is the Epistle to the Hebrews. Here the institutions of Judaism are displayed as a divinely given foreshadowing of the higher institutions and permanently valid spiritual principles of the Christian religion.

The church followed upon this track, though she was forced to embark upon the traditional distinction between the moral law of the Old Covenant, which is of permanent validity, and the ceremonial law, which was abolished in Christ. This clearly answers to the practical situation as it has existed in the Church. The Church has always reverenced the Jewish Scriptures as Christian Scriptures, not as an account merely of the historical origins of the Christian faith, but as a book authoritative for Christian doctrine, and for the guidance of the devotional and moral life. Nevertheless, the Church did not in point of fact literally obey the Scriptural commandments regarding the sacrifices, the festivals, the law of ceremonial cleanness, and the like. The desire of Christian theology to illustrate so far as possible the parallel between the lower and legal institutions of the Jewish religion, and the higher and spiritual institutions of the Christian religion, led many of the traditional theologians of the Church to describe the Christian faith as "the new Law." Just as, in particular, the Jewish Sabbath was a foretype of the Christian day of worship, so in general the whole institution of Judaism (the Law), was a foretype of the whole Christian institu-

tion. Difficulty which has been felt by some about this phrase illustrates a point of controversy which arose at the Reformation period.

In his effort completely to outlaw the "merit-earning" theology prevalent in many quarters in the mediaeval church, and to emphasize the principles of salvation "by grace *alone*" and "through faith *alone*," Luther fell back upon Paul's rugged antithesis, mentioned above as voiced in some passages, between "Law" and "Grace." It is therefore a characteristic theme of Luther, and of Protestant theology following him, that admission into the Christian Gospel of the religion of law (that is to say, the hope of a man that he may fit himself for God, and win divine favor, by self-imposed effort in obedience to the Law of God), is a radical corruption and a denial of the fundamental principle of salvation by grace alone. Thus "legality" is the opposite quantity to the Gospel. However, this evangelical principle, like other principles, can be perverted by partial and superficial minds into an error. The error in question is that of *antinomianism* (*anti*: "against"; *nomos*: "law"), which is the affirmation that the Christian who is saved by grace, and who walks by faith is on that account released from the duty of obedience to the moral law of God. This clearly is the evangelical principle falling into dangerous unbalance, and into an error of excess.

A fair and balanced reading of Luther makes it plain that he himself was not an antinomian. Yet in some passages in his works there are strong and paradoxical expressions of the antithesis between "law" and "grace" which speak of "the Law" almost as an enemy of "the Gospel." If such passages are isolated from the context they may be interpreted as a substantiation for antinomian doctrine. And some less wise evangelical teachers have at times fallen into this trap of misunderstanding. It may perhaps be said that antinomianism can exist in three degrees. There can be a very mild degree of antinomianism, in theoretical principle only. The believer may profess himself to have escaped altogether from the sphere of *duty* to obey the moral law of God into the Christian "liberty" of freely following the impulse of love. And on the basis of this he may live a strict moral life. Then there may be a moderate practical antinomianism, in which the believer deludes himself that the deep spiritual experience which he can profess, and the many devotional exercises which he enjoys, in some way compound for minor moral failings, in matters of truthfulness, honesty, self-control, or human kindness. Finally there is the outright antinomianism of the "lunatic fringe" of those who affirm that because they are accepted by God through the sole merits of Christ they are in principle free to indulge their vices if they wish. By contrast, it is surely the sound and long-established Christian position that the high purpose of the evangelical experience of salvation by grace is to enable man effectually and from the heart to carry out his unsparing duty of obedience to the moral law of God, sovereign over him, as over all men. The sure guide is that Christ came not to destroy the law, but to fulfill it (Matthew v, 17).

Wesley on the Law and the Gospel. It is plain from everything which he did and wrote that the fully evangelical Wesley, after the ALDERSGATE STREET experience, continued to be every inch the exponent of strict moral discipline. Anything which savored of antinomianism, or which by implication could be used as a religious excuse for moral compromise, was to him anathema. Antinomianism and quietism were to him "Satan's masterpieces," the using of the principles of religion to overthrow religion.

From an early date in 1739 Wesley was troubled in the FETTER-LANE SOCIETY by antinomian and quietist teaching, and it was this issue which caused him to separate from Fetter-lane, and so from the MORAVIANS, on July 20, 1740 (see Journal Nov. 1, 1739—July 23, 1740). Characteristic of the controversy are the notes for June 5, 1740, "I came to London; where finding a general temptation prevail, of leaving off good works, in order to an increase of faith, I began, on Friday the sixth, to expound the Epistle of St. James; the great antidote against this poison:" and for June 23, "I considered the second assertion, that there is but one commandment in the New Testament, viz. 'To believe;' that no other duty lies upon us; and that a believer is not obliged to do anything as commanded. How gross, palpable a contradiction is this to the whole tenor of the New Testament! Every part of which is full of commandments, from St. Matthew to the Revelation!" It was because Wesley had had fragments of Luther thrown at him in this controversy that he later reacted against Luther's *Commentary on Galatians* in a not altogether judicious manner (*Journal*, June 15, 1741). (See FAITH.)

Wesley's systematic teaching on the relation of the Law to the Gospel is largely contained in his *Standard Sermons*, XXIX, "The Original of the Law"; XXX, "The Law Established Through Faith, i"; XXXI, "The Law Established Through Faith, ii"; and also sermon XLIX, "The Lord our Righteousness," and his first and second "Dialogue Between an Antinomian and his Friend." (*Works*, vol. x). A summary of his authoritative teaching may be given from sermons XXIX and XXX. Christ set aside the Jewish ceremonial law, and established the moral law on a better foundation (XXIX 2,3). The moral law was declared to man at the creation, and is the glorious representation of the nature of God (XXIX ii). The law of God is pure (iii 2,3). It is certainly not of the nature of sin, but is the detector of sin (4). The keeping of it works the blessing of man (12). The first great use of the law is to trouble the conscience of man, and to convict him that he is a sinner (iv 1). The second is as a stern schoolmaster of divine punishment, to bring him to penitence (2). The third office of the law, forgotten or denied by many, is to keep the evangelical believer alert in his spiritual discipline (3). It reminds him of the sin yet remaining in his heart, and of the need for keeping close to Christ (4-7). The antinomian is sternly warned for his careless language: "Who art thou then, O man, that 'judgest the law, and speakest evil of the law?'—that rankest it with sin, Satan, and death, and sendest them all to hell together?" (8).

In sermon XXX, those who would abolish the sovereignty of the moral as well as of the Jewish ceremonial law over the believer have a zeal but not according to knowledge (3-6). The most usual way to make void the law through faith is not to preach it at all, as is the case with those deeply mistaken teachers who use the phrase "a preacher of the law" as though it were "a term of reproach, as though it meant little less than an enemy to the gospel" (i 1,2). Free forgiveness through "the sufferings and merits of Christ" is not to be offered to careless and impenitent men, but only to those who through the preaching of the moral law of God know themselves to be in need of forgiveness (3). This approach is the Scriptural and apostolic method (4-11). If the comfort of free forgiveness through the Cross is the only thing which is declared to the congregation, without the constant reminder of the unsparing demands of the moral law of God, the preaching of the Gospel will gradually lose its force (12). "A second way of making void the law through faith is, the teaching that faith supersedes the necessity of holiness" (ii 1). Any teaching is most dangerous which can be understood as implying that inward and outward righteousness of life is in some way less imperatively necessary for the "converted" Christian who lives by evangelical grace than it is for other men (2-4). This error, which is a mistaken reaction against Christian phariseeism, is entirely contrary to Scripture (5-7). Yet the most common way of making void the law is not to teach it, but simply to do it by a careless and easy-going life (iii 1). The evangelical principles ought to make the believer more zealous for right than he was before (2-4).

Wesley then seriously challenges his hearers to compare in detail the manner of their lives previously, when they were struggling outside the evangelical experience, with what it is now after evangelical conversion. Are they as abstemious, contemptuous of show, luxury, fashion, and the praise of this world, as economical of money and time, as austere and plain-spoken, and as careful to avoid gossip and flattery, as they were then? Are they as regular at Church service and private prayer now as they were then, or do they find themselves kept away by "a little business, a visitor, a slight indisposition, a soft bed, a dark or cold morning?" Are they as earnest in speaking to others of Christ? If any believer finds that he has insensibly "let up" on any of these duties since he came to the evangelical experience, he is on spiritually perilous ground (5-8). Clearly for Wesley sanctification and holiness were not emotional experiences, as an alternative to zealous churchmanship and strict morality. They were a life of unsparing devotional and moral discipline, but empowered by the evangelical experience and the indwelling Spirit. Christian liberty is not escape from the law, but power to obey it.

P. Allhaus, *The Divine Command*. Philadelphia, 1966.
W. Andersen, *Law and Gospel*. London and New York, 1961.
C. H. Dodd, *Gospel and Law*. New York, 1951.
W. Elert, *Law and Gospel*. Philadelphia, 1967.
John Fletcher, *Checks to Antinomianism*. New York: Soule and Mason, 1819.
G. A. F. Knight, *Law and Grace*. London, 1962.
W. B. Pope, *Compendium of Christian Theology*. 1880.
A. R. Vidler, *Christ's Strange Work*. London, 1963.
R. Watson, *Theological Institutes*. 1823-26.
J. Wesley, *Standard Sermons*. 1921.   JOHN LAWSON

LAWRENCE, JOHN (1824-1889), American United Brethren clergyman, soldier, jurist, was born in Wayne County, Ind., Dec. 3, 1824. Although educated in public schools with limited academic training, he was considered one of the most brilliant ministers in the Church. For a time he taught public school in northwestern OHIO. Married twice, his first wife died early in his ministry. In 1843 he joined the Sandusky Conference, Church of the United Brethren in Christ, and became a charter member of the Michigan Conference. He served first as a circuit preacher and later as presiding elder.

Lawrence became assistant editor of the *Religious Tele-*

scope in 1850, and two years later the sole editor. He continued in this editorial office until 1864, when he entered the Union Army as chaplain of the 15th U.S. Colored Troops, and later was made a captain of his regiment.

Following the Civil War he was appointed judge of a Freedman's Court, Nashville, Tenn., and afterwards practiced law in that city. He did not return to the active ministerial service.

A. W. Drury wrote, "He [Lawrence] was one of the most brilliant and most successful editors the *Religious Telescope* has had." Following Lawrence's death the Nashville *Daily American* paid him a glowing tribute recounting his many virtues as an attorney and honorable, liberal, patriotic citizen. He was a great writer. Some of his contributions were: *Manual of Rules of Order; History of the Church of the United Brethren in Christ* (2 vol.); *Slavery Question;* and *Plain Thoughts on Secret Societies.* He died in Nashville, Aug. 7, 1889.

A. W. Drury, *History of the UB.* 1924.
Religious Telescope, Aug. 14, 1889.   JOHN H. NESS, SR.

LAWRENCE, KANSAS, U.S.A. **First Church** has a history which parallels the history of the state. The stand of Methodist citizens on the question of slavery in the 1840's caused the name "Methodist" to be practically synonymous with "Free State," and many of the immigrants sent out by the North were Methodists. The first such groups arrived in August and September of 1854, and in November of that year the first Methodist service was held in the "Hay Tent," so-called because it was made of hay. The first sermon was preached by a Methodist minister from MISSOURI. Early in 1855, the Methodist Church was organized as a local society and plans were made for building a stone church but these plans failed to materialize. Meetings were held regularly, however, in homes and other available buildings.

In 1856, a primitive church was erected of rough board sides, canvas roof, dirt floor, and black walnut seats. This building was called "The Tent." It was destroyed by a storm in less than a year. In 1857 a frame building was erected which the Methodists shared with other denominations. It was also used by the city school during the winter. Plans were started in 1862 for a larger church building, but on Aug. 21, 1863, Quantrell and his band of guerillas raided Lawrence, killing and wounding men and ruining buildings. The seats of the little Methodist church were removed and it was used as a morgue. One hundred fifty men were killed, many of them leading Methodists. In spite of this disaster, plans for a new church continued. This red brick building was much larger than its predecessor and it served Lawrence Methodists for twenty-five years. At the laying of the corner-stone in 1864, the *Kansas State Journal* reported, "this ceremony has eclipsed any other occasion in our history as a state."

By 1872 plans were made for a much larger church building which would be the largest and finest west of the Mississippi River outside of ST. LOUIS. Work progressed rapidly until the financial panic of 1873, when all construction stopped for fifteen years. But by 1891 the congregation was able to move into the beautiful stone church which with very few exterior changes is still in use. In 1959 the sanctuary was enlarged and a new heating and air-conditioning system was installed. An addition to the north side for religious education was built in

1962. Thus the church has tried to keep pace with the growth of the times and of the town. Membership in 1970 was 2,193.

BESSIE DAUM

LAWRENCE, MASSACHUSETTS, U.S.A., is situated on the Merrimac River and is a great manufacturing center on the Boston and Maine Railroad, twenty-eight miles from the city of Boston. That part of the city north of the Merrimac River is in the NEW HAMPSHIRE CONFERENCE.

Methodist work in Lawrence began in answer to a request made of the presiding elder, Elihu Scott, at the Methuen, Mass., Quarterly Conference, May 1846, asking that a preacher be sent to Lawrence. At the ensuing annual conference, James L. Slason was sent with a missionary appropriation of $125. There being no place to meet, Charles Barnes on 5 Broadway opened his own home for public worship. A concert hall was later secured. In 1845, L. D. Barrows became pastor with a $200 missionary appropriation and twenty-three members reported. Bridgeman's Hall on Oak Street was then used until a building was erected on the corner of Haverhill and Hampshire Streets, and the basement was finished for dedication March 26, 1848, with Barrows preaching on the theme, "Worship God!"

A second church appearing in 1853 on Garden Street showed a good growth of spiritual interest and the enthusiastic support of the people. The work was continued faithfully and this church had a good deal of evangelistic interest and missionary spirit. A Sunday school was early started on Bodwell Street, and Seth Dawson was superintendent for many years. In 1880 the church known as St. Mark's was organized, and continues to serve today.

Oaklands, in neighboring Methuen, was also a missionary product of the Garden Street Church, where at Cook's Corner, Miss Mary E. Cook had an important part. It later became the scene of growing Italian work with a church building, a pastor, and fifty-four members.

With the influx of French Canadians around Garden Street, a merger of this church was effected with the Haverhill Street Church in 1910. Both David B. Dow and George W. Farmer were appointed to the new Central Church Society. Preliminary plans were then made for a new church edifice. This was built on Haverhill Street opposite from the "Common," under the pastorate of Edwin S. Tasker, beginning in 1912. This church continues its great ministry in the heart of Lawrence.

For several years in the early 1880's a mission Sunday school was conducted by different denominations in a chapel belonging to the Y.M.C.A. of Lawrence, situated on Lake Street in the Arlington section of the city. With most having Methodist leanings, in April 30, 1891 at a meeting called to consider the matter, the presiding elder, George W. Norris of the Dover District, was asked to organize the society into a M. E. Church. This was done and is now St. Paul's. The Vine Street Church came into the New Hampshire Conference by transfer from the German Conference which had work there then.

Cole and Baketel, *New Hampshire Conference.* 1929.
Journal of the New Hampshire Conference.

WILLIAM J. DAVIS

LAWRENCE UNIVERSITY, Appleton, Wisconsin, was founded in 1847, one year before Wisconsin achieved

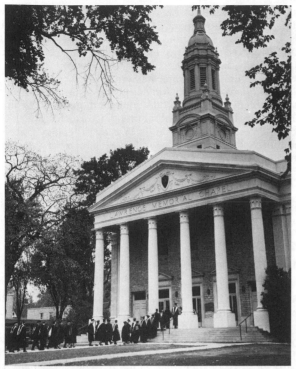

LAWRENCE MEMORIAL CHAPEL

statehood, as a joint effort of the ROCK RIVER CONFERENCE and Amos Adams Lawrence, a Boston merchant with wide philanthropic, educational, and political interests. The present charter makes the institution's forty-two member board of trustees a self-perpetuating body. Its ties with The United Methodist Church are through a board of twelve visitors, six elected by the EAST WISCONSIN Annual CONFERENCE and six elected by the WEST WISCONSIN CONFERENCE. At least nine are alumni members nominated by alumni.

In 1964 Lawrence College and Milwaukee-Downer College merged to form Lawrence University. It is made up of Lawrence College for Men, Downer College for Women, the Conservatory of Music, and the affiliated Institute of Paper Chemistry. A Phi Beta Kappa society was installed in 1914. Degrees offered are the B.A. and B.M. (Music).

JOHN O. GROSS

LAWRY, HENRY HASSALL (1821-1906), New Zealand minister, was born in New South Wales and was educated at KINGSWOOD SCHOOL, England, where he was converted. He became a local preacher and entered business in LONDON. Prompted by filial duty, he came to NEW ZEALAND with his father, WALTER LAWRY, arriving in 1844. In the same year, Henry was received on probation and studied Maori under JAMES BULLER at Tangiteroria.

After teaching at the Wesleyan Native Training Institution in AUCKLAND, he became the first missionary at the Pehiakura Station, and for five years covered a wide area of country around the Manukau Harbor. A second scattered circuit (Waima) undermined his health. He was brought back to Wesley Three Kings College, and in 1874 superannuated.

Subsequently, he served with the Auckland Auxiliary of the BRITISH AND FOREIGN BIBLE SOCIETY. He revised and re-edited a Maori book of services. He acted as interpreter in the Maori land court. He was a man of rich and varied experience, wide reading, and deep spirituality.

W. Morley, *New Zealand.* 1900.   WILLIAM T. BLIGHT

LAWRY, SAMUEL (1854-1933), New Zealand Methodist minister, was born in St. Mabyn, Cornwall, England, in 1854 and came to NEW ZEALAND at the age of eight. For thirty-four years he was a circuit minister, and then in 1911, he became connexional secretary. This position he held for sixteen years. He was secretary of Conference for seven years, and then president in 1904, and again in 1913, on the occasion of Methodist Union.

Steeped in Methodist tradition, thoroughly versed in Methodist polity and procedure, prominent in the philanthropic and social movements of his time, he gave fifty years of devoted service to his church. He died at Christchurch on July 26, 1933.

Minutes of the New Zealand Methodist Conference, 1934.
WILLIAM T. BLIGHT

LAWRY, WALTER (1793-1859), early missionary to AUSTRALIA, TONGA and NEW ZEALAND, was born at Rutheren, Cornwall, England, on Aug. 3, 1793. Converted in early age, he soon began to preach. He was accepted in 1817 as a candidate for the ministry by the Wesleyan Conference in England and was appointed as assistant missionary in NEW SOUTH WALES. He arrived in SYDNEY in May 1818, and became the colleague of SAMUEL LEIGH.

The situation which confronted them was such that they "agreed to live on two meals a day if they could have another missionary and a printing press." Lawry was stationed at Parramatta, and served there with conspicuous success for four years. He then went to Tonga to commence the Friendly Islands Mission. In 1822 the Tongan Islands had been abandoned by the London Missionary Society because of the ferocity of the natives. Lawry worked amongst them until his health compelled him to retire in 1825, when he went back to England.

For nineteen years he remained in English circuit work. He returned to the Southern Hemisphere in 1843, having been appointed General Superintendent of the Wesleyan Missions in New Zealand, and Visitor of those in Polynesia, an office he held for eleven years. He established the Wesleyan Native Training Institution in Auckland and founded Wesley College and Seminary.

In 1854 he retired from the duties of the ministry because of failing health and settled in Parramatta, New South Wales, where he died on March 30, 1859. His diary (as yet unpublished) is a classic description of life in early Australian history.

J. Colwell, *Century in the Pacific.* 1914.
W. Morley, *New Zealand.* 1900.
E. W. Hames, *Walter Lawry and the Wesleyan Mission in the South Seas.* Wesley Historical Society, New Zealand, 1967.
WILLIAM T. BLIGHT

LAWS, CHARLES HENRY (1867-1958), New Zealand minister, was born at Newcastle-upon-Tyne, England, in 1867, and was brought to NEW ZEALAND at the age of seven. He heard the call to the ministry at an early age, and became the leading preacher of the Methodist Church in New Zealand. Mainly through his advocacy, the New

Zealand Conference gained its independence from Aus-
TRALIA.

He insisted on better training for ministers and was
the driving force behind the building of Trinity Theological College and hostel in Auckland (1929). For a period
of eleven years (1920-31) he held the position of principal
of the theological college, first at Dunholme and then at
Trinity College. Earlier, he was secretary of Conference
six times, and president twice—in 1910, and again in
1922. As a leader and administrator he was without peer
and as a preacher he belonged to the very front rank. He
died in Auckland on Feb. 8, 1958.

Wesley Parker, *Rev. C. H. Laws, B.A., D.D., Memoir and
Addresses.* A. H. & A. W. Reed, 1957.   L. R. M. GILMORE

LAWSON, ANNA ELIZABETH (1860-1951), was a life-
long missionary to INDIA representing the WOMAN's
FOREIGN MISSIONARY SOCIETY of the M. E. Church. She
was born in Clio, Iowa, U.S.A., Feb. 2, 1860. At the age
of fourteen, she joined the M. E. Church and decided to
prepare for service in the church at home or abroad. In
1881, she graduated from IOWA WESLEYAN UNIVERSITY
and became a teacher in country schools. She was active
in church work, including teaching Sunday school classes.

In 1885, she went to India as the first missionary from
the Des Moines Branch of the Society. She was appointed
to the girls' orphanage in Bareilly. After furlough, she was
appointed principal of the Methodist Girls' School at
Meerut and remained there throughout her second term,
establishing a reputation as a skillful administrator and a
beloved servant of the church.

In the terrible famine that came late in the nineteenth century, and continued into the twentieth, she was
sent to Phulera, Rajputana, as manager of a home in
which hundreds of orphaned children were gathered. Returning from a second furlough, she was again appointed
to Rajputana and served as principal of the girls' school
in Ajmer. Many girls whose lives were saved by her efforts during the famine were then her students.

Miss Lawson had a flair for business. She early became
treasurer of the funds of the Woman's Foreign Missionary
Society within her annual conference. From her parents'
estate she received a legacy which, through her stewardship, became a great asset of the Kingdom. She purchased
property in the summer resort of Mussoorie, and made
it available for missionary recruits studying Indian languages. She engaged competent instructors to help the
missionaries, and was one of the founders of the Landour
Language School. She also purchased a cottage in Sat Tal
for use by women teachers in Methodist schools, so that
they might have the advantage of a rest away from the
summer heat of the Indian plains, and share in privileges
provided by the Ashrams of E. STANLEY JONES.

In 1951 Iowa Wesleyan University bestowed upon her
the honorary L.H.D. degree. A short time later that year
she passed away, in her ninety-second year.

J. WASKOM PICKETT

LAWSON, JOHN (1909-   ), the editor of the doctrinal articles in the *Encyclopaedia of World Methodism,*
is a minister of the British Methodist Church. He was
born in Leeds, Yorkshire, in which city his family have
been Methodists ever since his great-great-grandfather,
John Lawson, was converted there in 1802. While a

student of agriculture he received a call to preach, and
later entered the separated ministry in 1932, receiving
his theological education at Wesley House, Cambridge.
For twenty years he was employed in the pastoral min-
istry, chiefly in rural circuits in the eastern counties of
England. During this time he wrote his dissertation, *The
Biblical Theology of S. Irenaeus,* and a number of other
books, chiefly on Wesley doctrine and general theology.
Since 1955 he has taught church history, historical the-
ology, Wesley history, and Wesley theology, at the
Candler School of Theology, Emory University, Atlanta,
Georgia, U.S.A. Among his more recent publications is
A Comprehensive Handbook of Christian Doctrine. He is
a firm upholder of the Wesley heritage of doctrine and
devotion, and keenly interested in the movement for
Christian unity.

N. B. H.

LAWSON, MARTIN E. (See JUDICIAL COUNCIL.)

LAWTON, OKLAHOMA, U.S.A., **Centenary Methodist
Church.** Less than two weeks after the official opening
of Lawton, on Aug. 18, 1901, B. F. Gassaway, missionary
to the Kiowa, Comanche, and Apache Indians, organized
the M. E. Church, South, with funds provided by the
Board of Missions of that Church. The lot where the
congregation met was on the corner of 9th and D, and
a canvas tent housed the twenty-four original members.
In November, the charge was made a station and the
new minister, W. F. Dunkle, Sr., arrived, only to have
the tent blown down that very night. Members built a
box structure to house the church within the week and,
shortly, the new church had an organ, active commissions,
an EPWORTH LEAGUE, Women's Societies, a full slate of
officers, and a modest parsonage.

During the pastorate of A. J. Worley (1903-04), a new
frame structure was built and the canvas windows and
homemade seats were replaced by oak pews and stained
glass windows. R. S. Satterfield (1905-06) and the rapidly growing church were host to the Oklahoma Conference
in 1906, an ambitious project considering the fact that the
church had no electricity nor plumbing. Business meetings for the gathering were held in the Ramsey Opera
House. From this conference, Lawton sent forth her first
ordained minister, R. E. L. Morgan.

On Jan. 21, 1907, during the pastorate of A. L. Scales,
the present church site at the corner of 7th and D was
purchased. The church built a recreational building during
the years of World War I in order to better serve the
personnel at Fort Sill. With Wilmore Kendall (1918-21)
plans were made and funds procured for the new Centenary M. E. Church, South, so-named because of funds
used from the Centenary Fund of the Board of Church
Extension (MES) and the War Work Commission of the
same Church. Wilmore Kendall worked actively but,
because of his blindness, requested a new pastor for the
supervision of the actual building, J. D. Salter (1922-24).
The cornerstone was laid in 1922, and in 1924 the ladies
of the church contributed a pipe organ, kitchen and
parlor furnishings, stained glass windows, and church
pews.

In 1939, the Northern and Southern Methodist churches
of the city united and Centenary members took an active
part in the united annual conferences. By 1943, under the
pastorate of Forrest A. Fields (1941-48), all loans on

church properties were paid off. The Second World War gave an added incentive to the youth program, and it expanded to include junior and senior high groups and a flourishing college and career.

During the pastorate of J. W. Browers, Jr., beginning in 1952, the remodeled sanctuary was dedicated, and the old First Presbyterian Church at 8th and D was purchased to be used as the youth building. Under the leadership of Argus Hamilton, Jr. (1960-64), a modern education-office building was completed.

The 1970 membership of 2,874 continues to reflect the pioneer spirit and Christian concern of the original twenty-four men and women who met in August of 1901 with a dream and a commitment to the future.

Clegg and Oden, *Oklahoma.* 1968.
Chronicles of Comanche County, Vol. IV, No. 1, Spring 1968.
ELWYN O. THURSTON

LAY DELEGATION (U.S.A.). In the early days of American Methodism, indeed from 1784 until 1872 in the M. E. Church, and until 1866 in the M. E. Church, South, the Annual and GENERAL CONFERENCES consisted wholly of ministers. There was no representation from the laity of the church, and the great call and demand for "laity rights" and lay representation was a major one in bringing about the organization of the METHODIST PROTESTANT CHURCH. JAMES R. JOY, who was familiar with early Methodist procedures, stated once that in early Methodism no one was allowed in a conference when it was in session, save its own members. All members were, of course, preachers, and there was no "gallery" for visitors, nor indeed were any visitors allowed. The secrecy of conference proceedings as carried on by ministers alone helped to intensify the call for lay rights.

This was, of course, the Conference plan which the Wesleyans in England had been carrying on for many years before American Methodism originated. And it should be admitted that the business of the annual conferences was almost altogether ministerial, as few financial matters came under review. But as the Church grew in strength and in numbers, and as property in churches, in educational institutions, in publishing houses, and the like, was accumulated, the desire became more manifest that the laity of the church should have some voice in arranging its general plans.

Local preachers began the first agitation towards this end, as they felt that in the delegated General Conference—meeting first in 1812—they had been left without any representation, and of course without authority. As discussion spread in the Church a period of great turmoil ensued, and the laity rights movement finally brought about the organization of the Methodist Protestant Church.

During subsequent anti-slavery discussions in the General Conference (after the Methodist Protestants had withdrawn), various matters regarding laity rights also came up. In 1842 a number of persons seceded to form the WESLEYAN METHODIST CHURCH which, like the Methodist Protestants, introduced lay representation into their legislative bodies and rejected episcopacy and the presiding eldership.

When the M. E. CHURCH, SOUTH, was formed under the PLAN OF SEPARATION, there was no difference between the episcopal Methodisms in the matter of lay representation. But when the Southern Church reorganized following the Civil War in 1866, there was up for adoption a plan for lay representation to be acted on in the General Conference. That Conference created a special committee to report at the next General Conference (1870) upon the whole matter of lay representation.

The Committee duly recommended this in 1870 with a provision that would admit laymen to the General Conference in equal numbers with ministers; and also recommended that four lay representatives should be elected to each Annual Conference from each presiding elders's district; and that these four should be elected by the newly established District Conference—the District Conference being a strictly southern creation as of that date. It was specifically provided that the lay members were not to vote upon ministerial qualifications or character—and it may be said that lay members never have been allowed to vote upon such up to the present day. In spite of opposition by JOHN C. KEENER, NORVAL WILSON, and LEONIDAS ROSSER, HOLLAND N. MCTYEIRE—to be elected bishop by that conference—managed to get the report for lay representation adopted by a good majority.

Later on in the M. E. Church, South, the ratio of lay representation in the annual conferences was changed so that in 1914 eight delegates were allowed to be elected from each presiding elder's district; then in 1926 it became one lay delegate for every 800 church members. When the PLAN OF UNION was finally adopted, this became one lay delegate from every pastor's charge, no matter how large that charge should be, or how small.

In the M. E. CHURCH in 1860, the General Conference adopted a resolution expressive of a willingness to introduce lay delegation into the General Conference "whenever the Church desired it," and agreeing to submit the question to a vote of the lay members of the church, and also to a vote of the ministry. The vote was taken in 1861-62, in the midst of the excitement of the Civil War, and resulted in 28,000 members in favor and 47,000 against; 1,338 ministers for and 3,969 against. Thus it failed.

After the close of the war the subject was again discussed and the General Conference of 1868 submitted another plan for lay delegation to the consideration of the people. In spite of a great many technical matters which were involved in voting upon the proposed amendments, the result of the vote was a two to one majority for lay representation. The General Conference of the church in 1876—still not quite convinced—ordered the appointment of a committee who should consider, in the interim of the conferences, the question of the expediency of lay delegation. It reported favorably to the General Conference of 1880.

The plan of lay representation as proposed by the General Conference of 1872 and ultimately adopted provided for two lay delegates from each annual conference, except where a conference had only one clerical delegate, and in such cases only one lay delegate was allowed. Lay and clerical members were to deliberate in one body but to vote separately (vote by orders), if such separate vote should be called for by one-third of either order. In such cases both orders had to concur.

General Conference lay delegates were to be elected by an ELECTORAL CONFERENCE of laymen which was to assemble on the third day of the session of each annual conference held previous to a General Conference. The electoral conference was to be made up of one layman from each circuit or station, and there were certain specifications as to age and church membership for them before they could be recognized.

The above provisions continued with slight modifications until 1900, when the M. E. Church adopted a written constitution. This put the election of lay delegates in the hands of a regular lay conference which was then established. This lay conference, as called for in 1900, was something more than the old lay electoral conference which had only met once every four years. It was in effect, a parallel conference to that of the ministers, and was established for the purpose of voting on constitutional amendments—and also of considering and acting upon matters relating to lay activities and such other matters as the General Conference might direct. One lay member from each pastoral charge was to be elected to the lay conference. Clerical and lay members were to meet in united sessions for certain parts of the joint program.

When church union came about between the three Methodist Churches of the United States in 1939, it was evident that lay representation would be continued in much the same pattern as had been the case in the two Methodist Episcopal Churches. However, the Methodist Protestant plan of electing one layman from each charge was put into the Plan of Union, and followed out henceforth. The old electoral lay conference, and the conference of laymen which sat in parallel with the conference of ministers in the M. E. Church, was done away in favor of the plan which the Southern Church had always pursued—that of having laymen actual integrated members of the annual conference itself. At present, therefore, each annual conference is organized with its ministerial membership and its lay membership all sitting in a body and acting together upon all matters in general parliamentary proceedings.

The adoption of Amendment X in The Methodist Church allowed those churches which had more than one minister to send a lay delegate for each effective full-time minister in full connection appointed to their charge. This provision was continued in the Constitution of The United Methodist Church. "Each charge served by more than one minister shall be entitled to as many lay members as there are ministerial members" (*Discipline*, 1968, P. 36.)

When ministerial character is involved, as admission to Conference or voting to grant ordination to a minister, the lay members are not constitutionally allowed to vote.

Several JUDICIAL COUNCIL decisions came about since 1940 defining matters of lay participation in the annual conference. One of them holds that laymen have no right to call a conference of their own lay delegate membership apart from the annual conference itself unless this is to elect delegates to the JURISDICTIONAL or GENERAL CONFERENCE (decision 74 J.C.); also that the ministerial members of the annual conference may exclude from their meeting place (if they choose to do so) the lay members when a matter of ministerial character is involved (decision 42 J.C.). These decisions were made prior to 1968.

Present regulations. The Constitution of The United Methodist Church provides that whatever be the number of ministerial delegates to the General and Jurisdictional Conferences an Annual Conference is allowed to elect, there shall be "an equal number of laymen." It also provides that in electing laymen to the General Conference, the laymen of the annual conference shall sit and vote as a body in electing their delegates; while the ministerial members sit as a body electing their delegates. Recent

General Conferences provided that if a minister is selected to act as spokesman and leader of a delegation in one quadrennium, at the next quadrennium the lay leader of the delegation shall be the leader, and so on alternatively. In the General Conference the laymen and ministers sit together with each delegation assigned its own seats, and laymen and ministers are equally assigned to committees in accordance with the rules of the General Conference itself. Voting can be called for by "orders"—that is the lay members must be polled as lay members, and the clerical members as ministers. Such a vote can be ordered by one-third of either order when one of that order makes such an appeal. The vote by orders is, however, a blocking move, designed to defeat a pending measure. It is never made to further a measure since it is much more difficult in a close decision to carry each order by a majority than to carry the whole house.

Women delegates. Women have been given full laity rights in the Methodist Churches since early in the present century. Their admission to the conferences as lay persons followed the victory of lay representation in both Episcopal Methodisms. The struggle for full laity rights for women in the M. E. Church was concluded victoriously for them when the constitution of 1900 of that church was adopted. However, not until 1914 did the M. E. Church, South allow women to become stewards and enjoy all other lay rights except admission to the conference and ordination. Both these rights were subsequently given. Not until after union and in 1956 did the General Conference pass legislation declaring that "women are included in all provisions of the *Discipline* referring to the ministry" (*Discipline*, 1960, P. 303). This allowed women to become members of the annual conference and the traveling ministry if and when an annual conference shall elect such to membership. These rights were carried over into the United Methodist Church in 1968.

E.U.B. Church. The struggle for laity rights in the E.U.B. Church and its antecedent bodies followed much the same lines as it did in the Methodist Episcopal Churches. For the successive steps which led to full laity representation, see the synopses of the General Conferences of these Churches listed under General Conference.

E. S. Bucke, *History of American Methodism.* 1964.
Discipline, UMC.
N. B. Harmon, *Organization.* 1948, 1953, 1962.   N. B. H.

LAY LEADER is the name of an officer of The United Methodist Church. He is, of course, a layman who may be an Annual Conference Lay Leader in which case he is elected by the Annual Conference; or a Charge Lay Leader elected by the Charge Conference and serving in his own local church.

The office of Lay Leader grew out of a need felt by the Board of Lay Activities and kindred agencies in The Methodist Church—and its antecedent Churches—before the Union of 1939. The Constitution of The United Methodist Church makes the Conference Lay Leader a member of the Annual Conference by virtue of his office. He is chairman of the Conference Board of the Laity also by virtue of his office. Annual Conference Boards of the Laity, as they are now, have specified membership, and a definite assignment of work and program upon which they report at each session of the Annual Conference.

In the local charge the Lay Leader, who is elected by

the CHARGE CONFERENCE, has the following privileges and responsibilities: membership in the Charge Conference; in the Board of Administration; and in the Council on Ministries. In general, he represents the work of the laity in the local church in all manner of ways. In instances where more than one church is on a charge, the Charge Conference must elect additional Lay Leaders so that there will be one Lay Leader for each church. The Lay Leaders, both in the Local Charge and in the annual Conference, each have certain representative responsibilities which they are called upon to assume at the sessions of these respective bodies. Present duties and responsibilities are outlined in the *Book of Discipline*. (See also LAY MOVEMENT IN AMERICAN METHODISM.)

Discipline, UMC, 1968.   N. B. H.

LAY MOVEMENT IN AMERICAN METHODISM, THE, officially recognized at the organization of The Methodist Church in 1939 with the creation of a General Board of Lay Activities, is in reality as old as Methodism itself.

From the very beginning of Methodism in England, JOHN WESLEY made use of laymen as preachers and leaders. JOHN CENNICK, THOMAS MAXFIELD, JOHN NELSON and others were among the earliest and best known of these laymen. Furthermore, all the preachers Wesley sent to the new world, including FRANCIS ASBURY, were laymen. It was not until the organizing Conference (the CHRISTMAS CONFERENCE) of the M. E. Church in 1784 that the preachers of American Methodism received ordination.

The first three Methodist Societies organized in America on the Wesley plan were founded by laymen. PHILIP EMBURY, a carpenter and teacher, organized the JOHN STREET Society in NEW YORK. Captain THOMAS WEBB of the British Army formed the Society later called ST. GEORGE'S in PHILADELPHIA; and ROBERT STRAWBRIDGE, a farmer, began Methodist Societies in MARYLAND. Nor did the laymen cease their activities following the ordination of the preachers at the conference of 1784. ABEL STEVENS, the nineteenth century historian of American Methodism, comments on their value by writing, "Scores of other preachers and laymen of these times, faithful and invincible pioneers of Methodism . . . men who not only labored before the itinerants arrived, and afterward with them, but provided them food and homes and 'preaching houses,' should be commemorated forever by the Church."

Unfortunately, no official recognition was taken of these laymen. They were not members of the annual conferences and they had no place in the GENERAL CONFERENCES of the Church. They had no organization other than a makeshift "District Conference"—which in the pioneer period did not last long—through which they might exert an influence on the growing church.

Agitation for lay representation in the annual and General Conferences, however, was stirring the church. In 1821 a layman, WILLIAM S. STOCKTON, founded a paper called the *Wesleyan Repository and Religious Intelligencer*. It was later succeeded by a magazine entitled, *The Mutual Rights of Ministers and Members of the Methodist Episcopal Church*. Stockton, a man of progressive views, fearlessly set forth in his magazine his ideas in favor of lay representation and lay activities. He is said to have been the first person publicly to have advocated lay representation, and in this sense is the father of the

movement. EZEKIEL COOPER, second Book Editor of the M. E. Church, contributed to the *Repository* two articles favoring lay representation—one on the "Question of Lay-delegation" and the other on "The Outlines of a Proposed Plan for a Lay-delegation."

The General Conference of the M. E. Church meeting in 1828 rejected all memorials on the subject, and shortly thereafter the METHODIST PROTESTANT CHURCH was organized. That church provided for lay representation in each of the annual conferences and for an equal number of laymen and ministers in the General Conference.

In 1852, following the bisection of the Church in 1844, the M. E. Church was again agitated by laymen and ministers desiring lay representation. In that year a group of laymen met in Philadelphia to discuss the situation. The *Philadelphia Christian Advocate* was launched, and the question was debated in its pages. In 1860 the General Conference was swayed by appeals for lay representation to the extent that it passed a resolution stating approval of the general idea "when it shall be ascertained that the church desires it." Pastors were requested to take a vote among their male members over twenty-one years of age "for" or "against" lay representation. The measure was voted down by a ratio of almost two to one. Agitation, however, continued. In 1868 the General Conference approved a plan whereby each annual conference was to be represented at the General Conference by two laymen, and sent the plan to the annual conferences for possible approval. This plan became the law of the church, and in 1872 for the first time in the history of the M. E. Church, laymen sat in the General Conference (see LAY DELEGATION).

Two years previously in 1870 the Southern Church had granted equal representation to ministers and laymen in the General Conference, and had passed a law providing for four lay delegates from each district to sit with the ministers in the annual conferences and be an integral part of it.

The new law in the Northern Church, however, did not abate the clamor for greater lay representation; and agitation for equal representation in the General Conference as well as representation in the annual conferences reached hurricane proportions.

Laymen's Associations. In the meantime on Feb. 19, 1889 a group of Methodist laymen in Philadelphia met at the Arch Street Church in Philadelphia and organized "Philadelphia Laymen's Association of the M. E. Church." Membership was limited to residents of Philadelphia, and they dealt with the questions of "new church buildings," "equal lay representation," "the admission of women to the General Conference," and other kindred subjects. The Association, furthermore, corresponded with laymen throughout the country proposing a convention of laymen to take place in Omaha prior to the General Conference of 1872. The meeting was held, memorials were sent to the General Conference for equal lay representation, and to this end an amendment to the constitution was proposed. The General Conference approved the measure, but it failed to pass the annual conferences.

Another step, however, was now taken by the PHILADELPHIA CONFERENCE. A convention of laymen met in Norristown on March 9, 1893, where the annual conference was meeting, and formed the Laymen's Association of the Philadelphia Annual Conference, the former Association being formally dissolved. According to Charles F. Eggleston, writing in *Pioneering in Penn's Woods,* it was the "first Methodist Laymen's Association of any Annual Conference in the United States."

The Association actively promoted similar organizations in other conferences. These Associations continued to agitate for equal representation of laymen and ministers in the General Conference, and by 1900 this goal was achieved.

The next step was to secure equal lay representation in the annual conferences—a measure that was voted down by the annual conferences in 1920 and 1924, but became the law of the Church in 1932.

Southern Church. Ten years previous to this action of the Northern Church, the Southern Church, with a more progressive outlook, had organized a General Board of Lay Activities on Aug. 23 at Lake Junaluska, N. C. J. H. Reynolds was elected General Secretary but immediately resigned in order to continue his work as president of HENDRIX COLLEGE. GEORGE R. MORELOCK was elected to succeed him, and Morelock continued in this position until Methodist union in 1939, and then was elected the first executive secretary of the General Board of Lay Activities of The Methodist Church. He continued in this position until his retirement in 1948.

Northern Church. The Northern Church had not been totally lax in challenging its laymen, but had at the General Conference of 1908 also formed the Methodist Brotherhood. The first Executive Secretary was Fayette L. Thompson, 1908-1912. He was succeeded by WILLIAM S. BOVARD. The General Conference of 1916 placed the responsibility for this work on the Superintendent of the Adult Department of the Board of Sunday Schools and named Bovard as Director. He served until 1920, when he was elected Executive Secretary of the Board of Sunday Schools, and Bert E. Smith was elected his successor. In 1924 the General Conference formed four boards into the BOARD OF EDUCATION and Bovard was then elected as Executive Secretary of this board. Smith was elected as Superintendent of Adult Work of the Board of Education and served in that capacity from 1924-1934. He was also Director of Men's Work, an adjunct of the Board of Education. EDGAR T. WELCH was the first president of this commission. He was succeeded by Judge H. R. Snavely who served up to the time of unification in 1939.

Steps in Cooperation. On Feb. 28-29, 1928, in LOUISVILLE, Ky., an "All Methodist Conference on Men's Work" was held involving representatives of the M. E. Church, South, and M. E. Church. Out of this conference came the Joint Commission of Men's Work. This commission held its first meeting in Louisville on Dec. 27, 1928. JOHN R. PEPPER was elected president, Edgar T. Welch, vice president, and H. R. Snavely, secretary. This commission formed a Joint Men's Council which later became the Inter-Methodist Men's Council. The Inter-Methodist Men's Council held its first meeting in Louisville Dec. 5-6, 1929.

Toward Unification of Lay Work. When it became apparent that the M. E. Church, M. E. Church, South, and the M. P. Church would unite, a meeting of responsible persons in Lay Activities and Men's Work of the three denominations was called on April 6, 1938 in ST. LOUIS, Mo. At this meeting the group unanimously approved the idea of a General Board of Lay Activities as an autonomous administrative arm of the united church. Approval was also given to organize Boards of Lay Activities in annual conferences and districts. The Official Board was to be the arm of lay activities in the local church.

A Steering Committee on Lay Activities and Men's

Work was set up to direct further procedures toward union. The Steering Committee drafted a communication to the Commission on Union dealing with the matter of Lay Activities and Men's Work. On April 26, 1939 in KANSAS CITY, Mo., the Uniting Conference approved the organization of a General Board of Lay Activities as an official agency of The Methodist Church, U.S.A.

The General Conference of 1940 fixed the headquarters of the General Board in Chicago, Ill. In 1962 headquarters were moved to Evanston, Ill. George L. Morelock was elected the first executive secretary, a position he held until his retirement in 1948. Chilton G. Bennett was elected his successor, serving from 1948 until 1951. E. Lamont Geissinger served as acting executive secretary during 1951-52. ROBERT G. MAYFIELD was elected General Secretary in 1952, and served until 1968.

The General Board of the Laity. At the 1968 Uniting Conference, the General Board of Lay Activities (as it had been) of The Methodist Church and the Department of Christian Stewardship and the general organization of Evangelical United Brethren Men of the former E.U.B. Church were united under the name General Board of the Laity. (Paragraph 1183, *Discipline*, 1968.) This was mandated to operate under the charter of its own incorporation and the *Discipline* of The United Methodist Church "to hold and administer trust funds and assets of every kind and character . . . and to develop and promote a program in keeping with its objective and functions." These functions are stated to be "that all persons be aware of and grow in their understanding of God, especially of his redeeming love as revealed in Jesus Christ, and that they respond in faith and love—to the end that they may know who they are and what their human situation means, increasingly identify themselves as sons of God and members of the Christian community, live in the spirit of God in every relationship, fulfill their common discipleship in the world, and abide in the Christian hope." (Paragraph 1186, *ibid.*)

The organization of the new Board was provided for by the *Discipline* of 1968 and it was greatly enlarged over what the old Board had been. It was empowered to function through two divisions—the Division of Lay Life and Work and the Division of Stewardship and Finance. Lay Life and Work is directed to function through two sections: the Section of Lay Ministries, and the Section on United Methodist Men. Detailed directions for the proper administration of these and other divisions of the General Board of the Laity will be found in the current *Discipline*. Stewardship and Finance is heavily stressed.

In each jurisdiction there may be a Jurisdictional Board of the Laity auxiliary to the general board, as the Jurisdictional Conference may determine.

Annual Conferences are each directed to create a Conference Board of the Laity auxiliary to the general and jurisdictional board, and to follow through the general program of the whole Church in this field.

A Conference lay leader shall be elected annually by the Annual Conference on nomination of its particular Board of the Laity. The duties of this office are carefully outlined in the *Discipline* as are the duties of the Charge Lay Leader.

It is also directed that there shall be a Conference organization of United Methodist Men which is auxiliary to the general, jurisdictional, and conference Boards of the Laity. This organization is designed to supplant and enlarge the work of the old former Methodist Men as this organization was known in The Methodist Church.

District Boards of the Laity are called for in regarding the general plan of work for these. As with other boards of the Church, general regulations governing this board may be changed by succeeding General Conferences in minor particulars from time to time.

E. S. Bucke, *History of American Methodism*. 1964.
Discipline, UMC, 1968.
Pioneering in Penn's Woods, the Philadelphia Conference Tract Society, 1937.
ROBERT G. MAYFIELD

LAY PASTORS. In the late nineteenth century some British LOCAL PREACHERS were paid to assist circuit ministers, though without securing the training, status, allowances, and security of the ministers themselves. They were known variously as "hired local preachers," "lay agents," and "lay pastors," the latter becoming their official designation. Their employment was considered a necessary expedient in the Methodist Church after METHODIST UNION in 1932, though it was viewed with increasing misgivings. They were accepted and appointed by the HOME MISSION DEPARTMENT, usually from the ranks of accredited local preachers, and served four years on probation, pursuing a directed course of studies, before being accepted on an approved list. The lay pastor was expected to wear civilian attire, and was subject to the jurisdiction of the LOCAL PREACHERS' MEETING of the circuit to which he was appointed. After earlier attempts had been made to eliminate this "second class ministry," or at least to reduce its numbers, the Conference of 1947 urged circuits no longer to employ them, and this exhortation was re-emphasized by the Conference of 1963. Many of the former lay pastors were able through special training to gain acceptance to the regular ministry, and the *Minutes of Conference* no longer officially recognizes the standing of any except those who have retired in that work, whose names are listed. (See MINISTRY.)

FRANK BAKER

LAYMEN'S ASSOCIATION, FIRST. (See LAY MOVEMENT IN METHODISM.)

LAYTON, (MISS) M. E. (1841-1892), was the first missionary of the WOMAN'S FOREIGN MISSIONARY SOCIETY sent to an appointment in INDIA outside of the original India Mission field in Oudh and Rohilkhaud. She started the Calcutta Girls' School on its great career of service. Originally its students were mainly Europeans and Anglo-Indians. Now they represent many racial and creedal communities, and the school contributes powerfully to both the national strength and to church growth. She was born in Delaware, U.S.A., February 1841, and died at Cawnpore, India, April 28, 1892.

J. WASKOM PICKETT

LAZENBY, MARION ELIAS (1885-1957), American minister, missionary, editor, and church historian, was born at Forest Home, Butler Co., Ala. Feb. 8, 1885. He was licensed to preach in 1906; was admitted into the ALABAMA CONFERENCE in 1907, and was appointed at that Conference to CUBA, where he served as pastor of the Trinity Church, Havana. Returning to his home confer-

ence, he served as pastor of several churches. In 1922 he became editor of the *Alabama Christian Advocate*, and in 1928 he transferred to the NORTH ALABAMA CONFERENCE and continued as editor until 1935. After serving as district superintendent and as pastor, he went to CHICAGO in 1943 to become assistant editor of the *Christian Advocate*. Returning to ALABAMA in 1949, he was for one year superintendent of the Huntsville District before being recalled to the editorship of the *Alabama Christian Advocate*. In 1953 he retired and was asked to write the *History of Methodism in Alabama and West Florida*. This last—a monumental task—was accepted by the conference shortly before Lazenby's death on Sept. 12, 1957, at Montevallo, Ala.

Clark and Stafford, *Who's Who in Methodism*. 1952.
C. T. Howell, *Prominent Personalities*. 1945.

LEADERS, LEADERS' MEETING. The CLASS MEETING arose in BRISTOL in 1742 as financially expedient, and rapidly developed into a valuable pastoral instrument, with the leader of each class not only collecting small weekly contributions for society expenses, but admonishing and encouraging his (or her) members. Otherwise their title might well have become "collectors" rather than "leaders." By about 1744 the CLASS LEADERS were exercising this pastoral oversight, not chiefly by visits to the homes of those members on their class list, but by conducting a weekly fellowship meeting for them. Many who thus began as class leaders developed sufficient theological acumen and eloquence to become LOCAL PREACHERS. The office of class leader was one which offered large scope for women as well as men.

The leaders brought the money which they had collected to the STEWARDS of their society, and in early years this took place weekly. Gradually this led to a regular meeting of stewards and leaders with the minister or his preaching helpers in order to discuss the spiritual welfare of the society, and this became known as the Leaders' Meeting, comprising the preacher in charge (in the chair), the stewards (the executive officers), and the class leaders. Throughout Wesley's lifetime the leaders' meeting possessed only advisory powers, and Wesley himself, or his preaching helpers, made the real decisions. The conference of 1797 for the first time gave the leaders' meeting the right of veto in the admission of members and in the appointment of the leaders themselves, thus slightly reducing the prerogatives of the preachers. The spiritual influence of the class leaders was very high indeed, but their administrative power remained very limited. The undercurrent of dissatisfaction about this was one of the factors in the rise of most of the major disputes within Wesleyan Methodism. Most of the daughter bodies reduced ministerial prerogative and increased the power of the lay leaders, and gradually this liberalizing tendency affected the parent body also. At METHODIST UNION in 1932 this was unequivocally written into the constitution of the new Methodist Church. The local Leaders' Meeting now possesses much greater authority, having complete oversight of the spiritual welfare of the society, including the appointment of leaders and stewards, and the admission and discipline of members.

Davies and Rupp, *Methodist Church in Great Britain*. 1965.
W. Peirce, *Ecclesiastical Principles*. 1854.
Spencer and Finch, *Constitutional Practice*. 1951.
FRANK BAKER

LEBANON VALLEY COLLEGE, Annville, Pennsylvania, U.S.A., is a college of The United Methodist Church, formerly of the E.U.B. Five citizens of Annville attended the East Pennsylvania Conference, Church of the United Brethren in Christ, in 1866, and offered an Academy building there valued at $5,500, for an institution of learning. It was accepted, but no one could be found to operate the new school. There was no college graduate in the entire conference. G. W. Miles Rigor, who had attended college for three years, enlisted his neighbor, Thomas R. Vickroy, a Methodist minister and graduate of DICKINSON COLLEGE, to join him in a joint partnership and take over the lease. Thus on May 7, 1866, the school opened as scheduled with Vickroy running the school, Rigor as agent, and fifty-nine coeducational students.

Vickroy's term saw eleven acres added to the "lot and a half of ground" conveyed by the original deed. A spacious four-story building was erected. A charter was granted by the Commonwealth of Pennsylvania. A complete college curriculum was established, based on the classics but including music and art, and two classes were graduated before Vickroy gave up his lease and moved west in 1871. At that point, it was decided that the College would not be leased again but would be operated henceforth by a board of trustees.

The five presidents during the next twenty-five years had great difficulty in keeping the College afloat, due to lack of support ranging from open opposition to disinterested apathy. A library was established in 1874, and a college newspaper appeared in 1888. However in the fall of 1896, the school was debt-ridden, with an enrollment of only eighty.

The administration of President Hervin U. Roop, starting in 1897, marked the first real period of expansion. Under his leadership five new buildings were erected, including a library donated by Andrew Carnegie, and the administration building was re-built after the disastrous fire of Christmas Eve, 1904. By 1905, enrollment had soared to 470, with a faculty of twenty-three.

Loss of public confidence and financial support prompted Roop's resignation in 1905 and the College faced its darkest days. Bankruptcy was averted by the keen business sense and generosity of President Laurence Keister, who served from 1907 to 1912.

President George D. Gossard finally gave the College stability when he achieved for it accreditation and a million dollar endowment fund. By the end of his twenty-year term in 1932, there were 653 students and thirty-two members of the faculty.

Clyde A. Lynch, who came in 1932, faced a series of external crises during his eighteen years as president. The stock market crash shrank the handsome endowment raised by his predecessor; the Depression of the 1930's shrank the enrollment, followed by World War II; the post-war influx of returned war veterans then stretched it to more than capacity. Lynch's administration started the policy of buying property adjacent to the campus to allow for future expansion, and also raised over a half million dollars, part of which was to be used for a new physical education building. This building was named in Lynch's honor upon completion.

The twelfth and latest president of the College, FREDERIC K. MILLER, served for almost seventeen years. During his term, inflation caused mushrooming costs, but the so-called "Tidal Wave of Students" made possible selective admissions. The greatest physical expansion in the history of the College then occurred, with seven new buildings erected and several renovated. Two major fund-raising drives were successfully concluded. Enrollment increased by eighty percent, with a corresponding increase in faculty and administrative staff. The centennial of the founding of the College was observed by a year-long series of events. Miller became the first Commissioner for Higher Education in the State of Pennsylvania.

At the start of its second century, as a fully-accredited, church-related, coeducational college of the liberal arts and sciences, Lebanon Valley occupies a thirty-five acre campus and twenty-eight buildings, and has a full-time enrollment of 838 students and a faculty of seventy-two members. A Master Plan for its development has been adopted by the Board of Trustees.

Paul Wallace, *History of Lebanon Valley College.* 1966.

EDNA J. CARMEAN

W. EARL LEDDEN

LEDDEN, WALTER EARL (1888-   ), American bishop, was born in Glassboro, N. J., March 27, 1888, the son of Joseph Jackson and Miriam Risden (Higgins) Ledden. He graduated from Pennington, N. J., Seminary, Music Department (organ) in 1907. In 1910 he received the Ph.B. degree and in 1913 the A.M. from DICKINSON COLLEGE. He was awarded the B.D. by DREW THEOLOGICAL SEMINARY in 1913 and in 1913-14 did graduate work at Drew University. From SYRACUSE UNIVERSITY, in 1927, he received the D.D. degree and, in 1944 was given the LL.D. degree by Dickinson College. In addition to these degrees and honorary doctorates, he is widely recognized as an accomplished organist and an authority on church music.

Ledden was married to Lida Iszard July 2, 1913 (deceased October 1957). They had two sons and a daughter.

Bishop Ledden was on trial as DEACON, NEW JERSEY CONFERENCE, 1912, and received in full connection as ELDER in 1914. He served as pastor of the Goodwill Church, Rumson, N. J., 1910-14; the First Church, Belmar, N. J., 1914-19; State Street Church, Camden, N. J., 1919-20; Broadway Church, Camden, N. J., 1920-26; Richmond Avenue Church, Buffalo, N. Y., 1926-30; Mathewson Street Church, Providence, R. I., 1930-38; and Trinity Church, Albany, N. Y., 1938-44.

He was elected bishop and assigned to the Syracuse Area in 1944 and served as bishop of this area until his retirement in 1960. He was president of the COUNCIL OF BISHOPS, 1956-57, and has served in many other important capacities, including chairman of the Interboard Committee on Missionary Personnel; chairman, Interboard Committee on Materials for Training in Church Membership; vice-president, BOARD OF EVANGELISM; vice-president, COMMISSION ON WORSHIP; member, BOARD OF WORLD PEACE and BOARD OF MISSIONS; member of the executive committee of the Commission on Family Life.

He was on the Division of Christian Life and Work, NATIONAL COUNCIL OF CHURCHES; and from 1945 until 1949 he was president of the New York State Council of Churches.

He has been trustee of Drew University, Syracuse University, Folts Home for the Aged, Williamsville Home for Children, and Clifton Springs Sanitarium.

He represented the Council of Bishops in visitation in Central and South Africa in 1948, and in South America in 1954.

On Jan. 25, 1964, Bishop Ledden was married to Henrietta Gibson in the chapel of Christ Church, Methodist, New York. An unusual feature of the ceremony was that the marriage rites were performed by Bishop HERBERT WELCH, one hundred and one years of age, believed to be the world's oldest bishop, who was assisted by HAROLD A. BOSLEY, minister of Christ Church.

After his retirement Bishop Ledden joined the faculty of WESLEY THEOLOGICAL SEMINARY where he taught in the field of Ritual and Church Music. He has continued to work closely with the National FELLOWSHIP OF METHODIST MUSICIANS. He and his wife presently reside in Syracuse, N. Y.

Who's Who in America, Vol. 34.
Who's Who in The Methodist Church. 1966.

MARY FRENCH CALDWELL

LEDNUM, JOHN (1797-1863), American minister, historian and member of the PHILADELPHIA CONFERENCE, was born in Sussex County, Del., Nov. 15, 1797. He died in Philadelphia, Nov. 18, 1863. He was converted at nineteen years of age and became an itinerant in the spring of 1823. Considered by his colleagues as a "profitable preacher" and as a "theologian of the first class," he is, nevertheless, chiefly remembered for his book, *A History of the Rise of Methodism in America . . . from 1736 to 1785*. The book contains some errors, but, for the most part, it is accurate. Making no attempt at a literary style, Lednum presented his material in terse, factual statements. It is one of the recognized sources on early Methodism in America.

FREDERICK E. MASER

LEE, ADA HILDEGARDE JONES. (See CALCUTTA, India, Lee Memorial Mission.)

LEE, ANNA MARIA (1803-1838), American missionary pioneer, was born in New York City, Sept. 24, 1803, the daughter of George Washington and Mary (Spies) Pittman. With a group of missionaries she sailed from Boston, July 29, 1836, by way of Cape Horn to Honolulu, arriving the day before Christmas. In April she continued her voyage to OREGON, and arrived at Fort Vancouver, May 17, 1837.

She wrote many poems. When JASON LEE, founder of the first mission in Oregon, asked her to be his wife, she gave her answer in a poem, "Yes, where thou goest I will go."

Their wedding Sunday, July 26, 1837, was the first marriage of a white man and white woman in the Oregon Country.

In the spring of 1838 Jason Lee was urged to return to the United States to report on the work, and try to secure more support. Before he left, she gave him another poem, "Must my dear Companion leave me,/Sad and lonely here to dwell?"

Her son died soon after birth, and she died the next day, June 26, 1838. She was buried in the beautiful fir grove where she had taken her marriage vow. Her body has since been moved to the Lee Mission Cemetery at SALEM, Ore.

Theressa Gay, *Life and Letters of Mrs. Jason Lee, First Wife of Rev. Jason Lee of the Oregon Mission.* Portland: Metropolitan Press, 1936.
John Parsons, *Beside the Beautiful Willamette.* Portland: Metropolitan Press, 1924.   ORMAL B. TRICK

LEE, BENJAMIN FRANKLIN (1841-1926), American bishop of the A.M.E. Church, was born in Gouldtown, N. J., on Sept. 18, 1841. He graduated from WILBERFORCE UNIVERSITY in 1872 with the B.D. degree. He was ordained DEACON in 1870 and ELDER in 1872. He was a theological professor at Wilberforce University (1873-1875), and later was President of Wilberforce (1875-1884). He was also an editor of *The Christian Recorder* (1884-1892). He was elected bishop in 1892, and retired voluntarily in 1924. He was a delegate and member of the Permanent Committee of Arrangements of the ECUMENICAL METHODIST COUNCIL in 1881.

His voluntary retirement in 1924 was noted as remarkable since he was the only bishop of his Church ever to do so. He was austere in appearance but had a keen sense of humor; was a man of deep learning, impatient of petty ambitions and jealousies. Bishop Wright said of him, "He seldom sought honors. 'They are too empty,' he said, 'but I do seek service.'" He answered in the same manner when someone asked, "Dr. Lee are you running for the Bishopric?" His answer was, "No, but I *am* standing for it." He has churches named for him at Jacksonville, Fla.; Cincinnati, Ohio; Nashville, Tenn.; Little Rock, Ark.; Morgan City and Oak Grove, La. and Brownswood, Texas.

R. R. Wright, *The Bishops.* 1963.   GRANT S. SHOCKLEY

LEE, DANIEL (1807-1896), was an American missionary to the Indians of OREGON, 1834 to 1843. No account is given of his early life but in 1833, as a member of the NEW HAMPSHIRE CONFERENCE, he was commissioned by the Foreign Missionary Society of the M. E. Church as a missionary to the Indians of Oregon. The commission came from the Foreign Missionary Society because the

U. S. Claim to the Oregon country was not established until 1846. He was to work under the superintendency of his uncle, JASON LEE.

In the spring and summer of 1833 the mission party of five men made the arduous six-month journey across the plains and mountains to Oregon, travelling in company with Nathaniel Wyeth's fur traders.

In Oregon the main mission station was established in the Willamette valley about ten miles north from where SALEM, the capital city of Oregon, is now located. Here Daniel Lee carried his full share of the hard labor needed to build log houses for the mission, and prepare wild land for farming. The missionaries were largely dependent on their own efforts to feed themselves and the Indian children in their school.

In 1838 Jason Lee gave Daniel the difficult job of opening a second mission station at the Dalles of the Columbia River. Under his direction this station was the most successful of the missions in the Indian work. He continued his work there until 1843, when his own ill-health and that of his wife (in June 1840 he had married Marie Ware, a newly arrived mission teacher), forced him to return to New England. There he published, in collaboration with another returned missionary, J. H. Frost, a history of the Oregon mission, *Ten Years in Oregon* (N. Y.: 1844), a book which did much to inform the church about the Oregon mission.

After some years of labor in the churches of the New Hampshire Conference, ill-health caused him to relocate. Shortly after he followed his sons westward where in OHIO, KANSAS and ILLINOIS he served small churches as his strength permitted. He died in Illinois, and he and his wife, who died some years before him, are buried near Butler, Ill.

C. J. Brosnan, *Jason Lee*. 1932.
Erle Howell, *Northwest*. 1966.   ROBERT MOULTON GATKE

LEE, DAVID HIRAM. (See CALCUTTA, India, Lee Memorial Mission.)

LEE, EDWIN FERDINAND (1884-1948), American missionary bishop, was born in Eldorado, Iowa, July 10, 1884, son of Andrew and Carrie (Anderson) Lee. He received his education at NORTHWESTERN UNIVERSITY (B.S., 1909) and GARRETT BIBLICAL INSTITUTE (B.D., 1924). He was awarded five honorary doctorates. He married Edna Dorman on June 8, 1909.

Lee joined the UPPER IOWA CONFERENCE in 1908, and his appointments were: New Hampton, Iowa, 1908-10; missionary to Batavia, Java, and pastor of Wesley Church, Kuala Lumpur, MALAYA, 1910-12; Central Church, MANILA, Philippines, 1912-15; Rockford, Iowa, 1915-17; and chaplain in the U. S. Army in France, 1917-19. He was decorated by the French Government for his war service and by the government of Serbia for his relief work after the Armistice, and was given the King George V Jubilee Medal in 1935.

Lee was Associate Secretary of the Board of Foreign Missions in New York, 1919-24, and pastor of Wesley Church, Singapore, Straits Settlement, and superintendent of the Singapore District, 1924-28. Elected MISSIONARY BISHOP of Malaya and the Philippines in 1928, he served as such until he retired.

Bishop Lee was a delegate to the INTERNATIONAL MISSIONARY CONFERENCE, Madras, India, 1938; a Fellow

EDWIN F. LEE

of the Royal Geographic Society, London; member of the American Academy of Political and Social Science, New York.

Caught in Singapore when the Japanese attacked the city in December 1941, Bishop and Mrs. Lee and fifty missionaries held out as long as possible against leaving the country. Just before the city's fall, Lee broadcast a message of hope assuring the people of America's ultimate victory. The Lees were evacuated on Jan. 30, 1942, with the Japanese only seventeen miles from the city.

He served as director of the General Commission on Army and Navy Chaplains in 1944. He returned to Malaysia and the Philippines after the war and re-established Methodist churches and schools. He expressed great hope for the future of Christianity in that area.

Retiring in June 1948, after forty years of unusual service around the world, Bishop Lee died Sept. 14, 1948.

C. T. Howell, *Prominent Personalities*. 1945.
F. D. Leete, *Methodist Bishops*. 1948.
World Outlook, November 1948.   JESSE A. EARL

LEE, HANDEL (Li Han-to, 1886-1961), preacher and seminary president, was born in Kiangningchen, Kiangsu province, CHINA, and received his education at the University of Nanking, Nanking Theological Seminary, BOSTON UNIVERSITY SCHOOL OF THEOLOGY, and DREW THEOLOGICAL SEMINARY, receiving the Ph.D. at Drew in 1933. After pastorates in Wuhu and Nanking he was appointed district superintendent in the Central China Conference (later called the Mid-China Conference) in 1927, and was elected president of the union (Methodist, Presbyterian, Disciples, and Baptist) Nanking Theological Seminary in 1931. He held this position until his retirement in 1949.

Under his administration the seminary greatly enlarged its activities. During the Japanese War the seminary moved its main center to Shanghai, where it continued even after the attack on Pearl Harbor. Another branch of the seminary was opened in Chengtu, the educational center of Free China, and continued until the end of the war, when both branches were reunited on the Nanking campus.

Lee's wise leadership, both in his own church and in interdenominational activities, strengthened the church in central China to meet the difficulties of the Communist period, and the seminary which he headed for eighteen years is presently the only theological seminary still continuing in mainland China.

China Christian Yearbook, 1936-37.   FRANCIS P. JONES

LEE, JAMES WILDERMAN (1849-1919), American clergyman and author, was born in Rockbridge, Ga., Nov. 28, 1849. A graduate of Emory College, he joined the NORTH GEORGIA ANNUAL CONFERENCE, M. E. Church, South, in 1874. He married Eufaula Ledbetter in 1875. He served churches in this conference intermittently a total of nineteen years, among them, Trinity Church, ATLANTA.

Lee transferred to the ST. LOUIS CONFERENCE in 1893, and was appointed to St. John's Church, ST. LOUIS, where he served with distinction three separate appointments, 1893-97, 1901-05, 1911-15. He was presiding elder of the St. Louis District 1897-1901, and Chaplain of Barnes Hospital, 1916-19.

Lee joined with Dr. Wagner of the M. E. Church to edit and publish the short-lived *Illustrated Methodist Magazine* (1902-03), in expectation of promoting fraternity and the ultimate union of the two Episcopal Methodisms. Under his leadership the present magnificent St. John's Church was built (1902-03), which the city listed as something visitors to the St. Louis World's Fair should by all means see. It is one of the finest examples of classic Roman Temple architecture in the United States.

His journeys to Palestine for study, begun in 1894, resulted in Lee's writing *The Romance of Palestine, Footprints of the Man of Galilee*, and *A History of Jerusalem*. Three of his books received warm praise and wide circulation—*Robert Burns, The Geography of Genius, The Making of a Man*, which was translated into several languages, and *The Religion of Science*, the theme of which was the oneness of truth in science and religion. It placed Lee among the foremost "harmonizers" in the period of "science" versus "religion" controversy.

The catholicity of his spirit and his instinctive humanitarianism gave support to the many missionary, educational and charitable enterprises with which he was associated in the cities of St. Louis and Atlanta, and in the annual conferences of the Church. Lee died in St. Louis, Oct. 4, 1919, as the result of a fall at the home of his son, Ivy Ledbetter Lee, in Rye, N. Y. He was buried in Bellefontaine Cemetery.

Minutes of the St. Louis Conference, MES, 1920.
Who's Who in America, 1914.   FRANK C. TUCKER

LEE, JASON (1803-1845), American pioneer of Protestant Christianity and United States territorial aspirations in the area of the present states of Oregon and Washington. He was born near Stanstead, Lower Canada (thought at that time to be south of the boundary and part of the U. S.), June 28, 1803, the son of one of the Minutemen who fought at Concord and Lexington. His ancestral roots reached back 200 years in Massachusetts.

JASON LEE

At the age of twenty-three he was converted in a Wesleyan Methodist revival, and in 1829, in preparation for the ministry, he entered Wilbraham Academy, Wilbraham, Mass.

In response to a request from four northwest Indians who in 1831 travelled to ST. LOUIS asking about the white man's religion, a plea publicized through the church press, WILBUR FISK, President of WESLEYAN UNIVERSITY, recommended Jason Lee to lead a missionary journey to that area. Lee accepted an appointment from the Missionary Society of the M. E. Church and gathered a party including his nephew, DANIEL LEE, Cyrus Shepard, a teacher of Lynn, Mass., and two other laymen, P. L. Edwards and Courtney M. Walker, both of Independence, Mo. The expedition's goods were shipped around Cape Horn to the Columbia River, and the party, consisting of seventy men in all, plus 250 horses, mules, and cattle, was led overland by Nathaniel J. Wyeth, a fur trader of the Rockies.

At Fort Hall, near the present city of Pocatello, Idaho, Jason Lee preached the first Protestant sermon heard west of the Rocky Mountains on July 27, 1834. After a kindly reception by P. C. Pambrun, Hudson's Bay official at Fort Walla Walla (now Washington), on September 1, the party traveled by barge down the Columbia River, arriving at Fort Vancouver, 100 miles from the Pacific, September 15. Upon advice of John McLoughlin, Chief Factor of the Hudson's Bay Company on the Pacific coast, Lee established his mission on the east side of the Willamette River about sixty miles above its confluence with the Columbia.

Their desire to convert the Indians of the area was frustrated by difficulties of communication and, before long, by catastrophic illnesses which heavily decimated the tribal population. The INDIAN MANUAL LABOR TRAINING SCHOOL for the natives was established, and on its discontinuance in 1844 the building was sold to another institution also founded by Lee—the Oregon Institute, which later became WILLAMETTE UNIVERSITY, the first school of college rank west of the Rockies.

Lee opened Christian work at various places, including a mission at The Dalles, on the Columbia River, in 1837. He encouraged the emigration of Christian families to the OREGON country as a means of bringing civilized and Christian influences to that raw society.

Jason Lee early became involved in the political development of the northwest, urging measures which would settle in favor of the United States the long-standing dispute with England over the boundary. He was instrumental in drawing up a petition, signed by American citizens and Canadians who desired to become American citizens, asking that the laws of the U. S. be extended over Oregon. In the course of his journey east with this petition he learned that his wife, ANNA MARIE LEE, had died in childbirth, the child also perishing. After two years' absence from Oregon, time spent in persuading governmental and church leaders of the urgency of development of the Oregon territory, Lee returned west by ship, with thirty-one new missionaries, including his new wife, the former Lucy Thompson, of Barre, Vt.

As the Oregon mission grew, it became increasingly occupied with white settlers, the Indian population having substantially diminished. Lee was deeply involved in the political controversy over British or American possession of the territory. The dispute also divided the missionaries, and JOHN P. RICHMOND, a critic of Lee's political intervention, persuaded the Mission Board to replace Lee as superintendent of the mission. Lee learned of this action in November 1843, in the Sandwich Islands, to which he and his daughter (his second wife had died in 1842) had travelled in hopes of securing a ship to New York.

Lee continued his dual role as political pioneer and Christian missionary by going to Washington in an attempt to persuade officials of the need for urgent action to establish American sovereignty in the Oregon territory, and by appearing before the Mission Board and successfully defending the administration of the mission. In failing health, he returned to his boyhood home in Stanstead, Canada, where he died March 12, 1845.

Jason Lee must be counted as a strong influence in the spread of Protestant Christianity to the Pacific Northwest, and in the securing for the United States the area south of the 49th parallel—the Puget Sound Country, Cascade Mountains, and the great watershed of the Columbia River. Cornelius J. Brosnan has summarized these achievements:

Consider Lee's visit in 1838 to the East, with his lectures in 88 cities and towns, including the capital of the nation; his meetings and lectures promoted by a great and influential denomination . . . ; consider Slacum's widely quoted report; consider the Second Petition or Memorial of the Oregonians, framed at Lee's Mission House; the introduction of the Linn Bill; of Cushing's elaborate report, embodying two Lee documents, with a publication and distribution of 10,000 copies; consider the fact that Lee's widely attended and published lectures dwelt upon the desirability of the Pacific Coast as a place of settlement and thus assisted in awakening an interest that sent the Peoria Party to Oregon in the spring of 1839, and was a factor in bringing between eight hundred and a thousand settlers . . . ; consider the Provisional Government of Oregon and the important part Lee's Mission had in its inception and promotion; consider that experienced politicians saw in the movement for an American Oregon vitality enough to make it an issue in a presidential campaign on the basis of our claims to that territory. When all these contributions are appreciated one cannot doubt that, though incidental and not primary, the Lee Mission was a significant factor in the settlement of the Oregon boundary controversy.

A. Atwood, Conquerors. 1907.
C. J. Brosnan, Jason Lee. 1932.
John Martin Canse, Pilgrim and Pioneer: Dawn in the Northwest. New York: Abingdon Press, 1930.
H. K. Hines, Pacific Northwest. 1899.
—————, Jason Lee, Pioneer of Methodism. San Francisco: Hammond Press, 1896.
E. Howell, Northwest. 1966.
John M. Parsons, Beside the Beautiful Willamette. Portland: Metropolitan Press, 1924.   JOHN C. SOLTMAN

LEE, JESSE (1758-1816), early American preacher, father of Methodism in New England and commonly regarded as next to ASBURY in influence, was born on March 12, 1758, in Prince George County, Va., sixteen miles from Petersburg. His father was converted under DEVEREUX JARRATT, an evangelical Anglican who in the beginning days cooperated with Asbury and the Methodist movement. This led to the conversion of Jesse Lee. His education was limited but he attended a singing school and became a good singer.

He joined the Society in 1774 under ROBERT WILLIAMS, who was then serving the Brunswick circuit, which included Halifax and Bute Counties in NORTH CAROLINA as well as fourteen counties in VIRGINIA. Three years later Lee went to North Carolina to take temporary charge of the farm of a widowed relative, and there he became a class leader, exhorter, and local preacher. He preached his first sermon at a place called "the Old Barn" on Sept. 17, 1779.

JOHN DICKINS was on the Roanoke Circuit and in order to devote time to literary work he asked young Lee to take his place for a few weeks, and thus began Lee's career as a traveling preacher.

In July 1780, Lee was drafted into he army. He had scruples against war and refused to take the rifle that was offered him. Placed under guard, he prayed with his captors and was soon singing and preaching to them. He was willing to perform any unarmed duty and so he was made a wagon driver and became a sergeant of pioneers and unofficial chaplain. He was honorably discharged after serving three months.

In 1782 he rode a circuit in North Carolina and Virginia and was admitted to the Conference on trial the following year. He did not receive word of the CHRISTMAS CONFERENCE, which he always regretted and attributed to the fact that FREEBORN GARRETTSON, the courier sent to summon the preachers, had preached too much along the way.

His first appointment, in 1783, was to the Caswell Circuit, after which he served five years in North Carolina, Virginia, and MARYLAND. In 1785 he went from Salisbury, N. C., to meet Asbury at the home of Colonel Joseph Herndon in Wilkes County. Asbury had been a Superintendent (later called bishop) for only a month, and he appeared in "black gown, cassock, and band," whereupon Lee objected to the attire as unbecoming to Methodist simplicity. The rebuke caused Asbury to lay aside the regalia.

Asbury took Lee with him on his southern tour. At Cheraw, S. C., a young man from MASSACHUSETTS described the low state of religion in New England and Lee determined to go there. In 1790 he preached under "the Old Elm" on Boston Common and gave the next ten years of his life to New England, where he became the virtual founder of Methodism.

Jesse Lee weighed 250 pounds and on at least one occasion he used two horses, leading one and changing from time to time. He was elected to deacon's orders in 1786 but declined ordination; however, at the conference of 1790 in NEW YORK he was privately ordained

DEACON by Asbury, and publicly ordained ELDER the following day.

In 1797 Asbury called Lee to assist him in the work of the episcopacy and at the General Conference of 1800 he expected to be elected a bishop and had some reason to think that Asbury encouraged the hope. But he was defeated by RICHARD WHATCOAT. This he attributed to Asbury, to whom he later wrote a scathing letter of denunciation. He had previously made attempts to reduce Asbury's power and on one occasion THOMAS COKE objected to the passage of Lee's character. But when on May 10, 1816, the funeral procession of Asbury, including the whole GENERAL CONFERENCE and an immense throng of citizens, moved through the streets of BALTIMORE, among the leading marchers and mourners was Jesse Lee.

In 1801 Lee returned to the South as presiding elder in Virginia, and except for a roving commission as far southward as Savannah, he spent the next fourteen years in his native state, where he bought a small farm near his father.

In 1809 Lee was elected chaplain of the U. S. House of Representatives and was reelected four times. In 1814 he was elected chaplain of the Senate. The next year he was transferred to the BALTIMORE CONFERENCE and sent to Fredericksburg, a move which he considered to be a political maneuver to prevent his election to the General Conference. He refused to go to the appointment because it was not then in his conference.

Jesse Lee in 1810 published *A Short History of the Methodists in the United States of America*, the first ever written. The Conference would not sponsor it and the author secured subscriptions for its publication. It seems that Asbury was not favorably inclined, but when he had seen the book he wrote, "It is better than I expected. He has not always presented me under the most favorable aspect; we are all liable to mistakes, and I am unmoved by his."

Lee also wrote a life of John Lee, his brother, and he published two sermons. He kept a voluminous *Journal,* which was destroyed when the Publishing House in New York was burned in 1836; Asbury's *Journal* was lost in the same fire. Fortunately, much of Lee's work was preserved in the biography written by his kinsman, LEROY LEE.

Jesse Lee died on Sept. 12, 1816, while attending a CAMP MEETING near Hillsborough in Maryland. He was laid to rest in the old Methodist burying ground in Baltimore, but in 1873 his body was moved with others to Mount Olivet Cemetery where it rests today by that of Asbury, Bishops GEORGE, EMORY, and WAUGH, ROBERT STRAWBRIDGE and other stalwarts of early Methodism.

F. Asbury, *Journal and Letters.* 1958.
W. W. Bennett, *Virginia.* 1871.
Dictionary of American Biography.
William Larkin Duren, *The Top Sergeant of the Pioneers: The Story of a Lifelong Battle for an Ideal.* Emory University, Ga.: Banner Press, 1930.
L. M. Lee, *Jesse Lee.* 1848.
William Henry Meredith, *Jesse Lee, A Methodist Apostle.* New York: Eaton & Mains, 1909.
M. H. Moore, *North Carolina and Virginia.* 1884.
W. B. Sprague, *Annals of the Pulpit.* 1861.
M. Thrift, *Jesse Lee.* 1823.   LOUISE L. QUEEN

LEE, LAWSON (1918-   ), missionary to URUGUAY, was born in Homestead, Okla. He studied at Oklahoma North-

western College at Alva, SOUTHERN METHODIST UNIVERSITY, and the University of Southern California. He held pastorates at Alva, Arnett, Terral, Mutual, and Enid, all in Oklahoma.

Lawson and Sylvia Lee came to MONTEVIDEO in March, 1948. They worked one year as assistants in CENTRAL CHURCH while learning Spanish. In 1949 they went to Paysandu, Uruguay, where they took a dying church and made it into a going concern. They built a church and parsonage from Lawson's own plans. In an outlying district, St. Luke's Church was founded.

In 1962 the Lees were transferred to Montevideo, and he became executive secretary of The Methodist Church in Uruguay and later mission treasurer for Uruguay, as well as interim minister of Emmanuel Church. In 1966 he was appointed one of the two ministers of Central Church, keeping his two executive positions as well.

Lee's interests range from painting pictures to making plans for churches or assembling electronic organs.

EARL M. SMITH

LEROY M. LEE

LEE, LEROY MADISON (1808-1882), American minister, editor and leader of Southern Methodism, was born at Petersburg, Va., on April 30, 1808. He was the son of Abraham and Elizabeth Lee and was related to JESSE LEE, whose biography he was later to write. He was converted in Petersburg on April 1, 1827, under the preaching of W. A. SMITH and admitted to the VIRGINIA CONFERENCE in 1828, then in session at Raleigh, N. C., under Bishop SOULE. As eastern NORTH CAROLINA was then a part of the Virginia Conference, Lee served several appointments in that state, including New Bern, later being moved to Trinity, Richmond, where his parsonage was destroyed by fire in 1835. Never robust, he was recuperating from a spell of illness shortly after this in FLORIDA, and while there was elected editor of the *Christian Sentinel,* a paper which had just been purchased by the Virginia Conference. For reasons of health he dropped out of the editorship for several months, but eventually came back and resumed the editorship of the publication which was now named the *Richmond Christian Advocate* —a paper destined to last under that name until 1940 when it became the present *Virginia Christian Advocate.*

LeRoy Lee kept his name "at the masthead of this for nearly a quarter of a century." He became a stalwart champion of the Southern point of view, and was a member of the GENERAL CONFERENCE of 1844, which divided the Church; of the LOUISVILLE CONVENTION the next year; and of the first General Conference of the M. E. Church, South, in Petersburg in 1846. He declined reelection to the editorship in 1858 and was made presiding elder of the Norfolk District, but the Federal fleet taking possession of NORFOLK on May 10, 1862, ended his work there for a time.

Later Lee served Centenary Church, Lynchburg; Granby Street in Norfolk; Union Station, RICHMOND; and served as presiding elder two terms, and then spent one year at Ashland, in part acting as a chaplain of RANDOLPH-MACON COLLEGE there until he retired in 1881. Lee, besides his voluminous editorial writings, published in 1847, *Life and Times of Jesse Lee*, his distinguished kinsman.

Lee—who was given the degree of D.D. by Transylvania College in 1848—married first Nancy Mosely Butler of Elizabeth City, N. C., who died the following November. Afterward he married Virginia Addington in 1836 and to them were born nine children.

The action for which Lee became most famous was his move in the 1870 Conference of the M. E. Church, South, to so arrange it that the power of the Southern bishops to "check" an action of the General Conference was made a properly constitutional provision, and not (as it had been since its adoption in 1854) a merely statutory one. Lee's old pastor and mentor, W. A. Smith, had written and sponsored the adoption of the statutory resolution in 1854, but Smith himself realized the legislation was not constitutional and should have personally made a move to see that it was made constitutional had he not died. LeRoy M. Lee was chairman of the Committee on Episcopacy of General Conference of 1870, and brought in a statesmanlike report of which Bishop DuBose says, "The report of Dr. Lee on this provision has become one of the great State papers of Methodism. It is, in fact, a priceless dissertation on the constitution and particularly stresses the rights of the body of the elders, from whom the constitution was derived (or rather their successors, the clerical and lay members of the present-day Annual Conferences) to determine the processes by which unconstitutional acts of the General Conference may be arrested." (DuBose, p. 113-4.). The upshot was that this whole matter was passed by the General Confernce and referred for approval to the Annual Conferences. They adopted it and thus this constitutional provision as drawn up by Lee was firmly written into the organic life of the M. E. Church, South, to remain there until union with the M. E. and M. P. Churches in 1939. Lee acted as chairman of the powerful Committee on Episcopacy both in 1870 and in 1874. He died in Ashland, Va., on April 20, 1882, and was buried in Virginia's famed Hollywood Cemetery overlooking the James River in Richmond.

H. M. DuBose, *History of Methodism*. 1916.
Minutes of the Virginia Annual Conference, 1882.   N. B. H.

LEE, LIM POON (1910-   ), American lay leader among California Oriental United Methodists, was born in Hong Kong, Dec. 19, 1910. At the age of eight months he and his parents came to the United States to make their home. He was educated in the SAN FRANCISCO public

schools, graduated from the UNIVERSITY OF THE PACIFIC in 1934 with an A.B. degree, did graduate work at the University of Southern California from 1934 to 1936, and received a LL.B. degree from Lincoln University School of Law, San Francisco, in 1954. He was in the U. S. Army, 1943-46; and served with the Counter Intelligence Corps in the Philippine Islands and Hokkaido, Japan. From 1939 to 1963 he was in public welfare and juvenile court work in San Francisco. He was field representative for Congressman Phillip Burton, San Francisco, from 1963 to 1966. In 1966 he became acting postmaster of San Francisco and in 1967 was made postmaster, in which position he directs the work of over 10,000 postal workers. He has been a member and chairman of the board for the Department of Veteran Affairs in CALIFORNIA; as chairman he presided over the board that determined policies for 1,021 civil service personnel, and administered an annual budget of $15 million. He has been very active in the Veterans of Foreign Wars, and has served as vice chairman of the National Legislative Committee. He is a member of the Chinese United Methodist Church in San Francisco, and has been lay leader of the California-Oriental Provisional Annual Conference. He teaches a church school class each Sunday, and is the church's lay leader. He serves as board member for the Chinese Branch of the YMCA; Telegraph Hill Neighborhood Center; Columbia Park Boys' Club; the Greater Chinatown Community Service Association; the Multi-Culture Institute, and is a member of the Chinese Cultural Foundation which is building the Chinese Culture and Trade Center in San Francisco; he is the co-chairman of the Mayor's Committee on Survey and Fact-Finding in Chinatown. He and his wife Catherine were married in 1941, and have four children.

WALTER N. VERNON

LEE, LUTHER (1800-1889), American preacher, was born of illiterate parents in Schoharia, N. Y., Nov. 30, 1800. He joined the Methodist Church at the age of nineteen, and could barely read the Bible or hymn book, even after becoming a local preacher. On July 31, 1825, he married a school teacher, Mary Miller, and they had five sons and two daughters. She gave him all the education he ever received.

Joining the GENESEE CONFERENCE in 1827, when it extended into CANADA and the roads and trails could be traveled only on horseback, he was assigned to Malone Circuit. Ordained DEACON and ELDER a few years later, Lee served charges in Henvel, Lowville, Martinsburg, Watertown, and Fulton, N. Y., 1831-36. Transferring to the BLACK RIVER CONFERENCE in 1836, he rose rapidly to a place of leadership. A fighting reformer, a powerful debater, the growing anti-slavery agitation captured his interest. After the assassination of Luther Lovejoy at Alton, Ill., in 1837, he declared himself an abolitionist. In 1838 he located and became an agent in NEW YORK for the Massachusetts Anti-Slavery Society. In 1840 he took part in organizing the Liberty Party.

At the organization of the WESLEYAN METHODIST Connection in 1843, he entered their traveling ministry and was president of their first General Conference in Cleveland, Ohio, in 1844. He was editor of the *True Wesleyan* for eight years, and served as pastor of Wesleyan churches in Syracuse, and Fulton, N. Y., and Felicity and Chagrin

Falls, Ohio. His last Wesleyan position was professor in ADRIAN COLLEGE, 1864-67.

With many others he returned to the M. E. Church in 1867, and for ten years served the Court Street Church, Flint; Ypsilanti; Northville, and Petersburg charges in Michigan.

Luther Lee was the author of several valuable books which had a large sale. Among these were, *Universalism Examined, Systematic Theology, Immortality of the Soul,* and *Autobiography of Luther Lee, D.D.*

Superannuated in 1877, Lee died in Flint, Mich., Dec. 13, 1889.

Dictionary of American Biography.
National Cyclopedia of American Biography.
M. Simpson, *Cyclopaedia.* 1878.   JESSE A. EARL

LEE, THOMAS (1727-1786), British Methodist, was born at Keighley, Yorkshire, in 1727. As a young man, while working only half-time as an evangelist, he was able to establish societies where no itinerant had yet been. Eventually he became one of WILLIAM GRIMSHAW's preachers in the Haworth round, and then a regular itinerant from 1755 until his death in 1786, traveling around the huge northern circuits. He was one of the most heroic of the early preachers, and often he and his wife suffered terrible persecution and hardship.

T. Jackson, *Lives of Early Methodist Preachers.* 1837-38.
                                N. P. GOLDHAWK

UMPHREY LEE

LEE, UMPHREY (1893-1958), American preacher, educator and author, was born in Oakland City, Ind., March 23, 1893. He went to Texas when his father, Josephus Lee, transferred there in 1910. He was educated at Trinity College (A.B., 1914), SOUTHERN METHODIST UNIVERSITY (M.A., 1916), and Columbia University (Ph.D., 1931). He served several pastorates before going to the University of Texas to establish the Wesley Bible Chair in 1919.

In 1923 he became pastor of Highland Park Methodist Church, DALLAS, Texas, on the campus of Southern Methodist University; it became one of *The Christian Century's* "Great Churches of America," and by 1960 was the largest in the denomination. During this time he also served as professor of homiletics of S.M.U.'s School of Theology and from 1937 until 1939 he was dean of the VANDERBILT UNIVERSITY School of Religion.

In 1939 he became president of Southern Methodist University and by 1954, when he left the presidency to become chancellor (because of health problems), the university's endowment had increased by $20,500,000 and eighteen new buildings had been erected. He was credited, more than any other individual, with molding the university into the great institution it had become at the time of his death June 23, 1958.

Above and beyond his official posts, he was a member of the GENERAL CONFERENCES of 1934, 1940, 1944, 1948, the Uniting Conference of 1939, and the ECUMENICAL CONFERENCES of 1946 and 1951. He was the Cole Lecturer at Vanderbilt University (1946); Quillian Lecturer at EMORY UNIVERSITY (1947); Fondren Lecturer at Southern Methodist University (1957). Also he was President of the Civic Federation of Dallas, President of the Dallas Rotary Club, and President of the Philosophical Society of Texas.

Umphrey Lee was author of the following books: *Jesus the Pioneer* (1926); *A Short Sketch of the Life of Christ* (1927); *The Lord's Horseman: John Wesley* (1928), which was revised in 1954; *The Bible and Business* (1930); *Historical Backgrounds of Early Methodist Enthusiasm* (1931); *John Wesley and Modern Religion* (1936); *The Historic Church and Modern Pacificism* (1943); *Our Fathers and Us* (1958).

During the years that Umphrey Lee was pastor of the Highland Park Church he was engaged in research projects in Europe toward his volumes pertaining to JOHN WESLEY. At home and abroad he was recognized as one of the interpreters of the Arminian tradition and the Wesleyan movement.

He held membership in the Medieval Academy of America, the American Historical Society, the American Society of Church History, and the Philosophical Society of Texas. Excelling as scholar, author, preacher, speaker, lecturer, and columnist, he was universally acclaimed by his colleagues for his pre-eminence among the ministers of Texas in his generation.

Clark and Stafford, *Who's Who in Methodism.* 1952.
Journal of the North Texas Conference, 1959.
Who's Who in America.   WALTER N. VERNON

LEE, WHAN SHIN (1902-   ), a bishop of the Korean Methodist Church, was born in Kang-Dong, near Pyeng-yang, in what is now North KOREA, Jan. 8, 1902. After study in the local Methodist Mission schools, he graduated from the Union Methodist Seminary in SEOUL (high school level at that time) in 1927, and from Chosun Christian College, Seoul, in 1931. He received the B.D. degree from VANDERBILT UNIVERSITY in 1933, M.A. from the University of Pennsylvania in 1935, and D.D., Yonsei University, Seoul, 1963.

From 1935 to 1938 he served as Director of Youth Work of the Korean Methodist Church. Ordained in 1938, he became President of the John Bible Institute in Pyeng-yang and served until the purge of all American-trained men in 1943.

He served as Professor of Chosun Christian University, 1945-1951, as General Secretary of the National Association of the Y.M.C.A., 1951-1954; and Professor, Methodist Theological Seminary, Seoul, 1955-1962.

He was elected bishop of the Korean Methodist Church in 1962 and served one four-year term. He was a delegate to the East Asia Christian Conference, Bangkok,

WHAN SHIN LEE

1964, and to the E.A.C.C. Working Committee, Ceylon and Manila, 1965, and Y.M.C.A. World Committee, Geneva, 1953.

He is the author of *Principles of Youth Guidance* (1931); *Visiting Europe and America after World War II* (1947).

He lives in Seoul.

Who's Who in The Methodist Church, 1966.

CHARLES A. SAUER

LEE, WILLIAM BOWMAN (1864-1955), American preacher and missionary to BRAZIL, was born in Newbury County, S. C., on July 16, 1864, son of a Methodist preacher. Having lost both parents in childhood, William Lee was forced to work for a living early in life. He united with the Methodist Church at sixteen; studied at Painesville, S. C., then moved to Durham, N. C., where he continued his studies while working with the Duke industries. He was esteemed by the Duke family and married a niece of the family, Mamie Fonville, on May 28, 1891. Deciding to become a preacher, he earned his B.D. degree in theology from Trinity College, and was ordained a deacon at the NORTH CAROLINA CONFERENCE in 1893.

Accepted by the Board of Missions (MES), the Lees sailed for Brazil in 1895. Through long years in Brazil, Lee served as pastor, presiding elder, professor of mathematics at INSTITUTO GRANBERY, and later as Reitor (principal) of the same school; and he was for a time editor of the official weekly, *Expositor Cristão.* He also translated articles, hymns, and the Methodist *Discipline* of 1910, and the *History of the Church,* by Williston Walker. He was author of a book of sermons and a volume on *The Teachings of the Prophets.* He served on several church-wide committees, including the one on autonomy of the Methodist Church of Brazil. At first he had difficulty mastering Portuguese, but he later became the most fluent and eloquent of all missionaries, and was especially loved for his close identification with the Brazilians.

Mamie F. Lee, his wife, taught for some years at Instituto Granbery, and was a director of Colegio Mineiro. She is best remembered as the founder in June 1900, of the Joias de Cristo (Christ's Jewels), the first missionary society for children in Brazil. Under her inspiration and leadership, these children's societies helped raise funds to support Hipolito de Campos, Brazil's first missionary to Portugal.

Four children were born to the Lees—Wesley, Mary, Lucy, and William. After his wife's death in July, 1944, Lee married the widow of Michael Dickie—Julia Coachman, also an effective worker in the church. Before her death in 1956, she edited *Aleluias,* a new hymnal which the Methodist press published. Lee retired in Brazil, died in São Paulo in his daughter Lucy's home, and was buried in the Santo Amaro Cemetery.

Expositor Cristão, Aug. 9, 1944. JOÃO GONCALVES SALVADOR

LEE, WILSON (1764-1804), pioneer American preacher, was born in Sussex County near Lewes, Del., in November 1764. He was converted at the age of seventeen and entered the traveling ministry in 1784. He was probably a member of the CHRISTMAS CONFERENCE, and was Bishop WHATCOAT's assistant for one year. On the Allegheny circuit in 1784, situated among the mountains of WEST VIRGINIA with no defined limits, he crossed the lofty ranges many times.

Redford wrote of him: "Reared in the midst of refinement and surrounded with the luxuries of life, his manners polished and possessing talents of a high order, Lee might have achieved eminence in any profession." His neatness of attire and habits, his love, his consuming zeal and excellent voice commanded respect. With an ardent spirit but with slender physical resources, Wilson Lee hazarded his frail body for nine years in the roughest frontier circuits of West Virginia, PENNSYLVANIA, KENTUCKY and TENNESSEE.

His early charges were Allegheny circuit, 1784; Redstone circuit, 1785; and Talbot, 1786. Spending six years in Kentucky and middle Tennessee, Lee's frontier circuits were from the Monongahela to the banks of the Ohio—Kentucky, Slat River, Green River, Great Barrens, and Cumberland River—in which stations there was great savage cruelty and frequent deaths. Wilson Lee apparently had great success in the vicinity of NASHVILLE, Tenn. The first church building was erected of stone in 1789 or 1790—now McKendree Church, Nashville. Two of Lee's converts were General James Robertson, the founder of Nashville, and his wife.

In 1793 Lee came east, and in 1794 went to New England. He was pastor of JOHN STREET CHURCH, New York, 1795; ST. GEORGE's, Philadelphia, 1796-99, and presiding elder of the Baltimore District, 1801-03. A fervent spirit, he lost his health in 1804 and was superannuated, dying October 11 of that year. He was buried in Anne Arundel County, Md.

Henry Boehm wrote, "I heard Lee preach in 1797 at St. George's when he was stationed there. He was a tall, slender man, had a musical voice and his delivery was very agreeable. He was one of the great men of Methodism and a great favorite of Mr. Asbury."

H. Boehm, *Reminiscences.* 1875.
E. S. Bucke, *History of American Methodism.* 1964.
J. F. Hurst, *History of Methodism.* 1901-04.
A. H. Redford, *Kentucky.* 1868-70.   JESSE A. EARL

LEE, JESSE, PRIZE was established by the Association of Methodist Historical Societies to encourage research and publication in the field of American Methodism. It is part of the program of awards, which includes grants-in-aid, administered by the Awards Committee of the COMMISsion on Archives and History. In response to annual announcement of competition for the prize, numerous manuscripts of book length have been submitted. Awards were made as follows: in 1967 to Lewis M. Purifoy, "Negro Slavery, the Moral Ordeal of Southern Methodism"; in 1968 to Lester Scherer, "Ezekiel Cooper, an Early American Methodist Leader," and in 1970 to William B. Gravely, "Gilbert Haven, Racial Equalitarian." The prize was made a biennial affair in 1970.

FREDERICK A. NORWOOD

LEE MEMORIAL MISSION. (See CALCUTTA, India, Lee Memorial Mission.)

LEEDS, England. In 1740 JOHN NELSON heard JOHN WESLEY preach in Moorfields, London, and returned to Birstall, near Leeds, to share his experience. By 1742 his evangelism had spread to Armley; and here WILLIAM SHENT heard him, brought by his wife, Mary, who had been converted at John Nelson's door. Shent invited Nelson to Leeds, and there he preached outside Shent's barber's shop in spite of threats to kill him. This shop, at the bottom of what is now Briggate, became the headquarters of a society that numbered fifty when John Wesley first visited it on April 8, 1743. The house was licensed for Methodist worship on April 7, 1746, and remained the center of Methodism until the first chapel was built in 1751. This chapel was built around the house of a basket-maker, Mathew Chippendale; and when it was roofed over, the old house was pulled down and the debris thrown through the chapel window. It got the name of the "old Boggart House" because it was supposed to be built in a haunted area. Shent continued his barber trade; his preaching and accounts exist today (in the handwriting of the steward, Thomas Hey, the eminent surgeon), noting payment to Shent of 7/6 a quarter for shaving the preachers, and a similar sum was spent on kneecaps for John Wesley. John Nelson died in 1774.

After his wife's death Shent "fell into sin" and was turned out of the society. An eloquent letter to the Keighley society restored him, but in 1787 he died a drunkard. Methodism had taken firm root in Leeds, however; one hundred years later the vicar of Leeds wrote "the de facto established religion is Methodism." The Boggart House was the only chapel until Albion Street (1802); then Isle Lane (1815), Wesley Meadow Lane (1816), Brunswick (1825), St. Peter's (1834), and Oxford Pace (1834) were built. Of these only BRUNSWICK remains as it was. For about a hundred years these chapels remained fairly full, and revivals kept them so. In 1794 a thousand members were added, and another thousand in 1838, under the preaching of John Rattenbury. Numbers rose between 1797 and 1840 from 2,460 to 8,079.

There were also reversals. Leeds took part in the controversies which followed Wesley's death, and added a few of its own. Most Leeds Methodists were originally "Church Methodists" and held their services at 7 A.M. and 5:30 P.M. to avoid the hours of service of the parish church. It was freedom from establishment which led the builders of Albion Street out of the Wesleyan connection in 1802. ALEXANDER KILHAM's reforming party sent seventy of its members to the Wesleyan Conference which met in Leeds in 1797. Not being able to agree, they withdrew to Ebenezer Chapel (bought from the Baptists)

and began an independent existence as the METHODIST NEW CONNEXION.

A more severe reversal began with the proposal in 1826 to build an organ in the new Brunswick Chapel. This was the start of the Leeds Organ Case. When the Conference of 1827 overruled an adverse vote of the District Meeting, seventy of the Leeds local preachers and leaders went on strike against the plan, and in the end more than a thousand members left the Leeds circuits and set up the PROTESTANT METHODISTS. When controversy broke out again in 1849 as a result of the FLY SHEETS agitation, the WESLEYAN REFORMERS began in Leeds with a huge tea meeting, in which "a thousand persons partook of the beverage." Two thousand members left the Wesleyan Methodist societies in the course of this controversy. In 1857 these joined with the Protestant Methodists and others to form the UNITED METHODIST FREE CHURCHES. At about the same time the Church of England, under the leadership of the famous Vicar of Leeds, Walter Farguhar Hook, reorganized and reanimated itself. Hook rebuilt the parish church, and with it twenty-one other churches, twenty-seven schools, and twenty-three vicarages. He won many back to the Established Church.

PRIMITIVE METHODISM first entered Leeds on Nov. 29, 1819, when WILLIAM CLOWES opened a mission. In a single year the membership of the Primitives was 984, but it was three years before the first chapel was built at Quarry Hill. By 1830 forty preaching places were on the plan, and by 1932 there were nine circuits, though some of these were single-minister stations. As a consequence of the FORWARD MOVEMENT, Oxford Place Chapel became the head of a new circuit in 1891, and three years later SAMUEL CHADWICK was sent to be superintendent of the "new mission." Thirty thousand pounds was spent on remodeling the premises, and in his twelve-year ministry the membership rose from 294 to 957. Aggressive evangelism and social work went hand in hand, and tracts were distributed every week to 2,500 houses. Chadwick went to Cliff College in 1907, and in 1910 George Allen began another great ministry of ten years.

Brunswick Chapel had an Indian summer dating from the ministry of A. E. Whitham, who began to preach there in 1918. He had musical and poetic gifts which enriched his sermons. Brunswick began to grow, and in 1925 LESLIE D. WEATHERHEAD began there a ministry of eleven years, in which it was necessary to be at the church door an hour before time if one wanted a seat. He removed to the London City Temple in 1936 and was succeeded by WILLIAM E. SANGSTER. On the day that war started in 1939, Sangster began his term in London. None of the large Leeds city congregations survived the war intact, and Brunswick was no exception. In an effort at reorganization, Brunswick and Oxford Place Chapels were placed together in a new central circuit. A team ministry, committed to serve the city, hopes in the redevelopment of the city center to build premises fit for mission to the twentieth century. But Leeds has been no exception to the rule that the Methodist churches in the inner belt of the industrial cities have declined sharply since 1932, and this decline has been only partly compensated by growth among the suburban societies.

JOHN BANKS

LEESBURG, VIRGINIA, U.S.A., thirty-eight miles northwest of Alexandria, is the county seat of Loudon County.

Settled in 1749 and incorporated in 1758, it was probably named for Francis Lightfoot Lee and Philip Ludwell Lee, local landholders who were among the town's first trustees. The town still has some old houses of stone and brick with ivy-clad walls shaded by elms and oaks, and doorways with massive knockers.

Prior to 1769 Methodism flourished in four places in America—NEW YORK; PHILADELPHIA; Sam's Creek, MARYLAND; and Leesburg, VIRGINIA. The Methodist Society in Leesburg is regarded as the oldest in the state, and presumably it began under the leadership of ROBERT STRAWBRIDGE or some of his local preachers. In the early days Leesburg was one of the towns nearest to Sam's Creek where Strawbridge, according to Asbury's *Journal* (April 30, 1801), built the first Methodist chapel in America.

SITE OF OLD STONE CHURCH, LEESBURG,
FIRST METHODIST CHURCH PROPERTY IN AMERICA

The Old Stone Church. On May 11, 1766, the Methodist Society purchased a half-acre lot in Leesburg for "no other use but for a church and meetinghouse and graveyard." The Old Stone Church, as it came to be known, was begun in 1766, completed in 1770, and dedicated free of debt, June 24, 1790. The earliest dated tombstone in the Old Stone Church cemetery is 1777. It stands at the grave of Captain Wright Brickell who was converted at Norfolk under JOSEPH PILMORE. Brickell was one of the original BOOK STEWARDS of the Methodist Societies in America. RICHARD OWINGS, the first native-born Methodist local preacher in America, died at Leesburg in 1786, and he and a number of other prominent Methodist preachers are buried in the cemetery.

When the 1796 GENERAL CONFERENCE designated six annual conferences with geographical boundaries, the "northern neck of Virginia," including Leesburg, became a part of the BALTIMORE CONFERENCE. When the M. E. Church divided over slavery in 1844, the Baltimore Conference adhered North. However, in 1848 more than half the members of the Old Stone Church in Leesburg decided to affiliate as a congregation with the VIRGINIA CONFERENCE (MES). For a few years the two groups worshiped alternately in the Old Stone Church, but in 1850 a lawsuit ensued and the court ruled that the church belonged to the M. E. Church because that body had held title to it since 1766. In 1853 the members who adhered South built their own church.

As time passed the Northern membership in Leesburg dwindled, and in 1894 the Old Stone Church was abandoned. In 1897 the Negro congregation of the WASHINGTON CONFERENCE (ME) in Leesburg instituted and

lost a lawsuit for possession of the Old Stone Church. In 1900 the parsonge adjoining the church was sold for $416.05, and in 1902 the Old Stone Church was torn down. The communion table was then given to the Leesburg Southern church as the descendant congregation of the Old Stone Church group which adhered South in 1848.

Today the Old Stone Church Site and Cemetery, designated as one of the historic SHRINES of American Methodism by the 1964 General Conference, is the property of the Virginia Methodist Historical Society.

Recent History. The Leesburg Southern Church continued as an appointment in the Virginia Conference until 1861 when the Baltimore Conference (ME) divided into northern and southern branches. The Leesburg church then adhered to the Old Baltimore (southern) part of the conference. As is well known, that wing of the Baltimore Conference was officially received into the M. E. Church, South at the 1866 General Conference and it continued as the Baltimore Conference of that denomination until unification in 1939.

As a strategic town in northern Virginia, Leesburg was involved in the Civil War, and the church suffered, but in after years it grew, had distinguished pastors, and was regarded as a strong, cultured, conservative appointment in the Baltimore Conference (MES). One feature of the church program in comparatively recent years has been a summer union Sunday evening service in front of the Loudon County Courthouse with the square largely filled with worshipers, some of them passersby who stop for the service at the county crossroads.

At unification, Leesburg and all of the Virginia territory of the Baltimore Conference (MES) became a part of the Virginia Conference (MC), and when the Arlington District was formed in 1962, Leesburg, which had been in the Alexandria District for many years, fell within the new district.

In 1969 the Leesburg Church reported 725 members, property valued at $274,500, and $32,836 raised for all purposes.

Columbia Lippincott Gazateer, 1952. Columbia Univ. Press.
General Minutes, MEC, MECS, MC, and UMC.
Frederick E. Maser, *The Dramatic Story of Early American Methodism.* Nashville: Abingdon Press, 1965.
Melvin L. Steadman, Jr., *Leesburg's Old Stone Church* (pamphlet, 1964).
W. W. Sweet, *Virginia Methodism.* 1955.
Virginia, A Guide to the Old Dominion, 1940. Virginia Writers' Project, 1947, Fourth Printing. ALBEA GODBOLD

LEETE, FREDERICK DELAND (1866-1958), American bishop, was born at Avon, N. Y., Oct. 1, 1866, of English Puritan and French Huguenot ancestry. He was the son of Menzo Smith Leete, under whom he was converted in a revival at thirteen. A grandson of Alexander Leete, the bishop was the eighth descendant from William Leete, Colonial governor of Connecticut. Frederick Leete was educated at SYRACUSE UNIVERSITY (A.B., 1889; A.M., 1891), and held the honorary D.D., L.H.D., and LL.D. degrees. He married Jeanette Fuller on July 28, 1891, and they had three children.

Leete united with the NORTHERN NEW YORK CONFERENCE in 1888 and was appointed to Dryer Memorial Church, Utica, 1888-91. He served as Y.M.C.A. Secretary, Utica, 1891-94; First Church, Little Falls, 1894-98; Monroe Avenue, Rochester, 1898-1903; University Church,

FREDERICK D. LEETE

Syracuse, 1903-06; Central Church, DETROIT, Mich., 1906-12. He was elected bishop in 1912 and assigned to the ATLANTA Area, 1912-20; the INDIANAPOLIS Area, 1920-28; and the OMAHA Area, 1928-36, when he retired.

Bishop Leete was a member of three ECUMENICAL METHODIST CONFERENCES, 1911, 1921, 1931, and was president of the Ecumenical Council of the Americas and Orient, 1931-44. He was a life member of the American Historical Association; a Fellow of the Royal Society of Arts, London.

Bishop Leete served on every commission that dealt with church union prior to 1939, and was said to be one of the most creative minds of the Northern commission. Bishop Moore wrote, "Bishop Frederick D. Leete was one of the most valuable members of the Commission. He spoke always with directness and understanding, and his suggestions, motions and decisions contributed greatly to working out the plan of Union. By his long ministry in prominent pastorates in the Northland, his discerning episcopal service in the Atlanta area, he had acquainted himself not only with the mind of his own church but with the necessary position and requirements of the Church, South. . . . He met the issues with deep insight, clear vision, broad churchmanship, calm courage and genuine statesmanship." (*Long Road to Methodist Union*, p. 128.)

Leete's *Methodist Bishops*, published in 1948, contains interesting facts about 250 Methodist bishops. Though the accounts are not always accurate in minor matters, it is a valuable collection of biographies.

Bishop Leete's personal "Methodist Bishops' Collection," containing nearly all the books and pamphlets written about the 250 bishops covered in his book and including some 4,000 letters from bishops, has been housed at SOUTHERN METHODIST UNIVERSITY, along with his rare library of Methodist historical material.

Bishop Leete died on Feb. 16, 1958.

C. T. Howell, *Prominent Personalities*. 1945.
F. D. Leete, *Methodist Bishops*. 1948.
J. M. Moore, *Long Road to Union*. 1943.   JESSE A. EARL

LEEWARD ISLANDS (district of the METHODIST CHURCH IN THE CARIBBEAN AND THE AMERICAS), formerly referred to a group of British islands in the Eastern Caribbean, including St. Kitts (properly called St. Christopher), Nevis and Anguilla, Antigua and Montserrat. St. Kitts, Nevis and Anguilla form a self-governing associated state within the British Commonwealth, though Anguilla in 1968 refused to recognize the connection with St. Kitts and Nevis. Antigua is also an associated state. The term "the Leeward Islands" also includes Guadeloupe which is an overseas department of France.

The Methodist district includes the above mentioned, though there is no work on the island of Guadeloupe, and also St. Eustatius, which forms part of the Netherlands Antilles, and St. Martin (St. Maarten), which is partly a French possession, and partly within the Netherlands Antilles. In addition, the district includes the British associated state of Dominica, geographically the most northerly of the Windward Islands; the American and British Virgin Islands and Aruba and Curaçao, in the Netherlands Antilles, 500 miles to the southwest off the coast of Venezuela. Its work is carried on in English.

Antigua, the headquarters of the district and of the MCCA, is the subject of a separate article.

The broad lines of development throughout the district are similar, though there are variations from one island to another. In most places, lay Methodist initiative preceded the visits of THOMAS COKE and the stationing of the first British ministers. A period of rapid expansion despite opposition, was followed in the 1820's by a decline in membership. The liberation of the slaves in British colonies in 1834, occasioned some political disturbance from which the church suffered, and in the mid-nineteenth century, economic depression in the West Indies led to emigration from the smaller islands, while the internal struggle of the Wesleyan Methodist Church in Britain led to the withdrawal of some missionary staff. Nevertheless, the church gradually expanded during the late nineteenth and twentieth centuries, and in some islands, such as Tortola in the British Virgin Islands, Methodism came to form the largest Christian community. The Leeward Islands District (then known as the Antigua District) was incorporated into the autonomous West Indian Conference in 1884, despite the opposition of its chairman and a majority of members of the synod.

Methodism entered **Curaçao** about 1930, when a local preacher named Obed Anthony began preaching in a hired hall, and in the open air. He and his followers later entered the Dutch Protestant Church, but a Methodist minister was stationed in Curaçao from 1945. Meanwhile, in **Aruba,** Methodist services and prayer meetings had been begun by Thomas Markham, a local preacher from Montserrat, and others. The first minister, W. J. Barrett, was appointed in 1939, and was transferred to Curaçao in 1945. The first Methodist minister in **St. Croix,** American Virgin Islands, was appointed in 1967.

In 1967 the district became a founder member of the METHODIST CHURCH IN THE CARIBBEAN AND THE AMERICAS. It has maintained throughout its history connections with other parts of the Caribbean area and of world Methodism.

Methodism was introduced into St. Kitts by Lydia Seaton, a servant who had lived in the house of Frances Turner, one of NATHANIEL GILBERT's converts in Antigua. The first Methodist community, which Thomas Coke visited in 1787, 1789 and 1805, included the editor of the local newspaper, named Cable, and a jeweller named Bertie. WILLIAM HAMMET was stationed in St. Kitts by Coke, and followed by THOMAS OWENS and others. A schism, led by an Anabaptist local preacher and a former missionary, divided the church in 1806, but a revival took place about 1815. The church contained at this time an unusually high proportion of white members. Relations with Anglicans in the 1820's were tense, but the Methodist community was by far the largest denomination on the island. Education made slow progress, and support by missionaries from Britain diminished. A second revival took place in 1870, after a long period of decline, but lives and property were lost from time to time through fire (1867), hurricane (1871) and flood (1880). The first Kittitian minister, Alban E. Belboda, began work in 1913. During the period of the West Indian Conference (1884-1904), the St. Kitts District became distinct from the Antigua District. From 1904, when the Leeward Islands District was created, to 1950, the chairman of the district resided in St. Kitts.

Coke's first visit to **Nevis** in 1787 was unsuccessful, but the island was visited soon after by William Hammet, and Thomas Owens was stationed there after Coke's second visit in 1789. On this occasion, Coke held in Nevis a conference of West Indian staff. A chapel was built in Charlestown, the main town, in 1790, with the support of prominent planters such as the cousins Richard and Walter Nisbett and William Brazier. By the time of Coke's third visit, in 1793, the church had 400 members in Charlestown alone. In 1797, controversy on moral issues between the minister and some planters led to an attempt to burn down the church, and there were further attacks on the church in 1816. Local leadership was difficult to maintain, and membership ebbed and flowed in Nevis as elsewhere. Wesleyan Methodist discipline aroused some opposition. The abolition of slavery caused less disturbance in Nevis than in St. Kitts, and churches were crowded by the mid-1830's. A further period of decline in mid-century was followed in 1861 by a revival of the Obeah cult. Under a succession of capable ministers, the Church was steadily built up until the period of the autonomous West Indian Conference (1884-1904). It was from Nevis that William Claxton and William Powell emigrated to Guyana in 1802, to establish Methodism there.

Methodism was brought to **Anguilla** by one of its own citizens, John Hodge, who returned home in 1813, to find no minister of any denomination on the island. Two years later, a missionary from St. Barts (St. Bartholomew) visited Anguilla, to find that Hodge had gathered around him a Methodist community of 250 members. The deputy governor of the island paid public tribute to his work in 1817, and he was ordained in 1822. During the years of economic depression, most Methodists remained faithful to the church, and the island has made a disproportionately large contribution to the ministry and deaconess order.

Before Coke's first visit to the Dutch Island of **St. Eustatius** (Statia) in 1787, a class of twenty Methodist members had been gathered by a Negro slave, converted in North America, and known as "Black Harry." At first he was allowed to preach freely, and the Dutch governor went to hear him, but later his influence over his fellow-slaves aroused the apprehension of the white planters, and public preaching was forbidden. Coke preached privately to the authorities, and organised six classes dur-

ing a two weeks' visit. On his return at the end of 1788, Coke found that Black Harry had been banished, and an edict prohibiting public prayer was in force. Nevertheless, Coke baptised 140 people. William Brazier of St. Kitts was sent to lead the Methodist community, but he was soon driven from the island. Within a year Coke returned, to receive a personal rebuff from a new Dutch governor, though Methodists were allowed to meet privately. No minister was appointed to the island until Myles Coupland Dixon arrived in 1811, but under his successor, Jonathan Raynar, (1815-1818), St. Eustatius became a separate circuit, and relations with the Dutch authorities greatly improved. The church was destroyed by earthquake in 1842, but the church's work was helped by government grants.

St. Martin is an island of thirty-nine square miles, divided between Dutch and French administration. John Hodge of Anguilla visited both parts of the island in 1847. He was driven from the French sector after one successful meeting, but found a more friendly reception in the Dutch colony. At first, the island was visited by the missionary stationed in St. Bartholomew, but in 1819 a new circuit of St. Martin's and Anguilla was constituted. The attitude of the French authorities changed, and they gave an annual grant to the mission. Emancipation of the slaves came in 1849 to the French part of the island, and in 1863 to the Dutch part, as to St. Eustatius and other Dutch possessions. The French government later pressed for the appointment of French-speaking ministers, and few local preachers were to be found, so that although the church enjoyed a good reputation, its pulpits were sometimes unfilled.

When Coke visited Tortola, the largest of the **British Virgin Islands,** with William Hammet in 1789, he found no church there, though he was well received by the authorities, and the MORAVIANS had been at work in the neighboring island of St. Thomas for over fifty years. The church grew rapidly, until in 1796, it included among its members almost half the slave population. The Wesleyan missionary John Brownell was assaulted in 1806 by one of a group of white men whose conduct Brownell had attacked in print, and in 1814, a schismatic movement was led by an ex-missionary named Stewart. Nevertheless, there was no official opposition to the church. In the early years of the nineteenth century, the islands had been served by a staff of three ministers, but by 1884 these had been reduced to one. Nevertheless, by the beginning of the twentieth century, the Methodist community included more than eighty percent of the inhabitants. The proportion has since declined, but a majority of the people are still Methodists. Methodism has played a prominent role in education, and women's and youth organizations are active.

Methodism was a relatively late arrival to the United States Virgin Islands. St. Thomas, then a Danish possession, became a center of Moravian work in 1732, and, with St. Croix, was brought within the Anglican diocese of Antigua in 1848, but it was not until 1891, during the period of the autonomous West Indian Conference, that the first Methodist minister, J. B. Foster, was stationed there. Work is expanding in St. Thomas and in St. Croix, and a Methodist minister was stationed in St. Croix for the first time in 1967.

A Methodist society with a dozen members existed in **Montserrat** as early as 1793, and Coke already planned to establish a circuit there, but it was not until 1820 that the first missionary, John Maddock, arrived. He died within a year, and although he was immediately replaced, the growth of the church was steady rather than spectacular. Many of the settlers were Irish Roman Catholics, and among the indigenous inhabitants, there were periodic revivals of the Obeah cult. There has been close cooperation with government, particularly in educational work.

Dominica was visited by Coke in 1787 and 1788. The small Methodist community, led by a Mrs. Webley, received its first minister, an Irishman named William Mc-Cornock, in 1788. Within six months, he had died. The early history of Dominican Methodism, until 1817, is marked by a high rate of mortality and sickness among missionaries, and consequently by periods during which the station was left vacant. Controversy about church property in 1810 severely reduced the membership, but by 1833 it had risen to almost 1,000. Roman Catholicism was well established in Dominica before the beginning of Methodist work, and its influence has continued to predominate. (See also WEST INDIES.)

Kindling of the Flame, British Guiana District, 1960.
G. E. Lawrence, *The Wesley of the West Indies*, Montserrat, 1938. PAUL ELLINGWORTH

LEFFINGWELL, CLARA (1862-1905), American FREE METHODIST missionary, was born at Napoli, N. Y., Dec. 2, 1862. In 1886 she was licensed to preach, and served churches in NEW YORK and PENNSYLVANIA. In 1896 she went to CHINA under the China Inland Mission. She was there during the Boxer riots. Her concern was the evangelization of the Chinese and in having her own denomination share in it. After a term she returned home to crusade for the establishment of Free Methodist missions in China. The General Conference and Missionary Board were persuaded. She was appointed superintendent for China with the authority to raise the needed funds, and secure recruits for the field. In less than two years she had done both—breaking her health through overwork. However, she went to the field with several new missionaries. Within a few weeks, she had located a field for the Free Methodists in Honan Province. Stations were opened at Chengchow and Kaifeng. She lived only a few months afterward and died in China, July 16, 1905.

B. S. Lamson, *Venture!* 1960.
Sellew, *Clara Leffingwell, A Missionary.* N.d.
BYRON S. LAMSON

LEFLORE, GREENWOOD (1800-1865), American Indian chief and strong supporter of Methodist mission work among Indians, was born on June 3, 1800 near what is now JACKSON, Miss. He was the son of a French-Canadian trader and merchant, and of a French-Indian mother. When twelve years old he went to NASHVILLE, Tenn., where he was educated, living in the home of Major John Donly whose daughter, Rosa, he married. Returning to MISSISSIPPI he became one of the chiefs of the Choctaws and was soon very influential among them. He opened his home as headquarters for Alexander Talley in his preaching tours, and also served as interpreter. He was one of the chief leaders in the signing of the treaty of Dancing Rabbit Creek, which caused much bitterness among the Choctaws who opposed leaving their old home for the lands of OKLAHOMA. Leflore decided to stay in Mississippi rather than to migrate west, and became a prosperous land and slave owner. He served four years

in the state senate, built a magnificent mansion near the town later named for him—Greenwood, in Leflore County. The Civil War brought him great financial loss as he remained loyal to the Union until his death on Aug. 31, 1865. Other members of the Leflore family moved to Indian territory. A half-brother, Forbis Leflore, served as an assistant Methodist preacher and interpreter for preachers. For a time there was a Methodist appointment called Leflore, and a county in Oklahoma named for the family.

Babcock and Bryce, *Oklahoma.* 1937.
Angie Debo, *Rise and Fall of the Choctaw Republic.* Norman: University of Oklahoma Press, 1934, 1961.
Dictionary of American Biography, Dumas Malone, ed. Vol. XI, pp. 143-44. Charles Scribner's Sons. 1933.
Publications of the Mississippi Historical Society, Vol. VII, pp. 141-51. WALTER N. VERNON

LEGAL HUNDRED. The name used in the Wesleyan Methodist Church for the select hundred preachers and their successors to whom Wesley assigned the legal conduct of CONFERENCE business by his DEED OF DECLARATION, 1784.

FRANK BAKER

LEGION OF SERVICE was a Youth movement started by the UNITED METHODIST CHURCH in Britain in 1922, and intended as an advance on both the CHRISTIAN ENDEAVOUR and the Scouting movement. Some idea of its mood may be gathered from the Aspiration of its highest grade of membership, the Guides:

> As the shepherd counted the flock
> And through the night sought high and low
> The missing sheep, so let me seek
> The lost until I find;
> Nor the lost man alone,
> But Heaven's ideal of all he may become,
> The mother-thought of God for every life,
> Giving myself with joy to win his best,
> Believing still, though failures oft recur,
> Drinking the cup Christ drank,
> 'For their sakes,' saving with Him,
> 'I sanctify myself.'

A Fellowship of Service was also created, to serve the leaders of the Legion, and those who did other types of Youth work. At the time of Methodist Union, the Legion of Service reported twenty-two Senior branches with 687 members, and fourteen Junior branches with 363 members. The United Methodist Church had about 139,000 members at the time.

JOHN KENT

LEIFFER, MURRAY HOWARD (1902-   ), American clergyman, educator, JUDICIAL COUNCIL member, was born at Albany, N. Y. He was educated at the College of the City of New York and the University of Southern California, receiving also the B.D. degree from GARRETT THEOLOGICAL SEMINARY, M.A. from the University of Chicago and Ph.D. from NORTHWESTERN UNIVERSITY. He was ordained and joined the SOUTHERN CALIFORNIA-ARIZONA CONFERENCE, 1927, but has since served as an educator.

As a teacher he has been instructor in sociology at Chicago Training School, 1929-32; associate professor of sociology and social ethics at Garrett, 1929-32; associate professor, 1932-35; and professor since 1936. He organized and directed the Bureau of Social and Religious Research, making surveys that were of great value to church bodies, general and local. Among these was a study of the Methodist episcopacy, carried on with the aid of the COUNCIL OF BISHOPS.

His membership on church board and committees has included the Board of Temperance, the Board of Christian Social Concerns, and the General Conference Committee on correlation and editorial revision, which last helped in editing the *Discipline* (TMC) in 1952, 56, 60 and 64. He was elected to the Judicial Council of the church in 1964 and in 1968 became its president.

Dr. Leiffer has written: *Manual for the Study of the City Church, City and Church in Transition* and *The Effective City Church*. He edited *The Urban Fact Book* and *Crowded Ways*. Two of his books centered about laymen—*The Layman Looks at the Minister* and *In That Case*. His involvement with the ministry and training ministers spurred his authorship of *The Methodist Ministry; Retirement and Recruitment in the Methodist Ministry, The Role of the District Superintendent;* and *The Episcopacy in the Present Day*. After and while teaching at Singapore and Manila in 1961 and 1965 he wrote *The Methodist Church in Singapore*, and *Methodist and Other Protestant Churches in Manila*.

He is a member of a number of learned and professional societies.

In 1924 he married Dorothy Corinne Linn and they had one son, Donald John, a teacher of sociology.

Who's Who in The Methodist Church, 1966.   T. OTTO NALL

SAMUEL LEIGH

LEIGH, SAMUEL (1785-1852), first Australian Methodist minister, was born on Sept. 1, 1785, at Milton, Staffordshire, England. Associated with the Independent Church at Hanley, he enrolled in a Theological School conducted by the Rev. Dr. Bogue, a strict Calvinist. Leigh favored Arminianism and quietly withdrew. He then joined the Wesleyan Society at Portsmouth, England and assisted JOSEPH SUTCLIFFE. Appointed to the Shaftesbury Circuit, he interested himself for two years in Christian Education. He was deeply influenced by an interview he had with THOMAS COKE, who was then setting out for missionary fields in CEYLON.

On Oct. 3, 1814, he was ordained and his authority "to feed the flock of Christ and to administer the holy sacraments" was signed by ADAM CLARKE, SAMUEL BRADBURN, THOMAS VASEY and John Gaultier.

Leigh left Portsmouth on Feb. 28, 1815, enroute to New South Wales, AUSTRALIA. He arrived in SYDNEY in the "Hebe" on August 10, and the following day presented his credentials to Governor Macquarie who, suspicious of "sectaries," gave Leigh the opportunity to become a servant of the Government. To the credit of Macquarie, Leigh's sincerity and forthrightness won his admiration and practical support.

Leigh held services in the Rocks area, Sydney, and pioneered work at Castlereagh, Parramatta, Windsor, Lower Portland and Liverpool. By 1819 he had established the first Methodist circuit with fourteen preaching places. This involved riding horseback over 150 miles each week. He visited and preached in Newcastle on several occasions. He befriended and was supported by Samuel Marsden, who held the position of Senior Chaplain (C of E), and became an active member in the Society for Promoting Christian Knowledge and Benevolence.

Leigh helped establish the Colonial Auxiliary Bible Society in 1817. On Marsden's suggestion and with his support, he was able to visit NEW ZEALAND. He returned for health reasons to England in 1820 and married Catherine Clewes.

In 1821 he established a mission in Hobart, leaving William Horton in charge. In February 1822, he founded the first Wesleyan mission at Whangaroa. Returning to New South Wales he became acting superintendent of Sydney Circuit and later was stationed at Parramatta. It was there his wife died on May 15, 1831, and was buried in St. John's cemetery. Because of indifferent health he again returned to England. He died May 2, 1852.

He has an honored place in Australasian history and his work is perpetuated in New South Wales by the Leigh Theological College, Enfield, and the Leigh Memorial Centenary Church, Parramatta.

Australian Dictionary of Biography. Vol. II, 1967.
J. Colwell, *Illustrated History*. 1904.
C. H. Laws, *Toil and Adversity at Whangaroa*. New Zealand, Wesley Historical Society, 1945.
Rita F. Snowden, *The Ladies of Wesleydale*. London: Epworth Press, 1957.
Alexander Strachan, *Remarkable Incidents in the Life of the Rev. Samuel Leigh*. London: James Nicholls, 1855.

                                    STANLEY G. CLAUGHTON

LELIÉVRE, MATTHIEU (1840-1930), French pastor and historian, was the son of Jean Leliévre (1793-1861), who was born in Normandy of Roman Catholic parents. On his return from fighting in Napoleon's armies, Jean Leliévre was converted at the age of thirty-eight and became a Methodist minister. Three of his sons entered the Methodist ministry. Matthieu, born circa 1840, though he entered the ministry quite young, quickly became one of the leading men. Succeeding one of CHARLES COOK's sons, he became secretary of the French Sunday School Union. He started a teacher's paper, which was an immediate success, and continues to this day.

He was known, not only as a preacher, but also as an author. He wrote lives of several of the early French Methodist ministers, of JOHN HUNT of Fiji fame and of WILLIAM TAYLOR of California. His volume on the pioneer preachers of the West in the United States does them justice. His life of JOHN WESLEY ran through five editions, carefully revised and improved. It was translated into five languages: English, German, Italian, Spanish, and Tamil. He also edited, with D. Benoit, Crespin's *Livre des Martyrs,* the French equivalent of Foxe's *Book of Martyrs,* his share being two large quarto volumes. Several volumes on French Huguenot history show the breadth of his interests. His last book was on Wesley's theology, written only a couple of years before he died, well over eighty years old, a labor of love.

With others he started a Home Missionary Society, after the 1870 war with Prussia, in order to revive the churches of all denominations.

For years, he was editor of the French Methodist paper, *l'Evangéliste.* Though Methodism was a small minority compared to the Reformed and Lutheran Churches, Leliévre made this journal one of the most influential religious papers.

He was several times President of the French Conference and was awarded the D.D. (*honoris causa*) by the University of Ohio.

Théophile Roux, *Matthieu Leliévre.* 1932.   H. E. WHELPTON

LENHART, JOHN L. (1805-1862), American clergyman and Navy chaplain, was born Oct. 29, 1805, to a well-known Pennsylvania family. In 1830 he entered the PHILADELPHIA CONFERENCE, though his membership subsequently was in the NEW JERSEY and NEWARK CONFERENCES. Illness came while at Cross Street, Paterson, N. J. His physician recommended a seashore appointment, whereupon he became a chaplain in the U. S. Navy. Retaining membership in the Newark Conference when it was set off from the New Jersey Conference, he was the first chairman of the conference board of stewards.

The Civil War found Lenhart serving aboard the *Cumberland.* Eligible for retirement, he chose to serve further. He was the first Navy Chaplain to die as the result of enemy action, when the *Cumberland* was rammed and sunk by the Confederate ship *Virginia* (formerly the *Merrimack*) at Hampton Roads, Va., March 8, 1862. "When it was seen that the Cumberland must go down all the officers in charge of the wounded were ordered on deck and to bring with them such of the wounded as there might be some hope of saving, which order was obeyed by the surgeons and others. The Chaplain, instead of coming on deck, went into his room and shut the door when in a few minutes he met his fate, the ship going speedily down." It was thought the door swung shut after the chaplain entered the room and that he was unable to open it due to damage to the vessel. Writing to a friend before the fatal attack he said: "It is just as near my heavenly home from the Cumberland as from any other place."

V. B. Hampton, *Newark Conference.* 1957.
History of the Chaplain Corps, U. S. Navy.
Minutes of the Newark Conference, 1862.
EDGAR R. ROHRBACH

LEONARD, ADNA BRADWAY (1837-1916), American pastor, presiding elder, missionary secretary, was born at Berlin, Ohio, on Aug. 2, 1837, the son of John and Nancy (Davis) Leonard. Educated at Union College in Alliance, Ohio (A.M., 1881; Hon.D.D., LL.D.), he entered the PITTSBURGH M. E. CONFERENCE in March, 1860. From then until 1886 he served churches in OHIO and the Leavenworth District in the KANSAS CONFERENCE. He was elected corresponding secretary of the Missionary Society and Board of Foreign Missions in 1888, serving as such until 1912.

Leonard's pastorates were characterized by revivals. During his three years at Central, Springfield, Ohio, the membership rose from 590 to 805. As presiding elder in KANSAS at the first and fourth rounds he would preach and hold Quarterly Conference on Saturday, then preach twice on Sunday, administer Communion, and hold a love feast. On the second and third rounds he would preach and hold Quarterly Conference. As far as was possible, he aided pastors in revivals during the fall and winter. In 1885 Adna Leonard was a candidate for Governor of Ohio on the Prohibition ticket. He was elected a delegate to the GENERAL CONFERENCE eight times, and was sent to three ECUMENICAL METHODIST CONFERENCES, 1891, 1901, and 1911.

On Feb. 19, 1861, he married Caroline Amelia Kaiser and they had seven children, one son, ADNA WRIGHT LEONARD, in time becoming a bishop.

A. B. Leonard was elected corresponding secretary of the Missionary Society of the M. E. Church and served longer than any of his predecessors, or from 1888 to 1912. He visited twenty-five foreign countries one or more times on five missionary tours, 1893, 1901, 1904, 1906, and 1907. On the 1907 trip, lasting eight months and eighteen days, he preached forty times and transacted the business of the Missionary Society. Financial expenditure for foreign missions in 1888 amounted to $244,000. By 1912 it increased to $822,000, having reached its highest peak in 1906, which was $831,000. The 1912 General Conference unanimously adopted a resolution stating that Leonard had set an example of devotion to the cause of missions and that he be made Secretary-emeritus for life, empowering the Board to make him a grant annually as it should judge advisable. After writing his autobiography, *The Stone of Help,* in 1915, he died April 22, 1916.

A strong figure in the Church, Dr. A. B. Leonard was an outstanding preacher and great Missionary Secretary.

A. B. Leonard, *The Stone of Help, Autobiography.* Cincinnati, Ohio and N. Y.: Methodist Book Concern, 1915.
C. F. Price, *Who's Who in American Methodism.* 1916.
JESSE A. EARL

LEONARD, ADNA WRIGHT (1874-1943), American bishop, was born in Cincinnati, Ohio, on Nov. 2, 1874. He was educated at New York University, DREW THEOLOGICAL SEMINARY, and The American School of Archeology, Rome, Italy. He was received on trial in the CINCINNATI CONFERENCE in 1899 and ordained deacon the same year. He was united in marriage to Mary Luella Day, Oct. 9, 1901.

Churches served by A. W. Leonard include Green Village, New Jersey; First Church, San Juan, Puerto Rico; American Methodist Church, Rome, Italy. He returned to America in 1903 and afterwards served Grace Church, Piqua, Ohio; Central Church, Springfield; Walnut Hills Church, Cincinnati; and First Church, Seattle. He was elected bishop of the M. E. Church in 1916. As bishop he served the following areas: San Francisco, 1916-1924; Buffalo, 1924-1932; Pittsburgh, 1932-1940; and Washington, D. C., 1940-1943.

The following colleges and universities conferred honor-

ADNA W. LEONARD

ary degrees upon him: OHIO NORTHERN UNIVERSITY, College of Puget Sound, University of Southern California, SYRACUSE UNIVERSITY, ALLEGHENY COLLEGE, WEST VIRGINIA WESLEYAN COLLEGE, The AMERICAN UNIVERSITY, and WESTERN MARYLAND COLLEGE.

Bishop Leonard died in an airplane accident over Iceland in 1943, while on an inspection tour of the American forces in Europe and Africa, at the request of President Franklin D. Roosevelt, and in the interest of the Commission on Chaplains of the FEDERAL COUNCIL OF CHURCHES of Christ in America. He was buried in Iceland. His children were Adna Wright Leonard, Jr., and Mrs. Henry G. Budd, Jr.

Bishop Leonard was an impressive soldierly looking man of great force of character. He was a stickler for parliamentary order and saw that his conferences followed out exactly the procedures outlined in the *Discipline,* and drove ahead with the programs of the church. His tragic death in the line of duty for both his church and nation was deeply felt by his brethren.

Journals of Puget Sound Conference, 1910-16; Pacific Northwest Conference, 1943.
C. F. Price, *Who's Who in American Methodism.* 1916.
ERLE HOWELL

LESLIE, DAVID (1797-1869), an American missionary, circuit rider, and leader in Christian education in the Pacific Northwest.

A member of the NEW ENGLAND CONFERENCE, he volunteered for service in the OREGON mission to the Indians in 1836. He and his family reached Oregon in September 1837, completing an eight-month voyage from BOSTON around the Horn. For two years, when the superintendent, JASON LEE, was seeking reinforcements from the east coast, Leslie was acting-superintendent.

Before the United States and Great Britain settled the Oregon boundary in 1846, there was no legal government in Oregon established by a sovereign state. In 1838 the settlers near the mission appointed Leslie a justice of the

peace. In this capacity he conducted the first trial by jury held in Oregon, a trial in which one of the settlers was acquitted from the charge of murder. He prepared a memorial for the American settlers, petitioning the U.S. Congress to extend protection to the settlers in Oregon. He joined with the settlers to establish a temporary government, which served the pioneers as their only government until the U.S. established the territorial government of Oregon in 1848.

After the close of the Indian mission in 1846, Leslie remained in Oregon to work among the white settlers. Never a man of robust physical strength, the work of the circuit rider left him broken in health and, at the early age of fifty-two, he took the supernumerary relation. But his labors for the church never ceased until death closed his work in March 1869.

Living on his land claim near SALEM, he served the church in many ways, but the service which gave him a large place in the history of Methodism in Oregon was his long service to WILLAMETTE UNIVERSITY, the Methodist school which is the oldest university in the Pacific Northwest. He was a member of the original board of trustees in 1842 (known as Oregon Institute until its charter in 1853), and continued a member until his death in 1869. He was president of the board, succeeding Jason Lee, until his death, a period of twenty-five years. It was a period when the work to maintain the struggling pioneer university required his full devoted efforts, best described as a full-time, but non-salaried position. The Oregon Conference committee on education said in its report the year of Leslie's death, concerning Willamette University and Leslie's relation to it, "much of the honor of its place in the history of the church in Oregon will arise from the part he bore in laying its foundations, and carrying it through its earliest struggles and difficulties."

R. M. Gatke, *Willamette University.* 1943.
ROBERT MOULTON GATKE

LESLIE, ELMER ARCHIBALD (1888-1965), American clergyman and educator, was born in Tolono, Ill., April 8, 1888, the son of Robert and Mary (Campbell) Leslie. He received the A.B. degree from the University of Illinois in 1910; the S.T.B. degree in 1913 and the Ph.D. degree in 1916 from BOSTON UNIVERSITY. He also studied at Leipzig, Glasgow, Halle, Berlin, Oxford and Jerusalem.

Admitted on trial to the MAINE CONFERENCE in 1911, he was ordained a DEACON in 1912, joined the NEW ENGLAND CONFERENCE in full connection in 1913, and received his ELDER's orders in 1915. He served Methodist churches in Urbana and Savoy, Ill.; Kittery, Me.; Arlington, Medford, Cambridge and Brookline, Mass. He founded and directed the WESLEY FOUNDATION at Harvard University in Cambridge from 1918 to 1921. From 1921 until 1957 he was professor of Hebrew and Old Testament literature at Boston University. He was widely known as a lecturer and writer.

His numerous published works include *Old Testament Religion* (1936), *The Psalms* (1949), *Jeremiah* (1954) and *Isaiah* (1963). He was a contributor to *Abingdon Bible Commentary* and *The Interpreter's Bible.*

Beloved by colleagues and students alike, he was not only a scholar whose work was marked by carefulness and thoughtfulness, he was also one who never lost the pastoral touch. His deep faith and prayer life profoundly influenced his associates.

On June 26, 1913 he married Helen Fay Noon, daughter of a New England clergyman, by whom he had four children: Jean Taylor (Mrs. A. Donald Hackler), Robert Campbell, James S. and Donald William (deceased).

Elmer A. Leslie died at his winter retirement home in Winter Park, Fla., Feb. 26, 1965.

Minutes New England Annual Conference, 1965.
Nexus, Alumni Magazine, Boston University School of Theology, May 1965.
Who's Who in Methodism, 1952.　　　ERNEST R. CASE

LESSEY, THEOPHILUS (1787-1841), British Methodist and one of the most noted Wesleyan preachers of his time, was born at Penzance, Cornwall, and was baptized by JOHN WESLEY himself. He was educated at KINGSWOOD SCHOOL, entered the ministry in 1808, and became president of the Conference in 1839, the first son of a Methodist minister to be elected to that office. He died in London on June 10, 1841.

G. Smith, *Wesleyan Methodism*. 1857-61.
G. West, *Sketches of Wesleyan Preachers*. London, 1849.
　　　　　G. ERNEST LONG

LEVERT, EUGENE VERDOT (1795-1875), American minister and colorful character who was one of the "founders of Methodism in Alabama," was born Oct. 20, 1795, King William County, Va., the son of Dr. Claudius Levert, who was surgeon of Count Rochambeau's French fleet when it came to help the Americans win their independence. Dr. Levert married about 1785, Ann Lea Metcalfe, of one of the old families of Tidewater, Va. Eugene Levert came to ALABAMA first in 1818, and joined the Methodist church near Huntsville in 1819. In 1821 he joined the MISSISSIPPI CONFERENCE which then extended over the western part of Alabama, and was appointed to the Tuscaloosa Circuit, with Samual Patton as his senior minister.

In 1822 he was sent to the Alabama Circuit with Joshua Boucher, but in 1823 was located by the Conference against his desire, because he had married on Jan. 23, 1823, Martha Patton. (She subsequently became the mother of fifteen children.) The feeling in that day against young ministers marrying was very strong, hence the unwilling location. However, in 1825 he was readmitted and assigned to the New River Circuit, and in 1826 to the Cahaba Valley Circuit, but in 1827 he was forced to locate again, this time voluntarily due to his own health. In 1828 he was readmitted a second time, and served the Tuscaloosa Circuit, being one of the original presiding elders at the organization in 1832 of the ALABAMA CONFERENCE. Thereafter he served several appointments in his Conference including the Selma District and the Demopolis District. He was elected delegate to the GENERAL CONFERENCE of 1840, and was one of the original trustees of Centenary Institute at Summerfield, in Dallas County, Ala. A zealous Mason, he became Grand Master of the Grand Council of the Masonic Lodge for Alabama in 1866-67. It is said that more children were named for Eugene V. Levert than probably for any minister in Alabama. *The History of Methodism* by West (page 613), gives some interesting facts in connection with Eugene V. Leveret's connection with the Tarrant family.

Levert died April 19, 1875, and was buried at Marion, Ala.

Greene County Democrat, Eutaw, Ala., March 3, 1955.
　　　　　F. S. MOSELEY

HYUNGKI J. LEW

LEW, HYUNGKI J. (1897-　　), Korean bishop and author, was born in Hichyun, North Pyeng-An Province, KOREA, Nov. 17, 1897. He attended a Methodist Mission school, graduated from Aoyama College in TOKYO, OHIO WESLEYAN UNIVERSITY, BOSTON UNIVERSITY SCHOOL OF THEOLOGY, and then received his M.A. from Harvard in 1927.

Returning to Korea that year he began work in religious education for the M. E. Church Mission. In 1932 he became general secretary of the Department of Education of the newly organized Korean Methodist Church. During these years he produced thirty volumes, including a translation of the Abingdon one-volume *Bible Commentary*.

Pressure of Japanese military authorities forced Lew and other American trained personnel out of church leadership in 1941, and he endured severe persecution until the end of World War II. In 1945, the American Military Government of Korea placed him in charge of the largest Japanese printing plant in Korea.

In 1948 he was made President of the Theological Seminary, where he continued until 1953. When Bishop Yu-Soon Kim was kidnapped by the Communists after the invasion of 1950, Lew was elected to succeed him. His two terms involved care for thousands of refugees at Pusan, and rehabilitation of some 400 churches under the Bishop's Appeal Fund.

In 1958, due to constitutional limit of two terms, he returned to editorial work. A large Korean Bible Dictionary came off the press in 1960. A Korean Bible Commentary in four volumes, averaging some 1,200 pages each, covering the entire Bible, was completed in 1968. Work has begun on a biography of church leaders.

Who's Who in The Methodist Church, 1966.
　　　　　CHARLES A. SAUER

LEWES, DELAWARE, U.S.A., the site of the first Methodist Society in America, formed by GEORGE WHITEFIELD. Whitefield visited the place, then known as Lewiston or Lewis Town, on Oct. 30, 1739 and remained two days.

He was met in the evening by two or three leading persons and on the following day "preached at two in the afternoon to a serious and attentive congregation." "Persons of different denominations were present," he wrote, "and the congregation was larger than might be expected in so small a place, and at so short a notice. After sermon, the High Sheriff, collector, and chief men of the place came and took leave of me; and by their means we were provided with horses and a guide for our journey at a reasonable expense."

In April 1741, William Becket, Anglican rector at Lewes, wrote: "It is surprising to observe how the vulgar everywhere are inclined to enthusiasm. Mr. Whitefield (the early minister of Methodism) had a vast crowd of hearers in May last when he preached four or five times from a balcony. They continued, unknown to me, to set up a religious society."

The Society had seventeen members and survived only three years. It was revived in 1779 by FREEBORN GARRETTSON. A frame church building, known as old Ebenezer, was erected in 1788 and Bethel Church was built about two years later. In 1970 Bethel reported a membership of 556.

G. Whitefield, *Journals*. 1960.   ELMER T. CLARK

LEWIS, EDWIN (1881-1959), American theologian, lecturer, author, and professor, was born on April 18, 1881, in Newbury, England. He was the son of Joseph and Sarah (Newman) Lewis. He married Louise Newhook Frost (deceased 1953) on Jan. 5, 1904, and their children are Olin Lewis, Velva (Mrs. Kenneth B. Grady), and Faulkner Lewis (vice-president of the MacMillan Company). He married a second time Josephine Stults, who survives him. When Edwin Lewis was nineteen years of age, he went to Labrador with Sir Wilfred Grenfell and joined the Newfoundland Methodist Church of Canada, 1900-03, and then went into the NORTH DAKOTA Conference where he served from 1904-05. He was educated at Sackville College, Canada; Middlebury College; United Free Church College, Glasgow; DREW SEMINARY (B.D., 1908; Th.D., 1918); New York State College for Teachers (B.A., 1915), and DICKINSON COLLEGE (D.D., 1926). He transferred to the TROY CONFERENCE in 1910 and served North Chatham, 1913-16; First Church at Rensselaer, New York; and then became an instructor in Greek and Theology at the Drew Seminary, 1916-18. He became adjunct professor of Systematic Theology there in 1918 and in 1920 became a professor, which position he occupied until he retired in the early 1950's.

Lewis publicly stated that his theological attitude changed somewhat as he progressed in his work, and he challenged certain extremely liberal teachings in his book, *A Christian Manifesto*, published in 1934. He also wrote *Jesus Christ and the Human Quest*, 1924; *A Manual of Christian Beliefs*, 1927; *God and Ourselves*, 1931; *Great Christian Teachings*, 1933; *The Faith We Declare* (the Fondren Lectures for 1938); *A Philosophy of the Christian Revelation*, 1940; *A New Heaven and a New Earth* (which were the Quillian Lectures at EMORY UNIVERSITY, 1941); and *The Creator and the Adversary*, in which he opposed the rather widely held idea that there was no positive spirit of evil in the universe and that the goodness of God was everything. "We have gone too far toward a benevolent monism," he told the writer of these lines. He was one of the co-authors of the *Abingdon Bible*

Commentary, 1929, a work which is still held in high repute.

Upon his retirement from Drew, he taught for a time in Temple University in PHILADELPHIA, though he continued to maintain a home in Madison, N. J. He died in the winter of 1959.

E. S. Bucke, *History of American Methodism*. 1964.
C. T. Howell, *Prominent Personalities*. 1945.
Journal of the Troy Conference, 1960.   N. B. H.

LEWIS, FELIX L. (1888-1965), twenty-third bishop of the C.M.E. CHURCH, was born on Sept. 4, 1888, at Homer, La. He was licensed to preach in 1901 and was admitted to the Louisiana Conference in 1906. He received a B.S. degree from WILEY COLLEGE and attended GARRETT BIBLICAL INSTITUTE. He served churches in TENNESSEE and LOUISIANA, and was appointed presiding elder for fifteen years. In 1934, he was elected general secretary of the Kingdom Extension Department, where he served until 1946 and his election to the office of bishop. He retired from service in January 1960, and died in August 1965.

Harris and Patterson, *C.M.E. Church*. 1965.
The Christian Index, May 16, 1946.   RALPH G. GAY

LEWIS, THOMAS HAMILTON (1852-1929), American Methodist Protestant president and church statesman, was born in Dover, Del., on Dec. 11, 1852. His father died in 1853 and the family moved to MARYLAND where he lived until he moved to WASHINGTON, D.C. in 1920.

He entered WESTERN MARYLAND COLLEGE in 1871 and was graduated in 1875. Entering the MARYLAND CONFERENCE of the M. P. Church in 1875, he served two pastorates: the first at Cumberland, Md., 1875-6; the other at St. John's Church in Baltimore, Md., 1876-81.

On Dec. 11, 1877, he married Mary Ward, daughter of J. T. WARD, president of Western Maryland College.

In 1881 he organized the WESTMINSTER THEOLOGICAL SEMINARY (now WESLEY SEMINARY) and served as its first president from 1881 to 1885. He then became president of Western Maryland College, which he served until 1920, a period of thirty-four years. In the meanwhile he was elected president of the GENERAL CONFERENCE of the M. P. Church, serving one four-year term. In 1920 he was again elected president of that body, serving eight years as its first full-time president.

In 1928 he was elected Contributing Editor of the combined denominational papers, *The Methodist Protestant* and *The Methodist Recorder*, continuing in that capacity until his death in 1929. To the last he was in full possession of his extraordinary mental and spiritual gifts. He was buried in the Westminster city cemetery after a service in the Baker Chapel of the College.

"Such in brief outline is the life story of the most remarkable man the Methodist Protestant Church has produced." (1930 *Maryland Conference Journal*, p. 133). He was a superb preacher, a great orator. His presidency of the College gave it a firm educational and financial foundation. His three terms of president of the General Conference were conspicuous in administrative grasp of denominational policies and programs, giving to the Church a sense of unity and direction it greatly needed. Much of this focused in the great centenary celebration (Methodist Protestant) in BALTIMORE in 1928.

Perhaps his greatest achievement was in relation to

Methodist unification. In 1908 he was elected president of the General Conference of his church. The General Conference of the M. E. Church, in session in Baltimore, sent a delegation, consisting of Bishop WARREN, JOHN F. GOUCHER and Senator J. P. DOLLIVER, to the General Conference of the M. P. Church, in Pittsburgh, with a proposal to "renew organic fellowship with the Methodist Episcopal Church." Their coming was enthusiastically received and their message referred to the committee on union. This latter committee acted in reply: "That a commission consisting of nine members be appointed by this Conference for the purpose of meeting with a like commission of the Methodist Episcopal Church, of the Methodist Episcopal Church, South, and of other Methodist Churches in this country to promote as far as possible the reunification of Methodists in America."

A deputation of three—T. H. Lewis, A. L. Reynolds, J. W. HERING—was sent to Baltimore. It was here that he made his remarkable appeal for Methodist union. He was at his best in voice and material. At the close, referring to his Church, the smallest body—"Brethren, if little Benjamin may but beat a drum or carry a flag while Judah and Ephraim once more march on to the same music of peace, joyfully we will say, Amen, God wills it."

The editor of the *Advocate* wrote of the event: "At the appealing climax, they (the Conference) were on their feet again—laughing, cheering, saluting, singing—delegates and spectators alike swayed by the fraternal impulse."

It happened, however, that the Conference took no further action for union and no meetings were ever held.

Undaunted, T. H. Lewis made his way to the 1910 session of the M. E. Church, South, and had a similar response as at Baltimore. That Conference also reached no conclusive decision with reference to union.

Fortunately, both of the other Churches had appointed commissions to deal with the problem of overlapping areas. It was at a meeting of these two groups that he appeared, whether by invitation or voluntarily, for he was not a member of either body. But out of it all developed a tri-church movement for organic union. Several meetings of the three commissions were held, resulting in a body of "Suggestions" for union. And though he did not live to see it, the movement for Methodist unification, for which Thomas Hamilton Lewis labored, continued in various phases, culminating at Kansas City, Mo., in 1939.

JAMES H. STRAUGHN

LEWIS, WILLIAM BRYANT (1891-1956), American missionary medical pioneer of the M. E. Church, South in the Belgian Congo, was born in Vicksburg, Miss., Oct. 24, 1891. Educated at MILLSAPS COLLEGE, and the Medical School of VANDERBILT UNIVERSITY, he practiced medicine in LOUISIANA, 1913-16. He was with the Louisiana National Guard on the Mexican border, 1916-17, and then in France 1917-19 as a medical officer of the A.E.F. during World War I. He afterward continued medical studies at Tulane University, but the call to Christian service was overwhelming and he was appointed a medical missionary to the CONGO in 1923.

Lewis received permission from the Belgian government to establish a leper colony in association with the hospital and medical service he directed in Tunda Station. He also pioneered in the opening of rural dispensaries in outlying and remote villages in a wide area surrounding Tunda.

These were served by trained native hospital attendants. Mrs. Lewis, the former Zaidee Hunter Nelson of Jackson, Miss., assisted her husband in the Tunda Hospital and in the organization of an evangelistic and health ministry in the mission area. On retirement they returned to MISSISSIPPI. A large and commodious hospital, the Lewis Memorial Hospital, has been built at Tunda and named in honor of the Lewises.

Ann L. Ashmore, *The Call of the Congo.* Nashville, 1947.

W. W. REID

WILSON S. LEWIS

LEWIS, WILSON SEELEY (1857-1921), American educator and bishop, was born near Russell, N. Y., June 17, 1857. Although raised in poverty and with little formal education, he started teaching rural school at age sixteen. He worked his way through three years at St. Lawrence College at Canton, N. Y., and went to Iowa in 1880 to teach in the public schools. He felt he was called to preach and joined the UPPER IOWA CONFERENCE in 1885. He was appointed pastor at Blairstown. In 1888 he became principal of Epworth Seminary, a Methodist preparatory school at Epworth, Iowa. After notable success there he was elected president of MORNINGSIDE COLLEGE, Sioux City, Iowa, in 1897 and transferred to the NORTHWEST IOWA CONFERENCE.

He travelled a year in Europe before assuming his post. The conference had recently taken over Morningside College from a group of local promoters. It had one small building, a large debt, no assets and no public goodwill. Under President Lewis its academic standards were raised, the debt and the main building which now bears his name was erected. He secured financial support from near and far, including gifts from Andrew Carnegie and the General Education Board which formed the beginning of an endowment fund.

National attention was attracted to his ability and in 1908 he was elected bishop. His assignments were eight years at Foochow, CHINA, and four years at Shanghai. He and Bishop JAMES W. BASHFORD superintended the work in China during the downfall of the Manchu dynasty and through the First World War. He was called back to the U.S.A. in 1913 to participate in a nationwide campaign for finances to save GOUCHER COLLEGE in Baltimore, Md. He came home again to give leadership in raising the CENTENARY FUND for Missions in 1919. He strongly supported the ill-fated Interchurch World Movement for missions which followed.

A self-devised philosophy of missions guided his work. He made himself accessible to the Chinese pastors. He strengthened the local churches by increasing their self-dependency. He schemed to create among the Methodists an all-China awareness and loyalty in contrast to the local and regional fragmentations typical of that land. He insisted upon the steady up-grading of the church's educational institutions. The church membership grew from 22,000 in 1903 to 77,000 in 1920.

His son, John, served as a missionary in China. His daughter, Ida Belle, eventually became President of Hwa Nan College at Foochow under the WOMAN'S FOREIGN MISSIONARY SOCIETY. In 1920 he was assigned to the Peking area. His health broke soon afterward and he returned to Sioux City, where he died on Aug. 24, 1921. He is buried there in Graceland Cemetery under an impressive stone monument erected by the citizens. A boulevard and a city park also bear his name.

S. N. Fellows, *Upper Iowa Conference.* 1907.
F. D. Leete, *Methodist Bishops.* 1948.
Ida Belle Lewis, *Bishop Wilson Seeley Lewis*, Sioux City, Ia.: Morningside College, 1929.
Minutes of the Northwest Iowa Conference, 1921.
B. Mitchell, *Northwest Iowa Conference.* 1904.

FRANK G. BEAN

LEXINGTON, KENTUCKY, U.S.A. (population 107,944) is a city situated in the heart of the famous blue grass region of Kentucky, and Lexington itself is sometimes called the "capital of the blue grass." For the origin and the development of early Methodism in Lexington see the history of the FIRST METHODIST CHURCH there in the article below.

Centenary Methodist, now located in north Lexington, celebrated its 100th anniversary in 1966. It dates its origin from the latter part of December 1865, when 133 members withdrew from the Hill Street M. E. Church, South —now First Church—and met and organized on Jan. 3, 1866, a new church which adhered to the M. E. Church. The first unit of this church's building was upon the corner of Broadway and Church Street and was dedicated on Oct. 14, 1866. The sanctuary was added in 1870. In 1955 the congregation moved to the present location and remained there until it combined with Trinity Church which had been established under the district superintendency of A. G. Stone in 1940-46. Trinity itself was established as a church in 1945 when a pastor was appointed there.

Old Centenary in its downtown location had by that time begun to face problems of limited space and inadequate parking facilities, and its members were moving out to suburban areas. So Trinity and Centenary worked out a combination—"the most beautiful church wedding that has ever been held" states the Centenary brochure celebrating this event. The new Centenary is quite commodious and has a new educational building attached to the church. Centenary members claim that it "has the vitality of a young church and the stability of a mature church." Donald W. Durham was the pastor of the church on the 1966 centenary occasion. In 1970 the membership was 1,984.

Recent statistics indicate that total membership of the Methodist churches in the Lexington district is 19,109 and property values are of $9,438,065 last reporting.

Centenary Methodist Church. Published by the Church Directory of Publishers. Louisville, Ky., 1966.   N. B. H.

First Church is the historic downtown church of Lexington. Here the first Lexington Society was organized in 1789 while Lexington was still a frontier village. Five miles from Lexington in 1790 Bishop ASBURY held the first Annual Conference west of the Alleghenies. In this conference plans were made for the starting of BETHEL ACADEMY, the first Methodist institute of learning west of the Alleghenies. In 1804 the society of Lexington became the first station west of the Alleghenies. In 1815 Bishop Asbury preached his last sermon in KENTUCKY in this church from the text found in Zephaniah 3:12-13. In 1819 the church consisted of 113 white and seventy colored members.

The first session of the newly formed KENTUCKY CONFERENCE was held here in 1821. All three of the Bishops —WILLIAM McKENDREE, ENOCH GEORGE, and ROBERT R. ROBERTS—were present. The Conference also met here in 1822. The second location of the church was on Church Street between Upper and Limestone. On this lot a sturdy brick church 60x50 feet was built with a gallery above for colored people.

Colored people continued to be listed as members of the church until the period following the Civil War, when the number greatly decreased. Stephen Chipley should be mentioned. He was an apprentice to Maddox Fisher, Lexington businessman and member of the Methodist Church. Fisher taught him the bricklayer's trade and reading, writing, and arithmetic. Stephen Chipley served on the Board of Trustees of the Methodist Church for fifty years.

H. H. KAVANAUGH was pastor in 1833 and 1834. In the summer of 1833 the epidemic of Asiatic cholera caused nearly 500 deaths in less than three months time. Every family was affected and business was paralyzed. Under Kavanaugh's ministry, however, a revival began in January 1834 and lasted two months, and 200 people were added to the Methodist Church. He was elected bishop in 1854.

The increasing membership of the Lexington congregation made it necessary to select a new location. Property was acquired on High, or Hill Street, from the German Lutheran Community and here was built a church long known as the Hill Street M. E. Church, South. This was in 1841. In 1842 the Annual Conference was entertained here and H. B. BASCOM dedicated the new church in that same year. H. H. Kavanaugh was pastor again in 1847-48. In 1842 H. B. Bascom became president of TRANSYLVANIA UNIVERSITY, at that time a Methodist institution.

Through the efforts of Kavanaugh and Bascom another great revival was held with far reaching effects that greatly strengthened the local church. R. K. HARGROVE, later a bishop, was pastor in 1867. In 1878 H. P. Walker was pastor. During that time the Hill Street Auxiliary of the WOMAN'S FOREIGN MISSIONARY SOCIETY, authorized by the GENERAL CONFERENCE in May of that year, was organized in the Hill Street Church. Their first annual session was held in the Hill Street Church in March 1879. F. W. Nolan was pastor from 1882-86. Under his pastorate the church was fully remodeled, and he was assisted in a notable revival in 1884 by HENRY CLAY MORRISON. Bishop R. K. Hargrove, former pastor, presided at the Annual Conference session at Hill Street Church in 1890.

Under the pastorate of E. G. B. Mann, 1907-11, the present First Methodist Church was built. Mrs. Scola Inskeep Chenowith left by will $10,000 toward the building of the new stone church. She made three provisions: "The church was to raise $25,000. The new building was to be completed in two years. It was to be without debt when dedicated." These stipulations were carried out and the new church was dedicated on Jan. 10, 1909. The old name Hill Street M. E. Church, South was changed to First M. E. Church, South, Lexington. Following unification in 1939, the church became known as the First Methodist Church of Lexington.

First Church in its long history has always assisted in starting other Methodist churches in Lexington. E. L. Southgate, pastor in 1894, with H. P. Walker, presiding elder, assisted in the organization of the Sunday school in the north section of the city. This later became Epworth Church. U. G. Foote, pastor in 1902-06, assisted in the establishment of the church that later became Park Church. For several years it was a mission under the Quarterly Conference of the Hill Street Church.

In September 1907, O. B. Crockett was appointed as the first regular pastor of the Park Church.

Under the ministry of Gilbert Combs in 1922-28 the WESLEY FOUNDATION of the University of Kentucky met in First Church. The Wesley Foundation continued here until it moved to the new location in 1964.

On Oct. 10, 1940 the Woman's Society of Christian Service was organized here. The new Educational Plant was dedicated free of debt on Oct. 24, 1965. Present membership is 1,306, constituting a cross section of the city of Lexington.

RUSSELL R. PATTON

LEXINGTON CONFERENCE (ME), was organized at Harrodsburg, Ky., March 2, 1869, with Bishop LEVI SCOTT presiding. A Negro conference, it was formed by dividing the KENTUCKY CONFERENCE (ME) along racial lines. The conference began with two districts, Lexington and Louisville, twenty-six charges, and 3,526 members. The 1872 GENERAL CONFERENCE added OHIO and INDIANA to the territory of the Lexington Conference, and in 1873 it reported an Ohio District with twelve charges. In 1876 the conference boundaries were extended to include ILLINOIS. That year the conference had an Indianapolis District, and it reported fifty-eight charges and 6,871 members. Later MICHIGAN, MINNESOTA, and WISCONSIN were added, while southwest Illinois was surrendered to the Central Missouri (later CENTRAL WEST) Conference.

The Lexington Conference continued with two districts in Kentucky, one in Ohio, and one in Indiana, and for some years there was little growth in membership. In 1900 the conference reported 9,182 members. In 1914 the Chicago-Indianapolis District was formed, and the conference reported 12,506 members that year. In 1917 the Chicago District was organized with ten charges. During the First World War Negro migration to the north increased, and by 1920 the conference membership had risen to nearly 17,000. In 1938 the conference had 124 charges, and nearly 25,000 members.

The Lexington Conference's St. Mark Church in CHICAGO was known widely for years as one of the strongest congregations in Methodism. From 600 members in 1915, it grew to nearly 3,500 by 1930. From 1939 to 1964 the church regularly reported 4,000 to 4,700 members every year. In more recent years the St. Mark membership has greatly decreased.

At unification in 1939, the Lexington Conference became a part of the Central Jurisdiction.

Two members of the Lexington Conference were

elected bishops in The Methodist Church, M. W. CLAIR, JR. (1952) and M. LAFAYETTE HARRIS (1960).

The Lexington Conference supported PHILANDER SMITH COLLEGE at LITTLE ROCK, Ark. In 1942 the churches of the conference raised about $1,100 for the college. GAMMON THEOLOGICAL SEMINARY was commended as the one institution in the Central Jurisdiction for training ministers.

In 1964, its last year, the Lexington Conference reported 124 charges, 130 ministers, 40,689 members, property valued at $10,522,390. At that time the Kentucky churches of the conference were merged with the Tennessee Conference (CJ) to form the TENNESSEE-KENTUCKY CONFERENCE, and the remainder of the conference was absorbed by the overlying conferences of the North Central Jurisdiction.

General Minutes, MEC and MC.
Minutes of the Lexington Conference.
M. Simpson, Cyclopaedia, 1882.   ALBEA GODBOLD

LEYLAND, ARTHUR STANLEY (1901-   ), British minister, was born Nov. 25, 1901, in St. George's, Shropshire, England. Accepted for the ministry in the PRIMITIVE METHODIST CHURCH in 1922, he was sent for theological training to Hartley College, Manchester, and served in circuits in different parts of the kingdom until 1945, when he came to the London area for the first of four terms there in Highgate, Barnet, Brixton Hill, and Streatham. From 1940 onward he acted as Assistant Secretary of the British Methodist Conference, and for many years conducted a weekly feature in the Methodist Recorder.

Dr. Leyland pioneered the ministerial exchange program of the WORLD METHODIST COUNCIL in 1946, when he exchanged pulpits with Dr. Theodore C. Mayer of The Methodist Church, U.S.A. Since that time he has served as chairman of the British Committee on Ministerial Exchanges in the World Methodist Council. He is also a member of the British Council of Churches Visiting Preachers and Exchange Committee. He has been a delegate from British Methodism to the WORLD CONFERENCE on several occasions.

FRANK BAKER

LIBERIA is a country on the southern "bulge" of West Africa. Methodism is as old as the country. Both Methodists and Baptists share honors in having had outstanding leaders among the original settlers. When the colonists gained foothold in present-day Liberia in January 1822, the Methodist leader, Elijah Johnson held the little group together in a critical hour. During a revival in 1824, "upwards of twenty persons, all professing Christ for the first time," were added to the Methodist Society. A few days later they were given a lot for a church, which was built and finished in 1825.

When the first Methodist missionary, MELVILLE B. Cox, arrived in Liberia in 1833, he helped stabilize the Methodist work and brought it under episcopal supervision from America. Although Cox lived only four and one-half months after his arrival, he had carried the work beyond the boundaries of Monrovia. An Annual Conference was organized on Jan. 10, 1834, by Rufus Spaulding and S. O. Wright; however, formal authorization had to wait until the General Conference of 1836. There were three ministerial members at that conference: Spaulding, Wright, and the Liberian, Anthony D. Williams. Williams had been ordained in 1833 at the Oneida Conference. Wright is buried in Monrovia. Spaulding had to return home because of health. Late in 1834, John Seys arrived to assume leadership of the mission. Born in the West Indies, he was able to stand the tropical climate better than others. The Liberia Conference Seminary was opened in 1839, with Jabez Burton as principal. On March 19, 1837, a new Methodist church was dedicated in Monrovia. Built of stone, sixty-six by fifty feet, it is still in use today.

The period 1833 to 1844 has been called the "Golden Age" of Methodist Missions in Liberia. Because of the toll in lives and broken health among the missionaries, the local leadership gradually shifted over to the Liberians. A turning point in the life of the church came in 1851, for the conference had to decide whether to disband or go on under their own leaders; at this time FRANCIS BURNS was acting as President of the conference. In 1853 Bishop LEVI SCOTT visited Liberia for the Annual Conference session held in Cape Palmas. There, for the first time in the country, an ordination service was held. Eleven men were ordained as DEACONS and eight as ELDERS. For the first time since its founding the conference had ministers set apart to perform the ordinances and sacraments of the church. In 1856 Francis Burns was elected the first Liberian missionary bishop by the General Conference of the M. E. Church. He was the first "missionary bishop" ever elected, the office largely being created to take care of the type of supervision Burns was to give. He gave leadership until his death in April 1863. He was followed in the episcopacy by another well qualified Liberian, JOHN W. ROBERTS, brother of the first President of Liberia, JOSEPH J. ROBERTS. By 1868 the Liberia Annual Conference was given full status in the M. E. Church with representation in the General Conference. Bishop Roberts served until his death in 1875, when again the episcopal supervision was assigned to bishops from America. In 1876 the conference had five districts and twenty-one appointments. In 1877 the membership reached 2,488.

In 1884 the General Conference elected the veteran missionary, WILLIAM TAYLOR, as bishop for Africa. Taylor's plan was to establish self-supporting mission stations in a chain across Africa. After having started the work in the Congo he brought a number of missionaries to Liberia. Soon seven stations were established along the Cavalla River, six along the Kru Coast, and ten in Sinoe and Grand Bassa Counties and on the St. Paul River. Over fifty missionaries, the majority of them women, were taken by Bishop Taylor to Liberia. During the period the Mission Board sent out nineteen men to do district and educational work. When Bishop Taylor retired in 1896 his methods had been criticized and many casualties had been reported. But though a number of stations had closed, his work has in several places brought permanent results. It should be noted that the great membership strength of the Methodist Church today lies in the areas where his work was established. Most of the men entering the ministry today come from this Kru Coast area.

After having been without a resident bishop for thirty years, Liberia received Bishop ISAIAH B. SCOTT, an American Negro elected by the General Conference of 1904. A period of progress followed. The membership rose from 3,301 to 10,959 by 1916 when Bishop Scott retired. During this period special emphasis was given to self-help and self-support, education, and evangelism among the Grebo and Kru tribal groups.

A visit by THOMAS S. DONOHUGH, secretary of the M.E.

METHODIST CHURCH, GANTA, LIBERIA

Mission Board, in 1923 brought about a reorganization of the mission work. An important decision was to begin a new station at Ganta in the interior. After a two weeks' trek through the jungle, GEORGE W. HARLEY and his wife arrived at Ganta in 1926. The Ganta station became one of the largest Methodist stations in Africa; it includes the hospital, elementary and junior high schools, girls' and boys' dormitories, evangelism department, literacy work, nursing school, and industrial work with a fine carpenter's shop, where mahogany furniture is built. The Harleys retired in 1960. Thousands of treatments are given in the clinic every year; two new hospital wings were equipped for modern surgery with a staff of three doctors; the leprosarium with 700 patients and twelve out-stations was set up; and evangelistic work in over seventy villages was started. Another important project following this 1923 visit was the strengthening of the COLLEGE OF WEST AFRICA.

The assignment of Bishop Willis J. King (1944-56) as resident bishop assured the work in Liberia of more stability and expansion, as there had been no resident bishop since 1928. New work was begun at Gbarnga, located 120 miles inland at an important crossroad. A significant step forward was taken when a Conference Board of Missions was organized to assume in part the responsibility for the new mission. Cooperation with Cuttington College was started with the providing of a Methodist professor on the staff. The Woman's Division (TMC) opened a well-equipped hostel for girls attending the College of West Africa, and has since provided a home economics teacher for the school. The academic standards of the school were raised considerably and the position of the College of West Africa as the leading college preparatory school in the country was further strengthened.

Under Bishop Prince A. Taylor, Jr. (1956-64), much was done to strengthen the administration of the Annual Conference and to bring the Liberian Church to the point of self-sustenance. This has partly been brought about due to the foresight and vision of WILLIAM V. S. TUBMAN, President of Liberia, and a dedicated layman in the Methodist Church.

In 1964 the General Conference (TMC) voted an enabling act which would permit Liberia to become either an autonomous church or a CENTRAL CONFERENCE. At the Annual Conference session in February 1965, the Liberia Annual Conference voted unanimously to establish a Central Conference, and to elect a Liberian as bishop. This historic conference was held Dec. 8-12,

MT. SCOTT CHURCH, CAPE PALMAS, SITE OF
FIRST SESSION OF LIBERIA CENTRAL CONFERENCE

1965, at Mt. Scott Memorial Methodist Church in Cape Palmas, the same place where the first Liberian ministers were ordained by Bishop Levi Scott in 1853. STEPHEN TROWEN NAGBE, SR., is the first Liberian to be elected bishop and consecrated in Liberia. He conducted his first Annual Conference and service of ordination at Caldwell, near Monrovia, the place where Melville Cox held his first camp meeting 133 years before.

Among important developments after World War II was cooperation with Cuttington College in theological training, and a mission and church were organized in Gbarnga—the joint theological training program at Cuttington is no longer in effect.

The Church in Liberia has started to train a full-time indigenous ministry. Admission to Conference membership has been raised from eight to twelve years of schooling. By 1962 three congregations had full-time pastors with college degrees. A Pastors' School has been established at Gbarnga which takes men who have completed tenth grade in school and gives them two or three years theological training.

W. C. Barclay, *History of Missions.* 1949-57.
Ivan Lee Holt, *Methodists of the World.* 1950.
J. F. Hurst, *History of Methodism.* 1901-04.
W. J. King, *Liberia.* N.d.   WERNER J. WICKSTROM

LIBERIA ANNUAL CONFERENCE organized in that land (see LIBERIA) was given authority by the General Conference of 1964 to become organized into a Central Conference during the quadrennium ending in 1968 provided that it should have a minimum of twenty ministerial members on the basis of one delegate for every four ministerial members of the Annual Conference. Pursuant to this requirement during the quadrennium, Liberia became a Central Conference of The United Methodist Church through the actions which have been outlined above in the general account of Liberia.

N. B. H.

LIBERTY CHURCH, Greene County, Georgia, U.S.A., cradle of Methodism of Central Georgia and one of the oldest Methodist churches in continuous operation. Around 1786, John Bush erected a brush arbor as a community center for CAMP MEETINGS in what was then called Crackers Neck. It became a preaching place for Methodists and from this grew Liberty Chapel. In 1797, JAMES JENKINS, a pioneer Methodist itinerant, served the Washington Circuit which included Greene, Wilkes, Taliaferro, Lincoln, Elbert, Hart, Franklin, Madison, and Oglethorpe Counties. After preaching at Liberty, Jenkins reported in his journal that following a fiery exhortation, a man in uniform came down the aisle and fell at his feet crying for pardon. Others came after him, and according to Jenkins, this occurrence at Liberty Chapel was the origin of the Methodist custom of penitents coming to the altar. "The meeting became so noisy," he continued, "that it was a wonder the horses did not take fright."

Many of the great men of early Methodist history were connected with Liberty. Bishop ASBURY preached there several times. "In Liberty there is life," he wrote in 1801, "and many souls have been brought to God, even children." Again he preached there on Christmas Day, 1806, noting that the new chapel measured thirty by fifty feet.

In December of 1808, the twenty-third session of the SOUTH CAROLINA CONFERENCE, which also served GEORGIA, met at Liberty. Bishops Asbury and McKENDREE attended, and Asbury estimated that between 2,000 and 3,000 people were present, for one of the first winter camp meetings in America was held in conjunction with the annual conference. LOVICK PIERCE was ordained an ELDER, and WILLIAM CAPERS was admitted a preacher on trial. Liberty continued to serve the rural area in which it was located, and in 1966 it was on the White Plains Circuit in the Augusta District of the North Georgia Conference.

F. Asbury, *Journal and Letters.* 1958.
A. M. Pierce, *Georgia.* 1956.   DONALD J. WEST

LICENSES, PREACHERS' AND PREACHING HOUSES'. The Act of Uniformity (1662) was followed by the Conventicle Acts of 1664 and 1670, whereby anyone attending "any unlawful assembly, conventicle or meeting under colour or pretence of any exercise of religion" would be fined or imprisoned. The Toleration Act (1689) gave relief to bona fide Dissenters, but did not provide for Methodists, who were recognized by neither Anglicans nor Dissenters. The only way out of the dilemma was for Wesley to license his itinerants as "preachers of the Gospel," though against their will they had to accept licenses in which they were described as "Dissenting Preachers." They were accused of "acting under a lie" (see Wesley's letter to Thomas Adam, July 19, 1768), i.e., while professing themselves members of the Church of England, they licensed themselves as Dissenters. To obtain a license a preacher had to take the oaths, make certain declarations, and generally comply with the Act of Toleration.

As persecution set in, it became increasingly necessary for Methodist buildings to have the protection of being licensed. They were registered as buildings "for the worship of God and religious exercises as Protestant Dissenters." The New Room, Bristol, was the first to be thus registered (October 17, 1748). The Large Minutes (*Minutes* i. 602) of 1763 lays down the proper form for such a license. In 1812 the Methodists played a large part in the events which led up to the repeal of the Conventicle Act.

F. Baker, *Wesley and the Church of England*. 1970.
Wesley Historical Soc. *Proceedings*, xi, 82, 103, 130.

JOHN C. BOWMER

LICHFIELD PLAN was drawn up in 1794, three years after Wesley's death. April 1 and 2, THOMAS COKE consulted at Lichfield with ALEXANDER MATHER, THOMAS TAYLOR, JOHN PAWSON, SAMUEL BRADBURN, JAMES ROGERS, HENRY MOORE, and ADAM CLARKE about the future organization of Methodism. The plan recommended: (1) preachers be received into FULL CONNEXION by being ordained deacon; (2) preachers approved by the Conference be ordained elders; (3) an order of SUPERINTENDENTS be instituted.

The plan went on to suggest geographical "divisions," listed the personnel to be appointed superintendents (largely the same as the authors of the plan!), and outlined the extent of their authority. The Conference that year "treated" the Lichfield Plan as "tending to create invidious distinctions among brethren and those who attended the meeting were considered as aspirants after honour." Thus it was rejected, though doubtless its authors argued that it accorded with Wesley's intentions when he "set apart" Coke and Mather by the laying on of hands to be superintendents.

V. E. VINE

J. SCOTT LIDGETT

LIDGETT, JOHN SCOTT (1854-1953), British Methodist, once called "the greatest Methodist since John Wesley," was born at Lewisham, Kent, on August 10, 1854, and entered the Wesleyan ministry in 1876. His services to the church were recognized by his election to the LEGAL HUNDRED in 1902, and he became PRESIDENT of the Wesleyan Conference in 1908 and first president of the reunited Methodist Church in 1932.

His main life work was the Bermondsey Settlement, which he founded in 1891 with WILLIAM FIDDIAN MOULTON, and of which he remained warden until 1949. Lidgett's services to the borough were acknowledged when he was made an honorary freeman, but his influence extended into the life of the whole of London, especially in educational matters. He became an alderman on the London County Council in 1905, and was a member of the senate of London University from 1922-32. In 1931-32 he was vice-chancellor of the university.

He was a member of many interdenominational organizations, and in 1913 served on a royal commission. From 1907-18 he edited *The Methodist Times*, and from 1911 was the joint editor of *The Contemporary Review*. In addition he was a distinguished theologian, his main works being a FERNLEY LECTURE, *The Spiritual Principle of the Atonement* (1898); *The Fatherhood of God* (1902); *The Christian Religion* (1907). He died at Epsom, Surrey, on June 16, 1953.

R. E. Davies, *John Scott Lidgett*. 1957.
Minutes of the Methodist Conference, 1953.

H. MORLEY RATTENBURY

LIEBNER, OTTO (1879-1946), missionary and statistician, was born Feb. 3, 1879, to Jewish parents in Vienna, Austria. After graduation from high school he attended the University in Vienna. Shortly after his graduation he came to New York City, was converted, and enrolled in the Biblical Seminary of New York. He graduated in 1914 and was accepted by the Board of Missions of the M. E. Church as a missionary. From 1919 to 1928 he served in South America. In 1929 he was put in charge of the work of the Baltic countries, Bulgaria and Jugoslavia. In 1933 he returned to America and served as a pastor at Evansville, Ind. From 1936 to 1939 he served as a professor of Biblical Interpretation at the Biblical Seminary in New York. The final seven years of his life were spent doing statistical work for the Chicago office of the General BOARD OF PENSIONS of The Methodist Church.

ROBERT CHAFEE

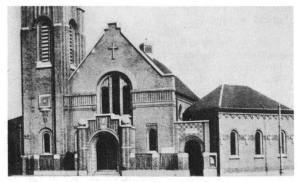

EGLISE EVANGELIQUE METHODISTE
DE LA REDEMPTION, LIEGE, BELGIUM

LIÉGE, Belgium, The Methodist Church (French) began in 1925 as an annex of HERSTAL Church. In 1930 a beautiful church building was erected by H. H. STANLEY, overlooking the Meuse River at Pont Maghin. The church was twice damaged by the blowing up of a bridge in 1940 and 1944. During the Nazi occupation, Pastor Henri van Oest was arrested and sent to a death camp in Germany. He died in Siegburg on March 10, 1945. Pastors have been F. Cuenod, 1924-37; H. van Oest, 1938-41; P. Spranghers, 1944-46; A. Wemers, 1947-58; J. Coviaux, 1959-64; and L. Berchier since 1965.

WILLIAM G. THONGER

LIGHTWOOD, JAMES THOMAS (1856-1944), British pioneer in the study of Methodist music and hymnology, was born in Leeds, the son of a Wesleyan Methodist minister. He was educated at KINGSWOOD SCHOOL. After some experience in trade, with his brother Edward in 1879 he opened a boarding school at Lytham St. Annes, Lancashire. He was one of the founding members of the WESLEY HISTORICAL SOCIETY, and in 1910 began the Methodist musical monthly, *The Choir*. In 1892 he published thirty-two *Tunes with Hymns for use in Day and Sunday Schools*, and continued to write hymn tunes throughout his life; five of them were included in the *Methodist Hymn Book* (1933). Of his many books the following are probably the most useful: *Methodist Music in the Eighteenth Century* (1927), *Stories of Methodist Music* (1928), *Samuel Wesley, Musician* (1936), and especially the standard reference work, *The Music of the Methodist Hymn Book* (1935).

FRANK BAKER

LIM SI SIN (1910-   ), bishop for two terms of the autonomous Methodist Church of Lower Burma, whose election was the highlight of the Conference (Oct. 5-10, 1965), at which the Burma Annual Conference of The Methodist Church became the Autonomous Methodist Church of Lower Burma. Previous to his election, he had been the pastor for sixteen years of the Christ Methodist Church in Rangoon, and superintendent of the Chinese District of the Conference for almost the same period. He and his wife are the parents of seven children——three daughters and four sons, one of whom is Dr. Lim Toh Bin, a graduate of Northwestern Medical College (Illinois) and now practicing medicine in Canada. Bishop Lim was born in CHINA in 1910 and came to BURMA from Amoy in 1949 as pastor of the Chinese-language Christ Methodist Church.

The consecration of Bishop Lim was presided over by Bishop HOBART B. AMSTUTZ. A purple stole was presented to Bishop Lim by Bishop Amstutz. At the same moment Bishop Amstutz said, "I hereby dissolve the Burma Annual Conference of The Methodist Church and declare the establishment of the Autonomous Methodist Church of the Union of Burma."

Among the distinguished guests who attended this consecration were the Roman Catholic Archbishop Bazin; Anglican Bishop of Rangoon, H. V. Shearburn; Rev. John Thet Gyi, general secretary of the Burma Christian Council; representatives of the Baptist Church, and the Rev. Vulchuka, fraternal delegate from the Upper Burma Methodist Church which became autonomous in 1964. Bishop Lim's two terms as bishop ended in September 1969.

N. B. H.

LIMA, Peru, is the capital of that nation and is one of the most interesting cities in the world. It is one of the oldest cities of the Americas and contains within it both Indian and Spanish colonial tradition, as well as modern buildings

LA VICTORIA CHURCH, LIMA
THE OLDEST EVANGELICAL CHURCH BUILDING

and processes. In it there is the oldest university in the Americas—the University of San Marcos, founded in 1551. The city's population in 1970 is given as 2,415,700.

There are today about ten regular Methodist Sunday schools and preaching places in Lima, as well as the several institutions whose work is described below. Three congregations are near self-supporting. The First Methodist Church is perhaps the strongest of these.

Colegio Maria Alvarado is a school for girls formerly known as Lima High School. Founded in 1906, it was one of the first girls' schools in PERU to offer secondary education. At the present time it has both elementary and secondary departments. It offers college preparatory, commercial and home economics courses. Enrollment in 1968 was 645.

The school is located near downtown Lima in a building provided in 1932 by the WOMAN'S DIVISION OF CHRISTIAN SERVICE and added to in 1954. Funds for the building were secured and administered through the service of Gertrude Hanks, who was principal for many years. The school is directed by Mrs. Olga Vanderghem, a graduate of Maria Alvarado and its first Peruvian principal.

Escuela America de La Victoria is an elementary school in the La Victoria section of Lima. Begun in 1916 as the parochial school of a Methodist church, Escuela America in 1966 enrolled 700 students. The director, Moises Huaroto, and the entire faculty were Peruvian.

La Florida Methodist Center is a social center in Lima, founded in the early 1950's by Martha Vanderberg, missionary of the Woman's Division of Christian Service. It was the first project of its type undertaken by any Protestant church in Peru and stimulated similar projects in Chincha, Miramar, Pedregal, and other places.

By the year 1950, villages of squatters had begun to spring up on the hills across the Rimac River from Lima. Miss Vanderberg learned of the needs of families there, beyond the reach of churches, schools, and social services. She was a teacher at Colegio Maria Alvarado and recruited a student to help her conduct a small vacation church school.

The interest continued, with students donating books for a reading room. Additional vacation schools were held, and Sunday classes were begun. Church services were added. Miss Vanderberg directed the work while continuing to teach, later becoming full-time director. A building was erected with the aid of the BOARD OF MIS-

SIONS in New York and was occupied in 1954. By 1959 more than 1,300 persons were registered for various services of the center.

Activities included child care, a kindergarten, club work, distribution of clothing and other emergency supplies, and health services.

Panamericana Normal School is a Methodist teacher-training school, established in 1961. The normal school was started in order to help alleviate a chronic shortage of trained teachers in Peru, and especially to increase the number of Evangelicals (Protestants) qualified to teach in the day schools affiliated with Evangelical churches. Many Methodist local churches maintain day schools, and the thirteen Methodist schools in Peru enroll more than 3,500 pupils. The school hopes to train future teachers in new educational methods, stressing participation by the child in the learning process as opposed to a traditional emphasis upon memorization.

The first graduation exercise was held on Dec. 12, 1964—just one week after long-delayed official recognition was given by the government. The student body is coeducational, and the course of study is for four years. Enrollment runs around fifty.

Barbara H. Lewis, ed., *Methodist Overseas Missions*. New York: Board of Missions, 1960.　　　EDWIN H. MAYNARD

LINCOLN, England. Methodism was securely rooted in the county of Lincolnshire some forty years before the city of Lincoln itself heard JOHN WESLEY, and before Sarah Parrott and Dorothy Fisher became the first two members. It was in the year 1787 that Mrs. Fisher came from Gonerby to live in Lincoln, and she came in response to a pressing invitation from the small society at Sturton by Stow, where Sarah Parrott was a member. Two years later the first chapel was built in the city, and from that time the cause moved forward with vigor. By the end of the century there were close to a hundred members. By 1815 the little Waterside Chapel became too small, and the Bank Street building was erected; and if the first generation of Wesleyans was growing a little old by 1836, they were sufficiently enterprising to launch the big Wesley Chapel, and over 500 members joined a cause which had connectional fame.

This chapel stood for 125 years while Methodism expanded into all parts of the city. Before "Big Wesley" was built, a society had started in the north in Newport, and two chapels preceded the present Gothic-style Bailgate Chapel, erected in 1880, dominating the more ancient Newport Arch of Roman fame. In the south, the Wesley members established a society in 1864 which resulted in the building of Lincoln's famous Hannah Memorial Chapel, and still later St. Catherine's Chapel. In 1859 they started the Rosemary Lane Day School, but there had already been twenty years of educational activity on the Big Wesley premises. Bailgate and St. Catherine's in turn pioneered the fringes of the town north and south, and chapels were built in the new housing estates. Various Lincoln business firms were connected with Wesleyanism, such as Mawer and Collingham, drapers; Ruddocks, printers; Bainbridge, another draper; Stokes, confectioner; besides many influential men in industry, and a large number of aldermen and councillors. A number of Lincoln's mayors were men from Wesley Chapel. RICHARD WATSON, an early president, was brought up at Wesley. JOHN HANNAH entered the ministry from here, and be-

came the first tutor at Hoxton, the start of Wesleyan Methodist ministerial training. FREDERICK J. JOBSON was a Lincoln man; he laid the foundation stone of the Hannah Memorial Chapel and himself became president. John Hornabrook also entered the ministry from Lincolnshire Methodism.

The Wesleyan Conference met at Big Wesley on two occasions, in 1909 and 1925; and the large premises housed all kinds of civic, cultural, and social functions. When at last the building had to be demolished, a brass tablet telling of the efforts of Sarah Parrott and Dorothy Fisher was carefully removed, and is now located in the new chapel at Sturton, where Lincoln Methodism really began.

PRIMITIVE METHODISM began in Lincoln about the year 1818, when WILLIAM CLOWES visited the city and held a meeting in Castle Square. In 1819 a chapel was erected in Mint Lane, and twenty years later the first of the Portland Place causes. Primitive Methodist enterprise in Lincoln, as elsewhere, reached out to other areas; and though it was centered in Portland Place for a long period, by the middle of the century societies were established at Rasen Lane in the north, Carholme Road in the west, and Newark Road in the south. One notable feature of Lincoln Primitive Methodism was the appointment of Mary Birks as the third minister in 1824; and in 1828 another woman, Ann Tinsley, was minister. One of Ann Tinsley's converts was Edward Chapman, who served the cause for half a century.

To Joseph Broadberry, another lifelong member, belongs the distinction of having been a working man who climbed to the city magisterial bench. In later years, Alderman C. T. Parker, who gave distinguished service to Lincoln Primitive Methodism, was mayor of the city three times. Portland Place, now named Lincoln Central Methodist Church, remains alone of the Primitive Methodist churches, combining the work of Hannah Memorial and other once flourishing chapels in the city center.

The Reform movement of the early 1850's affected the Wesley and Newport societies to the extent of their losing some 250 members; yet in 1863 both these societies had fully recovered these losses. The WESLEYAN REFORMERS worshiped in the Corn Exchange until they bought Zion Chapel, where members of the COUNTESS OF HUNTINGDON's connection had recently ceased to meet. By 1864 the Silver Street Free Methodist Chapel replaced the old Zion, and for almost a century its witness was as strong as any in the city. Elsewhere the Reformers, now known as the Free Methodists, built chapels in the city, which in their prime were greatly progressive. The UNITED METHODIST FREE CHURCHES Annual Assembly met in the Silver Street Chapel in the year 1898, when the Rev. J. C. Brewitt, a Lincolnshire man, was appointed secretary. He became president the following year. Honored names in the Free Methodist world in Lincoln were the Allmans, Crosbys, and the Meltons, besides the still more honored name of WILLIAM C. JACKSON, the last of the United Methodist Church presidents, and president of the Methodist Church in 1935.

With the union of Methodism in 1932, the task of circuit realignment began, and the fusion of societies. Not until 1957, however, was a position reached in circuit arrangement which satisfied the many differing traditions. The three circuits into which the city and villages are divided make for administrative purposes a well-defined ordering, and Methodism in Lincoln today is worthily maintained.

WILLIAM LEARY

LINCOLN, NEBRASKA, U.S.A., the capital of the state, with a population of 148,092 (1970), is a city surrounded by fertile farms. Settled in 1856 and incorporated as a city in 1877, Lincoln was the home of the orator, William Jennings Bryan, three times Democratic candidate for president of the United States. Bryan Memorial Hospital, started with a gift of Bryan's home to the Methodist Church in 1922, is one of Lincoln's outstanding hospitals. The original Bryan home, "Fairview," a museum on the hospital grounds, is visited by thousands each year.

Lincoln is the seat of the University of Nebraska, NEBRASKA WESLEYAN UNIVERSITY, and Union College. The Lincoln statue, replica of the monumental Washington, D. C. statue by Daniel Chester French, is located here.

Methodism's mother church in NEBRASKA was organized in 1854 by William Goode, first superintendent in Nebraska. A Reverend Gage was the first pastor in Nebraska City in nearby Otoe County.

Salt Creek Mission, started in 1857, is now St. Paul Church in Lincoln. In 1866 the M. P. Church started a school for children here. It became the first public school in Lincoln. Nebraska Wesleyan University moved from York to Lincoln in 1887. The episcopal headquarters of the Nebraska Area are in Lincoln.

Bishop DWIGHT LODER, a native Nebraskan, was born in the small village of Waverly near Lincoln. He was elected bishop in 1964. Bishop GERALD KENNEDY was pastor of St. Paul Church in Lincoln at the time he was elected to the episcopacy in 1948.

In 1970 Lincoln had nineteen churches with a membership of 17,157.

First Church was organized Nov. 18, 1888, in Nebraska Wesleyan University's "Old Main" at the call of the chancellor. Services were held weekly in the chapel and the chancellor or one of the professors provided the sermon. It was not long before the annual conference appointed a pastor to the rapidly growing new charge. The congregation met in Old Main for several years and then erected a parsonage. Plans to build a church were delayed by the severe droughts and national panic of the nineties, when the college suffered severely.

By 1900 two lots were purchased at the corner of 50th and St. Paul, University Place. Two years later men of the congregation built a basement, covered with a flat tin roof, which was first used in February 1903. Leaks and noise made it unsatisfactory. However, increased population and college enrollment gave the college priority in building, and the church moved back to the new auditorium on the campus in 1907.

Construction of the church attracted the town's attention, the problem being how the great steel framework and large pillars could be raised. The financial drives and costs were greater than expected. On dedication day, Dec. 12, 1909, the bishop in charge took three dramatic collections, from three capacity congregations, to raise enough money for the dedication service. Although St. Paul, Trinity, and Grace were older, the new church took the name First Church.

From the beginning the congregation had been evangelical in spirit and behavior. The new church proved more restrained emotionally. The basement of First Church was used by the Ladies Aid Society to feed the Student Army Training Corps of World War I.

After the drouth-stricken thirties and war-anxious forties, a new educational building seemed imperative in the early fifties. Several financial campaigns resulted in a structure for the church school.

Throughout its history First Church has been a focal point in the community, trying to meet the social and spiritual needs of all its members and constituents. In 1970 First Church had 2,237 members and church property valued at $941,279.

ST. PAUL CHURCH, LINCOLN, NEBRASKA

St. Paul Church was started in 1857 when Zenos B. Turman was appointed to the Salt Creek Mission and preached probably the first sermon in Lancaster County, Neb., in the cabin of James Eatherton about twelve miles south of Lincoln. It was one of sixteen preaching places embracing seven counties.

In 1867 Lincoln was made the state capital. The population increase led the Methodists to build a church under the leadership of R. S. Hawks. In this building a reception was held for the first Governor of the state, David Butler, Jan. 18, 1868.

The first pastor assigned to Lincoln was H. T. Davis in the spring of 1868. He dedicated the church in June, when the population was about 200, with sixteen Methodists. By the end of the year the church building was outgrown and the congregation accepted a free lot from the Capital Commission and erected another church, costing $3,000. This was located on the present church site and was dedicated Sept. 26, 1869.

By 1871 the membership was 202. The next year it reached 300, and a parsonage was built. A wing was added to the church under W. B. Slaughter in 1874-77. Subsequently what became known as the Old Stone Church was erected and completed Aug. 23, 1885. It burned in 1899, and the present edifice was built and finished Nov. 17, 1901.

During the twenty-two-year pastorate of Walter Aitken 1920-42, the church experienced considerable growth. The next pastor was Gerald Kennedy, 1942-48. His pastorate doubled the membership and more than doubled the budget. In 1945 the Second Methodist (German) Church and St. Paul merged. Kennedy was elected bishop in 1948. In 1954 a needed educational building was completed.

From the beginning St. Paul has tried to serve the

spiritual needs of the community. While other churches have moved out to the residential sections, it has remained a down-town church within walking distance of hundreds of University students. A complete renovation of the sanctuary took place in 1968. In 1970 the church property was valued at $1,875,000, and the membership was 2,644.

Trinity Church was formed in 1887 by the union of Bethel and Second M. E. Churches. Its edifice depicts its history and its name, for it is three buildings in one. The first, which houses Great Hall, Youth Center, the offices and some of the classrooms, was completed in 1893. The second, which contains the sanctuary, more classrooms, and the heating plant, was dedicated in 1911. The third, housing most of the classrooms, the church parlor, the fellowship hall, and the kitchen, was erected in 1957.

Two of Trinity's ministers were chosen to head Nebraska Wesleyan University—D. W. C. Huntington in 1891. and Vance Rogers in 1957. The church provides a large share of the support of a missionary, and within the last six years has given seven of its young people to full-time Christian service.

With a membership of 2,384 in 1970, situated near the Nebraska state capitol building and in the heart of the older residential section of the city, Trinity ministers to statesmen, business leaders, and people from all walks of life.

Ethel Booth, *First Methodist Church of Lincoln, Nebraska.* 1963.
A Brief History of St. Paul Methodist Church. Published by the church, 1957.
General Minutes.
E. E. Jackman, *Nebraska.* 1954.
Bartlett L. Paine, Memorial Parlor Dedication Program and Booklet, St. Paul Methodist Church, Lincoln, Nebraska, Dec. 17, 1967.　　　　　　　　TOM McANALLY
JESSE A. EARL
PAUL D. SISLER

LINCOLN CONFERENCE. (See CENTRAL WEST and SOUTHWEST CONFERENCES.)

LINDSEY WILSON COLLEGE, Columbia, Kentucky, was founded by the LOUISVILLE CONFERENCE in 1904 as a secondary and normal school. Junior college work was added in 1923, and secondary and normal offerings were discontinued in 1932.

The school carries the name of Lindsey Wilson, the deceased nephew and stepson of the late Mrs. Catherine Wilson of Louisville, Kentucky, who contributed $6,000 toward the erection of the administration building, the central building of the campus. Through the years the college has served youth from the Cumberland plateau section of Kentucky. The governing board has twenty-four members elected by the KENTUCKY and Louisville Annual Conferences.

JOHN O. GROSS

LINEBERRY, FRANK WATSON (1883-1949), American Methodist Protestant minister, was born at Plymouth, Ind. Aug. 7, 1883. He graduated from ADRIAN COLLEGE in 1908. In 1910 he married Mable Fordyce and the same year was admitted on trial in the Indiana M. P. Conference. He served as Conference President from 1929 to 1939, when Methodist Union was consummated. He

was a member of the Commission on Union. He died at Port Angeles, Wash., Jan. 9, 1949.

HAROLD THRASHER

LINKS, JACOB (? -1825), first South African Wesleyan minister and martyr, was a Namaqua Hottentot, who had some schooling at Klamiesberg mission station. He learned from both Dutch and English and became a schoolteacher and interpreter for the missionaries. In 1818 he was accepted as the first African minister. He worked with another Namaqua, Johannes Jaager, and the English Wesleyan missionary, WILLIAM THRELFALL, among the bushmen. In 1825 all three crossed the Orange River to pioneer among the bushmen; but during that autumn, all were murdered at the instigation of their guide.

J. Whiteside, *South Africa.* 1906.　　　　CYRIL J. DAVEY

LINTHICUM HEIGHTS, MARYLAND, U.S.A. **Holly Run Chapel,** constructed in 1828, was the first building ever erected by members of the nascent METHODIST PROTESTANT CHURCH. These included the Linthicums, Shipleys and Hammonds who had left Patapsco M. E. Church during the MUTUAL RIGHTS controversy. The 27 x 33 foot structure of British ship ballast brick stood until 1966 at Annapolis and Camp Meade Roads, south of BALTIMORE. Then it was painstakingly reassembled brick by brick adjacent to the present third edifice of the congregation now called the Linthicum Heights United Methodist Church. By the time of its rededication, May 19, 1968, some original furnishings of the long disused structure had been reacquired and installed.

EDWIN SCHELL

LINZELL, LEWIS EDWIN (1868-1927), was a M.E. missionary in INDIA from 1899 to the time of his death in 1927. He was born in LONDON, England, but migrated to CANADA in his teens and then to the United States. He attended OHIO WESLEYAN UNIVERSITY and in 1896 obtained a bachelor's degree. He married a fellow student, Phila Keen, daughter of Methodist minister and author, Samuel A. Keen. Linzell joined the CINCINNATI CONFERENCE, served several Ohio churches, and then in 1899 went to India as a missionary. After a fruitful pastorate at Bowen Church in BOMBAY, and a term as superintendent of the Bombay District, he became a charter member of the GUJARAT ANNUAL CONFERENCE, and principal of the Florence B. Nicholson School of Theology.

In 1912, and again in 1924, Linzell represented Gujarat Conference in the GENERAL CONFERENCE. As a speaker on India and Methodist missions, he proved to be unusually popular. A writer of the day described him as "a vivacious, virile, vivid and veracious reporter and advocate of Missions." He died in Ohio.

J. WASKOM PICKETT

LIPPITT, CHRISTOPHER (1744-1824), officer in the American Revolution, pioneer manufacturer, and Methodist layman, was born in Cranston, R. I., the son of Christopher and Catherine (Holden) Lippitt and the great-grandson of John Lippitt of England who settled in RHODE ISLAND in 1638.

After holding several public positions he was commissioned Lieutenant-Colonel on Jan. 18, 1776, joined the continental army and served in the battles of White Plains, Trenton and Princeton. Brevetted a Brigadier General by Washington, he commanded the state forces in the Battle of Rhode Island, Aug. 29, 1778. During the Revolution his brother in New York made him aware of the spirituality and enthusiasm of the Methodists. Thereafter, Christopher Lippitt's home in Cranston became, as frequent visitor FRANCIS ASBURY said, "an open house for Methodists." In 1791 JESSE LEE preached there; a class was formed in 1794 with the General, his wife and daughter as members. Largely at his own expense Lippitt erected a chapel near his home in 1800 in which, two years later, Asbury and WHATCOAT ordained preachers. The General often conducted services, frequently reading a Wesley sermon. He was a member of the Providence Peace Society. As a businessman he built the third cotton mill in Rhode Island.

General Lippitt was married to Waite Harris on March 23, 1777. They had twelve children. On June 17, 1824, he died in Cranston, where his house still stands.

Dictionary of American Biography.   ERNEST R. CASE

LIPSCOMB, WILLIAM CORRIE (1792-1879), American advocate of reform and modification in M. E. church government, and a prominent leader in the establishment of the M. P. Church, was born Sept. 13, 1792, in King William County, Va., and grew up in Georgetown, D. C. He joined the M. E. Church and took an active role in church work. He attended the Convention of Methodist Reformers from Maryland and the District of Columbia in BALTIMORE in November 1826, and came to be an outstanding member of the General Convention of reformers which met on Nov. 12, 1828, also in Baltimore. It was Lipscomb who offered the resolution calling for the appointment of a committee to prepare a "Constitution and Discipline" to be submitted to the General Convention in Baltimore in November 1830. Because he attended the convention, he was stripped of all his official positions in the M. E. Church. In June 1829, he was licensed to exhort in the M. P. Church; he was licensed to preach in October 1829, and was ordained a deacon in 1832. He was one of the founders in 1832 of the Ninth Street M. P. Church in Washington, then a station in the MARYLAND CONFERENCE. At the request of the quarterly conference, he was placed "in charge of the society" until a pastor was appointed in 1833. He was secretary of the Convention of 1830 and of the GENERAL CONFERENCE of 1834, and was a member of the General Conferences of 1838, 1842, 1850 and served as President of the General Conference that met in May 1858, at Lynchburg, Va. Despite President Lipscomb's efforts to prevent a split at this conference, the M. P. conferences divided bitterly over the issue of slavery. He was a member and served as temporary chairman of the convention which met in Montgomery, Ala., on May 7, 1867. He served as a lay delegate to the Maryland Conference in 1840, 1844, 1845, 1850, 1853. 1859, 1861 and 1865 and was Chairman of the Electoral College which met in Philadelphia in April 1858. He was often a contributor to *The Methodist Protestant*, the official church periodical, where he exhibited "a strong, logical intellect and uncompromising adherence to his convictions." "As a preacher he was clear, forcible, and tender, though his close attention to secular pursuits made his ministrations in later life unfrequent." One of his sons, A. A. Lipscomb, D.D., LL.D. (1816-1890), taught for

many years at VANDERBILT UNIVERSITY and served as an unstationed minister to the M. P. Church in Montgomery, Ala.

William Corrie Lipscomb died on Dec. 6, 1879, and was buried in Oak Hill Cemetery in Washington, D. C.

A. H. Bassett, *Concise History.* 1877.
T. H. Colhouer, *Sketches of the Founders.* 1880.
E. J. Drinkhouse, *History of Methodist Reform.* 1899.
The Methodist Protestant, May 16, 1928.
    RALPH HARDEE RIVES

LITERATURE, BRITISH METHODISM IN. A short entry on this theme cannot attempt to be exhaustive nor to distinguish finally between enduring literature and mere mention in print. Not even all the works of JOHN and CHARLES WESLEY would qualify for this former category, but certainly John Wesley's *Journal* and a number of the hymns by John and Charles and a few of their followers should be included. The hymns have their own reference; the *Journal* is an unequaled picture of the eighteenth century and of the birth and growth of a movement during fifty years of heroic missionary travel. With these should certainly be mentioned Robert Southey's *Life of Wesley* (1820), the first of the biographies to win a place in literature, though some of the *Lives of Early Methodist Preachers* (collected edition, 1837-38) have their own claims to remembrance.

Apart from these, Methodism made its first appearance in English literature through numerous satirical and unflattering references in the works of novelists and dramatists. GEORGE WHITEFIELD was much more target of caricature than the Wesleys at this stage, notably in Fielding's *Tom Jones* (1749) and in Samuel Foote's play, *The Minor* (1769). More general accounts of Methodist conversions are given in Richard Graves' *Spiritual Quixote* (1773) and Smollett's *Humphrey Clinker* (1771). Horace Walpole's *Letters* contain a brief description of Wesley as a preacher ("wondrous clean . . . as evidently an actor as Garrick"), and Boswell's *Life of Johnson* includes the doctor's famous complaint that John Wesley could talk well on many subjects but was never at leisure. George Crabbe in *The Borough* describes a Methodist sermon.

In the novels of the nineteenth century it is not always easy to distinguish whether Methodism is referred to or some other evangelical Dissenting body. Those which cannot be identified are therefore omitted. The Dissenting pastors of both Dickens and Thackeray, for instance, are caricatures of anonymous denomination who have had a long progeny in the English novel, through H. G. Wells and J. B. Priestley right into our own time. But among more definite references, Jane Austen makes Mary Crawford in *Mansfield Park* (1815) assign the clergyman hero slightingly to "some great company of Methodists," and Disraeli mentions Methodism not unsympathetically in *Sybil* (1845). With the Brontës, however, we are on firmer ground; the references are those of familiarity. G. Elsie Harrison has pointed out that Emily's picture in *Wuthering Heights* (1847) of the Rev. Jabes Branderham is certainly inspired by the celebrated JABEZ BUNTING; and the revival at Briarmains Chapel represents, from the outside, something that was well-known or remembered in the West Riding. Charlotte Brontë makes unmistakable and unflattering comments about Methodism in both *Shirley* (1849) and *Villette* (1853), and the former novel has the unforgettable saga of the clash between the church and chapel Sunday school processions. Mrs. Gaskell, as befits the wife of a Dissenting minister, is gentler, both in her vivid account of Wesley's friend, Parson Grimshaw of Haworth (*Life of Charlotte Brontë*, 1857), and in her amusing account of a Methodist proposal of marriage in *Ruth* (1853).

But the most important presentation of Methodism in nineteenth-century literature is undoubtedly that of George Eliot in *Adam Bede* (1859). Here for the first time in fiction Methodists are fully and sympathetically shown; both Seth Bede and DINAH MORRIS are drawn from life, and Dinah's preaching on the green and mission to the condemned girl are based on actual happenings in the life of George Eliot's remarkable Methodist aunt, ELIZABETH T. EVANS.

Toward the end of the nineteenth century the references in novels become more numerous, including many of little literary value, now forgotten. Among the more memorable are those in Arnold Bennett's novels of the Five Towns (e.g., *The Old Wives' Tale*, 1908); these are based on a close and critical acquaintance with respectable Victorian chapel going in the industrial towns. After this the task of distinguishing between ephemeral and enduring literature becomes difficult, and only a few pointers can be given. Among others, references of varying length and interest can be found in the works of Quiller-Couch (*Hetty Wesley*), John Buchan (*Midwinter*), Sheila Kaye-Smith, Howard Spring (*Fame is the Spur, And Another Thing*), Joyce Cary, Robert Graves, etc. In biography, the unhappy reminiscenses of Peter Fletcher (*The Long Sunday*, 1958) may be added to M. K. Ashby's picture of a nearly vanished village Methodism in *Joseph Ashby of Tysoe* (1961) and Herbert Palmer's account of a manse childhood in *The Mistletoe Child* (1935). Early Methodism's lack of educational privilege is reflected throughout this summary, in the dearth of specific dramatic or poetic references, if we exclude, as before, the possible evangelical references in poems by Browning and Masefield. Perhaps the most famous certain reference in drama is W. S. Gilbert's to the King of Barataria, who influenced the whole plot of *The Gondoliers* (1889) by becoming "a Wesleyan Methodist of the most bigoted and persecuting type."

MORWENNA R. BIELBY

LITERATURE OF DEVOTION. (See DEVOTION, THE LIFE AND LITERATURE OF.)

LITHUANIA. (See BALTIC STATES.)

LI T'IEN-LU (1886-   ), educator, was born in Taian, Shantung province, CHINA, and was educated at Peking University and VANDERBILT UNIVERSITY, where he received his Ph.D. in 1916. He was successively principal of Peking Academy, and dean, vice-president and president of Cheeloo University. From 1930 until 1950, when he retired, he was dean of Nanking Theological Seminary. (See HANDEL LEE.)

Dr. Li was Secretary of the Chinese delegation at the Washington Conference of 1922, and was awarded the Fourth Order of Chia-ho in recognition of his services. He was the author of *Congressional Policy in Relation to Chinese Immigration*.

He is retired and living in Shanghai, but continues as a member of the Board of Managers of Nanking Theological Seminary.

China Christian Yearbook, 1936-37.
Who's Who in Modern China, 1954.   FRANCIS P. JONES

LITTLE, CHARLES JOSEPH (1840-1911), American clergyman and college professor, was born at Philadelphia, Pa., Sept. 9, 1840. The University of Pennsylvania awarded him the A.B. in 1861 and the A.M. in 1864. After beginning his ministry in the M. E. Church as a member of the PHILADELPHIA CONFERENCE, he spent the academic year 1870-1871 in study at the University of Berlin. During this period of study he met Anna Marina Schultze, whom he married Dec. 3, 1872. To this union four children, a son and three daughters, were born.

After continued service in the Methodist ministry following his study abroad, he became professor of mathematics in Dickinson Seminary. After two years of teaching, he returned to the pastorate, but before a year had passed he was back at DICKINSON COLLEGE as professor of philosophy and history. After eleven years (1874-1885) in this position, he became professor of logic and history at SYRACUSE UNIVERSITY and continued there until 1891.

With this somewhat unusual background, Charles Joseph Little became professor of historical theology at GARRETT BIBLICAL INSTITUTE in 1891. Four years later he was made president of the school though this election, fortunately for several generations of students, did not mean that he ceased to teach. He continued this dual role of teacher and administrator until his death in 1911.

Technically, Little was not a trained theologian but he was in a very real way a comprehensive scholar and this masterful ability served him in good stead in those turbulent days when faculties and church conferences were often involved in bitter controversy over the issues of science, especially evolution and the higher criticism in biblical studies. If he did not enjoy a good fight, he did not shrink from controversy. He once said to the writer, "I do not know much Hebrew" (as a linguist, he did know Greek, Latin, Italian, German and French), but he added defiantly, "I do know enough Hebrew so that these experts cannot bamboozle me." An intimate colleague said this about him: "He appeared to be an inexhaustible fountain of information, giving the impression of encyclopedic knowledge available at a moments notice."

Delegates to the several M. E. GENERAL CONFERENCES to which he was elected promptly recognized him as one who could state the reason for the faith that was in him promptly and vigorously. His leadership in American Methodism at home was recognized by British Methodism in an invitation to give the celebrated FERNLEY LECTURE in 1900. In addition to the published Fernley Lecture, we have *Christianity and the Nineteenth Century, The Angel and the Flame*, a volume of sermons, and *Biographical and Literary Studies*. The contents of this last volume represent the wide range of his scholarship. There are essays entitled: The Apostle Paul, Hildebrand, Dante, Savonarola, Galileo, Ibsen, The Place of Christ in Modern Thought, etc. Eight of his addresses are printed in the memorial volume edited by his successor, CHARLES MACAULEY STUART. His address on Lincoln at the centennial of that man's birth deserves perpetuation as a model of character analysis and oratory at its best.

Little served the church in the PHILADELPHIA and ROCK RIVER CONFERENCES. He died March 11, 1911.

HORACE GREELEY SMITH

LITTLE ROCK, ARKANSAS, U.S.A., is the capital of and is situated in the center of the state on the Arkansas River. In 1970 the city had a population of 128,880. The city has registered a rapid growth in industry and new business in recent years. Although predominately agricultural, the city is also the seat of a large number of home offices for insurance companies and other firms. Its cultural and educational growth is reflected in Little Rock University, the Arkansas Arts Center, and various historical museums and sites.

There are 17,939 members of The United Methodist Church in Little Rock. The A.M.E. CHURCH and the C.M.E. CHURCH also have representative bodies.

The office of the Bishop of the Arkansas Area and Area Headquarters are located here. The Arkansas Methodist Children's Home is situated in the western part of the city. PHILANDER SMITH COLLEGE, a Methodist institution, is near the heart of the downtown area. Camp Aldersgate, operated by the Board of Missions of The United Methodist Church, lies just outside the city.

First Church, "The Cathedral of Arkansas Methodism," is the mid-city church of Little Rock and houses the office of the Bishop of the Arkansas Area. The church was organized in 1831, five years before Arkansas was admitted as a state into the Union. It has occupied three buildings in its 135-year history: the first was a small brick chapel built in 1836. The ground on which the present church stands was purchased in 1879 and a stately brick structure then erected. This building was destroyed by fire in 1895. A new red brick building (seating 1,000) was erected in 1899 and is still in use. In 1951 a $500,000 educational building was completed. Usually general sessions of the Arkansas Area of The Methodist Church are held in First Church. During the Civil War the pastor, Richard Colburn Butler, was deposed by Federal authorities and a minister of the M. E. Church placed in charge for a brief period.

In 1958 all property on the block was purchased for future expansion, together with a large parking lot across the street. An activities building contains a gymnasium, recreation rooms, Boy Scout room, craft department, and other facilities for serving all ages in a weekday downtown program.

Three former pastors of First Church have been elected to the office of bishop: H. BASCOM WATTS, WILLIAM C. MARTIN, and AUBREY G. WALTON, the latter being elected in 1960 when serving as pastor. With a staff of thirteen persons, including three ordained ministers, and a membership of 2,646, First Church continues as a vital force in the city of Little Rock, and in its laity furnishes some of the prominent leaders in civic and business affairs in the state and city. Three governors of the state have been members of the congregation. The church also serves parishioners residing in every section of Little Rock, North Little Rock, and many in Pulaski County.

The church has assisted in the organization of a large number of new Methodist congregations in the city, and has supported them financially and by supplying members.

Miles Chapel was organized under the leadership of her first pastor, John Peyton, before the C. M. E. Church was born (1870).

MILES CHAPEL C.M.E., LITTLE ROCK, ARKANSAS

In the church's infancy it was denominationally independent. Bishop W. H. MILES took the congregation into the C. M. E. Church in July 1873, and named it Miles Chapel.

Miles Chapel was host to the C. M. E. General Conference of 1890. It is the oldest C. M. E. Church west of the Mississippi. Miles Chapel has always housed the members in a brick church. It has had three locations: 3rd and Ferry; 5th and Rector; and 5th and Bender, the present site.

Pulaski Heights Church is the largest Methodist church in membership in the state of Arkansas. Needing a church in the rolling hills section of western Little Rock, Pulaski Heights was organized in 1912. The church grew rapidly and as early as 1923 it became apparent that additional facilities would be needed. The depression and World War II prevented the congregation from carrying out plans for a new building, but in 1948 plans were put out for bids for a beautiful Gothic church. The bids far exceeded all expectations and the Board gloomily faced the prospect of further delay in achieving the dream of this congregation; then the voice of one woman stood out as she said, "A church is not built with dollars and cents, a church is built with faith! . . . I move we begin construction immediately." Today the church stands just three blocks from the original building, ministering to the children, youth and adults in this section of the city. To the sanctuary have been added an educational building and a youth building. Church school classes meet during the week as well as on Sunday. Family night programs; a Mothers' Day Out each week, where young children are cared for in the church as mother has a day out; a choir program for all ages; a community service program called "opportunities for action," and many other weekday as well as Sunday programs make this church a vital part of Methodism.

Full or part time support is given to missionaries serving HONG KONG and OKINAWA. The T. J. and Inez Raney lectures given each May in the church bring distinguished ministers to the city of Little Rock to enrich and revitalize the spiritual and cultural life of the community. Many young men have gone from this church to serve as ministers and today are giving outstanding leadership to The United Methodist Church.

Pulaski Heights Church has had a great past and looks to the future with an effective approach to programming related to our world today. Its 1970 membership was 3,957.

H. Jewell, *Arkansas*. 1892. ROBERT E. L. BEARDEN

LITTLE ROCK CONFERENCE was created in 1866 by changing the name of the Ouachita Conference. No mergers, divisions, or rearrangement of conference boundaries were involved. The Little Rock Conference covers the south half of the state of Arkansas. (See ARKANSAS for history of early Methodism in state.)

It was said jokingly that the name of the Ouachita Conference was changed because the preachers did not know how to spell it, but the real reason was the decreasing influence of streams in the lives of the people and the rising importance of cities. The first three conferences in Arkansas—Arkansas, Ouachita, and White River—were named for rivers. By 1914 all of the river names had disappeared. Little Rock was not only the capital city, it was and still is the chief metropolis in the state. Many conferences were and still are named for the largest city within their boundaries, and most of the episcopal areas of the church today are identified by the names of the cities in which the bishops reside.

The church at Washington, ten miles west of Hope, is historically important. The Washington Male and Female Academy flourished in Washington for fifteen years before the Civil War, and the town itself served as the capital of Arkansas during the last two years of that conflict. Methodism was established in the vicinity of Washington in 1817 by WILLIAM STEVENSON, a local preacher from MISSOURI. Washington was the center from which Methodism first made its way into both TEXAS and OKLAHOMA. The Washington Church was organized in 1822, and its present building, a large well preserved colonial style edifice, was erected in 1860. The conference historical society has published a pamphlet on the church, and it has assisted the congregation with the renovation of the building and restoration of original fixtures. The church has been recommended for designation as a historical landmark or shrine in the denomination.

The Methodist Children's home in Little Rock is supported by both Arkansas Conferences. The *Arkansas Methodist*, long the official paper for Arkansas Methodism, is published in that city.

When created in 1866 the Little Rock Conference had about fifty-one appointments and approximately 7,000 church members. In 1970, the conference had 173 pastoral charges, 83,758 members, and its churches, parsonages, and other property were valued at more than $34,824,683.

J. A. Anderson, *Arkansas Methodism*. 1936.
S. T. Baugh & R. B. Moore, Jr., *Methodism's Gateway to the Southwest* (Pamphlet). Little Rock: Epworth Press, 1966.
Minutes of Little Rock Conference.
W. N. Vernon, *William Stevenson*, 1964. ALBEA GODBOLD

LITTLEJOHN, JOHN (1756-1836), pioneer American preacher, was born in Penrith, Cumberland County, England, Dec. 7, 1756. Emigrating with his family to America about 1767, he was awakened under the ministry of JOHN KING in MARYLAND in 1774.

Entering the conference in 1777, he traveled two years and then married, returning to the local ranks. After location he settled in LEESBURG, Va., and remained there until 1819, when he moved to LOUISVILLE, Ky. Later Littlejohn went to Warren County and finally to Logan County, Ky. In 1831 he was readmitted to the BALTIMORE CONFERENCE, transferred to the KENTUCKY CONFERENCE, and was placed on the superannuate list, where he remained until his death.

As early as 1775 Littlejohn, while traveling from Annapolis to Montgomery County, Md., was taken before a magistrate for not having a pass. He was opposed to the oath required by VIRGINIA and Maryland during the Revolutionary War. The Maryland oath was obnoxious to both pro-British and pro-American persons. Later he escaped being tarred and feathered because a magistrate protected him.

Only a few American ministers were as able as Littlejohn in his day. During his brief itinerancy he was one of the most efficient and useful pastors. Noted for his intellectual ability, piety, and devotion to the church, thousands were converted under his eloquent preaching.

He earned a name for himself in the national annals when in the War of 1812, President James Madison—who had to flee Washington—committed to Littlejohn the original Declaration of Independence and other priceless documents for safekeeping.

Littlejohn died on May 13, 1836, during the GENERAL CONFERENCE.

W. E. Arnold, *Kentucky*. 1935-36.
E. S. Bucke, *History of American Methodism*. 1964.
G. H. Jones, *Guidebook*. 1966.
Journal of the General Conference, 1836. JESSE A. EARL

LITTLETON FEMALE COLLEGE, Littleton, N. C., opened in January 1882, as Central Institute for Young Ladies. In the following month it was chartered by the General Assembly of NORTH CAROLINA when Littleton civic leaders formed a corporation to operate the school "for the intellectual, moral and religious development and training of young ladies." A number of substantial three-story frame buildings were erected on the grounds of the College. The charter was amended in 1888 to change the name of the institution to Littleton Female College. In 1912 the "Female" was dropped from the name, although only women continued to be admitted.

In 1889, JAMES MANLY RHODES, who, with the exception of two years, was President of the College during its entire history, purchased Littleton Female College from its stockholders and immediately began an extensive program of improvements. In the administration of the College, Rhodes was assisted by a faculty and staff noteworthy for their character, ability and scholarship. Littleton College offered a wide variety of courses. In addition to the Preparatory Department, there was a Training School for nurses, a Practice and Observation School for prospective teachers, and a Business School.

A natural result of Rhodes' affiliation with the M. E. Church, South, was a strong religious influence at Littleton College. Special emphasis was placed on religious training and on the formation and growth of character. Bible was a required course for every student. As a result of the religious atmosphere which characterized the academic program and due to the moderate tuition fees charged, many daughters of itinerant Methodist ministers attended Littleton College. The College was enthusiastically endorsed by resolutions passed at the annual conferences of the M. E. Church, South, and the NORTH

CAROLINA CONFERENCE of the M. P. Church. News of College activities frequently appeared in *The Raleigh Christian Advocate* and *The North Carolina Christian Advocate*. The Charter provided that all bequests and donations were to become the property of the M. E. Church, South. A large number of alumnae became teachers in North Carolina's public schools and in various colleges. Many former students entered the foreign mission field. The editor of *The Raleigh Christian Advocate* once observed that from Littleton College were "going forth positive moral, mental and social influences which must play an important part in developing the Christian womanhood of the South."

The college enrollment was impressive with more than 200 students attending each session for many years. There were 274 students enrolled in 1907. Governor Charles B. Aycock, North Carolina's famous educational governor, was a trustee of Littleton Female College; it was the only educational institution except the University of North Carolina of which he served as trustee.

Fire destroyed the Littleton College buildings on the night of Jan. 22, 1919, with a loss estimated in excess of $50,000. Due to his advanced age and poor health, and the fact that the College was not endowed, President Rhodes decided not to replace the buildings and Littleton College closed.

The Littleton College Memorial Association was organized in 1927 by alumnae and friends of the former college who have met annually since then to keep alive the spirit and work of the college. At the annual meeting in July 1961, held at Pullen Park, Raleigh, N. C., President Thomas A. Collins of NORTH CAROLINA WESLEYAN COLLEGE, Rocky Mount, N. C., extended an invitation to the members of the Association to meet in the following July on the grounds of the new Methodist college which serves the same general area as that of Littleton College. "North Carolina Wesleyan College is in a very real sense a spiritual outgrowth of Littleton College," stated President Collins, and noted that the flame lighted by the earlier institution was still very much alive. He invited the alumnae of Littleton College to consider themselves the first "alumni organization" of the new college. Annual reunions since 1961 have been held at North Carolina Wesleyan College.

Ralph Hardee Rives, "Littleton Female College," *The North Carolina Historical Review*, XXXIX (July, 1962), 363-377; see, also, The Littleton College Memorial Collection, North Carolina Wesleyan College and in The Southern Historical Collection, University of North Carolina, and *North Carolina Wesleyan College Bulletin*, 1965-1966, pp. 85-86.

RALPH HARDEE RIVES

LITTLETON COLLEGE MEMORIAL COLLECTION, Rocky Mount, N. C., U.S.A., is an extensive collection of memorabilia of the former Littleton Female College. In 1960 the Littleton College Memorial Association (organized in 1927) voted to establish a Littleton College Memorial Collection of books to be presented to the library of the new NORTH CAROLINA WESLEYAN COLLEGE at Rocky Mount. In addition to these resource books, material consisting of catalogues, annuals, literary magazines, literary society pins, diplomas, numerous photographs and clippings and various other items specifically associated with the history of Littleton Female College was assembled. This collection was presented to the North Carolina Wesleyan College Library and duplicates were placed in the

Southern Historical Collection in the library at the University of North Carolina, Chapel Hill.

The Association has also established the Vara L. Herring Scholarship at SCARRITT COLLEGE and the Littleton College Memorial Loan Fund at North Carolina Wesleyan College.

The Littleton College Memorial Collection is a valuable assemblage of information for the researcher interested in the history and development of education in the late Victorian era and the early twentieth century.

Ralph Hardee Rives, "Littleton Female College," *The North Carolina Historical Review*, XXXIX (July, 1962), 363-377; see, also, The Littleton College Memorial Collection, North Carolina Wesleyan College and in the Southern Historical Collection, University of North Carolina, Chapel Hill.

RALPH HARDEE RIVES

LIVERMORE, MELVA A. (1869-1941), was a missionary in INDIA appointed by the WOMAN'S FOREIGN MISSIONARY SOCIETY of the M. E. Church. She was born in Chanton County, Mo., April 9, 1869, and was educated in NORTHWESTERN UNIVERSITY (B.A.) and Columbia University (M.A.).

Miss Livermore was outstanding as an educator, an evangelist, and a worker for the public welfare. She began her career as an educator in KANSAS at the age of sixteen, by teaching in a country school. She pursued her own education zealously, graduating and taking teacher's training. Going to India in 1916, she served as principal of a girls' boarding school in Meerut and of Ingraham Institute in Ghaziabad. She contributed much to the developments that have placed both of those institutions in the front ranks of church and mission schools. The former is now an intermediate college for girls, and the latter is one of India's best known and most successful vocational high schools and centers for extension education.

As an evangelist, she often spent weeks touring by ox cart in the villages without returning to her home. Her associations were with the poor, the oppressed, and the illiterate. She established and supervised many primary day schools and woman's societies, wrote a life of Christ in simple Hindustani for newly literate villagers, and entered into the life of those humble people as one who delighted to serve.

She won the admiration of all classes and was appointed a member of the municipal board of Ghaziabad. She retired in 1936, but was in demand as a speaker about missions and people in India until her death on July 31, 1941.

Journals of the Northwest India and Delhi Conferences.

J. WASKOM PICKETT

LIVERPOOL, England. Methodism was bound up with the rapid growth of southwest Lancashire in the nineteenth century, when the area changed from a county of few parishes and scattered population into one of the greatest manufacturing centers in the world. The city of Liverpool grew from almost nothing at the same swift rate, and most of the people who built Methodism there came from outside. JOHN WESLEY often used the port, and the old Lancashire North Circuit dated from 1766; a Liverpool Circuit first appears in 1771. The Liverpool North and Liverpool South Circuits were formed in 1826, though by that time Mount Pleasant Chapel had long been built (1789) and also Brunswick, the most famous of these early chapels. This was the scene of the Wesleyan Conference of 1820, at which the Liverpool *Minutes* were drawn up, to remain, with alterations made in 1885 and 1944, the standard description of the ideal Methodist minister.

The advance of Methodism was interrupted by the controversies of 1834-37. SAMUEL WARREN was warmly supported in the Liverpool South Circuit. It was in Liverpool that David Rowland, a class leader, was charged before his leaders' meeting with "assisting with the formation of a certain Association," and with taking part in public meetings to advocate its views. He and some others were expelled from Wesleyan Methodism for their part in this agitation, and it was actually at a meeting in Liverpool that the WESLEYAN METHODIST ASSOCIATION was formed and its constitution adopted. When the UNITED METHODIST CHURCH was formed in 1907, there were four circuits in Liverpool; these were united into a single circuit in 1929, shortly before METHODIST UNION in 1932.

As for PRIMITIVE METHODISM in Liverpool, WILLIAM CLOWES preached in the city in 1813, but does not seem to have established any regular work. When John Ride, another Primitive Methodist itinerant, preached there in 1821, he was arrested by a civil officer and lodged in the prison; it is said that ADAM CLARKE, the Wesleyan Methodist preacher, intervened with the magistrates to obtain his release. The Tunstall Circuit was missioning Liverpool at this time; and through the preaching of James Bonser, who arrived in Liverpool in January 1822, enough progress was made for the establishment of a separate Liverpool circuit in 1823.

For some years vigorous Welsh Methodist churches (see WALES) were found on Merseyside, and a circuit seems to have existed as far back as 1803. There was large nineteenth-century immigration from WALES, and so a strong group of societies emerged, which were for a time grouped in the Liverpool District but later transferred to the First North Wales District. A number of men entered the Wesleyan Methodist ministry from these churches, including the grandfather of HUGH PRICE HUGHES. Little of this work now remains, however. The children and grandchildren of the early immigrants have lost the Welsh language; they attended English schools, married into English families, and have gradually been assimilated for the most part into the English religious world. The future would seem to hold little promise for this part of Methodist work.

The most striking figure in later Liverpool Methodism was the Wesleyan Methodist minister CHARLES GARRETT, a famous early leader of the Methodist teetotal movement. He became the first superintendent of the new Liverpool Central Mission, an offshoot of the FORWARD MOVEMENT, in 1882, the year in which he was also elected president of the Wesleyan Methodist Conference. He remained at Liverpool until his death in 1900, and made the mission the center of Methodist evangelism and social work in the city.

Liverpool Methodism suffered badly during the air raids made on Merseyside during the Second World War. Churches were damaged or destroyed; the dispersal of population affected the older churches, for many people never returned to their old homes and did not pick up the threads of their old religious lives. After the war an extensive building program had to be undertaken to restore damaged churches and to build new ones, and to put new churches on the large housing estates which were a feature of the reconstruction of the area. All the same, it may be said that Liverpool has suffered less than many other areas of the industrial North from the general religious decline of the past fifty years. Careful planning of the work and the redeployment of the ministry have helped to relate the church afresh to the town and surrounding country. A regular service has been set up to meet all immigrants entering the port. In 1954 one of the first Methodist INTERNATIONAL HOUSES was opened for overseas students; this has been enlarged and two other hostels have been added. A former missionary is presently employed among the large West Indian population in the city. Unlike many other districts, Liverpool has been able to report some increase of membership in the years since 1945.

GILBERTHORPE HARRISON

LIVERPOOL MINUTES. At the British Wesleyan Methodist Liverpool Conference of 1820 a decrease in the membership of the connection was reported for the first time since annual returns of membership had been instituted. Moved by a sense of responsibility, the preachers passed a series of resolutions, pledging themselves to renewed devotion to their pastoral and preaching duties. These were known as the 'Liverpool *Minutes*,' and it was directed that they should be read in every May Synod and once a year in a meeting of the ministers in every circuit. In 1885 the 'Resolutions on Pastoral Work' were substituted, but the bulk of the earlier document was retained.

W. L. DOUGHTY

LIVES OF EARLY METHODIST PREACHERS. JOHN WESLEY required of his preachers that they set down an account of their "call to preach and present religious experience," a practice which survives in the public testimony of candidates for ordination. Many of these accounts were printed in the *Arminian Magazine*. As connexional editor, THOMAS JACKSON compiled a selection of thirty-seven of them under the title *The Lives of Early Methodist Preachers* (3 vols., 1837-38). In the third edition (6 vols., 1865-66), he added an introductory essay and four additional lives. A later connexional editor, JOHN TELFORD, published a two-volume annotated selection of thirteen of the lives under the title *Wesley's Veterans* (1909), to which subsequently (1912-14) he added five more volumes containing twenty-three additional lives. A table correlating Telford's seven-volume arrangement with Jackson's six is given in *Proceedings of the Wesley Historical Society*, xxii, 102-5.

J. C. BOWMER

LIVINGSTON, G. HERBERT (1916-   ), American FREE METHODIST and ordained elder of the Kentucky-Tennessee Conference of his church, was born at Russell, Iowa, and married Maria Saarloos, in 1937. He was educated at WESSINGTON SPRINGS COLLEGE, South Dakota (B.A.), Kletzing College, Oskaloosa, Iowa (A.B.), ASBURY THEOLOGICAL SEMINARY (B.D.), and DREW UNIVERSITY (Ph.D.). He served as a pastor for fifteen years in Wisconsin, Iowa, New York and South Dakota, was dean of Wessington Springs College for two years and has been professor of Old Testament at Asbury Theological Seminary since 1953. He has participated in archaeological excavations in Israel and Jordan. Dr. Livingston holds membership in the Academy of Religion; Society of Biblical Literature; National Association of Professors of Hebrew; Evangelical Theological Society and Wesley Theological Society. He is the author of *Genesis and Jeremiah, Aldersgate Biblical Series;* Psalms 73-150 in *Wesleyan Bible Commentary;* Genesis, in *Beacon Bible Commentary;* and Jonah and Obadiah in *Wycliffe Bible Commentary.*

BYRON S. LAMSON

LIVING EPISTLE, THE, a holiness magazine, was first introduced to Evangelicals in January 1869, as an independent piece of journalism. REUBEN YEAKEL, later bishop, and Elisha Hoffman, a song writer, were co-editors. It was a twenty-four page monthly during its first year, which was increased to thirty-two pages in the second year. Supported by a group of ministers and laymen as a private venture to teach holiness in accordance with the Bible and the Evangelical Discipline, it was offered to and accepted by the EVANGELICAL ASSOCIATION GENERAL CONFERENCE in 1871. Under the auspices of the Publishing House at least two-thirds of its pages were used for family and Sunday school purposes. By 1875, it had lost its primary purpose and was serving the Sunday schools of the church. By the end of 1907 its usefulness had disappeared, even as a Sunday school paper, and it was discontinued.

R. W. Albright, *Evangelical Church,* 1942.
J. H. Ness, *History of Publishing.* 1966.   JOHN H. NESS, JR.

LIVINGSTONE COLLEGE, Salisbury, North Carolina. (See SALISBURY, NORTH CAROLINA.)

LLOYD, JOHN SELWYN BROOKE (1904-   ), British statesman and Methodist layman, was born on July 28, 1904. His father and grandfather were both called John Wesley Lloyd, and his great-grandfather was a Methodist minister. He was educated at Fettes School and at Magdalene College, Cambridge. In 1927 he was president of the Cambridge Union. His later career was divided between law, politics, and the army. A barrister of Gray's Inn, he joined the Northern Circuit in 1930, and in 1951 became a Master of the Bench, Gray's Inn. He served throughout the Second World War in the army, rising from second lieutenant to brigadier in 1944. He was also staff officer on H.Q. Second Army until the surrender of Germany. After the war he entered the House of Commons as M.P. for the Wirral Division of Cheshire; he was minister of state at the Foreign Office from 1951 to 1954, and then within a period of fifteen months he was successively minister of supply, minister of defence, and secretary of state for foreign affairs, all in Conservative cabinets. He was foreign secretary, 1955-60, a period including the Suez crisis, which led to the resignation of Anthony Eden as prime minister. After an unusually long period at the Foreign Office, Lloyd was chancellor of the exchequer, 1960-62, when he instituted his famous "wage pause" and set up the National Economic Development Council. When he left office in 1962, he was asked to prepare a report on the organization of the Conservative party. He returned to office in 1963 in Sir Alec Douglas-Home's government, as lord privy seal and leader of the House

of Commons. He was made a privy councillor in 1951 and a companion of honour in 1962.

PETER STEPHENS

LOCAL PREACHERS IN AMERICA. (See MINISTRY IN AMERICAN METHODISM, THE.)

LOCAL PREACHERS. Early History. As early as 1738 JOHN WESLEY recognized the value of a layman who was prepared to witness publicly to his Christian experience, and to exhort others to a similar acceptance of saving faith. Such was JOSEPH HUMPHREYS when Wesley first sponsored him, though later he turned from "exhorting" to the authoritative exposition of scripture, and was ordained. Similarly Wesley accepted the services at BRISTOL in 1739 of JOHN CENNICK. He was also happy to use THOMAS MAXFIELD as an exhorter in LONDON, but was both distressed and angry when Maxfield stepped over the narrow line dividing exhorting from expounding— the latter (in Wesley's view) the prerogative of a DEACON who had been episcopally ordained to the ministry of the Word of God. By 1741, however, Wesley had accepted Maxfield as his first "son in the gospel," i.e. a layman commissioned to a full time preaching ministry. Others speedily followed, and the term "preacher" was soon applied equally to exhorters and expounders, the subtle distinction almost forgotten. The expounders or preachers, however, were the forerunners of the Methodist MINISTRY, and the exhorters of the order of Methodist Local Preachers.

Wesley continued to emphasize the difference in the years that followed, although this left little trace in the official *Minutes* of the Methodist conferences. Those lay preachers whom he recognized as possessing suitable gifts and graces he usually called to itinerate among the Methodist societies as his HELPERS, and with the development of defined CIRCUITS one of these helpers in each was designated to oversee the others as Wesley's ASSISTANT. After Wesley's death these achieved the title which he had resisted, that of "minister." Sometimes the itinerant or travelling preacher was prevented from fulfilling a preaching engagement, and on such occasions his place might be taken by a substitute—possibly a Methodist who had already gained some pastoral experience as a CLASS LEADER, possibly a recent convert who was urged to relate his Christian experience in place of a regular sermon.

In 1747 Wesley carefully examined the situation in Cornwall, an area of rapidly expanding societies and insufficient itinerants. He found that of eighteen "exhorters" (this term was used) five were unfitted or unworthy, three were "much blessed in the work," and the remaining ten "might be helpful when there was no preacher in their own or the neighboring societies." These latter were the type of men whom he came to recognize as "local preachers," or preachers in their own locality as opposed to the itinerant preachers who travelled around wherever they were sent by Wesley. The 1747 Conference listed twenty-three travelling preachers and thirty-eight men who "assist us only in one place." Of these thirty-eight eleven later served for at least an interval as itinerants. At the 1753 Conference sixteen local preachers were present, of whom four later became itinerants.

CHARLES WESLEY urged his brother John in 1751 to make the following specific regulations about the admission of local preachers to full time service:

"With regard to the preachers, we agree:

    1. That none shall be permitted to preach in any of our societies, till he be examined both as to his grace and gifts, at least by the assistant, who sending word to us may by our answer admit him a *local* preacher.

    2. That such preacher be not immediately taken from his trade, but be exhorted to follow it with all diligence.

    3. That no person shall be received as a *travelling* preacher or be taken from his trade by either of us alone, but by both of us conjointly, giving him a note under both our hands.

Something of this kind may well have been agreed at the 1752 English conference (whose minutes have not survived), as in fact it was at the first Irish conference, held that year in Limerick. If so, these regulations were not incorporated into the "Large Minutes," which contain only a casual reference to local preachers. In the Deed of Declaration of 1784 they are not mentioned at all.

Although (unlike the itinerant lay preachers) the local lay preachers were the subject of very little legislation during Wesley's lifetime, they nevertheless remained an important part of the Methodist system. As early as the 1760's regular preaching plans were prepared in some circuits to organize their activities the most usefully, and the larger a circuit became the more need there was for local preachers to supply pulpits on Sundays. With a few exceptions the local preachers were regarded as temporary substitutes who must carefully be prevented from aggrandizing themselves at the expense of the travelling preachers, and Wesley occasionally advised his assistants to "clip their wings." At the same time the "locals" were seen as potential itinerants, whose home circuit was both their training ground for the itinerancy and the more limited field of ministry to which they could return if for one reason or another either they or Wesley felt it necessary for them to leave the full time itinerancy, as many did: of two hundred itinerant preachers, accepted between 1741 and 1765, only eighty-one actually died in the full time work or as "supernumeraries."

In 1780 John Crook, the founder of Methodism in the Isle of Man, and Wesley's assistant there, met forty-five local preachers serving in the island, and the "Local Preachers' Minute Book" recording their deliberations and decisions at Pell on that occasion remained in use until 1816. Their business was conducted by the method of question and answer, as in Wesley's annual conference for the travelling preachers. Wesley's *Journal* for Feb. 6, 1789 speaks about "the quarterly day for meeting the local preachers" as if it were a normal thing, in London at least. Not until 1796, however, were quarterly local preachers' meetings formally incorporated into the printed legislation as a universal feature of Methodist polity. The systematic training and organization of local preachers came much later still.

The Local Preachers in Early Methodism, by Duncan Coomer, in *Proc.* of the W.H.S., xxv, pp. 33-42 (Burnley, 1945).
Rupp and Davies (eds.) *Methodist Church in Great Britain.* Vol. 1. pp. 236-38.

                              Frank Baker

Later History. One of the causes of Methodist disunity in the early nineteenth century was the tension which developed between the local and itinerant preachers as the latter settled down into a normal ministry. This tension was largely resolved when laymen were admitted to the Wesleyan Methodist Conference in 1877. But even at Methodist Union in 1932 it was still necessary to allow for the possibility that in extraordinary circumstances laymen—who were in practice local preachers—should administer Holy Communion.

From an early date women also were allowed to preach. Even John Wesley himself occasionally used women preachers. Primitive Methodism prided itself—from 1803—in having "no sex limitation in church work." The Wesleyans were much slower in recognizing that women lay preachers as well as men had a legitimate call and place in the life of the church, and did not officially acknowledge this until 1918. Since that date the number of women preachers in Methodism has steadily risen, and particularly since Union—this despite the shrinkage in total membership. In 1963 one out of every five local preachers in the active work was a woman.

The systematic training of local preachers has only become general in the present century. The first written examinations were in 1927, and these became general and obligatory only after Union (1936). The Local Preachers' Department—which is answerable to the Conference for all matters relating to local preachers, particularly their training and standards—came into being only in 1937, and the first ministerial secretary to be specially responsible for this work was appointed that year. Since then the department has steadily grown in size and scope, in its activities and its influence throughout Methodism. In other communions, where the value and distinctive contribution of lay preachers is becoming increasingly recognized, the Methodist organization with its Order of Local Preachers and its facilities for training them, is both coveted and emulated.

In Methodism in Great Britain there are now about 22,000 fully accredited local preachers, and about 4,000 at various stages of their preliminary training. Three out of every four Sunday services are taken by local preachers.

Annual Reports of the Local Preachers' Department.
The Preacher's Handbook.
R. F. Wearmouth, *Methodism and the Working Class Movements.* 1937.
                              David N. Francis

LOCAL PREACHERS OF THE METHODIST EPISCOPAL CHURCH, NATIONAL ASSOCIATION OF, grew out of an 1858 New York City convention of local preachers. There persons from twelve annual conferences largely in the northeast organized the "Local Preachers' Association of the M. E. Churches of the U. S.," with provision for auxiliary conference and district associations. In 1859 at Baltimore the name was changed to "National, etc." The group was able to secure listing of local preachers in the annual conference minutes, held an annual convention, and also promoted historical observances such as the 1866 Centennial, and the erection of the Embury monument at Ashgrove, N. Y. Following incorporation in Baltimore, Md., Jan. 12, 1833 for "fraternal intercourse, brotherly cooperation, the advancement of education, etc.," the Association in 1890 gained control of Ft. Wayne College from the North Indiana Conference, renamed it Taylor University and elected its trustees until the Alumni Association of the school took control in 1922.

Despite its name, the organization enlisted few supporters outside the northeast. The last known officers were elected for 1917-18.

Methodist Year Book, 1919.   Edwin Schell

LOCAL PREACHERS MUTUAL AID ASSOCIATION

LOCAL PREACHERS MUTUAL AID ASSOCIATION was started in Britain as the General Wesleyan Methodist Local Preachers Mutual Aid Association in July, 1849. In 1839 Wesleyanism celebrated its Centenary by raising £300,000 in a special appeal. At this time, many Wesleyan Methodist LOCAL PREACHERS were receiving Poor Law Relief while others were living in workhouses and ending their days in a pauper's grave. The Wesleyan Methodist Conference was asked to allocate a small portion of the Centenary Fund to the relief of these local preachers. The Conference not only refused to allocate any of this money but also refused to give approval to the launching of a special appeal for this particular purpose. Two local preachers, Francis Pearson and Joseph H. Marsden, met in a Matlock village and decided to call a number of local preachers together for fellowship and to consider forming a society for the benefit of the poor and sick among their number. Many difficulties were placed in their way by official Wesleyanism; but a group of them met in Aldersgate Street in July 1849, and decided to launch the association at a meeting in BIRMINGHAM later that year.

Members paid an entrance fee of ten shillings and a subscription of twopence per week. At the end of twelve months 1,260 members had enrolled, and the contributions amounted to £1,276. In the first fifteen years the membership doubled, and the income rose to £30,000, of which £22,000 was distributed to the sick and poor. Progress continued; membership grew; the scope of benefits was widened; and in the 117 years of its existence the association has distributed almost £2,000,000 in relieving those local preachers, widows, and dependents "in necessitous circumstances." The help takes various forms: weekly allowances, sickness benefits to those very elderly members who were members before the National Insurance Act came into operation, lump-sum grants, and, during the last twenty years, the provision of five Eventide Homes at Westcliff on Sea, Woodhall Spa, Minehead, Grange over Sands, and Barleythorpe (Oakham). At the last named, nursing care is given to residents in need of more care and attention than can be provided in ordinary Eventide Homes. A sixth home at Rickmansworth (Hertfordshire) was opened at the end of 1966, and here again, nursing care is provided.

The association was established on a basis of mutual aid, but as the years passed many Methodist societies expressed a wish to make grants toward the association's work as a tribute to the services of local preachers. Today almost every Methodist church in Britain allocates the whole of one Sunday's collections, or a part of that one Sunday's collections, to the association as a thank-offering. As times and circumstances change, the association— honored by Royal Patronage since 1922—has adapted changes in its methods and its work. When METHODIST UNION came in 1932 the doors were opened to all Methodist local preachers, and thousands joined from the non-Wesleyan Methodist bodies. In 1962 the association agreed to make its benefits available to all Methodist local preachers even though they had not contributed to the association's funds. All this work—apart from a small staff at the head office—has been voluntary. Local Preachers' Mutual Aid workers never ask for or receive expenses; they give freely of their time, money, and ability to help their less fortunate brethren. The association has never taken sides in church or national controversies. It is a charitable organization, registered as such with the Registrar of Friendly Societies. There are 615 branches,

divided into thirty-four districts. The district committee elects delegates to the annual aggregate meeting, which any member may attend, but the 350 delegates are given hospitality and take preaching appointments in the district where the aggregate is held. The honorary officers consist of a president, a treasurer, and two secretaries; and they, with the former presidents, the ten trustees, and seventy elected members, constitute the General Committee of the association, which meets in different parts of the country nine or ten times a year. At the end of 1965 the association had 18,329 members: it was making weekly allowances to 834 local preachers, widows, and dependents; and more than 120 elderly local preachers, their wives, and widows were resident in the five Eventide Homes. During the year collections from Methodist churches provided £34,377. The total expenditure on charitable gifts, administration, and the maintenance of the homes was £99,674. Legacies were always placed in reserve, and from these the association received £20,000 in interest and dividends in the course of the year. The association is completely autonomous, administered entirely by local preachers.

ALBERT E. SHAW

LOCATION

LOCATION is formal cessation from the traveling ministry of the Methodist connection by one who thereby is no longer under the appointment of a bishop, but who does not lose his status as a LOCAL PREACHER. Location may be granted by a formal vote of an Annual Conference when a member requests it; but an annual conference has a right to locate a man against his own volition if it feels it proper to so terminate his membership in its body. This sometimes comes about when a man proves to be unacceptable in the traveling ministry, or is so patently unfitted for it that a suitable appointment can no longer be found for him, and thus he is requested or forced to "locate."

Many otherwise acceptable and useful men find it necessary to locate for personal reasons—for instance, family conditions, such as the invalidism of a wife, sometimes by reason of a man's own health, or the like, and when he has not reached an age when he may ask for formal superannuation or retirement. After location, one takes his place in the ranks of the local preachers, and his membership goes into the local church where he continues to work under the direction of his pastor or the district superintendent in such ways as may be possible. When an ordained minister locates, he does not lose his ordination status (except as explained below).

Each annual conference looks to its Committee on Conference Relations to pass upon a request for location when such request comes from one of its members, or when a name is referred to the Committee by a district superintendent with his own recommendation that a man be located. The annual conference is sovereign in all matters of conference relationship, and while a man located against his will formerly had the right in the M. E. Church to appeal to a Judicial Conference (*Discipline*, 1908, P. 160), the unchallenged principle that every organized body shall be the judge of the qualifications of its own members holds in The United Methodist Church with reference to annual conference membership.

"When a member of an Annual Conference in good standing, shall demand a located relation, the Conference shall be obliged to grant it to him." (*Journal*, General

Conference, 1840, ME.) "This is the only relation in the church which can be changed solely by the will of the person concerned," said Bishop McTyeire.

The *Discipline* (1968, P. 368) states that a man may be located when found "unacceptable, inefficient, or indifferent in the work of the ministry," and the conference may by count vote on recommendation of the Board of the Ministry locate such a man without his consent. In such instances "the authority to exercise the ministerial office shall be suspended" (P. 368). He has today no right of appeal. Disciplinary regulations outline the duties, obligations, and responsibilities of local preachers and indicate to what body they are amenable for character and conduct.

Discipline, 1968.
H. N. McTyeire, *Manual of the Discipline.* 1920. N. B. H.

LOCKE, CHARLES EDWARD (1858-1940), American bishop, was born in Pittsburgh, Pa., Sept. 9, 1858. The son of William H. Locke, a chaplain in the Union Army, his ancestors were of historical colonial stock. He was educated at MOUNT UNION COLLEGE and ALLEGHENY COLLEGE. He married Mina J. Woods on Dec. 27, 1882, and they had a son and a number of daughters. He joined the EAST OHIO CONFERENCE in 1881.

After eight years in small town pastorates, Locke was appointed to the famous Smithfield Street Church in PITTSBURGH, Pa., and thereupon began a career as a pastor of notable churches. For thirty years he was in the most famous and influential pulpits of the denomination. These appointments included Smithfield Street, Pittsburgh, 1888-92; First Church, PORTLAND, Ore., 1892-97; Central, SAN FRANCISCO, 1897-99; Delaware Avenue, BUFFALO, N. Y., 1899-1904; Hanson Place, BROOKLYN, 1904-08, and First Church, LOS ANGELES, 1908-20. He conducted the funeral services of President WILLIAM MCKINLEY and of IRA D. SANKEY, a Methodist evangelistic singer connected with Dwight L. Moody.

Elected bishop in 1920, he served in the PHILIPPINE ISLANDS, 1920-24; St. Paul, Minn., 1924-32, retiring in May 1932. He was a delegate to the NEW ZEALAND Methodist Centennial and also to AUSTRALIA in 1922. He was elected president of the CALIFORNIA Anti-Saloon League in 1933, and was active in it and other civic and reform movements.

Bishop Locke was the author of thirteen books, which were read by devout preachers with appreciation.

He died on March 4, 1940, in Santa Monica, Calif. and was buried in Forest Lawn, Glendale, Calif.

Journal of the Southern California-Arizona Conference, 1940.
F. D. Leete, *Methodist Bishops.* 1948.
Who's Who in the Clergy. JESSE A. EARL

LOCKHART, RICHARD ARTHUR (1893-1963), Irish minister, was born in BELFAST and educated at the Methodist College there. He was ordained in 1922, appointed to Mfantsipim School, Gold Coast (now GHANA), and three years later became Principal. The early development of that school, and the important place it took in the community, is due more to him than to any other person. After fourteen years he returned to IRELAND for a short period of circuit work, but in 1943 by Government invitation he went to KENYA as Principal of Kagumo College for teacher-training. He spent twelve years there, living through the perils of the Mau Mau period.

His influence on African education made an unrivaled contribution to the development of Ghana and Kenya. With his wife he was invited by the Government of Ghana to the celebrations of independence, and he was again invited when autonomy was granted to Ghana Methodism. His last ministerial appointment was at Centenary Church, DUBLIN, and he died in retirement in his native Belfast.

Cole, *Methodism in Ireland.* 1960.
F. Jeffery, *Irish Methodism.* 1964. FREDERICK JEFFERY

LOCKWOOD, J. H. (1837-1916), American pioneer preacher in northwest KANSAS, serves as an example of the men who built Methodism in his time and area. Born in PHILADELPHIA, Pa., on March 10, 1837, he moved to ILLINOIS as a youth and attended MCKENDREE COLLEGE. He was licensed to preach in 1858 and, except for three years as CHAPLAIN of the 49th Illinois regiment, spent the first fourteen years of his ministry in the SOUTHERN ILLINOIS CONFERENCE.

In 1872 he came to Kansas, serving first in the KANSAS CONFERENCE and, after it was divided, in the NORTHWEST KANSAS CONFERENCE. His Kansas years were spent largely at Salina and Beloit where he was presiding elder (for fifteen years) and pastor. He served as a presiding elder at the origin of the Northwest Kansas Conference and was its first delegate to the GENERAL CONFERENCE. There is a heavy listing in the conference journals of committees of which he was a member. In 1883 he was appointed to the Board of Trustees of BAKER UNIVERSITY at the same time that he became one of five ministers on a board of trustees to locate and charter what later became KANSAS WESLEYAN UNIVERSITY. In 1884 he was president of the conference board of church extension, as well as a member of the conference camp-meeting committee and of the conference boundaries committee. The conference was small and J. H. Lockwood had the pioneering spirit. For six years he served as district superintendent of the AMERICAN BIBLE SOCIETY for Kansas, and for eight years was a member of the general missionary committee. He became supernumerary in 1904, and moved to California where he died on Feb. 6, 1916.

Minutes of the Kansas Conference, 1875-82.
Minutes of the Northwest Kansas Conference, 1883-1904, 1916.
W. H. Sweet, *Northwest Kansas.* 1920. INA TURNER GRAY

LODER, DWIGHT ELLSWORTH (1914-   ), American college president and bishop, was born in Waverly, Neb., on July 8, 1914, the son of William and Alice C. (Snyder) Loder. He graduated from the University of Nebraska with the A.B. degree in 1936. After a year of graduate work there in the College of Law, in which he obtained honors, he was diverted by a call to the ministry and transferred to BOSTON UNIVERSITY SCHOOL OF THEOLOGY, where he received the S.T.B. degree in 1939. He was awarded the D.D. degree from Hamline University, 1951, from Garrett Theological Seminary, 1955, and from Albion College, 1968. He received the L.H.D. from Willamette University, 1966, and the S.T.D. from Dickinson College, 1966. He married Mildred Ethyl Shay on Sept. 17, 1939, and to them were born Ruth (Mrs. James Burnecke), William and David.

Dwight E. Loder served as associate pastor of the First Congregational Church, Stoneham, Mass., 1937-39. He was ordained to the Methodist ministry in the CENTRAL NEW YORK CONFERENCE in 1939, and served two pastor-

Dwight E. Loder

ates in PENNSYLVANIA—North Towanda, 1939-41; and Blossburg, 1941-47; and then joined the Hennepin Avenue (MINNEAPOLIS) Church staff in 1947. There he served as pastor from 1950 until 1955 when he was elected to the presidency of GARRETT THEOLOGICAL SEMINARY where he served until 1964, becoming a member of the ROCK RIVER CONFERENCE in 1957. He was elected to the episcopacy by the North Central Jurisdictional Conference in 1964, and put in charge of the MICHIGAN Area.

Bishop Loder was a delegate to the North American Faith and Order Study Conference of the WORLD COUNCIL OF CHURCHES in 1957, and participated in the WORLD METHODIST COUNCIL Ministerial Exchange in 1959. His lectureships include: Eighth annual Ministers' Convocation of Southern California, 1956; Glide lecturer, Glide School of Evangelism, San Francisco, 1960; and Fondren lecturer, SOUTHERN METHODIST UNVIERSITY, 1965. He attended the World Methodist Convocation on Theological Education, 1961; and was a delegate to the GENERAL CONFERENCES of The Methodist Church, 1960 and 1964; and of the North Central Jurisdictional Conferences, 1960 and 1964. He was a member of the Methodist Commission on Ecumenical Consultation, of the Commission on Chaplaincy, the subcommittee on theological education, proposed E.U.B.-Methodist merger; a member of UNIVERSITY SENATE of The Methodist Church, 1963-65; and a member of the North Central Jurisdictional Commission on Higher Education. He has been president of the Association of Methodist Theological Schools, 1960, and of the Chicago Theological Faculties Union, 1961. He received a distinguished Alumni award from Boston University School of Theology in 1964. He has been a member of the Michigan Governor's Ethical and Moral Panel, since 1965; and a former member of the Board of Directors of Asbury Hospital, of HAMLINE UNIVERSITY, of the Minneapolis Young Men's Christian Association, and

since 1964 has been a trustee of ALBION COLLEGE and of ADRIAN COLLEGE.

Who's Who in America, Vol. 34.
Who's Who in The Methodist Church, 1966.   N. B. H.

LOEPPERT, HENRY VERNE (1893-   ), American businessman and lay leader of the ROCK RIVER CONFERENCE, was born in Sandwich, Ill., on Sept. 2, 1893, the son of Henry C. and Elizabeth J. (Dieterich) Loeppert. He was educated in Chicago, Ill. and Appleton, Wis., and did further work at the University of Chicago, NORTHWESTERN UNIVERSITY, and in the graduate school at Harvard. On June 25, 1919, he married Ellen Sophia Waterman, and their children are H. Verne and Marilyn Elizabeth (Mrs. Bruce A. McLeod).

Mr. Loeppert entered business in 1922, and thereafter became prominent in various business interests and corporations in and about the CHICAGO area. For fifty years he was a member of the first German Methodist Church of Chicago and its successor, the Armitage Avenue Methodist Church. Since 1958, he has been a member of the First Methodist Church, EVANSTON, Ill. He was elected Rock River Conference Lay Leader, 1943-52.

His other church interests have been the Chicago Wesley Memorial Hospital, the Church Federation of Greater Chicago, the Board of Publications of The Methodist Church, of which he was a member for twelve years; director of the National Mutual Church Insurance Company of Chicago; and treasurer of the Executive Committee of the Board of Lay Activities of The Methodist Church, 1944-52. He has also been a trustee of the Methodist Ministers Pension Fund; KENDALL COLLEGE, Evanston; and president of the Conference Board of Missions, 1956-60. The United Churchmen of Chicago honored him as Layman of the Year on April 2, 1957, and a resolution in his honor was passed by the Board of Publication of The Methodist Church on Oct. 30, 1963. In 1961, he resigned from his business as president of the Boyd Wagner Company to accept, at the urging of Bishop BRASHARES, the Executive Directorship of the Methodist Old Peoples Home (Chicago, Ill.) of the Rock River Conference. He has been a member of the GENERAL CONFERENCE of The Methodist Church in all of its sessions from 1940 to 1964, with the exception of the Conference of 1956, when he accepted status as a delegate to the JURISDICTIONAL CONFERENCE in deference to his wife who had been elected a delegate to the General Conference of that year, since she was president of the Conference WOMAN'S SOCIETY OF CHRISTIAN SERVICE. He was elected a member of the General Conference Entertainment and Program Committee, 1964-68. He is presently engaged in promoting the Methodist Community of Services, an expansion of the Methodist Home on Foster Avenue, Chicago, and the planning of a new retirement complex on the South Side of Chicago in connection with property owned by St. Mark's Church. In 1966 he was nominated by the Methodist Old Peoples Home board and honored by the mayor of the City of Chicago for his contribution to Senior Citizens of Chicago.

Who's Who in The Methodist Church, 1966.   T. OTTO NALL

LOFTHOUSE, WILLIAM FREDERICK (1871-1965), British minister, was born in South Norwood, LONDON, and educated at the City of London School and Trinity College,

Oxford. He entered the Wesleyan Methodist ministry in 1896, training at Richmond College, London, where he also served as assistant tutor, 1896-98. He was appointed in 1899 assistant tutor at Handsworth College, BIRMINGHAM (see THEOLOGICAL COLLEGES); and there, apart from three years in circuit (1901-04), and three as a chaplain in the armed forces (1916-19), he spent the whole of his ministry until his retirement in 1940.

An Old Testament specialist, but widely read in other branches of theological study, he exercised a profound influence on his students. He lectured in the Old Testament from 1904 to 1916, and again from 1919 to 1925. From 1925 to 1940 he was principal of the college and tutor in systematic theology and philosophy of religion. He was elected president of the Wesleyan Methodist Conference in 1929, and in 1932 was chosen president of the Society for Old Testament Study.

His deep concern for social justice was seen in his work for the Methodist Union for Social Service. He was present at the COPEC conference on social Christianity in 1924, when he proposed the report on *The Relation of the Sexes*. On the same general subject he published *Ethics and the Family* (1912), *Altar, Cross and Community* (1921), *Purity and Racial Health* (1920), etc. His more strictly Old Testament writings included *Jeremiah and the New Covenant* (1926) and *Israel after the Exile* (1928). Keenly ecumenical, he played a part in the Faith and Order movement. His last published work was an essay on CHARLES WESLEY in *A History of the Methodist Church in Great Britain* (ed. Rupp and Davies, 1965). He died in Croydon on July 5, 1965.

JOHN NEWTON

LOGAN, JACOB TAYLOR (1854-1946), American minister and ordained elder of the Pittsburgh Conference of the FREE METHODIST CHURCH, was pastor and superintendent in Pennsylvania and Editor of *The Free Methodist*, 1907-1923; 1927-1931. He was an evangelistic pastor, an eloquent temperance lecturer, an attractive writer. He had tremendous vitality and carried on a heavy speaking schedule at the age of ninety. He died at Winona Lake, Ind.

BYRON S. LAMSON

LOMAS, JOHN (1798-1879), British minister, was born in Hull on Dec. 13, 1798, the son of Robert Lomas, a Wesleyan Methodist minister. He was educated at KINGSWOOD SCHOOL, of which he was headmaster from 1820 to 1823. In 1820 he was accepted for the ministry; and after leaving Kingswood he traveled in Bath, MANCHESTER, BRISTOL, HULL, and LONDON. In 1853 he was elected President of the Conference by an almost unanimous vote. He delivered the third FERNLEY LECTURE, *Jesus Christ: The Propitiation for our Sins*. From 1861 to 1867 he was the tutor in theology at Richmond College (see THEOLOGICAL COLLEGES), and held the same position at Headingley College from its opening in 1868 to 1872. He never married. As a preacher he was highly esteemed, especially by the more cultured of his hearers. He died on Aug. 20, 1879.

G. J. Stevenson, *Methodist Worthies*. 1884-86.

W. L. DOUGHTY

LONDON, England, the metropolis of Great Britain and the commanding city of the British Empire and now center of the British Commonwealth of Nations, has from the beginning been at the center of the Methodist movement. JOHN WESLEY was converted in London, established his headquarters there, and is buried there, as are his brother Charles and his mother Susanna. The organized work of The Methodist Church and Conference has always centered in London and most of its general offices are there now. Various historic shrines and places of Methodist work in the city are as follows:

Aldersgate Street runs north from St. Martins le Grand as far as Goswell Road. Number 28 on the east side is said to mark the probable site of the building where John Wesley felt his "heart strangely warmed" on May 24, 1738. The actual room may have been in the Hall House which was entered from Nettleton Court (now built up). It is doubtful if any part of the original building remains.

Bunhill Fields, City Road. The Dissenters Burial Ground opened in 1665. SUSANNA WESLEY was buried there on Aug. 1, 1742. Her son John preached the funeral sermon "to an immense multitude." Among others buried in Bunhill Fields are William Blake and his wife, John Bunyan, Daniel Defoe, and ISAAC WATTS. A memorial to Susanna Wesley erected in 1870 stands in Wesley's Chapel opposite.

Fetter Lane. Between Ludgate Circus and the Law Courts, Fetter Lane runs north from Fleet Street to Holborn. The first society met in the bookseller JAMES HUTTON's house at the sign of the Bible and Sun in Little Wild Street. About September, 1738, the meeting place was changed to a room in Fetter Lane where the society met until July 20, 1740.

THE FOUNDERY

The Foundery was situated near the northeast corner of Finsbury Square. A dilapidated iron foundry, Wesley leased it in 1739 and made it into the headquarters of the Methodist movement until 1778. Out of this "vast uncouth heap of ruins" he made a chapel which would accommodate fifteen hundred people, a smaller meeting room for about three hundred people, and a book room. Here were the first free dispensary in London (since the dissolution of the monasteries), a free school (with two masters and sixty children), an almshouse for widows. Here also were the private apartments of John Wesley's preachers, and here his mother died.

Kennington Common. GEORGE WHITEFIELD preached near the gallows on April 29, 1739, to a congregation estimated at thirty thousand. John and CHARLES WESLEY also preached there regularly in the open air in 1739 and 1740.

Little Britain is to the west of Aldersgate Street (near where it is joined by St. Martins le Grand). No. 12 is the site of the house of JOHN BRAY, the brazier. It was frequented by the Wesley brothers, and Charles Wesley was staying there at the time of his evangelical conversion.

Marylebone, Parish Church of. Wesley's parents were married in the old church on Nov. 12, 1688. The church was rebuilt in 1741 and demolished in 1949. Charles Wesley is buried in the graveyard near the site of the church in Marylebone High Street.

Moorfields. This was reclaimed low-lying marshland, laid out as a park in 1605 and later built upon. In the north of the district was the Foundery and nearby was Whitefield's first tabernacle, dating from 1741, giving the name to the present Tabernacle Street. Regular open-air services were held in Moorfields from 1739 to 1777. On March 2, 1777, John Wesley recorded: "There were thousands upon thousands; and all were still as night. Not only violence and rioting, but even scoffing at field-preachers is now over."

Snowfields. Here stood the third building John Wesley acquired for worship in London. He first preached there on Aug. 8, 1743. Thereafter services were regularly held for over twenty years. It was built by Madame Ginn, a lady of Unitarian leanings, in 1736.

Spitalfields. Originally this was "hospital-fields," the open space around St. Mary's Hospital on the north side of what is now Spital Square. Samuel Annesley lived in a house in Spital Yard, and there his daughter Susanna was born on Jan. 20, 1669. This house still stands.

West Street Chapel dates from about 1680. It was built by French Protestant refugees, and first called La Tremblade. John Wesley obtained the lease of it in 1743. It appears on the London Plans of 1754 as "The Chapel" to distinguish it from the Foundery. The original building still stands and is at present used as a warehouse.

Wesley's Chapel (City Road). The Mother Church of World Methodism is in City Road, London, opposite Bunhill Fields. Built to replace the old Foundery, which stood on a nearby site, it was known as Mr. Wesley's Chapel, or the "New Chapel," or more often the City Road Chapel. The foundation stone was laid on April 21, 1777, and the chapel, built to Wesley's design, was opened by him on Nov. 1, 1778.

Architecturally it is, in Wesley's words, "perfectly neat but not fine." It stands foursquare, east-west. It held "far more people than the Foundery." Within, it is surrounded on three sides by a large gallery—the front of which is decorated with the repeated motif of Wesley's choice, the dove surrounded by a serpent. The gallery was for a hundred years supported by wooden pillars made from the masts of King George III's men-of-war. These pillars have been preserved in the vestibule. They have been replaced by pillars of French jasper, gifts of representative Methodist churches overseas. In 1800 the west end of the gallery was made oval in form. The original mahogany pulpit still stands in the central position. Behind it is the communion table and mahogany communion rail. The Adam ceiling—in gold and white—was, at the time, the largest centrally unsupported ceiling in any building in England.

The original windows have been replaced by a number of commemorative windows in stained glass, notably (in 1892) in the apse (above the reredos), "The Adoration of the Magi," presented by the WESLEYAN REFORM UNION; "The Apostolic Commission," presented by the UNITED METHODIST FREE CHURCHES; and "Solomon's Porch," presented by the PRIMITIVE METHODIST connection. In the gallery on the north side is "The Wesleys' Conversion" window. On the reredos, under the words "Holy Holy Holy," the Apostles' Creed and the two commandments of the Lord Jesus are inscribed on a gilt background.

WESLEY'S CHAPEL, CITY ROAD, LONDON, ENGLAND

The font belonged to JOHN FLETCHER's church at Madeley, Shropshire, and was placed in Wesley's Chapel in 1891. The chapel contains memorial tablets to many notable servants of the Church. The most famous are in the sanctuary, to John and Charles Wesley, John Fletcher, JOSEPH BENSON, THOMAS COKE, and ADAM CLARKE. In the vestibule is the bronze memorial to all the Methodists who gave their lives in the two world wars.

In the graveyard behind the chapel, John Wesley is buried. The funeral took place at 5 A.M. on March 9, 1791. The vault was subsequently opened for eight others; his sister, MARTHA HALL; his preachers, DUNCAN WRIGHT, Thomas Bradshaw, JOHN RICHARDSON, JOHN MURLIN, THOMAS OLIVERS, Walter Griffith; and his physician, Dr. JOHN WHITEHEAD. Also buried in this graveyard are PETER JACO, JABEZ BUNTING, Adam Clarke, and George Whitefield, and many other well-known early Methodist preachers. The burial register for the graveyard contains over five thousand names.

A small vestry adjoining the chapel has been set aside as a prayer room to commemorate the Foundery. Here is the pipe organ which belonged to Charles Wesley, also some forms from the original "Foundery"—the lectern from the band room, and the pewter communion plate which John Wesley used. In the forecourt of the chapel stands the statue (by Adams-Acton) of John Wesley, erected at the centenary of his death by the subscriptions of the children of Methodism. The portico in front of the chapel was erected in 1815.

Wesley's Chapel was severely damaged by fire on Dec. 6, 1879. The restoration was carried out in keeping with the original style of the building. Impressions were carefully taken of what remained of the ceiling, so that the present is a careful replica. The chapel stands in one of the most badly war-damaged areas of London. On the night of the greatest fire raid in 1940, buildings all round were gutted and the chapel was saved only by the wind changing. New buildings on the adjacent sites are now complete, and the surrounding district is being rebuilt.

Although the local membership is small, the chapel exercises a wide ministry. There are thousands of visitors annually from all parts of the world. Commemorative and memorial services are fittingly held here, and regular worship services are faithfully maintained. Recently, sound and television broadcasts have given a contemporary significance to this "Church of the World Parish."

Wesley's House, 47 City Road, stands on the south side of the forecourt of Wesley's Chapel. John Wesley took up residence there on Oct. 9, 1779, and it was his London home for the last twelve years of his life. He died in this house on March 2, 1791. The house was opened as a museum on November 10, 1898. It has been extensively repaired, the most recent restoration being the entire building of the west wall in 1963.

The house contains a large and valuable collection of John Wesley's personal possessions and other early Methodist mementos. In the study on the first floor are his writing desk, bookcase, and study chair (which had belonged to a cock-fighting bookmaker who was converted through Wesley's preaching). Also his long-case clock (made in 1693 by Claudius de Chesne), his traveling robe and three-cornered hat, his shoes and buckles. A recent addition is the large umbrella which he left behind at Guisborough. His conference chair also stands in this room. The portrait of Wesley painted by FRANK O. SALISBURY hangs in the study. The rear room on the first

floor was Wesley's bedroom, which contains some of the original furniture. Leading out of it is the small prayer room where, it is said, he spent an hour between 4 A.M. and 5 A.M. each morning. There are his kneeling stool and his Greek New Testament. The second floor is largely set out as a museum of Wesleyana. Here can be seen many of his personal possessions. Notable among them are his traveling writing desk and the bronze lantern from his carriage; also the famous teapot given to him by JOSIAH WEDGWOOD. The most remarkable exhibit is his electrical machine, which he designed and found so effective in the treatment of "melancholia."

FIRST DAY COVER OF UNITED NATIONS STAMP
FEATURING CENTRAL HALL, LONDON

Westminster Central Hall, the administrative headquarters of British Methodism, housing, as well as a vast worship area, the offices of the Secretary of Conference, the HOME MISSION DEPARTMENT, the CHRISTIAN CITIZENSHIP DEPARTMENT, the Finance Board, the LOCAL PREACHERS Department and the Methodist Homes for the Aged. It was built on the site of the old Aquarium, directly opposite Westminster Abbey. The architect was A. B. Richards, and the building is said to have consumed over 10,000 tons of Portland stone, 5,000 tons of cement and over 1,000 tons of steel. The poet and architectural critic, John Betjeman, has described it as "by far the best example in London of Viennese baroque conceived by an Edwardian architect."

The idea of a Methodist equivalent of the Anglican Church House (also in the vicinity of Westminster Abbey), was the dream of Sir ROBERT PERKS towards the end of the nineteenth century, though it is true that he conceived it as the headquarters of Wesleyan Methodism, rather than of Methodism as a whole. He was able to convert his dream into bricks and mortar by means of a grant of £250,000 from the "Million Guineas Fund," a project launched by the Wesleyan Methodist Church to mark the advent of the twentieth century, and a scheme in which Robert Perks was deeply involved. The Subscribers' Roll is displayed in the vestibule of the Hall, and every name represents a "thank-offering of one guinea, neither more nor less." The Hall was officially opened on Oct. 3, 1912, in the presence of representatives of world Methodism and civic heads of many London and provincial boroughs. A service of dedication was conducted by MARSHALL HARTLEY, Simpson Johnson and John Hornabrook. After a civic luncheon, the President of the Wesleyan Methodist Conference, LUKE WISEMAN, led divine worship and preached. At a great evening meeting, presided over by Sir Robert Perks, the speakers were Bishop NUELSEN of American Methodism and WILLIAM L. WATKINSON, one of the most famous Wesleyan preachers of his day. As a place of worship, Westminster Central

Hall has been the pastorate of a distinguished series of ministers: John E. Wakeley (1911-1914), Dinsdale T. Young (1914-1938), F. Luke Wiseman (1938-1939), W. EDWIN SANGSTER (1939-1955), Derrick Greeves (1955-1964), and Maurice Barnett from 1964. As a church, it has suffered from the social decay of central London and from the decline in popularity of preaching as such. After the Second World War, in 1946, the Central Hall was chosen to be the venue of the first meeting of the General Assembly of the United Nations organization. A plaque was fixed to the south wall in commemoration of this historic occasion; it was unveiled by the Prime Minister of the day, Clement Atlee, later Lord Atlee. The Hall continues to serve Methodism both as preaching center and administrative center: a new department is a Pastoral Care and Counselling unit, begun under the direction of the Rev. William Kyle.

F. Baker, *Methodist Pilgrim in England.* 1951.
F. C. Gill, *John Wesley.* 1962.
J. H. Martin, *Wesley's London Chapels.* 1946.
G. J. Stevenson, *City Road Chapel.* 1872.
E. H. Sugden, *Wesley's London.* 1932.
J. Telford, *Wesley's Chapel and House,* 1906.

MAX WOODWARD
JOHN C. BOWMER

LONDON QUARTERLY REVIEW, THE (See MAGAZINES AND NEWSPAPERS, Br.).

LONG, ALBERT LIMERICK (1832-1901), was a distinguished American scholar and missionary representing Methodism in the territory of the Eastern Orthodox Church. He was born at Washington, Pa., on Dec. 4, 1832, the son of Warner Long of the Pittsburgh Conference. He graduated from ALLEGHENY COLLEGE in 1852, and that institution later conferred upon him the D.D. degree. In 1853 while principal of Green Academy, Carmichaels, Pa., he married Mary E. Rice of Meadville, Pa. His bride lived only a few weeks. In the shadows of his bereavement he heard and heeded the call to the Christian ministry and enrolled in the Theological Seminary at Concord, N. H. Upon graduating he was admitted to the PITTSBURGH CONFERENCE in 1857, and at that session was appointed a missionary to BULGARIA. Before sailing he married Mrs. Persis S. Loveland of Concord, N. H., who became the mother of their three children.

Methodist work was just beginning in Bulgaria when Albert Long arrived in 1857. In 1863 he was appointed Superintendent of the entire Mission to the Orthodox people and moved to Constantinople. He translated the Bible into the Bulgarian language, during which work he returned to America for a couple of years. Returning to Constantinople he established and edited a family religious paper in Bulgarian, and translated hymns and books, including *Pilgrim's Progress,* into that language in his efforts to provide a Christian literature for the Bulgarian people.

In July, 1872, he was invited to take the professorship of Natural Science in Robert's College in Constantinople, and after the step was approved by The Missionary Society, he accepted. For nearly thirty years he taught and witnessed for his Lord in that influential institution in which he was loved and his scholarship was widely respected. Being in failing health, in 1901, he was granted a year's leave of absence by the College and started for America on July 8th. Reaching Liverpool, England on July 27th he was too weak to continue. Taken to the Royal Infirmary, he died on July 28, 1901 and was buried in St. James cemetery. Albert Long's name was on the rolls of The Pittsburgh Conference of the M. E. Church from 1857 to 1901 and his distinguished labors in a difficult mission field make him one of the most eminent contributions of that great Conference to world Methodism.

W. GUY SMELTZER

LONG, CHARLES ALEXANDER (1881-), American preacher and missionary to BRAZIL, was born near Alto, Texas on Aug. 22, 1881. He graduated in 1905 from the University of Oklahoma, joined the OKLAHOMA CONFERENCE in 1906, and was ordained deacon in 1908. After some years in Oklahoma, he graduated from VANDERBILT with a B.D. degree. While there, he married, on July 8, 1911, Lucy York, then a student at SCARRITT COLLEGE. They sailed for Brazil, arriving in RIO DE JANEIRO on August 6. He was ordained elder by the Brazil Annual Conference then in session and at once appointed pastor and superintendent of the Instituto Central do Povo, then located on Rua Acre.

During his years in Brazil, Long served as pastor, district superintendent, professor of theology, and dean (reitôr) of the INSTITUTO GRANBERYENSE, Director of the Seamen's Mission in Rio, Secretary of the Board of Social Action of the Methodist Church of Brazil; representative of the Church on the COMMISSION OF COOPERATION IN LATIN AMERICA, and as builder of churches and parsonages. In JUIZ DE FORA, he built one of the handsomest Protestant churches in Brazil.

He also pioneered in the far interior of the State of Goiás, where the church owned one small lot. Long left five houses of worship, four residences, and several lots. In all his work, his wife was a consecrated, efficient helper, especially in connection with the ANNA GONZAGA HOME, near Rio de Janeiro.

The Longs retired to the United States after forty years of service, in February 1952, settling in Ardmore, Okla. There they continued active service in church work. Mrs. Long died in March 1970.

J. L. Kennedy, *Metodismo no Brasil.* 1928.
Voz Missionaria, 1960 (last quarter).

EULA K. LONG

LONG, EULA LEE KENNEDY (1891-), was born of pioneer American Methodist missionaries, in Taubaté, State of São Paulo, on Sept. 25, 1891. She studied at mission schools in BRAZIL and at Mackenzie College, São Paulo, after which she graduated from RANDOLPH-MACON WOMAN'S COLLEGE in the U.S.A. Returning to Brazil, she met on shipboard FRANK M. LONG, a missionary and Y.M.C.A. secretary. They fell in love, were married on Oct. 13, 1914, and of this union, five children were born.

In Brazil, between 1913 and 1934, Mrs. Long served actively, becoming secretary and president of the Methodist Women's Societies in the Rio Grande do Sul Conference and one of the founders of the Methodist women's official magazine, the *Voz Missionaria.* She was a charter member and organizer of the Liga Pro-Abstinencia (Woman's Christian Temperance Union) in Porto Alegre, and taught a course in scientific temperance to a group of city teachers.

For helping her husband introduce Mothers' Day to

Brazil in 1918, she received special honors (1954) from her native city, Taubaté, at which time the City Council named a street "Kennedy," honoring both her and her father, J. L. KENNEDY. Her most influential work was in the literary field—writing a Sunday column for a state newspaper, and writing also a number of influential books including her father's biography and *Coracões Felizes* (Happy Hearts), which went into ten editions and was also translated into Spanish in MEXICO. In recognition, Eula Long was named corresponding member of three academies of letters in Brazil.

Returning to the United States with her family in 1934, she lectured and taught courses on South America, and published articles in nationally known magazines. In 1945, she received a second national award in poetry from the Edwin Markham Memorial Association; in 1959 a citation from Randolph-Macon Woman's College for outstanding religious leadership; an honorary life membership in the Woman's Society of Christian Service; and was named VIRGINIA Mother of the Year. She is editor for Brazil and the Brazilian articles and personalities in this *Encyclopedia of World Methodism*. Mrs. Long lives in Roanoke, Va.

Clark and Stafford, *Who's Who in Methodism*. 1952.
Who's Who Among American Women.   JAMES A. LONG

LONG, FRANK MILLARD (1883-1958), American layman, secretary of the International Committee of the Y.M.C.A. in BRAZIL, was born in Comiskey, Kan., on Nov. 18, 1883. He early moved to OKLAHOMA and graduated from the State University (B.A. 1908; M.A. 1909).

An opening for mission work came with a call to INSTITUTO GRANBERY in JUIZ DE FORA, Brazil, and by a mutual agreement between the Methodist Church and the International Y.M.C.A., he was sent to organize "Y" work and to teach Bible, English, and athletics. He sailed in July, 1913. On the ship, he met EULA LEE KENNEDY who was returning to Brazil after graduation from RANDOLPH-MACON WOMAN'S COLLEGE. They fell in love and were married on Oct. 13, 1914.

After two years at Granbery, Long was called to serve the Y.M.C.A. in Recife (Pernambuco) during an emergency; from then on he continued in this organization. He was in RIO DE JANEIRO one year, and then sixteen years in PORTO ALEGRE (Rio Grande). In this last, according to Dr. Kenneth Latourette, the success of the Y.M.C.A. work was "phenomenal," and Long's record "striking." Among other things he trained athletes for the continental Olympics, some of whom won first places, and for this he was named "Father of Athletics" in Rio Grande do Sul.

He served on the board of trustees of the College, now Instituto Porto Alegre; and initiated the first death-benefit plan for Methodist preachers in that state. In May 1918, with Mrs. Long's help, he introduced Mothers' Day to Brazil, possibly a first in all South America. The day was later officialized by government decree. In a posthumous celebration in 1961, the city council of Porto Alegre named a public square the "Praca Frank M. Long," and in 1968 held special commemorations and issued a stamp folio in his honor.

Recalled to the United States in 1934, because of the depression, Long served in the Memphis and Roanoke Y.M.C.A.'s until 1942; then in Y-USO's in Dublin and Hampton, Va. Upon retirement in 1952, Frank Long

and his wife spent three years in Norman, Okla., where they enrolled in university classes. He died in Roanoke, Va., on May 31, 1958, of congestive heart failure. Survivors included his wife and four children—James, a geophysicist; Lewis, a psychologist; Eulalee Anderson; Edith Schisler, who married a second generation missionary to Brazil; and fourteen grandchildren. A son, Frank Millard, Jr., was killed in the Second World War.

J. EARL MORELAND

LONG, JOHN WILLIAM (1882-1956), American preacher and educator, was born in Sussex County, Del., Nov. 3, 1882. The son of Richard Wilson Long, public school teacher and Methodist preacher, he attended the public schools of Wicomico County, Del., graduating from the Delmar High School. He was graduated from Wesley Junior College, Dover, Del., in 1904, and DICKINSON COLLEGE in 1907.

Following a series of pastorates in the CENTRAL PENNSYLVANIA CONFERENCE, the last at St. Paul's Church, State College, Pa., he was elected president of Williamsport Dickinson Seminary, Williamsport, Pa., in 1921. Under his leadership the institution became a Junior College in 1929, and a four-year degree granting college, LYCOMING COLLEGE, in 1947.

Lycoming College is his living memorial. It reflects the devotion of his spirit and the dedication of his life. His service to education and to the church was recognized by a D.D. degree conferred by Dickinson College, and a LL.D. from WESTERN MARYLAND COLLEGE. Wesley Junior College made him the recipient of its Wesley Award in recognition of a half century of service.

He was married to Mildred Lee Lewis and they became the parents of four sons and four daughters. He retired in 1955 from the institution which he served as president for thirty-four years, and died within the year on May 5, 1956.

Journal, Central Pennsylvania Conference, 1956.

D. FREDERICK WERTZ

LONG, JOSEPH (1800-1869), American Evangelical preacher and bishop, was born Oct. 2, 1800 in Berks County, Pa. In 1818 he was converted in OHIO where his family had moved. He entered the ministry of the EVANGELICAL ASSOCIATION at the conference session held in New Berlin, Pa., in June 1822. On Jan. 10, 1826, he was married to Catherine Hoy, but his salary was very small, so he had to locate to earn a living for his family, his parents and the family of a helpless brother.

In 1841 he returned to the itinerancy. At the GENERAL CONFERENCE in 1843, held in Greensburg, Ohio, he was elected bishop and served in this office until his death in Forreston, Ill., June 23, 1869.

Bishop Long was an outstanding preacher in his day. Many men declared they never heard his equal. He was witty and sometimes sarcastic. Bishop S. P. SPRENG writes that "he was profound and overwhelmingly powerful . . . a son of thunder." Lacking the best of education himself, Long fostered educational institutions within the church, even applying part of his estate to the maintenance of Greensburg Seminary at Greensburg, Ohio.

He was a strict disciplinarian, understanding both the doctrine and the law of the Church. Yet he was progressive, quietly adapting himself to changing conditions and ideals. He was kind and helpful in his relations with young ministers of the church. In him the Church had a wise counsellor, far-seeing and prudent, and a staunch defender of the fundamental doctrines of the Evangelical Church.

R. W. Albright, *Evangelical Church.* 1942.
R. M. Veh, *Evangelical Bishops.* 1939.　　　Howard H. Marty

ISAAC LONG BARN

LONG BARN, ISAAC, located near Neffsville in the Landis Valley of Lancaster County, Pa., is the site of the meeting between Martin Boehm and Philip William Otterbein on Pentecost Sunday 1767, from which evolved the former Church of the United Brethren in Christ.

As was the custom in those days, a crowd of German residents of central and eastern Pennsylvania had gathered together for a "Great Meeting." The preacher for the occasion was Martin Boehm, a Mennonite minister from the southern part of Lancaster County. In his audience was a German Reformed pastor who had once served a congregation in Lancaster, but who was now located at York, Pa., Philip William Otterbein.

Otterbein was so moved by the fervor of the sermon he heard that he rushed forward and embraced the preacher with the greeting *Wir sind Bruder*, "We are brethren."

Although other meetings of a similar nature were conducted in this sturdy stone and wood barn and the woods adjacent to it, none has been as significant in the history of the E.U.B. Church as was this meeting in 1767. On June 16, 1960, the Pennsylvania Historical and Museum Commission erected one of its historical markers near the Isaac Long Barn in recognition of its importance in the religious history of the state.

Although it has been enlarged, the original building with its wooden pegs holding the timbers in place still stands. The land surrounding it was farmed in 1968 by the Jacob B. Landis family, direct descendant Mennonites from Isaac Long, who have been most cooperative with the historical agencies of the church and have always welcomed visitors to their premises.

On May 14, 1967, the 200th Anniversary of the meeting of Boehm and Otterbein at the Isaac Long Barn was commemorated with a service that had to be conducted due to inclement weather in the auditorium of the Manheim Township High School before an audience of 1,100.

Bruce C. Souders

LONG BEACH, CALIFORNIA, U.S.A., with a population of 346,975 (1970), is situated on the Pacific Ocean and noted for its port and naval activities, its oil and varied industries, its international beauty pageants and year-round mild climate. Long Beach is also an important center for Methodism. "The Methodist Resort Association" was formed in 1884, sponsoring tent meetings and tabernacle assemblies. Out of this came First Methodist Church of Long Beach, and later the Long Beach District Union to aid church extension. First Church was organized in 1884 before the city was incorporated or chartered. It was destined to be the "mother church" of Methodism locally, and the host for numerous Annual Conference sessions across the years.

From its founding Long Beach has looked to Methodist clergy and laity for significant leadership, the latter especially having been prominent in the economic, political, social, cultural, and educational life of a fast growing city. Early Methodist names in Long Beach in 1884 were Bishop Cyrus D. Foss; Presiding Elder R. W. C. Farnsworth; and G. W. Elwood, first pastor. Prominent names of laity near the turn of the century were Charles J. Walker, E. Vance Hill, Fell Lightburn, Dr. D. W. Cuthbert, M. H. LaFetra, E. E. Buffum, R. J. Craig, S. A. Stone, E. M. Lyman, F. D. Bishop, S. Townsend, F. W. Stearns, J. W. Hand and C. F. Van de Water.

While there have been several mergers and relocations of local churches to better serve residential needs, Long Beach Methodism now has thirteen local churches with a combined membership of 9,884. The three largest churches are Los Altos, California Heights, and Grace. The Los Altos church was organized in 1954 and grew to 2,569 members by 1970. The former First M. E. Church, South is now known as Moore Memorial. The organizational chronology of Long Beach churches follows: First, 1884; Moore Memorial, 1901 (formerly First M. E. S. and Centenary M. E. S.); Grace, 1911 (formerly Alamitos Park, 1903); Atlantic, 1925 (merger of Central, 1905 and Trinity, 1913); East, 1922 (formerly Zaferia, 1913); Belmont Heights, 1914; North, 1930 (formerly Virginia City, 1923 and Spaulding, 1929); California Heights, 1930; Silverado, 1944; Los Altos, 1954; Latin American, 1956; Dominguez, 1959. Methodism is also represented in long Beach by a former E.U.B.; A.M.E.; C.M.E.; and Free Methodist churches.

The Long Beach District of the Southern California-Arizona Conference has fifty-one local churches with 26,546 members (1970 *Journal*).

Donald R. O'Connor

LONGACRE, JAMES BARTON (1794-1869), American layman, who became a world famous engraver, was born in Delaware County, Pa., on Aug. 11, 1794. He was apprenticed to an engraver in Philadelphia and obtained early notice by an engraving he did of President Andrew Jackson. In 1831 he was employed in the illustration of the money which was then reproduced in certain American works being published. At first in conjunction with James Herring, of New York, and later independently, he planned and published the *National Portrait Gallery of Distinguished Americans* (1834-9). Among the engravings in this group were some sketches done by himself. The *Portrait Gallery* yet is of interest and he held in high esteem.

Descended from Swedish ancestors, he was early trained in religious life, and when young became a member of old St. George's Church at Philadelphia, filling the offices of class-leader, steward, and trustee for many years. He left St. George's with others to form the Central Church, Philadelphia, and served it also in the same positions until his death. He was one of the first trustees of DICKINSON COLLEGE, one of the first managers of the Philadelphia Conference Tract Society and Publishing House, and for thirty years was a vice-president of the American Sunday-School Union.

In 1844, Longacre was appointed engraver to the United States mint, and from that time until his death designed all new coins. He was also called upon to remodel the coinage of CHILE—which he did.

He died in Philadelphia, Pa., on Jan. 1, 1869.

Americana Encyclopedia, The. Vol. 17. New York: American Book-Stratford Press, Inc. 1950.
M. Simpson, *Cyclopaedia.* 1878.   N. B. H.

LONGACRE, LINDSAY BARTHOLOMEW (1870-1952),
American educator and hymnist, was born on Jan. 26, 1870, in Pottsville, Pa. He was educated at Columbia University, at DREW THEOLOGICAL SEMINARY, and at the University of Jena in Germany, 1905-10. He received the Ph.D. degree from New York University in 1908. For a time he served in the NEW YORK CONFERENCE, but then went to the ILIFF SCHOOL OF THEOLOGY in 1910, where he was destined to spend most of his life. Considered an authority on liturgy and church music, he wrote the *Riverdale Hymn Book,* published by Revell in 1912, and was the composer of songs, hymns, and tunes. He served on the Commission on Ritual and Orders of Worship of The Methodist Church, 1940-44, which Commission created the first Book of Worship of The Methodist Church, and in this Longacre wrote the entire section of daily devotions. After his retirement from Iliff, Longacre returned to New York where for a time he served in a pastoral way as an assistant to RALPH W. SOCKMAN at Christ Church. He died on Sept. 18, 1952.

C. F. Price, *Who's Who in American Methodism.* 1916.
Minutes, Colorado Conference, 1953.   N. B. H.

LONGSTREET, AUGUSTUS BALDWIN (1790-1870),
American jurist, author, educator, and minister, was born at Augusta, Ga., Sept. 22, 1790. He graduated from Yale University in 1813 and followed the example of his friend, John C. Calhoun, by studying law at Litchfield, Conn., In 1815 he was admitted to the bar at Augusta, Ga., and located at Greensboro, Ga., where he married Eliza Parke and became judge of the circuit court. Judge Longstreet was elected to the GEORGIA legislature in 1821. He was a religious skeptic, but the death of his eldest child so affected him that after a long struggle, he joined the M. E. Church in 1827. He returned to Augusta and resumed his law practice. There he edited *The States Rights Sentinel,* which gave him a national reputation when HARPER AND BROTHERS published the sketches in book form in 1840.

In 1836 Longstreet became a member of the first board of trustees of WESLEYAN COLLEGE at MACON, Ga. In 1838 at the age of forty-eight he entered the Methodist ministry. Two years later he was elected president of Emory College at Oxford, Ga. One of the students, L. Q. C. LAMAR, married Longstreet's daughter. In 1841 Yale conferred upon him the LL.D. degree.

At the GENERAL CONFERENCE in 1844, Longstreet delivered the Declaration of the Southern Delegates which stated that the vote against Bishop ANDREW had made it impossible for the General Conference to continue to legislate for the Methodist Church in the slaveholding states. He played a prominent role in the LOUISVILLE CONVENTION of 1845, where because of his legal experience, he was called upon to help draft the rules for the proceedings of the Convention. He was also elected to the first General Conference of the M. E. Church, South, in 1846.

During 1849 Longstreet was president of CENTENARY COLLEGE which was then operated by the Methodist Conferences of MISSISSIPPI and LOUISIANA. From 1849 to 1856 he was president of the University of Mississippi, but his political writings against the "Know-Nothing" movement aroused such controversy that he retired from public life. In 1857, however, he accepted his fourth college presidency at the University of South Carolina. In 1865 Longstreet settled again in Mississippi and wrote extensively to justify the lost cause of the South. His greatest companion in his old age was his (by then famous) son-in-law, Senator and Justice Lucius Quintus Cincinnatus Lamar. Longstreet died in Oxford, Miss., on July 9, 1870.

Dictionary of American Biography.
Thomas English, *Emory University.* 1966.
A. M. Pierce, *Georgia.* 1956.
A. H. Redford, *Organization of MES.* 1871.
G. G. Smith, *Georgia.* 1913.   DONALD J. WEST

LONGVIEW, TEXAS, U.S.A., **First Church** is a three-million dollar church plant located in Longview's business district, with a graceful church tower joining with tall office buildings to make the city's skyline.

First Church had its beginning about 1840 in a log meeting house, which the congregation made available for use by other early Protestant denominations of the community. The evangelistic membership steadily grew, progressing from the log house to a one-room frame structure by 1860, a brick church in 1875, and a much larger brick building in 1900, with the addition of the church's first educational building in 1909. The cornerstone for the present-day church was laid in 1951 by Bishop A. FRANK SMITH.

Today's modern plant is of modified Romanesque architecture and situated on a landscaped square. The churchly sanctuary, seating 724, has stained glass windows designed to give a complete, connected story of the earthly ministry of our Lord Jesus Christ. Equipment includes a 3-manual, 32-rank pipe organ. A prayer room, near the main street entrance, is open at all times.

Complete facilities provide for the educational and social life of the church. The three-story Children and Youth Building is widely recognized throughout the Southwest as a model of efficiency and beauty. Functional, attractive adult classrooms, a well-stocked library, chapel and parlor, large banquet hall, fully equipped kitchen, modern staff offices, and an adjoining, hard-surfaced parking lot are features of this building.

A distinctive music program characterizes First Methodist. There are eight choirs with more than 200 members. The Chancel Choir sings each Sunday morning, and presents special programs with symphonic accompaniment during the year.

The School for Little Children is a highly successful week-day school for three- to five-year olds. Enrollment is presently limited to 150.

Present church membership exceeds 2,200, and church school attendance averages about 700. First Methodist is mission-minded, and gives approximately $10,000 in World Service and Conference benevolences from its annual budget of $190,000. Two worship services are held each Sunday morning and one on Sunday night. Wednesday night meetings frequently follow a general membership supper. The church staff is headed by its first minister, an associate minister, a director of Christian education, day school director, two choir directors, an organist, and five secretaries. First Methodist calls itself, "The Church at the Heart of the City with the City at Heart."

Longview News Journal, Oct. 6, 1957.

DERWOOD L. BLACKWELL

LON MORRIS COLLEGE, Jacksonville, Texas, was founded in 1873 at Kilgore, Texas, as Alexander Institute. Two years later it became the property of the EAST TEXAS CONFERENCE of the M. E. Church, South. It moved to its present location in 1894, became a junior college in 1912, and assumed its present name in 1924. The great growth and development occurred during the administration of Cecil E. Peeples, who has been president since 1935. The governing board consists of forty-one members elected by the TEXAS CONFERENCE.

JOHN O. GROSS

LOOFBOUROW, LEONIDAS LATIMER (1877-1969), American minister and historian, started life at Atlantic, Iowa, Dec. 5, 1877, but was destined to roam widely in the service of Methodism. He was admitted on trial in the CALIFORNIA CONFERENCE of the M. E. Church in 1903. His California pastorates included Eighth Avenue, Oakland (1906-11); First, Burlingame (1919-25); and Coop Parish, Richmond (1949-59); but he also was stationed at First, Honolulu (1915-19); and Union, Balboa, in the Canal Zone, Panama (1937-41). From 1925 to 1931 he served as superintendent of the Redwood-Shasta District, and was a member of various boards and commissions of the M. E. Church.

Loofbourow was an outdoorsman in his youth and combined poetry with nature study while in the high Sierras, as did his contemporary and fellow Californian, John Muir. He won Phi Beta Kappa honors and a B.A. degree at Stanford, a B.D. degree at BOSTON UNIVERSITY, and an honorary D.D. at the UNIVERSITY OF THE PACIFIC. His publications, mostly in church history, include *In Search of God's Gold* (1950) and *Steeples Among the Sage, A Centennial Story of Nevada's Churches* (1964). He also wrote a two volume account, *Cross in the Sunset*.

"He lived his history as he wrote it" stated the *Together* news edition for the San Francisco Area (UMC) as it announced his death on May 13, 1969. "In 1952 at age 75 he rode horseback nearly one hundred miles around the southern arm of San Francisco Bay . . . telling the deeds of this Conference and its people." He and Mrs. Loofbourow (Anna Hart Robertson) celebrated their golden wedding anniversary with 1,600 guests several years before her passing at age 93.

Loofbourow was a helpful contributor to this *Encyclopedia* covering much California history for it.

Clark and Stafford, *Who's Who in Methodism*. 1952.

LELAND D. CASE

LOPES, JOSÉ LEONEL (1868-1920), Brazilian preacher, was born in Santa Barbara do Mato Dentro, state of Minas Gerais, on Sept. 18, 1868, the only child of staunch, traditionally Roman Catholic parents. As a youth in Ouro Preto, Minas Gerais, he heard for the first time the Gospel preached by JOÃO E. TAVARES. He began to inquire, then was convinced, converted and gave himself utterly to Christ.

He was one of the first students of GRANBERY COLLEGE, now Instituto. In 1897, he married Jovita de Araujo, and they had eight children.

Lopes served many churches in the state of Minas Gerais, SÃO PAULO, RIO DE JANEIRO, and Rio Grande do Sul. He was always a hard worker, courageous, and compelling evangelist. It was said that when the bishop needed a man for a difficult or remote station, the unanimous recommendation always was, "Get Leonel Lopes."

Stricken with diabetes, he was taken to the Hospital Samaritano in São Paulo. Relatives and friends wanted to secure a private room for his greater comfort, but Leonel refused, commenting, "In a ward, I can speak of Christ to many others." And this he did. Though both legs had to be amputated, Leonel never faltered in faith or courage. He died on Sept. 19, 1920.

ISNARD ROCHA

LORD, JOHN WESLEY (1902-), American bishop, was born in Paterson, N. J., on Aug. 23, 1902, the son of John James and Catherine (Carmichael) Lord.

He graduated from the Montclair State Normal School, Montclair, N. J., in 1922. He was a teacher and principal in the NEW JERSEY schools from 1922 until 1924. He received the B.A. degree from DICKINSON COLLEGE in 1927, and the B.D. from DREW THEOLOGICAL SEMINARY in 1930. He matriculated for his Ph.D. at the University of Edinburgh, Scotland, in 1930 and 1931, and did graduate work at Rutgers University in the field of education. He received a D.D. from Dickinson College in 1943 and LL.D. in 1949; and S.T.D. from BOSTON UNIVERSITY in 1949.

On April 29, 1931, he was united in marriage to Margaret Farrington Ratcliffe. They have one daughter, Jean Phillips Lord (Mrs. Arnold C. Cooper).

He was admitted on trial and ordained DEACON at the NEWARK CONFERENCE in April, 1929; admitted to full connection and ELDER in 1931. From 1927 until 1930 he was an assistant pastor of the Emory Methodist Church in Jersey City, N. J.; then pastor of the Union Community Church in Union, N. J., while it was under construction with volunteer labor, 1931-34. Subsequently he held pastorates at the First Church in Arlington, N. J., 1935-38; and at the First Church in Westfield, N. J. 1938-48.

At the Northeastern JURISDICTIONAL CONFERENCE in session at Albany, N. Y., on June 18, 1948, he was elected bishop and was consecrated on June 20 in Trinity Church, Albany, N. Y. He was assigned to residence in the BOSTON Area and served as presiding bishop there until June 1960, when he was assigned to the Washington Area. This embraces the District of Columbia, DELAWARE, most of MARYLAND, and a small part of WEST VIRGINIA.

In 1950-56 he was president of the New England Deaconess Hospital; and in 1953-55 of the Massachusetts Council of Churches. He was a member of the Board of Lay Activities, Northeastern Jurisdiction.

Bishop Lord is a Trustee of CLAFLIN COLLEGE; New

England Deaconess Hospital, Boston; AMERICAN UNIVERSITY; Sibley Memorial Hospital, Washington, D. C.; Wesley College, Dover, Del.; WESTERN MARYLAND COLLEGE; Dickinson College; Morgan Christian Center, MORGAN STATE COLLEGE, Baltimore. He is Chairman of the Board of Governors, WESLEY THEOLOGICAL SEMINARY; President of The Methodist Corporation, Washington, D. C.; President of the General BOARD OF PENSIONS, and Chairman of the Interreligious Committee on Race, Washington, D. C. He is a member of the Commission on Ecumenical Affairs and General BOARD OF CHRISTIAN SOCIAL CONCERNS of The United Methodist Church; General Board of the NATIONAL COUNCIL OF CHURCHES of Christ in the U.S.A.; National Council for a Responsible Firearms Policy; U.S. Interreligious Committee on Peace; Clergy and Laymen Concerned About Vietnam; and Honorary Chairman of The Committee of Responsibility (to save war-burned and war-injured Vietnamese children).

Who's Who in America, Vol. 34.
Who's Who in The Methodist Church, 1966.   N. B. H.

LORD'S SUPPER. (See COMMUNION, THE HOLY.)

LORE, DALLAS D. (1815-1875), American missionary and editor, born in New Jersey in 1815, who joined the PHILADELPHIA CONFERENCE of the M. E. Church in 1837. In 1840 he was nominated as a missionary to Africa, but circumstances prevented his entering upon the work. He subsequently served as a pastor in Lancaster, Pa., but in 1847 he went as a missionary to BUENOS AIRES, where he remained seven years. During that time he successfully supported the work of the mission in Buenos Aires. Upon his return from Buenos Aires, he was sent upon a tour of observation in NEW MEXICO with a view to the establishment of a mission in that territory. His letters back to the Board of Missions from Sante Fe in 1855 were not encouraging, and while he was able to organize a class of nine persons at Socorro, and one of fourteen members at Peralto, and a circuit of four appointments, he did not feel that the work should be continued. After receiving his report, the Board decided to discontinue the mission.

Lore then was elected editor of the *Northern Christian Advocate* by the GENERAL CONFERENCE of 1864, and re-elected in '68 and '72. He was active in calling the New York Methodist State Convention which met at SYRACUSE in 1870, and which determined upon the establishment of SYRACUSE UNIVERSITY. Dallas Lore died near Auburn, N. Y., on June 20, 1875.

W. C. Barclay, *History of Methodist Missions*. 1957.
M. Simpson, *Cyclopaedia*. 1878.   N. B. H.

LORENZ, EDMUND SIMON (1854-1942), American United Brethren hymn writer, composer, and publisher of religious music, was born at North Lawrence, Ohio, in the home of a United Brethren minister, July 13, 1854. After graduating from high school in Toledo he taught German in the public schools of that city (1870-74). In 1874 Lorenz went to work for the United Brethren Printing Establishment in DAYTON, Ohio, where he edited *Hymns for the Sanctuary* (1874). For several years he alternated between his college education and serving churches, having joined the Miami Conference, United Brethren in Christ, in 1877.

On Oct. 1, 1878 he married Florence Kumler. He graduated from OTTERBEIN UNIVERSITY (1880) and Yale Divinity School (1883). Following study at Leipzig and Berlin, Germany, he served as pastor in Dayton until 1887, when he was called to be president of LEBANON VALLEY COLLEGE (1887-89).

Ill health forced him to leave the college, and he then turned to the work for which he became famous. In 1890, he founded the Lorenz Publishing Company in Dayton, Ohio, which became widely renowned for the publishing of church music. As editor and head of the company, he not only wrote hymns and composed music but served many denominations by providing music publications used by countless local churches and Sunday schools. In his later activities he functioned primarily as a lay businessman, but his contributions were always church oriented. His many publications of religious music included the editing of the *Otterbein Hymnal* (1890) and the *Church Hymnal* (1935) for the United Brethren in Christ. He died July 10, 1942, in Dayton, Ohio.

William Coyle, ed., *Ohio Authors and Their Books*. Cleveland, World Publishing Co., 1962.
Religious Telescope, Vol. 108, No. 30 (July 25, 1942).
DONALD K. GORRELL

LORENZ, JUSTINA. (See SHOWERS, JUSTINA L.)

LOS ANGELES, CALIFORNIA, U.S.A., a city of 2,781,829, now ranks third city in the nation in population. The Pueblo de Nuestra Senora la Reina de los Angeles was founded in 1781 and given its name by the Spanish governor of CALIFORNIA. The Pueblo soon discarded most of its name and became known as the "City of the Angels" because of the beauty of its situation and excellent climate.

Los Angeles was incorporated in 1850. At that time its twenty-eight square miles held a population of 1,610. In 1853 Bishop EDWARD R. AMES, presiding at the CALIFORNIA CONFERENCE in SAN FRANCISCO, appointed Adam Bland a "missionary" to Los Angeles. Bland's first move was to lease El Dorado, a saloon located on Main Street, near the town's Plaza, and transform it into a chapel where he held services and where his wife conducted a school for girls.

The "City of Angels" was anything but that in those early days. The backwash of the gold rush brought unsavory characters to town and launched a period of general lawlessness. Conditions were made worse by the divided loyalties of the Civil War period. For a time, the representatives of all Protestant denominations abandoned their work in this area. Bland left Los Angeles and became the presiding elder of the Santa Clara District in northern California.

In 1866, after the Civil War was over, Adam Bland came back to reorganize the work he had left earlier. It was not until 1867 that Columbus Gillet was appointed pastor and thirty people attended a Quarterly Conference and Love Feast in Los Angeles. This was the beginning of an unbroken appointment of ministers to the Fort Street, later known as the First Methodist Church.

In 1868 the Fort Street Church was built. It was a brick building on the west side of what is now called Broadway, between Third and Fourth Streets. When it became too small for its growing congregation, a larger frame structure was erected next door. In 1876 the Fort Street Church established a school for young people and called it "The Los Angeles Academy." This was the forerunner of the University of Southern California. MARION M. BOVARD became pastor of the Fort Street Church in 1878, and two years later resigned to become the first president of the University of Southern California, which opened its doors in 1880 with fifty-three students enrolled.

The Southern Pacific ran its tracks into the city in 1876, joining Los Angeles to the rest of the continent. When the Santa Fe extended its tracks into the city in 1885, there resulted a rate war for patronage marked by a large influx of newcomers. Los Angeles, which had 1,610 people in 1850, had 8,453 in 1875. The population of Los Angeles County during that same period rose from 3,530 to 24,344. In September of 1876, with Bishop WILLIAM L. HARRIS presiding, the Southern California Conference (M.E.) was organized with thirteen buildings, nine parsonages, 1,257 members, twenty-seven ministers in full relationship, and three men on trial.

In 1891 the Fort Street Church paid $37,500 for lots at Sixth and Hill Streets. On Easter Sunday, 1900, the new First Church was dedicated. It cost more than $73,-000. The report that year showed 984 members and forty-four probationers.

From 1902 until 1963 the ministers of First Church were drawn directly from different parts of the country. ROBERT C. MCINTYRE, widely known for his eloquence, having served distinguished pastorates in CHICAGO and DENVER, came in 1902. He was elected bishop in 1908. CHARLES EDWARD LOCKE, who served pastorates from OREGON to NEW YORK and had the distinction of conducting the funeral service for President WILLIAM MCKINLEY, came in 1908. During his pastorate, in 1913, the present location of 8th and Hope Streets was purchased. In 1920 he was elected bishop. That same year Elmer E. Helms came from Calvary Church, PHILADELPHIA. He was the leader in the building of the present $1,500,000 church edifice at 8th and Hope, which was dedicated free of debt on July 8, 1923. ROY L. SMITH, for twelve years pastor of Simpson Methodist Church, MINNEAPOLIS, served from 1932 to 1940 when he was appointed editor of the *Christian Advocate*. DONALD H. TIPPETT came from the Bexley Church, COLUMBUS, Ohio, and served from 1940 to 1948, when he was elected bishop. Richard Sneed came from the Court Street Church of Rockford, Ill., in 1948 and served until 1963, carrying on a modernization program designed to meet a changing environment and a changing constituency. John A. Zimmer (1963-64) and Don R. Boyd (1964-   ) were the first ministers in more than half a century who served other churches in the Conference before becoming pastors of First Church, Los Angeles.

Today both First and Trinity face problems arising from financial supporters who pass away or move to more desirable residential areas and take their church letters with them. In 1940 Trinity had 4,944 members and First Church, 4,934. In 1970 Trinity had 437 members and First Church 619. With every decrease in church membership there has been an increase, per member, in the cost of property maintenance. A plan for merger of these two churches, set forth by a Committee representing both, failed to be approved by Trinity. The hope and expectation is that both of these downtown churches, perhaps working together, will find avenues of service and financial support comparable to earlier days.

In 1887 the Fort Street Church organized a Chinese Mission which operated as a Sunday school. Six years later seventy-five Chinese were enrolled with an average

attendance of forty-five. The Church licensed the first Chinese local preacher in the United States. Chan Kin Lung later became the pastor of the local Chinese Church.

In 1880 the Committee on Missions of the Fort Street Church rented a small building for eight dollars a month, and started a chapel for Spanish-speaking people. This was the forerunner of the Spanish American Institute, the Plaza Community Center, and the Frances DePauw Home and School for Mexican girls, the latter sponsored by the WOMAN'S HOME MISSIONARY SOCIETY.

On March 31, 1904, the Los Angeles City Missionary Society was organized. Most of the Methodist churches in Los Angeles area have received help, at one time or another, from what is now called the Los Angeles Missionary and Church Extension Society.

One section of Los Angeles which formerly had been a choice residential area became the home of thousands of foreign-born people. Properties were run-down and rents were low. Immorality was widespread and juvenile delinquency was at a high level. Only one small church, the Newman Methodist Church, remained to minister to the people. It was here, in 1917, while serving as pastor of Newman Church, that G. BROMLEY OXNAM got the vision that resulted in the All Nations Foundation. In 1936 Oxnam was elected a bishop, the only bishop who spent his entire parish ministry in the Southern California Conference.

EDGAR J. EVANS

First A.M.E. Church in Los Angeles holds the distinction of being the first Negro church in the city. African Episcopal Methodists were in Los Angeles as early as 1870. In 1872 the church was organized with twelve members in the home of a Mrs. Biddie Mason. The first edifice was built on a lot costing $700 at Fourth and Grand Avenue. The earliest pastor of First A.M.E. was Jesse Hamilton. In 1887, under the leadership of Jordan Allen, the church removed to a second site on Agusa Street where it remained for about a dozen years. The present structure was completed in 1903 on the corner of Eighth and Towne. Bishop Frederick D. Jordan, who was pastor of First A.M.E. from 1940 to 1949, was elected bishop in 1952.

GRANT S. SHOCKLEY

Holman Church is the church with the highest rate of growth in the SOUTHERN CALIFORNIA-ARIZONA CONFERENCE over the past twenty years. The church was organized in 1945. Seven persons met in the first regular meeting. At the first Quarterly Conference, forty-three persons were listed as charter members. Membership in 1970 stood at 2,688.

In the early days of Holman, before a church home was purchased, services were held in a dance hall called Music Town; in a Seventh Day Adventist Church; and in a Japanese Methodist Church. A Jewish Synagogue was the first church home purchased, and Lanneau L. White was appointed minister in 1947. He is now the senior of a ministerial staff of three, and around him the growth of Holman has evolved. The ministerial staff is integrated. The predominantly Negro congregation has provided the example for all to see, as the two Negro and one Caucasian ministers guide the in-depth program of the church and provide leadership in the community.

White is in charge of preaching and church administration; Edward S. Williams is the associate minister whose emphasis is on membership and evangelism; Victor Hand was later appointed associate minister, and is officially the minister of education and community affairs.

In 1958 a new sanctuary was dedicated, for which Holman received an award for excellence from the Architectural Guild of America. Educational facilities are now under construction.

Holman Methodist Church is nationally known for its relevant preaching, beautiful music, inspiring worship, and its warm friendliness and outreach of service to others. It has many firsts to its credit, and is noted for its creative approach to the problems of the present day church and the inner city.

The Church leadership—both ministerial and lay—insures for Holman many years of effective Christian witness in the immediate community, in the Conference and over the nation.

E. D. Jervey, *Southern California and Arizona.* 1960.
Journals of the Southern California-Arizona Conference.
M. Simpson, *Cyclopaedia.* 1878.
R. R. Wright, *Encyclopedia.* 1947.

Pacific Homes is a non-profit corporation of The United Methodist Church (U.S.A.), operating seven retirement homes in Southern CALIFORNIA, ARIZONA and HAWAII, also six convalescent hospitals. With a background of over fifty years of operation, it is the largest as well as one of the most experienced organizations in the retirement field. Admission is without discrimination as to race, color or creed.

The first of the Pacific Homes, Kingsley Manor, was built "in the country" between Los Angeles and Hollywood and opened in January 1912, on a site formerly used for Methodist CAMP MEETINGS. For many years it was known as "Pacific Home." Construction of the home was aided by a Mrs. Margaret Ammann's bequest to the GERMAN METHODIST CONFERENCE. Following the merging of the German Methodist and M. E. Churches a new corporation was formed which ultimately became the present Pacific Homes Corporation. Through the years additional homes have been built or acquired in Claremont, Pacific Beach, La Jolla, and Chula Vista in California; in Phoenix, Arizona, and in suburban Honolulu in Hawaii. These represent a variety of locations—the seashore, the desert, a small college town close to the mountains, an Island of the Pacific, and well known Hollywood.

Today these seven retirement facilities provide a total capacity of 2,200, or approximately twelve percent of the total accommodations included in the seven score and more Methodist Homes in the United States. The convalescent hospital facilities include 500 beds and several of the units also serve patients from the community at large. The Sparr Convalescent Hospital in Los Angeles serves mainly community patients.

The concept of full life care has gained wide acceptance and Pacific Homes plan of organization has served as the pattern for many homes throughout the nation. A unique feature is the fact that fees are never increased during the tenure of a resident in the home. Fifty years operating experience makes it possible for costs to be projected quite accurately. Retirement home funds are subject to constant scrutiny under California laws.

While prepaid life care is the general requirement, the financial arrangements are sufficiently flexible to meet the needs of those who can only partially prepay; and for those who have mainly monthly income from Social Security, or from pension, or annuities, full monthly payments are approved.

Pacific Homes is also concerned that members of The United Methodist Church in the SOUTHERN CALIFORNIA-ARIZONA CONFERENCE who do not have adequate funds to permit them to be residents of Pacific Homes, shall receive some assistance from the earnings of the Endowment Fund. Approximately 150 accommodations have been reserved for these Methodists with limited means.

Methodist ministers and laymen compose the Corporation, the Board of Directors, and the individual home Boards of Management. They give of their talents and many hours of their time to Pacific Homes. Dr. Edward P. O'Rear, General Manager since 1953, with a staff and more than 700 employees, is responsible for the management of Pacific Homes.

ABBIE E. SARGENT

WESTWOOD CHURCH, LOS ANGELES, CALIFORNIA

Westwood Community Church is the Methodist church most nearly related to the University of California at Los Angeles with its 25,000 students. The church and the University have grown together. When in 1926 the University began to make plans to move to the Westwood hills, G. BROMLEY OXNAM, then the secretary of the Los Angeles Missionary and Church Extension Society, later a distinguished bishop of the church, arranged with Conference Church Extension support, to buy the present property on Wilshire Boulevard.

By 1928 the first unit was begun with funds raised by the First Methodist Church of Los Angeles under the leadership of Elmer Ellsworth Helms. The fifteen charter members were enrolled by certificate of transfer from First and other Methodist churches. By 1940 the educational wing, containing classrooms, parlor and a social hall, was added. In 1948 the administration unit was constructed. The beautiful Memorial Sanctuary, with its Glory Window, was completed by 1951. The parking area was increased so that the property now extends 535 feet along the boulevard.

With the burning of the mortgage, July 1961, the church became free of debt, with property valued at over two million dollars and an annual budget of more than a quarter of a million. Plans are on the drawing boards for a million dollar replacement and refurbishing program. The staff includes four ministers, four lay directors, and a total of thirty persons. Membership is reported in 1970 as 2,306.

F. HAROLD ESSERT

LOSEE, WILLIAM (1757-1832), Canadian preacher, was the first regular itinerant to be sent from the M. E. Church to CANADA in 1790. He was born June 30, 1757, in Dutchess County, N. Y. He was a Loyalist and served in an unofficial regiment known as the Westchester Loyalists. After his conversion he was received on trial by the NEW YORK CONFERENCE in May 1789. Immediately after the conference sessions he was sent to the Lake Champlain circuit—a most difficult appointment because the settlements were widely scattered and the people were indifferent to religion. He applied for permission from his presiding elder to minister to Methodists living on the north bank of the St. Lawrence River, and FREEBORN GARRETTSON permitted Losee to proceed with this missionary journey.

During the winter of 1790 he crossed the St. Lawrence River, probably at St. Regis, and proceeded westward toward Kingston, visiting and preaching at Matilda, Augusta, Elizabethtown, Kingston, and finally Adolphustown, where he remained for the rest of the winter, renewing acquaintances and holding services. As a result, petitions asking for an ordained itinerant were prepared and sent with Losee to the annual meeting of the New York Conference, held in New York in October. The conference agreed that he should form a circuit in Canada.

Returning to Upper Canada in the winter of 1791, he organized a circuit in the Kingston district. The first regular classes were established in February and March of that year at HAY BAY, and in Ernestown and Fredericksburgh respectively. Within a year plans were drawn for the erection of the first Methodist chapel in Upper Canada. This building still stands on land provided by Paul Huff, a member of Losee's original class. Hay Bay Church is one of the few shrines of Canadian Methodism.

At the New York Conference in 1792 Losee reported the reception of 165 members. The conference appointed him to the Oswegatchie circuit, east of Kingston, but in 1793 he was located because of ill health. Never again does his name appear in the Minutes of Conference. His creative, spirited, and fruitful ministry covered only four years.

Losee was tall, active, and excitable. Although he suffered from a withered arm, he was a fearless horseman, who covered great distances and yet seemed to have sufficient physical strength to preach with fire and power. He could be classified as the exhorting type—fluent, passionate, and prophetic in his bold denunciation of evil.

There are a few random references to his subsequent life. After his recovery from a mental breakdown, usually attributed to the marriage of his beloved to his colleague, DARIUS DUNHAM, he entered business in New York, frequently serving as a lay preacher. He returned at least once to visit his friends in Adolphustown, and S. Stewart tells of hearing William Losee preach at the New York Conference held in Troy in 1821.

Losee died on Oct. 16, 1832, and was buried in the cemetery of the M. E. Church, Hempstead, New York. On Jan. 30, 1834, his wife Mary died, at the age of eighty, and was buried beside him. In 1914 this cemetery was coverd with soil, after the grave markers had been laid flat, in order to constitute a lawn for the church.

In 1969, as the result of the city of Hempstead taking a strip of land from the church yard in order to widen the street, it became necessary to remove the graves of some of those buried in this area. The graves of William and Mary Losee were among the five requiring removal. The Hempstead church gave the Losee grave stones to the Bay of Quinte Conference, The United Church of Canada, and they were removed to Old Hay Bay Church. There a cairn, in which the stones were embedded, was erected at the church which Losee built in 1792.

J. Carroll, *Case and His Cotemporaries.* 1867-77.
Methodist History, October 1970; January 1971.
G. F. Playter, *Canada.* 1862.　　　　A. E. KEWLEY

LOTHI, MEYI, son of Marashane's chief Induna in the Lulu Mountains of the Northern Transvaal, was converted in the Cape through the London Missonary Society. He returned in 1880, preached, taught, erected a church building and appealed to the Wesleyan METHODIST MISSIONARY SOCIETY to take over his Society. The Chairman of the District visited the area in 1885, baptized fortynine adults, forty-eight children and solemnized forty marriages. Lothi was blind in one eye.

Journal of the Methodist Historical Society of South Africa. Vol. III, No. 2 (October 1958).
Minutes of South African Conference, 1939.　　　D. C. VEYSIE

LOTT, CLIFFORD BARNETT (1919-　　　), American minister and son of Jesse Jackson and Savannah (Collins) Lott, was born in Groveton, Texas, Jan. 26, 1919. He obtained degrees from the following schools: B.S., North Texas State University, 1941; B.D., GARRETT THEOLOGICAL SEMINARY, 1944; and D.D., IOWA WESLEYAN COLLEGE, 1964. On Dec. 27, 1941, he was married to Betty Louise Corson, and they are the parents of three children.

Mr. Lott was ordained deacon by the SOUTH IOWA CONFERENCE in 1945 and elder in 1947. For four years he served an Iowa pastorate, then was director of the WESLEY FOUNDATION, Texas A. and I. for a year before becoming Instructor in Bible, SIMPSON COLLEGE, 1949-54. For the next ten years he was associate pastor, Grace Church, DES MOINES, Iowa. From 1964-66, he was DISTRICT SUPERINTENDENT, Burlington District. He became Administrative Assistant, Board of LAY ACTIVITIES, 1966, and with the formation of The United Methodist Church, he was elected Associate General Secretary, Division of Stewardship and Finance, General Board of Laity.

He has been trustee of Halcyon House, Hillcrest Children's Services, and Iowa Wesleyan College. He served as Dean of the Iowa Pastor's School and a number of conference responsibilities.

Who's Who in The Methodist Church, 1966.
JOHN H. NESS, JR.

LOUISBURG COLLEGE, Louisburg, North Carolina, began in 1787 as Franklin Academy for men. Its first principal was Matthew Dickenson, graduate of Yale, who was the maternal uncle of Cyrus W. Field. Louisburg Female Academy was added in 1813, to be reorganized as Louisburg Female College in 1857. Operated as a Methodist institution since 1907, it became a junior college for women in 1915 and a coeducational junior college in 1931. The governing board consists of thirty-six members elected by the NORTH CAROLINA CONFERENCE.

JOHN O. GROSS

LOUISIANA, sometimes called the "Pelican State," is in the south central part of the United States. It is bounded on the north by ARKANSAS, on the east by MISSISSIPPI, on the south by the Gulf of Mexico, and on the west by TEXAS. It averages about 100 feet above sea level, and its climate is semi-tropical. Originally settled by the French, Louisiana was ceded to Spain in a secret treaty in 1762, but in 1800 it was returned to France, and Napoleon sold it to the United States as a part of the Louisiana Purchase. In 1804 Congress designated the area below the thirty-third parallel as Orleans Territory, and on April 30, 1812, the territory was admitted to the Union as Louisiana.

Industries in Louisiana include farming, minerals, petroleum, natural gas, salt, sand, gravel, and sulphur. In addition, the forests of the state produce some of the finest lumber, and there are extensive coastal fisheries. With an area of 48,523 square miles, the state has a population of 3,564,310 in 1970.

Eccentric evangelist LORENZO DOW may have been the first Methodist to preach in Louisiana. LEARNER BLACKMAN, presiding elder at NATCHEZ, 1805-07, was the first regular itinerant to visit Louisiana. In 1805 Elisha W. Bowman was appointed as "missionary to Louisiana" with instructions to begin at NEW ORLEANS. Unsuccessful in that city, he pushed on to other communities. In 1806 he established the first Methodist circuit in Louisiana, and organized a congregation at Opelousas. In 1808 JAMES AXLEY who endured persecution on the Catahouchee and Wichita Circuits, erected with his own hands the first Methodist church building in Louisiana. It was called Axley Chapel.

At first the Louisiana work was a part of the MISSISSIPPI CONFERENCE. In 1836 the part of the state west of the Mississippi River was included in the newly created ARKANSAS CONFERENCE. In 1840 all of Louisiana was again in the Mississippi Conference.

The LOUISIANA CONFERENCE (MES) was created by the 1846 GENERAL CONFERENCE. The first session of the conference was held at Opelousas in January 1847. The conference included the part of Louisiana west of the Mississippi River and the cities of New Orleans and BATON ROUGE on the east side. The remainder of Louisiana east of the river continued in the Mississippi Conference until 1894. Thereafter the Louisiana Conference covered the entire state.

In 1869 the M. E. Church formed a Louisiana Conference by dividing the Mississippi Mission Conference. This conference included both white and Negro ministers and churches. In 1893 the conference was divided along racial lines and the white work, along with that in east Texas, became the Gulf Mission. In 1897 it became the Gulf Mission Conference, and in 1904 the Gulf Conference. When it became a full conference it also included the white work of the M. E. Church in Mississippi. In 1926 the Gulf Conference was absorbed by the SOUTHERN CONFERENCE which until two years before had been the Southern German Conference covering Texas and Louisiana. The merger enlarged the boundaries of the Southern Conference to include the white work in Mississippi.

Methodist work among German immigrants in New Orleans began in the 1840's. In 1860 the Louisiana Conference (MES) had four German missions in that city and one in Franklin. The Germans chose to align their churches with the Louisiana Conference (ME) when it was organized in 1869. They were placed in the Southern German Conference (ME) when it was formed in 1874. Never strong in Louisiana, the German work consisted of only two churches in New Orleans when the Southern German Conference was absorbed in 1924.

At unification in 1939, the Louisiana part of the Southern Conference (ME) brought eighteen preachers, fourteen pastoral charges, and 3,278 members into The Methodist Church. The Louisiana Conference (ME) continued in the Central Jurisdiction of The Methodist Church and temporarily in the South Central Jurisdiction of The United Methodist Church.

The Methodist Protestants organized a Louisiana Conference in 1846 which merged in 1870 to form the Arkansas and Louisiana Conference. In 1884 the work was strong enough to justify setting off another Louisiana Conference which continued until unification in 1939 when it brought forty-eight preachers, thirty pastoral charges, and 3,529 members into The Methodist Church.

The three large Negro Methodist denominations—A.M.E., A.M.E. Zion, and C.M.E.—have relatively strong conferences in Louisiana. The C.M.E. Church reports about 40,000 members and the A.M.E. Church about 11,000 members in the state.

The Louisiana Conference (SCJ) supports CENTENARY COLLEGE at Shreveport, Glenwood Hospital at West Monroe, Methodist Hospital in New Orleans, and the Louisiana Methodist Children's Home at Rustin. The *Louisiana Methodist* is published for the conference in Little Rock in conjunction with the *Arkansas Methodist*. The conference maintains WESLEY FOUNDATIONS at eight state and private colleges and universities.

In 1970 the two Louisiana Conferences reported a total of 489 ministers, 137,521 members, and 603 churches valued at $75,797,535.

R. H. Harper, *Louisiana Methodism.* 1949.
C. H. Phillips, *History of the C.M.E. Church.* 1925.
G. A. Singleton, *The Romance of African Methodism.* New York: Exposition Press, 1952.
Journals of the Louisiana Conferences.   J. HENRY BOWDON, SR.

LOUISIANA CONFERENCE (A) was created by the 1846 GENERAL CONFERENCE by dividing the MISSISSIPPI CONFERENCE. The new body was organized at Opelousas, Jan. 6-13, 1847. John Powell, the only presiding elder present, acted as president of the conference until the arrival of Bishop JOSHUA SOULE. The boundaries of the conference included NEW ORLEANS and BATON ROUGE and all of the state of Louisiana west of the Mississippi River. The east part of LOUSIANA continued in the Mississippi Conference until 1894.

When organized the Louisiana Conference had five districts, fifty effective elders, forty-three pastoral charges, and 8,101 members, 3,329 of them colored. (See LOUISI-

ANA for early Methodist history in the state.) At its seventh session in Baton Rouge in 1853, the Louisiana Conference made history by adopting a resolution favoring lay representation in the conferences. It was one of the first steps made in that direction in Southern Methodism.

During its history the Louisiana Conference supported educational projects such as Mansfield Female College, Homer College, Pierce and Paine College, and other schools, some of which were stillborn or lived at most only a few years. The only permanent Methodist institution of higher learning established in Louisiana is CENTENARY COLLEGE at Shreveport. As early as 1825 an academy was started at Jackson, La. By 1845 it had failed, and the Mississippi Conference, of which Louisiana was then a part, bought the property. Meantime, in 1841 the Mississippi Conference had inaugurated Centenary College at Brandon Springs, Miss. Regarding Jackson, La., as a better location for a college, the conference proceeded to move Centenary into the academy property it had bought. During the Civil War Centenary College was closed and its buildings were used as a hospital for Confederate soldiers; later in the conflict it was occupied by Federal troops. The college reopened in 1865. In 1908 Centenary was moved to Shreveport where it continues as one of the strong Methodist colleges in America.

The *New Orleans Christian Advocate* was established in 1850 and continued publication until 1946. The paper was launched by a joint committee of the ALABAMA and Louisiana Conferences, and the Mississippi Conference soon joined in its support. In 1883 the Alabama Conference withdrew in order to establish its own paper. The first editor of the New Orleans paper was HOLLAND N. McTYEIRE, later bishop and able church historian. Four other editors of the publication also became bishops— JOHN C. KEENER, LINUS PARKER, CHARLES B. GALLOWAY, and J. LLOYD DECELL. In its day the *New Orleans Christian Advocate* was a strong and influential church paper. It failed in 1946 because Mississippi Methodism withdrew support in order to establish its own paper. Since 1949 the *Louisiana Methodist*, issued in Little Rock in conjunction with the *Arkansas Methodist*, has served Louisiana Methodism.

The Louisiana Conference operates the Louisiana Methodist Children's Home at Ruston; the Methodist Home Hospital in New Orleans, an institution for unmarried mothers and for the adoption of their children; St. Mark's Community Center in New Orleans; the Dulac Indian Mission at Houma; and the Sager-Brown Institute at Baldwin. The conference supports the Methodist Hospital in New Orleans and the Glenwood Hospital at West Monroe. Wesley Foundations are maintained at eight private and state colleges and universities in Louisiana.

At unification in 1939, the Louisiana Conference (MECS) brought 189 ministers, 171 pastoral charges, and 70,787 members into The Methodist Church. In 1970 the conference reported 398 ministers, 279 pastoral charges, 121,302 members, and 456 churches valued at $69,775,590.

R. H. Harper, *Louisiana Methodism*. 1949.
General Minutes, MECS and MC.
Journals of the Louisiana Conference. J. HENRY BOWDON, SR.

LOUISIANA CONFERENCE (B) traces its lineage to the Louisiana Conference (ME) which was organized Jan. 18, 1869 at Wesley Chapel, New Orleans, with Bishop MATTHEW SIMPSON presiding. Composed of Negro and white ministers and churches at the outset, it was formed by dividing the Mississippi Mission Conference. (See LOUISIANA for early history of Methodism in the state.) At its organization in 1869 the conference had three districts which were increased to five by the end of the session, twenty-seven churches, forty-three charges, and 10,662 members. In 1893 the conference was divided along racial lines, the white work becoming a part of the Gulf Mission.

At unification in 1939, the Louisiana Conference became a part of the Central Jurisdiction. With the abolition of that Jurisdiction in 1968, the conference, pending merger, was placed in the South Central Jurisdiction of The United Methodist Church.

In 1968 the conference was sponsoring a newspaper, the *Christian Explorer* which centered on Christian education. The conference had an interest in Gulfside Assembly, Waveland, Miss. (badly hurt by the great hurricane of 1969), the People's Community Center in New Orleans, and the Lafon Protestant Home in the same city. It supported a deaconess at the Sager Brown Home in Baldwin.

In 1970 the Louisiana Conference (B) reported 91 ministers, 89 charges, 16,219 members, and 147 churches valued at $6,021,945.

General Minutes, MEC and MC.
Journal of the Louisiana Conference, MEC and MC.
F. E. MASER

LOUISIANA CONFERENCE (MP) was organized in 1846. Its territory included LOUISIANA and TEXAS when it began. George W. Johnson who had moved to Louisiana from OHIO two years before, took the lead in organizing the conference; later he served as its president.

Because Methodist Protestantism in Louisiana and ARKANSAS was weakened by the Civil War and its aftermath, the work in south Arkansas was linked with Louisiana about 1870 to form the Arkansas and Louisiana Conference. It was divided in 1884 to form separate Arkansas and Louisiana Conferences, except that a small portion of northern Louisiana continued as a part of the Arkansas Conference until unification in 1939.

The Louisiana Conference (MP) brought forty-eight preachers, thirty pastoral charges, forty-four churches, and 3,529 members into The Methodist Church in 1939.

A. H. Bassett, *Concise History*. 1882.
R. H. Harper, *Louisiana Methodism*. 1949.
Discipline of the M. P. Church.   F. E. MASER

LOUISVILLE CONFERENCE (MES) was created by the 1846 GENERAL CONFERENCE. It was organized at Hopkinsville, Ky., Oct. 14, 1846 with Bishop JAMES O. ANDREW presiding. Its territory is western Kentucky, except the part west of the Tennessee River which is in the MEMPHIS CONFERENCE. The eastern boundary of the Louisville Conference is a line running south and east from LOUISVILLE to the Tennessee River. When it began the conference had fifty-six preachers, and 14,495 white and 2,225 colored members.

The Louisville Conference came to unification in 1939 with seven districts, 173 charges, 524 societies, 73,618 members, and churches and parsonages valued at $4,831,-188. At that time it was merged with the Louisville District of the M. E. Church and three charges of the M. P.

Church to form the Louisville Conference of The Methodist Church. The M. E. Church brought 28 charges and 9,996 members to the merger.

During its history the Louisville Conference has contributed leaders to the larger church. Edward Stevenson was the first secretary of the Missionary Society (MES). DAVID MORTON organized the Board of Church Extension (MES) and served as its corresponding secretary for sixteen years. Four Book Editors of the Southern Church were members of the Louisville Conference: A. H. REDFORD, JOHN J. TIGERT, GROSS ALEXANDER, and FRANK M. THOMAS. While serving as secretary of the Board of Missions, H. C. MORRISON was elected bishop in 1898. ROY H. SHORT served as editor of *The Upper Room* and was elected bishop in 1948. Though not a member of the Louisville Conference, Bishop JOHN M. MOORE, the architect of Methodist union, was born at Morganton within the bounds of the conference.

The Louisville Conference supports jointly with the Kentucky Conference, KENTUCKY WESLEYAN COLLEGE at Owensboro, UNION COLLEGE at Barbourville, LINDSEY WILSON JUNIOR COLLEGE at Columbia, and the Methodist Home, Inc. (for children) at Versailles. The conference is related to the Methodist Hospital at Henderson and the Methodist Evangelical Hospital in Louisville. It has two retirement homes, Wesley Manor at Louisville and Lewis Memorial Home in Franklin.

In 1968 when the Tennessee-Kentucky Conference (CJ) was merged with the overlying conferences of the Southeastern Jurisdiction, the Louisville Conference received some of the ministers and churches from that conference.

The Louisville Conference in 1970 reported six districts, 290 pastoral charges, 321 ministers, 103,400 members, property valued at $45,178,925, and $4,283,547 raised for all purposes during the year.

General Minutes, MECS and MC.
Minutes of the Louisville Conference.
Jubilee Addresses at the Louisville Conference, 1896.

HARRY R. SHORT

LOUISVILLE CONVENTION, THE, was the meeting in 1845 in Louisville, Ky., of the delegations from the Southern Conferences, who there agreed to form the **Methodist Episcopal Church, South.** Their assembly was in response to the PLAN OF SEPARATION adopted the previous year by the GENERAL CONFERENCE of the M. E. Church, which had met in NEW YORK and provided for a division of the M. E. Church should the Southern Conferences so desire. The delegations of the various Southern Conferences met before they left New York just after adjournment of the General Conference and agreed to present to their own Annual Conferences the question as to whether or not they should have a conference, or convention, the next year in Louisville, to discuss and arrive at a final conclusion regarding their separation from the M. E. Church.

Pursuant to this, the several Annual Conferences including KENTUCKY, MISSOURI, HOLSTON, TENNESSEE, NORTH CAROLINA, MEMPHIS, ARKANSAS, VIRGINIA, MISSISSIPPI, TEXAS, ALABAMA, GEORGIA, and SOUTH CAROLINA agreed to meet in such a convention, and provided funds to support the expenses of their delegations in traveling to Louisville.

The annual conferences in the "slave holding states," as they frankly called themselves, proved to be one-minded regarding the holding of the convention in Louis-

ville in May 1845, and the meeting there was clearly and completely representative of the conferences above mentioned. In addition to the conferences above named, the FLORIDA CONFERENCE sent two men, and the INDIAN MISSION CONFERENCE two. The leaders of Southern Methodism were almost all present in the meeting which convened on the first day of May 1845, in the old Fourth Street Church in the city of LOUISVILLE.

Bishop JAMES O. ANDREW was present and Bishop JOSHUA SOULE likewise was there, but Bishop THOMAS A. MORRIS, who was also present, declined to preside over the convention itself, engaging only in what the *Minutes* called "religious exercises." The Convention adopted a resolution declaring that they, "acting under the provisional plan of separation adopted by the General Conference of 1844, do solemnly *declare* the jurisdiction hitherto exercised over said Annual Conferences, by the General Conference of the Methodist Episcopal Church, *entirely dissolved;* and that said Annual Conferences shall be, and they hereby *are constituted,* a separate ecclesiastical connexion, under the provisional plan of separation aforesaid, and based upon the Discipline of the Methodist Episcopal Church, comprehending the doctrines and the entire moral, ecclesiastical, and economical rules and regulations of said Discipline, except only, in so far as verbal alterations may be necessary to a distinct organization, and to be known by the style and title of the Methodist Episcopal Church, South." (*History of American Methodism,* Vol. 2, p. 118.)

The Louisville Convention was not, properly speaking, a General Conference, but a *convention*—which however, did make provision for a General Conference to be held the next year in Petersburg, Va. It also made provisions for mission work and publishing interests, looked toward the formal organization planned for the next year and adjourned on May 19, 1845.

E. S. Bucke, *History of American Methodism.* 1964.
History of the Organization of the Methodist Church, South: Comprehending all the Official Proceedings of the General Conference; the Southern Annual Conferences, and the General Convention. (Nashville, Tennessee: Compiled and Published by the Editors and Publishers of the South Western Christian Advocate for the M. E. Church, South, by order of the Louisville Convention. William Cameron, Printer, 1845). N. B. H.

LOUISVILLE, KENTUCKY, U.S.A. The first Methodist Society in Louisville was formed in 1806. It met first in a private home, then in a log schoolhouse. In 1809 a building was erected on Market Street between Seventh and Eighth Streets. FRANCIS ASBURY records in his *Journal* on Oct. 22, 1812, "I preached in Louisville, Kentucky, at eleven o'clock, in our neat brick church 30 x 48 ft. I had a sickly congregation. This is a growing town, a handsome place."

In 1816, a new church was built on Fourth Street near Jefferson. It was a large brick church with a wide gallery on each side. Louisville at that time was a part of the OHIO CONFERENCE and the conference session of that year was held in this church. Bishop McKENDREE dedicated the building before the conference convened. The Louisville church became a station in 1818 and HENRY B. BASCOM, later bishop, became its pastor. One hundred and twenty white members and thirty-seven colored were reported. In 1835 two other congregations were formed from the membership of the Fourth Street Church on Brook Street and on Eighth Street.

After the division of American Methodism at the GENERAL CONFERENCE of 1844, the Constitutional Convention which formed the M. E. Church, South, met in the Fourth Street Church. As the city expanded, churches were organized on Shelby Street and Twelfth Street, and in 1852, the Fourth Street Church was moved to Fifth and Walnut Streets, and the Eighth Street Church to Chestnut near Eighth. The M. E. Church organized Trinity Church at Third and Guthrie Streets in 1865; and the German Methodists, under the leadership of Jacob Shumaker, organized a congregation on Jackson Street in 1844. In 1907 the Walnut Street and the Chestnut Street churches united to form the Methodist Temple at Sixth and Broadway, and following unification the Methodist Temple and Trinity Church merged to form Trinity Temple on the site of the later institution.

The A.M.E., the A.M.E. Zion and the C.M.E. denominations have built a strong constituency among the Negro population and seven congregations of the former Central Jurisdiction of The Methodist Church are also to be counted here. These however have been merged into the LOUISVILLE CONFERENCE in connection with the dissolution of the Central Jurisdiction.

With the growth of the city, Methodism has attempted to serve the expanding population. It now has seventy congregations and approximately 35,000 members within the metropolitan area.

Through the years these churches have been served by some of the outstanding ministers of Methodism, and Louisville Methodism has given to the larger circles of the Church many strong leaders, both lay and clerical.

HARRY R. SHORT

Fourth Avenue Church. Methodism was the first of all organized religions in the city and the first Methodist Society, dating from 1806, and has enacted its fascinating history in six different homes, under five distinct names.

The first building in 1812 was a primitive sanctuary only 34 by 38 feet on Market Street, where Bishop Asbury once preached. Though he called the group a "sickly congregation," it grew rapidly; in 1816 a larger, better house was erected nearer the town center. Here for thirty-six years the Fourth Street Church was blessed with a gifted array of highly talented pastors, many of whom became widely known throughout the connection. Among them were three destined to be elected bishops: Henry B. Bascom, 1818-20; THOMAS A. MORRIS, 1828-30; and HUBBARD H. KAVANAUGH, 1835-36.

Other early pastors of note: William Burke, later Cincinnati's first postmaster: Charles Holliday, Marcus Lindsey, William Adams, Edward Stevenson, Edmund W. Sehon, and John H. Linn.

In 1845 the church was host to delegates from all the southern conferences to the historic LOUISVILLE CONVENTION, gathered to plan the establishment of the M. E. Church, South, as a separate denomination.

After 1852 the congregation spent fifty-five notable years in a new home called the Walnut Street Church, again served by some of Methodism's finest preachers— men like Charles B. Parsons, Thomas Bottomley, H. C. Settle, SAMUEL A. STEEL, FRANK M. THOMAS, and the fourth pastor to become a bishop, HENRY C. MORRISON.

A great gathering of Methodist leaders from all over the land, north and south, came to the Church in 1876 for the first churchwide meeting held in connection with the CAPE MAY COMMISSION plans for the restoration of fraternal relations between the two major divisions of the original M. E. Church.

Unique and massive was the congregation's next home, occupied in 1907 at Sixth and Broadway. It was built by the Jews in 1857, but constructed in the traditional shape of a Christian cross! Taking back a branch which had left in 1835, First Church remodelled the old temple and took the legal name, Union M. E. Church, South, but was popularly called "The Methodist Temple." For thirty-three years "The Temple" continued faithful through increasing vicissitudes; yet in this period alone 2,126 new members were received. Outstanding evangelistic pastors were U. G. Foote, J. W. Weldon, and H. H. Jones.

In 1940 the congregation merged with the Trinity M. E. Church, organized in 1865 near the site where the First Church began. The merged congregations, now called Trinity Temple Church, moved into this forty-year-old edifice and enjoyed a great ministry.

In order to provide a stronger evangelistic program for the city and a surer financial base for itself, Trinity-Temple's 600-strong membership gave up its home, and in 1962 erected on a downtown corner an imposing structure of eighteen floors, providing apartments for elderly in addition to handsome church quarters on the first three floors, with a roof garden and "Chapel in the Sky" at the top.

ELBERT B. STONE

Parkview Church is the oldest continuous Methodist congregation in Louisville. One must go back to 1780 and the early days of the Falls of the Ohio River to discover that the area was crowded with flatboats of those who had drifted down to KENTUCKY from the settlements of Pennsylvania Dutch. A number of these people did not stop in Louisville but pushed on to the banks of Mill Creek and the wilderness trail to the Salt Licks. Among these families we would have found Christian and Jacob Shively, who purchased from the governor of VIRGINIA a thousand-acre tract of land at the junction of Mill Creek and Man's Lick Trail. Here they built a mill and did a thriving business with the settlers.

It is not known when Methodism was first brought into this section of Kentucky. About 1811, however, the Jefferson Circuit was established and in 1816 ANDREW MONROE was appointed preacher over the Jefferson Circuit. It was under his ministry that the Mill Creek Church was built. In the Jefferson County records one can find that Christian Shively gave one acre of ground on which the church was built. The deed is dated June 17, 1816, and is made out to Isaac Miller, Hugh Logan, Phillip Shively, Alexander Smoot, James W. Thornsberry and Matthew Love, who were trustees for the church to be erected and known by the name of Mill Creek Church.

JOHN LITTLEJOHN, a pioneer Methodist preacher in Louisville and vicinity, whose journal is preserved in the archives of the Louisville Conference Historical Society, records on Jan. 20, 1822: "I drove from Louisville in a sleigh to Shively's Stone Meeting House and preached to a large and inspiring crowd."

For a time the church was used by all denominations but about the time of the Civil War it was restored as a Methodist building and it has continued with a regular pastor and congregation until the present time.

A change in the residents of the community reduced the membership and attendance about the middle of the eighties, but a small and faithful few continued having regular services until a turn of the tide of residents brought new members and interest in the church.

In 1920 this church was the first appointment of ROY H. SHORT (later bishop), then in his teens. When he appeared for his first service, the Sunday school superintendent inquired if he might show him to the youth class. The reply was: "I'm your new minister."

The church was moved in 1945 to a location on Stowers Lane, and it was moved again in 1965, due to construction of a highway, to its present location at 2020 Garrs Lane. The church which has been known as Parkview since 1945 is a thriving suburban church that is growing in the service of Christ, through its work in the community of Shively.

JOHN C. BRINSON

Quinn Chapel A.M.E. Church. In 1833 Bishop MORRIS BROWN transferred WILLIAM PAUL QUINN to the Ohio Annual Conference of the A.M.E. Church and assigned him to the Pittsburgh Circuit as a missionary. In the course of his travels he organized a congregation of African Methodists at Louisville about 1838. Between 1838 and 1844 another A.M.E. itinerant, George Johnson, "put up a little frame building on the lot they bought in the city." Quinn refers to this in the famous missionary report that he made to the General Conference of 1844:

Also the church erected in the city of Louisville, Kentucky is in a flourishing condition. I am fully persuaded (that) this mission, if faithfully conducted, will at no distant period, accomplish wonders for our people settled in these western states in their moral and religious elevation.

Including its founder, Quinn, for whom it was later named, this church has had as its pastors five men who eventually became bishops: William P. Quinn (1844), REVERDY C. RANSOM (1924), NOAH W. WILLIAMS (1932), FRANK M. REID (1940) and ERNEST L. HICKMAN (1956).

GRANT S. SHOCKLEY

St. Paul Church, Bardstown Road at Douglass Boulevard, began its life as an outpost Sunday school early in 1915. This was a missionary enterprise of the Highland Methodist Church, and Professor Henry A. Smith was assigned to lead this endeavor. He became its first Sunday school superintendent and held that office until his death, forty-three years later.

In 1921, the present church lot on the corner of Bardstown Road and Douglass Boulevard was bought. M. L. Dyer was then pastor of the church. The building was moved from Woodbourne Avenue and placed over a basement, on the present lot, in 1923. The name was changed from Woodbourne Avenue to St. Paul. This structure was used until the present sanctuary was built in 1931, during the pastorate of J. C. Rawlings.

In 1941, Roy H. Short (now bishop) came to be the pastor of St. Paul Church, from which pulpit he went to the editorship of *The Upper Room* in 1944. Howard W. Whitaker, of the KENTUCKY CONFERENCE, was appointed pastor of St. Paul in 1944. Under his ministry the church school plant, including the chapel, was erected in 1949.

In July, 1949, Bishop WILLIAM T. WATKINS appointed Ted Hightower as minister of St. Paul, effective September 1. He was installed as the executive minister on Sept. 3, 1949 and remained in the position until June 1, 1966.

St. Paul Church has had a steady and highly useful history. Following the consolidation of its own position and buildings in 1949, St. Paul launched its first missionary offensive. In 1950 funds were raised for the building of St. Paul in CAMAGUEY CUBA, on the campus of PINSON COLLEGE. In 1951, the Rev. and Mrs. Victor L. Rankin went to this church as missionary pastor and completed its building. The Rankins were supported by St. Paul.

From this beginning, several other churches were established in Cuba, parsonages were built, school buildings were erected, and our largest missionary endeavors were centered there until the Castro Revolution necessitated the withdrawal of our missionaries.

The Woman's Society supports Dr. Mildred Shepherd in INDIA. A medical jeep has been purchased for work in the PHILIPPINES. Both interest and money have gone to PAKISTAN, the CONGO, SCARRITT COLLEGE, American Indian work, and many other causes, as well. "St. Paul In India," located at Bidar, has now been completed and paid for and is one of the largest Methodist churches in that section of India.

At home, St. Paul Church has been a sponsoring church, establishing four suburban churches, some of which are now, after twelve years, almost as large as the parent church. They are Christ Church, Buechel, St. Mark and Walker Memorial, all in Louisville.

In 1962, the church purchased property at 2006 Douglass Boulevard, adjoining the original church property. This is a three-story apartment building which has been renovated as "Fellowship House" and put into service for the young people and multiple uses of the church. The Deaf-Oral School meets in this building.

In 1963 a generous gift of $100,000 made possible the installation of stained glass windows in the sanctuary, and twenty-two outside windows of St. Paul church. This remarkable fenestration carries a continuous iconography of biblical and church history, beginning with the Creation at one end of the sanctuary and closing with the building of the Church Center for The United Nations in New York, at the other end. It also has the headstone for a large renovation program which is now being completed with the installation of a new pipe organ at a cost of more than $75,000. This organ is being dedicated in honor of Ted Hightower.

A Brief History of Fourth Avenue Methodist Church, Louisville, Kentucky, 1888-1968.
W. F. Lloyd, *History of Methodism in Louisville.* 1901.
W. I. Munday, *Louisville Methodism Yesterday, Today and Tomrrow.* 1949.
D. A. Payne, *History* (AME). 1891.
J. C. Rawlings, *History of Louisville Methodism.* 1927.
A. H. Redford, *Kentucky.* 1868-70.
R. R. Wright, *Encyclopedia.* 1947. WALTER B. WHITE, JR.

LOVE, EDGAR AMOS (1891-), American bishop, was born in Harrisonburg, Va., Sept. 10, 1891, the son of Julius C. and Susie Carr Love. His early educational training was received in the public schools of VIRGINIA and MARYLAND. In 1909 he was graduated from the Academy of MORGAN COLLEGE and in 1913 he received the B.A. degree, Cum Laude, from Howard University.

The B.D. degree was awarded him by Howard University School of Religion in 1916, and the S.T.B. from BOSTON UNIVERSITY SCHOOL OF THEOLOGY in 1918. For two sessions he did graduate work at the University of

Chicago. He was awarded the D.D. by Morgan College in 1935; by GAMMON THEOLOGICAL SEMINARY in 1946, and by Boston University in 1956.

His marriage to Virginia Louise Ross, of Staunton, Va., took place on June 16, 1923. They have one son, Jon Edgar Love.

Admitted on trial in the WASHINGTON CONFERENCE (ME) in 1916, he received full connection as elder in 1918. His pastorates include: Grace Church, Fairmount Heights, Md., 1916; John Wesley Church, Washington, Pa., 1921-25; Asbury Church, Annapolis, Md., 1925-28; Simpson Church, Wheeling, W. Va., 1928-31; and John Wesley Church, Baltimore, Md., 1931-33.

His pastoral work was interrupted in 1917 when he began his service as CHAPLAIN in the United States Army, with the 368th Infantry and the 809th Pioneer Infantry, serving a total of two years and three months, fourteen months of which was overseas. After his Army service he became a member of the American Legion and attended, as a delegate from the State of MARYLAND, the first American Legion Convention, MINNEAPOLIS, Minn. in 1919. Years after when he had become a bishop, he and Bishop WUNDERLICH of Germany discovered that they had been in the directly opposing armies of one of the late battles of the World War. The daily papers where the COUNCIL OF BISHOPS was meeting photographed Bishops Wunderlich and Love standing together and featured this story.

From 1919-21 he was an instructor at Morgan College.

He became superintendent of the Washington District in 1933 and served in this capacity until 1940, when he became the Superintendent of Negro work, BOARD OF MISSIONS and Church Extension, of The Methodist Church, New York City, a position in which he served until 1952, when he was elected bishop and assigned to the Baltimore Area, Central Jurisdiction, of The Methodist Church.

He served as Secretary of the College of Bishops and President respectively, Central Jurisdiction, and at various times served in other important capacities. After 1940 he was a member of the Board of Temperance and the Board of Missions of The Methodist Church. During his active service he held membership in the following: the Methodist Commission on Chaplains; the General Commission on Chaplains; the NATIONAL COUNCIL OF THE CHURCHES OF CHRIST in the U.S.A.; the Y.M.C.A. (Baltimore, Md.); The International Frontiers Club of America —Baltimore Chapter; the National Association for Advancement of Colored People, Baltimore Branch; 33° Mason, Southern Jurisdiction; METHODIST FEDERATION FOR SOCIAL ACTION; the Southern Conference Educational Fund.

He has served as trustee of the following: Morgan College Corporation, Baltimore, Md.; BENNETT COLLEGE; and of Gulfside Assembly, Waveland, Miss. He was president of the Fraternal Council of Churches, Inc., and in October and November, 1954, visited Methodist work in MALAYA on invitation of the Malayan Board of Evangelism. By appointment of Governor Ritchie, he served at one time as a member of the Maryland Interracial Commission. He was appointed by Mayor McKeldin of Baltimore, to the Police Advisory Committee, and by Governor J. Millard Tawes of the Committee to Study the Penal Institutions of the State of Maryland.

One of the outstanding sermons of his career was delivered in 1959 in connection with the 175th Anniversary of Methodism. In it he made a stirring appeal to an audience of young ministers—all of whom were under thirty-five—not to conform to the status quo, but to have the courage to push forward to new horizons of their own. He reminded them that the founders of Methodism were, like themselves, young men. Following retirement at the Jurisdictional Conference of the Central Jurisdiction in 1964, he continues to reside in Baltimore.

Who's Who in The Methodist Church, 1966.

MARY FRENCH CALDWELL

LOVE FEAST or **AGAPE.** The oldest known document on the orders of the church is the *Didache* and it is here that the primitive Christians spelled out the first regulations for the Agape. Several things seem to be established from examination of this document: (1) The Agape was not the Eucharist, or Communion, though it did prescribe prayers of thanksgiving before and after the celebration of The Lord's Supper; (2) It was conducted in the absence of a settled ministry by the laymen who belonged to the little bands of gathered Christians; it obviously was the Christian carryover of the Jewish customs observed by families when a blessing was said before the meal, and a thanksgiving following the meal.

The Eastern Orthodox Church and the Coptic Christians are credited by most scholars for continuing the practice of the Love Feast during the remaining centuries until the German pietists revived the custom in Europe in the late 1600's. JOHN WESLEY met the Agape for the first time in 1737 when he was in Savannah, Ga., and attended a Moravian Love Feast. (Wesley's *Journal,* Aug. 8, 1737). FRANK BAKER indicates in *Methodism and the Love Feast* that shortly after Wesley's heartwarming at ALDERSGATE in 1738, the FETTER LANE Religious Society, to which he then belonged, listed among its rules the fixing of regular times for observance of the Love Feast. At this point the feasts began at 7 o'clock and ended at 10:00—but one record shows a Fetter Lane Love Feast starting at 9:00 p.m. and ending at 3:00 a.m.! Wesley records in his *Journal* for Dec. 31, 1738 that he, his brother CHARLES, WHITEFIELD, and others attended such a feast at Fetter Lane and that "about three in the morning . . . the power of God came mightily upon us."

As Methodism grew in America and established itself as a church in 1784, the Love Feast was an integral part of its pattern. The Love Feast and the Lord's Supper were immediately identified as the proper places to receive offerings for the poor. By 1789 the *Discipline* not only listed as a required duty for the preachers the regular watch night services, the prayer services, but also the Love Feast. To strengthen the evidence of the role of the Love Feast, the clear directions of Wesley contained in his *A Plain Account of Christian Perfection* were included in the *Disciplines* of 1792, 1794, 1796, and 1797. They also ruled, "Suffer no Love Feast to last above one hour and a half."

The *Discipline* of 1852 shows a liberalizing trend in the matter of who could attend the Love Feast. In Section III of that *Discipline,* question 5 reads, "How often shall we permit strangers to be present at our Love Feasts?" The answer, "Let them be admitted with utmost caution; and the same person on no account above twice or thrice, unless he become a member."

Patterned on the *agape* of New Testament and apostolic times, the Love Feast became an important devotion among Methodists in the days of John Wesley, and has been observed on occasions by Methodists ever since.

When possible, worshipers were to be seated in a circle or around a table. Bread was broken into small portions, or a common loaf passed from hand to hand. Traditionally a loving cup with two handles was provided for water. The usual order for a modern observance might run:

A Prelude
A Hymn of Praise
The Scripture, St. John 6:26-35
Voluntary Prayers and the Lord's Prayer
An Address
A Hymn of Christian Fellowship
The Passing of Bread with Blessing
The Passing of the Cup with Blessing
A Thanksgiving in unison
An offering for the poor
Testimonies
A Hymn of Thanksgiving
A Blessing
A Postlude

In both British and American Methodism there have been attempts to revive interest in observance of the Love Feast. American Methodists have included the form for observance in their official *Book of Worship* and many Annual Conferences set a time in their programs for a Conference Love Feast. The *Discipline* has continued all through the years to list as a duty of the pastor, "To hold or appoint prayer meetings, love feasts, and watch-night meetings, wherever advisable." (Discipline 1964, Par. 352.8) In honesty it must be reported that more often than not, Twentieth Century Methodists are probably unaware of the Love Feast, but there is a great value in this tradition that many churchmen seek to revive. (See also WORSHIP.)

F. Baker, *Methodism and the Love Feast*. 1957.
Discipline, 1784, 1797, 1853.   EMORY S. BUCKE

LOVELY LANE CHAPEL, Baltimore, Maryland, U.S.A. The historic building in which the M. E. Church in America was organized in 1784, was the second Methodist Church built in BALTIMORE, but FRANCIS ASBURY loved it, and had a great hand in its building. It was built in 1774 with two of Asbury's converts, William Moore and Philip Rogers, playing a key part in erecting it. When Francis Asbury laid the foundation for the building he wrote in his *Journal*, "Who could have expected that two men, once among the chief of sinners, would ever have thus engaged in so great an undertaking for the cause of the blessed Jesus?" Further mention of the building is seen in Asbury's *Journal* earlier in the year. Asbury himself proved anxious to be sent to Baltimore that he might be pastor of Lovely Lane, where the people were eager that he might come and serve with them. THOMAS RANKIN, however, then Wesley's superintendent, insisted on sending him to PHILADELPHIA. Finally, however, late in February, 1775, Rankin agreed that Asbury might go and become pastor in Baltimore, and especially at Lovely Lane.

When the epochal meeting took place between COKE and Asbury late in 1784, and they decided to call a conference of the preachers to consider Wesley's instructing Coke that he come to America and ordain Asbury (and the furnishing of the American Methodists with a *Sunday*

Service), it is not strange that Asbury wanted Lovely Lane in Baltimore to be the meeting place.

The chapel was down by the harbor (inner harbor now) of old Baltimore town, and was a small rectangular brick building. For many years, and even today, the site upon which Lovely Lane stood was occupied by the Merchants Club (206 East Redwood Street), upon which a bronze tablet reads, "Upon this site stood from 1774 to 1786, the Lovely Lane Meeting House, in which was organized December, 1784, the Methodist Episcopal Church in the United States of America." In Lovely Lane, of course, Coke was taken as bishop, and Asbury consecrated as one, and the Church organized. The successor to Lovely Lane in Baltimore was the first Light Street Church at Light Street and Wine Alley, begun in August, 1785, and dedicated by Asbury on May 21, 1786.

Within recent years the First Methodist Church in Baltimore, as it was long known, standing at the corner of St. Paul Avenue and 22nd Street, decided to adopt the name "Lovely Lane," and henceforth will be known under that title. This Church today carries on a full-time, aggressive ministry, as befits a large and influential city church. In connection with the present Lovely Lane is the Methodist Museum, and offices of the Methodist Historical Society of Maryland.

E. S. Bucke, *History of American Methodism*. 1964.   N. B. H.

LOVERN, JAMES CHESS (1909-   ), American minister, was born in Morgan County, Ga., Aug. 21, 1909. He received the B.A. and B.D. degrees from SOUTHERN METHODIST UNIVERSITY, and the D.D. from SOUTHWESTERN UNIVERSITY. Admitted on trial in the SOUTHWEST TEXAS CONFERENCE in 1935, he served pastorates in San Angelo, La Feria, Edinburg, and Harlingen before going to Laurel Heights Church, SAN ANTONIO, 1949-54. Transferring to the NORTHWEST TEXAS CONFERENCE, he served the 5,000-member First Church, LUBBOCK, 1954-64, and then succeeded Bishop W. McFERRIN STOWE at St. Luke's Church, OKLAHOMA CITY, Okla. He has been a member of the General BOARD OF MISSIONS since 1964, and has been elected to and served five times in the GENERAL and JURISDICTIONAL CONFERENCES.

Who's Who in The Methodist Church, 1966.   N. B. H.

LOVETT, WILLIAM (1800-1877), British Methodist, was born in Newlyn, Cornwall. He was one of the leaders of the CHARTIST Movement in 1838, became secretary of the convention, which it was hoped might prepare the way for Parliamentary reform, and edited a newspaper *Chartism, a New Organ of the People*. He suffered imprisonment for criticizing police action against demonstrators, but he had no sympathy with O'Connor and Stephens, the "Physical Force Chartists." Lovett's moderate policy estranged him from other Chartists, and he was not involved in the fiasco of the monster petition of 1848. In 1846 he transferred his allegiance to the antislavery movement, retired from active politics, and spent his last years in teaching.

William Lovett, *Life and Struggles*. London, 1876.
                                                    JOHN KENT

LOWE, THOMAS G. (1815-1869), American minister, was born between the towns of Halifax and Enfield, N. C., near the historic Hayward's Chapel Methodist Church, on

Aug. 10, 1815. He received his early education in the "old field schools" of the day, and became a local preacher for the M. E. Church before he was twenty-one years old. Although he never entered the annual conference, he preached and had stated appointments in many areas of eastern NORTH CAROLINA and VIRGINIA. He was frequently called upon "to deliver funeral discourses and Masonic addresses, in both of which he very greatly excelled." His sermons always attracted large audiences. In a eulogy to Lowe presented in 1882, Theodore B. Kingsbury observed that Lowe's name "should be added to that roll of illustrious American preachers who were eminent for a rich, glowing, and inspiring eloquence." Lowe never wrote out his sermons, made an outline, or used notes, feeling that he lost all inspiration and fervor when he resorted to a pen. His sermons, which usually lasted thirty to forty minutes, were mentally organized while he was working or fishing and he would memorize the language he wished to use. His "finest oratory," however, was usually heard when there had been no previous preparation and he spoke extemporaneously. He spoke with a clear, musical voice and always used pure, correct English. He had "a splendid imagination but under the control of reason and taste and allied to wisdom and discretion. He was a very sound piece of American timber." He "spoke fine poetry, although presented in the garb of prose." Once, he spoke at the JOHN STREET CHURCH in New York City and afterward was invited to preach there for the then unheard of salary of $12,000 a year. He chose, however, not to leave his home and labors in North Carolina.

Lowe married Maria J. Wade of New Bern, N. C., in August, 1842, and to this union two daughters were born. He died on Feb. 13, 1869.

W. C. Allen, *History of Halifax County*. Boston, 1918.
Theodore B. Kingsbury, *An Oration on the Life and Character of the Late Rev. Thomas G. Lowe, Delivered at Hayward's Church, Halifax County, on June 24th, 1882.*

RALPH HARDEE RIVES

LOWE, TITUS (1877-1959), American bishop, was born in Bilston, England, Dec. 17, 1877, and came to the United States at the age of fourteen. The Lowe family settled near PITTSBURGH, Pa., and Titus, the youngest of six children, worked in a steel mill as a boy.

He was educated at OHIO WESLEYAN (A.B., 1900; A.M., 1908) and Western Theological Seminary (B.D., 1902), and received honorary degrees from Ohio Wesleyan, NEBRASKA WESLEYAN, and the College of Puget Sound. He married Anna B. Creed on Oct. 18, 1901; she died April 4, 1911, and he married Edith E. Egloff on Jan. 6, 1913. She died after Bishop Lowe retired, and in 1957 he married Ellen Louise Stoy.

Titus Lowe joined the PITTSBURGH CONFERENCE in 1900. His pastorates were: Fourth Street, Braddock, Pa., 1900-03; Thoburn Church, CALCUTTA, India, 1903-08; South Fork, Pa., 1908-09; First Church, Cedar Falls, Iowa, 1909-13; First Church, OMAHA, Neb., 1913-21; Y.M.C.A. Lecturer in France, 1917-18; and Corresponding Secretary of the Board of Foreign Missions of the M. E. Church in 1921.

He was elected bishop in 1924, and was assigned to SINGAPORE, 1924-28; PORTLAND, Ore., 1928-39; and to INDIANA, 1939-48. In 1942, Bishop Lowe organized the School of the Prophets while serving the Indiana Area.

TITUS LOWE

It was a week-long annual refresher training program for the state's 1,000 Methodist pastors and was still conducted at DePauw University when Bishop Lowe died.

A big athletic man, Bishop Lowe was a college football player in his youth and later an avid golfer. His greatest relaxation was found in playing the piano, and it was his familiarity with church music that caused his church to put him on the Hymnal Commission of 1930-34.

A week after retirement, Bishop Lowe was appointed director of METHODIST OVERSEAS RELIEF, and he served in this capacity, 1948-52.

He died at Indianapolis, Ind., on Nov. 27, 1959. His funeral was conducted on November 30 by Bishops RICHARD C. RAINES and J. RALPH MAGEE. The remains were cremated.

Who's Who in the Clergy.
World Outlook, January 1960.

JESSE A. EARL

LOWELL, LEROY M. (1894-   ), an ordained elder of the Southern Michigan Conference of the FREE METHODIST CHURCH, was born at Cortland, N. Y. He received the A.B. degree (Magna Cum Laude) at GREENVILLE COLLEGE, 1923, and the A.M. degree from the Winona Lake School of Theology, 1933; SEATTLE PACIFIC COLLEGE conferred the Litt.D. in 1943. He was pastor of Free Methodist churches in CALIFORNIA, KANSAS and MICHIGAN. Dr. Lowell served as president of SPRING ARBOR (Michigan) Junior College, 1935-44 and 1955-57. He was the first speaker of the denomination's Light and Life Hour broadcast. He is author of *Building the House Beautiful*. He was editor of denominational youth papers, 1941-56. Dr. and Mrs. Lowell live near Lakeland, Fla. since retiring.

BYRON S. LAMSON

LOWES, MATTHEW (1721-1795), British Methodist, was born in Whitfield, Northumberland. As a young man he was deeply influenced by CHARLES WESLEY's sermon, "Awake, thou that sleepest!" published in 1742, and a visit of CHRISTOPHER HOPPER to his home about 1748 led to his conversion. JOHN WESLEY confirmed the urging of his friends that he should become an itinerant preacher, but he remained a LOCAL PREACHER until he could discharge his father's debts. His first appointment was to the LEEDS circuit in 1751. The arduous work of the itinerancy proved too much for his indifferent health, and after intervals of serving as a "half-itinerant" in 1771, Wesley regretfully accepted his resignation because of his "asthmatic complaint." He remained in Newcastle as a supernumerary, whence he made occasional preaching expeditions as his health permitted.

On his preaching rounds Matthew Lowes had sometimes sold a family remedy, "Lowes' Balsam." This method of supplementing his meager income to support a large family was stopped when the 1768 conference strongly urged itinerant preachers not to engage in trade, an exhortation followed up in 1779 by a specific prohibition. After his retirement, however, the position was different, and in November 1771, John Wesley wrote to Lowes: "Certainly there is no objection to your making balsam while you are not considered as a travelling preacher." Lowes' Balsam apparently provided sustenance for Lowes and his family until his wife's death in 1793 and his own on Feb. 8, 1795. The recipe has continued to serve the farming community since, passing into the hands of a Methodist chemist in Alston, George Thompson, who sold the preparation as "Lowes' Veterinary Oil." At a change of ownership on Thompson's death in 1890, it became "Laws' Oil," and is still manufactured by a firm of Carlisle chemists.

Arminian Magazine, 1795.
Methodist Magazine, March 1947.   FRANK BAKER

LOWRY, HIRAM HARRISON (1843-1924), American missionary, church builder and educator, was born in Zanesville, Ohio, May 29, 1843. He served in the 97th Ohio Infantry, 1862-63. In 1867 he graduated from OHIO WESLEYAN, married Parthenia Nicholson, and went to Foochow, China. He was the first Methodist missionary to cross the Pacific in a steamship.

In 1869, the Wheelers and Lowrys were sent to Peking to open a mission there. In 1873, when Wheeler had to return to the United States because of ill health, Lowry became superintendent of the mission, a position in which he continued until 1893. When Peking University was opened in 1894, he was named its president and continued until 1918, when it was reorganized to become a union institution and renamed Yenching University. He died in Peking on Jan. 13, 1924.

He was an able, broad-minded, unselfish and diligent administrator, and the North China Annual Conference often recognized its debt to this pioneer missionary.

W. C. Barclay, *History of Missions.* 1957.
Dictionary of American Biography.
W. N. Lacy, *China.* 1948.
Who's Who in America, 1918-19.   FRANCIS P. JONES

LOWSTUTER, WILLIAM JACKSON (1871-1958), American minister, teacher and New Testament scholar, was born in Brownsville, Pa., on Oct. 19, 1871. His family inheritance was German and English. His early religious life was in the Protestant Episcopal Church of his mother. But Methodism early appealed to him and he turned toward her strong educational stress. He received a M.A. degree for public school teaching from California Normal

School, California, Pa., in 1890. He received his A.B. degree from ALLEGHENY COLLEGE in 1898, and was received into the PITTSBURGH CONFERENCE and fully ordained in 1902.

He served Methodist Churches in Vanderbilt, Pa., and Braddock, Pa., and then decided on further education and entered BOSTON UNIVERSITY.

He was married to Lida Vance Moore on Sept. 15, 1903. One son, William Robert Lowstuter, and three grandsons survive.

He received the S.T.B. degree from Boston University in 1908, the Ph.D. in 1911, and the D.D. from Allegheny in 1915. Elected the Jacob Sleeper Fellow from Boston University, he spent two years of study in Berlin and Marburg, Germany.

From 1911 to 1918 he taught at the ILIFF SCHOOL OF THEOLOGY, and from 1918 until his retirement in 1941 at the BOSTON UNIVERSITY SCHOOL OF THEOLOGY.

He died at St. Petersburg, Fla., in 1958. After Mrs. Lowstuter's death he married a friend of many years, Mrs. Anna Taylor, who died in 1965.

Lowstuter's love of the parish ministry never left him, and there is a Memorial Room in his honor in the United Church of Norfolk, Mass., where he served many years. He had a superb ability in the classroom to unite the study of the New Testament text to the living church. He was an able lecturer, but most of all he was a teacher of ministers! No man ever had a higher respect for his calling. "My students are my books," he would say, and this was his standard for faculty efficiency at the professional level. Few men, if any, ever trained more men for the schools and churches of American Methodism.

WALTER G. MUELDER

LOYNE, SOPHIA D. (1845-1917), was the wife of an American clergyman, and a pioneer in founding institutions to help the needy. She was born in Yorkshire, England, a daughter of James and Hannah Drinkwater, and came to the United States during the period of the Civil War. She married William A. Loyne in October 1870, while he was a local preacher in St. John's Church, Dover, N. H. She had five children, four of whom survived her.

After her husband went into the traveling ministry and during her residence in Portsmouth, N. H., Mrs. Loyne became interested in the poor of the city, the needy sailors, and the aged people. She then helped found a home for the aged, the first institution of its kind in that state. Also through her prayers and influence came into existence the Manchester (N.H.) Children's Home and Dispensary and the Mercy Home for the Care of Girls. During residence in Colebrook, N. H., her heart bled for the neglected lumbermen of the North Country, and from her small beginnings the work grew rapidly until it was a nation-wide service of the Woman's Christian Temperance Union. At the head of this movement, first as State Superintendent of the Department of Lumbermen and then as National Superintendent of the Department of Lumbermen and Miners, Mrs. Loyne held both offices throughout the rest of her life.

This work embraced over four million men and many thousands of families, and was one of the largest departments of Christian activity to be found anywhere in the world in those days. While living in Woodsville, N. H., she felt moved to aid the woodmen and the railroad men, and through that interest the Woodsville Cottage Hospital was born, designed to alleviate the sufferings not only of woodsmen and railroad men but of a multitude that continue to this day to need its services. The city of Laconia, N. H., owes to Mrs. Loyne, as much as to any one else, the founding of Laconia's Home for Old People. At Mrs. Loyne's death on July 14, 1917, more than ordinary loss was felt.

Journal of the New Hampshire Conference, 1918.

WILLIAM J. DAVIS

LO YUN-YEN (R. Y. Lo) (1890-), writer and public official, was born in Kiukiang, Kiangsi province, CHINA. He was educated in William Nast College (see article on CARL F. KUPFER), BALDWIN-WALLACE COLLEGE and SYRACUSE UNIVERSITY, where he was awarded a Ph.D. for his thesis, *The Social Teaching of Confucius*. On his return to China he became editor of *The Chinese Christian Advocate* and *The Young People's Friend*. He was also active in public affairs and was for many years a member of the Legislative Yuan. He was a delegate to the Jerusalem Conference of the INTERNATIONAL MISSIONARY COUNCIL in 1928 and to the Methodist GENERAL CONFERENCES of 1928 and 1940.

Besides several books on the opium problem, he was author of: *The Chinese Revolution from the Inside* (1930); *What is Democracy?* (1924); and *Christianity and New China* (1922). As far as is presently known, he is still living in Communist China, but nothing has been heard from him since about 1950.

China Christian Yearbook, 1936-37.
Who's Who in China, 1950.
Who's Who in Modern China, 1954.

FRANCIS P. JONES

LUBBOCK, TEXAS, U.S.A. (1970 population 146,379). Methodism was first organized in Lubbock on March 3, 1892, by R. M. Morris, with worship on one Sunday a month. The first church building, a frame structure, was completed in 1905 and cost $1,500. Services were then held twice a month.

A modern nine-story hospital was opened in August 1954, near Texas Technological College. It was valued at $3,581,197 and was acquired by the NORTHWEST TEXAS CONFERENCE about six months later and named Methodist Hospital. Recent improvements include a $200,000 coronary care unit which is one of the largest and most completely equipped units of its type in existence. A school of nursing and a nurse's dormitory are an important adjunct to the hospital.

There are presently twelve United Methodist churches in Lubbock, including Mount Vernon (Negro) and La Trinidad (Spanish). Also, there is Bethel, a church of the A.M.E. Church, and one of the C.M.E. Church.

Lubbock's twelve United Methodist churches are valued at $7,637,444 and reported 14,538 members in 1970. First Church, described below, is the largest and oldest with 5,960 members. A disastrous tornado struck Lubbock on May 11, 1970, destroying Wesley Church, a frame building whose congregation numbered 120, blowing away the roof of St. John's, and damaging the windows of First Church.

First Church, sometimes called "The Cathedral of the West," is of contemporary Gothic design based on the English Gothic style of architecture. The buildings, including the educational building, have a present valuation of approximately $2,700,000.

FIRST CHURCH, LUBBOCK, TEXAS

The church was first organized on March 3, 1892, with services in the courthouse, and twelve charter members. At last reporting in 1970 the membership was 5,960 and the church school enrollment exceeded 3,000. The church claims the second largest church school average attendance in Methodism.

In 1900 a church and parsonage were built by volunteer labor. The church was destroyed by fire in February, 1917. The church built at Broadway and Avenue M (location of present building) was dedicated on Oct. 17, 1920. The present building was opened on March 6, 1955.

The impressive stained glass in the windows in the sanctuary was imported from England. The magnificent Rose Window is twenty-six and one-half feet in diameter, one of the four largest rose windows in the world. It depicts in part "The Creation." The windows at the lower level are of famous Methodist leaders of the early days, and leading Biblical characters. The window at the rear of the sanctuary adumbrates "Worship," with appropriate symbols. The art glass windows in the chapel were brought over from the old sanctuary. Of symbolic interest in the church is a wood sculpturing of "The Last Supper" (made of solid quartered white Appalachian oak)—an exact replica of Leonardo da Vinci's painting and set in the altar at the head of the chancel. There have been twenty-three pastors since the organization of the church.

The Avalanche Journal, Lubbock, Texas: March 6, 1955.

St. Luke's Church is said to be the fastest growing church in the Northwest Texas Conference. The church began on Aug. 7, 1955, with the Village Theatre as a meeting place. Only fifty-four people were present for the first worship service and charter membership was closed in November 1955, with 187 members. Leo K. Gee, just graduated from PERKINS SCHOOL OF THEOLOGY, was the new pastor of this new church. The community was growing rapidly and the church was able to keep step with it. In 1970 St. Luke's reported 2,250 members and it continues its growth.

The completion of the first unit of building was on April 3, 1957. Since then there have been three additional building programs. St. Luke's rates among the highest of the churches paying into World Service. One of the most important aspects of the church is the Ministry to Children and Youth. The Church School is large and well staffed by dedicated laymen. There are presently a senior pastor and three associate ministers serving St. Luke's.

J. O. HAYMES

LUCCOCK, HALFORD EDWARD (1885-1960), American minister, author, and educator, was born in Pittsburgh, Pa., March 11, 1885, the son of NAPHTALI and Etta Anderson Luccock. Luccock's high school years in St. Louis Mo., included the one athletic feat of his life, a mile run in which he defeated T. S. Eliot—who later became the renowned poet.

On June 17, 1914, Luccock married Mary Louise Whitehead. They had two children, and their son Robert became professor of preaching at BOSTON UNIVERSITY SCHOOL OF THEOLOGY. Luccock entered the old NEW YORK EAST CONFERENCE on trial in 1908, was ordained a DEACON in 1909, and was ordained an ELDER and taken into full connection in 1910. He served pastorates in NEW YORK and CONNECTICUT until 1913 when he became an instructor at Hartford School of Missions. From 1916 to 1918 he was registrar and instructor at DREW THEOLOGICAL SEMINARY. He was editorial secretary of the Board of Foreign Missions from 1918 to 1924, and contributing editor of *The Christian Advocate* (New York) from 1924 to 1928.

In 1928 Luccock became professor of preaching at Yale Divinity School where he did his major work of teaching, preaching, and writing, and befriending generations of students until his retirement in 1953. He completed twenty-six books and a mountain of journalistic writing. His son estimated that his father spent the equivalent of eight years in the itinerant travels of preaching from coast to coast.

Luccock became famous for his dry humor. Until his death he contributed a column to *The Christian Century* called "Simeon Stylites."

It was said that Luccock broke every rule of preaching, but he had his own style and thrilled and inspired countless numbers of people. He was considered one of the great authorities on preaching. He was a warm human being, and wherever he traveled made an effort to contact his former pupils. He maintained an interest in the affairs of the New York East Conference, and in 1926 he collaborated with Paul Hutchinson in writing a popular history of American Methodism. In 1953 he delivered the famous Beecher Lectures at Yale.

Luccock received honorary degrees from SYRACUSE, WESLEYAN, Vermont, Yale and NORTHWESTERN universities, and a Litt.D. from ALLEGHENY COLLEGE. He died in his sleep of terminal cancer at Hamden, Conn., Nov. 5, 1960.

Christian Century, Dec. 14, 1960.
C. T. Howell, *Prominent Personalities*, 1945.
Journal of the New York East Conference, 1961.
Who's Who in Methodism, 1952.

DONALD J. WEST

LUCCOCK, NAPHTALI (1853-1916), American bishop, was born at Kimbolton, Ohio, Sept. 28, 1853. He graduated from OHIO WESLEYAN (A.B., 1874; A.M., 1877) and the University of Pittsburgh (Ph.D., 1886). He was a life-long student, with a keen and discriminating appreciation of the best in literature, history and science.

Entering the PITTSBURGH CONFERENCE in 1874, he gave several years to the pastorate and then became professor of Greek at ALLEGHENY COLLEGE, 1885-88. He was then pastor of First Church, Erie, Pa., 1888-93; Smithfield Street, PITTSBURGH, 1893-97; Union Church, ST. LOUIS, Mo., 1897-1909; Hyde Park Church, KANSAS CITY, a new church which he organized, 1909-12. In 1910 he was

fraternal delegate to the GENERAL CONFERENCE of the M. E. Church, South.

Elected bishop in 1912, Luccock was assigned to HELENA, Mont. With cheerful diligence and unswerving devotion, he took up the task but his health soon failed. Exposure because of a delayed train brought on pneumonia, the occasion of final collapse, and he died in LaCrosse, Wis., April 1, 1916, and was buried in Bellefontaine, St. Louis, Mo.

He had married Etta Anderson on Sept. 27, 1876. She and a son died before the bishop did. Two daughters and one son survived their father. The son, HALFORD E. LUCCOCK, became a gifted preacher, a distinguished writer, and a noted professor of preaching at Yale for more than a quarter of a century.

Among the books written by Naphtali Luccock were, *Christian Citizenship, Living Words from the Pulpit*, and *Sermons, Royalty of Jesus*.

Bishop F. J. McCONNELL said, "Bishop Luccock, in his own way made a most helpful contribution to the inner workings of the Board of Bishops during the brief time that he lived after his election . . . He had the power to use an intellectual surgical needle, with humor for an anesthetic, so that the puncturing was all over before the patient knew what had happened."

F. D. Leete, *Methodist Bishops*. 1948.
F. J. McConnell, *Autobiography*. 1952.
Pittsburgh Christian Advocate, April 6, 1916.   JESSE A. EARL

LUCKNOW, India, has long been regarded as the capital city of that part of Indian Methodism which was founded by American Methodist missionary enterprise.

Lucknow had earlier been the capital of the Muslim kingdom of Oudh, and chief rival to Delhi as the center of Indian Islamic culture. The Urdu language, derived largely from Arabic and Persian, still spoken by Muslims in this part of India, was the official court language of the Moghala.

Two hundred miles southeast of Lucknow is the Hindu holy city of Varanasi (Benares), so that the area was both a Muslim and a Hindu stronghold. Those who founded a Methodist mission center in Lucknow in the mid-nineteenth century thus faced formidable opposition. Yet in planning the mission to India, the BOARD OF MISSIONS and WILLIAM BUTLER considered Lucknow the most strategic center.

The Butlers arrived in Lucknow on Nov. 29, 1856, a time of immense importance for both the political and the religious history of India. In that year, Oudh came under British rule. Many of the complex causes of the Indian Mutiny (now sometimes called the "first war of independence"), which broke out in May 1857, were already in fermentation both in Lucknow itself, and throughout North India. Lord Dalhousie's social reforms, which included the abolition of "suttee" or the suicide of widows, were exciting suspicion that the aim of British rule was to subvert Indian faiths and traditional religious customs.

Within a few months of the Butlers' arrival, North India was aflame, and Lucknow itself besieged. But before that the Butlers had been cordially received, and entertained in the Residency for a week. However, they were advised against establishing a mission in Lucknow at that time, and found themselves unable to buy or rent property there. They therefore established their first center at

BAREILLY. Soon after the Mutiny, the Commissioner wrote to Butler advising the immediate opening in Lucknow of the proposed mission. Property was quickly found and purchased. The Commissioner and his friends contributed two thousand rupees for repairs and supervised the work. Mr. and Mrs. Ralph Pierce were the first missionaries to be appointed to Lucknow. Pierce and JOEL JANVIER began immediately an active program, including bazaar preaching, three primary schools, an English weekly service for British soldiers, and class meetings in English and Urdu. The following June Hossin Beg, his wife and their daughters were baptized as the first Methodist converts from a non-Christian religion in Lucknow.

Since 1936, Lucknow has been the official residence of a Methodist bishop.

British Methodist work in Lucknow began in 1864 when Daniel Pearson, a Wesleyan minister, visited the city. He was told that the American missionaries were prepared to hand over a congregation of two hundred Europeans, in order to concentrate on work among Indians. Joseph Broadbent was stationed in Lucknow from 1866 to 1873, for military and English work. In 1879, the Lucknow and Benares (later Varanasi and Lucknow) district was set up, with a total of only sixty-one full members, divided between congregations in Lucknow and Faizabad. By 1968 the district had thirty-two places of worship, 1,966 full members and a community of 4,819. It had three secondary schools with 2,398 students, and one teachers' training college with fifty-six students. (See also LUCKNOW ANNUAL CONFERENCE.)

J. WASKOM PICKETT
D. B. CHILDE

Nur-Manzil Psychiatric Institute, located at Lal Bagh, Lucknow, was founded in 1955 by E. STANLEY JONES, a missionary of the Board of Missions of the Methodist Church. Jones began his missionary career in 1907 at Lucknow. His experience as an evangelist and counselor, combined with his Bible study, led him to regard psychiatry as a field of knowledge that could contribute substantially to the welfare of people. He was troubled by the signs of hostility between certain psychiatrists and churchmen, and sought to bring into a practical synthesis or working partnership the insights and therapies of psychiatry and Christian discipleship. Patients now treated come from a wide range of creedal and racial communities in India and other countries of Asia. The superintendent is now James Stringham.

B. T. Badley, *Southern Asia.* 1931.
J. N. Hollister, *Southern Asia.* 1956.
A. D. Hunt, ed., *Seventy Years on the Lucknow and Banaras District of the Methodist Church, 1880-1950.* Mysore City: Wesley Press, n.d.   J. WASKOM PICKETT

LUCKNOW CHRISTIAN COLLEGE. In 1866, the centennial year of American Methodism, two members of the India Conference discussed until late at night the opening of a college by the conference as a worthy recognition of this special anniversary. The suggestion was approved, and by 1868 an endowment fund of 10,000 rupees had been received. The school was opened on Feb. 1, 1877, with HENRY MANSELL as principal, in a small house on the mission compound.

The following year, B. H. BADLEY became principal. Fifteen of the nineteen years of his service in INDIA were given in Lucknow, largely in developing the Christian

College. He saw the school become the Centennial High School in 1882, and then raised to college grade when affiliated, on July 2, 1888, with the Calcutta University under the name of the Lucknow Christian College. In response to appeals to the government, Badley secured a desirable triangular plot of land just across from the high school building, on which the new building was erected. The foundation stone was laid by Bishop JAMES M. THOBURN on Aug. 6, 1891, and it was formally opened on Oct. 31, 1892. Badley did not live to see the fulfillment of his dreams.

More than literary education was provided, for as early as 1892, the business department was opened and for two generations trained men in various commercial subjects. Then it had to be closed for financial reasons. In 1920-22, the complete reorganization of the institution was effected, involving the separation of the college, high school, and school of commerce. The organization of the Lucknow University by the government in 1920 reserved to that institution the right to confer the B.A. and B.Sc. degrees; leaving other institutions the "Intermediate College" level of only two years beyond high school. In 1946, degree classes were restored.

The College of Arts, Science, and Commerce is the largest and main unit of the institution. The most important service the college renders as a four-year institution is in science, with more than two-thirds of the students in this department. The Teacher Training College was opened in 1952, the first nongovernment training college in the state. This was a two-year course leading to the certificate of teaching, but when this was abolished by the government, the college was upgraded for the Licentiate Teaching Diploma. It is among the leading teacher-training colleges of the state. The College of Physical Education is recognized as a pioneering institution in its field. In 1955, a one-year course for graduates, leading to the Diploma in Physical Education, was added under the Lucknow University. This was the first university diploma in physical education to be given in the state.

The first Indian principal, appointed in 1921, was one of its own alumni, J. R. CHITAMBAR, who left the position in 1930 when he was elected a bishop of the M. E. Church. One of the buildings in the later years of an extensive building program is the Bishop Chitambar Memorial Chapel. The second Indian principal, C. M. THACORE, has been at the helm since 1949, and is responsible for much of the expansion of the present time.

JOHN N. HOLLISTER

LUCKNOW CONFERENCE, in India, whose area begins about 300 miles from CALCUTTA and extends on both sides of the Ganges River for over 300 miles. Methodist work was opened there in 1858. Portions of the conference have been included at various times in the NORTH INDIA, Northwest India, and BENGAL ANNUAL CONFERENCES. The Lucknow Conference was organized in February 1921, by Bishop FRANK W. WARNE. There are five districts in the conference. The Arrah-Buxar District has ten circuits. BUXAR is a town of 35,000 inhabitants where there is a church of 882 members, which is largely self-supporting. The Buxar Brides' School is also located there.

The Ballia District has a church in Ballia, and there are reported to be 3,917 members in the district. The Gonda District, where work began in 1865, has about 1,583 Methodists in eight circuits. These center in Gonda, a town of about 46,000, seventy-three miles east of Lucknow on the North-Eastern Railway. It is in the midst of an agricultural area. There is a partially self-supporting church in the town with a membership of 579, a considerable number of whom are students and teachers at the Chambers Memorial Girls' School there, which is largely supported by the Woman's Division of Christian Service.

The Kanpur District includes six civil districts. There are approximately 7,732 Methodists and thirteen circuits on this district.

Allahabad, where there is a church with almost 1,000 members, is largely self-supporting, and there is also a Methodist Primary School supported by the Woman's Division of Christian Service with an enrollment of 326 boys and 58 girls. The ALLAHABAD AGRICULTURAL INSTITUTE is across the Ganges River.

KANPUR, head of the district by that name, is a city of 895,106, situated on the right bank of the Ganges River, fifty miles southwest of Lucknow, and is the largest city in Uttar Pradesh. There are two self-supporting churches in Kanpur. There are several other centers where church groups are organized. Kanpur also has the Methodist High School supported by the Woman's Division of Christian Service, and the Hudson Memorial Girls' School, supported by this same division.

In the Lucknow District there are 2,951 members in six circuits. The Lucknow Conference in its five districts reports 23,211 members, including those of baptized children. The bishop of the Area lives in Lucknow.

Discipline, UMC, 1968. P. 1901.
Project Handbook Overseas Missions. 1969.   N. B. H.

LUCKNOW PUBLISHING HOUSE. In January, 1860, WILLIAM BUTLER faced a problem: orphan boys had been gathered together in BAREILLY, but he knew that not only food but employment was necessary. He felt there was no other means within reach but printing. And for this, J. W. WAUGH's experience as a practical printer seemed providential—the very help needed for the enterprise, and for the printing of hymns, tracts, and catechism. Funds were made available by seven missionaries who gave $100 each as loans for two years, and the press was set up in Bareilly. It was at first called the India Book Concern.

In 1866, the press was moved to Lucknow and set in a small room near the home of the superintendent. The staff consisted of six men, with only one hand-press. Christian literature was made available, however, and for more than a century the Lucknow Publishing House, as it came later to be known, has made its impact on Christian teaching through its publications. From its humble beginnings the publishing house now occupies its own building with rooms for all departments, as well as a large book-sales room. Modern facilities, including an offset press, have been added to the equipment in recent years and literature can be produced in all the languages of INDIA, but especially in English, Urdu, and Hindi.

From the beginning, the agents (managers) of the publishing house have been missionaries, only a few of whom had practical training for the work. WILLIAM W. BELL, with both technical and business ability, was appointed agent in 1954, and brought the publishing house to a state of production and financial stability not exceeded in all its previous years of service. In recent

LUCKNOW PUBLISHING HOUSE

years, the BOARD OF MISSIONS has departed from its old practice of making no appropriation for publishing, and has given grants to help meet the need of making literature available, not only for the Christian community, but for others who ask for good literature.

JAMES THOBURN felt the need of some communication with the public and started *The Witness* with the help of JAMES MESSMORE. It was published first in May 1871, every two weeks, but the following year it became a weekly. It was aided at first by special subscription but very soon became self-supporting. In more recent years it has been subsidized by the publishing house. Now called *The Indian Witness*, it has a full-time editor, trained in Journalism. The *Kaukab-i-Hind* (Star of India), a bi-weekly in Roman Urdu, meets a need felt by many village pastors and leaders.

JOHN N. HOLLISTER

LUGG, THOMAS BRANSFORD (1889-1967), American church executive, was born in Salem, Wis., Dec. 11, 1889. His education was received at NORTHWESTERN UNIVERSITY and GARRETT BIBLICAL INSTITUTE. Joining the ILLINOIS CONFERENCE in 1915, he served pastoral charges until 1932. He was a chaplain in World War I. His administrative ability was recognized, and he became superintendent of the Quincy and Jacksonville districts of the conference. He served the Methodist Church as a whole in the position of Executive Secretary and Treasurer of the WORLD SERVICE and Finance Commission for sixteen years, from 1944-1960. As treasurer of The Methodist Church, he brought to bear in the councils of the church, a quiet sincere sagacity and administrative ability which had marked effect. A leader of the Southern section of the church said that one of the finest things about the unification of American Methodism in 1939 was "getting to know and work with Tom Lugg."

He died in Evanston, Ill., on Sept. 1, 1967.

Who's Who in The Methodist Church, 1966.

HENRY G. NYLIN

LUKE, BENJAMIN R. (? -1918), an orphan boy from an upper-caste family, came to the orphanage run independently by Louisa H. Anstey, a former missionary of the London Missionary Society, at Kolar, in Mysore State. When Miss Anstey made over her mission to the M. E. Church in 1890, and it became an institution of the SOUTH INDIA CONFERENCE, Benjamin Luke and his wife joined the Methodist Church. He went to help C. B. Ward in pioneer work at Sironcha in the Central Provinces. In 1889, he was appointed preacher-in-charge. His circuit became larger in area than many annual conferences now are. The work prospered. In 1917, he became district superintendent. Under his leadership, church membership and local support gained rapidly. The failure of the rains the next year brought the threat of famine. Cholera broke out and was quickly followed by the arrival of the influenza epidemic that was then sweeping the world. It overtook Luke while he was on tour. He died Oct. 21, 1918, and his body was brought home and buried in Sironcha.

Mrs. Luke remained in Sironcha until 1930, actively working as an evangelist. Their only son, J. R. Luke, has served as pastor of large churches and as district superintendent. A daughter, Dr. Jaya Luke, has been in charge of medical work since 1925, mostly at Sironcha. Another daughter, Ada Luke became the first Indian principal of the co-educational Methodist High School of Bidar.

B. T. Badley, *Southern Asia*. 1931.
J. N. Hollister, *Southern Asia*. 1956.   J. WASKOM PICKETT

LUKE, CHARLES MANLEY (1857-1946), NEW ZEALAND Methodist layman, was born in St. Ives, Cornwall, England, and brought up in nearby Penzance. He came to New Zealand and soon won a place in the business life of Wellington. He possessed great gifts as a platform speaker and local preacher. He served for many years as chairman of the hospital board, and became mayor of the city. He was a member of the executive of two exhibitions and a member of the royal commission to consider the federation of New Zealand with the Australian states. He served for many years on the Legislative Council, where he was a strong advocate of temperance reform. Twice president of the PRIMITIVE METHODIST Conference, he was also vice-president of the Union Committee in 1913.

ARCHER O. HARRIS

LUKE, JOHN PEARCE (1858-1931), New Zealand layman, was the son of Samuel Luke, who emigrated with his family from Cornwall in 1874. Settling in Wellington, Samuel Luke founded Luke's Foundry, an engineering firm. His son John became a prominent citizen, serving on the City Council continuously from 1898 to 1921. For the last eight years of that period he was mayor. He was a member of Parliament from 1908 to 1911, and again from 1918 to 1928. He was knighted in 1921. He and his brother Charles were actively connected with the Trinity Methodist Church, Newtown, Wellington.

Who's Who in New Zealand. 3rd Ed. (The Rangatira Press, Wellington, 1932).   COLIN D. CLARK

LUMB, MATTHEW (1761-1847), was a British missionary pioneer to the WEST INDIES. He was born near Halifax, Yorkshire, in October 1761, and was brought up as an Independent. But he became a Methodist LOCAL PREACHER in 1780 and an itinerant in 1783, being appointed to Barnard Castle. In 1788 he offered as a missionary and was stationed in ANTIGUA, then moved to St. Vincent in 1789. Here the law forbade unlicensed preaching, with fines rising from £18 for a first offense to death for a third. Lumb was imprisoned; and when Negroes rioted against the injustice, he preached through his cell window. THOMAS COKE brought his case to the Privy Council and gained repeal of the laws. On his release Lumb went to Barbados. He died, after later ministering in England for thirty-three years, on March 2, 1847.

T. Coke, *West Indies*. 1808-11.
P. Duncan, *Jamaica*. 1849.
Findlay and Holdsworth, *Wesleyan Meth. Miss. Soc.* 1921.
CYRIL J. DAVEY

LUMBER RIVER ANNUAL CONFERENCE OF THE HOLINESS METHODIST CHURCH was organized as the Lumber Mission Conference of the Holiness Methodist Church by several M. E. Church, South, ministers of NORTH CAROLINA who became interested in their local situation. They organized Oct. 26, 1900, at Union Chapel Church, Robeson County, N. C., with a special emphasis on home missions and scriptural holiness.

Doctrinally, the church is Wesleyan with an emphasis on the universality of the atonement, the witness of the spirit, and holiness. They retain the CLASS MEETING structure and require a probationary period of six months for prospective members.

A bishop presides over the six congregations and 1,000 members in their annual conference meeting. Ministers are not itinerant and, hence, have no time limit on the length of their pastorate. The *Yearbook of American Churches* of 1968 lists Bishop M. L. Lowry of Pembroke, N. C. as the bishop.

Census of Religious Bodies, 1936.
Yearbook of American Churches, 1968.   J. GORDON MELTON

ROBERT F. LUNDY

LUNDY, ROBERT FIELDEN (1920-   ), American missionary and bishop, is the son of Clyde E. and Elizabeth (Teilman) Lundy. He was born at Stilesboro, Ga., on March 29, 1920. He is a graduate of EMORY AND HENRY COLLEGE, and CANDLER SCHOOL OF THEOLOGY, EMORY UNIVERSITY, and holds the honorary D.D. degree from Emory and Henry.

He married Elizabeth Hall of Pulaski, Va., on June 15, 1944, and they have three children.

From 1944 to 1948, Robert Lundy was pastor of First Church of Oak Ridge, Tenn., and during one year at Yale he was pastor of East Pearl Street Church in New Haven, Conn.

Going to MALAYSIA in 1950 as a missionary, he served in a variety of capacities. His pastorates included Klang, Kuala Lumpur, Kuantan, Ipoh, Barker Road and Wesley Churches in SINGAPORE. While pastor of the Kuantan Church he organized and served the Eastern Malaya District. For four years he was district superintendent of the Perak District. In addition to his other work, Lundy was editor of *The Methodist Message*, the official organ for Southeast Asia, and served as Methodist News Correspondent for Malaysia. He served for a term as President of the Council of Churches of Malaysia and Singapore.

He was elected bishop in 1964 to head the work in the Singapore area for a four year term. At that time the Singapore area of The Methodist Church had four annual conferences with diverse languages. After serving his terms as bishop, R. F. Lundy resumed his place in the autonomous church recently organized in Malaysia.

Going simultaneously to Southeast Asia with Bishop Lundy were his brother, John Thomas Lundy, later Field Treasurer for Singapore and a cousin, Dr. Gunnar Teilmann, a leading minister in Malaysia.

Who's Who in The Methodist Church, 1966.
                                         CLYDE E. LUNDY

LUNN, HENRY SIMPSON (1859-1939), British, medical missionary and railway and shipping agent, was born on July 30, 1859, at Horncastle, Lincolnshire, and entered the Wesleyan ministry in 1881. After training as a minister, he qualified as a medical doctor with a view to service overseas; and in 1887 he went to INDIA, but returned the following year because of ill health. Service at the West London Mission was interrupted in 1890 by controversy with the Mission House over missionary methods in India, and this led to Lunn's resignation from the ministry in 1893 and the resumption of his business career. He became involved in Liberal politics and discussions of church unity, and was knighted in 1910. His publications include *The Love of Jesus, The Secret of the Saints*, and *Reunion and Lambeth*. He edited *Review of the Churches* from 1892-96, 1920-30. He died on Feb. 16, 1939.

H. S. Lunn, *Chapters from My Life*. London, 1918.
————————, *Nearing Harbour*. London, 1934.
                                   H. MORLEY RATTENBURY

LUTON INDUSTRIAL COLLEGE in England, was founded in 1957. Its charter laid down the following principles: to make the Christian faith relevant in the realms of industry and commerce; to give practical training in industrial mission; and to give training in leadership and corporate responsibility. The College was founded through the initiative of a Methodist minister, William Gowland, who left the Albert Hall, Manchester, in 1954, to make his headquarters in Luton, Bedfordshire, a car manufacturing town in the south of England. The Conference stationed him in charge of a church called Chapel Street, built to seat 2,000, and then on the point of closure. Gowland developed the premises as a community-center, the Luton Industrial Mission, and was soon acting as industrial chaplain in eight factories. He started the College itself in the Chapel in 1957, and during the first ten years 6,000 students attended short courses. The main aim was to train laymen but theological students also attended. In September 1959, the College became a division of the Methodist HOME MISSION DEPARTMENT. The British Methodist Church now has about two hundred ministers who serve as industrial CHAPLAINS; they all receive an induction course before they start, and are invited back every third year for retraining. An annual study conference for the chaplains is part of their three-tier training. The College is ecumenical in terms of staff and students. It was the first industrial college of its kind in the world. One important emphasis of industrial chaplaincy in British Methodism has been that chaplains should only be appointed where both management and trade unions are in agreement: no ecumenical work is possible within industry where the unions in particular oppose the

LYDIA PATTERSON INSTITUTE, EL PASO, TEXAS

coming of the chaplain. There has been a tendency in Britain for chaplains to be set up through management alone. A second emphasis has been on the need for continuity in the chaplain's work: men should not be sent and then taken away again within two or three years.

WILLIAM GOWLAND
FRANK BAKER

LYCETT, FRANCIS (1803-1880), British businessman and benefactor of the church, was born at Worcester, the son of a glovemaker, and was converted in his youth. In 1832, following a slump in his father's business, he became manager of a glove firm in LONDON and prospered. From 1866-67 he was sheriff of London and Middlesex, and was awarded a knighthood in 1867. He refused the honor of meeting Emperor Napoleon III because the meeting was to have been on a Sunday.

Lycett was generous in support of the Wesleyan Theological Institution, the Leys School, CAMBRIDGE, home and overseas missions, and the BRITISH AND FOREIGN BIBLE SOCIETY. With GERVASE SMITH he was largely responsible for the Metropolitan Chapel Building Fund, launched in 1860, and personally promised £50,000 for the building of fifty chapels in twenty years, provided an equal sum was raised in the provinces. He died on Oct. 29, 1880.

G. J. Stevenson, *Methodist Worthies.* 1885.

H. MORLEY RATTENBURY

LYCOMING COLLEGE, Williamsport, Pennsylvania, was established in 1812 as Williamsport Academy. It became Williamsport-Dickinson Seminary in 1848, Williamsport Dickinson Junior College in 1929, and Lycoming College in 1948. The college is the property of the Preachers' Aid Society of the CENTRAL PENNSYLVANIA CONFERENCE.

Lycoming is the Indian name for the region around Williamsport. The college offers the B.A. degree. The governing board has thirty members elected by the Preachers' Aid Society of the Central Pennsylvania Conference.

JOHN O. GROSS

LYDIA PATTERSON INSTITUTE, El Paso, Texas, originally a school for Mexican boys, now coeducational, was made possible by a gift of $75,000 on Dec. 4, 1913, by an El Paso attorney, Millard Patterson, who was not a Methodist. Patterson stipulated that the money was "to be used under the auspices of the Methodist Episcopal Church, South for the education and religious training of boys and young men to preach the gospel in Mexico." The school was named Lydia Patterson in memory of Patterson's wife who was for many years a member of Trinity Church, El Paso. The original gift was used to erect a building to house the school. From the beginning the institute received support as a missionary project, and today it is related to the National Division of the General BOARD OF MISSIONS while at the same time it enjoys a special relationship to the SOUTH CENTRAL JURISDICTION whose annual conferences accepted quotas and raised some $750,000 for its building program in the 1960's. The institute has a special English department, an intermediate school, a high school, a preministerial department, and a night school for adults. Young men preparing for the ministry may live in the institute's dormitories while attending college in El Paso. The institute is closely affiliated with the RIO GRANDE CONFERENCE, many of whose ministers are among its alumni. Lydia Patterson Institute is accredited by the Southern Association of Colleges and Schools and by the University Senate. It is managed by a board of trustees elected by the South Central Jurisdictional Conference. In the main its support is derived from tuition, individual donations, and advance specials from the churches of the South Central Jurisdiction. In 1969 the institute reported 25 teachers, 582 regular students, a library of 10,200 volumes, a plant valued at $1,600,000, an annual budget of $262,000, and an endowment of $17,000.

Bulletins of Lydia Patterson Institute.
1970 Yearbook, General Board of Education.
Project Handbook Section of Home Fields (National Division, Board of Missions of The Methodist Church).   N. B. H.

LYNCH, JAMES (1775-1858), Irish preacher and missionary pioneer in CEYLON and INDIA, under the British Wesleyans, was born in Londonderry, in the north of

IRELAND, and grew up as a Roman Catholic. He was converted under Methodist preaching 1802 and entered the ministry in 1808.

In 1812 he was one of the volunteers who joined THOMAS COKE'S missionary venture to the East. When Coke died on this journey, James Lynch was one of those with qualities of leadership to take over the difficult situation that ensued. The strategic stations the little company of six young preachers established in Ceylon have remained important centers of witness through all the years since. Not being good at languages, Lynch himself ministered mainly to British civil and military personnel.

Once the work was firmly begun in Ceylon, the chance came to fulfill something of Coke's original plan. In 1817 James Lynch became a pioneer missionary to Madras, and was welcomed by a group of serious-minded people who met for Bible study in Royapettah. He built the first chapel there in 1817, and continued a ministry mainly amongst Europeans until a breakdown in health necessitated his return to Ireland in 1825.

In Ireland he threw himself again into circuit work, mainly in the north. Increasing physical weakness led to his retirement from active ministerial life in 1842. Most of his closing years as a supernumerary were spent in England, at LONDON and LEEDS, and he died March 21, 1858.

A junior colleague on one occasion was WILLIAM BUTLER whose missionary zeal was so kindled by James Lynch, that in later years he was the founder of American Methodism's missions in INDIA and MEXICO.

C. H. Crookshank, *Methodism in Ireland*. 1885-88.
Findlay and Holdsworth, *Wesleyan Meth. Miss. Soc.* 1921.
W. M. Harvard, *Ceylon and India*. 1823.   CYRIL J. DAVEY
                                                FREDERICK JEFFREY

LYNCH, JAMES D. (1839-1872), American Negro minister and politician, was born on Jan. 8, 1839 in BALTIMORE, Md. His father was a free man who had purchased James' mother from slavery. After he graduated from the Kimball Union Academy in NEW HAMPSHIRE in 1857, Lynch became a Presbyterian minister until 1859 when he joined the A. M. E. Church. He served parishes in ILLINOIS and INDIANA before his transfer to the Baltimore Conference in 1860.

In May 1863, Lynch became a missionary to former slaves in SOUTH CAROLINA under the auspices of his church and the National Freedmen's Relief Association. Two years later he and four other preachers, with Bishop DANIEL A. PAYNE, formed the South Carolina Conference of the A.M.E. Church. Returning to PHILADELPHIA in February 1866, Lynch became editor of *The Christian Recorder*, the official A. M. E. paper. In June 1867, he resigned that post to join the M. E. Church, convinced that it was, he wrote, "God's chosen power to lift up my race from degradation." Immediately Lynch went to MISSISSIPPI where he helped to organize a new conference for the M. E. Church in 1869.

A popular orator and respected spokesman for black Mississippians, Lynch pleaded so effectively for racial harmony that he maintained the respect of his white ecclesiastical and political opponents. In 1868 and 1872 he was a delegate to the Republican National Convention. Educational work with the Freedmen's Bureau and election in 1870 as Secretary of State for Mississippi involved

him further in politics. He continued, however, as a presiding elder in the MISSISSIPPI CONFERENCE and served as one of the first Negro delegates in a M. E. GENERAL CONFERENCE in 1868, and again in 1872. From 1868 until his death Lynch published the *Colored Citizen's Monthly* "to defend the interests of the Negro, the Republican Party and the M. E. Church." His death from pneumonia on Dec. 18, 1872 in Jackson, Miss., cut short a brilliant career of racial, political and ecclesiastical leadership.

James M. McPherson, ed. *The Negro's Civil War. How American Negroes Felt and Acted During the War For the Union.* New York: Pantheon Books, 1965.
Ralph E. Morrow. *Northern Methodism and Reconstruction.* East Lansing, Michigan: Michigan State University Press, 1956.
Alexander W. Wayman. *Cyclopedia of African Methodism.* Baltimore: Methodist Episcopal Book Depository, 1882.
Vernon L. Wharton. *The Negro in Mississippi,* 1865-1890. Chapel Hill, North Carolina: University of North Carolina Press, 1947.   WILLIAM B. GRAVELY

LYNCHBURG, VIRGINIA, U.S.A., on the James River in the foothills of the Blue Ridge Mountains with a population of 53,134 is a shipping and trading center for a rich agricultural region. Founded by John Lynch in 1757, Lynchburg was incorporated as a town in 1805 and city in 1852. During the Civil War the Confederates held Lynchburg to the end as one of their vital supply bases. Lee surrendered at Appomattox Court House twenty miles east of the city.

Three schools are located here: RANDOLPH-MACON WOMAN'S COLLEGE, Lynchburg College, and Virginia Theological Seminary. Sweet Briar College is twelve miles away.

Bishop FRANCIS ASBURY frequently visited Lynchburg and held several conferences there. Both Bishops Asbury and WHATCOAT preached and celebrated holy communion in the city in 1805.

In 1811 Lynchburg was mentioned in the *Minutes*, with John Weaver as pastor who reported 207 members for the circuit. At the division of the M. E. Church in 1845, the society of course adhered to the M. E. Church, South. After the Civil War the M. E. Church organized a society of colored members before 1876. That year Lynchburg had three Southern Methodist Churches: Centenary with 402 members; Court Street, 388; City Mission, 108; and the M. E. Church (colored) had 617 members.

Memorial Church was organized in 1883 with eighty-nine charter members who transferred from Court Street, among whom were C. V. Winfree and John Bell Winfree, leaders of church and civic life.

RANDOLPH-MACON WOMAN'S COLLEGE, chartered in 1891, opened its doors in 1893 with William Waugh Smith as founder and first president.

In 1900 there were six M. E. Church, South, congregations: Court Street, Centenary, Memorial, Trinity, Cabell Street, and Southview.

The unification of Methodism in 1939 brought two former M. P. churches (First Church and Park View) into the VIRGINIA CONFERENCE (SEJ). Jackson Street Church, organized in 1866 as a Negro M. E. Church, became a part of the WASHINGTON CONFERENCE (CJ).

Chestnut Hill Church was organized in 1951 in a building purchased from the Congregational-Christian Church with a small group of the original members remaining as charter members.

In 1965, a group of dissenting Methodists, reacting against the position of The Methodist Church on civil rights, withdrew and organized the First Southern Methodist Church as a "segregated church without bishops."

Other Methodist bodies in Lynchburg in 1965 were: the C. M. E., organized in 1872 (membership, 160); and the Wesleyan Methodist Church, organized in 1929 (membership, 56).

Lynchburg has been the host to many history-making sessions of both the Virginia Conference and the Washington Conference.

In 1970 Lynchburg reported thirteen United Methodist Churches—Fort Hill with 1,454 members and Centenary with 1,114 members being the larger. Court Street had 910 and the Lynchburg District 23,529.

Collier's Encyclopedia (Crowell-Collier Publishing Company, 1965).
Roberta D. Cornelias, *The History of Randolph-Macon Woman's College.* Chapel Hill, N. C.: University of North Carolina Press, 1951.
General Minutes (U.M.C.), 1970.
Alfred A. Kern, *Court Street Methodist Church, 1851-1951* (Richmond, Va.: Dietz Press, 1951).
Minutes, Lynchburg District Conference, 1891-1965.
Minutes, North Carolina-Virginia Annual Conference (CJ), 1965.
Minutes, The District Stewards, Lynchburg District, 1853-1965.
M. Simpson, *Cyclopaedia.* 1878.   THOMAS J. HAWKINS

LYNCHBURG COLLEGE, Lynchburg, Virginia, U.S.A., also called "Lynchburg Military College," the first Methodist Protestant College in the American South, developed from the tense political situation of the mid-1850's and was destined to close soon after the outbreak of the War Between the States. Due to the slavery issue, the entire faculty at MADISON COLLEGE, Uniontown, Pa., resigned at the commencement of 1855 and announced that a new M. P. college would open that fall. Lynchburg was chosen as the site for this college not only because it was centrally located and in VIRGINIA but because of its healthy climate and easy accessibility. Lynchburg College opened on Oct. 1, 1855, with a faculty of five and eighty-one students. It was enthusiastically endorsed by local citizens who raised $20,000 toward its expenses. The college was incorporated by an Act of the Virginia Assembly passed on Dec. 17, 1855, and the forty trustees were empowered "to confer literary degrees and distinctions upon such persons as in their opinion shall merit the same." Among the trustees was WILLIAM HENRY WILLS of NORTH CAROLINA.

During the first term of the college there were 108 students and in March, 1857, there were 135 students from ALABAMA, TENNESSEE, North Carolina, MARYLAND and Virginia. Samuel K. Cox was president of Lynchburg College until 1858, when Robert L. Brockett accepted the office. In 1860 Robert Boyd Thomson became president. The college adopted a military system of training, at first conducted on a voluntary basis but, after 1860, compulsory for all students over the age of fourteen. Uniforms were worn by the cadets who drilled in regular military fashion.

The GENERAL CONFERENCE of the M. P. Church which met in Lynchburg in 1858 focused denominational attention on the new school. Lynchburg College was forced to close in 1861 when most of the faculty and students enlisted in the Confederate Army. During the War Between the States the buildings were used as a hospital by the Confederate government and, after the war, as barracks by the Federal army. Due to the financial difficulties following the war, Lynchburg College was never reopened.

Acts of the Virginia Assembly, 1855-56.
A. H. Bassett, *Concise History.* 1870.
J. T. Oakey, "The Story of the Old Lynchburg College," ms. copy in Jones Memorial Library, Lynchburg, Va., dated 1936.
                                    RALPH HARDEE RIVES

LYNCHBURG FEMALE COLLEGIATE INSTITUTE (1858-c. 1861), Lynchburg, Va., U.S.A., known also as "Lynchburg Female Seminary," was established and operated by the faculty of the Lynchburg Methodist Protestant College. The Institute was opened on Feb. 1, 1858, with Samuel K. Cox, President of Lynchburg College, as president. Both the College and the Institute were forced to close when their joint faculty resigned in 1861 to join the Army of the Confederate States of America. Neither school was ever reopened.

J. T. Oakey, "The Story of the Old Lynchburg College," manuscript copy in the Jones Memorial Library, Lynchburg, Virginia, dated 1936.   RALPH HARDEE RIVES

LYNN, MASSACHUSETTS, U.S.A., with a population (1970) of 87,817, located eleven miles northeast of Boston, was first settled in 1629. Primarily known as a shoe manufacturing center, the city's industry today includes two large General Electric plants. Here Virginia-born JESSE LEE, "Apostle of Methodism to New England," preached in December 1790, at the corner of present Market and Essex Streets in the home of Benjamin Johnson. On Feb. 20, 1791 with eight members, Lee organized the first Methodist Church in Massachusetts in the Johnson barn. The following June a building was erected; here BISHOP ASBURY conducted the first Methodist conference in New England, Aug. 3, 1792.

On March 3, 1968, the third structure built of red brick in 1879 at the original location on City Hall Square was vacated; the property was sold and the building demolished. The historic First Church congregation, now relocated and united with St. Paul's, claims to have established the first Methodist Sunday school in New England in 1816; organized the first Methodist Missionary Society in the United States, Feb. 21, 1819; released WILLIAM BUTLER, pastor in 1856, to become the first native New England Methodist missionary and the father of Methodist missions in INDIA and MEXICO. Four ministers of this church became bishops: SOULE, HEDDING, MALLALIEU, and GROSE. The Paul Revere bell from the tower of First Church, to which Longfellow referred in his poem, "Bells of Lynn," has been re-hung in St. Paul's Church.

At the present time besides the merged congregations of First Church-St. Paul's, there are eight other Methodist churches in Lynn, the first four of which are offshoots of "the church on the Common": Boston Street, South Street, Maple Street, Trinity, Broadway, Lakeshore Park, Lakeside and St. Luke's. All the Methodist churches in the city have an aggregate membership of 3,977 persons (1970). In order to meet the complex problems of the changing city of Lynn three churches in the west section—Boston Street, South Street, and Trinity—though retaining their original identity have pooled their resources in "a group ministry" for effective Christian action. More mergers will undoubtedly be consummated in the near future.

Encyclopedia Americana (International edition), Vol. 17
Minutes, New England Annual Conference.
165th Anniversary Book, First Methodist Church, Lynn, Mass.
M. Simpson, *Cyclopaedia.* 1878.　　　ERNEST R. CASE

LYONS, ERNEST SAMUEL (1868-1948), American missionary to the PHILIPPINES and leader—in his later years—of the CALIFORNIA ORIENTAL MISSION, was born at Howell, Mich., on May 12, 1868. Lyons was educated at Puget Sound Business College and the GARRETT BIBLICAL INSTITUTE, from which he received the B.D. in 1899, and the D.D. in 1925. He obtained a law degree from Washington State College in 1893. In the Philippines itself he took the bar examination in 1913 so that he could take care of the increasing legal business having to do with Methodist properties in the Philippines at that time. He married Harriet Elenor Ewers on Dec. 4, 1900, and to them were born five children.

He was received into the ROCK RIVER CONFERENCE in 1899 and ordained elder in 1901. After student pastorates in the United States, he went overseas as headmaster of the Anglo-Chinese School, SINGAPORE, in 1899. He was appointed Field Missionary to the Philippines in 1903; district superintendent of the Northern District (Philippines) in 1905; superintendent, Manila District, 1912; and pastor of the Students' Church in MANILA in 1914. He left Manila with Mrs. Lyons on March 21, 1937, with an official tribute paid to them in these words, "These two veteran missionaries have had a remarkable service in the Philippines and have seen in their thirty-four years of residence here a most phenomenal growth of the evangelical Christian movement and especially of the Methodist Episcopal Church, whose missionaries they are."

After Lyons and his wife had come back to California, he was called back into active service to be superintendent of the California Oriental Mission. It was through his work that the mission became organized as a Provisional Conference in 1945, after which time he again retired. He was a member of the American Bar Association, a life member of the Royal Asiatic Society, Straits Branch. One of the most versatile men in his activities and one of great usefulness to the church, Ernest S. Lyons left an enduring memory with those who knew and worked with him in the Philippines and in California. He died in 1948.

Mrs. Harriet Elenor Lyons died in Los Angeles on Oct. 4, 1966.

Journal of the California Oriental Provisional Conference, 1949.
The Methodist Bulletin, M. E. Church in the Philippines, No. 5, May 1937.
World Outlook, January 1967.　　　N. B. H.

McANALLY, DAVID RICE (1810-1895), American church editor, was born in Granger County, Tenn., Feb. 17, 1810, the son of Charles and Elizabeth (Moore) McAnally. He was twice married, first to Marie Thompson, and later to Julia Reeves.

Admitted on trial in the HOLSTON CONFERENCE in 1829, he served various charges in TENNESSEE, NORTH CAROLINA, and VIRGINIA during the next fourteen years. Taking the presidency of East Tennessee Female Institute at KNOXVILLE in 1843, he held that post until 1851 when he was elected editor of the *St. Louis Christian Advocate*. Except for brief periods, he continued in that position until his death in 1895.

McAnally was an effective editor. In presenting the news he sought to keep his readers informed on the march of events, and in his editorials he tried to ground them in sound doctrine. As the Civil War approached he was frankly pro-Southern, upholding states' rights and defending (without praising) the institution of slavery. In 1862 he was arrested, his paper was suppressed for treasonable and subversive statements, and for some weeks he was held in Myrtle Street Military Prison in ST. LOUIS. Throughout his editorship he was recognized both in his own denomination and in the M. E. Church as a strong voice speaking in and for MISSOURI and Missouri Methodism.

In 1852 McAnally was chairman of the convention which founded CENTRAL METHODIST COLLEGE and he cooperated with other Missouri Methodist leaders in raising an endowment for it. While in Tennessee he was interested in the common school system and joined Horace Mann and others in an effort to improve it. He was a delegate to five GENERAL CONFERENCES of the M. E. Church, South, 1854, '58, '66, '70, and '82, leading his delegation to the last three.

McAnally wrote several books, including *Life and Times of Rev. William Patton* (1858), *Life and Times of Rev. Samuel Patton* (1859), *Life and Labors of Bishop E. M. Marvin* (1878), and *History of Methodism in Missouri* (1881). His primary interest was in the church, and most of what he wrote dealt with it, but some chapters in his works were devoted to an interpretation of the life and thought of the times.

Dictionary of American Biography.
M. Simpson, *Cyclopaedia.* 1878.
F. C. Tucker, *Missouri.* 1966.   ALBEA GODBOLD

McARTHUR, ALEXANDER (1814-1909), British Wesleyan Methodist industrialist and politician in AUSTRALIA and Britain, was born in IRELAND on March 10, 1814. In 1841 he went to Australia for his health. His brother, WILLIAM McARTHUR, encouraged him to set up as an export merchant, and during the gold rush the business prospered. He became a member of the Sydney Legislative Assembly and, later, of the Legislative Council. In 1863 he returned to England, and became M.P. for Leicester from 1874-92. In 1883, he gave £5,000 toward a new fund for building chapels in London. He died on Aug. 1, 1909.

H. MORLEY RATTENBURY

McARTHUR, WILLIAM (1809-1887), British Wesleyan Methodist, merchant, alderman, and politician, was born in County Donegal in IRELAND on July 6, 1809. He became manager of a woolen drapery business which prospered when his brother ALEXANDER McARTHUR went to AUSTRALIA. Already an alderman of Londonderry, in 1857 he moved to LONDON, and in 1867 became sheriff of London and Middlesex, in 1872 an alderman, and in 1880 lord mayor. From 1868-85 he was Liberal M.P. for Lambeth and was a leading advocate of the annexation of FIJI to the British crown. He was knighted in 1882. A Sunday school teacher for forty years, he supported the church in many ways, giving £10,000 in 1883 to a new fund for building fifty chapels in London and, with his brother, £3,000 toward the building of WESLEY COLLEGE, BELFAST, whose foundation stone he laid in 1865. In 1881, as lord mayor, he entertained the first ECUMENICAL METHODIST CONFERENCE at a reception at the Mansion House, London. He died on Nov. 16, 1887, in London.

T. McCullagh, *Sir William McArthur.* London, 1891.
G. J. Stevenson, *Methodist Worthies,* iv. 1885.
H. MORLEY RATTENBURY

M'AULAY, ALEXANDER (1818-1890), British Wesleyan evangelist and missionary, was born in Glasgow on March 7, 1818, and, though his father had been baptized by JOHN WESLEY, had a Presbyterian upbringing. He and his brother Samuel were both converted at a mission prayer meeting in 1835, and both entered the Wesleyan ministry, Alexander in 1840. He became known as an anti-Socialist, but also as a leader of a forward movement and evangelist. As secretary of the Metropolitan Chapel Building Fund, he was responsible for the erection of several chapels, and in 1876 he succeeded CHARLES PREST as general secretary of the HOME MISSION DEPARTMENT. In 1867 he was elected to the LEGAL HUNDRED, and in 1876 became president of the Conference. After his retirement he fulfilled a lifelong ambition to preach the gospel overseas, traveling at his own expense to the WEST INDIES and Africa. He died on Jan. 1, 1890, at Somerset East, Cape of Good Hope.

G. J. Stevenson, *Methodist Worthies,* iii. 1885.
H. MORLEY RATTENBURY

McBRIER, EDWIN MERTON (1865-1956), American mercantile executive, churchman and philanthropist, was born July 16, 1865, on his father's farm near Russell, N. Y.

As a young man of twenty-two, he taught day school

and at the same time taught a Sunday school teachers' Bible class in the local Methodist church. In 1887, he opened a variety store in Lockport, N. Y., over the door of which read "Woolworth & McBrier." The "Morning Watch" movement stimulated him to systematic Bible study and prayer, and in late 1889 he sold his business and went to CHINA as a missionary under the China Inland Mission, intending to spend his life in this calling. The fatal illness of his brother, with whom he had been in partnership, impelled him to return to the States, to save his business.

In 1894, McBrier opened a five and ten store for S. H. Knox and Company in DETROIT. During this period, he taught the Bible class in the Woodward Avenue Methodist Church. In January 1912, five chains of five and ten stores merged to form the F. W. Woolworth Company. Six of the principal executives, including E. M. McBrier, F. W. Woolworth, F. M. Woolworth and S. H. Knox, had one parent or the other who was a McBrier. E. M. McBrier continued to rise in responsibility, becoming buyer of merchandise for the merged stores, and retiring on Aug. 1, 1921.

In 1912, the McBrier family had moved to Montclair, N. J., and in 1914, McBrier was elected a member of the Executive Committee of the Board of Foreign Missions of the M. E. Church. In Montclair, he cultivated the intimate friendship of JOHN R. MOTT and other Y.W.C.A. leaders. He continued on the BOARD OF MISSIONS until 1949. In 1917, he became treasurer of the United Board of Christian Colleges in China, and continued in this capacity until 1949, during which period he hired his own secretary and rented his own office space, serving with no compensation.

He was a member of the Board of Directors and the Board of Trustees of the Montclair Y.M.C.A. from 1916 to 1948, and led the campaign to liquidate the indebtedness of the Methodist Home for the Aged in OCEAN GROVE, N. J. Among the many honors accorded him for his leadership and benevolence, were the "Order of the Jade" tendered by the Republic of China in 1940, a citation by SYRACUSE UNIVERSITY in 1944 (on whose Board he served from 1923 to 1944), and a citation by St. Lawrence University in 1949. His service from his retirement to his death accounted for thirty-three years of unremunerated leadership for missions and the Church.

He died in 1956 and is survived by two daughters. He is interred in Montclair, New Jersey.

Bible Studies of Edwin Merton McBrier from 1887 to 1952. Private Printing, 1952.
E. M. McBrier, *Some Reminiscences.* Private Printing, 1955.
GORDON E. MICHALSON

McCABE, CHARLES C. (1836-1906), "Chaplain-Bishop" of American Methodism, was born Oct. 11, 1836, at Athens, Ohio, a grandson of Robert McCabe, class leader and adviser of JOHN STEWART, pioneer American Methodist missionary to the Delaware and Wyandott Indians of OHIO. In 1847 McCabe's family moved to Chillicothe, Ohio, and, from thence, to BURLINGTON, IOWA, in 1850. For a short time he farmed at Mt. Pleasant, Iowa, and clerked in a Cedar Rapids store. He was converted at the age of eight, under the ministry of JACOB YOUNG; later, in 1850, after his removal to Iowa, he went to the altar at a watch night service conducted by Levin B. Dennis in Burlington's Old Zion Church, afterward ex-

CHARLES C. McCABE

plaining: "I was born in Ohio, and born again in Burlington." He joined Old Zion in 1851.

McCabe attended school at Athens, Ohio, and at Burlington, Iowa, before entering preparatory school at OHIO WESLEYAN UNIVERSITY (1854). For two years he was high school principal in Ironton, Ohio. He married Rebecca Peters on July 5, 1860. Also, in 1860, having been previously a local preacher, he was ordained DEACON, was admitted to the OHIO CONFERENCE of the M. E. Church, and was assigned to Putnam (now in Zaneville), Ohio.

In 1862, the Civil War having broken out, he became Chaplain of the 122nd Ohio Volunteer Infantry and, being captured June 16, 1863, spent four months in Libby Prison, Richmond, Va.; later, he went into the Christian Commission movement to obtain assistance for wounded soldiers. His singing, in this position, popularized the "Battle Hymn of the Republic," while his addresses crystalized into his lecture, "The Bright Side of Life in Libby Prison."

In 1865 McCabe became pastor at Portsmouth, Ohio, building a church there, and served as Conference Centenary and Educational Agent (1866). He was financial agent of Ohio Wesleyan University (1867), before being called to PHILADELPHIA in 1868 as assistant to A. J. KYNETT in the Methodist Extension Society, where he continued as a secretary for sixteen years. His battle cry in promoting church extension, "we're building two a day," became famous throughout the church.

McCabe transferred to the NEW YORK CONFERENCE in 1870. This "apostle of optimism" was elected Corresponding Secretary of the Missionary Society by the GENERAL CONFERENCE in 1884 and soon began sounding the slogan, "a million for missions." "Chaplain" McCabe was elected to the Methodist episcopacy in 1896. This missionary promoter, evangelist, and gospel singer, known to many as the "Methodist missionary millionaire," became Chancellor of AMERICAN UNIVERSITY, Washington, D. C., in December 1902. He died Dec. 19, 1906, in New York City and was buried in Rose Hill Cemetery, Chicago, Ill.

Bishop McCabe's writings include *Final Report on Salt Lake City Church* (pamphlet, 1880); *A Glance Backwards* (pamphlet, 1886); *The Open Door in Latin Countries* (First General Missionary Convention Address, Cleveland, 1903); *The American University—Taking Our Bearings* (pamphlet, 1903); *Shouting* (pamphlet about Christian rapture, n.d.); and "Dream of Ingersollville" (an allegory). He edited *Winnowed Hymns*, assisted by D. F. McFarlane.

Burlington Hawk-Eye, Sept. 5, 1907.
Christian Advocate, Dec. 27, 1906.
Dictionary of American Biography.
The Epworth Herald, Dec. 29, 1906.
J. B. Finley, *Wyandott Mission.* 1840.
F. D. Leete, *Methodist Bishops.* 1948.
Northwestern Christian Advocate, Jan. 2, 1907.
Zion's Herald, Dec. 26, 1906.   MARTIN L. GREER

McCAINE, ALEXANDER (1768-1856), American preacher and one of the founders of the METHODIST PROTESTANT CHURCH, was born in DUBLIN, IRELAND, of Roman Catholic parents and designed for the priesthood. When he was about twenty years of age he came to CHARLESTON, S. C., where he was converted under the ministry of WILLIAM HAMMETT, who led one of the earliest secessions from the M. E. Church.

McCaine began preaching in Charleston and attracted the favorable attention of Bishop FRANCIS ASBURY, who took him as a traveling companion. He joined the Conference in 1797 and served circuits in the Carolinas and Virginia. He located in 1806 to educate his children, but after the death of his wife in 1815 and at the solicitation of Asbury he re-entered the active ministry. Although he was not a member of the GENERAL CONFERENCE, he was elected secretary of that body in 1820. He again withdrew in 1821 and became the head of a boys' school in BALTIMORE.

He was appointed by Asbury to prepare a commentary on the Bible but did not complete the work. In 1827 he wrote a book under the title of *The History and Mystery of Methodist Episcopacy*, in which he opposed episcopacy and espoused the cause of the Reformers, whose agitation led to the formation of the M. P. Church. JOHN EMORY, the BOOK AGENT in NEW YORK, published a reply, *A Defense of Our Fathers*, which called forth from McCaine a rebuttal entitled, *A Defense of the Truth*, which was published in 1829. In 1850 he published a book under the title of *Letters on the Organization and Early History of the Methodist Episcopal Church*. Among his other writings were a series of thirty-six letters in the Pittsburgh *Christian Advocate*, and forty letters in the *Boston Olive Branch*, which appeared also in book form. In all of these he upheld the principles of the Reformers. He also wrote in defense of slavery and published in 1842 a work called *Slavery Defended Against the Attacks of the Abolitionists*. He contributed numerous articles to the *Western Recorder* on the same theme.

McCaine was active in the M. P. Church to the end of his life. He was a member of the General Conventions at Baltimore in 1827 and 1828 and of the General Conference of 1830, and a member of the committee which prepared the Constitution and the *Discipline* of the new denomination. He was also a delegate to the General Conferences of 1842 and 1854.

He worked mainly in the South and died in the home of his daughter, Mrs. James Brett, in Augusta, Ga., on June 1, 1856.

F. Asbury, *Journal and Letters.* 1958.
T. H. Colhouer, *Sketches of the Founders.* 1880.
Dictionary of American Biography.
E. J. Drinkhouse, *History of Methodist Reform.* 1899.
M. Simpson, *Cyclopaedia.* 1878.   ELMER T. CLARK

McCALLUM, DUNCAN (? -1834), was JOHN WESLEY's apostle-general in SCOTLAND, commissioned to convert the heathen there. Self-taught, he mastered four languages and extensive scientific knowledge. McCallum preached in Erse and English. He commenced as an itinerant in 1775 and labored indefatigably until 1829, becoming then supernumerary. He traveled forty years in Scottish circuits, serving long, broken terms at Aberdeen, Inverness, Edinburgh, and Dumfries, and eleven years around Newcastle, Shields, and Morphet. He was named in the DEED OF DECLARATION. Wesley ordained him DEACON and ELDER in August 1787. A celebrated preacher, disciplinarian, and frequently chairman of the district, he experienced hardship among Calvinistic and unresponsive fellow countrymen. He died July 21, 1834.

City Road Magazine. London, 1875.
L. Tyerman, *John Wesley.* 1870-71.   GEORGE LAWTON

McCLEARY, PAUL (1930-   ), missionary to BOLIVIA, was born in ILLINOIS, received his A.B. degree from Olivet Nazarene College, attended the University of Illinois, and earned a B.D. degree from GARRETT THEOLOGICAL SEMINARY. He married Rachel Timm, a science teacher, and they have four children. Since he began work in Bolivia in 1957, he has served as pastor in Cochabamba, both of the Union Church (English-speaking) and the Spanish-speaking Methodist church, and of the Methodist church in Santa Cruz. He was superintendent of the Central District. In 1962 he was appointed executive secretary of the annual conference.

                    NATALIE BARBER

McCLELLAND, CLARENCE PAUL (1883-   ), American college president, was born at Dobbs Ferry, N. Y., on Jan. 18, 1883. He was educated at WESLEYAN UNIVERSITY, DREW THEOLOGICAL SEMINARY, and SYRACUSE UNIVERSITY. He joined the NEW YORK CONFERENCE in 1908, serving churches until 1917. From then until 1925 he was president of Drew Seminary for Young Women.

Transferring to the ILLINOIS CONFERENCE, he became president of Illinois Woman's College, later named MACMURRAY COLLEGE, in Jacksonville, Ill. During his twenty-six-year term, until retirement in 1952, the college was greatly expanded in every way. The religious emphasis of his administration was exemplified by the new Annie Merner college chapel, erected in 1949.

Dr. McClelland served as a director of the Association of American Colleges, and as a member of the National Council of the Y.M.C.A. He is the author of *Question Marks and Exclamation Points*. Upon retirement he and Mrs. McClelland continued to live in Jacksonville, Ill.

C. T. Howell, *Prominent Personalities.* 1945.
Who's Who in Methodism, 1952.   HENRY G. NYLIN

JOHN McCLINTOCK

M'CLINTOCK, JOHN, JR.

M'CLINTOCK, JOHN, JR. (1814-1870), American clergyman, educator, editor, was born in PHILADELPHIA, Pa., on Oct. 27, 1814, the son of John and Martha (M'Mackin) M'Clintock, both born in County Tyrone, IRELAND. He was educated in the Grammar School of the University of Pennsylvania. At fourteen he started clerking in his father's retail dry goods store; at sixteen he became a bookkeeper in the Methodist BOOK CONCERN in NEW YORK CITY. While here he was soundly converted and considered entering the ministry. He entered the University of Pennsylvania in 1832, completing the required course with honors in three years. During his last year at the University he preached regularly. In April 1835, he was admitted on trial in the PHILADELPHIA CONFERENCE of the M. E. Church and appointed to JERSEY CITY, N. J. Never physically strong, his health broke in 1836 and he gave up the pastorate.

With the help of friends he turned to education, becoming assistant professor of mathematics at DICKINSON COLLEGE, and two years later (1837) full professor. Here he remained for twelve years, transferring in 1840 to the chair of classical languages. He published *A First Book in Latin* (1846), and with George R. Crooks, *A First Book of Greek* (1848). "Second Books" in both subjects appeared a few years later. These are noteworthy in that they started a method of teaching the classical languages which is still used.

Improving health enabled him to preach more frequently and on April 19, 1840, he was ordained an ELDER by Bishop ELIJAH HEDDING.

In 1848 the GENERAL CONFERENCE elected him editor of *The Methodist Quarterly Review* and he resigned his professorship to accept. During his eight-year term the *Review* became a scholarly exponent of the best Christian thought, and for the first time, self-supporting. His analytical essays on the positivist philosophy of Auguste Comte, and his detection of its errors attracted the French philosopher's notice and led to a correspondence between them.

He declined the presidencies of two universities to which he was elected, Wesleyan (1851), and Troy (1855).

In 1853, with JAMES STRONG, he began the *Cyclopaedia*

of *Biblical, Theological and Ecclesiastical Literature,* a work in twelve volumes, still authoritative in many fields, which took much of his time for the rest of his life. Other publications included *The Temporal Power of The Pope,* (1855); a volume of sermons; a translation of *A History Of The Council Of Trent,* from the French of L. F. Bungener (1855); and from the German, with Charles E. Blumenthal, *The Life of Christ,* by August Neander.

In 1856, resigning from the *Review* he accompanied Bishop MATTHEW SIMPSON as a delegate to the British Wesleyan Conference and the Conference of the Evangelical Alliance at Berlin. On his return he became pastor of St. Paul's M. E. Church, New York City. This appointment expiring by limitation in 1860, he was appointed pastor of the American Chapel, Paris, France.

During the Civil War he was a most effective representative of the Northern interests through his speeches, writings, and personal contacts, removing apprehensions abroad, and through *The Methodist,* of which he was corresponding editor, giving correct information at home. In 1864 he returned to the pastorate of St. Paul's from which ill health forced his resignation.

As chairman of the General Conference Centenary Committee (1864-1868), he kept busy planning the celebration of the CENTENNIAL OF AMERICAN METHODISM (1866). DANIEL DREW, financier and philanthropist of New York City, desired to found a "Biblical and Theological School" in connection with this event, and in accordance with his wishes M'Clintock became the first president of DREW THEOLOGICAL SEMINARY, now part of DREW UNIVERSITY, in 1867. Less than three years later (March 4, 1870), he died and is buried in Madison.

In 1837 he married Caroline A. Wakeman, to whom was born one son, Emory. In October 1851, he married Catherine W. Emory, widow of his friend, ROBERT EMORY. The University of Pennsylvania honored him with a D.D. (1848), and Rutgers University conferred the LL.D. on him in 1866.

American Annual Encyclopaedia. D. Appleton & Co., 1870.
George R. Crooks, *Life and Letters of the Rev. John M'Clintock, D.D., LL.D., Late President of Drew Theological Seminary.* New York: Nelson & Phillips, 1876.
Dictionary of American Biography.
Minutes of the Newark Conference.   WILLIAM M. TWIDDY

McCOLL, DUNCAN

McCOLL, DUNCAN (1754-1830), Canadian preacher, the apostle of Methodism in southwestern New Brunswick, was born in Argyllshire, SCOTLAND. His parents belonged to the Scotch Episcopal Church, which he later left to become "a hearty and zealous Wesleyan." At an early age he enlisted as pay sergeant in the British army. In 1778 his regiment was ordered to Halifax, and at the battle of Penobscot Bay he was under fire for the first time.

His military experiences caused him to think deeply about religion, to set aside a day for prayer, and to slip away with his Bible to a quiet retreat in the woods. While in Bermuda in the winter of 1784 he met a Methodist woman from PHILADELPHIA, who told him about Methodism. She later became his wife and a help to his ministry.

When his regiment was disbanded in the spring of 1784, he settled at St. Andrews, New Brunswick, and during the next year he entered business at St. Stephen. Because the people were without a place of worship, he opened his home for service. So many were drawn to his services that the magistrate threatened to suppress them, and in consequence McColl was certain that it was his duty to preach.

At this stage he gave up his business, formed a Methodist society, and devoted his time to preaching. It was not easy, nor did he have full cooperation. "I had also to provide a house, seats, and a fire for people in the winter, for no one took it into his head to help me," he wrote. In 1790, however, he induced his supporters to build a church.

WILLIAM BLACK met Duncan McColl in 1792 and encouraged him to become a Methodist itinerant. He helped to found societies in Fredericton and in other parts of the St. John valley. Ordained in 1795 by ASBURY, McColl returned to St. Stephen where he remained the rest of his career.

For thirty-five years of his ministry, Duncan McColl labored hard to win souls to Christ and to form Methodist societies. He had to endure many hardships, provocations, and discouragements and the numerical results were not great. Nevertheless he left a deep impression on the religious life of the region.

In 1829 he became superannuated, but was unable to assist his successor greatly. He finished his diary Dec. 5, 1830, and on December 17 he died. He was buried in the St. Stephen and Milltown Protestant Cemetery where, in 1885, a substantial monument was erected in his honor.

Duncan McColl was a brave soldier, Loyalist, settler, and preacher of Jesus Christ. He symbolized the fact that the strength of the Methodist movement in the Loyalist period depended on the spontaneous response of converted and deeply concerned persons to the profound religious needs of the new communities. As a lay preacher he emerged to meet the challenge of spiritual destitution on the frontier. He introduced Methodism to New Brunswick and, to his distinguished colleague Matthew Richey, "he was second to none of the earlier Provincial itinerants in mental power."

The Autobiography of a Wesleyan Methodist Missionary. Montreal: E. Pickup, 1856.
British North American Wesleyan Methodist Magazine, 1841-42.
G. S. French, *Parsons and Politics.* 1962.
T. W. Smith, *Eastern British America.* 1877-90. A. E. KEWLEY

McCOMBS, VERNON MONROE (1875-1951), American missionary and eventually leader in Spanish-American missions in the far west, was born at Parkers Prairie, Minn., in July, 1875. Licensed to preach in 1902, he attended St. Cloud Teachers College and taught for a short time. Later he graduated with the B.A. degree from HAMLINE UNIVERSITY, 1903, and then from DREW THEOLOGICAL SEMINARY, 1906. In the same year he received the M.A. degree from New York University. In 1906 also he married Eva M. White, and he and his young wife, both Student Volunteers, sailed for the mission field in PERU, where he engaged for a time in teaching. Later he was appointed as superintendent of North Andes Mission, covering PERU and ECUADOR. After a few years of work, he broke in health and had to return to America. A physician in NEW YORK advised him to go to the Southwest for rest, and thus he went to southern CALIFORNIA.

As early as 1879 the SOUTHERN CALIFORNIA CONFERENCE had interested itself in mission work among the Mexicans. The first Sunday that McCombs was in Los

ANGELES he made his way to the Mexican Sunday school on Bloom Street. There he found one teacher struggling with a small class. The visitor was invited to speak to them and this he did in perfect Spanish. This was his introduction to new work, for that same year he was named superintendent of Spanish work in Los Angeles. By his deep interest in and love for the Mexicans, he gathered about him a growing number of them, and by Conference time the work was so well established that in 1912 he was appointed superintendent of Spanish and Portuguese work and later, after some years, he was appointed superintendent of the Latin American Mission.

To secure help for the expanding work, he had to secure two ministers from MEXICO, and the new impact on the Mexican population soon made it necessary to move from the Bloom Street building to an adequately planned church on the old Plaza, the center of the Spanish speaking community. In a comparatively short time, a long-time hoped for school for young Mexicans was started. Earlier in the century, the WOMAN'S HOME MISSIONARY SOCIETY of the Conference had established a school for Mexican girls in Hollywood. In 1909 a group of interested Methodists had organized and incorporated The Spanish American Training School for Boys, but little happened until McCombs revived the project, and since in southern California he had been fortunate in meeting former friends from his Hamline student days, many of whom had prospered, he readily found cooperators.

Ten acres of land was secured on Fifueroa Street on the outskirts of Gardena, and here in October 1913, the school became a reality in newly erected buildings. Its aim was "to educate and give industrial and spiritual training to Mexican boys." Today the school is known as the Spanish American Institute.

The plight of the Mexican people demanded that well planned social work should go hand in hand with the religious activities, and this resulted in the organization of the Plaza Community Center. This actually began in the Bloom Street quarter, and in a way was the forerunner for the GOODWILL INDUSTRIES, for bags were given out to interested people to be filled with cast-offs. This gave employment to a few needy people. However, that method was changed with the coming of the better equipped Goodwill. The center developed an Employment Office, a Medical, and a Legal Clinic, a Dental Clinic and a General Welfare Office. The Center has followed the Mexicans as they moved from the Plaza area to other homes on the East side of the city. The work, however, is the same. Today several of the leaders in both church and social service have come from the Gardena School and from the influence of the Plaza Church and the Community Center. Both the Superintendent of the School and of the Center are Mexicans today. These institutions are living and growing memorials to the love, devotion, and tireless labors of Vernon Monroe McCombs, who died in Los Angeles, Calif., on March 15, 1951, and is buried in Forest Lawn Cemetery, Glendale, Calif.

E. D. Jervey, *Southern California and Arizona.* 1960.
Journals of the Southern California Conference, ME, 1911, 1912, 1920, and of the Southern California-Arizona Conference, TMC, 1951. JOHN GABRIELSON

McCONNELL, CHARLES MELVIN (1886-1957), an American clergyman and educator, son of Israel and Nancy Jane (Chalfant) McConnell and brother of Bishop

FRANCIS J. MCCONNELL, was born on Jan. 16, 1886. He was educated at OHIO WESLEYAN (B.A., 1907) and BOSTON UNIVERSITY SCHOOL OF THEOLOGY (S.T.B., 1910). CORNELL COLLEGE honored him with the D.D. in 1941. In the NORTH-EAST OHIO CONFERENCE, he was received on trial in 1909 and in full connection, 1911. His appointments were as follows: Middlefield, 1910-12; Berea, 1913; Lakeville-Newkirk, 1914-20; Board of Sunday Schools, 1921-23; representative of the General Board of Home Missions and Church Extension, 1924-25; professor, Boston University School of Theology, 1926-54.

He married Grace Dimmick in 1911 and to them were born four daughters. Mrs. McConnell died in 1949. In 1953 McConnell married Mrs. Margaret Brown and they made their home in Deering, N. H., where he died, Sept. 6, 1957. Burial was in Delaware, Ohio.

His career included teaching at Andover-Newton Theological School, staff membership with the Interseminary Commission for Training for the Rural Ministry, and activities as a founder of the Methodist Rural Fellowship. *The Methodist Rural Fellowship Bulletin* (Winter, 1957) was dedicated to "Pat" McConnell and carries wonderful tributes to him. He had an unerring sense of the values of rural life and of the need to nourish, to conserve, and to enhance them. In both Methodist and in ecumenical circles he played a leading role in giving spiritual depth and practical expression to the great movement for rural betterment.

Journal of the New Hampshire Conference, 1958.

WILLIAM J. DAVIS

McCONNELL, DOROTHY (1900-   ), American editor and author, was born at Ipswich, Mass., Sept. 18, 1900, daughter of FRANCIS JOHN and Eva (Thomas) MCCONNELL.

She received the A.B. degree from OHIO WESLEYAN UNIVERSITY in 1920, and the M.A. degree in 1922 from Columbia University.

She was a social worker, 1922-26, and an editor, 1926-32. From 1940 to 1966 she was editor of *World Outlook*, periodical of the BOARD OF MISSIONS of The Methodist Church, New York, New York.

Miss McConnell has served as a member of the Board of Higher Education in Asia, on the executive committee of the WORLD METHODIST COUNCIL, on the national board of the Y.W.C.A., committee member of the NATIONAL COUNCIL OF THE CHURCHES OF CHRIST in the U.S.A., and of the WORLD COUNCIL OF CHURCHES.

She is the author of *Friends of Nippon, Sugar is Sweet, Focus on Latin America, Pattern of Things to Come, Contemporary Man and the United Nations,* and co-author of *Sharing The Gift.* She continues to reside in New York.

Who's Who in the Methodist Church, 1966.   J. MARVIN RAST

McCONNELL, FRANCIS JOHN (1871-1953), American bishop, was born on a farm about five miles from Trinway, Ohio, on Aug. 18, 1871, the son of I. H. and Nancy J. (Chalfant) McConnell. His father and one of his brothers were Methodist preachers. He was educated at OHIO WESLEYAN (A.B., 1894) and BOSTON UNIVERSITY (S.T.B., 1897; Ph.D., 1899). Eleven institutions, including Harvard, Yale, Boston, and Ohio Wesleyan Universities, awarded him honorary degrees. On March 11, 1897, he

FRANCIS J. MCCONNELL

married Eva Thomas, and they had two sons and one daughter.

McConnell joined the NEW ENGLAND CONFERENCE in 1894. He had four appointments in MASSACHUSETTS— West Chelmsford, 1894-97; Newton Upper Falls, 1897-99; Ipswich, 1899-02; and Harvard Street, Cambridge, 1902-03—and was pastor of New York Avenue Church, BROOKLYN, 1903-09. He served as president of DEPAUW UNIVERSITY, 1909-12, and was elected bishop in the latter year. His episcopal residence was in DENVER, Colo., 1912-20; PITTSBURGH, Pa., 1920-28; and NEW YORK, 1928-44. He retired in 1944.

He was president of the FEDERAL COUNCIL OF THE CHURCHES OF CHRIST IN AMERICA, 1929, and was president of the Religious Education Association in 1916. He was a leader in the METHODIST FEDERATION FOR SOCIAL ACTION from its founding in 1912 to his retirement in 1944.

Bishop McConnell and Edgar S. Brightman were recognized as the two most famous students of BORDEN P. BOWNE, the personalist philosopher of Boston University. Bowne once told McConnell that if he planned to enter the ministry, he should pursue the study of philosophy long enough to earn the Ph.D. degree, and then concentrate on economics and political theory. Later McConnell said that he could work any problem in mathematics ever given him, but still he might make a mistake "in the additions and subtractions."

A great preacher, more intellectual than emotional, McConnell was one of the eleven American Methodists who up to his time delivered the Lyman Beecher lectures at Yale (1930). In 1931 he was the Barrows lecturer in INDIA. He served as visiting professor at Columbia University, 1932-33, at DREW and GARRETT SEMINARIES in 1934, and at Yale in 1946. His sermons were simpler than his lectures.

While president of DePauw, McConnell attended more to the spiritual development of the students than to the finances of the institution. He astounded church people by urging the Indiana legislature to appropriate more money for state schools because, he said, it would result in more money being given to DePauw.

During McConnell's episcopal residence in Denver, the area included MEXICO, a nation then undergoing revolution. In administering the area, he traveled an average of 42,000 miles a year.

McConnell received both praise and condemnation for serving as chairman of the Interchurch World Movement Committee to investigate and report on the Pittsburgh steel strike in 1919. A strong champion of human rights on moral and religious grounds, he disregarded the pressure brought to bear on him to repudiate the committee's report. In the end the report proved helpful in eliminating the twelve-hour day in the steel mills, and some of the industrialists later became McConnell's friends. After the steel strike McConnell was recognized as an ecclesiastical leader of the first rank.

In a debate with Clarence Darrow, the famous agnostic lawyer, Bishop McConnell granted so many of the attorney's contentions that it surprised Darrow. Then in a masterful way McConnell showed that there is intelligence in the universe. Taking Darrow's premises and leading the man into what for him was a new field of thought, McConnell presented impressive and all but unanswerable arguments in favor of theism.

In writing a 1,000-word weekly article for *The Church School Journal* for thirty years, Bishop McConnell published about 3,500,000 words. In addition, he produced twenty-four books. Some of them were: *Is God Limited?* 1924; *The Christlike God*, 1927; *Borden Parker Bowne*, 1929; *The Prophetic Ministry*, 1930; *John Wesley*, 1939; and *By the Way*, 1952, which was his autobiography.

As was the case with John Wesley, Bishop McConnell met the needs of the people at the place of their greatest need. He was one of the foremost American prophets of neighborly concern during his generation. In intellect, in religious insight, and in world-wide sympathy, he stood forth as a scholarly seer, a practical theologian, and a prophet of the social gospel. He died at his home in Lucasville, Ohio, on his eighty-second birthday, Aug. 18, 1953, and was buried there. Bishop FREDERICK B. NEWELL of New York officiated at the funeral, and two masterful addresses by Bishop HERBERT WELCH, then past ninety, and HARRIS F. RALL, were read by sponsors, with Bishop U. V. W. DARLINGTON among those in attendance.

Eva Thomas McConnell (July 23, 1871-Feb. 19, 1968), the wife of Bishop McConnell, was a remarkable woman in her own right and enjoyed wide esteem over the whole church. For some years she was vice-president of the WOMAN'S FOREIGN MISSIONARY SOCIETY of the M. E. Church and traveled widely with her husband. Speaking at a final dinner given in his honor by the New York Area on his retirement, Bishop McConnell said that his wife had asked him a few days before just what was meant by a "realist." The bishop said, "I'm not sure I know, but if there ever was one, she is." She died at Lucasville, Ohio, in her ninety-seventh year.

Homer J. Chalfant, "The Golden Links." Ms., 1962.
The Christian Advocate, Sept. 3, 1953.
F. J. McConnell, *By the Way*. 1952.   ALBEA GODBOLD
N. B. H.

McCORMICK, THOMAS (1792-1883), a charter member of historic St. John's Church, BALTIMORE, Md., was one of eleven preachers in Baltimore who were expelled from the M. E. Church because of their advocacy of reform in the church government. He was born in Loudoun County, Va., on Jan. 5, 1792, but following the death of his mother he was reared by his uncle, Thomas Moore, in Montgomery County, Md., and brought up in a Quaker atmosphere. He visited Methodist churches, however, and in 1811 joined the M. E. Church. He was licensed to exhort in 1816 and in the following year was licensed to preach. On April 21, 1822, he was ordained deacon by Bishop McKENDREE. McCormick served as a pallbearer at Bishop FRANCIS ASBURY's funeral in 1816. He attended the GENERAL CONFERENCES of 1816 and 1820. An early advocate of ecclesiastical reform, McCormick joined the first Union or Reform Society in Baltimore, and following the establishment of the Associated Methodist Church, later known as the METHODIST PROTESTANT CHURCH, he was ordained an elder by NICHOLAS SNETHEN on April 5, 1829. Following a long and active career in the M. P. Church, he was elected as a supernumerary member of the MARYLAND CONFERENCE (MP) in 1869. He later served as a member of the famous Union Convention of 1877 in which the two branches of the M. P. Church re-united.

He died on Feb. 20, 1883, and was buried in Mount Olivet Cemetery in Baltimore.

A. H. Bassett, *Concise History*. 1887.
T. H. Colhouer, *Sketches of the Founders*. 1880.
E. J. Drinkhouse, *History of Methodist Reform*. 1899.
RALPH HARDEE RIVES

JAMES H. McCOY

McCOY, JAMES HENRY (1868-1919), American bishop, was born in Blount County, Ala., on Aug. 6, 1868. He received the degrees of B.A., M.A. and D.D. from Southern University, Greensboro, Ala., now BIRMINGHAM SOUTHERN COLLEGE. He joined the NORTH ALABAMA CONFERENCE in 1889, and served the Ensley Circuit and churches in New Decatur, Dadeville, Alexander City, BIRMINGHAM, TUSCALOOSA and Huntsville.

He was editor of the *Alabama Christian Advocate* for one year and was president of Birmingham College from 1906-1910. He was elected bishop of the M. E. Church, South, by the GENERAL CONFERENCE in 1910. He served as president of the EPWORTH LEAGUE Board and trustee of various institutions of learning. He died March 22, 1919.

Bishop McCoy was a man of singularly modest demeanor. His strength was in his sincerity and the utter trust his brethren of North Alabama had come to repose in him. He did not live to become widely known over the whole church, dying in an untimely way when he was only fifty-one years of age. He presided only once back in and over his own home conference held in Anniston, Ala., in 1913. "From his election to the episcopacy until his death," says Lazenby, "his name was carried at the head of the clerical roll of the Conference as an honorary member."

M. E. Lazenby, *Alabama and West Florida.* 1960.
Who Was Who in America.   ELMER T. CLARK

McCOY, LEWISTINE M. (1918-   ), American missionary to CHINA and BRAZIL, and now Executive Secretary for Brazil, MEXICO, PANAMA and COSTA RICA of the BOARD OF MISSIONS of The United Methodist Church. He was born on March 9, 1918 in Lexington, Ky., and graduated from KENTUCKY WESLEYAN COLLEGE in 1940. In 1943 he married Jessie Marion Wall of NORTH CAROLINA, a graduate of DUKE UNIVERSITY. They have five children.

After receiving his B.D. in 1944 from the Divinity School at Duke University, McCoy joined the KENTUCKY CONFERENCE. For a year he taught Bible and Religion at Kentucky Wesleyan; then, planning to go to China as a missionary, he spent a year at Yale studying the Chinese language and culture. The McCoys sailed for China, and arrived in Shangahi on Dec. 31, 1946. He was ordained elder in the East China Conference, served as co-pastor at Huchow Institutional Church and as Relief Administrator until forced to leave China because of the Communist take-over. The McCoys moved to HONG KONG, and there he opened the first American Methodist office; helped some 400 missionaries to leave China, and find other work; served as treasurer of Church World Service, of the American Mission to Lepers, the United Board of Christian Colleges, and some Brethren and Mennonite groups.

In 1951 he came back to the United States on furlough and in 1952 was appointed to Brazil. During the next ten years there, McCoy served as church pastor, treasurer for the old Division of World Missions, and for the Woman's Division of Christian Service. He was president of the Social Security Department of the Methodist Church of Brazil and of its JUDICIAL COUNCIL; as president of the Board of Directors of the Interdenominational Language School in Campinas (São Paulo), and a member of other church Boards. He was twice elected delegate to the General Conference of the Methodist Church of Brazil. In 1961 he was named delegate from Brazil to the Second Latin-American Protestant Conference in LIMA, PERU; and in 1962, was made Executive Secretary of the first Latin American Methodist Consultation, held in BUENOS AIRES. In 1958 Kentucky Wesleyan awarded him the honorary title of D.D.

McCoy was called to NEW YORK in 1963 to be the Executive Secretary of the Joint Commission on Missionary Personnel. In September 1965, he was elected Executive Secretary for Brazil, Mexico, Panama and Costa Rica in the Division of World Missions. He also serves on the Administrative Committee of the Latin America Department of the Division of Overseas Ministries of the NATIONAL COUNCIL OF CHURCHES, and is Chairman of the Supporting Committee on Brazil within that department. Recently, he was elected to the Board of Trustees of Santiago College, CHILE.

Minutes of the East China Conference, 1946-49.
Minutes of the Third Annual Conference in Brazil, 1952.
Who's Who in the Methodist Church, 1966.   EULA K. LONG

M'CULLAGH, THOMAS (1822-1908), British Wesleyan Methodist, was born at New Inn, Galway, IRELAND, on Feb. 17, 1822. He was brought up in the Established Church of Ireland, but became a Methodist in Kilkenny in 1839. He was employed by the Ordnance Survey; and in 1841 his work took him to Yorkshire, where his increasing devotion to Methodism led him into the Wesleyan ministry in 1845. He soon became a preacher known all over the country and was a respected superintendent and chairman. In 1875 he was elected to the LEGAL HUNDRED, and the presidency of the Conference followed in 1883. His literary work appeared mostly in journals, and revealed his considerable interest in Methodist history. He died on Nov. 11, 1908.

Minutes of the Wesleyan Conference, 1909.
G. J. Stevenson, *Methodist Worthies,* iv. 1885.
                          H. MORLEY RATTENBURY

McCULLOCH, JOSEPH FLAVIUS (1856-1934), American educator, minister, and editor, was born in Guilford County, N. C., Jan. 24, 1856. He received his education at ADRIAN COLLEGE, Johns Hopkins University, and Clark University. He served on the faculty of Adrian College and the University of Michigan, and later returned as President of Adrian College.

McCulloch had one supreme purpose in his life, and that was to see the establishment in NORTH CAROLINA of a college for members of the M. P. Church. He worked toward that goal for forty years.

In 1893 McCulloch moved to GREENSBORO, N. C., and established a church paper, *Our Church Record,* which first appeared in 1894. It was later called the *Methodist Protestant Herald.* His reason for starting the paper was to create sentiment for the building of a M. P. college in North Carolina. He saw his dream realized when the cornerstone of Roberts Hall, the first building on the campus of HIGH POINT COLLEGE, was laid in 1924. The boy's dormitory was named McCulloch Hall in recognition of McCulloch's patient crusade.

A quiet, determined man who was so engrossed in his work and purpose that he allowed few people to get to know him well, McCulloch was respected as a man of deep conviction and high ideals.

He died in Greensboro, N. C., Oct. 1, 1934.

J. Elwood Carroll, *History of the North Carolina Conference of the Methodist Protestant Church.* Greensboro, 1939.
Minutes of the North Carolina Conference, MP, 1934.
                                    J. C. MADISON

McCULLOCH, MARY ELIZABETH BARROW (1858-1924), outstanding leader in the woman's work of the M. P. Church, was born near Oberlin, Ohio, on April 9, 1858. She attended school at Blissfield, Mich., and at ADRIAN COLLEGE where she and her husband-to-be, Joseph F.

McCulloch, graduated in 1883. They were married in September of that year. Mrs. McCulloch took an active role in supporting the work of her husband while he served as President of Adrian College, and as minister in churches in Fairmont, W. Va., and GREENSBORO, N. C. She did pioneer work in organizing, expanding, extending and strengthening the North Carolina Branch of the WOMAN'S FOREIGN MISSIONARY SOCIETY of the M. P. Church. The women of this organization paid the following tribute to her: "To Mrs. McCulloch's far-sighted leadership, her quiet suggestion and her spirit of hopefulness we owe much that we have gained. For nearly twenty years she led us, always forward, steadily upward, pushing toward the great objective with that active faith that must achieve even if conditions were unfavorable." She served (1902-1920) as the editor of *The Woman's Missionary Record*, a M. P. paper aimed toward creating a missionary spirit by letting its readers know the need and work being accomplished in the mission field. She died in November 1924, and was buried in the cemetery at Tabernacle Church, Greensboro, N. C.

J. Elwood Carroll, *History of the North Carolina Conference of the Methodist Protestant Church.* Greensboro, 1939.
Mrs. E. C. Chandler, *WFMS of the MP.* 1920.
Journal of the North Carolina Conference, MP, 1924.

RALPH HARDEE RIVES

McCULLOH, GERALD OTHO (1912-   ), American minister and church official, was born at Auburn, Kan., Sept. 10, 1912, son of Otho John and Eva (Skaggs) McCulloh.

He was graduated with the A.B. degree from BAKER UNIVERSITY in 1932, and by that University he was awarded the D.D. degree in 1954. He received the M.A. degree from BOSTON UNIVERSITY in 1934 and the S.T.B. there in 1935. In 1938 he received the Ph.D. degree from the University of Edinburgh (Scotland). He was awarded the D.D. degree by HAMLINE UNIVERSITY, and the L.H.D. by OHIO NORTHERN UNIVERSITY.

Admitted on trial into the KANSAS CONFERENCE, M. E. Church, and ordained DEACON in 1934, he was received in full connection and ordained ELDER in 1936.

He was professor of philosophy in Hamline University, 1938-42; minister, Hamline Church, ST. PAUL, Minn., 1942-46; professor, systematic theology, GARRETT THEOLOGICAL SEMINARY, 1946-53. Since 1953 he has been director of the Department of Ministerial Education of the General BOARD OF EDUCATION of The Methodist Church, known now as the Department of the Ministry, in which he continues at NASHVILLE, Tenn.

He was a delegate to the WORLD METHODIST CONFERENCE, 1951, 1956, 1961, 1966; to the World Conference on Christian Education, Tokyo, Japan, 1958; and to the WORLD COUNCIL OF CHURCHES, New Delhi, India, 1961, and Uppsala, Sweden, 1968. Since 1956 he has been a member of the department of ministry, and since 1962 of the triennial assembly and the General Board of the NATIONAL COUNCIL OF CHURCHES.

Since 1953 he has been a trustee of GAMMON THEOLOGICAL SEMINARY; and since 1957 he has been a trustee of the Interdenominational Theological Center, Atlanta, Ga., and of ST. PAUL SCHOOL OF THEOLOGY. He is also a trustee of Hamline University. He is a member of the American Society for Church History and of the American Philosophical Association.

On June 8, 1939 he was married to Evelyn Belle Butler, and they have two children.

Who's Who in the Methodist Church, 1966.   J. MARVIN RAST

McCULLOUGH, WILLIAM (1759-1840), American layman, who named Asbury, N. J., was born near Bloomsbury, Warren Co., N. J., on Dec. 18, 1759, the son of Benjamin and Hannah Cook McCullough. Both father and son served in the Revolutionary Army, the former as a captain, and the latter, seventeen years old when he enlisted in 1776, as a private, later becoming brigade quartermaster.

In 1784, William settled in Hall's Mills, N. J. In 1793 he became a lieutenant colonel of the Sussex County Militia, and thereafter was called "Colonel." He was a member of the New Jersey State Assembly, 1793-1799, the State Council, 1801-1803, and County Judge, 1803-1838.

McCullough was converted and joined a Methodist society in 1786 under the preaching of John McClaskey and EZEKIEL COOPER. His mansion on a bluff overlooking the Musconetcong River was a place of entertainment and preaching for the preachers, and there he welcomed Bishop ASBURY in 1789. The meeting house at Hall's Mills was erected in 1796, and Asbury laid the cornerstone on August 9. Colonel McCullough named both the church and the town for the bishop; Hall's Mills was the first community in America to be called Asbury, and the same was true of the church. He had the Warren County community of Mansfield renamed Washington, in honor of George Washington. He aided in the establishment of a Methodist society there and gave the property on which the First Methodist Church was erected in 1825.

McCullough died on Feb. 9, 1840, and was buried in the cemetery at Asbury, N. J.

V. B. Hampton, *Newark Conference.* 1957.
History of Asbury Church. n.d.   VERNON B. HAMPTON

McCUSKEY, ROY (1883-   ), American pastor, district superintendent, and college president, was born four miles from Cameron, W. Va., on June 19, 1883.

He entered the WEST VIRGINIA CONFERENCE of the M. E. Church and after serving a number of appointments became President of WEST VIRGINIA WESLEYAN COLLEGE, 1931-41. Then he served St. Paul's, Parkersburg from 1941 until his retirement in 1949.

He was a delegate to the GENERAL CONFERENCES of 1924, 1932, 1936, and 1940.

Roy McCuskey did more than any man to save the college during the depression of the early thirties. After unification, he kept the institution in Buckhannon, W. Va., where it is said to have the most beautiful campus in America. Under McCuskey one-half the members of the West Virginia M. E. Conference were then trained at Wesleyan. Dr. McCuskey resides in Parkersburg, W. Va.

Methodist Ministers of the West Virginia Conference.
Roy McCuskey, *All Things Work Together for Good to Them That Love God.*   JESSE A. EARL

McCUTCHAN, ROBERT GUY (1877-1958), American musician, hymnologist and editor of *The Methodist Hymnal* (U.S.A.) of 1935, was born Sept. 13, 1877, at Mt. Ayr,

Iowa. He graduated from SIMPSON COLLEGE, Iowa, Bachelor of Music, 1904, and Doctor of Music in 1927. He began teaching music in BAKER UNIVERSITY, Kansas, 1904, but in 1911 became dean of the School of Music of DE-PAUW UNIVERSITY Indiana. In 1939 McCutchan went to Claremont, Calif., becoming a lecturer in the Claremont Graduate School in 1940 and there he remained until his death in 1958.

His first wife was Carrie Burns Sharp whom he married on Nov. 23, 1904 (deceased 1941), and they had one son, Robert John. He married again on Dec. 11, 1944, Helen Laura Cowles.

A skilled choral conductor, Robert McCutchan developed wide interest in congregational singing throughout the country and lectured on church music to church groups and at colleges and universities. He made a practice of collecting church hymnals, commentaries, and early American writings on religious music beginning with the seventeenth century. He left 3,000 such items to Claremont College in 1957. This collection is considered to be the finest of its field in the west.

McCutchan once observed: "Hymns have always filled the common need of human beings to praise God, give thanks, meditate or speak in penitence. When you want to discover the essential spirit of Christianity, turn to a hymn." He edited *The Methodist Hymnal* of 1935 and wrote *Our Hymnody*, 1937—an annotated enlargement of this hymnal. He also wrote *Hymns in the Lives of Men*, 1945; *Music in our Churches*, 1925, and *Music in Worship*, 1927. In 1957 he wrote his last book, *Hymn Tunes: Their Sources and Significance*. He died on May 15, 1958, at Pilgrim Place, Claremont, Calif., and was buried in Greencastle, Ind.

Pomona Progress Bulletin, The. Pomona, California: May 15, 1958.
Who's Who in Methodism. Chicago: A. N. Marquis Co., 1952.
JESSE A. EARL

MACDONALD, FREDERIC WILLIAM (1842-1928), British Methodist, was born at LEEDS, Feb. 25, 1842, the son of George Browne Macdonald, a Wesleyan Methodist minister, and grandson of James Macdonald, one of John Wesley's preachers. Frederic was educated at St. Peter's Collegiate School, London, and at Owens College, Manchester, the earliest form of what was to become the present Manchester University. He entered the Wesleyan Methodist ministry in 1862, and served as circuit minister, theological tutor at Handsworth College, BIRMINGHAM (from 1881), and secretary of the Wesleyan METHODIST MISSIONARY SOCIETY (from 1891). He was a fraternal delegate to the GENERAL CONFERENCE of the M. E. Church at CINCINNATI in 1880 and was elected president of the Wesleyan Conference in 1899. He superannuated in 1914, and died in Bournemouth, Oct. 16, 1928. He was most famous as one of the preachers of his time; he also wrote biographies of WILLIAM MORLEY PUNSHON and JOHN W. FLETCHER of Madeley.

Macdonald came from a remarkable family. His sisters Georgiana and Agnes married respectively the painters Sir Edward Burne-Jones and Sir Edward Poynter; and Alice and Louisa became the respective mothers of Rudyard Kipling, poet and novelist, and Earl Stanley Baldwin of Bewdley, Conservative leader and prime minister. One result of this relationship, we are told, was that

Kipling sometimes made suggestions about the phrasing of Baldwin's speeches.

Methodist Recorder (1899). *Wesleyan Methodist Minutes*, 1929.
JOHN NEWTON

McDONALD, WILLIAM (1820-1901), American holiness minister, writer, and editor, was born March 1, 1820, at Belmont, Maine. He was converted and received his call to the ministry in 1838 and was licensed to preach in 1840. In 1843 he joined the MAINE CONFERENCE of the M. E. Church. During his sixty-one years of active service he was pastor of charges in MAINE, WISCONSIN, PROVIDENCE, NEW YORK EAST, and NEW ENGLAND CONFERENCES, some twenty-six charges in all.

McDonald stated that he experienced entire SANCTIFICATION in 1857 at the Kennebunk (Maine) CAMPMEETING, and as the holiness movement progressed he came quickly to the front. He was one of the founders of the National Campmeeting Association for the Promotion of Holiness and served as vice-president for sixteen years and president for twelve. He was the first editor of the *Advocate of Bible Holiness*, the Association's national periodical, and later edited the *Christian Witness*.

He wrote numerous books in a variety of fields. His most popular were his holiness books, *The New Testament Standard of Piety* and *The Scriptural Way of Holiness*. He wrote a history of Methodism in Providence, R. I., where he had organized the Trinity Church. While he lay dying, his last book, *Young Peoples' Wesley*, was at the press. He passed away Sept. 11, 1901.

Zion's Herald, Sept. 11, 18, 1901.
J. GORDON MELTON

MacDONELL, GEORGE NOWLAND (1879-1953), an American missionary to CUBA and MEXICO, was born in Savannah, Ga., the son of George N. and Margaret Walker MacDonell. He was graduated from Emory College, Oxford, Ga., in 1893, then studied theology for three years at VANDERBILT UNIVERSITY. He was first appointed for work in CHINA, and studied the language and customs of the Chinese people. Although his reservation had been made to sail from SAN FRANCISCO, Bishop WARREN A. CANDLER, in charge of both China and Cuba, recognizing the strategic need for workers to go immediately to Cuba, canceled the trip to China and ordered MacDonell to go to Cuba.

Accordingly, he arrived in Havana on Dec. 31, 1898, and the following day the Spanish flag went down and the United States flag went up. The day marked the end of the era of Spanish colonization in the Western Hemisphere. Since there were many American soldiers stationed at Camp Columbia, in Havana, for some months after the end of the War with Spain, he assisted chaplains while studying Spanish.

There was then raging an epidemic of yellow fever with a heavy death toll, which MacDonell noted in his diary. He and his room-mate, Thaddeus E. Leland, came down with the dread disease, and both were nursed back to health by Mabel Kenerly Thrower, a teacher in the Colegio Central of which Leland was principal. While the two men were still sick, they were visited by Major W. C. Gorgas, head of the Army department of sanitation, and Dr. Carlos J. Finlay, Cuban physician who first advanced the theory that the disease was transmitted by the mosquito. They formed a lasting friendship. As associates, MacDonell soon had Hubert W. Baker and H. W. Penny.

He was married in 1900 by Bishop Candler to Mabel K. Thrower, and their first child, George MacDonell, Jr., was born in Havana. Two other sons, Thomas and Robert, and a daughter, Margaret, were born after they left Cuba.

Recognizing the need for medical missions, he asked for leave of absence to study medicine and graduated from Atlanta Medical College, now a part of EMORY UNIVERSITY. On finishing his medical course he engaged in practice as surgeon at the Minas Viejas, near Villaldama, and later conducted the American hospital in Monterrey, Nuevo Leon, Mexico.

After ten years in Mexico, he retired from that field due to severe revolutionary conditions which forced American citizens to be recalled to the U.S. He moved to Miami, Fla., where he became head of the city health department. He was awarded the Carlos J. Finlay medal by the Cuban government for his continued interest in Cuba, and his research with Finlay on the transmission of yellow fever by the mosquito.

His widow continued the missionary zeal of her partner and for many years was vitally interested in the missionary work of The Methodist Church. She passed away in Miami, on Feb. 23, 1968.

S. A. Neblett, *Methodism in Cuba.* 1966. GARFIELD EVANS

MacDONELL, ROBERT WALKER

MacDONELL, ROBERT WALKER (1857-1888), pioneer missionary to MEXICO of the M. E. Church, South, was born in Savannah, Ga., on Oct. 11, 1857, the son of George G. N. MacDonell. His primary education was in the public schools of SAVANNAH and then he attended EMORY COLLEGE at Oxford, Ga., graduating in 1877. He was converted in a CAMP MEETING near Springfield in October 1872, and received into the church in November of that year. Having finished college, he taught school for a time and was then licensed to preach in 1877 and admitted to the SOUTH GEORGIA CONFERENCE on trial. For a time he served a circuit in South GEORGIA. He felt the call to the mission field in 1880, and Bishop GEORGE F. PIERCE presented his name to the BOARD OF MISSIONS for that work. He was accepted in May 1880, but was permitted by the Board of Missions to remain in Georgia for the rest of that year, serving at Savannah in place of a pastor who had been injured in a railroad accident. He was ordained DEACON and ELDER in December 1880, by Bishop Pierce. On December 28 of that year, he was united in marriage with Fachie Williams, the daughter of W. D. M. Williams, president of the State Institute for the Blind. They traveled to Mexico early the next year.

He served in several places in Mexico—for a time as superintendent of the District of Leon and in April 1884, was transferred to the American Church in EL PASO. He maintained his interest in and contact with the Mexican believers during this time, however. In 1885, he was charged with opening a new mission in the city of Durango, capital of the state of the same name. He was well-received and soon a school was opened with the cooperation of Catherine McFarren, a Presbyterian. He obtained the right to be known as the "Apostle of Methodism" in the state of Durango. His influence widened and he was respected throughout the area.

At a conference in SAN ANTONIO in 1885, the missions in the far-reaching territories of the area were formed into an Annual Conference and MacDonell was named secretary of this body. This organization was the forerunner of the RIO GRANDE CONFERENCE of the present. At times, the district superintendent did not arrive when scheduled for conferences and other meetings and MacDonell presided in his absence. In 1886, at the Annual Conference in Monterrey, H. C. Hernández was named assistant to MacDonell and his help proved most valuable in maintaining the work established at Nombre de Dios and San Juan del Río as well as in the capital. At the following session of the Annual Conference in 1887, a new District was formed of the work in Durango, Chihuahua, Sonora and Sinaloa in Mexico and of the American territories of NEW MEXICO, ARIZONA and the mission at El Paso. MacDonell was named District Superintendent. He died at Nombre de Dios on Dec. 21, 1888, after a hard ride on horseback to keep a preaching engagement.

N. B. H.

McDOUGALL, GEORGE MILLWARD

McDOUGALL, GEORGE MILLWARD (1821-1876), Canadian Methodist missionary, was born in Kingston, Upper Canada, Ontario, on Sept. 9, 1821. Educated at VICTORIA COLLEGE, he was received on trial in 1850. As a probationer he worked with WILLIAM CASE at Alderville and subsequently served at the Garden River and Rama missions. Ordained in 1854, he was appointed in 1860 as chairman of the Hudson's Bay and Rocky Mountains district and missionary at Rossville, Manitoba.

After a 1,200-mile exploratory trip to Fort Edmonton in 1862 with his son John and THOMAS WOOLSEY, he established a new mission about eighty miles east of Edmonton. Here he worked with Woolsey, H. B. STEINHAUER, and John as a lay assistant. In 1867-68 he visited eastern CANADA to raise money to recruit men for his field. George and Egerton Ryerson Young and Peter Campbell responded to his appeal.

Following a great smallpox epidemic in 1871, during which he lost two children and many of his Indian charges, he established a permanent mission at Edmonton, a post first occupied by R. T. RUNDLE in 1840. Two years later he opened a new mission on the Bow River to the Stoney and Blackfoot Indians. In 1874-75 he returned to the east and to Britain. His mission was exceptionally successful in arousing enthusiasm for the Indian missions and in persuading the federal government to improve the condition of the Northwest.

Upon his return to the west, McDougall was asked by Lieutenant-Governor Morris of Manitoba to pacify the western Indians. They accepted his advice and did not block the work of surveyors and other federal officials.

While he was engaged in January 1876, in putting up new buildings at Morleyville on the Bow River, McDougall perished on the plains. He was buried at the mission site.

George McDougall was the effective founder of Methodist and indeed Protestant Christianity in Alberta. To Principal Grant of the Queen's University, he was "one of our simple great ones." Governor Laird acclaimed him as "one of the most devoted and intelligent advisers the Indians ever had."

J. McDougall, *George Millward McDougall, Pioneer, Patriot and Missionary.* Toronto: Briggs, 1888.
J. McLean, *The Hero of the Saskatchewan.* Barrie, 1891.
J. E. Nix, *Mission Among the Buffalo.* Toronto: Ryerson, 1960.
J. E. NIX
F. W. ARMSTRONG

McDOUGALL, JOHN (1842-1917), Canadian Methodist missionary to the Indians, was born at Owen Sound, Ontario, Dec. 27, 1842, and was married in 1864 to Abigail, daughter of HENRY B. STEINHAUER, and after her death in 1871 to Elizabeth, daughter of S. C. Boyd. His parents were the GEORGE M. McDOUGALLS, also missionaries to the Canadian Indians. His education was acquired in mission and village schools in Ontario, and two sessions at VICTORIA COLLEGE, Cobourg. He left college to accompany his father to his mission station in Manitoba, where young John taught school. Moving with his father's family to Victoria Mission, near Fort Edmonton, he continued as his father's lay assistant and interpreter, being stationed at Pigeon Lake as a lay supply. He was ordained July 30, 1872, at the missionary conference held at Winnipeg, Manitoba. In 1873 he began a new mission to the Stoney and Blackfoot Indians at Morleyville, then in unsettled territory. On the death of his father in 1876, he became chairman of the Saskatchewan district in the Methodist Church, a position he held until 1896.

He served as president of the Manitoba and North West Conference in 1893 and of the Alberta Conference in 1906, and as delegate to General Conference in 1886, 1890, and 1894. He was granted the doctorate of divinity by Victoria College, Toronto. After retirement in 1906, he was appointed by the Canadian government as commissioner to the Doukhobors and Indian commissioner for British Columbia, Alberta, and Saskatchewan.

Between 1888 and 1912 he wrote a biography of his father, a series of six volumes of personal memoirs, a novel, and many newspaper and magazine articles on the west.

An ardent Canadian nationalist, he advised the Indians at the signing of Treaties 6 and 7 with the federal government and acted as guide, scout, and chaplain during the Northwest Rebellion in 1885. His missionary career had spanned the transition of the Canadian West from a Hudson's Bay fur-trading empire to a peaceful agricultural settlement, and the Indians' transition from nomads dependent on the buffalo to a new life on the reserves. He died in Calgary on Jan. 15, 1917.

J. McDougall, *On Western Trails in the Early Seventies.* Toronto: Briggs, 1911.
————————, *In the Days of the Red River Rebellion.* Toronto: Briggs, 1903.
John Maclean, *McDougall of Alberta.* Toronto: Ryerson, 1927.

J. E. NIX

McDOWELL, WILLIAM FRASER (1858-1937), American bishop, was born at Millersburg, Ohio, Feb. 4, 1858, the son of David A. and Rebecca (Fraser) McDowell. His father, a devoted layman, was a member of the 1904 GENERAL CONFERENCE. Young McDowell was educated at OHIO WESLEYAN UNIVERSITY (A.B., 1879, and Ph.D., 1893), and BOSTON UNIVERSITY (S.T.B., 1882). AMERICAN, DENVER, NORTHWESTERN, Ohio Wesleyan, Vermont, and WESLEYAN UNIVERSITIES conferred honorary degrees on him—D.D., LL.D., and L.H.D. He married Clotilda Lyon, Galion, Ohio, the daughter of a Methodist minister, Sept. 20, 1882. They had one daughter, Olive, who died while still a young woman. Mrs. McDowell, president of the WOMAN'S FOREIGN MISSIONARY SOCIETY (ME), 1908-21, died Dec. 27, 1930.

McDowell was admitted to the NORTH OHIO CONFERENCE in 1882, and was ordained DEACON in 1883 and ELDER in 1886. He served three charges in the conference:

Lodi, 1882-83; Oberlin, 1883-85; and Tiffin, 1885-90. In the latter year he was named Chancellor of the University of Denver, serving nine years. While in that position he delivered the first series of university extension lectures ever given in the state, using the subject, "Some Studies in the French Revolution." Also, while in Denver he served on the state board of charities and correction.

In 1899 McDowell became Corresponding Secretary of the BOARD OF EDUCATION (ME). In 1900 he was a delegate to the GENERAL CONFERENCE from the COLORADO CONFERENCE, and in 1904 he led the North Ohio Conference delegation to the General Conference. At that time he was elected bishop and served in CHICAGO, 1904-16; and in WASHINGTON, D. C., 1916-32, retiring in the latter year. In 1910-11 he made episcopal visits to INDIA, CHINA, JAPAN, and the PHILIPPINES.

Widely recognized as a great preacher, McDowell was invited to deliver the prestigious Lyman Beecher Lectures on Preaching at Yale Divinity School in 1917. He gave the following lectures at educational institutions: Cole, VANDERBILT, 1910; Mendenhall, DEPAUW, 1922; Merrick, Ohio Wesleyan, 1926; Earl, Pacific School of Religion, 1926; Alumni, GAMMON, 1927; Wilkin, WESLEY FOUNDATION, Illinois, 1928; and Drew at Drew, 1933. When in his eightieth year, just two months before his death, McDowell delivered a series of lectures at BOSTON UNIVERSITY which were later published under the title, *In All His Offices.* Commenting on the man and the occasion, President DANIEL L. MARSH said, "After eleven years, I do not recall that I ever witnessed anything quite comparable to that week at Boston University. Bishop McDowell had the spirit of a patriarch and the bearing of a kindly king. Students wept unashamed. After each lecture, students gathered and talked in a reverent and subdued manner about the things the great bishop had said." Bishop EDWIN H. HUGHES said McDowell was the "most distinctive in manner and speech" of all the bishops, and added, "He specialized in the devotional life. His prayers swung us into God's orbit. His benedictions became equal to a complete service." Others declared that there was hardly a speaker on the American platform in McDowell's day who could equal him in the power to sway an audience.

McDowell was dedicated to the cause of the union of American Methodism and he gave much time and energy to it. He served on his own denomination's commission on union from 1916 until his death in 1937. After the death of Bishop EARL CRANSTON in 1932, McDowell was chairman of the commission. In referring to McDowell's contribution, Bishop JOHN M. MOORE called him "that prince of men, that master of assemblies, that apostle of union, that untiring toiler in the creation of an acceptable and adequate plan of union." Edwin H. Hughes declared that at a meeting of the joint commission in LOUISVILLE, Bishop McDowell "lay in agonized wakefulness until five o'clock in the morning" praying and pondering a solution to the race issue in relation to Methodist union. When the PLAN OF UNION was completed, Bishop McDowell considered it a high privilege to present it to the 1936 General Conference for adoption.

Tall and dignified in bearing, McDowell was impressive in appearance. He looked the part of a church leader, and he always brought statesmanlike qualities to bear on ecclesiastical problems. He was at home in any company; in conversation his wit was brilliant. Withal he was humble. He said, "When I hear men talk about the bishop being the 'chief minister,' and 'chief pastor,' I always think not of the word 'chief' but of being chief '*minister*,' chief '*pastor*' to my brethren."

Between 1910 and 1933 Bishop McDowell wrote eight books: *In the School of Christ, A Man's Religion, Good Ministers of Jesus Christ* (Yale Lectures), *This Mind, Making a Personal Faith, That I May Save Some, Them He Also Called,* and *Father and Brethren.*

On Sunday April 25, 1937, Bishop McDowell preached at Morganton, N. C., and died the next day in Washington, D. C. A funeral service was held at Foundry Church with Bishops McConnell and Hughes as the principal speakers. There was a second service in the chapel at Ohio Wesleyan University with President EDMUND D. SOPER in charge. Burial was in Delaware, Ohio. A handsomely carved pulpit was later installed in the historic Foundry Church in memory of Bishop McDowell.

Christian Advocate, Jan. 16, 1941.
E. H. Hughes, *I Was Made a Minister.* 1943.
F. D. Leete, *Methodist Bishops.* 1948.
W. F. McDowell, *In All His Offices.*
JESSE A. EARL
ALBEA GODBOLD

McFARLAND, JOHN THOMAS (1851-1913), American minister, educator and editor, was born at Mt. Vernon, Ind., on Jan. 2, 1851. His family moved to IOWA in 1853 and he soon enrolled in the preparatory department of IOWA WESLEYAN UNIVERSITY, where he remained until his senior college year. After a year at the BOSTON UNIVERSITY SCHOOL OF THEOLOGY, he served as student pastor in the IOWA CONFERENCE (ME) before returning to Boston University, from which he was graduated in 1878. Accepted into the Iowa Conference, he served a year at Eddyville and in 1879 filled the combined position of the University charge, Mount Pleasant, and adjunct professor of natural science at Iowa Wesleyan. In 1880 he was transferred to the CENTRAL ILLINOIS CONFERENCE for a year each at Elmwood and Peoria. Returning to Iowa Wesleyan in 1882 as Vice President and Professor of Belles Letters and History, he was elected President in 1884. His dynamic leadership until 1891 increased the endowment fund, raised the enrollment, expanded the science and music curricula, developed the museum and laboratories, and initiated work on the Hall of Science and Chapel. He attracted attention in national educational circles and served as a delegate to the 1888 GENERAL CONFERENCE and the 1891 ECUMENICAL METHODIST CONFERENCE.

In 1891 he returned to pastoral work in the ILLINOIS CONFERENCE; in 1895 in the NEW YORK EAST CONFERENCE at the New York Avenue Church, BROOKLYN, and in the KANSAS CONFERENCE at First Church, TOPEKA, 1899-1904. In 1905 he became Corresponding Secretary of the SUNDAY SCHOOL UNION and Tract Society, and in 1909 Editor of the Sunday School Publications. To the task of editing multiple materials for a vast circulation change, he brought learning, insight and flexibility in spite of criticism from ultra conservative areas of the church. He died at Maplewood, N. J. on Dec. 22, 1913. During his career he received an honorary D.D. from the UNIVERSITY OF THE PACIFIC in 1885, an LL.D. from SIMPSON in 1903 and an L.H.D. from Iowa Wesleyan in 1905.

General Minutes, 1880-1914.
Minutes of the Iowa Conference, 1873-1891.
The Methodist Yearbook, 1915.
LOUIS A. HASELMAYER

McFERRIN, JAMES (1784-1840), American pioneer preacher, was born in Washington County, Va., March 25, 1784, of Irish Presbyterian ancestry. He was brought up as a farmer. At age twenty he married, settling in Rutherford County, Tenn.

James McFerrin was a captain in the War of 1812 under General Andrew Jackson; and subsequently suffered great privations in the campaign against the Creek Indians. He was elected Colonel and for several years led the best-trained regiment of state troops.

In 1820 he was converted and immediately began to preach. He was admitted to the TENNESSEE CONFERENCE Nov. 25, 1823. His ministry was in ALABAMA after 1828, and in western TENNESSEE after 1834. He filled a number of prominent appointments and traveled extensively. He reported the following in 1839: "Since I joined the Conference, I have preached 2,080 times, baptized 573 adults and 813 infants, and have taken into society 3,965 members." As a preacher he was somewhat peculiar in his manner, but possessed an indescribable influence over the multitude. He had three sons who entered the ministry. One was JOHN BERRY MCFERRIN, able Southern leader. James McFerrin died in Tipton County, Tenn., Sept. 4, 1840.

Appleton's Cyclopedia of American Biography.
M. Simpson, *Cyclopaedia.* 1878.
JESSE A. EARL

JOHN B. MCFERRIN

McFERRIN, JOHN BERRY (1807-1887), American preacher, editor, and administrator, was born June 15, 1807 in Rutherford County, Tenn. His father, JAMES MCFERRIN, was a Methodist preacher who, before his conversion, had been a farmer and soldier, having served as an officer with General Andrew Jackson in the Creek Indian war.

John McFerrin was converted in 1820, and the next year at the age of fourteen he was called on more and more frequently to deliver prayer during meetings. At sixteen he was appointed a CLASS LEADER, gaining from this experience what he called the best theological training ever organized by the Methodists.

At Cambridge, Ark., Oct. 8, 1825, McFerrin was publicly examined, licensed to preach, and recommended for admission on trial as a traveling preacher in the TENNESSEE CONFERENCE. He was assigned to Franklin Circuit, and delivered his first sermon at Tuscumbia, Ala., as northern ALABAMA was then a part of the Tennessee Conference.

After his ordination as DEACON by Bishop JOSHUA SOULE, McFerrin was sent as a missionary to the Cherokee Indians —a highly responsible assignment to be laid on the shoulders of a young man not yet twenty years old. He preached and conducted a school for the Indian children until 1829, when he was ordained by Bishop ROBERTS and assigned to the Limestone Circuit in north Alabama. He was only twenty-four when he was appointed to Huntsville (Ala.) Station. From there he went to NASHVILLE, Tenn.

Despite his protests about being unready for its responsibilities, McFerrin was appointed presiding elder for the Florence (Ala.) District in 1836. In 1837 he was named presiding elder of the Cumberland District in TENNESSEE.

McFerrin was transferred from the pastorate to the editorial field in 1840, when he was asked to edit the *Christian Advocate*. What was intended as a temporary assignment lasted for eighteen years.

When the split between the Northern and Southern Methodists occurred in 1844, McFerrin supported the position of the South, and provided strong guidance in the organization of the GENERAL CONFERENCE of the M. E. Church, South.

Its General Conference in 1858 elected McFerrin BOOK AGENT, a post he served effectively.

With the outbreak of the War Between the States, he was placed in charge of all Methodist missionary work in the Army of Tennessee (C. S. A.), frequently preaching to the troops.

In 1866 at the General Conference held in NEW ORLEANS, which practically reorganized the M. E. Church, South following the war, he was elected Secretary of Domestic Missions. When this post was combined with that of Secretary of Foreign Missions in 1870, McFerrin won the election to head the work of the Missions board.

For eight years he was Secretary of the BOARD OF MISSIONS, until he was returned to the post of Book Agent at a time when the department was in grave financial difficulties. His experienced management enabled the department to regain its former strength and extend its influence.

An honor that stood out for McFerrin was his election as a delegate to the 1881 ECUMENICAL METHODIST CONFERENCE in LONDON. He also attended the important CENTENNIAL OF AMERICAN METHODISM held in 1884 at BALTIMORE, Md.

So beloved was McFerrin that even in 1886, when his hearing and sight had failed very much, he was named overwhelmingly as the leader of the Tennessee delegation to the General Conference, where he was again elected as Book Agent.

This big, sharp-featured man with prodigious memory and rapier-like wit sat in more General Conferences and occupied connectional offices longer than any man of his day. He was widely known for his ability as a rough-and-tumble debater, and rarely was he defeated.

Although he was best known for his work as an administrator, McFerrin excelled as a preacher. His distinctive, somewhat nasal voice and simple, direct style created a deep impression on his listeners.

One example of the effect McFerrin's preaching had on people is seen in the fact that when U.S. President JAMES KNOX POLK was dying, he sent for J. B. McFerrin. Polk had never before united with a church, but had been Methodist in sentiment since hearing McFerrin preach at a CAMP MEETING in 1833. At the request of the dying ex-President, McFerrin baptized him and received him into the church. When Polk died June 15, 1849, McFerrin delivered the sermon at the funeral.

John B. McFerrin died on May 10, 1887, and was buried in Nashville, Tenn.

O. P. Fitzgerald, *John B. McFerrin, A Biography*. Nashville: Publishing House of the M. E. Church, South, 1888.
Minutes of the Tennessee Conference, 1887.
J. P. Pilkington, *Methodist Publishing House*. 1968.

H. D. WATTS

MacGEARY, JOHN SAMUEL (1853-1931), a missionary bishop of the FREE METHODIST CHURCH, was born near PITTSBURGH, Pa. In early life he taught in rural schools. Converted when about twenty-two years of age, he joined the M. E. Church, and later the Free Methodist Church. Called to the ministry, he was admitted to the Genesee Conference in 1876. He was a charter member of the Pittsburgh Conference, 1883, where he served as pastor and superintendent, and also a charter member of the Oil City Conference of 1899. He served as field secretary for GREENVILLE COLLEGE for several years. In 1911 he was elected the first (and only) missionary bishop of the Free Methodist Church. He travelled in INDIA, CHINA, JAPAN and Africa. He was General Missionary Secretary, 1915-19; pastor and district elder of the California Conference until his death at Oakland, Calif., Jan. 20, 1931. He was the author of: *Outline History of Free Methodist Church*. He was Corresponding Editor of *The Free Methodist* for twenty-two years. John S. MacGeary was a progressive thinker, aggressive church builder, and outstanding pulpiteer.

BYRON S. LAMSON

McGEHEE, EDWARD (1786-1880), prominent American layman of early MISSISSIPPI and LOUISIANA, was born in November 1786 in GEORGIA, but went into Mississippi and settled in Wilkinson County when he was quite a young man. He became wealthy and was a benefactor of the Colonization Society and the AMERICAN BIBLE SOCIETY, and established an academy near his home. He gave largely to CENTENARY COLLEGE when that was founded.

He came to NEW ORLEANS with Mark Moore and WILLIAM WINANS in 1819, and helped to secure a preaching place for these Methodist ministers in the loft of a flour inspector's office. Later on he gave some $40,000 for the church which was first known as Poydras Street, and later Carondelet Street. The official title of the latter church was in time fixed as "The McGehee M. E. Church, South."

Judge McGehee, as he became, served in the Mississippi legislature and was, it is said, offered the place of Secretary of the United States Treasury by Zachary Taylor, then President. McGehee, however, declined to so serve. His handsome residence, Bowling Green, near Woodville, Miss., was burned during the Civil War. He helped to build the first railroad and first cotton factory in the deep South, and is said to have invented the cattle guards which kept cattle from attempting to go upon the railroad trestles and bridges of that day. He was the last survivor of a family of thirteen children, his brothers Abner, Abram, John, and William becoming planters in Mississippi and Louisiana.

Judge McGehee died on Oct 1, 1880. A memorial sermon was delivered by Bishop JOHN C. KEENER at the

Carondelet Street Church on October 31 of that year. Although one son, Micajah, died in an untimely way, the Judge was survived by seven children and many grandchildren.

N. B. H.

McGOVERN, GEORGE STANLEY (1922-   ), United States senator and member of the WORLD METHODIST COUNCIL, was born in Avon, S. D., on July 19, 1922, the son of Joseph C. and Frances (McLean) McGovern. He was educated at DAKOTA WESLEYAN UNIVERSITY and NORTHWESTERN UNIVERSITY, from which he received the M.A. degree in 1949 and the Ph.D. in 1953. His wife was Eleanor Stegeberg, whom he married on Oct. 31, 1943, and they have five children.

For a time Senator McGovern taught history and political science at Dakota Wesleyan University, but in 1956 he was elected to the U.S. House of Representatives from the First District of his state. He was the Food-for-Peace Director in the Kennedy Administration, 1960-62; and was elected a member of the U.S. Senate from SOUTH DAKOTA in 1963. He served as a pilot of the U.S. Air Force in the second World War, and was decorated with the Distinguished Flying Cross. He is the author of *The Colorado Coal Strike, 1913-14*, 1953; *War Against Want*, 1965. He was a candidate for nomination as the Democratic nominee for the Presidency of the United States at the 1968 Democratic Convention, and that same summer served as a delegate to the WORLD COUNCIL OF CHURCHES meeting at UPPSALA, SWEDEN. In 1972 he was the Democratic candidate for the Presidency but was defeated by Richard Nixon.

Who's Who in America, Vol. 34.
Who's Who in the Methodist Church, 1966.   N. B. H.

McINTYRE, ROBERT (1851-1914), American bishop, was born in Selkirk, SCOTLAND, of solid Presbyterian parents, on Nov. 20, 1851. His father was a weaver and brought his family to PHILADELPHIA in America in 1858. His mother died not long after this move, and the father married again, but died, leaving the support of the family to Robert who was then seventeen. The future bishop learned the trade of bricklayer and, at the age of twenty, moved the family to CHICAGO where the great fire just at that time made his services much in demand. McIntyre never forgot his laboring days, and kept a trowel hung in his office the rest of his life as a reminder.

Becoming a book salesman, he was converted in a revival meeting in ST. LOUIS and decided for the ministry. He was received into the ILLINOIS CONFERENCE in 1878, and his unusual preaching ability opened to him some of the largest churches in the Conference. Leaving the Illinois Conference, he became pastor of Trinity Church in DENVER, St. James in Chicago, and finally the great First Church, LOS ANGELES, which almost doubled its membership in the six years of his ministry. He always drew great congregations to his churches and was likewise a popular lecturer. He had an unusual gift for painting word pictures, some of them becoming famous, and his early background made him sympathetic to social problems and kept him in touch with common people. He was judged by many to be the greatest Methodist preacher of his day.

He attended VANDERBILT UNIVERSITY for one year and was given the D.D. degree by the UNIVERSITY OF DENVER in 1896. In 1908 he was elected to the episcopacy of the M. E. Church, but served only a few months more than six years. While on his official journeys, he was taken acutely ill in Chicago and died there on Aug. 30, 1914. He lies buried in Inglewood, Los Angeles.

The following incident is told of Robert McIntyre, indicative of his character: Once when Bishop WARREN was presiding over the SOUTHERN CALIFORNIA CONFERENCE, a minister guilty of a very serious indiscretion was required to stand before the brethren to be reprimanded by the Bishop. There he stood alone in humiliation before the bar of the Conference, while Bishop Warren with trembling voice visited the rebuke upon him. Unexpectedly, a brother minister arose, went forward and took his stand close beside the offending brother as if he would share with him his shame. As a result of the unpremeditated, Christlike deed, the Bishop and the entire Conference were in an instant weeping. Such a man was Robert McIntyre. "When he came to Los Angeles he was known as Robert McIntyre, the orator; when he left he was known as Robert McIntyre, the saint."

Journals of the Illinois and Central Illinois Conferences, 1914.
F. D. Leete, *Methodist Bishops*. 1948.

RICHARD D. LEONARD

McKAY, ORVILLE HERBERT (1913-   ), American minister and seminary president, was born at Croswell, Mich., on Oct. 9, 1913. His parents were Herbert Washington and Iva M. (Perry) McKay. He was educated at ASBURY COLLEGE, receiving the A.B. in 1934; at DREW UNIVERSITY, B.D., 1937, and the Ph.D., 1941; and did postgraduate work at OXFORD, England, in the summer of 1949. ADRIAN COLLEGE awarded him the D.D. degree in 1962. He was awarded an S.T.D. by MACMURRAY College in 1965, and LL.D. by MCKENDREE COLLEGE in 1966. His wife was Mabel Coppock, whom he married on Aug. 19, 1935, and they had three children.

Dr. McKay joined the DETROIT CONFERENCE and was ordained DEACON in 1936 and came into full connection and was ordained ELDER in 1938. He served as associate minister at the Nardin Park Church, Detroit, 1941-43, and 1946-47; was the minister of First Church, Highland Park, Mich., 1947-51; First Church, Midland, Mich., 1951-65, in which year he was elected president of GARRETT THEOLOGICAL SEMINARY at Evanston, Ill. He has been the chairman of the Board of Hospitals and Homes of the Detroit Conference; the chairman of the Board of the Ministry of that Conference and a member of its Commission on Ecumenical Affairs, and on that of The Methodist Church since 1965; and The General BOARD OF EDUCATION of the Church. He was a delegate to the North Central JURISDICTIONAL CONFERENCE, 1956, '60, '68; and to the GENERAL CONFERENCE of 1960 and '64, '66 and '68. He was chaplain of the U.S. Army Air Force, 1943-45.

Who's Who in the Methodist Church, 1966.   N. B. H.

McKAY, WILLIAM JOHN (1847-1921), American preacher, born at Belfast, Ireland, May 29, 1847. At five years of age he came to the United States where he lived in Port Washington, Horicon and near DeSoto, in WISCONSIN.

At seventeen years of age, he enlisted in the Fourth Wisconsin Infantry and served during the last year of the Civil War. He was converted and at once felt the call to preach, in answer to which he joined the WEST WISCON-

SIN CONFERENCE in 1870. His appointments included Mt. Sterling, LaCrosse, Eau Claire and Madison and he was also presiding elder of the Eau Claire and Madison Districts. He was a member of the GENERAL CONFERENCES of the M. E. Church in 1884, 1888 and 1896.

LAWRENCE COLLEGE of Appleton, Wisconsin conferred upon him the honorary D.D. degree in 1895. Besides his Conference activities, he was very active in the affairs of the Grand Army of the Republic and was for many years Commander of the G.A.R. Post in Madison, Wis. He was a man of great effectiveness in prayer and one who made a deep impress on his Conference.

Yearbook of the West Wisconsin Conference, 1922.

JOHN W. HARRIS

McKECHNIE, COLIN CAMPBELL (1821-1896), British PRIMITIVE METHODIST, was born at Paisley, SCOTLAND. He began his ministry in the Primitive Methodist Church in Ripon, in Yorkshire, and continued his years of circuit ministry in the Sunderland district until 1870. During this period he inaugurated the Sunderland Ministerial Association for the stimulation of ministerial studies, and this movement spread throughout Primitive Methodism. In 1855 he became the editor of the *Christian Ambassador* (founded in 1854, the forerunner of the *Primitive Methodist Quarterly Review*), and continued in the post until his death. He was general connexional editor from 1876 to 1887. Deeply interested in ministerial education, he was the first secretary of the SUNDERLAND THEOLOGICAL INSTITUTION founded in 1868, the earliest Primitive Methodist experiment with a theological college, later superseded by Hartley College at MANCHESTER. In 1880 he was elected President of the Primitive Methodist Conference. He was also responsible, in 1892, for the revision of WILLIAM ANTLIFF's *Life of the Venerable Hugh Bourne.* He died in September, 1896.

JOHN T. WILKINSON

WILLIAM MCKENDREE

McKENDREE, WILLIAM (1757-1835), the first native American bishop, was born on July 6, 1757, in King William County, Va., the son of John and Mary McKendree.

He served in the Revolutionary War and was present at the surrender of Cornwallis at Yorktown.

He was reared in the Anglican faith but joined a Methodist society when he was about nineteen years old. Ten years later he was converted under the preaching of JOHN EASTER. He was received on trial in the VIRGINIA CONFERENCE in 1788 and appointed with Philip Cox to the Mecklenburg Circuit. His succeeding annual appointments until 1794 were the Cumberland, Portsmouth, Amelia, Greenville, and Norfolk Circuits.

For four years his presiding elder was JAMES O'KELLY, who became disaffected and withdrew to form a separate body called the REPUBLICAN METHODIST CHURCH. When the GENERAL CONFERENCE in 1792 refused to adopt O'Kelly's resolution providing for an appeal by any preacher who was dissatisfied with his appointment, McKendree went with him for a brief period and declined to take a circuit for one year. Then he traveled briefly with Bishop ASBURY and became convinced that O'Kelly was in error, and again took his place in the Conference. In 1795 he served the Bedford Circuit and the following year he became a presiding elder, a post which he filled for eleven years until he was elected bishop.

In 1801 he was sent to the KENTUCKY District of the vast WESTERN CONFERENCE, which covered OHIO, Kentucky, TENNESSEE, WESTERN VIRGINIA and part of ILLINOIS. He later served two years on the Cumberland District. Thus be became identified with the western area.

In 1808 he was asked to preach before the General Conference, although unknown to most of its members. So powerful was his deliverance that Asbury predicted his election as bishop, a prophecy which was fulfilled a few days later.

As a bishop he introduced some new features which did not meet with Asbury's wholehearted approval. One of these was consultation with the presiding elders in making the appointments, from which emerged the "CABINET," which persisted in the Church. Another was a formal report to the General Conference, which gave rise to the EPISCOPAL ADDRESS at all succeeding conferences. McKendree usually traveled with Asbury and the latter made the appointments, but at the TENNESSEE CONFERENCE in 1815, the aging bishop said, "My eyes fail. I will resign the stations to Bishop McKendree—I will take away my feet." McKendree was then practically alone in the episcopacy, for Asbury did not hold another conference and died the following March.

McKendree did not have much formal education but he became a great preacher and ecclesiastical statesman. In 1820 he opposed vigorously a movement in the General Conference to limit the power of the bishops in assigning the preachers to their charges.

Because of physical infirmities he was largely relieved of his work after 1820 but he continued to travel over the connexion and assist in the superintendency until his death. In 1830 he gave 480 acres of land to the Lebanon Seminary in Illinois, and its name was changed to McKENDREE COLLEGE.

He died at the home of his brother, Dr. James McKendree, in Sumner County, Tenn., on March 5, 1835. He was buried nearby, but his body was later transferred to the campus of VANDERBILT UNIVERSITY at Nashville.

J. M. Buckley, *Constitutional and Parliamentary History.* 1912.
Dictionary of American Biography.
R. Paine, *William M'Kendree.* 1869.

M. Simpson, *Cyclopaedia.* 1878.
W. B. Sprague, *Annals of the Pulpit.* 1861.
T. O. Summers, *Biographical Sketches.* 1858.
J. J. Tigert, *Constitutional History.* 1894.   ELMER T. CLARK

McKENDREE CHAPEL

McKENDREE CHAPEL, three miles east of Jackson, Missouri, was designated as a Methodist Historic SHRINE by the 1960 GENERAL CONFERENCE. Built in 1819, it is the oldest Methodist and the oldest Protestant church building west of the Mississippi River.

In 1801, William Williams, a Methodist layman, moved from Kentucky to Missouri and soon set aside two acres of his farm to be used for CAMP MEETINGS. The site was first used for that purpose probably in 1806. A Methodist class or congregation was organized there in 1809. Williams served as class leader from the beginning until his death in 1838. Bishop WILLIAM McKENDREE attended a camp meeting there in 1818, and the chapel which was begun that year was named for him. The Missouri Conference met in the chapel in 1819, its first session west of the River. Also, the conference convened in the chapel in 1821, 1826, and 1831, an indication that McKendree was an important church with an adequate building for that period.

When the M. E. Church divided over slavery in 1844, a majority of the McKendree Chapel members voted to adhere South, but the pastor on the charge, Nelson Henry, strongly favoring the Church North, managed to align the chapel with that body. As time passed the Church North grew weaker in the region and the chapel regularly received missionary aid. About 1890 it ceased to exist as an organized church. However, the building was not forgotten. In September 1910, the ST. LOUIS CONFERENCE (MES) met in Jackson and took occasion to go out in a body and hold a special session in the old chapel. In 1916, the same conference met in Cape Girardeau and went out to conduct a service at McKendree Chapel commemorating the organization of the MISSOURI CONFERENCE in 1816.

In 1925, William Stewart was appointed pastor at New McKendree Church, Jackson. Finding Old McKendree in desolation and disrepair, he led a movement for its restoration. He aroused the interest of the St. Louis Conference (ME), and in 1926 that body voted to deed a one-half interest in the chapel to the M. E. Church, South with the request that it appoint one-half of the trustees and share in the upkeep of the property. Laymen donated money and physical labor to clean up the grounds and repair and restore the chapel. A right of way from the public road to the chapel was purchased. In time a steel canopy was built over the chapel, and later still a home for a curator was erected on the grounds. Since 1933 an annual service of commemoration featuring an outstanding speaker has been conducted at the chapel with several hundred people attending.

Singularly, Old McKendree Chapel might not have survived had not Nelson Henry managed to keep it in the hands of the minority of members who adhered North in 1845. Also, it is significant that the new deed for the chapel dated July 22, 1927, providing that thereafter half the trustees would be members of the Church South, became a point of reunion of the two churches formed by the division of the M. E. Church in 1844.

William Stewart, *Mindful of Man.* Cape Girardeau, Mo.: Missouri Litho and Printing Co., 1964.
Frank C. Tucker, *Old McKendree Chapel.* Cape Girardeau, Mo.: Missouri Litho and Printing Co., 1959.   ALBEA GODBOLD

McKENDREE COLLEGE, Lebanon, Illinois, was opened in 1828 as Lebanon Seminary with EDWARD R. AMES, later a bishop, as the principal, and with a Miss McMurphy as the other teacher. In 1830, the name was changed to McKendree College in honor of Bishop WILLIAM McKENDREE. He later deeded 480 acres of rich Shiloh Valley land to the college.

The legislature of the State of Illinois granted a charter to McKendree College on Feb. 9, 1835. A second charter, more detailed, under which the college still operates, was approved by the state legislature on Jan. 26, 1839. The first three members of the faculty were graduates of Wesleyan University. PETER CARTWRIGHT was an active supporter of the college and served as chairman of its board of trustees. PETER AKERS, an able preacher of the ILLINOIS CONFERENCE, was its first president, and was recalled to the office on two later occasions.

The institution has limited accreditation by the UNIVERSITY SENATE of The United Methodist Church. It offers the B.A. and B.S. degrees. The governing board has thirty-six members, a majority of whom must be active members of The United Methodist Church: twelve elected by the Southern Illinois Conference, twenty-four elected by the board but confirmed by the Southern Illinois Conference.

JOHN O. GROSS

McKENNA, DAVID L. (1929-   ), American FREE METHODIST educator and ordained elder in the Pacific Northwest Conference, was born at Detroit, Mich. He was educated as follows: A.A., SPRING ARBOR (Junior) COLLEGE, 1949; B.A., Western Michigan University, 1951; B.D., ASBURY THEOLOGICAL SEMINARY, 1953; M.A., University of Michigan, 1955; Ph.D., University of Michigan, 1958. He married Janet Ruth Voorheis in 1950. His service includes: pastor, Vicksburg, Mich., 1950-51; Dean of Men; Academic Dean; Vice-president, Spring Arbor (Junior) College, 1953-60; Assistant Professor of higher education, Ohio State University, 1960-61; President, Spring Arbor College, 1961-68; President, SEATTLE PACIFIC COLLEGE since 1968. He has been a member, Board of Administration, Pacific Northwest Conference; president, Association of Free Methodist Colleges and Secondary Schools; member of denominational Board of Administration; member of Resolution and Education Committees, National Association of Evangelicals. He holds membership in Phi Kappa Phi, Association of Higher Education, and Phi Delta Kappa. His community interests include United

Community Service, Jackson, Mich.; Michigan Commission on College Accreditation; Metropolitan (Detroit) YMCA Board of Directors; Seattle Chamber of Commerce, Education Committee; Seattle Rotary Club. He is the author of *Concept of the Christian College*, 1963; editor *The Urban Crisis*, 1969; contributing editor, *United Evangelical Action*, and articles in *The Free Methodist* and *Christianity Today*.

BYRON S. LAMSON

McKENZIE, JOHN WITHERSPOON PETTIGREW (1806-1881), American preacher and educator, was born on April 26, 1806 in Burke County, N. C. He founded a school at Columbia, Tenn., in 1831 and was admitted to the TENNESSEE CONFERENCE in 1836. He transferred at once to the ARKANSAS CONFERENCE and his first appointent was to the Choctaw Indians in what was later Indian Territory. In 1839 he was appointed to a circuit extending from western ARKANSAS to Preston Bend, near Denison on Red River in the Republic of TEXAS. In 1841 he started a small school in a log house with sixteen children, the beginning of McKenzie College located near Clarksville, Texas. In a few years the school became the most prosperous and vigorous institution in the southwest, if not west of the Mississippi River, during the period up to the Civil War. McKenzie continued to preach on request and officiated at many weddings, funerals, and church dedications, but his major work was conducting the school. Originally the school was chiefly a preparatory one but in 1845 a "female department" and a "collegiate department" were added. In 1848 the first A.B. degree was conferred. By 1846 there were sixty-three students and in 1848 eighty-six were reported in the college, with even more in the preparatory department. By 1859-60 there were 405 students taught by nine faculty members. The war years cut enrollment, and severe economic conditions, plus McKenzie's advancing age, resulted in the closing of the school in 1868. A total of about 3,300 students attended the school, and McKenzie reported that about 2,200 of these "made public profession of religion" while there. Many of the later leaders in the area and the state attended the college. In 1853 four large new buildings, erected at a cost of $30,000 provided almost unrivaled facilities among nineteenth century schools, at least in the South and the Southwest. In 1878 McKenzie was awarded an honorary D.D. degree by EMORY College (now UNIVERSITY). He died on June 20, 1881.

"McKenzie College" by John D. Osburn in *Southwestern Historical Quarterly* (April, 1960).
M. Phelan, *Texas*. 1924.   WALTER N. VERNON

MACKENZIE, PETER (1824-1895), British Wesleyan Methodist evangelist and humorist, was born at Glenshee, Perthshire, SCOTLAND, Nov. 11, 1824, but migrated to England to become a pitman in Haswell Colliery, Durham. He was converted in 1849. He entered the Wesleyan ministry in 1859 and, after many successful years in a number of circuits, was in 1886 relieved of circuit work for work in the connection at large. In great demand as a preacher because of his racy, humorous style, he is described on his epitaph at Dewsbury, Yorkshire, as "the Greatheart of Methodism." He died on Nov. 21, 1895.

J. Dawson, *Peter Mackenzie*, 1896.
D. T. Young, *Peter Mackenzie*. 1904.

H. MORLEY RATTENBURY

McKINLEY, WILLIAM (1843-1901), the twenty-fourth President of the United States of America and a staunch Methodist, was born in Miles, OHIO on Jan. 29, 1843. At the age of ten he was baptized and received into membership in the M. E. Church by the Rev. Aaron D. Morton. During the American Civil War he served with distinction in the Northern Army, rising from a private to the rank of major. Following the war he studied law and in 1867 opened an office in Canton, Ohio. Here he met and in 1871 married Ida Saxton. They had two children who died in infancy. While in Canton, McKinley was active in the local M. E. Church and for a time served as superintendent of the church school. The pew he occupied in First Church, Canton, is specially marked by an appropriate metal plate.

In 1876 McKinley was elected to the Congress of the United States as a representative from Ohio. Defeated in 1882, he was re-elected in 1884. All together he served six two-year terms between 1876 and 1890. As a congressman he was known for his advocacy of a high protective tariff. In 1890 he sponsored a tariff bill bearing his name which became law. While a congressman McKinley and his wife attended the Foundry M. E. Church in WASHINGTON, D. C. In 1891 he ran for governor of Ohio and was elected.

In 1896 McKinley was nominated by the Republican Party for the office of President of the United States. In the election he defeated his Democratic opponent, William Jennings Bryan, and was inaugurated on March 4, 1897. In 1900 he was re-elected. During his first administration the United States engaged in a brief war with Spain. As a result of this war the PHILIPPINES, Guam, and PUERTO RICO were ceded to the United States and the island of CUBA became an independent country. While President, McKinley attended the Metropolitan M. E. Church, the national Methodist church which had been erected during the administration of ULYSSES S. GRANT by contributions from Methodists throughout the country. His pastors during this time were HUGH M. JOHNSTON and FRANK M. BRISTOL.

Included among his private papers is a signed statement declaring: "My belief embraces the Divinity of Christ and a recognition of Christianity as the mightiest factor in the world's civilization." In Buffalo, N. Y., on Sept. 6, 1901, William McKinley was shot by Leon Czolgosz. Eight days later he died. He is buried in Canton, Ohio.

Dictionary of American Biography.
Hampton, *Religious Backgrounds of the White House.*
Kane, *Facts About the Presidents.*
Leech, *In the Days of McKinley.*   H. ALDEN WELCH

McKINNEY, JOHN WESLEY (? -1946), sixteenth bishop of the C.M.E. CHURCH, was born in Texas. He received his education at Prairie View Normal School and Austin College. He began preaching in 1883 and served as a local preacher for several years before entering the itinerant ministry. McKinney served as pastor, presiding elder, and Secretary of Church Extension before being elected to the office of bishop by the General Conference in 1922. He and Bishop ROBERT TURNER BROWN led in the establishment of a church in Trinidad, WEST INDIES. Bishop McKinney was noted as a man of conviction and high moral standards. He retired in 1942 and died on Aug. 28, 1946.

Harris and Patterson, *C.M.E. Church.* 1965.
The Mirror, General Conference, CME, 1958. RALPH G. GAY

MACKINNON, SALLIE LOU (1889-1973), American missionary and Mission Board executive, was born at Maxton, N. C., on Oct. 27, 1889, the daughter of Alexander James and Virginia Lee Mackinnon.

She graduated from RANDOLPH-MACON WOMAN'S COLLEGE, 1911, and at SCARRITT Biblical Institute (then in Kansas City, Mo.). She volunteered and was sent to CHINA, where she served as a missionary under the BOARD OF MISSIONS of the M. E. Church, South, for ten or twelve years. She then became the executive secretary of the WOMAN'S FOREIGN MISSIONARY SOCIETY of the M. E. Church, South, whose headquarters then were in NASHVILLE, Tenn. After the unification of Methodism in 1939-40, she went to New York City where she served as executive secretary for China, Africa and Europe under the Woman's Division of Christian Service of The Methodist Church. Later with the changing situation in China, she remained in charge of Africa and Europe for the Woman's Division. She retired in 1956, and after living in Nashville, Tenn., for several years, took up her residence in the Brooks Howell Home in ASHEVILLE, N. C., in 1964. In her tenure as executive secretary, she served on many important committees and was quite influential in interdenominational and international mission groups in their wider plans and moves.

She died in Asheville on March 16, 1973.

The Methodist Woman, Vol. 15, No. 6, February 1955.

N. B. H.

McKNIGHT, GEORGE (? -1813 or 1814), American pioneer layman, at whose home on the Yadkin River in NORTH CAROLINA, the three important frontier conferences of 1789, 1790, and 1791 were held, was one of the earliest settlers on the Yadkin River. His land grant is dated 1762, and there is evidence that he had occupied the land near the mouth of Linville Creek, where the Great Wagon Road from PENNSYLVANIA crossed, at least as early as 1758.

In the years before the Revolutionary War he was connected with the MORAVIANS of the Wachovia settlement, and opened his house to them for preaching in English. Sometime about 1783 a Methodist society was organized in his community, and in 1786 Bishop FRANCIS ASBURY found a living society there, and a chapel at McKnight's. Located just below where the Yadkin turns south, the place was admirably located for gathering the preachers from all directions, and Asbury took full advantage of it.

The 1789 Conference was attended by the preachers from the Holston country of East TENNESSEE, who crossed the mountains by way of the Flower Gap. "We had weighty matters for consideration before us," wrote Asbury. The most important such matter was the launching of the *Arminian Magazine*, which the BOOK STEWARD, JOHN DICKINS, edited and published at PHILADELPHIA. The preface to the first volume was signed by Asbury and THOMAS COKE at "North Carolina, April 10, 1789."

After the 1791 Conference the growing Methodism on the Holston side of the mountains made conferences there desirable, and McKnight's faded into the background.

The home and chapel of McKnight were located about where the present U. S. Highway 158 crosses the first branch east of the Yadkin River just south of the Interstate 40. It is now in Forsyth County, but at the time of George McKnight it was in Rowan County, almost on the Surry County line. McKnight died at the home of a son-in-law in Surry County in 1813 or 1814.

In 1808 and 1809 the society there, led by McKnight's sons and sons-in-law, built a new church by the name of Mt. Pleasant, some two miles to the south. This, in turn, gave way to a church and school at Clemmonsville, a mile east of the original site. The old Mt. Pleasant, however, has been restored and stands as a shrine in Tangelwood Park, a public park donated by some of the Reynolds family of that section.

W. L. Grissom, *North Carolina*. 1905.
Moravian Records.
Rowan and Iredell Counties (North Carolina), Records.

HOMER M. KEEVER
LOUISE L. QUEEN

McLAUGHLIN, JOHN RUSSELL (1905-   ), American minister, and general secretary of the Commission on Chaplains, was born at Blue Mound, Kan., May 24, 1905, son of William and Mattie (King) McLaughlin.

He received the A.B. degree from BAKER UNIVERSITY in 1930, and was awarded the D.D. degree by Baker in 1952. From DREW UNIVERSITY he received the B.D. degree in 1932 and the M.A. degree in 1934. He pursued postgraduate study at Columbia University, 1934-35; at GARRETT THEOLOGICAL SEMINARY, 1938-40; and at New York University, 1946-48.

He was admitted on trial into the NEWARK CONFERENCE, M. E. Church, and was ordained DEACON in 1933. He was received into full connection and ordained ELDER in 1935.

His pastorates were: Baldwin, Kan., 1926-28; Edwardsville, Kan., 1929; Woodrow, Staten Island, N. Y., 1932-35; Jersey City, N. J., 1935-41; Leonia, N. J., 1941-49. He was superintendent of North District, Newark Conference, 1949-55. From 1956 for more than two quadrennia he was general secretary, Commission on CHAPLAINS, Washington, D. C. He served to become chaplain-major in the U.S. Army Air Force.

He married Ada Frances Richard on June 10, 1928, and they had two children. She died in Berchtesgaden, Germany, in 1961.

He was married to Iona S. Henry on June 15, 1963. They continue to reside in Washington, D. C.

Who's Who in the Methodist Church, 1966.   J. MARVIN RAST

McLAUGHLIN, WILLIAM PATTERSON (1849-1921), missionary pastor in ARGENTINA, was born in CINCINNATI, Ohio. He was graduated from OHIO WESLEYAN UNIVERSITY and BOSTON UNIVERSITY SCHOOL OF THEOLOGY and entered the OHIO ANNUAL CONFERENCE. After eleven years of service in several churches, McLaughlin and his wife, the former Rebecca Long, accepted an appointment in NEW ORLEANS, LA., where he organized a missionary district among French- and Italian-speaking people. After seven years he accepted the call to South America.

Arriving at Christmas 1892, he served as pastor of First Methodist Church, BUENOS AIRES for twenty-nine years, until his death in February 1921. His pastorate was distinguished by a widening influence and deepened relationships which left enduring marks. His social insights were particularly effective during the years of the First World War. "He went about doing good," are words on a marble monument erected to his memory.

W. C. Barclay, *History of Missions*. 1957.   HUBERT R. HUDSON

MACLAY, CHARLES (1821-1890), American businessman and Methodist benefactor, joined the BALTIMORE CONFERENCE but in 1851 transferred to the CALIFORNIA. In 1859 he asked for location on medical advice. He prospered in business, and was one of the chief financial supporters of the church. He served in both the State Assembly and Senate from Santa Clara County. His interest in an educated ministry led him to be active in supporting the UNIVERSITY OF THE PACIFIC. Later he endowed the Maclay College of Theology in connection with the University of Southern California.

The collapse of the land boom in that part of the state brought a series of financial crises. Finally the endowment and the university were lost to the church. But Maclay's loyalty to Methodism never wavered. He was one of California's distinguished laymen.

C. V. Anthony, *Fifty Years.* 1901.
H. H. Bancroft, *Chronicles of the Builders,* II, p. 307.
E. D. Jervey, *Southern California and Arizona.* 1960.

LEON L. LOOFBOUROW

ROBERT S. MACLAY

MACLAY, ROBERT SAMUEL (1824-1907), pioneer missionary of the M. E. Church in CHINA, JAPAN and KOREA, was born in Concord, Pa., on Feb. 7, 1824. After graduation from DICKINSON COLLEGE in 1845, he was ordained and sailed for China in 1847. His fiancee, Henrietta Caroline Sperry, followed him two years later, and they were married in HONG KONG in 1850. He was appointed superintendent and treasurer of the mission and continued until 1872.

His first plan for developing Methodist work in China was to move steadily westward, from Fukien to Kiangsi, and then to West China and possibly to Tibet. In furtherance of this plan he sent VIRGIL HART and Elbert Todd from Foochow to Kiukiang on the Yangtze River in 1867. But, by the following year, he was ready to sidetrack further westward advance for a time, in favor of establishing work in North China. In 1869, Lucius N. Wheeler and Hiram H. Lowry were sent to Peking to begin work there.

In 1861, Maclay published his interesting book, *Life Among the Chinese,* and in 1871 he collaborated with C. C. Baldwin in a massive dictionary of the Chinese language in the dialect of Foochow.

By this time his thought was reaching out even beyond the bounds of China. On Dec. 16, 1870, he wrote to the missionary society, urging that work be established in Japan. The following year he returned to America—his second furlough in twenty-three years—and while away the bishops transferred him to Japan to found the mission he had advocated.

He arrived in Japan in 1873, and was superintendent of that mission until 1888, serving also in TOKYO as president of Ei Wa Gakko, a college which embraced the Anglo-Chinese Academy and the Philander Smith Biblical Institute. He was delegate from Japan to the ECUMENICAL METHODIST CONFERENCE in London in 1881. While there he made a strong plea for the closest possible cooperation of the various Methodist mission boards throughout the world.

His continuing statesmanlike concern for the whole East Asia area showed itself in a visit to his old home in Foochow in 1881, when he helped to establish the Anglo-Chinese College; and also in a visit to the king of Korea in 1884, when he obtained permission for the establishment of Methodist work in that country.

In 1888, he was ministerial delegate from Japan to the GENERAL CONFERENCE of the M. E. Church held in New York. After the Conference he resigned from mission work and became dean of the newly opened Maclay College of Theology in San Fernando, Calif., a post which he held from 1888 to 1893, when he retired.

W. C. Barclay, *History of Missions.* 1957.
W. N. Lacy, *China.* 1948.
Who's Who in America, 1906-07. FRANCIS P. JONES

McLEAN, JOHN (1775-1861), Justice of the Supreme Court of the United States, who among other things is remembered for his thirty-one-year tenure on that Court. He was the first Ohioan to become a Justice of the highest court in the land.

A native of Morris County, N. J., born March 11, 1775, he settled with his family in what became Warren County in southwestern OHIO. He worked on the family farm until he was eighteen, then went to CINCINNATI to work in the Hamilton County Clerk of Court's office and to read law. He was admitted to the bar in 1807, and began his practice in Lebanon, county seat of Warren County.

Almost immediately he began his long political career, first as U.S. Congressman in 1812, re-elected in 1814. In 1815 he was elected to the Ohio Supreme Court bench. In 1822, President Monroe named him Commissioner of the General Land Office. The next year be became Postmaster General. Although he disagreed with President Andrew Jackson, Jackson appointed him to the U.S. Supreme Court.

Justice McLean dissented from Chief Justice Roger Taney in the Dred Scott case, holding that slavery "had its origin in power, was contrary to right and upheld only by local law."

His peers described him as "conscientious, thorough, inherently just. . . . inclined to reject the opinion of others."

For many years he was a communicant member of the M. E. Church, and one historian said of him, "His private life was in perfect harmony with his profession." He once was president of the American SUNDAY SCHOOL UNION,

Despite his lack of formal higher education, four colleges conferred upon Justice McLean the honorary LL.D. degree. Harvard was one and WESLEYAN UNIVERSITY in Connecticut another.

A tall and commanding figure, Justice McLean was a man of simple habits; his manners were genial and courteous, and he was distinguished by his intellectual versatility. It was said that he was as regular in attending class meeting as Chief Justice Taney was in attending mass.

Few men in political life enjoyed such broad support. In 1836 the Whigs favored him for presidential nomination; he was considered a possible nominee of the Liberty party in 1848, and later the same year at the Free Soil Convention. In 1856 the Ohio delegation favored him for the presidential nomination at the first national Republican convention. He was of great help in acting as mediator in the suit the Southern Church (MES) brought against the Northern (ME) to obtain its share of the BOOK CONCERN's worth after the Northern Church had repudiated the PLAN OF SEPARATION which in 1844 had been agreed upon. However when the suit of the South finally came before the Supreme Court, Justice McLean excused himself because he was a Methodist, and let his fellow justices decide the issue—as they did for the South.

He also entered the field of Methodist biography, writing a life of PHILIP GATCH and of JOHN COLLINS.

Justice McLean died April 4, 1861. The next day the *Ohio State Journal*, Columbus morning newspaper, said: "Justice McLean was a profound jurist, a citizen justly esteemed for his excellent social qualities, and an exemplary Christian."

Dictionary of American Biography.
M. Simpson, *Cyclopaedia.* 1878.   JOHN F. YOUNG

MACLEAN, JOHN (1851-1928), Canadian Methodist missionary to the Indians and historian, was born in Kilmarnock, SCOTLAND, Oct. 30, 1851, and was educated at the Burgh Academy, Dumbarton. In 1873 he emigrated to CANADA. He attended VICTORIA UNIVERSITY (B.A., 1882; M.A., 1887) and ILLINOIS WESLEYAN UNIVERSITY (Ph.D., 1888).

Received on trial in 1875, he was ordained in the Methodist Church in 1880. From 1880 to 1889 he was a missionary to the Blood Indians near Fort Macleod, in what is now Alberta. During this period he was also a public-school inspector. Subsequently he had pastorates at Moose Jaw, Saskatchewan; Port Arthur, Ontario; Neepawa and Winnipeg, in Manitoba; in the last of which he founded the Maclean Mission. In 1895 he was president of the Manitoba Conference, and from 1902 to 1906 he was editor of *The Wesleyan*. For many years he was the historian of the Manitoba Conference, and from 1918 to 1922 he was archivist of the Methodist Church.

Maclean's interests were extensive. He was a member of the Canadian Institute, the American Folklore Society, and the Manitoba Historical Society. Widely regarded as an authority on the Western Indians, he wrote numerous ethnological pamphlets and a variety of books. These included *Canadian Savage Folk* (1896), *James Evans* (1890), and *McDougall of Alberta* (1927). He did much to interpret and to preserve the culture of the Western tribes and to strengthen Methodism in the prairie provinces.

G. H. Cornish, *Cyclopaedia of Methodism in Canada.* 1881.
L. E. Horning and L. J. Burpee, *A Bibliography of Canadian*

Fiction. Toronto: Victoria University Library, 1904.
W. S. Wallace, ed., *Macmillan Dictionary of Canadian Biography.* London: Macmillan, 1963.   J. E. NIX
F. W. ARMSTRONG

McLEAN, JOHN H. (1838-1925), American clergyman and educator, was born in Hinds County, Miss. He attended (and taught for two years at) McKenzie College, Clarksville, Texas, and entered EAST TEXAS CONFERENCE in 1860; went into Trinity (later named NORTH TEXAS) Conference when organized in 1867. He served leading churches and districts; was head of Paris Female College, 1869-71; vice-regent of SOUTHWESTERN UNIVERSITY at Georgetown, Texas, 1880-91; and regent, 1891-97. He was manager of Texas Methodist Orphanage, 1908-12; and a member of the ECUMENICAL METHODIST CONFERENCE in Washington, 1891, and in New York in 1901.

WALTER N. VERNON

McMAHAN CHAPEL, organized in 1833, is the oldest Methodist church and the oldest continuing Protestant congregation in the state of Texas. The chapel is located on Spur 35 two miles south of Route 21 some twelve miles east of San Augustine. There in what was then the San Augustine Municipality of the Mexican Government, Samuel D. McMahan (d. 1854) who came from Tennessee, settled in 1831.

At the MISSISSIPPI CONFERENCE in Vicksburg, November 1832, James P. Stevenson was appointed to the Sabine Circuit in LOUISIANA, a few miles east of where McMahan had settled. In the spring of 1833 at Nachitoches, La., Stevenson met some Texans who asked him to come across the line and preach to them, even though Protestant services were forbidden in Mexican territory. Assured by the laymen of protection from prosecution, Stevenson went over and held a two-day meeting in a private home near what is now Milam, Texas. McMahan attended the services and invited Stevenson to come and preach at his home also. Stevenson did so, returning several times during the year to hold services. The people requested Stevenson to organize a church, but he, knowing that organizing a Methodist church would be against the law, formed instead in September 1833, a "religious society" of forty-eight members and named McMahan the "CLASS LEADER." Such was the beginning of McMahan Chapel. Then in July 1834, Henry Stephenson, successor of J. P. Stevenson on the Sabine Circuit, formally organized a Methodist society in McMahan's home, and it was soon called McMahan Chapel.

Following the Texas War of Independence in 1836, the McMahan congregation grew rapidly, and there was need for a church building. In December 1838, the Mississippi Conference appointed LITTLETON FOWLER as presiding elder of the Texas Mission District. Fowler built a home near Samuel McMahan's place and made it his headquarters. Also, in 1839 Fowler assisted with the building of a log chapel forty by thirty feet for the McMahan congregation.

The McMahan log structure was replaced by a frame church in 1872, and another of similar material was erected in 1900. The present brick edifice, valued at $49,500, was built in 1949 and was dedicated in 1956 by Bishop A. FRANK SMITH.

The 1970 GENERAL CONFERENCE designated McMahan Chapel as one of the first three official United

Methodist Landmarks because of its historic significance.

A cemetery containing the graves of Samuel D. Mc-Mahan, Littleton Fowler, and other early Methodist leaders in Texas, adjoins McMahan Chapel. The chapel is the head of a four-point work with the pastor residing in a brick parsonage beside the church. In 1969 McMahan Chapel reported twenty-nine members.

Texas Christian Advocate, Sept. 18, 1880.
Walter N. Vernon, "McMahan's Chapel: Landmark in Texas," in *Methodist History*, October 1970.
Walter Prescott Webb, ed., *The Handbook of Texas*. Austin, 1952.
C. A. West, *McMahan's Methodist Chapel*. Pamphlet, n.p., n.d.
Henderson Yokum, *History of Texas*. II, 221. New York: Redfield, 1856.
ALBEA GODBOLD

McMILLAN, ETHEL (?-1954), a New Zealand Methodist missionary sister, was born in Victoria, Australia. After qualifying as a midwife, in 1915 she became a missionary nursing sister under the Methodist Church of Australasia, on the island of Choiseul in the Western Solomons. When the New Zealand Conference took over the Solomon Islands field in 1922, she continued to work on Choiseul for a further twenty years. For a good part of that time she was the only European worker on the island. Hundreds of orphans owe their lives to her unremitting care, and through her influence, hygienic and domestic conditions were revolutionized in many of the villages. She retired in Melbourne, where she died on Jan. 19, 1954.

ARTHUR H. SCRIVIN

M'MULLEN, JAMES (17?-1804), British Methodist pioneer missionary to GIBRALTAR, entered the Wesleyan ministry in IRELAND in 1788 and answered an appeal to go to Gibraltar in 1804. The society consisted of about twenty members, both soldiers and civilians. Yellow fever was raging on his arrival, and his wife died almost immediately. He himself visited the sick and preached, but died on Oct. 17, 1804, only a week or so after landing, the first Wesleyan missionary martyr of the European field.

Findlay and Holdsworth, *Wesleyan Meth. Miss. Soc.* 1921-24.
W. Moister, *Wesleyan Missionaries.* 1878. CYRIL J. DAVEY

McMULLEN, WALLACE (1819-1899), Irish minister, was born in Ards, County Down, in the north of IRELAND, and entered the ministry in 1841. He soon showed administrative gifts, and in 1859 he began his connection with Home Mission affairs as Assistant Secretary of the Contingent Fund. His connection with this work lasted until he died, and for the last twenty years of his life he was the General Secretary of the Home Mission Fund. This was the department through which the whole organization and finance of the Irish Methodist Church was guided. He advocated and helped carry through the plan for lay representation in the Irish Conference in 1877. Much of the work for Methodist Union in Ireland in 1878 was his responsibility, and he helped to consolidate united Irish Methodism by his constructive financial genius. As a member of the LEGAL HUNDRED, he was four times called to the highest office in the Church in Ireland, Vice-President of the Conference, in 1874, 1878, 1888 and 1895.

FREDERICK JEFFERY

MacMURRAY COLLEGE, Jacksonville, Illinois, was chartered as Illinois Conference Female College in 1846. The name was changed to Illinois Woman's College in 1899, and in 1930 to MacMurray College for Women in honor of the late James E. MacMurray, former Senator from Illinois, whose devotion to the college was reflected by his large gifts. The college is related to the CENTRAL ILLINOIS CONFERENCE. A coordinate college for men was established in 1955. Degrees offered are the B.A., M.Ed. (Education), and M.S. The governing board has thirty-three members; it is self-perpetuating.

JOHN O. GROSS

McMURRY, WILLIAM FLETCHER (1864-1934), American bishop, was the son of a Methodist preacher, William Wesley McMurry, and was born in Shelby County, Mo., June 29, 1864. His father was a very influential leader in MISSOURI Methodism and sent his son to St. Charles College (1880-1882) and to CENTRAL COLLEGE at Fayette (1882-1885). A few years after he left Central College he was married to Frances Byrd Davis, Oct. 9, 1888, and they had three children. He was ordained in the M. E. Church, South, in 1886. He held several pastorates between 1886 and 1897 and was a presiding elder from 1897 to 1902. He then became pastor of Centenary Church in ST. LOUIS and served in that important downtown church until 1906. These were the World Fair years in St. Louis and his pastorate at Centenary was one of the most successful evangelistic pastorates in the long history of Missouri Methodism. In 1906 he was elected Secretary of the Board of Church Extension of his denomination and served until 1918, when he was elected a bishop at the GENERAL CONFERENCE in ATLANTA.

His first assignment as bishop took him to the Orient, and then in subsequent years he served several Episcopal areas in Southern Methodism. For years he was President of the Board of Finance of the M. E. Church, South, was a member of the Joint Commission on Unification of American Methodism, and he was twice a delegate to the ECUMENICAL METHODIST CONFERENCE, in 1901 and 1921. In addition to his work as bishop he served as President of Central College from 1924 to 1930.

He presided over a great meeting of his Episcopal Area, including the BALTIMORE, the KENTUCKY and the WEST VIRGINIA CONFERENCES, at Staunton, Va., on Jan. 9, 1934. He returned home with an attack of influenza, was taken to Barnes Hospital in St. Louis and died there of a heart attack on the morning of Jan. 19, and he was buried at Shelbyville, Mo., in his native county.

Bishop McMurry, measured by any standard, was a big man. He was as able an administrator as Methodism in the United States ever produced, and he would have gone to the top in any field of endeavor. He was an indefatigable worker, and he demanded of all who served under him the same kind of devoted and energetic work. Because the tasks committed to him by his church required such drives and strength, he seemed at times to be overpowering.

I. L. Holt, *Missouri Bishops.* 1953.
C. F. Price, *Who's Who in American Methodism.* 1916.
IVAN LEE HOLT

McMURRY COLLEGE, Abilene, Texas, was established in 1920 and named for Bishop WILLIAM F. McMURRY who presided over the conference that ordered the founding. Its founder was James W. Hunt, a minister of the Northwest Texas Conference.

McMurry is the legal and spiritual successor of four educational institutions of West Texas and New Mexico: Stamford College, Clarendon College, Seth Ward College, and Western College of Artesia. McMurry College received the first endowed lectureship given by Mr. and Mrs. J. M. Willson of Floydada, Texas. Willson lectureships have been given by them to thirty educational institutions. Degrees offered are the B.A. and B.S. The governing board has sixty trustees elected by the NORTHWEST TEXAS and NEW MEXICO ANNUAL CONFERENCES.

JOHN O. GROSS

MACNAUGHTON, NORMAN (1880-1951), American preacher, lecturer and teacher, was born March 3, 1880 in Glengarry, Ontario, CANADA, the son of Alexander and Sarah (McDonald) MacNaughton. He earned his A.B., B.Th., and B.D. degrees at McMaster University, Toronto, Canada, and received the M.A. degree at Yale in 1912. Further graduate work was taken at the University of Chicago, 1925-1929. ADRIAN COLLEGE conferred upon him the degree of LL.D. in 1945.

He married Kathleen Mabel Chalk on Sept. 20, 1910, in Toronto, Canada. He served congregations in New Westminster, British Columbia; Southfield, CHICAGO, Ill.; and Tecumseh, Mich. He joined the Adrian College faculty in 1930, where he held the Chair of Christian Philosophy for twenty years until his retirement in 1950. He was in constant demand as a speaker for various special occasions. As a teacher of college students he had few superiors. The *Michigan Christian Advocate* said, "Over a period of years his wit, wisdom, and common sense had been a source of inspiration. Dr. MacNaughton was both humble and great in spirit." His conference relationship was with the ILLINOIS and MICHIGAN CONFERENCES of the M. P. CHURCH, and then into the DETROIT CONFERENCE of The Methodist Church at the time of union in 1939. His death occurred July 12, 1951, and he was buried in Adrian.

Detroit Conference *Journal*, 1952.
Daily Telegram, Adrian, Mich., July 12, 1951.
Michigan Christian Advocate, July 26, 1951.
Who's Who in Methodism, 1952. FRANK W. STEPHENSON

MACON, GEORGIA, U.S.A. In 1803, white settlers in GEORGIA purchased a tract of land from the Creek Indians. At the top of the hill on the east side of the Ocmulgee River, Fort Hawkins was built, and on the west side, the streets for Macon were laid out. Circuit riders from adjoining territory came to the settlement to preach and hold revivals.

The first Methodist Society was organized in the home of R. R. Evans in 1826. On Dec. 23, 1826, Governor G. M. Thorpe signed a bill passed by the Georgia Legislature, authorizing the Commission appointed to plan the town of Macon, "to lay off a suitable piece of ground for the Methodist Episcopal Church." The granite marker on this building site (which is Mulberry Street Methodist Church) says, "No building has ever stood on this spot except a Methodist Church dedicated to the worship and service of Almighty God." The first building was erected in 1828.

First Macon appointments read: 1827, SOUTH CAROLINA CONFERENCE, Milledgeville District, Macon and Clinton, Thos. Darly, P.C. In 1828 the circuit was rearranged to read—South Carolina Conference, Milledgeville District, Milledgeville and Macon, Samuel K. Hodges, sup., Charles Hardy. In 1829 Macon was made a station with IGNATIUS A. FEW, preacher-in-charge. At the end of that first year as a station the membership was 120 white and 36 colored.

In 1828 the GENERAL CONFERENCE authorized the South Carolina Conference to be divided, and in January 1829, the division was made at the Savannah River, with the Carolinas in one conference, and GEORGIA with FLORIDA in the other. The GEORGIA CONFERENCE was organized in Macon in January 1830.

WESLEYAN COLLEGE, under the name of Georgia Female College, received its charter from the Legislature of the State of Georgia on Dec. 23, 1836; began construction in 1837; faculty elected in 1838; opened its doors Jan. 7, 1839, and issued the world's first college degrees for women, July 16, 1840, GEORGE F. PIERCE, President. Today Wesleyan College is located on a 240-acre campus and is supported by SOUTH GEORGIA, NORTH GEORGIA, and FLORIDA CONFERENCES and the BOARD OF EDUCATION of The United Methodist Church.

Additional Methodist churches have been organized in Macon, beginning with Vineville, 1849, followed by First Street, East Macon, South Macon, and then Centenary. Today there are twenty-six congregations with 14,710 members out of a population of 118,764 people. The A.M.E., A.M.E. ZION, and C.M.E. CHURCHES are represented in congregations numbering more than 1,000 members. Macon is the strongest Methodist center in South Georgia.

KING VIVION

Mulberry Street Church, Macon, located in the heart of Georgia, in 1826 had a population of about 800 people and this was the third year of the community's life. There were stores, a school, a Masonic lodge hall, a hotel, but no church building. Occasional religious services were held in a temporary court house located on Mulberry Street.

The first regular services of Christian worship began in Macon when a Methodist society was organized in 1826 with seventeen members. Named the "Macon Methodist Episcopal Church," the congregation was a part of the South Carolina Conference.

By special act of the Georgia Legislature a tract of land was granted the young congregation at the corner of Mulberry and First Streets adjacent to, but outside, the city limits. On this site the first building for Christian worship in the City of Macon was erected in 1828. The church has remained on this site during all its life. In the first simple frame structure built there the Georgia Conference, including the churches in Georgia which had formerly been a part of the South Carolina Conference, was organized. Because of this historic event Mulberry Street Church has been known as the "Mother Church of Georgia Methodism." In the year 1847 the name of the church was changed from "Macon Church" to "Mulberry Street Church."

In 1850 a second and larger church building, this one of brick construction and more handsome than the first, was erected. As the congregation grew there was a need for still further expansion, and in 1882 the third sanctuary building was constructed. The walls of this building are still in use.

By the time Mulberry Street Church was ready to celebrate its centennial it had "mothered" eight congregations in the growing city of Macon. At the time of the centennial a new expansion program was begun, and in 1929 a large educational building and a remodelled sanctuary were completed at a cost of $250,000.

The economic depression of the 1930's found the church in serious financial difficulties with a large debt. In 1937 a legal agreement was reached with holders of bonds on the church's debt by which only a portion of the indebtedness was to be paid. But the moral obligation to pay 100 percent of the value of the bonds was never forgotten by the church, and in 1945 this was done. The dedication of the educational building followed. In the early 1950s plans were made and funds raised for a new activities building, a chapel, a new organ, and the renovation of the sanctuary. Before the end of that decade the task was completed at a cost of more than $400,000, and in 1960 the Stevens-Taylor Chapel was dedicated.

On an April morning in 1965 a disastrous fire destroyed all but the walls of Mulberry's sanctuary. With courage and devotion the congregation made plans for rebuilding. The new construction was done within the same walls of the old sanctuary and was completed in 1968 at a cost of $560,000.

Through the years the Mulberry congregation has sought to set a pace for the churches which it has sponsored in evangelism, missions, education, social concerns, and stewardship. At a time when the growth of cities and suburban churches has weakened many congregations in the downtown areas, Mulberry has maintained a vigorous strength and leadership.

In 1970 it reported 2,091 members, property valued at $2,469,458, and $134,940 raised for all purposes.

FRANK L. ROBERTSON

Swift Creek Church, situated in Bibb County, near Macon, is an old country church which was founded in 1867. It was organized by William Capers Bass of Wesleyan College as Swift Creek Mission. When first entered in the minutes of the South Georgia Conference, 120 white and two colored members were reported. A century later the membership is approximately double that number, this still being a rural community.

The men of the community built the Swift Creek church on a lot of three and one-half acres deeded by Mrs. Elisha Davis to the first trustees, William Hanover Donnan, James Duke and Lunce Riggins, Nov. 5, 1868. The original building is still the sanctuary. Wings have been added and extensive improvements made.

For ninety years Swift Creek was on a circuit with one pastor serving several churches. By 1933 the depression had nearly depopulated the community, the membership had dwindled to six active members and the church was closed. In 1936 it was reopened with twenty-five members. Membership and attendance steadily increased. In 1957 a parsonage was bought and it became a station with a full-time pastor.

WILMUTH DONNAN

R. F. Burden, *Historical Sketch of Vineville Methodist Church.*
J. W. W. Daniel, *The 150th Anniversary, Mulberry St. Church.* Macon: J. W. Burke Co., 1951.
Bessie L. Hart, *Pastors of Mulberry.* Macon: Southern Press, 1965.

Methodism in Macon, Georgia from 1826 to 1903, 75th Anniversary of Macon Methodism.
Minutes of the Annual Conferences, 1773-1839.
O. A. Park, *The Centennial Celebration—1826-1926.* Macon: J. W. Burke Co., 1926.
G. G. Smith, *Georgia and Florida.* 1877.

McPHEETERS, JULIAN CLAUDIUS (1889-   ), American evangelist, pastor and educator, was born at Oxley, Mo., on July 6, 1889, the son of William Garland and Edna (Greer) McPheeters. Educated at Marvin College, MISSOURI, he later taught Latin and Greek and studied at Meridian College, MISSISSIPPI, 1910-11, and was at SOUTHERN METHODIST UNIVERSITY for one year, 1916. Honorary degrees were later conferred upon him. He married Ethel Chilton on Jan. 28, 1914, and they had two children, Chilton Claudius and Virginia Wave.

Licensed to preach in 1908, he held summer revivals and then was received on trial in the ST. LOUIS CONFERENCE (MES). He was ordained deacon and elder and went into full connection in 1921. His appointments were: Oran, 1909-10; evangelist, 1912-16; Williamsville, 1917; Mellow Memorial, ST. LOUIS, 1918; Summersville, 1919-21; Missoula, Mont., 1921-23; University Church, TUCSON, Ariz., 1923-30; Glide Memorial, SAN FRANCISCO, 1930-48. He became president of ASBURY THEOLOGICAL SEMINARY, 1942-62 (1942-48 serving both Glide Memorial and the seminary), and he retired in 1962.

In 1918 an authoritative medical report indicated that he had tuberculosis and would never be able to preach but might find it possible to do light work in five years. By faith, prayer and following his physician's directions (he slept on an open porch for three years), he was preaching twice on Sunday within one year. During his pastorate at Missoula, the membership doubled in two years.

He was the founder and builder of Glide Memorial Institutional Church in San Francisco, then called the most pagan city in America. When Glide Church purchased the Californian Hotel, McPheeters did away with the bar, and within one month the hotel's average rate of occupancy became the highest in the city.

A leader of the holiness movement, McPheeters restored the academic accreditation of Asbury Theological Seminary; paid off its debt; and increased the annual enrollment from sixty to 250 students. He was also founder and president of the Redwoods Camp Meeting near Santa Cruz, Calif. From 1942 to 1962 he was editor of *The Herald,* successor of *The Pentecostal Herald,* edited by H. C. MORRISON. After retirement McPheeters continued to edit *The Herald.* He wrote eleven books and was a delegate to the UNITING CONFERENCE in 1939, the JURISDICTIONAL CONFERENCE in 1940, and the ECUMENICAL METHODIST CONFERENCE, 1947.

The Asbury Seminarian, Spring-Summer, 1962.
Who's Who in Methodism, 1952.   JESSE A. EARL

McPHERSON, HARRY W. (1879-1957), American education executive, was born in rural Cumberland County, Ill. His college education was at ILLINOIS WESLEYAN UNIVERSITY, and his theological training at BOSTON UNIVERSITY. Joining the ILLINOIS CONFERENCE in 1904, he served churches until 1932, with a term as superintendent of the Springfield District, 1923-25. His social and ecumenical outlook led him to be one of the founders of the Illinois Council of Churches.

As president of Illinois Wesleyan during the difficult depression years, 1932-36, he saved it from financial losses by his firm and wise administration. His plan of accepting farm produce as tuition kept many students in college, and gave Wesleyan much good publicity. The larger church called him in 1936 as Executive Secretary of its BOARD OF EDUCATION, and gave him charge of the Division of Educational Institutions. He was continued in this position in The Methodist Church from 1940 to 1948, in which position he served with distinction.

C. T. Howell, *Prominent Personalities*. 1945.
Journal of the Illinois Conference, 1958.
Elmo Scott Watson, *The Illinois Wesleyan Story*, 1850-1950. Bloomington, 1950.   HENRY G. NYLIN

McQUIGG, JAMES, Irish preacher and scholar, had an outstanding knowledge of the Irish language and was one of three General Missionaries along with CHARLES and GIDEON OUSELEY appointed in 1799. Owing to the hardships he had to endure, he broke down in health and had to return to circuit work. Here also his evangelistic success led to the formation of many new Societies. Trinity College, DUBLIN, offered him a Readership in Irish, but he refused this attractive academic post, choosing to remain a Methodist preacher. In 1815, after twenty-six years as a preacher, he was expelled by the Conference on the grounds of immorality, despite his strong denial of the charge. He continued the work he had begun of editing the Bible in Irish for the BRITISH AND FOREIGN BIBLE SOCIETY. Not until after his death, a few years later, was his innocence proved and his name cleared by the confession of the guilty party.

C. H. Crookshank, *Methodism in Ireland*. 1885-88.
R. H. Gallagher, *Pioneer Preachers* (Irish). 1965.
F. Jeffery, *Irish Methodism*. 1964.   FREDERICK JEFFERY

MacROSSIE, ALLAN (1861-1940), American pastor, district superintendent, educator, was born of Scotch parentage at Kingston, Ontario, Canada, the son of William and Althea (Hershey) MacRossie, both devout Methodists. He married Edith M. Weston on Oct. 18, 1888, and they had two sons, William and Allan, Jr.

Educated at Queens University, Kingston, Ontario (A.B.) and DREW THEOLOGICAL SEMINARY, B.D., 1887, and later the D.D., he entered the NEW YORK EAST CONFERENCE in 1888. His appointments were: Corona, N. Y., 1888-91; South Park, Hartford, Conn., 1891-93; Mamaroneck, N. Y., 1893-94; Grace, Brooklyn, N. Y., 1894-99; Sand Street, Brooklyn, 1900-01; St. James, New York, 1901-11; Superintendent, New York District, 1911-17; St. Andrew's, New York, 1917-21; Commissioner, War Council, American Red Cross, 1917-18; then he became educational director, General Conference Commission on COURSES OF STUDY, 1921-39, and proved a commanding leader in the field of ministerial training.

A member of the Board of Home Missions, Board of Foreign Missions, and Commission on Conservation and Advance, he was also a trustee of Drew and Drew Seminary for Young Women. MacRossie was a manager of the New York Federation of Churches, the New York Deaconess Home, and the Methodist Hospital in Brooklyn. Several times he was a delegate and reserve delegate to the GENERAL CONFERENCE.

MacRossie's excellent training in Biblical perspective at Queens University and Drew Seminary prepared him

in the beginning for the so-called higher criticism which was then starting to stir theological circles and causing confusion and bitterness. Young MacRossie found his way between "the stagnation of reactionaryism and the over-rashness of radicalism." As pastor and district superintendent he was an inspiring counsellor.

A dynamic executive, he completely revolutionized the method of training young ministers in the Conference Course, establishing virtually a system of adult education through correspondence. He developed what might be called a college of preachers which met once a year at Evanston, Ill., to listen to religious leaders from the most important pulpits and theological schools. The ministers in the Conference Course constituted what was sometimes called the largest theological school in the world.

Bishop McCONNELL said in his memoir of MacRossie in 1940:

He had to be on his guard constantly against other administrative agencies which would, if they could, have taken over his commission as a secondary part of some other organization. He had need of all his Scotch sturdiness before he came to the end. During the past two decades, the influence of Dr. MacRossie has played more directly upon the majority of younger ministers than that of any other educational official during his time. Dr. MacRossie was a marvel of industry, of presistent persistence in working toward an end, of shrewdness of discernment as to men's capabilities and peculiarities, of loyalty to his friends and his ideals.

He died on March 2, 1940, and his funeral was conducted in Christ Church Methodist, New York City, on March 5. Bishops E. H. HUGHES and F. J. McConnell delivered the addresses. Burial was in Kingston, Ontario. He was survived by his wife and two sons.

Alumni Record, Drew Theological Seminary, 1867-1925.
F. J. McConnell, *By the Way*. 1952.
E. H. Hughes, *I Was Made a Minister*. 1943.
New York Conference Journal, 1940.
C. F. Price, *Who's Who in American Methodism*. 1916.
JESSE A. EARL

H. N. McTYEIRE

McTYEIRE, HOLLAND NIMMONS (1824-1889), American bishop, editor, educator, and the great figure in Southern Methodism during the crucial years following the Civil War, was born in Barnwell County, S. C., on July 28,

1824. He was educated at the old COKESBURY SCHOOL in his native state and at RANDOLPH-MACON COLLEGE in VIRGINIA, remaining there as a tutor one year after his graduation. In 1845 he was admitted on trial to the VIRGINIA CONFERENCE of the M. E. Church, South, and appointed to Williamsburg. Two years later, he became pastor of St. Francis Street Church in Mobile, Ala. He was sent to NEW ORLEANS in 1849 and in 1851 he founded the *New Orleans Christian Advocate*. He became editor of the central organ of his Church, the *Christian Advocate* at NASHVILLE, Tenn., in 1858 and continued in that influential position for four years, becoming an intense Southern protagonist as the Civil War came on. He attacked abolitionists, Republicans, and the North generally until 1862 when Nashville was taken over by the Union Army and the METHODIST PUBLISHING HOUSE property occupied. McTyeire bitterly criticized the withdrawal from Nashville under General Joseph Johnston and wrote: "The tameness of surrender, without a blow, must have made the bones of Andrew Jackson turn in his grave at the Hermitage."

The McTyeires refugeed in southern ALABAMA at a cabin built in the woods near Mobile. The effectiveness of the Northern blockade was such that McTyeire could buy no shoes for his wife in all Mobile.

Later McTyeire was appointed pastor in MONTGOMERY, Ala., where he served until the GENERAL CONFERENCE of 1866. There was some question just after the war among the Southern bishops of abandoning the Church's status as an independent organization, but they asked McTyeire to draft an address which would summon the annual conferences to elect delegates to a General Conference to decide on these matters. He did so and in this General Conference, the first the South had had in eight years, McTyeire took the lead, being the champion of lay representation and for an increase in the pastoral time limit from two years to four. He also championed plans for organizing the COLORED METHODIST EPISCOPAL CHURCH and took the lead in calling for the reestablishment of the missionary program of the Church, and for rehabilitating the Publishing House in Nashville.

He was elected bishop by this conference and at this critical time when he was forty-two years of age. As Bishop SOULE died in 1867, this threw great responsibility on him as one of the new bishops. He lived in Nashville, but conducted 125 annual conferences, an average of five and one-half for each year he served as bishop.

McTyeire was the virtual founder of VANDERBILT UNIVERSITY in Nashville in 1872. He secured from Cornelius Vanderbilt the original gift of $500,000, which was later increased to $1,000,000 and which has been added to by other members of the family in later years. Vanderbilt provided that Bishop McTyeire should be president of the Board of Trustees with full veto power.

In his later years he lived on the grounds of the University. He died there on Feb. 15, 1889, and is buried on the campus.

McTyeire's greatest literary contribution was his *History of Methodism*. He also wrote a work called *Duties of Christian Masters*, dealing with the question of slavery. He was the foremost authority on Church law and published *A Manual of the Discipline* and *A Catechism on Church Government*. He was one of the strongest bishops of the Church in an era of strong bishops. Bishop ATTICUS HAYGOOD wrote of him: "He was no mere ecclesiastic. He

was in his Church, its first statesman, as well as chief pastor."

G. Alexander, *History of the M. E. Church, South*. 1894.
C. T. Carter, *Tennessee Conference*. 1948.
Dictionary of National Biography.
Journal of the General Conference, 1890.
J. J. Tigert, *Holland Nimmons McTyeire*. 1955.

ELMER T. CLARK

MACY, VICTOR W. (1910-   ), American FREE METHODIST ordained elder of the Southern California Conference of his Church and a mission executive, was born at LOS ANGELES, Calif. He was educated at SEATTLE PACIFIC COLLEGE, B.A., D.D.; Biblical Seminary in New York, S.T.B., and S.T.M. He married Susan B. Blain in 1936, and became a missionary, under appointment of the General Missionary Board for MOZAMBIQUE, Africa, 1936-60. He has been Area Secretary for Africa since 1960. His foreign travels include Africa, Asia and Latin America areas.

Dr. Macy has specialized in production of mission films, developing near-professional levels in color-sound filming. His sound-color films are: *Africa Fellowship; Beauty for Ashes; Cheeza; High Calling; Missionaries are Human; Ziuko; African Harvest; Eastern Harvest; Four Seasons; The Mountains Sing; World Parish; Conquerors for Christ; World Fellowship; Beautiful Feet;* and a film for Seattle Pacific College. He is the author of *History of Free Methodist Mission in Portuguese East Africa*. He resides in Bukavu, CONGO.

BYRON S. LAMSON

MADAN, MARTIN (1726-1790), Anglican Evangelical, was the elder brother of Spencer Madan, Bishop of Peterborough, and cousin to William Cowper, the poet. Educated at Westminster School and Christ Church, OXFORD, Madan was called to the bar in 1748. Shortly afterward he was converted under JOHN WESLEY's preaching and was ordained in the Church of England. In 1750 he was appointed chaplain of the Lock Hospital in London, a post which he held for thirty years. He itinerated for the COUNTESS OF HUNTINGDON from 1757. He also associated with the Methodists and attended the Conference of 1762.

Gentleman's Magazine, 1790, part i, 478.
Gospel Magazine, iv, 196.   A. SKEVINGTON WOOD

MADHYA PRADESH ANNUAL CONFERENCE is a conference of INDIA which was named for and covers a central and the second largest state of India. Bhopal is its capital, and the state is located between the Narbada and Godavari Rivers, and touches the states of the Deccan, as well as of the northern part of the country. It is rich in minerals and has extensive forests. Hinduism is the predominant religion and Hindi the chief language. There are many tribal languages and dialects. The state covers an area of 171,217 square miles and has a population of about 32,000,000.

The Madhya Pradesh Conference was organized in 1913 out of what had been the Central Provinces Mission Conference. The name was changed after independence to Madhya Pradesh Annual Conference, which has the same meaning.

The conference has four districts, namely Balaghat,

Bastar, Jabalpur, and Khandwa. Of these the largest is the one centered in Jabalpur, a city of 295,375, and perhaps the most centrally located city in India, with a healthful climate and high altitude. It is about 616 miles from Bombay and 733 miles from Calcutta. Jabalpur contains two Methodist churches and the Leonard Theological College. The conference supports a membership of 15,901 (1968) served by approximately thirty-two ordained and fifty supply pastors.

Disciplines.
Barbara H. Lewis, *Methodist Overseas Missions.* 1960.
Project Handbook Overseas Missions, The United Methodist Church. New York: Board of Missions, 1969.   N. B. H.

MADISON, WISCONSIN,

MADISON, WISCONSIN, U.S.A., the state capital, population of 170,073, was planned as a community by Steven Mason and James Doty in 1836 and was named for President James Madison. Incorporated as a city in 1856, it is the seat of the University of Wisconsin (chartered in 1848) and of Edgewood College.

Methodist services were first held in Madison in November 1837, "in the Barroom of the American House, then owned by James Morrison." Salmon Stebbins, a presiding elder, preached that night, and then received an offering totaling $11. During 1838, a Mr. Pillsbury preached in Madison about once a month. Salmon Stebbins also is reported to have stopped by occasionally that year, as presiding elder.

The first Methodist building was begun in 1849, and completed in 1853. The second building, on the present site at Wisconsin and Dayton, was built in 1876. Madison first appears in the minutes in 1843, with Thomas L. Bennett as pastor. In 1845 the church had only forty-six members. By 1876 the Madison M. E. Church reported 230 members and church property appraised at $43,590. Then the German Methodist Church had sixty-five members and property worth $4,500.

During the 1890's the membership grew rapidly to about 400. As early as 1908 the church employed an assistant pastor to work with the University students, and in 1912 a WESLEY FOUNDATION was started near the campus. A few years later First Church sponsored the forming of a mission in the city's Italian district, and this was merged with a neighborhood church in the early 1960's. In 1919, First Church started Methodist Hospital, which today is a modern 150-bed institution.

The greatest period of expansion into the growing suburban areas came after World War II, when new congregations were established in each new major development in the city.

Madison also has two WESLEYAN METHODIST churches, a FREE METHODIST CHURCH, and an A.M.E. CHURCH.

Madison had eleven United Methodist churches in 1970 with a combined membership of 7,481 and property appraised at $3,549,862. First Church with 2,302 members had property worth $1,292,739.

General Minutes
History of First Methodist Church, Madison, Wisconsin. 1937.
JESSE A. EARL
J. ELLSWORTH KALAS

MADISON COLLEGE,

MADISON COLLEGE, Uniontown, Pennsylvania, the third college established in the United States under the auspices of the M. E. Church. It was a project of the PITTSBURGH CONFERENCE launched at the initial session of that Con-

ference in 1825. It opened for students and was chartered by the Legislature of PENNSYLVANIA in 1827. The first President was HENRY B. BASCOM, later a bishop of the M. E. Church, South. Bascom had been Chaplain of Congress in 1823 and named the College for President James Madison.

Madison only continued as a M. E. College for five years, until 1832, at which time the patronage of the Pittsburgh Conference was transferred to ALLEGHENY COLLEGE at MEADVILLE, Pa., and the faculty and students of Madison were transferred to Allegheny. Since the first Methodist college, COKESBURY, had been discontinued after the fire that destroyed it in 1795; and since the second college, AUGUSTA, established under the patronage of OHIO and KENTUCKY CONFERENCES in 1822, was abandoned in the 1840s, this continuity of Madison in and via Allegheny gives to Allegheny College the claim to be the oldest Methodist college in the United States.

The Madison College buildings in Uniontown were occupied for a time in the 1830s as a Cumberland Presbyterian college, and then they went under the control of the M. P. Church. At the meeting of the GENERAL CONFERENCE of that church in 1850, GEORGE BROWN reported that the trustees of Madison College had offered the institution to the conference. Since the location was at a central point between the northern and southern conferences of the M. P. Church, the offer was accepted.

A Board of Trustees was appointed and Madison College commenced operations again in the summer of 1851. In 1853, the NORTH CAROLINA CONFERENCE of the M. P. Church recommended Madison College "as the most suitable place at which the sons of Methodist Protestants may be educated." In 1854, JOHN SPEIGHT was appointed to act as agent for the North Carolina Conference and solicit funds for the college. R. H. Ball, FRANCIS WATERS, and Samuel K. Cox each served as President of Madison College for short periods of time. However, since the various presidents, faculty members, commissioners and trustees of the college were largely selected from the southern conferences of the M. P. Church, some tension was created. As a result of the controversial political atmosphere of the period, the faculty and president resigned at the commencement of 1855 and announced that a new M. P. college would open in Lynchburg, Va., in September of that year. Eighty-five students also withdrew from Madison College to enroll at Lynchburg College. Brown, who had served as President of the Board of Trustees, became President of Madison College that fall, and remained in that position until 1857 when, due to indebtedness, small enrollment, lack of financial support and endowment, the trustees decided to close the college.

A. H. Bassett, *Concise History.* 1877.
Minutes of the Pittsburgh Conference, ME, 1876.
Our Church Record, June 23, Sept. 29, 1898.
W. G. Smeltzer, *Headwaters of the Ohio.* 1951.
RALPH HARDEE RIVES
W. GUY SMELTZER

MAGARET, ERNST CARL

MAGARET, ERNST CARL (1845-1924), German-American minister and hymn writer, was born at Anklam, Pomerania, Germany on July 6, 1845. Educated in the classical Gymnasia at Anklam and Greifswald, he emigrated to America in 1864 and became a teacher at CENTRAL WESLEYAN COLLEGE, Warrenton, Mo. In 1869 he was admitted to the Southwest German Annual Conference of the M. E. Church. From 1868-1883 he served various churches in IOWA and ILLINOIS. From 1883-1884 he was a professor at the MOUNT PLEASANT GERMAN COLLEGE. He then served important German churches in BURLINGTON, IOWA; Warsaw, Pekin and Belleville, Illinois; and in ST. LOUIS until his retirement in 1917.

He was noted for his writings, particularly poetry, and the editorship of the *Jubiläumsbuch der St. Louis Deutschen Konferenz*. His greatest achievement was in the translation and composition of original hymns for every important German Methodist hymnal: *Deutsches-Gesang-und Melodienbuch* (1888); *Die Perle* (1894); *Lobe den Herrn!* (1895) and *Die Pilgerklänge* (1907). He edited himself *Die Kliene Palme* (1895) which contained fifty-six translations and twenty-one originals. He died in Omaha, Neb., on July 3, 1924.

Jubiläumsbuch der St. Louis Deutschen Konferenz; Minutes of the St. Louis German Conference 1924; Hymnals and Memorabilia in Z. F. Meyer Collection of German-American Methodism (Iowa Wesleyan).   LOUIS A. HASELMAYER

MAGATA, DAVID, was born in the Magaliesberg, was captured by the Matabele and became a personal attendant of Mzilikazi. He escaped when Mzilikazi was attacked by the Boers and went to Thaba 'Nchu Wesleyan Mission. Converted he returned to the Magaliesberg to find his family had disappeared. He settled in Potchefstroom and preached every morning on the market square to the Bantu and colored people. Some whites laid a charge of disturbing the peace against him. The local magistrate ordered a public lashing and banished him from the Republic. After receiving his lashing, Magata went to Natal and then to Sekukuniland. On the border he met Commandant Paul Kruger who listened to his story sympathetically and gave him written permission to return to Potchefstroom. He was to be allowed to preach and no one was to interfere with him. Blencowe appointed Magata as a lay agent of the Wesleyan MISSIONARY SOCIETY at an annual salary of £12.

Journal of the Methodist Historical Society of South Africa. Vol. III, No. 2 (October 1958).
Minutes of the South African Conference, 1939.

D. C. VEYSIE

MAGAZINES. American Methodism. The general story of the publication of magazines and newspapers in American Methodism will be found in the account of the METHODIST PUBLISHING HOUSE and the Book Concern which it succeeded. Certain distinctive and significant magazines which have been and may now be published as official organs of the Church will be found listed under their own names, as *Arminian Magazine, Methodist Review, Southern Quarterly Review, Religion In Life*, etc.

British Methodism. Wesleyan Methodism. The first Magazine of Methodism, *The Arminian Magazine* (q.v.) was started by JOHN WESLEY in 1778 and continued under various titles until 1969 (vide *Methodist Magazine*). The nineteenth-century controversies within the Connexion, together with the growing literacy of the people, created a great demand for more reading matter, and the number of Methodist magazines and newspapers multiplied. *The Watchman* (see below), *The Illuminator* (1835-36), and *The Wesleyan Vindicator* (1850-52) defended the official Wesleyan policy and polity against left-wing reformers.

Learned comment on events and current literature was catered for in *The London Quarterly Review* (1853-1932), later to be amalgamated with *The Holborn Quarterly* (see below) to form *The London Quarterly and Holborn Review* (1932-68) and now allied with *The Church Quarterly Review* to form the present *Church Quarterly*.

LOCAL PREACHERS were served by *The Preachers Magazine* (1890-1927) and *The Preachers and Class Leaders Magazine* (1928-54) which has now been superseded by *The Preachers Quarterly*. An earlier publication, *The Methodist Pulpit* (1871-73), simply reproduced sermons by well-known preachers.

For Sunday school teachers there were *The Wesleyan Sunday School Magazine* (1857-89), *The Methodist Sunday School Magazine* (1890-1901), *The Teacher and Preacher* (1909-13) and *The Teachers Magazine* (1930-47).

Many magazines for children and young people were issued: *The Child's Magazine* (1824-45), *Early Days* (1846-1916), *The Kiddies Magazine* (1917-57), *Our Boys and Girls* (1887-1905), *Youth's Instructor* (1817-55), and *The Guild* (1897-1901). *The Choir* (1910-64) catered for musicians, and was superseded by a general magazine on the arts, *Mosaic* (1965-67). *The Church Record*, under various similar titles (1892-1957) provided an inset for local church magazines. Magazines for home reading included *The Cottager's Friend*, later entitled *The Christian Miscellany and Family Visitor* (1846-1900), *The Wesleyan Tract Reporter* (1841-49), *The City Road Magazine* (1871-76), *The Methodist Messenger* (1871-72), *The King's Highway* (1872-1927, "A Journal of Scriptural Holiness"), *Experience* (1881-1927), *The Monthly Greeting* (1890-92), *Hope* (1909-11) and *Home and Empire Magazine* (1924). Special interests were met in *The Methodist Temperance Magazine* (1868-1906), *The Wesley Naturalist* (1887-89), *The Journal of the Wesley Bible Union* (1914-27).

The Methodist New Connexion. The first real rival to *The Methodist Magazine* was one of the same title, started by the METHODIST NEW CONNEXION in 1798, but in 1812 the title was changed to *The New Methodist Magazine* and in 1833 to *The Methodist New Connexion Magazine*. Thus it continued until 1907. *The Methodist Monitor* had appeared in 1796-97 as an organ for disseminating the views of the Kilhamites who, under the leadership of ALEXANDER KILHAM and WILLIAM THOM, separated from the Wesleyans in 1796 to form the Methodist New Connexion. This connexion also published *The Sunday Scholars Magazine* (1850-98) and *Young People* (1899-1907).

The Reform Movements. The Reform Movements produced an abundance of literature. *The Tent Methodist Magazine* (1823), *The Wesleyan Protestant Methodist Magazine* (1829-34), *The Wesleyan Association Magazine* (1828-57), *The Watchman's Lantern* (1834-35), *The Wesley Banner* (1849-54) (q.v.), *The Wesleyan Review and Evangelical Record* (1850-51), *The Wesleyan Reformer* (1851-52), all expressed the thought and traced the development of the reform agitation within Methodism during the first half of the nineteenth century, but when the UNITED METHODIST FREE CHURCHES was formed in 1857, *The United Methodist Free Churches Magazine* held the field until 1907—from 1892 to 1907 the title was *The Methodist Monthly*. Other magazines of this body were *The Sunday School Hive* (1849-91), *Welcome*

Words (1867-91), and *The Brooklet* (1885-94). *The Wesleyan Methodist Penny Magazine* ran from 1853 to 1857. Those who did not enter the United Methodist Free Churches formed The WESLEYAN REFORM UNION, and as such exist to this day. They published *The Wesleyan Reform Union Magazine* (1861-65), which in 1866 assumed the title *Christian Words* which it still carries.

The Bible Christians. This small Connexion published *The Bible Christian Magazine* (1822-1907) and a *Young People's Magazine* which began about 1825 and ran, under various titles, until 1907.

The United Methodist Church. This body published *The United Methodist Magazine* (1907-32), *Young People* (1907) and *Pleasant Hour* (1908-12).

The Primitive Methodist Church. This, the largest non-Wesleyan body, published its own magazine from 1819 to 1932. From 1819 to 1899 its title was *The Primitive Methodist Magazine*, and from 1900 to 1932 *The Aldersgate and Primitive Methodist Magazine*. Of high quality, especially under the editorship of A. S. PEAKE, was *The Holborn Review* (1910-32), previously known as *The Christian Ambassador* (1863-77) and *The Primitive Methodist Quarterly Review* (1878-1915). Teachers and preachers were catered for by *The Primitive Methodist Preachers Magazine* (1832-?) and later by adapting the Wesleyan periodical of the same title, *The Teachers Assistant* (1873-95), *The Sunday School Journal and Preachers Magazine* (1896-1907), *The Teacher and Preacher* (1908-13), *The Primitive Methodist Sunday School Magazine* (1914-32). Young people were provided for in *Springtime* (1886-1929), *Joyful Tidings* (1892-1903), *Advance* (1923-32), and *The Child's Friend* (1865-1914).

Interdenominational. A magazine intended to serve all branches of Methodism, *The Methodist Quarterly*, ran from 1867 to 1872. It claimed to be "independent and unsectional," sympathetic to liberal tendencies in Church polity and without bigotry. It believed that the days of controversy over ecclesiastical polity were past. Of shorter duration were *The Methodist World* (1870) and a *Methodist Times* which ran from 1867 to 1869 and is not to be confused with a newspaper of the same title which ran from 1885 to 1932 (see below).

Newspapers in British Methodism. The first Methodist newspaper to appear was *The Watchman* (1834-85) (q.v.), intended to defend Wesleyan policy and polity against the attacks of left-wing reformers (as Protestant Methodists, *The Warrenite Controversy* and *The Fly Sheets* agitation). Although it was not an official Conference publication, it exerted a strong influence on Wesleyan Methodists. Conservative in tone, it reported and commented on ecclesiastical and political events. The newspaper of the Wesleyan Reformers was *The Wesleyan Times* (1849-52), but there were others of short-lived duration—*The Wesleyan Chronicle* (1840), *The Wesleyan and Christian Record* (1841), and *The Wesleyan* (1843-48). In 1861 *The Methodist Recorder* (q.v.) appeared, and is still in circulation. In 1885 a new publication, representing more liberal tendencies, was started under the editorship of HUGH PRICE HUGHES—*The Methodist Times* (1885-1932). The PRIMITIVE METHODISTS had *The Primitive Methodist* (1868-1905) which incorporated *The Primitive Methodist World* (1883-1908), and, in turn, became *The Primitive Methodist Leader* (1905-25) and *The Methodist Leader* (1926-32). With the consummation of METHODIST UNION this newspaper amalgamated with *The Methodist Times* to become *The Meth-*

odist Times and Leader (1932-37) and in 1937 this was incorporated with *The Methodist Recorder*. Other newspapers representing the smaller denominations were *The United Methodist* (1903-1932) and *The Free Methodist* (1886-1907). *The Methodist* (1874-84) endeavored to serve all branches of Methodism and was of wide culture, politically liberal and was the predecessor of *The Methodist Times* which it commended in its last issue. *The Wesleyan Methodist* (1923-24) promulgated the views of a party within Wesleyan Methodism which protested against Methodist Union.

The Joyful News was a lively weekly journal with an emphasis on evangelism. The first issue, edited by THOMAS CHAMPNESS, appeared in February 1883. It greatly extended its influence under SAMUEL CHADWICK, Principal of CLIFF COLLEGE. As the magazine of this college, it continued under its original title until 1962, when it appeared as *Advance* (not to be confused with an earlier magazine of this title). In 1964 it was succeeded by *The Cliff Witness*.

JOHN C. BOWMER

J. RALPH MAGEE

MAGEE, JUNIUS RALPH (1880-1970), American bishop, was born in Maquoketa, Iowa, June 3, 1880, the son of John Calvin and Jane Amelia (Cole) Magee. He received his early educational training in his native state. He graduated from the Iowa State Teachers College in 1901 with the B.D. degree. In 1904 he received the Ph.B. degree from MORNINGSIDE COLLEGE and the LL.D. degree there in 1931. He graduated at BOSTON UNIVERSITY SCHOOL OF THEOLOGY in 1910, receiving the S.T.B., and the D.D. in 1947. He held a number of other honorary degrees.

He was ordained and served as a deacon in 1904 and as elder in 1906. His pastorates were: Rustin Avenue Church, Sioux City, Ia., 1902-04; Paulina, Ia., 1904-07; Falmouth, Mass., 1907-11; First Church, Taunton, Mass., 1911-14; Daniel Dorchester Memorial, BOSTON, 1914-19; St. Mark's Church, Brookline, Mass., 1919-21; and First Church, SEATTLE, Wash., 1921-29.

He became superintendent of the Seattle District,

serving in this capacity until 1932, when he was elected and consecrated bishop. He was resident bishop of the St. Paul (Minn.) Area from 1932 until 1939; president of Hamline University, St. Paul, 1933-34; resident bishop of the Des Moines Area, 1939-44, and resident bishop of the Chicago Area from 1944 until 1952, when he retired. He was director of the Crusade for Christ, 1944-48 and president of the Council of Bishops, 1950-51.

Bishop Magee was married to Harriet A. Keeler on Sept. 10, 1902. Their children are J. Homer Magee, Associate Secretary of the Council on World Service and Finance; and Dorothy J. Magee of the American Hospital Supply Corporation. Mrs. Magee died on Oct. 31, 1943.

In 1944 a portrait of Bishop Magee was presented by Iowa Methodists to the Iowa State Department of History and Archives. Bishop Magee was the first native Iowan ever to be made a bishop and to serve in Iowa as such from any denomination.

Bishop Magee served in an official capacity in a number of important church-wide organizations. He was named by B. C. Forbes in the Hearst Newspapers, as one of the sixteen most influential persons in Seattle.

He was the chairman of the committee to combine the Puget Sound Conference and Columbia River Conference into what is now the Pacific Northwest Conference, and presided at the Northwest German Conference when it was integrated into nine other conferences. This meant considerable work with pension funds, equalization *in re* ages of members, etc.

He served as trustee of the following organizations: Chamber of Commerce, Seattle, 1925-32; University of Puget Sound; Simpson College; Cornell College; McKendree College; Iowa Methodist Hospital; Hamline University; Northwestern University; Greater Chicago Federation of Churches; Garrett Theological Seminary; Kendall College; Illinois Wesleyan University; Wesley Foundation, University of Illinois; Wesley Memorial Hospital, Chicago; and the Lake Bluff, Illinois, Children's Home.

He died Dec. 19, 1970, in Morton Grove, Ill.

Who's Who in The Methodist Church. 1966.

Mary French Caldwell

MAGIC METHODISTS, a nickname given to the followers of James Crawfoot in addition to the more widely accepted title of Forest Methodists.

John T. Wilkinson

MAHABANE, EZEKIEL EGBERT (1900-   ), South African minister, was born at Thaba 'Nchu, Orange Free State (brother of Z. R. Mahabane), on Feb. 21, 1900. He received primary education at Besonvale Practising School and high school education at Morija in Basutoland (now Lesotho). He then trained as a teacher at Lovedale Missionary Institution and thereafter entered the Methodist ministry in 1925. After theological training at Wesley House, Fort Hare, he travelled in the following circuits: Douglas, Kilnerton, Pretoria, Randfontein, Vereeniging and Johannesburg. In 1962 he became the first African Superintendent of the Witwatersrand (African) Mission. Offices held: General Secretary of the Temperance and Social Welfare Department of the Methodist Church 1939-56; General Missionary Secretary 1957-62; Ministerial General Officer of the Missionary Department 1963 to present time; Vice-President of the Christian Council of South Africa 1960-61; President of the Witwatersrand

E. E. Mahabane

Christian Council 1965 to present time. He represented the Methodist Church of South Africa at the 1956 World Methodist Conference at Lake Junaluska, and at the Third Assembly of the World Council of Churches at New Delhi in 1961. He is a member of the World Council of Churches Central Committee.

S. P. Freeland

MAHABANE, ZACCHEUS RICHARD (1881-   ), South African minister, was born on Aug. 15, 1881 at Thaba 'Nchu, Orange Free State. His parents were converted from heathenism when he was ten years old and his father began to preach immediately. Zaccheus was a herd boy until he went to school. He trained for the teaching profession at Morija, Basutoland, but after two years' teaching became a court interpreter. Accepted for the ministry in 1908, he was trained at Lesseyton, Queenstown and served in the following circuits: Cape Town, Vrede, Kimberley, Winburg, Kroonstad, Brandfort. He became the first African official member of the Methodist Conference in South Africa when he was appointed Secretary of the Board of Examiners (1935-40), and served as a member of the Revision, Church Union and Sessional Committees. He also became the first African President of the Triennial Convention of the Young Men's Guild, held a number of positions on national bodies, and attended gatherings in Belgium (1926), Accra (1957) and Ibadan, Nigeria (1958). He retired from active work at the end of 1957, but continues to preach and undertake supply work.

S. P. Freeland

MAHIN, MILTON (1824-1916), pioneer American clergyman, was born in Green Co., Ohio, on Oct. 22, 1824. He moved to Indiana and was admitted on trial in the North Indiana Conference in 1841. He married Eliza Dorsey, Oct. 31, 1843. Milton Mahin had an enviable and unique record in that the Conference *Minutes* show that he served a total of seventy-five years as pastor and presiding elder. He was elected to the General Conference in 1868. He died Oct. 7, 1916.

Harold Thrasher

MAHON, ROBERT HENRY (1840-1929), American minister, was born in Crockett County, Tenn., on Oct. 22, 1840, the son of Jackson H. Mahon, a Methodist minister. He was received on trial in the MEMPHIS CONFERENCE in 1860, and appointed junior pastor with his uncle, Robert Burns, to the Trenton Circuit. After two years he was sent to Paris, Tenn. He served also as pastor at Grenada, Miss., at Mayfield, Ky.; Broadway, in Paducah, Ky.; First and Central Churches, MEMPHIS; and at Brownsville, Dyersburg and Union City, Tenn.; presiding elder of Memphis, Dyersburg and Brownsville Districts. Seven times he was a delegate to the GENERAL CONFERENCE and two other times alternate; several times he received a considerable vote for bishop. He published a book, *The Token of the Covenant or The Meaning of Baptism.* R. H. Mahon was one of the outstanding scholars and ecclesiastical statesmen of his conference, and was well-known as interpreter of the Scriptures.

In 1864 he was married to Annie Vaulx Blakemore of Trenton, Tenn., who died in 1876; in 1878 he was married to Mrs. Sue Hobson Senter of Nashville, Tenn.; she died in 1912. This same year he took the supernumerary relation after fifty-two years of active ministry. Thereafter he lived in the home of his daughter, Mrs. Ruth Hay of Brownsville, Tenn. He died May 28, 1929. He taught a ladies' Bible class regularly during his years of retirement.

While pastor of First Church, Memphis, he secured the appointment of JOHN R. PEPPER as Sunday school superintendent, a world figure in Sunday school work.

F. H. PEEPLES

IDABELLE LEWIS MAIN

MAIN, IDABELLE LEWIS (1887-   ), missionary educator in CHINA and BRAZIL, was born in IOWA and studied at MORNINGSIDE COLLEGE and Columbia University. Her first teaching was at Tientsin, in the Keen School for Girls. She also taught English in Nankai University, where for one semester she had Chou En-lai in her class.

In 1924, she was appointed assistant secretary of Methodist education for all China, and assisted in editing *The China Christian Educational Review.* In 1926, she became president of Hwanan College in Foochow, but resigned in 1929 to make way for a Chinese president, and in the following year she returned to Shanghai as a secretary of the China Christian Educational Association.

In 1932, she was married to W. A. Main, treasurer of the China missions of the M. E. Church. They remained in China until 1941, editing *The China Christian Educational Review* and *The China Christian Advocate.* In 1941 they retired and lived in America, but after Mr. Main's death in 1945, she returned to Hwanan College where she taught until the Communist occupation in 1949. In 1950 she was appointed to Colegio Bennett in RIO DE JANEIRO, and taught there for five years. She is now retired and living in Robincroft Home, Pasadena, Calif.

FRANCIS P. JONES

MAINE is the extreme northeastern state of the Union. It is bounded on the east, north, and west by CANADA, on the southwest by NEW HAMPSHIRE, and on the southeast by the Atlantic Ocean. The forty-fifth parallel divides the state into almost equal northern and southern sections. The extreme north is free of killing frost about three and one-half months of the year, and most of the state is spared for about four and one-third months. The largest of the New England states, Maine's area is 33,215 square miles, and its population is about 977,260.

The Province of Maine was granted to Ferdinando Gorges and John Mason in 1622. Gorges became the sole owner; after his death the Colony of Massachusetts Bay gradually encroached, and finally in 1677 bought the province from Gorges' heirs for 1,250 pounds. Maine continued as a part of Massachusetts until it was admitted to the Union as a state in 1820.

Methodism entered Maine when JESSE LEE was appointed to the Province of Maine and Lynn, Mass., at the session of the NEW ENGLAND CONFERENCE in Lynn in August 1793. On September 10, of that year, Lee delivered the first Methodist sermon in Maine at Saco. He soon visited eighteen towns in the province. In 1794 Lee was named presiding elder, and his district included MASSACHUSETTS, New Hampshire, and Maine. On November 13 that year, Lee preached at MONMOUTH, Maine, and found that a man named Wagner had formed a class of fifteen members there; it was the first Methodist class to be organized in Maine. During the conference year 1794-95, Lee dedicated a Methodist meetinghouse at (East) READFIELD, the first one to be erected in Maine. The next year a chapel was dedicated at Monmouth.

In 1798 BISHOP ASBURY conducted the New England Conference at (East) Readfield. At the 1799 session of the same conference in New York City, JOSHUA SOULE was admitted on trial; he was the first native of Maine to become a member of the New England Conference. Asbury appointed Soule a presiding elder in 1804. As a member of the 1808 GENERAL CONFERENCE, Soule drafted the plan for a delegated General Conference, one of the most important pieces of legislation ever adopted by the supreme law-making body of Methodism (see RESTRICTIVE RULES). Elected bishop in 1824, Soule was a dominant figure in the office for more than two-score years. He adhered South after the division in 1844. Two other bishops were born in Maine, DAVIS W. CLARK and EDGAR BLAKE, elected in 1864 and 1920, respectively. All three men were serving in other states and conferences when elevated to the episcopacy.

For several years Maine formed one district in the New England Conference, and in time it grew to three districts. The MAINE CONFERENCE was created by the 1824 General Conference, and was organized in 1825. In 1848 the Maine Conference was divided to form the East Maine Conference. After seventy-five years the two conferences were merged to form again the Maine Conference covering Maine and part of New Hampshire.

As soon as the Maine Conference was organized it became affiliated with a school called the Maine Wesleyan Seminary which had opened at Kent's Hill in February of that year. The institution had difficulties, but it kept going and in time was named the Maine Wesleyan Seminary and Female College. The conference board of education declared in 1880 that Maine Wesleyan was the leading institution of learning in the state and said that many young men were going directly from the school into the ranks of the itineracy. In 1900 the same board said there were few churches in the conference which had not felt the uplifting influence of the college. About 1910 Maine Wesleyan became a secondary school and was called KENTS HILL SCHOOL. Under that name it is today an accredited Methodist secondary school with an endowment of some $750,000, a plant worth $1,000,000, and about 300 students.

The *Maine Wesleyan Journal* was published from 1832 to 1841, and was then merged with *Zion's Herald*.

In 1970 the Maine Conference reported three districts, 134 pastoral charges, 142 ministers, 33,257 members, and property valued at $16,366,666.

Allen & Pillsbury, *Methodism in Maine*. 1887.
General Minutes, MEC and MC.
Minutes of the Maine Conference.   ALFRED G. HEMPSTEAD

MAINE CAMP MEETINGS. The first CAMP MEETING in MAINE is believed to have been held at Buxton in 1806. About twenty preachers, traveling and local, were present. Bishop ASBURY preached on Saturday and Sunday to a crowd estimated to be 5,000. Two years previously Asbury was in Buxton for a session of the NEW ENGLAND CONFERENCE. At that time he preached and ordained ministers in a grove, using a hay cart for a pulpit.

From this beginning at Buxton, camp meetings spread throughout the State, becoming a powerful influence in the life of Methodism. Evangelism was the prime purpose; however, not only were souls converted but also for several generations many preachers in the Conference were men converted at camp meetings. Here, too, the moral reform movements, especially the abolition of slavery and the temperance cause, were powerfully presented.

In the earlier development of the camp meeting, not much equipment was required—a speaker's stand, plank seats for the congregation, straw for mattresses, a place for tents and perhaps some sort of fence with a gate. As time went on, refinements were added, such as a "tabernacle," a boarding house for meals, and cottages built by individuals or by local churches on ground rented from the local camp meeting association.

There are known to have been forty or more locations in Maine where, for a longer or shorter time, camp meetings were held. Some changed from one site to another. The greatest crowds on record were those at Littleton. "Some of the Presiding Elders," wrote A. A. Callaghan,

"reported great crowds, one reported an attendance of 15,000 and said that if anyone had any suggestion as to how the situation could be handled he would be glad to consult."

East Livermore Camp Meeting was established in 1847; one of the organizers was a man who came to be known as Camp Meeting John Allen. He was converted in 1825 at the camp meeting at Industry. He used to take his granddaughter to the camp meeting at Strong, a few miles from her home at Fairbanks, where she often sang as a girl. Later she was known in world opera as Madame Nordica. Camp Meeting John Allen fittingly preached his last sermon at the age of ninety-three at the East Livermore Camp Meeting, and the next morning went "home to glory." The East Livermore Camp Meeting is still active, though for several years has not been under Methodist auspices.

Two outstanding camp meetings deserving particular mention are Old Orchard and Northport. The former, which ran from 1872 to 1934, at one time attracted national attention. The Northport Camp Meeting, which served the churches up and down the Penobscot River, had a landing for the Bangor-Boston steamships which was an added convenience and attraction. The association sponsoring this camp disbanded in the 1920's. Many of the cottages were privately owned; the others were acquired by individuals, and the place became a summer resort.

At present only two camp meetings continue to hold services and to preserve their organizations. The Empire Grove Camp Meeting at East Poland draws considerable support from the Portland District, holds a week of services and a Church Vacation School. The cottagers who spend the summer on the grounds for the most part have Methodist membership or traditions. Several Conference ministers own cottages, and one retired minister "winterized" his cottage and lives there the year round.

The other camp meeting still in operation is at Jacksonville located in Washington County on the Bangor District. It has a week of services and a youth program for those who cannot get to the Methodist Camp at Winthrop. For several years there has also been a camp for underprivileged youth.

As the camp meetings gradually disappeared, especially from about 1910 to 1918, the work with adults in the field of evangelism of the revival type has declined almost to the vanishing point. Beginning with about 1920, several EPWORTH LEAGUE Institutes were held across the state in preparatory schools and teacher's colleges. After much experiment and with the increased availability of automobile transportation for delegates, it seemed wise to establish only one organization and to secure a desirable camp site for the newer approach to youth work. Such a camp with a dozen buildings and a waterfront was purchased on a lake in Winthrop in 1948. There a series of different age groups of children and youth attend camps of one or two weeks duration from mid-June until September, followed by a camp for the Conference Lay Activities. Many young adults as well as youth who are active members of local churches, and several young ministers in the Conference, answered the challenge of Christ at the recent Methodist Camp and this seems to have taken over some of the function of the camp meeting of former times.

A. A. Callaghan, "Camp Meetings in Maine," Maine Conference *Year Book*, 1951, pp. 59-63.   ALFRED G. HEMPSTEAD

MAINE CONFERENCE (ME) was created by the 1824 GENERAL CONFERENCE. Its territory at the beginning was MAINE and the part of NEW HAMPSHIRE east of the White Hills and north of Ossipie Lake. The Maine Conference was carved out of the NEW ENGLAND CONFERENCE. The new conference was organized at Gardiner, Maine, July 6, 1825, with Bishop ENOCH GEORGE presiding. It began with three districts, thirty-two charges, forty-two preachers, and 6,960 members. (See MAINE for beginning of Methodism in the state.)

By 1840 the membership of the Maine Conference had trebled, and in 1843 it reported 27,400 members, the high water mark in membership for a century. In the next three years the net loss was nearly 7,000 members. The total membership in 1847 was 20,448.

In 1848 the Maine Conference was divided to form the EAST MAINE CONFERENCE. The division left 10,773 members in the Maine Conference.

From the beginning the Maine Conference supported a school at Kent's Hill called the Maine Wesleyan Seminary (see KENT'S HILL SCHOOL). Also, the conference supported the BOSTON SCHOOL OF THEOLOGY, and it had close ties with WESLEYAN UNIVERSITY in Connecticut as long as that institution was related to the church. The conference owns and operates a 180-acre Camp and Conference Center at Winthrop. Instead of maintaining WESLEY FOUNDATIONS, in more recent years the conference has supported an ecumenical ministry on college campuses. In 1968 the conference established the Methodist Conference Home, Inc. at Rockland, Maine.

The 1920 General Conference adopted an enabling act permitting the Maine and East Maine Conferences to merge during the quadrennium if both should so vote. The Maine Conference rejected the merger in 1921, but in 1922 both conferences voted for it, and it was consummated in 1923. The first session of the enlarged Maine Conference was held at Bangor, April 18-23, 1923. At that time the conference had four districts, 271 charges, and 23,234 members. By 1930 the conference membership had declined to 21,880, but thereafter it increased. In 1935 there were 25,908 members, and in 1945 the total was 28,425.

In 1966 MARGARET K. HENRICHSEN was appointed superintendent of the Bangor District, the first woman district superintendent in Methodism.

In 1970 the Maine Conference reported three districts, Augusta, Bangor, and Portland, 134 charges, 142 ministers, 33,257 members, property valued at $16,366,666 and $2,067,918 raised for all purposes during the year.

Allen & Pillsbury, *Methodism in Maine.* 1887.
General Minutes, MEC and MC.
Minutes of the Maine Conference.   ALFRED G. HEMPSTEAD

MAITLAND, New South Wales, Australia, was originally known as the Hunter River Circuit and included the settlement at Newcastle. SAMUEL LEIGH visited the penal establishment at Newcastle in 1821. A second visit was made later. JOSEPH ORTON passed through Newcastle in August 1839, sailing up the Hunter River to Morpeth and travelling across country to Maitland. Here he found a Methodist Society and a chapel in course of construction, due largely to the labors of a local preacher from IRELAND named Jeremiah Jedsam. Later the same year, NATHANIEL TURNER preached and met members of the Society during a brief visit. The first missionary stationed at Maitland, Jonothan Innes, arrived the following year (1840); the circuit then extended from Newcastle to Singleton. For several years previously, meetings for Christian fellowship had been held in Newcastle, led by William Lightbody, later employed by the Wesleyan Conference as a local preacher and school teacher. In 1854 Rev. W. Curnow resided in Newcastle for a short period. In 1856 it was separated from the Maitland Circuit, with William Clarke as the first minister. Singleton Circuit was created the same year. The mother-circuit, Hunger River, was in 1855 renamed Maitland.

J. Colwell, *Illustrated History.* 1904.
"Glory Be," Brochure of Centenary of Newcastle Methodism, 1945.   AUSTRALIAN EDITORIAL COMMITTEE

MALAYSIA is a constitutional monarchy comprised of the nine Sultanates and two British Straits Settlements of the former Federation of Malaya (Malay Peninsula), together with the former British Colonies of SARAWAK and Sabah (North Borneo) situated on the Island of BORNEO. SINGAPORE (city and island) had been a constituent element of Malaysia when it was established in 1963, but it withdrew in 1965, because of racial and political tensions, to become an independent country. Both Malaysia and Singapore are members of the United Nations and the British Commonwealth.

The area of present Malaysia is approximately 138,000 square miles, of which 78,000 stands in the elements on Borneo (Sarawak and Sabah). The population is about 8,350,000, of which 1,250,000 live in Sarawak and Sabah. In the population, Malays predominate in all sections except Singapore, where Chinese are at least seventy-five percent. There are sizeable groups of Tamils from INDIA, as well as Indonesians. The capital is Kuala Lumpur (300,000 people), twenty-five miles inland from Port Swettenham on the Straits of Malacca.

The aborigines of Malaya were never left alone. Varied peoples came from far to trade and settle, bringing their gods and their cultures with them. A hardy group of the Singh clan of northwest India, forced from their homes, settled on the island at the southern tip, building a town which they called "Lion City"—Singapore. Others from South India and CEYLON, speaking Tamil, came in such numbers as to form an enclave with Hinduism and its culture. The teachings of Buddha entered by way of a strong dynasty out of Siam (Thailand). CHINA seems always to have been overpopulated, and thousands have poured into Malaya, revering Confucius—sturdy peasants, astute businessmen, wise legislators. Early Arab traders dominated the eastern seas, Islam appearing in their communities in every port city.

Catholic Christianity arrived with the ships of PORTUGAL, Spain and FRANCE, soon to be followed by the Protestantism of the Dutch and British. Portugal proved unable to maintain any sizeable area. Spanish influence centered in the PHILIPPINES. France consolidated what became French Indo-China—now Viet Nam, Laos and Cambodia. The Dutch achieved an island empire of over 1,500 miles from Sumatra to Celebes—now INDONESIA. Britain's foothold was the cosmopolitan focal center, Singapore, and the supporting peninsula, producing great quantities of rubber and tin. Singapore and environs became a Crown Colony, while Protectorates were established for the Peninsula Sultanates.

After Pearl Harbor and the decimation of all Allied

Tamil Church, Kuala Lampur

naval units between India and Australia, early in World War II, Japanese forces swarmed down the coast and along the Malay Peninsula. Singapore fell without a siege, its strong defenses having been constructed against sea-attack, and requiring supporting naval power. After the ultimate defeat of Japan, British sovereignty was restored, the Federation of Malaya was established and independence achieved. A wearisome and costly struggle against Communist infiltration and sabotage has practically eliminated that menace from the Peninsula.

The British-protected Sultanates and Settlements of the Malay Peninsula, together with the separate city-island, Singapore, were constituted a limited monarchy in August 1957, becoming a member of the United Nations. In September 1963, following two years of negotiations, this Federation in turn became the sovereign state, Malaysia, including the former British colonies, Sarawak and Sabah (North Borneo), located on the northwest coast of Borneo. Malaysia was duly admitted to membership in the United Nations, occupying the seat of the former Federation of Malaya. Indonesia, under Sukarno, had consistently challenged the procedure, entering upon forceful attack. Numerous military invasions of the Borneo elements were repulsed by the Malaysia armed forces, aided by some British troops. The Philippines also entered a legal claim to the Borneo territories.

Early in 1966 a military coup occurred in Indonesia, toppling the Sukarno regime. Lieut. Gen. Suharto assumed leadership of the new military junta, designating the experienced Adam Malik as Foreign Minister to succeed Dr. Subandrio who was arrested on charges of treason.

Sukarno was retained as a figurehead of government, stripped of all essential powers. The Indonesia Provisional People's Consultative Congress unanimously approved overthrow of the Sukarno regime, and ordered the complete realignment of the foreign policy. After careful negotiations, on Aug. 11, 1966, Abdul Razak, Malaysia Vice-President, and Adam Malik, Indonesia Foreign Minister, signed a formal accord and treaty, declaring the cessation of hostilities between the two countries. The accord also provided for the restoration of normal diplomatic relations, and pledged to the citizens of Sabah and Sarawak (North Borneo) the right to a plebiscite to determine their future status as between Indonesia and Malaysia. The restoration of normal trade and cultural relations is implicit in the accord.

On Feb. 7, 1885, William F. Oldham (later bishop) arrived at Singapore with James M. Thoburn (later bishop), to establish work under appointment of the South India Annual Conference of the M. E. Church. Within a month Oldham had organized a church and quarterly conference, including English, Eurasians, Tamils and Chinese in membership. The Municipality granted land, and the first church building was erected that year. The Chinese colony provided several thousand dollars for a school. The Tamils developed their own church and school. In 1887 the Woman's Foreign Missionary Society appointed Sophia Blackmore of Australia, under support of the Minneapolis Branch. She arrived July 18 and promptly opened a school for Tamil girls. Miss Blackmore gave forty years of service in Malaya.

The Malaya work passed to the Bengal Conference

at its organization in 1887. In 1889 the work became the Malaya Mission, and the Malaysia Mission Conference in 1894. Annual Conference status was gained in 1902. The extensive growth of work among the Chinese prompted separate organization for that element, as the Malaysia Mission Conference 1936, Provisional Annual Conference 1940, and Malaysia Chinese Annual Conference, 1948.

Among the early missionaries in Malaya, William G. Shellabear should be named. English by birth, an officer in the Royal Engineers, ordered to Singapore, he met Oldham. Catching the gleam of missionary service, Shellabear went back to England, resigned his commission, married, and returned to the new line of duty among the Malays. A born linguist, he acquired several dialects as well as the basic language, translated and printed much literature in Malay tongue, as he studied, loved and served that fascinating people. Unable to remain on the equator in the later years, Shellabear came to America. He taught oriental languages at DREW THEOLOGICAL SEMINARY, and also at Kennedy School of Missions, Hartford, Conn., until his death. "He was a distinguished linguist and scholar, an authority on the Malays and their language, a wise and devoted missionary, and a sincere Christian."

The Methodist Church has grown steadily on the Peninsula, with over eighty churches and about 12,000 members. The chief centers are the capital, Kuala Lumpur, and Klang, Malacca, Seremban, Raub, Ipoh, Sitiawan, Telok Anson, Penang, Taiping. The schools, however, with registration of many thousands, constitute the distinguishing mark of the Mission. Statements concerning Methodist work in Singapore, and Sarawak-Sabah, will be found in separate articles under those titles.

Methodist Church of Malaysia and Singapore. In response to the felt need of an autonomous Methodist Church in Malaysia, and pursuant to permission given by the GENERAL CONFERENCE of The United Methodist Church in 1968 to effect the same, such a Church, denominated the Methodist Church of Malaysia and Singapore, was officially constituted on Aug. 9, 1968. Upon that same day, the first national of that land to be elected a bishop, Dr. YAP KIM HAO, was by ballot elected as the first bishop of the new autonomous Church.

The Malaysia Chinese Annual Conference, the Singapore-Malaya Annual Conference, and the Tamil Provisional Annual Conference in West Malaysia and Singapore, and the Sarawak Annual Conference and the Sarawak Iban Provisional Annual Conference in East Malaysia comprise the new Church. In its structure it has been provided that there shall be a president for each annual conference who will be the administrative head. Not all such presidents will receive remuneration, but will serve in other capacities in the Church. The bishop is looked to as the spiritual leader of the whole Church and his voice is to be the voice of the Church. He makes appointments in each annual conference with the help of an advisory board, and will ordain those who seek ordination as DEACON or ELDER when proper authorization is given.

The early life of the new Church is being guided by eight ministers and eight laymen forming the Executive Council of its General Conference. These will share with Bishop Yap the important task of fashioning policies and procedures, and of establishing the guidelines by which the autonomous Church will function under the new *Discipline.* "New Life for the New Church" has become the theme for this autonomous Methodist Church as it "faces with vitality and a new commitment the opportunities for effective witness and mission in newly developed nations."

W. C. Barclay, *History of Missions.* 1957.
Encyclopaedia Britannica.
Barbara H. Lewis, *Methodist Overseas Missions.* 1960.
National Geographic, September 1961.
World Methodist Council *Handbook of Information,* 1966-71.
World Parish, Vol. VIII, No. 6, March 1969.
ARTHUR BRUCE MOSS
N. B. H.

MALDEN, MASSACHUSETTS, U.S.A. **Centre Church,** located five miles north of BOSTON, was organized in 1821, largely through the work of shoemaker James Howard in whose home a class was formed. Prior to this time the Methodist influence had been at work through the preaching of GEORGE WHITEFIELD (in 1740 and 1770) and JESSE LEE (1790). Although a class was formed on Cross Street at the time of Lee's preaching, no permanent results followed.

The Malden congregation, outgrowing two earlier buildings, each one at different sites (one erected in 1826, the other in 1856), constructed the present large, red brick edifice on Washington and Pleasant Streets in 1874. A three-story brick building was added in 1911.

The congregation numbering in 1970, 1,071 members has been influential in civic, educational and philanthropic circles. Four pastors of this church have become bishops: ERASTUS O. HAVEN, GILBERT HAVEN, JR., EDWIN HOLT HUGHES, and LAURESS J. BIRNEY. Another pastor, LUCIUS BUGBEE, became the editor of Methodist church school publications. From this church eighteen men have gone into the ministry.

Centre Methodist Church's 125th anniversary, 1946 (pamphlet).
Minutes of the New England Conference. ERNEST R. CASE

MALLALIEU, WILLARD FRANCIS (1828-1911), American bishop, was born at Sutton, Mass., Dec. 11, 1828, and was educated at WESLEYAN UNIVERSITY in Connecticut.

He joined the New England CONFERENCE of the M. E. Church in 1858 and was pastor at Grafton, Mount Bellingham, Chelsea, Lynn, Monument Square, Charleston; Bromfield Street, BOSTON; Walnut Street, Chelsea; Trinity in Worcester; Broadway in South Boston; and presiding elder of the Boston District. He was a member of the GENERAL CONFERENCES of 1872, 1880, and 1884. At the last he was elected bishop. He served for nine years as bishop in NEW ORLEANS, four years in Buffalo, N. Y., eight in Boston. He retired in 1904.

Bishop Mallalieu received honorary degrees from East Tennessee Wesleyan University and New Orleans University. He was the author of the *Why, When and How of Revivals, The Fullness of the Blessing of the Gospel of Christ,* and *Words of Cheer and Comfort.* He died on Aug. 1, 1911 at Auburndale, Mass., and was buried in Bay View.

F. D. Leete, *Methodist Bishops.* 1948.
Journal of the General Conference, 1912.
Who's Who in America. ELMER T. CLARK

MALLINSON, WILLIAM (1854-1936), British layman and philanthropist, was born at Whitechapel, LONDON, July

6, 1854. He was a timber merchant and prospered in business. Brought up a member of the UNITED METHODIST FREE CHURCHES, be became treasurer of the London Church Extension and Mission Committee in 1893 and held office for forty years. During this period the United Methodist Free Churches—and after 1907 the UNITED METHODIST CHURCH—built under his leadership in London thirty chapels and thirteen schools. He endowed the Mallinson Trust for the benefit of London churches, and carried through a scheme for the extinction of all debt on United Methodist chapels in London and the home counties, the amount totaling £66,000. He held other connectional offices, was a magistrate, and was created a baronet in May, 1935. He died on May 5, 1936, at Walthamstow, London.

H. Smith, J. E. Swallow, and W. Treffry, *The Story of the United Methodist Church.* London, 1933.

OLIVER A. BECKERLEGGE

MALTBY, WILLIAM RUSSELL (1866-1951), British Methodist, was born at Selby, Yorkshire, on Dec. 5, 1866. A Wesleyan Methodist minister's son, he qualified as a solicitor in 1892, but in 1893 entered the Wesleyan ministry. He was warden of the WESLEY DEACONESS ORDER from 1920-40. He was President of the Wesleyan Conference in 1926. In 1928 he gave the Burwash Memorial Lecture, on *The Significance of Jesus.* He delivered the first Cato Lecture in AUSTRALIA in 1935, *Christ and His Cross.* He strongly supported proposals to admit women to the Methodist ministry.

JOHN KENT

MALVERN, ARKANSAS, U.S.A. **Rockport Church** is one of the earliest churches organized west of the Mississippi River, established in 1816 by JOHN HENRY. The first Rockport Church was built of logs and heated by a large stone fireplace with split log benches for seats and a split log table. It was situated on the Ouachita River on the north side of the Military Road, which was then the Southwest Indian Trail. One of the first bridges across the Ouachita River was built at this point about two miles northwest of Malvern.

One of the earliest settlers was Christian Fenter, and most of the preachers in early days stayed in his home when they preached or traveled by. The township in which Rockport is located is named after him.

In 1877 the Rockport Methodists decided to move their church building to Malvern, because the railroad had come through that place in 1871, and most of the members at Rockport moved into Malvern. At Malvern itself a new church building was erected in 1888. During the time the building was going on in Malvern, the Methodists who remained at Rockport reassembled and held services in the public school building at Rockport. When the congregation at Malvern did build their new church, the church at Rockport bought back their old church building for $50, moved it back to Rockport where it stands today.

During the Centennial celebration of ARKANSAS in 1936, which was also the centennial of the Rockport Church having been established as a preaching circuit, the church received a visit from President Franklin D. Roosevelt and his wife. The President delivered an address to several thousand people from the porch of this old church, and the sermon for the occasion was preached by Bishop JOHN M. MOORE of Dallas, Texas.

Rockport Church has been remodeled and repaired many times and is today a neat frame building sitting at the intersection of two well-traveled, paved highways. The people in that section consider it a monument to the religious devotion and endeavors of their pioneer ancestors.

Mrs. Bennie Finch, *History of Malvern Methodist Church.* N.d. Malvern *Daily Record,* 25th Anniversary Edition, 1942; 50th Anniversary Edition, 1967.

RAY N. BOYLE

MANCHESTER, ARKANSAS, U.S.A. The first Methodist church east of the Ouachita River was organized in 1837 by Jacob Custer. It was located on one acre of land given by George S. Wimberley. The chartered members of this church included the following: Thomas C. and Jamima Hudson, Nathan and Nancy Strong, Miss Tennessee Hudson, Miss Mariah Strong, and one colored member, Laney. Later came the Joneses, the Bullocks, the Littlejohns, and the Sims. The Manchester Chuch was the strongest church in the south ARKANSAS area during the days of its prosperity. Preaching was held in homes of the members until a log cabin of one room was built in 1844. It was named the Manchester M. E. Church.

About 1850 the Princeton Circuit was set off, embracing nearly all the territory between the Ouachita River on the west, Saline on the east, Camden on the south, Hot Springs on the north, of which Manchester was the principal church. In 1863 the Manchester Church, due to the problem of slavery, changed its name to the Manchester M. E. Church, South, which it remained until unification in 1939.

In 1888 Manchester Church was divided due to a growing community called Dalark. At this time the Manchester M. E. Church, South moved from the one-room log building to its present location, which was given by Mr. and Mrs. W. F. McCaskell, and two sons, Joe and Charlie Neal. This deed is recorded in the Circuit Court Clerk's office in Arkadelphia, Ark., Sept. 20, 1910.

In 1910 and 1911, under the capable leadership of J. H. McKelvy, the first part of the present building was constructed. It continued in use till 1938 under the capable leadership of A. J. Bearden. The present sanctuary was added to the old part of the original church. The original church was made into class rooms for the church school. At this time it was placed on the Dalark Charge. In 1970 Manchester had a membership of 74 with an average attendance of seventy at its morning service.

J. J. McKNIGHT

MANCHESTER, CONNECTICUT, U.S.A. In August 1790, GEORGE ROBERTS, assistant to JESSE LEE, organized a Methodist Society in Manchester in the home of Thomas Spencer. Four years later Bishop ASBURY found a neat house of worship on Spencer Street. In 1821 a larger church was built at the Center, which was used for thirty years.

Three preaching points developed: one in the north section which started its first Sunday school in 1826 and developed into a separate church in 1851. This is today known as St. Paul's in Manchester. One developed in Buckland's Corners and flared up in a revival, but never managed to become an enduring church. The Center congregation moved to the south and built its church in 1854 and this last was destined to endure and to become known today as South Methodist Church.

SOUTH CHURCH, MANCHESTER, CONNECTICUT

South Church today has an elegantly appointed sanctuary and the largest membership of any church in the NEW ENGLAND SOUTHERN CONFERENCE. The style of the church is Tudor Gothic and is of local grey field stone with trimmings of grey case stone and with English cathedral glass windows leaded in small panes. The building is now covered with ivy. A square tower, sixty-seven feet high and surmounted by turreted battlements, is placed at the southwest corner of the main building and contains a bell from the first Methodist church in Manchester and a memorial set of chime bells ranging in size from 275 to 2,000 pounds. Because of its unique design and setting the South Church has long been a familiar and famous landmark of Manchester, Conn.

Throughout the interior, there are carved oak antique decorations. Julian S. Wadsworth, a former pastor and wood carving enthusiast, carved the Twelve Apostles in oak to form panels in the reredos screen. Guido Mayr of Oberammergau, who portrayed the part of Judas in the "Passion Play," carved a bas-relief of the famous Leonardo da Vinci painting of "The Lord's Supper" across the top of the screen. Other wood carvings decorate the pulpit and lectern and depict the lives of Christ and His Disciples.

The lectern itself is bronze and represents an eagle standing on a globe, a symbol of St. John in his capacity as an Evangelist where "He soared in the Spirit and saw God."

The Pulpit has five carved oak panels representing Biblical references to Christ and His Church. The central panel, carved by Wesley B. Porter, a former member of South Church, symbolizes Christ—The Rose of Sharon and the Cross forming what is known as the "Rose-Croix." At the base of this panel is the inscription, "As a Lily Among Thorns," taken from the Song of Solomon.

The music of South Church has been emphasized for many years with vocal choirs of all ages and a rhythm choir which interprets ideas through rhythmic motion. The large window in the sanctuary, facing east has been given the name of "Creation," for here in the ivy-covered panes, the birds nest year after year and raise their young.

The baptismal font made of Carrara Italian marble is located in the west arm of the cruciform building. The handcarved antique silver lamp which hangs above the font came from one of the ancient churches of Jerusalem and was presented by Mrs. Mattie Case.

Across the street from the Church proper are ten acres of land known as the "South Church Campus," where two Cheney mansions are located. Today, these two mansions provide class space for all the church school below junior high school age, a church parlor for group meetings and a hundred-car parking lot.

From the original membership of six, the church has now grown to 2,397 members, making South Church the largest as well as the most influential church in the New England Southern Conference.

Almond, *Methodism in Manchester*. N.d.
Hibbard, *History of the North Methodist Church of Manchester, Conn.*
R. C. Miller, *New England Southern Conference*. 1898.
                                              HARVEY K. MOUSLEY

MANCHESTER, England. Manchester's growth into one of the greatest industrial and commercial centers of modern England dates from the industrial revolution of the eighteenth century.

JOHN WESLEY visited Manchester on three occasions before his evangelical conversion to see his friend JOHN CLAYTON. GEORGE WHITEFIELD paid the first of seven visits there in December 1738; and BENJAMIN INGHAM preached in Long Millgate in May 1742. The first Methodist sermon was delivered by JOHN NELSON at Manchester Cross in either 1742 or 1743; but not until CHARLES WESLEY's visit in January 1747 was a society formed. JOHN BENNET, who had already pioneered Methodism in the surrounding villages, added the society to his round in March of that year; and John Wesley came in May 1747, when he preached at Salford Cross. This new society had several homes, including a garret by the river Irwell and a Baptist chapel in Shudehill, before a chapel was begun in Birchin Lane in 1750. Completed in 1751, it was, with Liverpool, the first Methodist chapel in Lancashire.

In 1752 Manchester became the head of a circuit covering much of Lancashire and Cheshire. The following year, despite the defection of John Bennet, there were 250 members, and the chapel had to be enlarged. In 1765 the Conference met in Manchester for the first time, a sign of the town's growing connectional importance. In 1781 Birchin Lane was replaced by the Oldham Street Chapel, which was "about the size of that in London." For some years later after 1788 there was a close link with the nearby St. James' Church, and the Oldham Street congregation attended services there in a body. The Wesleyans also played a part in setting up interdenominational Sunday schools in Manchester in 1786.

After 1751 John Wesley usually visited Manchester every year. On Easter Day, 1790, his last visit, he described 1,600 communicants at Oldham Street. The membership grew with the rapid rise in the town's population—in 1799 there were 2,225 members in Manchester and Salford. More chapels were built: Gravel Lane, Salford, 1791; Great Bridgewater Street, 1801; Swan Street, 1808 (closed, 1826); Chancery Lane, 1817; Grosvenor Street, 1820. In 1826 four large chapels were built: Irwell Street, Salford; Ancoats; Oxford Road; and Oldham Road, Wesley.

In 1824 a second Wesleyan circuit was formed, with Grosvenor Street at its head. For some years this was the wealthiest chapel and circuit in the British connection, as may be seen from its contributions in THE CENTENARY FUND, 1839. Despite the Warrenite secession of 1834-35 (see below), Wesleyan Methodist membership reached 10,000 in Manchester in 1883. The second Wesleyan theological college, Didsbury, was built there in 1842. In 1886, when the central area was beginning to lose ground, the first Wesleyan Central Mission was begun in Manchester under SAMUEL COLLIER. The failing Oldham Street Chapel, now surrounded by warehouses, was closed in 1883, and the Central Hall was erected on the same site.

Collier built up what he called "the largest congregation in the world," which met for more than twenty years in the famous Free Trade Hall until the Albert Hall was built in 1910 as its permanent home. This is still the preaching center of the mission. The first General Chapel Committee met in Manchester in 1790; from this grew the Wesleyan Methodist Department for CHAPEL AFFAIRS, which was established in Manchester in 1855. It remains the only British Methodist departmental headquarters outside London.

The METHODIST NEW CONNEXION started in the city in 1797, when a secession took place, mainly in Salford. Manchester formed one of the first seven Methodist New Connexion circuits. Mount Zion Chapel, Nicholas Croft, was built in 1800, but had to be relinquished in 1808 for a smaller building in Oldham Street. The cause made little progress until 1835, when a new chapel was opened in Peter Street. The Methodist New Connexion Book Room was in the city from 1827-44, and the Jubilee Conference of the denomination was held there in 1846. Salem Chapel, Strangeways, was opened in 1851 and the following year became the head of a Manchester North Circuit. Apart from strong churches at Pendleton and Newton Heath, the New Connexion made slow progress; in 1906 the total membership of the two circuits was fourteen hundred.

On the other hand, the secession of 1834-35 under SAMUEL WARREN was much more serious, as Warren was then superintendent of the Wesleyan Oldham Street Circuit. About a thousand members left the four Manchester circuits and formed the Wesleyan Methodist Association. Their chapels were often built as close as possible to those of their Wesleyan rivals. Sunday school teachers seem to have played an important part in the division. Membership fell slightly after the initial excitement, but in 1851 there were eleven Association chapels in the Manchester registration district, compared with eighteen Wesleyan, five Methodist New Connexion, and two PRIMITIVE METHODIST chapels. These Association chapels entered union with the Wesleyan Reformers in 1857, and membership then increased. In 1876 the resulting UNITED METHODIST FREE CHURCHES opened their ministerial training college in Manchester at Victoria Park.

As for Primitive Methodism, evangelism probably reached Manchester late in 1819. By October 1820 there were 130 members, and in 1821 Manchester was constituted a separate circuit. The first chapel was in Jersey Street, Ancoats, opened in 1823, followed by one in the Oxford Road, and in King Street, Salford. The main expansion came between 1850 and 1900, when several large chapels were built, including Great Western Street, in Moss Side, and Higher Ardwick. The Primitive Meth-

odist theological college, Hartley, was set up in Manchester in 1868, not far from Great Western Street. In 1932 there were twelve Primitive Methodist circuits in the city area, with thirty-eight churches. These circuits, together with the Wesleyan circuits, joined the six UNITED METHODIST CHURCH circuits (formed in the union of 1907) in 1932. The strength of the Wesleyans was approximately equal to that of the other two bodies combined.

Despite the decline in religious observance in England and the fall of Manchester's population, it was more than twenty years before the rationalization of the city's circuits neared completion. Membership has fallen steadily since 1932; and although the number of chapels has been reduced from about one hundred in 1932 to about fifty-six in 1965, some overlapping remains. Other changes included the removal of Didsbury College to BRISTOL in 1945 and the closure of Victoria Park College in 1932, when it was amalgamated with Hartley to become HARTLEY VICTORIA COLLEGE. The Central Hall in Oldham Street was damaged by bombs in the Second World War, but reopened in 1954. The offices of the Chapel Affairs Department remain in the building.

E. A. ROSE

MANCHESTER, NEW HAMPSHIRE, U.S.A., is situated on the east bank of the Merrimack River and on the Boston and Maine Railroad in the south central portion of the state. Its territory was traversed by the early pioneers of Methodism, although because of its connection with older appointments, the name appears first in the conference minutes in 1819. Services were occasionally held at the Town House by Reuben Peaslee of Hampstead, and later by John Haskell, a member of the Legislature, both local preachers. Orlando Hines, here a few years on a part-time basis, was the first Methodist to administer the ordinance of BAPTISM in this town, having baptized Mrs. Edna Procter and Miss Rhoda Hall by immersion about 1827. Made a part of the Poplin Circuit, embracing Popkin, Chester, Sandown, and Manchester in 1828, it was the scene of a great revival a year later, with meetings conducted by JOHN BRODHEAD and Caleb Lamb, preachers on the circuit. Eighty were converted, among them James M. Young and James McCaine, who entered the Methodist ministry.

On Sept. 29, 1829 the first Methodist society was organized in the kitchen of Israel Morrill on Huse Road with eighty members. A church commenced at the Center was completed the following year at a cost of $1,800. This building was used for ten years. On Dec. 16, 1839, a new church society was organized and building erected on the corner of Hanover and Chestnut Streets. This was soon removed to the corner of Pine and Merrimac Streets and was transferred later to another denomination. In 1842 a brick church on Elm Street was built at a cost of $16,000 when John Jones was pastor. The lower part of this Elm Street Church was occupied by stores. In 1856 a third society was organized as the North Elm Street Church, which first met in a hall up the street. It continued in existence until 1862, when it was united with the old church and Bishop OSMON C. BAKER named the new organization St. Paul's and appointed JAMES MONROE BUCKLEY as pastor. In 1875 a society known as The Tabernacle was organized and held services in Smythe's Hall. It continued six years, but gradually growing weaker it finally favored re-uniting with St. Paul's to help build a new church.

At the north end a new society was organized in 1886 called The People's Church. W. A. Loyne was appointed pastor. The City Hall, the Y.M.C.A. parlor, and homes were. the scenes of services, until a lot at the corner of Pine and Penacook Streets was secured and a chapel built. Later the name was changed to St. James' Church and during M. V. B. Knox's pastorate, 1891-92, a fine new church was built. This was merged with St. Paul's during the pastorate of Franklin P. Frye, Oct. 1, 1951.

Feeling itself no longer at the center due to population shifts, Center Church considered the need for moving. While J. W. Bean was pastor, 1885-87, a lot was bought on Valley and Jewett Streets and a house built, later to be used as a parsonage though at first this was used for chapel services. When Claudius Byrne became pastor, the Center Church was moved to a location next to the parsonage, raised, and a story built beneath it for a vestry and the house finished for a parsonage. Here the membership remained until 1920, when with Centenary aid they erected a splendid modern plant, now known as First Church. New pews, a new chancel, and a change of the choir loft was made during the pastorate of Ray H. Cowen in 1953-54, at a cost of $14,200. In 1960, $12,400 was spent on redecorating the sanctuary, installing new light fixtures, covering the floor with tile and laying asphalt driveways to church and parsonage.

From 1891-1911 some work was carried on in a chapel at Massabosic Lake, which for a time was a Methodist Church served by the pastor at First Church, but because of lack of growth the work was given up. In 1888, Louis N. Beaudrey, a French missionary, began work in Manchester among French people. This subsequently was carried on by Thomas A. Dorion in 1889, and by Emile J. Palisoul for many years. In October 1895, a church society was organized on the west side with sixteen members. This was called Trinity Church. The following year there were thirty-nine members, a congregational average attendance of 150 and a Sunday school of sixty students. With the purchase of a schoolhouse on School Street and much sacrifice, a desirable house of worship was made in 1897. This served nobly until with the gradual weakening a merger was effected with St. James Church in 1940.

The 1970 statistical report gives: Manchester, First, 644 members, 359 church school members, and property valued at $403,175. St. Pauls, 444 members, 147 church school, and $301,000 property values.

Cole and Baketel, *New Hampshire Conference.* 1929.
Journals of the New Hampshire Conference.
M. Simpson, *Cyclopaedia.* 1878.   WILLIAM J. DAVIS

MANEFIELD, ALBERT GEORGE (1896-1963), Australian minister, was born at Wallsend, New South Wales, AUSTRALIA. He was accepted as a candidate for the ministry in 1919, trained at LEIGH COLLEGE, and ordained in 1925.

Prior to appointment as Assistant Home Mission Secretary in 1934, he ministered in the Far West and North West Missions of New South Wales. He was appointed Home Mission Secretary in 1940 and became General Superintendent in 1949, which position he held until retirement in 1962.

He was elected President of the NEW SOUTH WALES CONFERENCE in 1954. It is recognized that his work and vision made possible the Methodist Nursing Service in the Far West of New South Wales. He was responsible for the establishment of the Deaconess Order in New South Wales.

He was an able administrator, a competent preacher and a significant leader. He was the Convenor of the Federal Home Missions Council and the Canberra Consultative Council in the Australian Capital Territory.

AUSTRALIAN EDITORIAL COMMITTEE

MANGUNGU, Northland, NEW ZEALAND, situated on the Hokianga River, was the site of the re-establishment of the Wesleyan mission following the forced withdrawal from Wesleydale, and the return of the missionaries to NEW SOUTH WALES in January, 1827.

The mission party, led by JOHN HOBBS arrived at the Hokianga Heads on the "Governor Macquarie" on Oct. 31, 1827. They settled temporarily at Horeke under the protection of the great chief, Patuone. Shortly afterward, land was secured but not occupied at Te Toke.

Final choice fell on Mangungu, where an area of 850 acres was purchased. The missionaries moved in on March 28, 1828, and established a base from which the work spread throughout the whole country. It continued to be of importance until the late 1850's, when as a result of population movements, it was largely abandoned in favor of Waima.

C. H. Laws, *First Years at Hokianga.* Wesley Historical Society, New Zealand, 1945.   L. R. M. GILMORE

MANHATTAN, KANSAS, U.S.A., **First Church,** is a large church serving not only the community but the Kansas State University of Manhattan. It records for itself an interesting and colorful past. The Kansas-Nebraska Bill of 1854, with its doctrine of "Popular Sovereignty," which left the slavery question up to the settlers, created a rush of emigrants hurrying to settle the West and taking one side or the other of the slavery issue. The groups that came to the junction of the Blue and Kansas Rivers were predominantly Northern Methodists, and were there to keep KANSAS a free state. ISAAC T. GOODNOW, professor at the Providence Seminary at East Greenwich, R. I., was the leader, along with his wife's brother, JOSEPH DENISON. Denison was to be the first regular minister of the M. E. Church in Manhattan.

These folk came to Kansas in 1855, built a church, established Bluemont Central College (which later became Kansas State University), and helped to make Kansas a free state. Charles H. Lovejoy held the first Methodist church services on March 25, 1855. The Church was really first established on the *Hartford,* a steamboat bringing a group of ardent free-staters from CINCINNATI, Ohio, to Kansas. This group was organized under the leadership of Judge John Pipher on April 30, 1855. On its return the *Hartford* burned, but the bell, known as the "Hartford Bell" is still a museum piece in Manhattan First Church. The name "Manhattan" was chosen because money was given to the settlers by donors from the island of Manhattan, NEW YORK CITY, with the understanding that this would be the name. Nearby is the famous "Beecher Bible and Rifle Church" at Wabaunsee.

Bluemont Central College, chartered in 1858 under the auspices of the Kansas-Nebraska Conference of the M. E. Church, began classes in 1859. Washington Marlatt was its promoter and first president. He was joined by

Isaac T. Goodnow and Joseph Denison in the establishment of the Kansas State Agricultural College. This received the first land grant provided for Kansas under the Morrill Act. Bluemont Central College was turned over to the State, and eventually became Kansas State University.

The University has several buildings named after former Methodist ministers, including Goodnow, Washington Marlatt, and Joseph Denison. First Church in 1970 had 2,635 members, and property valued at $947,000.

General Minutes, UMC.   Kenneth R. Hemphill

MANILA, Philippines. The city of Manila, on Luzon Island in the Republic of the Philippines, is the cultural, commercial, industrial, educational, and religious center of this relatively new nation. It is the governmental capital, though Quezon City, a former suburb of Manila, is technically the governmental capital of the Republic. Manila's population is approximately one-twentieth of the 35,000,000 people on the whole archipelago.

Manila was the first city in the Philippines entered by Methodist missionaries in 1899, and it has continued to be the "headquarters city" for Methodism and its principal institutions since that time. There are thirty-five Methodist churches in Manila and its immediate environs. The two largest Methodist churches in the Islands are in the heart of Manila, and there are two English-speaking congregations.

Harris Memorial School, Manila

Serving the entire archipelago are the following specialized institutions founded by Methodist missionaries, and now largely operated by Filipino pastors, teachers, and technical personnel: the Harris Memorial School, training young women from all east and southeast Asia as deaconesses and kindergarten teachers; Mary Johnston Hospital, which was destroyed by fire during World War II, and later rebuilt with American and Filipino funds; the Mary Johnston School of Nursing; Eveland Hall, a residence for graduate nurses; Methodist Social Center, including Hugh Wilson Hall, a college girls' dormitory, and pre-school and kindergarten classes, and a dental clinic; and the Methodist Book Room, providing educational and religious reading materials for Methodists and the general public. In cooperation with other Protestant groups in the Philippines, Methodists are engaged in the support and administration of these institutions in Manila: Philippine Christian College; Protestant Chapel and Fellowship Hall at the University of the Philippines; the Sampaloc University Center; and the activities of the National Council of Churches of the Philippines.

Mary Johnston Hospital, Manila

Mary Johnston Hospital began with the dream of Dr. Rebecca Parish when she volunteered to go to Manila in 1906 to put her life into the task of saving babies, children, mothers, and to help bring health to the Philippines. By December 10 of that year she had opened Despensaria Betania and the project was underway.

D. S. B. Johnston of St. Paul, Minn., gave $12,500 for a hospital to be a memorial for his wife. Located on a sea beach in Manila the hospital was inaugurated on Aug. 18, 1908, with rooms and wards for thirty-five patients. There were three missionaries on the staff, which was headed by Dr. Rebecca Parish, and eleven nursing students.

In 1911, the hospital burned but it was repaired and a third floor for nurses' dormitory was added. In 1913, the Philippine government gave funds for an additional building to house the maternity ward, dispensary and milk station.

At the outbreak of World War II, the hospital became an emergency hospital where the wounded from air raids were hospitalized. The Imperial Japanese Army allowed work to continue under the supervision of the Filipino staff. The hospital burned on Feb. 5, 1945, during the liberation of Manila.

On Sept. 3, 1949, the cornerstone of the new building was laid. On Aug. 26, 1950, the new building was inaugurated with President Elpidio Quirino as the main speaker. The new 137-bed hospital was designed to serve as a general hospital, accommodating men, women, and children. As in the past, crowds still throng to the hospital, seeking health, hope and happiness. After the war until his death in 1964 the administrator of the hospital was Dr. Gumersindo Garcia, Sr.

Project Handbook Overseas Missions, UMC, 1969.

W. W. Reid
Byron W. Clark

MANLEY'S CHAPEL, located in Henry County, Tenn., U.S.A., was the first church in the territory now embraced by the Memphis Conference of The United Methodist Church. In 1820 a local Methodist preacher, John Manley, organized the church and the first pastor was Benjamin Peeples, who had been sent by the Kentucky Conference to organize Methodist work in the territory. The original log church was built in 1821, but was soon replaced by a larger log building, as Manley's Chapel became the head church and center of the Sandy River Circuit.

In 1823 the Manleys donated land and John Manley, in conjunction with Richard and Hamlin Manley, William and Abraham Walters, T. F. Lilley, Johanan and Robert Smith, James and John Randle, Henry Wall, Joel, John and W. T. Hagler, the Moodys, the Lowrys and a few others organized a camp ground around the church. The annual CAMP MEETINGS became a vital part of Manley's Chapel and were held every year but one until 1912.

The old log church was replaced by a frame structure in 1857, when W. H. Gillespie was pastor, and in 1934, when the site of Manley's Chapel had become inaccessible to automobiles, a church built largely of materials salvaged from the old building was constructed on a location donated by Melvin Carter. On this site about seven miles from Paris, Tenn., on Reynoldsburg Road, a new brick church was erected and dedicated on Nov. 2, 1958.

Journals of Memphis Conference.   MARY SUE NELSON

MANNING, CHARLES (1714-1799), British Anglican, was the son of a Norwich painter. He graduated from Caius College, Cambridge, and from 1738 to 1757 was rector of Hayes, Middlesex. He supported the Wesleys and attended the Conferences of 1747 and 1748. He is said to have officiated at John Wesley's wedding in 1751, but there is no entry in the parish register to confirm this statement.

A. SKEVINGTON WOOD

MANSELL, HENRY (1833-1911), pioneer M. E. missionary in INDIA, was a graduate of ALLEGHENY COLLEGE. He then married Annie Benschoff, and they arrived in India in 1863. He founded a boys' school at Pauri, Garhwal, out of which has grown the Messmore College, named for JAMES MESSMORE, one of his colleagues who was associated with the institution for many years.

Mansell was the first principal of the Centennial School at LUCKNOW, forerunner of LUCKNOW CHRISTIAN COLLEGE. He was principal of Bareilly Theological Seminary, 1884-85, and of Philander Smith College at Naini Tal.

Mansell acquired a mastery of Hindu and Urdu; and in addition to preaching often in these languages, he wrote many articles and a number of books, including commentaries on the Old Testament prophecies, as well as adaptations and translations of English language commentaries.

His children became the first second-generation M.E. missionaries in India. A daughter, Hattie, was sent to India by the WOMAN'S FOREIGN MISSIONARY SOCIETY and, after brief service in Moradabad, joined ISABELLA THOBURN as a professor in the Woman's College at Lucknow. She later married David C. Monroe, and their son, Harry Monroe, served as a missionary in India. A son, William Mansell, became principal of Lucknow Christian College during the furlough of the founder, and later was principal of the Bareilly Theological Seminary.

J. WASKOM PICKETT

MANSFIELD, RALPH (1799-1880), early missionary to AUSTRALIA, was born at Liverpool, England on March 12, 1799, the son of Ralph and Ann Mansfield. He was ordained in 1820, designated as a missionary to NEW SOUTH WALES, and received into full connexion at the Conference of 1823. After an eventful voyage in the *Surry*, anchor was cast at Hobart Town where he "was graciously received by His Honour, Lieutenant-Governor Sorrell with permission to preach and with a guard of constables to prevent disturbances." Arriving in SYDNEY, he was appointed Secretary of the auxiliary of the Wesleyan Missionary Society. He had a first-class flair for journalism and co-edited the *Australian Magazine* which showed interest in secular matters. It was successful but its policy disturbed the Wesleyan Committee in England who prohibited its publication.

In July 1823, he was appointed to Van Diemen's land and in Hobart Town presided at the first business meeting of the Hobart Town Society on Aug. 11, 1823. In 1824 Lieutenant-Governor Arthur desired to form a native establishment for the education and civilization of the aborigines. Mansfield was keen to establish a training school for young men in this missionary enterprise. Nothing concrete seems to have developed.

The Lieutenant-Governor assisted in the building of a chapel and asked that a chaplain be nominated for Macquarie Harbour. Again the London committee rejected local suggestions. Mansfield was transferred to Sydney in June 1825. He became the District Secretary. The London committee was unsympathetic toward suggestions from Mansfield, and he was disciplined for preaching during church hours and administering Holy Communion. In 1838 the committee refused to increase or consider New South Wales requests for increased living allowances. Mansfield, incensed at their parsimony, resigned in October 1828. He wrote, "I formally resign but am virtually expelled. I do not resign the Ministerial office but simply that of a Wesleyan missionary. As a local preacher I hope that I may still be useful to the cause of God."

His resignation and slight obstinacy was a serious loss to the connexion. He became joint-editor with Robert Howe of *The Sydney Gazette* in January 1829. A month later Howe was drowned and Mansfield became sole editor. He was editorially involved in political concerns and supported Governor Darling. In 1831 he printed the first issue of the *Government Gazette* and for eight years contributed to *The Colonist*. Keenly interested in education, he became the Secretary of the Protestant committee opposed to Governor Burke's "Irish system of National Education."

In 1836 he was director and secretary of the Australian Gaslight Company, secretary of the Sydney Floating Bridge Company and Royal Exchange Company. In 1841 he was appointed Editor of *The Sydney Morning Herald* of left-wing politics.

Deeply attached to the church, he felt it an honor to hold the position of first secretary to the Baptist Church in New South Wales.

He died at Parramatta on Sept. 1, 1880, remembered as a man of courage, a layman who never lost his missionary vision, a man of rare ability who served God and man.

S. G. CLAUGHTON

MANSO, JUANA (1819-1875), was an Argentine educator and writer. In 1836 she went into exile in MONTEVIDEO, URUGUAY, because of political persecution by partisans of the Argentine dictator Juan Manuel de Rosas. When Rosas partisans dominated that city also, her family fled to BRAZIL. There Miss Manso married a Brazilian musician, Francisco Paula de Noronha, whom she accompanied to the United States. There he deserted her. Probably sometime during her stay in the United States she became a Methodist. Shortly after Rosas had fallen, she returned to Buenos Aires (in 1854) and became active in the Methodist church there.

The great Argentine educator, President Domingo F. Sarmiento, charged her with organizing public libraries. She was one of the very few persons who joined Sarmiento in his revolutionary ideas on public education. She was founder of the government publication, *Los Anales de la Educacion Comun* (Annals of Common Education). She wrote books on pedagogy, but also wrote in the fields of history and sociology and was the author of novels and plays.

One of Miss Manso's novels, *La hija del comendador* (The Commander's Daughter), was a cry against slavery —obviously written under the influence of Harriet Beecher Stowe's *Uncle Tom's Cabin*, published two years before. Miss Manso was concerned with social problems and the advancement of young women. Already, during her stay in Montevideo, she had founded the Young Ladies' Atheneum, and in Buenos Aires she started one of the first women's magazines in the country, *Album de Señoritas* (Young Ladies' Album).

Her life in the United States stirred in Miss Manso a desire to establish Sunday schools in her mother country. In 1870 she published in Argentina a booklet describing Sunday schools in North America.

Miss Manso confronted many hardships and persecutions because of her Protestant profession, extending even to her death bed. She was buried in the British (Protestant) Cemetery in Buenos Aires, but in 1920 her remains were transferred to the National Mausoleum of the Teaching Profession.

El Estandarte Evangelico de Sud America, 75th anniversary edition, 1911.
Ismael A. Vago

MANTRIPP, JOSEPH CLOSS (1867-1943), British Methodist, was born at Lowestoft in 1867. He entered the Primitive Methodist ministry in 1891. He became secretary of the Derby Conference in 1913, and from 1926 to 1931 served as Connexional Editor. After Methodist Union in 1932 he was deputy editor. His publications included *The Faith of a Christian* (Hartley Lecture, 1931) and, later, *The Devotional Use of the Methodist Hymn Book* and *The Great Good News*. He was a valued member of the Methodist Union Committee, and high tribute was paid to his editorial work as a member of the Methodist Hymn-Book Committee. He died on Feb. 3, 1943.

John T. Wilkinson

MANUAL LABOR SCHOOL, west of Covington, Newton County, Georgia, was a forerunner of Emory University in Atlanta, and of Emory College (later called Emory-at-Oxford and now again Emory College). The Manual Labor School was established in 1834 but was absorbed by Emory College in 1840. Emory College was named in memory of Bishop James O. Andrew's episcopal classmate, Bishop John Emory, who was killed in a carriage accident in 1835. Manual labor was a part of the college (chartered Dec. 19, 1836) program but was doomed to failure. One year after absorption of the Manual Labor School, the system was dropped.

Because the latter school was not as successful as it had been hoped, the 1836 General Conference noted that Randolph-Macon College in Virginia was too

distant for Georgia youth who might want an education under Methodist auspices. So the Conference acted on Ignatius Few's suggestion to establish a Methodist college in Georgia. Samuel Bryan and Thomas Benning were appointed agents to raise $100,000 for it. Few was chairman, and then became the college's first president. It is significant that he was also the prime mover in plans for the Manual School.

Few inspected land purchased by the Manual Labor School lying one to three miles north-northwest of Covington. The college and the 330 acres of that land laid out for the college town of Oxford are both named for "the seat of learning of John and Charles Wesley."

E. J. Hammond, *M. E. Church in Georgia.* 1935.
Ouida Wade Roton

MAORI KING MOVEMENT. In 1858 a confederation of powerful inland tribes in the Waikato area of the North Island of New Zealand "elected" an aged chief, Potatau Te Wherowhero, as the first Maori king. The purpose was threefold: to oppose further sales of land to European settlers; to secure law and order among warring tribes, in which it was felt that the European administration had failed; and to seek to recapture the dwindling prestige of the Maori people.

Through the intervening years "the king movement" has lost much of its early political significance, and remains as a cultural and spiritual link between all the Maori tribes of New Zealand. The Movement's headquarters is the Turangawaewae Pa, at Ngaruawahia, and the present leader is Queen Te Ata-i-rangi-kaahu, sixth in line of direct descent from the first Maori king. Ngatete Kerai Kukutai, a New Zealand minister, was a respected friend and adviser of the Movement.

M. P. K. Sorenson, "The Maori King Movement," *Studies of a Small Democracy,* ed. by R. Chapman and K. Sinclair. Paul's Book Arcade for the University of Auckland, 1963.
L. R. M. Gilmore

MARIETTA, GEORGIA, U.S.A., **First Church,** was organized in 1833 in the home of George W. Winters with thirty-seven charter members, John P. Dickinson serving as pastor. Shortly thereafter a building was erected on Husk Street at Whitlock Avenue.

Under the pastorate of Charles R. Jewett in 1848 a new sanctuary was dedicated on Atlanta Street at Waverly Way. Here the first Sunday school was organized. The first railroad in Cobb County began operations Sept. 15, 1845, from Marietta to "Marthasville"—renamed "Atlanta" two years later. Marietta was directly in the path of Sherman's march-to-the-sea and was all but destroyed by the ravages of that terrible conflict. Although the parsonage was burned, the church building was spared and is still standing.

In June 1878 the first Woman's Foreign Missionary Society in Southern Methodism was organized by this congregation. Some years later it merged with the Woman's Home Missionary Society and, after unification in 1939, became known as the Woman's Society of Christian Service.

At the turn of the century a new building on Atlanta and Anderson Streets was built during the pastorate of J. W. Quillian and dedicated by W. W. Wadsworth. This plant, with subsequent additions, served admirably for some sixty years. During World War I, sixty-three of its members entered the armed services and during World War II a service flag with seventy-seven stars was proudly displayed. At the Atlanta Street location the membership grew from 455 in 1896 to 2,115 as reported in 1965. Numerically it had then become the fifth largest in the NORTH GEORGIA CONFERENCE and had long since outgrown its physical capacity.

In September 1909, Dr. Fred P. Manget, with a M.D. degree from EMORY, returned to Marietta and married Louise Anderson, daughter of W. D. Anderson, a beloved former pastor of this church. This dedicated young couple left immediately for the Orient, founded, and for almost four decades operated the Huchow General Hospital, one of Methodism's great missionary outposts.

In the early 1960's a movement was started for a complete new church facility. Prevailing sentiment was that it should continue as a "downtown" church. During the pastorate of Gordon Thompson (1957-61), enough money was raised to buy several acres within two blocks of the Public Square, and to have left a substantial start on a building fund. It is interesting to note that this tract of land included the site of the original church built in 1835.

Under the able leadership of Charles B. Cockran the building program was brought to a successful conclusion. On Jan. 16, 1966, Bishop J. OWEN SMITH with District Superintendent W. Candler Budd consecrated the present plant—said to be one of the finest in GEORGIA Methodism. A church school of thirty-two class rooms, a fellowship hall, administrative offices, library, parlor, and chapel are all air conditioned and tastefully decorated. The sanctuary seats 1,046. Membership in 1970 was 2,103.

George D. Anderson, Jr., *The M. E. Church, South, of Marietta, Georgia.* Marietta: Brumby Press, Inc., 1933.
Journal of the North Georgia Conference.
S. B. G. Temple, *The First Hundred Years.* Atlanta: Walter R. Brown Pub. Co., 1935.   GUY NORTHCUTT

MARIETTA, OHIO, U.S.A., an old historic city situated at the confluence of the Ohio and Muskingum Rivers, was the first organized settlement in the Northwest Territory. Methodism began in the new settlement in 1799, when Robert Manley crossed the Ohio River and organized classes. "He was welcomed to the log cabin of Robert McCabe, a shoe-maker-settler, who with his wife and two other couples professed faith in Christ and were constituted the first regular Methodist Church in Ohio." A circuit was organized before the close of the year.

It was with difficulty that Methodism gained a foothold in Marietta. In 1805 JACOB YOUNG, one of the famous frontier preachers, held a successful CAMP MEETING. A number of persons were converted and a class was formed under the leadership of Jones Johnson, who had been a follower of Thomas Paine before his conversion. This class marks the beginning of real growth of Methodism in Marietta.

In 1806, during the pastorate of the famous PETER CARTWRIGHT, a camp meeting was held and a number of influential persons converted. Marietta was at that time a part of the Marietta and Kanawha circuit which extended along the Ohio River for 150 miles and far into (West) Virginia. In 1808 the Marietta Circuit was formed. In 1816 JOHN STEWART, a dissipated black man, was converted and went out as a missionary to the Indians, thus inaugurating the great missionary movement of American Methodism.

For the ten years after their first organization, the Methodists worshiped in private homes and schoolhouses. In 1815 a church building was erected. It was twice enlarged before the erection of the Centenary church in 1839. In this new brick structure the society prospered greatly. In a revival held in 1842 there were 187 new members brought into the membership. The greatest revival in its history swept the church in 1856 when 210 persons were converted. In 1859 Whitney Chapel was formed, mainly from the membership of the Centenary Church. Two bishops, DAVID H. MOORE and EARL CRANSTON, were among the pastors of this church. In 1875 Whitney Chapel and Centenary Church were consolidated to form the First M. E. Church in Marietta. First Church today is still located on the site of the newly formed church and has a membership of 1,383.

Crawford Chapel was erected on the Fort Harmar side of the Muskingum River in 1833. This church and Centenary were a circuit until 1848 when both became stations. In 1895 Crawford Chapel was rebuilt and became the Gilman Avenue M. E. Church. It has sent two missionaries to the foreign field—Miss Carrie Jewell to CHINA, and Miss Esther Devine to INDIA. The Gilman Church today has a membership of 429.

The German Methodist Church was founded in 1839. Many of the early settlers in Marietta came from the northern part of Germany. A number were converted and joined the English Methodist church and organized a class within the church. In June 1839, a mission was organized for the German Methodists when Carl Best was sent to Marietta. The first German Methodist church building was purchased from the English church in 1840, services being held in private homes before this. The congregation continued to worship in this building until 1876 when they relocated and built a new building. The name was changed to Trinity Church during the first World War in 1918. In 1933 the Central German Conference was disbanded and Trinity Church became a part of the Zanesville District of the Ohio Conference.

Other churches in Marietta include the Norwood Church which has 568 members, the John Stewart Memorial Methodist Church with eight members (this is a Negro church which carries the name of Methodism's first missionary to the Indians); there is also a Wesleyan Methodist Church in Marietta.

J. M. Versteeg, *Ohio Area.* 1962.   FLOYD W. POWELL

MARION, OHIO, U.S.A. **Epworth Church,** the "mother church" of Methodism in Marion County, Ohio, traces its history back to 1820 when a sturdy group of eight devout pioneers organized the first Methodist class. The first building was erected in 1831, and, becoming speedily outgrown, was replaced in 1845 by a new building known as Centenary M. E. Church. The closeness of the railroad made this location undesirable, and in 1854 the congregation moved to another site where it remained for thirty-five years. In 1890, when the membership had grown to over 600, the present building was erected, which at that time was one of the largest and best church buildings in OHIO.

Four great revivals have made Epworth what it is today: 1854-55, 1869-70, 1893, and 1896. Literally hundreds of members were received into the church, making Epworth the largest church then in the conference. The longest pastorate was that of Jesse Swank, who endeared himself to the entire city. He served from 1915-25. Two former pastors became college presidents: Albert E. Smith, President of OHIO NORTHERN UNIVERSITY for twenty-five years, and JOHN L. HILLMAN, President of SIMPSON COLLEGE. Among the many outstanding laymen who have served Epworth, mention should be made of John H. Clark (1872-1960), for over fifty years a trustee of Ohio Northern University, a delegate to four GENERAL CONFERENCES, a member of the General BOARD OF MISSIONS, and of the Book Committee. He taught a Sunday school class for young men which grew to be one of the largest in the state. The membership of Epworth in 1970 was 2,013.

JOHN F. YOUNG

MARKEY, M. BELLE (1875-1961), American missionary to CUBA and MEXICO, was born at MacClenny, Fla., Dec. 8, 1875. Her education was at Polytechnic College, Fort Worth, Texas, SCARRITT COLLEGE and George Peabody College, Nashville, Tenn. After finishing college she taught for two years at Clarendon College, Clarendon, Texas.

In 1902 she was accepted by the Board of Missions (MES) and arrived in Cuba the same year. She was appointed teacher at Irene Toland School, Matanzas, where she remained until 1920 when she was transferred to Colegio Buenavista, Marianao. In 1926 she was transferred to the Centro Cristiano at Chihuahua, Mexico. After forty-one years of service she retired in 1943.

On a visit to Mexico in 1944 she decided to remain for another year as a helper in Chihuahua. Although retired and while living in California she assumed positions of responsibility as a leader and teacher in the local churches. She passed to her reward Feb. 1, 1961 at Pasadena, Calif.

Her work was always characterized by a faithful sense of duty and carefulness in all details.

GARFIELD EVANS

MARKHAM, EDWIN (1852-1940), American poet, author of "The Man with the Hoe," was a teacher by profession. He was born in OREGON, but in early life moved to a CALIFORNIA farm. Here he developed his love of nature, and in an ungraded school had a teacher who introduced him to the world of poetry. After graduating from the San Jose Normal School he taught in Coloma, Calif., famous as the site of the discovery of gold. Placer mining had given out, but he, as he said, discovered spiritual gold through the visits of the Methodist presiding elder. It was in Coloma that he saw in a magazine a reproduction of Millet's picture and wrote the opening lines of his great poem. For a time he was licensed as a local preacher. His last teaching was as principal of an Oakland, Calif. school. Here he saw the original Millet canvas, and finished his poem.

"The Man with the Hoe" immediately caused nationwide—almost worldwide—controversy. His other best-known poem was "Lincoln, Man of the People." He continued to write and lecture until over eighty years of age.

He was the poet of the social awakening that stirred the church in the early years of the twentieth century. By pen and voice he did much to aid reform movements, as in legislation to prohibit child labor. He was the poet of social reform.

A large man physically, with rugged features crowned with ample white hair and beard, he was to the last an impassioned pleader for "Bread, Beauty, Brotherhood."

William L. Stidger, *Edwin Markham*. Nashville: Abingdon Press, 1933.
Who's Who in America. LEON L. LOOFBOUROW

MARKSMAN, PETER (? -1892), a Chippewa Indian missionary in the nineteenth century in WISCONSIN and MICHIGAN, was a member of the MICHIGAN CONFERENCE. He grew up among the Chippewa, his father a medicine man, his mother a nominal Roman Catholic. Although little is known about his early life and conversion, he was brought into Methodist circles in 1833 by the Indian missionary John Sunday and JOHN CLARK, who in the 1830's was organizing work among the Indians, and was trained in mission work by ALFRED BRUNSON.

In 1835 he was sent by Clark to establish a mission at Lac Court Oreille in northwest Wisconsin. He accompanied Brunson on a project among the Sioux. From 1840 on he served under appointment in various missions in the Michigan and DETROIT CONFERENCES. He was ordained DEACON in the Michigan Conference in 1842 and ELDER in 1862. In 1844 he married a French-Indian woman, Hannah Morien. He served at various times at Sault Ste. Marie, Fond du Lac, Janesville, Kazier, Grand River, Pesahgening, Saginaw Bay, Iroquois Point, and Sugar Island.

One of the most successful enterprises was work with Indians at Kewawenon mission, a Methodist station at the head of Keweenaw Bay on Lake Superior. Between 1843 and 1847, owing to a mysterious lapse in his life, he was expelled from Michigan Conference, but restored, first on trial, then in 1850 into full connection. In his later years he was highly regarded as an able senior missionary for Indian work, and was recognized in a full obituary in the Conference *Minutes* when he died, May 28, 1892.

R. A. Brunger, "Peter Marksman—Chippewa Indian Missionary," *Michigan Christian Advocate*, March 3 and 10, 1966. Frederick A. Norwood, "Peter Marksman, Chippewa Missionary," *Adult Student*, August 1959. FREDERICK A. NORWOOD

MARKWOOD, JACOB (1815-1873), American United Brethren bishop, son of John and Margaret (Durst) Markwood, was born Dec. 26, 1815, near Charleston, W. Va., and died Jan. 22, 1873, at Luray, Va. He attended public school about one year, but devoted his life to study, reading copiously, becoming scholarly in languages, logic, metaphysics, medicine, and the Bible. He married Arbeline Rodeffer on Sept. 3, 1837.

Converted at seventeen, he joined "Old Stone Church," a congregation of the UNITED BRETHREN IN CHRIST in Green Springs, Va. He was licensed to preach and received into the Virginia Annual Conference in 1837, ordained in 1841, and elected presiding elder in 1843, holding that office until he was elected bishop by the GENERAL CONFERENCE of 1861. Re-elected bishop in 1865, his ill-health prevented re-election in 1869. He was a member of every General Conference from 1841 to 1869. From 1855-1861, he was a member of the denomination's BOARD OF MISSIONS and was sometime Trustee of Mt. Pleasant College and OTTERBEIN UNIVERSITY.

Weak in health, he threw himself without reserve into the work of the Church and the causes he espoused. He was strongly opposed to slavery and this opposition made him *persona non grata* in his home state of VIRGINIA during the Civil War. An example of a man who burnt himself out for his Lord, he died with the conviction that the Lord had no more work for him to do.

A. W. Drury, *History of the U.B.* 1924.
Koontz and Roush, *The Bishops.* 1950.
H. A. Thompson, *Our Bishops.* 1889. HOWARD H. SMITH

MARLATT, WASHINGTON (1829-1909), American pioneer preacher of the western prairies, was born June 28, 1829, in Wayne County, Ind. He graduated at Asbury University (now DePauw) at Greencastle, Ind., in 1853. He studied theology at this university, was licensed to preach, and went to Manhattan, Kan., in 1856. It is said that he came the entire distance on foot and alone.

Marlatt was present at the first Methodist Conference held at Lawrence, KANSAS Territory, in November 1856. He was admitted on probation to the Kansas-Nebraska Conference at Nebraska City in April, 1857. He became a circuit preacher and was assigned to the Wabaunsee Circuit, which included that county, Davis County (later Geary County) and all of the territory west to Pike's Peak in COLORADO. His salary was $100 per year. He traveled over his circuit on horseback. When Bluemont Central College (now Kansas State University) was organized at MANHATTAN in 1859, Marlatt became the first principal. A building on the campus is named for him. Marlatt was instrumental in obtaining much of the land for the first college. He died in Manhattan, Kan., on Sept. 27, 1909, and is buried there.

KENNETH R. HEMPHILL

MARRIAGE. As the foundation of both Church and State rests upon the family, and the family on marriage, it is easy to understand that the marriage relation everywhere should be regarded with the highest respect. In almost all tribes and nations marriage has been considered as a religious rite, and its celebration is universally accompanied by a social sanction and public observance which even among the most primitive peoples may be termed religious. Among the Hebrews this was especially true. In the first book of the Hebrew Scriptures, outlining this relation of man and woman, it is written: "For this cause shall a man leave his father and his mother, and shall cleave to his wife; and they shall become one flesh" (Genesis 2:24). This passage the Lord not only referred to, but sealed unto His people by adding to it, "What therefore God hath joined together, let not man put asunder." By the creation of man and woman together in Eden; by the laws written (Levitical code) and unwritten which guard this estate; by the family relationships of our Lord and His Apostles; by His teaching respecting the matrimonial tie—the divine seal has been set on the marriage institution. With the growth of the priesthood this class always took over the celebration of this Rite.

Matrimony was raised to the dignity of a SACRAMENT by the Roman Church during medieval times, and is still so regarded by that Church. That marriage itself is a Sacrament was denied by the Reformers. In following the Church of England's teaching in this regard, Methodism in its ARTICLE ON RELIGION XVI, after explaining the two Sacraments ordained of God (BAPTISM and the LORD'S SUPPER) this Article goes on to name matrimony as an "allowable estate." However, marriage has been regarded among all Christian people as something more than a mere "allowable estate," and "it is not too much to say that after the convenanting together of man and woman in the sight of God and their solemn promise each to the other, the pronouncing them man and wife together in the Name of the Father, and of the Son and of the Holy Ghost approximates a sacramental act, in the old English sense of a 'making sacred'." Bishop R. J. COOKE put it: "The solemnization of matrimony is a religious service, and levity or lightness of a manner of any description on the part of the minister should receive a severe rebuke."

Until those comparatively recent times when the Church and State became separate—certainly in America —the whole matter of marriage was left entirely in the hands of the Church, or its ministry. However, eventually the civil power took over and began to regulate the matter of marriage, since marriage is as necessary to its own existence as it is to the life of the Church. The relation of Church and State has nowhere come into stranger complexity than in the "concurrent" jurisdiction which they thus have over the marriage state. In the view of the State, the minister is empowered to authorize and execute a special type of contract between man and woman when they marry each other; and ministers are forbidden to marry persons unless, or until, they procure a civil license.

The Methodist Church for a time followed rather strictly the age-old Christian teaching which warned Christians against being united in marriage with unbelievers or irreligious persons. This was because of the influence which a married partner exercises over the whole of life. The following rules are found in early Methodist *Disciplines:* "Many of our members have been married with unawakened persons. This has produced bad effects; they have been either hindered for life or have turned back to perdition. To discourage such marriages, 1. Let every preacher publicly enforce the apostle's caution, 'Be ye not unequally yoked together with unbelievers,' II Cor. vi.14. 2. Let all be exhorted to take no step in so weighty a matter without advising with the more serious of their brethren. In general women ought not to marry without the consent of their parents. Yet there may be exceptions. For if, 1, a woman believes it to be her duty to marry; if, 2, her parents absolutely refuse to let her marry any Christian; then she may, nay, ought to marry without their consent. Yet even then a Methodist preacher ought not to be married to her. We do not prohibit our people from marrying persons who are not of our church, provided such persons have the form and are seeking the power of godliness; but we are determined to discourage their marrying persons who do not come up to this description." (*Discipline,* M. E. Church, 1864, p. 35.)

These regulations were in time dropped from the *Discipline,* though the danger that prompted them is still felt by many a good pastor and parent.

Methodism has never raised any question concerning the ceremony or rite by which sincere persons marry each other. However, a "civil marriage," in the view of the Roman Catholic Church is no Christian or Sacramental marriage at all, since it is not celebrated by one of her priests, though it is an honorably binding social engagement. This standpoint, however, is not adopted by Protestants, and any properly licensed marriage, whether solemnized by a Justice of the Peace or a minister, is taken as fully valid spiritually in our connection.

Early American Methodist *Disciplines,* until as late as 1844, directed that the Banns or "ecclesiastical License" for any proposed marriage should be proclaimed in Methodist churches, as they were in the Church of England. But the power of the State to regulate and license the proposed relation of the parties soon superseded the Church's attempt to do so. At present properly ordained ministers who are empowered to solemnize matrimony are simply directed to see that the parties are "qualified according to Law."

Who May Celebrate. As marriage in view of the church has always been a religious rite or observance, its conduct has always been in the hands of the priestly class. In the Middle Ages, when marriage became a sacrament, the priest or bishop had charge of this matter, especially since he joined to it the service of the Mass. In the English Prayer Book, from which we borrowed our office, the officiating minister is commonly termed "the Priest," though there are places where he is termed "the Minister."

When the M. E. Church organized in 1784, the celebration of matrimony in the *Sunday Service* and *Discipline* was committed to DEACONS as well as to ELDERS. Within recent years, however, "supply" preachers, even though they may not be ordained, have been allowed to marry couples, but this must only be within their own pastoral charge. When a minister becomes fully ordained, he is entitled to conduct all rites of the church wherever he is.

The Position in Britain. Originally the only way in which it was possible legally to be married in England was in the Established Church, though Scottish law made some provision for "common law" marriages. This strictness was felt to be a disability and hardship by Nonconformists, particularly by Quakers, who professed conscientious scruple at going to the Parish Church, yet who found that their own ceremonies were not recognized by the law. Early Methodists as a matter of course were married in the Church of England, and this custom still continues to some extent, particularly in rural areas. During the last century legislation was passed for the relief of Nonconformity, to make provision for weddings in churches other than the Church of England, and also for purely civil ceremonies at which the law forbids prayers to be said. British Methodist marriages proceed under these Marriage Acts. The legal marriage consists in the presence in the legally registered building of the couple, duly qualified by Registrar's Certificate and by residence, who shall make the declarations required by law in the presence of the Authorized Responsible Person recognized for that building by the Registrar-General, and in the presence of two witnesses. The declaration is one of "no lawful impediment," and of consent to the marriage, and the Authorized Responsible Person must write up the record in the official marriage registers, which he and the witnesses must sign. The law takes no cognizance of what religious ceremonies may be performed, nor does it require that the Authorized Responsible Person be an ordained minister. It is, however, the almost universal custom for the local Trustees of the Church to nominate the minister to the Registrar-General as the Authorized Responsible Person. Thus at the normal Methodist wedding the minister stands in a distinct dual capacity, both as a public legal official performing a civil ceremony, and as a minister performing a Christian marriage at the same time. Yet he does not perform the legally-binding ceremony because he is an ordained minister, but because he is the Authorized Responsible Person under the Marriage Acts. A visiting minister who is not the Authorized Person can and often

does come to take the religious service, but the Authorized Person (or a public Registrar), who does not as such have anything to say, must be present to hear the legal declarations, and make and sign the entry in the Registers.

Who May Be Married. From ancient times there have been certain degrees of blood kin which prevent the marriage relation, and in time the medieval church developed a body of canon law which set forth prescribed conditions preventing matrimony, or in case an actual ceremony was had, declaring that the marriage was invalid. The general principle of "forbidden degrees of consanguinuity" followed the law of Leviticus, but extended by the sacramental principle that the man and his wife are "one flesh," with the effect that relations by marriage as well as blood relations are included within the "forbidden degrees." In particular, it was against the canon law to marry one's deceased husband's brother (one's "brother"), or one's deceased wife's sister (one's "sister"). The effect of this was to create a very various complication of technical impediments to marriage, which could if necessary be dispensed with by the ecclesiastical courts, or which could give rise to proceedings for nullity. So while there was technically no divorce there were ways of dissolving marriages in cases of pressing necessity. Methodists, with Protestants in general, do not proceed in this way, but follow the civil law. They feel that since the granting of a license now is in the hands of the State, that power can be looked to to follow its own laws, and will refuse a marriage license to persons who cannot be properly qualified. Furthermore, as is well known, the qualifications that the State does make for marriage and annulment, rest heavily upon the laws and customs the Christian Church has long inculcated.

Divorce. Persons who have been divorced present a special problem when they come and ask to be married again by their own minister. The traditional Christian standard from ancient time has been to forbid a second Church marriage to a person who has been party to a divorce, whether "innocent" or "guilty," on the ground that the sacramental union is in principle indissoluble (Mark x:2-9). Divorce is indeed allowable on the ground of adultery (Matthew xix:9), but it is only a legal permission to live apart, and does not bring the right to remarry, as the marriage still in principle exists (Mark x:11-12). However, in the modern period the Protestant Churches have tended to modify this discipline by accommodating it to the mores and laws of the civic community. They have in general been reluctant to call in question the validity of a divorce pronounced by the law of the state. The M. E. Church for many years forbade its ministers to marry any couple where a divorce was involved, unless this divorce was for adultery—"the one scriptural cause," as the M. E. Church, South (which had the same regulation) termed it in its *Discipline*. However, of recent years The Methodist Church recognized the fact that causes other than adultery may break a marriage, and present regulations in the *Book of Discipline* so indicate. "Divorce is not the answer to the problems that caused it. It is symptomatic of deeper difficulties," —so states the 1964 *Discipline* in its paragraph 1821 dealing with the Christian family. Present regulations provide that "a minister may solemnize the marriage of a divorced person only when he has satisfied himself by careful counseling that (a) the divorced person is sufficiently aware of the factors leading to the failure of the previous marriage, (b) the divorced person is sincerely preparing to make the proposed marriage truly Christian, and (c) sufficient time has elapsed for adequate preparation and counseling. The usual minister endeavors to decide upon each case on its own merits when there is a divorce involved, sometimes refusing to perform the ceremony, sometimes judging that it is right and proper for him to do so after he has looked into the entire situation.

British Methodism. Cases where divorced persons seriously apply for marriage in a Methodist Church are not in general very numerous, for a common feeling is that a civil marriage is the appropriate step in such cases. This is probably the least unsatisfactory solution to a painful and compromised business, for the unfortunate in life are not forbidden to marry, but the Church is not asked publicly to compromise the admitted Christian ideal of life-long and indissoluble marriage. There is also the somewhat invidious problem that the Church of England, which nominally comprises the bulk of the nation, in general adheres to the traditional strict standard, and refuses to marry divorced persons. Thus some who are in fact not Methodist people may at times come making enquiry whether some other Church is more accommodating. The rule is that if a minister is approached to marry a divorced person he shall communicate the matter to the Chairman of the District. If there is any doubt he shall consult with his colleagues in the Circuit, and if there is still doubt the Chairman shall call together a special advisory committee to consider the case. A reasonable interpretation of this procedure is that if there is some person of Christian integrity, well known, who has been the victim of wrongdoing by an erring partner, and who wishes for a second marriage in Church, he or she should not be refused by the Church. But other people, less known to us, and of whose understanding of Christ's marriage law we are less sure, ought not to be encouraged to come for Church weddings, particularly in cases where the divorced party has been guilty of the matrimonial offense. There must be special reason for confidence that the person in question has come to a real change of mind and life. There is on the one hand the possibility of the forgiveness and restoration of sinners, but the Church must be on guard against adjusting her standards to the conventional mores of society, or using her services to give an air of respectability to impenitent sinners against the Christian marriage law of a life-long union. The Church ought to give full moral support to the minister who undertakes the invidious and painful task of upholding the Church's standards in personal pastoral contact. Thus the Standing Orders rightly guarantee the position of a minister who has conscientious scruples against marrying divorced persons.

The Marriage Rite. The rite of matrimony as found in the Methodist *Discipline* and sent over to American Methodism by JOHN WESLEY himself is an abridgment of the Form of Solemnization of Matrimony in the English Prayer Book. It is a beautiful office, skillfully put together, so as to join devotion and liturgical excellence with a stately and yet gracious service. John Wesley did not change the matrimonial office of the Prayer Book in any way, except to leave out the "wedding"—commonly called the "ring ceremony." In omitting the ring, and all mention of it in the wedding prayer, Wesley followed the Puritan idea, as the Puritans objected bitterly to the wedding ring, which to them savored of the old unreformed ritual.

In American Methodism, however, in the middle of the nineteenth century, the M. E. Churches both put back the ring ceremony, and at present there is a provision for a double ring where the parties each desire to give the other such a token. The word "wed" in old English meant a pledge, or something given in pledge, and "with this ring I thee wed" meant that with this ring I thee *pledge.* John Wesley sent to American Methodism a marriage service, without a wedding!

In the revision of the marriage rite through the years, not too many changes have been made, though since 1940 the challenge to the parties ("If either of you know any reason why ye may not be lawfully joined together, ye do now confess it") has been omitted, since it is said the parties have already responded to that question before the clerk of the court in order to obtain their license, and satisfied him that they are ready to be married, and therefore, the Church need not stop to challenge them. The omission of this challenge, however, has been to the distaste of some, who feel that it not only belongs in the formal wedding drama, but that the church or minister ought not to pronounce a man and woman husband and wife in the name of the Holy Trinity unless and until he has publicly asked them himself, if they know any reason why they may not be lawfully joined.

A recent revision of the Ritual has clarified certain of the rubrics at the beginning of the wedding service, but no other great change has been made. The British Methodist marriage service has been less revised away from the Anglican original, and has never been without "the giving and receiving of a ring," though the continental custom of the bride also giving a ring to the bridegroom is uncommon. (See also ETHICAL TRADITIONS, British.)

Disciplines.
N. B. Harmon, *Rites and Ritual.* 1926.   N. B. H.

MARRIAGE OF MINISTERS. (See ARTICLES OF RELIGION, Article XXI.)

MARRIOTT, WILLIAM (1753-1815), one of JOHN WESLEY's executors, was born in LONDON on Dec. 16, 1753. Both his parents were among the earliest members of Wesley's society at the FOUNDERY. He was educated first at the school which Wesley started there, and then at Madeley by JOHN FLETCHER. Marriott entered his father's business as a baker but later became a wealthy stockbroker. In 1801 he was nominated as sheriff of London but declined the office. He was a generous philanthropist and a treasurer of the STRANGER'S FRIEND SOCIETY. He died in London on July 15, 1815.

L. F. Church, *More About the Early Methodist People.* 1949.
G. J. Stevenson, *City Road Chapel.* 1872.   G. ERNEST LONG

MARSH, CHARLES FRANKLIN (1903-   ), American college president, was born at Antigo, Wis., Aug. 18, 1903, son of Charles O. and Mae (Barnett) Marsh. He was graduated from LAWRENCE COLLEGE, A.B., 1925; University of Illinois, M.A., 1926; Ph.D., 1928.

He was an examiner with the U.S. Civil Service Commission the summers of 1929-30; a member of the faculty of the College of William and Mary, 1930-58; chancellor, professor of economics and business administration, 1941-54; dean of the faculty, 1952-58. In 1958 he became president of WOFFORD COLLEGE, Spartanburg, S. C., serving in that capacity until retirement in 1968.

He has been active in educational, church, and civic affairs, serving as a member of the UNIVERSITY SENATE, on the Commission on Church Union, Commission on Ecumenical Affairs, and CONSULTATION ON CHURCH UNION. Also he was deputy administrator of the NRA, 1935-36, principal economist (Federal) Board of Investigation and Research, and was active in various councils of the Commonwealth of Virginia, being chairman of the Williamsburg Postwar Planning Commission, a member of the City Council, and president of the Williamsburg Chamber of Commerce. He has been president of the Council for Spartanburg County and chairman of the commission for long range planning of the City of Spartanburg. He has served as member of the American Economics Association, of state and regional education associations, as president of Phi Beta Kappa.

In The Methodist Church he has been a delegate to the JURISDICTIONAL CONFERENCE, 1960, and to the GENERAL and Jurisdictional CONFERENCES of 1964 and 1968.

He is author of various books and publications in the line of his own interests. Also he wrote "Contributions of Wofford College to Methodism," *Methodist History*, 1965.

He was married to Chloro Nancy Thurman, Sept. 8, 1928, and they have two children.

Who's Who in the Methodist Church, 1966.

J. MARVIN RAST

MARSH, DANIEL L. (1880-1968), American minister, church leader, and university president and chancellor, was born in West Newton, Pa., on April 12, 1880. He was the son of George W. and Mary (Lash) Marsh. He received the A.B. degree from NORTHWESTERN UNIVERSITY in 1906, the A.M. in 1907, and S.T.B. from BOSTON UNIVERSITY in 1908. Thereafter he studied at GARRETT BIBLICAL INSTITUTE, the University of Chicago, University of Pittsburgh, University of Geneva and at Oxford University. He received the Ph.D. from the University of Bologna in ITALY in 1931, and was the recipient of numerous honorary degrees.

On Aug. 22, 1906, he married Harriet Truxell, who died on July 15, 1937. Their children are Mary (Mrs. Ronald W. Ober); Marjorie (Mrs. Paul N. Otto); Madeline (Mrs. Harold DeWolf—wife of the Dean of Westminster Theological Seminary in Washington); and Harriett (Mrs. Robert H. Murray). He married Mrs. Arline Woodford McCormick on Nov. 24, 1938, and their adopted daughter Nancy Arline is Mrs. Mason N. Hartman.

Marsh served pastorates in the PITTSBURGH CONFERENCE for a time and then became president of Boston University in 1925, where he served until 1951, when he became chancellor for life. He was a member of the GENERAL CONFERENCE of the M. E. Church in 1916, '20, '24, '28, '32, '36; a member of the Uniting Conference of The Methodist Church in 1939, and of the General Conference of The Methodist Church in 1940, '44, '48. He was a member of the BOARD OF EDUCATION from 1929 to 1952, and belonged to various scientific and honorary groups. He was the author of numerous books including *The House of Seven Pillars; Life's Most Arresting Question* (1950); *The True Church* (1958); *Religion in Education in a Time of Change* (1962). He died May 20, 1968, and a funeral service was held for him in the Marsh

Chapel at Boston University on May 25. At his death *Time* magazine commented: "There was no argument about the near miracle he worked at Boston University where he took a moldering collection of brownstones for 9,600 students in 1926 and built a multiversity that today boasts 23,000 students and thirteen graduate schools."

New York Times, May 23, 1968.
Who's Who in America.   N. B. H.

MARSHALL, CHARLES KIMBALL (1811-1891), distinguished American minister and leader of Southern Methodism, was born in Durham, MAINE, of French Huguenot ancestry. His parents removed to BOSTON for several years where he was educated. Then later they moved to NEW ORLEANS, La., where he carried on his studies, and also began to hold religious meetings. In May 1832, he was licensed to preach by the Methodist Conference at New Orleans. In that year he went to NATCHEZ, Miss., to fill a vacated pulpit, and there became a member of the MISSISSIPPI CONFERENCE. Always handsome and eloquent, the young minister found himself famous at once and in demand for the best pulpits. Later he served in BATON ROUGE, La., and in JACKSON and VICKSBURG, Miss. He was known throughout the south and the nation as the "silver tongued orator" of Methodism.

In 1836 he married Miss Amanda Maria Vick, daughter of NEWITT and Elizabeth Clarke VICK. Newitt Vick was the founder of Vicksburg, and in this town Marshall and his wife made their home. Sargeant S. Prentiss, also a native of Maine, lived in Vicksburg, and he and Marshall became fast friends. Both known as great orators, they each ranked high in popular esteem throughout the nation.

Marshall continued his Methodist ministerial work with zeal and energy to the end of his life. Much of his time was spent in helping those in distress and danger. He went through thirteen yellow fever epidemics, ministering night and day to the ill and dying—especially in the dreadful one of 1878 in which Bishop CHARLES B. GALLOWAY came so near death when he was pastor at Vicksburg.

During the War Between the States, 1861-65, C. K. Marshall devoted his time and strength and finances to aiding the sick and wounded on the field. To him the Confederate government was greatly indebted for a system he provided, or planned for, of depots and hospitals, and its factory for making wooden legs, the model for which he drew up.

In 1880, Marshall gave especial attention to the Negro problem, and the future of the colored race in relation to the southern states. He wrote many pamphlets on the subject. He never refused to join in aggressively upon the issues of any day and time.

After an attack of pneumonia, he died at his home in Vicksburg, on Jan. 14, 1891. Bishop Charles B. Galloway, a close friend, conducted the funeral services.

Dunbar Roland, *Mississippi*. Atlanta, 1907.

MRS. N. VICK ROBBINS

MARSHALL, WILLIAM (1811-1846), was born in England and joined the Methodist ministry in 1838. From June, 1839, to May, 1842, he served on the Western Shore mission, which stretched for almost two hundred miles along the south coast of Newfoundland. During the first year he visited fifty-two coves and harbors, in some of which the people had not seen a minister before. In that year he baptized 150 children. In his second year on the mission he visited sixty places by boat. In June, 1842, he was appointed to the Green Bay mission with Twillingate as his headquarters. On this mission also, he travelled extensively. By his devotion and zealous labors he laid the foundation on which Methodism was built in the northern part of Newfoundland. Not surprisingly, he died at the early age of thirty-five.

W. Wilson, *Newfoundland and Its Missionaries*. Cambridge, Mass.: Dakin & Metcalf, 1866. N. WINSOR

MARSHALL SCHOLARSHIPS are offered, under the will of the late Miss Marshall of Glasgow, to ordained ministers of the Methodist Church of Great Britain who have completed not more than ten years of their ministry after ordination. The Major Scholarship is of the value of £20, and the Minor Scholarship is of £5. The Minor Scholarship is open only to those candidates who at the time of the examination possess no university degree; the Major Scholarship is open to all candidates without restriction. The scholarships are awarded on the results of an examination held each year in May. The papers are set on the language and exegesis of the New Testament, and on the history and criticism of the New Testament. The examination is concerned primarily with translation, grammar, and interpretation, but candidates are expected to show a general grasp of the critical questions involved.

W. F. FLEMINGTON

L. R. MARSTON

MARSTON, LESLIE RAY (1894-   ), American ordained elder of the Central Illinois Conference and bishop-emeritus of the FREE METHODIST CHURCH, was born at Maple Ridge, Mich. He received the A.B. degree from GREENVILLE COLLEGE, 1916; the A.M. degree from the University of Illinois in 1917; and the Ph.D. degree from the University of Iowa, 1925. Houghton College conferred the LL.D. degree in 1939, and Greenville College the D.D. in 1942.

Dr. Marston is the author of *The Emotions of Young*

Children, 1925; *From Chaos to Character*, 1935; *Youth Speaks*, 1939; and *A Living Witness*, 1960. He was Executive Secretary for the National Research Council's Committee on Child Development, 1926-28. He served as a member of the 1930 White House Conference on Child and Health Protection. He was president of the National Association of Evangelicals, 1944-46, and chairman of its World Relief Commission, 1950-59. He is a fellow of the America Association for Advancement of Science and the Society for Research in Child Development. As Dean and President of Greenville College, he served the institution a total of fifteen years. Bishop and Mrs. Marston make their residence at Greenville, Ill.

BYRON S. LAMSON

MARTHA'S VINEYARD CAMP MEETING ASSOCIATION, Oak Bluffs, Mass., U.S.A. For many years this Association sponsored an annual camp meeting which became an institution on this island off the Massachusetts coast. The first of these CAMP MEETINGS was held in 1835 in what was then called the Wesleyan Grove. Only a few hundred people were in attendance. By 1851 the congregation on the Sabbath of camp-meeting week numbered between 3,500 and 4,000; in 1858 there were some 12,000 Sabbath worshipers.

A feature of the camp ground was the appearance of small family tents which sprang up around the large church tents, and which were occupied year after year by certain families who made a habit of attending, and whose social life was largely dominated by camp-meeting occasions. In 1846 there were thirteen church tents and one family tent; by 1860 the number had increased to over 500 tents of all kinds. Gradually the family tents were replaced by cottages, which many of the families occupied for the entire summer. Cottage City, now Oak Bluffs, grew up around the camp grounds. In 1869 there were more than 30,000 visitors, many of them attracted by the Grand Illumination. This event traditionally climaxed the summer season, when parks, avenues, cottages and the camp grounds were decorated with Japanese lanterns. Elaborate fireworks were displayed at Ocean Park, in Oak Bluffs.

The camp-meeting program changed gradually from a type of revival service, but its religious usefulness did not diminish. In 1878 Trinity Church was built, and in 1879 the present steel Tabernacle was erected, to take the place of the large canvas circus tent, seating 4,000 people, which had been in use during the preceding years. Grace Chapel, in back of Trinity Church, was constructed in 1885.

During the summer services are held every Sunday morning in the Tabernacle, with a "Community Sing" every Wednesday evening. The delightful custom of "Illumination" is still observed on the camp grounds and surrounding cottages one night a year, in August.

The unique character of the camp grounds, a heritage from quite a different day, has been wonderfully preserved by the many generations of cottage owners. To keep the outward appearance of serenity and charm, and at the same time to enjoy the modern conveniences of a mechanized age is the desire of those who have chosen this place for a summer retreat.

Joseph C. Allen, *Tales and Trails of Martha's Vineyard*. Boston: Little, Brown & Co., 1938.
Charles Edward Banks, *The History of Martha's Vineyard*. Boston: George H. Dean, 1911.

Henry Beetle Hough, *Martha's Vineyard, Summer Resort, 1835-1935.* Rutland, Vt.: Tuttle Publishing Co., 1936.
A. K. Lobek, *Brief History of Martha's Vineyard Camp-Meeting Association.* Oak Bluffs, Mass.: 1956.
R. C. Miller, *New England Southern Conference.* 1897.
Hebron Vincent, *A History of the Wesleyan Grove, Martha's Vineyard Camp Meeting.* Vol. 1, 1835-1858, Boston: George C. Rand and Avery, 1858; Vol. 2, 1859-1870, Boston: Lee & Shepard, 1870.
Vineyard Gazette, various numbers.   MABEL E. WARING

MARTIN, ISAAC PATTON (1867-1960), American preacher and historian, was born near Strawberry Plains, Tenn., on Dec. 11, 1867. He joined the HOLSTON CONFERENCE on trial in 1889, and was sent as a supply pastor to Lebanon, Ore., for one year. He then returned to Holston, where he spent the rest of his life.

His appointments there in order were Louisville, Maryville, Pocahontas, Tazewell, Lebanon, Sweetwater, Morristown, KNOXVILLE district, Church Street Church in Knoxville, Big Stone Gap district, Abingdon district, conference educational secretary, Morristown district, Knoxville district, Fountain City Church in Knoxville, agent for EMORY AND HENRY COLLEGE. He retired in 1940.

On Jan. 1, 1890, he married Bettie Lee Trent and they had four children. He received the honorary D.D. degree from Emory and Henry College in 1911.

Martin was a delegate to seven GENERAL CONFERENCES (MES), including the Uniting Conference in 1939, and also to the ECUMENICAL METHODIST CONFERENCES in 1911 and 1931. He was co-author with JOHN STEWART FRENCH of legislation creating the JUDICIAL COUNCIL of first the M. E. Church, South, and then The Methodist Church.

Martin was the historian of the Holston Conference and wrote *History of Methodism in The Holston Conference,* (2 vols., 1944) and a biography of Bishop E. E. Hoss (1942). He died at Knoxville on March 9, 1960, and was buried in the conference cemetery at Emory, Va.

Journal of the Holston Conference, 1960.
Who's Who in Methodism, 1952.   ELMER T. CLARK

J. S. MARTIN

MARTIN, JOHN S. (1815-1888), American minister and Conference Secretary, was born at Alexandria, Va., Sept. 7, 1815. At the thorough school of Benjamin Hallowell

he obtained a scholastic training which served as a sufficient basis for continuous study during the years of his ministry. He was converted at the age of sixteen, licensed to preach at the age of nineteen, and received into the BALTIMORE CONFERENCE in 1835. Recognizing his ability, his brethren sent him to General Conference in 1856 at Indianapolis, and in 1860 at Buffalo. Adhering to the South at the division of the Baltimore Conference, he became a commanding figure at every General Conference of the M. E. Church, South, from 1866 on. In 1882 and 1886 he was secretary of the General Conference. At the Methodist Centenary held in BALTIMORE in 1884 he was elected secretary by acclamation of all parties. He was systematic in his methods and a fine organizer, a faithful pastor and to the last a constant student. His intimate acquaintance with the Scriptures and his fine memory gave accuracy and beauty to his apt and frequent quotations. His burning zeal often swept the assemblies and brought multitudes to repentance and salvation. No place was too exalted, none too humble for him willingly and gladly to serve. He was appointed to his last charge at Saint Paul's in Baltimore, and although in his seventy-third year entered upon his work with an enthusiasm and activity that seemed to renew his youth. J. E. Armstrong said, "He preached to crowded houses as if his tongue had been touched with a live coal from off the Altar." He died July 8, 1888.

J. E. Armstrong, *Old Baltimore Conference.* 1907.
    W. W. MCINTYRE

MARTIN, JOHN THOMAS (1816-1897), American capitalist, philanthropist, and churchman, was born in BALTIMORE, Md., on Oct. 2, 1816. He was the son of John and Maria (McConkey) Martin. His ancestors were natives of England. They settled in MARYLAND in 1633. The house built by Thomas Martin in the 1600's at Island Creek Neck, Talbot County was in the possession of the family until 1866.

John Martin received his education at St. Mary's School in Baltimore and then entered the mercantile house of Birckett & Pearce. At the age of sixteen he joined the Light Street M. E. Church in Baltimore.

In 1835, he moved to ST. LOUIS, Mo., where, with his brother, he built up a large clothing business. He associated himself with the Fourth Street Church in St. Louis and served for fourteen years as its recording steward and secretary of the Sabbath school.

In 1844, Martin went to NEW YORK CITY to start a manufacturing branch of the company. He settled in BROOKLYN and became a member of the Pacific Street Methodist Church. He later served as president of its Board of Trustees for many years, and was instrumental in securing a larger building for the congregation when the former one became too small.

Ill health forced his retirement for a time, but in 1862, he returned to business and became the main supplier of clothing to the Federal government during the Civil War. It is reported that he sold over $50,000,000 worth of clothing to the government, and that there were times when the government owed him from $8,000,000 to $13,000,000. His success in business enabled him to buy up large tracts of water front property and to invest heavily in banks and railroads. Martin was one of the founders, and first treasurer, of the Brooklyn Polytechnic

Institute, a member of the Brooklyn Historical Society and a Director of the Mercantile Library.

In 1866, the centennial year of American Methodism, Martin gave $25,000 for the erection of a building at the Theological Seminary at BREMEN, GERMANY. The school was under the direction of LUDWIG S. JACOBY, an American sent out by the Mission Board and supported by the German missions in America, whom Martin had gotten to know years before in St. Louis. Before the building was erected in Bremen, it was decided to move the school to FRANKFURT-ON-MAIN. At Frankfurt a building was erected with Martin's money, and, in honor of his gift the name of the school was changed to "Martin Missions Anstalt." It is today the PREDIGERSEMINAR der Methodisten Kirche, or Theological Seminary at Frankfurt.

In the later years of his life, Martin lost his interest in Brooklyn Methodism. This was due to the fact that his church, Pacific Street, found itself caught in urban change. Differences of opinion arose as to the best methods of maintaining the church. Martin apparently did not agree with the decisions which were made and, for nearly twenty years prior to his death, attended the "Church of Pilgrims." On April 10, 1897, John Thomas Martin died in New York City.

Christian Advocate, May 27, 1897.
New York Times, April 12 and 15, 1897.
M. Simpson, *Cyclopaedia.* 1878.   C. WESLEY CHRISTMAN, JR.

MARTIN, JOSEPH C. (1865-1939), fourteenth bishop of the C. M. E. CHURCH, was born in Gibson County, Tenn., on Feb. 8, 1865. He attended Howe Institute in MEMPHIS, Tenn., and Roger Williams University in NASHVILLE, Tenn. Martin began preaching in 1887 and was pastor of churches in TENNESSEE, WASHINGTON, D. C., and SOUTH CAROLINA. In 1912, he was elected publishing agent and as such became noted as an organizer and financier. At the General Conference in 1922, he was elected to the office of bishop. He gained a reputation for his organizational and financial leadership. Bishop Martin died on Feb. 6, 1939.

Harris and Patterson, *C.M.E. Church.* 1965.
The Mirror, General Conference, CME, 1958.   RALPH G. GAY

MARTIN, PAUL ELLIOTT (1897-   ), American bishop, was born on Dec. 31, 1897, at Blossom, Texas, the son of Charles E. and Willie (Black) Martin. He received the following degrees: SOUTHERN METHODIST UNIVERSITY, A.B., 1919; LL.D., 1945; SOUTHWESTERN UNIVERSITY, D.D., 1938; HENDRIX COLLEGE, D.D., 1945; OKLAHOMA CITY UNIVERSITY, S.T.D., 1968.

On June 29, 1920, he was united in marriage to Mildred Helen Frayar, who has accompanied him in all his church-wide activities.

During the first World War, he served as a lieutenant in the United States Army. For a time, he was principal of the Blossom High School, 1919, and then the Superintendent of Public Schools there from 1920 until 1922. Entering the ministry of the M. E. Church, South, in 1922, he was ordained DEACON in 1924, and an ELDER in 1926. All of his pastorates were in the NORTH TEXAS CONFERENCE: Cedar Hill Church, DALLAS, 1922-24; Maple Avenue, Dallas, 1924-27; Henrietta, 1927-29; Iowa Park, 1929-30; Kavanaugh Church, Greenville, 1930-35; district superintendent, Wichita Falls District, 1935-38;

PAUL E. MARTIN

First Church, Wichita Falls, 1938-44. He was elected a bishop at the South Central JURISDICTIONAL CONFERENCE in 1944 and assigned to the ARKANSAS-LOUISIANA Area, where he served until 1960, when he was assigned to the HOUSTON Area.

From 1960 to 1968 he was president of the Methodist Council on WORLD SERVICE AND FINANCE. He was chairman of the American Section of the WORLD METHODIST COUNCIL, 1956-61. He was president of the Board of Temperance and vice-president of the BOARD OF EDUCATION, president of the COUNCIL OF BISHOPS, 1962. He was a delegate to the GENERAL CONFERENCE of the M. E. Church, South, in 1938, the Uniting Conference in 1939, and the General Conference of The Methodist Church in 1940 and 1944. He is a trustee of Southern Methodist University, Southwestern University, and Western Methodist Assembly.

Since 1949, Bishop and Mrs. Martin have visited the following mission fields: ALASKA, FORMOSA, JAPAN, the PHILIPPINES, MALAYA, INDIA, PAKISTAN, South America, and Africa. In Africa in 1957, they studied Methodist work in the CONGO, Southern RHODESIA, SOUTH AFRICA, ANGOLA, and LIBERIA. Bishop Martin has lectured at various colleges and elsewhere. He delivered the Fondren Lectures at Ministers' Week at Southern Methodist University, 1968; he was elected to serve as a professor at PERKINS SCHOOL OF THEOLOGY, S.M.U., upon his retirement in 1968. He is the author of *My Call to Preach,* 1946, and of a booklet, *Humanity Hath Need of Thee.*

Bishop Martin at his formal retirement in 1968 was administering the work of The Methodist Church in the TEXAS and RIO GRANDE ANNUAL CONFERENCES, comprising about 730 churches with a total membership of more than 220,000. He resides in Dallas.

Who's Who in America.
Who's Who in the Methodist Church, 1966.   N. B. H.

MARTIN, WILLIAM CLYDE (1893-   ), American Methodist bishop, was born in Randolph, Tenn., July 28, 1893. His parents were John Harmon and Leila (Ballard) Martin.

On July 1, 1918, he was married to Sally Katherine

WILLIAM C. MARTIN

Beene, of Blevins, Ark. Their children are: Donald Hankey, Mary Catherine, and John Lee.

He attended the University of Arkansas in 1913-14; received his B.A. degree from HENDRIX COLLEGE in 1918 and his D.D. in 1929. He was a student at the United Free Church, Aberdeen, SCOTLAND, 1919. In 1921 he received his B.D. degree at SOUTHERN METHODIST UNIVERSITY. Honorary degrees conferred on him are: LL.D., NEBRASKA WESLEYAN UNIVERSITY, 1940; BAKER UNIVERSITY, 1944; Southern Methodist University, 1958; D.D., CENTRAL COLLEGE, 1947; DENVER UNIVERSITY, 1953; and Texas Christian University, 1963.

He was ordained to the ministry in the M. E. Church, South, in 1921 and was pastor of the Grace Methodist Church, HOUSTON, Texas, 1921-25; First Methodist Church, Port Arthur, Texas, 1925-28; First Church, LITTLE ROCK, 1928-31; First Church, DALLAS, 1931-38.

He was elected bishop of the M. E. Church, South, May 3, 1938, and assigned to its Pacific Coast Area, 1938-39. He was bishop of the Kansas-Nebraska Area 1939-48 and of the Dallas-Fort Worth Area from 1948 until his retirement in 1964.

He has been a member of the BOARD OF EDUCATION; Board of Lay Activities; the Peace Commission; the Rural Life Commission (chairman 1944-48); Committee on Study of the Ministry; and the Advance for Christ.

Among other groups in which Bishop Martin has been a member and often occupied important positions of leadership have been: The NATIONAL COUNCIL OF CHURCHES, of which he served as president during the biennium of 1953-54, representing a membership of 35,000,000 Protestants; President of the South Central COLLEGE OF BISHOPS, 1956; General BOARD OF EVANGELISM, 1956-64; President, Commission on Promotion and Cultivation, 1952-64; President, Association of Methodist Historical Societies, 1956; President, COUNCIL OF BISHOPS for 1953; trustee of Southern Methodist University since 1939; Southwestern University since 1948; a vice-president of the Methodist BOARD OF MISSIONS and president of the Board's Division of World Missions, 1960-64; vice-president, Division of World Missions, 1956-60; General Board of National Council of Churches since 1952; board of Lub-

bock Methodist Hospital since 1954; and Central Committee of the WORLD COUNCIL OF CHURCHES since 1954. He is also a Mason.

He is author of *To Fulfill This Ministry* and *Proclaiming the Good News.* Bishop Martin retired in 1964. He served on the faculty of PERKINS SCHOOL OF THEOLOGY as Lecturer in Church Administration, 1964-68. He resides in Dallas.

Who's Who in America, Vol. 34.
Who's Who in the Methodist Church, 1966.
MARY FRENCH CALDWELL

MARTIN COLLEGE, Pulaski, Tennessee, was founded in 1870 as Martin Female College. It was named for Thomas Martin, an attorney residing in Pulaski who made the original gift to found the institution. Ownership was transferred to the M. E. Church, South, in 1908. The junior college program began in 1914, and the school became coeducational in 1937. The governing board consists of thirty-two members elected by the TENNESSEE ANNUAL CONFERENCE.

JOHN O. GROSS

MARTINDALE, WILLIAM J. (1841-1916), American minister, son of Moses and Margaret Martindale, was born Oct. 18, 1841, in Miami County, Ind. and died in Wichita, Kan., Aug. 18, 1916. His parents were devoted Methodists and under this influence he felt the call to the ministry early in life. He preached his first sermon as a local preacher Oct. 25, 1862, and joined the NORTHWEST INDIANA CONFERENCE in 1863. He transferred to the MISSOURI-ARKANSAS CONFERENCE in 1865, where he served as a pastor sixteen years and as presiding elder five years. He was a delegate to the GENERAL CONFERENCE of the M. E. Church in 1876 and was reported as the youngest member of that body.

He transferred to the SOUTHWEST KANSAS CONFERENCE in 1887, where he served twenty-six years before retiring in 1913. He served as a presiding elder eighteen years, twelve of these years in western KANSAS where new settlers were coming in and where new churches were being organized. These districts were lands of great distances where in six years on the Dodge City District he travelled 83,000 miles by horseback, buggy, walking or train. Such men as Martindale made the Methodist Church strong in that part of Kansas.

His brethren honored him by electing him three times as a delegate to the General Conference. He was a delegate to the Centennial CHRISTMAS CONFERENCE in BALTIMORE in 1884, and to the World Sunday School Convention in Rome in May, 1907.

He was an evangelist, a builder of churches and a builder of men.

Journal of the Southwest Kansas Conference, 1917.
Western Methodist, March 26, 1896. WILLIAM F. RAMSDALE

MARVIN, ENOCH MATHER (1823-1877), American bishop, was born near Wright City, Warren County, Mo., June 12, 1823, the son of Wells and Mary (Davis) Marvin. His parents came from New England. Marvin had little schooling other than instruction given him by his parents who had taught school in the east. His father belonged to no church; his mother was an unaffiliated Bap-

ENOCH M. MARVIN

tist; he himself attended Methodist services in the home of a neighbor and was converted in 1840. He married Harriet Brotherton Clark in October 1845, and they had five children. Their son Fielding became an itinerant in the MISSOURI CONFERENCE.

Marvin joined the Missouri Conference in 1841, and was ordained deacon in 1843 and elder in 1845. In the latter year he adhered South as the M. E. Church divided. His appointments were: 1841, Grundy Mission; 1842, Oregon Circuit; 1843, Liberty Circuit; 1844, junior preacher, Fourth Street, St. Louis; 1845, Weston Circuit; 1846-47, Hannibal Station; 1848-49, Monticello Circuit; 1850, Palmyra Station; 1851, St. Charles Circuit; 1852-53, St. Charles District; 1854, agent, St. Charles College; 1855, transferred to the St. Louis Conference and stationed two years at Centenary, St. Louis; 1857-58, First, St. Louis; and 1859-61, Centenary, St. Louis.

Tall, angular, and dressed in homemade clothes, Marvin made less than a prepossessing appearance as a young preacher. After a year in the conference three of his brethren, believing him unsuited to the ministry, advised him to drop out. Fortunately he did not heed their advice. Ten years later, at the request of the conference, he preached the memorial sermon for one of those men, and twenty-five years afterward he returned to MISSOURI as the presiding bishop and made the appointment of another!

Notwithstanding his homely appearance, Marvin quickly won recognition as a pulpit preacher of great power. W. W. Redman, his presiding elder the first three years, said on the conference floor, "Bishop, he is a green looking boy, but I tell you he can preach, and if he lives he will be a star!" An assiduous student, an indefatigable worker, and endowed with what today is called charisma, Marvin was widely recognized as the premier preacher in Missouri Methodism before he was thirty. He was a delegate to the 1854-58 GENERAL CONFERENCES and led his delegation to the one that did not meet in 1862. Appointed presiding elder at twenty-nine, he constantly assisted his preachers in revivals, formed two new circuits, and at the end of his two years showed a net gain of fifteen percent in church members.

Marvin was notably successful in his ST. LOUIS pas-

torates. A skilful debater, he used his pulpit to answer a Roman Catholic priest who delivered and published lectures critical of Protestantism. Marvin's twenty-three rebuttal messages appeared in the newspaper each week and then were brought out as a book, *Errors of the Papacy*. The volume had a good sale and made him widely known.

When the Civil War began, Marvin was unwilling to take the oath of allegiance required in St. Louis. Sending his family to his boyhood farm home, he slipped out of the city at night in February 1862, and made his way south. He supplied the Methodist church at Woodville, Miss., for some months, and then became unofficial chaplain to General Sterling Price's army, serving in MISSISSIPPI and ARKANSAS. He held revivals among the troops and organized an undenominational army church to conserve the results. Also, he conducted revivals in churches in the region in which Price's army maneuvered. For the last year and a half of the war he made the home of Rev. W. E. Doty, Greenwood, La., his headquarters. In February 1865, he began supplying the Methodist church at Marshall, Texas, and continued there until August 1866. His wife and children joined him in Marshall in March 1865, thanks to a pass provided by President Lincoln.

Though still a member of the ST. LOUIS CONFERENCE, Marvin was not elected a delegate to the 1866 General Conference which met in NEW ORLEANS. However, many if not most of the delegates knew him by reputation, and since there was talk that at least one of the new bishops to be elected would come from west of the Mississippi River, his name was prominently mentioned. Moreover, his friend Doty on his own motion went to New Orleans and advocated Marvin for the episcopacy. Therefore, it was not surprising that Marvin, though not a delegate and not even present at the General Conference, was elected a bishop on the first ballot. He appeared at the conference the next day; he had arranged his travel schedule so as not to arrive in New Orleans until the balloting for bishops was over.

Marvin's first episcopal assignment was the Indian Mission. Finding the preachers discouraged and ready to disband, he fired them with new enthusiasm, personally pledged $5,000 for their support, and then traveled over the church and raised it. Marvin probably did more than any other one man to rouse Southern Methodism from defeatism after the war. He opposed Methodist union at the time, saying amicable relations must first be established between the two churches. However, he believed that union would come in fifty years. He defended the right of the M. E. Church, South to expand in any geographical direction. Also, he supported the Southern view of the episcopacy, maintaining that the bishops in caring for all the churches had a pastoral function as well as administrative responsibility.

Moving back to St. Louis, Marvin gave strong leadership to Methodism in the city and the state. He led in collecting $100,000 to establish the influential St. John's Church in St. Louis in 1868, and he helped to raise a similar amount for the endowment of CENTRAL COLLEGE. He spent seventeen months on the west coast strengthening Southern Methodism in that region.

The 1874 General Conference voted that one of the bishops should visit the Orient. Chosen for the assignment, Marvin looked upon it as a means of dramatizing and inspiring support for the missionary movement. Sailing from San Francisco in November 1876, the ten months' journey took him around the world, and it was a pronounced success. His book, *To the East by Way of the West,* sold 20,000 copies.

Marvin began writing for the *Western Christian Advocate* as a young preacher, and in time he contributed to the *St. Louis Christian Advocate* and to every periodical in the church. His books in addition to those already mentioned were: *The Work of Christ, The Life of William Goff Caples, Sermons,* and *The Doctrinal Integrity of Methodism.*

Marvin's contemporaries declared that he had more than ordinary endowments. Certainly he had a quick, keen, and exceptionally retentive mind, and he was motivated by a strong inner drive to succeed at whatever he undertook. He was a powerful pulpiteer; D. R. McANALLY who heard him often believed that if he could have been accurately reported when at his best, the frame of his sermons would not have been surpassed in his day. Withal Marvin was dedicated and devout; he constantly practiced the presence of God. He died in St. Louis, Nov. 26, 1877, and was buried in Bellefontaine Cemetery there.

General Minutes, MEC and MECS.
Thomas M. Finney, *Life and Labors of Enoch Mather Marvin.* St. Louis: James H. Chambers, 1880.
Albea Godbold, "Bishop Enoch Mather Marvin," *Methodist History,* April, 1964, pp. 1-22.
Ivan Lee Holt, *The Missouri Bishops.* 1953.
D. R. McAnally, *Life and Labors of E. M. Marvin.* St. Louis: Advocate Publishing House, 1878.　　ALBEA GODBOLD

MARYLAND is a Middle Atlantic state south of the famous Mason and Dixon line boundary with Pennsylvania and north of the rambling Potomac River which separates it from the Virginias. Known as "America in miniature," Maryland's 10,577 square miles include most of the vast Chesapeake Bay, a drowned estuary, and extend from Atlantic beaches westward 235 miles over coastal plains and piedmont plateau into the Appalachian Mountains. Flora and fauna run the gamut from cypress swamps and aquatic bird refuges, to Frostburg's subarctic winters, with oyster fisheries and rich farmland in between. Megalopolis cuts a northeasterly swath from the national capital, but burgeoning high income bedroom suburbs are matched by declining highland and rural counties. Outside the latter areas, the populace has become a cross section of the ethnic, socio-economic melting pot which is America.

As an English colony settled in 1634 by the Catholic proprietor Lord Baltimore, Maryland's Assembly in 1649 became the first in America to enact religious toleration. However, Catholic worship was later proscribed, and in 1692 the Church of England was "established" and was supported until 1776 by levies from all taxables irrespective of religion. Non-Anglican Protestants found a haven in the colony, and both Quakers and Presbyterians trace some of their American origins to Maryland soil.

About 1760 an Irish Methodist local preacher, ROBERT STRAWBRIDGE, settled in what is now Carroll County near the present New Windsor and began to preach over a wide area, including much of northern Maryland. He built log meetinghouses near his home and at Bush now in Harford County. The body of his loyal followers included WILLIAM WATTERS and RICHARD OWINGS who became the first native American traveling and local

preachers. JOHN KING preached in Baltimore in 1771, and on June 22, 1772, John Wesley's missionary, JOSEPH PILMORE, organized the first Methodist classes there. By 1773 some 500 of the 1,160 American Methodists were in Maryland, and four preachers were appointed to the Baltimore Circuit.

During the Revolutionary War an oath of fidelity was required in Maryland, and numerous nonjuring Methodist preachers suffered prosecution. Despite the turmoil, the withdrawal of Wesley's mission force, and the death of Strawbridge, the numbers in the Methodist societies greatly increased. By the first Federal census of 1790, 4.4 percent of Maryland's population were Methodist members, twice the 2.2 percent in Virginia, which was second. Circuit preachers found their greatest hearing on the "eastern shore" which has remained the "garden of Methodism" for two centuries. Methodism took a leading place among the churches in all but the southern part of the state.

The Methodist Episcopal Church was organized at BALTIMORE in 1784 and its quadrennial GENERAL CONFERENCES met there 1792 to 1808 and 1816 to 1824. COKESBURY, the first Methodist college in the world, was founded at Abingdon in 1787 and continued operation until 1795, when it was destroyed by fire. A second Cokesbury College was started in Baltimore in 1796, only to meet a like fiery fate within the year.

The United Brethren Church was formally organized at the Kemp home near Frederick in 1800 and flourished among German speaking Marylanders.

From the first, Negroes were objects of Methodist concern and great numbers became followers. Splits elsewhere in 1796 and 1816 gave rise to the A. M. E. and A. M. E. ZION CHURCHES, but despite the fact that DANIEL COKER, co-founder of the A. M. E. Church, was from Baltimore, most Maryland Negroes remained in the M. E. Church.

The MUTUAL RIGHTS controversy from 1820 to 1827 largely centered in Baltimore, and it was there that the ousted Reformers held their conventions of 1827, 1828, and 1830 which resulted in the organization of the METHODIST PROTESTANT CHURCH. At Holly Run in Anne Arundel County the new denomination erected its first church building, while at Baltimore it sustained the secession of the mother church, St. John's, from the M. E. Church in 1843. From the beginning a portion of M. P. publishing was conducted at Baltimore. In 1867 the denomination founded WESTERN MARYLAND COLLEGE at Westminster, adding the Westminster Theological Seminary in 1882. A short-lived schism in the M. P. Church was healed at Baltimore on May 16, 1877, when the northern and western group of conferences known as "the Methodist Church," reunited with the M. P. Church. It was the first union of Methodist denominations in America.

When the slavery issue divided the M. E. Church in 1844, the part of the PHILADELPHIA CONFERENCE which extended into the nine eastern counties of Maryland, and the BALTIMORE CONFERENCE on the western side of Chesapeake Bay adhered North even though a majority of the general population in the region was proslavery. The sincerity of the historic Maryland Methodist proclamation that slavery was a "great evil" was attested by the financial support given by Maryland Methodists for the colonization of Negroes in LIBERIA and by the numerous manumissions of slaves, so many in fact that by 1860 the number of free Negroes in Maryland almost outnumbered the slaves.

Prior to the Civil War, the VIRGINIA CONFERENCE of the M. E. Church, South succeeded in organizing circuits at Potomac and Rock Creek in Montgomery County, Md., and the proslavery members of the Gatch Church near Baltimore organized Andrew Chapel.

The "new chapter" on slavery, adopted by the 1860 General Conference, urged preachers and laymen to seek the extirpation of slavery by all lawful and Christian means. Strongly opposed to such legislation, the Baltimore Conference in its 1861 session disowned the General Conference. Though not in favor of the "new chapter," the Philadelphia Conference and the East Baltimore Conference (the latter formed in northern Maryland and central Pennsylvania in 1857 by dividing the Baltimore Conference), remained relatively calm. The onset of the Civil War in April, 1861 forestalled the impending rupture in the Baltimore Conference, but the hostilities of four years utterly disorganized church life and work. Rival "original" Baltimore Conferences contended with each other, while a group of pastors who sympathized with the South but who were caught in Baltimore organized several independent churches. The "original" Baltimore Conference (which always called itself "Old Baltimore") which sympathized with the South, was visited in 1865 by Bishop JOHN EARLY of the Southern Church, and in 1866 it became the Baltimore Conference of the M. E. Church, South. Its territory included Maryland, except Garrett County, and northern Virginia, the District of Columbia, and a small part of WEST VIRGINIA.

Negro Methodists in Baltimore secured separate district conferences for their local preachers in 1856. In 1864, the DELAWARE CONFERENCE on the eastern shore and the WASHINGTON CONFERENCE west of Chesapeake Bay were organized for Negroes. White and Negro Methodists of Baltimore, assisted by the FREEDMEN'S AID SOCIETY, began Centenary Biblical Institute in 1867. It became MORGAN COLLEGE. Later a branch of the institution was started at Princess Anne.

Civil War losses to the economy and the church were never fully retrieved. The bitter aftermath of lawsuits and recrimination resulted in church extension which was more competitive than cooperative. However, by 1884 Methodists North and South came to Baltimore for the CENTENNIAL METHODIST CONFERENCE. Subsequent celebrations were held in the same city in 1934 and 1966 to mark the SESQUI-CENTENNIAL of the CHRISTMAS CONFERENCE and the BICENTENNIAL OF AMERICAN METHODISM.

Methodist institutions in Maryland included two homes for the aged at Baltimore begun in 1868 and 1870, and two at Westminster which opened in 1896 and 1926. The two latter institutions have since merged with the outstanding Asbury Home at GAITHERSBURG which was founded in 1926. The Kelso Home for Girls, started in 1873, and the Strawbridge Home for Boys, launched in 1923, merged to become the present Board of Child Care at Rockdale. Maryland General Hospital at Baltimore was acquired in 1911, and the Woman's College of Baltimore, now the front rank GOUCHER COLLEGE, was begun in 1884. Other institutions include two Baltimore homes for business girls, a deaconess home, and the Baltimore GOODWILL INDUSTRIES which was established in 1919.

In 1970 there were about 1,000 Methodist churches in Maryland with more than 284,000 members, as compared with 199,686 members in 1950, about eight per cent of the state's population in both periods.

E. M. Amos, *An Official Souvenir Book, American Methodist Bicentennial.* Baltimore, 1966.
J. E. Armstrong, *Old Baltimore Conference,* 1907.
E. C. Hallman, *Garden of Methodism.* 1948.   EDWIN SCHELL

MARYLAND CONFERENCE of the M. P. Church was the largest in the denomination. This was due to several factors. The M. E. Church was organized in BALTIMORE in 1784 and "the seed sown on Maryland soil reproduced in marvelous increase." Among advocates of lay rights— "Reform"—after 1820 were such prominent traveling preachers as NICHOLAS SNETHEN and ALEXANDER MCCAINE, not to mention several able Baltimore local preachers. These men became contributors to the *Wesleyan Repository* and its successor *Mutual Rights* through which they agitated effectively for lay representation. Also, "the first Union Society was formed in Baltimore, and the first to feel the prosecution encountered in the cause of reform was a Maryland minister, DENNIS B. DORSEY, who was denied appointment at the Baltimore Conference." Then the Baltimore Union Society which included eleven local preachers and twenty-two laymen was expelled from the M. E. Church for disturbing its peace. After their appeal was denied by the 1828 GENERAL CONFERENCE, widespread sympathy added to their ranks. Colhouer's *Founders of the Methodist Protestant Church* mentions thirty-one Marylanders who constituted more than one-third of the total. Seven of the first thirteen presidents of the M. P. General Conference were from Maryland. Finally, Baltimore had become a "storm center," and the three preliminary national conventions of the Reformers were held in the city in 1827, 1828, and 1830. In 1828 they organized as the Associated Methodist Churches, and in 1830 they took the METHODIST PROTESTANT name.

The Maryland Conference was organized in April, 1829 under the presidency of NICHOLAS SNETHEN. Admitted at that time were the first thirteen of the 611 traveling preachers who were enrolled in the 110-year history of the conference. By 1831 some 2,256 members were reported in eleven appointments. Largely as a result of CAMP MEETINGS and revivals, the number doubled by 1839 and doubled again by 1843.

Among early churches were St. John's, Baltimore, organized in December, 1828 in a former Protestant Episcopal Church on Liberty Street; Georgetown, D. C., begun by forty members on Dec. 2, 1828; Reisterstown Circuit and Centreville in December, 1828, Deer Creek and Pipe Creek Circuits, January, 1829. At Uniontown on the latter circuit the entire membership of the M. E. church joined. Holly Run Meetinghouse, still standing at LINTHICUM HEIGHTS, was finished in the spring of 1829 and is said to be the first church building erected by the new denomination. Savage, Brookeville, Magothy and Union Chapel near Roxbury Mills, along with Kent Island, Chestertown and Easton were other pioneer societies. Ninth Street Church, Washington, was built in 1835 with aid from other churches throughout the connection.

The infant conference had sent missionaries to PENNSYLVANIA and NEW JERSEY by 1831, and had recorded itself as opposed to slaveholding and in favor of abstinence. THOMAS HAMILTON LEWIS, the conference historian from 1879 to 1929, chronicled only one controversy. It involved pastoral tenure, sought by St. John's

Church, Baltimore, for August Webster beyond the two-year limit which obtained in the denomination at that time. The quarrel eventuated in 1844 in loss of control of St. John's and appointments in PHILADELPHIA, along with the withdrawal of Webster and THOMAS S. STOCKTON from the conference.

The Maryland Conference adopted many of the practices of the mother church. A full time conference president was elected annually. He visited the charges and made the appointments of the preachers subject to conference approval, and to appeal by any pastor to a committee on appeals.

In 1829, the conference started a fund for worn out preachers and widows. Within half a century the corpus had grown to $76,000 while some $90,000 had been distributed to claimants. A home missionary society was started in 1831, a foreign mission society in 1837, and a women's missionary society in 1881. The denomination's first missionary to the foreign field was sent out in the latter year. Institutions within the bounds of the conference were: WESTERN MARYLAND COLLEGE, WESTMINSTER THEOLOGICAL SEMINARY, Aged Peoples Home, Working Girls Home, and Book Concern Property. The first three were established in 1867, 1882, and 1896, respectively.

At the time of Methodist union in 1939, JAMES H. STRAUGHN of the Maryland Conference was one of two bishops elected from the M. P. Church. The Maryland Conference brought into The Methodist Church in 1939 some 169 ministers, 240 Sunday schools with 35,946 pupils, 255 churches with 37,225 members, and property valued at $6,695,420. The benevolent giving of the conference in that year totaled $630,000.

T. H. Lewis, *Maryland Conference.* 1879.
E. J. Drinkhouse, *History of Methodist Reform.* 1899.

JAMES H. STRAUGHN

MASER, FREDERICK ERNEST (1908-   ), American minister and historian, was born at Rochester, N. Y., Feb. 26, 1908. His parents were Herman A. and Clara M. L. (Krumn) Maser. In 1930 he received an A.B. degree from Union College, Schenectady, N. Y.; in 1933 a Th.B. from Princeton Theological Seminary, and also in 1933 an M.A. in English from Princeton University. DICKINSON COLLEGE awarded him an honorary D.D. degree in 1957 and McKENDREE COLLEGE a LL.D. in 1964. He married Mary Louise Jarden on Dec. 25, 1959. He joined the PHILADELPHIA CONFERENCE on trial in 1933, and went into full connection in 1935. His appointments were Birdsboro, 1933-38; Central, Frankfort, PHILADELPHIA, 1938-45; St. James Church, Philadelphia, 1945-53; District Superintendent of the Northwest Philadelphia District, 1953-58; Old ST. GEORGE'S CHURCH, Philadelphia 1958-67; Sabbatical leave, 1967-68; Dean of Students and Assistant Professor of Homiletics, Conwell School of Theology, Philadelphia, 1968-

He was Chairman of the Division of Evangelism of the Pennsylvania Council of Churches, 1950-58; a delegate to the Northeastern JURISDICTIONAL CONFERENCE, 1952, to the GENERAL CONFERENCE of 1956, and to the WORLD METHODIST CONFERENCES, 1956 and 1961. He has been a member of the Advisory Council of WESLEY THEOLOGICAL SEMINARY since 1961. He served as a member of the executive committee of the Association of Methodist Historical Societies, 1956-68, and was Vice-President, 1960-68. He has been a member of the International Association of Methodist Historical Societies since 1966. He belongs to the Colonial Philadelphia Historical Society, Penn's Towne Historical Society, Academy of Fine Arts, the Pennsylvania Historical Society, Church History Society, and numerous other historical organizations. He wrote *The Dramatic Story of Early American Methodism,* 1965, and was a member of the editorial Board and a contributor to the three volume *History of American Methodism,* published in 1964. He was a member of the editorial board of the *Methodist History* magazine, editor of *Discovery Magazine,* 1960-64, editor of the *Journal of Joseph Pilmore,* 1969, and has contributed articles to various church publications. He has written extensively in the field of Methodist history. He was a consulting editor and a contributor to Corpus Dictionaries, 1967-68. He was cited by Temple University, Philadelphia, for his gift to the Sullivan Library of First Editions, signed copies and manuscripts of Joseph Conrad, and in 1967 he was the recipient of the St. George's Gold Medal Award for "distinguished service to the Methodist Church." He is a collector of rare Bibles, Prayer Books, Wesleyana, and Early American Book Bindings. He is a member of the supervisory board of the *Encyclopedia of World Methodism.* In 1971 he was elected the first executive secretary of the World Methodist Historical Society (formerly the INTERNATIONAL METHODIST HISTORICAL SOCIETY).

Who's Who in the East, 1968.
Who's Who in the Methodist Church, 1966.   N. B. H.

MASHABA, ROBERT, was born in the Tembe tribe in Portuguese East Africa, went to Durban as a youth to work in the sugar plantations, and then to Port Elizabeth in 1875. Here he was converted in the Wesleyan church and baptized by the Reverend Robert Lamplough, whose Christian name he adopted. He went to Lovedale Training Institution for three years and became fluent in English. In 1885 he returned to Lourenco Marques to preach. He worked for a time on the construction of the railway to the Transvaal, as he received no financial support from the church. The Roman Catholic Church, the Swiss Mission and the Anglican Church offered to take him and his converts into their work but Mashaba demurred. He wrote to the Wesleyans in the Cape Colony telling them that some 200 converts awaited baptism. This letter was brought to the attention of the Rev. EZRA NUTTALL and the Rev. William Mtembu was sent to establish the Society. The South African Conference recommended that the work be taken over by the Transvaal District. In 1892 the Rev. GEORGE WEAVIND, acting Chairman, went to Lourenco Marques. He found a day school with about fifty children, four local preachers, a congregation of 200, a church building three miles from the town and other preaching places. In 1893 Weavind opened a new church at Mabota, eight miles from Lourenco Marques. It seated 400 and cost £100 which was raised by the congregation. In the same year Mashaba was accepted as a candidate for the ministry. In October 1894 a rebellion against the Portuguese broke out in the neighborhood of Mashaba's church and he was accused of complicity with the rebels. Mashaba moved his church from the area in order to disassociate himself and his people from the rebels. Notwithstanding his plea of innocence, Mashaba was arrested on Jan. 7, 1896 and deported to Cape Verde. It was six years before he was released. The Portuguese authorities would not permit him to return to Lourenco Marques so he continued his ministry on the Witwatersrand and in Swaziland. Mashaba made a valuable contribution to Christian literature in his native tongue. He had two reading books printed for use in his school, translated the Gospel of Matthew into Seshona and translated and composed ninety hymns. He retired in 1934 and was allowed to return to his birthplace, Nkasana, where he died on May 20, 1939.

Journal of the Methodist Historical Society of South Africa. Vol. III, No. 2 (October 1958).
Minutes of South African Conference, 1939. D. C. VEYSIE

MASIH, DAULAT (1872-1949) and **MANOHAR** (1906-), were father and son, both born in the village of Phatgali in the Katyur Valley of the Kumaun foothills of the Himalayas. Masih is a surname adopted after their conversion. Before they became Christians they, like all their neighbors, used the surname Singh. Daulat's older brother, Deb Singh, was the first convert of the family and suffered rough treatment at the hands of relatives and neighbors. But Daulat Singh was so much impressed by his brother's witness to Christ in words and behavior that he, a widower at the time, was converted and put his sons in the boarding school maintained by the London Missionary Society at Almora.

Daulat Masih was thirty-nine years old when converted in 1911. After more than a year of residence in Almora, he returned to his village, leaving the sons in Almora. He undertook to win to Christ his kinsmen and neighbors throughout the valley, and to that end he began preaching and composing Bhajans (Hindi religious lyrics) in Kumauni, the dialect of Hindi commonly spoken in villages of Almora District. He obtained help from a senior, well-educated Indian minister, U. S. Rawat, in editing the songs. Rawat lauded Daulat Masih as a man of faith and devotion. In Phatgali and in other villages, his relatives and friends turned to Christ.

On Jan. 1, 1926, the London Missionary Society officially withdrew from the Almora District and made their responsibilities and property over to the M. E. Church. The congregations and scattered Christians united with the Methodists, retaining strong love and respect for those who had brought them to Christ. Daulat Masih continued his work as a singing evangelist and personal witness.

Manohar Masih, the older son in the boarding school, made an excellent record there and afterward graduated from the government medical school at Agra, becoming a Licentiate of Medical Practice. He later took special training in the treatment of leprosy; and, shortly after the Methodist Church accepted responsibility in Almora, he was named as superintendent of the Almora leper asylum, which is believed to be the first institution in India established to help sufferers from Hansen's disease.

Henry Ramsey, commissioner of the Almora District when the Methodist Church began work in India, and a great benefactor of the church, had started this project at his own expense. Manohar Masih soon became one of India's most able leprologists. He has been superintendent of the Almora Home for more than forty years. In 1956, he was invited to help the mission to lepers and the United Mission to NEPAL in recommending to the Government of Nepal plans for opening leprosy work in that country.

After twenty years of work for sufferers in Almora and in a network of village clinics established to discover and treat cases of the disease in early stages, Masih decided that he could be more helpful as an ordained minister than as a layman. He took the conference course of study and joined the NORTH INDIA ANNUAL CONFERENCE. He was ordained deacon and elder by Bishop J. WASKOM PICKETT. More than a thousand people with leprosy have confessed faith in Christ and been baptized through the work of the Almora institution.

A protegé of Masih, also from a village home, is now associate superintendent of leprosy work in the North India Conference, and Masih serves as secretary to the medical council of the Methodist Church in Southern Asia. He gives three days each month to a primary school and a dispensary operated by the church in Phatgali. In that village there are now forty-four resident families. Thirty-eight of these families are active members of the church. The remaining six families cooperate in many church activities, though calling themselves Hindus. From Phatgali have come eight ordained ministers, two physicians, six nurses, eight teachers in Indian schools, a district woman evangelist, the wife of an Indian surgeon, a university lecturer in home economics, a college professor in the United States and more than a dozen men and women holding responsible positions in India's defense forces or in civilian government employment.

B. T. Badley, *Southern Asia.* 1931.
J. N. Hollister, *Southern Asia.* 1956.
Journal of the North India Conference. J. WASKOM PICKETT

MASON, HAROLD CARLTON (1888-1964), American FREE METHODIST and an ordained elder of the Wabash Conference. He married Alta E. McFate in 1909. He received his education at Huntington College, B.S., 1907; A.B., 1913; honorary D.D., 1924; ADRIAN COLLEGE, A.B., 1916; University of Michigan, M.A., 1924; Indiana University, Ed.D., 1945. He was ordained in the CHURCH OF THE UNITED BRETHREN IN CHRIST in 1907. His teaching service included Chesbrough Seminary, North Chili, N. Y.; principal of schools, Whitmore Lake, Mich.; superintendent of schools, Horton, Mich. until 1911; pastor, Adrian, Mich., 1911-12; instructor, Huntington College and pastor, 1912-13; pastor, Blissfield, Mich., 1913-18; Central Church, Montpelier, Ohio, 1918-21; bishop, 1921-25; professor of philosophy and dean, Adrian College, 1925-29; superintendent of schools and Lenawee County Normal School, 1929-32; president, Huntington College, 1932-39; professor of philosophy, Winona Lake School of Theology; pastor, Winona Lake Free Methodist Church, 1939-43; special lecturer, Grace Theological Seminary, Winona Lake, 1943; professor, Northern Baptist Theological Seminary, 1943-48; professor, ASBURY THEOLOGICAL SEMINARY, 1948-1961.

He was a member of several learned societies and educational associations. He wrote *The Teaching Task of the Local Church,* 1960; *Abiding Values in Christian Education; Reclaiming the Sunday School,* and contributed to *Light and Life Press* Sunday school publications, and to the American Sunday School Union. He was an eloquent gospel preacher, a Christian gentleman with great capacity for friendship.

BYRON S. LAMSON

MASON, JOHN (1780?-1864), British Methodist, entered the Wesleyan ministry in 1811. He had a natural aptitude for business and finance, and was commercially trained before entering the ministry. In 1824 he was a general secretary of the Missionary Society. He was BOOK STEWARD from 1827 to 1864—the longest period of service so far. He faced an appalling debt, the business having been for years drained of its capital in the interests of Methodist work (an endemic Book Room disease). He laid the foundations of great prosperity and sought to create a distinctively Methodist literature. RICHARD WATSON wrote much of his work at Mason's request. In the 1832 Conference he declared, "I, as Book Steward, am not under the Book Committee"—a declaration of independence not infrequently occurring in Book Room politics. Mason preached twice a Sunday and led a society class at City Road Chapel. He died, age eighty-three, on March 1, 1864.

FRANK CUMBERS

MASON, WILLIAM (1790-1873), British BIBLE CHRISTIAN minister, was born at Stepleton, Cookbury, North Devon. A champion wrestler, he was converted through WILLIAM O'BRYAN in 1816 and opened missions in Kent, Northumberland, and West Somerset. In 1827 Mason married Mary Hewitt (1803-53), a maiden preacher of breeding and Quaker extraction from Milverton. Immensely strong, he could walk great distances and quell an interrupter; at the age of sixty-six he was called out of superannuation to reopen the Portland Mission, closed through persistent hooliganism, and was triumphantly successful. He died at Holsworthy May 30, 1874, and was buried in the Bible Christian Chapel Yard.

Bible Christian Magazine, June 1873.
Lois Deacon, *So I Went My Way: William Mason and His Wife, Mary, 1790-1873.* London: Epworth Press, 1951.

GLYN COURT

MASON CITY, IOWA, U.S.A. **First Church,** of colonial architecture, is the fourth largest United Methodist congregation in the state of IOWA. It was once served by WILLIAM H. SPENCE, whose son, Hartzell, wrote *One Foot in Heaven* and *Get Thee Behind Me* as memoirs of his life in a Methodist parsonage, part of which were experienced in Mason City.

Judge Elisha Randall, the pioneer Methodist in Mason City, came from NEW YORK in 1855, carrying a preacher's license from his home church. A man of clear vision, he erected a saw mill on the banks of the Winnebago. The winter of 1855-56, which is recorded as one of the worst on Iowa's prairies, left great choking white drifts which in springtime melted to carry havoc before them. The saw mill was swept away. Undaunted Elisha Randall and his neighbors built a new saw mill on the ruins of the old. Randall and ten companions soon afterward started a Methodist class on March 8, 1857, the first religious organization in the little settlement of Masonville.

In 1866 it was decided to build a church. The deed was in the name of the Congregational Society. All helped to build the stone structure, now a part of the Congregational Church.

The first Methodist church building was constructed in 1869, a flat-roof structure costing $3,000. The congregation is now worshipping in its third building, valued in excess of $1,000,000. A large cross-section of the city's populace, 3,000 persons in a city of 32,500 population, are members of the present-day church, and many others turn to it for spiritual help and guidance.

General Minutes.
Mason City *Globe-Gazette,* Oct. 21, 1968.   LEROY E. BAUMAN

MASSACHUSETTS, one of the five smallest states in the Union with an area of 8,257 square miles and a population of 5,630,224 in 1970, has, from its Puritan beginning at Plymouth in 1620 to the present, made a distinctive imprint upon the character and culture of the United States. The nickname "Bay State" characterizes the eastern shoreline bordering the Atlantic Ocean. It suggests a great history of fishing, shipbuilding, and commerce. The Indian word "Massachusetts," meaning "near hills," characterizes the intervening 140 miles to the Berkshire Hills near New York State; it suggests small farms, diversified industry, and the tourist trade. Into this territory Methodism made a late organizational thrust in the final decade of the eighteenth century.

To be sure, GEORGE WHITEFIELD impressed thousands throughout Massachusetts with his preaching during the evangelical revival from 1740 onward. In Boston CHARLES WESLEY, stormbound en route from Georgia to England, had preached in 1736; there RICHARD BOARDMAN organized a class in 1772; there WILLIAM BLACK served Methodism briefly in 1784, and there FREEBORN GARRETTSON did the same a few years later. But all of those early efforts were without permanent results.

To JESSE LEE history appropriately accords the title, "Apostle of New England Methodism." Having been appointed at JOHN STREET CHURCH in NEW YORK CITY on May 28, 1789 to "the Stamford Circuit," as yet without boundaries or organization, Lee began his New England work the following month in Norwalk, Conn. By the summer of 1790 he had penetrated Massachusetts, preaching in Wilbraham on May 3 and in Boston, July 9. His first organizational success was the establishment of a society in LYNN on Feb. 20, 1791. The following year a small society was organized in BOSTON. As time passed, Lynn became the stronghold of Massachusetts Methodism.

Bishop ASBURY made his first visit to Massachusetts in 1791. He was disappointed because Methodism was being so poorly received throughout New England. Methodism's difficulty in Massachusetts, as in other parts of New England, was threefold. (1) Congregationalism and Anglicanism were already well established; in many communities the established clergymen were supported by taxation; and the coming of itinerant enthusiasts threatened the social and economic status of the community. (2) The "experimental nature" of Methodism with field preaching, extempore prayers, and testimonies was viewed suspiciously by conservative Yankee Calvinists. (3) Methodist leaders, including Asbury, had deliberately postponed work in Massachusetts and the other New England states, concentrating first on the South and the West, erroneously believing there was no "dearth of religion" in New England because of the "Edwards-Whitefield evangelical revival."

In spite of difficulties Methodism moved forward. In 1796 the NEW ENGLAND CONFERENCE was created. Originally including all the New England states, the boundaries of this conference were altered several times. By 1840 the words "the New England Conference" were synonymous with Massachusetts Methodism alone, minus sections not only in the extreme west but also in the southeastern and northeastern portions of the state.

There were 824 Methodists in Massachusetts in 1796. Between 1800 and 1820 there were nearly 600 conversions a year in the New England Conference. In 1900 the conference reported 40,667 members. Still numerically few in comparison with the total population of the state (about two percent were members of The Methodist Church in 1968), Massachusetts Methodists have exerted a liberalizing influence on the Christian church in Massachusetts and beyond out of all proportion to their numbers. This claim is substantiated by the work of ORANGE SCOTT, Henry Helms, and LEWIS O. HARTMAN in the field of social concerns; by the service of WILLIAM BUTLER, CLEMENTINA BUTLER, and GILBERT HAVEN in missions; by the ministry of JOHN DEMPSTER, WILBUR FISKE, and JAMES PORTER in education; and by the contribution of ALBERT C. KNUDSON and EDGAR F. BRIGHTMAN in theology. At the present time Massachusetts Methodists are striving to relate the pragmatism and piety of the Wesleyan revival to urban renewal, church extension, and ecumenicity.

The Methodist Protestants organized a small Boston Conference in 1830. It became a mission conference in 1880 and disappeared soon after 1900.

The Methodists began the publication of *Zion's Herald* in Boston in 1823. It changed names and combined with other papers for brief periods. Now a monthly it has been published under the original name for more than 140 years.

In 1970 The United Methodist Church had about 100,000 members in Massachusetts.

Boston Area Study, Church Surveys, Boston Univ., 1963.
Encyclopaedia Britannica Junior, Vol. X, 1960.
Jones, George H., *Methodist Tourist Guidebook*, 1966.
Minutes of the New England Conference.
Simpson, *Cyclopaedia*. 1878.
W. W. Sweet, *Methodism in American History*.
                                                   ERNEST R. CASE

MASSEY, ALABAMA, U.S.A. **McKendree Church,** located in the far southwestern corner of Morgan County, north ALABAMA, is an old historic Methodist church.

Named for an early Methodist leader, Bishop McKENDREE, the McKendree Church was established in the 1820's as a society, where meetings were held in an old threshing barn, on Crowdabout Creek. The old barn, weatherproofed and renovated, was used as a house of worship, which was served by visiting circuit-riders, until 1840. In that year, land was donated by Augusta Hewlett, grandfather of the late Roy Hewlett, Methodist minister of the NORTH ALABAMA CONFERENCE. On this land a log church was built and this remained in use until the need for a larger church necessitated the building of a third structure across the road in the year 1887.

This sanctuary was used until the present church was built in 1947. Throughout these years, the McKendree Methodist Church has remained a vibrant witness to a faith as strong as its pioneer founders.

Decatur (Alabama) *Daily*, Dec. 12, 1964; Dec. 19, 1965.
                                                   JIMMY E. HOWARD

MASTER, VIRJIBHAI KHOJABHAI (1892-1953), and **ITHIELBHAI VIRJIBHAI** (1912-   ), Gujarati Methodist ministers, were father and son.

Virjibhai, the father, was born at Uttarsanda, a village five miles from Nadiad. His education began in a Salvation Army primary school in his village. He came to the Methodist Boys' School at Nadiad when he was about nine years old. He passed the Vernacular Gujarati Final Examination, equivalent to the sixth grade, and then entered the Florence B. Nicholson School of Theology in Baroda, where he was known as an intelligent and studious young man and a fervent Christian. He served acceptably in rural appointments; and, while not neglecting any part of his pastoral duty, he continued his Bible study and acquired considerable freedom in the use of English.

He became a teacher in the school of theology, and a missionary colleague said of him, "He studies harder than any of his students." While teaching in the seminary, he began editing a Gujarati language paper. He translated into Gujarati the Methodist *Book of Discipline* and a number of English hymns. For a few years, he was principal of the school of theology. Other appointments were the pastorate of two strong city churches, the superintendency of three districts, and the chaplaincy of the Nadiad Methodist Hospital. He died on April 15, 1953, in Baroda.

Ithielbhai, his son, is a graduate of LEONARD THEOLOGICAL COLLEGE. As a CRUSADE SCHOLAR he took advanced training in the United States, earning a Master's Degree from SOUTHWESTERN UNIVERSITY at Georgetown, Texas, and a B.D. at ASBURY SEMINARY. He has served with distinction as a pastor and a district superintendent and has been prominent in interdenominational activities. For five years, he was vice-president of the India Christian Endeavor Union and was a delegate to the world convention of that body at London in 1950. For years he has been secretary of the Gujarat Regional Christian Council. He has represented his Annual Conference in the CENTRAL CONFERENCE OF SOUTHERN ASIA repeatedly, and has been delegate to the GENERAL CONFERENCE of The Methodist Church three times.

Journals of the Bombay and Gujarat Annual Conferences.
                                                   J. WASKOM PICKETT

MASTERSON'S STATION, near Lexington, Ky., U.S.A., was the seat of the first Methodist Conference in KENTUCKY in 1790. Richard Masterson came from VIRGINIA and in 1784 built a log dwelling five miles northeast of Lexington. A Methodist class was organized in his home and soon a log meetinghouse was built, the first Methodist meetinghouse in Kentucky.

In the spring of 1790 FRANCIS ASBURY called the preachers who had come into Kentucky to meet him at this place in the first Methodist Conference to be held in the Kentucky territory. Bishop Asbury came through the wilderness from NORTH CAROLINA accompanied by RICHARD WHATCOAT (later Bishop), HOPE HULL, and John Sewell. At Masterson's Station they met with the six preachers, FRANCIS POYTHRESS, James Haw, WILSON LEE, Stephen Brooks, Barnabas McHenry, and Peter Massie. Thomas Wilkerson arrived later. The conference lasted for two days; Wilson Lee, Thomas Wilkerson and Barnabas McHenry were ordained elders. Bishop Asbury writes in his Journal: "We had preaching noon and night and souls were converted and the fallen restored."

There were no separate minutes taken of the conference. The only records we have are from the testimony of those who were present. To the two circuits in the state, two new circuits were added and four new preachers were assigned. Francis Poythress was appointed as presiding elder. The membership of the church was reported as 1,265 whites and 107 colored. Plans for BETHEL ACADEMY were adopted. No other church had at that time undertaken such an enterprise. A subscription of 300 pounds in land and money was taken and the preachers sent out with instructions to "Beg for Bethel Academy."

W. E. Arnold, *Kentucky*. 1935-36.
F. Asbury, *Journal and Letters*. 1958.
A. H. Redford, *Kentucky*. 1868-70.   HARRY R. SHORT

MASTERTON, New Zealand, **Homeleigh Children's Home,** sixty-four miles northeast of Wellington, was established in 1921 as a Methodist home for children denied normal home care. It serves the southern half of the North Island. The home is a single unit, three-story concrete building to which a recreation wing was added in 1959. Funds for the establishment and partial maintenance of the home were provided from income from trust lands granted to the Wesleyans in 1852 by the colonial governor, George Grey. The home stands on fourteen acres of ground that produce vegetables, milk, and eggs for home use.

The first matron was Sister May Moriarty, and James Cocker was secretary-manager until his death in 1935. N. H. Prior, a foundation member of the board of management and honorary physician to the home, served for a record term of forty-two years before retirement in 1962.

JOHN B. DAWSON

MATHABATHE, SAMUEL, was born in Secocoeni's tribe, went to Pietermaritzburg in Natal to look for work in 1866 and was converted through the Rev. JAMES ALLISON. In 1873 he returned to his own people with a Christian companion, Johannes. The chief, Pahlala, threatened to kill him if he preached, so he went from house to house teaching the Bible. Four years later the chief died and his successor, his chief wife, a sister to Secocoeni, granted permission for services and a school. The work prospered. A church was erected. Converts were baptized by Dr. Hofmeyr of the Dutch Reformed Church who honored their wish to remain Wesleyans, and even gave them the Holy Communion. Two men were sent to the French Mission in Basutoland for training as teachers and on their return, worked under the direction of Mathabathe. In 1882 Mathabathe resisted an order of the chieftainess that a twin child should be killed according to heathen custom. In consequence, the church was burned to the ground and 200 Christians were ordered to leave. Mathabathe arranged for some to go North with Johannes while he took the rest to a farm in the South called Good Hope. Watkins purchased this farm 165 miles north of Pretoria, on behalf of the Wesleyan Missionary Society in 1883 and it became an influential mission station.

Journal of the Methodist Historical Society of South Africa. Vol. III, No. 2 (October 1958).
Minutes of South African Conference, 1939.   D. C. VEYSIE

MATHER, ALEXANDER (1733-1800), British Methodist, was born at Brechin, SCOTLAND, in February 1733. His account of his early life, written in 1780, includes the

ALEXANDER MATHER

story of how as a boy he joined the rebellion of 1745 and was lucky to escape with his life. The autobiography also contains an important description of his experience of CHRISTIAN PERFECTION in the years 1757-60. He had been converted under JOHN WESLEY's own preaching in LONDON in 1754 and became an itinerant in 1757. He was one of Wesley's closest confidants and lieutenants during the last ten years of Wesley's life, and in 1788 became the first of the itinerants to be ordained by Wesley for the English work.

Mather believed that Wesley had intended him to assume a guiding role in the government of the Methodist societies after his death and, together with THOMAS COKE, to exercise some kind of episcopal oversight of the whole body. The Conference of 1791, however, did not want an episcopal system, and both Mather and Coke were passed over in the election of the first president of the Conference, though Mather was chosen in 1792 as the second president. In 1794 Mather was associated with other leading preachers in the LICHFIELD PLAN, another attempt to graft an episcopal order onto the connection, but this scheme was also rejected by the Conference of 1794.

Mather was personally involved in the dispute which led to the expulsion of ALEXANDER KILHAM in 1796, and published a pamphlet defending the action of the Conference. He was perhaps the leading figure in the group of itinerants who would have liked to mold the Methodist system more closely on the Anglican pattern, but he never won the full confidence of the preachers as a leader, though he was greatly respected as "a perfect master of all the minutiae of the doctrines and discipline of Methodists." He died on Aug. 22, 1800.

T. Jackson, *Lives of Early Methodist Preachers*. 1837-38.
Minutes of the Wesleyan Methodist Conference, 1801.
G. Osborn, *Outlines of Wesleyan Bibliography*. 1869.
JOHN NEWTON

MATHEWS, GEORGE MARTIN (1848-1921), American United Brethren bishop, was born east of CINCINNATI, Ohio, on the Mathews' homestead, Aug. 22, 1848. He graduated from OTTERBEIN COLLEGE, anticipating a legal profession. In 1872, he married Clara Belle Hopper, and had one son, Milton. Without consulting him, his home church recommended him for license to preach in 1878. The next year he was licensed by the Miami Conference, UNITED BRETHREN IN CHRIST, and ordained by the same Conference in 1882. He graduated from Union Biblical Seminary (now UNITED THEOLOGICAL SEMINARY) also in 1882. He was pastor of the Summit Street Church, DAYTON, Ohio, 1884-89; served as presiding elder of the Miami Conference, 1889-94; was pastor of the First Church, Dayton, Ohio, 1894-98; and was associate editor of the *Religious Telescope*, 1898-1902.

At age fifty-three, he was elected bishop in 1902 where first he had residence in Dayton, Ohio, then in Chicago, Ill., for twelve years, but was back in Dayton for the last quadrennium. During this time he wrote two books: *Justification* (1902) and *Christ in the Life of Today* (1916).

Bishop Mathews touched every part of the church. He served on the executive committee of the FEDERAL COUNCIL OF CHURCHES. He was distinguished for the tenderness and strength of his emotional nature, at once genuinely human and thoroughly Christian.

He died after a short illness at Dayton, Ohio, April 3, 1921. Orville Wright, the famous inventor, served as one of the honorary pallbearers. Interment was in Woodland Cemetery, Dayton.

A. W. Drury, *History of the U.B.* 1924.
Koontz and Roush, *The Bishops.* 1950.   GALE L. BARKALOW

JAMES K. MATHEWS

MATHEWS, JAMES KENNETH (1913-   ), American missionary and bishop, was born on Feb. 10, 1913, at Breezewood, Pa., the son of James Davenport and Laura Mae Wilson Mathews. He grew up in OHIO and TEXAS.

He received his A.B. degree from Lincoln Memorial University in 1934; his S.T.B. in 1937 from the Biblical Seminary in New York. He did graduate work in 1937-38 at the BOSTON UNIVERSITY SCHOOL OF THEOLOGY. In 1957 he received his Ph.D. from Columbia University, his thesis being a study of the religious teachings of Mahatma Gandhi. In 1955 he spent a four-month leave in special studies on INDIA at Cambridge University in England. He holds honorary degrees from Lincoln Memorial University, D.D., 1954; WESLEYAN UNIVERSITY, D.D., 1965; LYCOMING COLLEGE, L.H.D., 1966; OHIO WESLEYAN UNIVERSITY, L.H.D., 1967.

Following a brief pastorate in NEW YORK CITY, he was commissioned a missionary of the M. E. Church in 1938 and assigned to service in India. He served as pastor of Bowen Memorial Church in the city of BOMBAY.

On June 1, 1940, in Naini Tal, Northern India, he was united in marriage to Eunice Treffry Jones, an only daughter of Dr. and Mrs. E. STANLEY JONES. They have three children, Anne Treffry, Janice Virginia and James Stanley.

In 1941 he was transferred to Dhulia, West Khandesh district, north of Bombay, where he was superintendent of the Dhulia-Pantamba district, until he volunteered for military service. He was a major with the American Army in India during World War II, 1942-46. In 1946 he was elected to the staff of the Methodist BOARD OF MISSIONS in New York City as Secretary for Southern Asia. In 1952 he became associate general secretary of the Division of World Missions of the Board. In that position, he shared general administrative responsibility for the denomination's missionary program in forty-four countries.

In 1956, he was elected a bishop of The Methodist Church by the SOUTHERN ASIA CENTRAL CONFERENCE (India), but resigned before consecration, believing that at that stage Indian Methodism was mature enough no longer to require non-Indians for its episcopacy. Two Indian national bishops were subsequently elected, MANGAL SINGH and GABRIEL SUNDARAM. In Washington, D. C., on June 17, 1960, he was elected a bishop of The Methodist Church by the Northeastern JURISDICTIONAL CONFERENCE and consecrated on June 19, 1960. He was assigned to residence in the BOSTON Area.

Bishop Mathews has been active in the INTERNATIONAL MISSIONARY COUNCIL and in the WORLD COUNCIL OF CHURCHES; he is a member of its Central Committee and chairman of the Structure Committee. He has served as a member of the General BOARD OF EVANGELISM; and of the General BOARD OF EDUCATION of The Methodist Church and its Division of Higher Education, as well as chairman of the Department of College and University Religious Life. He has been chairman of the Interboard Committee on Missionary Education, the METHODIST COMMITTEE FOR OVERSEAS RELIEF, the Crusade Scholarship Committee, and the COORDINATING COUNCIL. He is a member of the General Board of Missions and of the Commission on Ecumenical Affairs of The United Methodist Church. He was chairman of the CONSULTATION ON CHURCH UNION, 1968-70. He was a member of the Executive Committee and of the Structure and Program Committee of the WORLD METHODIST COUNCIL and of the Advisory Committee for a World Conference on Religion and Peace. He has been a delegate to numerous international ecumenical gatherings of the World Council of Churches, the International Missionary Council and the World Methodist Council. He is a Vice-President of the NATIONAL COUNCIL OF CHURCHES of Christ in the U.S.A., a member of its Executive Committee and General Board, as well as chairman of its Division of Christian Unity.

Bishop Mathews is chairman of the Board of Directors of North Conway Institute and of the Board of Trustees of SANTIAGO (Chile) College. He is also a Trustee of BOSTON UNIVERSITY, where he is a member of the Executive Committee; of the New England Deaconess Hospital; KENTS HILL SCHOOL; TILTON SCHOOL; CLAFLIN UNIVERSITY, and Bangor Theological Seminary.

Bishop Mathews is the author of *South of the Himalayas*, 1955, a popular study of India and Pakistan and the story of Methodism in those lands; *To the Ends of the Earth*, 1959; *Eternal Values in a World of Change*, 1960; *A New Church for a New World* (1968); and of many articles and papers for presentation.

Who's Who in America, Vol. 34.
Who's Who in the Methodist Church, 1966.   N. B. H.

MATHEWS, JOHN (1826-1907), colorful American pastor, was born in Philadelphia, Pa., June 13, 1826, the son of Scotch-Irish parents. As a youth he moved to Shelbyville, Tenn., where he joined the Presbyterian Church but soon transferred to the M.E. Church, South. He was licensed to preach in 1845 and was admitted to the TENNESSEE CONFERENCE in 1846.

In the spring of 1852, after serving several charges and while pastor at Andrew Chapel in NASHVILLE, Mathews responded to the call for volunteers for CALIFORNIA. Finding that the M. E. Church was already well entrenched in California, and perceiving that of necessity he would be compelled to defend the M. E. Church, South against the charge that it was a slave church, and knowing that in so doing he would have to say things that would not harmonize with his own convictions, he soon concluded that he had made a mistake. In the spring of 1853 he requested a transfer back to the States, but the bishop (JOSHUA SOULE) refused to grant it. Determined, Mathews boarded the next steamer out of SAN FRANCISCO and returned to Tennessee. That fall Bishop WILLIAM CAPERS broke church law and appointed him as supply preacher at Fayetteville, Tenn., even though he was still a member of the PACIFIC CONFERENCE. In 1854, that conference located Mathews and he was then readmitted to the Tennessee Conference. He married Mary A. Menefee, April 30, 1857, and they had five children.

Mathews soon gained recognition as an able pastor-evangelist. He preached to great audiences wherever he served and won thousands of converts in his long ministry. He was unique. He had the capacity to arouse enthusiasm for himself and the cause he represented. In the pulpit he used five or six sheets of paper filled with notes. Grasping the sheets at the lower lefthand corner, he would fan them out at the top as he preached. His hearers observed that when the sermon was well fanned out, so to speak, Mathews was through preaching. Mathews was so popular that at the end of his first pastorate at Centenary Church, ST. LOUIS (1890), a testimonial was presented to him by the mayor of the city, the judges of the criminal courts, the prosecuting attorneys, and the heads of the police department. After three years at St. John's Church in St. Louis, Mathews returned as pastor at Centenary in 1893 and, contrary to the law of the church which limited pastorates to four years at that time, stayed five years. During the fifth year his appointment was listed in the conference jour-nal as "Sunday school Agent and member of Centenary Quarterly Conference."

Mathews served about thirty charges in his long career. In addition to those already mentioned, some of his more important assignments were: Franklin, Decatur, Gallatin, Spring Hill, and McKendree (Nashville) in Tennessee; Auburn, Florence, MONTGOMERY, TUSCALOOSA, Tuskegee, and Wetumpka in ALABAMA; Carondelet Street, Felicity Street, and Rayne Memorial in NEW ORLEANS; and Walnut Street and Washington Street in KANSAS CITY, Mo. He was appointed to the important McKendree Church, Nashville, when seventy-two years of age. During his fourth year there his health suddenly failed and he retired at once.

Mathews' autobiography, *Peeps Into Life*, published in 1904, shows that he was a dedicated minister, a keen observer of life, an able preacher, and an interesting writer. He died in St. Louis, Sept. 1, 1907, and was buried there. A great crowd attended his funeral.

General Minutes, MECS.
John Mathews, *Peeps Into Life*. Published by the Tennessee Conference, 1904.   JESSE A. EARL
                                ALBEA GODBOLD

MATHIAS, REX (1907-   ), Australian church leader, was born at Maldon, Victoria on Jan. 9, 1907. He is a graduate of the University of Melbourne. He served for nine years as a journalist on the staffs of *The Herald* and *The Argus*, both of MELBOURNE. In 1932 he was accepted as a candidate for the ministry and entered the Theological Hall, Queens College, and secured his M.A. degree in 1934. He gained the Selly Oaks Colleges' Diploma of Religious Education and for two years was a lecturer in the Westhill Training College, Selly Oak, BIRMINGHAM, England. On his return he was appointed as a staff member to the VICTORIA AND TASMANIA Methodist Young People's Department and in 1940-44 was Chaplain at WESLEY COLLEGE.

He became the First Director of the Council for Christian Education in Schools (Victoria), 1944-46, followed by an appointment as First Director of the Methodist Federal Board of Education and Co-Director and Editor-in-Chief of the Joint Board of Graded Lessons of AUSTRALIA and NEW ZEALAND. Always interested in mass media, he was first Chairman of the Australian Religious Film Society, 1945-64. He was a popular and regular speaker on Melbourne's famous Yarra Bank on the "Voice of Methodism" platform, 1946-61. Deeply involved in Evangelism, he served as Secretary to "The Mission to the Nation," 1953-56.

Elected as Secretary of the Victoria and Tasmania Conference, he became President in 1962-63. In 1965-69 he was Superintendent of the Canberra Circuit, Australian Capital Territory, and is now Chairman of the Geelong Synod District, Victoria and Tasmania Conference.

He is the Secretary-General and President-General elect of the General Conference of the Methodist Church of Australasia, 1969-72.

S. G. CLAUGHTON

MATIU and **RIHIMONA**, New Zealand Methodist Maori laymen, were the first martyrs for Christ among their people. During 1837, the two young men, accompanied by Wiremu Patene and Hohepa Otene went to preach the Gospel to a Chief Kaitoke, who lived near Mangamuka (Northland).

Kaitoke had threatened to kill anyone who dared to preach the Gospel to him and fired on the party, killing Matiu and Rihimona, and wounding the others. The relatives of the martyrs attacked and captured Kaitoke, who, after receiving instruction, professed a desire to become a Christian.

W. Morley, *New Zealand*. 1900.　　　L. R. M. GILMORE

MATLACK, LUCIUS C. (1816-1883), American minister and organizer of the WESLEYAN METHODIST CONNECTION in the United States, was born in BALTIMORE on April 28, 1816. Having been licensed to preach, he was recommended for reception into the PHILADELPHIA ANNUAL CONFERENCE in 1837. He was refused admission by a unanimous vote because of his abolitionist sentiment, and in 1838 he was rejected a second time for the same reason. In 1839 his license was withheld, whereupon he accepted an invitation from ORANGE SCOTT and went to New England. There he was relicensed by the Quarterly Conference at Lowell, Mass., and was received on trial into the NEW ENGLAND CONFERENCE in 1840. In protest against the ambiguous position of various Methodist conferences on the matter of slavery, Matlack in 1842 joined with Orange Scott, La Roy Sunderland, and Jothan Horton in a statement of withdrawal from the M. E. Church and agreed to call a convention to organize a new denomination, "free from episcopacy and slavery." Thus began the Wesleyan Methodist Church in America.

Matlack filled many offices of trust in the new organization, at one time serving both as Connectional Agent and Editor, and as president of the General Conference. In 1860 he was appointed chaplain of the 8th Illinois Cavalry but was soon transferred to the fighting ranks of the Union Army as a major, and for heroic services in the field he was breveted colonel of the 17th Illinois Cavalry.

In the fall of 1866, however, Matlack along with Luther Lee, John McEldowny, and Cyrus Prindle withdrew from the Wesleyan Connection in disappointment over the failure of merger considerations with the M. P. Church. Matlack reunited with the M. E. Church, being received by unanimous vote and with great cordiality into the Philadelphia Conference in 1867.

He served appointments on the Wilmington District until 1869, when he transferred to the LOUISIANA CONFERENCE. He was presiding elder of the NEW ORLEANS District until 1873, when he transferred to the WILMINGTON CONFERENCE which had been formed out of the Philadelphia Conference. Matlack continued to serve appointments in Wilmington and Easton Districts, with four years as presiding elder of the Wilmington District, until his death at Cambridge, Md., June 24, 1883.

Matlack was married twice. First to Miss Maria Ruhl of Philadelphia, who died in New Orleans; and in 1873 to Miss Roberta H. Stephenson, who, with a son, survived him.

General Minutes, 1884.
E. S. Bucke, *History of American Methodism*, 1964.
The American Wesleyan for July 11, 1883 and October 3, 1966.　　　LOUISE L. QUEEN

MATTOON, ILLINOIS, U.S.A. (population 19,616). **First Church** is a large church in a small city with approximately ten percent of the people in its membership. As early as Jan. 5, 1856, there is a filed record naming "trustees of the M. E. Church of Mattoon, as of the 18th day of August last." In 1856 W. R. Howard, a circuit rider, gathered together eight people and organized the first Methodist Society of Mattoon. The first meetings were held in the homes of the people, and among the first members was Clemm Goar, who was the moving spirit of the group. The first resident pastor was Benjamin Newman, who came in 1857.

In 1859 the first church building, a brick edifice with ceiling eighteen feet high and costing $10,000, was dedicated at what is now 1318-1320 Champaign Avenue. A great storm did much damage to the church building in 1864.

By 1871 the town's population had shifted, so the congregation erected a larger brick church at the northwest corner of Charleston Avenue at First Street (now 17th). This cost $12,500. E. D. Wilkins was then pastor. In 1878-79 the membership was 463 and average Sunday school attendance was 321. Mr. and Mrs. Dudley Hopper deeded their home to the church for a parsonage, and it was used by J. B. Horney, 1900-03.

The second church building was completely destroyed by fire June 15, 1901, and the cornerstone for the present church was laid April 10, 1902. The new church on a new site was dedicated in February 1903. It cost $42,500, and had a membership of 750.

After some improvements, a rededication service was held in 1910 with Bishop WILLIAM A. QUAYLE preaching. Value of the property then was $60,000. Under G. W. Oliver, 1913-15, the membership reached 1,640. THOMAS B. LUGG was pastor from 1928 to 1931, and he later became general treasurer of WORLD SERVICE AND FINANCE of The Methodist Church.

During the pastorate of Leland L. Lawrence, 1946-49, remodeling and improvements were made costing $140,000. Under the present pastor, Clifford C. Brown, 1964-　　, remodeling for new classrooms was done. Also a building was purchased in the church block for educational purposes costing $63,000.

Forty-two pastors have served First Church. It has entertained three annual conferences, the first in September 1874. In 1970 First Church had 1,839 members and the property was valued at $651,066.

Mrs. H. E. Champion, "History of First Church," ms. 1968.
General Minutes.　　　JESSE A. EARL

MAVIS, W. CURRY (1905-　　), American minister, is an ordained elder of the Kentucky-Tennessee Conference of the FREE METHODIST CHURCH and a professor at ASBURY THEOLOGICAL SEMINARY. He was born at West Salem, Ill. He secured the A.B. degree at GREENVILLE COLLEGE, and the A.M. at New York University. He also holds the Th.M. and Ph.D. degrees from the University of Southern California. He was pastor of Free Methodist churches in IOWA and CALIFORNIA and a superintendent of the Iowa Conference of the Free Methodist Church. Dr. Mavis was president of Los Angeles Pacific College and is now professor at Asbury Theological Seminary, Wilmore, Kentucky. He is author of *Advancing the Smaller Local Church; Beyond Conformity;* and *The Psychology of Christian Experience*. Dr. and Mrs. Mavis make their home at Wilmore, Ky.

BYRON S. LAMSON

MAXEY, ELIZABETH (1846-1924), was a Methodist deaconess in CALCUTTA for many years. She was closely associated with the ministry of FRANCIS WESLEY WARNE while he was pastor of Thoburn Church, Calcutta. Before leaving for INDIA in 1888, she had taught in OHIO schools for twenty-one years.

Miss Maxey succeeded in helping a vast number of people, moving easily and often between the palaces of the wealthy and the hovels of the poor. Among those who bore witness to her helpfulness were the renowned merchants and their wives, Sir Thomas and Lady Lipton and Sir Robert and Lady Laidlaw. The former invited her, after she returned, to their home in Britain and provided the expenses of her return to India. The latter were members of Thoburn Church and conferred with her often about the needs of poor Anglo-Indians and Indian Christians.

Bishop Warne testified to her rare ability to move well-to-do people to assist the needy, and credited her with an influence upon Robert Laidlaw that contributed largely to his magnificent benefactions to Calcutta Boys' School and to other English-language schools in India.

Miss Maxey died in Urbana, Ohio, May 30, 1924.

J. N. Hollister, *Southern Asia*. 1956.   J. WASKOM PICKETT

THOMAS MAXFIELD

MAXFIELD, THOMAS (*d*.1784), British Methodist, was converted as a young man under JOHN WESLEY's preaching at BRISTOL on May 21, 1739, and was soon made the leader of a BAND there. The following year he accompanied CHARLES WESLEY to LONDON, where he was given pastoral responsibility as a trusted assistant leader. It was almost certainly in the winter of 1740-41 that John Wesley left him in pastoral charge of the FOUNDERY society while he went to Bristol. During that period Maxfield gradually progressed from speaking of his Christian experience and giving general exhortations to preaching, *i.e.* expounding a text from the Bible. In Wesley's view this was the prerogative of an ordained DEACON, to whom alone was committed the ministry of God's Word. When news of this indiscretion was relayed to him in Bristol, therefore, he hastened to London, complaining to his mother (who spent her last years at the Foundery), "Thomas Maxfield has turned preacher, I find."

She replied, "Take care what you do with respect to that young man, for he is as surely called of God to preach as you are. Examine what have been the fruits of his preaching, and hear him also yourself." Having followed her advice, Wesley's "prejudice bowed before the force of truth: and he could only say, 'It is the Lord: let him do what seemeth him good.'" (Coke and Moore, *Life of the Rev. John Wesley*, pp. 219-20.)

Maxfield made a similar deep impression upon Selina, COUNTESS OF HUNTINGDON. Thus convinced, in the early months of 1741, John Wesley began to employ Thomas Maxfield as a full time lay preacher, his first "son in the gospel," the forerunner of the many more without whose assistance it would have been impossible to extend and sustain the Methodist societies throughout the British Isles.

For many years Maxfield remained one of Wesley's most trusted itinerant preachers, present at many conferences, and from 1745 onwards named one of the ASSISTANTS, although the minutes for 1755 listed him for the time being as one of the chief LOCAL PREACHERS. At the 1758 conference his name followed immediately those of the Wesleys, a position which would have been especially appropriate if (as is likely) he had already been ordained priest by Dr. William Barnard, bishop of Derry 1747-68. This ordination was on Wesley's recommendation, and the bishop told Maxfield: "Mr. Maxfield, I ordain you to assist that good man, that he may not work himself to death."

Maxfield was an emotional preacher, and somewhat inclined to exaggeration. In the early 1760's he became the leader of a group of London visionaries (including GEORGE BELL) who rejected normal Methodist discipline. Disowned by Wesley (or disowning Wesley, depending on the point of view) in 1763 he set up as an independent minister in London. In 1766 he published for his congregation *A Collection of Psalms and Hymns*, with a companion *Collection of Hymns for the Lord's Supper*. The following year he issued *A Vindication of the Rev. Mr. Maxfield's Conduct in not continuing with the Rev. Mr. John Wesley, and of his behaviour since that time*, which Wesley belatedly answered in print in 1778.

Maxfield married a wealthy lady, Elizabeth Branford, one of GEORGE WHITEFIELD's converts, by whom he had a large family. She died in 1777. Maxfield himself was seized with a paralytic stroke on Dec. 21, 1782, and died March 18, 1784. His breach with Methodism was to some extent healed during his later years.

C. Atmore, *Methodist Memorial*. 1801, 1871.
Dictionary of National Biography.
J. Wesley, *Journal*. 1909-16.
————, *Letters*. 1931.
Wesley Historical Soc. *Proceedings*, xxi, xxvii.   FRANK BAKER

MAXWELL, D'ARCY, Lady Maxwell (?1742-1810), Scots Methodist, was the youngest daughter of Thomas Brisbane of Brisbane, Ayrshire, SCOTLAND. Educated in Edinburgh, at sixteen she went to live in London with her aunt the Marchioness of Lothian, by whom she was presented at court. Shortly afterwards she married Sir Walter Maxwell, fourth baronet of Pollok, Scotland, but at the age of nineteen lost both her husband and their baby son. Personal tragedy led to a deepened spiritual life, conversion, and an unceasing spiritual pilgrimage. Later she testified: "God brought me to himself by afflictions." In January 1762 she entered into a solemn covenant with God, which she put into writing in 1764 and frequently renewed, especially at Holy Communion.

Shortly after her husband's death Lady Maxwell had moved to Wariston's Close, Edinburgh, and became a member of the West Kirk (St. Cuthbert's). Although at first she employed a private chaplain of the Church of Scotland to care for the spiritual needs of her household, after a few years she herself conducted daily worship for them, a practice which she kept up for about forty years.

D'Arcy, Lady Maxwell, was much more sensitive and saintly than her friend, the somewhat imperious LADY GLENORCHY, yet she retained the attributes of Martha as well as of Mary. Named as Lady Glenorchy's executor, she faithfully prosecuted her friend's chapel-building and other religious projects. On her own account she also founded in 1770 and continued to maintain a charity school in Edinburgh, where by her death over 800 poor children had been trained. She was a keen advocate of SUNDAY SCHOOLS, of which she founded at least three, two in Scotland and one in England.

Membership of the Methodist Society was open to those who wished also to continue as churchmen or dissenters, and in 1764 Lady Maxwell seems officially to have become a Methodist, remaining such until her death, although her name does not appear in the earliest extant Society Book, dated 1806. The Society Book does record, however, that the Methodist preachers in Edinburgh were still holding a special CLASS MEETING in the evenings as at first. She also met in a Methodist BAND, and was one of the most generous and enthusiastic supporters of Methodist principles and causes. During the bitter Calvinistic controversy of the 1770's Lady Maxwell remained loyal to Wesley, even in a stronghold of Calvinism.

She had first become friendly with JOHN WESLEY in 1764, and maintained a regular correspondence with him until his death in 1791, when she inserted a notice of his death in the Edinburgh newspapers, pleading for belated justice "to one of the greatest characters that has appeared since the apostolic age." At least twenty-five of Wesley's letters to her are known. He constantly urged her to eke out her frail health by exercise and travel, advice which she followed. She died July 2, 1810, respected and beloved by Methodists and Presbyterians alike.

John Lancaster, *The Life of Darcy, Lady Maxwell*, 2nd ed. London, Kershaw, 1826; see also the revised 3rd ed., by William Atherton, London, John Mason, 1838. FRANK BAKER

MAYFIELD, ROBERT GREENLEAF (1911-), American lay leader, was born at Lebanon, Mo., on July 31, 1911. He was educated at the University of Missouri where he got his LL.B. degree; he was given the honorary LL.D. from ILLINOIS WESLEYAN UNIVERSITY, 1958. His wife was Frances Margaret Odom, whom he married on Jan. 12, 1943, and they have two children.

Dr. Mayfield was admitted to the MISSOURI bar in 1935, and practiced in his native town of Lebanon for some seven years, at which time he became associate secretary of the GENERAL BOARD OF LAY ACTIVITIES of The Methodist Church with offices in Evanston, Ill. He became General Secretary in 1952 and served in that capacity until 1968. He served with the Army of the United States, 1942-46, and again from 1950-52.

He was a member of the Board of Managers of the United Church Men during the period 1952-68, and was a lay member of the Third Assembly of the WORLD COUNCIL OF CHURCHES at New Delhi, India, 1961, and

of the Fourth Assembly at Uppsala, Sweden, in 1968. He was also a delegate to the WORLD METHODIST CONFERENCES of 1956, '61, and '66, and was a member of the executive committee of the WORLD METHODIST COUNCIL. He is presently Assistant to the President in stewardship at ASBURY THEOLOGICAL SEMINARY.

Who's Who in the Methodist Church, 1966.   N. B. H.

MAYSVILLE, KENTUCKY, U.S.A. The area of Mason County, formerly Bourbon County before statehood was granted, was touched by Methodism after Bishop FRANCIS ASBURY at the 1786 Conference in BALTIMORE created a KENTUCKY Circuit. Two years later he visited the settlement of Limestone (now Maysville), and created the Limestone Circuit. BENJAMIN OGDEN and James Haw, said to be the first itinerant Methodist preachers to set foot on Kentucky soil, organized the second Methodist Church in Kentucky in 1786. This was in a cabin occupied by Mr. and Mrs. Thomas Stevenson. Mrs. Stevenson had united with a church in MARYLAND in 1768, and she became a member of this second Methodist church organized in Kentucky. This church was located within a few miles of Maysville, or Limestone. When Limestone was a trading post and Indians lingered in the area the first Methodist church was built in Maysville. Samuel Tucker and Joseph Lillard were the first pastors assigned to Limestone Circuit. Returning from a trip with friends, Tucker was the only person to survive an attack by Indians, but expired soon after reaching Maysville and was buried in an unmarked grave located in the area of Front and Market Streets.

In 1813 the first Methodist church, a small frame building, was erected on the south side of Second Street adjoining Graces Alley. Four different buildings occupied this site, the last of which was dedicated in 1891. This building was dismantled in 1966 and the site is now occupied by a car lot.

In 1844, pursuant to provisions of the PLAN OF SEPARATION for churches in the border states to the Mason-Dixon Line to determine whether they would identify with the M. E. Church or the M. E. Church, South, 109 members of the Maysville Church voted to go to the new church, and ninety-seven to remain with the M. E. Church. The group with the majority vote claimed possession of the building and the M. E. group brought suit for possession of the property. This became a test case and went to the Court of Appeals in Frankfort, Ky., which decided in favor of the M. E. Church, South. Maysville Methodism thus became bitterly divided.

In 1847, John Armstrong, a wealthy merchant and a strong supporter of the old church, bought a parcel of land on Third Street and the Third Street M. E. Church was erected thereon. In 1946, following the Uniting General Conference in Kansas City in 1939, these two churches were united and Trinity Methodist Church was born. In 1955 a new sanctuary was erected.

Methodism has traditionally been a vital religious movement in Maysville and in later years Seddon Church and Central Church were organized. Few other towns of comparable size have more than one Methodist church. The Seddon Church was organized in 1888 and the Central Church in 1886. Scott Church, which gets its name from Bishop LEVI SCOTT, was organized in 1864, by a Rev. Talbert, and the first active pastor, Adam Nunn, was appointed in 1869. The LEXINGTON ANNUAL CONFERENCE

(ME) was entertained at the Scott Church in 1872, 1877, 1895 and 1910.

The total membership of the four churches in 1970 was 1,873.

W. E. Arnold, *Kentucky*. 1935-36.
J. B. Finley, *Sketches of Western Methodism*. 1854.
Frank C. King, *History of First Methodist Church, 1790-1941*.   ROBERT L. ANDERSON

MAZE, MATTHEW T. (1857-1940), American bishop of the EVANGELICAL CHURCH, was born near Lewisville, Ind., on Nov. 16, 1857. In 1881 he married Katie Goar. They farmed in NEBRASKA from 1883 until 1888, when he was licensed to preach by the Nebraska Conference of the Evangelical Association. In the subsequent denominational division, Maze joined the minority group, which created The UNITED EVANGELICAL CHURCH. He served his denomination as presiding elder in the Kansas Conference (1895-1903), pastor (1903-06), and presiding elder again (1906-14). He also served (1914-18) as Treasurer of Western Union College in LeMars, Iowa, of which he had been a founder. His episcopal tenure extended from 1918 to 1934. He died in Lincoln, Neb., on Oct. 28, 1940, survived by his wife and two children. An outstanding administrator, Maze gave prominent support to the reunion which, in 1922, created The Evangelical Church. He also served for a time as President of the PENNSYLVANIA Council of Churches and gave active support to the FEDERAL COUNCIL OF CHURCHES.

R. W. Albright, *Evangelical Church*. 1942.
The Evangelical Messenger, Nov. 9 and 16, 1940.
K. JAMES STEIN

CHARLES L. MEAD

MEAD, CHARLES LAREW (1868-1941), American bishop, was born in Vienna, N. J., on July 20, 1868, the son of Joshua and Alice A. (Hough) Mead of the NEWARK CONFERENCE. Charles Mead was educated at the Centenary Boarding School in Hackettstown, N. J., and later took his B.A. degree at New York University in 1896. While attending school in Hackettstown he met Eleanor M. Smith of Mauch Chunk, Pa. They were married in June 1896, after he had been ordained by the Newark Conference in the year 1895. Five children were born to them.

Bishop Mead served the following churches as pastor before his election to the episcopacy: Rutherford (1895-99); Hoboken (1899-1904); NEWARK, Centenary (1904-08); Hoboken (1908-09); BALTIMORE, First (1909-13); NEW YORK CITY, Madison Avenue (1913-14); and DENVER, Trinity (1914-20). He was elected bishop May 20, 1920 at the GENERAL CONFERENCE in Des Moines, Iowa. He served as bishop of the Denver Area from 1920-32. He then moved to KANSAS CITY where he was the presiding bishop from 1932 to 1941. He was the resident bishop of the area at the time of the Uniting Conference of Methodism.

Bishop Mead during the First World War felt the responsibility of aiding American soldiers and thus served with the Y.M.C.A. for six months on the front lines in France.

His ministry was recognized far and wide, SYRACUSE awarding him a D.D. in 1907 and the UNIVERSITY OF DENVER awarding him an LL.D. in 1920. Never a great intellectual, Bishop Mead was one of the "pastoral bishops" of Methodism during this period. His sermons were brilliant with pertinent illustrations and he knew the secret of touching people where they lived. He closely identified himself with those pastors under his care, and many of them regarded him not only as their bishop but as their counsellor and friend.

Bishop Mead died May 17, 1941, and is buried in Denver, Colo.

CHARLES L. MEAD, JR.

MEAD, STITH (1767-1834?), American preacher, was born in Bedford County, Va., the son of wealthy Colonel William Mead, and was educated at Augusta Academy in GEORGIA. He was converted in 1789 and three years later entered the VIRGINIA CONFERENCE.

Mead in his journal set down the happenings at this conference, including his admission: "Monday, May 21, 1792. We rode over Peter's Mountain by the Sweet Springs, to brother Edward Keenan's at REHOBOTH CHAPEL, Sinks of Greenbrier county, where I was glad to meet with the bishop, REV. FRANCIS ASBURY; HOPE HULL, Philip Cox, Jeremiah Abel, elders; Salathiel Weeks, John Lindsey, Bennett Maxey and John Metcalf, deacons. . . . James Ward and Stith Mead admitted on trial, as probationers. . . . Bennett Maxey and JOHN KOBLER, by requests of the bishop, related to the Conference their religious experience, and then the Conference adjourned until Tuesday, at 8 o'clock A.M., at which time J. Kobler, Geo. Martin, S. Mead were examined by the bishop before the Conference, first, of our debts; secondly, of our faith in Christ; thirdly, of our pursuits after holiness" (Armstrong, pp. 108-9).

In 1797 Stith Mead, WILLIAM McKENDREE and LeRoy Cole were harbingers of a great Gloucester Circuit revival with marked power. Along with 500 conversions came persecution and Mead was strongly opposed, as he was later by his own relatives while founding Methodism in Augusta, Ga., 1798. His revival preaching was greatly useful elsewhere in VIRGINIA and Georgia—one convert being JOHN EARLY. W. W. Sweet says that Stith Mead was "the father of the Virginia camp meeting."

Mead served six years on the Georgia and RICHMOND Districts as a presiding elder, and in the 1808 GENERAL CONFERENCE. He located in 1816 but was readmitted as a superannuate. His journal, which was unfortunately consumed in the burning of Richmond at the evacuation of the Confederate troops in 1865, was of considerable assistance to William W. Bennett when he was writing *Methodism in Virginia*.

J. E. Armstrong, *Old Baltimore Conference*. 1907.
W. W. Sweet, *Virginia Methodism*. 1955.   EDWIN SCHELL

MEADOWS, CLYDE WILLIAMSON (1901-   ), American United Brethren (Old Constitution) bishop and youth leader, was born at Pamplin, Appomattox Co., Va., Jan. 3, 1901. His parents were both ministers, serving home mission fields.

He began high school in VIRGINIA and was graduated with an A.B. (1925) from Huntington College. The Lutheran Theological Seminary, Gettysburg, Pa., conferred upon him the B.D. and S.T.M. degrees. He was awarded the D.D. (1940) by Huntington College.

He definitely answered the call to the ministry under the influence of Christian Endeavor at the age of nineteen. He was licensed to preach in 1920. He has served in the pastoral ministry for thirty-nine years in INDIANA, PENNSYLVANIA and Ontario. He also was pastor-conference superintendent for twenty-eight years.

His pastorate of thirty-three years at the King Street Church of Chambersburg, Pa., saw church membership increased from 450 to over 1,300.

He was elected to the bishopric and served his denomination from 1961 to 1969, when he was retired as bishop emeritus. He has served on general church boards and for many years has been a trustee of the Milton Wright Memorial Home, Inc., which operates two institutions, one serving children and the other elderly people.

He was president of the International Society for Christian Endeavor from 1959 to 1962 and was vice-president before his election to the presidency. He was elected president of the World's Christian Endeavor Union at the convention in SYDNEY, AUSTRALIA in 1962.

He is the author of the books, *Why We Choose Christ*, *Music in Christian Education*, and *A Christian and His Church*, and numerous pamphlets on evangelism. He served as editor of three editions of *The United Brethren Hymnal*.

He likes to fly, holds a private pilot's license and has been labeled the "flying pastor."

Contact, May 14, 1967.   J. RALPH PFISTER

MEADVILLE, PENNSYLVANIA, U.S.A., the seat of Crawford County, the center of farm and oil producing land thirty-three miles south of Erie on French Creek, was settled about 1788 by Major David Mead as a Revolutionary outpost.

Steps to establish ALLEGHENY COLLEGE, located here, were first taken in 1815. On March 24, 1817 this college was incorporated. Later that year a Presbyterian minister, Thomas Alden, was inaugurated as its first president. Originally controlled by Presbyterians, the college later (1833) was managed by the PITTSBURGH CONFERENCE of the M. E. Church and subsequently by additional affiliated conferences. With an enrollment (1970) of 1,634 and a faculty of 121, almost sixty percent of the students continue academic work in graduate and professional schools. Influential far beyond the community of Meadville, distinguished names associated with the college have been MARTIN RUTER, LUCIUS H. BUGBEE, Bishop MATTHEW SIMPSON, Bishop CALVIN KINGSLEY and JAMES THOBURN.

In 1806 ROBERT R. ROBERTS brought Methodist preaching to Meadville. The first service was held in a hotel bar room. Strong opposition to Methodism delayed the establishment of Meadville as a regular appointment on the Erie Circuit until 1818. In 1824 a class was formed; in 1825, under Robert C. Hatton, religious interest was stimulated and a church formed. The congregation met first in the upper story of a blacksmith shop. Joseph S. Barris, the first stationed pastor, reported 155 members in 1832. In 1867, through the generosity of Allegheny College friends, as well as townspeople, a beautiful stone edifice was erected to house the Methodist congregation. Three years later another Methodist congregation built and occupied what was then known as the State Street Methodist Church. Today the Stone Methodist Church has a membership (1970) of 1,542 and a church school enrollment of 628. Two smaller groups, Bethany and Centerville, are associated with Stone Church. The other large congregation, Grace Church, has a membership (1970) of 663.

Allegheny College Handbook.
General Minutes.
M. Simpson, *Cyclopaedia*. 1878.   ERNEST R. CASE

MEANS OF GRACE is a theological expression which has been much used by Methodists and indicates those services through which spiritual influences usually reach a Christian heart. UMPHREY LEE explains in his book, *Our Fathers and Us:* "And WESLEY's notion, which persisted for many years in this country as well as in England, was that men should attempt to use the grace of God as it came to them through the means. The phrase 'means of grace' is an old ecclesiastical phrase"—coming, he explains, into the English Prayer Book in 1662 in the General Thanksgiving. There thanks are given "for the means of grace and for the hope of Glory." The expression was of common usage so far as Wesley was concerned, and in one of his standard sermons, Wesley preached on "The Means of Grace." He defines these as "outward signs, words, or actions, ordained of God, and appointed for this end, to be the ordinary channels whereby He might convey to men, preventing, justifying, or sanctifying Grace."

Methodists do not teach that Grace is limited to participants in particular services but believe that it is freely given to the obedient heart through the operation of the Holy Spirit. They do, however, attach great importance to the faithful observance of the Means of Grace as these have been prescribed in Scripture, and as they are emphasized in John Wesley's General Rules. In the General Rules are emphasized the attendance upon the public preaching of God's word; private, family and public prayers; Christian conversation and testimony, in class or social meetings; reading the Holy Scripture; Baptism, the Lord's Supper and certain of the ordinances.

The chief of these means are prayer, whether in secret or with the great congregation; searching the scriptures (which implies reading, hearing and meditating thereon); and receiving the Lord's Supper, eating bread and drinking wine in remembrance of Him; and these we believe to be ordained of God, as the ordinary channels of conveying His grace to the souls of men. (Wesley, *Sermon*)

John Wesley omitted BAPTISM in his sermon on the Means of Grace. Sugden thinks that was because those to whom Wesley was preaching the sermon had already been baptized in infancy. Wesley, however, put the greatest emphasis upon using the Means of Grace, and had no sympathy for those who thought that people might know what is in the Bible simply by some inspiration of the Spirit, or that they must "wait for the Spirit" to impel them before they begin to utilize the Means of Grace. This was his quarrel with the enthusiasts—those who said that it was not right to use the Means of Grace unless ones' heart felt "inclined" to use them.

Wesley reacted heatedly against this. He said that we "must trample under foot that enthusiastic doctrine of devils that we are not to do good unless our hearts be free to it" (Rules of the Society, 1743). That is to say, when one does not feel like using the Means of Grace, Wesley believed that one was the very person who ought to use them. If anyone did not feel like praying, Wesley said he, of all people, needed prayer. Methodists in part got their name from their regularity in going to Communion—no matter how they felt—and for meticulously observing habits and acts taught by Scripture and put into practice by Christian life.

Lee calls attention to the fact that Methodists believe that the Sacrament of the Lord's Supper was a converting ordinance, and that SUSANNA WESLEY herself was said to have been converted during her reception of the Lord's Supper. The BOARD OF EVANGELISM of The Methodist Church within recent years referred to certain practices devolving on Christians as "the Holy habits," but this expression does not seem to have been generally adopted and cannot quite be equaled with the Means of Grace. It refers more to acts of personal participation, to the purely human regimen found helpful, rather than to the objective divinely established procedures which may properly be called God's Means of Grace. "Our Methodists do not believe that any special form of worship is absolutely prescribed," said Bishop SIMPSON. "They do believe that wherever there is a sincere desire to please God, the person will engage in these varied exercises; and where these are neglected, Methodists have always felt that delinquent members should be instructed, admonished and warned." Simpson with the stern authoritarianism of his day added, "If willfully and persistently negligent, they shall be expelled from the Church." Modern Methodism is not as strict as this last injunction seems to imply, but it can be asserted that wherever the Means of Grace are neglected and are persistently ignored, the result is always a forgotten Church and a forgotten God. Methodists gladly join the Church of England and the Protestant Episcopalians in formally thanking God for "the Means of Grace and the Hope of Glory."

J. Wesley, Standard Sermons. 1921.   N. B. H.

MEARA, WILLIAM (1871-1959), Methodist minister and twice President of the SOUTH AFRICAN Conference, was the son of a small farmer and was born at Dunmanway, West Cork. His boyhood ambition to become a sailor was overruled by his conversion and call to the ministry. After theological training in BELFAST, Meara served in three Irish circuits before coming to the Transvaal in 1899. Soon after his arrival the Anglo-Boer War broke out, and he interrupted his ministry at Barberton to serve as a chaplain to the British forces. During the years that

WILLIAM MEARA

followed, he served with great acceptance in Pretoria and other towns of the Province. He once again served as a chaplain to the forces during World War I, first in the South West Africa campaign, and later in France where he had a narrow escape from death on the day Armistice was declared.

William Meara's greatest ministry was at the Methodist Central Hall in the heart of Johannesburg, South Africa's largest city. Here for fifteen years he wielded a great influence upon the life of the brash, young and growing metropolis of the Witwatersrand Gold Reef, and again, as in previous ministries, many people were led to know Christ as Saviour through his preaching and pastoral work.

In 1936 he was appointed to the Trinity Methodist Church, East London, and at the same time assumed the Chairmanship of the Queenstown District. A thriving work in both European and African circuits brought many problems, and he proved a wise and efficient administrator and a father-in-God to his ministerial brethren. It was during his East London ministry that he was elected twice to the Presidency of the Methodist Conference, the first man to reach this high office on two occasions for over forty years.

After a year's furlough and a brief three-year ministry in Pietermaritzburg, William Meara retired to Umkomaas, Natal, where he died on May 5, 1959. He is remembered by many with respect and affection as one of the outstanding figures of South African Methodism in the twentieth century.

S. P. Freeland, Fighter for God—the Story of William Meara. Stockwell, Ilfracombe, Devon, n.d.   S. P. FREELAND

MEEK, ROBERT ABNER (1867-1949), American minister and editor, was born on Dec. 7, 1867, at Black Hawk, Miss. He was the son of Robert Drayton and Martha Anne (Johnson) Meek. He graduated from the University of Mississippi in 1888, and received the D.D. degree from

EMORY AND HENRY COLLEGE in 1910. His wife was Cornelia C. Crippen (b. Dec. 10, 1868), whom he married on Dec. 7, 1893. They had one son, Robert Edwin Meek.

Meek entered the NORTH MISSISSIPPI CONFERENCE in 1890 and served at Carrollton, Vaiden, Coldwater, Tupelo, Starkville, West Point, Greenville (all in MISSISSIPPI), and then in 1906 went on the Greenville District as presiding elder, 1906-09. In 1910 he became editor of the *New Orleans Christian Advocate*, the organ of the LOUISIANA and the Mississippi and North Mississippi Conferences (MES) and served until 1918. On leaving the *Advocate*, he served for the next four years as presiding elder of the Sardis District, North Mississippi. Meek was a born editor, knowing not only what to publish but how to give guidance with strong editorials in which he set forth well reasoned convictions with great strength and ability. He was a member of the GENERAL CONFERENCE (MES) of 1910, '14, '18, and '22. Locating in 1922, he was subsequently elected a lay delegate from North Mississippi to the General Conferences of 1926 and 1930. After he retired from the editorship of the *New Orleans Christian Advocate*, in his later years (1922-30) Meek edited an independent paper, *The Southern Methodist*, devoted largely to fighting what he considered to be harmful, modernistic trends in the church. He never failed to attack by name church leaders whom he felt were leading the people amiss, and as a Southerner bitterly opposed union with the M. E. Church. When he died, the editor of the *Baltimore Southern Methodist* in commenting on his life said that no church editor dared to evaluate R. A. Meek "until they were sure he could not reply." He was, however, greatly respected by his brethren and had many devoted followers. He was a trustee of MILLSAPS COLLEGE, serving for a time as vice-president of the Board; and also a trustee of the Methodist Hospital in MEMPHIS. He died on Feb. 4, 1949 in Lexington, Miss.

C. F. Price, *Who's Who in American Methodism*. 1916.

N. B. H.

MEHARRY, JESSE (1806-1881), American farmer and philanthropist, son of Alexander and Jane (Francis) Meharry, was born Aug. 15, 1806, near Manchester, Adams County, Ohio. In 1827 he came to INDIANA and took up 240 acres of land at Shawnee Mound in Tippecanoe County. He was a very successful farmer. He was converted in 1828 at a CAMP MEETING. He was a life member of the Missionary Society of the Methodist Church. In 1869 he offered his 394-acre farm at Shawnee Mound as a gift to the state if the new agricultural college were located there. In 1876 he made his first gift of $11,000 to Indiana Asbury University. Meharry Hall in East College at DEPAUW UNIVERSITY bears his name. He was a delegate to GENERAL CONFERENCE in 1876. He married Jane Love Francis Aug. 10, 1831. There were no children, but eight homeless children made this their home and received a good start in life. He died Aug. 20, 1881.

History of the Meharry Family in America, 1925.
Minutes Northwest Indiana Conference, Committee on Education, 1881.

W. D. ARCHIBALD

MEHARRY MEDICAL COLLEGE, Nashville, Tennessee, began as the medical department of Central Tennessee College in 1876, an institution founded by the FREEDMEN'S

MEHARRY MEDICAL COLLEGE

AID SOCIETY of the M. E. Church. In 1900, Central was reorganized as Walden University, and the medical department was named to honor the Meharry family of Illinois, substantial contributors toward the expansion of the school.

The institution is one of two medical schools in the United States dedicated to the education of Negroes as physicians, dentists, and nurses. Through the assistance of the General Education Board (Rockefeller), Carnegie Foundation, and other benevolent agencies, it has been able to erect a modern plant for medical education. Forty percent of all the Negro physicians and dentists in the United States are graduates of this institution. Hubbard Hospital is also owned and operated by Meharry Medical College. The governing board has thirty-two trustees, elected by the board. The charter requires representation from The United Methodist Church but does not specify the number of persons.

JOHN O. GROSS

MEISTER, KARL PHILIP (1886-1965), American pastor and executive, and the first full-time executive secretary of the Board of Hospitals and Homes of The Methodist Church following unification. Born in Caledonia, Ohio, on Oct. 31, 1886, he was the son of Philip and Georgetta (Boyles) Meister. He married Jessie Irene Kinnamon on June 24, 1909, and there was one son, Herbert H. Meister.

He was a student at Ohio Wesleyan Prep. School, 1912-14; B.A. *Cum Laude*, OHIO WESLEYAN, 1918; D.D., in 1942; a student at BOSTON UNIVERSITY SCHOOL OF THEOLOGY, 1919-23. He was admitted on trial in the NORTHWEST OHIO CONFERENCE in 1917; and into full connection in 1922; became a DEACON in 1920, ELDER 1922. He served as field secretary of the Ohio Methodist Children's Home, Worthington, Ohio, 1914-18; office manager, Cincinnati Area, Columbus, Ohio, 1919; as pastor of Centralville Church, Lowell, Mass., 1920-23; field secretary Board of Hospitals, Homes and Deaconess Work of the M.E. Church, Chicago, 1923-24; secretary, church relations of Ohio Wesleyan University, 1924-30; the superintendent of Elyria Methodist Home and Hospital for Aged, 1930-39; superintendent, Norwalk District, 1939-43; superintendent, St. Luke's Methodist Hospital, Cedar Rapids, Iowa, 1943-44; and executive secretary, Board of Hospitals and Homes, 1944-56.

He was an official delegate to the National Health

Assembly in 1948; a member of the Advisory Committee, Children's Bureau, 1948-52; member Advisory Committee, Division of Aid to Dependent Aged, 1948-52; Mid-Century Conference on Children and Youth, 1950; Delegate to the National Conference on Aged and Aging, 1958; a charter member of the National Committee on Aging; a writer of articles for church and other publications.

Meister was an undisputed leader in health and welfare matters. He promoted the highest standards of care and service in the spirit of Christian compassion. He won for the Board of Hospitals and Homes a recognized place in the Church and in the nation.

He died on Feb. 13, 1965, in Elyria, Ohio.

Clark and Stafford, *Who's Who in Methodism.* 1952.

MELBOURNE, Australia, capital of Victoria, was founded by John Batman and is AUSTRALIA's second largest city, with a population of over 2,000,000. Since the second World War European migration has accounted for Melbourne's population increase. Today this city is looked upon as Australia's financial bastion in addition to being a center of culture and learning. (For the beginning and development of Methodist work in and about Melbourne see VICTORIA AND TASMANIA CONFERENCE.)

WESLEY CHAPEL, MELBOURNE, AUSTRALIA

The Methodist Ladies' College in Melbourne was founded in 1882 by W. H. FITCHETT and is a primary and secondary school for girls. It began with sixteen pupils and now has an enrolment of 2,000 in the main school. Fitchett encountered much opposition to his plan for a church school, largely because the governments of the Australian states had their own systems of education, and because of the financial outlay involved. However, his commanding influence in the church, his reputation as an author, and his personality prevailed and the school was established. During his forty-six years at the school

(where he died in 1928), he saw the school grow and achieve good academic rating.

Fitchett was succeeded as principal by the late J. W. Grove, and A. HAROLD WOOD was principal from 1939 until his retirement in 1966.

Buildings now include a very beautiful chapel, an assembly hall of modern design with a seating capacity of 1,100, laboratories and other special buildings. The school has won distinction for its music under the leadership of Miss Ruth Flockart. A branch of the school was established in the Melbourne suburb of Elsternwick in 1929. This has an enrolment of over 500 and became an independent school in 1961.

Wesley College is a well-known boys' school in Melbourne, and is one of a group of independent boys' schools in that city. It was founded at a time when the discovery of gold was bringing great prosperity to Victoria, and it owed a great deal to the planning and enthusiasm of two great Methodists of those early days in the state, DANIEL J. DRAPER and Walter Powell.

The college was opened in January 1866, with J. S. Waugh as president and James Corrigan as headmaster. Subsequent headmasters include M. H. Irving and H. M. Andrews, A. S. Way, L. A. Adamson, Harold Stewart, Neil McNeil, W. H. Frederick, and T. H. Coates.

In 1933 the college was entirely rebuilt and enlarged through the gift of two generous laymen, A. M. and G. R. Nicholas, and it became one of the best equipped schools in Australia. From an original enrolment of eighty boys, Wesley College now has 930. Because of increased enrolment, accommodation and playing fields have proved inadequate and a fine property has recently been purchased in an outer suburb of Melbourne on which further playing fields are to be developed and a junior section of the school opened. The college is governed by a council of ministers and laymen appointed by the Victorian and Tasmanian Conference of the Methodist Church. Now over a century old, Wesley has a splendid scholastic and sporting record and numbers many outstanding jurists, statesmen, teachers, scientists and leaders of the church among the "old boys."

C. I. Benson, *Victorian Methodism.* 1935.

AUSTRALIAN EDITORIAL COMMITTEE

MELLARD, JAMES HENRY (1778-1855), pioneer American minister and one of the four original presiding elders of the ALABAMA CONFERENCE, first joined the old SOUTH CAROLINA CONFERENCE in 1801. He served as an itinerant in GEORGIA, SOUTH CAROLINA, and NORTH CAROLINA, and was one of the first two missionaries (1808) to the Negroes ever sent out by the M. E. Church. On June 1, 1809, he married Ann Rumph, and located the next year. In 1821 he was still a local preacher in Autauga County, Ala. Mellard contributed greatly to the spread of Methodism in MONTGOMERY, for he preached Aug. 26, 1821, in the Montgomery County Court House, and is said to have organized the FIRST METHODIST CHURCH in MONTGOMERY, Ala., on Sept. 25, 1829.

Mellard joined the MISSISSIPPI CONFERENCE in 1827 and was appointed to the Alabama Circuit. In 1828 he became presiding elder of the Alabama District. He was thus one of the original presiding elders in 1832 when the Alabama Conference was established. He was also appointed one of the first trustees of LA GRANGE COLLEGE, chartered in 1830 as the first college in Alabama.

In 1833 he located again, but he continued to labor as a local preacher for twenty-two years, while rearing a large family. By his first wife, Ann Rumph, he had five children. On Nov. 5, 1822, he married Mrs. Sophie Addison, and they had five children. By Mrs. Rachel M. Rumph, whom he married May 2, 1837, he had one child. He died Nov. 17, 1855, at the age of seventy-seven years, having been a preacher of the gospel in connection with the Methodist Church for fifty-six years. He was buried near Three Notch in Bullock County, Ala.

Alabama Christian Advocate, Jan. 18, 1955.
M. E. Lazenby, *Alabama and West Florida*. 1960.

DONALD J. WEST

F. OTTO MELLE

MELLE, F. H. OTTO (1875-1947), German bishop, the first one to be so elected by the GERMANY Central Conference, was born at Liebengruen (now East Germany). His parents were devoted Methodists, his father a lay preacher. After studying at Frankfurt Methodist Theological Seminary and one year as pastor at Dresden, he was appointed to serve in the then united AUSTRIA and HUNGARY as missionary and superintendent (1900-20). Through his work missionary conferences were founded in these countries and in the YUGOSLAVIA of post World War I. He married Hanna Eckardt in 1907; they had one son and two daughters.

In 1920 he was elected President of Frankfurt Theological Seminary. As an able educator he trained men from the BALTICS, Germany, and SWITZERLAND to Southeast Europe; numerically the Seminary has never again reached the peaks of the twenties. His asset in dealing with young men was a heart full of understanding. When the 1936 GENERAL CONFERENCE consented to the formation of a Germany Central Conference, F. H. Otto Melle was elected its first bishop and served until 1946, when he retired.

Bishop Melle was a superb leader of men, an extremely versatile administrator, and a pastor of pastors. His vision of a worldwide Methodist family with special emphasis on the United States and of German Methodist Free Church life challenged his students and his pastors. He was one of the foremost leaders of the German Evan-

gelical Alliance; his struggle for total abstention and for local administrative control of breweries and saloons, when put to a nationwide popular vote, failed to win a majority of the German people but was indicative of what he stood for and how he would fight for matters he considered essential.

He was a very powerful speaker and a popular preacher. Evangelism was near to his heart. He was in charge of the Germany Central Conference in years of the most difficult home situation and of nearly six years of total warfare. In responsibility before God he undertook the precarious task of steering clear of the various cliffs that threatened church and society during the Nazi regime. He did better than has been accredited to him at times, and the Methodist Church in Germany owes him more than can be expressed.

C. ERNST SOMMER

MELLO, JOEL JORGE DE (1914-1963), Brazilian lay leader, engineer, and businessman, was born in SÃO PAULO on Nov. 1, 1914. Though poor, Joel was able to graduate in engineering from Mackenzie University, an evangelical school, in 1936. Before graduation, he had been working for the Ingersoll-Rand Corporation of BRAZIL, and through them he was given an opportunity to study in the United States. On his return to São Paulo, he taught for several years in the Mackenzie Engineering School, and later became a director of the E.B.E.—Brazilian Engineering Enterprises.

In 1943 he married Arcília Rocha, by whom he had seven children. Though he went through more than one financial crisis in his business, he always succeeded in rehabilitating himself.

He worked with great consecration in three different Methodist churches in São Paulo, one of which he founded. He later became a supply pastor and worked without salary.

He was for some years secretary of Missions in the Third Region Conference. Deeply impressed with the possibilities of Christian witness by radio and television, Mello initiated a television program, "Songs of my Faith," which became popular. Not long before his death, he headed a campaign for the acquisition of an evangelical broadcasting station in São Paulo, and in time bought the Radio Cometa. Because of his sudden death, he was unable to liquidate all his commitments; but interested persons carried on, and today, Radio Cometa is a reality.

On his farm in nearby Guararema, he built an adequate camping site for young people, whatever their denomination, for study and relaxation. Also into his large country home, he and his wife cared for abandoned children, paying the support of a couple engaged to look after them. On Nov. 11, 1963, while traveling to a church meeting in Resende, state of São Paulo, he suffered a heart attack, which led to his death. He was buried in the Campo Grande Cemetery in São Paulo.

Numberless tributes were paid to his character. The city council of São Paulo gave his name to the street on which stood the Vila Mariana Church, which he had shepherded for two years.

Expositor Cristão, Dec. 1, 1963.   ISNARD ROCHA

MEMBERSHIP IN METHODIST CHURCHES. When early Methodist Societies were formed, they made no claim to be churches, but simply associations of Christians which enabled persons who belonged to them to increase their piety and usefulness. JOHN WESLEY, in outlining his GENERAL RULES for the United Societies stated that there was only one condition "previously required" for those who desired admission into these Societies, "a desire to flee from the wrath to come, and to be saved from their sins." (Paragraph 95, *Discipline*, 1968.) Admission into the Society was gained by showing a proper spirit, and by being approved by a minister or class leader after undergoing a system of probationary trial. Under this method of probation, the person was allowed all the privileges of the meetings, though was not received into full fellowship until after a period of six months acquaintance —or some definite time of trial. Receiving a member into one of these Societies or dismissing him from it, did not affect his membership in the Church of England, or other Church, to which he may have belonged. Indeed, there were members of the Societies who did not belong to any church at all when they were admitted.

When the Methodist Episcopal Church was organized in the United States, and later when the Wesleyan Church in Britain was organized, what had been a group of Methodist Societies became a Methodist Church. This had an immediate bearing upon the life and discipline of individual members. For when a person was turned out of an early Methodist Society, he did not thereby lose his standing in his Church nor his claim upon the Sacraments of the Church. But when church membership was entirely in a Methodist church which administered the Sacraments, and this was his sole ecclesiasticism, it was soon found that the church could not be as strict in expelling people and cutting them off from all churchly ordinances as the societies had been in holding members to the original special Methodist disciplines. There are those who say today that yet the marks of a society are deeply ingrained in all the Methodist churches.

Reception of Members. In the early days of the Societies and indeed during the formative period of the M.E. Church in America and elsewhere, the manner of receiving members into the Church was exceedingly simple. Those who wished to unite with the church gave their names to the ministers and were placed in classes, and if at the end of six months these were recommended by the class leader or by the pastor who had charge of training them, they were eligible to be received by the church as full members. There was, however, in American Methodism no regular ritualistic **Form for the Reception of Members** (as it was later called) either in the M.E. Church, or its cognate branches until past the middle of the nineteenth century. This was largely due to the fact that Wesley did not send over any office for Confirmation in the SUNDAY SERVICE (Prayer Book) which he sent to American Methodism. Eventually in the M.E. Church and the M.E. Church, South, forms for the reception of members were drawn up, which forms were greatly influenced by the Office of Confirmation of the Protestant Episcopal Church in America. These forms were revised from time to time, and when the three Methodist Churches united in 1939, a new form was drawn up which was used until 1964 when a further revision of this office was ordered.

This form now in the *Ritual* (see Book of Worship) and known as "Order for Confirmation and Reception into the Church" is the first time the name "confirmation" has been given frankly to this office in the Methodist Church. Disciplinary regulations provide that a person

must be baptized before he or she may be received into the Church, but quite often when a person has not been baptized, baptism may be administered to such person just previous to or sometimes as part of the Office for Confirmation. The office itself calls for a public profession of faith on the part of the applicant, an affirmation of belief in the teachings of the Church, and a promise to conform to its Discipline. The vows thus taken pledge the one being admitted to obey the rules and regulations of The United Methodist Church. Within recent years the congregation present is made to participate in the reception of members by expressing an intent to assist and help the person being received (see the *Ritual*, in loc).

Present regulations in The United Methodist Church insist that admission to the Church shall be "without regard to race, color, national origin or economic condition." The membership of a local church is defined as consisting of all persons who have been received into its fellowship on profession of their faith, by transfer from some other church or by restoration, and whose membership has not been terminated by death, transfer, withdrawal, expulsion, or action of the Quarterly Conference. A member of a local Methodist church is a member of The United Methodist Church anywhere in the connection. (*Discipline*, 1964, Paragraphs 107-111.)

Further regulations provide that when anyone offers himself for membership, it is the duty of the pastor, or proper persons appointed by him, to instruct such persons in the meaning of Christian Faith and the history, the organization and teaching of The United Methodist Church, to explain the baptismal and membership vows and to lead them to commit themselves to Jesus Christ as Lord and Savior. When the minister is convinced that such persons have given proof of the genuineness of their faith, and their desire and ability to assume the obligations and become faithful members of the church, he is to bring them before the congregation, administer the vows and receive them into the fellowship of the church, and enroll them as members.

Children, as members, should be brought by their parents for Baptism at an early age. A roll of baptized children of the church constitutes a "preparatory membership roll" of the church (*Discipline*, 1968, Paragraph 122). When children are received into full membership, of course their preparatory period ends.

Various disciplinary regulations give instruction regarding preparatory membership, and as such regulations change from time to time, it will not be possible here to set forth the various changes which have occurred in them. Regulations regarding "probationary members," as those on trial were formerly termed, have also been altered from time to time.

Affiliate Member is a member of The United Methodist Church who resides for an extended period in a city or community away from his home church, but does not wish to take (change) his membership from his home church. He may, however, on his request be enrolled as an Affiliate Member of a Methodist church located in the vicinity of his temporary residence. The *Discipline* provides that the home pastor shall be notified of such affiliate membership, and the membership itself entitles the person to the fellowship of the church he attends, and to its pastoral care and oversight, and to participation in its affairs. He must however continue to be counted as a member of his own home church. Persons of other denominations may become associate members of a local Methodist church under much the same conditions as these outlined above.

Associate Members are often nominal members of another denomination, usually of a State church in lands outside the United States, who under rules adopted by a Central Conference, have been permitted certain of the privileges and responsibilities of membership in a local Methodist church. Such associate membership came about in certain lands where the support and fellowship of members of other Churches who were willing to give needed support and fellowship were made welcome. Regulations provided by the former *Discipline* of The Methodist Church held that no action should be taken in this regard contrary to the Constitution and to the General Rules of The Methodist Church. (*Discipline*, 1964, Paragraph 562.) Certain JUDICIAL COUNCIL decisions were made within recent years defining more particularly the powers of the Central Conferences in this regard.

Termination of Membership. Membership in the Methodist Church is considered to be a precious possession not to be terminated except by death, transfer, withdrawal, expulsion or action of the Quarterly (Charge) Conference (in British Methodism by the LEADERS' MEETING). The pastor must report the loss of any members at each Quarterly (Charge) Conference, and indicate the reason for such. One of the RESTRICTIVE RULES binding upon the General Conference prevents that body from making any regulation which would deprive a person of church membership without a due trial "before the church, or by a committee, and of an appeal." (*Restrictive Rule* 4, Paragraph 18, *Discipline* 1968.) Rather minute directions are given today guiding and directing the pastor as to what he shall do when a member wishes to transfer to another denomination, or finds that such a person, without prior notice has united with another denomination. Pastors also are carefully directed as to how they may furnish a letter of transfer to a member wishing to move to another church.

The Charge (Quarterly) Conference of the Church has the right to remove from the roll the name of a person if such person cannot be located, and if the Commission on Evangelism of the local church together with the pastor so recommends.

The duty, power and privilege of receiving members according to the *Discipline* of The United Methodist Church is in the hands of the pastor of each charge and of him only. This has been the case since the beginning of American Methodism. No conference, no bishop, no official board may forbid the pastor to receive any person whom he feels is properly qualified. But while only the pastor may receive, he may not expel, once a member is admitted. Only by procedures carefully outlined in the *Discipline,* the processes of a church trial—if one be asked or by action of the Quarterly Conference when a person's whereabouts cannot be located, may a name be dropped from the roll, death or withdrawal of course excepted. (See also THEOLOGY, BRITISH.)

Disciplines.
Judicial Council Decisions, TMC.
M. Simpson, *Cyclopaedia.* 1878.   N. B. H.

MEMOIRS AND MEMORIAL SERVICES. A memoir, in common parlance, may be an official note or report, or something to be remembered, but in Methodist practical usage, the term usually has to do with the biographical material covering the life of a deceased minister and published in the official *Journal* of his Annual Conference. Formerly such memoirs were read one after another at the Annual Conference in a formal memorial service. However, the great growth of the Conferences in later years, and the time which the reading of such memoirs consumed, well nigh forced the abandonment of such time honored procedure.

Of late years it has become customary in the Conferences of The United Methodist Church to have a formal memorial service in charge of a Committee on Memoirs at each Annual session, and to have a single address given by some selected person. This deals in general terms with the life and effectiveness of those whose memoirs are being presented. The separate memoirs are usually prepared by persons who are formally requested to do so by the Committee on Memoirs, which usually consults beforehand the deceased minister's family. The names of the departed brethren are all read at the memorial service with special places reserved for the families of the deceased who may be able to attend. The written memoirs are later published in the Conference *Journal.* These memoirs may be referred to for many important matters in connection with the life of the men memorialized.

A listing of the memoirs of all deceased ministers of the M.E., M.E. South, and M.P. Churches is kept in the library of the Publishing House in Nashville, so that when the name of one memorialized is given, it is possible to ascertain at once the Conference *Journal* and year in which the memorial appeared.

N. B. H.

MEMPHIS, TENNESSEE, U.S.A. The first Methodist to preach in Memphis was probably Uncle Harry Lawrence, a Negro who preached to his people. The first society was organized in February 1826, nine months before the town was chartered. This became in time the First Methodist Church. T. P. Davidson was the first pastor, and there were three charter members, Mrs. Pauline Perkins, Elijah Coffee, and a Portuguese named Dickens. The church was part of the Wolfe River charge, a six-week circuit. In 1831 Bishop ROBERTS, presiding over the TENNESSEE CONFERENCE, appointed Francis A. Owen to organize a station. For a time they met in the "Blue Ruin Tavern." In 1832 land was purchased and the first church building of any kind in Memphis was erected, a frame building with split benches for pews. A Sunday school was organized the following year. By 1843 there were 300 white and more than 200 Negro members.

In 1840 Davidson's Chapel was organized near Fort Pickering, two miles south of the city limits. Asbury began in 1843, Forest Chapel and Edgewood in 1853, Central (St. John's) in 1859. The Civil War touched Methodism heavily. Several churches were used as hospitals by Union troops, two were burned, and Wesley Chapel (First) was assigned a Union chaplain as pastor.

Yellow fever in 1878 almost destroyed Memphis, but by 1900 there were fourteen churches. During the next twenty years, six more were organized. Then came a drouth with no new Methodist church for twenty-six years. In 1946 Grimes Memorial was begun with thirty members, named for C. C. Grimes, district superintendent at the time. By 1970 there were two districts and sixty-nine churches in the city and county. The statistics report 46,-

750 members in the Memphis and Memphis-Shelby Districts.

ROY D. WILLIAMS

Christ Church was organized in the Poplar Plaza Theatre on June 26, 1955, with 600 charter members. The present membership is 2,610. While located in the affluent East Memphis residential area, it draws members from all over the city. The church was organized under the leadership of Charles W. Grant. Three additional ministers are on the staff.

There are two educational buildings and a sanctuary, with a seating capacity of 1,510, located on more than ten acres of ground. The sanctuary contains stained glass windows, much admired, with Scriptural symbols. Presently, plans are being drawn for a fourth and final building with additional classrooms, a gymnasium, and another library.

Due to a vital interest in missions, supporting missionaries in BRAZIL, JAPAN, Africa and Borneo, MALAYSIA, Christ Church ranked third in American Methodism in ADVANCE SPECIAL giving, 1966-67. Christ Church has sponsored two new churches—Scenic Hills and Good Shepherd. It also sponsors a week day school, comprised of junior kindergarten, kindergarten, and grades one through six. State standards are met.

Christ Church is deeply interested in and is generously contributing to a Memphis renewal program, presently giving full support to an "Inner-City Worker." Total giving for all purposes in 1969-70 Conference year was $450,335. Church property is valued at $2,773,913.

Methodist Hospital, located at 1265 Union Avenue, was founded in 1918. The institution has grown from sixty-five beds to 900 beds, but its purpose, to serve as a haven of rest and treatment for the sick and needy—usually those of the Mid-South—has remained the same.

Ownership of the vast enterprise rests with the NORTH MISSISSIPPI, NORTH ARKANSAS and MEMPHIS CONFERENCES of The United Methodist Church, and is held in trusteeship. Trustees (six from each of the three conferences) are elected annually. The trustees in turn elect a Board of Managers to handle (under delegated power only) the actual operation of the hospital.

Methodist Hospital was incorporated in the state of Tennessee as a non-profit institution in 1922. On Sept. 17, 1924, the hospital moved to its present location with a capacity of 120 beds. Two and a half years later, the Lucy Brinkley Annex was completed, increasing the patient capacity to 185.

The West Wing, opened in November 1940, raised patient occupancy to 300. Construction in 1950 included the North Wing, a new laundry and storeroom, and additions to the Doctor's Office Building and Pharmacy.

The hospital acquired and began operating Memphis Eye, Ear, Nose and Throat Hospital with a patient capacity of sixty on Jan. 1, 1943.

Another major addition to Methodist Hospital, the East Wing, opened in June 1958. Ten stories high, the East Wing houses 246 patient beds. Also completed in 1958 was a new service wing constructed in connection with the East Wing. This service wing houses, among other things, a surgical suite and obstetrical suite.

On Jan. 13, 1966, the fifteen-floor William Green Thomas Wing, providing an additional 364 beds, was opened. Three additional service wing floors were also added. This new service area affords new X-ray, laboratory, physical therapy, surgical and intensive care unit facilities.

Another new feature of the Thomas Wing is the teenage patient floor located on the thirteenth floor. This new unit is manned by specially trained staff to care for children between the ages of twelve and eighteen. The floor provides a special recreation room for use of ambulatory patients. With the opening of the Thomas Wing, all operation of the Memphis Eye, Ear, Nose and Throat Hospital was moved to Methodist Hospital.

The Hospital maintains several educational programs. The School of Nursing is probably best known, and maintains the reputation of being one of the finest schools in the land. Other programs include schools for X-ray technicians, medical technologists, and inhalation therapists. In addition to the educational programs for interns and residents, the Hospital also has intern programs for administrative residents and graduate students in pharmacy.

Probably the largest and most extensive home mission program is carried on at Methodist Hospital through the Golden Cross Service Program, with contributions coming from the three owning conferences.

Both the Women's Auxiliary and the Volunteer Pink Lady Program make major contributions of time and financial support.

FRED MUNSON

St. Luke's Church has for many years enjoyed a unique position among the churches of the city.

The growth of the City of Memphis and expansion of Memphis State University have combined to make St. Luke's the largest Methodist church in the city and one of the most significant in the state. It is a church that always gives special attention to education, mission and youth.

St. Luke's began as an unattached preaching point, and then as Bethel Church on the corner of Prescott and Barron, where shortly after the Civil War a small, one-room, frame church was built on a lot given by D. R. S. Rosebrough.

In 1888 the church moved to the population center of East Memphis, a community called Buntyn. For sixteen years the church was known as the Buntyn Methodist Church. From 1875-1911 this church, known first as Bethel and then as Buntyn, was a part of the Springdale circuit, which circuit was Methodism's attempt to keep step with the eastward movement of the city in these years.

In 1911 the church, with 200 members, became a new appointment known as "The Buntyn Station."

In 1925 the property, at the center of the community on which St. Luke's now stands, was given to the church by John T. Fisher, a prominent Memphis Methodist business man. During the months while the congregation worshipped at West Tennessee State College, a small brick church was erected. This building is now the center for a Boy Scout program that reaches about 500 boys. In 1930 the present sanctuary of the church was built and the name changed to St. Luke's.

Since 1930 the story has been one of expanding program and increased membership. The area once served by St. Luke's now has ten Methodist churches—some of the most impressive churches in the City of Memphis. St. Luke's, with 3,082 members, continues to make plans for

ST. LUKE'S CHURCH, MEMPHIS, TENNESSEE

growth in membership, budget and building. It has been served by some of the most distinguished ministers of the MEMPHIS CONFERENCE. The longest pastorates have been those of James D. Jenkins, William C. Aden and James A. Fisher.

The goal assumed by the church and pursued vigorously centers in youth with a determination to make the service of St. Luke's Church relevant to college young people today and across the years.

MEMPHIS CONFERENCE (ME) was organized at Jackson, Tenn., Nov. 4, 1840, with Bishop J. O. ANDREW presiding. It was formed from portions of the TENNESSEE and MISSISSIPPI CONFERENCES. When organized its territory included west TENNESSEE, west KENTUCKY, and north MISSISSIPPI. At the beginning the conference had 12,680 white and 1,995 colored members. Named for the City of Memphis which, though on the west side of the conference territory, was about equidistant from its northern and southern ends, the conference included what was and still is an important cotton producing area. After the division of the church in 1844, the Memphis Conference adhered South under the PLAN OF SEPARATION.

The conference grew rapidly. Starting with three districts and twenty-eight charges, it had ten districts and some 29,000 white and 7,000 colored members in 1850. In 1869 there were about 40,000 white and 235 Negro members. Notwithstanding the loss of the Mississippi territory to the NORTH MISSISSIPPI CONFERENCE in 1870, the Memphis Conference had grown to more than 58,000 members by 1900, and at unification in 1939 it had more than 98,000 members.

In 1939 there was a determined effort to place the Kentucky section of the Memphis Conference in the LOUISVILLE CONFERENCE, in accordance with the plan to make annual conference lines conform as nearly as possible with state lines. Objection on the part of the Memphis Conference and its Kentucky members thwarted the move. In 1964 the Memphis Conference, knowing that one new episcopal area would be created in the Southeastern Jurisdiction, asked that it be so designated with the provision that the bishop reside in Memphis. But the Jurisdictional Conference after some debate awarded area status to the NORTH CAROLINA CONFERENCE, the bishop to reside in RALEIGH.

Notwithstanding its record of growth, the Memphis Conference has been somewhat straitened through the years by the fact that the City of Memphis is in the extreme southwest corner of Tennessee. The Mississippi River on the west and the Mississippi state line immediately on the south constrict the conference. In working for expansion and growth the conference cannot cross the river into Arkansas or the state line into Mississippi; it can work only in the wedge of Tennessee territory. It is to the credit of the conference that notwithstanding this geographical constriction, it has done well through the years.

The Memphis Conference gave The Methodist Church its first GENERAL CONFERENCE Secretary (1939-1956), LUD H. ESTES, who also served many years as secretary of his own conference and as Secretary of the General Conference (1930-1938) of the former M.E. Church, South. Bishop WILLIAM C. MARTIN, who was elevated to the episcopacy in 1938, the last bishop elected by the former M.E. Church, South, was born at Randolph, Tenn., within the bounds of the Memphis Conference.

The Memphis Conference supports LAMBUTH COLLEGE at Jackson, and in 1968 it voted to endow a Methodist Chair in Memphis Theological Seminary (Cumberland Presbyterian), when and if that institution is accredited. The conference is justly proud of the great Methodist Hospital at Memphis. Plans for building a retirement home are in progress.

In 1970 the Memphis Conference had eight districts, 370 ministers, 294 charges, 119,696 members, and property valued at $63,024,619.

General Minutes, MEC, MECS, and MC.
Minutes of the Memphis Conference.   N. B. H.

MENDENHALL, MARMADUKE H. (1836-1905), American preacher and philanthropist, was born in Guilford, N.C., May 13, 1836. Upon moving to Union City, Ind., he joined the NORTH INDIANA CONFERENCE in 1856. He is remembered as an effective preacher and pastor, being elected to the GENERAL CONFERENCE in 1880. In addition to his pastoral work, he engaged in numerous business ventures which proved quite successful. He endowed the Mendenhall lectureship at DEPAUW UNIVERSITY. This lectureship has attracted some of the keenest minds and best known ministers and theologians in the country as the annual lecturers. Mendenhall died Oct. 9, 1905.

HAROLD THRASHER

MENDOZA, VINCENTE (1875-1955), one of the most brilliant men in Mexican Methodism, was born in Guadalajara, Dec. 24, 1875. He studied with the famous teacher Aurelio Ortega and was looked after by David F. Watkins, a Congregational missionary. He first entered work at a printing plant but heard the call for the ministry and entered the Presbyterian Seminary. It was closed temporarily, and he went to the School of Theology in Puebla. He entered the Annual Conference on trial in 1899, and served churches in Tezontepec, Pachuca, Puebla, and Gante. From 1915 to 1921, because of the revolution, he went to CALIFORNIA and became a member of the SOUTHERN CALIFORNIA CONFERENCE. There he lost his first wife, by whom he had four children. Then he married Natalia García Bravo. From 1922-38 he was part-time pastor, and also teacher at Union Evangelical Seminary. Also he acted as a newspaper editor. From 1947-48 he devoted his time to the Seminary. He retired in 1949 but was active until illness and death came on June 14, 1955.

Mendoza was a strong speaker, good writer and poet, lecturer and teacher. Large congregations and numerous audiences outside the church gathered to listen to his interpretation of the Bible and to his prophetic word. At institutes, conventions, ministerial assemblies, and all kinds of gatherings, his Bible classes were enjoyed by both adults and young people. He served the same in small as well as in large churches.

He was successful in his pastorates but even more so with his pen. From 1910 to 1914 he was director of the *Christian Advocate*, from 1922-27 of *El Mundo Cristiano* (an interdenominational paper). He was director of *El Evangelista Mexicano* (1935-38), a new name for the Methodist official paper which is still published, and from there on he was a contributor to it until his death. His writings were strong, stimulating and controversial. Mendoza's memory will long live as the best hymn writer in Latin America. Throughout his life he assembled a growing collection of hymns for all occasions. *Himnos Selectos* finally appeared as a hymnal in which he included original works, words and music, or translations and selections of good music for church use in various departments. He enabled the Christians of MEXICO to sing their faith with joy and power.

GUSTAVO A. VELASCO G.

MENGEL, CHARLES H. (1879-1964), a bishop in the American Evangelical Congregational Church, was noted for his aggressive leadership. Born at Summit Station in Schuylkill County, Pa., May 8, 1879, he became a pastor in The United Evangelical Church in 1899. Starting as a "breaker boy" in the anthracite coal mines, his education had to be secured wherever possible with some

studies at Temple University in PHILADELPHIA, and other studies by correspondence. However, he was greatly interested in education, and in time (1953) led the Board of Education of his church in starting the Evangelical Congregational School of Theology in Myerstown, Pa. He also helped found and was president of the trustees of the Burd and Rogers Home for aging people (first located at Herndon, Pa. [1924] and later at Myerstown).

He was elected a presiding elder in the East Pennsylvania Conference and served from 1922 to 1930, then served as bishop for eight years, 1934-42 (the limit in his church). He was a leader in opposing the merger of The UNITED EVANGELICAL CHURCH with the EVANGELICAL ASSOCIATION in 1922, and thus was a dominant figure in organizing the Evangelical Congregational Church. Bishop Mengel died Jan. 14, 1964, at Allentown, Pa. His body was laid to rest in the Greenwood Cemetery, Allentown.

ROBERT WILSON

MENTOR, OHIO, U.S.A., celebrated 150 years of Methodism in 1968. OHIO was visited by Methodist preachers as early as 1790, but credit for establishing Methodism in Mentor must be given to Ira Eddy who organized a society in 1818. He had eight charter members, four pioneer men and their wives. His circuit was called Grand River. It consisted of forty-three townships and appointments so arranged that he could preach in each of them every twenty-one days.

Eddy was a preacher and organizer of great ability, serving in time as pastor of almost every charge in Northeastern Ohio and one who doubtless accomplished as much for the beginnings of Methodism along the lake shore as any other man.

In the early years of the church's history services were held in homes and later in school houses. The pioneer preachers were men of great courage. Their exposure to storms and floods, wild beasts and Indians through the almost trackless forest that was then the Mentor community, made them all become heroes. One official board sent a petition to conference asking for "a preacher who could swim," as the one appointed to Mentor the year before had drowned in trying to cross a swollen stream.

An early example of Christian cooperation was the building of the first church in Mentor. This was a brick building erected in 1838 by the Methodist and Disciple congregations.

The first Board of Trustees was elected in April 1842, for the purpose of erecting a distinctly Methodist church. A frame building was completed in 1844 on a half acre of ground purchased for $50 at the site of the present church. The contractor accepted his pay in cattle due to the scarcity of cash. When the first services were conducted, the building had not been lathed or plastered. The worshippers brought in blocks of wood on which planks were laid for seats. The building was completed in 1848. In 1866 extensive repairs were made to the "audience room."

When Frank Dunbar was appointed to the Mentor Church in 1900, he was asked after his first service if he had been sent by the Lord to build a new church. He affirmed that he had. When a building fund had been raised and a plan selected, the old church was moved to the rear of the property, and worship continued to be held in it until the new building was completed. Farewell services in the frame church were held in January 1906, and the new church was dedicated the following Sunday. During the dedication service the small deficit in the building fund was subscribed, and the building dedicated free of debt. Its construction price was $11,000. Later improvements included installation of electric lights and a pipe organ.

Anticipating rapid growth—for Mentor is located in the center of one of Ohio's most rapidly growing counties —the congregation, in 1955, adopted an over-all plan providing that an education building be the first phase of the building program, with a new sanctuary the second phase. Other steps would include a new social hall and more educational facilities.

As soon as the Christian education center was constructed in 1957, it was necessary immediately to begin plans for a new sanctuary. The present sanctuary, completed in 1962, accommodates 1,200, not including the choir, and there are two services each Sunday. Duplicate sessions of the church school are also held. Present church membership is reported as 2,017.

"History of Mentor Methodism," *The Quarterly Bulletin,* Vol. I. Mentor, Ohio, September 1894.
"Mentor Methodist Church," *The Telegraph,* Painesville, Ohio, Nov. 21, 1953.   MAE BOOTH

MERIDIAN, MISSISSIPPI, U.S.A. **Central Church.** Organized Methodism began in Lauderdale County, Miss., in January 1839, when the ALABAMA CONFERENCE, of which the region was then a part, appointed William Howie to the Lauderdale Mission. A year later the mission reported 358 white and twenty-nine colored members, and in 1841 it became the Lauderdale Circuit.

Dearman Chapel, erected in 1852 on what is now Ninth Street near Eleventh Avenue, was the first Methodist church building in the Meridian community. In 1859 Meridian appeared for the first time in the conference appointments, JUNIUS E. NEWMAN preacher in charge. The next year the charge reported 150 white and fifty colored members. The Mobile Conference, formed in 1863 by dividing the Alabama Conference, met in Meridian in 1868.

The 1870 GENERAL CONFERENCE readjusted annual conference boundaries and placed Lauderdale and some other counties on the eastern edge of Mississippi in the MISSISSIPPI CONFERENCE. The Meridian District, formed in 1868, was continued. The Meridian church had 208 white and no colored members in 1870.

In 1886 a new church building, said to be "the best in the conference," was erected in Meridian. For a time it was called First Church, but in 1890 it was officially named Central Church. The building was destroyed by fire in 1913, and the congregation then relocated at Tenth Street and Twenty-Third Avenue. An impressive new sanctuary was erected in 1923. In 1951 an education building was added, and in 1960 the interior of the church edifice was remodeled.

A Woman's Missionary Society was organized in 1879, and in 1887 Central Church sent Betty Hughes as a missionary to China. The church claims to have had the first organized Adult Bible Class in the Mississippi Conference.

As the downtown church, Central is one of sixteen United Methodist congregations in a city of about 45,000. In 1970 it had 1,636 of the 7,186 members of The United

Methodist Church in Meridian. The value of its property was $917,390, and it raised $10,539 for all purposes during the year.

General Minutes, MEC, MECS, MC, and UMC.
B. M. Hunt, *History of Central Methodist Church, Meridian.* (Typescript). 1958.
M. E. Lazenby, *Alabama and West Florida.* 1960.
Minutes of the Mississippi Conference.   NORMAN U. BOONE

MERITON, JOHN (1698-1753), British Anglican, hailed from East Anglia, where his father was an incumbent. He graduated from Caius College, Cambridge; and after serving as a curate at Oxburgh, moved to the Isle of Man, where he was converted. JOHN WESLEY met him in 1741 and invited him to join the Methodists. He accompanied Wesley on numerous preaching tours and acted as a secretary. He attended the first Conference in 1744.

Wesleyan Methodist Magazine (1900), 495-501.
                         A. SKEVINGTON WOOD

MERKEL, HENRY M. (1889-1960), American minister and historian of UTAH Methodism, was born Feb. 14, 1889 at Tamaroa, Ill. He was educated in the schools of southern Illinois, the Academy of McKENDREE COLLEGE, the New Mexico State Normal University, and the ILIFF SCHOOL OF THEOLOGY.

He was ordained DEACON in 1917, and ELDER in 1920, at the SOUTHERN ILLINOIS CONFERENCE, transferring to the NEW MEXICO MISSION in 1920, and to the COLORADO CONFERENCE in 1925, after which he served in the Utah Mission from 1926-1935. Returning to the Colorado Conference, he retired in 1954.

Henry Merkel is best known for his authorship of the book, *History of Methodism in Utah,* which has become a source book of facts, not only on Methodism in Utah, but of much in the religious, social, economic and political development of the West.

His ministry was marked by deep friendships, an evangelistic message, and a warm heart. He died June 15, 1960, speaking to the ROCKY MOUNTAIN CONFERENCE meeting in Denver, Colo., on behalf of McKendree College, an institution which had conferred upon him the D.D. degree. He is buried in Wiley, Colo., near the ranch he owned and loved.

Journal of the Utah Mission and the Rocky Mountain Conference.
H. M. Merkel, *Utah.* 1938.   WARREN BAINBRIDGE

MERRIFIELD, GEORGE (1854-1929), American minister, was born in Sutton, County of Surrey, England, Aug. 13, 1854. He came to America with his brother in 1873, coming to DETROIT where he planned to secure employment. He later worked as a miner in the MINNESOTA iron range and in the coal fields of PENNSYLVANIA. He mined silver in COLORADO and there "made a strike" which enabled him to enter GARRETT BIBLICAL INSTITUTE to prepare for the ministry. Almost all of his ministry was spent in the WEST WISCONSIN CONFERENCE. Dodgeville, Darlington, Lake St. Eau Claire, and Trousdale in Madison were among his appointments. He was also superintendent of the Platteville District, 1903-1909. Death came on March 5, 1929, in Platteville.

He was an excellent preacher, having a fine literary

style. An expression often used concerning him was, "a perfect Christian gentleman."

Yearbook of the West Wisconsin Conference, 1929.

JOHN W. HARRIS

MERRILL, ANNIS (1810-1905?), American attorney at law and Methodist pioneer in CALIFORNIA. Son of a member of NEW ENGLAND CONFERENCE, he graduated at WESLEYAN UNIVERSITY in 1835, studied law, and practiced in BOSTON. Coming to SAN FRANCISCO in 1849, he was a member of the first board of trustees of First Church, and of the UNIVERSITY OF THE PACIFIC. He drew up the charter for the university, and was president of its trustees for many years. He handled more legal cases for the church during its first half century than any other attorney in the state. A Sunday school teacher for forty years, at ninety he rode his bicycle in Golden Gate Park for his morning constitutional. He was regarded as one of the partriarchs of California Methodism, both in his local church and in the Conference. The date of his death is uncertain as it occurred shortly before the great earthquake and fire of 1906 in San Francisco which destroyed the official records.

C. V. Anthony, *Fifty Years*. 1901.
F. K. Baker, *History of First Methodist Church, San Francisco*.
N.d.   LEON L. LOOFBOUROW

MERRILL, STEPHEN MASON (1825-1905), American bishop, was born the fifth in a family of eleven children at Mount Pleasant, Ohio, on Sept. 16, 1825. The grandson of a Revolutionary Minuteman, he joined the church at seventeen and entered the OHIO CONFERENCE in 1846. His father was a farmer and shoemaker and his mother the daughter of a Revolutionary soldier, both strict Methodists.

After learning the shoemaker's trade and then teaching, he gave up both for the ministry. His first appointment was Georgetown, Ohio, a "hardscrabble" circuit with twenty-two preaching places. On July 18, 1848, he married Anna Bellmire, who survived him by only a few days. They had one son. Ordained DEACON, 1849, and ELDER, 1851, he rode hard circuits and read hard books for eleven years. Though without academic training, Indiana Asbury (now DePauw) University gave him an honorary A.M. in 1864. He had only a term or two in a rural academy.

For many years before receiving a station church, his salary was only $216 annually, and "table exercises". Before transferring to the KENTUCKY CONFERENCE in 1859, he was presiding elder in OHIO. Returning to the Ohio Conference in 1863, Merrill overcame a tendency to pulmonary disease and enjoyed good health. A close student of the doctrines and polity of Methodism, and having naturally a fine legal mind, he won recognition on the public forum and in the church press as a powerful speaker. Serving as presiding elder on the Marietta (Ohio) district, he was elected to GENERAL CONFERENCE, 1868.

Developing into a great church lawyer, Merrill won recognition in the General Conference for his wide knowledge of church constitutional law. Although he was a strong Union man and against slavery, he was not in the troubled post-Civil War-period a radical agitator. In the General Conference, with lay representation a key issue, he delivered a strong argument to the effect that laymen could not be admitted to that body without duly amending the constitution of the church. He so impressed the General Conference with his ability as a newcomer that he was at that session, 1868, elected editor of the *Western Christian Advocate*.

Four years later (in 1872) he was elected bishop, and assigned to the ST. PAUL, Minn. Area, 1872-80; and then to CHICAGO until he retired in 1904. He died suddenly while on a visit to Keyport, N. J., on Nov. 12, 1905. He was buried in Rose Hill, Chicago.

Bishop Merrill traveled widely over the United States and MEXICO. He wrote: *Christian Baptism; A Digest of Methodist Law; The Organic Union of American Methodism* (1892); *Mary of Nazareth and Her Family*, and eight other lesser known books.

Bishop Merrill was no revivalist or popular speaker—as is the case quite often with strictly legal minds. But in the forum of any great conference, his "massive argument, which his admirers likened to that of Daniel Webster, bore down all opposition." A walking encyclopedia on Methodist law, he was to his brethren a calm and useful counselor. He ranked next to Bishop JOSHUA SOULE in his knowledge of the Methodist Constitution and law. A great parliamentarian, his humor and calm made him a good presiding officer.

Dictionary of American Biography.
F. D. Leete, *Methodist Bishops*. 1948.
M. Simpson, *Cyclopaedia*. 1878.   JESSE A. EARL

MERRITT, KINSEY NEWTON (1891-1967), American conference lay leader and business executive, was born in BALTIMORE, Md., June 5, 1891, the son of John J. and Mary Ellen (Nellie) Merritt. Educated in the public schools of Baltimore, he married Helen Brown Maynadier Jan. 15, 1916. He worked for a time with what was then the Railway Express Company, and going to New York City, became vice president of that company in 1958.

Merritt joined the M. E. Church in 1900, and served in his local church faithfully as long as he lived. He was Sunday school superintendent of St. Mathew's Church in PHILADELPHIA, Pa.; president of the Sunday School Superintendents' Association, Philadelphia; and later on moving to northern NEW JERSEY, became lay leader of the NEWARK CONFERENCE, as the NORTHERN NEW JERSEY CONFERENCE was named then. He was president of the OCEAN GROVE CAMP MEETING ASSOCIATION, 1953-63, and contributed articles to various religious and business magazines. He was a lay delegate from his conference to the GENERAL CONFERENCE in his later years.

Kinsey N. Merritt was a dominant personage and proved to be an orator with unique talents. He is said to have been a public lecturer of power and persuasion, and exerted great influence in his whole section of The Methodist Church. In retirement he lived at Meadow Lakes, Hightstown, N. J. He died in June 1967.

Who's Who in The Methodist Church, 1966. JESSE A. EARL

MERRITT, TIMOTHY (1775-1845), American preacher and writer, was born in CONNECTICUT just prior to the Revolution and was directed into the ministry by ENOCH MUDGE. From 1797 to 1801 he was associated with Joshua Taylor, presiding elder of the district of MAINE lying between the Penobscot and Saco Rivers. In 1822 he had charge of a class of twenty-five members at Wood End, Lynn. From

1817 to 1819, and again from 1825 to 1827, he served the First Methodist Society in BOSTON.

The New England Methodist historian, JAMES MUDGE, writes of Timothy Merritt: "Christian perfection was his favorite theme, and he was a living exemplification of that Wesleyan doctrine. . . . His favorite topics were those which pertain to experimental and practical piety."

As a writer, Merritt was well known. For a time he was one of the editors of *Zion's Herald;* he was also an assistant editor of the *Christian Advocate* for a four-year period. He launched, in July 1839, a periodical called *Guide to Christian Perfection.* He was elected first vice-president of the third general convention of the Methodist anti-slavery movement which met in Lowell, Mass., in November 1838. This well-loved personality in the NEW ENGLAND CONFERENCE died in Lynn, Mass., on May 2, 1845.

J. M. Buckley, *History of Methodists.* 1896.
J. Mudge, *New England Conference.* 1910.
New England Historical and Genealogical Register, Vol. I, 1847; Vol. XV, 1861. ERNEST R. CASE

MESSMORE, JAMES H. (1836-1911), was an early M. E. missionary in North INDIA. A Canadian by birth, he was educated at ALLEGHENY COLLEGE, as were so many of the early Methodist missionaries to India. He arrived in India in 1860, and was married in 1861 to Elizabeth Husk, the first unmarried woman missionary sent to India by an organization of the M. E. Church. The Methodist Board of Foreign Missions sent three women to India early in the 1860's, in the expectation that they would be transferred to the proposed Woman's Missionary Society as soon as it was organized. The other women soon returned to America.

James Messmore made a distinguished record as a Hindustani scholar, seminary instructor, publisher, editor, English-church pastor and presiding elder. With JAMES M. THOBURN, he founded *The Lucknow Witness* in 1871, and was its editor for years. Its name was changed to *The Indian Witness,* and it became the official organ of the Methodist Church in Southern Asia. Messmore spent many years in Garhwal and gave much to the principalship of the boys' school, the first high school in Garhwal. After his death, it was named the Messmore High School by public request. It is now an intermediate, or two-year, college. So much was the veteran missionary revered that the Brahman teachers, senior students, and community leaders, nearly all former students of the school, insisted on carrying his coffin to the cemetery for interment.

J. WASKOM PICKETT

METHODISM is a term usually applied to that system of doctrine and general plan of economy held and professed first by the Wesleyan Methodists in England and then by the organized Methodist Church bodies there and in America and now in almost all the nations on the earth. In its wider significance, it is applied to the religious movement which commenced under the labors of the WESLEYS and WHITEFIELD in the first half of the eighteenth century.

The origin and development of the movement may be found narrated in other parts of this *Encyclopedia,* in the biographies of its founder and his helpers, and in the story of Methodism as it has developed in the many lands where it is today at home. Although each one of these present-day organized Methodist bodies may have certain characteristics which may cause it to differ somewhat from the others, all are one in the idea and practice of a "connexion," as Wesley liked to call it.

"Methodism is a family of Churches." This statement by the nineteenth century Wesleyan, WILLIAM ARTHUR, goes to the root of the matter, for the ties that bind this world communion together are neither legal nor constitutional, but they are those of a common origin, a common growth, and above all they bind together churches which primarily consist not of institutions, but of persons. Despite all the differences which race and culture and geography impose, there is a recognizable Methodist character, and Methodists from ZAMBIA, CORNWALL, CALIFORNIA, GERMANY, CUBA, INDIA, HONG KONG would find that they had a common spiritual inheritance. That this bond is "in the spirit" is not a fact to be under-rated, for of all institutions, it is the family with its informalities and its personal relationships which proves to be tough and enduring when more pretentious entities have passed away. The family too is the place of growth and change; sons and daughters grow up, tensions develop between age groups, and one by one the members of families make their own lives, get married, settle down elsewhere, so that there is in the strict sense an "organic unity" between them, capable of constant modification. The rise and development of Methodism from a number of societies within the Church of England into a world-wide communion justifies and exemplifies this "family" analogy.

The eighteenth century was a century of reaction against a century and a half of religious zeal, intolerance and dogmatic strife. It was itself tolerant, almost indifferent to supernatural claims, preferring to appeal to reason, and expressing its religion in an accommodating moralism. It was a ferment too, of critical ideas, of dissolving certainties, with attacks on current orthodoxies, centering on the doctrines of the Trinity and of the Person of Christ. One notable feature of the Evangelical Revival and especially of the sermons of John Wesley and the hymns of his brother Charles is their kerygmatic character, their joyful and confident proclamation of the Holy Trinity and of the Nicene faith.

Modern historians emphasize that the brothers Wesley did not inaugurate an awakening which had already begun in America and in Wales before their conversion, and have drawn attention to the eminent and various Anglican Evangelicals, some but loosely associated with the Wesleys and some explicitly dissociated from them, in whose parishes there were the fruits of converted souls, and renewed Christian communities. Nonetheless, the work of the brothers Wesley is central to the revival, and to their efforts we owe the emergence of the Methodists, not as masses of converted individuals, but as societies with their own coherent pattern of discipline and worship.

The Wesleys brought with them their own spiritual heritage: several generations of clerical ancestors, who handed down to them through SAMUEL and SUSANNA WESLEY all that was richest in the English religious tradition, Puritan and Catholic, as well as the more recent awareness, through the Non-Jurors of the spirituality of Jansenism and of seventeenth century Catholic mysticism.

To a tired English religion John Wesley brought the blood transfusion of German Pietism and of Moravianism, a warm affective piety, closely linked to study of the Bible and finding expression in noble philanthropy. The rise of Methodism John Wesley was wont to trace to the HOLY CLUB originated by his brother and a few academic companions in the University of Oxford. It may be that it was from their programmed and patterned integrity of worship and study that the nickname "Methodist" arose. Their search after holiness was in the main along traditional high church lines. It was later and above all during their missionary experience in GEORGIA, that the Wesleys made first-hand contact with the exiled Lutherans and MORAVIANS at Ebenezer and SAVANNAH and drew from them lessons and clues for what they had so far sought in vain. Despite the comparative failure of their mission in Georgia, they had learned much in their own private and personal lives, and in an extraordinary way John Wesley had improvised means of growth in piety for his people which were later to become embodied in the structure of Methodism.

After their return to England, and especially in the summer of 1738, things began to happen quickly. Both brothers underwent conversion experiences. Both found their preaching unwelcome in the fashionable churches of LONDON. It was a turning point when their companion, George Whitefield, summoned Wesley to join him in preaching in the open air outside BRISTOL, and from this point on the revival became evident, as their preaching drew crowds who would not enter churches to hear them.

But Wesley's converts were not, like those of Whitefield, "ropes of sand," for from the beginning he organized them in BANDS, CLASSES, societies, a simple yet intricate discipline with their own means of grace, love feasts, vigils, fasts, etc. The sacramental services at the beginning of the Revival were a notable feature of the religious awakening, but these centered on the few occasions when the Wesleys and their small band of ordained clergy could assist them. For the most part the Methodists were driven to the sacramental and liturgical pattern of the Established church, and it was at such points that tension and hostility grew. By his constant travelling, and assisted by a splendid band of laymen, dedicated, tough, enduring all manner of hardness, he covered the land in constant journeys, though there were areas and places which he revisited more often than others, following his own injunction, "Go not only to those who need you, but to those who need you most."

In the 1740's the Methodists were often greeted with hostility from both mobs and magistrates, but by the end of their lives the Wesleys had become honored and respected national figures. It was among the uncared-for proletariat, the miners of Cornwall and WALES, the moving populations of the new industrial area that the Methodists found their strength. The Church of England was involved in its own past, and in an alliance with the State,

THE FIRST METHODIST CONFERENCE, JUNE 25, 1744

politically fruitful, but paralyzing in the end to the pastoral machinery of the church. Its deliberative Synods, the Houses of Convocation, were in abeyance during this critical period, with the result, as Newman observed, that the Church of England as a whole never met Methodism as a whole, never made up its corporate mind about it, came to no decision about it. The result was that the growing difference in ethos between the Methodists and the Establishment was unchecked, and after the death of Wesley this led to the separation of the Methodists from the Church of England, a singularly painless schism.

In the nineteenth century the Methodists in England were driven to institute their own ordinances of Word and Sacrament, to introduce ordination (with laying on of hands after 1836) and to exist as a separate communion until the 1830's, rather self-consciously thinking of itself as "the Body" and distinct from either the Church of England or the older Dissent. The Catholic revival, the Oxford Movement and the renewal of Roman Catholicism in England drove the Methodists into the alliance with the historic Free Churches which marked the latter part of the nineteenth century. During that century other Methodist bodies arose—the BIBLE CHRISTIANS in the West of England, and the PRIMITIVE METHODISTS mainly in the midlands and north, themselves originating in revivals, but in their polity and discipline giving a larger place to the laity than the more clerical Wesleyan organization, and unattached by any tradition to the Church of England.

The famous four "Our's" of the first Methodists signify their characteristic ethos: "Our doctrines." These were the scriptural doctrines of JUSTIFICATION by Faith, Assurance, NEW BIRTH, a combination known as "Evangelical Arminianism," but which had little to do with the theology of the Dutch ARMINIUS. It was rather the offer of free grace to all mankind, and the universal scope of the gospel which marked them off from the Calvinist evangelicals. None the less, it is probably best to see both sides of the Revival, Arminian and Calvinist, as within a common Augustinianism, and emphasis on the triumphant power of divine grace.

"Our hymns" were the hymns, in the main, of Charles Wesley which put into rousing, forthright, and unsentimental verse the doctrines of the gospel.

"Our literature" marks a whole educational revival, in which John Wesley took the lead, of which his schools at KINGSWOOD were a first fruit, and which educated his people by means of cheap tracts and pamphlets, as well as with the formidable library of classics, the CHRISTIAN LIBRARY in fifty volumes which he edited for his preachers.

"Our discipline" was the entirely characteristic polity, the result of a series of inspired improvisations by Wesley himself: wheels within wheels of Christian companies, from the band and class and society, to the district synod and the annual conference of preachers—this last, after Wesley's death becoming the sovereign body among the British Methodists; the itineracy of the preachers, going back to Wesley's own incessant journeyings, resembling those of a judge on "circuit"; the use of lay preachers and the growing opportunities for lay ministries within the Church.

During Wesley's own lifetime the Revival had spilled overseas, and in North America and in the WEST INDIES, there were revivals of similar pattern and with similar fruits to those in England. In the early nineteenth century a series of heroic and costly missionary adventures resulted in Methodist communities in West and SOUTH AFRICA, and in AUSTRALIA and the Pacific Islands. It was in North America, however, that the greatest development took place. Following the liberation of the colonies from English rule, the new American nation found room for the Methodists with their flexible organization and enterprising spirit, and as the great extension of American life westward began, the Methodists were always in the van. The result was a great Church which in numbers and in extent, and in the size of its mission fields, greatly outnumbers the rest of Methodism. Here, too, as in Africa and INDIA and Australasia, the institutional pattern followed of orphanages and hospitals, and above all schools and colleges and universities. The size of the American church, the nature of its growth and its expansion, resulted in structural differences from British Methodism, above all in that the American Methodist churches are episcopal.

For the history and development of the separate Methodist Churches, see each one under its own name in this *Encyclopedia.* All are marked in their professed doctrinal statements by a general adherence to Arminian doctrine as opposed to Calvinism, and the feature of the polity of each one is the itinerant system for ministerial placement. This is almost universally practiced save in certain small Congregational Methodist bodies.

In the last half of the nineteenth century the size and diversity of the Methodist churches throughout the world called for some kind of explicit link between them, and from 1881 onwards ECUMENICAL METHODIST CONFERENCES have been held at regular intervals, where matters of common concern might be deliberated. In the most recent years this has been strengthened by regular meetings of a WORLD METHODIST COUNCIL.

Methodism across the world has been active in the Ecumenical Movement, and Methodists share in the work of the WORLD COUNCIL OF CHURCHES at all levels. One of the effects of the Ecumenical Movement itself has been to throw back to the various communions questions about their own inheritance. They too, however, are conscious of the impulse towards a closer manifestation of Christian unity in a divided world. They are taking part, unilaterally and in company with other churches in dialogues and conversations with Roman Catholics, Orthodox and other Christian traditions. In many lands they too have been involved in discussions, plans and schemes for Christian unity, which in South India and in the United Church in CANADA have already come to fruition.

These, then, are the two marks of the last half century. The growth to autonomy and independence of churches in Australia, NEW ZEALAND, South Africa and in one African state after another, resulting in a new partnership between the churches of the Methodist family, the usefulness and fruit of which has still to be explored. And second, the call to unity, which faces Methodist churches in many lands and continents. Methodists are aware that this brings problems about their future relations with one another: they realize that it is important to take counsel with one another about these things, and to keep one another informed about common problems and opportunities. But they know that their loyalty to Christ and to His one Church, and their common dedication in mission to one world must always be the over-riding consideration. In His providence God raised up the Methodist people: He has greatly blessed them in their journeyings through

two and a half centuries. They take heart from these things, and go forward on their providential way.

Bibliographical note: The Methodist bibliography published in this *Encyclopedia,* as well as the reference citations under many institutions and biographies, may be referred to for a closer study of Methodism at any point of interest.

E. GORDON RUPP

METHODISM IN THE UNITED STATES.

THE METHODIST EPISCOPAL CHURCH, 1784-1939

The beginning of American Methodism is closely associated with immigrants arriving shortly before the War for Independence. PHILIP EMBURY, an Irish exhorter and local preacher of German descent, preached in NEW YORK in 1766. In 1767 the New York Methodists formed a society, and in the same year they were joined by THOMAS WEBB, a British army captain then stationed in America who had been converted by JOHN WESLEY. Webb extended his preaching to PHILADELPHIA (1767 or 1768), Long Island and DELAWARE, and formed societies in NEW JERSEY. Embury and the generous Captain Webb are known, respectively, as the founders of Methodism in New York and Philadelphia. To come to the distinctive character of American Methodism, however, one has to appreciate the kind and extent of Methodist activity in the area south of Philadelphia.

Methodist work in America may well have been underway before 1766. ROBERT STRAWBRIDGE quite possibly had been preaching in MARYLAND before 1763. This independent-minded Irishman made preaching journeys into Delaware, VIRGINIA and PENNSYLVANIA. He organized societies, built a preaching house, raised up preachers, and in time administered the sacraments among his followers, who welcomed his ministrations and strongly supported him later when Wesley's assistants took him to task for his irregularities.

Three young men converted in the wave of evangelistic activity initiated under Strawbridge and his followers were outstanding among the first native Methodist preachers. These were PHILIP GATCH, WILLIAM WATTERS, and FREEBORN GARRETTSON. Each was born and reared in the general vicinity of BALTIMORE, and each had been a communicant of the Church of England.

To the names of these independent lay preachers must be added that of the young Irish itinerant, ROBERT WILLIAMS, who came with the reluctant approval of Wesley. Wesley was irritated by Williams' preaching against the clergy and made him promise to work in subordination to the appointed missionaries. Williams' preaching in the parish of the friendly evangelical clergyman, DEVEREUX JARRATT in tidewater Virginia, was to mark the real beginning of the Methodist revival in that commonwealth. Even ASBURY was later to pay tribute to this "son of thunder," who came to be known as the founder of Virginia Methodism. But Williams, like Strawbridge, was to create problems for Wesley's assistants.

The Question of Discipline. Those who heard the Methodist itinerants probably found nothing strange in the continuation of a pattern of freelance preaching already made familiar by the revivals of the time. Wesley, however, would have no truck with freelance preaching which left nothing more behind than "a rope of sand." If there were to be Methodist converts in North America, Wesley held, they should be under the same rigid connectional discipline that he maintained in England.

Consequently, at the British conference of 1769 Wesley appointed RICHARD BOARDMAN and JOSEPH PILMORE as missionaries to America. Two years later Francis Asbury and RICHARD WRIGHT came out as missionaries. They were followed in 1773 by THOMAS RANKIN and GEORGE SHADFORD.

Wesley looked to Rankin to correct the defective discipline of his predecessors. Rankin's first conference, convened six weeks after his arrival in Philadelphia, laid bare the problems confronting the missionaries. Neither Strawbridge nor Williams was present. Moreover, of Methodists now reported "in society" (1,160), the preponderance were in those very areas to the south dominated by the two Irish preachers, Strawbridge and Williams, and their followers. However, the preachers attending Rankin's conference agreed that the American preachers and societies should be under the authority of Wesley, and that acceptance of the English *Minutes* (the LARGE MINUTES) as the standard of doctrines and discipline should be the basis of the connectional fellowship.

Rankin continued the yearly meeting of the preachers, but after the 1777 conference, with the War for Independence on, he returned to England, as had all the other missionaries save Asbury. With the outbreak of war, suspicion toward the Methodists had increased because of their relation to the church, and because of Wesley's Toryism and the pacifism of some of the preachers and members. Most Methodists, however, moved toward an alignment with the Baptists and the Presbyterians in opposition to the established Church.

By 1777 the number of Methodists in society had increased fivefold to 6,968, with the bulk of the membership still in the south. Only 488 members were reported from Pennsylvania, New Jersey and New York. When the preachers met in 1778 at LEESBURG, the first yearly conference on Virginia soil, Asbury was already in seclusion at THOMAS WHITE's in Delaware, and the young native preachers appeared in unquestioned control of the movement.

The Ordinance Controversy. The encounter between the sectarian native movement and the old-plan Methodism reached a crisis in the Fluvanna conference of 1779. Noting that the Episcopal establishment was now dissolved, the preachers established a presbytery from among their own number, accepted ordination from each other, and began to administer the sacraments. Meanwhile, Asbury, operating from his base in Delaware, undertook to win over the dissidents and preserve what he could of old-plan Methodism. Assuming *de facto* the office of "general assistant," he was able to muster sufficient support to heal the schism; and the Virginia preachers agreed to await further direction from Wesley. In the four years intervening before the arrival of Wesley's authoritative emissaries, Asbury not only assured the survival of much of the Wesleyan heritage but also laid foundations that, as it turned out, greatly facilitated the transition to an independent church. By 1784 the minutes showed 14,988 members and eighty-four itinerants, and Asbury had emerged as leader of the movement.

On Sept. 1, 1784, John Wesley, assisted by two other presbyters of the Church of England, THOMAS COKE and JAMES CREIGHTON, ordained as deacon RICHARD WHATCOAT and THOMAS VASEY. On the next day the two were ordained elders, and Wesley, assisted by Creighton and Whatcoat, "set apart" Thomas Coke as "superintendent" for America. The three emissaries, bearing Wesley's instructions, arrived in New York on November 3.

What Wesley envisaged for American Methodism is not clear. In his letter to "Our brethren in America" he mentioned "a little sketch" he had drawn up in response to the request of "some thousands of the inhabitants of these States" for his advice. (Apparently the "little sketch" was either lost or destroyed. A reasonable assumption is that what actually happened in the CHRISTMAS CONFERENCE soon to be held did not conform altogether to Wesley's intentions.) "I conceive myself at full liberty," Wesley's letter continued, "as I violate no order and invade no man's right by appointing and sending labourers into the harvest. I have accordingly appointed Dr. Coke and Mr. Francis Asbury to be Joint Superintendents over our brethren in North America; as also Richard Whatcoat and Thomas Vasey to act as elders among them, by baptizing and administering the Lord's Supper. And I have prepared a Liturgy little differing from that of the Church of England (I think, the best constituted National Church in the world), which I advise all the travelling preachers to use on the Lord's Day in all the congregations, reading the Litany only on Wednesdays and Fridays and praying extempore on all other days. I also advise the elders to administer the Supper of the Lord on every Lord's Day." (J. Wesley, *Letters*, vii, 237-39.)

Wesley explained the difficulties attendant upon his further attempts to persuade the English bishops to ordain ministers for America. Even if the bishops should ordain, their action would entangle the Americans with both the state and the English hierarchy. Besides, Wesley had long been persuaded "that bishops and presbyters are the same order, and consequently have the same right to ordain." He considered, therefore, that the American Methodists were "now at full liberty simply to follow the Scriptures and the Primitive Church." (*Ibid.*)

A third document sent over by Wesley was his Letter Testimonial of Coke's ordination. (J. Wesley, *Journal*, vii, facing 16.) In it he referred to the desire of the Americans "to continue under my care and still adhere to the doctrines and discipline of the Church of England" and to receive the sacraments "according to the usage of the said Church." This document, which came to light only after Coke's death, does not in itself support the view that Wesley intended that the Americans form an independent church.

The Christmas Conference. Coke first met Asbury at BARRATT's CHAPEL in Delaware on Sunday, Nov. 14, 1784. Asbury wrote in his *Journal:* "The design of organizing the Methodists into an Independent Episcopal Church was opened to the preachers present, and it was agreed to call a General Conference, to meet at Baltimore the ensuing Christmas." (F. Asbury, *Journal and Letters*, I, 471-72.) Freeborn Garrettson was dispatched to summon all the preachers. Some sixty or more were present when the conference convened at LOVELY LANE CHAPEL on December 24. Wesley could hardly have understood the mood of the Americans at the end of their long conflict with England, nor the extent to which the ties with English Methodism had been weakened. The American preachers were of a mind to make their own decisions. (See CHRISTMAS CONFERENCE.)

Asbury noted that all things were determined by majority vote. After the reading of Wesley's letter the preachers agreed to form themselves into an Episcopal Church and adopted the name proposed by JOHN DICKINS—The Methodist Episcopal Church. Asbury had declined to accept the office of Superintendent merely on the basis of Wesley's appointment, but both he and Coke were unanimously elected superintendents by the conference. Assisting in Asbury's consecration at Asbury's invitation, was PHILIP WILLIAM OTTERBEIN, later to become a founder of the UNITED BRETHREN CHURCH. Designation of the two superintendents by vote of the conference symbolized the new constitutional base, yet to be perfected, of the American church. It marked the transfer of the personal power of Mr. Wesley into the hands of the American preachers assembled in conference.

The form of *Discipline* adopted at Baltimore in 1784 was heavily dependent upon Wesley's *Large Minutes,* the alterations reflecting the changed situation of the American Methodists. The conference adopted twenty-four ARTICLES OF RELIGION which Wesley had adapted from the Thirty-nine Articles of Religion of the English Church, and added an Article entitled *Of the Rulers of the United States of America.* The conference also adopted *The Sunday Service,* the liturgy sent over by Wesley. Although *The Sunday Service* was, after a few years, to fall into desuetude, its importance as a bridge between American Methodism and the Church of England, not to mention the whole Western Latin tradition, cannot be overemphasized. In both doctrine and liturgy American Methodists were thus held in the great Christian tradition.

Other actions taken by the Christmas Conference included the decision to establish COKESBURY COLLEGE; a stringent rule prohibiting preachers from drinking intoxicating liquors (except as medicine); and the acceptance of a detailed plan "to extirpate the abomination of slavery."

There is evidence that not all the preachers were pleased with what was done at Baltimore. THOMAS HASKINS, for instance, felt that more consideration should have been given to the opinion of the mother church. Indeed, three leaders of the American clergy met with Coke and Asbury after the Christmas Conference had convened, and discussed with them a plan whereby the Methodists might retain organic relation with what was to be The Protestant Episcopal Church, plans for which were then only in the discussion stage. But the Methodist superintendents were not responsive to these informal overtures.

Organization Still Incomplete. With adjournment of the founding conference the preachers could present the new Methodist Episcopal Church to their constituency as apostolic in character, founded upon scripture, loosed from its questionable connections, no longer a group of "societies," but a church firmly dedicated to its divine vocation. In his sermon at the ordination of Asbury, Thomas Coke said to the new superintendent: "[God] will carry his gospel under thy direction from sea to sea, yea, perhaps, from one end of the Continent to the other." (T. Coke, *Sermon . . . at Ordination of . . . Asbury,* 22.)

The new church, however, was not yet able to give a clear definition of its corporate structure. Its organization remained tentative and partial. Its most distinctive structures were to emerge in the next generation as a means of controlling and extending the phenomenal expansion begun in the 1780's. Expansion was to push toward the West, the North and the South. In 1784 Asbury was traveling in southwest Pennsylvania, and by 1790 he was in KENTUCKY. In 1801 there were eight circuits in the

PITTSBURGH District and nine in the Kentucky District.

In 1788 Freeborn Garrettson presided over six circuits between New Rochelle (New York) and Lake Champlain. In 1789 JESSE LEE had begun his work in New England, and WILLIAM LOSEE was ranging "at large" in CANADA. Three years later missionaries were at work on the New York frontiers and near what is now Kingston, Ontario.

Asbury appointed a preacher to "range" in GEORGIA in 1785, and the next year he sent HENRY WILLIS to "Holston." By 1787 three circuits had been formed in Georgia. Most often the conference itinerants probing the frontier found that they had been preceded by local preachers who had already organized societies. In its first quarter-century the new Church increased the number of circuits seven-fold, to 324, and the number of members eleven-fold, to over 163,000.

The office of PRESIDING ELDER took form in these early years of expansion. The duty of the twelve elders elected and ordained at the Christmas Conference was to be present at all the quarterly meetings of the circuits under their charge in order to administer the sacraments. In 1786 the *Discipline* added to the elder's duties the exercising "within his own district, during the absence of the superintendents, all the powers invested in them for the government of the Church." The first GENERAL CONFERENCE, in 1792, employed the term "presiding elder" for the first time, thus distinguishing between preachers, ordained ELDERS, and those of their number bearing special administrative responsibilities.

Conference System Develops. The ANNUAL CONFERENCE as such developed after considerable experimentation. The yearly meeting of the preachers was basic in the Methodist discipline, but the widening deployment of preachers made a single yearly meeting impracticable. Asbury met the preachers in three sections in 1786 and 1787. Thereafter the sections increased and varied in number from year to year. These "district" conferences, as they were called, "collectively, or in the final session, were competent to exercise in any year the full legislative powers of the Church." (J. J. Tigert, *Constitutional History,* 222.)

A brief experimentation with an administrative COUNCIL was an attempt to meet the need for a centralized structure to overcome the awkward problem of processing legislation through the several "district" conferences. Asbury wished to avoid calling or depending upon a general conference of the preachers. The Council failed to win general acceptance, however, and after only two sessions, in 1789 and 1790, it was quietly abandoned. Turning next to his less-favored alternative, Asbury called the preachers to meet in 1792 in what was to be the first General Conference. At its second meeting, in 1796, the General Conference fixed the boundaries of six Annual Conferences which were to take the place of the various sectional conferences. By 1804 the Annual Conference had assumed its distinctive features as the self-contained ecclesiastical unit in which the preachers held their membership, in which appointments were made, and in which the work of the denomination had its regional organization. The Annual Conference thus became basic to the whole organization of the church as the *Discipline* of the present United Methodist Church declares it to be. (Constitution of The United Methodist Church, Division Two, Section vii, Art. II.)

The first General Conference was composed of all the preachers in full connection and was regarded as holding in itself the full power of the church. It bound itself not to modify any received rule of Methodism without a majority of two-thirds. It resolved to meet every four years. When, four years later (in 1796), the General Conference defined the Annual Conference, the basic conference system of the Methodist Episcopal Church was complete.

Embraced within this system was the QUARTERLY CONFERENCE, which was the organizational focus of the connection on the circuit level. Even before the arrival of Wesley's missionaries, the lay preachers in the Chesapeake area had conducted "quarterly meeting conferences," and the first American *Discipline* assumed the continuation of the quarterly meeting as a part of the Methodist economy. More stable in operation than the local society, the Quarterly Conference consisted of the preacher in charge, all the local preachers and class leaders, and the circuit stewards. Presiding over its sessions was the Elder, who functioned as "eyes, ears and mouth" of the episcopacy. The Quarterly Conference was the occasion on which the Methodist people, especially in the newer sections, had opportunity to experience most completely their participation in the church. Inasmuch as the Presiding Elder then in charge was often the only ordained minister present, many Methodists found the HOLY COMMUNION only at the Quarterly Conferences. Since the Conferences were occasions of much preaching, they also became centers of revival activity, and, beginning about 1802, the summer quarterly conference often coincided with a CAMP MEETING. From time to time the *Book of Discipline* assigned additional administrative and judicial functions to the Quarterly Conference, but it was not until 1848 that a separate section of *The Discipline* was to deal with the conference.

Period of Controversy. Controversies during this period left their mark upon the church. JAMES O'KELLY challenged Asbury on his exercise of the episcopal power. Strongly imbued with revolutionary ideology and popular rationalism, O'Kelly appealed to scripture in his opposition to episcopacy. He vigorously opposed the Administrative Council, and gained the support of Coke and Jesse Lee in pressing Asbury to call the first General Conference. When the Conference met, O'Kelly introduced a proposal that a preacher dissatisfied with his appointment might appeal to the conference for another than the one fixed by the bishop. The conference failed to support this further attack upon the bishop's power, and O'Kelly with several followers withdrew from the church. Against the continued preaching and writing of O'Kelly, Asbury defended the episcopacy as essential to the unity of the church and as especially necessary for the preservation of the itinerant system.

Asbury sensed another threat in the constituting of The Protestant Episcopal Church in 1789. This event, a surprise to some in view of the weakened state of the Church of England parishes in America, put an end to the hope entertained by some that the Methodists might absorb the remnants of the Established Church. More serious in the view of Methodist leaders was the loss of some preachers who accepted orders from the Episcopal bishops. The threat was dramatized in 1791 with Asbury's discovery that Coke had privately approached Episcopalians relative to bringing the Methodists into The Protestant Episcopal Church (see COKE-WHITE CORRESPONDENCE). Asbury's response was to intensify that self-conscious differentiation

from the Episcopalians which was to characterize much of American Methodism down to the present.

Against Protestant Episcopal claims of apostolic succession, the Methodists now began to emphasize their "succession" from John Wesley, "the most respectable divine since the primitive ages, if not since the time of the apostles." (R. Emory, *History of Discipline*, 282.) These words may seem strange in view of Wesley's known disapproval of the American Methodists' use of the designation "bishop" in the place of "superintendent" and in view also of American resentment toward Wesley's attempts in 1787 to have Richard Whatcoat and Freeborn Garrettson elected superintendents.

Because the American preachers did not fully trust Coke's administration, the whole burden of supervision had fallen upon Asbury. Coke spent little time in America, his function being restricted largely to presiding at conferences. (See THOMAS COKE AND AMERICAN METHODISM.) After his departure in 1806 he was not to return to America. Richard Whatcoat was elected bishop in 1800, in his sixty-fifth year. With Whatcoat's death in 1806 and the final departure of Coke in the same year, Asbury, himself now in declining health, became the sole episcopal administrator. The General Conference of 1808 provided some relief for Asbury by electing WILLIAM McKENDREE to the episcopacy. McKendree, already prominent because of his work as Presiding Elder in the WESTERN CONFERENCE, became the first native-born bishop and was to carry on strongly the Asburian episcopacy.

The Delegated General Conference. The 1808 General Conference also adopted legislation that came to be regarded as the constitution of the Church. Until that year a simple majority in the General Conference might have radically altered or abolished any Methodist standard. Not only that, but factors of distance had made for unequal representation of the Annual Conferences in the General Conference. In 1804, for instance, three of the seven Annual Conferences—Philadelphia, Baltimore and Virginia—because of their proximity to the traditional seat of the General Conference, supplied over three-fourths of the conference membership.

To correct this imbalance and to provide for a safer center of power, it was determined that the General Conference should become a delegated body, operating under carefully defined restrictions. This was accomplished, and the delegated conference was forbidden to change the Articles of Religion or the GENERAL RULES; to do away with the episcopacy or the general itinerant superintendency; to do away with the right of trial and appeal; or to divert the profits of the BOOK CONCERN or CHARTERED FUND to other than the benevolent objects to which they had been devoted. Strict procedures were defined in time for altering these "RESTRICTIVE RULES," as they came to be called.

Bishop McKendree's election symbolized the new importance of the West. The great camp meetings of the first years of the new century soon became largely a Methodist enterprise, and a "harvest time" for the frontier preachers. The whole Methodist system was remarkably adapted for expansion in the new sections. The Methodist bishop, not a diocesan but a general superintendent, directed the deployment of a corps of itinerant preachers, establishing circuits, expanding circuits into districts and districts into new annual conferences. PETER CARTWRIGHT was typical of the rugged group of Presiding Elders, directly responsible to the bishops, commanding the cadres of itinerants, training young preachers on the job, and representing all the connectional interests of the church. ROBERT R. ROBERTS, elected bishop in 1816, the first married bishop of the church, established his home in INDIANA, thus becoming the first bishop to itinerate from a permanent base in the West.

The message of the itinerant preacher was congenial to the hardy character of the frontiersman; and Methodist literature (circulated by every preacher), and Methodist singing served the purposes of the expanding revival. For the Methodists the revivalism of America's Second Great Awakening was converted to a system of expansion, subservient to the hierarchical organization of the church. Camp meetings moved from the frontiers back to the older sections of the East, and, with the growth of towns and cities, became the "protracted meetings" of the settled communities. Philip Schaff, young German scholar who had migrated to America, observed at mid-century that the Methodist movement had "next to Puritanism, the greatest influence on the general religious life . . . . It has uncommon energy and activity, and enjoys an organization eminently fitted for general enterprises and systematic, successful cooperation."

The Great Expansion. The years between the death of Asbury in 1816 and the outbreak of the Civil War marked the heyday of Methodist expansion in America. A new generation of circuit riders moved out in advance of the Pony Express, and before there was a solid line of states, Methodist conferences reached to the Pacific. JASON LEE preached the first Methodist sermon west of the Rockies in 1834. In 1837 MARTIN RUTER entered TEXAS. ISAAC OWEN was appointed to CALIFORNIA in 1853, and in the following year WLLIAM H. GOODE entered Kansas. Annual Conferences already organized in the great central valley served as bases for the new drive into the Far West. This same period saw the beginnings of Methodist foreign mission work in Africa (1833), South America (1836), CHINA (1847), and INDIA (1856). There were also special appointments for work with Indians and immigrant groups. In 1864 three German conferences were organized, consolidating Methodist missions serving the many Germans who had come to America.

A wave of benevolent interest and activity, drawing support from the revivals and contributing to further expansion, now spread over America. Following Asbury's death, a new generation of younger preachers, including such men as NATHAN BANGS, WILBUR FISK and Martin Ruter, moved into the leadership of the various benevolent enterprises and contributed to the building of new institutions. The General Conference of 1820 officially committed the denomination to the support of education; and the two decades following came to be known as the great college building era of the church. By 1865 Methodists had started schools in thirty-three of the thirty-four states. In the 1840's and 1850's JOHN DEMPSTER, though encountering much opposition, stirred an interest in theological education. To Dempster belongs credit for the founding of two theological schools, the Methodist General Biblical Institute at Concord, NEW HAMPSHIRE, and GARRETT BIBLICAL INSTITUTE at Evanston, Illinois.

Zion's Herald, appearing in 1823, was the first of a distinguished line of weekly religious journals. By the opening of the Civil War the General Conference had authorized nine *Advocates* to serve various geographical areas from New York to California. (See ADVOCATES, CHRISTIAN.)

Methodists in general did not support the large number of interdenominational benevolent societies growing up in the first quarter of the century. They were apprehensive of the control of the so-called "benevolent empire" by the older churches, and suspicious of what they considered its Calvinist orientation. Moreover, Methodists shared with the frontier churches a certain resentment toward missionary and benevolent enterprises directed from the Eastern seaboard. Consequently, Methodists preferred their own benevolent societies. A Methodist Tract Society was founded in 1817, and in 1820 the General Conference endorsed the Methodist MISSIONARY SOCIETY. The Methodist SUNDAY SCHOOL UNION was established in 1827, and the Methodist Bible Society in 1828. DANIEL P. KIDDER, elected corresponding secretary of the Sunday School Union in 1844, laid the foundations for the Christian Education program of the Church.

Ferment and Division. The M. E. Church could not avoid the swell of religious and social ferment and the sectarian controversy that swept over the country in this period. Because of the structure of Methodist polity, most of the controversy within the church eventually took the form of criticism of the episcopal system. Agitation for the election of presiding elders and lay representation in the annual conferences eventuated in the schism of 1830 and the organization of The METHODIST PROTESTANT CHURCH. Deep cultural differences contributed to the divisions involving the slavery question and racial attitudes. Discrimination against Negro Methodists in Philadelphia and New York led to the founding of the AFRICAN METHODIST EPISCOPAL ZION CHURCH (1820). Radical antislavery Methodists founded the Wesleyan Connection (now designated the WESLEYAN METHODIST CHURCH), in 1843; and the largest rupture in the history of American Methodism occurred with the constituting of the METHODIST EPISCOPAL CHURCH, SOUTH, after the General Conference of 1844.

A revival of interest in the Wesleyan teaching on CHRISTIAN PERFECTION in the 1830's soon led to an unfortunate polarization in the church between ardent defenders of the renewed form of the doctrine, and those who considered the emphasis to be divisive. Defenders of HOLINESS teachings made common cause with a growing number who feared for the loss of old and familiar ways in the church. The FREE METHODIST CHURCH emerged (1860) out of the holiness controversy.

Factors other than the slavery question contributed to the tragic division of 1844. Chief among these was a difference in interpretation of the nature of the episcopal office. With the moderates in the church no longer able to set a course between the more extreme parties, deeply rooted hostilities flared into the open in the General Conference of 1844, which at length agreed upon a PLAN OF SEPARATION to be followed in the event of separation. Southern leaders moved at once to lay plans for a separate church, and in May 1846, the first General Conference of the Methodist Episcopal Church, South, met in PETERSBURG, Virginia. Great bitterness ensued, particularly in the border conferences. The whole course of events subsequent to the 1844 General Conference gave rise to such a wave of revulsion in the Northern conferences that the 1848 General Conference voted to repudiate the Plan of Separation, which both sides had four years before considered fair and equitable. The act of repudiation added to the heritage of bitterness affecting relations between the two churches long after the conclusion of the Civil War.

The Civil War Years. At the outbreak of the Civil War, each of the two Churches produced by the division in 1844 was the largest and the wealthiest denomination in its own geographical area. Both churches now supported their governments and turned to the work of ministering to their troops, supplying chaplains and providing Bibles and tracts. The great revival fervor that had stirred the nation immediately before the war moved into the army camps in both North and South.

The Northern Church suffered far less dislocation from military operations. Its institutions were stronger and its resources more ample. Northern bishops, editors and preachers set about mobilizing public opinion, encouraging recruitment and raising funds to support both Methodist and interdenominational ministries in camp and field. The church's extensive wartime activity reflected and encouraged a growing sense of responsibility on the part of the church for the moral quality of the whole of public life. This understanding of the scope of the church's responsibility was not altogether new, but it found forceful expression in new leadership emerging during the war, represented by men such as Bishop MATTHEW SIMPSON and the wartime denominational editors. Bishop Simpson, who enjoyed wide contact with political leaders, especially with Abraham Lincoln, and swayed multitudes with his oratory, also represented a new concern among Methodists that their church be fully recognized in the ecclesiastical affairs of the nation. *Harper's Weekly* referred to the Methodists in 1866 (Oct. 6) as "the predominant ecclesiastical fact of the nation." In contrast to the disorganization, demoralization and impoverishment of the Southern Church, the Northern Church came to the end of the war with its institutions intact and its leadership steering it into the mainstream of American political life.

Mission to the South. Cultural imperialism, ecclesiastical conquest and sincere motives of compassion were strangely mixed in the mission of the Northern Church to the South after the war. Bitterness, resentment and violence met the often heroic ministries of Northern Methodists entering the South to assist with the education of the emancipated Negro slaves. Northern bishops looked upon the South as missionary territory. Northern Methodist expansion began behind the Federal lines in 1863 and pressed forward as military operations opened the way, with Northern preachers proselyting freely and laying claim to church property. Ten new Annual Conferences of the Methodist Episcopal Church were organized in the South by 1869.

Work with freed slaves began in 1862. Methodists at first cooperated with various interdenominational organizations concerned with relief of the freemen; but in 1866 the Society was supporting twenty-nine institutions for Negroes and sixteen academies for whites.

Changes in Methodism following the Civil War paralleled in many respects similar changes in the nation. Both the church and the nation responded to the movement and growth of the population, to radical alterations in social and political life, and to profound changes in the intellectual climate. The forces of industrialization and urbanization and the flood of immigrants, the rise of a boisterously competitive capitalism, the rapid increase of wealth, and the stirrings of labor brought sometimes violent social conflict, political corruption, social stratification, and the problems of the slum. There was need for the

consolidation of institutions and the forming of new structures to cope with the growing complexities of life. The nation faced increasing involvement in foreign relations. All these developments had their parallels in the growth of Methodism after 1865. Young, aggressive, jealous of its new-found status and confident in its future, the Methodist Episcopal Church now entered into a period of "rugged denominationalism." The CENTENNIAL OF AMERICAN METHODISM celebrated in 1866, was the first church-wide program to raise funds for planned improvement and expansion, and appropriated Methodist experience gained in fund-raising for benevolent causes during the war. It symbolized the transition to a new way of doing things. The Centennial campaign raised nearly $9 million, a large part of which was directed toward education.

Missions and Church Extension. Both branches of the Church had continued their missionary interests following the division of 1844, but it was not until after the war that organization and financial support was provided for an expanding missionary enterprise. In the last decades of the century, missionary activity was integrated into the whole life of the church. Machinery for the administration of missionary endeavors followed roughly parallel lines in the Northern and Southern churches. Geographically speaking, American Methodism had for the most part completed its overseas expansion by the end of World War I. In the same period the church established a program of national missions to serve within the borders of the nation and its dependencies.

American Methodism committed half of its missionaries to its two largest mission fields, CHINA and INDIA, where work had begun before the war. Methodist missionaries entered JAPAN in 1873 and began work in KOREA in 1885. From its base in India the Church established missions in Southeast Asia. Methodist missions expanded steadily in Latin America after the Civil War and, after 1885, in various parts of Africa. By 1921 American-related Methodists in Europe outnumbered those in Latin America and Africa; but the earlier American missionaries in Europe were usually nationals who had returned to their homeland.

As expansion continued the Church developed new patterns of organization for overseas work. In 1858 the Northern Church elected FRANCIS BURNS the first of its missionary bishops. In 1868 the General Conference gave all former Mission Annual Conferences the status of Annual Conferences. Growing self-sufficiency of the overseas mission was registered in the rise of the CENTRAL CONFERENCES (authorized by General Conference in 1884), the affiliated autonomous churches (e.g., BRAZIL, 1930) and the independent Methodist churches (e.g., Japan, 1907).

Facing the surge of growth in newly opening areas in the West, the Northern Church organized in 1864 its General Extension Society, chiefly to raise capital funds to lend to new congregations. Under leadership of the colorful C. C. "Chaplain" McCABE, the Extension Society (see CHURCH EXTENSION) was an important factor in establishing Methodism in the prairie and Rocky Mountain states. In the wake of the swelling tide of immigration, work with various non-Anglo-Saxon groups rapidly increased. In 1907 the church created the Board of Home Missions and Church Extension. Organization of the Department of City Work (1912), and the Department of

Rural Work (1916) reflected the growing importance of specialized ministries.

Language Conferences. Methodism was significantly enriched by its language conferences (as they were often called), ministering to Germans, Swedes, Norwegians and Danes in the United States. Most effective was the work among the Germans. An outstanding German leader, himself an immigrant, was WILLIAM NAST, who became the prototype of the Methodist leader engaged in language work. By 1915 there were ten M. E. German language conferences. The first of four Swedish language conferences was organized in 1877. The Norwegian Conference (later changed to NORWEGIAN-DANISH) was organized in 1880. Bilingual missions were developed also among Chinese, Japanese and Mexicans in the 1870's, and among Italians in the last decade of the century. By 1924 some 740 effective pastors were engaged in foreign language work. The last of the language conferences was dissolved in the early 1940's.

Women's agencies for the support of missions made their appearance shortly after the Civil War. The WOMAN'S FOREIGN MISSIONARY SOCIETY was formed in BOSTON in 1869 to support women missionaries and national Christian teachers. The WOMAN'S HOME MISSIONARY SOCIETY was organized in 1880. The General Conference officially recognized the DEACONESS movement in 1888, and by 1920 the Northern Church had almost 900 deaconesses.

Christian Education. In 1858 the General Conference committed the Church to the religious instruction and nurture of children preparatory to reception into full membership. This official stand, taken after several years of debate over the significance of Christian nurture prior to conversion, led to more clarity of thought and consistency of practice in reference to the Church's task in the nurture of its children.

The most revolutionary development in Christian education began during the term (1868-1888) of JOHN H. VINCENT as secretary and editor of the Sunday School Union. Vincent's administration brought radical improvements in teacher training and the refinement of methods, and introduced such modern things as age grouping and building plans adapted for religious instruction. Vincent sought to introduce many of the standards and practices of public education. By 1876 almost every Methodist Church had a Sunday School, and the number of students was reported to exceed the number of church members. Contributing to this growth was the multiplication of printed materials furnished for teachers and students. Methodist literature constantly increased in diversity and adequacy, and in general was popular, well-balanced, and adapted to the needs of the churches.

The Methodist educational program also reflected the wide-spread interest in the development of youth leadership. Youth organizations appeared in various conferences. In 1889 several of these organizations were absorbed in the EPWORTH LEAGUE, which was to become the official youth organization in both the Northern and Southern churches. As Methodist work expanded among college students, WESLEY FOUNDATIONS appeared on the campuses of state and non-Methodist institutions. By 1920 student work at state colleges and universities had extended to fifty centers.

Publishing Interests. For a brief period after the war both the Publishing House of the M. E. Church, South and the BOOK CONCERN of the M. E. Church suffered from mismanagement and questionable business practices. However, with the appointment of more laymen to management positions, and the introduction of improved administrative practices, the publishing enterprises soon entered a period of prosperity. With the marked increase in demand for Sunday School materials, new sales records were established, additional buildings were acquired and modern equipment installed. In the early 1900's the Book Concern entered into cooperative projects with other Protestant publishers. The Graded Lesson Series, introduced in 1908, enjoyed surprising popularity. Of continuing significance for the health of the publishing venture as well as the moral and spiritual improvement of the Methodist people was the system of distribution, with every minister continuing to serve as local agent of the Book Concern.

Methodist editors in the latter half of the nineteenth century rose to high places of influence in the life of the church. Most of them plain and self-made men, they were fiercely loyal to the denomination. Three war-time editors were elected bishops in 1864. After the war Methodist editors wrestled with most of the social problems of their day. Repeated attempts were made to merge the various *Advocates*. Merger was finally accomplished in 1932 with the establishing of a single national weekly (see ADVOCATE, CHRISTIAN) with six regional editions.

With the founding of the COKESBURY PRESS by the Southern Church and the ABINGDON PRESS in the Northern Church, the two larger churches countered a decline in the sale of strictly denominational books with expansion into the general religious field.

Higher Education. Of some 200 colleges established by Methodists before 1865, only thirty-four continued to exist up to 1939. Limited finances, poor location and internal dissensions contributed to this high mortality. Methodist colleges founded after the Civil War reflected, on the whole, a much sounder condition. Although enrollments were greatly reduced in the war years, none of the Northern colleges closed. Postwar expansion was confined largely to the North and the West. Methodist schools were established in some western states before the admission of these states into the union. This period also saw the beginning of the Methodist universities, only NORTHWESTERN having started before the war.

Many of the Negro institutions established in the South were at first hardly more than primary schools or academies. The Negro schools of collegiate grade, strengthened by the gifts of philanthropists and later by foundation grants, pioneered in training ministers, teachers, physicians and other leaders. Efforts to upgrade Methodist institutions serving Negro youth were intensified after 1920. Although educational work among white people in the South was more limited, four colleges had been firmly established by the time of Union in 1939. Contributing immeasurably to the improvement of academic and business practices of Methodist schools was the work of the UNIVERSITY SENATE, organized in 1892.

The scope of educational and professional concern in the Methodist institutions was constantly broadened even as their strictly Methodist character tended to diminish. In certain cases there was a loosening of ties between the church and its institutions. At the time of unification, however, Methodism's list of schools was considered the strongest of all the Protestant groups. The three Methodist branches brought into their union in 1939 nine universities, nine theological schools, sixty-seven colleges and twenty-seven junior colleges. (See EDUCATION IN METHODISM.)

The creation of theological schools had profound implications for the changing character of the church and its ministry. It was only after the founding of two such schools that the General Conference, in 1856, gave formal approval to theological education of its ministers. In these earlier years no formal academic training was required of candidates for the traveling ministry. The historic four-year Conference COURSE OF STUDY was considered adequate preparation. Although theological education was theoretically the concern of the whole church, the theological schools resulted from efforts independent of the General Conference. As the church matured there was increasing demand for a ministry equipped with broad theological training. Even so, as late as 1939 less than half the ministers entering Annual Conferences on trial had professional training in theological schools.

A Changing Constituency. The story of Methodism after the Civil War was, in the popular sense of the term, a success story. Success led to considerable complacency. There was little evidence before 1880, either in the church press or in official pronouncements, of the questioning of conventional attitudes toward economic and social questions. This was Methodism's age of affluence, and affluence was generally taken as confirmation of the rightness of the social order that produced it. The system magnified the traditional virtues of thrift, sobriety and hard work, the same virtues that enabled Methodists to climb up the economic and educational ladder.

Theodore Roosevelt, then the running mate of President WILLIAM MCKINLEY, a Methodist, and later President himself, spoke "these warming words" of "the most representative church in America. . ." at the M. E. General Conference in 1900: "The Methodist Church plays a great part in many lands; and yet I think I can say that in none other has it played so great and peculiar a part as here in the United States. Its history is indissolubly interwoven with the history of our country for the six score years since the constitutional convention made us really a nation. Methodism in America entered on its period of rapid growth just about the time of Washington's first presidency. Its essential democracy, its fiery and restless energy of spirit, and the wide play that it gave to individual initiative, all tended to make it peculiarly congenial to a hardy and virile folk, democratic to the core, prizing individual independence above all earthly possessions, and engaged in the rough and stern work of conquering a continent."

All the while, the constituency of the church was rapidly changing. Their increasing middle-class orientation made Methodists less able to understand and identify with the poor. The church found itself more and more alienated from the working classes and especially from those immigrant groups that were not responsive to Methodism's standards of conduct. Moreover, the style of Methodist piety was also undergoing alteration. Among the old familiar ways abandoned in many places were the class meeting, probationary membership, the enforcement of discipline, revivals and camp meetings, and simplicity in dress, worship and congregational life.

A revival of the Holiness movement had followed the war, and many conservatives in the church, including some bishops and editors, supported that movement, thinking that its teachings and the earnestness that it inspired might preserve Methodism against the erosion of affluence, urban culture and theological liberalism. The Holiness movement, which possessed some affinity with the romantic idealism of the period, turned many of its converts into evangelistic and missionary work and various forms of social service. Unfortunately, however, a more radical wing of the Holiness revival introduced fanatical and divisive tendencies which by 1900 resulted in the loss of many preachers and members to scores of independent Holiness congregations and various sectarian groups. The chief complaint against the more radical Holiness leaders was their criticism of episcopal authority, and their determination to keep their widespread activities independent of the bishops' control.

During the 1880's there were increasing signs that the church was awakening to its responsibility toward the larger social, economic and political problems. The episcopal address of 1888 devoted a long section to the problems of labor. If the Methodist interest was tardy, its growth was to be vigorous and extensive. The SOCIAL CREED, adopted in 1908, gave expression to the Methodist conscience for the ills of modern society. Shortly, the social emphasis was registered in the teaching materials of the Sunday schools, in the Conference Course of Study and the seminary curricula.

Methodist confrontation with social change was encouraged by many of the church's teachers of theology, who sought to understand the new intellectual currents influencing the mind of the nation, and to state the faith in terms more relevant to the times. The questioning of old formulations brought inevitable criticism and controversy, and two professors in BOSTON UNIVERSITY were accused of heresy. However, the charges were not sustained. Neither heresy charges nor the fundamentalist-modernist controversy was to bring the disruption in Methodism that troubled some other churches. Methodist fundamentalists in the 1920's launched an attack on the books listed in the Course of Study, but the General Conference declined to act upon the charges.

Lay Representation. Laymen were first seated in the Northern and Southern General Conferences in the 1870's. After the great controversy that led to the Methodist Protestant division, "lay delegation" ideas were generally under suspicion; but by mid-century prominent laymen were supporting the cause of more democratic representation. An independent paper, *The Methodist,* championed the cause, and among the sympathizers was Bishop Matthew Simpson. The Southern Church seated an equal number of laymen and preachers in their 1870 General Conference. Two years later the Northern General Conference seated laymen on the basis of two from each Annual Conference. It was not until 1900 that laymen were admitted to the Northern General Conference in equal number with ministers.

Lay representation in the Annual Conferences came more slowly. The Southern Church introduced legislation in 1866 to seat four laymen from each district in the Annual Conferences. The Northern Church established a "Lay Conference" at the Annual Conference level in 1900, and finally admitted laymen into the Annual Conference in 1932. (See LAY DELEGATION AND LAY MOVEMENT IN METHODISM.)

The Road to Union. "The long road to Methodist union" began before the wounds of war were healed. When Bishops JANES and Simpson met with the Southern bishops in ST. LOUIS in 1869, it became clear that organic union could not be discussed until full fraternal relations had been established. The two churches exchanged fraternal delegates in 1874 and 1876, and in the latter year a Joint Commission on Fraternal Relations meeting at Cape May, N. J. (The CAPE MAY COMMISSION), drew up a "Declaration and Basis of Fraternity," which acknowledged each church as a legitimate branch of episcopal Methodism. In effect the Cape May Declaration put an end to the discussion of the Plan of Separation. It stands as the first great milestone on the road to union.

Twenty years were to pass before discussion of actual steps toward union, but other events were to make the question of union inescapable. The First and Second ECUMENICAL METHODIST CONFERENCES in 1881 and 1891 raised the question of Methodist federation. Leaders of both the Northern and the Southern churches participated in the planning for the Centennial Methodist Conference in Baltimore in 1884. Methodists in other countries were discussing union, and in 1883 the four Canadian Methodist groups united to form The Methodist Church in Canada.

A "period of federation" was initiated in 1898 with a joint meeting of commissions appointed by the Southern and Northern General Conferences. Resulting from the work of the Joint Commission on Federation were a common hymnal, catechism and order of worship.

The three churches actually came to grips with the possibility of organic union in 1910, when a commission of Methodist Protestants met with the Joint Commission on Federation. This enlarged group produced a proposal plan of union, the so-called "Chattanooga Report" of 1911, which was to be the real basis upon which unification was eventually accomplished. Methodist Protestants, feeling now that the union question was at this stage a matter to be settled by the two larger groups, stood aside to await the outcome. The two General Conferences set up a Joint Committee on Unification, which got down to work in 1916. Its first proposed constitution was turned down by both General Conferences. This plan called for six white Jurisdictional or Regional Conferences and one embracing "the work among colored people in the United States," with each Regional Conference retaining full power over distinctly regional affairs within its jurisdiction. (See JURISDICTIONAL CONFERENCES.)

Returning to its work, the Joint Commission next offered a proposal establishing one General Conference with two Regional or Jurisdictional Conferences, one composed of the Annual Conferences of the Northern Church and the other composed of the Annual Conferences of the Southern Church. Although both General Conferences in 1924 (there was a called session of the M. E. South Conference) gave approval to the plan, it failed to carry the required three-fourths of all votes cast in the Southern Annual Conferences. The final count was 4,528 in favor and 4,108 against.

But union was really closer than the disappointing vote of 1925 seemed to indicate. A younger generation, impatient with inherited resentments and more objective in their assessment of history, demanded union. The three churches, never differing in basic doctrines, had now drawn closer together in spirit and practice and in various cooperative enterprises. Above all, the men who had gained much experience and insight in long discussions in the union commissions refused to resign their hopes.

Methodist Protestant leaders, catalysts from the beginning in the union discussions, initiated the final drive toward union. After each of the three churches had

authorized a commission for union, the Joint Commission met in August 1934, and a year later completed work on the PLAN OF UNION. The Plan passed all three General Conferences and their Annual Conferences by tremendous majorities. The UNITING CONFERENCE convened in KANSAS CITY, Mo., on April 26, 1939. (For a more detailed account of the above moves, see UNIFICATION OF AMERICAN METHODISM.)

THE METHODIST CHURCH, 1939-1968

The Methodist Church born in the Uniting Conference of 1939 found itself in a world unbelievably changed, not only from that of the early Methodist fathers, but also from that in which the separated branches had come to maturity. For one thing, the population of the United States had, between 1845 and 1940, increased over sevenfold. What was more, the new problems that had challenged the churches after the Civil War seemed almost simple in comparison with the crises, convulsive and worldwide in scope, that the two decades after 1940 were to bring. Moreover, the whole Christian enterprise was in the midst of a re-examination of the statement of its message and the understanding of its mission. Therefore, the new church faced the dual task of consolidating its inherited structures and of girding itself for mission in the radically altered environment to which it would become increasingly sensitive.

The reorganization, and in some cases relocation, of general church boards and agencies called for much discussion and compromise. The new structures were more complicated and sophisticated, requiring expansion in personnel. Understandably, the early changes were in general conservative. The new jurisdictional system was a source of uneasiness. Although it offered the possibility of a desirable regional diversity, the jurisdictional system carried within it—at least in the eyes of its critics—the threat of division into regional churches. The existence of the Central Jurisdiction, which symbolized the whole struggle of the church with the problem of racial segregation, evoked a controversy that mounted in intensity until the dissolution of that structure in 1968.

Responding to growing criticism of duplication and overlapping of programs, the General Conference of 1948 ordered a comprehensive survey by a management consulting firm. Although the 1952 Conference largely rejected the Church Survey Report, several important changes resulted either directly or indirectly, from the recommendations of the survey commission. These included the establishment of a COORDINATING COUNCIL, charged with the task of review and coordination of the work of the general boards and agencies; and a COMMISSION ON PROMOTION AND CULTIVATION to promote and interpret the programs of the benevolence agencies. The emerging administrative structure placed long-term church-wide program planning under the COUNCIL OF BISHOPS, the COUNCIL OF SECRETARIES (organized in 1940) and the Coordinating Council, with the Commission on Promotion and Cultivation responsible for general promotion of the unified program. In view of the achievement of the quadrennial programs instituted in 1944 and 1948, the 1952 General Conference wrote into the law of the church a provision for continuation of these programs. The quadrennial emphases brought direction and stimulation to the work of the church and contributed to the increase in benevolent giving.

In its first two decades after unification The Methodist

Church registered steady if not dramatic expansion in all areas of its work. This was a period of unprecedented mobility in the American population, of rapid growth in the metropolitan areas and acceleration of the movement from the inner city to the suburbs. By 1960 Methodist membership had increased by a fifth, although the general population had grown by a third. The number of pastoral charges increased from approximately 21,000 to over 24,000. Most of the new congregations were in the rapidly growing suburbs. With the merger or closing of many small churches, the number of preaching places declined, but the average membership per congregation increased from 174 to 252. In these twenty years the value of local church and parsonage property quadrupled, and the over-all per capita giving to benevolences increased by 136 percent.

The Ministry. Expansion of its organizational structure after 1940 tended to magnify the connectional character of Methodism. This was reflected in developments in the offices of bishop and district superintendent—as the presiding elder of earlier days was now called. With more and more administrative involvement, the bishop was increasingly judged in terms of his administrative skills. Although the constitutional description of the episcopal office had not been altered, the traditional authority of the bishop faced subtle challenge by other power centers. The large coordinating bodies, for instance, were exercising prerogatives in program planning formerly claimed exclusively by the bishops. More and more the district superintendent became the key person in the connectional program. An extensive amount of administrative detail was added to his responsibilities.

The rising educational level of the general population emphasized more than ever the importance of adequate professional training for the minister. Pressure increased to set uniform minimum standards for admission to the Annual Conferences. The General Conference in 1944 placed the church on record as normally expecting a Bachelor of Arts degree or its equivalent as the minimum academic qualification of a candidate for the ministry. The Commission on Ministerial Training made available a variety of opportunities for ministers to study for professional advancement. In the meantime, a study ordered at the time of unification to investigate the whole program of ministerial supply revealed disturbing facts about the age of ministers, the rate of retirement and the adequacy of new recruits. One result of this continuing study was the provision of more liberal financial support for theological education. In 1956 the General Conference authorized two new theological seminaries, bringing the total number then to twelve.

The Local Church. Perhaps at no point was progress more notable after unification than in the organization and work of the local church. Responding to the report of its Commission on the Local Church, the 1952 General Conference provided for a more functional organization to include required program commissions in EVANGELISM, EDUCATION, MISSIONS, and Finance. In 1960 a fifth required local church commission, on Christian SOCIAL CONCERNS, was added. The new plan for the local church did away with much overlapping of interests and responsibilities, increased lay initiative, and at the same time bound the work of the local church to the general program of the denomination.

The years following unification brought a reorganization of all aspects of the church's Christian education program.

Beginning in 1947 the CURRICULUM COMMITTEE initiated intensive studies leading to the revision of all Church school curriculum materials. The new materials were characterized by firm grounding in the teaching of the church, and by employment of sound educational procedures. With facilities crowded and leadership taxed in the wake of the high birth rate after World War II, the Board of Education of the Church devoted much attention to leadership training. New programs were developed in weekday education, family life, camping, and work with older persons. Programs for youth, sponsored by various agencies in the church, were gradually co-ordinated, and emphasis placed upon guiding youth and their counselors in developing their own programs and projects. A Board of Missions program of short-term assignments for youth opened challenging new avenues of service for young people. The great interest in the use of audio-visual facilities and techniques led eventually to the establishing of an independent agency, the TELEVISION, RADIO AND FILM COMMISSION (TRAFCO), to produce motion pictures and filmstrips for use on television and in the local church.

Lay Activities. Laymen moved into wider participation in all areas of the life of the church. In time, lay delegates were given full membership in the Annual Conferences, a status they had not achieved in the former M. E. Church. Lay representation on the general boards was approximately equal to that of ministers, and laymen were increasingly elected to major staff positions. The General Board of Lay Activities sponsored work with Methodist Men's organizations and gave special emphasis to STEWARDSHIP and Finance. The Board was not as successful in reaching its special constituency, however, as was the WOMAN'S SOCIETY OF CHRISTIAN SERVICE. A complete realignment of the church's work and the interests of women, far beyond the traditional limits of the LADIES AID and the missionary societies in the uniting churches, brought great numbers of women into broad participation in the church's work.

Reinforcing the work of these organizations charged specifically with development of lay programs was a deepening understanding of the ministry of the laity. This new interest in "lay Christianity," which revived a distinctive emphasis of early Methodism, was inspired in part by ecumenical emphases upon Christian vocation and church renewal, and in part by a deeper appreciation among Methodists of the meaning of church membership. Methodist churches had a wider and more varied program of evangelism in 1960 than in 1940, and in most instances laymen assumed the major responsibility for recruitment. "Joining the church" was to be taken far less casually than before 1940, and pastors were more insistent that new members be adequately instructed. An abundance of devotional literature, such as *The Upper Room*, circulated in the churches, and groups for the cultivation of spiritual life stimulated fresh and serious interest.

Theological Renewal. Supporting this new seriousness and affecting the witness of the church in all areas of its work, both at home and abroad, was the theological renewal that had begun in the years leading up to Methodist reunion. Some Methodist leaders in the mid-1930's were sensitive to the theological revival in Europe and were growing more critical of the evangelical liberalism which at that time was perhaps dominant among Methodist theologians. Issues raised by these men were sharpened in the next decade. Moreover, the impact of ecumenical conversations was leading Methodists to re-capture Wesley's theological orientation and to re-examine the theological heritage of American Methodism. The work of a younger generation of theologians led to a theological renaissance which penetrated the seminaries and began to reach laymen as well. Coextensive with the theological revival was a new interest in biblical studies, which also flowered in the seminaries and found expression in the preaching and teaching of the church. (See the Doctrinal articles in this *Encyclopedia;* and also ETHICAL TRADITIONS IN AMERICAN METHODISM.)

Its deeper theological interest helped Methodism to think more critically about the church and its mission, about the relation of faith to culture, and the meaning of Christian vocation.

Christian Social Concerns. After the adoption of its Social Creed in 1908 American Methodism wrote an enviable chapter of compassion and persistent courage in social witness. The wide-ranging social justice program advocated in 1908 still seemed radical a quarter-century later when much of it was written into law. Other problems—race relations, peace and world order—which had claimed less attention in earlier years, moved into the center of the church's concerns. All the while the METHODIST FEDERATION FOR SOCIAL SERVICE, an unofficial organization founded in 1907, guarded the church against complacency. Bishops of the church, such as HERBERT WELCH, FRANCIS J. McCONNELL and FREDERIC B. FISHER, were prominent in the leadership of the social movement.

Even as it moved toward greater social responsibility, however, Methodism, like most of American Protestantism, was disturbed by anxieties. At the beginning of the century the Methodist Episcopal Church, successful, numerous and relatively wealthy, enjoyed the favored position of senior partner, so to speak, in the national culture. With its middle-class, rural and Anglo-Saxon orientation it lent sanctity to the traditional values of the older America. When the church did move to champion the cause of labor and to defend the Negro and the immigrant, it created for itself a disturbing problem of identity. As the "new Americans" began to claim a place of their own in the national life, Methodists saw their former position of influence eroding. The story of the prohibition crusade and Methodist involvement in the 1928 presidential election, illustrated both the changing character of American culture and the declining power of the older Protestantism. Almost at the moment of its triumph over the "wets," Methodists found that they no longer were senior partners. The experience of the 30's and 40's would make clearer what the failure of the prohibition crusade had implied: Methodism (indeed, all of Protestantism) must function in a plural society; it must distinguish carefully between the standards of its culture and the ethical demands of its inherited faith; and its social witness would be no less demanding, but more wisely and realistically conceived.

When the wave of conservative reaction after World War II directed fierce attacks on Methodist social teachings in general, and the Methodist Federation for Social Action (its new name) in particular, the church's response was not to surrender its position, but to bring the program of social education and action more completely under the oversight of the General Conference. The Conference in 1952 set up a Board of Social and Economic Relations to deal with questions in the areas of economic life, race relations and civic and social welfare. Early in the follow-ing year Bishop G. BROMLEY OXNAM, on his own request and with unanimous support of the Council of Bishops, appeared before the House Un-American Activities Committee in Washington to answer charges that he was "soft" on Communism. Although the charges were not formally withdrawn, Bishop Oxnam's brilliant defense blunted the point of much of the irrational attack upon the churches. In 1960 the General Conference further strengthened its base for social witness by consolidating the work of the Board of Social and Economic Relations with that of two older agencies, the Board of Temperance and the Board of World Peace, under a single agency, the Board of Christian Social Concerns. For the first time the Church now had strong and effective co-ordination of its social concerns at the highest level and auxiliary means to bring these concerns to the attention of every member. Methodists did not speak with one voice on the crucial social issues of the mid-20th century, but the church was prepared to guide its people in the study, discussion and action required of responsible Christians.

Higher Education. Methodist institutions for higher education underwent considerable change after unification because of a phenomenal increase of tax-supported institutions and radical changes in what the public expected of education. Church institutions placed heavy emphasis upon improvement of standards and strengthening of faculty and endowments. The number of unaccredited senior colleges was reduced from thirty-four in 1940 to two in 1960. A few Methodist-founded institutions, in their search for funds, broke their ties with the denomination. However, in 1960 eight universities, twelve schools of theology, seventy-seven senior colleges, and twenty-one junior colleges retained their Methodist ties. Although higher education was then receiving a larger proportion of the Methodist benevolence dollar than ever before, concerted emphasis was placed on developing within the Annual Conferences increased support for institutions in their areas. A Department of College and University Religious Life in the Division of Educational Institutions of the Board of Education was maintaining contact with students in non-Methodist as well as in Methodist schools, and was instrumental in raising the standards of work with students.

New Publishing Ventures. Of all the enterprises inherited by the united church in 1939 none expanded more effectively in service than did the publishing interests. Six printing and manufacturing plants were consolidated into two plants, and the administrative and organizational structure was completely revamped. By 1960 sales had grown fivefold, and capital assets had increased to $21 million. By 1967 the Publishing House had seventeen retail outlets in major metropolitan areas. Abingdon Press had become one of the major book publishers of the nation. Publication of *The Interpreter's Bible,* completed in 1957 at a cost of $2 million, was the most notable achievement of its kind in the church's history. Another impressive publishing venture was a new periodical for the Christian family, called *Together,* which by 1960 reached a circulation of a million. Other general church periodicals were the bi-weekly *Christian Advocate* for Methodist leaders; and *Religion in Life,* a quarterly published for the Christian scholar. The Publishing House, in cooperation with the Editorial Division of the Board of Education, coordinated the church school literature of the three uniting churches and continued work on improvement of these materials.

Social Services. Changes in other Methodist institutions reflected shifts in population patterns and the marked growth in federally-assisted welfare services. The number of homes for the elderly increased from the thirty-seven established before union to ninety-six in 1960. This growth stood in contrast with the small increase in hospitals, and that in homes for children. The number of hospitals increased from sixty-eight to seventy-six. Of the forty-four homes maintained for children in 1960, only one had been opened since unification. More of the Methodist homes were adapting their programs to serve troubled children and children from broken families. The church also sponsored several residences for business women and two homes for unmarried mothers. GOODWILL INDUSTRIES, devoted to employment and rehabilitation of handicapped workers, were in 1960 operating in 141 cities. Some of these centers were maintained on an interdenominational basis.

Hardly had the Uniting Conference adjourned when the churches received urgent calls for CHAPLAINS to serve in the armed forces. In 1942 the Council of Bishops established the Commission on Chaplains to develop standards and recruit candidates. By 1944 over 1,300 Methodists were serving as military chaplains. The Commission, established as a permanent agency in 1948, continued to maintain liaison with Methodist chaplains during the Korean War and in the enlarged peace-time military services. In 1956 the Commission was authorized to recruit and endorse chaplains to serve in industry and in certain public and private institutions. (See CHAPLAIN AND COMMISSION ON CHAPLAINS.)

The Inner City. In the area of national missions the problems overshadowing all others as Americans moved past mid-century were those associated with the inner core of the large cities and industrial areas. The church entered a variety of ventures, many of them on an interdenominational basis, in the inner city. Assisting in the development of new strategies for national missions, urban and rural, were research personnel in the various boards and the seminaries, whose work was co-ordinated by an Interagency Committee on Research established in 1960.

The urban ghettos, created at least in part by the flight of the middle classes to the suburbs, caused Protestants to look afresh at the social stratification of their churches. A new urgency had now entered the picture, too, in the wake of America's Negro revolution; and white churchmen began to recognize that they could no longer think in terms of ministering "to" Negroes. Symbolizing this change in perspective was the dropping of the Department of Negro Work from the organizational structure of the Division of National Missions. Yet the task of building a racially inclusive church was hardly more than begun.

Meanwhile, the Department of Town and Country Work continued its interest in the small church and rural communities, as the nation was becoming more sensitive to the presence of rural poverty. The Woman's Division also continued to work in rural areas, particularly in the maintenance of schools, and in providing Christian education workers in rural areas.

Boards and agencies of the church found themselves intricately involved in the work of interdenominational agencies which had grown steadily in number since the beginning of the century. From the time of its organization in 1908, Methodist leaders were actively engaged in the life of the FEDERAL COUNCIL OF CHURCHES of Christ in America. In 1950 the Federal Council joined with a number of other interdenominational agencies in which Methodists had participated to form the NATIONAL COUNCIL OF CHURCHES of Christ in the United States of America. The comprehensive program of united work and witness launched by the National Council drew frequently from Methodist leadership for officers and staff. Countless other Methodists worked in state and local councils and in special conferences related to the National Council.

World Outreach. Nowhere were Methodists made more aware of the passing of the world of their fathers than in the area of world mission. Not only had the world changed. The church itself was gaining a new understanding of its mission and learning that mission had to be undertaken in cooperation with other denominations. If World War II disrupted the usual work of the missionaries in every field, it also accelerated a whole range of world-wide developments, long since underway, but now intensified with inescapable urgency. Administrators of the missionary enterprise had to confront the rise of a new nationalism and the end of western colonialism, the revival of non-Christian faiths and the insistence upon cultural integrity, the extension of Communism and the evolution of socialistic political and economic systems, the explosion of population and the impact of new communications media.

The church's mission required new strategies, new policies of recruitment and deployment of personnel, new ways of assisting indigeneous leadership, and new relations between the overhead agencies and the workers in the field. Of no less urgency was the need to help members of the local churches gain a better understanding of "the church in mission." The quadrennial programs of the General Conference emphasized more personal contact between the missionary on the field and the members of the home congregation. Response to the promotion of "mission specials" was so extensive that by 1960 over half of the receipts by the Division of World Missions was from this source. Two decades after unification, despite the vast changes that had intervened, the number of missionaries representing the Division of World Missions and the Woman's Division of Christian Service in the Christian enterprise outside the United States and its territories had increased by approximately thirty percent.

Closely related to mission in the twentieth century was Methodist involvement in the ECUMENICAL MOVEMENT. It was a Methodist layman, JOHN R. MOTT, who more than any other one man, laid the groundwork for this movement. Mott in 1910 presided over the first WORLD MISSIONARY CONFERENCE at Edinburgh, which is often called the fountainhead of the Ecumenical Movement. Methodist missionary leaders helped guide the INTERNATIONAL MISSIONARY COUNCIL, organized to follow up the Edinburgh Conference. American Methodist theologians and ecclesiastical leaders also participated in the Faith and Order and Life and Work Movements prior to the founding of the WORLD COUNCIL OF CHURCHES; but it was really at the first assembly of the World Council in Amsterdam in 1948 that Methodist leadership began to appear in strength. American Methodists had a closer view of ecumenical conversations in 1954 when the second assembly of the World Council met on the campus of Northwestern University of Evanston. Since 1954 an increasing number of Methodists have participated in World Council assemblies, in various ecumenical study commissions and in writing and teaching in the field of ecumenics.

One of the fruits of Vatican Council II has been the

friendly discussions and positive relationships between Protestants and Roman Catholics. Methodists were among the official observers at the Council in Rome, and the Methodist Council of Bishops when in session dispatched a letter of greetings to the Council.

Changes in Worship. As the Methodist Church broadened its participation in the ecumenical movement and increased in its own self-understanding it was also influenced by the liturgical renewal that moved through many of the churches. Too long accustomed to the ways of free worship to give way to radical changes or imposed uniformity, Methodists had nevertheless, since the Civil War, manifested growing interests in church architecture, in the improvement of its resources in music, and in achieving greater dignity in its services. At times this interest proved more cultural and esthetic than distinctively religious. With the rediscovery of its theological heritage, however, the church was moved to give more deliberate consideration to the meaning and use of historic forms of worship. Interest developed especially among youth and student groups. A department of Ministry of Music under the Board of Education, the National Fellowship of Methodist Musicians, the Department of Architecture of the Board of Missions, and the general Commission on Worship offered guidance and provided resources. Courses in worship found place in the seminary curricula. A revision of *The Hymnal,* prepared by the Commission on Worship and officially adopted in 1964, drew more extensively than its predecessor upon both the Wesleyan hymnody and the heritage of ecumenical hymnody, while retaining many of the hymns long cherished in various sections of the church. New services prepared by the Commission and placed in *The Hymnal* and *The Book of Worship* brought contemporary Methodist worship more fully into the tradition of its own Wesleyan heritage as well as that of Western Christianity in general.

On the eve of the General Conference of 1968 The Methodist Church made ready to merge its relatively brief institutional life into a larger union. It then joined hands with the Evangelical United Brethren Church and formed The United Methodist Church. In its twenty-nine years The Methodist Church had labored in one of the most critical periods in the life of the nation and perhaps of the world. With all the changes in its exterior life, however, and despite a humbling awareness of unfinished tasks, one may fairly claim that it had not been unfaithful to its heritage. That heritage had been shared by the Evangelical United Brethren. To the United Methodist Church has been handed not only the stewardship of a common heritage, but also a parish reaching to the ends of the earth in which Christians of many heritages will—one devoutly hopes—discover their unity as disciples of one Lord.

James W. May

(Ed.—An enormous bibliography may be referred to for further study at any point of interest in the above account. The general bibliography of Methodist historical works listed in this *Encyclopedia* will indicate many of these. *The History of American Methodism* in three volumes, edited by Dr. Emory Bucke (Abingdon, 1964) will provide a sweeping and accurate account of the general development of American Methodism up to 1964. The many persons and institutions whose names are printed in small capitals in the above account may be referred to in their alphabetical listing in this work for a deeper and more detailed study of such persons and institutions.)

THE UNITED METHODIST CHURCH (1968-   )

In late November of 1946, just seven years after the 1939 union which formed The Methodist Church, and just a few days after the union which formed the Evangelical United Brethren Church, a definite move toward the union of these two churches began. Bishop G. Bromley Oxnam of The Methodist Church brought a fraternal address to the first General Conference of The Evangelical United Brethren Church. In it he mentioned the naturalness and possibility of such a union.

First Moves Toward Union. Prior to the Evangelical United Brethren General Conference of 1958 several persons sent petitions to the conference asking that E.U.B. leaders explore the possibility of union with The Methodist Church. That 1958 conference, meeting in Harrisburg, Pa., directed its Commission on Church Federation and Union "to further study and explore the possible advantages and the potential problems involved in organic union with The Methodist Church, and "to continue exploratory conversations with the Commission on Church Union of The Methodist Church."

Bishop Reuben H. Mueller of the Evangelical United Brethren Church went as fraternal delegate to the 1960 General Conference of The Methodist Church in Denver, and spoke there about the possibility of union. That conference authorized The Methodist Commission on Union to negotiate a Plan of Union with a similar commission from the Evangelical United Brethren Church. It was not until 1962, however, that the E.U.B. Commission was authorized by the Grand Rapids General Conference of that church to negotiate such a plan. Union was the dominant theme of the Grand Rapids meeting where the subject was literally prayed through the legislative committee first and later through the plenary session.

By early 1964 the Joint Commission on Union had negotiated a proposed Constitution for The United Methodist Church. The preamble to that Constitution said,

The prayers and intentions of The Methodist Church and The Evangelical United Brethren Church have been and are for obedience to the will of our Lord that His people be one, in humility for the present brokenness of the church, and in gratitude that opportunities for reunion have been given. In harmony with these prayers and intentions these churches do now propose to unite, in the confident assurance that this act is an expression of the oneness of Christ's people.

Conversations concerning union between the two churches and their constituent members have taken place over a long period of years, and the churches have a long and impressive history of fellowship and cooperation.

Therefore, we, the Commissions on Church Union of The Methodist Church, and of The Evangelical United Brethren Church, holding that these churches are essentially one in origin, in belief, in spirit, and in purpose, and desiring that this essential unity be made actual in organization and administration in the United States of America and throughout the world, do hereby propose and transmit to our respective General Conferences the following Plan of Union and recommend to the two churches its adoption by the processes which they respectively require.

This Plan of Union or constitution was presented to the General Conference of The Methodist Church at Pittsburgh, Pa., in April of 1964. That conference did not adopt or approve the constitution, but it did approve the union *in principle* and voted to hold an adjourned session of the Methodist General Conference at the same time and in the same city as the 1966 General Conference of the E.U.B. church. This proved to be CHICAGO.

Following this affirmative Methodist action of 1964, seventeen joint committees involving almost 200 persons were appointed to share in the work of negotiating a total Plan of Union. At that time Bishop LLOYD C. WICKE of The Methodist Church and Bishop Reuben H. Mueller of The Evangelical United Brethren Church were co-chairmen of The Joint Commission on Union, and Mr. CHARLES C. PARLIN of The Methodist Church and Bishop J. GORDON HOWARD of The Evangelical United Brethren Church were co-secretaries. In November of 1964 Dr. PAUL WASHBURN was called from a pastorate at First Evangelical United Brethren Church in Naperville, Illinois, to become executive secretary of the E.U.B. Commission.

Early in 1966 The Plan of Union, a book of 361 pages, was mailed to delegates to The General Conferences of the two churches which were to meet in Chicago, Illinois, in early November. The book included a Letter of Transmittal, an Historical Statement, The Constitution, Doctrinal Statements and The General Rules, Social Principles and Organization and Administration. It was in reality the Plan of Union lacking only The Enabling Legislation.

The Chicago Conferences. At Chicago, the two conferences meeting Nov. 8-12, 1966, in back-to-back ballrooms of the Conrad Hilton Hotel, elected an Inter-Conference Committee to negotiate different positions held by the two conferences regarding the published plan. By Friday morning, November 11, the negotiating was ended and the two conferences were ready to vote. The Methodist conference needed a two-thirds majority, and the Evangelical United Brethren conference needed a three-fourths majority to adopt the Constitution and The Enabling Legislation. At high noon, an hour after the conferences had paused to honor America's military men who died in wars, it was announced that both conferences had voted and cast the required number of affirmative votes to send the Constitution and Enabling Legislation on to the Annual Conferences for their approval. On the afternoon of that day the two conferences met together for a Service of Thanksgiving. Bishops Mueller, RAINES and Wicke spoke, and the joint conference sang "Blest be the Tie That Binds."

During the following months The Plan of Union was republished as it had been amended at Chicago. An editorial committee—EMORY S. BUCKE, CURTIS A. CHAMBERS, Charles C. Parlin and Paul Washburn—had responsibility for this republication.

By June 26, 1967 enough affirmative votes had been cast in the Annual Conferences of the two churches to assure the union. On that day Bishop DONALD TIPPETT, President of the Methodist Council of Bishops, and Bishop Reuben Mueller, President of The Evangelical United Brethren Board of Bishops, made formal public announcement that the union had been approved.

The Uniting Conference. The celebration of the union took place in DALLAS, Texas on April 23, 1968. During the service of worship Dr. ALBERT OUTLER preached on "The Unfinished Business of an Unfinished Church." Some of his poignant lines follow:

The essence of the event is self-evident: it is the accomplished fact of The United Methodist Church. Where once, scarcely a generation ago, there were five churches, now there is one. Where once our differences kept us apart—with dif-

ferent languages and folkways—now they are overcome or else at least contained within a larger circle of committed fellowship. We have been Christian brethren, after a fashion, for the better part of two centuries—but *separated* brethren. Now our memberships and ministries have been mingled without compromise or indignity; our separate traditions have been sublated and made one.

. . . This, then, is our birthday—a day to celebrate, a day to remember, a day for high hopes and renewed commitments. This is a day when the eyes of the whole Christian community are focused on us and especially those of our Methodist brethren in Britain who are with us in spirit. This is the day that the Lord has made. Let us really rejoice and be glad in it— glad for the new chance God now gives us: to be a church united in order to be uniting, a church repentant in order to be a church redemptive, a church cruciform in order to manifest God's triumphant agony for mankind,

Till sons of men shall learn his love
And follow where his feet have trod
Till glorious from the heavens above
Shall come the city of our God!

Following the sermon Bishop Mueller and Bishop Wicke made declaration of the union in the following words:

I, Reuben H. Mueller, a bishop of The Evangelical United Brethren Church, hereby announce that the Plan of Union with The Methodist Church has been adopted by The Evangelical United Brethren Church in accordance with the procedures prescribed in its constitutional law, namely, by an affirmative vote of more than three-fourths of the members of the Chicago General Conference present and voting on November 11, 1966, and by more than a two-thirds affirmative vote of the aggregate number of members of all the annual conferences in North America present and voting thereon.

I, Lloyd C. Wicke, a bishop of The Methodist Church, hereby announce that the Plan of Union with The Evangelical United Brethren Church has been adopted by The Methodist Church in accordance with the procedures prescribed in its constitution, namely, by vote of more than a two-thirds majority of the members of the Chicago General Conference present and voting on November 11, 1966, and by more than a two-thirds majority of all members of the several annual conferences present and voting thereon.

We now jointly declare that the Plan of Union between The Evangelical United Brethren Church and The Methodist Church has, by its terms and by the terms of the Enabling Legislation, become effective and henceforth The Evangelical United Brethren Church and The Methodist Church shall go forward as a single entity to be known as The United Methodist Church.

After the Declaration of Union the two bishops, then two children, then two youths, then two adults, then six ordained ministers from five continents, then two church officers, and finally all the 10,000 persons present joined hands and said,

Lord of the Church, we are united in thee, in thy Church, and now in The United Methodist Church. Amen.

and the union was a fact.

Near the close of the celebration Bishop Tippett led the congregation in an impressive Covenant.

We are no longer our own, but thine. Put us to what thou wilt, rank us with whom thou wilt; put us to doing, put us to suffering; let us be employed for thee or laid aside for thee, exalted for thee or brought low for thee; let us be full, let us be empty; let us have all things, let us have nothing; we freely and heartily yield all things to thy pleasure and disposal.

And now, O glorious and blessed God, Father, Son, and Holy Spirit, thou art ours, and we are thine. So be it. And the covenant which we have made on earth, let it be ratified in heaven. Amen.

Following the act of union, the Uniting Conference turned to the work of perfecting *The Discipline* for the new United Methodist Church. While such perfecting was accomplished, it could not be said that the conference was totally occupied with the new church's structure. It was much more concerned about the situation in the United States, and focused its attention again and again upon how to be a church on relevant mission to the world of 1968 and beyond. It therefore established a new Commission on Religion and Race. It adopted a Quadrennial Program under the theme, "A New Church for a New World"; it voted to secure $20,000,000 to be used in ministering to the crisis in the nation. Bishop JAMES K. MATHEWS, who was elected to head the Quadrennial Program said, "The Uniting Conference was a renewal conference and will be known as one of the great Christian gatherings of this century."

PAUL WASHBURN

METHODIST, THE, was an independent church paper, published weekly in NEW YORK beginning June 14, 1860. Often called "The New York Methodist," it was at first the organ of conservatives in the M.E. Church who protested a new disciplinary provision against slavery passed at the GENERAL CONFERENCE of 1860. Earlier, leading members of the NEW YORK EAST CONFERENCE had formed a Laymen's and Ministers' Union to lobby against revisions in the chapter on slavery in the *Discipline,* which had been unchanged since 1816. At the General Conference the Union sided with border Methodists, some of whom, clergy and laity, were slaveholders. They threatened to secede from the church because of attacks from antislavery Methodists. After the passage of the new legislation, and with the defeat of ABEL STEVENS, the incumbent editor of the *Christian Advocate and Journal* in New York, the Union no longer had direct access to the official church press. Its members decided to issue *The Methodist* in order to prevent a disruption of border Methodism and to provide a journal of conservative opinion for the church.

The leading supporters of the new paper included Stevens, later an eminent historian of Methodism; Oliver Hoyt, a New York banker; Daniel Ross, a New York leather merchant; and its first editors, JOHN M'CLINTOCK, a professor and former editor of the *Methodist Quarterly Review,* and GEORGE R. CROOKS, later a professor at DREW THEOLOGICAL SEMINARY. Crooks went to work immediately to keep the BALTIMORE CONFERENCE in the northern church. He argued that the new antislavery rule was merely advisory, and not prohibitory. Crooks' campaign was partially successful, despite the withdrawal of sixty-six ministers and twenty-five thousand members in MARYLAND and VIRGINIA who formed an independent Central Methodist Episcopal Church which merged with southern Methodism after the war. While southern states were forming their confederacy in 1860 and 1861, Crooks cultivated Union sentiment in Maryland and western Virginia to support a loyal Methodist church on the border.

During the war *The Methodist* abandoned its toleration of slavery and supported President Abraham Lincoln's policies, including the edict of emancipation. Its editorial position was a barometer of northern public opinion, which, at first, backed the war as necessary to preserve the union, and only later supported it as a means to end slavery. Editorial correspondent M'Clintock, who was pastor of the American Church in Paris from 1861 to 1864, published a regular series of articles on European political and public attitudes toward the American war. His reports were informative documents about the competition for foreign support between the Confederacy and the United States.

Early in the war *The Methodist* took up a new cause. Its offices became headquarters for the lay representation movement in northern Methodism. Crooks sent out lecturers to promote the cause and published 250,000 tracts urging Methodists to end clerical domination of church conferences. The final success of lay representation in 1872, was due, in large measure, to the work of Crooks and his associates.

After the Civil War, *The Methodist* promoted the reunion of northern and southern Methodism. Throughout the reconstruction period, the paper was the leading voice in the North calling for fraternal relations which were finally consummated between the M.E. Church and the M.E. Church, South, in 1876. Crooks and his successor, David H. Wheeler, who became editor in 1875, opposed radical reconstruction in the South and consistently criticized racial equalitarians in the northern church.

Even though it was not an official paper supported by the GENERAL CONFERENCE, many outstanding Methodists wrote for and subscribed to this journal. Weekly circulation grew to nearly 22,000 by 1873. Bishop MATTHEW SIMPSON, nationally known orator and preacher, regularly published sermons in *The Methodist.* After the bishop's death, Crooks edited a volume of his selected sermons which were first published in the paper. Simpson's Lyman Beecher lectures on preaching at Yale University also appeared in the columns of *The Methodist* during the fall and winter of 1878-1879.

In 1881, DANIEL CURRY, former editor of the *Christian Advocate* in New York, became Wheeler's associate, but the paper's future was doubtful. It no longer had any special cause to promote. On Oct. 7, 1882, therefore, the final issue appeared, after which time *The Methodist* consolidated with the New York *Advocate.*

Robert D. Clark, *The Life of Matthew Simpson.* New York, 1956.
G. R. Crooks, *Matthew Simpson.* 1890.
Zion's Herald, Sept. 21, Oct. 5, 19, 1859.

WILLIAM B. GRAVELY

METHODIST ADVOCATE, THE, a weekly periodical published in 1868 and for some years afterward in ATLANTA, Ga., under the controlling patronage of the M.E. Church, when that Church was enlarging its work strongly in the Southern States following the Civil War. The GENERAL CONFERENCE (ME) of 1868 authorized the BOOK AGENTS at CINCINNATI to publish such a periodical, either at KNOXVILLE, Atlanta, or NASHVILLE, with the editor to be appointed by the bishops of the Church with the concurrence of the Book Agents. It was understood that these were at liberty to discontinue the paper if its publication should involve a greater loss to the concern than $2,000 per annum. After a time the Book Agents selected Atlanta, and the first number of the paper appeared on Jan. 6,

1869, E. Q. Fuller having been appointed editor by the bishops. The subscription list, however, averaged a little less than 3,000 per year, and as there was considerable tension between the "Northern Methodists," as the M.E. Church was called in the deep South, and the reorganized M.E. Church, South, the *Methodist Advocate* did not grow rapidly.

At the General Conference of 1872, N. E. Cobleigh was elected editor, and upon his death in 1874, E. Q. Fuller was again appointed to fill the place, and he was duly elected to it by the General Conference of 1876. The circulation as reported to that General Conference was 3,102.

The Methodist Advocate did not prosper and was discontinued at the direction of the Book Committee, the last number being issued on Feb. 24, 1883. At the 1884 General Conference, it was reported that T. C. Carter, former missionary to China, had purchased the printing plant and furnishings and had reestablished the paper in Chattanooga, Tenn., under the same name.

The Book Concern at the General Conference of 1888, secured the adoption of a resolution to subsidize *Methodist Advocate* and to recognize it as "the official organ of the Church in its patronizing territory in the Southern States," the subsidy not to exceed $500 per quarter. The resolution provided for church control over the "general tone and editorial conduct" of the paper, but denied any responsibility for its financial obligations.

At the 1892 General Conference the Book Committee reported that the obligations of the paper were too great for its resources, even including the subsidy, and the Publishing and Book Committees had deemed it wise to purchase the property and franchises. After negotiating for two years, the Book Committee closed a contract with T. C. Carter on Nov. 15, 1891, securing his resignation as editor. The agreement included filling the unexpired subscriptions of *Methodist Advocate* with the *Western Christian Advocate*.

Journal of the General Conference, ME, 1868, 1884, 1888, 1892.

M. Simpson, *Cyclopaedia.* 1878. N. B. H

METHODIST BOOK AND PUBLISHING HOUSE, THE

(1829-1925), at Toronto, CANADA, was organized on authority granted by the Canada Conference of the Methodist Episcopal Church meeting at Ancaster, Upper Canada, Ontario, in August 1829. It was resolved:

That a weekly paper should be established under the direction of the Conference, of a religious and moral character, to be entitled *The Christian Guardian.* That the place of its location be the Town of York (now Toronto). That the sum of $700 is sufficient to purchase all the apperatus for a printing establishment. That the sum of $2,050 will meet the annual expence of such a paper. . . . That the stock to the amount of $2,000 be raised by dividing it into 100 shares of $20 each, half of which to be paid immediately, and the remainder subject to the call of the persons who may be appointed to superintend the publishing of the paper; the said stock to be repaid with interest as soon as the avails of the concern will admit of it. That . . . the members of the Conference . . . take up the shares among themselves, but if all be not disposed of in that way, that they use their influence with their friends to have the remainder taken up immediately. That a committee of 5 persons be appointed annually by the Conference to superintend the publishing of the paper and other printing that may be done in the office. (Canada Conference, Ms. *Minutes,* 1829.)

EGERTON RYERSON was elected book steward and editor, and was furnished with the following handwritten certificate which is still preserved in the offices of the Publishing House: "This may certify that the Bearer, Rev. Egerton Ryerson, is appointed Agent for procuring a printing Establishment for The Canada Conference, and is hereby commended to the Christian confidence of all, on whom he may have occasion to call for advice and assistance for the above purpose." It is signed, "William Case, Superintendent, Ancaster, Upper Canada, Sept. 4, 1829."

The first publication of the church press was entitled *The Doctrines and Discipline of the Methodist Episcopal Church in Canada* (1829). This was followed in 1835 by the first book, a Canadian edition of *The Village Blacksmith, or Piety and Usefulness Exemplified,* a memoir of the life of SAMUEL HICK, by JAMES EVERETT, published by Matthew Lang for The Wesleyan Methodist Church in Canada. *Minutes* of Conferences, special reports, a few sermons and addresses, an early book of poems, pamphlets on temperance, a cookbook entitled *The Frugal Housewife's Manual,* by A. B. of Grimsby (1840), and a variety of writings by Egerton Ryerson himself mark the lists of the early years of the Publishing House. In 1860 there was an experiment in publishing a missionary biography, *The Life and Journals of Rev. Peter Jones.*

During the last quarter of the nineteenth century *The Canadian Methodist Magazine,* edited by W. H. WITHROW, which ranked with the best literary publications of that period, was issued by the Publishing House. In addition, it began to prepare Sunday school publications for Canadian church schools. *The Sunday School Banner* made its first appearance as a teacher's assistant in 1868 (editor, ALEXANDER SUTHERLAND). Illustrated story papers for recreational reading began with *The Sunday School Guardian* (1846), *The Sunbeam* (1880), *Pleasant Hours* (1880), *Onward* (1891). These have been revised, enlarged, succeeded by new publications, until today the Publishing House issues four such story papers with a total weekly circulation of more than 300,000.

The name of WILLIAM BRIGGS is important in the record of the development of the Methodist Publishing House. He served as book steward from 1879 until 1918, and during this time the volume of business increased enormously. He acquired printing contracts, notably from the provincial government, which enabled the plant to enlarge its equipment, until it became the largest printing as well as publishing concern in Canada. Briggs acquired Canadian publishing rights from a number of British authors and publishers, and began to import books from the United States. The Methodist Book Room, as it was popularly called, became a depository and a publishing house for books of all kinds. William Briggs used his own name as publisher. A trade name was adopted shortly afterward.

General book publishing, in the modern sense of the term, in addition to official church publishing, began with the appointment of a book editor in 1920. Lorne Pierce (1890-1962), who came into the office as literary adviser to the book steward, was to review books and periodicals for the official church paper. But his passion for Canadian literature, born out of his studies at Queen's University, Kingston, and fed by a simultaneous flowering of Canadian literary expression after the First World War, compelled him to think of building a publishing program which was destined to make a great house greater. The house adopted as its trade name The Ryerson Press, in honor of its founder, and under that imprint undertook seriously to publish the best by Canadian authors, artists, poets and historians. Some of the significant items published in the twenties were: *Our Canadian Literature; Representative Prose and Verse* by Albert Durrant Watson (1859-1926); *Methodism and the New Catholicism,* by Lorne Pierce; *Makers of Canadian Literature,* a series of thirteen volumes of biographical and critical studies of early Canadian authors; *Ryerson Essays,* a series of pamphlets written by Canadian churchmen on religious topics and heresies; *Canadian History Readers,* a series of brief biographies of Canadian pioneers; and the *Ryerson Poetry Chapbooks,* a series of inexpensive publications to record the current output of verse.

When the Methodist, Presbyterian, and Congregational Churches of Canada united in 1925 to form The United Church of Canada, the Methodist Book and Publishing House became The United Church Publishing House (The Ryerson Press). The original church paper, *The Christian Guardian,* published without interruption for ninety-six years, became successively *The New Outlook* (1926) and *The United Church Observer* (1939), which is still being published. The Sunday school publications have become *The New Curriculum,* a series of annual study books for teachers and pupils of all grades. Book publishing, including a full range of educational text books for elementary and secondary schools and trade books in all categories, continues to give the church Publishing House a unique place among its counterparts in other countries. Through the medium of publishing, Methodism in Canada produced a lively and imaginative mission to the church and the nation. (See also THE CHRISTIAN GUARDIAN.)

A. Green, *Life and Times.* 1877.
L. A. Pierce, *Chronicle of a Century.* 1929.
C. B. Sissons, *Egerton Ryerson.* 1937.   C. H. DICKINSON

METHODIST COLLEGE, Belfast, Ireland, was opened in 1868 as a school providing higher education leading to university entrance, and as a theological college for the Methodist Church in IRELAND. From the beginning the school was open to boys and girls of all denominations, and a boarding department for boys was an integral part of the institution. One special feature was to provide for the education of the children of Methodist ministers. A boarding department for girls was established in 1891 in McArthur Hall, provided by the munificence of Sir WILLIAM McARTHUR. The school pioneered in developments in secondary education, particularly after the creation of the Ministry of Education in Northern Ireland, following the Government of Ireland Act, 1920. In 1919 the theological department was transferred to Edgehill, and an Act of Parliament in 1926 completed the legal separation. The original site of about fourteen acres is now almost wholly occupied by the new buildings modern developments have made necessary, especially in science laboratories, but in 1932 a site of almost forty acres was obtained at Pirric Park, Belfast, for playing fields. One of the two junior schools, Downey House, was established there; the other, Fullerton House, is beside the main college. Methodist College now has 2,149 pupils—1,288 boys and 846 girls—of whom 1,609 are in the secondary grammar department, eleven to eighteen years of age, while there are 301 in Fullerton House and 239 in

Downey House in the two preparatory departments, five to eleven years of age. Of the total number there are 203 boarders. Principals and Heads of the Theological Department have been WILLIAM ARTHUR, 1868-71; Robert Crook, 1871-73; Robinson Scott, 1873-80; Joseph McKay, 1880-91; Oliver McCutcheon, 1891-95; William Nicholas, 1895-1908; Joseph Campbell, 1908-20; then see Edgehill College. Headmasters have been Robert Crook, 1868-71; Henry R. Parker, 1871-90; Henry S. McIntosh, 1890-1912; Ernest I. Lewis, 1912-17; John W. Henderson, 1917-43; John Falconer, 1943-48; Albert H. R. Ball, 1948-60; and A. Stanley Worrall, 1961- .

R. L. Cole, *Methodism in Ireland.* 1960.
J. W. Henderson, *Book of M.C.B., 1868-1938.*
F. Jeffery, *Irish Methodism.* 1964.
R. Marshall, *Centenary Volume.* 1968.   FREDERICK JEFFERY

METHODIST COLLEGE, Fayetteville, N. C., was chartered Nov. 1, 1956, as an institution of higher education under the auspices of the NORTH CAROLINA CONFERENCE. The citizens of Fayetteville and Cumberland County assumed responsibility for providing a campus and for contributing $2,000,000 to match a like amount from the conference, plus $50,000 annually for current operations. The campus of 577 acres, with 12 modern buildings acquired since 1957, is valued at a higher figure than many institutions which have been in existence 100 years or more. The college was admitted to membership in the Southern Association of Schools and Colleges in 1966 and was accredited by the UNIVERSITY SENATE of The Methodist Church in 1967. Degrees granted are the B.A. and B.S.

The governing board has a minimum of twenty-four and a maximum of thirty-six trustees, nominated by the board, approved by the North Carolina Conference Board of Education, and confirmed by the annual conference.

JOHN O. GROSS

METHODIST COMMITTEE FOR OVERSEAS RELIEF. (See UNITED METHODIST COMMITTEE FOR OVERSEAS RELIEF.)

METHODIST EPISCOPAL CHURCH, THE. (See METHODISM IN THE UNITED STATES.)

METHODIST EPISCOPAL CHURCH, SOUTH, the second largest American Methodist denomination prior to Unification in 1939, grew out of constitutional questions related to slavery. The law of the Church then provided that Methodists should not hold slaves in those states where the laws allowed emancipation and where emancipated slaves could enjoy freedom.

Bishop JAMES O. ANDREW of GEORGIA became connected with slavery through his marriage to a woman who owned slaves. Since the laws of the state did not permit emancipation, Andrew executed a document in which the ownership was secured to his wife, and which provided that the slaves would be assisted to go to a state where emancipation was legal if they chose to do so.

The situation led to a notable debate in the GENERAL CONFERENCE of 1844. The Northern delegates insisted that a bishop's connection with slavery would be harmful to the Church in the North, while the Southern delegates took the position that the Church would be practically destroyed in the South by punitive action against a slave-holder in a state where emancipation was forbidden by law, and who had violated no rule of the Church. Furthermore, it was claimed that the General Conference proposed to pass on the constitutionality of its own action.

The Northern majority adopted a resolution which requested Bishop Andrew to desist from exercising the functions of his office so long as the impediment remained. In the *impasse* a PLAN OF SEPARATION was adopted. This provided that if the Southern Conferences deemed it advisable to organize a separate General Conference the assets of the BOOK CONCERN would be divided proportionately, conferences and churches should decide to which branch they would adhere, and neither body would continue or organize work in areas which adhered to the other. All this was mutually and amicably agreed upon.

Under the Plan of Separation the Southern Conferences elected delegates to a Convention which met at LOUISVILLE, Ky., and there decided to organize a separate Church. In 1846 the first General Conference of the M.E. Church, South met in PETERSBURG, Va., and held its sessions in a Negro church building, as the Washington Street Church had not been completed. The new Church retained the same law on slavery.

Bishop JOSHUA SOULE of MAINE, who in 1808 had been the author of the CONSTITUTION of the Church, adhered to the South because he believed that the action of the General Conference deposing Andrew broke the Third RESTRICTIVE RULE and was in violation of the Constitution. The Conference of the M.E. Church, South gladly accepted Bishop Soule as bishop, and elected WILLIAM CAPERS of SOUTH CAROLINA and ROBERT PAINE of TENNESSEE to the episcopacy. Further moves of this important conference may be seen in the brief synopsis of its work under GENERAL CONFERENCES.

A change of sentiment occurred in the North, however. The General Conference of the M.E. Church in 1848 repudiated the Plan of Separation, declined to receive LOVICK PIERCE, the fraternal delegate from the Southern Church, and refused to divide the assets of the Book Concern. A long period of estrangement followed and Northern conferences were organized in the South. The Plan of Separation was, however, upheld by the U. S. Supreme Court. In 1876 the CAPE MAY COMMISSION, appointed by both Churches, unanimously declared that both were legitimate branches of Episcopal Methodism and fraternal relations were established.

The M.E. Church, South grew greatly and later established conferences on the West Coast and in the Northwest, which was not a part of the United States at the time of the division. In 1939 there were thirty-four annual conferences with 6,500 pastoral charges and a membership of over 3,000,000. There were organized missions among the Orientals, Indians and Mexicans in the West and Southwest, and these had around 12,000 members. Foreign missions had been established in ten countries, and these had a total membership of approximately 150,-000. (See also METHODISM IN THE UNITED STATES.)

G. Alexander, *History of the M. E. Church, South.* 1894.
History of the Organization of the M. E. Church, South. 1845.
Missionary Year Books, MES.
M. Simpson, *Cyclopaedia.* 1878.   ELMER T. CLARK

METHODIST FEDERATION FOR SOCIAL SERVICE was an unofficial group formed in 1908 within the M. E. Church to work, as its name implies, for social justice in American life. Some extremely able church leaders were among its first organizers, including Bishop F. J. McCONNELL, Bishop HERBERT WELCH, and others. For the account of its involvement and pronouncements in matters that caused the withdrawal of support from it by the 1952 GENERAL CONFERENCE, see ETHICAL TRADITIONS IN AMERICAN METHODISM.

N. B. H.

METHODIST HISTORY is a 64-page quarterly periodical published by the COMMISSION ON ARCHIVES AND HISTORY of The United Methodist Church, LAKE JUNALUSKA, N. C. Volume I, Number 1 of the journal appeared in October 1962, with ELMER T. CLARK as editor, under the auspices of the then Association of Methodist HISTORICAL SOCIETIES. The magazine carries both scholarly and popular articles on Methodist history. It fills a need in that it prints and preserves valuable Methodist historical material.

ALBEA GODBOLD

METHODIST HOMES FOR THE AGED (Br.). Through the initiative of the Rev. Walter Hall, the last twenty years of whose active ministry were spent in the LONDON area, the British Methodist Conference of 1942 founded the Methodist Homes for the Aged. This organization was designed to aid at least a few of the many who retire on fixed incomes of dwindling value because of the rising cost of living, and was in the tradition of JOHN WESLEY's provision of homes for poor widows. Large houses were secured, and subdivided into bed-sitting-rooms for the residents, who share a communal dining room and lounge. Residents must be over sixty-five, and they contribute to the expenses of the Home according to their means. Hall and his successors, the Revs. William Stoate and Richard J. Connell (the present General Secretary), have been successful in raising money from many sources, mainly in gifts from individuals. The Homes available have increased from three in 1947 to twenty-six in 1969, and others are in the planning stage. One of the earliest residents in the Bognor Home was Mrs. E. Rhein, a descendant of CHARLES WESLEY. There is always a long waiting list of people seeking accommodation. (For Methodist Homes for the Aged in American Methodism, see HEALTH AND WELFARE MINISTRIES, Board of, and HOMES AND FACILITIES FOR THE AGING (EUB).)

FRANK BAKER

METHODIST INFORMATION (U.S.A.), whose full title is the Commission on Public Relations and Methodist Information of The United Methodist Church, is the official news bureau and public relations office of that Church. It was begun in 1940 at the GENERAL CONFERENCE (TMC) of that year and owes its origin to the Bishops of the Church at the time of the reorganization of their Methodism in 1939. They had observed that social service organizations were establishing strong publicity departments, and that there were successful public relations operations in other religious bodies. Therefore, in their EPISCOPAL ADDRESS to the Uniting Conference, the Bishops, under the heading "An Intelligent Church," said that "Methodism in this great day finds itself with large numbers of communicants and adherents who have little knowledge of its activities, plans, purposes, happenings and movements. They are not, except in the most meager way, methodistically informed. The Church must keep them in touch . . . The greatest modern agencies for taking the messages of this church to its own people and to all people must be called into full action . . . A department of Methodist Intelligence . . . adequate in equipment, capable in management, and vigorous in action will have extraordinary possibilities for the United Church."

This recommendation resulted in the adoption of a report which called for the establishment of a Commission on Public Information. In 1952 the General Conference changed the Commission's name to the present title as given above, but all through the years it has been popularly known by the shortened title—Methodist Information. This has become a familiar trademark in hundreds of newspaper, radio and television offices over our land.

This agency is "to gather news of public interest concerning Methodist activities and opinion, and disseminate it through the secular press, the religious press, radio, television and other legitimate media of public information." (Discipline, 1964, ¶ 1586) It is also charged with certain responsibilities for training in church public relations. Successive Disciplines carry full details and directions concerning the Commission's work.

The top executive officer of Methodist Information for the first six quadrennia of its existence (twenty-four years) was Dr. RALPH STOODY of NEW YORK. He retired in 1964. An annual fellowship of $3,000 for graduate study in religious journalism has been provided by the Commission to honor Dr. Stoody, and to help perpetuate the high standards epitomized by him.

The Headquarters office was maintained during its first years in New York. Following the reorganization of the Commission on Public Relations and Methodist Information in 1968 in The United Methodist Church, the Headquarters office was moved to DAYTON, Ohio. The decision to establish a new headquarters office in Dayton was based on that city's more central location with reference to the church constituency and other general offices; and the fact that Dayton had been the location of the administrative offices of the former E.U.B. Church. Other national-level offices are maintained in cities where the principal boards and agencies are located: at NEW YORK CITY, NASHVILLE, Tenn.; EVANSTON, Ill.; and WASHINGTON, D. C.

Affiliated with the national offices is a network of some thirty-five area offices of Methodist Information. While these offices are autonomous and answerable to the bishop and governing commissions in their respective episcopal areas, they do cooperate with the general office of Methodist Information, and many of them were established with the help of modest grants-in-aid from the national office.

Methodist Information nationally is governed by a twelve man commission, nominated by the Council of Bishops and elected by the General Conference. The current chairman of the commission is Bishop EUGENE M. FRANK of ST. LOUIS.

Dr. ARTHUR WEST in the Dayton Headquarters office is the present general secretary of the commission.

Disciplines.
N. B. Harmon, Organization. 1953.   ARTHUR WEST

METHODIST LAY PREACHERS' ASSOCIATION (New Zealand) is an organization recognized by the Conference, its duties being to foster the interests of lay preachers, until recently known as "local" preachers. Control is vested in an elected executive, with branches in each synodal district. All lay preachers who have been granted full status by their quarterly meetings are members of the association.

This association was formed in 1921, but before that time the Local Preachers' Mutual Aid Association served the needs of preachers in all branches of Methodism. While much of the work of the executive is of necessity administrative, the chief aim, both at national and district levels, is the improvement in the standard of preaching by lay men and women.

Accredited status is granted by quarterly meetings when a candidate has been successful in written and oral examinations, and has shown satisfactory ability in the conduct of public worship. Since 1922 the written examinations have been conducted by the board of examiners of the New Zealand church. However, schemes of study and written examinations were earlier approved through the Mutual Aid Association, and were operated from 1908 on behalf of the Wesleyan and Primitive Methodist churches.

The lay preacher has played an effective part in the work of church extension since the early settlement days of this country. In place after place they have prepared the way in the organization of societies before the appointment of a local minister. Experienced preachers from England were to be found in the work of evangelism in all the main settlements of the 1840-50 era. Even in the church settlements of Canterbury and Otago, Methodist local preachers were among the settlers arriving on the first immigrant ships. Again they were to be found in the military establishments during the Maori Wars.

The gold rushes of the 1860's brought to New Zealand an influx of men of all classes of life seeking fortunes from the icy waters of high-country gullies—gold! Among them were many who had already found that which is of more value than gold, and soon local preachers were given the Christian message in hastily erected tent churches in the many mining settlements. Their evangelistic fire prepared the way for the ministers who were later appointed to work in these difficult fields.

The early days were times of many small and scattered settlements. With the turn of the century came the breaking up of the large land holdings, and with this the number of small settlements greatly increased. This was the day when the "circuit buggy" carried the preachers far and wide over unpaved roads with mud and potholes in abundance. The "clip-clop" of the horse and buggy was a familiar sound to settlers in a hundred townships as the "local" traveled about to preach the Word of God.

Increasing industrialization and city growth, combined with modern transport, have reduced somewhat the demand on the services of lay preachers. However, in the true spirit of Methodism new doors are opening, and the lay preacher still finds large fields in which to serve.

WILLIAM T. BLIGHT

METHODIST MEN'S FELLOWSHIP, official association of Methodist laymen in New Zealand, was formed in 1931 with the idea of enlisting the cooperation of the men of Methodism in the promotion of the work of the church at home and abroad in the spiritual, mental, and social aspects of Christian living. Branches have been formed in many circuits, and where the movement is strong, district executives have been set up. At the head of the organization is the national executive, which carries out the policy of the movement as decided at the annual meeting held during the Church Conference.

In recent years, the movement has placed emphasis on the provision of a wide variety of resource materials and ideas to prepare for the tasks confronting the men of the church.

E. L. F. BUXTON

METHODIST MEN AND UNITED METHODIST MEN. (See LAY MOVEMENT IN AMERICAN METHODISM.)

METHODIST MISSIONARY SOCIETY. Origins. THOMAS COKE was the impassioned visionary first responsible for British Methodist missionary work. In 1784 he published *A Plan of the Society for the Establishment of Missions amongst the Heathen,* and followed this in 1786 with a financial appeal, *An Address to the Pious and Benevolent.* WESLEY, sharply critical because he felt British Methodism to be already overstrained, gave Coke his support from the 1787 Conference. On Christmas Day, 1786, on the way to America with the preachers, Coke had landed at St. John's, ANTIGUA. Here he found a thousand Negro slaves gathered for worship, shepherded by JOHN BAXTER, a shipwright, who had continued the work of preaching to slaves begun in 1760 by NATHANIEL GILBERT on his own plantation. Coke left the three preachers in the WEST INDIES, and WILLIAM WARRENER was officially stationed at Antigua in 1787. Coke poured time and money into the West Indies circuits; and despite bitter persecution, the work grew steadily throughout the islands.

Coke's plea for a mission to Africa and the East met unyielding opposition until 1813, when at the Liverpool Conference he offered £6,000, the remainder of his fortune, for its establishment. The mood of Methodism was changing. Suspicion of Coke had given away to affection. GEORGE WARREN had already been appointed to SIERRA LEONE in 1811—the first missionary outside the West Indies and the colonies. JABEZ BUNTING founded the first District Missionary Society at LEEDS in October, 1813, and other districts quickly followed suit. Coke finally sailed for CEYLON on Dec. 31, 1813, with seven other volunteers. On May 3, 1814, he died on the Indian Ocean and was buried at sea.

Advance and Withdrawal to the Mid-Nineteenth Century. An era of spectacular advance followed Coke's death. In 1816 the Missionary Committee was formally constituted by the Wesleyan Conference—all noncolonial missionary work was done by the Wesleyans until the 1850's. Within ten years almost all British Methodism's main fields were entered. In the West Indies membership leapt to twenty thousand in 1820, and was over forty thousand by 1840. Warren died within a year of landing in Sierra Leone; but although the "White Man's Grave" claimed 110 missionaries of all denominations in thirty years, volunteers were always ready to fill the gaps. GAMBIA was occupied. JOSEPH DUNWELL went to the Cape Coast, followed by THOMAS BIRCH FREEMAN, who pioneered into Ashanti and pressed on to DAHOMEY. In 1816 BARNABAS SHAW went to Cape Colony, and a year or so later began to open up the hinterland, with WILLIAM SHAW. JAMES LYNCH moved from Ceylon to INDIA in 1817. In 1815 SAMUEL LEIGH was sent to AUSTRALIA and then, in 1822, to NEW ZEALAND. In the same year WALTER LAWRY landed in TONGA, and soon afterward, NATHANIEL TURNER, DAVID CARGILL, WILLIAM CROSS, JOHN HUNT, and others began preaching in SAMOA and FIJI.

In Europe, CHARLES COOK began his work in FRANCE in 1821, and British Methodist missions were established in GERMANY, SWEDEN, GILBRALTAR, Malta, the Ionian Islands, Palestine, and Alexandria.

But by the middle of the century the apparently glorious picture had completely changed. In 1840 the Canadian Conference was constituted, and in 1855 the new Australasian Conference took over responsibility for the South Seas. Even so, the Wesleyan society could not meet all the needs that were left. Too much had been attempted too quickly, and withdrawals were inevitable. In Europe only France and a small society at Wurtemburg remained. That too much attention had been given to making converts and too little to training them had resulted in a sharp membership decline in the West Indies. A natural response to such existing areas as Ashanti and the South Seas had left harder fields, such as India and Ceylon, almost unmissioned. Missionaries were frustrated by the lack of financial support and new recruits, even when prospects were at their brightest; and in Africa, Thomas Birch Freeman withdrew from the ministry for some years. Financial stringency was inevitable. British Methodism, already sadly divided for almost half a century, was stricken once more. At a time when missionary work needed full support, the Wesleyans lost a hundred thousand members as a result of the FLY SHEETS agitation against clerical autocracy. Many of these united to form the UNITED METHODIST FREE CHURCHES in 1857. The midcentury was a time for "rethinking missions." Priorities, strategy, motive, and approach all had to be reconsidered.

New Beginnings. By the Jubilee of the Wesleyan Methodist Missionary Society in 1863, it was clear that despite failures much had been achieved. More careful attention was given to pastoral care, as well as evangelism, in the West Indies. West Africa had ten thousand members. Though only two were found in Ashanti, human sacrifice there was fast disappearing. The last cannibal feast had already been held in Fiji. France, like CANADA and Australasia, had its own Conference. Income began to rise again, augmented by the "Children's Offerings" (later to be known as the Juvenile Missionary Association) begun in 1841. Haphazard response to any call for help was giving way to planned advance. In India and Ceylon a more genuine encounter with the historic Eastern faiths was taking place; and though the Madras and Mysore districts had less than four hundred members between them, a real advance had been made through the establishment of high schools and later primary schools for boys. New missionary societies, agencies, and fields were a feature of the second half of the nineteenth century.

1) *New Societies.* Up to this period the non-Wesleyan societies had missioned only in the colonies. The PRIMITIVE METHODISTS had sent missionaries to the United States and Canada as early as 1829, and others in 1844 to Australia and New Zealand. John Addyman had gone to Canada for the METHODIST NEW CONNEXION. The BIBLE CHRISTIANS had workers in Canada and Australia, and the United Methodist Free Churches sent men to Australia

and New Zealand as soon as their Conference was formed in 1857. From the midcentury they took their share in full missionary work. (a) The United Methodist Free Churches undertook some work in Sierra Leone in 1859; responded to appeals from J. Lewis Krapf, a German explorer, and sent men to KENYA in 1862; and in 1864 began Chinese work at Ningpo which soon extended to Wenchow. (b) The Methodist New Connexion also turned to CHINA (Tientsin) in 1859. (c) Primitive Methodists concentrated on Africa. R. W. Burnett and Henry Roe went to Fernando Po in 1870, and it later became the springboard for the Mendeland Mission in Sierra Leone. In the same year Henry Buckenham began work at Aliwal North, in SOUTH AFRICA. (d) The last in the field, the Bible Christians, began work at Yunnan in 1844—a hard ground until the Miao "mass movement" in SAMUEL POLLARD's time.

2) *New Fields.* Wesleyans, after so many withdrawals in Europe, were hesitant to enter China when it was opened to Western influence. The first missionary, GEORGE PIERCY, was a layman who paid his own charges in 1851. The Wesleyan Methodist Missionary Society appointed JOSIAH COX to Hankow in 1853. All the other societies, except the Primitive Methodists, quickly followed (see above). The last field entered was BURMA, in 1881, where a chaplain began work among the Buddhists. The Wesleyan Missionary Society had stationed ministers in ITALY, SPAIN and PORTUGAL in the 1860's.

Though women had worked alongside their husbands from the beginning, it was not until 1858 that the Wesleyans set up "The Ladies' Committee for the Amelioration of the Condition of Women in Heathen Countries." From this essentially Victorian beginning has grown Women's Work. Though the first women missionaries were regarded as freak products of the missionary movement, it soon became clear that they were essential to the missionary effort, especially among women and children. They served at first as evangelists and teachers, later as nurses and doctors, and later still in many kinds of "social" work.

3) *Medical Work.* Dr. Porter Smith was the first medical missionary on his appointment to Hankow in 1864. "Healing" was soon seen to be an essential means of evangelism, at first especially in China and then in India. African medical work was aided by the WESLEY GUILD, which first undertook work in Ilesha, sending Dr. Stephens in 1912. The first Leper Home was opened in Mandalay in 1898, and early leprosy work owes much to Dr. Isobel Kerr, who went with her husband to Hyderabad in 1907.

Twentieth Century Developments. All the societies have faced the same kind of problems in this period. Methodist UNION came easily in 1932 to societies already much accustomed to consultation, especially as few of their fields overlapped. Women's work was integrated into the new Methodist Missionary Society at this period. Established means of evangelism—preaching, village tours, colportage —have continued, and so, to less degree, have pioneering efforts, notably in Northern Burma, the Zambezi area, and under EPHRAIM ALPHONSE in British Guiana. Education has been basic to the work, and many leaders in church and nation have come from mission schools. State control has tightened in India and Ceylon, where specifically Christian education has become less possible. In Africa south of the Sahara the church still makes the major contribution to education through schools or personnel, but there is much leeway in girls' higher education. General medical work has grown rapidly in scope, in-

fluence, and experiment. Growing literacy emphasizes the need for Christian literature, and such established printing presses as that at Mysore and bookshops as in Accra help to meet this. So do Methodist writers on the field, who normally write for a larger-than-Methodist constituency. Social and "reconstruction" work is widely undertaken, and lately this has been considerably helped by the cooperation of the Methodist Relief Fund and the Methodist-inspired Fund for Human Need. Typical examples are HONG KONG housing for refugees, famine relief in South India, flood relief in Kenya and Bengal, and the Rastafarian project in Jamaica. Orphanages have long been part of Methodist missionary effort.

It is impossible to give comparative figures of membership during this period owing to (1) the withdrawal from China; (2) the integration of Methodism into united churches, such as the EGLISE RÉFORMÉ in France (1940), and the Church of South India (1947). In the earlier part of the century, membership was greatly increased through the phenomenon of mass movements—in the Gold Coast, in Southwest China under Samuel Pollard and F. J. DYMOND, in Hyderabad under CHARLES POSNETT, and in the Ivory Coast through "Prophet" WILLIAM HARRIS— in which whole villages and tribes asked for baptism. The danger was that so broad a stream rushing into the church could not but be shallow in experience and training. Adequate manpower remained the great need.

The main developments have stemmed from the transition from mission to church. The missionary has ceased to be the accepted leader in most fields, but is accepted as the colleague of national workers. This has been the aim of missionary work at its best, but it has been accentuated by nationalist movements, with their emphasis on the value of the indigenous. Architecture, music, forms of worship, the expression of the faith must be more and more in national terms. Administrative leadership in this situation passes naturally to indigenous nationals. One difficulty for the church arises because extreme nationalists have suspected that "colonial" interests may still affect the church. In financial affairs most of the Missionary Society budget is spent on the support of missionaries and their work; but though many districts have long been self-supporting (e.g., GHANA, Ceylon, the West Indies), other low-income areas (e.g., South India) still need support. In "advance projects" and missionary activity undertaken by overseas districts and conferences, the Missionary Society shares fully, but "plant" and "property" appeals can seldom be adequately met.

Full cooperation between overseas churches and the home base is now normal, but recent examples are the "Skegness Conference" (1961), at which representatives of all Methodist districts and churches overseas met with Missionary Society officers; and the appointment of the first non-European field secretary at Missionary Society headquarters.

The transition from mission to church is seen most fully in the inauguration of new conferences in Ghana (1961), NIGERIA (1962), Italy (1962), and Ceylon (1964). These conferences are fully autonomous, but maintain links, through both missionary personnel and official representation, with the British Conference.

Official cooperation with other churches has been part of missionary policy since the Edinburgh Conference of 1910. The Missionary Society has been a major partner in the Conference of British Missionary Societies. Overseas it has participated in united medical work (e.g.,

Vellore, South India), united schemes of evangelism (e.g., Cooper Belt Mission, Northern RHODESIA), and joint theological training (e.g., Bangalore, South India; Caenwood, Jamaica; and Nigeria).

The outstanding example of cooperation leading to actual church union is, of course, the Church of South India (1947), which included a quarter of a million Methodists, and in which over a hundred Missionary Society missionaries are still at work.

The Methodist Missionary Society today is regarded as the Overseas Missions Department of the Methodist Church in Great Britain, but at the same time it is the partner in mission of the autonomous conferences born of its labors. At the headquarters the officers are responsible individually for the care of the four zones: (1) the United Kingdom, (2) Asia, (3) the Western Area, and (4) Africa, while one officer is responsible for coordination across the zones. A great deal of attention has to be given to the ecumenical relationships which are developing rapidly in all parts of the world.

The present financial commitment of the society is above £1,000,000 annually in home income. With grants from governments and other overseas income, the total annual expenditure never falls below £4,000,000 (1963).

Women's Work. Prior to Methodist Union in Britain (1932) each denomination had its own women's society for the support of missionary work and the provision of women missionaries. These were Wesleyan Methodist Women's Auxiliary (founded 1858); Bible Christian Women's Missionary League (1892); Ladies Missionary Association of the United Methodist Free Churches (1897); the Methodist New Connexion Ladies Missionary Association (1899); and the Primitive Methodist Women's Federation (1909). In 1834, David Abeel, an American missionary invalided home from China, began a "Society for the Promotion of Female Education in the East." Suitable women who applied were recommended as "helpers" to missionaries unable to tackle zenana work themselves. Mary Twiddy, sent by this society to Ceylon in 1840 and then to India, urged the need of a more official Methodist approach which would give women "helpers" a proper status and gain greater support for work which they alone could do. As a result there was formed on Dec. 20, 1858, with fifteen members, "The Ladies Committee for the Amelioration of the Condition of Women in Heathen Countries, Female Education, etc." Its task was to select, train, and station women missionaries, mostly teachers, and to raise money for their support. In an age when women's place was in the home, early attitudes were critical and financial support comparatively slight, but within fifteen years twenty-one women were appointed. Early appointments were haphazard, in response to calls for help. Policy needed to be developed, financial support increased, and closer links made with the Wesleyan Methodist Missionary Society. In 1874 Mrs. LUKE WISEMAN joined the committee, providing the leadership and insight needed for these changes for almost forty years. At her death in 1912 the early patronizing title had been changed to the Women's Auxiliary; the Girl's League had been started in 1908; ninety-three women missionaries were overseas, many of them in medical work. The other Methodist organizations were set up on similar lines, benefiting from the longer Wesleyan experience. At Union, in 1932, the various auxiliaries took the name of "Women's Work," and though it has three General Secretaries and its own committees

at every level, it is an integral part of the Methodist Missionary Society. In 1965 there were about two hundred women missionaries. (See MISSIONS, AND ORGANIZED METHODIST MISSIONARY WORK for American missionary history.)

CYRIL J. DAVEY

METHODIST NEW CONNEXION was a British Methodist denomination which was started in 1797 and which finally became part of the UNITED METHODIST CHURCH in 1907. The founders were WILLIAM THOM and ALEXANDER KILHAM; and their earliest followers were Wesleyan Methodists, chiefly from cities in the north of England in the industrial areas. They withdrew from the old connection because after JOHN WESLEY's death in 1791 the Wesleyan Conference was unwilling to grant to the laity the right to choose their own class leaders, to decide who should become and who should cease to be a member of society, and to send their own elected representatives to the annual conference to decide all business in conjunction with the itinerant ministers.

The New Connexion also thought that Methodism should unite with the nonconformist churches rather than with the Anglican Establishment. About 5,000 Wesleyans seceded in 1797; by 1815 there were about 8,000 members; the connection did not grow very rapidly, and in 1907 the membership was 37,000. The first New Connexion Conference was held at LEEDS in 1797, when William Thom was chosen president; the second, at SHEFFIELD in 1798, adopted a constitution which treated the laity and the ministry as equally responsible for church government; this included lay representation in the Annual Conference, which Wesleyan Methodism did not accept until 1877.

One of the most famous early ministers was RICHARD WATSON, the theologian, who served as a New Connexion minister from 1803 to 1811, when he returned to the Wesleyan connection. In the first half of the nineteenth century leadership was provided by THOMAS ALLIN (1784-1866), but the course of the New Connexion was deflected by the career of JOSEPH BARKER, whose gradual retreat from orthodoxy into Chartist politics caused the loss of about 4,000 members when he was expelled from the ministry in 1841. The litigation which followed these withdrawals led to the legal embodiment of the New Connexion by a Deed Poll signed by all the members of the Conference of 1846; this provided for the septennial revision of the constitution by the Conference with the approval of the circuits; a Model Trust Deed was also drawn up; and District Meetings, in which the laity were represented as well as the itinerancy, had been started in 1844.

The New Connexion seemed fated not to retain its most unusual servants: "General" WILLIAM BOOTH had joined the WESLEYAN REFORMERS in 1851; he became a hired preacher in 1852; he was dissatisfied with the chaotic state of the new body, however, and so became a New Connexion probationer minister in 1854. He was actually ordained in 1858. It was during his ministry at Gateshead (1858-61) that his wife Catherine began to speak in public. Booth, however, was unwilling to be restricted to the work of a single circuit, and in 1861 he resigned, becoming an independent revivalist.

In 1862-64 the New Connexion established a theological

college at Ranmoor, Sheffield, which was used until the First World War and then sold in 1919. It was in 1860 that John Innocent and W. N. HALL arrived in CHINA to start a mission; Innocent lived to be president of the Centenary Conference held in Sheffield in 1897. Between 1837 and 1874 the New Connexion established a Canadian Mission, which had about 8,000 members when it united with other Methodist bodies and ceased a separate existence. In England, however, the New Connexion did not grow tremendously; after the Wesleyan schism of 1849, the reforming impetus was taken up by the UNITED METHODIST FREE CHURCHES, whose members were not attracted by the New Connexion—they wanted a still looser constitution and a more revivalistic style of piety. As late as 1889 negotiations between the New Connexion and the United Methodist Free Churches broke down completely over the status of the circuit minister, which the New Connexion felt was insufficiently guarded by the proposals for a union.

The negotiations which led to the union of 1907 may be traced back to the third ECUMENICAL METHODIST CONFERENCE, which met in LONDON in 1901. The negotiations which followed this brought an approach to the New Connexion from the Wesleyan Methodist Church. The New Connexion Conference of 1905, however, rejected the Wesleyan approach and united with the Bible Christians and the United Methodist Free Churches in 1907. At that time the New Connexion had 37,000 members, 204 ministers, 1,123 local preachers, and nearly 88,000 Sunday school scholars.

METHODIST PROTESTANT, THE. (See METHODIST PROTESTANT-RECORDER.)

METHODIST PROTESTANT CHILDREN'S HOME (1910-1941), located first at Denton, N. C., U.S.A., and after August 1913, at High Point, N. C., was established by the WOMAN'S HOME MISSIONARY SOCIETY of the NORTH CAROLINA ANNUAL CONFERENCE and was the only denominational orphanage of the METHODIST PROTESTANT CHURCH. Mrs. W. C. (MINNIE LEE HANCOCK) HAMMER recommended the establishment of a children's home in a presidential address in May 1910, and the Rev. G. L. Reynolds, who became interested in the project, offered an old, discarded school building located on the M.P. Church property in Denton. The Methodist Protestant Children's Home was opened on Aug. 22, 1910. Mrs. R. S. (Mabel Williams) Russell, who served as the first matron, Mrs. J. W. (Etta Auman) Austin, and Mrs. Fannie Page operated the home until it was removed to HIGH POINT.

ARMINIUS G. DIXON took an active role in having the home established in High Point (considered to be a more central location), and J. R. Reitzel, A. M. Rankin, George T. Penny and W. P. Pickett gave financial assistance toward making the move. A thirty-eight-acre farm was purchased from Mr. and Mrs. J. J. Welch near High Point and both Mr. and Mrs. Welch gave substantial gifts on the price of the land. Mr. and Mrs. H. A. Garrett became superintendents of the home on Aug. 1, 1913, and upon their resignation in 1924 the property was valued at more than $200,000. Rev. and Mrs. E. G. Lowdermilk and Dr. and Mrs. E. F. Allman supervised the home prior to 1928 when Dr. Dixon and his wife, MARGARET MINERVA KUHNS DIXON took charge. There were seventy-two children in the home at this time.

The Children's Home made steady progress throughout its existence and received the cooperation and support of the North Carolina Conference, to whom the property was deeded, and in 1912 it was endorsed by the GENERAL CONFERENCE from which it also received annual financial assistance. The Sunday Schools of the North Carolina Conference donated approximately fifty percent of the home's operational costs and additional funds came from the DUKE ENDOWMENT, private gifts and the women of the North Carolina Branch of the Home Missionary Society.

In 1939 the property was valued at approximately $350,000, and there were some 115 children being cared for in the home. Following the unification of the M.P. Church, the M.E. Church and the M.E. Church, South, the Children's Home was closed in 1941.

Mabel Williams Russell, *History of the Methodist Protestant Children's Home, 1910-1935*. High Point, 1935.
J. Elwood Carroll, *History of the North Carolina Annual Conference of the Methodist Protestant Church*. Greensboro, 1939.
The Methodist Protestant, May 16, 1928.

RALPH HARDEE RIVES

METHODIST PROTESTANT CHRISTIAN ENDEAVOR UNION (1892-1939), the official youth organization of the METHODIST PROTESTANT CHURCH, assisted local churches in training young people "to conduct meetings, lead public prayers, make addresses, do Christian service, give systematically and develop their spiritual natures in private meditation, prayer and Bible study." The organization was an affiliate of the Interdenominational Union of the Christian Endeavor. The GENERAL CONFERENCE of the M.P. Church of 1892 recognized young people's societies as a general agency of the church and at a meeting held in Trinity Church, Brooklyn, in July 1892, the Methodist Protestant Christian Endeavor Union was established. At the General Conference of 1908, a Board of Young People's Work was formally established to promote the religious education program of the M.P. Church through the expansion of Sunday schools and Christian Endeavor societies. CHARLES H. HUBBELL served for seven years as the first General Secretary of the Board and traveled throughout the various M.P. conferences enlisting and training young people for more efficient church service. Upon his death, HARLAN L. FEEMAN was appointed his successor and in 1917, when Feeman became the President of ADRIAN COLLEGE, A. G. DIXON became Secretary. Under the leadership of E. A. Sexsmith, who succeeded Dixon, a leadership training program of summer conferences, institutes and schools of methods was inaugurated. Sexsmith was followed by Lawrence Little. The Board of Young People's Work directed the religious educational program not only of the Christian Endeavor Societies but of Sunday schools, vacation church schools, week-day schools of religion, leadership training schools, institutes and summer conferences, conventions, vocational guidance and various other phases of the children, young people and adult's work. Free organizing literature for Christian Endeavor Societies was furnished by the Board. The individual societies were organized on the senior, intermediate and junior levels and used *The Christian Endeavor World* and *The Junior Work* (a monthly publication), published by the United Society in Boston, Mass. John F. Cowan, an active M.P. editor, founded *Our Young People*, which

became the official organ of the Christian Endeavor Societies until it was discontinued. *The New Guide* (originally known as *Our Morning Guide*) was oriented toward both Sunday school and Christian Endeavor constituency.

The Methodist Protestant, May 16, 1928.
J. Elwood Carroll, *History of the North Carolina Annual Conference of the Methodist Protestant Church*. Greensboro, 1939.
Scattered issues of the *Journal of the North Carolina Annual Conference of the Methodist Protestant Church*, 1892-1939.
RALPH HARDEE RIVES

METHODIST PROTESTANT CHURCH.

A major division of Methodism which united in 1939 with the Methodist Episcopal Church and the Methodist Episcopal Church, South to form The Methodist Church.

Beginnings. The Methodist Protestant Church was organized in BALTIMORE, Md., 1830, as a result of dissatisfaction with the episcopacy and the lack of lay representation in the conferences of the M.E. Church. Such dissatisfaction had existed for some time. It was part of the American thinking following the Revolution. One of the "Reformers," ALEXANDER MCCAINE, wrote a preamble to his *History and Mystery of Methodist Episcopacy* which was very much like the opening words of the Declaration of Independence. THOMAS HAMILTON LEWIS, in a fraternal message to the GENERAL CONFERENCE of the M.E. Church in 1908, spoke of the inherent differences within Methodism as exemplified by FRANCIS ASBURY and NICHOLAS SNETHEN. "They represented two principles of government radically different . . . Asbury believed that men must be ruled, Snethen that they might be developed to rule themselves . . . Snethen laid the ax to the root of the tree of ecclesiastical absolutism by the simple expedient of giving unofficial Methodism the right to vote."

In 1816, and again in 1820, there was attempt to make the presiding eldership elective. A resolution to that effect was passed by the General Conference of 1820 by vote of 65-25, and in the same session it was suspended for four years by vote of 45-35. The following General Conference, 1824, it was declared that the resolution providing for election of presiding elders was void because it had not been sustained by a majority of the annual conferences. The mounting suspicions of the Reformers became convictions, that episcopal power had worked behind the scenes to defeat the will of the General Conference.

On the failure of this piece of legislation, a prominent layman, WILLIAM S. STOCKTON, began publication of a paper called the *Wesleyan Repository* at Trenton, N. J., for the promotion of the ideas of the Reformers. Its utterances were aggressive and radical, but since the official *Methodist Magazine* had announced that it would publish no articles on controversial subjects, the *Repository* gained wide circulation.

A petition for a change in the form of Methodist government was sent to the General Conference in 1824, and when it was rejected, a convention of the Reformers was held. This group established a periodical called the *Mutual Rights of the Ministers and Members of the Methodist Episcopal Church*, to succeed the *Wesleyan Repository*, and took steps to organize societies throughout the country. In an attempt to suppress this movement, the BALTIMORE CONFERENCE expelled DENNIS B. DORSEY, W. C. Pool, and thirty-three others "for spreading incendiary publications." A test case was made in the appeal of

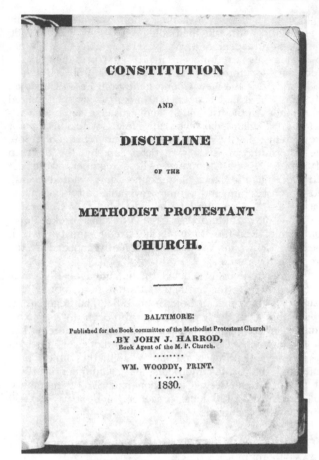

TITLE PAGE, FIRST DISCIPLINE

Dorsey and Pool to the General Conference of 1828, which appeal was denied.

Prior to 1828 the expelled members and others formed a society known as "Associate Methodist Reformers," and two years later at the 1830 convention adopted a Constitution and Discipline and took the name Methodist Protestant Church. In doctrine it did not depart from accepted Methodist standards, but it eliminated episcopacy and the presiding eldership, and admitted laymen to both annual and general conferences. Each annual conference had a president and there was also by election a president of the general conference. The appointment of ministers was generally made by a "Stationing Committee," made up of ministers and laymen, though very significantly, in the MARYLAND CONFERENCE, the appointments were made by the president, just as they were by the bishop in the M.E. Church.

Development. The first General Conference of the M.P. Church met in Georgetown, D.C., May 6, 1834. Nicholas Snethen was elected president. There were representatives from thirteen conferences which reported a membership of 26,587, not including ministers. The outstanding ministerial leaders of the church were Alexander McCaine, ASA SHINN, Nicholas Snethen, Dr. SAMUEL K. JENNINGS, GEORGE BROWN, Cornelius Springer, John French, William C. Lipscomb. Lay leaders of note were John Chappell, Thomas McKeever, Spier Whitaker, PHILEMON B. HOPPER, and William S. Stockton. THOMAS H. STOCKTON, son of William, was one of the eloquent preachers of his day. He served as Chaplain of the House of Representatives in Congress and made the dedicatory prayer at

Gettysburg at the time of Lincoln's famous address. The quality of this leadership was attested by ABEL STEVENS when he spoke of them as "men whose character, talents and prestige . . . rendered their loss to the parent church a deplorable misfortune."

The reform movement had begun by the publication of its principles in the *Wesleyan Repository* and the *Mutual Rights.* Considerable literary ability had been shown in promoting the cause of reform. The young church saw the need of continuing publication. The *Methodist Correspondent* appeared in CINCINNATI in 1830, with Moses M. Henkle as editor, and among its distinguished contributors were Asa Shinn, Nicholas Snethen, and Cornelius Springer. The *Mutual Rights and Methodist Protestant,* of Baltimore, shortened its title and as the *Methodist Protestant* became the official organ of the church in the East. At the General Conference of 1834 a stock company was organized to establish a Book Concern, which was incorporated by the General Assembly of Maryland in 1835. In 1854 there was a division, and the Western Methodist Protestant Book Concern was set up at Springfield, Ohio, and with it the publication of the *Western Methodist Protestant.*

The church launched out on an educational venture almost from the start. Nicholas Snethen migrated to the West and started Dearborn College at Lawrenceburg, Ind. It was an unfortunate enterprise, for the buildings were destroyed by fire in 1839 and never rebuilt. The MICHIGAN CONFERENCE took steps to establish the Michigan Literary Institute at Leoni, Mich., in 1847, but before buildings could be built the movement was absorbed by ADRIAN COLLEGE, a Congregational institution at Adrian, Mich., which in turn was taken over by the M.P. Church at the General Conference of 1862. MADISON COLLEGE, at Uniontown, Pa., came over to the M.P. Church in 1849, but never prospered, due to North-South factions within student body and faculty. It was closed in 1855, with faculty and students transferring to Lynchburg College, Virginia. WESTERN MARYLAND COLLEGE was organized at Westminster, Md., in 1867, taking over the location of the Buell Academy, and has had an immensely successful career.

The General Conference of 1834 set up a Board of missions, with Dr. Samuel K. Jennings as president. The first missionaries were sent to the western part of the United States, principally to Oregon. In 1836 a Negro minister from Maryland, David James, was appointed superintendent of a mission at Cape Palmas, Africa, but the venture seems to have been a failure, since no further notice was given to it.

Division. Even while the M.E. Church was involved in the controversy over lay representation, the slavery question was also troubling the church. After the separation of episcopal Methodism in 1844, the M.P. Church continued the debate. In the eastern part of the church Alexander McCaine of Maryland was writing tracts in support of slavery while Asa Shinn of the Pittsburgh-Ohio area was opposing it. The Cincinnati Convention of 1857 prepared an anti-slavery memorial for the General Conference which met in Lynchburg, Va., May, 1858. The memorial was not adopted, a resolution declaring that the General Conference should never legislate on questions of morality taking its place.

A "General Convention of Delegates from the Northern and Western Conferences of the Methodist Protestant Church" was held in Springfield, Ohio, November 1858,

to which delegates from nineteen conferences had been elected. The action of the Convention was to dissolve relations with such conferences which practiced or tolerated slave-holding, "until the evil of slavery complained of be removed." In 1862 the "General Convention of the Methodist Protestant Church" met in Cincinnati. In 1871 the "Second General Conference of the Methodist Church (formerly Methodist Protestant)" was held in Pittsburgh. Under the same name the General Conference met in Princeton, Ill., May 1875, and adopted a report on "Methodistic Union," naming commissioners to meet with like commissioners of the M.P. Church. The Civil War being over and the slavery issue settled, the two divisions, North and South, met in Baltimore, May 11, 1877, and the M.P. Church was re-united, "inasmuch as the cause for suspension of official relations . . . is now entirely removed by the providence of God."

Maturity. The last General Conference of the M.P. Church before uniting with the two Episcopal bodies was held in High Point, N. C., May 20, 1936. It had as president JAMES H. STRAUGHN of Maryland, and as secretary, C. W. BATES, of North Carolina. The Board of Missions, organized in 1834, had now expanded to include both Home and Foreign boards, and had incorporated the WOMEN'S FOREIGN MISSIONARY SOCIETY. The Board was carrying on missions in JAPAN, CHINA, and INDIA. The Board of Christian Education had two divisions: (1) Educational Institutions, promoting Adrian College, Adrian, Mich.; High Point College, High Point, N. C.; Western Maryland College, Westminster, Md.; Westminster College, Tehuacana, Texas; and the Westminster Theological Seminary, Westminster, Md.; (2) Division of Religious Education, promoting the work of Church Schools and continuing the activities of the former Board of Young People's Work.

In 1929 the *Methodist Recorder,* published in Pittsburgh and successor to the *Methodist Correspondent* and the *Western Recorder,* was merged with the *Methodist Protestant,* of Baltimore, to form the *Methodist Protestant-Recorder,* thus in a way bringing together the Western and Eastern sections of the church. However, the church still maintained two Book Directories, one in Pittsburgh, one in Baltimore.

The General Conference of 1936 reported a total membership of 191,863 for the M.P. Church. The Maryland Conference, with 35,758 members, had not only been at the center in founding of the denomination, but at the forefront throughout its history. But the phenomenal growth of which EDWARD J. DRINKHOUSE frequently spoke was not maintained. The General Conference of 1877 reported 169,405 members and there was a wave of enthusiasm over the union of slavery and anti-slavery factions. It was proclaimed that the church had entered upon a "tide of prosperity unexcelled in the history of denominations." But the gains were not remarkable from 1877 to 1936. The original cause of separation from the M.E. Church had been resolved. The M.P. Church had become another Methodist Church.

Union of Methodism. The General Conference of 1908, held in Pittsburgh, appointed its president, Thomas Hamilton Lewis, together with A. L. Reynolds and J. W. HERING, as fraternal delegates to the M.E. General Conference meeting in Baltimore. Lewis was chairman of the Commission on Union of the M.P. Church, and in a memorable address to the General Conference he made a long remembered plea for the union of divided Methodism. His telling argument was that the M.P. Church was a child separated from divorced parents and wanted to come back to a united home. Tremendous applause was reported and the high inspiration of the occasion was carried through the years. At the General Conference of the M.P. Church in 1936 a PLAN OF UNION was approved. The church set about securing ratification of the Plan among its annual conferences. The President of the General Conference, James H. Straughn, played a very significant part in this work of ratification of the Plan.

At the UNITING CONFERENCE, held in KANSAS CITY, 1939, the M.P. Church by vote of its delegates elected as bishops of The Methodist Church, James Henry Straughn and JOHN CALVIN BROOMFIELD. The matter of lay representation had been settled years before in the Episcopal branches of Methodism and it was now demonstrated that the episcopacy was no longer a stumbling block. The controversy of the Reformers was ended. Bishop JOHN M. MOORE, when presiding, spoke facetious and suggestive words when he presented Bishop-elect Straughn to the Uniting Conference: "Once a totalitarian leader and now a colleague in the ranks of benevolent democracy." (See also METHODISM IN THE UNITED STATES.)

Centennial. The M.P. Church observed its Centennial Anniversary in Baltimore, Md., May 16-17, 1928. The celebration was held in connection with the twenty-fifth quadrennial General Conference of the church. The conference sessions were conducted in St. John's M.P. Church and at the Lyric Theater, and were attended by some 3,000 persons, the largest number of Methodist Protestants ever to gather in one place in the history of the denomination.

The program was prepared by a committee appointed by the 1924 General Conference. President Thomas H. Lewis served as chairman; he was assisted by the presidents of seven annual conferences. A 300-member chorus organized by E. D. Stone, pastor of Hampden Church, Baltimore, provided special music for the celebration. Young ladies representing twenty-four annual conferences presented the offerings for the "Centennial Gratitude Gift" which amounted to more than $100,000. James H. Straughn directed the promotion for the Gratitude Gift. LYMAN EDWIN DAVIS wrote a special "Centennial Hymn." President Lewis presented an "Address of Salutation," and representatives of the Protestant Episcopal Church, the Presbyterian Church, the M.E. Church, and the FEDERAL COUNCIL OF CHURCHES brought greetings. Addresses were delivered by HUGH LATIMER ELDERDICE, HARLAN L. FEEMAN, CUTHBERT W. BATES, FRANK T. BENSON, and John C. Broomfield.

The Centennial Anniversary was preceded by a five-day M.P. Centennial Young People's Convention which used the theme, "Christ Preeminent." Several denominational leaders, including A. G. Dixon, FRANK W. STEPHENSON, and Robert M. Andrews, addressed the young people. A special "Centennial Edition" of *The Methodist Protestant* was published May 16, 1928.

Memorial Collection. The M.P. Church Memorial Collection was established in 1963 at NORTH CAROLINA WESLEYAN COLLEGE, Rocky Mount, N. C., by a number of friends and members of the former M.P. Church who were interested in the preservation of research materials connected with that branch of Methodism. The collection includes a wide assortment of books, bulletins, pamphlets, newspaper articles, and varied other memorabilia. There

are portions of the private libraries of several distinguished members of the North Carolina Conference of the M.P. Church, including J. F. Dosier, JOHN F. SPEIGHT, N. G. BETHEA, and C. W. Bates. There are a number of religious treatises and denominational publications of significance.

All of the published histories of the M.P. Church are in this collection, including: James R. Williams, *History of the Methodist Protestant Church* (Baltimore, 1843); John Paris, *History of the Methodist Protestant Church* (Baltimore, 1849); Ancel H. Bassett, *A Concise History of the Methodist Protestant Church* (Pittsburgh, 1882); J. Elwood Carroll, *History of the North Carolina Conference of the Methodist Protestant Church* (Greensboro, 1939); Edward J. Drinkhouse, *History of Methodist Reform*, 2 vols. (Norwood, Mass., 1899). There is a complete file of the *Journal* of the North Carolina Conference for the years 1894-1939 and miscellaneous copies of the *Journal* of the General Conference dating back to 1850. Of special interest to historians and rhetoricians are the handwritten copies of several sermons given by John Paris, as well as other personal correspondence and published works of this well known nineteenth-century minister and author. There are also records of the Board of Trustees of the North Carolina Annual Conference of the M.P. Church, and a number of M.P. *Disciplines* dating from 1834, and hymnals dating from 1851.

Other valuable Methodistica connected specifically with the former M.P. Church may be found in the library at High Point College, at the library of the COMMISSION ON ARCHIVES AND HISTORY, Lake Junaluska, N. C., and at Westminster Theological Seminary.

Washington Conference. This significant gathering was held in Washington, D.C., May 12-15, 1931. It had been called by the Executive Committee of the M.P. Church at a time critical both for the church and the government, and its goal was to strengthen interest in denominational obligations and church activities and to discuss the Christian church and its place in world affairs. The motto of the conference was "Forward Together." Over 2,600 persons, representing a large number of the 2,000 M.P. churches and 200,000 members of the denomination, registered for the conference, which held its sessions in the Memorial Continental Hall of the Daughters of the American Revolution. John Calvin Broomfield, President of the General Conference, gave the opening address. Others who spoke included GEORGE W. HADDAWAY, Mrs. C. W. Bates, J. W. Hawley, E. A. SEXSMITH, CHARLES E. FORLINES, Frank W. Stephenson, Lawrence C. Little, and James H. Straughn. There were over 1,400 persons present for the Fellowship Banquet held at the Mayflower Hotel on Friday, May 15.

At the conclusion of the conference, A. NORMAN WARD, chairman of a forty-member "Committee of Findings," reported some twelve points set for the denomination by the Conference, including the placing of greater emphasis on evangelism and on the enlarged fields of Christian service opened by religious education, raising in full church assessments, and the awakening of the denomination "to a new sense of its importance and obligation in the spreading of 'scriptural holiness' throughout the lands, and for the great work . . . in carrying forward . . . the plans and purposes of the Kingdom of God. . . ." Following the Washington Conference a series of "Echo Meetings" were held on the grass roots or local level of the denomination in order to make known these goals. The

Conference had great effect in mobilizing the work of the M.P. Church at that time.

Centennial Anniversary of the Methodist Protestant Church, 1828-1928. Memorial Volume. Baltimore, 1928.

E. J. Drinkhouse, *History of Methodist Reform.* 1899.

S. K. Jennings, *Exposition of the Late Controversy.* 1831.

Journals of the General Conference, ME, 1796-1836, 1908.

Journals of the General Conference, MP, 1827-1858, 1939.

Journal of the Uniting Conference, TMC, 1939.

A. McCaine, *History and Mystery of Methodist Episcopacy,* 1827.

Methodist Protestant-Recorder, May 19, 1931.

The Mutual Rights of the Ministers and Members of the Methodist Episcopal Church, Vol. II, Baltimore: R. J. Matchett, 1826.

News and Observer, Raleigh, N. C., Dec. 30, 1962; July 20, 1963.

The North Carolina Christian Advocate, Jan. 11, 1962; July 25, 1963.

N. Snethen, *Essays on Lay Representation.* 1835.

A. Stevens, *History of Religious Movement.* 1858-61.

W. W. Sweet, *Methodism in American History.* 1933.

RALPH HARDEE RIVES

N. B.H.

METHODIST PROTESTANT CHURCH (1939-   ). The continuing Methodist Protestant Church was formed by ministers and members of the Mississippi Conference of the former M.P. Church who did not wish to join in the 1939 Methodist merger because of what they termed the liberalism of The Methodist Church. They emphasize the Bible as the literal word of God, the indwelling of the Holy Spirit subsequent to regeneration, and the premillennial return of Jesus Christ. They are a racially segregated church, believing this serves the best interests of both black and white. Their motto is, "Earnestly contend for the faith which was once delivered to the saints."

The church has congregations in MISSISSIPPI, ALABAMA, MISSOURI, LOUISIANA, and OHIO in three conferences. Mission work has been established in KOREA and in two locations in British Honduras. A liberal arts school, Whitworth College, is operated in Brookhaven, Miss. They are members of the American Council of Christian Churches and the International Council of Christian Churches. They are affiliated with the SOUTHERN METHODIST CHURCH, the Fundamental Methodist Church, and the Evangelical Church in America in the International Fellowship of Bible Methodists.

The government is a representative democracy modeled on the United States government. Equal representation is given laymen in all functions of the church. There are no bishops.

W. L. Hamrick, *The Mississippi Conference of the Methodist Protestant Church.* 1957.

"The Methodist Protestant Church", a tract.

J. GORDON MELTON

METHODIST PROTESTANT HERALD, THE (1894-1939), was a weekly denominational periodical maintained by the NORTH CAROLINA CONFERENCE of the M.P. Church. It was an outgrowth of *The Central Protestant* and was the only publication sponsored by a specific conference in the M.P. Church. J. F. McCULLOCH started *Our Church Record* in 1894 with the view of arousing interest in the need for a conference educational institution. The name was changed to *The Methodist Protestant Herald* in 1910.

The paper was published throughout its existence in GREENSBORO, N. C. In 1896-97 the M.P. Publishing House was built in Greensboro and the income was used for the support of the paper until the opening of HIGH POINT COLLEGE in 1924, when the income went to it. The M.P. Publishing House was sold for $30,000 in 1938, a profit of $20,000 for the college.

McCulloch possessed considerable mechanical skill and not only edited *The Methodist Protestant Herald* but personally printed it. The subscription price was one dollar a year until 1916, when it was raised to $1.50 and in 1929 it was raised to two dollars. A subsidy based upon size and ability to pay was levied against all the churches and organizations in the North Carolina Annual Conference in order to support the paper. Despite severe financial difficulties, the paper survived the economic depression of the 1930's. McCulloch died in 1934 and J. E. PRICHARD, who had assisted McCulloch, assumed the editorship for the remainder of 1934 and through 1936. R. M. ANDREWS served as editor from 1937 until 1939 when the paper was merged with *The North Carolina Christian Advocate,* the official organ of the two conferences of the M.E. Church, South.

The North Carolina Annual Conference was rendered an impressive service by *The Methodist Protestant Herald* during the forty-five years of its publication. "Editor McCulloch, in addition to seeing High Point College opened and in operation, which was the primary purpose of the establishment of the paper, saw the METHODIST PROTESTANT CHILDREN'S HOME brought into being largely through the work of his paper. McCulloch also rendered a great service in the development of the entire Conference program through the years."

J. Elwood Carroll, *History of the North Carolina Annual Conference of the Methodist Protestant Church.* Greensboro, 1939.

Scattered issues of *Our Church Record* and *The Methodist Protestant Herald* and the *Journal of the North Carolina Annual Conference of the Methodist Protestant Church.*

RALPH HARDEE RIVES

METHODIST PROTESTANT-RECORDER, the official periodical of the M.P. Church at the time of Methodist union in 1939, was an outgrowth of the merging of two papers: *The Methodist Protestant,* issued from Baltimore, Md., and *The Methodist Recorder,* published at Pittsburgh, Pa.

The origin of *The Methodist Protestant* may be traced to *The Wesleyan Repository and Religious Intelligencer* (1821-1824), a bi-monthly in large octavo form with sixteen pages, initially issued from Trenton, N. J., by WILLIAM H. STOCKTON, an influential layman of the PHILADELPHIA CONFERENCE, M.E. Church. When *The Methodist Magazine,* the only Methodist periodical in America at the time, refused to publish controversial subjects that might disturb the harmony of the church, William Stockton published this liberal periodical to expose the abuses of clerical power and urge more lay representation in the governing bodies of the church.

After several years of controversy *The Wesleyan Repository and Religious Intelligencer,* of which the second and third volumes were issued monthly at Philadelphia, was succeeded by *The Mutual Rights of the Ministers and Members of the Methodist Episcopal Church,* which appeared from Baltimore as a monthly in August 1824. It was authorized by the Baltimore Union Society of reformers whose constitution in the first issue became the model for other similar societies and an important guide in creating the Constitution of The Methodist Protestant Church. A committee of ministers and laymen edited the paper with Dr. SAMUEL K. JENNINGS, chairman. The title was changed in 1828 to *The Mutual Rights and Christian Intelligencer*, edited and published by D. B. DORSEY as a semi-monthly folio of four large pages. From Jan. 7, 1831 it became *The Mutual Rights and Methodist Protestant* until the words "Mutual Rights" were dropped from the title in June 1834.

Mutual Rights, as it was often referred to, like its predecessor and early successors, was frankly controversial and pledged to open debate about forms of church government. Favorite themes were: equal representation by laymen and ministers in all church conferences; election of presiding elders as opposed to their appointment by the bishops; local preachers' rights including membership in annual conferences; rights of trial and appeal by ministers and members of the church. Most of the writers were anonymous "for prudential reasons," but the names of many were revealed in 1850 by Stockton. The list included EZEKIEL COOPER (whose ideas were later used in the Constitution and Discipline of The Methodist Protestant Church), HENRY B. BASCOM, JOHN EMORY, ASA SHINN, ALEXANDER MCCAINE, THOMAS E. BOND, CORNELIUS SPRINGER, and Gideon Davis. NICHOLAS SNETHEN was the most able and prolific of the contributors. Because it was the chief propaganda organ of the Methodists agitating for reform in the 1820's, the possession, circulation, and use of *Mutual Rights* became grounds for expulsion from the M.E. Church.

The Methodist Protestant, as the paper was called from June 1834 to its merger with *The Methodist Recorder* in 1929, had several distinguished editors during the nineteenth century, including E. YEATES REESE and E. J. DRINKHOUSE. It continued to be issued from Baltimore during that period.

The Methodist Recorder had its origin when CORNELIUS SPRINGER in 1839 issued an independent paper from Zanesville, Ohio entitled *Western Recorder*. He continued it for six years. Then in 1845 A. H. BASSETT became the editor, issuing it from the same place under the same title. In 1855, this independent paper was accepted by the northern and western annual conferences as an official paper, to express more adequately their views on slavery and abolition. Its name was changed to *Western Methodist Protestant* and issued from Springfield, Ohio. During the years when the northern section of The M.P. Church withdrew to become The Methodist Church, 1866-1877, this paper served exclusively as its denominational voice. Its name was changed to *Methodist Recorder*. In 1871, the publishing house was established at Pittsburgh, and this paper was issued from that location.

Following church union in 1877, both *The Methodist Protestant* (Baltimore) and *Methodist Recorder* (Pittsburgh) were accepted as official church papers until they were united Nov. 1, 1929 as *The Methodist Protestant-Recorder*, issued from Baltimore. The two editors, FRANK T. BENSON (*Methodist Protestant*) and LYMAN E. DAVIS (*Methodist Recorder*) were retained as editorial associates. Shortly before the merger Benson died and Davis became editor-in-chief, the paper being located at Baltimore. H. H. Price succeeded Davis and was followed by

RICHARD L. SHIPLEY, who continued until Methodist union in 1939, when the paper was discontinued.

A. H. Bassett, *Concise History*. 1887.
E. J. Drinkhouse, *History of Methodist Reform*. 1899.
Methodist Protestant, May 16, 1928.
Methodist Recorder, Oct. 25, 1871, p. 4.

DOUGLAS R. CHANDLER
RALPH HARDEE RIVES

METHODIST PUBLISHING HOUSE

METHODIST PUBLISHING HOUSE, THE. Official publishing agency of The United Methodist Church; oldest and largest of Methodist connectional agencies; publisher, printer, and retail distributor of books, church and church school supplies, periodicals and audio-visual aids; nonprofit, self-sustaining, appropriates from its earnings monies for the retirement and pension funds of annual conferences for conference claimants; headquarters in Nashville, Tennessee; retail branches and other operations in thirteen other cities, coast to coast; governed by the Methodist Board of Publication; John E. Procter, present President and Publisher; employs 1,865 persons; annual sales in excess of $40,000,000 for 1970-71 fiscal year.

The Methodist Book Concern. The Methodist Publishing House, America's oldest continuing publisher, traces its official history to 1789 when the M.E. Church appointed two of its preachers, JOHN DICKINS and Philip Cox, to the post of BOOK STEWARD. The *Minutes* of the Church for 1789 record these appointments, implying that Cox served as a traveling book steward while Dickins was stationed in Philadelphia as the minister of ST. GEORGE'S CHURCH. By August of 1789, Dickins was issuing books bearing his own imprint, the earliest reputed to have been Wesley's translation of Thomas á Kempis' *Imitation of Christ*, entitled *An Extract from The Christian's Pattern*. Soon the publishing enterprise was being spoken of as the Methodist Book Concern, the name under which it was incorporated in 1836.

Although for more than a century and a half 1789 has been accepted as the official founding date of the Methodist Book Concern, it should be noted that publishing has, since the earliest days, been associated with Wesleyan Methodism. JOHN WESLEY himself employed both pen and pulpit in his evangelical efforts in England even before sending preachers to America. As the movement developed on the North American continent in the 1760's,

Wesley's publications, especially those defining his theological position, and the Wesleyan method of salvation, were needed and sought by those who came into the Methodist societies. Prior to the American Revolution, officially these publications—sermons, *Notes*, hymnbooks, and *Large Minutes*—were forwarded to America by Wesley himself for distribution by the early preachers. In the late 1760's and early 1770's, one of the preachers presumed on his own to publish Wesley items in this country. He was ROBERT WILLIAMS, who came to America in 1769 and preached in the colonies from VIRGINIA to NEW YORK. Effective though Williams was in the spread of Methodism, his private publishing venture did not meet with Wesley's approval and at the first American Conference, held in 1773, he was instructed to publish no further items. For the next several years, presumably, such Methodist books as were distributed by the preachers were imported from England, specifically from John Wesley. Evidence exists of a rather brisk business in these items and the supervision of their sale by persons called Book Stewards. All this, however, transpired before the establishment of the M.E. Church.

The story of Methodism during the years of the Revolution belongs in another portion of this volume, but it should be borne in mind that the vicissitudes of wartime affected the distribution of Methodist books as they did other aspects of the Methodist movement. During the war, when FRANCIS ASBURY desisted from traveling and remained at the White farm in DELAWARE, there is evidence in his *Journal* that for a time he was engaged in the distribution of books, packing them for shipment to other sections. These volumes, it is to be presumed, were manufactured in England.

With the coming of peace, and the independence of the American colonies, American Methodism changed from a movement within the Church of England to a church, separately organized and established in its own right. This occurred, as will be noted elsewhere, at the CHRISTMAS CONFERENCE of 1784. In accord with the Wesleyan tradition, American Methodism at its organizing Conference stressed the importance of reading, and immediately following published as its first official work the minutes of this Conference. Also published soon thereafter was the sermon preached by THOMAS COKE on the occasion of Francis Asbury's ordination. These publications appeared in 1785 and bore the imprint of the church, but not a distinct publishing agency.

The years 1786, 1787, and 1788 are significant in the history of Methodist publishing in that during each one distinct references are made to publishing as a specific activity of the church. In Asbury's *Journal*, the entry for April 26, 1786, reference is made to accounts of the "Book Concern," with specific reference to BALTIMORE as its location. In 1787 there first appeared in the *Discipline* a separate section devoted to publishing. This section, in accord with Wesley's English pattern, provided that publishing should be a connectional enterprise, to the extent that items published "in this country" bear the approval of the conference ("if it can be gotten") and that profits from such activities be devoted to Methodist causes. In 1828 EZEKIEL COOPER, the second Book Steward of the Methodist publishing activity, recalled that John Dickins, the first Steward, while the minister in New York, in 1787 "commenced printing some books, the small pocket hymnbook, and some others." The year 1788 is significant as some argue that the action

in which Dickins was officially made Book Steward, was taken in that year, although not recorded until 1789. The fact that publishing was much in the minds of the Methodists during these years is borne out by the fact that Asbury's ill-fated COUNCIL of 1788 and 1789 was called to deal with, among other things, "our printing business." In fact, JESSE LEE implied that publishing perhaps began in New York as early as 1783, when Dickins first went there as a stationed minister.

Significant though all these dates are in a consideration of the history of The Methodist Publishing House, the fact remains that the title Book Steward first appears in the 1789 minutes, and that the earliest imprints bearing the name of a steward, so far found, bear also the date 1789, and PHILADELPHIA as the place of publication. Thus 1789 must remain as the official date for the founding of this agency, until other evidence is produced. Earlier activities, however, should not be overlooked.

The Book Concern in Philadelphia. The man credited with the founding of The Methodist Publishing House, John Dickins, was born in England in 1747. Except for his own record of his birth date on a page in his family Bible, he enters history in the year 1774 as a Methodist in Virginia. In 1777 he was admitted to the Conference on trial, and until 1779 preached on circuits in southern Virginia and NORTH CAROLINA. In 1779 he was married to Elizabeth Yancey, the daughter of a landed gentleman of Halifax County, N. C. In 1781, with the Revolutionary War for the most part concentrated in that section of the country, Dickins located and until the end of the war lived in North Carolina, near Fishing Creek, at the Edgecombe County line, on property evidently in his wife's dower. In April 1783, Francis Asbury records his successful persuasion of Dickins to return to the ministry and accept an assignment in New York, at Wesley Chapel—later JOHN STREET CHURCH. By June of that year Dickins and his family (two of his six children had been born by this time) were in New York, where he remained—except for the conference year 1785-1786, which he spent in North Carolina—until sent to Philadelphia in 1789.

It was Dickins who first met Thomas Coke on his arrival in America, he who first heard Wesley's plan for the new church, and he who suggested the name for this church when it was organized at the Christmas Conference. Dickins was further distinguished by being regarded as the best educated of the early Methodist preachers (tradition says he was educated at Eton), and the originator of the idea for a KINGSWOOD SCHOOL in America, which was founded as COKESBURY COLLEGE. That he was a well-educated man, with literary inclinations, seems doubtless.

Arriving in Philadelphia in June 1789, Dickins immediately turned his attention to publishing, with several books appearing during that year and in the spring of 1790. These volumes included, besides á Kempis already mentioned, *Saints Everlasting Rest* (the work of JOHN FLETCHER), the *Arminian Magazine* for 1789 (evidently published in one volume, late in the year), John Wesley's *Primitive Physic,* and the Pocket Hymnbook. Philip Cox, the traveling book steward, apparently coordinated the sale of these items to the people through the Methodist circuit riders. John Dickins' first book list, like those which came later, consisted of items originally published in England, which through the emphasis of Wesley had come to be recognized as "Methodist" books. For the most part they fell in the category of practical theology.

From 1789 to 1798 Dickins operated the publishing agency that, in the course of time, came to be known as the Book Concern. Publishing at several different Philadelphia addresses throughout the decade, Dickins employed others to print his books and, contrary to legend, never himself operated a print shop. Considerable evidence remains of his sales efforts, however, including records of shipments to the "West" and South, and efforts to collect payment for the items.

For more than a century and a half tradition was held that Dickins began the Book Concern on his life's savings; and while exact record of the transaction of the founding of the Book Concern has yet to be found, it can be said with certainty that Dickins, like his successor, Cooper, used his own finances in the venture. At the first GENERAL CONFERENCE of the Church, in 1792, oversight of the Book Concern and supervision of Dickins' work, became an assignment of the PHILADELPHIA CONFERENCE, especially the three-man Book Committee of that Conference.

Although surviving the yellow fever epidemics that ravaged Philadelphia in 1783 and again in 1787, Dickins, in 1798, contracted the disease and on September 27 of that year died. His oldest daughter, Betsy, was also stricken and preceded her father in death by one day.

Immediately Francis Asbury summoned Ezekiel Cooper, a minister of the Philadelphia Conference, and chairman of the Book Committee, to superintend the Concern. Reluctantly, Cooper agreed, although for several months John Dickins' older son, Asbury, managed the business. When the Philadelphia Conference met in the summer of 1799, Cooper was officially elected Book Steward and Editor. It is interesting to note that young ASBURY DICKINS, as well as his mother, continued in literary pursuits, with the result that their names have a place in the history of American literature as co-publishers, after 1800, with Joseph Dennie, of the *Port Folio,* the literary magazine of Philadelphia's intellectual circle in a day when Philadelphia was the cultural center of American society.

At the time of John Dickins' death, the Methodist publishing agency was $4,500 in debt, largely, it appears from records, to the Dickins estate. Cooper, however, by careful management and the investment of some of his own money, set the Concern on its feet, reorganizing it and concentrating its attention on the publishing of strictly Methodist items. For the most part, however, it continued as a small, one-room enterprise, in straitened circumstances.

In 1803, just as the Book Concern was beginning to enjoy a modest prosperity, difficulty arose among the Philadelphia Methodists at their conference ostensibly over Cooper's being allowed to stay in one place for so long. Cooper, along with his Book Concern, was requested by the Book Committee to leave the city. Asbury, ever vitally interested in the business, desired that Cooper should go to Baltimore. The General Conference of 1804, however, directed him to New York, which was much more favorable to Cooper. The summer of 1804 found him operating the business under the direction of the NEW YORK CONFERENCE in the Battery section on Gold Street.

Early Years in New York. By 1808 Cooper was able to report that the Concern was out of debt and valued at $45,000. At this Conference he refused election to the Steward's post, thus setting a precedent of eight-year tenure that for many years was the policy of the church,

and turned the job over to his assistant, John Wilson. Upon the death of Wilson in 1810, DANIEL HITT, who had been one of the most successful book-selling circuit riders in Dickins' day, became Book Steward, with THOMAS WARE as his assistant. Hitt remained in charge of the Concern through the years of the War of 1812, which, while marked by tremendous growth of the church, were not prosperous for the Book Concern. The lists during these years remained much the same as they had under Dickins—reprints of English volumes published to define the tenets and teachings of Methodism.

In 1816, at the end of Hitt's term as Book Steward, the General Conference elected to the post JOSHUA SOULE, then a young minister of the denomination. Soule had already won recognition as the composer, in 1808, of the document that for many years served the M.E. Church as a constitution. Like Ezekiel Cooper, Joshua Soule did not relish assignment to the post of Book Steward. He accepted it, however, and following the direction of the Conference, in 1818 published the first number of *The Methodist Magazine,* which was immediately successful. This periodical, which soon had a circulation of 10,000— a phenomenal circulation for its day—had been preceded by two unsuccessful efforts in the line of periodical publications. In 1789-90 and again in 1797-98, John Dickins had attempted to publish a duplicate of Wesley's *Arminian Magazine* for circulation in America. Composed largely of excerpts from the English publication, with a few American articles, these ventures had proved unsuccessful for the Book Concern, with its staff of two or three (at various times) persons. *The Methodist Magazine,* however, largely emphasizing "the work of God on *this* continent" won favor right away, and was the first real basis of hope for the future of the Book Concern. Despite this success, however, Soule refused reelection as Steward in 1820, and the post went to a New York minister later famous as a M.E. editor, author, and organizer. His name was NATHAN BANGS. Thomas Mason served as his assistant.

The Era of Nathan Bangs. Nathan Bangs, a man of the optimistic 1820's, thought big; and under the insistent urgings of his hand, the little Book Concern grew. For a time it seemed as if the forced flowering would prove fiscally fatal for the tender enterprise, but under the careful management of later Stewards it grew roots to sustain the ambitious program conceived and executed by Bangs. In 1821 the Concern, after having moved all over the lower end of Manhattan Island, rented the basement of the Wesleyan Seminary building on Crosby Street, and here Bangs installed a bindery, the first of the Concern's own book manufacturing departments. In 1824 Bangs opened a print shop; and when the Seminary moved to White Plains, on his own initiative he bought the New York property. This done, Bangs proceeded to enlarge the list of publications. In 1823 a periodical entitled *The Youth's Instructor and Guardian* had been started. This was followed, in 1826, by the *Christian Advocate,* and in 1827 by the *Child's Magazine. The Methodist Magazine* was also continued. Besides enlarging the list of periodicals, Nathan Bangs revised the book lists, adding to them more works by American Methodists. In 1824 the Concern began issuing Adam Clarke's commentary, entitled *The Holy Bible,* and, the next year, Watson's *Theological Institutes.* Of all Bang's innovations, however, nothing excelled the *Christian Advocate* in popularity.

By 1828, with 25,000 subscribers, it had the largest circulation of any publication, religious or secular, in the entire country. After Bangs had served eight years as Senior Book Agent, in 1828 he became editor of the paper, filling this position until 1836.

The Opening of the First Branch House. The General Conference of 1820, which elected Bangs Book Steward, authorized the opening of a branch of the Book Concern in CINCINNATI, Ohio, and elected MARTIN RUTER, a minister distinguished as a teacher and scholar, to direct the affairs of the new undertaking. The difficulty of transporting goods from the east to the Mississippi Valley region, and the difference in currency values between the two sections, prompted the western venture. Begun as a subsidiary of the New York Concern, the operation in Cincinnati soon proved itself and in 1836 was incorporated as a separate enterprise, under the name of the Western Methodist Book Concern. Until 1912 this organization functioned separately from the Concern in New York, for many years even being guided in its affairs by a separate Book Committee from the one which had oversight of the New York operation. Even after consolidation of the Book Committees in 1868, two separate local committees had immediate responsibility for the two houses.

Although at first primarily concerned with circulating reprints of New York publications in the western country, the Western Book Concern soon began a book list and later a list of periodicals, distinct from those published in the east. Most notable of these were the German publications, books and periodicals, which began to issue from the Western Book Concern in 1839; and the elaborate monthly, entitled the *Ladies' Repository*, published from 1841 to 1876. The *Western Christian Advocate*, a weekly newspaper similar to but not a duplicate of the New York paper, first made its appearance in 1834.

Expansion of the New York Concern. The decade of the 1830's, during which the Book Concern moved positively to the publication of books and materials for the Sunday schools, was marked by expansion of the Concern's real estate holdings in New York. In 1833, at 200 Mulberry Street, the Concern erected its first building designed and built for its own use. A multi-story brick edifice, accommodating all departments for book manufacture as well as the Concern's retail and mail-order sales departments, this building was destroyed by fire in February 1836. Later in that year, partly financed by donations from Methodists and members of other churches, another building was constructed at the same address. It was used by the Concern until 1889, when a structure was erected at 150 Fifth Avenue.

During the 1840's the publishing programs of both the eastern and western Concerns developed extensively as the church grew and as her Sunday schools flourished. By 1844, when the church divided North and South, impressive catalogs of Book Concern publications were being issued, encompassing not only traditional theological titles, church requisites, hymnbooks, and volumes of moral and ethical value, but also list after list of Sunday school books, grouped as libraries (in the Wesleyan manner) or offered for sale as separate volumes. These Sunday school items were nearly all directed to children.

The Book Concerns and the Division of the Church. When the M.E. Church split in 1844, division of the property of the Book Concerns (in the east and in the west) came to be one of the main points at issue between the M.E. Church and the newly formed M.E. Church, South. According to the famous PLAN OF SEPARATION approved by the General Conference of 1844 (the last one attended by both the Northern and Southern factions), the holdings of the Book Concern, along with other church properties, were to be divided proportionately with the Southern group, should the annual conferences vote to establish a separate Southern church. In 1845, at the LOUISVILLE CONVENTION, the M.E. Church, South, came into being. Between 1844 and 1848 discord between the two churches rather generally prevailed, especially in the border conferences between the two sections. In 1848, when the General Conference of the M.E. Church met for the first time following the split, the Plan of Separation agreed to by the Conference of 1844 was repudiated, on the grounds that it had not been approved by a majority of the annual conferences. By this time the separation of the Southern group, approved in 1844, was viewed in the North as a secession, in which the Church, South, had no claim on the property of the Book Concern. The Southern Church promptly filed suits in the civil courts for its share of the holdings. Ultimately, late in 1853, the Supreme Court of the United States, to which the decisions of the lower courts were finally appealed, ruled in favor of the Southern Church, awarding it $254,000 as its share of the Book Concerns. With this money the M.E. Church, South, in 1854 began its own publishing house in Nashville, Tenn.

The Book Concerns in the Last Half of the Nineteenth Century. Despite the heavy financial burden imposed by the court decision, the Book Concerns of the M.E. Church continued to grow in size and program during the decades of the 1850's and 1860's. Except for a slight setback in the first year of the Civil War, the Concerns prospered during the war years. Their Agents (in 1844 the title Book Steward was changed to BOOK AGENT which had been informally used for many years) arrived at the General Conference of 1868 with reports of growth, expansion, and financial solvency. The New York Concern, as had always been the case, was the larger of the two; but the Concern in Cincinnati was likewise a sizable operation, complete with manufacturing and sales departments, and branches in other cities. By 1868 the New York Concern had branches in BOSTON, BUFFALO, PITTSBURGH, SYRACUSE, and SAN FRANCISCO; the Cincinnati Concern had branches in CHICAGO and ST. LOUIS. Of all these branches the one in Chicago was by far the most solid. Since its establishment by the General Conference of 1852, the Chicago operation had experienced steady growth.

During the twenty years from 1852 to 1872, the commanding figure in the Book Concerns of the M.E. Church was THOMAS CARLTON, Senior Agent in New York, a Methodist minister with a gift for administration and financial management. Under his direction the Methodist Book Concern in New York moved into the front ranks of American publishing houses, weathering even the severe financial depression of 1857 that closed many other firms. An ambitious publishing program, embracing both books and periodical publications, became characteristic of the Methodist Book Concern, which annually issued extensive catalogs heavily slanted to the Sunday school and including a wider variety of subjects than had initially been typical of Book Concern lists. Perhaps the outstanding periodical publication of these years was the *Sunday School Advocate*, begun in 1841 and published in New York, Cincinnati, and Chicago.

As it had done since 1852, the General Conference in

1868 reelected Thomas Carlton to the position of Senior Agent in New York. JOHN LANAHAN, a minister of the BALTIMORE CONFERENCE, was elected Junior Agent. It was an unequally paired team, and the next four years in the history of the Methodist Book Concern were wracked with dissension and scandal. Amid the scandalous hubbub of American life of the 1870's, discord issued also from the Methodist Book Concern. Suspecting mismanagement of the business, Lanahan shortly after taking office, began investigations into the several departmental operations in the New York organization. In the printing department, he found evidence that seemed to justify his fears; and in some manner these discoveries came to the attention of the secular press, notably the *New York Times*. A front page story in this paper in September 1869, announced to the world that the Methodist Book Concern was tainted with fraud. Thus began a season of turmoil that lasted until the meeting of the General Conference of 1872. Lanahan's actions left him open to the charge of slander and insubordination. The actions of the Book Committee, ultimately responsible for investigating the matter, left this body open to the charge of whitewashing corruption in the name of public relations. Thomas Carlton, who very unwisely had engaged in financial speculation in oil companies worth millions of dollars, and who even more unwisely had done so in partnership with other employees of the Concern and on the Concern's premises, became the subject of hot debate between those who considered him a martyr and those who considered him the prime offender. Finally the General Conference of 1872 took action, appointed a special committee to investigate the matter, and approved the committee's report, in which both Agents were exonerated of the charge of fraudulent actions. Declaring that minor fraudulent practices had been perpetrated by certain employees in the Concern, but stating that they had not endangered the financial position of the House, the report called for a reorganization of the accounting procedures, which in their laxity left the way open for fraud should such be attempted. Needless to say, neither Carlton nor Lanahan was re-elected to the Agency in 1872.

In their stead REUBEN NELSON, a minister from the WYOMING CONFERENCE, and JOHN MILTON PHILLIPS, a layman from Cincinnati, were elected Agents for New York. Phillips has the distinction of being the first layman ever to be elected to the top position in the Methodist Book Concern. It should be said in passing that the General Conference of 1872, when Phillips was first elected, was the first General Conference of the M.E. Church to be composed of lay, as well as clerical delegates. Besides his significance as the first layman to hold the position of Book Agent, Phillips is also significant as the first man from the west to head the Book Concern in the east. The son of a former assistant editor of the *Western Christian Advocate*, Phillips was employed at the Western Book Concern in his early youth and rose to a position of responsibility there before being elected Book Agent in New York.

Following the so-called Era of Frauds, the Methodist Book Concerns, east and west, both prospered, and the eastern Concern together with the Missionary Society of the M.E. Church, in celebration of its 100th Anniversary in 1889, erected an impressive headquarters building at the corner of Fifth Avenue and Twentieth Street in New York City to house all its operations. In 1869, the Concern and Missionary Society had jointly purchased a build-

ing at 805 Broadway, and it was occupied by office and sales operations for the ensuing twenty years. The manufacturing departments remained at 200 Mulberry Street. Opened with elaborate ceremonies, the structure at 150 Fifth Avenue served as headquarters of the Methodist Board of Missions and the Book Concern (later the Publishing House) in New York until the late 1950's.

In terms of publications, the twenty years following the Civil War were distinguished for the Methodist Book Concerns by their publication of uniform Sunday school lessons (the first ones issued as "the Berean Series"), and publications for Chautauqua. Phillips and Hunt, Agents for the New York Concern, were the first publishers of Chautauqua texts designed specifically for that purpose. Notable advancement of the printing industry in these years resulted in increased book production both in the eastern and western houses. This carried over into the 1890's, when publications and other materials for the EPWORTH LEAGUE formed a significant part of the publishing program. These years also saw an increase in the number of theological books published by the Concerns.

Stepped-up production, resulting in sharpened competition, together with the depression of 1893, so severely affected the Book Concern in New York that at the turn of the century, this house, which had been the unquestioned leader in Methodist publications for more than a century, fell behind its counterpart in Cincinnati, not so directly affected by the economic fluctuations of the more heavily industrialized east. For many years consolidation of the two publishing houses had seemed fiscally desirable, especially as the two chief reasons for the existence of the Cincinnati Concern, lack of cross-country transportation and sectional differences in currency, had disappeared. This union was approved in 1908 and accomplished by 1912. At this time Chicago, along with New York and Cincinnati, became a headquarters city for the unified Concern.

In 1914, following the union of the two houses, ABINGDON PRESS was selected as the imprint of the Book Concern on those books designed for wider use than simply within the M.E. Church. Up to this time, and since the days of John Dickins, publications of the Concern had been issued in the name of the Book Agents, a practice also followed, because of copyright restrictions, in the publishing house of the M.E. Church, South. This practice, which continued until a decade ago, often makes difficult the identification of items published by the official publishing agencies of Methodism. The first line of Abingdon Press books, although consistently of high moral tone, extended beyond the bounds of the strictly religious.

Enjoying the general prosperity of the times, in the mid 1920's, the Methodist Book Concern extended its real estate holdings and erected a printing plant in suburban Dobbs Ferry, N. Y., moving its manufacturing operations out of New York City. This, along with other factors, left the Concern in weakened condition to weather the big depression of the 1930's. As a result the organization arrived at the end of the decade in serious economic condition. Thus its affairs were somewhat disordered at the time of unification in 1939.

Publishing House of the Methodist Episcopal Church, South. When Nathan Bangs began the *Christian Advocate* in 1826, so popular was this publication that local Methodist papers, modeled after the New York periodical, began to spring up throughout the settled portions of the country. Further impetus was given them when the Book

Concern in 1833 approved the publication of a "Christian Advocate" for the Mississippi Valley Region (the *Western Christian Advocate*). Sectional feeling was rather generally characteristic of the country, and the desire for special sectional papers sprang up in smaller and smaller regions. One of these was begun in NASHVILLE, Tenn., in 1833; and there were others elsewhere, both within and outside the South. The General Conference of 1836 accorded official sanction, including Book Concern sponsorship, to six of these papers, one of which was the Nashville publication. Thus began Methodist publishing in Tennessee's capital city.

By the time of the split in the M.E. Church, the Nashville paper, titled the *South-Western Christian Advocate*, was being ably edited and managed by JOHN B. McFERRIN, a Methodist minister of the TENNESSEE CONFERENCE. In 1845, the first book published by the M.E. Church, South, a history of its organization, was issued in Nashville under the direction of McFerrin. The organizing convention in Louisville provided for a Southern Book Concern, and at the church's first General Conference in 1846, JOHN EARLY, later bishop, was named Book Agent. Located in RICHMOND, Early gave direction to such book publishing as the Church, South undertook in its early years. THOMAS O. SUMMERS, in CHARLESTON, S. C., was named editor of the Church's Sunday school publication, the *Sunday School Visitor*, and *Advocates* were approved for all three cities. More formalized publishing plans were to be laid when the property of the Book Concerns of the Northern Church was divided. As has already been seen, this required ten years, during which interval the Southern publishing program was carried out in a scattered fashion.

The General Conference of 1854, anticipating a large sum of money to be received from the M.E. Church in accordance with the terms of the Plan of Separation and the decision of the courts, voted to establish a full-blown publishing house, complete with print shop, in Nashville, Tenn. This city was already identified with Methodist publishing; was nearer the center of the South than either CHARLESTON or RICHMOND; and was neither a border town, such as LOUISVILLE, nor a river town, such as MEMPHIS. Thus to it fell the honor of being the site of the first real publishing house south of the Mason-Dixon line. The whole section, other denominations as well as Methodists, took pride in it. As its first quarters, a tobacco warehouse on Nashville's public square was secured, and with the aid of a Philadelphia binder who relocated his shop in Nashville, the Southern Methodist Publishing House got under way late in 1854. Edward Stevenson and F. A. Owens were elected Book Agents.

To make up for lost time, the Southern House immediately launched a full-scale publishing program, duplicating insofar as possible that of the two Northern Book Concerns. During its first year, the BOOK EDITOR, as the title had become, again T. O. Summers, said that 150 titles were issued by this house. Some were traditional Methodist items, while others were reprints of English books, quickly "revised" by Summers—who was born in England—and pushed through the press. By 1858 it was obvious that the new enterprise had overextended itself, and John McFerrin, editor of the *Nashville Christian Advocate,* was elected Book Agent. From the outset his task was to correct the fiscal mistakes the House had made in its first four years.

McFerrin was well on the way to accomplishing his assignment when, in 1861, the Civil War erupted, unsettling conditions throughout the section. Nashville, the carefully chosen site of the Publishing House, was the first major Southern city to fall. It was occupied in February 1862 by the federal army, in advance of which McFerrin and most of the officials of the House (all staunchly Confederate in their sympathies) fled farther south to escape capture. From this time until the end of the war, activities of the Southern Methodist Publishing House were at a standstill, especially after the property of the House was confiscated in 1863 for use as a U. S. Government printing house.

During the late spring and summer of 1865, McFerrin and other departed Publishing House officials returned to Nashville to begin their work anew. Securing from President Andrew Johnson a release of the property, badly damaged during the federal occupancy, McFerrin resumed publication of the *Nashville Christian Advocate* in the late fall of 1865. Prior to the war, in the interest of economy, the Nashville paper had been made the sole official organ of the denomination, the other papers such as the *Southern Christian Advocate* in Charleston and the *Richmond Christian Advocate,* reverting to the support of their related annual conferences.

When the first postwar General Conference of the M.E. Church, South met in NEW ORLEANS in May 1866, continuation of the Publishing House, despite all odds, was voted. A. H. REDFORD, a minister of the LOUISVILLE CONFERENCE, was made Book Agent, while editorial responsibilities were largely assigned to T. O. Summers.

Recovering with rather amazing speed from the plight in which it found itself in 1865, the Southern House by 1872 felt itself to be sufficiently strong to undertake the erection of a new office building and plant in Nashville. Hardly had the new structure been completed than faults in the construction made immediate repairs necessary if the building was to be safely occupied. This unexpected cost, coupled with poor financial management and the overextending of credit, so sapped the life of the enterprise that by 1878 bankruptcy appeared the only choice. However, at the General Conference that year, McFerrin, since 1866 the church's Mission Secretary, was recalled to the post of Book Agent, and with the Book Committee was authorized to make whatever disposition of the House seemed best. Determined that the Southern Methodist Publishing House should not fail, McFerrin and the Book Committee devised a plan whereby low interest bonds could be sold to pay off high interest loans the House had previously made. The sale of these bonds across the South, largely accomplished by John B. McFerrin himself, a tough, consecrated campaigner as well as a master of oratory, comprises one of the most dramatic chapters in the history of The Methodist Publishing House. Within less than two years the bonds, totaling $300,000, were sold; and by 1884, when McFerrin died, the House was declared free from debt.

The careful and cautious management required by these circumstances somewhat inhibited the program of the Southern Methodist Publishing House during these years, throughout which its major efforts were concentrated on production of the *Christian Advocate,* edited by the able and popular O. P. FITZGERALD, and items for the Sunday school. In the latter field (although elsewhere the program of the organization was weak), obvious efforts were made to keep abreast of the times.

The decade of the 1890's was a period of significant

growth for the southern organization which, as the century turned, was further benefited by money appropriated by the U. S. Senate to pay off the long-standing war damage claim occasioned by federal occupancy of the Nashville property during the Civil War. This claim was based on the declaration of the Lincoln administration that restitution would be made for war damage to property of churches, educational institutions, and other eleemosynary enterprises. In 1898, after more than thirty years, the U. S. Senate acted favorably on the claim of the M.E. Church, South. In the final days—indeed in the final hours—of the Senate's consideration, a question was raised concerning the size of the fee the House had agreed to pay its lawyer for handling the case. A hasty exchange of letters and telegrams between the Agents and Washington officials on this point (which was judged to have no bearing on the justice of the claim), resulted in a charge that the Agents, J. D. BARBEE and D. M. SMITH, had been deliberately misleading in their answers to certain questions. Considerable furor was caused throughout the Southern Church, with the result that the General Conference of 1902 staged a full-fledged investigation of the matter. Assured by the U. S. Senate that the Church would not be expected to return the money—$288,000—paid on the claim, the General Conference exonerated the action of the Agents. Barbee, however, was not re-elected Book Agent, although Smith was returned to the position of Junior Agent. In 1903, upon the resignation of Barbee's elected successor, R. J. Bigham, Smith became Senior Agent. Like John Milton Phillips in the M.E. Church, Smith was the first layman to hold the post of Book Agent in the Southern Church.

The generally favorable condition of the Southern Methodist Publishing House in the early 1900's led to expansion of the enterprise and real estate improvements in Nashville. In 1899 a branch was begun in DALLAS, Texas, and in 1902, together with the Missionary Society of the M.E. Church, the Southern House opened a branch in Shanghai, CHINA, which functioned for several years. This bold step was in accord with a tradition of assistance to missionary endeavors for many years practiced by the Methodist Book Concern in New York. During the middle years of the nineteenth century a missionary publishing house in Bremen, GERMANY, had to a certain extent been sponsored by the Methodist Book Concern. The program of German publishing in Cincinnati and that of Spanish and Portuguese publishing in the Southern House were in the same tradition. In 1912 a branch was officially opened in Richmond, Va., where through colporteurs and other channels Methodist books had been sold for many years.

In 1907 the Nashville operation of the Southern Methodist Publishing House moved from the public square location to a building erected for its use at 810 Broadway in Nashville. For many years this building, since it also housed several general agencies of the church, was informally regarded as the headquarters of the M.E. Church, South. After unification in 1939, 810 Broadway, Nashville was official headquarters for the Publishing House of The Methodist Church until 1957.

Following a steady though undramatic course during the years between 1910 and 1920, the Southern Methodist Publishing House in 1924 adopted a policy of publishing books of general Christian appeal as well as issuing titles bearing specifically on Methodism. At this time the House selected the imprint COKESBURY PRESS, which until unification was used on these items. The venture was immediately successful, and was partly responsible for the healthy condition in which the Southern Methodist Publishing House emerged from the depression of the 1930's. Well patronized by the church and accustomed to weathering adverse times, the Southern House at the time of Methodist union in 1939 was the soundest publishing enterprise of any of the three churches.

As a manufacturer of books since 1854, the Southern Methodist Publishing House had been a leader in this industry. In 1924 a separate printing plant was erected on Demonbreun Street in Nashville, which in 1957 formed the core of a new structure now headquarters of Methodist publishing. Since 1935 the Methodist printing plant in Nashville has employed as its trade imprint The Parthenon Press. This imprint, since unification, has also applied to printing done in the Cincinnati plant.

The Methodist Protestant Book Concern. Within bounds it might be said that the formation of the Methodist Protestant Church commenced in 1828 had as its basis the desire on the part of the Methodist Reformers for a free press. Claiming with some justification that they had only limited access to the columns of *The Methodist Magazine,* then under the editorship of Nathan Bangs, certain Methodist ministers independently began publication of a periodical entitled *Mutual Rights.* This publication, issued from Baltimore, advocated equal lay and clerical representation in the conferences of the church, together with restrictions on, if not elimination of, the powers of the episcopacy. Reprimanded for fostering a schismatic movement within the Methodist Episcopal Church, the leaders were expelled. As a result the Methodist Protestant Church was organized in 1830.

The importance of publications, especially periodicals, was recognized by the church at its organizing convention. JOHN JOLLY HARROD, a Baltimore book dealer, was named Book Agent and, it was said, like John Dickins before him, began the enterprise with his own funds. Prominent among its publications was the *Methodist Protestant,* a weekly newspaper which succeeded *Mutual Rights.* For a time Harrod attempted to publish and sell books for the denomination, but as the response in this area was limited, he relinquished his commission, and the church attempted to establish a book concern through contributions from the church members. This effort was never successful, but publication of the *Methodist Protestant* was continued.

In the 1850's dissatisfaction arose in the northern and western conferences of the church over the policy governing the *Methodist Protestant's* refusal to admit discussions of slavery in its columns. By action of the General Conference of 1854, permission was given for each section of the church to have its own periodical, if the conferences desired, with responsibility for the publications to rest on the annual conferences, not the General Conference. While meeting to discuss the beginning of a western publication, the western anti-slavery conferences decided to withdraw entirely from the eastern and southern conferences. As a result there were two churches from 1866 to 1877, as well as two publications. The *Methodist Protestant,* published in Baltimore, continued as the organ of the southern and eastern sections of the church, while the *Western Methodist Protestant* became the organ of the western conferences. Published for a time at Zanesville, Ohio, and later at Springfield, Ohio, the *Western Recorder* as it was ultimately named, along with the Western Methodist Protestant Book Concern, in the early

1870's came to rest at Pittsburgh. Although neither of the Book Concerns was a large operation, the Book Concern of the western Methodist Protestant body operated its own print shop.

In 1877 when the two sections of the church again came together, a Board of Publications was established, with separate local "directories" in charge of the Baltimore and Pittsburgh operations. By this time the Pittsburgh Directory was publishing not only the *Recorder,* but also a Sunday school periodical entitled *Our Morning Guide,* similar to the *Sunday School Advocate* of the Methodist Episcopal Church and the *Sunday School Visitor* of the Southern Church. The Baltimore Directory was publishing the *Methodist Protestant* and a series of uniform Sunday school lessons, both edited by EDWARD J. DRINK-HOUSE. In 1884 all Sunday school publications were transferred to the Pittsburgh Directory, from which point they were distributed as well as printed.

Maintaining distinct identities for many years, the two Methodist Protestant publishing enterprises came closer together in 1929, when the two papers, the *Methodist Protestant* and the *Methodist Recorder,* were merged as the *Methodist Protestant Recorder,* published in Baltimore, where by this date a print shop was also being operated. This printing establishment employed as its trade name The Stockton Press, in commemoration of THOMAS STOCKTON, early denominational leader.

Methodist Protestant publishing, while never carried out on so extensive a scale as the publishing programs of the Methodist Episcopal Church and the Methodist Episcopal Church, South, is notable for its consistent production of both general and Sunday school periodicals. These publications did much to establish and maintain the identity of the relatively small denomination.

Since Unification. When the three Methodist Churches came together in 1939, Nashville was chosen as headquarters of what all agreed should be called The Methodist Publishing House. At this time the organization had mail-order branches in thirteen cities in addition to six printing plants. Each of the three uniting churches had its own system of Sunday school literature, and each its own assortment of periodicals. Consolidation of these operations, greatly affected by the entry of the United States into World War II in December 1941, was not completely achieved until the late 1940's. When finally accomplished The Methodist Publishing House consisted of thirteen mail-order locations, two printing plants (one in Nashville and one in Cincinnati), one system of Sunday school (by this time called "church school") literature, one general church periodical (the *Christian Advocate*), and one quarterly publication as successor to *The Methodist Magazine* and the old *Quarterly Reviews* (under the title *Religion in Life*). Except for official Methodist items, the House was using the imprint Abingdon-Cokesbury Press on its books, and The Parthenon Press as the trade name of its manufacturing department. It was headed by two Publishing Agents, one lay and one clerical, and governed by the Methodist Board of Publications.

Blessed with financial success during the war years and the years of the religious boom following the war, the newly unified operation was enabled to move forward despite almost constant organizational changes necessitated by the continuing process of unification. The decade of the 1940's was distinguished by initiation of the project to publish a Bible commentary, which appeared in twelve volumes published between 1951 and 1956 as *The Interpreter's Bible,* now a classic of biblical scholarship.

In 1956 the *Christian Advocate* became two publications: *Together,* a handsome monthly family magazine rivaling in technical perfection and editorial content elaborate secular publications of the period; and the *New Christian Advocate,* a professional journal for Methodist ministers and laymen intimately involved in the affairs of the local and general church. (In 1960 this publication reassumed the original title *Christian Advocate.*) In 1957 the House completed and occupied a new headquarters building at 201 Eighth Avenue, South, in Nashville, and in that same year undertook studies leading to a reorganization of its retail and mail-order departments and distribution points. In 1960 it adopted the trade name Cokesbury, for this aspect of its services, and changed the name of its book publishing department to Abingdon Press.

The recurrence of these names throughout the recent history of Methodist publishing deserves explanation. Both are related to the first educational endeavor of Methodism in America. Cokesbury College, the first Methodist school in this country, was opened in 1787 at Abingdon, Md. The name Cokesbury combines syllables from the names of the first two Methodist bishops: Thomas Coke and Francis Asbury. The idea for Cokesbury College, it will be remembered, was first set forth by John Dickins, who is recognized as the founder of The Methodist Publishing House. Reminiscent of the days of the mounted circuit rider is the present circuit rider colophon or trademark of The Methodist Publishing House, a tribute to the men who first circulated the books and periodicals published by the organization.

Today The Methodist Publishing House has operations in fourteen metropolitan areas across the nation. In Nashville are offices of its five central divisions: Retail Sales, Publishing, Manufacturing, Accounting, and Personnel and Public Relations. In Nashville also is the larger of its two printing plants, one of the largest complete printing operations in the nation; its Southern Regional Service Center (mail order); and one of its Cokesbury Book Stores. In Chicago and suburban Park Ridge, Illinois, are editorial offices of *Together;* the *Christian Advocate;* the North Central Regional Service Center; and a Cokesbury store.

In New York City and suburban Teaneck, New Jersey, are the Northern Regional Service Center, a Cokesbury store, and a Cokesbury book depository, in the Church Center near the United Nations Building. Other regional service centers and book stores are in Richmond, Virginia; Dallas, Texas; and San Francisco, California. Cokesbury stores are likewise operated in Atlanta; Boston; Baltimore; Cincinnati (where is located the second of the Methodist printing plants); Detroit; Kansas City, Missouri; Los Angeles; and Pittsburgh.

Some indication of the book publishing activity of The Methodist Publishing House may be seen in the catalogs of Abingdon Press, which annually list more than a hundred new titles, including religious books, children's books, and books of general interest to youth and adults. A sizable portion of the publishing program of the House is concerned with the publication of teaching materials for the Church school, bearing the Graded Press imprint, editorially prepared by the Editorial Division of the Methodist Board of Education on outlines devised by the church's CURRICULUM COMMITTEE.

A Nonprofit, Self-Sustaining Organization. From its inception The Methodist Publishing House and its predecessor organizations have been nonprofit but self-sustaining. Even before the Methodist Book Concern officially came into being, the *Discipline* of 1787 specified that profits arising from the sale of books should be directed to denominational causes at the discretion of the bishop and the Council. The 1792 *Discipline* directed the Book Steward to pay monies out of the book fund for Cokesbury College, district schools, and "distressed preachers." From the outset, success was so presumed for the publishing activity that no provision was made for its own sustenance other than such monies as would come from its own operation. For a time, in the early 1800's, an effort was made to collect money for a Tract Fund to enable the Concern to sell at less than publishing cost evangelistic and moralistic tracts. This effort, however, was notably unsuccessful. Therefore, it can be truthfully said that The Methodist Publishing House has been self-sustaining since its founding.

The practice of drawing support for church causes from book sales, early established by the church, continued almost uncontrolled during the early years of the Book Concern. Despite the passage of the sixth Restrictive Rule in 1808, forbidding the General Conference to use the surplus funds of the Book Concern for any other purpose than the support of worn-out preachers, the Concern for many years paid the salaries and expenses of the bishops and underwrote the expenses of the General Conferences, besides supplying money for other less obvious expenses of the church. In 1860, Thomas Carlton said, "The Concern has paid the general expenses of the whole church, . . . at an average of nearly $38,000 per annum since 1836." It is calculated that during this period about $300,000 was actually distributed to the annual conferences for the relief of the retired ministers, their widows and dependent children. Between 1860 and 1868, $132,609 went for this purpose.

At the turn of the century, the Methodist Book Concern, including the Concern in Cincinnati, began making larger appropriations for the conference claimants. By 1939, it was reckoned that a total of nearly $9,000,000 had been appropriated by the Methodist Book Concern for this purpose.

The precedent established by the M.E. Church of drawing money from its publishing house for the miscellaneous expenses of the church was followed from the first by the M.E. Church, South. By 1866, it was figured that $233,000 of Publishing House money had been spent in "outside enterprises" of the M.E. Church, South. Because of the straitened financial circumstances of the Southern Methodist Publishing House, no appropriations were made to the conference claimants of the Church, South during the 1870's and for most of the 1880's. Resuming the practice in 1888, the Southern Methodist Publishing House by unification had appropriated a total of $1,848,290 for the conference claimants of the Southern Church.

The Book Concerns of the M.P. Church, although basically organized in a different manner from those of the episcopal churches, were from the first hopefully considered a source of revenue for the denomination. This hope never materialized, however, as the concerns at best only met their own expenses.

Since unification, The Methodist Publishing House, has operated strictly in conformity with the church's Fifth Restrictive Rule, which provided that the income of the organization could only be used for the business itself, with proceeds above operating expenses and proper reserves going only to the conference claimants. A total of $12,365,000 was appropriated for these beneficiaries between 1940 and 1968.

In the aggregate, since its organization in 1789, the publishing agency of The Methodist Church has provided more than $23 million for the denomination's retired ministers, widows, and orphaned children.

In The United Methodist Church. At the union of The Methodist Church and the Evangelical United Brethren Church in 1968, the publishing interests of both Churches were put under one General Board of Publication, similar to, and for practical purposes an extension of, the Board of Publication of The Methodist Church as it had been up to that time. The General Board, comprising all the publishing interests of The United Methodist Church, functions as The Methodist Publishing House. The Board consists of forty-five members including two bishops selected by the Council of Bishops, five members at large, elected by the Board, and thirty-eight members elected by the Jurisdictional Conferences, the number from each Conference determined by the membership of the Jurisdiction.

The E.U.B. Church brought into the union the Otterbein Press, located in Dayton, Ohio, and the Evangelical Press in Harrisburg, Pa. Centralization of the entire printing operation in the interests of efficiency and economy brought all publishing to the Nashville plant. In view of this, the Cincinnati, Dayton, and Harrisburg plants were sold. (See also PUBLISHING HOUSE CONTROVERSY.)

F. Asbury, *Journal and Letters.* 1958.
N. Bangs, *History of the M. E. Church.* 1838-41.
J. Minton Batten, *The History of the Methodist Publishing House.* Nashville: Personnel and Public Relations Division of The Methodist Publishing House, 1954.
A. H. Bassett, *Concise History.* 1877.
Centennial of the Methodist Book Concern and Dedication of the New Publishing and Mission Building, a memento volume. New York: Hunt and Eaton, 1890.
Disciplines.
E. J. Drinkhouse, *History of Methodist Reform.* 1899.
Fifteen Years and an Idea. A Report on Cokesbury Press. Nashville: Cokesbury Press, 1938.
H. C. Jennings, *Book Concern.* 1924.
Journals of the General Conferences.
J. Lanahan, *Era of Frauds.* 1896.
Jesse Lee, *Short History.* 1810.
J. P. Pilkington, *Methodist Publishing House.* 1968.
Millard George Roberts, "The Methodist Book Concern in the West." Unpublished dissertation, The University of Chicago, 1947.
Ralph Stoody, "Religious Journalism: Whence and Whither?" Unpublished thesis, Gordon College of Theology, 1939.
W. F. Whitlock, *Book Concerns.* 1903.   JAMES P. PILKINGTON

METHODIST QUARTERLY REVIEW. This title covers the publishing history of a periodical which began in 1818 as *The Methodist Magazine,* and continued to appear under various titles (except 1829) until its demise in 1931: *The Methodist Magazine,* monthly, 1818-28; *The Methodist Magazine and Quarterly Review,* quarterly, 1830-40; *The Methodist Quarterly Review,* 1841-84; and *The Methodist Review,* bimonthly, 1885-1931. In addition to English predecessors (beginning with *The Arminian Magazine* from 1778) two abortive efforts had already been made: the reprinting of the first two volumes

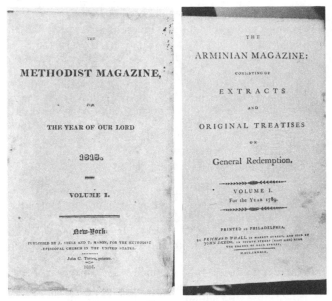

METHODIST QUARTERLY REVIEW

of the English magazine by JOHN DICKINS in 1789-90 as enterprises of the newly founded Methodist BOOK CONCERN, and the distribution in 1797-98 of a few numbers of a proposed *Methodist Magazine* authorized by the GENERAL CONFERENCE of 1796.

In 1816 the General Conference instructed "the book steward and his assistant," who turned out to be JOSHUA SOULE and Thomas Mason, to begin anew the project of publishing a serious religious periodical. Accordingly in 1818 appeared the first issue of *The Methodist Magazine*. "The great design of this publication," averred the editors, "is to circulate religious knowledge—a design which embraces the highest interests of rational existence, as the sum of individual and social happiness increases on a scale of proportion with the increase of spiritual light and information." The subsequent editors were: NATHAN BANGS, 1820-36; Samuel Luckey, 1836-40; GEORGE PECK, 1840-48; JOHN MCCLINTOCK, 1848-56; DANIEL WHEDON, 1856-84; DANIEL CURRY, 1884-88; James Mendenhall, 1888-92; WILLIAM KELLEY, 1892-1920; GEORGE ELLIOTT, 1920-30.

During the early years the little monthly subsisted on reprints of articles drawn chiefly from the *Arminian Magazine* and pious accounts of divine providence and saintly deaths. Bangs accomplished much with little until his election as Missionary Secretary in 1836, when Samuel Luckey took over for a quadrennium. During this period book reviews became a part of the regular features. The change from small monthly to substantial quarterly in 1830 marked the emergence of a true theological review. Not until the era of George Peck, however, did the magazine assume mature status as a serious journal. Interpretations of new trends in philosophy and theology began to appear. German works were reviewed.

The *MQR* entered an exciting period with the appearance of John McClintock as editor. Taking up his duties as General Conference complained against the scholarly standards in favor of more popular treatment, he forthrightly stood firm for yet higher standards. Long intensive review articles appeared on religious and secular books like Butler's *Analogy* and Ticknor's classic on Spanish literature. Several articles took up cudgels against prevailing liberalism of the Channing-Parker-Comte varieties. Throughout the whole century contributions followed in regular succession on aspects of Wesleyan theology and Methodist church order.

During the long decades between 1856 and 1884 Daniel D. Whedon spent his tremendous energy on building the *MQR* into a journal unsurpassed by any other of the time. Its influence was felt not only within the circle of Methodism but throughout American Protestantism. Many contributions came from non-Methodists, among them Philip Schaff. Whedon was not afraid of controversy. The pages sparkled with fires of debate on lively issues. Schleiermacher and Bushnell came off rather well in critical articles; but Theodore Parker and Ralph Waldo Emerson were severely mauled. The *Review* took account of the appearance of a new generation of Methodist theological writing—Whedon's own *Freedom of the Will*, Miner Raymond's *Systematic Theology*, John Miley's *Atonement in Christ*. In addition it sought to interpret for its readers the broader aspects of nineteenth century culture, especially in the field of literature. A few voices were raised in favor of original American art.

With Whedon's retirement, the new editors, Daniel Curry and, more important, James Mendenhall, expanded the review to a fat bimonthly, including several added features designed to win a wider audience, the "Arena" and "Itinerants' Club." The doughty old editor turned his journal into a veritable fortress against the attacks of "agnosticism, Old Testament criticism, and all the cognate upheavals in the path of Christian culture and progress." He was already struggling to prevent the nineteenth century from becoming the twentieth. Nevertheless new voices were heard and different points of view were expressed. Culturally a reaction set in against the romantic vagaries of Berlioz and "the unspeakable Zola."

The next period, the long editorship of William V. Kelley, carried the *MQR* into the twentieth century. Names like RALL and LEWIS and KNUDSON appeared, to say nothing of the perennial BOWNE. Kelley suited well the spirit of the turn-of-century with his combination of serious theological and broad cultural interests. The furious battles of modernists and fundamentalists were muted in the magazine. There was a respite from the fiery crusades of Whedon and Mendenhall.

The last decade was controlled by George Elliott, who died suddenly in 1930. The *MQR* died almost as suddenly, doubly stricken by the death of its editor and the Great Depression, and expired with the third issue of volume 114 in 1931. It had been born three years after the venerable *North American Review*, which managed to survive eight years longer. It continued in unbroken vigorous publication far longer than any other scholarly religious periodical in America. It was reborn in 1932 as the ecumenical review, *Religion in Life*, different in title and scope but of the same parentage.

FREDERICK A. NORWOOD

METHODIST QUARTERLY REVIEW (M.E. Church, South). This magazine was launched in 1847, with H. B. BASCOM, President of Transylvania University, LOUISVILLE, Ky., as editor and JOHN EARLY the publisher.

The introduction in the first issue stated the magazine's policy. Following are excerpts. "It is intended as a general Church organ, authorized by the Methodist Episcopal Church, South, at Louisville, Kentucky . . . Ours is an age of nominal opulence, commercial greatness, varied mechanical activity and rapid progress . . . This review is designed to explore theology, philosophy, science, education and literature. It is written primarily for the south, to encourage southern authors . . . Honest search for facts of theology and historical reality are always to be sought and fairly presented . . . As a Nation, we are one, and God grant that we shall forever continue to be."

The first volume featured a defense of "State Rights," and a plea for "Adequate Religious Education of the Negro." A department of "exegesis" and a generous editorial section were carried throughout its history. The *Quarterly* of the M.E. Church, South, during the nineteenth century, carried articles titled "Is A Classical Liberal Arts Education Essential To An Effective Minister?" "The Merits of the Property Settlement of the Divided Methodism," "Proper Female Education," "Missions," "Biographies of Eminent Ministers" (many of other denominations), and many other subjects.

In 1851 DAVID S. DOGGETT became the editor and John Early continued as publisher, in RICHMOND, Va. By 1858 the *Quarterly* was moved to NASHVILLE, Tenn., with THOMAS O. SUMMERS the editor. In 1859 the Southern Methodist Publishing House was listed as the publisher.

The *Quarterly* of the M.E. Church, South, was discontinued in 1860, with the outbreak of the Civil War. It was some years before that Church recovered from war enough to publish a journal again, but in the meanwhile the GENERAL CONFERENCE of 1870, struggling to get the Church back after the ravages its people had suffered, adopted the *Southern Review* as their official journal. This was edited by ALBERT TAYLOR BLEDSOE and became the "representative connectional publication" of the Church, South.

Bledsoe had begun this quarterly journal in BALTIMORE in 1867 and it soon obtained a wide and powerful influence "over the southern half of the continent," as Bishop HORACE DUBOSE expressed it. Bishop DuBose termed Bledsoe "a demiurge who seemed to have concreted all masteries into a single brain and taken his place upon the tripod. Its editor being a Methodist layman who a little later entered into the local ministry, the people called Methodists felt a peculiar loyalty to the *Review*." The *Review* and the church's support of it continued to the close of 1877 when Bledsoe died. Bishop DuBose properly observed that the numbers of this magazine "are a repository of theological and philosophical thought of such excellence as to constitute a library in themselves." This is true, and the forty-eight issues of the *Southern Review* are today highly prized, cherished and often referred to in many important libraries, especially over the South.

Two years after Bledsoe's death, in 1879, the old *Quarterly* of the M.E. Church, South was revived. J. W. Hinton of MACON, Ga. was editor and J. W. Beck of CHATTANOOGA and BIRMINGHAM the printers, under contract with the Southern Methodist Publishing House until 1887, when the "new series of the Quarterly Review" was first printed in the Nashville plant.

The Southern Methodist Publishing House was severely handicapped by the Union Army of Occupation in Nashville, when it commandeered their new building and equipment, for five years, as Army Headquarters. "The Federal War Claims Committee" appraised the damage at $500,000 but the Church could not secure an act of Congress for payment until 1897, when a compromise settlement was made for $288,000, thirty-five percent of this amount going for attorneys' fees, and cost the Church another long controversy.

In 1886 appeared the first two of many articles on "Union of the Methodist Churches." W. P. Harrison was editor from January 1887 through 1902, when JOHN J. TIGERT gave distinction to the magazine until 1906. GROSS ALEXANDER was listed editor during 1906, however, E. E. Hoss edited the quarterly for 1907 when Alexander took over the editorship until 1915. Horace DuBose gave editorial luster to "The Review" for 1916-18. Frank Thomas was editor for 1919-21, to be succeeded by GILBERT ROWE from 1921-28. WILLIAM PETER KING became the thirteenth and last editor in 1928 until the General Conference of 1930 decreed that the "Honorable Methodist *Quarterly Review* of the Methodist Episcopal Church, South, be discontinued with the current volume." The depression also helped to terminate the *Quarterly Review* of the M.E. Church in 1931. Subsequently *Religion in Life* began to be published under the auspices of the M.E. Church, and this journal was adopted and provision made for its continuance in The Methodist Church.

Before and after 1860 brief experiments were made to publish the magazine as a monthly and a bi-monthly. During the nineteenth century the most frequently listed topics were on Methodist polity, ministerial education, Methodist schools and colleges, the place of women in the church, lay representation in the annual and general conferences. Less frequent articles explored English Literature, biographies and missions.

The "dawn of the golden century" was hailed in 1900. Articles reflected new issues in the twentieth century such as secularism, modernism, fundamentalism, the "status of the Negro," labor, temperance, peace and woman suffrage. By 1966 many of these once issues have been resolved, or are now rapidly moving towards some adjustment.

H. M. DuBose, *History*. 1916.
Methodist Quarterly Review, complete file on microfilm in the Library of the Methodist Publishing House, Nashville, Tenn.

J. RICHARD SPANN

METHODIST RECORDER, THE, a Wesleyan newspaper, first issued on April 4, 1861, under G. T. PERKS and W. MORLEY PUNSHON, was more liberal and cheaper than *The Watchman*. Its editors or managing-editors have been W. T. DAVISON, NEHEMIAH CURNOCK, J. B. Watson, F. D. WISEMAN, R. G. Burnett, and the present editor, W. E. Pigott. It is vigorously independent and not the property of the denomination or the Conference. It reports foreign and general news and comments thereon in "Notes of the Week." Having absorbed *The Methodist Times and Leader* and *The United Methodist*, it is the only Methodist newspaper circulating today in England. A series of "Winter Numbers" issued annually at Christmas from 1892 to 1907 are rich in articles on Methodist history. (See photo, p. 1593.)

The Methodist Recorder, Centenary supplement, April 6, 1961.

JOHN C. BOWMER

METHODIST REVIVAL FELLOWSHIP was formed in 1952 by a few evangelical British Methodist ministers and laymen who had begun to meet together annually for prayer and Bible study shortly after the Second World War.

METHODIST Recorder

5,874   THURSDAY, JULY 2, 1970   PRICE 9d.

Conference ready now for Stage One

SEVENTY-NINE PER CENT SEAL ON 1969 DECISION

BY THE EDITOR

Whitworth Hall,
University of Manchester,
Saturday, June 27

The Representative Session of the 1970 Conference this morning served notice on the Church of England that it is ready to proceed with Stage One of the plan for Unity.

It was made clear that a simple majority would have been enough. In the event, on a show of hands, 485 representatives voted in favour with 124 against, a majority of 79.64 per cent.

Earlier in the year twenty-nine Synods had given approval to the 1969 decision in the following terms:

The Conference, affirming its faith that the Holy Spirit will lead us into a new Church, gives approval to the inauguration of Stage One of the Anglican-Methodist proposals.

Conference is no picnic and there are long periods when members have to listen intently to serious debate. There are, however, lighter moments when the wit of the speaker gets a ready response and one such moment has been caught by the Recorder photographer in this shot of the representatives.

METHODIST RECORDER

Since that date it has grown (1963) to a fellowship of some two hundred ministers and over a thousand laymen, whose membership is scattered not only in British Methodism but through the mission field. It also has branches in AUSTRALIA and NEW ZEALAND. Its aims are to encourage study of the ways in which the Holy Spirit has worked in past revivals, and to stimulate prayer for a revival in the present age, believing that this is a most desperate need. In order to prepare for revival, the fellowship believes that there is a need to stress not only prayer, but also dependence upon the Scriptures and in particular the doctrines of assurance and scriptural holiness.

ROBIN J. O. CATLIN

METHODIST SOCIETY (Stillwellites), U.S.A., was formed in 1820 in NEW YORK when SAMUEL STILLWELL, a prominent politician in New York City and leader of a class of Negroes, and WILLIAM M. STILLWELL, his nephew and traveling preacher in charge of two Negro congregations in New York City, led over 300 people out of the M.E. Church. The cause of the schism was a resolution passed by the 1820 GENERAL CONFERENCE concerning the trust clause in the deed. The Conference said it would henceforth admit no charter for any house of worship not in keeping with the *Discipline* of the M.E. Church. This resolution offended many of the independently-minded

New York Methodists, who then left to form the Methodist Society in the City of New York.

The new church was congregational: bishops and presiding elders had no place in the organization. The Bible was to be the guide of discipline, and any rules were to be made by the members' vote. A *Discipline* was published in 1821 and a periodical, *The Friendly Visitor*, began. In 1826 disagreement over whether the church was to be purely congregational or somewhat connectional caused a split. The 2,000 member body had spread to CONNETICUT, NEW JERSEY, and Long Island. After the split, the church died out, though William Stillwell continued to preach in an independent Methodist church until 1851.

Frederick E. Maser and George A. Singleton, "Further Branches of Methodism are Founded," in *History of American Methodism,* 1964.   J. GORDON MELTON

METHODIST STUDENT MOVEMENT. (See YOUTH MOVEMENT.)

METHODIST THEOLOGICAL SCHOOL IN OHIO, Delaware, Ohio, was authorized by the GENERAL CONFERENCE of 1956, when that body called for expansion in the education of ministers. For several years prior to this date, OHIO Methodists, under the leadership of Bishop HAZEN G. WERNER, had been studying the possibilities for a seminary in Ohio. Between 1956 and 1960, Ohio Methodists raised $3,500,000 in a state-wide campaign. Later, $2,000,000 was added. OHIO WESLEYAN UNIVERSITY gave the school fifty-seven acres for a campus, and an additional fifteen-acre plot was obtained. The physical plant, dedicated October 14, 1960, was erected at a cost of $4,000,000. Instruction began in September, 1960. The seminary gives a B.D. degree. The governing board is made up of forty-four trustees, twelve each elected by two Ohio conferences; nine from bordering annual conferences, nominated by the bishops and elected by the conferences; ten at large; and the bishops of the two Ohio areas.

JOHN O. GROSS

METHODIST UNION FOR SOCIAL SERVICE, an organization founded by S. E. KEEBLE in 1905, and dissolved in 1926 when its functions were taken over by the Temperance Department of the Wesleyan Methodist Church.

Maldwyn L. Edwards, *S. E. Keeble*, London, Epworth Press, [? 1950].
FRANK BAKER

METHODIST UNITARIAN MOVEMENT, THE, (1806-58) forms the only real example of Methodist deviation upon doctrinal grounds. It was founded by JOSEPH COOKE (1775-1811), and gave birth to vigorous churches on the borders of Lancashire and Yorkshire. Because of two sermons preached at Rochdale in 1805, Cooke was expelled from the Methodist Society on grounds of doctrinal error. Although he never reached a Unitarian position, he appeared to have Socinian leanings, and the Methodist Unitarian Movement was the logical outcome of his methods in the study of the Scriptures. His followers became known as "Cookites," and their first chapel was built in Rochdale in 1806, followed by one at Newchurch-in-Rossendale in 1809. The earliest extant plan (1812) shows eighteen preachers and prayer leaders and sixteen places.

Closely associated with Cooke was John Ashworth. The introduction of the Cookites to organized Unitarianism arose as a result of their preachers occasionally supplying the pulpit of the Elland Unitarian Chapel, at that time in a straitened condition. The first annual meeting of the Methodist Unitarian Association, which existed until 1844, was held in Rochdale in 1818. In the following years Richard Wright (1764-1836), an itinerant of the Unitarian Fund, a missionary society established by the Unitarians in 1806, stimulated and encouraged the Methodist Unitarian congregations. About 1838, however, their organization began to dissolve. The leaders of the movement died; John Ashworth in 1851; James Taylor in 1856; James Wilkinson, the last of the faithful band of Cookite preachers, in 1858. Henceforth the congregations became independent in government and discipline, and passed into the main stream of Unitarian Christianity. Ashworth was the author of *Ten Letters: Giving an account of the Rise and Progress of the Unitarian Doctrine in the Societies . . . formerly in connection with the late Joseph Cooke* (1817; 2nd ed., 1829; reprinted, 1870).

The government and discipline of the movement was Methodist; the annual meeting of the association was a Methodist conference in miniature. The movement strongly supported the growth of Sunday schools, an outstanding example of which was at Todmorden, where

John Fielden (1784-1849), M. P., was superintendent. The half century during which the movement flourished was a period of social and political unrest. The Methodist Unitarians were, in the main, weavers, colliers, and artisans, and their ministers belonged to the same class. Fielden threw himself into the crusade for factory reform, and many Methodist Unitarians were behind the Todmorden Political Union, formed in 1831 to obtain radical reforms, the abolition of slavery and oppression. Of the political council, numbering twenty, seven were prominent Methodist Unitarians. The Methodist Unitarians also numbered in their ranks some of the earliest advocates of cooperation in England.

H. McLachlan, *The Methodist Unitarian Movement*. Manchester, 1919.
JOHN T. WILKINSON

METHODIST WOMEN'S FELLOWSHIP in New Zealand came into being on Feb. 1, 1964, for the first time combining all women's work in the church into a single, nationwide movement. The former WOMEN'S MISSIONARY UNION and the WOMEN'S GUILD FELLOWSHIP thereupon ceased to exist; and in addition many local groups, variously known as Fireside Clubs, Young Mothers' Groups and so on, were affiliated to the movement. The result has been a great increase in efficiency and a considerable saving in overhead expenses.

The new movement has taken over the programs and responsibilities of the former separate organizations. Its executive powers are vested in a national convention which meets annually in October. Membership is approximately ten thousand, and the amount raised for national objectives (year ending August 31, 1966) was £18,000. In addition, local fellowships raised a further £20,000 for circuit and trust objectives.

New Zealand Methodist Conference Minutes, 1964-66.
L. R. M. GILMORE

METHODIST WOMEN'S MISSIONARY UNION in New Zealand was formed in 1915. For many years auxiliaries or groups of missionary minded women had been working for missionary advancement: in Dunedin from 1902, in Christchurch from 1907, in Auckland and Wellington from 1908. Representatives of these and other auxiliaries —twelve in all—met in Christchurch in 1915 and formed the Methodist Women's Missionary Union and annual conferences have been held ever since.

In 1962, the union reported 226 auxiliaries with a total membership of 6,363. The income for 1960-61 was £17,302. Since 1906, gift parcels have been sent periodically to home and overseas sisters engaged in missionary work. Kurahuna, a hostel for Maori girls was opened by the union and is still supported by members of the Methodist Women's Fellowship. Each year, a special objective was accepted by the union; and in 1960-61, £2,750 was raised and sent to the Home and Maori Mission Department to assist in replacing furniture and amenities in one of the department's hostels for Maori girls.

The "Gleaners' Circle" has always endeavored to enlist support for missions from women living in isolated places. Gleaners have been sent regular missionary letters from the national president and from missionary sisters. Used stamps are sold too; and in 1960-61, £1,486 was raised in this way.

District conventions have been a feature of the union

program, and the movement has been singularly used of God to enrich the spiritual life of the church.

In 1964, the union united with the Women's Guild Fellowship to form a single movement known as the Methodist Women's Fellowship. All former activities of the union are continued by the new fellowship movement.

Kurahuna, a Maori girls' school hostel, at Onehunga, Auckland, New Zealand, owned and operated by the Women's Missionary Union (and now by the new Fellowship Movement), was opened on January 26, 1931, as the Kurahuna School of Domestic Science and Hygiene for the training of adolescent Maori girls. Union members raised most of the money to purchase a house and land and have maintained the work by instituting a penny-per-week-per-member fund. In 1944 the policy was changed to take younger Maori girls who live at the hostel and receive Christian and domestic training, while attending the local primary and secondary schools.

Methodist Women's Missionary Union Souvenirs and Reports.
WILLIAM T. BLIGHT

METHOPRESS. (See ARGENTINA.)

METHVIN, JOHN JASPER (1846-1941), American preacher and missionary to the Indians of OKLAHOMA, was born in Jeffersonville, Ga., Dec. 17, 1846. Educated in the schools of GEORGIA after serving two years in the Confederate States Army, he became a lawyer, then a teacher in the public schools, and then became president of Gainesville College and also of Butler Female College.

He was licensed to preach in the M. E. Church, South in 1870, ordained deacon in 1874, admitted on trial in the INDIAN MISSION CONFERENCE and ordained elder in 1885, and admitted to full membership in 1887, supernumerary in 1905, and retired in 1908.

In 1885 John Methvin heard the call of the church for missionaries to the Indians and went out to be Superintendent of New Hope Seminary for girls among the Choctaws. The next year he had similar work at Seminole Academy. During this year he made a tour of the Western Tribes in Oklahoma Territory, and wrote a report of conditions among these Indians urging that missionaries be sent. At the Annual Conference on Oct. 12, 1887, he was appointed "Missionary to the Western Tribes."

Immediately, he and his wife and children began the long journey west to Anadarko, Okla., where the Indian Agency for these tribes was located. He spent two years visiting the tribes from KANSAS to TEXAS, and decided to concentrate on the Kiowa, Comanche and Apache tribes. A parsonage was built with an annex for public worship, and the Indians were invited to join in the "New Worship."

He visited in teepees and tents, held prayer services, talked with individuals, speaking through interpreters. He made it clear he wanted nothing other than the opportunity to tell them of the love of God for all men. Among the very first converts was an Indian chief, To-hau-sin, and many followed his lead. Churches and Sunday schools were started, and in 1890 a day school was opened. This was known as "Methvin Institute" and for twenty years it was one of the great civilizing agencies. A ready writer, many articles and books came from his pen. Among them are: *Our Brother in Red, Andele or the Mexican-Kiowa Captive, Fig Leaves or Else,* and *In the Limelight.*

He died Jan. 17, 1941, and his body was laid to rest in the cemetery at Anadarko, in the land and among the people he loved.

Clegg and Oden, *Oklahoma.* 1968.
Journals of the Oklahoma Conference and the Indian Mission Conference.
C. E. NISBETT

MEXICAN BORDER CONFERENCE. (See RIO GRANDE CONFERENCE.)

MEXICO (Estados Unidos Mexicanos) is located in North America, bordered by the U.S.A. and GUATEMALA, and has an area of 1,972,545 square kilometers. The population is 48,600,000 (1970) and increases at the rate of 1,400,000 a year. It is fifteen percent white of European extraction, twenty-nine percent indigenous, fifty-five percent mixed races (mestizos), and one percent of other races. The official language is Spanish.

México has a variety of climates. The main sources of its economy are agriculture, livestock and mining.

As early as eight to ten thousand years B.C., nomad tribes wandered through its territory. The Maya-quiché and the Náhuatl groups were outstanding. They were highly developed, but they were in a period of decline, and were conquered by the Aztecs, a warrior people. During this period, in 1519, Hernando Cortéz landed in Vera Cruz.

The conquest of México was done by Spanish adventurers interested in gold, not in God. The natives, according to their traditions, took them to be descendants of their god (Quetzalcoatl). Assisted by Franciscan, Dominican and Augustinian monks, the conquerors took over all power, imposed their civilization and established a social life according to the feudal system from Europe. Big haciendas were built; slavery and exploitation were effected in the name of the new religion.

Europeans destroyed the native idols, substituting for them statues of Mary and of the infant Jesus. They evangelized them, imposing ideas and rituals by force, and baptized them by thousands. Conversion was made to forms, therefore the result was syncretism, and the natives were made to live in darkness, superstition, and ignorance. A few priests, like Bartolomé de las Casas and Fr. Pedro de Gante, are remembered for their good intentions and efforts to protect the defenseless, innocent natives. Such was the colonial period for 300 years.

México fought its war of independence from Spain in 1810, led by Miguel Hidalgo y Costilla, a priest. A period of chaos followed. By 1857 there was in existence a liberal party. It was composed of men who were not under the control of the traditional church; they were free to think and to act for themselves. Through the assistance of this party the President Benito Juarez, an Indian, was able to consolidate the Republic and to strengthen it. Under his leadership there was formulated the progressive constitution of 1857 and the famous laws of reform were enacted. These two documents established freedom of religion, the separation of Church and State, the nationalization of cemeteries and of the property of the clergy, lay teaching in the official schools, and civil marriage.

Following Juarez there was a thirty-four year period of dictatorship under Porfirio Díaz. In 1910 México was again involved in a much bigger revolution, social in essence and purpose, started by Francisco I. Madero. This revolution is even going on today, and has provided for a new nation. The Constitution was revised and a new one made in 1917, which provided justice for all, established national sovereignty, safeguarded individual rights, and recognized the rights of the manual worker and the need of agrarian changes. Through the years major developments have been in industry and commerce, education for all, new content and meaning in international relations, and self-determination for a new nation, old though it be.

It is recognized that the natives of México were very religious. There was, however, not much progress, due to the type of Christianity brought by the *conquistadores* and lived by the colonizers. The Bible was practically unknown by the priesthood and forbidden to be read or owned by lay people. Roman Catholicism was the official religion. An effort to evaluate the effect of the church in Mexico at that time shows that much of the misery, illiteracy, backwardness, and unrest of the people was due to the inability of the clergy to see the needs of the people as they ought to have done.

The reform movement under Juarez favored freedom of worship. Liberalism permeated different levels of society. The Inquisition was forbidden, therefore it was possible to strengthen colportage. Work of the BRITISH and AMERICAN BIBLE SOCIETIES started in 1827. By 1860 Protestant missionary work was being done along the U. S. border and missionaries were even sent south into the country.

It is no wonder that President Benito Juarez said, "I could wish that Protestantism would become Méxican by conquering the Indians; they need a religion which will compel them to read and not to spend their savings on candles for the saints." He also said, "Upon the development of Protestantism depends the future happiness and prosperity of my nation."

The Methodist Episcopal Church in Mexico. Two main branches of Methodism from the United States opened work in México. The GENERAL CONFERENCE of the M. E. Church appointed a committee in 1836 to consider the advisability of establishing work in México and South America. In November 1871, under the leadership of Bishop MATTHEW SIMPSON, an appropriation for the work was made. In 1872 WILLIAM BUTLER was selected to be superintendent of the work in México. Bishop GILBERT HAVEN preceded him and arrived at the port of Vera Cruz in December of 1872, and on Christmas day he was a passenger on the first through train of the newly constructed railroad to México City.

William Butler has been called "the founder of two missions," because twenty years before he came to México, he had gone on a similar work to INDIA. He arrived in México City, Feb. 23, 1873, and remained there seven years, after which he returned to the United States. He was an efficient and skillful worker. Soon after arriving in México City, he managed to buy a property. It happened to be the cloister of the first Franciscan monastery erected in the Americas. It is located on Gante Street, No. 5, the place in which Fr. Pedro de Gante had established the first grammar school in the continent and had opened it for the Indians. The place was dedicated, and consecrated as a Methodist Church, and opened to public worship on Christmas day of 1873.

Southern Methodism. In 1873 the LOUISIANA CONFERENCE met at NEW ORLEANS. Bishop GEORGE F. PIERCE was presiding, and invited Bishop JOHN C. KEENER to

make a few remarks. In his speech he mentioned interest in México, the closest neighbor, and thrilled his hearers with an account of the conversion of Alejo Hernández, a political exile from México then living in Brownsville, Texas. When he finished, a voice from the rear of the church called out, "If there were sufficient money, could you go to México?" To this Bishop Keener responded, "Of course I could go." A collection was raised, and so the first missionary of the M. E. Church, South was Bishop Keener. He embarked on the steamer *Tabasco* for Vera Cruz.

By 1875 he had secured a property in México City to be used as a church. It was the San Andrés Chapel which had been a part of the Capuchin monastery. They called it "The Messiah" in México City, and it later became the Church of El Mesías. Alejo Hernández was then appointed pastor of the newly organized church, and Sostenes Juárez, a man distantly related to the famous president, preached the first sermon in Spanish to a Spanish congregation of seven persons. Before returning to the States, the founder appointed J. L. Daves the first superintendent of that Méxican Mission.

Protestant work in México during that time was very difficult for the Methodists, as for all Protestants. The people were divided into two classes, the rich and the poor, and the poor were very poor. Fanaticism created great opposition. Persecution was almost everywhere. Families were divided on account of faith. New converts were ostracized by their relatives and friends. However, the work was carried on courageously by both the missionaries and the congregations. With firm resolution they planted the seed.

In accord with the times, the work was led by missionaries, mainly from the U.S.A.: men and women, preachers and teachers. They established churches, day schools, seminaries, orphanages and medical clinics in some of the most important cities, such as Chihuahua, Durango, Torreón, Monterrey, Guadalajara, General Terán, Saltillo, Guanajuato, Querétaro, Pachuca, Puebla, Caxaca, San Luis Potosí and the Federal District.

TEMPLO METODISTA, DURANGO, MEXICO

Very soon because of the readiness in many ways of the country and its people, there were converts and naturally national leaders began to share in the work, taking upon themselves important duties.

Long would be the list of that legion of faithful workers from both countries who witnessed to their faith in Christ and tried to help others to find peace, happiness and salvation. It would be impossible to forget such missionaries as John W. Butler and his wife, Sarah; J. P. Hauser and Mrs. Gould C. Hauser; Jackson B. Cox; Frank S. Onderdonk; Mr. and Mrs. Lemuel Newberry. In the field of education Dr. and Mrs. Matthew D. Smith, Ethel Thomas, Laura Temple, Helen Hewith, Grace Hallister and Mae B. Seal. In the training of the ministry, Milton C. Davis; in medical work, Miss Edna Pathoff and Dr. Leví B. Salmans; in social work and evangelism, Hattie L. Ayres, Lillie Fox, Leila Roberts, Helen M. Hodgson, Bishop W. P. THIRKIELD, and Bishop GEORGE A. MILLER.

Some outstanding nationals ought to be mentioned. Ministers: Agustin Palacios, Justo M. Euroza, Pedro Flores Valderrama, Victoriano D. Báez, Vincente Mendoza, Epigmenio Velasco, Eduardo Guerra S., Agapito C. Coronado, Gaspar Garza y Garza, Benjamín Fernández, Felipe Rincón, Raúl Ríos León, Eucario M. Sein, Ernesto M. Villansana, J. T. Ramírez, and Manuel V. Flores. In the field of education, Juan Díaz Galindo, Manuela Vargas, Antonio Carro, Agustín Romero López, Francisco Cruz Aedo, Benjamín N. Velasco, Francisco Cepeda C. and María González. Women active in denominational and interdenominational work, Mrs. Josefina G. de Velasco, Elisa S. de Pascoe, María Q. de Frausto, Guadelupe S. de Perales, Elizabeth M. de López, Mercedes Fernandez, Maclovia Garza Flores, Victoria Reyes, and Carmen Dávila.

Mexican Methodism United. Methodist unity came true in México on Sept. 16, 1930, even before the union in the U.S.A. From the beginning the M. E. Church and the M. E. Church, South in Mexico were somewhat related and very much in parallel. Each worked independently and attained triumphs and successes or faced dangers on its own, but often there was coordination. They supported enthusiastically the "National Convention," an interdenominational annual gathering for inspiration and spiritual growth. From it much fruit has come about.

In 1917-19 there was a joint effort in which several Missionary Boards proclaimed the "Cincinnati Plan." This plan expressed the desire and the imperative need to establish not only fraternal relations between the two Methodist churches, but also intimate and organic forms of cooperation with each other. The Central Area Latin American Conference of the M. E. Church was held in PANAMÁ. México was worthily represented by Bishop Wilbur P. Thirkield, VINCENTE MENDOZA, Victoriano D. Báez, and EPIGMENIO VELASCO. Those men were commissioned to work towards the unification of the two branches of Methodism before the next General Conference. The following Annual Conference of the M. E. Church, meeting in México City and presided over by Bishop George A. Miller, approved unanimously the idea, and asked the Bishop to write a project for unification. There was similar support at the Conference of the M. E. Church, South, presided over by Bishop WILLIAM B. BEAUCHAMP.

Duly representative committees were appointed to study and work on the project. Approval was given by the General Conference of the M. E. Church in Kansas City, Mo., May 25, 1928, and by the General Conference of the M. E. Church, South at Dallas, Texas, May 14, 1930. The four official committees met in México City on July 7 and 8, 1930, with twenty representatives from each Conference. Bishop W. A. CANDLER presided and uni-

fication was accomplished in the Iglesia Metodista de México, an autonomous entity, affiliated with the mother churches.

On Sept. 16, 1930, on the day of the celebration of the independence of México, with a solemn service, the session of the First General Conference was opened to establish the Methodist Church of México. Victoriano D. Báez

IGLESIA METODISTA EL DIVINO SALVADOR, JUAREZ, MEXICO

presided. Legislation was enacted and promulgated in the original *Discipline*. Plans for work were formulated and JUAN NICANOR PASCOE was elected the first bishop of the Iglesia Metodista de México. He was consecrated the following Sunday, Sept. 21, 1930.

Medical work was most urgent when Methodism began. Dr. Leví B. Salmans established in Guanajuato an important center which no longer exists. There were others in Monterrey, San Luis Postosí and México City. The people lacked knowledge, and illness and suffering were abundant. There was very little application of hygienic measures. Medicines and hospital care were very expensive. Much work was done through teaching, campaigns, lecturing, and practical service, through improvised clinics and movable staff. Now that the Social Security program of the Government has taken the major responsibility for medical care for working men and their families, the church tries to help in areas where the need is not met by the government program.

SANATORIO PALMORE, CHIHUAHUA, MEXICO

An important Methodist medical center exists in Chihuahua. The Sanatorio Palmore, with a plant valued at four million Mexican pesos, a school for nurses, a combined staff of evangelical and non-church-related doctors, is recognized as one of the most important medical centers in the north of the country. There is still a ministry to be carried on in producing Christian nurses and Christian doctors, not only trained with the best of knowledge but with the love of Christ.

Education. The first missionaries of the Methodist Church recognized the great need for schools and education for the underprivileged masses, and schools of higher learning, especially for the training of teachers. In most cases a day school was built by the side of the church. The pastor was at the same time teacher in the school. Even through the revolutionary years, up to 1930, Protestant schools were recognized as among the outstanding centers of education, because of their quality and moral contribution. One emphasis of the Mexican Revolution still in process is a strong program of education, which includes school buildings with the best of equipment, the training of teachers, a program of development to take care of the needs of a fast-developing country, and facilities for students to study for a career to be trained abroad in technical fields.

The Protestant schools still have a place. Colegio Palmore in Chihuahua, under the leadership of Francisco Cepeda, in celebrating its seventy-five years of service, finds its graduates in key positions in government, industry, commerce, education, as well as members of a society where Christian ideals and standards learned at the school find a place of operation. There is Colegio Elliot Torreón, Instituto "Dr. Andrés Osuna" in Piedras Negras, and Colegio Juarez in Guanajuato.

Querétaro, a city full of history, still feels the impact of the Instituto Benjamin N. Velasco, a militarized school. Augustín Romero Lopez has rendered service to the church, the community and the country in assisting parents in the education of their boys.

Pachuca will long live, although Manuela Vargas retired from active work and Antonio Carro Zempualteca has been called home to his deserved reward. The Hijas de Allende and the Julian Villagran schools will live on with a high record for their services. Ministers, school teachers, outstanding professional men, and active workers in many organizations found training, inspiration and backing at these important schools.

Puebla is another important state capital where two schools were established. The life of the city has been affected in more than one way. Juarez School, Instituto Normal Mexico, and Instituto Mexicano Madero will remember names like Blanche Betz, Juana Palacios, Adela Palacios, Angela Lozano, Altagracia Juarez. María Robles, and Consuelo Vargas de Romero, Pedro Flores Valderrama, Gonzalo Báez-Camargo, Carlos Laguna, Juan Díaz Galindo, Francisco Cruz Aedo and Miguel Sarmiento and many more who taught at these institutions. No matter where they are living or working such mottoes as "the best culture for the best service," along with the inspiring personalities and living examples, will enlarge the action of such schools. Many of their students have been active leaders in the progress of their home towns. Some are authors of text books, some are active church leaders. Deaconesses and ministers trained in Methodist schools are now the pride of the two Annual Conferences. Some are serving the church in other countries. Through education, the Methodist Church has made a great contribution to Mexican life.

In Mexico City, Laura Temple's vision still holds on.

Ethel Thomas, Sara Alarcón, Delfina Huerta and many others have carried since 1906 the school for girls, which even today is an important asset for the activities of the Methodist Church.

Methodism could not have carried on as successfully as it has without training girls to become deaconesses. Such a school is now directed by Miss Carmen Dávila, a graduate from it. The school cooperates with the Union Evangelical Seminary in training boys and girls for service to the Master. Seminary training was first started in Puebla by the M. E. Church, in Saltillo and in Mexico City by the M. E. Church, South, in efforts to provide the much needed leadership. Since 1917, just having celebrated fifty years of service, the Methodist Church, with Congregationalists and Disciples of Christ, has cooperated in the Union Evangelical Seminary where their ministers are trained. Manuel V. Flores is at present the Principal. He carries forward the memories that John Howland, Milton C. Davis, F. J. Huegel, and Juan Díaz have left, in this field of service.

Social Centers. México has been a country of revolutions, a mixture of the old with the new and of rapid social changes. Half the population is now under fifteen years of age. People's needs vary much from place to place and from one person to another. Christian environment and guidance for growth and adjustment is sought by those at a disadvantage. A combined effort of the Woman's Division of Christian Service in the U.S.A. with national leaders made possible the creation of Christian Social centers.

The Centro Social Cristiano in Chihuahua was founded in 1919 and developed under the experienced leadership of Lillie F. Fox. At present it has a modern plant with a gymnasium, a day nursery, a program for personality development, and a complete commercial study course, thanks to the devoted ministry of Irene Nixon, who led it from 1951 to 1965. The director today is Horacio Ríos.

Monterrey is an important industrial city, second to the Federal District, fast growing with a large floating population seeking employment or entrance to the United States as braceros (seasonal workers). It was blessed by the Centro Social, founded by Sara E. Warne in 1921. Helen M. Hogdson made of this place a true life investment in every sense. The results will long be felt. She discovered and made possible training for leaders now serving the centers. María González, a worthy successor, learned by her side the art of serving in the name of our Master. The Centro has a full program for every day in the week and supports the church program. Classes in English, cooking, clubs, work with children, young people, and adults, sports and playground, community service, extension work at needed barrios, and personal guidance keeps them busy. Camping is done at a beautiful site in the mountains—a dream came true through Anna Belle Dyck's consecrated work.

Other centers with similar work are located in Durango, Centro MacDonell; Saltillo, Centro Social Roberts; and Cortazar, Centro Social Rural.

The Country and the Church Today. No doubt México is fast developing. It makes headway among underdeveloped nations growing and strengthening its life, and even marks routes for international understanding and cooperation for universal peaceful survival. Religion finds it difficult to follow that speed. The Church as an institution is caught amid the fast changing moves, and yet, the Methodist Church in México recognizes that it has responsibility to its members, to its tradition, but more so to the country and to the people living there.

Bishop ALEJANDRO RUIZ MUÑOZ aims to recover the youthful power and the strength with which Methodism was born and is trying to relocate the message and its proclaimers amid the modern roads of needs and conflicts and is studying the ways and means to make it live according to the times.

The Methodist Church in Mexico is organized in two Annual Conferences constituted by three districts each. It has 296 congregations and pastoral charges. It has 194 church buildings and 342 preaching places. It has 156 pastors, 40 women workers and deaconesses, and 26 missionaries. The membership is 27,463 and 7,825 probationers, making a grand total of 35,288 (1969 figures).

The Methodist Church of México is now planning its one hundredth anniversary. Plans are underway and much effort is being put forth to make of this date a strong goal to double the membership, to deepen its life in Christ and to widen its influence in the power of the Spirit of Christ in service to humanity and in witness of the faith among the Mexican people.

The FREE METHODISTS have for some time had work in Mexico, though the 1917 constitution severely restricted all church work in that country. Both church and government made concessions in 1929, but anti-church riots broke out in 1931. Against this background, Gonzalo Cisneros, Free Methodist minister, went to Mexico in the early thirties as a missionary from the California Latin Conference. He established churches in the states of Sinaloa and Sonora. A Bible Training School was located at Nogales, Arizona. Here young people were prepared for service in Mexico. The school has now been relocated at the University City of Hermosillo, and the program modified to give Bible instruction to young people preparing for any of the professions. In 1965 a church constitution meeting the provisions of Mexican law, was adopted. The Mission superintendent resides at Nogales, Arizona. He is liaison between the conference and the mission board. Membership is reported at 721.

J. W. Butler, *M. E. Church in Mexico*. 1918.
Mrs. John Wesley Butler, *Historic Churches in Mexico*. New York and Cincinnati: Abingdon Press, 1915.
Gonzalo Baez-Camargo, *Biografia de un Templo*. Mexico: Ediciones Luminar, 1953.
————— and Kenneth G. Grubb, *Religion in the Republic of Mexico*. World Dominion Press, 1935.
Cincuentenario de la Fundacion de la Iglesia Metodista Episcopal en Mexico. Casa Unida de Publicaciones S.A., 1924.
Ada M. C. Drees, *Thirteen Years in Mexico*. New York: Abingdon Press, 1915.
Elizabeth M. Lee, *He Wears Orchids*. New York: Friendship Press, 1951.
—————, *Methodism in Mexico*. New York: Board of Missions, n.d.
————— and Alfred W. Wasson, *The Latin American Circuit*. New York: Board of Missions, 1942.
Libro Conmemorativo de las Bodas de Diamante de la Iglesia Metodista de Mexico. Imprenta Nueva Educacion, 1948.
Los Primeros Veinticinco Anos del Metodismo en Mexico. Imprenta de la Iglesia Metodista Episcopal, 1899.
Frank S. Onderdonk, *A Glimpse at Mexico*. Nashville, 1930.
Andres Osuna, *Por La Escuela y por La Patria*. Casa Unida de Publicaciones S.R.L., 1943.
Horacio Westrup Puentes, *Paladines del Evangelio en Mexico*. Casa Unida de Publicaciones, 1953.

Olga Vela and Margaret Wade Campbell, *Cinco Centros*. Cincinnati: Board of Missions, n.d.   GUSTAVO A. VELASCO

MEXICO, NEW YORK, U.S.A., Mexico Methodist Church, oldest continuous church in the Black River-Ontario District, began about 1808 when a Methodist circuit rider preached the first sermon. That year he organized the first class at the home of Leonard and Minerva Ames with five members. The Ames home was used for church services until about 1820.

In 1810 the Mexico Circuit extended from Camden and Redfield to the Oswego River. The Methodists and the Congregationalists for some years used a schoolhouse built in 1820. Mexico M. E. Church was legally organized in 1833 and a brick building was erected that year. A parsonage was built in 1840.

The brick church was burned in 1840. Then for years the Methodists worshipped in Town Hall. The present church was constructed in 1851. From 1883 to 1885 the church was repaired and enlarged, adding memorial windows. The present parsonage was received as a legacy from Dr. Harriet Ames Rundell in 1897.

When the centennial was celebrated in 1908, the church had grown from five to 332 members, with twenty descendants of Minerva Ames present. In 1926 a new chapel costing $15,000 was added. In 1943 the church had four missionaries in CHINA and JAPAN. In 1947 the sanctuary was repaired and renovated.

For two separate periods the Sunday school rooms were used by the Mexico Academy and Central School while erecting new school buildings. Again in 1957 the church was remodeled, and rededicated Nov. 3, 1957.

In 1970 Mexico First Church had 566 members and church property valued at $236,623.

General Minutes.
History of Mexico Methodist Church. Leaflet published by the church, 1958.
Mexico Methodism—The Centennial Celebration—1808-1898.
Elisabeth M. Simpson, *Mexico, Mother of Towns.* N.d.
                                                JESSE A. EARL

MEYER, LUCY RIDER (1849-1922), founder of the Chicago Training School for Mission and Social Service and of the Deaconess Order of the M. E. Church, was born Sept. 1, 1849, in New Haven, Vt., the daughter of Richard D. and Jane (Child) Rider. She held degrees from Oberlin College (A.B., 1872; A.M., 1880), and the Woman's Medical College of NORTHWESTERN UNIVERSITY (M.D., 1887), and she did graduate study in the Divinity School of the University of Chicago. On May 21, 1885, she married Josiah S. Meyer, and they had one son.

At fourteen Lucy joined the Methodist church at Weybridge, Vt. As a young woman she taught school in several places, including one year at GREENSBORO, N. C., in a freedmen's school supported by Quakers. She later wrote a number of Negro Spirituals which won recognition.

After graduating from Oberlin she entered medical school because her fiancé was training to go out as a medical missionary. Because of his untimely death in 1875 she returned to her parents' home in VERMONT. As a teacher in the local Sunday school she prepared Bible readings and lists of questions for her pupils, and soon was contributing to Methodist Sunday school periodicals, a practice she continued through the years. Her signature, "Lucy J. Rider," became a familiar name in church and

Sunday school papers. She copyrighted twenty "Whisper Songs" for children, the words and music bearing her initials.

In 1876 she became "Lady Principal" in the Troy Conference Academy, Poultney, Vt., teaching natural science. After one year she entered Boston School of Technology for further training. Her first book, *The Fairy Land of Chemistry,* financially her most successful literary effort, was published about that time.

In 1879 she went to McKENDREE COLLEGE, Lebanon, Ill., as professor of chemistry. While there she spent many weekends going to distant towns and cities to address or to help organize Sunday school conventions. In June 1880, she was a delegate to the World Sunday School Convention in London, and returned to become Field Secretary of the Illinois State Sunday School Association, a post that called for travel, speaking, and writing. It was soon said that her presence made any Sunday school convention a notable event. In 1883 she published *Children's Meetings,* a book that had a large sale for many years.

While serving (four years) with the Sunday School Association, Lucy Rider dreamed of starting a permanent school to train young women for leadership in Christian work and often spoke of the need in public addresses and in private conversation. Disappointed because no school materialized, she resigned from the Sunday School Association and spent the winter of 1884-85 teaching Bible study and music in Dwight L. Moody's school at Northfield, Mass. Also, while in the east she tried unsuccessfully to interest church leaders in New York in helping to found a school. Returning to Chicago in May, she was married. Shortly afterward the Chicago Preachers' Meeting invited her to speak on her plan for a training school. Following her enthusiastic address, a committee composed of ministers and representatives of the two women's missionary societies of the church was appointed.

Assisted by her husband, Lucy Meyer worked and planned feverishly through the summer of 1885 and in October the Chicago Training School for Christian Women, as it was first called, opened with four students. Well informed on the deaconess movement in Europe, Lucy Meyer aimed to train Christian young women who, assured of board, room, laundry and $8 per month, would give full time in ministry to the poor, the orphan, the sick, and the aged. The school's monthly paper, the *Deaconess Advocate,* told of its work and encouraged financial contributions. As finances permitted, new buildings were erected, and an orphanage, a hospital, and a home for the aged were established. The 1888 GENERAL CONFERENCE recognized deaconess work and provided for a board of deaconesses in the annual conference. A General Board of Deaconesses was set up in 1900, and in 1908 the Methodist Deaconess Association was established with Lucy R. Meyer as secretary. The Chicago Training School reached a peak enrolment in 1910 of 256 and a graduating class of eighty-four.

Controversy swirled around Lucy Meyer through the years. Some objected to her school saying the church and Sunday school could fit young women for such service. The deaconess uniform which she designed was criticized as a step toward Roman Catholicism. Her biggest difficulty was with the WOMAN'S HOME MISSIONARY SOCIETY. Early in its history that organization employed deaconesses, and with some logic it argued that the institution and the movement headed by Lucy Meyer should be under its care and guidance. A capable, independent,

strong-minded woman, Mrs. Meyer would not agree. A long struggle, damaging to both sides, ensued for the control of the deaconess movement in the church. In 1903 bishops met with representatives of both sides to no avail. In the 1912 General Conference an impassioned speech by Mrs. Meyer (she was a delegate three times beginning in 1904) won an overwhelming vote for the minority report which kept the work independent. The friction began to subside in 1924 with the formation of the Board of Hospitals, Homes, and Deaconess Work.

Lucy Rider Meyer felt divinely called to educate young women for Christian service. The training school she established in Chicago was her life. All she did and suffered was to the end that the school and the deaconess movement might prosper. At a banquet in New York she was humorously, and yet appropriately, introduced as the "Archbishop of Deaconesses." For more than thirty years she and her husband, a former YMCA secretary whose business ability and practical sagacity complemented her enthusiasm and consecration, gave themselves sacrificially to the school.

A writer of ability, Lucy Meyer published, in addition to the books already mentioned, *Deaconesses, Biblical, Early Church, European, American,* 1890; *The Shorter Bible,* 1895; *Deaconess Stories,* 1900; and a novel, *Mary North,* 1903. Also, she compiled poems and hymns and wrote a number of articles which were published. In 1918 she was made president emeritus of the training school. She died in Chicago, March 16, 1922.

General Conference Journals, 1904-12.
Isabelle Horton, *High Adventure, Life of Lucy Rider Meyer.* Cincinnati: Methodist Book Concern, 1928.
Lucy R. Meyer, *Deaconesses, Biblical, Early Church, European, American.* Cincinnati: Cranston and Stowe, 1890.
C. F. Price, *Who's Who in American Methodism.* 1916.
Who Was Who in America, Vol. 1, 1897-1942.

ALBEA GODBOLD

MIAMI, FLORIDA, U.S.A., today is the largest city in FLORIDA, the county seat of Dade County, and is known the world over as a resort center. About 1870 the first settlers built on the site where Fort Dallas had stood during the Indian War.

The first Methodist service to be held in Miami was in Pierce's sponge warehouse on the banks of Biscayne Bay sometime in 1892. C. W. White, who served the Indian River Mission and who came to Miami monthly by stagecoach or boat, helped this congregation to build a church in 1893. The church was located on the Military Trail at an Indian trail crossing. At this site a little community was emerging known as Lemon City, so the new church took the name of Lemon City Methodist Church, by which it was known until 1934 when its name was changed to Grace Methodist. The first service was held in this church on Easter Sunday, 1893. At this time the present downtown Miami was little more than a jungle where only seven white people lived. Lemon City, however, had a thriving population of 300 inhabitants.

On April 15, 1896 the last spike was driven on the Henry Flagler railroad line to Miami. Pioneers began to pour into the area and the pines and palmetto scrub gave way to a city of tents and rough pine board houses. In October of 1896, Levi L. Fisher, the presiding elder of the Jacksonville District of the St. JOHN'S RIVER CONFERENCE of the M. E. Church, arrived in Miami to take a boat to Key West. While he was waiting passage on the boat, he began talking with some fishermen who were mending their nets. While chatting with them he asked, "Are there any Methodists living along the River?" A houseboat was pointed out belonging to Bill Wilson, who they said was a Methodist. The presiding elder visited the Wilsons and stirred them up about starting a Methodist Church. A month later, on Nov. 15, 1896, fifteen persons met on Wilson's houseboat and organized the M. E. Church in Miami. E. V. Blackman was appointed as pastor of this work. Shortly after he arrived he went to Henry M. Flagler, the capitalist, and persuaded him to donate a lot for the building of a M. E. Church and at the same time he secured donations of land for a Baptist Church and for the M. E. Church, South. Flagler had several years earlier given $200 to help build the Lemon City Church.

In December of 1896, James Bolton was sent to Miami by the M. E. Church, South to the Biscayne Mission embracing Lemon City, Miami and Coconut Grove; however, that year nothing was done to organize a church in Miami itself. It was a year later when Fred Blackburn was appointed to Miami in 1898, that the M. E. Church, South was organized. He visited through the community trying to ride through the wagon-rutted sand roads on a bicycle.

The M. E. Church and the M. E. Church, South both began their work under the name of First Methodist Church. In 1912 a new church and parsonage was built by the M. E. Church at a cost of $87,000. This new church was named White Temple. In 1914 the M. E. Church, South erected a new building at a cost of $44,100, and its name was changed to Trinity. Lemon City, Trinity and White Temple became mother churches for numbers of mission churches as the Miami area grew. By 1939, at the time of Methodist union there were eleven appointments in the greater Miami area made by the M. E. Church, South and six by the M. E. Church. Both churches had a Miami District.

As the city grew, the number of Methodist churches increased. By 1945 there were twenty-one churches with a total membership of 11,152. By 1970 the number of appointments had increased to thirty-seven with a total of 30,645 members.

First Church. Trinity Church was for sixty-eight years the historic downtown church of southern Methodism, mother church to a number of thriving Miami area churches and one of the most prolific churches in giving of her sons and daughters to the ministry. In 1966, Trinity Church united with White Temple Church which was located just two blocks away, to form the First Methodist Church of Miami. The name is significant in that both Trinity and White Temple were originally organized as First Methodist Church, White Temple in 1896, and Trinity in 1898. The "new" Church has 1,916 members and is presently engaged in a building program to erect a center of Methodism and Protestantism for downtown Miami which will cost in excess of a million dollars.

General Minutes.
Glenn James, *Golden Anniversary*, pamphlet issued by White Temple Church, 1946.
Miami Herald, April 2, 1960.   WILLIAM E. BROOKS
                                        CLARENCE M. YATES

MICHALSON, CARL (1915-1965), American theologian, author and teacher, was born in Waverly, Minn., June 29, 1915, son of Carl D. and Gertrude K. (Leuzinger)

Michalson. He was educated at John Fletcher College, B.A., 1936; DREW UNIVERSITY, B.D., 1939, M.A., 1940; Yale University, Ph.D., 1945.

He was admitted on trial into the MINNESOTA CONFERENCE, M. E. Church, 1938, ordained deacon 1939, received in full connection and ordained elder 1940.

He was a pastor in Iowa, 1935-36; Teabo, N. J., 1938-40; New Hyde Park, N. Y., 1941-43, and then became professor in DREW THEOLOGICAL SEMINARY in 1943. He soon came into prominence as a theologian and lecturer. He was visiting lecturer in SOUTHERN METHODIST UNIVERSITY the summer of 1955, and in Tokyo Union Theological Seminary, JAPAN, 1958. He served as a member of the Board of Governors of the Council for Clinical Training, Theological Foundation for Southeast Asia; as member of the American Theological Society, American Philosophical Association, and of the Society for Theological Discussion. He wrote during these years *Faith for Personal Crises*, 1958; *The Hinge of History*, 1959; *Japanese Contributions to Christian Theology*, 1960; *The Witness to Kierkegaard* (Editor), 1960; *The Rationality of Faith*, 1963.

He was married to Janet Aloyse Merrill, May 30, 1944. Their children are Karen and Steven.

Michalson was tragically killed in a plane accident on Nov. 8, 1965, while enroute to address an educational gathering. In 1967 a collection of his essays was published posthumously under the title *Worldly Theology—The Hermeneutical Focus of an Historical Faith*. His work and influence were outlined and evaluated in appreciative articles and reviews in such journals as *The Christian Century* and *Religion in Life* following his untimely demise.

Who's Who in the Methodist Church, 1966.   J. MARVIN RAST

MICHALSON, GORDON ELLIOTT (1911-   ), American educator, was born at Waverly, Minn., Aug. 22, 1911, son of Carl D. and Gertrude Kathryn (Leuzinger) Michalson.

He received the B.A. degree from the University of Minnesota, 1937; M.A., 1939; B.D., DREW UNIVERSITY, 1941; Ph.D., 1947. He did postgraduate study in Union Theological Seminary the summer of 1941 and in Edinburgh (Scotland) University the summer of 1951. In 1962 he was awarded the L.H.D. degree by Bradley University, and the same by MACMURRAY COLLEGE in 1968.

He was engaged in business and commerical aviation, 1929-36. In 1938 he was admitted on trial into the North Minnesota Conference, M. E. Church, was received in full connection and ordained deacon in 1939, and ordained elder in 1941.

His pastorates were in Norwood and Kimball, Minn., 1935-38; East Orange, N. J., 1939-42; Montclair, N. J., 1946-52; Westfield, N. J., 1952-57. He was professor of historical theology in GARRETT THEOLOGICAL SEMINARY, 1958-60. From 1960 to 1968 he was president of MacMurray College. In 1968 he became president of the SCHOOL OF THEOLOGY AT CLAREMONT, Calif.

He was a member of the Board of Education of the NEWARK CONFERENCE, 1948-50; chairman of the Board of Pensions, 1952-58. He was a trustee of Centenary Junior College, 1952-54; of the Methodist Home for the Aged, Ocean Grove, N. J., and of Methodist Hospital in BROOKLYN, N. Y., 1956-58; of Lincoln Academy in Illinois; and member of the Lincoln Society of Illinois. He served to Lieutenant Commander, United States Naval Air Corps, 1942-45. He is a member of the American Association of Colleges and Universities, and American Theological Society, the Union League Club of Chicago, and the University Club of St. Louis. He is contributor of articles to religious and educational journals.

He was married to Louise Buckley Card on Aug. 16, 1939. Their children are Kathryn Louise and Gordon Elliott.

Who's Who in America, Vol. 34.
Who's Who in the Methodist Church, 1966.   J. Marvin Rast

MICHIGAN, one of the north central states, is divided into two peninsulas, and is nearly surrounded by the Great Lakes. The name is derived from the Indian "Mishigamaw," which means "Great Water." The state ranks eleventh or twenty-third in size, 96,720 square miles or 57,022, according to whether one includes that part of the Great Lakes over which the commonwealth has undisputed possession. It has 3,121 miles of coastline, more than any state save Alaska.

During the colonial period Michigan was explored and settled by French missionaries and fur traders. They established settlements at Sault Ste. Marie (1668), the Straits of Mackinac (1671), and Detroit (1701). In 1760-61, during the French and Indian War, Michigan passed from French to British control. Title to what is now Michigan went to the United States at the close of the Revolution.

At first a part of the Northwest Territory, then of Indiana Territory, Michigan was organized as a separate Territory in 1805, and was admitted to the Union in 1837. On the completion of the Erie Canal in 1825, a tide of immigration flowed into Michigan. In 1830 the population was 31,639.

Michigan ranks high in agriculture, tourism, mining, and manufacturing. With the rise of the automobile industry in the twentieth century, the population grew rapidly—2,800,000 in 1910, over 5,000,000 by 1940, and 8,778,187 in 1970. Michigan was called the "arsenal of democracy" in the second world war.

The first Methodist preacher in Michigan was Daniel Freeman who came from Canada in the spring of 1804 and preached several times. Later in the same year Nathan Bangs delivered several sermons in Detroit. Methodism was established in the Territory by William Case of the New York Conference in 1809 when he made Detroit a regular preaching point on his circuit which covered southwestern Ontario. In the fall of 1810, William Mitchell, a member of the Western Conference, organized a class of seven members in Detroit. The Detroit Circuit of the Upper Canada District reported 134 members in 1812, of whom about fifty were in Michigan.

During the war years of 1812 and 1815 there was no Methodist preacher in Michigan and the work became disordered. In 1815 when Joseph Hickcox of the Genesee Conference was appointed to the Detroit Circuit, he found the original seven members in the town still faithful but he declared that even so the place was a "sink of iniquity." His three-weeks circuit, 300 miles around, had three preaching places in Michigan.

The first Methodist church edifice (the first Protestant church) in Michigan was built in March 1818, on the River Rouge six miles west of Detroit in what is now east Dearborn. The structure, some 24 by 30 feet, was of logs, and it had rough benches for seats; it was in use for ten years.

The Methodist work in Michigan was in the Upper Canada District of the Genesee Conference until 1820, when the General Conference placed Michigan Territory in the Ohio Conference. By 1824 the Detroit Circuit had 242 members. In 1835 two districts were established in the Territory.

In 1836, the Ohio Conference was divided to form the Michigan Conference which included the two districts in Michigan and four in northern Ohio. The conference was organized Sept. 7, 1836 at Mansfield, Ohio, with Bishop Joshua Soule presiding. At the outset the conference had two stations and twenty circuits. The two Michigan districts had 4,044 members. A few appointments in southwestern Michigan were in the La Porte District of the Indiana Conference from 1832 to 1840.

In 1840 the Michigan Conference was limited to the state of Michigan and at the time it had seventy-eight ministers and 11,523 members.

John Clark of the New York Conference began mission work among the Indians in the upper peninsula in 1832. The conference took charge of the mission in 1837. Copper mining began in the state in 1844, and in 1847 John Pitezel, an Indian missionary, was appointed to work among the miners. In time there were five appointments in the Indian Mission District, including one at Sandy Lake, Minnesota. Judson Collins went from Albion as a missionary to China in 1847.

In 1835, on the request of several Michigan Conference leaders, the state legislature issued a charter for a college. Wesleyan Seminary opened at Albion in 1843 and became Albion College in 1861.

In 1856, the Michigan Conference was divided to form the Detroit Conference which covered the eastern half of the lower peninsula and all of the upper peninsula. At the time the state had 21,378 Methodists.

The Michigan Christian Advocate, a weekly, was established in 1874. With a circulation of nearly 30,000, it is today the only independent Methodist paper in the North Central Jurisdiction and the only Protestant weekly in Michigan.

In 1876 the two conferences chose Bay View as the location for an annual state-wide camp meeting, and it continues as an important summer religious and cultural center. In 1906 the Michigan Conference established the Clarke Memorial Home for the Aged in Grand Rapids, and the Detroit Conference started a similar institution at Chelsea. In 1962 the latter conference established another home in Detroit. The two conferences acquired Bronson Hospital in Kalamazoo and the Methodist Children's Village near Detroit in 1920. In 1939 with Methodist unification the conferences acquired Adrian College, a former Methodist Protestant school. There are now ten Wesley Foundations in Michigan. Both conferences have camps and extensive camping programs.

In 1900 there were approximately 100,000 Methodists in Michigan rather evenly divided between the two conferences. After that date, due in part to the rapid rise of the automobile industry, the Detroit Conference forged ahead. By 1929 it had some 103,000 members to about 65,000 for the Michigan Conference.

In 1933, when the Chicago Northwest Conference (German) was absorbed by the English-speaking conferences in several states, the two Michigan conferences received seventeen of the German churches. Methodist unification in 1939 brought fifty-seven Methodist Protestant pastoral charges with 3,426 members into the conferences. In 1942 some eleven Swedish churches came in when the Central Northwest Conference (Swedish) was absorbed. In 1958, two churches from the LEXINGTON CONFERENCE, Central Jurisdiction, were received into the Detroit Conference, and nine more came in 1964 when the Lexington Conference was absorbed.

Between 1940 and 1955 the population of Michigan increased 37.7 per cent and the Methodist membership grew 31 per cent. The rapid growth of suburban areas, the decline of inner city areas, and the loss of population in the lumbering, mining, and agricultural areas of the state, have posed problems for Michigan Methodism. The conferences had campaigns for funds for church extension in 1953 and 1955. In 1962 they projected a united crusade for money to undergird Albion and Adrian Colleges and GARRETT THEOLOGICAL SEMINARY.

In 1970 the two Michigan conferences had a total of thirteen districts, 1,014 churches, 163,541 church school pupils, 300,428 church members, and property valued at $201,359,752.

Willard Baird, *This Is Our Michigan*. Battle Creek: Federated Publications, Inc., 1959.
Robert Gildart, *Albion College, 1835-1960*. Albion: Albion College, 1961.
Minutes of the Detroit and Michigan Conferences.
E. H. Pilcher, *Michigan*. 1878.　　　RONALD A. BRUNGER

MICHIGAN CHRISTIAN ADVOCATE. The town of Adrian, Mich., was the birthplace of two *Michigan Christian Advocates*. In 1851 J. V. Watson published a paper by that name. Shortly thereafter he moved to CHICAGO, taking with him the paper which became the *Northwestern Christian Advocate*.

Twenty-two years later in 1873, another clergyman by the name of Orrin Whitmore, presiding elder of the then Adrian District, broadened the scope of his *Adrian District Methodist*, a monthly publication, into a paper for all of Michigan Methodists entitled *The Michigan Christian Advocate*. By a striking coincidence the second *Michigan Christian Advocate* was edited in the same Adrian office as the first. Whitmore's monthly paper did not seem to meet the need or come up to the expectations of Michigan Methodists. Finally the matter was brought before the Annual Conference which recommended by a strong vote that a *weekly* paper be published.

The next question was: Who would publish it? After considerable discussion among prominent laymen and ministers it was decided to form a stock company to be known as The Methodist Publishing Company whose purpose was to print a religious newspaper called the *Michigan Christian Advocate*. Book and job printing were also a function of that company. DETROIT was to be its headquarters. Capital stock totaled $10,000 and was divided into 100 shares of $100 each. Two days before Christmas in 1874 final organization of the company was effected at Detroit and the *Michigan Christian Advocate* was launched upon its illustrious career.

Ten years after the Advocate was born a campaign boosted its circulation from 6,000 to 10,000. From there it went to 14,000, 15,000 and finally 18,000. In those days subscriptions were carried many months beyond expiration date. It was a common practice until postal regulations outlawed it. So the 18,000 was hardly comparable to a similar figure today, but it was a noteworthy attainment.

From 1886 until the end of the First World War the Publishing Company made money and gave its profits to the retired ministers' pension fund. Associate editor, Elmer Houser, wrote in 1933 that the gifts to the pension fund totaled $93,000.

All this time the paper was actually under the direction of the private corporation, run by dedicated laymen and ministers who had the interests of the church at heart, and regarded the *Advocate* as a service they were glad to perform. However, following the First World War in 1919, it seemed fitting that the stock company be dissolved. This was done and the *Advocate's* equipment, assets and subscription list were given outright to the two annual conferences of the Michigan Area, namely, the DETROIT and MICHIGAN CONFERENCES. A board of eight ministerial trustees, four from each conference, were elected by the conferences and became responsible for publishing and operating the job printing business which augmented the *Advocate's* income.

For many years *Zion's Herald*, published in BOSTON, and the *Michigan Christian Advocate* were the only "independent" weekly Methodist periodicals published in the Northern part of the Church. The others were under GENERAL CONFERENCE control. *Zion's Herald* continues as a monthly, leaving the *Advocate* the only one in the North publishing with weekly frequency. (Some years ago the *Advocate* started publishing forty-six issues a year, skipping every other week during the summer period. This policy continues.)

The editors of the *Advocate* invariably have been ministers. Yet it must be said that the longest and perhaps the most distinguished service ever rendered the *Advocate* was by a consecrated layman.

The first editor after the Publishing Company was formed was Orrin Whitmore, who continued in this capacity until his appointment in 1876 to a pastorate in Saline, Mich.

There were at least two in those early days who were called "Editor-in-Chief." One was L. R. FISKE, one-time president of ALBION COLLEGE, and J. M. ARNOLD. The latter managed a private bookstore in Detroit, which was later purchased by the Methodist BOOK CONCERN, probably in November of 1886. Today the Detroit Cokesbury bookstore of the METHODIST PUBLISHING HOUSE is the outgrowth of that original purchase. In addition to managing his bookstore, Arnold became Business Manager and Assistant Editor of the *Advocate* and finally its Editor-in-Chief.

To J. H. POTTS belongs the distinction of being editor for the longest period. He was a towering figure of over six feet in height—a member of the Michigan Conference. For forty years (1877-1917) his pen worked overtime for the *Advocate*, and his trumpet-like voice resounded throughout the state as he was called upon to speak in its various pulpits. He was also a strong liberal voice in the General Conference and crossed verbal swords with another distinguished editor, JAMES M. BUCKLEY, on the issue of seating women in that body. Potts won.

The next editor was picked from the Detroit Conference and served briefly during the difficult years of the First World War. He was Frank F. Fitchett, who was stricken in health and was forced to retire in 1920.

The *Advocate* trustees again turned to the Michigan

Conference for someone to fill the vacancy. This time their choice was William H. Phelps, who had served as pastor and district superintendent, and is remembered by many Michigan Methodists for his kindly spirit and unquenchable wit. His editorship covered a period when Biblical controversy raged, and when the devastating depression took a heavy toll of church papers. For nineteen years (1920-1939) he stood serene amid these storms which he made easier to endure by his never-ending sense of humor. Like his predecessor, he retired because of ill health and died shortly thereafter.

Following him is the present editor, John E. Marvin, who came to the editorship in 1939 from three years' experience as Associate Editor. He is a son of the Methodist parsonage and served several churches in the Detroit Conference before joining the *Advocate* staff.

In its Associate Editors, the *Advocate* has always been blessed with both editorial and business ability. Only the following are mentioned: JOSEPH F. BERRY, who became editor of the *Epworth Herald* and later a bishop; James E. Jacklin, who was the moving spirit in founding Chelsea Home, a Detroit Conference institution for the elderly, and who served the *Advocate* for twenty-four years; Elmer Houser, a Methodist layman who served for a total of fifty years as circulation manager, bookkeeper, business manager and finally as Associate Editor.

In the summer of 1941 the *Advocate* returned to Adrian, the place of its birth, after a Detroit sojourn of about sixty-seven years. The circumstances of this return represent a unique undertaking in Methodist history. The biggest influence leading up to this event was the unification of the Northern, Southern and M. P. branches of Methodism in 1939. Two M. P. institutions played a major role in the *Advocate's* transition—the former M. P. Publishing House in PITTSBURGH, and Adrian College.

After unification it was decided to discontinue the Pittsburgh publishing plant and to give to Adrian College certain pieces of printing equipment. This seemed natural because both institutions had been affiliated with the M. P. branch of the now united Church. It was Samuel J. Harrison, then president of Adrian College, who saw the possibilities of setting up a printing plant carried on by the College as a part of the student self-help program. He also saw the possibility of bringing the *Advocate* to Adrian's campus and pooling the equipment of both printing establishments to form what came to be known as the Adrian College Press.

A change in college administration in 1959, and the lack of adequate space for printing facilities and editorial offices resulted in the ADVOCATE moving to a new location in the same town. A Methodist layman, Robert Tuttle, who had managed the Adrian College Press, joined with another layman, Donald Swenk, to form a printing business which leased certain pieces of *Advocate* equipment, and continued to print the paper under a contractual arrangement.

As time passed, the *Advocate* board was enlarged to include an equal number of laymen and ministers from both the sponsoring conferences. Circulation reached its lowest point in the depression of the 30's when it dropped to 8,000. Since then, it has climbed slowly but surely to reach its current listing of over 28,000—the highest in its 93-year history.

The content of the publication is described by its statement on the cover, "The Newsmagazine of Michigan Methodists." While it majors on local, state, national and world news of Methodism in particular, and of Christendom in general, it is also an opinion magazine dealing with current issues, many of them highly controversial. The policy is thoroughly democratic, however, allowing for the widest possible latitude of opinion on a variety of moral and religious subjects.

This liberal editorial policy has kept the *Advocate's* editors in the center of current debate whatever the issue. When Phelps was editor, he was accused of heresy, and actually investigated by a committee from his conference—but given a clean bill of theological health. In characteristic humor he boasted to his last days that he was the only minister in his conference who was orthodox because he had a committee's report to prove it! This incident will illustrate the freedom practiced by *Michigan Christian Advocate* editors through the years of the modernist-fundamentalist controversy, and in the more recent times of social and political turmoil. Besides news and opinion, the *Advocate* has carried a limited amount of promotional material, but has always been careful to avoid becoming a purely promotional type publication.

JOHN E. MARVIN

MICHIGAN CONFERENCE was formed in 1836 by dividing the OHIO CONFERENCE. (See MICHIGAN for account of early Methodism in the state.) At the beginning the conference had two districts in Michigan and four in OHIO. The two Michigan districts had 4,044 members. The first session of the conference was held at Mansfield, Ohio, Sept. 7, 1836, with Bishop JOSHUA SOULE presiding. Beginning in 1840, the conference was limited to Michigan, and at that time it had seventy-eight ministers and 11,523 members.

In 1856, the DETROIT CONFERENCE was formed by dividing the state and thereafter the Michigan Conference was limited to the west half of the lower peninsula. The division left the conference with ninety-one ministers and 10,623 members. Down to 1900 the two conferences were about equal in numerical strength, but thereafter the increasing population in the Detroit area, due largely to the rise of the automobile industry, caused the Detroit Conference to forge ahead.

In 1931 when the Michigan Conference had approximately 64,000 members, it reduced the number of its districts from six to five. In 1968 with a membership of more than 105,000 a sixth district was again created. The names of the districts are: Albion, Kalamazoo, Lansing, Grand Rapids, Central Michigan, and Grand Traverse.

In 1969 the name was changed to West Michigan Conference and in 1970 the Conference reported 464 churches, 110,906 members, 67,401 enrolled in Church schools, and property valued at $73,632,842.

General Minutes, ME and TMC.
M. B. Macmillan, *Michigan.* 1967.   ALBEA GODBOLD

MICHIGAN CONFERENCE (EUB) was organized in Grand Rapids, Mich. in June 1951, following the 1946 union of The EVANGELICAL CHURCH and the Church of the UNITED BRETHREN IN CHRIST. It brought together the work of the former denominations in MICHIGAN.

The work of The Evangelical Church had begun in Michigan in 1838, when Solomon Altimos, a minister of the East Pennsylvania Conference, settled in Ash Township near Flat Rock, in the southeastern corner of the state. He began to preach in the area and also traveled across southern Michigan as far as St. Joseph County. In 1845, a mission was formed near Ann Arbor by the Ohio Conference. About this time, work was started in southwestern Michigan by both the Indiana and Illinois Conferences. The GENERAL CONFERENCE of The Evangelical Church, meeting in Buffalo, N. Y., in 1863, ordered the organization of the Michigan Conference, its boundaries to include all of the state of Michigan, that portion of the state of Ohio lying north of the Maumee River, and a narrow strip from the northern edge of the state of Indiana. The organization was accomplished in May, 1864, at the session of the Ohio Conference, meeting in Carey, Ohio, with the first regular session of the Michigan Conference being held in April, 1865, in the Beagle Church, near Blissfield. This infant conference of sixteen churches and 1,414 members (1865) enjoyed steady growth through the years, first in the rural areas and later spreading to the rapidly growing urban centers. By 1950 there were 124 organized congregations and 14,946 members. The conference boundaries remained virtually unchanged during this period.

In 1831, the Wabash Conference of the United Brethren Church assigned William Davis to travel the St. Joseph Circuit, which included St. Joseph, Cass, and Berrien Counties in southwestern Michigan, along with some territory in northern INDIANA. Shortly thereafter, a group was meeting in Brown's Tavern in Berrien Springs but no permanent work was established until 1845. In 1838, the Ohio Sundusky Conference appointed Stephen Lillybridge to the Michigan Mission, an area in the southeastern corner of Michigan; but no permanent work was established here until 1848.

The General Conference of the United Brethren Church across the years took a number of actions affecting conference boundaries in Michigan; but these actions involved only the lower peninsula of the state, for no work was ever begun in the upper peninsula. In 1845, the territory of Michigan was divided east and west, that part lying north of Ohio being given to the Sandusky Conference, and the part north of Indiana to the St. Joseph Conference. Work progressed so that by 1853, the Michigan Conference, a mission conference including all of the state except the southwest corner, was authorized. The southwest corner, including St. Joseph, Berrien, and Cass Counties, remained with the St. Joseph Conference. In 1857, Michigan became a self-supporting conference. 1861 saw a major revision of boundaries as Michigan Conference was given the bottom two rows of counties in the state plus the Maumee District of the Sandusky Conference. St. Joseph Conference maintained its corner while all the state north of the two rows of counties was organized as the North Michigan Conference. This arrangement held until 1869, when the Michigan Conference became the North Ohio Conference and was given only the southernmost row of counties in Michigan. The rest of the area was assigned to the northern conference which was renamed Michigan. In 1877, the state was again divided north and south with the division line running through Grand Rapids and Flint. The southern portion was named the Michigan Conference and the northern portion was called the Saginaw Mission Conference, a name which was changed four years later to North Michigan Conference when it became self-support-

ing. Following the division of the United Brethren Church (1889), Michigan and North Michigan were consolidated into one Michigan Conference (1897) and, in 1901, St. Joseph Conference gave its corner of the state to the Michigan Conference. This boundary was then maintained until the conference union of 1951, but the many divisions over the years contributed to slow growth. By 1950, there were 39 organized congregations and 4,993 members.

The Michigan Conference of The Evangelical United Brethren Church had 21,830 members in 1968. There were 113 charges and a total of 133 churches. Ministerial membership was 180 in all classes. The conference was divided into two districts, with a residence for the East District Superintendent in Detroit, and a residence for the West District Superintendent in Grand Rapids. The conference office was maintained in Lansing. The total value of church property in Michigan was $14,009,626. $2,732,510 was paid out for all purposes in 1967.

In 1969, the conference united with the Detroit and West Michigan Conferences of the former Methodist Church to form the present Detroit and West Michigan Conferences.

Watson: *History of the Michigan Conference of the Evangelical Church,* 1942.
Watson and Spafford: *History of the Michigan Conference of the Evangelical United Brethren Church,* Vol. II, 1961.

ARTHUR L. SPAFFORD

MICHIGAN CONFERENCE (MP) was organized in July 1842, with five itinerant ministers from the Ohio Conference, three circuits, and some 250 church members. James Gay was the first president. In 1858 the conference was divided to form the West Michigan Conference which continued as a separate body until 1908 and was then absorbed by the Michigan Conference.

The Michigan Conference was strongly opposed to slavery. It refused to elect delegates to the M. P. GENERAL CONFERENCE in 1850 because to do so would mean complicity with the evil of slavery. In 1864 the conference passed a strong resolution in support of the Federal government as it prosecuted the war against "rebellion."

Apparently some members of the conference believed that Methodist Protestantism in its enthusiasm for democracy had developed a connection that was too loose for effective church life. In 1873 the conference formed eight subdistricts of five to seven churches with a pastor as chairman of each. The chairman visited the circuits and the quarterly conferences in his subdistrict and was expected to act as the conference president would if he were present. The chairman had no control over the appointments of the preachers unless he was a member of the conference stationing committee. The subdistrict plan proved helpful in promoting missions and finances. There was some opposition to the subdistrict plan; over a period of several decades it was adopted in some years and rejected in others.

Perhaps Methodist Protestantism's most important venture in Michigan was ADRIAN COLLEGE. Chartered in 1839, it became a Wesleyan Methodist school in 1852. In 1859 it was moved from near Jackson to Adrian. In 1862 the trustees voted to invite the Methodist Protestants to cooperate at Adrian. The move seemed logical because at that time there was serious talk of uniting the nonepiscopal Methodists in the north and west and because the Methodist Protestants in Ohio, Illinois and Michigan had for some time desired to start a college.

The union plans failed, but the Adrian trustees, caught in a financial crisis, wanted help with the college debt and a proposed endowment fund. The college was put in the hands of the Methodist Protestants by the simple expedient of electing a majority of the trustees from that church. The Methodist Protestants did not pay off the debt nor did they raise the endowment fund, but they took charge of the college. In succeeding decades the institution had a precarious existence, but it managed to survive. At unification in 1939, Adrian College came into The Methodist Church with no debt, an endowment of some $152,000, and a plant valued at $340,000. It has grown to be a first-rate church college.

The Methodist Protestants in Michigan were never numerous, as compared with the membership of the M. P. Church. Their churches were almost altogether in the rural areas and small villages. A congregation of more than 100 members was rare. Simpson's *Cyclopaedia*, fourth edition, published in 1882, reported two Methodist Protestant conferences in Michigan, 104 itinerant ministers, seventy-two unstationed preachers, 4,352 members, thirty-three churches and thirty-one parsonages valued at $82,490. As a denomination probably the Methodist Protestants exerted an influence beyond what might be expected in view of their small constituency in the state.

In 1938 the Michigan Conference journal reported seventy ministers, fifty-seven churches, 7,630 enrolled in the Sunday schools, 1,038 in the women's societies, and 4,176 church members.

E. S. Bucke, *History of American Methodism*, 1964.
Margaret B. Macmillan, *The Methodist Church in Michigan*, 1967.
Michigan Conference *Journals*, 1932-1938. ALBEA GODBOLD

MIDDLEBURG, FLORIDA, U.S.A. **Middleburg Methodist Church,** a pioneer FLORIDA church, is located twenty-six miles southwest of JACKSONVILLE on State Highway 21. A historical marker gives directions to the church which is located just east of the highway at the place where Highway 21 crosses Black Creek.

The Methodist Church at Middleburg is one of Florida's oldest Protestant congregations with an unbroken line of pastoral appointments dating from 1823, two years after Florida became a Territory of the United States. The local records indicate that Methodist people met prior to that time but no organized church is noted until 1823. It must be remembered that no Protestant worship was permitted under Spanish rule in Florida. The Middleburg Church was cited by the 1963 FLORIDA CONFERENCE for 140 years of continuous service. The building is the oldest in the Florida Conference. It remains an excellent example of church construction in Florida during the pre-Civil War period. As one visits this church and the adjoining cemetery, one feels that one has been transferred back a century and a quarter.

The church structure is of wide clapboards on the exterior and wide random width tongue and grooved ceiling on the inside, all painted white. The nails were wrought by hand at a then nearby forge. The pews are mahogany. All of the lumber was cut from neighboring forests and was dressed by hand. The visible evidence of the drawknife can be observed by all. The labor in

the cutting of lumber and the construction of the church was by slaves owned by members of the church.

No major change has been made in the interior of the building since the 1850's. There is a wide center aisle which was designed to separate the men and the women. Two back pews were reserved for the use of the slaves, "that they might have the privilege of joining in the common worship."

Descendants of the early settlers in the Middleburg area, who had received land grants from the King of Spain, are represented in the church membership.

GORDON N. CRAIG

W. VERNON MIDDLETON

MIDDLETON, WILLIAM VERNON (1902-1965), American bishop, was born in Baltimore, Md., Dec. 25, 1902, the son of William F. and Stella (Fort) Middleton. He was educated at DICKINSON COLLEGE (A.B., 1928), New York University (A.M., 1932), and DREW UNIVERSITY (B.D., 1931, and Ph.D., 1946). His honorary degrees were: D.D., LL.D., L.H.D., J.U.D., and Litt.D. He married Miriam Kathleen Horts, June 13, 1931, and they had two children, Patricia Jean and William H. L.

Received on trial in the PHILADELPHIA CONFERENCE in 1928, Middleton was ordained both deacon and elder in 1930. His pastoral appointments were: Dauphin and Heckton Circuit, 1924-28; Hulmeville, 1928-31; associate, First Church, Germantown, 1931-33; Canadensis, 1934-35; and Narberth, 1935-39. He was pastor of Covenant Church, Philadelphia, and executive secretary of the Philadelphia Missionary and Church Extension Society, 1939-42. From 1942 to 1944, he gave full time to the work of the society. From 1944 to 1960, he served with the Division of National Missions in Philadelphia, first as secretary of the church extension section, 1954-56; and finally as general secretary of the Division, 1956-60.

Middleton was a delegate to the 1956 and 1960

GENERAL CONFERENCES, leading his delegation to the latter. He was a trustee of three Pennsylvania colleges: Dickinson, ALLEGHENY, and LYCOMING. He published two books, *Methodism in Alaska and Hawaii,* and *The Arm of Compassion.* Elected bishop in 1960, he was assigned to the Western Pennsylvania Area, renamed the Pittsburgh Area in 1964.

Middleton was recognized as an able administrator. His work as secretary of church extension promoted the growth of Methodism in PUERTO RICO, and today it is the largest Protestant church in the island. As bishop he conducted two successful financial campaigns for church extension in his area. He made a favorable impression as host bishop of the 1964 General Conference at Pittsburgh. He died Nov. 12, 1965 at Minneapolis while en route to a meeting of the COUNCIL OF BISHOPS in Seattle. Burial was at Chambersburg, Pa.

Methodist Story, January, 1966.
Who's Who in the Methodist Church, 1966.   JESSE A. EARL

MIDDLETOWN, OHIO, U.S.A. **First Church** is the direct descendent of the first religious group organized there when a little band of devout Methodists met for worship in the fall of 1805 in the log cabin home of James Grimes, a Methodist local preacher who had migrated from VIRGINIA after serving in the Revolutionary War. Itinerant preachers and such circuit riders as PETER CARTWRIGHT served the growing society, which soon became a member of the Miami Circuit, the first in OHIO. On Sept. 17, 1815, at the OHIO Annual CONFERENCE held in Lebanon, James Grimes, the founder of the Society, was ordained a local preacher by Bishop FRANCIS ASBURY. Participating in the ordination service was WILLIAM McKENDREE, then the only other American Methodist bishop.

The group outgrew the Grimes cabin and for a time beginning in 1815 met in a new one-room brick school house, the first to be erected in the hamlet. The congregation built its own one-room house of worship in 1829, the first brick church in Middletown. It was dedicated by Bishop JOSHUA SOULE.

In 1849 the group outgrew the one-room church and a two-story brick building forty-two by sixty-seven feet was built at a cost of $3,900. It was dedicated Jan. 20, 1850, by George W. Walker, the presiding elder, and was named Walker Chapel in his honor. The Ohio Annual Conference met in this church in 1880, with Bishop JESSE T. PECK presiding.

After forty years the two-story brick church became inadequate and the present handsome one, the first stone church in Middletown, was erected in 1890, at a cost of over $50,000, and dedicated May 3, 1891, by Bishop ISAAC W. JOYCE.

The church immediately opened Middletown's first public library in one of its rooms. About 1,000 books had been contributed and members served as voluntary librarians.

The Ohio Annual Conference was entertained again in 1892, with Bishop WILLIAM X. NINDE presiding. During its 161-year existence many dedicated ministers have served Middletown church, and one of them, WILBUR E. HAMMAKER (1904-1908), later became a bishop.

Additions and improvements have been made from time to time, the latest in 1953, when a modern three-story educational building adjoining the church was built at a cost of $102,600. The membership in 1970 was 2,190 and the annual budget at that time was in excess of $153,000.

Wilfred D. Vorhis, *The 150 Year History of the First Methodist Church of Middletown, Ohio.* 1956.   WILFRID D. VORHIS

MIDLAND, MICHIGAN, U.S.A. **First Church** is located in what is called the "City of Beautiful Churches." The present building, the only downtown church, was started in 1950. The sanctuary—a brick, steel and glass structure with balconies—seats 1,000 worshipers. The attention of the worshiper is drawn upward toward the skylighted altar and cross. Through the side walls of plain glass, accentuated by smaller colored panes, the congregation looks out on one side to a landscaped pool and on the other to a cloistered garden. Individual panes in memorial windows express personal concepts of Christian faith.

Fellowship Hall and classrooms are in the lower level. The educational wing and the chapel were consecrated in 1953. The final phase, the construction of improved office, choir, church school, library and caretaker facilities, was completed in 1967. The church complex covers a city block.

Midland became a part of a circuit in 1857 with four members and nine probationers. In 1868 the 40 by 70 frame building was started. This building with renovation and additions served the church until a fire in 1936 forced the 547 members to a new decision.

The membership tripled in the period from 1950 to 1965 and in 1970 stood at 3,427. The church school and youth programs have an average attendance of 1,000. Outstanding is the young leadership in the church and the wide participation in community affairs by many of its members.

The church is a center for Methodist district and conference meetings and also community religious meetings. The architecture and natural setting of the church was arranged to inspire in its membership the concept of growth—growth beyond themselves, beyond walls, beyond this earth, beyond time.

LOUIS WOOD

MIDLAND, NORTH CAROLINA, U.S.A. **Bethel Church** in Cabarrus County was organized in 1782 in Yadkin Circuit, and was put in Salisbury Circuit in 1783-1814. Among the first members were Alexander McLarty and family, by certification from "South End of Kinlyse (or Kintze) (SCOTLAND), 29 July 1773." Margaret McLellan joined in 1783, and David and Mary Taylor, David White and John Garmon in 1784.

"Taylor's Meetinghouse" became "Bethel" about 1808 with the first deed and a new log church. Under the VIRGINIA CONFERENCE until 1815, Bethel was then put on Sugar Creek Circuit and its successors in the SOUTH CAROLINA Conference until 1870. Then it went into the NORTH CAROLINA CONFERENCE until 1890, when the WESTERN NORTH CAROLINA CONFERENCE was organized. Associated with Clear Creek Circuit until 1906, Bethel was then on two-point charges with Mill Grove, Big Lick, and Bogers until it became a permanent station appointment in 1946.

Bethel was rebuilt about 1850 and in 1924. The 1970 membership was 274 and the property is valued at

$121,300. Nine men have gone into the ministry from Bethel.

F. Asbury, *Journal and Letters.* 1958.
W. L. Grissom, *North Carolina.* 1905.
Minutes of the Conferences, 1773-1813.
Charlotte Circuit Quarterly Conference Minutes, 1815-67.

G. W. BUMGARNER

MIDLAND, TEXAS, U.S.A., is the only city or town in Midland County. The county was organized in 1885. It is traditionally ranching country, but in recent years vast oil resources have been discovered, and today several major oil companies maintain regional offices in Midland. The First Methodist Church was organized in Midland in August 1885, with seven charter members, six women and one man. There are now five Methodist churches in Midland with a total membership of 6,225. **First Church,** the mother church, is the largest, with a membership of 2,288 and a Church school enrollment of 1,374. The first building was a small frame structure erected in 1889. The present church building is valued at $900,000 and the parsonage at $64,000. A new sanctuary, built in 1967-68, is considered one of the most beautiful in TEXAS.

J. O. Haymes, *Northwest Texas Conference.* 1962.

J. O. HAYMES

MIDWEST CITY, OKLAHOMA, U.S.A., **Wickline Church.** Twenty-five years ago a town sprang up on a wheat field across from Tinker Air Force Base. A few months later, June 13, 1943, the first Methodist church in this area started in a tent. In the struggling early days of the church, an elderly woman, Mrs. Jeffie Wickline, left all she had to this church in memory of her husband for whom the church was named. The money derived from the estate was a little over $18,000, but the new church found the money and the sacrificial gift an inspiration for a renewed stewardship. Over the next fifteen years, four building projects completed the church plant worth $500,000. The membership has grown from four the first Sunday to 2,417 today.

Seven pastors have given their encouragement to this progress. The pastors were: D. Allen Polen, C. E. Nisbett, Lee Bowles, D. Wesley Doak, Don F. Harrel, Elwyn O. Thurston, H. Ray Baker. Seventeen young men have gone into full-time Christian service.

The church has been known for its progressive ideas. There are no traditions that have to be followed. Wickline Church has assisted in the organization of four new churches in this area. When the new day in education was presented, leaders in children and adult education prepared themselves. Presently youth leaders are pushing the new youth ministry. Wickline is still a young church and eager to find new ways to serve her community.

MRS. ROBERT CARLISLE

MIGUEZ-BONINO, JOSE (1924-), Argentine theologian and educator, was born in Sante Fe, ARGENTINA, to staunch Methodist parents. He received theological training at the FACULTAD EVANGELICA DE TEOLOGIA in BUENOS AIRES. Upon graduation he went to Union Theological Seminary in New York, where he earned B.D., M.A., and Ph.D. degrees.

Prior to launching into a teaching career, he was pastor of the Ramos Mejia (Buenos Aires) and San Rafael

(Mendoza) churches. After some years as a professor in the seminary at Buenos Aires, he became president in 1960. Currently he writes articles for theological journals, and he was invited to teach for one semester at Union Seminary, New York, in 1967. He was one of the Methodist observers at the first and third sessions of the Vatican II Ecumenical Council of the Roman Catholic Church.

He is married to the former Noemi Niewenhuyze, and they have three sons.

EDWIN MAYNARD

MILBURN, WILLIAM HENRY (1823-1903), blind chaplain of the United States Congress, was born in PHILADELPHIA, Sept. 26, 1823, the son of Nicholas Milburn. When five years of age, the sight of his left eye was destroyed by a piece of glass thrown by a playmate. The other eye became inflamed and its vision was seriously impaired. By the age of thirty he was totally blind. His family moved to Jacksonville, Ill., in 1838. He entered Illinois College in 1841, but was obliged to leave in 1843 because of poor health. He had been able to read only by holding a book very close to his eyes.

Pioneer Methodist preachers, including the famous PETER CARTWRIGHT, frequented the Milburn home, and young Milburn decided to become a preacher. As an exhorter, in 1843, he accompanied PETER AKERS on a 500-mile circuit. They slept on shuck mattresses laid on cabin floors and ate the food the people offered. Milburn claimed that thereafter he never liked fried chicken, hog, hominy, or corn bread. On Sept. 13, 1843, Milburn was admitted to the ILLINOIS CONFERENCE and appointed to the Winchester Circuit. Two years later he was ordained deacon and appointed agent to raise money for McKENDREE COLLEGE and a female seminary which later became MacMURRAY COLLEGE. While en route from Wheeling to Cincinnati by boat, he met a group of congressmen whom he reproved for drinking, card playing, and profanity. Impressed, they raised a purse for him and almost immediately (1845) secured his election as chaplain of the House of Representatives. Milburn married, Aug. 13, 1846, and moved to BALTIMORE, though he continued as financial agent for his conference.

Because of poor health, Milburn moved South in 1848, transferred to the ALABAMA CONFERENCE, was ordained elder, and in January 1849, was appointed to Montgomery. After serving there and in Mobile, he went back to Congress as chaplain for one term (1853), and then settled in New York. There he supplied churches, including historic JOHN STREET, and lectured widely in the United States, Canada, and England. About 1862 he took orders in the Protestant Episcopal Church, but in 1878 he was readmitted to the Illinois Conference. Resuming as chaplain of the House of Representatives in 1885, he served until 1893, when he became chaplain of the U.S. Senate. He resigned the latter position in 1902 because of failing health. In 1893 he offered the invocation at the World's Columbian Exposition, and in 1897 he led the opening prayer at Queen Victoria's Diamond Jubilee.

Milburn wrote four books, including *Ten Years of Preacher Life,* and *The Pioneers, Preachers, and People of the Mississippi Valley.* As a speaker and writer, his style was simple and undecorated, but it was enlivened by humor and illustration. He traveled 1,500,000 miles lecturing and preaching, and he was the most distinguished blind man of his time. He died at Santa Barbara, Calif., April 10, 1903.

General Minutes, MEC and MECS.
Christian Advocate, June 22, 1944.
Dictionary of American Biography, Vol. 12. JESSE A. EARL

MILES, WILLIAM H. (1828-1892), first bishop of the C. M. E. CHURCH, was born on Dec. 26, 1828, at Springfield, Ky. He was born a slave and owned by Mrs. Mary Miles, who freed him in her will. In 1855, William Miles joined the M. E. Church, South and was licensed to preach in 1857. When the C. M. E. Church was formed in 1870, he was the first to be elected to the office of bishop by the first General Conference. His consecration to the episcopacy was by Bishops McTYEIRE and PAINE of the M. E. Church, South. Bishop Miles served for twenty-two years as the Senior Bishop and was noted as an eloquent preacher. He died on Nov. 14, 1892, at Louisville, Ky.

Harris and Patterson, *C. M. E. Church.* 1965.
I. Lane, *Autobiography.* 1916.   RALPH G. GAY

MILES COLLEGE, Birmingham, Ala., named for Bishop WILLIAM H. MILES, is a co-educational liberal arts institution. It is the result of early efforts put forth by the C. M. E. CHURCH to establish an educational institution of collegiate rank. The college is considered to have been a development from two high schools—one at Thomasville, established in 1898, and the other one at Booker City (now Docena) established in 1902. These high schools were organized and maintained by the ALABAMA and North Alabama conferences. The college received its charter from the State of Alabama in 1909.

It grants the Bachelor of Arts and Bachelor of Science degrees.

The governing board consists of twenty-six members, three-fourth of whom must be members of the C. M. E. Church, and three members from the Board of Missions of The United Methodist Church.

Total enrollment is 1,029; total faculty is 105; value of physical plant, $2,740,224; and endowment, $235,447.

MILEY, JOHN (1813-1895), American minister and theologian, was born in Butler County, OHIO, on Christmas day, 1813. He was graduated at Augusta College (A.B., 1834, A.M., 1837), and entered the Church's ministry through the OHIO CONFERENCE of the M. E. Church in 1838. He was minister to numerous local churches in Ohio until 1825, when he transferred to the NEW YORK EAST CONFERENCE where he remained until 1873, when he was called from his pastorate at Washington Square Church, New York City, to the chair of systematic theology at DREW THEOLOGICAL SEMINARY. In this position he served as professor and author until his death on Dec. 13, 1895; his funeral was held in the chapel at Drew.

During his years at Drew, Miley not only met the classroom responsibilities attendant upon his professorship, but also assumed the task of propounding a Methodist theology for his day. That theology was set forth in a host of published articles but especially in two discursive works: *The Atonement in Christ* (1879) and *Systematic Theology* (in two vols., 1892 and 1894). The former was an explication of the dominant theories of the atonement and a defense of the "Governmental Theory" (which

aimed to preserve the justice of God's moral demands) of Grotius, a seventeenth century Arminian statesman and theologian. Miley's *Systematic Theology* was his effort to present a "Methodist Arminianism" which would theologically differentiate Methodism from Calvinism and Romanism and which would acknowledge the insights and limitations of the science and scientific method of his time. Both of the above books were included in the Conference COURSE OF STUDY of the M. E. Church, the work on the atonement occupying this honor from 1880 to 1908.

Despite his active life as teacher and theologian, John Miley served as a member of four GENERAL CONFERENCES and in 1886 was fraternal delegate to the General Conference of the M. E. Church, South.

J. R. Joy, *Teachers of Drew.* 1942.
Lamb's Biographical Dictionary of the United States.
Miley, *The Atonement in Christ,* and *Systematic Theology.*
          CONRAD CHERRY

PAUL W. MILHOUSE

MILHOUSE, PAUL WILLIAM (1910-   ), American E.U.B. bishop, churchman and author, was born on Aug. 31, 1910, at St. Francisville, Ill. His formal education was received at INDIANA CENTRAL COLLEGE, A.B., 1932, Magna Cum Laude, and at American Theological Seminary, B.D., 1937, and Th.D., 1946. Honorary degrees were conferred on him by Indiana Central, D.D., 1950, and WESTMAR COLLEGE, L.H.D., 1965. On June 29, 1932, he married Frances Noblitt; they have three children.

Ordained in the ILLINOIS CONFERENCE, Church of the UNITED BRETHREN IN CHRIST, in 1931, he served churches at Elliott, Olney, and Decatur. He has been statistician, secretary, director of student work, director of youth and young adult camps in the Illinois Conference (EUB). He conducted a religious news television program at Harrisburg, Pa., for one year. Wider churchmanship has been expressed in his presidency of the Ministerial Association and Council of Churches in Decatur; associate editorship of the *Telescope-Messenger,* 1950-59; executive secretaryship of the General Council of Administration, 1959-60; election to the bishopric in 1960; membership in General Assembly of the WORLD COUNCIL OF CHURCHES, 1961, and in the General Assemblies of the NATIONAL COUNCIL OF CHURCHES, 1960, '63, and '66. He was a member of the Arbitration Panel in Decatur labor strike, and of the Board of Directors of the Illinois State Council of Churches.

An interest in writing from high school days has found expression in several widely used books. They include *Enlisting and Developing Church Leaders,* 1946; *Come Unto Me,* 1947; *Except the Lord Built the House,* 1949; *Doorways to Spiritual Living,* 1950; *Lift Up Your Eyes,* 1955; *Christian Worship in Symbol and Ritual,* 1953; *Laymen in the Church,* 1957; *At Life's Cross Roads,* 1959; and *Otterbein, Pioneer Preacher,* 1968. He edited *Growing Together,* 1959, and *Facing Frontiers,* 1960. Additional writings of his have appeared in numerous periodicals. In The United Methodist Church Bishop Milhouse was assigned to the OKLAHOMA Area.

Builders, Dec. 18, 1960.
The Telescope-Messenger, Dec. 9, 1950; Nov. 8, 1958; Dec. 10, 1960.   ARTHUR C. CORE

A. C. MILLAR

MILLAR, ALEXANDER COPELAND (1861-1940), American clergyman, educator and editor, was born at McKeesport, Pa., on May 17, 1861, the son of William John and Ellen (Coven) Millar. He attended CENTRAL COLLEGE in Missouri, receiving the A.B. degree in 1885, and the A.M. in 1889; Wesleyan College, Winchester, Ky., D.D., 1907; HENDRIX COLLEGE, Conway, Ark., D.D., 1940; University of Arkansas, LL.D., 1922. He married Elizabeth Harwood (deceased, May 22, 1924) of Brooksfield, Mo., on June 27, 1887, and they had two sons and a daughter. Millar

married a second time Susie McKinnon of Jacksonville, Texas, on Oct. 15, 1925.

He was ordained to the ministry of the M. E. Church, South in 1888, after serving for a year as professor of Latin and philosophy at the Neosho, Mo., Collegiate Institute, 1886-87. He became president of the Central Collegiate Institute of Altus, Ark., which was moved later to Conway, Ark., and renamed Hendrix College in 1890. He served as professor of history and economics, Central College, Fayette, Mo., 1902-04; presiding elder, Little Rock District, 1906-10; president of Hendrix College (second time), 1910-13; president of Oklahoma Methodist College, Muskogee, Okla., 1913-14; associate editor of the *Western Methodist* (now *Arkansas Methodist*), 1904-14. He was editor-in-chief of the *Arkansas Methodist,* 1914-40, also serving as presiding elder of the Arkadelphia District, 1931-32.

Millar was head of the good-roads-movement in Arkansas which resulted in the adoption in 1899 of an amendment to the Arkansas Constitution, authorizing counties to levy a road tax. He led a movement to secure legislation regulating college degrees. In the larger church, he was delegate to the Ecumenical Conference on Foreign Missions; a member of the General BOARD OF EDUCATION (MES), 1898-1902; a member of the Educational Commission; of the Arkansas Historical Commission, 1909-13, and again in 1927. He led a special investigation of the Arkansas Penitentiary in 1908; was president of the Arkansas Education Association, 1911. He was a delegate to the GENERAL CONFERENCE, MES, five times including 1930; secretary of the Arkansas Forestry Commission, 1924-40; president of the Arkansas Anti-Saloon League, 1923-40; president of the Western Methodist Assembly, 1922-33; vice-president, 1933-40. He was vice-president of the JUDICIAL COUNCIL (MES), 1934-39. He traveled in Latin America, 1920. He died in Little Rock, Ark., on Nov. 9, 1940. He is the author of *Twentieth Century Education Problems,* 1901; *Together* (poem), 1910; "My Own Loved Arkansas" (song), 1937.

Journal of the Little Rock Conference, 1940.
Who's Who in America, 1938-39.   KENNETH L. SPORE

MILLER, ADAM (1810-1901), American German preacher, was born in MARYLAND, of Mennonite ancestry, having a grandfather and two uncles who were Amish preachers. He grew up in an Amish colony at Shanesville, twenty-five miles from Canton, Ohio. His father, impressed by Joseph McDowell, later an itinerant in the OHIO, ROCK RIVER, and IOWA CONFERENCES, sent Adam to McDowell for English instruction. Influenced by McDowell's preaching, Miller was the first of his family to embrace Methodism. He received an exhorter's license and spent almost two years with McDowell, going to school in summer and teaching in winter. Licensed to preach in 1830, he entered the Ohio Conference of the M. E. Church, in 1831, and was assigned to Nicholas Circuit, VIRGINIA, traveling 350 miles around thirty-one appointments. Also, serving Guyandotte and Point Pleasant circuits, then in Virginia, Miller traveled in Kanawha District for four years.

Removing to INDIANA, he was assigned to Greenville Circuit (1835), West Union Circuit (1836), Milford Circuit (1838), and then to the German Methodists in CINCINNATI and on Lebanon District (1839). In 1840 he was appointed to a regular German District of the CINCINNATI CONFERENCE. Miller, who was the first native

American to join WILHELM NAST's ministry to German settlers, helped establish churches in BALTIMORE, NEWARK, Rahway, Poughkeepsie, Albany, and BUFFALO.

In 1858, transferring from the Peoria Conference to the Iowa Conference, Adam Miller began teaching in the German Language and Literature Department of IOWA WESLEYAN UNIVERSITY. Granted "superannuated or wornout" status in 1861, he removed to Springfield, Ill.; he then resided almost a decade in CHICAGO and was living in DENVER, Colorado Territory, in 1873. His Iowa Conference membership was terminated by location in 1874. Adam Miller was effective as a preacher for twenty-two years, eight on circuits, one on a station, and thirteen in other appointments, while having fifteen non-effective years.

P. F. Douglass, *German Methodism.* 1939.
A. Miller, *German Methodist Preachers.* 1859.
————————, *German Missions.* 1843.
A. W. Haines, *Makers of Iowa Methodism.* 1900.
Minutes of the Cincinnati Conference, 1909.
Minutes of the Iowa Conference, 1858-74.
J. M. Versteeg, *Ohio Area.* 1962.   MARTIN L. GREER

MILLER, ELIZABETH KUMLER (1835-1908), outstanding American church woman, was born on a farm near Millville, Ohio, Feb. 1, 1835. Her father, Daniel C. Kumler, was one of the three men sent to Africa in 1855 to begin United Brethren Mission work in SIERRA LEONE, West Africa.

She attended the village school, Oxford Female Seminary (now Western College for Women, Oxford, Ohio) and OTTERBEIN COLLEGE, graduating in 1858. One of her classmates at Otterbein College was BENJAMIN R. HANBY, the famous song writer.

After teaching in an integrated village school in Ohio, in 1859 she married John S. Miller and began housekeeping in a log cabin. In 1862 she was called to be principal of the Ladies Department of Otterbein College. She accepted and they moved to Westerville, where her husband died a year later.

In 1880 she came to DAYTON, Ohio to serve the Women's Missionary Association of the Church of the UNITED BRETHREN IN CHRIST. She served in various capacities—as trustee, editor of the *Woman's Evangel* and national president. It was said of her during these years that "she was the best known and the best loved woman in the Church."

She was a sensitive woman with remarkable insight into the total task of the Church and with a worldwide concern. She was also a poet and a book of her poems was published after her death. Early on Oct. 23, 1908, she died and was laid to rest in Woodland Cemetery, Dayton, Ohio.

Woman's Evangel, December 1908.   MRS. S. S. HOUGH

MILLER, EMORY (1834-1912), American minister, was born in Mount Pleasant, Pa., on Dec. 23, 1834. He attended Mt. Pleasant College and after moving to IOWA enrolled at the Iowa Conference Seminary (Cornell College) and later took some work at the GARRETT BIBLICAL INSTITUTE.

He was admitted to the IOWA Annual CONFERENCE of the M. E. Church in 1858 and served churches, until retirement, in the Iowa Conference, the UPPER IOWA

CONFERENCE, the DES MOINES CONFERENCE, with the years 1860-1861 in the MISSOURI CONFERENCE, and 1882-1885 in the MINNESOTA CONFERENCE. Outstanding pastorates were filled at Cedar Rapids 1863-1864; Davenport 1871-1872; Iowa City 1880-1881; Des Moines 1884-1886; 1905-1907 and Indianola 1887-1891. He was presiding elder of the Davenport District 1868-1870; Cedar Falls District 1875-1879; Des Moines District 1892-1897.

His preaching and expositions of Holy Scripture were especially effective in large urban congregations. Recognized by IOWA WESLEYAN UNIVERSITY with an M.A. in 1856, he was twice honored by the State University of Iowa with a D.D. in 1877 and an LL.D. in 1888. A book, *The Evolution of Love* (1892), received many commendations. During his pastorate at Indianola and after retirement, Miller was a member of the teaching staff at SIMPSON COLLEGE.

He was a delegate to the GENERAL CONFERENCES of 1876, 1880, 1892, 1896, 1904 and to the ECUMENICAL METHODIST CONFERENCE in Washington, 1891. He died in Des Moines on July 3, 1912.

Des Moines Conference, Official Minutes 1912, pp. 83-85.
LOUIS A. HASELMAYER

MILLER, FREDERIC K. (1908-   ), Commissioner of Higher Education for PENNSYLVANIA, was born Nov. 28, 1908, in Lebanon, Pa., to United Brethren parents, the Rev. HARRY E. and Laura (Keiper) MILLER. He earned his A.B. degree at LEBANON VALLEY COLLEGE (1929) and his M.A. (1931) and Ph.D. (1948) at the University of Pennsylvania, where he was an Assistant in History from 1931 to 1933.

After serving as a teacher of social sciences and basketball coach at Lebanon High School (1933-39), he became Chairman of the Department of History at Lebanon Valley College. From 1948 to 1950, he added to his teaching responsibilities the duties of Assistant to the President; and following the death of President Clyde A. Lynch, he served as the Acting President from 1950 to 1951. In 1951, Dr. Miller was elected President of Lebanon Valley College, a position he held until 1967, when he assumed his present post with the Department of Public Instruction of Pennsylvania.

Dr. Miller's tenure as President of Lebanon Valley College was marked by great growth in assets, faculty strength, and academic quality. In addition to the leadership he supplied his Alma Mater, Dr. Miller found time to participate in numerous religious, community, and educational affairs.

He was a delegate to the GENERAL CONFERENCE of the E.U.B. Church from 1954 to 1966; a member of the Board of Publications and Trustee of the OTTERBEIN PRESS, 1955-60; and President of the Historical Society of The Eastern Conference, 1950-66. He holds his membership in the Annville United Methodist Church.

In educational circles, he was a member of the Commission on Higher Education of the Middle Atlantic States Association of Colleges and Secondary Schools, 1960-66; President of the EUB College Administrators, 1957-60; Secretary (1957-61), Vice President (1961-62), and President (1962-63) of the Pennsylvania Association of Colleges and Universities; and Chairman of the Board of the University Center at Harrisburg, 1961-63 and 1966-67.

His participation in community affairs ranges from membership on the Board of Trustees of the Good Samaritan Hospital, Lebanon; the Board of Directors of the Lebanon County Chamber of Commerce; and the Lebanon County Unit of the American Cancer Society; the Board of Directors of the Lebanon YMCA to membership on the Student Services Committee and the Executive Committee of the Pennsylvania State YMCA.

Dr. Miller is married to the former Marion Stover of Philadelphia and is the father of a daughter, Janet Louise, wife of Robert N. McLeod. Dr. Miller served with the U.S. Army in the European Theater of Operations, 1943-45. He has been awarded honorary degrees as follows: Litt.D., Muhlenberg College, L.H.D., DICKINSON COLLEGE, LL.D., Lebanon Valley College, and Ped.D., Geneva College.

Who's Who in America.   BRUCE C. SOUDERS

MILLER, GEORGE (1774-1816), was one of the first two ordained men to become associated with JACOB ALBRIGHT, founder of the "Evangelische Gemeinschaft" in PENNSYLVANIA at the opening of the nineteenth century. The other of the two was JOHN WALTER.

George Miller was born Feb. 16, 1774, at Pottstown, Montgomery Co., Pa., and died April 5, 1816, in Union township, Union County of that state. He is buried at New Berlin, Pa.

In his childhood, the parents, Jacob and Elizabeth Miller, moved to Alsace township, Berks County, where the father died when George was but eleven years of age. He had erected and was operating a grist mill at the time of his death. The business proved to be a valuable source of income for the family. There were two other sons in the family, John and Solomon. The family was of the Lutheran faith.

George Miller suffered a confining illness at the age of twelve. He reported that this experience resulted in a new sense of respect for his mother and led him to read through the entire Bible by the age of eighteen. Regaining his health, he received catechetical instruction from a Lutheran pastor of Reading, Pa. Although sensing an urgency toward the abiding spiritual values of life, he was also at times beset with temptations common to youth of his age.

At the age of nineteen, Miller took up residence with his brother John and soon became a master millwright, fully informed on the construction of grist mills and the milling business. In 1798 he purchased a tract of land in Brunswick township, Schuylkill County, where he erected and operated his own mill. In 1800 he was married to Magdalena Brobst, at which time they erected their own home near the mill site.

It was in the years of early 1796 that Jacob Albright began his itinerant preaching in eastern Pennsylvania. In 1798, Miller first heard Albright speak and was deeply impressed. In 1802, while Miller was operating his own milling business, Albright called one evening and asked for night's lodging. He was invited to preach in the Miller home.

On June 2, 1802, while at work in his own mill, George Miller made a complete surrender to God. Both his wife and brother Solomon embraced the Christian faith under the early influences of Jacob Albright and John Walter. A class was established of which he became the leader.

In 1805 Miller sold his land and mill properties and entered into full-time itinerant Christian work under the direction of Albright and Walter. His first assignment covered work in Lancaster, Dauphin and Berks counties.

The first Annual Conference of the newly emerging church was held at Muhlbach (now Kleinfeltersville), Lebanon County, in 1807. At this session Miller was ordained elder.

In the early 1800's Miller became afflicted with intermittent illness. After 1809 he could accept no definite assignment to the pastorate. Having some literary ability and upon the urging of his fellow pastors, he accepted the responsibility of writing the newly projected *Discipline* which Jacob Albright had not been able to carry through. This historic original draft of seventy-five pages was completed in 1809. Shortly thereafter he compiled a "book of rules" for Conference business. In succession he wrote *Practical Christianity*, a short biography of Jacob Albright, and then his own autobiography. Much of this work was done on a small printing press in his own home.

WILLIAM C. F. HAYES

MILLER, GEORGE AMOS (1868-1961), American bishop, was born in Mendon, Ill., July 8, 1868, the oldest of four children of Martin and Ardalissa Dryer Miller. The family moved to CALIFORNIA, where the father became a pioneer in early California Methodism, serving churches in the Sacramento and San Joaquin Valleys, farming virgin soil to support his family.

George Miller attended the University of Southern California and later graduated from Stanford. In 1895 he married Margaret Ross and they had two daughters.

He was ordained in 1896 and served pastorates in Hanford, Calif. (1896-1900) and Fresno First Church (1900-04), a church founded by his father. He went to Central Church in MANILA, P. I. (1905-07), returning to the States to lecture and do field work with the AMERICAN BIBLE SOCIETY (1907-08). He served Hamilton Church, SAN FRANCISCO (1908-09), and First Church, SAN JOSE (1909-14), Grace Church, San Francisco (1914-16), and then, sent by California Epworth Leaguers, he went to PANAMA as Mission Superintendent (1917-19), pioneering Methodist work in COSTA RICA. He then became Executive Secretary of Mission Work in South America for the M. E. Church. In 1924 he was elected to the episcopacy at the GENERAL CONFERENCE of that church held in Springfield, Mass., though he was not a delegate to the Conference.

Bishop Miller served one quadrennium each from headquarters in MEXICO CITY, BUENOS AIRES, and SANTIAGO. He retired in 1934, served a local church in Lafayette, Calif., and continued his interest in Spanish American missions. He raised funds for and established the Training School for Christian workers in Costa Rica. He died Oct. 12, 1961, his wife, who had greatly helped him through the years, predeceasing him.

Bishop Miller's service, in line with nationalistic trends the world over, spanned the years when Methodism moved into an era of increasing self-administration, self-extension and self-support, on the mission field. He turned over to "national" bishops, one by one, the three episcopal areas in Spanish America, bringing to a close the period of church administration from the United States.

Before modern travel facilities, Bishop Miller traveled up and down the hemisphere on burro-back, by cattle boat, through tropical jungles and over blizzard swept mountains, enduring at times the miseries of altitude sickness. He was a gifted and prolific writer, some thirty books in English and Spanish and several blank verse dramatizations of Biblical stories coming from his pen. He was also a musician, playing both string and wind instruments; an artist, who created exquisite wood carvings and charcoal sketches. Many a church benefitted from his versatile skills as organ-builder, expert mechanic, able carpenter, photographer, and printer. His sense of humor never failed, nor did his calm acceptance of life, a prime requisite for a difficult administration with tensions of decreasing depression appropriations and the growing pains of a church moving toward self-direction and maturity.

Among the books written by Bishop Miller were: *Interesting Manila; The Life Efficient; China Inside Out; Prowling About Panama; Adventures With Christ in Latin America; Restlessness and Reality; Missionary Morale; Mexico and the Mexicans;* and his autobiography, *Growing Up,* which he wrote when he was ninety-one years of age.

C. F. Price, *Who's Who in American Methodism.* 1916.

EVELYN MILLER BERGER

MILLER, HARRY E. (1873-1947), American clergyman, pastor of the Salem United Brethren Church, Lebanon, Pa., from 1904 to 1945, one of the longest pastorates on record in the former United Brethren Church.

The son of Isaac and Frederica Schach Miller, Harry Miller was born at Orwin, Pa., June 5, 1873. After moving to Lebanon with his parents, he was converted at the age of twelve in the Memorial United Brethren Church; but he later transferred his membership to the Salem Church, which recommended him for the Quarterly Conference license in 1893. He was ordained in 1899, by the East Pennsylvania Conference, CHURCH OF THE UNITED BRETHREN IN CHRIST, the year he received his A.B. degree from LEBANON VALLEY COLLEGE.

In 1903, he graduated from Bonebrake Theological Seminary (now UNITED THEOLOGICAL SEMINARY), Dayton, Ohio, and returned to PENNSYLVANIA where he served as pastor of the Zion Church, Myerstown, for a year before assuming the leadership of his home congregation in 1904. In 1912, he took a M.A. degree at Lebanon Valley College; and in 1916 he was honored with a D.D. degree by the same institution.

During his pastorate, Miller received 1,078 members into the Salem congregation on profession of faith. He was known throughout the denomination as a masterful, sincere preacher and to his congregation as a devoted pastor. He was active in a number of responsible positions in both the East Pennyslvania Conference and the denomination as a whole. Beginning with 1909, he represented his annual conference at GENERAL CONFERENCE eight times; but illness prevented his accepting election to the merging conference of the Church of the United Brethren in Christ and THE EVANGELICAL CHURCH in 1946. He was a Trustee of Lebanon Valley College for twenty-seven years, and a member of a number of agencies of his annual conference throughout his active pastorate.

Miller died Feb. 4, 1947, two years after the Salem congregation had honored him by electing him as Pastor Emeritus. He is buried at the Mt. Lebanon Cemetery, Lebanon. He had been preceded in death in 1941 by his wife, the former Laura Keiper. The Millers were the parents of two sons. Dr. FREDERIC K. MILLER, President of Lebanon Valley College from 1950 to 1967, and the Rev. Paul A. Miller.

P. B. Gibble, *East Pennsylvania Conference.* 1951.

BRUCE C. SOUDERS

MILLER, LOIS C. (1918-   ), daughter of an E.U.B. minister in the Kansas Conference, was born in Wichita, Kan. She received her collegiate education from York College (now WESTMAR COLLEGE), where she received the B.A. degree. Westmar College later gave her an honorary doctorate.

Miss Miller served briefly as a teacher in the NEW MEXICO MISSION and ten years in weekday religious education in CALIFORNIA and OHIO. Then followed a three-year service as bookstore manager for the OTTERBEIN PRESS, prior to becoming in 1955 secretary of missionary education for children and youth in the Women's Division, BOARD OF MISSIONS. From 1963 to 1968 she was secretary of Interpretation and Education for the E.U.B. Board of Missions. With the formation of the United Methodist Church in 1968, she became associate general secretary of the Joint Commission on Education and Cultivation, Board of Missions.

A delegate to the 1968 Assembly of the WORLD COUNCIL OF CHURCHES (Uppsala), Dr. Miller was elected to the World Council Central Committee. She has also been active as a member of the Department of Education for Mission, NATIONAL COUNCIL OF CHURCHES in America.

JOHN H. NESS, JR.

MILLER, WILLIAM (1775-1846), American bishop of the A.M.E. ZION CHURCH, was born in Queen Anne County, Md., Aug. 23, 1775. He was converted March 4, 1788, and was licensed to preach in New York City in 1808. He joined the conference June 21, 1821 and was ordained deacon June 22, 1821. He received his elder's orders in 1823 and was elected a superintendent (full) in 1840. He died June 10, 1846. Flood has his death listed in PHILADELPHIA in 1849, while Moore reports his death in the twenty-sixth Conference (New York, 1846). We feel that the first account (June 10, 1849) is therefore incorrect.

DAVID H. BRADLEY

MILLS, ALFRED AVERY (1877-1963), Australian minister and President of the QUEENSLAND CONFERENCE 1930 and 1947, was born in Bendigo, Victoria. He was a diligent minister from 1907-1948. He served as circuit minister, military chaplain, Secretary of Home Missions and Connexional Secretary. He established many circuits, extended the work of the Church and inspired and directed new and aggressive enterprises. He was statesmanlike and zealous in determining the future pattern of the Church in Queensland.

AUSTRALIAN EDITORIAL COMMITTEE

MILLS, EDWARD LAIRD (1875-1959), American minister and church leader, was born on March 30, 1875, at Ryegate, Vt. He was reared and partly educated in the western United States. He graduated from WESLEYAN UNIVERSITY in 1898, and from BOSTON UNIVERSITY SCHOOL OF THEOLOGY in 1902. Following his ordination in the same year he went to MONTANA where he served various churches until 1910, when he was appointed superintendent of the Butte District of the MONTANA CONFERENCE. In 1914 he became superintendent of the UTAH Mission.

Edward L. Mills was elected superintendent of frontier work under the Board of Home Missions and Church Extension (ME) in 1916, which office he held until 1920, when he was elected editor of the *Pacific Christian Advocate,* a position he filled admirably until his retirement.

He was author of the book, *The Advancing Church,* and also *Plains, Peaks and Pioneers.* The D.D. degree was conferred upon him in 1911 by WILLAMETTE UNIVERSITY and by Wesleyan University, his alma mater, in 1921.

He was a wise and efficient leader, a fearless advocate of civic righteousness, and a keen and constructive ecclesiastical statesman. He died on Nov. 7, 1959.

H. M. Merkel, *Utah.* 1938.
Minutes of the Oregon Conference, 1960.
C. F. Price, *Who's Who in American Methodism.* 1916.
WARREN S. BAINBRIDGE

MILLS, JACOB (1842-1925), American minister, was born Nov. 18, 1842, near Topham, Vt. He lost an arm in the Civil War, then served eleven years in internal revenue and customs. He married Jennie Forrest, Nov. 17, 1870. They had three children: EDWARD LAIRD, George, and Edith. Answering an advertisement by Col. Wilbur F. Sanders, he invested in a horse ranch in Montana. After he was called to preach in 1881, he responded to an appeal by F. A. RIGGIN for ministers for MONTANA, went west in 1882, became the first resident pastor at Fort Benton, built the Benton parsonage and the Sun River church (the first Methodist buildings in northern Montana), and was ordained elder in 1885. He was presiding elder of Bozeman District, 1887-93, and of the Helena District, 1899-1905. He secured the organization of the Great Falls District, later North Montana Mission, and the organization of Kalispell Mission. He was twice delegate to GENERAL CONFERENCE; was conference evangelist, 1907-14, and died at a cottage prayer meeting, Oct. 28, 1925. Burial was at Forestvale Cemetery, Helena.

E. L. Mills, *Plains, Peaks and Pioneers.* 1947.
Roberta Baur West, "How They Brought the Good News of Methodism to North Montana." Mss. ROBERTA BAUR WEST

MILLS, JOB S. (1848-1909), American U.B. minister and bishop, was born Feb. 28, 1848, in Washington County, Ohio, of Quaker ancestry.

He received a license to exhort in 1867, a quarterly conference license to preach in 1868, and joined the Scioto Conference, CHURCH OF THE UNITED BRETHREN IN CHRIST, in 1870. He became college pastor at Westerville, Ohio, in 1874, and served a six-year term, and another two-year term later. For a period of time Job Mills was a presiding elder of the Central Ohio Conference. In 1887 he became professor of English literature and rhetoric in Western College, at Toledo, Iowa, when two years later he was made president of that institution, serving three years. This was followed by one year as professor of philosophy there.

Mills was elected bishop in 1893 and re-elected quadrennially until his death in 1909. In 1896, and again

in 1903, he embarked on visitation tours to the mission fields in Africa and GERMANY. In 1902 he visited PUERTO RICO. In 1907 he visited the missions in JAPAN, CHINA, and the PHILIPPINES.

Largely through private study and upon examination he received A.M. and Ph.D. degrees. One of his friends said of him, "His messages were backed by the force of clear thinking, full information, and an impressive personality." In 1870 he married Sarah A. Metsgar, who died in 1874. In 1876 he was married to Mary Keister, of Scottdale, Pa. To them were born two sons and three daughters.

Bishop Mills died at Annville, Pa., Sept. 16, 1909.

A. W. Drury, *History of the U.B.* 1931. CLAYTON G. LEHMAN

MILLSAP, KATHRYN ANNA (1890-   ), American deaconess, was born in Benton, Kan., on Jan. 30, 1890, the daughter of John Riley Millsap, a Methodist minister in the SOUTHWEST KANSAS CONFERENCE, and Katie E. Dugan.

Miss Millsap attended the Wichita (Kansas) College of Music but, having decided to become a Methodist deaconess, she enrolled in the Kansas City National Training School for Deaconesses and Missionaries (later NATIONAL COLLEGE) and graduated in 1914. She first served as pastor's assistant in ST. PAUL, Minn., then as missionary on the Carthage (Missouri) District for four years. In 1926-27 she was pastor's assistant at Bethel Church, Wichita. In 1927 the Southwest Kansas Conference appointed her chaplain of Wesley Hospital, Wichita, and she served there continuously until her retirement in 1959. She received specialized training at Wichita University; ILIFF SCHOOL OF THEOLOGY; took clinical training under Dr. Anton Boisen, Elgin (Illinois) State Hospital; and studied at Columbia University and Union Theological Seminary, New York City.

She pioneered in the midwest in new concepts of pastoral care and counseling in hospital ministry, and her work received national recognition. She initiated the organization of Ministers and Physicians Clinic at Wesley Hospital which has met annually since 1944. She was a charter member of the Protestant Hospital Chaplains Association and served as member of hospital committees of national import; she has been called on for addresses at Conferences of Ministers, National Hospital Organizations, Mental Hygiene Societies, Ministers and Physicians Clinics, and other groups.

She was lay delegate from the CENTRAL KANSAS CONFERENCE to the GENERAL CONFERENCE (TMC) and the South Central JURISDICTIONAL CONFERENCE of 1940. Upon retirement from active service she was appointed Chaplain Emeritus and Consultant to the Chaplain's Department by the Central Kansas Conference.

Minutes of the Central Kansas, Minnesota, St. Louis, and Southwest Kansas Conferences.
Wichita Beacon-Eagle, various numbers, 1927-59.
World Horizons, 1940-65. MARY F. SMITH

MILLSAPS, REUBEN WEBSTER (1833-1916), American layman and philanthropist, was born May 30, 1833, in Copiah County, Miss., a son of Reuben and Lavinia Clowers Millsaps. Young Reuben left his home at the age of seventeen, walked to Natchez, a distance of about sixty miles, where he took passage on a steamboat for

Madison, Ind., to enter Hanover College. After two years at Hanover he transferred to DePauw University, from which he graduated in 1854. He went back to Mississippi and taught school for two years, saving every penny he made so he could go to Harvard Law School. After receiving his law degree at Harvard, he practiced law in Pine Bluff, Ark., from 1858 to the beginning of the Civil War. He saw extensive service in the Confederate Army and came out at the close of the conflict with the rank of major. After his discharge, he returned to south Mississippi and entered the business of cotton buying and transporting. From that he entered merchandising at Brookhaven. In 1880 he sold his business and went to St. Louis, Mo., where he established a wholesale grocery and cotton commission business. In 1885, he returned to Hazlehurst, Miss., and established the Merchants and Planters Bank, then moved to Jackson, Miss., in 1887 and became president of the Capitol State Bank.

In 1869 he married Mrs. Mary F. Younkin, daughter of Horace Bean, a wealthy banker of New Orleans. They had no children, but reared a niece whom they adopted.

Major Millsaps was a stalwart Methodist and a loyal churchman. He was a constant attendant at the business meetings of the church from the local Church Conference to the General Conference. No layman in Mississippi was more frequently elected a delegate to the General Conference than he.

His great work was in laying the foundation for Millsaps College with an initial gift of $50,000, in 1889. All told, he gave more than ten times that amount to the college which bears his name and took a prominent part in its first Board of Trustees. In addition, he gave the property on which the Mississippi Methodist Children's Home is located, and gave financial help to other educational and religious institutions.

He died on June 28, 1916, and was buried in a mausoleum on the campus of Millsaps College.

Journal of the Mississippi Conference, 1916.
New Orleans Christian Advocate, 1916.　　J. A. Lindsey

MILLSAPS COLLEGE, Jackson, Mississippi, was chartered in 1890. It was named for its chief benefactor, Major Reuben W. Millsaps, a graduate of DePauw University, who offered $50,000 for endowment, provided Methodists of Mississippi matched it, and who gave to the college additional amounts totaling over $100,000. Its first president was William Belton Murrah, later a bishop of the M. E. Church, South. Bishop Murrah, Bishop Charles Galloway, and Major Millsaps are generally recognized as the founders.

During the 1930's a study of the educational work of Mississippi Methodists resulted in consolidating with Millsaps College the two junior colleges under control of the Methodist Conferences in Mississippi—Grenada College and Whitworth College. In 1966, the Ford Foundation made a challenge grant of $1,500,000 to the college which the college more than met in the subsequent months. It now offers the B.A., B.S. and B.M. (Music) degrees. The governing board has sixteen members elected by the Mississippi and North Mississippi Conferences.

John O. Gross

MILNE, ANDREW MURRAY (1838-1907), pioneer missionary and South American Bible agent "from Cape Horn to Quito," has been called "the most noted Bible agent of his generation."

Born in Scotland in a pious home, he entered upon a life of consecration to Christ during the religious awakening of 1857-58, and became an active member of the United Presbyterian Church. He came to Buenos Aires in secular work and was sent to Gualeguay, where he, "though unable to speak the language of the country, embraced early opportunities for distributing gospels and tracts to the lightermen with whom he had to deal." Back in Buenos Aires, Milne was recounting his experiences to William Goodfellow, whose church he had joined upon arrival in Argentina, when the latter suddenly turned to him and said: "How would you like to be engaged in such work all the time?" Milne replied that it was just the work he would delight in. The American Bible Society had been in correspondence with Goodfellow about opening Bible work in the River Platte region; Milne applied and in February 1864, was appointed agent of the society.

The appointment indicated Montevideo, but since an agency of the British and Foreign Bible Society was already there, Milne established himself at Rosario, Argentina. From that up-river port he visited new towns and cities. Later (1869-79) he spent eleven years in Montevideo, then came back to Buenos Aires to establish the River Platte Agency in 1880. He wrote in a letter in 1904:

Since the establishment of this agency, there has fallen to the agent the very distinguished honour of planting the flag of the society's permanent operations in all the capitals and in many of the chief cities of the ten republics of South America. . . . In carrying out the instructions of the managers, the agent has circumnavigated South America once, crossed the Cordilleras [the Andes] ten times, and passed from the Atlantic to the Pacific or vice versa still oftener, and with his own hands sold tons of Scriptures. . . . Many years ago we expressed a desire to see Ecuador opened to the Gospel; to see the American Bible Society's work established in every country of South America, to see the work of this agency efficiently established from Ecuador to Cape Horn, and to have a hand in the opening of the Fountain of Life to the 3,500,000 Quichua Indians of Bolivia, Peru and Ecuador. In His amazing grace God has permitted us to see all of these desires realized.

On the last day of 1864, Milne had been married to Harriet Leggat, born in Aberdeenshire. She lived to complete forty years of joint service with her husband, taking full charge of the agency during his long absences on Bible work. Milne died in Buenos Aires on Aug. 22, 1907.

Ines Milne, *From Cape Horn to Quito with the Bible*. Rosario, Argentina, 1942.
Adam F. Sosa, *Desde el Cabo de Hornos hasta Quito con la Biblia*. Buenos Aires: La Aurora Press, 1944.

Daniel P. Monti

MILWAUKEE, WISCONSIN, U.S.A., the largest city in the state, was founded by Solomon Juneau in 1818 and was incorporated in 1846. Mark Robinson was admitted on trial in the Illinois Conference in 1835 and was appointed to the "Milwaukee Mission." The Wisconsin region was then included in the Chicago District. Robinson preached the first Protestant sermon in Milwaukee and organized a class with four members. At the 1836 conference session Robinson reported fifty-three members for Milwaukee, the figure including members at other points on the circuit. In 1837 the Milwaukee District was formed with Salmon Stebbins as presiding elder. That year a board of trustees was appointed for the Milwaukee church, and in 1841 a church building was dedicated. It was rebuilt in 1844 at a cost of $10,000. Originally called Spring Street, it later became First Church. In 1847 some members withdrew and formed a Wesleyan Methodist church. In the same year a second M. E. congregation called Walker's Point was formed with nine members. Two years later it had thirty members. In 1848 the WISCONSIN CONFERENCE was organized.

In 1880 the M. E. Church had four English-speaking churches in Milwaukee with a total of 839 members and three German-language congregations with 475 members. In 1920 there were eleven English-speaking churches and six German with 4,047 and 909 members, respectively.

In 1969 The United Methodist Church had twenty-five congregations in Milwaukee, twelve of them from the former Methodist Church and thirteen from the former E.U.B. Church. The first group reported 5,904 members, property valued at $7,705,881, and a total of $214,213 raised for all purposes during the year. The former E.U.B. churches reported 4,949 members, property valued at $3,958,727, and $509,246 raised for all purposes during the year.

First Church is the city's oldest congregation. The first Methodist service was held in the Solomon Juneau trading post in 1835, and the church was organized in 1836. During its history, First Church has occupied church facilities in eight locations, and it is presently in the process of building the first major downtown church edifice to rise in a metropolitan area of more than a million people within twenty-five years.

First Church "established" the government of Milwaukee and housed the first city hall. The city council met in the sanctuary and the city offices were in the church basement. First Church claims to have started the first kindergarten in the world, and it had the first public library in Milwaukee. The church has long exerted great influence in the city.

When an expressway removed its older building, First Church purchased a complete block in the center of the city, a site valued at more than $2,000,000. Present plans call for the erection of an impressive church edifice with adequate parking facilities. In 1969 First Church reported 712 members and $26,462 raised for all purposes during the year.

Kingsley Church is the largest Methodist congregation within the city limits. Its stately nave in German Gothic is impressive. The church began as a store-front mission at Lisbon Avenue and 28th Street in 1891 and it grew rapidly. The first building was erected at 29th and Brown Streets in 1893. In 1907 the cornerstone of a new edifice was laid at 33rd and Walnut Streets, and the present sanctuary was erected. As the years passed the area around the church developed into a thriving residential district. In 1908 the church had 246 members.

With changing times and an altered environment the mission of Kingsley Church changed. The area to the east became the inner core of the city inhabited largely by Negroes. The residential area in the immediate neighborhood of the church became a "port of entry" for white families from the rural districts and from the South, as well as for young couples starting out in married life. The church has steadily tried to serve the needs of the population around it. A large and well-equipped gymnasium offers recreation to city boys and girls who are without playground space and who are often, because both parents work, without much parental care. A day care center is maintained. Various activities are provided for teenagers. The congregation aggressively seeks out new couples and others in need of guidance, encouragement, fellowship, and Christian nurture. It has been successful in training these newcomers for church leadership. Many of them, as they acquire more economic resources, move out to the suburbs and strengthen the churches there. Methodist churches west of Milwaukee have many former Kingsley Church members as leaders in their congregations.

In 1969 Kingsley Church reported 979 members, property valued at $728,641, and $40,033 raised for all purposes during the year.

General Minutes, MEC and UMC.
M. Simpson, *Cyclopaedia.* 1878.

ALBEA GODBOLD
ENSWORTH REISNER

MINISTERIAL CALL. It is the acknowledged position in the Church that "only Christ can make a minister." Therefore the indispensable qualification for a man to take upon himself the ministry of the Word and Sacraments is that he be called by the Holy Spirit. This traditional Christian doctrine is reflected plainly in the Ordinal of the Church of England, where the first question addressed to him who presents himself to be ordained Deacon or Priest, or consecrated Bishop, is to this effect: "Do you trust that you are inwardly moved by the Holy Ghost to take upon you this office and ministration—?" and this question is retained in this leading position in the Ordinals of the Methodist Churches.

The reason for this is plain. No man is good enough or wise enough to become a Christian minister on the ground of personal qualification. The minister is not one who has mastered the subject of religion, and who on this account offers good advice to those who have not. In this he is in a position fundamentally different from the practitioners of other learned professions. Though the minister certainly ought to be inwardly devoted to Christ, and outwardly of upright conduct, yet in the end he is in as great need of the Gospel as those who listen to him, or who receive the sacraments at his hands. As he preaches he is offering to the people good counsel which he himself finds it desperately difficult to take, and he is aware that unless he constantly watches unto prayer, self-examination, and the discipline of the moral life, he will shamefully compromise the standards which he holds out to others. Thus the man who preaches or gives spiritual counsel, or who administers the sacraments, because he imagines that his own spiritual, theological, or moral attainments entitle him so to do, is convicted of the basest hypocrisy. There is only one possible honest reason for offering for such a task, and that is a deep sense that God has chosen one to be His messenger and agent, and that to refuse the task would be to do despite to the Spirit of grace.

No minister, however devout, or eloquent, or learned, can "convert" one of his hearers to God, or evoke in him the gift of saving faith, for faith is the gift of God alone. Thus when the preacher stands in his pulpit he is inviting

God to use him to work a miracle. If this be so, he cannot go as a well-intentioned volunteer, but as a man impelled by God.

Biblical Doctrine. This is the position of the Bible. Though the sense of personal divine call is most clearly expressed in the case of the more individual ministry of the prophets (Isaiah vi 8, lxi 1, Jeremiah i 4-10, xx 7-9, Ezekiel iii 4-11, xxxiii 7-9, Amos vii 14-15), yet the same is true in principle of the continuous hereditary priesthood, for the house of Aaron owed its position to the circumstance that it was chosen by God from among Israel to be priests before Him (Numbers xvi 4-11, ff., Hebrews v 4). The New Testament Church, likewise, lived under a very distinct sense of the guidance of the Holy Spirit in all its actions, and in nothing was this more plain than in the choice and commissioning of the Christian ministry (Mark iii 13-19, John xv 16, xx 19-23, Acts i 21-6, ix 15, xiii 2-3, Galatians i 1, 11-17, 1 Corinthians ix 16-17).

There is, however, another important spiritual principle complementary to the above. The true and profitable servant of Christ is not an autonomous Christian individualist, but a loyal member of the disciplined and ordered Body of Christ. His concern in Christian service must always be not to please himself, or merely "to express himself," but to do that which is useful for the building up of the whole Body (1 Corinthians xiv 1-5, 13-18, 26-8). In bestowing the gift of the ministry upon the church, God has granted a great variety of spiritual office and equipment, which are complementary one to another. It is most necessary, therefore, for all Christ's servants to cooperate with one another in due order for the advantage of the whole church, behaving one towards another with unselfish modesty and corporate loyalty, forswearing the natural instincts of rivalry, and the sinful desire for status and pre-eminence (Luke xxii 24-6, 1 Corinthians xii 28-31, Ephesians iv 7-8, 11-16, 1 Peter v 1-6, 3 John 9-10).

There thus rests upon the disciplined corporate church both the right and the duty to make careful examination of those who profess to have received a call to the Christian ministry, to determine both their integrity of purpose and their suitability to particular tasks. JOHN WESLEY, himself, emphasized this duty of examining those who "think they are moved by the Holy Ghost to preach." Among other things, Wesley said that inquiry should be made, not only regarding their own religious experience, but also, "Have they gifts (as well as grace) for the work? Have they (in some tolerable degree) a clear, sound understanding? Have they a right judgment in the things of God? . . . A just conception of salvation by faith? And has God given them any degree of utterance? Do they speak justly, readily, clearly?" (*Wesley's Works*, Vol. V, p. 230).

These questions are yet kept in the present *Book of Discipline of The United Methodist Church* and will be seen to be sensible, as well as practical.

It is sadly possible for one who has a distinct sense of "call" to be the victim of delusion. Thus the man who perhaps quite sincerely feels himself called of God, yet whose general moral reputation may be called in question, is clearly the victim of a dangerous self-deception, and his call must be rejected (1 Timothy iii, 1-12). Likewise, no man can be accepted into the position of a public teacher in the church if his doctrine subverts the given and fixed principles of the divine revelation in Christ (Galatians i 8, ii 4-5, 1 Timothy vi 3-5). Further-

more, that a man is authentically called to the ministry does not involve that he is the sole judge of the kind of ministry to which he is called. This choice depends to a large extent on what practical tasks there are to do in the church at the time, and what talents and equipment of personality are possessed by the available ministers. Not all have the gifts which make good preachers, or teachers, or administrators, or pastoral counsellors, or choristers, though all these functions are necessary in their place, as equally are those gifts which are less conspicuous in public, such as prayer, attendance at worship, and kindly aid to one's neighbors. The church cannot send a man to a task of which he is incapable simply because he feels a desire to do it. His sense of "call" needs to be educated and guided by the advice of his fellow-Christians. In making acknowledgement that the Holy Spirit has called a man, the church has to exercise the duty, also under the guidance of the Holy Spirit, of deciding to what form of ministry he is to be sent. And one of the leading marks of the man who is truly called is cheerful loyalty to the church in this matter.

The Examination of the Call. Thus in the Anglican Ordinal the leading question regarding the divine call is coupled with another, no less searching, regarding ecclesiastical Order: "Do you think in your heart that you be truly called, according to the will of our Lord Jesus Christ, and the order of this Church of England—?" The same effect is conveyed in the question in the Methodist Ordinal, reflecting as it does (in the British office), a characteristic phrase of Wesley: "Will you submit yourselves as sons in the Gospel, to those whom the Methodist Church shall appoint to have the rule over you?" However, this balance between the individual call and the corporate order is not always easy to maintain in practice, because the church and her servants are not always and everywhere fully guided by the Spirit, being frail and human. Therefore all too often the peace and spiritual health of the church have been wounded by sad collision between the zeal of someone who wishes to serve in some perhaps novel or irregular way, and the prudential conservatism of authority within the established church. The one can easily fall into impatience and self-pleasing, the other into defensive jealousy for status, and self-seeking. This, the chief cause of the crippling divisions of the church, is a tragedy of church life. The welfare of the Christian church largely depends upon keeping this just balance between the rightful claims of prophetic zeal and of church order.

It may be well to consider the way in which this has worked out in practice within the church, and within Methodism. In the great institutional churches, such as the Roman Catholic, the balance has tended to come down heavily in the direction of institutional loyalty and regular ecclesiastical order. Thus the activity of the Spirit of Christ in making a minister has been interpreted chiefly as the due selection of candidates to go into the seminary, their proper training, and the regular act of ordination. An overwhelming conscious personal impression that one *must* be a minister of Christ has been considered rather as the characteristic of a few outstanding saints. In the "revivalist" denominations and religious societies, on the other hand, the balance has come down in the opposite direction of individual prophetic call. It has often been assumed that any man who feels within himself an urge to preach, and who shows the ability to draw after him a group of followers, has a Christian right to form his own congregation, and give to it what standards of doctrine and discipline he sees fit. Methodists feel that both these positions are defective, the one by swallowing up the sense of a conscious personal call, the other by swallowing up ecclesiastical discipline and cohesion.

It may without immodesty be claimed that *authentic* Methodism, such as reflects the true spirit of Wesley, has found a salutary balance in this important matter. The standard has been upheld before the people that he who offers himself as a candidate for the ministry should have as his indispensable qualifications a genuine conscious experience of saving faith in Christ, showing itself in a morally strict and upright life, and a whole-hearted devotion to Christ, a faithful and loving zeal for the welfare of the church, and some degree of evident divine blessing upon the witness he has already made for the Gospel, and upon the service he has already rendered to the church. And to this must be added some real measure of inward spiritual compulsion to offer for the work of the ministry, though it need not be supposed that this must necessarily come through the medium of some sudden and startling spiritual impression. The growing sense of a task before one crying to be done may be sufficient to bring a genuine sense of call, and such a candidate should not be deterred from offering because he has not "heard a voice."

At the same time it has always been made clear within Methodism that this ministry is to be exercised within the controlling and sustaining discipline of a closely-knit connexional polity. The man offering for the ministry is to be prepared to lay aside all self-pleasing and self-seeking, to put the welfare of the church and her people first in his loyalties, and to give himself cheerfully to that part of the work not which he would choose, but which the church shall choose. And he is to be a preacher not of his own notions but of the church's faith, revealed authoritatively in Christ, recorded in Scripture, and interpreted according to the mature wisdom of the church.

The Call to the Ministry in Methodism. It has not always been easy even within Methodism to keep this balance. During the long years when, at any rate in British Methodism, there were normally more candidates for the ministry than could be found room for in the connexion, the natural custom was to examine all candidates carefully, and to choose the required number on the basis of the selection of those who had already been most blessed by fruits to their work, or who appeared to have the most promising personality and gifts. There was no particular evidence that many of the rejected candidates were not just as sincerely devoted to Christian service, and authentically called, as those accepted. Thus it could be objected by the critic that the church was in fact inconsistent with her professed principles, and made acceptance to the ministry a matter of ecclesiastical expediency, rather than of recognition of the work of the Spirit. This is indeed a hard question, and it often caused bitter disappointment to good men.

There is perhaps no completely satisfactory solution which will resolve all hard cases, for the reconciliation of elevated spiritual principle with practice can never be complete in an imperfect church operating in an imperfect world. First it must be said that no man has a *right* to become a minister of a particular church so that if the right be denied by the church he has a cause for umbrage. The ministry is not a matter of human right,

but of divine duty. The notion that the right to preach the Word and administer the Sacraments in the congregation is in effect a sort of professional status-symbol conferred upon the fully accomplished Christian worker is a revolting profanation of sacred things, and an idea to be fought tooth and nail in the Church. The office is an obligation laid upon one of the servants of God, and involves, if rightly understood, a call to self-sacrifice such as will certainly be shunned by the man who is in fact seeking his own gratification.

Furthermore, a call to the ministry does not necessarily mean admission to the ministry of the church in a particular place, or even of a particular branch of the church. Thus many candidates for whom there was in former years no room in England went abroad and entered the ministry of Methodist and other churches in the dominions overseas, or in America. This is surely a wise administration of the church's talents, fully in keeping with the doctrine of the divine call. Finally, failure on account of family or other circumstances, or age, or health, or gifts, to be eligible for the separated and ordained ministry does not involve in Methodism exclusion from the ministry of the Gospel. There is also the ministry of the laity, and the consecrated and qualified Methodist layman can normally preach or teach as often as he will, knowing full well that there are parts of the Gospel message which can be declared with more effect by a dedicated lay preacher who is known to earn his living in the world, than by the separated minister. It is most necessary to resist the very un-Methodist notion that lay preachers are in some way "amateur" or "stop-gap" preachers. The ministry of the laity and the separated and ordained ministry is all one colleagueship together in the service of Christ. Thus a lay preacher of perhaps modest gifts and education, who understands the message of the Bible, and who faithfully declares the Gospel, has exactly the same divine Gospel-authority as the ordained minister, and may be used by God to do as much good in the church, though he may not be equally qualified for every pulpit. Conversely, he who stands in the pulpit and is so taken up speaking of his own notions that he forgets to declare God's revelation in Christ has forfeited his Gospel-authority, even though he may have had hands laid on him in ordination, and be a member of a conference, and be appointed by a bishop, and the possessor of ecclesiastical vestments and a Ph.D.

If we turn to modern conditions, particularly in the large and institutionally secure American Methodist Churches, another problem can present itself. There is a very rightful desire to improve the educational standards of the ministry, as well as its technical standards in professional training. This is in keeping with the doctrine of the call, for the man who is authentically called by God will certainly want to do everything in his power to improve his talents, and to be as widely useful a servant of Christ as he may. Nevertheless, in these circumstances the idea can creep in unawares that the accepted practical qualification for the Christian ministry is a degree in theology, and that the higher the degree the more dignified the ministry for which a man is qualified. This is to look upon the ministry as a professional occupation comparable to other professional occupations, the status of which depends upon membership of some body which alone has the right to practice some skill, on account of some special training. There is a dangerous invasion of the church by unspiritual ideas of status derived from the usages of secular society.

An attempt to fortify the position of the church by establishing a system of "secure professional status" for the Christian ministry is foredoomed to failure, because the true minister of Christ may expect often to find himself an object of contempt in the eyes of the men of this world, not on account of his incompetence but on account of his competence. This is because the Gospel itself is an object of offense to those who are foolish enough to account themselves wise, or capable, or sophisticated—as was our Lord Himself despised. Accidental circumstance may indeed from time to time have brought the church and its ministry into a position of communal prestige, but these have generally proved to be occasions of spiritual peril. The true status of the Christian minister is one only to be discerned by those awakened souls who are seeking for God, and to these the minister of the Gospel has a status which cannot be enhanced by professional qualifications, prestige in society, or money. The office of speaking to men and women on behalf of God Himself, and of giving to needy souls the sacrament of the body and blood of the Lord, is a privilege far above any human deserving, which far out-tops any distinction of birth, or rank, or public office, or academic degree, or wealth, though this can only be seen to be so by those having eyes to see.

The Call of Women. A question which has been much discussed in some circles is how far the church can rightly recognize a call to the ministry in a woman. One issue which is often forgotten in this discussion must first be clarified. This is that in the Order of Deaconesses the Methodist Church already has for long had a ministry of women, ordained (the *Book of Discipline* used the word *consecrated*) by laying on of hands, who can be pastors of congregations, and who, if qualified so to do, can preach, and who in certain appointments (in Britain) are by regular custom given by the conference a special dispensation to administer the sacraments. Thus the distinction between such a ministry and the itinerant ministry of men is not in any clear sense a theological or spiritual distinction. It is a distinction chiefly consisting in conference membership and sphere of administration, i.e. a distinction of Order. However, what is meant in the present discussion is the issue as to whether women can be called into the same Order of ministry as the separated and ordained ministry of men.

It would certainly seem that this is a matter of the due Order of the Church, rather than of theological principle, because the efficacy of the preached Word and of the Sacraments depends upon the action of God, and not upon the personal characteristics of the minister. The church has in fact had a very long and dignified tradition of the ministration of women in the church, as deaconesses, but more particularly, in the monastic Orders. The custom whereby women have not been admitted to the priesthood clearly goes back to the religious and social ideas prevalent in and natural to the Jewish background of Christianity. That this custom has so largely endured into a modern world in which women have made good their claim to enter many occupations and callings is a mark of the traditionalism and conservatism which is natural to organized religion. This conservatism is almost as manifest in those parts of the church which have officially admitted women into the separated ministry, because it must be admitted that in these cases church leaders have generally been more willing to ordain women than have local congregations to accept them as pastors. On the other hand, those institutional churches which are furthest from admitting women to the priesthood have in point of fact experienced more of the ministry of consecrated women!

Though there does not seem to be any spiritual or theological reason why a call to the ministry should not be recognized in a woman, the common argument of "sex equality" can hardly be admitted as a theological or spiritual reason why it should be recognized, because, as has been observed above, admission to the ministry is in no sense a mark of Christian status. The woman who tacitly says, "I am willing to devote my full time to the service of the church on condition that I can be given equal status with the men, but I am not prepared to serve in a different Order of ministry, such as a deaconess," clearly does not fully understand what is involved in the conception of the call to the ministry. This form of argument almost answers to the notion (just as wrong in a woman as in a man!) that one is doing a favor to the church by offering for Christian service, and a favor which ought to be "recognized." And this manner of thought, derived from the standards and customs of the world, is totally opposed to the conception of the ministry as a divine call. The true minister of Christ is not primarily rendering a service to man, but fulfilling an obligation to God.

However, one must have the deepest sympathy with a devoted Christian woman who is moved by a strong sense of call to the ministry, yet who finds her call tragically frustrated by a difference of judgment expressed in the order of her church, which is not prepared to accept her. Yet she is in the same position as many men who have felt this call, yet who have not been accepted by the church into the separated ministry. The chief argument against the admission of women to the separated ministry would appear to be one of expediency, namely, that for particular denominations to do this apart from the general body of Christendom increases occasions of ecclesiastical separation within the church, and is an unecumenical action. Admission is something which ideally ought to be done by the whole church together. A salient example of this is the situation in British Methodism, where the main reason for delay in admitting women to the itinerant ministry is undoubtedly that to do so would present added difficulty in the establishment of a common ministerial order with the Church of England. And the reason in turn, though often unavowed, why the Church of England is so far from admitting women to the priesthood is that this would occasion a further degree of separation between Anglicanism and the Roman Catholic and Eastern Churches.

Prospective Ministerial Calls. It has been noticed that in some parts of the church there has during the mid-century years been a decline in the number of those professing a call to the ministry. This is a token of something seriously wrong in the church, either in the past, or else in the present. It can be argued that in some parts of the church entrance upon the Christian ministry was formerly a way in which young men lacking money and position could rise to a place of honorable status in the community, and that this made it easier for them to respond to the sense of call. Nowadays, however, with wider education opportunities open to the people, and a much greater variety of professional and semi-professional occupations in which a Christian can render useful service to the community, this incentive has been relaxed. It has in short became harder for young men to resolve to enter upon a calling which has little to offer in advancement, or worldly status, or income. In so far as this is indeed the case, here is a condemnation of the past, and a sign that the church has not always succeeded in living up to the principle she has professed. And if this be so, the church may have to get used to organizing herself with fewer separated ministers. From the spiritual point of view this might prove to be no bad thing, because the ministry of the laity is just as vital for the welfare of the church as is the separated ministry. Furthermore, these many occupations of public responsibility and welfare are often in fact important parts of the ministry of the laity. And in any case, the church is certainly better off if its official ministry is rid of the type of man who can be moved by considerations of worldly advantage and status. In considering the supply of candidates for the ministry, the church must consider first and foremost the welfare of the Gospel, and not the institutional convenience of her established organization.

There is some ground for fearing, however, that when there is a decline in number of candidates for the ministry this may sometimes be due to more serious causes. That is to say, the sense of divine calling may have disappeared, and the Christian ministry appeared as a mere human occupation. Some of the Christian laity have perhaps been too much inclined to speak of their minister as though he were a lecturer on miscellaneous subjects of his own choosing, airing his own opinions in the pulpit with the aim of "keeping the people interested," and as such, a fair target for criticism. His pastoral activity has been represented as though he were the "organizing secretary" employed by a little local organization, whose chief concern was to keep "the going concern" going. And it is sadly to be admitted that some ministers have at times fallen into attitudes, policies, and preaching which have encouraged their people to suppose that all this is indeed the case. If so, the spiritually earnest and sensitive man, who of all men most ought to become a Christian minister, will certainly not feel called to enter upon so ignominious and compromised an occupation. In the last resort a church gets the ministry it deserves. If the Christian community evidently and sincerely looks upon the minister of the Gospel, even though he be modestly paid and of no importance in the sight of the world, as a *man of God*, summoned by God Himself to the most august task in human experience, and if the ministers by the whole course of their life and preaching make this exalted view credible to their people, then the church will never lack a sufficiency of men called into the ministry. The whole history of the church plainly shows that what matters for the welfare of the Gospel is not how numerous, or how clever, or how endued with prestige are God's servants, but whether they are the sort of men and women whom God can use to perform His own work.

Discipline, UMC, 1968, P. 301, 305.
Large Minutes.
W. E. Sangster, *The Approach to Preaching.* London, 1954.
Spencer and Finch, *Constitutional Practice.* 1958.

JOHN LAWSON

MINISTERIAL SUPPORT. The early Methodist preachers went forth to preach the gospel moved by a divine impulse, and without at first having societies upon which to depend. JOHN WESLEY supported himself by a fellowship which he held in Oxford University, and by the profits on books which he published from time to time. He also aided his ministers by giving away all that he could possibly spare, limiting himself merely to the supply of his own wants. Many of the early preachers were engaged in business employment. They were called "lay preachers," and simply gave their Sabbaths or week-day evenings for service, acting as the "LOCAL PREACHERS" in America came to do later. As Methodist societies were organized, and as they became strong, they contributed for the support of their ministers, who were thus in time enabled to devote their whole time to their specific calling.

The support of the early preachers in the United States was exceedingly meagre. The membership was generally poor, and the ministers were unmarried men, who traveled from place to place, living among the people, and subsisting on small contributions. In 1774, before the M.E. Church was organized, we find an enactment that each preacher should have $64 per year and traveling expenses; indeed, the earliest preachers did not receive this sum. Captain WEBB, who founded many of the societies, and who, more than any other person, gave great help to American Methodism, supported himself as an army officer and by other means, besides contributing to the erection of church edifices. EMBURY and STRAWBRIDGE were married men, but were local preachers—called "lay preachers"—the one being a carpenter and the other a farmer, and they were in part supported by their labor. ASBURY, BOARDMAN, PILMORE, RANKIN, ROBERT WILLIAMS, and SHADFORD were single men. Williams subsequently married and located, and of him it was said, "He was the first American Methodist preacher that published a book, got married, and died" (Simpson, p. 616).

In 1774 the stipend for an itinerant in full connection was set at six pounds per quarter. The preacher had the right of ownership and use of his horse, even though the animal may have been provided and provisioned by the circuit.

In 1778 paper money had during the war depreciated, and the ministerial salary was thereupon raised to thirty pounds per year, which was nearly equivalent to eighty dollars. As some ministers, being greater favorites, received gifts which added to their support, the Conference of 1782 desiring to equalize the allowances adopted a resolution that "all the gifts received by the preachers, whether in money or clothing, should be brought into the quarterly meeting and valued by the preachers and stewards, and the preacher who had received the gifts should be considered as having received so much of his quarterage, and if he is still deficient he shall carry to the account such deficiency, that if possible he shall have it made up out of the profits arising out of the sale of books and the annual collections" (Simpson).

In 1780 the first notice occurs of the wives of preachers, the fourteenth question reading, "What provision shall be made for the wives of married preachers?" A. "They shall receive an equivalent with the husband if they stand in need." In 1783 we find the answer to the question, "How many preachers' wives are to be provided for?" is "Eleven, and the sum needed for their support is 260 pounds." As regards this sum it was said, "Let the preachers make a small collection in all the circuits." That purpose was to equalize the support, or rather that all the circuits should combine in sustaining the families. In 1784 thirteen preachers were reported as married, and

302 pounds were apportioned to different charges. A collection was also ordered to be taken up in every charge, prior to Conference, to meet the deficiency. This was called the "Conference collection," a name that was destined to last in American Methodism for a long time, but to be more broadly applied. A year after the organization of the church this collection amounted to 300 pounds, which was applied to making up the quarterly deficiency and sending out two missionaries.

The English Wesleyans for a time had a system of equalization so that large families could be supported by small circuits; the Children's Fund and the Educational Fund was taken up on all the charges, and was distributed according to the number of the family. This system did not prevail in the United States. In 1785 the thirty-seventh question of the minutes reads, "What shall be the regular salary of the elders, deacons, and helpers?" To which answer is made, "$64, and no more; and for each preacher's wife $64; and for each preacher's child, if under the age of six years, there shall be allowed $16; and for each child over the age of six and under the age of eleven years, $21.33." This rule in reference to children created dissatisfaction, and the Conference of 1787 resolved that no provision should be made in future for the children of married preachers, and this appears to have been the practice of the church until 1800.

In those early days they were strict, even beyond propriety, in reference to all financial matters. One of their rules reads, "We will on no account whatever suffer any deacon or elder among us to receive any fee or present for administering the ordinance of marriage, baptism, or the burial of the dead; freely we have received, freely we give." It is probable that this rule was adopted to prevent jealousy among the ministers, as but few at first were elected to orders. A few years subsequently it was agreed that a present might be received for the marriage ceremony, but it must be reported to the stewards of the circuit, to be applied to the quarterage. This rule continued in force until 1800. At this day it seems surprising how so great a work could have been sustained on such small means. Brave and self-denying were the men who laid the firm foundations of the edifice of Methodism; yet it became almost impossible for men with families to remain in the traveling ministry, and hence nearly all of them located. The loss of so much talent and experience out of the ministry of the church by location greatly grieved Bishop Asbury and other leading minds. In part to remedy this evil, in 1796 the GENERAL CONFERENCE organized the CHARTERED FUND, appointing for it a board of trustees. Its design was to supplement the salaries, and to afford some support for the worn-out preachers, their widows and orphans. Prior to that time an effort had been made to support a Preachers' Fund, by requiring every person when admitted to pay $2.67, then one pound American currency, and to contribute annually $2. This organization was on the principle of a mutual aid society; but in 1796 it was merged into the Chartered Fund. An appeal was issued on behalf of this fund, in which we find the following paragraph: "It is to be lamented, if possible with tears of blood, that we have lost scores of our most able married ministers; men who, like good house-holders, could upon all occasions bring things new and old out of their treasury, but were obliged to retire from the general work because they saw nothing before them for their wives and children, if they continued itinerant, but misery and ruin."

Until 1860 the salary of a preacher was fixed at $100, and $100 for his wife, and a small allowance was made to the children. The circuits or stations were also required to estimate a sufficient amount for the family expenses. But in 1860 in the M.E. Church the rule for specific allowances was removed from the *Discipline,* and the stations and circuits were allowed to determine what they considered necessary for ministerial support. The same plan was followed by the M.E. Church, South, which in 1854 directed that "the claims of preachers shall be estimated by their respective Boards of Stewards" (Peterson, p. 102), and this was followed by clarifying legislation along the same line in succeeding General Conferences. Thus by stages came the system which has prevailed in American Methodism since that time, of each local charge whether circuit or station fixing and paying the salary of the minister appointed to them. Bishop MATTHEW SIMPSON felt that this created great inequality in the charges, and added to the embarrassment of arranging the appointments. In too many cases the estimate made was not fully met; but even then the preacher had no claim upon the property of the church as a compensation for his services. The *Discipline* expressly provides that the church property shall not be mortgaged or encumbered for current expenses.

The difference in the salaries paid by the various charges has been criticized as establishing a financial grading for ministers and ministerial appointments, thus making money somewhat the measure of ministerial evaluation which it should not be. From time to time a move is made in present-day American Methodism to equalize salaries as they were equalized in the earlier days, and this move has been largely successful in the matter of the district superintendents' salaries in the respective annual conferences. In conferences where these salaries have not been equalized, the district stewards decide what their district shall pay their superintendent. Where a conference equalizes the superintendents' salaries, these are paid out of a general fund raised by the conference as a whole, the amount being decided by the conference following the report of its World Service Commission.

Recent disciplinary regulations provide that the salary which is to be paid the preacher-in-charge be fixed by the charge conference and made a matter of record before each annual conference year begins. It is the duty of the official board in each local church "after consultation with the Committee on Pastoral Relations, or with the pastor if there is no such committee, and after all matters pertaining to his efficiency, to recommend to the Quarterly [now Charge] Conference, at the session next preceding the Annual Conference, the salary and expense allowance of the pastor, and of the associate pastor or pastors if any." (*Discipline,* 1964, Paragraph 215.2.) The fixing of the salary in advance gives the appointive power and the preachers involved, a sure commitment as to what may be counted upon as each appointment is made. It may be noted that any additional income, as for instance fees for preaching and even wedding fees, must be counted by each minister as taxable income by the U. S. Internal Revenue Service.

In early days, due to the smallness of the remuneration paid preachers, the people made up something of this by a certain generosity in gifts of produce. A "pounding" was the somewhat colloquial word used to describe concerted gifts on the part of the people of provisions, produce, etc. At the same time merchants began to allow a "ministerial discount" to ministers and their families in the purchase of goods, and physicians usually refused to accept payment for their services to the parsonage family. As better salaries began to be paid, "poundings" and ministerial discounts, etc., have become less and less in evidence. The ministry as a whole expresses satisfaction over this, preferring an adequate salary and housing, with the responsibilities that go with these, to the well-meant but desultory support of former days.

E. S. Bucke, *History of American Methodism*. 1964.
Disciplines, ME, MES, TMC, UMC.
P. A. Peterson, *Revisions of the Discipline*. 1889.
M. Simpson, *Cyclopaedia*. 1878.   N. B. H.

MINISTERIAL TRAINING (British). The *Minutes* of the first Conference (1744) includes: "Q. Can we have a seminary for labourers? A. If God spare us until another Conference." In 1745 to the same question the answer was: "Not till God give us a proper Tutor." Lists of books were drawn up to guide the preachers' reading, and they were expected to read as well as sell the *Christian Library*. Courses were sometimes held for preachers in London, at KINGSWOOD SCHOOL and at the Orphan House, Newcastle. It was not until the Conference of 1834, however, that the Wesleyans resolved to set up "The Wesleyan Theological Institution for the Improvement of the Junior Preachers." After some controversy (see SAMUEL WARREN) this led to the inauguration of several THEOLOGICAL COLLEGES, and nearly all candidates accepted for the ministry are sent to one of them. Each college is closely linked with its local university, and those students who are qualified to do so usually take a degree locally or else take the divinity degree of London University, which one may do as an external student.

The curriculum of the colleges stresses biblical studies, church history, and systematic theology; in recent years there has been more emphasis on homiletics, pastoral theology, etc. In his fourth and final year, the student normally spends two months gaining practical experience in circuits. Each college is a community, with its devotional life centered in its chapel, and the students preach frequently in nearby circuits. On leaving college a probationer is stationed in a circuit under the supervision of a superintendent for the remaining years of his probation, usually not more than two in number; he also engages in courses of study under the direction of another minister in the district. On the successful completion of his probation, he proceeds to ordination and full connexion. The Ministerial Training Department in London, which has a full-time ministerial secretary, supervises the whole system.

A. RAYMOND GEORGE

MINISTRY, American Methodist. The M.E. Church in America organized with and was organized by a ministry as set forth in actions published in the *Minutes* of the CHRISTMAS CONFERENCE. The words are historic: "We will form ourselves into an episcopal church under the direction of superintendents, elders, deacons and helpers, according to the forms of ordination annexed to our liturgy and the form of discipline set forth in these *Minutes*." The word "preachers" was not used in this connection, though Methodist ministers everywhere have been known by the term *preacher*, as they were in Wesley's day in England.

The ministry in America stemmed from the ordinations of JOHN WESLEY himself and whatever may have been the view regarding these ordinations in other lands, American Methodist ministers have always been proud to trace their ecclesiastical descent back to the founder of Methodism. He ordained THOMAS COKE to be a superintendent, and RICHARD WHATCOAT and THOMAS VASEY to be elders, and instructed Coke to ordain ASBURY also a superintendent, and provided him and the American Methodists forms for the ordination of superintendents, ELDERS and DEACONS, which forms were used at the Christmas Conference and ever afterwards. The word "helpers" which occurs in the Christmas Conference *Minutes*, was really the equivalent of "preachers," and was absorbed and lost in the term *preacher* in a very few years.

In early American Methodism, there was for a time a bit of uncertainty on the part of some churchly elements because of the influence of the Church of England, and that of the Protestant Episcopal Church, its successor in America. For a time these denied the validity of Methodist orders since Wesley was not a bishop. Thomas Vasey himself, whom Wesley had ordained, on his return to England, later besought orders from and was ordained by a bishop of the Established Church. However, the great success of early Methodism, and the signs of spiritual strength and of God's effective presence in its work, soon swept away any criticism on ecclesiastical grounds. Methodist orders established themselves not by resting upon past descent, but by immediate strength and power. "The test of Apostolic Succession is apostolic success," some Methodists have liked to put it.

In American Methodism from the day when Francis Asbury refused to allow himself to be consecrated a bishop unless and until his brethren should elect him to that position, all ordinations whether of bishops, elders or deacons, have depended upon the enabling vote of a Conference. In the case of bishops, electing was always to be done by a GENERAL CONFERENCE, or, as it is at present, by JURISDICTIONAL or CENTRAL CONFERENCES. In the case of elders and deacons, the clerical members of an Annual Conference itself before the Union of 1939 sometimes voted orders for men, as was shown by its direction known as the "missionary rule" by which those to go as missionaries might be ordained by special appointment; and also by the empowerment given to the War Work Commission (MES) in the first World War to authorize the ordination of CHAPLAINS for the armed services in a time of emergency. However, with these rare exceptions no General Conference has ever endeavored to take away from the Annual Conferences their right to vote orders for deacons and for elders. Under the present Constitution of The United Methodist Church, this right is specifically granted to the annual conferences. Also no power to elect a bishop can inhere in the General Conference, but only in the Jurisdictional, or Central Conferences.

Wesley sent over three forms of ordination, and while that for the bishop or "superintendent" is an exact replica of that "For the Ordaining and Consecrating of a Bishop or Archbishop" in the Church of England, the Methodist Churches in America, following and stirred by the episcopal controversy of earlier years, decided that the bishop in Methodist polity is not a member of a third order, but simply an elder who has been set apart for a special type of administrative work. Various actions by General Conferences have strengthened and certified this principle, and a rubric at the beginning of the office for the consecration of a bishop in the M.E. Church during its later years stated flatly "this service is not to be understood as an ordination to a higher order in the Christian ministry beyond and above that of Elders or Presbyters, but as a solemn and fitting consecration for the special and most sacred duties of Superintendency in the Church" (M.E. *Discipline*, 1920, paragraph 533).

Francis Asbury, anxious to strengthen Methodist episcopacy by every means possible, not primarily for its own sake but to have the power to establish itinerancy firmly in American Methodism, leaned a bit toward the idea that a bishop did possess something of unusual status in regard to orders. However, in the unremitting struggle carried on through the years to limit Methodist episcopacy, not because of its name or status, but because of its absolute power in making appointments, it came about that even in the M.E. Church, South, where the bishop was traditionally in much stronger position than he was in the M.E. Church, bishops were never held to be a "third order." (See EPISCOPACY.)

The Methodist eldership, comparable to the priesthood in the Church of England, has ever been held in high repute among American Methodists, and to be ordained elder is the ultimate goal of each minister who gives himself in life service to the church. And just here comes in the unusual relationship which has existed between Conference membership on one hand, and ministerial orders on the other, which has been a marked feature of American Methodism, and which has, at times, led to embarrassing involvements. Conference membership, or the admission into an Annual Conference by vote of the Conference, is a process entirely apart from ordination. Yet this was—and still is in many ways—the rule for long years in all American Methodism. This situation stemmed from John Wesley's own policy of admitting men to Conference long before he agreed to allow them the privileges of the ordained. As it was, in actual practice in American Methodism, once a man was formally admitted to the Conference, after progress had been made in certain studies or sometimes in work accomplished, the brethren would vote that that person should be ordained, first deacon and then elder. Thus there have always been two distinct types of initiation for Methodist ministers. One is when a Conference is entered by vote of the ministers of that Conference and after answering the questions which Wesley said all should answer who joined his own "connexion." The second is when one has been voted orders, and takes the vows of ordination, and by the imposition of hands of a bishop, and other presbyters, is made a deacon or elder. For well over the first hundred years of Methodism in America, preachers might belong to a Conference and yet never be ordained; and in time some could be ordained as "local elders" who never joined the Conference at all or came within the traveling connection. Also ordained conference members may "locate" without losing their orders. Instances, however, have been known when such a person no longer under the control of the Conference has presumed upon his orders and this has led to embarrassment. This situation in time caused confusion, not only in the keeping of Conference records, but in the whole matter of Conference relationship and orders. To clarify ministerial status at least two different Commissions have been appointed within recent years (TMC) to study the ministry and make appropriate recommendations. The study has been continued by The United Methodist Church.

Also, within recent years, in order to enforce more firmly the regulation that each minister must complete a certain COURSE OF STUDY, it was provided that one must be ordained a deacon before he may be admitted on trial in an Annual Conference.

Ordained ministers of the Methodist churches are recognized as of equal status with the ordained ministers of other Christian denominations everywhere; and in turn, provision is made for admitting into an Annual Conference ministers from other denominations who have themselves been ordained, provided that they take the requisite vows. They are not, however, asked to submit again to the imposition of hands. It is thus clear that admission to an Annual Conference thereby putting a man into the traveling preacherhood is one thing—a special Methodist situation; while ordination as a deacon or elder really puts a man into the ministry of the general worldwide Church, and his ordination is so regarded by other Christian brotherhoods.

As part of the fight against the strong Asburian episcopacy of early days, an attack was made upon the Methodist diaconate. It was asserted to be no ministerial order but an "office"—as Baptists for instance hold. Indeed, the M.P. CHURCH when organized (with, of course, no bishops) decided also that they would have no deacons but simply one order of ministers, namely elders. The Methodists in GERMANY also decided that they would not have deacons as a separate order, but elders only. The JUDICIAL COUNCIL of the Methodist Church, when the right of the General Conference to agree that in the Germany Central Conference the ordination of an elder might be one's final ordination, and ordination as a deacon might be omitted, decided that granting this power to the Germany Conference was a constitutional right of the General Conference and did not break fundamental Methodist law. (Decision 58, May 6, 1948.)

At the 1964 General Conference a strong effort was made to declare the Methodist diaconate simply an office, and not an order. There was a minority and majority report from the Committee on Ministry presenting opposite views upon this matter. The situation was deferred by referring the whole matter to a commission empowered to further study the ministry.

The influence of other great ecclesiasticisms which have only one order—but not of course the Protestant Episcopal Church—is very strongly felt in American Methodism, and this tends to hold the deacon to be more of a lay officer than a ministerial order. The move to denature the traditional Methodist diaconate has also been abetted by the argument that many supply ministers—now local pastors—might be allowed to hold the office of deacon and be called deacons with no ordination, if the diaconate shall ever be called an office. It is worthy of note however that in the episcopal controversy of 1810-1830, Bishop ROBERT EMORY in his *Defence of Our Fathers* defended the order of deacon by saying that whatever happened to Methodist episcopacy, the deacon should be left untouched in his own order.

Local Preachers was the name given to those assistants of Wesley who "assisted us only in one place" as over against those who traveled about at Wesley's command. The local preacher was usually termed a "lay preacher" in Britain.

In American Methodism, the term local preacher historically came to be given to those who are licensed to preach but not members of an Annual Conference and so not under the appointment of a bishop. When a Conference member dropped out of the traveling connection, he was said to "locate" and became again a local preacher not subject to appointment. However, "location" always was at the vote of the Conference which alone had the right to grant location when this was requested; or which could "locate" a man against his will if it found him unacceptable. Occasionally men were forced to locate or located by Conference action as a disciplinary measure against them for certain improper actions not deemed worthy of a trial. However, Bishop COLLINS DENNY said that the status of a local preacher was so estimable that "location" should never be used as a penalty since the local preachers of Methodism have done such heroic ministerial service. In The United Methodist Church, the Uniting Conference of 1968 changed "local preacher" to "local pastor," keeping the status itself much as it had been. When a man is first licensed to preach, he becomes a local pastor and holds such status until he is admitted to Conference membership, and thus goes into the traveling connection. As a pastor, he is under the direction of the minister over him, and he must make a report of his activities from time to time as the *Discipline* provides.

Men who have been Conference members and locate because of health or family reasons, or for other valid reasons, continue to hold their orders if they have been ordained. It should be said that regular Conference men who are retired or superannuated on account of age or infirmity are not considered local preachers—or local pastors—as are those who have never joined a Conference, or who have dropped out before they reach the age of retirement.

Supply Pastor. A supply pastor is a preacher appointed to a pastoral charge, usually as a substitute either because of an emergency between sessions of the Annual Conference, or because there is a shortage of Conference ministerial members at the time of the Conference, and the appointment otherwise could not be filled. (The name "Lay Pastor" was given to this type of minister at the Uniting Conference of 1968, but we describe the development here under the old name of Supply Pastor.)

The use of supply preachers came about gradually and was usually due to some aforementioned emergency when the bishop or, as was frequently the case, the district superintendent, put into a local pulpit a man who was asked to "supply it" until the next session of the Annual Conference. When that time came it was expected that a regular Conference member would be appointed and usually was. But with the great growth of the Church and the proliferation of many small and circuit charges for which regular ministers could not be secured, there grew in the Methodist Churches a large, and to a certain extent, a permanent body of "supply preachers." The most of these have been men who could not get into the actual Conference membership by reason of stipulated educational or other requirements which the General Conference in later years has seen fit to enact. They have been, nevertheless, men of ability and consecration, and the usual Annual Conference has a great number of "supplies." In The Methodist Church, before its reorganization as The United Methodist Church, there were Approved Supply Pastors. These were local preachers who on recommendation of the Board of Ministerial Training and qualifications of each annual conference—or a similar body—were approved by the annual conference as eligible

for an appointment during the ensuing year as "supply pastor" of a charge. In 1968 the name Approved Supply was dropped in favor of Local Pastor, though the office itself can scarcely be. Indeed it is generally admitted that The United Methodist Church could not do its work nor man its charges were it not for these men. Their aim is of course, when possible, to secure membership in the annual conference itself, and within recent years less stringent regulations have been passed regarding educational requirements, so that more of the better qualified local pastors, as they are now to be called, may be admitted by conference vote.

Superannuates, or Retired Ministers, are those who are officially placed in the retired relationship and have thereby "ceased to travel." A superannuated minister in The United Methodist Church "is one who at his own request, or by action of the ministerial members in full connection (in his Conference) on recommendation of the Board of the Ministry has been placed in the retired relation" (*Discipline* 1968, Paragraph 359). Every ministerial member of an annual conference whose seventy-second birthday precedes the first day of the regular session of his annual conference must be automatically retired from the active ministry at the said conference session; and at his own request and by vote of the annual conference, any ministerial member who has attained age sixty-five or has completed forty years of full-time approved service prior to the date of the opening session of the conference, may be placed in the retired relation with the privilege of making an annuity claim upon the pension funds of the church (Paragraph 362). An annual conference has the right to place any ministerial member in the retired relation, with or without his consent and irrespective of his age, if such relation is recommended by the conference Board of the Ministry (Paragraph 360).

It is possible and quite frequent for a superannuate minister, if he is willing, to be assigned to active duty by the bishop, and thereby to be known as a "retired supply." Every Superannuate is a member of the local charge conference and has all the privileges of membership in the local church where he resides, except as the *Discipline* may set forth otherwise. He must report to the charge conference and to the pastor all marriages performed and baptisms administered, if any. If he resides outside the bounds of his annual conference, he must forward annually to his conference a certificate of his Christian and his ministerial conduct, must tell something about the number and circumstances of his family, and the district superintendent or the pastor of the charge within whose bounds he resides must sign his report. (*Discipline*, 1968, Paragraph 364.)

In the early days, retirement or superannuation entailed great hardship upon ministers since there was then small provision for their support. At a very early period in English Methodism, a collection was taken in the various societies for the support of the superannuated preachers and the American Christmas Conference of 1784 adopted the same provision. This was long continued. After a time there was organized a CHARTERED FUND for the purpose of aiding the retired ministers, but the income from these sources was so scanty that those who could manage their own support either from property or by business which they were able to follow were not considered claimants on the conference funds.

Later on, in the growing Methodist churches, much better provision was made for the support of retired men, and in time a BOARD OF PENSIONS was created to look after this matter on the part of the general church; each annual conference came to set aside in its annual budget each year a certain amount for conference claimants. The annual conferences within recent years have been making much better provision for their claimants, including superannuates, basing the annuity amount usually upon years of active service.

Superannuated ministers continue to hold membership in their annual conference and often take an active part in its deliberations and in voting at each annual session. Every ministerial member, active or retired, is "active" until the conference session ends, and his status announced or reannounced in the appointments or minutes. As is the case with all conference members, their retired relation depends upon the vote of the conference, though the provision retiring men automatically at seventy-two years of age is fixed law of the whole church.

Bishops often use the superannuate ministers when they are willing to fill pulpits made vacant by death or for other reasons, or sometimes use retired men for appointments where their services will greatly help the work. Incidents have been known, however, where a man in a strong pulpit who reached the retirement age but wished to be reappointed to his same pulpit as a "retired supply" was not allowed to do so. The COUNCIL OF BISHOPS itself has acted upon this matter in certain instances and stated that "a bishop could not do by indirection what the General Conference said could not legally be done *in re* a man's retirement at seventy-two."

The annual conference pauses usually at each of its sessions to pay tribute to the men who are at that time retiring, and the superannuates are held in high honor in every Methodist conference.

Supernumerary Minister is one who by reason of impaired health, or other equally sufficient reason, is temporarily unable to perform full work. (*Discipline* 1968, Paragraph 358.) The relation, of course, is one to be granted by the man's Annual Conference and cannot be granted for more than five years in succession, except by a two-thirds vote of the conference, and on recommendation of the Committee on Conference Relations. A supernumerary minister may receive an appointment or be left without one, according to the judgment of the Annual Conference of which he is a member. He is subject to all limitations of the *Discipline* in respect to reappointment and continuance in the same charge as those that apply to effective ministers. If he is given no pastoral charge, he has a seat in the local Charge Conference, and all the privileges of membership in the place where he resides. He must report to the Charge Conference and to the pastor, all marriages performed and all baptisms administered. Should he reside outside the bounds of his Annual Conference, he must forward to it annually a certificate telling of his work, and the like, and if he fails to make such a report, the Annual Conference may locate him without his consent. A supernumerary minister has no claim on the conference funds except by vote of the conference itself.

The English *Minutes* originally defined supernumerary preachers to be "those who can preach four or five times a week" (Simpson's *Cyclopaedia*). This definition was adopted when ministers were expected to preach not only three times on the Sabbath, but almost as often on every day of the week. In the M.E. Church in the United States, the first definition of those who are super-

numeraries came in 1792 when it was affirmed that a supernumerary preacher was one "so worn out in the itinerant service as to be rendered incapable of preaching constantly: but at the same time is willing to do any work in the ministry which the conference may direct, and his strength enable him to perform." In 1800, on motion of Thomas Coke, supernumerary preachers, their widows and orphans, were to have the same support which was then accorded to effective preachers.

In early days the supernumerary relation gave the M.E. Church little trouble, as there was no tendency to remain in the Conference unless one had the ability to labor effectively. Indeed, in those days the great embarrassment of the Church was the constant tendency in the ministry to seek location. However, as the funds of the Conferences increased, and as a connection with the Conference became more desirable, some who desired to seek rest for a few years, for travel or to engage in various work—even in business—desired to maintain their connection with the Conference but to be placed on the supernumerary list. Because of the difficulties this caused, the 1860 M.E. General Conference abolished the relationship so far as the Annual Conferences were concerned, but the phrase still remained in the RESTRICTIVE RULES in relation to the General Conference appropriating the produce of the PUBLISHING HOUSE "to any purpose other than for the benefit of the traveling, supernumerary, superannuated, and worn-out preachers, their wives, widows and children." In 1864 the former relation was restored, however, but with the definition which has lasted to the present and the provision that the supernumerary preachers "shall have no claim upon the beneficiary funds of the church, unless by vote of the Annual Conference." (*Discipline* 1968, Paragraph 358.)

The supernumerary relationship is one not often sought today, as superannuation, even for those who are disabled physically, will usually be granted by the Annual Conference if the Board of the Ministry so recommends. Since a supernumerary minister has no claim on Conference or general church funds except by special vote of his Conference, and since a regularly retired or superannuated minister does have a claim when the Conference grants him superannuation, the latter status is usually sought rather than the supernumerary relationship. Five hundred and forty-three supernumeraries were reported in the ministerial membership of the five Jurisdictions of The United Methodist Church in the United States in the *General Minutes* of 1970.

N. B. H.

MINISTRY, British Methodist. JOHN WESLEY's initial reluctance to allow laymen to expound the Scriptures was overcome in 1739. In 1744, at the first Conference, he and his brother and four other clergymen of the Church of England began by inviting four of the laymen to join them. The business included the following: "Q. Are Lay Assistants allowable? A. Only in cases of necessity." There followed an account of their office, "in the absence of the Minister," and the "Rules of an Assistant," later known as the "Rules of a Helper."

The Minutes of 1745 contained a list of these assistants. The Minutes of 1745 contained the following: "Q. In what view are we and our helpers to be considered? A. Perhaps as extraordinary messengers, designed of God to provoke the others to jealousy." The tests of those called of God to preach were said to be grace, gifts, and success (later called fruit). The Minutes contains the stationing of the assistants in circuits. In 1747 a distinction was drawn between "our present Assistants" and "those that assist us only in one place." Thus arose the distinction between the Traveling Preachers and the Local Preachers.

The traveling preachers, who were the forerunners of the Methodist ministry, were eventually divided into the Assistants (the assistant being the traveling preacher in charge of each CIRCUIT) and the other traveling preachers, who were called helpers, a term which did not long survive. The traveling preachers included preachers on trial, also called probationers. The term "probationer" was also used occasionally for local preachers on trial. When they had successfully completed this period of probation, which at first was one year, but was later extended to four years, they were received "into Full Connexion" with John Wesley and the Conference. They received allowances for themselves and their wives and were forbidden to engage in trade.

Wesley insisted, especially in his "Korah" sermon on the ministerial office, that they were not priests and had no right to administer the Sacraments; but he was equally emphatic, in the face of much opposition, in asserting their right to preach and to exercise an itinerant rather than a parochial ministry. The principle of itinerancy was expressed in two ways: they traveled around the large circuits, often spending each night in a new place, and they were not stationed in the same circuit for many years together. But when a preacher was too worn out to travel any longer, his name was printed in the circuit in which he resided, with the title of Supernumerary.

In 1784, to meet the needs of the people of North America, Wesley ordained deacons and elders by the imposition of hands, and by the same method set apart as a superintendent THOMAS COKE, who like himself was a priest of the Church of England. Wesley had been persuaded by the works of Lord Chancellor PETER KING, which he read in 1746, and by other books, that presbyters have the right to ordain, and he defended his action by claiming it was scriptural. He also sent to America *The Sunday Service of the Methodists in North America*. This was in reality an abridgment of *The Book of Common Prayer* and included services of ordination for deacons, elders, and superintendents. In the following years he ordained men for SCOTLAND and other places, and after 1788 for England. He ordained men as deacons and as elders (or sometimes as presbyters), and probably ordained ALEXANDER MATHER as superintendent for England. In all Wesley ordained at least twenty-seven men, and many of the certificates survive.

After his death some ordinations were performed by those whom he had ordained, but ordinations were soon stopped, and the distinction between ordained and unordained preachers was dropped. Coke, however, and later others, often ordained by the imposition of hands those who were going as missionaries overseas. The title of the chief preacher in each circuit, which in Wesley's lifetime had been assistant, was changed a few years after his death to Superintendent. Certain preachers were chosen as chairmen of districts, and eventually overseas some of these were given the status of general superintendent.

In 1795 by the PLAN OF PACIFICATION the traveling preachers in Full Connexion were permitted to administer the Sacraments where this was desired locally, subject to the control of the Conference. Hitherto, this had been permitted only occasionally amid much controversy, but now quickly it became the universal practice. Thus the connection acknowledged that its traveling preachers performed the usual function of Christian ministers and so claimed its independent place within the universal Church. Reception into full connexion received even greater emphasis and came to be described as "virtual ordination."

In 1836 the Wesleyan Conference resolved that the men to be received into full connexion should be ordained by the Scriptural method of the imposition of hands; in subsequent years the reception into full connexion and the ordination were separated by a few hours. In 1846 the three ordination services, which had survived in most editions of *The Sunday Service*, were replaced by a single service.

The other Methodist bodies all followed the same pattern. At the end of his probation a candidate was voted "into Full Connexion," "to the approved list," or the like, by the Conference; or, among the PRIMITIVE METHODISTS, by the District Meeting. The public ordination which followed the same evening usually included some outward sign, such as the giving of the ordination Bible, or the right hand of fellowship, but not the imposition of hands.

The ministry in Great Britain is heir to all these traditions. Generally speaking, those who have completed their probation are received into full connexion by the Representative Session of the Conference, which resolves that they shall be ordained by the imposition of hands the same evening; and this is done by the president or his representative, assisted by other ordained ministers. The itinerancy has been somewhat modified, in that ministers change circuits less frequently, and to some extent concentrate on particular churches within a circuit. Chairmen of districts are now recognized as *pastores pastorum*.

J. H. S. Kent, *Age of Disunity*. 1966.
A. B. Lawson, *John Wesley*. 1963.
London Quarterly & Holborn Review, April 1951.
Ministry, Baptism and Membership in the Methodist Church (Official Conference Statements).
J. L. Nuelsen, *Ordination im Methodismus*. 1935.
E. W. Thompson, *Wesley: Apostolic Man*. 1957.
Wesley Historical Soc. *Proceedings*, xxx-xxxiii.
C. W. Williams, *Wesley's Theology Today*. 1960.

A. RAYMOND GEORGE

MINNEAPOLIS, MINNESOTA, U.S.A., in 1970 had a population report of 431,977. Greater Minneapolis takes in several suburbs of considerable size and increases the population to more than one million. The city is a grain, flour and trades center, for Minnesota is a strong agricultural grain state. The State University of Minnesota is located in Minneapolis, one of the very largest in the United States. Besides the University, there are numerous business, trades, technical and other training schools in the city. There are numerous articles and machines manufactured in Minneapolis; and many of the Northwest offices for distributing companies are located in the downtown loop. Minneapolis is known as the City of Lakes with its scenic drives around the lakes, along the Mississippi River and through some of the finest residential areas in America.

The first Methodist Mission was located at St. Anthony and was established in 1849. After the first small log structure was outgrown, a much larger stone church was erected on the same site, and in 1955 a $500,000 addition was added which made all parts of this historic church up-to-date and beautiful in its many serviceable parts. A WESLEY FOUNDATION is housed here, and has pretty well taken over the occupancy of the entire building. Whereas this used to be a strong residential church, it is now used by students at the University of Minnesota, for it is centrally located on the campus.

Wesley Church was the second church organization and building in the city. It is located at Marquette and Grant Streets and is now considered an inner-city church. In the past fifteen years, the membership of Wesley Church has decreased to its present membership of 691 (1970 *Minutes*). There is a large office building built by the Wesley Church Corporation located next to this handsome, red stone church and the complex is known as The Wesley Temple. This church has been a strong influence in the building of Minneapolis, its government and high standards.

Richfield Church, located at 58th and Lyndale Avenue, was a pioneer Methodist church in 1854. In the past twenty years, this church has grown to 2,579 members and is still a powerful church in the city's life.

North Church, located on the north side of Minneapolis confronting one of the city's beautiful parks, was another early church with its history beginning in 1854. It has a membership of 754. Their building has been modernized and made usable for worship, educational programs, social relations, office facilities and many serviceable contributions to people in North Minneapolis.

Aldersgate in St. Louis Park, West Minneapolis, has a membership of 1,392, a fine church edifice with facilities for worship, Christian education, administrative work and a beautiful chapel.

Brooklyn Center is another early pioneering church that began in a truck-farming suburb of Minneapolis in 1854. Like these other churches described, this one-time rural church has been modernized and made into one of our most attractive suburban churches with a membership of 1,213.

Columbia Heights is a well situated church in Northeast Minneapolis that has grown with strides to 860 members in the past twenty years.

Hillcrest Church, likewise, has sprung forward in leaps and bounds possessing a beautiful church property which enables them to serve their 1,093 members with great efficiency and strong leadership.

Simpson Church is another inner-church that has decreased in membership to 413 members after an illustrious past giving strong leadership to all phases of the city's life and growth.

Hobart Church was named for CHAUNCEY HOBART, who was appointed the first district superintendent of the Minneapolis district in 1853. Hobart is known as the father of MINNESOTA Methodism. Hobart Church is located in a fine residential part of Minneapolis and is considered one of the finest of the smaller metropolitan churches. Its membership is 445.

Lake Harriet Church is another larger church with a membership of 1,368. It has a church property of great value to enable it to carry forward the best type of Methodist church program—which it is doing.

Hennepin Avenue Church is one of the architectural and religious landmarks of the city. An unusual octagonal Gothic structure, with its slender spire rising more than 200 feet above the hillside on which it stands, it is one of the commanding religious edifices of Minneapolis. Members of the congregation have historically been active in the life of the city, giving the church an equally impressive place in the community.

The church was first organized in 1875. It was formed as a Sunday school, organized by seventy-six members of an already-existing Methodist church. Apparently there had been some dissension concerning the doctrine of SANCTIFICATION.

In 1911, the members of the congregation were talking about the wisdom of relocating. They were given a piece of property on Lowry Hill, a prominent location in the growing city, but very close to Fowler Methodist Church, which had been organized in 1892. The two congregations agreed to merge and build a new structure on the donated property. The present buildings were dedicated on Oct. 22, 1916, and a modern church school building was added in 1950.

The Walker Art Gallery in the Hennepin Avenue Church is a renowned assembly of religious art of great value. The collection was presented to the church by Mr. and Mrs. T. B. Walker in 1914, and includes a series of more than two hundred lithographs. These are displayed on the stone walls and corridors and rooms of the church buildings, and are said to be the only set in America of the famous engravings of the Holy Land, Arabia, Egypt, and Nubia done by Louis Haghe from water colors painted in 1838-39 by David Roberts of the Royal Society.

Families of the church have been active in instituting and developing such Methodist institutions as Walker Home for the Aging, the Methodist and Asbury Hospitals.

Four bishops have been elected from among its pastors: CHARLES BAYARD MITCHELL, CHARLES WESLEY BURNS, RICHARD C. RAINES and DWIGHT E. LODER.

The congregation has numbered approximately four thousand for more than a quarter century. Its membership is inclusive of all races, particularly since 1956 when members of the Border Methodist Church (Negro) became members of this congregation. The church has long been numbered among the denomination's leaders in WORLD SERVICE and ADVANCE SPECIALS giving. Membership in 1970 was 4,158. Chester A. Pennington has been senior pastor since 1955.

There are forty-three United Methodist churches in greater Minneapolis with a total membership of 22,293. Methodism claims a strong fifteen percent of the population of greater Minneapolis, and, with the population gains through the years, has kept pace. Methodism is well thought of in Minneapolis by people in all walks of life and from its beginning has given strength and power to the religious life of the city.

Walker Methodist Residence and Nursing Home, Inc., began in 1945, under the auspices of the MINNESOTA CONFERENCE of The Methodist Church. What is now known as the "A Building," a three-story brick building conveniently located in South Minneapolis, had formerly served as a maternity home and hospital. From the beginning of this Home, it was decided that never would a lack of finances be a deterrent in the admission of any worthy Methodist. Consequently the financial structure was established on a monthly payment basis, with a membership fee of $300. Residents were encouraged to furnish their own rooms, in order that this might be a building of many homes. There were only a few double rooms, indicating that privacy was an attribute recognized and appreciated by the official family.

The Administrator, who had a medical casework background before going into administration, recognized the need for a Social Service Department and an occupational therapy program, and as a consequence these two ancillary services were immediately available to residents.

It was originally requested that the applicant be a member of a Methodist church for the past five years, and because the rate was set at $50 a month, the recipients of Old Age Assistance were able to enjoy the same benefits and privileges as those of greater financial resources. The Elim Home, the property of the Norwegian-Swedish-Danish Conference of the Methodist Church, was closed, and its occupants became the first residents of the Walker Methodist Residence. A waiting list developed immediately. Consequently in 1951 the "B Building," adding one hundred beds, each with an individual half bath, was erected. At this time a recreational director was added to the staff, and a dietitian.

In 1957 the "C Building," containing nineteen apartments for gracious living (but not light housekeeping), in addition to sixty private rooms, was built and occupied.

The need for a Health Center facility was recognized, and so in 1964 ground was broken for the present Health Care Center, which was occupied for the first time as of May 25, 1966. Here again privacy was recognized as a form of therapy, and there are double rooms provided for couples, where the hale spouse may occupy the room with the one who is ill, or if both are ill, they may receive care together. Three of the five floors are carpeted, and there is air conditioning on these floors also.

A basic premise of the Board of Trustees has been that those who have attained maturer years need and deserve recognition, understanding and the opportunity for creative living. The Residence has participated actively in community programs in the geriatric field, and has served as a center for activities for older people.

E. F. Baumhofer, *Trails in Minnesota*. 1966.
Hennepin Avenue Methodist Episcopal Church, *Dedicatory Exercises and Historic Statement*. 1916.   ORVAL CLAY DITTES
MRS. CAMPBELL KEITH

MINNESOTA, the twelfth largest state in the Union, is located in the north central section of the United States. It is bounded by CANADA on the north, Lake Superior and WISCONSIN on the east, IOWA on the south, and SOUTH and NORTH DAKOTA on the west. It was admitted to the Union in 1858, and in 1970 its population was over 3,760,-000. Its area is 84,000 square miles. There are more than 10,000 lakes and thirty-four major parks in the state. Its sandy soil is very fertile. While primarily an agricultural state, Minnesota leads the nation in the production of iron ore. It also has considerable deposits of marble, limestone, granite, jasper, sandstone, mica, feldspar, travertine and clay. Among its most important industries are livestock, meat packing, grain, flour, machinery, printing and publishing.

Minnesota was originally occupied by the Ojibway and Chippewa Indian tribes in the north and by the Dakota or Sioux tribes in the south. The first whites to enter the region were Frenchmen, P. E. Radisson and M. Chouart, who may have visited the territory as early as 1655. In 1679 Father Louis Hennepin accompanied the explorer Dulhut (Duluth) into the area and later wrote the first published book describing the state. In 1762 the land was ceded by France to Spain in a secret treaty, but English leaders explored the eastern section where they established trading posts. The British ceded the territory to the United States after the Revolutionary War, although the English flag flew from the trading posts until after the War of 1812. In 1803 the United States purchased the western section of the country from France which had regained the territory from Spain.

The first Methodist mission in Minnesota was opened in May, 1837 at the Sioux village of Kaposia (now South St. Paul) by ALFRED BRUNSON of the ILLINOIS CONFERENCE. Here the first Methodist society in Minnesota was organized in 1837 with thirty-four members. One of the converts, Jacob Folstrom, a Swedish fur trader whose wife was an Indian, was said to be worth the whole cost of the mission. Folstrom became a local preacher and proved to be an invaluable guide and interpreter for the missionaries. In 1838 a mission was begun among the Chippewa Indians at Elk River on the Upper Mississippi by G. W. Brown, and in 1839 and 1840 missions were opened at Sandy Lake and Fond du Lac by Samuel Spates and John Johnson. In 1853 missions were started at Millie Lac and other places. Though these missions were productive of much good among the Indians, all were eventually abandoned.

The first Methodist work among the whites in Minnesota began in 1844 when the ROCK RIVER CONFERENCE appointed Joseph Hurlburt to the St. Croix Mission which included all the settlements of the Mississippi and its tributaries above the head of Lake Pepin. Hurlburt preached at Fort Snelling, RED ROCK, Stillwater, Marine, Osceola, and St. Croix Falls. In 1846 Hurlburt was succeeded by Jonathan W. Putnam who added Point Douglas and St. Anthony Falls to the circuit. Three years later Minnesota became a district in the WISCONSIN CONFERENCE, and in June, 1849 CHAUNCEY HOBART, called the "Father of Minnesota Methodism," was appointed presiding elder of the Minnesota District and pastor at ST. PAUL. Methodist churches were organized in 1849 at both St. Paul and MINNEAPOLIS, and in that year Hobart built the brick Market Street Church in St. Paul, the first Methodist church building in the territory of Minnesota.

In 1852, a treaty with the Indians opened the rich country between the Mississippi and Minnesota Rivers for settlement, and thereafter the Minnesota District expanded rapidly. In 1855 the Minnesota District of the Wisconsin Conference was set off as the MINNESOTA CONFERENCE. In 1856 the Jackson Street Methodist Church was erected in St. Paul. Now used only for business, it is the oldest standing Methodist church building in Minnesota. The church at Montecello, built in 1857, is the oldest Methodist church edifice in continuous use in the state.

In 1894 the Minnesota Conference was divided to form the NORTHERN MINNESOTA CONFERENCE, the latter comprising about two-thirds of the state. The two bodies continued separately until 1948 when, after prolonged study by a merger commission, they united to form again the statewide Minnesota Confererence.

In 1859 the Minnesota Conference formed a Scandinavian Mission District, but as time passed all foreign language work was assigned to foreign language annual conferences. In 1877 the Swedish churches became a part of the Northwest Swedish Conference which covered ILLINOIS, IOWA, and some other states. This conference later divided to form several Swedish conferences, one of which, the NORTHERN SWEDISH CONFERENCE, was fairly strong in Minnesota. The Northwest Norwegian Conference, covering Minnesota, Illinois, Wisconsin, and other states, was formed in 1880. Five years later it became the NORWEGIAN AND DANISH CONFERENCE which continued until 1943. The NORTHERN GERMAN CONFERENCE, including work in Minnesota and North Dakota, was formed in 1886, which continued until 1924.

The M.P. CHURCH organized a Minnesota Conference in 1858 with five ministers and four laymen. It was never strong; in 1877 the denomination had only 300 members in the state. The work dissolved after 1908. The Minnesota Conference of the WESLEYAN METHODIST CHURCH was organized in 1859. As time passed the conference was unwilling to abide by the denomination's stand on secret societies. About 1903 the conference dissolved, and the congregations which remained loyal to the denomination were attached to the Iowa Conference. The FREE METHODISTS operate in the state through their Northern Iowa-Minnesota Conference. In 1970 the conference had ten churches in Minnesota.

The United Methodists in Minnesota support one Methodist related college, WESLEY FOUNDATIONS, several hospitals, homes for the aged, and other institutions. United Methodism is the largest Protestant denomination in the state. In 1970 the Minnesota Conference reported eight districts, 505 ministers, 319 pastoral charges, 139,224 members, and property valued at $79,469,636.

E. F. Baumhofer, *Trails in Minnesota*. 1966.
T. C. Blegen, *Building Minnesota*. 1938.
C. Hobart, *Minnesota*. 1887.   EARL F. BAUMHOFER

MINNESOTA CONFERENCE (ME) was organized August 7, 1856 in HAMLINE UNIVERSITY Chapel, Red Wing, Minn., with Bishop MATTHEW SIMPSON presiding. At the outset the conference had four districts, St. Paul, Minnesota, Red Wing, and Winona. There were forty-seven itinerants, forty-five local preachers, fifty-three charges (seven in WISCONSIN), and 1,761 members.

Methodism in MINNESOTA began with mission work among the Indians in 1837. Work among the whites started in 1844 when the ROCK RIVER CONFERENCE appointed Joseph Hurlburt to the St. Croix Mission. Five years later there was a Minnesota District in the WISCONSIN CONFERENCE.

In 1850 there was Methodist sentiment in favor of establishing a school or seminary in Minnesota, and on March 3, 1854 Hamline University was chartered by the legislature. The school opened with 139 students at Red Wing, Goodhue County, in November 1854. Bishop L. L. HAMLINE, for whom the institution was named, donated $25,000. In 1855 a brick building containing a chapel, school room, library, reading rooms, laboratory, recreation rooms, and dormitory quarters was erected.

By 1859 the Minnesota Conference had grown to seven districts. The next year it lost one district to the WEST WISCONSIN CONFERENCE and one to the DETROIT CONFERENCE, but at the same time it added a Scandinavian Mission District. As time passed Swedish, German, and Norwegian-Danish annual conferences were organized, though none was limited to the state of Minnesota alone. (See Minnesota, and the Table of Methodist Annual Conferences).

In 1877 NORTH DAKOTA was attached to the Minnesota Conference, an arrangement which continued until 1884 when the NORTH DAKOTA CONFERENCE was organized. In 1894 the Minnesota Conference was divided to form the NORTHERN MINNESOTA CONFERENCE. Fifty-three years later the two merged to form again the state-wide Minnesota Conference. At the time of the merger the Minnesota Conference had 42,490 members and the Northern body 47,481.

Because of the generosity of one Mrs. S. H. Knight, the Minnesota Conference was able to establish Asbury Methodist Hospital and the Rebecca M. Harrison Deaconess Home in MINNEAPOLIS in 1892.

In 1968 Minnesota Methodism was giving support to three hospitals, Asbury in Minneapolis, Methodist Hospital just outside Minneapolis, and the Rochester Methodist Hospital. It had one Methodist related college, Hamline University in St. Paul, and it conducted WESLEY FOUNDATIONS at the University of Minnesota, St. Paul College, St. Cloud Teacher's College, Duluth College, and at the state teachers' colleges in Bemidji, Mankato, and Winona. The conference established Walker Home for the aged in Minneapolis, the Paul Watkins Memorial Home in Winona, and homes at Fairmont and Montevideo, along with the Tourelotte Memorial Deaconess Home for retired nurses. In addition, the GOODWILL INDUSTRIES in Duluth, St. Paul, Minneapolis, and St. Cloud, and the Methodist Girls Club in St. Paul (a home for working girls) receive support.

Minnesota Methodism has furnished a number of leaders for the church, including three bishops, CHARLES WESLEY BURNS, RICHARD C. RAINES, and T. OTTO NALL.

In 1970 the Minnesota Conference had eight districts, 505 ministers, 319 pastoral charges, 139,224 members, and property valued at $79,469,636.

E. F. Baumhofer, *Trails in Minnesota*. 1966.
C. Hobart, *Minnesota*. 1887.
Minutes of the Minnesota Conference.
    EARL F. BAUMHOFER

MINNESOTA CONFERENCE (EUB) had its origin in two conferences. The Minnesota Conference of the CHURCH of the UNITED BRETHREN IN CHRIST was organized by Bishop LEWIS DAVIS, Aug. 5, 1857, at Marion, near the present city of ROCHESTER, Minn. One year later a membership of 201 was reported. The first minister was Edmund Clow, who came to Winona County from the Rock River Conference in the fall of 1854. Two years later the Home, Frontier and Foreign Missionary Society sent J. W. Fulkerson from VIRGINIA, who became presiding elder when the Conference was organized.

The second original conference is the Minnesota Conference of THE EVANGELICAL ASSOCIATION of North America. It was organized by Bishop J. J. ESCHER on April 24, 1868, in Emmanuel's Church, Dakota County, near Farmington, Minn., and numbered 1,536 members. From 1856 to 1860, the Minnesota congregations had been a part of the Wisconsin Conference, and from 1861 to 1868, of the Iowa Confernce. The first minister was Andrew Tarnutzer, who came to Winona County in the fall of 1856 from the Wisconsin Conference. He organized the first congregation on March 2, 1857, in what is now Inver Grove Heights. The second building of this congregation (1874) still stands five miles south of the State Capitol. It is located, with the cemetery, on Salem Church Road and is known locally as Salem Church Memorial

Shrine. Minnesota ministers established congregations in Dakota Territory between 1874 and 1884. The Dakota Conference was organized in 1884 with about one thousand members. The German language was used for worship services in most of the congregations in the Dakota and Minnesota Conferences until 1914.

After a minority group from the Evangelical Association formed THE UNITED EVANGELICAL CHURCH in 1894, congregations were established in Minnesota by the Des Moines Conference (UE). In 1899, these were placed in the newly formed Northwestern Conference (UE). In 1922, The United Evangelical Church and the Evangelical Association united to form THE EVANGELICAL CHURCH. At the session of the Minnesota Conference in 1923, nine fields and ten ministers from the Northwestern Conference became a part of the Minnesota Conference of The Evangelical Church. At that time there were 7,980 members.

The Minnesota Confernce of the E.U.B. CHURCH was organized in Rochester, May 2, 1951, when the two original conferences united. At the time of this union there were 14,485 members. Of these 2,235 were former United Brethren and 12,250 were former Evangelical members. At the beginning of 1969 there were in the Conference 15,286 members in eighty-three congregations served by sixty-two ordained and one non-ordained minister. Most of the churches are located in the southern one-half of Minnesota and about twenty-two percent of the membership lives in the seven-county Twin City metropolitan area of MINNEAPOLIS and ST. PAUL. Union with the former Methodist conference in Minnesota was effected in 1969.

Minutes of the Minnesota Conference (UB), 1951.
Albert H. Utzinger, *History of the Minnesota Conference of The Evangelical Association, 1856 to 1922.* Cleveland, 1923.
ROY S. HEITKE

MINNIS, JESSE F. (1895-   ), American M. P. Missionary to INDIA, was born in Orange County, N. C., on June 10, 1895. He was educated at Elon College (B.A.), WESTMINSTER THEOLOGICAL SEMINARY (B.D.), DREW UNIVERSITY (M.A.), and had a year of graduate study in Cornell University. He married Meryl Stokes of MARYLAND shortly before going to India in 1922.

His first appointment was as superintendent and treasurer of the Methodist Protestant Mission at Dhulia, West Khandesh District, Bombay Province. Except when on furlough, he remained superintendent of the mission until it was united with the BOMBAY ANNUAL CONFERENCE of the Methodist Church in Southern Asia. He was then named superintendent of the Dhulia-Puntamba District.

After unification his appointments included, besides the one already mentioned, superintendent of the Nagpur and Bombay districts, and supervisor of building construction in the Bombay Annual Conference. He wrote a booklet in English entitled *Financing the Rural Church.* In 1955 Mrs. Minnis became ill, and physicians ordered the return of the family to America. Although she recovered, it was thought inadvisable for them to try again to work in the tropics. Jesse Minnis joined the NORTH CAROLINA CONFERENCE and served various churches as pastor. He retired from the missionary ranks in 1961 and from the Annual Conference in 1963.

Minutes of the Bombay and North Carolina Conferences, 1961-63.
J. WASKOM PICKETT

MINOR DISTRICT SYNOD. The Wesleyan Methodist Conference of 1793 made provision for a court of appeal for preachers accused of immorality or at odds with their colleagues. This consisted of two preachers chosen by the accused and two chosen by the accuser, presided over by the Chairman of the District, who had a casting vote. This "Minor District Meeting" was empowered to act on behalf of the District Meeting comprising all the preachers, either by suspending the preacher accused or by arbitrating in the dispute. Any preacher thus subject to discipline had the right of appeal to a full District Meeting or to the Conference itself. In 1894 the court was increased to six (apart from the chairman) by the addition of two preachers nominated by the Chairman of the District or (if the Chairman himself was a party in the dispute) by the President of the Conference.

In 1835 the principle of appointing a small group to adjudicate disputes between preachers was extended by the Conference to lay members of the Wesleyan Methodist Society who felt that they had been unjustly expelled. They also were empowered to nominate two preachers to a Minor District Committee which had "the power of modifying, reversing, or confirming the sentence." At the same time and in a similar manner the Superintendent Minister was also given the right of appeal against any LEADERS' MEETING which he felt was obstructing his work. Because these provisions were sometimes misunderstood, sometimes abused, the Conference of 1852 provided for a second hearing of disciplinary cases within the CIRCUIT itself by a "special circuit meeting" consisting of not more than twelve lay members appointed by the QUARTERLY MEETING, to be presided over by the Chairman of the District.

The Wesleyan Methodist Conference of 1892 officially altered the title of what had been called both District Meetings and District Committees to "District Synods," and as a consequence the Minor District Meeting was renamed a Minor District Synod. Under this designation the court has been continued with provisions almost unaltered into the Methodist Church.

FRANK BAKER

MINUTES OF CONFERENCE, quite often termed *Journals* in connection with the reporting of the General and Annual Conferences in American Methodism, have always been carefully kept by a Secretary and his assistants in each Conference involved.

JOHN WESLEY called the first Methodist Conference in 1744 and JOHN BENNET—then a lay preacher—kept the *Minutes* of this gathering. WILLIAM MYLES—one of Wesley's preachers and an intimate friend of the founder of Methodism—states, "The subjects of their deliberations were proposed in the form of questions, which were amply discussed, and with the answers, written down and afterwards printed under the title '*Minutes of Several Conversations Between the Reverend Mr. Wesley and Others*' but now commonly called the 'Minutes of the Conference'". (William Myles, *Chronological History of the Methodists*, London, Third Edition, 1803, p. 23, quoted by Thomas B. Neeley, *History of the Origin and Development of the Governing Conference in Methodism*, Cincinnati: Cranston & Stowe, New York: Hunt and Eaton, 1892).

John Bennet's *Minutes* quoting Mr. Wesley in the record of the 1744 Conference stated, "It is desired . . .

that we may meet with a single eye and as little children who have everything to learn; that every point may be examined from the foundation; that every person may speak freely whatever is in his heart; and that every question proposed may be fully debated, and bolted to the bran." This last expression "bolted to the bran" was the common one at that day, and referred to the sifting of wheat—bolting—until nothing but bran·was left.

The question and answer pattern of the *Minutes* of 1744 and afterward was continued until this became fixed in the LARGE MINUTES, and eventually in the *Book of Discipline* in American Methodism. The "minute questions" must yet be called and answered in quarterly and annual conferences.

The minutes of all Methodist Conferences—as in all organized bodies—are kept by a Secretary, and these *Minutes* are usually read and approved by the body as a whole if time permits. The General Conference of The Methodist Church usually has a "Committee on the *Journal*" which it elects and holds responsible for seeing that the *Minutes* have been properly kept by the Secretary, and reporting that fact to the General Conference itself. In the case of the Annual Conference, there is sometimes a similar Committee on Minutes, though when time allows, the Minutes of the preceding session are publicly read by the Secretary, and then approved by the Conference with such corrections or amendments as seem needed, with the bishop putting the question, "Are the *Minutes* correct?" If he hears no objection, he declares them approved as read.

This is also the procedure in District and Quarterly Conferences though quite often the District Superintendent after holding a Quarterly Conference, will adjourn that body stating that as the Secretary has not had time to prepare the *Minutes* of the particular session, these will be subject to approval by a subsequent conference or by a Committee. Occasionally the Conference simply agrees to trust the secretary for completing an accurate account.

In American Methodism it has been the custom for many years to publish the proceedings of the General Conference under the title of *The Journal* of such and such Conference. With the Annual Conferences the same nomenclature in a great many instances is followed and thus the Minutes become the *Journal of the Kentucky Conference*, or *Journal of the New York Conference*, etc., of such and such a date.

The Journal of the usual Annual Conference carries beside the minutes, the conference roll or directory; the memoirs of the deceased preachers, and sometimes wives of preachers; tables of statistics and reports of various kinds, together with resolutions and reports adopted; and sometimes of speeches or addresses which the Conference orders to be printed in its *Minutes* or its *Journal*. A file of the *Minutes* or *Journals* of any Annual Conference will provide much material for the history of that Conference, as the successive *Journals* of the General Conference also provide a history of the undertaking and work of the general Church.

It may be mentioned in connection with the General Conference and the Jurisdictional Conferences that a *Daily Christian Advocate* is published at such quadrennial sessions, and the exact record of everything said on the floor of the Conference, as well as all actions taken is minutely transcribed for each daily issue. (For *Minutes* in the British Methodist Church, see CONFERENCE, MINUTES OF; see also LARGE MINUTES for the general pattern of Methodist Conference procedures.)

Journals of successive Annual and General Conferences.

N. B. H.

MIRANDA, BERNARDO DE (1863-1891), pioneer Brazilian preacher, was born in Paranaguá, Province of Paraná, BRAZIL. Reared a Catholic, he was converted under the preaching of J. W. TARBOUX. Miranda bought his first Bible in 1883, and became one of four founding members of the Methodist church in São PAULO, when it was organized by J. W. Koger. Almost immediately he began preaching on the São Paulo Circuit. In 1886, he received an appointment from Bishop GRANBERY when the bishop organized Brazil's first annual conference. Miranda was admitted as a local preacher on July 14, 1887, and in December 1889, he helped E. A. Tilly organize the Methodist church in Taubaté, state of São Paulo. Miranda was ordained DEACON in August 1890, when the first such ordination took place in Brazil.

By the end of that year, however, severe illness forced his retirement, and he died of yellow fever on Feb. 13, 1891—the first Brazilian preacher to die in the service.

J. L. Kennedy, *Metodismo no Brasil*. 1928.   ISNARD ROCHA

MIRANDA, LUDGERO LUIZ De (1864-1892), Brazilian Methodist preacher, was born in what was then the province of São PAULO. At the age of thirteen, he left home to work in Santos, and there he lived for three years. In a short autobiographical sketch written in 1892, he told of hearing the Gospel for the first time in August 1884, on the invitation of his older brother, BERNARDO DE MIRANDA. He was converted after hearing JOHN W. TARBOUX's sermon on "The Strait and Wide Roads," and was so moved that he at once resolved to become a preacher as was his brother, Bernardo. He went to RIO DE JANEIRO where he studied some months under J. J. RANSOM. In August 1886, Ransom sent him to JUIZ DE FORA, state of Minas Gerais, to sell Bibles and other books in anticipation of opening Methodist work there.

Ludgero worked in two or three small stations in the state of Minas Gerais, one being Rio Novo. There in August 1886, as he preached and sold Bibles with FELIPE DE CARVALHO, another young preacher as companion, both were arrested, marched through the streets like common criminals, and ordered to leave town within forty-eight hours. But JAMES L. KENNEDY, coming through at this time with Bishop J. O. GRANBERY, went to the police authorities, claimed their right to speak, and had them freed with permission to continue the services. In 1891, Miranda was ordained DEACON, and this, he wrote, "was the most glorious day in my life."

Tragedy, however, cut short his career in the ministry early in 1892. His wife, Herminia, died of yellow fever on January 2; his little girl on January 5; and Ludgero himself died on January 17. Thus, within a period of two weeks, a whole family was wiped out by this dread disease.

Though only twenty-eight years of age, Ludgero had won many to Christ, and he died victoriously.

J. L. Kennedy, *Metodismo no Brasil*. 1928.   ISNARD ROCHA

MISSION BOATS, or Canadian West Coast marine missions, began in the year 1874 when THOMAS CROSBY was sent to Port Simpson on the northwest coast. From this center he traveled some three thousand miles yearly in dugout canoes, sailboats, and steamers, bringing the Gospel to isolated Indian villages.

In 1883, Crosby went East and managed to raise $7,000. With this money the "Glad Tidings" was built in New Westminster by a recently converted shipwright and seaman called WILLIAM OLIVER. A wooden vessel of forty tons, she was seventy-one feet over-all with a fourteen-foot beam and a depth in the hold of eight feet. She was fitted in Victoria with a 323 nominal horsepower steam engine. When the "Glad Tidings" arrived in Port Simpson in the winter of 1884 on her maiden voyage, the natives welcomed her by firing cannons, raising flags at every pole, and calling out the brass band. Reputed to run on "porridge and prayers," she was known to the natives as the "Come-to-Jesus Boat" because of Crosby's habit of standing on the bow and singing the hymn with these words as they approached a village. In 19 years of service the "Glad Tidings" logged 78,041 miles. She carried missionaries, teachers, and medical aid to countless outposts, and assisted in the building of more than thirty churches, schools, and mission houses. She carried mail and materials for lighthouses, remote villages, and logging camps; but her prime cargo was the Gospel powerfully preached by Crosby, assisted by Captain William Oliver. The "Glad Tidings" was blown ashore and wrecked in 1903. She had never been insured.

The "Udal," a fifteen-ton, forty-five-foot, diesel-powered boat was built by Captain Oliver at his own expense and presented to the church in 1908. Trimmed with fancy brass fittings from Scotland, the "Udal" (Haida for "The Dearest Thing I Possess") struck the shore in northern waters and sank before she had sailed a year.

Following the loss of the "Udal," a forty-five-foot, gasoline-engined boat called the "Homespun" was purchased. Skippered by Captain Oliver, she carried on the work for about three years.

In 1912, the "Homespun" was sold and an 83-foot, 166-ton steamship was built and named the "Thomas Crosby." During the First World War she was commandeered by the government to do patrol work. Then, following the war, even though she earned $1,000 a year by dropping off mail at the lighthouses, she was found to be too costly. She was sold in 1919 and replaced by three smaller boats: the "Iwyll," which was run out of Cape Mudge by Captain Robert Scott; the "William Oliver," which worked out of Alert Bay, but which later was moved to the Queen Charlotte Islands; and the "Thomas Crosby II," which was blown ashore and wrecked at Sandspit on December 5, 1920. The "Iwyll" was replaced by the "Edward White," which eventually became a medical launch used by G. E. DARBY at Bella Bella. In 1923, the "Thomas Crosby III" was built by Captain Oliver, backed by the home mission board. Powered with the old Miller engine from the wrecked "Crosby II," this boat carried on the work around the Queen Charlotte Islands and the Northern mainland coast for nearly fifteen years. By this time the Methodist Church had been incorporated into The United Church of Canada, which, in 1966, still operated a fleet of boats as well as one seaplane.

T. Crosby, *Up and Down the North Pacific Coast.* Toronto: Methodist Publishing House, 1914.

R. C. Scott, *My Captain Oliver.* Toronto: United Church Publishing House, 1947.

Mrs. F. C. Stephenson, *Canadian Methodist Missions.* 1924.

HUGH W. McKERVILL

MISSIONARY BANDS OF THE WORLD was formed in 1885 by Vivian A. Dake, a minister of the Free Methodist Church, as a society for missionary recruitment and fellowship among the youth of his charge. It was originally called the Pentecost Band. Other similar groups were formed, and after a short time they declared independence as the Pentecostal Bands of the World. The name Missionary Bands of the World was adopted in 1925. In 1958 they merged with the WESLEYAN METHODIST CHURCH.

Clark: *Small Sects in America.*   J. GORDON MELTON

MISSIONARY BISHOPS. A Missionary Bishop was a bishop in the M. E. Church elected for a specified foreign field with full episcopal powers there, but with his episcopal jurisdiction limited to the foreign mission field for which he was elected. (*Discipline*, 1888, Paragraph 166.)

This grade of bishop, with supervision limited to a special field, was somewhat the outgrowth of the contention regarding the episcopacy which was maintained by the (Northern) majority of the GENERAL CONFERENCE of 1844, which decided that the office of bishop was completely under the control of the General Conference. (See PLAN OF SEPARATION.) The action in 1844 (against which the Southern delegates contended strongly) in effect said that the Methodist bishop had no constitutional status but only a statutory one, whose powers could be fully determined by the majority vote of a General Conference.

It seemed good, therefore, to the M. E. Church, as mission fields grew and there was need of episcopal supervision there, to put a bishop in each one of these lands, but to avoid giving him *general* superintendency. "A Missionary Bishop is not, in the meaning of the *Discipline*, a General Superintendent." (Paragraph 167, *Discipline*, 1888.) The legislation creating this office, however, held Missionary Bishops not to be subordinate to the true General Superintendents, but co-ordinate with them in authority in the special field for which they were elected, and each one was amenable for his conduct to the General Conference, just as were the General Superintendents. It was further provided by the 1888 General Conference that the election of one to be a Missionary Bishop carried with it the assignment to the specified foreign mission field; and that such a bishop could not thereafter become a General Superintendent except by a distinct election to that office.

Missionary Bishops of this distinct type were continued in the M. E. Church up until the time of Church union in 1939. The Constitution of that year made no provision for the election of this distinct type of bishop. When such supervision for the overseas missions fields was found to be needed (as was the case after Church union with Southern Europe and a large part of the African work), the General Conference requested specific JURISDICTIONS to elect bishops whom it was understood would be full General Superintendents, and assign them to these regions. Pursuant to this, Bishop PAUL N. GARBER was elected a General Superintendent by the Southeastern Jurisdiction and assigned to the GENEVA Area in 1948; Bishop NEWELL

BOOTH was elected a bishop by the Northeastern Jurisdiction for the CONGO and assigned to that Area. Both these men subsequently were brought back to the United States and placed in charge of Episcopal Areas in their respective Jurisdictions.

The Constitution of The United Methodist Church made no provision for electing this distinct type of bishop, though statutory legislation in the *Disciplines* of The Methodist Church, and now in The United Methodist Church, defines the office and powers thereof. However, upon the death of Bishop GOWDY and the other missionary bishops who were such at the time of union in 1939, the office had seemingly disappeared from life in The Methodist and The United Methodist Church. (See also EPISCOPACY.)

Disciplines.
N. B. Harmon, *Organization.* 1962.
D. Sherman, *Revisions of the Discipline.* 1890.   N. B. H.

MISSIONARY METHODIST CHURCH, THE, was formed in 1913 by members of the WESLEYAN METHODIST CHURCH who withdrew in a dispute over a number of rules and regulations. The organization of the church, originally called the Holiness Methodist Church, was at Forest City, N. C., on July 28. Henry Clay Sisk, Thomas A. Sisk, James C. Stafford, and J. B. Sisk led in the church's formation, along with Miss Lillie Hardin, the first secretary. The doctrine of the church is Wesleyan, with a strong doctrine of SANCTIFICATION and ESCHATOLOGY. Three sacraments are observed, baptism, the Lord's Supper, and foot washing. The church's government is connectional, with property held jointly by the local church and the annual conference. The pastor is called by the local congregation. Ministerial education is by a course of study, an annual Bible Institute, and a correspondence course given by Union Bible Seminary, Westville, Ind.

In 1970 the sect reported twelve churches, being served by thirty-two ministers, with 1,200 members. Mission work is carried on through the Oriental Missionary Society.

Discipline of the Missionary Methodist Church of America. 1969.   J. GORDON MELTON

MISSIONARY RECORD, THE (1885-1939), was the monthly denominational periodical sponsored first as *The Woman's Missionary Record* by the WOMAN'S FOREIGN MISSIONARY SOCIETY of the M.P. Church and after 1928 by the Board of Missions of the M.P. Church. It was published in BALTIMORE, Md. Its purpose was to create a missionary spirit by informing readers of the mission work of the denomination and its needs. It contained news of both home and foreign missions, colleges, leadership training schools and the various benevolent interests of the M.P. Church. It offered constructive program materials for the use of individual church auxiliaries, and during 1938-1940 gave information containing the missionary implications of the Methodist union. *The Missionary Record* was an outgrowth of *The Methodist Missionary,* published by T. H. COLHOUER, who, because of pastoral duties, was forced to discontinue the publication. It was then taken up by C. H. Williams, Corresponding Secretary of the Board of Missions, who called the paper *The Methodist Protestant Missionary.* At the meeting of the Executive Board of the Woman's Foreign Missionary Society in 1885 the Board of Missions offered the publication to the society to be used as its official organ. The paper was adopted and its name changed to *The Woman's Missionary Record.* Mrs. Mary A. Miller, the first editor, served in that position for ten years. The motto, "I can do all things through Christ which strengtheneth me," was adopted. In later years the motto, "Not by might nor by power, but by My Spirit saith the Lord of hosts," was used. The first issue of *The Woman's Missionary Record* appeared in July 1885. Mrs. F. C. Huling, who was editor from 1898-1903, introduced the magazine form of the periodical that was used thereafter. Mrs. J. F. McCULLOCH was editor for some twenty years beginning in 1903 and her husband published the magazine for ten years. When the periodical became the official organ of the Board of Missions of the M.P. Church following the GENERAL CONFERENCE of 1928, the "Woman's" was dropped from the name. Mrs. Marie W. Thompson, who served as editor of *The Missionary Record* for five years, was followed by Miss BETTIE S. BRITTINGHAM, formerly Dean of Women at Westminster College, Tehuacaua, Texas, who served as editor from 1933 until the merger of *The Missionary Record* into a new magazine, *The Methodist Woman,* in September 1940.

Mrs. E. C. Chandler, *History of the Woman's Foreign Missionary Society, 1879-1919.* Pittsburgh, 1920.
J. Elwood Carroll, *History of the North Carolina Annual Conference of the Methodist Protestant Church.* Greensboro, 1939.
Scattered issues of *The Missionary Record* and *The Woman's Missionary Record.*   RALPH HARDEE RIVES

MISSIONARY RULE is the disciplinary proviso commonly referred to by this name which allows persons to be ordained (*Discipline,* TMC, 1964, Paragraph 403.3) as a special privilege for those going to the mission field. This obviates the necessity of serving as deacons under appointment for the length of time the normal minister must before ordination in the homeland. The Board of Missions, however, has its own specifications for approving carefully such persons, and the bishop who ordains them is only empowered to conduct such ordination when it is certified that such persons will be under appointment immediately for foreign work by the Board. Regulations regarding this matter have been changed in minor particulars through subsequent *Disciplines* within recent years, but the missionary rule is still in use.

Discipline of The United Methodist Church, 1968, *in loc;* see ELDERS.   N. B. H.

MISSIONARY SOCIETIES, Am. (See WOMEN'S SOCIETY OF CHRISTIAN SERVICE; WOMAN'S HOME MISSIONARY SOCIETY; and WOMAN'S FOREIGN MISSIONARY SOCIETY.)

MISSIONS, CENTRAL, Br. (See FORWARD MOVEMENT, Br.)

MISSIONS, DEPARTMENT OF OVERSEAS. (See METHODIST MISSIONARY SOCIETY.)

MISSIONS, HOME, Br. (See HOME MISSIONS, Br.)

MISSIONS AND BOARD OF MISSIONS OF THE E.U.B. CHURCH. History of Evangelical Missions.

The Eastern Conference of the EVANGELICAL ASSOCIATION organized the first missionary society at its session in 1838. In order to broaden the scope a subsequent meeting was held March 1, 1839 near New Berlin, Pa. and the General Missionary Society of the Evangelical Association was formed and constitution adopted. The General Conference that year sanctioned the society and introduced a section into the *Discipline* on "support of missions." The first missionaries assigned under the Society were sent out in 1839 to the Mohawk Valley in NEW YORK, to Ontario (CANADA), and New York City.

A Board of Missions was created by the GENERAL CONFERENCE in 1859, whereby mission work assumed by the Society was managed by the Board. A full-time Missionary Secretary was elected. Earlier, in 1850, the annual conferences had cooperated in establishing a GERMANY Mission, although the Eastern Conference gave more direct support. A Japanese mission was opened in 1875, followed in 1904 with one in CHINA.

With the formation of The UNITED EVANGELICAL CHURCH in 1894 a Missionary Society was established, but the Church did not elect a full-time secretary until the General Conference of 1906. A mission field was formed at Changsha, China with the arrival in that city of the first missionary couple, Nov. 27, 1901.

When the Evangelical Association and The United Evangelical Church united in 1922, the Missionary Society of The EVANGELICAL CHURCH became the legal successor. It later added work in NIGERIA to the foreign fields already established.

United Brethren in Christ. In 1841 General Conference established the "Parent Missionary Society of the United Brethren in Christ" to extend the Gospel both on the frontier and in foreign lands. In 1845 a Board of Missions was formed to supervise the work of the Society. Then in 1853 the General Conference organized the Home, Frontier, and Foreign Missionary Society. Two missions were located (Southern Missouri and Canada) and arrangements made to send missionaries to Africa in that same year. Generally, however, home mission work was left to the management of the self-supporting annual conferences. In 1905 Home Missions were made independent and a Home Missionary Society was formed. In 1921 the Home Mission Board and the Church Erection Board were brought together.

Starting with work in SIERRA LEONE, West Africa in 1853, fields were opened in China (1889), JAPAN (1895), PUERTO RICO (1899), and the PHILIPPINE ISLANDS (1901). The work begun in Germany in 1869 was turned over to the M.E. Church in 1905. Cooperative work was also initiated in the Dominican Republic.

Evangelical United Brethren Church. In 1946 the Board of Missions was established, successor to the several missionary and church extension societies which operated in the two churches. Then the Board of Missions was reorganized in 1966 with the following Divisions: World Missions; National Missions; Women's Service; Missions Resources. A General Secretary was elected for the entire Board with executive secretaries for each Division. One office of Treasurer operated for the entire Board.

At the time of the formation of The United Methodist Church mission fields were being conducted, either cooperatively with other denominations or singly, in Nigeria, Sierra Leone, BRAZIL, ECUADOR, HONG KONG, Japan, IN-DONESIA, SARAWAK, the Philippine Islands, and Puerto Rico.

LOIS MILLER

MISSIONS, AND ORGANIZED METHODIST MISSIONARY WORK.

There is a sense in which Methodism itself was a missionary movement, and the same in an even larger way may be said of Christianity. Certainly the sense of mission was always to the fore in all the movements of the first Methodist Societies, and afterward in all the growth and organizational work of the various Methodist branch churches as they came to be. JOHN WESLEY himself came to America as a missionary in 1735, and later on as the head of the Methodist movement he sent men to preach in various places who were understood to be not only preachers but missionaries of gospel light. The beginnings of Methodist work in America has been told in other places in this *Encyclopedia*. The M.E. Church in America was organized under that name in December 1784, and immediately began expanding mission-wise almost in parallel with the expansion of the westward-growing nation.

The expansion of American Methodism and its separate organizational moves can best be told under the following divisions:

Methodist Episcopal Church (undivided), 1784-1844.
Methodist Episcopal Church (separated), 1845-1939.
Methodist Episcopal Church, South, 1845-1939.
Methodist Protestant Church, 1830-1939.
The Methodist Church, 1939-1968.
The United Methodist Church, 1968-

Note: The material which appears herewith is in large part the adaptation of an article on Methodist Missions taken from the *Encyclopedia of Modern Christian Missions*. The general editor of this was Burton L. Goddard, and it was published in 1967 by Gordon College and Gordon Divinity School, Thomas Nelson and Sons being the publisher. We make grateful acknowledgment to Thomas Nelson and Sons for the use of this copyrighted material. In certain instances the material has been adapted and edited to bring it up to date, and certain sections of the original article have been omitted since these have been treated under the respective nations and regions where Methodist missions were carried on. Also, the section on the present United Methodist Church and its Board of Missions organization has been added to the original article, as The United Methodist Church under that name was not in being when the article for the *Encyclopedia of Modern Christian Missions* was written.

METHODIST EPISCOPAL CHURCH, 1784-1845

One year after the Church organized at the CHRISTMAS CONFERENCE, or in 1785, it set apart FREEBORN GARRETTSON and JAMES O. CROMWELL to go to Nova Scotia. It also appointed a missionary to ANTIGUA, though he died before leaving for that field. It commenced missionary activity in CANADA in 1790 through WILLIAM LOSEE. The Nova Scotia mission ended about the turn of the century and the Canada missions divided formally from connection with the M.E. Church in 1832, the constituencies of these two regions becoming affiliated with British Methodism.

The *Missionary Society* of the M.E. Church was organized in New York on April 5, 1819, and became an official agency of the Church by General Conference action in 1820. Its first full-time executive was NATHAN BANGS, drafter of the Society's constitution, who was elected in 1836. The original purpose of the organization was "to enable the several annual conferences more effectually to extend their missionary labors throughout the United States and elsewhere."

The first mission under the aegis of the Missionary Society was founded in LIBERIA by MELVILLE B. COX in 1833.

Soon afterwards, representatives of the Society established English-speaking missions in South America: FOUNTAIN E. PITTS in ARGENTINA in 1835, JUSTIN SPAULDING in BRAZIL in 1839. The Brazil and URUGUAY missions were suspended in 1842.

MARTIN RUTER and two assistants established a mission in the independent Republic of TEXAS in 1837, following sporadic forays by Methodist preachers into the territory while it was still under Spanish and Mexican jurisdiction.

Two splits in the Church reduced the Missionary Society's supporting constituency. A reform group protesting against the exclusively clerical and episcopal control of the denomination finally withdrew, and in 1830, after two years' organizing activity, formally established the METHODIST PROTESTANT CHURCH. The other and much more deep-seated division came as a result of controversies centered in the slavery question and following the PLAN OF SEPARATION in 1844, resulted in the establishment of the M.E. CHURCH, SOUTH in 1845-46. The three Methodist denominations remained in separation until they were merged in 1939 after many years of negotiation. We give now the development of organized missionary activity in each of these three Churches.

METHODIST EPISCOPAL CHURCH (SEPARATED), 1845-1939

The Northern section of the newly divided church retained the name and status of the M.E. Church. The Missionary Society remained its official missionary agency until 1907. The chief cooperating organizations were the WOMAN'S FOREIGN MISSIONARY SOCIETY, founded in 1869; the WOMAN'S HOME MISSIONARY SOCIETY, founded in 1880; and the CHURCH EXTENSION SOCIETY, which was established in 1865 and superseded by the Board of Church Extension in 1872. During most of this period, the Missionary Society administered its work through a Board of Managers and its Corresponding Secretaries, subject to the General Missionary Committee, which met annually to make appropriations and to establish policy.

In 1907, the Missionary Society, which had promoted both foreign and domestic missions, was replaced in a reorganization of the Church's benevolence agencies. A new Board of Foreign Missions undertook the administration of foreign missions, and a consolidated Board of Home Missions and Church Extension assumed direction of domestic missions. The Board of Foreign Missions maintained headquarters in NEW YORK CITY, as had the Missionary Society.

Among the more notable Corresponding Secretaries of the Society and the Board were JOHN P. DURBIN (1850-72), John M. Reid (1872-88), ADNA B. LEONARD (1888-1912), Henry K. Carroll (1900-08), FRANK MASON NORTH (1912-24), S. Earl Taylor (1912-20), and RALPH E. DIFFENDORFER (1924-39; 1939-49, Executive Secretary, Division of World Missions, The Methodist Church).

From $95,000 in 1845, the receipts for foreign mis-

sions slowly increased to $1,320,000 in 1907, and $2,216,-000 in 1918. In 1919, a hundred years after the founding of the Missionary Society, the Board, cooperating with other Methodist agencies, conducted an intensive financial drive known as the Centenary campaign. (See CENTENARY FUND.) Its immediate aim was a radical increase of giving for a period of five years. Pursuing the central purpose of the Centenary Movement, and relying on pledges made, the Board planned major extensions and developments in foreign work based on estimated total yearly receipts of $10 million. However, payments fell far short of pledges; total receipts were forty-six percent below the expected income. Corresponding retrenchments had to be made in the planned world program; results on the field were calamitous; the Board's affairs were in severe crisis. Nevertheless, total receipts for the Centenary period (1919-23) average about $5,500,000 a year, compared with about $2 million from 1914 to 1918.

By 1928, the year before the economic depression began, receipts had dropped, however, to about $2,975,-000; and by 1939, they were down to about $1,417,000, yielding planned appropriations for the field that were lower than those made in 1918.

Until 1920, the Board of Foreign Missions conducted the regular financing of its operations independently of other denominational agencies. In that year, the Board came under limited jurisdiction of a commission authorized to correlate promotional appeals, unify budgeting, and maintain a central appropriations treasury for all benevolence boards. Foreign missions thus became a part of what was known, from 1924, as the denomination's WORLD SERVICE program.

After the Separation of 1845, the M.E. Church entered foreign mission fields on five continents.

In Asia, the first mission was established in CHINA by JUDSON D. COLLINS and MOSES C. WHITE, who arrived there in 1847. A China missionary, ROBERT S. MACLAY, was influential in founding a mission in JAPAN in 1873, becoming its first superintendent. Maclay also became the first superintendent of the KOREA mission, which was organized in 1885, with HENRY G. APPENZELLER and WILLIAM B. SCRANTON as the Society's missionaries, and with Scranton's mother, Mary F. Scranton, serving as a W.F.M.S. worker. Work was started in OKINAWA in 1892 as part of the Japan mission, and continued into the period of World War II.

By expansion from the INDIA mission, which was founded in 1856 by WILLIAM BUTLER, another group of Asian missions was developed. The first entry into Indian territory, later to become part of PAKISTAN, was accomplished by the founding of a mission in Karachi in 1873. JAMES M. THOBURN, superintendent of the Calcutta District, organized a mission in Rangoon, BURMA, in 1879, and another in SINGAPORE in 1885, with WILLIAM F. OLDHAM, a native of India, as the leader of the latter enterprise. The mission centered in Singapore (the Malaysia Mission) reached out, in turn, into the (then) Federation of MALAYA by establishing work in Penang in 1891. In the same year, it projected a brief, abortive mission into British North Borneo. Thoburn, by virtue of his jurisdiction over the Malaysia Mission Conference, inaugurated a mission in the PHILIPPINE ISLANDS in 1899. Bishop FRANK W. WARNE, in 1901, organized a group of Chinese immigrants to SARAWAK into a circuit of the Singapore District.

INDONESIA (then the Netherlands East Indies) also

was entered by workers from the Malaysia jurisdiction—Sumatra (1905) by Solomon Pakianathan; Java (1905) by John R. Denyes; W. Borneo (1906) by Charles M. Worthington; Bangka (1911) by Mark Freeman. In 1928, the Board of Foreign Missions concentrated the work in this area in Sumatra, withdrawing from Java and W. Borneo, and shortly afterwards cutting its ties with Bangka.

The Missionary Society opened evangelistic work in Europe in 1849, when LUDWIG S. JACOBY arrived in GERMANY from the United States as a result of a missionary impulse arising among German immigrants converted to Methodism in America. Preachers from Germany extended the work to SWITZERLAND in 1856. The North Germany Conference acquired a small mission in AUSTRIA by transfer from the British Wesleyans in 1897. The following year, the pastor in charge in Vienna began Methodist work in HUNGARY. Most of it was in the southern area, Backa, which became a part of YUGOSLAVIA when the new state was established after World War I.

A second European development also grew out of Methodist foreign-language missions in the United States. OLE P. PETERSEN, converted in the BETHEL SHIP mission in New York, returned to NORWAY as a missionary in 1853. John P. Larsson, a Swedish convert, returned to his homeland and became the Society's first missionary in SWEDEN in 1854. CHRISTIAN B. WILLERUP, superintendent of the new Scandinavian mission, opened work in DENMARK in 1858. In 1881, the Sweden Conference incorporated into its appointments evangelistic work in FINLAND already begun by Methodist emigrants from Sweden. In 1889, a mission was started in RUSSIA under the Finland District of the Sweden Conference.

Methodism reached the BALTIC STATES by extension from European missions. A German pastor from Königsberg, East Prussia, started work in Kaunas, Lithuania, in 1903. The Russian District of the Finland and Russia Mission Conference organized a mission on the island of Oesel, Estonia, in 1910, and in Riga, Latvia, in 1911.

Four other, unrelated missions emerged in Europe—in BULGARIA (1858), ITALY (1873), FRANCE (1907), and SPAIN (1919). In South America, the M.E. Church continued the Argentina mission started before the Separation of 1844. It also reopened in 1868 and 1885 the two suspended pre-Separation missions—Uruguay and Brazil, respectively. (All but a fragment of the Brazil work was transferred to the M.E. Church, South in 1900.) THOMAS B. WOOD, superintendent of the South America mission, established a new enterprise in PARAGUAY in 1886, which continued until 1917. Evangelistic work begun in Callao, PERU, by FRANCIS G. PENZOTTI, a Methodist employee of the AMERICAN BIBLE SOCIETY, became a Methodist mission in 1890. In the same year, the Church acquired a CHILE mission when the CINCINNATI ANNUAL CONFERENCE adopted as its Chile District an unofficial Chile mission enterprise begun in 1878 by WILLIAM TAYLOR, the free-lance Methodist founder of independent, "self-supporting" missions in South America, India, and Africa. For a dozen years, beginning in 1898, there was a mission in ECUADOR. From 1900, it was composed chiefly of teachers supplied by the Board and supported by the government of Ecuador. Karl G. Beutelspacher opened a mission in BOLIVIA in 1901.

Elsewhere in Latin America, William Butler, founder of the India work, became the first appointee to a mission in MEXICO founded in 1873 under the direction of

Bishop GILBERT HAVEN. Bishop THOMAS B. NEELY, resident in BUENOS AIRES, organized a mission in PANAMA in 1905. GEORGE A. MILLER, superintendent in Panama, extended the work to COSTA RICA in 1917.

In Africa, the pre-Separation mission in Liberia remained in operation under the Northern church. In 1896, the Missionary Society granted official status to three independent missions established earlier by William Taylor, MISSIONARY BISHOP for Africa—ANGOLA (1885), CONGO (1886), and MOZAMBIQUE (1893). Methodism penetrated Southern RHODESIA in 1898. In the same year, Bishop JOSEPH C. HARTZELL, Taylor's successor as Missionary Bishop for Africa, received by transfer an independent mission on the island of Madeira, which was administered with Africa work until Madeira was given up in the 1940's. A missionary also served in the Cape Verde Islands for part of 1901. North Africa was entered in 1908, when missions were started in ALGERIA and TUNISIA. The Mozambique mission extended its evangelistic ministry into the Union of SOUTH AFRICA in 1919, following up the mine workers imported from Mozambique.

Several outposts classified as domestic missions were developed outside the United States. Work in HAWAII was conducted from 1855-62 in association with the CALIFORNIA ANNUAL CONFERENCE, and was reopened in 1888 among emigrants from Japan to Hawaii. Evangelistic effort in ALASKA began in 1897. CHARLES W. DREES established a mission in PUERTO RICO in 1900, and Methodist work began in the DOMINICAN REPUBLIC in 1921 in a united effort with the mission boards of the Presbyterian Church (U.S.A.) and of the United Brethren.

Integration of the foreign fields and their converts and members into the ecclesiastical structure of the Church based in the United States early became the practice—and before long, the fundamental policy—of the M.E. Church. Beginning with Liberia (1836), Germany (1856), and India (1864), Mission Conferences and Annual Conferences were gradually established by GENERAL CONFERENCE legislation, until by 1900 there were seven Mission Conferences, sixteen full-fledged Annual Conferences, and four affiliated formal Missions in Europe, Asia, Africa, and Latin America. By that time, the denomination was well on the way to making itself a world church.

The General Conference of 1884 provided for the organization on foreign fields of what were called "CENTRAL CONFERENCES" composed of Annual Conferences, and of Missions on certain larger fields, to which should be given autonomy in supervising educational, publishing, and other regional connectional interests. Six such Central Conferences were organized: Southern Asia, 1885; Eastern Asia, 1897; Southeastern Asia, 1923; South Africa, 1921; Latin America, 1924; Germany, 1936.

The first two Central Conferences (India and China were the two permanent core countries) became significant administrative units; and according to some commentators, their existence provided sufficient autonomy on the field to avert Methodist participation in church union projects insofar as those movements were motivated by the desire for national autonomy in church life. The legislation providing for Central Conferences was originated not to meet demands for indigenization of the Church on the foreign field, but to provide relevant and effective supervision. When demands for indigenization emerged, however (as in India in the 1920's), the Central

Conference apparatus afforded practical expression to the movement towards those goals.

In addition to its pattern of Annual Conferences, the Church extended to the foreign fields its system of episcopal supervision. The practice of visitation by regular bishops (General Superintendents) began in 1853, when Bishop LEVI SCOTT visited Liberia. In 1858, FRANCIS BURNS, a member of the Liberia Conference, was consecrated in the United States as a bishop for Liberia, after his election by his Conference. JOHN W. ROBERTS (like Burns, an American Negro) was similarly elected and consecrated, in 1866.

In 1884, the General Conference began electing a series of Missionary Bishops with jurisdiction limited to specific fields, almost all of them having served previously as missionaries. To Liberia were assigned ISAIAH B. SCOTT (1904-16) and ALEXANDER P. CAMPHOR (1916-19), both born in Negro slavery in the U.S.; to Africa (general), William Taylor (1884-96), Joseph C. Hartzell (1896-1916), and EBEN S. JOHNSON (1916-20); to India and Malaysia, James M. Thoburn (1888-1908), Frank W. WARNE (1900-20), EDWIN W. PARKER (1900-01), JOHN E. ROBINSON (1904-20), William F. Oldham (1904-12, resident in Singapore), JOHN W. ROBINSON (1912-20), and WILLIAM P. EVELAND (1912-16, resident in MANILA); and to Japan (1904-08) and Korea (1908-12), MERRIMAN C. HARRIS.

Between 1900 and 1920, supervision by visiting bishops and by Missionary Bishops was supplemented—in China, Europe, and Latin America—by the assignment of Bishops of the category of General Superintendent to residence in foreign fields. Most notable among them was JAMES W. BASHFORD, stationed in China from 1904 to 1919. In 1920, the missionary episcopacy was abolished in favor of supervision by General Superintendents in foreign residence. This policy, which removed a point of distinction between the Church abroad and the Church in the United States, was later modified when the General Conference elected EDWIN F. LEE Missionary Bishop for Southeast Asia in 1928, and JOHN M. SPRINGER for Africa in 1936.

In 1929 occurred an important broadening of the base of the episcopacy and of the power of Central Conferences, when by Constitutional amendment it became possible for Central Conferences to elect Bishops for their own jurisdictions. The Eastern Asia Central Conference elected (1930) John Gowdy, a Board missionary born in Scotland, and CHIH PING WANG; Southern Asia elected (1930), JASHWANT R. CHITAMBAR; Latin America elected (1932), JUAN E. GATTINONI, an Argentinian born in Italy; Germany elected (1936), F. H. OTTO MELLE.

Three mission constituencies withdrew from the M.E. Church to become components in autonomous Methodist churches. In 1907, the two Conferences in Japan (5,000 members) joined with the Japan missions of the M.E. Church, South and of the Canadian Methodist Church in founding the Japan Methodist Church. In 1930, the Mexico Conference (5,000 members) merged with the mission of the M.E. Church, South to found the Methodist Church of Mexico. In the same year, the Korea Conference (11,000 members) united with the Southern Methodist mission to establish the Korean Methodist Church. The Board of the home church, however, continued sending funds and personnel to the now independent churches.

By 1939, there were fifty-one foreign Annual or Mission Conferences, with 352,000 full members of the Church.

The four numerically strongest fields had half the Conferences and seventy-two percent of the members—India, with ten Conferences and 101,000 members; China, with eight Conferences and 63,000 members; the Philippine Islands, with two Conferences and 53,000 members; Germany, with five Conferences and 36,000 members. (At this time, the membership of the Church in the United States was 4,443,000.) The Board had 571 foreign missionaries; and the W.F.M.S., making field expenditures of more than $900,000, had 475 missionaries.

METHODIST EPISCOPAL CHURCH, SOUTH
1845-1939

The LOUISVILLE CONVENTION of 1845, composed of representatives of the Conferences about to establish the Southern church, designated the Missionary Society of the M.E. Church in the City of Louisville as the provisional central missionary agency for the emerging denomination. The first GENERAL CONFERENCE, in 1846, established the Missionary Society of the M.E. Church, South to facilitate "missionary labors at home and in foreign countries."

The Society maintained headquarters in LOUISVILLE until 1856, and from then on, permanently and almost continuously in NASHVILLE. In 1866, the Church divided its missionary operations between a Board of Domestic Missions and a Board of Foreign Missions. But in 1870, the entire work was reunified, under a general Board of Missions, with combined financing of foreign and domestic projects. The General Conference of 1874 again revised the missions system, assigning basic responsibility for domestic missions to the Annual Conferences, and assigning the operation of all other missions to the General Board. The effect of this change was to make foreign, bilingual, and frontier missions a connectional interest under the Board, and to leave the support of underdeveloped areas within the established Conferences to the efforts of the Conferences themselves.

The first connectional auxiliary of the Board was the Woman's Missionary Society, founded in 1878 to unite the women of the Church "in the work of sending the gospel to women in heathen lands" through women workers, and renamed the Woman's Foreign Missionary Society in 1894. The Board of Church Extension was established in 1882. In 1886, it organized a Woman's Department, which in 1890 began home missionary work as the Woman's Parsonage and Home Missionary Society. This society, renamed the Woman's Home Mission Society, became independent of the Board of Church Extension in 1898.

The General Conference of 1910 effected a major reorganization of the Church's missions apparatus. Separate departments for foreign and for home missions were established in the general Board of Missions. The connectional Woman's Foreign Missionary Society and Woman's Home Mission Society were merged, becoming the Woman's Missionary Council, whose administrators and work (for women and children) were integrated into the structure of the Board. The Council reached its auxiliary home and foreign societies through its own Home and Foreign Departments. The first President of the Woman's Council (1910-22) was BELLE H. BENNETT, who earlier (1898-1910) had been President of the Woman's Home Mission Society.

In 1914, promotion of evangelism throughout the denomination was added to the major functions of the Board.

The executive leadership of the earlier Missionary Society and of the Board of Missions was concentrated perennially in the Secretary (from 1910, the General Secretary). Among the most notable incumbents were Edmund W. Sehon (1850-68), JOHN B. McFERRIN (1870-78; also Secretary of the Board of Domestic Missions, 1866-70), ALPHEUS W. WILSON (1878-82), Isaac G. John (1886-94), WALTER R. LAMBUTH (1894-1910), and WILLIAM W. PINSON (1910-22). (Considering his long ministry as a missionary, a Board secretary, and a bishop in charge of foreign fields, successively, Lambuth was the outstanding missionary leader of the Southern church.) In 1922, the Board was reorganized according to a pattern that dispersed executive responsibility among eight Administrative Secretaries, the office of General Secretary being abolished. The General Secretaryship was restored in 1926, and WILLARD G. CRAM, who had been a missionary in Korea, served in that office from 1926 to 1939.

The Southern church retained no foreign mission from the pre-Separation period, but carried over a large proportion of the domestic missions, including all of the Negro work and most of the American Indian work. The new denomination's missionary resources were devoted chiefly to domestic fields until late in the 1870's.

From that time on, current contributions to the Board for foreign work gradually rose to $721,000 in 1918 (not including Woman's Council income). Cooperating with the Northern church in the CENTENARY Movement of 1919-23, the Board radically increased its income during the five-year period. New foreign fields were entered, and appropriations were sharply increased. But less than fifty percent was paid on the total Centenary pledges by the end of the fifth fiscal year. At the close of 1925, the total operations of the Board showed a deficit of more than a million dollars. Regular contributions for foreign missions in that year were more than a third lower than in 1918, and were approximately the same in 1939.

The Board's first foreign venture was a mission to China established by CHARLES TAYLOR and BENJAMIN JENKINS in 1848.

Three missions were established in Latin America. Bishop JOHN C. KEENER organized one in Mexico in 1873. The Board of Missions began a second, in Brazil, by recognizing as a missionary (in 1875) JUNIUS E. NEWMAN, who was already resident there, and by sending from the United States JOHN J. RANSOM, who arrived in 1876. Missionary work in CUBA, begun in 1883, grew out of the interest of the FLORIDA CONFERENCE in domestic missions for Cuban immigrants, and developed for fifteen years in close association with that Conference, receiving a fresh stimulus in 1899, after being brought under the administration of the Board, following the Spanish-American War and liberation of Cuba.

The first missionaries to Japan—JAMES W. LAMBUTH, WALTER R. LAMBUTH, and O. A. Dukes—began their work in 1886. Ten years later, CLARENCE F. REID, a China missionary, became the first Southern Methodist missionary to Korea. Chiefly to reach emigrants across the northern borders of Korea, a Siberia Korean mission was begun in 1920. It developed work in Manchuria and in Siberian Russia. A decade later, the work in Russian territory was given up because of difficulties under the Soviet regime. The Manchurian work was transferred in 1930 to the Korean Methodist Church.

Bishop Walter R. Lambuth organized a mission in the Congo in 1914, with Charles C. Bush, D. L. MUMPOWER, and J. A. Stockwell as the first missionaries.

In Europe, permanent missions emerged from relief and social service work begun in BELGIUM, CZECHOSLOVAKIA, and POLAND in 1920.

Some of the foreign fields, beginning with Mexico in 1885, were organized into regular Annual Conferences of the Southern church. Bishops from the United States made supervisory visits abroad from time to time. During part of the quadrennium beginning in 1922, four bishops were in residence abroad—in BRUSSELS, Shanghai, SÃO PAULO (Brazil), and SEOUL. In 1926, bishops were assigned to Brussels and Shanghai only; and in 1930, such assignments were discontinued. From 1934 to 1939, foreign administration was handled mostly by a single bishop, ARTHUR J. MOORE. In 1906, the General Conference formalized the status of less advanced fields by constituting them Missions, with limited supervisory functions and (after 1910) limited General Conference representation.

In the quadrennium prior to 1930, three supervisory Central Conferences were organized—in Mexico, Europe, and Brazil. This was a minor development compared with the emergence of the Central Conferences in the Northern church.

The Japan Conference became a component of the autonomous Japan Methodist Church in 1907. The Board of Missions continued work in Japan both through the new denomination and through Board-controlled supplementary activity. In 1918, the latter work was designated the Japan Mission. In 1930, the Mexico Conference (3,700 members) and the Korea Conference (7,600 members) entered, respectively, the Methodist Church of Mexico and the Korean Methodist Church, both of them autonomous. In the same year, the three Brazil Conferences (15,000 members) became the autonomous Methodist Church of Brazil. The Board continued sending funds and personnel to the three churches founded in 1930.

By 1939, the Belgian, China, Cuba, and Czechoslovakia Conferences and the Congo and Polish Missions had a total of 29,000 church members, nearly half of them in China. (The membership of the Church in the United States was 2,953,000.) The Board was maintaining, through its general program, 111 foreign missionaries (including those associated with autonomous Methodist churches). The Section of Woman's Work, operating under appropriations of over $400,000, had 169 foreign missionaries.

METHODIST PROTESTANT CHURCH
1828-1939

The first GENERAL CONFERENCE (1834) founded a Board of Foreign Missions, with headquarters in BALTIMORE, later (1850) in PITTSBURGH. For nearly fifty years, despite its name, the Board concentrated almost entirely upon domestic missions.

The Pittsburgh board was continued from 1858 to 1877 by a group of Conferences in the North and West which withdrew after failing to persuade the M.P. Church to ban slaveholding by its members and to remove the Constitutional provision restricting church suffrage to whites. The seceded group merged in 1866 with certain Wesleyan and other non-episcopal Methodists, to form The Methodist Church. The Methodist Church and the South and East Conferences of the original M.P. Church united as the Methodist Protestant Church in 1877, the newly united Church establishing a Board of Missions as successor to the Pittsburgh board (removed at times to Springfield, Ohio; most recently in 1875).

The WOMAN'S FOREIGN MISSIONARY SOCIETY of the church was organized in Pittsburgh in 1879, and was recognized by the General Conference in 1880 as a permanent agency of the denomination. It worked autonomously, but in cooperation with the Board of Missions.

In 1888, the work of domestic missions was assigned to a new Board of Home Missions, the earlier board being renamed the Board of Foreign Missions. The WOMAN'S HOME MISSIONARY SOCIETY (later sometimes called the Woman's Board of Home Missions) was organized in Bridgeton, N. J., in 1893, and was recognized by the General Conference in 1896.

The Board of Foreign Missions and the Woman's Foreign Missionary Society were merged in 1924 as the Union Board of Foreign Missionary Administration, with headquarters in Pittsburgh. In 1928, the Union Board, the Board of Home Missions, and the Woman's Home Missionary Society were merged in a Board of Missions.

Among the Executive Secretaries for foreign missions were FRANK T. TAGG (1884-92), T. J. Ogburn (1896-1908), FREDERICK C. KLEIN (1908-26), and GEORGE W. HADDAWAY (1928-1939).

The denomination began its official foreign mission work in 1880 in Japan, when Harriet G. Brittain opened a school for girls in Yokohama. After some years of informal work in China, the Woman's Foreign Missionary Society undertook a regular mission in Kalgan, North China, with the cooperation of the American Board (Congregational). Charles S. Heininger, the first missionary, reached his post in 1910. The Kalgan project came under the control of the Board of Foreign Missions in June, 1919. Two years earlier the Board had taken over an independent mission in Dhulia, India, developed by Florence Williams and Mattie Long, who went to India in 1903.

The M.P. Church erected two of its foreign missions into Mission Annual Conferences—Japan (1892), China (1919)—with representation in the General Conference, and with administration assigned to the Foreign Board.

In 1939, the M.P. Church, which numbered about 197,000 members in the United States, had 6,000 members on its three foreign fields. It maintained fourteen foreign missionaries.

THE METHODIST CHURCH
1939-1968

The missionary interests (both home and foreign, both general and women's) of the three uniting denominations were merged into a single agency organized in July 1939, as the Board of Missions and Church Extension of The Methodist Church. The name was changed by order of the General Conference of 1952 to the Board of Missions of The Methodist Church.

The Constitution of the Board was grounded in a Disciplinary statement of the aim of missions—

The supreme aim of missions is to make the Lord Jesus Christ known to all peoples in all lands as their divine Saviour, to persuade them to become his disciples, and to gather these disciples into Christian churches; to enlist them in the building of the Kingdom of God; to cooperate with these churches; to promote world Christian fellowship; and to bring to bear on all human life the spirit and principles of Christ.

The Constitutional functions of the Board included the following—

(1) to help persons come to a knowledge of Jesus Christ as Savior and Lord of individuals and society; (2) to seek, as an agency of the Christian Church, to respond to God's action in Christ through engaging in religious, educational, social, medical, and agricultural work, in every part of the world, and to promote and support all phases of missionary and church extension activity in the United States and in other countries; (3) to aid persons to live and act as Christians in personal life and in the social order of all lands and among all peoples; (4) to foster, strengthen, and promote missionary understanding, interest, and zeal throughout The Methodist Church. . . . [Daily Christian Advocate (1960), 191].

The Board's administrative authority resided in the Board of Managers—a large body (nearly 150 persons) of bishops, ministers, and laymen which met annually, and whose interim powers were delegated to a General Executive Committee. The Board's chief officers were a president, General Secretary, and a treasurer.

The major activities of the Board were conducted through three divisions—the World Division, the National Division, the Woman's Division—and through a Joint Commission on Education and Cultivation. These groups were raised from among the Board members, were formally organized, and were under the executive leadership of their respective Associate General Secretaries.

Each Annual Conference maintained a Board of Missions auxiliary to the General Board, and each local church had a Commission on Missions auxiliary to the General and the Annual Conference boards. Auxiliaries of the Woman's Division (WOMAN'S SOCIETIES OF CHRISTIAN SERVICE) were organized in the respective Jurisdictions, Annual Conferences, and local churches.

The foreign missions were administered by the World Division. Until reorganization of the Board in 1964, the Department of Work in Foreign Fields of the Woman's Division also administered foreign missions. The basic financing of the work of the World Division was derived from a budgeted share of the Church's apportioned general benevolences (which are administered by the COUNCIL ON WORLD SERVICE AND FINANCE) and from special gifts. The latter, commonly called Advance Specials, account for about fifty-four percent of the Division's current income. The basic income of the Woman's Division was derived from gifts originating in local-church Woman's Society of Christian Service units. The two Divisions conducted their promotional and missionary education activities in cooperation with the National Division through the Joint Commission. Missionary recruitment was conducted by the Board's Joint Committee on Missionary Personnel.

The Board published two general monthly periodicals, which included presentations of the world missions cause—World Outlook (Joint Commission) and The Methodist Woman (Woman's Division).

Since 1940, the METHODIST COMMITTEE FOR OVERSEAS RELIEF (MCOR), an agency including members representing the Board, supplemented the Board's continuing foreign program by relief, rehabilitation, and refugee resettlement activities. Within the span of years since it came into being it resettled 15,000 refugees in the U.S., and distributed more than $24 million in aid abroad.

The World Division and the National Division were represented on the Church's Crusade Scholarship Committee, which provided financial assistance to train (in the U.S. and elsewhere) future leaders of churches in mission fields. After World War II, and up to 1964, 1,400 students from sixty countries were beneficiaries of the program. The basic financing was provided by the annual One Great Hour of Sharing offering.

For mission work in the several countries references must be had to the general articles under these countries. It will be understood that changes are rapidly taking place, not only due to the reorganization of The Methodist Church when it became The United Methodist Church, but epochal moves into autonomy which have taken place in various nations and are yet taking place.

The work in Europe, Asia, Africa, and Latin America will be found listed under the various nations. Cuba, Brazil, and Mexico have now autonomous Churches, and in Puerto Rico and the Dominican Republic the National Division of Missions administers work. This is likewise true of Alaska and Hawaii. Africa and the various mission fields of Africa are treated under such centers as Algeria and Tunisia, Liberia, the Congo, and certain of the new nations which have arisen within recent years. The Africa Central Conference has two bishops, resident in Salisbury and in Lubumbashi (former Elisabethville), respectively, the latter being a bishop of the Northeastern Jurisdiction.

Field Work. The patterns of field work done by Board missionaries have always been varied. The chief categories were church development, educational, medical, social-economic-industrial, agricultural-rural, literature and communications, and administrative. Some of the missionaries did several kinds of field work; many were specialists. Young people were assigned to some fields for three-year terms prior to commissioning as regular missionaries. Nearly 1,500 missionaries were assigned to overseas service. Under The Methodist Church until 1964, about one-third of them were under the direction of the Woman's Division.

Institutions. The Methodist Church participated in over a score of colleges and universities. Among those of Methodist origin are Aoyama Gakuin (Tokyo), Ewha University (Seoul), Soochow University Law School (Taipei), Lucknow Christian College, and Isabella Thoburn College (Lucknow), the first Christian college for women in Asia. There were several junior colleges in Asia and South America, Colegio Ward (Buenos Aires) and Santiago College (Chile) being among those founded by the Methodists. The Church was active in twenty-four interdenominational theological seminaries, and maintained several Methodist seminaries. It supported college-level teachers' colleges and normal schools in India and one each in Japan, Korea, and Pakistan. It participated in interdenomination vocational colleges—Allahabad Agricultural Institute, Ludhiana Medical College (India), Yonsei University Medical College (Seoul), Vellore Christian Medical College, and the nurses' training colleges of the last two institutions.

The Methodist enterprise included a score of schools for Christian workers below seminary level, Deaconess training schools, teacher training schools on the secondary level or below, and about 300 secondary or pre-secondary schools or school districts in twenty-four countries. Almost all of these were solely Methodist in operation.

There were thirty-nine Methodist-sponsored hospitals (a quarter of them interdenominational) located in Africa, Korea, Okinawa, the Philippines, Sarawak, India, Pakistan, Nepal, Bolivia, and Mexico, half of them maintaining nurses' training schools. Clara Swain Hospital (Meth.), Bareilly, India, founded in 1870, was the first hospital in Asia for women and children. There were also clinics, dispensaries, and medical centers, and colonies for leprosy patients (two-thirds were non-denominational).

Methodist institutional work overseas also included urban social centers, rural center projects, and a dozen printing and publishing enterprises. Their publications included periodicals in more than a dozen languages.

Cooperative Activity. The Methodist missionary movement participated extensively, both at home and on the foreign field, in many types of interdenominational activity and cooperation, and in the major phases of interchurch endeavor out of which the ecumenical movement has grown and continues to express itself. The Methodist Church was a charter member of the National Council of Churches of Christ in America, and of the World Council of Churches; its missionary agencies cooperated with the relevant agencies of these councils. The United Methodist Church continues this cooperation.

THE UNITED METHODIST CHURCH
1968-

In 1968 when The United Methodist Church was organized and took over the work of the former Methodist and Evangelical United Brethren Churches, an enlarged new organization was called for. This follows rather generally—and in the main rather closely—the organization of the Board of Missions of The Methodist Church as it has been delineated above. As the correlation of work in the various mission fields is still proceeding, the *Book of Discipline* must be referred to for all organizational changes and for future ones as these may be called for. The mission work is organized under the name of the Board of Missions of The United Methodist Church, and its headquarters remain in New York, and represent an enlargement of the Board's offices there as these were carried on for The Methodist Church.

The name of the Woman's Division has been changed to Women's Division and the Methodist Committee for Overseas Relief to the United Methodist Committee for Overseas Relief. The entire organization of this Board, as well as of other boards of the Church, is presently under study and structural changes may be anticipated in the next and future General Conferences. The correlation of the mission work of the E.U.B. Church and that of The Methodist Church is now proceeding, and that is causing administrative changes especially in the mission fields overseas from the United States. The autonomous Methodist churches which are organizing in various lands also have great bearing upon missionary activity, though in almost all instances a close tie is kept between the autonomous Methodist churches of these lands and the respective boards of missions which formerly sponsored and supported them.

Annual Reports of the various Missions bodies.
W. C. Barclay, *History of Missions.* 1949-57.
E. S. Bucke, *History of American Methodism.* 1964.
J. Cannon, *Southern Methodist Missions.* 1926.
Disciplines of the various branches of Methodism.
Journals of the General Conferences.
B. H. Lewis, *Methodist Overseas Missions.* 1960.
Minutes of the various Conferences.
Burton L. Goddard, ed., *Encyclopedia of Modern Christian Missions.* New York: Thomas Nelson and Sons, 1967.

N. B. H.

MISSISSIPPI, sometimes called the "Magnolia State," is in the south central part of the United States. Its name is derived from the Mississippi River, which means "Father of Waters." The state is bounded by TENNESSEE on the north, ALABAMA on the east, the Gulf of MEXICO and LOUISIANA on the south, and Louisiana on the west. Its area is 47,716 square miles, and in 1970 its population was 2,158,872.

Originally inhabited by three strong Indian tribes, the Natchez in the southwest, the Choctaws in the center and southeast, and the Chickasaws in the north, Mississippi was partly explored in 1540 by de Soto, a Spaniard, and in 1673 by Jacques Marquette and Louis Joliet of France. In 1682 la Salle reached the mouth of the Mississippi River and claimed for France all the territory drained by the river. He called it Louisiana for Louis XIV. In 1699 the French established Biloxi, the first white settlement in Mississippi.

At the end of the Seven Years War in 1763, France ceded to Great Britain its territory east of the Mississippi River with the exception of NEW ORLEANS, which with the vast Louisiana territory of the west went to Spain. Following the Revolutionary War England relinquished her part of that region to the United States. However, Spain took military possession of the land in 1781 and did not withdraw its troops until 1798. The Mississippi Territory of the United States was then organized, and in 1804 it was extended to the state of Tennessee on the north and to the Gulf of Mexico on the south; it was restricted on the east by the creation of the Alabama Territory. In 1817 Mississippi was admitted to the Union as a state, and, after a series of settlements with the Indians culminating in 1832, the entire state was opened to settlers who then poured into the area. On Jan. 9, 1861, Mississippi became the second state to secede from the Union. It suffered great losses during the Civil War. The fall of its important stronghold of VICKSBURG on July 4, 1863 was a disaster for the South and an important victory for the North.

Methodism began in Mississippi in 1799 when TOBIAS GIBSON traveled the hazardous trail from his home in SOUTH CAROLINA to preach to a few settlers in and around Natchez. In the village of Washington, near Natchez, Gibson organized the first Methodist congregation west of GEORGIA and south of Tennessee. In 1813 the MISSISSIPPI CONFERENCE was organized. At the time it included all of Mississippi below the Indian settlements in the north, a part of western Alabama, and the main portions of Louisiana. ELIZABETH FEMALE ACADEMY, operated under the direction of the Mississippi Methodists at Washington from 1818 until 1847, may have been the first chartered institution exclusively for the higher education of women in America. In 1832 the Alabama portion of the Mississippi Conference, along with Mississippi's eastern tier of counties, was placed in the newly formed ALABAMA CONFERENCE. From 1837 to 1839 all Methodist work in TEXAS came under the direction of the Mississippi Conference. Following the division of the church in 1844, the Mississippi Conference adhered South. In January, 1847 the LOUISIANA CONFERENCE of the M.E. Church, South was organized. However, the east portion of Louisiana, except New Orleans and BATON ROUGE, remained in the Mississippi Conference until 1894.

Methodism in northern Mississippi began in 1819 when EBENEZER HEARN was appointed by the TENNESSEE CON-FERENCE to the Buttahatchie Circuit. The exact boundaries of the circuit are not known, but it covered five counties in Alabama and extended into northeast Mississippi. A barrier of Indians in north Mississippi kept the work of the Mississippi Conference from extending farther northward in the early years. Beginning in 1821, however, circuit riders from the Mississippi Conference penetrated the northern part of the state. In 1870 the NORTH MISSISSIPPI CONFERENCE (MES) was formed.

After the Civil War the M.E. Church followed the occupation forces into the South, forming churches among Negroes and among some of the whites. In 1865 the Northern church organized the Mississippi Mission Conference, which was made up mostly of Negroes; its territory included Mississippi, Louisiana, and Texas. Four years later this body was divided to form the MISSISSIPPI CONFERENCE which included only the state of Mississippi. The Negro work grew rapidly, and in 1891 the Mississippi Conference itself was divided to form the UPPER MISSISSIPPI CONFERENCE. Both conferences were continued in the Central Jurisdiction in 1939.

In 1870, the year the C.M.E. CHURCH was organized, it formed a conference in Mississippi. Today this denomination has two conferences in the state—Mississippi and Upper Mississippi. The A.M.E. CHURCH and the A.M.E. ZION CHURCH have established work in Mississippi. Organized in the north in 1816 and 1820, respectively, these churches moved into the South following the Civil War and vigorously evangelized among the Negroes. Today the A.M.E. Zion Church has two conferences in Mississippi—South Mississippi, and West Tennessee and Mississippi. The A.M.E. Church also has two conferences in the state—North Mississippi and Mississippi.

METHODIST PROTESTANTISM began in Mississippi as early as 1828, and it organized a Mississippi Conference in 1841 with Elisha Lott as president. The Texas Conference was set off from the Mississippi Conference in 1848, and the North Mississippi Conference in 1854. In 1870 the Mississippi Conference voted to unite with the Mississippi Conference (MES), and seven M.P. preachers were received as itinerants in that body. The next year the MISSISSIPPI CONFERENCE (MP) started over again with one itinerant and four laymen, and thereafter it grew steadily if slowly; within a decade it had about 1,000 members and by the turn of the century about 3,000. The two conferences continued until unification in 1939. Shortly before unification, the North Mississippi Conference reported eleven charges, twenty churches, and 1,340 members. The Mississippi Conference had fifty ministers, twenty-six charges, seventy-two church buildings, and 4,898 members. However, twenty-one preachers and sixteen churches chose not to enter The Methodist Church.

Today the Mississippi and the North Mississippi Conferences of The United Methodist Church divide the state between them. On the abolition of the Central Jurisdiction in 1968, the Mississippi and Upper Mississippi Conferences were placed temporarily in the Jackson Area of the Southeastern Jurisdiction pending merger.

Mississippi Methodism supports three colleges: MILLSAPS at Jackson, WOOD JUNIOR COLLEGE at Mathiston, and RUST at Holly Springs. It also maintains a number of hospitals, homes, camps, and WESLEY FOUNDATIONS. In 1968 the four Mississippi conferences had a total of twenty districts, 671 charges, and approximately 219,618 members. Their church property including parsonages was valued at $81,287,316.

J. B. Cain, *Mississippi Conference*. 1939.
General Minutes, ME, MES, TMC.
W. L. Hamrick, *Mississippi Conference* (MP). 1957.
J. G. Jones, *Mississippi*. 1908
W. B. Jones, *Mississippi Conference*. 1951.
J. A. Lindsey, *Mississippi Conference*. 1964.
G. R. Miller, *North Mississippi*. 1966.
Minutes of the Mississippi and North Mississippi Conferences.

J. B. CAIN

MISSISSIPPI CONFERENCE was organized at the home of NEWIT VICK, a preacher who was not a conference member at the time, on Nov. 1, 1813. The location was about five miles southwest of Fayette in Jefferson County. It was planned that either Bishop ASBURY or Bishop MCKENDREE would come from the TENNESSEE CONFERENCE, which met on October 3, and preside at the organization of the new conference which was to be composed of the MISSISSIPPI and LOUISIANA preachers, but because of Indian troubles in ALABAMA and Mississippi the brethren in Tennessee practically forbade the bishops to risk the journey. Consequently Samuel Sellers presided at the first session of the Mississippi Conference and WILLIAM WINANS acted as secretary. Ten preachers were present. As it turned out, due to the War of 1812 and danger from the Indians, no bishop attended a session of the Mississippi Conference until Oct. 10, 1816 when it met at the home of William Foster on Pine Ridge seven miles north of Natchez, with Bishop ROBERT R. ROBERTS presiding. During those first three years conference members served as president, substituting for the bishop in every capacity except the ordination of preachers.

When Methodist work began in Mississippi it was a part of the WESTERN CONFERENCE. Beginning in 1806 there was a Mississippi District in the conference, LEARNER BLACKMAN serving as the first presiding elder. In 1812 the Western Conference was divided to form the Tennessee Conference, the latter to include the Mississippi District and several other districts to the north. In creating the Tennessee Conference, the 1812 General Conference authorized the bishops to form another annual conference "down the Mississippi" any time during the next four years "if they find it to be necessary." Such was the authority for the formation of the Mississippi Conference in 1813.

According to the 1816 *Discipline*, the Mississippi Conference included "all the state of Louisiana south of the Arkansas [River], and all the Mississippi Territory south of the Tennessee River." What is now Alabama was a part of the conference. When formed in 1813 the Mississippi Conference reported seven charges and 1,067 white and 240 colored members. The total membership nearly doubled the next year, but in 1816 the figures were 1,531 white and 410 colored members.

By 1819 the Mississippi Conference had grown to three districts, Mississippi, Louisiana, and Alabama, and it reported 2,170 white and 361 Negro members. In 1832 the Alabama Conference was organized to include Alabama south of the Tennessee River and the eastern tier of counties in Mississippi. In 1837 the Mississippi Conference was enlarged to include TEXAS within its bounds, an arrangement which continued until 1840 when the TEXAS CONFERENCE was formed. When the M. E. Church was divided in 1844 the Mississippi Conference of course adhered South.

In December, 1845, the districts were rearranged and the appointments made in readiness for the creation of the LOUISIANA CONFERENCE by the 1846 General Conference. Louisiana, east of the Mississippi River, except for the cities of New Orleans and Baton Rouge, remained in the Mississippi Conference until 1894.

In 1853 when the Mississippi Conference was forty years old it had fifty-six charges and 14,258 white and 10,071 colored members. In that year JAMES W. LAMBUTH, father of Bishop WALTER R. LAMBUTH, joined the conference, and volunteered as a missionary for CHINA; he did pioneer work in the Orient for nearly forty years.

The M. E. Church, South began publishing the *New Orleans Christian Advocate* in 1851. It soon became the official organ of the Mississippi and Louisiana Conferences and continued as such until 1946 when the Mississippi Conference joined the NORTH MISSISSIPPI CONFERENCE in publishing the *Mississippi Methodist Advocate*. Through the years several Mississippi preachers served as editor of the New Orleans paper, among them CHARLES B. GALLOWAY and J. LLOYD DECELL, who later became bishops.

The Mississippi Conference was interested in education, supporting or patronizing through the years prior to 1870 some sixteen academies and colleges. ELIZABETH FEMALE ACADEMY (1818-1847) at Washington near Natchez, may have been the first school in America chartered exclusively for the higher education of women. In recognition of the academy's priority the Daughters of the American Revolution have placed a marker on its original site. Port Gibson Female Academy began in 1826 and continued until 1929. Sharon and Madison Colleges flourished before the Civil War. CENTENARY COLLEGE, now at SHREVEPORT, La., was started by the Mississippi Conference at Brandon Springs, Miss., in 1841. It was soon moved to Jackson, La., which was within the bounds of the Mississippi Conference until 1894. The two conferences jointly supported Centenary until 1892, when Mississippi Methodism established MILLSAPS COLLEGE. The Mississippi Conference operated Whitworth College for women at Brookhaven from 1859 to 1938 when it was merged with Millsaps.

In 1888 the Mississippi Conference appointed a committee to confer with the North Mississippi Conference on establishing a Methodist college in Mississippi. Four years later the school, named for R. W. MILLSAPS, whose liberal donations helped to launch it, opened at Jackson. Today it is a strong Methodist college. Two of its presidents, both members of the North Mississippi Conference, have been elected bishop, W. B. MURRAH in 1910 and H. ELLIS FINGER, JR. in 1964. Another president, A. F. WATKINS, was secretary of the GENERAL CONFERENCE from 1910 to 1926. The conference has given support to PAINE COLLEGE, Augusta, Ga.

In 1913 at the end of its first century the Mississippi Conference had seven districts, 160 charges, 568 churches, and 55,133 members. At unification in 1939 there were 194 preachers, 161 charges, 521 churches, and 81,470 members. These joined with seventeen preachers, seventy-three churches, and 4,816 members of the Mississippi Conference (MP) to form the Mississippi Conference of The Methodist Church.

Through the years the Mississippi Conference has had a number of able leaders. Prior to the Civil War the two outstanding men in the conference were William Winans

(1788-1857) and BENJAMIN M. DRAKE (1800-1860). Drake was a member of every General Conference from 1828 until his death. He worked in the General Conference for higher educational standards for the Methodist ministry. CHARLES B. GALLOWAY, elected bishop at thirty-six, was the premier pulpit orator in American Methodism. J. T. Leggett, presiding elder for twenty-two years, and Bishop J. LLOYD DECELL were outstanding conference leaders in the twentieth century. Bishop NOLAN B. HARMON, though not a member of the conference, was born at Meridian and graduated from Millsaps College.

At the present time the conference supports Millsaps College in JACKSON and WOOD JUNIOR COLLEGE at Mathiston; the Methodist Hospital at Hattiesburg and the proposed Mississippi Methodist Hospital at Jackson; the Methodist Children's Home at Jackson; the SEASHORE METHODIST ASSEMBLY and the Seashore Manor on the Gulf coast; Camp Wesley Pines; and WESLEY FOUNDATIONS at the state schools.

In 1970 the Mississippi Conference had six districts, Brookhaven, Hattiesburg, Jackson, Meridian, Seashore, and Vicksburg. It reported 335 ministers, 302 charges, 105,431 members, and property valued at $44,750,264.

General Minutes, ME, MES, TMC, UMC.
Minutes of the Mississippi Conference.
J. G. Jones, *Mississippi*. 1908.
J. B. Cain, *Mississippi Conference*. 1939.   J. B. CAIN

MISSISSIPPI CONFERENCE (ME, 1868) was created by the 1868 GENERAL CONFERENCE by dividing the MISSISSIPPI MISSION CONFERENCE. The new conference was organized at Canton, Miss., Jan. 7, 1869 with Bishop MATTHEW SIMPSON presiding. This conference is not to be confused with the Mississippi Conference which was organized in 1813 and which became the Mississippi Conference of the M. E. Church, South after the division in 1844.

At its organization in 1869, the Mississippi Conference reported two districts—Jackson and Holly Springs—twenty-seven charges, 8,732 members, 2,219 probationers, and sixteen church buildings and five parsonages valued at $32,035. By 1872 there were over 28,000 members including probationers. Thereafter growth was moderate; in 1890 the conference reported 152 charges and a total of 31,603 members. The next year the conference was divided to form the UPPER MISSISSIPPI CONFERENCE. The division left the Mississippi Conference with three districts and about 15,000 members.

In 1939 the Mississippi Conference became a part of the Central Jurisdiction of The Methodist Church. At that time it had five districts, 102 charges, and 21,981 members. The conference supports RUST COLLEGE at Holly Springs. In 1967 the appropriation for the college from conference funds was $975.

Gulfside Assembly at Waveland, Miss., is within the bounds of the Mississippi Conference. Gulfside has served as the summer assembly of the Central Jurisdiction. It is a thirty-acre tract on the Gulf of Mexico. The facility has a three-story inn with dormitory accommodations and a cafeteria, a two-story hall, two lodges, five cottages, a snack shop, and an auditorium which will seat 1,000. Also, there is an administration building with offices, class rooms, and a library. All of this property was badly damaged, and some of it destroyed by the great hurricane of the late summer of 1969.

In 1967 the Mississippi Conference reported four districts, 69 ministers, 82 charges, 22,191 members and property valued at $3,357,404. On the abolition of the Central Jurisdiction in 1968, the conference was placed in the Jackson Area of the Southeastern Jurisdiction pending merger.

General Minutes, ME and TMC.
Minutes of the Mississippi Conference. FREDERICK E. MASER

MISSISSIPPI METHODIST ADVOCATE, THE a sixteen-page weekly newspaper, is an integral part of MISSISSIPPI Methodism. Published in JACKSON, Miss., it is the official organ of the Jackson Area composed of the MISSISSIPPI and NORTH MISSISSIPPI CONFERENCES.

The *Advocate* is used by the bishop, the cabinets, conference boards and commissions, pastors, laymen, the WOMAN'S SOCIETY and the METHODIST YOUTH FELLOWSHIP for promotion of the work of the church in Mississippi. It gathers news of Methodist activities from all over the world and records the progress, efforts and achievements of churches at home. Through its pages, the aims, purposes, needs and activities of Mississippi Methodist institutions, colleges, hospitals and homes, are constantly kept before the readers. Church school teachers gain help through the lessons prepared by ministers from the area. The paper memorializes the honored dead.

The *Mississippi Methodist Advocate*, the successor to the *New Orleans Christian Advocate*, which served Methodism in the South for more than one hundred years, was established in June 1947. C. T. Howell of Birmingham, Ala., was the first editor (1947-1955). The new paper was sixteen pages (44 x 60 picas) and published by Oliver Emmerick of McComb. Later the printing contract was taken over by Tombigbee Printing Company of Jackson. The organ struggled under financial difficulties during its growing years.

In 1955, Samuel E. Ashmore of the North Mississippi Conference was appointed editor. The Advocate office was located in the Science building at MILLSAPS COLLEGE. In 1957 the office moved to the new Methodist Building. Today Thornton Publishers do the printing and mailing of the periodical which is 57 x 81 picas.

ANN L. ASHMORE

MISSISSIPPI MISSION CONFERENCE (ME), composed largely of colored ministers and churches, was organized at NEW ORLEANS, La., Dec. 25, 1865. Its territory included MISSISSIPPI, LOUISIANA, and TEXAS. At the beginning the conference had four districts—New Orleans, Opelousas, Mississippi, and Texas—and there were sixteen preachers, 2,692 members, and five churches valued at $47,000. The next year the Texas work was set off as the Texas Mission Conference, though that group did not meet to organize until January 1867.

The 1868 GENERAL CONFERENCE divided the Mississippi Mission Conference to form the Louisiana and Mississippi Conferences of the M. E. Church. When they met for organization in January 1869, the two conferences together reported a total of more than 23,500 members including probationers, an indication of how rapidly the M. E. Church grew among the Negroes in the South following the Civil War.

General Minutes, MEC.   FREDERICK E. MASER

MISSOULA, MONTANA, U.S.A. **First Church** was one of the pioneer churches of the northwest. The first Methodist minister to reach Missoula was George Comfort, who came in 1869; and his successor as superintendent was J. A. Van Anda. But the first regularly appointed pastor was THOMAS C. ILIFF, in 1871. He served three years, organized a church for the one or two hundred whites there, and built a church which was dedicated on Sept. 15, 1872. The cost was $2,300; and $500 of that amount was the gift of the pastor, and another $500 was borrowed from the CHURCH EXTENSION SOCIETY. At the time, it was the only Protestant church building between Helena and Walla Walla. Hugh Duncan was the next pastor; he stayed only one year, and the church was then without a pastor for a period, served by supply pastors from time to time; among them FRANCIS RIGGIN and W. W. VAN ORSDEL (Brother Van).

Brother Van reorganized the church on May 22, 1892. Only one of the original members was there, Mrs. W. H. H. Dickinson. She lived to participate in the semi-centennial celebration in 1921. She was the first school teacher in Missoula county, and her marriage to Mr. Dickinson was the first Protestant marriage ceremony in western MONTANA. One of Missoula's public schools is named for her.

During the 90's, the financial crisis nearly ended the life of the church. A heavy debt finally led the Church Extension Society to vote to sell the property to the Protestant Episcopal Church; but Francis Riggin made the trip to PHILADELPHIA at his own expense and persuaded the Society to abandon this plan, to accept one-half of the amount as full payment, and persuaded the preachers at the Conference session to contribute the money to pay off the debt.

J. W. Bennet returned to Missoula for a second pastorate in 1910 and pushed through a plan to build a new church. It was built at a cost of $50,000 and dedicated by Thomas C. Iliff, forty years after he had built the first church. At the time, it was the most pretentious structure yet erected by Montana Methodists. It was an Akron-plan structure, and served the congregation until 1956. Trinity M. E. Church, South was merged with First M. E. Church in 1939; and at about the same time, the WESLEY FOUNDATION at the University of Montana was organized and has continued to be a major emphasis of the church program.

In 1957, a new sanctuary was built at the same site and using the lots formerly occupied by the parsonage. The cost of the new parsonage, new pipe organ and remodeled building was nearly $400,000. Eight years later the present plant was completed by the erection of an educational wing at the cost of $1,000,000. The present membership of First Church is 1,455; a new church, St. John, has been organized by Missoula Methodists and is serving a growing congregation in the city.

E. L. Mills, *Plains, Peaks and Pioneers.* 1947.

HUGH S. HERBERT

MISSOURI is in the center of seventeen states located in the great MISSISSIPPI Valley. The state takes its name from its largest river which in turn was named for a tribe of Indians that once lived near the river's mouth. The state's area is 69,674 square miles, and in 1970 its population was over 4,630,000.

The first white settlers in Missouri were the French. They established St. Genevieve in 1735 and ST. LOUIS

in 1764. Spanish rule began in 1771. In 1800 the region went back to France, and the United States acquired it in the Louisiana Purchase of 1803.

Missouri became a territory in 1812 and, under the Missouri Compromise, it entered the Union as a slave state in 1821. As a border state in the Civil War, about 50,000 of its men were in the Southern armies and some 100,000 in the Northern forces.

Methodism entered Missouri in the late summer of 1798. JOHN CLARK, a Scotsman who came to ILLINOIS via GEORGIA, preached the first Methodist sermon in Missouri near Herculaneum from a boat tied to a rock on the west bank of the Mississippi River. In 1805, following a CAMP MEETING conducted at Spanish Pond, Clark formed a Methodist class, and in January of the following year he organized a second class at Patterson. Clark later joined the Baptists.

In 1805, WILLIAM McKENDREE, presiding elder in the WESTERN CONFERENCE, sent JOSEPH OGLESBY into Missouri on a reconnaisance tour. On his return Oglesby reported that there were 200 likely prospects for Methodism in the region. Encouraged by Oglesby's report, the Western Conference appointed John Travis to the Missouri Circuit in 1806. After a year of work Travis reported the establishment of two circuits, the Missouri and the Meramec, with 100 white and six colored members.

The first Methodist church in Missouri was organized in 1807 at Coldwater near St. Louis by William McKendree, John Travis, and JESSE WALKER. There were thirty-nine members, most of them coming from the two classes previously formed by John Clark. Methodist classes were organized at Mt. Zion near St. Louis in 1806, CAPE GIRARDEAU and the site of McKENDREE CHAPEL in 1809, NEW MADRID in 1810, and Fredericktown in 1811. New Madrid and Fredericktown are the two oldest continuing Methodist congregations west of the Mississippi River. By 1811 there were five Methodist circuits in Missouri with 480 white and thirty-two colored members.

Shiloh Church, the first Methodist meetinghouse west of the Mississippi River, was built between 1810 and 1814 in Bellevue Valley some seventy-five miles south of St. Louis. In 1819 McKendree Chapel, made of hewn poplar logs, was erected near Jackson. The original structure still stands, and it is recognized as the oldest Protestant church building west of the Mississippi River. The 1960 GENERAL CONFERENCE designated it as a national Methodist HISTORIC SHRINE.

The MISSOURI CONFERENCE was organized by Bishop McKendree at Shiloh Meetinghouse near Belleville, Ill., in 1816. At the time the conference included Missouri, ARKANSAS, Illinois, and eastern INDIANA.

The early circuit riders bypassed St. Louis for several reasons. For one thing, the Protestant immigrants, the people most receptive to Methodism's evangelistic message, were settling mostly on farms in the rural areas, and there was plenty of work to do among them. Second, the Methodist preachers of that day felt unprepared educationally or otherwise to win converts and establish churches in the cities generally. Third, the prospects in St. Louis were particularly discouraging because many of its citizens were Roman Catholics while many others were godless adventurers given to vice and lawlessness. To assault such a citadel of wickedness seemed inadvisable if not foolish. But avoidance of St. Louis was not to continue indefinitely. In 1811, five years after John Travis had been appointed as the first Methodist itinerant in

Missouri, George Colbert preached occasionally in St. Louis, as did Jesse Walker in the years immediately following. Then in 1817 JOHN SCRIPPS made St. Louis a preaching point on the Coldwater Circuit which he was serving. Finally, in 1821 the Missouri Conference, deciding that it was time to make a serious attempt to establish a church in St. Louis, appointed Jesse Walker as conference missionary. The intrepid Walker organized a congregation and erected a building on Fourth Street in 1822, the first Protestant church edifice in the city. The Missouri Conference met in St. Louis that year for the first time in its history. Walker reported ninety-five white and thirty-two colored members. In 1839 the Negroes built their own church in St. Louis, probably the first Negro Methodist church in Missouri.

In 1830 the Missouri Conference organized a missionary society and sent two of its ablest men, Thomas Johnson and his brother William, as missionaries to the Shawnee and the Kansa Indians, thus beginning a successful work among Indians which led to the organization of the INDIAN MISSION CONFERENCE in 1844.

After the division of the M.E. Church in 1844, the Missouri Conference adhered South. For the time being this left the M.E. Church with no organized work in the state. In 1846 the Missouri Conference (MES) was divided, the area south of the Missouri River becoming the ST. LOUIS CONFERENCE. In 1871 the southwest quarter of the state was set off as the West St. Louis Conference, the name being changed to the SOUTHWEST MISSOURI CONFERENCE in 1874. These three conferences were continued intact until Methodist unification in 1939.

In 1848 the M.E. Church re-entered Missouri, forming the MISSOURI CONFERENCE which included Missouri, Arkansas, and territory to the west. In 1852 the name was changed to the Missouri and Arkansas Conference. The next year this body was divided to form an ARKANSAS CONFERENCE and a Missouri Conference, the latter including most of Missouri, and KANSAS and NEBRASKA. In the next few years several changes in names and boundaries of conferences were made. Then in 1869 the work in north Missouri was designated as the Missouri Conference and that in south Missouri and Arkansas as the St. Louis Conference. There was an Arkansas Conference from 1873 to 1920, when it merged with the St. Louis Conference. Then from 1931 to 1939 the Missouri Conference again included all of Missouri and Arkansas. In 1886 the M.E. Church organized the Central Missouri Conference to include its Negro work in the state. In 1928 this conference absorbed a part of the Lincoln Conference (the latter had covered several states) to form the CENTRAL WEST CONFERENCE.

The M.E. Church, South established the *St. Louis Christian Advocate* in 1851. An influential paper, it continued until 1928. The *Central Christian Advocate* began as a private enterprise in 1854 and was made an official organ by the M.E. Church GENERAL CONFERENCE in 1856. It continued until Methodist unification.

Other branches of Methodism had work in Missouri. The METHODIST PROTESTANTS came into Missouri as early as 1836, and formed in 1850 the Missouri Conference which continued until unification in 1939. In 1852, however, the M.P. work was divided to form the Platte Conference in the northwest part of the state. In 1867 the Platte Conference was superseded by the North Missouri Conference which in 1916 merged with the Iowa Conference to form the Iowa-Missouri Conference. At the

time of unification there were sixty M.P. churches in Missouri with some 4,000 members.

German Methodism began in Missouri in 1841 when the M.E. Church appointed LUDWIG S. JACOBY as a missionary among the Germans of St. Louis. In spite of persecutions from the secular Germans of the city, Jacoby organized a congregation of forty and soon had it housed in a small frame church. Opposed to slavery, the Germans adhered North after the division of 1844. Between 1845 and 1850 German work in Missouri developed rapidly. There were about 50,000 Germans in the state, and German circuits were established in communities along the Mississippi and Missouri Rivers. In later years St. Louis became an important center of German Methodism.

These German churches were in the English-speaking conferences until 1864 when the General Conference authorized German language conferences. In 1879 the ST. LOUIS GERMAN CONFERENCE, including east Missouri, south Illinois, and south Iowa, was organized by dividing the Southwest German Conference. In 1925 the St. Louis German Conference merged with the overlying conferences of the M.E. Church.

The A.M.E. CHURCH, the A.M.E. ZION CHURCH, and the C.M.E. CHURCH began work in Missouri in the nineteenth century. In 1840 the A.M.E. Church organized the Indiana Conference which included Missouri and several other states north and south in its boundaries. The conference territory was too vast for effective work, especially since it included both free and slave states, a situation which created problems for free ministers appointed to churches in the South. In 1852, the Missouri Conference was created to include all churches of the denomination in the slave-holding states of the West and South. The work prospered and by 1956 there were three A.M.E. conferences operating in Missouri: Missouri, North Missouri, and Southwest Missouri.

The A.M.E. Zion Church organized the Missouri Conference in 1890. By 1906 it had eleven churches and 1,765 members. Ten years later there were sixteen churches and over 4,000 members. In mid-century the conference had about twenty churches in the state and a vital community program in St. Louis.

The C.M.E. Church, though not as strong as either of the other Negro bodies, is active in Missouri. Parts of two conferences, the Kansas-Missouri and the Southwest Illinois, operate in the state.

In 1835 the first Methodist college in Missouri was established at St. Charles. After a long career of service it closed in 1915. From 1835 to the present about 100 academies, schools, and colleges have been established in Missouri under Methodist auspices. Only about ten could be called colleges. Many were short lived. CENTRAL METHODIST COLLEGE in Fayette, founded in 1855 by the M.E. Church, South, is the only Methodist college in the state today. The institution has about 1,000 students, an endowment of more than $4,250,000 and buildings worth over $7,000,000.

At unification in 1939, the five conferences in Missouri were reduced to three which conformed to the boundaries of the three conferences of the former Southern church. In 1960 these were consolidated into the MISSOURI EAST and MISSOURI WEST CONFERENCES.

Following the division in 1844 and until long after the Civil War, ill feeling between the two branches of Episcopal Methodism was perhaps more intense in Missouri than in any other state. This was due in part to the fact that Missouri was a border state. It is not too much to say that during the war, civil, social and religious life fell apart. Churches were closed, some preachers were imprisoned, and some were exiled. Methodists on both sides suffered indignities of various kinds. When the war was over immigration brought in many people from north and east who enabled the M.E. Church to grow rapidly. As a result the two branches of Methodism built altar against altar in many parts of the state.

After the report of the CAPE MAY COMMISSION in 1876, however, prayer and tentative efforts on behalf of Methodist unity began in Missouri. The annual conferences exchanged fraternal messengers; competing churches united in revivals and other activities; and after 1905 conference committees "exchanged churches," a procedure which resulted, in many places, in only one Methodist church where formerly there had been two in competition. From 1890 on the annual conferences of both churches in Missouri urged their General Conferences to prepare plans for unification, and as the years passed they overwhelmingly approved each proposal which was presented. The final plan which actually brought unification was approved almost unanimously in Missouri. When actual unification was effected, the northern and southern branches of Methodism in Missouri were more evenly divided—three Southern Methodists to two Northern ones —than in any other state. Yet it is claimed that nowhere else in American Methodism was unification more smoothly arranged, nor as the years passed was it more successful than in Missouri.

In 1970 the two Missouri conferences supported a children's home in St. Louis, a home for the aged in Marionville, four hospitals, four youth camps, and WESLEY FOUNDATIONS at the nine state schools. Between them the conferences had 664 charges, 805 ministers, 252,443 members, and church property valued at $115,340,770.

General Minutes, ME, MES, TMC, UMC.
Minutes and Disciplines of denominations and annual conferences.
F. C. Tucker, Missouri. 1966.   FRANK C. TUCKER

MISSOURI CONFERENCE was organized at Shiloh Church near Belleville, Ill., on Sept. 13, 1816 with Bishop WILLIAM McKENDREE presiding. Its territory included western INDIANA, ILLINOIS, MISSOURI, and ARKANSAS, an area so large that it now contains more than a dozen conferences. The first session of the conference in Missouri was held at McKENDREE CHAPEL near Jackson in September 1819. The importance of McKendree Chapel in the early years is indicated by the fact that the conference met there three more times—1821, 1826, and 1831. In 1817 the conference reported 3,100 white and seventy-three colored members. (See MISSOURI for beginnings of Methodism in the state.) In 1824 the conference was divided to form the ILLINOIS CONFERENCE, and in 1836 the Arkansas Conference was set off from Missouri.

The first missionary endeavor of the Missouri Conference was in 1830 when it sent Thomas Johnson and his brother William as missionaries to the Shawnee and the Kansa Indians. In 1835 the conference established St. Charles College which continued until 1915.

In 1845 the Missouri Conference reported 23,781 white and 2,529 colored members. The church having divided, the conference voted overwhelmingly that year to adhere

South. Since there was some northern sentiment in the conference, the M.E. Church soon organized a conference in the state which continued until unification in 1939. (See MISSOURI CONFERENCE [1848-1939].)

In 1846 the Missouri Conference (MES) divided to form the ST. LOUIS CONFERENCE which included the part of the state below the Missouri River. This left the Missouri Conference with 9,704 white and 1,025 colored members. By 1860 the membership had more than doubled— 17,717 white and 2,006 colored members. The Civil War brought disaster; in 1866 the conference had only 11,551 white and 346 colored members. However, recovery was rapid; in 1869 the conference reported more than 19,000 members.

In 1900 the Missouri Conference had 170 charges, 498 churches, and 44,431 members. In the next thirty-nine years the membership grew a little, but since its territory was largely rural with a decreasing farm population, the number of charges and churches declined. The conference came to unification in 1939 with 136 charges, 340 churches, and 49,421 members.

The Missouri Conference owned or was affiliated with eight educational institutions in 1900, including St. Charles College, CENTRAL COLLEGE and Howard-Payne College at Fayette, and Central College for Women at Lexington. By 1920 the number of schools had dropped to three, and by 1930 to one—Central College which, though within the bounds of the Missouri Conference, was supported by all of Southern Methodism in Missouri.

One member of the Missouri Conference, EUGENE R. HENDRIX, was elected bishop in 1886 while serving as president of Central College. Two other men who attained the episcopacy, ENOCH M. MARVIN and WILLIAM F. McMURRY, began their ministry in the Missouri Conference but were not members of it at the time of their election.

After unification in 1939, there was sentiment in Missouri Methodism for consolidating the three conferences into two or possibly into one. Over the years several interconference commissions drafted plans which proved unacceptable to one or more of the conferences. Merging into two conferences seemed logical, but there was no agreement on how to divide the state. As the "mother conference," the Missouri body was reluctant to agree to any realignment that would bisect its territory or do away with its name. But in the end, that conference, concluding that the other two would agree on no other plan, concurred, and by authority of the 1960 South Central JURISDICTIONAL CONFERENCE, the three conferences were consolidated into the MISSOURI EAST and MISSOURI WEST CONFERENCES, effective in 1961.

At its last session in 1961, the Missouri Conference reported six districts, 212 charges, 77,676 members, and property valued at $32,416,418.

General Minutes, ME, MES, TMC.
Minutes of the Missouri Conference.
F. C. Tucker, Missouri. 1966.   FREDERICK E. MASER

MISSOURI CONFERENCE (ME, 1848), which was organized in 1816, adhered South in 1845 by a vote of eighty-six to fourteen. According to the 1844 GENERAL CONFERENCE PLAN OF SEPARATION, the entire conference was obligated to go the way the majority voted. But the 1848 Northern General Conference repudiated the Plan of

Separation, and it proceeded to establish another Missouri Conference that year which included MISSOURI and ARKANSAS and territory to the west. This Missouri Conference was organized at the session of the Illinois Conference in Belleville, Sept. 13, 1848. The printed minutes show that the conference had two districts in Missouri and one in Arkansas, twenty-two charges, and a total of 1,538 members. The next year the conference met at Ebenezer Church in ST. LOUIS, a congregation of 140 members which had erected a church building in 1846. Preachers from Missouri, Arkansas, TEXAS, KANSAS, and NEBRASKA were present at the conference.

In 1852 the Missouri Conference was divided to form the Arkansas Conference, the latter to include the southern part of Missouri as well as Arkansas. Two quadrenniums later the two states were placed together again as the Missouri and Arkansas Conference. Then in 1868 north Missouri was designated as the Missouri Conference, while south Missouri and Arkansas formed the St. Louis Conference. Four years later Arkansas was set off to itself again as a conference, an arrangement which continued until 1920 when the Arkansas Conference was absorbed by the St. Louis Conference. In 1925 the absorption of the ST. LOUIS GERMAN CONFERENCE brought nearly 5,000 members into the two Missouri Conferences. In 1932 the St. Louis Conference was merged with the Missouri Conference, an arrangement which continued until unification in 1939.

In 1869 the St. Louis Conference reported six districts, 107 charges, and 13,401 members. In 1920, the year Arkansas was again made a part of the St. Louis Conference, it reported 47,146 members. In its last year, 1931, the St. Louis Conference reported 52,845 members. In 1932, when all of Missouri and Arkansas were again included in the Missouri Conference, the statistics were eleven districts, 330 charges, and 83,184 members.

During their existence the Missouri and St. Louis Conferences established and supported a number of schools. Carleton College operated at Farmington from about 1879 to 1924. In 1871 the St. Louis Conference accepted a school at Carthage which became Ozark Wesleyan College; the institution closed about 1932. A school started at Cameron in 1883 became Missouri Wesleyan College in 1897. It achieved accreditation, but ultimately financial difficulties forced its closure and in 1930 all of its resources were merged with BAKER UNIVERSITY in Kansas. A training school which in time became NATIONAL COLLEGE was started by the WOMAN'S HOME MISSIONARY SOCIETY of the M.E. Church in Kansas City, Kan., in 1899. It soon moved to Kansas City, Mo., and later offered liberal arts courses. Lacking financial support and patronage from the surrounding annual conferences, National College was never able to achieve full accreditation. The college closed in 1964, and its property was acquired by and became the campus of the ST. PAUL SCHOOL OF THEOLOGY, Methodist.

The number of hospitals and homes established by the M.E. Church in Missouri is impressive. The following, with date of establishment and location, are still serving as Methodist or Methodist related institutions: Epworth School for disturbed girls, St. Louis, 1909; Missouri Methodist Hospital, St. Joseph, 1897; Freeman Hospital, Joplin, 1925; Ozark Manor (Methodist Home for the Aged), Marionville, 1925; and Burge Hospital, Springfield, 1906.

In 1939, its last year, the Missouri Conference reported eight districts (one of them in Arkansas), 314 charges, 92,362 members, and property valued at $6,820,860.

General Minutes, MEC.
Minutes of the Missouri Conference.
F. C. Tucker, *Missouri*. 1966.   FREDERICK E. MASER

MISSOURI CONFERENCE (EUB). The first United Brethren preaching in MISSOURI was in the southwestern corner of the state prior to 1850 when a few families had arrived from the east. In 1851 the Sandusky Conference gave Bishop GLOSSBRENNER money to employ a suitable missionary for Missouri. When the new Missionary Board was formed in 1853, Josiah Terrel was appointed missionary to Missouri. The following year, Nov. 3, 1854, the Missouri Conference was organized in Jasper County, with five mission fields.

Since 1847 the IOWA conferences had cultivated work in the northern tier of counties in Missouri. These were eventually turned over to the Missouri Conference, whereas the former charges in the southwest were united with work in KANSAS. Thus an old conference acquired a new constituency.

In 1881 the GENERAL CONFERENCE formed the Southwestern Missouri Conference, taking from the Osage Conference that part of its territory in Missouri, south of the Missouri River. Four tiers of counties in ARKANSAS were added in 1885 and the name was changed to Southern Missouri Conference. A statewide conference was constituted in 1897 by uniting Southern Missouri and Missouri Conferences. Then in 1921, with the closing of the Louisiana Conference, the few remaining churches were added to Missouri Conference.

When the E.U.B. Church was formed in 1946, there were no former Evangelical churches within the three states of LOUISIANA, Arkansas and Missouri. Conference membership in 1946 was listed at 4,152 persons. Then when The United Methodist Church was established in 1968 there were 2,787 members. A year following church union the congregations of the conference had been received into those former Methodist conferences within the several states.

JOHN H. NESS, JR.

MISSOURI EAST CONFERENCE was organized at Fayette, Mo., May 30, 1961 with Bishop KENNETH W. COPELAND presiding. The conference was formed by merging the ST. LOUIS CONFERENCE with the east half of the MISSOURI CONFERENCE as the three conferences in Missouri—the SOUTHWEST MISSOURI CONFERENCE was the third one—were consolidated into two. Its territory includes the east half of Missouri. When organized the conference had eight districts: Cape Girardeau-Farmington, Hannibal-Mexico, Jefferson City, Kirksville, Poplar Bluff, Rolla, St. Louis North, and St. Louis South. There were 276 ministers, 285 pastoral charges, 117,216 members, and property valued at $51,523,300.

When the CENTRAL WEST CONFERENCE (CJ) was merged in 1966, the Missouri East Conference received twenty-two charges, fifteen ministers and 5,281 members from that body.

The Missouri East Conference supports the Methodist Children's Home in ST. LOUIS. It maintains a chaplain at Barnes Hospital and directs its Golden Cross funds to that institution. It supports the summer assembly called

Epworth Among the Hills at Arcadia, Blue Mountain Camp at Arcadia, and Camp Jo Ota at Clarence. The conference in cooperation with the MISSOURI WEST CONFERENCE supports Ozark Methodist Manor at Marionville, CENTRAL METHODIST COLLEGE at Fayette, ST. PAUL SCHOOL OF THEOLOGY Methodist at KANSAS CITY, and WESLEY FOUNDATIONS at nine state institutions of higher learning.

The Missouri East Conference raised nearly $800,000 in capital funds for St. Paul School of Theology Methodist by 1963. From its beginning in 1961, the conference has laid an apportionment on its churches each year for higher education, the amount raised being distributed on a quota basis to Central Methodist College, St. Paul School of Theology Methodist, and PHILANDER SMITH COLLEGE at LITTLE ROCK, Ark. The amount collected for these schools in 1968 was $221,416.

In 1967 the two Missouri conferences projected the Missouri Methodist Foundation, Inc., through which interested persons may donate or bequeath money to the Methodist Church in Missouri for the support of its religious, charitable, and educational work.

In 1970 the Missouri East Conference reported seven districts, 352 ministers, 287 charges, 113,800 members, and property valued at $58,533,466.

Minutes of the Missouri East Conference.
F. C. Tucker, *Missouri.* 1966.   A. STERLING WARD

MISSOURI WEST CONFERENCE

MISSOURI WEST CONFERENCE was organized May 30, 1961 at Fayette, Mo., with Bishop EUGENE M. FRANK presiding. The conference was formed by merging the SOUTHWEST MISSOURI CONFERENCE with the west half of the MISSOURI CONFERENCE as the three conferences in Missouri—the ST. LOUIS CONFERENCE was the third one—were consolidated into two. Its territory includes the west half of Missouri. The conference began with ten districts, Chillicothe, Fayette-Marshall, Joplin, Kansas City North, Kansas City South, Maryville, Nevada, St. Joseph, Sedalia, and Springfield. In 1962 the conference reported 368 pastoral charges, 384 ministers, 144,609 members, and property valued at $43,885,095.

When the CENTRAL WEST CONFERENCE (CJ) was merged in 1966, the Missouri West Conference received twelve charges, nine ministers, and 2,786 members from that body.

The ST. PAUL SCHOOL OF THEOLOGY Methodist, KANSAS CITY, is within the bounds of the Missouri West Conference. The seminary, founded in 1957 by authority of the GENERAL CONFERENCE, has been strongly supported by the annual conferences in MISSOURI, KANSAS, and NEBRASKA; in the first few years they raised capital funds for the institution in the amount of nearly $5,000,000, and in addition they contribute annually to its operating budget.

The Missouri West Conference maintains conference camps at Eldorado Springs and Lawson. It supports the Methodist Hospital at St. Joseph, Cox Medical Center at Springfield, and Freeman Hospital at Joplin. Jointly with the MISSOURI EAST CONFERENCE it contributes to CENTRAL METHODIST COLLEGE at Fayette, St. Paul School of Theology Methodist at Kansas City, Ozark Manor at Marionville, the METHODIST CHILDREN'S HOME in ST. LOUIS, and the WESLEY FOUNDATIONS at nine state institutions of higher learning. From its beginning in 1961, the Missouri West Conference has laid an apportionment on its

churches each year for higher education, the amount raised being distributed on a quota basis to Central Methodist College, St. Paul School of Theology Methodist, and PHILANDER SMITH COLLEGE at LITTLE ROCK, Ark. The amount collected for these schools in 1968 was $279,183.

In 1970 the Missouri West Conference reported ten districts, 453 ministers, 377 charges, 138,643 members, and property valued at $56,807,304.

General Minutes, UMC.
Minutes of the Missouri West Conference.
F. C. Tucker, *Missouri.* 1966.   A. STERLING WARD

MITCHELL, BENNETT (1832-1922), American pioneer preacher, was born in Monroe County, Ind., Feb. 18, 1832. After two years at Indiana Asbury College he moved to Lucas County, IOWA, where he joined the IOWA CONFERENCE in 1855. His first four appointments moved him steadily westward across Iowa. The Conference was divided in 1860 and he found himself a member of the Western Iowa Conference, which in 1864 was named the DES MOINES CONFERENCE. In 1862 he became presiding elder of the Council Bluffs District at the western boundary of the state. In 1865 he was appointed to the Chariton District. In 1869 he was sent northward to the Sioux City District, which comprised ten counties in northwest Iowa and all of the Dakota Territory. There was only a handful of churches in the whole district. In 1872 the Conference again was divided and then he was a member of the NORTHWEST IOWA CONFERENCE. He belonged in all to four Conferences yet never transferred. In 1873 he was appointed to the Algona District.

In 1877 ended this unusual record of four consecutive terms as presiding elder in four different districts. He then served as pastor to various local churches, managed the Conference Claimants Fund for a year, and retired in 1903. After his retirement he wrote a history of the Northwest Iowa Conference. His son, Charles B., became a minister of this Conference.

Bennett Mitchell advanced with the church across 500 miles of frontier, founding and nurturing scores of churches. He helped to found SIMPSON and MORNINGSIDE COLLEGES and started a college at Algona which did not survive. He was elected five times to GENERAL CONFERENCE and was a director of the National Anti-Saloon League. He died Aug. 12, 1922 and is buried at Sioux City, Iowa.

Minutes of the Northwest Iowa Conference, 1922.
B. Mitchell, *Northwest Iowa Conference.* 1904.
                                          FRANK G. BEAN

MITCHELL, CHARLES BAYARD (1857-1942), American bishop, was born Aug. 27, 1857, in PITTSBURGH, Pa., the son of Daniel Patrick and Anna Elizabeth (Baker) Mitchell. He was a charter member of the SOUTHWEST KANSAS CONFERENCE which he entered in 1880.

On July 6, 1882, he married Clara Aull.

In 1884 he transferred to the KANSAS CONFERENCE where he was financial secretary for a few years. Transfers to other conferences followed as it was evidently his desire to serve but one church in an annual conference: 1887, Pittsburgh; 1888, NEWARK; 1892, ST. LOUIS; 1897, MINNESOTA Northern; 1901, EAST OHIO; 1908, ROCK RIVER.

A delegate to the GENERAL CONFERENCES of 1904, 1908, 1912 (alternate), and 1916, the latter Conference elected him a bishop and assigned him to ST. PAUL, Minn., where he served for two quadrennia. In 1924 he was assigned to the PHILIPPINE ISLANDS. In 1928 he retired from the episcopacy.

While at St. Paul, he instituted a campaign for $1,750,-000, in those days a large amount, and the success of the campaign materially aided the several Methodist educational institutions in his area; LAWRENCE COLLEGE, HAMLINE UNIVERSITY, Parker College, DAKOTA WESLEYAN, and the WESLEY FOUNDATION at Madison, Wis.

A graduate of ALLEGHENY COLLEGE, he held the B.A., M.A., Ph.D., and D.D. degrees from that institution. BAKER UNIVERSITY granted him the LL.D. He was the author of a book of sermons, *The Noblest Quest*, and *A Little Bundle Of Letters from Three Continents*.

He died in Pasadena, Calif., Feb. 23, 1942, and was buried in Forest Lawn, Glendale.

Journal of the General Conference, 1944.
F. D. Leete, *Methodist Bishops*. 1948.   WILLIAM M. TWIDDY

MITCHELL, ERIC A. (1917-   ), bishop, was born at Madras, INDIA, July 7, 1917. He was educated at Baldwin Boys' School, Bangalore, and Leonard Theological College, Jabalpur, where he won the theological diploma in 1942. As a CRUSADE SCHOLAR he attended Union Theological Seminary in New York where he was awarded the B.D. and S.T.M. degrees, the latter in 1957. He served as pastor at Madras, 1937, and at Asanol in the Bengal Conference, 1942-49. At the latter place he was married in 1946, and he and his wife have one son.

Mitchell was chaplain of Vellore Medical College at Madras, 1958, and from 1959 to 1969 he was pastor of Taylor Memorial Church at BOMBAY and also district superintendent. He has attended a number of conferences and consultations, including the 1964 and 1968 GENERAL CONFERENCES (TMC), the consultation on structure (COSMOS) at Green Lake, Wis., the Assembly of the WORLD COUNCIL OF CHURCHES at UPPSALA, Sweden, and the World Family Life Conference at LONDON in 1966, where he was elected vice-chairman of the body. He is a member of the board of directors of the Y.M.C.A., and vice-chairman of the Bombay Samaritans, which is an organization that ministers to people who are tempted to commit suicide. Also, he is a leader in other organizations which help working boys and aged spinsters.

At the Central Conference of the Methodist Church in Southeast Asia, Mitchell was elected bishop on Jan. 2, 1969. He was assigned to the Hyderabad Episcopal Area which includes the HYDERABAD and SOUTH INDIA ANNUAL CONFERENCES. As an episcopal leader he serves as chairman of the Council of Evangelism, the Board of Missions, and the Commission on COURSES OF STUDY.

Daily Indian Witness, Bangalore, India, Jan. 3, 1969.
ALBEA GODBOLD

MITCHELL, HINCKLEY GILBERT (1846-1920), American educator and theologian whose "trial" for heresy became a *cause celebre* in the M. E. Church, was born on Feb. 22, 1846, in Lee, N. Y., to James and Sarah Gilbert (Thomas) Mitchell. His educational achievements were many: Falley Seminary, Fulton, New York, 1867; WESLEYAN UNIVERSITY, A.B., 1873, A.M., 1876, and D.D., 1901; BOSTON UNIVERSITY SCHOOL OF THEOLOGY, S.T.B.,

1876; Leipzig University, Ph.D., 1879; and MT. UNION COLLEGE, D.D., 1888. He married Alice Stanford on June 29, 1880.

Mitchell served as Director of the American School of Oriental Research in Jerusalem, 1901-02; member of Alpha Delta Phi fraternity; member of 20th Century Club; Secretary of the Society of Biblical Literature and Exegesis (editor of its *Journal*, 1882-88); member of the Harvard Biblical Club. He was the author of: *Hebrew Lessons*, 1885; *Amos—Essay in Exegesis*, 1893; *Theology of the Old Testament* (trans.), 1893; *Isaiah I-XII*, 1897; *The World Before Abraham*, 1901; *Genesis*, 1909; *Tales Told in Palestine* (with J. E. Hanauer), 1904; "Haggai and Zechariah," *International Commentary*, 1912; *Ethics of the Old Testament*, 1912.

He became pastor of the Methodist church in Bearytown (or Fayette) of the CENTRAL NEW YORK CONFERENCE in 1879. He then taught Latin and Hebrew at Wesleyan University, 1880-83; was professor of Hebrew and Old Testament exegesis, at Boston University School of Theology, 1883-1905; and after that was professor of Hebrew and Old Testament exegesis at Tufts College, 1910 until his death.

The Mitchell Case. He championed, in his classes, the higher criticism as it was beginning to be called, especially in the study of the Old Testament. In 1895 he was charged with "Unitarian" tendencies on account of his denial of the Mosaic authorship of the Pentateuch. He became a theological storm center in the M. E. Church. A collection of articles edited by W. W. Shenk, entitled *Shall Methodism Remain Wesleyan in Type, and Evangelical?*, presented many accusations directed toward Mitchell. The articles were addressed to the bishops, ministers, and members of the M. E. Church, to present "the departures of Professor H. G. Mitchell of Boston University School of Theology, as set forth by certain men who have been students in his classroom work." The contributors felt Mitchell ought not be permitted to remain in the seminary, for his rationalistic theology encouraged denial of authority of the Word of God, tended toward Unitarianism, and sought to revolutionize Methodist doctrine. Mitchell's idea of evolution, they said, denied that man ever had a fall, contended that man had inherent in himself the full power for his own development, and repudiated God's plan for Christ to die that men might live.

The GENERAL CONFERENCE of the M. E. Church therefore passed a resolution in 1900 that required, as a condition for the recognition of any theological school of the M. E. Church, that its professors be confirmed by a majority vote of the bishops present and voting at any regular meeting of their Board. Another resolution in 1904 stated that when specific charges of misteaching in Methodist theological schools were made in writing by responsible parties, members or ministers of the M. E. Church, the bishops were to appoint a committee from themselves to investigate charges. Their subsequent report, if adopted by the Board of Bishops, was to be transmitted to the trustees of the theological school involved for proper action.

Attempts were made to prevent Mitchell's confirmation in 1900, but failed. In 1905, when Mitchell was again up for re-election, he was attacked for "misteaching," based mainly on his book, *The World Before Abraham*. The bishops' committee said the book contained statements about the historic character of the Book of Genesis that seemed unwarranted, objectionable, and tended to invalidate the authority of other portions of Scripture. Mitchell's view of the fall of man and his assertion that the deluge was local were declared to invalidate Jesus' reference to Noah, and Paul's reference to the death of all in Adam. This, they felt, destroyed the authority of Jesus and the inspired writers of the New Testament. Thus, in 1905, charges of heresy were formally brought to the bishops, who voted not to confirm Mitchell's re-election to Boston. They sent their reasons and decision to the trustees, saying they had examined the charges made by responsible parties, and that the trustees should take responsible action.

Six months later the trustees asked the bishops to reconsider their refusal to confirm. The bishops refused, saying the trustees had not taken, or made known, any "proper action." "There had been no explanation from Professor Mitchell, much less modification or withdrawal of the statements objected to by the bishops and which created a 'reasonable doubt.' There went from the trustees, so far as the bishops knew, no request to Professor Mitchell even to consider whether the parts of his book referred to by the bishops ought to be reconsidered, revised or withdrawn." (*The Independent*, Nov. 16, 1905, p. 1179.)

In self defense, Mitchell requested that he be tried by the Central New York Conference of the M. E. Church, of which he was a member. The Conference appointed a committee to investigate the case, and after hearing the committee's report, refused to institute a formal trial. The Conference did, however, pass a resolution of censure for teachings which were contrary to the Holy Scriptures and to the doctrinal standards of Methodism. A trial was refused, because Mitchell no longer held the chair at Boston, and because a trial would cause too great a disturbance. F. J. McCONNELL (later bishop) demanded an immediate trial for Mitchell, but was refused.

The Judiciary Committee of the General Conference of the M. E. Church, in 1908, held that the Central New York Conference action was illegal. They ruled that there was no disciplinary provision for the report of the investigating committee, or for the action of the Central New York Conference in adopting the committee's report. The report of the committee was said to have reflected upon the character of Mitchell, and it was therefore the duty of the Conference to have granted him a trial upon his demand, or to have struck from the report all reflections upon his character. The Conference had refused or neglected to do so, and therefore the action of the committee and the Conference was declared null and void.

The Judiciary Committee of this General Conference also ruled that the bishops had the legal right to investigate reported charges of erroneous teaching in the seminaries of the M. E. Church.

Mitchell devoted the years 1906-08 to literary work, and in 1909 traveled in Europe. He left teaching in the M. E. Church and was appointed to the chair of Hebrew (and after 1915, New Testament also) at Tufts College (a Universalist seminary) in 1910, where he remained until his death. He left unfinished an autobiography, *For the Benefit of my Creditors*, published after his death, in 1922.

E. S. Bucke, *History of American Methodism*. 1964.
George Albert Coe, "A Crisis in Methodism," *The Outlook*. Dec. 16, 1905.
Dictionary of American Biography.

The Independent, "Professor Mitchell's Case," Nov. 16, 1905.
Minutes of the Central New York Conference, 1906-08.
C. F. Price, *Who's Who in American Methodism*. 1916.
W. W. Shenk, ed., *Shall Methodism Remain Wesleyan in Type, and Evangelical?* N.p., n.d.
Reports of the Committee on Judiciary, ME, 1924.
Who Was Who in America, Vol. 1.   STEPHEN G. COBB

MITCHELL, ISAAC GREEN (1810-1881), American pioneer preacher, was born near Madison Springs, Madison Co., Ga., on May 27, 1810. He was ordained as an ELDER in the M. P. Church on Nov. 12, 1843. He is credited with having officiated at the first wedding ceremony held in Marthasville, now ATLANTA, Ga. He served as a circuit rider until 1856 when he moved to Atlanta. When a mortgage foreclosed on the property of the M. P. Church located at the corner of Garnett and Forsyth Streets in Atlanta, Mitchell purchased it for $2,900 and had the portion of the lot occupied by the church building deeded to the M. P. Church. On the remaining portion, he built a home where he resided until his death.

He married Mary Anne Dudley on Jan. 15, 1829; she died on Feb. 12, 1856. It is of historic interest that Mitchell was the great-grandfather of Margaret Mitchell, author of *Gone With the Wind*.

Mitchell is buried in the family lot at Panola, Rockdale Co., Ga. Funeral services were held in the M. P. Church next door to his residence.

The Atlanta Historical Bulletin (Margaret Mitchell Memorial Issue), May 1950.   RALPH HARDEE RIVES

MITCHELL, PAUL DENNY (1912-1946), an American missionary to CUBA, was born in Mangum, Okla., Aug. 29, 1912, son of C. F. and Anna M. Welch Mitchell. After attending public schools in his home state he attended SOUTHERN METHODIST UNIVERSITY, where he received both A.B. and B.D. degrees. For one year he served as pastor at Duke, Okla., and in 1937 accepted work in Cuba where his first work was in Camaguey.

For eight years he was teacher and director of the nascent Methodist Seminary in Havana. During these years at different times he also served as pastor of three congregations in and around Havana, and when a missionary at Holguin became sick exchanged work for several months.

He was the author of *Grounds for Gratitude*, which was translated into German; *Teepees to Towers*; *Mision y Comision del Metodismo*; and *Cuba Calling*. He gave the proceeds of the sales of his books for Christian literature in Latin America.

Because of illness in his home, he retired from Cuba and accepted appointments at Verden and Noble, Okla. Taking his young people on a picnic one of the girls, Jeanette Harris, ten years of age, was caught in the current when swimming. He was a good swimmer and attempted to rescue her but both were drowned.

When only a youth he became possessed of the idea that he should be a missionary, and veritably to the ministerial manor he was called. Wherever he went he was popular and at the same time quiet, dignified and unselfish. No one has ever excelled his record in learning the Spanish language so rapidly, to the degree that he could preach with power in both Spanish and his native tongue. His death left a tragic void.

GARFIELD EVANS

MITCHELL, THOMAS (1726-1785), British itinerant, was called "the poor man's preacher." He was born at Bingley, Dec. 3, 1726, to godly parents. By temperament religious, by trade a mason, he was converted under JOHN NELSON'S and WILLIAM GRIMSHAW'S ministry. About 1747-48, he became itinerant; and WESLEY arranged numerous brief spells for him, but after 1768 Mitchell kept most circuits for two years. In Lancashire, Yorkshire, and Lincolnshire, he was frequently mobbed—at Wrangle being repeatedly ducked and painted. Few preachers suffered more. In 1760 he and others caused a stir by administering Holy Communion at Norwich. He became supernumerary in 1784 and died in 1785.

T. Jackson, *Lives of Early Methodist Preachers.* 1837-38.
J. W. Laycock, *Methodist Heroes.* 1909.   GEORGE LAWTON

MIYAMA, KANICHI (dates uncertain), the first Japanese Christian convert in America. In JAPAN during the 1870's Miyama sought to enroll in an army academy but failed the entrance exams. Despondent over his failure, he came to the United States in 1876 to seek new hope and life. Providentially, his friend in Japan had given him a letter of introduction to Otis Gibson, a missionary to CHINA who was then the superintendent of the Chinese Mission in SAN FRANCISCO. From Gibson the young Miyama learned not only the English language but also about God as revealed in Christ. He was baptized in 1877, thereby becoming the first Japanese Christian convert in America. Subsequently "The Japanese Gospel Society" was organized. This group gathered regularly in the Chinese Mission. Out of this small Christian gathering grew the San Francisco Japanese M. E. Church, the mother church of all Protestant churches among the Japanese people in the United States.

After serving eight years in the San Francisco Church, as the first Japanese Methodist minister in America, Miyama was brought by the Holy Spirit to HAWAII and there he started the Methodist work among the Japanese people in the islands. One of the Christian fruits gathered in by Miyama was the conversion of Taro Ando, the Consul General of the Japanese government stationed in Honolulu. Ando later became the father of the Christian Temperance Movement in Japan.

TARO GOTO

MOBILE, ALABAMA, U.S.A., a port city in the southeastern United States, is located near one of the deepest natural harbors on the Gulf of Mexico. The present site was settled by the French in 1711. Its name originates from an Indian Tribe, the "Maubila," which once inhabited the area.

The first attempt at Methodist beginnings in the city was in 1821 when Alexander Talley was appointed by the MISSISSIPPI CONFERENCE as a "missionary to PENSACOLA, Mobile, Blakely and adjoining territory." After one year of disappointing labor, Talley located. The Mississippi Conference discontinued the appointment for the next two years.

During these interim years, Nicholas McIntyre, a presiding elder, secured a lot for a Methodist church in Mobile. The deed was made May 10, 1824, to five Methodists who were members of congregations on the Chickasawhay Circuit.

In 1825 the Mississippi Conference sent Henry P. Cook to serve the "Mobile and Pensacola Mission." Cook had worked in Pensacola (FLORIDA) the previous year, but requested that Mobile also be included in his work. A few months later he died of yellow fever.

Cook's successor, John Russell Lambuth, reported on Dec. 14, 1826, a membership of eighteen white and seventy-eight Negro members, the first tangible evidence of Methodist growth in Mobile. During 1827 the first Methodist house of worship was completed. Receiving no pay from the Methodists in Mobile, Lambuth supported himself by establishing a school.

Although the first Society was officially listed by the Mississippi Conference as the Mobile Mission, local citizens, observing the congregation's zeal and activity, referred to it as the "Bee Hive" church.

In 1830 the Mobile Mission reported a loss in membership resulting from the organization of the M. P. Church. Following the leadership of Peyton S. Graves, a sizeable group withdrew from the mission.

In 1832 Mobile was listed as an appointment within the newly organized ALABAMA CONFERENCE of the M. E. Church. R. L. Walker, who had served as host-pastor of the organizational conference in Tuscaloosa, was appointed pastor of the church in Mobile.

From 1826 until 1841 there was only one Methodist church in Mobile. At the annual conference, beginning Dec. 30, 1840, Bishop JAMES O. ANDREW directed Greenberry Garrett, presiding elder of the Mobile District, to enlarge the work. As a result, two new charges were formed: (1) Second Charge and (2) Seaman's Mission. The "Bee Hive" Church was listed as First Charge.

In 1842, First Charge was renamed Franklin Street, and the following year Second Charge became St. Francis Street, after having been known as Jackson Street for one year.

Two new churches were organized in 1843; (1) West Ward, an addition to the Franklin Street appointment, and (2) Little Zion, later named the Big Zion A.M.E. Zion Church.

Recognizing serious educational needs, Franklin Street and St. Francis Street Churches cooperated in the formation and support of a free school that continued until ALABAMA enacted the free public school law.

The first session of the Alabama Conference following the PLAN OF SEPARATION adopted in 1844 was held in Mobile during February 1846. Until the PLAN OF UNION in 1939 most of the Methodist work in Mobile continued under the M. E. Church, South, and the various Negro Methodist churches. Neither the M. P. Church nor the M. E. Church were ever numerically strong in Mobile.

In October 1845, a new church, forerunner of the Toulminville Methodist Church, was established. A one-room frame building was completed in 1846, and was used by all Protestant denominations in the area.

Yellow fever claimed a terrible toll in lives throughout Mobile in 1853. Every Methodist preacher in the city died of the dread disease within three weeks' time.

The Civil War years, 1861-1865, were difficult years for Methodism in Mobile. Many charges were left "to be supplied," others were served by supernumerary preachers. In 1863 the Mobile District itself was marked "to be supplied." The Alabama Conference divided itself into two conferences, the Montgomery and the Mobile, hoping to facilitate the work. The General Conference (MES) in 1866 countenanced the division, and it continued until 1870.

In 1874 an outgrowth of a Mobile City Mission Circuit was organized as the Four Mile Post Church. A one-room frame building was constructed and was ready for occupancy by 1881. After being known as the Crichton Church from 1898 until 1925, its name was changed to the Spring Hill Avenue Church.

During the pastorate of A. J. Lamar, the Franklin Street Church, Mobile's oldest, relocated. In 1890 the new building was completed and was renamed the Government Street Church.

In 1896, the Alabama Conference met in the new Government Street Church. At this session another church, called Oakdale Mission, was formed, making the fifth church serving within the city limits of Mobile.

Materials from a saw mill shed were used to build the first Dauphin Way Church in 1913. Officially organized a year later, the congregation had a charter membership of twenty-six. By 1965 its membership had grown to 2,155. During twenty-five years of this remarkable growth, A. Carl Akins was the church's pastor.

The churches of Mobile had difficulty meeting their "benevolent apportionments" during the depression years of early 1930's. All pastors, serving churches not having paid these apportionments, were required to make a complete canvass of every member, securing, if possible, a pledge to benevolences.

After unification in 1939 two churches in Mobile were members of the Central JURISDICTION: Warren Street and Wesley.

As the city of Mobile grew, suburbs became numerous around the city's perimeter. To meet this challenge twelve new congregations were organized between 1925 and 1965. Simultaneously, shifting populations resulted in difficult problems for the inner city. Two efforts have been undertaken, moving toward a confrontation of these problems: the Inner City Mission, an effort by the Church to meet the pressing needs of poverty; and the Toulminville—Warren Street Methodist Parish, a cooperative effort involving a Negro church and an ALABAMA-WEST FLORIDA CONFERENCE white church.

Big Zion A. M. E. ZION CHURCH came to life in 1842. The growth of the membership of a white Methodist church located at the corner of Franklin and St. Michael Streets, Mobile County, caused the members of this church to seek a way to relieve a growing condition of racial contact.

After a length of time, the white church placed S. H. Cox, white, in charge of the Negro congregation and the services were held in a little house on the southeast corner of Church and Dearborn Streets.

They remained in this place free of charge with Cox as pastor until 1848, when they decided to purchase it with funds donated them.

Under the law of Alabama, they were prohibited from holding property under their own names. Therefore, the property was deeded to the following white trustees: Viz: A. H. Ryland, R. S. Baker and R. L. Watson.

Local preachers at this time were Ferdinand Smith, Charles Lee, and Battas Dayes. They were permitted to pray during services.

Shortly after this place was purchased, it was burned to the ground, and the little band went from there to a carpenter's shop which was also burned down. After the burning of the carpenter's shop, they worshipped in the Burden's Mill, at St. Francis and Wilkinson Streets. From there they moved to the Medical College on St. Anthony at Lawrence Street. The first Quarterly Conference was held.

Now appeared the first A.M.E. Zion bishop to come South—Bishop J. J. CLINTON, who brought with him Wilbur G. Strong, who persuaded them to vote to transfer their membership from the M. E. Church, South, to the A.M.E. Zion connection. The property, however, remained under the ownership of white trustees until 1867.

In 1860, while still worshipping in the Medical College, the members of the Church purchased lots on the northwest corner of Church and S. Bayou Streets from Henry Turner and constructed a shed building in which they held their services. Charles Lee, a local preacher, was the pastor while worshipping in this shed.

In 1865 Ferdinand Smith was ordained by Bishop J. J. Clinton of the A.M.E. Zion connection. He was the first Negro minister to be ordained by a Negro bishop in the state of Alabama. On July 29 of the same year he was authorized to take charge of the church. He was pastor until 1867, when E. D. Taylor succeeded him.

Samuel Wilson served until 1880; William Spencer, 1880-1885; A. J. Warner, 1885-1891; H. R. Gaines took charge of the church in 1891 and served until 1893; C. H. Smith succeeded Gaines in 1893; Richard A. Morrisey, 1899-1904; A. J. Rodgers, 1904-1908; L. W. Kyles, 1908-1914; G. W. Johnson, 1914-1921; J. R. White, 1921; F. W. Riley, 1925; M. F. Gregory, 1931-1932; A. A. Garvin, 1933-1934; R. H. Collins Lee, 1934-1935; William Bascom, 1935 through 1936; D. G. Garland, 1936; A. E. Ellison, 1937-1941; Felix S. Anderson, 1941-

Dauphin Way Church is the stately mid-city church of the port city. It is not Methodism's oldest in Mobile, but it is the largest and one of the most influential. Like the congregation of an early Christian church, Dauphin Way had its beginning in the homes of those who desired a church fellowship in this new area of the city. The year was 1913. A site was given and an old sawmill shed was torn down and rebuilt to house this fledgling congregation. In 1922 the church was moved several blocks and in a short time merged with St. Stephens Road Church. In 1925 the building on the new site was completed, and this facility served well until 1957, when Dauphin Way opened its new sanctuary, diagonally across Dauphin Street from the old.

Twenty children gathered for the first Sunday school class meeting in a home in 1913. Fifty years later over 2,000 composed the fellowship of Dauphin Way. That number continues to grow year by year.

The beautiful colonial sanctuary, dedicated in 1964, is one of the most impressive church structures in the Azalea City. It seats 1,200 worshippers and provides an atmosphere of stately simplicity. Its cross, high above the city, brings a fitting peak to its tapering spire, calling all who pass by to look up in adoration.

In 1970 Dauphin Way reported a membership of 2,177, property valued at $1,769,910, and $200,283 raised for all purposes.

Journals of the Alabama Conference, ME, MES, TMC.
Journal of the Alabama-West Florida Conference.
M. E. Lazenby, *Alabama and West Florida*. 1960.
A. West, *Alabama*. 1893.   FRANK THOMAS HYLES, JR.
                                DAVID H. BRADLEY
                                JOEL D. MCDAVID

MODEL DEED. (See DEEDS, TRUST.)

MOFFATT, ELBERT MARSTON (1884-1966), was born in Le Sueur, Minn., and graduated from Dartmouth. He arrived in INDIA, Feb. 19, 1911, as a Y.M.C.A. secretary. He served first as business secretary at headquarters in CALCUTTA, and then as general secretary of the Y.M.C.A. in Allahabad. Returning to America in 1916, he became secretary of the Bowery Y.M.C.A. in New York.

In September 1920, he again arrived in India, but as a missionary of the M. E. Church, and began a new career in which he achieved distinction. He was appointed manager of the school of commerce of LUCKNOW CHRISTIAN COLLEGE. The next year, 1921, Lucknow University invited him to be dean of commerce, and he served both institutions until 1926 when he took furlough. Subsequent appointments included treasurer of Lucknow Christian College, 1927-30; superintendent, Kumaun and Sitapur Districts, 1927-30; secretary of the executive board, 1931-46; and branch treasurer for India, Board of Missions. He was the originator of the All-India Provident Fund for ministers and other employees of the Methodist Church and its agencies in India. He took the lead in organizing the inter-mission business office in BOMBAY and in securing the participation of seventy-two missions.

He left India on furlough in 1946 and was held there as a secretary of the Board of Missions, working on a study of deeds for property owned by the board in various countries. He served as secretary of the GENERAL CONFERENCE Commission on the Structure of Methodism Overseas (COSMOS), 1946-50.

In the autumn of that year he returned to India and became agent of the LUCKNOW PUBLISHING HOUSE and held that position for four years. He represented the Board of Missions in deputation work for two years or more. He retired in 1956, but in retirement was called back to India to make a study of the state of property records and to devise plans for the transfer of properties owned by the Board of Missions to the church in India. He died in October 1966.

Minutes of the North India Conference. J. WASKOM PICKETT

MOKITIMI, SETH MOLEFI (1904-   ), Methodist minister in SOUTH AFRICA, was born at Quthing, Basutoland

SETH M. MOKITIMI

(now Lesotho) on Jan. 15, 1904, and began life as a herd boy on the hills of his native country. He later attended school and then proceeded to the HEALDTOWN MISSIONARY INSTITUTION where he received his high school education and qualified as a teacher. Candidating for the ministry of the Methodist Church of South Africa, he was trained in theology at Wesley House, Fort Hare and ordained to the work of the ministry. After a period of service at Zastron in the Orange Free State he was appointed chaplain to the students at Healdtown. Thereafter he served in the Transkeian circuit of Osborn, at the Bensonvale Missionary Institution in the Northern Cape as Governor, and at Bloemfontein. He was Secretary of the Methodist Church's Board of Examiners (1941-62) and became General Missionary Secretary in 1963. After being runner-up for the Presidency of the Methodist Conference for five years, he was elected as President of the 1964 Conference, the first African to hold this position. In 1966 he was elected President of the Christian Council of South Africa.

S. P. FREELAND

MOLEMA, son of the Barolong chief Tauane, gained his Christian experience at Thaba 'Nchu. Tauane died in 1850 and was succeeded by his son Montsioa but Molema became the spiritual leader. He had moved with the tribe from Thaba 'Nchu back to their homeland in the vicinity of Maquassie, thence to Lotlakana and Moshaneng and finally to Mafeking. For forty years he was their leader and preacher, with occasional assistance from missionaries from the Kimberley and Bloemfontein District. In January 1882 Molema died—just ten months before the Chairman of the new Transvaal District visited Mafeking. The Chairman found a thriving church and Sunday school of 500 children and adults led by Joshua, Molema's son. A thousand people attended the services held under a large tree. There was a church building but it was too small for the congregation.

Journal of the Methodist Historical Society of South Africa. Vol. III, No. 2 (October 1958).
Minutes of South African Conference, 1939.   D. C. VEYSIE

MOLING, FRANCES (1871-1945), American missionary to CUBA, was born in Havana, Mo., May 11, 1871. A school for girls had been started in Havana with Hattie G. Garson, who had been transferred from MEXICO, 1898, director; and another school in Cienfuegos in 1900, with J. D. Lewis. The latter began with five pupils and Lewis worked without salary for ten months. The two schools were united and settled at Cienfuegos.

Fortunately, in 1898 a Mrs. Dora Bowman, from the NORTH TEXAS CONFERENCE, became very much interested in what she had heard of the needs of Cuban children and collected $18,000 to help with a school for Cuban children. Mrs. Bowman requested that the school be named for her sister-in-law, Eliza Bowman.

On taking charge of the school in 1902, Miss Moling secured valuable property on one of the main streets in down-town Cienfuegos, where for more than twenty years the school functioned as a co-educational day school. With her wise leadership the school soon grew to the capacity of its class rooms.

About 1924 buildings located on a hill in the highest point in town, where the city reservoir had been previously located, were offered for sale. Miss Moling bought them and added a commodious class room building and chapel. The small space for dormitory purposes was always filled to capacity and buses were required to bring the day pupils that crowded the class rooms.

To properly evaluate her work and character it was said, "one needs a pen of gold dipped in imperishable ink." With a vision, a lover of the beautiful, a tireless worker, she possessed all the virtues that make a noble and refined person and at the same time a quiet sweetness and patience.

Not only was she an excellent business administrator but her quiet sweet disposition affected everyone that ever knew her. She retired in 1937 and died March 28, 1945.

S. A. Neblett, *Methodism in Cuba*, 1966.   GARFIELD EVANS

MOLTHER, PHILIP H. (1714-1780), Moravian, was born at Burtweiler, Alsace, on Dec. 26, 1714. As tutor to Count ZINZENDORF's son, he became a Moravian; and at FETTER LANE in LONDON he propounded the doctrine of "stillness," which asserted that those who believed themselves converted should abstain from the means of GRACE, especially from the Lord's Supper, until all their doubts were removed. This doctrine and Molther's objections to the Methodist "scenes" were largely responsible for the disruption of the Fetter Lane group and the formation of the first Methodist society in 1740. The doctrine of "stillness," though supported by August Spangenberg and others at the time, was soon dropped. Molther died at Bedford on Sept. 9, 1780.

Daniel Benham, *Memoirs of James Hutton*. London: Hamilton, Adams & Co., 1856.
C. W. Towlson, *Moravian and Methodist*. 1957.
G. A. Wauer, *The Beginnings of the Brethren's Church in England*. London, 1901.
J. Wesley, *Journal*. 1909-16.   C. W. TOWLSON

SHOT K. MONDOL

MONDOL, SHOT KUMAR (1896-   ), Methodist bishop, was born in Murshidabad, West Bengal, INDIA, on Oct. 11, 1896. His father was an ordained Methodist minister in the BENGAL ANNUAL CONFERENCE. His formal education was acquired entirely in India. He studied in the Scottish Churches College and in St. Paul's College, both in CALCUTTA, and was graduated with a B.A. degree

from the University of Calcutta. His theological education was obtained through the Conference COURSE OF STUDIES.

Early he acquired a reputation as an instructive and spiritually helpful preacher. In his early thirties he was appointed the first Indian superintendent of the Calcutta District, and at forty-four years of age became the second citizen of India elected to the Methodist episcopacy. For sixteen years he supervised the HYDERABAD Area. At the end of 1956, he was transferred to the DELHI Area, where he remained until his retirement in 1965. When the Central Conference of the PHILIPPINES asked the COUNCIL OF BISHOPS to assign one of their number to the MANILA Area to serve until that Conference elected an additional bishop, his colleagues of the Council unanimously chose Bishop Mondol.

His leadership has extended far beyond the boundaries of his own church. He has served as President of the National Christian Council of India, 1949-1956; President of the National Missionary Society of India, 1943-1958; President of the India Sunday School Union, 1948-1964; President of the World Council of Christian Education and World Sunday School Association, 1958-1962; President, United Mission to NEPAL, 1958-1964; President, North West Indian Christian Council, 1958-1962; President of the Delhi Y.M.C.A., 1960-1965; Chairman of the Managing Committee of the Christian Medical College at Vellore; and member of the Executive Committees of the Council of Bishops of The Methodist Church and of the WORLD METHODIST COUNCIL. He participated in public affairs often. In Asansol he was a municipal commissioner and in Hyderabad a fellow of Osmania University.

He maintained cordial relations with Prime Minister Nehru and members of his cabinet and with Doctors Rajendra Prasad and Radhakrishnan, the first and second Presidents of the Republic of India.

He has been awarded honorary degrees from American institutions as follows: ASBURY SEMINARY, D.D.; BOSTON UNIVERSITY, S.T.D.; AMERICAN UNIVERSITY, LL.D.; ALBION COLLEGE, LL.D.; and WILEY COLLEGE, LL.D.

Bishop Mondol married Carolyn Belle Osburn, a missionary of the WOMAN'S FOREIGN MISSIONARY SOCIETY. Her parents were also missionaries in India. Among their children is one son who is a member of the MICHIGAN ANNUAL CONFERENCE.

Who's Who in The Methodist Church, 1966.
                                        J. WASKOM PICKETT

MONMOUTH, MAINE, U.S.A., where the first Methodist church in MAINE was established. In 1793 JESSE LEE visited in Monmouth and came again on Oct. 22, 1794 after he had been made presiding elder of MASSACHUSETTS, NEW HAMPSHIRE and Maine. That year Philip Wagner had been appointed to Maine. When Lee came to Monmouth, he found that Wagner had gathered a group of fifteen people. The organization of the class on Nov. 1, 1794, by Philip Wagner, gives Monmouth the distinction of being the first Methodist church established in Maine. December 25 of that year Holy Communion was observed for the first time in Monmouth at Capt. Peter Hopkin's tavern, with Jesse Lee presiding and preaching on the text Isaiah 9:6.

On Oct. 28, 1795, the church at old Meeting House Corner was well under way. Some work had been begun the previous year on land donated by Major David

Marston. It was dedicated on May 31, 1796, making it the second chapel in Maine. This group started work on their church earlier than the work at (EAST) READFIELD, but were held up by lack of funds. This building burned in 1843. The new church was erected at the present site in 1846. The steeple was dedicated in 1866. In 1930 the Congregational Church united with the Methodist Church, forming what is called the Monmouth United Church. The services are held in the Methodist church; the Congregational church was sold to the Masonic order.

A member of the Monmouth Church, Harry Cockrane (1860-1946), an artist, mural painter, and decorator of churches and other public buildings, painted (about 1924) a mural of Bishop ASBURY fording a wilderness stream and holding an open book in his hand. This work, entitled "The Man on Horseback," was reproduced on the cover of the Methodist magazine *Together* on the occasion of the 175th Anniversary of Methodism in America. The painting is on the wall of the Methodist Church of Monmouth together with another painting by Mr. Cochrane of St. John on Patmos, writing on a tablet. The inscription is "In memory of the First Methodist Class in Maine," with these words of scripture: "And I heard a voice from Heaven saying unto me 'Write Blessed are the dead who die in the Lord'." Mr. Cochrane was a member of the Monmouth church all of his life and honored as a saintly man. He commemorated in art the historical fact that the church at Monmouth was the first Methodist church organized in Maine.

The minister at Monmouth also serves the church at East Monmouth. The Methodist society here was formed in 1794 and joined with three other denominations in building a meeting house, still in use, about 1800. It was agreed that the society that outlasted the others was finally to own the property. This is now the East Monmouth Methodist Church. Visitors today admire the "punkin" pine floor boards, oil reflector lamps, forty-pane windows, pews with hinged doors, old balcony and Christian cross doors. Weekly services are held and a union service annually on the Sunday afternoon following Thanksgiving Day that is attended by people from a large area. Jesse Lee preached in East Monmouth on Aug. 5, 1800, but it is not known whether this church had then been built.

Allen and Pilsbury, *Methodism in Maine.* 1887.

ALFRED G. HEMPSTEAD

MONROE, ANDREW (1792-1871), American pioneer preacher, was born in Hampshire County, Va., Oct. 29, 1792. He accompanied his parents on their moving, first to TENNESSEE, and later to OHIO where he grew to maturity. He was one of four preachers born to his parents.

Monroe was licensed to preach by the Zanesville, Ohio, Circuit in 1815 and was admitted on trial to the OHIO CONFERENCE that year. He served appointments there and in KENTUCKY, and transferred to the MISSOURI CONFERENCE in 1824. The western edge of the American frontier lay in MISSOURI at that time. After two pastorates in ST. LOUIS (1824-25; 1828-29), Monroe's decisive leadership placed him repeatedly in the presiding eldership—a total of twenty years—over districts that were expanding westward with an ever increasing number of circuits. He bought and operated Prairie Lawn Seminary, Danville, Mo. (1831-38), the first Methodist-related school in Missouri. He was further identified with educational endeavors by serving as Agent for St. Charles College in

whose behalf he made a tour of eastern conferences. On the eve of the Civil War he served as Agent for CENTRAL METHODIST COLLEGE. In this community he spent the war years in both the pastorate and the presiding eldership.

At division of the Church, Monroe led and largely influenced the Missouri Conference to go into the M.E. Church, South. The Civil War in Missouri with its accompanying disorders prevented the bishops of the Church, South from attending the sessions of the Annual Conference. Twice Monroe was chosen President of the Conference and virtually became "substitute bishop." The leadership of his voice and pen largely prevented the disintegration of the Southern Church in Missouri. In 1865 he rallied ministers and laymen by calling a Convention to undertake the rebuilding of the church. From this Convention came the PALMYRA MANIFESTO, a declaration of faith in the future which was widely circulated in the Southern Conferences and which considerably influenced the GENERAL CONFERENCE of 1866.

Monroe was a member of eleven General Conferences; five of the undivided M.E. Church and six of the M.E. Church, South. He knew personally the leaders in both branches of the church who gave him their confidence and esteem. He died Nov. 17, 1871, and was buried in Mexico, Mo.

M. L. Gray, *Missouri Methodism.* 1907.
Andrew Monroe, "Recollections." Typescript, Commission on Archives and History, Lake Junaluska, N. C.

FRANK C. TUCKER

MONROE, DAVID SOLOMON (1833-1910), American minister, was born April 15, 1833, in LEESBURG, Va. He was educated in the BALTIMORE public schools and in Baltimore City College.

In 1854 he was admitted into the BALTIMORE CONFERENCE of the M.E. Church and, by reason of boundary changes and its division at the time and following the Civil War, was subsequently a member of the East Baltimore and CENTRAL PENNSYLVANIA Conferences. Upon the organization of the Central Pennsylvania Conference in 1869, he was elected its first secretary and served with unique distinction in that capacity for twenty-five years, resigning when appointed presiding elder of the Altoona District.

Elected a member of the GENERAL CONFERENCE of the M.E. Church in 1876, he was named assistant secretary of that body. In 1880 he was first assistant secretary, and in 1884 became secretary. He held this office of Secretary of the General Conference until 1904, when he declined to be a candidate, having been a member of seven General Conferences.

After serving for fifty-seven years in the ministry, he died in Altoona, Pa., Nov. 15, 1910, leaving his entire estate to the church he loved. His body is interred in Mount Olivet Cemetery, Baltimore, Md., where Bishop ASBURY and a number of other heroes of Methodism also lie at rest.

He was known as an outstanding pastor, an eloquent and scholarly preacher, and a princely giant among his brethren.

The Christian Advocate (New York), Dec. 1, 1910.
Journal of the Central Pennsylvania Conference, 1911.

CHARLES F. BERKHEIMER

MONROE, JOSHUA (1786-1874), American preacher, was born in Allegany County, Md., and spent his ministry in western PENNSYLVANIA where he became a charter member of the PITTSBURGH CONFERENCE when it was formed in 1825. He was admitted in the BALTIMORE CONFERENCE in 1808. He served as a presiding elder for thirteen years. One of the founders of Beaver College, he served as president of its Board of Trustees for many years. He was a delegate from the Pittsburgh Conference to the GENERAL CONFERENCES of 1828, 1832, and 1836. He wrote a series of twenty-nine articles titled *Recollections of the Past*, which were published serially in the *Pittsburgh Christian Advocate* from Dec. 23, 1856 to Sept. 21, 1858. They are autobiographical, covering the years 1791 to 1836, and run to a total of over thirty thousand words.

Pittsburgh Christian Advocate, Dec. 23, 1856 to Sept. 21, 1858, and July 17, 1869.
W. G. Smeltzer, *Headwaters of the Ohio*. 1951.

W. GUY SMELTZER

MONROE, SAMUEL YORKE (1816-1867), American clergyman and church extension secretary, was born at Mount Holly, N. J., July 1, 1816. Converted in youth in Union Church, PHILADELPHIA, Pa., under the labors of Charles Pitman, he was admitted to the NEW JERSEY CONFERENCE on trial in 1843. All of Monroe's pastorates were in NEW JERSEY. He was presiding elder two terms in the New Jersey Conference. His last pastorate was Trinity Church, Jersey City.

Upon the organization of the CHURCH EXTENSION SOCIETY in 1865, Monroe was chosen by the bishops to be the first Corresponding Secretary. Due to excessive labors over the church his health was weakened. During the first year as Corresponding Secretary he raised over $60,000. He was elected to three GENERAL CONFERENCES—1856, 1860, 1864—"at the last of which he received a very flattering vote for Bishop." Leaving home in Camden, N. J., to attend a meeting in Sands Street Church, BROOKLYN, N. Y., he fell or was thrown from the rear platform of a railway car near Jersey City, and was thus dashed against the rocks and instantly killed. He was buried in Evergreen Cemetery, near Camden, N. J., Feb. 13, 1867.

Appleton's Cyclopaedia of American Biography.
Minutes of the Newark Conference, 1867.

EDGAR R. ROHRBACH

MONROE, LOUISIANA, U.S.A., **Bartholomew Church**, a frontier meetinghouse, is located in Monroe District, LOUISIANA CONFERENCE, on the present Bastrop-Bonita highway, Morehouse Parish.

Masons and Methodists constructed and jointly owned the rectangular frame building dedicated June 25, 1835. Virgin timber sills were secured by wooden pegs to notched, hand-hewn tree trunks two stories high. The outside boards of heart pine were fastened with square hand-forged iron nails. The upper floor housed independent Masonic lodge meetings until Bartholomew Lodge, Free and Accepted Masons #112, operated under charter from the Louisiana Grand Lodge (1853-1899). The lower floor provided a candle lighted place of worship for both master and slave. Membership never exceeded 150.

Tombstones in the thirteen-acre cemetery trace pioneer hardships through exposure, epidemics, and the pestilence of war. Buried in 1853, as yellow fever victims, were the pastor, John B. Eddins, his wife and son. The Rev. Samuel Haws and most of his family died from typhoid in 1860.

Since organization of the Louisiana Annual Conference (1847), Bartholomew Church has been on the following circuits: Bastrop, Bonidee, Colony Mission, Lind Grove, Plantersville, and Washita.

In 1958, complete renovation preserved the architectural style of the church but included modern improvements. Sunday school rooms replaced the early lodge rooms. The congregation continues to bear Christian witness.

Journals of the Louisiana Conference.
Grand Lodge Archives, New Orleans, La.
Quarterly Conference Minutes. MILDRED NIXON NOLAN

MONTANA, sometimes called "the Treasure State" or "the Land of the Shining Mountains," is in the northwest section of the United States. It is bounded on the north by CANADA, on the east by the Dakotas, on the south by IDAHO and WYOMING, and on the west by Idaho. With 145,878 square miles, it is fourth in size among the fifty states. Mountainous in the west and southwest, the remaining three-fifths of the state is mostly plains. Organized as a territory in 1864, Montana became the forty-first state in 1889. In 1970 its population was 682,133.

Partially explored by Lewis and Clark in 1805, Montana was soon afterward settled by whites. The first immigration of consequence, however, came following the discovery of gold in 1858. Bannock was founded in 1862, Virginia City about 1863, and HELENA in 1864.

Both branches of Episcopal Methodism had work in Montana. The ministry of the M.E. Church began with a sermon delivered Jan. 10, 1864 at Bannock by a preacher named Craig. During the same winter William Florkey organized a Methodist class at Virginia City. In June 1864 a group of men under the leadership of an ordained local preacher named William James built a church in Junction City, about three miles from Virginia City. A church costing $1,500 was erected at Virginia City that same summer.

The M.E. Church's greatest leader in Montana in the early days was WILLIAM WESLEY VAN ORSDEL, known as "Brother Van." He preached the first sermon at Fort Benton in north Montana June 30, 1872. Van Orsdel did more than any other man to keep alive the frontier churches and to promote the institutions of his denomination in the region. The denomination developed two conferences in Montana—Montana which was carved out of the ROCKY MOUNTAIN CONFERENCE in 1876, and North Montana which was formed by merging the Kalispell and Montana Missions in 1907. In 1924 the two united to form the MONTANA STATE CONFERENCE.

The pioneer preacher of the M.E. Church, South in Montana was L. B. STATELER. Accompanying a large number of emigrants for the northwest, Stateler and his family arrived in Bozeman July 7, 1864. Stateler first visited Virginia City July 10, but for lack of a house in which a congregation could gather he did not begin preaching at once. About the middle of July he went to Norwegian Gulch on the headwaters of Willow Creek, some thirty-five miles northeast of Virginia City, where he met a Southern Methodist local preacher named Hardgrove. Assisted by laymen, they erected an arbor, covered it with brush, and began preaching services. Later Stateler preached in various homes to which he was invited. He organized the first Southern Methodist society in the home of Richard Reeves in January 1865. Reeves lived near a settlement on Willow Creek where there were a number of church members from MISSOURI. Other Southern Methodist preachers who came soon after Stateler were J. H. Pritchett and B. R. Baxter. The one began preaching at Helena in 1865 and the other a year later.

The Montana Conference of the M.E. Church South was organized and held its first session at Helena, Sept. 19-22, 1878 with Bishop W. M. WIGHTMAN presiding. L. B. Stateler was secretary. Prior to that time the Montana work had been a part of the DENVER CONFERENCE. At the beginning the new conference had two districts, Helena and Deer Lodge, six preachers, ten charges, and 232 members. The conference grew slowly, and in 1917 when it had 969 members and thirteen appointments, it merged with the Columbia and East Columbia Conferences to form the Northwest Conference. In that year the Montana Conference of the M.E. Church, which began in 1876 with 295 members, reported over 11,000.

At unification in 1939, all of Methodism in Montana became the Montana Conference. In 1964 Lehmi County, IDAHO was added to the conference.

During its history the M.E. Church established a church paper, a college, several hospitals, a children's home, and a school.

In 1968 the Montana Conference had 118 ministers, 80 pastoral charges, 26,831 church members, 16,865 church school pupils, and property valued at $11,252,-500.

In 1969 the Big Horn Basin of WYOMING, with seventeen churches, was added to the Montana Conference, and the name was changed to Yellowstone Conference.

General Minutes, ME, MES, TMC.
Minutes of the Montana Conference.
E. J. Stanley, *Montana*. 1884.
Roberta B. West, "How Methodism Came to North Montana," *Methodist History*, April 1967.   JOHN F. REAGAN

MONTANA CONFERENCE was organized at MISSOULA in June 1939, with Bishop WILBUR HAMMAKER presiding. It included the churches of the Montana State Conference (ME) and the Montana churches of the NORTHWEST CONFERENCE (MES). At the time of organization the conference had eighty-five preachers, 144 churches, and 16,411 members. (See MONTANA for account of beginnings of Methodism in the state.)

Originally the work of the M.E. Church in Montana was administered as a mission and was centered almost exclusively in the southwest corner of the territory. Early leaders included Hugh Duncan, F. A. RIGGIN, J. A. Van Anda, and WILLIAM W. VAN ORSDEL, who was known as "Brother Van." Montana with UTAH formed the ROCKY MOUNTAIN CONFERENCE in 1872, but in 1876 the body was divided to form the Montana and Utah Conferences. Four years later Montana was reduced to mission status again, and then in 1887 it became once more a conference.

Methodism was established in north Montana by Van Orsdel, who preached his first sermon at Fort Benton, June 30, 1872. Also, he conducted services among the Indians at the Blackfoot and Piegan Agency. In 1890 a 60,000 square mile section of north Montana became the Great Falls District of the Montana Conference with Van Orsdel as presiding elder. Under his leadership the work progressed. The mission had twenty-three preachers, thirty churches, and 1,191 members.

In 1900 the Kalispell Mission was founded in what was known as the Flathead Valley in northwest Montana. It had nine preachers, fourteen churches, and 584 members. In 1907 the Kalispell and North Montana Missions merged to form the North Montana Conference. In 1924 the North Montana and Montana Conferences merged to make the Montana State Conference which continued until unification in 1939.

Today the Montana Conference and the Presbyterian and Congregational churches of the state support ROCKY MOUNTAIN COLLEGE at Billings, the only Protestant institution of higher learning in Montana. Also, they maintain hospitals in Billings, Bozeman, and Great Falls, and a Children's Home at HELENA. The conference has a two-million dollar retirement home, Hillcrest Retirement Apartments, in Bozeman. A mission to the Blackfoot Indians has been maintained for many years at Browning on the Blackfoot Reservation.

The Montana Conference is part of the Denver Area of the Western Jurisdiction. In 1968 the conference reported 118 ministers, eighty pastoral charges, 26,831 church members, 16,865 church school pupils, and property valued at $11,252,500.

By action of the 1968 Western JURISDICTIONAL CONFERENCE, effective in June, 1969, the Big Horn Basin of WYOMING with seventeen churches was to be added to the Montana Conference and the name changed to Yellowstone Conference.

General Minutes, ME, MES, TMC.
Minutes of the Montana Conference.
Roberta B. West, "How Methodism Came to North Montana," *Methodist History*, April 1967.   JOHN F. REAGAN

MONTANA CONFERENCE (EUB) brought together at its founding in 1948 two separate conferences of identical name but of different denominational affiliation prior to this date. The oldest of these conferences was the one belonging to the CHURCH OF THE UNITED BRETHREN IN CHRIST.

The congregation at Carlyle, Mont., is the mother church of the United Brethren in Christ in the Montana Conference. It originated in the home of Mr. and Mrs. Briley Douglas, who organized a Sunday school of eight members on May 6, 1907. On Sunday, July 25, 1909, G. W. Emerson completed the organization of the church itself. By 1919 the conference reported twenty-six organized United Brethren churches. Throughout the history of the conference, there have been sixty-five different pastors. The average length of pastorate has been two and one-half years. The rapid change in pastors was due to the low salaries and the smallness of the conference, which limited the opportunities for advancement.

At the time of uniting with the Montana Conference of THE EVANGELICAL CHURCH in 1948 there were nine organized congregations with a total property value of $113,-300. There were seven ordained ministers and a total membership of 776 persons. Total money paid for all purposes was $35,627.

Evangelical work in MONTANA was started almost simultaneously by two separate conferences. In 1908, S. B. Dillow, presiding elder of the Platte River Conference (NEBRASKA) came to visit his brother near Broadview.

Bishop W. F. HEIL announced that the General Board of Missions of The UNITED EVANGELICAL CHURCH was ready to give support on that field. In the northwestern section of the state, two years later, Presiding Elder William Suckow preached in the home of his brother; and from that meeting there grew what later became known as the Inverness Mission of the Dakota Conference (EVANGELICAL ASSOCIATION). H. A. Ritter was assigned to the field June 17, 1910.

The Montana Mission Conference was organized June 23, 1927, at Reedpoint, with John Oehlerking, presiding elder, and Bishop JOHN F. DUNLAP, Chairman. There were eight ministers; namely, H. S. Tool, W. C. Lasater, W. Isley, H. A. Thiele, N. A. Eller, E. C. Hicks, O. L. Peckenpaugh, and F. R. Witmer.

At the time of uniting with the Montana Conference of the United Brethren in 1948, there were fifteen organized congregations with total property value of $185,300, and fifteen ordained ministers.

The united conference covered the entire state of Montana, but with the small state population and the unfamiliarity of the population to The E.U.B. Church, the growth of the conference was quite small.

In 1967 membership amounted to 2,561 persons in twenty-three organized congregations. Total giving for all purposes was $232,493. Property was valued at $1,199,-567. The conference owns its summer camp grounds.

With the formation of The United Methodist Church in 1968, most of the E.U.B. congregations refused to enter the union. Those that did vote to unite became a part of the Montana Conference of the former Methodist Church which was renamed the Yellowstone Conference.

Stine O. Douglas, *History of the Montana Conference of the United Brethren in Christ* (1909-1945).
Proceedings of the Montana Conference, E.U.B., 1968.
Robert E. Strutz, *History of the Montana Conference of the Evangelical Church, 1908-1954,* unpublished manuscript.

E. J. BOTT

MONTERO, Bolivia, is a small, growing town north of Santa Cruz, the center of an extensive and very rapid agricultural development. Considerable Methodist work is centered there. The Church of the Sower, organized in 1958, maintains four of the preaching places in outlying communities. This has been served by missionary pastors for some time.

Medical Work. Montero is a center for public-health work in a lowland jungle area of eastern BOLIVIA. Lack of medical facilities in the Montero area in 1955 gave concern; and two nurses, graduates of the American Clinic in LA PAZ, at first held daily clinics at the Rural Institute and made weekly visits to surrounding villages. In 1961 PABLO MONTI, Methodist missionary from ARGENTINA, took over the clinical medical work and was a pioneer in preventive medicine. James Alley, Methodist missionary and public-health doctor, who had received a Master of Public Health degree from Harvard in 1962, came in 1965.

In August of that year a census and health survey was taken in Montero, organized by Alley. Students from Wesley Seminary canvassed the homes of 11,150 persons. From the census were discovered such statistics as: fifty-five percent of the houses had mud floors; seventy percent did not have running water; thirty-three percent had no toilet facilities; more than half of the population was under twenty years of age; only 2,392 persons were reported having received any type of vaccination. Within a year more than 32,000 vaccinations had been given. The census showed a need for a basic public-health program with emphasis on nutrition, infectious diseases, and environmental sanitation.

Alley's work in preventive medicine has been oriented on a community rather than denominational basis. A public-health board composed of seven Roman Catholics and four Protestants has responsibility for administration of the local hospital (which the government had asked The Methodist Church to administer), the development of an educational program which includes a public-health workers' school (inaugurated in 1966 with twenty-eight students), and provision of extension service. Four health centers, located in the outlying four sectors of Montero, facilitate attendance by persons in all parts of the town.

The public-health project carried out its first campaign in November and December of 1965 by vaccinating 3,500

RURAL INSTITUTE, MONTERO, BOLIVIA

of the children of Montero against polio. Later there was a tuberculosis control program. Of about 12,000 persons tested, twenty-one percent showed positive reaction to the tuberculosis test.

A rehabilitation center is presently being planned for malnourished children. This will be a cooperative project between the Roman Catholic and Methodist Churches.

This health project in 1966 was serving some 18,000 persons living within five miles of Montero. By extending aid to the colonies located north of Montero, probably between 40,000 and 50,000 may be reached.

Rural Institute, a school and base for community development work in Santa Cruz Province of Bolivia, began in 1958 in Montero under a palm-thatched roof with six boys and one girl. About that time Aymara and Quechua Indians from the valleys of Cochabamba, and the high plains near La Paz began to pour into the area, and within eight years Montero grew from 3,000 to a busy city of 12,000 persons.

Methodist leaders foresaw this development and planned accordingly. In addition to the vocational high school which was established at the Rural Institute, medical work was started at Montero, and in 1963 a radio station was set up. A broad community development program in the zone of homesteading settlers became one of the central programs stemming out of the Rural Institute.

The institute provides secondary education for 180 boys and girls in a six-year vocational program. The school farm furnishes quality animals for distribution to local farmers. There are also programs of community development and public health. Close cooperation is maintained with government officials in the development of rural elementary education, and opportunities are provided for students to take part in agricultural extension activities. The real focus of the work on Montero is not on Montero itself, but on the pioneer communities and on the local congregations which have been established there.

Robert and Rosa Caufield and James and Evelyn Pace were pioneer missionaries in Montero area work.

Highlands Echoes, Sept. 10, 1962.
B. H. Lewis, *Methodist Overseas Missions.* 1960.

EDWIN MAYNARD
JAMES PACE

MONTEVIDEO, Uruguay, situated on the Rio de la Plata at its mouth, is the capital and metropolis of the Republic of URUGUAY. The city is said to have been named for an explorer who saw, or thought he saw, a mountain on that part of the lower bay. ARGENTINA and BUENOS AIRES have traditionally been united by many ties with Uruguay and Montevideo, and these two countries were once a part of the Spanish vice-royalty of Rio de la Plata.

Argentina and Uruguay were put together first in the Eastern South American Conference of the M. E. Church, and then in the La Plata Conference of The Methodist Church in 1948. In 1954 the two conferences were separated and are today under their own respective names.

There are nine Methodist churches in the city, including Central Church, and other institutions such as CRANDON INSTITUTE, Evangelical Hospital, and GOODWILL INDUSTRIES.

Central Church is the principal Methodist congregation of Uruguay. In a profound sense, the history of Central Church is the history of Uruguayan Methodism. Earliest Methodist efforts resulted in the establishment of Central, and it has been the backbone of the church here ever since. It is sometimes called the Protestant Cathedral of Uruguay.

The first Methodist missionary to Uruguay, WILLIAM H. NORRIS, arrived Oct. 12, 1839, and was authorized to buy a lot and build a church to cost not more than $12,000, if the people of Montevideo would pay half. It took two years to get a building permit, and then only with the understanding that it would be for the worship of people from SWEDEN, England, and the United States, and as a school for their children.

Because of financial difficulties at home and a war between Uruguay and Argentina, the Board of MISSIONS in New York recalled Norris in 1842. Efforts to reopen the mission failed until 1870, when JOHN FRANCIS THOMSON was sent to Uruguay from Argentina. Between the withdrawal of Norris and the arrival of Thomson, some work was carried on by laymen, and several missionaries visited the area. Thomson himself had made regular trips from Argentina from 1868 on, to conduct worship services in homes. Uruguayan Methodism considers that year as the date of the permanent establishment of its work.

The first contacts had been with foreign elements, but with the coming of Thomson the work in Spanish was emphasized. However, for many years an English-speaking congregation met with the Uruguayan group and used the same building. It was an important factor in the support of the work and in the construction of what is now Central Church.

The first building was a hall purchased on Dec. 2, 1869. Thomson remained as pastor until succeeded by THOMAS B. WOOD from Argentina in May 1877. In that year the first official board for Central Church was elected and the government recognized its baptismal certificates as legal documents.

In 1883 Wood bought land for a new church in what was called the new city (in contrast to the old city, once walled). The first section of the building there was completed in 1905. In 1910 JUAN E. GATTINONI (later bishop) became pastor. The present church building was constructed, and at its completion in 1913 it was one of the outstanding buildings in Uruguay. It is still the largest Protestant church in the country. The educational plant was completed in 1925.

Present pastors are Miguel A. Brun and Lawson Lee, who share equal responsibility for direction of the church under the group ministry plan. Other pastors in recent years have been ENRIQUE C. BALLOCH, 1921-32; Daniel Hall, 1933-45; CARLOS GATTINONI, 1946-57; and EMILIO CASTRO, 1958-65. These last two were elected Bishops in 1969, Gattinoni for the new autonomous church in Argentina; Castro for that in Uruguay.

Evangelical Hospital is operated by an interdenominational group with large Methodist participation. It is the only hospital of its kind in Uruguay. It was inaugurated Sept. 14, 1964, nearly thirty years after the movement to build it began. The hospital has forty beds on two floors to care for general surgery, traumatology, and maternity cases. It offers services in radiotherapy, physiotherapy, orthodontics and dentistry, and has a blood bank, most of whose donors are members of Evangelical churches. The hospital serves a large number of outpatients, many of whom are members of one of the several health insurance programs which the hospital offers.

The idea of erecting a hospital which would emphasize the Christian witness came from a group of members of The Methodist Church and was later supported by the Waldensian Church. Then other denominations came into the movement. Planning began in the 1930's under a Methodist physician, RAFAEL R. HILL.

The first offerings were collected through women's societies of the churches, and a person of humble social position left her small house as a legacy. This was the first sum of importance that the hospital received. Then a larger legacy made it possible to acquire the lot of 5,000 square meters where the hospital now is located. The cornerstone was laid on May 2, 1949, in a ceremony presided over by Methodist Bishop SANTE UBERTO BARBIERI.

The hospital has a high percentage of occupancy. Its evangelistic effort comes through daily contact with the sick (and those who accompany them) by the chaplain and hospital personnel. Those who make their first contact with the Christian faith here receive New Testaments, Bibles, and other Christian literature. On the teaching level, its mission is to prepare Christian technicians (doctors, nurses, and practical nurses) to do medical work where there was none, or where it had been poorly done.

Friendship House is a social center in the stockyards district. The work grew out of a tiny Sunday school in the home of a family named Sosa. Several missionaries of the WOMEN'S FOREIGN MISSIONARY SOCIETY, including Elizabeth Hewett, director of Crandon Institute, and Stella Long, broadened the program to include English and cultural classes with occasional preaching services.

In 1918 ARTHUR F. WESLEY was appointed pastor of the church and director of the social center, which he called Pan-American Institute. The program was enlarged to include charity for the poor, recreation for young people, and day schools for the children. Six schools were set up, with a Sunday school in connection with each.

In December 1924, EARL M. SMITH was appointed pastor of the Cerro Church and director of the Pan-American Institute, which was soon renamed Friendship House. As public schools sprang up, the mission schools were discontinued and effort was redirected to Christian education and social services, including the GOODWILL INDUSTRIES and social casework. The program was enlarged to include a daily game room, sports, free public library, Boy Scouts, dramatics, camps, gymnastics, work camps, vacation Bible schools, and evening classes.

In 1953 a functional new Friendship House was built. Now under Uruguayan leadership, the institute carries on an enlarging religious, social and cultural program.

Goodwill Industries of Montevideo are the first Goodwill Industries outside the United States. The work was started on June 1, 1925, as a part of the social service program of Friendship House. There was no capital, but a room eight by twenty feet was available between Sundays. The Goodwill bags of used clothing and articles for repair were brought in first on pony-back, then on the platforms of street cars.

In 1931-32 Antonio Loureiro spent five months with E. L. HELMS in BOSTON, studying the operation of the mother Goodwill Industries. When he returned, he took over management of the Montevideo Goodwill Industries. A British company offered part of an abandoned packinghouse, greatly enlarging the quarters. An old truck was purchased, and Goodwill in Montevideo was on its way. A great boost was a stand in the National Industries

Exposition of 1933, where 2,000 Goodwill bags were distributed, doubling the number of contributors. In 1950 a new truck was purchased. In 1966 it was still bringing in bags, though a second truck was hired frequently.

The 1953 Week of Dedication offering in the United States designated $50,000 to the Montevideo Goodwill Industries for a new building. This was completed and inaugurated in 1959. Thereafter Goodwill was separate organically from Friendship House.

At first the principal purpose of Goodwill in Montevideo was to alleviate suffering from the seasonal unemployment experienced each year in the meat-packing industry. Unemployment insurance and other social legislation has largely eliminated this evil. In recent years the purpose of the Goodwill Industries has changed to that common in the United States: work and wages for the physically and mentally handicapped.

About thirty persons now work in the Montevideo Goodwill Industries.

Journals of the Uruguay Conference.
B. H. Lewis, *Methodist Overseas Missions.* 1960.

LAWSON LEE
EARL M. SMITH

MONTGOMERY, ALABAMA, U.S.A. The first Methodist Society was formed in Montgomery in late 1828 or early 1829. The Society numbered ten people—nine women and one man. In 1970 there were 12,138 members of The United Methodist Church in Montgomery, seventeen church plants, one college (HUNTINGDON), with a total value of more than $10,000,000.

During the early years of the little village of Montgomery, so named in honor of General Richard Montgomery, worship services were conducted by circuit riders, many of whom were Methodists. James King of NORTH CAROLINA, a Methodist, came in 1819 and was the first minister to visit Montgomery. JAMES MELLARD arrived in 1821. Bishop ENOCH GEORGE of the M. E. Church came through Montgomery in January 1822, enroute to preside over the MISSISSIPPI CONFERENCE. He was invited to preach at the Court House, and inasmuch as this was the first visit of a high church dignitary, the entire town turned out to hear him.

Until 1825 the only house of worship was the Old Mills and Westcott Meeting House located about two miles from the village. In 1825 a church was completed on a lot provided by the Alabama Company, dealers in real estate. The frame building was forty-eight by twenty-four feet. It was called Union Church and Methodists used it along with members of other denominations. In 1832 the Alabama Company liquidated its assets. The Methodist church was given option to buy Union Church, but the congregation failed to raise the necessary funds. General John Scott, a member of Alabama Company, whose wife was a Methodist, bought the property for $500 at public auction and gave it to the Methodists. It was named Court Street M. E. Church, and the second session of the newly formed ALABAMA CONFERENCE was held in this church, with the opening service for the Conference on Dec. 11, 1833.

Montgomery became a station Dec. 17, 1829, when B. A. Houghton was appointed pastor by the Mississippi Conference. At the end of the Conference year 1832, S. B. Sawyer reported 237 members—110 white, 127 colored—for Court Street. In 1835 a larger building— sixty by forty-five feet—was dedicated under the pastorate of Henry W. Hilliard. This building served until 1853 when a large brick structure was erected. This building was dedicated March 3, 1856, by Bishop GEORGE F. PIERCE. The Negro members took the materials from the frame building and erected their own church on Holcombe Street. There are at the present time two Negro Methodist churches in Montgomery. They are Metropolitan Church and St. Paul Church with a total membership of 194.

(no longer in existence) was founded in 1858 by some members of Court Street. Dexter Avenue Church was founded in December 1886. J. P. Roberts was appointed as first pastor. Clayton Street Church, now Frazer Memorial, was formed in 1889, and a Mr. Howell, a local preacher, was placed in charge.

Perry Street Church, now St. Mark's, began with a union Sunday school in 1887, and became a Methodist congregation in 1893. Fifth Avenue, now Burge Memorial,

FIRST CHURCH, MONTGOMERY, ALABAMA

The Court Street Church served for a century until the property was sold in 1937 to the United States Government for $120,000. The congregation moved to Cloverdale Park, and became First Methodist Church of Montgomery. It presently reports a membership of 2,715.

In 1842 the M. P. Church of Montgomery was organized. A. A. Lipscomb was the first pastor, and the first building was dedicated in 1844. It was located on the corner of Bibb and Molton Streets, and the congregation worshipped at that location until a new building was erected in 1924. The new location was on Winona and Florida Streets, and the name became Capitol Heights M. P. Church. Among the ministers of this church was T. C. Casaday, who served as pastor for eighteen years. He was a delegate to the uniting conference which brought the three branches of Methodism together in 1939.

CHURCH EXTENSION was a concern of Methodists in Montgomery from the beginning. Herron Street Church

resulted from the efforts of the Dexter Avenue congregation, and the first Quarterly Conference was held March 13, 1899. Forest Avenue resulted from action taken in a Quarterly Conference at Dexter Avenue in January of 1903. St. Luke organized 1938, St. James 1948, Dalraida 1949, Whitfield Memorial 1951, Normandale 1954, St. Paul 1954, Asbury 1954, Perry Hill 1956, and Boylston 1956.

At the present time there is a Montgomery District Board of Missions financed by regular annual income from each church. The primary purpose of this District Board is helping to establish and maintain new congregations of The United Methodist Church.

Blan, *A Brief History of the First Methodist Church*. N.d.
Blue, *History of Montgomery, Alabama*. N.d.
M. E. Lazenby, *Alabama and West Florida*. 1960.
Owen, *The Methodist Churches of Montgomery*. N.d.

WILBUR LATIMER WALTON

MONTI, DANIEL PABLO (1902-   ), author and minister in ARGENTINA, was born in ITALY, the son of a shoemaker who was an elder in a Plymouth Brethren church. He was brought by his family to Argentina, arriving Jan. 1, 1905. Young Daniel learned to read and write and learned his father's trade, working for some time in a shoe factory that to this day belongs to the Monti family.

As a boy he began attending a nearby Methodist church and in time became a member. He entered the BUENOS AIRES Methodist Seminary and upon graduation entered the ministry of the Eastern South America Annual Conference. He has served several pastoral charges, including Bahia Blanca, Flores, Rosario Tala, and Liniers. He was a district superintendent for several periods.

Mr. Monti has been a student of the history of the churches in Latin America and has written several books. Among them: *El pensamiento religioso de los hombres de Mayo* (*The Religious Thinking of the Men of May*—meaning the Argentine patriots of 1810); *Historia del Metodismo Rioplatense* (*History of River Plate Methodism*, 1968); and *Asi brille vuestra luz* (a biography of CARMEN CHACON, a young lady pioneer in the educational work of The Methodist Church in Brazil). Among his other books are *Edelweiss, Contrastes* (children's tales); *Entre cielo y cuchillas* (*Between Sky and Hills*, a romance from the Argentine countryside); *Sal de la tierra* (Salt of the Earth); *En la montaña del Maestro* (*On the Master's Mountain*, studies on the Sermon on the Mount); and *Voces del pasado* (*Voices of the Past*, studies on the Hebrew prophets).

He married Maria de Carlo, daughter of a staunch Methodist layman. Two of the Montis' four children (Daniel E. and Emilio) are pastors in the Argentine Methodist Church. The second son, Pablo, is a medical doctor and has worked for more than ten years as a missionary doctor to BOLIVIA.

ADAM F. SOSA

ST. JAMES CHURCH, MONTREAL

MONTREAL, Canada, **St. James Street Church.** At the beginning of the nineteenth century, Montreal was essentially a French community, dominated commercially and socially by an English minority, among whom the leading figures were the great fur traders. In this inhospitable environment Methodist services were held as early as 1802 by missionaries from the M. E. Church, who found in the city former Methodists from NEW YORK.

Despite their American background, these persons appear to have favored Wesleyan Methodism, for as early as 1807 they asked THOMAS COKE for assistance. The War of 1812 completed their disenchantment with the American Church, and in 1815 they welcomed John Strong as a representative of the English Conference. Six years later, a new chapel was built on St. James Street, at the instance of Robert Lusher.

The first St. James Street Church was a classical building which would seat about 1,200 persons. The Society prospered under the direction of such men as Robert Alder, JOSEPH STINSON, William Harvard and MATTHEW RICHEY, all of whom achieved wide distinction in Canadian and British Methodism. By 1844 there were 770 members of the Society, and a new building was necessary. In 1845, a church which would seat 3,000 people was opened in the presence of the Governor-General, Lord Metcalfe. Matthew Richey preached at this first service.

For the succeeding forty years, the St. James Street congregation and its ministers exerted a powerful influence on the development of new Methodist congregations and educational institutions in Montreal. As in the past, it attracted some of the most outstanding Canadian Methodist orators, including WILLIAM BRIGGS, GEORGE DOUGLAS, and JOHN POTTS.

In the 1880's, confronted by great changes in the city, the St. James congregation bought a new site fronting on St. Catherine Street. The cornerstone of the building was laid in June 1887, by Senator James Ferrier, who had laid the stone of the former church. In June 1888, the last services were held in the old church; a year later the vast and imposing new St. James was opened.

Since 1888, St. James Church has continued in being, as a Methodist Church until 1925; and since that date, as a United Church congregation. Despite the gradual loss of its people to the suburbs, it has been a site of great preaching and of continuous missionary effort. In its life and its history are mingled the streams of American, English, and Canadian Methodism.

Chronicles of the St. James Street Methodist Church, Montreal. Toronto, 1888.
The 150th Anniversary of St. James United Church, 1803-1953. Montreal, 1955.   G. S. FRENCH

MOOD, FRANCIS ASBURY (1830-1884), American preacher and educator, was born in CHARLESTON, S. C., June 23, 1830. He was licensed to preach in 1849, and joined the SOUTH CAROLINA CONFERENCE and graduated from Charleston College the following year. In 1854 he organized a conference historical society; he made a tour of Europe in 1857. He served leading appointments and the presiding eldership, and was elected secretary of the conference. During the Civil War he served as chaplain in the Confederate hospitals in Charleston. At the close of the war, since the impoverished people could ill support him as presiding elder, he launched a weekly family newspaper, *The Record*, and also served as part-time pastor in a Unitarian church. In 1868 he was offered the presidency of Soule University, Chappell Hill, TEXAS, a struggling institution which he soon decided must be superseded by a stronger one in a better location. Mood drew up a statesmanlike proposal for a central university for the whole of Texas Methodism, and personally persuaded each of the five Texas conferences to adopt it in 1869. It was 1874 before the new institution opened its doors on October 6, with thirty-three students, under the title of The Texas University. In 1876 the state legislature insisted that the name Texas University be used only by a state institution, and so the Methodist school became SOUTHWESTERN UNIVERSITY. Because it is the successor to several earlier schools it can rightfully claim to be the oldest university in the state. Mood served as regent for twelve years. In 1881 he was appointed as a delegate to the first ECUMENICAL METHODIST CONFERENCE, held in LONDON, where he gave an address on "The Higher Education Demanded by the Necessities of the Church in Our Time." He died on Nov. 12, 1884, at Waco, following the session of his annual conference there.

Cody, *The Life and Labors of Francis Asbury Mood.* New York: Revell, 1886. WALTER N. VERNON

MOODY, GRANVILLE (1812-1887), versatile American preacher and colorful soldier, was born at Portland, Maine, Jan. 2, 1812, the son of William Moody. An ancestor, William Moody, was a native of SCOTLAND and settled in Plymouth Colony in 1632. Granville's father, a graduate of Dartmouth College in 1798, moved to BALTIMORE when Granville was four, and became the principal of the first female seminary in Baltimore in 1816. Educated at Baltimore, Granville became a clerk in his brother's store in Norwich, Ohio in 1831, and was licensed to preach in the M. E. Church on June 15, 1833. Received into the OHIO CONFERENCE, he held various appointments in the state. In 1860 he was pastor of Morris Chapel in CINCINNATI.

At the outbreak of the Civil War, he was invited to take command of the 74th Ohio regiment, receiving the cordial approval of his colleagues who called it providential. He resigned his pastorate and entered the military services. He had a burning zeal for the Union and served until May 16, 1863, when illness forced him to resign. Colonel Moody, as he was called, assisted the regimental chaplain and preached often, baptizing nine soldiers one evening.

By Moody's bravery at Stones River he won the title, "the fighting parson." A colorful and gallant colonel, he was struck four times with bullets. His own horse was shot, but he refused to leave the field. On recommendation of the Secretary of War, the U. S. Senate conferred upon him the rank of brigadier general, by brevet, March 13, 1865, for distinguished services at the Stones River Battle.

Moody was a delegate to the GENERAL CONFERENCE of his Church in 1864. After his retirement from the Army, he became an itinerant again and served with acceptance in various localities until 1882, when ill health caused him to take the supernumerary relation. Moving to his farm near Jefferson, Ohio, he resided there until his death on June 4, 1887, which was caused by an accident while he was on his way to preach a memorial sermon before a part of the Grand Army of the Republic at Jefferson.

Appleton's Cyclopaedia of American Biography.
E. S. Bucke, *History of American Methodism.* 1964.
JESSE A. EARL

MOORE, ARTHUR JAMES (1888-   ), American bishop, evangelist and long-time president of the Board of

ARTHUR J. MOORE

MISSIONS of The Methodist Church, was born at Argyle, Ga., on Dec. 26, 1888, the son of John Spencer and Emma Victoria (Cason) Moore. His great grandfather early moved to GEORGIA, and his grandfather, a Confederate soldier, was killed in the battle of Gaines Mill, 1862.

Arthur Moore was a student at Emory College, Oxford, Ga., for a time, but was converted in his twenty-first year and began to preach at once. He subsequently received the following educational degrees: from EMORY UNIVERSITY, D.D., 1934; CENTRAL COLLEGE, Fayette, Mo., D.D., 1924; ASBURY COLLEGE, Wilmore, Ky., D.D., 1922; FLORIDA SOUTHERN COLLEGE, LL.D., 1942; RANDOLPH-MACON, LL.D., 1939; SOUTHWESTERN UNIVERSITY, Georgetown, Texas, LL.D., 1935; and Mercer University, LL.D., 1968.

He was married to Mattie T. McDonald of Waycross, Ga., on April 26, 1906. Their children are the Rev. William Harry, Wilbur Wardlaw, Dorothy Emma (deceased), Arthur James, Jr. (the present editor of *World Outlook*), and Evelyn Moore Means. Mrs. Moore died in 1964.

He entered the SOUTH GEORGIA CONFERENCE of the M.E. Church, South in 1909, was ordained deacon in 1912, and elder in 1914. He was a general evangelist for eight years, 1912-20; and then became minister of Travis Park Methodist Church, SAN ANTONIO, Texas, 1920-26; and of First Church, BIRMINGHAM, Ala., 1926-30. He was elected bishop by the GENERAL CONFERENCE of the M.E. Church, South, on May 20, 1930, and assigned to the Pacific Coast Area, which he served until 1934. From 1934 until 1940 he was the bishop in charge of missionary activities of the Methodist Church in CHINA, JAPAN, CZECHOSLOVAKIA, BELGIUM and Belgian CONGO, POLAND, and KOREA. ("I have three continents to supervise," he remarked genially.) He was then assigned to the ATLANTA Area in 1940 by the Southeastern JURISDICTIONAL CONFERENCE of The Methodist Church. From 1952-54, he also supervised the GENEVA (Switzerland) Area with Conferences in Central Europe and North Africa.

In 1937 Bishop Moore led a "Bishop's Crusade" which rekindled missionary spirit and cleared the Mission Board (MES) of $7,000,000 debt. He was given a certificate of honor by the Chinese Government in 1938 in recognition of distinguished service rendered the Chinese nation in the field of human relief. At the 1952 General Conference he was presented the Korean National Medal of Honor from President SYNGMAN RHEE in recognition of his service to the people of Korea. He delivered the FONDREN Lectures at SOUTHERN METHODIST UNIVERSITY in 1953, and the Jarrell Lectures, Emory University, 1945.

Since 1945, Bishop Moore has been sent by the COUNCIL OF BISHOPS on five emergency missions to disturbed areas of the world: Korea, 1946; Europe, 1948; the Orient, MALAYA, Borneo and BURMA, 1949-50; Korea, 1951; GERMANY, 1953. He represented The Methodist Church at the Centennial of Methodism in INDIA in 1956.

In 1941 he was interim president of WESLEYAN COLLEGE, Macon, Ga. From 1934-39 he was a member on the committee of Interdenominational Relations and Church Union. He was president of the Council of Bishops of The Methodist Church, 1951-52. Bishop Moore also served as a member of the COORDINATING COUNCIL, the Board of Social and Economic Relations, the METHODIST COMMITTEE FOR OVERSEAS RELIEF, and the WORLD METHODIST COUNCIL.

He is or has been a trustee of Emory University, PAINE COLLEGE, Wesleyan College, Andrew College, YOUNG HARRIS COLLEGE, AMERICAN UNIVERSITY, LAGRANGE COLLEGE, GAMMON THEOLOGICAL SEMINARY, CLARK COLLEGE, REINHARDT COLLEGE, SCARRITT COLLEGE, Warren Candler Hospital (SAVANNAH, Ga.), and the LAKE JUNALUSKA, N. C., Methodist Assembly. He was chairman of the Southeastern Jurisdictional Council of The Methodist Church, 1940-60. In 1940 he became president of the Board of Missions of The Methodist Church in which commanding position he served until 1960—during the war and post-war years of that period.

Bishop Moore is the author of *The Sound of the Trumpets*, 1934; *Central Certainties*, 1943; *Christ After Chaos*, 1944; *Christ and Our Country*, 1945; *The Mighty Savior*, 1952; *Immortal Tidings in Mortal Hands*, 1953; and *Fight On! Fear Not*, 1962.

He retired as an active bishop in 1960, but at once took up again the status of a church-wide evangelist, and continues traveling and preaching widely over the whole connection. He has a residence in Atlanta, and also one on St. Simons Island, Ga.

Who's Who in The Methodist Church, 1966. N. B. H.

MOORE, DAVID HASTINGS (1838-1915), American bishop, was born at Athens, Ohio, Sept. 4, 1838. A son of Congressman Eliakim Hastings Moore, David Moore was graduated from Ohio University in 1860, A.B.; A.M., 1863; honorary D.D. and LL.D. He united with the OHIO CONFERENCE in 1860, having been converted in 1855.

He was Lieutenant-Colonel of the 125th Regiment, Ohio Volunteer Infantry, in the Civil War, a regiment which was dubbed the "Ohio Tigers" by General Thomas of Chickamauga. Having been wounded, Moore returned to civilian life broken in health.

His appointments (all in Ohio) were: Second Street, Zanesville, 1855-68; St. Paul's, Delaware, 1868-70; Wesley Chapel, Columbus, 1870-72; Trinity, Cincinnati, 1872-75; and president of the Cincinnati Wesleyan Female Seminary, 1875-80.

He followed EARL CRANSTON to COLORADO to become president of Colorado Seminary and one of the founders and first Chancellor of the UNIVERSITY OF DENVER, 1880-

89. His labors there are among the treasures of the ROCKY MOUNTAIN CONFERENCE's traditions. His genius for friendship was a short cut to the hearts of the plainsmen and mountaineers and this made him and the young university a power. He rode the buckboards and stages, bumping through canyons of Colorado and WYOMING, a builder of a civilization of strong western men.

Moore became editor of the *Western Christian Advocate*, 1889-1900, and his editorials rang clear and strong. He championed the rights of women regarding membership in the GENERAL CONFERENCE and the rights of the FREEDMEN. There was never "a dull line" where David Moore's pen had wrought.

Moore was elected bishop in 1900 and assigned to CHINA, JAPAN and KOREA for four years, and that was at the time of the Boxer uprising. He wrote a vivid description of the war between Japan and RUSSIA. In 1915 he wrote the life of Bishop JOHN MORGAN WALDEN. His other episcopal areas were: PORTLAND, Ore., 1904-08; CINCINNATI, 1908-12, when he retired.

On June 21, 1860, Moore married Julia Sophia Carpenter of Athens, Ohio. She died in 1911, leaving six children. Bishop Moore died on a train going to Cincinnati, Nov. 23, 1915. His body was laid to rest in the quiet churchyard at Athens.

A man of great strength of character, David Hastings Moore had a vivid imagination, a rich and copious vocabulary, and an analytic and synthetic mind. He was an example of outspoken loyalty to his principles, his friends and his fellowmen around the world.

Central Christian Advocate, Dec. 1, 1915.
F. D. Leete, *Methodist Bishops*. 1948.
National Cyclopedia of American Biography.
M. Simpson, *Cyclopaedia*. 1878. JESSE A. EARL

HENRY MOORE

MOORE, HENRY (1751-1844), British Methodist, was born near DUBLIN on Dec. 21, 1751. He entered the Methodist itinerancy in 1779. In 1787 he and his wife suffered at the hands of a mob when he was attempting to hold an open-air service in Dublin. On or near this very site was erected thirty-four years later the first Abbey Street Methodist Church, the site of the Dublin Central Mission. Moore was a close friend of JOHN WESLEY, who on Feb. 27, 1789, ordained him "a presbyter in the Church of God," the second man to be ordained for the English work. Wesley made him one of the three custodians of his manuscripts, and with THOMAS COKE he produced in 1792 a *Life of the Rev. John Wesley*. Moore was involved in the controversy over the administration of the SACRAMENTS by the itinerants in BRISTOL in 1794; he opposed the concessions made to the laity in 1797. He was elected President of the Wesleyan Conference in 1804, and again in 1823. He published *A Discourse . . . Romans* (1815); *Thoughts on the Eternal Sonship* (1817), a reply to ADAM CLARKE; a two volume *Life of the Rev. John Wesley* (1824-25); the first part of an *Autobiography, with Sermons*, etc. (1830). He died on April 27, 1844.

R. H. Gallagher, *Pioneer Preachers*. 1965.
F. Jeffrey, *Irish Methodism*. 1964.

JOHN KENT
FREDERICK JEFFERY

MOORE, JOHN H. (? -1957), American minister and nineteenth bishop of the C.M.E. CHURCH, was born in ALABAMA. He was educated at RUST COLLEGE in Holly Springs, Miss. Bishop Moore served as pastor and presiding elder and was elected General Secretary of Missions in 1914. During his episcopacy, he was known as a preacher, fund raiser, and church builder. He had a strong interest in missions and helped establish a mission in the BRITISH WEST INDIES. He died on Jan. 27, 1957.

Harris and Patterson, *C.M.E. Church*. 1965.
The Mirror, General Conference, CME, 1958. RALPH G. GAY

MOORE, JOHN JAMISON (1818-1883), American bishop of the A.M.E. ZION CHURCH was born in Berkeley County, W. Va., of slave parents, about the year 1818. His mother was born free, but at the age fifteen years was kidnapped in MARYLAND and sold into slavery in WEST VIRGINIA, where she married John's father, a slave. Her maiden name was Reidoubt and her husband's name was Hodge, but a change of owners caused him to adopt the name of Moore. When John Moore was six years old his parents, by the advice and assistance of friendly Quakers, attempted a flight from slavery with their six children, of whom the future bishop was the youngest. They were recaptured, however, and the oldest four children were sold South. A second attempt to gain their liberty was successful, and the parents, with their remaining two children, after many hardships and sufferings, reached Bedford County, Pa. Here a friendly farmer gave them employment and the two boys, William and John, were bound out for a term to his son, also a farmer. Owing to the pursuit of their former owner, the parents were obliged to leave the settlement, but John remained secure on the farm. He was taught to read and write by his employer, and acquired a knowledge of farming. The last part of his apprenticeship was served to a brother-in-law of his former master, who exacted six months over the proper time, and did not furnish the schooling or clothes and the cash he required by law after the expiration of the term.

After leaving his ungenerous master, he worked for six months for a farmer in the settlement at seven dollars per month. Having saved about fifteen dollars, he concluded to visit Harrisburg, and walked the 106 miles to that place in two days. In 1833 he became religiously impressed and experienced a change of heart. Leaving Harrisburg he visited his old home in the mountains where he remained some time, having obtained employment as a porter in a store. He was licensed as an exhorter on

returning to Harrisburg in 1834 and a year later received his license to preach. He joined the Philadelphia Conference (AMEZ) in 1839. John Jamison Moore was one of the great pioneering circuit riders of his denomination, serving not only in PENNSYLVANIA and OHIO but going as far west as SAN FRANCISCO, where he established a Zion Church. He was elevated to the bishopric in 1868 and died in 1883.

DAVID H. BRADLEY

MOORE, JOHN MONROE (1867-1948), strong and able bishop in The Methodist Church and leader in the unification of American Methodism, was born in Morgantown, Ky., Jan. 27, 1867.

The son of Joseph A. and Martha Ann Hampton Moore, he was of Virginian and English ancestry. Phases of his life included the pastorate, church journalism, education, missions, episcopal leadership and administration, as well as authorship of books, especially on Methodism.

There were early years of ample and painstaking preparation, including the Morgantown, Ky., public schools; Lebanon University, Ohio; Yale University; Leipzig and Heidelberg, Germany. Yale University conferred on him the Ph.D. degree (1895) and also the honorary D.D. degree; WESLEYAN UNIVERSITY at Middletown, Conn., the Litt.D. (1935); SOUTHERN METHODIST UNIVERSITY, the LL.D. degree (1938); Central College in Arkansas a D.D. (1908), and SOUTHWESTERN UNIVERSITY at Georgetown, Texas, a LL.D. (1928).

Moore's pastoral work began when he was licensed to preach in 1887 by the M.E. Church, South, ordained DEACON (1894), ELDER (1898). His pastorates included Marvin Church, ST. LOUIS, Mo. (1895-1898); Travis Park, SAN ANTONIO, Texas, (1898-1902); First Methodist, DALLAS (1902-1906). He was pastor of St. John's Church, St. Louis (1909-1910); Secretary of Home Missions of the M.E. Church, South, Nashville, Tenn. (1910-1918). He was elected bishop at the 1918 GENERAL CONFERENCE of his church. While pastor of the church in San Antonio, he was married to Miss Bessie Harris of that city.

When he was elected bishop on May 14, 1918, he was assigned to work in BRAZIL (1918-1922), following which he was in charge of conferences in OKLAHOMA and the east half of TEXAS (1922-1926); in charge of the west half of Texas and NEW MEXICO (1926-1930); GEORGIA and FLORIDA (1930-1934); MISSOURI and ARKANSAS (1934-1938). He was officially retired in 1938.

Besides his episcopal duties, Bishop Moore had various other responsibilities, such as Chairman of the General Board of MISSIONS; Editor of the *Nashville Christian Advocate* (1906-1909); member of the Joint Hymnal Commission to prepare the Methodist Hymnal (1904-1906); and also twenty-five years later a member again of the Joint Hymnal Commission (1931-1934). He was a member of the Joint Committee on Unification, composed of representatives of the M.E. Church, the M.E. Church, South, and the M.P. Church. Upon the death of Bishop MOUZON, he became chairman of the M.E. Church, South representatives. He was a member of the World Conference on Faith and Order held at Lausanne, and the one held at Edinburgh (1937); and was a member of the ECUMENICAL METHODIST CONFERENCE held at Atlanta, Ga. in 1931.

Bishop Moore was Chairman of the Department of Schools and Colleges of the M.E. Church, South (1934-1938); and Chairman of the Board of Trustees of Southern Methodist University (1932-1938). He endowed a Chair for a Traveling Fellowship for graduates of the School of Theology of the university.

He was author of the following books: *Etchings of the East* (1909); *The South Today* (1916); *Brazil: An Introductory Study* (1920); *Making the World Christian* (1922); *The Long Road to Methodist Union* (1943); *Methodism in Belief and Action* (1946).

Perhaps his most noteworthy contribution to Methodist history was his constructive work on the Unification Commission. He with Bishop E. H. HUGHES of the M.E. Church, and Bishop JAMES H. STRAUGHN of the M.P. Church, formed the great triumvirate of leaders as this momentous work came to completion.

He died Aug. 1, 1948, in Dallas, Texas, and was buried there.

C. T. Howell, *Prominent Personalities.* 1945.
Journal of the North Texas Conference, 1949.
MRS. JOHN H. WARNICK

JOHN Z. MOORE

MOORE, JOHN ZACHARIAH, II (1874-1963), American missionary to KOREA, was born in PITTSBURGH, Pa., Jan. 8, 1874. Son and grandson of Methodist ministers, he alternatively taught school and attended Scio College in eastern OHIO, and then entered DREW SEMINARY where he graduated in 1903.

With characteristic zeal he was on his way to Korea and even being ordained by Bishop DAVID H. MOORE in SEOUL before commencement time. His entire missionary career was centered in north Korea at Pyengyang, so that he could call most of the Methodist leaders from north Korea his "boys." At various times he had been presiding elder over all the work of his mission in north Korea and had founded scores of churches and primary schools as well as two high schools and two Bible schools.

He was a most effective speaker in the Korean language as well as English. His talks were filled with anecdotes and stories gleaned from his reading, especially of WESLEY, Lincoln, and Theodore Roosevelt. He was also a prolific writer about Korea, publishing numerous articles in magazines and newspapers. During forty years' work in either America or in Korea, he helped raise approximately half a million dollars for the work.

He was cited by the Japanese government in 1925 for his efforts in promoting educational work, and later by the Korean government for his distinguished missionary service. He died in LOS ANGELES, Calif., Aug. 6, 1963. Inurnment was at Richland Cemetery, near St. Clairsville, Ohio, the scene of his boyhood and youth.

CHARLES A. SAUER

MOORE, MORRIS MARCELLUS (1856-1900), American bishop of the A.M.E. CHURCH, was born in Quincy, Fla., on Nov. 15, 1856. His education was self-acquired. He was converted in 1861, licensed in 1876, and admitted into the Florida Annual Conference of the A.M.E. Church in 1878. He was ordained DEACON in 1880 and ELDER in 1881. He held pastorates from 1881 to 1896, and the General Office of Financial Secretary, 1896-1900. In 1900 he was elected bishop. He died in 1900 without ever having held an annual conference.

R. R. Wright, *The Bishops.* 1963.   GRANT S. SHOCKLEY

NOAH W. MOORE, JR.

MOORE, NOAH WATSON, JR. (1902-   ), American bishop, was born March 28, 1902, at Newark, N. J., the son of Noah Watson and Eliza A. (Boyce) Moore. He received the following degrees: MORGAN STATE COLLEGE, A.B., 1926; LL.D., 1961; DREW UNIVERSITY, B.D., 1931; GAMMON THEOLOGICAL SEMINARY, D.D., 1951; and SOUTHERN METHODIST UNIVERSITY, D.D., 1968. On Nov. 27, 1926, he married Carolyn W. Lee, and they have one daughter, Carolyn (Mrs. Arthur D. Weddington).

Noah Moore was admitted on trial in the DELAWARE CONFERENCE of the M.E. Church in 1930, and ordained elder in 1932.

His ministry includes in the Delaware Conference: New Rochelle, N. Y., 1930-31; Upper Hill, Md., 1931-35; Fairmount Circuit and Upper Hill, Md., 1935-37; Camphor Memorial, PHILADELPHIA, Pa., 1937-41; Zoar Church, Philadelphia, 1941-43; St. Daniels Church, Chester, Pa., 1943-47; superintendent of the Easton District, 1947-49; Tindley Temple, Philadelphia, 1949-60.

He was elected bishop at Cleveland, Ohio, on July 14, 1960, by the Central JURISDICTIONAL CONFERENCE and consecrated on July 17, 1960. This conference assigned him to its NEW ORLEANS Area.

Bishop Moore has served as a member of the COUNCIL on WORLD SERVICE AND FINANCE; the Committee for Overseas Relief; vice-president of the Morgan Christian

Center, Morgan College, Baltimore, Md. He is a trustee and vice-president of the Morgan College Corporation; on the Board of Managers of the Christian Street Y.M.C.A. in Philadelphia; a board member and secretary-treasurer of the Philadelphia Housing Authority; a trustee of the United Fund, Philadelphia and vicinity; on the Board of Directors of the Urban League, Philadelphia; Health and Welfare Agency, Southern Area, Philadelphia.

He is presently a member of the WORLD METHODIST COUNCIL; of the General BOARD OF EDUCATION; the Commission on WORSHIP; and on the Interboard Committee on Christian Vocations of The United Methodist Church. He is a member of the Board of Trustees of DILLARD UNIVERSITY, Gammon Theological Seminary, HUSTON-TILLOTSON COLLEGE, MORRISTOWN COLLEGE, and president of the Board of Trustees of WILEY COLLEGE.

Bishop Moore administered the LOUISIANA, TEXAS, and WEST TEXAS Annual CONFERENCES of the Central Jurisdiction of The Methodist Church until in 1968, when with the dissolution of the most of the Central Jurisdiction, he was by the South Central Jurisdiction assigned to the superintendency of the NEBRASKA Area. His episcopal residence is in LINCOLN, Neb.

Who's Who in America, Vol. 34.
Who's Who in The Methodist Church, 1966.   N. B. H.

THOMAS A. MOORE

MOORE, THOMAS ALBERT (1860-1940), Canadian Methodist and United Church of Canada minister, was born in Acton, Canada, West, June 29, 1860. He was educated at Acton public school, Georgetown Academy, and McGill University. In 1884, he was ordained in the Methodist ministry.

Although he was a highly successful preacher, he had also great administrative ability and a very keen interest in social and moral reform. For several years he was secretary and general secretary of the Ontario Lord's Day Alliance; he was president from 1910 to 1921. In the same years he took an active part in the work of the Ontario Temperance Federation.

From 1914 to 1925, Moore was secretary of the Joint Committee on Church Union, in which post he contributed substantially to the formation of The United Church of Canada (see CANADA). Thus, he became the first general secretary of the new church, and continued in office until 1936. One of his successors has said that "during the critical and formative time just after Church Union, he did much to shape and fashion the whole legal and administrative structure of our Church's life. . . . But he was more than a detached executive officer. He was guide, philosopher and friend, to ministers and laymen throughout the whole connexion." (Hamilton Conference, *Proceedings*.)

In recognition of his great work, Thomas A. Moore was elected Moderator in 1932. He served also on the Ecumenical Methodist Committee, as a member of the World Conference on Faith and Order, and president of the Canadian Brotherhood Federation. Among the honors he received were a D.D. from Wesley College, and an LL.D. from MOUNT ALLISON UNIVERSITY.

After his retirement, Moore devoted himself unceasingly to his first love—preaching. Unfortunately he was stricken with heart disease, and after 1938 had to desist from this work. He died in Toronto, March 31, 1940, and was buried in Acton cemetery.

G. H. Cornish, *Cyclopaedia of Methodism in Canada*. 1903. *Record of Proceedings*, Hamilton Conference, United Church of Canada, 1940.   G. S. FRENCH

MOORE, WALTER HARVEY (1886-1961), American preacher and missionary to BRAZIL, was born in Foster, Ky., Oct. 18, 1886. He received his B.A. in science and letters and a B.D. from Wesleyan College, Winchester, Ky.; and a second B.D. from CANDLER SCHOOL OF THEOLOGY. He married Nell Profitt, a teacher, on June 30, 1919, and they went to Brazil as missionaries that year. His first appointment was to INSTITUTO GRANBERY, JUIZ DE FÓRA, state of Minas Gerais. He was ordained DEACON in September 1920, by Bishop JOHN M. MOORE. In 1922, he was named Reitor (principal) of Granbery Institute, beginning thus a career that made him one of the most loved and influential citizens of the city. He remodeled the establishment, and in the year of the catastrophic flood in Juiz de Fóra, he took a leading part in the work of helping its victims, sheltering them in the school.

He next spent several years away from Granbery, directing the Methodist seminary near SÃO PAULO City, during what was a most difficult period in that institution's life. When he returned to Granbery in 1951, many Roman Catholic leaders were among those who met and honored him. He remained there until retirement in 1956, when he was highly honored by the community. A street was named for him and the city council of Juiz de Fóra declared him an honorary citizen. After his return he travelled to Washington, where he was decorated, at the request of Brazilian friends, with the Order of the Southern Cross, at the Brazilian Embassy (1957).

Active, energetic, consecrated, his life was one of constant service, of purity, and of love for his neighbor. To the vigor of his personality, he added the noble qualities of a magnanimous heart and a fine Christian spirit. That was one of the tributes paid to Walter Moore.

He died suddenly on July 17, 1961. His wife died in 1963. Their two children are Emeline Koppel and Walter Harvey, Jr., a sculptor in Washington.

J. B. PANISSET

MORADABAD ANNUAL CONFERENCE is a conference of INDIA with five districts, covering the area of about 4,000 square miles. There is a population of approximately 3,000,000, and the Christian population of the whole conference is 53,835.

The conference was organized in 1958, when the North India Conference was divided. Its districts are Bijnor, Chandausi, Garhwal, Moradabad, and Rampur.

Moradabad, the city, has a population of about 180,100. The Parker Intermediate College (enrollment, 844), the Methodist Girls Higher Secondary School (enrollment, about 600), and the Titus Elementary School (enrollment, 400), are located here, each with a hostel for Christian students. There are two self-supporting churches in the city.

Pauri is the headquarters of the Garhwal civil and ecclesiastical district. The Messmore Intermediate College is located here. It has recently become coeducational. The enrollment is about 900. Two miles away from the college is the Mary Ensign Gill coeducational primary and junior high school with 156 students.

Pauri is in the Himalayan Mountains, elevation 5,390 feet. Garhwal District borders on NEPAL and was a part of Nepal until ceded to British India in 1817. It was one of the earliest appointments of JAMES MILLS THOBURN, who years later became the first Methodist bishop in India.

Disciplines.
Project Handbook Overseas Missions, The United Methodist Church. New York: Board of Missions, 1969.

J. WASKOM PICKETT

MORAVIANS. The ultimate ancestors of the eighteenth-century Moravians were the Bohemian Brethren of the fifteenth century, advocates of a simplified Christianity, who eventually aligned themselves with the Protestant Reformation. Most of them were expelled from Bohemia and Moravia in 1621. In 1722 Moravian and other refugees (some of them of Brethren descent) settled at HERRNHUT under the patronage of Count ZINZENDORF. Zinzendorf developed the group into a complete religious and civil community, at first as a Pietist Lutheran society within which men of different churches could live. (He himself was both a Lutheran minister from 1734, and a Moravian bishop from 1737.) Pressure of circumstances led to the development of a separate church which in some respects was a revival of the Bohemian past. The society ideal persisted for years, however, and perhaps hindered the Moravian influence, although they quickly developed overseas Moravian activity. In general, Moravianism marks a further development of the Pietist type of Lutheranism begun by Spener and Francke in seventeenth-century GERMANY to an emphasis on conversion, and a personal religious experience centered (sometimes excessively) on a childlike devotion to Christ and his passion.

Within post-Reformation Protestantism as a whole, Moravianism represents a kind of domestic Protestant monasticism. The community was divided into "choirs" organized according to sex, age, and marital status, with a variety of unusual means of GRACE, under a partriarchal

discipline. In England, Moravianism was one element in the many-sided Evangelical Revival, and for a time promised to have a wide influence—e.g. through societies taken over from BENJAMIN INGHAM in Yorkshire and from JOHN CENNICK in the west in the 1740's. They were probably hindered by vacillations in Zinzendorf's policy and by overcentralization. In 1749 they achieved Parliamentary recognition as an episcopal church; and in 1755 were organized as the English province of Moravianism.

JOHN WESLEY first met Moravians on the way to GEORGIA in 1735; from them he learned about JUSTIFICATION and conversion which helped toward his conversion of 1738; he visited Herrnhut in the same year. But in 1740 he and his followers broke with the Moravians, and disagreement was sharpened by literary controversy and the bad reputation of the Moravians for emotional excesses in the 1740's. An attempt at Methodist-Moravian unity in 1785-86 by THOMAS COKE proved abortive. The original break was precipitated in some cases by the "stillness" doctrine of the Moravians (i.e., the belief that the use of the means of grace erodes justification by faith alone), and aggravated, it is alleged, by the conflicting ambitions of John Wesley and Zinzendorf as religous leaders. There were, however, clear doctrinal differences. Wesley accused the Moravians of dwelling exclusively on the doctrine of justification, neglecting the law and zeal for SANCTIFICATION. The Moravians accused Wesley of "having mixed the works of the law with the gospel as means of grace" (quoted in Renham, *Memoirs of James Hutton,* 1856, p. 47). A conversation of 1741 between Wesley and Zinzendorf makes clear the latter's Lutheran views, which underlay the controversy; he maintained that perfection along with justification was "imputed" in Christ once for all; no actual and growing perfection in men is possible.

Methodism owed a good deal to the Moravians; the initial rediscovery of justification, conversion, and ASSURANCE, some devices for the cultivation of religious experience, e.g. LOVE FEASTS and WATCH NIGHTS. Yet equally important and distinctive Methodist institutions (societies, covenant services, field preaching) came from other sources. Nor was the "monastic" organization of Herrnhut and the English Fulneck settlement ever a feature of Methodism. In its methods of extensive itinerant evangelism, and the rapid spread of self-supporting yet connected societies, English Methodism's development was strongly contrasted with the eventual stagnation of English Moravianism.

JOHN KENT

MORE, HANNAH (1745-1833), the famous evangelical Anglican writer, was born at Stapleton in Gloucestershire, the fourth of five daughters of Jacob More, who came from a Norfolk family. Removing to LONDON in her late twenties (circa 1773), she became associated with the literary world there, and was fascinated especially by the theatre. She came under the influence of David Garrick, as is shown by her letters to her family.

The pattern of her life began to change about 1785, owing to the possession of a "growing conviction of the unsatisfactoriness of all enjoyments which are not in accordance with scripture, and in unison with prayer." In consequence, she was responsible from 1789 for the establishment of schools for the poor at Cheddar, and other villages in Somerset, where there were soon three hundred children under her care. In this she followed the work of ROBERT RAIKES, but went beyond the pioneer in her concern that the newly literate should have worthwhile reading matter. This led to her writing a series of "Cheap Repository Tracts," the first of which was entitled *Village Politics*. The tracts came out at the rate of three each month and contained stories, ballads, and Sunday readings written in a popular style. Two million were produced in the first year; and they were vigorously attacked, one writer urging that her writings should be burned. In part the message of her tracts was that Englishmen should not follow the example of the French Revolution.

In 1802 she moved to Barley Wood, and now began the period of her writing of books: *Hints Towards Forming the Character of a Young Princess* (1805), *Coelebs in Search of a Wife* (1809), *Practical Piety,* and *Christian Morals* (1811). A biographer regarded her as an accomplished conversationalist. Her religion was moral in character, and she had a dislike of controversy. She had no particular contact with English Methodism, but was an example of the powerful Anglican Evangelical world which formed another contributing stream to the whole Evangelical Revival of the eighteenth and early nineteenth centuries.

Ford K. Brown, *Fathers of the Victorians: The Age of Wilberforce.* London: Cambridge University Press, 1961.
William Roberts, ed., *Memoirs of the Life and Correspondence of Mrs. Hannah More.* 4 vols.; London: R. B. Seeley, 1834.
Henry Thompson, *The Life of Hannah More.* London, 1838.

B. J. N. GALLIERS

MORELAND, JESSE EARL (1897-   ), American missionary and college president, was born at Commerce, Texas, on Oct. 2, 1897, the son of Royal Bert and Mary Emma (Long) Moreland. He received his A.B. degree from SOUTHERN METHODIST UNIVERSITY in 1918; the A.M. in 1921; the L.H.D. *causa honoris* in 1950. He did postgraduate work at Peabody College, Nashville, Tenn., in 1927. Other honorary degrees which came to him were the LL.D. from MORRIS HARVEY COLLEGE, 1941; from EMORY AND HENRY COLLEGE in 1942; from the UNIVERSITY OF CHATTANOOGA in 1955; and from the University of Richmond in 1964. The PORTO ALEGRE COLLEGE in BRAZIL recorded him Dr. Humanidades in 1948.

His wife was Helen Elizabeth HARDY and they married on Nov. 18, 1924. Their children were Jane Long (Mrs. Ben Vaughan Branscomb); Helen (Mrs. Clare Cotton, Jr.); Mary (Mrs. Thomas Ellison Smith); and Frances (Mrs. Lawrence Fossett).

Dr. Moreland went as educational missionary to Porto Alegre College, Brazil, 1921-22; was professor and vice-president there, 1922-26; and president from 1927-34. Then he returned to America and became the vice-president of SCARRITT COLLEGE, 1936-39. In 1939 he was elected president of RANDOLPH-MACON COLLEGE in Ashland, Va., and in that capacity served until his retirement in 1967.

Dr. Moreland has been a member of the Southeastern JURISDICTIONAL CONFERENCE of The Methodist Church, 1940, '44, '48, '52, '60, and '64; a member of the General BOARD OF EDUCATION of that Church and a member of the GENERAL CONFERENCES of 1944, '52, '56, '60, and '64. He was a member of the first Assembly of the WORLD COUNCIL OF CHURCHES in Amsterdam, 1948; of the second and third Assemblies at EVANSTON, Illinois, 1954, and in

NEW DELHI, India, 1961; a member of the Central Committee of the World Council of Churches, 1948-54. He was also a member of the Executive Committee of the FEDERAL COUNCIL OF CHURCHES of Christ in America, 1940-50, and a member of the first organizational meeting of the NATIONAL COUNCIL OF CHURCHES which supplanted that organization. He has been president of the National Association of Schools and Colleges of The Methodist Church and was the recipient of the ST. GEORGE'S Award, 1962. Also he received the Virginia Award from the National Conference of Christians and Jews, 1966. As a trustee he has been on the Board of PHILANDER SMITH COLLEGE, BENNETT COLLEGE, PENNINGTON SCHOOL; is a member of various academic and learned societies, and has served as a Director of the Hanover National Bank, Ashland, since 1961. Upon retirement in 1967, he continued to live in Ashland, Va.

Who's Who in The Methodist Church, 1966.   N. B. H.

MORELOCK, GEORGE L. (1880-1967), the first General Secretary of the BOARD OF LAY ACTIVITIES of The Methodist Church after church union, was born in Franklin, Tenn., on Jan. 8, 1880, the son of William L. and Tennessee Adeline (Jackson) Morelock. He married Ruth Murphy on June 6, 1906, and their children are Mrs. W. A. Jenkins, Elizabeth, and George L., Jr. He was educated at the University of the South (Sewanee), receiving the A.B. degree in 1913, and did graduate study at Stanford University, 1913-14. MILLSAPS COLLEGE gave him the LL.D. degree in 1937.

When the General Board of Lay Activities of the M. E. Church, South, organized in 1922, he became its first General Secretary, serving in that capacity until 1940 when he became Executive Secretary for the entire reunited Church. He was a member of the Uniting Conference in 1939 and of the JURISDICTIONAL CONFERENCE of 1940. He served on the BOARD OF EVANGELISM of The Methodist Church and on the FEDERAL COUNCIL OF CHURCHES of Christ for some years. He was delegate to the Oxford World Conference on Life and Work in 1937, and a visitor of Lay Work to CZECHOSLOVAKIA, to BELGIUM, BRAZIL and ARGENTINA in 1937. He wrote *A Steward in The Methodist Church; The Board of Stewards; The Way to Spiritual Life; The Ideal Layman;* and several other pamphlets in the same field. He retired in 1948 as General Secretary, and made his home thereafter in Miami, Fla. He died in Miami on Aug. 21, 1967.

C. T. Howell, *Prominent Personalities.* 1945.   N. B. H.

MORETON, ROBERT HAWKEY (1844-1917), British minister and missionary, was born in BUENOS AIRES, ARGENTINA, Jan. 10, 1844, son of Robert Moreton, who had emigrated from Cornwall, England, some time before 1830. The family returned to England in 1861, to avoid military service for Robert Hawkey, and settled in Helston, Cornwall. Robert Hawkey began to study medicine at St. Bartholemew's, LONDON, but hearing a call to the ministry he entered Richmond College, London, in 1864, and after three years there was appointed first to Helston, and then to St. Colomb, Isles of Scilly, where he met his future wife, Agnes Banfield. In 1870 his offer for overseas service was at first not accepted, but later that year, in November, the Wesleyan METHODIST MISSIONARY SOCIETY invited him to take up work in PORTUGAL because of his knowledge of Spanish, which he had already used in tract distributing work among Spanish sailors in the Thames side docks.

He arrived in Oporto, Portugal, on Feb. 16, 1871, with his bride whom he had married three weeks before. Here he ministered until his death in 1917, forty-three years in the active ministry and three years as a supernumerary minister. He knew what it was in the early days to suffer persecution at the hands of the populace, at times arriving home from some attempt at preaching "covered with mud," but he outlived this phase and became much respected and esteemed. Through the years his gifts as preacher, teacher, administrator and organizer were well exercised. His Methodism was of the classic variety; he built on the basis of the CLASS MEETING, and only admitted into membership after due, and sometimes lengthy, trial of each candidate; CLASS TICKETS in his own meticulous hand date from the first year of his ministry in Portugal. His preaching and pursuit of CHRISTIAN PERFECTION attracted many, including some devout Roman Catholics who were looking for the same way.

He translated a number of hymns into Portuguese and shared in the compilation of a succession of hymnaries; he introduced the tonic-sol-fá system of music into Portugal. He also translated some popular, and semi-polemical works, such as *The Convent Unmasked* by an ex-nun, Edith O'Gorman, and *Priest, Woman and Confessional*, by an ex-priest Chiniquy. He wrote several articles and treatises of a controversial nature. For four years he edited and produced the weekly, *A Reforma*. His son Robert was for some years secretary of the BRITISH AND FOREIGN BIBLE SOCIETY in Lisbon, and a grandson was a Methodist minister, dying in World War II. Robert Hawkey Moreton is buried, with his wife, in the British Cemetery of St. James, Oporto.

ALBERT ASPEY

MORGAN, JAMES HENRY (1857-1939), American minister and educator, was born near Concord, Del., Jan. 21, 1857. He was educated at Rugby Academy and DICKINSON COLLEGE, Carlisle, Pa. (A.B., 1878). He taught at Pennington Seminary and Rugby Academy for four years, and in 1882 he was elected Principal of Dickinson College Preparatory School.

In 1884 he was made adjunct professor of Greek in Dickinson College and in 1890, full professor, continuing in this chair until 1915. In 1903 he was elected Dean of the College; in 1914 he was acting president; and in 1915 he became President. His administration extended to 1928 when he retired, although he was pressed back into service as acting president for two more brief terms.

His administration at Dickinson was noteworthy. When he became acting president in 1914, the trustees were considering liquidating its scanty assets. In 1928 when he retired the college was free of debt, the endowment was almost $1,000,000, and a limit of 500 had been placed in student enrollment. Educational facilities, admission standards, quality of faculty, all had been raised. For sixty-five years he poured his energy into Dickinson College.

For forty-five years he was a pillar of the CENTRAL PENNSYLVANIA CONFERENCE of the M. E. Church, serving as a trustee from 1905 to 1926. Joining this conference in 1893, he was recognized as a pre-eminent leader among its members. For decades he was active in the training of ministers of the church, serving as Chairman of the Board of Ministerial Examiners. He was a member of the GENERAL CONFERENCE of 1916.

He was a force in the Pennsylvania Anti-Saloon League for many years, and bore heavy responsibilities unselfishly in the field of moral reform and in the temporal and spiritual affairs of the Church.

He was the author of *Dickinson College 1783-1933*, published in 1933.

Journal of the Central Pennsylvania Conference, 1940.
C. F. Price, *Who's Who in American Methodism*. 1916.
Who's Who in America.   CHARLES F. BERKHEIMER

MORGAN, JOHN (1792-1872), was a pioneer British missionary to GAMBIA. He was born at Torquay, Devonshire, on May 13, 1820. Appointed to begin work on the Gambia River, West Africa, he was joined by John Baker from SIERRA LEONE. Two attempts to establish work up the river were defeated by the unhealthy climate, and eventually Morgan established a station at St. Mary's, ten miles from the river mouth, where he built a church and school. He planned work at McCarthy's Island, later to become the main base in Gambia, but had to return to England owing to ill health. His *Reminiscences* are useful. He died on June 14, 1872, at Teignmouth, Devonshire.

CYRIL DAVEY

MORGAN, RICHARD (Senior), **WILLIAM,** and **RICHARD** (Junior), British Methodists. Richard Morgan, Sr. (1679-1752), held a post in the DUBLIN Court of Exchequer. His son William (1712-32) was one of the four original members of the Oxford HOLY CLUB. It was he who led the WESLEYS to visit the sick and prisoners. His father disapproved of his association with "that ridiculous society" and partly blamed it for the illness which resulted in William's early death, Aug. 26, 1732. John Wesley's reply, which allayed the father's suspicions, provides a valuable account of the Oxford Methodists. The younger son, Richard (1714-85), was entrusted to Wesley's care. He succeeded his father in Dublin and was visited by Wesley as late as 1769. It is uncertain whether he retained any vital interest in Methodist work.

M. Schmidt, *John Wesley*. 1966.
L. Tyerman, *Oxford Methodists*. 1873.   A. S. WOOD

MORGAN STATE COLLEGE AND THE MORGAN CHRISTIAN CENTER, BALTIMORE, Maryland. The Centenary Biblical Institute was founded in Baltimore in 1867, under the leadership of Bishop LEVI SCOTT. This name was retained until 1890 when it was changed to Morgan College. In 1939 the name was changed for the third time to Morgan State College, when the Trustees agreed to transfer all physical holdings to the State of Maryland.

Bishop Scott called a meeting of interested ministers and laymen of the BALTIMORE CONFERENCE on Christmas Day, 1866. The Bishop prepared and signed a draft upon the treasurer of the MISSIONARY SOCIETY of the M. E. Church for $5,000. At a second meeting on Jan. 3, 1867, a Board of Trustees, thirteen in number, was named, and a committee was appointed to draft a charter. Bishop Scott offered this prayer as the meeting closed: "May God prosper the work of our hands and enable us to do something that shall tell favorably and powerfully on the improvement and elevation of a people long neglected and oppressed."

The Charter was signed, sealed and recorded on Nov. 27, 1867, the Preamble of which states:

"Whereas, Thomas Kelso, John Lanahan, Henry W. Drakeley, William Harden, Hugh L. Bond, James H. Brown, William B. Hill, Charles A. Reid, William Daniel, Isaac P. Cook, Francis A. Crook, Robert Turner and Samuel Hindes have been designated by the Bishops of the Methodist Episcopal Church in the United States of America as Trustees to become organized into a body politic and corporate for the education of such pious young men, especially colored, for the ministry of the M. E. Church as shall have been judged by a Quarterly Conference to be divinely called thereto."

In order to meet the demands for training teachers, the Trustees added a normal department in 1874 and admitted female students. The demands on the Institute continued to grow. In 1890 the Trustees amended the Charter so that courses of study on the college level could be offered, the number of Trustees was increased from thirteen to twenty-four and the name was changed to Morgan College, which honored Lyttleton F. Morgan of the Baltimore Conference and Chairman of the Board of Trustees.

Again the Trustees faced the need for expansion. They sold the College to the State of Maryland in November 1939, on condition that the name Morgan be retained, that all previous graduates be recognized, that the State provide adequate budgets and construct required buildings. The Trustees then purchased land adjoining the campus on which they constructed a commodious building, which includes a chapel, meeting rooms, recreation room and other facilities. The Board, known as the Morgan College Corporation, sponsors a dynamic religious program on campus with Chaplains for the various denominations and employs a Methodist minister as Director and who is appointed by the Bishop of the Baltimore Conference.

When the school opened in 1867, it had nine students and two part-time instructors. In 1967 its enrollment was 4,140, with a faculty of 250.

EDWARD N. WILSON

MORLEY, MABEL (? -1954), New Zealand Methodist deaconess, was the eldest daughter of WILLIAM MORLEY. In 1907 she was appointed a deaconess of Durham Street Church and Superintendent of the Deaconess House which opened in the same year. Six years later, on grounds of health, Sister Mabel had to retire from the work, but in 1914 she was appointed the first matron of the newly opened South Island Children's Home in Harewood Road, Papanui. This position she held for fourteen years. During the years of the depression in the 1930's, and for many more years, Sister Mabel spent herself in the service of the poor and needy of Christchurch. She was a valued member of the mayor's Coal and Blanket Committee.

Sister Mabel was also closely involved in many forms of church work, serving on the boards of the orphanage and of the deaconess institution, and taking a leading part in the Methodist Women's Missionary Union.

Her last years were spent in quiet retirement, until in 1954 she passed away, one of the most dearly loved women of New Zealand Methodism.

New Zealand Methodist Deaconess Order Records.
WILLIAM T. BLIGHT

MORLEY, WILLIAM (1842-1926), New Zealand Methodist minister, was born at Orston, Nottinghamshire, England. Converted at the age of eighteen, he was received as a candidate for the ministry when he was twenty. He came to New Zealand at the age of twenty-two and entered the ministry there, serving leading pulpits and being secretary of the Conference on four occasions and president twice. In 1894 he was president of the historic General Conference of the Methodist Church of Australasia when it was agreed to give to the Annual Conferences permission to unite the various branches of Methodism in their own territories, according to a plan of union laid down by the General Conference. Morley in 1891 was a member of the Ecumenical Conference in Washington, D. C.

For ten years he was secretary of a committee charged with the revision of the Model Deed, and thus assisted in securing the present legal basis of the Australasian churches. In 1902, he was appointed managing treasurer of the Australasian Supernumerary Ministers' and Ministers' Widows' Fund, and he moved to Melbourne. He held the position for twenty-one years, until he himself superannuated. He died at Kew, Victoria, on May 24, 1926.

Bernard Gadd, *William Morley, 1842-1926* (Wesley Historical Society, New Zealand, 1964).
BERNARD GADD

MORNINGSIDE COLLEGE, Sioux City, Iowa, was chartered as the University of the Northwest in 1889. It was purchased by the North Iowa Annual Conference in 1894 and incorporated under the present name. WILSON SEELEY LEWIS, the second president, was elected a bishop of the M. E. Church. In 1914, Charles City College, an institution founded by German Methodists, merged with Morningside.

The institution has been one to which the Board of Missions of The Methodist Church has sent many students from Africa for work in higher education. Degrees offered are the B.A., B.S., B.M. (Music), and B.M.E. (Music Education). The governing board has thirty-six trustees elected by the NORTH IOWA CONFERENCE.

JOHN O. GROSS

MOROKA INSTITUTION, Thaba 'Nchu, Orange Free State, SOUTH AFRICA, has grown up on a Mission with a romantic past. In October 1833 JAMES ARCHBELL and JOHN EDWARDS, accompanied by Chief Moroka and several thousand Barolong, trekked from Platberg down the Modder River Valley to Thaba 'Nchu (the Black Mountain) where, on Dec. 17, 1833, they obtained a grant of approximately twenty-five square miles from Moshoeshoe, the Basuto "Moses," and other local chiefs. The chiefs were paid nine head of cattle and seventeen head of sheep and goats. The missionaries regarded the contract as an outright purchase, whereas Moshoeshoe (in accordance with African custom) was simply granting "a place to sit." The missionaries erected a school and church and launched an attack on Barolong illiteracy. By 1837 a hand-operated printing press in the church vestry was producing catechisms, scripture passages, school lessons and a Tswana Grammar.

A succession of faithful missionaries served and sacrificed to meet the growing educational and expanding evangelical needs of the people. Thirty primary schools and many churches were established. In 1937 a gift of land from Chief Fenyang and Dr. J. S. Moroka was accepted by the Methodist Church for the purpose of establishing an Institution with High School, Teacher-Training, Carpentry and Building Courses. During the first six years the Wardens were H. Greenwood, C. Crabtree and T. L. Sadler, and for the ensuing eighteen years W. Illsley filled this post. The present Warden (1961-   ) is L. G. S. Griffiths. The average number of students (male and female) in the period 1962-66 was 500, from whom there is a continuous flow of candidates for the ministry.

In 1938 a clinic was opened and an African nurse employed to serve the students and local community. Within a few years, with government assistance, buildings were erected to accommodate sixty in-patients. Financial assistance from the Orange Free State Provincial Administration, generous help from public bodies and from private individuals, and the sacrificial labors of medical, nursing and administrative staffs have brought the hospital beddage to 134, with sixty-eight nurses in training, ten African staff nurses and two African Sisters, both trained at Moroka. Dr. J. G. A. Scott, Miss Doris Tamblyn, Miss Rosalie Taylor, Dr. Prudence Barrett and E. F. B. Rose (the present Medical Superintendent), have served with distinction and devotion.

W. ILLSLEY
L. G. S. GRIFFITHS

MORRELL, THOMAS (1747-1838), pioneer American preacher and Revolutionary soldier, was born in New York City on Nov. 22, 1747. His father, Jonathan Morrell, was converted about 1765, while his mother's conversion was under the preaching of PHILIP EMBURY. The Morrells moved to Elizabethtown, N. J., in 1772, where the elder Morrell opened a store in which Thomas worked.

Thomas Morrell served in the Revolutionary War, and after the battle of Lexington in MASSACHUSETTS he became a captain of NEW JERSEY militia at Elizabethtown. He was severely wounded at the battle of Long Island in 1776, and was taken to New Providence, N. J., where he was nursed back to health. Thereafter he was in battles at Brandywine, Chadd's Ford, and Germantown (near Philadelphia), where he was again wounded. In the regular Continental Army he was successively Captain and Major of the 4th New Jersey Brigade.

In 1785 he was converted under the preaching of JOHN HAGGERTY in Elizabethtown. He gave up his business and began preaching within three months of his conversion. He was licensed as a LOCAL PREACHER in June 1786, and in 1787 was serving a circuit with Robert Cloud. Following his ordination as an ELDER in 1789 at NEW YORK, he was assigned to that city, with the specific charge to build a second Methodist church there. He organized the congregation which became the Forsyth Street Church, and erected a new house of worship.

Morrell was intimate with ASBURY, COKE and other leaders and frequently corresponded with JOHN WESLEY. On June 1, 1789, he arranged an audience with George Washington, who had just been inaugurated as President of the United States, in order that Asbury and Coke might present a congratulatory address which had been adopted by the conference then in session in New York, and with JOHN DICKINS he accompanied the two superintendents to present it personally to the Chief Executive. Coke, as an Englishman, was criticized for his action, but Asbury,

also an Englishman, was so identified with the American cause that no adverse comment was directed toward him. The Methodists were the first church group to take such action, and it drew favorable comment from the New York press.

Morrell served the leading churches of the denomination in New York, PHILADELPHIA, BALTIMORE, CHARLESTON and elsewhere. He was in New York nearly five years and later returned to that appointment, and he alternated with FREEBORN GARRETTSON in Philadelphia. In 1804 he was assigned to his home town of Elizabeth. In 1806 he located, but continued preaching on a circuit in Union, Essex and Morris Counties.

Major Morrell married Lydia Frazer of Westfield, N. J., in 1802, Bishop Abury performing the ceremony. One of their children was Francis Asbury Morrell, who became a Methodist preacher and joined the NEWARK CONFERENCE on its organization in 1857, but transferred to the NEW JERSEY CONFERENCE the next year.

Thomas Morrell died in Elizabethtown on Aug. 9, 1838, and was buried there.

V. B. Hampton, *Newark Conference.* 1957.
J. B. Wakeley, *Lost Chapters.* 1858.   VERNON B. HAMPTON

MORRIS, BERT JASPER (1875-1959), American minister, educator and editor, was born March 17, 1875. His family moved from Watseka, Ill. to Salina, Kan., in 1877. Morris graduated from KANSAS WESLEYAN UNIVERSITY in 1903, and married a classmate, Della Pearl Miller, on Commencement Day. They moved to Berkeley, Calif., that autumn, where Bert enrolled at the Pacific School of Religion. With a B.D. degree he returned to Harvard and BOSTON UNIVERSITY, receiving a M.A. degree at Harvard and a Ph.D. at Boston.

The College of Pacific, then at San Jose, Calif., engaged him as professor of philosophy. For eight years he served as Dean of students, and one year as acting president. In World War I Morris served for two years at Harvard in the Federal Bureau of Vocational Guidance. In 1920-25 he directed the WESLEY FOUNDATION Center of Trinity Church, Berkeley, for University of California students. The University honored him with membership in the Faculty Club. He then became religious editor of the *Pacific Rural Press* for seventeen years.

His last work was an eight-year pastorate of the Portola Church in the Sierra where he built a notable structure, "The Cathedral of the Mountains." He then retired to Berkeley, where he died on April 29, 1959, and was buried in the Oak Knoll Cemetery, San Jose.

L. L. Loofbourow, *The Cross in the Sunset.* 1961.
Minutes of the California Conference.   JOHN W. WINKLEY

MORRIS, CECIL VAN HORNE (1897-   ), American missionary to CUBA, was born April 28, 1897, at Clifton Forge, Va., the son of William Thomas and Minnie May Morris. He was educated at RANDOLPH-MACON COLLEGE with the A.B. degree and at Princeton Theological Seminary with the B.Th. degree.

In 1920 he went to Cuba as a contract teacher, but joined the Annual Conference there in 1924. His pastorates covered six cities in addition to the time he served as district superintendent of the Central District.

While president of COLEGIO PINSON, the hurricane of 1932 crossed over the island and over Camaguey where his school was located. He had married Margaret Fleming in 1924 and they always worked together as a team. In order to help the school she even worked in the kitchen. Their two sons, Cecil Lee and Richard, were both born in Cuba.

For health reasons they retired from the field in 1939, but continued to be active where he served as supply pastor and officer and teacher in his local church. They reside in Newport News, Va.

Anuario Cubana de la Iglesia Metodista.   GARFIELD EVANS

MORRIS, DINAH, a character in George Eliot's novel *Adam Bede,* almost certainly based on a real female preacher, George Eliot's aunt by marriage, ELIZABETH (TOMLINSON) EVANS.

FRANK BAKER

MORRIS, JAMES SAMUEL (1848-1931), South African Wesleyan Methodist missionary, was born at Fort Beaufort, Cape Colony, on Aug. 31, 1848. He was the son of 1820 settlers and educated at Lovedale. Converted at Queenstown under Bishop WILLIAM TAYLOR, he offered for the ministry in 1872. A perfect Xhosa linguist, he did mission work in the Wodehouse and Tsomo Circuits before moving to Buntingville, Western Pondoland, in 1875. Here he gained the confidence of the Paramount Chief Nqwiliso and helped to prevent the Mpondo from siding with the Mpondomise in their 1880 Rebellion. Instead, he himself led a column of 400 Mpondo warriors which Nqwiliso dispatched at his suggestion to relieve the Colonial magistrate at Tsolo, who was besieged in the local gaol. Grateful for his advice, the Chief and his people made gifts of cattle for the erection of the New Kilner Institute at Buntingville. In spite of previous assurances, the Cape Government refused maintenance grants because Pondoland was outside the colony, and in 1887 Morris broke down under the resultant strain. He then spent fifteen years among the migrant laborers in the Diamond Fields Compounds at Kimberley and a short but worrying period at Edendale, Natal, before returning to Western Pondoland. After four years at Palmerton, he returned in 1909 to Buntingville where the Institution had been reopened with government assistance after the annexation of Pondoland to the Cape. Morris retired in 1919 and died in East London on Feb. 23, 1931. He was revered for his personal bravery, wise counsel, administrative talent, practical evangelical preaching and deep understanding of the African people.

E. H. Hurcombe, *For God and the Bantu* (life story of J. S. Morris). N.d.
Minutes of South African Conference, 1931.
J. Whiteside, *South Africa.* 1906.   G. MEARS

MORRIS, PERCY F. (1879-1943), prominent American layman, was born in Bloomington, Ill., on July 20, 1879. He grew up on a ranch in CALIFORNIA, later moving to SAN FRANCISCO where he eventually owned a food brokerage firm. He married Lillie Gaddy in 1910 and they had two daughters and a son.

Percy Morris participated in nearly every phase of church work, but his chief interests were youth and missions. He was a founder (1907) and early president of the California Conference EPWORTH LEAGUE, and organized

the first Epworth League Institute in California. At the Asilomar Institute of 1916, he took a leading part in raising the necessary money to send GEORGE A. MILLER (later bishop) to PANAMA and COSTA RICA. His continuing interest led to his chairmanship of the Panama-Costa Rica Cooperating Council.

He served on numerous CALIFORNIA CONFERENCE boards and commissions, and was chairman of the WORLD SERVICE AND FINANCE Commission. He was a lay delegate to the GENERAL CONFERENCE in 1932, and to the Western JURISDICTIONAL CONFERENCE, 1940.

As a Trustee of the College of the Pacific for many years, he recognized the need for a chapel there. He made the initial gift and was Building Committee chairman for the Gothic chapel, dedicated in 1942, which today bears his name.

He died in Oakland of a heart attack on Nov. 22, 1943.

L. L. Loofbourow, *Cross in the Sunset.* 1961.
Who's Who in Pan-Methodism.   MARJORIE MORRIS BAYHA

MORRIS, THOMAS ASBURY (1794-1874), American bishop, was born on April 28, 1794, in Kanawha County near Charleston, W. Va. He was reared under Baptist influence and was converted in 1813 and made a Methodist class leader. The following year he became an exhorter and was licensed to preach.

In 1816 he was admitted on trial in the OHIO CONFERENCE and in due course was ordained a deacon by Bishop GEORGE and an elder by Bishop ROBERTS. His first appointment was to the Marietta circuit where he remained two years. In 1818 and in 1819 he served the Zanesville circuit and in 1820 he was sent to Chillicothe and then to Lancaster.

In 1822 he was transferred to KENTUCKY and sent to the Christian circuit, which covered two counties and parts of five others in Kentucky and TENNESSEE. He was then appointed to Hopkinsville and in 1824 he served the Red River circuit in Tennessee, which had twenty-one appointments, the nearest being twenty miles from his home. In 1825 he was made presiding elder of the Green River district in Kentucky, where he served two years. His succeeding appointments were LOUISVILLE, Lebanon circuit in Ohio, COLUMBUS, CINCINNATI, and presiding elder of the Cincinnati district. In 1834 he became editor of the *Western Christian Advocate.*

Morris was a member of the GENERAL CONFERENCE of 1824 and all of the succeeding conferences until elected bishop at the General Conference in Cincinnati in 1836.

As bishop he presided over conferences in Tennessee, TEXAS, ARKANSAS and in other areas, including the INDIAN MISSION in OKLAHOMA. He adhered to the North when the Church was divided in 1844. Morris was of course a bishop during the tension and disruption of the Church during the eighteen-forties. There is evidence that he endeavored to stand between the two irreconcilable forces. He attended the LOUISVILLE CONVENTION called by the southern delegates in 1845 but declined to preside at any session. He with Bishop JANES expressed a desire to go and hold the conferences assigned him in the South as the plan of visitation had been worked out by the bishops of the as yet undivided Church. However, the other bishops did not agree and worked up another plan of visitation in which Morris and Janes were excluded from any southern conference visitation. At one time he was charged in the press with having married a woman who owned slaves, but this was not the case. His second wife's first husband owned slaves but on his death they became the property of the son of his first wife.

In 1814 Morris married Miss Abigail Scales of VIRGINIA. They had two children and the son, Francis Asbury Morris, became a member of the MISSOURI CONFERENCE of the M. E. Church, South, and was a professor in St. Charles College. In 1844, his first wife having died, he married Mrs. Lucy Merriwether of Louisville, Ky.

In 1853 Morris published a book called *Miscellany, Consisting of Essays, Biographical Sketches, and Notes of Travel;* and in 1856 he wrote *Discourses on Methodist Church Polity.*

Bishop Morris died on Sept. 2, 1874, at Springfield, Ohio, and was buried in the Fern Cliff Cemetery there.

E. S. Bucke, *History of American Methodism.* 1964.
F. D. Leete, *Methodist Bishops.* 1948.
John F. Marlay, *The Life of Rev. Thomas A. Morris.* Cincinnati: Hitchcock & Walden, 1875.
M. Simpson, *Cyclopaedia.* 1878.   ELMER T. CLARK

MORRIS, WILLIAM EDWARD (1876-1952), American minister and long-time conference secretary, was born in Greensboro, Ala., June 22, 1870, the son of Joseph Terry and Mattie A. Williams Morris, while his father was finishing his education in old Southern University. As a boy he attended the public schools and then Oxford College, Oxford, Ala. He then entered Southern University, Greensboro, Ala., graduating with a B.S. degree in 1893, planning at the time to enter the medical profession. He attended Mobile Medical College, 1893-94, and Birmingham Medical College, 1894-95. However, he later responded to the call to preach and in 1895 was admitted on trial into the NORTH ALABAMA CONFERENCE. Bishop CHARLES B. GALLOWAY ordained him DEACON in 1897. Bishop WARREN A. CANDLER ordained him an ELDER in 1899. On May 18, 1898 he married Miss Fannie Sheldon.

From his very entrance into the Conference, Morris was asked to serve at the secretary's table. From 1895 to 1908 he served as first assistant to John W. Newman, long-time secretary of the Conference. He gave up his assistant's place when he was appointed to the Huntsville District in 1908. Upon the death of Newman in 1913, Morris was elected Conference secretary, which office he held till his retirement in 1942. He served as presiding elder of Huntsville, Birmingham, and Anniston Districts. He had a total of forty-seven years of service at his retirement, and had served many of the leading churches of the conference. He was greatly loved as a pastor.

He was a delegate to the GENERAL CONFERENCES (MES) of 1922, 1926, 1930, and to the Uniting Conference of 1939.

In 1925 BIRMINGHAM-SOUTHERN COLLEGE conferred upon him the D.D. degree. Upon his retirement, he moved to Birmingham to live in the Norwood community, where he had served the Norwood Church so effectively some years before. He died Nov. 15, 1952. Funeral services were conducted at the Norwood Church and his body was laid to rest in Elmwood Cemetery, Birmingham, Ala.

GEORGE FREDERICK COOPER

MORRIS BROWN COLLEGE. (See ATLANTA, GEORGIA, Morris Brown College.)

MORRIS HARVEY COLLEGE, Charleston, West Virginia, was founded in 1888 in Barboursville, W. Va., and named for Morris Harvey, its chief benefactor. The college was related to the Western Virginia Conference of the M. E. Church, South. Because of financial difficulties, the college abandoned its first location and moved to Charleston in 1939.

After the union of the three branches of Methodism in 1939, the newly organized West Virginia Annual Conference of The Methodist Church asked the UNIVERSITY SENATE to make a study of the educational needs of the conference, particularly with the view of determining the conference's ability to support two institutions. The senate, in 1941, recommended that the annual conference concentrate its support upon one college—WEST VIRGINIA WESLEYAN at Buckhannon. The conference released the property that it held, and Morris Harvey became a private college of liberal arts. It continues to have warm, friendly relationships with West Virginia Methodists.

JOHN O. GROSS

MORRISON, HENRY CLAY (1842-1921), American bishop of the M. E. Church, South, was born May 30, 1842, in Montgomery County, Tenn. He states in his autobiography that he was born in a plain small cottage five miles from the town of Clarksville, Tenn. His father was a small farmer with a large family and it was necessary for his son to work in the fields in order to support the family; therefore, Henry was prevented from attending school except for one eight month's term in a small country school. He professed religion in the Baker's CAMP MEETING near his home at the age of fourteen.

In 1857 the family moved to Graves County, Ky., and here despite the handicap of little formal education he took advantage of every opportunity to learn and was licensed to teach in the rural schools. During this time he responded to the call to the ministry and was licensed to preach in April 1863, at Pleasant Hill Church in Ballard County. He began his ministry on the Clinton Circuit of the MEMPHIS CONFERENCE. The circuit covered 150 miles and had twenty-seven preaching places. From here he joined the Confederate States Army and served both as soldier and spiritual advisor to the troops. After peace was declared he resumed his ministry on the Logan Circuit. He joined the LOUISVILLE CONFERENCE in 1865, and was assigned to Millerstown. His reputation as a preacher soon brought him to the leading pulpits of the conference, including four quadrennia in LOUISVILLE, Ky.

In 1886 he was transferred to the NORTH GEORGIA CONFERENCE and stationed at the First Methodist Church, ATLANTA. At the GENERAL CONFERENCE of 1890 he was elected as one of the secretaries of the Board of MISSIONS, and in 1894 became its Senior Secretary. Following the panic of 1893, the Board found itself with a debt of $132,-000. Morrison accepted the challenge of this indebtedness and by personal solicitation and correspondence raised $150,000. He was elected to the episcopacy in 1898. In the twenty years of his episcopal supervision, he served forty-one of the fifty-four conferences of the Southern church. He continued to raise money and at the time of his retirement in 1918, it was estimated that he had raised $3,000,000 for the church. After retirement he made his home in Leesburg, Fla., until his death on Dec. 20, 1921. The church there is named the Morrison Memorial.

A strong forthright leader, not in the least afraid of

controversy, he belonged among those awe-inspiring Southern Methodist bishops whose fiat made law in the conferences over which they presided; and who had no doubts as to the rectitude of their convictions. Withal he was fundamentally a kindhearted minister, and the editor of this *Encyclopedia* states that he has always been proud to have been ordained by H. C. Morrison.

George H. Means, ed., *Autobiography of Bishop Henry Clay Morrison*. Nashville: Publishing House, M.E. Church, South, 1917.
                                        HARRY R. SHORT

H. C. MORRISON

MORRISON, HENRY CLAY (1857-1942), American pastor, evangelist, educator, journalist, was born on March 10, 1857, at Bedford, Ky. His Baptist father, James S. Morrison, died when Henry was four; his mother, born Emily Durham, died when he was two. When Henry was three weeks old, his mother dedicated him to the ministry at a Methodist Quarterly meeting.

Educated at Ewing Institute, Perryville, Ky., and VANDERBILT UNIVERSITY for one year, he passed his examinations in all but one subject. However, later in life he was given an honorary D.D. by Vanderbilt. Converted at the age of thirteen, licensed to preach in 1878, admitted on trial in the KENTUCKY M. E. South CONFERENCE, 1881, he was ordained DEACON in 1886 and ELDER in 1887. He located in 1890, requesting the Conference to give him a local relationship in order to give full time to evangelism.

From 1879 to 1882 Morrison served four circuits: Floydsburg, Jacksonville (both as junior preacher), Westport, and Concord. From 1882 to 1890, he served five stations: Stanford; Eleventh Street Church, Covington; Highlands; Walnut Street, Danville, and Frankfort.

An evangelist from 1890 to 1910, his oratorical ability reached pinnacles of greatness while preaching to audiences numbered by the thousands. However, he never became what was sometimes called a "commercial evangelist." During 1908 he preached 471 times. It is estimated that he held 1,200 revivals, preached 15,000 times, traveled 500,000 miles, and had thousands of converts at his altars. Morrison's evangelistic zeal in camp meetings and revival preaching brought him into conflict with the authorities of his Church. The period from 1896 through

1904 was a stormy one. He was brought to trial in September 1897, in the Kentucky Conference, for "contumacious conduct." Upon his statement that he had "no intent" to violate church law "he was restored to his former position in the church and the case was closed." The church subsequently elected him to five General Conferences and the Ecumenical Methodist Conference in London, 1921.

Founder of the *Pentecostal Herald* about 1890, he was its editor for about thirty-five years, stressing holiness, and aiding and promoting ASBURY COLLEGE and ASBURY THEOLOGICAL SEMINARY. He wrote some twenty-five popular books, though he was not a scholarly writer or preacher.

Returning from a tour of world evangelism, Morrison accepted the presidency of Asbury College, and served from 1910-25. He served again as president from 1933-40, dominating the school for most of the time. He was made president *emeritus* and continued to hold this title until his death. He founded Asbury Theological Seminary in 1923. He was its first president and his administration continued until his death.

Dramatic, picturesque, magnificent in appearance, Morrison was considered one of the fifty great preachers of America by *The Christian Century*. He was also held to to be the greatest defender in Methodism of what he thought to be the Wesleyan teaching of Christian Perfection (SANCTIFICATION) within Methodism. ROY L. SMITH in *The Christian Advocate*, April 9, 1942, said: "There were those who disagreed with him on matters of theology, but no man surpassed him in devotion to the Christian evangel." E. STANLEY JONES said: "Morrison was one of the great men of the religious life of America, the last of the old Southern orators."

He married Laura Bain on June 20, 1888, and they had three children. Mrs. Morrison died Nov. 29, 1893, and he married Geneva Pedlar on April 9, 1895. They had five children. She died on March 23, 1914, and he married Mrs. Bettie Whitehead on Feb. 17, 1916. She died in 1945.

After preaching sixty-three years, Morrison preached his last sermon on his life theme, "How to win sinners to Christ." The next day, March 24, 1942, he died at Elizabethton, Tenn. Bishop U. V. W. DARLINGTON gave a tribute at his funeral in Asbury College and said: "We shall not see his like again. He was just about the last of the old group of great towering preachers who do not 'water down' anything but just plainly preach Christ, Savior from sin." He was buried at Wilmore, Ky.

P. A. Wesche, *Henry Clay Morrison "Crusader Saint."* Nampa, Idaho: n.p., 1963.
Who's Who in America.
Who's Who in the Clergy, Vol. 1.
C. F. Wimberly, *A Biographical Sketch of Henry Clay Morrison*. Chicago, 1922.   JESSE A. EARL

MORRISTOWN, NEW JERSEY, U.S.A., **Morristown Church** in the NORTHERN NEW JERSEY (former Newark) CONFERENCE is a suburban church with a historic past—a church which "offers a dynamic ministry today in a community and area rich in Methodist tradition, and in New Jersey history." Methodism began there in 1811 when Bishop ASBURY preached in the Presbyterian Church— the Presbyterians, then, as now, being strong in northern New Jersey. Preaching by circuit riders and prayer and CLASS-MEETINGS organized in homes eventually led to the establishment of a permanent society. A NEW YORK Methodist family, the Samuel Bonsalls, moved to Spring Valley in 1813 and opened their home to Methodist circuit riders twice a month. This link which Morristown had to the city of New York proved quite beneficial, and resulted in the formation of a Methodist church building in 1827.

The first church, a small rectangular red brick building, was dedicated on Oct. 14, 1927. On that occasion the building was packed three times by neighboring people, some of whom had walked seven miles to participate in the services. An 1828 revival added 200 members to the original thirteen. Nathaniel Porter, the first pastor, was appointed to Morristown in 1829 by the PHILADELPHIA CONFERENCE.

The congregation outgrew the first edifice by 1841, and a second building was erected, this time "on the Green." The new building was a white, wooden, colonial structure and is being used today by the A.M.E. CHURCH congregation. It was removed to its present site by a team of white oxen, after the present building had been erected on property given by George T. Cobb, Mayor of Morristown.

The cornerstone of the third building was laid in 1866 by Bishop JANES, who returned to dedicate it four years later in 1870. This church is the present imposing structure located on the east side of the Morristown Green. It is a stone edifice, of solid Norman architecture. The masonry is purple puddingstone trimmed with Maine granite. The spire terminating in a granite cross rises 150 feet. The interior is trimmed with butternut and black walnut.

Through the years the clock in the spire has been known by all in the community as the "Town Clock," and at one time the churchbell was used as the town fire alarm. In 1964 the Tucker Memorial Carillon was installed in the Tower as part of the $450,000 modernization program which renovated the structure and added a three-floor matching wing of educational, office and social facilities.

The first session of the NEWARK CONFERENCE was held in the second building in 1858. It was in the third and present handsome structure that the fourteenth session of the Newark Conference convened in 1871, and through the century outstanding anniversary sessions have been held there marking the thirty-fifth (1892); the fiftieth (1907); and the centennial (1957) sessions of the Newark Conference.

The church has grown consistently through the years. It has been served by some of the great preachers and leaders of the Northern New Jersey (Newark) Conference, including David W. Bartine, JONATHAN TOWNLEY CRANE, HENRY A. BUTTZ, GEORGE P. ECKMAN, JESSE L. HURLBUT, RALPH B. URMY, J. Edgar Washabaugh, Henry L. Lambdin, and William L. Lancey.

In 1970 it reported 1,354 members, property valued at $2,250,841, and $194,697 raised for all purposes.

M. ECKMAN
VERNON B. HAMPTON

MORRISTOWN COLLEGE, Morristown, Tennessee, began in 1881 as an elementary and secondary school for Negroes under the auspices of the FREEDMEN'S AID SOCIETY of the M. E. Church. It was founded by Judson S. Hill, a Methodist minister from New Jersey.

The school was started in a one-story frame building which had served previously as a slave mart. One of the students who was graduated from the school and later served for forty-four years as a teacher remembered having been sold at the front of the building in the days of slavery.

Junior college instruction began in 1923. In 1960 the name was changed to the present one. The college was granted full accreditation and membership in the Southern Association of Colleges and Schools in 1961. The governing board has thirty-three members elected by the board. Ownership of the college properties is vested with the Board of Education of The Methodist Church.

JOHN O. GROSS

DAVID MORTON

MORTON, DAVID (1833-1898), American preacher and executive, was born June 4, 1833, in Russellville, Ky., the son of Marmaduke B. and Nancy Caldwell Morton. He was baptized in infancy by JOHN LITTLEJOHN, an associate of FRANCIS ASBURY in the early days of American Methodism. He was educated at Russellville Academy and early entered public service where he developed outstanding executive ability. This served him well in later years when he became the first Secretary of CHURCH EXTENSION of the M. E. Church, South. He early felt the call to the ministry and in 1853 joined the LOUISVILLE CONFERENCE (MES). His promotion from circuits to stations was rapid and he soon became one of the most popular preachers of his conference. During the trying period of the War Between the States, 1861-65, David Morton had a part in the stormy sessions of his conference, when the conference was prevented from meeting as a whole and held its separate sessions under the watchful eyes of both Confederate and Union soldiers.

In 1867-68 he was instrumental in establishing two colleges in his conference—Logan College in his home town of Russellville and Warren College in Bowling Green. He was elected a delegate to the GENERAL CONFERENCE in 1870 and re-elected to each of the eight succeeding conferences. His death occurred just prior to the meeting of the General Conference of 1898 to which he had been elected.

In 1876 he was sent to the Pacific Northwest to help strengthen and establish churches. He visited every congregation of Southern Methodism in his territory and as a result of his work, the need of funds for building churches came to the attention of the General Conference of 1882. This led to the establishment of the Board of Church Extension and Morton was selected as its Corresponding Secretary. For sixteen years he piloted the course of this new board, extended its services, and built it into one of the most efficient agencies of the Church. He continued in this office until his death. During this time 3,817 churches were aided, nearly a million dollars was raised and the rate of church building averaged nearly one church for each day of the year.

In a tribute to him at the General Conference following his death, it was fitly said, "What Church Extension is among us, he made it." He was buried in Maple Grove Cemetery in his home town of Russellville, Ky., on March 15, 1898.

Elijah E. Hoss, *David Morton, A Biography*. Nashville: Publishing House, M.E. Church, South, 1916.
Journal of the Louisville Conference, 1898.
J. C. Rawlings, *Century of Progress*, N.p., 1946.
HARRY R. SHORT

MOSES, HORACE AUGUSTUS (1862-1947), American Methodist layman and philanthropist, was born April 21, 1862 on a farm in South Ticonderoga, N. Y., the son of Henry H. and Emily (Rising) Moses. He attended local schools and the two-year commercial course at Troy Conference Academy in Poultney, Vt., now GREEN MOUNTAIN JUNIOR COLLEGE. His business career began as an errand boy in the Springfield, Mass., paper mills where, in successive steps, he arose to manage. Eventually he founded his own mill, the Strathmore Paper Co., which became internationally known.

Moses was a "tither" all of his life. His many benefactions included the Eastern States Farmers Exchange; the Junior Achievement Movement which he conceived and first organized; the 4-H Clubs which he helped found and supported; the Green Mountain Junior College in Vermont; sixty-one major gifts to his home town of Ticonderoga, N. Y.; eighty-five gifts to educational institutions, including numerous buildings, permanent scholarships and endowed academic chairs; the Valley View Chapel in Springfield, Mass., one of America's most beautiful Gothic cathedrals.

He died on April 22, 1947, and is buried in Springfield Cemetery. His wife, Alice (Elliot) Moses, died in 1962, after being a member of Trinity Church for seventy-five years. Their daughter, Madeline Moses, presently lives in New York City.

H. HUGHES WAGNER

MOSSMAN, FRANK E. (1873-1945), American college president, a builder of institutions and of men and women, was born in Urbana, IOWA, on Aug. 26, 1873. On March 27, 1895, he married Zoa Foster and they were the parents of four children. He was admitted on trial in the NORTHWEST IOWA CONFERENCE in 1899. Frank Mossman graduated from MORNINGSIDE COLLEGE in 1903 and earned an M.A. there in 1905. He received honorary doctorates from Upper Iowa University and SOUTHWESTERN COLLEGE, Winfield, Kan.

Twice he was president of Southwestern College— 1905-1918, and from 1931 until he became president-emeritus in 1942. Between these two terms he held the presidency of his alma mater, Morningside College. During his first term as president at Southwestern he bought back the campus land which had been sold during the lean years and built Richardson Hall, the chief campus building. When he returned in 1931 he was the dean of college presidents of Methodism. Eight times he was elected a delegate to GENERAL CONFERENCE, and for many years he was a member of the UNIVERSITY SENATE. He died on June 12, 1945 and was buried in Winfield, Kan.

Mossman's ability to read the faces of students and to discern when they were disturbed by financial or other problems, as well as his wise counsel in the time of need, won for him the loyalty of students, faculty and supporters of the college. He thus molded many lives, easily but surely bending them toward a higher goal.

ROY L. SMITH, the editor and author, who was always grateful to Mossman for encouraging him to finish college, characterized "Prexy" as a great man with devotion, faith, enthusiasm, capacity for entering into the lives of others, and administrative ability.

Christian Advocate, June 18, 1942.
B. Mitchell, *Northwest Iowa Conference*. 1904.
Who's Who in America.
INA TURNER GRAY

MOTT, JOHN RALEIGH (1865-1955), American church statesman and world-wide leader in missionary enterprises and in the international Y.M.C.A., was born May 25, 1865, at Livingston Manor, N. Y. When he was four months old the family moved to Postville, Iowa. At the age of sixteen Mott entered the Upper Iowa College at Fayette, Iowa. At graduation he continued his work at Cornell University at Ithaca, N. Y., because he thought the religious life should speak more to the mind. In his junior year at Cornell, Mott became President of the Christian association. He came to the attention of the national Y.M.C.A. leaders when he succeeded in raising the money for a new college "Y" building.

His life of service in the Y.M.C.A. and on international and missionary levels was launched from this college platform. In the winter of 1886, J. Kynaston Studd, one of the "Cambridge Seven," came with his young wife to the Cornell campus. Mott heard him speak and found his Christian life, begun under Iowa Y.M.C.A. auspices,

JOHN R. MOTT

directed into full-time Christian service. In the same year he went as a delegate to the first International Christian Student Conference, held under the eyes of Dwight L. Moody at Mount Hermon, Mass. At this meeting, he helped organize the STUDENT VOLUNTEER MOVEMENT— whose missionary motto became, "The world for Christ in this generation." Mott became chairman and served in this capacity for thirty-two years.

Assigned to the executive committee of the Student Volunteer Movement in his capacity as a representative of the International Committee of the Y.M.C.A., he became chairman of this committee also and served for thirty-three years.

From these two relationships, a steadily increasing influence in the world movements of Christendom characterized his life. From 1888 to 1915 he was General Secretary of the Intercollegiate Y.M.C.A. movement of the United States and CANADA. In 1895 he became General Secretary of the World's Student Christian Federation. In 1898 he became Secretary of the Foreign Department of the International Committee of Y.M.C.A.'s. In 1901 he was elected Associate General Secretary of the International Committee. He was shortly chairman of the World's Committee of Y.M.C.A.'s. Several of these posts he held concurrently as the influence of both the Y.M.C.A. and the student missionary movement extended outward.

It was logical, therefore, that in 1910, when the WORLD MISSIONARY CONFERENCE was called in Edinburgh, Mott should be chosen chairman of Commission I, and presiding officer of the day sessions. Nearly 2,000 delegates from 159 societies and from fifty-four nations gathered to set their sights upon the world missionary target. As the session closed, Mott was chosen chairman of the Continuation Committee. He was therefore central to the leadership of the Jerusalem Missionary Council in 1928 and the Madras Missionary Council in 1938.

He presided at the Oxford Conference on Life and Work in 1937 and was one of the vice-presidents of the Edinburgh Conference of Faith and Order in the same year. When he resigned as chairman of the International Missionary Council in 1942, he continued at seventy-seven years of age several posts of outstanding significance, as president of the World's Alliance of the Y.M.C.A.; vice president for the Western Hemisphere of the Provisional Committee for bringing into being the WORLD COUNCIL OF CHURCHES, and several other offices. When the World Council of Churches came into being, he was named an honorary president.

During this extremely active and global life of service, Mott made four round-the-world trips, served in seventy-three countries, was decorated by sixteen nations, and received honorary degrees from eight distinguished universities, including Cornell, Yale, Princeton, Edinburgh, and Brown.

Confidant of bishops, statesmen, wealthy industrialists and Christian leaders the world over, Mott found time to write at least fifteen volumes, including six volumes of *Addresses and Papers* published in 1946-47. Three presidents of the United States—Roosevelt, Taft and Wilson— called upon him for service. During World War I, he was chairman of the United War-Work Committee which sought to raise $170,500,000 and raised more than $190,-000,000. Three times, he was offered the ambassadorship of CHINA by President Wilson, who described him as "certainly one of the most nobly useful men in the world." He indeed did serve the President as a member of the American deputation to MEXICO and as one of Wilson's appointees on the American Mission to RUSSIA.

Such was the life of one who in his early twenties, preparing for a legal career, heard a Cambridge athlete speaking for Christ put the challenge, "Seekest thou great things for thyself? Seek them not. Seek ye first the Kingdom of God." And said Mott, "on these few words hinged my life-investment decisions."

Mrs. Mott passed away in the early 1950's, and two years later, Mott married a second time. In 1937, he had been named an honorary canon of the Episcopal Church. And, although a life-long Methodist he was, upon his death on Jan. 31, 1955, interred in the Washington Cathedral, Washington, D. C.

Among his fifteen or more published books, are: *The Strategic Points in the World's Conquest; The Evangelization of the World in this Generation; The Pastor and Modern Missions; The Future Leadership of the Church; The Present World Situation; The Decisive Hour of Christian Missions; Addresses and Papers of J. R. Mott*, six vols.

E. M. McBrier, *Reminiscences*. Private Printing, 1954.
John R. Mott, *Addresses and Papers*. 6 vols. New York: Association Press, 1946-47.   GORDON E. MICHALSON

MOULTON, JAMES HOPE (1863-1917), British Wesleyan Methodist and distinguished scholar, was born on Oct. 11, 1863, at Richmond, Surrey. He was one of the first sixteen boys at Leys School, CAMBRIDGE, of which his father was headmaster. He entered the Wesleyan ministry in 1886, and for the next sixteen years was himself a master at the Leys.

In 1902 he was appointed to Didsbury College, Manchester, and later became professor of Hellenistic Greek and Greenwood lecturer in the Greek Testament at the University of Manchester. He was elected to the LEGAL HUNDRED in 1904. In 1912 he was Hibbert Lecturer on *Early Zoroastrianism*, and in 1913 FERNLEY LECTURER on *Religions and Religion*. He was also a fellow of King's College, Cambridge, the first Wesleyan minister to obtain a fellowship at Oxford or Cambridge. His study of oriental languages made him the greatest English authority of Zoroastrianism. With Deissmann and Milligan he was concerned with applying the new evidence on the papyri to the study of the New Testament, and with Milligan published *A Vocabulary of the Greek Testament, Illustrated from the Papyri*. Also he published *Grammar of New Testament Greek* (1906, 1929), and *From Egyptian Rubbish Heaps* (1914). He died in the Mediterranean through submarine action on April 7, 1917.

H. M. RATTENBURY

MOULTON, WILLIAM FIDDIAN (1835-1898), British Wesleyan Methodist and outstanding scholar, was born in Leek, Staffordshire, on March 14, 1835. After a brilliant career at London University he entered the Wesleyan ministry in 1858. He was appointed to Richmond College, Surrey, first as assistant and then as classical tutor, until in 1874 he was made the first headmaster of Leys School, CAMBRIDGE. In 1873 he was elected to the LEGAL HUNDRED, and became President of the Conference in 1890. In 1891, with J. SCOTT LIDGETT, he founded the Bermondsey Settlement. From 1870-81 he was secretary of one of the New Testament committees for the Revised Version of

W. F. MOULTON

the Bible. His publications include the English translation of Winer's *Grammar of New Testament Greek* (1870) with A. S. Geden, *Concordance of Greek New Testament* (1897), commentaries, and *History of the English Bible* (1878). He died on Feb. 5, 1898.

G. G. Findlay, *W. F. Moulton, the Methodist Scholar*. London, 1910.
W. F. Moulton (son), *Memoir*. 1899.

H. MORLEY RATTENBURY

FAWCETT MEMORIAL HALL, MOUNT ALLISON UNIVERSITY

MOUNT ALLISON UNIVERSITY (Sackville, New Brunswick). Methodists in Eastern British America (now the Maritime Provinces of Canada) waited for decades for an opportunity to start a program of higher education. Other denominations had their institutions of learning, but how were they to find the money to start and maintain one of their own? The opening came in a letter to the annual meeting of the New Brunswick District held in St. John in the spring of 1839. It was written by CHARLES FREDERICK ALLISON, a merchant living in Sackville, a small town almost on the Nova Scotia border. He suggested a school "in which not only the elementary, but higher branches of education may be taught," and "in which pure religion is not only taught, but constantly brought before the youthful mind," and which would be under the control of the Wesleyan districts of New Brunswick and Nova

Scotia. His offer to purchase a site in Sackville, to erect a suitable building, and to give a hundred pounds a year toward its upkeep was gladly accepted by the District, and was ratified quickly by the Nova Scotia District. In July, 1840, Allison laid the foundation stone of the Male Academy. Until his death in 1858 he continued to interest himself in the school and to increase his donations.

When the first young men entered in January, 1843, they were greeted by the first principal, HUMPHREY PICKARD, a native of New Brunswick, who had gone to the United States for his university education. Under his guidance the student body rapidly increased, and the range of work offered was expanded steadily. In 1854 a "Female Branch" was opened in a second building some distance from the first, and large numbers of young women came to take classes suited to their needs. In 1858, by act of the New Brunswick Legislature, the trustees of the Wesleyan Academy (Male and Female) were incorporated, and were given a charter conferring full degree-granting power. Thus began the three separate, yet interdependent, parts of Mount Allison, all of which were under the presidency of Humphrey Pickard.

Mount Allison Academy continued until 1953. A boarding school leading to university matriculation, it later acquired a coeducational commercial department. Young men whose education had been interrupted could here make up what they had missed, and those with little money in their pockets were accommodated in one way or another. In the years when high schools were remote from large sections of the population, it was a haven for ambitious adolescents; its discontinuance came only when regional high schools had become general. Three wooden buildings in which the academy was housed, were burned, and the fourth, a stone structure, is now a university women's residence.

The Ladies' College was the name early given to the Female Branch. Though it began as a high school, the curriculum was broadened to include many subjects then called for in the proper education of a young lady. In 1890 the cornerstone of the Conservatory of Music was laid, and within twenty years ten specialists were teaching in this department. In 1893 John Hammond was appointed director of art, and soon paintings from the collection of John Owens of Saint John, came into the new Owens Museum of Fine Arts. In 1904 the School of Household Science, equipped by Mrs. Lillian (Massey) Treble and named after her, was opened. In later years these and other departments were gradually integrated with the university, and by 1936 the school was reduced to a matriculation course, which was terminated in 1946.

The university has grown steadily through the years. From the two who formed the first graduating class in 1862, the number of students increased to some twelve hundred a century later, and it is becoming increasingly difficult to hold the enrollment at that figure. From its inception Mount Allison has been favored with some excellent teachers who could not be drawn away to positions which seemed to have much more to offer. The first university degree granted a woman in the British Empire was a bachelor of science, conferred upon Grace Annie Lockhart, in 1875; and in 1884 Miss Harriet Starr Stewart became the first woman to win a bachelor of arts degree from any Canadian university.

Instruction in theological subjects began in 1860, and in 1875 a Faculty of Theology was formally established with Charles Stewart as its first dean. This part of the university moved to Halifax in 1926, when it was amalgamated with the Presbyterian College to form Pine Hill Divinity Hall, a seminary of the newly formed United Church of Canada. Since that time candidates for the United Church ministry from eastern Canada have taken their arts at Mount Allison, and their theological studies at Pine Hill.

In 1903 the McClelan School of Applied Science was opened. From this developed the Engineering Department, which gives a three-year course leading to a degree after two additional years at a technical college. In contrast, commerce and education have been added recently.

The Mount Allison crest carries the words, *Litterae, Religio, Scientia,* and throughout its history a serious attempt has been made to integrate all three in the development of the whole man.

Though the building erected in 1854 to house the Female Branch still stands (1966), most of the early structures have disappeared and have been replaced by many fine new buildings. One of the latest is a chapel in the form of a symmetrical cross in the center of the campus. The stained-glass windows are unique in design, and of exceptional quality.

The university is governed by a board of regents, twenty of whom are appointed by The United Church of Canada, twenty by the Federated Alumni, two by the faculty, and four by the board. In 1960 the first chancellor, Ralph Pickard Bell, was installed. The presidents have been: Humphrey Pickard, 1862-69; David Allison, 1869-78, 1891-11; J. R. Inch, 1878-91; B. C. Borden, 1911-23; G. J. Trueman, 1923-45; W. T. R. Flemington, 1945-62; and L. H. Cragg, 1963-

G. S. French, *Parsons and Politics.* 1962.
D. W. Johnson, *Eastern British America.* 1924.
T. W. Smith, *Eastern British America.* 1877, 1890.

E. ARTHUR BETTS

MOUNT BETHEL ACADEMY (1794-1820) was an early Methodist school located in Newberry County, S. C., U.S.A., the first such institution of the Methodists in that state. The building, erected in 1794, stood on thirty acres of land given by Edward Finch, and was dedicated by Bishop FRANCIS ASBURY on March 20, 1795. It was twenty by forty feet in size, divided by partitions, with chimneys at each end. The second floor was a dormitory for students, and several cabins served as boarding houses and residences for the teachers.

Mark Moore was the principal for six years, being succeeded by one Mr. Hammond. The school was largely patronized by students from GEORGIA and both the CAROLINAS. It began to decline in the second decade of the nineteenth century and closed its doors about 1820, being succeeded by the Mount Ariel and COKESBURY SCHOOLS in that section. Nothing remains on the site.

A. D. Betts, *South Carolina.* 1952.
C. F. Deems, *Annals.* 1856-58.
A. M. Shipp, *South Carolina.* 1883.

LOUISE L. QUEEN

MT. GILEAD CAMPGROUND, located at Ben Hill, Near ATLANTA, Ga., U.S.A., is the offspring of the oldest Methodist church in Fulton (originally DeKalb) County, Ga. Mt. Gilead Church was planned for in 1824 in the home of John M. Smith by several families from Franklin Coun-

ty and was then organized by William J. Parks, pastor of the Lawrenceville Circuit.

A newspaper article written in the late 1800's, "The Story of Old Mt. Gilead," records: "The first Campground was established on what is now Jackson St., then Old Sandtown Road. Because of the fact that it was located on the highway leading to the Sandtown Ferry on the Chattahoochee River, connecting the Creek and Cherokee nations, it was called Sandtown Campground. Those good old Scotch-Irish pioneers held annual camp meetings here from as far back as 1824 until 1835. In that year, Rev. John M. Smith and Old Father Fain cut down the brushes for the 'Old Brush Arbor.' "

P. P. Smith (John M. Smith's oldest son) wrote for the *Southern Christian Advocate* in October, 1860: "I preached the first sermon at the new Campground on the 22nd Oct., 1835."

Thus the beginnings of this historic place. The center of the campground was a crude pineboard tabernacle with brush roof (later replaced with more substantial material), encircled by temporary living quarters called "tents." So phenomenal was the growth that, in 1860, sixty families with their livestock encamped there. The great influence of Aaron and James Turner, "Venerable Fathers in Israel," JESSE and Isaac BORING, GEORGE F. PIERCE, Charles Dowman, and others was renowned throughout the area.

The first tabernacle, destroyed by a heavy snow in 1880, was replaced that same year with the present tabernacle, under the supervision of James Barrett. The spiritual fervor of these CAMP MEETINGS climaxed in a great revival in 1900 under the preaching of W. A. Dodge. Preachers of that day vied for camp meeting preaching privileges, and often the "preachers' tent" had twenty preachers available for the four services per day. Preachers of a later day were S. R. Belk, JAMES E. DICKEY, the Jenkins brothers, and the Eakes brothers.

As the area rapidly became urbanized, the campground lost its appeal for "tent holders." A motel was erected in 1946; deteriorated tents were replaced with modern cottages; a new water system and other improvements were made under the long and faithful leadership of Erby McGee.

Today revival preaching by distinguished evangelists is still heard here the first two weeks in August each year. Some of the present trustees are descendents of the original trustees, who were: J. J. Fain, Lewis Peacock, Isaac Sewell, John B. Holbrook, and John M. Smith. These grandsons of the pioneers, with other young and zealous leaders, have the challenge to transform "The Old Campground" into a place of greater influence and glory for the Kingdom of God.

RUTH B. MOODY

MOUNT PLEASANT GERMAN COLLEGE, Mount Pleasant, Iowa (1873-1909), was founded in 1873 by the Southwest German Annual Conference of the M. E. Church under Rudolph J. Havighorst in association with IOWA WESLEYAN UNIVERSITY under President JOHN WHEELER. It offered academy, college and theological courses in the German language. The affiliation with Iowa Wesleyan permitted the students to enroll for a B.A. degree and many collegiate courses were not offered independently by the German College. The professors formed, in return, the German Department of Iowa Wesleyan. Associated with the college were such German-American Methodist scholars as F. WILHELM BALCKE, E. CARL MAGARET, FRIEDRICH MUNZ, EDWIN STANTON HAVIGHORST and KARL STIEFEL. Some 400-500 students attended the college and about 235 received diplomas. A three story college building and later a chapel were erected. The major contribution of the college was training ministers for the German Methodist Conferences. In 1909, the college was merged with Central Wesleyan College, Warrenton, Missouri by the sponsoring conferences of both schools, the St. Louis German and the West German. The land, the buildings and one half of the endowment fund reverted to Iowa Wesleyan. The Chapel was razed in 1926 and the College Building in 1961. Bricks and the inscribed granite lintel from the latter building were turned in a memorial marker on the site. The archives, originally moved to Warrenton, are now the core of the Zwingli F. Meyer Collection of German-American Methodism at Iowa Wesleyan College.

P. F. Douglass, *German Methodism*. 1939.
Louis A. Haselmayer, *The History and Alumni List of the Mt. Pleasant German College.* N.d.
Jubiläumsbuch der St. Louis Deutschen Konferenz.
Methodist History, July 1964.   LOUIS A. HASELMAYER

MOUNT ROYAL COLLEGE, Calgary, Alberta, was founded in 1910 under the sponsorship of the Board of Colleges of the Methodist Church of CANADA and through the efforts of a group of citizens under the leadership of GEORGE W. KERBY of Central Methodist Church in Calgary. In December 1910, the college was incorporated by an act of the provincial legislature to provide elementary and secondary education for both sexes, and instruction in music, art, speech, drama, journalism, commercial and business courses, technical and domestic arts. W. H. Cushing was appointed chairman of the board of governors and Kerby the first principal.

The college opened in September, 1911, with 154 students enrolled in all departments. By 1965 several thousand students were enrolled in the various departments.

In 1925, Mount Royal College came under the supervision of the Board of Colleges and Secondary Schools of The United Church of Canada, and Kerby continued as its principal. In 1931 a university department was established in the junior college division, and the elementary school program was discontinued. The university department offered the first two years of the arts and science courses as prescribed by the University of Alberta.

John H. Garden succeeded Kerby as principal in 1942 and served until 1959. The college charter was amended in 1944 and 1950 to provide broader base, and engineering courses were begun in the university department. The facilities of the college were enlarged with the erection of the Kerby Memorial Building and the G. D. Stanley Gymnasium in 1949. In the fall of 1956 a business administration department was established.

In January, 1959, W. John Collett, who had been dean since 1948, was appointed principal on the retirement of Garden. The college continues to grow and fill a need for high-school and post-high-school education as a community college. It has been reorganized as a cooperative community junior college controlled by the community and financed from the public treasury.

Massey Foundation Commission, *Report.* Toronto: Massey Foundation, 1921.
J. H. Riddell, *Middle West.* 1946.   J. E. NIX

MT. SEQUOYAH, ARKANSAS, U.S.A., a large camp and assembly ground near Fayetteville, is maintained by the South Central Jurisdiction of The United Methodist Church, and is officially known as the Western Methodist Assembly. It began in 1920 when a group of church leaders met at LAKE JUNALUSKA, N. C., and decided to challenge the annual conferences west of the Mississippi River to establish an Assembly Ground. East Mountain, at Fayetteville, Arkansas (later called Mt. Sequoyah), was selected as the site. Fifty buildings were thereafter erected, the first programs being given in the summer of 1923. It was soon found that the financial situation was to prove difficult, and so lots were sold, annuity bonds were arranged for, and the support of Methodist people earnestly solicited.

Sam Yancey was elected superintendent of the Assembly in due time and served faithfully and well for twenty-three years. Other buildings were erected during this time, including the large Clapp Auditorium which seats 600 persons and is still being used. A cafeteria was also built, unique in that four oak trees growing where it was built, were "incorporated" in its structure, their trunks and limbs spreading through and beyond the roof.

Elmer H. Hook succeeded Yancey in 1949. During his tenure as superintendent, all the cottages were modernized, Hook himself making many pieces of furniture in his wood-working shop. The PAUL E. and Mildred MARTIN building (named for Bishop and Mrs. Martin) was made possible by contributions from all the Conferences of the South Central Jurisdiction and by gifts from the T. L. James family of Ruston, La., and from J. J. PERKINS of Dallas. In the Martin building is a lovely chapel, as well as ten large classrooms, including an audio-visual room. A gift from the J. M. Willsons of Floydada, Texas made possible a small infirmary.

In June 1959, E. H. Hook retired to be succeeded by E. G. Kaetzell, who like Hook, proved to be a builder as well as an administrator. Under his leadership the architectural firm of Hare & Hare, of Kansas City, was employed to prepare plans for the rebuilding and construction of all needed facilities for the ongoing of the Assembly.

Pursuant to these and other plans, a financial goal was adopted by the bishops and Jurisdictional Council and voted into effect by the Annual Conferences of the Jurisdiction. As funds were provided, two new ten-room lodges were built, eleven motel-type units were erected, and a new modern cafeteria designed to serve and seat 350 persons came into being. The Woman's Building—built early in the life of the Assembly by the contributions of interested women, and owned and governed by them—was given to the Assembly in 1963, so that every building on the ground might be owned by the South Central Jurisdiction. Approximately 400 people can presently be housed at one time.

The grounds and buildings of the Mt. Sequoyah Assembly are now worth well over half a million dollars, and it provides an attractive meeting place for groups and leaders in all phases of Methodist work. Attendance has grown to 4,000 per year, and it is expected that this will increase as more heated buildings are provided, so that sessions may be held in winter as well as in summer.

A governing Board of Trustees for the Assembly meets once each year. This Board is composed of all the bishops of the Jurisdiction, a representative from each Annual Conference, the Jurisdictional president of the W.S.C.S.

and the District Superintendent of the Fayetteville District, as well as the Superintendent of the Assembly.

During the year of 1965 a new house was built, known as the Bishops' Cottage. This was made possible through the efforts of the resident Bishop of Arkansas, PAUL V. GALLOWAY. Contributions were made by Conferences and by a number of individuals, especially in Arkansas. This house is available to any bishop and/or his family who wants to come to the mountain at any time during the year.

MOUNT UNION COLLEGE, Alliance, Ohio, was established in 1846, and the Conservatory of Music (now the music department) in 1865. Scio College merged with Mount Union in 1911. The institution, which began as coeducational, was one of the first colleges in the world to enroll both men and women. In addition to having the patronage of the two Methodist conferences in Ohio, it has had the support of the Pittsburgh Annual Conference since 1864. Degrees offered are the B.A., B.S., B.M. (Music), B.M.E. (Music Education). The governing board has fifty members, twelve elected by the Northeast Ohio Conference, three by the Western Pennsylvania Conference, four by the Ohio Conference, fifteen by the board, six by alumni, six honorary; the three bishops and the president of the college, ex officio.

JOHN O. GROSS

MOURNER'S BENCH, which was also called the "anxious bench," was a term used in CAMP MEETINGS and early revivals referring to a certain number of benches directly in front of the speaker's stand or pulpit, which were enclosed by low rails on three sides (the platform or pulpit forming the fourth side). Persons seeking salvation were invited to come within the enclosure to kneel by or sit on the benches where they were made objects of prayer by the preacher and the congregation. Here they "mourned" for their sins until they were transformed by the "joy of salvation." Sometimes the enclosed space was referred to as the "altar" or, by the irreverent, as "the pen." B. W. Gorham in his *Camp Meeting Manual* suggests that this "altar" or "mourner's bench" "should be at least 25 feet square, with an aisle between the benches and with entries only at the two front corners by the speaker's stand." The men were usually separated from the women in the mourner's benches of the early camp meetings.

It is difficult to say when or where this arrangement or term first originated. It seems to have been used very early in the history of camp meetings, which began around 1800. It was used with dramatic power, however, by the evangelist Charles Finney during his revivals in Rochester and northern NEW YORK 1824-27. He writes of his work in Rochester, "I made a call, I think for the first time, upon all that class of persons whose convictions were so ripe that they were willing to renounce their sins and give themselves to God, to come forward to certain seats, which I requested to be vacated, while we made them subjects of prayer." Under his leadership the custom came to be universally used for a time at revival meetings and the term "anxious bench" began to displace the term "mourner's bench." The custom of inviting people forward in this way was also referred to as the "altar call."

The "mourner's tent" in early camp meetings was an outgrowth of the mourner's bench. It was a tent on the grounds provided for the same purpose as the bench. It was kept lighted all night so that at any hour of the day or night the "mourners" or "anxious ones" might come in for prayer. A curtain was hung to separate the men from the women.

See: W. F. P. Noble, *A Century of Gospel Work*, Philadelphia: H. C. Watts & Co., 1876, p. 361, where the above quotation from Finney can be found;
R. Weiser, *The Mourner's Bench, or an humble Attempt to Vindicate New Measures* (Bedford about 1844), pp. 1-4;
B. W. Gorham, *Camp Meeting Manual* . . . Boston: H. V. Degen, 1854;
C. A. Johnson, *The Frontier Camp Meeting* . . . Dallas: Southern Methodist University Press, 1955. FREDERICK E. MASER

MOUZON, EDWIN DU BOSE (1869-1937), American bishop, was born in Spartanburg, S. C., May 19, 1869. His parents, Samuel Cogswell and Harriet Peurefoy Mouzon, were descendants of devout Huguenot families, colonial day settlers.

All of his formal education was received in the public schools of Spartanburg, and in WOFFORD COLLEGE, where he received the A.B. degree in 1889. From early youth to the end of his life, he was an assiduous student.

In 1888 he was licensed to preach, and became the fourth minister in his family for four successive generations. After graduating from college, he was appointed supply preacher in Bryan, Texas. In 1890 he was married to Mary Elizabeth Mike. There were three daughters and three sons. The sons have attained distinction as university teachers and authors.

From 1889 to 1908, Mouzon served pastorates in TEXAS, with an interim of three years in KANSAS CITY, Mo. In 1908 he left the largest church in the then WEST TEXAS CONFERENCE, Travis Park in SAN ANTONIO, taking a greatly reduced salary, to organize a theological department at SOUTHWESTERN UNIVERSITY, in order to help prepare better ministers. After he was elected bishop in 1910, he gave vigorous leadership in helping to establish SOUTHERN METHODIST UNIVERSITY in DALLAS, Texas. His embryo professorship of theology at Southwestern University, where he taught Bible, systematic theology and homiletics, was transferred to Southern Methodist University, in 1915. He became the acting dean and organizer of what is now PERKINS SCHOOL OF THEOLOGY.

Bishop Mouzon presided over most of the annual conferences of the M. E. Church, South from 1910 to 1937. In 1930 he presided over the organization of the BRAZIL Methodist Church, and turned the GENERAL CONFERENCE there over to the native officials. He also held the Japanese, the Korean and the Cuban Conferences.

As a member of the Board of MISSIONS and also of the board of trustees of SCARRITT COLLEGE for Christian Workers, Mouzon was influential in the transfer of that institution from Kansas City to NASHVILLE, Tenn. From 1911 to 1931 he was a delegate to the decennial ECUMENICAL METHODIST CONFERENCES. In 1931 he spoke to this body on "The Basis of Confidence in Christian Thinking." He delivered the EPISCOPAL ADDRESS at the 1930 General Conference of the M. E. Church, South, when "fundamentalism" and union with the two other American Methodist Churches were featured in this address.

He was a versatile minister. One of his contemporaries called him "the preacher to his generation." Another declared that "the pulpit was his throne." In 1929 he gave the Yale University Lyman Beecher Lectures on Preaching. His title was "Preaching with Authority." His FONDREN Lectures at Southern Methodist University were "The Missionary Evangel," and his Cole Lectures at VANDERBILT UNIVERSITY were on "The Program of Jesus." In these last two lecture treatises, delivered the same year, he emphasized the unity of the personal and the social aspects of the gospel. In 1918, following a series of four deaths in his family, including his wife, he published *Does God Care?* as his theology of suffering. In the midst of the "fundamentalist" discussions in 1924, he wrote *The Fundamentals of Methodism*. There were many articles in periodicals from his pen, as specific issues arose. Four universities bestowed honorary degrees on him.

As a conference presiding officer, Bishop JOHN M. MOORE said of Bishop Mouzon that he had three admirable qualities: "(1) He was never hasty in making decisions; (2) he was sensitive to the needs of his ministers; (3) he never uttered a bitter word towards those who differed with him."

Bishop Mouzon was chairman of the Methodist Committee on Unification when the first plan was rejected. He wrote to Bishop EARL CRANSTON of the M. E. Church, Jan. 20, 1925, "We will not stop. The unification of our two churches must be. The men who are vociferous today cannot speak the word tomorrow. There is a higher voice that brings peace to troubled waters. So long as I live I shall plead this cause."

Bishop Mouzon died suddenly on Feb. 10, 1937, of a heart attack in CHARLOTTE, N. C., where he then resided in charge of the Charlotte Area. He was buried in Dallas, Texas.

Journals of General Conference, MES, 1910-38.
F. D. Leete, *Methodist Bishops*. 1948.
Nashville Christian Advocate, March 12, 1937; Feb. 26, 1939.
Edwin R. Spann, "Biography of Edwin D. Mouzon." Unpub. thesis, Duke University.   J. RICHARD SPANN

MOW COP is the summit of a ridge a thousand feet high bordering the counties of Cheshire and Staffordshire, England, where the first PRIMITIVE METHODIST CAMP MEETING was held on May 31, 1807.

The name, formerly written "Mole," may be the slightly disguised "meol" or "mel" meaning a bare, chalk hill. More probably however, the name is derived from Anglo-Saxon "mow" meaning "stack" or "heap," "cop" being the word for summit or top. An artificial tower, erected in 1754 as a landmark, crowns the hill.

JOHN T. WILKINSON

MOZAMBIQUE is a province of PORTUGAL in southeast Africa, the name applying to all of Portuguese East Africa. It is a large irregularly shaped region extending for 1,600 miles along the coast between Tanganyika and Natal (SOUTH AFRICA). The area is 297,659 square miles, and the population is 7,376,000. The capital is Lourenco Marques.

The European history of Mozambique began in 1498 when Vasco da Gama discovered the mouth of the Zambesi River. Portuguese colonization followed in 1505 at Sofala where there was a flourishing trade in gold and slaves. Hostilities immediately broke out with the Arabs who for centuries had dominated the coast southward to Sofala.

During the third quarter of the nineteenth century Portuguese traders and explorers strove to establish an east-west corridor from Mozambique to ANGOLA on the Atlantic. This was frustrated by Cecil Rhodes in bringing the central area under British control.

In the late 1870's, Ndevu Mashaba, a native of Lourenco Marques, was converted in the British Wesleyan Mission while he worked in the mines in South Africa. He studied at the Lovedale Training Institute of the Free church of Scotland Mission. Returning to Mozambique in 1885, Mashaba established a school at Komatipoort close to the Transvaal border west of Lourenco Marques. Several congregations were formed. Working in the Tonga dialect, he prepared a Tonga-English vocabulary, several school readers, a hymnbook, and parts of Scripture.

GEORGE WEAVIND of the British Wesleyan Mission at Pretoria, Transvaal, superintended Mashaba's activity, occasionally visiting the area. The work grew, despite difficulties with government and Mashaba's imprisonment for a time on false charges. By 1893 a chapel stood beside the school and the membership was 200, with four local preachers. In 1904 there were 850 members and other hundreds on probation. H. L. Bishop of the Wesleyan Mission was appointed in 1906 to reside on the circuit, extending from the Limpopo River to the Transvaal border. Agreement was reached with the adjacent mission of the M. E. Church that the Limpopo River should be their common boundary. The membership grew to 1,500, with a community of 5,000.

The American Board (Congregational) had entered Mozambique in 1881, but by the end of the decade decided to concentrate elsewhere. Bishop WILLIAM TAYLOR of the M. E. Church found the situation ready-made for his "self-supporting missions." During 1888 to 1890 he secured the American Board stations at Chicuque (Gikuki) overlooking Inhambane Bay, and Cambine (Kambini) twenty miles northwest. E. H. Richards, formerly of the American Board, remained in charge. The work progressed under Bishop J. C. HARTZELL who followed Taylor. The Hartzell School at Chicuque and the Leprosarium and hospitals there and at Cambine are notable.

Growing from a District in the Congo Mission (1888), this work emerged as the Southeast Africa Mission Conference (1920), and the Southeast Africa Annual Conference (1954), with seven districts, fifty-three circuits, 787 places of worship, 6,100 members and 25,000 in constituency. Forty-six African members of Conference and thirty-one supplies with twenty-three members on trial constituted the native ministry as of 1968.

Cooperative work with other missions appears in the Christian Center at Lourenco Marques, the Center at Beira, one of the port cities, and the Union Theological School at Ricatla. At Johannesburg, Transvaal, a strong evangelistic work is conducted among the Mozambique men working in the mines. The Methodist Central Mission Press moved from Cambine to Johannesburg in 1924, serves several missions of southeast Africa.

Free Methodist Church. G. Henry Agnew, pioneer missionary of the Free Methodist Church, reached Inhambane in 1885. With the help of E. H. Richards of the American Board, property was secured at Mabile on Inhambane Bay. Agnew served in Mozambique for eighteen years, and then in Transvaal and Natal. This station was eventually moved southward to Inhamachafo, a short distance inland from Inharrime. The station had a farm of

825 acres, with extensive agricultural and industrial training facilities, a school for pastors, dispensary, girls' school, missionary residences, Christian native village and central church. The northern center is at Nhaloi, 140 miles above Inhamachafo, occupying an old plantation. A new hospital stands there. Intensive work developed through the region between Massinga and the Rhodesia boundary. With this territory as his base, Ralph Jacobs pushed into Southern RHODESIA in 1938-39. The 1969 report indicated the Free Methodist membership as 7,500, although some bush circuits were unreported. Cooperation exists with The United Methodist Church in the training of nurses and medical technicians.

Findlay and Holdsworth, *Wesleyan Meth. Miss. Soc.* 1921-24.
Free Methodist World Missions, 1962 Report.
B. S. Lamson, *Free Methodist Missions.* 1951.
Project Handbook, Overseas Missions, 1969.
World Methodist Council, *Handbook.* ARTHUR BRUCE MOSS
BYRON S. LAMSON

MUDGE, ENOCH (1776-1850), American minister, was born at Lynn, Mass., on June 28, 1776, and became an itinerant minister in 1793. From that date until 1799 he traveled on various appointments in MAINE until the hardship of travel affected his health, and he settled in Orrington, Maine, from 1799 to 1816. During this period he was twice chosen State Representative, and was active in the passage of the "Religious Freedom Bill." Having resumed the itinerancy in 1816, he was stationed at BOSTON, Lynn, Portsmouth, Newport and other New England appointments. From 1832 until his retirement from active life in 1844, he was pastor of the Seaman's Chapel at New Bedford.

Enoch Mudge was a member of the Constitutional Convention of 1819. He wrote *Camp-Meeting Hymn-Book,* 1818; *Notes on the Parables,* 1828; a poem, *Lynn,* 1830; and published his *Lectures to Seamen* in 1836. He died on April 2, 1850.

Americana Encyclopedia, The, Vol. 19, New York: American Book-Stratford Press, Inc., 1950.
M. Simpson, *Cyclopaedia.* 1878. N. B. H.

MUDGE, JAMES (1844-1918), American minister and author, was born in West Springfield, Mass., on April 5, 1844. His great-grandfather, ENOCH MUDGE, was the first member, CLASS LEADER, STEWARD and LOCAL PREACHER in the Methodist Society of Lynn, Mass. His grandfather, James Mudge, was the first itinerant preacher raised on New England soil; his father James was also a Methodist minister.

He was received into the membership of the Lynn Common Church on his thirteenth birthday. He studied at Lynn High School, WESLEYAN UNIVERSITY, and BOSTON UNIVERSITY SCHOOL OF THEOLOGY. In 1868 he joined the NEW ENGLAND CONFERENCE on trial and two years later was received into full connection. During the course of his ministry he served ten churches. From 1878 to 1883 he served as a missionary to INDIA; from 1908 to 1912 he was editor of *Zion's Herald.* He was secretary of the New England Conference for thirty sessions—from 1889 through 1918. He was also the author of books dealing with Methodism, notably: *History of the New England Conference of the Methodist Episcopal Church 1796-1910; The Doctrines of God's Holy Word as Held in the Methodist Episcopal Church;* and *Handbook of Method-*

ism. He compiled several religious anthologies, including: *Honey From Many Hives; Poems With Power to Strengthen The Soul,* and *Spiritual Songs.*

In 1913 Mudge retired from active ministry. He died on May 7, 1918, leaving a son and two daughters. *Minutes* of the New England Conference, 1917, 1919.

ERNEST R. CASE

MUELDER, WALTER GEORGE (1907-   ), American author and Dean of BOSTON UNIVERSITY SCHOOL OF THEOLOGY, was born at Boody, Ill., March 1, 1907, son of Epke Hermann and Minnie (Horlitz) Muelder.

He was graduated with the B.S. degree from Knox College in 1927; S.T.B., BOSTON UNIVERSITY, 1930; Ph.D., 1933; D.H.L., WEST VIRGINIA WESLEYAN COLLEGE, 1960; L.H.D., CLAFLIN UNIVERSITY, 1963.

He was admitted on trial into the Chicago Northwest Conference in 1928, received in full connection and ordained elder in 1931. He was a professor at Berea College, 1934-40; professor of Christian Theology and Christian Ethics, University of Southern California, 1940-45; and since 1945 he has been professor of Social Ethics and dean of Boston University School of Theology.

He was a consultant at the Second Assembly of the WORLD COUNCIL OF CHURCHES, Evanston, Ill., 1954; delegate to the Third Assembly, NEW DELHI, India, 1961; delegate, World Conference on Faith and Order, Lund, Sweden, 1952; North American Conference, Oberlin, Ohio, 1957; World Conference, Montreal, Quebec, 1963; Protestant Observer, Second Vatican Council, 1964; chairman, Commission on Institutionalism, Department of Faith and Order, World Council of Churches, 1955-61; chairman of the Board of the Ecumenical Institute, 1961-68; and delegate to the Fourth Assembly, World Council of Churches, UPPSALA, 1968. He was Lowell Lecturer, 1951, and lecturer, Boston University, 1954.

His membership in various organizations includes: American Association of Theological Schools, Association of United Methodist Theological Schools, American Theological Society, NATIONAL COUNCIL OF CHURCHES (Division of Christian Life and Work), Massachusetts Council of Churches, Massachusetts Civil Liberties Union, Fellow, American Academy of Arts and Sciences.

He is the author (with E. S. Brightman) of the *Historical Outline of the Bible,* 1936; (with L. Sears and A. V. Schlabach) *The Development of American Philosophy,* 1940, revised 1960; *Religion and Economic Responsibility,* 1953; *In Every Place a Voice,* 1957; *Foundations of the Responsible Society,* 1959; *Methodism and Society in the Twentieth Century,* 1961; (with N. Ehrenstrom) *Institutionalism and Christian Unity,* 1963; *Moral Law in Christian Social Ethics,* 1966.

On June 28, 1934 he was married to Martha Grotewohl. Their children are: Sonja Jane (Mrs. Paul Devitt), Helga Louise (Mrs. Kenneth Wells), Linda Ruth (Mrs. William Schell).

Who's Who in America, Vol. 34.
Who's Who in The Methodist Church, 1966. J. MARVIN RAST

MUELLER, CHRISTOPH GOTTLOB (1785-1858), was the founder of Wesleyan Methodism in GERMANY. He emigrated to England in 1806 to escape conscription under Napoleon, and was converted in LONDON under Methodist preaching. He became EXHORTER, CLASS LEADER, and

CIRCUIT LEADER, and CIRCUIT STEWARD. He married Anne Claridge of Finchley in 1813. In that same year he visited his aged father in Winnenden (Kingdom of Württemberg, Germany), and in a MORAVIAN meeting in his father's house he gave a testimony of his experience of personal salvation through faith in Christ. As it was the time of rationalism and liberalism in European thought, this message was entirely new for many people in Germany. A revival started, and the Wesleyan METHODIST MISSIONARY SOCIETY (London) was asked by the new converts to send a minister. The London committee hesitated but finally acceded and sent Mueller to work as lay missionary (1831). He regarded his meetings in and around Winnenden as religious societies within the Lutheran State Church. Still he could not avoid troubles and persecutions. He was partly supported by the London committee (seventy pounds a year) and partly earned his living as a farmer. Year by year during the winter Mueller went on big preaching tours through Württemberg, like WESLEY riding on horseback or walking. At his death in 1858 the Methodist returns for that year showed fifty-seven preaching places, thirty-four class leaders and exhorters, and 1,040 members. LUDWIG S. JACOBY, superintendent of the Methodist Episcopal Church in Germany and John C. Link, pioneer of the EVANGELISTIC GEMEINSCHAFT in Germany, E.U.B. since 1851, belonged among his friends.

P. N. Garber, *Continental Europe*. 1949.
J. W. E. Sommer, *Christoph Gottlob Mueller von Winnenden.*
Bremen: Verlag des Traktathauses, n.d.   LUDWIG F. ROTT

REUBEN H. MUELLER

MUELLER, REUBEN HERBERT (1897-   ), American E.U.B. minister, general church officer, and bishop, was born in ST. PAUL, Minn., June 2, 1897, the son of Reinhold Michael and Emma (Bunse) Mueller. Seminary and college trained, he was licensed to preach in 1916 by the EVANGELICAL ASSOCIATION, ordained deacon in 1922, and elder in 1924. Pastorates were served in MINNESOTA

and INDIANA before he became a district superintendent in 1937. In 1943, R. H. Mueller was chosen executive secretary of the Board of Christian Education, THE EVANGELICAL CHURCH, and later of the E.U.B. CHURCH, and in 1954 he was elected bishop.

Mueller was married to Magdalene Stauffacher, Dec. 26, 1919. A daughter, Margaret (Mrs. Armin C. Hoesch, missionary to NIGERIA for thirteen years), was born to this union.

In addition to many denominational offices, Bishop Mueller has served as chairman of the Board of Managers of the World Council of Christian Education; president of the NATIONAL COUNCIL OF CHURCHES of Christ; member of WORLD COUNCIL OF CHURCHES Assembly and its Central Committee; chairman of BOARD OF BISHOPS (EUB); chairman of Commission on Church Union (EUB); recipient of THE UPPER ROOM Citation and the Distinguished Alumni Award, NORTH CENTRAL COLLEGE; and honorary degrees from WESTMAR COLLEGE (D.D.), North Central College (LL.D.), INDIANA CENTRAL COLLEGE (L.H.D.), Union Theological Seminary, Tokyo (D.D.), Indiana University (LL.D.), OTTERBEIN COLLEGE (S.T.D.), OHIO WESLEYAN UNIVERSITY (L.H.D.), and WEST VIRGINIA WESLEYAN UNIVERSITY (D.D).

Bishop Mueller has written numerous articles and books, the latest two being *His Church* and *The Living Word*. In The United Methodist Church he was assigned to the INDIANA Area in 1968 and became president of the COUNCIL OF BISHOPS in 1969, for a period of one term.

Who's Who in The Methodist Church, 1966.
                                                                JOHN H. NESS, JR.

MUKERJEE, H. L. (? -1931), and **NOLIN KUMAR** (? -1943), of INDIA, were father and son, who led unusual careers. H. L. Mukerjee was a Bengali Brahman, who was converted and radically changed. He married a daughter of JOEL THOMAS JANVIER, first Indian minister of the M.E. Church, and entered the ministry. In 1885, Mukerjee became an instructor in Bareilly Theological Seminary, and served on its faculty for thirty-eight years. He deeply influenced an entire generation of seminary students. He died Jan. 6, 1931, and was buried in Bareilly.

Nolin Kumar, his elder son, became a leading educator of the United Provinces and principal of the Government Teacher Training College at LUCKNOW. He was later deputized by the government to organize and direct the teacher-training college at the Muslim University, Aligarh.

Nolin Kumar Mukerjee was a member of two GENERAL CONFERENCES of the M.E. Church and a popular and effective local preacher. He died in Indore in 1943, and is buried there.

J. N. Hollister, *Southern Asia*. 1956.
J. E. Scott, *Southern Asia*. 1906.   J. WASKOM PICKETT

MUMMART, CLARENCE ALLEN (1874-1959), American United Brethren in Christ (Old Constitution) bishop and educator, was born of German ancestry, July 14, 1874 near Welsh Run, Franklin County, Pa. Home conditions were such that as a boy of nine or ten he was hired out to work on a farm. Schools were of a low standard and an education was considered unnecessary. By the age of seventeen his education was very limited, but he resolved that he would be ready to teach school by the time he was twenty. He received his first contract on his twentieth birthday and taught public school for six years. He was graduated from Huntington College with the A.B. (1907) and the B.D. (1908). He received the S.T.M. from NORTHWESTERN UNIVERSITY in 1925. The honorary D.D. was bestowed by Huntington College in 1912.

In his early life he had been associated with the UNITED BRETHREN CHURCH. At the age of fifteen he was working on a farm near Fairview, Md., and living with a Lutheran family. He made his confession of faith and affiliated with the Lutheran Church. When he felt called to the ministry he was aware of the Lutheran demand for an educated ministry, which came into conflict with his early training. He returned to the United Brethren Church and entered the gospel ministry in the Pennsylvania Conference where he was a member for nearly sixty-four years.

He was married to a United Brethren girl, Lillie Zimmerman, and was the father of four children, one son dying in infancy. The other son and two daughters have been engaged in educational work.

Mummart served as a pastor for a total of thirty-two years in Pennsylvania, Indiana and Ohio. He was conference presiding elder for five years. He served as the first general secretary of the United Brethren Christian Endeavor. He also was editor of the *Christian Conservator* for five years on two different occasions. He served as bishop two different terms for a total of eight years. His educational service to the church was as head of and professor in the theological department of Huntington College for seventeen years, during which time he also served as president for ten years on two different occasions.

He was an able executive and was always interested in the best interests of the church. He had abounding energy and frequently served the church in a dual role. Because of his early background he was sympathetic to those who served in the midst of hardships.

His death occurred at Greencastle, Pa., on Dec. 2, 1959. Burial was in the cemetery adjoining the Macedonia Church near Greencastle.

Contact, July 2, 1967.
United Brethren, Dec. 16, 30, 1959.   J. RALPH PFISTER

D. L. MUMPOWER

MUMPOWER, DANIEL LEEPER (1882-   ), a medical missionary to the CONGO and one of the pioneers in that field for the M.E. Church, South, was born at Fayette,

Mo., on Oct. 22, 1882, the son of Thomas Gray and Mollie Leeper Mumpower. He received the B.A. degree from CENTRAL COLLEGE (Fayette, Mo.) in 1902; and M.A. from Yale in 1903; and an M.D. from VANDERBILT in 1912. He resided in Doniphan, Mo., from 1903-08, teaching and working in a drugstore to get a pharmacist's license in order to work his way through Vanderbilt. He and his wife, Edith, were married in 1911, and three children were born to them.

Dr. Mumpower went to the Congo in 1913 under the Board of MISSIONS of the M.E. Church, South. He was appointed superintendent of the mission there by Bishop WALTER LAMBUTH even before he left the United States, and was stationed at Wembo Nyama the whole time he was in Africa. In 1920 he arranged for the building of a mission boat, named the "Texas," since Texans gave the funds for this river steamer.

Dr. Mumpower returned to the United States in 1922 because of the illness of his wife and settled in NASHVILLE in 1923 where he continued for a time his connection with the Board of Missions of his Church, or until 1932. He then went back into the practice of medicine. Illness forced him to retire on Aug. 1, 1965, and he had to be hospitalized there at the age of eighty-five.

Bishop Walter Lambuth, writing in the Dec. 28, 1917, issue of the *Christian Advocate* (Nashville), said of Mumpower, "The doctor is the same calm, sensible, earnest fellow. . . . Dr. Mumpower has just put through the press at Luebo a new edition for a school book in the Batetela language, and I find him at work translating the gospel of Matthew. . . . naturally, Dr. Mumpower's medical work has been limited because of great pressure of other duties and the absence of a trained nurse." With other pioneer missionaries, D. L. Mumpower left the mark of great accomplishment in the heart of the Congo.

Bulletin, Inglewood Methodist Church, Homecoming Welcome Issue, Nov. 29, 1964.
Christian Advocate (Nashville), Dec. 28, 1917.
The Epworth Era, January-April, 1915.   N. B. H.

MUNCIE, INDIANA, U.S.A. **High Street Church** heard its first Methodist sermon in 1829 delivered by Charles Downey, a circuit rider. In 1836 the first Methodist society was organized, becoming a part of the Munceytown Circuit with preaching in the homes. The members of the first class were: Eli C. Green, leader; Mary Green, Hannah Watton, John and Eleanor Smith, Samuel W. and Juliette Harlan, and Matilda, John, and Camelia Beeks.

On Aug. 18, 1838, Mr. and Mrs. Goldsmith C. Gilbert gave the Methodist church a building site. The first church building was erected in 1839, costing $450. In 1851 the membership had grown to more than 200. A new two-story brick church was built in 1856 and that fall the annual conference met there. The edifice cost $4,467 and Bishop AMES dedicated it on July 20, 1857.

The discovery of natural gas in Muncie in the fall of 1886 resulted in an industrial boom which brought many Methodists to the town. A revival in the winter of 1886-87 added about 300 new members. A new church site was purchased on High Street and Adams. The new church was named High Street. It was built under the pastoral leadership of C. U. Wade (father of Bishop R. J. WADE), 1886-91, made of red brick with sandstone trimming, and costing $40,000. C. H. Payne, former president of OHIO WESLEYAN, dedicated the church on June 2, 1889.

High Street Church promoted the spread of Methodism in Muncie. Wade organized Avondale Church in 1891, and it was dedicated Nov. 8, 1891, with High Street's assistant pastor, George A. Wilson, in charge.

During the pastorate of L. U. Naftzger, 1897-1900, FRED B. FISHER, then a high school student, later a distinguished Methodist bishop, was converted. In 1938 one-third of the ashes of Bishop Fisher were sealed in a niche prepared for them in the wall of the new sanctuary near the pulpit he had occupied on various occasions.

H. D. Ketcham, a brother-in-law of Bishop WILLIAM ANDERSON, was pastor of High Street from 1921 to 1924. High Street's growing congregation in time needed a new sanctuary. Claude H. King, pastor, 1925-34, served during the construction of the new church. At the request of the church and with his consent, King was sent to Europe to study church architecture. The new church was to be Gothic, made of Briar Hill sandstone, with imported glass windows. This sanctuary, a thing of beauty, was dedicated Oct. 5, 1930, and cost approximately $400,000. However, the coming of the depression delayed the payment of a $220,000 debt until March 1, 1948. This amount was paid during the pastorate of A. WESLEY PUGH, 1937-49. On Oct. 10, 1948, the church was rededicated by Bishop RICHARD RAINES and the mortgage was burned.

In 1970 the High Street Church was valued at almost $2,000,000, and had 2,158 members.

General Minutes.   JESSE A. EARL

MUNHALL, LEANDER WHITCOMB (1843-1934), American soldier, evangelist, and conservative editor, was born June 7, 1843, at Zanesville, Ohio, the son of David and Abigail (Rice) Munhall. He was educated in the public schools and the University of Chattanooga, Tennessee, A.M. In August 1862, he enlisted in Company C, 79th Indiana Infantry. Promoted to major and adjutant of the regiment, he took part in over a score engagements of the Civil War, mustering out June 7, 1865.

While a local deacon in the Philadelphia Conference, he became an evangelist. Beginning in 1874, he preached for more than fifty years. Munhall carried on evangelistic campaigns in cities of the United States and Canada. He preached to Panama Canal workers for two months. He was elected to six General Conferences of his Church from 1904 to 1928. He wrote these books: *Lord's Return and Kindred Truth; Higher Criticism vs. Higher Critics; Anti-Higher Criticism, or Testimony to the Infallibility of the Bible; Breakers, Methodism Adrift; A Convert and His Relations.* Munhall also edited *Word and Work* for three years, besides pamphlets and tracts.

A Methodist bishop said of Munhall: "He was a very conservative Methodist editor who was anathema to the main leadership of the Church whom he did not hesitate to criticize for their liberal ideas, especially the theologians whom he thought were leading the Church astray."

Munhall married Mary E. Thomas, Sept. 21, 1871, and they were the parents of five children. For many years Munhall's home was in Germantown, Philadelphia. He died Jan. 7, 1934.

C. F. Price, *Who's Who in American Methodism.* 1916.
Who Was Who in America.   JESSE A. EARL

MUNICH, Germany, the historic capital of Bavaria and one of the famous and influential cities of Central Europe,

had a 1968 population of 1,300,000. In 1873 the Wesleyan METHODIST MISSIONARY SOCIETY in LONDON appointed the first minister, P. Beutenmueller, to Munich. At that time the city was predominantly Roman Catholic. Thirty years later there were about 100 Methodists in Munich. In 1915 the present church in the Frauenlobstrasse was dedicated by Bishop J. L. NUELSEN. It had a membership of 500 in 1968. A second church, Enhuberstrasse (formerly independent), joined the Methodist Church in 1942. Its membership was reported at 800 in 1968. A third church, Paul-Heyse-Strasse (formerly E.U.B., founded in 1919) joined The United Methodist Church (Evangelisch-methodistische Kirche) in 1968, reporting 330 members.

Four ministers and two deaconesses are doing their work in the city at present. The first Methodist deaconess station (now a hospital) was opened in 1889 (organized by the NUREMBERG motherhouse "Martha-Maria"). The "Martha-Maria-Hospital" München-Solln until 1968 had some 100 beds and forty nurses, being enlarged to 150 beds in 1969. Church work is active, and church attendance is good, though it is difficult to gain new members, because practically everybody belongs to one church or the other; it is not easy to convince Roman Catholics, and the Protestant minority is active anyhow. The future depends on powerful preaching, a true family spirit in the churches, and intensive pastoral care.

HERMANN NEEF

MUÑOZ Y GALBAN, JUAN GUALBERTO (1882-1966), a Cuban pastor, was born in Fomento, Las Villas Province, July 12, 1882. Married in 1908 to Rosa Fernandez, their children were, Elisa, Alfredo, Virginia, Blanca and Evangelina.

He was converted in 1902 under the influence of W. E. Sewell at a service "where he went to scoff but remained to pray."

Entering the ministry in 1905, he served sixteen pastoral appointments and retired in 1954 after fifty years of service. Although retired he continued to work until a few days before his death.

For many years no Annual Conference was complete without the reading of the Resolutions Committee report by Juan Muñoz.

His life was characterized by his sense of humor, unselfish abnegation and humility. These were manifested in his home as well as in the church and among his friends.

Anuario Cubano de la Iglesia Metodista.   GARFIELD EVANS

MUNSEY, WILLIAM ELBERT (1833-1877), American minister of the M.E. Church, South, who while introspective and at times even morbid, was a brilliant and colorful preacher whose sermons made a deep impression on all who heard them. He was born in Giles (now Bland) County, Va., on July 13, 1833, the son of David Munsey and grandson of Zachariah Munsey, the latter being a local preacher of the M.E. Church in that part of VIRGINIA. He had an unusual mother, Mrs. Parmelia P. Munsey, who outlived him and who was called by Bishop JOHN C. KEENER, "wise, prudent and a good manager of home affairs." William Munsey was licensed to preach on Sept. 1, 1855, and received into the HOLSTON CONFERENCE (MES) in October 1856. Thereafter he was ordained DEACON in 1858 by Bishop ANDREW, an ELDER in 1860 by Bishop PAINE. He was married to Miss Virginia A. Blair at Jonesboro, Tenn., on May 17, 1860.

After serving a few years in minor charges of the Holston Conference, he was sent to CHATTANOOGA where he served, 1858-59; then to the well-known Church Street Church in KNOXVILLE, in 1860; to Abingdon, Va., in 1861; Chattanooga, 1862-63; back to Abingdon in 1864; then to Bristol (Tenn.-Va.) in 1865. He was then transferred to the BALTIMORE CONFERENCE and stationed at Alexandria, Va., in 1866, and then at Central Church, BALTIMORE, in 1867-68.

Munsey was made secretary of Foreign Missions early in 1869, which post he held for a few months, but not liking executive work, he was located at his own request and removed to Jonesboro, Tenn.

By this time he had become well known as a lecturer and preacher and being admitted to the Holston Conference again in 1875, he was transferred at once to the LOUISIANA CONFERENCE and stationed at the St. Charles Avenue Church (now Rayne Memorial), in NEW ORLEANS. In this church he made a great name for himself as he did everywhere by the forceful, unusual and electrifying powers of his delivery. His sermons (as may be seen in their printed form today) were florid and effulgent in the extreme and can be viewed as an example of that type of oratory which was then much admired over the South and, indeed, the nation. Bishop Keener said after hearing him preach at ASHEVILLE, N. C., "The impression made upon our mind at the time was that of the constant surging of the billows of an ocean of light." It was probably after hearing him preach that Bishop Keener brought him to New Orleans where he instantly won appreciation from wide audiences.

Munsey's sermons on Eternal Death, on the Resurrection, on the Creation and such themes gave him an opportunity for expanding the scope of his particular talent in preaching. "His description of the lost soul was Miltonic," said Bishop Keener after hearing that sermon.

Munsey was transferred to the ST. LOUIS CONFERENCE in 1876, but shortly after that, fell into ill health and died in Jonesboro on Oct. 23, 1877.

Describing him in the preface to the volume of his published sermons, Bishop Keener said, "As he plodded through his arguments, one could but admire the acuteness of his logic. . . . But when his conclusions had been reached, he would leave premises and conclusions behind, and upon the wings of imagination, would dart into illimitable fields of beauty and grandeur. He careered through the universe of fancy with a momentum that was positively wonderful, and sometimes even terrific. Wherever he soared and carried his audience with him, new worlds, new beauties, new sublimities, new horrors sprang into being on all sides. He could then easily descend from his flights, fold his wings, and then plod through his reasoning process as patiently as if he were totally destitute of imagination."

Following Munsey's death, his sermons were collected and published in a volume which old ministers of the Southern Methodist Church continue to treasure. From the preface and introductory articles in the front of this book, most of the information about Munsey can be obtained.

William Elbert Munsey, *Sermons and Lectures.* Nashville: Southern Methodist Publishing House, 1882.   N. B. H.

MUNZ, FRIEDRICH (1865-1916), German-American minister, professor and editor, was born in Heslach near Stuttgart, Germany, on March 24, 1865. Educated at Esslingen, he emigrated to Farmington, Iowa and attended the MOUNT PLEASANT GERMAN COLLEGE. He was admitted to the West German Annual Conference of the M.E. Church and served churches in NEBRASKA and Iowa City, IOWA. In 1891 he became pastor of the German Methodist Church in Mount Pleasant and president of the Mount Pleasant German College (1893-1897). In the latter year he became assistant editor and in 1900 editor of *Haus und Herd,* a popular monthly German Methodist family publication. To this he contributed many devotional and historical articles. He resigned in 1912 and in 1914 became professor of theology, CENTRAL WESLEYAN COLLEGE, Warrenton, Mo. He died suddenly on Sept. 14, 1916. He received an honorary M.A. from Central Wesleyan in 1892 and a D.D. from German Wallace College, Berea, Ohio in 1900. He edited two famous German Methodist hymnals, *Lobe den Herrn!* (1905) and *Die Pilgerklänge* (1907); wrote a well known treatise on preaching, *Homeletik* (1897), books on Biblical exegesis and translations of popular religious novels into German. He was a major intellectual force in German-American Methodism.

P. F. Douglass, *German Methodism.* 1939.
Haselmayer, *The History and Alumni List of the Mt. Pleasant German College.*
Jubiläumsbuch der St. Louis Deutschen Konferenz.
Minutes of the Annual Conferences 1885-1916.
                                LOUIS A. HASELMAYER

MURCHISON, ELISHA P. (1907-   ), twenty-ninth bishop of the C.M.E. CHURCH, was born at Fort Worth, Texas, on June 18, 1907. He received an A.B. degree from CLARK COLLEGE, a B.D. degree from GAMMON THEOLOGICAL SEMINARY, an M.A. degree from BOSTON UNIVERSITY, and an honorary D.D. degree from PAINE COLLEGE. He entered the ministry in 1920 and served churches in GEORGIA, TEXAS, MASSACHUSETTS, and ILLINOIS. From 1932 to 1935, he was a professor at Texas College in the department of religion, and from 1935 to 1938 was director of Leadership Education of the C.M.E. Church. He was editor of *The Christian Index,* the major publication of his denomination, from 1946 to 1954. He was elected to the office of bishop in 1958. At the first assembly of the WORLD COUNCIL OF CHURCHES in Amsterdam, he represented his Church, and he has also worked as a missionary in Africa. Presently, he is chairman of Public Resolutions of the C.M.E. Church in addition to serving his episcopal area. He presently resides in Birmingham, Ala.

Harris and Patterson, *C.M.E. Church.* 1965.
E. L. Williams, *Biographical Directory of Negro Ministers.* 1966.   RALPH G. GAY

MURFREESBORO, TENNESSEE, U.S.A., **First Church** was organized in 1820 as a result of a CAMP MEETING held at Windrow's Camp Ground. Soon after its close those who lived in Murfreesboro organized a church with approximately forty members. Services were conducted in a residence on College Street until a house of worship could be erected. The Annual Conference was held in this city in 1828, in the upper room of the Rutherford County Court House. It was attended by a large group of Cherokee Indians and it was here that JOHN BERRY

McFERRIN delivered his first missionary address. This Conference was also attended by Bishop JOSHUA SOULE.

Around 1840, a building sixty feet long and thirty feet wide was erected on Maple Street—later the site of Soule Female College. To the south of this building was the Methodist graveyard. Negroes worshipped in the church each Sunday afternoon at 3 o'clock. When a new church was erected in 1843 just across the street from the present structure, a gallery in the southern end was given over to Negroes for preaching and Sunday school. They continued to worship there until 1862 when the Northern Methodists assisted the Negroes in building a church on East College, known as Key Memorial Chapel.

When the Union army came to Murfreesboro in 1863, they took over the church for a hospital until July 1865, when it was turned over to the church officials by order of President Andrew Johnson. The third church building was begun in 1886 and dedicated three years later. In 1910 the church school building and the parish house were built next to the church. The parish house was razed in 1954 in order that a new educational building could be constructed. It became apparent in 1960 that additional space for the church school was imperative. The original building, erected in 1910, was razed and a three-story structure containing class rooms, nursery, scout, choir and additional office rooms built for these needs.

The Christian influence of this great church has touched the lives of nine generations of Methodism in Murfreesboro. Through its pulpit have passed Bishop ROBERT PAINE, its first minister; John B. McFerrin, leader of the Southern Church during the post-Civil War years, and Bishop PAUL B. KERN. It stands as a memorial to those who, with dedication and foresight, devoted themselves to the great work of Methodism, and as an inspiration and challenge to those still to come.

C. T. Carter, *Tennessee Conference.* 1948.
O. P. Fitzgerald, *John B. McFerrin, A Biography.* Nashville: Publishing House, M.E. Church, South, 1888.
News-Banner, Murfreesboro, Tenn., Oct. 16, 1928.

MRS. WALTER HUGHEY KING

MURLIN, JOHN (1722-1799), British itinerant, emotional preacher called "the weeping prophet," was born at St. Stephen Branwell, Cornwall, in August 1722. He prospered in business; and when converted in 1749, under JOHN DOWNES' ministry, he reluctantly began preaching. In 1754 WESLEY called him out, placing him frequently in BRISTOL and LONDON.

A man of fortune, apt to dictate his station, he was, Wesley acknowledged, gifted and successful. Murlin was involved in the sacramental controversy at Norwich and the pulpit-angel trouble at Halifax. He wrote *Sacred Hymns* (1781) and *Elegy on Fletcher* (1788). He died in retirement, at High Wycombe, on July 7, 1799, and shares Wesley's tomb.

G. LAWTON

MURLIN, LEMUEL HERBERT (1861-1935), American minister, educator, university president, was born in the village of Mendon, Ohio. His father was an itinerant Methodist minister. Being a supply pastor, the father's salary was so small that it became necessary for the son, even while in public school, to get part-time work to augment the family income. During vacation time, he "rode the circuit" with his father.

Lemuel entered DEPAUW UNIVERSITY, paying his way with money earned as a supply at nearby churches. He was graduated from DePauw in 1891, when he married Ermina Fallass. He served as a Methodist pastor for three years, and then was elected president of BAKER UNIVERSITY in 1894, which position he held until 1911, when he was elected president of BOSTON UNIVERSITY. He carried the burden of his office through the First World War.

Failing health and the advice of his doctor caused Murlin to tender his resignation to the Trustees of Boston University in 1925. On invitation from DePauw, he accepted its presidency, but retired at the end of three years. Then he and Mrs. Murlin traveled abroad until 1935, the year he died.

C. F. Price, *Who's Who in American Methodism.* 1916.

DANIEL L. MARSH

MURPHY, MRS. ANN (1731-1814), pioneer American church leader, moved from near Ellicott's Mill, Md., the probable place of her birth, and settled in 1780 near UNIONTOWN, Pa. She "was possessed of some means." Her home was the regular stopping place of the early Methodist itinerants. During eighteen of the twenty times Bishop ASBURY passed through the PITTSBURGH CONFERENCE territory, he stopped at or preached at Uniontown. ROBERT AYRES on the REDSTONE CIRCUIT, 1786-87, stopped at Ann's home on each round of the circuit. The preachers at the Quarterly Conference held in Uniontown in 1787 were lodged at "Widow Murphy's," as also at the first group conference, 1788, and probably in 1790 and 1792.

Jacob Murphy, son of Ann, continued the devotion of his noble mother. He was a trustee of the first Uniontown church and served as a local preacher. Asbury preached in Murphy's barn and ordained William Page as elder and Andrew Hemphill as deacon in Murphy's home in 1804. Jacob married the daughter of Colonel Isaac Meason.

As a personality, Ann Murphy was the most influential among the founders of Methodism in Uniontown, a stronghold of pioneer and present-day Methodism.

F. Asbury, *Journal and Letters.* 1958.
J. S. Payton, *Our Fathers Have Told Us.* 1938.
W. G. Smeltzer, *Headwaters of the Ohio.* 1951.

JESSE A. EARL

MURPHY, JOHN (1740-1813), a Presbyterian layman in Salem County, N. J., who later became active in Methodist work in southern NEW JERSEY. Murphy, a resident of Friendship, Salem County, was an Elder of the Pittsgrove Presbyterian Church at Daretown in Salem County. Being attracted by the spirit of the Methodist pioneer preacher, ABRAHAM WHITWORTH, Murphy invited him to hold meetings at his house. It was here that Whitworth preached the Word which ultimately became the means of BENJAMIN ABBOTT's conversion.

Murphy's interest in Methodism grew until at his house was formed possibly the first Methodist Society south of Burlington (Friendship, 1773). Later it was Murphy who gave generously to build the first place of worship at Friendship. This was known as the Murphy Meeting House. In it were conducted at least three far-reaching revivals of religion which did much to establish Methodism in southern New Jersey.

Both Methodist churches in Salem have their roots in the Murphy Meeting House. Murphy was also one of the founders of the M. E. Church in Salem in 1784, and is spoken of as a founder of Methodism in Fairton and Bridgeton, N. J. Affectionately known as "Father Murphy and as "the venerable" John Murphy, his befriending of the Methodists aided their cause strategically in an hour when their enemies were numerous and determined.

He died in 1813 and was buried in the cemetery of First Methodist Church, Bridgeton, N. J.

G. A. Raybold, *Reminiscences of Methodism in West Jersey.* New York: Lane & Scott, 1849.
Howard F. Shipps, "The Forgotten Apostle of Methodism." S.T.D. Thesis, Temple University, 1955.

FRANK BATEMAN STANGER

MURRAH, WILLIAM BELTON (1851-1925), bishop, was born in Pickensville, Ala., in May 1851. He was educated at Southern University, CENTENARY COLLEGE and WOFFORD COLLEGE. He joined the NORTH MISSISSIPPI CONFERENCE of the M. E. Church, South, in 1876, and served churches in Oxford, Winona and Aberdeen. He was vice president of Whitworth College, Brookhaven, Miss., for four years, and then became the first president of MILLSAPS COLLEGE at JACKSON, Miss., chartered in 1890, with the first session in 1892. Murrah, Bishop CHARLES B. GALLOWAY and Major REUBEN W. MILLSAPS are usually credited as the founders of this college.

Murrah was elected bishop of the M. E. Church, South, by the GENERAL CONFERENCE of 1910. His publications include addresses, lectures, sermons, and contributions to religious periodicals. A large, impressive-looking man, W. B. Murrah exerted quite an influence in church and educational circles. A large framed likeness of Bishop Murrah, with the other Alabamans who have been elected bishop, is kept in the episcopal office at Birmingham, Ala. Bishop Murrah died on March 5, 1925.

Who Was Who in America. ELMER T. CLARK

MURRAY, GRACE (1718-1803), who became a Methodist at the outset of the revival, served as a band leader at the Foundery, LONDON, and after the death of her husband, Alexander Murray, returned to her mother's home in Newcastle upon Tyne. Here she was appointed housekeeper of Wesley's Orphan House headquarters, and in that capacity nursed JOHN BENNET through a lengthy illness in 1746, after which they corresponded affectionately with each other. In August 1748, JOHN WESLEY also fell ill in Newcastle and was nursed by Grace Murray. He proposed marriage to her, took her south on a journey with him, and then left her at Chinley in the care of Bennet, who also wooed her, being assured that she had no commitment to Wesley. During the spring and early summer of 1749 she travelled with Wesley in IRELAND, and in DUBLIN they were betrothed by a contract *de praesenti.* After their return to England in July a jealous spasm propelled her once more to Bennet. Wesley decided to let John Bennet have her, though he had "a piercing conviction of his irreparable loss." Grace protested, however, that she loved Wesley "a thousand times better than [she] ever loved John Bennet." She pressed Wesley for a public ceremony, but after a renewal of the contract *de praesenti,* this time in the presence of a

GRACE MURRAY

witness, CHRISTOPHER HOPPER, Wesley continued his preaching tour.

Meantime Wesley wrote to his brother CHARLES about Grace. Charles, apparently not realizing the depth of John's commitment, persuaded Grace and John Bennet to marry, only too late to discover his misunderstanding of the situation. John Wesley forgave Bennet and Grace, but two years later Bennet left Methodism, and then became the pastor of a Calvinistic church at Warburton. Grace Bennet continued conducting weekly meetings for prayer and fellowship long after the death of her husband. Only once more, in their old age, did John Wesley and Grace Bennet meet. She died in her eighty-fifth year, and her biography was written by one of her five sons.

Frank Baker, "John Wesley's First Marriage," *London Quarterly Review,* October 1967.
William Bennet, *Memoirs of Mrs. Grace Bennet,* Macclesfield: Bagley, 1803.
J. A. Leger, *Wesley's Last Love.* 1910.
G. E. Harrison, *Son to Susanna.* 1937.

MALDWYN L. EDWARDS

MURRAY, JOHN JACKSON (1824-1905), American minister and president of the GENERAL CONFERENCE of the M. P. CHURCH in 1867, was born in Hagerstown, Md., on May 8, 1824. He was converted in 1839 and was licensed to preach on Dec. 25, 1841, and began itinerating on Queen Anne's Circuit in the MARYLAND CONFERENCE in April 1842. He filled all the prominent appointments in the Maryland Conference, including St. John's Church, BALTIMORE, and in 1873 was loaned to the PITTSBURGH CONFERENCE. He served on the committee chosen to compile the hymnbook of the M. P. Church published in 1859. He and his brother, J. T. Murray, conducted *The Methodist Protestant* editorially in 1870. While he was pastor of the M. P. Church in PHILADELPHIA, he organized a church in NEWARK, N. J., in 1859, with thirty-seven members. In 1860 he was appointed to serve as the first regular pastor of this church, a position he held for three years. He served as president of the General Conference of 1867 which met in Montgomery, Ala. In 1872 he was fraternal messenger to the General Conferences in 1858, 1862, 1866, 1870, 1874, and a delegate to the historic uniting convention of May 1877. At the 1866 General Conference, he offered a resolution which led to reunion with the northern branch of the church which had split over slavery in 1858. The resolution was passed by the conference.

Murray received the M.D. degree from Washington University in Baltimore in March 1850.

A. H. Bassett, *Concise History.* 1887.
E. J. Drinkhouse, *History of Methodist Reform.* 1899.
M. Simpson, *Cyclopaedia.* 1878.   RALPH HARDEE RIVES

MURRAY, THOMAS HOLT (1845-1916), American lawyer, orator and distinguished Methodist layman, was born April 5, 1845 in Girard Township, Clearfield Co., Pa. He was educated at the common schools near his farm home and at Williamsport Dickinson Seminary, from which he graduated in 1867. As a law student at Dickinson Seminary, he continued his education for this profession in a local law office and was admitted to the bar of Clearfield County in 1869. He soon became not only "the unquestioned leader of this bar," but the most sought after trial lawyer of western PENNSYLVANIA.

His maternal great grandfather, Philip Antes, had given the land for the first Methodist church in Clearfield County, and Thomas H. Murray became the most distinguished layman of his day in the CENTRAL PENNSYLVANIA CONFERENCE of the M. E. Church. He was elected to eight successive GENERAL CONFERENCES of that church (1888-1916), and to the ECUMENICAL METHODIST CONFERENCE of 1901. One of the most eloquent and influential laymen on the floor of the General Conference, he was designated by that body to be its spokesman in replying to the welcome to Lincoln, Neb. in 1892, given by the governor of the state and the mayor of the city. From 1896 to 1906 he was a member of the Joint Commission on the Federation of Methodism. He also served as a member of the Committee on Judiciary of the General Conference and of the Book Committee for a time.

Three volumes of his most notable addresses on various occasions, both civic and ecclesiastical, have been published. He was a member of Trinity M. E. Church, Clearfield, Pa. He died Dec. 8, 1916 at Clearfield.

Christian Advocate (New York), Jan. 11 and 18, 1917.
Journal of the Central Pennsylvania Conference, 1917.
The Pennsylvania Methodist, June 30, 1904.
The Progress, Clearfield, Pa., Nov. 12, 1966.
                                        CHARLES F. BERKHEIMER

MURRELLS INLET, SOUTH CAROLINA, U.S.A., **Belin Memorial Church,** started in 1836 as Oatland Methodist Church, was built a few miles from its present site by JAMES LYNCH BELIN, who preached there about twenty-three years. He was at that time the "missionary" in charge of the Waccamaw Mission.

In 1925 the building at Oatland was torn down, taken to Murrells Inlet and rebuilt to the exact specifications with the same lumber, and given the name of Belin Memorial Methodist Church. It was rebuilt on the same property as the old "Cedar Hill" Mission House which

was used as a home for James Belin for twenty-three years, and then by other ministers until 1960. At that time "Cedar Hill" was made into the educational building of the church and a new parsonage was built.

                                        THOMAS KEMMERLIN

MUSGRAVE, WALTER EMMETT (1880-1950), American United Brethren in Christ (Old Constitution) bishop, was born near Stockport, Ohio, Sept. 7, 1880. He had the advantage of a common school education, and received the equivalent of high school education by tutorial method. He made theology and church history his specialty. In 1928 he was awarded the D.D. from Huntington College.

He was married to Anna Yarnell and was the father of two sons and one daughter. One son died in infancy and the other, Wilford P. Musgrave, was dean of Huntington College for a number of years.

He was converted at the age of nineteen in a M.P. CHURCH, and soon received an exhorter's license. Since his early church experience had been United Brethren, he returned to that and joined the Scioto Conference. He served fourteen years as pastor and five years as presiding elder. During his ministry he was especially interested in young people, and organized CHRISTIAN ENDEAVOR societies in his churches. He was a successful evangelist and conducted a number of campaigns in the United States east of the Mississippi as well as in Ontario, CANADA. He was also interested in the temperance cause and was associated with Daniel A. Poling in this work in Ohio.

The GENERAL CONFERENCE of 1921 elected Musgrave as executive secretary of the Otterbein Forward Movement, and he moved to Huntington, Ind., where he resided the remainder of his life. He was elected bishop in 1925 and served that office for twenty-four years. While bishop he was president of many general church boards, but was especially interested in education and missions. He was an effective fund raiser and assisted the financial program of Huntington College many times. He was commissioned by the 1945 General Conference to write a history of the CHURCH OF THE UNITED BRETHREN IN CHRIST (OLD CONSTITUTION). A preliminary draft was mimeographed under the title, "The Church of the United Brethren in Christ: Its Teachings and Progress." He was devoting time to research for the amplification of the history at the time of his death, May 6, 1950, at Huntington, Ind. The memorial service was held at College Park Church and burial at Pilgrim's Rest Cemetery, Huntington.

Christian Conservator, May 31, 1950.
Contact, June 25, 1967.   J. RALPH PFISTER

MUSIC in American Methodism. The study of Methodist music before 1850 is primarily the study of hymns, particularly Wesleyan hymns. One writer stated in 1856 that even hymn singing among Methodists ". . . existed only in its rude and uncultivated state" (Willis, p. 41). Another commented in 1865 that Methodists have been attractive singers but poor musicians, fearful of "scientific music" and convinced that all instruments were a liability in the church.

Early Methodists frowned upon the use of anything other than the human voice. The playing of organs was a vanity, and the violin an incarnation of the devil. However, during the 1840's writers were advocating the use of the organ. By 1855 the organ was gaining considerable acceptance and in 1875 was in general use in larger churches. Smaller churches were content with small reed organs or melodeons. In a few instances other instruments, including the cornet, were used in special situations. The prominence of instruments is shown by the publication of numerous favorable and unfavorable comments about their use.

Methodist choirs came into existence when the better singers began sitting together, perhaps for their own enjoyment, and, incidentally, to lead the congregation. In 1850 a number of city churches in the east had regular choirs for which special seating was provided. An 1856 floor plan for a Methodist church in PITTSBURGH included a special area for choir members.

The quality of congregational music, according to writers of the time, was generally poor except in the occasional church that had competent leadership. The M. E. Church recognized the problem and appointed an editor to take charge of the music department of the Methodist BOOK CONCERN during the late 1860's. Hymnal introductions and numerous articles mentioned the need for increased emphasis upon the congregation and less upon the choir. SUNDAY SCHOOL singing during the last quarter of the century was said to be particularly poor and usually unrelated to the worship service.

Competition between choirs and congregations developed early. Complaints about professionalism in church music appeared in publications of the late fifties. There were those who believed that professional singers and organists belonged only on the stage and never in church. An organization called the Associated Choirs of New York prepared an excellent evaluation of the place of musicians and the use of music in worship. All phases of vocal and instrumental music in the church and Sunday school were included in the study. Activities of the Association were discussed by the 1864 GENERAL CONFERENCE of the M. E. Church and a committee was appointed to work with the musicians.

By 1875 almost all Methodist churches of any size had choirs of sorts. The "quartette choir" had also made its appearance even in small churches and was attaining considerable prominence. The M. P. CHURCH gave attention to the use of choirs in its hymnal of 1892 (a republication with little change of a private collection first published in 1872). A large part of the long Introduction is entitled "Choir and Congregational Singing." Mention is made of methods, materials and procedures for organists and choirs, including children's choirs. The mechanics of worship are carefully described.

During the last half of the century organ builders concentrated upon producing an orchestral rather than a church instrument. Organists were accused of being concerned with developing concert virtuosity while neglecting the basic purpose of their playing—leading the congregation in worship. Considerable antagonism developed between organists and ministers as a result.

The American Guild of Organists was established in 1896, partially for the purpose of breaking down this antagonism. Occasional articles in Methodist and other church publications discussed the proper use of the organ in worship but the situation showed little change until well into the twentieth century.

Prior to 1850, the few choirs in existence had one responsibility—to lead the rest of the congregation in

hymn singing. Choir "specials" were a gradual development, but by 1875 the original purpose of the choir seemed to have been lost since little attention was being given to the singing of hymns. Around 1900 certain congregations were asked to participate "silently" in the worship service in order that nothing should detract from the singing of the choirs.

Between 1875 and 1920 choirs changed very little. Many churches had only a mixed quartet, often well paid, while others had both quartet and choir. The "perfect" choral composition of the period included a solo for each member of the quartet and several "choruses" which could be sung by the quartet or by the supporting choir if one were maintained. (Only recently has the paid quartet within the choir ceased to exist to a significant degree.) No great concern was shown by churchmen for the development of effective music in the church and Sunday school. Some excitement was engendered by the publication of the new joint Methodist hymnal in 1905, but this interest was of brief duration. Writers occasionally discussed the place of the choir and often criticized the concertizing of organists, the operatic performances of soloists, and the annoying brilliance of choral groups in general.

The situation remained stagnant until several incidents of great importance occurred in the early 1920's: (1) series of three conferences on church music were held, beginning in 1921 at Rushville, Ind.; (2) the Methodist Book Concern published the lectures presented at these conferences (1923); (3) numerous thought-provoking articles on Methodist music appeared in church magazines; (4) consideration was given to the concept of a Ministry of music; (5) a Methodist Commission on Music was appointed (1924); (6) a highly significant book on Methodist music and worship was published (1924), expressing many concepts not generally accepted or applied for another thirty years.

By 1925 all but the very smallest Methodist churches had some sort of choir and an organ or piano. Some had Sunday school orchestras. The quality of music ranged from excellent to very poor. Congregational music was frequently neither good nor meaningful. Unfortunately, organ construction was entering a period when that majestic instrument became more suited for the funeral parlor than for the church. A few choirs wore robes, and some participated in services that were true worship experiences.

The twenties were a time of great activity. Ministers and musicians examined attitudes, procedures, methods and materials. The place of music in worship and education was debated, often with considerable heat. Attempts were made to develop an understanding of the responsibilities of all who were concerned with and affected by the music of the church. Conscientious church musicians showed concern for the poor state of congregational music and were eventually to provide much of the leadership that brought all church music into better balance. The organist/pianist was increasingly accepted as the person most able to improve hymn singing. The emergence of great college and university choral organizations inspired the church choir to seek its place as leader, teacher, and source of encouragement for better congregational singing.

The most significant result of this time of enthusiasm was The Methodist Hymnal of 1935, a cooperative venture of the three principal branches of Methodism. Church union which followed is believed by many to have been strongly affected by the joint publication of a successful hymnal.

Another important development was the growth of interest in children's and youth choirs and in the total program of music in Christian education. The Sunday school music of past generations was under careful scrutiny, but it was difficult to replace.

The movement for better church music was slowed by the depression and brought to a halt by World War II. One war-time development—the widespread use of the electronic organ—has had a strong and lasting effect. During the early fifties many varieties of electronic keyboard instruments appeared and some have made a significant place for themselves, especially in medium-sized and smaller churches.

Despite the thousands of electronic instruments sold during the last twenty years, pipe organ builders are unable today to keep up with the demand for their products. There has been a return to the construction of an organ that combines the best features of the preceding three hundred years of organ building. Organists, too, have a better understanding of their opportunities and responsibilities in the church and Sunday school.

Present trends in Methodist music are a direct outgrowth of action taken in 1952 by the General Conference at which the BOARD OF EDUCATION of The Methodist Church was instructed to examine the music of the church and to take any action needed to promote the better use of music in worship and Christian education. To implement these instructions a planning conference of church musicians, ministers and educators was held at Estes Park in 1955. The NATIONAL FELLOWSHIP OF METHODIST MUSICIANS (NaFOMM) grew out of the conference and was chartered the following year at Williams Bay, Wis.

NaFOMM had much to do with the progress made by Methodist music toward attaining its proper place in the church. (For an account of this organization see it under MUSICIANS, FELLOWSHIP OF UNITED METHODIST. The *Discipline* of 1968 directs that the Division of the Local Church under the Board of Education shall cooperate with this organization [Paragraph 1065.4].)

Music Ministry, a monthly magazine, was first published by the Editorial Division in 1960; the Publishing House was a full-time church music manager, and has published many books on music in worship and Christian education. Biennial convocations are held by NaFOMM and, in alternate years, by each jurisdiction; dozens of local, district and conference workshops on church music are held each year. A completely new approach is being made to music in the church school with emphasis upon excellent audio-visual materials. Theological seminaries are doing a more effective job of training ministers in the use of music. The revised Methodist Hymnal (1966) is adding its great influence.

Oliver S. Baketel, *Concordance of the Methodist Hymnal.* New York: Eaton and Mains, 1907.
Charles Newell Boyd, *The Organist and the Choirmaster.* New York: Abingdon Press, 1936.
B. F. Crawford, *Theological Trends.* 1939.
D. Creamer, *Methodist Hymnology.* 1848.
Nathaniel D. Gould, *Church Music in America.* Boston: N. Johnson, 1853.
Earl Enyeart Harper, *Church Music and Worship.* New York: Abingdon Press, 1924.
——————, *The Methodist Minister and the Music of the Church.* Nashville: Abingdon Press, 1959.
Stanley Armstrong Hunter, *The Music of the Gospel.* New York: Abingdon Press, 1932.
James T. Lightwood, *Methodist Music of the Eighteenth Century.* London: Epworth Press, 1927.
——————, *Music of the Methodist Hymn-Book.* 1950.
——————, *Stories of Methodist Music.* London: Epworth Press, 1928.
Austin C. Lovelace and William C. Rice, *Music and Worship in the Church.* Nashville: Abingdon Press, 1960.
Robert G. McCutchan, "A Singing Church," *Methodism: A Compendium.* Cincinnati: Methodist Publishing House, 1947.
——————, *Our Hymnody.* 1937.
C. S. Nutter, *Hymn Studies.* 1884.
Nutter and Tillett, *Hymns and Hymn Writers.* 1911.
C. F. Price, *Music and Hymnody.* 1911.
William C. Rice, "A Century of Methodist Music: 1850-1950." Unpublished Ph.D. dissertation, State University of Iowa, 1953. (Contains a bibliography of books, articles, etc. on church music: 339 items, all published before 1950.)
——————, "The Church Musician's Library," *Music Ministry,* Vol. 5 (August 1964), p. 8. (A list of books on church music published between 1950 and 1964.)
W. F. Tillett, *Our Hymns and Their Authors.* 1889.
Erastus Wentworth, "Methodism and Music," *Methodist Quarterly Review,* Vol. 47 (1865), p. 359.
Richard Storrs Willis, *Our Church Music.* New York: Dana and Co., 1855.
Worship in Music, Edwin Holt Hughes, et al., New York: Abingdon Press, 1929. WILLIAM G. RICE

MUSIC, British Methodist. The early Methodists in England inherited the tradition of metrical psalms which had dominated seventeenth century worship, but the varied meters adopted by CHARLES WESLEY demanded tunes outside the conventional long and common meters. JOHN WESLEY's first tune book, *The Foundery Collection* (1742), contained tunes of several types: Psalm tunes, German chorales (which he had learned from the Moravians), adaptations from popular melodies, and a few tunes specially written. Hymn singing became characteristic of Methodist worship, and was so effective as to arouse the envy of Anglicans.

At first the singing was unaccompanied, though occasionally the bass was reinforced by a bass viol. Later, orchestras became common, sometimes to the annoyance of the preachers. Anthems were popular, especially Edward Harwood's "Vital Spark," of which John Wesley spoke with admiration. Late in the century hymn singing became overornamented, with graces, trills, passing notes, repeats, and choruses. Against this practice John Wesley protested, but with little effect.

Organ music was introduced much later, new installations being forbidden by CONFERENCE until 1820. The split in English Methodism through the introduction of a large organ in Brunswick Chapel, LEEDS, was more a matter of disputed authority than of musical propriety. There was no organ in Wesley's chapel on City Road, LONDON, until the 1880's; for a long time there, as still in the Methodist Conference, the singing was led by a precentor.

The Anglican chant was never widely used in Methodism, except in the Canticles. There was, however, a revival in its use, and the influence of the Methodist Church Music Society encouraged the adoption of speech rhythm. Hymns, however, four or five in each service, have remained the staple diet of British Methodist worship; though anthems, and choral works at special seasons, are frequently given, sometimes by combined choirs (see HYMNODY).

A. S. Gregory, *Praises with Understanding*. 1936.
James T. Lightwood, *Methodist Music of the Eighteenth Century*. London: Epworth Press, 1927.
————, *Music of the Methodist Hymn-Book*. 1935.

C. W. TOWLSON

MUSIC SOCIETY, METHODIST CHURCH (British), arose from a meeting of British Methodist musicians and ministers in January 1934, to explore the new *Methodist Hymn Book* of December, 1933. Since then the society, formed in 1935, has widened its purview "to foster and develop all the musical resources of Methodism for Public Worship and Evangelism." It reports to Conference, and holds an Annual Conference and local conferences and supports local Festivals of Praise.

C. W. TOWLSON

MUSICIANS, FELLOWSHIP OF UNITED METHODIST (known until August, 1969 as the National Fellowship of Methodist Musicians—NaFOMM), is an organization sponsored by the Division of the Local Church, General BOARD OF EDUCATION of The United Methodist Church. Its membership is open to all persons who are working through music in the church.

This organization began in 1955 with an invitation to Methodist musicians to come together to discuss how The Methodist Church could better communicate the role of music in Christian education. Walter Towner gave leadership here and the idea of a fellowship was born. There were two significant ideas: to have a national Methodist music publication; and to set up standards for proper certification. NaFOMM, as it was at first called, was organized on July 13, 1956 at Williams Bay, Wis., with 110 persons signing its constitution. Walter Towner served as interim executive secretary until Bliss Wiant was appointed on May 1, 1957. Four years later, Wiant retired and Cecil E. Lapo, who had been the first president of NaFOMM, became its executive secretary. The organization presently has over 3,000 members.

Its objectives and goals may be stated as follows:

To make more positive the role of music in Christian nurture, worship and witness; to create among church musicians a fellowship of service to the church; to stress the importance of each Christian musician being a "churchman"; to encourage the composition of new music; to encourage and counsel educational institutions, particularly the seminaries, to plan greater emphasis on the training in, and appreciation of, great church music; to assist students interested in the ministry of music to become educated for full time Christian service in this field; to cooperate with Annual Conference Boards of Education, Commissions on WORSHIP and other similar groups in establishing workshops, institutes, conferences and study courses.

Publications: *FOUMM News Notes* is published bi-monthly and there is extensive cooperation with *Music Ministry*, the music magazine of the Editorial Division of the General Board of Education. Periodic pamphlets appear aimed at informative help for the local church in the field of vocational guidance and use of *The Methodist Hymnal*.

NaFOMM had a representative on the Methodist Hymnal Commission during the 1960-64 quadrennium, and enjoyed reciprocal representation on the General Commission on Worship. All bishops of The United Methodist Church are members of the Fellowship. Particular guidance in the formative years was given by Bishop EARL LEDDEN. The Fellowship is governed by an Executive Council consisting of current officers, and there are representatives from each JURISDICTION of The United Methodist Church, as well as consultative members including the editor of *Music Ministry*. The organization meets biennially for educational exchange, fellowship and enrichment of ideas.

Journal of Church Music, Vol. 10, No. 10, November 1968.
Music Ministry, Vol. 6, No. 11, July 1965.
William C. Rice, *A Concise History of Church Music*. Nashville: Abingdon Press, 1964.   WILLIAM K. BURNS

MUSKEGON, MICHIGAN, U.S.A., **Central Church,** is a strong church in the MICHIGAN CONFERENCE of The United Methodist Church. The first organized Protestant society in Muskegon became in time the present Central Church. In 1843, six years after the first sawmill was built on Muskegon Lake, a Protestant religious service was held in the Martin Ryerson boarding house with a "large" attendance and a collection of $7.50. A flourishing Methodist group at White Lake then began early to include Muskegon as a mission station. By 1855 regular services were being held in the public school house. The White River circuit was organized in September 1855, with L. M. Bennett in charge. Bennett came to preach in Muskegon every two or four weeks, walking along the shore of Lake Michigan from his White Lake home. Morning preaching at the school house was followed by afternoon services at the new lighthouse at the entrance to Muskegon Harbor.

In November 1856, the church was formally organized as a member of the Michigan Conference and John M. Pratt was named first resident minister. When the school house was no longer available for services a drive was initiated early in 1857 to raise funds for a church building. To this the community responded with gifts of money, labor and material. Dedication was held in June 1859.

The Civil War years were years of crisis for Muskegon's Methodists. The membership dropped to thirteen persons. For twenty-eight years the first structure served well the church and community. It was replaced in 1888. In December 1923, a move was designed to seek a location some distance from the center of the city, property was purchased, and a new building started under the leadership of Raymond Johns. On March 16, 1930 the new sanctuary was ready for use. The present edifice is of Gothic style and is built of Indiana limestone.

Central Methodist has sponsored the other Methodist churches in the community. One pastor, D. STANLEY COORS, was elevated to the episcopacy. At present Central has a membership of 1,700 and serves the community well from its mid-town location.

Central's Centennial in Christian Service, 1956.

MRS. ISABEL HORSLEY

MUSKINGUM CONFERENCE. (See OHIO CONFERENCE (MP).)

MUSKOGEE, OKLAHOMA, U.S.A. **First Church** had its beginning when Sam Checote, principal chief of the

Creek Indian tribe and presiding elder of the Methodist INDIAN MISSION CONFERENCE, in 1877 secured land from his tribe to give to the conference on which to build a church in the village of Muskogee (population 400). The Mission Board at NASHVILLE (MES) and the people (partly in work) gave $500 each. Young Theodore F. Brewer, teaching in the Asbury Training School at Eufaula, was appointed the first pastor in 1878 and remained until 1886. He came over to preach once a month until a parsonage was built in Muskogee, when he moved in.

Theodore F. Brewer organized the church in 1878 and built the original "Rock Church" the same year. Immediately after the church was organized, a Sunday school was started. (This school was destined to be served as Sunday school superintendent by A. E. Bonnell for thirty-five years.) Brewer also established a school, Harrell Institute, which met in the church until it grew so large that it had to build its own building.

In 1903 the church was destroyed by fire and the bishop ordered the church divided (money and property). Those living east of the "Katy" railroad were to form one congregation, and those living west of it another congregation. First Church acquired land six blocks east of the Rock Church, and this became the location of present First Church.

The second building was erected in 1904 under M. L. Butler, pastor, and was called First M.E. Church, South. In 1950 a new educational building was erected, Finis Crutchfield being pastor. Later, in 1958, D. Wesley Doak, pastor, led in the construction of the present sanctuary at a cost of about $300,000. Presently the church plans to build another educational unit, estimated to cost $200,000. Jack S. Wilkes, pastor, 1950-54, was elected president of OKLAHOMA CITY UNIVERSITY, which he served from 1957-63.

First Church is the "Mother of Methodism in Muskogee." St. Paul Church with 2,473 members, grew out of First Church. The other four churches of the community were helped by First Church. Three laymen have served the general Church: H. E. Newton on the Board of Missions for some thirty years; Jim Egan, the Board of Education; and R. B. Lazenby, the Board of Evangelism.

During First Church's ninety years of history more than thirty young men and women have entered the ministry and gone to mission fields. In 1970 First Church had property valued at $872,150 and 2,348 members.

The story of First Church and its relation to the Indians, other city churches, and education, together with recruiting more than thirty persons for the ministry and mission field, and the services of many distinguished laymen, provides a remarkable and relevant account of Methodist advance.

St. Paul Church was organized in 1903. It moved into its first permanent home, a structure at Seventh and Boston, in 1906. The work prospered and St. Paul's became one of the leading churches in the Conference.

In 1929 fire destroyed the entire building. The congregation was undecided whether to rebuild on the same location or move farther west. When two lots at the corner of 23rd and Okmulgee were donated, the congregation agreed to build there. A beautiful and adequate building was erected in 1930. As the west side of Muskogee developed, St. Paul grew also.

In 1960 the Rowsey Memorial Chapel was built at the other end of the block. All the residential property on this large block was purchased. In 1962 an educational unit was built, uniting the original building and the chapel. The entire area was cleared to provide adequate parking. Today St. Paul's has one of the commanding church properties in OKLAHOMA. Membership presently (1970) stands at 2,473 and with property valued at $1,316,894, the church considers itself challenged to carry on a well-rounded program of activities.

General Minutes.
Our First Methodist Church, Its First Seventy-Five Years.
Brochure, October 1953.   JESSE A. EARL

MUTO, TAKESHI (1893-   ), Japanese educator, pastor, and church leader, received his early education in Aomori Prefecture in northern JAPAN, where he was baptized at the age of ten in a Methodist church. After graduation from the Theological Department of AOYAMA GAKUIN in TOKYO, he did three years of study in the Tokyo Imperial University, specializing in ethics. This was followed by a year at NORTHWESTERN UNIVERSITY in the United States, where he majored in philosophy and received an M.A. degree in 1923. From 1924 to 1936 he was teaching at his alma mater, Aoyama Gakuin. He began preaching in 1934, and in 1936 became pastor of Chuo Kaido (Central Methodist Church) in Tokyo. He has held this pastorate ever since except for a period of about four years (1942-1946) when he was president of Kwassui Girls College, a Methodist school in Nagasaki. In 1954 he was elected Moderator of the United Church of Christ in Japan (the church into which the Japan Methodist Church had merged in 1941). After his first two-year term, he was reelected for a second term. While Moderator he represented the Japanese Church at the Methodist GENERAL CONFERENCE in MINNEAPOLIS in 1956. In 1959 he was elected Chairman of the National Christian Council of Japan.

JOHN B. COBB, SR.

MUTUAL RIGHTS was a publication (1824-1834) with the Methodist Protestant Reformers. (See METHODIST PROTESTANT RECORDER.)

MUTTAYYA and **MUNAYYA** (dates uncertain), were pioneer converts in the Bidar District of the SOUTH INDIA ANNUAL CONFERENCE. They were baptized by Joseph Henry Garden on January 1, 1892. Muttayya was a retired soldier and pensioner. He had worked under William Marrett, an engineer and a local preacher of the English church in HYDERABAD. By caste Muttayya was a Madiga. He and his entire family developed Christian faith and earnestly desired to be recognized as Christians and admitted to fellowship. Consultations between British and American Methodist missionaries led to an agreement that the Americans would work in Bidar and the adjoining territory in which this family lived. Munayya was a grandson of Muttayya and fully shared the old man's eagerness for Christian fellowship.

These men guided Garden and others to groups of their relatives, and many of them were converted. This launched a revival that has occasionally slowed but has never stopped. These two were no less responsible than the ordained ministers for the beginning of the strong church in Bidar District.

B. T. Badley, *Southern Asia.* 1931.   J. WASKOM PICKETT

MUZOREWA, ABEL TENDEKAYI (1925-   ), bishop of The United Methodist Church in the RHODESIA Area, was born on April 14, 1925, at Old Umtali Methodist Centre in Rhodesia, the son of Philemon Hadi and Hilda (Munangatire) Muzorewa. He studied at the Old Umtali Methodist Centre, 1950-52, and then came to America where he received an A.B. degree from CENTRAL COLLEGE in Fayette, Mo., in 1962. He was given the M.A. by SCARRITT COLLEGE, Nashville, Tenn., in 1963. On Aug. 11, 1951, he married Maggie Chigodora, and their children are Blessing Tendekayi, Philemon Dairayl, Wesley Tanyaradzwa, Scarriter Charles Chido. He taught in primary schools, 1944-47, and was a lay preacher, 1948-59. He was received on trial in the Rhodesia Conference in 1953, and into full connection with his elder's ordination in 1955. He was associate conference evangelist, 1952-55, and then became the pastor of the Chiduku North Circuit in Rhodesia, 1955-58. He was pastor of the Old Umtali Methodist Centre, Umtali, 1963-64, and then became the conference director of youth work at Umtali, 1965. He was in 1966 the youth secretary of the Student Movement and the traveling secretary of the Christian Council of Rhodesia.

At the African Central Conference of The United Methodist Church held Aug. 24-31, 1968, at Gaberones, Botswana, Abel Muzorewa was elected a bishop to succeed Bishop RALPH DODGE, who at that Conference announced his retirement. Bishop Muzorewa at forty-three years of age became one of the youngest Methodist bishops ever to be elected. His election came on the sixth ballot and he was assigned to the Rhodesia Area (presently comprising 28,661 members and 181 churches).

Who's Who in The Methodist Church, 1966.   N. B. H.

MYLES, WILLIAM (1756-1828), was an Irish Methodist, born in Limerick, on July 9, 1756. He heard WESLEY preach there in 1773. He itinerated in IRELAND, 1777-82, at his own expense, and became the first Irishman to be received into full connexion (1782). Thereafter his circuits were almost entirely English until 1823-24, when he became a supernumerary.

Myles was a self-taught linguist. As a student of theological controversy, he was the first historian proper of Methodism, his *Chronological History* appearing in 1798 (enlarged in 1803 and 1812). He published sermons, tracts, and an account of WILLIAM GRIMSHAW. He was named in Wesley's *Deed of Declaration* and in the deed for Bath. William Myles died at Liverpool on April 17, 1828.

C. H. Crookshank, *Methodism in Ireland.* 1885-88.
Methodist Magazine, 1797, 1828, 1831.   GEORGE LAWTON

Stephen T. Nagbe

NAGBE, STEPHEN TROWEN, SR. (1933-1973), resident bishop of the Monrovia Area of The United Methodist Church, was born on Oct. 23, 1933, in Betu, Sinoe County, Liberia.

He received his early schooling in Ghana, returning to Liberia to complete elementary school in Barclayville. He attended the College of West Africa where he graduated in 1951. His undergraduate work was done at Cuttington College and Divinity School. In 1958 he was ordained elder by Bishop Prince A. Taylor, Jr. That same year he married Melvena Morris and the Nagbes proceeded to the United States for further theological study.

He received the B.D. degree from Gammon Theological School in Atlanta in 1961 and returned to Liberia where he served in the pastorate until the summer of 1964. At that time he returned to the United States where he studied and received the S.T.M. degree from Boston University School of Theology in 1965.

On Dec. 10, 1965, he was elected by the first session of the Liberia Central Conference as the Methodist bishop to be elected and consecrated in Liberia on December 12, Harper, Cape Palmas. He was the first native Liberian ever elected as bishop of The Methodist Church.

He died Feb. 2, 1973, in Liberia, after a six-month illness.

N. B. H.

NAGORI, "TUAN" (Musa Manurung) (?-1927), Malaysian Christian leader, was born near the close of the nineteenth century. As a village chief, one of seven rajas, he lived in the heart of the jungles of Asahan, Sumatra, Indonesia. The beginning and the establishment of the Christian faith here centered definitely around him. He it was who issued the "Macedonian Call" for Christian missionaries to enter this Perdembanan jungle area where no one could even read or write. His first encounter with Batak Christian evangelists in 1907 was characterized by disdain. He was haughty and conceited, being the son of the Raja of all that region. He turned away from animism and took up with a hybrid religion called "Permalim." He even added the use of opium to his other vices. He later on embraced Islam. However, in spite of himself, he had been impressed by the humility and patience of the Batak evangelists who had visited him.

Later on he made the long journey on foot to the shores of Lake Toba to visit the old "Grandfather" Lutheran missionary, Nommenson. He tried to persuade him to send a teacher to his people, but there was none to spare. In 1912 he learned about the American Methodist Mission in Malaysia through a relative of Lamsana L. Tobing, an ordained Methodist minister from the West Coast of Sumatra then serving on the island of Java. Lamsana on furlough visited the village. Eight years later, under the superintendency of Leonard Oechsli, Tobing was appointed in 1921 to Asahan. It was not until July 17, 1921, that the baptismal service of Tuan Nagori and family was arranged, even though Tuan Nagori had himself baptized his own mother before she died, there being no other professing Christian there to do so.

During the years that followed, even to the time of his death on Dec. 13, 1927, Tuan Nagori continued his personal witnessing. As the first resident Methodist missionary in Asahan from America, this writer walked hundreds of miles with Tuan Nagori visiting people and villages in the Asahan jungles. Always he was found to be like the Apostle Paul, speaking a word for his Lord wherever opportunity afforded. A son, Djaleb; a daughter, Soulima; and a nephew, Philemon Sirait, are missionaries in Sarawak; and a grandson, Hasaoetan, is preaching in Sumatra.

Minutes of North Sumatra Mission, 1923-24.
Stephanus L. Tobing, *Toean Nagori Moesa Manoeroeng.* N.d.
Newton T. Gottschall

NALL, TORNEY OTTO, JR., (1900-   ), American editor and bishop, was born in Terre Haute, Ind., on May 23, 1900, the son of Torney Otto and Alta Mae (Stokes) Nall. While still a boy he moved with his family to St. Paul, Minn. He attended Hamline University, receiving the A.B. degree in 1921, did graduate work at the University of Minnesota in 1921-22, and studied journalism at Northwestern University, 1923-24. From Garrett, he received the B.D. in 1925, and received the D.D. degree from Garrett and Hamline in 1936 and 1939 respectively. ADRIAN COLLEGE awarded him the Litt.D. in 1943, as did Union College, 1949, and AMERICAN UNIVERSITY, 1950, and ILLINOIS WESLEYAN UNIVERSITY honored him with the LL.D. in 1951.

He was united in marriage to Frances Marie Mahaffie on Feb. 2, 1929, who has worked closely and efficiently with him in both his editorial and episcopal assignments.

During the first World War, Otto Nall served with the United States Army. His editorial career began with *The Epworth Herald* in 1922, and he wrote also for *The Classmate* and youth publications of several denominations. He became managing editor of *The Christian Advocate* in 1940. Methodist unification had then brought about the merger of seven regional *Advocates* into one official weekly, with ROY L. SMITH elected editor. Otto Nall, on the retirement of Roy Smith, became acting editor. He was elected by the Board of Publication to the editorship of *The New Christian Advocate* in 1946 when this publication became specifically a "trade paper" for ministers. He has continued as one of the columnists for *Together,* writing answers on "Your Faith and Your Church." He served as president of the Methodist Press Association from 1944-48, and as president of the Interdenominational Associated Church Press from 1945 to 1947.

T. O. Nall was ordained in the ministry of the M. E. Church in the MINNESOTA CONFERENCE, 1924. He was elected a bishop at the North Central JURISDICTIONAL CONFERENCE, Grand Rapids, Mich., in July 1960, and was assigned to the Minnesota Area where he served until 1968, when he was continued as an active bishop and assigned to the HONG KONG-TAIWAN Area.

Bishop Nall was chairman of the ASSOCIATION OF METHODIST HISTORICAL SOCIETIES (1964-68), which sponsored the *Encyclopedia of World Methodism.* In 1958 he made a trip into RUSSIA, studying the status of religion there. In 1962-63, he made a three-month study trip to INDIA, NEPAL, and PAKISTAN for the COUNCIL OF BISHOPS. He had a civilian assignment in Africa in 1966. He was a member of the ECUMENICAL METHODIST CONFERENCE, OXFORD, England, 1951; that at LAKE JUNALUSKA, N. C., in 1956; and in OSLO, Norway, 1961. He is a trustee of Hamline University and of Evanston Institute Ecumenical Studies.

Bishop Nall is the author of several books, including *Youth's Work in the New World,* 1936; *New Occupation for Youth,* 1938; *Move On, Youth,* 1940; *Jobs for Today's Youth,* 1941; *Young Christians at Work,* 1949; *Making Good As Young Couples,* 1953; *The Bible When You Need It Most,* 1957—a paperback in the popular Reflection Series. He was editor of *Vital Religion,* 1938; and of *These Prophetic Voices,* 1941. His present residence is in Clearwater, Fla.

Who's Who in America, Vol. 34.
Who's Who in The Methodist Church, 1966.   N. B. H.

NANCE, WALTER B. (1868-1964), American missionary to CHINA, was born at Cornersville, Marshall Co., Tenn., April 16, 1868, the son of James Washington and Mary Frances Amis Nance. He received his secondary education at Webb School, Bell Buckle, Tenn. He graduated with honors in arts and theology at VANDERBILT UNIVERSITY and later took graduate work at the University of Chicago. He was admitted to the TENNESSEE CONFERENCE in 1895

W. B. NANCE

and was sent as a missionary to China in 1896. In 1898 he was joined by Florence Rush Heiser, a Vanderbilt graduate whom he married in Kobe, JAPAN.

He soon became involved in the organization of Soochow University, which was started in 1901. His early years in China were spent in the mastery of the Chinese language and classics, which led to his being recognized as pre-eminent among American students of the Chinese language. He was professor of ethics and philosophy in the University which he helped to found and was its president, 1922-27, when he resigned in favor of a Chinese president.

He was interned by the Japanese during World War II, repatriated in 1943 and later retired by the Board of MISSIONS.

At the insistent demand of the university alumni, he was sent back to China in 1946 to rehabilitate the university devastated in the war, a task which was interrupted by the Communists who took over in 1949. From 1949 until his death at the age of ninety-six, he lived with his son in Oak Ridge, Tenn.

He was the author of *Soochow University,* published by United Board for Christian Colleges in China, 1956. In the 1920's he established a language school where newly arrived missionaries of all denominations were taught the dialect of East China. Hundreds learned the language through the phonetic system he pioneered.

His greatest contribution to the missionary enterprise was his conviction that if China was to be won for Christ, it would have to be through higher education with the melding of the best of classical oriental thought into modern Christian theology.

DANA W. NANCE

NANEZ, ALFREDO (1902-   ), American clergyman and educator, was born Feb. 28, 1902 in Monclova, Coahuila, MEXICO. He received the A.B. degree from SOUTHWESTERN UNIVERSITY, Georgetown, Texas (1930); B.D. degree from SOUTHERN METHODIST UNIVERSITY (1932); and was given a D.D. by Southwestern University (1950). He served as pastor, district superintendent (eleven years), and executive secretary of the RIO GRANDE CONFERENCE Board of Education (twenty years) before assuming his present position as president of LYDIA PATTERSON INSTITUTE, EL PASO, Texas, in 1966. He has edited a Spanish edition of *The Methodist Hymnal* and of the Methodist Ritual. He has served as a member of churchwide boards, including BOARD OF MISSIONS, 1934-38, and METHODIST COMMITTEE ON OVERSEAS RELIEF, 1956-68. He has been a delegate to general and jurisdictional conferences, a member of the Texas Methodist Foundation since 1960, and of the Board of Trustees of Southern Methodist University, 1960-68. He is married to the former Clotilde Falcon, and they have three children.

WALTER N. VERNON

NANTUCKET ISLAND, MASSACHUSETTS, U.S.A., has its antecedents in an eighteen-day preaching mission of JESSE LEE in April 1797. The following year Joseph Snelling, stationed in MARTHA'S VINEYARD, visited Nantucket and conducted open-air meetings on Mill Hill. On July 25, 1799, the first Methodist Society was organized by WILLIAM BEAUCHAMP. When the congregation's original building, completed on Fair Street in 1800, became inadequate, the present structure, with a seating capacity of 1,000, was erected in 1823.

With gable roof and six Ionic pillars under the portico added in 1840, the imposing edifice suggests the sturdy character of the nineteenth-century seafaring people who built it. The ceiling, supported by 12 x 12 timbers sixty feet long, the paneled balconies, and the historic Appelton pipe organ create within the structure a distinctive, early American atmosphere.

Two pastors of the Nantucket congregation, JOSHUA SOULE (1803) and ELIJAH HEDDING (1812), later became bishops. Two sessions (1820 and 1837) of the NEW ENGLAND CONFERENCE, and one session (1842) of the Providence Conference (later called the NEW ENGLAND SOUTHERN CONFERENCE) were held here. An ordination service was held in this church on Sept. 18, 1966, by Bishop JAMES K. MATHEWS—the first such service on Nantucket Island for more than a hundred years.

Bulletin 1966, Centre Street Methodist Church, Nantucket.
R. C. Miller, *New England Southern Conference.* 1898.
Minutes of the New England Southern Conference, 1966.

ERNEST R. CASE

NAPERVILLE, ILLINOIS, U.S.A., **Community Church** (First EUB Church) in 1962 celebrated 125 years of continuous existence. This began in 1837 but not until 1841 were the sturdy German pioneers at Naperville able to build a small church home for themselves. In 1858-59 they erected a substantial building on the corner of Franklin and Center Streets where the present church now stands.

There has always been a warm relationship between this church and NORTH CENTRAL COLLEGE even before the union in 1910 of the College Chapel Church with this "Zion Church," as it was called for many years. The quality of the church's music became greatly enriched when a gifted music professor took over the direction of the church choir, composed almost entirely of college students. He also played the new pipe organ, the organ being an innovation in the church in 1912. The sanctuary soon began to be used as a concert hall by the college.

To this day the same collaboration continues and marks Community Church as outstanding in the field of music.

The personnel of the membership was also affected by the close association of these two organizations and that of the EVANGELICAL THEOLOGICAL SEMINARY. There have always been many more students, professors, college and seminary presidents—and even more bishops—than are to be found in the usual congregation. Naturally the church has been a leader in the cultural life of the community.

Through the years of the depression and the second World War, and subsequent years, this church participated in countless projects of mercy. Carloads of food and clothing were packed and shipped under the personal supervision of the pastor and church leaders. From 1945-1948 the church raised a total of $11,628 for relief work overseas. PAUL WASHBURN, elected a bishop of The United Methodist Church at the Uniting Conference in 1968, was pastor of Naperville 1952-1964. The church's emphasis upon social concern and action has been increasingly sustained through the years.

Four sessions of the GENERAL CONFERENCE have been held in Naperville: 1859, 1871, 1927 and 1942. At each time some very important church policy was uppermost on the agenda. In 1942 it was the proposal for the union of The EVANGELICAL CHURCH and the UNITED BRETHREN CHURCH. The church today manifests a consciousness of good heritage and hard labor, has a continually increasing enrollment of over 1,100, and expresses a dynamic dedication to social action and to faith and beauty in its worship services.

ELIZABETH WILEY

NASCIMENTO, NATANAEL INOCENCIO Do (1910-   ), a bishop of the Methodist Church in BRAZIL, was born on July 12, 1910, in Cordeiro, Minas Gerais, Brazil. He received his secondary education at the INSTITUTO GRANBERY (Juiz de Fora, Minas Gerais), the University of São Paulo, and the theological seminary then at Granbery.

He was ordained DEACON in 1938 and ELDER in 1940. He has served as pastor; as district superintendent for thirteen years; as professor for twelve years at the theological seminary in Rudge Ramos, SÃO PAULO, and as its Reitor (principal) for seven years. From 1950 to 1960, he was president of the General Board of Missions of the Methodist Church of Brazil. He was among the first to draw up a plan for ministers' pensions.

He married Eunice Patricio, and they had four daughters. He was elected bishop in July 1965, and his region comprised the states of Rio de Janeiro and Guanabara (the former Federal District). He retired at the General Conference in July 1970.

EULA K. LONG

NASH, GEORGE (1905-   ), Australian minister, and president of QUEENSLAND CONFERENCE, 1964. He has been superintendent of the Central Missions, BRISBANE, since 1952, during which time its activities have been considerably developed. He established a hospital for the chronic ill and inaugurated Methodism's only mission to urban-dwelling Aborigines. He was chairman of the Queensland Council of Churches, chairman of the Presbyterian and Methodist Schools Association, Chairman of the Billy Graham Crusade, and has been active in the leadership of many conference committees. He is widely known for his work in both church and community life. He served for five years as chaplain in the Royal Australian Air Force in the second World War in New Guinea, Britain, and the United States.

NASH, RICHARD "BEAU" (1674-?), was born at Carmarthen on Oct. 18, 1674, the son of a glass manufacturer. Having been sent down from Jesus College, OXFORD, for riotous behavior, he became a professional gambler and Master of Ceremonies at the fashionable health resort of Bath during the first half of the eighteenth century. He dressed splendidly, and drove around Bath in semi-royal state in a post-chaise drawn by six grey horses, honored with outriders, footmen, and French horns.

There was a celebrated confrontation between Nash and JOHN WESLEY when the latter preached at Bath on June 5, 1739. Wesley's *Journal* notes: "There was great expectation at Bath of what a noted man was to do to me there; and I was much entreated not to preach, because no one knew what might happen. By this I report I also gained a much larger audience, among whom were many of the rich and the great. I told them plainly the Scripture had concluded them all under sin—high and low, rich and poor, one with another. Many of them seemed to be a little surprised, and were sinking apace into seriousness, when their champion appeared, and, coming close to me, asked by what authority I did these things, I replied, 'By the authority of Jesus Christ, conveyed to me by the (now) Archbishop of Canterbury, when he laid hands upon me, and said, "Take thou authority to preach the gospel." ' He said, 'This is contrary to Act of Parliament: this is a conventicle.' I answered, 'Sir, the conventicles mentioned in that Act (as the preamble shows) are seditious meetings; but this is not such; here is no shadow of sedition; therefore it is not contrary to that Act.' He replied, 'I say it is; and, beside, your preaching frightens people out of their wits.' 'Sir, did you ever hear me preach?' 'No.' 'How, then, can you judge of what you never heard?' 'Sir, by common report.' 'Common report is not enough. Give me leave, sir, to ask, Is not your name Nash?' 'My name is Nash.' 'Sir, I dare not judge of you by common report: I think it not enough to judge by.' Here he paused a while, and, having recovered himself, said, 'I desire to know what this people comes here for': on which one replied, 'Sir, leave him to me; let an old woman answer him. You, Mr. Nash, take care of your body; we take care of our souls: and for the food of our souls we come here.' He replied not a word, but walked away." (*Journal*, Vol. 2, pp. 211-213).

Though worsted in this verbal duel, Nash retained his dignity, and there is little doubt that his concern for law and order was genuine, for his code of Rules—applied as impartially as Wesley's—had long served to curb the boisterous society of Bath. "He enforced his rules with equal impartiality on the duchess or the farmer's wife and he made Bath an agreeable city to live in. He introduced music, turned dances into balls, abolished swords, riding boots and aprons, cleaned up the pump room, made special privileges for invalids, secured decency and good order, yet . . . preserved considerable freedom. Gambling and intrigue still flourished but discreetly and subject to convention." (J. H. Plumb, *Men and Places*, p. 120). G. M. Trevelyan's encomium might seem to place Nash in the same bracket as Wesley—"Nash

did perhaps as much as any other person even in the Eighteenth Century to civilize the neglected manners of mankind" (*English Social History*, p. 316)—and no doubt rebellious bucks trembled at Nash's appearing as much as recalcitrant society stewards did at Wesley's.

JOHN NEWTON

NASHVILLE, TENNESSEE, U.S.A., sometimes called "The Capital of Southern Methodism," had several significant names. From an unrecorded date, it was known as "Salt Lick," near present-day Sulphur Dell ball park. Monsieur Charleville, a French trader and explorer from NEW ORLEANS in 1714, seems to have been the first white man to settle at Salt Lick. Therefore, Salt Lick was changed to "French Lick" in honor of the explorer. In 1769, Uriah Stone, Gasper Mansker, and Isaac Bledsoe, who were explorers and hunters from VIRGINIA, made French Lick their base of operation in Middle TENNESSEE. Jan. 1, 1780, James Robertson, seven whites and one Negro from Watauga settlement, arrived at French Lick. The other part of the settlers came by boats down the Tennessee, up the Ohio and up the Cumberland Rivers, arriving at French Lick, April 24, 1780. After the arrival of the Robertson and Donelson settlers, the name French Lick was changed to the "Bluffs." With the increase of population, the name Bluffs was changed to the "Cumberland Settlement," which name was kept until the Revolutionary War.

General Nash was killed in the Revolutionary War. Soon after the close of the war, the Cumberland Settlement was changed to Nashborough, in honor of General Nash. "Borough" being an English word and the Revolutionary War making British nomenclature unpopular, the Legislature of NORTH CAROLINA in 1784 changed the name Nashborough to Nashville. It is a city of many universities, colleges, private and professional schools, and is affectionately called the "Athens of the South."

The KENTUCKY Circuit (in the newly organized M.E. Church) was organized in 1786. After one year, 1787, the circuit was divided into the Kentucky and Cumberland Circuits. BENJAMIN OGDEN was appointed by Bishop ASBURY to the newly organized circuit. It included Middle and West Tennessee, Logan, Warren and Simpson Counties in southern Kentucky. The new pastor made Nashville his headquarters.

It is not known how many Methodist churches Benjamin Ogden organized in his new circuit in 1787. Two churches are in operation today that are known to have been organized by him that year—**McKendree** on Church Street in Nashville, and Walkers Chapel on Walkers Creek four miles northwest of present day Goodlettsville, Tenn. The building that finally became McKendree in 1839, was erected on the public square in Nashville in 1790 or 1791. Bishop Asbury described this building upon his first visit to Nashville, Oct. 20, 1800, in company with Bishop WHATCOAT and the presiding elder, WILLIAM McKENDREE, as follows: "Not less than a thousand people were in and out of the stone church, which if floored, ceiled and glazed, would be a grand house."

The GENERAL CONFERENCE of the M.E. Church, South, in 1854, recognized the strategic location of Nashville and located the first METHODIST PUBLISHING HOUSE of that Church in this rapidly growing city. The original location was on the northeast corner of the public square where it remained until 1906. The second Publishing

House was erected at 810 Broadway in 1906. The third and present Publishing House was erected at 201 Eighth Avenue, South. First an enlarged printing plant had been placed there in 1924; a present office building was erected in 1957; and the present printing plant building greatly enlarged to its present size in 1961.

With the coming of unification in 1939, the BOARD OF EDUCATION, the Commission (now BOARD) OF EVANGELISM of The Methodist Church (and of course the Publishing House) were placed in or remained in Nashville. Subsequently, enlarged headquarters buildings were erected by the Board of Education and the Board of Evangelism. The TELEVISION, RADIO and FILM COMMISSION has also been established there. The chapel of *The Upper Room*, housed in the Board of Evangelism's building, is a show-place of the city. VANDERBILT UNIVERSITY, SCARRITT COLLEGE, and MEHARRY MEDICAL COLLEGE are among the educational institutions located in Nashville. The city has been the seat of an episcopal area and officially designated as such from 1940 to the present.

Nashville is not only a Methodist headquarters but the Southern Baptist Convention has its printing plant and publishing house there and many interests of other denominations are centered there.

The two Nashville districts (UMC) in 1970 reported 52,080 members and list 104 churches—all of which are in the city or very close by. The largest of these is Belmont, 2,621; West End, 2,512; McKendree, 2,201; with Calvary reporting 1,835, Belle Meade, 1,904; and Andrew Price Memorial, 1,991.

BELMONT CHURCH, NASHVILLE, TENNESSEE

Belmont Church, on Twenty-first Avenue, South, at Acklen Avenue, is on the southern edge of the University Center area involving George Peabody College, Scarritt College for Christian Workers, and Vanderbilt University and draws on the faculty and students of these schools for some of its leadership. Founded July 10, 1910, with thirty-four members, the church now has 2,621; and its facilities have expanded from a small frame structure to four commodious units extending a full block on Acklen Avenue. The sanctuary, completed in 1929 and seating approximately 1,200, is one of the largest and most impressive in the city. The other units, added 1951-55, contain a chapel seating 175, with reception facilities, offices, a library, classrooms, and a youth center which includes a gymnasium.

With the growth of Nashville many Belmont members now live in suburban areas around the southern rim of the city and drive many miles to participate in the full and varied program of a larger church. Special emphasis

is given to missions, Christian education, and music. Belmont partially supports two missionary couples who went from its own membership into overseas service, and also the pastor of a mission church in the city; and individuals and groups give time as well as money to other local mission causes. Leadership from the faculties of the nearby colleges and from the general agencies of the church has made possible training for almost all of the teachers of children and youth in the church school, and for the director and teachers of the weekday kindergarten. The adult classes also enjoy professional participation. Regular programs for retired adults and for handicapped persons are among the weekday activities.

Youth and adult choirs provide music in the two regular Sunday morning worship services. Graded choirs for younger ages, beginning with the kindergarten, meet weekly and present several programs each year. Youth and adult handbell ringers play with the choirs on festival occasions, as do guest instrumental soloists. The forty-six-rank organ, installed in 1961, is one of the largest in the city and makes possible bringing guest organists of national reputation for concerts two or more times a year.

Pastors of Belmont have included BACHMAN G. HODGE (1935-39), later a bishop, John L. Ferguson (1939-50), John W. Rustin (1950-59), Faris F. Moore (1959-69), and C. Glenn Mingledorff (1969-   ).

McKendree Church, the historic downtown church and long-time citadel of Nashville Methodism, is a civic landmark of Nashville. It was begun as early as 1787 when a group of Nashville's pioneers banded together in the first Methodist society in the then new settlement. They erected a small church on what is now known as "the Public Square."

In 1812 the society moved to the site now occupied by the Hume Fogg High School, and erected a building which for some time served as a meeting place of the TENNESSEE CONFERENCE and also of the Tennessee Legislature.

The congregation in time decided that this church building was too far from the center of town, so in 1818 a new structure was erected on Spring Street where the Noel Hotel Garage now stands. Nashville's first church-related Sunday school was started at the Spring Street Church.

Later there came a need for more space and this necessitated the purchase of the present location, on Church Street, Nashville. A stately sanctuary was raised there in 1833 and was dedicated by—and named for—Bishop William McKendree in 1834. New buildings were erected on this property in 1879 and 1882, but both were destroyed by fire. The present McKendree Church was completed in 1910, and to it has been added through the years an educational plant. The church has recently constructed new educational facilities and a sub-building under its own famous lawn in the heart of downtown Nashville in order to get more space for its present day requirements.

Among the vicissitudes of life in McKendree have been the two fires and the seizure of the McKendree edifice by federal troops during the Civil War. As to the fires, of course the complete destruction of the buildings constituted crises in the lives of the congregations. The turmoil incident to the Civil War was a challenge to faith.

A list of pastors who have served this church reads like a Who's Who of Southern Methodism in the United States. Among them have been JACOB YOUNG, 1806-07;

ROBERT PAINE, 1824-25; A. L. P. GREEN, 1832-33; FOUNTAIN E. PITTS, 1833-34; J. B. McFERRIN, 1835-36; J. W. Hanner, 1839-40; D. C. KELLEY, 1869-72; R. K. HARGROVE, 1872-74; WALTER R. LAMBUTH (assistant pastor), 1876; J. D. BARBEE, 1882-86; WARREN A. CANDLER, 1886-87; S. A. STEEL, 1889-92; JOHN MATHEWS, 1897-1901; E. B. CHAPPELL, 1901-06; COLLINS DENNY (acting pastor), 1906; J. S. FRENCH, 1910-14; O. E. GODDARD (associate pastor), 1919-22; H. B. Trimble, 1922-28.

Five of the above were elected bishops of the M.E. Church, South, namely, Robert Paine, R. K. Hargrove, Warren A. Candler, Collins Denny and Walter Lambuth.

McKendree is as much a part of Nashville as the famous Capitol, or the Cumberland River itself, and is so recognized by the people of Tennessee. The church presently (1970) numbers 2,201 members and employs three pastors.

West End Church is on West End Avenue facing the campus of Vanderbilt University, beyond which are Scarritt College for Christian Workers and George Peabody College for Teachers. The church fellowship is enriched by the participation of faculty members and students from all three schools in its life and worship. For a time before completion of the present sanctuary—a time which because of the depression stretched to over ten years (1929-40)—the congregation worshipped in Neely Auditorium on the Vanderbilt campus. The church has 2,512 members, with property occupying a city block and valued at well over $2,000,000.

In 1868 members of McKendree Church, "the mother church of Nashville Methodism," began a mission Sunday school on Church Street at Fifteenth Avenue, in a building so dilapidated that the coming of cold weather brought the project to a stop. The next year it was reactivated and organized as a mission church, called the West Nashville Mission and later West End Mission. The church became self-supporting in 1873 and worked toward a building, which was erected on Broadway at Sixteenth Avenue and opened for worship Feb. 9, 1875. Fifteen years later the congregation occupied a large new brick building on the same site, which was used until the move into the first section of the present educational building on Oct. 27, 1929. The present sanctuary was opened for worship March 10, 1940. On Sept. 15, 1968, occurred the formal opening of a five-story addition containing educational, social, and recreational facilities, including a gymnasium, which make possible for the church a full program of worship, education, fellowship, and service.

West End has many historic associations. Tablets and stained-glass windows reveal its close relation with the leaders of Methodism stationed in Nashville for a century. The church has yielded two successive pastors to the episcopacy: COSTEN J. HARRELL (1944) and JAMES W. HENLEY (1960).

Cullen T. Carter, ed., *History of Methodist Churches and Institutions in Middle Tennessee, 1787-1956.* Tennessee Conference Historical Society, 1956.
General Minutes.

CULLEN T. CARTER
FARIS F. MOORE
GORDON B. DUNCAN
C. A. BOWEN

NAST, WILHELM (1807-1889), founder of German Methodism, was born in STUTTGART, GERMANY on June 15, 1807. His father and mother died in his early youth but he

WILLIAM NAST

was reared in a good family atmosphere by an older sister. In his later youth he enrolled in Blauberen Seminary to prepare for the Lutheran ministry. His roommate chanced to be the well known radical materialist, David Frederick Straus, whose effect upon him was to produce mental doubts and weakened convictions. However William Nast's serious nature and scholarly disposition served to hold him steady as he matured.

In 1828, at the age of twenty-one, while in this restless state of mind, he came to America, and there continued to seek a well founded faith. He found for a time employment as private instructor in an English family near Harrisburg, Pa. Next he served as librarian and professor of German at West Point, the United States Military Academy. He then went to the Lutheran College at Gettysburg, Pa. Here Bishop McIlvaine proved a friend to him by securing for him a professorship of Greek and Hebrew in Kenyon College, Gambier, Ohio.

Nast formed a friendship with a shoemaker named John Smith whose faith impressed him, and on the occasion of the coming of the Methodist presiding elder, ADAM POE—afterward Book Agent at CINCINNATI—Nast went at Smith's invitation to meet the visitor. Poe was favorably impressed with young Nast and encouraged him in his pursuit for spiritual certainty. It is thereafter recorded that on Jan. 11, 1835, at Danville, Ohio, he came into a satisfying experience, one characteristic of the evangelistic and missionary happenings then in German Methodism.

On Aug. 18, 1835, at Springfield, Poe proposed to the OHIO CONFERENCE that William Nast be received on trial. His appointment was then announced, "Missionary among the German immigrants in and near Cincinnati." Nast at once began his work, preaching his first sermon in Wesley Chapel to a congregation of twenty-four Germans and twelve English hearers. He made extensive contacts with German-speaking groups, but at the next session of the Conference results seemed meager since only three persons had been converted. However one of these was John Zwahlen, later to be founder of Central (German) congregation in Wheeling, W. Va. The one and only German church in the WEST VIRGINIA CONFERENCE has been in the PITTSBURGH, OHIO, and West Virginia Conferences.

On Aug. 1, 1836, he married Margaret McDowell and they had five children. One daughter, Fanny Nast Gamble, established a "Nast Theological Professorship" (1899), which expanded, in 1902, into Nast Theological Seminary.

In 1836-1837 Nast served on the Columbus District, consisting of twenty-two appointments. In every direction the German Mission established contacts with German-speaking groups throughout much of the nation. Nast sent John Zwahlen to Wheeling to take subscriptions for the German publication "Christliche Apologete," and to investigate the possibility of organizing a class there. Cincinnati deserves the high honor of having the "Mother Church of German Methodism," but the congregation of the Central Church in Wheeling erected and dedicated there the first German Methodist church building in the world. Nast dedicated it March 22, 1840, the climax of John Zwahlen's leadership over the Christmas season of 1838, Zwahlen then serving as the first of a series of forty-two German pastors. Almost a hundred years later, in 1934, Central Church transferred to the West Virginia Conference.

Nast traveled widely in his evangelistic efforts among immigrant Germans. He spread the work of German Methodism to MISSOURI, KENTUCKY, ILLINOIS, WISCONSIN, and IOWA. He won thousands of converts and organized them into churches.

In 1839 he became editor of Der Christliche Apologete, a position he held for fifty-three years. The GENERAL CONFERENCE, after adopting this as an official organ of the church, elected Nast again and again. In addition to editorial duties, he engaged in translating, writing, distributing tracts, and preaching. He helped establish German Wallace College, Berea, Ohio (see BALDWIN-WALLACE COLLEGE), and became its first president. He made several European journeys and founded a successful Methodist mission in Germany. Wilhelm Nast's important publications include *Das Leben und Wirken des Johannes Wesley und Seiner Haupt-mitarbeiter* (1852) and *Die Aufgabe der Christlichen Kirche im neunzehnten Jahrhundert* (1857). He died May 6, 1889, at Cincinnati, Ohio.

W. C. Barclay, *History of Missions.* 1949-57.
Dictionary of American Biography.
P. F. Douglass, *German Methodism.* 1939.

MARTIN L. GREER
OTTIS RYMER SNODGRASS

NATCHEZ, MISSISSIPPI, U.S.A. The word "Natchez" in early records meant not a city but an area, sometimes called the "Natchez country." Methodism had been in the area a good number of years before any definite Methodist activity had taken place in the city itself. It is assumed that TOBIAS GIBSON, who came from SOUTH CAROLINA in 1799 and landed at Natchez, must have preached in the city, but there is no record of it. LORENZO DOW mentions preaching there a few years later, but reports little interest and spiritual concern.

The first churches in the Natchez area were organized in small towns and rural communities. The earliest and oldest is the church at Washington, organized in 1799 with eight members: William and Mary Foster, Randal and Harriett Gibson, Edna Bullen, Caleb Worley, and a colored man and his wife. The second congregation was organized at Kingston, sixteen miles southeast, in 1800; it was here that Lorenzo Dow sold his watch and bought a lot on which to build a Methodist church, the first Methodist property in the MISSISSIPPI Territory. The Methodists at Kingston have had three church buildings—a small building on the Dow lot, a brick building erected some years later, and the present building constructed in 1855-56 and dedicated on the first Sunday in May 1856. The church at Washington worshipped first in a schoolhouse, then in a union building on College Street, then in the building inside the Jefferson College campus in which the Constitutional Convention of 1817 was held, and since 1828 in the present building, which is the second oldest building in Mississippi and houses the oldest congregation. The oldest building is at Woodville, built in 1824.

No one knows when the first Methodist congregation was organized in the city of Natchez itself. The first church property in Natchez was acquired on March 25, 1807, a lot on Union Street north of Main, for the sum of $150. Since the Board of Trustees named in the deed were mainly nonresidents of Natchez, it seems probable that no organization had as yet taken place. Nor is it known just when a church was erected on this lot. It lasted a dozen years or more, when it was replaced by a new church on a different location and soon after the Civil War by the present Jefferson Street Church, which is at the present time the oldest building in use by Methodists in the major cities of the state.

Methodism in the Natchez area has had a long and honorable history. The first Sunday school in the southwest was established in Natchez by Richard Abbey and Miss Eliza Lowe, and the first organization of women in Mississippi took place in the Washington Methodist Church on July 23, 1823, with Mrs. John C. Burruss as president and Mrs. Caroline Matilda Thayer as corresponding secretary.

ELIZABETH ACADEMY at Washington opened in 1818 and was chartered by the legislature in 1819 to give degrees to women, and is said by many to have been the first chartered institution in the world to give degrees to women.

Other Methodist congregations in the immediate vicinity of Natchez, in addition to Washington and Kingston, have been Pine Ridge, Bethel, Sandy Creek, Selsertown, Locust Grove, and Pine Grove; while in Natchez Wesley Chapel, Pearl Street, Maple Street, Wesley, Grace, and Lovely Lane Churches have served the Methodist people.

Jefferson Street Church. Tobias Gibson came to Natchez as a missionary from South Carolina around 1800 and organized churches in the Natchez area. It is not known when the Methodist congregation in Natchez was formally organized. On March 25, 1807, under the leadership of LEARNER BLACKMAN, the first lot was obtained for the building of a church. It was called Cokesbury Chapel and was in use until 1823, when a new church was built on Union Street. This was sold in 1866 and the present church lot, bought in 1857, was not in use until 1872, when the first service was held in the present building on August 30. A parsonage was secured in 1850 and the church has had a parsonage since that time.

The first Sunday school southwest of PHILADELPHIA was organized in Natchez before 1829, and a missionary organization of the women of the Natchez and Washington churches was in existence before that time. Fourteen sessions of the annual conference have been held in the Natchez church.

Grace Church and Lovely Lane Church share with the original Jefferson Street congregation the responsibility of Methodism in Natchez.

Henry G. Hawkins, *Methodism in Natchez*. Jackson, Miss.: The Hawkins Foundation, 1937.
J. G. Jones, *Mississippi Conference*. 1908.   J. B. CAIN

NATIONAL CHILDREN'S HOME AND ORPHANAGE, Great Britain, was founded by THOMAS BOWMAN STEPHENSON, a Wesleyan Methodist minister, in 1869. Stephenson received two boys in a house he had rented in Church Street, Lambeth, London, and these were forerunners of some 43,000 children who have subsequently come under the care of the home. The home's purpose has from the earliest days been to minister to all categories of children in need; and the home's policy was, and is, to create substitute homes which approximate as nearly as possible a child's own home.

The home, which has some forty branches in England, Wales, Scotland, and the Isle of Man, also has a program of foster care, adoption, and family aid. Its child-care staff includes an Order of Deaconesses, or sisters, who are trained and ordained for their special tasks.

Though the home is a Methodist foundation, it receives children from all Protestant denominations, and many from none. The home furthermore is supported by the general public, to which it makes national appeals of various kinds.

The scope of the service rendered by the home to its three thousand children in care is very wide, including schools for backward, physically handicapped, and delinquent youngsters. For senior boys there is a very well equipped Printing Technical School. The Staff Training College, Stephenson Hall, is in London.

The National Children's Home is one of the most significant and widespread undertakings of the Methodist Church in Great Britain. Its headquarters are at Highbury Park, London, N. 5, and the present principal is the Rev. John Waterhouse, O.B.E.

JOHN WATERHOUSE

NATIONAL COLLEGE, Kansas City, Missouri, began as a deaconess training school in 1899 with special emphasis on biblical studies and social work. In 1946 the liberal arts program leading to a B.A. degree was adopted, and in 1954 it became a coeducational college. Plans were completed in 1964 for it to discontinue its work as a liberal arts college and merge with the SAINT PAUL SCHOOL OF THEOLOGY. This merger made possible a larger emphasis upon graduate work in religious education.

From 1899 until 1939 National was under the control of the WOMAN'S HOME MISSIONARY SOCIETY of the M.E. Church, and after Unification, of the Woman's Division of Christian Service of the Board of Missions. Its last year of academic work was 1963-64. In 1965 Saint Paul School of Theology moved to the campus.

JOHN O. GROSS

NATIONAL COUNCIL OF THE CHURCHES OF CHRIST IN THE U.S.A., with headquarters at 475 Riverside Drive, New York City, is a cooperative agency of thirty Protestant and Orthodox churches who propose "to show forth their unity and mission in specific ways and to bring them into living contact with one another for fellowship, study, and cooperative action." Four American Methodist church bodies are among the thirty "constituents" (or denominations) that comprise the Council: The UNITED METHODIST CHURCH, the AFRICAN METHODIST EPISCOPAL ZION CHURCH, the AFRICAN METHODIST EPISCOPAL CHURCH, and the CHRISTIAN METHODIST EPISCOPAL CHURCH. The cooperative work of the churches through councils in states, cities, and counties (in which Methodism generally has an important share) is represented on the Council's divisions, departments, and committees.

The National Council of Churches grew out of and continues the mission, witness, and service of twelve historical interdenominational bodies which began their united service and study early in the century. The "core" of this united ministry was the FEDERAL COUNCIL OF CHURCHES in the early organization and maintenance of which Methodism was a major factor. Among the Methodists who were presidents of the Federal Council before its merger into the National Council were: Bishop E. R. HENDRIX, FRANK MASON NORTH, S. PARKES CADMAN (a local preacher of British Methodism), Bishop FRANCIS J. McCONNELL, Bishop IVAN LEE HOLT, Bishop G. BROMLEY OXNAM. Two Methodists who have served as presidents of the National Council are Bishop WILLIAM C. MARTIN and ARTHUR S. FLEMING.

The thirty denominations in the National Council have a total membership of 42,000,000 persons. But, says the Council, "whereas the Council does not speak for its member churches, the churches through the Council do speak to one another and to the general public. What is said through the Council is determined altogether by the elected representatives of the churches."

The Council is governed by a General Assembly of 875 people, meeting once in three years, chosen by member communions. The General Assembly elects a General Board of 275 of its members; and this Board, meeting three times a year, is charged with the program and administration of the Council. On behalf of the churches and participating organizations, the Council currently carries on some seventy-five cooperative projects in the United States and overseas. These are the concerns of four divisions. In the Division of Christian Life and Work are departments promoting parish and community life, evangelism, stewardship, concern for race relations, religious liberty, economics, international affairs, and ministries to areas of special need—American Indians, migrant farm workers, etc. The Division of Christian Education is concerned with educational institutions and ministries, the pastoral ministry, vocation, and the development of the lay ministry. The Division of Overseas Ministries helps in the cooperation of all mission agencies of the churches in lands outside the United States—continuing the earlier services of the Foreign Missions Conference of North America—and has as its special charge the work of Church World Service in concern for relief, rehabilitation and reconstruction in war-torn and disaster areas, and in social and economic development. It also has a number of specialized ministries—literacy, literature, radio, medical, union churches, rural missions, military service personnel, etc.—in some forty countries. The Division of Christian Unity works for "ecumenical response" in the U.S.A. by study, organization of local councils of churches, promotion of dialogue, and the services of United Church Men, United Church Women, and Youth Ministry.

The United Methodist Church contributes to the support of the National Council and to the activities of its divisions and agencies largely through an appropriation made by the GENERAL CONFERENCE.

W. W. REID

NAUVOO, ILLINOIS, U.S.A. Methodism was established in Nauvoo shortly after the departure of the Mormons, following the assassination of their leader, Joseph Smith, and his brother Hyrum in the jail at Carthage on June 27, 1844. In October 1846, G. G. Worthington was transferred from the Knoxville circuit in ROCK RIVER CONFERENCE to begin work in Nauvoo. A few days after his arrival on October 20 he preached the first Methodist sermon in Nauvoo in the recently abandoned Mormon Temple.

"The desolate appearance of the 'City of the Saints'," he wrote in his report to the Missionary Society of the M.E. Church, 1847, "and the country around for five miles, at least, beggars all description, and can never be erased from my mind. The 'troubles' war, and strife, were just over, and a remnant of the 'regulators" left by the Anti-Mormon party still lingered in the great Mormon Temple, with the mouths of three great guns in the portico of the Temple, looking down upon those remaining in the deserted city."

With the arrival of troops under Governor Ford order was restored in the city, and Worthington began rounding up a few Methodist families. After the first Sunday services were held in the Music Hall nearby the Temple. This hall was purchased from the Mormons at a great loss to the latter. A church building was erected in 1853, which served until merger with the German Methodist congregation in 1904.

German Methodist work dates also from 1846, when Jacob Haas was appointed minister. A building was provided in 1855, and the charge was related later to the ST. LOUIS GERMAN CONFERENCE.

When the two Methodist congregations merged in 1904, the "English" building was sold and the German building was transferred to the CENTRAL ILLINOIS CONFERENCE. In 1913 this building was razed, and the present frame structure was erected. A membership of 148 was reported in 1970.

FREDERICK A. NORWOOD
HENRY J. NYLIN

NAVAJO METHODIST MISSION, Farmington, NEW MEXICO, was founded in 1891 by two missionaries—Mrs. Eldridge and Miss Raymond—who gave up positions in Government Schools in Lawrence, Kansas, to teach the gospel to the Indians.

The first mission was built at Jewett, about twenty miles west of Farmington, but in 1911 this mission was completely destroyed by flood.

In 1912 the present mission was established on thirty acres of land two miles from Farmington. More buildings have been added through the years, and the present value is estimated at $1,000,000 with an enrollment of thirty day students and 205 boarding students. This mission has classes from the first through the twelfth grades. There are church services, a Sunday school, a Methodist Youth Fellowship, and regular medical care for the Indians.

MRS. D. W. THORNBURG

NAWAB, PHILIP ANDREW, was an early convert from Islam in LUCKNOW. He was descended from the royal family of Oudh. The aura of royalty never forsook him. He was soundly converted, and spoke with an eloquence and winsomeness that commanded attention whether in church worship services, the drawing room of the elite, or the crowded bazaars. He began his ministry in the 1880's and continued it into the early years of the twentieth century.

J. WASKOM PICKETT

NAYLOR, GEORGE DENT (1880-1959), American missionary to CUBA, was born Nov. 15, 1880 in MARYLAND, where he joined the BALTIMORE CONFERENCE. Graduating from VANDERBILT UNIVERSITY, where he belonged to a group of STUDENT VOLUNTEERS, he was accepted as a missionary to Cuba in 1915. His first appointment was to the Isle of Pines, Havana Province. On occasional visits to HAVANA he met and married the talented Effie Wright Chastain, who had been born in MEXICO, the daughter of a Baptist missionary.

Their children were George Dent, Jr., Mary Jean, Kathleen Wright, William Chastain, Marguerite, and Annie Lee. Knowing Spanish from childhood, Mrs. Naylor became a prodigious writer and translator in Spanish. Her pen produced many translations, original plays, and for many years the children's page in church publications.

At every pastoral charge they were particularly loved, and their home and congregations knew no boundary of color. Also several homeless young people found a haven in their home.

After leaving the field in 1932, George Naylor served various appointments in the Baltimore Conference until his retirement in 1953. But after retirement, and with his wife in poor health, they returned to Cuba serving as substitute pastor in Guantanamo and Holguin until the political situation made it impractical to remain. They both died within a few weeks of each other in 1959.

GARFIELD EVANS

NAZREY, WILLIS (1808-1875), American bishop of the A.M.E. CHURCH, was born in the Isle of Wight, VIRGINIA, on March 5, 1808. His education was self-acquired. He was converted and licensed in 1837 and admitted into the New York Annual Conference in 1840. He was ordained DEACON in 1841 and ELDER in 1843. He held pastorates in Lewiston County, Pa.; PHILADELPHIA, Pa.; and NEW JERSEY. He was elected bishop in 1852. He withdrew from the A.M.E. Church to become first bishop of the British Methodist Episcopal Church (the A.M.E. churches in Canada and the B.W.I., etc.), which formed a separate denomination until a reunion in 1884. Nazrey died in 1875.

R. R. Wright, *The Bishops.* 1963. GRANT S. SHOCKLEY

NEBLETT, STERLING AUGUSTUS (1873-1969), American missionary to CUBA, was born in Union City, Tenn., on Sept. 11, 1873. In 1894 he became the first graduate of the American Temperance University, Harriman, Tenn. While working as an accountant for the Southern Express Company he had an experience of conversion and one year later (1900), he felt called for foreign missionary service. He arrived in Cuba in 1902 and became prin-

S. A. NEBLETT

cipal of a Methodist school in Cienfuegos, working with two teachers and fifty students.

In 1903 he was appointed by Bishop W. A. CANDLER to Matanzas, the first of an impressive list of pastoral charges which he filled. In 1905 he helped organize and became chairman of "The Protestant Conference," the first interdenominational body in Cuba. He was also one of the main inspiring forces behind the founding of the periodical *El Evangelista Cubano* and of the Union Theological Seminary in Cuba.

He was married to Lillian Richards, June 22, 1898, and their children were William, John and Lucy. After the death of his wife he married Myrtle Hargon, who was teaching in Cuba, and their children were Robert, Mary Frances and Samuel.

In the late 1920's his health began to fail and after doctors advised a change of climate, the BOARD OF MISSIONS sent him to conduct training schools for leaders in Europe. Later, his health having improved, he returned to Cuba.

For a period of fifty years he was a part of almost every forward movement of the church, both in his own denomination and in interdenominational activities. In the Council of Evangelical Churches he was one of the first vice-presidents. Every Methodist book of *Discipline* for many years was Neblett's translation into Spanish. He also translated into Spanish hymn books and other related material for the church schools. Over a long period he directed an evangelical book depository in Havana. As the organizer of the Conference Board of Christian Education he was called on to visit other countries and to consult with the parent boards in the States. As a result of his leadership Cuba led all the Latin American countries in Christian education.

After retiring he remained in Cuba for several years

continuing to teach in leadership schools. When he finally left Cuba he continued to translate Christian literature into Spanish while living in Nashville, Tenn. He then moved to Southport, Fla., where he died Nov. 9, 1969.

S. A. Neblett, *Methodism in Cuba.* 1966.

JUSTO L. GONZALEZ
GARFIELD EVANS

NEBRASKA is located in the north central part of the United States. Its name comes from the Indian words "Ni," meaning water, and "Bthaska," meaning flat. It is bounded on the east by the Missouri River, on the west by the states of WYOMING and COLORADO, on the north by SOUTH DAKOTA and on the south by KANSAS. With 76,522 square miles, Nebraska had a population of 1,468,-101 in 1970. It was admitted to the Union, March 1, 1867. The Platte River crosses the state from west to east. A part of the Louisiana Purchase, Nebraska was also a part of the Kansas-Nebraska Territory until 1861 when Kansas entered the Union. Following the Civil War, immigrants pushed into Nebraska seeking land in accordance with the Homestead Act of 1862. The population of the state grew rapidly after the coming of the Union Pacific Railway in 1869. Cattle, hogs, and grain are among chief products of the state. Industries include the manufacture of farm implements, parts for motors, airplanes, and telephone and electronic equipment. Also, Nebraska has a large cement industry made possible by large limestone deposits. The Strategic Air Command Base south of OMAHA controls American military defense operations all over the world.

The first Methodist sermon in Nebraska was preached by Harrison Presson in what is now Omaha on April 12, 1850 to members of his wagon train and some local Indians. In 1854 a Kansas and Nebraska Mission District was organized and attached to the MISSOURI CONFERENCE; WILLIAM H. GOODE who came from Richmond, Ind., served as presiding elder. Goode appointed William D. Gage to Nebraska City where he organized the first Methodist congregation and built the first Methodist church in Nebraska. Gage later became the first chaplain of the Nebraska Territorial Legislature.

The Kansas and Nebraska Conference was organized in 1856 at Lawrence, Kan., and in 1861 Nebraska became a separate conference. In 1880 the West Nebraska Mission was formed, comprising the territory west of Grand Island. In 1881 the NEBRASKA CONFERENCE was divided to form the NORTH NEBRASKA CONFERENCE which was comprised of the territory north of the Platte River and east of the West Nebraska Mission. In 1885 the WEST NEBRASKA CONFERENCE superseded the West Nebraska Mission, and in 1893 this conference was divided to create the NORTHWEST NEBRASKA CONFERENCE.

With the passage of time and the development of swifter means of communication and travel, there were no impelling reasons for four Methodist conferences in Nebraska, and they began to merge. In 1913 the North and West Nebraska Conferences were absorbed by the Nebraska Conference, and in 1924 the Northwest Nebraska Conference was included. Thereafter there was one conference covering the whole state.

The German Methodists, the Swedish Methodists, and the METHODIST PROTESTANT CHURCH operated in Nebraska. In 1864 the GENERAL CONFERENCE established a system of German Conferences, and in 1879 the West German Conference was organized at St. Joseph, Mo., to include churches in Missouri, Kansas, Nebraska, and Colorado. This conference continued until 1922 when the German churches in Nebraska were absorbed by the appropriate English-speaking conferences.

The Swedish Methodist churches in Nebraska were part of the Western Swedish Conference which was organized in Omaha in 1894 to include the Swedish work in Nebraska and several surrounding states. In 1928 this conference merged with two other Swedish conferences to form the CENTRAL NORTHWEST CONFERENCE (Swedish) which continued until 1942 when the Swedish churches and ministers were absorbed in the appropriate English-speaking conferences. There were ten Swedish pastoral appointments in Nebraska in 1927 and five in 1941.

The Methodist Protestants organized a small Nebraska Conference in 1860. For some years the conference received aid from the denominational board of missions. In 1866 the group felt strong enough to establish Lancaster Seminary at what is now LINCOLN, but after a few years the institution was sold to Lincoln for its first public school. The conference was strong enough to send delegates to the General Conferences during the last quarter of the nineteenth century, but the Methodist Protestant work in the state was dissolved in 1908.

As time passed, Nebraska Methodism came to support one college, NEBRASKA WESLEYAN at Lincoln; three hospitals; three retirement homes; and four youth camps.

In 1970 the Nebraska Conference had 480 ministers, 290 pastoral charges, and property valued at $53,797,267.

E. E. Jackman, *Nebraska*. 1954.
D. Marquette, *Nebraska*. 1904.

E. E. JACKMAN

NEBRASKA CONFERENCE was organized in Nebraska City, April 4, 1861 with Bishop THOMAS A. MORRIS presiding. (See NEBRASKA for beginnings of Methodism in Nebraska.) At the time it had twenty-one preachers including seven on trial, twenty pastoral appointments, four churches, and 948 members. There were two districts, Omaha and Nebraska City. During its history the Nebraska Conference divided several times to form other conferences in the state but by 1927 all of Nebraska Methodism had been incorporated again in the Nebraska Conference. At that time it had 464 charges and 101,593 members.

Nebraska Methodism has always been interested in schools and colleges. The first attempt to found an educational institution preceded the formation of the conference. In 1853 Cass County University was organized at Oreapolis, but it survived only three years. In 1879 J. H. Fleharty founded NEBRASKA WESLEYAN UNIVERSITY in Osceola, and Edward Thompson started York Seminary at York. In 1884 North Central Methodist College was opened in Central City. In 1886 Mallalieu University was launched in the town of Bartley, and Orleans College opened in Orleans. The two latter institutions survived about three years, but the others continued longer.

After five years in Osceola, Nebraska Wesleyan was moved to Fullerton, and three years later to York. In 1887 York Seminary and North Central College were absorbed by Nebraska Wesleyan, and the next year the institution moved to University Place, a suburb of LINCOLN, where a forty-acre campus was available and where the school is still located.

The conference supports three large hospitals—Nebras-

ka Methodist, Omaha, which opened in 1891; Bryan Memorial, Lincoln, which was established in 1924 and named in honor of its chief contributor, William Jennings Bryan; and West Nebraska General, Scottsbluff, founded in 1924.

Epworth Village, a children's home at York, was founded in 1896. Retirement homes include Crowell Memorial at Blair (1906) named in honor of the C. C. Crowell's who gave the land; the Sarah Anne Hester Home, Benkelman (1944), named in honor of the mother of the chief contributor, E. E. Hester; and Memorial Homes, Incorporated, Holdredge, a former community project which was purchased by the Methodists in 1956. The WOMAN'S HOME MISSIONARY SOCIETY organized the Omaha City Mission in 1876, and it continues to serve as the Wesley Community House. The conference supports four youth camps—Fontanelle near Fremont; Comeca near Cozad; Norwesca near Chadron; and Riverside near Milford.

In the groupings of conferences and states required by unification in 1939, the Nebraska Conference though "northern," became a part of the eight-state South Central Jurisdiction which was overwhelmingly "southern." At first Nebraska with Kansas formed an episcopal area, but in 1952 Nebraska alone became an area with the episcopal residence in Lincoln.

In 1970 the Nebraska Conference reported 480 ministers, 147,900 members, 290 charges, and property valued at $53,797,267.

E. E. Jackman, *Nebraska*. 1954.
Journals of the Nebraska Conference.
D. Marquette, *Nebraska*. 1904.

E. E. JACKMAN

NEBRASKA WESLEYAN UNIVERSITY, Lincoln, Nebraska, was established in 1886 when a commission appointed by the several Nebraska annual conferences merged three small colleges then in existence within the state. Since it was chartered on January 20, 1887, this date has been fixed in the college's calendar as Founders' Day. The college opened in September, 1888.

The schools that were merged into Nebraska Wesleyan were York College, York, Nebraska; Nebraska Central College, Central City; and Mallalieu University, Bartley. York was founded in 1879 by the Nebraska Conference. Nebraska Central College was the product in 1884 of the North Nebraska Conference. Mallalieu's founding date is unknown. It was considered a product of the West Nebraska Conference, though never officially adopted by that conference. Degrees offered are the B.A., B.S., B.S. in Education, B.M. (Music), B.M.E. (Music Education).

The governing board has sixteen persons elected to the Board of Governors by the Board of Trustees: three Methodist ministers, a representative of the alumni association, eleven other persons, and the resident bishop of the Nebraska Area as an ex officio member with vote. All must be members of the board of trustees. The board of trustees has fifty-six persons including the resident bishop of the Nebraska Area, twenty persons elected by the NEBRASKA ANNUAL CONFERENCE, fifteen persons elected by the alumni association, twenty elected by the Board of Trustees of Nebraska Wesleyan University.

JOHN O. GROSS

NEELY, THOMAS BENJAMIN (1841-1925), American bishop, was born at PHILADELPHIA, Pa., on June 12, 1841.

T. B. NEELY

A fifth-generation Methodist, he was the son of Thomas and Frances (Armstrong) Neely. He was educated at Dickinson Seminary and DICKINSON COLLEGE, receiving the honorary A.M. in 1875 and also the D.D. and LL.D.

Joining the PHILADELPHIA CONFERENCE in 1865, Neely rose rapidly in the Conference. He held thirteen pastorates chiefly in Philadelphia and vicinity and was presiding elder, 1889-94. In March 1882, he married Elizabeth Cheney Hickman.

Elected to GENERAL CONFERENCE in 1884, his deliberative talents were conspicuous. He was subsequently re-elected to five other General Conferences. His years of hard study of the history, law, constitution, and underlying principles of the Methodist Church, made Thomas Neely admittedly the greatest parliamentarian and expositor of church law in the M.E. Church.

He was a conservative and his caution increased with the years. In 1900 he was made Secretary of the Sunday School Union and Tract Society which included editorship. His travels and writings showed that he was an intelligent and robust executive. In 1904 Neely was elected bishop and assigned to BUENOS AIRES, ARGENTINA. He also opened a new mission in PANAMA and BOLIVIA. He held that the episcopacy was an office and not an order. His bishopric was a troubled one, partly due to altitude, climate, travels, age, and his unequivocal assertion of authority. His transfer to NEW ORLEANS, La., in 1908, did not help much, for the climate there probably hastened the death of his wife in 1912.

While Neely was a powerful champion of the idea that episcopacy is an office not an order, his uncompromising assertion of episcopal authority in its appointing power in certain northern conferences added to dissatisfaction with him as bishop. Against his bitter protest but according to his own interpretation of the law in maintaining the supremacy of the General Conference over the episcopacy,

Bishop Neely was retired by the 1912 General Conference. One of the historic and most dramatic and touching scenes of any General Conference took place when Bishop Neely rose from his sick bed and made his protest and last address to an unsympathetic Conference which nevertheless gave him a lordly welcome. His voice almost utterly failed but silently for an hour the overcrowded auditorium listened while only about one-fifth of those present could understand a word. It was a perfect tribute to a good man and great leader who did not know his own episcopal weaknesses. However, the vote was 496 to 297 to retire him, "no reason being formally stated." Ironically, it was noted that he had published in 1892, *The Governing Conference in Methodism, . . . Especially the General Conference of the Methodist Episcopal Church.*

During retirement he studied and wrote. He opposed the League of Nations, the Centenary Missionary Program, and Unification. He was an acute parlimentarian and learned historian and wrote twenty-one books dealing largely with Methodist history, doctrine, law, episcopacy, and the itinerancy. Among these were: *The Evolution of Episcopacy and Organic Methodism; Parliamentary Practice; Young Workers in the Church.* In 1911 he was a member of the Fourth ECUMENICAL METHODIST CONFERENCE. He died in Philadelphia, on Sept. 4, 1925, and was buried in West Laurel Hill, Philadelphia.

Dictionary of American Biography.
F. D. Leete. *Methodist Bishops.* 1948.
Who's Who in America.　　　　　　　JESSE A. EARL

NEGRO METHODISM IN THE UNITED STATES. (With special reference to The Methodist Church and its former Central Jurisdiction.)

Previous to 1939. To properly appraise the Central Jurisdiction in The Methodist Church, the structural arrangement set up in 1939 to accommodate the 300,000 Negro Methodists of The Methodist Church, it must be seen as a symbol of the past and present history of the Negro in the Methodist Church during the nearly two centuries of its existence in America; but more important still, as a practical demonstration of the efforts of a close-knit ecclesiastical organization, under most difficult social and political conditions, to include in its membership the most diverse racial groups.

The Methodist movement, from its beginning, made a special appeal to people in the lowest brackets of society. When its leaders, JOHN and CHARLES WESLEY, and their associates were excluded from the pulpits in LONDON and other cities in England, they took to the open fields and preached to the colliers and peasants in Kingswood and New Castle, and other mining communities in England. Their message was to the lowly and neglected classes. It was this same type in America to whom they made their greatest appeal.

To no group could their message have evoked a more enthusiastic response than among the African slaves. These people joined the movement in large numbers and were cordially welcomed, at least at first, by the leaders of the movement.

The missionaries sent by Wesley to America spoke appreciatively of the presence of the slaves in their meetings. In a letter to Wesley dated Nov. 4, 1769, Richard Boardman writes: "The number of the blacks that attend the preaching affects me much."

In his *Journal* of Nov. 17, 1771, Francis Asbury wrote:

"To see the poor Negroes so affected is pleasing, to see their sable countenances in our assemblies and to hear them sing with cheerful melody their dear Redeemer's praise, affected me much, and made me ready to say, 'of a truth I perceive God is no respecter of persons.'"

At the CHRISTMAS CONFERENCE in Baltimore in 1784, of the fifty-one churches which gave reports of their membership, all but fifteen reported Negro members. From the beginning of its history, therefore, Negroes were a part of the Methodist movement. According to Wade Crawford Barclay, the historian of Methodist Missions, the Negro membership in the church in 1786 numbered 11,280; in 1810-11, 34,724; in 1825-26, 47,433; and in 1844-45, 150,120.

Interracial Relations in Early Methodism. Despite the fact that Negroes were given what amounted to a "token" welcome into the movement, it soon became evident that they would be subject to caste distinctions and indignities. This was, doubtless, inevitable due to their status as slaves, but was also due to the social attitudes which prevailed in all the Colonies relative to class and social status. Seating in the churches, in some of the Colonies, was based on wealth and social prestige. The fact that Negroes, whether slaves or "free," were in the lowest bracket, meant that even when, and if, they were permitted to come into the churches for worship, they were given scant consideration as to seating. "They either sat on benches in the rear, or in an 'African corner.'"

The Methodists, because of their own relatively low social status at that time, could not hold the same degree of caste distinction as did the older and more exclusive churches of New England and the Atlantic Seaboard. Nevertheless, they too, soon began to make distinctions where Negroes were concerned. Barclay quotes from letters found in the *Journal* of one of Wesley's missionaries, JOSEPH PILMORE, in which he spoke of forming "a separate class for Negroes," and "after preaching, meeting with the Negroes apart." This trend was also evident early in Asbury's experience in America. In his *Journal* of Dec. 8, 1772, Asbury writes: "In the evening the Negroes were collected and I spoke to them in exhortation."

While the membership of the JOHN STREET CHURCH was interracial from the first, in the lists of membership published in 1787 whites and Negroes were listed separately. The ST. GEORGE'S CHURCH in Philadelphia also had separate listing. In addition to the separate seating arrangements, discrimination was shown in other ways. Barclay quotes from a letter by Pilmore dated Aug. 9, 1772, relative to a service where the church was not large enough to accommodate all who desired to attend.

"As the ground was wet they persuaded me to try to preach within, and appointed men to stand at the doors to keep all the Negroes out until the white persons were got in, but the house would not hold them." (Barclay, Vol. II, p. 55.)

In the southern section of the church, the problem was accentuated by fear of revolt on the part of the slaves. It was therefore deemed advisable, in some areas, to disallow religious services to the slaves; or where it was permitted, to provide a separate section for the Negro worshipers. There still exist, in many of the older churches of the South, balconies, where the slaves were seated during religious services.

In the light of these conditions, it is not surprising that there should have developed a feeling of unrest, especially among free Negroes in the northern section of the church, and a desire to have more freedom of expression. This was primarily responsible for the rise of the independent Negro Methodist denominations, and a great deal of credit deservedly belongs to men like RICHARD ALLEN who led their people in setting up first, independent local congregations, and finally, independent Churches. (See AFRICAN METHODIST EPISCOPAL CHURCH and AFRICAN METHODIST EPISCOPAL ZION CHURCH listings.)

In our appreciation of these men, however, we should not forget the leaders of the lowly Negro group who remained with the "Mother Church," and rendered yeomen service. One thinks especially of two such men: HARRY HOSIER, better known as "Black Harry," and JOHN STEWART. "Black Harry" accompanied both Asbury and Thomas Coke on a number of their preaching tours, and preached acceptably to both white and Negro audiences.

Stewart was converted at a camp meeting on the Marietta Circuit near Marietta, Ohio, sometime between 1814 and 1816, and became a missionary to the Indians.

There were other Negro leaders in every section of the church who were helping to carry the Word of God to their benighted fellowmen whose names never reached the public print, but nevertheless, are written in the "Book of Life."

In Episcopal Methodism (North and South) from the Division (1844) to Unification (1939). One of the very strange and interesting developments which followed the division of 1844 was the passionate interest shown by the Southern Church in the evangelization of the slaves. This is especially true when it is remembered that the immediate occasion for the Division of the Church in 1884 was the question of the ownership of slaves by one of the bishops from the southern section of the church. However, it was the Southern Church which showed the greatest zeal for the evangelization of the slaves, from 1844 to the beginning of the Civil War in 1861. This movement was led by WILLIAM CAPERS (later a bishop in the Church) from South Carolina. "He developed a type of organization," writes Willis J. Weatherford, "for serving the slaves, which swept over the entire South." (Weatherford, p. 91.)

In 1847, the church in the South reported 124,961 Negro members; in 1848, 127,241; in 1853, 146,949; in 1860, 171,857. The figures on this score are impressive and prove that the leaders of the church, South, showed a real evangelistic interest in the slaves.

The situation, however, changed with the Civil War. The change in the status of the Negro, following the Civil War, and the inability of the former masters to accept the new status of their former slaves, plus the activity of the independent Negro denominations in recruiting them into their churches, resulted in a rapid decline in the membership of the M.E. Church, South, during the war years. By 1866 the Negro membership had shrunk to 78,742.

At the General Conference of that church in 1866, a resolution was adopted which made possible the setting up of its Negro ministry and membership as an independent church. In 1870, this action, which had also the sanction of the Negro membership of that church, was taken. From that time until 1939, the two groups maintained close fraternal relations, but as distinctively separate denominations. During this period, the Southern Church made annual contributions to the new church (first named the Colored Methodist Episcopal Church —later changed to the CHRISTIAN METHODIST EPISCOPAL CHURCH)—from its benevolence budget; and took major responsibility for the support of PAINE COLLEGE, in Augusta, Ga., maintained for the training of Negro students. This was the situation in 1939 when the unification of the three Methodist denominations was effected.

In the Methodist Episcopal Church. We now turn to the situation in the M.E. Church—the northern branch of the Methodist Church—which, of course, is our major interest since the ministers and members of what became the Central Jurisdiction are now, and always have been, members of that branch of the church.

The division of the Church after 1844 did not have the same challenging effect in the north as in the South, at least not immediately. Despite their espousal of the freedom of the slaves, local attitudes against the admission of the Negroes into the churches changed slowly; and in a number of cases Negroes were encouraged to set up their own local congregations, even to join the independent Negro denominations. There was the added fact that the Negro population in most Northern cities was, in the early days, both small and economically insecure; and many joined the independent denominations on the basis of the racial appeal.

By 1850 (the last year of keeping separate lists of white and Negro members in the Annual Conferences of the Church) the total enrollment of Negroes in the M.E. Church was 26,309 which, as we have noted, was in great contrast to the Negro membership of the Southern Church in the same period. The Civil War, however, brought a greatly increased interest in the development of work among Negroes by the Northern Church. The passionate loyalty with which the Methodists of that Church had supported the Federal Government in the prosecution of the War, and their basic evangelistic and educational interest in the uplift of the underprivileged, made them the logical leaders, following the War, in "the fight to really make these people free." Thus the General Conference of 1864 authorized the organization of one or more Negro Mission Conferences. Under this provision, two Negro Mission Conferences were organized immediately following that General Conference: The DELAWARE, July 38, 1864; the WASHINGTON, Oct. 27, 1864. Also the Mississippi Mission Conference, composed of both white and Negro ministers, was organized in New Orleans, La., Dec. 25, 1865, with four districts: One for Mississippi, two in Louisiana, and one in Texas.

In the Episcopal Address at the General Conference of 1868, the bishops reported that nine Conferences had been organized in territory not previously included in Annual Conferences. These had a membership in 1871, as follows: Travelling Preachers, 630 (260 whites, 370 Negroes); Lay members, 135,000 (47,000 whites; 88,000 Negroes).

In 1868 the General Conference changed the status of the Conferences. Previously authorized as "Mission Conferences," they were then made full-fledged Annual Conferences with all the rights and privileges usual to Annual Conferences. Negroes elected by two of these "Mission Conferences" sat for the first time as delegates in the 1868 General Conference. The 1868 General Conference also authorized the bishops to organize new Annual Conferences in the South. By the close of the 1872-76 quadrennium, twenty Conferences—white, Negro, or mixed—

had been organized on the border and in the South. Three—Delaware, Washington, and Lexington—were all Negro; one, Kentucky, white; six—Holston, St. Louis, Arkansas, Virginia, West Virginia, and Missouri—predominantly white; six—South Carolina, Florida, Mississippi, Louisiana, Texas and North Carolina—predominantly Negro; three—Alabama, Georgia, and Tennessee—about equally divided between white and Negro members; and one, West Texas, bi-racial.

Racial Composition of Annual Conferences and Episcopal Leadership of the Negro Membership. As early as 1869, the division of Annual Conferences on racial lines was advocated. This agitation was begun in Georgia when a resolution was introduced by nine Negro preachers asking that the Negro Churches be formed into separate Negro districts under Negro presiding elders. A step in that direction was made by the setting up of one exclusively Negro district. A memorial to the General Conference of 1872 requested the formation of a separate Annual Conference for the Negro membership. No action was taken on this proposal at the General Conference of 1872, due to the fact that the Negro delegates were not unanimously in favor of setting up Annual Conferences on a racial basis. But the agitation for such action continued, led in some Conferences by whites; in others by Negroes. Thus it came about that at the General Conference of 1876, it was voted that where a majority of both whites and Negroes requested division, the presiding bishop was authorized to organize the new Conference, or Conferences.

By 1895, mixed Annual Conferences, composed of both white and Negro ministers, no longer existed in the Methodist Church. As Barclay observes, "By 1895 the developing process of segregation, first given official sanction by the General Conference of 1864, was complete." (Barclay, Vol. III, p. 321.)

Another issue which emerged rather early in the administration of work among Negroes was that of episcopal leadership for this particular group. Some critics (mainly outside the Church) asserted that the Church would never elect a Negro to the bishopric. A partial answer to this was given when the General Conference of 1856 made provision for the election of a Liberian as Missionary bishop (a distinct status) of that country. This provision was put into effect with the election of FRANCIS BURNS of Liberia (in 1858); this policy was continued in the selection of his successor, J. W. ROBERTS in 1866. But since both of these men were citizens of Liberia, and their service was limited to that particular field, this action did not and could not satisfy the demands in the home field.

In 1904, an American Negro, ISAIAH B. SCOTT, was elected a missionary bishop for service in Liberia. He had the same limitations as to the scope of this area of service, as did his predecessors in the office of "Missionary bishop."

It was not until 1920, that two full-fledged General Superintendents, equal in rank, official responsibility, and salary (including other financial perquisites) were elected in the M. E. General Conference. The fact that it was necessary at that late date to elect them on a separate ballot, is evidence that the Church had not completely overcome the barrier of color.

The Freedmen's Aid Society and Its Successors. One of the most constructive steps taken by the M. E. Church, following the Civil War, was the setting up of schools for the training of leaders among the Freedmen, both for special leadership in the work of the Church and nation, and for the responsibilities involved in the newly-attained citizenship in a democratic nation.

The program for this type of work was first begun as a cooperative venture among several of the major denominational groups, but there soon developed a tendency on the part of the several church bodies to set up their own denominational Boards. In line with this trend, a group of Methodist leaders, ministers and laymen, met in Cincinnati, Ohio, Aug. 7-8, 1866, to determine a program for the Methodist Church. The meeting resulted in the organization of the FREEDMEN'S AID SOCIETY with the objective "to labor for the relief and education of the freedmen, especially in cooperation with the missionary and Church Extension Societies of the Methodist Episcopal Church." (Barclay, Vol. III, p. 322.)

The Freedmen's Aid Society began its operations in the South in the Fall of 1866. In the very first year schools were set up in Georgia, Tennessee, Alabama, Mississippi, Kentucky, Louisiana, West Virginia, Virginia, and Florida. Three thousand pupils were enrolled the first year, under the tutelage of forty teachers. The Society, while authorized by the General Conference of 1868, was not given the status of a General Conference organization. By 1872 the Society was given full official approval and annual conference apportionments were sent down to the local churches for the support of the Society. In 1880 the General Conference directed the Society to aid the schools for whites in the South, and in 1888 the name of the Society was changed to the Freedmen's Aid and Southern Education Society, to more fully express the work of the Church among both races in the South.

By 1895 educational institutions under the patronage of the Society numbered forty-four, including, for Negroes a theological school, ten colleges and universities, and eleven academies, and for whites, three collegiate institutions and nineteen academies.

Early in its history the Freedmen's Aid Society had set a policy of inclusiveness of all its schools, regardless of color, but the steady pressure for segregation in both the Churches and schools in the South resulted finally in a complete separation of the two racial groups in the schools operated by the Society.

In 1924, the name of the Society was changed to the Board of Education for Negroes. Still later it was set up as one of the divisions of the general Board of Education, with the name, the Division of Negro Institutions. In The Methodist Church after 1939 it continued its work under the title, "Negro Higher Education in the Division of Educational Institutions." But by whatever name it has been called, this Society has, for more than a century, rendered great service to the cause of Negro education in the Church and nation.

Negro Membership an Issue in Methodist Unification.
The vigorous educational and evangelistic program carried forward by the Methodist Church, among the Negroes, expecially in the South, from the close of the Civil War, until 1939, when the Plan of Union was adopted, had both its advantages and disadvantages to those interested in Methodist Unification. To those who had believed in the possibility of the evangelization of people of all racial and national origins, and their inclusion in one Church of Jesus Christ, the plan of the Northern Church, while not ideal, had proven that the idea could be made to

work. For those with the other point of view, namely that the two racial groups should remain in separate denominations, on the basis of race, the Negro membership in the M. E. Church was a definite obstacle to Methodist Unification. The fact that the Negro membership in the Church numbered more than 300,000 did not make the problem any easier. It became evident that one of the major issues in the negotiations on Methodist Unification from 1916, when the active discussions on the subject began, until 1939, when the Plan of Union was adopted, was the status of the Negro membership in the re-organized Church.

To appreciate the total problem, we must see the issue from the standpoint of all the groups concerned: the M. E. Church, South, the white membership of the M. E. Church (Northern Branch), and the Negro membership of the M. E. Church.

From the standpoint of the Southern Church, with its history and social background since the Division in 1844, and its definititive action of 1870, in which it set up its Negro membership into an independent denomination, the logical status of the Negro in any plan for the re-organized Church, seemed to be the establishment of the Negro group into a separate denomination, either alone, or with other Negro church groups, with no organic relation to the white membership of the Church. Leaders of the Southern Church argued for that position for many years during the period of negotiations.

In the case of the M. E. Church, whatever might have been the individual preferences and even the practices of many of its members and local congregations, the Church officially had a long tradition in welcoming, theoretically at least, all groups into its fellowship. Further, there were still fresh memories among the older members of the Church of the vigorous educational and evangelistic programs which had been carried forward among the freemen since the Civil War. Thousands of Methodists were committed to that program. Also there was the legal fact that the Negro membership was as definitely a part of the Church as was any other group, and could not be eliminated from its membership except by their own choice. And finally, the Negro membership, although a minority group both numerically and in standing in the Church, was nevertheless conscious of its rights and prerogatives in the Church, and was not disposed to relinquish those prerogatives.

More important to them, however, than rights and prerogatives was the instinctive conviction, evident from their earliest connection with the people called "Methodists," that this Fellowship represented a communion that was seriously seeking to build a brotherhood among all men. They believed that their membership in such a Fellowship would help in the achievement of world brotherhood.

It was these varying views which over the period of nearly a quarter of a century of negotiations, had to be resolved before a Plan of Union satisfactory to a majority of Methodists could be agreed upon.

This meant compromises on all sides. For the Southern section of the new church, it meant giving up the insistence on a separate and independent church for the Negro membership, and accepting an arrangement which would leave them full-fledged members, albeit in a separate racial jurisdiction.

For the M. E. Church, it meant giving up the concept of a strongly centralized General Conference and accepting a regionally structured church.

For the Negro membership it meant accepting an arrangement by which the Annual Conferences of the Negro group would be set up as a regional group, or JURISDICTION, known as the "Central Jurisdiction," and based on a racial basis rather than geographical, as was true of the Jurisdictions for the white membership.

The Central Jurisdiction was by definition composed of the "Negro Annual Conferences, the Negro Mission Conferences and Missions in the United States of America." (*Constitution of The Methodist Church*, Section VIII, Article I.) This obvious racial distinction was never popular among the vast majority of Negroes in the church and ultimately had to end. However, the Central Jurisdiction did function as a coordinate Jurisdiction of the Church from 1939 until 1968 when it was dissolved into the five geographic jurisdictions under the United Methodist Church Constitution.

The Central Jurisdiction held sessions quadrennially (see record of these under JURISDICTIONAL CONFERENCES), elected bishops and Board members, and functioned exactly as other Jurisdictions. It was, however, a separate racial structure and wrote into the Constitution of a Christian denomination a definite segregated arrangement. Its existence proved to be an embarrassment to the whole Church, and feelings ran high over the very existence of this Jurisdiction at successive General Conferences. Amendment IX of the Constitution of The Methodist Church was passed by the General Conference and adopted by the Church as a whole during the 1956-60 quadrennium, in the effort to make easier the transition by local churches and annual conferences across and into the geographic jurisdictions. Such transfers proved desultory and hard to arrange, and posed great difficulties upon all Conferences involved. The General Conference of 1964 in passing the Plan of Union with the E.U.B. Church requested that the Central Jurisdiction be not mentioned, or allowed for, in the then pending plan of union. Pursuant to this, the Plan of Union set before the Church and adopted by the called General Conference of 1966, made no mention of the Central Jurisdiction, and it was understood on all sides that when this Constitution should be put into effect in 1968, the separate Negro Annual Conferences would go into their respective geographic jurisdictions. Some Conferences had already made this type of transfer (under Amendment IX), some conferences had completely merged, but the Constitution of The United Methodist Church effactually did away with the Central Jurisdiction as such. Its last session was held in Nashville, Tenn., Aug. 18-19, 1967.

There were bitter debates in the Negro Conferences and among Negro church leaders prior to the adoption of the Plan of Union in 1939, and, indeed, that Plan failed to carry in the majority of Negro Annual Conferences. It was, however, adopted by a majority of those present and voting in the white Conferences, both in the North and South, and as is stated above, became part of the constitutional structure of the Church.

Admittedly, the plan did have certain advantages, such as proportionate representation on all of the Boards of the Church; membership in its highest Councils, with members of its group being eligible to hold the highest posts in the Church, without discrimination as to salaries and other perquisites.

More important than these material benefits was the fact that the Central Jurisdiction made possible the beginning of the full-fledged brotherhood which has since been evolving, not only in The Methodist Church, but among Christians of every denominational persuasion, both Protestants and Catholics. Dr. M. S. DAVAGE representing the Negro Conferences at the Uniting Conference in 1939, made a declaration which The Methodist Church has not forgotten. "We want to be in a Church which embraces all mankind, and is big enough for God."

F. Asbury, *Journal and Letters*. 1958.
W. C. Barclay, *History of Missions*. 1949-57.
Daily Christian Advocate, Central Jurisdiction, 1967.
J. B. F. Shaw, *The Negro*. 1954.
Willis J. Weatherford, *American Churches and the Negro*. Boston: Christopher Publishing House, 1957. WILLIS J. KING

NEGRO METHODIST UNION NEGOTIATIONS (U.S.A.). During the past 150-year history of the three major Negro Methodist denominations in America—AFRICAN METHODIST EPISCOPAL, AFRICAN METHODIST EPISCOPAL ZION and CHRISTIAN METHODIST EPISCOPAL (formerly Colored Methodist Episcopal)—there have been many attempts at union or merger.

In 1864 the A.M.E. General Conference sent a delegation to the A.M.E. Zion General Conference suggesting that a commission on union be formed and empowered to call a convention and draw up articles of consolidation. The Zion connection favored this proposal and a convention was held in PHILADELPHIA on June 14-16, 1864. A platform and articles of agreement were formed which were then be sent to the annual conferences of each denomination for vote. If a favorable vote was received, the union would then be the order of business for the 1868 General Conferences. However, confusion arose as to whether or not the A.M.E. church had indeed sent the proposal to all local churches and annual conferences for a vote, and as a result, the Zion connection refused to consider this or any other proposal at their General Conference in 1868.

In 1885 union negotiations were revived. A joint commission of the A.M.E. and A.M.E. Zion Churches met in Washington, D.C., on July 15-17. A new name was proposed, First United Methodist Episcopal Church, and fourteen other articles of agreement. Disagreements arose over the proposed new name and the article concerning the episcopacy, however, and when only one bishop from the Zion connection was present at a scheduled meeting at Atlantic City, N.J., in August 1887, negotiations were postponed indefinitely. The next serious attempt at union occurred in 1892, but again a joint commission became deadlocked over the name to be given the new church.

On Feb. 16-17, 1918, a Tri-Council of bishops met at LOUISVILLE, Ky., and appointed a committee to draw up a plan of union. The committee met in BIRMINGHAM, Ala., on April 3, 1918, and in one day drew up a plan to be presented to the General Conferences of the three denominations. The so-called "Birmingham Plan" became a bone of contention, especially within the C.M.E. church. Though the plan was adopted at their General Conference in 1918, it was overwhelmingly defeated by the local congregations and annual conferences of that church, so that the A.M.E. and A.M.E. Zion General Conferences meeting in 1920 had nothing to consider.

A General Commission on Union was organized again in 1965. This Commission is committed to meeting at least twice a year and has set 1972 as a target date for merger among themselves, and 1980 as a target date for merger with The United Methodist Church. At this time, the Negro Methodist denominations are also involved in union talks with the Consultation on Church Union, an ecumenical body.

D. H. Bradley, *A.M.E. Zion Church*. 1956.
J. T. Jenifer, *Centennial Retrospect*. 1916.
C. H. Phillips, *History* (CME). 1898.
D. A. Payne, *History* (AME). 1891.
J. B. F. Shaw, *The Negro*. 1954.   Roy W. Trueblood

NEIDIG, JOHN, SR. (1765-1844), one of the founders of the United Brethren Church at Oberlin, Pa., was an associate of Otterbein and Boehm beginning about 1791.

The son of Abraham and Elizabeth Neidig, immigrants from Switzerland, John Neidig was born in Berks County, Pa., April 10, 1765. When he was about five years old, his family moved to Dauphin County, where they had close fellowship with the Mennonites. Despite the fact that his family had originally been German Reformed, John was chosen to be a preacher among the Mennonites when he was about twenty-five; but about a year later, he began his fellowship with the group of preachers who were to form the Church of the United Brethren in Christ.

Those neighbors and friends who became associated with John Neidig in the Highspire—Oberlin (then called Churchville) area became known as *Neidig's Leute* (Neidig's People); and in 1793 they erected their first church building on the spot where the present Neidig Memorial Church stands.

The home of John Neidig had a reputation for its deep spirituality and was a frequent stopping place for Christian Newcomer, who records twenty-four visits there in his *Journal*. The six sons and two daughters of John and Mary (Bear) Neidig grew up to give notable leadership to the church of their youth in Cumberland and Dauphin Counties of Pennsylvania, Frederick County, Md., and the area around Muscatine, Iowa.

John Neidig himself was faithful to the doctrine and practices of Otterbein and his followers and was a regular attender at the sessions of his conference. In 1812, 1820, and 1826, he was assigned an "overseer" of the work east of the Susquehanna River; and at camp meetings and worship services, he was in demand as a powerful preacher. He was named to the pastorate of Old Otterbein Church, Baltimore, Md., in 1828 and remained there until 1831.

John Neidig, Sr., died at his home near Highspire, Jan. 11, 1844, and is buried in the Highspire General Cemetery, located near the Harrisburg East Exit of the Pennsylvania Turnpike.

P. B. Gibble, *East Pennsylvania Conference* (UB). 1951.
                                        Bruce C. Souders

NEIGHBORS, WILLIAM SAMUEL (1860-1957), American minister, was born in Clay County, Ala., March 5, 1860. One of twelve children, his boyhood was a time of hardship, but his family worked together to see that he went to college. When he got off the train at Sweetwater, Tenn., he walked the nine miles to Hiwassee College with his trunk on his shoulder. From the moment he set foot on the campus of Hiwassee, he knew he was to be a Methodist preacher. He joined the church at Hillobee Campground in September 1875. Four years later he was licensed to preach at Notasulga, Ala. He was admitted on trial to the Holston Conference Oct. 17, 1887, ordained

a deacon in 1889, and elder in 1891. He graduated from Emory and Henry College in 1887.

He served as pastor of nearly every important church in the Holston Conference. He also was pastor of Greene Memorial Church, Roanoke, Va., and First Church, Baltimore, Md.

He was presiding elder three times of Holston Conference districts, and was for some time president of Sullins College, Bristol, Va. He led in the Centenary Fund promotion and contributed much to the success of the 1899 financial campaign for Emory and Henry College, which college awarded him an honorary D.D. degree in 1898. He was a delegate to four General Conferences (MES).

Neighbors was an able preacher and wise counselor. Reporting to the Holston Conference at a session in the early 1950's, a young minister said, "I've got Dr. Neighbors to preach for me next Sunday." "Well," replied Bishop Paul B. Kern, who was presiding at that session, "They'll get *one* good sermon."

It had been generally agreed that in the annals of Holston Conference no name ever stood higher as a preacher and man of God than that of William Samuel Neighbors. He died May 23, 1957, and was buried in Forest Hills Cemetery, Chattanooga, Tenn.

Journal of the Holston Conference, 1958.   L. W. Pierce

NEILL, JOHN LAMBERT (1882-1972), American preacher, missionary to Central Europe, and conference leader, was born at Montrose, Miss., on Jan. 17, 1882. He was educated at Millsaps College, receiving the B.S. in 1906. In 1908 he married Edith Reed (deceased April 1953). To them was born a daughter, Nellie (Mrs. Frank McKenzie Cross). J. L. Neill became first secretary of the Y.M.C.A. which was established at the Georgia Institute of Technology in 1906. The following year he joined the Mississippi Conference, and thereafter served as pastor in Pass Christian, 1907-08; Magee, 1909; Lorman, 1910; Hattiesburg, 1911-13; and Laurel, 1913-15. Upon the call of the M.E. Church, South, then beginning its work in middle Europe, he became superintendent of the Methodist work in Prague, Czechoslovakia, shortly after the first World War. He served in that capacity from 1922-25, and acted also as president of the Biblical Seminary in Prague during the same time. Upon his return to America, he became pastor of Yazoo City, 1926-27; Vicksburg, Crawford Street, 1928-31; Gulfport, 1932-33; Meridian, 1933-34; Brookhaven, 1936-39, Natchez, 1940-41; superintendent of the Meridian district, 1942-43; of the Seashore District, 1944-47; pastor of First Church, Philadelphia, Miss., 1948-54; retiring in that year. He also served as president of the Mississippi Anti-Saloon League from 1937 to 1950. After retirement, he lived in Decatur, Miss., where he died in 1972.

Who's Who in The Methodist Church, 1966.   N. B. H.

NEITZ, SOLOMON (1821-1885), American Evangelical minister and renowned pulpit orator, was born April 2, 1821, in South Whitehall Township, Lehigh Co., Pa. He became a member of the East Pennsylvania Conference, Evangelical Association in 1840 and held many official positions in annual and general conferences. He wrote the *Life and Labors of John Seybert*, the first bishop of the Evangelical Association. Solomon Neitz' visit to the mission field in GERMANY (1863), added much to the status of the work, since large state churches were opened to him and overflowing audiences gave him rapt attention. Philip Schaff declared "There are only two such German orators in the world, Krumacher in Germany, and Neitz in America."

With no training beyond three months in a common country school, his preparation had to be through personal application. This was possible, for he was richly endowed with unusual native talents, a craving for knowledge, and a will to use every spare moment for self-improvement. Furthermore, studying the Bible and catechism, with regular attendance at prayer-meeting, and worship services (at his father's insistence) laid a firm foundation of religious faith, resulting in an epochal conversion at age fourteen.

Contemporaries wrote of his magnetic personality, pronounced convictions, and ability to inspire vast audiences, not only with his skill in drawing word pictures, but by the unctuous power that characterized them. He died of apoplexy, May 11, 1885, in Reading, Pa.

Das Evangelische Magazin, Vol. 18, 1886.
The Evangelical Messenger, Vol. 16, 1863.
Journal of the General Conference, EA, 1887.
The Living Epistle, March 1886.
A. Stapleton, *Evangelical Association.* 1896.
————, *Flashlights.* 1908.
R. K. Schwab, *Christian Perfection in the Evangelical Association.* 1922.
R. Yeakel, *Evangelical Association.* 1896.   ROY B. LEEDY

NELLES, SAMUEL SOBIESKI (1823-1887), Canadian minister and educator, was born at Mount Pleasant, Upper Canada, Oct. 17, 1823. He was educated at Lewiston Academy and the Genesee Wesleyan Seminary in New York, VICTORIA COLLEGE, and WESLEYAN UNIVERSITY (Connecticut), from which latter institution he graduated with the B.A. in 1846.

Samuel Nelles was taken on trial in 1847, but in 1850 he was appointed principal and professor of classics at Victoria College. Four years later he became president and held this office until his death in 1887.

The years during which Nelles presided over Victoria's destinies were crucial ones. When he took office, the college was seemingly on its last legs, having few students, no staff, and no money. Under his skillful and tenacious leadership, the college gradually increased its enrollment; new faculties were added; the debts were paid; and a modest endowment was accumulated. All this was accomplished in the face of great uncertainty about the college's future, generated by the intermittent efforts to establish a satisafctory working relationship between the University of Toronto and the various church colleges.

Throughout his career, President Nelles had two great aspirations—to make Victoria a great Christian university, and to assist in building a great provincial university in which each college would preserve its distinctive traditions. It may be said that he accomplished the first to such a degree that the second became possible under his successor, NATHANEAL BURWASH.

Although he was devoted to his duties as Victoria's president, Nelles was equally concerned for the welfare of his church. As was customary, he preached regularly in college and elsewhere. He was not a great orator, but his sermons were characteristically thoughtful, philosophical, and well-illustrated from literature and science. On occasion, "in a certain giant majesty of movement, he reached

an altitude and amplitude of power that placed him side by side with the noblest of his time."

Nelles was keenly interested in missions and in church union, to both of which he contributed his breadth of judgment, his insight, and his zeal. For these and other services he was given a D.D. by Queen's University, and an LL.D. by Victoria.

At his death, Oct. 17, 1887, he was described as one whose

broad and generous sympathies gave him a loving nearness to everybody. He saw good in everything. Inspiration flowed with his kindness, which lifted the troubled into peace. Indeed, the keen insight which he had of truth, and that hush of spirit, as if the unseen was upon him, is the best evidence that his mind was habitually fixed upon high and sacred things.

He requested that his tombstone should bear these words: "Now we see through a glass darkly."

G. H. Cornish, *Cyclopaedia of Methodism in Canada.* 1881.
Minutes of the Bay of Quinte Methodist Conference, 1888.
C. B. Sissons, *Victoria University.* 1952.   G. S. FRENCH.

JOHN NELSON

NELSON, JOHN (1707-1774), British preacher, was born in BIRSTALL, Yorkshire, in October 1707, and brought up to be a stone mason like his father. From the age of ten he was hypersensitive about his sins, and he regarded the fatal illness of his father when he was sixteen as God's punishment upon himself. At nineteen he sought marriage largely as an antidote to sexual temptation, but continued to be fitfully unhappy because he "loved pleasure more than God." He was especially addicted to hunting, but rather than destroy his gun he left home to follow his trade in different parts of the country. LONDON proved a constant magnet to him. A few years' residence there, however, proved detrimental to the health of his wife and children, so that they returned to Birstall. Nelson himself, however, stayed on, being convinced—as he told those who reproved him for not returning home—"I have something to learn that I have not yet learned." In London he went from church to church, denomination to denomination, seeking spiritual peace. He was greatly impressed by WHITEFIELD's open air preaching in May 1739, but even more so with Wesley's first sermon in Moorfields on June 17, 1739. He became a constant hearer of the Wesleys, and in October experienced conversion, mainly through the influence of JOHN WESLEY and one of his soldier converts. He immersed himself in devotional reading, fasted every week-end, and urged others to be religious, even paying one of his fellow-workers to go and hear Wesley.

Meanwhile Nelson was happy to hear that some of his relations in Birstall were attending the preaching of BENJAMIN INGHAM, the Wesleys' colleague in OXFORD and GEORGIA. In the winter of 1740 he returned home expecting to find them also sharing his own radiant joy in a personal religious experience, but found them spiritually lifeless. He began to speak of his own far different experience, of *knowing* that his sins were forgiven. Increasingly large groups gathered in his home, some to listen sympathetically, some to dispute. Within a few days his brother was converted, then six of his neighbors, and eventually his wife Martha. Within three weeks the number of converts had increased to seventeen. It became clear that a rival fellowship was being created, owing allegiance to Nelson and through him to the Wesleys. Ingham sought unavailingly to restrain his enthusiastic preaching, although for some time they worked together in a group of societies many of which became Moravian.

In May 1742, John and CHARLES WESLEY stayed with Nelson in Birstall for a week, and from that time he unhesitatingly gave his full allegiance to them. He introduced Methodism into many towns and villages in Yorkshire and Lincolnshire, continuing to support himself and his family by intermittent labors as a stone mason, often hewing stone during the day and preaching in the evening. On May 4, 1744, a long-hatched plot to press him for a soldier succeeded, and he was sent north for military training, though he continued to preach to his captors and the jeering populace, often with remarkable success. After nearly three months he was set free, largely through the intervention of the COUNTESS OF HUNTINGDON, urged on by the Wesleys. Shortly afterwards John Wesley employed Nelson fully as a regular itinerant preacher, and in that capacity he travelled for almost thirty years in many parts of the country, often as Assistant in charge of a Circuit. He spent much time in the circuits of BRISTOL, MANCHESTER, and LEEDS, in addition to his native town of Birstall. Indeed he seems to have been especially successful in the areas most affected by the Industrial Revolution, where his direct homely preaching continued to make a great impression upon working people. His last circuit was Leeds, where he had introduced Methodism a generation earlier. Here he died of apoplexy on July 18, 1774. Thousands of admirers accompanied his coffin through the streets of Leeds, singing or weeping, as he was taken for burial in his native Birstall.

Nelson's homespun narrative of his arrest by the press-gang, and of his brief sojourn in the army, proved to be rousing material for Methodist gatherings. Charles Wesley read a manuscript copy of this aloud to the Bristol society in September 1744, and John Wesley prepared it for publication the following month. It was entitled *The Case of John Nelson*, sold for threepence, and was snapped up so rapidly that a second edition was called for during that same month of October, and two more before the end of the year. In 1767 Nelson himself published a much larger work, in effect an expansion of this earlier one, for it took his story no further than April 1745. This was entitled *An Extract from John Nelson's Journal*, and became a best-seller, especially as edited and slightly abridged by John Wesley. Indeed this is probably the best known of the many autobiographies of Wesley's preachers, and has largely served to make Nelson Wesley's best known lay preacher.

F. Baker, *William Grimshaw*. 1963.
T. Jackson, *Lives of Early Methodist Preachers*. 1837-38.

FRANK BAKER

NELSON, JUSTUS H. (1851-1937), American preacher and missionary to BRAZIL, was born in 1851, probably in WISCONSIN. He studied at LAWRENCE UNIVERSITY at Appleton, Wis., and at the BOSTON UNIVERSITY SCHOOL OF THEOLOGY, from which he graduated in 1879. In 1880, he was admitted on trial in the Providence, later NEW ENGLAND SOUTHERN CONFERENCE.

By this time, WILLIAM TAYLOR had made his last voyage to South America (1877-78), and had returned to the United States to recruit missionaries who were to serve on a self-supporting basis. Nelson was one of his recruits.

While awaiting his appointment, Nelson studied a year at Boston University, taking an "electic Course in Medicine." This, plus a course in practical nursing taken after going to Brazil (in Belém, province of Paraná), enabled him to be of great usefulness in administering simple treatments to the poor.

Mr. and Mrs. Nelson with William Taylor arrived in Belém on June 19, 1880, Taylor remaining only long enough to get a school successfully started. This school prospered and new recruits were sent out, including Justus' brother. But when yellow fever took the lives of two recruits and fire destroyed the school building, Nelson was forced to close it. He remained on the field, however, supporting himself and family by teaching English, German, and Portuguese.

When on his first furlough, leaving GEORGE NIND in charge of his work, Nelson asked that Brazil be organized into a district of the Providence Annual Conference, which was so done, with Nelson named presiding elder. He continued in this capacity until the Brazil Mission was organized into the South American Annual Conference (ME), to which he was then transferred.

Nelson organized the first Methodist church in Belém on July 1, 1883. In addition to pastoral work, he edited a religious publication which he called *O Apologista Cristão Brasilerio* (The Brazilian Christian Apologist). For this, he translated many hymns by Wesley and others. In one issue, he referred to the "idolatry prevalent in Brazil," and for this was sentenced to jail for "4 months, two days and 12 hours, being released April 8, 1893."

Nelson had hoped to stay in Brazil fifty years, working mainly in the Amazon region. But a depression forced his retirement in 1926, after forty-six years. He returned to the United States that year and died in 1937. He was survived by one son, Luther T. Nelson.

W. C. Barclay, *History of Missions*. 1949-57.
Annual Report, Board of Missions (ME), 1893.   D. A. REILY

NELSON, REUBEN (1818-1879), American minister, educator and publisher, was born in Andes, N. Y., Dec. 16,

1818. One of twelve children of Abraham and Huldah Nelson, he became a Christian at fifteen, a local preacher at eighteen and joined the ONEIDA CONFERENCE at twenty-one, becoming a fully ordained member in due course. Meantime he served as third preacher on the Otsego and Westford circuits. He also was principal of Otsego Academy, Cooperstown, N. Y. In his youth he lost his lower right arm in a woolen mill. Because of a throat affection he stepped aside temporarily in 1843. He married Jane Scott Eddy, daughter of Col. and Mrs. Asa Eddy of Milford, N. Y., in 1842.

In 1844 the Oneida Conference established Wyoming Seminary, in Kingston, Pa., naming Reuben Nelson its first president, a position he held twenty-eight years, excepting two years (1862-63 and 1863-64), when he was presiding elder of Wyoming district. In 1868-69 he filled both responsibilities. Becoming a member of the WYOMING CONFERENCE in 1852, Nelson was elected to the quadrennial GENERAL CONFERENCE five times, beginning with 1860. In 1876 he was chairman of the Committee on Episcopacy. In 1872 and 1876 the General Conference elected him senior Agent of the Methodist BOOK CONCERN, with offices in NEW YORK. His second election was by acclamation in recognition of his successful administration at a time when many business enterprises were being ruined. He also was made treasurer of the church's Missionary Society. He held honorary degrees from Union College and DICKINSON COLLEGE.

Nelson was an able preacher, educator and business man. He died in New York City, Feb. 20, 1879, and was buried at Forty Fort, Pa.

A. F. Chaffee, *Wyoming Conference*. 1904.
Dictionary of American Biography.
Journal of the General Conference, 1880.
Methodist Quarterly Review, October 1879.

LOUIS D. PALMER

NELSON, WILLIAM HAMILTON (1878-1956); American minister, author, and editor, was born at NEW ORLEANS, La., on April 6, 1878. He was educated at CENTENARY COLLEGE, now at Shreveport, La., SOUTHWESTERN UNIVERSITY, and the University of Chicago. He joined the WEST TEXAS CONFERENCE of the M.E. Church, South, in 1902. He served churches in SAN ANTONIO, 1902; Palacios, 1903; Port Lavaca, 1907. In the TEXAS CONFERENCE he was appointed to Angleton, 1908; HOUSTON, 1909; President, Chapel Hill Female College, 1910. He transferred to the PACIFIC CONFERENCE (MES) in 1911 and was appointed to Santa Rosa. In 1913 he became superintendent of the Children's Home of CALIFORNIA. In 1915 he went to the Cartwright Church in PHOENIX, ARIZ., in the Los Angeles Conference. As a member of the Pacific Conference in 1916, he served Chico and Yuba City. From 1918 to 1934, he edited the *Pacific Methodist Advocate* in SAN FRANCISCO, traveling extensively over the Western States until publication ceased. He served Woodland, Calif., from 1935 until 1939 when he retired in the newly formed CALIFORNIA CONFERENCE. He was Western agent, correspondent and general representative of the *Christian Advocate* of NASHVILLE from 1934 to 1939, and was a member of the GENERAL CONFERENCE of his church in 1922.

In 1931, Nelson wrote a history of Centenary College, entitled *Burning Torch and Flaming Fire*. His *Alluring Arizona* appeared in 1927. Seven other volumes were published over a period of sixteen years: *Tinker and Thinker —John Bunyan* and *Blood and Fire, William Booth* were biographies. Nelson was a master of picturesque and pungent phrase.

After retirement he supplied several churches including Knight's Landing and Boulder Creek. He resided mostly at San Francisco, San Diego, and Santa Barbara, where he died Nov. 1, 1956, and was buried there.

Journal of the California-Nevada Conference, 1957.
The Pacific Conference Annual, MES, 1939.

MAURICE B. CHEEK

NELSON, New Zealand, **St. John's Church,** the central Methodist Church, began its history when SAMUEL IRONSIDE conducted the first Methodist services in the open air before a congregation of newly arrived settlers. The first services organized by the settlers themselves were held in 1842 in a house built after the Maori manner, a local preacher conducting worship.

In 1843, JOHN ALDRED found the Wesleyans meeting in a place of worship built by public subscription for use by all denominations. It was called Ebenezer.

Later, a large brick schoolroom was built, and the Wesleyans moved there for their services and meetings.

In 1845, a brick church, forty-seven feet, costing £260 was opened. It seated two hundred persons, and was opened free of debt.

During the eloquent ministry of JOHN WARREN (1855-59), the church became too small. An acre of land was bought in Hardy Street, and the old church, with the land on which it was built, was sold. A new church was built on the new site and was opened in June, 1858, with a debt of only £145. A new parsonage was added later, then a gallery across the end of the church. By this time WILLIAM KIRK was the minister, and there was perpetual revival.

About thirty years later it was found that there were signs of decay in the church building. A new church to seat 550 people was opened in 1890. The cost of this building was £2,250, the minister at the time being William C. Oliver.

In 1899, during the ministry of J. S. Smalley, the parsonage, which had served for forty years, was replaced with a new one, toward the cost of which the congregation raised £1,144 in 1900.

Further buildings, a Sunday school hall and an infant school, were opened in 1912, J. J. Lewis being the minister. Bible class rooms followed in 1924, these being added to the old church building which had been shifted to the rear of the church site and was doing excellent service as a gymnasium. Youth work was flourishing at this time.

The membership of the circuit of which St. John's is the "mother church" was 482 in 1966.

Spring Grove Church was originally in the Nelson Circuit. It was built on a site of three acres, and was opened on April 18, 1858, P. Calder, D. Dolamore, and John Warren conducting the services. The building had cob walls consisting of an earthen formation. For many years there was a flourishing rural work, but with the changing character of the community, the work gradually declined, and for a number of years the building was not used. Shortly after centennial celebrations in 1958, the building was demolished.

The following entry in its baptismal register is of interest: "Ernest Rutherford, born 30th August, 1871, baptized 5th August, 1873. Son of James and Martha Rutherford, Wheelwright. Minister, Rev. W. Cannell."

Ernest Rutherford later became the first Baron Rutherford, eminent British chemist and physicist. Lord Rutherford won the Nobel Prize in chemistry in 1908. Later he effected the splitting and transmutation of the atom. He was made a peer in 1931 and died in 1937.

MATTHEW ALEXANDER McDOWELL

Photo: Alexander Turnbull Library
TAMATI WAKA NENE (1780-1871), FAMOUS MAORI CHIEFTAIN, AND FRIEND AND PROTECTOR OF EARLY MISSIONARIES TO NEW ZEALAND.

NENE, TAMATI WAKA (1780-1871), NEW ZEALAND Methodist layman and Maori chieftain and warrior, with his brother Patuone protected early Wesleyan missionaries from hostile attacks. When the brothers became Christians, Nene was baptized by a Wesleyan missionary and took the name of Tamati Waka (Thomas Walker). Patuone was baptized by an Anglican missionary and took the name of Eruera Maihi (Edward Marsh).

Nene was a good friend to the government as well as to the missionaries, and was one of the most convincing supporters of the Treaty of Waitangi, signed in 1840, by which sovereignty over New Zealand was ceded to the British Crown.

His services were recognized by the government, and he was granted a pension of £100 per year. In his later years he was greatly respected both by Maoris and Europeans. A government memorial erected in the Russell Anglican churchyard in his honor describes Nene as "the first to welcome the Queen's sovereignty to New Zealand: a consistent supporter of the Pakeha (white man)."

G. H. Scholefield, ed., *Dictionary of New Zealand Biography.* New Zealand Department of Internal Affairs, 1940.

L. R. M. GILMORE

NEPAL is an independent constitutional monarchy in south central Asia, the world's only Hindu kingdom. It became a member of the United Nations in 1955. Nepal stands as a geographical and political buffer between the Republic of INDIA and Tibet, which is controlled by Communist CHINA. The area is over 54,000 square miles, the contour being a rectangle 525 miles long, averaging 120 miles wide, oriented northwest-southeast. The population is 10,-294,000. The capital is Katmandu, population, 195,260.

Until 1960, the Himalayas, constituting Nepal's northern border, were considered impassable. However, the Communist Chinese, conquerors of Tibet, have thrust two effective roads across the vast massif to Nepal's border.

In the mid 1700's the land was conquered by hardy Hindu Gurkhas forced northwards from India by overpowering Moslems. Treaties were undertaken with Great Britain, commercial in 1791, political in 1801. A British Resident was admitted, to advise government. Britain also secured the privilege of recruiting a certain number of Gurkhas for the British Army in India. The Gurkha units remained loyal to Britain in the Sepoy Mutiny, 1857, and were the focal forces in overcoming that uprising. The valor of the Gurkha regiments in both World Wars was notable. The Republic of India inherited these units and the right of recruiting. The Gurkha battalion in the United Nations Force in the CONGO, 1962-63, proved very effective.

King Mahendra ascended the throne of Nepal in 1956, being markedly liberal in attitude. The country is governed under a democratic constitution promulgated in 1959, adapting to Nepal the Panchayat form of village government in Hindu India. Britain has provided specialists for advice in forestry and agriculture. United States governmental aid has been directed to roads and communications, irrigation, and simple industries.

A ROYAL PALACE WAS PROVIDED BY THE KING OF NEPAL TO HOUSE THE FIRST HOSPITAL, CALLED SHANTA BHAWAN, AT KATMANDU.

United Mission to Nepal. With thirty denominational groups now affiliated, The United Mission to Nepal was actually organized as a Methodist project under the leadership of Bishop J. WASKOM PICKETT in 1953. The following year medical services were begun under the direction of Dr. BETHEL FLEMING. In 1955 two additional doctors, Edgar and Elizabeth Miller, were sent out by the Methodist Board of MISSIONS. A palace belonging to the royal family was given to the mission for its hospital and has been in use since 1954 operating as Shanta Bhawan Hospital.

The United Mission operates four basic services: an educational program involving some 2,000 people; a technical institute for training skilled workmen; field hospitals; and dispensaries.

Nepal is dominated religiously by the Buddhists and Hindus, but there are increasing numbers of Christians throughout the country and they organize themselves ecumenically for work and worship. They may not legally seek converts to their Christian fellowships.

An indication of the growth and importance of this program is the appreciative recognition given by the King of Nepal to both the Flemings and the Millers. Their work began with eight staff members, ten hospital beds, and no nurses; the United Mission now has nearly 200 workers in the various aspects of the program. Nepal, until a change of regime in 1951, had been closed to all mission efforts. Some Roman Catholic mission work was begun in 1662, but this was expelled 100 years later. The remarkable and rapid development since 1953 by the United Mission has been the result of a progressive attitude on the part of the government and the willingness of Christian workers from thirty denominations to work together without denominational labels. The very difficult travel problems in Nepal have made it necessary to establish field service both for teaching public health and for actual medical treatment. A twenty-bed hospital has been built in Bhatgaon, east of Katmandu, where tuberculosis is their chief concern, but general medical care is also provided. A fifty-five-bed hospital has been built in Tansen.

There are now nine mission-managed schools, plus the technical and agricultural training centers. Increasingly the Nepalese are being trained to become leaders of these various programs. Natives are eventually to be in full charge. Nurses and doctors are being trained and extensive plans are under way for a very much enlarged central hospital and United Mission headquarters to be built in Katmandu.

Eleanor Preston Clarkson, *Medics in the Mountains: The Story of Edgar and Elizabeth Miller*. New York: Friendship Press, 1968.
Grace Neis Fletcher, *The Fabulous Flemings of Nepal*. New York: E. P. Dutton & Co., 1964.
J. N. Hollister, *Southern Asia*. 1956.
Edgar R. Miller, *Medical Mission in Nepal*. Board of Missions of The Methodist Church. N.d.
Minutes of the United Mission to Napel.
World Outlook, August 1962; April 1963.

ARTHUR BRUCE MOSS
EMORY STEVENS BUCKE

NESBITT, SAMUEL H. (1821-1891), was an important American leader of the PITTSBURGH CONFERENCE of the M.E. Church during the last half of the nineteenth century. Born in Butler County, Pa., of Seceder parentage, Sept. 30, 1821, he died at the Methodist Parsonage at New Brighton, Pa., April 5, 1891. His early life was passed in PITTSBURGH where he learned and followed the trade of a nailer. Converted in 1842, he entered ALLEGHENY COLLEGE. Graduating with honors in three years, in 1847 he was admitted on trial in the Pittsburgh Conference. He was principal of the Wellsburg Female Seminary 1853-1856, and President of Richmond College 1857-1859. From 1859 until 1872 he was the editor of *The Pittsburgh Christian Advocate*. He served as presiding elder on two districts for six years. He was a delegate to the

GENERAL CONFERENCES of 1864, 1868, 1872, and 1876, leading the Pittsburgh Conference delegation each time. A book from his pen, *The Sabbath of the Bible*, was published in 1890.

W. GUY SMELTZER

NESS, JOHN HARRISON (1891-   ), American E.U.B. pastor, conference superintendent, and denominational executive, was born Oct. 23, 1891 in Yoe, York County, Pa., to John Jefferson and Elizabeth Snyder Ness. He prepared for the ministry in LEBANON VALLEY COLLEGE (A.B. 1915) and continued his schooling in Princeton Theological Seminary, completing his work in 1919. Graduate studies in history and philosophy were taken in Johns Hopkins University. In 1925 Lebanon Valley College honored him with the D.D. degree.

In 1918 Dr. Ness was married to Miss Myra Grace Kiracofe, a college class-mate. To their union two sons were born: JOHN HERBERT and Robert Kiracofe Ness.

John Harrison Ness entered the Pennsylvania Annual Conference, CHURCH OF THE UNITED BRETHREN IN CHRIST, in 1911, and was ordained in 1919. Following several student pastorates, he was appointed to First Church, York, Pa., in 1919, serving there until elected to the superintendency of the conference in 1931. Many times a member of the GENERAL CONFERENCE of his church, Dr. Ness served on numerous important boards and commissions. He was elected publisher by the 1945 General Conference, which position he declined in order to remain in the superintendency. Later he did accept an election to serve his Church as Associate Secretary of the Board of Pensions (1948-1957), and Executive Secretary of the Board of Pensions (1957-1963).

Following retirement in 1963, Dr. Ness rendered special ministries to the United Church, Ponce, PUERTO RICO; the Ybor City Mission, TAMPA, Florida; the RED BIRD MISSION in KENTUCKY; and the Otterbein Home near Lebanon, Ohio.

Dr. Ness served on the central committee that prepared the details for the union of The EVANGELICAL CHURCH and the Church of the United Brethren in Christ to form the E.U.B. Church in 1946.

In The United Methodist Church he holds his membership with the CENTRAL PENNSYLVANIA CONFERENCE. He makes his home in Dayton, Ohio.

Journal of the General Conference, UB, EUB.
Minutes of the Pennsylvania Conference, UB.

PAUL E. HOLDCRAFT

NESS, JOHN H., JR. (1919-   ), American E.U.B. minister, was born in Hagerstown, Md., Sept. 29, 1919, to Myra Kiracofe Ness and JOHN HARRISON NESS. John, Jr. received his quarterly conference license from First United Brethren Church, York, Pa., in 1936; annual conference license from Pennsylvania Conference, CHURCH OF THE UNITED BRETHREN IN CHRIST, Oct. 8, 1940; and was ordained by the same conference, Oct. 3, 1944. Appointments were filled in MARYLAND and PENNSYLVANIA for fourteen years until he was elected the administrative leader of The HISTORICAL SOCIETY of The E.U.B. Church, DAYTON, Ohio, in September 1958. He held this position at the time of the formation of The United Methodist Church (1968). He married Lucille Hull, Feb. 26, 1944, and they had three children.

The following institutions conferred degrees upon him:

LEBANON VALLEY COLLEGE, Annville, Pa., A.B. (1940), and L.H.D. (1964); University of Pennsylvania, M.A. (1942); and Bonebrake (now UNITED) THEOLOGICAL SEMINARY, B.D. (1945). He also received certificates from the 18th Institute of Modern Archival Administration, AMERICAN UNIVERSITY, 1964, and the Institute of Archival Administration, UNIVERSITY OF DENVER, 1967. His book, *One Hundred Fifty Years*, a history of publishing in The E.U.B. Church, was issued in 1966. Since 1963 Ness has served on the Church Records Committee, Society of American Archivists.

With the union of The Historical Society and the Association of METHODIST HISTORICAL SOCIETIES in 1968, Dr. Ness became the executive secretary of the COMMISSION ON ARCHIVES AND HISTORY of The United Methodist Church. He retains his membership in the CENTRAL PENNSYLVANIA CONFERENCE.

HAROLD S. BROWN

NEVADA, called both the "Silver State" and the "Sagebrush State," is in the western part of the United States. Its Spanish name means "snow-clad." It is bounded by OREGON and IDAHO on the north, UTAH and ARIZONA on the east, and by CALIFORNIA on the south and west. With an area of 110,540 square miles, it is seventh in size among the states. Its population in 1970 was 481,893.

A large part of Nevada is called the Great Basin, a tableland 4,000 to 5,000 feet above sea level. Much of the state is arid, its rivers ending in "sinks" where the water is absorbed by the dry air or seeps into the ground.

Among the early pioneers who explored parts of Nevada was the young Methodist trader JEDEDIAH S. SMITH who in 1827 crossed the state from west to east. In 1848, at the end of the war with MEXICO, Nevada, then known as the Washoe Territory of California, became a United States possession. In 1850 it became part of Utah Territory. In 1861 Utah was divided and the western part was called Nevada. In 1863 Nevada was admitted into the Union.

Permanent settlement in Nevada began in 1859 with the discovery of the Comstock Lode. Thousands of people then flocked to what proved to be one of the richest deposits of precious metals ever found. By 1881 the original mines were exhausted, and while other deposits were discovered they too were soon depleted. By 1920 the mining industry had lost its original importance. As time passed, some agriculture and cattle ranching developed; irrigation made the valleys very productive. Tourism is a large source of income for the state.

Gambling was legalized in Nevada in 1931, and the residence requirement for divorce was reduced to six weeks. Nevada has since become a resort center for gambling, and for marriage and divorce. Under the circumstances, church life has not flourished, and church membership among the population is about one-half what it is in the rest of the country.

The first Methodist preacher to come to Nevada was Jesse L. Bennett. Ordained in 1829 in ILLINOIS, he went to California with the gold rush. By 1858 he was preaching in Virginia City, Nev., and the communities in Carson Valley. Among others who came to Nevada was Warren Nims; he built four churches and six parsonages. The first deed for a religious meetinghouse was recorded by the Methodists, Aug. 13, 1860, for a church building in Virginia City. One of the men involved in the transaction was a Methodist layman, HENRY G. BLASDEL, who became the first governor of the state.

The churches in Nevada were organized into a conference at Virginia City, Sept. 7, 1865 with Bishop CALVIN KINGSLEY presiding. The conference had two districts—Washoe and Humboldt, eleven preachers, seventeen pastoral appointments, four church buildings, and 267 members. In 1884 the Nevada Mission superseded the Nevada Conference. In 1917 the mission was abolished, and the Nevada work was divided between the two California Conferences (MEC).

Today White Pine County, Nev., is a part of the ROCKY MOUNTAIN CONFERENCE. The part of the state below the thirty-seventh parallel (chiefly Clark County and Las Vegas) is in the SOUTHERN CALIFORNIA-ARIZONA CONFERENCE. The remaining and larger portion of Nevada is in the CALIFORNIA-NEVADA CONFERENCE.

Since 1920 Nevada's population has grown, and Methodism's increase in the state has been proportionate. In 1968 about 2.5 per cent of Nevadans were members of The Methodist Church. Methodism has built new churches in the RENO-Lake Tahoe area, and in Las Vegas the denomination has been especially vigorous in expansion and building programs.

In 1970 The United Methodist Church had twenty-one pastoral appointments, 6,622 church members, and property valued at $4,906,795 in Nevada. The distribution of appointments, members, and property among the three conferences serving the state was as follows:

California-Nevada	13	2,842	$2,150,769
Rocky Mountain	1	254	95,576
Sou. Calif.-Ariz.	7	3,526	2,660,450

L. L. Loofbourow, *Steeples Among the Sage.* 1964.
Journals of the California-Nevada, Southern California-Arizona, and Rocky Mountain Conferences.
General Minutes, ME, TMC, UMC.   LEON L. LOOFBOUROW

NEW BEDFORD, MASSACHUSETTS, U.S.A., located fifty miles south of BOSTON on the west side of Buzzards Bay with a population (1970) of 101,262 has, since its founding in 1652, been known as one of the foremost Atlantic seaports. Its federal period whaling, well known through Herman Melville's *Moby Dick,* has given way to twentieth century diversified industries.

JESSE LEE preached there on Jan. 30, 1795, but a number of years elapsed before a strong Methodist society was formed. Originally attached to the Warren circuit in the state of RHODE ISLAND, a Methodist congregation with thirty members and Epaphras Kibby as pastor was founded in New Bedford in 1807. Fifty years later there were five congregations with 715 members and 509 Sunday school students. Today there are three churches in New Bedford; in order of present size they are: St. Paul's, Trinity, and Wesley. These churches have an aggregate of 1,214 members and 461 church school students (1970).

Encyclopedia Americana.
General Minutes, UMC, 1970.
M. Simpson, *Cyclopaedia.* 1878.   ERNEST R. CASE

NEW BERN, NORTH CAROLINA, U.S.A. The city of New Bern has long been a center of Methodist activity in the state of NORTH CAROLINA and its "Mother Church," CENTENARY, was cited in 1966 as the oldest Methodist Church in continuous service in the NORTH CAROLINA

CONFERENCE. The earliest mention of Methodism in New Bern is found in a 1760 letter from James Reed, Anglican missionary for the Society for the Propagation of the Gospel, who noted the great number of dissenters in his parish, among whom were some Methodists whom he described as "ignorant, censorious and uncharitable." Later, Reed recorded a visit by GEORGE WHITEFIELD to New Bern and quoted him as saying that the Methodists previously referred to were not "regular Methodists," as none were Methodists who did not follow either JOHN WESLEY or himself.

In the closing days of 1772, JOSEPH PILMORE, who was sent by John Wesley to the American colonies, preached in New Bern and observed: "In all my travels through the world I have met with none like the people of New Bern." Bishop FRANCIS ASBURY visited New Bern on several occasions, as recorded in his *Journal*: On earlier visits he was obliged to preach in the local Episcopal Church, but he noted in an entry on Feb. 20, 1804: "We moved a subscription to raise one thousand dollars to enlarge and finish the chapel; we have obtained six hundred dollars. Brother M'Caine preached, and there was something of a shout." LORENZO DOW visited New Bern in 1804.

The Methodist Society at New Bern was originally a part of the Carolina and Tar River Circuits of the VIRGINIA CONFERENCE. In 1786 the appointment was called "New Bern, New River and Wilmington." In 1796 the New Bern Society, including both whites and Negroes, consisted of some 100 members. The New Bern Methodists were organized into a congregation in 1802 and soon thereafter purchased a lot on the corner of what is now Hancock Street and Church Alley. The plain wooden structure was called "Andrew's Chapel." M. S. Bulchard was assigned to serve the charge prior to 1800, but there is no record of the New Bern station until the visit of Bishop Asbury in 1803 when he made plans for the establishment of a permanent church.

Following a twenty-day revival conducted by John Edwards, the membership of Andrew's Chapel grew so rapidly that a larger church building became necessary. In 1843-1844 a new church was constructed on the south side of New Street between Hancock and Metcalf Streets, and the name was changed to "Centenary." The third and present building, located on the corner of New and Middle Streets, was completed in 1904. Though an extensive fire on Sept. 15, 1935, destroyed much of the structure, it was soon rebuilt. The eight German stained glass windows in the sanctuary are valued at $30,000 each. The Centenary Church Sunday school became, in 1920, the first one in the North Carolina Conference of the M. E. Church, South, to be organized into departments so as to more adequately meet the needs of all ages. The John A. Russell Christian Education Building, named in honor of the minister who guided the building program and supervised its construction, is valued at nearly $200,000. It was completed in 1956; and ten years later a major renovation project for the church was undertaken.

When, in 1802, the M. E. Church was further divided into conferences, New Bern became the center of the New Bern District of the Virginia Conference; it is today the headquarters of the New Bern District of the North Carolina Conference of The United Methodist Church. The North Carolina Conference of the M. E. Church, organized in 1838, held its third session in New Bern in January 1840. Following the establishment of the North

Carolina Conference of the M. E. Church, South, its annual sessions were held in New Bern in 1846, 1858, 1888, 1900, 1907, 1921, 1936. The North Carolina Conference of The Methodist Church met in New Bern in 1957.

There are four Methodist churches in New Bern today: Centenary, Garber, Riverside and Trinity Churches. Trinity Church developed as a result of the establishment of the U.S. Marine Corps Air Station at Cherry Point near New Bern, and by the expansion of the city limits. It was chartered with forty-one members on Sept. 13, 1953. A cornerstone-laying service was held in September 1964, and the new sanctuary was first used on Feb. 14, 1965. Trinity Church has 512 members and a plant valued at $189,500. Garber Church was organized in November 1959. Its first unit was constructed in January 1961, and in 1970 it had a membership of 199. It was named in honor of Bishop PAUL N. GARBER. The Riverside Church has a membership of 441. The Centenary Church has a membership of 1,376.

Grady L. E. Carroll. *Francis Asbury in North Carolina*. Nashville: 1964.
George H. Jones. *The Methodist Tourist Guidebook*. Nashville: Tidings, 1960.
Journal of the North Carolina Annual Conference, 1967.
Eleanor Marshall Nelson and W. R. Stevens. *Centenary Methodist Church*. 1964.   RALPH HARDEE RIVES

NEW CASTLE, PENNSYLVANIA, U.S.A., located forty-three miles southwest of PITTSBURGH at the point where the Shenango and Mohoning Rivers meet to form the Beaver, has a population (1970) of 38,457. The community, settled in 1798, is situated in an area of abundant natural resources—coal and limestone.

Although the first Methodist meetings were held four miles north of the city by exhorter William Richard in 1804, services during the same year were also held in the city itself. James Watts in 1810 brought together a class of ten persons. Five years later the first structure, a log building, to house a Methodist congregation in New Castle was erected; the following year, 1821, New Castle appears in the Minutes of the Church as a distinct appointment with S. R. Brockunier as pastor. In 1836 a frame building replaced the log structure; later a brick building was constructed.

Another Methodist society was organized in 1847 with a building erected in 1850. Thereafter, Methodism continued to grow. According to the *General Minutes* of 1970 there are eight Methodist churches in New Castle with a total membership of 3,223 persons, and a total church school enrollment of 1,637 students.

Encyclopedia Americana.
General Minutes, UMC, 1970.
M. Simpson, *Cyclopaedia*. 1878.   ERNEST R. CASE

NEW CONGREGATIONAL METHODIST CHURCH was formed in 1881 by members of the Waresboro Mission and others involved in a rural church consolidation enforced by the Board of Domestic Missions of the GEORGIA CONFERENCE of the M. E. CHURCH, SOUTH. In protest of the consolidation, the group withdrew and formed the new body at Waycross, Ga., using the Constitution of the CONGREGATIONAL METHODIST CHURCH as their model. They adopted a loosely connectional system, rejecting particularly the system of annual conference assessments.

They also baptized by immersion and allowed foot washing at communion.

An early growth was stopped by the death of several leaders and the withdrawal of a number of congregations who joined the Congregational Methodist Church. At the present time, they have thirteen congregations, seven in GEORGIA and six in FLORIDA. They have no connections with any ecumenical bodies.

J. GORDON MELTON

NEW ENGLAND CONFERENCE originally included all of the New England states and a portion of CANADA. It was one of the six original conferences with definite boundaries created by the 1796 GENERAL CONFERENCE. The first session of the New England Conference was held at WILBRAHAM, Mass., Sept. 19, 1797.

As time passed other conferences were carved out of New England Conference territory as follows: the NEW YORK CONFERENCE in 1800, the MAINE CONFERENCE in 1825, the NEW HAMPSHIRE and VERMONT Conference in 1830, and the PROVIDENCE CONFERENCE in 1840. The setting off of these conferences finally reduced the New England Conference to those sections of MASSACHUSETTS surrounding the district centers of Springfield, Worcester, Lynn, and BOSTON. In 1962, however, the churches in extreme western Massachusess which had been linked with the TROY CONFERENCE and the New York Conference were returned to the New England Conference.

Though reduced in size geographically as time passed, the influence and service of the New England Conference increased. Between 1830 and 1840 some 150 men were received on trial in the conference. WILBRAHAM ACADEMY, WESLEYAN UNIVERSITY, and the Methodist Biblical Institute (forerunner of BOSTON UNIVERSITY) came into being before 1840. At Tremont Street Church, Boston, the WOMEN'S FOREIGN MISSIONARY SOCIETY was organized in 1869. In 1913 there were thirty-eight deaconesses working in Boston. These women organized associations that brought into being the New England Deaconess Hospital and the retirement homes at Concord and Magnolia. Within the New England Conference the GOODWILL INDUSTRIES which now encircle the globe were organized in 1912.

Urbanization and changes in population and transportation have altered the structure and strategy of the twentieth century New England Conference. Between 1900 and 1960 only three new Methodist churches were organized within the conference, while in the same period forty-three churches were closed, sixteen of them in Boston. However, fourteen federated parishes came into being and twenty-four merged congregations formed "new" churches. Corporate ministries, inner city work in Springfield and Boston, as well as an ad hoc Boston Metropolitan Methodist Planning Commission, are seeking to grapple with contemporary problems.

The New England Conference Commission on Archives and History is one of the strongest in the denomination. In cooperation with the BOSTON UNIVERSITY SCHOOL OF THEOLOGY Library, it maintains a good collection on Methodist history.

In 1970 the New England Conference had 201 charges, 289 ministers, 31,247 Church school pupils, 71,643 church members, and property valued at $60,093,539.

In 1970 the New England Conference and the NEW ENGLAND SOUTHERN CONFERENCE merged to form the Southern New England Conference.

General Minutes, ME, UMC.
Minutes of the New England Conference.
J. Mudge, *New England Conference.* 1910.   ERNEST R. CASE

NEW ENGLAND SOUTHERN CONFERENCE was organized at Fall River, Mass., April 13, 1881 with Bishop JESSE T. PECK presiding. It superseded the PROVIDENCE CONFERENCE in accordance with an enabling act adopted by the 1880 GENERAL CONFERENCE permitting that conference to change its name. The territory of the New England Southern Conference was the part of CONNECTICUT lying east of the Connecticut River, RHODE ISLAND, and southeastern MASSACHUSETTS. In 1881 the conference reported three districts, Providence, Providence North, and New Bedford. There were 186 charges and 22,564 members. The conference came to unification in 1939 with three districts, 172 charges and 34,374 members.

Among the earliest churches organized within the bounds of what came to be the New England Southern Conference were: Tolland, Thompson, Manchester, and New London in Connecticut; Acushnet, Scituate, Somerset, and Truro in Massachusetts; and East Greenwich and Portsmouth in Rhode Island. The first Methodist society in Rhode Island was organized at Warren in 1791. The first session of an annual conference in the region, and indeed in all New England, was held at Tolland, Conn. in 1793. The first Methodist parsonage in Connecticut, and possibly the first in New England, was built at Square Pond (now Crystal Lake) in 1795. During the celebration of the BICENTENNIAL OF AMERICAN METHODISM in 1966, plans were projected for restoring the old parsonage. One of the first CAMP MEETINGS in New England was conducted at Square Pond in 1806. Other camp meetings were held at different times in Willimantic, Yarmouth, and Oak Bluffs on MARTHA'S VINEYARD.

During its history the New England Southern Conference developed service institutions. Deaconesses began work among needy children in Fall River, Mass., in 1893, and about the same time a home for working girls was established in Providence. Fleidner Hall, a boarding home for young women, was built in Pawtucket in 1911. A home for the aged was projected in East Providence in 1966. East Greenwich Academy (see RHODE ISLAND) was maintained by the conference. In 1945 Camp Aldersgate was established on a one hundred-acre tract at Glocester, Rhode Island. An administrative office for the conference was set up in Providence in 1956.

In 1970 the New England Southern Conference reported three districts, Connecticut, New Bedford, and Providence. There were 114 charges, 159 ministers, 147 congregations, 35,097 church members, 17,035 Church school pupils, and property valued at $29,734,075.

In 1970 the New England Southern Conference and the NEW ENGLAND CONFERENCE merged to form the Southern New England Conference.

Camp Aldersgate, Scituate, Mass., is a camp originally owned by the New England Southern Conference of The Methodist Church. Purchased from Grace Protestant Episcopal Church of Providence, R. I., in 1944 for $13,000, it consisted of 100 acres of land, containing houses and an artificial, spring-fed lake covering seventeen acres of the land. In addition to its use as a children's camp, youth institutes and assemblies were held during the early years.

Sponsored by both the New England Southern and the New England Conferences and directed by the executive secretary of the Boards of Education of both Conferences, the program moved from an emphasis upon institute and assembly programs, to a stress on the significance of outdoor camping and small-group living as a means for Christian nurture. Camp Aldersgate is presently used for a twelve-week summer camping program designed for whole families, children, junior high and high school youth. By purchase or legacy, the camp now owns more than 250 acres of woodland. It is now under the reorganized New England Conference of The United Methodist church.

General Minutes, ME, UMC.
Minutes of the New England Southern Conference.
Howard E. Tower, *Brief History of Camp Aldersgate.* 1965.

DAVID CARTER
MABEL E. WARING

NEW GUINEA is, next to AUSTRALIA itself, the largest island in the Southern Hemisphere. The western half, West Irian, now controlled by INDONESIA, is not the responsibility of Australian Methodism. The eastern half is divided into two sections although these are controlled jointly by Australia.

In this eastern half the northern section was German territory from 1884 to 1914 and is now an Australian Trust Territory. The southern section has been a direct Australian Government responsibility since 1884; it is this section which is called Papua.

The islands of New Britain, NEW ZEALAND, and smaller islands to the east of the mainland of New Guinea are part of the Trust Territory of New Guinea.

These regions comprise people of many types, mainly Melanesian, with about 500 different languages. For the organization of the work in these islands into one administrative body see UNITED CHURCH OF PAPUA, NEW GUINEA AND THE SOLOMON ISLANDS.

Highlands Challenge: Nov. 28, 1950 was the official opening of the first mission station in the New Guinea Highlands. In a completely new, unevangelized area, the Methodist Church of Australasia is at work among people whose existence was unknown to the world before World War II. Estimates of their numbers vary up to one million people. Mendi was the first area chosen for the pioneer missionaries and because of the aggressive nature of the inhabitants, no women were allowed to accompany them for the first twelve months. The great barrier proved to be language and many varied dialects were identified.

It was eleven years before the first conversions and baptisms were recorded but since then, the gospel has spread vigorously through the villages. New circuits at Tari and Nipa have been opened. Native pastors and local preaches have been trained and are transported by helicopter, over the mountains, to speak to their own people in nearby valleys. Churches, schools, hospitals have been established and agricultural guidance given to these primitive people. Language translation work, both for school books and scriptures, is being undertaken. Maternal and infant welfare work and the Hansenide Centre established at Tari have been received gratefully by the people in this newest twentieth century mission.

Malmaluan Youth Training Centre, established in 1964 was constructed by a work party of voluntary assistants from Australia in 1963. It provides one Long Course per year for up to sixty students from all denominations in the Territory desiring to participate. In addition, Short Courses, Student Conferences, Weekend and Weeklong Conferences are conducted for up to 300 students. Courses are provided in Christian Education for all ages, Youth Leadership, Group Dynamics and Community Development from the Christian View. Guest lecturers from overseas are invited.

Malmaluan is the first lay or youth leadership center in New Guinea with a full-time director, the Rev. John Mavor, and two lay assistants. It serves the whole of Papua, New Guinea and the Solomon Islands. During each year, thousands gather at the center for its special services, at Easter, Pentecost, etc.

The director also travels around the islands for a part of each year, conducting regional courses in all fields of Christian Education. Malmaluan (a New Guinea name meaning "Deep Peace") Training Centre is a liaison point between parent churches of Australia and New Zealand and the younger Pacific Churches.

Missionary Martyrs: The heaviest blow received to the work of the Australian Methodist Overseas Missions came when ten of their finest missionaries, including eight ministers, were killed in 1942. As prisoners of war they were herded together on a Japanese freighter which was sunk by an allied submarine.

They had been stationed together in New Britain, but as the enemy thrust came further south towards Australia and the territory, the danger drew nearer and all women and children from the missionary homes throughout New Guinea were recalled home. However, the men chose to remain with the people they were serving and were consequently trapped by the Japanese advance to disappear into prisoner of war camps. For three years there was complete silence about their fate. Only after the cessation of hostilities were the facts learned concerning one Sunday in June 1942, when they were crowded with hundreds of soldiers and civilians on to the "Montevideo Maru" to be transferred to a prison camp in JAPAN. Some time between June 22 and July 1, the vessel was torpedoed off the coast of Luzon in the PHILIPPINES. There were no survivors. When the news reached Australia in 1945, a Service of Remembrance was held in Wesley Chapel, SYDNEY and at this service, four of the wives of the men killed, announced their intention of going back to New Guinea as soon as possible.

The names of those who perished were: L. A. Macarthur, W. L. I. Lingood, W. D. Oakes, H. J. Pearson, J. W. Poole, H. B. Shelton, T. N. Simpson, J. Trevitt, S. C. Beazley, and E. W. Pearse.

G. Brown, *Autobiography.* 1908.
J. W. Burton, *Call of the Pacific.* 1912.
Benjamin Danks, *In Wild New Britain.* 1933.

A. HAROLD WOOD

NEW HAMPSHIRE, a New England state and one of the original thirteen colonies, was named after Hampshire, England. Called the "granite state," New Hampshire has 182 mountains over 3,000 feet high, including Mt. Washington (6,288 feet), the highest mountain in the northeast. New Hampshire ratified the constitution of the United States on June 21, 1788, being the ninth and deciding state to do so. Forty-fourth among the states in size, New Hampshire has 9,304 square miles, about eighty-four per cent of it covered by forests.

Among the early explorers who visited New Hampshire

were Martin Pring (1603), Samuel de Champlain (1605), and Captain John Smith (1614). In 1641-79, 1689-92, and 1699-1741, New Hampshire was joined to the MASSACHUSSETTS Colony, but during the intervening years and until 1775, it was under royal governors. A provisional government was formed in 1776 and a state constitution was adopted in 1784.

The earliest authenticated Methodist service in New Hampshire was held at the home of James Robertson in Chesterfield in 1772. At the request of Robertson, PHILIP EMBURY preached on that occasion. In the next eighteen years there were were numerous unsuccessful attempts to establish Methodism in New Hampshire. Then in 1790, JESSE LEE was appointed to New England. On his first trip to BOSTON in that year, Lee went as far north as Portsmouth, N. H. In the following year he visited the state again and wrote, "We had a meeting in a private house. At Mr. Lindsay's request I preached on Psalm 1:6. I found it to be a time of much life and love and some of the people appeared to be much affected. When the service was ended some of the people blessed God for our meeting; all seemed friendly." In 1794 Lee became presiding elder in New England, and John Hill was appointed to New Hampshire under him.

Presumably John Hill gave attention to Chesterfield, because it had sixty-eight members in 1796 and the Chesterfield Circuit was formed that year. Lee wrote of Chesterfield, "It lay in the southwest corner of the State, near the Connecticut River. . . . The first society formed in the State was in Chesterfield, some time in 1795, at which time there were but a few that felt the freedom to unite with us. After some time a few more cast in their lots, and other societies were soon formed in other places. The circuit was entered upon the annual minutes in the year 1796. Some time after this there was a circuit formed higher up in the State called Landaff, and in that place religion prospered very much." The records confirm Lee's statement. By 1799 CHESTERFIELD had 131 members.

In 1804 the New Hampshire District was formed, and JOHN BRODHEAD was appointed presiding elder. In 1809 when MARTIN RUTER was appointed to succeed Brodhead, there were 1,673 members in New Hampshire.

The New Hampshire and Vermont Conference (NEW HAMPSHIRE CONFERENCE after 1831) was organized on June 19, 1829 at Portsmouth. The next year the conference reported 11,757 members, of whom 7,750 were in New Hampshire. In 1844, the New Hampshire Conference was divided to form the Vermont Conference.

The first Methodist seminary (secondary school) in New England was located in that part of Newmarket which is now Newfields, opening on Sept. 1, 1817. Newmarket was the first *permanent* educational institution founded by the Methodists in America. Soon a branch of the academy was located in Kingston, but because of continual financial deficits, it was transferred to WILBRAHAM, Mass., and in that location it was the beginning of Methodism's Wilbraham Academy. Another Methodist academy was started at Franklin, but soon afterward it was merged with the seminary at Tilton. The first meeting of the board of trustees of the TILTON SCHOOL was held in May, 1845. The institution was chartered by the General Court in 1852. Supported by the New Hampshire Conference, the Tilton School continues to serve as a junior college. It dedicated a new chapel in 1966. The Wesleyan Biblical Institute was started in Newbury, Vt., and was relocated in Concord, N. H. in 1847 and was incorporated

as the Methodist General Biblical Institute. In 1868 it was moved to Boston where it later became the School of Theology of BOSTON UNIVERSITY.

New Hampshire Methodism has furnished two men for the episcopacy, OSMON C. BAKER and EDGAR BLAKE. Many of its ministers have served as chaplains in the armed service of the nation, in hospitals, homes, the state legislature, and state prisons, and as campus ministers and missionaries abroad and at home. In 1967, several were serving in Africa, JAPAN, and MALAYA.

Since 1844 the boundaries of the New Hampshire Conference have changed little. Today it includes all of the churches in New Hampshire, ten in Massachusetts, and one in Vermont. In 1968, it had two districts, 97 ministers, and 19,272 members.

Cole and Baketel, *New Hampshire Conference*. 1929.
Journals of the New Hampshire and New England Conferences.
M. Simpson, *Cyclopaedia*. 1878.   G. BENNETT VAN BUSKIRK
WILLIAM J. DAVIS

NEW HAMPSHIRE CONFERENCE began as the New Hamshire and Vermont Conference in 1829. In 1831 it was incorporated by the state legislature as the New Hampshire Conference. Formed by dividing the NEW ENGLAND CONFERENCE, the New Hampshire and Vermont Conference was organized on June 19, 1829 at Portsmouth during the regular session of the parent conference, Bishop ELIJAH HEDDING presiding.

As one of the original conferences, the New England body dates from 1796. At the beginning it included the state of NEW YORK. In 1800 the New England Conference was divided to form the NEW YORK CONFERENCE, and at the outset the latter body included all of CONNECTICUT and parts of MASSACHUSETTS, NEW HAMPSHIRE, and VERMONT. In 1804 New Hampshire and Vermont were placed in the New England Conference where they remained until the formation of the New Hampshire and Vermont Conference in 1829.

The first session of the New Hampshire and Vermont Conference following organization was held at Barre, Vt., in June, 1830. Becoming the New Hampshire Conference in 1831, the body met alternately in New Hampshire and Vermont until 1844 when it was divided to form the Vermont Conference.

The first authenticated Methodist preaching service in New Hampshire was held at CHESTERFIELD in the home of James Robertson who had come from SCOTLAND in 1762. At his request PHILIP EMBURY came and preached in his house in 1772 and organized a class of five members. The religious zeal of those members gave the road through the town the name of "Christian Street" which it still bears. JESSE LEE preached in Chesterfield in 1793, and on June 20, 1803, Bishop ASBURY came and delivered a sermon in Robertson's house. In 1796 Chesterfield had sixty-eight members, and at the conference that year Philip Wager was appointed to the Chesterfield Circuit.

At its session in 1830, the New Hampshire and Vermont Conference had three districts, forty-two ministers, fifty-four appointments, and 11,757 members, some 7,750 of them in New Hampshire. In 1845, the year following the formation of the Vermont Conference, the New Hampshire Conference had 10,621 members.

There have been few changes in the boundaries of the New Hampshire Conference since the Vermont Conference was set off from it in 1844. The conference now includes all of the churches in New Hampshire, ten in Massachusetts, and one in Vermont.

In 1970, the New Hampshire Conference had two districts—Northern and Southern—ninety-seven ministers, seventy pastoral charges, 19,272 church members, and churches, parsonages and other property valued at $12,405,347.

Cole and Baketel, *New Hampshire Conference*. 1929.
Journals of the New Hampshire and New England Conferences.
M. Simpson, Cyclopaedia. 1878. G. BENNETT VAN BUSKIRK
WILLIAM J. DAVIS

NEW HAVEN, CONNECTICUT, U.S.A., population 133,-543 (1970), is situated at the mouths of the Quinnipiac, Mill and West Rivers, and at the head of New Haven Harbor. The city was settled on April 10, 1638, by immigrant Puritans. It is the seat of Yale University and has over 1,000 large and small manufacturing concerns. Industrial development was begun on a large scale in 1798 when Eli Whitney, inventor of the cotton gin, returned from GEORGIA and started a gun factory.

JESSE LEE visited New Haven and preached the first Methodist sermon on June 21, 1789, in the court house. The president of Yale and many students were present. Lee returned on July 5, 1789 and was allowed to preach in the Congregational Church. "Some told me they were much pleased with the discourse," he said, "but no man asked me home with him." However, a gentleman later came to Lee's hotel and invited him to his home.

In 1790 New Haven Circuit was formed and extended from Milford to Hartford. John Lee was the first pastor and formed a class of nine people. The city was connected with surrounding churches until 1814 when it became a station. In 1800 a house was bought and used until 1807 when a building was erected on Temple Street. In 1820 a larger building was erected on the public green, and in 1848 the church moved to its present location on the corner of Elm and College Streets.

Congregationalism had a strong foothold in New Haven, and it was difficult for Methodism to grow. However, East Pearl Street Church was established in 1833 and St. Andrews in 1883. In 1954 Grace merged with the Howard Avenue Church to form Wesley; and Summerfield and Hope were put on a two point charge in 1965. Park Church remained a station church.

After the War between the States, immigration increased from the Roman Catholic countries of Europe, and all Protestant groups were vastly outnumbered in New Haven. Moreover, there has been the tendency as the city becomes more industrialized, for the older settled families to move to the suburbs and affiliate with churches there. However, the Negro migration from the South to the Northern cities has greatly increased the membership of the Negro branches of Methodism. Several old Negro Methodist churches are located in New Haven. Varick A.M.E. ZION was begun in 1818. Bethel A.M.E. CHURCH was begun in 1837, and St. Paul's U.A.M.E. Church was established in 1849. Evers A.M.E. Zion Church has flourished, and Scott Tabernacle was organized in 1965.

Encyclopedia Americana.
M. Simpson, *Cyclopaedia*. 1878. DONALD J. WEST

NEW JERSEY, one of the thirteen original states, is located between PHILADELPHIA and NEW YORK, two im-

portant population and business centers times. With 7,836 square miles and a 7,084,992 (1970 census), the state rank size and eighth in population. New Jersey the Dutch early in the seventeenth centu the scene of much action in the Americ The state has vast shipping facilities, and concentration of factories, highways, railro It ranks first in the value of chemical pr a leader in many other fields. Princeton an outstanding universities.

New Jersey has been identified with Meth beginning in America. In 1739-40 GEORG preached in ten places in New Jersey and Island, New York, which was long associa Jersey Methodism. JOHN EARLY, a lay pre from IRELAND in 1764 and settled at Pen Wrightstown). After Whitefield, Early was odist preacher in New Jersey. John and W gave a tract of land to the Methodists at 1761, and there, though the exact date is n of the earliest Methodist meetinghouses was first edifice was replaced by a larger FRANCIS ASBURY preached at Penny Hill in and 1795.

Captain THOMAS WEBB organized the fi class or society in New Jersey. He went fr to Philadelphia in 1767 or 1768 and prea Mills, Trenton, and Burlington en route. visited those places several times, and he f at Burlington in 1770 with JOSEPH TOY, his as the leader. It is believed that Webb org at New Mills and Trenton about the same PILMORE and RICHARD BOARDMAN, who c WESLEY's first official missionaries to Ame traveled extensively across New Jersey.

Asbury made eighty-six recorded tours of and he and his compeers developed scores societies. Asbury preached first at Burlingto 1771, a few days after his arrival in Ameri crossed the province to Staten Island, N. Y. Amboy ferry and preached at Peter Van P November 9 and 10, his first sermons in th New York. In the early years New Jersey M heard JESSE LEE, RICHARD WHATCOAT, W KENDREE, EZEKIEL COOPER and scores of ot

THOMAS RANKIN conducted the first M ference in America at Philadelphia in July 1,160 Methodist members in America at t were in New Jersey. At that conference ten assigned to six circuits, one of the circui Jersey and Staten Island. From 1781 to 17 two circuits in New Jersey—West Jersey a Trenton was added as a circuit in 1786. were 2,439 Methodists in the state. The Phi ference dates from 1788, and New Jersey in that conference. A presiding elder and fi were assigned to the New Jersey Distric 1803 the Jersey District reported eight fifteen preachers, and 4,463 members. In Jersey and West Jersey Districts reported members with twenty-four preachers assi appointments. In 1829 the East Jersey, W Asbury Districts, representing the entire sta three appointments, fifty-one preachers, an o bers.

In 1836 the New Jersey Conference was formed by dividing the PHILADELPHIA CONFERENCE. At the time the new conference included New Jersey, Staten Island, and some adjacent New York and Pennsylvania territory. The 1856 GENERAL CONFERENCE created the NEWARK CONFERENCE by dividing the New Jersey Conference. At the beginning the Newark Conference included the northern part of New Jersey, Staten Island, and parts of Pennsylvania and New York. With some changes in boundaries these conferences have continued, but in 1965 their names were changed to SOUTHERN NEW JERSEY and NORTHERN NEW JERSEY.

The METHODIST PROTESTANT CHURCH had work in New Jersey. At the beginning in 1830, Methodist Protestantism in New Jersey was divided between the New York and Pennsylvania Conferences of the denomination. In 1838 the General Conference designated the part of New Jersey that had been attached to Pennsylvania as the New Jersey Conference, but the journals of the New Jersey Conference say it was not organized until 1841. Apparently all of Methodist Protestantism in New Jersey considered itself a part of the New York Conference from 1838 to 1841. In 1877 the New Jersey Conference reported twenty-one preachers and 2,121 members. This conference continued until October 1912, when it was merged with the Eastern Conference. At the time of the merger the New Jersey Conference had thirty-six preachers, thirty-six charges, and 4,284 members. The New Jersey part of the Eastern Conference merged with the Newark and New Jersey Conferences of The Methodist Church at unification in 1939.

The A.M.E., A.M.E. ZION, and C.M.E. CHURCHES have work in New Jersey. The first is represented by two annual conferences, New Jersey and South Jersey; the second has a New Jersey Conference, while the New Jersey work of the third is a part of its New York-Washington Conference.

New Jersey Methodism has contributed leaders to the church. THOMAS WARE, THOMAS MORRELL, and JEREMIAH LAMBERT stood out in the early days. Six men have been elected bishops while serving as members of the Newark Conference: ISAAC W. WILEY (1872), JOHN F. HURST (1880), JAMES N. FITZGERALD (1888), HENRY SPELLMEYER (1904), JOHN WESLEY LORD (1948), and FRED G. HOLLOWAY (1960). Six bishops served part of their ministry in New Jersey, but were conference members elsewhere when elected: EDMUND S. JANES (1844), JOHN H. VINCENT (1888), CHARLES B. MITCHELL (1916), CHARLES L. MEAD (1920), W. EARL LEDDEN (1944), and LLOYD C. WICKE (1948). Two bishops were born in New Jersey, but served no part of their ministry there prior to their election: THEODORE H. HENDERSON (1912), and FRED P. CORSON (1944). One could compile a long list of prominent preachers and leading laymen who have served Methodism in New Jersey.

In 1840 the New Jersey Conference appointed a visiting committee to the Methodist Episcopal Male Seminary, now PENNINGTON SCHOOL, at Pennington. In the same year the conference agreed to pay $500 to DICKINSON COLLEGE from the conference education fund, and requested each preacher to raise $5 during the year to reimburse the fund. CENTENARY (junior) COLLEGE FOR WOMEN was established at Hackettstown in 1867. DREW THEOLOGICAL SEMINARY began in 1866.

Today there are Methodist Homes for the Aged at OCEAN GROVE, Ocean City, Branchville, and Collingswood, as well as the Bancroft-Taylor Rest Home at Ocean Grove for deaconesses and missionaries, and another Deaconess Home at Camden. Also, in New Jersey are the famous religious resort at Ocean Grove and the Pitman Grove Camp Meeting in Gloucester County not far from Philadelphia.

The ratio of the total membership of the two New Jersey Conferences to the population of the state in 1810, 1840, and 1967 is shown in the table below. Percentagewise 1840 was the peak year. The reader will remember that in the early years parts of Pennsylvania and New York were in the New Jersey Conference and that a small portion of New York is still attached to the NORTHERN NEW JERSEY CONFERENCE.

Year	Total Membership of N.J. Conferences	New Jersey Population	Methodist Percentage
1810	6,839	245,562	2.8
1840	23,275	373,306	6.2
1967	204,853	7,004,000 (est.)	2.9

In 1970 the two New Jersey Conferences reported eight districts, 538 charges, about 654 ministers, 197,693 members, property valued at $158,654,875, and a total of $13,947,895 raised for all purposes during the year.

General Minutes, ME, UMC.
V. B. Hampton, *Newark Conference.* 1957.
Minutes of the New Jersey Conference.
F. B. Stanger, *New Jersey.* 1961.   VERNON B. HAMPTON

NEW JERSEY CONFERENCE. (See SOUTHERN NEW JERSEY CONFERENCE.)

NEW LONDON, CONNECTICUT, U.S.A. JESSE LEE preached at the Court House at New London on Sept. 2, 1789, as he was making his first visit to the towns along the shores of Southern New England. Bishop ASBURY followed him in 1791. In 1793, a circuit was formed, including Windham, Hebron, Glastonbury, Lyme, and into Rhode Island, with GEORGE ROBERTS the first presiding elder. Organizing as a church in 1793, the people held services in the Court House at the head of the main street. The first church building was erected in 1798 with both Jesse Lee and Francis Asbury present. This was the church home of Epaphras Kibby, who served sixty-seven years in the ministry. Bishop Asbury held Annual Conference here on July 5, 1795 with nineteen preachers present. On April 17, 1808 Conference assembled here for the second time with fifty preachers present, and held ordination services in the Congregational Church. The second church building was dedicated in 1817. Bishop Asbury wrote his last will and testament at New London in 1813, which contains the words "I will give it all to the Book Concern." In 1840 many members withdrew to organize a WESLEYAN METHODIST CHURCH, but they were granted the use of the same church building. However, in 1842, a new church building was erected by the remaining Methodists. In 1925 a new church building was constructed. A WESLEY FOUNDATION for students at nearby colleges, and for servicemen at the U.S. Coast Guard Academy and U.S. Submarine Base, is an important part of the life of this church.

R. C. Miller, *New England Southern Conference.* 1898.
New London Telegram, Oct. 30, 1893.   DAVID CARTER

NEW MADRID, MISSOURI, U.S.A., the site of the oldest active Methodist church in the United States west of the Mississippi River, was first known as an Indian settlement in 1786. Twelve white men joined the Indians in 1787. The settlers were mostly Frenchmen but the territory was Spanish and in 1788 a grant was secured from Spain, and then about sixty others joined the inhabitants and the New Madrid name was adopted from the Spanish capital. The area passed into French hands and the name became Louisiana and New Madrid was the capital. It was Roman Catholic by law.

In March, 1810, after the Louisiana Purchase, JESSE WALKER and JOHN SCRIPPS crossed the Big Swamp and formed a Methodist Society as a part of the CAPE GIRARDEAU Circuit. Two years later it became a circuit under its own name and since that date has never lost its identity. The church today is small but loyal and devoted.

The town was the center of the New Madrid earthquake of 1811-1812, one of the worst recorded and the greatest ever known on the American continent. It was felt over an area of 60,000 square miles, sank 6,000 square miles from three to nine feet, changed the course of the Mississippi River, damaged houses in Cincinnati, Ohio, 400 miles away, and formed Reelfoot Lake in Tennessee.

Elmer T. Clark, *One Hundred Years of New Madrid Methodism.* New Madrid: the author, 1912.
Louis Houck, *A History of Missouri. . . .* 3 vols. Cape Girardeau, Mo.: the author, 1908.   ELMER T. CLARK

NEW MEXICO (population 998,257 in 1970), is one of the mountain group states. It is west of TEXAS and north of MEXICO, and it is a part of the land ceded by Mexico in 1848. SANTA FE is its capital, so designated by the Spanish governor de Peralta in 1610. The state was under SPAIN until 1821, then under Mexico until the war of 1846. Many citizens are of Spanish-Mexican descent. Among the non-Spanish Americans are certain Indian tribes. Large areas of New Mexico's 121,666 square miles have been made fertile by irrigation with dams and reservoirs on the Rio Grande, Pecos, Canadian, and other rivers. The climate is dry and invigorating. ALBUQUERQUE, the location of the state university, is the largest city. New Mexico, including what is now ARIZONA until 1863, became a territory in 1850, and it was admitted as a state in 1912. Among its products are uranium, oil, potash, copper, lead, and gold. The Federal government's nuclear and space research projects at Los Alamos, White Sands, and Albuquerque have contributed greatly to the state's growth since 1945.

Both the M.E. Church and the M.E. Church, South pushed into New Mexico with mission work after it became a territory. In 1876 the Northern Church organized the New Mexico Mission, and in 1881 the DENVER CONFERENCE (MES) organized a New Mexico District with eight charges.

The New Mexico Mission (ME) had a checkered history. It began with sixteen charges and 319 members. In 1885 it was divided to form the New Mexico Mission and the New Mexico Spanish Mission. The latter became the New Mexico Spanish Mission Conference in 1892. In 1915 the New Mexico English Mission and the New Mexico Spanish Mission Conference were merged to form the NEW MEXICO CONFERENCE. In 1928 the conference became again the New Mexico Mission which merged at

unification in 1939. When the New Mexico Conference (ME) was formed in 1915 it had fifty-four charges and 4,073 members. In 1939 the New Mexico Mission brought twenty-four charges and 5,630 members into the New Mexico Conference of The Methodist Church.

The M.E. Church, South organized the New Mexico Conference in 1890. In 1893 it reported seventeen charges and 868 members. In 1915 there were fifty-one charges and 8,128 members. Thereafter the conference grew rapidly, coming to unification in 1939 with 24,253 members.

THOMAS M. HARWOOD established a school for boys in Albuquerque in 1887 with the aim of preparing Mexican youths for ministering to Spanish-speaking people. The school continued until 1931. Also, in 1887 the WOMAN'S HOME MISSIONARY SOCIETY (ME) established the Harwood School for Girls in Albuquerque, and in 1891 the society projected the NAVAJO METHODIST MISSION School at Farmington. Both institutions are still operating. The same society started the Houchen Settlement House in 1893, the Freeman Clinic in 1920, and the Newark Methodist Hospital in 1921, all of them in EL PASO, Texas. In 1911 the society established a sanitorium in Albuquerque which in 1952 became the Bataan Memorial Methodist Hospital. On October 31, the hospital was transferred to the Lovelace Foundation for Medical Research. The M.E. Church, South established LYDIA PATTERSON INSTITUTE at El Paso in 1914 to educate Mexican young people fleeing to the United States during the revolution in their country. Receiving strong support from the South Central JURISDICTION, the institute continues its ministry to Spanish-speaking students.

The New Mexico Mission (ME) and the New Mexico Conference (MES) merged at unification in 1939 to form the New Mexico Conference (TMC). New Mexico Methodism grew rapidly with the state after the second World War. In 1944 The Methodist Church had approximately 16,000 members in the state of New Mexico. In 1968 the number of members was about 62,000.

General Minutes, ME, MES, TMC.
T. Harwood, *New Mexico.* 1908, 1910.
Minutes of the New Mexico missions and conferences.
IRA E. WILLIAMS, JR.

NEW MEXICO CONFERENCE was organized at EL PASO, Texas, Oct. 20, 1939 with Bishop IVAN LEE HOLT presiding. The conference was formed by merging the New Mexico Mission of the M.E. Church which began in 1880, and the New Mexico Conference of the M.E. Church, South which was organized in 1890. The territory of the conference includes the state of NEW MEXICO and extreme west TEXAS through the counties of Winkler, Ector, Crane, Pecos, Terrell, and Val Verde (part). Prior to unification the New Mexico Conference (MES) included twelve charges in Colorado with some 2,600 members. These churches with their pastors were transferred to the COLORADO CONFERENCE (TMC) in 1939. When organized, the New Mexico Conference of The Methodist Church had four districts, Albuquerque, Clovis, El Paso, and Roswell. In 1941 there were eighty-nine charges and 25,464 members. (See New Mexico for beginning of Methodism in the state and for accounts of the New Mexico Mission (ME) and the New Mexico Conference (MES).)

The New Mexico Conference was in the DALLAS Area, 1939-44, and in the OKLAHOMA CITY Area, 1944-68. In

1968 the conference became a part of the Northwest Texas-New Mexico Area with the episcopal residence in ALBUQUERQUE. While in the Oklahoma City Area the conference was under the supervision of Bishop W. ANGIE SMITH.

During and following the second world war, the Federal government built nuclear and space research and testing plants and facilities at Los Alamos, White Sands, Holloman, Kirtland, and Sandia in New Mexico. These developments greatly accelerated the growth of the state's economy and its population. The 1940 population was 532,000; it had grown to 998,257 in 1970. The Methodist Church grew even more rapidly than the population in this period. Between 1944 and 1968 the number of preaching places in the New Mexico Conference rose from 121 to 152, the pension annuity rate from $16 to $72, contributions to world service and conference benevolences from $44,305 to $216,184, property value from $1,858,358 to $25,149,761, and church membership from 25,815 to 92,932.

The New Mexico Conference supports a number of institutions. Fifteen of its ministers and laymen serve as trustees of McMURRY COLLEGE at Abilene. Along with Texas Methodism the conference contributes to the Methodist Children's Home at Waco. Methodist institutions in El Paso are LYDIA PATTERSON INSTITUTE, Newark Methodist Hospital, and Houchen Community Center. Bataan Memorial Methodist Hospital and the Harwood School for Girls are in Albuquerque. The NAVAJO METHODIST MISSION SCHOOL is at Farmington and the Landsun Manor (for the aged) at Carlsbad. The conference supports eight Wesley Foundations within its bounds, maintaining full time directors at five of them. Conference camps are maintained at Sacramento and Glorieta. The conference established the *New Mexico Methodist* in 1966, placing upon its board of education the responsibility for publishing and promoting the paper.

In 1970 the New Mexico Conference reported four districts, Albuquerque, Carlsbad, Clovis, and El Paso. It had 166 ministers, 122 charges, 81,446 members, and property valued at $31,537,795.

N. B. H.

NEW ORLEANS, LOUISIANA, U.S.A. In 1718 New Orleans was founded by the French explorer Bienville, and the first efforts at teaching in this community were carried on by the Ursuline nuns for girls and a priest for boys. When the city was deeded to SPAIN in 1763, its exclusiveness towards Roman Catholicism was intensified. With the LOUSIAINA Purchase in 1803, Americans came to the territory, and for the first time, Protestant clergymen entered the once forbidden land.

In 1805 Bishop ASBURY sent Elisha W. Bowman to New Orleans. A modest amount of money was given to him to sustain him until he could get a work going which could help care for his needs and those of the Church. The conditions he found, however, were so bad that he was defeated on every hand. After repeated attempts at finding a place to preach and being promised the use of the Capitol building only to find that someone had arranged to have it locked when he arrived, he finally gave up the effort. He wrote to friends back in KENTUCKY on Jan. 29, 1806, "I shook off the dust of my feet against this ungodly city of New Orleans."

JACOB YOUNG, presiding elder of the MISSISSIPPI District, then made sincere efforts at establishing the work. By 1810 forty-three members were reported; and in 1811 Miles Harper was appointed the first regular Methodist pastor to the city of New Orleans.

In 1813 WILLIAM WINANS came to the city as a missionary. It was very difficult to find a place for a meeting, but he managed to secure facilities in the home of Methodists, Mr. and Mrs. Jacob Knobb, which he could use for living quarters. In this he ran a school during the week and preached on Sunday.

The Church lacked both money and missionaries. It was several years later that a building was secured. The next Methodist preaching place was in the loft of a flour inspector's office at the corner of Poydras and Carondelet Streets. Through the generosity and effort of a great Methodist layman, Judge EDWARD McGEHEE of Mississippi, this crude place was converted into a usable sanctuary. Out of this beginning came the first real church in 1825, a frame building on Gravier Street between Baronne and Carondelet. This is the predecessor to the great First Church now located on Canal Street.

While progress in New Orleans has never been as easy for Methodism as in some other cities, still by comparison the Church was having better times. In a few years it became necessary to build both a larger and more imposing building. In the year 1836, Bishop ANDREW preached the dedicatory sermon for a splendid edifice on the corner of Carondelet and Poydras Streets.

During the next dozen years, new names appeared as churches and preaching places and Sunday schools: the Good Hope Sunday School, later Algiers Methodist Church; Seaman's Bethel; Moreau Street Church, later to combine with the Krapp Street Church to form the present Second Methodist Church; the Lafayette Mission; McDonaughville Church; and others.

When the division of the Church occurred in 1845 New Orleans, along with the LOUISIANA CONFERENCE, adhered to the Church, South, and it so remained until the close of the Civil War. At that time the M.E. Church reorganized, chiefly under the superintendency of J. P. NEWMAN. Three Northern Churches remained until Unification in 1939; Napoleon Avenue, a leading Church today; Eighth Street, no longer present; and Church of the Redeemer, an Italian mission on Esplanade Street in the Vieux Carré.

It was in New Orleans that the M.E. Church, South practically reorganized in April 1866, after the Civil War. The city was then occupied by Northern troops, and for a time it was doubtful whether the Southern Methodists could get hold of a church in which to hold their GENERAL CONFERENCE called to meet there. However, the General Conference was held—the first time in eight years—and "the peeled and scattered hosts," as Bishop McTYEIRE puts it, "discouraged and confused by adversities and adverse rumors, rallied: . . . . and never did delegates meet in general conference from centers and remotest posts more enthusiastically; of 153 elected, 149 were present." This epochal New Orleans Conference adopted lay representation, and elected four bishops, WILLIAM M. WIGHTMAN, ENOCH M. MARVIN, DAVID S. DOGGETT, and HOLLAND N. McTYEIRE, the last having been for a time a pastor in New Orleans.

As early as 1842 there were several strong Negro Methodist churches in existence. Soule Chapel was built on Marais Street between Bienville and Conti Streets;

Wesley Chapel, located on Gravier Street, was also a strong colored church. In 1868 a literary institution was founded, which is now DILLARD UNIVERSITY.

Serious epidemics of yellow fever occurred with terrifying frequency between 1810 and 1909. In these epidemics the Methodist Church suffered a loss of twenty percent of its members. Highest praise and appreciation are due the faithful ministers who stood steadfast in all such times of hardships and danger, ministering alike to the spiritual and physical needs of a distressed and discouraged people.

Gambling has always been a problem in New Orleans. It had been used as a source of funds for many things, including religion. It reached its height in the Louisiana Lottery, which became so entrenched late in the nineteenth century that the State looked to this as one of its chief means of support. The united and determined effort of Protestant clergymen and laymen went far toward breaking the back of this legalized gambling. Despite the offer by the lottery company of a million and a quarter dollars a year to the State, an act prohibiting the sale of tickets was passed in 1894.

New Orleans Methodism has produced many able ministers. At one time four future bishops answered the roll of the Louisiana Conference from this area—LINUS PARKER, CHARLES B. GALLOWAY, J. C. KEENER, and H. N. McTYEIRE. FRANKLIN N. PARKER, who always claimed New Orleans as his city, was one of the few men who declined the office of bishop. John B. Matthews, John Hannon, and WILLIAM E. MUNSEY were among the great leaders of the New Orleans churches.

Other strong early Southern churches must be named to make this study accurate. Rayne Memorial Church located on St. Charles Avenue is still a leading Church. Felicity, one of the earliest and greatest, lives now largely on sentiment regarding its noble past; Louisiana Avenue was once a beautiful building on Louisiana and Magazine, but gave way when its membership moved out of the declining neighborhood.

Now there are over 20,000 Methodists in forty churches in Greater New Orleans, and the future is limited only by the manpower and financial resources available to develop this great and growing area.

Carondelet Street Church (whose successor is now First Methodist Church), one of the oldest churches in the city, occupied a building on Gravier Street near Carondelet from 1824 until 1835, when the financial assistance of Judge Edward McGehee enabled the congregation to build a church at Carondelet and Poydras Streets. On Jan. 18, 1851, sparks from a fire which destroyed the St. Charles Hotel ignited the church and it was damaged beyond repair. Undaunted, the membership purchased ground on Carondelet between Girod and Lafayette Streets, where a fine church building was erected, which was to serve the Methodists of New Orleans for fifty-three years.

In 1906, it was decided to move to a new location on St. Charles Avenue near Lee Circle, and the name was changed to the First Methodist Church. The Grand Consistory (A.F. & A.M.) of Louisiana purchased the Carondelet Street property, and it is now known as the Scottish Rite Cathedral. In the years that followed, two of the pastors of the church became bishops, Linus Parker and John C. Keener.

In 1956, First Church found itself in the path of the new bridge to be built over the Mississippi River, and merged with Canal Street Church to purchase a site at Canal Street and Jefferson Davis Parkway. There the congregation moved into a new church plant in October 1960, and a great church has come into being. First United Methodist is now meeting the challenge of a growing and changing city. Its ministry reaches over a twenty-mile radius, and shut-ins and a bi-state area are served through a television ministry once a month. The church has two services each Sunday morning and is largely visited by travelers and visitors who are in New Orleans on Sunday. Present membership is 1,115.

Felicity Church enjoys the distinction of having had three of its former pastors elected to the episcopacy. Bishop Holland Nimmons McTyeire, eminent historian of Methodism, was the church's founder and first pastor. Bishop Linus Parker served as the second pastor, and while there lost his bride of three months as a victim of yellow fever. Bishop John Christian Keener, strong leader of Methodism in Louisiana, filled the pulpit just prior to the American Civil War.

It was in December 1848 that Holland N. McTyeire was sent from the ALABAMA CONFERENCE, M.E. Church, South, to effect the union of three struggling mission stations in New Orleans from which Felicity was born. These were Andrew Chapel, whose pastor was killed en route to his charge with the burning of the steamboat on which he was a passenger; Elijah Steele Chapel, known as the "flatboat" church because it was built of lumber from dismantled Mississippi river flatboats; and the St. Mary Street Church.

On Christmas Day, 1850, the fifth session of the Louisiana Conference and the first to be held in New Orleans, was convened in the new red brick Felicity church. Bishop WILLIAM CAPERS dedicated the building.

This first building was destroyed by fire on Saturday afternoon, April 16, 1887. A new building, valued at $50,000, was erected on the original foundation and was dedicated by Bishop Keener June 3, 1888. Felicity is the oldest Methodist church in New Orleans remaining on its original site. At one time in its history it ranked as one of the most important churches in Louisiana Methodism. The conference *Journal* for 1874 indicates that the pastor's salary was $300 per annum, the second largest salary reported for the conference. The first EPWORTH LEAGUE chapter in Louisiana was organized at Felicity on Jan. 11, 1891.

FRANKLIN N. PARKER, son of Bishop Linus Parker, was licensed to preach by the Quarterly Conference of Felicity, and the father of Bishop NOLAN B. HARMON, editor of this *Encyclopedia*, was converted there. Parker was twice elected bishop by the General Conference, but declined the honor in order to continue his service to the church as a teacher of young ministers at EMORY UNIVERSITY.

Felicity was harassed by deadly epidemics of yellow fever, by fire, and by hurricane. Two of the most devastating hurricanes ever to strike New Orleans were those of 1915 and 1965, both of which left their angry marks upon the church. Battered and weather worn by time and the elements, the building has once more been renewed and, on Sunday, Oct. 9, 1966, Bishop AUBREY G. WALTON rededicated the sanctuary.

Felicity is now one of five churches comprising the New Orleans Inner City Methodist Parish. Church school and worship services are held every Sunday morning and a special ministry is provided for Cuban refugees by its bi-lingual pastor.

RAYNE MEMORIAL CHURCH, NEW ORLEANS, LOUISIANA

Rayne Memorial Church, formerly the St. Charles Avenue Church and now popularly known as the "Church of the Lighted Steeple," is a stately, impressive building and "the Cathedral of New Orleans Methodism." It was erected in 1875 and its Tudor-Gothic sanctuary was erected and cleared of indebtedness before the church itself was officially organized.

The generous gifts of Robert W. Rayne, a local preacher, made the building possible. Rayne was born in Sunderland, England, in 1808. His parents were members of the Methodist society, and he embraced religion and united with the church in 1824. He immediately became an active worker in visiting the poor in work-houses; and was a visitor for the Benevolent Strangers' Friend Society, dispensing alms, and holding prayer-meetings on Sunday evenings among the poor in their dwellings. He was shortly afterwards licensed to exhort and preach. In 1832 he emigrated to the United States, and, after a short residence in NEW YORK and PHILADELPHIA, settled in CINCINNATI, where, at the invitation of the Methodist Protestant Church, he accepted an appointment in the ministry. In 1835 failing health compelled him to locate, and business arrangements led him for a short time to MASSACHUSETTS. In 1842 he removed to New Orleans, and united with the M.E. Church. At the separation he adhered to the M.E. Church, South. He continued in mercantile business till the breaking out of the war. At its close he returned to the city, and was an active and consistent member of the M.E. Church South, living in harmony and fellowship with all denominations.

The first services were held in the completed sanctuary on the morning of Jan. 2, 1876, with Bishop John C. Keener presiding, and W. E. Munsey appointed its first pastor. In the afternoon the church was organized with

108 members, and in the evening Munsey, a gifted orator, preached a notable sermon on "Elijah." The church was named the St. Charles Avenue Methodist Church. Following the death of Mr. and Mrs. Rayne, the name was changed on May 2, 1877, to Rayne Memorial Methodist Church and dedicated as a memorial to Rayne's son, William, who was fatally wounded at Chancellorsville in the War Between the States.

The Church has the further distinction of having a WOMAN'S FOREIGN MISSIONARY SOCIETY organized in it on April 26, 1877, with Mrs. Robert W. Rayne as its first president. This antedates the organization by the General Conference of the M.E. Church, South, of a Woman's Board of Foreign Missions, by more than a year.

In 1925 an educational building and fellowship hall were erected, and a modern children's building was built in 1962. The Rayne Memorial Organ Series annually presents from two to four organists of world fame in concerts. Its C. I. Jones Memorial Lectures attract visitors from across the Southland, and annually present well known lecturers.

Rayne Memorial has always been missionary-minded. Its first local preacher, James D. Parker, organized a church on Nashville Avenue within the city, later named Parker Memorial Church. It also purchased and donated the lots upon which the Carrollton Avenue Church is located, and it assisted in the organization of that congregation. It participated in the great missionary conference of the M.E. Church, South, held in Tulane Hall in April 1901. The worship services and several committee meetings of that Conference were held in its sanctuary. Young J. Allen preached at Rayne Memorial on April 28 on the subject, "Come Over Into Macedonia and Help Us."

On Dec. 22, 1968 Hannah Chapel of Rayne Memorial was dedicated with appropriate ceremonies presided over by Bishop Aubrey G. Walton. The Chapel was named for Hannah Graham Lehde, wife of Pendleton E. Lehde, long time member of the church. The windows on the front of the building are of faceted red-yellow glass with eight side windows of stained glass with Christian religious symbols.

Rayne Memorial has traditionally been the church home of the families of the presiding bishop of Louisiana and the New Orleans district superintendent. Among its outstanding pastors have been W. E. Munsey, John Hannon, John Matthews, J. B. Walker, Franklin N. Parker, John A. Rice, Felix R. Hill, W. L. Duren, W. W. Holmes, H. L. Johns, B. C. Taylor, and Adrian M. Serex. Its tall and stately lighted-steeple, clearly visible to visitors arriving by riverboat or automobile, is an inspiration to the city; and despite the damaging hurricanes of 1915 and 1965, it points the Methodists of New Orleans godward.

St. James A.M.E. Church. JORDAN W. EARLY was the founder of African Methodism in New Orleans. He established a mission there as early as 1842. Permission to organize a Negro church in this city required an act of the Legislature. Early accomplished this through his Masonic contacts, and the charter, which was granted, named the church the "African Methodist Episcopal Church." Later, a lot on Roman Street was purchased, a church erected and dedicated as "St. James Chapel." In 1848 St. James requested a pastor from the Indiana Conference. Charles Doughty, one of their own members, was ordained and returned as the pastor. In 1858 all Negro churches in New Orleans were closed by the civil authorities. Following the Civil War this ban was lifted and St. James eventually became a leading appointment in the state.

Robert Alan Cross, *The History of Southern Methodism in New Orleans.* N.p., n.d.
R. H. Harper, *Louisiana.* 1949.
The Louisiana Methodist, Dec. 19, 1968.
Minutes of Board of Trustees, The Elijah Steele Church (Felicity Street M.E. Church, South), 1848-1918.
M. Simpson, *Cyclopaedia.* 1878.
C. S. Smith, *History* (AME). 1922.

JOLLY B. HARPER
CLYDE S. CLARK
MRS. ARTHUR C. KERR
BENEDICT A. GALLOWAY
GRANT S. SHOCKLEY

NEW ORLEANS CHRISTIAN ADVOCATE was published in NEW ORLEANS, La., from 1852 until its publication was discontinued in 1946. When the GENERAL CONFERENCE met in ST. LOUIS in 1850, a resolution was presented to that body by Jefferson Hamilton and B. M. DRAKE: "Resolved that the Louisiana, Mississippi, Alabama, and Arkansas Conferences establish a paper at such point as they may select and that the bishop presiding in said Conferences appoint an editor when requested to do so." The General Conference adjourned the following day without taking any action on the resolution. However, on their return journey, which began on May 14, 1850, on the steamer *James Hewitt*, a meeting was held of the delegates from these four Conferences, at which meeting a committee was appointed to consult upon the establishment of a church paper. The committee, WILLIAM WINANS being chairman and Jefferson Hamilton secretary, reported favorably upon the enterprise and it was provided that a paper should be published as soon as 3,000 subscribers and a suitable editor could be obtained. It may be correctly said that the New Orleans *Advocate*, like many worthy pioneers, was born on a Mississippi River steamboat!

On July 10, 1850, the committee issued a specimen number from New Orleans, with B. M. Drake serving as editor; it can be said that he was the first editor, though his term of office ran through only one edition. Copies of this publication were evidently mailed to all the preachers in the four Conferences.

The first regular edition of the *Advocate* appeared on Feb. 8, 1851, with HOLLAND N. McTYEIRE as editor in addition to his duties as pastor of Felicity Street Church in New Orleans. The publication was issued by a joint committee of the LOUISIANA and ALABAMA CONFERENCES, consisting of Richard H. Rivers, William E. Doty, and JOHN C. KEENER of Louisiana, and Jefferson Hamilton, William Murrah, and T. W. Dorman of Alabama. Neither the ARKANSAS nor MISSISSIPPI CONFERENCES were official sponsors of the project. The Arkansas Conference never did participate and the Mississippi Conference did not assume any responsibility until 1858, seven years later, though many people in both states subscribed for the paper. One suspects that leaders of Mississippi Methodism looked with disfavor on the dominance of the paper by the New Orleans triumvirate, H. N. McTyeire, J. C. Keener, and LINUS PARKER. The Alabama Conference continued as one of the supporting Conferences until 1880, and the NORTH MISSISSIPPI CONFERENCE began its official support in 1883.

When McTyeire was elected editor of the Nashville *Christian Advocate* in 1858, his successor at New Or-

leans was Clayton C. Gillespie. He came from the editorship of the *Texas Christian Advocate*, though his early ministry was spent in the Alabama Conference, where he was associated with Keener and McTyeire, now both in New Orleans. Gillespie edited an excellent paper until the outbreak of the Civil War. There are no files of the *Advocate* for the pre-war period in 1860, though it is generally assumed that publication was continued until some time in 1861, when the situation made it impossible to continue. There is a tradition that Gillespie went into the Confederate Army, but after the war his name appears no more in the records.

After the war the *Advocate* resumed publication in 1866 under the editorship of John Christian Keener, who brought the paper through its post-war difficulties and up to its former standard. He continued in that position until his election to the episcopacy in 1870. His predecessor, H. N. McTyeire, had been elected bishop four years earlier at the General Conference of 1866.

Then Linus Parker served for twelve years as editor of the *Advocate* and continued the excellent character of the paper as it had been under his predecessors. This was in spite of some difficulties occasioned by the period of reconstruction in the South, and particularly in LOUISIANA. After twelve years of splendid leadership, Parker was himself elected a bishop, but died soon after taking over that responsibility.

When Linus Parker was elected a bishop his successor at New Orleans was the youthful CHARLES B. GALLOWAY of the Mississippi Conference, only a little more than thirty years of age, and the first Mississippian to serve as editor. He was not able to give full time to the work, since he served as pastor in JACKSON and Brookhaven during the four years he was editor. In the first issue after taking over the editorship, Galloway quoted a writer who said that the New Orleans *Advocate* was "a training school for the episcopacy," to which the new editor modestly replied that "all episcopal material had been used already." Nevertheless, Galloway himself was elected bishop in 1886—the youngest bishop in Methodism—and once more the editorial chair had to be filled.

His successor was Charles W. Carter of the Louisiana Conference. He held the office a number of years, giving it up without notice in the early 1890's because of the financial situation and the failure to have his salary paid and the paper supported. J. M. Beard, chairman of the Publishing Committee, then took over the editorship and business management of the paper for four months, during which time he succeeded in solving a number of problems and in turning over the paper to his successor in much better financial shape.

Warren C. Black, a native Mississippian, and for many years a popular pastor and pulpit orator, served as editor from 1894 until 1900, with his son, M. M. Black, as his assistant for part of that time. In July 1900 the *Advocate* observed the fiftieth anniversary of its establishment. At the close of the year, Black resigned and was succeeded by John W. Boswell, who held the position until the latter part of 1909, though he had resigned in 1907. Then T. B. Holloman was elected editor, and at his refusal to accept the office, Boswell was persuaded to continue for two more years. He was a brilliant and scholarly man and served for a number of years as associate editor of the general church organ, the Nashville *Advocate*.

R. A. MEEK of the North Mississippi Conference succeeded Boswell and continued until June 1918, when he resigned. Meek was vigorous and aggressive in his editorial policies, and never failed to take sides in any issue before the church. He was particularly involved in the controversy over VANDERBILT UNIVERSITY and also the question of unification of the divided branches of Methodism, which he greatly opposed.

The Publishing Committee in June 1918 elected Henry T. Carley, a native Mississippian but a member of the Louisiana Conference and a teacher at CENTENARY COLLEGE, as editor to fill the vacancy until the committee met again in October. At this later meeting he was formally elected editor and continued in that office for ten years. Carley was a scholarly man and piloted the *Advocate* through difficult years. He was progressive in his thinking and held the confidence and respect of those who did not agree with him on such issues as unification of Methodism. Later he served as associate editor under W. L. DUREN.

R. H. Harper, a lifelong member of the Louisiana Conference and an honor graduate of Centenary College, succeeded Carley as editor. Unfortunately he came into the office just at the beginning of the depression, which affected the financial stability no little. Harper was a brilliant and capable editor, but he found the financial responsibility irksome, in spite of the outstanding service of C. O. Chalmers, for a long time the paper's business manager, and Harper resigned as editor after not more than two years in that responsibility. J. LLOYD DECELL, then presiding elder of the Brookhaven District in Mississippi, assumed the responsibility of the editorship in connection with his duties on the district, commuting, as Bishop Galloway had done, from Brookhaven to New Orleans. Decell served only one year, 1930-31, after which he went to the pastorate of Galloway Memorial Church, Jackson, from which he was elected to the episcopacy, the fifth editor of the *Advocate* to be elected to that office after serving as editor.

Daniel B. Raulins, a native Mississippian but a member of the Louisiana Conference, served as editor for several years. His service was significant and appreciated. After some three years, Raulins returned to the pastorate until his death.

Following Raulins, the final duties of editing this historic publication fell into the worthy hands of W. L. Duren, then of the Louisiana Conference but a former member of the North Mississippi and North Georgia Conferences. He spent twelve years as editor, through all of which he earned the respect and confidence of the readers of the paper. Part of the time he had as associate editor H. T. Carley, and for a period of time he had an associate from each of the three supporting Conferences: Carley from Louisiana, A. P. Hamilton from the Mississippi Conference, and Hugh Clayton and B. P. Brooks from the North Mississippi. Milton Chalmers succeeded his father as business manager.

Significant changes took place during Duren's editorship, all of which he viewed with calmness and discernment. The long-discussed union of the churches took place in 1939, and the *Advocate's* territory was then divided, the Louisiana Conference being placed in the SOUTH CENTRAL JURISDICTION and the Mississippi and North Mississippi Conferences in the SOUTHEASTERN JURISDICTION. This was the beginning of the end. There had been a persistent effort for many years to establish a Methodist paper in Jackson or Meridian, Miss., and at least one or two efforts in that direction had come to naught. Duren had served twelve years with fidelity and

effectiveness, and on Nov. 28, 1946, the last issue of the New Orleans *Advocate* came from the press. The *Mississippi Methodist Advocate* for the Mississippi Conferences and the *Louisiana Methodist* for Louisiana have since been published in its place.

The files of the *Advocate,* with the exception of a very few years, have been placed in the Methodist Room at MILLSAPS COLLEGE. A joint committee from the Louisiana, Mississippi, and North Mississippi Conferences supervise their use.

J. B. CAIN

NEW PLYMOUTH, New Zealand, **Whiteley Memorial Church** was built as a memorial to JOHN WHITELEY, who was killed by Maori warriors at the White Cliffs, Pukearuhe, on Feb. 13, 1869, and whose death virtually brought an end to the Maori Wars. The church which it replaced had been occupied by the congregation since 1856.

The decision to build a Whiteley Church was made in 1897, during the ministry of C. H. Garland. The idea of a memorial caught the imagination of the community, and a church designed to seat 500 people was completed within a year. An exceptionally beautiful pipe organ was later installed, as a memorial to Methodists serving in the First World War. This historic edifice, the mother church and cathedral of Taranaki Methodism, whose foundation stone had been laid by the governor of NEW ZEALAND, the Earl of Ranfurly, was completely destroyed by fire on Feb. 18, 1959, while repairs and renovations were in progress.

It was rebuilt under the superintendency of W. H. Greenslade as a noble stone building, modern ecclesiastical in appearance, chaste in design and most convenient in appointments. Its lofty tower and illuminated cross dominate the surroundings.

R. LAURIE COOPER

NEW PROVIDENCE, NEW JERSEY, U.S.A., first called Turkey or Turkey Hills, was first visited by Bishop ASBURY in July 1806, who referred to it in his *Journal.* Long before the CAMP MEETING era, it was a prominent preaching place of the Methodists, and from it Methodism spread throughout the area. EZEKIEL COOPER preached there in 1786 and THOMAS MORRELL was there the following year.

The first Society was organized in 1789 by Johnny Robertson. Meetings were held at the home of Waters Burrows, Sr. The first meeting house was erected in 1803 on a lot donated by George Corey. LORENZO DOW in 1802 and Bishop Asbury in 1806 preached in this chapel. Asbury missed the first camp meeting at Turkey Hills in August 1806, but he was again at New Providence in 1811, always being entertained by Stephen Day. In 1816, Lorenzo Dow preached there six times. The original chapel at Turkey was replaced by a larger edifice in 1857 and a new educational building was added in 1954.

V. B. Hampton, *Newark Conference.* 1957.

VERNON B. HAMPTON

NEW SOUTH WALES CONFERENCE, Australia. There is reason to believe that the first class meeting in New South Wales was held in the residence of one Thomas Bowden, headmaster of the Male Orphan Institute, SYDNEY, on

March 6, 1812. It is believed that two classes were formed, the second supervised by John Hosking, headmaster of the Females' Orphan School. It is known that at Windsor, thirty-six miles northwest from Sydney, one Edward Eagar, who had been sentenced to transportation for forgery, regularly held a class meeting early in 1812.

In a letter to the Preachers and Members of the Committee of the METHODIST MISSIONARY SOCIETY (British Conference) dated April 3, 1812, Bowden and Hosking addressed a strong and telling appeal for the appointment of a "single legally qualified Preacher." Consequently SAMUEL LEIGH arrived in Sydney, New South Wales, in the *Hebe* on Aug. 10, 1815.

In an "Address of the Methodist Societies in New South Wales to the Committee," dated March 2, 1816, Edward Eagar, Steward; Thomas Bowden, James Scott and John Hosking, Leaders, stated that Leigh was "kindly received by our excellent Governor, General Macquarie, as well as by the Rev. Chaplains of the Colony." They stressed the need of an additional appointment, "but we are under the painful necessity of stating that our present circumstances will not enable us to support two preachers unassisted by the Committee . . . and what adds to our difficulties . . . is the total impossibility of borrowing money in this Colony on any interest or security whatever."

Services in Sydney were first held in a house, but Leigh was encouraged when through the generosity of John Lees, a retired soldier, the first Wesleyan Chapel at Castlereagh, on the Nepean River, was dedicated on March 7, 1819.

By 1826 the first New South Wales District Meeting reported eleven churches and one in Tasmania. The first New South Wales Conference of the Methodist Church of Australasia was held in 1902. The Centenary of Australasian Methodism was celebrated in August 1915. The Bi-Centenary of JOHN WESLEY's conversion was celebrated in 1938. The 150th Anniversary of the founding of Methodism was celebrated in 1962.

When the "Nineteenth Annual" District meeting met in Sydney in January 1839, the following were the stations and appointments: Sydney, John McKenny, Superintendent and James Watkin, Secretary; Parramatta, Daniel Draper; Lower Hawkesbury, William Schofield; Windsor, Samuel Wilkinson; and Bathurst, Frederick Lewis.

"The Missions in Australia, Van Diemen's Land, the Friendly Islands and Feejee" were constituted by the British Conference of 1854, "a distinct Connexion to be denominated the Australasian Wesleyan-Methodist Connexion" with "an annual Conference affiliated to the Parent English Conference." The first Australasian Conference was held in Sydney in January 1855, and in an address to the parent Conference said, "We have to rejoice in the gradually increasing prosperity of the work of God, both in the colonies and in the missions . . . We have now in connection with us 116 Ministers besides a number of Native Assistant Missionaries, nearly 800 chapels, 19,897 Church members, and 1,958 on Trial."

In 1873 a scheme of Annual and General Conferences was determined upon and in the following year the first New South Wales and Queensland Conference was held. The setting apart of the QUEENSLAND District into a separate Conference was carried out by the General Conference of 1890. The first New South Wales Conference was held in 1893.

The first PRIMITIVE METHODIST Annual Assembly in New South Wales was held in 1859 and that of the UNITED METHODIST FREE CHURCHES in 1890. By a Plan of Union agreed upon after lengthy negotiations, the various branches of Methodism united as part of the Methodist Church of Australasia in 1902.

At the General Conference held in Perth, Western Australia, May 1966, the following statistics were recorded: Ministers in Active work, 1,231; Supernumeraries, 286; Probationers, 186; Students in Training, 256; Theological Colleges, 10; Home Missionaries, 779; Deaconesses, 66; Local Preachers, 12,892; Class Leaders, 15,691; Confirmed Members, 250,010; Members under Nurture for Confirmation, 243,600. Number of Sunday Schools, 4,465; Teachers, 37,492; Scholars, 285,554; Membership in Youth Organizations, 102,609; Churches, 4,912; School Halls, 1,844; Parsonages, 1,274; Colleges, 65; Book Depots, 11; Publishing Houses, 4; Hospitals, 25.

Methodism in Australasia is indebted to the pioneers of the nineteenth century who in an environment never made easy by officialdom established and consolidated in these lands the cause of Jesus Christ.

Several departments of the work of the Methodist Church have assumed considerable social and religious significance and the most important of these are as follows:

Department of Christian Citizenship. This Department has grown from a staff of one in 1948 to a functioning instrument of the church employing over fifty people. It has developed homes, schools, and other services designed to meet the needs of the people.

Homes. The special work being done at the girls' home is to be expanded. A second home is being opened for particular work in cooperation with the New South Wales University. This represents a tremendous forward move in this highly important work with problem girls in the fifteen to eighteen year age bracket.

The boys' home is actually a mansion set on a farm of 800 acres. This particular venture, undertaken twelve years ago, has seen over 200 boys pass through its doors. Most of them have been helped to resolve the difficulties which they brought to the home. A maximum of twenty boys are taken at any one time and they and the staff live in one massive home. Most of the cost for running this place is derived from the varied activities on the farm, sheep, wheat, dairy, pigs and poultry.

Schools. Three years ago the Department opened the first school in this country for mildly mentally handicapped girls. One hundred girls can be accommodated at the delightfully situated school eighty miles south of Sydney. The aim is to train each girl to the maximum of her capacity and then find her employment in the community. This school caters for girls over sixteen years of age who previously have not had this opportunity. Already some girls have been placed in employment.

Children's Courts. In addition to conducting these special homes and school, the day to day operation of the Department involves attendance at the Children's Courts. A qualified social worker makes contact there, not only with the boys and girls before the court, but with the families. We deal with over 300 such children and families each year.

Family Needs. From this particular work and the insights derived from twenty years work in the Marriage Guidance field, plus the understanding gained through the Chaplaincy work mentioned above, we are convinced that the family and not just one member contacted in these special areas, needs our service. As society becomes more and more industrialized and population density rises steeply, the family must be given top priority if we are to prevent personal and group maladjustment.

Team Work. The Department has already begun to move in on this important front. In doing so, we do not "go it alone." We work with the State Health Department and other community organizations to discover how we can cooperate to meet the real needs of given communities. The action programmes that emerge are consequently different but they are meaningful to the people in the area where we operate.

This particular approach to our work has special significance for church congregations. They are being helped to see their mission to the local community. Through training and this kind of practical involvement, they are having their gaze turned outwards from the church building to the people who must always be the first concern of the Christian.

WAYSIDE CHAPEL, NEW SOUTH WALES CONFERENCE

Counselling. While heavily engaged in these special areas of work, the Department has always been deeply involved in counselling a wide range of disturbed individuals. Neurotics, psychotics, drug takers, alcoholics; the inadequates have always been our concern and in dealing with them, we have had the fullest support from the medical profession in all branches, the legal fraternity and other specialist groups.

Pioneers. All of this work has been undertaken not in any mood of monopoly but that the Department might demonstrate how missions and local churches can and must come to grips with the real problems of people. It is one of the true roles of church departments to pioneer ways of contacting and serving all sorts and conditions of people and then to leave it to local churches to get on with the job while it does more pioneering and discovering.

Rehabilitation of ex-Prisoners. The Department helped inaugurate the Civil Rehabilitation organization in this state which works in the difficult area of attempting to rehabilitate persons released from prison.

National and International Affairs. Wider affairs of the nation and of international concern are additional items on our charter. The vexed question of peace and war, the population explosion, the food problem of the world, the use of nuclear power for peaceful purposes, and race

relations are big issues that are constantly being studied. From the Department material is distributed to the church across the state. In addition the Director has been the national leader in efforts which have raised millions of dollars for United Nations Children's Fund, Refugees and Freedom From Hunger projects.

Church at Mission. Through this Department the church is at mission in the community in a host of ways. We are always prepared to experiment in new methods of work. We never settle back content or think we have found all the answers. We move into each day prepared to serve the living God who we believe is as modern as the task he asks us to undertake with Him for the sake of people. Enthusiastically we daily apply ourselves to work with people and their problems.

Department of Christian Education. The Department of Christian Education had its beginnings in 1904 when the Conference of that year established the Sunday School Department. The first General Secretary, Harold Wheen, was appointed in 1912.

At the same time, beside the Sunday schools, the participation of young people in the worshipping life of the church was receiving attention, and in 1914 the Young Worshippers' League was established. This organization provided some incentives for young people to attend worship to provide a record of their attendance and text cards.

The next development was that of youth organizations. This began in 1915 when a Methodist Boys' Group, later to grow into the Methodist Order of Knights, was started at Hurstville, a suburb of Sydney, by Alec Bray. Two years later the Christian Endeavour Society became an integral part of the Sunday School Department, and the same year saw the Methodist Order of Knights sponsored officially by the Department, and a sister organization, The Methodist Girls' Comradeship, formed. As a result of these developments the name of the Department was changed in 1917 to the Young People's Department. This name was retained for the next forty-seven years. In 1920 Australian Sunday school lessons were produced and in 1923 Methodist Sunday schools were linked with the Presbyterian and Congregational churches with the introduction of Graded Lessons prepared jointly by these churches.

In 1924 the Mail Bag Sunday School was initiated to serve children living in distant parts of the state and unable to attend a Sunday school.

The Harold Wheen Kindergarten was opened in 1929 in Redfern, a depressed suburban area of Sydney. This was a free kindergarten to serve the children of this area and is still currently operating. The same year saw the development of another new movement, that of camping, with the holding of the first Methodist Crusader Camp at Camden about thirty miles out of Sydney. The Crusader Movement as a camping organization quickly grew to cover metropolitan and country districts conducting camps regularly on holiday weekends, and currently conducting up to twenty camps per year.

In 1930 there began a move to include in the life of the church mixed clubs for young people. Some years later the Methodist clubs received their constitution and later in 1958 they were incorporated in the Methodist Youth Fellowship established that year.

A sub-department of Religious Instruction in Schools was developed in 1939. Stan Barrett was appointed to this sub-department to assist ministers in their task of giving religious instruction in day schools across the state. Ten years later this sub-department became a full department for Religious Instruction in Schools.

In the early 1950's there developed a movement to establish a Methodist Bible College. In 1955 an evening college was established and in 1959 the Department purchased a residence at North Sydney as the center for a regular Bible College.

In 1957 Sir Frederick and Lady Stewart donated a gift of twenty acres of land on the near north of Sydney as a Methodist campsite. This was developed as the Methodist Youth War Memorial Conference Center. In the same year the Department purchased a property next door to Gowanlea to be used as a Methodist girls' hostel. In 1958 a Pacific Island Scholarship in memory of JOHN DIXON was inaugurated to bring students from Papua New Guinea and the Pacific Islands to train in Australia. In the same year the M.Y.F. constitution was approved and this youth organization was established across the state. In 1959 the Young People's Department undertook supervision of the North Sydney circuit as a part of its work in conjunction with the Methodist Bible College established there.

In 1964 the N.S.W. Conference decided to bring together the Young People's Department and the Department of Religious Instruction in Schools to form the Department of Christian Education.

With the development of this new department the whole range of Christian Education work among children, youth and adults within the home and local church and the public school was incorporated. The Department has functioned in this way to the present time; in 1968 the Conference approved a new policy providing for a general director of the Department with an Associate Director for each of three divisions namely, Schools and Sunday Schools work, Youth Work, and Adult Work.

Alongside the Department's work has been the development of camping properties owned by youth organizations or district synods of the church. The Methodist Christian Endeavour Association, Methodist Order of Knights each have their own site in Sydney and in addition there are district sites established at Kilaben Bay at Newcastle, at Bonny Hills near Port Macquarie and Ballina on the far North Coast. Further campsites will be developed as camping becomes a more important activity in the life of the church.

The Methodist Bible College has remained a small college which at present has no resident student body, maintaining only an evening college and correspondence division.

Connexional Journal. *The Methodist,* traditionally described as the Connexional Journal, has now entered upon its 111th year of continuous publication, the centenary having been fittingly celebrated in July 1958.

Originally known as *The Christian Advocate,* it first saw the light of day in July 1858, and in its original and present forms has not failed to appear (except for a brief period of industrial upheaval) on the date of publication. It also has the distinction of being the oldest religious journal in Australia, a distinction of which the Church has some cause for pride.

Editorial policy has sought to bring before readers a balanced coverage of news from at home and abroad together with feature articles from any sources including the Australian Methodist Press Association. An editorial policy which reflects the mission and witness of the Church in the whole world in this ecumenical age is one that commends itself to thoughtful readers.

Department of Home Missions. The relationship of the Church in Australia to the British Methodist Conference in 1855 eventually brought to birth the New South Wales Department of Home Missions. In 1858 there were nineteen circuits in the New South Wales District, with thirty ministers, four supernumeraries and four Home Missionaries. The contributions of the circuits to the funds amounted to £359. This meagre amount was too small to meet the needs of a rapidly growing Church in a young and flourishing country. At a District meeting in 1857, permission was sought to form a Sustentation and Extension Fund, "after the model of the Missionary Society," to take over the work and objectives of the Church Extension and Chapel Fund. At an historic Conference which met at York Street, Sydney, on Jan. 20, 1859, it was resolved "that permission be given to the New South Wales District to form the proposed society, and that its constitution be approved." The Society was formed officially at a general meeting of Wesleyan Church officers in the school room at the Centenary Chapel on March 21, 1859.

The minutes of the first Annual Meeting of this new Society in 1859, reveal the critical process through which the Church was passing. The financial report indicates that in the first year the sum of £1,243.8.7 was raised from circuits, and a Government Grant of £670. was accepted and a deficiency was incurred of £52.19.6. The Society included in its objectives the following:

To defray the current working expenses, of the Society, and the ordinary necessary connexional expenses which belong to the Wesleyan Methodist Church in New South Wales.

To assist in sustaining ministers in neglected or scattered populations where the full support of a minister cannot be obtained.

To grants in aid of the erection of new Chapels, ministers' residences and school rooms, and towards liquidation of debt on such Methodist property as may have been already acquired.

The first grants amounting to £530 was paid by way of grants to circuits as far apart as Camden, Newtown, Newcastle and Brisbane, which is now the capital city of Queensland.

Evangelism. The early documents describe the primary task of the Church as being that of evangelism and the development of the spiritual life of the colony. The following quotation reveals the mind of the Department in its early history:

The committee have learned from various sources that much spiritual destitution exists in many parts of the colony, and as a consequence of this, much darkness of mind, and immorality of life unhappily afflict the people. Thousands of our fellow colonists never hear a Gospel sermon, or frequent the house of prayer.

Between Singletown and Warwick a distance of about 400 miles on the Great Northern Road, on which are situated some 15 or 16 townships. . . . no Wesleyan Methodist ordinances exist, and in many of them there is an utter dearth of evangelical ministrations.

The records which follow indicate an enthusiastic concern for the evangelization of this early colony. So much has happened since 1859. New South Wales has developed into one of the most prosperous States in the Southern Hemisphere. Today the capital, Sydney, is a booming city of near three million people; Newcastle is the industrial metropolis of Australia, and rich rural areas have developed on the coast and western plains. The whole atmosphere is one pulsing with life and vigorous plans are developed to match the population growth which now nears twelve and a half million.

Expansion. The first Home Missionary, W. H. Thompson, was appointed to Tweed River Station on the Queensland border, in 1889. In 1968 the Home Mission Department in this State appointed twenty-five Home Missionaries, supported lay agents in circuits, made progressive loans for properties, had formed the Far West and Inland Missions, developed the Women's Home Mission League, the Woolnough Sites and Church Extension Fund, a Deaconess Order, a Methodist Nursing Service, a Department of Church Development, a Division of Mission and Evangelism, employed full time Hospital Chaplains, undertook the development of Stewardship throughout the Church and staffed a Division of Immigration. Methodism in New South Wales is the story of a young Church staking a claim for the Faith and meeting every opportunity with a dedication and zeal, representative of that authentic missionary faith so clearly defined in the best pages of Christian history, and in the spirit of New Testament Missionary outreach.

The progress of the Home Missions Department has been undertaken by the Church across the State, working as a Conference unit. Conference has given to some of the Church's most able ministers the task of leading and planning the ministry of this Department. General Secretaries have been: W. Hessell, 1859-61; G. Hurst, 1861-64; 1866-68; 1869-80; B. Chapman, 1864, 1868; J. Oram, 1865; G. Woolnough, 1880-82; G. Lane, 1882-88; G. Sellors, 1888-96; J. Woolnough, 1896-1915; J. G. M. Taylor, 1915-23; W. H. Jones, 1923-40; R. H. Campbell, 1940-49; A. G. Manefield, 1949-62; W. Whitbread, 1962-69; R. R. Smith, 1969.

Over the past three years the Department has undertaken vigorous research into the place and relevance of this Department in a time of rapid change. In 1970 the Department moved to a suburban regional center at Chatswood, where new forms of ministry and renewal will be undertaken as a pilot project for the whole State.

Deaconess Order. The N.S.W. Department of Home Missions, under the far-seeing Superintendency of the late A. G. MANEFIELD, brought into being this Ministry in 1945, conscious of the leading of God. Four candidates entered into training, two of these being multi-certificated nurses. The latter went at the close of the year to their first appointment at Brewarrina, in far west of the State, to minister to farmer families and the native people that were attached thereto.

The college period for other than nurses was set at two years; and the probation for both types of Deaconesses, at five years, followed by ordination. Some applicants have been received in full connection as Deaconesses without the prescribed formal training owing to particular experience or educational qualifications.

The LEIGH MINISTERIAL THEOLOGICAL COLLEGE, Enfield, Sydney was the first place of this resident training of up to eight students per year. The onerous project here was wisely and kindly shepherded by the Principal, S. R. Bowyer-Hayward.

Within a few years, because of the influx of post-war men students, the Deaconesses were trained at the All Saints College, Haberfield, Sydney, run conjointly by the Methodist, Presbyterian and Congregational Churches,

primarily for the purpose of Overseas Missionary Students —(previously it was the George Brown Methodist Missionary Training College). Later, the Deaconess College had its own building in Leichhardt, Sydney until 1967, then the students were transferred, joining the Methodist Bible College, Brisbane in 1968, where students in training for various spheres of influence in the Church numbered up to seventy.

In N.S.W., lecturers were drawn from Leigh College, from among senior ministers and ministers with relevant scholastic advantage. The subjects studied included Bible, Theology, Psychology, Sociology, English, Homiletics, Church History, Ethics, Teaching Methods.

The N.S.W. Women's Home Mission League continue, as at first, to identify themselves with the work and personnel of the Deaconesses; constantly with fellowship, labor and finance.

Deaconesses serve in the State's city missions, ordinary circuits, and in the far "outback" with those of the Methodist Nursing Service. Deaconesses have been appointed to the chaplaincy of hospitals and the Methodist Ladies' College, Burwood, Sydney. A deaconess has served a term as Home Missionary. In 1968 sixteen deaconesses were in appointments, and that same year the Third General Convocation of the Order was held in Sydney, to which forty ordained deaconesses from all parts of Australia came. The first woman to be accepted as a candidate for the Methodist ministry was Deaconess Kay Edwards. She was accepted at the 1969 Conference.

First Australian Mission. This amazingly enlightened venture which began in Sydney in 1821, is linked forever with the name of William Walker (1800-1857). He sailed from England with Samuel Leigh and the Rev. and Mrs. William Horton and arrived in Sydney on Sept. 16, 1821. In October in company with Joseph Hassall he visited aborigines at Blacktown, after which he wrote, "all they require is a few clothes, agricultural implements and a supply of food until their crops be reaped . . . I left them with a consciousness of having never been favoured with a more profitable or serious season during my ministerial career." On another occasion he wrote, "they are idle and vagrant and the colonists too often encourage their vices. If they cut wood or do any other trifling work they are rewarded with a mixture of spiritous liquors . . . quarrelling ensues, and if ever incarnate devils appeared in this world, surely the natives are at such times their representatives."

In 1823 the Wesleyan missionaries of New South Wales met in Conference and decided to recommend to the overseas General Committee that an institution for aborigines be set up under the superintendence of a local committee consisting of all the missionaries in the colony and twelve laymen to be elected annually by the District Meeting.

Statistics for the New South Wales Conference as of May 1969, are as follows: Ministers in active work, 271; churches, 739; members, 52,404.

AUSTRALIAN EDITORIAL COMMITTEE

NEW YORK, the "Empire State," has an area of 49,576 square miles and a population of 17,979,712 (1970). Called New Netherlands by the Dutch who settled it, the British renamed it in honor of James Stuart, Duke of York, when they seized it in 1664. One of the original thirteen states, New York is noted today for industry, commerce, education, agriculture, and the arts. It is the leading manufacturing state, and New York is the nation's largest city and port as well as the headquarters of the United Nations, and the location of the head offices of many of the greatest national corporations and insurance companies. The state has 207 institutions of higher learning which enroll over 645,000 students.

Methodism was brought to New York City in the 1760's by the Irish immigrants PHILIP EMBURY and BARBARA HECK. Impetus was given the cause by Captain THOMAS WEBB. With his encouragement and financial help, a Methodist meetinghouse, Wesley Chapel, was constructed in 1768 and later renamed JOHN STREET CHURCH. The church, still active at the same location after 200 years, is one of the national historic SHRINES of American Methodism. FRANCIS ASBURY opened up work on STATEN ISLAND in 1771, and a visit to New Rochelle in the same year by JOSEPH PILMORE (who with RICHARD BOARDMAN was sent by JOHN WESLEY as a missionary team to New York and PHILADELPHIA in 1769) resulted in a society of thirteen members in 1774. After the arrival of Boardman in New York, Embury moved upstate to Camden in Washington County and organized the ASHGROVE Church in 1770. When the first Methodist conference in America was held at Philadelphia in 1773, New York reported 180 members, and the number was 222 in 1774.

During the Revolutionary War the Methodist movement in New York was retarded, but after 1788, as FREEBORN GARRETTSON led in opening the Hudson River Valley to Wesleyan influence, Methodism advanced. The movement then spread north and west following the river route of the Hudson and Mohawk, as well as the lake system—Lake Champlain to the east, the Finger Lakes in the central section, and the Great Lakes to the north and west. Methodist societies or churches were organized in the following places or regions in the years indicated: Newburgh, 1789; Albany, 1790; Wyoming Valley, extending into PENNSYLVANIA as well as Otsego and Saratoga counties, 1791; Herkimer County, 1793; Delaware County, 1794; Seneca County, 1796; Mohawk and Oneida Counties, 1799; and Cayuga County, 1800. The expansion of Methodism over New York state in so short a period of time was phenomenal. By 1855 the Methodist Church was the largest Protestant denomination in the state.

When the 1796 GENERAL CONFERENCE designated six annual conferences with geographical boundaries, the part of New York east of the Hudson River was placed in the NEW ENGLAND CONFERENCE and the remainder of the state in the PHILADELPHIA CONFERENCE. Then in 1800 the NEW YORK CONFERENCE was formed by dividing the New England Conference. At the beginning the New York Conference included the part of the state east of the Hudson River, the state of CONNECTICUT, and parts of MASSACHUSETTS, NEW HAMPSHIRE, and VERMONT. The boundaries were soon extended west to include more of New York. In 1810 the bishops formed the GENESEE CONFERENCE from parts of the New York and Philadelphia Conferences. The Canada Conference was formed in 1824 by dividing the Genesee Conference. In 1828 the New Hampshire and Vermont Conference was set off from the New York Conference. In 1829 came the ONEIDA CONFERENCE which included central New York and a part of Pennsylvania. It was formed by dividing the Genesee Conference. In 1833 the New York Conference was again divided to form the TROY CONFERENCE which included northern New York and a part of Vermont. In

1836 the BLACK RIVER CONFERENCE in northern New York was carved out of the Oneida Conference. In 1848 the Genesee Conference was divided to form the EAST GENESEE CONFERENCE in western New York and northern Pennsylvania. The 1848 General Conference divided the New York Conference again to form the NEW YORK EAST Conference which included Long Island, part of Connecticut, and a part of New York City. In 1852 the Oneida Conference was divided again to form the WYOMING CONFERENCE. The 1868 General Conference created the CENTRAL NEW YORK CONFERENCE from parts of the Oneida and Black River Conferences. In 1872 the NORTHERN NEW YORK CONFERENCE superseded the Black River Conference, and the WESTERN NEW YORK CONFERENCE was created by merging all of the Genesee Conference and part of the East Genesee Conference. Unhappy because their conference was abolished in 1872, the preachers from what had been the East Genesee Conference asked the 1876 General Conference to re-create the body. The General Conference complied, but the new East Genesee Conference which it decreed did not include all of the old territory. Whereupon, in the fall of 1876, instead of organizing as the East Genesee Conference, the preachers, with the consent of the bishops, approached the Western New York Conference about a merger, and the two bodies immediately united to form a new Genesee Conference.

Beginning in 1876 the M.E. Church had seven English-speaking conferences in New York: Central New York, Genesee, New York, Northern New York, New York East, Troy, and Wyoming. The latter three contained more or less territory from surrounding states. There was not another change in the names of these seven conferences until 1964 when the New York Conference absorbed the New York East Conference, and the Genesee Conference again became the Western New York Conference.

Methodism had foreign language work in New York. In 1866 the EAST GERMAN CONFERENCE (called Eastern German Conference for the first two years) was formed. Including all of the German work east of the Allegheny Mountains, it continued until 1943 and was the last of the German language conferences in the denomination to be absorbed. The EASTERN SWEDISH CONFERENCE was formed in 1901 to include all of the Swedish work in the northeastern states. It continued until 1941 before being absorbed. In 1908 the General Conference created the Italian Mission to include all Italian work east of a meridian drawn through Indianapolis. The Italian language work continued until 1916.

The METHODIST PROTESTANTS had work in New York from the beginning. Before the M.P. denomination was organized, a secedent group in northern New York called itself the Rochester Conference. In February 1830, the name was changed to the Genesee Conference. At the time it had about 442 members. The conference continued until 1908 when it was absorbed by the Onondaga Conference (MP). The Onondaga Conference, which then included western, central, and northern New York, continued until unification in 1939. In 1936 it reported forty-four churches, twenty-five preachers, and 2,135 members. On April 21, 1830 the New York Conference (MP) was organized in New York City with a total of ten itinerants and local preachers. Never a strong conference, it merged with the Pennsylvania Conference in 1911 to form the

Eastern Conference. At that time the New York Conference had 2,133 members.

The work of the WESLEYAN METHODIST CHURCH in New York is divided between its Champlain, Middle Atlantic, and Rochester Conferences, while that of the FREE METHODIST CHURCH is included in its Genesee, New York, and Susquehanna Conferences. The A.M.E. CHURCH has a New York Conference, the A.M.E. ZION CHURCH has a New York and a Western New York Conference, while the New York work of the C.M.E. CHURCH is included in its New York-Washington Conference.

In the early years all of the New York conferences of the M.E. Church supported schools and colleges. Nearly all of them had for longer or shorter periods a "conference seminary" or academy. The Genesee Wesleyan Seminary continued for more than 100 years. Such institutions as WESLEYAN UNIVERSITY, SYRACUSE UNIVERSITY, and the BOSTON and DREW THEOLOGICAL SEMINARIES were commended and supported as they came into existence. In more recent years the conferences have been contributing substantial sums for the support of WESLEY FOUNDATIONS and campus ministries at many state institutions of higher learning. In 1968 Syracuse University was the only Methodist institution of higher learning in the state, though the Troy Conference was giving support to Methodist related GREEN MOUNTAIN and Vermont (junior) Colleges in Vermont.

New York Methodism has furnished leadership for the larger church. Eighteen members of New York annual conferences have been elected bishops: BEVERLY WAUGH (1836), EDMUND S. JANES (1844), JESSE T. PECK and EDWARD G. ANDREWS (1872), CYRUS D. FOSS and ERASTUS O. HAVEN (1880), DANIEL A. GOODSELL (1888), CHARLES C. McCABE (1896), WILLIAM F. ANDERSON (1908), THEODORE S. HENDERSON (1912), ERNEST G. RICHARDSON and FREDERICK T. KEENEY (1920), WALLACE E. BROWN (1924), RALPH S. CUSHMAN (1928), CHARLES W. FLINT (1936), W. EARL LEDDEN (1944), and FREDERICK B. NEWELL (1952) and ROY C. NICHOLS (1968). Six men who served as members of the New York Conference at sometime in their career were not members of that conference or any other in New York at the time they were elevated to the episcopacy: ELIJAH HEDDING, JOSHUA SOULE, JOHN EMORY, DAVIS W. CLARK, RANDOLPH S. FOSTER, and LORENZO H. KING. Sixteen other men were either born in New York, or began their ministry there, but were serving elsewhere when elevated to the episcopacy: HENRY B. BASCOM, FRANCIS BURNS, CALVIN KINGSLEY, LINUS PARKER, WILLIAM X. NINDE, JOHN P. NEWMAN, BURTON R. JONES, HENRY SPELLMEYER, FRANK M. BRISTOL, WILSON S. LEWIS, RICHARD J. COOKE, FREDERICK D. LEETE, HERBERT WELCH, ERNEST L. WALDORF, FRED P. CORSON, and DWIGHT E. LODER. Two of the men in the latter list, Henry B. Bascom and Linus Parker, were elected bishops in the M.E. Church, South. Six bishops of the Free Methodist Church and two of the Methodist Episcopal Church in CANADA were born in New York. In addition to bishops, New York Methodism has furnished many leaders in other areas of the work of the church.

A number of service institutions in New York State bear witness to the outreach of Methodism's influence. Homes for the aged include Bethany Methodist Home, Brooklyn; Bethel Methodist Home, Ossining; Blocher Homes, Williamsville; Elizabeth Church Manor, Endwell; Folts Home, Herkeimer; Frontier Methodist Home, Niag-

ara; Methodist Church Home of New York, Bronx; Methodist Church Home, West Haven, Conn.; Methodist Home, Rochester; Methodist Retirement Center, Shelton, Conn.; and New York Deaconess Home, 1175 Park Avenue, New York City. Homes for children and young people include Methodist Home, Williamsville; St. Christopher's School, Dobbs Ferry; and Alma Mathews House for young women, 273 West 11th Street, New York City. Methodism has three hospitals in the state: Bethany Deaconess Hospital, and METHODIST HOSPITAL in BROOKLYN; and the hospital at the University of Syracuse. The Methodist Hospital in Brooklyn is the oldest Methodist hospital in America. John H. Vincent, later bishop, led in establishing the CHAUTAUQUA Institute at Lake Chautauqua in 1874. Chautauqua and a number of camps and conference centers are in operation every summer. An Indian Mission is maintained at Hogansburg.

In 1939 the Central New York, Genesee, New York, Northern New York, New York East, Troy, and Wyoming Conferences had a total of 27 districts, 1,773 charges, 458,635 members, and property valued at $79,707,369.

In 1970 the Central New York, Northern New York, Western New York, New York, Troy, Erie, and Wyoming Conferences reported 28 districts, 1,459 charges, 1,989 ministers, 593,724 members, property valued at $396,-789,444, and a total of $38,288,712 raised for all purposes during the year. These totals are not the exact statistics for Methodism in the state of New York. About one-half of the Wyoming Conference is in Pennsylvania; the New York Conference includes a part of Connecticut; the Troy Conference includes all of Vermont; and the Northern New Jersey Conference takes in a small part of the state of New York.

The Methodist Church had approximately 480,000 members in the state of New York in 1968.

Ray Allen, *History of the East Genesee Annual Conference.* Rochester: Hart Brothers Printing Co., 1908.
E. S. Bucke, *History of American Methodism.* 1964.
General Minutes, MEC and MC.
Minutes of the New York Conferences.
M. Simpson, *Cyclopaedia.* 1878.   ERNEST R. CASE
ALBEA GODBOLD

NEW YORK CITY, U.S.A. At the suggestion of Mrs. BARBARA HECK the first Methodist sermon in New York was preached in September 1766 by PHILIP EMBURY in his home on what was then known as Barracks Street. A growing congregation moved successively to an upper room ten doors from the barracks, the famed Rigging Loft on Horse and Cart Street in 1767 and, with the assistance of Captain THOMAS WEBB, into a chapel of its own on John Street Oct. 30, 1768. During the Revolutionary War the membership dwindled from 200 to sixty. Seven annual conferences were held with no appointment made to JOHN STREET CHURCH, which was isolated from the rest of American Methodism by the military situation. John Mann, converted under the ministry of BOARDMAN, occupied the pulpit through the war. In 1783 JOHN DICKINS was appointed and gathered the fragments together. The first session of the annual conference held in New York was in 1788.

As the membership of John Street grew, and as the population of Manhattan moved north, John Street Church began to establish new places of worship on the city's frontier. The first such was the Forsyth Street Church dedicated Nov. 8, 1789. During the next few years, the following additional Manhattan churches were erected: Willett Street, Allen Street, Second Street, Bowery Village (Seventh Street), Twentieth Street (18th Street), Bedford Street, Greene Street, Duane Street.

In 1832, when Methodist membership in New York was 5,433, an administrative decision to divide the churches into an East Circuit and a West Circuit was made. Prior to that, appointments had been made to John Street with its ministers rotating among the churches. Now there were two appointments and two quarterly conferences. A further division took place in 1836, when each church became a separate charge.

Growth in the city. With the abandonment of the circuit system and the deeding of property to local churches, it was inevitable that each newly independent church would be preoccupied with its development to the neglect of other areas of the city. Established churches flourished. Churches at Allen Street, Willett Street and Second Street were overcrowded, but several years elapsed before any new churches were established.

Church extension responsibilities were engaged in by the churches cooperatively through special organizations created for that purpose. Several years earlier, about 1820, the "Sunday School Society" had been established. It appears to have been reorganized as The New York City Sunday School Society about 1838. About 1842 the "Asbury Society" was organized "for the purpose of increasing the number of churches where they were most needed."

The Asbury Society established the Asbury Church in Norfolk Street in 1843 and later the Asbury Church on Jane Street in 1844. It also was instrumental in establishing a floating chapel—"BETHELSHIP John Wesley"—in 1845 which ministered to Scandinavian seamen and immigrants, and became the mother church of all Scandinavian Methodism in America and in Europe.

In 1844 the Ladies Missionary Society was founded. This organization established "Drydock Mission" on Ninth Street, now Eleventh Street, "Second German Church" on 40th Street, and FIVE POINTS MISSION.

Gradually church extension interests were consolidated with the New York City Sunday School Society. The constitution and by-laws which had been adopted in 1838 were amended in 1864 to include missionary as well as Sunday School work, and its name changed to "The New York City Sunday School and Missionary Society of the Methodist Episcopal Church." Under this name it was incorporated by act of the legislature in 1866. In 1871 the name was changed to "The New York City Church Extension and Missionary Society of The Methodist Church."

The Brooklyn Church Society of the M. E. Church was incorporated on May 28, 1878 to "aid churches, to give on church indebtedness, incumbrances on property, location of churches and church buildings, and to promote Sunday schools and missions in the city of Brooklyn and the vicinity." In 1917 its charter was amended to include Long Island.

North New York. The establishment of Methodist churches to the north, including Yorkville, Harlem, Bronx, Riverdale, began modestly about 1830 and accelerated in the period 1850 to 1870. The "Harlem Mission" first appears in the conference minutes in 1830, and includes all of Manhattan Island north of 23rd Street. Prior to this more than half of Manhattan Island was without regular Methodist preaching. The Seventh Street Church, and the Eighteenth Street Church, were on the frontier. The area

above 23rd Street was served by only two Dutch Reformed churches and perhaps four Protestant Episcopal churches. Here, however, Methodism developed some of its strongest churches among which were St. Paul, St. Andrews, Madison Avenue (now Christ Church) and Park Avenue.

The first Methodist church established in the area now known as Harlem was St. James, about 1830. After worshipping in several buildings, the present location on Madison Avenue at 126th Street was obtained in 1869. A strong Negro congregation continues a noble tradition in this building under the name Metropolitan Community Church. Negro people have held an important place in New York Methodism since the first meeting of the small group of five to which Philip Embury preached in the autumn of 1766. One of the five was a woman identified only as Betty, an African servant. The conference journal for 1786 reports 178 whites and twenty-five colored members in New York. In 1871 the most successful Methodist church for Negroes, St. Mark's, was established on Broadway, between 36th and 37th Streets. It was later relocated to St. Nicholas Avenue and 137th Street, Harlem, and shares with Salem Church in Harlem the honor of being the strongest churches of New York Methodism.

Even before the Harlem Mission, and the early spread of Methodism through the northern half of Manhattan Island, a Methodist church appears to have been established in Kingsbridge, north of the Harlem River, in 1826. It was known by various names: South Yonkers, Kingsbridge, North New York Mission, and in 1876, became St. Stephen's Church.

In the period between 1850 and 1865 several churches were established in the Bronx—Morrisania 1850, Fordham 1854, Tremont 1855, and Willis Avenue 1865.

Brooklyn. Attention was given Brooklyn early in Methodist history. Captain Webb, while riding the Long Island circuit in 1768, had occasionally preached a sermon in the home of a friend in Brooklyn. Prior to the revolution the few Methodists living in Brooklyn ferried to Manhattan to attend services first at the Rigging Loft and later at Wesley Chapel. FRANCIS ASBURY records a visit to Flatbush, a part of Brooklyn, Sept. 7, 1774, when he "heard Mr. Peabody preach." Woolman Hickson, who was assigned to New York in 1787, and who died in 1788, preached his first sermon in Brooklyn in the open air, standing upon a table in Sands Street, at the location upon which the Sands Street Church was later built. Peter Cannon accepted Hickson's invitation to make a regular meeting place available. This was his coopers shop. A class was soon formed, the first in Brooklyn, and NICHOLAS SNETHEN was the first leader.

By 1790 Brooklyn had become a regular preaching appointment, and was attached to the Long Island circuit. This circuit was served by two preachers. They alternated preaching a month in Brooklyn and a month elsewhere on Long Island. Those serving during the early years were Jacob Brush, John Eagan, James Boyd, Joseph Totten, and George Straveck.

Formal organization took place in the home of Peter Cannon on May 19, 1794. Property on Sands Street was purchased and a church erected and dedicated by Joseph Totten on June 1, 1794 as the "First Methodist Episcopal Church in the town of Brooklyn, Kings County, Nassau Island." Brooklyn became a separate station in 1795 and Joseph Totten became the first station preacher with thirty-five members.

Methodism was first established in the Borough and County of Queens, in New York City, with the organization of a church in Newtown (now Middle Village) in 1784. It was then the western point on a Long Island circuit with Commack the eastern point. These two accounted for twenty-four Methodists. Sixteen years earlier, 1768, Captain Thomas Webb first conducted Methodist services in this community at the home of James Harper, whose sons founded the publishing firm of HARPER & COMPANY. Meetings were held in the kitchen of his home in what is now Metropolitan Avenue. Later Newtown was a stop on the "circuit riding route" of JOSEPH PILMORE (1769-71) and Francis Asbury (1771-73). The first frame church was erected in 1785 at the corner of Dry Harbour and Junifer Roads.

Early Methodism in Jamaica is also associated with Captain Webb. The kindred of his wife lived in Jamaica. When retirement offered more leisure for travel "he went thither, hired a house and preached in it, and twenty-four persons received justifying grace." However, it was not until 1807 that a church was organized. It was a part of a circuit until 1843 when Joseph Ensign became its first resident pastor.

The old Long Island circuit was divided into two circuits in 1810—one in Suffolk County, on the east, and the other the Jamaica circuit on the west. This arrangement lasted until the Flushing circuit was organized in 1824.

Staten Island. The first sermon Francis Asbury preached in the State of New York was on Staten Island. His diary notation for Nov. 6, 1771 states: "In the way from thence [Philadelphia and Burlington] to New York I met with one, Peter Van Pelt, who had heard me preach at Philadelphia. After some conversation, he invited me to his house on Staten Island; and as I was not engaged to be at New York on any particular day, I went with him and preached in his house." PETER VAN PELT's family settled on Staten Island in 1687. He was a prominent citizen and a Methodist. His house was on Wood Road, about one half mile from the place where the Wood Road Church was built in 1787.

On Nov. 10, 1771, Asbury again preached at the home of Van Pelt, and in the evening a large congregation had gathered at the home of Justice Hezekiah Wright. He was Justice of the Court of Common Pleas of the Province of New York, and a prominent citizen who operated a fleet of vessels in coastal trade. Obviously, the seeds of Methodism had been sown on Staten Island earlier. Pilmore, Williams, and probably Boardman and Webb, had preceded Asbury in preaching on this Island. The Woodrow Church was organized May 5, 1787 in the home of Abraham Cole. The frame church was built and dedicated that year. Thomas Morrell was assigned as the first settled minister. The present Colonial church was dedicated Dec. 25, 1842—the earlier church having been destroyed by lightning.

The second Methodist church to have been established on Staten Island was Asbury in 1803 on what is now Richmond Avenue, New Springfield. Until 1806 it was known as both North End and Bold Neck Church. The present church was built on the same site in 1849. HENRY BOEHM was the first settled minister, 1802-3.

The Kingsley Church in Stapleton was organized in 1835. It was located at a private home until a frame church was dedicated Sept. 1, 1838 on the site of the present church.

Those three churches established outposts which was the pattern by which Methodism spread on Staten Island. Woodrow Church established Bethel Mission in Tottenville in 1822, St. John's Chapel at Rossville in 1854 and Pleasant Plains Church in 1854 (originally a class in 1837).

Asbury started Mariners Harbour Church in 1839, Dickinson Church in 1842, and Bloomfield Church in 1884. Kingsley established Quarantine Mission in 1840 and took on St. James of Rosebank as a mission as late as 1910.

Bethel A.M.E. Church. In the fall of 1817 Bishop RICHARD ALLEN, desiring to establish work in New York City where the A.M.E. ZION CHURCH had already made substantial progress, commissioned William Lambert, a member of the Philadelphia Conference, to go to New York City as an A.M.E. missionary. After arriving in New York Lambert secured the use of a school room on Mott Street in which he held services often, consecrating it for that purpose. Later in that same year (1818), Henry Harden was appointed to New York City. The young society remained at the Mott Street location until 1827 and continued to grow under Harden's leadership. Between 1827 and 1836 Bethel moved to locations on Orange Street, Centre Street, Elizabeth Street and Second Street, where they remained until about 1860. In 1860 Bethel moved to Sullivan Street where it grew to become one of the largest and most influential churches in the city. Between the First and Second World Wars it followed the Negro population of the city to its present uptown location.

Christ Church, Methodist, at Park Avenue and Sixtieth Street, is the denomination's central and leading church in America's metropolis. Standing at the heart of New York City and at "the gateway of the continent" it approximates in aim and influence JOHN WESLEY's concept, "the world is my parish."

It had its beginning in 1881 as the Madison Avenue M.E. Church. It was organized by a group of Methodists who wished to provide a Christian ministry for the increasing number of families who were establishing homes on the east side of Central Park, then a newly occupied part of the city.

From 1882 to 1917 the church had eight pastors: O. H. Tiffany, Charles Putnam Masden, Ensign McChesney, Sylvester F. Jones, Andrew Longacre, Wallace MacMullen, CHARLES L. MEAD (later bishop), and WORTH M. TIPPY. In 1915 RALPH W. SOCKMAN joined the staff and became pastor in 1917.

Sockman's fifty-year record of active service in the single metropolitan parish is unique in the annals of the ministry: lay member, 1911-13; student assistant, 1913-15; associate minister, 1915-17; senior minister, 1917-61. Under his guidance and radio ministry Christ Church became known throughout the Christian world. He was succeeded as senior pastor by HAROLD A. BOSLEY.

The new church building located at Park Avenue and Sixtieth Street was planned in 1929. Meanwhile, the present name, Christ Church, Methodist, had been adopted. The cornerstone was laid in November 1931, and the building was dedicated Nov. 26, 1933. Effective Nov. 15, 1933 the East Sixty-First M.E. Church was consolidated with Christ Church. This was pursuant to agreement and the order of Bishop FRANCIS J. McCONNELL with Sockman and Benjamin F. Saxon, who had been pastor of the East Sixty-First Church since 1909, as associate pastors.

The desire to build a beautiful sanctuary, as well as a structure adequate to its program, led to the selection of Ralph Adams Cram as architect, and his design was strongly influenced by the older Byzantine and Romanesque churches of the Mediterranean area. He recognized the limitation of the site in a mid-city area and created a church building with a restrained and well-proportioned exterior. Within he gave maximum space to the sanctuary, using glittering mosaic and rich marble for heightened color, with Christ as the central figure. Today the mosaics in Christ Church are regarded as among the best in America. The cost of land and building was over $3,000,000 in the 1930's, and the value has been greatly enhanced by the growth of the city.

In its physical form the church blends the East and the West. In its ministry and its work, it seeks to transcend man-made boundaries. Its membership includes leaders in the professional, economic and political life of the city. a large number of business and professional women and many students. Because of its pulpit, its beauty, and its central location, Christ Church attracts many week-day visitors as well as Sunday worshippers.

The Church Center for the United Nations is a twelve-story edifice on the U. N. Plaza—directly opposite the U. N. Headquarters Building—in New York City. It is an ecumenical building for the programs and services of interdenominational and denominational agencies concerned with humanitarian, peace, and social welfare interests. The edifice was erected by the BOARD OF MISSIONS and by the BOARD OF CHRISTIAN SOCIAL CONCERNS of The Methodist Church—both boards combining their programs of seminars and study of subjects and projects related to the U. N. Other organizations have headquarters in the building. It was opened for occupancy in May 1963, and consecrated the September following.

Notable in the Center are the Walter Van Kirk Memorial Library, the Dag Hammarskjöld Memorial Lounge, the Charles F. Boss Conference Room, and the Sadie Wilson Tillman Chapel.

Interchurch Center, the principal center of united Protestant and Orthodox witness and outreach in the U.S.A., is a modern nineteen-story edifice in New York City, bearing the address "475 Riverside Drive," and facing onto the Hudson River in upper Manhattan Island. It is in the area known as the City's cultural "Acropolis" which includes Columbia University and related institutions.

The site was donated by John D. Rockefeller, Jr., and many church organizations and individuals contributed to the erection of the edifice. The cornerstone was laid by President Eisenhower on Oct. 12, 1958, and the dedication was on May 29, 1960.

The Interchurch Center houses many tenant organizations, and these employ about 2,200 persons. About 30,-000 persons "sight-see" the Center each year; and many more thousands visit for church and related business. Besides denominational offices, exhibits, etc., visitors are interested in the Chapel and its sculptured ceiling, the Orthodox Room and its display of ancient icons, the Treasure Room which has many rare manuscripts of hymns and church music, and the original manuscript of the RSV Bible; and throughout the building tablets and other memorials to church leaders of recent years—men who contributed to the ecumenical movement.

The Board of Missions of the United Methodist Church occupies three floors in the Interchurch Center. Other Methodist agencies, presently housed there include: the A.M.E. CHURCH; the Foreign Missions Department of the A.M.E. Zion Church; the Interboard Committee for Christian Work in JAPAN, OKINAWA, the PHILIPPINES; the METHODIST COMMITTEE FOR OVERSEAS RELIEF; the New York City Society; the Brooklyn and Long Island Church Society; the New York Area Episcopal Office; the TELEVISION, RADIO, AND FILM COMMISSION; the New York Area Planning Commission.

Interdenominational and ecumenical organizations there with which the United Methodist Church works closely include: Agricultural Missions, Inc.; the Hymn Society of America; the Japan International Christian University Foundation; the Congo Protestant Relief Agency; Ludhiana Christian Medical College Board; the John Milton Society; the NATIONAL COUNCIL OF CHURCHES of Christ; the Protestant Council of the City of New York; the WORLD COUNCIL OF CHURCHES; the World Council of Religious Education; Vellore Christian Medical College Board; and the United Board for Christian Higher Education in Asia.

John Street Church (See JOHN STREET).

St. Mark's Church, in upper Manhattan, is one of the largest churches in the United Methodist connection, having presently approximately 4,700 members. It was organized on June 12, 1871, but moved to the present site on Nov. 22, 1920. The building is a stately one and acts as a center for the community about, serving many of its needs. It has an unusually active youth program, and is a member of the Harlem Interfaith Housing Corporation—a non-profit organization for the development of housing for community residents in that part of New York. A staff of four ministers serves St. Mark's.

Salem Church is a large church far up on Seventh Avenue, which ministers to a congregation of 2,600 members in the heart of Harlem. It was begun in April of 1902 in a storefront at 250 St. Nicholas Avenue as a mission of St. Mark's Church under the ministry of Williams H. Brooks. F. A. Cullen of the DELAWARE CONFERENCE was appointed to develop the new work. In August that year Salem moved to 232 West 124th Street in a private home previously used as a club and gambling center. In February of 1904 fire destroyed the worship area of Salem. With the help of the New York City Society, FRANK MASON NORTH, Secretary, six houses were purchased in 1911 at 133rd Street and Lenox Avenue. In 1908, Salem became an independent charge, and its rapid growth continued. In 1924 when Old Calvary M.E. Church, on Seventh Avenue and 192th street decided to relocate, Salem was ready to occupy the 2,000 seat sanctuary.

Dr. Cullen led Salem Church for forty-two years. He was succeeded by Charles Y. Trigg whose thirteen years of distinguished service witnessed a major renovation and won the fight that saved the facilities from threatened demolition to make way for city housing. Dr. Trigg retired in 1955, and is presently Minister Emeritus. In 1955 Joshua O. Williams became pastor of Salem until his death in 1963. During his pastorate major plans for an exterior renovation and a new community center were made. Samuel Sweeney served as interim pastor until June, 1964. In July Dr. ROY C. NICHOLS became pastor and by November 1967 the new community center had been completed and exterior renovation realized at a cost of over $800,000. The complete plant of Salem is valued at $1.3 million. Salem continued its outreach and service to the Harlem community. In July 1968, at the Northeastern JURISDICTIONAL CONFERENCE, Dr. Nichols was elected bishop. F. Herbert Skeete was thereupon appointed as pastor in August 1968.

Salem was the first Negro work organized in Harlem by a major denomination. Other older churches moved to Harlem from downtown in later years. The outstanding ministry of Salem to the social problems of its people continues with faithful support given the National Association for Advancement of Colored People and the New York Urban League. The latter was organized in Salem's dining room on 133rd Street.

Salem is located in the midst of St. Nicholas Housing project, and eighty percent of its membership live in Central Harlem. This cross-section congregation combines enthusiastic worship with twenty-eight John Wesley type classes, and these classes have accounted for the warmth and vigor of Salem from it inception. Six choirs serve the musical needs of Salem, with five directors and 240 members. Three ministers serve the pastoral needs of Salem and its community.

Paul Blakeney, *The 95th Anniversary Journal* (St. Mark's Church), October 1966.
Frederick A. Cullen, *Barefoot Town to Jerusalem*. New York: n.p., n.d.
J. T. Jenifer, *Centennial Retrospect* (AME). 1916.
D. A. Payne, *History* (AME). 1891.
S. A. Seaman, *New York*. 1892.
A. Stevens, *Memorials of Introduction*. 1848.

HENRY C. WHYMAN
GRANT S. SHOCKLEY
W. W. REID
F. HERBERT SKEETE
N. B. H.

NEW YORK CONFERENCE (ME) was created in 1800 by dividing the NEW ENGLAND CONFERENCE. Its territory at the outset was NEW YORK east of the Hudson River, the state of CONNECTICUT, and parts of MASSACHUSETTS, NEW HAMPSHIRE, and VERMONT. The conference was organized at NEW YORK CITY, June 19, 1800 with Bishop ASBURY presiding. Forty preachers attended, and appointments were made to twenty-eight charges. In 1803 the conference reported 11,458 white and 391 colored members.

As the years passed the boundaries of the New York Conference were altered many times. The most important boundary changes occurred when other conferences were carved from it or merged with it. The following conferences were set off from New York Conference territory in the years indicated: GENESEE, 1810; NEW HAMPSHIRE and VERMONT, 1828; TROY, 1833; and NEW YORK EAST, 1849. The latter merged with the New York Conference in 1964, thereby making the new New York Conference one of the strongest in the denomination. After the division into two conferences in 1849, the New York Conference was left with about 25,000 members. When the two conferences merged in 1964, the total membership was about 198,000.

Credit is due PHILIP EMBURY, BARBARA HECK, RICHARD BOARDMAN, JOSEPH PILMORE, and Francis Asbury for establishing Methodism in New York City and its immediate environs. (See New York.) In 1788 FREEBORN GARRETTSON began work as presiding elder in the region that stretches from New York City to CANADA and from Connecticut to Utica, and in the next thirty

years he more than any other man was responsible for establishing Methodism in that area. At RHINEBECK up the Hudson is the house in which Garrettson and his wife, Catherine Livingstone, lived until he died in 1827. In that year the New York Conference reported 30,223 members.

In 1841 a mission to German-speaking people was founded in New York City. In time there were two German districts in the conference, and in 1866 the EAST GERMAN CONFERENCE was organized.

Responding to the directive of the 1820 GENERAL CONFERENCE that annual conferences found colleges, the New York Conference established WESLEYAN UNIVERSITY at Middletown, Conn., in 1831. It is the second oldest permanent college in America founded by the Methodists. Wesleyan received strong support from the New York Conference and other surrounding conferences for more than a century until it ceased to be a Methodist related institution. A number of secondary schools which continued for longer or shorter periods were established throughout the New York Conference, the more prominent ones being Charlotteville Seminary at Charlotteville, Amenia Seminary at Amenia, Hedding Literary Institute at Ashland, Hudson River Institute at Claverack, and Drew Seminary for Young Women at Carmel.

In 1881 the METHODIST HOSPITAL in BROOKLYN, the oldest Methodist related hospital in America, was established in response to a challenging editorial in the *Christian Advocate* by the editor, JAMES M. BUCKLEY. GEORGE I. SENEY, the son of a Methodist minister, read the editorial which asked, "Is it not time that somewhere we built a hospital?" Seney then gave property and cash totaling $410,000 for launching the hospital. The institution started a school for training nurses in 1888. The hospital now covers a city block and there are plans for its further enlargement.

Other service institutions within the bounds of the New York Conference are: St. Christopher's Home for Children, Dobbs Ferry; Bethany Deaconess Hospital, Brooklyn; Bethel Methodist Home, Ossining; Methodist Church Home of New York, Bronx; Methodist Church Home, West Haven, Conn.; Bethany Methodist Home, Brooklyn; New York Deaconess Association Home, 1175 Park Ave., New York City; Methodist Retirement Center, Shelton, Conn.; and the Alma Mathews House for young women, 273 West 11th Street, New York City.

The New York Conference Center and Business Offices are located on a twenty-acre tract at Rye, N. Y. The Board of Missions of The United Methodist Church is domiciled at the Interchurch Center, 475 Riverside Drive, and the Church Center for the United Nations is at 777 United Nations Plaza in New York City.

The New York Conference operates four camps for children, youth, and adults: Quinipet at Shelter Island, Long Island; Sessions Woods at Bristol, Conn.; Epworth at High Falls; and Kingswood at Hancock.

Throughout its history the New York Conference has been affected by, and has endeavored to wield some influence on, the large number of immigrants entering the United States through New York. Starting with the German-speaking people in 1841 there have been ethnic churches down to the present. (See East German and Eastern Swedish Conferences, and Italian Mission). In recent years Negroes from the South and Spanish-speaking people from PUERTO RICO have come to New York in large numbers. Much of the conference's effort to minister to ethnic groups in the inner city is channeled through the New York City, Brooklyn, and Long Island Methodist Societies. These societies join with the National Board of Missions and with other denominations in the work. In recent years the New York Conference has raised $5,000,-000 to strengthen its ministry in the inner city, the suburbs, and the rural areas of the conference. The New York Conference has had some Negro members in its churches from the beginning, and it has had some large Negro congregations in New York City for many years. In 1959 Bishop FREDERICK B. NEWELL appointed a Negro minister to the church at Modena, New York, and beginning in 1962 the conference has had at least one Negro district superintendent in the bishop's cabinet. In 1968 ROY C. NICHOLS of the New York Conference was elected a bishop by the Northeastern Jurisdictional Conference, the first Negro ever elevated to the Methodist episcopacy "without regard to race" by a white JURISDICTIONAL or GENERAL CONFERENCE.

Over the years the New York Conference has provided the larger church with a number of bishops, missionaries, educators, theologians, editors, and other leaders. (See New York for a partial list of the bishops.)

The New York Conference came to unification in 1939 with four districts, 218 charges, 65,165 members, and property valued at $18,592,899. In 1963 the conference had 185 charges, and 74,129 members.

In 1968 the New York Conference reported eight districts, 441 charges, 709 ministers, 201,257 members, property valued at $165,637,374, and a total of $16,061,871 raised for all purposes during the year.

Fred H. Deming, ed., *The Onward Way, Story of the New York Annual Conference.* Saugerties, N. Y.: Catskill Mountain Publishing Corp., 1949.
General Minutes, ME, TMC, UMC.
Minutes of the New York Conference.

C. WESLEY CHRISTMAN, JR.

NEW YORK CONFERENCE (EUB) traces its origin to 1812, when the EVANGELICAL ASSOCIATION first gained a foothold in NEW YORK State. Although this mission failed, Christian Wolf then was sent into the state where he worked patiently around Fayette, Seneca County, N. Y., until he had established a nucleus for the denomination. Help arrived later and a circuit was formed. While Jacob Kleinfelter served the field, JOHN DREISBACH made regular visits as presiding elder. The work became organized as the "Seneca Circuit" and was a part of the Williamsport, Pa., District. The "Mohawk Circuit" was established in 1833 to minister to the Mohawk-German people along the Mohawk and Canajoharie Valleys.

The GENERAL CONFERENCE meeting at New Berlin, Pa., Sept. 29, 1847, decided that the work in New York and CANADA should be formed into a conference. The following February, at the session of the East Pennsylvania Conference, the New York Conference was formally organized with Bishop JOHN SEYBERT presiding. This conference brought the missionary efforts of the Canada, Buffalo, Rochester, Syracuse, and Albany Districts into one body with eleven circuits and 1,856 members. The first separate session was held in Buffalo on April 25, 1849. The work in Canada was separated from the New York Conference in 1865 and continued as the Canada Conference until January 1968, when it merged with the United Church of Canada.

Following favorable votes for conference union, the New York Conference churches were united with former Methodist conferences, Sept. 14, 1968. Eleven congregations were received into their respective conferences by the TROY, WYOMING, NORTHERN NEW YORK, and CENTRAL NEW YORK CONFERENCES. The remaining twenty-two churches united with the WESTERN NEW YORK CONFERENCE.

In 1966 there were thirty elders with thirty-four organized congregations and 6,929 members. Total money raised for all purposes that year amounted to $599,546, while congregational property was valued at $3,886,996.

R. W. Albright, *Evangelical Church.* 1942.
Journals of the New York Conference.
William Wagner, *History of the New York Conference of the Evangelical Church.* 1948. CLARENCE C. VAN

NEW YORK CONFERENCE SEMINARY AND COLLEGIATE INSTITUTE was a co-educational school, located in Charlotteville, Schoharie Co., N.Y., established in 1850. Though financed by private funds, it was endorsed by the NEW YORK CONFERENCE. Under the principalship of Alonzo Flack success was almost immediate, necessitating the addition in 1852 of two wings attached to the main building. Students by 1854 had increased to 1,253.

It was in 1854 that the original Seminary building was completely destroyed by fire. A single building had been in the meantime erected about a quarter of a mile away, designed to house the collegiate portion of the institution. Into this building the Seminary moved.

The original intent of the founders had been to operate the Seminary in conjunction with a collegiate department and also with a university, located in Troy, N.Y., and known as Troy University. This latter institution was built and operated long enough to graduate one class, but financial reverses faced by the promoters of this enterprise brought about failure, and the property was sold to one of the Roman Catholic orders.

A second fire, in 1867, reduced the Seminary to ashes, yet the trustees and faculty persisted in endeavoring to continue the life of the school. A large hotel in the community was purchased and fitted for school purposes, under the management of Solomon Sias, the son of the Rev. Solomon Sias, associate of ASBURY and later publisher of *Zion's Herald.* Charlotteville Seminary closed some time in 1875 and was not revived.

The significance of this Seminary is not to be measured in terms of its disasters, not the least of which was the decimation of much of the male portion of the students by the Civil War. The school offered an impressive curriculum. Literally hundreds of teachers went out from this school and an uncounted number of Methodist preachers received formal training there. Academically, Charlotteville Seminary rated among the best.

New York State Education Department markers have been placed to mark the site of the Seminary, beside the country road passing through Charlotteville.

WILLIAM R. PHINNEY

NEW YORK EAST CONFERENCE (ME). The 1848 GENERAL CONFERENCE created the New York East Conference by dividing the NEW YORK CONFERENCE. A list of appointments for the New York East Conference was read out at the 1848 session of the New York Conference which was held in the Washington Street Church, BROOK-LYN, beginning June 14. However, the New York East Conference did not hold its first separate session until May 30, 1849 when it met at Middletown, Conn., with Bishop THOMAS A. MORRIS presiding. The conference began with four districts, New York East, Long Island, New Haven, and Hartford. It had 114 charges and 21,485 members. At the beginning the territory of the conference was a part of New York City, Long Island, and the part of CONNECTICUT west of the Connecticut River, and its boundaries remained essentially the same throughout the conference's 115-year history.

The New York East Conference came to unification in 1939 with four districts, 259 charges, 96,874 members, and property valued at $20,265,241.

In 1964 the New York East Conference merged with the New York Conference to form again the larger New York Conference. In its last year the New York East Conference reported four districts—Brooklyn North, Brooklyn South, New Haven, and New York—262 charges, 390 ministers, 124,090 members, property valued at $74,553,-701, and a total of $8,791,480 raised for all purposes during the year.

Minutes of the New York East Conference.
General Minutes, MEC and MC.   ALBEA GODBOLD

NEW ZEALAND. This favored land consists of eight islands in the South Western Pacific, 1,200 miles across the Tasman Sea from the east coast of AUSTRALIA. The two main islands, the North and the South, are separated by the narrow Cook Strait (fourteen miles across at its narrowest part), and are inhabited by 2,808,590 people (1970). Though the South Island is the larger, two thirds of the people live in the North Island.

The large majority are Europeans, or "Pakehas" as they are often called to distinguish them from the Maoris. The latter number about 160,000, and were here before the Europeans. They claim that the islands were fished up out of the sea by Maui, the god-man. The geologists offer a similar explanation. Three hundred million years ago the land rose out of the sea, and since then has sunk beneath the waves again and again. This claim is supported by the rocks of the Southern Alps, the mighty backbone of the South Island, by the petrified forests on the coast line, and by fossil remains in many places.

Present-day Maoris trace their descent from those who came to New Zealand by canoe during the fourteenth century. They mark the southern limit of the Polynesian advance in the Pacific, the northern limit of which is Hawaii. After reaching New Zealand, the Maoris multiplied here until there were, perhaps, 200,000 in all.

They are a noble people, and evolved an impressive culture, though they possessed only bone and stone implements. Sinclair, in *A History of New Zealand*, says of them:

In some of their crafts they produced objects not yet surpassed in beauty of design or decoration by the works of their successors. They excelled in carving in wood, on their canoes, on their ornate meeting houses, on their boxes and tattooing funnels, and in stone. (p. 19)

The Maori recognised vast numbers of gods: but some recognised a supreme God who created the other gods and the universe. His name was Io; Io the parentless, Io of the hidden face, Io the giver of life. (pp. 20-21)

Religion pervaded the life of the Maoris. Debate and war were the great excitements of the Maori public, and the greater of these was war. The Maoris were the greatest of the Polynesian peoples. (p. 24)

In 1642, the Dutchman Abel Tasman sailed down the west coast of New Zealand. In 1769, Captain James Cook sighted the east coast of the North Island, and sailed right round the two islands. In 1773 for the second time, and in 1777 for the third time he visited the land. Many other explorers followed Cook, and then the sealers, missionaries, whalers, and traders appeared, much in that order.

Christian Mission. In 1814, Samuel Marsden, an Anglican clergyman from SYDNEY, NEW SOUTH WALES, preached the first Christian sermon, and in 1822 SAMUEL LEIGH, the first Methodist missionary in the same state, came to New Zealand, and began work at Kaeo in the far north of the North Island. In 1827, the station (Wesleydale) was destroyed by a Maori war party, and the missionaries narrowly escaped with their lives. The following year they began again on the opposite, or west, coast of the far north, at Mangungu on the Hokianga Harbor. It proved a successful venture, and by 1840 there were fifteen to twenty missionaries throughout the two islands.

The Maoris were most responsive to the Christian message. One missionary declared at that time that ninety percent of the people were disciples of Christ.

In 1840 the Treaty of Waitangi was signed. In this, Queen Victoria extended her protection to the Maori people, and reserved to them their fishing and other rights. Thus, without bloodshed, New Zealand passed under the control of Britain. The treaty played, and still plays, an important part in the development of the land. Without the influence of the missionaries, this treaty would probably not have been signed. This applies especially to the Anglican and Wesleyan missionaries. The Roman Catholic Bishop Pompallier and his French priests were present; they played no leading part in persuading the chiefs to sign.

At this time the Methodists had eight stations, two of them in the South Island: fifteen missionaries, with 1,300 members, and there were good working arrangements with the Anglican mission to prevent overlapping.

Unfortunately, the growing influence of the Pakehas and disputes regarding land led to fighting between the two peoples. The Maori Wars, as they were called, lasted sporadically from 1845 to 1869, and with one exception, they gravely affected the Methodist mission. One of the missionaries, JOHN WHITELEY, was killed in 1869 by the Maoris, and his death so shocked them that they would fight no longer.

Until the turn of the century it was thought that the Maoris were a dying people, but then there was a renaissance under Maori leadership, and ever since, the Maoris have increased, so that today their birth rate is much higher than that of the Europeans. The Methodist mission has not prospered to the extent that seemed likely in the early days, largely through resistance on the part of the Maori people—an unhappy legacy of bitterness from the Maori Wars. According to the 1970 census, there are today 225,435 Maoris and about 7½ percent of the Maori population claim to be Methodists.

There has been a revival of nationalism among the Maori people. Movements have combined old Maori pagan beliefs, a blend or mixture of Old Testament and New

Photo: Alexander Turnbull Library
THE MISSIONARY SHIP "TRITON" WHICH BROUGHT
STRONG REINFORCEMENTS TO NEW ZEALAND IN 1840.

Testament teaching, and a strong national sentiment. "Ratana" is the strongest of these movements, and it ranks as the third largest Maori denomination and the eighth largest in the country. The Methodists have privileges in Ratana Pa and among the children granted to no other church. This is due to the foresight and devotion of some of the missionaries thirty and more years ago.

The great majority of the Maoris today are under twenty-one years of age. There is a gradual fusion of the two peoples. Not a great many full-blooded Maoris are left even now.

Nowadays, Maori ministers are being trained in the same theological classes as European students, and some of them have won university degrees. Deaconesses are doing a splendid work among the women and children. Other denominations and sects are now at work among the Maoris, and some of them are right up alongside the Methodist stations. Others are in hitherto unoccupied areas.

Figures for other denominations in the 1961 census were: Anglican, 51,000; Roman Catholic, 28,500; Ratana, 22,000; Methodist, 12,611; and Mormon, 12,000.

The Methodist mission to New Zealand has been a noteworthy one. At the signing of the Treaty of Waitangi, Methodist chiefs played a leading part in persuading the other chiefs to sign. In large areas Methodist influence prepared the way for the white settler. In Otago, for instance, when the pioneers from Southland began negotiations with the Maoris for the purchase of land, the Maoris opened proceedings each day with prayer. These are some of the indications of the value of the mission to New Zealand at large.

The European Mission. Gradually the emphasis of the work changed from the Maori to the European. At first the work was administered from England. It was financed largely by the mission committee in London, both by direct grants and by providing the missionaries with articles for barter. From first to last over £200,000 was devoted to

the mission. In 1844 the grants began to grow smaller, though the needs were greater. During these years the missionaries were poor. They lived in homes meanly furnished. At times they were severely handicapped in their work by the shortage of money.

In 1854 New Zealand was transferred to the Australasian Conference. In 1869 the grants from England ceased altogether, and the New Zealand circuits took over the cost of the Maori work, as well as paying their own expenses. Ever since, the home and Maori missions have been closely linked.

As for barter, the mission society in London sent out articles like axes and tobacco to be paid to the Maoris for services rendered, or in return for food bought from them. It was a cumbersome system, for the missionaries had to provide storerooms, often costly to build. Moreover, the extravagance of some missionaries encouraged idleness among the Maori lads, who, as one missionary wrote, "share no little of the property."

In 1873 New Zealand became a separate conference in the Australasian church, and sent representatives every three years to a General Conference. In 1896, the UNITED METHODIST FREE CHURCHES and the BIBLE CHRISTIAN CHURCH in New Zealand joined with the Wesleyan Methodists. On Jan. 1, 1913, the Wesleyan Methodist Church in New Zealand separated from the General Conference of Australasia, and on the following February 6, the PRIMITIVE METHODISTS joined the Wesleyans to form "The Methodist Church of New Zealand," the first Conference of which met at once in WELLINGTON.

Until 1869, every minister in the Methodist churches of New Zealand had been born overseas. Slowly the proportion of New Zealand-born men began to increase, until, by the turn of the century, nearly all the candidates for the ministry were New Zealanders. It is probable that Methodists would have been a stronger church had they continued to receive a larger number of overseas men into the ministry.

The training of the men for the work was inadequate in those early years. Not until 1912 did Methodists possess a theological college proper (Dunholme), and then it was a rented building. In 1929, a worthy college with a hostel for students (university and other) attached, was opened in AUCKLAND (Trinity), and since then the standard of training has consistently risen, until today that standard is high.

Much of the pioneering work of the earlier years was carried out by consecrated home missionaries, who took the message into every corner of the land, and laid the foundations of what are today the circuits. For example, in 1913 Methodists had forty-four home missionaries, all untrained, but their witness was most effective. In 1966 there were only two home missionaries and four home missionary "supplies." It is now the policy of the Conference to man the stations either with ministers or supplies, the idea of offering men a life service as home missionaries having been abandoned. The country is still developing, and "supply" appointments will still be needed for some time to come.

Education. The early missionaries attached great importance to their Maori schools. There were, of course, no other schools. The government began to make grants to the schools of different denominations, the Methodist share being, all told, about £20,000. The missionary society expended about an equal amount. In 1853, there were 88 day schools, 188 Sabbath schools, and 5,846 scholars.

Some of the schools were boarding schools, but through the Maori Wars they were closed. In 1877, the government began to establish state schools, but even then the day schools had been closed. The Methodist missionaries were convinced that the work of educating should be left to the state.

Meanwhile the missionaries in the South Pacific had established a school for their own children in Auckland, Wesley College and Seminary, which later became Prince Albert College, but in 1906 even this college was closed.

There were also some Wesleyan schools for European children, but one by one they were all closed. Then in 1876, the work of the former Wesleyan Native Institution was resumed under the name of Wesley College at Three Kings (an Auckland suburb), and the training of the ministers began there. Gradually it built up a roll of scholars, and today, as Wesley College, Paerata, thirty miles south at Auckland, with an enrollment of two hundred boys, it is the one secondary school.

There can be no doubt that Methodism is weaker today than it should be because its record in education is poor.

RANGIATEA MAORI GIRLS' SCHOOL HOSTEL, SPOTSWOOD, NEW PLYMOUTH

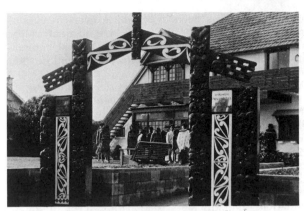

"TE RAHUI TANE," HOSTEL FOR MAORI BOYS, HAMILTON, NEW ZEALAND

Sons and daughters of Methodist farmers and professional men have been lost to the schools and colleges of other denominations. Methodists do not have their proportion of leaders in the professions. Despite these facts, there is still solid support among Methodist people that education should be left to the state, because of its greater resources in men and money, and that the churches should have the right to enter the schools, through their ministers and others, to teach the story told in the Bible.

Missions. Until 1913, the year of union with the Primitive Methodists, New Zealand Methodists were sharing with Australian Methodists the work in the South Seas: TONGA, FIJI, NEW GUINEA, and SAMOA, to name the chief fields.

When New Zealand became an independent Conference New Zealanders asked to have their own field, and in 1912 accepted responsibility for the Western Solomons. Here a vigorous mission has been carried on, and in 1966 ministered to 22,000 people. The depression years in the mid-nineteen-thirties, when it was necessary to withdraw some of the staff, and the years of the Second World War, when the Japanese occupied the islands, meant temporary setbacks. Today New Zealand Methodists have joined forces with the Australian Methodists in an additional mission to the highlands of New Guinea. These missions have become a precious part of the interests, and their reflex influence upon the Church in New Zealand has been most valuable.

Of late years New Zealanders have found themselves part of the Southeast Asian group of nations, and there is a growing interest in the Christian witness in these lands.

Missionary interests are shared by the Solomon Islanders themselves, for they have sent eighteen workers to the New Guinea Highlands, proving the genuineness of their own Christian experience.

Publication. The Methodist Board of Publications, carries on the work of a Publications Committee, set up in 1940 to issue pamphlets "setting out in popular form the teaching of the Methodist Church." At the beginning, its policy was somewhat timid, largely through lack of funds.

A bolder frame of mind emerged with the constitution of the Board of Publications in 1946, pledged "to carry through a vigorous policy of publications." It was planned to have a full-time director of publications who would also edit *The Methodist Times*. Widespread advertising in 1947 failed to attract a suitable candidate and the editor-manager policy has been in abeyance ever since. An appeal for £5000 in 1951 failed to receive adequate support, and this left the board hampered for lack of capital. In spite of this a useful supply of instructional and devotional material has been issued.

With the commencement of a widely circulating, free, fortnightly newspaper, *The New Zealand Methodist*, 1966, with Alun Richards as editor, the editor-manager policy still awaits realization, and the board continues with a part-time director.

Social Concerns. The Methodist Social Services Association was established in 1950 and succeeded in coordinating the various social services in New Zealand Methodism. This department surveys and makes recommendations annually on a nationwide level to the Conference and gives publicity to, and administers funds for, social service work. Its members consist of city missions, orphanages, eventide homes, hospitals, hostels and Maori Mission relief work.

Statistics. These tell their own story, which, probably runs parallel to the Methodist story in other lands. The following figures are taken from government census returns:

	1896	1926	1961
New Zealand population	703,360	1,334,469	2,414,984
Anglican	40.11%	43.45%	34.6%
Presbyterian	22.83%	25.93%	22.3%
Roman Catholic	14.23%	13.60%	14.4%
Methodist	11.1%	7.94%	7.2%

1. During these years an increasing percentage of people have availed themselves of the opportunity of "objecting to state their religious beliefs." The law allows them to do so. In 1926 there were 62,567, about four percent of the population. In 1956 there were 173,569: roughly eight percent. This exercises no little effect upon the figures in the above table, though one would suppose that the Methodist figures were not greatly affected.

2. It appears from these figures that, like the other Protestant churches, the Methodists have not kept their proportionate place in the community. It also appears that the Roman Catholic Church, in the period 1896-1926, declined, while the two largest Protestant churches increased. In the 1926-61 period, the reverse was the case. Over the last sixty years the Roman Catholic proportion has not altered significantly.

3. If to the table above we add some figures for Methodism, taken from the *Minutes* of the annual conferences, we learn that the year 1914 marked a high-water mark, that is, proportionately. Wesleyan and Primitive Methodists had just united: and in 1914 the First World War broke out, and hundreds of young men went overseas.

	1914	1944	1966
Churches	442	437	445
Other preaching places	487	380	213
Ministers in active work	163	176	248
Home missionaries in active work	47	32	6
Total agents in active work	210	208	254
Members	22,226	25,315	32,496
Sunday school scholars	30,191	18,913	21,458

In 1914, 81,713 attendants to public worship were reported. This figure was the largest ever returned. By 1931 it had dropped by 13,000, and the column was eliminated from the *Minutes*.

It would appear that Methodist Union was followed, whatever the reason, by a falling away. This was undoubtedly due in some measure to the impact of war. In 1939 war again weakened the church (this time by slowing up considerably the rate of increase), and only lately have Methodists begun to resume something of the earlier rate of advance. In the thirty years, 1914-44, the membership increased only 3,089. In the next sixteen years it grew almost 6,000.

But in thirty years (1880-1914) the membership grew from 3,542 to 22,226. The conditions now are different from those of the young pioneering days; but, by careful training of our ministers, and by keeping the evangelistic note in its proper place, and by avoiding another global war, the Methodist witness will fully justify itself in the life of New Zealand.

Trust Board. The Methodist General Purposes Trust Board is incorporated under the provisions of the Charitable and Educational Trusts Act, 1908. Its objects are to hold and administer any real or personal property transferred, devised, or bequeathed to the board, or in any other manner vested in the Board for special purposes or trusts in connection with any Methodist Church in New Zealand, or any church trust, organization, or department of the church. The personnel of the board is identical with that of the Supernumerary Fund.

In 1966 over a hundred different trusts and accounts were being administered, covering funds amounting to some £140,000—evidence of the growing importance of this fund in the general work of the church.

Other Methodist Bodies: Bible Christian Church. BIBLE CHRISTIAN work in New Zealand was started in 1841 at New Plymouth, with the arrival of a local preacher, Henry Gilbert. A small church was built and the Bible Christian Conference was asked to send a preacher. A long-delayed favorable reply came too late—the little congregation joined with the PRIMITIVE METHODISTS. A second beginning was made at Christchurch in 1877 by Edward Reed, a local preacher, who opened several preaching places. The first minister, W. H. Keast, arrived during the following year. With passing years, churches were built in Palmerston North, Wellington, Christchurch, Dunedin, and several smaller places. The two outstanding ministers of the connection were JOHN ORCHARD (superintendent, 1886-95) and WILLIAM READY, whose work in Dunedin was a spectacular success. Like the UNITED METHODIST FREE CHURCHES, the Bible Christians were too small to survive for long as a separate denomination, and they united with Free Methodists and Wesleyans in 1896. In the year of the union there were eleven ordained ministers and 609 members in full connexion.

Primitive Methodist Church began its work in New Zealand when ROBERT WARD arrived at New Plymouth from England in 1844. He visited from door to door, began to preach in the open air, and formed a society class of four members. A small congregation of Bible Christians joined with him, and the denomination was off to a good start. The work continued until 1913. Then the church united with the Methodist Church of Australasia in New Zealand to form the Methodist Church of New Zealand. By that time the Primitives were at work in every city and large center in New Zealand, and its laymen were playing a worthy part in the development of the country. Primitive Methodist statistics at the time of Union were: Members, 3,291; ministers and probationers, 43; churches, 81; other preaching places, 91;

home missionaries and deaconesses, 5, and local preachers, 208.

Scandinavian Mission was formed in 1872 by the appointment of Pastor Edward Nielsen, a probationer of the M. E. Church of NORWAY, who came to New Zealand to minister to a large community of his fellow countrymen who had immigrated to New Zealand. This mission covered an area in Southern Hawkes Bay and Manawatu. It was continued with the appointment of other workers (among whom was Otter Christoffersen) until 1893, when the work was merged with the neighboring circuits.

United Methodist Free Churches in New Zealand began effectively in 1868 with the arrival of MATTHEW BAXTER in the South Island city of Christchurch. He gathered some others about him, and churches were soon built at St. Asaph Street and the suburb of Addington. Six years later his health failed, and the virtual leadership of the young connection passed to Samuel Macfarlane, who became connectional secretary. In the years that followed, churches were founded in various places, notably in Auckland, Wellington, Napier, Westport, and Rangiora. From the beginning Free Methodism was hampered by lack of finance and manpower, but the real difficulty in the path of progress was that it could not compete with the larger Wesleyan Methodist body, from which it differed only by inclining to a congregational form of polity. Union between Wesleyans, Bible Christians, and Free Methodists was effected in 1896. At that time the United Methodist Free Churches reported 23 churches; six other preaching places; fourteen ministers; 34 local preachers; 941 church members; 208 Sunday school teachers; 1,880 Sunday school scholars; and 2,143 attendants at worship.

Wesleyan Methodist Church. Organized Methodism in Australasia began in 1815 with the appointment of Samuel Leigh to New South Wales by the British Conference. Seven years later Leigh pioneered the Wesleyan Mission in New Zealand. At first work was chiefly among the Maori people, but from 1840 on, churches mainly for Europeans sprang up in the larger centers. When the direct link with the British Conference was severed in 1854, New Zealand continued to be administered as a district of the Australasian Wesleyan Methodist Conference. From 1874 onward, New Zealand had its own annual conference, but continued to send representatives to the triennial General Conference in Australia.

Union with two small Methodist bodies—the Bible Christians and the United Methodist Free Churches—was consummated in 1896. Primitive Methodism stood aloof pending separation from Australia, and the name of the church was changed to the Methodist Church of Australasia. The direct link with Australia was severed in 1913, except for partnership in overseas mission enterprise, which continued until 1922, when the Solomon Islands field became a distinct New Zealand responsibility. Separation from Australia removed Primitive Methodist objections, and union with that body was consummated in 1913. Thus was the Methodist Church of New Zealand born.

At the time of the 1913 Union, the statistics of the Methodist Church of Australasia in New Zealand were: 19,753 members, including 2,052 Maori members; ministers and probationers, 146; Maori ministers and probationers, 10; churches, 372; schoolrooms and other preaching places, 239; home missionaries and deaconesses, 57.

Church Union. New Zealand Methodism has always been well to the fore in church union discussions. In 1900, union sentiment was so strong that for ten years the Presbyterian, Methodist, and Congregational churches combined their denominational newspapers. However, no enduring and positive action resulted at that time.

Conversations continued sporadically "between the Wars," and then in 1942 and 1948 two successive votes were taken on a basis of union. These resulted in a majority declaring for church union. However, it was agreed by the negotiating churches that on neither occasion was the majority large enough to warrant proceeding with organic union at that stage.

In 1953 the joint committee of the three churches took the initiative in inviting interested churches to join in fresh conversations. The Associated Churches of Christ responded favorably, and later, in 1964, the Anglican Church joined the negotiations.

In 1966 a joint Declaration of Faith was given general approval by all five churches, and progress was made toward a basis of union. Meanwhile the five negotiating churches were conducting many local experiments in co-operative working—reciprocal membership, union parishes, and joint use of buildings.

L. R. M. Gilmore, *The Bible Christian Church in New Zealand.* Wesley Historical Society, New Zealand, 1947.
Guy and Potter. *Primitive Methodism in New Zealand.* 1893.
G. I. Laurenson, *The Scandanavian Mission in New Zealand.* Wesley Historical Society, New Zealand, 1955.
S. G. Macfarlane, *Free Methodism in New Zealand.* Wesley Historical Society, New Zealand, 1958.
Minutes of the New Zealand Methodist Conferences.
W. Morley, *New Zealand.* 1900.
Keith Sinclair, *A History of New Zealand.* London: Penguin Books, 1959.
W. J. Williams, *New Zealand.* 1922.   WILLIAM T. BLIGHT
                                        L. R. M. GILMORE
                                          A. EVERIL ORR
                                      HERBERT L. FIEBIG
                                    GEORGE I. LAURENSON

NEWARK, Hokianga, NEW ZEALAND, was the site of a mission station at Pakanae, near the Hokianga Heads. The station was founded in 1836, by JOHN WHITELEY, who named it Newark after the town in England from which he came as a candidate for the ministry. It was never a large station because it was only a few miles from the head station at Mangungu. The site is still marked by several lofty Norfolk pines planted by Whiteley.

W. Morley, *New Zealand.* 1900.   L. R. M. GILMORE

NEWARK CONFERENCE. (See NORTHERN NEW JERSEY CONFERENCE.)

NEWCOMER, CHRISTIAN (1749-1830), pioneer bishop of the Church of the UNITED BRETHREN IN CHRIST, was born in a Mennonite home, nine miles from Lancaster, Pa. In the spring of 1775, Newcomer married and moved to Beaver Creek, near Hagerstown, Md. He came under the influence of PHILIP WILLIAM OTTERBEIN and GEORGE ADAM GEETING. He then joined one of the little groups of *Otterbein people,* who were referred to as "Dutch Methodists."

In 1777, Newcomer began to preach. He was a member of the first conference of the United Brethren, which met in Otterbein's parsonage, BALTIMORE, Md., 1789. He was elected bishop in 1813 and served until his death.

He was the foremost organizer of the United Brethren, bringing life and organization to the young church. Not satisfied merely to convert people, Newcomer insisted upon organizing classes and keeping records.

A half-century was spent as a circuit rider, Newcomer travelling as far west as INDIANA and KENTUCKY, and north into CANADA. He crossed the Allegheny Mountains thirty-eight times on horseback, the last trip at the age of eighty-one. A faithful record of his last thirty-five years was kept and this *Journal* was published following his death. He died at his home, March 12, 1830 as the result of a fall, and was buried in Beaver Creek Cemetery, near Hagerstown.

Christian Newcomer constantly urged union of the United Brethren with the Evangelicals and the Methodists. His references to the Methodists appear more than 125 times in his *Journal*. The United Methodist Church of the present can look back upon Christian Newcomer as one of its true fathers.

John Hildt, trans., *Life and Journal of the Rev. Christian Newcomer.* Hagerstown, Md.: F. G. W. Kapp, 1834.

D. HOMER KENDALL

FREDERICK B. NEWELL

NEWELL, FREDERICK BUCKLEY (1890-   ), American bishop, was born in Hartford, Conn., on March 11, 1890, the son of William Henry and Ellen L. (Brewer) Newell. He received the following degrees: B.A. from WESLEYAN UNIVERSITY, 1913, and the D.D. in 1936; M.A. from Columbia University, 1916; B.D., Union Theological Seminary (New York) in 1916; D.D. from MOUNT UNION COLLEGE, 1931; LL.D. from the AMERICAN UNIVERSITY, 1955, SYRACUSE UNIVERSITY, 1957, and D.D. from West VIRGINIA WESLEYAN COLLEGE, 1968. On Jan. 15, 1919,

he married Emily Louise Lewis of Jersey City, N. J. Their children are Eleanor L. (Mrs. Kenneth W. Steere) and Frederick Buckley.

Frederick Buckley Newell was admitted on trial and ordained deacon in the NEW YORK EAST CONFERENCE in 1917; full connection, 1920; and elder in 1922. He has been pastor of the People's Home Church and Settlement, NEW YORK CITY, 1917-20; assistant executive secretary, New York City Society of Methodist Churches, 1920-30; and executive secretary, 1930-52. He was elected bishop in 1952 and served the New York Area, retiring in 1960. On the death of Bishop MIDDLETON in 1965, he was put back into active service by the COUNCIL OF BISHOPS and put in charge of the PITTSBURGH Area for the rest of the quadrennium.

Bishop Newell has served as a member of the executive committee on the Board of Managers of Church World Service since 1960, acting executive director, 1961; and a trustee and member of the Curriculum Committee of Wesleyan University. Since 1945 he has been director of the Union Theological Seminary, and has been also a director of Charlton Industrial Farm School. He is a trustee of Wesleyan University, of DREW UNIVERSITY, and CENTENARY COLLEGE FOR WOMEN; a trustee and member Board of Trustees of the JOHN STREET CHURCH; trustee and member of the Executive Committee, a member and on the Board of Directors of the AMERICAN BIBLE SOCIETY since 1952, and a member of the Executive Committee of the New York City Society of The Methodist Church.

Who's Who in The Methodist Church, 1966.   N. B. H.

NEWMAN, JOHN PHILIP (1826-1899), American pastor, church organizer, chaplain, bishop, was born in New York, N. Y., Sept. 1, 1826. John Philip's father died when he was only eight years of age leaving his wife, Mary D'Orfey Allen, a vivacious and richly intelligent woman of Huguenot ancestry, with seven children.

At sixteen John Philip was converted and, after a few terms in Cazenovia, N. Y., Seminary, began to preach with rustic eloquence in country churches. He did not take a college course, and entered the Oneida Conference in 1849.

At Fort Plain, N. Y., a blunt schoolmaster told him that his grammar and pronunciation were abominable. Immediately he began zealously to remedy these and other faults. He married Angeline Ensign, an inspiring companion, in 1855. After filling a number of appointments, he was transferred in 1855 to the TROY CONFERENCE. Beginning to write out and memorize his sermons, his rich musical voice and imagination attracted the attention and admiration of the Governor of New York when Newman was stationed in Albany. In a short time he was transferred to the NEW YORK CONFERENCE where he crowded the largest churches in New York City-Bedford Street Church in 1859, and Washington Square, 1862-64.

In 1860 he made an extensive tour of Europe and of the East which resulted in a book, *From Dan to Beersheba,* 1864. He published six other books and some smaller booklets. From 1864 to 1869 he was responsible for establishing the M. E. Church in the South. He was stationed in NEW ORLEANS, La., and succeeded in building a fine church in that city, opening a seminary and an orphanage, and starting a paper.

In 1869 Newman was appointed to the new Metropolitan Church, WASHINGTON, D.C. President GRANT, Vice-President Colfax, Chief Justice Chase, Major-General Logan, and other notables, were members, as was later President McKINLEY. Newman was chaplain of the U.S. Senate three terms. President Grant made him Inspector of U. S. Consulates in Asia, 1874-76, and by Grant's appointment, he made a trip around the world. His report was valuable and he published *Thrones and Palaces of Babylon and Nineveh*. Newman served Metropolitan Church a second time, 1876-79. His next pastorate, 1879-82, was Central Church, New York City, of which Grant became a trustee. He was a member of the first and second ECUMENICAL METHODIST CONFERENCES. For the third time he was appointed to the Metropolitan Church.

A delegate to several GENERAL CONFERENCES, Newman was elected bishop in 1888. His episcopal residences were OMAHA (Nebraska), 1888-96, and SAN FRANCISCO (California), 1896-99. Bishop Newman made visits to JAPAN, South America and MEXICO.

Bishop Newman was not a distinguished administrator but his fine spirit and broad sympathy redeemed some of his weaknesses. His rehearsed gestures and literary illustrations pleased the prevailing taste of his day. The friend of Grant, Bishop Newman watched by his hero's bedside and pronounced the official eulogy.

Childless himself, he and Mrs. Newman educated scores of young men. He died at Saratoga, N. Y., his summer residence, July 5, 1899, and was buried in Mechanicville, N. Y. His estate was divided between DREW THEOLOGICAL SEMINARY, New Jersey, and a school in Jerusalem.

Dictionary of American Biography.
F. D. Leete, *Methodist Bishops.* 1948.
M. Simpson, *Cyclopaedia.* 1878.   JESSE A. EARL

NEWMAN, JUNIUS E. (1819-1895), American preacher and founder of permanent Methodist work in BRAZIL, was born near Point Pleasant, W. Va., on Oct. 16, 1819. He was licensed to preach in 1843, and in January 1848 was received in full connection into the ALABAMA CONFERENCE. Until 1867, Newman worked mainly in eastern MISSISSIPPI. Having lost most of his moderate fortune in the War Between the States, he decided to follow many of his Southern friends who were leaving the Reconstruction South for Brazil. He was therefore regularly accredited and appointed by Bishop W. M. WIGHTMAN for missionary work in Central America or Brazil.

Paying his own way, he arrived in RIO DE JANEIRO on Aug. 5, 1867, lived there for a period and then moved into the then province of SÃO PAULO, where many of his countrymen had settled, and bought a farm which served as a means of livelihood. He preached regularly to these transplanted North Americans; and on Aug. 17, 1871, organized a church with nine members, all Americans, in the community around Santa Barbara do Oeste, São Paulo. Until 1879, he served as superintendent of this mission. Finally, broken in health, he returned to the United States in the fall of 1889.

Newman's was the only voice raised for Methodism during the twenty-five-year silence that followed the Spaulding-Kidder Mission (1836-1845). He not only organized a work that became permanent; but his letters to the NASHVILLE and NEW ORLEANS *Christian Advocates,* addressed to the bishops and others of the M.E. Church, South, presented the urgent need of Brazilians, and resulted in the definite and official founding of the Brazil Mission, by act of the GENERAL CONFERENCE of 1874. In 1876, JOHN JAMES RANSOM was sent to initiate this work.

Junius Newman's two daughters, Mary Phillips and Annie Ayres, founded the Newman School in PIRACICABA, province of São Paulo, in 1879. Because of Mary's illness and Annie's marriage to J. J. Ransom, the school was closed. But it became the precursor of the Colegio Piracicabano, later called Instituto Educacional (see PIRACICABANO), opened in September 1881, by Martha H. Watts—the oldest Methodist educational institution in Brazil.

J. E. Newman died in Point Pleasant, W. Va., in May 1895.

J. L. Kennedy, *Metodismo no Brasil.* 1928.   D. A. REILY

NEWPORT, RHODE ISLAND, U.S.A. Before the Revolutionary War of 1775, Newport was one of the largest cities on the Atlantic coast, having grown rich with trade in molasses, rum, and slaves. It was the capitol of the State until 1900, and has long been a favorite watering place of the wealthy as well as a strategic naval station. JESSE LEE preached there, soon after the Revolution, in 1790. It was included in the Greenwich circuit, and Joshua Hall was appointed in 1800, and the society organized as the First Methodist Church. The church building, of colonial architecture, erected in 1806 was still being used in 1966, and is said to be the first Methodist church in the world with a steeple and a bell.

Bishop ASBURY preached in this building, and frowned upon the church having a steeple. His journal records, "we crossed Narragansett Bay on Friday, May 28, 1809, and came into Newport—grand house, steeple, pews; by lottery; the end is to sanctify the means. Ah, what pliability to evil." Actually, the lottery never worked out, and the money was returned to the people. Bishop COKE was in Newport in 1804. The present church is the mother of the Thames St. Church (1856-1923) which reunited with First Church in 1923 to form St. Paul's. The church building was partially burned in 1881, and renovated in 1882. In 1910 the building was enlarged, and in 1960 an educational unit was added.

Methodism in adjacent Middletown on Newport's Aquidneck Island at Portsmouth began in 1790 with Jesse Lee, and is the oldest church on the island, the society being organized in 1793 with Bishop Asbury preaching.

Lucius D. Davis, *History of the Methodist Episcopal Church in Newport, R. I.* 1882.
R. C. Miller, *New England Southern Conference.* 1897.
Zion's Herald, August 1960.   DAVID CARTER

NEWPORT NEWS, VIRGINIA, U.S.A., on the VIRGINA Peninsula, has a good harbor and is a foreign and coastwise shipping point. The Newport News Shipbuilding and Dry Dock Company plant covers 150 acres and is one of the largest in the world. The city was laid out in 1882 and incorporated in 1896. The population in 1970 was 137,348. The Civil War engagement between the *Monitor* and the *Merrimac*, March 9, 1862, off Newport News, was the first ironclad naval engagement in history.

Trinity Methodist Church was organized Dec. 8, 1886, with ten members under the first pastor, J. T. Bosman, who served 1886-88. The first services were held in the Union Chapel, and the first building was erected on Washington Avenue in 1887. The name was changed from Washington Avenue to Trinity in 1900 when a new building was constructed. During the pastorate of W. W. McIntyre, 1945-49, the membership was 1,429. In 1970 the membership was 901 and the property valued at $680,000.

First Church is the largest Methodist church on the Virginia Peninsula. It was designed originally to serve Hilton Village, an early experiment in suburban living during World War I. The Village was built far away from the city of Newport News, contact was made by streetcar. Since that time the city has surrounded the village, and First Church has become a central church for the city.

Started in 1920, its first buildings were of stucco design, but with the rapid growth during World War II, these buildings were demolished and replaced with buildings of modern colonial design. It now has a membership of 2,129, and a church school membership of 1,344.

The last church organized in the city was Asbury, which was established in 1961 in an area adjacent to Fort Eustis. There are plans for immediate establishment of two more Methodist churches.

In 1905 St. James Church was established by Negro Methodists. In 1970 St. James reported seventy-six members. There are two other Negro churches here: Walter's Temple A.M.E. Zion and St. Paul's A.M.E.

The twelve United Methodist churches in the city had 7,774 members in 1970, and property valued at $4,059,220.

Collier's Encyclopedia.
General Minutes.   R. BEVERLY WATKINS

NEWSPAPERS, British Methodist (see under MAGAZINES AND NEWSPAPERS, Br.). For American Newspapers, see under ADVOCATE, CHRISTIAN, and METHODIST PUBLISHING HOUSE for treatment of the general church publications. Certain significant American publications will be found treated under their own names, as *Zions Herald, The Methodist Protestant, Star of Zion,* etc.

NEWTON, MINNIE E. (1878-1944), was an eminently successful educational missionary in Gujarat State, INDIA. She was born in East Aurora, N. Y., Sept. 14, 1878, graduated from the New York State College for Teachers and later from Columbia University, earning the B.S. and M.A. degrees.

She went to India as a M.E. missionary in 1912. Her first appointment was to a small girls' school in Godhra, Panch Mahals District, which had been opened in 1900 to care for orphans saved from the terrible famine of that year. Out of that unpromising beginning she developed a highly successful junior-high school and a training school for women teachers of primary classes.

Her services were appreciated by her own and other churches and missions, and by the educational department of the Government of Bombay State, with which Gujarat was then associated. She was appointed chairman of the government school board for Panch Mahals District. It has been said that she trained more women teachers for service in India than anyone else had ever done.

Miss Newton died at Godhra, where she had served during most of her thirty-two years in India. She is buried in Godhra.

J. N. Hollister, *Southern Asia.* 1956.   J. WASKOM PICKETT

ROBERT NEWTON

NEWTON, ROBERT (1780-1854), British Methodist, was born at Roxby, North Yorkshire, April 8, 1780, the son of a farmer. Converted in 1798, he began to itinerate almost immediately, and was received into full connexion in the Wesleyan Methodist ministry in 1803. He was a famous preacher and advocate of overseas missions. He was elected president of the Wesleyan Conference in 1824, 1832, 1840, and 1848; between 1821 and 1847 he was secretary of the Conference on nineteen occasions. In 1840 he was fraternal delegate to the GENERAL CONFERENCE of the Methodist Episcopal Church in BALTIMORE.

Newton was prominent in all the internal Methodist controversies of his lifetime; as chairman of the Manchester District in 1833-35, he had to cope with both J. R. STEPHENS and SAMUEL WARREN. After JABEZ BUNTING he was the most distinguished of the conservative Wesleyans, and as such he was one of the chief targets of the FLY SHEETS. He superannuated in 1852 and died at Easingwold on April 30, 1854.

T. Jackson, *Robert Newton.* 1855.
Dinsdale Young, *Robert Newton, The Eloquent Divine.* c1910.
                                    JOHN KENT

NGAROPI, HAMIORA (1809-1887), was a pioneer Methodist Maori minister of New Zealand. Little is known of this man except that he became a Christian in 1835 and entered the ministry in 1856. His work is commemorated, along with others, on a granite monument on the site of the Mangungu Mission Station. The inscription concerning him reads: "Hamiora Ngaropi, who laboured among the Waikato tribes, he being the first Maori to be ordained to the ministry."

C. H. Laws, *First Years at Hokianga* (Wesley Historical Society, New Zealand, 1945).
New Zealand Methodist, July 23, 1887.   L. R. M. GILMORE

NIAGARA FALLS, NEW YORK, U.S.A., a large city and a tourist resort on the Niagara River, is surrounded by the Niagara fruit belt. The present city includes three former villages—Niagara Falls, Niagara City and La Salle, which was annexed in 1927.

The Scenic Gateway to America, Niagara Falls has the Niagara Falls Museum, and the Peace Memorial, honoring John the Baptist, John the Evangelist, Pope John and John Kennedy.

Methodist missionaries preached throughout the Niagara Frontier in 1788. George Neal seems to have been the first of these circuit riders, followed by WILLIAM LOSEE in 1791; Capt. WEBB, NATHAN BANGS, Joseph Sawyer, James Coleman, 1794; Andrew Prindle, 1810; Joseph Gatchell and Elder Loring Grant, 1811. Each of these men traveled about 300 miles in a circuit, touching each spot only about once a month.

They left CLASS LEADERS in their wake and held meetings in the private homes. The earliest of these class leaders at Niagara was known as Brother Post. Regular circuits followed in the beginning of the nineteenth century. Some seventy-seven circuit riders traveled the local circuit which at one time included a part of CANADA.

In 1815 Methodism was organized in the village of Niagara Falls. (This was the beginning of present St. Paul's Methodist Church.) The first house of worship was purchased in 1824 by civic-minded citizens and it served all denominations as Union Chapel until 1839 and later as Methodist Chapel. In 1839 the first Methodist Sunday school was organized with seventy-eight pupils, and the society was incorporated as First Society of the Methodist Episcopal Church of Niagara Falls Village.

The Methodists purchased the frame Presbyterian building in 1849. It was used until 1865 when a new building was planned and completed in 1872, dedicated by Bishop PECK Oct. 2, 1872.

In July 1865 the corporate name of this old church in Niagara Falls was changed to St. Paul's M. E. Church. The old St. Paul's building was in continuous use until July 1919, when it was sold. During the two and a half years of construction, the Y.W.C.A. edifice was used.

St. Paul's new church cost $276,764. The church was dedicated Aug. 12, 1923. The mortgage was not burned until Nov. 7, 1948. At this celebration, Bishop F. J. McCONNELL delivered the morning sermon and WILLIAM L. STIDGER, the evening sermon.

From 1943 to 1965, St. Paul's had sixty-four Lenten speakers, all outstanding clergymen of different denominations. The first was MERTON S. RICE. This was his last service. The following Sunday he died of a heart attack. The speakers included Charles R. Brown, HENRY HITT CRANE, BISHOP G. BROMLEY OXNAM, and Martin Niemoeller.

First Church was organized in September 1855, in the La Salle section of the city. This became a part of Niagara Falls in 1927. A church was dedicated in February 1856, on the River Road (Buffalo Avenue). Several renovations were made in the original building prior to its being razed in 1916 to make room for a Community Hall. The present church building and parsonage were dedicated on July 1, 1924.

Although the church had been called First Methodist for many years, the legal change to First Church from La Salle was not made until 1939. A new educational facility was dedicated in March 1953.

St. James Church first met Dec. 25, 1892, in a small wooden structure and was organized March 13, 1893. In 1913 a much larger new brick church was erected and dedicated in June. The church moved to a new location in an educational building in the late 1950's which was dedicated in 1963.

Wesley Church was started as a Sunday school in 1929 and assigned a supply pastor in 1941 as a mission post of First Church of La Salle. Officially organized in March 1948, and with help from other local churches and the conference, a modern church was dedicated Oct. 15, 1961.

The membership of the four Methodist churches in the city in 1970 totaled 2,516 and property was appraised at $2,316,153.

Encyclopedia Americana, 1962.
General Minutes, 1970.

JESSE A. EARL

NICENE CREED. (See CONFESSION OF FAITH.)

NICHOLAS, WILLIAM (1838-1912), Irish minister, was born at Wexford, and graduated at TRINITY COLLEGE, DUBLIN. He travelled some of the most important circuits in Irish Methodism, including three terms in Portadown, and was twice Vice-President of the Conference (1894 and 1903), the highest office in the Church. In 1893 he delivered the FERNLEY LECTURE of the British Conference, on the subject "Christianity and Socialism," and in 1895 became President (Principal) of the METHODIST COLLEGE, BELFAST. He was Secretary of the Education Fund for many years, and had a special interest in candidates for the ministry and in junior ministers. His personal friendship for these young men meant much to them in later life.

FREDERICK JEFFERY

NICHOLLS, MARGARET WAIATA (1894-), NEW ZEALAND deaconess, was born at Normanby, Taranaki, and brought up in Te Kuiti. Many gracious influences of home and church which surrounded her in childhood and youth led her to enter the Methodist Deaconess Order in 1920. Her whole life was then spent in the service of the Maori people, in the Waikato, King Country, and AUCKLAND circuits.

She made a special study of Maori religions, language, and customs, and was active in promoting social, educational, and religious welfare among the Maori people. Her outstanding service was recognized when she was made a Member of the Order of the British Empire in 1962.

It was largely through her influence that the famous Maori leader, the late Maharaia Winiata, entered the service of the Methodist Church.

Though interested in a wide variety of activities, Sister Nicholls claims that the preaching of the Gospel of Christ remains the most important factor in her life. She retired in 1967, after forty-six years' service.

L. R. M. GILMORE

NICHOLS, DECATUR WARD (1900-), American bishop of the A.M.E. CHURCH, was born in CHARLESTON, S. C., on Oct. 15, 1900. He earned the A.B. degree from Howard University in 1923 and the B.D. degree from DREW THEOLOGICAL SCHOOL in 1926. He was admitted to the New Jersey Annual Conference in 1925, ordained deacon in 1926 and elder in 1927. He held pastorates in RHODE ISLAND and NEW YORK having served also in the metropolitan New York Area. Several A.M.E. colleges granted him the D.D. degree and WILBERFORCE granted

D. WARD NICHOLS

him the LL.D. He was elected bishop in 1940. Bishop Nichols was instrumental in the organization of the Pension Department of the denomination.

R. R. Wright, *The Bishops*. 1963.   GRANT S. SHOCKLEY

NICHOLS, FLORENCE (1865-1958), American missionary who was twice principal of the ISABELLA THOBURN COLLEGE at LUCKNOW, INDIA. She was appointed to Lucknow in 1894 to assist Miss THOBURN in her effort to establish the pioneer Christian Woman's College in Asia. She was highly qualified, holding B.A. and M.A. degrees from BOSTON UNIVERSITY and having been trained for Christian service in the Deaconess Training School in BOSTON.

Persistent health problems interrupted her service. The doctors urged her to return to America in 1898. She went reluctantly, but less than a year later returned and was able to resume a heavy schedule of teaching and administration. In the emergency created by the tragic death of Miss Thoburn from cholera, Sept. 1, 1901, Miss Nichols became principal, and met the exacting need with great courage and ability. In 1908, health problems again made her departure from India necessary.

In another emergency in 1921, when the college had grown so that its separation from the high school and location in a new site was necessary, she accepted the call to leadership; and in the next four years, she put the college firmly in a position to achieve growth in service to the church and the nation. During her second principalship the college became an integral but semi-independent part of the new University of Lucknow, acquired a choice location, had excellent buildings constructed, and extended its service into many new fields of education.

Miss Nichols was born in Lynn, Mass., Oct. 27, 1865. Throughout her life, Boston and its suburbs were the center of her America. On retirement in 1925, she returned to the environs of her youth and continued both her Chris-

tian witness and her advocacy of educational opportunity for the youth of India. She died on Feb. 4, 1958.

M. A. Dimmitt, *Isabella Thoburn College*. 1963.

J. WASKOM PICKETT

NICHOLS, MILTON HAROLD (1872-1958), American pastor of the Arch Street Church, PHILADELPHIA, for twenty-one years, was born in Vineland, N. J. He was educated at DICKINSON COLLEGE and joined the PHILADELPHIA ANNUAL CONFERENCE. He served various pastorates, but his greatest work began in 1933 at Arch Street Church, which he molded into one of the commanding churches of the East. During his first year as pastor he began one of the first, regular religious radio broadcasts in the city; during his second year, he began Noonday Lenten Services, for which the church became noted, as well as the three-hour Good Friday services. Under his leadership the church became the virtual headquarters of the Philadelphia Conference, which began holding the annual sessions of the Conference in its spacious sanctuary. An orator noted for his poetic style in preaching, and for his simple presentation of profound theological truths, M. H. Nichols attracted large congregations. During World War II he brought an especially helpful ministry to the youth in the Armed Forces. He died May 12, 1958.

Minutes of the Philadelphia Conference, 1958.

FREDERICK E. MASER

NICHOLS, RAYMOND HOWARD (1888-   ), American newspaper editor and lay leader in the M.E. Church, South, and later in The Methodist Church, was born in Lampasas, Texas, on Oct. 6, 1888. His wife was Ethal Rhoads, whom he married on Jan. 29, 1914. He joined the Methodist Church in 1902, serving on the official board of his local church and then becoming district lay leader, 1932-34, a member of the World Service Commission of the NORTHWEST TEXAS CONFERENCE, 1960, and lay leader of that Conference, 1934-60.

He has been a member of every GENERAL CONFERENCE from 1938 to 1970, the president of the General BOARD OF LAY ACITIVITIES (TMC), 1944-60, a member of the General BOARD OF PUBLICATION, 1960-68. In national life, Mr. Nichols was director and vice president of the U.S. Chamber of Commerce, 1953-62, and a member of the National Labor-Management Manpower Policy Committee, 1952-60. He is a trustee of SOUTHWESTERN UNIVERSITY, Georgetown, Texas, elected to that position in 1950; also a member and past president of the Texas Press Association.

At the 1952 General Conference in SAN FRANCISCO when the reorganization of the various agencies of the Church was under consideration, Nichols was named as one of a six-member committee to consider and report back recommendations concerning the proposals which had come in dealing with the Church's reorganization. The General Conference accepted practically all the recommendations of his committee. He resides in Vernon, Texas.

Who's Who in America, Vol. 34.
Who's Who in The Methodist Church, 1966.   N. B. H.

NICHOLS, ROY CALVIN (1918-   ), American bishop, was born in Hurlock, Md., on March 19, 1918. He

ROY NICHOLS

was educated in the schools of PHILADELPHIA and received his B.A. degree from Lincoln University; the B.D. from the Pacific School of Religion; and an honorary D.D. degree from the same school in 1964, and also one in 1959 from the UNIVERSITY OF THE PACIFIC. His wife was Ruth Richardson, and they have three children, Melisande, Allegra, and Nathan.

He began his pastorate in Berkeley, Calif., serving the Downs Church. A member of the Berkeley Board of Education, he served as its president in 1964. For seven years while minister of Downs Church, he was a radio pastor of "The Christian Answer" broadcast in Berkeley and in Oakland. He was the organizing pastor of South Berkeley Community Church (one of the first interracial churches with biracial co-pastors in the nation), 1943-46. In 1964 he was transferred to NEW YORK CITY to assume the pastorate of Salem Church, a 2,800-member Negro church. This church became deeply involved in direct services to the Central Harlem Community under Dr. Nichols' leadership, constructing an $800,000 community center, which presently includes in its program all manner of helpful counselling and vocational interests.

Dr. Nichols was elected a delegate to the GENERAL CONFERENCE of The Methodist Church in 1960, '64, '66, and '68, and at the 1968 session of the Northeastern JURISDICTIONAL CONFERENCE, he was elected a bishop of The United Methodist Church, assigned to supervise the PITTSBURGH Area.

He is presently chairman of the Section on Project Development of the BOARD OF EVANGELISM of The United Methodist Church; a member of the Board of Managers, METHODIST HOSPITAL OF BROOKLYN, New York, 1964-68; vice-chairman, Advisory Board, Harlem Hospital, New York City, 1966-68; and of the executive committee of the New York City Society of the NEW YORK CONFERENCE, 1968. He is a member of the WORLD COUNCIL OF CHURCHES, on its Executive Committee and Central Committee. He was the lecturer at the Convocation on Medicine and Theology, 1967, and the Frank S. Hickman lecturer on the Ministry at DUKE UNIVERSITY, in 1968. He is the first Negro to be elected a bishop by a Jurisdiction other than the Central in which he served for a time but which now is no longer in existence.

Who's Who in America.   N. B. H.

NICHOLS, SIDNEY R. (1921-   ), American layman, son of Sidney A. and Lucy (Beach) Nichols, was born in Merrill, Wis., Aug. 16, 1921. He was married to Miss Vivian Helen West, June 14, 1942, and they have three children.

Enrolling at the University of Buffalo in 1941, he enlisted in the United States Air Force serving in the European Theatre of War. Upon his return to college he graduated from the University of Buffalo with B.A., cum laude, 1948 and M.A., 1952. Special studies were also taken at NORTHWESTERN UNIVERSITY.

From 1948-52 Mr. Nichols was Associate Mathematician for Cornell Aeronautical Laboratory, Buffalo, and from 1952-63 he was Chief Engineer and Technical Marketing Advisor for Firewel Co., Buffalo, a division of ARO, Inc. In 1963, he was appointed Associate Executive Secretary, Men's Work, General Board of LAY ACTIVITIES for The Methodist Church. With the 1968 union he became Associate General Secretary, Division of Lay Life and Work, General Board of the Laity.

Mr. Nichols is a past president of the East Aurora, New York Association of Churches, a former trustee of the Silver Lake Institute, and has been a member of the WESTERN NEW YORK CONFERENCE Board of Laity as well as dean of the annual conference Lay Retreat.

Who's Who in The Methodist Church, 1966.

JOHN H. NESS, JR.

MRS. THOMAS NICHOLSON

NICHOLSON, EVELYN RILEY (1873-1967), wife of American bishop THOMAS NICHOLSON and a leader in women's work in the United States and in international causes. She was president of the WOMEN'S FOREIGN MISSIONARY SOCIETY of the M.E. Church for nineteen years, 1921-1940. She became widely known for her interest in the WORLD FEDERATION OF METHODIST WOMEN, and in the cause of world peace.

Born Evelyn Riley in a parsonage in Jackson, Minn., on June 30, 1873, she received her A.B. degree from

DePauw University in 1897, and the next year a Master's degree from the same school. Later she received three honorary doctorate degrees in 1928 and 1939. After college Mrs. Nicholson taught Latin in Florida and Indiana high schools, and then became Professor of Latin at Cornell College, Mt. Vernon, Iowa, from 1901-17, when she married Bishop Thomas Nicholson, a widower who had been elected bishop in 1916. During this period of teaching she spent one year in Rome at Crandon Institute, 1903-04.

Helen Kim of Korea suggested in 1923 that the Christian women of the world should unite to work for peace and the betterment of all mankind. Mrs. Nicholson joined with Dr. Kim in this idea and in 1939 the World Federation of Methodist Women was founded. Mrs. Nicholson became the first president, 1939-44. Today this organization has over six million members in fifty-five countries.

Mrs. Nicholson became active in other international organizations also and was a member of the International Missionary Council, and World Alliance for International Friendship through the Churches. She attended many international conferences, such as: Conference on Cause and Cure of War, and the International Conference at Oxford (1923), at Budapest (1927), and at Jerusalem (1928). She was a delegate to General Conference of the M.E. Church in 1928 and 1936, and of The Methodist Church in 1940. Her book, *The Way to a Warless World,* was placed in the cornerstone of The Church Peace Center at the United Nations Plaza, New York. Upon retirement Mrs. Nicholson lived in Chicago until her death on Feb. 15, 1967.

Frances Nall

NICHOLSON, ROY S. (1903-   ), American Wesleyan Methodist minister, was born July 12, 1903 in Walhalla, S.C. He was ordained by the North Carolina Conference (W.M.C.) in 1925 and was a pastor in it eleven years. He served the denomination as general secretary of Wesleyan Youth (1924-1935), editor of Sunday school literature (1935-1939), secretary of Home Missions (1939-1943), editor of *The Wesleyan Methodist* (1943-1947), first supervising president of the denomination (1947-1959), and delegate to the World Methodist Council/Conference (1956). He served on the boards of the National Holiness Association and of the National Association of Evangelicals. He is the author of *Wesleyan Methodism in the South, History of the Wesleyan Methodist Church* (two revised editions), *Notes on True Holiness* (also translated and published in Korean and Japanese languages), and *Studies in Church Doctrine,* as well as of numerous articles for religious periodicals. He has been evangelist and special lecturer at camp meetings, conferences, seminaries and colleges. He was a member of a number of Church Commissions, such as the Hymnal Commission and the Commissions on Church Merger with the Free Methodist and Pilgrim Holiness Churches. He was honored by his election as General Conference President Emeritus in 1959, after serving in that office for twelve years. He continues to serve his Church as Chairman of the Department of Religion at Central Wesleyan College.

Who's Who in America, Vol. 34.

George E. Failing

Thomas Nicholson

NICHOLSON, THOMAS (1862-1944), American educator and bishop, was born at Woodburn, Ontario, Canada, on Jan. 27, 1862, the son of James, a farmer, and Hannah (Burkholder) Nicholson. He was educated at Toronto Normal, Northwestern University (A.B., 1893, A.M., 1895); Garrett Seminary (B.D., 1892; and later honorary D.D. and LL.D.). He married first Jane Boothroyd, on Aug. 20, 1885 (who died on May 10, 1915), and they had two daughters. He married Evelyn Riley on June 19, 1917.

He joined the Michigan Conference in 1884. After teaching high school in Canada, 1878-83, he served various charges in Michigan until 1889; pastor Big Rapids, 1893-4; principal and professor, Philosophy and Biblical Literature, Academy of Cornell College, Iowa, 1894-03; president and professor of Philosophy, Dakota Wesleyan University, 1903-08; secretary of the General Board of Education (M.E. Church), 1908-16 (New York City).

Under Nicholson, the Jubilee Educational Movement raised $35,000,000 for educational purposes. He was elected bishop in 1916, and served the Chicago area, 1916-24, and the Detroit area, 1924-32, when he retired.

Bishop Nicholson supervised the building of Boulevard Temple Church, Detroit, and took a leading part in national and international affairs. In 1912 he was chairman of an association of Board Secretaries out of which was developed the World Service Commission. He was the founder and first president of the Council of Church Boards of Education. In 1920 he was chairman of the reorganization Committee of the Interchurch World Movement and President of the Board of Sunday Schools, Board of Hospitals and Homes and Deaconess Work, 1924-28.

A delegate to three General Conferences, 1908-16; the fourth Ecumenical Conference, 1911; and fraternal delegate to Irish and British Wesleyan Conferences, 1923, he attended many international conferences officially. A Bible lecturer in many states, he was president of the Anti-Saloon League of America, 1921-32; staunch supporter of the 18th Amendment and a "great leader in the cause of temperance." In opposition to the election of Alfred A. Smith to the presidency of the United States, in the bitter campaign of 1928, Bishop Nicholson with Bishop JAMES CANNON of VIRGINIA, was considered a strong leader of the dry forces.

Physical affliction compelled Bishop Nicholson's retirement in 1932, but he was mentally alert until his death in Mt. Vernon, Iowa, on March 7, 1944, where he was buried.

F. D. Leete: *Methodist Bishops.* 1948.
National Cyclopedia of American Biography, The.
Who's Who in the Clergy.   JESSE A. EARL

NIEBEL, HENRY (1784-1877), American Evangelical minister, was one of the early and influential leaders of the EVANGELISCHE GEMEINSCHAFT. He was born in Berks County, Pa., March 16, 1784 and died near Sycamore, Ohio, May 2, 1877.

The family in his early youth moved from Berks County to Dry Valley, Union County, Pa. By 1806 he had become a public school teacher at Winfield in the Susquehana valley where the influences of the emerging Evangelische Gemeinschaft were rapidly expanding in the area. He considered the ministry in the Reformed Church, but was dissatisfied with what he felt was a spiritual dearth in that fellowship. Making his home with the Abraham Eyer family, he there met and heard JACOB ALBRIGHT and his associates in their interpretation of the Christian faith, had a new religious experience and became a charter member of the Eyer Class in 1808.

At the second conference of the emerging church in 1809, held in the home of GEORGE MILLER at Albany, Berks County, Niebel was granted credentials as a minister on probation. At that time the church numbered but 426 members served by six itinerant ministers.

Early appointments served by the young Niebel included the following: 1809-10 (with another assistant, M. Betz, under JOHN DREISBACH), the Schuylkill Circuit; 1810-11, the Schuylkill-Lancaster circuit with JOHN WALTER in charge. In 1811 he was ordained deacon and with M. Becker, another assistant, they served the York Circuit with John Dreisbach in charge; 1812-13, he traveled the Schuylkill circuit; in 1813 he was ordained elder and assigned to the Franklin circuit. In 1815 he was elected the second presiding elder of the emerging church. During the years 1815-21, he presided over two Conference sessions of the church, and served seven sessions as secretary. He was elected secretary of the GENERAL CONFERENCE of 1816.

In 1821 Henry Niebel for health reasons found it necessary to relinquish for a time the active work of the ministry. In 1829, however, he re-entered active work with the Western conference. At a critical time of need in 1833, he was sent to OHIO and elected a presiding elder to replace Joseph Long who had been supervising the work in that state. Niebel served in this capacity until 1843. The trip from PENNSYLVANIA to Ohio was made by covered wagon with his wife and seven children, the youngest at that time being but four months of age. Mrs. Niebel was the former Mary Eyer from Pennsylvania. Niebel was a brother-in-law of John Dreisbach, with whom he shared many responsibilities in the early church.

Niebel made definite contributions in the early literary and liturgical fields of the church. In 1816 he served as assistant publisher of the first printing establishment of the church at New Berlin, Pa. In 1816 he and John Dreisbach were appointed by the church to prepare a suitable hymn book and to amend the *Discipline* which had been previously compiled by George Miller. It was the first hymn book (German) of the church and served many years as the only such hymnal of the denomination. It was named "Das Geistliche Saitenspiel."

Henry Niebel was superannuated in 1848. He died at the home of his son Enos, near Sycamore, Ohio, May 2, 1877, his wife having preceded him in death. Nine children, all worthy supporters of the church, survived their father. He was buried at Bibler Cemetery, a few miles south of McCutchenville, Ohio.

R. W. Albright, *Evangelical Church.* 1942.
R. B. Leedy, *Evangelical Church in Ohio.* 1959.
                                         WILLIAM C. F. HAYES

NIGERIA is a country of West Central Africa located at the eastern end of the Gulf of Guinea. It is a member of the United Nations and the British Commonwealth of Nations. The coastline is approximately 400 miles, from Badagry (west) to Calabar (east) where the African coast makes a 90° turn from east-west to north-south. The area is 356,669 square miles, and the population is 61,450,000 (UN 1967 estimate), making Nigeria the most populous nation of Africa. The capital is Lagos, on an island of the same name, separated from the mainland by a superb harbor.

Portuguese navigators were the first Europeans to report contact with this sector of the African coast, sailing as far as the Niger Delta in the late 1400's. French, British and others also came and went. By the close of the eighteenth century, the British had displaced others as traders and pioneers from Lagos to beyond the Delta. Mungo Park, noted explorer and geographer, died on the upper Niger River in 1805.

Lagos and the adjacent mainland, annexed by Britain in 1861, was first administered from SIERRA LEONE. In 1874 control passed to the Gold Coast colony, and a Protectorate was established in 1896. Meanwhile, in 1886, the Royal Niger Company had been chartered to govern the older Oil Rivers Protectorate at the Niger Delta, as well as other areas. In 1900, that enterprise surrendered its rights and properties to the Crown. The country was then reorganized as The Protectorate of Northern and Southern Nigeria. In 1914, these jurisdictions were amalgamated as the Crown Colony of Nigeria. An elected Council was established in 1923, a long step towards self-government. Independence was granted in 1960, Nigeria then entering the United Nations and the British Commonwealth. The adjacent narrow strip of British territory in Cameroons, under the United Nations, joined independent Nigeria by virtue of a plebiscite in 1961. In 1966, a military government assumed power in the North and West, but was not recognized by the military governor of the East. The Eastern Region declared itself an independent republic, and from 1967 to 1970, there was civil war.

In 1838, several Africans who had been wrenched from this area as slaves were freed and taken to the British depot for free Negroes at Sierra Leone. They made their way to Lagos, recognizing it as the port from which the slave-runners had taken them. Venturing up the Ogun River, they came to Abeokuta, a town of the Yoruba people, where they were reunited with their families. Returning to Sierra Leone, they organized a company of other Yoruba recaptives, securing permission to leave for Abeokuta. Among these were several Methodists of Sierra Leone, these being the first Methodists of whom we have knowledge to settle in the Lagos-Niger territory. They reported arrival and begged for mission assistance.

FIRST MISSION STATION AT BADAGRY

In September 1842, THOMAS BIRCH FREEMAN, pioneer Wesleyan Methodist missionary, left his port in the Gold Coast, landing at Badagry near Lagos. He proceeded to Abeokuta, receiving hearty welcome from the chief, Shodeke, the entire city, and the Methodists he had known. Freeman established stations at Abeokuta and Badagry.

At first the work was administered from the Gold Coast. Under the leadership of John Milum such gain was made as to warrant setting Lagos apart as a separate District in 1878, the membership approximating 1,000. In 1913, the Centenary year of West Africa Methodism, the Wesleyan Methodist community included eleven missionaries, twenty-two African ministers, eighty-six catechists, and over 6,000 members on the District. By 1919, the membership had risen to 9,000. Meanwhile, PRIMITIVE METHODISM had entered Eastern Nigeria, and developed centers at Umuahia, Oron and Chewhee.

Steady growth marked Nigerian Methodism, with constant emphasis on Biblical instruction and personal religious experience. The school program is integrated into the government's system of education. Medical work is of a high standard, the church superintending the outstanding government supported leper settlement in the Uzuakoli area.

In July 1962, the Conference of the Methodist Church, Nigeria, was inaugurated, under the leadership of its Nigerian president, Joseph Soremekun. The Conference consisted in 1968 of seven districts, on both sides of the division caused by civil war. It had 1,540 places of worship, 54,332 full members and a total constituency of 146,640. The Conference had under its care fifteen medical institutions, including hospitals at Ilesha and Ituk Mbang, 522 primary schools with 121,482 pupils; eighteen secondary schools with 3,412 students. Ministers are trained in joint theological colleges: Immanuel College, Ibadan and Trinity College, Umuahia. Church union negotiations between the Anglican, Presbyterian and Methodist churches broke down in 1965. Civil war, beginning in 1967, caused serious disruption to the life of the nation. The Nigerian Methodist Conference met with-

out Biafran representatives, while in Biafra, a Methodist Assembly was constituted to carry on essential business.

American Methodism is represented in Nigeria by the small mission of the A.M.E. CHURCH.

E.U.B. Church. In 1904 the principal free churches of Nigeria united to form the Sudan United Mission. The first Evangelical member to work in this mission was Miss Rose Boehning, a deaconess from ILLINOIS. Miss Boehning sailed for Africa in 1905 to work in industrial missions. In 1906, Rev. C. W. Guinter, a member of the Central Pennsylvania Conference (United Evangelical) went to Africa to work among the Jukin and Chamba tribes. It was not until 1922 that the merged Evangelical churches assumed a mission support work in Africa. At that time Rev. and Mrs. I. E. McBride of the Platte River Conference (NEBRASKA) joined the Guinters in Nigeria.

With Guinter as teacher, a primary school was opened in Bambur in 1925. Other schools were started in surrounding areas. Since there were no reading books, the mission sponsored the publication of a Hausa Grammar.

At about the same time, temporary chapels were being constructed in the area. The first church building was dedicated in 1925 in Bambur.

It was not until 1932 that medical work was begun in a mud-wall dispensary. In this humble building African young people were trained to carry on dispensary work among their people. Other dispensaries were soon to be erected in strategic places. Because there were no doctors on the field every missionary was required to have six months' training in tropical diseases.

In 1965 there were 131 preaching places with nineteen organized congregations, 128 evangelists, and ten ordained ministers. There were eleven primary schools and one secondary school, one hospital with 110 beds (dedicated in 1951) and nineteen dispensaries.

The major emphasis in Nigeria has always been at the point of developing national leadership through training schools for evangelists, dispensary training, and teacher training.

J. F. A. Ajayi, *Christian Missions in Nigeria, 1841-1891: The Making of a New Elite.* London: Longmans, 1965.
F. W. Dodds, *Our Nigerian Field.* London: Hammond, n.d.
Findlay and Holdsworth, *Wesleyan Meth. Miss. Soc.* 1922.
A. J. Fox, *Uzuakoli: A Short History.* Ibadan and London: Oxford University Press, 1964.
A. E. Southon, *Ilesha and Beyond.* London: Cargate, n.d.
F. D. Walker, *A Hundred Years in Nigeria.* London: Cargate, n.d.
W. J. Ward, *In and Around the Oron Country.* London: Hammond, n.d.
World Outlook, December 1962.   ARTHUR BRUCE MOSS
                                     LOIS MILLER

NILES, DANIEL THAMBYRAJAH (1908-1970), Asian minister, author and ecumenist, was born near Jaffna, North CEYLON. He was educated at the United Theological College, Bangalore, India, and the University of London.

Before coming to the position as President of the Methodist Church in Ceylon, Niles held various Methodist and ecumenical positions. He was chairman of the North District of his Church, served for many years as the general secretary of the EAST ASIAN CHRISTIAN CONFERENCE, and at his death was President of the Conference.

He also served as principal of Jaffna Central College; pastor of St. Peter's Church in Jaffna; chairman, World's

D. T. NILES

Student Christian Federation; and secretary, Department of Studies in Evangelism of the WORLD COUNCIL OF CHURCHES.

Niles delivered many lectureships, among which are the Lyman Beecher Lectures on Preaching at Yale University Divinity School; and lectureships at NORTHWESTERN UNIVERSITY, as well as in colleges and universities in SCOTLAND and AUSTRALIA.

He was the preacher at the opening service of the World Council of Churches at its organizing session in Amsterdam in 1948, as well as the preacher for the opening session of the 1968 Assembly in UPPSALA, SWEDEN. He also was a speaker at the 1954 and 1961 Assemblies. In 1968 he was elected one of the six Presidents of the World Council of Churches.

D. T. Niles made one of the principal addresses at the WORLD METHODIST CONFERENCE in London in 1966 and led in a movement for the restructuring of the World Methodist Council of which he became a Vice-President. He was a prolific author and among his most recent volumes are *Buddhism and the Claims of Christ* and *Who Is This Jesus?*

He died very suddenly in Velore, India, on July 17, 1970, while at the height of his power and influence. "Though he became known as a symbol of Christian unity," the *New York Times* said of him, "both within his native Ceylon and on the international level, Dr. Niles always remained essentially a preacher with strong evangelical convictions."

New York Times, July 18, 1970.   LEE F. TUTTLE

NIND, GEORGE BENJAMIN (1860-1932), American lay preacher and missionary to BRAZIL and to Portuguese-speaking people, was born in St. Charles, Mo., on Nov. 23, 1860, of devout Christian parents. He received his education at NORTHWESTERN UNIVERSITY and went to Brazil through the influence of WILLIAM TAYLOR, later bishop, who had opened work there in 1880, with the plan of enlisting self-supporting missionaries. Nind arrived in Recife, capital of the then province of Pernambuco, in 1880.

Nind made a living by teaching music but held preaching services in his house and on city streets, even organizing a congregation. Licensed only as an exhorter, he repeatedly appealed for an ordained minister to come and take charge of the work, but Bishop JOHN H. VINCENT in the States refused to send any on the grounds that they were needed at home.

Nind remained in Recife twelve years until in September 1892, the illness of his wife forced a return to the United States. Here he was asked to take the place of a missionary who had been working with the Portuguese in New Bedford, Mass. About a year later, Nind was asked to go to the Cape Verde Islands. From there he went in 1900 to the island of Madeira, where he served about nineteen years as pastor and as editor and publisher of a religious paper, *A Voz de Madeira* (The Voice of Madeira). Authorized by Bishop J. C. HARTZELL, he compiled a book of hymns in Portuguese, some of his own authorship, some translated by himself or by JUSTUS H. NELSON, his brother-in-law. These were published together with a *Manual of Doctrine and Worship* for Portuguese Methodists.

After his first wife died he was married to Mary Elizabeth Foley.

When he finally returned to the United States, Nind edited for eight years a paper called *Aurora* (Dawn), designed to spread the Gospel among the Portuguese in the United States. He also taught Portuguese in BOSTON UNIVERSITY and in the Kennedy School of Missions in Hartford, Conn.

Nind died after a brief illness on June 1, 1932. He was survived by his wife and a daughter, Gretchen, a trained nurse.

W. C. Barclay, *History of Missions*. 1957.
Journal of the New England Southern Conference.
                                        D. A. REILY

NINDE, WILLIAM XAVIER (1832-1901), American bishop, was born at Cortlandville (Cortland), N. Y., on June 1, 1832. He was the oldest son of the Rev. William Ward Ninde, who was the oldest son of the Rev. William Ninde. This apostolic succession in the Ninde family goes back to a lay preacher mentioned with esteem in JOHN WESLEY's *Journal*, James Nind. This man came to America to serve with Bishop ASBURY.

William Xavier Ninde was only twelve years old when his preacher father died. The son united with the BLACK RIVER CONFERENCE in 1856. In time he ministered to the church at Adams, N. Y., where his father had served before him. He was appointed to Rome, N. Y., and twice to Central Church, DETROIT, Mich., before he accepted the presidency of GARRETT BIBLICAL INSTITUTE. He was known for his regular habits of study and for his dependence on prayer. In preaching he always used the right word in the right place, and careless phraseology "caused him positive pain." He brought great comfort to the sick.

He was elected bishop in 1884 and assigned residence at TOPEKA, Kan. He lavished on the whole church the same patient love for which he had become noted in his relation to his own children and to the people in the local churches. He became known as "The Saint John of the Episcopacy."

Among Bishop Ninde's writings we note his "Report

on the great cities of South America," and his authorship of introductions to various books such as O. J. Perrin's *Manual of Christian Ethics*. He was a member of the first and second ECUMENICAL METHODIST CONFERENCES in 1881 and 1891.

He travelled extensively throughout the church. He spent almost five months in INDIA and visited JAPAN and KOREA; and his daughter's work in CHINA won his heart to that land. Many costumes, curios and gifts which he received from overseas were presented to the Chicago Art Museum. His noted daughter, Mary Ninde Gamewell, represented the Church in Christian mission work in China, and wrote interdenominational mission study books. She is author of the biography of her father, entitled, *William Xavier Ninde . . . a Memorial*. The bishop also rejoiced in the ordination and work of his preacher son, Edward S. Ninde.

Bishop Ninde died in his sleep, Jan. 3, 1901. Memorial addresses were given and published by Bishops ANDREWS, JOYCE and WALDEN. Burial was in Woodland Cemetery, Detroit, Mich.

Mary Ninde Gamewell, *William Xavier Ninde . . . a Memorial*. Privately printed, 1902.
The Methodist Review, 1903.
Henry S. Ninde, *The Ninde-Ward Families*. 1929.

CHARLES W. BRASHARES

NIPPERT, LOUIS (1825-1894), missionary and Methodist educator in GERMANY, was born on March 23, 1825, in FRANCE (Alsace). In 1830 the family emigrated to America and settled in Belmont County, OHIO. They were converted under the preaching of two German-speaking ministers and joined the German Methodist church there. In early 1840 Nippert became a printer's apprentice in the Methodist BOOK CONCERN at CINCINNATI. After some years of service as a lay preacher, he became a minister and joined the OHIO CONFERENCE in 1846. His first independent task was to found a mission among German immigrants in INDIANAPOLIS. After various other appointments, he was sent to Germany in 1850. One year later he started work at Heilbronn in the south and moved to Frankfurt the succeeding year to supervise the total work in the south and the southwest. After a brief appointment to Bremen, including a provisional half year as dean of the new seminary, he went to Berlin, where he founded the first Methodist church in that city (1858). After beginning Methodist work at Basel, Switzerland, he moved to Zurich in 1862 as a presiding elder, from where he returned to Heilbronn (1866-68). His essential contribution proved to be in his service as dean of the Frankfurt Theological Seminary (PREDIGERSEMINAR) from 1868 to 1886. The seminary had just moved from Bremen to Frankfurt. Nippert was a great educator and the author of many valuable books—among them an outline of doctrine, lives of Francis Asbury and JOHN W. FLETCHER, and the superb *Homiletics and Pastoral Theology*. After thirty-six years of service in Germany, Nippert returned to America, where he worked in several circuits before his death on Aug. 17, 1894.

C. ERNST SOMMER

NISHIZUMI, DANIEL M. (1901-1946), pioneer Japanese FREE METHODIST missionary to BRAZIL, was born in Osaka, JAPAN, Dec. 22, 1901. Graduated from Free Methodist

Seminary, Osaka in 1928, he migrated to Brazil in 1929, supporting himself by teaching in public schools and later by establishing his own Christian school in SÃO PAULO. He pursued advanced studies in the Methodist and Presbyterian seminaries of Brazil.

He married Miss Yoshie Fugita in 1931. He organized the first Free Methodist Church in Brazil, Oct. 1, 1936. He visited the United States in 1938, was ordained elder and was made the superintendent for Brazil.

The first American missionaries arrived in June 1946. Nishizumi met with a fatal accident, June 26, 1946. A strong church has developed in Brazil on the foundations he laid.

B. S. Lamson, *Free Methodist Missions*. 1951.
Missionary Tidings, September 1946.   BYRON S. LAMSON

NITSCHMANN, DAVID (1696-1772), was one of three MORAVIANS of the same name. He was born at Zauchenthal, Moravia, on Dec. 27, 1696. With Leonard Dober he was a pioneer missionary to St. Thomas. He was placed in charge of the Moravian settlers in SAVANNAH, and accompanied JOHN WESLEY on his journey to GEORGIA in 1736, where he protested against Wesley's determination to admit Mrs. Hawkins to Holy Communion. Wesley consulted him about his proposal to marry SOPHIA HOPKEY. Nitschmann became a bishop in 1735, and died at Bethlehem, Pa., on Oct. 8, 1772.

D. Cranz, *The Ancient and Modern History of the Brethren*, B. La Trobe, trans., 1825.
J. E. Hutton, *A History of Moravian Missions*. London, 1922.
A. J. Lewis, *Zinzendorf*. 1962.
C. W. Towlson, *Moravian and Methodist*. 1957.

C. W. TOWLSON

NOBLE, FRED B. (1883-   ), American lawyer, prominent lay leader and JUDICIAL COUNCIL member, was born at Preston, Md., April 17, 1883. He was the son of Isaac L. and Mary Elizabeth (Corkran) Noble. He was educated at Washington College, A.B. in 1902; LL.D. in 1953; a student at the University of Maryland, 1904-05; Harvard, LL.B. in 1907. He married Eva L. Wyand on May 20, 1910, and they have one daughter, Mary. He was admitted to the MARYLAND Bar in 1907, to the FLORIDA Bar in 1908, and thereafter practiced law in JACKSONVILLE, Fla. He has held various responsible positions in the State. He was a member of the UNITING CONFERENCE in 1939, as a representative of the M. E. Church of the then ST. JOHN'S RIVER Conference. He was a member of the GENERAL CONFERENCE of the M.E. Church in 1936, and of The Methodist Church in '40, '48, '52, '60, '64; a member of the BOARD OF EDUCATION from 1936-48; of the GENERAL BOARD OF LAY ACTIVITIES, 1948-52; and a lay leader of the FLORIDA CONFERENCE, 1940-52, and 1952-56. He became a member of the Judicial Council of The Methodist Church in 1952 and was automatically retired from the Council in time to serve on the Jurisdictional Conference (SEJ) of 1956. His activities in his local church have continued as he continues to reside in Jacksonville.

Who's Who in The Methodist Church, 1966.   N. B. H.

NOBLE, WALTER JAMES (1879-1962), British missionary leader, was born at Darlington, trained at Didsbury College and entered the Wesleyan ministry in 1900, when

W. J. NOBLE

AGUSTIN NODAL

he sailed for CEYLON. He remained there until 1922, when he became a secretary of the Wesleyan METHODIST MISSIONARY SOCIETY; after 1932 he remained a secretary of the Methodist Missionary Society until 1947. He was President of the Methodist CONFERENCE in 1942. He died on Feb. 21, 1962.

JOHN KENT

NOBLE, WILLIAM ARTHUR (1866-1945), pioneer missionary to KOREA, was born in Springdale, Pa., on Sept. 13, 1866. He entered the WYOMING CONFERENCE in 1892 after studying at Wyoming Seminary and graduating from DREW SEMINARY, and then set out for Korea, where he arrived with his bride of three months in October of that year.

For three years he taught in Pai Chai College in SEOUL, and then was assigned to take up the work of the newly opened Pyengyang mission station to succeed William James Hall. After fifteen years he was transferred to Seoul where he remained until final retirement twenty-four years later.

He was an outstanding administrator with an amazing capacity for constant work. He served as mission superintendent for two years and for forty years was a district superintendent, often over more than one district. For three years he served the Pyengyang and Seoul districts (1908-1910) comprising more than half of his mission area and seventy percent of its Korean membership. He had travelled over the entire mission area and at one time or another had been district superintendent of ninety percent of the districts. In his forty-two years he saw his Korean church grow from fifty full members centered in Seoul to an autonomous Methodist Church with a membership of over 20,000.

He did considerable writing for the *Korea Repository* and the *Korea Review* and wrote one novel, *Ewa, A Tale of Korea*. He was officially retired in March 1933, but continued in service in Seoul to December 1934. He died at Stockton, Calif., Jan. 6, 1945.

C. F. Price, *Who's Who in American Methodism*. 1916.

CHARLES A. SAUER

NODAL Y RUEDA, AGUSTIN (1882-   ), a Cuban pastor, the oldest of a family of eleven brothers and sisters, was born Aug. 28, 1882, in Remedios, Las Villas province, CUBA. At an early age he lost his father, mother and sister from tuberculosis due to his father having been held as a prisoner in Spanish concentration camps. With only a few months of formal education, he learned to fend for himself and became an expert in the sale and manufacture of tobacco products. With his brother he became the owner of a cigar factory in San Juan de los Yeras, where MANUEL DEULOFEU was pastor of the Methodist Church.

Nodal considered himself an atheist and would not allow his workmen to discuss religion in the factory, and put up signs to that effect. Observing the quiet fortitude of Deulofeu as he continued to witness his faith while lying on his death bed, Nodal attended Deulofeu's funeral and memorial service. As a result he was miraculously converted and asked for license to preach, 1913.

The same year he joined the Annual Conference and was assigned to Aguado de Pasajeros. At first his wife thought he had lost his mind when he professed conversion, but was soon reconciled. They were married in 1908 and had eight children.

In an active ministry of forty-seven years, he served twenty different pastoral charges and never missed a roll call at Annual Conference, although at one session he went with a high fever. For many years the government gave him a special permit for preaching in any jail and on the streets of any city in the island. As a result of his preaching several outstanding Christian leaders were converted.

Serving some of the most difficult places, he often had to be away from his family for weeks at a time, yet he never complained. Twice he served as District Superintendent of the Oriental District. Because of his evangelistic fervor he was often called on to hold revival services in opening work in new areas.

A Mason, he was instructor in the Grand Lodge of Cuba and was sought after for masonic lectures. One of his outstanding lectures was "Masonry and the Bible."

He was unsurpassed as a story teller and many of his stories appear in his book, *Para los Pequeños y Para los Mayores*. Although he had retired officially he continued to work in three different places before the communist regime forced him to leave Cuba. Retiring to MIAMI he was active among the Cuban refugees until he was past eighty years of age.

Annuario Cubano de la Iglesia Metodista.   GARFIELD EVANS

NOLLEY, RICHMOND (1785-1815), pioneer American preacher, was born in Brunswick County, Va. Left an orphan soon after birth, he was reared in Sparta, Ga., by a Methodist merchant named Captain Lucas. After a dramatic and enduring conversion experience in 1806, he decided to become a Methodist minister, and in 1807 was received into the traveling connection. He was sent to the Edisto Circuit in the SOUTH CAROLINA CONFERENCE. For five years he served in NORTH CAROLINA and SOUTH CAROLINA. He was long remembered there for his patience, and especially for his diligence. He was a wonderful pastor, ministering to the sick and the aged, and his work in training the children under his care put him far ahead of his time. He also ministered to the slaves and taught their children.

In 1812 Nolley and three other young missionaries were sent to the MISSISSIPPI and LOUISIANA territories, which had scarcely been opened to Methodism. Amid Indian insurrections, Nolley moved from fort to fort, preaching and teaching the people on the Tombigbee Mission.

He was appointed in 1814 to Attakapas and Opelousas in Lousiana, where he established Methodism in a field as difficult as any in the wilderness country. This was not only because of the problems of nature, but by reason of a hostile Roman Catholic community of French and Spanish descent. Returning from his annual conference in late November of 1815, with the entire southern portion of what is now the LOUISIANA CONFERENCE as his charge, he attempted to cross flooded Hemphill Creek near the town of Jena, La. He was washed from his horse but managed to reach the other shore by clinging to overhanging branches. He started up a country trail to the home of Methodists nearby, but died on the way. The next day a friendly Indian found his body along the trail, his knee prints in the soft wet mud, and his hymn book opened to a familiar hymn. Methodist friends buried him nearby.

In 1856 the Louisiana Conference erected over his grave a small monument, which later was carried to the Jena church, and the location of the untended grave site was then almost forgotten. In 1956 it was decided to rebury his remains on the lawn of the church in Jena named for him, the Nolley Memorial Church. Traveling the lonely trail Nolley had traversed from the creek to the place his body had been found, people from throughout the state participated in a commemorative service, led by Bishop PAUL E. MARTIN and District Superintendent Jolly B. Harper. A suitable marker slab on the lawn of the church now tells the story.

H. N. McTyeire, *History of Methodism*. 1884.
T. O. Summers, *Biographical Sketches*. 1858.
JOLLY B. HARPER

NORFOLK, NEBRASKA, U.S.A. **First Church** is the principal downtown Protestant church in a town of 16,500 population. Its chimes ring out over the downtown business district at regular intervals from a Gothic spire which rises nearly a hundred feet above the level of the street. The present edifice was planned during the pastorate of Harry E. Hess in 1943. The educational building was erected in 1953 during the pastorate of Everett E. Jackman, and the sanctuary during the pastorate of Melvon L. Ireland in 1959.

Methodism came to Norfolk with the circuit riders in the years following the Civil War. A surge of immigration then brought many homeseekers to the rolling hills and valleys of northeastern NEBRASKA. Courageous and hardy settlers survived drought, insect plagues and floods to establish a permanent community. In 1871 the first circuit rider, S. B. York, preached in Norfolk and a class was soon organized. He rode a wide circuit stretching across northeastern Nebraska to the Dakotas, a distance of more than fifty miles and covering a territory of 10,000 square miles. His visits were at intervals of a fortnight or longer. Norfolk became a station in 1882.

The first permanent home for the little congregation was erected during the pastorate of Charles F. Heywood, who before entering the Methodist ministry had practiced law and served a term in the Nebraska legislature. The membership enjoyed a remarkable growth under the leadership of Jesse W. Jennings, 1889-93, and this necessitated the building of a larger church edifice under the able leadership of William Gorst, 1896. This served the needs of the congregation until the building of the present structure.

During the last decade of the nineteenth century large evangelistic CAMP MEETINGS were held in the vicinity of Norfolk, and these profoundly shaped the moral and religious character of the community. To this day the Methodist congregation counts among its members many people of stature and leadership in the community, and these account for the strength of the church as a significant force in the city.

In the main stream of the population explosion and urban growth of the twentieth century, Norfolk found itself a center of trade, industry and education for northeastern Nebraska. The Methodist Church rose to the challege with a new and larger ministry, multiple services, a staff of professionally trained workers, and a broadened vision of its mission to the world. In 1970 First Church had a membership of 1,686.

Harry E. Hess, *Methodism in Norfolk—A History*. 1945.
J. GRAYDON WILSON

NORFOLK, VIRGINIA, U.S.A., one of the great ports of the United States, is also one of the most historic cities of the nation. In the Colonial, Revolutionary, Civil War and both World War periods, Norfolk was of prime importance. Its present population is listed as 268,331.

The credit of organizing the first Methodist Society in Norfolk has been generally accorded ROBERT WILLIAMS. However, the *Journal* of JOSEPH PILMORE states, under date of Nov. 16, 1772, "Having proposed to form a society in Norfolk, I went to the preaching house, a playhouse, and gave an exhortation on the nature and necessity of meeting together, to help and build up each other in the faith of the gospel. I then withdrew to Captain Carson's, where I laid the foundation of a society by joining together twenty-six of them." According to this account, it would appear that the first society in Norfolk was formed by Pilmore and not Williams. Two days later Pilmore wrote, "I went over the water, to Portsmouth, with Mr. Williams and Mr. Watters, who arrived here today, to meet the society."

Robert Williams is, however, universally called the pioneer and apostle of Methodism in VIRGINIA and the south. He was the first Methodist minister to come to Virginia, and for the time his active ministry lasted, the most successful. Robert Williams kept no journal or records of his work. When he first arrived in Norfolk, he is thought to have preached from the court house steps. His preaching was new and strange, sometimes with strong language, which aroused the curiosity and opposition of the people. At first he was treated with incivility and unkindness, but later, as he became better understood, some willingly received him into their homes.

Norfolk first appears in the minutes of the Annual Conference for 1773, and for several years thereafter as a circuit of Norfolk and PORTSMOUTH. From 1776 to 1782, this circuit was omitted from the lists of appointments. The conflict between the colonies and the mother country and the burning of Norfolk in 1776 very nearly extinguished Methodism for a few years. ASBURY left the circuit because of these conditions in 1775. When the circuit was reestablished, James Morris was the preacher. Norfolk was a circuit until 1805, when it was permanently made a station.

When Asbury took charge of the society, he found about thirty members, no plan of regular class meetings, and the meeting house an old shattered building which had been a playhouse. He attempted to take subscriptions for a building. Only about thirty pounds, or about $170 was pledged, but with the war coming on the undertaking was abandoned until about 1792.

When Asbury returned in 1791 and again in 1792, he found the state of religion among the Methodists encouraging. He writes, "The seeds which I have been sowing for twenty years, begin to spring up. Norfolk flourishes."

In 1793, although the society numbered only about fifty members, most of them poor, they were determined to have a house of their own, even though on the plainest and cheapest scale. A lot on Fenchurch Street, adjoining the Academy lot, was leased for sixty years, at the price of "ten pounds in specie." The property was conveyed to "Francis Asbury, Bishop of the Methodist Episcopal Church, and to each minister and member of the said church in the United States, individually and collectively."

The small wooden building erected on the lot was very plain and rude in form and finish, and was used by the society for six years. This was the second place of worship to have been erected in Norfolk, the first being St. Paul's Episcopal Church. It was the first one to be built by private or voluntary contributions.

Land was purchased in 1800 on Cumberland Street for the second church building, which was first occupied in March 1803. Bishop Asbury in his *Journal* under that date says, "I preached in the new house, the best in Virginia belonging to our society." This was the first Methodist church to be built on Cumberland Street, from which it derived its name. It was the scene of some of the grandest triumphs the gospel ever achieved in the city of Norfolk.

The second church built on the Cumberland Street site was dedicated in 1834. The building was destroyed by fire in 1848. In less than one year the third church was ready for the congregation, and served the Methodists until about 1900. The fourth and last church erected on

Cumberland Street was only about two blocks from the original site and was used until 1922, when the congregation again decided to build and in another section of the city. This was erected in three units and was completed about ten years ago.

The "Cumberland Street Church" had remained as such for about 118 years but it is now known as the **First Church** and is the Mother Church of Methodism in Norfolk.

A notable event occurred on Cumberland Street when on Sunday, Feb. 27, 1848, at the 11 o'clock service, two volunteer foreign missionaries, BENJAMIN JENKINS and CHARLES TAYLOR, of the SOUTH CAROLINA CONFERENCE, were ordained as elders for the CHINA mission. This was the last service held in that church building before it was destroyed by fire.

In 1848, WILLIAM A. SMITH, minister, advocated the building of another Methodist church as the congregation had become too large to be served by one minister. Subsequently, in 1850, the Granby Street Station was built and used for the first time in December 1850. The minister, John E. Edwards, who was then serving Cumberland Street Church, transferred to Granby Street. This second church in Norfolk is now known as Epworth Church.

Sometime prior to the year 1854, the A.M.E. CHURCH was organized in Norfolk. Details are missing. The preacher of this church was a member of Cumberland Street Church and was recorded in a membership ledger as a Chapter Leader. It is thought that the minister of this congregation was white.

In May 1892, the Union Mission was organized in Cumberland Street Church by S. Q. Collins, who in all probability was a member of the church. The Mission, which is still active, was to serve needy families of the city.

In 1970 there were seventeen United Methodist Churches within the city, with a total membership of 17,-788. There is a Norfolk District in the conference which lists 33,157 members.

Epworth Church occupies a physical position in this seaport city that is not excelled by any other church. At the heart of the great business and seaport metropolis, Epworth is easily accessible to the tens of thousands of military and naval personnel who pass through its life and program each year.

In an era when other downtown churches have closed their doors or moved to residential areas, Epworth maintains a unique position, with net increases in church school and church enrollment and attendance, a varied program of activities for all age groups, an evangelical ministry, and a missionary program that touches the faraway places of the world.

Epworth directs to the men and women of the Armed Forces and related groups a large portion of its annual budget, and a vast segment of its program. It has become a city-center for worship and recreation to the military representatives of many nations.

Epworth Church, dating from 1850, is also known for the twenty-two stained glass windows in the sanctuary, which rank among the finest examples of art-glass in the country. In equipment and properties, the church claims to be able to meet the variant needs of a changing, contemporary, urban generation of members and constituents. There is a membership of 2,279 people who are scattered throughout the Tidewater city-complex of Norfolk, Portsmouth, Chesapeake, and Virginia Beach. The "Y's," the

EPWORTH CHURCH, NORFOLK, VIRGINIA

hotels, and high-rise apartments that surround the church, are said to find a renewal spiritual oasis in its multi-faceted ministry.

Miles Memorial Church was organized in the year 1910 and was a part of the circuit then known as Bethel Pine Beach and Ocean View. In the year 1911 Pine Beach was dropped and in 1912 Ocean View was established as a station. The little church on the corner of Cherry and First View Streets was started in 1911 and the cornerstone was laid in 1911 with Masonic and church ceremonies.

Because of the rapid growth in population and after World War I, the congregation outgrew the small church and the Ocean View School was once more used as a Sunday school. Then in 1923, under the leadership of L. T. Hitt, a two-story building was constructed next door for educational purposes. In 1930 the large social hall on the first floor was converted into a worship sanctuary and remained as such until March 19, 1950. With the continual growth of Ocean View as a residential area, the church facilities became inadequate. The church received 526 members into its fellowship in 1956, setting a record for accessions in one church in one year.

Ground breaking ceremonies for the erection of a new church home at 9450 Granby Street was Easter Sunday, 1949. Rufus A. Miles, after whom the church was named, is credited with full support for his financial aid. An additional educational building was erected in 1955. This great plant has an evaluation of $732,531. The present membership of Miles Memorial is 2,170. Two ministers and one missionary to COSTA RICA have gone out from this church. The church has a unique ministry to the retired ministers of the Virginia Conference. Many homes for the retired brethren are located on Selby Place behind the church.

Park Place Church is an influential mid-town church,

with a large percentage of its members residing beyond the radius of five miles.

The church was organized in 1902 near the outer limits of the city in a public school building, with thirty-seven members, under Daniel T. Merritt. During the year they purchased a site and started their first building, to which they soon added. Their religious success in the new community of "Park Place" warranted the procurement of a larger site to provide for even greater expansion; therefore, the corner-stone of the present church was laid by Ruth Lodge of Masons in 1916, and it was dedicated in 1917 by Bishop E. R. HENDRIX. The church burned in February 1923, causing complete loss of the sanctuary, which was rebuilt to a larger capacity and rededicated in October 1923. It suffered another fire in 1949, with major loss to the sanctuary and extensive spoilage to the Sunday school facility. Then the entire institution was modernized, making it a more practical facility for church activities, and dedicated finally by Bishop WILLIAM WALTER PEELE and R. Orman Bryant, Pastor.

Great emphasis is placed upon religious education and character building and the training in the field of music in this church has been of importance to both the youth and adult talent. Park Place is among the top ten Methodist churches in the country in supporting mission; it plays an important part in the spiritual lives of the military and naval personnel stationed in Tidewater; and eleven of its men are serving as ordained ministers of the Gospel, three of whom are in other denominations. On July 15, 1960, Bishop WALTER C. GUM was elected to the episcopacy from this pastorate.

The religious influence of Park Place has permeated into state, city, civic and fraternal affairs, many of the members being chosen or elected to high offices of responsibility and recognition. Present membership of the church is 2,230.

General Minutes.
Peter A. Peterson, "History of Cumberland Street M.E. Church, South," *Richmond Christian Advocate,* Nov. 15, 1915.
Thomas J. Wertenbaker, *Norfolk, Historic Southern Port.* Durham, N. C.: Duke University Press, 1931.

CLAUDIA E. LAMBERT
GALELMA J. BUTCHER

NORMAL, ILLINOIS, U.S.A. **First Church** was organized by a small group of Methodists in 1865, eight years after the founding of Illinois State Normal University (now Illinois State University), the second teacher's college to be established west of the Alleghenies. The church and the university, neighbors for more than a century, have experienced a mutual growth. By its centennial year First Church had grown to a church with a resident membership of more than 2,500 and an average worship attendance of more than 900. The church's peculiar responsibility to students has been recognized from the beginning. The original church was built only a block from the campus. When it became necessary to build a new edifice, the site chosen was even closer. The new building erected included separate quarters for the WESLEY FOUNDATION program. It appears that within ten years the church will be completely surrounded by a university with an enrollment of 20,000 students.

The new church and educational building, completed in 1957, is of contemporary design. A cross thirty-eight feet high, extends above the stone tower at the entrance to the sanctuary. The bell, which was brought from the old church, calls resident members and students to three morning worship services. The sanctuary windows, made of imported French slab glass, one inch thick and set in concrete, are placed in large panels on either side of the nave. The symbolism in the windows is a richly colorful reminder of the Christian debt to the Jewish faith, and of the most significant experiences in the life of Christ. Hundreds of students, both from Illinois State University and from nearby ILLINOIS WESLEYAN UNIVERSITY, regularly join the resident members in Sunday worship. In 1970 the membership was 2,739.

The Baby Fold is an institution founded to care for the following multiple services: (1) adoption of infants and pre-school children; (2) counseling for unmarried parents, including provision for prenatal care; medical and legal services, financial aid if needed—all under case-work direction; (3) residential treatment center for emotionally disturbed pre-school children, living in a controlled setting with houseparents, daily medical attention, psychiatric counsel and continuing casework supervision; (4) interim care and training for mentally retarded infants, from birth to three years of age, including casework counseling with parents and long-range planning for the child's continuing care; (5) foster home placement and supervision for children uprooted from natural homes but not legally available for adoption.

The Baby Fold was founded in 1902 and is a non-profit corporation, sponsored by the CENTRAL ILLINOIS CONFERENCE of The United Methodist Church. Its Board of Trustees consists of thirty members—fifteen clergy and fifteen lay. The Illinois Department of Children and Family Services license it as a child care facility and a child placement facility and it is certified by the Board of Hospitals and Homes.

GORDON B. WHITE
WILLIAM A. HAMMITT

NORMAN, OKLAHOMA, U.S.A., **McFarlin Memorial Church.** In 1921, Mr. and Mrs. Robert McFarlin asked for the privilege of building a church as a memorial to their son, Robert B. McFarlin, who died at the age of two years on July 28, 1893. Thousands of lives have been touched through this House of God which bears the name of this brief life.

The Church was built during the years 1923 and 1924 and dedicated on Dec. 7, 1924. It covers a floor space of 130 x 180 feet and cost in excess of $700,000. It is of Gothic style architecture and is built of Indian Lithic Limestone. It took some seventy cars of stone for the construction of the ninety-plus rooms. The church tower is a landmark for the community; it is 112 feet above the ground and can be seen at a distance from all highways leading to the city.

In the early years the University of Oklahoma used the modern dining room and kitchen facilities as these were the only adequate accommodations for large meeting and dining groups.

The seating capacity of the sanctuary is 1,700, with accommodations for an additional hundred at the rear of the sanctuary. The classrooms were originally built to accommodate an enrollment of 1,700 in the Sunday school —currently, McFarlin has an enrollment of 1,933 in Sunday school, out of a total membership of 3,522. This has, of course, necessitated the remodeling of many areas.

The first Sunday school enrollment was a total of 441 in twenty-two classes in 1924. The present program is guided by 216 officers and teachers with an average attendance of 1,000. Many of the charter members are still active in the life of the Church.

A bronze memorial tablet in the sanctuary expresses the love and spirit of this memorial which states: "This House of Worship is built for the youth of Oklahoma and the people of Norman, and whomsoever may find it in his heart to worship here."

General Minutes.

NORRIS, WILLIAM H. (1801-1878), a pioneer missionary to URUGUAY and ARGENTINA, was born in MAINE. He was admitted on trial to the NEW YORK CONFERENCE in 1825, transferring to the MAINE CONFERENCE a year later.

In 1839, in response to a request by JOHN DEMPSTER, he was appointed as a missionary to MONTEVIDEO, Uruguay, the first permanent Methodist missionary appointment for that country. Because of unsettled conditions and war between Uruguay and Argentina, he was unsuccessful in erecting a church building, although he did organize a congregation and hold services for two years. He returned home in 1842, but later the same year was reassigned to BUENOS AIRES, Argentina, where he worked with John Dempster. There he ministered primarily to the English-speaking community, which was broken up by civil war and a blockade of the port by British and French warships. He returned to the United States in 1847.

In 1847 he visited MEXICO as a Bible agent, going to Vera Cruz with United States troops engaged in the Mexican War. During the military occupation he placed Bibles in thousands of homes in Vera Cruz, Jalapa, Puebla, and Mexico City. He then began to fill a series of appointments in the NEW YORK EAST ANNUAL CONFERENCE.

Norris then served in that conference until 1863, when he became agent of the AMERICAN BIBLE SOCIETY in PANAMA and Central America. A year later he returned to Buenos Aires to assist in raising funds and in superintending the building of a new Methodist church and school.

W. C. Barclay, *History of Missions.* 1957.

EDWIN H. MAYNARD

NORTH, CHRISTOPHER RICHARD (1888-   ). British scholar, was born in 1888. He became a Methodist in 1904, offered for the Wesleyan ministry in 1908; he served as a missionry in LUCKNOW, 1918-20. In 1925 he went to Handsworth College, BIRMINGHAM, as Old Testament tutor, and remained there until the college closed during the Second World War. After five years in circuit he became professor of Hebrew at Bangor, where he was also dean of the faculty of theology from 1948 until his retirement in 1953. He was secretary of the Society for Old Testament Studies (1928-48), president in 1949, and treasurer (1952-57). His writings include *The Old Testament Interpretation of History,* which was the FERNLEY-HARTLEY LECTURE for 1946, *The Suffering Servant in Deutero Isaiah* (1948), and *Isaiah 40-55* (1952).

PETER STEPHENS

NORTH, ERIC McCOY (1888-   ), American minister, teacher, and executive secretary of the AMERICAN BIBLE

SOCIETY, (1928-56), was born in Middletown, Conn. on June 22, 1888, the son of FRANK MASON and Louise J. (McCoy) NORTH. He was educated at WESLEYAN UNIVERSITY, receiving the B.A. in 1909, the M.A. in 1910, and the D.D. in 1931. He received the Ph.D. degree from Columbia University in 1914, and is also a graduate of Union Theological Seminary. He married Gladys Haven, daughter of WILLIAM I. HAVEN, on April 17, 1920, and their children are Theodora, Louise Haven and William Haven. He became assistant professor of the history of Christianity at OHIO WESLEYAN, 1915-17. At intervals, 1917-24, he was an associate editor of Methodist Sunday-school publications. He was ordained a minister of the M. E. Church in 1918, and served as a departmental secretary of the Board of Foreign MISSIONS of that Church from 1919 to 1924. He lectured at DREW THEOLOGICAL SEMINARY, 1919-1924. He was executive secretary of the China Union Universities, 1924-27; associate secretary of the American Bible Society, 1927-28; and general secretary from 1928-56. He served as Assistant Secretary of the General Wartime Commission of the Churches, 1918, and as CHAPLAIN in the U. S. Army, 1918-19. He was many years a trustee of the United Board for Christian Higher Education in Asia, the Harvard-Yenching Institute, and DREW UNIVERSITY. He was decorated with the order of Orange-Nassau by the Netherlands. He has written *Early Methodist Philanthropy*, 1915; *Organization and Administration of the Sunday School* (with J. L. Cuninggim) in 1917; *The Kingdom and the Nations*, 1921; *The Worker and His Church* (with Louise M. North), 1921. When he was general secretary of the American Bible Society, he edited *The Book of a Thousand Tongues*, 1939. He resides in Chatham, N. J., and continues as a consultant of the American Bible Society.

Who's Who in America, Vol. 34.   N. B. H.

NORTH, FRANK MASON (1850-1935), author of the hymn, "Where Cross the Crowded Ways of Life," was an American pastor and administrator, an ecumenical statesman. Born in NEW YORK CITY on Dec. 3, 1850, he received a total of four degrees from WESLEYAN UNIVERSITY: B.A. (1872, with high honors and Phi Beta Kappa), M.A. (1875), D.D. (1894), LL.D. (1918). He had two sons by his first wife, who died in 1878. In 1885 he married Louise McCoy, daughter of a Congregational minister, and they had one son, ERIC MCCOY NORTH, long-time general secretary of the AMERICAN BIBLE SOCIETY.

North served six pastorates in the NEW YORK CONFERENCE between 1873 and 1887, then transferred to Middletown, Conn., in the NEW YORK EAST CONFERENCE. From 1892 until 1912, as corresponding secretary of the New York City Church Extension and Missionary Society (later New York City Society), he supervised a network of urban parishes, immigrant congregations, and interracial centers, including the Church of All Nations. During this period he also directed the National City Evangelization Union and edited *The Christian City*.

After administering Methodist work in New York City, he turned his talents to Methodism around the world, as corresponding secretary of the Board of Foreign Missions from 1912 to 1924. North was a delegate to the GENERAL CONFERENCES of 1908, 1916, 1920, 1924, and 1928; to the ECUMENICAL METHODIST CONFERENCES of

1901, 1911, 1921, and 1931; and to the WORLD MISSIONARY CONFERENCE at Edinburgh in 1910. He served on the Methodist Committee on Unification from 1920 until 1928, and on the INTERNATIONAL MISSIONARY COUNCIL from its formation in 1921 until 1928.

As one of the founders of the METHODIST FEDERATION FOR SOCIAL SERVICE, he shared in the drafting of the SOCIAL CREED adopted by the General Conference of 1908. That same year he helped to organize the FEDERAL COUNCIL OF CHURCHES and, as chairman of its Committee on the Church and Modern Industry, secured the adoption of the modified Methodist Social Creed as "The Social Creed of the Churches." As chairman of the Executive Committee of the Federal Council (1912-16) and as its president (1916-20), he represented the American churches in several missions of reconciliation and relief during the war years. For these services he was decorated by the French and Greek governments.

Besides his famous "Where Cross the Crowded Ways of Life," North's poems include "O Master of the Waking World" and "The World's Astir!" in *The Methodist Hymnal,* as well as in many others.

C. Lacy, *Frank Mason North.* 1967.
Who's Who in America.   CREIGHTON LACY

NORTH AFRICA PROVISIONAL ANNUAL CONFERENCE. This is a Conference organized of the Methodist work in ALGERIA and TUNISIA. The beginnings of Methodist work in North Africa and its growth into a Provisional Annual Conference are outlined under Algeria with certain of the general centers noted. The work in these may be briefly described as follows:

Algiers with a population of about 1,000,000, counting its outlying suburbs, is the principal city, seaport, and educational center of Algeria. It began as a trading post of the Phoenicians. The church there began to meet in a rented hall, but now meets at a new center at El-Biar, a suburb now part of the city of Algiers. The Methodist congregation is composed of both European Christians and certain converts from Islam. A new chapel has been erected at La Palmeraie in El-Biar. Algiers also has a Youth Club, a Young Women's Hostel (Villa Elisabeth), a Social-evangelistic Center at El-Biar, where a visiting nurse ministers to numerous families, a Sewing School with sixty students, while other missionaries work with women and girls through various group activities. There is also a Christian Social Center at El-Biar, which includes a chapel for the Algiers congregation. A trained Algerian social worker is appointed to social service there. The Christian Center of Maghrebin Studies in which The Methodist Church has a part, is located at Le Polmeroit. Merston Speight, a Methodist minister, is one of the two men in charge of the Center. The C.C.E.M. offers training in Islamics to members of all churches and tries to conduct a dialogue with Moslems.

Constantine is one of the largest cities of eastern Algeria, about 280 miles east of Algiers. There are about 200,000 inhabitants, most of whom are Arabic-speaking Muslims. It is a very ancient city, formerly a fortress considered impregnable because of its situation.

The church in Constantine worshipped in a girls' home chapel until a new church building was erected. There is a Constantine Boys' Home, a Frances Nast Gamble Memorial Home, which is for Muslim girls as well as for girls who attend certain governmental and vocational schools. There is also a Hannah Bradley Goodall Memorial Evangelistic Center, supported by the Women's Division of Christian Service, which ministers to Arabic-speaking girls who attend classes and clubs and use the library.

Fort National is a strongly fortified village up in the mountains of Great Kabylia, eighty miles east of Algiers. Fortifications here were built by the French in 1857. Evangelistic work has been part of the program of both Divisions of the General Board of MISSIONS of The Methodist Church through the past years. A Home for Boys was the outstanding feature of the Division of World Missions and still is. The home is now under the direction of a Kabyle Christian.

Les Ouadhias is a growing market center thirty miles from Fort National, named for a tribe of Kabyles in Great Kabylia. A number of governmental administrative units were for a time installed there, and many Kabyles from surrounding villages have settled at this center, which has a dispensary as well as an evangelistic center in this location. There are also a library for the men in the village, a new athletic field for basketball, volleyball, and handball, and handicrafts for women.

Il-Maten is a Kabyle village where there is a station of The Methodist Church. It is located four miles from the railway and 150 miles east of Algiers, overlooking the Souman Valley. Provision is made to do evangelistic work, carry on a dispensary, as well as a social and recreational program for the young men. Since 1963 there is a surgeon at Il-Maten, and a very well equipped hospital was built in 1966. Now there are fifty beds and two operating rooms.

Oran is the capital city of western Algeria, and a very important seaport almost 400 miles west of Algiers. Its population is something over 400,000 with 380,000 of these registered as Muslims. The Methodist Church supports there a small congregation composed mostly of European Christians who worship in the local church. There is also a weekly church school.

Tunis, which is the capital of Tunisia, has an Arab population. It is situated about ten miles from ancient Carthage and is a sizeable seaport and the site of a large Muslim university and several other important schools.

A small congregation worships in one of the halls of the Methodist Center at Tunis, which is jointly supported by the Women's Division of Christian Service and the Division of World Missions. The missionaries conduct evangelistic meetings and visit in the Muslim homes and work shops, taking advantage of every occasion to share the gospel with the people. There is also a young men's center and a Christian Social Center in Tunis. A center for women and girls was opened in 1954.

Bizerte. In this city about forty miles away a weekly worship is conducted as well as meetings with young people. Methodist missionaries cooperate closely with Swedish lady missionaries whose work is mostly with women and girls.

North Africa Provisional Annual Conference is part of the CENTRAL AND SOUTHERN EUROPE CENTRAL CONFERENCE and is administered from Zurich with Bishop FRANZ SCHAFER as the present presiding bishop. Rev. Paul Bres, district superintendent, oversees all this area in his one district.

W. C. Barclay, *History of Missions.* 1957.
Barbara H. Lewis, *Methodist Overseas Missions.* 1960.
Project Handbook, Overseas Missions, 1969.   N. B. H.

NORTH ALABAMA CONFERENCE was created in 1870. Prior to that date, parts of the territory which comprised it had been included at one time or another in the following conferences: WESTERN, TENNESSEE, MISSISSIPPI, ALABAMA (ME), and ALABAMA (MES).

Following treaties signed with the Chickasaw Indians on July 23, 1805 and the Cherokee Indians on Jan. 7, 1806, ratified on May 22, 1807 and Dec. 13, 1808, respectively, people of wealth and culture poured into Madison County, constituted in 1808. According to Anson West, "The first white people who touched the soil of North Alabama were Methodist, and Methodist services were held before a preacher was assigned. Joshua Boucher, a class leader and exhorter, came in 1808. Methodist Societies were organized, leaders appointed, exhorters licensed. As early as 1811 Methodist Quarterly Conferences were being held."

The first Methodist preacher appointed to the part of ALABAMA now included in the North Alabama Conference was JAMES GWIN. A member of the Western Conference, Gwin was appointed as "a missionary to go to that section in the great bend of the Tennessee River and to any contiguous territory where he might find the opportunity to hoist the banner of Methodism." A year later Gwin reported to the conference that the Flint Circuit had been organized with 179 members, four of whom were Negroes. The Flint Circuit had many preaching places, among them State Line, Ford's Chapel, Shiloh, Blue Springs, Lebanon, and Hunt Springs. Such was the beginning of Methodism in North Alabama.

When Alabama became a state in 1819, there were some 1,600 white and 206 Negro Methodists in the area which later comprised the North Alabama Conference. In 1832, when the Alabama Conference was created, it had 8,196 white and 2,770 Negro members. Whites and colored usually worshiped together, but in some places, particularly in Tuscaloosa, separate services were held. By 1830 Alabama Methodism had won 1,028 Indian members. Five Indians were ordained as Methodist preachers. In the part of Alabama which belonged at that time to the Tennessee Conference, there were 3,607 white, 653 Negro, and 260 Indian members.

Apparently the METHODIST PROTESTANTS formed the first regular Methodist annual conference in Alabama. LYMAN DAVIS (*Democratic Methodism in America,* p. 239) says the organization "was a process rather than a clear-cut beginning on any single date." There was a preliminary organization on May 1, 1829. A second meeting in September of the same year resulted in the formation of the Alabama Conference of the M. P. Church. Many of the outstanding members of the old church became Methodist Protestants.

Alabama Methodists, like those in other Southern states, were involved in the controversy over slavery. Some Methodist slave owners sought to minister to the spiritual well being of their slaves. Two colored missions were established in North Alabama. The wives and daughters of some white masters taught Negroes in Sunday schools. But the efforts to ameliorate the lot of the slaves did not satisfy northern Methodists, and the M. E. Church divided over slavery at the GENERAL CONFERENCE of 1844. In 1845, the M. E. Church, South was organized, and the Alabama Conference adhered South.

Methodism in North Alabama suffered from the ravages of the Civil War. LAGRANGE COLLEGE, the oldest institution of higher learning in the state, was burned by Federal troops. The college was founded in 1829 by the Methodists, antedating RANDOLPH-MACON COLLEGE (chartered in 1830), which today has the distinction of being the oldest Methodist college still in existence. Before it was destroyed LaGrange College had served Alabama more than a quarter of a century and during that time it was regarded as one of the strong colleges in the United States. The loss of the school was a great blow to North Alabama Methodists. Generally the destruction of property in the sections of Alabama overrun by Federal troops was great. Vagabonds connected with the northern army committed outrages.

In 1867, the M. E. Church officially re-entered Alabama. Many Alabamians regarded that church as a political organization under the dominance of radical politicians. But it is fair to say that many good Alabamians believed that the M. E. Church could "more perfectly serve an important and respectable minority to whom the Southern Church would not be acceptable." (Lazenby, p. 365). Thus there came about the two branches of episcopal Methodism in the state, and each had an Alabama Conference. It should be said that in spite of Southern antipathy the Alabama Conference (ME) rendered sincere and honorable service.

At its first session in 1870, the North Alabama Conference had almost 100 ministers whose membership had been in other annual conferences serving the area, along with seventeen others who were admitted on trial. The new conference had 261 Sunday schools with 1,386 teachers and 9,952 pupils. There were seven districts and eighty-six appointments, including three in college presidencies—W. H. Anderson, Florence Wesleyan University; J. G. Wilson, Huntsville Female College; and B. F. Farrabee, Tuscaloosa Female College. The conference claimed Athens Female College which was founded in 1842, and it held a half interest in Southern University at Greensboro. At the time of organization the conference had 22,648 members, 188 of them Negroes.

In 1872, the districts of the conference were rearranged, and for the first time there was a BIRMINGHAM District. However, it contained only one appointment in the city of Birmingham—Birmingham-Elyton Station.

On May 25, 1881, the first issue of the *Alabama Christian Advocate* appeared; the paper was sponsored jointly with the Alabama Conference. The WOMAN'S FOREIGN MISSIONARY SOCIETY was organized at Tuscaloosa in 1879. In 1886, the conference *Minutes* carried the names of the officers of "the Woman's Department of the Board of Church Extension." The Conference Parsonage and Home Mission Society came in 1897; a year later the name was changed to the WOMAN'S HOME MISSIONARY SOCIETY.

Methodism grew rapidly in the Birmingham area. The 1887 *Minutes* included the Bessemer District with twelve pastoral charges.

In the field of education, the conference emphasized the maintenance of both colleges and high schools. By 1892, there was sentiment in favor of a "North Alabama Conference College for Men" to be located in Birmingham. The institution was opened under that name in 1898.

By the turn of the century, the North Alabama Conference had made considerable progress. There were 217 preachers (nineteen retired and four supernumerary), 617 Sunday schools with 3,903 teachers and 36,407 pupils, 802 congregations, 670 houses of worship valued at $715,802, and 161 parsonages.

Succeeding years brought advances along many lines. The laymen, led by J. E. Morris of Saganaw, began a movement to provide homes for superannuated ministers. A board was set up to raise a fund for conference claimants, and a conference agency on superannuate homes with a director in charge was established.

The WESLEY FOUNDATION movement was launched in 1904 at the Alabama State College for Girls at Montevallo, with the Methodist church in that community ministering to the spiritual welfare of the students. In 1912, the conference established a committee to consider plans for improving the temporal, moral, and religious conditions of the Negro population. An offering was taken for MILES COLLEGE in Birmingham. In 1913, seven missionaries were sent to the foreign field. In the same year, JOHN WESLEY GILBERT, president of Miles College, accompanied Bishop WALTER R. LAMBUTH as he established a new mission at WEMBO-NYAMA, Africa. Gilbert urged Alabama Methodists to support the new mission.

In 1917, Southern University and Birmingham College were consolidated to form BIRMINGHAM-SOUTHERN COLLEGE. In the same year the conference enthusiastically endorsed the Methodist CENTENARY MOVEMENT, accepted its quota of $1,249,083, and two years later reported it had been oversubscribed.

In 1929, the conference cast a majority vote against the proposed plan for the union of American Methodism, the laymen being more opposed to it than the ministers. Twelve years later the vote for union was 344 to 100.

The North Alabama Conference went into The Methodist Church in 1939 with 344 ministers and 89,297 church members. The Methodist Protestant conference, after 110 years in the state, had thirty-four pastoral appointments and property valued at some $250,000. The Alabama Conference (ME) had 156 preaching places, 136 church buildings, and property valued at $371,481.

The first session of the North Alabama Conference of The Methodist Church was held at Woodlawn Church, Birmingham in November 1939, with Bishop J. L. DECELL in charge. Bishop WALLACE BROWN, who had presided at the final session of the Alabama Conference (ME), and J. S. EDDINS, substituting for Bishop JAMES H. STRAUGHN from the former M. P. Church who arrived late, participated in the formal service recognizing union. The united conference had eleven districts, 340 pastoral charges, 957 organized congregations, and 165,667 church members.

The North Alabama Conference has grown with the state. In addition to the metropolis of Birmingham, the conference has within its boundaries such strong cities as ANNISTON, BESSEMER, DECATUR, GADSDEN, FLORENCE, HUNTSVILLE, Jasper, and TUSCALOOSA. The conference has magnified the program of the rural church, and it has established Camp Sumatanga. The two Alabama conferences have greatly enlarged the Methodist Hospital in Birmingham, and they joined in building Fair Haven Home for the Aging in the same city in 1961. In 1970, the North Alabama Conference reported 517 pastoral charges and 195,301 members.

General Minutes, UMC.
Journal of the North Alabama Conference.
M. E. Lazenby, *Alabama and West Florida*. 1960.
A. West, *Alabama*. 1893.

G. FRED COOPER
FOSTER K. GAMBLE

NORTH ANDOVER, MASSACHUSETTS, U.S.A. **Rolling Ridge,** Methodist Center for church-related activities, located at 660 Great Pond Road, was purchased in 1948 through the initiative of laymen, and is controlled by the New England Conference and its Board of Education. This thirty-eight acre estate, twenty-five miles north of Boston, can accommodate 125 people in a campus-type setting of buildings and spacious grounds on a lakeside location. Originally designed for summer youth programs, the facility is now operated year round for seminars, institutes, and week-end retreats for all age groups under the administration of a bishop-appointed "Dean-Director" and a small staff.

Minutes of the New England Conference, 1966.

ERNEST R. CASE

NORTH ARKANSAS CONFERENCE was formed in 1914 by merging the Arkansas and White River Conferences. (See ARKANSAS for dates of predecessor conferences and early history.) The territory included in the new conference was identical with that of the Arkansas Conference before it was divided in 1870 to form the White River Conference.

The two conferences were consolidated in 1914 for practical reasons. As matters stood, they were too small in men and resources for economy of administration and for the appropriate appointment of the preachers to the churches. Moreover, by 1914 improved means of travel made it possible for preachers to gather for annual conference sessions from over a wider geographical area. The new body was called the North Arkansas Conference because the name properly identified its location in the state.

The North Arkansas Conference includes the fertile farming territory in the northeastern part of the state, locally called the "bottom," and the Ozark Mountain region in the northwest which is referred to as the "hill country."

The WESTERN METHODIST ASSEMBLY, established by the M. E. Church, South, in 1923, is at MOUNT SEQUOYAH, Fayetteville. Traditionally the superintendent has been a minister from the North Arkansas Conference. HENDRIX COLLEGE, since 1934 the only Methodist institution of higher learning in Arkansas, is within the bounds of the conference at Conway. The conference works cordially with the LITTLE ROCK CONFERENCE in support of many area-wide and denominational causes.

When organized in 1914, the North Arkansas Conference had 180 pastoral charges and 58,163 members. In 1970, there were six districts, 213 pastoral charges, and 98,880 members. The churches, parsonages, and other property belonging to the conference were valued at more than $37,000,000.

J. A. Anderson, *Arkansas Methodism.* 1935.
H. Jewell, *Arkansas.* 1892.
Minutes of the North Arkansas Conference. R. E. L. BEARDEN

NORTH CAROLINA is one of the thirteen original states, lying between VIRGINIA and SOUTH CAROLINA and bordering on the Atlantic Ocean. The first permanent settlement in North Carolina was made in 1660. The land area of the state is approximately 50,000 square miles, and its population in 1970 was 4,961,832.

North Carolina's wide coastal plain is well suited to farming, and though the region has some industry, it is primarily agricultural, growing cotton and tobacco; it leads the nation in the production of the latter. The piedmont section has become highly industrialized and urbanized, making North Carolina the foremost state in the production of textiles, tobacco, brick, and household furniture. The scenic Blue Ridge and Great Smoky Mountains in the west make tourism an important industry. More than 125,000 students are enrolled in seventy senior and junior colleges and universities in the state, DUKE and the University of North Carolina being the strongest educational institutions.

Peculiar to the geography of North Carolina and dominating its history more than any other factor are the Carolina Banks—long sandbar-like islands along the coast which block the rivers of the piedmont and cause them to flow for the most part into large bodies of shallow water called sounds. These banks have left the state without a single outstanding port for oceangoing ships, and they account for the fact that until recently North Carolina was a state of small farms without large cities or towns.

The lack of a port tended, through much of North Carolina's history, to tie the northern part of the state economically to Virginia and the southern part to South Carolina, while the mountain region developed close ties with TENNESSEE. As a result, sectionalism became more dominant in the political and religious life of North Carolina than in most states. Sectionalism in the state became more pronounced because the settlement of the western piedmont was not effected by a westward movement of people from the coastal plain, but rather by a sudden influx of immigrants who came down the valley of Virginia, turned east through the gaps in the Blue Ridge, and spread over the piedmont. Later they were joined by Marylanders and Virginians moving west and turning south when they reached the Blue Ridge. Prominent among those who came from PENNSYLVANIA were the Scotch-Irish and the Germans.

Organized Methodism entered North Carolina from Virginia about the beginning of the American Revolution. To be sure, GEORGE WHITEFIELD made several trips across the colony between 1738 and 1770, and in late 1772 JOSEPH PILMORE preached in the sound region en route to CHARLESTON, but the impact of those two men was not enduring. The first permanent foothold of Methodism in the colony was in the western coastal plain and eastern piedmont just below Brunswick County, Va. It was made possible by the preaching of ROBERT WILLIAMS there in 1774. By 1776 there was a North Carolina Circuit with 683 members. From that time forward Methodism spread rapidly in North Carolina. By 1779 there were three circuits with 1,467 members totally within the state. These circuits extended from the Virginia line down past the center of the state, while at the same time Virginia's Pittsylvania Circuit was extending into the western piedmont and the upper Yadkin valley.

The Yadkin Circuit, organized in 1780 by Andrew Yeargan, spread Methodism around the foot of the Blue Ridge into upper South Carolina. The SALISBURY Circuit began the spread of Methodism down the Yadkin and Pee Dee Rivers under the leadership of BEVERLY ALLEN in 1783, and the large Bertie Circuit formed in the same year was indicative of the spread of Methodism eastward. In 1787 a Bladen Circuit was formed for the lower Cape Fear region, and in 1789 DANIEL ASBURY organized a group of Virginia Methodists who had moved to the lower Catawba

River. In 1793 SAMUEL EDNEY was sent across the mountains to organize the Swannanoa Circuit. Thus except for a few areas, Methodism succeeded in covering the entire state of North Carolina in a little less than two decades.

The spread of Methodism in the piedmont was most successful among the Marylanders and Virginians, many of whom were already Methodists when they moved south. Some of the Scotch-Irish people had been influenced in Pennsylvania by the preaching of George Whitefield and Jonathan Edwards and were therefore ready to join the Methodists, especially during the great revival of 1801-02. There were some followers of PHILIP WILLIAM OTTERBEIN among the Germans in North Carolina, but the CHURCH OF THE UNITED BRETHREN IN CHRIST which he organized did not appear in the state as a separate organization.

During the spread of Methodism over North Carolina, FRANCIS ASBURY often traveled through the central and eastern sections holding important conferences. The first annual conference in America, following the CHRISTMAS CONFERENCE at BALTIMORE, was conducted by Bishops Asbury and COKE at the home of MAJOR GREEN HILL near Louisburg, April 20, 1785. The house is now one of the historic SHRINES of American Methodism. Asbury held a conference at Salisbury in 1786 and conducted three at the home of GEORGE MCKNIGHT near Salem—1789, 1790, and 1791. With the development of conferences on the frontier across the mountains, the center for Methodism in the state shifted eastward, and conferences were again held at the home of Green Hill in 1792 and 1793, the last to be conducted in the state during the eighteenth century.

When the 1796 GENERAL CONFERENCE created conferences with fixed geographical boundaries, North Carolina was divided between the Virginia and South Carolina Conferences. Then when the HOLSTON CONFERENCE was formed in 1824, the section of North Carolina across the Blue Ridge went with that body. In 1836 the NORTH CAROLINA CONFERENCE was formed by dividing the Virginia Conference, thus beginning a long drawn out process whereby all of North Carolina Methodism was finally placed in annual conferences which were wholly within the state. Over much opposition the North Carolina Conference acquired the churches in the Cape Fear Valley in southeastern North Carolina from the South Carolina Conference in 1850, and it got the work around CHARLOTTE and west of the Catawba River from the same conference in 1870. During the 1850's there was a strong movement in the North Carolina Conference for independence from Virginia. The goal was achieved when the North Carolina Conference withdrew support from RANDOLPH-MACON COLLEGE and the *Richmond Christian Advocate*, the two institutions which the two conferences had held in common up to that time. By the end of the decade the North Carolina Conference had established the *North Carolina Christian Advocate*, and Trinity College near HIGH POINT (later moved to Durham), the forerunner of DUKE UNIVERSITY. During the same period the state line from the sounds to the mountains became the boundary between the Virginia and North Carolina Conferences. When the WESTERN NORTH CAROLINA CONFERENCE was formed in 1890 it included the mountain section of the state which had been in the Holston Conference since 1824, and in 1894 the four counties in the extreme northeastern section of North Carolina were taken from the Virginia Conference and placed in the North Carolina

Conference. This completed the process of unifying North Carolina Methodism in annual conferences wholly within the state.

Another factor which complicated the growth of Methodism in North Carolina was the demand for democracy in the church. It was first felt when JAMES O'KELLY and his associates walked out of the 1792 General Conference. O'Kelly had a strong following in the northern piedmont section of North Carolina which resulted in the formation of the Christian Church (now a part of the United Church of Christ). O'Kelly's followers established Elon College near Burlington, N. C., which still survives as an A-grade college.

Of course, the METHODIST PROTESTANT schism in the 1820's was a more important result of the demand for democracy in the church. On Dec. 19, 1828 a group of preachers and laymen met at WHITAKER'S CHAPEL in Halifax County, N. C., and organized the first M. P. Conference in the land. The movement spread to Guilford County the next year, and by the time of the Civil War there were Methodist Protestants in most of the rural sections of the state. As time passed the NORTH CAROLINA CONFERENCE became one of the stronger M. P. conferences in the United States.

While the North Carolina Conference and all others which included parts of the state within their boundaries adhered South after the division in 1844, there was some dissatisfaction with that action. Several congregations in the old Quaker section of Guilford and surrounding counties affiliated with the WESLEYAN METHODIST CHURCH and sustained a precarious relationship with that body until they were driven underground or out of the state during the Civil War. In 1870 the group reorganized at Colfax, Guilford County, and in 1879 they formed a North Carolina Conference of the Wesleyan Methodist Church with three circuits. Growth was slow until the turn of the century when their emphasis on HOLINESS drew many who thought the older churches were surrendering an important emphasis. In 1965 the conference had two districts, ninety-four preaching places, 4,639 members (a few of them in South Carolina), and a campground and central meeting place at Colfax.

Following the Civil War the M. E. Church reentered North Carolina, and in 1867 some of the mountain congregations were received into the Holston Conference (ME) which had been organized in 1865. The Northern Church formed a Virginia and North Carolina Mission Conference in 1867 which was composed of both white and Negro ministers and churches. Two years later the mission conference was divided to form the Virginia and North Carolina Conferences. In 1879 the white ministers and churches were set off from the North Carolina Conference into a conference which became the Blue Ridge Conference. In 1896 the Blue Ridge Conference was divided to form the Atlantic Mission Conference in eastern North Carolina, but in 1912 the two were merged to form the BLUE RIDGE-ATLANTIC CONFERENCE which continued until unification in 1939. The North Carolina Conference continued as a Negro body until unification when it became a conference in the CENTRAL JURISDICTION. Then in 1964 it was merged with the Virginia churches of the Washington Conference (CJ) to become the NORTH CAROLINA-VIRGINIA CONFERENCE. The latter was merged with the overlying conferences of the SOUTHEASTERN JURISDICTION in 1968.

Following the Civil War, many of the M. P. congregations in North Carolina joined "the Methodist Church" (1866-77) which was made up of the northern conferences of the M. P. Church. Shortly before the two branches reunited in 1877 as the Methodist Protestant Church, the "Methodist Church" reported an East North Carolina and a Western North Carolina Conference. There was friction between these two bodies and the North Carolina Conference of the M. P. Church, and the latter conference, while voting for the reunion of the northern and southern branches of Methodist Protestantism in 1877, seemed determined not to receive some of the preachers and churches of the East and Western North Carolina Conferences. As a result, some of the members of the East and Western North Carolina Conferences formed the Deep River Conference in 1878 which continued until 1891 and then disintegrated with most of its congregations going into the Blue Ridge Conference (MEC).

While the M. E. Church succeeded in gathering many Negro members from the M. E. Church, South into its fold immediately following the Civil War, many more were attracted to the Negro Methodist denominations. Soon after the Federal troops occupied the sound region of North Carolina, J. W. Hood began to organize the A.M.E. Zion Church there. The North Carolina Conference of the A.M.E. Zion Church was organized in 1868. Today it is the strongest Negro Methodist church in the state, with seven conferences and Livingstone College at Salisbury. A North Carolina A.M.E. conference was organized at Wilmington in 1868, and that church now has two conferences in the state. By 1873 the C.M.E. Church, fostered by the M. E. Church, South, had a North Carolina Conference. In 1965 it had 9,200 members in the state.

When American Methodists considered union in 1925, the Blue Ridge-Atlantic Conference (ME) and the North Carolina M. P. Conference almost unanimously favored the move, while the two Southern Methodist conferences failed to ratify it. By 1938, however, when another plan for unification was presented, the vote against it in the two Southern conferences was negligible. In the merger, the boundaries of the two conferences of the M. E. Church, South became the boundaries of the conferences of The Methodist Church in the state. The five North Carolina annual conferences—two MES, two ME, and one MP—brought into The Methodist Church in 1939 a total of 767 charges and 358,265 members.

The Lake Junaluska Methodist Assembly, Inc. near Asheville, which now belongs to the Southeastern Jurisdiction, is within the bounds of the Western North Carolina Conference. With some 2,500 acres, Lake Junaluska is the largest summer assembly in the church. It has a 250-acre lake, a large number of lodges, and some 500 private homes. The World Methodist Building at Lake Junaluska is headquarters for the World Methodist Council, the Commission on Archives and History of The United Methodist Church, and the International Methodist Historical Society.

Seven men have been elected bishop from conferences in North Carolina: James Atkins (1906), John C. Kilgo (1910), Robert E. Jones (1920), William Walter Peele (1938), Robert N. Brooks and Paul N. Garber (1944), and W. Kenneth Goodson (1964).

North Carolina Methodism owns and controls, or is affiliated with, eight strong educational institutions: Duke University and the Duke Divinity School; Bennett College at Greensboro; Brevard Junior College at Brevard; Greensboro College which is the second oldest permanent college for women in the United States; High Point College, which was founded by the former M. P. Church; Methodist College at Fayetteville; North Carolina Wesleyan College at Rocky Mount; and Pfeiffer College at Misenheimer. The total enrollment in the eight institutions in 1968 was more than 12,000.

In 1970 North Carolina Methodism had two episcopal areas (Charlotte and Raleigh), two annual conferences, twenty-five districts, 1,209 charges, 1,580 ministers, 494,-094 members, and property valued at $271,610,462.

General Minutes, ME, MES, TMC, UMC.
Minutes of the conferences in North Carolina.
A. M. Chreitzberg, *Early Methodism in the Carolinas.* 1897.
E. T. Clark, *Western North Carolina.* 1966.
W. L. Grissom, *North Carolina.* 1905.   Homer Keever

NORTH CAROLINA CHRISTIAN ADVOCATE was started at a session of the North Carolina Conference (MES) held at Pittsboro, N. C., in 1855. At that conference a resolution was passed approving the establishment of a book store and a religious newspaper.

A committee was appointed to carry out the proposal, and the first issue was produced at Raleigh, N. C., in January of 1856 under the editorship of R. T. Heflin. He continued as editor until 1861, when W. E. Pell took over. However, in the same year, the young paper suspended publication on account of the Civil War. It was revived in the next year and continued under great difficulty until March, 1865, when the prostrate economic condition of the state compelled a second shut-down.

The determination to have a Methodist publication in North Carolina persisted, and a semi-official journal called the *Enterprise,* and later the *Methodist Enterprise,* came into being also at Raleigh in 1865. It was published by L. Branson, a Methodist local preacher, who had the active and able assistance of H. T. Hudson, then pastor of Edenton Street Church in Raleigh.

The next year the North Carolina Conference voted approval of a direct successor to the defunct *North Carolina Christian Advocate* which was to be called *The Episcopal Methodist* and to be edited by Hudson.

Within a few months, however, the name *Advocate* returned to the masthead, with variations thereafter between the name *Christian Advocate* and *Raleigh Christian Advocate.* J. B. Bobbitt took over editorial duties in 1868 and continued in this capacity until 1878.

From 1868 until 1894 there was a rapid succession of editors and publishers. Upon formation of the Western North Carolina Conference in 1890 the offices of the paper were moved to Greensboro, under sponsorship of both conferences. The original name, *North Carolina Christian Advocate,* came back into use in 1896, but three years later the North Carolina Conference withdrew support and established the *Raleigh Christian Advocate,* with T. N. Ivey as editor. Eight years later he left this position to become editor of the church's general organ, the Nashville *Christian Advocate.*

Both publications, the *Raleigh Christian Advocate* and the *North Carolina Christian Advocate,* continued on parallel courses until efforts to merge the two into one publication finally met with success in 1919. The two editors, L. S. Massey of the *Raleigh Christian Advocate* and H. M. Blair of the *North Carolina Christian Advocate,* became co-editors, with the latter name being retained for the publication. The next year GILBERT T. ROWE was named editor, only to leave within a year to become BOOK EDITOR in Nashville.

Thereupon A. W. PLYLER of the Western North Carolina Conference assumed the editorship and began a long and fruitful service which extended for over twenty years. His twin brother, M. T. PLYLER, was elected co-editor in 1927. The two of them formed a remarkable journalistic team, which did not terminate until their retirement in 1945.

In 1927 the presently occupied building was erected in Greensboro. During the twenty years thereafter the paper made steady advances in circulation and influence.

Its editorial voice was heard widely over the Church, and it came to be recognized as one of the leading religious journals in the United States. Perhaps the most significant achievement of the remarkable Plyler twins was in resolving the inter-conference problems and the financial stresses which had hampered the paper's progress in past years.

Since 1945, the editorial chair has been filled by a series of able writers and interpreters of church affairs. Henry C. Sprinkle, Jr., served from 1945 to 1949 when he left to become editor of *The World Outlook*. Thereupon, Cecil W. Robbins took the editorial helm until his resignation in 1955 to become president of LOUISBURG COLLEGE. The next ten years were divided equally between R. P. Marshall and S. J. Starnes, each of whom served with distinction. The present editor, James C. Stokes, assumed the position in June 1966.

The *North Carolina Christian Advocate* continues as the official publication of the North Carolina Conference and the Western North Carolina Conference of The United Methodist Church and these conferences control its operation through a Methodist Board of Publication, Inc. In addition to publishing the weekly religious journal, the enterprise also does job printing under the trade name The Piedmont Press. The total assets of the corporation at present are valued at close to half a million dollars.

NORTH CAROLINA CONFERENCE (MP) was organized at WHITAKER'S CHAPEL, near Enfield, N. C., Dec. 19, 1828, with Eli B. Whitaker, a preacher, presiding. It was the first METHODIST PROTESTANT annual conference, even antedating the organization of the M. P. GENERAL CONFERENCE. Because of the conference's priority and because of the location of its organizing session, Whitaker's Chapel was regarded through the years as the historic SHRINE of democratic Methodism in America. The organizing session of the conference was composed of nine preachers, five local preachers, and twelve laymen.

For more than sixty years the M. P. Church in North Carolina was predominantly a rural denomination. All of the earlier churches were in the open country. Attempts to establish congregations in the cities failed until around 1890. By 1896 the conference had organized societies and built churches in nine cities, including GREENSBORO, Asheboro, and HIGH POINT.

For the first half century there was sentiment in favor of dividing the conference into eastern and western branches. The division was effected at the session at Yadkin College in 1878. The division left the North Carolina Conference with nine charges and 2,500 members, and the new Western North Carolina Conference with twenty-one charges and 8,500 members. At Tabernacle Church,

Guilford County, in 1880, the two conferences merged to form again the North Carolina Conference.

The North Carolina Conference was typically southern in its attitude toward slavery. Its delegates to the 1838 General Conference were instructed to say, if the subject of slavery was broached, that the North Carolina Conference did "not consider that a debatable subject."

In 1866 when the northern conferences of the M. P. Church withdrew and formed "the Methodist Church," some M. P. ministers and churches in North Carolina announced that they had suffered for their anti-slavery views and asked for affiliation with the new denomination. The Methodist Church then recognized the small group as the North Carolina Conference. In 1875 this North Carolina Conference divided to form the East North Carolina and the Western North Carolina Conferences which officially came back into the M. P. Church two years later when the Methodist Church merged with it. However, a few ministers and churches of the East North Carolina and Western North Carolina Conferences either felt unwelcome in or were unwilling to return to the M. P. Church, and they proceeded to form the DEEP RIVER CONFERENCE. The Deep River Conference continued until about 1891 when it dissolved and most of its churches entered the Blue Ridge Conference (ME).

As time passed, the North Carolina Conference was the only one in the M. P. Church to maintain its own official paper. It published a paper called the *Watchman and Harbinger* from 1862 to the end of the Civil War. Then in 1873 it maintained the *Central Protestant* for eighteen years. From 1894 to 1939 *Our Church Record* (*Methodist Protestant Herald* after 1910), a weekly, was published in Greensboro. J. F. McCULLOCH, former president of ADRIAN COLLEGE, Michigan, was the able editor of the paper for forty years. His proclaimed purpose in becoming editor was to educate the people to the need of a M. P. College in North Carolina, and after thirty years he achieved his goal. The paper merged with the *North Carolina Christian Advocate* at unification in 1939.

The North Carolina Conference gave much attention to education. During the early years it officially approved schools in other states which had M. P. connections. Between 1855 and 1860 the conference projected JAMESTOWN FEMALE COLLEGE, but unfortunately it was destroyed by fire in 1861. YADKIN COLLEGE, ten miles west of Lexington, began as an academy about 1853 and was chartered as a college in 1861. At the time it had about eighty boarding students. When the war began sixty students entered the Confederate Army. After the war the school resumed operations, and in spite of debts and difficulties it carried on until 1924.

In 1921 High Point gave eighty acres of land and $100,000 in money for a M. P. college. ROBERT M. ANDREWS, a member of the conference, led in raising additional funds, and was then chosen as the first president of HIGH POINT COLLEGE which opened in 1924. The college proved to be an asset to the conference. In 1938 it was said that practically every young man entering the conference in recent years had been educated at High Point College. Today High Point College is supported by the WESTERN NORTH CAROLINA and NORTH CAROLINA CONFERENCES. It has an endowment of more than $2,000,000, a plant valued at about $6,000,000, and over 1,200 students.

Largely through the efforts of the WOMAN'S HOME MISSIONARY SOCIETY of the North Carolina Conference, the Methodist Protestant Children's Home was opened at Denton, N. C., in 1910, and moved to High Point in 1913. It was the only such institution in the M. P. Church. At unification in 1939 arrangements were made to close the home and transfer its ninety-seven children to the homes of the two North Carolina Conferences of The Methodist Church at Winston-Salem and Raleigh.

WILLIAM H. WILLS, an outstanding minister, served the North Carolina Conference both as secretary and president (several times), and in 1867 was elected president of the M. P. General Conference.

In 1937 the North Carolina Conference reported 224 churches, 80 ministers, 30,604 members, and churches and parsonages valued at $1,775,900. At the time of unification it was one of the largest conferences in the Methodist Protestant connection.

Minutes of the North Carolina Conference.
J. E. Carroll, *History of the North Carolina Annual Conference, Methodist Protestant Church*. Greensboro: McCulloch and Swain, 1939.
E. J. Drinkhouse, *History of the Methodist Protestant Church*. 1898.
ALBEA GODBOLD

NORTH CAROLINA CONFERENCE was created by the 1836 GENERAL CONFERENCE. It was set off from the VIRGINIA CONFERENCE at the meeting of the latter in Petersburg, Va., in January 1837, and was organized at that time with Bishop BEVERLY WAUGH presiding. The appointments of the North Carolina Conference were made separately from those of the Virginia Conference at the Petersburg session. The new conference began with five districts, Raleigh, Newbern, Roanoke, Danville, and Salisbury; forty-four charges, and 15,062 white and 3,666 colored members. In January 1838, the conference met at GREENSBORO, N. C., with Bishop THOMAS A. MORRIS presiding. The territory of the conference was North Carolina east of the Blue Ridge Mountains, except the extreme northeastern counties which continued in the Virginia Conference until 1894, and the southern segment of the state including Wilmington, CHARLOTTE, and Lincolnton, part of which continued in the SOUTH CAROLINA CONFERENCE until 1850, and the remainder until 1870.

Though the North Carolina Conference was not organized until forty years after the General Conference created annual conferences with definite geographical boundaries, the first conference of Methodist preachers following the organization of the M. E. Church at the CHRISTMAS CONFERENCE was conducted by Bishops ASBURY and COKE in April 1785, at the home of MAJOR GREEN HILL near Louisburg within the bounds of what is now the North Carolina Conference. (See NORTH CAROLINA for beginnings of Methodism in the state.) The Hill House is now a national Methodist Historic SHRINE. There were Methodist societies near the Virginia line in eastern North Carolina as early as 1774, and there was a North Carolina Circuit by 1776. By the time the North Carolina Conference was formed in 1837 there were nearly 30,000 white and about 12,000 colored members of the M. E. Church in the state.

From its beginning the North Carolina Conference cooperated with the Virginia Conference in supporting the *Richmond Christian Advocate* and RANDOLPH-MACON COLLEGE (chartered in 1830). A few years later when GREENSBORO COLLEGE was opened (1846), the two conferences joined in its support. But in time the North Caro-

lina Conference took steps to make itself independent of Virginia. In 1855 the *North Carolina Christian Advocate* was launched. Then in 1856 when relations between the two conferences had become strained over a bitter quarrel between W. A. SMITH, president of Randolph-Macon College, and CHARLES F. DEEMS, a professor at the University of North Carolina, the North Carolina Conference withdrew support from Randolph-Macon and accepted Normal College (Trinity) near HIGH POINT as its college for men, and the Virigina Conference dropped Greensboro College.

The North Carolina Conference adhered South after the division of 1844, and thereafter it grew steadily. In 1860 it reported 28,822 white and 12,043 colored members. In 1890 the conference was divided to form the WESTERN NORTH CAROLINA CONFERENCE. In the preceding year the North Carolina Conference had reported fourteen districts, 212 charges, and 91,975 members.

Throughout its history education has been a major concern of the North Carolina Conference. In the 1890's reports of the conference board of education urged assessments on the churches to support the current budget of Trinity College which moved to DURHAM in 1892. In 1889 the conference had voted to transfer the college to RALEIGH, but in the end Durham outbid the capital city. JULIAN S. CARR gave sixty acres in Durham for a campus, and WASHINGTON DUKE donated $85,000 in cash. In 1896 Duke contributed an additional $100,000 to the college on condition that it open its doors to women as well as men. A committee of ladies appointed by Trinity College alumni in the conference then drew up a resolution commending Duke for recognizing "womanhood in her influence and possibilities" and honoring "her by proposing to open to her the equal opportunities of advancement in education and distinction with man." In the same year, on recommendation of a group which included JOHN C. KILGO, president of Trinity, the conference adopted a resolution objecting to free tuition at the state university on the grounds that it was taxing the many to educate the few.

Among the schools which had either the support or commendation of the North Carolina Conference before the turn of the century were LITTLETON FEMALE COLLEGE, Wesleyan Female College at Murfreesboro, LOUISBURG FEMALE COLLEGE, and academies at Burlington and Jonesboro.

In 1924 JAMES B. DUKE, son of Washington, gave $40,000,000 to Trinity College with the understanding that it would become DUKE UNIVERSITY, whereupon a new 5,600-acre campus, dominated by a magnificent Gothic style chapel, was developed. Today Duke, with a plant valued at $126,000,000, an annual budget of $70,000,000, an endowment of $60,000,000, a library of 2,000,000 volumes, about 1,000 professors, 8,000 students, and a strong Divinity School that offers graduate as well as seminary degrees, is one of the great universities of the land.

In the 1950's the North Carolina Conference established two new educational institutions within its bounds, METHODIST COLLEGE at Fayetteville and NORTH CAROLINA WESLEYAN COLLEGE at Rocky Mount, laying assessments of some $5,000,000 on the churches to launch them. Methodist College now has a plant valued at about $7,000,000, an endowment of about $500,000, and 1,000 students, while the corresponding figures for the other school are $6,000,000, $210,000, and 700 students.

In recent years the North Carolina Conference has apportioned annually some $500,000 to be raised for its college sustaining fund. The money is distributed to Duke Divinity School, and Bennett, Greensboro, High Point, Louisburg, Methodist, and North Carolina Wesleyan Colleges. The conference helps to maintain WESLEY FOUNDATIONS at eighteen educational institutions in the state.

In 1899 the North Carolina Conference established an orphanage at Raleigh. Now called the Methodist Home for Children, it has a plant valued at $2,000,000 and is ministering to more than 200 children per year. The conference maintains a Methodist Retirement Home at Durham with a capacity of about 200.

One member of the conference has been elected bishop, JOHN C. KILGO (1910).

The North Carolina Conference came to unification in 1939 with seven districts, 226 charges, 132,735 members, and churches and parsonages valued at $9,268,655. The conference merged with parts of the BLUE RIDGE-ATLANTIC CONFERENCE (ME) and the NORTH CAROLINA CONFERENCE (MP) in 1939 to form the North Carolina Conference of The Methodist Church. Some of the ministers and churches of the NORTH CAROLINA-VIRGINIA CONFERENCE (CJ) were received into the North Carolina Conference in 1968 as the former was merged with the overlying conferences of the Southeastern Jurisdiction.

In 1970 the North Carolina Conference reported eleven districts, 522 pastoral charges, 619 ministers, 211,089 members, and property valued at $96,889,398.

General Minutes, MECS and MC.
Minutes of the North Carolina Conference.
W. L. Grissom, North Carolina. 1905.   ALBEA GODBOLD

NORTH CAROLINA CONFERENCE (CJ) was organized at Union Chapel, Alexander County, not far from Statesville, N. C., on Jan. 14, 1869, with Bishop EDWARD F. AMES presiding. The conference was formed by dividing the Virginia and North Carolina Mission Conference which had been organized at Portsmouth, Va., Jan. 3, 1867 with Bishop LEVI SCOTT presiding. The territory of the new conference was the state of NORTH CAROLINA. The conference at the outset included both Negro and white ministers and churches. It began with one district, twelve charges, and 2,859 members. At its first session appointments were made to sixteen charges. In 1879 the white work of the North Carolina Conference was merged with the Asheville District of the HOLSTON CONFERENCE to form the Southern Central Conference (called Blue Ridge Conference beginning in 1881). By 1900 the North Carolina Conference had four districts, Greensboro, Western, Wilmington, and Winston; 68 charges, and 10,289 members.

The North Carolina Conference emphasized education. In 1909 each district superintendent in his report to the conference declared that he had stressed the need of education and the importance of patronizing Methodist schools. They praised BENNETT COLLEGE and urged the conference to support it. The conference also supported GAMMON THEOLOGICAL SEMINARY in Atlanta.

On reentering North Carolina after the Civil War, the M. E. Church started several schools for Negroes (see BLUE RIDGE-ATLANTIC CONFERENCE for white schools), two of which have survived—Allen High School in ASHEVILLE and Bennett College in Greensboro. Bennett College was founded in 1873 by Negro leaders during the time that the FREEDMEN'S AID SOCIETY was giving assistance. The WOMAN'S HOME MISSIONARY SOCIETY of the denomination built homes for girls on the campus, and in 1926 the school was reorganized as a college for women. Bennett has become an outstanding institution with full accreditation. Today it has a plant valued at more than $4,000,000, an endowment of $2,000,000, and nearly 700 students.

An interested couple from NEW YORK started a primary school for Negroes in Asheville about 1885. The Woman's Home Missionary Society became interested in it and in time the school was accredited by the state. In 1945 the name was changed to Allen High School. Today it has a modern plant and its enrollment of 130 is drawn from several states and from Africa.

The North Carolina Conference entered the CENTRAL JURISDICTION of The Methodist Church in 1939 with four districts, sixty-three charges, and 13,994 members. At its last session in 1964, the conference reported four districts, 93 charges, 63 ministers, 14,750 members, churches and parsonages valued at $3,989,407, and $634,072 raised for all purposes during the year.

In 1955 the East Tennessee Conference (CJ) requested the North Carolina Conference to consider merging the two bodies, but nothing came of the proposal. In 1964 when the WASHINGTON CONFERENCE (CJ) was being absorbed by the overlying conferences of the Northeastern Jurisdiction, the Virginia churches of that conference were attached to the North Carolina Conference (CJ), and the name of the latter was changed to the NORTH CAROLINA-VIRGINIA CONFERENCE. The territory of the enlarged conference included North Carolina and all of Virginia except the southwestern counties which remained in the East Tennessee Conference (CJ). The North Carolina-Virginia Conference was organized at Greensboro, N. C., Aug. 11, 1964 with Bishop CHARLES F. GOLDEN presiding. The next year the conference reported five districts, 129 charges, 19,025 members, and property valued at $7,137,112.

In 1968 the North Carolina-Virginia Conference was merged with the overlying conferences of the Southeastern Jurisdiction in Virginia and North Carolina. In its last year the North Carolina-Virginia Conference reported four districts, Central, Eastern, Virginia, and Western; 98 charges, 88 ministers, 18,706 members, property valued at $7,637,698, and $670,216 raised for all purposes during the year.

General Minutes, MEC, and MC.
Minutes of the North Carolina Conference and the North Carolina-Virginia Conference.
E. T. Clark, Western North Carolina. 1966.   ALBEA GODBOLD

NORTH CAROLINA-VIRGINIA CONFERENCE (CJ). (See NORTH CAROLINA CONFERENCE (CJ).)

NORTH CAROLINA WESLEYAN COLLEGE, Rocky Mount, N. C., is the result of a movement initiated in the North Carolina conferences to build two new senior colleges during the last part of the twentieth century. The proposal of Rocky Mount citizens to raise $2,000,000 and to provide a campus and $50,000 annually for operating expenses to match similar amounts from the NORTH CAROLINA CONFERENCE was accepted by the conference in May 1956. The college was chartered on Oct. 25, 1956, and construction of the new campus started in 1959. The college was admitted to membership in the Southern Association of Schools and Colleges in 1966 and accredited by the UNIVERSITY SENATE of The Methodist Church in 1967. Degrees offered are the B.A. and B.S. The governing board has twenty-four trustees recommended by the board, nominated by the conference Board of Education, and confirmed by the conference.

JOHN O. GROSS

NORTH CENTRAL COLLEGE, Naperville, Illinois, U.S.A., began as Plainfield College in Plainfield, Ill., founded in 1861 by the EVANGELICAL ASSOCIATION. The college moved to its present site in Naperville in 1870 when residents of the town raised $25,000 and donated eight acres of land.

On May 17, 1870, the cornerstone of the present Old Main Building was laid, and the following fall 120 students and six faculty members began classes. After moving to Naperville, the school became known as North Western College and continued under that name until 1926, when the present name of North Central was adopted.

In 1967 the campus encompassed fifty-three acres, fifteen buildings, and had an endowment of $3 million and total assets of nearly $9 million.

The college grants the degrees of B.A., B.M., and B.M.E. The course of study is in the liberal arts with majors developed in twenty-two departments. A Mid-Winter Study and Research Term, freeing the month of January from the routine of classroom study, and a core curriculum are special study programs.

North Central College has a governing board of thirty trustees, one-third of whom are elected from annual conferences, three from the alumni association and the remainder at large.

The College and Seminary Library has 100,000 volumes. The present student enrollment is 865 students with sixty-eight faculty members. Its alumni have contributed in all areas of life—in business, industry, education, religion, military, government service, medicine, law, journalism and social services.

ARLO L. SCHILLING

NORTH DAKOTA, population 610,648 in 1970, is in the central part of the nation and is bounded by CANADA on the north, MINNESOTA on the east, SOUTH DAKOTA on the south, and MONTANA on the west. It was a part of the LOUISIANA Purchase in 1803. Its 70,665 square miles contain no mountains or forests. Frenchmen from Canada were the first white people in the region. In 1804-05 Lewis and Clark wintered at Fort Madan in what is now North Dakota. American settlers began moving into the area about 1850. At first they had trouble with the Indians, but by 1864 the Red men had been driven to the Bad Lands west of the Missouri River. In 1861 Dakota Territory (including both North and South Dakota) was formed. In 1880 the Great Northern Railway entered the state and in time it was extended to the west coast. Settlers then came in large numbers, and in 1889 North Dakota was admitted to the Union as a state. Ninety per cent of the state is farm land, and wheat is the chief crop. The state now produces oil, and with the development of water power manufacturing has become a part of its economy.

The 1860 GENERAL CONFERENCE, alert to Methodism's

opportunity, made Dakota Territory a part of the UPPER IOWA CONFERENCE. In the same year the Iowa body sent S. W. INGHAM as missionary into what is now South Dakota. In 1871 the same conference sent James Gurley to the North Pacific Mission which included North Dakota and part of Minnesota. At Fargo in that year Gurley conducted the first Methodist service in North Dakota. The next year John Webb, Gurley's successor on the mission, organized a Methodist society in Fargo, and in 1874 the first Methodist church building was erected at a cost of $1,200, the site for the edifice being donated by the Northern Pacific Railroad. A second Methodist society was organized at Grand Forks in 1873, and by 1876 it had erected a church.

In 1877 the North Dakota work was attached to the Red River District of the MINNESOTA CONFERENCE with Joseph B. Starkey as presiding elder. Starkey made Fargo his headquarters, and under his leadership the work expanded rapidly. In 1884 the North Dakota Mission was formed by dividing the Minnesota Conference, and in 1886 the mission was elevated to the status of an annual conference. In the next thirty years the work grew rapidly. (See NORTH DAKOTA CONFERENCE.)

In 1876 Methodist work among the Germans in North Dakota was begun by the Northwest German Conference. Many of the German missions and churches were short-lived, and in 1924 when the NORTHERN GERMAN CONFERENCE (to which the North Dakota churches then belonged) was merged, there were only two German charges in the state to be received into the North Dakota Conference. Several Norwegian Methodist churches were also organized in North Dakota, the most prominent being what is now Wesley Church in Hillsboro which made the first contribution ($2,000) to the Norwegian Methodist theological seminary, Evanston, Ill. (See NORWEGIAN AND DANISH CONFERENCE.) When the Norwegian and Danish Conference was merged with the overlying English-speaking conferences in 1943, it had five charges in the state which entered the North Dakota Conference.

In 1892 North Dakota Methodism projected Red River Valley University at Wahpeton. In 1906 the school was moved to Grand Forks adjacent to the state university and was called Wesley College. The conference gradually severed connection with the college, but it still elects trustees to the Wesley Center of Religion at the university. Today there is no Methodist college in North Dakota. The conference supports Kenmare Deaconess Hospital at Kenmare, Wesley Camp near Valley City, and WESLEY FOUNDATIONS at the several state institutions of higher learning.

In 1970 The United Methodist Church had ninety-three pastoral charges, 141 ministers, 25,219 members, and property valued at $12,156,312 in North Dakota.

C. A. Armstrong, *North Dakota.* 1946.
General Minutes, ME, TMC, UMC.
Minutes of the North Dakota Conference.   E. O. GRUNSTEAD

NORTH DAKOTA CONFERENCE was organized at Grand Forks on Oct. 14, 1886 with Bishop WILLIAM L. HARRIS presiding. The conference superseded the North Dakota Mission which had been formed at FARGO on Oct. 2, 1884. The boundaries of the conference included only NORTH DAKOTA. At the beginning the conference had two districts, Fargo and Grand Forks, and there were forty-seven charges and 2,341 members. (See NORTH DAKOTA for an account of the beginning of Methodism in the state.) By 1888 some eighteen new churches had been organized. In the next three decades aid from the Board of Home Missions built many churches. In 1910 the conference had four districts, 150 charges, and 9,535 members. Thereafter the membership grew a little, but the number of districts and pastoral charges decreased. In 1939 there were three districts, seventy-seven charges and 16,065 members.

About 1900 there was a schism in the North Dakota Conference over the doctrine of HOLINESS. J. G. Morrison, leader of the holiness group, finally joined the CHURCH OF THE NAZARENE taking with him a few pastors and local preachers. A Laymen's Holiness Association which had been organized also went to the Nazarene Church. By 1940 the Nazarenes had thirty-two churches in the state with a membership of 1,127, many of them former Methodists.

Interested in education from the beginning, the North Dakota Conference projected a college in 1892, but it was short-lived. While there is no Methodist college in the state today, the conference commends DAKOTA WESLEYAN UNIVERSITY, at Mitchell, S. D. to its people, and it supports the Wesley Center of Religion at the University of North Dakota in Grand Forks. Also, it maintains a strong WESLEY FOUNDATION program at the university, at North Dakota State University at Fargo, and at other colleges.

In 1920 the conference assumed responsibility for a hospital at Mandan, which in 1926 was named the Methodist Deaconess Hospital. In 1958 the nurses home at the hospital was remodeled and became the North Dakota Methodist Home for the Aged. In 1964 the hospital and home were sold to the Heartview Foundation, and they have now become a center for treatment of alcoholism. A hospital at Kenmare was purchased in 1923, and it is now known as the Kenmare Deaconess Hospital. In 1951 the conference established Wesley Acres Camp on what is called Lake Ashtabula near Valley City.

Long a part of an episcopal area composed of MINNESOTA and the two Dakotas, the Dakota Methodists petitioned the 1952 GENERAL CONFERENCE of The Methodist Church for an area made up of the two Dakota Conferences, and it was so ordered. The episcopal residence is in Aberdeen, S. D.

In regard to total membership, North Dakota Methodism has fared better than the state population. Between 1930 and 1950 the state population decreased ten percent, but in that time the membership of the North Dakota Conference increased from 14,032 to 15,067. Between 1950 and 1960 the population of the state increased two percent, while the Methodist membership grew to 20,317, an increase of thirty-five percent.

Following merger of the E.U.B. and Methodist Conferences, the North Dakota Conference reported three districts in 1970, ninety-three charges, 141 ministers, 25,219 members, property valued at $12,156,312, and a total amount raised for all purposes of $2,119,994.

Wesley Acres Camp is situated on Bald Hill Creek, about twenty miles northwest of Valley City, N. D. It was started in 1951 on forty acres, an oasis of American elm and other trees in a prairie valley. The camp has facilities for housing and feeding over 200, a large central assembly, small prayer chapel, facilities for groups of forty to fifty in the winterized section, modern plumbing, heated swimming pool. Open the year round, Wesley Acres serves the North Dakota Conference and area for youth camps, school of missions, pastor's school, family camp, ashram site, and retreats.

C. A. Armstrong, *North Dakota*. 1960.
General Minutes, ME, TMC, UMC.
Journals of the North Dakota Conference.　　DAVID F. KNECHT
WAYNE M. McKIRDY

NORTH GEORGIA CONFERENCE (MES) was created during the session of the GEORGIA CONFERENCE at Americus, Nov. 28 to Dec. 5, 1866, Bishop HOLLAND N. Mc-TYEIRE presiding. The 1866 GENERAL CONFERENCE authorized the division of Georgia Methodism into two conferences, provided the Georgia Conference could agree on a dividing line. After prolonged debate the brethren voted for a dividing line that ran generally east and west a little north of MACON. The division put nearly two-thirds of the state in the SOUTH GEORGIA CONFERENCE, and almost exactly two-thirds of the church members in the North Georgia Conference. At the close of the 1866 session of the Georgia Conference, Bishop McTyeire read out the appointments to the North Georgia and South Georgia Conferences. The next year North Georgia met in ATLANTA and South Georgia in SAVANNAH. At that time the one reported 38,211 members and the other 19,626. (See GEORGIA for beginnings of Methodism in the state and an account of the Georgia Conference.)

The North Georgia Conference grew rapidly. By 1875 it had 58,520 members and by 1900 some 98,622. Growth was due in part to aggressive missionary work within the bounds of the conference. In 1886 the conference had twenty-four missions, laying assessments on the churches for their support.

In 1871 the Methodist Children's Home was established at Norcross and was later moved to Decatur. The conference cooperated with the South Georgia Conference in supporting the *Wesleyan Christian Advocate* and WESLEYAN COLLEGE at Macon. The journals show that as the years passed the North Georgia Conference commended or gave support to a number of schools and colleges within its bounds which existed for longer or shorter periods of time. However, its principal institutions of learning were EMORY COLLEGE which was established at Oxford in 1836 and LaGRANGE COLLEGE for women (now coeducational) which began as an academy in 1831.

In 1910 the Conference expressed regret over the misunderstanding between the church and the board of trustees of VANDERBILT UNIVERSITY and the legal battle being waged for its control. After losing Vanderbilt, the M.E. Church, South voted to establish two universities, one east and one west of the Mississippi. In 1915 Emory College was moved to Atlanta and became the nucleus of EMORY UNIVERSITY, while the conference continued with an Emory (junior) College at Oxford. The CANDLER SCHOOL OF THEOLOGY was inaugurated in connection with Emory University. Today Emory, with a total endowment in excess of $110,000,000, a plant valued at $60,000,000, a strong medical school, and Crawford W. Long Hospital, is an outstanding university.

Two junior colleges survived and continued to receive support from the North Georgia Conference. YOUNG HARRIS COLLEGE was established in the northern part of the state near the NORTH CAROLINA line in 1882, and REINHARDT COLLEGE began at Waleska in 1883. PAINE COLLEGE, which belongs in part to the C.M.E. CHURCH, was launched at Augusta in 1882 with the help of such

Southern Methodist leaders as Bishop GEORGE F. PIERCE, ATTICUS G. HAYGOOD, and WARREN A. CANDLER. Paine College has received some assistance from North Georgia Methodists.

The North Georgia Conference came to unification in 1939 with ten districts, 289 charges, 377 ministers, 156,-400 members, and churches and parsonages valued at $8,232,995. Merging with parts of the Georgia Conferences of the M.E. and M.P. Churches, it then became the North Georgia Conference of The Methodist Church.

In more recent years the North Georgia Conference has developed, in addition to the educational and other institutions already mentioned, a camp called Glisson and the Wesley Woods Retirement Community in Atlanta. The conference raised $251,000 in 1968 for higher education, using part of it to help maintain nine WESLEY FOUNDATIONS at educational institutions.

In 1970 the North Georgia Conference reported eleven districts, 505 charges, 656 ministers, 216,940 members, property valued at $130,559,033, and $19,988,148 raised for all purposes during the year.

General Minutes, MECS and MC.
Minutes of the North Georgia Conference.
A. M. Pierce, *Methodism in Georgia*. 1956.   ALBEA GODBOLD

NORTH INDIA CONFERENCE borders on NEPAL and Tibet and comprises much of the section of Uttar Pradesh east and north of the Ganges. The conference covers 32,938 square miles and has a population of over 55,000,-000.

Methodist work was begun at BAREILLY, a principal city of the conference, by the Rev. and Mrs. WILLIAM BUTLER in 1856. After the mutiny of 1857, work was started quickly in other nearby centers—in Budaun, Moradabad, Shahjahanpur, and Bijnor. William Butler was assisted by able co-workers, including JAMES L. HUMPHREY, JAMES M. THOBURN, JAMES W. WAUGH, JAMES H. MESSMORE, E. W. PARKER, and CLARA SWAIN. These founded some of the earliest Methodist institutions in INDIA, among them the Parker Intermediate College at Moradabad, and the Messmore Intermediate College at Pauri, as well as the Lodhipur School and orphanage at Shahjahanpur. The Bareilly Theological Seminary is the oldest theological college started by any agency in India.

A missionary conference was organized in 1864, and this became an annual conference in 1874. There are presently 57,884 on the conference roll and forty-five ordained pastors and seventy-three other workers are reported. The conference has fourteen schools with 268 teachers. Its districts are: Bareilly, Badaun, Kumaun, Shahjahanpur. Bareilly, where Methodist work in this region began, now has a population above 254,409. Kaumaun, on the southern edge of the Himalayas, is an important summer resort area to which many people flee in May and June when the heat on the plains becomes most intense. During British rule Naini Tal was the summer capital of the United Provinces, now called Uttar Pradesh. The Methodist Church maintained there quality high schools for many years, Wellesley for girls and Philander Smith for boys, but sold them to the government after independence. Almora in the Kumaun District is now the chief Methodist center in the Himalayas with an intermediate college (Ramsey) and a higher secondary school for girls (Adams), a leprosarium, the oldest in India, and with a self-supporting church of about a thousand

members, full and preparatory. There are also Methodist Intermediate Colleges in Ranikhet and Dwarahat and Pithoragarh in Bidaun District.

The Budaun District and Shahjahanpur are the other two Districts of the Conference. Shahjahanpur is headquarters of the civil district of that name and a railroad junction 768 miles from CALCUTTA, and 987 from BOMBAY. It was founded during the reign of Shah Jahan, who built the Taj Mahal at Agra, and for whom the city is named.

The Lodhipur Institute, in the suburb by that name, is a school of technology sponsored by the Division of World Missions. It has been subsidized by the Ford Foundation. Sitapur, headquarters of a civil district and a railway junction, has a primary boys boarding school and a girls junior high school.

Discipline, UMC, 1968, P. 1901.
Project Handbook Overseas Missions. 1969.
J. WASKOM PICKETT

NORTH INDIANA CONFERENCE was the result of the first division of Methodism in the state of INDIANA into two conferences. The northern half of the state had belonged to the missionary district in 1832 when the INDIANA CONFERENCE was organized, but by 1844 it had grown to six districts with a combined membership of 27,563.

Thus the North Indiana Conference was organized at Fort Wayne (where the Maumee Mission had been established only fourteen years before) on Sept. 24, 1844. Bishop BEVERLY WAUGH presided, and Bishop L. L. HAMLINE was present. The new conference consisted of 105 ministers (eighty-nine under direction of eight presiding elders, with four under special appointment and four superannuated) and more than 27,500 members, and was defined on the south boundary by the National Road through INDIANAPOLIS.

With Methodism continuing to grow, another division of the annual conferences was made in 1852. The NORTHWEST INDIANA CONFERENCE comprised the northwest quadrant of the state and the new North Indiana Conference consisted of the northeast section. The new boundary of the North Indiana Conference "included all of northeastern Indiana, bounded north by Michigan, east by Ohio, south by the National Road and west by the Michigan Road as far north as South Bend, thence down the St. Joseph River to the Michigan state line, also the town of Logansport, all the towns on the National Road east of Indianapolis, and so much of the city of Indianapolis as lies north of Market Street and east of Meridian Street." The only major boundary change, from 1844 until 1968, occurred in 1868 when Indianapolis and its vicinity became part of the South East Indiana Conference and the Marion County line became part of the southern boundary.

Several men were prominent in early North Indiana history. ALLEN WILEY, though not a member of the conference assisted Bishop Waugh in making appointments at the first session in 1844, and the North Indiana Conference took special note of his death five years later. Joseph Tarkington, S. R. Brenton and S. C. Cooper gave noted service at various tasks and appointments in the early years of the conference. THOMAS BOWMAN first became a member of the annual conference in 1864, several years after he was elected president of INDIANA ASBURY

UNIVERSITY, and was a leader of the conference until his election to the episcopacy in 1872.

Though Indiana Asbury University was the major educational concern for the entire state, it had close identification with the North Indiana Conference via the presidency and various faculty members who were members of this annual conference. Other schools were encouraged by the annual conference. Fort Wayne College had great support and encouragement from the conference as it struggled to gain academic status and financial solvency, but it finally transferred its debt and property to Taylor University, an institution founded by the Local Preachers' Association of the M.E. Church. In 1893 the school was rechartered and moved to its present location in Upland. Although Taylor University has never had any official relationship to The Methodist Church, the conference has recognized and commended it from time to time.

A similar enterprise, named Whitewater Female College and Academy, was undertaken at Centerville in 1848. In 1851 it was made co-educational and was supported by the Indiana Conference as well. With a spotted history of educational and financial success, it disappeared from the academic scene by the mid 1860's.

Women in the North Indiana Conference were quick to take advantage of the inception of the WOMAN'S FOREIGN MISSIONARY SOCIETY and the later WOMAN'S HOME MISSIONARY SOCIETY. A year after its organization in 1869, there was a W.F.M.S. in Goshen. It was in 1882, two years after national organization had occurred, that the W.H.M.S. was organized in the Annual Conference. When the WOMAN'S SOCIETY OF CHRISTIAN SERVICE organized in 1940, the merged women's work consisted of 440 societies and 21,000 charter members. Much of the leadership for the work of the North Central Jurisdiction has come from women of the North Indiana Conference. Three have been presidents of the Jurisdiction—Mrs. Julia Parr Naftzgar, Mrs. J. N. Rodeheaver, and Mrs. D. G. Woolpert. By 1968 the conference reported 391 Woman's Societies and sixty-one Wesleyan Service Guilds with a combined membership of 22,688.

Within two months of its creation in Cleveland in 1889, an EPWORTH LEAGUE charter was requested for the Ft. Wayne district, and in two years all districts of the conference had such organizations. Youth work, through the Epworth League and its successor, the METHODIST FELLOWSHIP, has shown a record of increased youth participation throughout its history. Of monumental influence is the Epworth Forest Institute grounds at Lake Webster, begun in 1924, where "thousands, whether youth or sage, have found a station on the way of their eternal pilgrimage." Thousands of youth over the almost half-century of its existence have been influenced by it, and the annual conference has invested time, energy, and repeated financial resources to perfect this contribution to youth ministry. Though open to a variety of programs and opportunities for all ages, it remains a stable setting along the lakeshore where young men and young women (as well as others) may find the challenge of Christian commitment.

North Indiana Methodism has viewed with pride the growth of Parkview Memorial Hospital in Fort Wayne, the Methodist Memorial Home for the Aged at Warren and the Bashor Children's Home at Goshen. Each has had a distinctive ministry to offer. Also, Neighborhood House in Fort Wayne and Goodwill Industries in the same community dealt with Metropolitan concerns and were related to the Annual Conference.

At the time of union in 1968 the North Indiana Conference numbered 372 ministers, 408 charges and 117,047 members, with property valued at $62,962,341.

JAMES J. BABBITT

NORTH IOWA CONFERENCE was organized at CEDAR RAPIDS, June 22, 1949 with Bishop CHARLES W. BRASHARES presiding. It was formed by merging the UPPER IOWA and NORTHWEST IOWA CONFERENCES. Its territory included approximately the north half of the state. Since the Northwest Iowa Conference appeared in 1872, while the Upper Iowa body was created in 1856, the North Iowa Conference claimed historical continuity from 1856. The new conference began with eight districts—Algona, Cedar Rapids, Davenport, Dubuque, Fort Dodge, Sheldon, Sioux City, and Waterloo. It had 120,-368 members in 429 churches.

The North Iowa Conference supported two strong colleges, CORNELL at Mt. Vernon and MORNINGSIDE at Sioux City. It had two hospitals, St. Luke's Methodist at Cedar Rapids and Methodist at Sioux City. The latter coordinated its work with the Lutheran Hospital in Sioux City in 1966 to form the St. Luke's Medical Center, the conference giving approval and support. The conference had three retirement homes, Friendship Haven at Fort Dodge, Methodist Manor at Storm Lake, and Meth-wick Manor at Cedar Rapids.

For some years the North and South Iowa Conferences supported Hillcrest Children's Services at Cedar Rapids and the Iowa Methodist Services to Youth at DES MOINES. In 1968 the two organizations coordinated their services under the direction of one board of directors, the new name to be Hillcrest Services to Children and Youth. The work was to be directed from new headquarters at Dubuque. The conference maintains three camps for youth.

The North Iowa Conference supported jointly with the South Iowa Conference WESLEY FOUNDATIONS at Drake University and the three state universities. The *Hawkeye*, a monthly publication for Methodists in the Iowa Area, was published jointly by the two conferences. In 1968 the paper had a circulation of 33,000.

In 1968 the North Iowa Conference had 418 ministers, 277 pastoral charges, 152,082 members, and property valued at $61,717,202. In that year the North Central JURISDICTIONAL CONFERENCE voted that in June 1969, the conferences in IOWA should merge into one conference to be known as the Iowa Conference.

Ruth A. Gallaher, *A Century of Methodism in Iowa*. Mt. Vernon, Iowa: Inter-Conference Commission, 1944.
Minutes of the North Iowa Conference.   F. E. MASER

NORTH MISSISSIPPI CONFERENCE was organized at Water Valley, Miss., Nov. 30, 1870 with Bishop DAVID S. DOGGETT presiding. It was formed by merging portions of the MEMPHIS, ALABAMA, and MISSISSIPPI CONFERENCES. At the beginning the conference had twelve districts, ninety charges, and 21,757 white and fifty-eight colored members.

Organized Methodism first entered North Mississippi in 1819 when the TENNESSEE CONFERENCE appointed EBENEZER HEARN to the Buttahatchie Circuit which extended into Mississippi from ALABAMA. Hearn preached in Columbus, Miss., as early as 1820, and the first Methodist society with about ten members was organized there in 1823 by Wiley Ledbetter. In 1820 the name of the work was changed to the Marion Circuit, and it became an appointment in the Mississippi Conference. In the next ten years the Marion Circuit grew from seventy-two to 469 white plus fifty-two Negro members.

In 1832 the Alabama Conference was carved out of the Mississippi Conference, its territory including Alabama, West FLORIDA, and the eastern tier of counties in Mississippi. In the same year a series of government settlements with the Indians was concluded, and all of northern Mississippi was then opened to settlers. Thereafter Methodist work in the region grew rapidly. In 1840 the GENERAL CONFERENCE created the Memphis Conference which included a large part of north Mississippi. This meant that three annual conferences then had parts of what is now the North Mississippi Conference within their boundaries. In establishing the North Mississippi Conference in 1870, the General Conference was seeking to make conference boundaries conform to state lines in so far as possible. Since 1870 Mississippi has been divided between the North Mississippi and the Mississippi Conferences.

From the beginning the North Mississippi Conference was interested in education and it rendered service to the people of its region in a period when public education was inadequate. The minutes refer to a dozen or more academies and colleges in the early years which were either owned or patronized by the conference. For a time the conference favored the position taken in the EPISCOPAL ADDRESS of 1874 that the denomination seek to establish a whole system of schools. At its first session in 1870 the conference commended several academies as worthy of Methodist patronage and it accepted Verona Female College as a conference institution. In 1879 the conference accepted a school at Grenada which was chartered in 1882 as Grenada Collegiate Institute. After 1890 the conference resolutions and reports on education refer only to the support of institutions of higher learning.

The North Mississippi Conference supported VANDERBILT UNIVERSITY which was established in 1875, the minutes proudly noting that two of its ministers and two of its well known laymen were serving as Vanderbilt trustees. The conference joined the Mississippi Conference in 1888 in projecting a first-rate Methodist college in the state, the plan being realized when MILLSAPS COLLEGE in JACKSON was chartered in 1890. Two North Mississippi Conference preachers who served as presidents of Millsaps have been elevated to the episcopacy—WILLIAM B. MURRAH in 1910 and H. ELLIS FINGER, Jr. in 1964.

In 1875 the North Mississippi Conference had 394 churches; in 1900 there were 525. Between 1880 and 1900 the conference had a membership gain of fifty-five percent, though the population of its area increased only twenty-nine percent during that time. In 1870 there were only fourteen parsonages in the entire conference. A few years later the women in the churches organized the Woman's Parsonage and Home Mission Society and by 1900 there were 121 parsonages in the conference. From 1875 to 1900, the giving to foreign missions increased from less than $1,500 to over $9,000 per year.

In 1867 a plan to merge the M.P. Church with the M.E. Church, South failed, but the next year twenty-two ministers and 1,300 members of the former church in north Mississippi joined the Memphis Conference of the

latter church. Even so Methodist Protestantism survived in the region and at unification in 1939 about eight M.P. churches came into the North Mississippi Conference of The Methodist Church. The North Mississippi Conference brought six districts, 163 charges, and 75,137 members to the merger in 1939.

Today the North Mississippi Conference supports a number of institutions both inside and outside its boundaries, such as the Methodist Hospital in MEMPHIS, the Methodist Home and Hospital in NEW ORLEANS, the Methodist Children's Home in Jackson, the North Mississippi Methodist Agency for the Retarded, Lake Stephens Methodist Camp near Oxford, and Traceway Manor Home for the aged which was established at Tupelo in 1967. It joins the Mississippi Conference in strong support of Millsaps College and the *Mississippi Methodist Advocate* which is published in Jackson.

In 1970 the North Mississippi Conference had six districts, Cleveland, Greenwood, New Albany, Sardis, Starkville, and Tupelo. There were 243 ministers, 220 charges, 77,361 members, and property valued at $34,456,337.

Minutes of the North Mississippi Conference.
General Minutes, Methodist Episcopal Church, South and The Methodist Church.
G. R. Miller, *North Mississippi.* 1966.   GENE RAMSEY MILLER

NORTH NEBRASKA CONFERENCE (ME) was organized at Fremont, Neb., Sept. 14, 1881 with Bishop RANDOLPH S. FOSTER presiding. It was formed by dividing the NEBRASKA CONFERENCE. Its territory included northeast NEBRASKA; the Platte River was the southern boundary. Since OMAHA was north of the river, it fell in the North Nebraska Conefrence. This caused ill feeling because many felt that Omaha as the state's largest city should have remained in the Nebraska Conference. At the outset the new conference had two districts, Omaha and Norfolk, thirty-six charges and 2,065 members.

In 1913 the North Nebraska Conference was absorbed by the Nebraska Conference. At its last session in 1912 the conference reported four districts, Grand Island, Neligh, Norfolk, and Omaha; 127 charges, 169 churches, and 15,987 members.

E. E. Jackman, *Nebraska.* 1954.
General Minutes, ME.   E. E. JACKMAN

NORTH OHIO CONFERENCE (ME) was organized at Norwalk on Sept. 30, 1840 with Bishop ELIJAH HEDDING presiding. The conference was formed by dividing the MICHIGAN CONFERENCE. The territory of the North Ohio Conference at the beginning was north central and northwest OHIO. The conference began with six districts, fifty-four charges, and 24,148 members.

In 1856 the North Ohio Conference was divided, the northwest part of the state then being designated as the DELAWARE CONFERENCE. This reduced the membership of the North Ohio Conference from 29,093 to 14,820. The conference then continued intact until 1912 when it was merged with the EAST OHIO CONFERENCE to form the NORTH-EAST OHIO CONFERENCE.

In 1853 the North Ohio Conference was supporting OHIO WESLEYAN UNIVERSITY and Baldwin Institute. It voted that year to accept ownership and control of Ohio Wesleyan Female College, and it agreed to accept Mansfield Female Collegiate Institute, provided the conference would not be required to raise any part of the funds necessary to purchase the premises or to erect buildings. At the conference session that year the members pledged over $1,300 for the Metropolitan Church in WASHINGTON, D. C.

In 1873 the North Ohio Conference voted to join the CENTRAL OHIO CONFERENCE in supporting the "Lakeside Camp meeting grounds" (see LAKESIDE), and elected ten trustees to serve with a like number from the other conference to control the property and direct the activities.

In 1910 the conference journal showed that St. Luke's Hospital had been rendering service in Cleveland for two years, that the Old Ladies' Home at Elyria had had a good year, and that Ohio Methodism wished to establish an orphanage.

In 1911 the North Ohio Conference reported five districts, 168 charges, 40,436 members, and property valued at $2,491,900.

The North Ohio Conference merged with the East Ohio Conference in 1912 to form the North-East Ohio Conference.

General Minutes, MEC.
Minutes of the North Ohio Conference.
John M. Versteeg, *Ohio Area.* 1962.   ALBEA GODBOLD

NORTH SHIELDS CHAPEL DISPUTE was an important incident in the development of the connectional principle in British Methodism. In 1783 the lease of the old chapel in North Shields, Northumberland, ran out, and the question of a new site led to the formation of two strongly opposed parties. Each group secured a site and proceeded to the erection of a chapel. One was known as the Milbourn Place or Upper Chapel, and the other as the Bank or Lower Chapel. The issue, which was the settlement of both chapels on the Conference Plan, came before the 1787 and subsequent conferences. WESLEY's idea was that both chapels being secured to the Conference should be served, one by the preachers from the Newcastle Circuit, and the other from the Sunderland Circuit. In 1788 Wesley preached in the morning in the Lower Chapel and in the evening in the Upper Chapel. The dispute continued, however, with bitter correspondence turning upon the refusal of the Milbourn Place trustees to settle the building on the Model Deed, or Conference Plan, as it was called. Ultimately, in April, 1789, Wesley wrote to the three preachers of the Newcastle Circuit with which the Upper Chapel was associated, instructing them that failing a satisfactory answer concerning the legal settlement of the chapel, they must cease to recognize it. A letter from Wesley to Edward Coates, the leader of this group, three weeks later, indicates their final refusal and the detachment of the Milbourn Place Chapel and those associated with it from the Conference. The Bank or Lower Chapel was settled in the approved way and continued in association with the Sunderland Circuit.

E. BENSON PERKINS

NORTH TEXAS CONFERENCE began as the Trinity Conference (ME) which was carved out of the EAST TEXAS CONFERENCE in 1867. The name was changed to the North Texas Conference in 1874. The Trinity Conference was organized Oct. 9, 1867 at Sulphur Springs with Richard Lane presiding in the absence of Bishop HOLLAND N. McTYEIRE, who arrived later. Its boundaries included all of the present conference territory plus the remainder of northeast TEXAS lying above the Texas and Pacific Railroad from Texarkana to DALLAS. Among the forty-three preachers in 1867 were several who were well known or would become so: J. W. P. McKENZIE, missionary to the Indians in OKLAHOMA before crossing to Texas; William F. Bates, pioneer in the western area; JOHN H. McLEAN, educator and church statesman; and William H. Hughes, a pioneer in Dallas County. The conference began with 7,495 white and 588 colored members, 128 local preachers, sixty-seven churches valued at $73,850, and fifty-five Sunday schools with 2,080 pupils. When the name was changed to North Texas in 1874, the conference met at Denton, Nov. 4-10, with Bishop McTyeire presiding. It reported fifty pastoral charges and 18,229 members.

The North Texas Conference established a number of schools which served well in their day but none have survived. McKenzie College at Clarksville (1848-1868) was in its day one of the best colleges west of the Mississippi River. The Paris Female Institute began in the 1850's and operated for twenty years or more. Central College at Sulphur Springs began in 1883 and operated about ten years. Kidd-Key College at Sherman had its beginning as a high school. An outstanding institution for several decades, it became a casualty of the economic depression in 1935. Wesley College began at Terrell about 1909, was moved to Greenville, and closed in 1934.

Today the North Texas Conference has a share in the ownership of SOUTHERN METHODIST UNIVERSITY (it is owned by the South Central Jurisdiction of the church). Southern Methodist is the greatest church institution of higher learning in the southwest and the only one with the word Methodist in its name. Its PERKINS SCHOOL OF THEOLOGY, named for its benefactors J. J. PERKINS and his wife Lois C. Perkins, is a strong theological seminary with an endowment of more than $9,000,000.

Six members of the North Texas Conference have been elected bishops: JOHN M. MOORE (1918), CHARLES C. SELECMAN and WILLIAM C. MARTIN (1938), W. ANGIE SMITH and PAUL E. MARTIN (1944), and ALSIE H. CARLETON (1968). Five other bishops were members of the North Texas Conference at some time in their career though not at the time they were elevated to the episcopacy: SAMUEL R. HAY (1922), A. FRANK SMITH and PAUL B. KERN (1930), KENNETH W. COPELAND (1960), and LANCE WEBB (1964).

Dallas, the largest city in the North Texas Conference, is one of the strongest Methodist centers in the United States. In 1964 when the two Dallas districts were limited to Greater Dallas, they had a total of 87,188 members. The Highland Park Church in Dallas, with 9,202 members in 1968, is the largest congregation in the denomination if not the largest Methodist church in the world. In Dallas are to be found the offices of *The Texas Methodist*, a COKESBURY Regional Center, the residence of the bishop of the area, the Methodist Hospital, the Methodist Mission Home, the C. C. Young-Blanton Gardens retirement home, and Southern Methodist University and Perkins School of Theology. Southern Methodist, which opened in 1915, is becoming a great university. Its plant is valued at more than $50,000,000, and it has an endowment of $21,000,000, a library of 1,000,000 volumes, and a total enrollment of 14,000 students.

In 1968 the North Texas Conference contributed $150,-000 to the Texas Methodist College Association and $85,000 for WESLEY FOUNDATION work in the state. In 1970 the conference had seven districts, 239 pastoral charges, 382 ministers, 151,632 members, and property valued at 68,187,075. The conference raised for all purposes that year $12,374,597.

General Minutes, MECS and MC.
Minutes of the North Texas Conference.
W. N. Vernon, *North Texas*. 1967.   WALTER N. VERNON

NORTHCOTT, HARRY CLIFFORD (1890-   ), American bishop, was born in Exeter, Ontario, CANADA, Oct. 16, 1890, the son of James Harvey and Emily (Patey) Northcott. In 1919 he received his B.A. degree from NORTHWESTERN UNIVERSITY and in 1921, his M.A. from the same institution. In 1952, Northwestern awarded him the S.T.D. He did graduate work at the University of Chicago and, in 1921 received the B.D. degree from GARRETT BIBLICAL INSTITUTE. He received D.D. degrees from Garrett in 1941 and from ILLINOIS WESLEYAN UNIVERSITY in 1929. In 1953 Illinois Wesleyan awarded him the LL.D. degree.

He was married on June 14, 1917 to Florence M. Engle. They have one child.

He was ordained in the ROCK RIVER ANNUAL CONFERENCE in 1918. He was pastor of the Adriel Church (CHICAGO) 1917-19 and, in 1919 served as chaplain in the U.S. Army. Other Chicago pastorates were: Parkside, 1921-23; Euclid Avenue, Oak Park, 1923-28. From 1928 until 1948 he served as pastor of the First Church, Champaign, Ill. This pastorate was concluded in July 1948, when he was elected bishop at the North Central JURISDICTIONAL CONFERENCE and assigned to the WISCONSIN Area.

He has served as a member of the Board of MISSIONS, the Board of EVANGELISM, the Commission on CHAPLAINS, the Commission on Promotion and Cultivation (Executive Committee), and the Commission on DEACONESS Work (Chairman).

He was a delegate to the 1936, 1944 and 1948 GENERAL CONFERENCES and to the 1940, 1944 and 1948 Jurisdictional Conferences.

Bishop Northcott has served as trustee of Northwestern UNIVERSITY, LAWRENCE UNIVERSITY, Methodist Hospital Madison, Wis., and Bellin Memorial Hospital, Green Bay, Wis.

In 1950 he made a four-month official visitation of Africa and Europe, upon request of the COUNCIL OF BISHOPS. He also made an official visitation of Southeast Asia in 1953 and, in 1957 was assigned to visit Latin America.

When the Council of Bishops visited the White House during their April meeting of 1959, Bishop Northcott received an especially warm greeting from President Eisenhower, who reminded him of the fact that he and Mrs. Northcott had been schoolmates during their school days in Abilene, Kan. Mrs. Northcott was then Florence M. Engle.

Among Bishop Northcott's writings was an article entitled: "If My Daughter Should Want to Marry a Catholic" which was printed in 1945 in the *Christian Advocate,* in *Together,* and, later, in pamphlet form. Fifty thousand reprints of this article were sold out very shortly after they were off the press.

In 1959 Bishop Northcott announced that he would retire in 1960 because of ill health. He presently resides in Evanston, Ill., and usually answers the roll call at the stated meetings of the Council of Bishops.

Who's Who in The Methodist Church, 1966.
                              MARY FRENCH CALDWELL

NORTH-EAST OHIO CONFERENCE was organized at Epworth Memorial Church, Cleveland, Sept. 17, 1912 with Bishop WILLIAM F. ANDERSON presiding. It was formed by merging the NORTH OHIO and EAST OHIO CONFERENCES. Comprising a little more than one-third of the state's area, it was at the time geographically the largest annual conference in OHIO, and incidentally the largest numerically in the M. E. Church. The conference began with twelve districts, 426 charges, 131,062 members, and property valued at $8,092,500.

When the North-East Ohio Conference was formed it had two colleges—BALDWIN-WALLACE and MT. UNION—and several service institutions within its bounds, while at the same time it was committed to assist in the support of others in the state. Baldwin-Wallace College, founded at Berea in 1845, now has a plant valued at more than $17,000,000, an endowment exceeding $4,000,000, and some 2,600 students. Mt. Union College, founded at Alliance in 1846, has an endowment of about $3,350,000, a plant valued at some $10,000,000, and about 1,300 students. The conference in 1914 pledged "earnest support and prayers" for AMERICAN UNIVERSITY which opened that year in WASHINGTON, D. C., and it commended the work of BOSTON, DREW, and GARRETT seminaries. The conference supports the WESLEY FOUNDATIONS in the state.

At the beginning the North-East Ohio Conference had the St. Luke's Hospital in Cleveland and the Methodist Home at Elyria which was then called the Elyria Old Ladies' Home. The conference has since established or acquired Cope Methodist Home at Sebring, Healthaven Nursing Home near Akron, and the Berea Methodist Children's Home.

The North-East Ohio Conference came to unification in 1939 with eight districts, 412 charges, 202,998 members, and property valued at $20,475,784. At that time it was merged with thirty-one charges representing about 9,000 members of the OHIO CONFERENCE (MP) to form the North-East Ohio Conference of The Methodist Church.

In 1964 the North-East Ohio Conference was designated as an episcopal area with the bishop's residence in Canton. FRANCIS E. KEARNS was named as the presiding bishop.

In 1968 the North-East Ohio Conference reported eight districts, 545 pastoral charges, 641 ministers, 273,959 members, property valued at $138,870,434, and $18,220,-224 raised for all purposes during the year. When Methodist-E.U.B. merger was fully effected in Ohio in 1970, the name of the conference became East Ohio Annual Conference.

General Minutes, MEC and MC.
Minutes of the North-East Ohio Conference.
J. M. Versteeg, *Ohio Area*. 1962.
W. Guy Smeltzer, *Headwaters of the Ohio*. 1951. N. B. H.

NORTHERN GERMAN CONFERENCE was organized at Sleepy Eye, Minn., Sept. 27, 1888 with Bishop JOHN F. HURST presiding. It superseded the North German Conference which began in 1886.

American Methodism's ministry to German immigrants in their own language began in 1835 when WILLIAM NAST was appointed by the OHIO CONFERENCE as a missionary to the German-speaking people within its bounds. By 1860 nine conferences had a total of eighteen German districts. The 1864 GENERAL CONFERENCE authorized the organization of German-speaking annual conferences and immediately established three—Central German, Northwestern German, and Southwestern German. The first included OHIO, INDIANA, western PENNSYLVANIA, WEST VIRGINIA, KENTUCKY, and TENNESSEE. The second took in northern ILLINOIS, MINNESOTA, WISCONSIN, and part of IOWA, and the third covered central and southern Illinois, KANSAS, MISSOURI, and part of IOWA.

The Northwestern German Conference held its first session in Galena, Ill., Sept. 7-10, 1864 with Bishop LEVI SCOTT presiding. It began with five districts, sixty-three charges, and 5,495 members, including probationers. In 1868 the name was changed to Northwest German Conference, and it continued as such until it was absorbed by the English-speaking conferences in 1923.

The North German Conference, whose territory included Minnesota, NORTH DAKOTA, and MONTANA, was carved out of the North German Conference in 1886. The name was changed to Northern German Conference in 1888, as indicated above, and it so continued until 1924 when it was absorbed by the English-speaking conferences.

When organized in 1886 the North German Conference had three districts, MINNEAPOLIS, ST. PAUL, and South Minnesota. There were forty-three charges, and 3,758 members including probationers. When designated as the Northern German Conference in 1888 there were 4,693 members. As the years passed, some ministers and churches transferred to the English-speaking conferences. In 1924, its last year, the Northern German Conference had only one district, Minneapolis, about twenty-five itinerants, thirty-one charges, 4,115 members, and property valued at $408,000.

P. F. Douglass, *German Methodism*. 1939.
General Minutes (ME).   F. E. MASER

NORTHERN ILLINOIS CONFERENCE dates from 1840 when the ROCK RIVER CONFERENCE of the M.E. Church was separated from the ILLINOIS CONFERENCE. At that time the Rock River Conference included IOWA, WISCONSIN, and MINNESOTA. Iowa was separated in 1844; Wisconsin and Minnesota in 1848. In 1856 the Peoria Conference (later CENTRAL ILLINOIS) was taken from it. It presently covers the northern third of the state of Illinois.

JESSE WALKER was the first Methodist preacher in northern ILLINOIS. In 1823 he began work as a missionary to the Pottawatomie Indians north of Peoria. The first appointment to the region was in 1828, when John Dew was assigned to the Galena Mission.

The UNITED BRETHREN also organized a Rock River Conference in 1853. In 1867, it united with the Central Illinois Conference to form the Northern Illinois Conference. The EVANGELICAL CHURCH had work in northeastern Illinois from 1834. The conference was organized in 1845. In 1946 the Northern Illinois Conference of the E.U.B. Church was formed by the merger of these two conferences.

Significant in the advancement of Methodism in northern Illinois was the growth of CHICAGO to become one of the largest metropolitan areas in the United States. The primacy of this area for the growth of Methodism is seen in the location of significant national, regional and conference institutions in the metropolis. In 1852 an office of the BOOK CONCERN (ME) was opened and publication of the *Northwestern Christian Advocate* began the following year. Also in the 1850's NORTHWESTERN UNIVERSITY and Garrett Biblical Institute (now GARRETT THEOLOGICAL SEMINARY) were founded in EVANSTON. At Naperville the Evangelical Church founded NORTH CENTRAL COLLEGE (originally Plainfield College) in 1861 and EVANGELICAL THEOLOGICAL SEMINARY (originally Union Biblical Institute) in 1875. The Chicago Training School was opened under the leadership of LUCY RIDER MEYER in 1885 for the training of women in foreign and home mission work. From the work at the school, Mrs. Meyer developed some forty institutions serving Chicago Methodism, including Wesley Memorial Hospital (of which she was the first resident M.D.), the Chicago Deaconess Home, and the Chicago Methodist Old People's Home. In 1934 Chicago Training School affiliated with Garrett Biblical Institute.

Besides the above, Northern Illinois is served by a number of other institutions: GOODWILL INDUSTRIES, Lake Bluff Chicago Homes for Children, The Methodist Home (Evanston), Rosecrance Memorial Home for Boys (Rockford), Kendall College (Evanston), Bethany Home and Hospital (Chicago), Newberry Center (Chicago), and Foster Street Home (Chicago). The Methodist Building in Evanston houses offices of several GENERAL CONFERENCE agencies, and the Publishing House maintains a book depository in Park Ridge. The *Christian Advocate* and *Together* editorial offices are also located at Park Ridge.

Mergers in 1932, 1939, 1942, and 1943 created the Rock River Conference of The Methodist Church. Making up the new conference were parts of the CENTRAL NORTHWEST CONFERENCE (Swedish), the NORWEGIAN-DANISH CONFERENCE, the CHICAGO GERMAN CONFERENCE, the ILLINOIS CONFERENCE of the M.P. Church, and the Rock River Conference of the M.E. Church. In 1969 the Rock River Conference of The Methodist Church united with the Northern Illinois Conference of the E.U.B. Church to form the Northern Illinois Conference of The United Methodist Church.

The Conference publishes a newspaper, the *Rock River Methodist*. In 1970 Northern Illinois reported 201,833 members in 393 pastoral charges being served by 688 ministers.

Journal of the Northern Illinois Conference.
Almer M. Pennewell, *The Methodist Movement in Northern Illinois*. Sycamore, Ill.: Sycamore Tribune, 1942.
John G. Schwab, *History of the Illinois Conference of the Evangelical Church, 1837-1937*. Harrisburg, Pa.: Evangelical Press, 1937.   J. GORDON MELTON

NORTHERN MINNESOTA CONFERENCE was formed by dividing the MINNESOTA CONFERENCE at its session in Duluth, Oct. 3-9, 1894. The first session of the new conference was held Oct. 2-6, 1895 in MINNEAPOLIS with Bishop CHARLES H. FOWLER presiding. The boundaries were so drawn as to include Minneapolis in the Northern Conference and leave ST. PAUL in the Minnesota Conference. The new conference began with four districts, Duluth, Minneapolis, St. Cloud, and Willmar. There were

136 preachers, 131 charges, and 10,912 members. The division left the Minnesota Conference with the southern one-third of the state and some 13,000 members.

The Northern Minnesota Conference grew steadily and in 1925 it reported about 32,000 members. The Asbury Hospital, started in 1892 in Minneapolis, was supported by the Northern Minnesota Conference. The institution was the outgrowth of the Methodist DEACONESS movement in Minnesota and the generosity of one Mrs. S. H. Knight. Mrs. Knight's purpose was to establish a hospital to which a deaconess could bring the sick and needy for care. Beginning with thirty-four beds, the hospital experienced difficulties and changes as time passed, but it continues and is still supported by Minnesota Methodism. Through the generosity of another woman, Mrs. Thomas B. Walker, the Walker Methodist Home for the aged was established in Minneapolis in 1875. It was supported by the Northern Minnesota Conference, and it continues as an institution of Minnesota Methodism. The conference gave strong support to HAMLINE UNIVERSITY in St. Paul. As early as 1921 the two Minnesota conferences established a WESLEY FOUNDATION at the University of Minnesota.

A commission to study the possible merger of the two Minnesota conferences was set up in 1941. After prolonged deliberation the merger was effected in 1948 and there was again a state-wide Minnesota Conference. The Northern Minnesota Conference brought 47,481 members to the merger. In its last year the conference had four districts—Duluth, Fergus Falls, Litchfield, and Minneapolis, 143 charges, and property valued at $6,653,034.

Minutes of the Northern Minnesota Conference.
C. N. Pace, *Our Fathers Built, A Century of Minnesota Methodism.* N.d.   F. E. MASER

NORTHERN NEW JERSEY CONFERENCE was authorized by the 1964 Northeastern JURISDICTIONAL CONFERENCE at the time NEW JERSEY was designated as an episcopal area. The Jurisdictional Conference recommended that the NEWARK and NEW JERSEY CONFERENCES change their names to Northern New Jersey and SOUTHERN NEW JERSEY. Both conferences concurred, effective in 1965. The new name was adopted by the Newark Conference in session at Madison, N. J., on June 17, 1965 with Bishop PRINCE A. TAYLOR presiding. At the time the conference had four districts, 267 charges, 322 preachers, 92,253 members, and property valued at $61,596,893.

The 1856 GENERAL CONFERENCE had created the Newark Conference by then dividing the New Jersey Conference. The new conference embraced northern New Jersey and parts of NEW YORK and northeastern PENNSYLVANIA. The inclusion of the adjacent areas of New York and Pennsylvania in the Newark Conference reflected the preaching stations in those states which were cultivated by Bishop ASBURY and other traveling preachers as part of the New Jersey itinerary.

In April 1856, when the New Jersey Conference requested the General Conference to divide it into two conferences, it asked that the two bodies be permitted to meet together in 1857. Permission was granted. But no sooner had the preachers convened at Trenton in April, 1857 than the question arose as to whether the gathering was "the New Jersey Conference" or "the New Jersey-and-Newark Conferences" meeting in joint session. Bishop LEVI SCOTT, the presiding officer, ruled that it was the

New Jersey Conference until the close of the session, at which time he read out one list of appointments for the Newark Conference and another for the New Jersey Conference. Thus the Newark Conference dates from April 17, 1857.

The first separate session of the Newark Conference was held at Morristown, N. J., March 31 to April 5, 1858 with Bishop E. R. AMES presiding. At that time the conference reported four districts, 119 charges, 132 preachers, and 16,373 members. The records show that there were substantial increases during that first year in church membership, Sunday school enrolment, and finances. Thus in its initial year the Newark Conference set a trend of growth that was to continue for many years.

In its 1858 session the Newark Conference voted that "in view of its geographical position" it would not sustain "the formal position of a patronizing conference" for DICKINSON COLLEGE. At the same time the conference pledged support to the PENNINGTON SCHOOL in the New Jersey Conference. CENTENARY COLLEGE for Women was established at Hackettstown in 1867. Today Centenary is a strong Methodist junior college with a plant valued at $8,000,000, an endowment of $250,000, and some 660 students. Before 1900 the Newark Conference accepted MORRISTOWN COLLEGE, a Negro school in Tennessee, as a part of its benevolent responsibility and the conference continues to give it some support. The conference cooperates with the Southern New Jersey Conference in WESLEY FOUNDATIONS at Princeton and Rutgers and in campus ministries at many of the state institutions of higher learning.

The Newark Conference came to unification in 1939 with 284 charges and 69,357 members. At that time a part of the Eastern Conference (MP) was merged with it. In 1940 the conference reported 70,914 members.

Through the years the Newark Conference developed many leaders (see NEW JERSEY), and it was in the forefront in promoting lay representation, adequate support for ministers, church extension, advances in denominational administration, foreign missions, an adequate ministry in the cities, education, and solutions to ethnic and racial issues.

In 1907, 1932, and 1957 the fiftieth, seventy-fifth, and one hundredth sessions of the Newark Conference were held at MORRISTOWN, N. J., the scene of the first session. The conference centennial commission, headed by the writer of this article, prepared a special program for 1957 in which four bishops participated.

From 1857 to 1965 the boundaries of the Newark Conference were not changed, but on Jan. 12, 1965, by order of the Northeastern Jurisdictional Conference, the twelve churches (some 3,800 members) on Staten Island were transferred to the NEW YORK CONFERENCE. This transfer of churches terminated a close association between STATEN ISLAND and New Jersey Methodism which dated back to 1771 when Francis Asbury preached in New Jersey and on Staten Island and developed his first circuit in America. The transfer of the twelve churches was formally observed in a service at Trinity Church, Staten Island, in which the bishops of the New Jersey and New York Areas participated.

The Northern New Jersey Conference helps to maintain a number of service agencies and institutions. GOODWILL INDUSTRIES serves 125 people daily. The Aldersgate Camp reaches many young people. The conference gives support to the METHODIST HOSPITAL in BROOKLYN, the oldest Methodist related hospital in America. The conference joins the Southern New Jersey Conference in maintaining Methodist Homes in New Jersey with branches in OCEAN GROVE, OCEAN CITY, Branchville, and Collingswood.

In 1964 and 1965 the conference received six ministers and some churches from the DELAWARE CONFERENCE as that body merged with the overlying conferences of the Northeastern Jurisdiction.

At its 1968 session the Northern New Jersey Conference projected a four-year Total Mission Crusade for urban renewal, world-wide reconciliation, and support of Camp Aldersgate. Asked for $1,155,000, the churches of the conference pledged $1,240,000.

In 1970 the Northern New Jersey Conference reported four districts, 227 charges, 332 ministers, 88,022 members, property valued at $79,760,680, and $8,465,216 raised for all puposes during the year.

General Minutes, MEC and MC.
Minutes of the Newark and Northern New Jersey Conferences.
V. B. Hampton, Newark Conference. 1957.
——————, Francis Asbury on Staten Island. 1947.
——————, Methodist Heritage and Promise in Staten Island, 1965.   VERNON B. HAMPTON

NORTHERN NEW YORK CONFERENCE was organized at Utica, April 16, 1873 with Bishop JESSE T. PECK presiding. The 1872 GENERAL CONFERENCE created the conference by merging the BLACK RIVER CONFERENCE with a part of the CENTRAL NEW YORK CONFERENCE. The conference began with eight districts, 179 charges, 237 preachers, and 24,963 members.

Originally what is now the Northern New York Conference was a part of the Genesee District of the PHILADELPHIA CONFERENCE. It descended through the GENESEE CONFERENCE (formed in 1810), the ONEIDA CONFERENCE (formed in 1829), and the Black River Conference (formed in 1836).

The church at Sauquoit, N. Y., established in 1788, is regarded as the oldest continuing congregation in the conference. From its beginning the Northern New York Conference demonstrated interest in evangelism, missions, higher education, church publication, and established two schools which continued for some years: Ives Seminary and Antwerp Liberal Institute; and it gave support to Cazenovia Seminary, SYRACUSE UNIVERSITY, and AMERICAN UNIVERSITY. In more recent years the conference has supported BETHUNE-COOKMAN COLLEGE in FLORIDA, and has helped to establish the Ledden Chair in Christian Education at Syracuse. It has joined other conferences and denominations in an ecumenical approach to campus ministries at state institutions of higher learning.

The Northern New York Conference joins in supporting the Methodist Home for Children (Gateway) at Williamsville; the Folts Home (Aged) at Herkimer; and the Charlton School for Girls at Burnt Hills. Camp Aldersgate, in the foothills of the Adirondack Mountains is the site of a varied camping program serving all ages and interests from May until October each year. Conference offices are in the Methodist Center in Watertown, established in 1960.

The Black River and Northern New York Conferences have furnished leaders in the larger church. Bishops who were born in the region or served in the conference are: Jesse T. Peck, LINUS PARKER, WILLIAM X. NINDE, and

FREDERICK D. LEETE. Peck led in founding Syracuse University in 1870. JOHN DEMPSTER, who served as a missionary to BUENOS AIRES and was influential in the founding of both the BOSTON SCHOOL OF THEOLOGY and GARRETT BIBLICAL INSTITUTE, served as pastor in Watertown, New York.

The Northern New York Conference came to unification in 1939 with four districts, 267 charges, 35,729 members, and property valued at $4,841,874. At that time it received a few ministers and churches from the Onondaga Conference of the M.P. Church.

In 1970 the Northern New York Conference reported three districts, 136 charges, 152 ministers, 47,051 members, property valued at $24,494,712, and $2,738,417 raised for all purposes during the year.

General Minutes, ME, TMC, UMC.
Journal of the Northern New York Conference.
JOHN J. KELLY

NORTHERN SWEDISH CONFERENCE was organized at Calumet, Mich., Sept. 6, 1900 with Bishop CHARLES C. McCABE presiding. It superseded the Northern Swedish Mission Conference.

Until the middle of the nineteenth century there were only a few Swedes in the North Central states, but thereafter they came in rapidly increasing numbers. Swedish Methodist work in that region was linked to earlier beginnings on the Atlantic seaboard. A Swede by the name of Peter Bergner came to America as mate on a Swedish ship in 1822. An accident hospitalized him in NEW YORK, and while there he was converted. Interested in the spiritual welfare of his fellow-countrymen who as sailors came by the thousands to this country every year, he appealed to the Missionary Society of the M.E. Church for help. In time OLAF G. HEDSTROM, a preacher of Swedish descent in the NEW YORK CONFERENCE, assisted Bergner in organizing work among the Swedes. In 1845 a group of Swedes in New York incorporated under the name of "The First North River Bethel Society of the Methodist Episcopal Church." In 1846 a brother of Hedstrom organized a Swedish Methodist Church in Victoria, Ill.

In 1859 the MINNESOTA CONFERENCE organized a SCANDINAVIAN Mission District with ten appointments. The next year the mission district reported 385 members, including probationers. In 1861 it was designated as the Scandinavian District. In 1872 the Scandinavian District was divided to form the Swedish District and the Norwegian District. In 1877 the Swedish churches in the Minnesota Conference became a part of the newly organized Northwest Swedish Conference, the first Swedish conference to be organized by the Methodist Episcopal Church. The 1880 Discipline says that the Northwest Swedish Conference was to include all Swedish churches in the west and northwest along with those in the ERIE CONFERENCE in New York. By 1893 the Northwest Swedish Conference had churches in twelve states from New York to Minnesota, and it reported nearly 10,000 members, including probationers. The conference had more churches in Illinois than in any other one state.

The Northern Swedish Mission Conference, mentioned above, was carved out of the Northwest Swedish Conference. The Mission Conference held its first session in MINNEAPOLIS, Sept. 6-10, 1894. Its territory was Minnesota, MICHIGAN, and WISCONSIN. It had more churches in

Minnesota than in either of the other two states. The Mission Conference began with three districts, forty-two charges, and 2,607 members, including probationers. When raised to the status of a full conference in 1900, it still had only three districts, forty-five charges, and 2,749 members.

In 1927 the Northern Swedish Conference merged with the Central Swedish and Western Swedish Conferences to form the CENTRAL NORTHWEST CONFERENCE. The latter continued as a Swedish Conference until 1942 when its ministers and churches were received into the English-speaking conferences in which they happened to be located. At its last session in 1927, the Northern Swedish Conference reported two districts, fifty-one charges, 2,729 members, and property valued at $380,900.

F. E. MASER

MEMORIAL CHURCH, KAEO, NORTHLAND, NEW ZEALAND

NORTHLAND, New Zealand, **Kaeo Memorial Church,** was erected and opened in 1923, near the site of the original pioneer Maori mission station of Wesleydale. The laying of the foundation stone of the building formed part of the centenary celebrations the previous year. It stands as a memorial to the pioneer missionaries and their wives, and to the first Maori ministers of the mission, their names being inscribed on a handsome roll of honor. RITA F. SNOWDEN, the famous Methodist writer, says:

In our Memorial Church, there stands a chaste baptismal font —fashioned, we think, to represent more closely than a plaque could do, the spirit and interest of these women [i.e., the missionary wives]. On a silver strip affixed are these words: "Their richest gifts they offered gladly." (*The Ladies of Wesleydale,* London: Epworth Press, 1957, pp. 5-6.)

GEORGE L. LAURENSON

NORTHRIDGE, WILLIAM LOVELL (1886-1966), Irish minister and scholar. He was born at Ballineen, County Cork, and entered the ministry in 1910. Included in his early circuit career were four years at the BELFAST Central Mission. In 1926 he was appointed tutor at EDGEHILL COLLEGE at Belfast for theological training, and in 1943 he became principal. For many years from 1923 he was chiefly responsible for the editorial policy of the *Irish Christian Advocate.* Publications include books on

WILLIAM L. NORTHRIDGE

the Old Testament and on Pastoral Psychology, on which subject he has lectured in the United States on many occasions. He retired in 1957, but on the sudden death of his successor, R. Ernest Ker, he took over the guidance of Edgehill College for the year 1961-62. His high qualifications in psychology made him much in demand for advice and guidance.

FREDERICK JEFFERY

NORTHWEST CANADA CONFERENCE, E.U.B., came into being because of the persistence of members of The EVANGELICAL CHURCH in eastern Canada. Early in the nineteenth century, a number of Evangelical families moved from the state of PENNSYLVANIA to Ontario, CANADA. In 1816, JOHN DREISBACH preached among them but was unable to establish an organized work. Later, in 1839, two missions were formed, one at Waterloo and one at Black Creek. During the same year a CAMP MEETING, at which BISHOP JOHN SEYBERT preached, resulted in the organization of two other congregations, one at Berlin and the other in the surrounding neighborhood. Other advances followed; and in 1863, the work in Ontario was formed into a separate annual conference known as the CANADA CONFERENCE.

In 1876, the Canada Conference sent a special delegation to the west under the leadership of Superintendent Peter Alles to investigate the possibility of missionary work. Their report was discouraging. The delegation saw no opportunity for church work in an area that was swampy and sparsely settled. However, the west did open and among the early settlers were members from Evangelical churches in the United States and Ontario. At first, the DAKOTA CONFERENCE responded to the appeal of these people and sent missionaries to Western Canada, but due to pressing needs at home, the conference soon withdrew this assistance.

In 1899 the Canada Conference, after much investigation, deliberation and prayer, took up this work. W. E. Beese was assigned as the first missionary to the west with appointment to both Winnipeg and Grenfell. He preached his first sermon in the J. J. Niebergall home fifteen miles north of Grenfell. In 1900, A. W. Sauer was appointed to Rosthern, Saskatchewan; and in 1901, C. G. Kaatz was sent to Didsbury, Alberta. In 1908, L. H. Wagner became the first resident superintendent of the work in Western Canada.

After twenty-eight years of missionary work in the Canadian West, upon petition of the Canada Conference, the GENERAL CONFERENCE granted permission to organize the Northwest Canada Conference of The Evangelical Church. This organization took place in June 1927, at Didsbury, Alberta; and in 1928 the Dominion Government granted a charter to the new conference. W. W. Krueger was appointed superintendent by the General Board of Missions, in which capacity he served for twenty years.

At the time of organization the membership of the conference was 1,433. By 1968 this membership had grown to over 3,600. There were fifty-three organized congregations, thirty-seven ministers under appointment as pastors, and four under appointment to the Hillcrest Christian College. There were fifty-two churches in the conference, valued at $1,249,000. Additional property owned by the conference included the Hillcrest Christian College, valued at $375,000, and three camp grounds with assets of $75,000. Nearly 1,500 miles separated the eastern and western boundaries of this conference.

In The United Methodist Church the Northwest Canada Conference was granted permission to operate under the procedures of the COMMISSION ON THE STRUCTURE OF METHODISM OVERSEAS.

F. E. VORRATH

NORTHWEST CONFERENCE (MES) was organized at Milton, Ore., Aug. 29, 1918 with Bishop H. M. DuBOSE presiding. It was formed by merging the Columbia, East Columbia, and Montana Conferences. (See OREGON and MONTANA for accounts of these conferences.) Its territory embraced Oregon, WASHINGTON, IDAHO, and Montana. The conference began with three districts, Portland, Inland, and Montana, and it had forty-five charges and 4,916 members. In the twenty-one years prior to Methodist unification the Northwest Conference did not flourish. In 1939 it reported two districts, Portland and Spokane, and there were thirty-four charges and 3,647 members.

F. E. MASER

NORTHWEST INDIANA CONFERENCE covered less than one-fourth of the state of INDIANA, but it was blessed with a diversification marked by metropolitan and rural areas, industrialization and agriculture. Prompted in its creation by the growth of Methodism in northern Indiana from 1844 until 1852, it was authorized by the GENERAL CONFERENCE of 1852 upon request of the existing NORTH INDIANA CONFERENCE. Meeting in Terre Haute, the new conference encompassed forty-eight circuits (consisting of fifty-nine churches) with 11,488 members, and there were sixty-five ministers. The conference included all the Methodist work west of the Michigan Road from INDIANAPOLIS north to the St. Joseph River at SOUTH BEND (with the exception of Logansport), thence north to the MICHIGAN state line. On the south it included the northwest portion of Indianapolis (west of Meridian Street and north of Market Street) and followed the National Road west from the capitol to the ILLINOIS state line. The states of Illinois and Michigan supplied the other two boundary lines. The conferences maintained these boundaries until unification with the North Indiana and the Indiana North (EUB) conferences in 1968.

The venerable JAMES ARMSTRONG had worked in the area of northwestern Indiana as early as 1825 along with his assistant, Hackaliah Vredenburg, and continued until his death to organize new congregations in the area. John Daniel, John Marsee and John L. Smith were early leaders of the conference—all three carrying presiding elder responsibilities into the new conference from the older one. Joseph C. Reed, Hilary A. Gobin, and Aaron Wood soon assumed memorable leadership for the smallest of the Indiana conferences.

With INDIANA ASBURY UNIVERSITY located within the bounds of the conference, the new Northwest Indiana Conference had added incentive in its educational work. At its first session the conference elected trustees and visitors to the Greencastle school and representatives to inspect other Methodist educational efforts in the state, but Indiana Asbury remained its favorite and imminent project. Repeatedly, the home conference of the Methodist University (renamed DePAUW UNIVERSITY in 1884) responded to its need. To augment the educational work at Greencastle, the Conference cooperated with the local congregation in 1926 in the building of a new Methodist church, the Gobin Memorial Church, adjacent to the campus.

Recognizing the growth of state colleges and universities, the Northwest Conference created one of the early WESLEY FOUNDATION units in the United States at Purdue University in 1917. Its pioneering work helped set the tempo for Methodist campus ministry everywhere. It has been a leader in innovative ministry and responsible stewardship to the campus for fifty years.

Early in the Conference's history, private academies were developed and maintained (with varying degrees of success) until public school education became stabilized in this rapidly growing area of the state. A few became "feeder-lines" to the Methodist University at Greencastle, though most were short-lived. The Monnett School for Girls at Rensselaer was the last—struggling for survival against the twin floods of expanding public welfare departments and depleted support from the annual conference. By the end of the depression in 1934, the school had closed.

The churches of the Northwest Indiana Conference were fruits of early missions, and only their material means (never their Methodist spirit) limited the conference's missionary response. Three members of the conference in 1852 declared themselves ready to enter the mission field. Both home and foreign missions commanded their response. The missionary zeal transformed the shift of the conference from a primarily rural setting to a highly industrialized one, with all of its accompanying problems, to a challenge rather than a burden. This was to express itself in increased involvement in community affairs.

Epworth Hospital in South Bend was founded under the benevolent guidance of Methodist women and maintained a quasi-official relationship with the conference for several years. The conference cooperated with the other Indiana conferences in establishing the Methodist Hospital at Indianapolis, and after 1919 took exclusive control of the hospital in Gary. Likewise, an orphanage was begun at Greencastle in the early 1920's and moved to Lebanon in 1924 because of better facilities. The Indiana Methodist Children's Home at Lebanon has an illustrious history of almost one-half century of service. A residency for older people was established in Frankfort (Wesley Manor), and as union of the conferences approached in 1968 the home absorbed the assets and liabilities of an independent home in Greencastle and renamed it Asbury Towers.

The missionary zeal was to find worthy supporters among the women of the conference. During the organizational period of 1884-85, 49 auxiliaries of the WOMAN'S HOME MISSIONARY SOCIETY were formed with 1,153 women enlisted. A decade earlier the WOMAN'S FOREIGN MISSIONARY SOCIETY was firmly entrenched and by 1877 was donating one-fourth of all the missionary giving of the conference. After the union of the women's groups in 1941, a tremendous increase in missionary giving was realized and women's work made another surge forward.

The youth were quick to rally to the old EPWORTH LEAGUE. By 1893 there were a total of 4,912 youth enlisted in ninety-one youth groups in the conference. The Battle Ground Campground began development in 1874 and was the scene of many successful CAMP MEETINGS. It was also to become the scene of Junior and Senior Youth training conferences. A wilderness camp was developed in the early 1960's at Pine Creek.

With the union of The Methodist and E.U.B. Churches, the Northwest Indiana Conference was absorbed into the new NORTH INDIANA and South INDIANA CONFERENCES. The Northwest Indiana Conference brought 253 ministers, 267 charges, 96,238 members, and property valued at $44,445,219 to the union.

JAMES J. BABBITT

NORTHWEST IOWA CONFERENCE (ME) was organized Sept. 18, 1872 at Fort Dodge, Iowa with Bishop EDWARD G. ANDREWS presiding. It was formed by dividing the DES MOINES CONFERENCE, and its territory included the northwest quarter of IOWA and Dakota Territory. At the beginning it had three districts, Fort Dodge, Sioux City, and Algona; twenty-three preachers, nine churches, and 3,392 members.

In 1875 the conference petitioned the GENERAL CONFERENCE to organize the Dakota territory into a separate annual conference, but nothing was done about that until 1880.

Soon after its organization the conference gave support to Algona Seminary, but the school failed about 1880. The conference supported CORNELL COLLEGE until 1894 when it projected MORNINGSIDE COLLEGE at Sioux City by buying for some $25,000 the buildings of the University of the Northwest. It gave excellent patronage and support to Morningside, and today it is a strong Methodist college.

The Northwest Iowa Conference continued until 1948 when it merged with the Upper Iowa Conference to form the North Iowa Conference. In its last year the conference reported 200 ministers, 205 churches, and 54,884 members.

B. Mitchell, *Northwest Iowa Conference.* 1904.
Minutes of the Northwest Iowa Conference.   F. E. MASER

NORTHWEST KANSAS CONFERENCE (ME) was organized March 9, 1882 at Abilene with Bishop H. W. WARREN presiding. It was formed by dividing the KANSAS CONFERENCE, and its boundaries included all that "part of the state of Kansas north of the south line of township sixteen and west of the sixth principal meridian, yet so

as to include the Solomon City Circuit." This meant that the boundaries included approximately the west two-thirds of the north half of the state. When organized the conference had three districts—Beloit, Kirwin, and Salina. In 1883 the conference reported seventy-four charges and 5,991 members.

At the outset the Northwest Kansas Conference pledged support to BAKER UNIVERSITY at Baldwin, but at the same time it felt the need of a college within its own bounds. As a result of that sentiment, KANSAS WESLEYAN UNIVERSITY was opened at Salina in the fall of 1886. Through the years the school experienced many difficulties, but it survived. In 1968 it had in round numbers an endowment of $1,000,000, a plant valued at $6,000,000, and an enrolment of 900.

During its history the conference established three hospitals—Boothray Memorial at Goodland, Asbury at Salina, and Hays Protestant at Hays. It joined other conferences in the state in supporting Methodist institutions.

In 1939 the Northwest Kansas Conference merged with the SOUTHWEST KANSAS CONFERENCE to form the CENTRAL CONFERENCE. The Northwest Conference brought to the merger 128 charges and 26,144 members.

D. W. Holter, *Fire on the Prairie.* 1969.
Minutes of the Northwest Kansas Conference.   F. E. MASER

NORTHWEST NEBRASKA CONFERENCE (ME) was organized at Kearney, Neb., during a session of the WEST NEBRASKA CONFERENCE, Sept. 28-Oct. 3, 1892, with Bishop H. W. WARREN presiding. It was formed by dividing the West Nebraska Conference. The conference was located in northwest Nebraska and it included less than one-fourth of the state. It had one district, Chadron, some twenty-six charges, and 1,417 members at the beginning.

Northwest Nebraska continued as a separate conference through 1924 and was then absorbed by the NEBRASKA CONFERENCE. At its last session in 1924 the conference reported one district, United, forty-three charges, and 9,258 members.

E. E. Jackman, *Nebraska Methodist History.* 1954.
General Minutes, MEC.   E. E. JACKMAN

NORTHWEST TEXAS CONFERENCE (MES) was organized at Waxahachie, Sept. 26, 1866, with Bishop ENOCH M. MARVIN presiding. The conference was formed by merging the northern parts of the TEXAS and the RIO GRANDE CONFERENCES. At the beginning the Northwest Texas Conference included all the territory in the present CENTRAL TEXAS and Northwest Texas Conferences. (The Central Texas Conference was set off from the Northwest Texas Conference in 1910.) When organized the Northwest Texas Conference had four districts, thirty-two charges, and 3,890 white and 526 colored members.

Though the Northwest Texas Conference had thirty-two charges in 1866, none of them was within the bounds of the present Northwest Texas Conference. Moreover, not any of the counties in the present Northwest Texas Conference were organized before 1870. In 1876 the Texas Legislature created fifty-four counties in northwest Texas, but even so it was ten to fifteen years before many of them had enough population to organize a county government. However, once a county was organized, one or more Methodist churches soon appeared within its bounds.

Probably the first Methodist sermon in the present Northwest Texas Conference territory was delivered a little before 1870 by one Milton Jones at Fort Griffin, a United States military post established in 1867. Fort Griffin was listed in the conference appointments in 1875.

Around 1880, the Texas and Pacific and the Fort Worth and Denver Railroads came into northwest Texas and immigration soon followed. Also, Methodist activity soon greatly accelerated. Methodism felt strong enough to start Belle Plain College in the Abilene District in 1881, but it closed after seven years, probably because of unprecedented drought in the region. By 1900 the conference had nearly 67,000 members, fully five-sixths of them in the area that was to become the Central Texas Conference. By 1910 when the division into two conferences took place, there were nearly 116,000 members in the conference, two-thirds of them in the region being set off as the Central Texas Conference.

On Nov. 9, 1910 the Northwest Texas Conference, having given one-third of its territory and two-thirds of its membership to the newly created Central Texas Conference, met at Clarendon with Bishop JAMES ATKINS presiding. The conference started its new era with six districts, 148 charges, 179 preachers, and 39,009 members. The Central Texas Conference met a week later at Waxahachie with the same bishop in the chair.

The Northwest Texas Conference had a net increase in membership between 1910 and 1920 of only 2,718, but in the next decade the net advance was 18,237 members, representing a growth of about twenty-eight percent. The conference came to unification in 1939 with nine districts, 217 charges, 73,182 members, and property valued at $4,523,987. It raised for all purposes that year $836,080.

When limited to its present boundaries in 1910, the Northwest Texas Conference had three junior colleges: Clarendon College at Clarendon, Stamford College at Stamford, and Seth Ward College at Plainview. Between 1916 and 1918 both Seth Ward and Stamford closed because of disastrous fires. Clarendon College closed in 1927. A movement led by J. W. Hunt, last president of Stamford, brought about the establishment of McMurry COLLEGE at Abilene in 1923. With good administrative leadership and support from the conference, the college has grown. Today it has an endowment of more than $2,500,000, a plant valued at $7,000,000 and an enrollment of more than 2,000.

Since unification the Northwest Texas Conference has increased in membership about forty-five percent. It supports the Methodist Hospital at Lubbock, two retirement nursing homes (King's Manor at Hereford and Sears Memorial Methodist Center at Abilene), two youth camps, and several WESLEY FOUNDATIONS. It joins the other Texas Conferences in support of the Methodist Children's Home at Waco, *The Texas Methodist* at DALLAS, and some other causes. The conference raised $201,428 for higher education in 1968, and it projected a fiftieth anniversary campaign for $3,500,000 for McMurry College.

In 1968 the Northwest Texas Conference reported eight districts, 237 charges, 338 ministers, 106,515 members, and property valued at $49,981,691. It raised for all purposes that year $8,241,712.

General Minutes, MECS and MC.
Minutes of the Northwest Texas Conference. ALBEA GODBOLD

NORTHWESTERN UNIVERSITY, Evanston, Illinois, was established in 1851. The city in which it is located perpetuates the name of its principal founder, JOHN EVANS. The city also has streets named for Bishops FOSTER and MATTHEW SIMPSON and for early university presidents, Noyes and Hinman. Orrington Lunt and John Evans located the university immediately north of CHICAGO on the shores of Lake Michigan. Evans himself carried through the purchase of the original 379 acres for $25,000.

The founders, reflecting Methodist antipathy to intoxicating liquors, placed an amendment in the charter forbidding their sale within four miles of the university. The university's charter contains a tax-exemption clause that grants freedom from taxation in perpetuity. This was upheld by the Supreme Court of the United States in 1879.

Though today a nondenominational, coeducational school, NORTHWESTERN UNIVERSITY, as its catalog states, "is historically a Methodist-related institution." Its first five presidents were clergymen, graduates of Methodist schools. The sixth president, HENRY WADE ROGERS, was a layman, and with the exception of a one-year interval the presidents since 1890 have been laymen. Three of the early presidents of Northwestern were elected bishops. The short terms of clergyman presidents and their tendency to give preference to ecclesiastical offices may account for the shift to laymen.

The close orientation of Northwestern University to The Methodist Church in the last half of the nineteenth century is reflected in the concern of President Cummings to get young Methodists to attend college. In 1884, he noted that there was only one Methodist student to every 1,000 members in the nation. The Congregationalists had one to every 413 members.

Northwestern University was founded with the vision of a Methodist university fed by a network of Methodist colleges. In addition, it was deeply concerned for the religious needs of students in its professional schools. President Edmund J. James believed that a student of medicine should not be less a Christian than a student in liberal arts.

The schools are the College of Arts and Sciences, Business, Dentistry, Education, Music, Graduate, Technological Institute, Journalism, Law, Medicine, Speech, Evening Divisions. The university has a cooperative academic arrangement with GARRETT THEOLOGICAL SEMINARY. Northwestern also has a Phi Beta Kappa chapter. The governing board has fifty-nine trustees eight of whom are elected from ROCK RIVER, CENTRAL ILLINOIS, MICHIGAN, and DETROIT ANNUAL CONFERENCES of The United Methodist Church.

JOHN O. GROSS

NORWAY is the northernmost part of the continent of Europe; and Hammerfest, the northernmost town in the world, is in the very north of Norway. It is a country of mountains, fjords, and deep valleys. There are many islands along the west coast, and there are also a number of large and small rivers and lakes. The shape of the country is long and narrow; the distance from the southernmost point to the northernmost point is 1,100 miles. It covers an area of 125,064 square miles. The Spitsbergen group of islands is a Norwegian possession. According to the latest population figures (1970) the population is

3,867,400. OSLO, the capital, has about 500,000 inhabitants.

The most important economic activities are shipping, agriculture, forestry, fisheries, industry, and tourism. Norway has the fourth largest merchant navy in the world. Some Norwegians have become famous far beyond the frontiers of their own country, e.g. the polar explorers Fridtjof Nansen and Roald Amundsen; in the world of letters, Henrik Ibsen and Björnstjerne Björnsen; and the novelists Knut Hamsun and Sigrid Undset, both of whom were awarded the Nobel Prize for literature; the sculptor Gustav Vigeland; the painters Edvard Munch and Henrik Sörensen; the composer Edvard Grieg. Trygve Lie, the first Secretary General of the United Nations, was also a Norwegian.

O. P. PETERSEN

The Founder. The Methodist Church in Norway grew out of a spiritual revival movement. The one chosen to realize this revival was a Norwegian seaman, Ole Peter Petersen (1822-1901), and the story of Norwegian Methodism during its formative years is really the story of this one man. He was born at Fredrickstad on April 28, 1822. His father, who was a ship's carpenter, lost his life at sea when young Ole was only four years old. When Ole was six, his mother died also. He was confirmed at the age of fourteen. In the church register, the entry against his name says: "Very good knowledge, exemplary conduct."

Ole was a quiet and thoughtful boy. His thoughts were often concerned with God and God's word. His wish was to become a minister of the church, but he abandoned that idea and became a seaman, as his father had been before him, sailing along the coast of America for many years. When in New York, he frequently used to visit the BETHEL SHIP Mission. This had been started by the

American Methodist Episcopal Church, largely for the benefit of seamen from Norway, SWEDEN, and DENMARK.

At a meeting of a small group, the pastor asked him: "Is your soul saved?" Petersen answered very solemnly: "I apologize for having taken the liberty of coming to this meeting. I am not fit to be here, I am only a poor sinner in search of God if He will have mercy on me." The pastor talked with him about God, and the young seaman went his way.

One night, Petersen, who was on watch, paced the deck thinking about God. And it was then that he clearly heard the words, "Rejoice, my son." And his soul was filled with indescribable bliss.

METHODIST CHURCH, STAVANGER, NORWAY

The Beginnings of Methodism in Norway—First Hundred Years. Ole Peter Petersen sailed along the coast of America for several years. In a letter to his fiancée, Anne Marie Amundsen, in Fredrickstad, his native town, he described what the Lord had done for him. The letter was of such a nature that she allowed her own family to read it. After that it was passed from house to house until it was almost in shreds. All who read it were deeply moved by the contents and by the profound seriousness that characterized it. The outcome was that Petersen's fiancée wrote to him on behalf of all those who had read the letter, and urgently asked him to come home to guide them onto the road to God which he himself had found.

Petersen had not been considering such an early return home, but the request made him restless, so he decided to go and to bear witness of what God had done for him. On June 30, 1849, he arrived at Fredrikstad and saw his fiancée. Her aunt wanted to celebrate Petersen's homecoming with a glass of wine, but he replied: "I have not come back to be with you for such occasions, but to tell you what the Lord has done for my salvation." This set the tone for his stay in Norway. It was the beginning of a revival movement of great consequence. People began beseeching him to hold public meetings, but he replied: "I am not a minister of the church, nor do I know if the law of the land permits me to hold public meetings." But the revival movement continued.

One day he visited the minister of the Norwegian Lutheran state church to ask if he was permitted to hold public meetings if people asked him to do so. At first the minister answered noncommittally, and said that, after all, people could go to the services in the state church. But having talked with Petersen for a while, the minister said that there was freedom of religion in Norway, adding fortunately: "You are fully within your rights to follow God's word and your own conscience."

So Petersen started to hold public meetings. He had not intended to stay in Norway for long, and made preparations for returning to America with a view to sailing on coastal vessels again. But the newly converted asked him so urgently to stay on at home that he did not dare to refuse. In addition to his work at Fredrikstad, he had also visited many of the surrounding districts.

On one occasion, Petersen went to see a well-known layman within the Norwegian State Church. When they parted, this man said to Petersen: "May God bless you. I could wish that you would stay on here among us. We need men like you in Norway."

Early in the winter of 1849, he married Annie Marie Amundsen, and on April 24, 1850, he and his bride sailed for America. Before leaving for Norway in 1849, he had joined the Bethel Ship Misssion. Some time after his return to America he was asked to take up the appointment of assistant with the Bethel Ship Mission. His work was to be the visiting of lodging houses, hospitals, and of Norwegian, Swedish, and Danish families. On June 10, 1851, he received authorization as LOCAL PREACHER.

In the autumn of 1851 he was asked to go to IOWA in order to work among the Norwegian pioneers there. He did so, and as a result became one of the founders of the NORWEGIAN-DANISH ANNUAL CONFERENCE of the Methodist Episcopal Church of America.

Simultaneously he pursued intensive studies for the ministry; and on July 1, 1853, he was ordained DEACON and ELDER by Bishop BEVERLY WAUGH. Concerning him the bishop said: "He is one of the most humble, self-sacrificing, faithful, and self-denying men I have ever known. He is gentle, loving, zealous, pure, conscientious."

Those who had been converted to God in 1849-50 during Petersen's visit to Norway sent several letters to the church in America asking for Petersen to return home to Norway again. And eventually the M.E. Church in America, of which he was now a minister, decided that he should go to Norway.

On Dec. 3, 1853, he arrived in Oslo, and immediately continued to his native town of Fredrikstad, where he started the activities which were to lead to the foundation of the Methodist Church in Norway. The revival movement began to flourish again.

After the first Methodist congregation in Norway had been organized at SARPSBORG on Sept. 11, 1856, by Ole Peter Petersen, he continued his activities by visiting many other places. Another congregation was organized by CHRISTIAN WILLERUP at Halden, then called Fredrikshald, on November 3 of the same year, and activity continued to expand steadily.

In 1859, and at his own request, Petersen was appointed to a position in America. For three years he was the leader of the work on Bethel Ship, and in 1863 he was appointed superintendent of the Norwegian Mission District in the WEST WISCONSIN ANNUAL CONFERENCE. During that time he worked tenaciously for the church, taking up work among the many Norwegians and Danes who had settled in CHICAGO. Chicago itself was of course beyond his district, but he nevertheless felt that it was up to him to take the initiative. And in June, 1868, the first Nor-

wegian-Danish Methodist congregation was founded in Chicago.

After serving six years as district superintendent in WISCONSIN, Petersen received a pressing request to return to Norway to take up the position of superintendent of the work of the church in Norway. He accepted, on condition that the appointment should be for two years only. Those two years were years of progress—several new congregations were founded, and activities expanded to many new places. Under Petersen's leadership the preachers came together for an annual meeting in 1870, where one of the decisions was to publish a catechism, a hymnbook, and a church monthly magazine. On April 28, 1871, he preached his valedictory sermon in Oslo prior to going back to America, where he had been appointed to the Norwegian-Danish church in Chicago.

In 1874 he was given an appointment in BROOKLYN, where he organized a Norwegian-Danish Methodist congregation. The Scandinavian Mission to Seamen in New York, including the Bethel Ship, was incorporated within the field of activities of the new congregation.

In 1878 Petersen became superintendent of the Milwaukee Norwegian District and subsequently of the Chicago Norwegian District. During his later years he officiated as pastor at Racine; Maplewood Avenue, Chicago; and MINNEAPOLIS.

As late as 1901, Ole Petersen, who by then had reached the age of seventy-nine, accepted an appointment in Brooklyn. He threw himself into the work with his customary energy, and founded yet another Norwegian-Danish congregation. He died in Brooklyn on Dec. 20, 1901, and was buried in Milwaukee, where his wife had found her last place of rest almost twenty years earlier.

Petersen was a man of utterly consistent character, willing and ready at all times to give advice, guidance, and consolation. He had an unshakeable sense of justice, which was a prominent feature of his character. He loved children and young people, and was filled with a fiery and untiring energy. He was a keen and discerning theologian. He wrote a number of books, articles for magazines, periodicals, and pamphlets. His most important work is *Betraktninger over Bibelens hovedlerdommer*. His hymns and chorales and translations are used in church to this day. They express a humble adoration of God, and a deeply felt desire to lead a life of sanctity for him.

Ole Petersen has been honored in his native town of Fredrikstad with a bust in one of the public parks, and by naming a street in the center of the town after him.

Development of Norwegian Methodism. As soon as the Methodist Church in Norway had become organized, new Methodist congregations were founded, one after the other. Sunday schools and youth work were started. In fact, work with Sunday schools had already begun in February, 1855, that is to say before the Church had become organized. Youth work was organized in 1889. Also choirs, brass bands (with choirs), women's societies, etc., were founded, and foreign and home mission work was started.

By and by, the number of preachers increased, and preachers' meetings were held at suitable intervals, until a regular Norwegian Annual Conference (now the Norway Conference) was organized in Oslo in 1876, under the leadership of Bishop E. G. ANDREWS.

In 1953, a member of the Methodist Church in Norway, ODD HAGEN, was elected Bishop of Northern Europe; and in 1964 a Norwegian missionary, HARRY P. ANDREAS-

SEN, was elected Bishop of ANGOLA (Africa). In 1961, the WORLD METHODIST CONFERENCE was held in Oslo. In 1966 the Norwegian bishop, Odd Hagen, was elected president of the WORLD METHODIST COUNCIL.

The development of the work done by the Methodist Church in Norway resulted in the foundation of several institutions.

Publishing. As early as 1856—the year in which the Methodist Church in Norway was founded—the first book was published. It was on church discipline. On May 21, 1867, a preachers' meeting took place, at which eight preachers were present. One of the subjects for discussion was the setting up of a company for the dissemination of Christian literature. That was the beginning of the publishing house, still in existence, of the Methodist church in Norway: *Norsk Forlagsselskap*. The first magazine to be published was a Sunday school magazine, which started in 1871. The present title of this magazine is *Barnevennen*. On Jan. 28, 1872, the first issue of the official church paper came out, which is now published under the name of *Kristelig Tidende*. The publications by *Norsk Forlagsselskap* include textbooks, scientific works, historical works, collections of sermons, books of chorales, fiction, and literature for edification, etc.

Social work began with a children's home, which was opened in Oslo in 1892. In 1922 a further children's home was opened in Oslo, and a children's home for northern Norway was opened at Finnsnes in 1923. An old-people's home was opened at Vadsö in northern Norway in 1924, another one in Oslo in 1925, and a third one in Bergen in 1954.

A home for young men was opened at Fredrikstad in 1960. Altogether these homes have places for forty-four children, twelve young men, and ninety old people.

Hospitals and deaconess work were started in Oslo in 1897, and continued in Bergen in 1904, and in Skien in 1939. These hospitals are called "Betanien" (Bethany houses), and at the Betanien hospitals there are now a total number of 358 beds. The institutions have 531 deaconesses, who serve in hospitals run by the Church, and also in state and local authority hospitals.

A theological school was started on May 27, 1873, in Oslo. In 1924 the Methodist Churches in Scandinavia (Sweden, Denmark, FINLAND, Norway) came together to establish the UNION SCANDINAVIAN THEOLOGICAL SCHOOL, and a piece of property was acquired for that purpose at Gothenburg, Sweden. It has had a great influence throughout all Scandinavia.

A Bible school was established in Oslo in 1941. This provides Bible courses and local courses for the congregations, and also arranges for instruction by correspondence.

Missionary work was properly organized at the Annual Conference in 1907, Southern RHODESIA being chosen as the first field for Norway missions. The Methodist Women's Society was established in 1931. The local congregations, the Youth Fellowship, and the Methodist Women's Society in Norway all now work together, and maintain missionaries at the following places: INDIA, HONG KONG, MALAYA, Rhodesia, CONGO, Angola, LIBERIA, ALGERIA and TUNISIA, a present total of thirty-three missionaries.

Present (1967) statistics of Norwegian Methodism: Number of churches, 89; other places of worship, 90; ministers, 85; missionaries, 33; local preachers, 107; number of Methodists in Norway, 22,000; number of children attending Sunday school, 6,900; youth work, 5,500.

Eilert Bernhardt, "The Beginnings of Methodism in Norway," *World Outlook*, August 1956.
——————, *Metodistkirken. Opprinnelse. Laere, Organisasjon.* Oslo: Norsk Forlagsselskap, 1933.
—————— og Aage Hardy, *Metodistkirken i Norge—100 ar.* Oslo: Norsk Forlagsselskap, 1956.
A. Haagensen, *Den norsk-danske Metodistkirkes historie—pa begge sider av havet.* Chicago: Den norsk-danske Boghandels officin, 1894.
Aage Hardy, *O. P. Petersen, Metodistkirkens grunnlegger i Norge.* Oslo: Norsk Forlagsselskap, 1953.
O. P. Petersen, *Betrektninger over Bibelens hovedlærdommer.* Chicago: Den norsk-danske Boghandels Trykkeri, 1900.
J. Thorkildsen, *Den norske metodistkirkes historie.* Oslo: Norsk Forlagsselskap, 1926.   EILERT BERNHARDT

NORWEGIAN AND DANISH CONFERENCE in the United States was organized at Cambridge, Wis., Sept. 10, 1885 with Bishop THOMAS BOWMAN presiding. It superseded the Northwest Norwegian Conference which was organized at Racine, Wis. in September 1880.

The responsibility of the Norwegian and Danish Conference was all of the Norwegian and Danish work between the Allegheny and Rocky Mountains, though the conference minutes show that practically all of its charges were in seven states—ILLINOIS, IOWA, MICHIGAN, MINNESOTA, WISCONSIN, and the DAKOTAS.

This conference is not to be confused with the Norwegian and Danish work in the Pacific northwest which began as the Northwest Norwegian-Danish Mission in 1888, became the WESTERN NORWEGIAN-DANISH CONFERENCE in 1896, and continued as such until unification in 1939.

Norwegians and Danes began emigrating to America in appreciable numbers in the 1840's and 1850's. In 1856 the WISCONSIN CONFERENCE formed a Norwegian Mission District with eight circuits located in the states of Wisconsin, Minnesota, and Iowa. In 1859 the MINNESOTA CONFERENCE organized a Scandinavian Mission District. In 1872 both conferences separated their work into Swedish and Norwegian Districts. The 1880 GENERAL CONFERENCE authorized the formation of a Norwegian Annual Conference, and that fall, as indicated above, the Northwest Norwegian Conference was organized. The conference began with four districts, Chicago, Milwaukee, Minnesota, and Iowa. There were thirty-one charges and 2,640 members. In 1885 when the name of the conference was changed there were forty-five charges and 3,380 members.

The Norwegians and Danes proposed the establishment of a school as early as 1866, and in 1870 a Norwegian-Danish seminary opened in Evanston, Ill. However, it was 1886 before classes were conducted regularly. The institution continued until 1934 when it merged with a Swedish school which in 1950 became KENDALL COLLEGE, an accredited Methodist junior college. The conference established the Elim Old People's Home in MINNEAPOLIS in 1914; the home and its assets were valued at $54,000 at the time of merger in 1943.

The Norwegian and Danish Conference was the last of all the language conferences in Methodism to be absorbed by the English-speaking conferences. The conference disbanded May 30, 1943. At the time its boundaries included all of the United States east of the Rocky Mountains. In its last year the Norwegian and Danish Conference had two districts—Chicago and Minneapolis—and it reported forty-eight charges, 4,737 members, and property valued at $710,088.

General Minutes, MEC and MC.
C. N. Pace, *Our Fathers Built, A Century of Minnesota Methodism*. N.d.
E. S. Bucke, *History of American Methodism*. 1964.

F. E. Maser

NORWEGIAN METHODISM IN THE U.S.A.

In 1851 Ole P. Petersen (see Norway), a native Norwegian, was sent by the M. E. Church as preacher to the Norwegian settlers in northeastern Iowa. As a result of his work in that district the first Methodist congregation among Norwegians in the United States was established at Washington Prairie, Winneshiek County, Iowa, in April, 1852. Methodist activity among Norwegian immigrants spread to more and more places. In 1856 it was decided that all Norwegian missions in Wisconsin, Iowa, and Minnesota were to be united into one district, the Norwegian Mission District. From the register of appointments for 1857 it appears that mission work was done at the following places: Cambridge, Racine, Hart Prairie, Primrose, Viroqua, and Richland, Wis.; Upper Iowa, Winneshiek County; St. Paul and Chisago Lake, Minn.

In 1863 the Danish brethren in Wisconsin were incorporated into the Norwegian District.

In 1870 the Norwegian-Danish District made an agreement with Northwestern University at Evanston, Ill., for the organization of a department for Norwegian and Danish students. A class was started the same year. On July 3, 1875, the Norwegian and Danish Educational Society of the M. E. Church was incorporated.

In 1879 the Minnesota Annual Conference was held at Winona, Oct. 1-6, under the chairmanship of Bishop Jesse T. Peck. This Annual Conference passed a resolution, or memorial, addressed to the coming General Conference; the closing paragraph reads as follows:

Although the relationship between the Norwegian and the American brethren at this Conference has for many years been as harmonious and brotherly as could be desired, we are nevertheless of the opinion that work amongst the Norwegians will be furthered to the best advantage if the Norwegians were to establish their own separate Annual Conference; and we would therefore humbly request this General Conference which is about to take place to consider the suitability of establishing such a separate organization.

Pursuant to this in 1880 the Norwegian and Danish preachers in the United States all met together in an Annual Conference of their own for the first time. At that date the connection with American Methodism had been in existence for twenty-nine years. This Annual Conference took place at Racine, Wis., Sept. 9-13, under the chairmanship of Bishop W. L. Harris. The Norwegian-Danish Conference had then 2,266 members, with a further 274 on probation, and there were forty-three churches.

At the annual Conference of 1883, at Racine, Wis., it was decided to establish a Norwegian-Danish School of Theology, and the session the following year decided that this school was to be at Evanston, Ill. In 1890 the foundation for publishing activities was laid in the Norwegian-Danish Publishing Society. This enterprise was merged with the Methodist Book Concern in 1914.

On Dec. 23, 1896, the Norwegian and Danish Methodist Preachers' Aid Society was established, and on Aug. 20, 1914, a home for elderly members was opened in Chicago. This bore the name of "Elim Home."

The Norwegian-Danish congregations thereafter steadily continued their work. But in consequence of the steady decrease in the number of immigrants coming from Norway and Denmark, and the fact that the early immigrants and their descendants had become Americanized, the number of Norwegian-Danish congregations grew smaller, until they were eventually all merged into American Methodism, according to a decision adopted by the Uniting Conference in 1939. The last Norwegian-Danish Conference convened in Trinity Church, Racine, Wis., on May 26, 1943, under the chairmanship of Bishop E. L. Waldorf.

Eilert Bernhardt

NORWICH,

Norfolk, England, has always been an important agricultural and manufacturing center in East Anglia. In the eighteenth century it was, as it is now, a city of churches and a stronghold of nonconformity. It was the third city in the country, and therefore it was natural that John Wesley's visits should be frequent. On his first visit, in July 1754, he was accompanied by his brother Charles, their host being Captain (later Colonel) Gallatin, in whose house the first recognized Methodist service was held. As John was far from well, Charles was the preacher; and it was he who a few days later took a seven-years' lease on an old brew house, on the site of a former bell foundry near the castle, in which building, known as the Foundery, the first regular society of eighteen members was formed. Services were held there for about seven years, and the society seems to have had a fairly steady existence, apart from some violent persecution by the Hell-Fire Club, composed of papists, Nonjurors, Jacobites and others.

In 1758 Wesley negotiated a seven-years' lease on the "Tabernacle," a fine meetinghouse designed by the famous Norwich architect Thomas Ivory and opened in 1753 by George Whitefield for the Countess of Huntingdon's connection. Here it was that the notorious Calvinistic Methodist preacher James Wheatley officiated. After his expulsion from Wesleyan Methodism in 1749 for immorality, he had established himself in Norwich, though also persecuted by the Hell-Fire Club, until misconduct again led to his disappearance. It is not surprising that at the Tabernacle Wesley found a congregation whose instability (many were Antinomians or Sandemanians) nearly drove him to despair, evoking such comments as: "I told them they were the most ignorant, self-conceited, self-willed, fickle, intractable, disorderly, disjointed Society in the three kingdoms" (*Journal*, iv, 351, Sept. 9, 1759); or "I have had more trouble with this Society than with half the Societies in England put together" (*Journal*, v, 36, Oct. 11, 1763). This state of things was reflected in the membership, which shrank from about 330 to 170 when the Tabernacle was vacated at the expiration of the lease.

In 1766 the society rented from the General Baptists a chapel in St. James' Parish and continued to worship there until 1769, when the members realized their long-cherished ambition to have a building of their own. The stigma caused by Wheatley's behavior had made it difficult for them to purchase a plot of ground, but eventually a site was procured in Cherry Lane, and the new chapel, to which Wesley contributed £270, was opened by him in October 1769. Here the Norwich Wesleyans worshiped for forty-two years; the cause prospered, the membership increasing from 160 to 250, the congregation rising to 500. This was partly due to preachers like GEORGE SHADFORD, JOSEPH PILMORE, RICHARD WHATCOAT (the American Methodist pioneer), and ADAM CLARKE, who were all stationed in Norwich in this period. John Wesley's last sermon in Norwich was preached in Cherry Lane in 1790, when he was eighty-seven. He wrote: "But the house would in no wise hold the congregation. How wonderfully is the tide turned. I am become an honourable man at Norwich."

By 1809 the problem of increasing numbers made a new place of worship necessary. A convenient site was found in nearby Calvert Street, and in June 1811 a capacious chapel was opened by THOMAS COKE. This building is still used for Methodist worship. A second chapel was soon needed, and in October 1824, St. Peter's Chapel, in Lady-Lane, was opened by ROBERT NEWTON, then president of the Wesleyan Methodist Conference. For some years it was said that no less than two thousand people attended Methodist services every Sunday; a third chapel, "New City," was opened in 1839, seating six hundred, in a populous district near St. Peter's. As a result, however, of the disastrous events of 1849 the Norwich Circuit was torn asunder. The excommunicated rebels, the WESLEYAN REFORMERS, made the Calvert Street Chapel their headquarters, taking over New City as well. Among their leaders were W. H. Cozens-Hardy, Robert Daws, and John Clarke, who left their mark on the public and religious life of Norwich.

The PRIMITIVE METHODIST connection had entered Norwich as far back as 1821; outstanding among them were ROBERT KEY and the woman traveling preacher ELIZABETH BULTITUDE. The Primitive Methodists divided the city among themselves, and in 1932 there were three separate circuits in Norwich.

From 1868 the WESLEYAN REFORM UNION, set up in 1859 by the Reformers who would not enter the UNITED METHODIST FREE CHURCHES in the union of 1857, has had a strong branch in the city.

Each section of Norwich Methodism for long had powerful Sunday schools. After the Union of 1932 there was a steady movement toward consolidation of Methodism in the city; the Primitive Methodist circuits disappeared as separate entities, and in 1966 there were only two circuits, the Calvert Street and St. Peter's Circuits, with sixteen and eighteen societies respectively. Norwich was a good example of the crippling effect which the mid-nineteenth century divisions had on the progress of Methodism; a new start has been made, however, since 1945.

W. A. GREEN

NORWOOD, FREDERICK ABBOTT (1914-   ), American minister, educator, and historian, was born in San Diego, Calif., on July 11, 1914, the son of Frederick A. and Florence (Abbott) Norwood. He received the B.A. degree from OHIO WESLEYAN in 1936; the B.D. from Yale in 1939; and a Ph.D. there in 1941. His wife, whom he married on June 14, 1943, was Florence Louise Corbett, and their children are Mary Beth and Pamela Zoe. Dr. Norwood joined the NORTH-EAST OHIO CONFERENCE in 1941, was ordained a deacon in 1943, and came into

full connection in 1944. He served for a time as a minister in OHIO, 1942-46, and then became the professor of history at BALDWIN-WALLACE COLLEGE, Berea, Ohio. 1946-52. He took the chair of church history at GARRETT THEOLOGICAL SEMINARY in Evanston, Ill., in 1952, and continues in that position.

He has been a member of the General Commission for the Methodist BICENTENNIAL, a Guggenheim Fellow, American Association of Theological Schools Fellow, and is the author of *The Reformation Refugees as an Economic Force*, 1942; *The Development of Modern Christianity*, 1956; *History of the North Indiana Conference, 1917-1956*, 1957; *Church Membership in the Methodist Tradition*, 1958; *Great Moments in Church History*, 1962, and *Strangers and Exiles*, a history of Religious Refugees, 2 vols. 1969. He was a member of the Editorial Board of *The History of American Methodism* and of *Methodist History*. He contributed the general article *Methodism* to the *Encyclopaedia Britannica* and numerous articles to professional Journals. He is upon the editorial board and supervisory committee of the *Encyclopedia of World Methodism*.

Who's Who in The Methodist Church, 1966.   N. B. H.

NOTSON, GARY THOMPSON (1865-1956), American M.E. minister and hospital administrator, was born near Lamoni, Decatur County, Iowa on Sept. 19, 1865. Educated in the public schools, he was active in the printing business until 1891 when he entered the ministry in the DES MOINES ANNUAL CONFERENCE. In 1893 he transferred to the DAKOTA ANNUAL CONFERENCE where he served churches at Flandreau, Sioux Falls, Elk Point, Centerville, Pierre and Alexandria until 1910. In that year he was appointed district superintendent of the Huron District, a position which he held until 1914.

Notson was active in the Church Federation of Dakota, the SOUTH DAKOTA Historical Society and as a trustee of DAKOTA WESLEYAN UNIVERSITY. His achievements were recognized in 1913 when Dakota Wesleyan conferred upon him an honorary D.D. In 1914 he became executive secretary for the newly organized Methodist State Hospital, Mitchell, S.D., and completed two financial campaigns for $100,000 and $80,000 so that the hospital was dedicated on Feb. 10, 1918. He continued in this position until 1920 when he transferred to the NORTHWEST IOWA ANNUAL CONFERENCE as superintendent of the Methodist Hospital, Sioux City. Here he raised some $500,000 for the work and remained in the post until 1938 when he accepted a retired relationship. In 1939 he returned to South Dakota as director of the Sanatorium and Hospital, a city institution in Chamberlain. He died on Dec. 2, 1956 in Sioux City, Iowa.

A Century of Methodism in South Dakota, 1860-1960. (Diamond Jubilee Booklet. Conference Historical Committee, 1960.)
M. D. Smith, *Circuit Riders of the Middle Border*. 1965.
C. F. Price, *Who's Who in American Methodism*. 1916.
Minutes of the North Iowa Annual Conference, 1957, pp. 259-260.   LOUIS A. HASELMAYER

NOTTINGHAM, England. One of England's smaller industrial towns, situated in the Midlands, Nottingham grew rapidly as a result of the eighteenth-century industrial expansion. The earliest record of Methodist activity there centers round a Mr. Howe, who preached at Nottingham

Cross and later at the house of Matthew Bagshaw in Crossland Yard, Narrow Marsh. The house had to be modified by removing the ceiling from the living room and allowing the men to sit upstairs and the ladies down, with the preacher perched on a chair on a table in the middle of the downstairs room.

JOHN WESLEY came himself to Nottingham in 1741, and though most accounts of that visit record his favorable impression of the countryside, few recall his observation made of the early Methodists in Nottingham: "I could not but observe . . . that when I began to pray there appeared to be a general surprise, none once offering to kneel down, and those who stood, choosing the most easy indolent posture which they conveniently could." However, Methodism grew considerably in the next twenty years and heard many of the well-known preachers, including JOHN NELSON and THOMAS COKE. In July, 1757, John Wesley remarked that what was needed most was a larger house. In 1764 the Octagon, or Tabernacle, was opened at a cost of £124. Nottingham at that time was under the Methodist direction of DERBY. In 1776 a separate Nottingham circuit was established. In 1777 there were 700 members; 1787, 800; 1791, 1,000; 1797, 1,400.

In 1783 the Tabernacle was sold to the General Baptists, and a new church at Hockley was opened. Linked to the opening of this church, which was to become the center of much controversy, is the name of a famous preacher in Nottingham, Thomas Tatham. Meanwhile, in 1796, ALEXANDER KILHAM was expelled from the Wesleyan connection for his publications regarding ecclesiastical polity. In 1797 the members of the Hockley church voted by 320 to 280 to follow him, and the trustees being in the majority group refused to receive preachers designated by the old connection. In a lengthy discussion between the friends of the METHODIST NEW CONNEXION and the friends of the old, the main object of the action taken by the trustees of the Hockley Church was to force the itinerant preachers to admit the People into the yearly Assembly. In spite of the threat of litigation, the Methodist New Connexion retained the use of Hockley Chapel, and the Wesleyan Methodists were obliged to meet temporarily at Beck Barn, and in 1799 to open a new church at Halifax place (thanks to Thomas Tatham). The two Methodist groups indulged in a great deal of wordy polemic through the next generation, but they thrived on it. In 1804 the new church at Halifax Place had to be enlarged; in 1816 the New Connexion built a new church in Parliament Street, and in 1818 Hockley was returned to the Wesleyans. In 1826 Parliament Street had to be enlarged, and in 1839 Wesley Chapel, Broad Street, was built. The controversial church at Hockley was then sold to the PRIMITIVE METHODISTS, who had entered Nottingham in 1815.

SARAH KIRKLAND, a famous woman evangelist, had first come to Nottingham to conduct open-air services in the forest. CAMP MEETINGS were held in Nottingham Forest (also known for its associations with Robin Hood), being led in by HUGH BOURNE and in 1818 by WILLIAM CLOWES. Room for the Primitive Methodists was found at the Old Factory, Broad Marsh (a room above a disused smithy); and there preparatory meetings were held before the Primitive Methodist Church was constituted formally in Nottingham in 1819. Nottingham remained a center of Primitive evangelism, William Clowes being sent from Hull to work there. In 1823 Canaan Street

Chapel was opened to seat nine hundred persons, built in what one commentator called the "barnic style." In 1839 they bought Hockley and created the second Nottingham circuit; Nottingham's third and fourth were created in 1877 (Forest Road), and 1889 (Mayfield Road), respectively, and by the time of METHODIST UNION in 1932 there were six Primitive Methodist circuits in and around the city.

In 1907, the Methodist New Connexion in Nottingham found added strength in union with the UNITED METHODIST FREE CHURCHES, which was fairly strong in the area. Perhaps the most important fact in their Nottingham history, however, was their loss, in the mid-nineteenth century, of the services of a young minister called WILLIAM BOOTH, who, either from inability to come to terms with the administration of the church, or through fear of being expelled from the connection as had been his former minister and friend, SAMUEL DUNN, resigned, and later became famous as General Booth, the founder of the Salvation Army.

By 1932 both the Wesleyans and the UNITED METHODIST CHURCH had four circuits in Nottingham, making fourteen in all with the Primitive Methodists. There were many small chapels that had been sponsored by businessmen for their employees; and though in 1935 the number of circuits was reduced to six, there still remained a problem of redundancy. None of the chapels existing today is of great age, and those with the longest history have been rebuilt since they were founded. Many have known a period of success when the seating was not adequate, and observers in the nineteenth century noted other inadequacies—for example, the ventilation: "What streams of condensed vapour, unable to escape into the common sewer of the open firmament, have been seen running down the chapel walls." The desire for greater comfort as the churches became more middle class—and in one case for "more commodious family pews"—led to the frequent modification and sometimes the demolition and reconstruction of the buildings. In 1902 the Wesleyan Methodists, moved by the FORWARD MOVEMENT, bought the Albert Hall to set up a Central Mission. Unfortunately, the building caught fire just after the purchase, and the project was almost dropped. However, money was found to restore the building and the hall finally opened in 1909.

Of all the churches in Nottingham the Albert Hall is now the best known. In 1956 a further improvement was the opening of Methodist International House to care especially for overseas students. The Methodist CONFERENCE was held in Nottingham in 1945 and 1957. The famous Faith and Order Conference—"Unity begins at Home"—which set before all the British churches the target of unification by 1980, was held at Nottingham in 1964.

Samuel Dunn, *Thomas Tatham.* 1847.
G. H. Harwood, *Nottingham.* 1872.　　　　JOHN DOLLING

NOVA SCOTIA. (See CANADA.)

NOYES, HENRY SANBORN (1822-1872), American scholar and University president, was born in Landaff, N. H., Dec. 24, 1822. While preparing for college at Newbury Seminary, Newbury, Vt., he served as assistant instructor in mathematics and Latin in 1845 and 1846. He graduated from WESLEYAN UNIVERSITY, Middletown,

Conn., in 1848, at which time he also was instructor at Springfield Wesleyan Seminary, Springfield, Vt. He returned to Newbury in 1850 to teach mathematics, Greek and German. In 1854 he became principal of Newbury Seminary and continued teaching Greek and moral philosophy. Henry Noyes and Harriet Verback, a student in the Seminary, were married Feb. 16, 1849. Mrs. Noyes subsequently became preceptress during her husband's administration.

Noyes was elected professor of mathematics at NORTHWESTERN UNIVERSITY, EVANSTON, Ill., in June 1854, but did not move to Evanston until June 1855. Noyes became the president of the University and held the post as manager, promoter and central figure of that institution for ten years. He died May 24, 1872.

As a scholar Henry Noyes was at home in several languages. He could recite long passages from Homer from memory, and it is said that at one time, while in Evanston, he heard a mathematics class in Greek. It was his custom to award diplomas to the graduating classes in Latin.

M. Simpson, *Cyclopaedia*. 1878.   ELDON H. MARTIN

NUELSEN, JOHN LOUIS (1867-1946), bishop, scholar and ecumenist, was the son of an American Methodist minister, Heinrich Nuelsen, who had emigrated from GERMANY in 1842 and served in Europe as a pastor from 1851-89. John Louis was born in ZURICH, SWITZERLAND, on Jan. 19, 1867. He shared in the itinerancy of the family and went to high school and junior college (Gymnasium) in Karlsruhe and Bremen, Germany. On the return to America, John Nuelsen started his studies at DREW UNIVERSITY, where he obtained his B.D. degree. After further academic training in the States, he pursued his study of theology at the German Universities of Berlin and Halle. There followed a period of ministerial work at Sedalia, Miss., after which he taught classical languages at the Methodist College in SAINT PAUL, Minn. Then for five years he taught exegetical theology at CENTRAL WESLEYAN COLLEGE, Warrenton, Miss. In 1899 he became theological professor at the Nast Theological Seminary in Berea, Ohio, where he taught both in German and in English for nine years, using both languages in his writings. Between 1896 and 1908 he published five books in German, and two in English—significantly one on Luther, and one, in 1908, on *Some Recent Phases of German Theology*.

By this time he had become widely known also through his addresses at SUNDAY SCHOOL and youth conventions and his Bible studies at CAMP MEETINGS. This may partially explain, why, at the age of forty-one, he was in 1908 elected bishop, being given episcopal supervision of the Omaha Area.

He proved to be an excellent administrator and parliamentarian. In 1912 he was sent to Europe to succeed Bishop WILLIAM BURT. With his office in Zurich he supervised the whole of Methodism in Europe and North Africa from that point. Two years later, World War I broke out and made work very difficult for him. He always regarded nationalism as a very real danger to Christianity. Even when he no longer had access to certain countries, he planned ahead what should be done after the war. It was then that his name became "known from Paris to Moscow, from Rome to Stockholm." His relief work, particularly for the children of the European coun-

tries, proved a magnificent contribution. This as well as his scholarly interpretation of the two continents each to the other, and his ecumenical spirit were the reasons why the University of Berlin conferred upon him the honorary degree of a theological doctor, through the hands of its famous dean and New Testament scholar, Professor Adolf Deissmann. This was a singular thing to happen to a Methodist and was the beginning of ecumenical acceptance. After the reorganization of Continental Methodism, Nuelsen became the bishop of the CENTRAL EUROPEAN CENTRAL CONFERENCE, which first met in 1925.

John Nuelsen was called a "Bridge builder" between Germany and America and a true ecumenist. In addition to his heavy load of administration and the traveling it demanded it is surprising how many books he published from 1920 onward. To a significant extent he wrote of Methodism and its role as a free church. But historical research engrossed him more and more. He edited and to a great degree himself wrote a fine volume in German on the history of Methodism (2 editions). Also valuable are his contributions on JOHN WESLEY and the German hymns; and on JOHN WILLIAM FLETCHER (1929). His book on the ORDINATION in Methodism (1935), suggested as a subject by J. W. E. SOMMER, became influential in molding German and European thought on the theology of ordination, and the concept of one ordination only. It is due to him and J. W. E. Sommer that the Germany Central Conference knows only one ordination (since 1948). As an ecumenist Nuelsen contributed largely to overcome state church prejudice against what had been called "sectarian" Methodism. As an excellent theologian, an aristocratic leader of people and a tireless pastor of pastors he possessed profile and gained admiration and affection. He retired in May, 1939, after the Uniting Conference held in Kansas City. Four years after he retired he died in Bethesda Hospital, CINCINNATI, Ohio.

F. Wunderlich, *Methodists Linking Two Continents*. 1960.
C. ERNST SOMMER

NUREMBERG, Germany, is one of the old historic cities of Europe. The circuits established there are in the South Germany Annual Conference. British Wesleyan and the Episcopal Methodism of the United States both started work about the same time in Nuremberg. In 1875 the Wesleyan ministers, Beutenmueller from Munich, and Boettcher from Kirchberg/Jagst, visited Nuremberg to give religious addresses. On Jan. 1, 1877, J. J. Sommer took over the Wesleyan mission, and a month and a half later founded a local church with seven members.

The M.E. Church (U.S.A.), after the GENERAL CONFERENCE of 1876, sent J. Zipperer to Nuremberg in order to find out whether the city was suitable for missionary enterprise. On Nov. 2, 1876, J. Kaufmann took over; and in February 1877, a church was founded and four people were received as members. At the Annual Conference of 1877, eighteen probationary members were reported. This evangelistic work radiated to many small towns and villages, but owing to state church opposition, only a few congregations were gathered.

The Wesleyan Church dedicated St. Paul's Chapel on Feb. 9, 1890, the first Methodist church building in Bavaria. It was within the bounds of this circuit that J. G. Ekert in 1889 founded the deaconess mother-house, Martha-Maria. The Zion's Church of the Episcopal Meth-

MARTHA MARY HOSPITAL, NUREMBERG, GERMANY

odist branch was dedicated in 1893. Both churches and the deaconess mother-house were destroyed during the Second World War on Jan. 2, 1945. The deaconess mother-house was rebuilt as Bavaria's most modern hospital (350 beds) from 1950-1969.

A new Zion's Church was dedicated on Nov. 5, 1950; a new St. Paul's Church on Jan. 31, 1954. The EVANGELISCHE GEMEINSCHAFT (EUB) also founded a congregation in Nuremberg. Members were looked after by the minister of Aalen from 1931 to 1948, and after 1948 by the minister of Munich. In February 1951, a congregation was founded by R. Kohlenbrenner and in 1956 a sanctuary was built at Humboldtstrasse. The congregation grew up to 100 members counting adherents. In connection with the union resulting in the United Methodist Church, this group became part of St. Paul's congregation. Both circuits are missionary minded, and at present have a total constituency of over 1,600.

Martha-Maria Deaconess Hospital (Mutter-haus Diakonie) at Nuremberg, is a well-equipped and well-staffed hospital and nursing home, situated on spacious grounds a little way out of the city. It has an excellent nursing corps and has quarters in its impressive main building for retired deaconesses as well as for those who give their lives in active service for their ministry of health and healing. Martha-Maria enjoys a deserved prestige both in its own community and all over Germany wherever its work has come to be known.

PAUL ERNST HAMMER
N. B. H.

NUTTALL, EZRA (1850-1915), South African Wesleyan missionary was born in England on Nov. 4, 1850. His family was Anglican and a brother, Enos, became Archbishop of the West Indies. Ezra Nuttall entered the ministry in 1871 and came to SOUTH AFRICA in 1875. He established a teachers' training and industrial institution for Africans at Edendale near Pietermaritzburg in Natal (which later became known by his name) and served in white circuits in Durban, Cape Town and East London. He was chairman in succession of the Natal, Cape of Good Hope and Queenstown districts, secretary of the South African Conference from 1901 to 1903, president of the Conference in 1895 and 1904, and was elected to be president of the Conference in 1916, the centenary year of South African Methodism, but died before assuming office on November 23, 1915. He was a powerful preacher, an able administrator and faithful friend of the African and Coloured peoples of South Africa.

Minutes of the South African Conference, 1916.

E. LYNN CRAGG

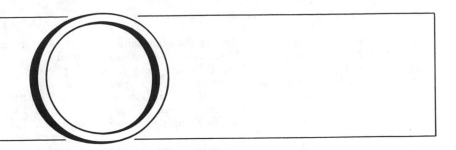

OAK RIDGE INSTITUTE, Oak Ridge, N. C., though not a denominational school, was for many years closely associated and identified with the NORTH CAROLINA CONFERENCE of the M.P. Church. From 1884 until 1915 it was owned and operated by Professors John Allen Holt and Martin Hicks Holt, brothers who were prominent Methodist Protestants. Most of the families in the Oak Ridge community were members of the Methodist Protestant faith and in 1889 a M.P. church was built on the grounds of the school.

The Institute was established in 1852 and prior to the War Between the States its course of study was largely oriented around the preparation of students for advanced classes at the University of North Carolina. In 1879 John Allen Holt was joined by Martin Hicks Holt, and not long afterward the trustees leased the school to the two brothers. In 1884 the Holts bought the school and in the same year a chapel and Literary Society Halls were built. In 1892 Holt Hall, with classrooms, a library, gymnasium, YMCA room and museum, was built. Benbow Hall for boarding students was built in 1905.

In 1889 there were 253 students of both sexes from several states and in 1908 there were nearly 300 students from many states and several foreign countries. The school was considered to be one of the best preparatory schools in the South and in 1898 was referred to as "the largest and best equipped Fitting School in the South." It trained hundreds of teachers for the public schools during the late nineteenth and early twentieth centuries, and there was a standing offer of free tuition to ministerial students of the M.P. denomination.

On Jan. 17, 1914, the Oak Ridge Chapel and many of the main buildings were burned. Following the deaths of Professor Martin Hicks Holt on Nov. 26, 1914, and Professor John Allen Holt on June 15, 1915, the alumni of Oak Ridge Institute rebuilt the school with each donor receiving a share or more of stock in a private corporation. The present-day institution, known as "Oak Ridge Military Institute," is governed by a board of trustees and its assets are operated through a nonprofit Oak Ridge Foundation.

J. Elwood Carroll, *History of the North Carolina Annual Conference of the Methodist Protestant Church.* Greensboro, 1939.
Journal of the North Carolina Conference, MP, 1906, 1910, 1915.
Our Church Record, June 23, 1898.
The Rocky Mount (N. C.) *Telegram*, Sept. 1, 1966.

RALPH HARDEE RIVES

OAKLAND, CALIFORNIA, U.S.A., population 358,486, was established in 1852, as a major port and transportation center at the east end of the SAN FRANCISCO Bay Bridge. Contiguous cities are Berkeley and Richmond to the north, Alameda, San Leandro and Hayward to the south. The first Methodist services were held in 1856

and the first Methodist church was organized in 1862 by C. E. Rich.

California College, established by Congregationalists and Presbyterians, became the University of California in 1868 under Oliver Fitzgerald, Methodist minister and state superintendent of public instruction. The East Oakland Church originated out of First Church in 1874 but was reunited in 1959 as First Church and became "one church with two locations" (913 members).

Southern Methodism came in fairly early and had one church. The fifteen Methodist churches extant in 1970 (5,034 members) include Chinese, Korean, Japanese, Filipino and two Negro congregations. Taylor Memorial (Negro) is largest in membership (1,342), Down's Memorial (Negro) is third in size (660). Neither was ever in the Central Jurisdiction. Former Portuguese, German and Norwegian-Danish congregations became the base for Good Shepherd, Montclair and Lake Park churches. Fred Finch Children's Home, seventy-five years old, is now serving disturbed teenagers. Two retirement homes are operated: Beulah and the new Lake Park. In 1863 the A.M.E. CHURCH purchased a former site of First Church. The Negro population was quite small until World War II but is now large and growing. There are two A.M.E., one C.M.E., one A.M.E. ZION churches. Forty percent of the city's population is composed of minority groups. There are no Free Methodists or Wesleyans at present.

Fred Finch Children's Home is a child care agency of the CALIFORNIA-NEVADA CONFERENCE of The United Methodist Church.

Captain and Mrs. Duncan Finch, active members of First Church, Oakland, gave the acreage on which it is built, known as the Brooklyn Fruit Ranch, in memory of their son, Fred. On Sept. 10, 1891, the California Conference and Lay Association of the M.E. Church officially received the gift and authorized the establishing of the Fred Finch Orphanage.

This agency of the Church has a distinctive record of changing services to keep pace with each transitional need of society. In 1936 the name was properly changed to the Fred Finch Children's Home. In 1961 the agency established a residential, psychiatric treatment facility for the emotionally disturbed adolescent, with consultation and therapy to the families of youth in residence.

CHARLES EDWIN LORD
HAROLD R. BARNES

OBERLIN, PENNSYLVANIA, U.S.A. **Neidig Memorial Church** is the oldest congregation of the former E.U.B. Church east of the Susquehanna, and one of the oldest in the entire denomination.

It is not exactly known when the people who were to be referred to as *Neidig's Leute* (Neidig's People) first gathered together in one another's homes for worship. Presumably this was about 1790, when JOHN NEIDIG, SR., was chosen by lot to be a preacher among the Mennonites. They erected their first house of worship in 1793, as documents prepared by Neidig himself record both the cost of the building and the subscriptions secured to pay for the building. However, the record of the transaction which secured their land from John Roop for five shillings was not filed in the Recorder's Office of Dauphin County until Aug. 4, 1803.

The building erected in 1793 was constructed of stone and measured about thirty by forty feet. The interior was plain and contained only a table along one wall, and chairs for the members of the congregation. It is said that as the building was going up, a cynical bystander remarked that "a house about the size of a corn crib would accommodate them for all time to come." It really appeared that this cynical remark might be fulfilled for as late as 1852 the Quarterly Conference minutes listed only twenty-four members in the class, in spite of the fact that a larger frame building had been erected in 1850 to replace the original building. However, by 1887 the situation had changed. What had once been open country was now a small town, and a new and larger building was erected in 1887. This has been added to on several occasions since then. The most recent addition is the education unit and children's chapel constructed in 1961. In 1970 Neidig Church had a membership of 381.

P. B. Gibble, *East Pennsylvania Conference*, UB. 1951.

BRUCE C. SOUDERS

O'BRYAN, WILLIAM (1778-1868), British founder of BIBLE CHRISTIANS was born Feb. 6, 1778, at Gunwen, Luxulian, Cornwall. He became a Wesleyan LOCAL PREACHER in 1802. His preaching was attended by extraordinary outpourings of spiritual power, and he established many causes. In 1814 he relinquished his business to devote himself entirely to preaching, and evangelized much of North Devon and Cornwall. Twice expelled from Methodism for excessive zeal, in October 1815, he formed an independent society thus founding the Bible Christian connection. In time, however, his authoritarian rule as president of the Conference aroused resistance, though he continued to be loved and revered. Leaving the connection, he went to America in 1831 and served in NEW YORK and CANADA. He paid six visits to England, the last in 1861, when he preached in many Bible Christian chapels. He died Jan. 8, 1868, and was buried in Greenwood Cemetery, Brooklyn, N. Y.

A. W. G. COURT

OCALA, FLORIDA, U.S.A. **First Church** probably originated in the work of John L. Jerry, who was sent in 1827 to serve St. Augustine and Alachua Mission. This was the official beginning of Methodist work in north central FLORIDA. The southern point of this circuit "250 miles around" was Fort King, which had been established in 1825 as an Indian agency, and became in 1827 a military post.

A post office was established in Marion County in 1845, and was designated Ocala in 1847. The Camp King Mission was set up by the GEORGIA CONFERENCE in 1844, in the Newnansville District. The Board of Managers of the Missionary Society of the FLORIDA CONFERENCE reported on April 4, 1845: "Camp King Mission: This mission was under the pastoral care of Rev. E. L. T. Blake;

has 74 white and 18 colored members, and promises much good."

The Ocala Circuit and Marion Mission were placed in the newly created TAMPA District in 1852. In 1867 the Ocala District was organized, and maintained for two years. In 1880, during the second year of the pastorate of H. E. Partridge, the Ocala church became a station appointment, with forty-nine members. This was increased to seventy-nine at the close of 1881.

The first church building was erected in 1850 to be replaced by a rather large church edifice in 1890. This served until the present sanctuary was erected in 1952, under the pastorate of George A. Foster. The Mabel Rich Educational Building was added in 1967, while Bruce F. Gannaway served as pastor.

First Church has grown to a membership of 2,308 with property valued at almost $1,000,000. It is credited with advance gifts of close to $25,000, including full support of a missionary couple.

BRUCE F. GANNAWAY

OCEAN CITY, NEW JERSEY, U.S.A., a resort town in Cape May County, was founded on Sept. 10, 1879, by a group of Methodists interested in establishing "a Christian Seaside Resort." On Oct. 20, 1879, the Ocean City Association was incorporated. The following year the Ocean City Tabernacle Association, a permanent organization which is still active, was established to preserve the "ideals of the founders."

In the same year, 1880, the present **First Church,** Ocean City, first called St. Peter's M.E. Church, was organized.

Church services were held from 1880 to 1883 in a hall, and later in the local school building. The cornerstone of the original frame church building was laid on Aug. 20, 1880. This building was replaced in 1908 by a stone structure which is still in use. Since 1956 a new educational building has been erected and the sanctuary greatly enlarged and renovated.

Through the years of Ocean City's history there has been a sincere attempt to retain the Christian atmosphere which characterized the original founding of the city. Moderate Sunday closing laws have been consistently maintained, though not without struggle and effort. The sale of alcoholic beverages has never been permitted within the city limits. Special religious services flourish during the summer season. Both the Ocean City Tabernacle Association and First Methodist Church sponsor services in Boardwalk Theatres on Sunday evening. The Tabernacle Association also holds two Sunday morning services in its own building and sponsors a week-long "CAMP MEETING."

Since 1942 the NEW JERSEY ANNUAL CONFERENCE has held its annual sessions in Ocean City. In 1944 Ocean City was the site of the Northeastern JURISDICTIONAL CONFERENCE of The Methodist Church.

F. B. Stanger, *New Jersey.* 1961.
J. Ellis Voss, *Ocean City.* A. Dhor Company, 1941.

FRANK BATEMAN STANGER

OCEAN GROVE, NEW JERSEY, U.S.A., was founded in 1869 and obtained a charter from the NEW JERSEY legislature as the Ocean Grove Camp Meeting Association of The M.E. Church. That charter empowered the original twenty-six trustees and their successors (thirteen ministers and thirteen laymen) to acquire land, build, and establish a "convenient and permanent" Christian seaside resort and camp meeting.

From early June until after Labor Day, the Ocean Grove program embraces youth meetings, Bible classes, preaching missions, Sunday school classes, religious and cultural movies, concerts, organ recitals, religious drama, and twice every Sunday worship services in the great auditorium. The season is climaxed by what has become famous as the Ocean Grove camp meeting—a ten day evangelic program, concluding Labor Day Sunday.

Many religious conferences hold their annual sessions here. One thing for which Ocean Grove is particularly well known is the Sunday rules. These include a rule barring traffic and all automobiles must be off the streets before midnight Saturday and until midnight Sunday so that on the Sabbath the twenty miles of Ocean Grove streets are devoid of cars. The calm and quiet are almost unimaginable! Most persons park their cars in the perimeter parking lots.

The title to all property within the limits of Ocean Grove remains with the Association. It does not sell property outright, but it does lease home lots to individuals under 99-year renewable contracts. These leases cannot be assigned except to persons vouched for as to good moral character and in sympathy with Ocean Grove's purposes. As a result, Ocean Grove reserves its lands for its chartered purposes—Christian experience.

V. B. Hampton, *Newark Conference.* 1957.
Mrs. W. B. Osborn, *Pioneer Days of Ocean Grove.* New York: Methodist Book Concern, n.d.　　　Kinsey N. Merritt

ODA, KANEO (1902-1965), first bishop of the Japan Free Methodist Church, was converted to Christianity while in high school. At the age of seventeen he felt called to the ministry. He graduated from Osaka Seminary, studied in Seattle Pacific College, and completed work for his doctorate at San Francisco Theological Seminary.

Appointed a missionary to China by the Japan Free Methodist Church in 1939, he established a thriving congregation in Peking. Repatriated in 1946, he was elected superintendent of the Japan Conference.

Conference superintendent and bishop, professor and college president, evangelist, able interpreter and translator, Oda made a valuable contribution to the Free Methodist Church and the Christian movement in Japan. He was one of the first to propose a world-wide organization of Free Methodist churches. He served on the planning committees and was the first vice-president of the Free Methodist World Fellowship which was organized Jan. 12, 1962. He died in Osaka, Japan, Feb. 28, 1965.

Byron S. Lamson

ODELL, DONALD A. (See Judicial Council.)

ODESSA, TEXAS, U.S.A. **First Church** has grown to become one of the greatest churches among the plains cities of western Texas. In September of 1900, a group of Methodists began holding services in a little Baptist church building in Odessa. The First Methodist Church was formally organized in January of 1901, with thirty-eight charter members, during the pastorate of T. L. Lallance. For a time services were held in the Ector County Courthouse, and then the members returned to

the Baptist church building, where services were held until the first Methodist building was erected on its present site in 1908. A new brick structure was erected in 1938, and an educational building added in 1948. In 1949 a new sanctuary was built at a cost of $150,000, and educational facilities expanded in 1962.

On Nov. 12, 1965, the entire church plant was completely destroyed by fire. The congregation banded together to meet the challenge of the days of hardship caused by the fire, have completed what they feel to be one of the most beautiful and serviceable churches in the southwest. The church listed 2,390 members in 1970.

General Minutes.

OESCHGER, OLIN EMERSON (1906-　　　), church administrator and General Secretary of the Board of Hospitals and Homes of The Methodist Church, was born on April 19, 1906, in Bay Port, Mich. He was educated at North Central College (A.B., 1927); University of Michigan (M.A., 1928); Illinois Wesleyan University (L.H.D., 1958). He married Marie M. Finkbeiner in 1932, and they have one daughter. He was for a time in the business office of the University of Michigan Hospital at Ann Arbor, Mich. Then he became the administrative assistant and personnel director of the Board of Hospitals and Homes of The Methodist Church from 1945-56, when he was elected General Secretary of that Board. He served on many important committees of his church and was chairman of the Joint Committee on Hospitals and Homes of The Methodist Church, and of the E.U.B. Church; on the Committee of Aging of the National Social Welfare Assembly; on the Association of Church Social Workers (former treasurer); American Hospital Association, and American Protestant Hospital Association.

As General Secretary Dr. Oeschger was responsible for administering the work of this coordinating, standardizing and consultative agency for more than 280 affiliated hospitals and homes located in forty-one states. He retired on March 31, 1969.

Who's Who in The Methodist Church, 1966.

OFFICIAL BOARD. This was the name of the administrative agency in each local church in the later years of American Methodism. It was composed of the stewards, trustees, and other church officials, and met apart from the Quarterly Conference and at more regular times —usually monthly. It was really the executive arm of the Quarterly Conference, and that Conference was counted on to approve actions of the Board that might need overall authority, since the members of the official board largely comprised the Quarterly Conference also.

In time, the Quarterly Conference was allowed to delegate some of its elective power to the Official Board, and in the latter days of The Methodist Church, the various commissions of the Church created by the Quarterly Conference were directed to report to the Official Board.

The name Official Board was done away in the *Discipline* of 1968—the term Administrative Board being adopted by The United Methodist Church. But the term "official board" is still freely used. Methodist bodies other than The United Methodist Church continue to use the name Official Board for the same type of local church agency.

Disciplines.   N. B. H.

OFFICIAL FORMS AND RECORDS, COMMITTEE ON, an office created within The Methodist Church in 1940 in order to correlate and produce a uniform system of records for reporting church statistics. Since 1952 it has been a committee of the COUNCIL ON WORLD SERVICE AND FINANCE. The membership has varied from five to the present eleven and includes a bishop, six Council members, an Annual Conference secretary, treasurer and statistician, and a district superintendent, with additional consultants. The initial work of the committee was correlating the different systems of records and forms of the churches forming The Methodist Church. The Committee meets annually, with an extended meeting at the beginning of each quardrennium to make major changes which may be necessary in report forms for the quadrennium.

The Committee cooperates with the General Agencies of the church in determining the contents of various reports, but final determination of the reports is the responsibility of the committee. This is true of all official reports except those in use in the local church school and by the Woman's Division. Official forms and records include quarterly conference reports, pastors' reports to the Annual Conference, local church financial and membership records and other forms helpful to pastors and bishops. The METHODIST PUBLISHING HOUSE prints all official forms and records.

OGDEN, BENJAMIN (1764-1834), American pioneer preacher of KENTUCKY and the Cumberland Valley, was born in NEW JERSEY, April, 1764. At an early age he was a soldier in the Revolutionary War. He embraced religion in 1784, the year the M.E. Church was organized. In 1786 he was one of the first two preachers appointed to Kentucky (both the same year). In 1787 he formed the Cumberland Circuit in the wilderness, the first preacher appointed there. At the end of the year he reported sixty-three members. The early Cumberland Circuit included NASHVILLE and all the forts and settlements on the north side of the Cumberland River, in the area between what later was Gallatin on the east and Clarksville on the west; it included some preaching points in adjoining sections of Kentucky.

In 1788 Ogden married Nancy Puckett of Mercer County, Ky., and went to VIRGINIA. He returned to the West in 1790 and continued to live there. For a while he withdrew from the Methodists.

However, he was again licensed to preach, re-admitted to the KENTUCKY CONFERENCE, and appointed in 1816 to Henderson Circuit. In 1817 he was again found in the traveling connection, but he soon sank a second time under the pressure of ill health but again reappeared in active service in 1824. For three years he did effective work on the Tennessee Mission, the Christian, and the Yellow Banks Circuits. In 1827 he took his place upon the superannuated list where he remained until his death.

Benjamin Ogden died, a member of the conference, at the residence of his son near Princeton, N. J., Nov. 20, 1834. Dying in peace after a life of suffering, he was buried near Princeton.

A plain, strong, effective preacher, Ogden did much to establish the Kentucky Conference. He engaged in missionary labors, and endured great hardship in preaching the gospel throughout the Mississippi Valley and to some of the Indian tribes.

The Kentucky Historical Society on Sept. 14, 1969, erected a highway marker to Benjamin Ogden. Harry R. Short, historian of the LOUISVILLE CONFERENCE of The United Methodist Church, provided a brochure to be used on that occasion. The marker is as follows:

BENJAMIN OGDEN
Methodism's First Western Cavalier
1764-1834
First Methodist Preacher
Sent To Kentucky
1786
"No man should be sent to this field
who is afraid to die."

W. E. Arnold, *Kentucky.* 1935-36.
E. S. Bucke, *History of American Methodism.* 1964.
Conference *Minutes,* 1836, p. 405.
Benjamin Ogden, Methodism's First Western Cavalier, 1764-1834. (Brochure, written to be read at the unveiling of a highway marker erected by the Kentucky Historical Society, September 14, 1969, Harry R. Short, Historian of the Louisville Conference.)
M. Simpson, *Cyclopaedia.* 1878.   JESSE A. EARL

OGLESBY, JOSEPH (1782-1852), American pioneer preacher, was born in Virginia. He was admitted to the WESTERN CONFERENCE on trial in 1803 and was appointed with John Sale that year to the Miami Circuit in OHIO. In 1804 he was assigned to ILLINOIS Circuit. While on this circuit, he crossed into MISSOURI and preached in the Murphy Settlement, now Farmington, Mo. He "reconnoitred the Missouri country to the extremity of the settlements and had the pleasure of seeing the mighty hunter, Daniel Boone."

In 1806 the Whitewater Valley was organized into a circuit called the Whitewater Circuit. Oglesby was appointed to that newly formed circuit in the Ohio District.

Located in 1809 on account of his poor health, Oglesby, a man of superior talent, reentered the conference in 1811 and located again in 1815. Readmitted to the INDIANA CONFERENCE in 1832, he was appointed presiding elder of the Bloomington District in 1834, serving for two years. Very popular among the early inhabitants, Joseph Oglesby traveled extensively through Indiana, Illinois and Missouri. An able administrator, acute thinker and effective preacher, he died in 1852.

E. S. Bucke, *History of American Methodism.* 1964.
M. Simpson, *Cyclopaedia.* 1878.   JESSE A. EARL

OGLETHORPE, JAMES EDWARD (1696-1785), British philanthropist, prison reformer, and founder and first governor (1732-33) of the colony of GEORGIA in North America, approached JOHN WESLEY in 1735 to go as Anglican minister to the new colony. Wesley went as a missionary for the Society for Propagation of the Gospel, while CHARLES WESLEY accompanied him as Secretary for Indian Affairs and personal secretary to Oglethorpe. During their stay in Georgia (1736-37) the Wesleys became personally unpopular with the colonists and their relationship with Oglethorpe was often strained.

T. SCOTT

OHIO is a north central state which is bounded on the north by MICHIGAN and Lake Erie, on the east by PENNSYLVANIA and WEST VIRGINIA, on the south by WEST Virginia and KENTUCKY, and on the west by INDIANA. Its area is 41,222 square miles and its population is 10,542,000 (1970). Ohio is the nation's third greatest industrial state, with countless industries which manufacture products that touch almost every American household. It leads in the production of tires, machine tools, business machines, glassware, and other items. It produces much steel, lime, coal, and coke. Also, Ohio is one of the wealthier agricultural states; its farm products are valued at more than $1,200,000,000 per year. The state has 100 institutions of higher learning, including four Methodist schools. Admitted to the Union in 1803, Ohio was the first state to be carved out of the Northwest Territory which was formed by Congress in 1787.

The first large scale settlement in Ohio was developed prior to 1785 in what was then Indian territory. Located near Martins Ferry, the village was declared illegal by the national government and the people were ordered to vacate the place. The settlers refused to leave; their situation was relieved when the Northwest Territory was formed.

The first Methodist sermon in Ohio was delivered by George Callahan in September, 1787. Callahan was one of the preachers on the Ohio Circuit located in VIRGINIA (now West Virginia) between WHEELING and PITTSBURGH. By invitation he preached in a log blockhouse at a place then called Carpenter's Station in Jefferson County, Ohio. Backwoodsmen armed with rifles, tomahawks, and scalping knives stood guard against a possible Indian attack while Callahan preached. Callahan promised to return. In 1793, Francis Clark, a local Methodist preacher who had served in Kentucky, preached to a few people at Fort Washington where CINCINNATI now stands.

The first Methodist society in Ohio was organized by Francis McCormick at Milford near what is now Cincinnati in 1797 or early 1798. Beginning with ten members, by fall the society grew to thirty-two; later it included the famous PHILIP GATCH and several of his family. McCormick held services in different places and soon organized two more classes. He appealed to the Kentucky preachers for help, but they had no ministers to spare. In 1798 Bishop ASBURY appointed JOHN KOBLER as presiding elder in Kentucky with instructions to go and form a circuit in Ohio. Kobler labored nine months and established a circuit up the two Miami Rivers toward DAYTON. In 1799 Lewis Hunt was appointed to the Miami Circuit, but his health failed and he was succeeded by Henry Smith whose name appears in the *General Minutes* as the first appointment in Ohio. Smith formed the Scioto Circuit some 400 miles in extent, and in 1800 he led in erecting the first Methodist church building in Ohio, a structure twenty-four feet square, located on Scioto Brush Creek in Adams County. The building was used for 20 years. The renowned PETER CARTWRIGHT was appointed to the Scioto Circuit in 1805, and to the Marietta Circuit in 1806. Appointed to a charge in Kentucky in 1807, he did not serve in Ohio again.

The Deerfield church in the Western Reserve, organized in 1801, is probably the oldest continuing Methodist congregation in Ohio. It was organized by Henry Shewell, a blind local preacher.

From the time Methodism began in Ohio down to 1812, the work in the eastern part of the state was attached to the BALTIMORE CONFERENCE, while that in the west was included in the WESTERN CONFERENCE. The 1812 GENERAL CONFERENCE created the OHIO CONFERENCE to include Ohio and eastern Kentucky. The first session of the Ohio Conference was held in October of that year at Chillicothe with Bishops Asbury and McKENDREE in charge. The conference began with sixty-one preachers and 23,644 members.

In 1816 the Salt River District of the Ohio Conference went to the TENNESSEE CONFERENCE. In 1820 the KENTUCKY CONFERENCE was formed. When the PITTSBURGH CONFERENCE was created in 1824 it included the part of Ohio east of the Muskingum and Tuscarawas Rivers. In 1836 the Ohio Conference was divided to form the MICHIGAN CONFERENCE, the latter including a part of northern Ohio as well as Michigan. In that same year extreme northeastern Ohio was taken from the Pittsburgh Conference and placed in the newly created ERIE CONFERENCE. In 1840 the Michigan Conference was divided to form the NORTH OHIO CONFERENCE.

In 1852 the Ohio Conference was again divided to form the CINCINNATI CONFERENCE which included southwest Ohio and such work as the M.E. Church then had in Kentucky. In 1856 the North Ohio Conference was divided to form the Delaware Conference, the territory of the new body being northwest Ohio. After four years the name of the Delaware Conference was changed to the CENTRAL OHIO CONFERENCE.

The next change in boundaries came in 1876 when the Ohio parts of the Erie and Pittsburgh Conferences were detached and merged to form the EAST OHIO CONFERENCE. In 1912 the East Ohio and North Ohio Conferences merged to form the NORTH-EAST OHIO CONFERENCE. In 1913 the Central Ohio and the Cincinnati Conferences merged to form the West Ohio Conference. Then in 1928 the West Ohio Conference was absorbed by the Ohio Conference. The Ohio and North-East Ohio Conferences continued in The Methodist Church in 1939.

In 1940 the two Ohio conferences became an episcopal area with the bishop's residence at COLUMBUS. Then in 1964 the North Central JURISDICTIONAL CONFERENCE designated each Ohio conference as an episcopal area, calling them the Ohio East and Ohio West Areas, with the episcopal residences in CANTON and Columbus. In 1964 the Ohio Conferences received some ministers and churches from the LEXINGTON CONFERENCE (CJ) as that body (excepting its Kentucky work) was absorbed by the overlying conferences of the North Central Jurisdiction.

The organization of the Missionary Society of the M.E. Church in 1819 grew out of missionary endeavor in Ohio. In 1816 JOHN STEWART, a free Negro from Virginia, felt impelled to go and preach to the Indians. Through an interpreter he preached to the WYANDOT INDIANS in Upper Sandusky. His work was so successful that it aroused interest in missions and led to the organization of the Missionary Society. The little church which the Wyandot Indians left when they were moved west in the 1840's is now a national Methodist historic SHRINE.

The work of the M.E. Church among the Germans began in Ohio. In January, 1835 WILLIAM NAST, the "Father of German Methodism," was converted in a revival meeting in Danville, Ohio. At the meeting of the

Ohio Conference in August of that year Nast was appointed a missionary to the Germans. The German work soon spread to other states, and in 1864 the General Conference authorized a system of German-speaking annual conferences which continued for about sixty years.

Ohio Methodism was in the forefront in establishing institutions of higher learning. Before the rise of public high schools, the church operated academies as well as colleges. Prior to 1884 the M.E. Church in Ohio owned and controlled eleven academies and was related to nine others. In 1968 Ohio Methodism had four colleges, three of them over 100 years old. OHIO WESLEYAN UNIVERSITY was founded at Delaware in 1842, and BALDWIN-WALLACE COLLEGE began at Berea in 1845. MOUNT UNION COLLEGE at Alliance opened in 1846. OHIO NORTHERN UNIVERSITY was established at Ada in 1871. The Ohio conferences now maintain WESLEY FOUNDATIONS at six state supported schools. The 1956 General Conference authorized the building of two new theological seminaries, and the METHODIST THEOLOGICAL SCHOOL IN OHIO opened at Delaware in the fall of 1960. Ohio Methodists contributed more than $4,000,000 to help launch the institution. Then in 1965 the Ohio churches gave $7,000,000 more for the four Methodist colleges and the six Wesley Foundations in the state.

The Western Edition of the *Christian Advocate* was published in Cincinnati from 1834 to 1940. Beginning with THOMAS A. MORRIS in 1836, several of its editors were elected bishops.

Ohio Methodism owns, operates, or is related to a number of service institutions. There are seven homes for the aged: Bethesda Home, Wesley Home on College Hill, and Wesley Hall in Cincinnati; Crestview at Sylvania; Elyria Methodist Home; Wesley Glen at Columbus; Cope Methodist Home at Sebring; and Healthaven Nursing Home near Akron. The conferences are related to six hospitals: Bethesda and the Christ Hospital in Cincinnati, Flower Hospital at Toledo, Lake Park Hospital at Sylvania, Riverside Hospital at Columbus, and St. Luke's Hospital at Cleveland. Two homes for children are maintained: Berea Methodist Children's Home, and the Methodist Home for Children in Worthington.

The Mill Men's Hostel in Steubenville is an unconventional means of evangelism. The hostel serves both labor and management at the entrance to a large steel company. Steelworkers come in to read, chat, or seek counseling from the minister-director.

Ohio Methodism supports LAKESIDE on Lake Erie, one of the largest summer assembly grounds in the church. Dating back to an old time camp meeting in 1842, Lakeside continues its tradition of combining religion, education, culture, and recreation in its program.

Ohio Methodism has furnished leadership for the larger church. Sixteen members of the Ohio conferences have been elected bishop: Thomas A. Morris (1836), LEONIDAS L. HAMLINE (1844), EDWARD THOMSON (1864), STEPHEN M. MERRILL and WILLIAM L. HARRIS 1874), JOHN M. WALDEN (1884), ISAAC W. JOYCE (1888), WILLIAM F. McDOWELL (1904), WILBUR P. THIRKIELD (1912), HERBERT WELCH (1916), E. L. WALDORF (1920), WILBUR E. HAMMAKER (1936), SCHUYLER E. GARTH (1944), HAZEN G. WERNER (1948), F. GERALD ENSLEY (1952), and LANCE WEBB (1964). Nineteen other men who were born in Ohio have been elevated to the episcopacy while serving as members of conferences in other states or on the mission field: MATTHEW SIMPSON, EDWARD R. AMES,

RANDOLPH S. FOSTER, JAMES M. THOBURN, EARL CRANSTON, CHARLES C. McCABE, DAVID H. MOORE, MERRIMAN C. HARRIS, NAPHTALI LUCCOCK, FRANCIS J. McCONNELL, ADNA W. LEONARD, FRANKLIN E. C. HAMILTON, LAURESS J. BIRNEY, RALPH A. WARD, BRUCE R. BAXTER, CHARLES W. BRASHARES, HOBART B. AMSTUTZ, LLOYD C. WICKE, and RALPH T. ALTON.

Ohio Methodism produced such able leaders as RALPH E. DIFFENDORFER, missionary executive, and ERNEST FREMONT TITTLE and RALPH W. SOCKMAN, outstanding preachers.

Several important Methodist movements originated in Ohio. The FREEDMEN'S AID SOCIETY was organized in Cincinnati in 1866, the WOMAN'S HOME MISSIONARY SOCIETY in the same city in 1880, and the EPWORTH LEAGUE in Cleveland in 1889.

METHODIST PROTESTANTISM was relatively strong in Ohio. The OHIO CONFERENCE was organized Oct. 15, 1829 at Cincinnati with ASA SHINN as president. Appointments were made to twenty-two charges at the first session. At the outset the conference comprised the entire west in its territory and it was thus the nucleus of a number of M.P. conferences. In 1833 the Ohio Conference reported 10,348 members, and at that time it was divided to form the PITTSBURGH CONFERENCE which included Ohio east of the Scioto and Sandusky Rivers. In 1842 the Ohio part of the Pittsburgh Conference (MP) was designated as the Muskingum Conference which continued until 1918 when it was absorbed by the Ohio Conference (MP). The Ohio Conference came to unification in 1939 with seventy-four charges, eighty-six ministers, 21,464 members, and property valued at $1,130,350.

Beginning in 1876 when the Ohio parts of the Pittsburgh and Erie Conferences were merged to form the East Ohio Conference, all of Ohio Methodism except the churches in the Lexington Conference was then embraced in five annual conferences wholly within the state. That year the five conferences reported 157,317 members. The five conferences were reduced to three in 1912 and to two in 1928, and they came to unification in 1939 with 454,665 members and property valued at $42,441,285.

In 1968 the two Ohio conferences reported nineteen districts, 1,247 charges, 1,561 ministers, 619,116 members, property valued at $294,930,229, and a total of $42,960,776 raised for all purposes during the year.

By authority of the 1968 North Central JURISDICTIONAL CONFERENCE, the two Methodist and four E.U.B. annual conferences in Ohio voted to merge into two conferences to be known as the East Ohio and West Ohio Conferences. In 1970 the Ohio Conferences of The United Methodist Church reported 737,643 members, 1,703 charges, 2,310 ministers, and property valued at $409,746,225.

J. M. Barker, *Ohio Methodism*. 1898.
General Minutes, ME, TMC, UMC.
Minutes of the Ohio Conference.
J. M. Versteeg, *Ohio Area*. 1962.   DeWayne S. Woodring

OHIO CONFERENCE (ME), was organized Oct. 1, 1812, at Chillicothe with Bishops ASBURY and McKENDREE in charge. Incidentally it was at this session that the presiding elders were first asked to assist the bishops in making the appointments, thus constituting what today is called the bishop's CABINET. The conference was formed by dividing the WESTERN CONFERENCE. According to the *Discipline,* when created the Ohio Conference included the "Ohio, Muskingum, Miami, Kentucky and Salt River Districts." Those districts covered OHIO, eastern KENTUCKY eastern INDIANA, and a part of present day WEST VIRGINIA. The conference began with sixty-one preachers and 23,644 members. (See OHIO for beginnings of Methodism and for the creation of other conferences in the state.)

The Ohio Conference has continued to the present day, but through the years its boundaries have changed a number of times. It gave up territory to the TENNESSEE CONFERENCE in 1816, to the KENTUCKY CONFERENCE in 1820, to the PITTSBURGH CONFERENCE in 1824, to the MICHIGAN CONFERENCE in 1836, and to the CINCINNATI CONFERENCE in 1852. After 1852 there was no major change in its boundaries until 1928 when it absorbed the WEST OHIO CONFERENCE. The membership of the Ohio Conference after each of the territorial alterations mentioned above was: 1816, 22,278; 1820, 34,178; 1824, 28,505; 1836, 47,874; 1852, 30,943; and 1928, 229,650.

From the beginning the Ohio Conference was interested in education. In 1822 it joined the Kentucky Conference in projecting AUGUSTA COLLEGE, Augusta, Ky., on the Ohio River. The school flourished for twenty-two years. As time passed a number of academies were launched, some under the control of the conferences and some conducted in the interest of the church under private ownership. In 1968 the Ohio Conference had two strong institutions of higher learning: OHIO WESLEYAN UNIVERSITY at Delaware, founded in 1842, which has an endowment of $20,000,000, a plant valued at $8,000,0000, and over 2,500 students; and OHIO NORTHERN UNIVERSITY at Ada, founded in 1871, which has some 2,400 students, a plant valued at $12,000,000 and an endowment of over $3,000,-000. Six WESLEY FOUNDATIONS in the state are supported jointly by the two annual conferences.

The Methodist Home for Children was established in Worthington in 1911. The Bethesda Home, first Methodist home for the aged in Ohio, was established in CINCINNATI in 1899 with the cooperation of all the conferences in the state. Other Methodist homes for the aged within the bounds of the conference are: Crestview at Sylvania; Methodist Home on College Hill, and Wesley Hall in Cincinnati; and Wesley Glen at Columbus. The Ohio Conference is related to Bethesda and the Christ Hospitals in Cincinnati, Flower Hospital at Toledo, and Riverside Hospital at Columbus.

The Ohio Conference came to unification in 1939 with eleven districts, 539 charges, 251,667 members, and property valued at $21,965,501. At that time it merged with forty-three charges (about 12,000 members) of the OHIO CONFERENCE (MP) to form the Ohio Conference of The Methodist Church. In 1964 when the LEXINGTON CONFERENCE (CJ) was merged with the overlying conferences of the NORTH CENTRAL JURISDICTION, the Ohio Conference received the work of that conference which was within its bounds.

In 1964 the Ohio Conference was designated as an episcopal area with the bishop's residence at Columbus. F. GERALD ENSLEY was named as the resident bishop.

In 1968 the Ohio Conference reported eleven districts, 702 charges, 920 ministers, 345,157 members, property valued at $156,059,795, and $24,740,552 raised for all purposes during the year. At the time it was the second

largest conference in the connection. In 1970 when Methodist-E.U.B. merger was fully effected, the name of the conference became the West Ohio Annual Conference.

J. M. Barker, *Ohio Methodism*. 1898.
General Minutes, ME, TMC, UMC.
Minutes of the Ohio Conference.
J. M. Versteeg, *Ohio Area*. 1962.   N. B. H.

OHIO CONFERENCE (EUB). Among the progressive measures of the ninth conference session of the EVANGELICAL ASSOCIATION in the historic year of 1816, was the appointment of Adam Henney and Frederick Shower to form circuits in the new state of OHIO. Shower abandoned his field but Henney established Canton Circuit, embracing eight or ten counties and a round of 400 miles. Meanwhile the church fathers in PENNSYLVANIA held the first session of a GENERAL CONFERENCE and adopted a permanent church name, Die Evangelische Gemeinschaft (Evangelical Association). Henney gave the first report of the work in Ohio in 1817: eight converts, thirty-three accessions, and a membership of fifty-five.

At this time Ohio was called "The Far Western Country." However, for eleven years (1816-27), thirty preachers made one or more long tedious trips on horseback over the Allegheny Mountains, traveling an average of approximately 800 miles to Ohio and return for the annual conference sessions.

In 1823, the western field was separated from Salem District of the Mother Conference and named the Ohio District. In 1826, it was constituted the Western Conference, and this conference saw a remarkable expansion from 1822 to 1839. From four circuits and five preachers on one district, it grew to thirty-nine men, twenty fields, and four districts; and its membership increased from 523 to 3,653. Operations by 1839 had extended over western Pennsylvania, Ohio, southern MICHIGAN, INDIANA, northern ILLINOIS, and into WISCONSIN.

The General Conference of 1839 reformed the two conferences into the East Pennsylvania, West Pennsylvania, and Ohio.

Editor W. W. ORWIG, commenting on the remarkable extension of the Ohio Conference bounds in these years, with five districts reaching into five states, declared, "This conference is now the largest in the Evangelical Association, both in the number of members and ministers, and the bounds of its territory." A change came in 1844, when the Ohio Conference session at Red Haw, Ohio, organized the Illinois Conference out of the Indiana and Illinois Districts.

Out of territory in western Pennsylvania developed by the Ohio men, the PITTSBURGH CONFERENCE was organized in 1851. The mission work in Michigan, carried on for nineteen years, was organized into the MICHIGAN CONFERENCE at the 1864 session of the Ohio Conference.

After the Ohio Conference changed to the use of English, the German congregations in the region of Lake Erie, still being replenished by new immigrants from Germany, were formed into a conference in 1876, called the Erie Conference. Many strong churches were developed by this conference but by 1923 they also had become English and were reunited with the Ohio Conference.

The Ohio United Conference (UNITED EVANGELICAL CHURCH) was organized in 1892 by a group which had withdrawn from the Evangelical Association. After thirty years of growth and effective service a happy reunion was effected with the Ohio Conference in 1924.

In 1951, after 135 years of notable history, the Ohio Conference, with 126 ministers and 160 churches, was dissolved and a membership of over 26,000 was transferred to three former UNITED BRETHREN conferences: Ohio East, OHIO SOUTHEAST, and OHIO SANDUSKY CONFERENCES of the E.U.B. Church.

Der Christliche Botschafter, 1839, p. 28; 1842, p. 22; 1874, p. 28.
R. B. Leedy, *Evangelical Church in Ohio*. 1959.
Original Conference Book, EA, 1800-58.
A. Stapleton, *Evangelical Association*. 1896.
Western and Ohio Conference Record Books.   ROY B. LEEDY

OHIO CONFERENCE (MP) was organized at CINCINNATI on Oct. 15, 1829 with ASA SHINN as president. The conference included most of the territory west of the Allegheny Mountains. The majority of the ministers who attended had been local preachers in the M.E. Church. At its first session the conference ordained two deacons and twelve elders, and it stationed twenty-two men. Most of the preachers were appointed to localities with the hope that they would be able to form circuits, because at the time only a few circuits and stations of the M.E. Church had cast their lot with the new denomination. In 1830 the conference reported 3,791 members. In the next three years between fifteen and twenty preachers were added to the itinerary, and in 1833 the conference reported 10,348 members.

In 1833 the Ohio Conference was divided to form the PITTSBURGH CONFERENCE, the Sandusky and Scioto Rivers to be the dividing line. In 1836 and 1839 the ILLINOIS CONFERENCE, and the INDIANA CONFERENCE, respectively, were set off from the Ohio Conference. Then in 1842 the Ohio part of the Pittsburgh Conference, save the extreme northeastern segment of the state, was designated as the Muskingum Conference. The Muskingum Conference was organized in September, 1843.

METHODIST PROTESTANTISM became relatively strong in Ohio, and the fourth (1846) and sixth (1854) GENERAL CONFERENCES of the denomination met in Cincinnati and Steubenville, respectively. Other General Conferences convened in the state in later years. In 1846 the Ohio Conference had 4,509 members and the Muskingum Conference 7,244. In 1896 the statistics were 14,586 for Muskingum and 6,099 for the Ohio Conference. In 1918 the Muskingum and Ohio Conferences united as the Ohio Conference. In the preceding year the Ohio Conference reported 34 charges, 34 preachers, and 7,875 members to 54 charges, 58 preachers, and 15,706 members for the Muskingum Conference.

Beginning in 1850, Ohio Methodist Protestants made several unsuccessful efforts to establish a school. Finally in 1900 the Muskingum Conference launched West Lafayette College which continued for sixteen years, and then by order of the General Conference the school was merged with ADRIAN COLLEGE in MICHIGAN.

The Ohio Conference came to unification in 1939 with 74 charges, 86 ministers, 21,464 members, and property valued at $1,130,350. As the merger was effected, forty-three of the charges fell within the OHIO CONFERENCE and thirty-one in the NORTH-EAST OHIO CONFERENCE of The Methodist Church.

A. H. Bassett, *Concise History*. 1877.
Minutes of the Ohio Conference, MP, 1939.
J. M. Versteeg, *Ohio Area*. 1962.
Yearbook of the M. P. Church, 1918.   ALBEA GODBOLD

OHIO EAST CONFERENCE (EUB) came into existence in 1951; but it traces its beginning back to June 2, 1817, when the first of its predecessor conferences was organized by the GENERAL CONFERENCE of the CHURCH OF THE BRETHREN IN CHRIST in session at Mt. Pleasant, Pa. The MUSKINGUM CONFERENCE, as the new conference was called, embraced all of the territory lying east and north of the Muskingum River as well as several counties in western Pennsylvania. The first session was held at Joseph Naftzgar's in Harrison County, Ohio, on June 1, 1818. Bishops CHRISTIAN NEWCOMER and ANDREW ZELLER presided; six ministers and three visitors attended. From this beginning, the conference grew in strength until 1853 when it was divided and the ERIE CONFERENCE was formed.

On Sept. 7, 1886, the Western Reserve Conference, which had been split away from the Erie Conference in 1861 and had its eastern boundary established at the Pennsylvania line in 1877, and the Muskingum Conference were reunited at Massillon, Ohio, to form the East Ohio Conference.

At the outset the East Ohio Conference had 8,000 members, 139 organized churches, and eighty-nine ministers. The forty charges in the Conference were divided into three districts, each under the supervision of a presiding elder. When the East Ohio Conference closed its record (1951), there were sixty-four charges, 100 organized churches, and 21,322 members.

Following the denominational merger in 1946, the state of Ohio was divided into four conferences. On Sept. 7, 1951, at Canton Ohio, Bishop FRED L. DENNIS presided at the uniting session that dissolved the East Ohio (UB) and the Ohio (Evangelical) and officially created the Ohio East Conference. Bounded on the north by Lake Erie, on the east by the Pennsylvania State Line, on the south by the OHIO SOUTHEAST CONFERENCE, the territory falling within the boundaries of the Ohio East Conference comprised about one-fourth of the geographical area of the state of Ohio.

The Ohio East Conference was divided into two districts, north and south, each under the supervision of a conference superintendent. Its 37,495 members worshiped in 142 churches and the conference was served by 123 active elders and seven probationers (1967). The total value of local church property amounted to $22,187,820 while the average per member contribution for all purposes was $92.47 (1967).

In 1969, the conference joined with the Northeast Ohio of the former Methodist Church and a number of congregations from the Ohio Southeast and Ohio Sandusky Conferences to form the East Ohio Conference.

B. S. Arnold, *History of the East Ohio Conference, United Brethren in Christ*. 1965.
D. Berger, *History of UB*. 1897.
A. W. Drury, *History of the UB*. 1924.
Journal of the Ohio East Conference, 1951, 1967.
L. R. CAROTHERS

OHIO GERMAN CONFERENCE (UB) was organized at Germantown, Ohio, Oct. 20, 1853, with Bishop DAVID EDWARDS presiding, and concluded its work on Sept. 28, 1930 in the session held at Zanesville, Ohio. Entirely German in its beginning, the church had become predominantly English by 1930. In the mid-nineteenth century, the need for a separate German Conference was keenly felt. The UNITED BRETHREN GENERAL CONFERENCE of 1853 authorized the formation of the Ohio Conference. This conference was given the responsibility of organizing German churches wherever such work was feasible. Mission churches were therefore established in OHIO, INDIANA, ILLINOIS, KENTUCKY, and NEBRASKA. The Women's Missionary Association of this conference was organized in 1868, antedating the national women's organization by several years. The OLD OTTERBEIN CHURCH in BALTIMORE, Md., was for many years an affiliate member of this conference. Numerous denominational leaders of the nineteenth century were members of the Ohio German Conference: William Mittendorf, Ezekiel Light, Edward Lorenz, G. Fritz, A. Schmidt, and Caspar Striech.

With the advent of World War I, the German language ceased to be popular and many of the formerly strong German churches became English-speaking and affiliated with the English conference in whose boundary they were located.

During the last twelve years of its history this conference was ably guided by E. F. Wegner as superintendent. At the conclusion of the work of this conference the remaining churches affiliated with the Illinois, Indiana, Miami, and East Ohio Conferences of the United Brethren in Christ.

D. Berger, *History of UB.* 1897.
A. W. Drury, *History of UB.* 1924. LOUIS O. ODON

OHIO MIAMI CONFERENCE

OHIO MIAMI CONFERENCE (EUB) was the successor to the Miami Conference of the CHURCH OF THE BRETHREN IN CHRIST. The change of name followed the union of the Evangelical and United Brethren denominations in 1946. The churches of the Ohio Conference of the EVANGELICAL CHURCH were transferred to the four United Brethren Conferences and the name *Ohio* was added to each former United Brethren Conference name.

The Ohio Miami conference covered all or parts of the following counties: Darke, Preble, Butler, Hamilton, Clermont, Brown, Highland, Warren, Montgomery, Miami, Champaign, Clarke, Greene and Clinton Counties. Harrison in Indiana, Newport in Kentucky, and Wrightsville and Liberty Chapel in Adams County were also in the Ohio Miami Conference, but outside the above boundaries. The OHIO SANDUSKY CONFERENCE bordered Ohio Miami on the north and the OHIO SOUTHEAST on the east.

United Brethren work began in OHIO with the coming of German-speaking preachers from PENNSYLVANIA and MARYLAND in 1804 and 1805. The first English-speaking preacher, John McNamar, arrived in 1813. The first church was organized in 1806 at Germantown. The Miami Conference was formed in 1810, when CHRISTIAN NEWCOMER met with fifteen preachers at Michael Kreider's in Ross County. Among those present were ANDREW ZELLER and Daniel Troyer, who became prominent leaders in the new movement.

In the first years the conference included most of Ohio and INDIANA. At successive GENERAL CONFERENCES, the area was reduced with the formation of other conferences. However, little change was made after 1830.

As the use of the German language became less common in the Miami Conference, German-speaking churches in Ohio and Indiana organized the OHIO GERMAN CONFERENCE at Germantown in 1853 with Bishop DAVID EDWARDS presiding. This conference continued until 1930,

when it was dissolved. Each of its congregations joined with the conference in which territory it was located.

The conference has had periods of rapid growth, while in some years it has recorded losses. At the end of 1967, it had 111 organized churches and 35,286 members. Elders numbered 123. Of these, 93 were under appointment. The value of church and parsonage properties was $17,463,240. The total paid for all purposes was $2,766,303.

The City of DAYTON, near the geographical center of the conference, has been the location of several denominational institutions. The denominational headquarters have been located here. The former U.B. Building was for some time the largest office building in the city. Here also was located The OTTERBEIN PRESS, the only publishing house of the United Brethren Church. Its only seminary has been continuously in Dayton, since its organization in 1871. The name of this school was changed from Bonebrake Theological Seminary to UNITED THEOLOGICAL SEMINARY when it merged with the Evangelical School of Theology from Reading, Pa., in 1954. The Otterbein Home, formerly a home for children and the aged and now only caring for older people, is located in the former Shaker property near Lebanon, Ohio.

The denominational Woman's Missionary Assocation of the United Brethren in Christ was organized in the Summit Street Church of the Miami Conference in 1872. Earlier than this, The Sisters Missionary Society was organized in the Ohio German Conference. The first three missionaries sent to a foreign country by the United Brethren in Christ were members of the Miami Conference: W. J. SHUEY, D. C. KUMLER, and D. K. FLICKINGER, all of whom went to SIERRA LEONE in West Africa in 1855.

When the camping movement became prominent, the conference purchased the property of the former Miami Military Institute in Germantown in 1945.

The area of the Ohio Miami Conference has been in a section of the state which became rapidly urbanized. Within the conference area, six cities of more than 42,000 population in 1960 accounted for a total population of 1,016,536. This change from rural to urban has been a problem for which the churches were slow to find a solution. In 1970 the conference united with the Ohio, Ohio Sandusky and part of the Ohio Southeast Conferences to form the West Ohio Conference of The United Methodist Church.

A. W. Drury, *History of the UB.* 1924.
Roy D. Miller, *The Miami Conference* (now Ohio Miami) *The Evangelical United Brethren Church, 1810-1860.*
Miami Conference *Minutes.* ROY D. MILLER

OHIO NORTHERN UNIVERSITY

OHIO NORTHERN UNIVERSITY, Ada, Ohio, is an undergraduate university with colleges of liberal arts, engineering, law, and pharmacy. Throughout its history this institution has emphasized professional education including teacher training along with liberal arts. Established in 1871 as Northeastern Ohio Normal, it was purchased by the CENTRAL OHIO CONFERENCE of the M. E. Church in 1898. Its present name was assumed in 1914. Theodore Presser, who founded the Presser Foundation, which has assisted in erecting "Presser Halls" for the instruction of music on many college campuses in the United States, began his work as a music teacher in Ohio Northern University in 1871.

Degrees granted are the B.A., B.S., B.S. in Education, B.S. in Pharmacy, B.S. in Civil Engineering, B.S. in Mechanical Engineering, B.S. in Electrical Engineering, LL.B., J.D. (Doctor of Jurisprudence). The governing board has forty-two members, half of whom are elected by the two Methodist annual conferences in Ohio.

JOHN O. GROSS

OHIO SANDUSKY CONFERENCE (EUB) was composed of territory in the northwest quarter of the state of OHIO. Its boundaries were Lake Erie on the north, Sidney, Ohio on the south, the INDIANA state line on the west and the western limits of Mansfield, Ohio on the east.

The Ohio Sandusky Conference was one of the largest conferences of The EVANGELICAL UNITED BRETHREN CHURCH, having 176 elders and 172 charges in 1967. The value of local church property and the annual conference holdings, which included Camp St. Marys, near St. Marys, Ohio, and Camp Sebroske, near Oak Harbor, Ohio, was in excess of 20 million dollars (1968). The conference membership was 42,720, and the average giving per member for missions and benevolences was $16.00. The total giving for all purposes was $87.00 per member.

The Sandusky Conference of the UNITED BRETHREN IN CHRIST had its beginning when Jacob Baulus moved from MARYLAND in 1822 and settled in the lower Sandusky area near the present city of Fremont, Ohio. He immediately began to evangelize the area and formed several classes. In 1829 Baulus reported to the Muskingum Conference for the Sandusky Circuit. In 1831 the Scioto Conference formed the Marion Circuit which extended into the Sandusky area, while the Miami Conference was developing the Maumee mission which was located in the area south of Lake Erie. It may be said that the eventual territory of the Sandusky Conference included some of the Muskingum, Scioto, and Miami Conferences.

The first session of the Sandusky Conference was held on May 12, 1834, in Seneca County, Ohio. At first the field of labor extended into Indiana and MICHIGAN, but by 1845 Sandusky had lost the Indiana territory with the formation of the St. Joseph Conference. In 1853, the Maumee work attained the status of a conference and continued under this name until the year 1857, when it became known as the Auglaize Conference. The year of 1853 also saw the rise of another conference, the Michigan, which later became the North Ohio Conference. Both the North Ohio and the Auglaize Conferences affected the course and growth of the Sandusky Conference, when in 1861 the Maumee district in Ohio was removed. This territory was regained for Sandusky forty years later when North Ohio and Auglaize Conferences were dissolved. The Sandusky Conference maintained rather stable territorial boundaries and growth for the next fifty years.

In 1951, following the merger of The EVANGELICAL CHURCH and the United Brethren in Christ, the Sandusky Conference of the former United Brethren Church merged with the western district churches of the Ohio Conference of the former Evangelical Church. The Ohio Sandusky Conference of The Evangelical United Brethren Church was formed.

The Flat Rock Children's Home was located within the bounds of the Ohio Sandusky Conference, but it received its support from additional conferences of the denomination. The Home was established in 1866 at Flat Rock, Ohio, to care for Civil War orphans. Since its founding, more than two thousand children of elementary school age have been cared for.

In 1969 the conference joined with five other conferences of The United Methodist Church in Ohio to form the West Ohio and East Ohio Conferences.

A. W. Drury, *History of the UB.* 1924.
J. L. Luttrell, *History of the Auglaize Annual Conference.* Dayton: U. B. Publishing House, 1892.
Journal of the Ohio Sandusky Conference, 1951, 1968.

C. DAVID WRIGHT

OHIO SOUTHEAST CONFERENCE (EUB). The first conference in OHIO of the CHURCH OF THE UNITED BRETHREN IN CHRIST was the Miami Conference, formed in 1810. Although it was state-wide in scope, most of the churches were located in the southern section of the state. As settlers came into the northeastern sector, the Muskingum Conference was created in 1818. Then in 1825 Scioto Conference was formed from the southeastern portion of the state, receiving its congregations from the Miami Conference. Expansion of the Scioto Conference was steady so that in 1873 there were 8,036 members.

In 1878 The GENERAL CONFERENCE established a Central Ohio Conference, taking most of its members from the Scioto Conference. A large portion of this conference was re-united with the Scioto Conference in 1901, when the Southeast Ohio Conference was formed with 13,534 members. By the time of union with The EVANGELICAL CHURCH the conference had grown to a membership of 23,975 persons.

In 1951 the only former Evangelical conference in Ohio, known as the Ohio Conference, was divided so that its churches went into each of the former United Brethren conferences in the state. The name of the conference formed by the churches in the southeastern portion of Ohio was Ohio Southeast Conference.

Following the formation of The United Methodist Church, conference unions took place in 1970. Two conferences, East Ohio and West Ohio, were formed from the six conferences of the two former denominations. Most of the 27,523 members of the former Ohio Southeast Conference were received into the new West Ohio Conference.

JOHN H. NESS, JR.

OHIO WESLEYAN UNIVERSITY, Delaware, Ohio, was founded by Methodist pioneers in 1841 and was granted its charter in 1842. In 1877, Ohio Wesleyan became coeducational when the Ohio Wesleyan Female College, an independent institution established in Delaware in 1853, merged with the university.

Ohio Wesleyan has educated many of Methodism's foremost leaders, including twenty-two bishops. In the early part of this century the university ranked so high in the training of missionaries that JOHN R. MOTT once said that Ohio Wesleyan was second only to Oxford in the number of missionaries sent into foreign fields. Today the tradition of Christian responsibility and service established by the missionaries of earlier years is continued by large numbers of students preparing for service careers and by hundreds of alumni holding service-oriented positions at home and abroad.

The university's curriculum emphasizes liberal arts and sciences and preprofessional courses. Its chapter of Phi

Beta Kappa was chartered in 1907. Degrees granted are the B.A., B.M. (Music), B.F.A. (Fine Arts), and the M.A. The governing board has forty-two members: twenty elected by two Ohio annual conferences, nine by alumni, ten at large; bishops of the Ohio areas and the president, ex officio.

JOHN O. GROSS

O'KELLY, JAMES (1757-1826), American preacher, was born in IRELAND but emigrated to America in 1778. He began his ministerial work during the Revolution which was then raging and in that same year, 1778, was admitted into the traveling connection. The CHRISTMAS CONFERENCE voted him orders, and he was ordained ELDER at the organization of the M. E. Church (1784) at that time. For several years he was presiding elder of the South VIRGINIA District, and was a member of the ill-fated COUNCIL which ASBURY tried to set up in place of frequent GENERAL CONFERENCES, but which withered away almost immediately.

He was early a champion of those who opposed the authority of the bishop, and while some judged that there was a personal antipathy against Asbury on his part, others saw him as a champion of the independent spirit of the American preachers. In the 1792 General Conference, O'Kelly offered a motion which became historic and about whose intent Methodists have never ceased to divide. His motion stated, "After the bishop appoints the preachers at conference to their several circuits, if any one thinks himself injured by the appointment, he shall have liberty to appeal to the conference and state his objections; and if the conference approve his objections, the bishop shall appoint him to another circuit." (*History of American Methodism*, Vol. I., p. 436).

Upon the defeat of the motion, O'Kelly resigned from the Church with a few of the brethren joining him, even WILLIAM MCKENDREE himself who was destined after Asbury to become the greatest champion of the strong episcopacy.

For his part, Asbury endeavored to treat O'Kelly kindly, and as he knew that he was advancing in years, proposed that O'Kelly should receive forty pounds; but meanwhile O'Kelly withdrew and organized a Church giving it the name of the REPUBLICAN METHODIST CHURCH, the name being suggested by the prevalence of Republican sentiments in Virginia. In this Church all the preachers according to their order were to stand on an equal footing, there were to be no degrees in the ministry, and greater freedom was promised to the people than they enjoyed in the M. E. Church.

The influence of O'Kelly became rather strong in the border counties of Virginia and NORTH CAROLINA, and the *Minutes* show from 1792 to 1798 a loss of about 8,000 persons, some of which can be attributed to O'Kelly's agitation. O'Kelly gave forth a pamphlet explaining his reasons for protesting against the M. E. Church. NICHOLAS SNETHEN, whom Asbury called his "silver trumpet," answered O'Kelly, though Snethen himself was destined to become a METHODIST PROTESTANT leader a few years later.

The controversy raged quite heatedly and James O'Kelly himself ordained such preachers as came to him, but it is said he was greatly disappointed in the number of those who did join his ranks. In 1801 he changed the name of the church to the Christian Church, and divisions and subdivisions followed until it gradually dwindled away. However, the writer of these lines heard Bishop COLLINS DENNY say as late as 1934 that he was surprised to find that there were still some Republican Methodist Churches belonging to the O'Kellyites here and there in isolated portions of Virginia. (Eventually the remnants of O'Kelly's Church merged with the Congregationalists in the Congregational Christian Church.)

James O'Kelly seems to have been one of those strong opinionated men who do not fit into an organization where someone else must definitely lead, and they must as definitely follow. He died in North Carolina, Oct. 16, 1826.

F. Asbury, *Journal and Letters*. 1958.
E. S. Bucke, *History of American Methodism*. 1964.
J. M. Buckley, *Constitutional and Parliamentary History*. 1912.
C. F. Kilgore, *James O'Kelly Schism*. 1963.
Life of the Reverend James O'Kelly, written by himself, N.d.
F. A. Norwood, "James O'Kelly, Methodist Maverick," *Methodist History*, April 1966. N. B. H.

OKINAWA is the central and most important island of the Ryukyu archipelago, which extends 400 miles southwestward from Kyushu island (JAPAN) to include the Yaegama group close to the northeast point of Taiwan. Naha is the capital. The Ryukyus, often called Loo Choo, form a chain of reefs and islets separating the Pacific Ocean from the East China Sea. The land area is 921 square miles, of which Okinawa holds 500. The Ryukyu population is 833,000, of which nearly 800,000 live on Okinawa. Resettlement from that overpopulated island is being carried out in the Amami group to the northeast, and in the Miyako and Yaegama groups to the southwest.

For long centuries Okinawa and the other islands paid occasional tribute to Chinese overlords. Commander Matthew Perry's fleet wintered at Okinawa while awaiting Japan's reply to his demands for commercial and political relations with the United States. At the time of the Sino-Japanese War, Japan annexed the archipelago. American forces captured Okinawa in the final phase of World War II. By virtue of the Treaty of San Francisco in September 1951, the United States assumed authority over the archipelago, under trusteeship of temporary character regularized by the United Nations, although Japanese "residual sovereignty" is recognized in the Treaty.

The M. E. Church entered the Loo Choo islands (Ryukyus) in 1904, under the leadership of Dr. and Mrs. H. B. Schwartz. A vigorous circuit was developed, fre-

KANESHI CHURCH, OKINAWA

quently visited by the missionaries stationed at Nagasaki, Japan. When the United Church of Christ in Japan was organized in 1941, before the outbreak of World War II, Methodist work in Okinawa became a part of Japanese Methodism.

In 1946, following World War II, the Okinawa-Ryukyu church became the United Church of Christ of Okinawa (*Okinawa Kirisuto Kyodan*).

Evangelistic work centers in the churches in Naha-Shuri, Ishikawa (close to the U.S. Naval and Marine base), Taira (north) and Ishigaki (southern Yaeyama group). From these centers, educational, agricultural and medical work moves out, particularly into areas of re-settlement. The Okinawa Christian Institute, junior-college level, interdenominational, located close to University of the Ryukyus, erected new buildings and equipment to train indigenous leadership for the church; the enrollment approached 100. Membership of the Okinawa *Kyodan* is over 1,500, of which the Methodists are the largest group. There are twenty-five organized churches with numerous other preaching places, under the direction of twenty ordained pastors and other workers in training. The Division of World Missions of The United Methodist Church (U.S.A.) provides seven married missionary couples, and PHILIPPINE Island Methodism supports a woman missionary.

Encyclopaedia Britannica.
Barbara H. Lewis, *Methodist Overseas Missions.* 1960.

ARTHUR BRUCE MOSS

OKLAHOMA, population 2,498,378 in 1970, is in the southwest section of the U.S.A. Acquired in the LOUISIANA Purchase of 1803, the United States set the territory apart in 1834 for the Indian tribes that were being moved from east of the Mississippi River. In 1889 the central section of the territory was purchased from the Indians for white settlement and 20,000 whites immediately rushed in to establish homes. In 1960 there were still 65,000 Indians in the state. Oklahoma was admitted to the Union in 1907.

The first Methodist and the first Protestant sermon in what is now Oklahoma was delivered by WILLIAM STEVENSON, a member of the MISSOURI CONFERENCE, at Pecan Point in 1818 while he was establishing Methodism in southwest ARKANSAS. Pecan Point became a charge in the Missouri Conference.

The main thrust of Methodism in what is now Oklahoma grew out of missionary work among the Indians. Ministry to the Indians was started by southern conferences of the M. E. Church before the tribes were moved west by the government in the decade 1829-39. As a result of the missionary endeavor there were several thousand Methodist converts among the Indians before they were moved west. Some missionaries accompanied the Indians en route west while some went ahead to be ready to minister to them when they arrived, Alexander Talley from the MISSISSIPPI CONFERENCE being one of the latter. In 1831 the Mississippi Conference appointed Talley as superintendent of the Choctaw Mission, and about the same time the Missouri and TENNESSEE CONFERENCES also sent missionaries into Indian Territory. In 1836 when the ARKANSAS CONFERENCE was organized, it had a district in Indian Territory which took over the Indian mission work from the other conferences. By 1844 the Arkansas Conference had twelve white preachers, three Indian preachers, twenty-one local Indian preachers, and over 3,000 members in Indian Territory.

The 1844 GENERAL CONFERENCE created the INDIAN MISSION CONFERENCE. The next year the conference adhered South, and it continued as the Indian Mission Conference until 1906 when it was superseded by the OKLAHOMA CONFERENCE (MES).

After the Indian Mission Conference adhered South in 1845, the M. E. Church had no work in Oklahoma until the Wyandotte Indians moved to Indian Territory. The OHIO CONFERENCE established a mission among the Wyandottes in 1819. In 1843 the Wyandottes moved from OHIO to KANSAS and from there to Indian Territory in 1871. Gradually the evangelizing work of the M. E. Church spread in Indian Territory, and in 1880 the denomination established the Indian Mission. The mission became the Indian Mission Conference in 1889, and three years later it was designated as the OKLAHOMA CONFERENCE.

The METHODIST PROTESTANTS established an Indian Mission in what is now Oklahoma in 1887. In 1896 they formed the Chickasaw Mission Conference on two Indian Reservations, and the same year they organized the Oklahoma Mission Conference in Oklahoma Territory by dividing the Fort Smith Mission. In 1900 they set up the Southwest Oklahoma Mission among the Indians, and four years later they formed the Choctaw Indian Conference. In 1908 all of these M. P. missions and conferences were either absorbed or superseded by the denomination's Oklahoma Conference which itself merged in 1916 to make the Fort Smith-Oklahoma Conference. The latter conference continued until 1939.

With the coming of white settlers into Oklahoma, the three major branches of Methodism organized churches and conferences for them which were soon stronger than the Indian churches and missions or mission conferences. In 1906 the M. E. Church, South therefore changed the name of its Indian Mission Conference to the OKLAHOMA CONFERENCE. The white work grew rapidly, and in 1911 the Oklahoma Conference was divided to form the East Oklahoma and West Oklahoma Conferences. Then in 1919 the Indian work was separated from the white to form the Indian Mission (MES) which continued in The Methodist Church in 1939. In 1930 the East and West Oklahoma Conferences of the Southern Church merged to form the Oklahoma Conference which continued until 1939.

By 1892 the Indian Mission Conference of the M. E. Church included many white ministers and churches, and its name was changed to the Oklahoma Conference which continued until unification in 1939. In 1904 the denomination separated the Indian work from the Oklahoma Conference and designated it as the Indian Territory Mission, changing the name to the East Oklahoma Mission two years later. In 1911 the mission was absorbed by the Oklahoma Conference.

In 1902 the M. E. Church organized the Okaneb Conference, a body that included all of the denomination's Negro work in Oklahoma, MISSOURI, Kansas, and NEBRASKA, changing the name one year later to the Lincoln Conference. In 1928 this conference was merged, part of it going with the Little Rock Conference to form the SOUTHWEST CONFERENCE, and the remainder going with the Central Missouri Conference to form the CENTRAL WEST CONFERENCE, all of them being Negro conferences.

At unification in 1939 the East and West Oklahoma

Conferences of the M. E. Church, South had a total of 91,795 members, the Oklahoma Conference of the M. E. Church had 58,704, and the Oklahoma part of the M. P. Fort Smith-Oklahoma Conference had 2,000, making a total of 152,499. The work of the three conferences was merged to form the East and West Oklahoma Conferences of The Methodist Church. In 1954 the East and West Conferences were combined to form the Oklahoma Conference.

In 1939 the Indian Mission of the M. E. Church, South and the Southwest Conference of the M. E. Church continued in The Methodist Church, the one in the South Central Jurisdiction and the other in the Central Jurisdiction. The Indian Mission became the Oklahoma Indian Mission Conference in 1959.

In 1970 the Oklahoma Indian Mission Conference, the Oklahoma Conference, and the Oklahoma District of the Southwest Conference reported a total of 534 pastoral charges, 575 ministers, 274,474 members, and property valued at $100,000,000.

Babcock and Bryce, *Oklahoma.* 1937.
H. E. Brill, *Oklahoma.* 1939.
Clegg and Oden, *Oklahoma.* 1968.
General Minutes, ME, MES, TMC, UMC.   OSCAR FONTAINE

OKLAHOMA CITY, OKLAHOMA, U.S.A. (population 363,225), is the capital of the state and its largest city. Methodism began in Oklahoma City the very week the city began. When on April 22, 1889, the territory was thrown open to white settlement and Oklahoma City became a city of several thousand overnight, Methodist services were held in a tent the very next Sunday. A Sunday school was organized and the church at once began her work.

Today there are seventy Methodist churches in the area, and growing at the rate of one new church each year. St. Luke's Church is one of the show places of the city. OKLAHOMA CITY UNIVERSITY enrolls four thousand students. The city is the episcopal residence of the bishop, who presently administers the work of Methodism over the entire state including the Indian Mission Conference. The South Central JURISDICTIONAL CONFERENCE of 1968 was held in Oklahoma City, and Bishop ALSIE CARLETON, elected at that conference, was consecrated in St. Luke's.

Deaconess Hospital (Free Methodist), organized in 1900 in Guthrie, Okla., moved to its present location in 1910. A general hospital service is maintained. The unwed mother program known as "Home of Redeeming Love" has served more than 8,000 girl patients. The main hospital building has recently been greatly enlarged. Several auxiliary buildings are located on the twenty-acre campus. It is an accredited institution of the FREE METHODIST CHURCH.

St. Luke's Methodist Church was born with the "Oklahoma Run" which opened this former Indian Territory for white settlers officially April 22, 1889. By nightfall on this turbulent Monday, an estimated 10,000 settlers (more modest reports say 3,000) had converged on the City's site and set about putting homes and businesses on the premises to which they had staked claims.

Varying accounts from the several churches which claim descent from the first Sunday of the City's birth indicate the likelihood that several religious services were held on the first Sunday, April 28, 1889. The one to which St. Luke's attaches her ancestry, was held under a white flag

ST. LUKE'S CHURCH, OKLAHOMA CITY, OKLAHOMA

on what became Third Street, between present North Broadway and North Robinson Streets, by a Methodist preacher, James Murry. St. Luke's has a portion of this historic flag under glass in her church halls.

The church which formed on this original site continued to meet at this spot, known locally as "Tabernacle (M. E., South) Church."

In June, Bishop EUGENE HENDRIX authorized the transfer of I. L. Burrows from the ARKANSAS CONFERENCE to become pastor of the First M. E. Church, South, in Oklahoma City, and promised $750 from the General Board of MISSIONS to purchase the three lots on which the church had been meeting. Despite the City's rapid growth, competition of other churches and commercial enterprise were strong in the new community. Fifty people were related to the congregation at this time. Stalwart Christian people were among the membership that saw the church through successive stages of growth: enclosure of the tabernacle before winter of 1889; a brick sanctuary added in 1903; a change of name to St. Luke's M. E. Church, South, in 1904; the purchase of lots for a new building at Eighth and North Robinson in 1905; the erection of a $90,000 building at the new site, completed in 1908; addition of a $75,000 Sunday School building (cir. 1923); purchase of lots for a new structure at Fifteenth and North Robinson in 1946; erection of the first unit for the new building in 1951; completion of the new sanctuary in March of 1957; periodic purchase and development of off-street parking lots, 1950-62, quarter million dollar expansion of facilities in 1961, providing new offices, classrooms, nursery, library, bride's room, and reception room.

Overcoming the severe struggles of the early years, including the panic of 1893, the growth and influence of St. Luke's have experienced a steady rise. Located close to the center of the originally compact City and challenging strong leadership from the community since its beginning, St. Luke's has become an increasingly important part of the City's life. Her membership (1970) stood at 7,292; her staff of thirty-three continues to grow and her budget for the coming year is $525,000.

From the earliest days, St. Luke's has been served by a very high calibre of ministerial leadership. The noted P. R. Knickerbocker became pastor (1906-1910). He was followed by E. C. McVoyl; ROBERT E. GOODRICH; Frank Barrett; and FORNEY HUTCHINSON (1918-32).

Dr. Hutchinson's pastorate, with his warm, outgoing spirit, his constant pastoral ministry, his interest in the life of the entire community brought this thriving, growing church to flower. After more than thirty-five years, his stamp of Christian love is still upon the character of St. Luke's and the memory of the City.

There followed Dr. Hutchinson, other distinguished pastors: PAUL W. QUILLIAN (1932-36); CLOVIS CHAPPELL (1936-41); W. B. Selah (1941-45); William H. Wallace, Jr. (1945-51); W. MCFERRIN STOWE (1951-64) (now bishop); and J. Chess Lovern, the present pastor, who followed Bishop Stowe in 1964.

Village Church, located in suburban Oklahoma City, was organized in 1951 and has grown to a membership of 2,750 (1970). The Oklahoma City District Board of Missions and Wesley Church were the original sponsors of the new church. The first meetings were conducted in Wiley Post Airport. With window curtains made of parachutes, airplanes coming and going, a pilot's room for a nursery, and the balcony for a place of worship, the young congregation began holding Sunday school and worship services. Richard Gibbens was appointed the first pastor. It is interesting to note that he had grown up in the sponsoring Wesley Church.

The sanctuary is contemporary in design with large wooden arches supporting the ceiling, and will seat 650 people. It was completed in 1963, twelve years from the date of the first ground breaking for the first unit.

Village Church has had a phenomenal growth in membership. In order to meet the needs of the congregation, two Sunday school sessions are conducted each Sunday and two worship services are conducted.

Wesley Church, a stately English Gothic sanctuary, today stands in the exact population center of the metropolitan city. In October 1910, F. A. Colwell was appointed by Bishop WILLIAM A. QUAYLE to the task of organizing a church in the far northwest section of Oklahoma City.

A hastily constructed tabernacle was built at Military and 32nd Streets and when Bishop Quayle preached the first sermon on Christmas Day, 1910, the furnishings consisted of a floor of sawdust, some donated chairs, and a square piano. In the spring of 1911 the tabernacle was moved to the corner of 25th and Douglas, the site of the present building. Wesley closed its first conference year with 136 members.

The present sanctuary was dedicated May 20, 1928, the membership then being 771. Depression years brought a crisis to Wesley, but church members managed interest payments on a towering mortgage by proceeds from doughnut sales. Church women spent long hours turning out thousands of doughnuts.

Wesley is located near the Methodist Oklahoma City University and is called the University Church. One of its pastors went from the church to the presidency of the University, and one of the University's presidents came to Wesley as minister. Since its beginning twenty minsters have served it, and the membership today is 3,282.

General Minutes.
History and Roster, St. Luke's Methodist Episcopal Church, South. Printed by the church, 1926.
Beth Prim Howell, St. Luke's: A Living History of a Unique Church—First 75 Years. Oklahoma City, 1964.
Look Magazine, 1957.
Together, February 1958.

OSCAR FONTAINE
BYRON S. LAMSON
JOSEPH T. SHACKFORD
WILLIAM R. HENRY
MRS. CHARLES R. THIGPEN

OKLAHOMA CITY UNIVERSITY, Oklahoma City, Oklahoma, was established as Epworth University in 1904 at Oklahoma City by the M. E. Church and the M. E. Church, South. It was moved to Guthrie, Okla. in 1911, and the name was changed to Oklahoma Methodist University. The college was moved back to Oklahoma City in 1919, and the name was altered first to Oklahoma City College and then, in 1924, to Oklahoma City University. The educational program includes arts and sciences, music, business, and law.

Its large growth and expansion came after 1940. In 1960 a program for creating a regional center of excellence was begun with the consultative assistance of the Massachusetts Institute of Technology. A $2,000,000 grant from the Ford Foundation was made to the university in 1962, to be matched by $4,000,000.

Degrees granted are the B.A., B.M. (Music), B.S. in Business, B.I.A. (Industrial Arts), LL.B., M.A.T. (Teaching), M.B.E. (Business Education), J.D. (Doctor of Jurisprudence). The governing board has forty-seven trustees, thirty-two members elected by the OKLAHOMA ANNUAL CONFERENCE, fourteen district superintendents of that conference, and the resident bishop.

JOHN O. GROSS

OKLAHOMA CONFERENCE (ME) was organized at OKLAHOMA CITY, Dec. 14, 1892 with Bishop DANIEL A. GOODSELL presiding. It superseded the INDIAN Mission CONFERENCE which included many white churches that had been organized after the territory was opened to white settlers in 1889.

When the Oklahoma Conference was created, the Indian work continued as a part of it. However, in 1904 the Indian charges were set off as the Indian Territory Mission, the name being changed to the East Oklahoma Mission in 1906. The mission began in 1904 with 27 charges and about 1,275 members, but as time passed it did not flourish. The Indians were poor, the pastors' salaries were low, and the churches had to contend with the hostility of the unconverted and the competition of the Church, South. By 1911 the prospects for the work were so discouraging that the mission asked the GENERAL CONFERENCE to make it a part of the Oklahoma Conference, and it was so ordered. Some Indian work continued in the Oklahoma Conference, but after 1912 it was largely neglected until unification in 1939.

The Oklahoma Conference began in 1892 with four districts, Ardmore, Eastern, Northern, and Southern; 94 charges, 35 preachers, 60 local preachers, and 3,129 members. The conference grew rapidly, reporting nearly 15,000 members in 1903.

At its first session in 1892 the Oklahoma Conference took a strong stand for the establishment of a college. Several schools were launched over the years, but in the end the only college to survive was what is now OKLAHOMA CITY UNIVERSITY. The two Episcopal Methodisms started Epworth University in Oklahoma City in 1901, but it failed in 1911 when the Northern Church withdrew support to start a college in Guthrie. Eight years later the institution at Guthrie was closed, and the denominational college was opened in Oklahoma City. In 1928 the Southern Church joined in its support, and Oklahoma City University was able to weather the depression years to become a strong Methodist college.

The Oklahoma Conference was merged in 1939 to help form the East and West Oklahoma Conferences of The

Methodist Church. At that time the conference reported 246 charges, 209 ministers, 58,704 members, and property valued at $675,314.

H. E. Brill, *Oklahoma*. 1939.
Clegg and Oden, *Oklahoma*. 1968.
General Minutes, ME.
Minutes of the Oklahoma Conference.   FREDERICK E. MASER

OKLAHOMA CONFERENCE (MES) was organized at TULSA, Nov. 14, 1906 with Bishop JOHN J. TIGERT presiding. It superseded the INDIAN MISSION CONFERENCE which had become overwhelmingly a body of white ministers and churches. The Indian preachers and churches continued in the Oklahoma Conference and its successor conferences until 1918 when they were set off as the Indian Mission.

The Oklahoma Conference began with twelve districts, 237 charges, and 38,529 members. In 1910 there were fifteen districts, 295 charges, and 52,267 members, and the body divided to form the East and West Oklahoma Conferences. At that time practically all of the Indian work was placed in the East Conference. The next year the East Conference reported 27,901 members and the West Conference 28,177. At Tulsa on Oct. 29, 1930 the two conferences merged to form again the Oklahoma Conference with twelve districts and 76,665 members, an arrangement which continued until unification in 1939.

Southern Methodism in Oklahoma was interested in schools and other agencies, and with the aid of the Federal government and the Indian Councils, the Indian Mission Conference built a number of schools for the Indians. The Methvin Institute at Anadarko (1890-1906) was the Southern Church's last school for Indians. As the conference became predominantly white, schools for the whites were established. When the Oklahoma Conference began in 1906 it had four colleges: Epworth University at Oklahoma City, Spaulding College at Muskogee, Willie Halsell College at Vinita, and Hargrove College at Ardmore. All failed within the next ten years. Finally in 1928 the Southern Church joined the Northern Church in support of the college in Oklahoma City which became OKLAHOMA CITY UNIVERSITY, a strong Methodist college today.

In 1919 the two Oklahoma Conferences started an orphanage at Oklahoma City and invited the Indian Mission, then one year old, to elect two members to the institution's governing board. Moved to TAHLEQUAH about twenty years later, the Oklahoma Methodist Home for Children has become an outstanding institution of its kind.

In 1882 the Indian Mission Conference began publishing a paper in Muskogee entitled *Our Brother in Red*. Between 1905 and 1920 Oklahoma Methodism joined first with ARKANSAS Methodism and then with TEXAS Methodism in publishing papers. In the latter year the *Oklahoma Methodist* began, flourished for ten years, and was then merged with the *Texas Christian Advocate* to form the *Southwestern Christian Advocate*.

In 1939 the Oklahoma Conference approached unification with ten districts, 257 charges, 364 churches, 91,795 members, and property valued at $7,583,752.

Babcock and Bryce, *Oklahoma*. 1935.
Clegg and Oden, *Oklahoma*. 1968.
General Minutes, MES.
Minutes of the Oklahoma Conferences, MES.

ALBEA GODBOLD

OKLAHOMA CONFERENCE (MC) was organized at TULSA, May 24, 1954 with Bishop W. ANGIE SMITH presiding. It was formed by merging the East and West Oklahoma Conferences. The latter two conferences were created at unification in 1939 when the Oklahoma Conference (MEC), the Oklahoma Conference (MECS), and the Oklahoma part of the Fort Smith-Oklahoma Conference (MP) were merged. (See OKLAHOMA, INDIAN MISSION, and OKLAHOMA CONFERENCES MEC and MECS for accounts of Oklahoma Methodism prior to 1939.)

The East Oklahoma Conference began in 1939 with six districts and 214 charges, while the West Conference had seven districts and 279 charges. The next year the one reported 57,313 members and the other 69,902. When they merged in 1954 to form the Oklahoma Conference, the East Conference had 222 charges and 90,028 members, and the West Conference 288 charges and 115,259 members making a total of 205,287 members in the Oklahoma Conference as it began. This represented an increase of sixty-one per cent in the total membership of the two conferences between 1940 and 1954.

Three Oklahoma pastors have been elected bishop: H. BASCOM WATTS and PAUL V. GALLOWAY from the pastorate of Boston Avenue Church, Tulsa, the one in 1952, the other in 1960; and W. MCFERRIN STOWE from St. Luke's Church, OKLAHOMA CITY, in 1964. Bishops DANA DAWSON and KENNETH W. COPELAND served as pastors in Oklahoma and were elevated to the episcopacy after moving elsewhere.

The Oklahoma Conference supports OKLAHOMA CITY UNIVERSITY which has over 2,000 students, a fourteen-million dollar plant, and an endowment of $2,000,000. The churches take offerings for PHILANDER SMITH COLLEGE in LITTLE ROCK. Fifteen WESLEY FOUNDATIONS are maintained with five full time campus ministers. The *Oklahoma Methodist* reaches nearly half the families in the conference.

The conference also supports the following institutions and service agencies: the Oklahoma Methodist Manor for the aged and the Frances E. Willard Home for Girls in Tulsa; the 400-acre Boy's Ranch near Gore; the Methodist Home for Children at Tahlequah; two nursing homes, one at Enid and one at Clinton; Camp Canyon near Hinton; Lake Texoma Camp near Kingston; and Camp Egan near Tahlequah.

In 1970 the Oklahoma Conference reported 14 districts, 468 charges, 549 ministers, 259,812 members, and property valued at $97,408,269. The total amount of money raised for all purposes that year was $9,454,322.

Clegg and Oden, *Oklahoma*. 1968.
General Minutes, TMC, UMC.
Minutes of the Oklahoma Conference.   FREDERICK E. MASER

OKLAHOMA-TEXAS CONFERENCE (EUB) consisted of two former annual conferences in OKLAHOMA and TEXAS plus two groups of churches previously belonging to two other annual conferences. The Oklahoma and Texas Conferences were united in 1956. A group of five UNITED BRETHREN Churches in the Oklahoma Panhandle were added to the Oklahoma United Brethren Conference when the North Texas United Brethren Conference was dissolved in 1913. Seven E.U.B. churches in Oklahoma belonging to the Kansas Conference became a part of the Oklahoma-Texas Conference in 1960.

The EVANGELICAL ASSOCIATION began work in Texas

in 1879. Bishop J. J. ESHER of the Evangelical Association was the man most instrumental in getting approval of his mission board to send men to preach the gospel in German in Galveston and SAN ANTONIO.

The first congregation was organized in San Antonio in 1879. Between 1880 and 1887, J. M. Gomer, who was in charge of the work at Galveston, made visits to the interior of Texas to seek opportunities for expanding the work among German-speaking Evangelicals who had migrated to Texas from northern states. The first session of the Texas Conference was held at Temple in October 1887. From 1894 to 1899, the conference existed as two Districts, "north" and "south." The conference continued as a single district from 1899 onward.

The membership of the seven charges comprising the Texas Conference at its beginning was 253. The greatest number of ministers for any one year was sixteen, in 1912, and these men served seventeen appointments.

The organizing Conference of the Oklahoma United Brethren Church was held at the Eden Chapel Church, ten miles southeast of Stillwater, in February 1898. Twenty-four ministers and twenty lay delegates made up the official membership.

The twenty-five charges totaling 1,500 members had been a part of the Arkansas Valley Conference preceding 1898. United Brethren people had been among those settlers securing property in the opening of the "Unassigned Lands" in 1889, and other openings of Indian lands in 1890's. By 1907, when Oklahoma became a state, the conference counted seventy-five churches, twenty-seven preachers, and 2,836 church members.

The Oklahoma Conference was principally an organization of rural churches. In 1900, the twenty-four churches averaged sixty-six members each; and in 1950, the average number of members in the thirty-one churches reporting was 130.

The North Texas Conference of the United Brethren Church existed from 1908 to 1913. At their final session in 1913, five churches in the Oklahoma Panhandle were transferred to the Oklahoma Conference.

The Texas Conference and Oklahoma Conference were united on May 29, 1956. Texas brought eight churches, 1,376 members, and eight pastors to the Union; Oklahoma brought twenty-two churches, 3,343 members, and nineteen pastors.

The Student Aid Society of the Texas Conference was continued in the united conference. Its purpose was to give financial assistance to ministerial students while attending Seminary.

Since Oklahoma-Texas union one mission church was begun—Cathedral Church now called Regency Park Church at Moore, Okla.—in 1963. Finances for the new church came largely from the Forward Fellowship program begun in 1959.

In 1960 the seven Kansas Conference churches located in Oklahoma were joined to the Oklahoma-Texas Conference and seven Itinerant Elders of the Kansas Conference transferred their credentials to the Oklahoma-Texas Conference.

From 1964 through 1967, Camp Redlands was leased by the conference from Oklahoma State University at Stillwater and was used chiefly as a site for Christian Education groups.

In 1968 churches in Texas joined former Methodist Conferences in that state and the twenty-five churches in Oklahoma became one with the former Oklahoma Methodist Conference.

MARVIN M. POLSON

OLD STONE CHURCH SITE AND CEMETERY, Leesburg, Va., is a national historic shrine of The United Methodist Church. (See LEESBURG, VIRGINIA.)

OLDHAM, WILLIAM FITZJAMES (1854-1937), missionary bishop of the M. E. Church in Southern Asia 1904-12; secretary of the Board of MISSIONS, New York, 1912-16; bishop (general superintendent), South America, 1916-28. He was born at Bangalore, INDIA, Dec. 15, 1854. His father was an officer of the army of the East India Company. He married Marie Mulligan, born in Poona. Both were of British and Indian ancestry.

Oldham was employed as a government surveyor, when in 1873 he heard D. O. Fox, an associate of WILLIAM TAYLOR, preach. He was converted and joined the Methodist Church, and a little later he went to America and entered ALLEGHENY COLLEGE. He joined the MICHIGAN ANNUAL CONFERENCE. In 1884, he was accepted as a missionary of the Board of Missions and sent to India.

Bishop THOBURN was looking for a man to open Methodist work in SINGAPORE. He chose Oldham, whom he ordained as an ELDER on Jan. 11, 1885, and the next day appointed him to organize and superintend a mission in Singapore. Thoburn and Oldham went together and held evangelistic services in the town hall. They quickly organized the first Methodist Church, with seventeen members, all British and Eurasians. A few days later a Chinese gentleman joined.

Oldham's work in Singapore was dramatically successful. He developed strong influence among the multi-racial people of the city, organizing congregations using Indian and Chinese languages as well as English. He opened schools and obtained support from well-to-do people of all races. At first, the Malaysia field was included in the BENGAL ANNUAL CONFERENCE, but on April 1, 1893, the MALAYSIA Mission Conference was formed.

Having laid the foundations of the Church in Malaysia, Oldham returned to America and first entered the pastorate and then became professor of missions and comparative religions at OHIO WESLEYAN UNIVERSITY. Bishop BASHFORD wrote of Oldham in this period, "I have wondered whether any pastor in Methodism ever accomplished a greater work than did Dr. Oldham in the last two years."

In 1904, he was elected missionary bishop for Southern Asia with residence in Singapore. In 1912, he was elected one of three co-ordinate secretaries of the Board of Missions and was in constant demand as a speaker and writer. But the 1916 GENERAL CONFERENCE elected him a regular bishop (general superintendent) and assigned him to South America with residence in BUENOS AIRES. He succeeded Bishop STUNTZ as the second resident bishop in Latin America. He came to Buenos Aires in 1917 and stood until 1928, when in turn he was succeeded by Bishop MILLER.

Bishop Oldham worked for an active cooperation among the Protestant denominations in the River Plate region. During his term of office the M. E. Church entered a cooperative agreement with the Disciples of Christ to work together in Colegio Ward and Union Seminary. Mrs. Mary Oldham, his wife, was a pious lady who was very much appreciated. Until today the Pastors' Wives Association of the Argentine Conference bears her name.

When Oldham was bishop in South America, he had to cross the Andes Mountains in the late fall with the last bank of muleteers to go before winter set in, an altitude of 18,000 feet and winter near. When the mule drivers arrived in late evening at an inn over the crest of the mountains, the bishop's mule was there but no Oldham. The men hurried back and found the bishop on the road unconscious, his clothes frozen to the ground. He is yet remembered in South America with admiration and affection. He retired in 1928, made his home then for several years in India before returning at last to the United States. He died in Glendale, Calif., March 27, 1937, and is buried in Forest Lawn. Among his writings are a sketch of Thoburn in *The Picket Line of Missions, The Study of Missions in Colleges; Malaysia: Nature's Wonderland; The Crucial Hour of Missions; India, Malaysia and the Philippines,* and *Thoburn—Called of God.*

F. D. Leete, *Methodist Bishops.* 1948.
F. J. McConnell, *Autobiography.* 1952.
National Cyclopedia of American Biography.

J. WASKOM PICKETT

OLDROYD, ROXANNA (1881-   ) is a notable pioneer in teaching science subjects to women college students in INDIA. She was born in Shreve, Ohio, Nov. 25, 1881. She was awarded B.S. and M.A. degrees by Kansas State University in 1904 and 1908.

In the summer of 1909, she went to India as a missionary appointed to teach science subjects in ISABELLA THOBURN COLLEGE. At that time very few Indian men or women cared to study science. Their interests were concentrated upon languages and philosophy. Miss Oldroyd taught physics, chemistry, and biology, but initially had fewer than a dozen students in college classes.

On furloughs, she pursued postgraduate studies in science subjects at the University of Chicago and in theology at GARRETT BIBLICAL INSTITUTE. Gradually but steadily, enrollment in her science classes grew, and many of her students became science teachers in other institutions. Many others developed an interest in medicine as a profession and eventually became physicians or surgeons. Of her many students who went on to distinguished achievements one, Evangeline Thillyampalam, became the principal of the college. Miss Oldroyd had a missionary career of almost forty years at Isabella Thoburn College.

M. A. Dimmitt, *Isabella Thoburn College.* 1963.

J. WASKOM PICKETT

OLDS, EDWIN THOMAS (1890-1966), NEW ZEALAND Methodist minister, was born in South Canterbury, New Zealand, on Aug. 1, 1890, one of a large family in a humble Methodist home. He was educated at Oamaru and Christchurch. Accepted for training for the Methodist ministry, he spent the years 1912 to 1914 at the theological college in Dunholme.

In 1915, during the First World War, he enlisted in the New Zealand Rifle Brigade and saw active service in France. He was given an officer's commission in the field. After being severely wounded in 1918, he was invalided home to New Zealand.

In 1919 he was ordained. His most important appointments were Napier, where he was sent in 1931 to help

restore confidence after a disastrous earthquake, and Pitt Street, the historic AUCKLAND church, where he built up a crowded congregation, ministering from 1935 to 1950. He was also chairman of the Auckland District from 1943 to 1949, and president of Conference in 1948. "Tom" Olds was an evangelist and a prophet of inspiration and hope. The young responded to his ardor, and the old found new courage. In the closing years of his life he suffered much weakness and pain, but his faith never wavered. He died in Auckland on Aug. 28, 1966.

New Zealand Methodist Conference Minutes, 1966.

ERIC W. HAMES

OLIN, JULIA M. (-1879), American editor and writer and wife of STEPHEN OLIN, whom she married in 1843 when he was president of WESLEYAN UNIVERSITY. She was born Julia M. Lynch, her father a person of consequence, in NEW YORK. Olin had come to Wesleyan as its president in 1842, and the next year married Julia Lynch, who was his second wife.

After his death, in 1851, she lived with her only surviving son, Henry. She decided to edit Olin's work, and being aided in this by some literary friends, she brought out in 1853, his *Life and Letters,* and his *Greece and the Golden Horn* in 1854. With the proceeds brought in by these writings she established a prize in the Wesleyan University.

Mrs. Olin herself wrote chiefly poems and certain material for daily devotions. She contributed to *The Ladies Repository, Western Christian Advocate,* and the *Methodist Quarterly Review.* It is said that she was a SUNDAY SCHOOL teacher all her life from the age of seventeen. She also is connected with the FIVE POINTS MISSION built on the site of the "old Brewery" in New York, and served as treasurer, directress or corresponding secretary for twenty-six years. She died in New York in 1879.

M. Simpson, *Cyclopaedia.* 1878.   N. B. H.

STEPHEN OLIN

OLIN, STEPHEN (1797-1851), American intellectual leader and college president, who exerted great influence during the first half of the nineteenth century. He was born in Leicester, Vt., on March 7, 1797, and was graduated at Middlebury College, taking honors of his class. His health being impaired, he went to the South and accepted the position of principal of an almost nondescript Tabernacle Academy near Abbeville, S. C. The new teacher boarded in the family of a local preacher by the name of James E. Glenn. After Mrs. Glenn asked him whether or not he opened his school with prayer, he was induced to begin doing so, and this resulted in his conversion.

Having become converted, he applied for license to preach, but the presiding elder, Joseph Travis, was in great doubt about him, and while he trusted Glenn's good judgment, would not look favorably upon Olin until he "put him up" to preach. The sermon was so good that Travis judged it to be a plagiarism. He was again put up and preached a better sermon than the first. A third time he was tried, and his effort excelled both of the others. Finally, on Sunday, before an immense congregation, he preached on the daughter of Herodias dancing before Herod and "swept the field." The presiding elder gave in and licensed him to preach. Two or three years later he entered the SOUTH CAROLINA CONFERENCE, but in 1826 went to the University of Georgia, where he taught English literature for seven years. While there he married a Miss Bostick of Milledgeville, Ga., who was his devoted companion for twelve years. She died in Naples, Italy, while they were on an extended journey in Europe.

In 1834 he accepted the presidency of RANDOLPH-MACON COLLEGE, then at Boydton, Va., and then for a time, from 1837-41, he traveled in Europe and the East, publishing a volume having to do with his travels. In 1842 he was elected president of WESLEYAN UNIVERSITY at Middletown, Conn., upon the death of WILBUR FISK. There had been a brief presidency there by NATHAN BANGS who resigned in order that Olin might take over.

In 1843 he married again, this time JULIA M. LYNCH who accompanied him in his travels and especially to the first meeting of the Evangelical Alliance in LONDON in 1846.

Olin was elected a delegate to the GENERAL CONFERENCE of 1844, and took a prominent part in the great debate which divided that body. Knowing the South, as well as the North, he attempted to reconcile the insurmountable differences between the two sections, and in a speech to the body seconded the motion of WILLIAM CAPERS of SOUTH CAROLINA, calling for a committee to see what plan might be worked out for the pacification of the Church.

Olin, however, voted with the majority of the Conference and was appointed one of the committee to draw up a "reply to the Protest" in order to answer the "protest" which had been formally put in by the southern delegations. However, when next year the M. E. Church began to repudiate the PLAN OF SEPARATION, Olin joined Nathan Bangs in saying that the "honor of the Church was at stake" and that the commitment of the General Conference with regard to the Plan of Separation should be kept.

As president of Wesleyan (which became the strongest institution of learning of the M. E. Church during the years of the presidency of Wilbur Fisk and Stephen Olin), Olin entered the field of theological discussion and became a champion of the Methodist viewpoint. He held that the great lack in the theology of Methodism was "the reduction of its tenets to a scientific system." It is said that many Methodists hoped that Olin himself would commit the Wesleyan motifs to such treatment, but his demands as an administrator in charge of Wesleyan, and more particularly the desperate situation of his health (bad health

plagued him all his life), kept him from doing so. Eventually his nervous power gave way, and he died in Middletown on Aug. 16, 1851. His wife edited his writings after his death and published also his *Life and Letters*. His was one of the rare minds of the Methodist Church.

E. S. Bucke, *History of American Methodism*. 1964.
A. M. Chreitzberg, *Methodism in the Carolinas*. 1897.
Encyclopedia Americana.
H. N. McTyeire, *History of Methodism*. 1884.
M. Simpson, *Cyclopaedia*. 1881.   N. B. H.

OLIN, WILLIAM H. (1821-1889), American minister and publicist, was born Jan. 5, 1821, in Laurens, Otsego Co., N. Y. He studied at Cazenovia Seminary, and afterward studied law, was admitted to the bar, and opened a law office in Oneonta, N. Y.

During revival meetings Olin heard A. B. Earle preach on "The Power of Prayer." Immediately he skeptically challenged the pastor to try prayer on him, but declined to cooperate by going forward. However, the minister urged people to pray for the young lawyer. A few nights later Olin yielded, was thoroughly converted and joined the church. Having been suggested as a candidate for Congress, and having been invited to enter partnership with a prosperous law firm in New York City, he declined. Instead, he entered the Methodist ministry and became a member of the ONEIDA CONFERENCE of the M.E. Church in 1851. With changes in district and conference boundaries he became a member of the CENTRAL NEW YORK CONFERENCE, and then in 1869 of the WYOMING CONFERENCE.

Olin was a presiding elder seventeen and a half years, and a member of the GENERAL CONFERENCE eight times, 1860-1888. While presiding elder of the Binghamton district (1884-87), he represented Broome County one term in the State Assembly, having been nominated by the Prohibition party and endorsed by the Republican. WESLEYAN UNIVERSITY conferred upon him the M.A. degree, and SYRACUSE UNIVERSITY the D.D. degree. He was married twice; first to Emily A. Reed, and in 1857 to Melissa E. Walker, both of Oneonta.

Olin had a striking personality, was an eloquent speaker and a contender for righteousness. He died in Dexter, Mich., on Sept. 16, 1889, and was buried in Oneonta.

A. F. Chaffee, *Wyoming Conference*. 1904.
Minutes of the Wyoming Conference, 1890.
                                        LOUIS D. PALMER

OLIVER, (CAPTAIN) WILLIAM (1849-1937), Canadian Methodist lay missionary, was born March 19, 1849, at Bishoptown-on-Clyde, SCOTLAND. His father was a farmer and tile-maker, his mother a servant girl who took William, strapped to her back, when she went reaping with a sickle in the fields. William went to work at the incredibly early age of five, driving the blind horse that powered the mill for crushing tile clay. At seven he was a rivet boy at Denny's shipyards. By going to night school, for which he paid a penny a week, he learned to write by the age of fourteen.

At twenty, William Oliver went to sea as ship's carpenter on the Norwegian sailing ship "Ebenezer," and for the next twelve years he sailed all over the world on a number of vessels. Once, when their sailing ship was caught in the doldrums crossing the Atlantic, he saved himself and the crew from starvation by scraping filthy grain off the keelson, washing it, and grinding it up for porridge.

At the age of thirty-two, and in an advanced stage of alcoholism, he arrived in Victoria, Vancouver Island, where he left the ship and went to work in the shipyards, transferring a year later to New Westminster on the Fraser. It was here in the year 1883, at the age of thirty-four, that he was dramatically converted.

Not long after his religious experience he met THOMAS CROSBY, who raised money in the East to purchase or build a mission boat for the West Coast work. William Oliver offered his services. Working for mere room and board, he built the first Methodist mission boat on the West Coast, "The Glad Tidings." When she was launched he accompanied Crosby as engineer, later as skipper. After "The Glad Tidings" was wrecked, Oliver entered the fish-oil manufacturing business on the Queen Charlotte Islands, but five years later he sold out, and using his own money, he built the "Udal," which he presented to the church with the stipulation that he be allowed to navigate her. In the closing years of his life he designed and built two more mission vessels, the "Thomas Crosby," and the "Melvin Swartout." At the age of eighty he retired from sailing and took the job of supervising the building, equipment, and maintenance of the marine mission fleet for The United Church of Canada.

Captain Oliver was a daring navigator, a master craftsman, and a fearless personal evangelist, whose reputation was unsurpassed along the coast from Vancouver to Alaska. He was for years the companion and friend of the renowned Thomas Crosby, and though intensely devout he was at home with loggers, fishermen, trappers, and lighthouse-keepers wherever he went.

In April, 1896, Oliver married Agnes Calder, the daughter of one of the first converts among the Haida people of Queen Charlotte Islands. They had no children of their own, but adopted one boy, Robert. Captain Oliver died Jan. 3, 1937, after fifty years of service on the coast.

W. H. Morris, *Captain William Oliver: A Fisher of Men.* Peru: N.p., 1941.
R. C. Scott, *My Captain Oliver.* Toronto: United Church Publishing House, 1947.   H. W. McKervill

OLIVERS, THOMAS (1725-1799),

OLIVERS, THOMAS (1725-1799), British itinerant—shoemaker, musician, poet, hymn writer, controversialist—was born at Tregynon, Montgomeryshire, and baptized Sept. 8, 1725. Converted at BRISTOL under WHITEFIELD, joining the Methodists at Bradford-on-Avon, Olivers began preaching about 1744. Associated with WESLEY from 1753, he traveled until 1772 in Lancashire, Yorkshire, SCOTLAND, IRELAND and LONDON. After 1777 he resided in London, where he lent £600 toward Wesley's Chapel, and subedited (badly) Methodist publications. In dignified, well-reasoned, sometimes caustic writings he championed Wesley's Methodism against AUGUSTUS TOPLADY, ROWLAND and Richard HILL, and Theophilus Evans. He wrote the hymn, *The God of Abraham Praise,* which yet remains in Methodist hymnals. He died at Hoxton, March 7, 1799.

GEORGE LAWTON

OLMSTEAD, B. L. (1886-1960), an ordained elder of the FREE METHODIST CHURCH, was editor of *Arnold's Com-* *mentary* (Free Methodist) for twenty-nine years. He held the degrees A.B. and A.M., Wheaton College, Illinois; B.D., McCormick Theological Seminary. He pursued graduate studies at Glasgow, Scotland on the Bernadine Orme Smith Fellowship. He was pastor of Free Methodist churches in MICHIGAN, INDIANA, and ILLINOIS. He served as Dean of Theology, GREENVILLE COLLEGE (1922-31). He then became editor of Free Methodist Sunday school literature, continuing until his death in 1960. He was a reverent scholar, clear writer, persuasive preacher. He died at Winona Lake, Ind.

BYRON S. LAMSON

OLMSTEAD, WILLIAM B. (1862-1941), an ordained elder of the California Conference of the FREE METHODIST CHURCH, was General Missionary Secretary. He attended Spring Arbor Seminary. He was pastor and superintendent in OHIO and MICHIGAN, and was elected editor of Sunday school literature in 1898 and General Sunday School Secretary in 1907. While President of Wessington Springs Junior College, he was elected General Missionary Secretary serving from 1919 to 1933. He was a pastor in the California Conference until his death, Sept. 22, 1941. He was a capable administrator, clear writer, forceful preacher and a great missionary statesman. His death occurred at San Jose, Calif.

BYRON S. LAMSON

OLSON, OSCAR THOMAS (1887-1964), American pastor, ecumenist, liturgist and authority on the Methodist ritual, was born at CHICAGO, Ill., Jan. 2, 1887, the son of Oliver W. and Hannah T. Olson. He received his A.B. from ALBION COLLEGE in 1911, his M.A. from Columbia University and Union Theological Seminary in 1913. He held several honorary degrees.

He married Edith Margaret Ketcham in 1912, and one of their three sons was John Frederic Olson, president of OKLAHOMA CITY UNIVERSITY. His pastorates included Trinity Church, DETROIT, Mich.; historic Mount Vernon Place Church, BALTIMORE, Md., where he exerted considerable influence in that city; Wilmette Parish Church, Wilmette, Ill., and from 1924 until his retirement in 1959, he served Epworth-Euclid Church, CLEVELAND, Ohio.

Olson early obtained a name for himself in the field of liturgics, and was a pioneer in calling the attention of Methodism to the proper use of forms of worship. He was a member of the Joint Hymnal Commission of the Methodist Churches, which brought out the *Methodist Hymnal* in 1935, and on its sub-committee which drew up the Responsive Readings published in that Hymnal. He was chairman of the Commission on Rituals and WORSHIP of the M. E. Church, and served as secretary and editor for the commission that published the *Book of Worship* in 1944. He also became chairman of the Commission on Worship of the FEDERAL COUNCIL OF CHURCHES, 1940-48. He was a delegate from the BALTIMORE CONFERENCE to the M. E. GENERAL CONFERENCE of 1932, the Uniting Conference of 1939, and to the General Conference of The Methodist Church in 1940, 1948, 1952, 1956, and 1960. In the last named quadrennia, he was a delegate from the NORTH-EAST OHIO CONFERENCE. He was put in strong nominations for the episcopacy several times by his conference brethren.

In 1947, he was made secretary of the ECUMENICAL

METHODIST COUNCIL, Western Section; in 1951 at the WORLD METHODIST COUNCIL in OXFORD, England, he was elected President of the American Section; in 1956 at the World Methodist Conference at LAKE JUNALUSKA, he became Vice-President of the World Methodist Council.

He died Nov. 23, 1964 and was buried in Forest Hill Cemetery, Ann Arbor, Mich.

C. T. Howell, *Prominent Personalities.* 1945.
Yearbook of the North-East Ohio Conference, 1965.

ROBERT H. COURTNEY

OMAHA, NEBRASKA, U.S.A., known as "the Gateway City," is on the Missouri River opposite Council Bluffs, Iowa, and is the industrial and commercial center of NEBRASKA. An important grain, livestock and meatpacking market, Omaha's major industry is food processing. Among other things, it manufactures farm machinery, fertilizer and insecticides. It has the nationally known "Boys Town," a famous symphony orchestra, Joselyn Museum, and Mormon Cemetery.

The site of a licensed Indian trading post in 1825, Omaha was founded in 1854 and incorporated in 1857. It is the seat of the Municipal University of Omaha, Creighton University, Duchesne College, the College of St. Mary, and of Nebraska's School for the Deaf.

Methodism was introduced into the Omaha region about 1851 when William Simpson was sent to Council Bluffs from the IOWA CONFERENCE. Omaha first appears on the M. E. Church records in 1854. It was listed (1855) in connection with the MISSOURI CONFERENCE. The next year it was included in the Kansas and Nebraska Conference. In 1861 it reported eighty-one members with property valued at $6,000, and then came to be in the NEBRASKA CONFERENCE which was organized in 1860.

Omaha had three churches in 1876 with 359 members, not including an A. M. E. Church with thirty-seven members. First Church then had 252 members.

Omaha was for many years Headquarters of the Omaha Area in the M. E. Church, including Iowa and Nebraska. After 1939 the JURISDICTIONAL system separated these states, and though Omaha continued as headquarters for a time, it served various territories—KANSAS, indeed, being added for one quadrennium. LINCOLN, Neb., is at present headquarters for the Nebraska Area as well as for the Nebraska Annual Conference. In 1891 the Nebraska Methodist Hospital (now the Omaha Methodist Hospital) was established. It is presently in process of moving to new and adequate modern facilities in the western suburbs of Omaha. GOODWILL INDUSTRIES came to Omaha in 1934 from St. Louis, Mo., with Ross Wesley Adair at the head. E. E. Hosman guided its development until his retirement when it moved to very modern facilities in a strategic location on South 42nd Street.

Stragetic Air Command headquarters to the south of the city offers special opportunities for Methodism to touch the lives of a select group of U.S. Airmen and their families. The Omaha Campus Ministry, an ecumenical project, has been directed by Leonard S. Barry, under Nebraska Conference appointment since 1963. He ministers to colleges and graduate schools of the city. Benjamin F. Schwartz also serves as Assistant Protestant chaplain of the Veterans Administration Hospital in Omaha. There are four congregations of the A.M.E. CHURCH, and one each of the FREE METHODIST, WESLEYAN METHODIST, and C.M.E. CHURCHES.

In 1970 there were seventeen United Methodist churches in Omaha with a total membership of 14,508, and property valued at $7,476,595.

First Church was the first church of any denomination to be organized in Omaha. The first Methodist sermon ever preached in Nebraska was delivered by Harrison Presson on April 21, 1850 to members of the wagon train with which he was traveling. Returning later, Presson was a member of the Nebraska Conference for many years. Omaha first appeared on the records of the M. E. Church in 1854.

On Aug. 13, 1854, Peter Cooper preached at the Snowden residence. In September 1855, Isaac F. Collins of Council Bluffs, Iowa, organized First Methodist Church in the Territorial Capitol Building with six members—twelve years before statehood. Omaha reported twenty-six members in 1855; eighty-one in 1861; and 232 in 1876.

Early in 1856 the first building was erected on the site given to the church by the Ferry Boat Company, whose president was William B. Brown, a true pioneer of Omaha and a Methodist. The Ferry Boat Company gave two lots. One was sold for $1,500 and the money was used in building the first sanctuary at a cost of $4,500. It was dedicated in 1856 by Moses Shinn, presiding elder.

In 1876 a frame church was constructed and occupied until June 8, 1890, when the basement of the third building was first occupied. The imposing edifice was of stone and brick, and seated 1,200 people. It cost approximately $100,000 and was dedicated May 24, 1890. This church was completely destroyed by fire on Jan. 11, 1954.

After the fire the present church was built at 69th and Cass Streets. The first service was held in it June 2, 1957. It is located on twelve acres of land. In 1970 First Church reported 3,796 members.

Omaha City Mission Society, as it is now constitued, is an agency of the WOMEN'S SOCIETY OF CHRISTIAN SERVICE of The United Methodist Church, and is a new organization, having been incorporated in January, 1959. However, the present organization is the successor to the oldest social agency in the state of NEBRASKA, the Christian Workers Association, which was founded Oct. 27, 1872, by a group of laymen of the First Methodist Church of the city of Omaha. In 1922 the Women's Home Missionary Society of The M. E. Church became interested in sponsoring the work of "The Mission," and soon assumed the responsibility for its operation.

The work of the Agency was originally that of relief to the poor, a shelter for the homeless, day care for children, and a dormitory for women and girls. The growth of the city and the changing of neighborhoods made the location at 1204 Pacific unsuited for the program of the Agency by the late twenties. The building was sold and the Agency moved in 1934 to a rented property at 2201 Cass Street. The new location and a new approach to human needs caused the program of the Agency to be that of a community or "settlement house" center. The building became known as Neighborhood House and served with great success for twenty-four years in a very needy section of the Near-North Side of Omaha.

A new modern community center called "Wesley House" at 2001 North 35th Street was erected in 1958-59. Wesley House is located in the center of an area of 16,000 persons in which there are no churches of major denominations, no recreation or community service facilities except a public grade school. It is an area in which there is an increasing number of minority peoples. The neighborhood shows some signs of change and deterioration, but is not past reclamation. A third community center program was begun at 30th and Grant Streets in the property of the Municipal Housing Authority in the city of Omaha in the summer of 1959.

Before Wesley House building plans were approved, a re-study was made of the services and the type program to be carried on by the Agency. The purposes of Omaha City Mission Society were set forth in the new constitution to be:

To provide Christian neighborhood centers which shall work cooperatively with the communities, schools, churches, and other religious and social welfare agencies to determine and meet the spiritual, intellectual, physical, moral and civic needs of the communities irrespective of race, color, or creed. This purpose shall be achieved through the provision for religious instruction, and services, recreation, group work, and education.

A professionally trained, dedicated staff of Christian workers is now actively engaged in fulfilling this purpose through the various groups, programs and activities of the Agency in three centers in three distinct communities. Those centers are: Wesley House, 2001 North 35th Street; Neighborhood House, 724 North 22nd Street; and Hilltop Homes, 3012 Grant Street.

St. Paul Church is a church situated midway between an inner-city situation and the suburbs and continues to demonstrate a deep concern for church extension. Involved in a building program and an enlarging local program, St. Paul has managed to invest significantly in the development of five new churches in the Omaha area during the past ten years.

St. Paul is the result of a merger of three churches— Centenary, Walnut Hill, and Benson Methodist churches, as these were during the days of economic depression. Their merger was accomplished in 1930 when the respective properties were transferred to the St. Paul M.E. Church. A new site was purchased—its present location— at the intersection of Country Club Avenue and Corby Street.

During the period since this merger the church has grown approximately four times its original membership. Its leadership is characterized by laymen and ministers who are concerned to identify the efforts of the church both with the community and with the larger reaches of world responsibility. The aim is to balance its local program with the investment of both money and personnel in new churches, and in world mission projects.

Throughout its history the church has emphasized a strong Christian education program. Wherever possible its program has also had a strong family emphasis, but the church has provided also for persons whose experiences are found mostly outside the family setting. The time of one staff member is devoted to programs reaching persons who do not feel at home in the traditional couple, or family-centered type of church life. Having been a pioneer in Omaha in the development of a program characterized by multiple-services and a staff ministry, St. Paul looks forward to continuing opportunities for improvements.

In 1970 St. Paul Church reported 3,205 members, property valued at $1,120,455, and a total of $213,952 raised for all purposes.

General Minutes, UMC.
M. Simpson, *Cyclopaedia.* 1881.
G. A. Steinheimer, *Centennial Bulletin, First Church History, 1867-1967.*

BENJAMIN F. SCHWARTZ
JESSE A. EARL
HAROLD G. CRUME
ALVA H. CLARK

ISAMU OMURA

OMURA, ISAMU (1901-   ), Japanese pastor and church leader, was born in Yamanashi Prefecture in central JAPAN, and was baptized as an infant in the Methodist Church. He graduated from the Theological Department of AOYAMA GAKUIN, TOKYO, in 1928. After serving for three years as a pastor, he came to BOSTON UNIVERSITY, where he received the S.T.B. degree in 1933, and S.T.M. in 1934.

On returning to Japan he became pastor of the Asagaya Methodist Church in Tokyo, and at the same time began teaching in the Theological Department of Aoyama Gakuin. He gave up his pastorate when he was made Dean of the Theological Department in 1937, but, when he resigned as Dean in 1940, he returned to the same church, of which he is still pastor. He has been active in the work of the United Church of Christ in Japan, in which the Japan Methodist Church merged in 1941. He has represented the church in various international meetings, including the GENERAL CONFERENCE of The Methodist Church in Denver in 1960. At that time he was serving as vice-moderator. In 1962 he was elected moderator of the United Church of Christ in Japan, and was re-elected in 1964.

JOHN B. COBB, SR.

ONDERDONK, FRANK SCOVILL (1871-1936), American missionary and leader in missionary work in MEXICO, was born in Mission Valley, TEXAS. Educated at SOUTHWESTERN UNIVERSITY, Georgetown, Texas, he was admitted to the WEST TEXAS CONFERENCE, and then went to Mexico in 1897 and was an active leader in the Central Mexico Mission. He was District Superintendent in San Luis Potosi (1897-1901), and in Mexico City (1901-

03); principal of the Colegio Wesleyan in Guadalajara (1903-07); and in San Luis Potosi (1907-14).

A large, genial, optimistic, and energetic man, he earned the affection as well as the support of those who knew him both in Mexico and in the missionary promotional visits he frequently made back to Texas and into other states, where he addressed large assemblies of Southern Methodists. In 1910, when the Mexican revolution started, Onderdonk went back to Texas to take charge of the work there. He wrote one book *A Glimpse at Mexico*.

Bodas de Diamante del Metodismo en Mexico, 1873-1928.
GUSTAVO A. VELASCO G.

ONEIDA CONFERENCE (ME) was organized at Cazenovia, N. Y., in June 1829. It was formed by dividing the GENESEE CONFERENCE. The 1828 GENERAL CONFERENCE voted to permit the Genesee Conference to divide into two bodies if it so desired. At its session in Ithaca, beginning July 24, 1828, the conference voted to divide, designated the part of its territory east of Cayuga Lake as the Oneida Conference and agreed to meet as separate conferences in 1829. The territory of the Oneida Conference included a part of central NEW YORK and a small part of northern PENNSYLVANIA. The conference began with six districts—Black River, Cayuga, Chenango, Oneida, Pottsdam, and Susquehanna. There were fifty-nine charges and 19,320 members.

At its 1835 session the Oneida Conference voted to ask the General Conference to divide it into two conferences. At that time the conference had nine districts, 119 charges, and 34,763 members. The next year the northern part of the conference territory was set off as the BLACK RIVER CONFERENCE. This left the Oneida Conference with six districts—Berkshire, Cayuga, Chenango, Cortland, Oneida, and Susquehanna—sixty-seven charges, and 19,164 members.

In 1851 the Oneida Conference had eight districts and 30,484 members. The next year three of those districts—Newark, Susquehanna, and Wyoming—were set off as the WYOMING CONFERENCE. This left the Oneida Conference with 19,207 members.

The 1868 General Conference abolished the Oneida Conference. Its territory was divided between the Wyoming Conference and the newly created CENTRAL NEW YORK CONFERENCE. The Chenango and Otsego Districts went to the Wyoming Conference, and the Auburn, Cazenovia, Cortland, and Oneida Districts to the Central New York body. The latter is regarded as the legal and historical successor of the Oneida Conference.

In 1868, its last year, the Oneida Conference reported 146 charges, 19,467 members, and property valued at $840,600.

F. W. Conable, *History of the Genesee Annual Conference.* New York: Nelson and Phillips, 1876.
General Minutes, MEC.
ALBEA GODBOLD

ONTARIO LADIES' COLLEGE, founded in 1874, is located in Whitby, Ontario, CANADA. The original structure, built by Sheriff Nelson G. Reynolds in 1859 and known as "Trafalgar Castle," is reputed to have been the finest private residence in Canada in its day. When it was learned that the palatial dwelling would have to be sold, a small group of men in the Whitby area acted swiftly to secure the building and its 100 acres of property

from the sheriff as a school for girls, in the name of the Wesleyan Methodist Church. J. E. Sanderson was appointed moral governor and J. J. Hare principal. In 1878, an extension known as Ryerson Hall, in honor of EGERTON RYERSON, was erected to provide for the increasing enrollment. In 1895 another extension, known as Frances Hall, in honor of Lillian Frances Massey Treble, a generous benefactress of the school, was built. Between 1911 and 1913 further extensions to the main structure were made, as there were in 1955.

The college has been administered by a board of directors, incorporated in 1878 as a private company with share capital under the statutes of the Province of Ontario. In 1961 this charter was amended to provide for a company without share capital.

The college has always maintained close ties with the church. At the time of church union in Canada in 1925, this relationship was substantially strengthened. The school is now classified as a secondary school operating under the Board of Colleges of The United Church of Canada, which makes an annual grant.

The first principal remained at his post forty-two years and was succeeded in 1915 by Francis L. Farewell. At his death in 1928, Charles R. Carscallen was appointed. Stanley L. Osborne became principal in 1948 and was succeeded in 1968 by R. C. Davis.

When the school was founded, it was primarily a finishing school. Today the curriculum embraces the five-year program of the arts and science branch of the department of education of the Province of Ontario, and offers English, history, geography, mathematics, science, Latin, French, German, and home economics. In the residence 125 students can be accommodated.

M. Macrae and A. Adamson, *The Ancestral Roof.* Toronto: Clarke Irwin, 1963.
J. E. Sanderson, *First Century in Canada.* 1908-10.
S. L. OSBORNE

ORANGE, New South Wales, Australia. **Wolaroi College** for boys is 200 miles west of SYDNEY. It was established as a Methodist school in 1926, being acquired from private interests, and has twenty-seven acres of land.

From 1950 modern buildings have been erected, such as Manual Arts, Classrooms and Junior School. The school has an agricultural trend, but also directs to University Entrance in all fields—Arts, Sciences, and Commerce.

Enrolment is 132, of whom 112 are boarders.

AUSTRALIAN EDITORIAL COMMITTEE

ORANGEBURG, SOUTH CAROLINA, U.S.A., **Methodist Home for the Aging.** On Nov. 2, 1953 the Board of Hospitals and Homes of the SOUTH CAROLINA CONFERENCE purchased 113 acres of land east of Orangeburg on which there were ten buildings, properly equipped to take care of aging people. The Home thus purchased was opened on Jan. 6, 1954 with ten residents. The property had formerly served as a training school for air cadets during World War II.

In 1956 the Costen Harrell Building was opened. In 1958 a modern infirmary was opened and in 1961 Harmon Hall opened. In 1963 extensive renovation was made to Capers Hall and a superintendent's residence was built. In 1964 there was a tenth anniversary celebration and a new wing was added to the infirmary. A new residence hall was opened the next year and the business manager's residence renovated. The infirmary has a capacity of fifty-one. The residence capacity, including the infirmary, is 200. The present value of property is $110,000 and that of buildings and equipment is $485,000. There is very little indebtedness.

Trinity Church is a church of the former Central Jurisdiction and is a haven of worship for a cross-section of the Orangeburg community, as well as for students and faculties of two colleges, CLAFLIN COLLEGE, a Methodist institution, and the South Carolina State College. Trinity has served people of all stations of life since T. Willard Lewis, presiding elder of the Charleston District, and Thomas Phillips organized the church the first Sunday in January 1866, in a schoolhouse built by the Freedmen's Bureau. The present edifice, located on Boulevard, is the third structure built since the church was organized. Its three levels house a sanctuary, parish hall, nine classrooms, a pastor's office, a fully-equipped kitchen, weekday kindergarten department, mid-week service chapel, lounges, scout room and utility compartments. Also facing Boulevard, directly across from the two colleges, is the parsonage, a brick structure erected in 1949.

Trinity Church provided conference lay leadership for periods longer than any church in the conference, and has a church school and Sunday attendance record greater than any church in the conference.

Over the years Trinity has served as a center for spiritual, civic, political, and educational activity. The Centennial Celebration was observed the month of January, 1966.

PIERCE EMBREE COOK

ORCHARD, JOHN (1838-1907), NEW ZEALAND minister, was born in Devonshire, England. In 1861 he became a probationer of the BIBLE CHRISTIAN CHURCH. Two years later he was transferred to Victoria. In 1886 he came to CHRISTCHURCH, New Zealand, where he served for nine years. Three years after coming to New Zealand he was appointed General Superintendent of the Church in the Colony, and in 1899 was president of the Wesleyan Methodist Church, three years after the union of the Wesleyans, the Free Methodists, and the Bible Christians. He was prominent in many public movements and was, at the time of his death, a member of the City Council, of the Licensing Bench, of the Charitable Aid Board, and was a governor of the technical college. He died on Jan. 6, 1907.

L. R. M. Gilmore, *The Bible Christian Church in New Zealand.* (Wesley Historical Society, New Zealand, 1947).

L. R. M. GILMORE

ORDER OF CALEB is the organization and continuous roll, past and present, of Methodist ministers who have served twenty or more years in MONTANA. It was instituted during the 1912 session of the North Montana Conference by Bishop LUCCOCK, Aug. 16, 1912, at the Grand Union Hotel, Fort Benton, at a Pioneer Banquet given to mark the fortieth anniversary of Brother Van's (VAN ORSDEL) arrival there in 1872. Brother Van refused to be honored alone and suggested that those who had served twenty years in Montana also be honored. This became the basis of membership, and the motto selected was Numbers 13:30. ("And Caleb stilled the people before Moses and

said, Let us go up at once, and possess it, for we are well able to overcome it.") Following Brother Van, the Montana Methodists have honored a distinguished list of their veteran preachers.

E. L. Mills, *Plains, Peaks and Pioneers.* 1947.
Minutes of the Montana Conference.
E. J. Stanley, *L. B. Stateler.* 1916.   ROBERTA BAUR WEST

ORDER OF ST. LUKE, originally named the Brotherhood of St. Luke, was organized in the American Methodist Church in 1946 by R. P. Marshall and William Esler Slocum, as a liturgical and pastoral fellowship, composed of Methodist ministers, seminary students and lay associates. It is not an Order in the strict sense, but a fellowship; however it does have a Rule of Life and Service which centers around the devotional life of the members, and an emphasis upon worship and the study of liturgy. Very similar to the Sacramental Fellowship in English Methodism, it maintains fraternal relations with this group, and some members hold membership in both.

The Order publishes a quarterly review, *Work Worship,* devoted to studies in the field of liturgy and ecumenical action. Yearly convocations are held in various Methodist seminaries, and the members have been active in the ecumenical movement, the president-emeritus, Romey P. Marshall, having been one of the organizers of the World Center for Liturgical Studies at Boca Raton, Fla. Chapters are organized in various conferences in the U.S.A.

R. P. MARSHALL

ORDERS OF WORSHIP, U.S.A. (See WORSHIP IN AMERICAN METHODISM.)

ORDINATION. This is the name for the solemn act whereby men are set apart for office in the Christian ministry. The Lord Himself chose His apostles, and sent them forth endowed with special gifts. The rite of ordination goes back in principle into the Old Testament, and was applied to the priests, Levites, and kings (Numbers viii: 10), anointing with oil being the practice. The "laying on of hands" was also a frequent practice in ancient days, and the communication of special spiritual endowment was connected with it (see IMPOSITION OF HANDS). Moses adopted this ceremony when he set apart Joshua as his successor (Numbers xxvii: 18; Deuteronomy xxxiv: 9). In the New Testament accounts are given of the selection of church officers (Acts xiv: 21-3; vi: 1-7; xiii: 1-4). The form of ordination in New Testament life came always to be the imposition of hands with prayer. When the apostles set apart the seven deacons, as told in Acts vi, they laid their hands upon them "and prayed."

In reaction against the Roman position making ordination a sacrament, many of the evangelical churches laid the chief emphasis upon the vocation, or divine call, rather than upon an outward ordination. Martin Luther appealed to the credentials of St. Paul when he exclaimed that "He who is called, he is consecrated, and may preach Him who gave the call. That is our Lord's consecration, that is the proper chrism." However, the Augsburg Confession in Article 14 states, "No one may teach publicly in the Church, or administer the sacraments except he be rightly called." Ordination is regarded as the church's solemn approval and public attestation of such inward call. This attitude has been continued in Methodist Churches. (See MINISTERIAL CALL.)

Just when the various "orders" of the ministry of the Church originated has been a matter of debate. It is generally admitted that there is not mentioned in the New Testament an order of clergy in the modern sense of the term. After a time, however, there came to be recognized an order—not simply an office—of DEACONS, and the origin of this is to be found, as stated above, in Acts vi: 17. There was also in early days a definite order of "presbyter-bishops" (Acts xiv 23; xx 17, 28), which order later divided into presbyters (priests; see ELDER) and bishops (see EPISCOPACY). Thus there came to be in the universal Church from an early time the three traditional orders of the ministry, namely, bishops, priests, and deacons, which orders have continued into the Church of England and the Protestant Episcopal Church of the United States. JOHN WESLEY, who sent to American Methodism three forms for ordination in the SUNDAY SERVICE, chose the name "elder" in place of "priest," and "superintendent" in place of "bishop."

At an early date the bishop took the power of ordination into his own hands, and was able to initiate persons into the diaconate, or priesthood (eldership), and also into the episcopate. One opinion is that "very early some of these *episcopi* were assigned the appointment and ordination of the new elders but there seems to have been no rule about it; e.g. in Egypt up to the first quarter of the third century, the presbyteries ordained without episcopal supervision" (Mejer-Jacobson quoted in *Rites and Ritual of Episcopal Methodism,* Harmon, p. 312).

Eventually bishops alone came to have the right to ordain (in association with the presbyters), as they now do in the Church of England, the Protestant Episcopal, and United Methodist Churches. In the United Methodist Church under certain circumstances district superintendents can do everything a bishop can do except ordain.

Ordination and John Wesley. Until well after his evangelical conversion, which itself made little difference to his views on ordination and the ministry, John Wesley held the Anglican beliefs of his day, stating that "bishops, priests and deacons were of Divine appointment" and that Episcopal ordination was necessary for valid sacraments. His field preaching—and more important in this context, his employment of LAY PREACHERS—constituted irregularities of practice. His reading in 1746 of Lord Peter King's *Primitive Church,* and, by 1755, of Edward Stillingfleet's *Irenicon* convinced him that the orders of bishops and priests respectively were essentially the same, though they performed different functions, and that no particular form of church government was prescribed by Christ or the Scriptures, and therefore none could be perpetually binding. As an ordained presbyter, Wesley accordingly claimed the right to ordain, but for a time refused to do so guarding against separation from the Church of England; another factor was undoubtedly the influence of his brother CHARLES, who did not share his new beliefs as to presbyterial powers.

John Wesley emphasized the distinction between the preaching and the sacramental office, maintaining definitely that ordination was required for the latter. In order to provide the Sacraments for his people, Wesley tried, but with little success, to secure regular ordination for some of his preachers from Anglican bishops, and, in one instance, illegal though his action strictly speaking was,

obtained ordination from ERASMUS, a vagrant Greek bishop, for one preacher. In 1775, in consultation with JOHN FLETCHER and JOSEPH BENSON, he drew up a scheme for the greater efficiency of the lay preachers, including proposals for ordination, but these proved abortive.

However, in America, where according to statistics Methodism had expanded rapidly, there were few Anglican priests (and no bishops) from whom the Methodists could obtain the Sacraments. He appealed in vain to Lowth, Bishop of London, under whose jurisdiction Anglican work in America lay, to ordain one of his preachers for Methodist work there. Possibly influenced by a schismatic step in 1783, when two of Selina, COUNTESS OF HUNTINGDON's chaplains separated from the Church of England and proceeded to ordain laymen, Wesley, on Wednesday, Sept. 1, 1784, "appointed Mr. Whatcoat and Mr. Vasey to go and serve the desolate sheep in America." On the next day, Thursday, he says he added three more, though no names are given. His *Diary* for Sept. 2 records that he "ordained Dr. Coke as a Superintendent by imposition of hands and prayer." THOMAS COKE was already a priest of the Established Church and therefore, according to Wesley's revised beliefs, required no further ordination to become a bishop or superintendent. The *Diary* has the word "ordained"; the Journal says "appointed"; and the certificate issued by Wesley has the words "set apart." (*Journal,* Standard Ed. vii; 15-16.) This "setting apart" seems to have been due as much to Coke's persuasion as to Wesley's own wishes— Coke and the Methodists in America interpreted it as episcopal consecration, though it is held by some that Wesley simply intended by this act to delegate his personal authority to Coke while in America, and also as a blessing upon his work of superintendence.

Ordinations for SCOTLAND, and for missionary work overseas successively followed. A complete list of those ordinations of which actual evidence exists may be found in the *Proceedings* of the WESLEY HISTORICAL SOCIETY (xxxiii, 118-19). This includes details of names, times of ordination, and respective orders.

Wesley's justification for these further ordinations was that these regions were outside the legal jurisdiction of the Anglican Church. This was a frail excuse based on a wrong assumption, as the Church of England had its representatives in these countries. Inevitably, ordinations for the English work followed. Pressure was brought to bear on Wesley by people and preachers alike, while some of the latter had taken upon themselves the right to administer the Sacraments without any authority deriving from Wesley at all. As his brother Charles, who had been the greatest restraint upon these moves, was now dead, John Wesley ordained the first of three men for England, ALEXANDER MATHER, deacon and presbyter on Aug. 6 and 7, 1788, respectively. HENRY MOORE and THOMAS RANKIN were similarly ordained on Feb. 26 and 27, 1789.

Together with the appointment of Coke, Wesley published his *Sunday Service* for the American Methodists, which was a revision of the Anglican *Book of Common Prayer.* The ordination services he prescribed therein were for the orders of deacon, elder, and superintendent, indicating his preference for the threefold order of ministry. After John Wesley's death, his followers in England placed little value on his opinions on this subject; the rite of ordination was for the meantime abandoned (apart from the ordination of men destined for service overseas), and when the laying on of hands was resumed in 1836, ordination was simply to the "office and work of a Christian minister"—a form unknown to Wesley.

The final attitude of Wesley to his ordinations, and related questions, is clearly that of a man with a mind deeply and painfully divided. He had set his heart upon preventing separation from the Church of England, yet in his old age he knew that his purpose was defeated, and that the cumulation of his own actions involved virtual separation. So in the *Journal* for July 27, 1786 he can register the determination of the British Conference not to separate "at least till I am removed into a better world" (cf. May 16, 1788). Yet on July 29, 1788 the *Journal* can still rehearse the "variations" from the Church of England as not involving separation. So also in his celebrated last bitter letter to ASBURY of Sept. 20, 1788: "But in one point, my dear brother, I am a little afraid both the Doctor [Coke] and you differ from me. I study to be little; you study to be great.—How can you, how dare you, suffer yourself to be called Bishop? I shudder, I start at the very thought." Wesley was not declaring regret that he set up an authoritative connexional Church government in America, exercising *episcope* under "General Superintendents." It was simply that he did not like the word "bishop," which for him had traditionalist and Anglican connotations it did not carry for most of his American followers. In summarizing the evidence that the aged Wesley had mixed feelings about his ordinations (*John Wesley and Christian Ministry*, pp. 172-3), the present writer states his judgment: Wesley "does regret, not so much the ordinations, as the circumstances necessitating them and the results of them."

Ordination in American Methodism. John Wesley for forty years after he held his first Methodist Conference in 1744, would let none of his preachers administer the Sacraments while they were unordained, although he licensed and directed them in preaching. Nor did Francis Asbury in America allow—when he could help it—any of the American preachers, unordained as they then were, to administer the Sacraments, although ROBERT STRAWBRIDGE and one or two others acted on their own. However, in 1784, Wesley sent over to America with Thomas Coke forms for ordination in the Prayer Book or *Sunday Service* which he had prepared, and which the CHRISTMAS CONFERENCE adopted. From that day to this in American Methodism the three respective forms of ordination which Wesley sent have been used to induct men into the diaconate, the eldership, and the episcopate. Preliminary to this move, as is narrated above, John Wesley himself had ordained Richard Whatcoat and Thomas Vasey as elders, and had ordained Thomas Coke a superintendent (see CHRISTMAS CONFERENCE, SUNDAY SERVICE, THOMAS COKE, FRANCIS ASBURY).

The ordination forms of the American Methodist *Ritual*—which were taken from the Book of Common Prayer almost *litteratim*—may be studied for the vows which the respective ordinands take, and the authority given to each person in these three separate investitures. In the Methodist Episcopal Churches, the "ordination of a bishop" was definitely changed by the GENERAL CONFERENCES of the respective Churches to "the consecration of a bishop," with the intention of indicating the teaching of these Churches, and that of The United Methodist Church, that the bishop is not a higher order than that of the elder. The Protestant Episcopal Church and the Church of England hold that there is an order of bishops

and another order of priests, but in episcopal Methodism the bishop is regarded simply as an elder who has been set apart by a special rite for an office of high administration. However, the M.E. Church, South always contended—and a strong opinion in present Methodist life contends—that "once a bishop always a bishop," and that men who have been inducted into this office have the right to ordain as long as they live. This right has recently been challenged by those Methodist bodies which elect a bishop for a stated term only, especially the CENTRAL CONFERENCES of the now United Methodist Church.

At the General Conference of 1964 (TMC) a strong effort was made to do away with the ordination of deacons, and make this simply consecration to an *office* rather than to an *order*. The same idea, namely, that there is but one ordination, was furthered by the E.U.B. CHURCH, when it came into union with The Methodist Church.

The EVANGELICAL branch of the E.U.B. Church had traditionally observed a dual ordination of deacons and elders while the UNITED BRETHREN IN CHRIST had only one ordination (elder) except for a few years (1818-25) in its early history. With the formation of the E.U.B. Church in 1946, one ordination was adopted—that for an elder.

However, at the 1968 Conference uniting The Methodist Church and the E.U.B. connection, there was a report of a quadrennial committee which had been directed in 1964 to study the ministry in The Methodist Church. This committee in turn consulted with the E.U.B. representatives and there was general agreement that there should be a recommendation that The United Methodist Church keep the diaconate as a separate order as it has been in Methodism since the time of Wesley and the Christmas Conference. This was done and so the two orders remain in The United Methodist Church. (See also, DEACON, ELDER, EPISCOPACY.)

N. B. Harmon, *Rites and Ritual*. 1926.
J. H. S. Kent, *Age of Disunity*. 1966.
A. B. Lawson, *John Wesley*. 1963.
J. J. Tigert, *Constitutional History*. 1894.   A. B. LAWSON
                                                       N. B. H.

O'REAR, EDWARD CLAY (1863-?), American jurist, who represented the M.E. Church, South in important litigation for many years, was born on Feb. 2, 1863, in Montgomery County, Ky. He was educated at the public schools of that state. Judge O'Rear, as he was usually called, was elected a member of the GENERAL CONFERENCE of his Church in 1910, and became chairman of the Vanderbilt Commission created by the General Conference of 1906 and asked to determine the relation of VANDERBILT UNIVERSITY to the M.E. Church, South. He, as attorney, represented the Church in the ensuing litigation. He became a judge in Montgomery County, Ky., and later became judge of the Court of Appeals of KENTUCKY. He was the Republican nominee for the governor of Kentucky in 1911. Judge O'Rear was a well-known figure in the general councils of the M.E. Church, South and earned the gratitude of that Church for his efforts in its behalf.

C. F. Price, *Who's Who in American Methodism*. 1916.
                                                       N. B. H.

OREGON, population 2,056,171 in 1970 is in the Pacific northwest. The area of the state is 96,981 square miles. Oregon was made a territory in 1848, and in 1859 it was admitted to the Union. In 1853 WASHINGTON Territory was carved out of Oregon Territory.

The first Methodist and the first American missionaries in Oregon were JASON LEE and his associates who in 1834 settled on the Willamette River between present day OREGON CITY and SALEM. In 1843 Lee was replaced by GEORGE GARY as superintendent of the mission, and Gary in turn was superseded by WILLIAM ROBERTS in 1847.

The Oregon and California Mission Conference, which also included the present states of NEW MEXICO, ARIZONA, WASHINGTON, and IDAHO, was created in 1849. The 1852 GENERAL CONFERENCE authorized the division of the Oregon and California Mission Conference so as to form the OREGON CONFERENCE and this then included Oregon, Washington and Idaho, and was organized in March, 1853. The 1872 General Conference authorized the formation of a conference in east Oregon. In 1873 the bishop in charge of the Oregon Conference appointed preachers to three districts in the newly formed East Oregon and Washington Conference, so named because it included the work in east Washington also. In 1876 the name was changed to the COLUMBIA RIVER CONFERENCE. The Oregon Conference lost the west Washington work in 1884 when the PUGET SOUND CONFERENCE was organized.

The M. E. Church had foreign language work (German, Norwegian, and Danish) in Oregon and the surrounding states. (See WASHINGTON.)

The M.E. Church, South began work in Oregon in 1858, and in 1866 the PACIFIC CONFERENCE (MES) was divided to form the Columbia Conference. The latter included Oregon, Washington, and the northern part of CALIFORNIA. The first session of the Oregon Conference was held at Corvallis, Ore., Oct. 26-30, 1866 with Bishop H. H. KAVANAUGH presiding. It reported twelve charges, fourteen preachers, and 526 members. The Southern Church persevered in the northwest, but it did not have as great success as the Northern Church. In 1890 the Columbia Conference was divided to form the East Columbia Conference, but prior to the division the conference had only thirty-five charges and 1,963 members. In the same year the Oregon and Puget Sound Conferences of the M.E. Church reported a total of nearly 15,000 members. Both the Columbia and East Columbia Conferences continued until 1917 when they merged with the MONTANA CONFERENCE to form the NORTHWEST CONFERENCE which continued until unification in 1939. In 1917 the Columbia, East Columbia, and Montana Conferences reported 1,905, 2,010, and 969 members respectively. The Southern Church established two schools which operated twenty years or more before closing— Corvallis College at Corvallis and Columbia College at Pendleton.

The M.P. CHURCH listed conferences or missions in Oregon from 1850 to the turn of the century, but it had no appreciable strength in the state. In 1968 the FREE METHODIST CHURCH had some 110 congregations and over 8,000 members in Oregon. Each of the three major Negro Methodist denominations has one or two churches in the state.

The M.E. Church projected ten or more academies and colleges in Oregon, but only one, WILLAMETTE UNIVERSITY, has survived. Today the Oregon Conference also supports a number of other service agencies and institutions.

The IDAHO CONFERENCE which began in 1884 has always included within its bounds several counties in eastern Oregon. In 1968 the Idaho Conference had thirteen charges and about 2,770 members in Oregon.

In 1968 the Oregon and Idaho Conferences merged to form the Oregon-Idaho Conference. At that time The Methodist Church had 158 pastoral charges and approximately 55,000 members in the state of Oregon.

General Minutes, ME, MES, TMC.
Minutes of the Oregon and the Idaho Conferences.
T. D. Yarnes, *Oregon.* 1957.   ERLE HOWELL

OREGON CITY, OREGON, U.S.A. **First Church.** The first pastor at Willamette Falls, later Oregon City, was Alvin F. Waller, assigned by JASON LEE in 1840. The work was to be solely among the Indians. By 1842 the Indians were disappearing and whites beginning to arrive. More came in 1843. That year the Methodists erected in Oregon City the first Protestant church on the Pacific Coast. The church was dedicated in 1844 by GUSTAVUS HINES who succeeded Waller that year. By 1848 DAVID LESLIE was pastor and mission superintendent, and WILLIAM ROBERTS took up his residence at the place. That year Oregon City and Clackamas, attached to the circuit, reported forty-seven members. The following year, JAMES HARVEY WILBUR and J. L. PARRISH were appointed to Oregon City and Portland.

In 1855, the Oregon City Seminary, originally set up as an interdenominational school in 1849, was sold to the Methodists. The original sponsors, headed by Congregational pastor George H. Atkinson, were unable to finance the school. The Methodists leased it to the City Council in 1860 and sold it in 1867.

GEORGE ABERNETHY, first Governor of OREGON, was a member of this church, a trustee and largest contributor. In 1846, the Territorial Fourth of July celebration was held in the church, and the Provisional legislature met there in 1847-48. In 1855 the OREGON ANNUAL CONFERENCE met in this church, with Bishop O. C. BAKER presiding.

In 1856 the building was moved to Seventh and Main Streets, and replaced by a new structure in 1890. In 1903 the building was raised and a store constructed under it. In 1919 the plant was destroyed by fire. The next building, a remodeled home, was dedicated by Bishop WILLIAM O. SHEPARD, March 20, 1921, while Melville T. Wire was pastor. The cornerstone for a new building was laid, Aug. 6, 1950 and the structure was dedicated Feb. 17, 1957.

C. J. Brosnan, *Jason Lee.* 1932.
Clackamas County Historical *Annual,* 1959.
H. K. Hines, *Pacific Northwest.* 1899.
T. D. Yarnes, *Oregon.* 1958.   ERLE HOWELL

OREGON CONFERENCE (MC), grew out of the mission established by JASON LEE and his associates on the Willamette River in September 1834. The group farmed, preached, and conducted a Sunday school and a day school. Additional personnel, including a physician and several women, arrived in 1837. In 1838 a branch was opened at The Dalles on the Columbia River, and in 1839 Lee returned east to ask for more help. He brought fifty-one men, women and children to OREGON. Stations were then opened in several more places. Meantime, adverse reports on Lee's management of the mission caused the Missionary Society in New York to send out GEORGE GARY in 1843 to replace him as superintendent. The original purpose of the mission was to minister to the Indians, but it soon became largely a ministry to the white settlers. WILLIAM ROBERTS, an able leader, succeeded Gary as superintendent in 1847. By 1848 there were seven circuits in Oregon with 443 members, and on Sept. 5, 1849 Roberts presided at the organization of the Oregon and California Mission Conference which had been authorized by the 1848 GENERAL CONFERENCE.

In 1852 the Oregon and California Mission Conference was divided to form the Oregon Conference which at the time included all of what are now Oregon, WASHINGTON, and IDAHO, and part of MONTANA. At the end of the first year the conference reported eleven charges and 706 members. As time passed new conferences were formed in the region (see OREGON), and finally in 1928 the boundaries of the Oregon Conference (ME) were limited to the state, except for six eastern counties which continued in the IDAHO CONFERENCE. In 1929 the Oregon Conference had 29,694 members. It came to unification in 1939 with 144 charges and 34,729 members. The Portland District of the NORTHWEST CONFERENCE (MES) brought thirteen charges and 1,835 members into the Oregon Conference of The Methodist Church in 1939.

Jason Lee and his associates started the Oregon Institute in 1842, the forerunner of WILLAMETTE UNIVERSITY at SALEM. Through the years the Oregon Conference fostered a number of other academies and colleges which lived and served for longer or shorter periods, but Willamette is the only Methodist institution of higher learning in Oregon which has survived. With an endowment of nearly $9,000,000, a plant valued at $10,000,000, a faculty of more than 100, and a student body of 1,500, Willamette rates high academically. It claims to be the oldest United States university west of Missouri.

The *Pacific Christian Advocate* of the M.E. Church was founded in 1855 at Salem, Ore., moved to PORTLAND in 1857, and continued publication for more than sixty years.

The Oregon Conference supported Willamette Methodist Hospital, Willamette View Manor, the Methodist Home in Salem, five WESLEY FOUNDATIONS, and several GOODWILL INDUSTRIES in the state. It joined the American Baptists in supporting Rose Villa at Milwaukie, and it cooperated with the Presbyterians and Episcopalians in maintaining Rogue Valley Manor at Medford.

One member of the Oregon Conference, BRUCE BAXTER, was elected bishop in 1940.

In 1968 the Oregon Conference had four districts, 145 pastoral charges, 213 ministers, 51,717 members, and property valued at $24,807,197. By authority of the Western JURISDICTIONAL CONFERENCE, in 1968 both the Oregon Conference and the Idaho Conference voted unanimously to merge in 1969 to form the Oregon-Idaho Conference.

General Minutes, MEC, MECS, and MC.
Minutes of the Oregon Conference.
T. D. Yarnes, Oregon. 1957.   ERLE HOWELL

OREGON MISSION. The Methodist mission to the Indians of OREGON under the leadership of JASON LEE was one of the most remarkable in the early history of such work. While it seemed to fail in the end, it did have certain enduring results.

The trigger that sent Lee to Oregon was the report of a plea in 1831 by four Indians in ST. LOUIS for Christian missionaries who would interpret to their people "the white man's God." Lee was a young member of an old New England family. He was recruited by WILBUR FISK, president of WESLEYAN UNIVERSITY, Middletown, Conn. Lee's nephew, DANIEL, agreed to go out as associate to Jason in the enterprise. Lee also recruited Cyrus Shepard as a teacher, and employed two lay assistants.

They went by boat to St. Louis and from there set out in April, 1834, with another party that invited them along. Altogether there were sixty men, 200 mules and horses, and twenty head of cattle. Lee soon discovered that the Indians were not waiting for the gospel with open arms or open minds. He also found the traders less than enthusiastic about missionary work. The travellers' route took them from Independence, Mo., to the Platte River, to Wyoming, to Fort Hall, Idaho, to Fort Walla Walla, Wash., to Fort Vancouver, and finally to the Willamette Valley.

Soon they had a mission house built—and three Indian orphans to care for. Lee began with a school and sought to train the Indians as farmers so as to encourage a settled way of life. The school made slow progress; the Indians were lukewarm toward it; the climate was hard on the New Englanders; Daniel Lee had to leave to recuperate and Cyrus Shepard had a leg amputated in 1839 and died in a few months.

To strengthen the work the supporting Board sent out reinforcements: a doctor (with a wife, daughter, and son), and a ship's carpenter, plus a large quantity of supplies. A few months later another group of missionaries arrived: a single minister, a minister with a wife and three children, and a woman teacher. Jason Lee married one of the new teachers.

In 1838 Lee decided to make a trip back to New England to enlist support for an expanded mission. He aroused great response: "never before had the Methodist Church experienced a missionary campaign equalling that led by Jason Lee between the early part of November, 1838 and May, 1839," writes Wade Crawford Barclay. A budget of $30,000.00 was appropriated, and plans made for nine mission stations, with farmers, mechanics, teachers, and physicians as well as ministers. A boat was chartered to carry to Oregon the fifty-one persons who had been recruited.

With more personnel and a larger budget the work expanded rapidly, with a total of six mission stations soon in operation. But some locations were poorly chosen, some of the new missionaries (or their wives) not fully committed to the work, and the Indians began to lose their first enthusiasm for the gospel. Some of the new staff wrote back to New England criticizing Jason Lee's leadership; the Board back home felt it was not getting as frequent reports as it should, and money for the Oregon mission (and for all mission work) was increasingly hard to secure.

The Board's Oregon committee first considered sending out a special agent to try to evaluate the situation, but finally sent out George Gary to take over the work from Jason Lee with orders to liquidate virtually all "non-religious" work, and to cut down on personnel as rapidly as possible. Gary went to work with a vengeance on his arrival at the mission on June 1, 1844, and by September 1847, the whole enterprise had been liquidated—five of the stations being closed down and the sixth one given to the American Board (Congregational) representative in Oregon, Marcus Whitman.

Jason Lee, in the meantime, had gone back to New England to defend his policies and was able to vindicate his actions. But his health failed and he died in 1845, only two years before the promising enterprise to which he had given his life came to an inglorious end. There were, however, some enduring achievements: the beginnings of a school that eventually became WILLAMETTE UNIVERSITY, and the laying of foundations for the settling of Oregon as a state.

W. C. Barclay, *History of Missions,* ii, 1950.

WALTER N. VERNON

O'REILLY, WINSTON DARCY (1913-   ), Australian church official was born at Roseville, NEW SOUTH WALES, on April 27, 1913. In 1939 he married Rotha Doreen Doyle. He has held the following appointments within the Church: Croydon, two years; Coonamble, four years; Peak Hill, three years; Home Missions Department (Assistant Secretary), four years; LEIGH THEOLOGICAL COLLEGE, twelve years, assistant Principal; METHODIST LADIES' COLLEGE, Burwood, five years as Principal; Connexional Secretary, Methodist Conference, five years; Secretary of Conference 1968-69; president 1969-70.

In addition he has given the following leadership to the Methodist Church: Convenor of the Board of Finance, New South Wales; Member of the management of the Property Department; Department of Christian Education; Home Missions Department; president of the War Memorial Hospital Board; editor of *The Methodist;* Member of the Australasian General Conference Standing Committee; General Conference Board of Finance; Laws Committee; and member of the Joint Constitution Commission for the Uniting Church in Australia.

At other times W. D. O'Reilly has had active engagement in the affairs of Good Neighbor Council; New South Wales Society for Health; Australian Council of Churches, and Council of Churches in New South Wales, of which he became president in 1967. He was also responsible for the establishment of chaplaincy services to the Mental Hospitals in New South Wales.

AUSTRALIAN EDITORIAL COMMITTEE

ORIGINAL SIN. The Wesleyan Doctrine. Included in WESLEY's abridgement of the Church of England's *Thirty-Nine Articles* is the following version of the Article on "original or birth sin" (the passages omitted being indicated by brackets): "Original sin standeth not in the following of Adam [As the Pelagians do vainly talk], but it is the [fault and] corruption of the nature of every man, that naturally is engendered of the offspring of Adam; whereby man is very far gone from original righteousness, and is of his own nature inclined to evil, and that continually, [so that the flesh lusteth always contrary to the Spirit, and therefore in every person born into this world it deserveth God's wrath and damnation. And this infection of nature doth remain, yea, in them that are regenerated]." Although Wesley's abridgement clearly represents a full acceptance of man's chronic, calculable involvement in sin, his excisions also suggest concern over the difficulties presented by the notions of original guilt and indwelling sin which were to prove so preoccupying to subsequent Methodist theologians.

The persistent, repetitious nature of man's inclination to evil—and the universal misery associated therewith—were, to Wesley, pragmatic evidence of universal moral corruption. Of this there was no question. His own *Doctrine of Original Sin, according to Scripture, Reason, and Experience* (1757) was directed against the writings of John Taylor, whose interpretations were considered by Wesley to compromise the view that the natural condition of man is diseased, corrupt, fallen, and "devilish"—and thus to cancel out the very essence of the plan of salvation itself. Through Adam, its federal head, mankind suffered not only the loss of "original righteousness" (the knowledge and love of God, its moral image), but a corruption in understanding, will, and liberty (the so-called "natural" image of God) as a consequence of Adam's alienation from vital fellowship with God (Sermon V, i, 1-9). Although Wesley denied (until clear Scriptural proof could be brought) that any man is liable to eternal punishment for Adam's sin alone, he held that the depravation attending mankind's collective participation in Adam's sin included the proper implications of guilt, except as graciously resolved through the universal impact of Christ's atoning grace (Romans v:18, often being cited at this point). The question of man's condition of guilt could not be discussed, insisted Wesley, apart from the integral acceptance of the universally-enlivening "prevenient" consequences of redemptive grace. As a doctrinal corollary to this, in definitive Wesleyanism, the baptism of infants remained an acknowledgement of the covenant of grace which had blessed, and continued to enlighten, universal men.

Wesley, of course, did distinguish between "original" (or "inbred," "indwelling") and "actual" sin (or sin properly so-called), thus indicating his own practical emphasis on associating guilt with direct, volitional involvement (eg. Sermon XV, *The Privilege of those that are Born of God,* ii, 2). However to place the Wesleyan doctrine of original sin more completely in its proper context one must also see the doctrine of entire sanctification as another direct corollary. Indeed, for Wesley the phenomenon of the reception of perfect love (as a gracious gift) constituted a restoration to that responsive communion with the divine will which defined holiness; there was release here, from man's "root" condition of unrighteousness. (See CHRISTIAN PERFECTION.)

[So CHARLES WESLEY can sing from 2 Corinthians v:17,

The original offence
Out of my soul erase,
Enter Thyself and drive it hence,
    And take up all the place (*Works,* xiii, 49.)

and

Take away the *power* of sinning,
Alpha and Omega be;
End of faith as its beginning
    Set our hearts at liberty. (*Works,* iv, 219.)

(cf. St. Augustine, *De Civitate Dei,* xxii, 30.)

J. L.]

Early American Methodism. Methodist preachers and authors in the early American period (late eighteenth and early to mid-nineteenth centuries) continued, for the most part, to sustain the Wesleyan position on the universal moral corruption of "natural man"—a condition whose properly-attendant guilt had been resolved, and whose deep depravity had been mitigated, through the universal efficacy of Christ's atonement. It was such a continuing doctrinal heritage which led the American Wesleyans to reject the moralisms of the Deists and Unitarians which they encountered. Indeed, it was such an emphasis on man's moral impotency (apart from gracious restoration) which led NATHAN BANGS, American Methodism's great theological editor in the early nineteenth century, to disavow the term "Arminian" as adequately designating that doctrinal position characteristic of Methodists (acknowledging that many "who have been denominated *Arminians,* have not always oiled their doctrine sufficiently with divine grace").

In his extended exchanges with Professor E. T. Fitch of Yale College (published in 1837 as *Calvinistic Controversy*), President WILBUR FISK of the WESLEYAN UNIVERSITY felt that the conflict between Calvinism's "new divinity" and the Wesleyan stance came to a head in this very matter of the moral corruption characteristic of "natural man." The question, Fisk concluded, was simply this: "Has fallen man, on the whole, the power to make a right choice, or has he not? We say without grace he has not. And therefore fallen man is not, in the responsible sense of that term, a free agent without grace."

There was tension, however, within early American Methodism as to the continued utilization of such a doctrine of "natural man's" moral corruption. Writing in *The Methodist Magazine* for 1820, one Methodist author anonymously expressed his concern over this ambiguity: "We have been warring against fatality and some other doctrines connected with it, until we have been driven, it is to be feared, into extremes on the other side," such as the concept that "the most vicious disposition [may be] reformed . . . by illuminating and directing it, in the free and proper exercise of its natural faculties and powers." "This language," continued this critic, "certainly contains the very marrow of Pelagianism. By adopting it, we fly into the face of the eighth article of our faith [Of Free Will]; and thereby, we deny the first and most important doctrine of revealed religion—the utter moral depravity of man through the fall, by which he is naturally rendered absolutely incapable of any liberty in the actions of his mind, respecting a choice of good in preference to evil."

Subsequent Transitions. Certainly the most important development in mid-nineteenth century American Methodist theological history occurred, not so much at the point feared in the article just cited, but in the consideration of the implications of "original guilt" (even as resolved by grace). ASA SHINN in his *Essay on the Plan of Salvation* (1813) had sharply rejected any penal consequences associated with the mere possession of "original corruption"; to hold otherwise was to deny one of the inescapable "first principles of morals," namely, that "no person is accountable for what is not his power." This type of concern was to be most influentially championed, in the theological mind of mid-century American Methodism, by DANIEL D. WHEDON. Whedon, who served as editor of the *Methodist Quarterly Review* from 1856 to 1884, was convinced that the unique position of Methodism, theologically speaking, lay in the clear affirmation

of man's freedom of contrary choice over against the "necessitarianism" of traditional Calvinism. This position led Whedon to be quite openly critical of what he took to be the carelessness of such British Methodist theologians as RICHARD WATSON and WILLIAM BURT POPE. The issue centered on the propriety of assessing universal guilt (except "presumptively") in relation to the condition of natural man prior to his own accountable action. Whedon cited, with approval, the statement of Wilbur Fisk that guilt "is not imputed until, by a voluntary rejection of the Gospel, man makes the depravity of his nature the object of his own choice." Here, insisted Whedon, there was no "hereditary guilt," only "a hereditary nature personally made guilty." Such a position was simply contradicted, according to Whedon, by W. B. Pope's statement (in his *Compendium of Christian Theology,* 1875) that the true doctrine of original sin is opposed "to every account of sin which insists that it cannot be reckoned such by a righteous God save where the will actively consents; and that none can be held responsible for any state of soul or action of life which is not the result of the will at the time. There is an offending character behind the offending will." (2nd. ed., 1880, Vol. II. pp. 83-4.)

THOMAS O. SUMMERS and JOHN J. TIGERT, influential theologians in the M.E. Church, South (and related to VANDERBILT UNIVERSITY in the 1880's), proved supportive of the tradition suggested by Pope which upheld universal man's "realistic" involvement in Adamic guilt *and* the expiation of Christ's atonement. Whedon's influence, on the other hand, was to be seen in the statement by Professor MINER RAYMOND (GARRETT BIBLICAL INSTITUTE, in his *Systematic Theology,* 1877) that the real tragedy consequent upon Adam's offense is not condemnation but the inheritance "by the natural law of propagation" of a corrupted nature.

Whedon's emphases were to be further elaborated, late in the nineteenth century, in the systematic concerns of Professor JOHN MILEY (DREW THEOLOGICAL SEMINARY, New Jersey) for a "consistent Arminianism" within American Methodist thought. Miley proved quite critical of the ambiguities regarding the nature of culpability associated with Wesley's doctrine of original sin. He insisted that the denial of original guilt, "native demerit," was the definitive theological contribution of Arminianism; indeed, Wesleyan interpretations should be clarified accordingly. The issue of injustice in the Divine economy—as related to a doctrine of universal Adamic guilt—was simply *not* relieved by any compensatory provisions of grace.

A somewhat different representation of the Wesleyan tradition, within mid and late-nineteenth century American Methodism, is to be found in the writings of WILLIAM FAIRFIELD WARREN, who became the first president of Methodism's BOSTON UNIVERSITY. In his Introduction to the study of systematic theology (Einleitung, *Systematische Theologie einheitlich behandelt,* published in 1865 while Warren was professor in the Methodist seminary at Bremen, Germany), Warren reiterated the traditional Wesleyan doctrine of the transformation of man's initial status and condition through atoning grace; none of Adam's descendants were held guilty (i.e., under actual condemnation) until they rejected the grace of Christ. Nevertheless, Warren was quite critical of any phraseology such as "infant justification," or the restoration of "gracious ability," which might suggest some element of condemnation prior—at least, logically—to the restorative intervention of grace. Rather, insisted Warren, it was the teaching of "consistent Methodism" that the graciously-unconditional benefits of the atonement were initially *constitutive* of man's moral condition; "the child stands on a level with every other new created being, a natural and equal object of divine care." Rather than abstracting the moral individual from the prevenience of redemptive grace, as was the *tendency* in Whedon and in Miley, Warren's theological anthropology often was characterized by an *unacknowledged* incorporation of the effects of prevenient grace into the descriptions of man's moral nature.

The Twentieth Century. The early twentieth century, in American Methodism, was to provide clear evidences that the consensus had by then swung away from the language and implications of inherited moral corruption *and* attendant guilt (*resolved by* universally-efficacious atoning grace) to the clear affirmation of natural man's given condition as simply being that of proper and immediate moral accountability. American Methodist hymnody and ritual saw less of the language of man's sinful corruption (or of its specific theological corollary, the prevenient grace consequent upon universal atonement). The emergent influence of critical-historical Biblical scholarship, with its reassessment of some of the traditional literalisms that had become associated with the story of Adam, contributed to the disenchantment with the language of "original sin," and its implications regarding mankind's Adamic involvement. Prominent Methodist theologians such as ALBERT KNUDSON (at BOSTON UNIVERSITY SCHOOL OF THEOLOGY for over three decades following 1906) emphatically concluded that there is "no such thing as inherited guilt or an inherited moral depravity"; only the free activity of the will originated sin (cited in Robert Chiles' important study of *Theological Transition in American Methodism*, 1965). Bishop FRANCIS MC-CONNELL, whose *John Wesley* was published in 1939, was frankly relieved to relegate the idea of "original sin" to an eighteenth-century frame of reference; rather, commented McConnell, man's nature and character is "the result of forces—physical and psychological—which have been at work for hundreds of thousands of years."

The *reevaluation* of the traditional doctrines of original sin and original guilt—together with the acceptance of the myth form for mankind's "Adamic" involvement—was, however, to prove part of the effect within Methodism of the psycho-theological reassessment of man's nature associated subsequently in this century with the emergent influence of Kierkegaard's existential critiques, Freud's depth psychology, Barth's Biblical theology, and the re-examination of historical theology. The *problem* of mankind's chronic perversity—and the compensatory givenness of redemptive grace—received new emphasis in the studies of Methodist scholars such as GEORGE CELL, DAVID SHIPLEY, ALBERT OUTLER, Harold Lindstrom, Colin Williams, and others. Williams' summary of the contemporary, "existential" relevance of Wesley's doctrine of original sin, for instance (in *John Wesley's Theology Today*, 1960), insisted that "its restatement in terms of modern Biblical understanding" left Wesley's essential position untouched: ". . . in the light of prevenient grace we can speak of every man being his own Adam, so that we become aware of our separation from God as incurring guilt, because of the possibility of the repair of that relationship con-

stantly offered by God." However, continued William's restatement, the truth that every man is his own Adam must not be stressed "to the point where the fallenness of the race for which the symbol of the First Adam stands is lost. It is only in the light of God's offer of a restored relationship (through prevenient grace) that every man *becomes* his own Adam."

It must also be added that mid-twentieth century Methodist literature *generally* continued to be marked by a now-recognizable ambiguity as touching the ground of man's moral accountability—whether it was a continuing provision of the natural order or a gift of gracious restoration. The ambiguity itself seemed to be a repetitious element in the theological anthropology of Methodism.

Developments in British Methodism. It is perhaps characteristic that in 1875, when as observed above, D. D. Whedon was in America assailing the notion of "original guilt," W. B. Pope, the most influential systematic theologian of British Methodism at that period, should be offering a learned defence of the traditional system. Since that time responsible British Methodist thought appears to have moved much more conservatively in relation to this matter than that of America, and therefore has remained much closer to Wesley, though serious account has been taken of the findings of natural science regarding the physical evolution of the human race.

Somewhat naturally, the prevailing tone has been set by the scholarship of the Church of England. Possibly the most constructive theological event was the publication in 1889, by a group of Oxford scholars coming out of the Anglo-Catholic tradition, of *Lux Mundi*, a set of powerfully argued essays which sought to vindicate the proposition that on the one hand the findings of natural science and of sober biblical criticism could be candidly accepted, and that on the other hand all the essential intention of traditional Christian doctrine could be maintained. This volume says little directly on the subject of Original Sin, but this approach was pursued in the most influential British books on this subject by F. R. Tennant, *The Origin and Propagation of Sin* (1901), and *The Fall and Original Sin* (1903). Here the case is argued for an "evolutionary theory of the origin of sin." During the moral probation of the evolving human race, in its first days, there was occasion for an event spiritually and morally analogous to the event described in mythological terms in the Genesis Fall-story. Thus evolutionary biology as an account of the physical origin of the race can be combined with the doctrine in theology of the fallen and sinful condition of the race.

The resultant attitude of "non-fundamentalist orthodoxy" is characteristic of most responsible Methodist theological thought in Britain at the present time. This attitude has been confirmed by various findings of modern New Testament exegesis. Thus it would be widely accepted that in such a text as 1 Corinthians xv:22, "as in Adam all die" St. Paul's essential thought is that of Adam as the spiritual "type" of the race, and is by no means entirely dependent upon an understanding of Adam as the physical ancestor of the whole race. So the Pauline theology can well survive the understanding of the Genesis Fall-story as an unhistorical myth. So also it is realized that the New Testament "wrath of God" is not so much the personal attitude of a punishing divine Judge to individual men, as a principle of divine nemesis in human affairs. So the traditional Christian doctrine that the whole fallen and guilty race is collectively under "the wrath" can be well maintained but without the morally dubious proposition that God will hold personally responsible for sin individuals who are not yet old enough or experienced enough to have made a voluntary and personally accountable choice.

The general consensus of British Methodist thought today, therefore, would be to allow the legendary character of the Genesis Fall-story, to dismiss the notion of "original guilt," yet to affirm the collective and individual moral and spiritual bondage of the race, together with the utter impossibility that man should save himself by self-improvement and education, apart from the saving grace of God.

W. B. Pope, *Compendium of Christian Theology*. 1889.
F. R. Tennant, *The Fall and Original Sin*. Cambridge, 1903.
——————, *The Origin and Propagation of Sin*. Cambridge, 1901.
R. Watson, *Theological Institutes*. 1832.

JOHN LAWSON
LELAND SCOTT

FIRST CHURCH, ORLANDO, FLORIDA

ORLANDO, FLORIDA, U.S.A. First Church had its beginning when the annual conference meeting at JACKSONVILLE, Fla., in January 1874, appointed O. W. Ransome to the Orlando Circuit. At that time Orlando was a village of 450 people. Since there was no church building, services were held in the court house. A CAMP MEETING near Zellwood in 1878 greatly strengthened the Methodist work in Orlando. In 1881-82 Orlando became a half-station served by Anderson Peeler, M.D. During this time a church building was erected at a cost of $1,000 on a site purchased for $200. Under C. E. Pelot a larger building was erected in 1888. The building was not finished, but it accommodated the Annual Conference session in January 1886. Existing records of the church date from January 1885. The building was remodeled in 1904-05, during the pastorate of R. V. Atkisson, at a cost of several thousand dollars.

Plans for a modern building were made during the

pastorate of Dr. Chapman, and the building was erected during the pastorate of Dr. Wray at a cost of $50,000. This structure served as the sanctuary until 1963. In 1924 during the pastorate of W. A. Cooper, Wesley Hall was built, and it serves as a part of the educational facility at the present time. In 1872 the church had a membership of 75; in 1938, 1,878; in 1944, 2,918; and 1970 the membership totalled 4,758 and it is the largest church in the FLORIDA CONFERENCE. Many of the twenty-two other Methodist churches of Orlando have been sponsored by this church. It was listed as one of the "Ten Great Churches of America" by the *Christian Century* magazine in 1950. Each year it is listed as one of the ten Methodist churches giving most to missions. Two pastors of the church have been elected to the episcopacy while serving here: JOHN W. BRANSCOMB in 1952 and E. J. PENDERGRASS in 1964.

General Minutes, UMC.
John B. Ley, *Souvenir and Year Book*. Orlando, Fla., 1916.
Frank A. Smith, *History of First Methodist Church, Orlando, Florida, 1859-1944*. Florida Methodist Centennial Edition.
A. Fred Turner, *Program for the Eightieth Anniversary Homecoming and Founders Day of First Methodist Church of Orlando*. 1938.

MILLARD C. CLEVELAND

ORMSTON, MARK D. (1890-1960), American FREE METHODIST minister, was born Dec. 17, 1890, at St. Johns, Mich. Converted at age fifteen, he early became a thorough student of the Bible and his life was a reflection of its message. He was a student at GREENVILLE COLLEGE. He entered the ministry of the East Michigan Conference of the Free Methodist Church, where he served as pastor and superintendent until 1936. He was a bishop, 1936-58; bishop emeritus, 1958-60. During his term as bishop, Ormston was also chairman of the Commission on Missions. He led a successful debt elimination campaign and placed the missionary program on a sound financial base. Bishop Ormston was an able administrator, a wise counsellor and trusted friend. He excelled as an eloquent, spirit-filled preacher. Great congregations were stirred to action by his prayers and sermons. He died at Jackson, Mich., June 23, 1960.

BYRON S. LAMSON

ORPHAN HOUSE, NEWCASTLE-UPON-TYNE, England, was built in 1743 to house the first Wesleyan society to be gathered in the town. It was intended to be an orphanage for forty poor children—hence its name—but this scheme was not carried out. Instead, it became a hostel for the Wesleyan itinerants in the north of England, a library, a preaching house, and the place where JOHN WESLEY himself lived when in the area. GRACE MURRAY was matron for some time. The Orphan House was outside the walls of the town, and in the 1745 rebellion was thought to be in danger from the invading army. Wesley held an impressive service in the House on Sept. 29, 1745, asking for divine help for King George of England. CHARLES ATMORE started a SUNDAY SCHOOL at the Orphanage in 1790. It remained the center of Wesleyan worship until 1821, when the Brunswick Chapel was built on a neighboring site, when the Orphan House ceased to function as a place of worship. In 1856 the Orphan House Wesleyan Day School was erected on the same site; this was demolished in 1957; a memorial plaque was attached to the building which replaced it. The

Orphan House is remembered, not only because of its link with Grace Murray, but also because in the eighteenth century it was for long the headquarters of Wesleyan Methodism in the north.

W. W. Stamp, *Orphan-House of Wesley*. 1863.   JOHN KENT

ORTON, JOSEPH (?-1842), British missionary pioneer to AUSTRALIA. The first notice of him that exists is his appointment in 1826 as a Wesleyan probationer to Falmouth and Montego Circuits, JAMAICA. Here he suffered violent persecution in the immediate pre-emancipation days, and was imprisoned with Isaac Whitehouse, another preacher, in the common jail for fourteen days, being released only on direct orders from the chief justice. Apparently broken in health he returned to England in 1828.

In 1831 he was sent to Australia, where Methodism was at its lowest ebb. He was made chairman of the New South Wales District, with a staff of five ministers. A strong, gracious, and far-sighted administrator, his appointment coincided with the beginnings of nonconvict immigration. Having brought new life to NEW SOUTH WALES, he was made chairman of the new Van Diemen's Land (Tasmania) District in 1835, from which he visited what was to become the state of Victoria. Then he interested the government in the support of a mission at Port Phillip, later to be the city of Melbourne. Australian Methodism owes a great debt to his leadership and courageous planning. He died at sea April 30, 1842.

CYRIL DAVEY

ORWIG, WILLIAM W. (1810-1889), American pathfinder-churchman of the EVANGELICAL ASSOCIATION, was born to Mr. and Mrs. Abraham Orwig, Sept. 25, 1810, near Orwigsburg, Pa. On May 24, 1832 he married Susanna Rischel; to them were born ten children.

He was received into the itinerancy of the EASTERN CONFERENCE (EA) in 1828; he was presiding elder in his mother conference at the age of twenty-two, and just before retirement was presiding elder of ERIE CONFERENCE; elected bishop in 1859, his poor health prevented his re-election in 1863.

He pioneered in publishing. Elected book agent and editor in 1836, he promptly bought the second printing press for the denomination and edited *Der Christliche Botschafter*, the first general periodical of the denomination. His *Geschichte der Evangelischen Gemeinschaft*, 1857, put into English in 1858, was so well done that all subsequent histories have been indebted to it.

The range of his theological concerns is reflected somewhat in his book titles: *Katechismus* (a catechism for youth), 1847; *Die Heilsfulle* (The Fullness of Salvation), 1873; and *Pastoral-Theologie*, 1877.

Other pioneering activities included his leadership in founding the Missionary Society, his advocacy of the Sunday school, and his bold fostering of higher education in the founding of Union Seminary at New Berlin, Pa., in 1856.

He contributed much toward the later development of his church before his death in Cleveland, Ohio, on May 29, 1889.

R. W. Albright, *Evangelical Church*. 1942.
David Koss, "Bishops of the Evangelical Association, United

Evangelical and Evangelical Churches." B.D. thesis, Evangelical Theological Seminary, 1959.
R. M. Veh. *Evangelical Bishops*. 1939.   ARTHUR C. CORE

GEORGE OSBORN

OSBORN, GEORGE (1808-1891), British minister, was born in Rochester on March 29, 1808. He entered the Wesleyan Methodist ministry in 1828. He took a prominent part in the internal controversies of Wesleyan Methodism between 1830 and 1857. He was a strong opponent of change in the Wesleyan system, and especially of the admission of lay representatives into the Conference; he was a vehement supporter of JABEZ BUNTING. In 1847 he persuaded the Wesleyan Methodist CONFERENCE to permit him to "test" the loyalty of Wesleyan ministers to the status quo by asking them to sign a document in which they affirmed that they had not contributed to the FLY SHEETS. More than a thousand ministers signed, but the number who refused to do so was sufficient to rob the "test" of its effectiveness. He was elected to the LEGAL HUNDRED at the Conference of 1849, at which he played a large part in the expulsion of the ministers accused of having written the Fly Sheets. In later years Osborn continued to maintain the conservative position, and he became increasingly isolated. He became one of the secretaries for Foreign Missions in 1851, retaining the post until 1867; he then was appointed as a Theological Tutor at RICHMOND COLLEGE, London (see THEOLOGICAL COLLEGES), remaining there until retirement in 1884. He was twice president—in 1863 and 1881. When the ECUMENICAL METHODIST CONFERENCE met in London in 1881 he gave the opening and closing addresses, and it was at this Conference that he met WILLIAM GRIFFITH again for the first time since 1849. Griffith received the communion from Osborn's hands (standing, as he objected in the true Puritan tradition, to kneeling). Among Osborn's literary works was *The Poetical Works of John and Charles Wesley* (xiii vols., London, 1868-1872), though this was not a definitive edition. He also published *Outlines of Methodist Bibliography* (1869). Osborn enjoyed great prominence in nineteenth century Methodism, but achieved very little.

B. Gregory, *Sidelights*. 1898.   JOHN NEWTON

OSBORN, THOMAS GEORGE (1844-1910), British Methodist educator, was the son of Thomas Osborn of Rochester and a nephew of the well-known GEORGE OSBORN. He was educated at Wesley College, Sheffield, and Trinity Hall, Cambridge, where he became a Fellow. Although studying for the Bar, in 1866 he was persuaded to accept a temporary emergency appointment as Headmaster of KINGSWOOD SCHOOL—where he remained for nearly twenty years. During that time he successfully introduced the best current public school practice to Wesley's foundation, and left it immeasurably stronger. During much of this period Woodhouse Grove served as a preparatory school for Kingswood, so that Osborn was in charge of both institutions, seeking to ensure for them a true family spirit as well as high academic standards and religious culture. Upon his resignation in 1885 (partly because of pressure to have a minister instead of a layman as headmaster), he founded Rydal School in Colwyn Bay. He remained one of the most prominent and influential laymen in Wesleyan Methodism, for long a member of every Conference from the first admission of laymen. At the centenary of Wesley's death in 1891, he delivered an address at Wesley's Chapel, City Road, London, in which he called for a Ladies' College for British Methodism. He did not marry until 1896, and died April 8, 1910.

FRANK BAKER

OSBORNE, DENNIS (1828-1902), was an Anglo-Indian who was soundly converted in LUCKNOW in 1871 under the preaching of WILLIAM TAYLOR. At the time he was superintendent of the chief engineer's office. One Sunday when the pastor was ill, Osborne was called upon to preach. That first sermon established his reputation as a preacher. Osborne and another layman held meetings in Allahabad and organized a church. When the church fell into trouble, having no pastor, Osborne went again for meetings, and this time remained as pastor, resigning his coveted post and accepting an uncertain salary of less than one-third of what the government had been paying him. He joined the Annual Conference in 1874. He and JAMES MILLS THOBURN started annual meetings in Lucknow at the time of the Dasehra Festival. People came from as far away as CALCUTTA, BOMBAY, MADRAS, and CEYLON. The meetings were held annually for more than fifty years.

Osborne went to the GENERAL CONFERENCE in 1884. His speeches in America generated so much interest in missions that he returned with funds to open a boys' school, the Philander Smith Institute at Mullingar, Mussoorie. He became superintendent of the Allahabad District, and organized English language congregations in Agra, Roorkee, Mussoorie, Meerut, and Ajmer. He was at the time of his death superintendent of the Bombay District. Osborne sponsored PHOEBE ROWE, the Anglo-Indian woman evangelist.

The Lucknow Witness, Sept. 5, 1873.　J. WASKOM PICKETT

OSHKOSH, WISCONSIN, U.S.A. **Evergreen Manor, Inc.,** is a church operated home for the aged, owned and operated by the WISCONSIN CONFERENCE of the United Methodist Church. Construction was completed in 1967 at a total cost of $1,750,000, which includes land, furnishings, and construction.

Evergreen Manor has a Health Center of forty-eight beds, licensed by the Boards of Health of the State of WISCONSIN and the city of Oshkosh, which gives skilled nursing care to the residents. The Health Center is Medicare certified.

Evergreen Manor is operated under a corporation of twenty-one directors, elected by the Wisconsin Conference. The functional operation of Evergreen Manor has as its one task the care of aging men and women. Adequate resident activities make homelife challenging. Evergreen Manor allows no discrimination on the basis of race, color or national origin.

Evergreen Manor is a member of the Wisconsin Methodist Homes Association and is currently under the direction of the Executive Director of the Association, George H. Palmer.

OSLO is the capital of NORWAY. It was founded about 1050 A.D. The number of inhabitants (in 1966) is about 500,000.

The revivalist movement, which was started at Fredrikstad in 1849 by Ole P. Petersen (see NORWAY), and which was preliminary to the first Methodist congregation being organized at SARPSBORG in 1856, spread to Oslo as early as 1857. Carl Nilsson Osterlund, who was a bricklayer by trade, and who had been saved at the time when CHRISTIAN WILLERUP and Petersen were active in Halden, came to live in Oslo. He immediately began to hold meetings, and founded a Sunday school in Oslo seven years prior to the organization of a congregation there.

In the autumn of 1862, Anders Olsen, a cobbler, settled in Oslo. Some more Methodists from the Halden district also moved to Oslo, and this made more urgent the desire that there be a permanent organization. Anders Olsen dominated the period of transition from organized activity to congregation, and it was he who laid the foundation for the congregation which was organized in Oslo in 1865.

In the autumn of 1870, MARTIN HANSEN was appointed pastor in Oslo. The meetings drew very large crowds, and it became obvious that a chapel would have to be built. Hansen secured a site for the congregation, where a two-story building was erected, with the meeting hall on the first floor. This began to be used on April 23, 1871. On the same site three years later a church was consecrated in 1874—the first Methodist church in the capital of Norway. This congregation continues today as the First Methodist Church of Oslo.

The work in Oslo expanded, and in 1877 a second

CENTRALKIRKEN, OSLO, NORWAY

congregation was organized and became known as "Methodist Congregation Elim." This congregation first built a small chapel, and then in 1896 a four-story business building with adjoining church was completed.

In 1887, a third congregation was founded in Oslo. In the beginning it made use of rented accommodations, but subsequently got its own church. This is the congregation which in 1961 took into use an eight-story business building with adjoining church. This church located in the center of the city is known as "Centralkirken."

One further congregation was founded in Oslo in 1895, and this also built a chapel. The chapel was demolished at a later date, and a five-story business building together with a church replaced it, and was taken into use in 1956. This is the Immanuel Church.

The tenth WORLD METHODIST CONFERENCE was held in Oslo, Aug. 17-25, 1961. The president of the Conference was HAROLD ROBERTS, of Great Britain. The theme of the Conference was "New Life in the Spirit." About

BETANIEN HOSPITAL, OSLO, NORWAY

two thousand delegates and foreign guests attended the conference, as well as great numbers of visitors from all parts of Norway and Sweden. His Majesty, Olav V, King of Norway, was present on the opening night of the conference to welcome and extend greetings to the delegates.

Immediately prior to the conference, the World Federation of Methodist Women had held their Sixth Assembly, the theme being "Jesus Christ Is Lord." Also at this assembly the attendance was very large.

EILERT BERNHARDT

OSTERHOUT, SMITH STANLEY (1868-1953), Canadian minister, was born of United Empire Loyalist stock in Cobourg, Ontario, on June 30, 1868. He graduated from VICTORIA COLLEGE, Toronto, and following ordination came to British Columbia in 1893 as a volunteer for the Indian work and was stationed on the Nass River in the northern part of the province.

After five years on the Nass he was moved to Port Simpson, the largest Tsimshian village on the coast. Here he served for another five years. He learned and spoke the language fluently, edited a grammar, and translated hymns and scripture into the Tsimshian. The provincial government made him a justice of the peace for Cassiar district.

After eleven years in Indian work, he ministered to white congregations in Victoria, Kamloops, Vernon, and Vancouver. In 1911 he was appointed superintendent

of Oriental missions for western Canada, and served in that capacity until his retirement in 1939. He was a member of the first General Council of The United Church of Canada, in 1925.

In 1929 he published *Orientals in Canada,* which was regarded as a valuable contribution to one of Canada's racial problems. In 1916 and 1939 he was president of the British Columbia Conference. He died on Oct. 7, 1953, in Vancouver, B. C.

Osterhout was a man of broad sympathy and understanding. Possibly his greatest contribution to the religious life of his day was his ability to interpret the values of the Oriental and Occidental, each to the other.

G. H. Cornish, *Cyclopaedia of Methodism in Canada.* 1881.

W. P. BUNT

OSTROM, EGON NILS (1903-1945), Swedish minister, evangelist, martyr, and missionary was born in Hälsingborg, SWEDEN, Nov. 27, 1903. A godly mother kindled the lamp of faith in his heart, and at the age of thirteen he had a transforming Christian experience which made him a "winner of souls."

He studied for the ministry at the UNION THEOLOGICAL SEMINARY in Gothenburg and was graduated in 1927. A spectacularly successful ministry in Mölndal, 1925-30, made his name known all over Sweden, and many tried to convince him to stay in Sweden as a minister and evangelist. But in 1930 he was transferred to SUMATRA for work among the Chinese of that island. He spent about ten months in CHINA to learn the Hokkien dialect, and upon his return to Sumatra he was able to speak the language. Large crowds gathered around his pulpit, for the Hokkien-speaking Chinese of Sumatra had never heard a white person so able to use their mother tongue.

In 1937 he returned from furlough, which included studies at DREW UNIVERSITY in the United States, and was appointed to Tebing Tinggi where he had some very successful years in spite of the war. Being a native of Sweden, he and his family decided (together with another Swedish family) to remain in Sumatra. He served as Methodist district superintendent and as Mission treasurer, besides his work as evangelist among the Chinese. When all neutrals were interned at the beginning of the Indonesian revolution, he used his time in camp as a Red Cross worker, and was appointed Acting Consul for Sweden. On Dec. 11, 1945 he decided to return to his home for some documents, though many of his friends warned him. He was picked up by some extremists, thrown into a river, and his body was never found. The story of Egon N. Ostrom is ably told by his wife, Vera Edborg Ostrom, in her Book *O Boksu*—the story of a man who gave his life for Sumatra.

Vera Edborg Ostrom, *O Boksu.* New York: Board of Missions, 1948.
Metodistkyrkans i Sverige. Arsbok, 1946.
Minutes of the Sumatra Provisional Annual Conference, 1948.

RAGNAR ALM

OSUNA, ANDRÉS (1872-1957), Mexican educator and outstanding layman, whose connection was with the M.E. Church South, in that land, but whose influence was felt in the realm of education over the whole country. He was born in a Christian home in Cd. Mier, Coahuila, and from childhood had the religious influence of his mother and of a missionary, Alexander M. Southerland. The Instituto Fronterizo (later Laurens Institute) in Monterrey, and the Methodist church the family attended also exerted great influence in his life. Adventurous, the child moved from one place to another seeking education, working his way ahead, learning English and teaching what he knew. He graduated as teacher from the Normal School in Monterrey in 1892, and the same year married Lugarda L. Treviño.

He established a private grammar school in Saltillo, Coahuila, and became one of the founders of the teacher's training school there, in 1894. Later he became director of that school. He was appointed general director of Elementary Education in the State. His influence was felt in a reorganization of the plan of studies, the program of work, the equipment used, the buildings, and the administration, for eleven years.

In 1909 a new door was opened to him through contact with WALTER R. LAMBUTH, secretary of Missions from the M.E. Church, South in the U.S.A. Osuna was invited to work in the editorial department for Spanish books in the Publishing House at NASHVILLE, Tenn. There, he carried on an important program of publication and was also able to study at VANDERBILT UNIVERSITY. He received the Ph.D. there in 1915.

President Venustiano Carranza appointed him General Director of Public Education in the Federal District in 1915. He was elected temporary Governor in his home state in 1918.

From 1920-27, along with other duties, he accepted the position of manager of the Union Publishing House (Protestant concern) in Mexico City, and in 1927 was appointed Director of Public Education in the state of Nuevo León. Osuna was most helpful to the Church in matters of finance, properties, governmental relationships, and education. He was a fine Christian, a true witness. His death occurred on May 17, 1957.

GUSTAVO A. VELASCO G.

OTTERBEIN, PHILIP WILLIAM (1726-1813), American bishop of the UNITED BRETHREN IN CHRIST, was born June 3, 1726 in Dillenburg, Nassau, GERMANY, where his father served as both minister and teacher in the Reformed Latin school. Of the ten chiildren born into this family three died in childhood, while six sons became ministers and the surviving daughter married a minister. With the death of her husband Mrs. Otterbein moved her family to Herborn, so that the children could better obtain an education at the Academy, nearly equivalent to a university schooling. The eldest son supported the family until the next in age, Philip William, could take over. Then Philip, in turn, supported the group until the son below him in age, had completed his education.

Following an examination before the Herborn faculty, May 6, 1748, Philip Willaim was approved as a candidate for the ministry and became a precepter in the Herborn school. The next year, June 13, 1749, he was ordained and filled the pulpit at Ockersdorf in addition to teaching. Opposition appeared from some who wanted to stop his preaching, about which his mother remarked, "Ah, William, I expected this and give you joy. This place is too narrow for you, my son; they will not receive you here; you will find your work elsewhere."

When Michael Schlatter, a missionary to PENNSYLVANIA, appeared in Germany looking for volunteers to accompany

PHILIP W. OTTERBEIN

him back to the New World to fill vacant pulpits among the German Reformed, Otterbein responded. He and five other recruits were examined by the Dutch Reformed Synod of Holland and approved. They landed in New York, July 28, 1752.

Otterbein was soon called to the congregation at Lancaster, Pa., the second most important Reformed church in America. During the six years he served in this city a new stone church was erected, internal order within the congregation assured, and he served one year, 1757, as president of the Reformed coetus. Following an earnest sermon on repentance and faith in 1754, a man under conviction came to Otterbein for advice. Philip William replied, "My friend, advice is scarce with me today." Then the preacher retired to his quiet place where he stayed until he had obtained the joy of his own conscious salvation.

Some years later, about 1767, attending a "great" meeting in the barn of ISAAC LONG in Lancaster County, Otterbein heard a Mennonite bishop, MARTIN BOEHM, preach a warm sermon on personal salvation. Following the message, Otterbein hurried forward, embraced the Mennonite, and exclaimed, "Wir sind bruder (We are brothers)." Here he had found one who knew spiritual truths through deep pangs and struggles which Otterbein himself had discovered under similar effort. This occasion furnished roots for a religious movement that eventually was to culminate in the formation of the Church of the United Brethren in Christ.

Pastorates were conducted in Tulpohocken, Pa. (near Reading), FREDERICK, Md., and YORK, Pa., during the next sixteen years. Within that period Otterbein was married to Miss Susan LeRoy of Lancaster, April 19, 1762, who died within six years, April 27, 1768. He remained a widower for the rest of his life.

Otterbein assumed charge of an independent Reformed congregation in Baltimore, Md., May 4, 1774, but after having refused the offer several previous times. Perhaps the change of decision was induced by a letter that FRANCIS ASBURY wrote Feb. 3, 1774 urging Otterbein, whom he had not yet met, to settle in BALTIMORE. In the forty years that followed, Otterbein and Asbury became close friends.

Otterbein, along with a number of Reformed ministers and laymen desirous of promoting a spirit of inward piety, began to meet with some regularity as early as 1774. They did not intend to create a new church but to form a little association within the Reformed Church that might serve "to leaven the whole lump." Ultimately most of the ministers of the group withdrew from this society, while the laymen remained. Otterbein became the leader under whom they worked. Their efforts were expanded chiefly in MARYLAND and VIRGINIA. where the Reformed Church had very little influence upon the German people. Eventually this group of "united ministers" did form a new church in 1800, known as the Church of the United Brethren in Christ (see UNITED BRETHREN). Philip William Otterbein and Martin Boehm, a former Mennonite, became the first bishops or superintendents.

In 1805, Otterbein suffered a serious illness, from which he never quite recovered. From then until his death he did not leave Baltimore, but the preachers of this new church came to him for counsel and assistance.

Upon the invitation of Francis Asbury, Philip William Otterbein assisted in the consecration and ordination of his friend to the office of bishop, Dec. 27, 1784. Their last visit together was on the evening of March 22, 1813. HENRY BOEHM, a traveling companion of Asbury and son of Martin Boehm, was present and wrote about the experience many years later: "That was an evening I shall ever remember; two noble souls met, and their conversation was rich and full of instruction. They had met frequently before; this was their last interview on earth —long ago they met in heaven."

Less than two months before his death, at the age of eighty-seven years, Otterbein had received a special request from the Miami Conference asking that he ordain several persons by the laying on of hands, so that these afterwards might perform the same for others. (Up to this time certain United Brethren preachers had been ridiculed as irregular by some persons in other denominations.) On Oct. 2, 1813, in the parsonage at Baltimore, in the presence of several members of the congregation, CHRISTIAN NEWCOMER, JOSEPH HOFFMAN, and Frederick Schaffer were duly ordained by Otterbein, assisted by WILLIAM RYLAND, an elder in the M.E. Church.

Death came to this churchman Wednesday, Nov. 17, 1813, at his home. At the funeral service a German discourse was preached by J. D. Kurtz, a Lutheran, followed by an English message delivered by William Ryland.

Asbury received the news of Otterbein's death while on one of his trips, and exclaimed, "Is Father Otterbein dead? Great and good man of God! An honor to his church and country. One of the greatest scholars and divines that ever came to America, or born in it. . . ." Four months later, in March 1814, by request of the BALTIMORE CONFERENCE of the M.E. Church, the conference adjourned to Otterbein's Church where Asbury preached in memory of his departed friend.

Otterbein was buried in the courtyard of the church in Baltimore where he had served for nearly forty years. Soon after his death the church became known as The Otterbein Church (later The OLD OTTERBEIN CHURCH), and continued to be an independent congregation supplied by ministers of the Church of the United Brethren in

Christ. In 1949 it was formally received into The E.U.B. Church.

F. Asbury, *Journal and Letters*. 1958.
A. C. Core, *Otterbein*. 1968.
A. W. Drury, *History of the UB*. 1924.
————, *Otterbein*. 1884.
Otterbein Collection in Commission on Archives and History.
                                                    JOHN H. NESS, JR.

OTTERBEIN CHURCH, "The Old Otterbein," Conway and Sharp Streets, BALTIMORE, Md., "Mother Church of the UNITED BRETHREN IN CHRIST," and a United Methodist Historic SHRINE, was erected 1785-1786 on the same site on which a temporary chapel had been erected in 1771, when the congregation was organized. Several other churches existed in Baltimore at the time Otterbein Church was erected, but all have either rebuilt or relocated, leaving Otterbein have the distinction of being the oldest church edifice in the city. Organized as an independent German Evangelical Reformed Church in 1771, the same congregation became United Brethren when the United Brethren denomination was launched in 1800, and pastor Otterbein was elected to the bishopric.

The first pastor of the congregation was BENEDICT SCHWOPE, who served from 1771 to 1774. He was a warm friend of Methodists ROBERT STRAWBRIDGE and FRANCIS ASBURY. Several Methodist histories state, "There is a strong tradition that Strawbridge received ordination from Rev. Mr. Schwope." On Monday, June 22, 1772, Schwope loaned his chapel to Francis Asbury as a place for the organization of the LOVELY LANE MEETING HOUSE congregation ("Mother Church of American Methodism").

Desiring to follow the frontiersmen into KENTUCKY, Schwope resigned his pastorate in 1774, but not before he, with assistance from Asbury, had prevailed upon PHILIP WILLIAM OTTERBEIN to accept the Baltimore pastorate. Otterbein preached his first sermon in the chapel on May 4, 1774, and remained as pastor until his death, Nov. 17, 1813. His ashes repose in the adjoining churchyard.

The temporary chapel of 1771 soon gave way to the present edifice, erected in 1785-1786, on the same site. Bricks for the massive walls were brought from England as ballast in the famous clipper ships. All nails used in the building were hand-made. The bells were cast in Bremen and were installed in 1789. The bells rang at the close of all America's wars since their installation. Before Baltimore had a fire alarm system, the bells called volunteer firemen to fight fires. The big bell tolled for the deaths of our martyred presidents: Lincoln, Garfield, McKinley, and Kennedy. In keeping with instructions from Otterbein, the bells have never been rung on Good Friday. When immigrant ships arrived from Germany, the bells rang a welcome while residents of "Little Germany" —the community around the church—rushed to the nearby docks to greet the newcomers. The German language was used in the services until 1918. Many outstanding citizens of Baltimore have been members of the church. Five pastors became bishops and several became editors of German literature.

In 1825 the cemetery surrounding the church was filled and ground was purchased for a new one "way out in the country"—eight blocks west.

In addition to loaning the Methodists the chapel in 1772, and the appeal to Otterbein by Asbury in 1774,

OTTERBEIN CHURCH, BALTIMORE, MARYLAND

there are other facts that indicate the close rapport of their respective groups in the late 1700's and early 1800's. When Asbury was consecrated as a bishop in 1784, he requested that Otterbein should have a part in the ceremony. Asbury and Otterbein had many consultations on ways and means of merging their groups into a united church, even to the working out of a proposed discipline. The long absences of Asbury from the city, the increasing age of Otterbein, and the barriers of language seem to have been the factors that prevented the union.

When Otterbein finally yielded to a demand by his German associates that he ordain them, he insisted that a Methodist preacher should assist him. Asbury was out of the city, so William Ryland, a nearby Methodist pastor, was brought in for the ceremony. This was in October, 1813. Several weeks later Bishop Otterbein died and the English sermon at his funeral was preached by Ryland. Asbury was out of the city and when he heard of the death of his friend, several weeks later, he wept like a child and delivered a classic eulogy. In March 1814, when the Methodist conference met in Baltimore, a memorial session was held in Otterbein Church, with Asbury delivering the sermon.

Otterbein Church is the only church building in the Baltimore area, still standing, where it is definitely known that Asbury preached—not once, but many times.

P. E. Holdcraft, *Pennsylvania Conference* (UB). 1938.

PAUL E. HOLDCRAFT

OTTERBEIN COLLEGE, Westerville, Ohio, first institution of higher learning established by the UNITED BRETHREN IN CHRIST. Otterbein University (changed to College in 1917), resulted from action taken by the old Scioto Conference in the fall of 1846. The first Board of Trustees met in Westerville, Ohio, on April 26, 1847, and decided to open on Sept. 1, in two small buildings purchased from the Blendon Seminary, a defunct Methodist institution. Otterbein claims to be the first college in America to *begin* as a coeducational institution, and the first to employ women on its faculty. The first two graduates of the university were women. No student has ever been denied admission to Otterbein on grounds of sex, race, color, or creed.

Nine conferences of The E.U.B. Church elected twenty-four trustees to the governing board. Ten trustees were elected by the Alumni Association, and ten at large. Otterbein secured a charter from the State of Ohio in 1849 and granted its first degrees in 1857. Graduating in the second class (1858) was BENJAMIN HANBY, the songwriter, son of Bishop WILLIAM HANBY, and one of Otterbein's most famous alumni.

For more than sixty years, Otterbein University fought a constant battle against debt, with student enrollment fluctuating between fifty and 200. The Civil War, a disastrous fire which destroyed the Old Main Building in 1870, and two national financial panics threatened to snuff out her feeble flame of learning. Due largely, however, to the heroic efforts of Presidents LEWIS DAVIS (1850-57 and 1860-71), Henry A. Thompson (1872-86), Henry Garst (1886-89), T. J. Sanders (1891-1901), and George Scott (1901-04), the university maintained an excellent faculty, produced outstanding graduates, and finally achieved economic stability.

Under the vigorous leadership of Presidents Lewis Bookwalter (1904-09) and Walter G. Clippinger (1909-39), Otterbein College enjoyed three decades of unprecedented prosperity and growth. Eight new buildings were erected, and an endowment of a $1,000,000 was created. Then the successive blows of world war and depression brought this era to a painful halt. President J. R. Howe (1939-45) struggled against dwindling enrollments and diminished resources to hold the college to its course. Under President J. Gordon Howard (1946-57), Otterbein began to share in the phenomenal growth of postwar American higher education. In 1967 the student body numbered 1,530, the faculty 103, the total number of college employees over 300. The operating budget was over $3,500,000; the endowment $3,051,973; and the physical plant $5,934,714 (forty-four acres and forty-one buildings).

When the Association of Ohio Colleges first adopted minimum standards for college work, Otterbein was one of fifteen Ohio institutions to meet the requirements. She became a member of the North Central Association in 1912 and of the Association of American Colleges in 1915.

LYNN W. TURNER

OTTERBEIN PRESS, a publishing house of The E.U.B. CHURCH, located at 230 W. Fifth Street, DAYTON, Ohio. The first publishing house of the Church of the UNITED BRETHREN IN CHRIST was established in a dwelling on the west side of North Court Street in Circleville, Ohio in 1834. The *Religious Telescope* and other church publications were issued from Circleville until 1853, when the U. B. Publishing House was moved to Dayton, Ohio.

A four story building was erected for publishing purposes on the northeast corner of Fourth and Main Streets in downtown Dayton. It was enlarged on numerous occasions (1869, 1884, 1891, and 1903). In 1905 the first section of a fourteen story office building was built on the original site. A second section was added in 1921 and included a tower with six additional stories. Early in the twentieth century land in downtown Dayton was too valuable to be used as a factory location. A site was purchased on West Fifth Street and the present structure, The Otterbein Press, was built in 1915.

The business for many years was handicapped with a heavy indebtedness, partly due to its own expansions and also from the erection and operation of the office building. The office building was eventually sold in 1952 and the assets were placed in an investment fund for ministerial pensions.

The profits of the publishing enterprise were designated solely for preacher pensions. Since 1947, a total of $2,071,-000 had been transferred from profits for this purpose. In each of the two years 1966 and 1967, The EVANGELICAL PRESS and The Otterbein Press gave jointly a total of $415,000 for pensions. After the formation of the Church Services Division of the Board of Publication in 1963, a sum of $1,370,000 was transferred from The Otterbein Press assets to erect and equip the three story office

building and historical wing at 140 South Perry Street, Dayton, Ohio. The net worth of The Otterbein Press (Aug. 31, 1967) amounted to $3,625,000 and there was an employment of 230 persons. Current sales were listed in 1967 at $4,700,000. The Press itself, as an agency of The E.U.B. Church, went under the Board of Publications of The United Methodist Church in 1968. In 1969 Otterbein Press was sold along with the Cincinnati and Harrisburg plants.

Records of the Board of Publication, EUB, in the Commission on Archives and History.　　JOHN H. NESS, JR.

OUR CHURCH RECORD (1894-1910) was the weekly periodical of the NORTH CAROLINA CONFERENCE of the M.P. Church published by J. F. McCULLOCH in GREENSBORO, N. C. It was an outgrowth of *The Central Protestant* and was the only publication sponsored by a specific conference in the M.P. Church. *Our Church Record* was started with the view of arousing interest in the need for a conference educational institution. In 1898 there were several issues devoted to the history of the Methodist Protestant Church in NORTH CAROLINA which provide valuable material for the researcher interested in the Methodist Protestant movement. In 1910 the name of the paper was changed to *The Methodist Protestant Herald.*

J. Elwood Carroll, *History of the North Carolina Annual Conference of the Methodist Protestant Church* (Greensboro, 1939); scattered issues of *Our Church Record.*

RALPH HARDEE RIVES

GIDEON OUSELEY

OUSELEY, GIDEON (1762-1839), Irish preacher. A fox-hunting, drinking, gambling country gentleman from County Galway, he was converted in 1791 through Methodist meetings begun in his home town of Dunmore by soldiers from the Royal Irish Dragoons. He became a LOCAL PREACHER, but his proficiency in the Irish language led to him being called out by the 1799 Conference with

CHARLES GRAHAM and JAMES McQUIGG as a General Missionary over the whole of Ireland. For forty years he exercised this unique public ministry, preaching in fairs and markets everywhere with great evangelistic success. Many other preachers were appointed from time to time to help in this Irish Mission, but most of them had to retire, broken in health by the hardships they had to endure. Ouseley continued to preach and travel until a few months before his death. A memorial church to him is in Mountmellick, County Laois, the town in which he preached his last sermon.

C. H. Crookshank, *Methodism in Ireland.* 1885-88.
R. H. Gallagher, *Pioneer Preachers.* 1965.
F. Jeffery, *Irish Methodism.* 1964.
William Reilly, *A Memorial of the Ministerial Life of the Rev. Gideon Ouseley, Irish Missionary.* London: John Mason, 1847.   FREDERICK JEFFERY

ALBERT C. OUTLER

OUTLER, ALBERT COOK (1908-   ), American minister and theologian, was born at Thomasville, Ga., on Nov. 17, 1908. He received his A.B. degree from WOFFORD COLLEGE in 1928, and the D.D. there in 1952. Other degrees are from EMORY UNIVERSITY, B.D., 1933; Yale, Ph.D., 1938; Kalamazoo College, D.D., 1962; LYCOMING COLLEGE, L.H.D., 1964; Notre Dame, LL.D., 1966; OHIO WESLEYAN, L.H.D., 1967; General Theological Seminary, D.S.T., 1967; Emory University, Litt.D., 1968. His wife is Carlotta Grace Smith, whom he married in 1931 and they have two children.

Dr. Outler served certain appointments in the SOUTH GEORGIA CONFERENCE and then took the post of instructor in theology at DUKE UNIVERSITY, 1938-39, becoming a full professor and serving there until 1945. He was an associate professor at Yale, 1945-48, the Dwight professor

of theology there, 1948-51, at which time he went to SOUTHERN METHODIST UNIVERSITY in Dallas, Texas, where he became professor of theology.

He has been a delegate to the Methodist Church's Third World Council in Faith and Order at Lund, Sweden; a Methodist delegate to the Third Assembly of the WORLD COUNCIL OF CHURCHES in New Delhi; vice-chairman of the Fourth World Council of Faith and Order, Montreal, 1963; observer at the Second Vatican Council; a delegate (NORTH TEXAS CONFERENCE) to the GENERAL CONFERENCE of The Methodist Church, 1960, '64, and '68; vice-president of the Commission on Ecumenical Affairs and the chairman of the Ecumenical Study and Liaison Committee of 1964. He is the past president of the American Theological Society and of the American Society of Church History.

Among his books are: *A Christian Context for Counseling,* 1946; *Colleges, Faculties and Religion,* 1949; *Psychotherapy and the Christian Message,* 1954; *The Confessions and Enchiridion of St. Augustine,* 1955; *The Christian Tradition and the Unity We Seek,* 1957; *That the World May Believe,* 1966; *A Methodist Observer at Vatican II,* 1967; *Who Trusts in God; Musings on the Meaning of Providence,* 1968. He is a member of the editorial committee of *A Library of Protestant Thought,* and also the author of *John Wesley* (1964). He is a member of the Editorial Board of the WESLEY WORKS PROJECT and currently is serving as chairman of the theological study Commission on Doctrine and Doctrinal Standards authorized to study Part II of the Plan of Union by the General Conference and other pertinent references in the *Discipline* and to bring back to the General Conference of 1972 its report on doctrine and doctrinal standards in The United Methodist Church. He delivered the uniting ceremony sermon at Dallas, Texas, before the combined General Conferences of The Methodist Church and the E.U.B. Church. He is a Fellow, American Academy of Arts and Sciences and a member of The Academy of Texas.

Who's Who in America.
Who's Who in The Methodist Church, 1966.   N. B. H.

OVERSEAS MISSIONARY SOCIETY, New Zealand, has its headquarters in Auckland. "Overseas" was formerly "Foreign." In 1856, when a Wesleyan Methodist Conference was constituted for Australasia, its responsibilities included the care of the existing missions in TONGA and FIJI. When Methodist work was reopened in SAMOA, and established later in New Britain (1875), Papua (1891), and the Solomon Islands (1902), Methodist men and women from NEW ZEALAND shared with Australians in the labors there. After a New Zealand Conference had been formed, affiliated with the Australasian General Conference, a minister in circuit work was regularly appointed as honorary Conference secretary for Foreign Missions. He and other representatives from New Zealand attended some sessions of the Board of Missions at Sydney.

In 1913, the various divisions of the Methodist Church in the country were united, and the Methodist Church of New Zealand became independent of the Methodist Church of Australasia. Plans then begun for a division of the overseas mission work were delayed by the First World War. In 1922, the centenary year of New Zealand Methodism, the Solomon Islands Mission District was separated to be the sole overseas missionary responsibility of the Methodist Church of New Zealand. In anticipation of this step, the Methodist Foreign Missionary Society of New Zealand was constituted. The first full-time General Secretary was W. A. Sinclair, set apart in 1919. He was succeeded by A. H. Scrivin in 1932.

Except for financial and staffing setbacks during the depression of the 1930's and for the occupation of the Solomon Islands by the Japanese during the Second World War, the work of the society has gradually extended.

In 1953, the missions boards in AUSTRALIA and New Zealand entered into an agreement for cooperation, which resulted in New Zealand Methodism taking an active share in a newly founded mission in the NEW GUINEA Highlands.

C. T. J. Luxton, *Isles of Solomon*. Methodist Foreign Missionary Society of New Zealand, 1955. STANLEY G. ANDREWS

OWEN, ISAAC (1809-1866), pioneer American clergyman in CALIFORNIA, began life in VERMONT but two years later was taken by his parents to INDIANA. Coming under the influence of Methodist circuit riders, he was converted at age seventeen, and admitted to the INDIANA CONFERENCE in 1835. While stationed at Greencastle, he took private instruction from professors at Indiana Asbury University (now DEPAUW), and also at Bloomington, seat of the state university. So tutored, he acquired a critical knowledge of the Greek Testament. Indiana Asbury recognized his abilities as an organizer and orator, employed him four years as financial agent and conferred on him an honorary D.D.

A second career opened for him in 1849 when he was appointed the first missionary of the M.E. Church to California. Joining the gold rush, he and Mrs. Owen, with an infant daughter, took the long overland trip westward to SACRAMENTO where they were sheltered in Sutter's Fort until a frame parsonage could be built. They lived in it a scant month before it was swept away by the flooded American River. Escaping to SAN FRANCISCO, they later established a home at Santa Clara where Mrs. Owen remained while her indefatigable husband ranged over mountain trails linking California settlements. So fruitful was his ministry, historian LEON L. LOOFBOUROW characterized him as "the Francis Asbury of California."

Isaac Owen called "a convention" of ministers and laymen Jan. 6-7, 1851 at the Methodist Church of San Jose "to consult and advise" on the "founding of an institution of the grade of a university." It soon came into being, was seated first at San Jose, then Santa Clara, and in 1924 at Stockton, and is now the UNIVERSITY OF THE PACIFIC—oldest chartered institution of higher learning in California.

Owen had planned to start a university in California before he had left Indiana, which was sheer audacity, for in 1850 California had but 699 Methodists. Nevertheless Owen's University of the Pacific dream became reality. Its historian, Rockwell D. Hunt, says that Isaac Owen "more than any other individual, as trustee, agent, and presiding elder, may with good reason be called the founder . . ." But closely associated with him were WILLIAM TAYLOR and EDWARD BANNISTER.

On Jan. 16, 1850 the ship *Arkansas* arrived in San Francisco Bay with $2,000 worth of books which Owen, in the honored Wesleyan tradition, had purchased before starting west. With the help of William Taylor, they were put on sale—establishing the first continuously existing bookstore in California.

In 1860 Owen was put in charge of the Sacramento District, and he and most of his family made the wearying four-day trip by wagon from Santa Clara to the state capital. There Mrs. Owen soon died. When Owen was elected to the GENERAL CONFERENCE of 1856, he could not spare time for the trip east, but upon his election again in 1864, he did go to PHILADELPHIA. Later, while in charge of the San Francisco District, what appeared to be a trifling wound on his hand became serious as erysipelas set in. He died Feb. 9, 1866, and Bishop SIMPSON later recorded, "no man did more for laying the foundation of the Church on the Pacific Coast than did Isaac Owen."

C. V. Anthony, *Fifty Years*. 1901.
R. D. Hunt, *College of the Pacific*. 1951.
L. L. Loofbourow, *In Search of God's Gold*. 1950.
M. Simpson, *Cyclopaedia*. 1881.   LELAND D. CASE

OWENS, THOMAS (17?-1808), British pioneer missionary to the WEST INDIES, was an Irishman, whose date and place of birth are uncertain. He became a Wesleyan traveling preacher in 1785, and was one of the earliest missionaries appointed to the West Indies. A man of high character and personal charm, he was offered the Anglican living (£800 per annum) at Carriacou by Governor-General Matthews, but refused it in order to continue ministering to the slaves. He served ably in Grenada, St. Vincent, Tortola, St. Kitts, etc., returned to Britain in 1803, and died in 1808.

OWENS, THOMAS (1787-1868), American pioneer preacher of the deep South, noted for his exuberant humor and irregular, colorful words and actions. He was born near CHARLESTON, S. C., on Jan. 8, 1787, the son of Thomas and Frances Owens. His parents, who were Methodists, removed to the MISSISSIPPI Territory, it is thought in 1803. Tommy Owens—as he was always called—led a rather wild life in his youth, addicted to profanity, Sabbath breaking, occasional drunkenness, and horse-racing. On one occasion, while riding an impromptu race, he was thrown over his horse's head and for a time his life was despaired of. He would frequently comment afterward, "The way of the transgressor is hard."

Through concerned prayers and later while attending a quarterly conference communion service, he was converted and entered upon his new life with great delight. He began to enjoy discharging churchly duties, then became an exhorter, knowing instinctively how to call for penitents, and how to manage the altar services—which he did with marked success. After a successful meeting in his own church, he and one of his co-workers decided to go to Greenville, Miss., not far away, and there they soon organized a church with about sixty members. The court house was used for worship.

Tommy Owens was small and thin, and when the MISSISSIPPI CONFERENCE was organized on Nov. 1, 1813, at the home of Newitt Vick, he was admitted, though over some opposition because of "his unusual flow of wit and humor." Also he seemed to lack requisite physical strength. He was, however, admitted and gave fifty-five years to the ministry—much longer than most of the robust brethren who had doubted his endurance in conference life.

His irrepressible humor often got him into trouble with

the more sober conference brethren. Taking part in a debate once and greatly opposing ministers marrying and bringing their young wives to conference, he ended by saying, "They come riding up to conference beside their young wives with all the importance of a Bishop."

Bishop R. R. ROBERTS, who was presiding, interrupted and said, "Brother Owens, please tell the Conference how important a Bishop is." "Well, as to that, Sir," Owens replied, "I do not know that I can decide; but they are very important *in their place*. To say the least of it, I think those who marry before they learn how to preach might have the prudence and modesty with their young wives that a cow has with her young calf; hide them out awhile before they bring them to conference." He himself later married Mrs. Rebecca Bass Calvit on Jan. 8, 1828.

On one occasion, the conference voted to have the bishop reprimand Brother Owens for his levity in the pulpit. The bishop did so and then kindly called upon Brother Owens to lead in prayer. Owens said, "O Lord, Thy knowest that this world's a whirligig—a whirligig, O Lord. Amen." (Lazenby's *History of Methodism in Alabama and Mississippi*, p. 88)

The grandmother of this writer said she heard him once when she was quite young and remembered that the congregation sang the hymn, "Oh How Happy Are They," with the lines (which Methodist Hymnal Commissions have long excised!), "I rose higher and higher on a chariot of fire, and the moon it was under my feet"; Brother Owens stopped the music and said, "Ah, Brethren, that was high flying for you."

On another occasion there was a debate concerning uniformity in dress for the preachers. "Most of the Southern preachers had already abandoned the short trousers, knee buckles, and long stockings which were still worn by both of our bishops now present with us." So wrote historian John G. Jones in 1826. Most of the older ministers continued to use and contend especially for the old-fashioned Methodist coat. "But," added Jones, "our younger ministers soon quietly gave up the keel-bottomed coat with its standing collar, for the neat-fitting frock coat. J. R. LAMBUTH and Thomas Owens were the first to venture into our Annual Conference with the ordinary frock coat. Some of the old brethren looked at them reprovingly. . . . They were soon followed by most of the young men in the Conference, and ultimately by most of the older ministers too." (Jones, ii, 119).

As the Mississippi Conference covered the western and southern part of ALABAMA in those days, Owens served appointments in Alabama, as well as in Mississippi, which later became a state in 1818. He lived to be eighty-one years of age, dying at his home at Rocky Springs, Miss., on July 1, 1868, and the Mississippi and Alabama Conferences are proud today to claim him as one of their pioneers.

J. G. Jones, *Mississippi Conference*. 1887-1908.
M. E. Lazenby, *Alabama and West Florida*. 1966.   N. B. H.

OWENSBORO, KENTUCKY, U.S.A. **Settle Memorial Church.** The first Methodist Society was organized in Owensboro (then Owensborough), in 1833. From this Society evolved the present Settle Memorial Church. ALBERT H. REDFORD, the second pastor of the Methodist Society in Owensborough in 1839, was a leading figure in KENTUCKY Methodism for forty years. He served as book agent for the GENERAL CONFERENCE and was the author of *The Life and Times of Bishop Kavanaugh* and a three-volume *History of Methodism in Kentucky*.

Owensboro's first Methodist church building was erected in 1851 and it was here that David Morton, later the first secretary of the Board of Church Extension of the M.E. Church, South, served from 1858 to 1860. Sixty-three years later BACHMAN GLADSTONE HODGE (elected bishop in 1956) became pastor of Settle Memorial.

Settle Chapel, the second building occupied by the Owensboro church, and Settle Memorial, the third and present edifice, were named for Henry C. Settle, who served the congregation from 1866 to 1870 and again from 1877 to 1881. Settle Chapel was completed in 1881, during Settle's second assignment to Owensboro, and Settle Memorial in 1907. The *Century of Progress*, published by the Historical Society of the LOUISVILLE CONFERENCE, used the one word "brilliant," to describe Settle.

In 1970 Settle Memorial reported 1,992 members, property valued at $1,026,795, and a total of $96,486 raised for all purposes.

General Minutes.   HUGH O. POTTER

OWINGS, RICHARD (1738-1786), first native born local preacher in American Methodism, was born in Baltimore County, Md., Nov. 13, 1738, son of Joshua and Mary (Cockey) Owings. In 1770 he accompanied ROBERT STRAWBRIDGE, under whom he was converted, on a preaching mission to Georgetown (now part of the District of Columbia), and "crossing the Potomac river, planted societies in Fairfax county, Virginia." When Strawbridge died in 1781, while visiting at the home of a convert, Joseph Wheeler, the funeral sermon was preached by Owings.

He was appointed in 1775 to the BALTIMORE Circuit. His name appears in the Minutes as "Owen" and "Owens," incorrect forms of the surname which he did not use. The family name is perpetuated in Owings Mill. The Minutes of 1786 list him as a deacon appointed to the Fairfax (Virginia) Circuit.

Thomas Scott recalls that Owings "was nearly six feet in height, slender, stooped in his shoulders, sandy hair and florid complexion." He died on Oct. 8, 1786 and was buried in the cemetery of Leesburg's "Old Stone Church." His will, dated Oct. 5, 1786, and probated five days later on Oct. 10, was witnessed by JOHN LITTLEJOHN, Samuel Murrey and Thomas Edwards.

Frederick E. Maser, *The Dramatic Story of Early American Methodism*. Lake Junaluska, N. C.: Association of Methodist Historical Societies, 1966.
Thomas Scott, "Journal." Ms. owned by Dr. Lawrence Sherwood, Oakland, Md.
Melvin Lee Steadman, Jr., *Leesburg's Old Stone Church*.
W. W. Sweet, *Virginia*. 1955.   WALTER M. LOCKETT, JR.

OWSTON FERRY CASE. In May, 1874, the perpetually smoldering relations between the Wesleyan Methodist connection and the Church of England once more burst into flame. The vicar of Owston Ferry, G. E. Smith, declined to allow the title "The Reverend" to appear on the tombstone of the daughter of a Wesleyan minister, the Rev. H. Keet (Anglican incumbents have some control over the form of memorials erected in their churchyards). The Archibshop of Canterbury, A. C. Tait, in a letter to *The Times* on Aug. 11, 1874, agreed with the Wesleyans that such an objection ought not to have been made, but the Bishop of Lincoln, Christopher Wordsworth, upheld Smith's action on the ground that the Wesleyan ministers, not being in what he called Holy Orders, had no right to the title of "Reverend," and that in any case this was contrary both to the wishes of JOHN WESLEY and of the Wesleyan Methodist Conference regulations of 1793. In the previous year the bishop had issued a "Pastoral to the Wesleyan Methodists in the diocese of Lincoln," inviting them to the return to what he called the Mother Church, according to the principles of their founder.

Very vehement controversy followed both these actions, and the Wesleyan Conference of 1874 manifested a great deal of anti-Anglican feeling. Smith's decision regarding the tombstone was upheld in the ecclesiastical court of arches but was overruled by the court of appeal, the privy council. One result of all this was Osborne Morgan's Burial Law Amendment Bill of 1880, which Bishop Wordsworth bitterly opposed as a bill which would "imperil the existence of the Church of England." One indignant rural rector armed his flock with pitchforks to keep the dissenters out of his churchyard. Nevertheless, the bill became law, enabling dissenting ministers to hold their own services, after due notice, in the parish churchyard. This act (43 and 44 Victoria c. 41) and subsequent clarifications in 1900, brought to an end what B. L. Manning called "the dreariest and most unedifying of all the campaigns in the long war between the Establishment and Dissent."

B. L. Manning, *The Dissenting Deputies*. London, 1952.

MALDWYN L. EDWARDS

OXFORD, England, **Wesley Memorial Church.** WESLEY severed his connection with the spiritual life of Oxford University when he "delivered his soul" to its members in Great St. Mary's Church, on Aug. 24, 1744. His private diary shows that at the time of his conversion he was in touch with small religious groups of townspeople in Oxford, where they probably formed the first Methodist Society. Oxfordshire was assigned to the London District by the Conference of 1746, but in 1748 it became a separate circuit. In 1765, Thomas Tobias was stationed as "travelling preacher" in the Oxford Circuit, since which time there has been a regular succession of Methodist preachers in the town. When Wesley visited Oxford, he usually preached in private houses, and his congregations must have been small. In 1773 it was said that Methodists in and around Oxford worshiped with the Baptists. Ten years later, however, the Methodists had acquired a meeting house, for Wesley records in his *Journal* for July 14, 1783, "I preached in the new preaching-house at Oxford, a lightsome cheerful place." This preaching-house is the building now (1969) numbered 32 and 34 New Inn Hall Street, which was then and still is the property of Brasenose College, from which it was rented by the Society for 23s. 8d. a year. Wesley preached in this building on some half-dozen subsequent occasions, but only in 1788 and 1789 was it too small to hold the congregation of both townspeople and students with comfort.

After Wesley's death the Society, which can never have been large, fell into decay, and there were less than twenty members in 1799. However, the cause recovered and in 1815 was strong enough for members to decide to build a chapel. Donations were solicited, but came in slowly, even though the Conference in 1816 considered

the case of the Oxford Chapel "extraordinary," and allowed the preachers of the Oxford Circuit to send a circular letter to every superintendent minister. There was strong opposition in Oxford to the building of a Methodist Chapel; eventually a site a short distance west of the meeting house was bought from Daniel Harris, one-time Keeper of Oxford Gaol. His relations tried, though unsuccessfully, to prevent the sale on the grounds that Harris was insane and incapable of managing his own affairs.

The architect of the new chapel was William Jenkins, who had taken up that profession after twenty-two years as a Methodist preacher. In May 1817, the foundation stone was laid and the Chapel was opened in February 1818. The building cost over £5,000, most of which was raised by loans and annuities, which left a heavy burden of debt. Nevertheless a schoolroom, used both as a Day School and Sunday school was added at a cost of over £200 in 1819.

Henry Goring, an Anglican resident in Oxford, presented the Chapel trustees with £2,000 towards liquidating the debt on the Chapel, and £500 towards the school, which was immediately improved; in 1831, a new school was built. Unfortunately Church records are sparse and little is known of this period though there was an active Tract Society and a Missionary Auxiliary. CLASS MEETINGS were still a regular feature of Church life; in 1846, there were six meetings on Sunday, the first at 7 A.M., three every Monday, Tuesday and Thursday, two every Friday and one every Wednesday. Unfortunately the Church was divided by the FLY-SHEET agitation; teachers seceded from the Sunday school, taking their classes with them, and the congregation was depleted, membership falling from 249 in 1845 to 180 in 1854. Much of the Chapel debt remained unpaid, annual income was usually less than expenditure, and in 1857 when BENJAMIN GREGORY took up his ministry at the church he found Oxford Methodism in a pitiable condition, ruined by dissension and on the verge of bankruptcy. Under his ministry, things began to change. Undergraduates, at the risk of offending the University authorities flocked to hear his sermons, and though local Anglo-Catholic Clergy were bitterly anti-Methodist, Gregory forged close links with local Evangelical Anglican clergy as well as with other nonconformist bodies. The financial position of the Church was further strengthened in 1859 by a legacy from its old benefactor, Henry Goring, but the millstone of debt was not cleared for another ten years. Originally, singing in the Chapel had been accompanied by an orchestra, but a small organ replaced this in 1862, and a larger and better instrument was installed in 1866. At this time, the Church had an active Young Men's Improvement Society; Day School and Sunday school now seem to have separated, but both flourished.

Until 1871, membership of Oxford University had been limited to Anglicans, but in that year the religious tests were abolished. Perhaps anticipating the growth of nonconformity within the University, the Conference of 1871 appointed a special committee to consider the building of a new chapel, since the old was dilapidated, and "inadequate to meet requirements of the times." The Conference sanctioned a general appeal for funds and work on the new chapel, built in front of the old, began in 1877 during the ministry of G. Maunder, the memorial stones being laid in July. The architect was Charles Bell of London, who adapted the Gothic decorated style for the new building. A striking feature is the carving of the arcade capitals and other ornamental stonework to represent English plants. There is a rose-window in the (ritual) east wall, and in the west a stained glass window representing flowers mentioned in the Bible and water plants, placed there by local Temperance Societies in memory of Maunder, who died before the building was complete. On the south side is a window representing Faith, Hope and Charity and another showing the Risen Lord between Simeon and Anna. The cost of the new building and of the conversion of the old into lecture and classrooms amounted to £13,000. For a time these classrooms were also used by a Girls' School, founded in 1800; the old Lancasterian School having now become a successful high grade boys' school, though the stages of its development are not clear.

Benjamin Gregory was prevented from fulfilling his preaching appointment at the Chapel during his Presidential year, and sent as his substitute HUGH PRICE HUGHES, who made an immense impression. As a result, Hughes accepted the ministry of Wesley Memorial Church in 1881, although he knew Maunder had said that Oxford was the poorest Methodism he had known and many people advised him against the move. Nevertheless Hughes spent three of the most fruitful years of his life at Oxford, despite the fact that both University and city were antagonistic to Methodism, while the countryside around was sunk in agricultural depression. Under Hughes' energetic leadership, Methodism became a strong force in the Oxford district. Hughes founded a Mission Band, which

visited surrounding villages in wagons called "Gospel Chariots," which gave new life to languishing causes and established new ones. A powerful preacher, Hughes increased the membership of the Church by over a hundred in his first year. He took a particular interest in undergraduates, as a result of which, a Wesleyan Society (now the John Wesley Society) was formed.

Hughes' successors were for the most part men of signal ability and scholarship. They included G. Stringer Rowe, later House Governor of the Ministerial Training College at Headingley; John Martin, who had served with distinction in the West African Mission Field, where he wrote grammars of local languages, for which he also devised alphabets; James Chapman, later principal of the Women's Teacher Training College, now Southlands College, Wimbledon. During Chapman's ministry, the Church celebrated the centenary of Wesley's death, an event which met with friendly support from the evangelical wing of the Anglican Church, but with bitter attacks on the "Wesleyan schism" from Anglo-Catholics. During the ministry of Enoch Salt (1893-6), Anglo-Catholic opposition was more bitter, but this drew Methodism closer to the older Dissent (Baptist, Congregational); a Nonconformist Church Council was formed in Oxford. A branch of the WESLEY GUILD, whose activities continue to the present, was also formed during Salt's pastorate. From the time of Hugh Price Hughes until the First World War missions to the city as a whole and open-air evangelical meetings were an important feature of church life.

A heavy program of restoration and renovation of the

WESLEY ROOM, LINCOLN COLLEGE, OXFORD, ENGLAND

church buildings was finished just before the outbreak of War in 1914. This event acted as a great stimulus on church life; work among young people was increased and there was a flourishing club for soldiers. Immediately after the War, the social activities of the church were re-organized and extended, and the Boys' School expanded. Unfortunately the Trade Depression which followed forced the trustees to close the school and sell the buildings in 1930, to St. Peter's College, which bought the old Chapel building in 1932. Thanks to this sale, it was possible to build a new block containing offices and rooms for smaller meetings, among which is the extremely attractive John Wesley Room.

The Bicentenary of Wesley's admission as a Fellow of Lincoln College was celebrated in 1926 when representatives of Methodist Churches in the British Isles and overseas attended a special service in Lincoln College Chapel. Rt. Hon. Walter Runciman unveiled a bust of Wesley in the College Quadrangle.

Wesley Memorial Church celebrated its Jubilee with special services in 1928, and in 1932 the Union of the three English Methodist Connexions was marked by a service at which representatives of these bodies, as well as the Anglican and Nonconformist Churches were present. Within the year, the congregation of the nearby UNITED METHODIST CHURCH was united with that of Wesley Memorial. The Church's Diamond Jubilee was celebrated in 1938, in a time of growing political uncertainty. When war broke out in 1939, troops were billeted in the Church Hall and in 1940, a Forces Canteen was opened; this did not close until 1945, during which time it served 204,000 meals, as well as countless cups of tea and other refreshments. Short services for the Forces were broadcast from the church during the war, and in spite of black-out restrictions, social organizations continued with renewed vigor.

In 1951, the church was the headquarters of the ECUMENICAL METHODIST CONFERENCE, and Methodists from all over the world became familiar with its precincts.

Although the post-war years were marked by financial stringency, church membership steadily advanced, and a new problem was created with the greatly increased number of Methodist students in the University. At first, these were met by the appointment of an assitant minister, who was also an officer of the Student Christian Movement, which shared with the Church the expense of his maintenance. However, a Commission was appointed in 1961 to consider the position of the church with regard to members of the University and to other chapels in the circuit. This decided that there should be two ministers, one of whom, as in earlier days, should be superintendent minister of the Circuit. In 1964, D. Rose was appointed to Wesley Memorial Church and became superintendent minister in 1965.

The Church celebrated the 150th anniversary of the opening of the old chapel and the ninetieth anniversary of the opening of the new chapel in May 1968 by special services. The president of Conference, Irvonwy Morgan, unveiled a plaque on 32 and 34 New Inn Hall Street, recording that it was the first Methodist meeting house in Oxford and that John Wesley preached there on several occasions. St. Peter's College plans presently to demolish the old Chapel, and replace it with new buildings.

J. E. OXLEY

OXFORD, MISSISSIPPI, U.S.A. The Methodist church in Oxford was organized in 1837 under the leadership of William Craig, pastor, with David O. Shattuck as presiding elder of the Holly Springs district. The first deed bears date of Aug. 23, 1838, the trustees being Richard R. Corbin, William Webb, Daniel Grayson, Nathanael S. Jennings, and William Gordon. On this lot, which cost $50, a frame building was erected in the fall of 1838, during the pastorate of A. J. S. Harris. Pastors who served in this building were E. J. Williams and William B. Walker, with others whose names are not available.

On July 4, 1851, a new lot was purchased on Jackson Avenue near the square and a new church built thereon, a handsome brick building with an auditorium upstairs and a substory beneath. The University of Mississippi had opened at Oxford, and this new building was evidently intended to serve the students as well as the townspeople. Trustees in 1851 were William Gordon, William Webb, John M. Boggs, Lewis T. Wynn, Hugh W. Rison, B. Walton, and William Jones. The following served as pastor in this church before it was burned in 1889: Lewis H. Davis, E. J. Williams, George W. Carter, C. N. B. Campbell, John Barcroft, John J. Wheat, Amos Kendall, S. R. Brewer, W. B. MURRAH, Kenneth A. Jones, W. T. J. Sullivan, E. B. Ramsey, R. M. Standifer, and Thomas W. Dye. Many outstanding students and faculty members worshipped in this building, among the former CHARLES B. GALLOWAY, later a Methodist bishop and JAMES W. LAMBUTH, one of the great pioneer missionaries in the Methodist Church, serving in China and Japan from 1854 until his death in 1892. There was a Methodist parsonage on South Lamar Street during most of this time.

A Gothic brick church was built on the same location in 1890 with a Sunday school annex, one of the first of its type in the area. The Sunday school during the college year was always too large for the building, and for a number of years the church used the public school building just across the street. The movement for a new church began in 1920 but it was not until fifteen years later the actual plans began to be put into effect. A building committee was appointed in 1935. The NORTH MISSISSIPPI CONFERENCE approved the building of the first unit at a cost of $60,000 and the MISSISSIPPI CONFERENCE promised to cooperate. A new location was secured from the Bank of Oxford in December 1936, and construction began on Feb. 1, 1937.

The new sanctuary was constructed in the fall and winter of 1949 and the spring of 1950. H. ELLIS FINGER, now a bishop, was pastor at that time. The cost was $90,000.

In addition to the enterprising local membership, which now reports 1,184 persons, the Oxford Methodist church has been primarily the church of the University of Mississippi. It is located nearer the campus than the church in any of the other college towns and is more influenced by the school than any similar church in Mississippi.

J. B. CAIN

OXFORD COLLEGE OF EMORY UNIVERSITY, Oxford, Georgia, occupies the old campus of Emory College established in 1836. When Emory College became the College of Arts and Sciences of EMORY UNIVERSITY, in 1915, the Oxford division continued as an academy. In 1929 a junior college was started. The institution is an integral part of Emory University, and library and assets are re-

OLD CHAPEL AT EMORY, OXFORD

ported by the university. For the governing board, see EMORY UNIVERSITY.

JOHN O. GROSS

OXFORD INSTITUTE ON METHODIST THEOLOGICAL STUDIES grew out of a concern that Methodist beginnings at Oxford University be memorialized through a living theological consultation. As early as the 1951 meeting of the WORLD METHODIST COUNCIL at OXFORD, some effort to mark this memorial was sought. At the World Methodist Council meeting at LAKE JUNALUSKA in 1956, the format of a theological institute was agreed upon. The first such Institute was held in 1958.

One hundred persons from over the world made up largely of Methodist theologians come together for a ten-day institute at Lincoln College, Oxford. The total membership is divided roughly as one-third U. S., one-third British and one-third the rest of the Methodist world. This institute has provided a meeting place for persons engaged professionally in theology in world Methodism. It has focused each time on a significant doctrine of the Church, and on some occasions has contributed to studies of these doctrines in the WORLD COUNCIL OF CHURCHES.

The first Institute was in 1958 and its theme *Biblical Theology and Methodist Doctrine*. The second Institute in 1962 was on *The Doctrine of the Church*. The third in 1965 was on *The Finality of Christ*, and the fourth in 1969 had as its theme, *The Living God*. Presiding as wardens in these respective sessions were the Rev. Reginald Kissack (1958), Principal HAROLD ROBERTS (1962) and Dr. DOW KIRKPATRICK (1965), and Principal Raymond George (1969). The first of the series was published in the July 1959, *London Quarterly and Hol-*

born Review and the others were published in book form by ABINGDON PRESS, NASHVILLE, Tenn., U.S.A. A fifth Institute is projected for the summer of 1973.

DOW KIRKPATRICK

OXFORD METHODISTS were the original followers of JOHN WESLEY at Oxford University. John Wesley himself described the beginning of the Oxford Methodists as follows: "In November, 1729, four young gentlemen of Oxford—Mr. John Wesley, Fellow of Lincoln College; Mr. Charles Wesley, Student of Christ Church; Mr. Morgan, Commoner of Christ Church; and Mr. Kirkham of Merton College—began to spend some evenings in a week together in reading, chiefly, the Greek Testament." (*Works*, viii, 334.) The "Mr. Morgan" mentioned was WILLIAM MORGAN, the elder of the brothers who were at Oxford, who died in tragic circumstances in DUBLIN on August 26, 1732. Robert Kirkham, who died in March 1767, was the son of the Rev. Lionel Kirkham of Stanton, Gloucestershire. Kirkham's place as the fourth member of the party is disputed, however, by V. H. H. Green, the historian, who forwards the claims of Francis Gore of Christ Church (see *The Young Mr. Wesley*, p. 151). By 1735 this group had grown to some fourteen or fifteen (*Works*, xiii, 288), and Luke Tyerman (*The Oxford Methodists*, 1873) lists the following as having been connected with it: Charles Morgan (born, 1714), Commoner of Lincoln College; John Clayton (1709-73), Brazenose; BENJAMIN INGHAM (1712-72), Queen's; JOHN GAMBOLD (1711-71), Christ Church; JAMES HERVEY 1714-58), Lincoln; Thomas Broughton (died, 1777), Exeter; John Boyce (born c. 1711), Christ Church; William Chapman of Pembroke; Charles Kinchin (died, 1742),

Corpus Christi; Richard Hutchins (died, 1781), Lincoln; Christopher Atkinson (1713-74), Queen's; JOHN WHITELAMB (1710-69), Lincoln; and WESTLEY HALL (died, 1776), Lincoln. As one would expect, it is not easy to be exact about membership, and Green in *The Young Mr. Wesley* quotes from a contemporary list which gives the following additional names: GEORGE WHITEFIELD, Pembroke College; Thomas Horne, Christ Church; Richard Smith and Henry Evans, Christ Church; John Robson and Gridsley (Christian name unknown), Lincoln; Matthew Salmon, Brazenose; Kitchen (Christian name unknown), Pembroke; Robert Watson, Henry Washington, John Bell, Roger (?) Wilson and John (?) Smith, Queen's. Green also lists men who "were on the periphery of the HOLY CLUB, who were at least interested in its activities": Bulman, Bingham, Morgan Graves, Cox, Watkins (Wadham College); Christopher Rhodes and John Spicer (Christ Church); and William Golburne. Others are named who fall into this category: Nash, Langford, Potter, Thomas Patten (Corpus Christi); William Nowell (Brazenose); Hudson Martin (Jesus); George Watson (Christ Church); William Haward (Merton); William Clements (Lincoln); Nicholls, William Smith, Thomas Greives, Robert Davison, and Matthew Robinson (the last four all of Lincoln).

V. H. H. Green, *Young Mr. Wesley*. 1961.
L. Tyerman, *Oxford Methodists*. 1873.　BRIAN J. N. GALLIERS

G. BROMLEY OXNAM

OXNAM, GARFIELD BROMLEY (1891-1963), American bishop was born at Sonora, Calif., Aug. 14, 1891, the son of Thomas Henry and Mamie (Job) Oxnam. He was educated at the University of Southern California (A.B., 1913), and BOSTON UNIVERSITY (S.T.B., 1915). He did graduate study at Harvard and other schools. During his career some twenty-one institutions, including AMERICAN, Boston, NORTHWESTERN, Princeton, Southern California, and Yale Universities, conferred on him a total of eight honorary degrees—D.D., S.T.D., Th.D., LL.D., Litt.D., L.H.D., D.Sc., and D.C.L. He married Ruth Fisher, Aug. 19, 1914, and they had three children, Robert, Philip, and Ruth (Mrs. Robert McCormack).

Admitted on trial in the SOUTHERN CALIFORNIA CONFERENCE in 1913, Oxnam was ordained deacon in 1915 and elder in 1917. His appointments were: 1916, Poplar, Calif.; 1917-26, Church of All Nations, LOS ANGELES; 1927, professor, BOSTON UNIVERSITY SCHOOL OF THEOLOGY; and 1928-35, president, DEPAUW UNIVERSITY.

In one year at Poplar, Oxnam built a new church and a new parsonage and more than doubled the church membership. In ten years at the Church of All Nations, he identified with the labor movement and other causes, and he organized activities including a boys' club of 1,000 members. As a result the area which had previously had the highest juvenile delinquency rate in Los Angeles attained a rate lower than the average for the municipality as a whole. While serving the church Oxnam was also professor of social ethics in the University of Southern California for four years.

A delegate to four GENERAL CONFERENCES, 1924-36, Oxnam was elected bishop in 1936. His episcopal assignments were: 1936-39, OMAHA; 1939-44, BOSTON; 1944-52, NEW YORK; and 1952-60, WASHINGTON.

The episcopacy gave full scope for Oxnam's abilities. He visited every parsonage in the Omaha Area which comprised IOWA and NEBRASKA. He traveled widely; usually his annual expense account was larger than that of any other bishop in the church. He wielded great influence as secretary of the COUNCIL OF BISHOPS, 1939-56, transforming the periodic meetings of the church leaders into a real Council which considered a full and challenging agenda at each session. He originated the plan which requires the bishops in turn to visit foreign fields so as to gain first-hand knowledge of world conditions. He conceived and led the Methodist Crusade for World Order, 1944-48. Under his leadership WESTMINSTER SEMINARY in MARYLAND was moved to Washington as WESLEY SEMINARY, and the School of International Service was established at American University with funds appropriated by the General Conference.

Endowed with a quick mind, a diversity of gifts, and a capacity for hard work, Oxnam developed competence in a number of fields. He filled ten or more important university lectureships, including the Lyman Beecher at Yale, Fondren at SOUTHERN METHODIST, Merrick at OHIO WESLEYAN, Earl at PACIFIC, Tipple at DREW, and Hoover and Tuthill at Chicago. His books, more than twenty in number, widened his influence. Among them were: *The Mexican in Los Angeles*, 1920; *Social Principles of Jesus*, 1923; *Preaching in a Revolutionary Age*, 1944; *The Church and Contemporary Change*, 1950; *I Protest*, 1954; and *A Testament of Faith*, 1958. He was a trustee of nine institutions, including Boston and American Universities.

Active in both denominational and ecumenical organizations and movements, Oxnam served as president of the FEDERAL COUNCIL OF CHURCHES, 1944-46; was a presiding officer at the organization of the National Council of Churches, 1950; was one of the presidents of the WORLD COUNCIL OF CHURCHES, 1948-54; and later was a member of the Central Committee of the latter. He chaired the division of educational institutions, General BOARD OF EDUCATION, 1939-44, and did the same for the division of foreign missions, General BOARD OF MISSIONS, 1944-52. During World War II he was a member of the Civil Advisory Commission to the Secretary of the Navy, official visitor for the Joint Chiefs of Staff to army and navy chaplains, chairman of the Commission to Study Post War Relief Conditions in GERMANY, and chairman of the Methodist Commission on CHAPLAINS.

Claiming that the Committee on Un-American Activities of the U.S. Congress had for seven years released so-called "files" containing false material which said or suggested that he was a communist, and pointing out that the Committee had ignored repeated requests to correct its files, Oxnam in July 1953, requested a hearing before the Committee. In a twelve-hour session he attempted to explain his beliefs and to refute the false accusations. The Committee did not apologize or retract, but afterward two individual congressmen said they did not believe the bishop was or ever had been a communist. The reaction in the press was favorable to the bishop. After Oxnam's death the 1964 Northeastern JURISDICTIONAL CONFERENCE adopted a resolution saying the bishop had "called the House Committee on Un-American Activities to public accounting" for the "irresponsible way" in which it had attacked and tried to intimidate him and other churchmen. Also, the resolution declared that Oxnam had "left the impress of his brilliant mind, courageous spirit, and tireless will on every level of the life of The Methodist Church as well as the National and World Council of Churches."

Broken in health, Oxnam retired in 1960. He died at White Plains, N. Y., March 12, 1963. On April 11, 1964, his ashes were interred in a solemn service of enshrinement beneath the chancel of the Oxnam Chapel, Wesley Theological Seminary, Washington, D. C.

Christian Advocate, March 28, 1963.
General Conference Journals, MEC and MC.
General Minutes, MEC.
Journal of the Northeastern Jurisdictional Conference, 1964.
G. Bromley Oxnam, *I Protest.* New York: Harper, 1954.
Service of Enshrinement of the Ashes of G. Bromley Oxnam. (Pamphlet). 1964.
Who's Who in America, Vol. 30.
World Outlook, June, 1963.   ALBEA GODBOLD

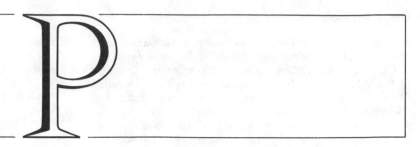

PACE, JAMES (1930-), missionary to BOLIVIA, was born in Brownsville, Texas. He received the A.B. degree from SOUTHERN METHODIST UNIVERSITY and the B.D. degree from Yale Divinity School. He married Evelyn Duponey, and they have four children. A missionary to Bolivia since 1957, he has served as pastor, superintendent of the Central District, conference executive secretary (1962), director of Wesley Seminary, and executive secretary of the conference committee on literacy and literature.

NATALIE BARBER

PACE, JOHN CAPERTON (1888-), and **MILDRED SMITH** (1893-), served with distinction as missionary educators in INDIA from late 1920 until July 1943. Pace was born in Palestine, Texas, and was educated at SOUTHWESTERN UNIVERSITY (B.A.), SOUTHERN METHODIST UNIVERSITY, and Yale Divinity School (B.D.). Mrs. Pace was born in Stirling City, Texas, April 17, 1893.

They were appointed to India and arrived there in 1920. Their first appointment was to a boys' industrial school at Aligarh, United Provinces, but in February 1922, they were put in charge of the only high school then in existence in the large NORTHERN INDIA CONFERENCE.

After furlough in 1925, they were sent to the now-famed Ingraham Institute at Ghaziabad, a few miles from DELHI. They remained in that key appointment until 1942, when they left India on furlough. The next year, for family reasons, they withdrew from service under the board; and, after a few years on a farm, John Pace accepted the presidency of a junior college in TEXAS.

While he was in the grip of the responsibilities of the principalship of Ghaziabad, Mrs. Pace was both his invaluable colleague and a very convincing adviser of other primary and second school officers. Their helpful influence was felt in hundreds of schools in India, penetrating into secular schools of government, and even into schools maintained by non-Christian groups.

J. N. Hollister, *Southern Asia.* 1956.   J. WASKOM PICKETT

PACIFIC CHINESE MISSION. Thousands of Chinese immigrants poured into CALIFORNIA following the Gold Rush of 1849. Nearly two decades passed before the M. E. Church began evangelizing them. With support from the CALIFORNIA CONFERENCE and the General Missionary Committee in New York, Otis Gibson, who had served as missionary in CHINA, became superintendent of missionary work among the west coast Chinese in 1868. He soon organized two Sunday schools in SAN FRANCISCO and one in SAN JOSE. In 1870, a headquarters building called the Chinese Mission Institute was opened in San Francisco. By 1878 Gibson reported that the work was opening up and expanding on every side.

Several factors served to hinder the ministry to the Chinese immigrants. In the early years there were no native Chinese preachers to assist the missionaries. The

white people soon developed strong race prejudice against the Chinese. It was not unusual for Chinese to be attacked, kicked, and beaten as they were on their way to Methodist services and language classes. Then in 1882 came the Chinese Exclusion Act which effactually stopped the rapid influx of immigrants from China.

Because of ill health, Gibson resigned as superintendent of Chinese missions in 1884 and was succeeded by F. J. Masters. Other leaders in the Chinese work were John Hammond, A. J. Hanson, George Hedley, Edward James, and George Pearson. Eventually Chinese missions were started in Berkeley, Gilroy, Monterey, Salinas, Watsonville, Hanford, and Marysville, California, and in such cities as PORTLAND, SEATTLE, DENVER, SAN ANTONIO, and TUCSON in other states. In 1907, superintendent James reported that he had traveled 6,000 miles in making the circuit of the work in the Pacific Chinese Mission.

The California Conference formed a Chinese District in 1893, and in 1904 the Chinese Mission was formally organized in San Francisco with Bishop LUTHER B. WILSON presiding. In 1908 the name was changed to Pacific Chinese Mission and it included all Chinese work in the western half of the United States. At unification in 1939, the Pacific Chinese Mission with eleven effective preachers, 428 members, and 773 Sunday school pupils became a part of the California Oriental Mission which also included Filipino and Korean work. The organization was designated as the California Oriental Provisional Conference in 1945. In 1952 the ministers and churches of the provisional conference were absorbed into the English-speaking conferences of the WESTERN JURISDICTION. However, sixteen years later there were still five Chinese Methodist churches in California—at San Francisco, Oakland, Sacramento, and Los Angeles.

W. C. Barclay, *History of Methodist Missions.* 1957.
E. S. Bucke, *History of American Methodism.* 1964.
Journals of the Pacific Chinese Mission.   EDWAR LEE

PACIFIC CONFERENCE (1852-1939) was the first organized work of the M. E. Church, South on the west coast. Sent by the bishops of the church, JESSE BORING and A. M. WYNN of the GEORGIA CONFERENCE and D. W. Pollock of the ST. LOUIS CONFERENCE arrived in SAN FRANCISCO in 1850. They distributed literature, organized circuits, enrolled members, and in April 1852, formed the Pacific Conference to include CALIFORNIA, OREGON, ARIZONA, and NEW MEXICO.

At the outset the work of the conference was limited to the vicinity of San Francisco, but in 1854 the presiding elder of the Stockton District learned that some members of a church on the LOS ANGELES Circuit of the M. E. Church, opposed to an abolition society in the congregation, had withdrawn and desired affiliation with the Southern church. He visited the group, organized a class of sixteen, and sent three preachers to the area in 1855.

Due to anti-Southern feeling, the work progressed slow-

PACIFIC GROVE, CALIFORNIA

ly in southern California. A Los Angeles District was formed in 1858 but was discontinued the next year. In 1866 and 1867, Los Angeles was the sole appointment of the Pacific Conference in the southern part of the state. However, in 1868, the Los Angeles Mission District was formed with five appointments.

The Pacific Conference organized an Oregon District in 1859, and in 1866 the GENERAL CONFERENCE designated Oregon and a part of northern California as the Columbia Conference (1866-1917).

In October 1870, the Pacific Conference was again divided to form the Los Angeles Conference (1870-1922). The new body included southern California and Arizona; at the beginning it had ten preachers and 475 members. Throughout its history the Los Angeles Conference was never large. In 1880 there were about 1,000 church members. By 1900 there were thirty churches and some 2,000 members, one-sixth of them in Arizona. When the conference was dissolved in 1922, it gave back to the Pacific Conference some 4,500 members and sixteen churches, while the remainder—about 2,800 members and twenty-one congregations—formed the Arizona Conference.

For lack of strength the Southern Methodist conferences in California were not able to establish a permanent college or seminary. However, they started several educational institutions which served varying periods of time. Among them were Bascom Institute at San Jose, Asbury Institute at Sacramento, Corvallis College in Oregon, and the Pacific Methodist College at Vacaville. The latter institution later moved to Santa Rosa; it began in 1861 and closed in 1887.

The Pacific Conference launched a church paper at San Francisco in 1852. Published under several different names, it finally became the *Pacific Methodist Advocate* in 1891 and so continued until 1934. The *Los Angeles Christian Advocate*, started in 1885 by the Los Angeles Conference, failed within three years. GROVER C. EMMONS, long a Southern Methodist leader in southern California, founded *The Upper Room* in 1934 and was its editor until his death ten years later.

The conferences laid strong emphasis on Sunday schools and youth work. Trinity Church in Los Angeles pioneered in the ministry to youth and prepared the memorial to the General Conference of 1890 which resulted in the establishment of the EPWORTH LEAGUE in the Southern church. Soon after 1900, the WOMAN'S HOME MISSIONARY SOCIETY began operating the Homer Toberman Deaconess Home in Los Angeles. It has continued as a settlement or neighborhood house ministering to the needy.

Trinity Church, organized in 1869, was the largest church in the Los Angeles Conference from 1880 onward, and in time it became one of the strongest congregations in Southern Methodism. In the decade from 1920 to 1930 the congregation quadrupled in size. The growth and dominance of Trinity Church were due largely to an intensive proram under the leadership of able pastors, such as H. M. DuBose, CHARLES C. SELECMAN, and ROBERT P. SHULER. At its peak strength the church had nearly 5,000 members.

Through the generosity of a Southern Methodist, LIZZIE H. GLIDE, the Glide Memorial Church was erected at Taylor and Ellis Streets, San Francisco, in 1929 at a cost of about half a million dollars. Beginning with seventy members, Glide Memorial took the place of the Fitzgerald Church a few blocks away. A program of continuous evangelism lifted the membership to about 1,350 by 1939. In the 1940's the membership began to decline. In 1967, the church reported something over 300 members.

The M. E. Church, South did not fare well in competition with the M. E. Church in California, particularly in the southern part of the state. The Southern church preachers were vigorous and determined, but their denomination did not invest as much money in church extension as did the Northern church. Moreover, the Northern church had a distinct advantage in that the majority of the immigrants into the region were from the northern states.

At unification in 1939, the Pacific Conference with 19,817 members constituted the total numerical strength of the M. E. Church, South in California. Some 11,308 of these members went into the California Conference and 8,509 into the SOUTHERN CALIFORNIA CONFERENCE of The Methodist Church.

General Minutes (MES), 1855ff.
E. D. Jervey, *Southern California and Arizona.* 1960.
J. C. McPheeters, *The Life Story of Lizzie H. Glide.* San Francisco: Eagle Printing Co. 1936.   PEARL S. SWEET

PACIFIC GERMAN CONFERENCE grew out of mission work among the German-speaking people in the northwest. Frederick Bonn joined the OREGON CONFERENCE in 1880 and gave himself to work among the Germans. He went to Puget Sound in 1882 and soon had German churches at TACOMA and SEATTLE. JAMES H. WILBUR started work among the Germans at Walla Walla.

In 1888 the North Pacific German Mission, including work in WASHINGTON, OREGON, IDAHO, and MONTANA, was organized. In 1892 it became the North Pacific German Mission Conference, and in 1905 the Pacific German Conference. The conference was organized Sept. 7, 1905 at PORTLAND, Ore., with Bishop WILLIAM F. McDOWELL presiding. At the time of organization it had two districts, Portland and Spokane, and there were twenty-two charges and 1,242 members. Twelve of the charges were in Washington.

The Pacific German Conference was the last of the German conferences to be organized in the M. E. Church in accordance with the plan for a system of such conferences adopted by the 1864 GENERAL CONFERENCE. The Pacific German Conference reached peak strength in 1910 when it had twenty-four charges and 1,539 members. Liquidation of the German conferences came rapidly after 1925 when the St. LOUIS GERMAN CONFERENCE merged into the overlying English-speaking conferences. The decrease in German immigration and the rapid Americanization of the German language churches after the first world war made the mergers inevitable. With few church services being conducted in German there was no logical reason for maintaining the German conferences. The Pacific German Conference merged in 1928, having at the time seventeen charges, nineteen churches, 1,256 members, and property valued at $107,350.

P. F. Douglass, *German Methodism.* 1939.
General Minutes, MEC.   FREDERICK E. MASER

PACIFIC GROVE, CALIFORNIA, U.S.A. At the southern tip of the Monterey Peninsula is situated this one-time capital of CALIFORNIA Methodism. The annual conference of 1875 was offered a gift of 100 acres of land at this place for a summer resort and retreat for Methodists. The offer was accepted and the area was developed as Pacific Grove Retreat. CAMP MEETINGS were held; Methodist families vacationed here in great numbers; many Methodists came here to live and to die; and the city of Pacific Grove came into being.

A church was built, far larger than the local membership required, to be serviceable for the sessions of the annual conference which met here twenty-seven consecutive times, 1886 to 1913. Preceding the session many of the ministers and their families were at Pacific Grove several days while the Itinerants' Club met each morning and provided intellectual stimulus for the ministers while the families enjoyed the vacation. Lectures on poetry, Bible themes, or other contemporary topics, discussions on church polity, Sunday school curriculum or other matters of interest filled the hours, and in the evening an illustrated lecture or musical program. Pacific Grove provided a Methodist cultural center for the people whose interests followed the annual conference sessions.

In time the church corporation lost all the property except that occupied by church and parsonage because of financial problems. Changing patterns of life shifted interest away from the former ways, and Pacific Grove ceased to be a dominant factor in conference life. The first pastor named was J. B. Chynoweth, in 1884. He reported twenty-five members. The church was a notable one for many years, and the conference cemetery at Pacific Grove was the place of interment of many Methodist ministers.

C. V. Anthony, *Fifty Years*. 1901.
California Christian Advocate.
L. L. Loofbourow, *In Search of God's Gold*. 1950.
J. C. Simmons, *Pacific Coast*. 1886.   DON M. CHASE

PACIFIC JAPANESE MISSION. The M. E. Church began work among the Japanese in CALIFORNIA in 1877 when some Japanese attended the Chinese mission being conducted by Otis Gibson. (See PACIFIC CHINESE MISSION.) In 1884, Kanichi Mieyama, a Japanese, was admitted on trial into the CALIFORNIA CONFERENCE. The conference formed a Japanese District in 1893, and in 1894 the first Japanese Methodist Church in America was dedicated in SAN FRANCISCO. Work among the Japanese extended north, south, and east from San Francisco.

The Pacific Japanese Mission was organized in 1900 with M. C. HARRIS as superintendent. The mission included the Japanese and Korean work on the Pacific slope and in HAWAII. Methodist work had flourished among the Japanese in Hawaii because Kanichi Mieyama went there as a missionary from California in 1885. In 1905 the Hawaii work became the Hawaii Mission, leaving the Pacific Japanese Mission with eight pastors, 699 church members, and 305 Sunday school pupils.

Beginning in 1897, the M. E. Church, South did oriental missionary work on the west coast, and there was some division of responsibility between the two Episcopal Methodisms. (See CALIFORNIA ORIENTAL MISSION.)

HERBERT B. JOHNSON was superintendent of the Pacific Japanese Mission from 1904 to 1925. That period was marked by the development of anti-Japanese feeling on the west coast and the rise of an English-speaking generation of Japanese. Many Japanese Methodist young people began to achieve places of leadership in the English-speaking communities. Frank Herron Smith served as superintendent from 1926 to 1944. He led in church

extension, in Christian training for young people, and in the promotion of good will among Americans and Japanese. Japanese churches were organized in CALIFORNIA, OREGON, WASHINGTON, ARIZONA, and COLORADO.

At unification in 1939, the mission was superseded by the Japanese Provisional Conference which also included the Japanese work from the California Oriental Mission of the M. E. Church, South. The promising work of the provisional conference was soon interrupted by the second world war. More than 110,000 Japanese people on the west coast were evacuated to the desert areas of western America. Though the doors of many Japanese churches were locked and other sanctuaries were rented, somehow religious services and activities were carried on among the Japanese in the relocation centers. Because of the illness of Smith, John B. Cobb was appointed acting superintendent in 1945. Channing A. Richardson led the mission from 1946 to 1948, and in 1949 Taro Goto became superintendent, the first Japanese in the United States to hold the office.

In the post-war years, the work of the provisional conference was notable in several ways. Leadership in the churches passed from Japanese-speaking to English-speaking members. There was progress in church building—ten new churches, thirteen education units, and seven parsonages, along with the purchase of fifteen parsonages. Also, there was a definite trend toward integration of the Japanese work with the English-speaking conferences. The merger finally was consummated in 1964, and the Japanese Provisional Conference was no more. At the time of integration the conference had forty-one ministers (eleven retired), thirty churches, 6,534 members, and property valued at $3,581,990.

E. S. Bucke, *History of American Methodism*, 1964.
Journals of the Pacific Japanese Mission.
Journals of the Pacific Japanese Provisional Conference.
TARO GOTO

PACIFIC NORTHWEST CONFERENCE, which includes the state of WASHINGTON and part of IDAHO, was organized as a conference of the M. E. Church, Sept. 17, 1929 at SPOKANE, Wash., with Bishop TITUS LOWE presiding. At the time of organization the conference also included the work in ALASKA, but that was set off as the Alaska Mission in 1939. The Pacific Northwest Conference was formed by merging the Puget Sound and COLUMBIA RIVER Conferences. The one covered west Washington, and the other east Washington and a part of Idaho. When organized the new conference had nine districts and 49,724 members. (See WASHINGTON for beginnings of Methodism in the state.)

The Columbia River Conference was formed in 1873 by dividing the OREGON CONFERENCE. It was first called the East Oregon and Washington Conference, the name being changed to Columbia River in 1876. The conference included east Washington, east OREGON, and the panhandle of Idaho. At the end of the first year it reported nineteen charges and 455 members. In 1922 the Oregon territory of this conference was given to the Oregon Conference. In its last year, 1928, the Columbia River Conference reported three districts, 115 charges, 20,449 members, and property valued at $1,853,050.

The Puget Sound Conference was formed in 1884 by dividing the Oregon Conference. Its territory was west Washington. In 1924 Alaska was made a part of the conference. The conference started with two districts and thirty-four charges. At the end of the first year it reported 1,638 members. In its last year, 1928, the Puget Sound Conference had four districts, 168 charges, 28,580 members, and property valued at $2,669,250.

The PACIFIC GERMAN CONFERENCE and the PACIFIC SWEDISH MISSION CONFERENCE were absorbed by the overlying English-speaking conferences in 1928, and a few ministers and churches from both bodies were received into the Columbia River and Puget Sound Conferences at that time. At Unification in 1939, three M. P. congregations with about 800 members, and two from the M. E. Church, South with 394 members, entered the Pacific Northwest Conference of The Methodist Church. The WESTERN NORWEGIAN-DANISH CONFERENCE was merged with the overlying English-speaking conferences in 1939. This merger brought nine churches with about 530 members into the Pacific Northwest Conference. The new Pacific Northwest Conference was organized at Bellingham, Wash., on June 14, 1939 with Bishop WALLACE E. BROWN presiding. It began with five districts; and in 1941 it reported 247 pastoral charges and 48,011 members.

Methodist work among the Japanese in Spokane began in 1902. The JAPANESE PROVISIONAL CONFERENCE was merged with the overlying English-speaking conferences in 1964. This merger brought four Japanese churches with 1,023 members into the Pacific Northwest Conference.

One member of the Pacific Northwest Conference, J. RALPH MAGEE, was elected bishop in 1932.

Methodism in Washington has supported schools and service agencies. The Columbia River Conference had the *Columbia Christian Advocate* in Spokane in the 1890's, and the Puget Sound Conference supported the *Pacific Christian Advocate* at Portland, Ore. Both conferences maintained several WESLEY FOUNDATIONS at the state schools. The College OF PUGET SOUND (now UNIVERSITY) was founded at Tacoma in 1888. With an endowment of over $5,000,000, and a plant valued at $13,000,000, the school has a student body of more than 2,300.

In 1968 the Pacific Northwest Conference was supporting the Deaconess Children's Home at Everett, Central Washington Deaconess Hospital at Wenatchee, Spokane Deaconess Hospital, Kadlec Methodist Hospital at Richland, Bayview Manor in Seattle, Wesley Gardens at Des Moines, Rockwood Manor at Spokane, Goodwill Industries at Aberdeen, Seattle, Spokane, and several camps.

The Pacific Northwest Conference reported in 1970 seven districts, 236 charges, 405 ministers, 101,718 members, and property valued at $52,416,524. In that year it raised for all purposes $7,914,835.

General Minutes, MEC, MECS, TMC, UMC.
Erle Howell, *Methodism in the Northwest*. Nasvhille: Parthenon Press, 1966.
Minutes of the Pacific Northwest Conference.   ERLE HOWELL

PACIFIC SWEDISH MISSION CONFERENCE (ME) grew out of Methodist mission work among the Swedish-speaking people in the northwest. The Swedes came to the region in large numbers in the 1880's. While most were Lutherans, some had been won to Methodism in the eastern part of the United States. Swedish Methodist work began on the west coast in 1873 when a group of Swedish and Norwegian friends organized a class in the Howard Street M.E. Church, SAN FRANCISCO. Two years later the class became an independent church, and the next year it received its first pastor. As time passed Swedish churches were organized in BERKELEY, PASADENA, SPOKANE, TACOMA, SEATTLE, PORTLAND, SALEM, and elsewhere.

In 1890 a Swedish District with ten charges was organized in the Puget Sound Conference. A year later the district reported only 108 members. In 1900 there were 225. Notwithstanding the low aggregate number of members in the Swedish churches, the Pacific Swedish Mission Conference was organized on Sept. 2, 1908, at Oakland, Calif., with Bishop HENRY W. WARREN presiding. It began with two districts, California and Washington, and there were eighteen charges and 950 members.

The Pacific Swedish Mission Conference continued only twenty years, holding its last session in 1928. At that time it had sixteen charges, 1,230 members, and property valued at $253,600. The Swedish churches and ministers were received into the overlying English-speaking conferences.

General Minutes, MEC.
Erle Howell, *Methodism in the Northwest*. Nashville: Parthenon Press, 1966.
V. H. Esllrniud and E. D. Olson, *A Short Story of Swedish Methodism in America*. Chicago, 1931.   FREDERICK E. MASER

PADUCAH, KENTUCKY, U.S.A., is a city on the Ohio River named for the Chief of an Indian tribe that occupied the area. The earliest religious meetings in Paducah are unrecorded, but in 1834 two circuit riders, George W. Martin and George W. Cayce, called together a group of their converts and organized the first Methodist church in the lower Ohio Valley. It was organized in the private school of Professor Robert Ball and was known as the Paducah charge. These were followed by Finley Bynum, G. W. Kelson, J. D. Fleming, J. W. Jones, E. M. Williams, E. W. Yancey, J. P. Stanfield, and George E. Young. In 1841 the first appointment was made to Paducah Station, in the person of James Young, and under his leadership the church building was completed.

Although in KENTUCKY, the charge was in the MEMPHIS ANNUAL CONFERENCE, which in 1883 changed the name of Paducah Station to Broadway Church. In 1888 a group of members formed a second mission in north Paducah, and in 1970 there were thirteen United Methodist churches in the city, with a total membership of 5,097. Broadway is the largest, with 1,054 members.

General Minutes.
Journals of the Memphis Conference.   JAMES A. FISHER, SR.

PAGE, JESSE HAYES (1831-1903), distinguished American minister and educator, was for almost a quarter of a century a leader in the NORTH CAROLINA CONFERENCE of the M. P. CHURCH. He was born May 23, 1831. In 1881 he united with the NORTH CAROLINA CONFERENCE of the M. E. CHURCH, SOUTH. He was a member of a prominent Wake County, N. C., Methodist family which included his nephew, the Honorable Walter Hines Page, Ambassador to Great Britain, 1913-1918.

Page was educated at South Lowell Academy and at RANDOLPH-MACON COLLEGE. In 1855 he came to Brinkleyville, N. C., where he and WILLIAM HENRY WILLS opened the HALIFAX MALE ACADEMY and later the ELBA FEMALE SEMINARY. He was licensed to preach at Bethesda Church at Brinkleyville in 1858, the same year in which he joined the North Carolina Conference of the M. P. Church. On Dec. 2, 1856, he married Martha Elizabeth Wills, daughter of Henry Wills. The Pages had one son and five daughters.

Page served as Secretary of the North Carolina Conference in 1859, 1861, 1866, 1867, 1875 and 1876. He was President of the Conference in 1878-1879. He was a member of the GENERAL CONFERENCES of the M. P. Church held in 1866, 1874 and 1880. Around 1870 he and RICHARD HENRY WILLS, his brother-in-law, held a protracted meeting near the residence of E. L. Lee in Halifax County and as a result "Lee's Chapel" was established.

Page served first as a private and later as chaplain in the Army of the Confederate States of America. In 1865, at the close of the war, he returned to Brinkleyville and in the following year was assigned to the Tar River Circuit of the North Carolina Conference. In 1867 and 1868 he taught again at Brinkleyville and from 1869-1871 he taught at "Whitakertown" near Enfield. During this period he also served the Roanoke Circuit. In 1871 he moved to Guilford County and taught until 1873 when he returned to his boyhood home, Cary, in Wake County and taught until 1877. In 1877-1878 he served the Halifax Circuit, which included Bethesda Church and Eden Church (which see), and in 1878 he was made President of the Conference. In 1880 he moved to Winston (now WINSTON-SALEM) and in 1881 he united with the M. E. Church, South. As a member of the North Carolina Conference of this branch of Methodism, he served the following circuits or stations: Lenoir, Rock Spring, Rockingham, Kinston, Concord, Statesville, Morganton, Aberdeen, Laurinburg. Page was "a man of strong individuality and lovable personality" and "one of the most able and distinguished ministers of the gospel in NORTH CAROLINA and one of her most beloved sons." He had an exceptionally good pulpit voice and he was well-acquainted with the Latin, Greek and Hebrew languages.

He was superannuated in 1899 and died in Henderson, N. C., on Dec. 10, 1903.

The Henderson (N.C.) Gold Leaf, Dec. 17, 1903.
Journal of the North Carolina Conference, MES, 1904.
Our Church Record, June 23, Sept. 29, 1898.
Manly Wade Wellman, Rebel Boast. New York, 1856.
J. E. Carroll, North Carolina Conference (MP). 1939.
                                          RALPH HARDEE RIVES

PAGE, JOHN (1766-1859), American pioneer preacher and presiding elder, was born in Fauquier County, Va., on Nov. 22, 1766. He married Celia Douglass in 1791.

Admitted on trial in the itinerancy, he was appointed to Livingston in 1792; Danville, 1793; Salt River, 1794; Limestone, 1795; Green (East Tennessee), 1796; Huckstone, 1797; Salt River and Shelby, 1798; Cumberland Circuit, 1799-1802.

On the Cumberland Circuit, John Page wrought mightily for four years and was peculiarly adapted to the work on that circuit. It was unusual in that day to continue a man on a circuit longer than one year. At the close of his four years he was appointed presiding elder of the Cumberland District. At the end of the first year he was broken in health and therefore located in 1804.

In 1800 Page had been placed on the Holston, Russell, and New River Circuit in VIRGINIA, but owing to dissatisfaction among the people of Cumberland Circuit at

his removal from that circuit, he was recalled and his place supplied in Holston.

Page was one of the prime movers and one of the most important Methodist leaders in the historic Great Revival which came about in TENNESSEE and KENTUCKY in the early years of the nineteenth century. Out of it came many denominations, Christian organizations, and movements during the Revival.

Readmitted to the Conference in 1811, Page was appointed to Goose Creek Circuit; and Caney Fork, 1812; again he located in 1813. He was readmitted and sent to Stone's River, 1825; Nashville Circuit, 1826; LEBANON, 1827; Smith's Fork as supernumerary, 1828; Goose Creek, 1829-30; Fountain Head, 1831-32; and Smith's Fork, 1833. He was either a supernumerary or superannuate from then on until his death.

When Page entered Kentucky and Tennessee, there were in that territory nineteen traveling preachers. At the time of his death there were 681. A man of faith and power, John Page died June 17, 1859, at the age of ninety-three and in the sixty-eighth year of his ministry.

E. S. Bucke, History of American Methodism. 1964.
R. N. Price, Holston Methodism.
Journal, Tennessee Conference.   JESSE A. EARL

PAGE, RODGER CLARENCE GEORGE (1878-1965), Australian minister, was a member of a devoted Methodist family at Grafton, on the Clarence River, northern New South Wales. One of his brothers was the late Sir Earle Grafton Page, for a time Prime Minister, and for many years Treasurer in the Federal Government.

Rodger Page went to TONGA in 1908 and became chairman of the small Methodist Church from which the majority of Tongan Methodists (the Free Wesleyan Church of Tonga) had seceded in 1885. With great patience and genuine affection for all Tongans he worked for re-union. Through the leadership of the late QUEEN SALOTE the hopes of re-union were largely realized. In 1924 the Methodists were legally united with the Free Wesleyan Church of Tonga of which R. C. G. Page became President, 1924-46. It was regrettable that about one-third of the seceding body refused to unite and has remained outside union ever since.

Page's devotion to Methodism and the people's interests, his cheerful spirit, and his influence with the Queen brought him very great respect. Though a widower he continued to labor in Tonga until ill-health compelled his retirement in 1947. He died in SYDNEY in 1965 and his ashes were taken to Tonga at his request. The Queen, not long before her own death, showed the high regard in which she held Rodger Page by ordering that the Tongan word reserved for royalty should be inscribed on his tomb; no greater recognition, in the opinion of Tongans, could have been given.

                                          A. HAROLD WOOD

PAGE'S MEETING HOUSE, near Radford, Va., was a log church built in 1774, some two and one-half miles south of Radford. The HOLSTON CONFERENCE Committee on History has erected a stone marker at this historic site. Edward Morgan, an Englishman by birth and reputed to have been licensed by JOHN WESLEY in England, is associated with Page's Meeting House. He preached there on Sundays and is said to be the first pastor of this earliest church within the bounds of what is now the Holston Conference.

FRANCIS ASBURY preached in this chapel several times, and David Morgan was ordained there, being the first man ordained in the whole area. Here also was held the first CAMP MEETING, which was one of the centers of a great revival. JOHN PAGE was a promoter of this revival in the Holston country at the close of the eighteenth century.

In 1874 Page's Meeting House was replaced by a frame building erected not far away by William H. Price. The old chapel disappeared and the land reverted to the original donors.

F. Asbury, *Journal and Letters*. 1958.
I. P. Martin, *Holston*. 1945.
R. N. Price, *Holston*. 1903-13.   E. E. WILEY, JR.

FEDERICO PAGURA

PAGURA, FEDERICO (1923-   ), Argentine bishop, was born in Arroyo Seco, ARGENTINA, and attended the Methodist-related Colegio Americano in Rosario in that country. He attended Union Theological Seminary in BUENOS AIRES, where he graduated in 1946. He is a former Methodist Crusade Scholar, having studied in that capacity at the Union Theological Seminary in New York, 1948-49.

Bishop Pagura entered the Methodist ministry in 1947. He served as pastor of the Church of the Resurrection in Rosario, and as district superintendent of the Central District of the Argentina Annual Conference. In 1960-61 he was on the staff of the World Student Christian Federation in GENEVA, SWITZERLAND, preparing a hymnal and a book of worship for students in SPAIN, PORTUGAL, and Latin America. He has been president of the Argentina Conference Board of Christian Education, vice-president of the conference's General Board, and president of the Evangelical Council on Christian Education and Curriculum in Latin America. He is married and the father of three children. He was elected bishop by the South America CENTRAL CONFERENCE, holding what was to be its last meeting in SANTIAGO, CHILE, in January 1969. The various Methodist annual conferences comprising the Central Conference of South America are expected to become autonomous Methodist churches during the 1968-72 quadrennium (see LATIN AMERICAN EVANGELICAL METHODIST CHURCHES, COUNCIL OF).

When elected bishop, Federico Pagura was professor of pastoral counseling and chaplain at the Union Theologi-

cal Seminary in Buenos Aires. He was assigned the Methodist work in PANAMA and COSTA RICA.

                                        N. B. H.

PAINE, ROBERT (1799-1882), American bishop, was born in Person County, N. C., on Nov. 12, 1799, the son of James and Mary A. Paine. The family went to Giles County, Tenn., in 1814, and Robert was educated in the neighborhood schools and at a private school near Culleoka, Tenn. In 1817 he was converted in a CAMP MEETING held at Pisgah campground and joined Bethesda Methodist Church under the ministry of THOMAS L. DOUGLASS, presiding elder of the NASHVILLE district. After he was licensed to preach, he spent one year as the colleague of Miles Harper on the Nashville circuit and was then admitted on trial into the TENNESSEE CONFERENCE, meeting at Nashville on Oct. 1, 1818, Bishops McKENDREE and GEORGE presiding. His first appointment was the Flint River circuit in TENNESSEE, followed by a year on the Tuscaloosa circuit in ALABAMA. After that he served successively Murfreesboro and Shelbyville, Franklin and Lebanon. In 1823 he was appointed presiding elder of the Forked Deer district. In 1824-25 he was pastor at Nashville, and in 1826-29 he was presiding elder of the Nashville district.

In 1829 he was appointed superintendent of a school at Tuscumbia, and from 1830 until his election to the episcopacy in 1846, he was president of LaGrange College in Franklin County, Ala. During this time he was awarded the D.D. degree by a college that is not known at the present time.

As a bishop, Robert Paine presided over all the conferences of Southern Methodism, serving as the presiding officer of the Tennessee Conference on six different occasions. He was the presiding bishop of the MISSISSIPPI CONFERENCE for nine sessions. After his election as bishop he moved to Aberdeen, Miss., where he remained until his death on Oct. 19, 1882. His wife died at Aberdeen on Jan. 3, 1904. At the time of his death the following children survived him: Mrs. J. H. Scruggs, Mrs. S. F. Hamilton, William M. Paine, and George C. Paine.

At the request of the GENERAL CONFERENCE of 1854, Bishop Paine was requested to write the life of Bishop William McKendree, which he did with great effectiveness, due largely to his early association with Bishop McKendree.

R. H. Rivers, *The Life of Robert Paine*. Nashville: Southern Methodist Publishing House, 1884.   J. B. CAIN

PAINE COLLEGE, Augusta, Georgia, an institution historically related to the needs of Negro youth, was established in 1883 as Paine Institute, through the joint efforts of the M.E. Church, South, and the C.M.E. CHURCH. The name was changed in 1903 to the present one. Bishops ATTICUS HAYGOOD, WARREN A. CANDLER, and CHARLES B. GALLOWAY were influential in getting the institution started and in securing financial support from the M.E. Church, South.

The school was named for Bishop ROBERT PAINE of the M.E. Church, South, who had been interested in plantation missions and organized the Negro members of his church into the C.M.E. Church. Southerners of both races planned for and supported the college from the beginning. It was the major concern of the M.E. Church, South, for Negro education and supported as such.

EPWORTH HALL, PAINE COLLEGE

Degrees granted are the B.A., B.S., and B.S. in Education. The governing board has thirty members: including six from The United Methodist Church at large; six from the Woman's Division of Christian Service; six from the C.M.E. Church; the Executive Secretary, Educational Work, National Missions; a representative of the staff of the Division of Higher Education, named by the division; one of the executive secretaries of the Southeastern Jurisdictional Council; General Secretary, Board of Christian Education of the C.M.E. Church; a representative of the Paine College National Alumni Association, elected by them; and the president of Paine College, ex officio.

JOHN O. GROSS

PAISLEY, CHARLES HENRY (1843-1908), Canadian Methodist preacher and theologian, was born in Fredericton, New Brunswick, Nov. 15, 1843. After taking his M.A. degree at the University of New Brunswick in 1866, he was received on probation as a Methodist minister. Before and after his ordination in 1870 he was stationed on several circuits in the Maritime Provinces.

In 1879 he was appointed principal of MOUNT ALLISON Academy and professor of New Testament Greek at the university. He was also one of the examiners of the University of New Brunswick. He left these positions in 1884, and obtained leave to study at Edinburgh and Cambridge. Returning in 1885, he served on circuits until 1896, when he returned to Mount Allison as professor of church history and New Testament exegesis. In 1902 he became dean of theology, a position which he held until his death.

During his ministry Charles Paisley held many responsible positions in the church. He was President of the New Brunswick and Prince Edward Island Conference in 1888, and a delegate to several General Conferences. At the time of his death he was a member of the General Conference Committee on Union with the Presbyterian and Congregational churches, and of its subcommittee on doctrine. He was honored by Victoria College with a D.D. in 1900.

Paisley made many contributions to *The Wesleyan* and other periodicals on both religious and scientific subjects. One of his papers, "Illustrations of the Harmony Between Scripture and Science," was published in *The Canadian Methodist Magazine.*

His sudden death at Sackville, Jan. 20, 1908, was a great loss to his church and to his university.

D. Johnson, *Eastern British America.* 1924.
T. W. Smith, *Eastern British America.* 1890.   E. A. BETTS

PAKISTAN. On Aug. 15, 1947 the British Crown Colony of INDIA was granted independence, and divided into two sovereign dominions according to religious predominance—India (Hindu) and Pakistan (Moslem). Both remained in the British Commonwealth, and also joined the United Nations. Pakistan decided in 1953 to become a Republic, in May 1955 adopted a new constitution, and in March 1956 inaugurated the new republic. The Moslems predominated in the west and that portion became West Pakistan. They also predominated in the east, and that became East Pakistan, separated by 1,000 miles of Hindu India. The name Pakistan was chosen because it means Holy Land.

A little more than one-fifth of prepartition India came into Pakistan, 365,529 square miles in all, of which West Pakistan had 310,403 square miles, the remaining 55,126 being in East Pakistan. The 1961 Census reports the population as follows: For all Pakistan 132,000,000, of whom Moslems are about eighty percent. Literacy figures for Pakistan total 15.9%; West Pakistan 13.6; East Pakistan, 17.6.

In West Pakistan the people are largely from the Aryan stock with some of Mongol and Central Asian ancestry. Very few Aborigines are in the land.

The ruins of Harappa, on the banks of the Ravi River 120 miles south-west of LAHORE, and of Mohenjo-Daro on the banks of the Indus 200 miles north of KARACHI belong to the Indus Valley Civilization of 5,000 years ago, and show their advanced culture (Dravidian).

The ruins of Taxila, some twenty miles north-west of Rawalpindi, reveal much early history, e.g. the coming of Alexander the Great in 327 B.C. and the lingering Greek influence. The beginning of the spread of Buddhism brought the famous Indian king, Asoka, 273-232 B.C., to Taxila and helped make a Buddhist Center in Taxila. Buddhist influence in India was great for several centuries.

The first Moslem invader of India came from the west, Persia, in 712. Through the following eight centuries frequent and incessant forays or invasions continued, ending in 1525 with Babar who set up the famous Moghul dynasty which ended with the death of Aurangzeb in 1707. Confusion reigned till the British era came after 1750. During the 200 years of Moghul domination the Moslems increased rapidly in numbers, particularly in the extreme east of India and even more in the west. South India remained very predominantly Hindu and the northern part of India was overwhelmingly Hindu, beginning from Amritsar and increasingly stronger to mid-Bengal.

In 1365 Firoz Shah, a Moslem king, imposed a poll tax on Hindus, with Moslems exempt, known as Jizya. Akbar, a Moslem, abolished the tax in 1569. In 1679 Aurangzeb, last of the famous Moslem kings of the Moghul dynasty, reimposed the Jizya tax. A few years later it was not enforced and has not been in force since.

The British control of India began in the 1750 decade, in the name of the East India Company. In 1857 the British Government took over the control of India, but Moslem majorities continued in the western sections and the eastern half of Bengal. After the first World War, the British Government came to the conclusion that India should get independence.

The rivalry between the Congress Party dominated by Hindus, and the Moslem League representing Moslems, led to the demand from the latter for separation at the time of independence. The nearer the promised day of independence came, the more adamant the Moslem League became. The British leaders feared the outbreak of civil war within all of India, particularly all of northern India, and so agreed to the separation. The Congress Party reluctantly accepted the plan. The Congress Party was never happy over the partition, and Moslem-established Pakistan was unwilling to accept India's action claiming the right to absorb Kashmir on the request of the ruler, a Hindu, ruling a nation predominantly Islamic. Fighting between India and Pakistan over Kashmir broke out in 1948, but was quickly muted into a cease fire urged by the United Nations. In September 1965, the fighting again broke out, and again the United Nations got a cease fire arranged and carried out. In January 1966, the Russian leader, Kosygin, arranged for a meeting in which the two leaders, Premier Shastri for India, and President Aiyub for Pakistan, signed the Tashkent agreement that eased matters considerably, but did not include a decision or agreement on Kashmir. The sudden death of Shastri, from a heart attack, an hour or two after signing the new agreement, brought a lull, and the election of another Premier, Mrs. Firoze Gandhi, *nee* Indira Nehru, daughter of Jawahir Lall Nehru. No definite agreement on the Kashmir issue was reached at Tashkent discussion. The Kashmir issue between India and Pakistan is still pending.

Important Towns in West Pakistan: (1969 population estimates shown). Karachi, (3,060,000); Lahore, (1,-823,000); HYDERABAD, (434,000); Rawalpindi, (455,-000); Multan, (225,000); Peshawar, (213,000); Lyallpur, (over 100,000); Sialkot, (over 100,000); QUETTA, (about 70,000); Murree (a Hill station in the Himalayas).

Methodism in Pakistan Prior to Partition. Methodist work began in Karachi in 1874 when a regiment of British troops had responded to the preaching of WILLIAM TAYLOR, later bishop to Africa. The regiment came to Karachi with summers in Quetta. D. O. Fox was the missionary sent to begin the organized work. The first church building was erected in Karachi for the English speaking group in 1874. Within a couple of years there was also an Indian congregation formed. A church building was also erected in Quetta. These two places were outposts of the BOMBAY CONFERENCE for almost fifty years, until the formation of the INDUS RIVER CONFERENCE in 1923.

The first Methodist congregation in Lahore was organized in 1881 by JAMES SHAW, and the first church building erected in 1883. The work in the Indian group was separated in 1886. The congregations continued, growing slowly until 1904. The North India Mass Movement quickened the work in and around Lahore, led by J. B. Thomas, then J. C. BUTCHER, followed by others. Miss Lily D. Greene was the first representative of the WOMAN'S FOREIGN MISSIONARY SOCIETY (M.E. Church, U.S.A.), to come to Lahore; she arrived in 1912. A primary school and hostel for boys had already been started, and Miss Greene soon got a primary school and hostel started for girls. The Urdu-speaking congregation had grown considerably and now grew more rapidly. Indian preachers and district workers were increasing rapidly in numbers, and local groups were organized in several towns. The boys' school was moved to Raiwind, twenty-five miles from Lahore, in 1922.

In 1922 the Indus River Conference was organized. It included from the BOMBAY CONFERENCE, Karachi and Quetta. From the NORTHWEST INDIA CONFERENCE, Lahore and Multan, together with other districts which in 1950, after partition since they were in India, joined the DELHI CONFERENCE. The Indus River Conference represented Methodism in all of West Pakistan.

The increasing numbers of poor people of the village coming into the Methodist Church in large numbers, and the need for securing land for many of them to settle made matters increasingly acute. The Government was then building an elaborate and intricate canal system to develop agriculture in the Punjab. CLYDE B. STUNTZ in 1924 was able to get permission for 200 Christian families to purchase land to settle on. A Christian village was formed, its official name being Chak No. 135/16/L. The grateful community gave it the name STUNTZABAD. Many other Christian families managed to secure land in neighboring villages, making possible the development of a fine rural church, composed of people who had come from a poor community, and had been unable to have schools to which their children could go.

Methodism Since Partition. Partition split the Indus River Conference, confining the conference to Pakistan. The leadership of the conference went with those on the India side. New leaders were needed in Pakistan. The conference that remained in Pakistan consisted of twenty-seven members of whom three were missionaries; one Pakistani member who had completed high school, eighteen Pakistani members who had not completed high school, and five retired Pakistani preachers. All Pakistani members had been through the seminary. The number of Methodists was a little over 25,000.

The latest figures show the number of Methodists to be 56,000. The conference members number fifty-five, of whom ten are missionaries; of the Pakistani members, eight are graduates; nineteen have passed high school; seventeen have not passed the high school; one is retired. All but two of the Pakistani members are seminary trained; both of the untrained are graduates.

New leaders have come to the front. There are nine districts in the area, all having Pakistani district superintendents. There are four high schools at work and one more expected to be fully accredited soon, making a total of five, two of whom are for boys, two for girls and one co-educational. Each high school has a qualified Pakistani principal, the two for girls having lady principals. Missionaries are helpers and associates, engaged in special work organizing new types of service.

Expansion of Work and Development of Conferences: The distance between Lahore and Karachi by train is 755 miles. Thirty-five miles from Lahore are considered Methodist fields; then a gap of 115 miles is served by other churches, followed by 120 miles more of Methodist field; another gap of work for other churches then comes and the last one hundred miles to Karachi are also in the Methodist field. These long distances made the work of conference committees expensive and time-consuming. The need for a separate conference to take care of Karachi and Quetta became evident. Up to 1954 the main effort had been in the Punjab section which included Lahore and Multan. The importance of Karachi as the first capital led to a strengthening of the Methodist force there.

The GENERAL CONFERENCE of 1956 gave authorization

for the necessary establishment of the Karachi Provisional Annual Conference which was duly organized in 1959. The General Conference of 1960 authorized the creation of the Provisional Central Conference of the Methodist Church in Pakistan, since membership in the CENTRAL CONFERENCE OF SOUTHERN ASIA had become unwise. Episcopal leadership had been provided, first when the Indus River Conference was included in the Delhi Area, with J. WASKOM PICKETT as resident bishop until May 1952; then for four years as part of the Lucknow area, with CLEMENT D. ROCKEY as resident bishop. In November, 1956, the Central Conference of Southern Asia retired Clement Rockey who had reached the age of retirement. On the request of the Indus River Conference, approved by the COLLEGE OF BISHOPS of the Central Conference in India, he was given authorization by the COUNCIL OF BISHOPS of The Methodist Church to serve in Pakistan until the end of September 1964. By action of the Council of Bishops in Pittsburgh in 1964 the retiring bishop of South East Asia Central Conference, was authorized to take over. Thus on Oct. 1, 1964, retired Bishop HOBART B. AMSTUTZ served as bishop in Pakistan.

Centers of Methodist Work in Pakistan. Partition provided Pakistan with a good nucleus of workers and institutions in The Methodist Church. Expansion into new centers of work, and opening of new institutions, as well as further development of existing institutions, have resulted in the following: Lahore, Lucie Harrison Girls High School (800); Stuntzabad, high school (600), and ten primary schools; Quetta, primary school, Bethel Church; Karachi, Drigh Road Church, Drigh Road High School (over 600),

The Trinity Girl's High School of the Methodist Church (234), The Methodist Primary School (301).

Churches in Pakistan have found it helpful and stimulating to work together to meet the needs of the developing country. The West Pakistan Christian Council was speedily organized, and has grown steadily in efficiency thus producing better relations between the denominations at work in the country: Anglicans, Presbyterians (of four different branches), Methodists, Salvation Army, and Pakistan Lutherans. Headquarters are in Lahore. The W.P.C.C., as it is called, selects fields for new groups to work in Pakistan, and provides for the exchange of new ideas, also for organizing institutions of comity, smoothing out denominational differences, enforcing rules for comity, and for providing an agency to approach government when necessary.

Institutions in which Methodists are cooperating: Lahore: United Christian Hospital, Forman Christian College, Kinnaird College for Women, Kinnaird Teacher Training Center. Gujranwala: Theological Seminary—one Methodist missionary on staff; two Pakistani students in each year's class, training for the Methodist ministry; United Bible Training Center for Village Workers—for Christian women workers and the wives of seminary students; Boys Industrial School—for Technological Education; Christian Adult Literacy Center.

The Central Conference of Pakistan in 1968 on the first and only ballot for bishop elected John Victor Samuel. Mrs. Shirin Samuel, his wife, is capable and well qualified to help him provide able leadership for Methodism in Pakistan.

THEOLOGICAL SEMINARY, PAKISTAN

In 1968 trouble in the Gujranwala Theological Seminary broke out. Methodism cooperates in the Seminary, providing staff and sending students, as other denominations also do. Staff members from other participating denominations, continued in teaching their classes. A few other Pakistani members of the United Presbyterian Church tried to control the Seminary. Failing to secure help as they wanted they applied to Dr. Carl McIntyre in America to provide finances and join in the effort to get village churches of rural groups, of any denomination, to join them. Dr. McIntyre gave money to enable weak rural churches to receive enough to pay their pastors three times as much as they had been getting. Very few of the rural ministers of other churches accepted the money and stayed with their congregations. The rebellious group continued to try to occupy their quarters and hold classes in the seminary buildings. The struggle to control continues. The classes of students of the main group and their teachers from other churches continue to receive their preparation for the ministry.

United Church Formed in Pakistan. In 1970 an epochal event for Protestantism came about in Pakistan by the formal consummation of church union and the birth of a new 200,000 member church in that land on November 1-3. The cooperative work of the different denominations in Pakistan has been described in previous paragraphs, but through historic ceremonies held in Lahore, the Pakistan United Methodist Central Conference, the Anglican Church of Pakistan, the Pakistani Lutheran Church, and the United Church of Pakistan became a united body. The new church encompasses both East and West Pakistan. Bishop John Victor Samuel took a prominent part in leading 60,000 United Methodists into this union.

The new Church was organized into five dioceses—four in Western Pakistan, each known by the name of its headquarters: Lahore, Multan, Sialkot, Karachi. Efforts at the time of this writing are being made to organize the northwestern part of the Lahore diocese into another diocese. Bishop Samuel became the chosen head of the Multan diocese.

B. T. Badley, *Southern Asia.* 1931.
W. C. Barclay, *History of Missions.* 1957.
Ghayur-ul-Islam, et al., comp., *A Handbook of Pakistan Economy.* Lahore: Ali Brothers, 1957.
J. N. Hollister, *Southern Asia.* 1956.
Barbara H. Lewis, *Methodist Overseas Missions.* 1960.
Minutes of the Indus River Conference, 1963; Karachi Provisional Conference, 1963-64.
Pakistan—1962-1963. Karachi: Pakistan Publications, 1963.
Short History of Hind-Pakistan. Pakistan Historical Society, 1960.
World Outlook, April 1963.   Clement D. Rockey

PALMER, EVERETT WALTER (1906-1971), American bishop, was born in Menomonie, Wis., on Jan. 25, 1906, the son of John Stephen and May (Sanders) Palmer. From Dakota Wesleyan University, he received the B.A. degree in 1932, the D.D. in 1952; he was a part-time graduate student at Drew Theological Seminary, 1935-39, where he received his B.D. degree in 1935; a graduate student at Oxford (England) University, summer of 1950; received the degree of S.T.D. from the University of Puget Sound in 1961; also a LL.D. degree from Morningside College, in 1963.

On June 30, 1927, he married Florence Ruth Wales, and they had three daughters, Joanne (Mrs. Clifford C.

Everett W. Palmer

Cate), Elizabeth (Mrs. A. Ross Cash), and Ruth (Mrs. John P. McKean).

Everett W. Palmer preached his first sermon on Nov. 15, 1929, and from 1929-30 was pastor in Artesian, S. D. He was admitted on trial at the Dakota Annual Conference (ME) in October 1930; ordained a deacon at Atlantic City, N. J., on Oct. 1, 1934; elder at Asbury Park, N. J., Sept. 22, 1935. His pastorates include: Artesian and Farwell, S. D., 1929-32; Silverton Circuit, N. J., 1933-34; Trinity Church, Highland Park, N. J., 1934-42; Centenary Tabernacle, Camden, N. J., 1942-46; First Church, Asbury Park, N. J., 1946-51; First Church, Glendale, Calif., 1951-60. He was elected bishop July 13, 1960 at the Western Jurisdictional Conference, and assigned to the newly created Seattle Area.

As a member of the General Board of Education, he was chairman of its Department of Ministerial Education; vice-president of the Commission on Ecumenical Affairs; and chairman of its Committee on Promotion and Interpretation of Ecumenical Affairs; he served also as a member of the Commission on Structure on Methodism Overseas; of the Commission on Interjurisdictional Relations; and was chairman of the 1966 Urban Life Convocation; also he was on the executive committee of the Methodist Educational Foundation. He was president of Pacific Homes Corporation, 1953-60.

Bishop Palmer was a member of the World Methodist Council, of the Assembly of the National Council of Churches, and was a Methodist delegate to the World Council of Churches in Uppsala, 1968.

He received the "Star of Africa: Grand Band," Liberia's highest decoration presented to a citizen of another country. Presentation was made by President W. V. S. Tubman, president of the Republic of Liberia.

His books include: *Spiritual Life Through Witnessing* (Tidings Press), 1955; *You Can Have a New Life* (Abingdon), 1959; *There is An Answer* (Abingdon), 1962; and

The Glorious Imperative (Abingdon), 1967. He delivered the Jarrell Lectures at EMORY UNIVERSITY at the CANDLER SCHOOL OF THEOLOGY (Atlanta, Georgia), in 1967. He travelled widely in carrying out various church-wide responsibilities including an episcopal visitation to South Asia in 1963; to Africa in 1967.

He served as resident bishop of the Seattle Area, including WASHINGTON State and Northern Idaho until his death in Palm Springs, Calif., on Jan. 5, 1971, of an apparent heart attack.

Who's Who in America, Vol. 34.
Who's Who in the Methodist Church, 1966.   N. B. H.

PALMER, FLORENCE (1904-   ), was a missionary in the GUJARAT ANNUAL CONFERENCE, 1930-59. In 1960, she became secretary for INDIA, Nepal, and PAKISTAN and in the Woman's Division of the BOARD OF MISSIONS in New York. In 1965 she returned to India and retired in 1968.

Miss Palmer was born in Carthage, Ill., April 8, 1904. She holds a B.A. degree from Carthage College, and has studied in Garrett Biblical Institute and SCARRITT COLLEGE. In India she was an effective evangelist and district administrator of primary schools. With the advantage of four years of secretarial service in the Board of Missions added to her previous fruitful experience, she assisted the church in India in a fruitful study of women's leadership training.

Minutes of the Gujarat Annual Conference.
                                                   J. WASKOM PICKETT

PALMER, PHEBE (1807-1874), American lay evangelist and exponent of Christian holiness, was born in New York City, Dec. 18, 1807, the child of Henry Worrall and Dorethea Wade.

Her father was born in Yorkshire, England. As a boy of fourteen, he heard JOHN WESLEY preach, was convinced of the truth of his preaching, and soon became a member of Society, receiving a ticket certifying his membership from the hand of Mr. Wesley. About the age of twenty-five, Mr. Worrall came to America and settled in New York City. After some spiritual struggle, he became a member of the M. E. Church, as had his wife before him. Phebe was their fourth child. In later years, Phebe expressed gratitude for the influence Christian parents and a Christian home had upon her life. She was converted at an early age. In spite of this experience she seemed not to have been completely satisfied with her religious experience or the depth of her spiritual life.

Phebe married WALTER C. PALMER, a New York City physician, on Sept. 28, 1827. Their life together was happy. They shared many common interests—and none more than their desire to promote spiritual holiness. Both were greatly influenced by a revival which took place in the Allen Street Methodist Church in 1832.

In subsequent years, Phebe gave birth to, and lost, several children—one tragically. She, herself, passed through a critical illness and was convinced that her life had been miraculously spared. All of these experiences, along with her spiritual hunger, led her to search for further light and understanding. On July 26, 1837, she had an experience, following much inner spiritual wrestling, which convinced her that she had experienced perfect love and had been sanctified.

Her home soon became a meeting place for a group of women who had been meeting regularly for prayer for a number of years. These meetings gradually grew in numbers and importance until they attracted ministers and laymen from all corners of the world. In later years, when Dr. and Mrs. Palmer were away on evangelistic tours, the meetings went on in their home in their absence and even after Mrs. Palmer's death.

Mrs. Palmer quickly became the leader of this group and an outstanding leader in the holiness movement both in and outside of Methodism, in this country and abroad. She was invited to speak at many church conferences, assemblies, camp meetings, and other gatherings. With her husband, she conducted meetings in Great Britain and Ireland over a four year period. She wrote a number of books, many of which were published by her husband. Among them are: *The Way of Holiness,* 1850; *Pioneer Experiences,* 1868; *Some Accounts of the Recent Revival in the North of England and Glascow,* 1859; and *Four Years in the Old World,* 1866 (with Dr. Palmer).

Excerpts from her letters and writings, published in *The Life and Letters of Mrs. Palmer* by Richard Wheatley, indicate that her interest in, and exposition of, holiness were not irrational or out of keeping with scriptural teaching. She may have been caught up in the tides of revivalism and perfectionism which dominated much of the religious life of the early nineteenth century in America. Yet her desire to love God with all her heart and mind and soul and strength was not divorced from her desire to love and serve her fellowman.

Mrs. Palmer took her stand against slavery; she worked for the liberation of women in the church and in society; she saw that just wages must be paid to domestic help; she recognized that a Christian must be a good and interested and active citizen; she opposed the liquor traffic and its degrading effects upon human life and the community.

Mrs. Palmer had her detractors and opponents. Yet the number and names of bishops and ministers who supported and encouraged her efforts read like a Who's Who of Methodism during the years of her lifetime. There can be no question but that her influence was great upon the people who were touched by her life. Indeed, she was one of the moving spirits in one of the important theological and doctrinal crusades of the nineteenth century.

Mrs. Palmer died Nov. 2, 1874.

E. S. Bucke, *History of American Methodism.* 1964.
Richard Wheatley, *The Life and Letters of Mrs. Phoebe Palmer.* New York: W. C. Palmer, 1876.
                                        C. WESLEY CHRISTMAN, JR.

PALMER, WALTER C. (1804-1883), American physician and lay evangelist, was born in NEW JERSEY on Feb. 6, 1804. After graduating from the College of Physicians and Surgeons in New York City, he engaged successfully in the practice of medicine in that city. He was converted at an early age and joined the Methodist Church.

On Sept. 28, 1827, he married Phebe Worrall. They lived happily together for nearly fifty years. During many of these years, Palmer supported and encouraged his wife in furthering the teaching of scriptural holiness. Through most of their married life meetings, devoted to this cause, were held in their home on Tuesday afternoons. These meetings were exceedingly popular and became models for similar meetings held around the country.

Dr. and Mrs. Palmer were members of the Allen Street

Methodist Church in New York City and faithfully supported the work there. They later transferred their membership to the Norfolk Street Church in New York City because they felt their help was needed there to strengthen the work. This desire to help undergird the Christian cause motivated all of their living.

Palmer accompanied his wife on many of her evangelistic tours, both in this country, Canada and Europe. One of their most extensive tours through Great Britain and Ireland lasted for four years. They gave an account of their experiences on this tour in their book *Four Years in the Old World*.

For thirty-seven years, Palmer edited and published the *Guide to Holiness*, a magazine devoted to advancing the cause of holiness. In 1870, the magazine had over 30,000 subscribers. Palmer published many of the books written by his wife to explain and further the cause to which they were both devoted.

He was a man of wide sympathies and deep religious conviction. He was thoroughly committed to the advancement of the spiritual life as this was understood and practiced by the holiness advocates of the nineteenth century—especially within the Methodist Church.

Palmer's full and useful life came to a close at Ocean Grove, N. J. He died there on July 20, 1883.

C. WESLEY CHRISTMAN, JR.

PALMORE, WILLIAM BEVERLY (1844-1914), for twenty-four years was Editor of the *St. Louis Christian Advocate*, the organ of the three annual conferences of the M.E. Church, South, in MISSOURI. He was born in Fayette County, Tenn., and as an infant was taken to Missouri by his recently widowed mother to a farm near Malta Bend. There he grew up and received an elementary education. At the onset of the Civil War, he enlisted in the Confederate Army of General Sterling Price, and served in General John S. Marmaduke's Brigade throughout the war. At war's end he operated a general store in Waverly.

Palmore was deeply religious. He was active in the Waverly church as a Sunday school teacher. In this exercise he felt and responded to a call to the ministry. To prepare for this vocation he entered VANDERBILT UNIVERSITY. Upon his return to Missouri he joined the SOUTHWEST MISSOURI CONFERENCE. He quickly came to leadership, recognized for his intelligence and ability in "the practical affairs" of the Church as well as for his forceful preaching.

In 1887 Palmore was appointed financial agent of Central College For Women, Lexington, to raise a debt of $16,000. This he did in one year's time. His attachment to the college became permanent and was expressed by his many benefactions; particularly, while Editor of the *Advocate*, by raising $10,000 to endow a scholarship to aid the daughters of ministers and other "worthy girls."

While serving Walnut Street Church, KANSAS CITY (1890), he was elected assistant editor of the *Advocate* to relieve the drain upon the strength of aged Editor McANALLY. Upon the latter's death in 1892, Palmore was elected Editor and Manager.

His personal financial resources, and his bachelorhood, enabled him to publish the *Advocate* at a small annual profit; to travel frequently to foreign mission stations throughout the world; and to give generously toward the education of young women. His gifts made possible the establishment of Palmore Institute, Kobe, JAPAN, and Colegio Palmore, Chihuahua, MEXICO.

Palmore often declared that he was led and guided by the Holy Spirit; that none of the changes and events in his life were of his planning. Perhaps the most startling instance he cited was fracturing his wrist by a fall upon the station platform as he was about to board the "boat train" to take passage on the *Titanic*. The delay enforced by the doctor caused him to miss the boat.

It was his editorial policy to cover events in social, political and economic affairs, local, state and national, in the perspective of the Christian religion. Articles and reports of missionary endeavors reflected his deep personal interest. He was notably successful in securing a wide coverage of local church news, often by attending district meetings and by preaching in local churches. He pushed the circulation of the *Advocate* to more than 20,000, with a large readership outside the state.

Palmore held moderate views on most of the contemporary social and economic issues, and was often a leader in reform movements in the state. But he was a steady and unintimidated foe of the "liquor traffic," the advocate of complete prohibition of all alcoholic beverages. He wrote many anti-tobacco articles. His articles on these subjects were generally without the smooth and polished style seen in his writings on other subjects. He wasted no fine rhetoric on them.

FRANK C. TUCKER

PALMYRA MANIFESTO, THE, is a 1,000-word document issued at Palmyra, Mo., in June, 1865, by ministers and laymen of the M.E. Church, South.

ANDREW MONROE, "the pioneer and patriarch of MISSOURI Methodism," called the meeting in Palmyra. Aware that the MISSOURI CONFERENCE (ME), meeting in St. Joseph in March 1865, had invited the Missouri Conference (MES) to unite with it, and mindful that many people north and south believed that the Church South, which had been closely identified with the Confederacy and which had suffered great losses during the war, would disintegrate when the conflict ended, Monroe felt that all should know that the M.E. Church, South was determined to carry on as an independent ecclesiastical body. Significantly his invitation said the purpose of the Palmyra meeting would be to ascertain the condition of the church and to consider means of advancing its welfare.

Twenty-four preachers and about half as many laymen convened at Palmyra in response to Monroe's call. Bishop HUBBARD H. KAVANAUGH of KENTUCKY, the only southern bishop who spent much time outside the Confederate lines during the war, arrived on the second day, and his presence inspired the group. Out of the meeting came the manifesto which declared that the M.E. Church, South claimed original paternity and coexistence as a Methodist Church with the other branches of the Methodist family, that the differences between the two episcopal Methodisms had not been swept away in the war, that the Church North was trying to gain by strategy what it failed to get by military order during the war, and that the Church South was determined to carry on as a separate and distinct ecclesiastical organization, while at the same time cultivating fraternal relations with other church bodies.

Quickly circulated over the South by both the religious and the secular press, the Palmyra Manifesto had an exhilarating effect on ministers and members alike in the region. Some said it was like life from the dead. The manifesto prompted the bishops of the M.E. Church, South, meeting at Columbus, Ga., in August 1865, to issue a pastoral address that was a trumpet call to action; it proclaimed that the M.E. Church, South still survived and that it would go forward with determination. The bishops called for a GENERAL CONFERENCE to meet in NEW ORLEANS the next year. That gathering, influenced directly and indirectly by the spirit of the Palmyra Manifesto, proved to be one of the most significant and forward looking General Conferences in the history of American Methodism.

Charles W. Ferguson, *Organizing to Beat the Devil: Methodism in the Making of America.* New York: Doubleday, 1971.
E. S. Bucke, *History of American Methodism.* 1964.
W. H. Lewis, *The History of Methodism in Missouri, 1860-70.* Nashville: Methodist Publishing House, 1890.
Frank C. Tucker, *The Methodist Church in Missouri, 1798-1939.* Nashville: Parthenon Press, 1966.   ALBEA GODBOLD

PALO ALTO, CALIFORNIA, U.S.A., population 55,413 (1970), about thirty miles southeast of SAN FRANCISCO on the Southern Pacific Railroad, was incorporated in 1894. The population more than doubled from 1950 to 1960. It was named Palo Alto (Spanish for tall tree), and is a residential city for Leland Stanford wished to have a residential community near Stanford University campus. It is a shopping center for some 160,000 people.

Methodist meetings in Palo Alto were held in the homes of pioneers by Wilbur W. Thoburn (a close friend of David Starr Jordan, first president of Stanford University), pastor of Mayfield Methodist Church, 1891-92. First Methodist Church was started as a mission church with twenty-four charter members by M. H. Alexander on Jan. 14, 1894. The site of First Church, on which three buildings have been erected, was assessed at $51. In 1896, despite the 1893 Panic, First Church erected a white-painted redwood church, with oil-skin windows and wood-burnings stoves costing $3,200 (the other two buildings were constructed in 1914 and 1963 on the original lot).

For the development of Palo Alto Methodism in a more complete way, see the accounts following of First Church, Aldersgate, St. Andrews, and Wesley. In addition to these, it should be added that the University A.M E. Zion Church was established in 1918. Their present building was erected and dedicated in 1965 at a cost of $135,000.

Aldersgate Church has had three names (Japanese Methodist, Page Mill Methodist, Aldersgate Methodist) and eight locations.

In November, 1909, young Japanese immigrants felt the need of Christian faith and fellowship and ten of them organized in Palo Alto a Japanese Methodist Mission group in 1909, under the leadership of the superintendent, H. B. JOHNSON, and Katahide Yoshioka, pastor of the church in San Jose. Stanford students and a few Japanese families organized a mission church in 1911 in the basement of G. Lkazawa's boarding house. Early part-time pastors were Atsuji Komuro and Otoe So.

In April 1940, a new $10,000 church building was completed and dedicated. Gifts included $1,500 from the Board of Home Missions, $2,500 from the Caucasian community and $6,000 from the Japanese community.

Church membership was thirty in 1933.

During World War II, all persons of Japanese descent were evacuated from the West Coast and placed in ten Relocation Centers, Palo Alto Japanese being removed to Harte Mountain, Wyo. During this trying period following 1942 Mr. and Mrs. Alon H. Wheeler, Sunday school teachers, kindly cared for their church and belongings until 1945. The church re-opened that fall. To help returned Japanese further at this time the Palo Alto Fair Play Committee was organized.

In 1950 the membership rose to seventy-four. The first full-time pastor, Sadao Masuko, was appointed in 1952 and served two years. In 1960 church membership was 171 and church school 162. The church was self-supporting in 1962.

Traffic and parking problems made it imperative that the church relocate and build new quarters. The congregation bought a three-acre site on Manuela Avenue. Groundbreaking took place on May 3, 1964. The new church, Aldersgate, was consecrated by Bishop DONALD HARVEY TIPPETT on Aug. 15, 1965.

The JAPANESE PROVISIONAL CONFERENCE was dissolved May 15, 1964, and the thirty-one Japanese Methodist churches joined the various geographical Conferences, the Aldersgate Church joining the CALIFORNIA-NEVADA CONFERENCE. Since 1945 the Aldersgate Church has been a bi-lingual church. Membership in 1970 was 251, and 170 students attended church school. The hillside setting of the new sanctuary, facing mountain rim sunsets, adds to the beauty of the Japanese architecture for these Japanese-American Christians.

First Church, whose new $1,350,000 modern-Gothic church with dramatic stained glass windows is often called the "West Coast Cathedral of Methodism," has 2,472 members and continues leading the California-Nevada Methodist Conference in benevolences.

This pioneer church was during the ministry of J. F. Jenness, 1901-03, the final home church for Bishop WILLIAM TAYLOR. Its lamp-lighted pulpit was sometimes filled on Sunday nights by Stanford University's famed president, David Starr Jordan.

Just before the 1906 earthquake and fire swept San Francisco, and did damage locally, the church gained its first parsonage when Rev. H. E. Milnes was pastor, 1903-06. During the pastorate of Carl Melvin Warner the outgrown wooden church was moved across the street for temporary use until the second place of worship, the $36,000 white stucco church with belfry was completed. The financial struggle for this building was climaxed by Bishop EDWIN HOLT HUGHES' three-hour fund rally and the church dedication before 900 people.

Layman fund drives under the ministry of R. MARVIN STUART during and following the second World War netted a $22,000 parsonage, a $55,000 sanctuary remodeling and the great cathedral church for the rapidly growing membership.

The church's physical plant today includes a small chapel and 14,000-square foot basement for the Edward D. Kohlstedt Memorial Hall, the Stuart Youth Center and choir, and church school rooms. Dedication day was June 2, 1963. This new building has been called a space-age decision to build a great "downtown church" at a time when other denominations were moving out into suburban neighborhoods. A future membership of 4,000 was then projected by this largest church of the Methodist California-Nevada Conference.

FIRST CHURCH, PALO ALTO, CALIFORNIA

GERALD KENNEDY was pastor in 1940-42, and awakened the congregation to needs in a growing and changing Palo Alto as this city was on the threshhold of becoming the major western center of university and industrial laboratories for electronics, genetics, medical and aerospace research.

During and following World War II, Church school attendance doubled and re-doubled several times. "Family Night" was proved feasible for even a big congregation and the original Fireside Fellowship evolved into seven fellowships. In addition to organized fund raising, zealous laymen learned a way of raising the annual operational budget on one "Loyalty Sunday." Retreats for yearly planning and summer church camp were important developments.

Music, with noted choir directors over the years, has been significant at this church, which has the unique Merritt C. Speidel Memorial Organ (two co-ordinated organs).

There are eight Circles of the WOMEN'S SOCIETY OF CHRISTIAN SERVICE and the WESLEYAN SERVICE GUILD. The Men's Club and the Commission on Missions have sponsored eight refugee families (Latvian, Polish, German, Chinese and Dutch-Indonesian) in new homes and jobs in Palo Alto.

University A.M.E. Zion Church began in 1918 when a small group of Palo Alto residents met in the home of Mrs. Melvina McCaw at 330 Cowper Street. Their desire for a church home led to the establishment that year of the A.M.E. Zion Church Mission directed by J. W. Byers. Early meetings were held at Fraternity and Ostranger Halls on University Avenue. The little Christian flock

with its eight original trustees was served by E. P. Bond its first minister.

By the fall of 1923 the twenty-two-member congregation, under the guidance of L. W. McCoy and Elder Byers, raised $1,254 for the church fund. Ground was broken for the $6,000 church on March 10, 1924, and in April 1925 the building, seating 200 worshippers, was dedicated. Church membership had increased to thirty-eight and average attendance was seventy-five.

The indebtedness through the Depression years of the 1930's was serious, but community efforts rescued the congregation from its distress. The church was helped by L. Offenhizer and Alexander Miller, associated with Stanford University, Dallas E. Wood, First Church layman, Oscar M. Green of All Saints Episcopal Church, Gerda Isenberg, president of the Palo Alto Fair Play Council, R. Marvin Stuart, pastor of First Church, authoress Kathleen Norris, and others.

The parsonage, an organ and a next door rental income property were acquired in 1945 when J. O. Hart was minister. By 1963 church membership had increased to 100 families and the congregation purchased the present site at 3549 Middlefield Road. The Ramona Street building was sold with final services held there on the Sunday of Aug. 9, 1964, prior to occupancy of the modern new $135,000 church which was dedicated in 1965.

Wesley Church. Earliest Methodism of the San Francisco Peninsula seems to have rooted this church, according to fragmentary records and yellowed newspaper files. The eleven-saloon town of Mayfield sprouted from the cattle trail and stage coach route long before Stanford University or Palo Alto were even anticipated. Yet there proved to be some few determined Methodists in the rough little Mayfield of the 1870's. The Alley-Bowen History of 1881 notes that a Methodist Episcopal Church was built in 1872, and a local paper refers to a Ladies' Aid Society of Mayfield Methodist Church in 1893.

By 1904 trustees of the Mayfield Methodist Church decided to tear down their old building at second and Sherman and build a new church and parsonage on lots in Evergreen Park. A white-painted wooden belfry church was completed the following May.

Since the pastorate of Thomas Bateman in 1924, the name Mayfield Community Church had designated this as the one Protestant church of the Town of Mayfield (South Palo Alto after 1925). In mid-summer 1941, the church trustees changed the name to College Avenue Church. Bishop JAMES C. BAKER was present for the church re-dedication on Nov. 22, 1942, following a $2,500 renovation of the building.

In 1959 First Church of Palo Alto gave a $30,000 debt-free adjacent building site to the College Avenue Church —soon to have its name changed to Wesley Church. The new $120,000 sanctuary and hall were dedicated in 1959.

First Methodist Church Service of Consecration, with History of the Church, June 2, 1963.
General Minutes.

CHARLES PAMLA

PAMLA, CHARLES (1834-1917), was one of the first four Africans ordained to the Wesleyan Methodist ministry in SOUTH AFRICA and the first African superintendent minister. His father, who belonged to a royal house in Natal, fled to Gcalekaland during the Shaka Wars and later migrated to the Peddie district. He was given the name Pamla—"a person of no fixed abode"—by the Gcaleka chief Hintsa. Charles was converted at an early age and accepted for the ministry in 1866. Almost immediately he became interpreter to Bishop WILLIAM TAYLOR, accompanying him through the native territories and learning much by precept and example. In 1867 he was enrolled in the first class at the Theological College, HEALDTOWN, and in 1871 he was ordained. Pamla's most significant ministry was at Etembeni (1890-1909) where he built up the membership from 300 to 5,000 and survived several attempts upon his life. He subsequently served as connexional evangelist, giving special attention to the preparation of laymen for evangelistic work. It is estimated that he was instrumental in 25,000 conversions.

He was an active preacher until the day of his death on June 24, 1917.

Minutes of South African Conference 1918.
Gordon Mears, *Charles Pamla*, Methodist Missionary Pamphlets No. 2—Cape Town.
W. Taylor, *Christian Adventures in South Africa*, New York, 1881.   G. MEARS

PANAMA, a republic occupying the 400-mile long S shaped isthmus connecting South America with Central and North America, is a charter member of the United Nations. Panama City is the capital. Exclusive of the Canal Zone, Panama's area is 28,753 square miles; and the population (1969 estimate) is 1,417,000.

As in many other regions, Methodism in Panama is much older than Methodist missionary work. According to tradition, a Methodist called Mother Abel landed at Bocas del Toro between 1815 and 1821, with some English settlers. She gathered Colombian fisherfolk for worship, taught them Methodist hymns, and preached salvation by faith.

Methodist missionary work began in March 1877, when WILLIAM TAYLOR (later bishop) went there. He encountered a number of Negroes who had migrated from Jamaica, some of whom were members of the British Wesleyan Methodist Church. They had no pastor in Panama. On returning home Taylor appointed Charles W. Birdsall to Panama, and he departed in November 1878. Birdsall succumbed to malaria in four months. E. L. Latham followed him, remaining long enough to organize a Methodist Society and erect a combined chapel, school and parsonage at Panama City. In 1881 Richard Copp went to Colón, effectively developing the work in both cities for about ten years.

Meanwhile Methodists in Jamaica were becoming interested in their Negro members who had emigrated to Panama. In 1884 the British Wesleyan Methodist missionary, Thomas Geddes, spent four months in Panama. He was followed by other missionaries and agents of the newly autonomous West Indian Conference, including his son, Alexander W. Geddes, who worked in Panama from 1887 to 1902.

Two Panamanians were called to the Methodist ministry during this period: Edward A. Pitt, who became the first Methodist worker in COSTA RICA, and Clifford M. Surgeon, who returned to Panama in 1913.

American Methodist work, which had lapsed since the end of Copp's ministry in Panama, was renewed when, in 1903, Panama became independent, and the United States took over the Canal. The republic decreed the separation of Church and State, so that neutrality between religious groups was implied by the constitution. A conference on Protestant missions was held in Panama in 1916. Two years later, a mission to the Valiente Amerindians was begun by EPHRAIM S. ALPHONSE. Surgeon and Alphonse reduced the Valiente language to writing, and Alphonse became the first national chairman of the Central American sub-District.

In January 1967, Panama and Costa Rica became a full district, under its West Indian chairman Felmin B. Cockburn. Later in the same year, it became a founder district of the autonomous METHODIST CHURCH IN THE CARIBBEAN AND AMERICAS. The district has a community of about 2,000. It has one secondary school in Colón, with 114 students. The district's youth work is reaching out into

Spanish-speaking homes as well as the West Indian families who form the majority of the Church's members.

In early 1969 in the general reorganization of American-related Methodism in South America, several of the annual conferences became autonomous churches each to have its own bishop. The Central American Provisional Annual Conference was given this right, and FEDERICO PAGURA was accordingly elected bishop, and assigned to the Costa Rica and Panama area to be the President of the Provisional Conference there.

COLON CHURCH, PANAMA

The American United Methodist Church has congregations in Panama City, Colón and Cristobal. The Panamanian Institute enrolls 1,500 students. A rural work center, in David, capital of Chiriqui Province. At Armuelles, a banana port on the Pacific coast, the United Fruit Company gave land for a chapel. Membership is around 600 with a much larger community.

Traditionally, American-related Methodism has worked mainly among Spanish-speaking Panamanians, and British-related Methodism with Negroes of Jamaican descent, and with the Valiente. The work of the Methodist Church in the Caribbean and the Americas is now largely self-supporting, apart from the Valiente work which is a mission. The MCCA and the Central American Provisional Annual Conference have co-operative ministries, especially in Colón.

E. S. Alphonse, *Among the Valiente Indians*. London: Cargate Press, 1938.
W. C. Barclay, *History of Missions*. 1949-57.

PANGGABEAN, WISMAR (1904-   ), head of the autonomous Methodist Church in INDONESIA, was born in Simasom, Pahae, Sumatra, Indonesia, March 15, 1904. His parents were first generation Christians and sent their son to the Mission School in the village. When he was sixteen years old he was called to become "help-teacher" in a small school. Two years later the Methodist Church asked him to go to Singkawan, BORNEO, to teach Indonesian in a Chinese school. From 1923 to 1927 he was a student in the Methodist Training School in Bogor, Java. After graduation he was appointed to do pioneer work among the jungle-dwelling Bataks in Asahan, Sumatra. His Annual Conference elected him for further training in 1941 and sent him to the Batak Seminary in Tarutung. On account of the war his ordination had to wait until 1949, when he was ordained deacon one day and elder the next. He served some large churches, became district superintendent in 1950, and also served as treasurer of

the Home Missionary Society, Conference Treasurer, and later principal of the large Methodist School in Medan. His Church sent him as delegate to a number of Ecumenical Conferences such as The Prapat Conference and The Indonesian Council of Churches. When the political situation in Indonesia called for an Indonesian assistant to the bishop, Panggabean was appointed to that position, and when, in 1964, the Methodist Church of Indonesia became autonomous, he was elected their first Ketua (Bishop), to which position he was re-elected in March 1967.

RAGNAR ALM

PAPUA, comprising the southeastern part of the island of NEW GUINEA and certain nearby islands, was annexed by Queensland, AUSTRALIA, in 1883 and by the British Crown in 1888. It came under the control of the Australian Commonwealth in 1901 and became the Territory of Papua in 1906. JAPAN invaded Papua in early 1942, but in December of that year Australian control was restored. It is presently considered Australian territory and United Nations territory. The dependency is about 90,540 square miles and a population in Papua itself of 620,000.

The London Missionary Society commenced operations in the Port Moresby district of Papua in 1871. After Australian Government administration began the policy of demarcation of missionary areas in Papua, Methodists took responsibility for the islands to the south-east of the mainland (D'Entrecasteaux, Trobriand, Louisiade groups) together with a small district at the tip of the mainland known as East Cape.

In 1891 Methodist missionaries entered this area, with GEORGE BROWN the inspiration here as elsewhere. The leader was W. E. BROMILOW, previously a missionary in FIJI. Patient in his dealings with primitive people, equally gifted in administration and translating Bromilow served in this malarial district for twenty-one years.

One of the chief difficulties was travelling through the islands over long ocean distances and through reef-strewn seas; because of the narrow entrances only small craft could be used.

The homogeneity and the tribal structure that mark Polynesian people (e.g. in TONGA and SAMOA) had no counterpart in Papua or in New Britain and adjacent islands. The people differed widely in language and lacking either chiefs or a sense of nationhood.

The first Missionary Sisters came from Australia to Papua to found an orphanage and care for babies who would otherwise have been buried alive with their dead mothers, according to native custom.

Bromilow's successor was M. K. Gilmour, boat-builder and preacher who served for thirty-three years. In his term medical work was established in this district where there had previously been no doctor for 40,000 inhabitants.

During World War II the authorities ordered the evacuation of the missionaries from these exposed islands. The mission was left to the faithful care of South Sea Islands workers.

Since the war evangelistic, educational and medical work have made marked progress, enabling the district to take a worthy place in the United Church of Papua, New Guinea and the SOLOMON ISLANDS.

J. W. Burton, *Papua for Christ*. 1926.
W. E. Bromilow, *Twenty Years Among Primitive Papuans*. 1923.   AUSTRALIAN EDITORIAL COMMITTEE

PARADISE, JOHN (1783-1833), American portrait artist, was born Oct. 24, 1783 in Hunterdon County, N. J., and died in September 1833, near Springfield, N. Y. Though modern critics regard him as an artist of limited talents, his drawings were correct in detail and he was popular as a portraitist of Methodist preachers of his day, his attachment to Methodism being further evidenced by naming his artist son, John Wesley Paradise.

John Paradise worked in PHILADELPHIA from 1803 until 1810 when he moved to NEW YORK, where he became a member of the National Academy of Design upon its organization in 1826. The History Society of New York owns his portrait of Henry Ten Brook. Other evidences of his art are held widely and many family portraits are believed to be unidentified as his work.

John Paradise painted an oil on canvas of Bishop FRANCIS ASBURY during the GENERAL CONFERENCE of 1812 in New York at the home of Mrs. Anne Grice (1760-1839), daughter of John Hammond, prominent Methodist at Annapolis. Bishop Asbury and HENRY BOEHM were her guests at the time. That portrait is believed to be the one for which the Board of Missions in 1844 paid John Paradise's widow $20, raised by private subscription. It now is on exhibition at the United Methodist Publishing House offices, in Nashville, Tenn.

E. Benezet, *Dictionnaire des Peintres, Sculpteurs, Dessinateurs, et Graveurs* (vol. VI, p. 515).
E. S. Bucke, *History of American Methodism.* 1964.
Mantle Fielding, *Dictionary of American Painters, Sculptors, and Engravers.* New York: James F. Carr, 1965.

LELAND D. CASE

PARAGUAY is an inland republic of South America. One of the smallest countries on the continent, Paraguay has an area of 157,000 square miles and a population of 2,303,000 (1969). It has extensive but undeveloped natural resources, and the economy is based upon farming and grazing.

Homeland of the Guarani Indians, the region along the Paraguay River received its first Spanish settlers in 1535. It became a part of the Spanish Empire in South America, until it gained independence in 1811. The Roman Catholic Church is established, but under law other religions are tolerated. The estimated Protestant community of 11,000 (1961) is considerably less than one percent of the population—as small a percentage as any country of Latin America except ECUADOR.

The first Methodist workers—and in fact the first Protestant ministers—to visit Paraguay were a Scotsman who came in from ARGENTINA, ANDREW M. MILNE, and a Uruguayan, Juan Correa, who were traveling together as colporteurs of the AMERICAN BIBLE SOCIETY and made a tour in Paraguay in 1881. Paraguay was visited again by Methodists in 1884, and in 1886, CHARLES W. DREES, superintendent of the South American Mission in BUENOS AIRES, Argentina, appointed a local preacher, Juan Villanueva, to establish a Paraguay Circuit. Because of anti-Protestant feeling, he was warned of the danger of assassins, but he proceeded boldly, making regular visits to Asuncion, Paraguari, and German colonies of Altos and San Bernardino. He was the only Protestant pastor in Paraguay. A girls' school was established in Asuncion, with Juana Villanueva as teacher. By 1891 the school enrolled more than 100 pupils. A boys' school was established in 1892 by Antonio Bandres.

When the South America Annual Conference was organized in 1893, there was a Paraguay District. Contacts during the first years were mainly with the European population, for none of the missionaries had learned the Guarani language, then spoken by most of the Paraguayan people. In 1894 and 1895, efforts to reach poor Paraguayan people in Asuncion and some small towns in the interior met with moderate success.

Following the Panama Congress of Protestant workers in Latin America (1916), comity agreements were signed between various mission boards in the United States. Under one of these agreements, the M.E. Church withdrew from Paraguay, leaving its work to the Disciples of Christ. The Disciples now have an important school, Colegio Internacional, in Asuncion.

The FREE METHODIST CHURCH OF NORTH AMERICA entered Paraguay in 1946. BYRON S. LAMSON, secretary of the General Missionary Board, visited Asuncion and purchased five acres and buildings that had been used previously as an orphanage by a nondenominational mission group. The Rev. and Mrs. HAROLD H. RYCKMAN were appointed, arriving in Asuncion in July of that year.

The orphanage building was remodeled for a Bible training school, which was operated for several years but then closed. A clinic was established in 1956 and carried on for ten years by Elizabeth A. Reynolds. The 1965 annual report listed two stations, ten outstations and five organized churches. They were organized as a provisional conference.

Colonies of Japanese have settled in newly opened agricultural regions. The Free Methodist Mission in BRAZIL, which has work among Japanese colonists there, has sent Minoru Tsukamoto to direct work among the Japanese in Paraguay.

In the summer of 1966, crusades sponsored by young people from the United States and CANADA were held in the Asuncion area. Two new churches have recently been opened here. Gospel distribution and cooperative evangelistic activity are recent developments. This still remains a provisional conference. Church growth has been slow.

W. C. Barclay, *History of Missions.* 1957.
W. Stanley Rycroft and Myrtle M. Clemmer, *A Factual Study of Latin America.* New York: Commission on Ecumenical Mission and Relations, United Presbyterian Church U.S.A., 1963.
Alberto G. Tallon, *Historia del Metodismo en el Rio de la Plata.* Buenos Aires: Imprensa Metodista, 1936.

EDWIN H. MAYNARD

PARIS, JOHN (1809-1883), distinguished M.P. minister and author, was the son of Henry and Mary Paris and was born in Orange County, N. C., on Sept. 1, 1809. He taught school for several years near Mount Hermon Church, Orange Circuit, of the NORTH CAROLINA CONFERENCE of the M.P. CHURCH and at Mount Hermon Church in 1832 Paris was converted and decided to enter the ministry. In November of 1843 he was received into the North Carolina Conference and assigned to the Roanoke Circuit.

At the meeting of the Annual Conference in 1848, Paris was authorized to complete a history of the M.P. Church in North Carolina begun by WILLIAM BELLAMY, who had died in 1843. This history, a valuable record of the reform movement among the Methodists in North Carolina during the 1820's, was published in BALTIMORE in 1849. For several years, Paris was not assigned a pastorate in order that he might devote his entire time to writing. In addition to his *History,* Paris wrote several books, and the magazine, *Our Living and Our Dead,* carried a series of chapters in 1875 written by Paris entitled "History of the War by an Army Chaplain," based on his experiences during the Civil War. At the age of fifty-two he volunteered and served the Confederate Army for four years as a chaplain.

Paris served many M.P. churches in North Carolina. He was President of the North Carolina Conference of the M.P. Church in 1879 and 1880.

John Paris married first a daughter of William Bellamy of Edgecombe County, N. C., and on Dec. 19, 1849, he married Maria Yancey of Mecklenburg County, Va. He died near Buffalo Lithia Springs, Va., on Oct. 6, 1883, and was buried at Fairview Cemetery, LaGrange, N. C.

The three-volume diary which Paris kept during the Civil War is preserved in the Southern Historical Collection at the University of North Carolina at Chapel Hill.

J. E. Carroll, *North Carolina Conference* (MP). 1939.
Journal of the North Carolina Conference, MP.
Our Church Record, June 23, Sept. 29, 1898.

RALPH HARDEE RIVES

PARIS, PERCY REGINALD (1882-1942), NEW ZEALAND Methodist minister, was born in DUNEDIN, and at the age of twenty-one became a candidate for the ministry, and entered PRINCE ALBERT COLLEGE for training. He began his ministry at Otaki in 1906 and served in a total of nine circuits.

His ministry was marked by a deep concern to increase the beauty and significance of public worship, and by a passionate interest in social questions. Often the center of controversy because of his pacifist convictions and liberal political views, Percy Paris was none the less universally respected for his utter integrity, the graciousness of his personality and the warmth of his preaching. He was president of Conference in 1938, and was for ten years editor of the *New Zealand Methodist Times.*

He collapsed while conducting evening worship in Wesley Church, WELLINGTON, on Palm Sunday, March 29, 1942, during the seventh year of his ministry there, and died almost immediately.

Ormond Burton, *Percy Paris* (friends of Percy Paris, Wesley Church, Wellington, 1963).   L. R. M. GILMORE

PARK, WILLIAM HECTOR (1858-1927), American medical missionary to CHINA, was born in Catoosa County, Ga., on Oct. 27, 1858. He was educated at Emory College, Georgia, graduating in the class of 1880. He studied medicine at VANDERBILT UNIVERSITY, but the Mission Board of the M.E. Church, South, had him go to New York for further study in Bellevue Medical College, and he took further work at Edinburgh, Scotland. He went to Soochow in 1882 and in the following year, 1883, he and WALTER R. LAMBUTH established the Soochow Hospital, which Park continued to serve nearly forty-five years. Besides the hospital work, he and Dr. Margaret Polk trained many young men and women to become successful doctors.

He compiled the book *Opinions of Over One Hundred Physicians on the Use of Opium in China.* This was published by the Anti-Opium League in Shanghai, China, by the American Presbyterian Mission Press in 1899. When the book was presented in the British House of Commons,

W. H. PARK

it helped to stop the British opium trade in China. It had been made possible by funds raised by missionaries and business men as well as certain wealthy Chinese friends.

Park was married to Nora Kate Lambuth, sister of Bishop Lambuth, who worked along with her husband, and was especially active in the Anti-Foot Binding Association. They had one daughter, Mrs Dwight Lamar Sheretz, the wife of a missionary to China and, within recent years, to RHODESIA. Park died in FLORIDA in 1927, but his ashes were taken back to Soochow for burial, and his wife, who died in Soochow in 1949, is buried beside him in the same cemetery.

FRANCIS P. JONES

PARK RIDGE, ILLINOIS, U.S.A., **First Church** well merits the tribute, "Church Undaunted." Actual construction of the first edifice began in 1857, only to be halted shortly afterward when a national money panic interfered with payment of subscriptions. A portion of the basement had been completed, however. Here the struggling congregation worshiped until the summer of 1859. Despite difficulties the pioneers did not lose sight of their goal. In October 1859 the first church was completed and dedicated at a cost of $6,000.

For a period of forty-two years, membership averaged fifty-one persons, not reaching 100 until 1912. During the same period the church had twenty-nine different pastors. The years between 1917 and 1936 saw remarkable improvement in the church's fortunes. Park Ridge grew; so did the church membership.

When it became evident in 1917 that a new church building was necessary, plans were made for a new edifice. After several years of discussion, committee meetings and attention to a volume of detail, work on the new church was ordered to proceed. A gift of $20,000 from F. C. Jorgeson was an important assist. Estimated cost of the new building was $120,000, of which it was necessary to borrow $60,000. Dedicatory services were Sunday, April 12, 1925, with Bishop E. H. HUGHES preaching the sermon. By 1947 a debt of $65,000 was liquidated.

The last twenty years mark an amazing growth in the

church both in membership and property. Adult attendance soared; so did Sunday school membership.

New and enlarged facilities for the church school became necessary. Committees promptly made preparations. The building project was completed in 1952 at a cost of $250,000 and was consecrated Sept. 21, 1952.

In recent years a third floor was added to the church school.

Now the church officiary and congregation have authorized a remodeling program to cost approximately $225,-000, providing for a new chancel, new choir loft, new organ console, new offices and social quarters. Thus from a modest membership of fifty-one in the early days, the church has grown to 2,377 members and a property valuation of $1,044,000

General Minutes.   EDWARD D. AKERS

PARKER, ALBERT AUSTIN (1871-1949), was a missionary to INDIA from 1904 to his retirement in 1936. He was associated helpfully with the recruitment and training of ministers throughout his missionary career. He was first an instructor, and then principal of the Florence B. Nicholson School of Theology at Baroda, and from 1928 was principal of the Leonard Theological College, Jabalpur. Between service in those institutions he gave dynamic leadership to the Council of Christian Education in all its varied service to the church and the nation. He was a forceful preacher, and many young people decided to accept Christ as Lord and Saviour as a result of listening to A. A. Parker's sermons. His presentation of the need for the preaching of the Gospel and of the sacred nature of the ministerial calling added significantly both to the number of candidates for the ministry, and to the Christian concern and purpose with which they asked for ministerial training.

He was born in Hamilton, IOWA, Jan. 27, 1871, and was educated at SOUTHWESTERN COLLEGE, Winfield, Kansas. He married Luetta Oldham of Wichita in 1896, and joined the SOUTHWEST KANSAS CONFERENCE in 1897. He was pastor of St. Paul's Church, Wichita when he responded to the call for missionaries in India. Mrs. Parker shared in all his labors, and in his happy years of retirement. Parker died in LOS ANGELES, CALIFORNIA, July 6, 1949, and Mrs. Parker in the same city several years later.

The Indian Witness, Aug. 4, 1949.   J. WASKOM PICKETT

PARKER, CHARLES EDWARD (1872-1933), American missionary to INDIA, became a fervent evangelist and perhaps the foremost minister of God in the "Mass Movement" that made possible the HYDERABAD and SOUTH INDIA ANNUAL CONFERENCE. He was born in Robeson County, N. C., on Feb. 13, 1872. His father died when he was a small boy.

Because of the poverty of the family, he rarely went to school more than two months in any year. He worked hard on a hilly farm, and at the age of nineteen he was converted, and determined to get an education. By home study he managed to learn enough to obtain entrance to the local high school. He was inspired by the example of two NORTH CAROLINA men who had obtained college education after reaching adult life although they were barely able to read when they started.

In his first year in high school he worked on the farm from daylight until nine or ten o'clock, then went to his first class. He studied during recess, while others played. When he had learned enough to teach in a primary school, he took a county examination and received a license to teach. He taught for eighteen months, and then entered Trinity College—from which DUKE UNIVERSITY later developed. Sometimes he fasted because he had nothing to eat. Eventually he graduated from Trinity College and DREW SEMINARY, and in 1901 was appointed to India.

In 1911 he became superintendent of Hyderabad District. In 1904, he married Sarah R. Turner of Braddock, Pa., then a missionary of the M.E. Church in Gujarat.

At his funeral, all creeds and castes were represented. His selfless service had convinced multitudes that he had fellowship with God, and many had come to Christian faith and experience, drawn by his influence.

J. WASKOM PICKETT

E. W. PARKER

PARKER, EDWIN WALLACE (1833-1901), was elected missionary bishop for Southern Asia by the GENERAL CONFERENCE of the M.E. Church in May 1900. He never presided as bishop over an Annual Conference. Until September 15 of that year he remained in the United States for a heavy schedule of preaching appointments and discussions with mission board secretaries. He was not well when he arrived in BOMBAY by ship on October 16, and there encountered a succession of problems.

He was warmly welcomed in his home at Shahjahanpur in LUCKNOW, which was to be his official residence, and also in every center he visited, but his health steadily worsened. On New Year's Day 1901, he arranged for Bishop F. W. WARNE to take charge of his conferences. He died on June 30 in Naini Tal, and is buried in the Kaladungi Cemetery near many other pioneer missionaries of Methodism in INDIA.

Parker was born in St. Johnsbury, VT., Jan. 21, 1833. He was of old Yankee stock, his Scotch-Irish ancestors having arrived in MASSACHUSETTS early in the eighteenth century. His father was a farmer, and he worked full-time on the farm during most of his boyhood, never going to school more than three months in any year, until after his twentieth birthday, he entered Newbury Seminary. In the previous year he had been converted, and almost immediately felt that he must "preach the Gospel of the Son of God." Until then his ambition had been to become a farmer. In prayer in the woods one day a deeper experience came to him, and he began to sense that God wished him to become a missionary. He fearfully told his fiancée, Lois Lee, of this growing conviction, and she replied that from childhood she had felt that she might be a missionary. They were married in 1856.

In 1857, he accepted a pastoral charge at Lunenburg, Vt., and he and Mrs. Parker both taught school. The next year, they learned that the BOARD OF MISSIONS wanted six married couples to go to India and they asked if they might go. Friends tried to dissuade them, but in December 1858, the appointment came; and early in March of 1859 they left Vermont for India. They arrived in Lucknow with three other couples and a single man, JAMES M. THOBURN, on Sept. 3, 1859.

Their first appointment was to Bijnor. Parker baptized his first convert, Guy Dayal, in June 1860. He was one of the first missionaries to contact the Mazhabi Sikhs, and of him it is said in the *Minutes* of the India Mission Conference, "No other missionary worked harder or longer for their uplift." His biographer, JAMES H. MESSMORE, says: "His capacity for work was exceptional. . . . He possessed the gift of leadership."

Throughout his forty-two years in North India, Parker was near the center of planning and direction for Methodist action. His counsel was invariably sought on all major projects, not only in his own church but in other, and in such interchurch activities as the British and Foreign Bible Society, the North India Book and Tract Society, and the United Missionary Conferences.

After Bishop Parker's death—he was sixty-seven when elected bishop—Mrs. Parker decided to continue to live in India. She was greatly honored and loved by Indian Christians and respected by people of all creeds, castes and races. She was a forceful public speaker with a strong voice that could be heard to the most distant corner of every assembly.

J. N. Hollister, *Southern Asia*. 1956.
J. H. Messmore, *The Life of Edwin Wallace Parker, D.D.* New York: Eaton and Mains, 1903.
J. E. Scott, *Southern Asia*. 1906.   J. WASKOM PICKETT

PARKER, FITZGERALD SALE (1863-1936), American pastor, presiding elder, editor, was born in Caddo Parish, La., March 16, 1863, the son of Bishop LINUS PARKER and Ellen Katherine (Burruss) Parker. Educated at University High School and University of Louisiana (now Tulane), NEW ORLEANS, La., he studied at the New England Conservatory of Music one year, not earning a degree. CENTENARY COLLEGE of Louisiana conferred upon him the D.D. degree in 1903. He was converted and joined the Felicity Street Methodist Church (New Orleans) about 1874, then entered the hardware business and for a time was clerk in the British and American Mortgage Company of New Orleans. Answering then the call to the ministry, he was admitted into the LOUISIANA CONFERENCE in January 1886.

His appointments were: Carrollton Avenue and Parker's Chapel, New Orleans, 1886-87; Santa Ana, Calif., one year; Trinity Church, EL PASO, TEXAS, 1889. Then again in LOUISIANA he served New Iberia, 1890-93; Dryades Street,

New Orleans, 1894-96; Lake Providence, 1897-98; Jackson, 1899; presiding elder, BATON ROUGE District, 1890-91; and Crowley, 1902-03. He went with the EPWORTH LEAGUE Board (MES) at Nashville, Tenn., in 1904, becoming the Board's General Secretary in 1910. Here he lived and worked until his death. He was secretary of the LOUISIANA CONFERENCE for twenty years, 1900-20.

Parker's pre-eminent and outstanding work was unquestionably his leadership of young people through the Epworth League. He was General Secretary for twenty years, 1910-30, and editor of the *Epworth Era*. Under him the League chapters practically trebled. After the merger of the Epworth League with the Board of Education in 1930, he remained editorial writer for the Board of Education, and for the BOOK EDITOR's office from 1930 until his death in 1936.

He was also a member of the BOARD OF MISSIONS of his Church for twenty-four years, 1906-30; a representative of the Board of Missions for a time in the Orient; one of the trustees of Mansfield Female College in Louisiana; and a delegate to the GENERAL CONFERENCES of 1906 and 1914.

Parker rendered notable service to the life and worship of the Church on the Joint Hymnal Commissions in 1905 and 1935. JOHN W. LANGDALE of the M.E. Church said of him: "He was easily the most spiritual member of the Joint Hymnal Commission . . . To have come to know him, is one of the rich rewards of the hymnal association."

On April 17, 1901, Parker married Lucy Irwin Paxton of Vicksburg, Miss., and they had two sons, Fitzgerald, Jr., and William Paxton. He died in Nashville on July 21, 1936.

Journal of the Louisiana Conference, 1936.
C. F. Price, *Who's Who in American Methodism*, 1916.
    JESSE A. EARL

PARKER, FRANKLIN NUTTING (1867-1954), American pastor, theologian and influential teacher of ministerial students and ministers, was born in NEW ORLEANS, La., on May 20, 1867. He was the son of Bishop LINUS PARKER and Ellen Katherine Burruss Parker.

Franklin Parker attended CENTENARY COLLEGE OF LOUISIANA (then at Jackson) in 1883-1884. Then he was a student at Tulane University in 1885. He never received an earned degree, but was the recipient of honorary degrees from Centenary College, and Trinity College (later DUKE UNIVERSITY in North Carolina). He married Minnie Greeves Jones of BATON ROUGE on Dec. 20, 1899, just as he concluded his tenure as a presiding elder on the Baton Rouge District, and on his move to be the pastor of Carondelet Street in New Orleans. To them were born two daughters, Mrs. Nell P. Stipe, and Mrs. Margaret P. Winn, both of ATLANTA.

Franklin N. Parker, although he greatly revered his father, made no profession of faith until he was seventeen years old. Then he joined the church under S. Holsey Werlein on Jan. 25, 1885, in the old Felicity Street Church in New Orleans. He was licensed to preach on May 11, 1885. His father, who had been elected a bishop in 1882, died between the time Frank Parker joined the church and the granting of his license to preach. He was admitted on trial in the LOUISIANA CONFERENCE on Jan. 6, 1886; ordained a deacon by Bishop KEY at Shreveport in 1888; an elder by Bishop DUNCAN in 1889.

After serving two or three small appointments, he was

sent to Carrollton Avenue, New Orleans in 1888; then to Rayne Memorial, New Orleans, 1892-1895. He was then appointed to Baton Rouge, 1896-1898; to Carondelet Street, 1899-1901; put upon the Baton Rouge District 1902-1903; and from thence he served in Monroe as pastor, then presiding elder of the Crawley District for a year, and then was sent to take over the New Orleans District, which he served 1906-1909. In 1910 he was appointed to Alexandria, La., but left there in 1911 to become the Professor of Biblical Literature at Trinity College in Durham, N. C. There he taught for three years. In 1914 he was sought by Bishop WARREN A. CANDLER to come to the newly founded CANDLER SCHOOL OF THEOLOGY at EMORY UNIVERSITY, where he was to remain the rest of his life. He occupied the chair of Systematic Theology from 1915 to 1918, and then became Dean of the School in 1919. In that capacity he served for eighteen years until in 1938, when he became Dean Emeritus. He continued teaching, however, until 1952.

He was a delegate to the GENERAL CONFERENCE of the M.E. Church, South, seven times, usually leading the LOUISIANA delegation. In 1918 at the General Conference in Atlanta, he was elected bishop, but refused the election explaining that he did this "solely on the ground that he deemed himself not qualified to serve in the office to which he had been elected." His refusal to accept the episcopacy was not always understood, though his unimpeachable sincerity carried conviction with it.

Parker did his greatest work as a teacher in the School of Theology at Emory. Though not having a formally earned theological degree, he could nevertheless take a leading place in theological circles because of his own wide reading and study and great competence in that which underlies all theology, namely a spiritual understanding of God, and of sure and orthodox Christian teaching.

In his later years Parker's pupils contributed $100,000 to endow a chair of theology at the Candler School of Theology and named it for Franklin N. Parker. One of his contributions as a member of the 1930 General Conference (MES) was to serve on the sub-committee which provided for the retirement of a bishop automatically at, or near, seventy years of age. Parker's formulation of the resolution in this regard was accepted by the larger committee, and voted by the General Conference, and thus became a law in the Southern Church.

He died in the home which his wife had planned and which they both took pleasure in building in Atlanta. Mrs. Parker predeceased him by some few years. Parker himself died on March 1, 1954, his funeral being held in the Durham Chapel of the School of Theology.

Clark and Stafford, *Who's Who in Methodism*. 1952.
Minutes of the Louisiana Conference, 1955.   N. B. H.

PARKER, GEORGE DANIEL (1872-1958), American missionary in BRAZIL, was born in NEW ORLEANS, La., on Aug. 17, 1872, and graduated from CENTENARY COLLEGE, then in Jackson, La. Though his mother was a Roman Catholic, George became a Methodist, but no information is available as to his ministerial training.

He went to Brazil in November 1901. His first appointment was to work in RIO DE JANEIRO. Later, he transferred to the Rio Grande do Sul Conference. On Feb. 10, 1908, during his first furlough in the United States, he married Ada Stewart, who had been seven years in Brazil as a

missionary and who had proven herself a consecrated missionary. During a calamitous epidemic of yellow-fever in Ribeirão, Preto, she had left the classroom for the hospital rooms, earning among Brazilians the title of "angel."

Parker served as pastor, presiding elder, agent for the publishing house, and president of Colegio União, now the Instituto, in URUGUAIANA, Rio Grande do Sul. Wherever he went, he left fine churches and parsonages. Perhaps his greatest work was in helping educate several girls to become teachers for Methodist schools, and in influencing five or six young men to enter the ministry, one of these being JOAO AMARAL, who in time became a bishop. Failing eyesight forced his retirement to JACKSONVILLE, FLA., where he died on Feb. 13, 1958, and was buried there. In memory of his wife who had died on July 12, 1948, he left a substantial bequest for the Gloria Church in PORTO ALEGRE.

EULA K. LONG

LINUS PARKER

PARKER, LINUS (1829-1885), American editor and bishop, was born on a farm near Vienna, Oneida County, N. Y., April 23, 1829, the son of devout Methodists, John and Alvira (Wadham) Parker. From six to sixteen he attended school six months each year and became an avid reader. Later he studied three months at Mandeville College, NEW ORLEANS. CENTENARY COLLEGE (Louisiana) awarded him the D.D. degree.

In 1845, young Parker went to New Orleans and worked in a store operated by an older brother. In 1846, he enlisted and served as a soldier in the Mexican War. Soon afterward he began the study of law, but his pastor, HOLLAND N. McTYEIRE, later bishop, and Richard Deering, the presiding elder in New Orleans, guided him toward the ministry. In March 1849, he began to supply Good Hope Chapel in Algiers, and two months later he abandoned the study of law and was licensed to preach. The following December he joined the LOUISIANA CONFERENCE, and was ordained DEACON in 1851 and ELDER in 1853. He rose rapidly, going to SHREVEPORT, the strongest church in the conference outside New Orleans, at twenty-one, and to Carondelet Street Church, the ranking congregation in LOUISIANA Methodism, at twenty-six. His appointments, all in Louisiana, were: Lake Providence, 1849; Shreveport, 1850-51; Felicity Street, New

Orleans, 1852-54; Carondelet Street, 1855-57; New Orleans District, 1858; Felicity Street, 1859-61; Shreveport, 1862-63; Caddo Circuit (because of the war), 1864-65; Felicity Street, 1866-69; New Orleans District and editor of the *New Orleans Christian Advocate*, 1870-73; and editor, 1874-81.

On June 7, 1853, Parker married Sallie F. Sale who died of yellow fever three months later, September 13. His second marriage, Jan. 20, 1858, was to Ellen K. Burruss. They had three sons, John B., Fitzgerald S., and Franklin N. The latter two joined the Louisiana Conference and became distinguished leaders in the church, the one as editor of the *Epworth Era* and the other as dean of CANDLER SCHOOL OF THEOLOGY.

As a young preacher, Parker was greatly interested in the *New Orleans Christian Advocate* which was established in 1851. Encouraged by McTyeire, the editor, he began contributing articles which showed marked journalistic ability. Later as editor of the paper, he was widely recognized as an able religious journalist. He wrote rapidly, easily, and with little need for revision or emendation. His polished, limpid style won him fame and made him known throughout the connection and beyond. As time passed his friends felt that he did his best and most lasting work with his pen.

Though born and reared in the North, Parker became southern in his viewpoint and sympathies. After the Civil War he agreed that slavery was evil and that it had to go. However, he believed that out of the sordid traffic had come good to the Negro and to Africa in that it brought both into contact with Christian civilization.

Parker was a delegate to four GENERAL CONFERENCES, 1866, '74, '78, and '82, and the latter elevated him to the episcopacy. For two years he gave episcopal supervision to the TEXAS conferences, and then was assigned to the conferences in MISSOURI, MISSISSIPPI, NORTH CAROLINA, and MARYLAND. He died rather suddenly in New Orleans, apparently of a cerebral hemorrhage, March 5, 1885, and was buried there.

Charles B. Galloway, *Linus Parker*. Nashville: Southern Methodist Publishing House, 1886.
General Minutes, MECS.
General Conference Journal, 1886, pp. 184-185.
M. Simpson, *Cyclopaedia*. 1878.

JESSE A. EARL
ALBEA GODBOLD

PARKER, RICHARD JOSEPH (1878-1960), an American missionary to CUBA, was born Feb. 14, 1878. He was married to Lottie Lee Barnes Dec. 21, 1904. They had five children. In 1908 he was accepted as a missionary to Cuba where he served efficiently as pastor and district superintendent for fourteen years. Because of health reasons he retired from Cuba in 1922 and for a number of years was superintendent of Latin work in FLORIDA. His last work was assistant pastor of Hyde Park Church, TAMPA, Fla. His evangelistic spirit characterized his work wherever he went, even when retired. In Cuba it was common for him to search out the cane workers and hold services for them when they would be resting in the fields at noon.

GARFIELD EVANS

PARKER, SAMUEL (1774-1819), American preacher, was born in NEW JERSEY about 1774 and became a member of the Methodist Church when he was fourteen years old.

In 1800 he received his license as a local preacher and in 1805 became a travelling preacher. In 1809 he received ELDER's orders and was appointed to serve as the first presiding elder in the Indiana district. He continued in this appointment for four years, at which time the district was divided. In 1813 he rode the Deer Creek circuit, in 1814 was appointed presiding elder of the Miami District, and in 1815 the presiding elder of the KENTUCKY District. He was then sent to the MISSISSIPPI CONFERENCE, where on Dec. 20, 1819, he died. His funeral sermon was preached on the Sunday following his death at WASHINGTON, Miss., by WILLIAM WINANS who had earlier preached at Vincennes, Ind.

ROBERT S. CHAFEE

PARKER, WHITE (1887-1956), American Indian minister, was born Oct. 20, 1887 near Cache, Okla., son of the famous Quanah Parker, last of the great chiefs of the Comanche Indians. He attended Cook Christian Training School in PHOENIX, Ariz. He was admitted on trial in the OKLAHOMA CONFERENCE in 1934, and served in some of the leading appointments of the INDIAN MISSION. He married Laura Esther Clark, daughter of M. A. Clark, early missionary among the Comanches. He was killed in an automobile accident on March 2, 1956, while returning home from the annual Indian Mission Pastors' School. He was a man of commanding appearance and gentle demeanor, greatly loved by those he served.

Clegg and Oden, *Oklahoma*. 1968.
Journal of the Oklahoma Conference. 1956.

WALTER N. VERNON

PARKERSBURG, WEST VIRGINIA, U.S.A., a city of about 43,000 in 1970, is located at the confluence of the Little Kanawha and Ohio Rivers. The Methodists were the first denomination to enter the region and later they were the first to build a church in Parkersburg. In 1790, Jacob Lurton and Thomas Boyd, Methodist circuit riders, were appointed to the Kanawha Circuit which included the region in which Parkersburg is located. It is believed that the first church in the area was built of logs near Fort Neal. The fort itself was erected in 1785 near the confluence of the rivers. Sometime before 1817, the Methodists constructed a brick church on Avery Street in Parkersburg, and the building was used as a school during the week.

In 1832, J. H. Power and B. L. Jefferson were appointed to the Parkersburg Circuit; it was the first time the name of the town which was chartered in 1820 appeared in the OHIO CONFERENCE minutes. The next year the circuit reported 812 members. In 1836 Parkersburg became a station, and in 1837 it reported 162 members. At that time a new church was built opposite the city hall. Asbury Academy, with Gordon Battelle as principal, flourished in Parkersburg, 1840-43.

In 1845, the church in Parkersburg, which had reported 207 white and nine colored members in 1844, cast a majority vote for adhering South, and the M.E. Church, South retained control of the building. A wealthy citizen gave lumber to the members who desired to adhere North, and in fourteen days they built a frame church on Fifth Street. The next year the new church reported 100 white and ten colored members, while in 1846 the congregation which adhered South had 129 white and no colored members.

In 1857, the trustees of the M.E. congregation in Parkersburg brought suit and recovered the building from the Southern Methodists. In 1862 the structure was torn down and a new and larger church was erected. That edifice was destroyed by fire in 1873, and another was built. The present First Church building was completed in 1911 when there were 642 members. Before and after the division of 1845, First Church had some distinguished pastors, such as PETER CARTWRIGHT, ASA SHINN, JACOB YOUNG, H. B. BASCOM (later bishop), and T. B. Hughes who was the father of Bishops E. H. and M. S. HUGHES. John L. Wolfe, who was reared in Parkersburg, served as pastor eighteen years, 1945-63.

After losing the church property in 1857, the Southern Methodist congregation worshiped for a time in the City Building. In 1858 the body, which then had 225 members, bought a lot at Seventh and Market Streets and at a cost of $10,000 erected the largest church building up to that time in Parkersburg. For nearly half a century thereafter it was the strongest congregation in the WESTERN VIRGINIA CONFERENCE (MES). In 1895 the building was sold and a new one, thereafter known as St. Paul's Church, was erected on Market and Eleventh Streets. Six of St. Paul's pastors were, or became, college presidents, and one of the six was elected bishop. They were U. V. W. DARLINGTON, R. T. Webb, Paul S. Powell, W. B. Campbell, T. S. Wolfe, and Roy McCuskey. The latter had previously been a minister in the M.E. Church. Darlington (later bishop) had two pastorates at St. Paul's, and he also led in building the Johnson Memorial Church in Huntington.

In 1900, First Church had 494 members to 421 for St. Paul's. At unification in 1939 the figures were 839 and 766, the difference being exactly seventy-three members in both years. In 1939 the M.E. Church had eight churches and 4,085 members in Parkersburg to five congregations and 2,073 members for the M.E. Church, South.

In 1872 the West Virginia Conference of the M.P. Church started a mission in Parkersburg with Benjamin Stout in charge. He conducted a revival in an abandoned schoolhouse near Lynn Street, and on Christmas Day organized a congregation of twenty-two members. They bought the schoolhouse and fitted it up as a place of worship. Within four years the church had 100 members. In the next three decades, Bethany Church, as it was called, experienced financial difficulties, but it carried on. In 1936 it reported 236 members and property valued at $27,000. It came into The Methodist Church at unification in 1939.

In 1970, there were fifteen United Methodist churches in Parkersburg proper, three of them being former E.U.B. congregations with an aggregate membership of 2,002. The fifteen churches had a combined membership of 7,949 and property valued at approximately $5,130,000, and they raised for all purposes during the year about $428,000.

I. A. Barnes, *The Methodist Protestant Church in West Virginia*. Baltimore: Stockton Press, 1926.
General Minutes, MEC, MECS, MC, and UMC.

JESSE A. EARL
ALBEA GODBOLD

PARKS, HENRY BLANTON (1856-1936), an American bishop of the A.M.E. CHURCH, was born in GEORGIA about 1856. He was educated in Atlanta University. He rose to be a General Officer (Connectional Missionary Secretary) during 1896-1908. He was elected to the episcopacy in 1908 and as a bishop served in the south and west. Bishop Parks was known as an eloquent and impressive preacher.

R. R. Wright, *The Bishops*. 1963.   GRANT S. SHOCKLEY

PARKS, WILLIAM J. (1799-1873), pioneer American preacher, was born in Franklin County, Ga., on Nov. 30, 1799. He was the son of Henry Parks, one of the first converts to Methodism in GEORGIA. Reared in the backwoods, unpolished, and with skin as dark as an Indian's, he was licensed to preach under the venerable ISAAC SMITH on the Athens District, Georgia. In 1822, Parks was admitted on trial into the SOUTH CAROLINA CONFERENCE which then served Georgia. Few men have left behind them such an impressive record of long and varied service to the Methodist Church. He was a missionary two years, presiding elder fourteen years, four years on a station, ten years agent of church institutions, and twelve years on circuits, a total of forty-two years of effective service.

Parks was elected a member of all GENERAL CONFERENCES of undivided Methodism from 1832 to 1844. He was elected to the LOUISVILLE CONVENTION in 1845, but was unable to attend. After the formation of the M.E. Church, South, Parks was chosen for every General Conference from 1846 to 1870, but he was not able to attend in 1846 and 1870. In 1836 he became a member of the first board of trustees of WESLEYAN Female COLLEGE at Macon, Ga.

Parks was married three times. He was widely loved and became affectionately known as Uncle Billy. He helped officiate at the funeral of Bishop JAMES O. ANDREW in Oxford, Ga., in 1871. On Dec. 16, 1873, Parks died at Oxford, Ga., just a few days before the meeting of the NORTH GEORGIA CONFERENCE.

H. N. McTyeire, *History of Methodism*. 1884.
A. M. Pierce, *Georgia*. 1956.
G. G. Smith, *Georgia*. 1913.
M. Simpson, *Cyclopaedia*. 1878.   DONALD J. WEST

PARLIN, CHARLES COOLIDGE (1898-   ), American lawyer, financier, and a president of the WORLD COUNCIL OF CHURCHES, was born on July 22, 1898, in Wausau Wis., the son of Charles Coolidge and Daisy (Blackwood) Parlin. He was educated at the University of Pennsylvania, received the LL.B. degree at Harvard in 1922, and has subsequently been the recipient of many honorary degrees. He served as a private first-class in the U. S. Army in the first World War. He was admitted to the New York Bar in 1923, and has since practiced law in NEW YORK CITY. He is the director of numerous corporations. He married Miriam Boyd on Oct. 11, 1924, and their children are Charles Coolidge, II, Camilla, and Blackwood Boyd.

Parlin was a member of the GENERAL CONFERENCES of 1940, '44, '48, '52, '56, '60, '64, '68, and '70. In 1944 he led the debate presenting a minority report from the Committee on the state of the Church calling for prayer for victory in the war then raging, which was against the majority report of that Committee presented by ERNEST F. TITTLE, its chairman. This great debate featured that General Conference, the minority report being substituted for the majority by a close vote in a vote by orders.

Parlin has served on the WORLD METHODIST COUNCIL (was president, 1970-71); was the secretary of the COMMISSION ON CHURCH UNION, 1948-64; chairman of the Committee to Study Jurisdictional System, 1956-60; chairman of the Committee on Interjurisdiction Relations, 1960-64; on the Ad Hoc Committee on the Union with the E.U.B. Church in 1964, at which General Conference at its adjourned session in 1966 he presented the report of the Committee calling for union. He has been a member of the General Board of NATIONAL COUNCIL OF CHURCHES since 1950, and the first vice president from 1958-61. He was chairman of the committee in the U.S.A. which raised the money for the founding of the World Council of Churches; attended the founding Amsterdam Assembly in 1948 and the succeeding Assemblies of 1954, 1961 and 1968; was a member of the Finance Committee, 1948-68; of the Central Committee 1954-58; and of the Presidium 1961-68. He was honored in October 1969 at the Citation Dinner of *The Upper Room* receiving on this occasion its annual award. He was especially honored at the General Conference of The United Methodist Church in St. Louis in 1970 by a testimonial dinner attended by almost all the conference.

Who's Who in America, Vol. 34.
Who's Who in The Methodist Church, 1966.   N. B. H.

PARR, WILLIAM DAVID (1855-1918), American minister, was born near Jolietville, Ind., Nov. 10, 1855. He was admitted on trial in the NORTH INDIANA CONFERENCE in 1878. He was pastor of several churches and was elected four times to GENERAL CONFERENCE in 1896, 1900, 1904 and 1908. He was active in civic and business affairs and became widely known as the "dedicator of new churches," being extremely efficient in raising money on the day of dedication. It is said that he dedicated more churches than any other Methodist minister during his lifetime. He married Cora Walton on Jan. 11, 1883. He died at Kokomo, Ind., Aug. 12, 1918.

HAROLD THRASHER

PARRAMATTA, New South Wales, Australia, was the second place of importance in the Colony when SAMUEL LEIGH visited it in 1815. Religious services were first held in the Government schoolroom. One of his converts was James Watsford, whose son, JOHN WATSFORD, became a notable missionary to FIJI.

WALTER LAWRY who had arrived from England in 1818 to become Leigh's colleague, may be regarded as the father of Methodism in Parramatta. He became the first minister there when it became a separate circuit in 1820. A chapel was opened on Good Friday, 1821, on a site granted by Governor Macquarie. When a new church was built by DANIEL DRAPER in 1839, this chapel was incorporated as the vestry. On the day of the opening of the church, the foundation stone of the Centenary Church at North Parramatta was laid. The present church, known as Leigh Memorial, was opened in 1887.

Several strong circuits have been formed from the original Parramatta Circuit which is now the head of a connexional district and the center of active church enterprises.

J. Colwell, *Illustrated History.* 1904.
AUSTRALIAN EDITORIAL COMMITTEE

PARRISH, JOSEPH LAMBERSON (1806-1895), American Indian missionary, U. S. Indian Agent, and leader in Christian education in the Pacific Northwest. Joseph L. Parrish heard the call to the Indian mission in OREGON in 1839. As JASON LEE, the mission superintendent, had filled his quota of ministers, Parrish, a conference member, reverted to his early trade and went to Oregon as the "mission blacksmith." He went with the mission reinforcement which had made the long voyage around Cape Horn, reaching Oregon in 1840.

After two years as blacksmith working at the main mission station, located in the Willamette Valley, Parrish was given charge of his own station to work among the coast Indians. After the close of the Indian mission in 1846, Parrish worked as a preacher among the white settlers, first as a lay preacher and later as a conference member in full connection.

From 1849 to 1854 he was a government Indian agent during the years the government was seeking to establish the Indians of the Pacific Northwest upon reservations. Among the Indian tribes, with whom he worked as missionary or Indian agent, he was known as "The Man of Peace." It was the kind of peace which resulted from great courage and faith that his own purposes were in harmony with God's will.

Parrish was keenly interested in public affairs and during his early years in Oregon he joined the other settlers in establishing the Provisional Government of Oregon which was to be the only government the settlers had until the United States established the Oregon territorial government in 1846.

In 1854 he was again a missionary to the Indians, this time being appointed by the OREGON CONFERENCE, but ill health forced his retirement in 1856.

His home, when he could be there, had been for many years on his Donation Land Claim in what is now Salem, Ore. In his retirement years he served for sixteen years as the volunteer chaplain of the state prison. These very active retirement years permitted him to perform his greatest service to Methodism. He had been a member of the original board of trustees of the Oregon Institute (1840) which was chartered as WILLAMETTE UNIVERSITY in 1853, and is the oldest university of the Pacific Northwest. He was continuously a member of the board until his death in 1895. For twenty-six years, he gave courageous leadership to the little band of men who struggled and succeeded, in keeeping their Christian university a living institution despite the poverty of the pioneer community. Upon his death, his fellow trustees inscribed upon their official minutes, "He has been a continuing and constant factor in the planting, nurturing and rebuilding of Willamette University, faithful in service, loyal in purpose, and helpful in executing, his name goes into history as the friend of Willamette University."

R. M. Gatke, *Willamette University.* 1943.
ROBERT MOULTON GATKE

PARSONAGES, a term that originally came from the rentals, or amount due to the parson (from "person") in England, and then came to mean specifically his house, was the name brought over early into American Methodism to represent the dwelling place of the preacher. Parsonages were never mentioned in the records of the earliest years after the organization of the M.E. Church in America, since most of the preachers were unmarried, and all of them moved so continually that the matter of a permanent dwelling place—as is needed for an extended pastorate—was not an issue. However, by the time of the General Conference of 1800, the question of renting or building houses for the preachers came under discussion, and that Conference recommended that the friends or people of any congregation purchase a lot of ground in each circuit, and build a house upon it for the preacher and furnish it with at least "heavy furniture." By 1816, a provision relating to the duty of the presiding elders concerning parsonages was added to the above provision. The part that the stewards or trustees should play in this was put in by the General Conference of 1828. By this time the ministry, while still itinerant and moving as frequently as every two years, was becoming "settled" enough to need a house in which the pastor and family could live while he was upon that special appointment.

In time the need of such a house was seen everywhere, and it became the duty, and eventually the pride of each quarterly conference to see that a parsonage was provided for their preacher. Sometimes such houses were furnished, quite often they were not—a condition that lasted through the better part of the nineteenth century. Eventually parsonages as well as the local churches were covered by the Trust Clause as directed by the *Discipline* in order to insure the unchallenged occupancy of the minister when properly appointed to each special charge.

The present *Discipline*—and the disciplines of most Methodist churches—has quite a few regulations having to do with parsonages and their care. In time special regulations have had to be drawn up for seeing that the equities in a particular parsonage, which is jointly owned by several churches on a circuit, shall be secured to each such church if they are put upon other circuits, or made into a station. The number of parsonages and their value must be reported at each session of the Annual Conference, and made a part of the General Minutes of that body. Present day parsonages are commodious and well equipped homes, and some of them vie with the better homes in any community.

Disciplines.
M. Simpson, *Cyclopaedia.* 1878.   N. B. H.

PARSONS, ELMER E. (1919-   ), American executive of the FREE METHODIST CHURCH and an ordained elder in the Columbia River Conference, was born in Asotin County, Wash. He was educated at SEATTLE PACIFIC COLLEGE, A.B., 1942; Biblical Seminary of New York, S.T.B., 1945; ASBURY THEOLOGICAL SEMINARY, M.Th., 1955. He received the honorary D.D. from GREENVILLE COLLEGE, 1958. He married Marjorie Carlson in 1942. He was Dean and Professor of Religion, WESSINGTON SPRINGS COLLEGE, South Dakota, 1945-47; missionary service, mainland CHINA, 1947-49; missionary, JAPAN, 1949-54; President, Central (Junior) College, McPherson, Kan., 1955-64; missionary, Japan, and President, Osaka Christian College, since 1964. He has been Asia Area Secretary since 1964. He contributed to *Arnold's Commentary*, Light and Life Press, 1962 and 1967, and was the author of *Witness to the Resurrection* (Baker), 1967. He organized the Asia Fellowship Conference in 1965 and was a delegate to the World Congress on Evangelism, Berlin, GERMANY, 1966. He resides in Osaka, Japan.

BYRON S. LAMSON

FIRST CHURCH, PASADENA, CALIFORNIA

PASADENA, CALIFORNIA, U.S.A. **First Church,** was established in 1874 in a city now of 111,826 on the west coast and noted for wealth and culture. For several years, including the current one, it has been among the top two or three churches of the nation in benevolence giving.

In 1875 at its beginning the church took a lead in ecumenicity—an unknown word then—in the form of union services with the Presbyterians, as the two denominations met jointly in the school house with the Methodist and Presbyterian ministers preaching on alternate Sundays. In 1888, when the church's parking space for horses and buggies proved to be inadequate, the church paid $10 a month to a neighboring rancher to allow members to park their buggies in his orange grove and tie their horses to the orange trees. By 1890 more churches were needed in the Pasadena area, and First Church took the lead in establishing them.

All seven churches in Pasadena today received all or part of their initial support from First Church. The present Lincoln Avenue Church was built by First Church in 1898 at a cost of $13,000, and First Church made its investment secure by transferring 200 of its members to the new congregation. In 1924 First Church gave to the Methodists on the east side of the city the beautiful stone church building it had outgrown. Then its members raised $25,000 to help them buy a lot, and assisted them in numbering and moving the stones one by one to the new location, so that the building could be reconstructed just as it had been. The Holliston Avenue Church still stands in that location today, the second largest Methodist Church in the Pasadena area.

The present First Church building was erected in 1924, and is an impressive Gothic structure with a sanctuary seating 2,000. It provides a setting for the preaching and outstanding music for which the church has become known on the west coast. Among the preachers whose ministry has brought distinction to the Pasadena pulpit have been MATTHEW S. HUGHES (later a bishop), Merle Smith, Albert Day, Harold Case and Morgan Edwards. At one time so many retired Methodist bishops resided in Pasadena and attended First Church that a special pew was reserved for them, which pew still bears the metal plaque that reads simply, "The Bishops."

In 1886 First Church engaged in a nine-year fight to establish strict liquor laws, and to prohibit the sale of cigarettes to minors. Feelings became so intense that patrols had to be stationed both outside the church and in the back pews to maintain order. Ministers were hung in effigy on the front of the church, and a big hostile sign was once placed by the front door: "This Is A Saloon. Come In."

The Pasadena Methodist Foundation, established by the leading members of First Church in 1939, has current assets in excess of $2,000,000. Largely through the foundation the church was able to purchase and equip a fine mountain camp in the San Bernardino mountains. Also through generous gifts First Church was able to do much for the establishing of The SCHOOL OF THEOLOGY AT CLAREMONT, Calif.—a rare instance where a Theological Seminary was largely established by a local church.

Now showing some of the battle scars of a downtown city church, First Church of Pasadena continues its work with a current expense and benevolent budget at present of over $345,000. It maintains a large staff, including five ministers some of whom are engaged in counseling, crisis intervention, youth work and in giving a ministry to the inner city. While continuing its world-wide mission interests, the church has also within the last year built a new parsonage, and launched a campaign to raise $500,-000 for the purchase of adjoining property for parking and expansion, and for assisting the work of other Methodist churches in the city. It currently lists a membership of 2,587.

FIRST CHURCH, PASADENA, TEXAS

PASADENA, TEXAS, U.S.A. **First Church** is the oldest church in Pasadena, being organized in 1896 at the then-thriving community of Deepwater by Peter E. Nicholson, a local preacher. The church was organized with twenty-five or thirty charter members, and the first pastor assigned by the annual conference was S. W. Warner, who remained for three years.

In the autumn of 1896 the organization was moved to nearby Pasadena, since most of the members had moved from Deepwater and a number of them had settled in Pasadena. This church became a part of a circuit composed of Harrisburg, La Porte, Seabrook, and Pasadena. A Sunday school was organized in 1900 with J. W. Collins as the first superintendent. Mrs. W. F. Weeks and Miss Maggie Guinn joined the church in 1903, and are still very active members.

For the first nine years after organizing in Pasadena, the congregation met in the school building since the first church building was not erected until 1907, during the pastorate of O. F. Zimmerman. This first church building was of frame construction, and was truly a credit to the small town. The original property for the church was bought in 1904 by W. B. Bailey, R. M. Guinn, and H.

Plum, each of whom paid for one lot, and then deeded these lots to the church.

Among the early twentieth century ministers who served the church full time were the young John Mills and the older H. B. Smith. In 1935 the original educational building was erected under the chairmanship of A. G. Whitman, during the ministry of George J. Evans. In 1937, under the ministry of Marvin Vance, the movement for a new church began, and in 1938 a stone church was built. This is the building which now is used as Wesley Chapel, and is very popular for weddings.

Richard S. Marshall served the church for four years after Marvin Vance, and proved effective in leadership and Sunday school organization and classification. An addition to the educational building was erected in 1948 while D.D. McGaughey was pastor. It was during the pastorate of Rev. Nance B. Crawford that the present, fully air-conditioned, sanctuary seating approximately 900 persons, was built, and it was first occupied during the summer of 1955.

The membership of First Church has grown to the present enrollment of 2,411. A new educational building has been added at a cost of $300,000.

THOMAS M. PRICE

PASCOE, JUAN NICANOR (1887-1962), first bishop of the Iglesia Metodista de México, was born in San Telmo Ranch, Edo. de MÉXICO, Aug. 18, 1887. He studied at Colegio Palmore in Chihuahua and graduated from VANDERBILT UNIVERSITY in 1916. GARRETT BIBLICAL INSTITUTE in Evanston conferred on him the honorary D.D. degree in 1932.

Juan Pascoe experienced trying and difficult times during his childhood. His father had many controversies with Roman Catholics. Pascoe was member of the M.E. Church, South, ordained in 1908. He served churches in Torreón, Durango, and Laredo, Texas. He then studied at NASHVILLE. Upon his return, he was pastor of Balderas, Chihuahua, Saltillo Allende, SAN ANTONIO, TEXAS, Monterrey, and then to México City.

The First General Conference of the Methodist Church of México, upon consummation of the union of the two branches, was held in the Iglesia "La Santísima Trinidad." It opened its sessions on Sept. 16, 1930. Juan N. Pascoe was elected bishop Sept. 19, and consecrated on Sunday, Sept. 21, by the five presiding elders already elected. The term of office was four years. Difficult, of course, was the first period. Time and effort were devoted to organization and interpretation, seeking understanding among ministers as well as among the congregations. He also had to do much deputation work in the country and abroad.

Pascoe married Elisa Steel and they were parents of four children. Mrs. Pascoe has also been active in women's organizations and was Vice-Chairman of the WORLD FEDERATION OF METHODIST WOMEN for one term. Together, Dr. and Mrs. Pascoe undertook the ministry of translating *The Upper Room* to Spanish. For twenty-five years they did that work which has been a blessing for the Spanish-speaking Methodist churches as well as other denominations in many countries. Pascoe asked for voluntary location from the Conference in 1943 to co-operate in the lay movement of the church. For three years he was Secretary for the Y.M.C.A. A few years later he returned to the itinerant pastoral ministry and even after retirement continued to be secretary of Social action in the Church.

He died Nov. 6, 1962.

GUSTAVO A. VELASCO G.

PASTORAL VISITING. From the beginning Methodism has urged its ministers to visit the people. The early CLASS LEADER was a sub-pastor who was required to see each member of his class once a week to inquire into his spiritual condition. One of the questions asked of a preacher when he seeks admission into full connection in the conference is, "Will you visit from house to house?"

Today pastoral visiting is more difficult than in former times. Both parents may work away from home, and members of the family may eat and sleep at varied hours. Extracurricular school activities, community meetings, and motoring and numerous other forms of recreation may take people away from home during hours that a minister might normally be expected to call. If the pastor tries to visit while some persons are viewing their favorite television programs, he may not receive a warm welcome.

But even so, visiting continues to be one of the pastor's duties. The 1968 *Discipline* says that the pastor is "to visit in the homes of the parish and community, especially among the sick, aged, and others in need." He "is responsible for ministering to the needs of the whole community as well as to the needs of the people of his charge," and "he shall give an account of his pastoral ministry to the charge and annual conference." The very name pastor originally meant shepherd, and the pastor is still the spiritual leader of his people.

Pastors still find ways and times to minister to the people. They use the telephone and the mails, and they make it known that they are available for counseling when anyone wishes to come to them. They are alert to the times when sickness, sorrow, and other crises strike in homes and in individual lives. At such times they are needed and their ministry is welcome.

In Methodist circles the reputation and work of a preacher as a pastor counts heavily in the total evaluation of his ministry.

Discipline, 1968, Paragraph 350.
Nolan B. Harmon, *Ministerial Ethics and Etiquette,* 1950.
M. Simpson, *Cyclopaedia.* 1878.

JESSE A. EARL
ALBEA GODBOLD

PATAGONIA PROVISIONAL CONFERENCE was organized during the quadrennium ending in 1964 and comprises the country of southern ARGENTINA through Neuquen, Rio Negro, and the Bahia Blanca region of BUENOS AIRES Province (see also ARGENTINA). BARILOCHE is headquarters of the conference.

Discipline, 1960, P. 2007.2; 1964, P. 1846.   N. B. H.

PATERSON, NEW JERSEY, U.S.A. (1970 population 142,641), is an industrial city situated on the Passaic River. Incorporated as a city in 1851, it is the seat of a state teachers college and branches of Rutgers State and Seton Hall Universities.

Paterson first appears in the M.E. Church *Minutes* in 1825, when J. Creamer was pastor. He reported 126 members the following year. By 1857 the city had two stations—Cross Street and Prospect Street, with a total of 1,647 members and $18,000 worth of property. In

1876 Paterson had five churches and "the Paterson Circuit." The membership of the six charges was 2,263, property appraised at $121,000.

Market Street Church, the largest Methodist church in that city, had 710 members and property estimated at $65,000.

Calvary, built in 1895, was razed by fire on Jan. 2, 1967.

Christ Church began in the home of Mrs. Louise Bosshardt, a converted German, in 1881, and later became a part of the Newark German charge. Antipathy to the German language church during World War I caused the EAST GERMAN CONFERENCE to be dissolved in 1940. The German Church then became a part of the NEWARK (now NORTHERN NEW JERSEY) CONFERENCE. Services continued in German, and in English, in this church until 1957. Calvary and Christ Churches held joint services in Christ Church after the Calvary fire, but due to the prevalent erosion of city churches, ceased to hold services until 1968. The Calvary trustees continue to exist, pending property settlement, and Christ Church has asked to disband as of this writing.

East Side Terrace was built in 1893. The first parsonage for this church was built in 1925. LLOYD C. WICKE, now bishop, was the first pastor to move into the parsonage.

Embury Church began in 1869. Its building was dedicated in 1886. In 1904 the present property was purchased. It was remodeled in 1955.

Epworth Church began around 1891, becoming a regular conference appointment in 1908. A new church was built in 1914. It merged in 1968 with the former Christ E.U.B. Church.

Grace Church, one of whose pastors, J. W. FITZGERALD, became a bishop, moved to Wyckoff after its property was taken for public housing. Madison Park (a former METHODIST PROTESTANT CHURCH) began in 1895.

Paterson Avenue is in the Totowa section of Paterson, and came out of a cottage prayer meeting in 1866. The present edifice was dedicated in 1928. Bishop JOHN WESLEY LORD as a young man belonged to this church.

The Church of the Saviour began under Italian leadership when Signor Vincenzo Barrecchia gathered a group of new Americans in his home and organized an Italian Bible class. Beginning in 1908 the group used a room in the Prospect Street Church, but after 1914 took over the whole church. When the building was condemned in 1922, the people met for a time in the home of Nicola Bruno and also with the Salvation Army. The present Church of the Saviour was erected in 1924.

Simpson Church originated in South Paterson with the old Market Street Church people helping to organize it in 1889. The church building was destroyed by fire on Jan. 10, 1969. It had become a yoked parish with Madison Park in the late 1960's.

Union, the Totowa Borough Church, had its building destroyed by fire on Jan. 11, 1967. It had its first official board chosen in June 1911, and was built in 1913, adding Sunday school and meeting rooms in 1940.

Trinity, another church founded by Market Street Church, was organized on Feb. 21, 1889, and dedicated on July 6, 1890. Many of the first families in Paterson began to attend this church, and a new brick structure was dedicated on Thanksgiving Day, 1905. Trinity became the Spanish-speaking church, and following a fire in the early 1960's was sold to Negro Baptists. Its congregation as of 1969 was worshipping in Wesley Church.

Wesley Church was built around November 1891. In the private home of Francis Huntington the first meetings of the congregation were held. The group finally organized a year later as the Wesley M.E. Church and built a chapel which later became Eastside Terrace. The present building was dedicated in 1907. Wesley and Eastside Terrace became a yoked parish in 1967.

Westside Church was started by Sunday school teachers from Gross Street Church; and became part of a circuit in 1890. It became West Paterson M.E. Church in 1893; and was made a separate charge. A new building dedicated in 1905 had three fires, the last of which in 1941 destroyed it. Around 1918 the Borough of West Paterson was established, the site of the present church, built in 1941, remaining within Paterson, and the name was changed to Westside. The church is not to be confused with the present West Paterson Community (Methodist) Church, which came into being later, in West Paterson Borough.

In 1970 Paterson had seven churches. The church with the largest membership is Embury with 426 and estimated value of its building, equipment and land $660,690. Total membership reported by the seven churches was 1,246. Their property was valued at $1,486,945.

General Minutes.
V. B. Hampton, *Newark Conference.* 1957.
M. Simpson, *Cyclopaedia.* 1878.   N. B. H.

PATRICK, HUGH McALLISTER (1888-1959), NEW ZEALAND layman, was born in AUCKLAND. He began work in the Takapuna post office at the age of thirteen, and became director-general of the Post and Telegraph Department in 1945. He was decorated Member of the Royal Victorian Order for his efficient arrangement of the tour of the Duke of Gloucester in 1931.

Patrick had many public interests—justice of the peace, member and sometime president of the English-Speaking Union in Auckland, organizer for Merchant Navy Welfare Appeal.

He was an outstanding Methodist layman, and was a very acceptable local preacher. In 1959 he was awarded the Local Preachers' Association Long Service (50 years) diploma. He was national organizer of the Peace Thanksgiving Fund Appeal in 1947, and was elected vice-president of Conference in 1953.

New Zealand Methodist Times, Nov. 7, 1959.

L. R. M. GILMORE

PATTERSON, DONALD STEWART (1897-   ), lay leader of WASHINGTON, D. C., and the BALTIMORE CONFERENCE and executive secretary of the Methodist Commission on CHAPLAINS, 1943-1956, was born on May 20, 1897, in Anderson, Ind., and served with the U. S. Army from 1917-19. He became assistant to the president of AMERICAN UNIVERSITY in 1942, and thereafter continued to live in Washington, where he took an increasingly prominent part in the work of The Methodist Church. During World War II he was elected executive secretary of the Commission on Chaplains of The Methodist Church and served as such until 1956. From 1956 to 1965, he was the chairman of the Commission on Camp Activities of The Methodist Church. He was president of the COUNCIL OF SECRETARIES of the Church, 1954-55; the vice-president of the General Board of LAY ACTIVITIES, 1944-52; the lay leader of the Baltimore Conference, 1938-52. He

has served as a trustee of American University and of the Asbury Methodist Home at GAITHERSBURG, MD. WESTERN MARYLAND COLLEGE awarded him the Churchmanship Award in 1951, and he was named Layman of the Year by the Methodist Union in Washington in 1965. He is the author of *A National Strategy for Temperance Education,* 1940; *Methodist Men at Work,* 1943; and *Be Ye Doers,* 1958. He has been a member of successive GENERAL CONFERENCES for a number of years. He continues to reside in Washington, D. C.

Who's Who in The Methodist Church, 1966.   N. B. H.

PATTON, JOHN (1823-1897), American lumberman, merchant, banker, philanthropist and layman of the M.E. Church, was born Jan. 6, 1823 in Tioga County, Pa. He was reared in Curwensville, Clearfield County, Pa., by poor but pious and industrious parents whose backgrounds go back to Colonial days in America. His grandfather, Philip Antes, founded Methodism in Centre and Clearfield Counties. With limited educational advantages himself, John Patton became an ardent advocate and supporter of schools and colleges.

A pioneer lumberman, he became the founder of the First National Bank at Curwensville, promoter of mining resources and land development, director of a railroad and a patriotic, public spirited citizen. Active in politics, he helped to select Abraham Lincoln as Republican candidate for President at the Convention of 1861. A congressman during the Civil War, he earnestly supported the war measures and generously contributed funds for the relief of suffering soldiers. His land company founded the town of Patton, Pa., and named it for him.

General Patton was for many years known as the leading layman of the CENTRAL PENNSYLVANIA CONFERENCE of the M.E. Church, and was president of its Layman's Association. He was a delegate to the ECUMENICAL METHODIST CONFERENCE in WASHINGTON, D. C. He was a director of Williamsport Dickinson Seminary and a trustee of DICKINSON COLLEGE and DREW THEOLOGICAL SEMINARY.

His generous benefactions to religious and educational objects were remarkable for his day. His local church and the Patton Public School at Curwensville are monuments to his generosity. Methodist educational institutions and the Church Extension Society received large donations from him.

He was held in highest esteem because of the depth of his Christian character and his loyalty to Christ and his Church. He died at Curwensville, Dec. 23, 1897.

The Christian Advocate (New York), March 13, 1884.
The Conference News, Harrisburg, Pa., March 15, 1884.
Minutes of the Central Pennsylvania Conference. 1898.

CHARLES F. BERKHEIMER

PATTON, SAMUEL (1797-1854), American pioneer preacher, was born in Lancaster District, S. C., on Jan. 27, 1797. In his career he served in three Methodist Conferences. First the TENNESSEE CONFERENCE (1819-1821), where he was ordained traveling deacon by Bishop McKENDREE, and served effectively the Sequatchie and then the Clinch circuits; next he was enlisted to serve the Tuscaloosa Circuit (1821-1823) in the newly organized MISSISSIPPI CONFERENCE, where he had a most successful ministry. On November 27, 1823, he was married to Nancy Morrison of Sullivan County, Tenn., and applied for the transfer of his membership to the HOLSTON CONFERENCE in 1824. He was received into this Conference, meeting in Jonesborough, Tenn. and in it he served as an effective leader until his death.

Fourteen of his first nineteen years in Holston Conference were as a presiding elder. In this role, he was most effective, manifesting a spirit of modesty and humility with a deep sense of responsibility and efficiency in pastoral care. Though not highly trained, Patton was self-educated beyond his early elementary schooling. EMORY AND HENRY COLLEGE conferred the honorary D.D. upon him. As pastor of the First Church in KNOXVILLE, at the urgent suggestion of leaders in the Conference, he single-handedly published *The Methodist Episcopalian*, which became *The Holston Christian Advocate*, and evolved into the official organ in the Southern Methodist Church after 1848. Originally of Presbyterian background, Patton was capable of answering the attacks of Frederick A. Ross, eminent Presbyterian divine and editor of *The Calvinistic Magazine* published in Rogersville, Tenn. Patton's serious nature, combined with regular habits of reading and study, and his natural ability in logical reasoning, especially in doctrinal matters, qualified him eminently to champion Wesleyan doctrine and polity. Serving his church at all of the GENERAL CONFERENCES from 1828 until his death, he proved an invaluable interpreter of the position of the Church, South, before and after the eventful year of 1844.

Patton suffered an illness in youth that impaired his lungs, and this deficiency along with periodic and serious dejection inherited from "Miss Nichols" (suffering mental afflictions) whom his father married, impeded his joy of living and serving his Lord throughout his life. He was a man of five feet, eight inches in height, slender and a bit stooped, with keen, deep-set gray eyes, who leaned a bit forward in the pulpit, using few gesticulations, but always well-prepared and thoughtful in his utterances. He was respected and loved throughout his ministry, which was full of well-deserved honor and noted for effectiveness, as is attested by his friend, W. G. BROWNLOW, editor of *The Knoxville Whig*, with whom Patton roomed; his family, which included four children, lived at the Spring Place Home in Sullivan County. During most of his ministry, he received between one and two hundred dollars per year as salary. Frugal living, hard work, and consecrated devotion characterized this leader of early Holston Methodism, whose converts and accessions in the church ran to multiplied thousands.

He died Aug. 1, 1854, in Knoxville, Tenn.

David Rice M'Anally, *Life and Times of Rev. S. Patton, D.D., and Annals of the Holston Conference.* St. Louis, Mo.: n.p., 1859.
R. N. Price, *Holston.* 1903-13.
M. Simpson, *Cyclopaedia.* 1878.   E. E. WILEY, JR.

PAUL QUINN COLLEGE, the oldest Negro liberal arts college in TEXAS, was founded by the A.M.E. CHURCH at Waco in 1872. It was granted a charter for operation by the State of Texas in 1881. The first president of Paul Quinn College, as well as its organizer, was Bishop JOHN M. BROWN. The GEORGE B. YOUNG Theological Seminary is related to Paul Quinn College, which was named for the famed A.M.E. missionary. Bishop L. H. McCloney is president of the college, while B. L. McCormick is dean of the seminary.

GRANT S. SHOCKLEY

JOHN PAWSON

PAWSON, JOHN (1737-1806), British minister, was born at Thorner, near Leeds, in November 1737. He became a Methodist preacher in 1762, and in 1785 he was ordained by JOHN WESLEY for SCOTLAND, where he said that he became "fully satisfied that it requires a far greater degree of Divine influence, generally speaking, to awaken a Scotchman out of the dead sleep of sin than to awaken an Englishman." He sympathized with the popular request for the Methodist preachers to administer the SACRAMENTS to the societies in their care, though he accepted John Wesley's ruling, when he left Scotland in 1787, that he must not himself administer the Sacraments in England. He exercised a mediating influence in the controversies on this subject which followed Wesley's death, both in 1792, when Pawson suggested drawing lots on the question, and again in 1793, when he was President of the Conference. He was also one of the sponsors of the Lichfield Plan, which proposed a form of episcopal government for British Methodism, a scheme which the Conference of 1794 rejected.

Pawson's revision of Wesley's *Large Minutes* in 1797 was accepted by the Conference as the authoritative statement of Methodist discipline. He was elected President again in 1801, a mark of the high respect in which his brethren held him. ADAM CLARKE called him an "upright and downright man" (*Lives of Early Methodist Preachers,* ed. T. Jackson, London, 1846, i, 392), and a strain of severity and narrowness is implied by Pawson's expurgation of Wesley's library: it was he who burned John Wesley's annotated copy of the plays of William Shakespeare. The autobiography which Pawson contributed to the *Arminian Magazine* (q.v.) and which may be found in *Lives of Early Methodist Preachers,* is similarly a solemn, rather unrevealing production. Letters of his which survive, however, suggest a rather crisper character in everyday life. He died on March 19, 1806.

JOHN NEWTON

PAYNE, DANIEL ALEXANDER (1811-1893), distinguished churchman and the first American Negro college president, was born in CHARLESTON, S. C., on Feb. 24, 1811 of free parents. He migrated to the North and attended the Lutheran Theological Seminary in Gettysburg, Pa., 1835-38. Payne, who later received two honorary doctorate degrees (D.D., LL.D.), was licensed to preach and ordained in the Lutheran Church. He was admitted into the Philadelphia Conference of the A.M.E. CHURCH in 1843. Earliest advocate of a trained ministry in the denomination and its first historiographer, publishing one of the earliest pieces of historical research among Negroes, *History of the A.M.E. Church* (Nashville, 1891), Payne was elected to the episcopacy in 1852. In that office he organized the NEW ENGLAND CONFERENCE in 1852, the MISSOURI CONFERENCE in 1855, and the KENTUCKY CONFERENCE in 1868; negotiated the purchase of WILBERFORCE UNIVERSITY for the A.M.E. Church (1863); rendered yeoman service in re-establishing the denomination in his native SOUTH CAROLINA and introducing the connection in the South after the Civil War. He claimed the longest episcopal tenure of his denomination, forty-one years.

GRANT S. SHOCKLEY

PAYTON, JACOB SIMPSON (1884-1963), American minister and publicist, was born at De Soto, Iowa, March 24, 1884, and was educated at Fort Worth University (A.B. 1908) and DREW THEOLOGICAL SEMINARY (B.D. 1911). He joined the PITTSBURGH CONFERENCE and served Christ Church, the Army YMCA in France, Ben Avon, Sewickley, Beaver, and Asbury, Pittsburgh, besides superintending the Allegheny and Pittsburgh Districts, 1926-31. From 1936-41 he was editor of *The National Methodist Press*, then assistant editor of *The Christian Advocate* and during the war, acting editor of *The Chaplain*. He closed his career as Washington correspondent for *The Christian Advocate*. He was the author of *Our Fathers Have Told Us*, a history of the Pittsburgh Conference, 1938, and with E. T. CLARK and J. M. POTTS edited *The Journal and Letters of Francis Asbury*, 1958. Rose Marsh, whom he married June 16, 1917, survived him. He died Oct. 4, 1963, at Falls Church, Va.

EDWIN SCHELL

PEACE FELLOWSHIP, METHODIST, is the association of pacifists within the British Methodist Church. It was founded on Nov. 3, 1933. Following a letter by HENRY CARTER to *The Methodist Recorder* earlier that year, over 500 ministers covenanted together "to renounce war and all its ways and works, now and always, God being our helper." In January 1934, laity took the same covenant; and by 1939 the membership had risen to over 4,000, of whom 900 were ministers. The present membership is 5,000. Methodist Peace Fellowship is part of the Fellowship of Reconciliation, the ecumenical pacifist body.

JOHN STACEY

PEACH, JOHN S. (1810-1891), was born in England. He was received on trial in 1840 and came to Newfoundland in the same year. He was ordained in 1844 and served several of the larger charges in the Newfoundland district. He was financial secretary from 1856 to 1862, and was chairman of the district from 1863 to 1870. He was a delegate to the General Conference, Montreal, in 1878, the year of his retirement. A delegate to the Ecumenical Congress in 1881, he was elected President of the Newfoundland Conference in 1882. He gave valuable leadership in the Newfoundland District and Conference.

G. H. Cornish, *Cyclopaedia of Methodism in Canada.* 1881.
H. M. Mosdell, *When Was That?* St. John's: Trade Printers, 1923.

N. WINSOR

PEAKE, ARTHUR SAMUEL (1865-1929), British biblical scholar of international reputation, was born at Leek, Staffordshire, Nov. 24, 1865. He entered St. John's College, Oxford, in 1883. In 1887 he became Casberd Scholar and took First Class in the Honours School of Theology. In 1889 he became Denyer and Johnson Scholar and the next year gained the Ellerton Essay Prize. In the same year he was appointed lecturer at Mansfield College, Oxford, and was elected to a theological fellowship at Merton College. He was greatly influenced by the work of Cheyne, Driver, Sanday, Fairbairn, and Hatch.

In 1892 through the foresight of WILLIAM P. HARTLEY, he was appointed tutor at the Primitive Methodist Theological Institute, later named Hartley College, MANCHESTER (see THEOLOGICAL COLLEGES) and remained in this post for thirty-seven years until his death. He was also lecturer at Lancashire Independent College (Congregational) and at the United Methodist College in Manchester. In 1904 he became the first Rylands Professor of Biblical Criticism and Exegesis in the University of Manchester, and was the chief formative influence in the newly founded faculty of theology.

His tremendous literary output included: commentaries on *Job, Jeremiah, Hebrews* in "The Century Bible" (1902-12); *Colossians* in the "Expositors Greek Testament" (1903); *The Problem of Suffering in the Old Testament* (Hartley Lecture, 1904); *The Religion of Israel* (1908); *A Critical Introduction to the New Testament* (1909); *The Bible: Its Origin, Its Significance, and Its Abiding Worth* (1913); *The Revelation of John* (Hartley Lecture, 1919). His most notable achievement was the editing of *A Commentary on the Bible* (1919), for which by his wide influence he secured contributions by the most eminent scholars. A successor to this work still boasts the title, *Peake's Commentary* (1962).

From 1919 he was editor of the Primitive Methodist *Holborn Review* and in 1925 coeditor of *An Outline of Christianity.* A man of wide ecumenical understanding as church leader, he helped to save England from a fundamentalist controversy. He was the first nonconformist layman to receive the Oxford D.D. (1920); he also held the D.D. of Aberdeen. He died August 19, 1929.

John T. Wilkinson, ed., *Arthur Samuel Peake, 1865-1929: Essays in Commemoration.* London: Epworth Press, 1958.

JOHN T. WILKINSON

PEARCE, WILLIAM (1862-1947), American FREE METHODIST bishop, was born in Hayle, Cornwall County, England, Oct. 15, 1862. He was converted in a revival similar to the Welsh Methodists. Called to the ministry, he joined the California Conference, and served as pastor and district elder until 1901. He transferred to the Oregon Conference and to Genesee in 1904 where he served as pastor and district elder. He was a bishop, 1908-47. Except for the training in the common schools of England, he was self-educated. He had one of the finest minds in the church; by instinct he was a scholar. He mastered New Testament Greek without a teacher. For sixteen years he was chairman of the Board of Administration and the Board of Directors of the Free Methodist Publishing House. He was the author of *Our Incarnate Lord* and numerous articles in *The Free Methodist,* all of high merit. An unusual preacher, unique in every way, his great sermons were the poetic overflow of a rich mind and soul. His influence was wide and long-continued. He served as bishop longer than any other.

BYRON S. LAMSON

PEARNE, THOMAS (18?-1901), American Indian minister. The Conference *Journal* of the COLUMBIA RIVER CONFERENCE in 1901 carried this note, "He was born about 65 years ago." He married Kate McKay in 1869. JAMES H. WILBUR performed the ceremony. Both Thomas and Kate attended the Fort Simcoe Indian School in the early 1860's under "Father" Wilbur. Thomas then attended the Chemawa Indian School near Salem, Ore., and later returned to his home near Fort Simcoe to be taught Bible and other pastoral skills by Wilbur.

He was admitted on trial in the OREGON CONFERENCE in 1869, was admitted to full membership and ordained deacon by Bishop E. S. JANES in 1871, and appointed that year to Simcoe Indian Mission. He became a charter member of the Columbia River Conference when it was formed in 1874.

Besides preaching in the churches on the Yakima Reservation, he conducted and assisted in many revival meetings among the Indians of WASHINGTON, OREGON and IDAHO. Notable among these meetings was the great revival among the Nez Percés when over 300 were converted and became members of the church.

Pearne owned and operated a large ranch in Medicine Valley near Fort Simcoe, the first irrigated ranch in Yakima Valley, much of the proceeds from which he used to help those in need.

Death came to him in September 1901, and he was buried in the White Swan Methodist Cemetery. (This Cemetery was a part of the land donation of Chief White Swan to the Methodist Church for church, campground, and revival meetings for the Indians.) He preached, visited among them and ministered to their every need. His death was regretted by his own people and by hundreds of his white brethren.

Journals of the Oregon and Columbia River Conferences.

C. T. HATTEN

PEARSE, MARK GUY (1842-1930), British Wesleyan and world-famous preacher, was born on Jan. 3, 1842, at Camborne, CORNWALL, and after considering a medical career, entered the Wesleyan ministry in 1863. Serving in various circuits, he was elected to the Legal Hundred in 1884, and then from 1887-1904 was associated with HUGH PRICE HUGHES in the West LONDON Mission. Here he was largely responsible for the building up of the West London Mission Sisterhood. Worldwide preaching tours and many books on Cornish and religious themes

MARK GUY PEARSE

gained him an international reputation. He died on Jan. 1, 1930.

H. M. RATTENBURY

PEARSON, BENJAMIN HAROLD (1893-   ), an ordained elder of the Arizona-Southern California Conference of the FREE METHODIST CHURCH, is a retired missionary. He was born at Los Angeles, Calif., and holds the A.B. and Th.M. degrees from the University of Southern California. The Litt.D. degree was conferred on him by SEATTLE PACIFIC COLLEGE in 1942. He was superintendent of the Pacific Coast Home Missions, 1919-39 and General Superintendent of the Young People's Missionary Society, 1935-43. He served as Superintendent and Director of the Colombia, South America field, Oriental Missionary Society, 1943-50; and of the Brazil field, 1950-55. He was executive secretary, World Gospel Crusades, 1955-59; and President, 1960-65. He is now president emeritus. He is the author of *Mexican Missions; Off to Panama; The Lost Generation Returns; Wings Over Aztec Land; The Monk Who Lived Again; Next; Adventures in Christ-like Living; Don Pedro; The Headhunter's Bride;* and *The Vision Lives.* Dr. and Mrs. Pearson reside in Los Angeles, Calif.

BYRON S. LAMSON

PECK, GEORGE (1797-1876), American clergyman, educator, editor, and author, was born in Middlefield, Otsego County, N. Y., Aug. 8, 1797. The son of Luther and Annis Collar Peck, he and four brothers became Methodist ministers, one being Bishop JESSE T. PECK. A Christian at fifteen, he joined the GENESEE CONFERENCE in 1816, continuing in effective service fifty-seven years. He became a member of the ONEIDA CONFERENCE when organized (1829), and of the WYOMING CONFERENCE when organized (1852), being a member of the NEW YORK CONFERENCE during his editorial years (1840-1852). He served seventeen pastorates, was presiding elder seven times, and a member of thirteen sessions of the GENERAL CONFERENCE, 1824-1872.

From 1840 for eight years Peck was editor of the *Methodist Quarterly Review;* then four years as editor of the *Christian Advocate.* He was Principal of Cazenovia

GEORGE PECK

Seminary, Cazenovia, N. Y., 1835-1838. Shortly afterward he proposed that a seminary be established at Kingston, Pa., which materialized in 1844. He also was the proponent of the General Conference course of studies for preachers. Peck published several books, including *History of Wyoming, History of Methodism within the Bounds of the Old Genesee Conference,* and *The Life and Times of Rev. George Peck, D.D.*

WESLEYAN UNIVERSITY granted George Peck the M.A. degree and AUGUSTA COLLEGE that of D.D. In 1846 he went to LONDON as a member of the Evangelical Alliance.

George Peck married Mary, daughter of Philip and Martha Myers, of Forty Fort, Pa., June 10, 1819. Of their four children George M. and Luther W. became members of the Wyoming Conference, Wilbur F. became a physician, and a daughter became the wife of T. J. Crane of the NEWARK CONFERENCE.

Peck died in Scranton, Pa., May 20, 1876, and was buried at Forty Fort.

A. F. Chafee, *Wyoming Conference.* 1904.
Dictionary of American Biography.
L. D. Palmer, *Heroism and Romance.* 1950.
George Peck, *The Life and Times of Rev. George Peck.* New York: Nelson & Phillips, 1874.
——————, *Old Genesee Conference.* 1860.
LOUIS D. PALMER

PECK, JESSE TRUESDELL (1811-1883), American bishop, was born at Middlefield Center, Otsego County, N. Y., the son of Luther and Annis (Collar) Peck, and a descendant of Henry Peck, one of the founders of New Haven, Conn. He was the youngest of five brothers, all of whom became ministers. Educated at Cazenovia Seminary, he married Persis Wing, Oct. 13, 1831; they had no children.

Peck joined the ONEIDA CONFERENCE in 1832, was ordained DEACON in 1834, and ELDER, in the BLACK RIVER CONFERENCE, in 1836. He served several pastorates, and in 1837-40 was principal of a high school which later became Gouverneur Wesleyan Seminary. From 1841 to 1848 he was principal of the Troy Conference Academy, Poultney, Vt., after which he had four years as president of DICKINSON COLLEGE, Carlisle, Pa. In 1852, he went to Foundry Church, WASHINGTON, but left after two years to become editor and secretary of the Tract Society. In 1856 he was appointed to Greene Street Church, NEW YORK, and two years later, because of his wife's health, transferred to CALIFORNIA, where he served

pastorates in SAN FRANCISCO and SACRAMENTO and was presiding elder of the San Francisco District for one year. While in the west he was a trustee of the UNIVERSITY OF THE PACIFIC and contributed to its support. In 1866 he returned east, supplied St. Paul's Church, Peekskill, N. Y., for a time, and in 1867 was appointed to Hudson Street, Albany, where he served three years. From 1870 to 1872 he was pastor at Syracuse where he led in founding SYRACUSE UNIVERSITY.

Peck was a delegate to five GENERAL CONFERENCES, 1844-48, and 1864-72. Though only thirty-three in 1844, his speech in the debate over the status of Bishop JAMES O. ANDREW brought Peck into wide and favorable notice in the north. He believed himself capable of doing great things, and he manifested great energy and persistence. Though he weighed over 300 pounds, his body was seldom at rest and his mind was always on the alert. When others doubted that Syracuse University could succeed, he was confident. When the school began he pledged $25,000, a sum greater than all his possessions, and paid it. In 1883, he gave $50,000 to the institution and had nothing left. He published several books, including *The Central Idea of Christianity, The True Woman,* and the *History of the Great Republic.* In addition, he wrote tracts and pamphlets and contributed to Methodist periodicals and holiness magazines.

In 1872, Peck was elevated to the episcopacy and in the next eleven years manifested zeal and vigor in the work. He presided over eighty-three conferences, including those in GERMANY, SWITZERLAND, DENMARK, SWEDEN, and NORWAY. He participated in the first ECUMENICAL METHODIST CONFERENCE in 1881. He died in Syracuse, May 17, 1883, and was buried there.

Dictionary of American Biography, Volume 14.
General Minutes, MEC.
General Conference Journal, 1884.
M. Simpson, *Cyclopaedia.* 1878.
JESSE A. EARL
ALBEA GODBOLD

W. W. PEELE

PEELE, WILLIAM WALTER (1881-1959), American bishop, was born at Gibson, N. C., on Nov. 26, 1881. He graduated from Trinity College, DURHAM, N. C., in 1903 and was awarded the D.D. degree by the same institution in 1928. The LL.D. degree was conferred upon him in 1941 by RANDOLPH-MACON COLLEGE. He was married to Elizabeth Lytch of Laurinburg, N. C., on Aug. 2, 1911.

From 1903 until 1938, Peele served as an educator and pastor in NORTH CAROLINA Methodism. He was professor of Mathematics at Rutherford College, 1903-1906, and from 1906 to 1909 was president of that school. He was headmaster of Trinity Park School from 1911 to 1915 and from 1915 to 1918 was professor of Biblical Literature in Trinity College.

As pastor Peele served important appointments in North Carolina Methodism such as Edenton Street Church, RALEIGH, 1918-1923; Trinity Church, Durham, 1923-1928; First Church, CHARLOTTE, 1928-1937; presiding elder, Greensboro District, 1937-1938.

He was elected a bishop at the GENERAL CONFERENCE of the M.E. Church, South, in 1938 and from 1938 to 1952 he served as bishop of the Richmond Area which comprised the VIRGINIA, BALTIMORE and NORTH CAROLINA Conferences. He retired as bishop at the Southeastern JURISDICTIONAL CONFERENCE of 1952.

Bishop Peele gave dynamic leadership to the Richmond Area, and in addition his work influenced many phases of World Methodism. During World War II, he was chairman of the Methodist Commission on CHAPLAINS and directed the work of nearly 3,000 Methodist Chaplains. He was also chairman of the Methodist Commission on Camp Activities, which agency gave special attention to the program of local Methodist churches located near military bases for the military personnel and their dependents.

Bishop Peele was very active in the field of Methodist higher education, serving as a member of the Board of Trustees of DUKE UNIVERSITY, Randolph-Macon College, RANDOLPH-MACON WOMAN'S COLLEGE, LOUISBURG COLLEGE, FERRUM JUNIOR COLLEGE, and RANDOLPH-MACON ACADEMY. He also served as president of the COUNCIL OF BISHOPS and vice-chairman of the BOARD OF MISSIONS.

Upon retirement in 1952, Bishop and Mrs. Peele made their home at Laurinburg, N. C. He died there on July 1, 1959 and was buried in the Lytch Cemetery at Laurinburg.

PAUL N. GARBER

PEEPLES, BENJAMIN (1797-1883), American preacher, was born in Carter County, Tenn., April 3, 1797. He professed religion and joined the M.E. Church when but a boy, felt the call to preach early, and was licensed to preach when eighteen years of age. He was admitted on trial into the TENNESSEE CONFERENCE in October 1816, ordained deacon in 1818, and elder in 1820. He had traveled several circuits and in 1820 the KENTUCKY CONFERENCE was organized. He and Hezekiah Holland were appointed to the Dover Circuit as co-pastors.

He was later sent as missionary to that portion of the Jackson Purchase lying in KENTUCKY and TENNESSEE along with LEWIS GARRETT. The two met at McLemoresville, Tenn., and agreed to divide the territory, Garrett taking the southern portion and Peeples the northern. A group of people led by John Manley, a local preacher, had been holding services in a community a few miles east of what is now Paris, Tenn. Shortly after the arrival of Peeples, he organized this group into a church and it was named MANLEY'S CHAPEL. This church is believed by many to

have been the first Methodist church organized in the MEMPHIS CONFERENCE. This was in 1820. With this church as a base, the Sandy River Circuit was organized.

In 1822 Peeples married Martha Davidson Randle, a sixteen-year old girl with three younger brothers looking to her for care. At the Conference that year he located, feeling that with his responsibilities and his meager allowance from the church he could not support his family. He settled in the wilderness three miles east of what is now Henry, Tenn., and from this home as a base he carried on the work of the church, preaching, organizing churches and otherwise ministering to the territory. He practiced medicine, served as judge of Henry County Court several years, and was one of the commissioners who surveyed the Kentucky-Tennessee line on the north. His wife's three brothers and five of their sons became traveling Methodist preachers.

In 1869, having reared and supported the family, he was readmitted to the Memphis Conference and served several years with success. He died on Aug. 22, 1883. Peeples and Garrett are regarded as fathers of the Memphis Conference.

F. H. PEEPLES

PEGLAR, GEORGE (1799- ?), an American WESLEYAN METHODIST pastor and church leader, was born in LONDON, England, on Oct. 11, 1799, and spent his early life as a sailor and world traveler. For a time he belonged to the Methodist Protestant Church, but severed his connection with that body over the slavery issue. He was pastor of the Wesleyan Methodist Church in UTICA, N. Y., where the convention met in May 1843 and perfected the organization of the new church. At the sixth General Conference of the Wesleyan Methodist Connection held in ADRIAN, Mich., in 1864, the new West Wisconsin Conference was represented by the doughty sailor-preacher George Peglar. Interesting to note, only twelve of the persons present in the organizing conference twenty-one years before were in attendance at this one. George Peglar presided in the anniversary celebration. He was the first president of the Rochester Conference of his church, being named to that office in 1844. After the 1867 General Conference authorized the union of the two conferences in WISCONSIN, Peglar was elected the first president of the united conference. He had emigrated from NEW YORK and was active in the work there. He held this office still in 1869.

McLeister and Nicholson, *Wesleyan Methodist Church of America.* 1959.
M. Simpson, *Cyclopaedia.* 1878.   GEORGE E. FAILING

PEHIAKURA, on the Manukau Peninsula, NEW ZEALAND, was the site of an early mission station. The local chief, baptized as Epiha Putini (Jabez Bunting) attended training school at Mangungu and became teacher and preacher to his own people, first at Pehiakura and in later years at Ihumatao, from 1838 until his death in 1856. Missionaries, traveling from Mangungu to stations in the south, frequently called at Pehiakura and conducted services in the large church Putini had caused to be built. Membership grew by 1844 to seventy-two, with a total of 150 attendants to worship.

William Woon was appointed to be resident missionary at Pehiakura in 1845, but was unable to take up his appointment because of tribal warfare in the area. The work continued to be supervised from Auckland by H. H. Lawry, until it was entirely disrupted by the Maori Wars of the 1860's.

C. T. J. Luxton, *Methodist Beginnings in the Manukau.* Wesley Historical Society, New Zealand, 1960.   L. R. M. Gilmore

PEKIN, ILLINOIS, U.S.A. **First Church,** is the oldest congregation in Tazewell County. It began in the cabin of Jacob Tharp in "Town Site," later called Pekin, when Jesse Walker, the founder of Methodism in both St. Louis and Chicago, preached there in 1826. The first building, a brick structure, was later referred to as Foundry Church because it was then used as a foundry.

Pekin first appears in the conference minutes in 1842 when Warner Oliver was appointed pastor. The Pekin Circuit reported 232 members in 1843. Pekin became a station in 1857; it then had sixty-four members and its property was valued at $2,500. A Sunday school was organized in 1846.

The congregation erected a second building at Capitol and Margaret Streets about 1846, and another costing $12,000 was constructed at Fourth and Broadway in 1867. The latter structure was remodeled in 1905 and was used by the members until 1954 when the present edifice was consecrated.

When the Southwestern German Conference was organized in 1865, there was a German-speaking congregation of 104 members and property valued at $5,000 in Pekin, and by 1876 it outnumbered First Church 187 to 154. Now called Grace Church, it reported 1,533 members in 1970, property valued at $852,597, and a total of $108,562 raised for all purposes. The statistics for First Church in 1970 were 1,762 members, property valued at $553,554, and $87,962 raised for all purposes.

General Minutes, MEC, and UMC.
Simpson, *Cyclopaedia of Methodism.*
Marie Kohlbacher, *Brief History of First Church,* Pekin. (typescript), 1968.   Jesse A. Earl

PEKIN, NEW YORK, U.S.A., **Centenary Park** near Pekin marks the site of the Layman's Convention where the Free Methodist Church was organized, Aug. 23, 1860. It is located on Hoover Road, one and one-half miles south of Pekin, adjacent to Schenck's Grove where laymen and ministers adopted a Constitution and Book of Discipline for the new denomination. The park is bounded by a substantial rail fence. There is a bronze marker affixed to a fifteen-ton granite boulder, and the grounds are appropriately landscaped. The creation of Centenary Park was a joint venture of The International Light and Life Men's Fellowship, in cooperation with the denomination. The park was dedicated with appropriate ceremonies in connection with the Free Methodist Centennial General Conference of 1960.

The Free Methodist, Aug. 9, 1910.
W. T. Hogue, *Free Methodist Church.* 1938.
L. R. Marston, *From Age to Age.* 1960.
Clarence Howard Zahniser, *Earnest Christian: Life and Works of Benjamin Titus Roberts.* Circleville, O.: Advocate Publishing House, 1957.   Byron S. Lamson

PELAGIANISM, a heresy advancing unacceptable views concerning sin and Grace particularly referred to in the seventh Article of Religion of The United Methodist Church. The "father" of Pelagianism was Pelagius (d. around 420). Of Pelagius' life little is known definitely. Even his birthplace is not certain, although it seems likely that his native home was Britain. Pelagius was a monk of learning and moral earnestness. He came to Rome around 400 and became popular as a preacher. He was shocked at the low point which Roman morals had reached, and sought to raise ethical standards. He was concerned to stir up moral endeavor among lax Christians who stressed the weakness of the flesh and the impossibility of fulfilling God's commands.

The famous "Pelagian controversies" (over sin and grace) began when Pelagius visited North Africa where Augustine was bishop. Among the first literary efforts of Augustine after he became bishop of Hippo had been a treatise, *Ad Simplicianum,* addressed to Simplicianus the successor of Ambrose as bishop of Milan. The work is important in the development of Augustine's thought because it is generally regarded as a significant stage in his understanding of St. Paul and the theology of grace. In this writing Augustine denies the possibility of human merit before God and stresses man's sinfulness. Indeed he provoked Pelagius by his statement ". . . all men are a mass of sin . . ." (*Augustine: Earlier Writings.* The Library of Christian Classics, Vol. VI. Edited by J. H. S. Burleigh. Philadelphia: The Westminster Press, pp. 398, 402, 404.) Pelagius felt that Augustine's view of human nature was faulty and lay in part behind the evident decline in morals.

Of the writings of Pelagius little is extant. However, much can be learned from what remains of his work and from his opponents, especially Augustine. Pelagius regarded it an affront to God to insist that man could not help sinning. To him this seemed to be a fatalistic view of man. Others shared his doctrine (e.g. Celestius and Julian of Eclanum), and developed a "Pelagianism" which not infrequently went further than some of the teachings of Pelagius himself. The main concern of Pelagianism was to emphasize that man is a responsible being, and that his actions depend entirely upon himself. Any form of predestination is rejected by Pelagianism; man in his own freedom determines how he will develop. The argument used to support this doctrine of the freedom of the will is that God does not command man to do what man is unable to do. The unassisted human will is regarded as decisive in the matter of salvation. Man is completely free to choose good or evil because there is no internal or external pressure on him—no internal pressure because native depravity is denied; no external pressure because predestination is rejected.

Pelagianism insists that there is no Original Sin which has been inherited from Adam. Man's flesh is not regarded as evil, and death is not seen as a result of the fall. Neither sin nor virtue is inborn in man, and any concept of the transmission of sin from parent to child by generation (*peccatum ex traduce*) is rejected. Each soul is seen as a new creation from God and completely untainted with original sin. Pelagianism did recognize that the mass of men are indeed bad, but only so because they have been ready to follow the bad example of Adam's sin.

Because all men have followed a bad example they are culpable and must change their manner of living. But this change is not to be accomplished in the traditional way by relying upon grace. Grace is not regarded as a divine influence upon man's soul, nor a divine work done in behalf of man. Grace is regarded as the enlightenment of man's reason. Enlightenment comes through the law, especially the law found in the New Testament given by Christ in precept and example. This enlightenment enables man to see the will of God so that he may use his own natural powers to choose the good. Grace is not the direct work of God, it is comprised of the natural endowment given to men as they are enlightened.

A corollary of this teaching of Pelagianism is man's perfectibility. If man wills, he can observe God's commandments without sinning. Pelagius argues that God commands perfection (Lev. 19:2; Matt. 5:48), and man can fulfill the requirement. This perfection comes about by man's diligent effort and the continuous exercise of the will. When men use the resources at hand, they can reach a perfection. Many Pelagians teach that man can live without sin if he so wills.

Pelagian tendencies from time to time have reoccurred in the Christian Church. Schools of thought which have placed primary emphasis upon education and a social transformed environment to the relative neglect of conversion and regeneration by the grace of God have been regarded by many as a near, if not a total, Pelagianism. Many saw a movement toward a modern Pelagianism in the rise of theological Liberalism during the mid-nineteenth century. Liberalism, sometimes called "Modernism," stressed man's free will, human moral endeavor, character development, and man's rational powers. This movement was called "Culture Protestantism" by Karl Barth; and he criticized, among other things, the notion that man could find God or attain salvation through human effort. This reaction gave rise to a movement often called "Neo-Orthodoxy" or "Crisis Theology." This rejection of "modern Pelagianism" by Barth and others stressed the sovereignty to God in initiating any Divine-human encounter.

Methodist theology has sometimes been accused of having "Pelagian tendencies." This is because of three emphases of Methodism: (1) The emphasis upon free grace for all men which implies the possibility of SALVATION for all. (2) The rejection of double predestination. (3) The emphasis upon CHRISTIAN PERFECTION. However, it may be fairly claimed that traditional Methodist theology is free from Pelagianism. Indeed, Methodism, along with other branches of the Church, has from its beginning rejected Pelagianism, regarding it as too extreme. Wesley and other early Methodist leaders have always insisted upon man's sinfulness and the necessity for God's grace in the life of man. For example, Wesley, in the Preface to his work on *The Doctrine of Original Sin*, strongly repudiates a Pelagian position. Elsewhere (e.g. sermons "Salvation by Faith" and "Justification by Faith") Wesley emphasizes the necessity for the grace of God in salvation.

Methodism, in harmony with historic Christendom, has criticized Pelagianism at the following points: 1. *The nature of sin*. Pelagianism sees sin as a series of separate acts with no basis in a depraved nature. Sin is regarded as an action which does not have any connection with an inherited sinful condition of the soul. Methodism regards man as sinful, both racially and individually. The notion that certain men may have been without sin is rejected, and the doctrine of original sin is maintained. 2. *The nature of grace*. Pelagianism sees grace as the enlightenment of the natural capacities of man and fails to see any direct work of God in the life of men. Methodism views grace as something quite outside of man.

Grace is from God alone, and it is the result of God's direct activity in the life of man. 3. *The tendency of legalism*. Pelagianism interprets the relationship between God and man in a legal fashion. Good works are the basis for salvation. Methodism insists that salvation is *sola gratia* (by grace alone) and that man's justification is based upon the grace of God, not on the works of the law.

Pelagianism has been condemned by the Church as a heresy. It was rejected at Carthage (418) and at Ephesus (431). A later modification of Pelagianism called semi-Pelagianism was also condemned at Orange (529).

J. F. Bethune-Baker, *An Introduction to the Early History of Christian Doctrine*.
John Ferguson, *Pelagius: A Historic and Theological Study*.
J. N. D. Kelly, *Early Christian Doctrines*.
W. B. Pope, *Compendium of Christian Theology*. 1880.
R. Watson, *Theological Institutes*. 1832.

KENNETH CAIN KINGHORN

PEMBERTON, NEW JERSEY, U.S.A., population 1,341, a town in Burlington County, in which was erected the third Methodist meeting house in New Jersey and the fifth in the U. S. A. It was originally known as New Mills, but the name was changed to Pemberton in 1828.

The exact date of the organization of the Methodist Society at New Mills is indefinite. However, Methodist itinerants preached here as early as 1769. THOMAS COKE visited the Society in 1785 and wrote, "This place has been favored with a faithful ministry for sixteen years."

Captain THOMAS WEBB preached here, perhaps as early as 1768 or 1769. An early leader in the New Mills Society was William Budd who preached here before Bishop ASBURY's first visit in 1772.

The first church structure was begun in 1775. It was a frame building, twenty-six by thirty-six feet, with galleries around three sides and a high pulpit.

Bishop Francis Asbury visited New Mills on numerous occasions: 1772, 1776, 1782, 1783, 1786, 1789, 1800, 1802, 1806, 1813. During the 1806 visit, he preached a funeral sermon for Bishop WHATCOAT who had died earlier in the year.

Among the early pastors were JOHN KING, WILLIAM WATTERS, PHILLIP GATCH, THOMAS RANKIN, WILLIAM DUKE, FREEBORN GARRETTSON, BENJAMIN ABBOTT, and HENRY BOEHM.

There have been three church edifices in Pemberton. The first, built in 1775-76, was sold in 1833, and is still in use as a dwelling. The second, built in 1833, was destroyed by fire in 1894. The present sanctuary, built in 1894, continues to serve a growing congregation.

F. Asbury, *Journal and Letters*. 1958.
G. A. Raybold, *Reminiscences of Methodism in West Jersey*. New York: Lane & Scott, 1849.
F. B. Stanger, *New Jersey*. 1961.
Woodward and Hageman, *The History of Burlington and Mercer Counties*. Philadelphia: Everts & Peck, 1883.

FRANK BATEMAN STANGER

PEÑARANDA, NESTOR (1889-), was the first Bolivian Methodist minister. He was accepted into the Bolivian Missionary Conference of the M.E. Church in 1916, its first year. He and his wife, Angelica, soon felt the need to study the Aymara language so they could work more effectively in schools and churches among the Aymara Indians. Within six months Peñaranda was preaching in their language. Later, with another man, he translated the four Gospels and the Book of Acts from Spanish into Aymara. He also compiled an Aymara hymnbook. He retired from the ministry in 1948, but continued to work in retirement.

NATALIE BARBER

EDWARD J. PENDERGRASS

PENDERGRASS, EDWARD JULIAN, JR. (1900-), American bishop, was born in Florence, S. C., on Sept. 24, 1900, the son of Edward Julian and Eula Ethel (Smith) Pendergrass. He did his college work at the University of North Carolina, receiving the A.B. degree; his seminary studies at EMORY UNIVERSITY'S CANDLER SCHOOL OF THEOLOGY, and additional work at GARRETT SCHOOL OF THEOLOGY and the Moody Bible Institute in Chicago. He also holds an honorary D.D. degree from FLORIDA SOUTHERN. He married Lois Mae Sheppard on June 26, 1929. They have three children—Amy Katherine (Mrs. John Miller), Edla Ethel (Mrs. Burton Barnes) and Edward Eugene.

He has been a minister of the FLORIDA CONFERENCE since 1929. He was ordained deacon in 1932, elder in 1934. His first pastorate was at Fort White, 1930-31; followed by High Springs, 1931-32; Cross City, 1932-34; Fort Pierce, 1934-38; College Heights at Lakeland, 1938-39; Seminole Heights Church, TAMPA, 1939-43; superintendent of the Tallahassee District, 1943-46; pastor of First Church, Tampa, 1946-52; First Church, ORLANDO, 1952-64—all of these in FLORIDA. He was elected bishop in 1964, and assigned to the JACKSON (Mississippi) Area.

He was secretary of the Conference BOARD OF MISSIONS and secretary of Evangelism, 1960, '63; delegate to the GENERAL CONFERENCES of 1948, '52, '56, '60, and '64; Southeastern JURISDICTIONAL CONFERENCE, 1944, '48, '52, '56, '60, and '64. He is a trustee of MILLSAPS COLLEGE, RUST COLLEGE, WOOD JUNIOR COLLEGE, and LAKE JUNALUSKA ASSEMBLY. He is an ex-officio trustee of the

Methodist Children's Home, Methodist Home Hospital, Seashore and Traceway Manor.

Bishop Pendergrass is now assigned to the following boards and committees of The United Methodist Church: General Board of EDUCATION, General Board of EVANGELISM, Interboard Committee on Town and Country Work, and the Quadrennial Program, 1968-72. He resides in Jackson, Miss.

Who's Who in America, Vol. 34.
Who's Who in The Methodist Church, 1966.   N. B. H.

PENINSULA CONFERENCE which superseded the Wilmington Conference of the M.E. Church was organized by the Uniting Conference in 1939. Its territory includes the state of DELAWARE and the counties of MARYLAND east of the Susquehanna River and Chesapeake Bay. The first session of the conference was held at WILMINGTON, Del., May 15-20, 1940, with Bishop EDWIN H. HUGHES presiding. At the time the conference had 244 ministers, 241 pastoral charges and 68,891 members.

Captain THOMAS WEBB preached the first Methodist sermon in Delaware at Wilmington in 1769. The first Methodist society in the colony was organized at New Castle in 1770. The record shows 150 members in Delaware in 1773 and 1,714 in 1783.

From the beginning Methodist work on the peninsula was a part of the PHILADELPHIA CONFERENCE. In 1868 the GENERAL CONFERENCE organized the Wilmington Conference to include Delaware and the parts of Maryland and VIRGINIA east of the Susquehanna River and Chesapeake Bay. At its last session in 1939 the Wilmington Conference reported 183 ministers, 180 pastoral charges, and 53,438 members.

When organized the Peninsula Conference included all the ministers and churches in its territory belonging to the three branches of Methodism which united to form The Methodist Church, except the Negro ministers and churches which continued in the DELAWARE CONFERENCE of the Central Jurisdiction until 1965. Though it covered a little less territory than the body it superseded, the Peninsula Conference immediately showed an increase of over sixty ministers and some 15,000 members. These came from the former MARYLAND CONFERENCE of the M.P. CHURCH and the former BALTIMORE CONFERENCE of the M.E. Church, South.

When the Delaware Conference was absorbed by the conferences of the Northeastern Jurisdiction in 1965, the Peninsula Conference at once showed another increase of some sixty ministers and about 15,000 members.

Peninsula Methodism established a paper in 1875 and maintained it for thirty-five years. Called the *Conference Worker,* the paper was first published at Easton, Md.; soon afterward it moved to Chestertown, Md., and then to Wilmington. From 1884 to its demise in 1910, the publication was called the *Peninsula Methodist.*

The Peninsula Conference supports Wesley College, a two-year coeducational school at Dover; two homes for the aged—Methodist Country House at Wilmington, and Methodist Manor House at Seaford, Del.; and Drayton Manor, Worton, Md., a retreat center or camp primarily for adults. The conference cooperates with the Baltimore Conference in the support of the Board of Child Care at Rockdale, Md., giving some $18,000 to the organization in 1968.

Aware of the importance of history, the Peninsula Conference has an active historical society. The society has erected a museum and a home for a curator adjacent to BARRATT'S CHAPEL, near Frederica, Del., one of the historic SHRINES of American Methodism.

In 1970 the Peninsula Conference had 324 ministers, 240 pastoral charges, 64,901 enrolled in church school, 100,600 church members, and property valued at $66,-109,683.

General Minutes, ME, TMC, UMC.
Minutes of the Wilmington and Peninsula Conferences.
M. Simpson, *Cyclopaedia*. 1878.   ALBEA GODBOLD

PENNINGTON, CHESTER ARTHUR (1916-   ), American minister, was born in Delanco, N. J., on Sept. 16, 1916, the son of Chester Arthur and Emily (Lush) Pennington. He was educated at Temple University where he received the A.B. degree in 1937 and at DREW UNIVERSITY, receiving the B.D. in 1940, the Ph.D. in 1948. He did postgraduate work at Oxford in England. Ohio University gave him the L.H.D. degree in 1961. MCKENDREE COLLEGE awarded him the D.D. degree in 1968.

He married Marjorie Elizabeth Bruschweiler, on Sept. 13, 1941, and their children are Celeste Ann and Lawrence Arthur. Dr. Pennington joined the NEW JERSEY CONFERENCE in 1938, was ordained elder in 1940. He served as pastor in Neptune City, 1938-41; then in Spring Lake, N. J., 1941-43, and was chaplain in the U.S. Navy, 1943-46. He became assistant minister Calvary Church, EAST ORANGE, N. J., 1946-47, and thereafter was professor of philosophy at CENTENARY COLLEGE in New Jersey and the pastor in HACKETTSTOWN, N. J., at the same time, 1947-51. He then transferred to the NEW YORK CONFERENCE and became pastor of St. Paul and also St. Andrew Churches in New York City, 1951-55, and in that year was transferred to the MINNESOTA CONFERENCE and put in charge of the large Hennepin Avenue Church in MINNEAPOLIS. He is a member of the Commission on CHAPLAINS, a trustee of HAMLINE UNIVERSITY, a member of the American Theological Society, and is a director of the Ministers Life and Casualty Union of Minneapolis. He is the author of *Even So . . . Believe* (1966); and *With Good Reason* (1967), both published by Abingdon Press.

Who's Who in America, Vol. 34.
Who's Who in The Methodist Church. 1966.   N. B. H.

PENNINGTON SCHOOL, Pennington, New Jersey, a secondary school for boys, was founded in 1838 by the NEW JERSEY ANNUAL CONFERENCE. Included among its long list of graduates are many influential leaders of Methodism, such as J. M. BUCKLEY, editor of the New York *Christian Advocate;* BORDEN P. BOWNE, distinguished professor of Boston University; and the late Bishop ADNA W. LEONARD, who was killed in a plane crash in Greenland during the Second World War. In the 1880's it was said that a third of the ministers of NEW JERSEY were graduates of Pennington School. The governing board has twenty-four members elected by the New Jersey Annual Conference on nomination of the board of trustees.

JOHN O. GROSS

PENNSYLVANIA, called the "Keystone State" because of its central location among the thirteen original colonies, is thirty-third in size but third in population, according to the 1970 census (11,669,565). It was settled by the

Swedes in 1638, by the Dutch who conquered the Swedes, and by the English who overpowered the Dutch in 1644. In 1682 Charles II granted the land to the Quaker William Penn who named it Penn's Woods or Penns-sylvania. Noted for its agricultural and dairy products, Pennsylvania is also one of the largest mineral producing states; it supplies all of the anthracite and much of the bituminous coal for the nation. Industries include iron and steel, foundry and machine works, printing, knit goods, electrical supplies, and railway manufactures.

GEORGE WHITEFIELD was the first Methodist to visit Pennsylvania, preaching in PHILADELPHIA as early as 1739. A major influence in the Great Awakening, Whitefield nevertheless failed to organize his converts into societies. However, he made the word "Methodist" well known in the colonies.

Several of Whitefield's converts in Philadelphia began meeting informally in a sail loft on Dock Street. The loft belonged to Samuel Croft; the leaders of the meetings were James Emerson and Edward Evans. In 1767 Captain THOMAS WEBB came to Philadelphia and formed the sail loft group into a Methodist society which eventually became ST. GEORGE'S CHURCH, now one of the historic SHRINES of American Methodism.

In 1769 JOHN WESLEY sent his first two Methodist missionaries to America—RICHARD BOARDMAN and JOSEPH PILMORE. They arrived in Philadelphia October 21 and discovered that the society organized by Webb was meeting at 8 Loxley Court; it then numbered about 100 persons. Pilmore remained to minister to the group in Philadelphia while Boardman went on to NEW YORK. About a month later the Philadelphia society purchased the shell of the church building named St. George's from a German Reformed group.

Between 1769 and 1773, Wesley sent eight official missionaries to America, and on landing all of them came first to Philadelphia. FRANCIS ASBURY arrived in 1771 and THOMAS RANKIN and GEORGE SHADFORD in 1773. In 1773 and in the two succeeding years the first three Methodist conferences held in America were conducted at St. George's Church by Thomas Rankin, John Wesley's General Assistant for America. By 1800 numerous societies and circuits had been organized in Pennsylvania. Some of the early circuits and the dates of their beginning were: Chester, 1774; York, 1781; Lancaster, 1782; Redstone, 1784; Juniata, 1784; Ohio, 1787; Huntingdon, 1788; Pittsburgh, 1788; Bristol, 1788; Wyoming, 1791; Northumberland, 1792; Tioga, 1792; Carlisle, 1794; Shenango, 1800; and Erie, 1800.

In 1803 Pennsylvania was divided between two conferences, the Baltimore and Philadelphia. The BALTIMORE CONFERENCE had three districts, Alexandria, Pittsburgh, and BALTIMORE, which covered western MARYLAND and western Pennsylvania and extended into OHIO and western VIRGINIA. The conference reported thirty appointments and 18,927 members. The PHILADELPHIA CONFERENCE had six districts, Delaware, Chesapeake, Jersey, Albany, Genesee, and Susquehanna, and it covered eastern Pennsylvania, NEW JERSEY, a part of New York, and the eastern shore of the Chesapeake including DELAWARE. It had forty-three appointments and 33,187 members.

Not only was Pennsylvania one of the mother regions of American Methodism, it was also the place where the evangelical movement began among the Germans. The religious zeal kindled by PHILIP WILLIAM OTTERBEIN,

MARTIN BOEHM, and JACOB ALBRIGHT and which eventually produced the EVANGELICAL UNITED BRETHREN CHURCH, took its rise in Pennsylvania.

ALLEGHENY COLLEGE at Meadville, founded in 1817, has been under Methodist control since 1833. DICKINSON COLLEGE at Carlisle, established in 1783, has been Methodist since 1834. LYCOMING COLLEGE at Williamsport was started as an academy in 1812, came under Methodist patronage in 1848, was elevated to a junior college in 1929 and a four-year college in 1948. Title to Lycoming is held by the Preachers' Aid Society of the CENTRAL PENNSYLVANIA CONFERENCE. The Methodists started several academies or seminaries which were in reality secondary schools before the rise of public high schools. A number of hospitals, homes for children, and homes for the aged were also established.

Other Methodist bodies arose in Pennsylvania, some of them offshoots of the Methodist Episcopal Church. The A.M.E. CHURCH was organized in Philadelphia in 1816, and presently has two conferences in the state, Philadelphia and York. Part of the Philadelphia-Baltimore Conference of the A.M.E. ZION CHURCH is in Pennsylvania. The PRIMITIVE METHODIST CHURCH which came from England in 1829 has a conference extending from MASSACHUSETTS to the midwest and some of its churches are in Pennsylvania. The Methodist Protestant Church developed considerable strength in western Pennsylvania. Its PITTSBURGH CONFERENCE was one of the strongest in the connection. The WESYLEYAN METHODIST CHURCH, organized at UTICA, N.Y., in 1843, merged with the PILGRIM HOLINESS CHURCH in 1968 to form the Wesleyan Church. Before the union the Wesleyan Methodists had the Penn-Jersey Conference operating partly in Pennsylvania. The FREE METHODISTS, organized in 1860, have four conferences in Pennsylvania, Oil City, Pittsburgh, and parts of the New York and Susquehanna Conferences. Several smaller Methodist bodies have a few congregations in the state.

After the Philadelphia and Baltimore Conferences, which were original conferences, the M.E. Church developed four more conferences in Pennsylvania which continued until unification in 1939 and after. The PITTSBURGH CONFERENCE (ME) was formed in 1824 from parts of the Ohio and Baltimore Conferences. The ERIE CONFERENCE, composed of territory in Pennsylvania and New York, came in 1836 by dividing the Pittsburgh Conference. The WYOMING CONFERENCE was formed in 1852 by dividing the ONEIDA CONFERENCE (New York). The Wyoming Conference has always been made up about half and half of territory from Pennsylvania and New York. The Central Pennsylvania Conference was formed in 1868 from parts of the Philadelphia and East Baltimore Conferences. In 1962 the Erie and Pittsburgh Conferences combined to form the WESTERN PENNSYLVANIA CONFERENCE. After 1960 the Baltimore Conference had no Pennsylvania territory within its bounds.

About five per cent of Pennsylvania's population belonged to The Methodist Church in 1968. While this does not compare favorably with 10.7 per cent in Iowa, nevertheless the total number of Methodists in Pennsylvania, 540,201 in 1968, make it numerically one of the largest Methodist states in the nation. In 1968 there were 1,936 Methodist churches in Pennsylvania and they were valued at $345,248,677. At the time Pennsylvania Methodism was divided among three episcopal areas, Pittsburgh, Harrisburg, and Philadelphia, with a resident bishop in each of the cities named.

E. S. Bucke, *History of American Methodism.* 1964.
General Minutes, ME, TMC.
Minutes of the Pennsylvania Conferences.
M. Simpson, *Cyclopaedia.* 1881.   W. GUY SMELTZER

PENSACOLA, FLORIDA, U.S.A., is an important harbor city on Pensacola Bay, off the Gulf of Mexico. It was settled in the early 1500's by the Spanish, has been under the rule of five flags: Spain, France, England, Confederate States, and the United States. Pensacola was the site of the formal transfer of the FLORIDA territory to the United States in 1821, and now is headquarters for the Pensacola Naval Air Station.

Methodism was the first Protestant denomination to establish a mission in Pensacola. From 1781 to 1821, Protestant denominations were not permitted in the territory of Florida, but upon purchase of Spanish territory by the United States this restriction was removed and in 1821 the MISSISSIPPI CONFERENCE established the Pensacola Mission and appointed Alexander Talley as missionary.

Thus First Methodist Church, mother church of Protestantism in northwest Florida, was organized and although burned twice and moved several times, it was finally located in 1881 on its present site in downtown Pensacola.

Thirteen years later Navy Yard Mission was added to Pensacola Mission, and Green Malone became pastor. Navy Yard was later to become Warrington.

The Civil War years from 1861-1866 show no statistics nor appointments, for Pensacola was occupied by Federal troops; however, in 1861 there were sixty-six white and nine colored Methodists, with fifty-three white and six colored on probation. Post war years reflect in 1866 sixty-five white Methodists only.

The year 1891 marked the phenomenal spread of Methodism in Pensacola after years of yellow fever epidemics, hardships, and the Civil War interruptions. Now a group of preaching places were named: Malaga Square Mission, Muscogee Wharf Mission, Reed's Chapel, and Warrington. In 1902 Gadsden Street Church was built in East Pensacola. Reed's Chapel later became the present Richard's Memorial in West Pensacola.

Prior to 1861 the records show that Negro and white Methodists worshipped together. In March 1888, First Presbyterian sold its old building to "the M.E. Church (colored) for $2,500." This was the beginning of St. Paul Church which retained its M.E. connection. In 1904 St. Paul was to be host to the Annual Conference but, destroyed by fire and too late to notify delegates, Tolberts's Chapel A.M.E Zion (now Big Zion) loaned its church for the session to be held.

The St. Paul congregation bought its property for a new start, worshipped for a time in an old dance hall, later in a tabernacle of rough boards and sawdust floors, until the present handsome brick church was finished with the cornerstone laid in 1908. Bishop MALLALIEU who was of great inspiration to this congregation, bought for the church a gift of a large brass bell which still hangs in the belfry. As a member of the Central JURISDICTION, St. Paul was in the CENTRAL ALABAMA CONFERENCE, while her sister churches belonged to the ALABAMA-WEST FLORIDA CONFERENCE, Southeastern Jurisdiction.

In Pensacola proper, United Methodism is now represented by sixteen churches with a membership of 10,525. Primary churches are: First Methodist, Gadsden Street, Myrtle Grove, St. Mark, Richard's Memorial and Warrington. First Church in 1970 reported 1,646 members.

General Minutes.
M. E. Lazenby, *Alabama and West Florida.* 1960.

RALPH WESLEY NICHOLS

PENSIONS, BOARD OF. The care of retired ministers has been a concern of Methodist Churches since the organization of the M.E. Church in 1784. There was at first provided a CHARTERED FUND—which even today continues to bring in modest returns; subsequently, showing that this matter was on the mind of the Church, the GENERAL CONFERENCE in 1808, by the RESTRICTIVE RULES drawn up then, was forbidden to give the "produce" or profits of the PUBLISHING HOUSE to any cause other than that of the "superannuated and worn-out preachers, their wives, widows and orphans." This was at best but meager support for "worn-out" preachers, and through the years there came to be an increasing call for something better than this early penurious effort had proved to be. Various annual conferences after a time began to set apart out of their own funds monies for the support of their retired brethren, and philanthropic laymen provided retirement homes for ministers of their respective conferences. After a time the whole matter was taken over by the separate General Churches whose union came about to form what is now The United Methodist Church.

In the M.E. Church, South, there was created in 1866 in each annual conference a powerful committee known as the Joint Board of FINANCE. This became an institution in each annual conference, and these conference committees exerted great power in collecting and distributing monies for the conference claimants, as well as for other needed causes. Each annual conference came to depend heavily upon its Board of Finance to look after this matter.

In the M.E. Church eventually the Church itself created a Board of CONFERENCE CLAIMANTS and began to build a "Connectional Fund" which was administered by its central agency. In 1916 the Board of Conference Claimants became the Board of Pensions and Relief of the M.E. Church, and all the general funds were put under the control of that Board. It was thus enabled to correlate in a better way the whole matter of caring for the superannuates.

In the M.E. Church, South, as it became increasingly clear that a better integrated overhead organization was needed to care for all conference claimants, the General Conference in 1908 created a General Board of Finance and directed that it should be incorporated under the laws of MISSOURI. This Board a bit later promoted a churchwide Superannuate Endowment Fund, which added to its holdings appreciably.

The M.P. Church cared for its retired ministers in the same way as the M.E. Church did, that is chiefly through local conference collections and appropriations. But in time a general Superannuate Fund was created and the executive committee of that Church was given control of the Fund.

In 1939 at the organization of The Methodist Church, this whole matter of supporting the conference claimants was put under a Board of Pensions. This was organized as the Board of Pensions of The Methodist Church, incorporated in ILLINOIS, but it continued to carry on for a time the work of the boards and agencies of the separate uniting churches in order not to lose the funds which already had been devised by will and otherwise to the respective agencies looking after this matter.

Through the years 1939-1968, a better correlation was worked out by the separate boards and continuing agencies, and in 1968 at the organization of The United Methodist Church, there was created a General Board of Pensions to take over and look after this whole matter for the new and greatly enlarged Church.

The E.U.B. Church. As early as June 10, 1836 The Charitable Society was formed for the relief and support of "the itinerant superannuated and worn-out Ministers and Preachers of the EVANGELICAL ASSOCIATION (in the United States of America), their Wives and Children, Widows and Orphans" (*Articles of Incorporation*). In these early years in the CHURCH OF THE UNITED BRETHREN IN CHRIST many annual conference pension programs were rapidly coming into existence.

This benevolent ministry had its beginning in the twentieth century, however, when Bishop S. C. BREYFOGEL decided that the Church should do something for the retired ministers and ministers' widows.

A legislative act of the 1911 GENERAL CONFERENCE of the Evangelical Association in session at CLEVELAND, OHIO, brought the SUPERANNUATION FUND into existence. In preparation for church union with the Evangelical Association in 1922, the UNITED EVANGELICAL CHURCH raised $312,750, thus making it possible for ministers of The United Evangelical Church to participate in benefits of the Superannuation Fund.

On Jan. 1, 1943, the Ministers Reserve Pension Plan came into existence. This plan became available for ministers of The Evangelical Church who were ordained after Jan. 1, 1943. A Pension Plan for Lay Employees of the Church was also inaugurated on Jan. 1, 1943.

Leaders in the denominational pension program of the Evangelical Association and since 1922 in The Evangelical Church were: Bishop S. C. Breyfogel, 1911-1935; George Johnson, 1911-1920; J. R. Niergarth, 1920-1938; and A. H. DOESCHER, 1934-1958.

While many worthy annual conference pension programs existed at a very early date in the Church of the United Brethren in Christ, it was not until 1921, when the General Conference was in session at INDIANAPOLIS, that the denominational Ministerial Pension and Annuity Plan was legislated into existence. This pension plan was the result of a study authorized by the 1917 General Conference.

Leadership in the Ministerial Pension and Annuity Plan was provided by H. H. Baish (1921-1939) and George A. Heiss (1939-1948).

The union of The Evangelical Church and the Church of the United Brethren in Christ brought all the assets and liabilities of the two former pension programs under the direction of the Board of Pensions of The E.U.B. Church on Jan. 1, 1947. Offices of the Superannuation Fund at 1900 Superior Avenue, Cleveland, Ohio, and the Ministerial Pension and Annuity Plan at 16 East Eighth Avenue, YORK, Pa., were moved to the U.B. Building, Fourth and Main Streets, DAYTON, OHIO, at that time. The Board of Pensions in July of 1960 was relocated in the new

Administrative Offices Building, 601 West Riverview Avenue, Dayton, Ohio.

Pension legislation at the 1962 General Conference united the Superannuation Fund and the Ministerial Pension and Annuity Plan into the Senior Pension Plan. These two former ministerial pension plans had been closed to new entrants on Jan. 1, 1947.

Men who have served in various places of leadership in the Board of Pensions of the E.U.B. Church since 1947, are: A. H. Doescher (1947-1958), George A. Heiss (1947-1948), JOHN H. NESS, SR. (1948-1962), H. E. HILLER (1959-   ), G. L. Fleming (1961-   ), and Sherman A. Cravens (1967-   ).

During the long history of this benevolent enterprise the Board has gained added financial strength by grants from the PUBLISHING HOUSES, the Board of PUBLICATION, gifts and bequests, as well as appropriations from the denominational Christian Service Fund.

The 1966 General Conference placed the assets of The Printing Establishment of the United Brethren in Christ in excess of $2,000,000 under the supervision of the Board of Pensions of The E.U.B. Church. The income from this Printing Establishment Fund is distributed annually for pension purposes in the annual conferences.

On Jan. 1, 1967, the assets of the Board of Pensions of The E.U.B. Church were in excess of $25,000,000. There were 3,166 ministers and lay persons enrolled in The Senior Plan (for ministers), The Ministers Reserve Pension Plan, and The Pension Plan for Lay Employees. In 1967 over $1,000,000 were distributed to over 1,200 annuitants.

The *Discipline* may be referred to at any time to ascertain such matters as the organization and membership of the Board, and the rules and procedures which govern the administering to the needs of the conference claimants are also set forth in detail. This particular section of the *Book of Discipline* has grown larger and larger through the years—necessarily so, as all manner of different cases affecting the claims and interests of various claimants must be ruled upon in an equitable way, thus establishing precedents which eventually become law.

The Board is directed to "compile and maintain complete service records of ministerial members in full connection, associate members, and probationary members of the Annual Conferences of The United Methodist Church and of lay pastors whose service may be related to potential annuity claims" (*Discipline*, 1968, P. 1377.10). While it is admitted that the General Church and annual conferences have yet to do much more than they are doing for their claimants—men worn out in the service of the Church, men compelled to retire at seventy-two years of age, and the widows and orphans of preachers, much has been accomplished to date. Efficient offices manned by able executives and secretaries with present headquarters at EVANSTON, ILL., are depended upon to look after this matter as it should be.

Discipline, UMC, 1968.
N. B. Harmon, *Organization*. 1962.

N. B. H.
H. E. HILLER

PENZOTTI, FRANCISCO G. (1851-1925), was a prodigious distributor of the Bible, whose evangelistic work touched almost all of the countries of South and Central America. During his lifetime he personally distributed 125,000 copies of the Bible. Under his direction more

F. G. PENZOTTI

than 2,000,000 copies were distributed, and under his influence churches distributed another million.

Born in Italy, he emigrated as a boy to MONTEVIDEO, URUGUAY, where he established a carpenter shop of his own. At nineteen he married Josefa Sagastilbensa, his warmth toward the Roman Catholic Church having been cooled in a quarrel with the bishop over papers and fees connected with the wedding. He stopped going to Mass and dedicated himself to his carpentry, to study, and to his new home. However, he felt ill at ease. While he was trying to cheer a mood of despondency at a public dance hall, somebody gave him a copy of St. John's Gospel. This was in December 1875. The gift stirred anew a childhood interest in the restricted book, and he hurried home to read it with his wife.

Hearing that the whole Bible could be had at the Protestant chapel, he went and there met the man who had given him the book and two great Methodist preachers with whom his life henceforth was to be interwoven: John F. Thomson and ANDREW M. MILNE.

Penzotti became a regular attender and brought his friends to the Protestant chapel. Yet he failed to feel the joy he saw in others, so he sought a pastoral interview with Milne. As they were talking, they were joined by THOMAS B. WOOD, who talked and prayed with them. During the prayer, Penzotti suddenly felt "a ray of divine light penetrate my soul." He called out: "I feel that Christ has entered my heart. I want to sing a hymn of gratitude to the Lord." The three rose and sang.

Penzotti became one of a team of fourteen young people who went from door to door in Montevideo, distributing Bibles and talking about Christ. The church grew as a result, but the greatest outcome was to prepare the young Penzotti for the work that was to immortalize his name. While he was trying to combine preaching with carpentry, someone one night set fire to his shop—his only source of support. Turning to prayer and the Bible, he found comfort in the words of John 13:7: "What I am doing you do not know now, but afterward you will understand."

The Methodist Church at Colonia Waldense needed a pastor, and Thomson and Milne saw that Penzotti was the person to fill the vacancy. At first he refused because of his lack of preparation, but he came to feel that it was the will of God and accepted.

He was in charge of the church there from 1879-87, but early he felt life too comfortable in the Waldensian colony and resolved to become a missionary to the entire continent. In 1883, at the age of thirty-two, he interrupted his pastoral work to make his first missionary journey, going to BOLIVIA with Milne. The eight-month journey was made by way of northern ARGENTINA and included travel into CHILE. The pair distributed 8,000 copies of the Scriptures. They were not the first Bible Society colporteurs to enter Bolivia, but they went knowing that a predecessor, Joseph Mongiardino, had been murdered by a fanatic crowd.

On his second journey, Penzotti was the leader, with two assistants. This was a thirteen-month trip reaching hundreds of villages in northern Argentina, Bolivia, and Chile. Events included a celebrated debate on the Scriptures with the Archbishop of Cochabamba (Bolivia), in which Penzotti came off the hero of the liberals and Masons. He returned to Uruguay exhausted.

Milne saw Penzotti's need for rest, and persuaded him that they should go together to LONDON. In November 1885, they set out, and in London conferred with officials of the BRITISH AND FOREIGN BIBLE SOCIETY about Scripture distribution in Latin America. Then they returned home on a long circuit through South America, spreading Bibles all the way. They visited Trinidad and Curacao in the Caribbean, then landed in VENEZUELA. They preached and distributed Scriptures there and in Colombia, then visited ECUADOR where in a famous incident their books were confiscated at the customhouse. Entering PERU, they were welcomed and preached freely, perhaps unnoticed by the authorities. They also worked in Chile and Argentina before at last returning to Uruguay in December of 1886.

In a few months Penzotti had completed his pastoral work at Colonia Waldense, and then he was a pastor briefly at Rosario, Argentina. But at this point he took up the work of Bible distribution permanently, entering the service of the AMERICAN BIBLE SOCIETY.

He was sent to open a new Bible agency in Peru. Arriving with his family at the port city of Callao in July 1888, he began to distribute the Bible and preach in Spanish. So successful was he that the Anglicans (who were allowed to hold services in English) put a vacant chapel at his disposal. But the Roman Catholic clergy threatened to have the site dynamited, so he rented a house instead. As he moved about Peru, his services were often attacked, and persons who received his books were persecuted, excommunicated, and finally even imprisoned. At Arequipa in 1890 he was apprehended, charged by the local clergy with "clandestinely introducing immoral and corrupting books [Bibles!]." His books were confiscated, and he had to spend two weeks in jail. He made the jail into a church, and under his preaching one of the guards was converted. He was released through personal intervention by the president of the Republic, General Cardenas.

After a trip into Bolivia, Penzotti was arrested on July 26, 1890, as he arrived at his home in Callao. He now had to spend eight months in Casas Matas, called the most frightful prison in America. But this time the consciences of liberal people were astir. In Peru and all over America and Europe the "Penzotti Case" was known as a case for religious liberty. The Peruvian constitution did not allow other faiths besides the Roman Catholic, but diplomatic pressures were applied. Worldwide distribution was given to a snapshot taken by a North American reporter, showing Penzotti behind the iron gate of Casas Matas. The widespread interest succeeded in

opening the prison door for him on Easter Eve, March 28, 1891.

The next year he was appointed to open a new Bible agency in Central America. After visiting PANAMA, he entered COSTA RICA, where he organized a party of six to visit all the Central American countries. Disease overtook the party, and by the time they reached Managua, Nicaragua, all but Penzotti were sick, three actually dying. After burying the dead, Penzotti sent the two survivors back to Costa Rica and continued alone to GUATEMALA. At Guatemala City he established the Bible agency and was joined there by his family.

In 1906 he received an appointment to supervise the Bible agency at BUENOS AIRES, ARGENTINA, succeeding his old friend, Andrew Milne. By the time he could take up the appointment, in January 1908, Milne had died.

Penzotti continued his work in the Rio de la Plata area until 1921, when he retired as executive secretary, to be succeeded by one of his two sons. (The son, Pablo Penzotti, served the agency from 1921-46.) Though no longer secretary, Francisco Penzotti continued to be the evangelist until his death, July 27, 1925.

He has been variously described as "a hero of the evangelical cause in Latin America" and "apostle of liberty and truth." Others have seen parallels with JOHN WESLEY in his personal conversion experience, his evangelistic spirit, and the thousands of miles he covered on foot and muleback. A fitting memorial was given to him when, in 1956, the Bible Society gave the name "Penzotti Institute" to the training program it set up to prepare men for the work of Bible distribution, two by two, from house to house.

Francis G. Penzotti, *Spiritual Victories in Latin America: the Autobiography of Rev. Francis G. Penzotti, Agent of the American Bible Society for the La Plata Agency,* tr. and ed. by the Society. Centennial Pamphlet No. 16 of the American Bible Society. N. Y.: American Bible Society, 1916.

Luis D. Salem, *Francisco G. Penzotti—apostol de la libertad y de la verdad.* Mexico City: Bible Societies of Latin America, 1963.

Adam F. Sosa, *Desde el Cabo de Hornos hasta Quito con la Biblia.* Buenos Aires: La Aurora Press, 1944.

DANIEL P. MONTI
EDWIN H. MAYNARD

PEOPLE'S METHODIST CHURCH was formed in NORTH CAROLINA by members of the M.E. Church, South, who did not wish to join the Methodist merger of 1939. They are a conservative and holiness group with approximately 1,000 members in twenty-five congregations. They operate a school, John Wesley Bible College, in GREENSBORO, N. C.

Mead: *Handbook of Denominations in the United States.*

J. GORDON MELTON

PEORIA, ILLINOIS, U.S.A., with a population of 125,736 (1970), is beautifully situated along and above the west bank of the Illinois River, in the heart of rich farm land.

Methodism began in Peoria as early as 1824, when JESSE WALKER was appointed "Missionary to the Indians" in the vicinity of Fort Clark. He had moved westward from VIRGINIA in 1806 with WILLIAM MCKENDREE (later bishop), first to Southern Illinois, then to the Peoria territory. In 1825 he started First Methodist Church of CHICAGO. The first permanent class was formed in 1833, with seven members. Stephen R. Beggs came as pastor in 1839 and held meetings in Daniel Brestel's carpenter shop. He led the settlers in erecting the first church building, made of logs, and travelled as far as St. Louis to raise $65 toward the costs. Shortly an addition was necessary, making the building 40 by 43 feet.

The second building was completed in 1849—a brick structure, 60 by 90 feet, at Fulton and Madison Streets. Peter Cartwright was an official preacher here. In 1856 Peoria ceased to be a part of the Rock River Conference and became a member of the new Central Illinois Conference. The third building, a two-story brick, costing $35,000 (including the site) was completed at Sixth and Franklin Streets in 1884 and enlarged in 1891. This now and since early days has always been called First Church.

In 1910 William E. Shaw was appointed pastor of First Church. Two long talked-of events matured under his leadership. First, Madison Avenue Church (started as a missionary project in 1855) merged its membership of seventy-five with First Church in 1914. Second, a splendid new building was erected of Bedford Stone at the corner of Perry Avenue and Hamilton Boulevard at a cost of $133,762 (for lot, building and equipment) and dedicated June 18, 1916. The twenty-two years of Shaw's ministry were years of large growth, for he was an able preacher, and a leader with sound judgment, tact, diplomacy and untiring zeal. The influence of his life was wide-spread, then and even today.

Many distinguished men have served First Church in its long years and its membership and staff and spiritual influence have increased accordingly. In 1957, under the leadership of Robert Harvey Bodine, a fine, new administration building was erected adjoining the main structure at a cost of $894,325. Appropriately, it is named The William E. Shaw Memorial Church House.

The First German Methodist congregation erected a building at Fifth and Monson Streets in 1854. A second building, costing $7,000, was built between 1865-68. This congregation helped organize and build a church for the Sanger Street Mission in 1889, and this had regularly appointed pastors until it disbanded in 1921, with its members uniting with the German Church. A third building was completed in 1890 at a cost of $20,000. In 1918 the name of the church was changed to the St. John's, and in 1925 this went into the Central Illinois Conference, (MEC), the German Conference being dissolved. In 1950 the congregation moved to the East Bluff, with services being held in a public school until the first part of a three phase building program was completed. In this same year the name of the church was changed to Forrest Hill. In 1952 one section was formally opened, and presently other units make provision for worship, education and administration, at a cost of over $100,000.

Grace Church started as a Sunday school in 1863 or 1864 at the outskirts of town. The first building was dedicated in September 1897. It was known for a time as the Forrest Hill Church, but in 1939 the name was changed to University Avenue Church. Other structures were erected. The present sanctuary was begun in 1951, and an educational unit, costing $147,000, called Cartwright Hall, was completed in 1960.

Hale Memorial Church was organized by members of First Church in 1868 and dedicated its first building at Main and High Streets Jan. 14, 1869. In 1901 a new stone structure replaced the old building. The congregation changed the name to Epworth Church in 1953 and completed a new building in 1954 on Columbia Terrace in a residential section, nearer Bradley University.

Wesley Church was begun as a mission in 1870 in the south end of the city. Its members affiliated with First Church in 1926.

The Averyville Church (organized in the north end of town in 1894) built a lovely edifice in 1930, under the pastorate of T. Reighton Jones, and took the name of Madison Avenue Church.

Bethel Methodist was begun in 1911 and has long been a part of the community, serving the Negro people. It is now a member of the Central Illinois Conference.

Membership in Peoria United Methodist churches, according to the 1970 *Minutes*, is: Bethel—235; Epworth—399; First—4,340; Forrest Hill—863; Grace—347; Madison Avenue—589; and University Avenue—2,202, a total of 8,975. First Church has long been the largest Methodist church in the North Central Jurisdiction. Its total budget in 1970 was $275,000, $55,000 of which was for benevolences. There are five ministers on the church staff.

Peoria District, in the Central Illinois Conference, reported 37,092 members in 1970. Methodism in Peoria observed its centennial in 1924 and looks forward to its one hundred and fiftieth year in 1974.

Methodist Hospital of Central Illinois is a general hospital of 550 beds, with great new construction presently underway. The hospital's early years were precarious and uncertain. The move that began the hospital was prompted in 1898 by three deaconesses of the M.E. Church who at first saw the need for a home for deaconesses, and later were persuaded by Peoria doctors to combine this project with a small hospital of eighteen-bed capacity. Until 1917 it carried the name "The Deaconess Home and Hospital." As the deaconess' effort waned, the need for full hospital services in Central Illinois grew. The small hospital was increased in capacity by additions in 1910, 1918, 1924, and 1953.

The Methodist Hospital is under the sponsorship of the Central Illinois Conference of The United Methodist Church, and is governed by a Board of Trustees of thirty-six members. As provided in the by-laws, eighteen trustees must be ministers in active relationship to the Conference. The lay members come from many denominations although at least nine are required to be members of The United Methodist Church. These trustees serve without pay or remuneration of any kind.

Methodist Hospital is classified as a "base hospital" and as such has full facilities and a staff competent to perform a full range of delicate and intricate surgical procedures. There are eighty-four physicians and surgeons on its active staff, and the courtesy staff numbers 240 men and women. More than sixty percent of the hospital is of the most modern construction, fully air-conditioned, this section being opened in 1953 and 1960. There are fifteen operating suites which offer every convenience to surgeons.

The hospital is fully accredited by all proper accrediting agencies. It maintains a series of schools as a part of its responsibility, including a School of Medical Technology, School of X-Ray Technology, School of Surgical Nursing, training for practical nurses, a fully accredited School of Nursing, and a school for resident physicians in various specialties. Located near downtown Peoria, the hospital properties occupy more than two square blocks and are valued at more than $11 million. A full-time chaplain, an ordained Methodist minister, gives spiritual oversight to more than 1,000 employees, several hundred students and approximately 480 patients.

General Minutes.

FLORA C. MOORE
W. V. HERRIN

JOHN R. PEPPER

PEPPER, JOHN ROBERTSON (1850-1931), American merchant and Sunday school administrator, was born in Montgomery County, Va., on April 6, 1850, and was educated in the public schools and Christiansburg Commercial College. In early manhood he entered the wholesale grocery business in MISSISSIPPI and was president of companies in Greenville, Greenwood, Yazoo City, and Rosedale. He then went to MEMPHIS, Tenn., and became president of the Memphis Machine Works.

A leading layman of the M.E. Church, South, Pepper was especially interested in Sunday school work and was for nearly fifty years a Sunday school superintendent. He was a student of methods of religious education and wrote and published five books between 1885 and 1929. These were *Modern Sunday School Superintendent, Quiver Tips for Lovers of Sunday School Work, Tried Plans for Sunday School Work, Thirty Years at the Superintendent's Desk,* and *Well-Nigh Fifty Years at the Superintendent's Desk.*

Pepper was one of the founders of the Southern Assembly at LAKE JUNALUSKA, N. C., and was one of the original thirteen cottage owners in 1913. In 1923 and again in 1928 he was chairman of the Board of Trustees. In the days of financial difficulty he made large contributions to the Assembly; he purchased stock and loaned money, and in 1929 he donated the stock and notes for $10,500 to the institution.

Pepper died at Memphis on March 31, 1931.

Who's Who in America.

ELMER T. CLARK

PEREZ, CARLOS (1911-   ), Cuban pastor and college president, was born at Cardenas, CUBA on July 24, 1911. He married Juana Maria Sardiña in April of 1935. He studied at "La Progresiva," at CANDLER COLLEGE in HAVANA and SCARRITT and Peabody Colleges, NASHVILLE, Tenn., and in the Methodist Seminary (Havana); and received the Ph.D. degree from Havana University in 1934. He served several pastoral charges in Cuba and PUERTO RICO and was a district superintendent twice in Cuba. He was director of Colegio Pinson, 1935-38; of

Havana Central School, 1940-46; and of Candler College, 1946-60. He organized Candler University, 1958, which was the first Protestant university in all Latin America. He was a clerical delegate from Cuba to the GENERAL CONFERENCE of The Methodist Church in 1964 and also to the special General Conference of 1966. At present he is serving in Ponce, Puerto Rico.

GARFIELD EVANS

ASUNCION PEREZ

PEREZ, ASUNCION A. (1893-1967), Filipino social worker and first woman cabinet member was born in Gasan, Marinduque, on Aug. 15, 1893. She was educated at the MANILA High School (1915), the University of the PHILIPPINES (B.A. in 1917), the San Francisco Training School, and received honorary degrees from the Philippine Women's University (doctor of laws in human welfare), the Central Philippine University, the University of Wisconsin and the UNIVERSITY OF DENVER (doctor of humanities). She also received the Presidential Merit Award. She was married to Cirilo Perez on Aug. 18, 1918, and they had three children: Ernesto, Rebecca, and Edwin.

Returning from the United States in 1920, she joined the Far Eastern College where she taught until 1924 when she started as a social worker in charge of civilian relief for the American Red Cross (Philippine Chapter). She received her first presidential assignment from Senate President Manuel L. Quezon who sent her to America to make representation with American leaders to convince them not to send Filipino workers back to Manila during the depression. In 1925 she was named the executive secretary of the Associated Charities of Manila (Family Welfare Agency) which was absorbed by the government in 1941 and named the Bureau of Public Welfare. She was made chief of the Public Assistance Office and, after six months, director of public welfare. When World War II ended she was appointed superintendent of the Relief Office for the Greater Manila Area, supervising the rehabilitation of war victims. With the re-establishment of the Philippine Commonwealth in 1945, President Sergio Osmeña designated her as the director of public welfare, a position which she held until 1947. In the following year (1948) President Manuel Roxas appointed her the social welfare administrator where she sat in the president's cabinet, a position she held under four succeeding presidents. Also in 1948, President Elpidio Quirino made her the chairman, with cabinet rank, of the President's Action Committee on Social Amelioration which was entrusted with the physical, social, and economic welfare of the displaced individuals arising from the Hukbalahap activities.

Together with her husband she joined Marking's Guerillas on Oct. 20, 1942, to fight the Japanese invaders of the Philippines. They were captured by the Japanese on Feb. 3, 1944, and incarcerated in Fort Santiago. Her husband was executed by the Japanese and after enduring severe torture she was set free on May 25, 1944.

After her retirement from government service Mrs. Perez continued her social work in various fields. She became president of the Philippine Wesleyan College in Cabanatuan City and served actively in several humanitarian and civic organizations including the Philippine Mental Health Association, Children's Garden (an orphanage), Friendship, Inc., and the Women's Christian Temperance Union.

BYRON W. CLARK

PERFECTION, CHRISTIAN. (See CHRISTIAN PERFECTION.)

E. BENSON PERKINS

PERKINS, ERNEST BENSON (1881-   ), British Methodist minister, was born July 14, 1881 in Leicester, and was educated at Alderman Newton's School there. Accepted for the Wesleyan Methodist ministry in 1903, he served in Jersey for a year before going for theological training to Handsworth College, BIRMINGHAM. He early distinguished himself by his forceful advocacy of social reform, which found wide scope both in his superintendencies of city missions in NOTTINGHAM (1916-20), Birmingham (1925-35), and SHEFFIELD (1935-39), and also in his five years of service as Assistant Secretary to the Temperance and Social Welfare Department (1920-25). In 1939 he was appointed one of the Secretaries for the Department of Chapel Affairs. He retained that office until 1952, a crucial period during which he exercised a very important influence in directing the postwar reconstruction of Methodist property. His indefatigable labors were recognized by his election as President of the METHODIST CONFERENCE in 1948.

Benson Perkins was always active outside as well as within his own church. He was a prominent member of many national organizations, such as the Churches' Committee on Gambling, the National Federal Free Church Council (of which he was elected Moderator in 1954), and the BRITISH COUNCIL OF CHURCHES, of which he was

Vice-President 1952-54. In 1952 he superannuated after almost fifty years in the active ministry, but until 1961 he ably fulfilled his duties as Joint Secretary (with ELMER T. CLARK) of the WORLD METHODIST COUNCIL, to which he had been appointed in 1951. His best known writings include *With Christ in the Bull Ring* [i.e. at Birmingham] (1935), *The Methodist Church Builds Again* (with Albert Hearn, 1946), *Gambling in English Life* (the Beckly Lecture, 1950), *Methodist Preaching-Houses and the Law* (Wesley Historical Society Lecture, 1952), and his autobiography, *So Appointed*, which appeared in 1963. He was awarded an honorary LL.D. by CENTENARY COLLEGE OF LOUISIANA in 1956.

E. B. Perkins, *Autobiography.* 1964.   FRANK BAKER

PERKINS, JOE J. (1874-1960), and **LOIS CRADDOCK PERKINS** (1887-   ), American Methodist churchmen and philanthropists, who have made significant contributions to TEXAS Methodism. Mr. Perkins was born on a farm in Lamar County, Texas, on March 7, 1874. In early life he moved to the cattle raising part of the state, in 1910 reaching Wichita Falls, his home for the remainder of his life. Mrs. Perkins was born in China Springs, Texas, on Feb. 8, 1887. She attended SOUTHWEST UNIVERSITY, and went to Wichita Falls in 1913 as a teacher. She married Mr. Perkins in 1918. Perkins' first business effort was a department store in Decatur, which eventually led to a chain of stores in North Texas. Later he engaged—usually with others—in mining activities, in ranching, in banking, and in the development of oil leases and property. Mr. and Mrs. Perkins' first loyalty, however, was to Methodist causes and projects. They have served their local church in many capacities, he as trustee and steward, she in educational and missions work. Both have been delegates to annual and GENERAL CONFERENCES. They have helped support many civic enterprises and especially youth character-building agencies. They have contributed generously to many Methodist agencies, such as the NORTH TEXAS CONFERENCE pension fund, DALLAS Methodist Hospital, Methodist Children's Home at Waco, ALASKA Methodist Church, Anchorage, WESTERN METHODIST ASSEMBLY at Fayetteville, Ark., Southwestern University, SOUTHERN METHODIST UNIVERSITY, and most of all to PERKINS SCHOOL OF THEOLOGY at Southern Methodist University. The latter gift has amounted to about $12,000,000 including a new plant and an endowment. Giving by Mr. and Mrs. Perkins was always a joint action by husband and wife, and it was a natural outpouring of their concern for the cause involved, and never a mere financial contribution, as evidenced by their giving much of their time as trustee, board and committee member, and chairmen to various causes. Bishop PAUL E. MARTIN, for many years pastor of Mr. and Mrs. Perkins, called Mr. Perkins "the greatest layman I have ever known." Mr. Perkins died on Sept. 15, 1960. Mrs. Perkins has continued the same concern for Methodist enterprises. She has been awarded an honorary L.H.D. by Southwestern University and the LL.D. degree by Southern Methodist University. She was a member of the executive committee of the WORLD METHODIST COUNCIL, 1961-68. Dean JOSEPH D. QUILLIAN, JR., of Perkins School of Theology, has written that Mr. and Mrs. Perkins have given more to Texas Methodism than any other two persons—not simply of their means but also of their spirit. The Perkins heritage of churchmanship and philanthropy continues to the third generation through their daughter Elizabeth (Mrs. Charles N. Prothro), and the Prothro sons and daughter.

Wichita Falls Record News, Sept. 16, 1960.
Fort Worth Star Telegram, Sept. 16, 1960.
Wichita Falls Times, April 28, 1970.   WALTER N. VERNON

PERKINS, WILLIAM CHRISTIE (1868-1955), American lay leader and business executive, was born Sept. 27, 1868 in BALTIMORE, Md.

Starting to work at the age of twelve, Perkins spent his entire life in the hardware business. In 1917 he became associated with the American Chain and Cable Company in PITTSBURGH, where he became a prominent participant in the work of the M.P. Church.

His outstanding service was as President of the Board of Publications of the M.P. Church. He was a delegate to many annual and GENERAL CONFERENCES. In 1943-44 he was President of the Methodist Social Union of the PITTSBURGH ANNUAL CONFERENCE.

In 1947 Perkins retired after thirty years service with American Chain and Cable and moved back to Baltimore, where he died July 28, 1955. He is interred in Woodlawn Cemetery, Baltimore.

Clark: *Who's Who in Methodism*, 1952.   J. H. STRAUGHN

PERKINS SCHOOL OF THEOLOGY, SOUTHERN METHODIST UNIVERSITY, Dallas, Texas, grew out of a desire for a Methodist theological school west of the Mississippi. Ministers serving that region had received their education at SOUTHWESTERN UNIVERSITY, Georgetown, Texas. When Southern Methodist University opened in 1915, as the official university for the church west of the Mississippi, a school of theology was included. In 1945, Mr. and Mrs. J. J. PERKINS made provision for gifts exceeding $10,000,000, and the school moved from its original location to a sixteen-acre tract on the Southern Methodist campus. In 1951, seven new buildings, including the Perkins Chapel, classroom buildings, library, and dormitories, were dedicated. Later another classroom building and dormitory were erected. This stands out as one of the most significant developments in the history of Protestant theological education. The Bridwell Library, given by J. S. Bridwell, is part of the theological campus.

The seminary's degree program includes the B.D., M.R.E. (Religious Education), S.T.M. (Master of Sacred Theology), and M.S.M. (Sacred Music) degrees. The Ph.D. degree is available in cooperation with the university.

JOHN O. GROSS

PERKS, ROBERT WILLIAM (1849-1934), British Methodist, industrialist, and politician, was born on April 24, 1849, at Brentford, London, qualified as a solicitor, and from 1876-1901 was in partnership with HENRY FOWLER. Specializing in railway law, he became associated with a firm which built railways and docks in many parts of the world. From 1892-1910 he was Liberal M.P. for Louth, Lincolnshire, and a firm supporter of Lord Rosebery's liberal imperialism. Perks was originator and, from 1906-8, chairman of a group of 200 Nonconformist M.P.'s in the House of Commons.

From 1902-6 he was chairman of the Metropolitan District Railway. He was created a baronet in 1908. In 1878 he was one of the first group of laymen admitted to the Wesleyan Conference. He was an originator and the senior treasurer of the TWENTIETH-CENTURY FUND. He worked for METHODIST UNION and was the first vice-president of the united Methodist Church in 1932. He died on Nov. 30, 1934, in London.

H. M. RATTENBURY

PERRILL, FRED MAXSON (1882-1946), American missionary to INDIA and noted editor there, was born at Mentor,

PERKINS SCHOOL OF THEOLOGY, DALLAS, TEXAS

Kan., Dec. 4, 1882. He attended KANSAS WESLEYAN and BAKER UNIVERSITIES, graduating from Baker in 1903, and from GARRETT BIBLICAL INSTITUTE in 1906. He came to India in October 1906, and joined the BENGAL CONFERENCE. He was ordained deacon and elder before his twenty-fourth birthday. His appointments were missionary to Muzaffarpur; missionary in Arrah; superintendent of Ballia District, superintendent of Cawnpore (now Kanpur) District; and editor of *The Indian Witness*. He married Mary Voigt (sister of Bishop EDWIN VOIGT) May 5, 1911.

From his earliest years in India Perrill was a popular correspondent for *The Indian Witness* and for the church papers in America. He became editor of *The Indian Witness* in 1929, and continued for seventeen years at the helm of that official organ of Methodism in Southern Asia. He suffered a heat stroke on a railway journey in North India while en route to the mountains after exhausting labor, and died at the Clara Swain Hospital in BAREILLY, June 12, 1946. He is buried in Bareilly. His only son, Charles Voigt Perrill was then, and for some years before and after, superintendent of that renowned institution, and is now superintendent of the Creighton-Freeman Hospital in VRINDABAN which he is relocating between Vrindaban and Mattrura.

J. WASKOM PICKETT

PERRONET, CHARLES, EDWARD, and **VINCENT,** were British Evangelicals. **Vincent Perronet** (1693-1785), vicar of Shoreham, Kent, first met JOHN WESLEY in 1746. Both John and CHARLES WESLEY visited him and preached in his church. He became their friend and adviser. He attended the Conference of 1747, and it was to him that John Wesley addressed *A Plain Account of the People Called Methodists.* Not for nothing was Perronet called "the archbishop of Methodism."

Edward Perronet (1721-1792), the hymn writer ("All Hail the Power of Jesus' Name"), was the eldest son of Vincent Perronet, and itinerated for Wesley until he joined the COUNTESS OF HUNTINGDON and her connection. His open antipathy to the Established Church led him finally to become the pastor of a dissenting congregation in Canterbury. It was at Edward Perronet's house that Charles Wesley met MRS. VAZEILLE, who had aroused the interest of his brother John. When Perronet told Charles that his brother was thinking of marrying the lady, Charles "refused his company to the chapel and retired to mourn with my faithful Sally."

John Wesley had great admiration for Edward Perronet and wanted to hear him preach, but Perronet seemed determined that he should not. Seeing Perronet in his congregation one day, Wesley calmly announced that the former would preach the next morning. Perronet, feeling he could not go against Wesley's wishes, appeared in the pulpit at the proper time, announced the hymn, led in prayer, and then explained that he had not been asked to preach and had not consented to do so, but would deliver at that service the finest sermon that had ever been preached. He then read the Sermon on the Mount with no word of comment, after which he brought the service to a close!

Edward Perronet and his brother Charles, both Methodist preachers, favored separation of their group from the CHURCH OF ENGLAND when that question was under discussion. This movement was opposed by the Wesleys.

Perronet had written *The Mitre, a Sacred Poem,* in 1757, sharply criticizing the Church. At Wesley's protest, he discontinued selling it, but continued giving copies of it away. This caused a break between Perronet and the Wesleys, and also led to an estrangement between Perronet and the Countess of Huntingdon, whose chaplain he had been at Canterbury. He then served an independent dissenting church in that city until his death, Jan. 2, 1792.

Charles Perronet (1723-1776), the second son of Vincent Perronet, also itinerated in Methodism until in 1754 his advocacy of separation from the Church incurred Wesley's displeasure.

A. SKEVINGTON WOOD

MRS. J. W. PERRY

PERRY, CLARA TUCKER (1870-1964), American missionary leader, was born at NASHVILLE, Tenn., on Jan. 4, 1870, and was educated at the Nashville College for Young Ladies. On Oct. 19, 1893, she was married to JOHN WILEY PERRY, member of the HOLSTON CONFERENCE and secretary of the Home Department of the Board of MISSIONS of the M. E. Church, South.

Mrs. Perry became a leader in the Woman's Missionary Society of her Church. In 1907 she was elected Vice President of the Woman's Board of Home Missions and in 1910 became a Vice President of the Woman's Missionary Council, which was formed by the union of the Home and Foreign Boards. In 1931 she was elected President of the Council and remained in this office until the unification of the three large branches of American Methodism in 1939.

She was President of the Holston Conference Home and Foreign Missionary Societies in 1911 and again in 1920. She was the only woman member of the Commission on Methodist Union, a delegate to the GENERAL CONFERENCE in 1922, the Uniting Conference in 1939, and the first General Conference of The Methodist Church after unification in 1940. Her other Church activities included membership in the ECUMENICAL METHODIST COUNCIL, delegate to the Foreign Missions Conference, president of the Board of Managers of the Woman's Christian College in CHINA and EWHA COLLEGE in KOREA, member of the board of Ginling College in China and of the executive committee of the FEDERAL COUNCIL OF CHURCHES of Christ in America.

After the unification of American Methodism, Mrs. Perry was for four years a member of the Board of Missions and Church Extension, serving on the Woman's Division and also the Division of Foreign Missions.

Mrs. Perry died on Aug. 4, 1964, at Chattanooga, Tenn., at the age of ninety-four. She was survived by one son, Wiley Perry, and one daughter, Katherine Perry.

ELMER T. CLARK

J. W. PERRY

PERRY, JOHN WILEY (1866-1954), American minister and missionary administrator, was born in Scott County, Va., on Feb. 8, 1866. He studied in the public schools and in a small private school called Shoemaker College. He served one year as a supply preacher on the Erwin Mission in 1886 and then went to VANDERBILT UNIVERSITY, from which he graduated in 1891.

In 1892 he joined the HOLSTON CONFERENCE of the M. E. Church, South, and was sent to West Radford for two years. His other appointments in order were Centenary Church in KNOXVILLE, Highland Park in CHATTANOOGA, Sweetwater, Abingdon, Church Street Church in Knoxville, Morristown, presiding elder of the Chattanooga District, Conference Missionary Secretary, presiding elder on the Morristown District and the Knoxville District.

In 1922 he was elected by the General Conference as secretary of the Home Division of the Board of MISSIONS, in which office he remained for twelve years. During this period he rendered important service in connection with PAINE COLLEGE, an institution for Negroes at Augusta, Ga. When he relinquished the position of missionary secretary in a reorganization of the Board of Missions he returned to the Holston Conference and served four years as presiding elder of the Chattanooga District and five years as pastor at Abingdon, Va. He retired in 1942.

As a leader of his Conference Perry was ten times elected a member of the GENERAL CONFERENCE, including the Uniting Conference in 1939 and the first General Conference of The Methodist Church in 1940.

On Oct. 19, 1893, he married Clara Tucker of Nashville, Tenn., who later became the president of the Woman's Missionary Council. They had two sons and one daughter.

Perry died at Chattanooga, Tenn., on March 5, 1954, and was buried in Emory, Va.

Journal of the Holston Conference, 1954. ELMER T. CLARK

PERSECUTION OF METHODISTS IN ENGLAND. It was inevitable that Methodism should be persecuted because it was opposed to so many aspects of eighteenth-century religious and social life. Dishonest tradesmen found that their livelihood was threatened; the gentry resented criticism by the Methodists and feared revolution; the clergy was enraged by the rebukes of the Methodists and feared a revival of "enthusiasm."

The Mobs. Usually "King Mob" was the tool used by Methodism's opponents. Mobs were easily hired, made drunk, and then directed to plunder Methodist homes, destroy meeting houses, and wound Methodist men, women, and children. The preachers bore the worst of the mobs' attacks and some of them were actually martyred by the rabble.

The Law. Many magistrates were furiously hostile toward Methodism and were prepared to lead the mobs. Methodists were frequently denied legal redress by the courts, and many of them were sent to prison or pressed into the armed forces. The law, far from repressing persecution, became another tool of the persecutors, although Methodism was never officially suppressed as a matter of government policy.

Literary Persecution. Methodism was satirized in pamphlets, while clergymen thundered anti-Methodist sermons from their pulpits and published their attacks as broad sheets. The press, the stage, and the pulpit became weapons in the hands of the persecutors.

Later Persecutions. This general pattern of persecution persisted after Methodism became divided. In the nineteenth century, many of the social and religious conditions against which Methodism had first protested still remained, and both the *Bible Christians* and the *Primitive Methodists* were persecuted, especially in the villages.

D. D. WILSON

PERSEVERANCE, FINAL. The doctrine of the Final Perseverance of the Saints, often popularly expressed in the maxim, "Once saved, always saved," is a natural part of the strict Calvinist system, and was a subject of controversy in the times of Wesley, and since. Clearly, if Election to salvation is unconditional, if a man once finds himself in a state of salvation he is bound to continue in it to the end of his life, and to arrive in heaven. He may appear to stumble upon the path of life, but he cannot finally fall. Wesley called this position in question, ". . . The Calvinists hold . . . that a true believer in Christ cannot possibly fall from grace. The Arminians hold, that a true believer may 'make shipwreck of faith and a good conscience;' that he may fall, not only foully, but finally, so as to perish forever." (John Wesley *The Question, 'What is an Arminian?' Answered.* 1770) (See also ARMINIUS.)

In his opposition to Calvinism's syndrome of sovereign election, irresistible grace, and the final perseverance of the elect, we see one of the properly "Arminian" emphases of John Wesley. The position that the elect believer cannot ultimately fall away from his condition of grace was considered an item for *assurance* within Calvin's theology. To John Wesley such a position could only contribute to gross carelessness on the part of the believers and there was such a thing as "falling from grace." Profoundly true though it was, that "God is at work" enabling the believer both to will and to do of His good pleasure, it was equally true that the believer must "work out" his salvation "with fear and trembling."

Indeed, continued Wesley, "a believer need never again come into condemnation," need never "come into a state of doubt, or fear, or darkness. . . ." (*Minutes* for the Conference of 1744, question 10 for Monday, June 25). Nevertheless, "a man may forfeit the free gift of God, either by sins of omission or commission." (*Ibid*, question 11) How important, therefore, for every believer to beware, "lest 'his heart be hardened by the deceitfulness of sin;' . . . lest he should sink lower and lower, till he wholly fall away, till he become as salt that hath lost its savour: for if he thus sin wilfully, after we have received the experimental 'knowledge of the truth, there remaineth no more sacrifice for sins' . . ." (Sermon on the Mount, IV, i, 8, 1747). Wesley contrasted that "heaviness through manifold temptations," which is the common experience of believers with the possible return to the "wilderness" state characterized by the absence of any vital communion with the living God.

John Calvin had based his confidence in the final perseverance of the elect on Scriptural promises; such "assurance," in the case of the individual believer, was Scripturally-derived. Wesley felt the testimony of Scripture, however, included circumstances wherein true believers could finally fall; "that one who is holy or righteous in the judgment of God himself may nevertheless so fall from God as to perish everlastingly." (*Serious Thoughts upon the Perseverance of the Saints;* standard reference, for instance, was to Ezekiel 18:24) "Assurance," for Wesley, was a much more empirical phenomenon—associated with the believer's present confidence in the gift of justifying grace, wherein the love of God was manifest to the believer through the inward workings of the Holy Spirit. (*Romans* 5:5)

For the comfort which Calvin saw in the doctrine of final perseverance (for the elect believer!), Wesley emphasized rather the assurance of salvation through the witness of the spirit (see ASSURANCE), and the exhortation to "go on unto perfection." In the Wesleyan theology of grace, the anticipation of entire sanctification (itself a gift of grace) served as a corrective to the believer's "falling away." Augmenting such expectancy, of course, was the prime importance of continuing in the way of the "means of grace," continuing to implement the workings of Divine grace through the disciplines of worship, Bible study, prayer, sacrificial service.

Perseverance in grace, therefore, was conditioned upon the believer's persevering! Although the believer continued dependent upon atoning, redeeming grace throughout the course of his salvation, nevertheless—for Wesley—such grace (as seen through Scripture) must be considered finally resistible, the Spirit could finally be quenched. Thus the believer is "saved from the fear, though not from the possibility, of falling away from the grace of God." (Sermon I. ii. 4.)

LELAND SCOTT

PERSSON, JOSEF A. (1888-1964), Swedish missionary to AFRICA, was born in Stockholm, Oct. 14, 1888. His mother had herself first felt the call to the mission field. A poor widow, she brought up her son and was glad to send him away when God's call came to him. As a young man of eighteen he was one of the first two missionaries sent out by the Sweden Annual Conference in 1907. His first place was a primitive printing plant in Cambini, Inhambane, MOZAMBIQUE. Persson picked up the foreign language from the lips of his native helpers. So he learned to know the native languages, Chopi, Tonga, and Tswa. He gave the natives a literature, beginning with a primer and a grammar, a Tswa-English dictionary, Bible studies, and several other books. He crowned his work with a translation of the Bible into Tswa, which he thoroughly revised before his death. He settled down in Johannesburg, Union of SOUTH AFRICA, acting as pastor and district superintendent, and during the Second World War he served also as bishop's deputy. He developed the printing office in Johannesburg, the Central Mission Press in Cleveland, Transvaal, to be an important help for several missions in South Africa. He was active for more than fifty years, and crowds of friends, black and white, followed him when he was laid to rest in a jungle grave in October, 1964. Two of his sons are active in the work of the church.

Minutes of the Sweden Annual Conference, 1965.
Josef A. Persson, *Vardagsliv och högtidsstunder i Inhambane.* Stockholm, 1933.
Svenska Folkrörelser. Stockholm, 1937.   MANSFIELD HURTIG

PERTH, Australia, is the capital of AUSTRALIA's largest state, Western Australia, whose population has not quite reached a million people. Because of the discovery of vast quantities of minerals in Western Australia in recent years, the potential of Perth would appear to know no limits.

Kingswood College is a University College for men within the University of Western Australia. It was opened in 1963 by the Prime Minister of Australia, Sir Robert Gordon Menzies. It occupies a site of over five acres in a commanding position on Stirling Highway, Nedlands, a southern suburb of Perth. It has accommodation for one hundred and thirty-three students, including tutors. It is planned to increase this number to 250. Men of all denominations and faiths are admitted. All faculties are represented in the College and it is also the training center for men studying for the Methodist ministry.

The governing body is a council of nineteen, with the President and Secretary of the Methodist Conference ex-officio members. Two members are elected from the University Senate, two from the Academic Staff of the University, and the remainder, ministers and laymen, are elected annually by the Methodist Conference. General supervision over studies is exercised by a staff of about twelve tutors. A restricted number of nonresidential students is permitted to join the tutorial classes.

The Theological Institution established in 1912, now named the Barclay Theological Hall, is located on the college grounds. The College was built by gifts from Methodist people throughout the State, from business houses and companies, and by substantial contributions from the Commonwealth and State Governments.

Methodist Ladies College, Claremont, a southern suburb of Perth, is situated on Stirling Highway on thirteen acres of land overlooking Freshwater Bay, a lovely reach of the Swan River. It was founded in 1907 and now has an enrolment of six hundred and seventy-three fee-paying scholars. In addition to preparing girls to enter the University, the school offers courses in Commercial Subjects and in Domestic Arts.

In 1951 a day school for girls in South Perth, St. Anne's, was purchased by the Council and developed as a branch of M.L.C. It has become a flourishing school under its principal, Mrs. M. B. Way. In 1964 its name was changed from Methodist Ladies College, South Perth, to "Penrhos" but as yet it has not achieved its independence. Both schools are controlled by the one Council, a rather large group appointed annually by the Methodist Conference.

The Principal of the College is Walter Shepherd, and the Chaplain is D. McCaskill. Two deaconesses have been appointed by the Church to work at the schools.

Wesley College in South Perth is a day and boarding school for boys situated on twenty-one acres of land on the south-eastern bank of the Swan River. The foundation stone was laid on Nov. 11, 1922 by the Premier of Western Australia, Sir James Mitchell and the school opened in February 1923 with J. F. Ward as its first Headmaster. The school grew so rapidly that the College Council soon realized that it could not meet the pressing needs of the school. In 1926 the Annual Conference of the Methodist Church of Western Australia considered the problem

WESLEY CHURCH, PERTH, AUSTRALIA

and requested the Trustees of the Wesley Church Central Methodist Mission, Perth, a group of very able and influential men, controlling considerable financial resources, to take over the financial responsibility and management of the College. The Trustees then became the College Council. In 1965 steps were taken to release the Trustees from sole responsibility and the College Council was enlarged.

The School provides tuition from Kindergarten to the School Leaving Certificate Standard (Martriculation) and prepares boys to enter the professions, the commercial and business life of the city and the university. It has an enrolment of six hundred boys of whom one hundred and fifty-eight are boarders.

The Headmaster is Clive Hamer, and the Chaplain is B. R. Angus.

The Theological Institution, Western Australia, was established by the Methodist Conference of 1912, with Brian Wibberley as principal. Accommodation was provided in the buildings of the Perth Central Methodist Mission. Local preachers and Christian workers were permitted to attend classes with the theological students. The first World War disrupted this work and it was not recommenced until 1923, when J. W. Grove was appointed principal. Wesley College became the training center in 1927 and theological students were prepared for the Diploma of the Melbourne College of Divinity. The growing need for ministers with University training eventually led the Western Australia Conference to send its matriculated theologs to the Theological Halls in the Eastern States. This policy was continued until Kingswood College was founded in 1963 within the University of Western Australia. The Theological Institution, now named the Barclay Theological Hall, was located within the College, with Robert Maddox as director. Here students are able to take degrees in secular disciplines as well as in Divinity. The cost of the maintenance of the Hall is met by a levy upon the whole of the Church in Western Australia. The Presbyterian and Congregational Churches in this State are cooperative and are contributing to it both teaching staff and students.

AUSTRALIAN EDITORIAL COMMITTEE

PERU is a republic on the west coast of South America, extending 1,400 miles from ECUADOR to CHILE. The capital is LIMA. The area is 514,059 square miles, and the population (1969) is estimated at 13,172,000. The north-south ranges of the Andes Mountains, having deep valleys between, separate the country into long strips of highly diversified characteristics, with only slight communications to bind them together. The inhabitants of the varied sectors are as diverse as the terrain. Ten peaks of the Peruvian Andes reach at least 20,000 feet, the highest, Huascaran, attaining 22,205 feet. The Cordillera of the Andes marks the continental divide; all rivers rising in the slopes east of that line flow into the Amazon to the Atlantic.

The Inca empire and culture dominated the west coast of South America from the late eleventh century to the Spanish conquest under Francisco Pizarro in the 1530's. Cuzco, in southern Peru, was the capital. Roads were built along the valleys between the Cordilleras and today long stretches of the Inter-American Highway follow these roads. The ruins of forgotten Machu Picchu, an Inca city seventy-five miles north of Cuzco, were discovered by Hiram Bingham in 1911.

Needing a capital close to the sea, Pizarro founded Lima in 1535. Revolt and bloodshed continued for decades, Pizarro himself being assassinated in Lima. Jose de San Martin proclaimed Peruvian independence from SPAIN in 1820. Bolivar and Sucre followed up San Martin's victory and completed the ouster of Spanish forces in January 1826. Frequent revolutions marked the next hundred years. A new constitution was adopted in 1933 and amended in 1939. Some advanced social legislation has been enacted, and elementary and higher education are emphasized.

Peru is one of the "Indian republics," and an estimated forty-six percent of the people are of pure Indian blood. Another forty-three percent are Mestizo (mixed), and eleven percent of European extraction. Indigenous religions continue among some Indian groups. The Roman Catholic Church claims 89.6 percent of the population and Protestant groups only 0.7 percent.

Methodism was taken to Peru in the late 1870's by WILLIAM TAYLOR, later bishop, of the M.E. Church. He projected what he hoped would be a series of self-supporting schools and churches in Callao, Lima, and other cities. He actually established workers in Iquique, then in Peru but soon lost to Chile in the War of the Pacific (1879-83). From 1886 to 1890, FRANCISCO G. PENZOTTI, agent of the AMERICAN BIBLE SOCIETY and Methodist preacher, made several visits to Peru from ARGENTINA. In July 1890, he was arrested for preaching in Callao, suffering imprisonment for eight months before the international repercussions over the question of liberty of worship forced his release.

In 1891 THOMAS B. WOOD, Methodist leader in Argentina and URUGUAY, arrived at Lima as superintendent of the newly projected Western District of the South America Conference. Prior to this no organized Evangelical work had been established by any Protestant church. With the aid of his daughter, Elsie Wood, several schools were organized that developed into outstanding institutions. The leading Methodist schools are the CALLAO High School (Colegio America), Lima High School (Colegio Maria Alvarado), Victoria School (Escuela America de la Victoria), and Colegio Andino at HUANCAYO. These with Methodist parochial schools have a total enrollment of 3,500. The Institute for Christian Workers in Lima trains pastors and social workers.

Evangelistic work remained very difficult for many years, with frequent persecution. In 1945 the churches had barely 400 members. Then rapid progress started as the preachers moved out from the chief centers. Approach was made to the Campa Indians of the eastern jungle area near Satipo on the Rio Negro. The church membership has grown greatly of late years and the Peru Provisional Annual Conference became a part of the Pacific Area.

To meet a need for qualified Evangelicals as teachers in the schools, which form a substantial part of the mission program, The Methodist Church established the Panamericana Normal School in Lima in 1961—finally winning government approval one week before its first commencement in 1964. Also new in the educational field is a student hostel related to historic San Marcos University.

In recent years the church in Peru has shown a decided interest in social work, largely as a result of the ambitious program of the WOMAN'S DIVISION OF CHRISTIAN SERVICE in the La Florida Social Center, founded by the late Martha Vanderberg and serving residents of a very poor section of Lima. As the barriadas, or squatters' settlements, have become a serious social problem (containing more than a million residents in 1965), the church has extended social services and evangelistic work to them. Best known is the Methodist Social Center at Pedregal, a settlement built near a former garbage dump, where vocational training, adult classes, club work, a kindergarten, and religious services are offered. There is work in several other barriadas, much of it carried on by lay volunteers from the older established Methodist churches in Lima.

Methodists in Peru are becoming known increasingly for their social witness. The 1965 annual conference adopted a "Manifesto to the Nation"—a document without precedent for any church in the country. The manifesto proclaimed the rightful interest of the church in the social and economical organization of the world. The Church believes that all change, renewal or effective revolution ought to spring from man regenerated by the power of God.

The Peruvian Methodist Church. As has been the case with other conferences of The United Methodist Church in South America, the Conference in Peru, pursuant to proper legislation adopted by the General Conference of 1968, decided to become autonomous and so organized itself as a church, Iglesia Metodista Peruana, on Jan. 19, 1970, in Lima. The Rev. Dr. WENCESLAO BAHAMONDE, fifty-four years of age, was elected its first bishop. The Church reports 2,753 members (full and preparatory) in twenty-eight organized churches. There are 2,830 Sunday school pupils. The administration of work in Peru has been through two districts—a District de la Costa, which centers about Lima; and a District Centro with its principal center at Huancayo in the Andes.

In the Peruvian Methodist Church, almost full autonomy has been given to the districts of the conference as these districts have a certain appointing power, especially of those ministers and laymen who are not under the supervision of the whole church. There is, however, a general committee in charge of all the ministers in full connection, and these are assigned in a block to the districts and these make their appointments within the geographical limits. The bishop or president in this newly organized church has by no means the full appointive power.

W. C. Barclay, *History of Missions*. 1957.
General Minutes, 1965.
Barbara H. Lewis, *Methodist Overseas Missions*. 1960.
W. Stanley Rycroft and Myrtle M. Clemmer, *A Factual Study of Latin America*. New York: Commission on Ecumenical Mission and Relations, United Presbyterian Church U.S.A., 1963.
World Methodist Council, *Handbook of Information*.
                                          EDWIN H. MAYNARD
                                          ARTHUR BRUCE MOSS

PETERS, BENJAMIN (1844-1898), early Indian minister of the SOUTH INDIA CONFERENCE of the M.E. CHURCH, was born in Madras, was converted from Hinduism in 1874, and was ordained as an elder in 1882. His mother tongue was Tamil, but he learned English so well that he sometimes ministered to English-language congregations. His theological studies were conducted under the guidance of CLARK P. HARD.

While serving as pastor of the Tamil congregation in BANGALORE, Peters zealously preached on the streets. This led to counterpreaching on the streets by the Moslems, and to fear that violence might result. A magistrate issued an order against street preaching. Peters felt obliged in conscience to disobey. He changed his preaching place. The police drove his would-be hearers away. He was arrested and imprisoned, but on appeal was released on bail. The judicial commissioner decided that there could be no sweeping prohibition of Gospel preaching in public places, and he was released. Peters promptly resumed street preaching and suffered no further interference by the courts.

His stand and its outcome made an important contribution to the freedom "to profess, to practice and to propagate" the religion of one's choice which is now guaranteed by the Constitution of the Republic of India. He died in Madras May 10, 1898.

J. N. Hollister, *Southern Asia*. 1956.   J. Waskom Pickett

PETERS, WILLIAM (1855-1915), a minister of the M.E. Church in India, was born Jan. 1, 1855. He was said to be of mixed British and Indian ancestry but was proudly Indian in his feelings. His family lived in the Budaun District before and during the Sepoy uprising and narrowly escaped assassination. He was a fervent evangelist, an able administrator, and a saintly character. In time He was appointed as the first Indian superintendent of the Budaun District, which during his superintendency was the most rapidly growing district in the North India Conference. He died Sept. 28, 1915.

J. Waskom Pickett

PETERSBURG, VIRGINIA, U.S.A., is an old historic town situated on the Appomattox River about twenty-two miles south of Richmond. Methodism was introduced into Petersburg by Robert Williams in February 1773. It is said that Gresset Davis and Nathaniel Young, who were merchants of Petersburg, met Robert Williams in Norfolk where they happened to be and invited him to come and preach for them. He came and preached in an old theatre fitted up for the use of all denominations. As it turned out, however, the infant church was severely persecuted. At one time when Hope Hull and John Easter were holding a meeting, a mob burst in upon them with lighted squibs and fire crackers. Then another band brought up a fire engine and played a stream of water into the house until every light was put out. This account states that "Soon the place was involved in darkness, save where a bursting firecracker gave a momentary gleam, and the whole congregation was routed and driven from the place."

The preachers, however, continued to preach as occasion furnished and a society was begun and Petersburg was included in the Brunswick circuit. The old theatre was abandoned and a church was built on Harrison Street; but during the Revolutionary War, it was occupied by the soldiers, first as a barracks, then as a hospital, and was finally destroyed by fire. After the loss of the church, several people opened their private dwellings for the preaching. Soon after the close of the war, a second Methodist church was built, started by Mr. Davis, who headed the subscription list with fifty pounds. This church is described as "very small and unique of its kind, and showing any amount of props, beams, and girders."

In 1792, Petersburg first appears in the annals of the M. E. Church, John Lindsay being appointed pastor and an annual conference was held there on Nov. 15, 1793.

The first General Conference of the M. E. Church, South, was held in Petersburg in 1846, an epochal conference in every way. The delegates assembled at the Union Street Church, though this had just recently been sold to a Negro congregation. The Washington Street Church, which continues to stand in stately grandeur in Petersburg, had almost been completed but was not then ready for general occupancy. That church since that date has been noteworthy in the Virginia Conference.

The original cornerstone of the old Union Street Church is still preserved in the Washington Street Church today,

Washington Street Church,
Petersburg, Virginia

bearing the inscription: "Cornerstone of Union Street M. E. Church laid by Blandford Lodge of the Masons, October 26, 1818." Also, Washington Street preserves the pulpit brought from Union Street Church—one from which Bishop Asbury is said to have preached.

An A.M.E. Zion Church, erected in 1879, with a present membership of something over 350 and known as the Oak Street A.M.E. Zion Church, is also found in Petersburg.

The present churches of the city are: Blandford, with a membership of 415; High Street, 585; Memorial Methodist, 953; St. Mark's 713; Trinity, 633; and Washington Street, 833.

Many distinguished pastors of the Virginia Conference have served Petersburg through the years, and it has long been the head of a district. The Petersburg District presently reports 24,700 members.

E. S. Bucke, *History of American Methodism*. 1964.
M. Simpson, *Cyclopaedia*. 1881.
W. W. Sweet, *Virginia*. 1955.   N. B. H.

PETTY, JOHN (1807-68), British Methodist, was born near Skipton, Yorkshire, on Dec. 27, 1807. He united with the Primitive Methodist society in 1823, and six months later began to preach, serving as a hired local preacher in the Keighley Circuit. He entered the itinerant ministry in 1826 and commenced in South Wales, covering large tracts of country. He was appointed Connexional Editor in 1851. He was the first governor of the Jubilee School (Elmfield College), York, in 1862, becoming the first connectional theological tutor for candidates for the ministry. In addition to being a sound administrator, he was also a historian, and in 1864 published his *History of the Primitive Methodist Connexion* (revised edition, 1884). A volume of his sermons was published in 1851. He died April 22, 1868.

John T. Wilkinson

PEW RENTAL is an expedient for raising funds for a church by renting pews to individuals or families for their sole use and the use of their guests. Never popular in Methodism as a whole, the custom of renting pews did however prove acceptable in some sections of Methodism, particularly New England, in spite of the admonitions in the *Discipline* against it.

In 1784 the answer to Question 74 in the *Discipline* read, "Let all our Chapels be built plain and decent . . ." to which was added in 1820, "and with free seats." Several other paragraphs were added to this section of the *Discipline*, one of which read, "As it is contrary to our economy to build houses with pews to sell or rent, it shall be the duty of the several annual conferences to use their influence to prevent houses from being so built in the future; and as far as possible to make those houses free which have already been built with pews."

These provisions were evidently not universally acceptable, for in 1852 the *Discipline* added, "wherever practicable" to the provision of 1820 so that the whole line read, "and with free seats, wherever practicable." Evidently the Methodists were finding that pew rents could be a lucrative source of income.

Bishop MATTHEW SIMPSON, in his *Cyclopaedia,* said that in New England, "free churches are almost unknown," and there are extant today actual contracts for pew rentals of Methodist churches in New England. Simpson closed his article by saying, "At present the churches throughout the Middle States, and throughout the East and South generally, have free seats, except a few in the larger cities. In New England, NEW YORK, Northern Ohio, and MICHIGAN a large proportion of the churches are pewed."

The provision about pew rentals remained in the M. E. *Discipline* until 1928. Today all seats in Methodist churches everywhere are free.

Disciplines, ME.
M. Simpson, *Cyclopaedia.* 1880.   FREDERICK E. MASER

PFEIFFER, HENRY (1857-1939), and **ANNIE MERNER PFEIFFER** (1860-1946). Henry Pfeiffer was born at Lewiston, Pa., March 3, 1857, son of Henry and Barbara (Kluftinger) Pfeiffer. He was reared in Cedar Falls, Iowa, where he received his early education in the public schools. After attending NORTH CENTRAL COLLEGE in ILLINOIS, he secured employment as a clerk in a retail drug store in Cedar Falls and later on became the owner. In 1891 he moved to ST. LOUIS, Mo., and entered the wholesale drug business. Ten years later he founded the Pfeiffer Chemical Company. In 1908 Pfeiffer expanded his business by purchasing control of William R. Warner and Company, Inc., of PHILADELPHIA, highly regarded manufacturers, wholesalers and retailers of NEW YORK CITY.

Parallel with Pfeiffer's success in business was his interest in philanthropies, particularly those related to the M.E. Church, of which he was a lifelong member. This interest was aided by Mrs. Pfeiffer (born Annie Merner in New Hamburg, Ontario, Canada, on Sept. 23, 1860), to whom he was wed on March 7, 1882. Mrs. Pfeiffer, from the beginning, took an active role in the WOMAN'S HOME MISSIONARY SOCIETY of the M.E. Church. Her interest in homes for children and the aged, and particularly in educational institutions at home and abroad, was shared by her husband. Their philanthropies amounted to more than forty million dollars to colleges alone. While Mr. Pfeiffer carried on a business that rapidly expanded across the country and into many foreign countries, Mrs. Pfeiffer was serving on numerous boards of trustees of Methodist colleges and other institutions of the church. Both were the recipients of many honorary degrees and, in 1935, a junior college near Charlotte, N. C., of which Mrs. Pfeiffer was a trustee, changed its name to PFEIFFER COLLEGE in recognition and appreciation for their benefactions. Mr. Pfeiffer died in his eighty-third year on April 13, 1939, and Mrs. Pfeiffer passed away in her eighty-fifth year on Jan. 8, 1946, but the monuments to their names and benefactions will long remain to bless generations yet to come.

PFEIFFER COLLEGE, Misenheimer, North Carolina, was established by Emily Pruden as the Emily Pruden School, near Lenoir, N. C., in 1885. In 1903 Miss Pruden deeded the property to the WOMAN'S HOME MISSIONARY SOCIETY, and the name was changed to Ebenezer Mitchell Industrial Home and School. In 1910 it was moved to Misenheimer, where it operated as a high school until 1928, when two years of college work were added. In 1935 the name was changed to Pfeiffer Junior College, honoring Mr. and Mrs. HENRY PFEIFFER of New York, whose generous gifts made possible five buildings. It became a senior college in 1954, and since then its growth has been phenomenal both in resources and enrollments.

In 1961 the WESTERN NORTH CAROLINA CONFERENCE of The Methodist Church voted to sponsor the college and to extend financial support in a cooperative arrangement with the Woman's Division of Christian Service. Pfeiffer grants the B.A. degree. The governing board has thirty-six members, elected by the Western North Carolina Conference.

JOHN O. GROSS

PFRIMMER, JOHN GEORGE (1762-1825), pioneer American United Brethren preacher, was born in Alsace, France. He was a surgeon in the French navy, who at the age of twenty-eight emigrated to America where he settled in Berks County, Pa.

There he came under the influence of PHILIP WILLIAM OTTERBEIN and became a preacher in 1790.

After preaching in eastern and western PENNSYLVANIA he moved to Harrison County, Ind., in 1808, eight years after the territory had been opened to settlers. He became a member of the Indiana district of the MIAMI CONFERENCE, CHURCH OF THE UNITED BRETHREN IN CHRIST, and later served as superintendent, then secretary, of that annual conference, as well as secretary of the GENERAL CONFERENCE of 1825.

He was appointed an Associate Judge of the state by Governor (later President) William Henry Harrison, and served effectively for two years.

Pfrimmer played an active part in establishing the United Brethren Church in Indiana. He organized a church which bore his name, Pfrimmer's Chapel, which was the first United Brethren Church built west of OHIO. He sensed the need for the religious instruction of children and organized the first Sunday school in the denomination in 1820. He was simultaneously a physician, jurist, and a musician as well as a good soldier of Jesus Christ.

Pfrimmer died Sept. 5, 1825 and is buried near Corydon, Ind.

D. Berger, *History of UB.* 1897.
A. W. Drury, *History of the UB.* 1924.
C. H. Keller, *A History of the Allegheny Conference of the Church of the United Brethren in Christ.* Youngwood, Pa.: All State Printers, 1943.
John Wilson Owen, *A Short History of the United Brethren Church.* Dayton: Otterbein Press, 1944.
John H. Ness, Jr., article in *Builders,* Oct. 31, 1965.
A. BYRON FULTON

PHELAN, MACUM (1874-1950), American minister and author, was born in Trenton, Tenn., Feb. 22, 1874. As a youth he came to TEXAS, and soon entered the State University at AUSTIN, where he received the M.A. degree in

1903. For a short time he taught in the public school system. Reaching a decision to enter the ministry, he was received into the NORTHWEST TEXAS CONFERENCE on Nov. 16, 1905, and was active from that time until his retirement. Starting on the Colorado Circuit he was, at different times, assigned to appointments including the presiding eldership of the Vernon District. Transferring to CALIFORNIA, he was assigned to the Sacramento District. On his return to Texas he was for several years editorial assistant on the *Southwestern Christian Advocate* (later the *Texas Christian Advocate*). He returned to the pastorate, serving Haslett as his last appointment, retiring from that charge in 1937. He established a home in Handley, Texas, where he spent his declining years.

He was married Nov. 9, 1905, to Mrs. Bonita Brennard, and to them were born six children.

An outstanding contribution of Macum Phelan was his two-volume set of *The History of Methodism in Texas*, covering the years 1817 through 1899. In the preface to that publication he stated: "All of the old files of the *Texas Christian Advocate* now in existence have been examined page by page, and almost item for item, and these have been drawn upon to a very considerable extent."

He also wrote sermons and addresses. While trying to complete the second volume of his book on Texas Methodism, he developed an eye infection which made it impossible for him to read the final proof of his manuscript.

Representatives of the five Texas Annual Conferences of the M. E. Church, South, met in Dallas, Dec. 5, 1933, and elected a committee to make plans for the 1936 Centennial Celebration of Texas Methodism. Phelan was a valuable member of that committee.

He died Aug. 4, 1950, and was buried in Handley, Texas.

Journal of the Central Texas Conference, 1951.
O. W. Nail, *Southwest Texas Conference*. 1958.
————, *Texas Methodism*. 1961.
Texas Christian Advocates.   MRS. JOHN H. WARNICK

PHILADELPHIA, PENNSYLVANIA, U.S.A. (1970 population 1,927,863). The first Methodist to preach in Philadelphia was GEORGE WHITEFIELD. He arrived in 1739. Two of his converts, EDWARD EVANS and JAMES EMERSON, soon began meeting informally with several other like minded persons. Through Charles von Wrangle, a missionary to the Swedes in Philadelphia, they heard of JOHN WESLEY and British Methodism. Von Wrangle recommended to one of their number, James Hood, that they give a warm welcome to any of Wesley's preachers who might visit Philadelphia. In 1767 Captain THOMAS WEBB, a British Methodist local preacher, arrived in Philadelphia and was enthusiastically greeted by the Philadelphia Methodists. He organized them into "The Religious Society of Protestants called Methodists." There were seven members in the new Society meeting in a sail loft near a drawbridge on Dock Creek (now Dock Street) at Front Street.

Through Webb's leadership and preaching the Society grew rapidly, and in 1769 when the Methodist preachers, JOSEPH PILMORE and RICHARD BOARDMAN, arrived from England they found a Society of 100 persons desiring to be in connection with John Wesley. Pilmore remained in Philadelphia as pastor of the growing group, and Boardman travelled to NEW YORK. They subsequently exchanged appointments about every four months.

By this time, also, the Philadelphia Methodists had moved from their Dock Creek meeting place to a former pot house (a kind of tavern where beer was sold at a penny a pot) at number Eight Loxley Court. Prayer meetings were held on the first floor, and preaching services were conducted from a balcony outside the second story window where the preachers addressed the congregations gathered in the courtyard below. The arrangement, however, was unsatisfactory, and in 1769 the Methodists began to look for larger quarters.

A splinter group from the local German Reformed Church had built the shell of a huge building at what is now Fourth and New Streets. They borrowed a large sum of money, but were unable either to complete the building or to pay off the indebtedness, and their trustees were put into the debtor's jail. The Assembly then auctioned off the building to pay the debt, and it was purchased by a mentally retarded youth for 700 pounds. His father decried the bargain, but he refused to sign an affidavit that his boy was not mentally responsible. Hearing that the Methodists were looking for a building he sold it to them for 650 pounds. On Nov. 24, 1769 the Society moved into the unfinished building which had neither windows nor doors and only a rough dirt floor.

ROBERT WILLIAMS came to the New World with a license from Wesley to preach occasionally under the direction of the regular preachers. His ship had been driven southward by storms, and he landed at NORFOLK. He preached in Norfolk for a short time, and then came to Philadelphia, the Methodist Society there paying his way. By 1769 he had gone to New York and was there to greet Richard Boardman.

In 1770 JOHN KING arrived from England but not having proper credentials from John Wesley, was refused a local preacher's license by Pilmore. King preached a sermon in "Potter's Field" (now Washington Square) and so impressed the Methodists who heard him that Pilmore permitted him to give a trial sermon at St. George's and subsequently licensed him.

In 1771 FRANCIS ASBURY and RICHARD WRIGHT arrived. Asbury preached his first sermon in America from St. George's pulpit. In fact, all of Wesley's itinerants with few exceptions preached their first sermons in the new world in St. George's. In Philadelphia also Asbury formed the acquaintance of Mr. Roberdeau who afterwards, as General Roberdeau, introduced Bishops COKE and Asbury to General Washington when they visited him in Mt. Vernon in 1785 to discuss slavery.

In 1773 THOMAS RANKIN arrived from Europe, having been appointed general superintendent of the work in America. He held the first American Methodist Conference in St. George's July 14—16, 1773. Ten preachers were present, possibly eleven, if we accept WILLIAM WATTERS' inference that he also was present. At this Conference 180 members were reported in the Society in Philadelphia and a few surrounding appointments. The second and third Conferences of American Methodism were also held in Philadelphia in 1774 and 1775. In the former year the membership in Philadelphia was 204, and in 1775, 190.

Notwithstanding its plain and unfinished condition, St. George's was frequented by many able men. Among these was JOHN ADAMS who noted in his diary in 1774 that he had listened to Captain Webb with high appreciation of his eloquence. St. George's still stands and historians consider it the oldest existing Methodist meeting house in America, and the world's oldest Methodist church edifice in continuous service.

The Revolutionary War seriously affected the work in Philadelphia. When the British occupied the city they used St. George's with its dirt floor as a cavalry school. The Methodists protested strongly, holding their meetings now in the home of Mary Thorne, the first woman class leader of American Methodism. In the year 1776, therefore, the Conference met in BALTIMORE, and in 1781 and 1782 the name of Philadelphia disappeared from the Minutes, although statistics were given for the State of Pennsylvania. In 1783 Philadelphia reappeared, reporting 119 members, and in 1784, the war having closed, Philadelphia reported 470 members.

In 1789 JOHN DICKINS was appointed Book Steward and was also placed in charge of the Philadelphia appointment. Philadelphia continued as the center of the publishing business until 1804 when it was moved to New York. In 1790 RICHARD WHATCOAT was appointed to Philadelphia and Dickins became "Superintendent of the Printing and Book Business." In that year, also, a small brick building called "Ebenezer," in Second Street below Catherine, was opened by the Methodists. It was the first house of worship erected by the Methodists in Philadelphia, and was not built until twenty years after the purchase of St. George's. It is no longer standing.

In 1794 on Sixth Street above Lombard a place of worship was erected for the colored people. It acquired a large membership, and was under the discipline of the M.E. Church until 1816. It then became independent and was organized with other colored churches into the "AFRICAN METHODIST EPISCOPAL CHURCH." RICHARD ALLEN, who had been licensed to preach by St. George's in 1784, and had been ordained as a deacon by Asbury in 1799, became the first bishop of the new denomination.

In 1796 in Brown Street a second place of worship was opened for the colored Methodists called "ZOAR." This Society still remains in connection with the Methodist Church.

In 1793 and also in 1794, 1796, 1797 and 1798 a yellow fever plague swept Philadelphia, and in 1798 John Dickins died of the epidemic. He was one of the few clergymen who remained at his post in the city during the plagues. He was succeeded in the book business by EZEKIEL COOPER.

In 1800 a number of families, leaving St. George's, purchased a part of Whitefield's Academy near Fourth and Arch Streets, and in 1802 founded "Union Methodist Church." The original building is gone but the successor congregation is now Union Methodist Church, Brookline, Pa., a suburb of Philadelphia. The subsequent growth of the Methodist Church in Philadelphia has been steady though not rapid.

Philadelphia has been the seat of an Episcopal Residence for over 100 years. In 1863 Bishop MATTHEW SIMPSON, a close friend of Abraham Lincoln, settled in Philadelphia at the request of interested laymen who presented him with a house. He was followed by Bishop CYRUS D. FOSS, Bishop CHARLES MCCABE and Bishop LUTHER B. WILSON respectively. Bishop JOSEPH F. BERRY, who served in Philadelphia from 1912 to 1928, was the first bishop appointed to Philadelphia under the area system. Bishop ERNEST G. RICHARDSON served from 1928 to 1944 and Bishop FRED PIERCE CORSON from 1944 to 1968.

The Home for the Aged in Bala just outside of Philadelphia, was built in 1898 and 1899 largely through the benefactions of a Colonel Joseph M. Bennett; the Deaconess Home was erected on Vine Street in 1893 through the further munificence of Colonel Bennett (it has since moved to West Philadelphia); the Methodist Hospital was built on South Broad Street in 1888 to 1892 through the generosity of Dr. Scott Steward and today is an enlarged and completely modernized institution; the Orphanage (now the Children's Home) was begun in 1887 through the help of the ever generous Colonel Bennett; the Historical Society of the Conference was founded in 1867 and today houses its 10,000 volume library, manuscripts and relics at St. George's.

In 1914 a site was purchased by the Tract Society of the Conference and in 1916 the Wesley Building was completed at 17th and Arch Streets and still houses the Methodist Book Store. The Book Store is not connected with the Publishing House but is a venture of the Tract Society of the PHILADELPHIA CONFERENCE. The profits are used for the Preachers' Aid Society. It has been in existence on various sites since 1864. Prior to this date an independent Methodist Book Store was in existence.

In 1922 part of the Wesley Building was purchased as a headquarters by the Home MISSION BOARD of the General Church (now the Division of National Missions) and subsequently the bishop's office and many of the Philadelphia Conference agencies were established here. In 1967 the building was purchased by the Philadelphia Annual Conference when it was sold by the Division of National Missions. The Division moved to New York.

In 1949 the General Board of EVANGELISM of The Methodist Church conducted in Philadelphia a pilot project for a United Preaching and Visitation Evangelistic Campaign; 240 churches joined in the venture, resulting in 9,000 accessions to the church.

In 1953 a World Convocation on Evangelism, celebrating the 250th Anniversary of the birth of John Wesley, was held in Philadelphia. Laymen and preachers from all over the world gathered in Convention Hall for meetings each day and evening for three days. On Sunday morning, June 28, many of the visiting preachers occupied pulpits in metropolitan Philadelphia. In the afternoon despite heavy rains, 35,000 people gathered in Franklin Field for a mass meeting. One thousand individuals were personally united to the church that afternoon under the leadership of Resident Bishop Corson.

The present strength of Methodism in Philadelphia includes ninety-five Methodist charges. There are ten former E.U.B. charges, thirty A.M.E. charges, seven A.M.E. ZION charges, and one WESLEYAN METHODIST CHURCH.

The Academy. This structure, originally located on the west side of Fourth Street below Arch in Philadelphia, was built as a tabernacle or preaching house for George Whitefield and other itinerant preachers who desired a hearing in the city. Begun in 1740, it was immediately used by Whitefield who preached to a large congregation when the walls were only partially erected. It was completed by 1744 and five years later Benjamin Franklin and Whitefield cooperated in procuring it for about 777 pounds to house an Academy, the first in Philadelphia. It was chartered under the name, "The Academy and Charity School." A section was still reserved, however, as a preaching center for itinerants. In 1753 it became the

"College" of Philadelphia and was incorporated as "The College, Academy and Charitable School." A year later Dr. WILLIAM SMITH became the first Provost. The school had an excellent reputation and in 1753 sixty-five boys were enrolled from near-by colonies. In 1779 it was converted into "The University of the State of Pennsylvania," out of which the present University of Pennsylvania has grown. In 1800 a group of about fifty dissidents left OLD ST. GEORGE'S METHODIST CHURCH and rented the north end of the Academy building in which to worship. In 1801 they purchased the south end, worshipping there for about thirty years. They organized Union M.E. Church which is still in existence, being located today in Brookline, a suburb of Philadelphia.

In 1802 The University of the State of Pennsylvania was moved from The Academy Building on Fourth Street to the President's House on the west side of Ninth Street, south of Market. The House had been built as a residence for the Presidents of the United States, but it had never been used for this purpose. It was purchased by the University for $41,650, about one half of its original cost. In 1874 the University was moved to its present location in West Philadelphia. Near the men's dormitories of the University there is today a bronze statue of Whitefield commemorating his part in the founding of the University.

The Academy building itself is no longer in existence, the site now being partly used as a parking lot for a nearby restaurant. At one time a bronze tablet could be seen on a wall near this site: "The Whitefield Meeting House erected in 1740 for George Whitefield and for a Charity School subsequently used until 1812 by the School, Academy, College and University of Pennsylvania successively." The University had moved in 1802.

Albert W. Cliffe in his book, *The Glory of Our Methodist Heritage*, adds this other word: It was "the first symbol of Religious Freedom in America as it was used expressly for the use of any preacher of any religious persuasion who might desire to say something to the people of Philadelphia."

Arch Street Church is the stately Italian white marble Gothic cathedral at the very center of the city of "Brotherly Love." The Romanesque Masonic Temple is next door and the French Renaissance City Hall is situated just beyond that with the famous Billy Penn statue on top of it.

This is the hub of the industrial, business, historical and social life of the city. Arch Street Church is the oldest building in this complex, dating from 1862. New highrise business offices and apartments contrast the new with the old—but the self-giving life of the church is ever expanding.

A full program for the college or graduate students in center city is maintained. An open chapel daily invites hundreds to pray away from the noise of the city. The social services rendered reach into every part of the city and government as well as to the many strangers who need a helping hand.

Weekly Sunday evening services and mid-week Hour of Power are still popular here serving a downtown transient people. The business community enjoys the outstanding preachers presented each noonday during Lent. One of the largest WESLEYAN SERVICE GUILDS in the East meets here, as well as a weekly noonday Business Men's spiritual luncheon.

The visitors at the Sunday morning service include every state in the Union and almost all the countries of

ARCH STREET CHURCH,
PHILADELPHIA, PENNSYLVANIA

the world during the course of a year. The church has the privilege of entertaining these transients and getting further acquainted at a Coffee Hour following the service.

The Bishop of the area considers this his family church. The ashes of Bishop Ernest G. Richardson are interred under the marble pulpit which has presented almost every great preacher of each generation to the city of Philadelphia. General Grant attended service regularly with Bishop Simpson and his family.

Besides being the Conference seat where the Philadelphia Annual Conference meeting is held, Arch Street is always employing new approaches to serve its great Center City populace, using as its motto "'Where Cross the Crowded Ways' men find their way by the Cross."

Bethel A.M.E. Church. The "Mother Church" of the A.M.E. denomination began in 1786 in St. George's M.E. Church, as a Prayer Band of forty-two Negroes under the leadership of Richard Allen. Following an incident involving racial discrimination in 1787, Allen and several other Negro members withdrew from St. George's and organized a "Free African Society." By 1794 an African meeting house (Bethel) had been built, dedicated by Francis Asbury and opened for worship with Allen as preacher. Between 1794 and 1816 the Philadelphia M.E. Conference sought to reclaim Bethel. The matter was settled when Bethel was granted legal independence from St. George's in 1816.

About 1840, the 1794 structure was replaced by a second brick church which remained until 1889, when the present structure was built on the original site purchased by Allen. Seven pastors have been elected to the episcopacy from the pastorate of Bethel: Richard Allen

(1816), MORRIS BROWN (1828), WILLIS NAZERY (1852), CORNELIUS T. SHAFFER (1900), LEVI J. COPPIN (1900), WILLIAM H. HEARD (1908) and JOHN D. BRIGHT (1964).

Methodist Home for the Aged was founded in the spring of 1865 in the era often referred to as "Victorian," and indelibly marks the year when Bishop Matthew Simpson and his wife used their talents and substance to bring the Home into reality. Having acquired an "old" mansion with a tract of land in 1867, located on Lehigh Avenue, between 12th and 13th Streets, it was opened as a residence in 1868 with twenty-five guests. This project, a pioneer in the concern and care for aging Philadelphia, grew so rapidly that within a very brief period a new building was erected, this time providing accommodations for 100 persons. This was the largest Home for Aging in Philadelphia at the time.

Finally, again through the intense interest of the Simpsons, in 1898 a new site was acquired in what is considered today Urban Philadelphia. This overlooks the famed Fairmount Park, and there now are impressive buildings with ample accommodations for 240 people. Through the years the Home has enjoyed a reputation for excellent management under the direction of a Board of Managers and the Trustees. In addition, the Home is supervised by a professional staff training in geriatrics care. In recent years a modern infirmary has been opened with a capacity of seventy-two beds. During the 101st Anniversary the new Barnes facilities building was dedicated.

The present value of the property is $3,038,300 and that of the contents and equipment is $335,616. Currently there is no indebtedness. The operating budget today exceeds $500,000.

Methodist Home for Children, The, serves as a home for approximately sixty-five school-aged children from Philadelphia and surrounding areas. It was founded as an orphanage in 1879 by Mrs. Ellen Simpson, wife of Bishop Matthew Simpson. In the years that followed it became evident that the children needing a Home most desperately were no longer orphans, but rather dependent and neglected children from broken, disturbed, and deprived families. The Home gradually shifted its program to meet that need, and the name was subsequently changed from Methodist Episcopal Orphanage to Methodist Home for Children. The Home today is more professionally staffed than was possible in the past, and includes two social workers, a part-time psychologist, and a part-time psychiatrist, in order to deal with the complex problems of individual children coming out of abnormal backgrounds.

Other concepts have changed through the years. Whereas originally the children of the Home participated in an internal religious and educational program, having school and church on the grounds, the emphasis is now based upon the hope of preparing the children to be a part of normal society rather than isolated from it. Now most of the children attend public schools, with supplementary tutoring at the Home, while religious education is given both within the Home and in local Methodist churches.

In 1966 two modern cottages were completed, each housing fourteen children and two houseparents in single and double rooms. These replaced the old two and three story dormitory-type buildings which had served since the early 1900's. Two other modern cottages are presently in process of being built. The beautiful old stone Administration Building, containing the chapel, dining hall, recreation room, infirmary, and offices, has been renovated. The aim of the Home is to give deprived children the personal, professional care necessary for them to develop into happy and useful maturity.

Old Ebenezer was the first church built by the Methodists in Philadelphia, St. George's having been purchased from another denomination. Erected in 1790, it is mentioned frequently in Bishop Asbury's *Journal*. On one occasion a crowd gathered around the church while Asbury was preaching. They began "fighting, swearing, threatening." Asbury wrote, "This is a wicked, horribly wicked city; and if the people do not reform, I think they will be let loose on one another. . . ." (Vol. 1, pp. 729, 730)

The church was moved three times in its history, and the successor church today is Ebenezer, Havertown at Eagle and Steel Roads outside of Philadelphia. The original building located on 2nd St. near Queen is no longer in existence.

St. George's Church (see under ST. GEORGE'S).

Zoar Church (African Zoar Methodist Episcopal) founded in 1794, represents the historic continuity of the Afro-American within the traditional stream of The Methodist Church. She represents the remnant of Negroes who in the early days of the Republic, although disliking the patterns of participation available to them, refused to separate themselves from the fold of the "JOHN WESLEY Methodists." The eighteen men and three women used an abandoned butcher shop as their first place of public worship at Brown and Fourth Streets. Later a lot was purchased, the first edifice erected and dedicated by Bishop FRANCIS ASBURY and JOHN DICKINS, Aug. 4, 1796. This was Methodism's third structure built in Philadelphia.

Zoar was not included in appointments separately under St. George's until 1811. She became a separate station under the Covenant of Assumption in April, 1835, and was listed in 1836 as having 450 members. Perry Tilghman, lay preacher, was the first Negro pastor-in-charge from 1835 to 1844.

The Zoar Church received its charter from the Commonwealth of PENNSYLVANIA on June 14, 1837. The congregation moved from Brown and Fourth Streets to the present site, 1204-08 Melon Street, in 1883.

The first Convention of Colored Local Preachers and Laymen met at Zoar, Aug. 23-27, 1852, and the second convention on June 28, 1855. The first Conference of Colored Local Preachers met on August 5 and 6, 1857, under the leadership of Bishop LEVI SCOTT, and by the authority of the 1856 GENERAL CONFERENCE. Among the nineteen local preachers who attended were James Davis, and David Tilghman, local elders; and Richard Crawford from Zoar. The third and sixth conferences were also held at Zoar, Aug. 10, 1859 and Aug. 7 and 8, 1862, respectively. This series of conferences (1857-1863) became the immediate forerunner of the DELAWARE ANNUAL CONFERENCE of the M.E. Church instituted by the General Conference of 1864 on recommendation of the "Committee on the State of the Work Among the People of Color."

At the General Conference of 1868, James Davis, charter member of the Delaware Conference and a son of Zoar, was the first Negro ever to be seated as a General Conference delegate.

Among the deaconesses commissioned early in this century was Shelly Jane Gale of Zoar who was consecrated by Bishop EDWARD G. ANDREWS, March 18, 1904.

TINDLEY TEMPLE, PHILADELPHIA, PENNSYLVANIA

Existing churches founded by Zoar are: Tindley Temple (John Wesley, 1837); Janes Memorial (1872); St. Thomas, Frankford (1872); Haven Memorial (1878); St. John's, Spring Lake, N. J. (1885); and Mt. Zion (1915).

Richard Allen, *Life Experience*. 1833.
F. Asbury, *Journal and Letters*. 1958.
A. W. Cliffe, *Our Methodist Heritage*. 1957.
William Colbert, "Journal," ms. St. George's Church.
William Douglass, *Annals of the First African Church in the United States of America*. Philadelphia: King and Baird, 1862.
M. Simpson, *Cyclopaedia*. 1878.
A. Stevens, *History of the M. E. Church,* 1864-67.
F. H. Tees, *Methodist Origins*. 1948.
Carter G. Woodson, *The History of the Negro Church*. Washington, D. C.: Associated Publishers, 1921.

FREDERICK E. MASER
JAMES M. HANEY
GRANT S. SHOCKLEY
ROBERT L. CURRY
H. DARREL STONE
JOSHUA E. LICORISH

PHILADELPHIA CONFERENCE (ME). The first three conferences of Methodist preachers in America were conducted by THOMAS RANKIN in Old ST. GEORGE'S CHURCH, PHILADELPHIA, in 1773, 1774, and 1775. These and indeed all of the conferences prior to the organization of the M.E. Church in 1784 were gatherings of all the Methodist preachers in the land, and each meeting was called, "Some conversations between the Preachers in Connection with Rev. Mr. Wesley." Except in 1779 there was only one such conference each year.

After the organization of the church in 1784, the meetings of the preachers over which Bishop ASBURY presided were called "annual conferences." From 1785 to 1787 inclusive, apparently the preachers in Philadelphia and vicinity traveled to the annual conferences which Asbury held in Baltimore or elsewhere. Then on Sept. 22, 1788 Asbury convened a conference in Philadelphia, and thereafter the Philadelphia Conference met annually. Thus it is proper to date the Philadelphia Conference from 1788.

In 1796 the GENERAL CONFERENCE designated six annual conferences with boundaries, and the Philadelphia Conference was one of the six. At the time it embraced NEW YORK west of the Hudson River, PENNSYLVANIA east of the Susquehanna River, NEW JERSEY, DELAWARE, and the remainder of the Peninsula. (See PENNSYLVANIA for beginnings of Methodism in the state.) The boundaries of the conference were altered a number of times as the years passed and eventually about a dozen conferences in whole or in part were carved from the territory of the Philadelphia Conference.

Through the decades the Philadelphia Conference was a strong and influential body. In 1808 when the denomination had about 152,000 members, some 36,000 of them were in the Philadelphia Conference. Thirty-two of the 129 preachers eligible to sit in the 1808 General Conference were members of the Philadelphia Conference. Ten members of the conference have been elevated to the episcopacy: GEORGE H. BICKLEY, CHARLES W. BURNS, JOHN EMORY, EDMUND S. JANES, W. VERNON MIDDLETON, THOMAS B. NEELY, ROBERT R. ROBERTS, LEVI SCOTT, HENRY W. WARREN, and ISAAC W. WILEY. Bickley and Neely were born in Philadelphia.

The conference supports the Methodist Hospital in Philadelphia, a Children's Home at Bala, and Homes for the Aged at Bala and Cornwall. Three camps are maintained—Innabah, Pocono Plateau, and Carson-Simpson Farm. While there are no Methodist colleges within the bounds of the conference, it cooperates with the BALTIMORE CONFERENCE in supporting DICKINSON COLLEGE at Carlisle, Pa. The office of the bishop of the Philadelphia Area, is at 1701 Arch Street, Philadelphia.

In 1952 the PUERTO RICO Provisional Annual Conference was added to the Philadelphia Area, and since that time the churches in the area have greatly aided the growing Puerto Rico work. The conference gave strong support to the World Convocation on EVANGELISM which was held in Philadelphia in 1953, capitalizing on the two hundred fiftieth anniversary of JOHN WESLEY's birth.

In more recent years the territory of the Philadelphia Conference has been southeastern Pennsylvania only. In 1968 the conference reported 394 ministers, 340 pastoral charges, 141,333 members, and property valued at $113,-314,138.

The Philadelphia Conference merged with portions of the EASTERN and CENTRAL PENNSYLVANIA CONFERENCES (former E.U.B.) on Jan. 1, 1970, to form the Eastern Pennsylvania Conference.

F. Asbury, *Journal and Letters*. 1958.
General Minutes, ME, TMC.
Minutes of the Philadelphia Conference.
Francis H. Tees, *History of Old St. George's Church, including Sketch of Philadelphia Conference*. Germantown, Pa.: Paramore Print Shop, 1934.   FREDERICK E. MASER

PHILADELPHIA METHODIST, THE, was a magazine published twice a month by the Tract Society of the PHILADELPHIA CONFERENCE from the year 1879 to 1916. It contained some news of the general church, but it was more of a local news sheet for the benefit of the friends and members of the churches of the Philadelphia Conference. Growing out of the *Monthly Messenger* of the Tract Society, it was an ambitious undertaking of eight newspaper-size pages of which the Corresponding Secretary of the Tract Society, J. B. McCullough, was the Editor. In 1885 McCullough became full time Editor of the *Philadelphia Methodist,* another person assuming the position of Corresponding Secretary of the Tract Society. The paper reached its largest size and subscription list when in 1894 it was increased to sixteen pages. It continued over twenty more years, changing its name toward the end of its life to the *Methodist Times*. Interest in the paper slowly waned, however, and in 1916 the Tract Society reported to the Conference, "financial returns [do] not warrant the continuance of the *Methodist Times*." The report added, "we rejoice in the beautiful spirit exhibited by the *Times* management" in sending to the New York *Christian Advocate* its subscription list.

Minutes of the Philadelphia Conference. FREDERICK E. MASER

PHILANDER SMITH COLLEGE, LITTLE ROCK, Arkansas, was established as Walden Seminary in 1877 and chartered in 1883 as Philander Smith College, in recognition of gifts from the Smith family of Oak Park, Illinois. The college is one of the institutions founded in the South for the education of Negroes by the FREEDMEN'S AID SOCIETY of the M.E. Church. Under the leadership of Bishop M. L. HARRIS, who served as president for twenty-four years, the college was accredited and its resources

greatly expanded. Degrees granted are the B.A., B.S. and B.S. in Home Economics. The governing board consists of twenty-eight members elected by the board. Ownership of the college and its holdings is vested with the General Board of Education of The United Methodist Church.

JOHN O. GROSS

PHILIPPINES, REPUBLIC OF THE, is the largest island group of the Malay Archipelago, discovered in 1521 by Magellan, conquered in 1565 by the Spaniards, and for 333 years a part of the Spanish overseas possessions. The islands were ceded to the United States in 1899 in the treaty after the Spanish-American War. On July 4, 1946 the independent Republic of the Philippines was formally recognized. The islands are 1,150 miles from north to south and 682 miles from east to west, with a total area of 115,707 square miles lying entirely within the tropics. The estimated population in 1970 was 37,158,000. The people are chiefly of the Malay race. Approximately one-third of the population speaks English and one-third speaks Tagalog, the national language since 1946. Tagalog, Spanish and English are the official languages for government and commerce.

Church and State are separate by constitution and there is freedom of worship and of conscience except to the degree that social and indirect political pressures are exerted by the dominant church. About 82 percent of the population is Roman Catholic. Aglipayans number 2,000,-000; Muslims, 791,000; Protestants, 500,000. For almost four centuries following Magellan's discovery of the archipelago he named the Philippine Islands, SPAIN dominated the political life of the people with a heavy hand, and Catholic missionaries—and later Catholic priests—dominated the religious life. People and taxes were for Spain's wealth; any religious group other than Roman Catholic was forbidden to carry on its religious services.

And then, suddenly, Dewey's defeat of the Spanish fleet in May 1898 changed the whole political, religious, social and economic situation in the Philippines. American rule and then self-rule (the latter on July 4, 1946) came quickly. Religious liberty was immediately proclaimed and practiced. Three months after Spain's dominance ended, the first Protestant service was held in the Islands —by Chaplain George Stull, a minister of the M.E. Church who arrived with the occupying forces. Though the service was primarily for the military, many Filipinos —freed from the old Spanish-Catholic prohibitions— joined the soldiers in worship.

In March 1899, Bishop JAMES M. THOBURN, Methodist missionary bishop for INDIA and elsewhere in Southern Asia, arrived in MANILA with letters from the Missionary Society in America appointing him to begin missionary services in the newly-liberated land. A year later, Bishop Thoburn ordained one Nicholas Zamora as the first Filipino Methodist preacher.

During the early years of the new century, a large number of newly-named Methodist missionaries arrived from the United States—and educational and medical services were developed along with a rapidly gathering and training of Methodist congregations both in the cities and in the rural villages. The WOMAN'S FOREIGN MISSIONARY SOCIETY sent several women missionaries to the Philippines. The women organized a boarding school for girls, and this was later to become the Harris Deaconess School. During 1900, also, the activities of the missionaries

NIPA CHURCH, PHILIPPINES

spread from Manila to San Fernando in Pampanga, and to Malolos in Bulacan; and the seven preaching places (with seven Filipino workers and 220 probationers) were organized as "the Philippine Islands District of the Malaysia Conference."

In the first ten years of the century, the Methodist Publishing House opened a press in Manila—publishing *The Philippine Christian Advocate* in English, Spanish, and four Filipino languages; Harris Memorial School was founded; Mary Johnston Hospital was established; Union Theological Seminary was founded by Methodists and Presbyterians; and several notable churches—including Central and Knox Memorial churches—were organized. By 1908 the membership had grown to the point that the work was organized into the Philippine Islands Annual Conference.

Methodist missionaries to the Philippines worked zealously in the development of indigenous leadership—for the church and its institutions. The long restlessness of the Filipinos under Spanish rule, the educational opportunities given by the American school system in the Islands, and the new spirit of freedom and achievement and search for "a place in the sun" all contributed to the churchmen's desire to conduct their own religious services and institutions free from anything that looked like American domination or tutorship. The spirit of nationalism rose high—and affected both the church and secular institutions. Unfortunately, the American Methodist Church, moving as fast as its machinery for organization permitted, was not speedy enough for some of the Methodists of the Philippines, and a considerable group of the latter broke away from the Annual Conference and formed "The Evangelical Methodist Church in the Philippine Islands." This new church was then led by the aforementioned Nicholas Zamora. Friendly and cooperative relationships exist between this new church and the Philippine Islands Central Conference—but the breach has not been healed.

Prior to the organization of the Central Conference (which elects its own bishops and is in many other ways self-governing), the Philippine Islands Annual Conference was divided into the Philippines Annual Conference, and the Northern Philippines Annual Conference; and more recently (1949) the Northwest Philippines Annual Conference was created, and (1955) the Mindanao Provisional Annual Conference was added. The first session of the still newer Middle Philippines Annual Conference met in 1961. This rapid growth in conferences reflects the rapid growth of Methodism in the Islands.

The Church had suffered heavily in men and in edifices of worship during the years of Japanese occupation

ST. JOHN'S CHURCH, QUEZON CITY

in the second World War—but the Christians had neither flinched nor knuckled under, and their post-war recovery was a remarkable chapter of history.

Methodism in the Philippines has been strengthened by the coming in of about fifteen United Methodist missionaries who came from the former E.U.B. Church in America and who had been serving in what was called The United Church of Christ in the Philippines. In 1929, the United Brethren joined the Presbyterian and the Congregationalists to form the United Evangelical Church. That Church was a major party in the formation of the United Church of Christ in the Philippines in 1948, with the Disciples being the other main group. With the Philippine Methodists and the United Brethren in the United Church of Christ in the Philippines, a rather interesting situation came about at the union of The Methodist Church with the E.U.B. Church in May of 1968. The net result has been a great strengthening of The United Methodist Church in the Philippines.

PHILIPPINE WESLEYAN COLLEGE

Outstanding institutions still serving the Filipino people include: Union Theological Seminary, Mary Johnston Hospital and School of Nursing, Harris Memorial School, Philippine Christian College, Methodist Social Center (Manila), Philippine Wesleyan College, Northern Philippines Academy, Thoburn Memorial Academy, Eveland Memorial Academy, Aldersgate Junior College, Asbury Junior College, Aurora Wesleyan High School, Bethel Girls' High School, Greene Academy, Jose L. Valencia Academy, San Mateo Farm Research Center, Methodist Rural Center at Kidapawan, three mobile clinics, and eight student centers.

The Methodist Church in the Philippines has for some time been administered by two Filipino bishops elected by the Central Conference. In 1968 Bishop JOSE L. VALENCIA retired at the Central Conference after twenty years of service in the episcopacy and Bishop BENJAMIN I. GUANSING died in June 1968, after a little more than a year of episcopal service. To replace these two bishops, CORNELIO M. FERRER and PAUL L. GRANADOSIN were elected by the Central Conference of The United Methodist Church of the Philippines in Manila at the Nov. 22-Dec. 1 Conference. They will serve four year terms.

A new conference, the SOUTHWEST PHILIPPINES PROVISIONAL ANNUAL CONFERENCE, was constituted in 1969 by Bishop Cornelio M. Ferrer, presiding. This comprises territory formerly in the Philippines Annual Conference, including many large and small islands between Luzon and Mindanao. Among these are Mindoro, Palawan, Cebu,

and others where Methodist work is either beginning or in the developing stage.

The Philippines Central Conference, as at present constituted, is comprised of the Philippines, the Northwest Philippines, Northern Philippines, Middle Philippines, and Mindanao, with the Southwest Philippines as the new conference. The Central Conference is one of two Church bodies in the Philippines related to United Methodism in America. The other is United Church of Christ in the Philippines. Bishop Ferrer's Episcopal Address at the constituting conference, held in the Knox Memorial Church in Manila, was entitled, "God is giving us a New Church in the Philippines." Latest reports indicate that there are 130,830 full and preparatory members in The United Methodist Church of the Philippines.

E.U.B. Church. As a "Silver Anniversary Memorial" the Board of the Women's Missionary Association of the United Brethren in Christ voted in 1901 to establish a mission in the Philippines. The first missionaries, Sanford B. Kurtz and Edwin S. Eby, arrived there in 1901 and took up their work in three provinces in the northwestern part of Luzon under the direction of a Comity Committee. The new work met with strong opposition from native superstition and Romanism. The arrival of H. W. Widdoes and his wife in 1903 and their successes at San Fernando marked the beginning of better things. By 1908 a mission conference was organized, schools were opened, the Scripture was translated, a weekly religious newspaper was published in Ilocano and, in 1920 Bethany hospital was erected at San Fernando. This mission became the most rapidly growing mission which the denomination supported.

The Japanese invasion of Luzon wrought havoc upon this enterprise in the Philippines. The church in an heroic manner rebuilt her work.

Just two years after the union of the Evangelical Church and the United Brethren in Christ Church, in 1948, the United Church of Christ in the Philippines brought together in union these churches: The Christian Churches (Disciples of Christ); The EVANGELICAL UNITED BRETHREN CHURCH; the Congregational Church (now United Church of Christ); the Presbyterian Church, and the Philippines Methodist Church. Through this union there have come additional ministries in higher education, hospitals, in the newly located Union Theological Seminary, and by means of the organization of the National Council of Churches in the Philippines, new steps in ecumenical endeavors. The E.U.B. Church provided about twenty missionaries in this United Church.

Free Methodist Church. On recommendation of the Philippine Church Federation, Free Methodist missionaries started work in 1949 on Mindanao, the second largest of the Philippine Islands. Main stations are on the Agusan River at Bunawan and Butuan. Missionaries Groesbeck and Schlosser (from China) found few roads. They traveled by coastal steamer, river boat or on foot. New converts became lay-preachers and assisted placing pre-tuned gospel radio sets and hand-wound phonographs with gospel recordings in the interior villages. Churches were organized on a self-support basis. A Bible School opened in 1955 now occupies a fine campus at Butuan. Each student spends one year in field work before graduation. Government high schools are open for Bible instruction. Primitive outlaw tribes have been converted and reconciled with the government. Some translation of Christian literature is done by the students.

A conference was organized in 1963. A new field is being opened on the island of Leyte, where the population is sparse.

The national conference superintendent is a member of the denomination's Board of Administration. There were about 1,000 members in 1969.

R. L. Deats, *Philippines*. 1964.

——————, *Nationalism and Christianity in the Philippines*. Dallas: Southern Methodist University Press, 1967.

Douglas Elwood, *Churches and Sects in the Philippines*. Dumaguete City: Silliman University, 1968.

Barbara H. Lewis, *Methodist Overseas Missions*. 1960.

Mississippi Methodist Advocate, Aug. 9, 1969.   W. W. REID
LOIS MILLER
BYRON S. LAMSON

PHILLIPPI, JOSEPH MARTIN (1869-1926), American editor and United Brethren clergyman, was born March 2, 1869, near London Mills, in Fulton County, Ill., the youngest of ten children of Martin and Caroline (Swartz) Phillippi. His advanced education was taken at Westfield College in Illinois (B.A., 1893), Union Biblical Seminary in Dayton, Ohio, (B.D., 1896), and ILLINOIS WESLEYAN UNIVERSITY (Ph.D., 1904). Westfield College also awarded him M.A. (1896) and D.D. (1906) degrees. In 1896 he was ordained by the ILLINOIS CONFERENCE, CHURCH OF THE UNITED BRETHREN IN CHRIST, and in 1897 he joined the faculty of Westfield College as professor of ancient languages. On Sept. 22, 1899, he married Marie Edna DeWitte, a student at the college.

In 1902 Phillippi moved to Dayton, Ohio, where he became assistant editor of the *Religious Telescope* (1902-1908). He became editor in chief of the denominational paper in 1908 and continued in that position until his death, Sept. 27, 1926. His continuous service as editor for more than twenty-four years was the longest in the paper's history. His writing was characterized by support of worthy civic causes and he often took definite stands on national political issues which had a moral aspect. Between 1909-13 he worked to establish the Otterbein Home, an institution for children and aged people established by the United Brethren Church on the site of a former Shaker colony. He wrote *The Sword Unsheathed, or The Bible for the Masses* (1911) and *Shakerism: or the Romance of a Religion* (1912).

A. W. Drury, *History of the UB*. 1953.

Religious Telescope, Oct. 9, 1926.   DONALD K. GORRELL

PHILLIPS, CHARLES HENRY (1858-1951), eighth bishop of the C.M.E. CHURCH, was born on Jan. 17, 1858, at Milledgeville, Ga. He joined the M.E. Church, South in 1868 and became a member of the C.M.E. Church when it was formed in 1870.

Phillips was licensed to preach in 1878 and was ordained deacon in 1879 and elder in 1883. He received an A.B. and M.A. degrees from Walden University and a M.D. degree from MEHARRY MEDICAL COLLEGE. Between 1883 and 1884, he was president of Jackson High School (later LANE COLLEGE). He served churches in TENNESSEE, WASHINGTON, D. C., and KENTUCKY. In 1894, he was elected editor of *The Christian Index*, where he served until 1902 when he was elected bishop by the General Conference. While bishop, he was noted as a scholarly writer and an eloquent speaker. He organized

the CALIFORNIA CONFERENCE and served as its bishop until his retirement in 1946. Bishop Phillips was designated "Church Historian" when he retired.

Harris and Patterson, *C.M.E. Church*. 1965.

I. Lane, *Autobiography*. 1916.

Religious Leaders of America, 1941-42.   RALPH G. GAY

PHILLIPS, GLENN RANDALL (1894-1970), American bishop, was born May 21, 1894, in Paulding County, Ohio, the son of Samuel Kepler and Iva Evelyn (Randall) Phillips.

He was married on Dec. 31, 1918 to Ruth Estella Clinger. They have one child, a son, Randall Clinger Phillips, a Methodist minister of Los Angeles.

He received his B.A. degree from OHIO WESLEYAN UNIVERSITY in 1915; studied at DREW THEOLOGICAL SEMINARY in 1916, and in 1917 received his S.T.B. at GARRETT BIBLICAL INSTITUTE. He received the D.D. degree from Ohio Wesleyan University, Garrett Biblical Institute, WESTMINSTER COLLEGE and ROCKY MOUNTAIN COLLEGE; the LL.D. from the UNIVERSITY OF SOUTHERN CALIFORNIA and UNIVERSITY OF DENVER.

He was ordained in 1920. During 1919-20 he served as pastor at Moorpark, Calif.; at Santa Maria, 1920-25; at North Hollywood, 1925-29; at First Church, PHOENIX, Ariz., 1929-30; and at First Church, Hollywood, Calif., 1930-48.

He was elected to the episcopacy by the WESTERN JURISDICTIONAL CONFERENCE in 1948 and was assigned to the Denver Area.

Among the memberships he held in various groups were: Board of Lay Activities, 1948; NATIONAL COUNCIL OF CHURCHES OF CHRIST IN AMERICA, 1952; WORLD METHODIST COUNCIL, 1956 and 1961; WORLD COUNCIL OF CHURCHES, Evanston, Ill., 1954; Board of MISSIONS; Board of PUBLICATIONS; Chairman, COMMISSION ON CHURCH UNION, 1960-64; Commission on Jurisdictional Study; Registrar, Board of Ministerial Training, Annual Conference, 1936-48; Chairman, Deaconess Work; Overseas Relief (MCOR); Los Angles Church Federation; Denver Council of Churches; Los Angeles and Hollywood Ministerial Association, (President in 1934).

He contributed articles to a number of religious publications: *A Preaching Mission*, 1949; *Young Men for Tomorrow's Service*, 1951; and *Strength for Service*.

He was a lecturer, School of Religion, University of Southern California, 1940-45 and has served as trustee of the ILIFF SCHOOL OF THEOLOGY, the University of Denver, and CALIFORNIA WESTERN UNIVERSITY.

He made official visits to the Methodist Mission Projects in INDIA in 1950; to the Methodist Mission Projects in Europe and North Africa in 1953; and served as the Council of Bishops' Representative to the CENTRAL JURISDICTIONAL CONFERENCE in 1952.

In 1957 he received a citation for his distinguished leadership in the DENVER Area. He was host bishop to the GENERAL CONFERENCE when it met in Denver in 1960 and ably discharged all duties then devolving upon him.

Bishop Phillips retired in 1964 but was recalled by the COUNCIL OF BISHOPS and put in charge of the PORTLAND (Oregon) Area in 1967 upon the death of Bishop RAYMOND GRANT. He served until 1968, when he again retired and lived in SAN DIEGO until his death Oct. 6, 1970. A man of singular sweetness of spirit, he was held in high and affectionate regard by all who knew him and especially by his compeers in the Council of Bishops.

Who's Who in The Methodist Church, 1966.

MARY FRENCH CALDWELL

PHILLIPS, JOHN MILTON (1820-1889), American book agent and Methodist layman, was born in Montgomery County, Ky., March 26, 1820, the son of William Phillips, a Methodist clergyman. Orphaned at the age of fifteen and left with the responsibility of rearing a younger brother, he began his career with the Methodist BOOK CONCERN in Cincinnati, Ohio, as office boy and factotum. He applied himself diligently to his work and became an accountant and guarded the business affairs of the Concern.

He was elected a lay delegate to the M.E. General Conference in 1872, at which time he was elected junior BOOK AGENT in New York. He was the first layman to be elected a secretary of the General Conference and also the first layman to become Book Agent. He became senior NEW YORK agent in 1879 and remained in that office until his death.

A quiet and unassuming man, he knew the business of publishing and brought to his post thirty years of experience with the Concern. JOHN M. PHILLIPS died at CINCINNATI, Jan. 15, 1889.

The New York *Christian Advocate* said of him, "Little has been done or organized on a large scale in Methodism for a quarter of a century without receiving the benefit of his unobtruded counsels and harmonizing spirit."

E. S. Bucke, *History of American Methodism.* 1964.
National Cyclopedia of American Biography.
M. Simpson, *Cyclopaedia.* 1878.

JESSE A. EARL

PHILLIPS, PETER (1778-1853), British founder of INDEPENDENT METHODISTS, was born at Warrington. Arising from a sense of pastoral neglect, a new movement was started, and the Friar's Green Chapel was built. An encounter with Wesleyan discipline led Phillips to a close study of the New Testament, and he became convinced that the Church should be self-governing and the ministry unpaid and unseparated. Under some Quaker influence for a while, the group was known as Quaker Methodists, and some, including Phillips, adopted the Quaker mode of dress and speech. His preaching secured the establishment of new societies throughout Lancashire and Cheshire, and the new denomination took the name of Independent Methodists in 1808. In 1816 Phillips was elected President of the Conference of the Independent Methodists, a post which he filled eight times. His wife, Hannah Phillips, became a female evangelist alongside her husband, and HUGH BOURNE was influenced by both in his early ventures. Phillips traveled some thirty thousand miles, mostly on foot during this preaching tour.

JOHN T. WILKINSON

PHILLIPS, PHILIP (1834-95), American gospel singer, hymn writer and musical editor of the METHODIST BOOK CONCERN, was born in Chautauqua County, N. Y., on Aug. 13, 1834. He early developed musical talent and at the age of nineteen devoted his whole time to musical science and practice. He was successful in publishing *Early Blossoms,* a collection of hymns; and *Musical*

Leaves, another brochure of the same type which sold over a million copies. During the Civil War, he entered into the work of the Christian Commission, and published *Hymn Songs* for the Soldiers' Orphan Home at Iowa, the proceeds of the sale of this book being used for the Soldiers' Home. In 1866 he became musical editor of the Methodist Book Concern in NEW YORK, and issued the *New Hymn and Tune Book* which was much used in the Methodist Episcopal Church. In 1868 he visited England, and again in 1872. On this latter trip, he proceeded by SAN FRANCISCO on a tour around the world. He held evenings of song in the Sandwich Islands, AUSTRALIA, NEW ZEALAND, Palestine, EGYPT and INDIA, sometimes in cities, sometimes beneath the shade of wide-spreading banyan-trees. Returning eventually to Naples, Rome, Florence, Genoa, and the leading cities of Europe, and coming back to England, he gave 200 nights of song for the SUNDAY SCHOOL UNION. He was one of the first of the "gospel singers," as others of that profession following Phillips subsequently made a career of singing for large church congregations, or in revival services, or in giving personal concerts. "Mr. Phillips has the honor of leading in introducing these evenings of song," according to Bishop SIMPSON, "and is the first who has thus belted the globe." He died in Delaware, Ohio, on June 25, 1895.

Encyclopedia Americana. 1950.
M. Simpson, *Cyclopaedia.* 1878.   N. B. H.

PHOEBUS, WILLIAM (1754-1831), American physician and minister, was born in Somerset County, Md., in August 1754. Little is known of his early life. While quite young, he joined the Methodist Society. He was admitted on trial to the travelling ministry in 1783 and was appointed to the Frederick Circuit. In 1784, he was appointed to East Jersey. He was one of the ones who attended the CHRISTMAS CONFERENCE in BALTIMORE in 1784, at which American Methodism was organized into a church under the leadership of COKE and ASBURY.

In 1785 he was appointed to the West Jersey Circuit; 1787 to Redstone; 1788 to Rockingham; 1789 to Long Island; 1790 to New Rochelle; 1791 to Long Island. In 1792 he located, possibly due to his marriage and to the necessity of making more adequate provision for his family. In 1796-97 he returned to the travelling ministry. However, he located once more in 1798 and took up the practice of medicine in the city of New York. He was readmitted to the NEW YORK CONFERENCE in 1806 and stationed at ALBANY. In 1808 he transferred to CHARLESTON, S. C. He returned to NEW YORK in 1811 and served there through 1812. He was sent to New Rochelle in 1813; to New York in 1814-15; to Albany in 1816; to Jamaica, L. I., in 1817; to Zion and Asbury Churches, New York, in 1818; and served as Conference missionary in 1819-20. In 1821 he was given the supernumerary relation and in 1824 was listed as superannuated. He remained in that relation until his death.

According to his contemporaries, Phoebus was a man of considerable intellectual ability and spiritual awareness. He was an effective physician and minister, as well as something of a linguist and historian. His eccentricities of speech and manner, according to NATHAN BANGS, made him on some occasions the object of ridicule—which he bore with patience and Christian grace.

Phoebus was a participant in some of the most significant events in the history of early American Methodism.

In addition to attending the Christmas Conference of 1784, he was a member of the GENERAL CONFERENCE of 1808 which voted that the Church should hold a delegated General Conference in the future. It is reported that Phoebus made the motion to take up the matter of regulating the General Conference, a matter forcibly brought to the General Conference by a memorial from the New York Conference.

In 1821, Phoebus was elected by the New York Conference of the A.M.E. connection to preside over its first yearly session, in the absence of the invited bishop (probably McKendree) from the M.E. Church. This Conference convened in New York City on June 21, 1821.

Phoebus was the author of two books which are important for the understanding of early American Methodism. The first, *An Essay on the Doctrine and Order of the Evangelical Church in America,* was published in 1817. It has been called "one of the finest summaries of the doctrinal and historical position of early Methodism. . . ." (Bucke, I, 337). The second, *Memoirs of the Rev. Richard Whatcoat,* was published in 1828. The first part of the book contains Whatcoat's incomplete *Journal.* The latter part of the book contains Phoebus' understanding and evaluation of Whatcoat and of his relationship to developing Methodism.

Phoebus died on Nov. 9, 1831. He is buried in Cyprus Hills Cemetery, Brooklyn, N. Y.

E. S. Bucke, *History of American Methodism.* 1964.
Discovery, Quarterly Journal of Methodist Historical Treasures, published by Northeastern Jurisdictional Association of Methodist Historical Societies, Spring 1963.
M. Simpson, *Cyclopaedia.* 1878.
W. B. Sprague, *Annals.* 1861.   C. WESLEY CHRISTMAN, JR.

PHOENIX, ARIZONA, U.S.A., the capital of the state, is surrounded by many tourist attractions, prehistoric villages, cliff dwellings, Papago Park, and the city's South Mountain Park. Phoenix was founded in 1870 and incorporated in 1881. It is the site of Phoenix Junior College, founded in 1920. Arizona State University is located at Tempe, ten miles away.

According to unverified tradition, N. M. Dyer, presiding elder of the NEW MEXICO District of the COLORADO CONFERENCE (ME), preached the first Methodist sermon in ARIZONA at a date and place not known. Alexander Gilmore of the NEWARK CONFERENCE was later appointed Army Chaplain and assigned to Arizona. He preached in the Southern Methodist Church in 1871. Southern Church work had begun, but evidently no regular work was conducted then. No report of Southern work is available from 1872 to 1875.

In 1880 GEORGE F. BOVARD, a probationer in the SOUTHERN CALIFORNIA CONFERENCE, was appointed to Phoenix. He held services in the George Coast home where the First Methodist Church was organized with eleven members in January 1881. Bovard held a revival in another home and forty-nine members were added to the church. Under Bovard a brick church was built, valued at $4,000 in 1883.

In 1870 the Los Angeles Conference (MES) appointed Alexander Groves a missionary to Arizona. He went to Phoenix, held services in the schoolhouse, and organized a Sunday school. M. M. Jackson hauled children from their adobe hut homes to and from Sunday school in a wagon drawn by oxen. Groves held a camp meeting in

the school and in the fall of 1870 organized a class of seven. Later a lot was secured in downtown Phoenix and a frame church was built in 1884. It is the present Central Church.

Other Methodist developments through the years include the establishment of Good Samaritan Hospital in 1912, and the organization of many new Methodist churches. Other branches of Methodism active in Phoenix today are: two C.M.E. Churches, one A.M.E., four Evangelical Methodist, and three Free Methodist. In 1970 there were twenty-two United Methodist churches in the city, with a total membership of 15,550.

Central Church (Mother of Methodism in the Valley), had its beginning in 1870 when two ministers, Alexander Groves and Franklin McKean, were appointed to the Arizona Territory. The Southern California-Arizona Conference *Journal* states that Alexander Groves was the first pastor assigned to the church. Services were held under cottonwood trees or brush ramadas, and sometimes in the homes of ranchers, in theaters and store rooms, until 1875 when the first church structure was erected at the corner of Second Avenue and West Washington.

In 1880 another church (adobe) was built on the southwest corner of Central Avenue and Monroe, on grounds donated by the city. The congregation grew rapidly and by 1902 the adobe church was replaced by an imposing brick structure which served for many years. The congregation was growing rapidly when the Arizona Territory became a state in 1912.

By 1920 it was evident that more room was needed, so property was purchased at the corner of Central and Pierce and another structure was begun. The cornerstone was laid in 1920 and the first service was held on May 4, 1924. Between 1942 and 1949 land was purchased at Central and Palm Lane and plans were initiated for the present two million dollar plant. Under the leadership of Charles Kendall, the present complex of buildings was realized. In 1949 the Sanctuary was begun and the fifth structure of Central Methodist Church was dedicated Sept. 24, 1950. The educational building followed in 1954, then Pioneer Chapel, and the administrative building in 1955. Kendall Hall, the fellowship facility, was consecrated on Jan. 20, 1957. Additional property was acquired in 1963 for future expansion. The membership in 1970 was 2,785. The peak membership was reached in 1961 at 4,654, however members from this church have started or helped to start several new churches in the Valley.

First Church is considered one of the most beautiful Methodist churches in the entire Southwest. Although officially organized with eleven members in January 1881, the first Methodists began meeting as early as 1874 when four of them came together under a brush-arbor in Phoenix and began worshiping regularly.

The townsite of Phoenix had just been established through a patent signed by President ULYSSES S. GRANT. The population was about 300. Business and town lots were selling for $7 to $11 each. In 1875, with prophetic vision, the M.E. Church through its church extension program, bought strategic lots in the heart of town.

The brush-arbor Methodists decided to rent a building for worship services. The selection was an adobe building with dirt floor and dirt roof, but capable of seating 100 people. The first official meeting was held Jan. 16, 1881, when the church organized with eleven members.

Through the years the church has had four sites—

FIRST CHURCH, PHOENIX, ARIZONA

three in downtown Phoenix and the present site, which is about five miles from the center of downtown Phoenix. For fifty-seven years prior to moving to the present site at Central and Missouri Avenues the church was located at Second and Monroe Avenues. As the city moved northward the membership and attendance began to dwindle until it was below 1000.

Ground breaking services for the educational plant, administration offices and Fellowship Hall were held on March 2, 1952. The first service at the new location was held Aug. 31, 1952. On June 30, 1957 ground was broken for the new sanctuary, and the first services were held in it on Christmas Sunday, Dec. 21, 1958.

The membership in 1970 was 3,193, which is the second largest membership in the SOUTHERN CALIFORNIA-ARIZONA CONFERENCE. The church and grounds are valued at $1,200,000.

First Church has a dynamic program for all age groups. It reaches out in service around the world. One college president, GEORGE F. BOVARD, and one bishop, GLENN R. PHILLIPS, have served as its pastors.

General Minutes.
E. D. Jervey, *Southern California and Arizona.* 1960.

JESSE A. EARL
WILSON O. TROXEL

PICKARD, BENJAMIN (1842-1904), British Methodist, was one of those Liberal trade unionists who strengthened the hold of Gladstone on the votes of the working class. Pickard was a Wesleyan LOCAL PREACHER who had started to work in the pit at the age of twelve, and who became general secretary of the Yorkshire Miners' Union in 1881, and the first president of the Miners' Federation in 1888. Outside Parliament he had fought for mines acts, antitruck acts, and the institution of a living wage; as Liberal M.P. for Normanton he pressed for an eight-hour day in the mines, and for the setting up of conciliation boards to settle disputes.

E. R. TAYLOR

PICKARD, HUMPHREY (1813-1890), Canadian minister and educator, was born in Fredericton, June 10, 1813, into a family which stemmed from the pre-Loyalist congregationalist settlement in New Brunswick. His mother was a member of the first Methodist society in Fredericton. He was educated at the WESLEYAN UNIVERSITY, in Connecticut, before returning home to enter his father's business.

Pickard was more interested in the ministry than in business, and in 1835 he sought admission to the Wesleyan ministry. Fortunately he was permitted in 1837 to return to Wesleyan University, from which he graduated in 1839. He was ordained in 1842, stationed in St. John, and appointed editor of *The British North American Wesleyan Methodist Magazine,* a forerunner of *The Wesleyan.*

By this time the new Sackville Academy was taking shape, and those in charge were looking for a principal. After considerable hesitation, the young and scholarly Pickard was offered the place. He was at the academy when it opened January 19, 1843, with a few students. Under his skillful management with the number of students quickly increased, and soon the "Female Branch" was added. By 1862, Pickard had secured the establishment of MOUNT ALLISON. The first class in Arts graduated in 1863, the beginning of a steady and increasing stream of trained people who were to find their way into all parts of our country and to the lands beyond the seas.

In 1869, Pickard decided to leave Mount Allison and return to editorial work. Until 1872 he was editor of *The Wesleyan* and book steward. Subsequently he returned to Sackville, to become Mount Allison's agent and minister of the Sackville Methodist Church. He retired in 1877 and died in Sackville, Feb. 28, 1890.

Apart from his regular duties, Pickard filled many responsible positions in the Methodist Church. The Conference of Eastern British America elected him secretary from 1857 to 1860, co-delegate in 1861, and President in 1862 and 1870. He was often a representative to the British Conference and a member of the second General Conference of the Methodist Church in 1886. Appropriately he was given the doctorate of divinity by Wesleyan University in 1857.

His successor at Mount Allison, David Allison, said:

Nature had endowed him too with vigorous mental powers which within certain ranges had been carefully cultivated. He did not aspire to the reputation of profound or versatile scholarship, but he was a clear thinker, with exceptional aptitudes for the exact sciences, for logic, and for philosophy. As a teacher he excelled in the lucidity of his prelection, in the emphasis with which he presented truth that he deemed important, and in the rare power he possessed of stirring up to intellectual activity the indifferent and the indolent. (*The United Churchman.*)

Elsewhere Allison concluded: "He was on the whole the most influential personal factor in determining the evolution of Methodist history in the Maritime Provinces."

G. H. Cornish, *Cyclopaedia of Methodism in Canada.* 1881.
G. S. French, *Parsons and Politics.* 1962.
T. W. Smith, *Eastern British America.* 1877.
The United Churchman, Jan. 12, 1966.   E. A. BETTS

PICKAVANT, JOHN (1792-1848), was born in Lancashire, England. He was converted to Methodism in 1808.

Initially a local preacher, he was put on trial and sent to Newfoundland in 1814. He was stationed first at Port de Grave, and in 1815 he moved to St. John's, to take charge of the new Methodist chapel, then under erection. In January, 1816, the new chapel was burned, and he went to England to solicit funds for a new one.

Pickavant served in Newfoundland for almost thirty years, and during many of these was chairman of the district and recognized head of the Wesleyan Methodist Church in the colony. He was described as "a master in Israel, gentle and gentlemanly, and in his pulpit an orator at once charming and subduing." His long ministry and his valuable leadership in the district gave inspiration and strength both to members and ministers who were devoted to, and anxious for, the growth of Methodism in Newfoundland.

D. G. Pitt, *Windows of Agates.* St. John's: Gower Street Church, 1966.
T. W. Smith, *Eastern British America.* 1877.
W. Wilson, *Newfoundland and its Missionaries.* Cambridge, Mass.: Dakin & Metcalf, 1866.   N. WINSOR

GEORGE PICKERING

PICKERING, GEORGE (1769-1846), a New England pioneer preacher, was born in Talbot County, Md., in 1769. Converted at eighteen in ST. GEORGE'S CHURCH, PHILADELPHIA, he became a Methodist in the face of opposition. He was admitted to the BALTIMORE CONFERENCE in 1790, and after two years was sent to New England. Over the years he was appointed to BOSTON, Lynn, Lowell, Cambridge, Salem, Marblehead, Newburyport, Gloucester, Roxbury, and other places. Four different times he was appointed presiding elder in Boston, serving a total of eleven years in that capacity. In addition, he was frequently engaged as financial agent for schools and embarrassed churches. On one occasion he made a tour through DELAWARE and MARYLAND collecting money for a chapel in Boston. He was known for tact, enterprise, and success. He had a tenacious memory, a sense of humor, and good judgment. He was a popular preacher and a successful evangelist. It was said that the children and the unlettered as well as the educated comprehended his brief sermons.

A leader in his conference, Pickering represented it at least nine times in the GENERAL CONFERENCE, 1804-32 and 1844. He led the delegation every time except in 1844 when he was the fifth and last member on his delegation. ORANGE SCOTT and others displaced Pickering in the 1836 and 1840 delegations, presumably because they were more vehemently opposed to slavery than Pickering.

In the 1808 General Conference, Pickering had the distinction of being a member of the committee which drafted the plan for a delegated General Conference.

Pickering married Mary Bemis, the daughter of Abraham Bemis, a wealthy and dedicated Methodist layman of WALTHAM, Mass. She inherited her father's estate, and she and her husband lived there the rest of their lives. However, a home in Waltham did not keep Pickering from itinerating as a Methodist preacher. He went where he was sent and visited his family occasionally. His biographer says that in half a century of married life he spent a total of about ten years at home. Pickering never retired, and when he died at Waltham, Dec. 8, 1846, it was claimed that he was the oldest effective Methodist preacher in the world.

M. Simpson, *Cyclopaedia.* 1878.
A. Stevens, *Memorials of Methodism.* 1849.   ALBEA GODBOLD

PICKETT, DEETS ELBERT (1885-1966), American temperance leader and managing editor of *The Clipsheet* and *The Voice,* was born in Dangerfield, Texas on Aug. 29, 1885, the son of Leander and Millie Dorough Pickett.

Pickett came to The Board of TEMPERANCE of the Methodist Church in 1912 as Research Secretary and Managing Editor of *The Clipsheet,* a weekly paper which was sent to all leading newspapers, and *The Voice,* a monthly magazine with a circulation at that time of about 75,000.

He was educated at Louisville Training School and ASBURY COLLEGE, both in KENTUCKY. He attended the Alcohol School of Studies, Yale University in 1943. He married Annie Belle Mingeldorff Oct. 25, 1907, and they had two children.

After his retirement in 1954 he lived near Fredericksburg, Va., until the family moved to SOUTH AFRICA, where Mrs. Pickett and the children presently live. Pickett passed away in September 1966, in Africa.

During his long career as a temperance worker Pickett was Secretary of The Internal Reform Bureau, (1912), and Executive Secretary of the Christian and Social Commission. He studied liquor control in Great Britain and FRANCE in 1919. He represented the government at the 16th International Congress Against Alcoholism in SWITZERLAND, 1921.

Pickett is the author of *Enemies of Youth* and other books, monographs, magazine articles and pamphlets.

So impressed with his ability were many governmental leaders that he was invited more than once to assume prominent White House responsibilities. Declining lucrative positions in the darkest days of the temperance movements, Pickett elected to stay on with the Board of Temperance, sometimes at less than half payment of his meager salary.

The Voice, February 1954.
Who's Who in America, 1953-54.

PICKETT, JARRELL WASKOM (1890-   ), American missionary to INDIA and bishop, was born near Jonesville, Texas, on Feb. 21, 1890, the son of Leander Lycurgus and Ludie (Day) Pickett. He was graduated from ASBURY COLLEGE, B.A., 1907; M.A., in 1908; and a D.D. in 1926. He received the LL.D. from OHIO NORTHERN UNIVERSITY in 1946, and the L.H.D. from OHIO WESLEYAN UNIVERSITY in 1966. He married Ruth Robinson on July 27, 1916. Their children are Elizabeth Day (Mrs. Henry Ankeny Lacy), Miriam Lee (Mrs. William E. Gould), Margaret Joy (Mrs. John Sagan) and Douglas Robinson.

In 1908 and 1909, J. Waskom Pickett was a teacher of Latin and Greek at Vilonia, Ark.; and from 1909-10, associate professor, New Testament Greek, Taylor University (Upland, Ind.). He was admitted on trial, ordained deacon, then elder in the NORTH INDIA CONFERENCE (ME) in 1911; full connection in 1913. He served as pastor in LUCKNOW, India, 1910-14; missionary at ARRAH BIHAR, India, 1917-23; superintendent of the Arrah District, 1918-23. He was editor of the *Temperance Clip-Sheet*, 1917-23; and editor of the *Indian Witness*, 1925-29. He was secretary of the National Christian Council of India from 1930 until 1936. He was elected bishop by the CENTRAL CONFERENCE of SOUTHERN ASIA in 1935-36 and assigned to the Bombay Area, 1936-45; and the DELHI Area, 1945-56, retiring in 1956.

Since retirement, Bishop Pickett has been professor of Mission, BOSTON UNIVERSITY SCHOOL OF THEOLOGY, and counsellor in evangelism, Methodist BOARD OF MISSIONS 1957-60, and counsellor in Finance, American Committee for Ludhiana Christian Medical College, New York City, since 1961. He is the organizer of the United Christian Mission to NEPAL, 1950, and its president, 1950-56; chairman, Methodist Church Councils on Christian Education and Medical Work, 1936-56; consultant on the Constitution of India, Indian Political Leaders, 1947-56; and consultant on Indo-American Relations by appointment of Presidents Truman and Eisenhower. He was the organizer, the first chairman of the National Christian Relief Committee, India, 1947; acting president of the National Christian Council, 1945-46; and is the past president of Boards of various colleges, hospitals, and regional Christian Councils.

Bishop Pickett is the author of *Mass Movements in India*, 1933; *Christ's Way to India's Heart*, 1938; (with Warner, Azariah, Van Doren, Jones) *Moving Millions: The Pageant of Modern India*, 1938; (with D. A. McGavran and G. H. Singh) *Christian Missions in Mid-India*, 1938; (with D. A. McGavran) *Church Growth and Group Conversion*, 1956; (with Smith, Barbier, Booth, Brewster, Brumbaugh) *Lands of Witness and Decision*, 1957; *The Dynamics of Church Growth*, 1963, and (with Elia Peter) a popular short book, *India*, a résumé of Methodist activities in India, 1965. He has acted as over-all editor and compiler of the India Methodist material in this *Encyclopedia of World Methodism*. He resides in Dearborn, Mich.

Who's Who in The Methodist Church, 1966.   N. B. H.

PIERCE, GEORGE FOSTER (1811-1884), American bishop, and one of the great leaders of southern Methodism, was born on Feb. 3, 1811, in Greene County, Ga., when his mother, Ann Foster Pierce, the wife of the distinguished LOVICK PIERCE, was staying at her father's home while Lovick Pierce was making his rounds of the district.

George Pierce had the great advantage of association with and training by his father. George was educated in Greensboro where certain distinguished leaders of the state then lived, and where a teacher of unusual ability took him in hand and taught him the fundamentals of sound learning. He entered the freshman class of Franklin

GEORGE F. PIERCE

College (ATHENS, Ga.), a state school, when he was a little over fifteen years old, and later went into what became the University of Georgia. His college days ended, he attempted to study law, but failed at that, and following an interview with JAMES O. ANDREW, felt called to preach and gave himself into the ministry. He married Ann M. Waldron in 1834 and was almost immediately thereafter sent to CHARLESTON, S. C.

He was elected president of EMORY COLLEGE in 1849, where he served until 1854. Meanwhile, he had been a delegate to the GENERAL CONFERENCE of 1844 and had taken part in the great debate which resulted in the PLAN OF SEPARATION and the division of Methodism. He was, of course, a champion of the South and while only thirty-three years of age "was a born ruler of men and bore the kingly look on his face" his biographer expressed it. The motion which eventually passed the General Conference by a strictly sectional vote to depose Bishop Andrew as a slave owner aroused Pierce, and his speech carried in the *Journal* of that Conference has served to set forth the Southern point of view in a powerful way.

Pierce took part in the organization of the M.E. Church, South, at both the LOUISVILLE CONVENTION in 1845 and the first General Conference in Petersburg in 1846.

George F. Pierce was elected bishop eight years later in 1854 by the M.E. Church, South in spite of a whisper campaign against him which stated that he was not sound in his views on CHRISTIAN PERFECTION. Pierce affirmed that they were substantially those held by the Methodist Church, but he admitted that they were not exactly those of Mr. Wesley nor his father. "The great difficulty has been," he stated long afterward, "not an actual disagreement upon the subject itself, but in the attempt to define what is undefinable." (Smith, *Life and Times*, p. 190.)

As bishop, he was sent into ARKANSAS and MISSOURI and in 1859 to the far west. He managed to hold the MISSISSIPPI, ALABAMA, and GEORGIA CONFERENCES in 1862 when invasion had already broken up the South, but through the war years could do very little, especially after Sherman had invaded GEORGIA. His only son, Lovick (there were four daughters), of the 15th Georgia Regiment C.S.A. was wounded in the fighting during the Gettysburg campaign, but lived to be the grandfather of the present LOVICK PIERCE, the publisher of The Methodist Church and now retired.

Bishop Pierce took part in what was really the reorganization of the M.E. Church, South, in 1866 at NEW ORLEANS and found himself the senior bishop in 1870. He was admittedly very conservative in his views, part of his antipathy to any involvement of the Church in politics being due to the aggressive attitude of the Northern bishops, especially Bishop SIMPSON, who had no hesitation in relying on Federal Armies to extend the sweep of the M.E. Church in the conquered South. Bishop Pierce opposed the move to establish a theological seminary, as Bishop McTYEIRE managed to do in his sponsorship of VANDERBILT at NASHVILLE. He objected to the extension of the "time limit" from two years to four in the matter of ministerial appointments, and observed in speaking of AUGUSTA, GA.: "The four years rule and the organized choir have well nigh ruined one of the finest churches in the state."

The General Conference of 1878 was held in ATLANTA where Bishop Pierce was much the senior bishop and was given all honor by his comrades. In 1884 he and his wife celebrated their golden wedding and there were many distinguished guests at his home "Sunshine" near Sparta, Ga.

He retired to "Sunshine" and knowing that he would not again make any Conference visitations, he called ATTICUS G. HAYGOOD (later bishop) to him and gave him directions to give Bishop McTyeire to take over his Conferences. To a venerable Christian minister, Dr. J. Rembert Smith, who was also a physician and sitting by his side, he asked, "What do you think about me? Will I get well?" The physician paused and then replied, "No bishop, your work is done, it is impossible for you to recover." He died as he had lived in quietness and peace, and was buried at the home of his son in Sparta. His biographer observed that what he had said beautifully of Bishop CAPERS in his memorial service could be said of him: "There were no sins to lament, no vices to deplore."

G. G. Smith, *George Foster Pierce*. 1888.   N. B. H.

PIERCE, LOVICK (1785-1879), prominent American minister, from 1804 until his death, both in the M.E. Church and, after its formation, in the M.E. Church, South.

Progenitor of a family productive of Methodist leadership in successive generations to the present day, Lovick Pierce was the father of GEORGE F. PIERCE, widely respected bishop in the M.E. Church, South, and of James L. Pierce and Thomas F. Pierce, ministers in that church; and great-great grandfather of LOVICK PIERCE, who from 1946 to 1970 headed The METHODIST PUBLISHING HOUSE.

Lovick Pierce was born March 24, 1785 in Martin County, N. C., where his parents Lovick Pierce, Sr. (son of Philip Pierce) and Lydia Culpepper Pierce settled after their marriage in Portsmouth, Va. Son of an humble household, Lovick Pierce was one of nine children born to his parents. Most of his formative years were spent in Barnwell County, S. C., where his family moved in his early childhood. Later described by their son as plain people who "lived by personal daily labor," Lovick, Sr. and Lydia Pierce reared their children under the general

LOVICK PIERCE

influence of the Baptist Church, predominant among the small farmers, hunters, and trappers of the frontier South, who composed the society of which the Pierce family was a part.

By 1802 the influences of Methodism were being strongly felt in the region of the Pierce farm, and in the summer of that year the entire family, including Lovick and his elder brother, REDDICK, joined the M.E. Church. This occurred despite the initial skepticism of the father, a militia captain, who at the outset had questioned the doctrinal soundness of the new denomination.

In 1803 under the preaching of JAMES JENKINS, a Methodist circuit rider, both Lovick and Reddick experienced conversion and indicated their interest in becoming Methodist preachers. Shortly thereafter the parents moved into GEORGIA, settling in Baldwin County, leaving the sons in SOUTH CAROLINA, where they began their ministry. Received into the SOUTH CAROLINA CONFERENCE in 1804, Lovick, then nineteen, was assigned to the Great Pee Dee Circuit in Eastern South Carolina, where for a time he was engaged in teaching. At this period the South Carolina Conference embraced all of South Carolina, part of NORTH CAROLINA and the settled portions of Georgia and FLORIDA.

In 1806 when the Conference met at Sparta, Ga., Lovick was assigned to the Apalachee Circuit, during the course of which assignment he took into the church a Miss Ann Foster, the gay and fashionable daughter of a wealthy Green County planter, Col. George Foster. Chastened by her conversion experience, which came, as was often the case in those days, during a camp meeting, the young lady renounced her frivolous ways and in 1809 became the wife of the handsome and fastidous, although as yet unschooled, young preacher. On Sept. 28, 1809, at the home of her father, Ann Foster and Lovick Pierce were married. This year was further made distinctive by Pierce's ordination as elder and his simultaneous assignment by Bishop FRANCIS ASBURY to the position of presiding elder of the Oconee District which included half the state of Georgia. At the time, it is said, Pierce was the youngest man ever to be named presiding elder.

From 1809 to 1812 he served in this capacity. In the latter year he was further honored by election to the denomination's first delegated General Conference.

During the War of 1812, Pierce was drafted and assigned as chaplain to the troops at SAVANNAH. It was during these years that the young preacher, because of a throat ailment, reluctantly resolved to give up the traveling ministry for a career more compatible with his responsibilities as husband and father. His son, George, later to become a bishop, was born in 1811, the eldest of Lovick and Anne Pierce's eight children, of whom there were four sons. Locating in 1814, Pierce (1815-1816) pursued a course of study at the medical college of the University of Pennsylvania in Philadelphia to qualify himself as a preaching physician, a career he followed successfully in Greensboro, Ga., until 1823.

Returning to the itineracy of the M.E. Church in that year, he soon re-established himself as a leader in the denomination, holding various pastorates in Georgia and serving as one of the first agents of Georgia Female Academy (later Wesleyan at Macon). In 1830, when the GEORGIA CONFERENCE was formed from the South Carolina Conference, Pierce was one of its charter members. (In 1867 this conference was further divided into the NORTH and SOUTH GEORGIA CONFERENCES, with Pierce's membership remaining in the latter.) In 1835 Pierce became a trustee of RANDOLPH-MACON COLLEGE in Virginia, receiving the D.D. from that institution in 1843.

Lovick Pierce was a delegate to all the GENERAL CONFERENCES of the M.E. Church from 1824 to, and including, the Conference held at New York in 1844 when the sectional division in the denomination occurred. In this division he went with the Southern group, with whose cause he was more than ordinarily identified, having himself been the man to recommend JAMES O. ANDREW in 1812 for conference membership when Andrew was a young unknown preacher. Successively Pierce was a delegate to the LOUISVILLE CONVENTION of 1845 at which the M.E. Church, South, was organized, and to the first General Conference of this church in 1846. At this conference he was elected the fraternal messenger of the M.E. Church, South, to the 1848 General Conference of the M.E. Church. But when this body met in PITTSBURGH, while accepting Pierce personally and unofficially as a friend, it rejected fraternal relationships with the newly formed Church and refused to recognize him in his official capacity. The conference recorded its action as follows:

". . . whereas there are serious questions and difficulties existing between the two bodies, therefore resolved that while we tender to Rev. Dr. Pierce all personal courtesies, and invite him to attend our sessions, this General Conference does not consider it proper at present to enter into fraternal relations with the Methodist Episcopal Church, South." (*Daily Christian Advocate*, May 6, 1848.)

To this Pierce replied: ". . . within the bar I can only be known in my official character." And he added:

"You will therefore regard this communication as final on the part of the M.E. Church, South. She can never renew the offer of fraternal relations between the two great bodies of Wesleyan Methodists in the United States. But the proposition can be renewed at any time, either now or hereafter, by the M.E. Church. And if ever made upon the basis of the Plan of Separation, as adopted by the General Conference of 1844, the Church, South, will cordially entertain the proposition." (*Ibid.*)

As Bishop Andrew in 1844 had become the embodiment

of the rift in Episcopal Methodism, so Pierce, in 1848, became the symbol of the uncordial feelings that existed between the two ecclesiastical bodies for nearly thirty years. Fortunately Pierce lived to see fraternal relations again established. In 1876, after the M.E. Church had made moves of reconciliation, he was again elected fraternal messenger to the General Conference of that denomination. Ill health prevented his presence at the gathering but the acceptance of his written message by the M. E. body did much to repair the damage caused by its action of 1848.

Up until the time of his death, Lovick Pierce, although never elected to the episcopacy, held a unique position of leadership in the Church, South. Invariably he was a delegate to its General Conferences, and for more than thirty years was a guiding influence in its affairs. Described as being not so rhetorically brilliant as his famous son, George, the "old Doc" in his day was considered by many "the ablest expounder of the Scriptures then living. He was truly a marvelous preacher, deeply spiritual, with a mighty sweep of thought and a vocabulary to match . . ." He was said to delight in "the grandest themes," delivering them in a diction marked by "the roll of evangelical thunder." For the rudest rustic as well as the most learned scholar, "the simple grandeur of his character had charm . . ."

Active in body and mind until the end of his life, Pierce died Nov. 9, 1879, in Sparta, Ga., at the home of his son, George, where he had resided during his declining years. Two days later his remains were buried at Columbus, Ga., by the grave of his wife, who died in 1850. His death was mourned throughout the Church and throughout the section with whose affairs he had so closely identified his long and fruitful life. His portrait is in the home of his great-grandson in Nashville, the present LOVICK PIERCE.

A. D. Betts, *South Carolina*. 1952.
Christian Advocate (Nashville), Nov. 15, 1879; Nov. 29, 1879.
O. P. Fitzgerald, *Sunset Views*. 1900.
R. Irby, *Randolph-Macon College*. 1899.
Journal of the General Conference, ME, 1848; MES, 1850.
Methodist Review, January-February 1897.
A. M. Pierce, *Georgia*. 1956.
G. G. Smith, *George Foster Pierce*. 1888.
——————, *Georgia and Florida*. 1877.

JAMES P. PILKINGTON

PIERCE, LOVICK (1903-   ), Publisher of The (United) Methodist Publishing House, was born on Oct. 17, 1903, in Sparta, Ga., the son of Walter Flournoy and Sarah (Alfriend) Pierce. He was a student at the Georgia Military College, 1920-21; MORNINGSIDE COLLEGE, D.B.A. in 1952; OHIO NORTHERN UNIVERSITY, Litt.D. in 1961. He married Florence Eugenia Couch on Jan. 30, 1926, and their children are Eugenia Carter (Mrs. Andrew W. Young, Jr.) and Lovick, Jr. Mr. Pierce is the grandson of Bishop GEORGE F. PIERCE and the great-grandson of LOVICK PIERCE—the Southern Church leader of a hundred years ago.

He joined The METHODIST PUBLISHING HOUSE and became its merchandise manager at the Richmond Branch, 1921-29; went to Dallas as manager of the Publishing House Branch there from 1929-46, when he was elected one of the PUBLISHING AGENTS—as they then were termed —of The Methodist Church. The Publishing Agents' title was changed in 1956, with one such to be appointed and to be known as Publisher of The Methodist Church and President of the publishing corporation. Mr. Pierce was elected and continued in this capacity until he retired in 1970.

He was steward in Ginter Park Church, RICHMOND, Va.; Highland Park Church, DALLAS, Texas, where he served as chairman; and in West End Church, NASHVILLE, Tenn. He has been the treasurer of the SOUTH CENTRAL JURISDICTIONAL CONFERENCE, 1940-46; a member of the Council of Secretaries since 1946; ex officio member of the CURRICULUM COMMITTEE of The Methodist Church; of the 1960-64 Hymnal Commission; the Commission on Worship; the ad hoc committee dealing with the Methodist-E.U.B. union; and director and executive of various Church organizations. Presently, Mr. Pierce serves on the Board of Trustees of SCARRITT COLLEGE. He also is one of the directors of the First American National Bank of Nashville; is a member of the American Booksellers Association, for many years upon its Board and at one time Vice-President; is a member of the American Book Publishers Council, and of the NATIONAL COUNCIL OF CHURCHES. He has been a member of the Board of Governors of the Nashville Area Chamber of Commerce. The present enlarged Publishing House, including its new building and printing facilities—among the largest in the world—came about under his administration.

Who's Who in America, Vol. 34.
Who's Who in The Methodist Church, 1966.   N. B. H.

PIERCE, RALPH (1827-1908) and Mrs. Pierce, with the Rev. JAMES L. and Mrs. HUMPHREY, were the first missionary recruits from America to join Dr. and Mrs. WILLIAM BUTLER in the INDIA Mission. On the day of the massacre in BAREILLY, May 31, 1857, a meeting was held in BOSTON to bid farewell to these two couples. When they reached CALCUTTA on Sept. 22, they were not allowed to depart for the north, but remained in Calcutta and studied Hindustani. On March 11, 1858, they joined Butler at the Taj Mahal in AGRA in well-furnished rooms in the building known as Jawab (or "answer"), a feature of Moghal architecture.

His first appointment was to Naini Tal. A school for girls was opened in the residence. A few months later the superintendent appointed him to LUCKNOW. (The appointments in those days were given only to the men, but the wives worked as devotedly as did their husbands.) The first converts in Lucknow from a non-Christian religion were from Islam—Hosein Beg, his wife, and daughter. They were baptized June 12, 1859.

In the fall of 1858 a girls' orphanage was opened in Lucknow under the care of Mrs. Pierce. In 1861-62, she was assisted by Miss Husk (later Mrs. Messmore). In Nov. of 1862, Mrs. Pierce died. The orphanage was then removed to Bareilly, and Pierce became its superintendent. He was assisted by Mrs. David W. Thomas. It became and remained for a generation the largest and most productive of the girls' boarding schools of Indian Methodism. In 1861, the orphan girls in the school numbered forty-one. Two years later they numbered 135. After furlough Pierce remained in America. He died in Washington, D.C., March 17, 1908.

B. T. Badley, *Southern Asia*. 1931.
J. N. Hollister, *Southern Asia*. 1956.
J. E. Scott, *Southern Asia*. 1906.

J. WASKOM PICKETT

PIERCE, REDDICK (1782-1860), a minister of the M.E. Church, and subsequently of the M.E. Church, South, was born in Halifax County, N. C., Sept. 26, 1782. Both he and his brother, LOVICK, his junior by two years, were admitted on trial into the SOUTH CAROLINA CONFERENCE at CHARLESTON in 1805, with Bishop ASBURY presiding. Reddick Pierce was sent as junior preacher on the Little River Circuit, GEORGIA. He then served the Sparta Circuit, Augusta station, and COLUMBIA, S. C., and was presiding elder of the Saluda District.

The two brothers differed markedly in appearance and temperament. Reddick was vigorous in body and mind, brave, daring. Lovick was somewhat more gentle and sensitive, with a taste for all the refinements of life.

Reddick was a man of extraordinary power in the pulpit. His brother, Lovick, records that scores fell senseless as Reddick preached. The brothers possessed no early literary advantages, but their ministry was characterized by lofty heroism and wholehearted dedication to the cause of Christ.

Reddick Pierce located in 1812, but returned to the work in 1822. He resided in Fairfield County, S. C., later moving to Mt. Ariel to educate his children. He became very deaf in later life and could communicate with his friends only by writing. He was asked once why he attended church so regularly, for "Uncle Redd, you can't hear a word" said the inquirer. "I go to fill my place" said the old minister simply.

The last twelve years of his lfe were spent in the home of Jacob Stroman in Orangeburg County, S. C. He died July 24, 1860, and his body was buried at Rocky Swamp Church. This tribute was paid to him by a friend: "A purer Christian never lived. His whole religious life was a rich development of the most guileless devotion to God, His Cause and Kingdom."

A. D. Betts, *South Carolina*. 1952.
M. Simpson, *Cyclopaedia*. 1881.
G. G. Smith, *Georgia and Florida*. 1877.   J. MARVIN RAST

PIERCE, ROBERT BRUCE (1917-   ), American minister and city pastor was born in Hancock, Mich., on April 11, 1917, the son of Ralph Milton and Nellie Payne Pierce. He was educated at NORTHWESTERN UNIVERSITY, A.B., 1939; M.A., 1944; GARRETT THEOLOGICAL SEMINARY, B.D., 1941; Hebrew Union College, and holds an honorary degree from UNION COLLEGE. His wife was Harriet Vivian White whom he married on Aug. 3, 1938, and they have four children.

Dr. Pierce was admitted on trial into the ROCK RIVER CONFERENCE in 1940 and into full connection and ordained elder in 1942. He served as pastor in Glencoe, Ill., 1941-49; Broadway Church, INDIANAPOLIS, Ind., 1949-57; Metropolitan Church, DETROIT, Mich., 1957-61, at which time he became pastor of the Chicago Temple or First Church of CHICAGO. He serves as a trustee of the Chicago Wesley Memorial Hospital, the Rock River Conference Foundation, the Board of Directors of the Chicago YMCA Hotel, and is a member of the Advisory Board of the Salvation Army. He was the recipient of the Freedom Foundation's George Washington medal in 1954. His office is in the imposing skyscraper building of the Chicago Temple, where of course he preaches each Sunday morning.

Who's Who in America, Vol. 34.
Who's Who in The Methodist Church, 1966.   N. B. H.

PIERCE, WILLIAM HENRY (1856-1948), Canadian minister, was born at Fort Rupert on Vancouver Island, of a Scottish father and a Tsimshian mother, on June 10, 1856. Three weeks later his mother died, and when the news of her death reached her father, he took the infant boy to Port Simpson where he was reared among the tribesmen of his mother.

His first teacher was William Duncan, an Anglican missionary, who founded Metlakatla, ALASKA. At twelve years of age he joined the crew of the "Otter," a Hudson's Bay Company steamer under command of a Captain Lewis, who saw signs of promise in the boy. At fifteen he was converted under the preaching of THOMAS CROSBY, the great Methodist missionary to the Indians of the Pacific Coast. For a time, he acted as an interpreter for Crosby when opening new missions on the coast and up the Nass and Skeena Rivers.

In 1877, Pierce was appointed to Port Essington, at the mouth of the Skeena, where he taught school and preached. Under the direction of Crosby, Pierce opened missions at Fort Wrangel, Alaska, at Lak-al-zap on the Nass, at Bella Bella on Campbell Island, and at Bella Coola on the mainland. In 1895 he was with Crosby on the mission boat, "Glad Tidings," when they visited thirty-two villages and travelled over seven thousand miles.

Pierce's next appointment was Kitseguecla on the Upper Skeena, but shortly thereafter he was sent further up the river to Kispiox, where he remained for fifteen years. In 1910 he returned to Port Essington—his first mission—and was there until his retirement in 1932.

Pierce, the first person of Indian blood to become a minister in British Columbia, was ordained in May, 1887, at the first meeting of the Methodist Conference. Gifted with an alert mind, compelling humor, shrewdness, and intense Christian devotion, he made an indelible mark on the lives of both Indians and Canadians. He was a staunch advocate of temperance, a leader in social changes, and a wise and trusted counselor.

W. H. Pierce, *From Potlatch to Pulpit*. Vancouver: Vancouver Bindery, 1933.
Mrs. F. C. Stephenson, *Canadian Methodist Missions*. 1925.
                                                                    W. P. BUNT

PIERCY, GEORGE (1829-1913), first British Methodist missionary to CHINA, was born at Pickering, England, February 27, 1829. After two voyages as a seaman he settled back to farming and was an effective LOCAL PREACHER. An interest in China, then newly opening to the West, resulted in his asking the Wesleyan METHODIST MISSIONARY SOCIETY for authority to go as a missionary, but they could not contemplate opening new work at that time. Piercy went to Hong Kong on his own charges in 1851, preached to soldiers and civilians, and moved on to Canton in 1852, when he offered himself again to the missionary society and was then accepted as a Wesleyan minister. In 1853 he opened the first Wesleyan preaching hall in Canton and was joined by W. R. Beach and JOSIAH COX. The Wesleyan Church had committed itself to the China Mission. In 1854 Mrs. Piercy began a school for girls; but in 1856, following the second Opium War, the missionaries had to withdraw to Macao. Here, February, 1857, the first Methodist converts were baptized. Piercy returned to Canton in 1858 and remained in South China until 1882. He died July 16, 1913.

                                                                    CYRIL J. DAVEY

PIERPONT, FRANCIS HARRISON (1814-1899), governor of the "restored" state of VIRGINIA, and M.P. layman, was born Jan. 25, 1814, near Morgantown, Monongalia County, Va. (now W. Va.), the son of Francis and Catherine (Weaver) Pierpont. He won the B.A. degree at ALLEGHENY COLLEGE in 1839. After teaching school two years in his home state and one year in MISSISSIPPI, he returned home and was admitted to the bar.

An ardent anti-slavery man, Pierpont supported Lincoln for president in 1860. When Virginia seceded from the Union in 1861, he organized a mass meeting at Wheeling in May which led to a convention that elected him provisional governor of Virginia. When WEST VIRGINIA was admitted to the Union in 1863, a new governor was chosen for that state, and Pierpont was granted a four-year term as governor of the "restored" state of Virginia, that is, governor of the few counties which were in Federal hands and not in West Virginia. Pierpont moved his capital to Alexandria and carried on under military protection. When the Confederacy fell, he went to RICHMOND and became in fact the governor of Virginia, carrying on until replaced by a military commander in 1868. He then returned to his home in Fairmont, W. Va., and resumed the practice of law. Known as the "father of West Virginia," the state placed a statue of him in the Capital at Washington in 1910. One biographer says that apparently Pierpont belonged to that large class of men who are selected as leaders in troubled times because they possess strength of conviction rather than strength of intellect.

As a Methodist Protestant strongly opposed to slavery, Pierpont was among those who withdrew from the WESTERN VIRGINIA CONFERENCE (MP) in 1866 and went into the PITTSBURGH CONFERENCE which became a part of the newly formed Methodist Church (See Table of Methodist Annual Conferences). He was elected president of the Second GENERAL CONFERENCE of the Methodist Church which met in Pittsburgh in 1871. Though a delegate to the 1875 General Conference, he did not attend. However he participated in the 1877 Convention at BALTIMORE when the Methodist Church and the Methodist Protestant Church reunited under the latter name, and he served as a delegate to the 1880 General Conference (MP).

Pierpont married Julia Robertson of New York in 1854. He died at the home of his daughter in Pittsburgh, March 24, 1899, and was buried at Fairmont, W. Va.

T. H. Colhouer, *Sketches of the Founders*. 1880.
Dictionary of American Biography, Volume 14.
E. J. Drinkhouse, *History of the Methodist Protestant Church*. 1898.
                                                                    ANN G. SILER
                                                                    ALBEA GODBOLD

PIERS, HENRY (1694-1770), British Anglican, figures in JOHN WESLEY's diary as a friend whom he often met in the period leading up to his conversion. Piers himself was led to Christ under the influence of CHARLES WESLEY and JOHN BRAY. A vicar of Bexley, Kent, Piers offered his pulpit to the Wesleys. Kezia Wesley was a paying guest in his home. He was a member of the FETTER LANE SOCIETY and attended the Conferences of 1744 and 1747.

                                                                    A. SKEVINGTON WOOD

PIETERS, ANDRE (1924-   ), a minister of the BELGIUM Conference of the Methodist Church, was born at St. Andres les Bruges (Belgium), on Dec. 31, 1924. He was

ANDRE PIETERS

given a Th.B. degree at the Brussels Protestant Theological School and a Ph.D. from Cambridge University (England) in 1965. He was pastor at VILVORDE—the William Tyndale Memorial Church—from 1950 to 1959 and at Uccle from 1962-63. He has been secretary of the annual conference since 1955, a district superintendent since 1961, a professor at the Protestant Theological School since 1961 and Dean in 1966, elected President of the Executive Council of The Protestant Church of Belgium at its organization in 1969. He married Andrée Deslé of Kain (Belgium) in October 1944, and they have two daughters.

WILLIAM G. THONGER

PIETISM AND METHODISM. Definitions. Continental Pietism arose in the seventeenth century as the older half-brother of eighteenth century Anglo-American Awakenings of which Methodism is a part. This explains (1) that Pietism was of greater influence on Methodism than vice versa. Yet (2) Methodism is distinct from Pietism because it also stems from other sources than Pietism. Concretely, (3) Pietism and Methodism, both originally mocking names ("Pietism" first used around Darmstadt 1677, "Methodism" at Oxford 1729) share the emerging Protestant emphasis on the piety of the people over against theological doctrine and church structure. They (4) differ because Pietism is embedded in Calvinistic-Lutheran soil while Methodism stems from Anglican-Puritan parentage.

History: Pietism *a. Roots.* Pietism claims (1) the Reformation. Calvin's concern for the third use of the law (the law as the scaffold for Christian living, *Institutes* 1559, 2, 7, 12) led the very defenders of orthodoxy to an ethically oriented *Precisionism* (Voetius 1589-1676). Luther's 1522 *Preface to the Romans* (with its emphasis on a living faith) motivated the Rostock Reform wing of Orthodoxy (H. Mueller 1631-1675, Scriver 1629-1693). They in turn led Spener (1635-1705) to claim the *Preface* again and again as the Magna Charta of Pietism. The real Father of Pietism, however, is Martin Bucer, the mediator among the Reformers. His program (cf. the *Tetrapolitan Confession* of 1530) intended a Protestant consensus on the basis of piety. Direct links connect Bucer with Calvinistic and Lutheran Pietists (Ames, Spener) and also with the Radicals (via Schwenkfeld). Anglican (Bradford) and Puritan (Perkins) piety is also in his debt.

Pietism blends (2) into the unbroken stream of Mysticism. It treasures among the ancients Macarios and among the medievals Tauler. Since the Reformation the Pietistic pedigree includes Protestant mystics like Weigel (1533-1588), Arndt (1555-1621) and Boehme (1575-1624). Nor is Pietism afraid to appropriate seventeenth century Romance Mysticism, particularly Quietism (Molinos 1628-1696/7, Fenelon 1651-1715, de Guyon 1648-1717).

b. Classical Forms. Pietism began around 1630 in the Netherlands as (1) Reformed Pietism, though not yet under this name. It grew out of the academic orthodoxy of the universities (Ames and the *Cases of Conscience* theology, 1630 ff., at Franeker; Voetius and legalistic Precisionism in conventicles at Utrecht, 1634 ff; Coccejus and evangelical covenant theology, 1648 ff., at Leyden). Pietism was carried out, however, by pastors. In Holland Lodensteyn in Utrecht (*Scales of Imperfections* 1664) stayed within the church, Labadie in Middelburg (*Reformation of the Church by the Ministry* 1667) broke with it (1669). In Northwest GERMANY (Muehlheim/Ruhr) Undereyck founded 1666 conventicles which later provided the setting for the devotion of Tersteegen (1697-1769).

Lutheran Pietism (2), which gave the movement its name, developed four main forms. First, there is the Pietism of the founder Spener. During his ministry in Frankfurt/Main (1666-1686) Spener instituted (1670) conventicles out of which grew his *Pia Desideria* (1675), the program of Pietism which made Spener into the head of the Pietistic party. Second, his student Francke (1663-1727) created Pietistic welfare and educational institutions in Halle. As professor he made the theological faculty of the university into the academic center of Pietism. Third, in Wuerttemberg Bengel (1687-1752) shaped Pietism exegetically-apocalytically (*Gnomon* 1742) and his student Oetinger (1702-1782) elaborated it systematically-philosophically (*Philosophia Sacra* 1765). From these three "pedestrian" forms ZINZENDORF (1700-1760) distinguished the (fourth form of) Pietism of the Moravian Brethren as "equestrian." This Pietism swings wider, first to the Radicals (Dippel, Sifting Period) then to Luther (since 1734). The MORAVIANS were criticized by Halle (Francke's son) and Wuerttemberg (Bengel, Oetinger).

Radical Pietism (3) on Calvinistic soil breaks with the church by external emigration, creating free churches (Labadie 1669, Church of the Brethren 1708). On Lutheran soil it goes into internal emigration. Sectarians withdrew into individualism. Some are loosely interrelated in Jane Leade's Philadelphian Society (founded 1694, Peterson, Breckling, Gichtel). Others represent extreme offshoots on the way to the Enlightenment (Dippel). Most important is G. Arnold (1666-1714). In his *Impartial Church and Heresy History* (1699/1700) he replaces dogmatic confessionalistic church historiography by the ethical approach of Pietism.

c. Subsequent Forms. Classical Pietism arose against the front of Orthodoxy and foreshadowed the Enlightenment. In the nineteenth century Neo-Pietism (1) emerged on the continent as it did in England and America in the form of revivalism (*Erweckung, Réveil*). Although it had representatives in universities (Tholuck) it was often anti-intellectual in its reaction to the Enlightenment. The classical Pietistic heritage appears in Neo-Pietism in three ways. In the territorial churches it took the form of *Inner* or *Home Mission* (Wichern, Hauge). It was soon expanded into evangelism (Schrenk, Keller), a concern the free churches joined. A special emphasis is found in the Holiness Movement (Rappard, Gebhard).

Neo-Pietism led to Neo-Orthodoxy and related movements. These are today under attack by (2) a contemporary Pietism which stands in a broken relationship to classical Pietism and only in an oblique relationship to Neo-Pietism. The traditional conventicles (classical Pietism) and movements (Neo-Pietism) are exceeded by a new *Confessional Movement No Other Gospel* (1693 ff.). Its distinguishing marks are a fundamentalism in the attitude toward Scripture and various forms of personalism in its efforts to create Christian life styles (Bergmann, Kuenneth).

History: Pietism and Methodism *a. Wesley and Pietism.* The founder of Methodism had various contacts with Pietism. (1) Literary Contacts. In his Oxford days (1733 ff.) Wesley read widely in Francke and was also acquainted with Arnold. In preparing his *Notes upon the New Testament* (1755) Wesley extensively excerpted from Bengel's *Gnomon* of 1742. In 1763 the *Notes* became a part of (the not yet repealed) doctrinal standards of Methodism. Thus the Lutheran Pietism of Wuerttemberg lives on in the confessional documents of Methodism. (2) Structural contacts are given with the Anglican Religious Societies (e.g. at Aldersgate Street). These were fostered by Anthony Horneck (1641-1696), a friend of Spener's. Wesley modelled his own societies (1739 ff.) more after these than the Moravian societies (e.g. at Fetter Lane) with whom he soon had conflicts. (3) Personal contacts seem to be restricted to meetings with Moravians: on the way to and in Georgia (1735 ff., Spangenberg) as well as after his return in England (1738 ff., Boehler) including a visit to Herrnhuth 1738, Zinzendorf). From these contacts rose his interest in translating German Pietist hymns. When the Methodists and the Moravians broke (1740 ff.) it also meant for Wesley a conscious decision for the classical Pietism of Spener, Francke and Bengel.

b. Early Methodism and Pietism. The contacts of other early Methodists with Pietism were also embedded in the situation which was marked by two facts. Works by Francke (particularly his *Pietas Hallensis,* 1705) were generally accessible in the translation of Anthony William Boehm(e). From 1740 on writings of Zinzendorf's became available in English, in addition to the personal influence which the Moravians exerted particularly through their London societies. *Some special points.* Charles

Wesley, like his brother John, was influenced by Pietistic hymnody (Neander, Tersteegen, Zinzendorf) in his frequent insistence that in the sight of God man is but a worm. A charismatic itinerant ministry in England and America led Whitefield into many contacts with Pietists, mainly Moravians, including an unsuccessful correspondence and personal meeting with Zinzendorf (1743).

c. Later Methodism and Pietism. Revivalistic Methodism and Pietism developed largely separately with only occasional meetings. English Methodism stimulated Pietistic publications on Methodism (Niemeyer, Burckhardt, Krummacher, Christlieb). American Methodism originally rejected German language work which led to the formation of the United Brethren Church (1787 ff.) and the Evangelical Association (1816 ff.) in both America and Germany. When later (1838 ff.) American Methodism supported German-speaking work contacts increased. In America Nast (1807-1899) continually built bridges to the immigrant Germans which led him into a literary controversy with Walther (Missouri Synod Lutheran) over communion (1847). In Germany the meeting ground for Pietism and Methodism became increasingly the Evangelical Alliance which had been founded in England 1846 and was introduced into Germany 1878.

d. Contemporary Methodism and Pietism. Today contacts are on restricted levels. Ecumenical relations of the larger Methodist Churches in America and Britain with the larger Reformed and Lutheran Churches on the continent relegate the Methodist-Pietist relations to inner-evangelical conversations. In Britain the former Primitive Methodists uphold the "Pietistic" stance of the dissenters, although this stance is partly social in origin. In America the smaller Methodist Churches of decidedly Arminian outlook (in the following of Fletcher, not of Wesley, although the position is claimed to be Wesleyan) relate to the descendents of the early immigration churches with pietistic background. On the continent rural sections of Methodism placed in traditional pietistic surroundings (Wuerttemberg, Lower Rhine, Saxony, parts of Switzerland and Scandinavia) continue old bonds of alliance.

Theology: Pietism. Pietism exists only in concrete geographical, confessional and later denominational forms, although it intends to overcome these. For these reasons Pietism possesses no unified theology. Yet all of its forms (including the Anglo-American Awakening relatives) share certain foundations, concerns and results of classical Pietism.

a. Foundations. (1) The norms of Word and Spirit. For ecclesial Pietism the Word of scripture (devotional book) is the historical vehicle for the Holy Spirit (Coccejus, Bengel). For radical Pietism the outer Word of the flesh only confirms the inner Word of the Spirit (Petersen). (2) The rules of faith and love. The act of faith is more important than the content of belief (Spener, Arnold). The doctrine of faith is exceeded by the life of love (Tersteegen). The mediator between faith and love is conscience (Ames).

b. Concerns. (1) The nature of piety is expressed by the new man who has his origin in the New Birth (Spener) and is edified in Sanctification and Perfection (Spener). (2) The conventicles of piety (*Collegia pietatis*) anticipate the future Kingdom of God within (for the Radicals: outside) the established churches of the present (Voetius, Bengel). As *ecclesiae in ecclesia* (respectively *extram ecclesiam*) they gather the true church in or from the many churches through the means of fellowship (Undereyck, Spener). (3) The practice of piety rests on specific suggestions for conduct (Voetius) but also moves out to tackle social evils (Francke). (4) A reformation of piety is called for as a second reformation building on the first reformation of doctrine (Teellinck). Spener's *Pia Desideria* outline the program: reforms are necessary because of the fallen state of the church (cf. also Arnold). Reforms are possible because of better times promised to the church (cf. also Bengel). Reforms are suggested as concrete measures to be taken up by the church, particularly the ministry (cf. also Labadie).

c. Results. (1) Pietism upholds an ambiguous attitude toward the world as both God's good creation and man's dominion in which he constantly fails. Therefore Pietism's relations to state and society vacillate according to the openness of the people concerned to cooperate with Pietism (Cf. Francke and Prussia). (2) Pietism accepts as special mandate mission work (e.g. Halle Missions in Tranquebar, Moravians in Greenland, both in America). This engenders an irenic spirit of ecumenism which transcends old party lines (cf. Zinzendorf's tropology and Arnold's *Church and Heresy History*). (3) The expansion of Pietism was effected geographically by outreach (Halle Pietism in Switzerland, Scandinavia, RUSSIA) or transplantation (Moravian colonies in England, Greenland and America). Socially Pietism spread by permeating the lower classes who had few or no worldly goods to lose and by entering the uppermost classes who could afford to. Classical Pietism was not at home in the middle classes. (4) Further effects reach into literature (Goethe, Romanticism, e.g. Scleiermacher) and influenced scholarship particularly in the areas of psychology and education (Francke, Pestalozzi).

Theology: Pietism and Methodism. Original Methodism (i.e. as it felt bound by its doctrinal standards) shared most foundations, concerns and results of classical Pietism. It differs (increasingly so) in some special points.

a. Foundations. (1) The (norming) norms of Word and Spirit are confirmed by the (normed) norms of reason, antiquity and experience. Reason is appropriated because Methodism had to respond to Deism while Pietism preceded the Enlightenment (Knowledge and piety in KINGSWOOD SCHOOL, Charles Wesley). Antiquity is emphasized in agreement with the Anglican mother church (Wesley's refusal to consider separation from the CHURCH OF ENGLAND). Experience is the modern scientific test to which both Methodism and Pietism are open (The legitimate practice of testimonies and the illegitimate invocation of Wesley's private warm heart experience as a model). (2) The rules of faith and love are clarified as suffering and doing the will of God, suffering what God does for us and doing what God does in us (Wesley).

b. Concerns. (1) The nature of piety shall lead the new man to perfection, not a sinless perfection but a perfection that frees from sin (Wesley). Contemporary Methodism has all but renounced this doctrine. (2) The Kingdom of God is an inward work (The life of God in the soul of man, Wesley with Scougal), realized in the Methodist societies (1739 ff.) whose conferences (1744 ff.) are prudential means of grace (Wesley; where two or three confer with each other). Conferences have since (1784 ff.) changed from sacramental to administrative means. Yet Methodism is basically still an *ecclesiola* (emphasizing fellowship instead of doctrine or structure) although it had to move to *ecclesia* functions with which

it has not yet come to terms. (3) Practical piety is shown by doing no harm, by doing good and by attending upon all the ordinances of God (Rules 1743). Because the third element increasingly tended to become problematic, the first two misled Methodism sometimes into moralism. (4) Reforms of piety are enacted within the societies (the early discipline of membership tickets, later given up) but also encouraged at large (Wesley's criticism of war and opposition to slavery, Methodism's Social Creed).

c. Results. (1) Originally the ambiguity of the world was felt more in personal than social categories. Therefore Methodism always supported (sometimes uncritically) the state (Wesley and the Crown, ASBURY and the outcome of the American Revolution) at least silently (under totalitarian regimes). Recently Methodism notices ambiguities in the social, yet hardly in the cosmic world. (2) Mission and ecumenism have been strong Methodist emphases since Wesley. Often mission and ecumenism were pursued with an optimistic activism which is today being challenged. (3) Methodism expanded geographically mainly among English speaking people through evangelism (at home) and mission (abroad). In the western world it appealed originally to the lower classes whom it soon lifted socially through the preaching of frugality (Wesley: On the use of money). Only rarely were entrances into higher classes achieved (Whitefield and LADY HUNTINGDON). Today Methodism is predominantly middle class, another reason for its rejection of Pietism. (4) Of the further effects of original Methodism few remained alive. Wesley's broad literary activity was soon overshadowed by dissenter position (in Britain) or revivalistic emotionalism (in America). Wesley's emphasis on learning was kept alive mainly among the Wesleyan Methodists in England. Others, especially in America, advocated a less complicated activism. Wesley's concern for education (Kingswood School) was replaced by evangelistic SUNDAY SCHOOLS (Cf. the late foundation of Methodist seminaries and their thorough practical emphases).

A new Wesley renaissance (Cannon, Lindstrom, Towlson, Monk, C. Williams, M. Schmidt) has promise to lead Methodism not only to a much needed reappreciation of Wesley's significance but also to an openness toward its Pietistic relations and affinities.

H. Bett, *Spirit of Methodism.* 1945.
B. L. Manning, *Hymns of Wesley and Watts.* 1942.
A. W. Nagler, *Pietism and Methodism.* 1918.
M. Schmidt, *John Wesley.* 1966.
C. W. Towlson, *Moravian and Methodist.* 1957.
F. Wunderlich, *Methodists Linking Two Continents.* 1960.

EGON W. GERDES

PIGGOTT, HENRY JAMES (1831-1917), leading pioneer missionary in Italy, was born July 18, 1831, at Lowestoft, England, the son of William Piggott (missionary in SIERRA LEONE, 1824-28) and Elizabeth Gadsden. Educated at KINGSWOOD SCHOOL (1842-44), at Wesley College Taunton, and London University (1848-50), he entered the Wesleyan Methodist ministry, and served in Newbury, Berks, OXFORD, Hastings, and Hammersmith. He married Mary Ellen Brown in 1859. He refused invitations to AUSTRALIA and INDIA with RICHARD GREEN, but accepted one as pioneer missionary to Italy in 1861. He arrived in ITALY in November, 1861; initiated work at Ivrea, and Milan, and assumed leadership of the mission when ill-health compelled Green's return in 1863.

HENRY PIGGOTT

In 1865 he moved his base to Padua, and then to ROME in 1873. In 1870 the work was divided into two districts, north and south, Piggott being the General Superintendent. He is regarded as the Father of Methodism in Italy, and his *Life and Letters* as its primary text book. He was a scholar, evangelist and administrator, wide in ecumenical vision, and a tireless worker in the cause of unity among Protestants in Italy. He retired from the Superintendency of the mission in 1902, and from active pastoral work in 1903. Thereafter he lived in Rome until his death on Nov. 30, 1917.

Findlay and Holdsworth, *Wesleyan Meth. Miss. Soc.* 1921.
Piggott and Durley, *Henry James Piggott.* 1921.
CYRIL J. DAVEY
REGINALD KISSACK

PILCHER, ELIJAH HOLMES (1810-1887), American minister, was born in Athens, Ohio, on June 2, 1810. He was admitted to the OHIO CONFERENCE on trial in 1829, and preached one year in WEST VIRGINIA. Then followed eight years on farflung pioneer circuits in MICHIGAN.

Beginning in 1838, he served terms as presiding elder of several districts, interspersed with prominent appointments in Michigan. In 1833 Pilcher was one of four Methodist leaders who began working to establish a Seminary in Michigan, later ALBION COLLEGE. He served Albion as trustee, agent, and professor. He helped to establish the University of Michigan, serving five years as regent. He promoted the establishment of Michigan State Agricultural College, and was co-founder of the *Michigan Christian Advocate.* He served nine times as Secretary of the Conference, five times as delegate to GENERAL CONFERENCE, as a trustee of NORTHWESTERN UNIVERSITY, and member of the BOOK COMMITTEE of the BOOK CONCERN. He organized at least thirteen churches.

Pilcher studied law and was admitted to the bar; later he studied medicine and was admitted to practice. He was the author of *Protestantism in Michigan,* published in 1878, and of many articles.

In 1877 he heeded the call to aid the Canadian Methodists. He was serving as presiding elder of the Hamilton District in 1882, when his health broke. Pilcher died April 7, 1887 at the home of his son, Lewis, in BROOKLYN, N. Y. Married three times, he had four sons and one daughter. A son, Leander, served as a missionary in CHINA.

Io Triumphe, November 1957.
Minutes of the Detroit Conference, 1887.
E. H. Pilcher, *Michigan.* 1878.
James Elijah Pilcher, *Life and Labors of Elijah H. Pilcher.*
New York: Hunt & Eaton, 1892. RONALD A. BRUNGER

PILGRIM HOLINESS. (See WESLEYAN CHURCH.)

PILLAR OF FIRE CHURCH, THE, is a Methodist oriented pentecostal group organized around the teachings of Mrs. Alma White. It was organized in 1901 at DENVER, Colo., as the Pentecostal Union. The name was changed in 1917 to Pillar of Fire. The movement was ruled charismatically by Mrs. White until her death in 1946, and has been headed by her son, Arthur K. White, since that time. Mrs. White had been converted under Methodist ministers in KENTUCKY and eventually married one from COLORADO. She preached from her husband's pulpit but eventually gathered an independent following. She withdrew from the Methodist Church after conflict developed with church authorities. Mrs. White became the first bishop of the new body.

The Pillar of Fire teaches the "second blessing" holiness doctrine and premillenarianism, as part of the program to revive primitive Wesleyanism and to re-establish the true "New Testament" church. The church is anti-Catholic and defends the Ku Klux Klan. In the 1940's three volumes entitled *Guardians of Liberty* were first published in order to highlight these views.

The Pillar of Fire operates a large number of day schools, elementary schools and academies. Two colleges, Alma White College at Zarephath, N. J., and Bellville College at Denver, Colo., are in operation. The Belleview Bible Seminary operates out of the Alma Temple in Denver. Home missionary work is carried on in most of the major cities across the United States and foreign work in England and LIBERIA. The church was among the first to enter the radio ministry, buying its first station in 1927. Two others were added shortly after.

A periodical, *The Pentecostal Union Herald* (changed to *Pillar of Fire* in 1905) appeared almost as soon as the denomination. It has been joined by seven others. The denomination also publishes numerous books, mostly by Mrs. White and her sons.

E. T. Clark, *Small Sects.* 1949.
Yearbook of American Churches, 1971. J. GORDON MELTON

PILMORE, JOSEPH (1739-1825), Methodist itinerant in Great Britain and one of the first two preachers sent to America by JOHN WESLEY. (There are four spellings of his surname: Pillmore, Pilmoor, Pilmoore, Pilmore.)

He was born in Tadmouth, Yorkshire, England, Oct. 31, 1739. His parents belonged to the Church of England. At the age of sixteen, under the influence of John Wesley, he was converted. He was educated at KINGSWOOD SCHOOL. In 1765 he was admitted into the Methodist Conference on trial, and the next year into full membership. For two years he preached in WALES.

In August 1769, he volunteered to go to America to preach and the Conference sent him. He and RICHARD BOARDMAN arrived at GLOUCESTER POINT, N. J., on Oct. 24, 1769. The following day they met with the Methodist

JOSEPH PILMORE

Society in PHILADELPHIA. From that date until May 1772, Pilmore and Boardman alternated their ministries in Philadelphia and NEW YORK City, exchanging every four months. In Philadelphia, Pilmore supervised the purchase of ST. GEORGE'S CHURCH and introduced the Intercession and the LOVE FEAST into American Methodism. From May 26, 1772, until June 2, 1773, Pilmore made an evangelistic tour into the Southern Colonies, going as far as SOUTH CAROLINA. He formed Methodist Societies in BALTIMORE, Md., and in PORTSMOUTH and NORFOLK, Va. Even though there were no appointments for Pilmore and Boardman at the first American Conference in 1773, they continued their ministries in Philadelphia and New York for a short time. During the winter of 1774 they returned to England. Pilmore received no appointment at the Conferences in England in 1774 and 1775. From 1776 to 1784 he received appointments at LONDON, NORWICH, Edinburgh (twice), DUBLIN, NOTTINGHAM, YORK.

Sometime after the Conference of 1784, Pilmore withdrew from the Methodist ministry. Many reasons have been suggested for this action. Basically there was a decisive conflict between him and Wesley. Perhaps this division is the "Paul and Barnabas episode" of early Methodism.

In 1785 Pilmore was ordained a deacon and a priest of the Protestant Episcopal Church in America. From 1786 to 1789 he served as rector of the United Parishes of Trinity (Oxford, Pa.), All Saints (Lower Dublin, Pa.), St. Thomas, Whitemarsh (Pa.). From 1789 to 1794 he was assistant rector at St. Paul's Church, Philadelphia. In 1794 he became rector of Christ Church, New York City. In 1804 he returned to Philadelphia and served as rector of St. Paul's Church until 1821, when he retired. In 1807 the University of Pennsylvania conferred upon him the honorary D.D. degree.

He died July 24, 1825 and is buried beneath the floor of the Sunday school room of St. Paul's Church, Philadelphia.

Norris Barratt, *Outline of the History of Old St. Paul's Church, Philadelphia, Pa.* Philadelphia: The Colonial Society of Pennsylvania, 1917.
Dictionary of American Biography.
Maser and Maag, *Journal of Joseph Pilmore.* 1969.
Joseph Pilmore, *Narrative of Labours in South Wales, Performed Partly in Company with the Rev. John Wesley in the Years 1767 and 1768.* Philadelphia: William Stavely, 1825.
Frank Bateman Stanger, "The Life and Ministry of the Rev. Joseph Pilmore." Unpublished thesis, Temple University, 1942.
FRANK BATEMAN STANGER

JOSÉ PEDRO PINHEIRO

PINHEIRO, JOSÉ PEDRO (1907-   ), a bishop of the Methodist Church in Brazil, was born on March 19, 1907, in Garibaldi, state of RIO GRANDE DO SUL, BRAZIL, the son of Pedro and Marieta (Krieger) Pinheiro. His education included a secondary course in the Methodist seminary at PORTO ALEGRE INSTITUTE, and one year at the CANDLER SCHOOL OF THEOLOGY at EMORY UNIVERSITY.

Pinheiro was ordained deacon in 1933 and elder in 1935. He always served in his native state, both in rural and urban areas, successively as pastor, district superintendent, principal (Reitor) of the Instituto Porto Alegre, and director for seven years of the Lar Methodista, the children's home, in SANTA MARIA. He has also been editor of the Methodist youth magazine, *Cruz de Malta;* regional secretary of the Boards of Christian Education and of Missions; and president of the Central Council, the key committee coordinating activities between the Methodist Church of Brazil and the Methodist Church of the United States. He has also strongly supported Instituto João Wesley in Porto Alegre—designed to train pastors and laymen.

José Pinheiro was elected Bishop of the Second Region in 1955, re-elected in 1960, and again in July 1965. He retired at the July 1970 General Conference.

Who's Who in The Methodist Church, 1966.   N. B. H.

W. W. PINSON

PINSON, WILLIAM WASHINGTON (1854-1930), American clergyman and missionary administrator, was born in Cheatham County, Tenn., on April 4, 1854, and joined the TENNESSEE CONFERENCE of the M.E. Church, South, in 1878. He served pastorates at Bell Buckle, Winchester, McMinnville, Tracy City and Franklin in TENNESSEE, at AUSTIN, SAN ANTONIO and Gonzales in TEXAS, COLUMBUS, Ga., and LOUISVILLE, Ky.

He was Assistant Secretary of the Board of MISSIONS from 1906 to 1910 and General Secretary from 1910 to 1926. He then became the editor of missionary literature for the Sunday schools, in which capacity he served four years.

In 1916 Pinson launched the Missionary Centenary, a successful campaign to raise $35,000,000 for Southern Methodist missions in celebration of the one hundredth anniversary of the founding of the Methodist missionary society, and he was chairman of the joint committee representing both branches of American Methodism.

Pinson received honorary degrees from the University of Georgia and SOUTHERN METHODIST UNIVERSITY, and traveled widely in visiting the foreign mission fields of the world. Pinson College in Camaguey, CUBA, was named in his honor.

Pinson was the author of *In Black and White; Missions in a Changing World; China in Action; Bishop Walter R. Lambuth, Prophet and Pioneer;* and *George R. Stuart, His Life and Work.*

He died on Oct. 7, 1930, at Nashville, Tenn., and was buried there.

Who's Who in America.
Journal of the Tennessee Conference, 1930.   ELMER T. CLARK

PIRMASENS, Germany, has the mother church of Palatine Methodism, founded in 1855 by Ernst Mann. While waiting for his ship to America, he was invited to a BREMEN Methodist meeting and converted. He returned to his home city and began to bear witness; many were awakened. Persecution followed; meetings were prohibited several times; one preacher, the father of Bishop JOHN L. NUELSEN, had to leave the city within three hours. It was only in 1883 that all this was stopped by royal decree. But the church was growing. In 1876 a meetinghouse was dedicated. At the same time congregations were founded in other Palatine towns and in neighboring villages. In 1898 a big church was built, soon proving too small; so in 1914 another meetinghouse was bought and a second minister appointed. In the Second World War the church was destroyed and its members dispersed, the city being evacuated two times. But new members were won, and the church was reconstructed in 1950. There were about six hundred members in 1967, served by one minister. There has been a certain decrease in membership owing to mobility of population, particularly young people leaving Pirmasens.

WOLFGANG HAMMER

PITEZEL, JOHN H. (1814-1906), American preacher, was born in Frederick County, Md., on April 18, 1814. The family moved to "the wilds" of OHIO when John was nine. He lived in Tiffin, Ohio from age fifteen to twenty, and was licensed to preach in April 1834. He attended Norwalk Seminary for a year, and in 1835 was assigned to the Lima Circuit in Ohio, and later in the year appointed to the Lower Sandusky Circuit as junior preacher. When the MICHIGAN CONFERENCE was formed at Mansfield, Ohio in 1836, John was appointed to the Tecumseh Circuit. After serving ADRIAN, Ypsilanti, Northville and Plymouth in southern Michigan, he was appointed to the SAULT STE. MARIE Indian Mission in Michigan's Upper Peninsula in 1843. He served the Kewawenon Mission during 1844-47, and the Eagle River Mission among the early copper miners during 1847-48. From 1848 to 1852 he served as Superintendent of the Indian Mission District of the Michigan Conference, in Michigan's Upper Peninsula. After leaving these appointments he wrote *Lights and Shades of Missionary Life* (1857), giving vivid accounts of Indian life, and of early copper mining activities and white settlers. From 1852 to 1859 he served Kalamazoo, Allegan, Edwardsburg, and Paw Paw, in southern Michigan. In 1859 he was made supernumerary and superannuated until 1870, when he was put on the active list again and appointed to Flowerfield. He retired again in one year, due to continuing frail health, and went to live at Three Rivers, his wife's home. She died in 1880, and in 1887 Pitezel married the widow of G. W. Breckenridge of the OHIO CONFERENCE. They went to live in Norwalk, Ohio, and when she died in 1901, Pitezel went to live with a daughter in Loraine, Ohio. He died at the daughter's home on May 4, 1906. Burial was in Three Rivers, Mich.

Michigan Pioneer and Historical Collections, Vol. 3, p. 241.
Minutes of the Michigan Conference, 1906.
J. H. Pitezel, *Lights and Shades.* 1883.   BYRON G. HATCH

PITHORAGARH, India, a subdivision headquarters town in the beautiful Shor Valley of Kumaun District, Uttar Pradesh, has been a center of Methodist church activities since 1873. The beginning was made by arrangement of Bishop JAMES THOBURN on the suggestion of the missionaries of the London Missionary Society in Almora, who had learned that they were not to be allowed to open work there.

The request was made that a doctor be sent from America for Pithoragarh. Richardson Gray was sent in response to the request. In preparing to open missionary work in that remote but strategic center, he spent considerable time in Almora, the governmental district headquarters, and in the home of the most experienced missionaries in the Indian Himalayas. Before his preparations were complete he became engaged to Margaret Budden, one of four daughters of that greatly respected family. They were married and began work in Pithoragarh in 1875.

While four fifths of the people of the valley were Brahmans, and some were prosperous, there were no schools.

Gray began medical work. Mrs. Gray, knowing the local language (Kumauni) well, invited the women to her home and began teaching them needlework. Out of these activities came a call for a girls' boarding school. Annie Budden came to visit her sister and accepted an invitation to take charge of the girls' school. She joined the Methodist Church and soon thereafter became a missionary of the WOMEN'S FOREIGN MISSIONARY SOCIETY.

One day, a Hindu widow named Sarli came with two sons and two daughters, asking for religious instruction. The whole family soon became zealous Christians. One of the boys, named Khuliya, adopted the surname Wilkinson and became the leading Indian minister of the district. The long-range results of missions are well illustrated by the record of the Wilkinson family since Sarli's conversion in 1877. A son of Khuliya, Richard Wilkinson, followed his father into the ministry and served as pastor of large churches and as superintendent of two districts, one of them Pithoragarh. One of Richardson's sons has been professor of sociology in the University of Nagpur and is an eminent Christian layman who represents the WORLD COUNCIL OF CHURCHES in a study project in the United States. Another son is doing important social work in NEW YORK, and a daughter has held very responsible positions in educational institutions in India and America. A daughter of Khuliya married a young minister who has been superintendent of two districts, one on the plains of the Uttar Pradesh, the other, Almora.

From the small primary schools started by the Grays have come in the intervening years and through the able missionary service of many men and women—Indian more than American—a co-educational intermediate college and a junior high school for girls. From the early emphasis on healing, a wonderful ministry to sufferers from leprosy has been developed on the mountain just above Pithoragarh.

Outstanding among the missionaries from abroad has been LUCY W. SULLIVAN, who with Annie Budden exercised tremendous influence on two generations of Hindus and Christians in the Shor Valley and adjacent areas.

B. T. Badley, Southern Asia. 1931.
J. N. Hollister, Southern Asia. 1956.
J. E. Scott, Southern Asia. 1906.   J. WASKOM PICKETT

PITMAN, CHARLES (1796-1854), American pastor, orator, evangelist, presiding elder, and denominational administrator, was born at Cookstown, Burlington County, N. J., on Jan. 9, 1796. Early in his youth he came under the influence of Methodist meetings in Wrightstown, N. J., walking six miles to attend them. In his sixteenth year he was converted. Later he attended the Methodist services in New Mills (PEMBERTON), N. J.

At the age of seventeen he began teaching in a country school near his home. After his marriage (around 1817), he taught in a school near New Mills.

In 1817 he was licensed as a LOCAL PREACHER and accepted a supply appointment on the Trenton Circuit (New Jersey). In 1818 he was received on trial in the PHILADELPHIA CONFERENCE. In 1820 he was ordained DEACON and in 1821 ordained ELDER.

Pitman's highly successful ministerial career may be summarized under three types of assignment: as pastor, as presiding elder, and as denominational administrator. He served local pastorates from 1817 to 1826: Trenton Circuit, Bergen Circuit, New Brunswick, Bridgeton, all in New Jersey; ST. GEORGE'S, PHILADELPHIA (twice); Union, Philadelphia; Eighth Street, Philadelphia; Green Street, Trenton (New Jersey).

He served as presiding elder on the West Jersey District (1826-1830), on the East Jersey District (1830-1833), and on the Trenton District (1841).

He served as special agent to raise funds for DICKINSON COLLEGE (1835-36). From 1841 until his forced retirement in 1850, because of illness, he served as Secretary of the Missionary Society of the M.E. Church.

In 1844 the University of North Carolina honored him with the D.D. degree.

He was a leader in the movement to have New Jersey Methodism become an Annual Conference, separate from the Philadelphia Conference. This was done by the General Conference of 1836.

He died in Trenton, N. J., on Jan. 14, 1854, and was buried in Mercer Cemetery in that city.

Both Pitman Grove Camp Meeting and the City of Pitman, Gloucester County, N. J., which grew out of the Camp Meeting, are named for him.

C. A. Malmsbury, The Life, Labors and Sermons of Rev. Charles Pitman, D.D. Philadelphia: M. E. Book Rooms, 1887. The New Jersey Conference Memorial. Philadelphia: Perkinpine & Higgins, 1865.   FRANK BATEMAN STANGER

PITMAN COMMUNITY CENTER, Methodist rural community institution, was established in 1921 by John S. Burnette. It is located on Webb's Creek in Sevier County, Tenn., and serves a large area of the mountain country. A school, physician, nurse, a store selling used clothing and furnishings at a small price, post office, and craft shop comprise the center. The property has twelve acres of land used as a demonstration farm.

L. W. PIERCE

PITTS, FOUNTAIN E. (1808-1874), American preacher and missionary to South America was born in Georgetown, Ky., July 4, 1808. Both parents died when he was quite young. Fortunately, relatives provided him a good home and education. At twelve, he joined the church; at sixteen he was licensed to preach; and in 1826 he was admitted into the KENTUCKY CONFERENCE, on trial. Four years later he was ordained an elder and transferred to the TENNESSEE CONFERENCE.

In 1835, while pastor of McKendree Church, NASHVILLE, Tenn., he was asked by the Board of Managers of the Missionary Society to make a survey of South America. This was in response to a resolution of the 1832 GENERAL CONFERENCE of the M.E. Church, asking for study of the possibility of the church entering South America.

Gone from home nearly a year, Pitts spent six months in South America and made lasting impact upon BRAZIL, URUGUAY, and ARGENTINA. At RIO DE JANEIRO, Brazil, he organized a Methodist class in two weeks and petitioned the board to send a permanent missionary. He also organized a class in MONTEVIDEO, Uruguay. In BUENOS AIRES, Argentina, he organized a Methodist society and made preliminary arrangements for building a church.

Direct results of his survey were the sending out of JUSTIN SPAULDING, founder of the work in Brazil, the first Methodist missionary appointed for permanent service in South America, and of JOHN DEMPSTER, founder of Methodist work in Argentina and Uruguay.

Mrs. Pitts' health required his early return to TENNESSEE, where he served as circuit preacher, station preacher, and district superintendent. He became one of the leaders of the M.E. Church, South, at its organization and afterward.

Fountain Pitts was gifted in mind, voice, and personality. Eloquence and imagination made him one of the powerful preachers of his generation. He was noted for his campmeeting preaching, at a time when distinguished preachers of all denominations were creating the notable Cumberland Valley revival epoch of the first half of the nineteenth century. The slavery controversy embittered many churchmen, both North and South, but Fountain Pitts consistently sought to temper the passions of all with Christian charity and understanding. Early in the first GENERAL CONFERENCE of the M.E. Church, South, Pitts moved that LOVICK PIERCE, a like-minded peace maker, be sent to the next General Conference of the M.E. Church, as a fraternal delegate "to convey the love and good wishes of the Southern brethren."

Pitts' consuming concern became the redemptive ministry and welfare of the church. At the General Conference of 1874, he co-authored a resolution which resulted in the formation of the Brazil mission. On Sunday, however, during that Conference in LOUISVILLE, Ky., having preached twice, he was fatally stricken and died on May 12 of that year. The first funeral service was before the General Conference; the second was in McKendree Church in Nashville, Tenn., before his own congregation and a multitude of friends from all faiths.

W. C. Barclay, *History of Missions.* 1957.
E. S. Bucke, *History of American Methodism.* 1964.
Cullen T. Carter, *Methodist Leaders in Jerusalem Conference, 1812-1962.* Nashville, 1961.
————, *Tennessee Conference.* 1948.
Journal of the General Conference, MES, 1846.

EDWIN MAYNARD
J. RICHARD SPANN

PITTSBURGH, PENNSYLVANIA, U.S.A. (population 512,-789), is the second city in the state in size. It was laid out in 1786 and its strategic location at the junction of the Monongahela and Allegheny Rivers which formed the Ohio gave it early prominence as a gateway to the West. Its proximity to large bituminous coal fields and certain deposits of iron ore led to the establishment of large steel mills which have formed the basis of its industrial life through the years. The coal and steel industry drew persons from almost every portion of the world to Pittsburgh, and it has been truly a melting pot of the nations.

The city is first mentioned in the minutes of the M.E. Church for 1788, when Charles Conway was appointed the first preacher in the circuit, embracing the region for many miles around the city. In 1790 there were ninety-seven circuit members, though not many in Pittsburgh itself. Bishop ASBURY first visited the city in 1789, and makes the following record: "I preached in the evening to a serious audience. This is a day of very small things; what can we hope? Yet, what can we fear? I feel great love to the people, and hope God will arise to help and bless them."

Methodism was finally established in Pittsburgh in the year 1796 through the work of JOHN WRENSHALL, who had been born in England where he was converted in a Methodist society and became a local preacher. He removed to PHILADELPHIA in 1794 and then in 1796 came to Pittsburgh to open a new store. A little society under the leadership of Wrenshall met variously in a large room at the old fort at the Point, and in Wrenshall's home. In 1808, the little congregation moved to the home of THOMAS COOPER where, for some two years, services were held until the first Methodist church building in Pittsburgh was erected on the corner of Front and Smithfield Streets on a lot purchased from Thomas Cooper. On Aug. 28, 1810, Bishop Asbury stood upon the cornerstone of this church and preached, and made this entry: "The society here is lively and increasing in numbers, and the prospect still is good in this borough." This was the only house of worship owned by the Methodists until 1817, when a church was erected at the corner of Smithfield and Seventh Streets, where there has been a continuing congregation to the present.

The growth of the Methodist Church was quite rapid until between 1824 and 1829 great controversy arose in reference to the economy and government of the Church. A great deal of controversy was centered in the Smithfield Street Church, and the M.P. Church, which separated from the M.E. Church, became very strong in Pittsburgh and had a glorious history until 1939 when Methodism was reunited.

The Methodist Church in Pittsburgh grew rapidly, serving the diverse areas of the city by the establishment of what came to be great churches. In 1970 there were three churches with memberships of over 2,000 members. They are: Baldwin Community Church, Christ Church in Bethel Park, and Mt. Lebanon Church. Time has taken toll of the membership of certain other great churches, and yet First Church (formerly Christ) in Shadyside, Calvary Church on the Northside of Pittsburgh, and Emory Church in East Liberty are rendering a great service in difficult neighborhoods of Pittsburgh.

One of the significant movements of Pittsburgh Methodism was the creation of a City Society organized in 1880. It was chartered in 1894 as the Methodist Church Union and it serves as the official Home Mission and Church Extension agency for Pittsburgh Methodists. Through its efforts, Methodism has been attempting to relate to the City of Pittsburgh in days of change and decadence.

Three GENERAL CONFERENCES have been held in the City of Pittsburgh. The first in 1828, again in 1848, and more recently in 1964. The General Conference of 1964 held its sessions in the Civic Arena, which is noted for the dome which can be opened so that the great arena becomes an open-air theater. The late Bishop W. VERNON MIDDLETON, resident bishop of the Western Pennsylvania Area, in welcoming the 1964 General Conference, welcomed them to "the Renaissance City" and pointed out that persons had come from fifty states and nearly two score lands to attend the sessions.

The churches of Pittsburgh are contained within two districts of the WESTERN PENNSYLVANIA CONFERENCE, the Pittsburgh District and the Pittsburgh East. There are at the present time 54,822 members in ninety-five churches in Pittsburgh and its immediate environs. These churches possess assets in the amount of $37,896,084. The Methodist Church, therefore, is one of the dominant Protestant groups in the City of Pittsburgh, and its influence and service in the city is very great.

Baldwin Community Church is a large church in the Whitehall, South Hills section of Pittsburgh, which grew rapidly after its organization on Mothers' Day, May 12, 1946, when it was organized with eighty-five charter members under T. R. Courtice, the superintendent of the Pittsburgh District of The Methodist Church, who was the first minister of the new church. In October 1947, Courtice retired as David J. Wynne was appointed pastor and served through 1961. The church grew so rapidly that by 1952 two separate services were unable to seat the congregation and a third service was called for. The third building, a sanctuary, was completed in 1955 and on Christmas Eve the first service was held in the new building. In November 1959, the ground was broken for the final educational building and the addition housed thirteen classrooms of public school room size, a visual aids room, additional rest rooms and storage areas, bringing the total cost of buildings and lands to over a million dollars.

One of the striking experiences in the life of this church was the entertainment of the PITTSBURGH CONFERENCE in May of 1959 under the direction of Bishop LLOYD C. WICKE.

The story of Baldwin Community Church is a chronicle of growth in numbers and property, but likewise it is one of growth to a spiritual maturity. Across her years, she developed into a church of 3,110 in 1970, in which a program of family centered nature has been developed from interests such as dramatic groups, ceramics groups, chess groups, choirs, photography and art interests as well as those inspirational and educational opportunities that are usually associated with the on-going process of a local church. A weekday nursery school was begun as a service to the local community and enrolls over sixty preschool youngsters in each semester and is an integral part of the program of the church.

The church members are divided into a circuit system with three circuits, three ministers, and under each minister is a circuit lay leader. In each circuit, there are section leaders who are members of the Commission on Membership and Evangelism of the local church. Under each section leader, there are various area leaders. Areas are groups of some ten to twelve families for the purpose of fellowship, concern and general pastoral care. The area system works extremely well as a mode of communication for the overall effectiveness of the pastoral responsibility of the church in the community and is one of the keys to the success of this intimate relationship that exists in an extremely large church.

Christ Church, Bethel Park. Located on Highland Road in Bethel Borough, this great Church, started in 1949, had become the largest church in the Western Pennsylvania Conference by 1967. The organizing minister was Harry N. Peelor. The site of the new church was purchased by the Methodist Church Union of the Pittsburgh

Conference in 1945, and the proposed church was listed as a new appointment at the Conference session in October 1949. The first service was held on Oct. 20, 1949 in a two-room office on the second floor of the Mitchell Building on Highland Road, Bethel Borough. The first twenty-seven members were received in November 1949. On April 13, 1950 the church was officially chartered by the Commonwealth of Pennsylvania with 200 charter members. On July 5, 1951 ground was broken for the first unit of the building which was occupied for the first service in it on Easter Sunday, April 13, 1952. In May, 1959 ground was broken for three additional units, a sanctuary, with administration and educational wings. The new sanctuary was opened for worship on April 3, 1960. The 1960 membership had grown to 1,805, and by 1970 it was 3,604, with a property valuation of $1,730,-387. Its total benevolent contributions in 1970 were $34,351 while the church continued carrying a heavy building indebtedness. A highly developed system of pastoral care was inaugurated in the fall of 1961 whereby the congregation is divided into three societies each functioning under the administration of an ordained minister of the church staff. This is said to maintain the warmth of a smaller church while retaining the power of the present large one.

First Church. The first record of Methodist preaching in the City of Pittsburgh shows that WILSON LEE of the Red Stone Circuit preached in the Triangle district in 1785, one year after Methodism was organized in America and twenty-seven years after the founding of Pittsburgh. The Pittsburgh Circuit was formed in 1788 with Charles Conway as the pastor. For the first seven years meetings were held in the First Presbyterian Church and the remains of old Fort Pitt. Later they were held in private homes until the first brick chapel was completed in 1810 on Front Street between Smithfield Street and Wood Street, with William Knox as the pastor. In 1817 the group moved to a larger church at Smithfield Street and Seventh Avenue. On March 5, 1828, this church was incorporated by the legislature of Pennsylvania.

First Church was divided over the issue of mutual rights of ministers and laymen. In May of 1829 opposing groups in the church, one known as the "Old Side" and the other as "The Reformers," were holding separate services in the Methodist Church at the corner of Seventh Avenue and Smithfield Street. On June 24, 1829, the church was placed under the "Conventional Articles," which had been adopted in Baltimore, Md., on Nov. 12, 1828. On May 25, 1831 ground was purchased for a new church building on Fifth Avenue near Smithfield Street. This church was dedicated June 3, 1833. Later it came to be known as "The Old Home." The Corporation owned the churches on Water Street, Smithfield Street and Fifth Avenue and also a cemetery where the Pennsylvania Railroad Station now stands. Litigation developed among the members of the original church over the ownership of this property. The Superior Court of Pennsylvania held all of these properties belonged to the majority group or the "Reformers," who retained the original charter. However, the court recommended an amicable settlement, and an agreement was reached in which the "Reformers" gave to the "Old Side" group the title to the property at Smithfield Street and Seventh Avenue and $2,000. On Feb. 6, 1838 this group was incorporated as The Smithfield Street M.E. Church. In 1893 the church located on Fifth Avenue, known as The First Methodist Protestant Church in the City of Pittsburgh and holding the original amended charter, built two churches belonging to the same corporation, The First M.P. Church and Trinity M.P. Church. Following Methodist Union in 1939, the First M.P. Church again amended its charter, changing its name to The First Methodist Church of Pittsburgh. In 1946 The First Methodist Church of Pittsburgh united with Christ Church under the name of The First Methodist Church of Pittsburgh and the original charter granted by the Pennsylvania State Legislature in March of 1828 was amended to that effect. First Church reported 1,207 members in 1970.

John Wesley A.M.E. Zion Church. In the spring of 1836, a small group of Christians began holding religious services in the home of Mr. and Mrs. Edward Parker on Roberts Street. In July of the same year, they were organized into an A.M.E. Zion Mission, the first of the denomination in Pittsburgh. Their numbers outgrew the Parker home in a few months, necessitating larger quarters which were found in the home of Obadiah and Charlotte Mahoney, two members living on Arthur Street.

Three years later under the leadership of a Rev. Mr. Tabbs, a lot was acquired in Peru Way upon which a one-story building was erected; it became popularly known as "Little Jim." It was dedicated and occupied in the year 1850. In 1865, during the tenure of Nick Williams, a great revival was held in which 100 souls "desired to flee from the wrath to come and be saved from their sins" united with Zion Methodism and the "Little Jim." From this epoch-making event, the Peru Way structure became increasingly inadequate.

In the year 1881, under the pastorate of Jehu Holliday, the membership acquired a site on Arthur Street and proceeded to build a new building which was completed and dedicated in October 1886. From that time the John Wesley Church became one of the metropolitan charges in Zion Methodism.

During the long history of the congregation, twenty-five ministers have served the church, each rendering some worthwhile contribution to the life and history of Zion Methodism in Pittsburgh.

Mount Lebanon Church is a commanding church of the Pittsburgh area, having a fine edifice, a million dollar education facility, and has known great growth since its beginning in 1912. At that date a modest chapel was erected named Sanner Chapel to honor the memory of N. H. Sanner, an early pastor. This chapel, still in use today, served until the present sanctuary was completed and dedicated by Bishop FRANCIS J. MCCONNELL on Nov. 23, 1924. In 1955 the sanctuary was remodeled. The Mount Lebanon Church reflects the phenomenal growth of the South Hills District of Pittsburgh, where more and more people have built residences away from the smoke of the city. Membership grew steadily and in 1970 numbered 2,887 in spite of the fact that many of the members living south of Mount Lebanon have transferred to, and helped develop, Christ Church. Mount Lebanon Church also substantially assisted Christ Church financially for a number of years.

The church gained considerable national attention in 1942 when a "Golden Chain Campaign" was proposed to liquidate a $50,000 mortgage. The campaign was so successful that nearly $80,000 was pledged, and the excess amount was returned to the subscribers. One of the leaders

of this campaign was LEON E. HICKMAN, a member of the church, and prominent in general church activities.

Two former pastors of the church were elected to the episcopacy: LLOYD C. WICKE, 1942-48, and W. RALPH WARD, JR., 1948-60.

The church ranks among leading churches of Methodism in its mission giving.

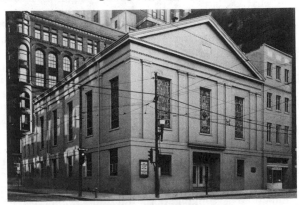

SMITHFIELD STREET CHURCH,
PITTSBURGH, PENNSYLVANIA

Smithfield Street Church. This is the old historic church of Pittsburgh Methodism. The original Society was established under the leadership of local preacher and merchant, John Wrenshall, in October 1796, and met from 1796 to 1803 in the historic "Blockhouse" of old Fort Pitt. Its first building was erected at Front and Smithfield Streets in 1810, and it became the first station appointment west of the Allegheny mountains in 1811. The present property at Smithfield Street and Seventh Avenue was purchased for $5,000 in 1817, and the first church building was erected on it in 1818. From 1812 to 1819 the membership grew from 167 to 357. A great revival in 1819 and 1820 increased the membership to 697 in 1821. One evening during the revival some young men put a paper of brimstone on the hot stove. The suffocating fumes, the character of the preaching, and the yellow painting of the building fastened the name "Brimstone Corner" upon the church.

The first GENERAL CONFERENCE west of the Allegheny mountains was held in this Church in 1828. It was the historic General Conference at which the appeal of "the Reformers" was rejected, and this resulted in the formation of the M.P. CHURCH. Consequently during 1829-33 Pittsburgh Methodism became greatly divided. The controversy split the Smithfield Street congregation and resulted in the formation of the First M.P. Church in 1831, and legal litigation over the Smithfield Street property ensued, the church site being retained by the M.E. congregation under an agreement reached in 1833.

Despite this disruption the church maintained its membership of about 750 until another controversy in the 1840's reduced the membership from 750 in 1843 to 360 in 1847. Seventy of the leading members withdrew at one time and joined new Methodist congregations being established in the growing city. Despite this decline, in 1848 it was determined to replace the inadequate old church. The present building was erected between May and December 1848, the chief initiative being by William Bingham, with Alexander Bradley providing financial guidance. It was dedicated on Christmas Day, 1848 by Bishop L. L. HAMLINE.

In the post Civil War period this historic church was one of the strong pulpits of Methodism and four of its pastors were elected to the episcopacy, namely: CHARLES W. SMITH, pastor 1876-1878, elected bishop 1908; CHARLES B. MITCHELL, pastor 1886-1888, elected bishop 1916; CHARLES E. LOCKE, pastor 1888-1892, elected bishop 1920; and NAPHTALI LUCCOCK, pastor 1893-1897, elected bishop 1912.

During the depression of the 1930's the property then in debt was saved for Methodism by the Conference Church Union assuming financial responsibility for. it. In 1942, under the leadership of the Church Union, a Pittsburgh Conference campaign produced the funds to pay off the indebtedness and renovate both the church and the adjoining building. The four story building was renamed Benedum Hall, for layman MICHAEL L. BENEDUM, a generous supporter of the project, and was made into the Pittsburgh Methodist Bookstore, and episcopal and other offices. This valuable corner is at present the last remaining piece of Methodist property in the "golden triangle" of downtown Pittsburgh. The Church continues as a functioning congregation, and the Center is a hive of activity.

Albert G. Curry, *Smithfield Street Methodist Church.* Pamphlet, 1953.
General Minutes.
Journal of the Western Pennsylvania Conference.
M. Simpson, *Cyclopaedia.* 1878.
W. G. Smeltzer, *Headwaters of the Ohio.* 1951.

ALLAN J. HOWES
MAHLON D. HURLBERT, JR.
W. GUY SMELTZER
JOHN W. HAWLEY
DAVID H. BRADLEY
W. E. FENSTERMAKER

PITTSBURGH CHRISTIAN ADVOCATE, THE. This weekly M.E. publication commenced on Feb. 1, 1834 and continued until June, 1932, when it was merged with *The Christian Advocate* published in New York. Its original name was *The Pittsburgh Conference Journal* and it was launched as a project of the PITTSBURGH CONFERENCE. In 1840 the GENERAL CONFERENCE gave its approval to the publication and its name was changed to *The Pittsburgh Christian Advocate.* Throughout its ninety-eight years of publication it continued to serve as the regional Methodist publication of the daughter Conferences of the original Pittsburgh Conference, namely: Pittsburgh, ERIE, NORTH EAST OHIO, and WEST VIRGINIA CONFERENCES. It was one of the leading publications of the M.E. Church with a circulation during the first quarter of the twentieth century of over 40,000. Its editors were among the most influential men of the denomination. They were: CHARLES ELLIOTT, WILLIAM H. HUNTER, Charles Cooke, HOMER J. CLARK, Isaac N. Baird, SAMUEL H. NESBITT, ALFRED WHEELER, CHARLES W. SMITH, John J. Wallace, and RALPH B. URMY. The bound files of this publication have been preserved and are the property of the Historical Society of the WESTERN PENNSYLVANIA CONFERENCE. They are housed in the Conference Historical Collection in the Library of the Historical Society of Western Pennsylvania in Pittsburgh. They have been microfilmed by the Board of Microtext of the American Theological Library Association and are available, in whole or in part, from them. They form a major source of the official history of the Pittsburgh Conference, *Methodism on the Headwaters of the Ohio,* by Smeltzer, where numerous significant items are preserved in quotations.

Pittsburgh Christian Advocate, Feb. 1, 1834 to June 1932.
W. G. Smeltzer, *Headwaters of the Ohio.* 1951.

W. GUY SMELTZER

PITTSBURGH CONFERENCE (ME) was created by the 1824 GENERAL CONFERENCE. It was composed of the original REDSTONE CIRCUIT and what might be called its daughter circuits. Its territory included western PENNSYLVANIA, eastern OHIO to the Muskingum and Tuscarawas Rivers, northwestern VIRGINIA (later WEST VIRGINIA), and the western tip of NEW YORK. The conference was carved mostly from the BALTIMORE and OHIO CONFERENCES, with small sections coming from the GENESEE and KENTUCKY CONFERENCES. At the beginning the Pittsburgh Conference had seventy-one preachers, forty-three appointments, and 20,355 members.

After the Fort Stanwix treaty with the Iroquois Indians in 1768, it became legally proper for white people to settle in southwestern Pennsylvania, and it is estimated that within seven years over 50,000 came into that area and northwestern Virginia. Among the newcomers were many Methodists from the STRAWBRIDGE region in MARYLAND, and there was some unofficial religious activity in their midst during the 1770's. Organized Methodism came into the region in the fall of 1783 when RICHARD OWINGS, Strawbridge's first local preacher, laid out the original Redstone Circuit, largely in the homes of relatives who had emigrated to the west. Bishop ASBURY appointed two itinerant preachers to the Redstone Circuit in the spring of 1784. By the end of the third year the Redstone Circuit had extended 300 miles and reported 756 members. In 1787 it was divided into three circuits, Redstone, Ohio (east of the Ohio River), and Clarksburg. By 1799 five circuits covered southwestern Pennsylvania and northwestern Virginia. They had a total of 1,649 members and about ninety-six societies, some eighty-seven of them centering in homes and the others meeting in small log cabin churches. Eight circuit riders ministered to the ninety-six societies.

After the defeat of the Indian Confederacy in 1795, northwestern Pennsylvania was opened to settlement. Many Methodists migrated to the region, and they became the nuclei for new Methodist societies. By 1804 the Redstone Circuit had expanded to include eight new circuits in northwestern Pennsylvania, eastern Ohio, and northwestern Virginia.

Such is the story of the rise of Methodism in the region which became the Pittsburgh Conference. After its organization the conference grew rapidly, and in 1836 it was divided, the northern portion becoming the ERIE CONFERENCE with four districts, fifty appointments, and 16,876 members, and the southern part continuing as the Pittsburgh Conference with five districts, fifty-eight appointments, and 25,615 members. In 1848 the WESTERN VIRGINIA CONFERENCE was organized, taking two districts from the Ohio Conference. In 1876 the EAST OHIO CONFERENCE was created by detaching the Ohio portions of both the Pittsburgh and Erie Conferences.

The original Pittsburgh Conference established Madison College at Uniontown in 1826. It continued until 1833 when it was merged with ALLEGHENY COLLEGE at Meadville, which came under the patronage of the conference at that time. Allegheny is still a Methodist institution of higher learning. In 1834 the conference launched a weekly publication, *The Pittsburgh Conference Journal*, which as the *Pittsburgh Christian Advocate* became an official organ of the denomination in 1840. It was merged with the *New York Christian Advocate* in 1932.

At unification in 1939 the Pittsburgh Conferences of the M. E. and M. P. denominations united within the boundaries of the Pittsburgh Conference (ME) to form the Pittsburgh Conference (TMC), the one unit bringing 395 churches and 120,622 members to the merger and the other sixty-three churches and 13,578 members.

In 1960 the NORTHEASTERN JURISDICTIONAL CONFERENCE readjusted a number of conference boundaries to make them conform more nearly to state lines, a preliminary step to the merger in 1962 of the major portions of the Pittsburgh and Erie Conferences into the WESTERN PENNSYLVANIA CONFERENCE. The Jamestown District of the Erie Conference became part of the Genesee Conference, some of the Genesee appointments came into the Western Pennsylvania Conference, and the churches in the northern panhandle of West Virginia were given to the West Virginia Conference.

In 1916 the Pittsburgh, Erie, and West Virginia Conferences were designated as an episcopal area with the bishop residing in Pittsburgh. This arrangement continued until 1960 when the West Virginia Conference became an area, the CENTRAL PENNSYLVANIA CONFERENCE taking its place in the Pittsburgh Area. Four years later the Central Pennsylvania Conference became an area with its bishop residing at Harrisburg, leaving Western Pennsylvania as the only conference in the Pittsburgh Area.

The Pittsburgh Conference existed 138 years as one of the strong conferences of American Methodism. In 1962, its last year, it reported five districts—Allegheny, Blairsville, McKeesport, Pittsburgh, and Washington—about 308 ministers, 345 pastoral charges, 163,861 members, and property valued at $76,317,442.

Minutes of the Pittsburgh Conference.
Minutes of the Western Pennsylvania Conference, 1963.
W. G. Smeltzer, *Headwaters of the Ohio*. 1951.

W. GUY SMELTZER

PITTSBURGH CONFERENCE (MP) was organized at the fifth session of the OHIO CONFERENCE (MP) in CINCINNATI in 1833. At the time the Ohio Conference included western PENNSYLVANIA as well as INDIANA and KENTUCKY. When formed the Pittsburgh Conference included the east half of OHIO, western Pennsylvania, and western VIRGINIA (later WEST VIRGINIA). The first session of the conference was held at Mt. Pleasant, Ohio, Sept. 9-16, 1834. At that time the conference had thirty-eight preachers, twenty-eight appointments, and 7,050 members. ASA SHINN served as first president of the conference.

Among other actions at its first session the Pittsburgh Conference voted to support the *Methodist Correspondent* which was launched by the Ohio Conference in 1830. The paper became the *Methodist Recorder* in 1866; it was published in Pittsburgh from 1871 to 1929 when it was moved to Baltimore and merged with the *Methodist Protestant* to become the *Methodist Protestant-Recorder*.

In 1842 the Ohio territory of the Pittsburgh Conference was set off as the Muskingum Conference, and in 1854 the Virginia part became the Western Virginia Conference. Due in part to this loss of territory, the Pittsburgh Conference grew slowly, as compared with its original numerical strength. In 1900 the conference had only 8,635 members, but even so it was the dominant conference in a region where the M. P. Church was relatively strong. Pittsburgh was next to Baltimore as a M. P. center; it was an important publication headquarters for the denomination.

The Pittsburgh Conference was a part of the Methodist Church (the name taken by one section of the divided M. P. Church), from 1866 to 1877. (See Table of Methodist Conferences.)

The Pittsburgh Conference strongly supported Allegheny Seminary until it closed in 1867. Then it gave generous support to ADRIAN COLLEGE in MICHIGAN which had become a M. P. institution in 1852. The conference assisted WESTMINSTER THEOLOGICAL SEMINARY from its founding in 1882, and it gave support to a home for the aged at West Lafayette, Ohio. A fairly strong Preachers' Aid Society was organized in the conference in 1852 on receipt of a gift of $25,000. Careful management and additional donations brought the fund up to $125,000, and the income from it made possible annual payments of $400 to the superannuates and $250 to the widows of ministers in the 1920's and 1930's.

Over the years several Pittsburgh Conference men were elected president of the M. P. GENERAL CONFERENCE, and some became president of Adrian College. JOHN CALVIN BROOMFIELD, president of the General Conference, 1928-36, was one of the two M. P. ministers elected to the episcopacy of The Methodist Church at the Uniting Conference in 1939.

In 1936 the Pittsburgh Conference voted seventy-two to seven in favor of Methodist union. In 1939 the conference brought sixty-three churches and 13,578 members into the Pittsburgh Conference of The Methodist Church.

A. H. Bassett, *History of the M. P. Church*. 1882.
Methodist Protestant Yearbook, 1918.
Minutes of the Pittsburgh Conference, 1936.   F. E. MASER

PLAN OF PACIFICATION (1795), together with the rules and regulations passed by the Wesleyan Methodist Conference of 1797, was the attempt of the Wesleyan itinerants after the death of John Wesley in 1791 to work out a constitution for the connection which would satisfy those who wanted the Wesleyan societies to become more like a religious denomination of a democratic kind (and that quickly), and those who were content with the position as John Wesley had left it. The Plan of Pacification, which was accepted by the itinerant conference in 1795, was a compromise on the subject of the Sacraments: one group, consisting especially of some of the more influential trustees, were not anxious to see the itinerants administer the Sacraments for the time being; a majority of the laity, and many of the itinerants themselves, thought that the itinerants should now be allowed to administer the Sacraments in virtue of their pastoral position. The plan provided that

the Sacrament of the Lord's Supper shall not be administered in any chapel, except the majority of the Trustees of the chapel on the one hand, and the majority of the Stewards and Leaders belonging to the chapel (as the best qualified to give the sense of the people) on the other hand, allow it. Nevertheless, in all cases the consent of the Conference shall be obtained before the Lord's Supper be administered.

Where there was a society but no chapel, it was sufficient for a majority of the stewards and leaders to say that the Lord's Supper should be administered. This decision meant that within a few years all the itinerants were administering the Sacraments without any local opposition, and this is often taken as marking the moment of separation between the Church of England and the Wesleyan Methodist societies.

The conference action was not based on a theory that the itinerants had received a presbyterian ordination in succession from John Wesley; the Conference of 1791 had forbidden any further ordinations by the imposition of hands and so prevented the emergence of a significant succession of this kind. The itinerants almost certainly regarded their reception into *Full Connexion* as a kind of ordination, "virtual ordination" as it is sometimes called. The chief architects of the plan were JOHN PAWSON, JOSEPH BENSON, and WILLIAM THOMPSON. It is not always realized that the plan also offered a solution to the problem of the place of the laity in the constitution. The section "Concerning Discipline" gave to a simple majority of trustees, or of the stewards and leaders, of any society authority to summon the pastors of the local district, together with all the trustees, stewards, and leaders of the circuit in which the society lay, in order to try any circuit pastor whom they considered "immoral, erroneous in doctrines, deficient in abilities," or an offender against the other rules contained in the plan itself. There was a lay majority in such a meeting, and it was empowered to act by a majority vote; a pastor found guilty had to withdraw from the circuit in question, though a district meeting, consisting of itinerants only, finally decided his fate. It is not surprising that in the "Addenda" to the *Minutes* of 1795 the itinerants said that "we have, to some degree, deposited our characters and usefulness in your hands, or the hands of your representatives, by making them judges of our morals, doctrines and gifts." This extraordinary regulation, however, was never appealed to, except perhaps when SAMUEL WARREN claimed, wrongly, that he ought to have been tried by this court in 1835, instead of by a district meeting.

As a first stage in the development of Wesleyan Methodism after John Wesley's death, the Plan of Pacification was important, but it was not as decisive as is sometimes suggested. The Constitution of 1797 had to add further clarification to the Wesleyan constitution, and the two sets of regulations were not in themselves sufficient to prevent the establishment of the METHODIST NEW CONNEXION in 1797. It was the position of the laymen in the Wesleyan Methodist connection which was the fundamental issue, not the question of the administration of the Sacraments. Further schisms took place between 1797 and 1849, and the matter was not finally settled until the admission of lay representatives to the Wesleyan Methodist Conference in 1878.

JOHN KENT

PLAN OF SEPARATION, THE. A plan adopted by the GENERAL CONFERENCE of the M.E. Church in 1844 after long and fruitless debate and heated division over continuing in the episcopacy a Southern bishop, JAMES A. ANDREW, who was a slave-owner, albeit an unwilling one. This Plan allowed the thirteen Annual Conferences in the slave-holding states to withdraw from the M. E. Church

"should the Annual Conferences in the slave-holding states find it necessary to unite in a distinct ecclesiastical connection" (*History of American Methodism*. Vol. II, p. 63). The whole report—later called the Plan of Separation—was a lengthy one containing twelve separate resolutions. Each of these was voted on separately with roll call votes on four of the separate resolutions, but the whole being finally adopted by the Conference with only eight members dissenting. In effect it allowed the Southern Conference representatives to ascertain the feelings of their people, and allowed "the Societies, stations and Conferences adhering to the Church in the south, by a vote of the majority of the members of the said societies . . . to remain under the unmolested pastoral care of the Southern Church" (*Ibid*). It agreed that there would be no attempt on the part of the M. E. Church to organize churches or societies within the limits of the Church, South, and the Church, South should reciprocally observe the same rule. It also agreed that the equity in the BOOK CONCERN should be divided in "the same proportions to the whole property of said Concern that the traveling preachers in the Southern Church shall be to all the traveling preachers of the Methodist Episcopal Church."

The text of this plan is given in full in Methodist histories. Pursuant to this Plan of Separation, the Southern Conferences and local churches did form their own ecclesiasticism—the METHODIST EPISCOPAL CHURCH, SOUTH. This Church organized formally in 1846 and existed as one of the two great branches of Episcopal Methodism until it, with the M. E. and M. P. Churches, reunited in 1939 to be The Methodist Church.

The Plan of Separation was repudiated by the next General Conference of the M. E. Church (1848) forcing the Southern Church, which had by that time organized, to go into court to secure its equity in the Book Concern and other general Church interests. The Supreme Court of the United States finally acted upon this matter, finding for the Church, South, and holding that the General Conference of the Church was competent to adopt the Plan of Separation and ordering the Book Agents and those in authority in the M. E. Church to pay over to the Southern Church the above mentioned equity. (Federal Reports, 16 Howard, 288; *Smith vs. Swormstedt*, 1853.)

E. S. Bucke, *History of American Methodism*. 1964.
C. Elliott, *Great Secession*. 1855.
Federal Reports, 16 Howard, 288, *Smith vs. Swormstedt*. 1853.
J. M. Moore, *Long Road to Union*. 1943.
Plan of Separation and Disruption of the Methodist Episcopal Church. Nashville: A. H. Redford, 1876.   N. B. H.

PLAUEN, Germany. About 1869 a Methodist family named Schneider re-emigrated from the United States to Plauen (Saxony) and gathered a group of people seeking salvation. Most of the first Plauen Methodists were women. The first official Methodist service was held on Whitsunday, 1870. For several years Plauen was served from other circuits; only after 1886, when two villages had been separated, was Plauen able to develop, and a big church was built in 1892. Three years later the Plauen-Reichenbach-Netzschkau Circuit was divided into three. Only 117 members were left in Plauen, but a steady increase led to about 800 adult members up to the time of the Second World War. Then the community suffered grievous losses from air-raid destructions and subsequent emigrations of members. The church property was de-

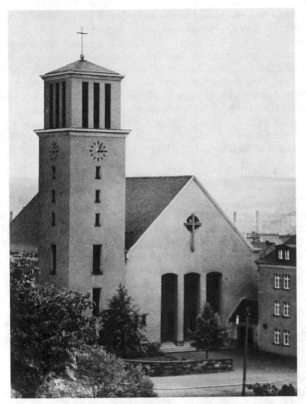

ERLOSERKIRCHE, PLAUEN, GERMANY

stroyed, but after the war the congregation gathered in a wooden, shed-like building, increasing again to about six hundred members. In 1954 the conspicuous *Erloserkirche* (Church of our Redeemer) with a seating capacity of 1,000, with numerous additional rooms was dedicated. The Plauen Circuit, today in the CENTRAL CONFERENCE of the German Democratic Republic and near the demarcation line between East and West and on the border of the CZECHOSLOVAK Republic, seems predestined to represent the world-wide Methodist task of reconciliation.

THEOPHIL FUNK

PLAYER, WILLA BEATRICE (1909-   ), American college president, was born at Jackson, Miss., on Aug. 9, 1909, the the daughter of Clarence C. and Beatrice (Day) Player. She received the A.B. degree from OHIO WESLEYAN UNIVERSITY, 1929, and the LL.D. from that institution in 1953. She became Doctor of Education at Columbia Teachers College; and has received the LL.D. from LYCOMING COLLEGE, 1962; from Morehouse College, 1963; and from ALBION COLLEGE, 1963. Miss Player went upon the faculty of BENNETT COLLEGE, N. C., in 1930, and after being an instructor and vice-president there, 1930-55, she was elected president of the college in 1955. She is a member of the Women's Planning Commission for the Japan International Christian University Foundation, Inc.; and the Ford Foundation; and is a member of the National Association of Schools and Colleges of the United Methodist Church (president, 1962-63); the North Carolina Council of Churches (secretary); the Southern Association of Secondary Schools and Colleges (Visiting Committee, 1953-54); American Association of University Women; the National Council of Negro Women, and of the United Church Women (upon its Board of Managers).

She is a member of the American Association of Colleges and has served on its Committee on Liberal Learning.

Who's Who in America, Vol. 34.
Who's Who in The Methodist Church, 1966.   N. B. H.

PLAYTER, GEORGE FREDERICK (1809-1866), Canadian minister and historian, was born in London, England. When he was twenty-four he emigrated to CANADA, and in 1834 he was taken on trial in the CANADA CONFERENCE. He was ordained in 1838.

For some years, Playter served on circuits in Upper Canada. At the same time his interest in writing was developing. After the union with the Wesleyans broke down in 1840, he issued two powerful letters entitled "A Voice from Canada" and "A Second Voice from Canada," in which he defended the Canadian Methodists. Thus from 1844 to 1846 he became editor of *The Christian Guardian,* but in this capacity his earlier promise was not fulfilled.

After he left *The Guardian,* Playter dropped out of the ministry temporarily to write and to operate a printing establishment. He took up circuit duties again in 1849, but became superannuated in 1858. In retirement he completed two volumes of his *History of Methodism in Canada,* of which only the first, covering the years before 1828, was published.

Playter's history was an admirable piece of work—well-informed, judicious, and comprehensive. The loss of the second volume, which would have continued the story to 1847, was a great misfortune for future historians of Methodism.

As a writer and as a preacher, Playter was honest, straightforward, and blunt. "His sermons were remarkable for their clearness. He uttered nothing at random, nor anything not worth the uttering. His professions were not loud, but he was a sincere, humble lover of the Saviour." (*Minutes of the Conference of the Wesleyan Methodist Church,* 1867, 16). He died on Oct. 24, 1866.

G. H. Cornish, *Cyclopaedia of Methodism in Canada.* 1881.
Minutes of the Conference of the Wesleyan Methodist Church, 1867.   G. S. FRENCH

PLUMMER, F. BERRY (1885-1957), American E.U.B. minister, was born to Charles W. and Sarah Eakle Plummer, Jan. 7, 1885, at Bridgeport, Washington County, Md. He joined the Pennsylvania Conference, Church of the UNITED BRETHREN IN CHRIST, in 1903 and was ordained by the same conference in 1908. He graduated from LEBANON VALLEY COLLEGE in 1905 with the B.A. degree and later received from his alma mater the D.D. degree. Plummer was married to Emma E. Flook of Myersville, Md., Nov. 11, 1907, who preceded him in death (Feb. 10, 1949).

He was one of the strongest figures in his annual conference, representing it in eleven GENERAL CONFERENCES. For thirty-five years Plummer served Hagerstown, Md., St. Paul's Church, one of the most important churches in the Conference. He served forty-one years as a trustee of Lebanon Valley College, receiving in 1955 the first citation that the college had issued to one of its trustees. For fifteen years he was a member of the executive committee of the FEDERAL COUNCIL OF CHURCHES of Christ in America. He served his denomination as a member of the General Board of CHRISTIAN EDUCATION, the Board of

Pensions, and the General Council of ADMINISTRATION, including its Executive Committee.

After an illness of eight weeks, Plummer died May 25, 1957 in Hagerstown, Md., and his remains were placed in the Mt. Zion Cemetery, Myersville, Md.

P. E. Holdcraft, *Pennsylvania Conference.* 1939.
Minutes of the Pennsylvania Conference, 1957.
The Telescope-Messenger, July 6, 1957.   JOHN H. NESS, JR.

PLYLER, MARION TIMOTHY (1867-1954), and **ALVA WASHINGTON** (1867-1956), American brothers, pastors, and editors. **Marion T. Plyler** was born on Sept. 14, 1867, in Iredell County, N. C., the son of Robert Conrad and Mary L. (Kimball) Plyler. His wife was Epie Duncan Smith, whom he married on June 20, 1900, and they became the parents of seven children.

He was educated at Trinity College (now DUKE), A.B. in 1892; A.M., 1897; and D.D., 1937; and at the University of Chicago where he did postgraduate work in 1898. He also received the M.A. degree from the University of North Carolina in 1905 and its D.D. in 1931.

Joining the NORTH CAROLINA CONFERENCE, he served Wilmington, Murfreesboro, Plymouth, Louisburg, Chapel Hill, Greenville, and Washington, 1892-1910. He was the presiding elder of the Elizabeth City District, 1911-14; of the Raleigh District, 1915; pastor, Grace Church, Wilmington, 1916-19; again the presiding elder of the Durham District, 1920-23; the Raleigh District, 1924-27. He became editor of the *North Carolina Christian Advocate* in 1928, and served in that capacity continually until his retirement in 1945.

Alva Washington Plyler, the twin brother of M. T. Plyler, began his ministry in 1892. Among other appointments, he served three times as presiding elder, the districts being ASHEVILLE, SALISBURY, and GREENSBORO in the WESTERN NORTH CAROLINA CONFERENCE. He became editor-manager of the *North Carolina Christian Advocate* in 1921 (seven years before his brother M. T. joined him). The Plyler Brothers, as they were always called, were always thought of together in connection with the editing and publication of the *North Carolina Christian Advocate.* Alva W. Plyler was the author of one book, *The Iron Duke of the Methodist Itinerancy* (John Tillett), which was published in 1925.

M. T. Plyler was a member of the GENERAL CONFERENCES (MES) of 1914, '18, '22, '26, '30, '34, and '38, and also of the General Conferences of The Methodist Church of 1940 and '44, as well as the UNITING CVNFERENCE of 1939. He attended the ECUMENICAL METHODIST CONFERENCE of 1921 and 1931; served on the General BOARD OF MISSIONS in his Church, 1918-25; was president of the Board of the Pastors' School at Duke University from 1918 for thirty-two years. He was president of the WESLEY FOUNDATION at the University of North Carolina also. He wrote *Leroy Lee Smith, Lawyer of the Old School,* 1916; *Men of the Burning Heart,* 1918 (in collaboration); *Bethel Among the Oaks,* 1925; *Thomas Neal Ivey—Golden Hearted Gentleman,* 1925; *Letters of Travel in America and Europe.*

He had considerable influence in his Conference as editor and church leader and was held in great respect by his brethren. He retired in 1945 and died in DURHAM, N. C., on March 24, 1954.

A. W. Plyler was a trustee of the Methodist Assembly (LAKE JUNALUSKA) at one time, and also a trustee of BREVARD COLLEGE. He married Grace Davis Barnhardt on July 20, 1901. (She is still living and resides in The Methodist Home, CHARLOTTE, N. C.). They had three daughters of whom only one survived infancy.

He was a member of the Southern Methodist Press Association and at one time was its president; also a member of the editorial council of the Religious Press of America. He received the honorary D.D. degree from both ASBURY COLLEGE and Duke University. He was a delegate to six General Conferences, including the Uniting Conference at Kansas City in 1939.

C. T. Howell, *Prominent Personalities.* 1945.   N. B. H.

PLYMOUTH, England. The first Methodist class to be formed in this famous Devon port was started in 1745, and twelve months later JOHN WESLEY paid the first of a score of visits to the city; the last of these was in 1789. His association with the city was not always a happy one, and on one of his last visits a better-than-usual reception occasioned the comment in his *Journal,* March 2, 1787: "What, is God about to work in Plymouth also." This uncertain beginning has been belied by later growth. Plymouth Methodism remained a part of the Devonshire Circuit until 1783 when the Plymouth Dock Circuit was formed. The first chapel was opened in Lower Street in 1780. Ker Street, the most famous of the early chapels, opened in 1787, was demolished in 1960's. By the time of John Wesley's death there were fifteen hundred members in the circuit. In 1819 a second circuit was carved out of the Dock Circuit and called Plymouth. In 1823 the Dock Circuit was renamed Devonport.

By 1871 Plymouth had to be redivided into the King Street and Ebenezer Circuits. The King Street Chapel, built in 1864, was claimed to be the finest outside London. It housed the Wesleyan Methodist conferences of 1895, 1913, and 1929, and remained in use until its destruction by German bombing in 1941. Ebenezer was built in 1816 and survived to provide a skeleton for the Plymouth Central Hall which was created after Wesley Church (1879) was destroyed in 1937 by fire. This reconditioned building would also have perished in the wartime blitz, but was saved largely due to the efforts of a team of students from RICHMOND COLLEGE who were holding a crusade at the hall at the time of the air attack. Their work in extinguishing dozens of incendiary bombs saved the building, which was the only large hall left standing in the city. And so it became, until 1959, the scene of the city's annual mayor-choosing ceremony, and of other important civic functions.

The Devonport Circuit was divided in 1893 to form the Gloucester Street and Belmont Circuits. These existed separately until 1926, when a single Devonport Circuit was again formed. The Belmont Chapel (1875) is still in use. The nineteenth century also saw the growth in the city of the other branches of the Methodist family. Primitive Methodism seems to have owed its origins to a local resident, William Driffield. By the middle of the century it had rooms in Plymouth and Devonport and village causes at Holberton and Dunstone to the east. From this work grew the societies at Millbridge, Herbert Street, Morice Town, and Cobourg Street. Of these city chapels only Millbridge survived the Second World War.

The UNITED METHODIST FREE CHURCHES had a society in Ebrington Street. The BIBLE CHRISTIAN movement was established in Plymouth Dock in 1818 by WILLIAM

O'BRYAN himself. It was at Stoke Damerell that a Bible Christian press was set up in 1822 to print a hymnbook. And it was in Stoke Damerell Church that O'Bryan's daughter Mary married William Thorne, the printer. The press moved to Shebbear in 1829, but the work in Plymouth grew. By mid-century there were half a dozen societies of which Greenbank and Embankment Road were the largest. It was to Elburton that Mary Thorne retired as a widow, and there spent the last ten years of her life.

The union of 1907 created three United Methodist circuits centered on Greenbank, Ebrington Street, and Morice Town. These three, together with the Primitive Methodist Circuit of Cobourg Street, and the four Wesleyan circuits—King Street, Ebenezer, Devonport, and Garrison were amalgamated after Methodist Union in 1932 to form King Street, East, Devonport, and Garrison Circuits. In the years before the Second World War the growth and movement of population in the city led to extension work in many of the suburbs. A new central hall was opened in the Garrison Circuit. At the outbreak of war the membership of the four circuits was over 5,000. The Second World War brought great naval and military activity in Plymouth, and between 1939 and 1945 Plymouth Methodism gave hospitality to thousands of servicemen from all over the world. The sailors' "Welcome" at Devonport, begun in 1908, and the Plymouth Central Hall were the focal points of this work. But in one week in April, 1941, the city center was destroyed by air attack, and a third of the population was made homeless. Eleven Methodist churches were destroyed and many others damaged. In Devonport on the Sunday morning after the blitz not one church was fit for worship. To deal with this emergency a single Plymouth Circuit was set up. This continued until 1945 when the Plymouth East Circuit separated itself. At the same time the Plymouth Central Hall joined the Garrison Circuit to form the Plymouth Mission Circuit. In 1952 the King Street and Devonport Circuits resumed their own existence.

Methodism in Plymouth has produced many famous men. HENRY CARTER, so long a creative figure at the Temperance Department, was born in the city. Three vice-presidents of the Methodist Conference came from Plymouth, including ISAAC FOOT. It was the generosity of John Beckly, a Plymouthian, which gave the Conference the annual lecture in social studies and Christianity which bears his name. Perhaps the city's greatest claim to fame in Methodism, however, will be that it was here in 1965 that the Methodist Conference took the historic decision to pursue the path of union with that Church of England from which John Wesley sprang.

DONALD MASON

POE, ADAM (1804-1868), American preacher and book agent, was born in Columbiana County, Ohio, July 21, 1804. His formal education was limited, but by dint of reading and study he became a well informed man. Baldwin University awarded him the D.D. degree in 1862. In 1825, he married Eliza Hosford, and they had a son and two daughters.

Brought up a Presbyterian, Poe embraced Methodism as a youth, and in 1827 joined the OHIO CONFERENCE. Following seven years on circuits, he received varied appointments. He served a total of nine years on four districts—Wooster, 1834-37; Tiffin, 1838; Norwalk, 1842 and 1847; and Elyria, 1848-49. There were five appointments

to two stations for a total of eight years—Mansfield, 1839, 1845-46, and 1850-51; and Delaware, 1840-41, and 1843. In 1844 he was appointed for one year as agent for OHIO WESLEYAN UNIVERSITY and Norwalk Seminary. In 1852, he became assistant agent at the Western BOOK CONCERN in CINCINNATI, and served as agent from 1860 to 1868.

Poe was pastor at DELAWARE when Ohio Wesleyan University began in 1842. A trustee from that time forward, he rendered notable service. At his funeral, Bishop DAVIS W. CLARK remarked that it could almost be said that Adam Poe was the founder of Ohio Wesleyan.

While Poe was preaching in a powerful revival at the Methodist Church, Danville, Ohio, in January 1835, WILLIAM NAST, who was to become the father of German Methodism in America, knelt at the altar with other penitents and was, according to his own testimony, "born again." It was Nast's Aldersgate experience. That September Poe introduced Nast to the Ohio Conference which admitted him on trial and appointed him as "German Missionary" in Cincinnati.

The FREEDMEN'S AID SOCIETY of the M. E. Church was organized Aug. 7-8, 1866, when eleven men, including Poe, met in Trinity Church, Cincinnati; he was elected as the first treasurer of the society.

A man of recognized ability and devotion, genial in nature, and equipped with a stock of reminiscences and anecdotes which he used effectively in conversation and preaching, Poe enjoyed the confidence of his brethren, as attested by the fact that they elected him to six GENERAL CONFERENCES, 1844-64. He died June 26, 1868.

E. S. Bucke, *History of American Methodism.* 1964.
P. F. Douglass, *Story of German Methodism.* 1939.
General Minutes, MEC.
Minutes of the North Ohio Conference, 1867-68.
M. Simpson, *Cyclopaedia.* 1878.   ALBEA GODBOLD

POL, GASTON (1924-   ), Bolivian educator, was born in Cochabamba. He studied at the university there, receiving a law degree in 1964. He took graduate courses at VANDERBILT, Peabody, and SCARRITT, all in NASHVILLE, Tenn. He married Julia Salazar, a teacher and director of the elementary sections of the American Institute. They have two adopted children. He was a professor in the school of law at the university. His positions in the Methodist Church included lay preacher, treasurer of the annual conference, executive secretary of finances, coordinator of educational work in BOLIVIA, and director of COLEGIO EVANGELICO METODISTA in La Paz (formerly American Institute).

In 1969 Dr. Pol was named as one of an eight-member Supreme Council on Education for Bolivia, which was created to guide sweeping educational reforms in Bolivia. He was one of five private citizens on this council, the other three being cabinet members. A United States missionary wrote: "the new and much-needed Comision Suprema de Educacion is charged with restructuring and unifying Bolivian education; this affords Dr. Pol a unique opportunity for service to his country."

NATALIE BARBER

POLAND, a country of eastern Europe, is bounded on the north by the Baltic Sea and the U.S.S.R., on the east by the U.S.S.R., to the south by Czechoslovakia, and to the west by GERMANY.

Polish history begins with 966 A.D., when Mieczyslaw I, duke of Mazowie, accepted Christianity for himself and his people. His son, Boleslaw the Brave, transformed his father's principality into a powerful and independent kingdom. With her everchanging frontiers and a prestige and political power that waxed and waned repeatedly, Poland played for the next seven centuries a vital role in European history. During the sixteenth century her rulers became elective. This democratic innovation weakened her to such an extent that her powerful neighbors, RUSSIA, AUSTRIA and Prussia, could partition her territory in three successive moves (1772, 1793, and 1795). Restored as a republic in 1918, Poland enjoyed a brief independence until she was divided anew by Germany and the U.S.S.R. in 1939. After the Second World War, she emerged as a republic again with sweeping changes in ideology, territory, and population.

Poland is recognized as traditionally a Roman Catholic country. Before the Second World War, sixty-nine percent of the population were Poles; of these seventy-five percent were Roman and Uniat Catholics. Today, ninety-eight percent is estimated as Polish, and of that ninety-four percent is Roman Catholic.

During the early days of the Reformation, Protestantism flourished in Poland, because of a prevailing religious tolerance, with Lutherans and Calvinists predominating. At one time a majority of the Polish nobles accepted the tenets of the Reformers. Due to a lack of unity and the extremism of some Protestant leaders, the educational activities of the Jesuits, and external political situations, the influence of the Reformation slowly waned until it became negligible. Today, Protestants represent between one and two percent of the population, with a predominance of the following denominations: Lutheran, Reformed, Methodist, Baptist and Evangelical.

Methodism. The Methodist Church in Poland grew out of the activity of the 1918-19 Centenary Commission of the U.S. M. E. Church, South. After the First World War, deputations were sent to Europe to investigate existing situations, and on June 5, 1919, the BOARD OF MISSIONS (MES) voted "that work be opened in Poland . . . as soon as the conditions will allow." This new activity sought to provide temporary physical relief to those in need, and religious services for those seeking spiritual guidance. The unique Polish Relief Campaign in the United States provided clothing and other supplies valued at $2,000,000. Daisy Davies was its director.

The first sessions of the "Poland and Danzig Mission" were held in Warsaw, Poland, Aug. 24-27, 1922, with Bishop W. B. BEAUCHAMP of RICHMOND, VA., presiding. It reported: districts, 2; charges, 9; churches, 7; membership, 800; probationers, 150; value of property, $67,000. The district superintendents were George W. Twynham and John Rasmussen, Sr. Other early missionaries and church workers were EDMUND CHAMBERS, Hiram King, Fred C. Woodward and THOMAS J. GAMBLE.

Klarysew School and Home. The first congregations were organized in the key cities of the country. To meet certain pressing postwar problems of the population, some institutions were opened. The best known of these was the school and children's home at Klarysew near Warsaw. This institution had three main goals: to provide a home and education for the most promising of the many orphans adopted by the church, to create a center that would be a base for the church's future development, and to help meet through education one of the fundamental needs of

METHODIST CENTRE, KLARYSEW,
NEAR WARSAW, POLAND

the country. Its first and only director was WLADYSLAW DROPIOWSKI, a well-known Polish educator. In 1933, due to budget restrictions, the mission was forced to close this institution. Reopened in 1965, it now serves as a conference center.

English Language School. Another unusual product of the early years is the English Language School in Warsaw. In 1921, E. B. McKnight and a Mr. Welch started free evening classes for teaching English and the Bible, and these gained immediate popularity. Reportedly from 1,500 to 2,000 persons attended during the first year. Soon these courses developed into an evening English language school for paying students. This gradually improved in teaching personnel, standards of instruction, physical facilities; it imported textbooks from London especially written for Poles. In the last decades it has been known as the best institution teaching English in Poland. Today it has over 5,000 students. Its directors were consecutively Thomas W. Williams, W. Winston Cram, Ruth Lawrence, Leonid Jesakow, and JOSEPH SZCZEPKOWSKI.

Woman's Work. On May 4, 1927, the Board of Missions of the M. E. Church South voted to close the Russian Mission in Harbin, Manchuria, and transferred the personnel and budget of the Woman's Department in that city to Poland for a program among White Russians. Constance Rumbough and Sallie Lewis Browne arrived from Harbin within a few months and established their headquarters in Wilno, Poland. Later their mandate was widened to include work among the women, youth, and children of the entire country.

Growth of the Methodist Church in Poland was slow. Legal restrictions, such as the lack of official recognition of the church by the state, made difficult any rapid expansion. The German-speaking congregations which had constituted an entire district in 1922 decreased rapidly in membership and influence. Even before the Second World War several of them conducted their services in Polish. After the war no German-speaking congregations remained.

In the 1920's, a program undertaken to establish new congregations and to open hostels for high school students among the White Russians in the northeastern provinces met with only limited success. The congregations disappeared when, in 1939, these provinces were annexed by the U.S.S.R. Attempts were made also (in the late 1920's) to open work among the Ukrainians in eastern Galicia. These efforts were fruitless. Church development received a serious setback from the depression in the United States, which between 1931 and 1936 brought drastic budget reductions and the recall of most of the American missionaries. Bishop U. V. W. Darlington of Huntington, W. Va., as the bishop in charge, sympathetically guided the young church during these difficult years. He was succeeded in 1934 by Bishop Arthur J. Moore of Atlanta, Ga. This tireless evangelist visited most of the Polish congregations and untiringly labored at deepening the spiritual life and increasing the missionary zeal of preachers and members.

The Second World War dealt a grave blow to Methodism in Poland. During this conflict one third of the congregations were lost because of territorial incorporation into the U.S.S.R. Over one half of the preachers were lost to the church, forced to leave the country by various circumstances. Many promising young Methodists perished in prisons and on battlefields. For six years the life of the church was totally disorganized.

Fortunately a vital core remained in Warsaw. Classes in church history and related subjects, usually given at theological seminaries, and covering a three-year course, were taught by university professors and other qualified persons. In this way some twenty men and several women were carefully prepared for future leadership in the church. When the war ended, most of the men students became the pastors of the rebuilt congregations.

Since 1945. With the coming of peace in 1945, Methodism experienced a period of substantial expansion. New congregations were organized in many parts of the country. Church membership grew rapidly. Some reasons for the increase were the official recognition of the Methodist Church in Poland by the Polish government; the uprooting and transfer to the west and north of a large segment of the population; the availability of young clergymen trained during the last few years of the war; the vigorous leadership of Konstanty Najder, the first general superintendent, and the material support from the church abroad under the energetic direction of Bishop Paul Neff Garber of the Geneva Area.

Much of this expansion was due to the situation that arose in former East Prussia, a considerable part of which fell to Poland in 1945. Since the German pastors and many of the members of the United Evangelical Church of this territory had fled to postwar Germany, their churches and parsonages stood empty. The constituencies that remained were leaderless. The Roman Catholic Church in Poland began to take over some of the church buildings. Najder, acting jointly with leaders of the Augsburg Evangelical Church (Lutheran), petitioned the Polish government to assign the still unoccupied churches to these two denominations. The Methodists were permitted to begin services and to organize congregations in over twenty of these parishes.

At the same time, new work was started in other parts of Poland. Numerically this period marked the high tide of Polish Methodism. For several years the annual reports showed over sixty pastors with appointments and memership above sixty thousand.

After the Second World War the Board of Missions sent another group of experienced missionaries to Poland. However, these were permitted to remain only a short time: in the fall of 1949, all foreign religious workers were ordered by the Polish authorities to leave the country. Seven dark years followed. No sessions of the annual conference were held. Dissensions and intrigues among the preachers abounded. Finally the traveling preachers expelled the general superintendent, Joseph Naumiuk, from the conference. Jan Ostrowski was elected his successor. Great losses in members and clergy occurred during these years.

After the radical political changes of 1956, a new day dawned for the church. Relationships between the preachers slowly improved. Communication with the church overseas became normal again. With the election of Joseph Szczepkowski as general superintendent, Methodism bound up its wounds and attacked energetically its organizational problems and missionary responsibilities. During these years Bishop Ferdinand Sigg of Zurich, Switzerland, in charge of the Central and Southern Europe Central Conference, visited the church regularly, ordained to the ministry those qualified, and supervised the appointments.

Today, though small in numbers, Methodism plays a vital role in modern Poland as a Protestant denomination. It has been active in the country's ecumenical organization and has sent delegates to numerous overseas religious and social action meetings. Its representatives have of course participated in the sessions of the Central and Southern Europe Central Conferences, and the General Conferences of the Methodist Church.

Annual Reports, Board of Missions, MES, TMC.
J. Cannon, *Southern Methodist Missions.* 1926.
P. N. Garber, *Continental Europe.* 1949.
Journals of the Annual Missions and Annual Conferences of the Methodist Church in Poland. Gaither P. Warfield

POLAND ANNUAL CONFERENCE embodies the Methodist work in Poland. It was a Provisional Annual Conference when in 1960 the General Conference of The Methodist Church gave permission to it to become an annual conference, if during the quadrennium a minimum of twenty-five ministerial members should belong. This condition was met and the conference was recognized as the Poland Annual Conference in 1964. It is in the Central and Southern Europe Central Conference and is currently presided over by the bishop of the Geneva Area.

Statistics of this conference at the 1969 reporting were: Number of districts, 5; charges or appointments, 36; organized churches, 36; preaching stations, 13 (total, 49); ordained ministers, 27; lay preachers serving as pastors, 8; members of the church, 6,519. Institutions of the conference as described above are the English-Language School at Warsaw, an orphanage at Klarysew, and a Bible school and youth center, "Warfieldowe," Klarysew.

Barbara H. Lewis, *Methodist Overseas Missions.* 1960.
N. B. H.

POLITICS AND BRITISH METHODISM. In the history of English party politics there has been a peculiar polarity. Underlying the shifting connections traced by the famous historian of the eighteenth century, Lewis Namier, and the altering attitudes to specific policies, there has remained a seemingly natural alliance between Tory and Anglican on the one hand and Liberal and Free Churchman on the other. From the days of Cavalier and Roundhead to those of Disraeli and Gladstone, and even to some extent to the present time, "Church and Queen" has been a Tory toast, while Whig-Liberal agents have relied on the support of the greater part of the Nonconformist vote. Neither party has been able to ignore religious loyalties; and when the Labour Party began to displace the Liberal

Party as the major party of political reform and radicalism, it too was seen to owe more to Methodism than to Marxism.

Within this pattern the part played by Methodism as an influence in English politics has been as equivocal as its own ecclesiastical development. JOHN WESLEY's authoritarian rule was as much a reflection of his Tory-Anglican traditions as of his undisputed supremacy over every part of the church he brought forth from its Anglican cradle, but at first he was anxious to keep Methodism out of politics as much as he could. Many of those to whom he preached had no votes; he was determined to avoid the dangers of allowing an evangelical movement to run out in the sands of political activity, as he feared some eighteenth-century nonconformity had done; he was anxious to avoid either Jacobite or Jacobin "smears," so he instituted a "no-politics rule" for his helpers.

In the troubled period which followed the death of Wesley this rule served to keep Methodists from unhappy association with some of the potentially revolutionary movements of the early nineteenth century, and the supposed atheism of some of the followers of Tom Paine horrified them. It is too much to claim that Methodism saved England from a revolution such as affected France, for conditions in the two countries were so different, but it is true that many to whom the new doctrines of the rights of men were being preached were finding them more clearly expounded in the Bible than in Rousseau or Paine. A no-politics rule normally works more favorably for conservatism than for radicalism, and two further tendencies in the post-Napoleonic War period worked toward keeping Methodists out of the old Whig-Dissenting alliance. There was a Tory government in office and the newly emergent church was anxious not to attract restrictions; the major public interest of Methodists was in humanitarian movements, and many of the leaders of these were Tories like WILLIAM WILBERFORCE and Shaftesbury.

The 1832 Reform Act did not much excite those whom Disraeli in *Coningsby* called the respectable Wesleyans who should be natural allies of his new-type Conservatives; they reacted in unmistakable aversion from Chartism; they might not like Anglo-Catholicism, but they would not support Liberal-Dissenters in trying to disestablish the Church of England. JABEZ BUNTING, in the mid-century, seemed to be the very incarnation of this new ecclesiastical-political entente between Methodism and Conservatism; even when the disasters of 1849-51 splintered the Wesleyan connection, his view still prevailed with the majority of his ministerial brethren, and with most Wesleyan laymen too.

Bunting's influence remained within Wesleyan Methodism strongly supporting authoritarian church government and conservative political sympathies; but outside the Wesleyan connection, there were other Methodist movements which were less fearful of contamination by liberal ideas. By 1797 ALEXANDER KILHAM's METHODIST NEW CONNEXION was avowing liberal principles in church and state alike. The appeal of WILLIAM CLOWES and HUGH BOURNE in PRIMITIVE METHODISM, and of WILLIAM O'BRYAN and his BIBLE CHRISTIANS was to a class socially lower than those who comprised the strength of the Wesleyan connection. It was small wonder that these connections were less circumspect in their political expression; among their members were to be found many who supported movements for cheap food and better working conditions. The Founding Fathers of English trade union-ism were often Methodist local preachers and class leaders, and the terms they used for some of their organizations they learned from the Methodism that first taught them the worth of ordinary men and also the way to organize them. Such men naturally turned to Liberals rather than to Conservatives; and as the franchise was widened, they were wooed first by the Radical-Liberals, and later by the Labour Party.

The parallel development of Wesleyan Tory and Primitive Methodist Radical was accompanied by the emergence of a Liberal Methodist type which was more middle class in composition, and which was particularly significant in the Gladstonian era. It was predominantly lay in character, and, while it was recruited in large numbers by the ecclesiastical conflicts of the nineteenth century, it may have owed its genesis to the consequences of the Municipal Corporations Act of 1835. Democratic institutions in England emerged first in the nineteenth century in local government, and it was here that Methodist laymen first found themselves in alliance with Nonconformist shopkeepers and manufacturers. So often in the old towns there had been an alliance between the squire, the parson, and the professional classes, respectable established citizens with a naturally conservative outlook. The new wealthy classes produced by the Industrial Revolution had to struggle against the privileges of this "establishment." Liberalism, with its substitution of election for inherited privilege and hierarchy, was the natural political creed for such protagonists. By the time of Gladstone and HUGH PRICE HUGHES, such Methodists had become a powerful ally of the Liberal Party when it claimed to speak with the voice of the "Nonconformist conscience."

In the twentieth century the interconnection between religion and politics had been blurred by greater emphasis upon class divisions. The three Methodist political types have all continued within the Methodist Church—reunited in 1932—but, as English Liberalism has declined in influence as a political party, many of the more radical Methodists have veered towards the Labour Party, which in England has been non-Marxist. Many of the more prosperous have joined their old Wesleyan brethren in supporting the Conservatives. It would be hard to estimate the proportion of each party within the Church today.

E. R. TAYLOR

POLITY, CHURCH. (See CHURCH GOVERNMENT; British Methodism, Organization of; and other articles dealing with various aspects of Methodist organization.)

POLK, CHARLES PEALE (1767-1822), American portrait painter, best remembered for his so-called "lost portrait" of Bishop FRANCIS ASBURY. He was a son of Robert Polk and Elizabeth Digby (Peale) Polk. His mother came from the famous Peale family of artists, was a daughter of Charles Peale, Jr., and a sister of Charles Willson Peale. After his father was killed in a naval action in 1777, Charles Peale Polk was trained in art by his uncle, Charles Willson Peale.

"The hard linear painting, well executed and attractive in Charles Willson Peale, was debased by his nephew, Charles Peale Polk," says critic J. Hall Pleasants in the *Maryland Historical Magazine*, pointing to "stiff handling by Polk of legs, arms, and figure . . ." But Polk painted Washington, Franklin, LaFayette, and other notables of the day. One canvas of Washington hangs outside the

State Dining Room at the White House and his work appears in exhibitions depicting the development of the portrait art in America.

The "lost portrait" of Asbury was done in 1794. He reluctantly agreed to sit for the artist only when James McCannon, a merchant tailor, proposed in exchange to give a warm waistcoat to each of his preachers. Asbury's *Journal* of June 18, of that year notes: "I once more came to BALTIMORE where, after having rested a little, I submitted to have my likeness taken; it seems they want a copy; if they wait longer, perhaps they may miss it. Those who have gone from us in VIRGINIA [i.e., followers of the schismatic JAMES O'KELLY] have drawn a picture of me which is not *taken from life*."

That portrait done in Baltimore was by Charles Peale Polk. For many years its whereabouts were unknown, but it was recovered by GEORGE C. M. ROBERTS, and is now owned by the Baltimore Conference Historical Society as a prized show-piece of the Lovely Lane Church Museum in Baltimore. That it once was used as a fire-screen was believed by Roberts, who made a study of the portrait's mysterious provenance. A hole was cut through the canvas where the right hand is uplifted, probably to admit a stovepipe. Now restored, this "lost portrait" was prominently exhibited, September-December, 1968, in Room 206 of the new National Portrait Gallery in Washington for the inaugural exhibit titled "This New Man." Now it is permanently on display at the Lovely Lane Museum, 2200 St. Paul Street, Baltimore. It offers an interesting comparison both in subject and technique with the Asbury portrait done in 1812 by JOHN PARADISE.

This 1794 portrait was done by Polk during a period when he was most popular as a painter of portraits and his own confidence in his talents ran high. He had advertised himself at Philadelphia as a house, ship, and sign painter in 1787. But from 1791 to 1793 he announced himself in Baltimore newspapers as a portraitist.

Apparently Polk for a while became a traveling artist, typical of the period, for he was in RICHMOND, Va., 1799-1800. In this he may not have been altogether successful for he became a government clerk in WASHINGTON and apparently lived there until his death in 1822. There is evidence that he married three times: 1) c. 1785, Ruth Ellison; 2) c. 1811, Mrs. Brockenbrough, and 3) c. 1816, Ellen B. Bowman,; and was father of fifteen children.

F. Asbury, *Journal and Letters*. II, p. 17.
Antiques Magazine, November 1968.
Maryland Historical Magazine, 1946.
J. Hall Pleasants, *Maryland Historical Magazine*, 1942.
Smithsonian Institution's *Catalog* of the exhibit "This New Man," 1968.
Together Magazine, November 1959.　　　　LELAND D. CASE

POLK, JAMES KNOX (1795-1849), the eleventh President of the United States and first President to be associated with the Methodist Church, was born on Nov. 2, 1795 near Pineville, N. C. In 1796 his family moved to TENNESSEE. In 1820, two years after his graduation from the University of North Carolina, he began the practice of law in Columbia, Tenn. In 1821 he became the chief clerk of the Tennessee Senate and two years later a member of the Tennessee House of Representatives. While a member of the state legislature he married Sarah Childess. They had no children.

From 1825 until 1839 Polk was a member of the U.S. Congress and for the last four years served as Speaker of the House of Representatives. In 1839 he was elected governor of Tennessee, but was defeated in his bid for reelection in 1841. In 1844 Polk was nominated by the Democratic Party for the office of President of the United States. In the November 5 election he defeated his opponent, Henry Clay, and on March 4, 1845 was inaugurated. During his administration TEXAS, IOWA, and WISCONSIN became states, the western part of the United States was acquired from MEXICO, and the OREGON dispute with Great Britain was settled.

While President, Polk usually attended the First Presbyterian Church in Washington, D. C. Early in his Presidency he wrote in his diary: "Mrs. Polk being a member of the Presbyterian Church I generally attend that church with her, though my opinions and predilections are in favor of the Methodist Church." When he attended church alone, he often worshiped at Foundry M. E. Church in WASHINGTON.

Polk declined to run for re-election in 1848. On June 9, 1849, shortly before he died, he was baptized and received into membership in the M. E. Church, South, by a long-time friend, JOHN B. MCFERRIN of NASHVILLE, Tenn. Polk died on June 15, 1849 in Nashville and is buried there on the State Capitol Grounds.

Fitzgerald: *John B. McFerrin, A Biography*.
Isely: *The Presidents, Men of Faith*.
Kane: *Facts About the Presidents*.
McCormac: *James K. Polk*.
Nevins, ed.: *Polk, The Diary of a President*.
　　　　　　　　　　　H. ALDEN WELCH

POLK, TRUSTEN (1811-1876), American layman, Governor of Missouri, and U.S. Senator, was born in Sussex County, Md., May 29, 1811. He attended Cambridge Academy and graduated from Yale University in 1831, with honors, completing a study there in 1833.

Polk opened a law office in ST. LOUIS, Mo., in 1835 to begin a notable career in the profession and in politics. Two years later he married Elizabeth Skinner, Dec. 26. In 1845 he was elected to the Convention to re-write the Constitution of the State of MISSOURI. His most important efforts were directed toward the establishment of public schools by constitutional provisions. This laid the foundation upon which the state's public school system has been built. Polk's interest in education was expressed by his becoming a founder and life-long supporter of CENTRAL METHODIST COLLEGE.

Thwarted in his desire to become a minister of the Gospel, his Christian commitment was expressed in his life and services to the Methodist Church. Trusten Polk held every office and performed every function open to a layman in his local church, Centenary, St. Louis; was actively engaged in district and annual conference affairs; and from 1866 until his death an influential member of the GENERAL CONFERENCE, M.E. CHURCH, SOUTH.

Polk ran successfully for the Governorship of Missouri against two politically powerful men, Robert Ewing and former U.S. Senator Thomas Hart Benton. He was inaugurated Governor on Jan. 5, 1857; but a week after that was elected to the U.S. Senate (January 13), and resigned the Governorship on Feb. 27. He served in the U.S. Senate until Jan. 12, 1862, when, the Civil War raging, he became Colonel of a Missouri regiment in the Confederate

States Army. He was appointed Judge Advocate General, Department of the Mississippi, but was captured by Union forces in 1864. Upon his release in 1865, he returned to St. Louis and resumed his law practice and church activities. His stature as a layman was recognized by his appointment as one of the two laymen to the CAPE MAY COMMISSION from the M. E. Church, South. His death April 16, 1876 occurred before the Commission met.

Hyde and Conard, *Cyclopedia of the History of St. Louis.* St. Louis: Southern History Co., 1899.
National Cyclopedia of American Biography.
Shoemaker, *Missouri and Missourians.* St. Louis: Lewis Publishing Co., n.d.   FRANK C. TUCKER

SAMUEL POLLARD

POLLARD, SAMUEL (1864-1915), British Methodist pioneer missionary to Southwest CHINA, was born at Camelford, England, April 20, 1864, the son of Samuel Pollard, a BIBLE CHRISTIAN minister. After five years in the civil service he offered for the Bible Christian ministry. Bible Christian missionary work had begun in 1884 when S. T. THORNE and Thomas Vanstone were sent to Yunnan, Southwest China, and Pollard and FRANCIS DYMOND joined Thorne at Chaotung in 1887. He spent four very hard years at Kunming from 1889-93, but was appointed chairman in 1895 and was sustained by more British workers. The main approach was to the Chinese people, but Pollard trekked into the hills, coming to know the aboriginal Miao people. His distinctive work began when four Miao tribesmen visited his house in 1904, after wandering five hundred miles in many directions "in search of truth." By 1905 Pollard had been visited by four thousand Miao and had begun to itinerate in their tribal areas.

The first church was built at Stone Gateway in 1905. The Chinese joined with the Miao's overlords, the No-su, in persecuting the new Christians; and in 1907 Pollard was attacked and almost killed, but before his death the Miao mass movement had been swelled by No-su and Go-p'u converts. Chapel building averaged three per year, with hundreds of cottage meetings, and twenty-three schools were opened. Pollard invented the "Pollard script" in committing the Miao language to writing, and translated the New Testament and many hymns. He died of typhus at Stone Gateway after heroic labors on Sept. 15, 1915.

CYRIL J. DAVEY

POLLOCK, CHARLES ANDREW (1853-1928), American jurist and prominent layman of NORTH DAKOTA Method-

ism, was born on Sept. 27, 1853 at Elizabethtown, N. Y., the son of John and Eunice Ellis Pollock. He received the A.B. degree (1878), M.A. (1881) and LL.D. (1908) from Cornell College. On Sept. 27, 1882 he married Martha Clinton. Four children were born to them: John C., Clara A., Lorine M., and Charles M. He migrated to the Dakota Territory in 1885 and became District Attorney of Cass County. He was Judge of the Third District Court of North Dakota from 1885 to 1905. He was elected a member of the GENERAL CONFERENCE of the M.E. Church from 1908-12. Here he served notably on the Committee on Judiciary which, in the M.E. Church, interpreted the constitutionality and effect of the General Conference enactments for the *Discipline.*

Judge Pollock was a firm believer in prohibition and became known as a mighty advocate of laws pursuant thereto. He was instrumental in writing the Prohibition Law of the State of North Dakota in 1889. He also wrote a *Manual of the Prohibition Law of the State of North Dakota* in 1910. He made his home in Fargo, N. D., where he died in July 1928.

DAVID F. KNECHT

POLWHELE, RICHARD (1760-1838), British Anglican, was born at Truro on Jan. 6, 1760, and educated at Truro School and Christ Church College, Oxford. Ordained in 1782, he was appointed in 1794 to Manaccan, near Helston, in Cornwall, a parish where he remained until 1821. He had already shown his interest in poetry, history and topographical studies. His study of Devonshire began to appear in 1793, and his more famous *History of Cornwall* in seven volumes from 1803 to 1808. He also published *Traditions and Recollections* (1826) and *Biographical Sketches in Cornwall* (1831). He comes into Methodist history because he was a vicious critic of the whole evangelical revival; in 1800 he published *Anecdotes of Methodism,* which contained the kind of material which LORD SIDMOUTH was to use against Methodism at the time of his abortive attempt to introduce anti-Methodist legislation. Polwhele was answered by SAMUEL DREW, who replied with *Observations on Polwhele's Anecdotes,* also in 1800. This controversy introduced the two men to one another, and they later became quite friendly. Polwhele cannot, however, be regarded as a very serious student of either Methodism or Evangelicalism in general. He died at Truro on March 12, 1838.

JOHN KENT

POMONA, CALIFORNIA, U.S.A., **Trinity Church** is a model of Tudor Gothic Cathedral of the fifteenth century and one of the most attractive churches in Pomona. The church began in May of 1877 when A. M. Hough organized the First M. E. Church of Pomona. The organization meeting was, appropriately, held in a carpenter's shop, owned by J. G. Reed. There were seven charter members of the new church. During that year the first church was built on land donated and the total cost of the building was $500, a goodly sum at that time.

During the early years the church was served by circuit pastors. In 1882 the church had grown to the point where it required a new building. This second church with a seating capacity of 300 cost $2,250. It was dedicated, debt free, on Sept. 30, 1883. In 1888 J. W. Phelps became pastor of the First M. E. Church, and a third building was built and dedicated Jan. 10, 1890. This building is still standing and is occupied by another denomination.

On Oct. 25, 1906 at a QUARTERLY CONFERENCE of First Church a motion was passed "that we recommend the building of a church on the north side of the Southern Pacific track." It was decided that the new church should be named Trinity M. E. Church. At a general meeting held on April 18, 1907, it was "voted" to build an edifice costing $21,000.

The year of 1935 brought about a great change for Methodism in Pomona. During the depression years, church pledges were materially reduced. In the interest of economy Bishop JAMES C. BAKER and District Superintendent Charles F. Seitler, promoted the merging of First Church and Trinity. This move resulted in the dissolution of the First M. E. Church Corporation, and the transfer to Trinity of its church property and most of its members.

In January 1953, ground was broken for the present sanctuary on the location of the old Trinity Church. Befitting God's house, the handsomest of materials have been used. Altar, reredos, paneling, and pews are of Philippine mahogany, richly carved. The front doors are hewn from solid oak.

Stained glass windows depicting the life of Christ, Old Testament history and contemporary events in Protestantism are memorial gifts installed by the famous Judson's Studios of LOS ANGELES, Calif. On Oct. 6, 1968 a new organ built by Abbot and Sieker was dedicated, one of the finest instruments in the Pomona Valley.

Trinity's building and equipment outlay is approximately $884,000 and is debt free. In 1970 it reported 1,741 members.

Trinity is Methodism's mother church in the Pomona Valley. It has been a church with a strong mission to foreign and local missions. Its church school and youth programs over the years have been responsible for youth entering the Christian ministry, youth work, mission field and other related church endeavors. The church serves the community with varied programs vital to youth in scouting and campfire groups; it serves its members through two worship services each Sunday, family night programs, WOMAN'S SOCIETY OF CHRISTIAN SERVICE, programs for Lent and Christmas, and church school classes for the children, youth and adults. The music program at Trinity is one of the most outstanding within the community.

First M. E. Church Quarterly Conference minutes, Oct. 25, 1906.
General Minutes, UMC.
John N. Strout, "History of Trinity Methodist Church, Pomona, California." Mimeographed, 1960.   JAMES R. McCORMICK

PONCA CITY, OKLAHOMA, U.S.A. **First Church** is a strong church in that section of OKLAHOMA. With the opening of the "Cherokee Strip" of Oklahoma Territory in 1893 and the subsequent establishment of Ponca City, the Methodists started with a "class" and within the year built their first church building. E. C. Harper was the first pastor. In 1921, under the pastorate of Clarence N. Hewitt, the present church edifice was erected and dedicated. An educational building was added in 1951.

Under the leadership of twenty-nine pastors who have served the First Church of Ponca City, membership has grown to 2,450 and a church school membership of 958 in 1970. Annual programming of its ministry exceeds

$125,000 in cost. Staff includes two full-time ministers, minister of music, two missionaries in CONGO, and secretarial assistance.

ARGUS J. HAMILTON, JR.

HENRY J. POPE

POPE, HENRY J. (1836-1912), British minister, was born at March, Cambridgeshire, Feb. 2, 1836. He entered the Wesleyan ministry in 1858. From 1876-97 he was secretary at the Chapel Office; he made this a center of religious aggression as well as a financial department. He was the inspiration of the Central Mission set up in Manchester in 1885-86, whose success was the key to the spread of the Central Hall idea throughout England. In recognition of his share in the FORWARD MOVEMENT, he was elected president of the Wesleyan Conference in 1893. In 1897 he became Home Missions Secretary, and worked constantly for expansion. He died in London on July 16, 1912.

JOHN KENT

WILLIAM B. POPE

POPE, WILLIAM BURT (1822-1903), British minister and scholar, was born at Horton, Nova Scotia, Feb. 19, 1822; his father was a Wesleyan Methodist missionary from Devonshire. Brought up at Plymouth, he studied for the ministry at the Theological Institution, Hoxton (1841-42). While on circuit, he built up a reputation by translating antirationalist German theologians: Haupt's *First Epistle*

John (1846); Stier's *Words of the Lord Jesus* (1854); Ebrard's *Commentary on the Johannine Epistles* (1859); Winer's *Confessions of Christendom* (1863). Pope became theological tutor at Didsbury College, Manchester, in 1867. In 1871 he gave the second FERNLEY LECTURE on *The Person of Christ;* in 1875-76 he published his *Compendium of Christian Theology.* In 1877 he was elected president of the Wesleyan Conference, and in 1878 published *Sermons, Addresses and Charges* delivered during his year of office.

A saintly man, Pope had immense prestige as a theologian in later nineteenth-century Wesleyanism; his aloof, scholarly conservatism probably explains why liberal theology developed so slowly in the Wesleyan connection. Blind in his later years, he died on July 5, 1903.

JOHN KENT

POPE, WILLIAM KENNETH (1901-   ), American bishop, was born Nov. 21, 1901, at Hale, Mo., the son of William Mumford and Victoria (LaRue) Pope. In 1917-20 he attended Clarendon College in Texas. He received his B.A. degree in 1922, and his B.D. in 1924 from SOUTHERN METHODIST UNIVERSITY. He attended the Graduate School at Yale University from 1927 to 1929. His honorary degrees include: D.D from SOUTHWESTERN UNIVERSITY (Georgetown, Texas) in 1937 and from HENDRIX COLLEGE in 1961; and the LL.D. degree from Southern Methodist University in 1964.

On March 16, 1930, he married Kate Sayle and they have two children, Katherine Victoria and Kenneth Sayle.

He joined the CENTRAL TEXAS CONFERENCE of the M.E. Church, South in 1924, deacon in 1925, full connection in 1926, elder in 1929. He was transferred to the SOUTHWEST MISSION CONFERENCE in 1936; to the SOUTHWEST TEXAS CONFERENCE in 1940; to the TEXAS CONFERENCE in 1949. His pastorates include: Milford, Texas, 1924-26; First Church, Breckenridge, 1929-33; First Church, GEORGETOWN, 1933-36; St. Paul Church, Springfield, Mo., 1936-40; First Church, AUSTIN, Texas, 1940-49; First Church, HOUSTON, 1949-60.

He was elected a bishop in June 1960 by the SOUTH CENTRAL JURISDICTIONAL CONFERENCE, and assigned to the Dallas-Fort Worth Area. He was a member of the South Central Jurisdictional Conferences of 1948, 1952, 1956 and 1960; a member of the General Conference (TMC) in 1952, 1956 and 1960. He served as secretary of the Commission to Study the Ministry of The Methodist Church 1949-56. He was a member of the General Board of EDUCATION of The Methodist Church, 1952-64, has been on the Board of Christian SOCIAL CONCERNS since 1960 and was elected on the Commission on Ecumenical Affairs by the Uniting Conference of 1968; also a member of the PROGRAM COUNCIL in 1968. He was a delegate to the World Conference on Life and Work in Oxford, England in 1937; and to the World Methodist Conference at Oxford in 1951. He was a visiting preacher to the General Conference of The Methodist Church in MEXICO in 1946, and represented The Methodist Church in the United States to the Centennial Celebration of Methodism in INDIA in 1956. Bishop Pope is a trustee of: Southern Methodist University, Southwestern University, TEXAS WESLEYAN COLLEGE, and of the Methodist Children's Home of Texas. He is a member of the Board of WESTERN METHODIST ASSEMBLY (MOUNT SEQUOYAH). He administers the work of The United Methodist Church in the NORTH TEXAS and the Central Texas Annual Conferences. The Area presently comprises more than 700 churches with a total membership of about 165,000.

Who's Who in America, Vol. 34.
Who's Who in The Methodist Church, 1966.   N. B. H.

PORT ARTHUR, TEXAS, U.S.A. **The Methodist Temple.** Many of the first settlers of Port Arthur were from KANSAS, ILLINOIS, IOWA and MISSOURI and many of these were Methodist. In January 1897, they held a meeting in Hotel Sabine and enrolled as a Methodist Class, after the original CLASS MEETINGS. Application for a charter was made and this was received in May of 1897. Material and work were solicited for the erection of a new house of worship. The Port Arthur Townsite Company donated a lot at the corner of Sixth Street and Savannah Avenue. One of the officials of the Kansas City, Pittsburgh and Gulf Railroad made the church a gift of eight dozen chairs. An organ was loaned to the little congregation. Charles K. Woodson was sent to the church in 1899, succeeding P. C. W. Wimberly, who had come into the Methodist Conference from the Presbyterian Church and was asked by the local Methodists to resign because of "inconsistency concerning Methodist discipline." A new organ was purchased while Woodson was at the charge. The church was without a pastor from 1900 until 1902. During this interval the Methodist congregation attended the Congregational Church services. In 1902 the church building was moved from Sixth and Savannah Avenue to Sixth near Beaumont Avenue.

On Oct. 28, 1902, the Trinity M. E. Church, South, was organized, taking a number of members from the First Church, North. The membership consisted of forty charter members. F. M. Bowles, who had been a successful lawyer and has just entered the ministry, was assigned by the Conference as pastor. Under his leadership 200 members were added to the church during the next four years and a church building at 836 Fifth Street was erected. A parsonage was added soon after. Several years later the church property in the 800 block was sold and the property at the corner of Nashville Avenue and Fifth Street with adjacent lots on Sixth Street was acquired by the church, which is known today as the Methodist Temple.

Twenty-nine pastors have served the pulpit of The Methodist Temple. One, WILLIAM C. MARTIN, was elected to the episcopacy. In 1970 the Temple reported a membership of 1,620.

General Minutes, UMC.   CARL G. OWENS

PORT ARTHUR COLLEGE, Port Arthur, Texas, was founded in 1908 by the Gulf Conference of the M. E. Church. The school practically came into existence with the city of Port Arthur itself. John Gates, a pioneer who developed the city, made provision for the campus and for assistance in erecting some of its buildings.

It began as Port Arthur Collegiate Institute. At present it is a vocational school specializing in business and electronics. The Board of Education holds title to the property and the school's endowment. The governing board of twenty-one members, elected by the board, is self-perpetuating.

JOHN O. GROSS

PORTER, HENRY PHILLIPS (1879-1960), seventeenth bishop of the C.M.E. Church, was born near Kilgore, Texas. He attended Texas College, where he finished the preparatory course in 1903. Bishop Porter began preaching in 1893 and became a member of the Central Texas Conference. In 1922, he was elected publishing agent, and while serving in that capacity he directed the building of a new publishing house and improved the church literature. At the General Conference in 1934, he was elected to the office of bishop. He presided over the episcopal areas of ALABAMA, OHIO, KENTUCKY, NORTH and SOUTH CAROLINA, and TEXAS. He retired in 1958 and died in 1960.

Harris and Patterson, *C.M.E. Church.* 1965.
The Mirror, General Conference, C.M.E. 1958.

RALPH G. GAY

PORTER, JAMES (1808-1888), American minister was born on March 1, 1808, in Middleboro, Mass., the son of William and Rebecca Porter. He attended Pierce Academy and KENT'S HILL ACADEMY. In 1827, converted under Ebenezer Blake, he joined the M.E. Church. He became a member of the New England Conference in 1830.

His early pastorates were within the bounds of the present SOUTHERN NEW ENGLAND CONFERENCE; later appointments included the cities of WORCESTER, BOSTON, and LYNN in MASSACHUSETTS. In 1844 he was presiding elder of the Worcester District and ten years later of the Boston District. From 1856 onward he was Assistant Book Agent in NEW YORK, retiring from that post and the active ministry in 1868.

As a result of a resolution introduced by Porter in the annual conference of 1855, laymen were admitted to NEW ENGLAND CONFERENCE committees. At the time of his death he was the only member of the New England Conference elected seven times to GENERAL CONFERENCE. Here he was a conspicuous leader in the anti-slavery struggle, especially in 1844. Evangelism, theological education, and promotion were his strong interests. Porter published sixteen volumes, including: *Compendium of Methodism, History of Methodism, Winning Worker, Chart of Life,* and *Helps to Officers of the Church.*

On June 17, 1838, he married Jane Tinkham Howard. Eight children were born to them. Porter died on April 16, 1888, in Brooklyn, N. Y. He was buried there in Greenwood Cemetery.

Minutes of the New England Conference, 1889.
J. Mudge, *New England Conference.* 1910.
M. Simpson, *Cyclopaedia.* 1878.   ERNEST R. CASE

PORTLAND, MAINE, U.S.A. JESSE LEE preached in Portland on his first visit to MAINE in 1793. On this occasion, and several other times, he preached in the second Congregational church, referred to in some accounts as "Rev. Kellog's meeting house." Once he preached in the court house. In 1794 Philip Wagner organized the class at Monmouth. He was appointed in 1795 to the Portland Circuit, where he organized the class at Portland. The population of the place then was 2,246. In December of that year the first Quarterly Meeting held in Maine assembled in Portland. Wagner formed a class of nine members who struggled along with great difficulty. At the end of nine years the class numbered eleven. The favorable turn came in 1804 when Enoch Elsley pur-

chased and presented to the society a house of worship previously used by the Episcopalians. The building was remodeled, moved to Federal Street, and was soon filled by a "respectable" congregation.

In 1797 Joshua Taylor was appointed presiding elder of the newly erected District of Maine and preacher in charge of the Readfield Circuit. It was in 1800, as he tried to preach in Castine, that he was rudely escorted from town by a clamorous mob. In 1804-5 he was appointed pastor of Portland. During that time the society grew from eleven members to sixty-four. Taylor was forced to give up his work because of ill health and opened a private school in Portland which he continued for sixteen years, preaching on the Sabbath in the vicinity as occasion required. He later was readmitted to the conference and in 1847 he retired in Portland. When he died in 1861 at the age of ninety-three years, the city of Portland went into mourning. The mayor and other dignitaries attended the service and during the funeral procession all the church bells of the city tolled. Methodism had made its place in the city and Joshua Taylor had been instrumental in bringing this about.

The Chestnut Street Church was completed and dedicated on Feb. 11, 1811. It prospered and, as the city extended its borders, became the mother of churches. In 1846 its members started the church on Pine Street; in 1851 they organized a church on Munjoy Hill, now known as Congress Street Church; later they established a church on Peak's Island in Casco Bay. For many years there was an Italian Mission which later became a church. A few years ago it was given up, its members joining other Methodist churches in the city as there was no longer need for services in the Italian language. For many years there was a Deaconess Home in Portland, but with changing conditions that, too, was given up.

For a considerable period Chestnut Street Church regularly received pastors transferred from other conferences, but of recent years members of the MAINE CONFERENCE have been appointed to it. Among its most distinguished pastors was Bishop MATTHEW SIMPSON HUGHES, brother of Bishop EDWIN HOLT HUGHES. This church has a present membership of 959, the largest in the Maine Conference. There are six United Methodist churches in the city of Portland, four in South Portland, four on islands in Casco Bay. Methodism in Portland and vicinity is stronger than anywhere else in the State of Maine.

Allen and Pilsbury, *Methodism in Maine.* 1887.
General Minutes, UMC.   ALFRED G. HEMPSTEAD

PORTLAND, OREGON, U.S.A., chartered in 1851, had a population of about 375,000 in 1970. JASON LEE, the pioneer missionary on the Pacific coast, and his associates introduced Methodism in the region in 1834. By 1848 there were eight mission employees, and in 1849 the Oregon and California Mission Conference was organized. In 1850, JAMES H. WILBUR was appointed to PORTLAND and OREGON CITY; he immediately began to build Portland Academy and what came to be known as "Father Wilbur's Chapel," the forerunner of First Church, on Taylor Street near Third. The next year Wilbur reported fifty-eight members on the charge. In 1852, the GENERAL CONFERENCE created the Oregon Conference, and that year Portland had forty-three members. The church had 109 members in 1860, 222 in 1870, and 296 in 1880, though by the latter year a second church, Hall Street, had been organized. In 1890, First Church had 631 members, while two other congregations and a Chinese mission accounted for some 500 more in the city. In 1912, when First Church had 1,250 members and Grace Church had 656, the two merged under the name of First Church which reported 1,670 members the next year.

In 1864, the East Portland Church was organized in the part of the city lying east of the Willamette River. Three years later it reported 326 members, including 127 probationers. After 1888 it was known as Centenary Church. In 1900, Portland had twelve churches with a total membership of 2,153. At unification in 1939, the M.E. Church had twenty-six churches and 11,149 members in Portland.

The *Pacific Christian Advocate* which began in Salem in 1855, was published in Portland from 1858 to 1929 when it was moved to SAN FRANCISCO.

In 1858, the M. E. Church, South organized work in OREGON, making it a part of the San Francisco District of the Pacific Conference. The Oregon District was formed in 1859 with ORCENETH FISHER as presiding elder. In 1860 he reported five circuits, one of them called Portland, with a total of 268 members. There are no records for the Civil War years, but in 1866 the Columbia Conference was formed with two districts, and a total of seven circuits in Oregon. However, the denomination had difficulty gaining a foothold in Portland. In 1868 there was a Portland Mission with forty-five members, but the next year the number had dropped to thirteen, and Portland did not appear again in the appointments until 1903 when C. A. Hyatt was appointed there. In 1904 he reported eighty-four members. From 1910 to 1919, the Portland church reported over 300 members each year, but thereafter it decreased in strength until 1931 when it closed.

The M. P. Church organized the Oregon and California Conference in 1850, but the denomination was never strong, and it disappeared from that region after 1908.

A few foreign language churches were organized in Portland, but with the passage of time they became churches in the Portland District of the Oregon Conference. Hughes Memorial, a Negro church with ninety-seven members in 1970, receives some financial aid from the Portland District Church Extension Society. That organization, composed principally of laymen, was formed in 1903. It helps to establish new churches and gives financial assistance to existing churches which are in need. The society helped to establish GOODWILL INDUSTRIES in Portland, and it has managed Leewood Camp. Portland Methodism assists with interdenominational inner city redemptional projects and helps to support Koinonia House on the Portland State College campus.

Portland was one of the sixteen cities selected by the 1904 GENERAL CONFERENCE of the M. E. Church for episcopal residences, and it has continued as such to this day.

In 1970, the Oregon-Idaho Conference had a Portland East and a Portland West District, the one having 43 charges and 15,203 members and the other 31 charges and 11,350 members. In the City of Portland proper The United Methodist Church in 1970 reported 26 churches, 11,742 members, property valued at $7,139,575, and $1,035,488 raised for all purposes during the year. Rose City Park and First are the two largest churches in the

city, the one with 1,652 members and property valued at $857,856, and the other with 1,313 members and property worth $1,519,937.

First A.M.E. Zion Church was organized in 1862 at the home of Mrs. Mary Carr on A Street (now Ankeny). It was then called "The People's Church." The first Trustees included Ned Simmons, a Mr. Johnson, and a Mr. Nichols. For some time the church held services at various homes of the members. Later, property was purchased on North Third Street, between B and C Streets (now Burnside and Couch Streets). Here, the cornerstone was laid, June 3, 1869. J. O. Lodge was the pastor at this time.

In 1883 the trustees of the church bought property on Main and Eleventh Streets (now Thirteenth Street), and erected a building. On Sunday, Oct. 11, 1891 the old cornerstone was relaid at 13th and Main Streets. A. Tilgham Brown was the pastor. The church remained at this location for more than twenty years.

The building of the church, at the present location, began in 1917, and was completed under the pastorate of W. I. Rowan; Bishop L. W. Kyles was presiding bishop at that time. The parsonage apartment was built in 1929 and was formally opened on May 12, 1929. With the opening of the enlarged Church plant, a more extensive program began, and the formal rededication of the new church and parsonage on Sunday, Sept. 15, 1929, by Bishop J. W. Martin, marked a new epoch in the history of this old Portland and Pacific Northwest Church. W. W. Matthews, a former pastor of First A.M.E. Zion of Portland, became a bishop.

There have been periods of great trial for Zion. During the period of 1911 to 1917 many members became dissatisfied and discouraged and joined other Churches. Again in the thirties, the church was faced with great financial problems, but overcame them by faith and by hard work of the members.

Rose City Park Church is a large residential church located half-way between downtown Portland and the city's international airport. Its brick edifice is best known for its memorial windows of traditional stained glass.

District Superintendent J. W. McDougall organized this congregation in the Rose City Community Club House on Feb. 1, 1913. The church soon bought nearby lots in this section which had just come into the city, a step which transformed a notorious horse racing track a few blocks away into a sedate municipal golf course. The new congregation soon moved from the club house into a large tent and, by the first winter, were housed in a bungalow-type wooden chapel, known as "The Little Brown Church on the Hill," which was used until 1925. By that time the first pastor, W. W. Youngson, had returned for a second pastorate after a term as district superintendent.

The present brick sanctuary was built in 1924-25, with an extensive educational unit and chapel added in 1951. Youngson Hall, honoring the first pastor, was dedicated in 1957. The nave was remodeled and enlarged with a new chancel added in 1965, with a new organ installed in 1966, bringing the total plant valuation to one million dollars.

In the mid-1950's the membership numbered over 2,000 and maintains a constituency of about twice that number. In 1970 it reported 1,652 members. It has a multiple staff and multiple Sunday morning services, served by five trained choirs. The chief emphasis has been on persons and their needs. During the Golden Anniversary Year in 1963, a count showed 85,000 people entering for worship, study or fellowship. Half of the twelve senior pastors who have served over the years, including this writer, have either been appointed to the church from the superintendency or have gone from this parish to a district assignment.

E. S. Bucke, *History of American Methodism.* 1964.
General Minutes, ME, MES, TMC, UMC.
Mildred P. Nye, *Portland's First Church.* Privately published, 1962.
M. Simpson, *Cyclopaedia.* 1878.
T. D. Yarnes, *Oregon.* 1959.
ALBEA GODBOLD
DAVID H. BRADLEY
DANIEL E. TAYLOR

PORTO ALEGRE, Brazil. The work of the Methodist Church in Porto Alegre, capital of Rio Grande do Sul, was begun by João C. Corrêa, lay preacher and homeopathic doctor. Born in Jaguarao, Rio Grande do Sul, he had moved to MONTEVIDEO, URUGUAY, where he first heard the Gospel. Converted, he became a volunteer worker for the Plate Conference of the M.E. Church, and was asked to return to BRAZIL. This he did in April 1875, selling Bibles and Christian literature. He was soon officially appointed by THOMAS WOOD, Superintendent of the Mission, to be a missionary in charge of the Province of Rio Grande do Sul.

Corrêa moved with his family and a young Uruguayan teacher, CARMEN CHACON, their protegée, to Porto Alegre. In September 1885, he organized the first congregation with six charter members; a Sunday school with twenty pupils, and a day school which he named the Colegio Evangelico Misto. Carmen was put in charge of the school, which eventually became the well-known COLEGIO AMERICANO of today. The little congregation grew into Central Methodist Church of Porto Alegre. Corrêa served until 1896, being succeeded by William Robinson, who came from Montevideo with his family, and with Miss H. M. Hegeman, a contract missionary teacher who was to direct the school. Due to illness and the death of a child, Robinson returned to the States, and JOHN W. PRICE took charge of the work. To this day the influence of the Prices is felt in the educational and evangelistic work of the Methodist Church in this region.

In 1900, the M.E. Church transferred its work in Brazil to the M.E. Church, South; and South Brazil was organized into a district of the Brazil Annual Conference. It is now the Second Ecclesiastical Region of the Methodist Church of Brazil.

Today there are seven self-supporting churches in Porto Alegre, plus Sunday schools and preaching points throughout the city and surrounding area. The Porto Alegre District supports a home for aged women, called the Ottilia Chaves Home. Other churches have developed fine welfare services, a girls' home, and mothers' clubs. Central Church, with its beautiful temple in the downtown area, has built a several-storied educational and office building.

There are two outstanding Methodist schools in the city. One is the Colegio Americano for girls, whose modern plant was designed by the missionary-architect, MARY SUE BROWN. The other is a boys' school, the Instituto Porto Alegre (originally called College), founded in 1923 with the support of Bishop JOHN M. MOORE. Its first principal or reitor was JOHN R. SAUNDERS. He was succeeded by EARL MORELAND, when he decided to continue in pastoral work.

A unique feature of Methodism in this city is a granite and bronze monument in its main park honoring JOHN WESLEY. Its sculptor was a Brazilian Methodist, Romano Reif. This is the first monument in South America that honors the founder of a leading Protestant denomination.

Porto Alegre College was founded in 1921 by the M.E. Church, South, with funds provided through the church's CENTENARY FUND. Its founders with Bishop John M. Moore, John R. Saunders and J. Earl Moreland. Bishop Moore chose the city and campus site, purchased the land and served as first advisor. Saunders served as first president, 1921-25; Moreland was vice-president, 1922-26, and president, 1927-34. Classes were held the first year in rented quarters in downtown Porto Alegre until the new campus buildings were completed in February 1924, on the site 400 meters above the level of the business section of the city. Enrollment was held to 350 men through the first fifteen years (1967 enrollment, 1,624; coeducational since 1945). Schools are Elementar (eight years), accredited by State, Rio Grande do Sul; Ginasio (six years), accredited by the Federal government since 1928; School of Theology (three years); business school (two years). Faculty and staff through 1934 numbered twenty-six. The name was changed in 1935 to Instituto Porto Alegre. The college was designed by its founders to serve the three Southern states, as GRANBERY COLLEGE served the Northern states. Trustees are nominated by the Board, but serve only after approval by the Concilio do Sul (So. Brazil Annual Conference). Presidents have been: Alan K. Manchester (1926-27); Dr. Oscar Machado (1934-49); Bishop JOSE PINHEIRO (1949-53); DANIEL L. BETTS (1953-55); Dr. Aslid Gick (1955-   ).

D. A. Chaves, *Methodism in Brazil.* N.p., n.d.
Enciclopedia Riograndense, IV, 1957.
E. M. B. Jaime, *Metodismo no Rio Grande do Sul.* 1963.
J. L. Kennedy, *Metodismo no Brasil.* 1928. OTTILIA CHAVES

PORTSMOUTH, NEW HAMPSHIRE, U.S.A., one of the oldest cities in New England, was settled in 1623 and incorporated in 1633. As early as 1767 GEORGE WHITEFIELD came here preaching the Word, but Methodism proper was introduced by JESSE LEE on July 18, 1790. On a second visit, there being no public building open to him, he preached to an eager throng from the court house steps.

In 1798 FRANCIS ASBURY noted in his diary that he found Portsmouth "well fortified against Methodism," but the seeds sown began to sprout almost eighteen years after Jesse Lee's first summer service, for a class of fifty-two active members made up the Methodist society organized April 27, 1808 by George Rich, missionary of the Boston District. He purchased for $2,000 an old meeting house on Vaughn Street, which had been the property of the Universalists, and it was used by Methodists for nearly twenty years.

Mentioned in the M.E. Church minutes first in 1806, Portsmouth, which was then in the Boston District, was served by Levi Walker, who was sent to RHODE ISLAND and Portsmouth. Previous to the organizing of a Sunday school in 1819, the LADIES AID SOCIETY had been formed and remained continuously active. After having been connected with various charges since its founding, it appears at the head of the New Hampshire District in 1820, with Josiah A. Scarritt as pastor. The Portsmouth society was incorporated by order of the General Court following occupancy on State Street of a newly built $9,000 sanctuary, dedicated Jan. 1, 1828. This was remodeled in 1868. The NEW ENGLAND CONFERENCE met at Portsmouth in 1829 and during the session organized the New Hampshire-Vermont Conference.

On May 4, 1839 the local fellowship adopted the following resolution: "Resolved that with John Wesley we believe that American slavery is the vilest that ever saw sun . . . Resolved that as slavery exists to an alarming extent in the Methodist Church, we ought by all constitutional means use our influence to clear the Church of this shocking abomination."

Attempts at forming a second society under the name of the Broadhead Church in 1859 were not successful and after a few years it was given up. An EPWORTH LEAGUE was organized in 1889 at the State Street Church. Upon completion of the present stone church on Miller Avenue in 1913, the old building was taken over for use as a Jewish Synagogue. In more recent years, due to the proximity of the Pease Air Force Base, additional facilities became imperative and an adjoining parish house and educational building was built and dedicated on Apr. 27, 1958. It is in the NEW HAMPSHIRE CONFERENCE and in 1970 reported 593 members, 160 preparatory members, a church school of 251, a Sunday school average attendance of 150, and estimated value of church building equipment and land of $296,600.

Cole and Baketel, *New Hampshire Conference.* 1929.
W. H. Daniels, *Illustrated History.* 1887.
Journals of the New Hampshire and New England Conferences.
M. Simpson, *Cyclopaedia.* 1878.
James Duane Squires, *The Granite State of the United States.*
New York: American Historical Co., 1956.
A. Stevens, *History of Methodism.* 1895.   WILLIAM J. DAVIS

PORTSMOUTH, VIRGINIA, U.S.A. (population 109,827), is one of the ports of Hampton Roads and an active seaport city. It has an important navy yard, is a rail and ocean shipping center. Laid out in 1750, it was the scene of conflict in the American Revolution and in the War Between the States.

JOSEPH PILMORE and ROBERT WILLIAMS were among the first evangelists sent to America by JOHN WESLEY. Williams, not an ordained preacher, left Ireland in 1766 and was licensed to preach at PHILADELPHIA in 1769 by Joseph Pilmore. In early 1772 Isaac Luke, a member of the Anglican Church in Portsmouth, heard Williams preach from the court house steps in NORFOLK and invited him to cross the river to Portsmouth. Williams accepted and preached from the porch of the Luke home on Court Street. He appointed Luke as leader of the group and Luke found an empty warehouse for a meeting place. Williams labored here two months before going elsewhere.

Joseph Pilmore preached in Portsmouth several times in July 1772, and on Nov. 14, 1772, organized the class into the first Methodist society in southeastern Virginia. Two days later he formed a society in Norfolk. These two groups formed the Portsmouth-Norfolk Circuit. At the first Methodist Conference in America, held in Philadelphia July 1, 1773, RICHARD WRIGHT, an ordained preacher, was appointed to the circuit. JOHN KING was the next pastor, followed by FRANCIS ASBURY in 1775. After Asbury arrived, a small chapel was built in Portsmouth on Effingham Street by the twenty-seven members.

The American Revolution brought troubles for Methodism. Wesley disapproved of rebellious colonists. Many preachers returned to Great Britain, among them Joseph Pilmore and Richard Wright. Asbury remained. He was on the circuit six months and conducted the funeral of Robert Williams while there. From 1777 until 1783, no preachers were appointed to the circuit. The British distrusted the Methodists and discouraged meetings. Class leaders continued the work, and membership increased during the war.

In Portsmouth the little chapel was outgrown, the society purchased a lot on Glasgow Street in 1792. The chapel building was moved to the new lot and enlarged. In 1792 WILLIAM McKENDREE became pastor of the circuit which had grown to 949 white and 693 Negro members. The Portsmouth church became a station in 1806. The first Sabbath school was established in 1818. The congregation moved to its present location on Dinwiddie and Queen Streets in October 1833.

In 1843 the congregation, interested in church extension, built a chapel on Gosport which became Wright Memorial Church. In 1843, because of the desires of the 342 Negro members, the church on Glasgow Street was turned over to these faithful members. This group was served for years by a white local preacher, George M. Bain, until a colored preacher, JAMES A. HANDY, was found. This church is now Emmanuel Church, a strong congregation of the A.M.E. Church. Also, Wesley Chapel was built on Effingham Street. It served that area until June 1966, when it was closed. Another chapel was erected which was to become Central Church.

The disastrous yellow fever epidemic of 1855 took the lives of many members.

The old church on Glasgow Street burned in 1856. George M. Bain asked Dinwiddie Street Church to help, and a large brick building was erected on North Street. The VIRGINIA CONFERENCE of 1858, presided over by Bishop KAVANAUGH, met there, and the building was then turned over to the Negro brethren.

During the War Between the States, Dinwiddie Street Church dropped from 600 to 197 members. The northern BALTIMORE CONFERENCE assumed control in 1862 with authority granted by Federal forces. Pastors appointed by the Virginia Conference were harassed by Federal troops and forced to leave. A notation in the conference annual listed Dinwiddie Street Church as being "in Federal hands." In 1864 the church burned, and the military commander gave St. John's Episcopal Church to the northern preacher, and that church was used by northern Methodists until the close of the war. During this period a small chapel was built at the rear of the Dinwiddie Street lot, and services were held there by the southern Methodists.

During its first century the Dinwiddie Street congregation had started four other churches: Wright Memorial, North Street, Wesley Chapel and Central. Three of its former pastors, Asbury, McKendree and EARLY, and one of its presiding elders, RICHARD WHATCOAT, had become bishops.

At the beginning of its second century Dinwiddie Street Church started rebuilding, and a new brick church was consecrated on Nov. 14, 1876. It was given the name Monumental as a monument to Robert Williams, the first Methodist to preach in Portsmouth in 1772, and the first to introduce Methodism into Virginia.

In 1881 the ladies of the church formed a Foreign Missionary Society, a new organization in Methodism, against the wishes of the pastor. He felt that women should not hold prominent positions in the church. His wife was the first president!

By 1907 Monumental was a prosperous city church with 869 members. It had become a leading church in Virginia Methodism, giving generously to missions, education and other Methodist causes. The first women stewards were elected in 1925. Many churches in Portsmouth were assisted in their early days by this "Mother" church. WILLIAM B. BEAUCHAMP, pastor 1915-1917, and WALTER C. GUM, pastor 1933-1936, later became bishops. Twenty-eight Methodist preachers came out of Monumental Church. Present membership is 1,158 (1970).

At the Annual Conference held in Norfolk in 1966, Monumental was awarded a certificate by the Conference Bicentennial Committee recognizing it as the oldest Methodist church in continuous existence in Virginia.

Journals of the Baltimore and Virginia Conferences.
J. J. Lafferty, *Sketches of Virginia Conference.* 1880, 1890, 1901.
Jesse Lee, *Short History.* 1810.
H. N. McTyeire, *History of Methodism.* 1884.
Dorothy Fleet Monroe, *The History of Monumental Methodist Church, 1772-1966.* N.d.
W. W. Sweet, *Virginia.* 1955.   JOHN RALLSON HENDRICKS

PORTUGAL (Igreja Evangélica Metodista Portuguesa, abbr. IEMP). Metropolitan Portugal occupies the western part of the Iberian Peninsula in Europe, being bounded on the north and east by SPAIN, and the south and west by the Atlantic Ocean. It covers an area of 35,466 square miles, and its population was estimated in 1968 as approximately nine million. Portugal is mountainous though about two-thirds of the land is cultivated. Lisbon, its capital, operates a major international airport.

In recent years marked industrialization has proceeded in all parts of the country, and in the overseas provinces, with a rapid growth of commercial and industrial activity, centering on the capital in the south, and on Oporto, the second largest city and seaport, in the north. This development not only has its important economic consequences, but is producing profound sociological effects on the life and ethos of the people.

As early as 1811, Methodist class meetings were being held among soldiers, with some officers, of the Duke of Wellington's Peninsular Army, winter quartered in Cartaxo, some forty-five miles north of Lisbon; but no known permanent results of this activity remain. Historically significant work began in 1853-54 when Thomas Chegwin, a Cornish mining engineer, inaugurated his class meeting among workers in the Palhal Mines in northern Portugal.

Another layman, James Cassels, born in 1844 of a British family resident in Portugal, introduced Methodism to Vila Nova de Gaia, a smaller neighbor of Oporto, situated on the southern bank of the River Douro. He was afterwards ordained a minister of the Lusitanian (Episcopal) Church, and became a naturalized Portuguese; he was decorated by the Portuguese Government in 1924 as a public benefactor, and a bust to his memory, "Diogo Cassels," stands in a public garden in Vila Nova. He built the first Wesleyan Church in Portugal, "Torne" in Vila Nova de Gaia (now the day-school building of the Lusitanian Church of St. John the Evangelist), which was dedicated in 1868 in a service conducted by H. H. Richmond, Methodist minister from GIBRALTAR, in which station the tiny work in Portugal was for a while included.

The first celebration of the Holy Communion and the first infant baptism (of James Cassel's daughter), also took place on this occasion.

In February of 1871 the first British Methodist missionary came to take charge of the work at Oporto and Palhal. He was Robert Hawkey Moreton, born in BUENOS AIRES in 1844, whose knowledge of Spanish helped him to a rapid acquisition of Portuguese, in which tongue he became an acknowledged master and into which he translated several hymns still widely used today in hymnaries both in Portugal and BRAZIL. He introduced the *tonic solfa* musical system into Portugal to enable his people, then mostly without culture, to learn to sing. He remained superintendent for forty-three years. His ministry was marked by the use of hymns and of the current Methodist liturgy in his own Portuguese liturgy, by his insistence on the class meeting and the due application of Methodist discipline, and by his own erudition and missionary zeal.

Aided by members of the British colony in Oporto, he designed and built the Mirante Church, opened in March 1877. This is the mother-church of Portuguese Methodism. Later, in 1934, the facade of this church was adorned with azulejos, the distinctive Portuguese glazed tiling used on exteriors, giving it an appearance almost unique in Methodism, with its two great evangelical texts seen regularly by the scores who pass by its doors. In the early days Moreton had the help of two converted Roman Catholic priests, Guilherme Dias and Santos Figueiredo, the former of whom had the distinction at that time of filling his unusual preaching place twice every Sunday morning with two distinct congregations.

Moreton's chief helpers for many years were ALFREDO DA SILVA, later (1914-48) General Superintendent, teacher, preacher and for a time member of the Oporto City Council, representative of international committees in the cause of peace, and a founder of the Portuguese YMCA; and José A. Fernandes, the first editor of the periodical *Portugal Evangélico,* founded in October 1920 and still being published. An earlier publication, *A Reforma,* a joint enterprise of Moreton and Dias, maintained a very high standard during its sixteen years of existence, 1876-92.

At the beginning of this century work was begun in Lisbon, superintended from Oporto, and under the charge, first of Arthur H. Wilks, and then of Thomas H. Simpson, both ministers of the British Methodist Conference. This venture met with great success, hundreds of people flocking to the services and meetings held in a hired basement room. In 1906 through lack of funds, this work was handed over to another evangelical mission.

Much of the work done in the past has contributed, directly or indirectly, to the life of churches, Methodist and others, in South America, notably in Brazil, where there are many Portuguese immigrants. Valuable contribution has also been made in this way to the work in ANGOLA, MOZAMBIQUE, and other parts of overseas Portugal, although there is no direct association with European Portuguese Methodism. Methodist work at one time existed in Madeira, but this has for many years been in the hands of the Presbyterians.

In 1968 there were five Portuguese ministers, with a British minister as General Superintendent and fraternal worker; there were also thirty local preachers and one Portuguese deaconess. The work is centered in Oporto, and covers mainly the northern half of the country, reaching to Coimbra, the ancient University town, and with the second largest of its churches at Aveiro, the so-called Venice of Portugal. The membership is upwards of 700, in a community of something over 2,500, being part of the estimated 65,000 in the non-Roman Christian community. There is good Sunday school work, as well as four small primary day schools. Other social and benevolent work is carried out, much of it in collaboration with other Protestant Churches; there is some ecumenical outreach. Large scale emigration has tended to keep numerical progress at a modest level, but there is positive growth.

The IEMP is an overseas District of the British Methodist Conference, and has a British missionary as its chairman. There is an Annual Synod with an elected permanent Executive Committee, which supervises the work now divided into two circuits, one centered on Oporto, the other on Aveiro. Plans for increasing autonomy are being studied. The IEMP is a full member of the WORLD METHODIST COUNCIL.

A Reforma, files of, 1876-92.
Diogo Cassels, A Reforma em Portugal. Oporto: privately published, 1906.
Findlay and Holdsworth, Wesleyan Meth. Miss. Soc. 1921.
E. Moreira, Vidas Convergentes. Lisbon: Junta Presbiteriane de Cooperacao em Portugal, 1958.
Portugal Evangelico, 1920.   ALBERT ASPEY

C. W. POSNETT

POSNETT, CHARLES WALKER (1870-1950), British missionary, was born in Sheffield, England, Oct. 7, 1870. Educated at KINGSWOOD SCHOOL and Richmond College, he sailed for India in 1895 and was appointed to Medak, Hyderabad District, in 1896. He was to become the great administrator in the Methodist Church in INDIA. Appointed chairman of the Hyderabad District and of the Provincial Synod in 1916, he established many of the district's most valuable institutions—Annuitant Society for Indian Ministers (1909), Pension Fund for Evangelists (1909), the "cathedral church" at Medak (opened 1924), the Training School for Evangelists (1926), the "Week of Witness" (1929), nursery schools (1936). A great evangelist and preacher, he shepherded tens of thousands of outcastes, mainly Madigas, who responded in the "mass movements" from 1916 onward and the smaller but equally important "caste movement," into the Church from 1926. He began work among Gonds (outcastes) in 1931. He worked constantly for Church union, and organized much relief work in times of famine, especially the great famine of 1918-21. He was decorated with the Kaiser-i-Hing gold medal by the government of India. On his

retirement in 1939 the Christian movement in Hyderabad numbered 109,000. He died on Sept. 30, 1950.

CYRIL J. DAVEY

POTTER, ANDREW JACKSON (1830-1895), American preacher, was born in Chariton County, Mo., April 3, 1830. In his day he was one of the best known pioneer preachers of West TEXAS. With only three months of schooling, he was left an orphan at ten years of age. He became a horserace jockey and a gambler, and then joined the army when sixteen. In the army he helped to fight Apaches and other Indians in NEW MEXICO and ARIZONA. He married and settled in West Texas in 1853. He was converted in 1856, and joined the Methodist Church in 1858, and became a local preacher in 1859. He served as a chaplain in the Confederate Army throughout the Civil War. In 1866 he joined the West Texas Conference of the M. E. Church, South.

Phelan summarizes Potter's career in these terms: He became "a noted character as an Indian fighter, a tamer of desperadoes and a popular preacher. . . . His rugged character, his courage and ready wit, common sense and sincerity made him a popular hero among the early settlers. In addition to his Bible, hymnbook, and saddlebags, a Winchester and six shooter were a part of Potter's equipment, and he was known on more than one occasion to use his fist as a quelling influence upon frontier toughs who were disposed to disturb public meetings."

Once a caller was sent through a pioneer settlement announcing Potter's preaching engagement that night in these words: "O yes, O yes, O yes. There is going to be some spang-up religious racket on Mr. F's gallery tonight by the fighting parson, a reformed gambler, but now a celebrated gospel sharp. The racket will begin in fifteen minutes."

Potter died in the pulpit at the close of a sermon at Tilman Chapel, near Lockhart, Texas, Oct. 31, 1895.

M. Phelan, Methodism in Texas. 1937.
O. W. Nail, The First 100 Years. 1958.
H. A. Graves, Andrew Jackson Potter, The Noted Parson of the
Texas Frontier. 1890.   WALTER N. VERNON

POTTER, JOHN (c. 1674-1747), Archbishop of Canterbury from 1737, previously Bishop of Oxford was a patristic and classical scholar. He approved of the ministrations of the Holy Club at the Bocardo Gaol, and ordained several of its members including JOHN WESLEY, BENJAMIN INGHAM, JAMES HERVEY, and JOHN GAMBOLD. Potter advised Wesley that it was possible for him to fulfill his ministry in other ways than as a parish priest. In 1739 Potter interviewed John and Charles Wesley, speaking with affection but warning them against rash speaking, and declaring himself to be against any kind of innovation. Potter was inclined to accept the validity of the Moravian episcopal succession. In 1750 Wesley abridged his Grecian Antiquities (2 vols., 1697-99) for the Kingswood scholars.

THOMAS SHAW

POTTERY, WESLEY. (See WESLEY POTTERY.)

POTTS, JAMES HENRY (1848-1942), American pastor and long-time editor of The Michigan Christian Advocate, was born June 12, 1848, near Simcoe, Ontario, CANADA.

He was the son of Philip and Fannie Ann (Buck) Potts. He received the A.B. degree from NORTHWESTERN UNIVERSITY, and ALBION COLLEGE in MICHIGAN awarded him the D.D. and LL.D. degrees in his later life. On Sept. 8, 1869, he married Alonsa C. Cole, and their children were James R., Florence A., and Alice E. As a pastor he served Ganges, Mich. 1869; Cedar Springs, 1871; Allen, 1872; and Plainwell, 1873. He became assistant editor of *The Michigan Christian Advocate* in 1877, and was with it until his retirement, as he became editor-in-chief in 1884, keeping his membership in the MICHIGAN CONFERENCE.

Potts was a member of the GENERAL CONFERENCES (ME) of 1888, '92, '96, 1900, and '04, and was appointed a fraternal delegate to the Canadian General Conference from the M. E. Church in 1894. He was also a member of the ECUMENICAL CONFERENCE of 1911. He served in the Civil War as a private in the 6th Michigan Volunteer Cavalry for fourteen months—from 1865-66 (being at that time but seventeen years of age). He was the author of *Methodism in the Field*, 1880; *Golden Dawn*, 1881; *Faith Made Easy*, 1888; *Back to Oxford*, 1903; *Upward Leading*, 1905; *My Gift to Thee*, 1909-10; *Every Day a Delight*, 1914. He was the editor of Perrine's *Principles of Church Government* brought out by the BOOK CONCERN in 1887; and *Living Thoughts of John Wesley*, 1891. He exerted great influence as an editor and his memoir in the Michigan Conference *Minutes* stated that "since his retirement he was a most loved figure in Algonac where he resided with his daughter."

Michigan Christian Advocate, March 26, 1942.
Minutes of the Michigan Conference, 1942.
C. F. Price, *Who's Who in American Methodism*. 1916.

N. B. H.

POTTS, JAMES MANNING (1895-1973), American minister, editor, and church executive, was born at Como, N. C., on July 14, 1895. He was the son of Reginald Harrell and Annie Christian (Moore) Potts. His education was at RANDOLPH-MACON COLLEGE, where he received the M.A. degree in 1920, and the D.D. in 1935. Princeton University granted him the Th.B. degree in 1924, the Th.M. in 1925, and he did postgraduate work at the University of Virginia and at the University of Chicago. The EWHA WOMAN'S UNIVERSITY in SEOUL, KOREA, gave him the Litt.D. in 1961.

His wife was Agnes Wright whom he married on Dec. 23, 1920, and their children are Reginald Harrell, James Manning, Joseph Christian, Katharine Coleman (dec.), Agnes Withers (Mrs. George Beck), and Ann Wilson (dec.).

Dr. Potts joined the VIRGINIA CONFERENCE in 1925, and went into full connection in 1927. He served as pastor in Berryman Church, Richmond, 1926-30; Trinity Church, Petersburg, 1930-32; Barton Heights Church, RICHMOND, 1932-35, was the superintendent of the Richmond District, 1935-40, and was pastor of Greene Memorial, ROANOKE, 1940-44—all in VIRGINIA. At this time he became the associate director of the CRUSADE FOR CHRIST with headquarters in CHICAGO, from 1944-48. He was then elected editor of *The Upper Room*, NASHVILLE, Tenn., where he served 1948-67, at which time he retired from its editorship.

He was a member of the TELEVISION, RADIO AND FILM COMMISSION, 1948-64; the Commission on EVANGELISM,

1940-48; the executive secretary of the Methodist Advance, 1948-50; a member of the General Board of the NATIONAL COUNCIL CHURCHES OF CHRIST, 1952-66; a member of the Broadcasting and Film Commission, 1952-65; a member of the General Assemblies of the Federal Council of Churches and the National Council of Churches from 1938; of the WORLD COUNCIL OF CHURCHES also. He was a member of the Advisory Council on Naval Affairs of the Sixth Naval District (U.S.) from 1956. He was a trustee of Randolph-Macon College, 1930-67, a Fellow in Methodist History, a member of the World Association of Christian Broadcasting, and his editorship of *The Upper Room* caused him to travel over world-wide Methodism where he acted as a liaison official between the Methodists in various countries and the Methodism of his own homeland and other denominations.

Dr. Potts wrote in conjunction with Dr. Asbury Smith, *Love Abounds, A Profile of Harry Denman*, 1965; edited the *Prayers of the Early Church*, 1953; *Prayers of the Middle Ages*, 1954; was editor-in-chief of *The Letters of Francis Asbury*, 1958; *Selections from Letters of John Wesley, Francis Asbury, John Woolman*, 1957; *Listening to the Saints*, 1962; *Grace Sufficient, The Story of Helen Kim*, 1964. He was associate editor of *The Journal of Francis Asbury*, three volumes, published in 1958; *History of American Methodism*, 1964; and was a contributor to articles on early Virginia Methodism in various historical and church publications.

Upon retirement in 1967, as editor of *The Upper Room*, he was elected by the trustees of the LAKE JUNALUSKA ASSEMBLY to serve as its executive director. He retired from this position in 1970 and resided in Crystal Springs, Fla., until his death on Jan. 31, 1973.

Dictionary of International Biography. London, 1968.
Who's Who in America, Vol. 34.
Who's Who in The Methodist Church, 1966.

N. B. H.

POTTS, JOHN (1838-1907), Canadian minister, was born at Maguire's Bridge, County Fermanagh, IRELAND. As a young man, he emigrated to CANADA and was for a time a student at VICTORIA COLLEGE. Taken on trial in 1858, he was ordained in the CANADA CONFERENCE in 1861.

From the outset Potts demonstrated striking oratorical abilities. A powerful man with a fertile, well-stocked mind, he rapidly gained a great reputation as an outstanding preacher. His talents were promptly put to use in the new Centenary Church (Hamilton), at St. James' Church in MONTREAL, and at the Metropolitan Church in TORONTO.

John Potts was, however, much more than a great pulpit orator. At an early stage, he became interested in the church's educational institutions. He was an active member of the governing bodies of Victoria University and the Wesleyan Theological College in Montreal. In 1886, he became Secretary of Education, which office he held until his death. In this capacity, he strengthened and amplified the Methodist Church's concern for the orderly development of all the educational institutions under its charge.

Potts, who received doctorates from OHIO WESLEYAN in 1887 and Victoria in 1894, was described by one of his contemporaries as a "Methodist of the Methodists." He was, indeed, a keen defender of his church's interests, a powerful orator, a temperance advocate, a man alert to changing trends in education and in politics. Yet he was not a sectarian. He was one of the first to make friendly gestures to the Episcopal Methodists, and he collaborated generously with representatives of other churches.

When he died in 1907, the Methodist Church lost one of the figures most representative of its late-nineteenth-century prosperity.

G. H. Cornish, *Cyclopaedia of Methodism in Canada.* 1881.
H. J. Morgan, ed., *Canadian Men and Women of the Time.* Toronto: Briggs, 1898.   G. S. FRENCH

POTTSVILLE, PENNSYLVANIA, U.S.A., First Church, is an important church of the PHILADELPHIA Area, and the first Methodist church established in what is known as the Anthracite Region of the PHILADELPHIA CONFERENCE. The city itself began in 1806 when a John Pott of Oley Berks County, Pa., came into the region and purchased a small iron furnace which had been built two years earlier by Lewis Reese and Isaac Thomas. The industry grew, a forge was added and houses were built for the workers. Other industries moved into the community and more families settled in the area, among whom were several Methodists. A local preacher, Jonathan Wynn, who also moved into the community, began holding religious services in the homes of the Methodists and has the honor of preaching the first Methodist sermon in Pottsville, although the exact date of its preaching is not known. During the winter of 1827 and 1828, however, the Methodists were visited by preachers from the Lancaster Circuit: GEORGE COOKMAN, David Best, Samuel Grace, and JOHN LEDNUM.

Preaching services began to be held regularly in a small log schoolhouse on North Center Street, and in 1828 a class was formed of thirteen members. Originally served by pastors from the Lancaster Circuit, the church was organized in 1829 with sixty-seven members as a separate appointment of the Philadelphia Conference. In October 1830, the first church building was dedicated, a stone structure 40 by 60 feet. The church continued to grow and some of its laymen assisted in the establishment of churches in neighboring anthracite communities, particularly Port Carbon and Minersville.

In 1854 a second church at 5th and Market Streets was begun in Pottsville by some dissident members of First Church, and it became known as Second M.E. Church. By 1857, however, the two churches had reunited.

First Church continued to grow, and the church building was enlarged. Finally in 1898 the site of the present huge gray stone edifice was purchased for $38,500. Ground for the new church was broken in 1907 and the cornerstone was laid in November of the same year. The entire cost of the building was $126,500, and was paid in full by 1916. It was a large sum to have been raised in those days. The church has had a widening influence in this section of the Anthracite Region. Its leadership is greater than one would expect of a membership of about 1,200 persons.

FREDERICK E. MASER

POWELL, THOMAS (1872-1949), Canadian Methodist and United Church of Canada minister, was born in Radnor, Herefordshire, England, on March 5, 1872. In 1876 he came to Canada with his parents and was educated at Almonte, Ontario. Originally an Anglican, he joined the Epworth League and became a Methodist.

He attended McGill University and Montreal Wesleyan College. Ordained in 1899, he was appointed to Olds in the Northwest Territories. Subsequently he served in various charges in Alberta until in 1918 he became superintendent of missions, a post which he continued to hold after Union. He retired in 1942, and died at Calgary on June 10, 1949.

Powell was president of his conference in 1913 and 1936. He was a commissioner to the first General Council of the United Church and to several subsequent ones. The doctorate of divinity conferred on him in 1928 by St. Stephen's College was indicative of the esteem in which he was held by the church in Alberta.

G. H. Cornish, *Cyclopaedia of Methodism in Canada.* 1903.
J. Riddell, *Middle West.* 1946.
The United Church Observer, July 15, 1949.   C. D. POWELL

POWER, JOHN H. (1798-1873), American minister, was born on March 15, 1798 in Montgomery County, Ky. and attended common schools there. He was admitted on trial to the KENTUCKY CONFERENCE of the M.E. Church in 1821 and to full connnection in 1823. He served churches in KENTUCKY, VIRGINIA, OHIO and IOWA for eighteen years and was an effective presiding elder in Ohio and of the Burlington, Muscatine and Keokuk Districts of the IOWA CONFERENCE for twenty-eight years. From 1848-52 he was assistant agent for the Western BOOK CONCERN and from 1854-55 he was in a supernumerary relationship because of ill health. He returned to active work in 1865 and continued vigorously until his death on Jan. 25, 1873. A member of the board of trustees of IOWA WESLEYAN UNIVERSITY 1860-72, he acted as president of the board 1868-72, and was influential in the expansion of the university and the public school system in IOWA. He was an official delegate to eight GENERAL CONFERENCES.

Gaining his education by individual effort, he taught himself both Greek and Hebrew. He was noted as a preacher of power and insight and as an administrator for methodical, exact attention to detail. He never missed a meeting of an annual conference in fifty-two years. Current religious and political controversy attracted his attention and he published pamphlets on: *Power on Universalism; Doolittle and Power; Domestic Piety* and *Letters to Dr. Smith on Slavery.* Ohio Wesleyan University granted him an honorary D.D. in 1853.

A. W. Haines. *Makers of Iowa Methodism.* 1900.
Iowa Wesleyan College Archives.
Journal and Reports of the Iowa Annual Conference, 1873.
E. H. Waring. *Iowa Annual Conference.* 1910.
                              LOUIS A. HASELMAYER

POYTHRESS, FRANCIS (1732-1818), American minister, was born in VIRGINIA in 1732 and converted there in 1772 under DEVEREUX JARRATT. He was received on trial in 1775, and after preaching ten years in Virginia and MARYLAND he served fifteen years (1786-1800) with distinction as a presiding elder. Although accustomed to settled life, he uncomplainingly endured frontier hardships to establish Methodism in KENTUCKY and to sustain BETHEL ACADEMY. Worn by his labors, he sank in 1801 into a tragic mental illness and died about 1818 in Jessamine County, Ky.

J. E. Armstrong, *Old Baltimore Conference*. 1907.
F. Asbury, *Journal and Letters*. 1958.
R. N. Price, *Holston*. 1906-14.   EDWIN SCHELL

E. W. PRAETORIUS

PRAETORIUS, ELMER WESLEY (1882-1966), American E.U.B. bishop, was born in Dayton, Ohio, Oct. 1, 1882. He was graduated from NORTH CENTRAL COLLEGE and EVANGELICAL THEOLOGICAL SEMINARY, Naperville, Ill. He was ordained a minister of the INDIANA CONFERENCE of The EVANGELICAL ASSOCIATION and through the course of denominational unions served in The Evangelical Church and The E.U.B. Church. He ministered as pastor of congregations in LOUISVILLE, Ky.; Terre Haute and Elkhart, Ind.

Sixteen years as Executive Secretary of the Board of Christian Education followed his service in the parish ministry. In 1934 he was elected bishop and quadrennially thereafter was re-elected by general conference until his retirement in 1954. He died in ST. PAUL, Minn., Feb. 2, 1966.

As pastor, educator and bishop he prosecuted his vocation with zeal, sincerity and joyous faith in God. His diligent efforts as a preacher, expounding the Word of God which he loved, were illuminating and dynamic and persuasive. He promoted programs of Christian Education which enhanced that cause at all levels of denominational life. He rendered inestimable service with his painstaking editorial work in the preparation and publication of successive denominational *Disciplines*.

Church and Home, April 15, 1966.   PAUL H. MILLER

PRAIRIE VILLAGE, KANSAS, U.S.A., **Asbury Church,** is located in a rapidly growing suburban area in Kansas City. Founded in October 1952, under the part-time direction of Mills M. Anderson, the first full-time minister, Al Hager was appointed in 1955 at which time the church

moved into its first unit or educational building. Asbury Church has now completed its facilities with a sanctuary, educational building, office-educational wing, and chapel unit. Its membership in 1970 was 2,575.

Asbury Church has been a pioneer in the small group movement. The life of the church is honeycombed with prayer groups, research groups, skeptic groups, and spiritual life encounter groups.

Asbury Church began the one-year lay-missionary program to the Inner-City in 1962-64, which was later adopted as the program of the 1964 GENERAL CONFERENCE.

The church is now in the process of developing a Clinical Pastoral Training program. It has a relationship to ST. PAUL SCHOOL OF THEOLOGY in terms of its supervisory capacity of seminary students in the life of the local church.

The original two-part saddlebag Bibles of Bishop FRANCIS ASBURY are owned and displayed in a special glass case at Asbury Church.

PRATHER'S MEETINGHOUSE in Iredell County, N. C. was organized before 1800. FRANCIS ASBURY visited it in 1797 and 1799, referring to it the first time as "the church in the Forks of the Yadkin," and the second time as "Prather's Meetinghouse." Land for the church was given by Bazil Prather in a deed dated 1800, as he, his family, and some neighbors were moving to southern INDIANA in which locality he became a leader in early Methodism. The name of Prather's Meetinghouse was changed to Mt. Bethel, and it continues as a work on the Harmony Charge, Statesville District. In 1969 Mt. Bethel reported fifty-six members and property valued at $20,695.

F. Asbury, *Journal and Letters*. 1958.
Minutes of the Western North Carolina Conference.
                                        HOMER KEEVER

PRATT, M. A. RUGBY (1875-1946), New Zealand minister, was born in Gisborne, New Zealand, but grew up in Tasmania. He served as a home missonary, entered the theological college in Melbourne, and then came to New Zealand. For twenty-five years he was a circuit minister and was known as a gifted organizer and also as a close and earnest student. In 1927 he began a term of nineteen years as connexional secretary, and during this time he considerably enlarged the scope of the service rendered by various departments to the church. In 1923, he visited Tonga and helped to reunite the church there in a spirit of harmony. He was keenly interested in the movement for Bible-in-schools and prohibition. He wrote *Pioneering Days in Southern Maoriland* (London: Epworth Press, 1932), and was a fellow of the Royal Historical Society. He died in Christchurch on March 6, 1946.

Minutes of the New Zealand Methodist Conference, 1947.
                                        WILLIAM T. BLIGHT

PRAYER. (See WORSHIP.)

PRAYER MEETINGS which began in early Methodism as informal gatherings of Christians, came in time to be in Methodist Churches, especially in those in America, stated, formal mid-week evening services. Some historians trace the origin of Methodism to a prayer meeting group (the HOLY CLUB), in which there were earnest inquirers after a more complete Christian life. The GENERAL RULES of The United Methodist Church state in their introduction, "In the latter end of the year 1739 eight or ten persons came to Mr. Wesley, in London, who appeared to be deeply convinced of sin, and earnestly groaning for redemption. They desired, as did two or three more the next day, that he would spend some time with them in prayer, and advise them how to flee from the wrath to come which they saw continually hanging over their heads. That he might have more time for this great work, he appointed a day when they might all come together, which from thenceforward they did every week, namely, on Thursday, in the evening. To these, and as many more as desired to join with them (for their numbers increased daily), he gave those advices from time to time which he judged most needful for them, and they always concluded their meetings with prayer suited to their several necessities." (*Discipline*, UMC, 1968.)

Wesley himself indicated that this was "the rise of the United Society first in Europe and then in America." The Methodist societies at first met apart from regular church hours for their preaching services, and also in general for their prayer services.

After organization of the M.E. Church in America, CLASS MEETINGS and prayer meetings continued of course to be held, though by now regular Sunday preaching services had begun. However, there grew in local churches as they were established at first the custom and then the rule to have a mid-week evening prayer service. This came to be on Thursday evening over a large section of the church, especially in the North, while Wednesday evening came to be the usual time in the South. Prayer meetings proved to be a great religious service to the church, as in them not only older members were expected and did take part but younger ones also frequently commenced publicly the exercise of their gifts and leadership in prayer and worship.

As the prayer meeting was held other than at the regular church service period, and was unknown in the older liturgical churches as a formal part of the church's program, Methodists were considered by some to be innovators and pioneers in thus dignifying a service of worship apart from the regular ordinances of the church. "In the United States and especially on its frontier where there was no ritualistic established church to preserve the 'dead forms,' the conventional means of grace and worship had little chance in competition with the prayer meeting and the revival." (Bucke, III, 610.) The same authority says that Philip Schaff was more horrified at the liturgical, than at the intellectual and doctrinal state of Methodism in America when he said, "In worship, Methodism is not satisfied with the usual divinely ordained means of grace. It really little understands the use of the Sacraments. . . . It has far more confidence in subjective means and exciting impressions, than in the more quiet and unobserved but surer work of the old church system of educational religion." (*ibid*). Schaff further states that he had been prepared to recommend that the formalized churches of Germany consider the adaptation of the prayer meeting to their needs, but after he came to America and saw the usual prayer meeting in action, he was not so impressed.

During the last half of the nineteenth century, the prayer meeting as an institution of Methodist Church life grew in importance, especially after class meetings as such had begun to die away. As travel became easier and the whole congregation could be centered about each individual church, it was easier to gather the congregation together for a mid-week prayer meeting than to continue to depend upon scattered classes as had been the case in early pioneer days, when Methodist families were separated—sometimes at a considerable distance—from each other. The prayer meeting thus came into rather full flower late in the nineteenth century, and Bishop SIMPSON says it was ". . . of great religious service to the church. . . . It has often been observed that wherever a genuine revival has prevailed the social means of grace have also more or less revived, and prayer meetings especially are at once established."

Methodism in America influenced other evangelical denominations with its prayer meetings, and these also adopted the prayer meeting plan on a nation-wide scale. However, with the increasing complexity and tensions of life which have come about toward the middle of the twentieth century, prayer meetings have declined greatly in influence, and indeed in many places have been entirely discontinued. Nevertheless, the *Book of Discipline* of The United Methodist Church still names as one of the duties of the pastor in charge "to hold or appoint prayer meetings, love feasts, and watch night meetings, wherever advisable."

Certain ministers make a feature of their prayer meeting services, and many are known to succeed well in conducting this type of worship. Others, especially in large churches, have discontinued the formal weekly prayer meeting, though encouraging local groups and organizations of the church to meet for prayer and worship in connection with their other duties.

E. S. Bucke, *History of American Methodism*. 1964.
M. Simpson, *Cyclopaedia*. 1878.   N. B. H.

PREACHING. British Methodism. One reason for the success of the eighteenth-century evangelical revival was a change in pulpit style. GEORGE WHITEFIELD and JOHN WESLEY and their imitators dropped the rather impersonal style which had developed in the time of Tillotson, and instead made a direct assault on the minds and feelings of their hearers, seeking to convert them on the spot. Simplicity returned: Wesley constantly advised his preachers to speak in the language of the common people.

At least one reason for this was that eighteenth century Methodist preachers often spoke in the open air, where elaborate periods and over-subtlety or argument were wasted. Open-air preaching was a novelty in the period; John Wesley began to preach outdoors when he was denied the use of the Anglican pulpits; much street preaching took place in the effort to form new societies in places where there was no Methodist building available; in the early nineteenth century the tradition was continued by the BIBLE CHRISTIANS and the PRIMITIVE METHODISTS who imitated the American CAMP MEETING, and spoke to country audiences from farm-carts in the fields; HUGH BOURNE stressed the importance of proclaiming the Gospel in the street, in order that those who refused to come to the chapels should have heard it; belief in the value of "open-air evangelism," as it is now often called, has remained even in twentieth century British Methodism. Nevertheless, most Methodist sermons have been preached indoors, in cottages as well as chapels, and the best eighteenth century Methodist preachers revived the Puritan tradition of preaching, in which the preacher developed his own spiritual experience for the spiritual benefit of his congregation. The eighteenth century sermon often lasted more than an hour; the shorter sermon seems to have come in the later nineteenth century, when HUGH PRICE HUGHES often spoke for about twenty minutes. Between 1791 and 1860 the style of Methodist preaching degenerated, often became very florid (cf. MORLEY PUNSHON). The reasons for the change remain obscure, but certainly early nineteenth century Methodist preachers suffered from their efforts at self-improvement. Thus, in *An Essay on the Christian Ministry* (1828), by Jonathan Edmundson, written as a guide to young preachers before the start of theological colleges, the author spoke of the necessity of studying rhetoric, which "will enrich your style, enable you to deliver your discourses with gracefulness, and fix the attention of your hearers." Edmundson recommended Claude on the *Composition of the Sermon* (this was probably the influence of the Anglican Evangelical Charles Simeon, who popularized the book in the Church of England); and Gibbon's *Rhetoric:* "Gibbon's Rhetoric claims your first attention. He gives you a clear account of the tropes and figures in their origin and powers; with a variety of rules to escape errors and blemishes and to attain propriety and elegance in composition. Examine his work with care, copy all his definitions, and commit them to memory."

The reaction against this tradition was part of the FORWARD MOVEMENT from about 1880. Hugh Price Hughes, SAMUEL COLLIER, LUKE WISEMAN, and others built up large popular audiences by a return to more direct, simple preaching; they also widened the scope of the pulpit, speaking on social and political themes more often than had been customary in the past. A modified version of the rhetorical tradition continued in WILLIAM WATKINSON and F. W. MACDONALD. At the close of the nineteenth century the day of the popular preacher reached its zenith; leading Methodist preachers had congregations which sometimes exceeded two thousand. At the same time thousands of Methodist ministerial and lay preachers continued to deliver sermons of a biblical and practical kind which would have seemed familiar in the eighteenth century. In the twentieth century the preacher's prestige and audience declined. Biblical criticism affected the situation deeply. The rhetorical tradition became rarer in a climate which grew more pragmatic and doubtful of authority. W. E. SANGSTER was the most recent Methodist in this tradition; he also wrote much on the technique of preaching. DONALD SOPER continued the tradition of commenting on social and political affairs. It was often said in the early 1960's, however, that the day of the popular preacher had ended. Television was replacing the church service as the preacher's medium of contact with society in general; it is too early to say how successfully Methodism would adapt to this new opportunity.

American Methodism. The establishment of Methodist Societies in America dates from the preaching of PHILIP EMBURY and Captain THOMAS WEBB in NEW YORK in 1766, and from JESSE LEE's work on the pioneer circuit in VIRGINIA in 1789. ROBERT STRAWBRIDGE, an Irish immigrant itinerating in MARYLAND, DELAWARE, PENNSYLVANIA, and Virginia, 1773-75, called forth the first native American preachers: PHILIP GATCH, FREEBORN GARRETTSON, and WILLIAM WATTERS. From the preaching of such devoted men, unordained and largely untrained, grew the Methodism which moved forward with the earliest settlers on every advancing frontier.

Until late in the nineteenth century, this preaching was almost exclusively evangelistic, designed to foster the three steps commonly accepted as structural to salvation— awakening, JUSTIFICATION, and SANCTIFICATION. The first two steps supplied the objective of preaching in mixed gatherings of believers and unbelievers; the last provided the substance of sermons at LOVE FEASTS and other more intimate services of the faithful. The preaching was biblical in method; the preacher was expected to "take a text" and to base both the structure and content of his message upon it. Addresses which did not meet this qualification were carefully designated "exhortations" or "discourses" to differentiate them from sermons.

Such preaching led to great revivals such as developed in Virginia in the years around 1772. The Virginia revival was traceable to the preaching of Devereux Jarrett, a minister of the Established Church who, having gone to England to be ordained, had come under the influence of JOHN WESLEY. Remaining in the Established Church, he preached in a manner largely Methodist in doctrine and spirit. These frontier revivals produced the "sacramental meeting," in which preaching continued daily for weeks on end and in which preachers became adept at reaching crowds of 10,000 or more. Following the revival of 1797-1805, the CAMP MEETING, a western development of the "sacramental meeting," achieved such popularity that by 1812 Methodists were holding at least 400 such meetings annually. Although there were extravagant emotional outbursts, these were discouraged by the circuit preachers, as by John Wesley and FRANCIS ASBURY before them.

Early American Methodist preaching was almost entirely the work of circuit riders, many of whom were assigned to territories requiring five or six weeks of continuous travel and daily preaching to cover. In 1803 a preacher was given the State of ILLINOIS as his charge; in 1806 another was assigned simply to MISSOURI. In such a ministry Francis Asbury traveled 270,000 miles and preached more than 16,000 sermons; on the East Jersey circuit, near the turn of the nineteenth century, EZEKIEL COOPER preached 345 times in a single year. In Illinois, at the same period, PETER CARTWRIGHT won a reputation for his witty, picturesque, resourceful extempore preaching and for his "muscular evangelism"—equally ready to struggle for a man's soul or to beat him in a fight if he interfered with the free expression of the gospel. Supplementing the circuit riders, frontier farmers, serving as LOCAL PREACHERS, shepherded congregations between circuit visits, or gathered the initial congregation in advance of the coming of the itinerant preacher.

With little formal schooling, these early preachers were uneducated only in the sense that Abraham Lincoln was uneducated, as WILLIAM WARREN SWEET observed. Carrying their few books in their saddlebags, they studied as they rode. Preaching his way around a circuit so far-flung that a dozen sermons a year would have guarded amply against repetition to the same congregation, Ezekiel Cooper recorded in his journal the use of seventy-three different texts in a single year. The outlines in his journal show a remarkable penetration in exegesis and an inventive variety in treatment. It was not until 1816 that the GENERAL CONFERENCE prescribed a course of study in which presiding elders were to supervise candidates for the ministry. Yet by 1878 the frontier had produced, in MATTHEW SIMPSON, a national figure known for his eloquence, who made a worthy contribution to the distinguished Lyman Beecher Lectureship in preaching.

Proclamation of CHRISTIAN PERFECTION declined after 1840, as the church found a more established life in cities and towns, with a somewhat more formal worship. In protest, organized emphasis on "HOLINESS" was promoted in many pulpits. A National Camp Meeting Association for the Promotion of Holiness, founded in 1867, had its principal strength among Methodists. A "holiness" revival swept considerable areas in 1880. Preaching tended to divide between this emphasis and the growing modernism, but the "holiness" movement left a limited influence within the church as it gave its strength to the establishment of separate denominational bodies devoted to this doctrine.

The opening of the twentieth century found a social message taking its place in Methodist pulpits, led by the notable preaching of such men as HERBERT WELCH, FRANCIS J. McCONNELL, FRANK MASON NORTH, and HARRIS FRANKLIN RALL. It was reflected in the adoption of the first SOCIAL CREED of the Church in 1908. In 1905-1906 Charles Reynolds Brown delivered his first series of Lyman Beecher lectures, devoting them to *The Social Message of the Modern Pulpit*. Within the span of a generation, other Methodists called to that important homiletic forum took up similar themes: Francis J. McConnell treating *The Prophetic Ministry;* G. BROMLEY OXNAM, *Preaching in A Revolutionary Age;* and ERNEST FREMONT TITTLE, *Jesus After Nineteen Centuries,* with a stress—always present in Tittle's preaching—on the social impact of Jesus. Such preaching fostered a new social conscience in the church.

With the development of electronic mass media, preaching took to the airways. RALPH W. SOCKMAN's long ministry in the National Radio Pulpit dramatized the use of that medium by great numbers of preachers across the country, who preached regularly through more local facilities. Led by the work of the TELEVISION, RADIO AND FILM COMMISSION (TRAFCO), ministers in the 1960's were learning to use the more difficult medium of television.

After a generation in which preaching had been mostly topical, the 1950's and 1960's saw the return of an emphasis on biblical preaching in theological seminaries; with the growing concern for the hermeneutic problem in the theological world there were indications that strong biblical preaching might dominate the pulpits of the final third of the twentieth century.

Batsell Barrett Baxter, *The Heart of the Yale Lectures.* New York: The Macmillan Company, 1947.
R. D. Clark, *Matthew Simpson.* 1956.
James McGraw, *Great Evangelical Preachers of Yesterday.* Nashville: Abingdon Press, 1961.
Lester Buryl Scherer, *Ezekiel Cooper, 1763-1847, An Early American Methodist Leader.* Unpublished doctoral dissertation: Garrett Theological Seminary Library.
W. W. Sweet, *Methodism in American History.* 1933.
Ernest Trice Thompson, *Changing Emphases in American Preaching.* Philadelphia: Westminster Press, 1943. JOHN KENT
MERRILL R. ABBEY

PREDIGERSEMINAR (The Theological Seminary of the United Methodist Church of Germany) is at Frankfurt/Main. Here in 1968 the Predigerseminar der Methodistenkirche and the Predigerseminar der Evangelischen Gemeinschaft (EUB Church) in Reutlingen were united.

The Predigerseminar der Methodistenkirche was opened in 1858 by L. S. JACOBY at BREMEN. The first students were two young Germans and one Swiss who felt the call to preach. After almost ten years in cramped quarters, the seminary was transferred to Frankfurt. The new build-

SEMINARY, FRANKFURT, GERMANY

ing was made possible by a gift of $25,000 by the New York textile merchant, John T. Martin, after whom the school was named "Martins Mission Anstalt." Frankfurt was chosen because of its central geographical position.

The last years of the nineteenth century proved fruitful for the seminary, which served the needs of a growing Methodism well. The faculty included German, Swiss, and American professors. W. F. WARREN served on the faculty from 1861-66 and went to BOSTON UNIVERSITY in the United States; his successor was J. F. HURST (1866-71), later to become bishop in the United States and the author of valuable publications. While the Frankfurt theological seminary was serving the needs of the M.E. Church, another theological school was training Wesleyan Methodist ministers in south GERMANY. When the Methodisms of American and British background were amalgamated (1897), the seminary in Frankfurt became the training center for all Methodist ministers. A fine new building was completed in 1914, but before it could be dedicated, the First World War broke out. German theological students were drafted into the army; only the Swiss men temporarily continued their work. A major part of the building was commandeered for a military hospital. Taking on new life in 1920, the seminary began one of its most fruitful decades. The new president, F. H. OTTO MELLE, was a superb administrator. Enrollments rose from twenty-three in 1920 to a high of eighty-eight in 1928. During this period the school trained not only Germans, Swiss, and Austrians, as it still does, but Bulgarians, Hungarians, Estonians, Finns, Lithuanians, Latvians, and Yugoslavs. There was even a Chinese graduate student. There have been exchange students also from ARGENTINA, the United States, JAPAN, Crete, and Great Britain in recent years.

Perhaps the seminary's most difficult period began in 1933 with the ascendancy of Hitler and the Nazis. Young men facing two years of army duty could make no plans for seminary training, and the theological course had to be shortened to four years. Apart from three men who did not become ministers, all students succeeded in holding to the church's viewpoint on public life and pastoral care. In 1936, Melle was elected the first German Methodist bishop; his successor at the seminary became J. W. E. SOMMER. Then came 1939 and war. After a few months the seminary found itself on an uncertain basis. Students attended only between campaigns when their military service permitted. Medical and dental military units took over some of the seminary rooms, thus safeguarding it from Gestapo control. Some damage was done to the buildings. After the war reconstruction proceeded slowly. Sommer having been elected a bishop in 1946, FRIEDRICH WUNDERLICH succeeded him as president. The seminary recovered with the help of American Methodist gifts. Enrollment reached fifty-four in 1951. Then in 1952 another blow fell. The seminary was cut off from serving the forty-five percent of German Methodists in the Eastern zone, as it had previously been cut off from Methodists in the Balkans. The East-zone Methodists, however, were able to set up their own theological school at Bad Klosterlausnitz, now under the leadership of Direktor Hans Witzel. Here both Methodist and EVANGELICAL UNITED BRETHREN students are trained. In 1952 Bishop Sommer died, and Wunderlich was elected to the episcopacy. In August 1953, C. ERNST SOMMER, son of the late bishop, became president of the seminary. In May 1968 C. E. Sommer was elected the first bishop of the United Methodist Church in Germany.

Predigerseminar der Evangelischen Gemeinschaft (EUB Church) in Reutlingen was opened July 25, 1877. The first director was John Kaechele. Until 1905 the attics of the Ebenezer-Church were used as classrooms and dormitories. Kaechele was succeeded by G. Heinmiller (1886-91). In 1891 John Schempp, Sr. was elected director. The character of the theological school was very much influenced by him during his almost thirty years of leadership. In 1905 a big and modern building was erected with large classrooms, library, dormitories for the students, flats for the teachers and adjoining rooms. When the building was dedicated in December 1905 the lord mayor declared the seminary on a hill overlooking the city to be an embellishment of Reutlingen, the old Freetown of the Reich. The seminiary trained the ministers of the Annual Conferences of Germany and SWITZERLAND and during some years after the First World War, also Estonians and Lithuanians. The most fruitful time of the school was during the years 1925-30 when fifty students were enrolled. During the Second World War the seminary was occupied for military purposes but in 1946 it was reopened under the directorship of John Schempp, Jr. with six students. In 1952 he was succeeded by Reinhold Kuecklich. With the help of the mother-church in the U.S.A. the buildings were enlarged and the enrollment was raised to thirty-four students. After 1954 the students of the German Democratic Republic had to do their studies in the east. Together with The Methodist Church, a new seminary in Klosterlausnitz was founded. When Kuecklich retired in 1966, Karl Steckel was elected director of the seminary in Reutlingen.

After several years of preparation and careful deliberations together at the union of the E.U.B. Church and The Methodist Church, the two seminaries were united, Sept. 15, 1968, in Frankfurt/Main. Karl Steckel was elected the new president. There were forty-one students and six full-time professors of whom two were Swiss. As a united seminary, the Frankfurt theological school has moved expectantly into its second century, ministering and witnessing to the indestructibility of the Christian faith, so that young men shall go forth, trained to meet every need a modern minister may encounter, and

strengthened in their faith and their sense of divine calling.

C. ERNST SOMMER
KARL STECKEL

PRESCOTT, C. J. (1857-1946), able scholar and educator, was born at Bridport, England, the son of a Wesleyan minister. He was educated at KINGSWOOD SCHOOL where he passed through the usual six years course, but being Head Boy was allowed to remain two additional years.

He won the Dux and Arithmetic Medals twice, and twice gained the Medal for Greek Testament. He passed the Junior Oxford Local Examination Twice and subsequently gained a scholarship for four years.

In 1873 he proceeded to Worcester College, OXFORD, where he completed his course in 1880, taking his B.A. degree and gaining honors in Mathematics. He received his M.A. degree in 1893.

He was accepted as a candidate for the ministry and appointed assistant tutor at HANDSWORTH THEOLOGICAL INSTITUTION.

In 1882 he accepted an invitation to join the Conference in NEW SOUTH WALES and was stationed at PARRAMATTA for three years, during which time he acted as tutor in Classics and General Literature at the Provisional Theological Institution at Stanmore.

In 1886 he was appointed Headmaster of the Methodist Ladies' College at Burwood and in 1900 was made Headmaster at Newington College, Stanmore, which position he held until his retirement.

In 1910 he was elected President of the New South Wales Conference.

When the new Methodist Hymn Book was under revision he gave valuable service as a member of the Revision Committee.

In 1912 he was honored with the D.D. degree by EMORY UNIVERSITY, U.S.A.

He was the author of three books: *Romance of a School, Matters for Methodists,* and *Methodist Churchmanship—Plaint and Plea.*

AUSTRALIAN EDITORIAL COMMITTEE

PRESIDING ELDER. (See SUPERINTENDENT.)

PRESS AND INFORMATION SERVICE, METHODIST (British) was formed as a result of a decision by the 1948 British Conference. Its function is to provide an authoritative channel of communication with the press when they are seeking information and guidance about Methodist affairs. It is responsible for providing newspapers with news about Methodism and with the views expressed by organizations of the church and its leaders on questions of current interest. The service is under the general direction of the CONNEXIONAL EDITOR, who presents its report to Conference, but a lay journalist carries out the actual work to ensure that matter submitted conforms to newspaper needs.

TOM GOODALL

PREST, CHARLES (1806-1875), British Wesleyan Methodist, had great influence in the organization of Wesleyanism after the mid-nineteenth century disputes. He was born on Oct. 16, 1806, at Bath, Somerset, and

CHARLES PREST

entered the Wesleyan ministry in 1829. President of the Conference in 1862, he is best known for his reorganization and extension of Home Missions during the last eighteen years of his life. He was also secretary of the COMMITTEE OF PRIVILEGES for nineteen years. As treasurer of the Schools' Fund, he was active in promoting the building of the new KINGSWOOD SCHOOL. He established district missionaries and encouraged the appointment of chaplains to the forces. He died at Lee, Kent, on Aug. 25, 1875.

JOHN KENT

PRETTYMAN, FORREST JOHNSTON (1860-1945), American minister and chaplain of the U.S. Senate during the Theodore Roosevelt and Woodrow Wilson administrations, was born at Brookeville, Md., on April 7, 1860. His father, E. Barrett Prettyman, had been Secretary of Education of MARYLAND, and his mother was Lydia (Forrest) Prettyman. He was educated at the Rockville (Maryland) Academy, at St. John's College at Annapolis, and in part at Washington and Lee University. RANDOLPH-MACON COLLEGE conferred upon him the D.D. degree later on in life.

On Oct. 17, 1888, he married Elizabeth R. Stonestreet, and to them were born two sons and two daughters, E. Barrett, Edith S., Charles W. and Martha B. The older son is Judge E. Barrett Prettyman, of the Fifth Circuit of the Court of Appeals in Washington, D.C. Prettyman served as pastor in the Old BALTIMORE CONFERENCE (MES) including St. Paul in BALTIMORE; Lexington, Va.; Martinsburg, W. Va.; Staunton, Va.; WASHINGTON, D.C. at Mount Vernon Place; and at Emory Church; also Trinity Church in Baltimore. He was the presiding elder of the Washington District for some years, and a member of the GENERAL CONFERENCE of the M.E. Church, South, 1906, 1910, and 1930; and a fraternal messenger to the M.P. General Conference of 1912.

Prettyman was a commanding preacher and after serving as chaplain of the Senate from 1913 until the beginning of the Harding administration in 1920, he was transferred to Church Street Church, KNOXVILLE, Tenn., where

he served for a time, and then went to the Gastonia Church in the WESTERN NORTH CAROLINA CONFERENCE. On his return to the Baltimore Conference, he was assigned to Wilson Memorial Church on St. Charles Avenue, Baltimore, in 1927, and then to Fredericksburg, Va., from which position he retired.

Prettyman had a presence which added distinction to any occasion in which he participated, and especially in the formal, diplomatic and congressional ceremonies and functions in Washington, D.C., he was able to represent his church and its ministry in an urbane, commanding way. He died at Rockville, Md., in the old family home there, on Oct. 12, 1945.

Journal of the Baltimore Conference, 1946.
C. F. Price, *Who's Who in American Methodism.* 1916.

N. B. H.

PRICE, CARL FOWLER (1881-1948), American layman, author, musician, organist, hymn composer, lecturer, historian and churchman, was born May 16, 1881, at New Brunswick, N. J. He was the son of Jacob Embury and Anne Bacon Ware Price. He was graduated from Centenary Collegiate Institute in 1898, and from WESLEYAN UNIVERSITY in 1902. On April 21, 1905, he married Leila A. Field of East Hampton. She died March 24, 1906. On June 19, 1913, he married Flora Draper Treat of New York. She died Aug. 30, 1919. They had one son, Sherman.

A man of great vitality, Carl Price was interested in, and served, Wesleyan University throughout his life. He helped found the Alumni Association in 1904, and the *Wesleyan Alumnus* in 1916. He edited a Wesleyan Song Book and wrote *Wesleyan's First Century,* a 400-page history of the college, in addition to many other articles and songs. In 1932 Wesleyan conferred upon him the honorary M.A. degree in recognition of his distinguished service to the University.

Carl Price served the church in many capacities. He was Secretary of the National Board of the EPWORTH LEAGUE, 1912-24; President of the Methodist Social Union, 1919-21; member of the ECUMENICAL METHODIST CONFERENCE in 1931; historian of the Methodist Historical Society, 1937-48; author of *Who's Who in Methodism* in 1916, and an active lay member of the NEW YORK CONFERENCE, serving as president of its Laymen's Association for over twenty-five years.

His greatest contribution to the church was in the field of music. Carl Price composed over 200 hymn tunes, as well as cantatas and canticles. He lectured on hymnody at Union Theological Seminary, New York, and at DREW UNIVERSITY. He was co-founder of the Hymn Society of America, serving as its president from 1922-26. He published many books on hymns, music, and worship. Among them are: *Music and Hymnody of the Methodist Hymnal, A Year of Hymn Stories, Curiosities of the Hymnal, More Hymn Stories, 101 Methodist Stories, Songs of Life, Hymns of Worship, 101 Hymn Stories, Hymns, Hymnologists and Their Stories.* In all he was the author of eleven books, editor of thirty music collections, published thirty-one songs, 200 hymn tunes, cantatas, festival services, booklets, and other miscellany, in addition to over 400 articles which appeared in various church and secular magazines and newspapers. He earned his living as an insurance broker, but his real vocation was church music.

Carl Price died April 12, 1948, following a stroke. He was buried at Kensico Cemetery, Valhalla, N. Y.

R. G. McCutchan, *Our Hymnody*. 1937.
Minutes of the New York Conference, 1948.

C. WESLEY CHRISTMAN, JR.

PRICE, FREDERICK ADOLPHUS (1879-1966), Methodist missionary and American consul-general of LIBERIA, was born on April 5, 1879, in Barbados, British West Indies. After receiving his early education in Barbados, Frederick Price traveled to the United States for special training in missionary service. After graduating from the Union Missionary Training Institute, BROOKLYN, N. Y., he was recommended by Bishop J. C. HARTZELL for appointment to Liberia. In late 1904 he began his mission service in Harper, Cape Palmas. Working along the Cavalla River, he established many mission schools.

Among the stations begun by Price was Barclayville, which remains today a strong center for Methodism and one of the fine schools in the Methodist system. In 1934 he became district superintendent of the Cape Palmas District and pastor of Mt. Scott Methodist Church, serving also as field treasurer for the Board of Foreign Missions. He served there until his retirement in 1945. His missionary pension he donated each year to the work of the church in Liberia.

Not content with one career of service, he then became a Liberian citizen and was appointed Liberian Consul General to NEW YORK CITY. This appointment included diplomatic assignments in WASHINGTON, D. C., and service on several delegations to the United Nations. After his retirement in 1958 (the second time), Dr. and Mrs. Price (nee Luna A. Jones) returned to Harper, Cape Palmas. Mrs. Price pre-deceased her husband in 1963. He was decorated several times by the Liberian government and his life remains an example of devotion to the service of his fellowman. He died in Monrovia, Liberia, on Jan. 5, 1966.

Official Gazette, Department of State, Republic of Liberia, Jan. 5, 1966.

PRICE, HIRAM (1814-1901), American congressman, banker and railroad president, was born Jan. 10, 1814, in Washington County, Pa. Removing to Mifflin County in 1819 and later to Huntingdon County, Pa., he was educated in local schools. He married Susan Betts in 1834 and they had five children. Price, described as a man "of determined perseverance, inviolate integrity, good business tact, temperate and conscientious," removed to Davenport, Iowa in 1844 and opened a store. He was school fund commissioner, 1847-56, and recorder and treasurer of Scott County, 1848-56. In the early fifties he occupied himself with railroad enterprises, building a railroad from Davenport to Council Bluffs. When Iowa's state bank was established in 1858, he represented the Davenport branch, serving as its president, 1860-65. Price, a Republican Party member, was U.S. Congressman, 1865-69 and 1877-81, and U.S. Commissioner of Indian Affairs, 1881-85.

He was a member of the Dubuque M.E. Church for over fifty-seven years, served as sexton, recording steward, trustee, class leader, and Sunday school superintendent. He was lay delegate of the UPPER IOWA CONFERENCE at two GENERAL CONFERENCE sessions and a trustee of

Mt. Vernon's Iowa Conference Seminary. Price, an advocate of temperance, organized a Grand Division of the Sons of Temperance in 1848; edited the *Temperance Organ* for several years; served as President of the "Maine Law Alliance," 1854; spoke on temperance at Iowa's first State Methodist Convention, 1871, and became the National Anti-Saloon League's first president. He died in Washington, D. C.

Annals of Iowa, April 1893, January 1894, January 1895.
Dictionary of American Biography.
S. N. Fellows, *Upper Iowa Conference*. 1907.
A. W. Haines, *Makers of Iowa Methodism*. 1900.

MARTIN L. GREER

PRICE, JOHN WATKIN (1870-1951), American preacher and missionary to BRAZIL, was born in Tamaqua, Pa., on Jan. 30, 1870. Price studied three years at Oberlin Academy then at the Christian Training School in Cleveland, Ohio, and the Christian and Missionary Alliance Training School in NEW YORK CITY. While studying in Cleveland, he met Elizabeth Wittman, a Bible student working among the underprivileged of that city. They were married June 18, 1895, and continued evangelistic work together in Cleveland.

Through reading Guiness' book, *The Neglected Continent*, Price felt definitely called to Brazil. He offered himself and was sent there in May 1896, by the Christian and Missionary Alliance. In 1898, however, he was moved to BUENOS AIRES, ARGENTINA, where he was received into the River Plate Conference of the M.E. Church, and was soon appointed to South Brazil, then a mission of that Conference. He was appointed pastor of the Central Methodist Church in PORTO ALEGRE, capital of the state of Rio Grande do Sul, in May 1899.

Price began expanding the work at once, established three suburban missions, and founded the first EPWORTH LEAGUE in the state. In 1899, when the South Brazil mission was transferred by mutual agreement to the M.E. Church, South, then operating in other areas of Brazil, Price elected to stay in Brazil. He served throughout the years as pastor, presiding elder, and superintendent of the mission. Though his strongest point was mainly in the field of evangelism, he also contributed to education by founding in 1908 the school in Uruguaiana, União Colegio, now Instituto. Later he also taught at Porto Alegre College.

After forty years on the mission field, the Prices retired to DENVER, Colo., and there continued a ministry to the Latin Americans of the area. In all his work everywhere, his wife was an invaluable helper. She was born in Ohio on March 19, 1872, and from the time she was sixteen, dedicated her life to the Lord's work. When John Price asked her if she was willing to go with him to a foreign country, she replied: "If there are souls to save, I'll go with you."

John Price died in Denver on May 21, 1951; and Mrs. Price in Englewood, N. J. (where she had moved to be with her daughter) on June 6, 1962. They were survived by three children—Thomas, a Harvard Ph.D.; Llewellyn, an archeologist; and Elizabeth Gorsuch, who, with her husband, served as a missionary in Brazil for a period. An older daughter, Margaret, had preceded them in death.

The Prices were considered among the most sacrificial and saintly of all missionaries. Mrs. Price's name lives on in an association of ministers' wives in the state of Rio Grande do Sul, named in her honor the Eliza Price Association.

E. M. B. Jaime, *Metodismo no Rio Grande do Sul.* 1963.
J. L. Kennedy, *Metodismo no Brasil.* 1928.   EULA K. LONG

PRICE, JOSEPH CHARLES (1854-1893), American Negro minister and educator, was born in Elizabeth City, N. C., on Feb. 10, 1854. His father was a slave, but Price followed the condition of his mother who was free born. Educated at first in freedmen's schools, Price studied for a time at Shaw University (Raleigh, N. C.) where he was converted during a revival. In 1875 he was licensed to preach in the A.M.E. ZION CHURCH. He began formal preparation for the ministry at Lincoln University in PENNSYLVANIA where he graduated in classics in 1879. Prior to the completion of his theological training there in 1881, Price was ordained elder. In 1880 he served for the first of four times as a delegate to the A.M.E. Zion General Conference.

While Price was abroad to attend the ECUMENICAL METHODIST CONFERENCE at LONDON in 1881, he toured Great Britain to raise funds for his church's Zion Wesley Institute in Salisbury, N. C. After obtaining pledges for nearly $10,000, he returned to America to assume the presidency of the school which was renamed to honor David Livingstone. During the next decade Price attracted national attention for his creative leadership in Negro education, which, he contended, should consist of liberal arts instruction as well as industrial training. He was largely responsible for establishing LIVINGSTONE's reputation as the first successful college in America founded, owned and manned by Negroes.

A nationally famous preacher and skilled orator, Price campaigned in behalf of prohibition and of racial justice. In 1890 the Afro-American National League, a Negro civil rights organization, named him its first president. In ecclesiastical affairs he earnestly supported a merger between the A.M.E. and A.M.E. Zion Churches. At the peak of his career Price was afflicted with Bright's disease to which he succumbed on Oct. 25, 1893 at his home in Salisbury.

W. J. Walls, *Joseph Charles Price.* 1943.
Carter G. Woodson, ed., *Negro Orators and Their Orations.* Washington: Associated Publishers, Inc., 1925.
                                                    WILLIAM B. GRAVELY

PRICE, RICHARD NYE (1830-1923), American minister and historian of the HOLSTON CONFERENCE, was born at Elk Garden, Va., on July 30, 1830. He was educated at EMORY AND HENRY COLLEGE, from which he received the B.A. and M.A. degrees and the honorary D.D. degree.

He joined the Holston Conference in 1850 and with the exception of one year's location he served continuously until his retirement in 1921. He held every type of appointment in the conference: circuit, junior preacher, presiding elder, conference secretary, college professor and president, editor of the conference paper, and chaplain in two wars.

He married Anne Edgeworth Vance of Marshall, N. C., on May 8, 1855, and was the father of ten children.

Price is best known as the author of *Holston Methodism,* a history in five volumes which was published in 1908 after ten years of labor devoted to its preparations.

He died at Morristown, Tenn., on Feb. 7, 1923, and

was buried there. He was "the oldest in years and longest in ministerial service" in the conference, having been a preacher seventy-three years, including three years as a local preacher.

Journal of the Holston Conference, MES, 1923.
I. P. Martin, *Holston.* 1945.   ELMER T. CLARK

PRICHARD, JESSE ELI (1880-1957), American M.P. minister and administrator, was born on Nov. 29, 1880, in Asheboro, N. C. He was the son of Isaiah Franklin and Nancy Ellen Conner Prichard. Upon graduation from WESTERN MARYLAND COLLEGE in 1909, he enrolled in WESTMINSTER THEOLOGICAL SEMINARY, where he received the B.D. degree in 1912. He was accepted on trial in the NORTH CAROLINA CONFERENCE of the M.P. Church in November 1911, and in November of the following year was ordained an elder and assigned to Halifax Circuit, which he served until 1915. He afterward served churches in NORTH CAROLINA as follows: Thomasville (1915-1916); Burlington (1916-1921); Henderson (1921-1926); Asheboro (1926-1931); WINSTON-SALEM (1931-1934; 1940-1941); GREENSBORO (1934-1938); Ramseur (1941-1945); and Mocksville (1945-1946).

In 1938 he became President of the North Carolina Conference of the M.P. Church, a position he held for two years. He was a member of the General Board of Education of his Church from 1924-1928 and served that body as Recording Secretary. In 1932 Western Maryland College conferred on him the D.D. Degree. He served for a number of years as a trustee of HIGH POINT COLLEGE and for twelve years as a trustee of the Methodist Children's Home of the WESTERN NORTH CAROLINA CONFERENCE in Winston-Salem. From 1934-1936 he was editor of *The Methodist Protestant Herald,* published at Greensboro, N. C., the official church paper for the North Carolina Conference.

Prichard was a delegate to three GENERAL CONFERENCES of the M.P. Church, a delegate to the Uniting Conference in 1939, and a delegate to the first SOUTHEASTERN JURISDICTIONAL CONFERENCE of The Methodist Church.

On Dec. 12, 1912, he married Laura Vestal of Siler City, N. C. Following his retirement in 1946, Prichard lived in Asheboro until his death on Aug. 10, 1957. He is buried in Asheboro City Cemetery.

J. E. Carroll, *History of the North Carolina Conference of the M. P. Church.* Greensboro, 1939.
The Dispatch, Henderson, N. C., July 27, 1957.
Who's Who in Methodism, 1952.   RALPH HARDEE RIVES

PRIMITIVE METHODISM, British Methodist denomination (1811-1932), was formed in 1811 by the coalescing of the CAMP MEETING METHODISTS and the CLOWESITES, both groups representative of the revivalism which marked the early nineteenth century. The beginnings were set in 1800, on the borders of Staffordshire and Cheshire, when HUGH BOURNE, a moorland carpenter, was working in the region. Converted three years before, he became concerned for the conversion of his cousin, Daniel Shubotham, of Harriseahead, to whom he gave a written account of his own conversion. Shubotham's spiritual deliverance soon followed, as also that of a collier, Mathias Bayley. By this "conversation-preaching" the work spread, and at Harriseahead a chapel was built. This revival, though nominally Wesleyan Methodist, went on without the recognition or direction of the Wesleyan Methodist authorities, though in 1802 the chapel and its associated classes were taken over by the Burslem Circuit. A second revival in 1804 arose at Tunstall, and in the Burslem Circuit, largely through a visit to Congleton by a revivalist group from Stockport. An important result was the conversion of WILLIAM CLOWES, a skilled potter who rapidly growing in Christian understanding, began evangelistic work.

The Harriseahead movement found vigorous expression in a CAMP MEETING held on MOW COP on May 31, 1807. Earlier, in 1805, a somewhat eccentric evangelist from America, LORENZO DOW, had labored in South Lancashire and East Cheshire. His utterances had often contained references to the camp meetings begun in America in 1799, and on a visit to Harriseahead he stressed this. Later, at Congleton, in April, 1807, Bourne bought certain pamphlets relating to these American meetings. Already Bourne had planned for a camp meeting to be held at Norton-le-Moors in August 1807, in order to counteract the evils of the local holidays or "wakes," but the Harriseahead people pressed to have "a day's praying on Mow." Official Wesleyan Methodist opposition began to appear on the one hand from the Burslem Circuit, and on the other from a master potter who declared camp meetings to be illegal. A second meeting was however held on Mow Cop on July 19, 1807.

Of these early camp meetings, however, the third held at Norton-le-Moors on August 25, is historically the most important, because the Liverpool Wesleyan Conference of 1807 had pronounced adversely upon such enterprises, and the preachers of the Burslem Circuit implemented the decision locally, with the result that supporters diminished in number. As Bourne was convinced as to the rightness of his judgment, the meeting was duly held and pronounced successful. The direct consequence was his expulsion from the Wesleyan society in 1808. Without complaint he continued his work on evangelization, and the following year engaged JAMES CRAWFOOT as an itinerant evangelist to labor in East Cheshire and Staffordshire. These "Camp Meeting Methodists" were not as yet a distinct community but rather a mission band whose labors were auxiliary to the regular churches. Because the Burslem Circuit refused to take over a new society at Stanley, which had been brought into being by their labors, by March, 1810, the Camp Meeting Methodists came to a separate existence. Written plans were now prepared, and these show some interchange between INDEPENDENT METHODISTS and the Camp Meeting Methodists.

In 1810, William Clowes was deprived of his Wesleyan Methodist membership. Many followed his leadership; and a home for those thus unchurched was found in the house of one Mr. Smith of Tunstall, where for some two years preaching services had been held. So this "house-church" soon became the center of a small circuit, and preparations were made for the building of a chapel at Tunstall. This new group became known as the "Clowesites," and before the opening of the Tunstall chapel they resolved to make common cause with the Camp Meeting Methodists. A joint meeting was held on May 30, 1811, at which union was agreed upon and tickets of membership were printed. In July, 1811, it was further decided that Crawfoot and Clowes should be separated as preachers and be supported

by the contributions of the members of the new denomination, now about 200 in number. At a further meeting on February 13, 1812, the name of the new denomination was determined: "The Society of the Primitive Methodists." The source of the name appears to be in the farewell address given by JOHN WESLEY to the preachers of the Chester Circuit in 1790, when, pleading for a ministry of universal evangelism, he declared: "If you have deviated from the old usage, I have not: I still remain a primitive Methodist." These words, recalled by Crawfoot, who had heard Wesley speak, determined the name. They were sometimes called "Ranters" because of their enthusiastic evangelism.

Owing partly to the social conditions of the time and partly to the sparse population of the region, the new denomination did not spread rapidly or widely, and until 1816 it was confined to the Tunstall Circuit. An issue now arose as to whether the policy should be one of consolidation or extension. The majority favored consolidation. Chapels were built, and Bourne became responsible in 1814 for framing regulations. The "Tunstall Nonmission Law" was the name given to the prevailing policy by those who disagreed, among them Bourne himself. Before long, however, the policy of extension reasserted itself, and more camp meetings were held in other counties, bringing spiritual revival especially in Nottinghamshire and beyond. Bourne became general superintendent of the connection and traveled widely. In 1819 Clowes entered Hull and began extension northward, later to be followed by a mission to Cornwall and the West Country. In 1820 the first conference was held in Hull, constituted of representatives from the circuits in the proportion of two laymen to one minister. By this time the membership of the new denomination had risen to 7,842; by 1824 it was 33,507.

The period 1825-28 proved to be a time of crisis, largely owing to the rapidity of growth. Through the courage and insight of Bourne a process of pruning took place. The following years were marked by geographical extension, so that by 1842 the membership had risen to nearly 80,000, with 500 traveling preachers and more than 1,200 chapels. This period of missionary extension was marked by much heroism, for the itinerant preachers had often to contend with hostility and persecution. A further feature in this process of evangelization was the extent to which women itinerant preachers shared in the work.

The decade 1843-53 was a period of transition. The superannuation of Bourne and Clowes in 1842 led to new leadership and far-reaching changes. The Connectional Book Room was moved to LONDON, and a proposal for a general missionary committee moved in the direction of greater coordination of the circuits, the period of circuit predominance gradually giving way to more centralization in missionary enterprise.

The death of the first leaders—Clowes died in 1851 and Bourne soon afterward in 1852—brought the beginning of the middle period of the denomination's history. By 1853 there were ten districts, and each tended to foster its own line of development. The annual District Meeting assumed great importance, and to no small measure at the expense of the overall Conference. Preachers were usually stationed within each district, the boundaries of which were rigidly held. This "districtism" made for an originality which brought denominational enrichment. The Hull District led the way in a bolder policy in chapel building; the Norwich District in overseas missions; the Sunderland and Manchester Districts in ministerial education; the Leeds District in Sunday school advance.

By the Jubilee year of the denomination in 1860 the connection reached a membership of 132,114; by 1875 it rose to 165,410, but the progress was not an uninterrupted one. The years 1852-55 were marked by decreases, largely due, however, to external causes including emigration, the Crimean War, and the FLY SHEETS controversy (1844-57) in Wesleyan Methodism.

Eventually "districtism" was bound to disappear, not least through a regulation of 1879 which encouraged circuit ministerial invitation irrespective of district boundaries. Further a new cohesion in Church polity upon a presbyterial basis was developing, and before the end of the century a more unified denomination had emerged. This is symbolized by the use of the word "Church" instead of "connexion" in the *Consolidated Minutes,* the codified laws of the denomination.

One feature of development was the expansion overseas. As far back as the Conference of 1820 in the Lincolnshire village of Scotter, it was decided to send a mission to the United States. In 1843 colonial missions were begun in AUSTRALIA and NEW ZEALAND. In 1870 missionaries landed in West Africa. In 1889 missions were begun in South Central Africa and in Southern Nigeria.

The last quarter of the nineteenth century saw great improvement in the general pattern and structure of church administration. Legislation regarding the safeguarding of chapel property was established. There was an expansion of interest in social questions, particularly in regard to London and the provincial centers of population. Orphanages were established. Particular emphasis was given to the uplifting of the working classes, and the trade-union movement derived many of its early leaders from the ranks of the local preachers especially in Northern England and in East Anglia. As early as 1832—under the deep conviction of Bourne—the Conference had emphasized the importance of the formation of temperance societies, and this strong temperance sentiment persisted throughout the denomination.

As early as the middle of the century some concern had been expressed regarding ministerial education, but it was not until 1865 that Elmfield House, in York, was acquired for the double purpose of providing a school for boys and also accommodation for ministerial training. In 1869, however, the latter arrangement was superseded by the purchase of a building in Sunderland for a separate theological institute. In 1886 the Theological College in MANCHESTER was opened, eventually to be known as Hartley College, its name chosen in acknowledgment of the two extensions (1897 and 1906) through the munificence of WILLIAM HARTLEY, and which was associated with the work of A. S. PEAKE, a biblical scholar of international reputation. Elmfield continued as a school for boys and, alongside it, a later foundation (1882) was Bourne College, on the outskirts of BIRMINGHAM.

At the time of the centenary of the denomination in 1907 a hundred thousand people attended the Centenary Camp Meeting on Mow Cop, and a fund of more than £270,000 was raised for the evangelistic, educational and social work. The spiritual results, tabulated in terms of addition to membership were, however, disappointing, though these were lean years for all churches in the land.

The 1914 war inevitably brought problems to Primitive Methodism, not least problems of conscience to many individuals, for Primitive Methodism has been perhaps the most pronouncedly pacifist of all the denominations save the Society of Friends. To meet the needs of the many thousands of Primitive Methodists who had enlisted, the resources of the Church were mobilized, and by the end of the war nearly fifty chaplains were at work in the services.

For some years it had become increasingly clear that some attempt must be made to bring together the differing groups within British Methodism. In 1912 the Wesleyan Conference declared its conviction that serious effort thould be made to this end, and in 1917 representatives met to discuss the possibilities; in 1920 a scheme in outline was presented to the three Conferences concerned. By 1925 sanction for such union was sought on the basis of a requirement of seventy-five percent majority vote. The Primitive Methodist Conference secured a ninety-three percent vote, but the Wesleyan Conference fell short of the required majority. Not until 1928 did the latter succeed in fulfilling the condition, but at each intervening Conference the Primitive Methodist vote continued heavily in favor of union. In 1932 the Union was achieved. Into the United Church, Primitive Methodism brought 222,021 members; 1,131 ministers; 12,896 local preachers, 277,792 Sunday school scholars; 4,356 church buildings.

H. B. Kendall, *Primitive Methodist Church.* 1905.

JOHN T. WILKINSON

PRIMITIVE METHODIST CHURCH (U.S.A.) arrived in the United States by way of migration of laymen from Great Britain. Concern for these members expressed at the 1829 British Conference by the Hull and Tunstall Circuits led to the sending of four missionaries to establish an American mission. Under the joint responsibility of these two circuits, William Knowles and Ruth Watkins from Tunstall Circuit and William Summersides and T. Morris from Hull Circuit sailed for NEW YORK on June 19, 1929. The Tunstall missionaries established work in New York, while the Hull missionaries founded classes at PHILADELPHIA and POTTSVILLE, PENNSYLVANIA.

At the American annual conference, meeting in 1840, it was "resolved that we consider ourselves from this time distinct from and unconnected with the English Conference." An attempt to re-establish ties with the English Conference was made in 1843; and HUGH BOURNE, even though he was over seventy years of age, traveled to the United States as an "Advisor from the English Conference." Relations on an informal basis were re-established, primarily through Bourne's own fatherly status as founder of Primitive Methodism; and with his death all relations ceased. The work continued to grow, although slowly, because of the overwhelming competition of a strongly evangelistic M.E. Church and the continued British-like structure of the Primitive Methodist worship.

Work formed itself very early into three conferences. A general conference was organized in 1889. It became the legislative body for the church, making all rules and regulations in its quadrennial sessions. It also has direct oversight of the general boards: the Foreign Mission Board, the Journal Board, the Publisher, the School of Theology, the Board of Temperance, and the Commission on Chaplains. There are at present four annual conferences: Eastern Wyoming, Schuykill, Pittsburgh, and Western. They provide administrative guidance along with the district and quarterly conferences. The conferences are presided over by a president, as there are no bishops or district superintendents; and laymen are equally represented at all levels.

Mission work is carried on in Guatemala, Kenya, and Brazil. An official organ, *The Primitive Methodist Journal*, is published monthly. At last report there were approximately 12,000 members in ninety churches.

The Primitive Methodist Church found its way to Canada through the efforts of Mr. William Lawson, a former layman in the Wesleyan Connection in England. Lawson had been expelled from the Connection because of his association with James Johnson, a Primitive Methodist. Lawson joined the Primitive Methodist Church in 1826 and preached in his home town of Bramton. In 1829 he migrated to CANADA and arrived in York (Toronto) on June 11. He gathered a class together and became their leader. In October a meeting home was secured. In 1830, at Lawson's request, William Watkins arrived as the first missionary preacher. Watkins left after a few months because of the weather, and William Summersides was transferred from the United States to take over the work. For the next several years Hull Circuit in England had direct responsibility for the Canadian mission. In 1833 the Niagara Station was set apart from York, and in 1838 the Brampton Station was given an independent status. Josiah Partington and William Lyle were sent from England to enlarge the work. By 1850 the total membership in the struggling church had risen to about 1,500 and nine appointments.

In 1853 the English Conference set the Canadian work apart and the first Canadian Conference met at Brampton, County of Peel. A hymnbook was approved, and plans were laid for a book room and a journal. In 1858 the semi-monthly *Christian Journal* was begun, and in 1860 the first *Book of Discipline* was authorized. In 1867 a theological institute was started with Thomas Crompton as tutor.

In 1870 a widespread move to unite all of Canadian Methodism held the attention of the conference. Primitive Methodists by this time were divided into six districts with fifty appointments. Although union was voted down at this conference, it was a continuing issue for future meetings.

In 1883 a plan of union was submitted to the membership and approved by an eighty percent vote. In 1884 final union was accomplished. The Primitive Methodist Church merged with the three other Methodist bodies to become the Methodist Church and thus ceased to exist as a separate body.

Discipline of the Primitive Methodist Church in Canada. Toronto: William Bee, 1873.
General Rules of the Primitive Methodist Church. London, 1922.
Mrs. R. P. Hooper, *Primitive Methodism in Canada.* 1904.
H. B. Kendall, *Primitive Methodist Church.* 1905.
Yearbook of American Churches, 1970.

J. GORDON MELTON

PRIMITIVE METHODIST CHURCH (1792-1803). Not to be confused with the still existing Primitive Methodist Church founded by LORENZO DOW, this church was the result of the preaching of WILLIAM HAMMETT. It was started by members of the M.E. Church in SOUTH CAROLINA who

had responded strongly to Hammett's preaching. Hammett had arrived in South Carolina after having several appointments in Jamaica and St. Christopher where his health had suffered. In 1791 the CHARLESTON congregation requested Hammett's appointment to their church. When ASBURY refused, Hammett developed his following, and they built their own church.

The main characteristic of the new church was its dissent with episcopal authority. The church grew for several years and established sizable congregations in GEORGIA and the Carolinas. A Rev. Meredith formed a large society of Negro members at WILMINGTON, N. C. The church suffered so much under the slipping reputation of its founder, who had difficulty in keeping peaceful relations with his ministers and became a slaveholder and a heavy drinker, that it returned to the M.E. Church soon after the death of its founder in 1803.

E. S. Bucke, *History of American Methodism.* 1964.
J. GORDON MELTON

PRIMITIVE PHYSICK. JOHN WESLEY's interest in medicine, fostered by wide reading of the available literature, enabled him to meet the desperate need of the poor for inexpensive and sensible guidance in matters of health and sickness. *Primitive Physick*, written by him and published in 1747, was of prime importance in furthering his purpose.

Wesley's approach to healing was by way of observation and experiment, in contrast to the generally accepted approach of eighteenth-century physicians by way of theory, e.g. Humoral, Brunonian. Wesley incisively castigates such theoretical approach in his Preface.

Primitive Physick defines in alphabetical order a variety of complaints, and applies to each disorder a number of simple remedies. These remedies form a wide selection from the plethora of eighteenth-century cures, many of which were nauseating, some dangerous, and most of which were useless.

Included in the Preface are excellent rules for maintaining health, and in the 1760 edition and thereafter, the use of electricity is recommended for some illnesses.

ARTHUR HILL

PRIMITIVE WESLEYAN METHODIST CONNEXION (Ireland) began in 1818 in IRELAND and consisted of those Methodists who wished to maintain the position of being a Society inside the Established Church. They opposed the 1816 decision of the Irish Conference to grant limited permission for Methodist preachers to administer the Sacraments. Their leader was ADAM AVERELL, a deacon of the Church of Ireland and a leading Methodist evangelist.

While the main body of Methodists ("Wesleyans") rapidly assumed the functions of an independent church, the Primitive Wesleyan Methodist Connexion remained officially a Society inside the Church of Ireland, though with its own Conference, District and Circuit organization. It was strongest in numbers in the Enniskillen and Clones area.

One effect of the Disestablishment of the Church of Ireland in 1870 was to re-emphasize the common Methodist heritage of the two Methodist bodies. After discussion, in 1878 the Primitives re-united with the main body, henceforth known as "The Methodist Church in Ireland."

R. L. Cole, *Methodism in Ireland*. 1960.
C. H. Crookshank, *Methodism in Ireland*. 1885-88.
F. Jeffery, *Irish Methodism*. 1964.
Wesley Historical Society *Proceedings*, 1963, 1964.

FREDERICK JEFFERY

H. T. PRIMM

PRIMM, HOWARD THOMAS (1904-   ), American bishop of the A.M.E. CHURCH, was born in Brentwood, Tenn., on June 23, 1904. He was educated at WILBERFORCE UNIVERSITY and Payne Theological Seminary (Ohio), from which institutions he received the A.B. and B.D. degrees in 1924 and 1927, respectively. He has received honorary degrees from Wilberforce and Allen Universities, and MORRIS BROWN, EDWARD WATERS, Payne, and Monrovia (Liberia, W. Africa) COLLEGES. He was ordained deacon in 1922 and in 1928, held pastorates in TENNESSEE, LOUISIANA, MISSISSIPPI and ARKANSAS. He was elected to the episcopacy in 1952 from the Union Bethel Church in NEW ORLEANS, La. He presently resides at NASHVILLE, Tenn. and supervises the work of the Fifth Episcopal Area District which includes the Puget Sound, California, Southern California, Colorado, Kansas-Nebraska, North Missouri and Missouri Annual Conferences.

GRANT S. SHOCKLEY

PRINCE OF WALES COLLEGE: PRINCE OF WALES COLLEGIATE (formerly Wesleyan Academy; Methodist College), St. John's, Newfoundland. In education, as in other areas, voluntary agencies were the first to attempt provision for the needs of the scattered people of Newfoundland. Schools were founded by the Society for the Propagation of the Gospel, and by the Newfoundland School Society, which were supplemented by Sunday schools and charity schools. Their efforts, however, were sporadic and unsystematic, and they reached comparatively few of the settlements.

As early as 1844, the provincial legislature passed an act to establish a non-denominational academy, but the institution was unsuccessful. This stemmed in large mea-

sure from the increasing clamor for the recognition of denominational interests in the schools, an attitude which was recognized by a new bill in 1850. The latter provided for three academies, representing the Roman Catholics, the Anglicans, and the other denominations.

At this juncture, the growing Wesleyan Methodist constituency protested against sharing the Protestant grant with other bodies. They regarded themselves as unfairly treated, in comparison with other groups. In their petition of 1857, they stressed that the Anglicans and Roman Catholics were receiving grants for their schools, but the 15,000 Methodists were lumped with minor Protestant bodies.

In response the legislature passed an act (1858) authorizing a Wesleyan Academy in St. John's, and an annual grant of £200. In September of that year the governor-in-council appointed the first board of directors.

When in 1874, the Wesleyan Methodist Church of Eastern British America was incorporated in the Methodist Church of Canada, the academy became the Methodist Academy. Under its third principal, R. E. Holloway, the school flourished in the next decade. New buildings were opened in 1887, leaving the old edifice as a home for boarders and ministers' children. In the same year a new charter was issued providing for the appointment of the board of governors of the St. John's Methodist College, by the Newfoundland Conference of the Methodist Church. The college remained subject to annual inspection by the relevant provincial superintendent.

Since 1887 the college has sustained much physical damage through repeated fires. The lost buildings have been replaced by a new main structure, known as Prince of Wales College, Pitts Memorial Hall, the Ayre Memorial Gymnasium, the Harrington building for elementary classes, and the Prince of Wales Arena.

Despite its difficult history, Prince of Wales College, as it was called after 1925, had an enviable academic and athletic record. Twenty of its students won Rhodes scholarships; many others secured various scholarly awards. Graduates of the college have acquired important places in the professions and in business.

From the start, the college balanced academic achievement with concern for the religious life. George P. Story, first chaplain and guardian of the home, was followed by Mark Fenwick, T. B. Darby, S. G. Garland, L. A. D. Curtis, W. E. Stanford, and J. A. McKim. All of these men gave outstanding service. The most recent was appointed religious instructor for all United Church schools in St. John's.

In 1962 the college system and the other United Church schools in St. John's were placed under a new board drawn from the college board of governors, the former United Church School Board and from local interested laymen. The new board, known as the St. John's United Church School Board, operates ten schools. The senior high school, called Prince of Wales Collegiate, is housed in a new building; the former Prince of Wales building is now known as United Junior High School. In these institutions the traditions of the Wesleyan Academy and the Methodist College are continued.

F. W. Rowe, *The Development of Education in Newfoundland*. Toronto: Ryerson, 1964.
T. W. Smith, *Eastern British America*. 1877, 1890.

W. F. BUTT

PRINTERS, John Wesley's, included William Strahan of London and Felix Farley of Bristol, William Pine of Bristol, and Robert Hawes of London (see BOOK ROOMS). For further information, see *A Charge to Keep,* by Frank Baker (London: Epworth Press, 1947).

JOHN KENT

PRISON MINISTERS (British). It may almost be said that Methodism began in prison; for the concern of JOHN WESLEY and his fellow members of the HOLY CLUB for those imprisoned in Oxford Gaol, and their methodical visits to and services in the jail partly led to their being called Methodists. CHARLES WESLEY frequently visited the prisoners in Newgate; and his work was carried on by other Methodists, such as Sarah Peters, who died of jail fever contracted during her visitations. SILAS TOLD became famous for his ministrations to condemned criminals.

Under the Prison Ministers' Act of 1863, denominations other than the Established Church were given the right to appoint ministers to visit their members in prison. Since that date Methodist ministers have been appointed to every prison and subsequently to every Borstal and detention center. Nominations are made by the Home Mission Department Prison Committee and submitted to the secretary of state, who makes the appointment of these ministers and thus ensures that they have the benefit of official recognition. The oversight of the work is the responsibility of the chaplain general of prisons, and of the Home Mission Department acting on behalf of the Methodist Church.

It is the duty of each visiting minister to visit his prison or institution at least once a week. He visits the prisoners in their cells in private; and, wherever numbers make it practicable, holds a regular service to which all under his care are permitted to come. This service is held either in the prison chapel or in some other conveniently arranged place. There is also opportunity for the regular celebration of Holy Communion, and the minister is permitted to use the prison communion vessels supplied by the prison authorities. By reason of his official appointment, the prison minister is in direct contact with the welfare and after-care agencies of the prison, both statutory and voluntary. Through these agencies he is often able to arrange visits to and aid for prisoners' families, to help in reconciliations, and to assist in providing contacts, work, and accommodation on release. In special cases he can also communicate direct with prisoners' families for the purpose of helping them and providing for the prisoners' after-care. All these tasks he undertakes as a spiritual ministry in order that he may effectively offer Christ and his saving power to those in need.

G. FRAZER THOMPSON

PRITCHARD, JOHN (1746-1814), British itinerant, was governor of KINGSWOOD SCHOOL from 1802-7. Born December 1746, at Arthbay, IRELAND, educated locally, afterward at Dublin Academy, he disappeared to London about 1763, suffering ague, poverty and spiritual despair. At the Foundery under PETER JACO in 1765 he found peace. Traveling with WESLEY in 1770-71, Pritchard was received into Full Connexion in 1772. After tramping four Irish circuits, he served in England—North, Mid-lands, East Coast, and West Country, from 1772-1802. Pritchard was frequently ill. Originally excessively nervous—leaving Norwich after only one week—he became a bold, undeterred preacher and pastor. He died in Bristol in 1814.

G. LAWTON

PROBATIONERS is the term by which those entering or endeavoring to enter into church membership, or into full annual conference membership are known. See MEMBERSHIP IN METHODIST CHURCHES; and also MINISTRY IN AMERICAN METHODISM.

PROBERT TRUST, at AUCKLAND, New Zealand, administers funds left to the Methodist Church by John Probert, an early Auckland settler who prospered with the growth of the city. He was also a loyal Wesleyan, being attached to Pitt Street Church. At his death in 1890 he left approximately £12,000 to be devoted to theological education in the City of Auckland. Invested in city property, the capital of the trust has multiplied in value, and the trustees are now able to contribute substantially towards the maintenance of TRINITY COLLEGE.

ERIC W. HAMES

PROCTER, JOHN ERNEST (1918-   ), American layman, was born July 23, 1918 in Gainsboro, Tenn. to Leon C. and Mary (Poteet) Procter. Schooling was obtained at Memphis State College, George Peabody College, VANDERBILT UNIVERSITY, University of Miami, and University of Tennessee. He was married to Jane Christine Sprott, May 23, 1941.

He rose to rank of captain while serving in the USAF, 1943-45, 1950-52. He was decorated with the Certificate of Valor and the Air Medal, receiving seven oak leaf clusters. Mr. Procter became manager of the Accounts Payable Department, the METHODIST PUBLISHING HOUSE, 1946-58; system analyst, 1958-64; vice-president of the Publishing Division, 1964-70; and Publisher from that date.

As a member of the NASHVILLE Administrative Management Society, he has held the offices of secretary, treasurer, vice-president and president, receiving the Outstanding Service Plaque for service to the national office, the Gold Merit Key (1961), and the Diamond Merit Key (1967). He has served as chairman of several committees for the Protestant Church-Owned Publishers Association. He is also a member of Nashville Chamber of Commerce, American Book Publishers Council, and the Publishers Section of the NATIONAL COUNCIL OF CHURCHES.

Who's Who in America, 1970-71.
Who's Who in The Methodist Church, 1966.

JOHN H. NESS, JR.

PROGRAM COUNCIL, THE, of The United Methodist Church. This organization, called for and created by the Uniting Conference of 1968, is new to American Methodism, but was known to the E.U.B. Church as part of their conference administrative work before union with The Methodist Church in 1968 (*Discipline* of the EUB Church, 1967, paragraph 1012-1017). As adopted and created for The United Methodist Church, it takes as its aim "to provide a consultation process wherein the

COUNCIL OF BISHOPS, the COUNCIL OF SECRETARIES, and the representative laymen and pastors may *discuss, choose, correlate* and *coordinate* program emphases of The United Methodist Church." It is also "to provide services to assist in the selection and coordination of the program emphases and in the interpretation and promotion of them in the Annual Conferences and local churches."

As organized this powerful body took over from The Methodist Church the functions of the Commission on PROMOTION AND CULTIVATION; the Coordinating Council; the Interboard Commission on Local Church; and the Department of Research of the COUNCIL ON WORLD SERVICE AND FINANCE; and incorporated the TELEVISION, RADIO AND FILM COMMISSION as a full division within its structure. It also took over and continues the former Program Council of the E.U.B. Church.

Fifteen bishops were made members of the Program Council—three from each JURISDICTION and four ministers from each Jurisdiction, at least three of whom are to be pastors at the time of their election; and seven laymen of whom at least one should not be over twenty-one years of age at the time of election. Two of these laymen also were to be women. All members of the Council of Secretaries were made members of this body but had no vote.

Lengthy disciplinary directions were given for the organization and functioning of this Council with specific directions regarding division of the body for purposes of administration, and further directions as to meetings, staff, secretariat, and the like.

In general the functions of the Program Council are to give leadership in and participate in the coordinate research and planning for The United Methodist Church, and to assist the general agencies of the Church in the interpretation and promotion of the cooperative program of all such agencies.

Since the Program Council takes over the work formerly done by the Coordinating Council, much of its work will be in the nature of correlating the different plans and moves of a Church as large as The United Methodist. Plans ahead, of course, will be made by the Council, especially when a new quadrennium is near. The Program Council must report directly to the General Conference upon its work.

A full secretariat is provided with executive officers who let the entire Church know of moves being made and planned for; and there is also a central promotional office for the purpose of advancing throughout the Church a program of World Service, Advance Specials, One Great Hour of Sharing, the Television-Radio Ministerial Fund, the Fellowship of Suffering and Service, the Interdenominational Cooperation Fund, and other general benevolence causes except as otherwise directed by the General Conference.

In each Jurisdiction, there may be a Jurisdiction Program Council designed to coordinate and make the work of the Boards and Agencies of the Church effective within such Jurisdiction. Likewise, in each Annual Conference, there must be organized an Annual Conference Program Council. This is to develop all recommendations from the local churches, the district agencies, the annual conference agencies, and the general Program Council and make all such available and useful in each Annual Conference.

In the local church, instead of a Program Council, a Local Church Council on Ministries is created which "shall consider, develop, and coordinate proposals for the church's strategy for mission. It shall receive, and where possible, utilize resources for mission provided by the District, Annual, Jurisdictional and General Conference Program Councils, boards, and agencies, and shall coordinate these resources with the church's plan for ministries in its local and other settings."

N. B. H.

PROGRAM-CURRICULUM COMMITTEE. When The United Methodist Church was formed in 1968 the responsibility for planning curriculum for the educational ministry of the local church was delegated to a Program-Curriculum Committee of the General Board of EDUCATION. It was similar to former curriculum committees in the uniting churches, with the significant addition to its scope of program elements related to curriculum.

The great growth of church schools and church school literature during the early years of the twentieth century, including various church school publications and lesson materials and the like, called in time for an over-all, authoritative, broadly based curriculum plan that Board staff alone could not properly develop. In the former M.E. Church the GENERAL CONFERENCE of 1928 authorized the Board of Education to "appoint a Curriculum Committee of such number and in such manner as it may determine, always including the BOOK EDITOR, the Editor of Church School Publications, and the Editor of *The Epworth Herald.*" The function of the committee was to "determine standard curricula for all church schools, including vacation and week-day schools, the EPWORTH LEAGUE, and other agencies within the local church, and to recommend to the Board books and other literature which may be found desirable for use in religious education and in the training of leaders and teachers." (Paragraph 500.4, *Discipline,* 1928.)

In the former M.E. Church, South, there was a staff Committee on Curriculum and Program after 1930 (*Discipline,* 1934, Paragraph 414), but at Union in 1939 a Curriculum Committee very much like that of the M.E. Church, and patterned after it, was established for The Methodist Church. The Committee consisted of seventeen voting members and of various important officials of the General Board of Education and The METHODIST PUBLISHING HOUSE, as well as representatives of the Board of MISSIONS, the Board of EVANGELISM, the Board of Christian SOCIAL CONCERNS, and the Board of LAY ACTIVITIES.

In the former E.U.B. Church there was a Church Curriculum Committee with twenty voting members representing the major boards and agencies of the church. Its function was to carry on curriculum research and to develop a curriculum design, including objectives, outlines, and courses of study. Writers and editors were responsible to the denomination's publishers.

In the current Program-Curriculum Committee there are thirty-five voting members. Among them are representatives of the major program agencies of the church, pastors, professors, lay workers, conference directors of education, and public school leaders. The committee meets semiannually, and is charged with planning a curriculum that "is graded, based on sound educational principles, and on the universal gospel of the living Christ . . . [and] related to the traditions, purposes, programs, and movements of the church." Resources based on these curriculum plans are developed by the

Board of Education through its Division of Curriculum Resources.

Discipline, TMC, 1940-64; UMC, 1968.

WALTER N. VERNON

PROMOTION AND CULTIVATION, COMMISSION ON, an agency of The Methodist Church was organized in 1952. The purpose of the commission was "that duplication, overlapping, and competition may be eliminated in the promotion of the general financial causes of the church, and to the end that our people may be informed about, and may adequately support the general agencies of the church," . . . and to promote "throughout the church the program of World Service, Advance Specials, Week of Dedication offerings, and other general financial causes except as otherwise directed by the General Conference." (1952 *Discipline,* Paragraphs 750-4)

The 1956 GENERAL CONFERENCE renewed this mandate and added specifically for promotion the Fellowship of Suffering and Service offerings, and the Television Ministry Fund. In 1960 the Week of Dedication offerings became the One Great Hour of Sharing offerings, and the Interdenominational Cooperation Fund was included for promotion. In 1960 and 1964 the General Conferences reaffirmed the mandate of the Commission to inform Methodist people that adequate support might be given the general agencies, and to promote the program of world service and other general benevolence causes.

Since 1952 the commission has informed Methodist people and encouraged their support of World Service and other general benevolences. The record written by Methodists during this sixteen year period shows that the total amount contributed to World Service, General Advance Specials, for Special Appeals such as Emergency Help for India, the Week of Dedication, and the One Great Hour of Sharing, the Fellowship of Suffering and Service, the Television-Radio Ministry Fund, Temporary General Aid and World Service Specials was $375,161,801.

A variety of means and materials were used by the commission to promote benevolence causes. *The Methodist Story,* a program journal, was sent free each month to ministers and key laymen in each local church. *The Methodist Story* and *Spotlight,* the program journal of the E.U.B. Church were merged in May of 1968. As *Methodist Story—Spotlight* it was mailed to over 315,000 persons in that month. Other printed materials include free Fourth Sunday World Service leaflets, leaflets about each general benevolence cause, World Service and general benevolence charts, and materials for special observances. Films and filmstrips have been developed as well to dramatize and pictorialize benevolences.

In 1952 the entire staff of the Advance For Christ and His Church office became the staff of the Commission on Promotion and Cultivation, with Bishop WILLIAM C. MARTIN serving as chairman and E. Harold Mohn as secretary and executive director. Related to the commission was the Advance Committee. From 1952-56 Bishop COSTEN J. HARRELL was chairman and Dr. Mohn was executive director. Bishop Martin served as chairman of the commission until his retirement in 1964 and E. Harold Mohn until his retirement in 1960. Bishop HAZEN G. WERNER became chairman of the Advance Committee in 1956, and was the chairman at the time of his retirement in 1968. In 1961 headquarters of the Commission were

located in Evanston, Ill., and ELLIOTT L. FISHER became general secretary. Howard Greenwalt was chosen general secretary of the Commission in 1966, following the death of Dr. Fisher. Bishop DONALD H. TIPPETT served as chairman of the Commission on Promotion and Cultivation from 1964 to 1968.

The General Conference of 1968 (The Uniting Conference) created an organizational union of the Commission on Promotion and Cultivation, the Coordinating Council, the Interboard Commission on the Local Church, and TELEVISION, RADIO AND FILM COMMISSION, and the Department of Research of the COUNCIL ON WORLD SERVICE AND FINANCE of The Methodist Church; and The PROGRAM COUNCIL of the Evangelical United Brethren Church. The Commission on Promotion and Cultivation became The Division of Interpretation of The Program Council.

Discipline, TMC, 1952-64; UMC, 1968.
Journal of the General Conference, TMC, 1952-64; UMC, 1968.

HOWARD GREENWALT

PROTESTANT METHODISTS, a British secession from the Wesleyan Methodist connection which took place in 1828. The affair began when a group of trustees from the Brunswick Chapel, LEEDS, applied to the Leeds District Meeting for permission to ask Conference to sanction the building of an organ in their chapel. (There still existed a residual Puritan objection to the use of such instruments in religious services, hence the complicated nature of the procedure.) The trustees were refused permission by a large majority, but nevertheless made their request to the Conference of 1827, which, despite the warning of the Leeds superintendent and a deputation of protest from the Leeds circuit involved, gave the desired permission. The trustees sent out orders for the building of the organ, but the local preachers and leaders who had originally objected to the idea on ritualistic grounds now decided to resist on constitutional grounds. The conflict soon turned on the rights of the ministry as opposed to the rights of the laity; at a special district meeting in Leeds, JABEZ BUNTING upheld the authority of the pastoral office as he saw it; in turn, he was supported by the Conference of 1828. The secession which followed was small; in 1830 there were 3,997 members, scattered thinly over Lancashire and Yorkshire, apart from 402 in the London South Circuit.

The *Rules of the Leeds Protestant Methodists* (Leeds, 1829; there was a final version in September, 1830) reacted so strongly against Wesleyanism that the ministry was replaced with an eldership, and the annual meeting was stripped of the enormous powers wielded by the Wesleyan Conference. The survivors of the secession joined the WESLEYAN METHODIST ASSOCIATION in 1837. The principal leader in Leeds was a local schoolmaster called James Sigston, who had written a biography of the revivalist, WILLIAM BRAMWELL. The Leeds secession was important because it marked the climax of Jabez Bunting's career; his autocratic behavior at Leeds was never forgiven by his opponents, and his refusal to make any significant concessions to the laity made inevitable an internal Wesleyan struggle which lasted until 1857. Many pamphlets were written at the time; see especially, three *Letters to the Protestant Methodists,* by Daniel Isaac (Leeds, 1830); *An Affectionate Address . . . to the South London Circuit,* Richard Watson (1829); the *Protestant*

Methodist Magazine, 1829-30; and *An Essay on the Constitution of Wesleyan Methodism,* John Beecham (London, 1829)—virtually a book, and a classic statement of Jabez Bunting's case, which was more coherent than is often allowed.

JOHN KENT

PROUTY, FLORENCE J. (1908-   ), American missionary to CHILE, was born in Ollie, Mont. She was sent to Chile as a nurse in 1940 to reorganize the medical work at Sweet Memorial Institute, SANTIAGO, which was a part of the program for training young women for work in the local church.

As a specialist in pediatric nursing, Miss Prouty was concerned about the high infant-morality rate in Chile and embarked on a campaign of educating the mothers on how to take care of their children. Under her leadership the kindergarten and day nursery were reorganized and have become the outstanding teaching center of its kind for all Latin America.

In 1946 Miss Prouty organized the medical work of The Methodist Church with the Mapuche Indians in southern Chile, a small clinic being set up in Nueva Imperial. The work has been extended into the nearby communities, and emphasis has been given to child care under the leadership of a missionary doctor and a Mapuche nurse.

The Bernardo O'Higgins Award was bestowed upon Miss Prouty in 1960 in recognition of her work and concern for the Chilean child. This is the highest award Chile gives to a foreign resident. In 1965 Miss Prouty received the Javier Spencer Award from the Association of American Women in Chile as the woman who had rendered outstanding service to the community during the year.

JOYCE HILL

PROVIDENCE, RHODE ISLAND, U.S.A., the state capital, had a population of about 177,000 in 1970. Founded by Roger Williams in 1636, it was incorporated in 1832. FREEBORN GARRETTSON preached the first Methodist sermon in the city in April 1787, and the second was delivered by JESSE LEE, July 4, 1790. Bishop Asbury visited the community as early as 1791, and in 1792 the Providence Circuit was organized. The circuit included Bristol, Cranston, Newport, and Warren along with some towns over the line in MASSACHUSETTS. Designated as Warren Circuit in 1792, it reported fifty-eight members.

In 1815 the first Methodist church building in Providence was erected with Van Rensselaer-Osborn as pastor. Following a successful revival in 1820, a new and larger building called Chestnut Street Church was dedicated in 1822. Chestnut Street sponsored Power Street Church in 1833, and in 1848 Mathewson Street sprang from the latter. In 1876 there were eight churches in Providence, including one in East Providence, with a total membership of 2,197. At that time the A.M.E. and A.M.E. Zion Churches had two congregations each in the city.

For many years during the first half of the twentieth century, Mathewson Street Church was one of the strongest and most influential churches in the NEW ENGLAND SOUTHERN CONFERENCE, reporting at one time more than 1,400 members. In more recent years it has declined in strength; in 1968 it had 768 members. Since that time Mathewson Street and Broadway Churches together have

been called Christ Methodist Parish. In 1970 the parish reported 894 members and property valued at $1,231,546.

In 1970, The United Methodist Church had, in addition to Christ Methodist Parish, four churches in Providence —Cranston Street, Friendship, Trinity Union, and Washington Park. The statistics for the five units were: 2,282 members, property valued at $2,582,986, and $165,090 raised for all purposes during the year.

General Minutes, MEC, MC, and UMC.
M. Simpson, *Cyclopaedia.* 1878.   ALBEA GODBOLD

PROVIDENCE CONFERENCE (ME), was organized June 9, 1841 at PROVIDENCE, R. I., with Bishop ELIJAH HEDDING presiding. The 1840 GENERAL CONFERENCE created the Providence Conference by dividing the NEW ENGLAND CONFERENCE. The territory of the new conference was the part of Connecticut east of the Connecticut River, RHODE ISLAND, and southeastern MASSACHUSETTS. The Providence Conference began with three districts, Providence, New London, and Sandwich. It had sixty-four charges, eighty-five preachers, and 10,664 members.

The successive divisions of the New England Conference to form the MAINE CONFERENCE in 1825, the New Hampshire and Vermont Conference in 1830, and the Providence Conference in 1840, reflect the statistical increase of Methodism in New England during that period, and the consequent advisability, under existing conditions, of organizing the several socio-economic parts of the region into separate annual conferences.

Two notable enterprises promoted by the Providence Conference were the East Greenwich Academy (See Rhode Island), and the MARTHA'S VINEYARD Camp Meeting. President U. S. GRANT had a "conversion experience" at Martha's Vineyard in 1874.

The Providence Conference was renamed the NEW ENGLAND CONFERENCE in 1881. In 1880 the conference reported 178 charges, 181 preachers, 23,147 members, and property valued at $1,669,250.

General Minutes, ME.
R. C. Miller, *New England Southern Conference.* 1898.
Minutes of the Providence Conference.
M. Simpson, *Cyclopaedia.* 1878.   ERNEST R. CASE

PRUSSNER, AUGUST HENRY (1884-1947), missionary, educator, writer, was born in Kreis Herford, Westphalia, GERMANY, April 23, 1884. As a very young man he emigrated to America, and settled down in Iowa. His desire for knowledge led him to Charles City College, from which he received his B.A. in 1914. In 1916 he was graduated with highest honors from GARRETT BIBLICAL INSTITUTE with a B.D. degree, and in 1917 he received his M.A. from NORTHWESTERN UNIVERSITY. Three years later he had completed his work for a Ph.D. from Chicago University in the field of Semitic languages.

In 1921 he had the choice of going to the Methodist Seminary in Frankfurt Am Main, Germany, or to a newly organized Theological Training School in JAVA, and decided in favor of the latter. He became Principal of the Training School, where he served 1921-1926. After his first furlough he was asked to go to SUMATRA and work as District Missionary, later District Superintendent, and in 1935-1940 as Principal of the Methodist Boys School in Palembang, where he built a beautiful new school building. Being a very able writer in the Indonesian (Malay) language, he translated a number of books and wrote several tracts and books, the most important of which was a scholarly study of Amos and Hosea (1935). Not able to return to Indonesia on account of the war, he transferred to the NORTHWEST INDIANA CONFERENCE. At the time of his death he was pastor of Immanuel and Sacred Heart Methodist Churches in SOUTH BEND, Ind., U.S.A. He died Dec. 13, 1947, and was buried in Highland Cemetery, South Bend.

RAGNAR ALM

THOMAS M. PRYOR

PRYOR, THOMAS MARION (1904-   ), American bishop was born in Cairo, Ill., on Feb. 28, 1904, the son of Thomas J. and Esther (Handley) Pryor. Later his family moved to MICHIGAN where he has lived and served the church.

His undergraduate work was taken at the University of Michigan, from which institution he also earned the M.A. and Ph.D. degree, the latter being in the field of Urban Sociology. He also earned the S.T.B. degree from BOSTON UNIVERSITY SCHOOL OF THEOLOGY, and took additional graduate training at the Sorbonne in France and the University of Heidelberg in Germany. ADRIAN COLLEGE awarded him an honorary degree in 1962.

He married Alice Wuerfel on Sept. 5, 1925. They have four children: Thomas H., a copywriter; David B., a clinical psychologist on the staff of the University of Michigan medical school; Nancy S. (Mrs. Karl Kienholz) and Mary Ann (Mrs. Roderick Daane).

Thomas M. Pryor is a member of Theta Phi (honorary theological fraternity) and Alpha Kappa Delta (honorary sociological fraternity). He has served as special lecturer at both the University of Michigan and Wayne University, Detroit.

He has served Methodist churches in both the DETROIT and MICHIGAN CONFERENCES. He was senior pastor at First Church, Kalamazoo, when elected to the episcopacy in 1964. Previously, he served for thirteen years as pastor of First Church, Royal Oak, Mich. His student pastorates

included Whitmore Lake, Montrose, Newberg, and Detroit, Whitefield.

Bishop and Mrs. Pryor have traveled widely throughout the nation and the world. He was with the Sherwood Eddy Seminar to Europe in 1951; journeyed through the USSR with the Board of Christian SOCIAL CONCERNS in 1961; made an around the world tour of Methodist missions in 1958, and has traveled twice for the I.R.O. and the Y.M.C.A. as an observer in displaced persons camps. In 1955 he spent three months in Nottingham, England as an exchange minister. In 1965 he and Mrs. Pryor made an episcopal visitation to missions in Africa.

Upon his election to the episcopacy in 1964, he was assigned to the CHICAGO Area where he is serving at present. He is a trustee of NORTHWESTERN UNIVERSITY, KENDALL COLLEGE, GARRETT SCHOOL OF THEOLOGY, NORTH CENTRAL COLLEGE, and Chicago Wesley Memorial Hospital. He was president of the Church Federation of Greater Chicago for the year 1968-69. He serves as a member of the WORLD METHODIST COUNCIL, the Commission for Ecumenical Affairs, the PROGRAM COUNCIL, and the National Board of EDUCATION.

Who's Who in America, Vol. 34.
Who's Who in The Methodist Church, 1966.   N. B. H.

PUBLICATION, BOARD OF (EUB), was the printing and publishing agency of the EVANGELICAL UNITED BRETHREN CHURCH in America with headquarters in DAYTON, Ohio. The Board was first organized immediately after union of the Church of the UNITED BRETHREN IN CHRIST and the EVANGELICAL CHURCH in 1946. From 1946 until 1962 the publishing work of the church was carried on by the two church publishing houses: The OTTERBEIN PRESS of Dayton, Ohio (United Brethren) and The EVANGELICAL PRESS of Harrisburg, Pa. (Evangelical). In 1962 the GENERAL CONFERENCE approved a plan of restructuring its Board of Publication to provide for all general church publishing by this Board under the administration of one publisher.

Publishing in the church has been an important function since the first years of the Evangelical and United Brethren Churches, beginning early in the nineteenth century. In The Evangelical Church the first publishing house was established in New Berlin, Pa., in 1817, being constructed side by side with the first church of that denomination which was erected in the same year. During the years other publishing centers for The Evangelical Church were located in Cleveland, Ohio, and Harrisburg, Pa. The original Harrisburg location of the publishing house was Second and Locust Streets (1894). A new, modern building was erected in 1918 at the corner of Third and Reily Streets which has been the site of The Evangelical Press from that time to the present. This is a three-story modern brick building with printing and binding equipment and administrative offices. An additional printing building (Plant No. 2) was erected in 1955 and is located a few blocks from Plant No. 1.

The United Brethren in Christ in its early years published disciplines, hymnals and church school literature, with printing being done by private printers. In 1834 printing equipment was purchased and a Printing Establishment opened at Circleville, Ohio. One of the first publications was the *Religious Telescope*, published Dec. 31, 1834. This publication was to continue without interruption until church union with The Evangelical

Church in 1946. The publishing house was incorporated in the State of Ohio in 1839, by an act of the General Assembly as the Printing Establishment of the United Brethren in Christ.

Within a few years there was a demand to move the publishing center to a larger city. After considerable heated discussion, the General Conference in 1853 authorized the Printing Establishment to be relocated in Dayton, Ohio. The first location was at Fourth and Main Streets. Publishing continued there in several different buildings until 1914. The publishing house was then removed to its present location at Fifth and Perry Streets. In 1935 The Otterbein Press was incorporated in the State of Ohio to become the successor to the Printing Establishment corporation as the official publishing agency of the United Brethren Church. The Printing Establishment corporation was continued as the holding company for the twenty-one-story office building which was erected at Fourth and Main in 1925. This building was sold in 1952 and the Printing Establishment corporation dissolved in 1966, after transfer of over $2,000,000 in assets to the Board of Pensions of the church.

Purpose and Objectives. The E.U.B. Church restated its publishing purpose and objectives in the General Conference of 1962 at the time the constitution of the Board was approved. The objectives as stated were as follows:

The primary publishing objective of The Evangelical United Brethren Church shall be to foster Christian thought and action through the wide distribution of Christian materials.

To accomplish this objective, the Board of Publication shall produce, publish, purchase and distribute Christian literature, printed, audio-visual and other materials for the church. The Board of Publication shall share with other agencies in the total Christian education program of the church, providing printing and publishing services to church boards and agencies in implementing the total program of the church.

Primarily, the publishing was for the churches and members of the denomination; however, from time to time the church had published religious books, periodicals, and additional material for other denominations and for the Armed Services Curriculum Committee.

Board Organization and Meetings. The Board of Publication was made up of eighteen members, two of whom were bishops of the church. Fourteen members were elected by the General Conference, seven of whom were laymen and seven ministers. Two members at large were elected by the Board of Publication. The Publisher of the Church, the General Conference-elected executive editors, and one representative from each of the following boards were advisory members: General Council of Administration, the Board of Christian Education, the Board of Evangelism, the Board of Missions, the Board of Pensions. All active bishops of the church were advisory members. All elected members of the Board constituted the Board of Trustees of The Evangelical Press and of The Otterbein Press.

The Board of Publication met annually or upon call. An Executive Committee of the Board met quarterly. The Board had the "responsibility for and supervision of all the publishing interests of The Evangelical United Brethren Church."

The Publisher was the chief executive officer and treasurer of the Board.

Church Publishing-Educational. The Board published a complete line of Sunday school literature for all ages,

including graded and uniform lesson materials. Supplemental materials were provided in the form of age level reading papers: *Builders* for senior high and above; *Friends* for junior high; *Boys and Girls* for juniors; *Children's Stories* for primary. *Power*, with daily meditations for youth, was printed and distributed for Christian Youth Publications to our church as well as several other denominations. Teacher's helps included materials for adults, youth, junior children, primary children and nursery-kindergarten.

Church and Home was a monthly magazine for the Christian home with a circulation of about 225,000.

Executive and administrative offices were located in the new Board of Publication Center building at Fifth and Perry Streets, Dayton, Ohio. The Publication Center also provided commodious quarters for a full staff of church school literature and *Church and Home* editors. The Board of Publication maintained an art department for its own publications and for art service to all of the departments of the church.

The Board held title for the church to several real estate properties, including two printing manufacturing buildings in Harrisburg, Pa., the five-story Otterbein Press building in Dayton, Ohio, and the new Board of Publication Center, with total assets aggregating over nine million dollars.

Grants for Pensions. The Board of Publication made annual grants from its net proceeds for the aid of retired ministers and their dependents. This had been a policy of both of the uniting churches since the beginning of publishing. These grants were made to the Board of Pensions and to the annual conferences. The annual grant for 1966 and 1967 each had been over $400,000.

Bibles, Books and Merchandise. The Board of Publication was responsible in the church for the promotion, sale and distribution of Bibles, religious books and other religious merchandise for the church and the home. Two modern bookstores were situated in Dayton, Ohio, and Harrisburg, Pennsylvania. A large part of this religious merchandising was carried on through a well organized mail order service.

In addition to church and religious printing, both of the printing plants did commercial work. This had been a policy of the church from its early years. The Board of Publication provided modern printing and binding equipment incorporating the latest printing processes and methods. Since much of the church printing was on a monthly or quarterly mailing basis, additional printing was required to keep employees and equipment busy throughout the year. The current dollar volume of the printing and publishing operation in 1967 was about $10,000,000 per year.

Throughout the years the church served its constituency and many others with Christian printed materials, challenging them to more active and meaningful Christian living.

With the formation of The United Methodist Church, the work of this Board was transferred to the new Board of Publication and the Methodist Publishing House.

J. H. Ness, *History of Publishing* (*EUB*). 1966.

L. L. Huffman

PUBLICATION, BOARD OF and **BOOK COMMITTEE.** The Board of Publication is the directing and controlling

Board or Agency of The United Methodist Church which manages and directs the METHODIST PUBLISHING HOUSE. This Publishing House "comprises the publishing interests of The United Methodist Church."

The Baltimore CHRISTMAS CONFERENCE in 1784 was the first ancestor of the Board of Publication, creating this role for itself by inserting the following paragraph in the Minutes of the Conference: " . . . the Advice of the Conference shall be desired concerning any valuable Impression, and their consent be obtained before any Steps be taken for the Printing thereof." The first Book Committee (so called in the M.E. Church and the M.E. Church, South, until unification) was appointed by the GENERAL CONFERENCE of 1792 and had three members: JOHN DICKINS, first Book Steward; Henry Willis and THOMAS HASKINS; and two duties: "to determine . . . . on the amount of the droughts which may be drawn from time to time on the book-fund," and "to publish . . . . such books or treatises as members of the Book Committee shall unanimously judge proper." The yellow fever epidemic of 1798 and Dickins' resultant death wiped out these brave beginnings of a book committee, since the *Discipline* for that year makes no mention of the Book Committee as originally set up, but lays the responsibility of the publishing interests of the church upon the PHILADELPHIA CONFERENCE, with a conference-appointed committee to examine quarterly the state of the Book Concern. No books or tracts were to be printed without the consent of one bishop and two-thirds of the Philadelphia Conference.

For nearly fifty years the annual conference in which the Book Concern was located appointed the Book Committees. In this responsibility, the NEW YORK CONFERENCE replaced the Philadelphia Conference when the Concern moved to New York under the stewardship of EZEKIEL COOPER in 1804. When "the Concern for the Western Country" was created in 1820 and located in CINCINNATI, the OHIO CONFERENCE appointed the Book Committees for the Western part of the church. Membership and responsibilities of the committee waxed and waned with the fortunes of the Concern, the general trend being onward and upward. By 1836, the Book Committee of the eastern Concern included all the preachers stationed in New York, including the editors of the periodicals and literature, the resident corresponding secretary of the Missionary Society and the presiding elder of the district. This arrangement held until 1844 when the General Conference ordered the first geographical distribution of the committee, specifying that both Eastern and Western Concern Committees be limited to six members each—two elected annually by each of these three conferences in the East: New York, Philadelphia, and NEW JERSEY— and two elected annually by each of the three Western conferences: OHIO, KENTUCKY, and INDIANA. The term "Book Steward" was dropped in favor of "Agent." The Western agent and assistant could be taken from any annual conference, not simply the Ohio Conference, and both Eastern and Western agents needed only the approval of the editors instead of that of the Book Committee to publish any new works.

In 1848 the General Conference assumed responsibility for appointing the Book Committees and gave the bodies expanded powers. In 1868, the two Committees were combined into one. In 1872, however, to assure local supervision, subordinate local committees were authorized for New York and Cincinnati. It was at the General Conference of 1872 that laymen, first elected delegates to that General Conference, became members of the Book Committee. In 1912, the Eastern and Western Concerns were unified under one charter and management and the Book Committee became a corporation.

The Book Committee of the M.E. Church, South, was created by the 1846 General Conference following the separation of the two Methodisms in 1844. From a membership of three, it grew to a thirteen-man body in 1878, with heavy lay representation: nine laymen and four ministers, reflecting this church's greater dependence upon the laity in business matters during the post-war and Reconstruction era. In 1890 the lay-clerical representation was adjusted to seven lay, six cleric. As the Eastern and Western Book Committees of the Methodist Episcopal Church were in the early years dominated by the annual conferences, in which its publishing houses were located, so was the Southern Book Committee membership made up largely of Nashvillians. Residential restrictions were instituted in 1898 when the *Discipline* specified that of the thirteen members, only five could be residents of Nashville and vicinity. In 1906 the Book Agents were made coordinate in rank, the title of the chief executive officer was changed to "Publishing Agent" and it devolved upon the Book Committee to determine their functions and prerogatives. In 1918 the Book Committee assumed the responsibility of electing the Publishing Agents, a responsibility of the General Conference since the founding of the church.

The Book Committee of the M.P. Church was created in 1830, following the 1828 split in the ranks of American Methodism over lay representation. The committee, accountable to the Maryland Conference in the interim of the General Conference, had both lay and ministerial members on it from its inception, more clearly defined duties than M.E. Church or M.E. Church, South, counterparts, but approximately the same powers. The rise of the North-West M.P. Book Concern, with headquarters ultimately at Pittsburgh, caused administrative problems, and at the 1854 General Conference a Plan of Division of the Book Concern was adopted, creating separate, self-sustaining Concerns, each operated by its own Book Committee, known as Directories. Four years later the church followed its Book Concerns into separation along the same geographical lines. Although the Church reunited in 1877, the publishing concerns continued to function separately, but under the control of the General Conference and a twenty-member Board of Publication, composed of the corporate bodies of the Pittsburgh and Baltimore Directories. The two M.P. Publishing Houses united in 1932.

The Present Board. At the time of church union of the three Methodisms in 1939, the term "Book Committee" was considered a bit archaic for the new union, and the "Board of Publication" supplanted "Book Committee" as the managerial group to control the Methodist Publishing House.

Regulations in the present *Discipline* call for the members of the Board of Publication to be elected largely by the Jurisdictional Conferences, and a ratio which provides for an equitable distribution among the various Jurisdictions has been worked out based upon their membership. The membership of the Board is equally divided, as far as practicable between ministers and laymen. Two bishops since 1952 have been members of the Board, selected by the COUNCIL OF BISHOPS; and five persons are put upon the present Board by election of the Board itself. Careful disciplinary regulations govern the proceedings and define the functions of the Board of Publication. These from time to time are changed, usually in minor ways that seem good to the directing General Conference.

The Board of Publication has since 1956 elected one general executive known as the president, who is the president of each corporation under the direction of the Board and who is also known as Publisher of The United Methodist Church. The Board also elects the Book Editor of the Church, the editor of Church School Publications —in conjunction with the action of the Board of Education—and elects also the editors of the general church periodicals, as the *Christian Advocate* and *Together*. Such editors are elected quadrennially.

The Board organizes, as do other Agencies, by electing its own president and officers and as it has traditionally had upon it laymen of unusual ability in the field of business and wide enterprise, its meetings are in the nature of the annual meeting of any other large manufacturing or business company.

This incorporated board functions through a chairman, vice-chairman, and secretary, an executive officer (the president already described), and a sixteen-member executive committee which exercises all the powers of the Board except those expressly reserved for Board action by the *Discipline* or by the corporate charter and by-laws. Board officers also serve as executive committee officers; the two bishops serving on the Board are ex officio members of the committee with vote; the president (publisher) is an ex officio member without vote.

In its directing and controlling of the Publishing House, the Board acts through the president (publisher) elected by the Board and answerable to it. For legal and historical purposes, the members of the Board of Publication are the successors of the incorporators named in the charters of the Methodist Book Concern (M.E. Church), the Publishing Agents of the M.E. Church, South, the Board of Publication of the M.P. Church, and the Board of Publication of the E.U.B. Church. The president (publisher) is the successor of the Book Agents of the M.E. Church, South.

Broadly speaking, it is the responsibility of the Board to direct the operations of the Publishing House in the channels laid down for it by the *Discipline*; to appropriate money from net income, above adequate reserves, and distribute this appropriation annually to the annual conferences for the conference claimants; to hold, use, manage, and operate all property and assets of the corporations that make up the body of the publishing operations of The United Methodist Church, and to see that all legal obligations of these corporations are fulfilled; and to make a written report of its action and proceedings to the church through the General Conference. The Board not only elects, but fixes the salaries of, and can suspend the following officers: president (publisher), book editor, editors of the official church papers, editor of church school publications, and other salaried officers provided for in the *Discipline*. It bonds the president and other corporate executive officers, and blanket bonds all staff personnel whose responsibilities justify such coverage, fixing the amount of the bonds and paying the premiums.

The Board of Publication controls an enormous business under the direction of the *Discipline*, which states that the

objects of the Methodist Publishing House shall be: "The advancement of the cause of Christianity by disseminating religious knowledge and useful literary and scientific information in the form of books, tracts, and periodicals; the promotion of Christian education; the transaction of any and all business properly connected with the publishing, manufacturing, and distribution of books, tracts, periodicals, materials, and supplies for churches and church schools; and such other business as the General Conference may authorize and direct." (See also METHODIST PUBLISHING HOUSE.)

Disciplines.
R. Emory, *History of the Discipline.* 1844.
J. P. Pilkington, *Methodist Publishing House.* 1968.

JAMES P. PILKINGTON

PUBLISHING HOUSE CONTROVERSY (1897-1902). The Union Army during the Civil War took over the relatively new M.E. Church, South Publishing House building and printing plant when NASHVILLE was occupied by the Union Army. They used and abused the building and equipment for approximately four years. In 1867 the War-Claims Committee appraised the rent and damage at $500,000. This claim was unsuccessfully pressed by various attorneys for over thirty years. Then Barbee and Smith, the Publishing House Agents, employed Major E. B. Stahlman, an eminent attorney in Nashville, "to secure the most favorable settlement possible." He was to receive thirty-five percent of the amount collected. The attorney spent much of 1896-97 in WASHINGTON seeking Congressional approval of the claim bill.

After the House voted in 1898 to pay $288,000 on the claim, it encountered opposition in the Senate. Senator Pasco of FLORIDA, the sponsor of the claim, wrote BARBEE that "there is a rumor in the Senate that Mr. Stahlman is to receive forty percent of the amount recovered. If this is so, I believe it will defeat the bill. I need a denial from you to read in the Senate." Before this letter could be answered, Senator Bates of MAINE made a request for denial or confirmation of the rumor. Barbee wired: "It is not true that Stahlman will receive forty percent." Stahlman gave the Senators the impression "that he was not interested in the case on account of monetary considerations."

After the Senate passed the bill and the $288,000 were paid, it became known that the attorney's fee was thirty-five percent. A Senate Investigating Committee was appointed on the grounds that the Senate had been deceived.

The Agents and their attorney insisted that "the Senate consider the claim on its merits: that the fee was a matter of the Publishing House Agents' discretion." Therefore the Agents felt that they were under no obligation to divulge the details of their contract with their attorney.

The Senate Investigating Committee summarized their findings as follows:

> First: That the Book Agents purposefully withheld facts.
> Second: That if there was any mistake or omission on the part of the Senate, it was in failing to protect the beneficiaries against the Book Agents.
> Third: The Committee deems it proper . . . that no censure should rest upon the Methodist Episcopal Church, South.
> Fourth: The Committee . . . suggests that no action be

taken by the Senate . . . but that the Church be allowed to take such measures as it deems proper.

W. P. Lovejoy, a member of the Book Committee (the Administrative management of the Publishing House) moved that the Book Committee ask the Agents to resign. This motion was rejected twelve to one.

This issue was debated all over Southern Methodism for over three years—in Annual Conferences, in the GENERAL CONFERENCE of 1902, and in the church papers. One side denounced the Agents for what they termed "unethical conduct." The defenders as vigorously denied the charges. They maintained that the Agents were victims of a chain of unfortunate circumstances. The facts are detailed by the Senate Committee Report No. 1416, and the Church Investigating Committees.

The College of Bishops, speaking for the whole Church, officially reported to the Senate "that if the Senate by official affirmative action, declare that the passage of the payment bill was due to misleading statements, we will . . . have the entire amount returned." The Senate however "refused to recommend any further action."

The 1902 General Conference Committee investigating the Agents, found no cause for trial, and the TENNESSEE CONFERENCE also found no grounds for trying J. D. Barbee. However, Barbee declined to be considered for reelection as BOOK AGENT. He was appointed PRESIDING ELDER of the Nashville District.

DuBose, in his *History of Methodism*, gave the General Conference summary of the controversy as follows:

> First: the Church had a historic, just and legal claim against the Government.
> Second: that the amount finally recovered and accepted as payment in full for the claim, was not equal to the loss sustained.
> Third: that in answer to the complaint that this payment had been secured through misleading statements of the churches representatives had not been substantiated by the Senate.
> Fourth: that the Church repudiates all acts of concealment.
> Fifth: that this action is declared to be a final settlement of the whole matter. (See the biography of J. D. BARBEE in this Encyclopedia.)

J. M. Batten, *Outline and Bibliographical Guide*. 1954.
H. M. DuBose, *Life of J. D. Barbee*. N.d.
—————, *History*. 1916.
Senate Report No. 1416: Methodist Book Concern.

J. RICHARD SPANN

PUBLISHING HOUSE OF UNITED EVANGELICAL CHURCH. (See EVANGELICAL PRESS.)

PUBLISHING HOUSES, Br. (See BOOK ROOMS, Br.)

PUERTO RICO, a hilly tropical island southeast of CUBA, is 105 miles long and 35 miles wide, and has a population of about 2,700,000. As a possession of the United States, it has commonwealth status and chooses its chief executive by popular vote. Puerto Rico's largest income is from manufacturing—textiles and apparel, electronic equipment, chemicals, etc. Spanish is the official language, but the study of English is compulsory in the schools.

When the United States received Puerto Rico from Spain in 1898, Protestant missionaries entered the island

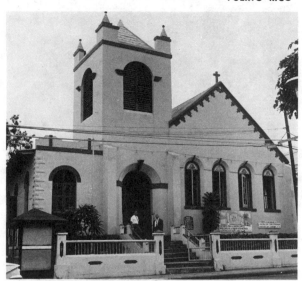

FIRST CHURCH, GUAYAMA, BUILT IN 1902, IS THE OLDEST METHODIST CHURCH IN PUERTO RICO

at once. The Methodist Episcopal Church transferred CHARLES W. DREES from URUGUAY in 1900, and he immediately organized English and Spanish-speaking churches in San Juan, the capital. Other Methodist missionaries soon arrived, and in 1902 the WOMAN'S HOME MISSIONARY SOCIETY of the denomination inaugurated several projects, including the George O. Robinson School for Girls in Santurce. By a comity agreement among several Protestant denominations, the Methodists were assigned a segment of territory running north and south through the center of the island and including the important cities of San Juan, Ponce, and Arecibo.

The Puerto Rico Mission (MEC) was organized at San Juan, March 7, 1902 with Bishop JOHN M. WALDEN presiding. The territory of the mission was Puerto Rico and adjacent islands. The mission reported 195 full members and 640 probationers. Appointments were made to ten charges.

The 1912 GENERAL CONFERENCE adopted an enabling act permitting the Puerto Rico Mission to become a mission conference, and it was organized as such at San Juan on Feb. 27, 1913 with Bishop WILLIAM BURT presiding. It began with thirty-five charges, eighteen ministers, twenty supply preachers, and 3,052 members plus 2,612 probationers. In 1939 the mission conference reported twenty-three charges and 2,800 members. In 1940 it became a provisional annual conference.

Today Methodism in Puerto Rico joins other denominations in supporting the Evangelical Seminary of Puerto Rico. The conference helps to maintain Middleton House, the Methodist student center which adjoins University Church in Rio Piedras. The George O. Robinson School has become coeducational, offering courses (English) from kindergarten through the twelfth grade. The pupils study religion as well as pursue a regular public school curriculum which is in Spanish.

In 1968 the Puerto Rico Provisional Conference reported two districts, fifty-six charges, sixty-nine ministers, 11,763 members, property valued at $4,994,780, and a total of $233,970 raised for all purposes during the year.

The 1968 General Conference elevated the Puerto Rico work to the status of a full annual conference. The Puerto Rico Conference was organized Jan. 23, 1969 at University

MOSAIC OF CHRIST ON FACADE OF
UNIVERSITY CHURCH, RIO PIEDRAS, SAN JUAN

Church, Rio Piedras, with Bishop J. GORDON HOWARD presiding.

E. S. Bucke, *History of American Methodism.* 1964.
General Minutes, ME, TMC.
Minutes of the Puerto Rico Provisional Conference.
Project Handbook, Section of Home Fields. National Division, Board of Missions, 1967.   ALBEA GODBOLD

PUGET SOUND CONFERENCE (MEC). See PACIFIC NORTHWEST CONFERENCE.

PUGH, ABRAM WESLEY (1894-   ), American minister, member of JUDICIAL COUNCIL, was born at Perkasie, Pa., June 7, 1894, son of Joseph M. and Harriett (Moyer) Pugh.

He received the A.B. degree from Taylor University in 1922, and was awarded the D.D. degree by that institution in 1936. DEPAUW UNIVERSITY also conferred the D.D. degree upon him in 1954.

He served as supply pastor in Cameron, Ohio, 1916; Marion, Home Park, Ind., 1920-22. He was admitted on trial into the NORTH INDIANA CONFERENCE, M.E. Church, 1919, and ordained deacon, 1921. He was received in full connection and ordained elder in 1923.

His pastorates were: Uniondale, 1922-26; Churubusco, 1926-28; Albany, 1928-32; Noblesville, 1932-36; superintendent, Richmond District, 1936-37, and again 1959-61; pastor, High Street Church, Muncie, 1937-49; superintendent, Fort Wayne District, 1949-55; pastor in Marion, 1955-59 (all Indiana). He was president of the Preachers Aid Society, North Indiana Conference, 1937-61; member of the GENERAL CONFERENCES, 1936-56; he was chairman of the committee chairmen, 1956, and chairman of the Rules Committee, 1948-56. He was a member of the Board of Publication of The Methodist Church, 1944-56, and a member of the Judicial Council of The Methodist Church, 1956-68 and secretary of the Council, 1960-64.

He has served as trustee of Taylor University, 1932-44; trustee and member of the executive committee of the Indianapolis Methodist Hospital, 1939-61; and as a member of the board of directors of Parkview Memorial, Fort Wayne, 1949-55. He served to 2nd Lieutenant, U. S. Army, 1918-19. In 1944 he was chairman of the Kiwanis International Committee on support of Churches in their Spiritual Aims.

He was married to Sarah Essa Pence on Aug. 24, 1920. Their children are: Geraldine Joy (Mrs. James C. Barr) and Miriam June (Mrs. Warren L. Bergwall). On June 6, 1967 he was married to Marguerite Deyo.

Who's Who in The Methodist Church, 1966.   J. MARVIN RAST

PULPIT ROCK, The Dalles, Oregon, U. S. A., is a slender basalt pillar, rising abruptly near the south boundary of the city of The Dalles, forming a natural pulpit from which the early Methodist missionaries were accustomed to preach to the Indians in pleasant weather. It was used first in 1838 when, on March 22, JASON LEE, DANIEL LEE, and H. K. W. Perkins arrived from the mission on the Willamette to found the mission at The Dalles.

The rock originally had two pinnacles rising about twelve feet from the base. Daniel Lee chiseled off one of the points for a table on which to place his Bible and the other was used as a seat by the minister.

An eye witness reported that customarily at dawn the minister mounted Pulpit Rock and blew a horn that could be heard across the Columbia. In response the Indians crossed the River in canoes while others came by foot to assemble about the rock to listen to the preaching of the Gospel.

The rock was dedicated and a memorial tablet set upon it, March 22, 1908, by the Old Fort Dalles Historical Society and the Good Intent Society of The Dalles Methodist Church. The tablet was unveiled by Miss Ethel W. Grubbs, granddaughter and only descendant of Jason Lee, first missionary in OREGON.

ERLE HOWELL

PUMPHREY, REASON (1736-1812), so far as is known was the first American Methodist to move west of the Appalachian Mountains after the Treaty of Fort Stanwix of 1768 opened the way to the issuing of land titles on the western PENNSYLVANIA and western VIRGINIA frontier. Pumphrey moved west from Anne Arundel County, Md., in 1772, accompanied by his wife, eight sons, seven servants, and four slaves. He first settled on a claim of 308 acres of land on the headwaters of Chartier's creek near the Indian village of Catfish within the bounds of the present city of Washington, Pa. Pumphrey had become a Methodist in one of ROBERT STRAWBRIDGE'S classes. He was accompanied to the west by Eli Shickle, one of Strawbridge's local preachers, who conducted religious services in the camp on Sundays en route west, and who preached in the Pumphrey and other frontier cabins until his return to Maryland in 1776.

Pumphrey was a cousin of RICHARD OWINGS, Strawbridge's leading local preacher. According to the *Journal* of JOHN LITTLEJOHN the BALTIMORE Circuit in MARYLAND in 1777-78 was an eight-week circuit with four preachers on it. Preaching points on it included the widow Ann Murphy; Edward Teal; the widow Pumphrey, Reason's mother; Joshua Owings, father of Richard; Hawkins; and William Ridgely, Pumphrey's father-in-law. In the early 1780's ANN MURPHY, Edward Teal, William Hawkins and others of the Maryland Methodists moved to western Pennsylvania. In the fall of 1783 Richard Owings visited these settlements west of the mountains and made plans for a Methodist circuit among them. In the spring of 1784 FRANCIS ASBURY appointed two preachers to the new Redstone Circuit.

In 1785 Pumphrey moved farther west to a bottom land farm on the Ohio River at Beech Bottom in Brooke County, Va., (now W. Va.), and almost immediately Methodism again followed him, a Society of the REDSTONE CIRCUIT being organized in his home in 1786. This Society became the Kadesh Chapel Methodist Church when the first church building was erected in 1788. This church continues today as one of the historic churches of the WEST VIRGINIA CONFERENCE.

W. GUY SMELTZER

PUNJAB UNITED CHRISTIAN SCHOOLS. These schools consist of two higher secondary schools—one for girls, the other for boys—and an industrial training center. They have been developed by the Punjab Synod of the United Church of North India, the Delhi Annual Conference of the Methodist Church of Southern Asia, and the related boards of missions. After years of delays caused by the Second World War and by the slow process of land acquisition, classes were opened in 1944. Initially 207 acres had been obtained, but the army took over the entire property for defense purposes during the war and has retained use of a large portion.

The enrollment figures for 1965 were: 333 (of which 137 were Christians) in the boys' high school; 218 (of which 151 were Christians) in the girls' high school; 34 (of which 18 were Christians) in the industrial center. Of the 306 Christians enrolled, 276 were in the boarding department and were under Christian supervision and instruction in the dormitories and in recreation.

The need for these schools has long been urgent, and their potential for service is immense. The master plan was drawn by a professional missionary architect. The first two stages of the building program have been completed.

Many students develop a strong sense of mission. This is helped by the Sunday school, which has an enrollment of 330. The school chaplain conducts weekly classes for teachers. During the last summer vacation fifty-five of the older students conducted daily vacation Bible schools in their villages. Some also had classes for illiterate Christians, teaching them to read and to witness to their faith.

J. WASKOM PICKETT

PUNSHON, WILLIAM MORLEY (1824-1881), British Methodist, was born at Doncaster, Yorkshire, May 29, 1824. The son of a draper, he entered the Wesleyan Methodist ministry in 1844. In the 1850's he established a reputation as the giver of highly rhetorical lectures: *The Huguenots, Wilberforce, Science, Religion and Literature, Daniel in Babylon,* etc.; the real subject of most of these was progress in the nineteenth century. In 1862-67 he raised £10,000 by lecturing, and built a series of Methodist chapels in seaside towns. He helped to found and edit the *Methodist Recorder.* From 1868-73 he was virtually the head of Canadian Methodism. In 1868 and 1872 he was fraternal delegate to the GENERAL CONFERENCE of the Methodist Episcopal Church. He returned to England, and was elected president of the Wesleyan Conference of 1874. He was appointed to the Home Mission Department in 1875; in 1876-78 he was the leader of those who

W. MORLEY PUNSHON

persuaded the Wesleyan Conference to admit lay representatives. Apart from his lectures and sermons, he published a series of devotional poems, *Sabbath Chimes* (1867), a Wesleyan imitation of Keble's *Christian Year.* He died at Brixton Hill, April 14, 1881.

F. W. Macdonald, *William Morley Punshon.* 1887.

JOHN KENT

PUNTAMBA, India, is the headquarters of a district of the same name in the BOMBAY CONFERENCE. It is located 200 miles east of Bombay City on the Godavari River, which is regarded by Hindus as sacred. Many thousands of pilgrims visit the town annually. It is within the civil district of Ahmednagar.

Methodism has a strong self-supporting church and operates a service program that includes (1) the Bowen Bruere Hospital, named for a greatly loved and fervent young second-generation Methodist missionary who died while serving here; (2) a rural high school, coeducational, which extends preferential treatment to boys and girls from villages and tries to maintain an atmosphere of rural simplicity; (3) hostels for selected boys and girls; and (4) an extension agency that promotes adult literacy, church membership, evangelism, and training for community service.

One of the circuits in the district centers in Sangamner, where Samuel Rahator and others representing The Methodist Church, British connection, carried on an active and productive evangelistic program for years. The work was made over to the Bombay Annual Conference in 1944.

"Puntamba-Sangamner," *The Gazette,* Board of Missions, 1960. J. N. Hollister, *Southern Asia.* 1956.   J. WASKOM PICKETT

PURCELL, CLARE (1884-1964), American bishop, was born on Nov. 17, 1884, at Columbia, Ala. He was educated at BIRMINGHAM SOUTHERN COLLEGE and the Divinity School of VANDERBILT UNIVERSITY, and received honorary degrees from three other institutions. He joined the NORTH ALABAMA CONFERENCE of the M.E. Church, South in 1906, and was appointed to Wedowee. His other appointments in North Alabama included Madison, Owenton Church in BIRMINGHAM, Sylacauga, Hartselle, Talladega, Tuscaloosa and Gadsden, and superintendents

CLARE PURCELL

of the Jasper District. He was a chaplain of the 131st Infantry, U.S. Army, with the American Expeditionary Forces during the first World War.

Clare Purcell was a member of the GENERAL CONFERENCE of the M.E. Church, South, 1930, 1934, and 1938 —at which last he was elected bishop and assigned to the CHARLOTTE Area. His brethren credited a speech he made in favor of unification during the debate on this matter as having much to do with his election, as this speech came at a critical moment and was noteworthy as coming from a delegate from the deep South. As bishop he served on the powerful COUNCIL ON WORLD SERVICE AND FINANCE, becoming its president in 1940. He also served on the Board of EDUCATION and Board of MISSIONS and then was chairman of the Trustees of LAKE JUNALUSKA ASSEMBLY, 1938-48. He was assigned to the Birmingham Area in 1948, where he served until his retirement in 1956. He was president of the COUNCIL OF BISHOPS, 1955-56. A man of great balance and sagacity, he enjoyed the respect and esteem of all his compeers.

After retirement, he continued to live in Birmingham until his death on Feb. 8, 1964, and is buried there.

Who's Who in America.
Clark and Stafford, *Who's Who in Methodism.* 1952.
ELMER T. CLARK
N. B. H.

PURITANISM AND METHODISM. The term "Puritan" may refer to any person concerned with renovation of religious thought and practice from the earliest centuries to the present. In late sixteenth-century England it referred to those who sought to continue the Protestant Reformation by establishing what they understood to be "pure" forms of doctrine, worship and church polity. Often these attempts to reform the church involved political action aimed at religious liberty and constitutional rights. Convinced that Christianity demanded a vibrant faith based on an experiential relationship with the God revealed in Christ, the Puritans took scripture as their primary guide of thought and action. Their ethical idealism, when rigidly practiced, tended to separate them from their neighbors.

Methodism's well-disciplined, circumspect, and sometimes austere mode of Christian living revived for many of JOHN WESLEY's contemporaries the spirit and practice found in Puritan models of the previous century. Bishop Warburton, Samuel Johnson, Horace Walpole, and others could, in Warburton's words, identify the "true character of Methodism" with that of the "old Precisians, Puritans, and Independents." This similarity in teaching and practice, so often recognized by friend and foe alike, denotes only one among several points of contact between the two movements.

The interconnection of Methodism with Puritanism has its origin in John and Charles Wesley's own Puritan heritage. Both their grandfathers and two of their great grandfathers had been Puritans of some renown. SAMUEL WESLEY's grandfather, Bartholomew Westley, and his father, John Westley, were ejected from their churches when they refused to accept the requirements of the Act of Uniformity imposed on Church of England clergy in 1662. SUSANNA WESLEY's maternal grandfather, JOHN WHITE, a member of the Long Parliament, took an active role in the examination and ejection of many Anglican clergymen during the Puritan regime. Her father, SAMUEL ANNESLEY, one of the most eminent ministers of London, unwilling to conform in 1662, became a leader of the disenfranchised Puritan community.

While Samuel and Susanna left this Nonconformist heritage to return to the Church of England, they carried with them many emphases of their early religious training. Samuel Wesley's disciplined daily scholarship concentrating in biblical study may perhaps be traced to his Puritan preceptors. Exposed in his Puritan home to the reality of a personal religious experience, Samuel proclaimed "the inward witness" to his sons even from his death bed. Susanna's influence through her typically Puritan regulation of the family household can hardly be overestimated. The rigid discipline; the careful timetable which left little room for "light" diversions; the insistence on personal and family meditation, devotion, and religious study; the expectation of genuine piety are all strikingly similar to Puritan prototypes. Influenced, perhaps unconsciously, by these Puritan emphases the Wesley brothers retained them throughout their own lives.

John Wesley readily admitted his public and university education had prejudiced him against the Nonconformists. Nevertheless, when his own study led him to Puritan writings he found there many qualities and teachings congenial to his own religious experiences. Overcoming his prejudices, he did not hesitate to abridge and publish numerous Puritan tracts and treatises for the instruction of the Methodists. Of the some fifty abridgments and abstracts published by Wesley as separate volumes, more than a third are by Puritan authors. In his *Christian Library*, designed specifically for guidance in Christian thought and life—termed by him "practical divinity"— Puritan authors predominate both in number and space allotted. Wesley's introductory comments to these works in the *Christian Library* expresses his opinion of their value: "The peculiar excellency of these writers seems to be, the building us up in our most holy faith . . . They lead us by the hand in the paths of righteousness, and shew us how we may most surely and swiftly grow in grace." Wesley found in the Puritan writings sound doctrine scripturally grounded and practical instruction in Christian living which might serve as guidance for his followers. Guided by the MORAVIAN pietists Wesley had come to an insistence on the priority of God's grace appropriated by man through faith alone and witnessed to by a believer's knowledge of his own relationship with God. When he looked for English material stressing these doctrines he found them among the Puritans. Supporting his position that a believer might enjoy personal assurance of God's grace, Wesley identifies this doctrine with that held by Puritans such as William Perkins, Richard Sibbes, and John Preston.

Wesley and the Puritans shared the conviction that SANCTIFICATION as well as JUSTIFICATION rested on faith alone. The Puritan doctrine which recognized sin and repentance even in believing Christians became one of Wesley's defenses against Moravian quietism for he saw it as "continually tearing up the roots of Antinomianism." Of course, Wesley rejected the Calvinistic predestinarianism accepted by most Puritans and corrected this in his abridgments, although he did find support for his own position in the works of Puritans Richard Baxter and John Goodwin. Richard Baxter also held a theory of "final justification" which is similar to that taught by Wesley.

Not only these theological affinities to the Puritans but also their practical instructions in daily living attracted Wesley to these works. JOSEPH ALLEINE's *An Alarm to Unconverted Sinners* and Richard Baxter's *A Call to the Unconverted* became standard Methodist evangelical publications. Wesley's insistence on self-examination and holiness found able representation in several Puritan works. For his explication of Christian conscience Wesley turns to that offered by his grandfather, Dr. Annesley. Christian family worship as delineated in Philip Henry's *Method of Family Prayer* became instruction for Methodists in this area. Wesley issued at least three editions of William Whateley's *Directions for Married Persons,* commenting, "I have seen nothing of the subject in any either ancient or modern tongue, which is in any degree comparable to it." Wesley's own educational philosophy certainly paralleled that of the Puritans and it may be that KINGSWOOD SCHOOL was patterned at least in part on the Dissenting Academies. A succinct abridgment of Richard Baxter's *The Reformed Pastor* incorporated in Wesley's *Minutes* became the standard outline for Methodist pastoral visitation and religious instruction.

In the independent Methodist worship services supplementing regular Anglican services, Wesley appropriated several distinctive Puritan forms of worship. His use of extemporaneous preaching and "free" prayers to appeal to those uncomfortable in formal worship had certainly been anticipated in Nonconformist worship. One of the unique services of Methodist worship—the service of covenant renewal—was patterned after JOSEPH and RICHARD ALLEINE's formula and directions for making a personal covenant with God. John and Charles Wesley found in the hymns of ISAAC WATTS a model for their own remarkable hymnody. Wesley's abridgment of *The Book of Common Prayer* for American Methodism may also have followed the suggested changes offered by the Presbyterian Divines at the Savoy Conference (1661). At least, most of their suggested changes are incorporated in Wesley's abridgment.

Wesley's Puritan selections constitute only a part of his genuine ecclecticism which drew from any source materials expressing a useful interpretation of the Gospel and offering practical instruction in Christian living. Nevertheless, Wesley's extensive appropriation of Puritan teachings and patterns guaranteed a significant Puritan impact upon later Methodism.

Many of Wesley's co-workers shared his appreciation of the Puritan tradition and teachings. JOHN FLETCHER, his chief ally in theological controversy, extensively quoted Baxter, Matthew Henry, John Owen, Daniel Williams, and others. Often dependent on the Biblical exposition of Matthew Henry, Charles Wesley also credited Baxter with helping him combat Antinomianism. THOMAS COKE acknowledged the influence of Alleine's *Alarm.* FRANCIS ASBURY's *Journal and Letters* make frequent reference to Puritan works and he, like Wesley, understood Baxter's *The Reformed Pastor* to be the pattern for Chistian ministers. Early American Methodists printed and sold many of Wesley's Puritan abridgments.

Later Methodists continued this interest in the Puritan tradition, as is seen in the extensive Puritan library amassed by THOMAS JACKSON, nineteenth-century editor of Wesley's *Works.* ADAM CLARKE, author of the most famous Methodist Biblical commentary, acknowledges his indebtedness to Henry Ainsworth's notes on the Pentateuch and recommends the interpretations of many Puritan commentators. A modern revival of Puritan study by Methodist scholars such as Gordon Wakefield, John Wilkinson, Gordon Rupp, FRANK BAKER, and John Newton indicates the continuing interconnection of the two traditions.

A common concern for a genuine personal religion dependent on God's grace and evidenced in a recognizable Christian mode of life brought the Puritan and Methodist traditions together. Perhaps, in the words of Horton Davies, Methodism revived "the evangelical passion and experiential religion" of Puritanism. Methodist interest in Puritanism has continued because of these central values found in the genuinely Christian life.

Frank Baker, "Wesley's Puritan Ancestry," *London Quarterly and Holborn Review,* 1962, p. 187.
J. Bishop, *Methodist Worship.* 1950.
Duncan Coomer, "The Influence of Puritanism and Dissent on Methodism," *London Quarterly and Holborn Review,* 1950, p. 175.
Horton Davies, *Worship and Theology in England: From Watts and Wesley to Maurice, 1690-1850.* Princeton: Princeton University Press, 1961.
R. C. Monk, *John Wesley.* 1966.
John Newton, *Methodism and Puritans.* London: Dr. Williams Trust, 1964.
————, *Susanna Wesley.* 1968.
F. C. Pritchard, *Secondary Education.* 1949.
Gordon Wakefield, *Puritan Devotion: Its Place in the Development of Christian Piety.* London: Epworth Press, 1957.

ROBERT C. MONK

PUSEY, GEORGE B. (1845-1933), American layman and philanthropist, was born at PITTSBURGH, Pa., on Oct. 22, 1845, the son of William B. and Jane H. Pusey. In his youth George Pusey learned the ways of business by serving as retail clerk, salesman, and manager in various mercantile businesses in Pittsburgh. As a young man he established his own wallpaper business. This business prospered and enabled him to accumulate a fortune estimated to exceed two million dollars at the time of his death.

Pusey never married. Beyond his business his chief interest was his church. He was a member of the former downtown Christ M. E. Church in Pittsburgh and a member of its board of trustees at the time the church was destroyed by fire in 1892. Along with other members of Christ Church residing in Pittsburgh's Northside area, he led in organizing Calvary M.E. Church, becoming one of the first trustees of the church. This congregation built a fine stone building in 1893 which remains as an excellent example of truly Gothic architecture. During his lifetime Pusey contributed liberally to his local church and to the conference and missionary organizations of Methodism. He died on Aug. 31, 1933 at his winter home in Orlando, Fla. After several bequests to employees and friends, the bulk of his estate was distributed to the charities he had supported during his lifetime. Chief beneficiaries were Calvary Church, the M.E. Board of Foreign Missions, the Methodist Church Union of Pittsburgh, the Y.M.C.A. and the Y.W.C.A. of Pittsburgh and several local hospitals. Pusey's bequest has enabled Calvary Church to continue an effective service in a neighborhood which has become an area of typical innercity bi-racial population.

FRANCIS M. KEES

PUTINI, EPIHA (c. 1816-1856), prominent NEW ZEALAND Methodist Maori layman, was born son of Chief Te Rangitaahua Ngamuka, was baptized in 1835, and took the name of Epiha Putini (JABEZ BUNTING). He was trained at Mangungu and became teacher and preacher among his own people at Pehiakura and Ihumatao until his death at about the age of forty in 1856. He was prominent in efforts to bring about cooperation between the missionary societies of the various churches and exerted himself for the welfare of his own people.

C. T. J. Luxton, *Methodist Beginnings in the Manukau.* Wesley Historical Society, New Zealand, 1960.

L. R. M. GILMORE

FRITZ HONG-KYU PYUN

PYEN, FRITZ HONG-KYU (1899-   ), a bishop of the Korean Methodist Church, was born in Chunan, KOREA, on May 28, 1899. He studied in Kongju Methodist Mission School, and finished high school at the German-Chinese High School in Tsingtao, China in 1919. He graduated from HAMLINE UNIVERSITY in 1926, and received the B.D. and Th.D. degree from DREW THEOLOGICAL SCHOOL in 1928 and 1931 respectively. While a student at Drew, Dr. Pyen was an instructor in German. The German language, as well as that non-Korean first name, was acquired while interned with a German Lutheran missionary in Tsingtao, China, during the first World War.

He was ordained in the NEWARK CONFERENCE in 1929, and then held pastorates in Honolulu, 1931-33, and Harbin, Manchuria, 1933-34. In 1934 he joined the faculty of the Methodist Theological Seminary in SEOUL, and four years later became its first Korean president (1938).

The anti-Christian government closed the seminary in 1940, and Dr. Pyen served as pastor of Chong-Kyo Church, Seoul, 1941-43, and East Gate Church, Seoul, 1943-46. In 1942 he was elected by the General Conference as the "Director-General" of the interim "Korean Methodist Block of the Japanese Christian Church in Korea" but was forced to resign after six months by the Japanese officials.

Shortly after the Japanese surrender, he reopened the Methodist Seminary which he headed until 1948 when he assumed the pastorate of South Mountain Church in Seoul. When the Seoul churches were closed by the Communist invasion he organized a church in Pusan. When Seoul was reopened in 1953, he resumed the pastorate of the South Mountain Church and continued to serve there until elected bishop of the Korean Methodist Church by the General Conference of that Church on March 4, 1967.

Bishop Pyen's first wife, Ban-Syuk Kim, perished in a tragic fire. She was the sister-in-law of Bishop J. S. RYANG and quite prominent. Bishop Pyen married Naptuk Kin on June 10, 1955.

Bishop Pyen was present and sat in and with the COUNCIL OF BISHOPS of The United Methodist Church at the Uniting Conference in DALLAS in 1968.

Having reached the age of retirement in 1970, he attended the General Conference meeting at St. Louis, and then stepped aside to accept the presidency of the Los Angeles Bible College and Seminary, newly established under Korean auspices.

CHARLES A. SAUER

PYKE, JAMES HOWELL (1845-1924), a pioneer missionary in NORTH CHINA, was born near Glenwood, Ind., July 9, 1845. He was educated at DEPAUW UNIVERSITY. In 1873 with Anabel Goodrich as his bride, he sailed for China, where he served as organizer of churches, as district and conference evangelist, and as missionary-in-charge of two districts. He was a charter member of the North China Conference when it was organized in 1893, and was a presiding elder (1884-1908). In 1903 he was decorated by the Emperor of China for his handling of the indemnity claims growing out of the Boxer Uprising.

W. W. REID

PYKE, RICHARD (1873-1965), British Methodist, was born at Sampford Courtney, Devon, in 1873. He entered the ministry of the BIBLE CHRISTIAN CHURCH in 1894, and his long and successful ministry was largely confined to the West Country. From 1915 to 1922 he was governor of Shebbear College, and from 1922 to 1949 bursar of Edgehill College. A tall, thin, commanding figure, he was chosen as President of the UNITED METHODIST CHURCH in 1927, and as president of the Methodist Church in 1939. He retired to BRISTOL in 1949 and continued to preach for many years. He died on Sept. 20, 1965.

JOHN KENT

QUAKER METHODISTS, the name by which the followers of PETER PHILLIPS of Warrington were known because they included many Quakers and adopted some of their customs. Later they came to be known as INDEPENDENT METHODISTS, the present name of the denomination.

JOHN T. WILKINSON

QUAKERS AND METHODISM. Like the Methodists, the Quakers had originated as a movement dedicated to the inculcation of personal religious experience and to securing the spiritual reform of the Established Church; they called themselves a "society," but accepted as their most familiar title a derisive nickname. It is not surprising, therefore, that in the early days of the revival it was frequently a friendly Quaker who gave protection and support to the persecuted Methodists. Although drawn together against their common enemies in the world, however, rivalry did develop between the two groups, who remained so far different in their views that they continued to seek proselytes from among each others' members. The Friends' quietist views on the MEANS OF GRACE especially distressed WESLEY, who maintained that because of this "a great gulf" was fixed between them. This was widened by the Quakers' formal insistence upon their peculiar and superficial "testimonies" in dress and speech, which Wesley termed "mere superstition."

Nevertheless the Society of Friends did exercise a beneficial influence upon Methodism. In himself insisting upon plain speech and simple dress Wesley acknowledged his debt to the Quakers. The Methodist QUARTERLY MEETING owed at least some of its inspiration (through JOHN BENNET) to the Friends, and they strongly influenced Methodist opposition to the slave traffic, just as Wesley's *Thoughts upon Slavery* was largely an abridgment of Anthony Benezet's *Some Historical Account of Guinea*—an abridgment warmly approved by the original author. Throughout the succeeding generations the Methodists and the Society of Friends have similarly maintained parallel courses, the social witness of Methodism enriched by that of the Friends, and they in turn gaining some warmth and flexibility in their spirituality in part at least from Methodist influences. Rarely, however, have Methodists been able to understand the more mystical aspects of Quaker teaching upon the "inner light," nor Friends to appreciate the sacramental emphasis which the Methodists derived from Wesley.

Frank Baker, *The Relations between the Society of Friends and Early Methodism.* London: Epworth Press, 1949.

FRANK BAKER

QUARTERAGE. The word "quarterage," meaning quarterly payments for the support of the ministry, is used in the 1796 *Discipline,* but it is not found in the book after that date. RICHARD BOARDMAN and probably ROBERT STRAWBRIDGE held quarterly meetings of societies and circuits.

In describing the work in 1772, JESSE LEE said the preachers regulated their business at different quarterly meetings. The quarterage was collected in preparation for the quarterly meetings and it was distributed or paid to the preachers at the meetings. Asbury's *Journal* for Dec. 22, 1772, says that at a quarterly meeting in MARYLAND, "Brother Strawbridge received eight pounds quarterage; brother King and myself six pounds each." Incidentally, that is the earliest known documentary reference to "quarterage" in Methodist writings. In explaining the word "quarterage" Simpson's *Cyclopaedia of Methodism,* published in 1876, says, "on stations and in cities this term is not so generally employed as formerly; but it is still in use on the circuits." Perhaps it is fair to say that as long as presiding elders were required to hold a QUARTERLY CONFERENCE on each charge every three months, and as long as it was the custom to divide the amount raised for the support of the ministry during the preceding quarter on a percentage ratio between the presiding elder and the preacher in charge, apparently the word quarterage was used on some circuits down to the beginning of the twentieth century and a little later.

F. Asbury, *Journal and Letters.* 1958.
Discipline, 1796.
E. S. Bucke, *History of American Methodism.* 1964.
M. Simpson, *Cyclopaedia.* 1878. ALBEA GODBOLD

QUARTERLY CONFERENCE, THE. The Quarterly Conference (renamed by the United Methodist Church in 1968 the Charge Conference) has been the traditional business and governing body of the local charge or station in American Methodism. It has continued to be so to the present time, though it may abrogate its rights in certain important particulars to the OFFICIAL BOARD of the church —or to a Church Conference—should it decide to do so. Recent changes have been made in this Conference—now the Charge Conference—under the Constitution of 1968, but it yet remains the sovereign and controlling body in each local charge.

Apparently called Quarterly Meetings at first in America —as the equivalent body is still called in Britain—in time the name came to be Quarterly Conference instead of Quarterly Meeting. ASBURY and COKE in their *Notes on the Discipline* indicated that the ruling elder, then becoming known as the presiding elder, should always preside at the several Quarterly Conferences under his charge, and this presidency came to be an established rule in Methodism as Quarterly Conferences grew in status and in standing.

The DISTRICT SUPERINTENDENT, however, as the presiding elder is now called, in presiding has no vote since he is not a member. He cannot even resolve a tie if there is a tie vote. In the absence of the district superintendent, an elder "designated by him" is empowered to preside. Sometimes the pastor himself is so designated. The Quarterly Conference is and in general always has been composed of all the traveling, supernumerary, and retired preachers residing within its circuit or charge. To these were added in time local preachers, exhorters, deaconesses, and thus this body has always been fully representative of the ministry. But making up the vast majority of the Quarterly Conference have always been local church lay officials—at first stewards and trustees, but in later years added to them, financial secretaries, treasurers, church school superintendents, and other ex officio members.

In the United Methodist Church, the members of the newly named Administrative Board—who are to all intents practically the same as those formerly known in The Methodist Church as stewards and official board members—now are members of the Charge Conference. The name steward, except that of the district steward, does not appear in the 1968 *Discipline* as the name of a church officer. The members at large of the administrative board are referred to by the *Discipline* of 1968 not as stewards, but as members of this board.

Traditionally no quorum has ever been required for a Quarterly Conference, as the members present at the time and place regularly appointed for a Quarterly Conference constitute a quorum. Occasions have been known where only the district superintendent and the pastor in charge were present, but if proper announcement had been made, a Quarterly Conference could be held and was valid. However, there has been a regulation within recent years that no property can be sold, purchased, nor any lien created upon church property unless ten days' notice has been given of such intent.

Also in a circuit where there are two or more churches, where real or personal property of a separate church is involved, or a merger of churches is to be considered, each local church shall organize a church local conference. This gives a local church a right to represent its own interests apart from the larger church conference of the circuit.

The Quarterly (Charge) Conference has electoral powers. It elects its own members once a year for the succeeding year, except the clerical or ministerial members who belong to the Annual Conference, and this automatically puts them in the Quarterly Conference. It elects stewards, trustees, and church school officials, and the like, though under certain circumstances it may provide for the election of these officials by a formal church conference. In addition to officers of the local church, the Quarterly Conference elects the church's lay representative to the Annual Conference, and to the District Conference when there is one.

For long years in Episcopal Methodism the preacher in charge had the sole right to nominate the lay officials of the church, and since these lay officials made up and make up, as they do now, the majority of the Quarterly Conference, to that extent the pastor exercised potential control of that body. However, in The Methodist Church after 1939, a nominating committee was created to nominate all the officials to be elected by the Quarterly Conference, though the pastor was made chairman of this committee and if there was no committee, he himself was to make all nominations. This power granted the pastor has been greatly criticized and has been so since earliest days of American Methodism. In their *Notes* appended to the *Discipline* of 1796, Bishops Asbury and Coke defended the pastor's right to name the stewards by himself, saying that the pastor was the one who "is

likely to be the best judge of the society at large and of each member in particular." Later on stewards came to be elected by the Quarterly Conference, but as described above, on nomination of the pastor.

The Quarterly Conference formerly had the right to license men to preach, but in The United Methodist Church this right has now been placed for many years in the hands of a committee of ministers headed by the district superintendent. However, no one can be licensed by this ministerial committee unless his Quarterly Conference has nominated or approved him.

In its supervisory powers, the Annual Conference creates many committees which have to do with the ongoing of the work. Up until 1968 certain commissions were obligatory in each local church, and these were to be elected by the Quarterly Conference though they were responsible to the Official Board. This regulation has been somewhat changed, though the Committee on Pastor-Parish Relations, that on Finance, and that on Nominations and Personnel are mandatory.

There can scarcely be a conflict between the Quarterly (Charge) Conference and the Official (Administrative) Board since they are both composed of the same persons and work generally in the same field. The Quarterly Conference, however, presided over by the district superintendent who represents the general Church, is the connectional link between each local church and the general Church. The district superintendent must ask the same questions at every Charge Conference which he asks at any one, and so connectional uniformity is maintained all up and down the line. The Official (Administrative) Board represents a local church only, and without the connectional bond of the Charge Conference may tend to keep the individual church somewhat isolated in its own plans and life. The Charge Conference "is the basic unit in the connectional system of The United Methodist Church." (*Discipline*, P. 144.)

The name Charge Conference was adopted in 1968 for Quarterly Conference in the United Methodist Church. All other Methodist Churches continue to use the name Quarterly Conference, which had been the name since the early days of Asbury. It is understood that each General Conference may make minor alterations in matters of membership, powers and specific duties of this body, as has always been the case, and may revise it at any session as was done in 1968.

Discipline, UMC, 1968.
N. B. Harmon, *Organization*. 1962.   N. B. H.

QUARTERLY REVIEW OF THE UNITED BRETHREN IN CHRIST was authorized by the GENERAL CONFERENCE in 1889. The first issue appeared in January 1890, with J. W. Etter, editor. It began with a circulation of 625 subscribers, but at the end of the quadrennium there were only 152 remaining. In mid-1891 the editor was elected professor of systematic theology in Union Biblical Seminary, Dayton, Ohio. He enlisted the support of his fellow faculty members, so that the General Conference of 1893 gave editorial responsibility to the faculty as a group. However, at the end of the year 1893, the Publishing House discontinued the magazine.

A group of nineteen church leaders organized "The Review Publishing Association" and revived the magazine without losing an issue. GEORGE M. MATHEWS, pastor of First Church, Dayton, voluntarily served as editor without renumeration for the remainder of the quadrennium. The General Conference of 1897 gave official recognition to the magazine with continued supervision by the Review Committee. When Mathews became associate editor of the *Religious Telescope* in 1898, he was replaced as *Review* editor by H. H. FOUT, pastor of Oak Street Church, Dayton.

The publishing house was directed by the 1901 General Conference to take full responsibility of the *Quarterly Review*. H. A. Thompson, associate editor of Sabbath School literature, became the new *Review* editor. In 1902 the magazine was increased to six issues and renamed the *United Brethren Review*. After continued losses, the publishing house discontinued the magazine at the end of 1908.

A. W. Drury, *History of the UB.* 1924.
J. H. Ness, *History of Publishing.* 1966.   JOHN H. NESS, JR.

WILLIAM A. QUAYLE

QUAYLE, WILLIAM ALFRED (1860-1925), American bishop and renowned orator, was born at Parkville, Mo., on June 25, 1860. His father was a miner and both parents were born on the Isle of Man. They had come to the United States in search of opportunities for more comfortable living. They were journeying to the west across MISSOURI when the baby was born a few miles from the KANSAS line. As the child grew he had the physical characteristics and the whimsical imagination of his Manx ancestors and was always proud to think he was a Manxman.

While his father was working in the mines of COLORADO his mother died, and there were years of search for her unmarked grave when he had grown to maturity. As a boy he found a home with a Kansas farmer. He went to BAKER UNIVERSITY at Baldwin, Kan., and there he graduated. Having been licensed to preach, his first pastorate was Osage City, Kan. He was called to the faculty of Baker University, and while he was still a young man, after a few years of teaching, he was elected to the presidency of his alma mater.

In many ways Quayle was a genius, and his preaching as he visited communities in behalf of the University gave him such a reputation that he was sought by large churches. He resigned the presidency of Baker to become pastor of Independence Avenue Church in KANSAS CITY. From there he went to the Meridian Street Church in INDIANAPOLIS. He returned to Kansas City to the pastorate of the Grand Avenue Temple. His fourth large city church was St. James in CHICAGO. He was so brilliantly gifted and such a unique phraser and preacher that one of the Chicago daily papers printed every Monday one of his Sunday sermons. He became a bishop in the M.E. Church in 1908 and served until retirement in 1924.

There was too much individuality in him for him to fit into any pattern, even that of the episcopacy. He was never at home in administrative tasks, but people would journey hundreds of miles to hear him preach at conference. At each conference session he gave a lecture for which tickets were sold for the benefit of some church fund. His famous lecture on "Jean Valjean" is remembered today by hundreds. Another remembered lecture of his was "Napolean Bonaparte—Democrat."

He loved books and acquired a large library. He would deny himself food and raiment to buy valuable books, and there is found today in the library of Baker University one of the most valuable collections of Bibles in the world which he brought together. In his pastorates he used once a month to give a lecture on a literary theme. One of his themes for such lectures in Chicago was "Shakespeare's Heroines." He loved nature, birds, flowers, and trees. This love was a heritage from the ancestors who lived on the picturesque Isle of Man. His descriptions of the beauties of God's out-of-doors were so thrilling that his greatest biographer, MERTON S. RICE, called him "The Skylark of Methodism."

Because of ill health he retired as bishop in 1924, writing to the General Conference, "Mine has been a sunny life, radiant as spring." He died on March 9, 1925.

Dictionary of American Biography.
Methodist Review, September 1925.
Merton S. Rice, *William Alfred Quayle, the Skylark of Methodism.* New York: Abingdon Press, 1928.
C. F. Price, *Who's Who in American Methodism.* 1916.
                                        IVAN LEE HOLT

QUEEN, LOUISE LEATHERWOOD (1923-   ), American lay woman, was born in Haywood County, N. C., on March 9, 1923, the daughter of William Pinckney and Margaret Kirkpatrick Leatherwood. She attended Woman's College of the University of North Carolina, Greensboro, N. C. She was married to Earl Wilson Caldwell (deceased 1947) on June 20, 1942, and to them were born two sons, William Earl and Wayne Wilson. In 1949 she married Kenneth A. Stahl (divorced 1962), and on July 9, 1963, she married Rufus G. Queen, who had two daughters, Pamela June and Dariacia Jan.

Louise Queen was employed as secretary to the Superintendent of Haywood County Public Schools from 1946 to 1951. She then assisted ELMER T. CLARK in setting up his office at Lake Junaluska, N. C., acting as his secretary in the work of the Association of Methodist HISTORICAL SOCIETIES and the WORLD METHODIST COUNCIL until his retirement as executive secretary of those bodies. She continued in the same office under ALBEA GODBOLD, who became executive secretary of the Association of Methodist Historical Societies in 1963, and she is now administrative and editorial assistant to JOHN H. NESS, JR., in the COMMISSION ON ARCHIVES AND HISTORY. She has served as illustration editor and copy editor of this *Encyclopedia,* in addition to preparing the general index for this work.

Mrs. Queen's local church membership is in Long's Chapel United Methodist Church, LAKE JUNALUSKA, where she has held numerous offices. She has served as secretary of the WESLEYAN SERVICE GUILD of the Western North Carolina Annual Conference, and has been active in numerous other church and civic organizations.

QUEEN'S COLLEGE, UNIVERSITY OF MELBOURNE

QUEEN'S COLLEGE, Melbourne, Victoria, Australia. As early as 1855, only a year after the Melbourne University was founded, the idea of a College affiliated with each of the universities of SYDNEY and MELBOURNE found voice in the first Australasian Wesleyan Methodist Conference.

Though ten acres in the University reserve at Carlton had been set aside by the Government for this purpose, over twenty years were to pass before the VICTORIAN AND TASMANIAN CONFERENCE took steps to utilize the concession.

The efforts to found a Central Theological Institution for the whole of Australia, made during subsequent years, broke down, on the matter of finance, and arrangements were made to train the men in existing establishments. In 1871 the Provisional Theological Institution for Victoria and Tasmania was linked up with Wesley College, Melbourne—students going into residence for both general and theological training.

In 1878 the Conference appointed a committee to raise

funds for the purpose of building a College for general educational purposes, and also "if possible to house theological students." W. A. Quick undertook the task of canvassing for money, and by December 1884, was able to report money in hand and promises amounting to £6,370. A small endowment fund was also provided, chiefly from a half share in the land of an earlier Wesleyan Immigrant's Home in Carlton. With further help from the Jubilee Thanksgiving Fund in 1886, the Conference resolved that the College should be erected in the Jubilee year of Queen Victoria's reign and for that reason, be called "Queen's." The foundation stone was laid on June 19, 1887, by His Excellency Sir Henry Brougham (later Lord Loch).

EDWARD HOLDSWORTH SUGDEN, an English Wesleyan minister, was appointed its first master. He arrived with his wife and family to take charge in January 1888. On March 14, 1888, the College was officially opened by the Governor.

The Council appointed by the Conference to administer the affairs of the College, elected W. A. Quick as its first chairman and E. W. Nye as its secretary. Quick was President of the Council for twenty-one years, contributing more than anyone else, outside the master, to the well-being of the College. Its first master, E. H. Sugden, gave outstanding service for forty years, from 1888-1928. He was followed by Rev. Kernwick from 1928-33 and Raynor Johnson from 1934-66. A. E. Albiston was Professor of Theology from 1920-38, followed by Calvert Barber, 1937-59 and Norman Lade, 1959-66.

Although the College was in financial difficulties in its early days, the gifts of many liberal benefactors have enabled it to steadily expand. In 1889 the College had thirteen students; by 1968 there was accommodation for 220 students and ninety non-resident students. Alongside it stands St. Hilda's Methodist-Presbyterian University College for girls.

The Theological Hall (founded 1871) is the organ of the Victorian and Tasmanian Conference charged with the training of men accepted as candidates for the ministry. It is not a separate College, but is associated with Queen's College where almost all of its students are in residence. It is under the direction of a principal, Professor Norman Lade; with whom are associated Professors of Biblical Studies and Systematic Theology. The Methodist Theological Hall works in close collaboration with that of the Presbyterian Church.

When Queen's College was founded the Conference resolved that "such College be made available, as far as practicable, for the training of our Theological students." Efforts were later made to establish a central Theological Institution for the whole of Australia. These broke down, and subsequently the provisional Theological Institution for Victoria and Tasmania was formed and linked, first with Wesley College (1871) and in 1889 with Queen's College. Here the students were under the direction of the Master, E. H. Sugden. In 1892 the Conference set up a separate committee to administer the Theological Institution. In 1920 A. E. Albiston was appointed as Theological tutor (later Professor of Theology) with full oversight of the curriculum of five years, three of which are spent chiefly in University studies and two in the B.D. course of the Melbourne College of Divinity and in other theological and pastoral studies.

AUSTRALIAN EDITORIAL COMMITTEE

QUEENSLAND CONFERENCE, Australia. Methodism in Queensland dates from 1847 when William Moore, Wesleyan Methodist minister from SYDNEY, began services in a hired hall in the main street of BRISBANE, at South Brisbane and in the nearby settlement of Zion Hill. Brisbane was then a struggling township of a few hundred people; today it is the capital city of the State and has a population of over 600,000. In less than a year Moore began the work at the mining township of Ipswich, twenty-five miles west of Brisbane. He was followed by a succession of ministers who established Wesleyan Methodist preaching places wherever possible.

In 1855 AUSTRALIA became an independent Conference with William B. Boyce as President, and headquarters at Sydney, New South Wales. Queensland then became a circuit in the New South Wales District. It was constituted a separate District in 1863. Complete autonomy was attained in 1893 when it became a separate Conference, having thirty ministers. Henry Youngman was the first President.

Its Jubilee was celebrated in 1897. By that time the church was represented in every important center and in a great many small townships throughout the State. There were ninety-four churches and seventy-seven other preaching places; thirty-two ministers and 139 local preachers; 2,742 church members, 18,109 adherents and 101 Sunday schools with 9,337 scholars and 938 teachers. A Thanksgiving Fund of £5,000 was fully subscribed.

The PRIMITIVE METHODIST CHURCH began in Queensland in 1860 under the auspices of the British Conference with W. Colley as minister. The first church was built in Brisbane in 1861. The work spread quickly and widely.

The UNITED METHODIST CHURCH was introduced in 1873, but its activities were limited. The BIBLE CHRISTIANS began in 1886 and soon had several churches in Brisbane and Ipswich. Before the turn of the century the Bible Christians and the United Methodist Church were merged with the Wesleyan Methodist Church. After some years of negotiation the Primitive and Wesleyan Methodist Churches were united in 1898, and HENRY YOUNGMAN was the first President of the Conference.

In 1905 Conference made the first organized effort to provide the ordinances of religion in the scattered communities in the vast inland of the State. A minister, equipped with a horse-drawn wagon, travelled extensively under difficult conditions, visiting the cattle stations, mining camps and sheep properties, conducting services and counselling the people in need.

As a result a number of home mission stations and circuits were created and young ministers appointed to them. Eventually three large mission areas were constituted and sturdy motor vehicles provided, making it possible to patrol thousands of miles and extend a ministry to lonely settlers, shearers, drovers and others.

The Centenary of Methodism in Queensland took place in 1947. The programme included a Crusade for the renewal of the Church and a Thanksgiving Fund of £100,000. The secretaries, C. A. Read and A. W. Preston, visited every circuit and home mission station, conducting evanglistic missions and quickening the interest of the members of the Church in the celebrations. R. S. C. Dingle compiled a history of the Church in Queensland, which was published in a 300-page book entitled *Annals of Achievement.*

At this time there were 126 ministers, 16,000 members of the Church, and 16,279 Sunday school scholars.

The Centenary ushered in an era of prosperity in which many handsome church buildings were erected and new activities introduced. Special emphasis was placed upon Christian education for young people. The programme was carried out in holiday camps, a Training College for Christian workers in Brisbane, in Teacher and Leader training courses, and through the mail bag Sunday school for the children of the inland. The work was under the direction of a succession of gifted ministers—H. A. Denny, H. W. Prouse, T. N. Deller, and I. W. Alcorn.

Statistics for the Queensland Conference as of May 1969, were as follows: 149 ministers in active work; 440 churches; 21,035 members.

The Home Mission Society was formed in 1864 for "the evangelization of Queensland without respect of colour, class or creed." This aim has been pursued persistently and is prominent today. The Society has been responsible for initiating numerous circuits and has provided from its agents many candidates for the ministry. It has been associated directly with the Methodist Inland Mission which is an activity of the General Conference for sending ministers into the vast areas in the central, western and northern parts of the country.

The Methodist work in many new housing settlements has been undertaken by the Society; it has administered hostels for students, homes for underprivileged children and homes for discharged men and women prisoners as well as supplying chaplains for hospitals and public institutions.

It introduced the Order of Deaconesses into the State and undertook the training of young women for the work.

Some of these activities are now conducted independently, while the Society turns its attention to other pressing needs—including a Mission to Aborigines and Islanders in North Queensland. A recent feature of the Home Mission work is its cooperation in new housing areas with the Presbyterian and Congregational Churches. The Society has been administered by a succession of competent superintendents—W. H. Harrison, A. A. Mills, J. A. Pratt, C. A. Read, N. H. Grimmett, and G. D. Smith.

Life Line is an organization which offers help to distressed people twenty-four hours a day. Thousands of men and women with fears and worries, beset by personal and domestic problems are counselled every year under the direction of the Rev. Alan Kidd, who is assisted by scores of voluntary workers. The well-known slogan is "Help is as near as the telephone." This social service enjoys public appreciation and support.

Inland Missions. In 1905 Conference made the first organized effort to minister to the scattered communities in the vast inland of the State. As a result of much sacrificial giving and prayer, a minister equipped with a horse-drawn wagon travelled extensively under difficult conditions over a wide area. This work was developed when young ministers were stationed at strategic centers. Eventually three large Mission areas were constituted. Today ten men with mobile units patrol thousands of square miles to minister to lonely settlers, shearers, drovers and others.

Church Schools. The Queensland Conference conducts six Church Schools in cooperation with the Presbyterian Church, which are administered by the Presbyterian and Methodist Schools' Association. They are Brisbane Boys'

College, Somerville House (girls), Clayfield College (girls), and Moreton Bay Girls' High School in the Brisbane area and Thornburgh College (boys) and Blackheath College (girls) at Charters Towers, North Queensland. They cater to students from primary classes to matriculation and are amongst the most reputable public schools in Australia.

Young People's Department H. A. Denny, first fulltime direction appointed in 1920, began an era of extraordinary development. He introduced teacher and leader training and modern equipment into Sunday schools; began a "Mail-Bag" Sunday school for out-back children; opened a holiday camp at the seaside where thousands of young people have received intensive Christian education at vacation times. There are now eight such camps serving the entire State. A Training College for Christian Workers is conducted by C. D. Alcorn and H. C. Krohn, where nearly 100 are in residence each year. The present Director, I. W. Alcorn, has two ministerial colleagues and one lay assistant. Young people constitute a large and lively part of the Church today. (See also BRISBANE.)

AUSTRALIAN EDITORIAL COMMITTEE

QUETTA, Pakistan. This city is about 550 miles west of Lahore and a similar distance north of Karachi and has train and air connection with both these important cities. There is also rail connection with Zahidan, a Persian frontier town to the West. Quetta is capital of Baluchistan Province, and the Administrative center for the Tribal Area. It has a large, well-organized Cantonment. Not far distant is a fine Thermal Plant completed in 1963-64. Quetta occupies a strategic location in case of an invasion from the West.

Methodist Work: The destructive Quetta earthquake of 1935 demolished the former church building. A temporary building then erected was replaced by the wellbuilt Bethel Church, in 1959. Its pastor, K. L. Peter (who serves also as district superintendent) is supported by the congregation, and his wife is principal of the thriving Primary School which meets in the old temporary church building. A well known and very popular Mission Hospital belonging to the Anglican Church is widely known because of two of its famous eye surgeons, father and son, the Drs. Holland.

CLEMENT ROCKEY

QUILLIAN, JOSEPH DILLARD, JR. (1917-   ), American minister and seminary dean, was born at Buford, Ga., Jan. 30, 1917, the son of Joseph Dillard and Jeannette (Evans) Quillian. He was graduated from Piedmont College, B.A., 1938; VANDERBILT UNIVERSITY, B.D., 1941; Yale University, Ph.D., 1951. On Dec. 15, 1944, he was married to Elizabeth Mary Sampson. Their children are: Suzanne Elizabeth, Alma Jeannette, Mary Shannon, Joseph Dillard III, Ellen Evans.

He was ordained to the ministry of the Congregational Church. In 1943 he was received in full connection and ordained elder in the TENNESSEE CONFERENCE of The Methodist Church. He was pastor of Hillsboro Circuit, Tennessee, 1938-41; NASHVILLE, 1941-42; Stamford, Conn., 1946-50; president of MARTIN COLLEGE, Pulaski, Tenn., 1950-54. In 1954 he went to be professor of worship and preaching at PERKINS SCHOOL OF THEOLOGY,

SOUTHERN METHODIST UNIVERSITY, and since 1960 he has been dean of that institution.

Since 1964 he has served as vice chairman of the Commission on WORSHIP. He served to lieutenant commander as chaplain, U. S. Naval Reserve, 1942-46. He is a member of the Association of Methodist Theological Schools, of the Association of American Theological Schools, and of the Council of Southwestern Theological Schools. He is the author (with H. Grady Hardin and James F. White) of *The Celebration of the Gospel*, 1964.

Who's Who in The Methodist Church, 1966.

J. MARVIN RAST

QUILLIAN, PAUL WHITFIELD (1895-1949), American pastor, was born Dec. 19, 1895, at Conyers, Ga., the son of John W. and Lucy (Zachry) Quillian. He was educated at EMORY COLLEGE, A.B., 1914, and SOUTHERN METHODIST UNIVERSITY, B.D., 1924. HENDRIX COLLEGE and Southern Methodist awarded him the D.D. degree, and FLORIDA SOUTHERN COLLEGE gave him the LL.D. On July 4, 1916, he married Eula Dupree in Sandersville, Ga., and they had one daughter.

After teaching school, 1914-16, Quillian entered business in 1917, and was president of the Arkansas Soft Drink Manufacturers, 1920-21. Feeling the call to preach, he entered the Southern Methodist ministry and was ordained in 1923. His appointments were: Camden, Ark., 1924-27; Winfield, LITTLE ROCK, 1928-32; St. Luke's, OKLAHOMA CITY, 1933-36; and First Church, HOUSTON, Texas, 1936-49. Under his leadership, First Church was then the world's largest Methodist church with 7,800 members and a staff of twenty-five.

Quillian was a delegate to the UNITING CONFERENCE, 1939, and to five GENERAL CONFERENCES, 1934-38, and 1940-48; to the 1947 ECUMENICAL METHODIST CONFERENCE, and to the 1948 Assembly of the WORLD COUNCIL OF CHURCHES. An able pulpit preacher, he served as a member of the National Christian Mission Team, 1941-42, and 1944. He contributed to the American Pulpit Series, 1945-46, and to Best Sermons, 1946.

He served on the Commission on Unification of American Methodism; was chairman of the Committee on Education in the Uniting Conference; and was a trustee of SOUTHWESTERN and DILLARD UNIVERSITIES, and of the Methodist Hospital in Houston. He was a member of the WESLEY FOUNDATION in TEXAS, the General BOARD OF EDUCATION of The Methodist Church, the National Advisory Commission on the Negro College Fund, and the Commission on the resettlement of the Japanese in the United States. He delivered the Thirkield Lectures at GAMMON THEOLOGICAL SEMINARY, 1945. A contributor to religious journals and books, he also wrote church school lesson material.

Quillian received large votes for the episcopacy in 1938, 1944, and 1948. In the latter year at the SOUTH CENTRAL JURISDICTIONAL CONFERENCE, he was one of the chief contenders for twenty-six ballots, after which he graciously withdrew. Since he had a brilliant mind and was an excellent preacher and an able administrator, many in the church were surprised that he was never elected a bishop. Bishop PAUL E. MARTIN said, "Paul Quillian was one of the most brilliant and dedicated men the Methodist Church has ever had . . . he was a great administrator, a gifted minister and a wise counselor."

Quillian died suddenly of a heart attack in Houston, March 28, 1949.

C. T. Howell, *Prominent Personalities.* 1945.
Who Was Who in America, 1942-1950.   ALBEA GODBOLD

QUILLIAN, WILLIAM FLETCHER (1880-1960), American college president and church executive, was born on Dec. 21, 1880, at Lithonia, Ga., the son of William Fletcher and Lucy Ann (Vail) Quillian. EMORY COLLEGE gave him the A.B. degree in 1901, the D.D. in 1921; at VANDERBILT he took post graduate courses, 1912-14. SOUTHERN METHODIST UNIVERSITY granted him the LL.D in 1931.

He married Nonie Acree on June 1, 1910, and their children are William Fletcher, Jr. (president, RANDOLPH-MACON WOMAN'S COLLEGE), Christine Mason (Mrs. Hubert Searcy).

Quillian, after serving in various posts including being missionary to MEXICO and editor of the *El Educaudo,* 1907-11, became president of WESLEYAN COLLEGE, Macon, Ga., 1920-31, at which time he became general secretary of the General Board of Christian EDUCATION of the M.E. Church, South. In 1940, upon Methodist union, he was elected Cultivation Secretary of the Board of MISSIONS and Church Extension of The Methodist Church and resided in NEW YORK from 1940-44. In that year he was elected executive secretary of the SOUTH-EASTERN JURISDICTION and moved to ATLANTA, Ga. Upon the sudden death of the president of Wesleyan College at Macon, in October 1950, Quillian acted again as president of that institution until the new president was elected and assumed charge in January 1952. During this time he commuted between Macon and Atlanta, continuing to hold his position as Executive Secretary of the Southeastern Jurisdiction. He occupied this position until his retirement in June 1952.

Quillian was a member of the GENERAL CONFERENCE of the M.E. Church, South, 1922, '26, '30, '34 and '38, and of The Methodist Church, 1940 and '44, representing the SOUTH GEORGIA CONFERENCE. He was also a member of the Uniting Conference in 1939.

He was on the Executive Committee of the FEDERAL COUNCIL OF CHURCHES, 1940, and of the ECUMENICAL METHODIST COUNCIL, 1930. He wrote *A New Day for Historic Wesleyan,* 1928; *Christ and the Coming Kingdom,* 1932.

On his retirement he continued to live in Atlanta, with a summer residence at LAKE JUNALUSKA, N. C. He enjoyed the complete confidence of his compeers in both the educational and executive world of American Methodism.

He died in Atlanta on Oct. 26, 1960.

C. T. Howell, *Prominent Personalities.* 1945.
C. F. Price, *Who's Who in American Methodism.* 1916.
N. B. H.

QUIMBY, SILAS EVERARD (1837-1913), American clergyman, was born in Haverhill, N. H., Oct. 19, 1837, the son of Silas and Penelope C. (Fifield) Quimby. Under the inspiration and guidance of his preacher father, Quimby made a public profession of his faith when he was fourteen years of age, and united with the M.E. Church at Unity, N. H., in 1852. He then attended TILTON SEMINARY, where his father had been a trustee

since its founding in 1845. He later attended WESLEYAN UNIVERSITY and graduated there in 1859.

Taking up the teaching profession, he taught Greek and Latin in the Newbury Seminary in VERMONT, and while there he went into the VERMONT CONFERENCE on trial and was ordained deacon by Bishop OSMON C. BAKER in April 1862. In 1863 he was transferred on trial to the NEW HAMPSHIRE CONFERENCE and stationed at Littleton, N. H. The next year he was again assigned to a professorship at Newbury Seminary. In 1866 he was ordained elder and received into full connection at Keene, N. H., by Bishop MATTHEW SIMPSON and was appointed president of Newbury Seminary.

When plans were made to transfer the school to Montpelier, Vt., Quimby was appointed to Lebanon, N. H., where he served two years. In 1869-70 he was appointed to Plymouth; 1871-73, Exeter; 1874-76, Sunapee. In 1877 he was appointed to Tilton, but the next year when the president of Tilton Seminary died, Quimby was sought to replace him. He held that office for seven years, 1878-85, during which time he raised the standard of the institution, organized the scientific department, instituted a special course of study in industrial science, and added a year to the course in preparation for college. During these years a spirit of revival was manifested among the students.

Resuming the pastorate, Quimby served the following New Hampshire appointments: Whitefield, 1886-87; Laconia, 1888-89; Newmarket, 1890; Exeter, 1891-93; Rochester, 1894; Penacook, 1895-96; Pleasant Street, Salem, 1897-1900; Conference evangelist, 1901; Milton Mills, 1902-03; Derry, 1904-07; Conference evangelist, 1908-12.

Silas Quimby was one of the great men of the New Hampshire Conference. He was twice elected delegate to the GENERAL CONFERENCE, 1880 and 1896; was for thirty-four years secretary of the New Hampshire Conference, 1877-1910; was a trustee of Tilton Seminary from 1871 until his death; and was recognized by SYRACUSE UNIVERSITY in 1910 with the D.D. degree.

He died on Feb. 23, 1913, at the home of his daughter in Bellefont, Pa., and was buried in Tilton, N. H.

Journal of the New Hampshire Conference, 1913.
WILLIAM J. DAVIS

QUINCY, PENNSYLVANIA, U.S.A. **Quincy E.U.B. Orphanage and Home** originated under the UNITED BRETHREN IN CHRIST, was incorporated Aug. 2, 1902, and started operation in 1903 in the farm home of Henry J. and Henrietta Middour Kitzmiller, who gave the home and 164 acres of land. Kitzmiller became the first superintendent and served until Jan. 25, 1936. Originally the home was opened only to children, and during the earlier half of the operation cared for as many as 155 youngsters at one time.

Z. A. Colestock opened his home in Mechanicsburg, Pa., to retirement residents early in the century as the first such home in the denomination. By 1913 it became evident that age would no longer permit him to care for those whom he served. Approaches were made and a building built, and in 1915 the Colestock residents became the first eleven occupants in the retirement section on the Quincy campus. The original capacity was thirty. Retirement population was increased by new buildings in 1927, 1954, 1961, 1963, and 1966, and today on the

Quincy campus and in the new Lititz, Pa. off-campus unit, Quincy Home is caring for 175 senior citizens.

At the inception of the retirement section of Quincy all programs were quite conservative, and all residents entered on what today is known as "life care." Applicants turned over to the home all assets and then the home accepted responsibility for the care of the person for the remainder of life. Today there is Plan II for persons with insufficient resources to meet the cost of care, and support is available to the resident from the State.

Care Programs today cover a much more complete medical and infirmary service, improved food service, recreation and activity facilities and direction, increased safety standards, higher staff ratio, and higher wages across the board. Some of these are dictated by the state and some by the times, and most are specific improvements and necessary; but they mark, in the history of the benevolent home, a move from a place to stay and be fed only, to a way of total life experience. The great increase in costs for such care in recent years has caused a great deal of concern for each applicant, as well as for the home administration, in working out equitable solutions for the retirement residents entering Quincy, or other homes.

S. FRED CHRISTMAN

JAMES QUINN

QUINN, JAMES (1775-1847), American preacher was born in Washington County, Pa., where his parents were among the earliest settlers west of the Appalachian mountains. In 1786 the family was received into one of the Methodist Societies of the REDSTONE CIRCUIT and the five children were baptized, James being the oldest. James was admitted to the BALTIMORE CONFERENCE in 1799. He married Patience Teal in 1803 and in 1804 followed his father-in-law, Edward Teal, to near Lancaster, Ohio. He served in OHIO, in the WESTERN CONFERENCE, until the OHIO CONFERENCE was organized in 1812. When the PITTSBURGH CONFERENCE was organized in 1825 he remained with the Ohio Conference. Much of his service, before 1825, had been in that portion of Ohio which was included in the original Pittsburgh Conference. James Quinn was a circuit rider for twenty-two years and a presiding elder for twelve years. He was a delegate to seven GENERAL CONFERENCES. John F. Wright of the Ohio Conference published a biography of Quinn in 1851 titled, *Sketches of the Life and Labors of James Quinn.* The volume incorporates a considerable section of autobiographical material written by Quinn himself and is a valuable portrait of early Methodism in western Pennsylvania and eastern Ohio.

W. G. Smeltzer, *Headwaters of the Ohio.* 1951.
John F. Wright, *Sketches of the Life and Labors of James Quinn.* Cincinnati: Methodist Book Concern, 1851.

W. GUY SMELTZER

QUINN, WILLIAM PAUL (ca. 1788-1873), American bishop of the A.M.E. CHURCH and instigator of the home missions movement in African Methodism, was born in Honduras, Central America, about 1788 of Roman Catholic parentage. He was taken to the United States at an early age, converted in 1808 in Bucks County, Pa., licensed to preach in 1812, and admitted in the Philadelphia Conference of the A.M.E. Church in 1816. He was ordained DEACON in 1818, but was not ordained ELDER until 1838.

Quinn, who was present at the organizing convention of the denomination at PHILADELPHIA in 1816, held pastorates in NEW JERSEY and PENNSYLVANIA before embarking on a missionary itinerary during which he founded seventy-two new congregations and organized forty-seven churches west of the Allegheny Mountains in OHIO, INDIANA, MICHIGAN, ILLINOIS, KENTUCKY, and MISSOURI between 1840 and 1844.

He was elected assistant bishop in 1841 and bishop in 1844. He died on Feb. 3, 1873, after having served the longest term as senior bishop in the denomination up until that time.

GRANT S. SHOCKLEY

RACE, JOHN H. (1862-1954), American preacher, educator, and publishing agent, was born at Paupack, Pa., on March 6, 1862. In 1858 his father, Ernest Race, came from England and settled within the boundaries of the WYOMING CONFERENCE.

As a young man, John H. Race thought of business as a career and took a position in a planing mill, where in an accident, he lost his left hand. This misfortune marked a turning point in his life. He entered Wyoming Seminary, where under the influence of LEVI L. SPRAGUE, he decided to enter the ministry and prepared for Princeton University. On graduation from college in 1890, he returned to Wyoming Seminary, where he taught in the English department for two years. Then he was sent to Centenary Church, Binghamton, N. Y.

In 1898 he became chancellor of Grant University in CHATTANOOGA, Tenn. During his administration the name was changed to Chattanooga University.

In 1913 the BOOK COMMITTEE of the M.E. Church elected him as one of the publishing agents of the BOOK CONCERN in CINCINNATI, Ohio. In June 1924, he was transferred to NEW YORK CITY, where he served as Senior Publishing Agent until his voluntary retirement in 1936 at which time he was elected Publishing Agent Emeritus by the GENERAL CONFERENCE.

He was a trustee of Wyoming Seminary from 1914 until the date of his death.

Leroy E. Bugbee, *Wyoming Seminary, 1844-1944.* N.p., n.d.
Minutes of the Wyoming Conference.   WILBUR H. FLECK

RADER, DANIEL LEAPER (1850-1910), American pioneer minister, was born Aug. 27, 1850, in Rose Hill, Johnson Co., Mo. He was converted in 1864, after his family had moved to Salina County, where, since there was no Methodist organization, Daniel joined the Presbyterian church. He studied under a Presbyterian minister before attending Shelbyville High School for two years, and after this he taught school briefly.

In 1866, he joined the M.E. Church, South; and, in 1871, became a minister and a member of the SOUTHWEST MISSOURI CONFERENCE of that church. He was immediately placed in charge of the Oskaloosa Circuit in KANSAS. Shortly thereafter he was sent to the Broadway M.E. Church, South, in Leavenworth, and then to Council Grove in 1873. He married Eugenia Shackelford on Sept. 18, 1872.

Returning to MISSOURI, Rader developed a respiratory ailment which compelled him to move to COLORADO in 1879. After a rest of more than two years he joined the DENVER CONFERENCE and was made presiding elder of the Denver District, a task he prosecuted with great vigor. Under his leadership, southern Methodism was established in the remote towns of Grand Junction and Fruita, substantially in advance of the work of the northern church.

Feeling that there was no need for two Methodisms in Colorado, he sought to transfer to the M.E. Church. The southern church, however, was unwilling to grant this request, so D. L. Rader located in 1885, and then entered the Colorado Conference of the northern church. Appointed at first to Cheyenne, Wyo., he became in 1888 the first superintendent of the Wyoming Mission Conference. Again, he distinguished himself, pushing the work of the church into the most isolated portions of the area assigned to him.

Later (1892), he became presiding elder of the Pueblo District of the Colorado Conference, and still later was associated with *The Rocky Mountain Advocate*, published briefly in DENVER. He was serving as editor of *The Pacific Advocate* at the time of his death in 1910.

I. H. Beardsley, *Echoes from Peak and Plain.* 1898.
Journal of the Puget Sound Conference, ME, 1911.
WALTER J. BOIGEGRAIN

RADHAKRISHAN, JOHN (1916-   ), is a minister in INDIA. He was born in an orthodox, priestly Brahman home, and was taught Brahmanic rites and discipline in his home. He attended a high school maintained by the Arya Samaj, did his undergraduate studies in a college run by an atheistic society, and did postgraduate studies in a Muslim college.

He developed an intense interest in religion, questioning and eventually rejecting the daily worship of gods and goddesses. His college principal, who was the founder of the atheistic society, hoped that he would join that organization. But Radhakrishan was led (in some way) to obtain a Bible for his own personal study. His first reaction was very unfavorable. He had begun his study with Genesis. With much difficulty, he met a Christian minister who advised him to study the New Testament. After two years of desultory reading, he developed a new and great interest in Christianity. He was nearing graduation, when he met a woman missionary who talked Hindustani beautifully and explained many passages that had puzzled him. Seeing his contact with Christians, many Hindus expressed shocked surprise that he would even consider becoming a Christian. On completing his B.A. examinations, he declared his Christian faith and was baptized. After gaining his Master's degree and teaching for three years in a Christian college, he was sent by the Presbyterian mission to Leonard Theological College and graduated at the head of his class.

Since there was no Presbyterian opening when John Radhakrishan completed his studies, he sought and obtained an appointment in a Methodist high school as warden of the hostel for Christian students. A call was made for CHAPLAINS to serve the needs of Christian troops in the army of India, and he volunteered. He was ordained and served as chaplain for five years. He then became a teacher in the BAREILLY Theological Seminary.

In 1949, he was awarded a scholarship for advanced study in the United States. He was accepted by BOSTON UNIVERSITY SCHOOL OF THEOLOGY as a candidate for the Doctor of Theology degree and was awarded that degree in the shortest possible time. His thesis on The Bhagavad-Gita and the Fourth Gospel was highly acclaimed. Again he went to Bareilly Seminary, but a year later he was appointed superintendent of the Shahjahanpur District, where he served for four years. In 1955, he was appointed to a professorship in Leonard Theological College. In March 1966, he became principal of the college. He is a member of the Faith and Order Commission of the WORLD COUNCIL OF CHURCHES, a member of the executive Committee of the National Christian Council's Board of Theological Education, vice-president of the Madhya Pradesh Christian Council, and a member of the CENTRAL CONFERENCE Commission on the Structure of Methodism and on Church Union. He has written many articles for church papers on India and abroad.

Minutes of the North India Conference, 1937-68.

J. WASKOM PICKETT

RAGSDALE, RAY WALDO (1909-   ), American minister, city pastor and church leader, was born at Washington, Ind., on Aug. 22, 1909, the son of Tilman L. and Clara E. (Johnson) Ragsdale. He was educated at DEPAUW UNIVERSITY, receiving the B.A. in 1931 and the D.D. in 1955; BOSTON UNIVERSITY, S.T.B., 1934; and the D.D. from the UNIVERSITY OF THE PACIFIC in 1951. He married Eleanor Hughes on Aug. 9, 1931, and they had two children.

He was admitted on trial in the INDIANA CONFERENCE in 1928 and after full ordination as elder in 1934, transferred to the west where he was pastor at Holbrook, Ariz., 1934-36; Flagstaff, Ariz., 1936-40; Fullerton, Calif., 1940-47; Westwood Church, Los ANGELES, Calif., 1947-54; superintendent of the Los Angeles District, 1954-60; pastor of the First Church, Whittier, Calif., 1960-63; and is presently at the Catalina Church, TUCSON, Ariz. He has been a delegate to the WESTERN JURISDICTIONAL CONFERENCE, 1944 to 1964 inclusive; and a member of the GENERAL CONFERENCE, 1952 to 1964 inclusive. At the General Conference of 1960, he was the "chairman of chairmen" of the various legislative committees, and thus the director of the presentation of all legislation of the Conference. He has been a member of the executive committee of the General Board of EVANGELISM, 1946-64; of the WORLD COUNCIL OF CHURCHES, Central Committee, Nyborg, Denmark, 1958; a delegate to the third Assembly of the World Council of Churches at New Delhi, India, 1961. He is a trustee of the Methodist SCHOOL OF THEOLOGY AT CLAREMONT, Calif. He is the author of *Self Help for Church Members* and *The Work of the Official Board.*

Who's Who in the Methodist Church, 1966.   N. B. H.

RAGSDALE, THOMAS CHARLTON (1863-1945), American pastor, was born Dec. 26, 1863, in Laurens County, S. C., the son of E. C. and Elizabeth Calhoun Ragsdale. While Thomas was still a child, the family moved to TEXAS. In 1888 he was admitted to the NORTHWEST TEXAS CONFERENCE and was appointed in succession to Temple, Cisco, and Missouri Avenue Church in Fort Worth. He married and had five children. The writer of his memoir

does not mention his education. It is known that in mature life he was awarded an honorary D.D. degree.

In 1894 Ragsdale transferred to the TENNESSEE CONFERENCE, and in the next forty-five years served thirteen appointments: Fayetteville, West Nashville, Madison Street in Clarksville, West End in NASHVILLE, Murfreesboro, Pulaski, McKendree and Tulip Street in Nashville, Murfreesboro District, Nashville District, East End in Nashville, Springfield, and Dickson. An able preacher with a good sense of humor, it was said that he served more leading churches in Nashville than any other preacher in his day. He was a member of the 1922 and 1926 GENERAL CONFERENCES, leading his conference delegation both times. After his retirement in 1939, Ragsdale lived at Springfield, Tenn. He died there, Dec. 22, 1945.

Cullen T. Carter, *Methodist Leaders in the Old Jerusalem Conference, 1812-1962.*
General Minutes, MECS, and MC.
Minutes of the Tennessee Conference, 1946. ALBEA GODBOLD

RAHATOR, SAMUEL (1866-1936), Indian minister, was born at Nasik, Western INDIA, and was converted at a mission conducted by Major Campbell of the Royal Engineers, 1885. Immediately Rahator gave up his work as a clerk on the railways and moved into the *chawls* (slums) of BOMBAY. He was accepted for the ministry in 1892; his work falls into three parts: in 1892-1911 in the slums of Bombay, where he founded the Marathi Methodist Church, opened orphanages, and often mediated in Hindu-Muslim disputes; in 1911-25, when he trekked through the Maharashtra villages beyond Nasik, and opened up the country circuit of the Methodist Marathi Mission under the Wesleyan METHODIST MISSIONARY SOCIETY; and in 1925-36 when, at the government's request, he worked among the criminal tribes in Maharashtra and helped to resettle many of them in Bombay. The first Indian minister to undertake pioneer missionary work to his own people under British Methodism, he died in Bombay, April 13, 1936.

CYRIL J. DAVEY

RAIKES, ROBERT (1735-1811), Sunday school promoter, was born in Gloucester, England, Sept. 14, 1735. He was the son of the proprietor of the *Gloucester Journal,* founded in 1722, and on his father's death in 1757 succeeded to the business. Raikes was a humanitarian member of the Church of England, but seems to have had very few direct links with the Methodist societies. HANNAH BALL had founded a SUNDAY SCHOOL at High Wycombe in 1769, and several years later Thomas Stock began one at Ashbury, Berkshire. Stock moved to Gloucester, and Raikes cooperated with him, in July 1780 opening his own Sunday school in the parish of St. Mary le Crypt, where GEORGE WHITEFIELD had been born and educated. One of the earliest Sunday school teachers employed and paid by Raikes later married the Methodist preacher SAMUEL BRADBURN. In November 1783 Raikes inserted in his *Gloucester Journal* a long letter describing the work of the Sunday school. This was reprinted in the *Gentleman's Magazine* for June 1784, and may be regarded as the beginning of the widespread Sunday school movement. JOHN WESLEY's *Journal* for July 18, 1784 describes his visit to a recently founded Sunday school in Bingley,

Yorkshire, noting: "I find these schools springing up wherever I go. Perhaps God may have a deeper end therein than men are aware of. Who knows but some of these schools may become nurseries for Christians?" In his *Arminian Magazine* for January 1785, Wesley printed an independent account by Raikes of the beginning of the Gloucester experiment. Raikes never claimed to be the founder of Sunday schools, though this title was accorded to him by Samuel Bradburn and others, but his advocacy undoubtedly led to their almost universal adoption.

Dictionary of National Biography.
Methodist Magazine, 1868, pp. 438-48.   FRANK BAKER

RICHARD C. RAINES

RAINES, RICHARD CAMPBELL (1898-   ), American bishop, was born at Independence, Iowa, Dec. 23, 1898. He was the son of Robert Bielby and Cora Belle (Curtis) Raines. He was educated at CORNELL COLLEGE, A.B., 1920; D.D., 1931; BOSTON UNIVERSITY, S.T.B., 1924, S.T.D., 1950; at Oxford University, 1924-25. He holds a number of honorary degrees including the LL.D. from Yonsei University, SEOUL, KOREA, in 1958. He married Lucille Marguerite Arnold on July 14, 1920, and their children are Rose Lucille, Robert Arnold, Richard Campbell and John Curtis.

He was ordained to the ministry of the M.E. Church in 1926, and after serving brief pastorates in MASSACHUSETTS and the Mathewson Street Church in PROVIDENCE, R. I., 1927-30, went to the Hennepin Avenue Church, MINNEAPOLIS, as pastor. There he served from 1930 to 1948 when he was elected bishop of The Methodist Church by the NORTHEASTERN JURISDICTION meeting that year. Bishop Raines was then assigned to the INDIANA Area of The Methodist Church, and was reassigned to this area for five quadrennia until he retired in 1968.

He was a delegate to the General and Jurisdictional Conferences of the Church, 1948; to the WORLD COUNCIL OF CHURCHES in Amsterdam in that same year; to the World Council of Churches in Evanston, 1954; to the WORLD METHODIST CONFERENCE at Lake Junaluska in 1956, and to the World Council of Churches, New Delhi, India. He served upon the COMMISSION ON THE STRUC-

TURE OF METHODISM OVERSEAS (COSMOS) 1956-64. He was one of the consultants to the Commission on WORSHIP for the revision of the Methodist Hymnal in 1960-64; member of the Commission on CHAPLAINS; of the Commission on Camp Activities; of the Executive Committee of the World Methodist Council; and of the Assembly of the World Council of Churches. He served as president of the Division of World Missions of the Board of MISSIONS of The Methodist Church, 1952-60; and as president of the Board of Missions, 1960-64. He was also the chairman of the Commission on PUBLIC RELATIONS AND METHODIST INFORMATION of The Methodist Church 1952-60.

Bishop Raines has been a trustee of Cornell College, Iowa; DEPAUW UNIVERSITY; and was in demand as a lecturer at various institutions of learning.

Bishop Raines was the first bishop to appoint a fulltime administrative assistant, which type of appointment later became a common and helpful procedure in many areas. He established the first full-time area program of public relations, and the first area program of pastoral care and counseling. He served as president of the COUNCIL OF BISHOPS of The Methodist Church, 1966.

His episcopal travel included two visits to South America in 1946, and 1963; and he was liaison bishop between American and Korean Methodists, 1952-60. He made an around the world tour, stopping in KOREA, while Korean churches were being rebuilt. In 1952 he visited Korea, JAPAN, and FORMOSA, conducting a series of seminars for chaplains in Japan and Korea on the invitation of the Chief of Chaplains' of the United States Army. He was also in Korea in 1954 and 1955, in Africa and the Near East in the same year, and in the spring of 1957, Korea and Japan.

Since retirement he and his wife reside in Pompano Beach, Fla. He has been assigned by the Council of Bishops to work in the area of recruitment.

Who's Who in America, Vol. 34.
Who's Who in the Methodist Church, 1966.   N. B. H.

RAIWIND CHRISTIAN INSTITUTE, Raiwind, Pakistan, is twenty-one miles south of Lahore. There are two departments included in the Institute. The high school has an enrollment of about 450. Of the twenty-five taking the final government examination in the high school graduating class of 1964, only one failed to pass. The high school enrollment is 427 of whom 351 are Christian. Fifty-three of these are girls. The second Department is the Training Class, preparing high school graduates to become teachers in primary schools, urban or rural. It is a one-year course finishing up with a government examination, and those passing receive a teaching certificate. This institute is the only approved non-Government training institution. Reporting the examination results conducted by government and noting that out of the 152 candidates for the high school and the Teacher's Training examinations only one failed, Inayet S. Mall, the capable principal, remarked: "These fine results bear testimony to the team work of the teaching staff."

CLEMENT D. ROCKEY

RAKENA, PIRIPI (c. 1860-1934), outstanding NEW ZEALAND Methodist Maori minister, was trained at Wesley College, Three Kings. Accepted for the ministry in 1882, he spent nearly the whole of his years in the ministry working among his own people at Mangamuka in the Hokianga district. He was noted as an effective temperance advocate, and for his eagerness in teaching his people the value of music in public worship.

New Zealand Methodist Conference Minutes, 1934.

L. R. M. GILMORE

RALEIGH, NORTH CAROLINA, U.S.A. FRANCIS ASBURY and JESSE LEE preached in Wake County, N. C., in 1780, twelve years before the city of Raleigh was founded as the capital of the state. JOHN KING, the first Methodist preacher to reside in the county, came there about 1790. A Scotsman, WILLIAM GLENDENNING, is credited with introducing Methodism into the village of Raleigh in 1799, and although he was not ordained, Glendenning built his own house of worship, thought by some historians to have been non-denominational, and officiated at its altar. Bishop Asbury preached at the North Carolina State House in Raleigh in 1800 and, assisted by Bishop WILLIAM McKENDREE, presided at the first Methodist conference held in Raleigh in 1811. Following this conference, the present-day Edenton Street Church was organized, although no specific date for its founding can be determined. The Raleigh Circuit was formed in 1807 by action of the VIRGINIA ANNUAL CONFERENCE of the M.E. Church which met in New Bern, N. C., and three years later the Raleigh District was established. Ten years later the Edenton Street Church became a separate station. Bishop Asbury last visited Raleigh in 1816. A mission chapel, later known as the "Central Church," was built in 1846 under the leadership of Bennet T. Blake, who also conducted a female seminary. Prior to 1852, when a PARSONAGE was first provided, Methodist ministers in Raleigh were obliged to room and board in the town. In 1849 the congregation of St. Paul's A.M.E. CHURCH was formed as an outgrowth of the Edenton Street Church. This congregation purchased its own church site in 1853 and since that date has served as the parent of several other Negro Methodist churches organized in Raleigh.

The NORTH CAROLINA CONFERENCE of the M.E. Church was organized in 1837 and met in Raleigh in October 1841. Following the establishment of the North Carolina Conference of the M.E. Church, South, annual conferences were held in Raleigh in 1853, 1862, 1865, 1874, 1882, 1897, 1909, 1922, 1927, 1937. Following the unification of the three major branches of Methodism in 1939, the North Carolina Annual Conference has been held in Raleigh in 1944, 1954, and 1965.

The Methodist Home for Children, supported by the North Carolina Conference, was established between Glenwood Avenue and St. Mary's Street, in 1899.

Raleigh Methodist churches in existence today are: Jenkins Memorial, established in 1907 from the former Brooklyn Church, which was established in 1878; Fairmont and Hayes Barton, both established in 1937; Person Street, established in 1939 from the Central Church which was established in 1846; and Epworth Church, established in 1893. Since 1945 the following new churches have been organized in Raleigh: Layden Memorial, Wesley Memorial, Westover, Highland, Longview, St. Mark, Cokesbury, Trinity, St. James, Wynnewood Park, Macedonia, Millbrook, Pleasant Grove. The Benson Memorial Church, located just outside the city limits, was organized in 1965.

For more than a quarter of a century, Raleigh has been the residence of the district superintendent of the Raleigh District. Following the SOUTHEASTERN JURISDICTIONAL CONFERENCE of 1964, it also became the episcopal residence of the Raleigh Area, including fifty-six eastern North Carolina counties.

On April 29, 1962, Bishop GARBER, president-elect of the COUNCIL OF BISHOPS, presided at the consecration of "The Methodist Building" on Glenwood Avenue. This building houses the bishop's offices and serves as the headquarters for the various boards and agencies of the North Carolina Conference.

In 1970 there were nineteen United Methodist churches in Raleigh, reporting a total membership of 14,230.

Edenton Street Church is the oldest congregation in North Carolina's capital city, and the present structure stands on the same spot Methodism has occupied in Raleigh since 1811.

In 1831 MELVILLE COX, its pastor, left to go to LIBERIA as a missionary. For several years the church has supported several missionaries on the foreign fields.

The original church building was destroyed by fire in 1839, and replaced in 1841. In 1881 a church school building was erected, and the sanctuary was torn down and replaced by a larger structure. In 1912 a new Christian education building was erected, which stood until 1937, when it was replaced by the present Poindexter Memorial Building. The sanctuary was renovated and enlarged in 1950-51, but it was destroyed by fire July 28, 1956. On Feb. 2, 1958, a new sanctuary, a distinctive new building, yet one in the spirit and form of the old building, was opened for worship.

BRAXTON CRAVEN, who served Edenton Street in 1864-65, commanded the Confederate Military Post at Salemburg and in the fall of 1865 became the president of Trinity College (now DUKE UNIVERSITY) until 1882. WILLIAM WALTER PEELE, who served the church from 1918-23, was elected bishop in 1938, the only minister of Edenton Street to become a bishop and the only native North Carolinian to enter the episcopacy from this state.

Among the prominent laymen who have been identified with Edenton Street Church were: JOSEPHEUS DANIELS, secretary of the Navy, 1913-21, and Ambassador to Mexico, 1933-42; and Willis Smith, president of the American Bar Association, 1945-46, and U. S. Senator, 1950-53. Although not a member of the church, Governor Clyde R. Hoey of Shelby, N. C., served as teacher of the Men's Bible Class during his gubernatorial administration, 1937-41.

The 200-foot, cross-tipped spire of Edenton Street Church is a prominent Raleigh landmark. Only two blocks from the Capitol Square and the principal downtown business district, this church continues to serve North Carolina's capital city. In 1970 it reported 3,339 members.

Methodist Home for Children is a multi-service agency for the care of orphan, dependent, and neglected children. It is owned, operated, controlled and financially supported by the North Carolina Conference of The United Methodist Church.

In 1873 the North Carolina Conference adopted a resolution authorizing the churches to raise money to assist the Masonic Orphanage at Oxford to care for orphan children, many of whom came from Methodist families. In 1898 the Conference decided to establish its own orphanage. As a result a corporation entitled "Trustees of the Methodist Orphanage" was incorporated by an act of the

State Legislature in 1899. A site was purchased in the city of Raleigh, the state capital. J. W. Jenkins was elected the first superintendent. J. B. Hurley was appointed "agent" to solicit money from the Sunday schools and churches of the conference. The first children were admitted in January 1901. In 1955 the name of the agency was changed from "Methodist Orphanage" to "Methodist Home for Children."

The Methodist Home, with a plant valued in excess of $1,600,000, occupies a sixty acre campus within easy walking distance of schools, churches and shopping areas. Children of school age, both boys and girls, may be served in group care at one time. Younger children are placed in foster homes. A competent staff provides professionally trained workers in social service, health, education and religion. Children attend public schools, go to a community church, participate in community life and live in family type cottages under the supervision of houseparents. The home cares for 150 children.

L. S. Burkhead, ed., *Centennial of Methodism in North Carolina.* Raleigh, 1876.
Edenton Street in Methodism, a memorial book published by Edenton Street Church, Raleigh, 1961.
General Minutes.
Journal of the North Carolina Conference.

RALPH HARDEE RIVES
GRADY L. E. CARROLL
H. ARTHUR PHILLIPS
J. W. LINEBERGER, SR.

RALEY, GEORGE HENRY (1864-1958), Canadian Methodist and United Church of Canada minister, was born in Yorkshire, England, on Feb. 14, 1864, and came to Canada in 1882. He was received on probation for the ministry in 1884 by the Bay of Quinte Conference, and ordained in 1889. On May 12, 1890 Raley married Maude Giles of Brockville, Ontario. After four years in Ontario pastorates, Raley volunteered for Indian work and came to British Columbia in 1893. He was the first ordained missionary in the northern village of Kitamat, one of the most isolated spots on the coast. During his thirteen years there, he served in many capacities—Christian minister, postmaster, lay doctor, justice of the peace, and trusted counselor. By taking a number of orphaned boys and girls into their home, the Raleys began what was to become the Elizabeth Long Memorial Home, a residential school.

Raley quickly mastered the language of the Kitamats, as well as other northern Indian dialects. He compiled the first dictionary. With a small hand press he turned out, in 1896, the North Coast's first newspaper, called *Nanakwa* (The Dawn). Raley also established the first meteorological station in northern British Columbia.

In 1906, he was transferred to Port Simpson—a large Indian village some thirty miles north of Prince Rupert. While here, he rebuilt the historic church after a fire. It had been built first by the veteran missionary, THOMAS CROSBY. A new mission house was also erected. After eight years at Port Simpson, Raley was appointed to the principalship of Coqualeetza Residential School at Sardis, B. C., an office he filled with distinction until his retirement in 1934.

In 1912 he was president of the Conference of British Columbia. He held a D.D. degree from Union College of British Columbia, as well as fellowships in the Royal Geographical Society and the Royal Society of Arts. He died in Vancouver on Sept. 14, 1958.

Raley wrote profusely. His writings covered almost every phase of Indian life, legend, and culture, on which he was a recognized authority. He was a collector of choice specimens of native art. His collection, said to be one of the finest in the province, now belongs to the University of British Columbia.

Records of the conference of British Columbia.
Mrs. F. C. Stephenson, *Canadian Methodist Missions.* 1925.
W. P. BUNT

RALL, HARRIS FRANKLIN (1870-1964), American theologian, was born at Council Bluffs, Iowa, Feb. 23, 1870, the son of a minister in the EVANGELICAL ASSOCIATION. He was a graduate of University of Iowa, and of the Divinity School of Yale University in 1897. He engaged in two years study abroad at University of Berlin, and of Halle-Wittenberg. A Ph.D. was granted him by the latter in 1899 magna cum laude.

Before going abroad, he married Rose St. John. Two daughters were born to them. Mary, the one surviving, holds an important position with the United Charities of Chicago.

After his return from Europe, Rall spent a year as student and lecturer at Yale and then served as pastor of the M.E. Church at East Berlin, Conn.; of Trinity in New Haven and the historic First Church of BALTIMORE, Md.

In 1910, Rall became president of ILIFF SCHOOL OF THEOLOGY, Denver, Colo., where he had to select and organize a new faculty, bring together a student body of promise, and establish the school on a substantial foundation. He accepted an invitation to the chair of Systematic Theology at GARRETT BIBLICAL INSTITUTE in 1915 in which position he was to continue his creative work until his retirement in 1945. Rall was made a member of the Commission on COURSE OF STUDY by the GENERAL CONFERENCE of 1916, became its recording secretary and in many ways its directing spirit. He prepared much of the necessary literature, helped organize the summer schools for the annual conferences, and the coaching conference for leaders held annually for many years at EVANSTON, Ill.

The bibliography of the writings of Harris Franklin Rall as given in a testimonial volume published in 1940 as part of the recognition of his twenty-five years of service at Garrett covers twelve pages. It lists, of course, all his books up to 1940, articles in scholarly journals, volumes to which he contributed a chapter or more, books reviews, etc. Not all the fourteen full length books he wrote can be listed here. Those best known are given in chronological order: *A Working Faith; New Testament History; The Life of Jesus and The Teachings of Jesus; Modern Premillenarianism and the Christian Hope; The Meaning of God* (Quillian Lecture); *A Faith For Today* (similar to his *Working Faith* of an earlier day); *Christianity; An Inquiry Into Its Nature and Truth* (this volume was selected out of over two hundred manuscripts submitted for the Bross Prize Award which in that anniversary year amounted to $15,000). Other books followed after 1940, chief of which were *Religion As Salvation; Paul and the Faith of Today; The God of Our Faith.* He ran a long series of articles in the *Christian Advocate* entitled "Doctor Rall Answers" and book reviews in the *Garrett Tower*, which journal he founded and edited for many years.

In 1949, Garrett established the Harris Franklin Rall Lectureship, a doubly appropriate recognition since he had given the Nathaniel Taylor Lectures at Yale as well as the Quillian and Ayer as noted above.

Rall's theology was discussed briefly in the December issue, 1964, of the *Garrett Tower* by his former colleague, GEORGIA HARKNESS. His social concern is discussed in the same issue of the *Tower* by his former student and colleague, MURRAY LEIFFER. This concern runs through all his writings as it did his teaching. He was active in the METHODIST FEDERATION FOR SOCIAL SERVICE as he was also in the early stages of the ecumenical movement. He attended the conference at Edinburgh and did much writing in preparation for the gathering at Lund.

Toward the end of his long ministry at First Church, Evanston, ERNEST F. TITTLE asked the official board to name Rall as adviser to the senior minister of that church. Tittle once said to a colleague: "I preach the gospel according to Frank Rall."

Harris Franklin Rall served the church in the following conferences, NEW ENGLAND SOUTHERN, BALTIMORE, COLORADO and ROCK RIVER. He died Oct. 13, 1964.

HORACE GREELEY SMITH

RALSTON, THOMAS NEELY (1806-1891), American minister, southern leader and theologian was born in Bourbon County, Ky., March 21, 1806, son of John Ralston and Elizabeth Neely Ralston. He was educated at Georgetown College, Ky. Converted at the age of twenty, he was licensed to preach the following year. He first joined the ILLINOIS CONFERENCE about 1833, and was ordained elder there in 1834. The following year he transferred to the KENTUCKY CONFERENCE. Strongly evangelistic, in one year on Mt. Sterling Circuit he brought 600 persons into the church. He was president of the Methodist Female High School in Lexington, Ky., 1843-47, and in 1851 he edited the *Methodist Monthly*. He was a delegate to the LOUISVILLE CONVENTION of 1845 of Southern Methodist Conferences. He was elected secretary pro-tem as the convention opened, later becoming assistant secretary; and at the first GENERAL CONFERENCE (MES) in 1846 he was chosen secretary. He was also a delegate to the General Conferences of 1850 and 1854. He was given the D.D. degree by Wesleyan University, Florence, Ky., in 1857. He edited four volumes of *Posthumous Works of the Rev. Henry B. Bascom* (1856 ff.), and was the author of *Evidences, Morals, and Institutions of Christianity* (1870), *Ecce Unitas, or a Plea for Christian Unity* (1875), and of *Elements of Divinity* (first edition, 1847, last one, 1924). For many years the latter book was in the minister's COURSE OF STUDY. Thomas J. Dodd of Kentucky and VANDERBILT called it "the first theological treatise in the way of a body of divinity that ever came from the American Methodist press," and GILBERT ROWE said that "it will long remain as the chief exponent of the religious thought of one of the most vital periods in the history of the Methodist Episcopal Church, South." Ralston died near Newport, Ky., on Nov. 25, 1891.

Appleton's Cyclopedia of American Biography (N. Y., D. Appleton and Co., 1888)
Christian Advocate (Nashville), Dec. 26, 1891.
General Minutes, MES., 1892, p. 30.   WALTER N. VERNON

RAMOS, RUY VITORINO (1909-1962), Brazilian layman and federal congressman, was born in Itaqui, state of Rio Grande do Sul, on Sept. 9, 1909. He was the son of Colonel Laurindo Ramos. While studying at the Methodist Instituto União, Ruy was converted and became an active Christian. He afterwards studied at the University of Porto Alegre, from which he received a bachelor's degree in law, and became a district attorney in Alegrete, where he lived the greater part of his life. He married Nehyta, and they had four children—Ecila, Cosete, Ruy, and Rosete.

Becoming interested in politics, and convinced that the evangelicals should take a more active part in government, Ruy campaigned for the office of Federal congressman from the state of Rio Grande do Sul, and was elected. In 1954 he tried for the Senate but lost due to very strong Roman Catholic opposition. He tried again in 1958, and was elected. Ramos was a leader in the Labor Party, the first president of the Movement for Landless Farmers, a strong advocate of the land reform in BRAZIL. Despite the fact that many disagreed with the principles he advocated, all admired Ramos for the fact that he was honest and not ashamed of his evangelical faith, and never bowed to the pressures of the ecclesiastical majority.

In the Methodist Church, he occupied several positions as layman. He was a member of the General Board of Social Action from 1950-60; was a delegate to the Latin American Evangelical Consultation in LIMA, PERU, in 1961; and was twice a lay delegate to the General Conference of the Methodist Church of Brazil (1946 and 1950). In 1962, he was promoting a plan for the development of Brazil's southwest frontier, in his native state, when an airplane accident took his life and that of his wife Nehyta.

Funeral rites were conducted in the Government Palace in Porto Alegre, capital of the state, with Bishop JOSE PINHEIRO officiating, and was attended by thousands including the highest state and local authorities.

ISNARD ROCHA

RAMSEY, FRED W. (1880-   ), American E.U.B. layman, was born Aug. 16, 1880. He was a member of Calvary Church, CLEVELAND, Ohio, and rendered distinguished service as executive director of the Forward Movement Campaign of the former EVANGELICAL ASSOCIATION in the early part of the century. The Campaign raised $1,000,000, a considerable sum at that time and the largest financial effort of the denomination to that date.

At that time, Dr. Ramsey was president of the Perfection Oil Stove Co., Cleveland, Ohio. He resigned this position to devote his time to philanthropic enterprises. He was chairman of the Cleveland Community Fund for years, raising millions of dollars for charitable institutions and enterprises. Then he served for three years as General Secretary of the International Council of the YMCA taking the place of the well-known JOHN R. MOTT. In this position he traveled to Europe and Asia continuously. OHIO WESLEYAN UNIVERSITY, Delaware, Ohio, honored him with the LL.D. degree.

Dr. Ramsey served as superintendent of Calvary Sunday school, Cleveland, Ohio, for forty-five years. For several decades this was the largest Sunday school in the former EVANGELICAL CHURCH, enrolling 1,800 pupils. When Dr. Ramsey's office as International YMCA Secretary was in NEW YORK, he would commute by pullman Saturday nights to be in this place of leadership in Sunday school, returning Sunday nights to New York. Over the years he has addressed many prominent gatherings within his own and other denominations.

RAYMOND M. VEH

RANCHHOD, KERSHAN, a bhagat, or leader of the Kabir Pant sect of reformed Hindus, was converted in BOMBAY in 1889 and baptized with three of his associates in the Grant Road Methodist Church by the pastor, HOMER C. STUNTZ (later bishop). Caste wise Ranchhod was regarded as very low in the social scale, but he was strong in personality, an able and energetic leader of his people, and had amassed some property. At the time of his conversion he was a labor contractor, recruiting and managing workmen for the conservancy department of the city of Bombay.

"With overflowing love for the Saviour and great eagerness for his people to know what he had learned," wrote *The Missionary Advocate* in 1874, he returned to Gujerat and urged his people to trust in Christ rather than in Kabir or any other. Several groups of his fellows in Gujarati towns and villages were converted. They were the first people to turn to Christ in considerable numbers, using group solidarity as a means of spreading the Gospel instead of allowing it to be an obstacle.

Another humble group had begun to learn of Christ through some of their number who were employed as house servants for members of the English-language Methodist Church that was established in Baroda in 1875. In 1895 a movement began among this second group, known as Dheds, also regarded as low-caste, but in their own thinking and in public esteem of higher rank than the conservancy group (commonly called sweepers). This second group is much larger in Gujarat than Ranchhod's people who first began moving together into Christian faith and purpose. And as the new movement grew in power, unfortunately caste prejudice prevailed over grace, and both the pioneer movement which began among the conservancy group and the later movement among the Dheds suffered serious retardation. Innumerable victories over the caste system have been won, but much remains to be done before this peculiar Indian form of segregation is completely overcome within the church in INDIA.

J. N. Hollister, *Southern Asia.* 1956. J. WASKOM PICKETT

RANDLE, BARTON (1796-1882), pioneer IOWA circuit rider, was born in Screven County, Ga., the son of a local Methodist preacher. In 1811 the family removed to the vicinity of Edwardsville, Ill. Barton was converted in 1812 and was licensed as exhorter and preacher. In 1831 he filled a vacancy on Spoon River Circuit, and that year he was ordained DEACON and received on trial into the ILLINOIS CONFERENCE of the M.E. Church, and assigned to Shelbyville Circuit. In 1832 he traveled the Henderson River Mission and organized a circuit with several societies. While on this charge he gave BARTON H. CARTWRIGHT, who was destined to plant Methodism in southern Iowa, his first preaching assignment.

Randle was ordained elder in 1833, received into the Conference in full connection, and assigned to Galena and Dubuque Mission. He was called the "Apostle of Iowa Methodism," and he introduced Methodism into northern Iowa. After preaching in Dubuque, on Nov. 6, 1833, he preached regularly during the winter of 1833-34 and established several appointments in Iowa. He organized

the first Methodist society in Dubuque, perhaps in Iowa, on May 18, 1834, and was the dominating force behind the erection of Iowa's first church building, the Dubuque Methodist log structure, which was raised July 25, 1834.

Described by PETER CARTWRIGHT as one of the best missionaries he knew, Randle subsequently preached on circuits, stations, and districts in southern Illinois until 1845, when he retired. In 1848 he resumed his itinerant ministry but was superannuated in 1850. He died on Jan. 2, 1882.

S. N. Fellows, *Upper Iowa Conference.* 1907.
R. A. Gallaher, *Methodism in Iowa.* 1944.
A. W. Haines, *Makers of Iowa Methodism.* 1900.
LeCompte, "Early Schools and Churches," *Proceedings in the House of Representatives* (Iowa Centennial—100 Years of Progress, 1846-1946).
E. H. Waring, *Iowa Conference.* 1910.   MARTIN L. GREER

RANDOLPH, FLORENCE (1866-1951) was born in Charleston, S. C., Aug. 9, 1866, a daughter of John and Anna (Smith) Spearing. At the age of eight years she was greatly impressed with Christianity through the teachings of a blind grandmother whom she led from house to house as the grandmother prayed with the sick and explained to them the Holy Scriptures.

In later years as Dr. Randolph became increasingly interested in social and religious endeavors, she began the study of Bible History under a private tutor who was a Yale graduate and an astute Greek and Hebrew scholar. Subsequently, Florence Randolph completed a course with the Moody Bible Institute in Chicago and further studied at DREW THEOLOGICAL SEMINARY.

Dr. Randolph's public work spanned fifty years. She began with the Woman's Christian Temperance Union in 1892 lecturing and organizing against the liquor traffic and remaining after in that organization for about forty years.

She was licensed to preach in Jersey City in 1897 and was ordained a deacon at Atlantic City in May 1900. During her active ministry, Dr. Randolph was pastor of five churches, the first being the A.M.E. ZION CHURCH on Pennington Street in Newark in May 1901, now Clinton Memorial Church. She was ordained an ELDER in 1903. For twenty-five years Dr. Randolph served as the president of the Women's Home and Foreign Missionary Society of the New Jersey Conference of the A.M.E. Zion Church and was the General President of the Society for four years. She was a member of the State Christian Endeavor Society and was the organization's only Negro state member for two years.

In 1915 Dr. Randolph founded the New Jersey State Federation of Colored Women's Clubs and served as president for twelve years.

Her inspirational leadership was responsible for the building of a beautiful $80,000 red brick colonial church, Wallace Chapel A.M.E. Zion Church, at Summit, N. J., together with a parsonage and a community house.

Dr. Randolph traveled abroad extensively. In 1901 she attended the ECUMENICAL CONFERENCE which met in London. In 1922 she again visited England enroute to the Gold Coast, British West Africa, now GHANA, where she spent two years bringing the Gospel to Africa as a foreign missionary. She spent time in SIERRA LEONE and Monrovia, LIBERIA. Upon her return to America she brought with her an African girl, Charity Zombelo, whom she educated in Summit High School and Hampton Institute. Upon her return to Africa, Miss Zombelo furthered the spread of the Christian principles through her teachings in African schools.

Dr. Randolph in 1931 made a trip to the Holy Lands including Palestine, Italy, Egypt, Turkey, Greece and several points in North Africa.

DAVID H. BRADLEY

RANDOLPH, JOSEPH BENJAMIN (1875-1961), American scholar and educator, was born in Shell Mound, Miss., On Sept. 9, 1875; he was one of two sons of John William and Mary E. J. (Berry) Randolph. He received the A.B. degree from New Orleans University in 1902 and the A.M. in 1905. He was a summer school student at Harvard University, 1907-11. He taught at WILEY COLLEGE, Marshall, Texas from 1902-10 and served as dean of Wiley College from 1910 to 1917. He was elected principal of Haven Institute, Meridian, Miss., in 1917 and held this position until 1920, when he was elected president of Samuel Huston (now HUSTON TILLOTSON) College in Austin, Texas. On the retirement of L. M. Dunton, J. B. Randolph was elected president of CLAFLIN COLLEGE, Orangeburg, S. C., and served in this capacity from 1922 to his retirement in 1945.

Joseph Benjamin Randolph married Gertrude Mattie Ramsey June 7, 1905. She preceded him in death Aug. 24, 1960.

Randolph was very active in the work of the SOUTH CAROLINA CONFERENCE of the M.E. Church. He was a member of the Uniting Conference of 1939 and the JURISDICTIONAL CONFERENCES of 1940 and 1944. Other religious activities included membership on The UNIVERSITY SENATE, 1920-24; and he was a member of the ECUMENICAL CONFERENCE of 1921.

He was laid to rest April 29, 1961 in the Fairmont Cemetery, Newark, N. J.

C. T. Howell, *Prominent Personalities*. 1945.
Yenser, *Who's Who in Colored America*, 4th ed.

J. W. CURRY

RANDOLPH-MACON ACADEMY, Front Royal, Virginia, was established in 1892 as a part of the Randolph-Macon system. Since 1953 it has operated under its own charter with its own board of trustees. It has always emphasized college preparatory work. The governing board has twenty members, is self-perpetuating, but election must be approved by the VIRGINIA ANNUAL CONFERENCE of the Methodist Church.

JOHN O. GROSS

RANDOLPH-MACON COLLEGE, Ashland, Va., a college of liberal arts for men, was chartered Feb. 3, 1830. The school was named for two of the distinguished congressmen of that day: John Randolph of Virginia and Nathaniel Macon of North Carolina. It was the first permanent institution of The Methodist Church to bear the name and do the work of a college.

During its first thirty-six years (1830-66) the college was located at Boydton, Va. It was closed during the Civil War, and most of its endowment, which had been invested in Confederate bonds, was lost. Removal of the college to Ashland took place in 1868.

Beginning in 1891, and continuing through 1930, the following institutions were included in the Randolph-Macon system: Randolph-Macon College, Ashland, Va.; RANDOLPH-MACON WOMAN'S COLLEGE, Lynchburg, Va.; Randolph-Macon Academy, Bedford, Va.; Randolph-Macon Institute (for girls), Danville, Va. RANDOLPH-MACON ACADEMY, Front Royal, Va. The school at Bedford was closed, and the one at Danville became an independent institution. In 1953 the charter of Randolph-Macon was modified and the three remaining schools—Ashland, Lynchburg, and Front Royal—were given separate boards of trustees.

While the beginning of a college is seldom the result of one man's efforts, JOHN EARLY must be placed at the top of the list of Randolph-Macon's founders. Associated with him in this enterprise were Hezekiah G. Leigh and Gabriel P. Disosway. John Early, a native of Virginia and a friend of Thomas Jefferson, joined the Virginia Conference in 1807 and was elected a bishop in the M.E. Church, South, in 1854. He was president of the board of trustees for forty-four years.

Randolph-Macon has been known for the high percentage of its graduates listed in *Who's Who in America*. It is doubtful that any small college can boast of more in Methodism's *Who Was Who*. Among these are Bishop HOLLAND N. McTYEIRE, founder of VANDERBILT UNIVERSITY, and Dean WILBUR F. TILLET of the School of Religion of the same university. Dean Tillet, as much as any leader, is responsible for his church's ability to keep its balance during the fundamentalist-modernist controversy.

Great teachers who at one time were associated with Randolph-Macon include STEPHEN OLIN, its first president and the second president of Wesleyan University; LANDON C. GARLAND, first chancellor of Vanderbilt University; Thomas R. Price, who attached as much importance to the teaching of English as to Latin and Greek and founded the first department for the teaching of English in the United States. He concluded his distinguished career as a professor in Columbia University.

Significant developments in the curricular program and expansion of the physical plant took place during the administrations of Presidents ROBERT EMORY BLACKWELL (1902-38) and J. EARL MORELAND (1939-67).

A Phi Beta Kappa chapter was established May 3, 1923. Degrees offered are the B.A. and B.S. The governing board has thirty-seven members, nominated by the board, approved by the Virginia Conference, and elected by the board.

JOHN O. GROSS

RANDOLPH-MACON WOMAN'S COLLEGE, Lynchburg, Va., was founded in 1891 under a charter granted to RANDOLPH-MACON COLLEGE for men in 1830. Although it was able to draw heavily upon the scholarly traditions developed by the men's college, in a short period the new woman's college was widely recognized for its own standards of educational excellence. In 1916 it became the first woman's college south of the Potomac to receive a Phi Beta Kappa chapter. The college's collection of paintings by American artists is one of the best owned by any college in the United States.

In 1966 Randolph-Macon Woman's College was chosen by the Ford Foundation for a challenge grant of $1,500,-000 as part of the foundation's Special Education Program designed "to advance the development of selected private institutions of higher education as national and regional centers of excellence." The college offers the B.A. degree. The governing board has thirty members, nominated and elected by the board with the approval of the Virginia Annual Conference. (The Randolph-Macon institutions operated under a single board until 1953 when separate boards were established for each.)

JOHN O. GROSS

RANGARAMANUJAM, PAUL (1893-1945), Indian minister, was born of Brahman parents at Mannargudi, South INDIA, and was converted as a scholar at Findlay College. Early desires for baptism were rejected by his family; and when he was baptized at eighteen, the age of consent, he was outcast by his family. He thought of becoming a *sannyasi* (wandering preacher) but entered the recently opened United Theological College at Bangalore in 1913, and was ordained in 1918, becoming a minister under the Wesleyan METHODIST MISSIONARY SOCIETY. After serving in Mesopotamia as a CHAPLAIN to Indian troops and acting as Student Christian Movement secretary in 1920-23, when he visited England and CHINA, he was appointed to Dharapuram in 1923. Here, as an ex-Brahman, his work among outcastes was greatly rewarding, and he constantly championed their rights. He was a man of high character, passionate evangelical zeal, and wide vision, with great gifts of leadership, and was greatly active in helping to create the Church of South India. He had been chairman of the Provincial Synod and of the Trinchinopoly District and was to preside over the Third General Synod of the Methodist Church in India, BURMA, and CEYLON at Mysore, when he died after a short illness, June 4, 1945, at Mannargudi.

CYRIL J. DAVEY

RANK, JOSEPH ARTHUR, Lord Rank of Sutton Scotney (1888-1972), British Methodist, was born on Dec. 22, 1888, the son of Joseph Rank, a Methodist and flour miller of Hull. He was chairman of Rank, Hovis, Mac-Dougall, one of the larger milling concerns in the world. In 1934 he pioneered the use of films for religious education and evangelism. He was personally involved in the production of religious films through Religious Films, Limited; among the films made are "John Wesley" and "The Promise." Lord Rank's part in the British film industry was through the Rank Organization, of which he was chairman from 1941 to 1962, and then president. In the church, Lord Rank was a Sunday school teacher and superintendent for almost fifty years; he held monthly film services in his village hall. He was chairman of the British Committee of the World Council of Christian Education and Sunday School Association; joint treasurer of the Home Mission Committee of the Methodist Church; and chairman of the Churches' Television Centre. He was made a baron in 1957, taking the title Baron Rank of Sutton Scotney.

R. A. Burnett, *The Life of Joseph Rank: Through the Mill.* London: Epworth Press, 1945.
Alan Wood, *Mr. Rank: a Study of J. Arthur Rank and British Films.* London: Hodden & Stoughton. 1952.

PETER STEPHENS

RANKIN, ALEXANDER MARTIN (1857-1940), distinguished American M.P. lay leader and benefactor, a manufacturer and industrial pioneer in HIGH POINT, N. C., was identified with the activities of the annual and GENERAL CONFERENCES of his denomination for forty years and was a prominent supporter of the M.P. Children's Home and the HIGH POINT COLLEGE. "Captain Rankin," as he was affectionately known, was born on Oct. 29, 1857, the son of William Wharton Rankin and Louise Roach Rankin of Benaja, Rockingham County, N. C. He attended YADKIN COLLEGE. He first married Mamie Belle Reece, who died in childbirth. They had one daughter who lived only three years. In 1898 he married Lena Blair and to this union were born six children. Rankin was engaged in many prosperous business interests.

"Captain Rankin" took an active interest in the establishment and maintenance of the M.P. Children's Home in Denton, N. C., and gave $500 when the home was later moved to High Point. He served as trustee of this home from its opening until his death, and after 1914 as secretary-treasurer. He was instrumental in the founding of High Point College and gave $10,000 to it; he served as a trustee from 1924 until his death. Rankin Memorial Methodist Church in High Point, founded about 1935, was named in his honor. He attended ten General Conferences, beginning in 1904, a distinction for which he was duly honored and recognized at the General Conference of 1936 which met in High Point.

"Captain Rankin" died on Jan. 23, 1940, in High Point and was buried in Oakwood Cemetery there.

J. Elwood Carroll, *History of the North Carolina Conference of the Methodist Protestant Church.* Greensboro, 1939.
High Point (N.C.) *Enterprise,* Jan. 23, 1940.
North Carolina Christian Advocate, February 1940.
S. M. Rankin, *The Rankin and Wharton Families and Their Genealogy.* Greensboro, n.d.　　RALPH HARDEE RIVES

RANKIN, GEORGE CLARK (1849-1915), American preacher and church editor, was born in Dandridge, Tenn. In ancestry the Rankins traced their line back to Scotland's Robert Bruce and rigid Calvinistic Presbyterianism. That inheritance continued through the days of George Rankin's father, who died when he was twelve. His mother was the first of the family to be of confident Methodist persuasion.

Rankin grew up during a period in which many people had little appreciation of "education" for the minister; but after one year in the annual conference he asked for "location" in order that he might go to school. On graduation from HIWASSEE COLLEGE in TENNESSEE he was admitted into the HOLSTON CONFERENCE (MES) where he labored until 1890. He later transferred to an appointment in KANSAS CITY, and then to Shearn Memorial Church in HOUSTON, Texas, and two years later to First Methodist Church, DALLAS. In 1898 he became editor of the *Texas Christian Advocate* and in that position made his greatest contribution to his church's life.

A great hulk of a man who "looked like a grizzly bear" one preacher said of him, he was powerful on the platform as well as in his forensic writing. He became best known for his attacks upon the liquor traffic and gambling. A common pattern, followed upon several different occasions, was for him to announce and preach a series of Sunday night sermons on these evils. During his editorship of the *Texas Christian Advocate,* 180 counties in

Texas outlawed the saloon, and the Legislature made gambling a criminal offense. Whatever else he might be writing of, his editorials almost always ended with the sentence "on with the battle"—and everyone knew he meant against the liquor traffic.

He died in the editorship, Feb. 2, 1915.

Journal of the North Texas Conference, 1915.
O. W. Nail, *Texas Methodism.* 1961.
George C. Rankin, *The Story of My Life.* Nashville: Smith and Lamar, 1912.
R. W. GOODLOE

LOCHIE RANKIN

RANKIN, LOCHIE (1851-1929), American missionary to CHINA, was born in Milan, Tenn., in 1851. In 1877 she responded to a call in the *Christian Advocate* (Nashville) for a volunteer to go as a missionary to China. She was commissioned by Bishop H. N. McTYEIRE in April, 1878, as the first unmarried woman missionary sent out under the auspices of women of the M.E. Church, South. She was sent to Shanghai to assist Mrs. J. W. LAMBUTH in the Clopton Boarding School. She quickly mastered the language and within a year opened a new grade school at Nanziang, fifteen miles away. Needing more help, she persuaded her eighteen-year-old sister, Dora, to join her in the work. Dora Rankin died six years after arriving, but this only intensified the efforts of her older sister, and soon she opened an Anglo-Chinese school. In 1901 she went to Huchow to open a boys' school. She lived in China through the defeat of China by JAPAN; the aggression by RUSSIA, Great Britian, GERMANY, and FRANCE; the fall of the Manchu Dynasty; the birth of the Chinese Republic in 1912; the Boxer Uprising; and the rise of Communism. She spent forty-nine years in educational missions in China. It was said that she had students in responsible positions in every province in China. Returning home in 1926 she retired on the campus of SCARRITT COLLEGE, Nashville. At her death on Sept. 13, 1929, her funeral was held in Scarritt's Wightman Chapel.

The Missionary Voice, December, 1929, pp. 21, 35
Mabel K. Howell, *Women and the Kingdom,* 1928, pp. 42, 129
Noreen Dunn Tatum, *A Crown of Service,* 1960, pp. 18, 24, 80, 81, 89, 93, 336
The Nashville Banner, September 13, 14, 1929
WALTER N. VERNON

THOMAS RANKIN

RANKIN, THOMAS (1738-1810), British Methodist preacher, was born at Dunbar, East Lothian. He came under the influence of Methodist dragoons and, after a business trip to Carolina, began to preach in 1759. He became an itinerant in 1761, in the Sussex Circuit. Later he became Wesley's traveling companion and in 1773 was sent out as "General Assistant and Superintendent" of American Methodism. He strove to enforce the Methodist discipline, but his brusque manner and lack of sympathy with the colonial cause led to strained relations. He returned home in 1778 and in 1789 was ordained by Wesley for England.

JOHN A. VICKERS

RANKIN, VICTOR LEE (1917-   ), was born in Alliance, OHIO, Oct. 2, 1917, the son of H. W. and Bertha Rankin. He graduated from FLORIDA SOUTHERN COLLEGE in 1941, BOSTON UNIVERSITY 1943, and obtained the M.A. degree from Union Theological Seminary in 1956.

He was married to Pearl Katherine Rankin on June 14, 1941 and their two sons are David and Larry.

His first appointment was assistant pastor to First Church, ORLANDO, Fla. In 1950 he was appointed pastor in Camaguey, CUBA, and later district superintendent of the Camaguey District. In 1960, because of communist pressure, he returned to the States and became assistant secretary for Latin America in the General Board of MISSIONS, 1960-62.

In 1963 he was appointed pastor of First Methodist Church, BUENOS AIRES, ARGENTINA, and the district superintendent of the Buenos Aires area.

GARFIELD EVANS

RANSOM, REVERDY CASSIUS (1861-1959), American bishop of the A.M.E. CHURCH, was born in Flushing, OHIO, on Jan. 4, 1861. He was educated at WILBERFORCE UNIVERSITY, where he graduated in theology in 1886, and at Oberlin College. He was converted in 1881, licensed to preach in 1883, ordained DEACON in 1886 and ELDER in 1888. He held pastorates in PENNSYLVANIA, Ohio, ILLINOIS, MASSACHUSETTS and NEW YORK. He was elected to the episcopacy from the editorship of the A.M.E. *Church Review* in 1924. Bishop Ransom was an outstanding exponent of the "Social Gospel." He delivered the invocation at the Democratic National Convention in 1940 and was a founder of the famous "Niagra Movement," the forerunner of the National Association for the Advancement of Colored People (N.A.A.C.P.).

GRANT S. SHOCKLEY

RANSOM, JOHN JAMES (1851-1934), American preacher and pioneer missionary to BRAZIL of the M.E. Church, South, was born in 1851, in Rutherford County, Tenn., the son of a Methodist preacher. He received his B.A. degree from EMORY AND HENRY COLLEGE, VIRGINIA, and his D.D. from the same in 1901. He was admitted to the TENNESSEE CONFERENCE in 1874. In response to urgent appeals made to the board by J. E. NEWMAN of Brazil, Ransom sailed for that country, arriving in RIO DE JANEIRO on Feb. 2, 1876. After a year studying at the Presbyterian Collegio Internacional in Campinas, state of São Paulo, Ransom traveled extensively to determine the best locations for establishing Methodist work. One trip took him to the state of Rio Grande do Sul, where the Methodist Episcopal Church had established work in 1875. From there he went to URUGUAY to confer with THOMAS B. WOOD, superintendent of the River Plate Conference. Returning to Rio de Janeiro, Ransom rented a house in which he held services—in English first, on Jan. 13, 1878, and in Portuguese two weeks later. This work aroused the hostility of the Roman Catholic hierarchy, which attacked him as an atheist and heretic through its magazine, *O Apostolo*. Ransom replied inviting them to come and listen.

He organized the first Methodist Church in Rio with six members, all Americans, one being the minister of the United States in Brazil. In March, 1879, Ransom received into membership the first Brazilians, one being a former Catholic priest, Antonio Teixeira de Albuquerque. By July he had received four other Brazilians. On Christmas day, 1879, Ransom married Annie Newman, who died six months later. He then came to the United States and authorized by the Board of MISSIONS, appealed for missionaries to Brazil. The result was that upon his return he took with him JAMES L. KENNEDY, JAMES W. KOGER, and MARTHA H. WATTS. They sailed via England in March 1881, and arrived in Rio de Janeiro on May 16, 1881.

Ransom worked mostly in the city of Rio de Janeiro, and in the states of São Paulo and Minas Gerais. In Rio, with Kennedy as associate, he did visitation work and supervised the construction of the first Methodist church in Brazil, the small but attractive Catete Chapel, which still stands. He also opened other preaching points in the city.

In 1882, Ransom returned to the United States for a visit; but was back for the July inauguration of the chapel, whose construction had continued under Kennedy's supervision.

In December 1882, when at a QUARTERLY CONFERENCE the work was divided into two districts, Ransom was named presiding elder of the Rio district, and Koger substituted for him as superintendent of the Mission. Ransom now devoted himself to itinerant work and to church journalism, though he returned to the United States in the fall of 1883. There, on September 2, he married Ella Crow and with her returned to Brazil. In 1884 he began publishing *A Escola Dominical* (The Sunday school), and a leaflet for children, *Nossa Gente Pequena* (Our Little People). On New Year's Day, 1886, he launched what was to become the official Methodist organ, *Metodista Catolico* (Catholic Methodist). It continued under this name until July 20, 1887, when by general consensus, and under the editorship of J. L. Kennedy, it was renamed *Expositor Cristão* (Christian Expositor) and so continues to this day (1969).

Brazil received its first episcopal visit on July 4, 1886, with the arrival of Bishop JOHN C. GRANBERY. He at once called a missionary Conference in Piracicabo, state of São Paulo, at which time a committee was named, consisting of Ransom and Kennedy, to regularize Methodist properties in Brazil. These, up to then, had to be held in Ransom's name and considered his personal property, since at that time the imperial government did not recognize the Board of Missions, or the Women's Missionary Council as juridical entities. Title to the property, however, had been guaranteed by a will executed in Brazil, and by legal documents held in NASHVILLE, Tenn.

At this meeting, for reasons never openly given, Ransom disassociated himself from the work in Brazil and asked for transfer back to the Tennessee Conference. Whatever the reasons his resignation was greatly regretted. After returning to the homeland Ransom served short periods in CALIFORNIA and CUBA from 1888 to 1890, going back and forth to his family in Tennessee. Finally, he served as associate pastor at McKendree Church in Nashville. There he died on Oct. 18, 1934, and was buried in Woodlawn Cemetery. He was survived by his wife and four children —Richard, Annie, Ellene, and John Crowe Ransom, the distinguished writer.

E. M. B. Jaime, *Metodismo no Rio Grande do Sul*. 1963.
J. L. Kennedy, *Metodismo no Brasil*. 1928.   EULA K. LONG

CHARLES W. RANSON

RANSON, CHARLES WESLEY (1903-   ), minister, educator, and former university dean, was born in Ballyclare, IRELAND, on June 15, 1903, the son of Henry John and Elizabeth (Clarke) Ranson. He studied at the METHODIST COLLEGE at BELFAST, Ireland, and Queen's University there, and at the EDGEHILL THEOLOGICAL COLLEGE—also at Belfast. He became a B.Litt. at Oxford (England) University, a Th.D. at Kiel University, Germany; and DICKINSON COLLEGE in America awarded him the S.T.D. in 1965.

Dr. Ranson was ordained in the ministry of the Irish Methodist Conference in 1929 and became a missionary to INDIA, 1929. After that he was the general secretary of the INTERNATIONAL MISSIONARY COUNCIL, 1948-58, coming to America in 1948 the better to manage the affairs of that International Council. He acted as a director of the Theological Educational Fund of the WORLD COUNCIL OF CHURCHES, 1958-63, and then became dean of the Theological School and the professor of Ecumenical Theology at DREW UNIVERSITY, Madison, N. J., in 1963. In 1968 he was appointed professor of Theology and Ecumenics at Hartford Seminary Foundation.

He was the president of the Methodist Church in Ireland, 1961-62, and is a member of the Board of Directors of the Fund for Theological Education, as well as a trustee of the Margaret Chambers Warnshuis Foundation. He received the King George V medal for public service in India in 1935. He has written *A City in Transition*, 1938; *The Christian Minister in India*, 1945; *That the World May Know*, 1953.

Who's Who in America, Vol. 34.
Who's Who in the Methodist Church, 1966.   N. B. H.

HARRY RANSTON

RANSTON, HARRY (1878-   ), NEW ZEALAND Methodist minister and noted Bible scholar, was born at Keighley, Yorkshire, in 1878. He began work in the worsted mills at the age of ten. By attending evening classes he won a scholarship to attend secondary school and another for Ruskin Hall, Oxford. Both had to be refused because of necessitous family circumstances.

In 1900, he trained for a year at Hartley College, MANCHESTER, under A. S. PEAKE, and then was appointed to Canning Town, East London.

In 1902, he came to New Zealand and served in a number of important circuits. While in full circuit work, and without being able to attend university, he gained the B.A. degree and the senior university scholarship in Greek of the University of New Zealand in 1913. The following year he graduated, M.A. with honors in Greek and Hebrew. He wrote two major books, the first securing him a doctorate of literature: *Ecclesiastes and the Early Greek Wisdom Literature* and *The Old Testament Wisdom Books* (London: Epworth Press, 1925, 1930).

For many years he was in close touch with the Auckland University, as degree examiner, part-time lecturer, and member of the senate. For twenty-two years he served on the staff of the theological college, both at Dunholme and Trinity, the last ten of them being as principal.

He retired in Auckland in 1941, but continued for some years as part-time lecturer at both Auckland University and Trinity College. In 1966 he was living at Tyler House, a home operated by Auckland Central Mission.

Minutes of the New Zealand Methodist Conference, 1941.
L. R. M. GILMORE

RAST, JOHN MARVIN (1897-   ), American minister, editor, and college president, was born at Bartow, Ga., on March 13, 1897, the son of Jeremiah Lawton and Susie Louise (Bearden) Rast. He was educated at EMORY UNIVERSITY and Columbia University (M.A. in 1924), Union Theological Seminary (1923-24), and CANDLER SCHOOL OF THEOLOGY (B.D., 1929). WOFFORD COLLEGE awarded him the D.D. degree in 1940. He taught three years at Emory University Academy and three at Wofford College. Going into the SOUTH CAROLINA CONFERENCE, he served three appointments until in 1936 he became editor of the *Southern Christian Advocate* and served as such from 1936 to 1941. At that time he became president of Lander College at Greenwood, S. C. He served in the first World War in the United States Army.

Dr. Rast has become well known as a writer of syndicated daily devotional newspaper features since 1925. His wife was Florence Olive Mays, whom he married on Aug. 24, 1927, and they have a son and two daughters.

For ten years he served as executive secretary of the Board of EDUCATION of the South Carolina Conference (after the Upper South Carolina and the South Carolina Conferences united). He became the associate editor of the *South Carolina Methodist Advocate*, 1963, and continues to write for the religious press. Dr. Rast has contributed several articles to this *Encyclopedia*.

Who's Who in America, Vol. 34.
Who's Who in Methodism, 1952.   N. B. H.

HAROLD B. RATTENBURY

RATTENBURY, HAROLD BURGOYNE (1878-1961), British, Methodist missionary to CHINA, was born at Witney in

1878, trained at Headingley College, and entered the Wesleyan ministry in 1902. He went to China in 1902, and served in the Hupeh district until 1935; he was a general secretary of the Wesleyan METHODIST MISSIONARY SOCIETY from 1935-50, and was president of the Methodist Conference in 1949. He was the son, grandson, brother, and father of Methodist ministers. His was the controlling voice in Methodist policy in China for many years. He died on Dec. 24, 1961.

JOHN KENT

RATTENBURY, JOHN ERNEST (1870-1963), British Methodist, brother of HAROLD B. RATTENBURY, and like him educated at Woodhouse Grove School. He entered the Wesleyan Methodist ministry in 1893, being trained at Didsbury College, MANCHESTER. Much of his ministry was spent in city missions, including eighteen years in the West London Mission, where he preached first in the Lyceum Theatre and then opened the Kingsway Hall. He was a founding member of the METHODIST SACRAMENTAL FELLOWSHIP, and an outstanding advocate of its ideals. The most important of his many publications appeared after his retirement in 1935; *The Conversion of the Wesleys* (1938), *The Evangelical Doctrines of Charles Wesley's Hymns* (the Fernley-Hartley Lecture for 1941), and *The Eucharistic Hymns of John and Charles Wesley* (1948). He died Jan. 19, 1963.

FRANK BAKER

RAYMOND, MINER (1811-1897), American minister and educator, was born on Aug. 29, 1811, at Rennselaerville, N. Y. With little education he turned to the shoemaker's trade, but in his eighteenth year felt called to a religious life. He entered Wesleyan Academy in WILBRAHAM, Mass., where, under the influence of WILBUR FISK, he moved from the role of student to that of helper and teacher. In 1838 he joined the NEW ENGLAND CONFERENCE, but continued at Wilbraham for three years.

From 1841 to 1848 he held pastorates in Worcester, BOSTON, and Westfield, Mass. He was elected principal at Wilbraham in 1848. The Academy under his administration prospered, with new buildings—Fisk, Binney, and Rich Halls being erected. He was elected professor of Systematic Theology at GARRETT BIBLICAL INSTITUTE of Evanston, Ill., in 1864, where he wrote a three-volume work, *Systematic Theology.*

Raymond was a delegate to six GENERAL CONFERENCES, representing the New England Conference five times and the ROCK RIVER CONFERENCE once. In 1856 he was General Conference Chairman of the Committee on Slavery. In 1872 he received over fifty votes for bishop.

He was married twice. By his first wife, Elizabeth Henderson, who died in 1877, he had five sons and a daughter. His second wife was Mrs. Isabella Hill Binney, widow of Amos Binney, one-time member of the New England Conference. Raymond died on Nov. 25, 1897, at Evanston, Ill.

J. M. Buckley, *History of Methodists.* 1896.
Zions Herald, Dec. 1, 1897.   ERNEST R. CASE

READER AT CITY ROAD CHAPEL, LONDON. In JOHN WESLEY's lifetime it had been the custom to use the services of the Book of Common Prayer at City Road Chapel,

and to employ Anglican clergymen to assist with the communion services. This continued after 1791, and in 1811 THOMAS VASEY was appointed as "Reader." He had been ordained by John Wesley in September, 1784, and sent to America and was later ordained in America by the Protestant Episcopal Bishop William White of PHILADELPHIA. His duty was to perform the liturgical service, which he did until the close of 1825. When he resigned, the trustees of the chapel made a vain attempt to find an Anglican clergyman to continue the succession; they then applied to the Wesleyan Methodist Conference for an itinerant to be stationed as Reader. This led to a quarrel with HENRY MOORE, who was still superintendent of the circuit in which the chapel lay, and who tried to claim the position of Reader in terms of John Wesley's will. Legal advice did not sustain Moore's claims, and from 1826 the Conference appointed itinerants to do the work of Reader at City Road, though not apparently using the title as such. By 1850, however, the City Road society had lost ground financially, and so in 1852 the trustees decided to save money by abolishing the office of Reader, and this decision came into effect from the Conference of 1853.

JOHN KENT

READFIELD, MAINE, U.S.A., is significant as the location of what is now called the Jesse Lee Memorial Church, the first Methodist meetinghouse erected in the state. JESSE LEE visited the region in 1793, and the following year was appointed presiding elder of the Lynn District and the Province of MAINE. Philip Wager was sent to the Readfield Circuit in 1794, and under Lee's direction he led in building the meetinghouse. In November Lee wrote that the edifice was almost completed, and on June 21, 1795, he dedicated the plain, rough structure.

On Dec. 12, 1794, Lee administered the communion to the society members at Readfield, the first time the rite was observed under Methodist auspices in Maine. With ten preachers present, Bishop ASBURY conducted the first Methodist conference in the Province of Maine at Readfield, beginning Aug. 29, 1798.

In 1825 the Readfield Church building was moved some thirty rods from its original location and was repaired and rededicated. In 1857 the structure was remodeled; the roof was raised and a steeple and bell were added. When the railroad came to Readfield, a new village grew up around the depot, and another Methodist church was established there. The original church was then called East Readfield.

About 1900, East Readfield was rededicated as the Jesse Lee Memorial Church. Today services are conducted in the building only at Easter, Christmas, and in the summer months; the members worship at the Kents Hill Church five miles away during the rest of the year.

In 1971 the Jesse Lee Memorial Church had twenty-nine members and its building was valued at $25,000.

Allen and Pilsbury, *Methodism in Maine.*
East Readfield Church. (Typescript), 7 pp., n. d.
General Minutes, MEC and UMC.
Minutes of the Maine Conference. WILLIAM T. BENNETT
BERTRAM F. WENTWORTH

READING, PENNSYLVANIA, U.S.A. **Memorial Church of the Holy Cross, Methodist.** This is the mother church of Methodism in Reading. The first Methodist sermon in

Reading was preached at the Court House by JOSEPH PILMORE May 27, 1772. He commented in his *Journal* on the wealth and prosperity of this city which then numbered about 400 persons. No Society was formed, however, and in 1803 when HENRY BOEHM attempted to preach in Reading he was prevented by the Commissioner. Five years later he and FRANCIS ASBURY passed through Reading and were ridiculed by the people. In 1822 two Methodist young men moved from Lancaster to Reading and organized a PRAYER MEETING or CLASS. The class grew and in the same year it was formally organized into a church (Ebenezer, now Holy Cross) by Henry Boehm. The organization took place in the old State House on the Northeast Corner of Fifth and Penn Streets. For the next five years the church met in the homes of its members, but in 1827 they erected a building on the East side of South Third Street which they called Ebenezer M.E. Church. In 1839 a larger brick structure was built on South Fourth Street below Penn which was remodeled in 1870 and again in 1884. A growing membership soon made this building inadequate, and the Trustees were instructed to look for a new site. The present site on North Penn Street was purchased and ten leading architects of the country submitted plans for the new building. A Philadelphia firm was selected. In 1890 ground was broken for the new church, and in 1893 the new structure was completed. It was called Memorial M.E. Church, which, in 1944, was changed to Memorial Church of the Holy Cross, Methodist. The building was considered by many to be one of the most beautiful in all of American Methodism. The Romanesque architecture was deviated by an arcaded cloister paved with mosaic. One entrance was marked by a stately tower supported by open groined columns. The interior walls were of white crystalline marble in combination with Portland Red Stone from Michigan. It is thought that the first vested choir began to serve here in 1893.

On Sunday, June 26, 1936 a fire broke out in the educational building and twelve fire companies fought the blaze to save the church proper. The sanctuary was saved but the educational building and the chapel were destroyed. By 1938 the educational unit and the chapel had been rebuilt and the sanctuary redecorated. Today the Church is one of the most influential Methodist Churches in the city. Directly or indirectly it has aided the organization and building of most of the Methodist churches in Reading.

Charles Yrigoyen, Jr., *History of Memorial Church of the Holy Cross, Methodist, in Reading, Pennsylvania,* manuscript in the archives of Old St. George's United Methodist Church, Philadelphia, Pennsylvania.   FREDERICK E. MASER

READY, WILLIAM (1860-1927), NEW ZEALAND minister, became an orphan at an early age. He lived as best he could until accepted into Muller's Orphanage at Bristol, England. Converted at seventeen, he was trained for the ministry at the BIBLE CHRISTIAN College. He came to New Zealand at twenty-seven and served some of the leading pulpits. He founded Dunedin Central Mission in 1890, where in a matter of two or three years he built up what was then the largest congregation in New Zealand. Famed as an evangelist, he was conducting a mission in Palmerston North when he suddenly took ill and died on Sept. 7, 1927. The story of his early life has been told in a book

by Lewis H. Court, *Ready, Aye Ready* (London: Epworth Press, 1935).

L. R. M. Gilmore, *The Bible Christians in New Zealand* (Wesley Historical Society, New Zealand, 1947).
L. R. M. GILMORE

RECIFE, Brazil, capital of the northeast state of Pernambuco. Methodism began in 1880, when WILLIAM TAYLOR made his second trip to South America. That year, in Recife, he laid the groundwork for a mission and sent out several "very strong men . . . but they set their plow too deep." All but one, GEORGE NIND, left soon, sick or discouraged. Nind, a licensed exhorter, established a congregation, taught music during the week to support himself; and on Sundays held Sunday school and worship services in his house, and preached outdoors in the public parks. Despite his constant pleas for help, no ordained minister was ever sent out. Finally, in 1892, he was forced by his wife's illness, to return to the United States—the Methodists in Recife were absorbed into other Protestant denominations that came in.

Recife, with a population of around one million, is the third largest city of BRAZIL and the capital of the northeast region. After decades of no witness, CESAR DACORSO, the first Brazilian bishop, made plans for the occupation of all Brazil, beginning with Salvador, state of Baia, in 1946. That year, the General Conference of Brazil considered Recife as a possible field; and in 1950, the General Secretary of Missions reported the existence of a small Methodist congregation which had resulted from the efforts of individual Methodists. It was, however, only in 1959 that Dorival Beulke, a Brazilian, was sent to Recife as a missionary.

His first service was held in a garage with an attendance of thirty-two. Since then, the work has spread to three other centers. These stress social service with literacy classes for adults, and instruction on nutrition and hygiene.

W. C. Barclay, *History of Missions.* 1957.
Minutes of Annual Conferences of the Methodist Church of Brazil, 1946, 1950, 1955, 1960.   D. A. REILY

RECORDS AND STATISTICS (U.S.A.). The Methodist Church has ever kept careful records of all its conferences and disciplinary actions. The *Large Minutes* as put together in the time of JOHN WESLEY, indicate how records first came to be formulated. Subsequently, when the *Discipline* began to be published in American Methodism, it contained within itself all sorts of recorded moves as well as disciplinary requirements.

It has always been the duty of the preacher-in-charge in the Methodist churches to keep correct records of all persons received on probation, or removed by letter, withdrawn from the church, and those who have deceased. Careful disciplinary directions have continued to be prescribed through the years instructing ministers how they must record enrollment, marriages, baptisms and deaths, and indeed all matters relating to the membership of the charge. One of the questions formally asked in quarterly conferences was, "Are the church records properly kept?"

Specific directions are given throughout the *Discipline* for the recording of work carried on, and for checking over work done. Every conference, from the Church Conference to the GENERAL CONFERENCE, has a secretary or secretarial staff whose duties are to keep careful records of all matters transpiring, and to see that these are properly preserved. The journal of each Annual Conference must be signed by the bishop or presiding president; and the bishops who preside over the General Conference must sign the minutes for the day or days upon which they preside.

The district superintendent signs the record of each charge conference. The minutes of the previous meeting are formally approved by the body creating them, after any member has an opportunity to propose corrections. Some conferences put the matter of checking and approving the minutes in the hands of a special committee.

It has long been the practice in the church for the minutes of each QUARTERLY (charge) CONFERENCE to be taken to the district conference (when there is one), and that conference appoints a committee to check over and report upon how the records of the several charges are kept. In turn, where there are district conferences, these send their records to the Annual Conference for approval. The Annual Conferences must send their four year printed journals to the succeeding JURISDICTIONAL CONFERENCE for its examination and approval.

The United Methodist Church has a Statistical Office which since reorganization of the general administrative offices of the church in 1952 has been put under the direction of the COUNCIL ON WORLD SERVICE AND FINANCE. Before that time there was an office of statistics under the BOOK EDITOR, and a statistician empowered to collect statistics from the entire church and to get these ready for the *General Minutes* as these were published.

The *General Minutes* of The Methodist Church have been published in one volume each year entitled the *General Minutes of the Annual Conferences of The Methodist Church in the United States and Overseas*. Such have been published since 1785. This now includes statistics for each local church in each annual conference. The Section of Research, Records and Statistics, which acts under the supervision of the Council on World Service and Finance, is authorized by the General Conference to put out each year the complete compilation of Methodist records.

The number of specific items having to do with the ongoing of all the activities of the church all of which must be reported on, and the necessity for the proper forms upon which to do this, forced The Methodist Church in time to create a Committee on Official Records and Forms. Something like 135 specific forms had to be prepared by this committee; everything from the proper baptismal certificate for an infant to the long list of questions which had to be called by the bishop at each annual conference.

Complete directions for keeping such records are outlined in the *Discipline* of The United Methodist Church, although such directions are not of course to be found together in any one place. The United Methodist Church prides itself, however, on keeping its records in better order and by a better system than any other large ecclesiasticism, although in older days the jibe was sometimes heard of the "Methodist Statistical Church."

The COMMISSION ON ARCHIVES AND HISTORY and Annual Conference HISTORICAL SOCIETIES have helped greatly in the preservation of old records and statistics. Each quarterly (charge) conference is now empowered to create a "committee on records and history" which "shall be responsible for assisting the pastor to see that all church and charge conference records are kept on the official record blanks provided for that purpose. This Committee is empowered to examine the charge conference records annually at the end of each conference year, and to report the result of its examination to the charge conference in the ensuing year." (*Discipline*, 1968, ¶ 1412.)

ROY A. STURM

RED BIRD MISSION. In 1919 the UNITED EVANGELICAL CHURCH, later the EUB Church, initiated a mountain mission on the Red Bird River at Beverly, Ky. Twenty acres in Bell County were donated for the mission by the Knuckle brothers.

Misses Myra Bowman (Pennsylvania) and Emaline Welsh (Illinois) were the first teachers, organizing a Sunday school for mountain people.

Elementary education in three locations and secondary education through a boarding school in 1931 became the first evidences of the growth of the mission.

J. J. DeWall of Iowa was the first evangelist and in 1920, a nurse, Lydia B. Rice, began a medical service. It was not until 1927 that a doctor, the Rev. Harlan S. Heim, M.D., joined the mission staff. The small hospital, erected in 1928, was replaced by a new structure located in Queendale in 1959.

The evangelistic witness also was manifest in the building of chapels and churches in Beverly, Jack's Creek, Beech Fork, Mill Creek and Greasy Fork, among others.

The mission work was carried on in 1970 by a staff of approximately eighty missionaries.

The rapid change in the mountains, including the strip mining process, and the advent of the Anti-Poverty government program in Appalachia have challenged the mission toward the significance of the church in its ministry to the people of the mountains.

LOIS MILLER

RED LION, PENNSYLVANIA, U.S.A., is a town where the United Brethren have always been strong. Red Lion was incorporated as a borough in the State of PENNSYLVANIA on Jan. 16, 1880. But as far back as May 10, 1729, when Lancaster County was established, there is record of white settlements in the area which is now known as York County. The soil was found to be unusually good. In a very short time industrious German immigrant farmers were clearing land and planting crops. Most of these German immigrants belonged to the Reformed and Lutheran faith; some were also Mennonites and Dunkards.

The areas now known as Freysville, Red Lion and Dallastown became settled with these German immigrants. In 1748 they built a log church and school—the only church that served this large territory. The St. John's Reformed Church was the first to establish a permanent church building with regular services for the town of Red Lion.

Since 1831 UNITED BRETHREN IN CHRIST missionaries had been preaching in the surrounding areas. In 1842 or 1843 Christian Crider urged the people to purchase a plot of land nearby and a place of worship was built. After the incorporation of the borough of Red Lion there was a strong urge for a town church of the United Brethren. The cornerstone for the town church was laid June 22, 1882. A new modern, architecturally beautiful Bethany Church was dedicated May 5, 1930.

St. Paul's Evangelical Church had its beginning in 1885 when Red Lion was a part of the Old York Circuit. An organization was effected but no regular preaching was maintained for lack of a place in which to worship. In 1894 a substantial brick church was built which had a membership of 125.

During the pastorate of J. Theodore Pettit, a new church school building was built and dedicated, debt free, in 1919. The church membership was 650 and a church school enrollment of 995.

St. Paul's Evangelical United Brethren Church, on Feb. 3, 1935, dedicated its Gothic Sanctuary. St. Paul's Church of Red Lion was one of the most beautiful and largest churches in the denomination. It had a membership of 1,700 members in 1967 and a few more than 2,000 church school members.

Although the population of Red Lion (1970) is 5,887, St. Paul's Church with its 1,656 members, Bethany with her 1,016 members, and Zion Church on the edge of town with 319 members accounted for more than one-half of the community's population.

Serving Red Lion are five other churches: St. John's United Church of Christ, Grace Lutheran, The Christian Missionary Alliance, Congregation of Jehovah's Witnesses and the Assembly of God.

But within a three mile radius of the borough of Red Lion are seventeen former Evangelical United Brethren Churches. In some of these areas thus served, there are no other denominations present.

ALFRED JOHN THOMAS

RED ROCK CAMP MEETING. In 1837 the first three Methodist missionaries—ALFRED BRUNSON, David King, and John Holton—went to MINNESOTA to minister to the Indians, to a Sioux village at Kaposia, now South ST. PAUL. Here in two and one-half years a church of thirty-three members had been organized—whites, Indians, and halfbreeds—and a farm of 150 acres placed under cultivation.

In the fall of 1839 B. T. Kavanaugh was sent as superintendent and built a log parsonage-meeting house-school on the east bank of the Mississippi at Red Rock. In 1843 the missions on both sides of the river were closed; others however, continued and white work extended.

John Holton, who came originally as a farmer, continued at Red Rock on his own farm. In 1868 he offered Pastor Bowdish of the Newport church, one mile south, ten acres of land for a CAMP MEETING. This included the log cabin and Red Rock. With neighboring pastors the offer was accepted, and the first camp held in June 1869. More land was purchased, extensive grounds developed, and camp meetings were held there continuously through 1937, with people coming by team, train, and steamer. The high point was 1886-88 under the ministry of Sam Small and SAM JONES when 20,000 passed through the turnstiles in a single day. Then came a gradual decline until 1899 when few attended.

In 1898 Bishop JOYCE assumed his residence in MINNEAPOLIS and brought evangelists Dunham and Baker for meetings. To conserve the results he organized in 1899 the Minnesota Pentecostal Association. For the year 1900 this new association was asked by the Red Rock Park Association to conduct the camp meeting, and this they did. Later they assumed the original charter and have conducted the camp since under the Red Rock name.

In 1938, due to encroaching industry and railroads, the camp was moved to Mission Farms, ten miles northwest of Minneapolis; and in 1961 to Lake Koronis, ninety miles west.

Noted evangelists and Bible teachers have appeared there. Missions have been emphasized and the voices of Bishops TAYLOR, McCABE, OLDHAM, and WARNE were heard. Other bishops have given forceful preaching— FOSS, McINTYRE, LEETE, CUSHMAN, NALL. Programs for children and youth have been well-planned; many have gone into the ministry and mission fields.

CHAUNCEY HOBART said: "What the State of Minnesota owes to Red Rock Camp Meeting can never be told. Nor can the waves of vital godliness that have flowed from it be estimated."

C. Hobart, *Minnesota.* 1887.
C. N. Pace, *Minnesota.* 1952.   BLAINE LAMBERT

REDFIELD, JOHN WESLEY (1810-1863), American leader in the organization of the FREE METHODIST CHURCH, was a medical doctor, a Methodist local preacher and an outstanding evangelist. He was prominent in the mid-century HOLINESS revival movement in ILLINOIS, and ultimately led this group to join with the reform movement in the GENESEE CONFERENCE (ME) to organize the new church. Redfield was the evangelist during an unusual revival on the campus at WESLEYAN UNIVERSITY, Middletown, Conn. B. T. ROBERTS, later founder of the Free Methodist Church, was a student there. He was greatly influenced by these events and became a life-long friend of Redfield.

BYRON S. LAMSON

A. H. REDFORD

REDFORD, ALBERT HENRY (1818-1884), American minister and historian, was born in St. Louis, Mo., Nov. 18, 1818. He was converted in his boyhood and was early impressed that he was called to preach. Through the assistance of an uncle he received a classical education and his uncle expected him to enter a career of business. Despite this opposition he acted upon his conviction of duty and was licensed to preach. He joined the KENTUCKY CONFERENCE in 1837. From mountain mission and hard circuits he moved on to the best circuits, stations, and districts of his conference.

Five times in succession he was elected as a delegate to the GENERAL CONFERENCE. He is best known for his work in historical research, and he left to the church three volumes of the history of Methodism in KENTUCKY to 1832, and a fourth volume entitled *Western Cavaliers,* bringing this history to the year 1846; also two other volumes entitled *The Life and Times of Hubbard Hines Kavanaugh* and *A History of The Methodist Episcopal Church, South.* These volumes have been a constant source of biographical and historical authority for Methodist historians. He searched the records of the church and availed himself of close examination of the *General Minutes,* the *Methodist Magazine, Quarterly Reviews,* and weekly journals of the church in order to bring together the details of the history of the Methodist Church in Kentucky. He rescued from oblivion the names of the pioneers and presented their characters in graphic briefness as only the wielder of a precise and eloquent pen could do.

In 1866, Redford was elected by the General Conference of the M.E. Church, South as BOOK EDITOR, and for twelve years he guided the METHODIST PUBLISHING HOUSE of the Southern Church through the most perilous period of its history, following the War between the States. He faced criticism, divisions, many times bankruptcy, but by reason of his deep devotion and excellent business ability, he was able to bring the publishing interests of Southern Methodism through this stormy period. At the General Conference of 1878 he was unable to continue further the arduous trials of his position and returned to a pastorate in Louisville, where he served until his death.

Journal of the Louisville Conference, 1884.
J. C. Rawlings, *Century of Progress.* 1946.   HARRY R. SHORT

REDRUTH PLAN as an episode in British Methodist history. After the death of JOHN WESLEY in 1791, disagreement about the future form of Methodism rapidly came to a head. The group of about fifty lay delegates who met in Redruth, Cornwall, on June 14, 1791, wanted a drastic revision of the Wesleyan constitution. They suggested, in a circular which was sent round the connection, that in future classes should choose their own leaders, and that members should not be expelled from or admitted to the societies without the consent of the majority of the existing members. The QUARTERLY MEETING should decide by a majority vote on such matters as the division of circuits and the admission of itinerants. If a case was brought against an itinerant, it should be heard by a court composed of equal numbers of itinerants and stewards. Such changes would have meant an end of the itinerants' virtual monopoly of Wesleyan government. The Redruth Plan had no immediate effect on the situation, but was important because it pointed forward to the kind of Methodist constitution which was to be set up by the METHODIST NEW CONNEXION in 1797, and shows that such attitudes were already rife in some areas of Methodism soon after John Wesley's death.

JOHN KENT

REDSTONE CIRCUIT. The original "mother Circuit" of American Methodism west of the Appalachian mountains in western PENNSYLVANIA and western VIRGINIA. The circuit was laid out in the homes of MARYLAND Methodists who had emigrated to the west in the Fall of 1783 by RICHARD OWINGS, and in the Spring of 1784 John Cooper and Samuel Breeze were appointed by FRANCIS ASBURY to organize the circuit. In its first three years the circuit expanded to about 300 miles in extent with thirty preaching places extending from Uniontown, Pa., to the Ohio River, and from just south of PITTSBURGH nearly to Fairmont, W. Va. In 1787 the circuit was divided into three circuits and the next year a fourth was added. By 1799 there were five circuits in the region with ninety-six preaching places: Clarksburg, twelve; Greenfield, twenty-four; Ohio, twenty-four; Pittsburgh, twelve; and Redstone, twenty-four. There were nine log meetinghouses in the region, the remainder of the preaching places being in homes.

After the Treaty of Greenville of 1795 opened the northwest Territories to legal settlement and Methodists moved into northwestern Pennsylvania and OHIO, circuits were laid out in the new regions, the impetus coming from the original Redstone Circuit region. Thus the Muskingum Circuit was organized in 1799; Shenango, 1800; Erie, 1800; West Wheeling, 1802; Hock-Hocking, 1803; and Deerfield, 1803. The name "redstone" derives from a small creek that flows west from the mountains through Uniontown to the Monongahela River at Brownsville in Pennsylvania. It gave its name to the early religious organizations that moved into the region of southwestern Pennsylvania and western Virginia after legal settlement was made possible by the Treaty of Fort Stanwix with the Iroquois Indians in 1768. Thus the Baptist Redstone Association was formed in 1776; the Presbyterian Redstone Presbytery in 1782; and the Methodist Redstone Circuit in 1784. The "redstone country" was an important stage in American westward migration where the advancing frontier was arrested for a quarter of a century, then burst westward in a flood with the end of the Indian wars.

Robert Ayres, manuscript journal for 1786-87.
Raymond Bell, *Methodism on the Upper Ohio before 1812.*
W. G. Smeltzer, *Headwaters of the Ohio.* 1951.
————, *The Story of Methodism in the Pittsburgh Region.*
W. GUY SMELTZER

REED, ELBERT E. (1896-   ), American agricultural missionary, was born at Wichita, Kan., and was reared in La Grange, Ill. He received a B.S. degree in horticulture from Iowa State College, 1920, and M.S. from Oregon State College, 1936.

In 1920 Reed was called to CHILE as horticulturist at EL VERGEL, 3,800-acre farm near ANGOL, acquired in 1919 by the M.E. Church. In 1925 he became general administrator, occupying this position until retirement in 1963.

The work Elbert Reed accomplished in building at El Vergel during these thirty-eight years became known all over Chile, and, indeed, to horticulturists over the world. He began with very little and with no encouragement or even belief on the part of the local Chilean landholders that he could do anything at all with the project he was starting. But in time there came to be gardens, orchards, finally a colony employing about 400 people, having its own grist mill and its own self-sustaining facilities with a chapel in which worship is regularly conducted, and an

ELBERT E. REED

amazing success in the planting of shrubs, flowers, fruit trees, and hardy trees for timber. The Chilean government after a time recognized this remarkable achievement by calling upon Elbert Reed for various types of services and authorities in horticulture over South America and foreign lands were accustomed to write him for advice on various matters connected with their work. With all the colony was a Christian one in every way, and practical Christianity was exemplified in all its attitudes and undertakings. El Vergel was struck by an earthquake and badly damaged in May 1960 and the Christians of Chile and Methodists of the world rallied to build back what had been destroyed in the chapel and facilities.

Reed contributed to the development of the fruit industries and to the beautification of city streets, parks, and gardens. His procedures in soil conservation and farm management were widely adopted and became important to food production.

In 1922 he was married to Marian Harrington, daughter of the Rev. and Mrs. FRANCIS M. HARRINGTON, missionaries in Chile and founders of The Methodist Church and schools in BOLIVIA.

For his work in Chile, Reed has received awards by the Government of Chile, Agricultural Missions, Inc., and the Alumni Association of Iowa State College. He retired to California to live.

EDWIN MAYNARD

REED, MARSHALL RUSSELL (1891-1973), American bishop, was born at Onsted, Mich., on Sept. 15, 1891, the son of Fred P. and Elsie A. (Russell) Reed. From ALBION COLLEGE he received the A.B. degree in 1914 and the D.D. in 1931; and from GARRETT THEOLOGICAL SEMINARY the B.D. in 1916 and the D.D. in 1940. NORTHWESTERN UNIVERSITY granted him the M.A. degree in 1917 and the S.T.D. in 1953; and ADRIAN COLLEGE, the LL.D. in 1959. He also studied at DREW UNIVERSITY.

He was ordained in 1917 and served pastorates in Gaines, 1917-18; Onaway, 1918-19; Calvary Church, Detroit, 1919-23; Jefferson Avenue, Detroit, 1923-28; Ypsilanti, 1928-34; Nardin Park Church, Detroit, 1934-48, all these being in MICHIGAN. He was elected a bishop of The Methodist Church at the NORTH CENTRAL JURISDICTIONAL CONFERENCE at INDIANAPOLIS, Ind. in July 1948, and was assigned to the Michigan Area.

He married Mary Esther Kirkendall on May 14, 1917, and they had three daughters, Elizabeth Jan (Mrs. Allan Gray), Elsie Mae (Mrs. John Ferentz), and Mary Louise (Mrs. William Ives).

Bishop Reed was a delegate to the GENERAL CONFERENCE of the M.E. Church in 1932, '36, and to that of The Methodist Church in 1940, '44, and '48—when he was elected bishop. He was also a member of the Uniting Conference in 1939. He served on the General Board of the NATIONAL COUNCIL OF CHURCHES, on the Board of MISSIONS, on the Board of PENSIONS (of which he was president), and on the Commission on Interjurisdictional Relations. He was chairman of the National Methodist Conference on Urban Life, 1962, and the president of the COUNCIL OF BISHOPS, 1962-63. He served as trustee of the Children's Home Society, the Chelsea Home for the Aged, of Adrian College, and of Albion College in Michigan. His official travel visitations as bishop took him to CHILE, 1950, and a four-month visitation to INDIA and the Orient in 1951, at the request of the Council of Bishops. He was the official visitor to Europe and North Africa in 1955. Upon his retirement in 1964, he continued to reside in Onsted, Mich. He died March 1, 1973, in Chelsea, Mich.

Who's Who in the Methodist Church, 1966.   N. B. H.

REED, MARY (1854-1943), an heroic missionary of the WOMAN'S FOREIGN MISSIONARY SOCIETY of the M.E. Church, was born in a prosperous family in Lowell, OHIO, and educated in that state. She came to Kanpur, INDIA in 1884, but became ill a few weeks later, and was sent to Pithoragarh in the Himalayas to recuperate and to study Hindi. On a ridge above her temporary home at the mission, she saw a colony of lepers, and felt that God wished her to serve them and would in time show her how. She returned to Kanpur and served there until she was appointed in 1889 to Gonda.

The next year she went to America on furlough. In her homeland she became ill again, and was treated in Christ Methodist Hospital in CINCINNATI. A tingling sensation in the forefinger of her right hand and a strange scar on her right cheek baffled the physicians. One day, "as clearly as if a voice had spoken," she learned that her disease was leprosy, and that she should return to India to serve the lepers at Pithoragarh. She told her physician of the "revelation" that she knew God had given her about her condition. He consulted other physicians who were acquainted with leprosy and they confirmed the diagnosis. Within her family she told only one sister before saying good-bye to parents and other loved ones and friends. In LONDON and Paris she consulted experts on leprosy, who confirmed her conviction and the diagnosis made in Ohio.

From BOMBAY she wrote to her sister and asked her to tell her mother. She proceeded to Pithoragarh with joy, fully persuaded that she was under God's compulsive guidance. With backing from her church and the British Mission to Lepers, she developed at Chandag Heights, two miles above Pithoragarh, a lovely home for the homeless and gave herself unreservedly to serving sufferers from leprosy. While she never doubted that the physicians were correct in diagnosing her illness, she lived in the assurance that God was holding it in check to enable her to serve others without fear. She alleviated the suffering of hundreds and led a great company of afflicted people to Jesus Christ and the joy of discipleship. She returned to America just once to say good-bye to her family and country. After 1912 she never departed from the hills of Eastern Kumaun.

Some of those whom she received into her home came out of NEPAL, and others from Bhot on the border of Tibet. She maintained a guest house near her house and many people from India, Great Britain, and America traveled to Chandag Heights to meet her. She had a well-stocked library and kept abreast of history—local, Indian, and world. Her book *The Unfailing Presence* tells the secret of how she lived alone and achieved so much.

Lee S. Huizenga, *Mary Reed of Chandag*. Grand Rapids, Mich.: Zondervan Publishing House, n.d.
E. Mackerchar, *Mary Reed of Chandag*. London: Mission to Lepers, n.d.　　　　　J. WASKOM PICKETT

REED, NELSON (1751-1840), American minister, was born in Anne Arundel County, Md., Nov. 27, 1751, and entered the traveling ministry on PETERSBURG (Virginia) Circuit, June 1778. He was ordained elder at the CHRISTMAS CONFERENCE and presided ten years over various districts before his marriage and location in 1800. In 1805 he re-entered the BALTIMORE CONFERENCE, where his comrades knew him for integrity and humble piety, and there served twelve additional years as a presiding elder before retiring in 1821.

Six times elected to GENERAL CONFERENCES (1808-28), he led the 1824 delegation. Although reputedly the world's oldest Methodist preacher, he remained active and in the closing year of life, as the sole surviving COKESBURY trustee, deeded the college property to Abingdon Church. He died Oct. 20, 1840 at BALTIMORE. His journal, 1778-82, is in the Methodist Historical Society, Baltimore.

J. E. Armstrong, *Old Baltimore Conference*. 1907.
E. S. Bucke, *History of American Methodism*. 1964.
　　　　　EDWIN SCHELL

REED, SETH (1823-1924), American minister, was born in Otsego County, N. Y., on June 2, 1823, of Puritan New England ancestry. The father died before his birth, leaving the mother and four children to struggle on a pioneer farm. In 1840, at seventeen years of age, he began to teach school.

In 1842 the family moved to GRAND RAPIDS, Mich. where he taught everything from alphabet to astronomy in rural schools, gaining his knowledge by home study. Expecting to enter the legal profession, he also studied law and became familiar with Blackstone's Commentaries.

His mother had been a Universalist and had brought up the boy in that faith; but before leaving New York he had undergone a conversion and joined the Methodists. In Grand Rapids he responded to the call of the ministry and entered the MICHIGAN CONFERENCE in the fall of 1844. For the next seventy-nine years he answered the annual conference roll call in person, a denominational

record. His early circuits were Flat River, Mapleton, Bennington and Genesee, circuits which covered entire counties, where the preacher followed trails, corduroy roads, and met deer and bear and pagan Indians.

In 1847 he married Harriett W. Russell, who was his companion for fifty-one years. To them four children were born. Among his city appointments were Mount Clemens, Pontiac, Flint, Ypsilanti, Ann Arbor, and DETROIT. For a period of eighteen years he served as a district superintendent. During the Civil War he served both Union and Confederate forces as a member of the Christian Commission.

When the DETROIT CONFERENCE was organized in 1856, he was elected its first secretary, a position he held for four years. In 1895 he was one of the organizers of the Anti-Saloon League at WASHINGTON, D. C. He also served as the first superintendent of the Methodist Home for the Aged at Chelsea, Mich.

After his retirement and his marriage to Henrietta Andrews, following the death of his first wife, he resided in Flint. His one hundredth birthday in 1923 was the occasion of a civic and Conference-wide celebration. He died March 24, 1924 and was buried in Glenwood Cemetery, Flint, Mich.

Minutes of the Michigan and Detroit Conferences.
E. H. Pilcher, *Michigan*. 1878.
Seth Reed, *The Story of My Life*. Cincinnati: Jennings & Graham, 1914.　　　　WILLIAM C. S. PELLOWE

REED, WALTER (1851-1902), noted American physician, head of the United States Army Yellow Fever Commission and the one generally credited with the discovery of the mosquito as the carrier of yellow fever. He was born in Belroi, Gloucester Co., Va., on Sept. 13, 1851, his father being Lemuel Sutlor Reed who served for forty years as a Methodist preacher in the VIRGINIA CONFERENCE (MES). Living in Charlottesville, he attended the University of Virginia, obtaining a medical degree in 1869 and a second degree from Bellevue Hospital Medical College (later merged with New York University's Medical School) in 1870. In 1874 he went into the Medical Corps of the U. S. Army.

Reed's work will always be associated with the work of the Yellow Fever Commission and with the consequent control of that disease. The Walter Reed General Hospital in Washington was subsequently named in his honor. He is said to have been "of a lively, happy disposition, enthusiastic and optimistic in everything to which he turned his hand." He is one of the few Methodists whose bust has been placed in the Hall of Fame of Great Americans in New York City.

Dictionary of American Biography.
Consult also H. A. Kelly, *Walter Reed and Yellow Fever*, 3rd Edition. 1923.
The Hall of Fame for Great Americans at New York University. Edited by Theodore Morello. New York: New York University Press, 1967.　　　　N. B. H.

REED, WILLIAM (1800-1858), British BIBLE CHRISTIAN minister, was born at Holwell, Buckland Brewer, North Devon, in October, 1800. His family united with WILLIAM O'BRYAN, and Reed accompanied JAMES THORNE on itinerary in 1819. Diffident and retiring as a youth, he developed remarkable powers of oratory, sustained prayer, and spiritual persuasion, and during his year at Holsworthy four hundred members were received on trial. In 1835 he helped to reconcile many who had followed O'Bryan out of the connection. He was four times president of Conference, and F. W. BOURNE considered him the greatest preacher of the denomination. Reed died at Barnstaple on May 9, 1858, and was buried at Lake.

ALYN W. G. COURT

ELI YEATES REESE

REESE, ELI YEATES (1816-1861), American preacher, poet, educator, singer, was for nineteen years the editor of *The Methodist Protestant*, the official organ of the M. P. CHURCH. Reese was born in BALTIMORE, Md., on Jan. 18, 1816, the youngest of four preacher brothers who were actively identified with the M. P. Church. These brothers were the sons of David and Mary Reese. John S. Reese, M.D. (May 15, 1790-Feb. 15, 1855) served as president of the MARYLAND CONFERENCE many times; Levi R. Reese was chaplain in the House of Representatives in Congress in 1837-38; Daniel E. Reese (Feb. 17, 1810-April 23, 1877) was president of the Maryland Conference from 1871-73. Eli Yeates Reese was elected editor of *The Methodist Protestant* on Oct. 13, 1838, retired on July 22, 1843, and served again as editor from July 25, 1846, until his death on Sept. 14, 1861. He was the principal compiler of the Hymn Book of the Methodist Protestant Church, published by authority of the GENERAL CONFERENCE of 1859.

Reese was popular as a public lecturer both in Baltimore and elsewhere in the United States and often spoke on the Lyceum circuit. His death resulted from a mental depression which came about as the War Between the States severely cut the circulation of his paper south of the Potomac River. Also the death of his wife a year earlier had a profound effect. He was buried in the Baltimore Cemetery.

A. H. Bassett, *Concise History*. 1877.
T. H. Colhouer, *Sketches of the Founders*. 1880.
E. J. Drinkhouse, *History of Methodist Reform*. 1899.

RALPH HARDEE RIVES

REESE, LEVI R. (1806-1851), American M.P. leader of considerable note in his connection and president of its GENERAL CONFERENCE for a term, was born in Harford County, Md., Feb. 8, 1806. At the age of seventeen he was employed as an assistant teacher in an academy, where he increased his literary attainments. He planned to enter the naval service, but the death of a young friend made a deep impression on his mind, and under the pointed exhortation of a preacher he was converted and united with the M.E. Church, being about twenty years of age. He espoused the cause of reform, then being agitated in BALTIMORE, joined the Union society, and became secretary to that body; and in the controversies which arose he was among the number excommunicated from the M.E. Church on the charge of "sowing dissension in the church and speaking evil of ministers." He immediately entered into the active ministry of the new METHODIST PROTESTANT CHURCH, and spent two or three years in NEW YORK and PHILADELPHIA. He subsequently served in every important station and in every official position in the body with which he was connected. For two successive years he was chosen president; was repeatedly a representative in the General Conference; and at one time presided over its deliberations. He was elected CHAPLAIN to the House of Representatives in Congress in 1837-38. During his chaplaincy a regrettable duel occurred which stirred public circles greatly, and Levi Reese delivered an impressive address which Bishop SIMPSON says was one of "delicacy, fidelity, and pathos." He also delivered in the Capitol a series of discourses on the obligations of the Sabbath, which were afterwards published. He was the author of *Thoughts of an Itinerant*. He died in Philadelphia, Pa., Sept. 21, 1851.

M. Simpson, *Cyclopaedia*. 1878.

N. B. H.

REEVES, HANNAH PEARCE (1800-1868), born in Devonshire, England, Jan. 30, 1800, became one of the first itinerant woman preachers in the M.P. Church and therefore a pioneer among women in the first half of the nineteenth century who sought the right to share the lecture platform and the pulpit with men. She began preaching among the BIBLE CHRISTIANS at the age of nineteen and traveled on circuits in England and Wales. Subsequently she came to America and on July 5, 1831, was married to William Reeves (Dec. 5, 1802-April 20, 1871). Reeves, a native of Staplehurst, Kent, England, had come to the United States in 1829 and become a minister in the OHIO ANNUAL CONFERENCE of the M.P. Church. At the division of the Ohio Conference in 1833, he continued in the newly formed PITTSBURGH CONFERENCE, which he later served frequently as president. He became a member of several GENERAL CONFERENCES and conventions of the denomination.

Upon arrival in America the couple immediately began their joint career in the reform movement of this church. Though Mrs. Reeves was offered an appointment on her own, she declined, preferring to accompany and assist her husband in his work. She was described as an "earnest and successful speaker, and was active in works of benevolence and philanthropy." Her health during the last nine years of her life kept her from regular public appearances, but she continued to be active in assisting churches, Sunday schools and benevolent societies. In 1848 her husband published at Putnam, Ohio, a defense of the ministry of women; and GEORGE BROWN wrote a book relating her life and services.

She died on Nov. 13, 1868, in New Brighton, Pa.

A. H. Bassett, *Concise History.* 1887.
George Brown, *The Lady Preacher; or, The Life and Labors of Mrs. Hannah Reeves* (Philadelphia: Daughaday & Becker, 1870).
T. H. Colhouer, *Sketches of the Founders.* 1880.
E. J. Drinkhouse, *History of Methodist Reform,* 1899.
M. Simpson, *Cyclopaedia.* 1882.

REEVES, JONATHAN (dates unknown), British Methodist, was one of John Wesley's earliest supporters. Reeves labored with success both in Cornwall and Ireland. He attended the Conferences of 1746, 1747, and 1748 and was appointed a trustee of the Orphan House in Bristol. He sought episcopal ordination and accepted the chaplaincy of the Magdalen Hospital, London, in 1758. He later served as a curate in Whitechapel and as rector of West Ham, Essex.

A. SKEVINGTON WOOD

REFORMED METHODIST CHURCH was formed in 1814 in Readsborough, Vt., by a group of Methodists led by Pliny Brett, a local preacher. At their first conference, Feb. 4, 1814, they adopted some Articles of Religion and rules for church government. The government was essentially congregational with no sharp distinctions being made between ministers and laymen. While the Methodist system of representative conferences was kept, ministers were delegates only if elected, not ex-officio. The local church was the focus of power, having the right to ordain elders, select their own ministers and do whatever else was necessary to carry on their work. Ministers, likewise, could pick their field of service.

Their doctrine was essentially Wesleyan though they emphasized divine healing and the possibility of attaining entire sanctification in this life. However, church membership did not rest upon assent to any particular doctrine, but in the fruits of righteousness obtained. They were anti-slavery and had an article against war.

From VERMONT, the church spread into the rest of New England, CANADA and NEW YORK. In 1837 it began publication of *The South Courtland Luminary,* which became the *Fayetteville Luminary* in 1939 and the *Methodist Reformer* in 1942.

In 1838 Pliny Brett, a large group in Ohio, and a large group in MASSACHUSETTS left the Reformed Methodists for the M.P. Church. Even in this weakened condition, the church continued to exist as a separate body until 1952 when it united with the Church of Christ in Christian Union and is now known as the North Eastern District of the Churches of Christ in Christian Union.

E. S. Bucke, *History of American Methodism.* 1964.
Vincent L. Milner, *Religious Denominations of the World,* 1872.
Yearbook of American Churches, 1967.　J. GORDON MELTON

REFORMED METHODIST UNION EPISCOPAL CHURCH.
The Reformed Methodist Union Episcopal Church was formed in 1885 by members of the A.M.E. CHURCH who withdrew after a dispute concerning the election of ministerial delegates to General Conference. William E. Johnson was elected the first president. A strong sentiment of

and for the non-episcopal nature of the new church was expressed. However, in 1896, steps were taken to alter the polity; and in 1919 after the death of Johnson, E. Russell Middleton was elected bishop. He was consecrated by Rt. Rev. Peter F. Stevens of the Reformed Episcopal Church. Following Middleton's death, a second bishop was elected and consecrated by the laying on of hands of seven elders of the church.

Doctrine was taken from the M.E. Church. The polity has moved in that direction and was fully adopted in 1916. Class meetings and love feasts are also retained. There were 16,198 members in thirty-one churches reported in 1967.

Frank S. Mead, *Handbook of Denominations in the United States.* Nashville: Abingdon, 1965.
Yearbook of American Churches.　J. GORDON MELTON

REFORMED NEW CONGREGATIONAL METHODIST CHURCH. The Reformed New Congregational Church was formed in 1916 by Earl Wilcoxen, a minister of the CONGREGATIONAL METHODIST CHURCH, and J. A. Sander, an independent minister. Using the doctrines of repentance, forgiveness and justification as their main points, they began a preaching tour through southern INDIANA and ILLINOIS and gathered converts into congregations.

The church is of the "holiness" type believing in the forsaking of sin by the sinner and the reception of divine light by God. They believe that war is contrary to Jesus' teaching and they condemn divorce, fancy wearing apparel, and secret societies.

As its name implies, the church is congregational in government and each elects its own pastor who is paid by freewill offering. No statistics later than 1936 are available at which time there were eight churches with 329 members.

Census of Religious Bodies, 1936.　J. GORDON MELTON

REFORMED ZION UNION APOSTOLIC CHURCH. The Reformed Zion Union Apostolic Church was founded by a group from the A.M.E. CHURCH interested in setting up a religious organization "to aid in bringing about Christian Union, whose fruit will be Holiness unto the Lord." Led by James Howell, the group met at Boydton, Va., in April 1869 and organized the Zion Union Apostolic Church with James Howell as the president. Harmony and growth prevailed until 1874, when changes in polity led to the election of Howell as bishop with life tenure. Dissatisfaction with this action nearly destroyed the organization even though Bishop Howell resigned. In 1882 a reorganization was effected, the four-year presidental structure reinstituted, and the present name adopted.

A representative conference structure is maintained with the law-making power invested in a quadrennial General Conference. Over the years the four-year presidency has again been dropped in favor of life-tenure bishops. A board of publication has control over church literature and publishes the church school material and the *Union Searchlight,* a periodical.

In 1965, the Reformed Zion Union Apostolic Church reported 16,000 members in fifty churches.

General Rules and Discipline of the Reformed Zion Union Apostolic Church, 1966.　J. GORDON MELTON

REGISTRATION FOR WORSHIP AND MARRIAGES. Following the eviction of over two thousand clergymen of the Church of England, under the Act of Uniformity, 1662, and the oppressive Conventicle Act, 1664, some relief was given to dissenters by the Act of Toleration, 1689, under which dissenting meetinghouses might be licensed. With the extension of Methodist preaching houses, as they were called, JOHN WESLEY was faced with a great difficulty. He rightly maintained that the Methodists were not dissenters but, many of them, members of the Established Church, and that the preaching houses were not used during church hours. He finally agreed, after taking legal advice, but under protest, that Methodist chapels might be licensed under the Act of Toleration. This was one factor which involved definite separation from the Church of England. It was not until toward the end of the nineteenth century that the continuing disabilities were removed. The present requirements in respect of all Nonconformist places of worship are as follows: (1) A building which is intended to be used for public worship must be registered for that purpose before use. Sketch plans may be required by the Superintendent Registrar, and a fee of 2/6 has to be paid. (2) A building registered for public worship must be further registered if it is desired that it should be used for the solemnization of marriages. A fee of £4.10.0 is payable to the Registrar General. The presence of the official registrar to witness and register the marriage is necessary unless otherwise provided as under (3). (3) An "authorized person"— minister or layman—may be certified on the appropriate form in triplicate to the Registrar General and when officially registered can take the place of the registrar in attendance at the ceremony and in registering the marriage. No fee is required in securing this appointment, but there are certain conditions including the provision of a suitable safe for the security of registers.

Registrations (1), (2), and (3) can all be undertaken at the same time if so desired.

E. BENSON PERKINS

REHOBOTH BEACH, DELAWARE, U.S.A., a seaside resort community, is situated on the Atlantic Ocean below the mouth of the Delaware Bay and forty miles from DOVER.

Because Robert W. Todd, a Methodist minister, suggested at a WILMINGTON preachers' meeting that an oceanside religious gathering might prove popular, a CAMP MEETING was begun at Rehoboth in 1872. When land was secured and lots laid out, Todd was made manager. The resort town, a direct outgrowth of the camp meeting, developed slowly. From the camp meeting program two churches were eventually organized: the first, nonsectarian under Methodist control, was built by summer residents and called "Bishop Scott's Church" after the bishop who presided at the 1880 dedication; the second, Epworth Church, was built in 1889. When fire destroyed Scott's Church in 1913 the two congregations united, using the site of the former church, rebuilding and enlarging the old structure, and taking the name of the latter church. In 1970 Epworth Church property was valued at $381,-260; its membership numbered 515, there were 260 church school students.

General Minutes.
E. C. Hallman, *Garden of Methodism.* 1948. ERNEST R. CASE

REHOBOTH CHURCH

REHOBOTH CHURCH, one of the national Historic SHRINES of American Methodism, located on a five-acre tract two miles east of Union, Monroe Co., W. Va., is the oldest Protestant church edifice west of the Alleghenies. A log structure some twenty-one by twenty-nine feet with a narrow gallery which will seat nearly as many people as the room below, the church was built in 1786.

Under the leadership of local preachers who lived among the settlers in the region, a Methodist society was organized there in 1784. The group met in a schoolhouse which stood near the site of the present church. About 1785, Methodist circuit riders by the names of WILLIAM PHOEBUS and Lasley Matthews visited the area, and under Phoebus' ministry, Edward Keenan, a former Roman Catholic, was converted. Keenan led in building Rehoboth Church. His tombstone northeast of the church reads, "Edward Keenan, born 1742, died August 11, 1826. He built Rehoboth Church, and gave the lot of ground."

Rehoboth Church gave Methodism a foothold in a region where there were still forts against the Indians. In 1787 the Greenbrier Circuit which included Rehoboth Church was formed, and JOHN SMITH was appointed to travel it. Setting out to organize Methodism in the territory, Smith used Rehoboth Church as his rallying point. Smith's journal shows that he visited Rehoboth Church the first time on July 29, 1787. Also, it indicates that he was ordained deacon there by Bishop ASBURY on July 5 or 6, 1788 in the first ordination ceremony ever conducted west of the Alleghenies. According to Asbury's journal, he conducted three conferences at Rehoboth Church— 1792, 1793, and 1796—and in addition he preached in the church in 1790 and 1797.

Rehoboth Church was used regularly as a place of worship for more than a century. From the early days people in the vicinity manifested concern for the log church and gave it protection and care. It is now the property of the Commission on Archives and History of the WEST VIRGINIA CONFERENCE. In recent years a steel canopy has been erected over the old log structure to protect it from the elements.

The 1960 GENERAL CONFERENCE designated Rehoboth Church as a national Historic Shrine of American Methodism.

F. Asbury, *Journal and Letters.* 1958.
Kibler, J. L., *A Historical Sketch of Rehoboth Methodist Episcopal Church, South Monroe County, West Virginia. Journal of John Smith.* Unpublished. At Garrett Theological Seminary.   LAWRENCE F. SHERWOOD

REID, ALEXANDER (1821-1891), NEW ZEALAND minister, was born in Edinburgh, SCOTLAND. As a young man, he became a teacher, both at OXFORD and at Bath. Fired with enthusiasm for the missionary cause, he offered for service in Africa and was sent for training to Richmond College, LONDON. He was there only twenty-four hours, for a letter came from WALTER LAWRY asking for two of the best men, and Reid was one of those chosen. Ordained and married in 1848, he reached New Zealand in 1849, and was appointed principal of Wesley College, Three Kings.

After eight years of strenuous teaching and preaching, Reid's health gave way and he was sent to the Te Kopua Mission Station. There he won the deep affection of the Maoris, who picked him up bodily and carried him to safety when the Maori Wars brought alien tribes to the district. After working among the British troops, he served in leading circuits until 1885, when he was again appointed to Three Kings, where he labored until his death on Aug. 25, 1891.

He helped to translate the Bible into the Maori language; he attended the first ECUMENICAL METHODIST CONFERENCE in London; he was president of the New Zealand Wesleyan Conference in 1876; he was a member of the Auckland University Council; he was a leader of men and a prince of preachers.

W. Morley, *New Zealand*. 1900.   WILLIAM T. BLIGHT

REID, CLARENCE FREDERICK (1849-1915), pioneer missionary of the M.E. Church, South, to CHINA and KOREA, and later secretary of the Laymen's Missionary Movement, was born in South Oxford, N. Y., July 19, 1849. As a member of the KENTUCKY CONFERENCE (MES), he was appointed missionary to China, arriving in Shanghai in 1878. He became presiding elder of the Soochow District, and was a charter member of the China Mission Conference, organized in 1886.

The Soochow missionaries were seeking a mission field with more suitable climate for those who found the Soochow area unbearable, and in 1895, Reid and Bishop EUGENE R. HENDRIX visited SEOUL for that purpose. Decision was made to open work, and Reid was named superintendent of the Korea District of the China Conference. The next year he established residence in Seoul, surveyed the Korea field and began work in both Songdo and Seoul. In 1897 he was made superintendent of the newly established Korea Mission by the Board of Missions of his church.

Failing health caused Reid to return to America in 1900, but he never forgot his zeal for work in China and Korea. His remarkable gifts as a platform speaker made him a favorite through southern Methodism, especially for his address, "The Old and New in China."

He had early made a promise of a hosptial for Songdo but it was left to his son, Wightman T. Reid, M.D., to fulfill that dream. A generous layman from Lynchburg, Va. gave $5,000, and in 1907, the son went to Songdo to erect the W. C. Ivey Hospital and begin the medical work which continued until Songdo was over-run by the Communists in 1950.

After returning to America, Reid became superintendent of work for Orientals on the Pacific Coast for his denomination, and in 1909 was named secretary of the Laymen's Missionary Movement. His energetic leadership secured among other things legislation in the 1914 GENERAL CONFERENCE giving official standing to the work of the laymen of the church.

Clarence F. Reid died in Erlanger, Ky., Oct. 7, 1915.

Journal, North Alabama Conference, 1915, p. 225.
The Missionary Voice, November, 1915, pp. 482-484.
      CHARLES A. SAUER

REID, FRANK MADISON (1898-1962), an American bishop of the A.M.E. CHURCH, was born in NASHVILLE, Tenn., on Aug. 11, 1898. He received the A.B. degree from WILBERFORCE UNIVERSITY (Ohio) in 1921, and the M.A., D.D. and LL.D. (honorary) from Wilberforce and Allen Universities respectively. He was converted in 1904, licensed to preach in 1918 and admitted into the West Kentucky Annual Conference in 1922. He was ordained DEACON in 1922 and ELDER in 1923. He held pastorates in KENTUCKY and MISSOURI. He was elected bishop in 1940 from the pastorate of St. Paul Church, ST. LOUIS, Mo. He served in South Africa and the southern United States. He died in 1962. Bishop Reid was active in the civil rights movement in SOUTH CAROLINA and known as an eloquent preacher.

R. R. Wright, *The Bishops*.   GRANT S. SHOCKLEY

REINHARDT COLLEGE, Waleska, Ga., was established in 1883 as Reinhardt Normal College with elementary and secondary schools. The college was named for Captain A. M. Reinhardt of Atlanta, who was the leading influence in its establishment. The elementary school transferred to the public-school system in 1925, and the secondary work was discontinued in 1956. Samuel Candler Dobbs, a nephew of Bishop WARREN A. CANDLER, was chairman of the board of trustees from 1926 to 1951 and the school's chief benefactor. The governing board consists of forty-two members elected by the board and confirmed by the North Georgia Annual Conference.

      JOHN O. GROSS

RELIEF FUND, METHODIST (British), began as a private appeal by HENRY CARTER to assist refugees in Europe; it has been administered since 1951 by the DEPARTMENT OF CHRISTIAN CITIZENSHIP. It gives help "in special cases of emergency, distress or need, in which the Methodist Church has a particular denominational responsibility." This is in practice interpreted to mean Methodists in distress, and also relief projects administered by Methodists. The fund now serves (1) to give immediate assistance to distress caused by natural catastrophes; (2) to sustain refugee relief work in GERMANY, AUSTRIA, HONG KONG, and ALGERIA; (3) to launch eventually self-supporting long-term relief projects, e.g. "Operation Friendship" in Jamaica, an orphanage in Uzuakoli, an agricultural development project in Kenya; (4) to provide personal assistance in cases of acute need. There is regular cooperation with the METHODIST COMMISSION ON OVERSEAS RELIEF (U.S.A.). Annual income grew from £1,500 in 1951 to £34,000 in 1965, an indication that the fund, though kept deliberately subordinate to Inter-Church Aid, exercises a growing ministry of practical compassion.

      E. ROGERS

RELIGION IN LIFE is a quarterly journal published by ABINGDON PRESS, a division of the METHODIST PUBLISHING

HOUSE of The United Methodist Church. It names itself "A Christian Quarterly of opinion and discussion" and makes its appeal to ministers and thinking laymen of all denominations. It was begun in the early 1930's by JOHN W. LANGDALE, the book editor of the M.E. Church who felt that since the old *Quarterly Review* had been discontinued, and the *Quarterly Review* of the M.E. Church, South, was about to be discontinued, a journal to take the place of these traditionally sponsored Church publications might well be published with success and profit. This should be not for Methodism alone, but for a wide reading Christian constituency among the major denominations of the United States and it was hoped over the English speaking world. The publication was begun by the Methodist Book Concern in New York and when a few years later at Church union in 1939 the Book Concern was merged into the Methodist Publishing House, the Uniting Conference itself—and subsequent General Conferences—have ordered and sponsored the publication of *Religion in Life*.

To further the interdenominational appeal, the editorial board chosen for this journal has always had in its membership scholarly and representative men of various Christian denominations. On its "advisory council" likewise are scholars, theologians, publicists and Church leaders of various denominations. The book editor of the Methodist Church is directed by the *Discipline* to edit *Religion in Life* as part of his duties, and the publication of the quarterly is entrusted to the Methodist Publishing House. The BOARD OF PUBLICATION of The United Methodist Church "at its descretion, may continue the publication of the quarterly *Religion in Life,* with the book editor responsible for its editorial content."

In keeping with its interdenominational character, *Religion in Life* does not promote specifically the fundamental Methodist emphases as did the old *Reviews* of the past generation. It is understood, however, that as it is underwritten and published by The United Methodist Church, it will and does set forth in many scholarly articles the teachings and trends and influential happenings in that Church, as well as reflecting significant movements in the modern Church world—both in theology and in life.

Religion in Life is necessarily somewhat eclectic for the reasons given above. The vast number of its subscribers are, however, Methodists. Within recent years each issue has been devoted specifically to a particular emphasis in the realm of Church life and thought, with three or four articles setting forth the special emphasis featured in that individual issue. Other articles are chosen for their merit in the general field of Church life, history, ethics, theology, and so forth, and as in the case with other scholarly publications, a book review section endeavors to keep the readers abreast of new and significant publications.

Religion in Life, like its *Review* predecessors (except possibly in their heyday) has never been entirely self-supporting, but is underwritten by the Publishing House of The United Methodist Church as a service to Christian scholarship and to enlightened thinking on the part of its readers. The journal is held in high repute in the United States, is on file in many libraries, and current and past volumes of *Religion in Life* are available on microfilm for those who wish to have its published material made thus available.

Following JOHN LANGDALE, who died just after Church union in 1939, NOLAN B. HARMON, book editor of the

Church, edited the journal until 1956 when he was elected bishop; and then EMORY S. BUCKE, the present book editor of The United Methodist Church, became editor-in-chief. The address is the Methodist Publishing House in Nashville, Tenn.

Files of *Religion in Life*
E. S. Bucke, *History of American Methodism*. Vol. III (pp. 295, 303, 307, 537).
J. P. Pilkington, *The Methodist Publishing House*, Nashville. Abingdon Press. (p. 160).   N. B. H.

RELIGIOUS SOCIETIES. Several voluntary groups were founded in later seventeenth-century England, to combat what many felt to be a breakdown of religion, morals, and social stability. This probably reflected the declining influence of traditional church doctrine and discipline, as well as a desire for active lay Christianity. Of these societies, the Society for Promoting Christian Knowledge (1698) promoted education, and the Society for the Propagation of the Gospel (1701) hoped to serve the colonies. The Societies for the Reformation of Manners (1690-91) wished to implement existing laws against vice; and in the eighteenth century both JOHN WESLEY and WILLIAM WILBERFORCE supported short-lived attempts to revive them. The "Religious Societies" proper were founded earlier (c. 1678) by ANTHONY HORNECK and Richard Smithies for young Londoners with a religious concern. They were wholly Anglican, under clerical direction; they used the *Prayer Book;* and discussion of personal problems was voluntary. Later, these societies spread to the rest of the British Isles and encouraged charitable work. Religious societies of this type still active in 1738 probably supplied personnel rather than methods or ideas to early Methodism. Under Methodist and Moravian influence, and in response to the preaching of WHITEFIELD and the Wesleys, these societies, and new ones, began to use free prayer, to emphasize justification by faith, and to concentrate on mutual confession of sins. The older type of society probably disappeared, while the specifically Methodist societies separated from the Moravians in 1740, and had their own distinctive rules from 1743.

HENRY RACK

RELIGIOUS TELESCOPE, official paper of the Church of the UNITED BRETHREN IN CHRIST, was authorized by the Scioto Conference in 1834, when the GENERAL CONFERENCE of 1833 requested that Conference to supervise the publishing venture to be formed at Circleville, Ohio. In June 1834 WILLIAM RHINEHART had begun a newspaper for the VIRGINIA CONFERENCE under the title *Union Messenger,* soon changed to *Mountain Messenger.* The trustees of the newly formed denominational publishing house, in order to discourage more than one periodical in the church, purchased the fonts of type from William Rhinehart in November 1834, and chose him to become their editor. Rhinehart also brought along his subscribers, small in number. The first issue, a semi-monthly, was released Dec. 31, 1834. Later it became a weekly.

When DAYTON, Ohio became the site of the publishing house in 1853, the *Religious Telescope* was issued from that city. The paper continued to serve the church until the time of union with The EVANGELICAL CHURCH in 1946. It was then united with *The Evangelical-Messenger* of that body to become The *Telescope-Messenger* of The

EVANGELICAL UNITED BRETHREN CHURCH, which paper received the volume numbering of the *Religious Telescope*.

JOHN H. NESS, JR.

RENNER, S. M. (1896-   ), E.U.B. minister in SIERRA LEONE, West Africa, was born Oct. 22, 1896. Educated in the mission schools of the Church of the UNITED BRETHREN IN CHRIST in Sierra Leone, he entered the ministry, January 1918, and was ordained by the Sierra Leone Conference, January, 1927. He served pastorates at Freetown and Moyamba, covering fifty-one years. For twenty-two years he also was conference superintendent. On June 2, 1921 he was married to Miss Martha Rosaline, to which union were born four sons, two of whom entered the ministry.

In addition to denominational responsibilities he has held membership as follows: general secretary and president of United Christian Council; president of Sierra Leone Ministers Fraternal; Freetown City Council; Chairman of Mining Wages Board; The Protectorate Assembly; Committee on return to Civilian Rule; WORLD COUNCIL OF CHURCHES Committee on Rapid Social Changes in Africa.

LEBANON VALLEY COLLEGE gave him an honorary D.D. degree in 1945. King George VI decorated him as an Officer of the Most Excellent Order of the British Empire (Civil Division) and Queen Elizabeth II decorated him as Commander of the Most Excellent Order of the British Empire.

JOHN H. NESS, JR.

RENO, NEVADA, U.S.A., is the educational, financial, and industrial center for the northern and central part of the state. The town was named for a Civil War General, Jesse Lee Reno.

Methodism and the Central Pacific Railway reached Truckee Meadows, now Reno, in the same year, 1868. The town grew steadily. When the mines closed and NEVADA turned to "tourism" for its support, Reno announced itself "The Biggest Little City in the World." Owing to Nevada' liberal divorce law in the years following World War II as many as 6,000 divorces were granted here annually, and 24,000 marriages per year were performed. As the downtown church, First Church was sought by many of the out of town couples who came from religious homes. An energetic pastor, Frederick H. Busher, arranged to have a minister of marriage, and announced that all fees, above expenses, would go to missionary work in the state. For several years this church reported the second largest number of marriages of any church in the United States.

Since 1950 Las Vegas has become more an amusement center than Reno, and attracts larger numbers.

The campus of the University of Nevada is in the city. President during its formative years, 1884 to 1904, was Joseph E. Stubbs, a member of the CALIFORNIA ANNUAL CONFERENCE.

The six Methodist churches in the Reno-Lake Tahoe area report (1970) 2,121 members.

General Minutes.
L. L. Loofbourow, *Steeples Among the Sage.* 1964.

LEON L. LOOFBOUROW

RENTOUL, THOMAS C. (1882-1945). Australian minister and church leader. After a sound evangelical conversion, T. C. Rentoul entered the ministry in Victoria in 1911. He soon became distinguished by his earnestness and his administrative ability. He was a CHAPLAIN in World War I, 1916-18, suffering the effects of gas. After a short experience in circuit work he was selected to assist A. T. HOLDEN in Home Missions work.

From 1932 to 1945 he was general superintendent of Home Missions in Victoria. Tall, with authority in his bearing, a master of detail, and tireless in pursuing progressive policies, T. C. Rentoul stamped his influence on the life of Methodism in Victoria, and also in the Federal Inland Misson. He travelled far and wide through the inland areas of the continent in supervising the pioneer work of the Church.

T. C. Rentoul's initiative was seen in organizing the work of the Deaconess Order, in the acquisition of church property, and in stimulating EVANGELISM. He served as chaplain in World War II and was Chaplain-General from 1937 until his death on Dec. 28, 1945, this resulting from an infection received while on duty in NEW GUINEA that year.

He was president of the VICTORIA AND TASMANIA CONFERENCE in 1940, elected secretary-general in 1945 and, but for his untimely death, would have become president-general.

A. HAROLD WOOD

REPENTANCE. Repentance in its generic sense signifies a change of mind (*metanoia* in the Greek New Testament), a wishing something were undone that has been done and signifying a change of mind and disposition. In a strictly religious sense it signifies a conviction of sin, and a godly sorrow for it. A real repentance differs from what has sometimes been called "repentance" when that has been caused by the knowledge of injuries sustained or penalties likely to come. It is not sorrow for being caught in wrong doing. Evangelical repentance is not only sorrow for something done—sometimes for a whole life recognized as wrong—but is a recognition of the sin as offensive to God, accompanied by an immediate intent to see that the act repented of is done no more. Frequently great moral dejection comes when man feels himself helpless in the power of temptation against the type of thing he is repenting of. This was St. Augustine's experience again and again before he actually was converted. He repented enough—as he tells the story in his *Confessions*—but could not by his own power keep from sin—until he really threw all on God.

"Repentance is a personal sorrow for personal sin as against a Holy God," wrote OLIN A. CURTIS (in *The Christian Faith*, p. 353). "We should place great emphasis upon the fact that repentance is *personal*. . . . repentance is not merely something done by a person, it is something done by a person when he is *self-conscious*. . . . no man can repent without real self-decision and there can be no self decision without full self-consciousness." The same authority goes on to define repentance more definitely as "a sinner's personal sorrow over his responsible sin, both in deed and in condition of heart; and involves a confession of the guilt of a sin, a purpose to get free from his sin, and an intense hatred of his sin against the Holy God."

For a time there was a debate between certain Calvinistic theologians who held that regeneration precedes faith and repentance; as, according to that view, only the regenerated could perform such religious acts. With them the process was first regeneration; second, faith; and third, repentance. Methodists have always believed that in the salvation of the sinner, the Holy Spirit first enlightens his understanding and causes him to feel his need of a Saviour; that under this spiritual influence and enlightening comes a sincere repentance and an intent to turn from sin; then comes belief and hope in the Lord Jesus Christ and a casting of the soul upon His mercy and leadership; and then as has been the case with many, there follows a sense of justification and of acceptance by God.

While repentance is, strictly speaking, the act of man, it is nevertheless also in another sense the gift of God. Without the Grace of God first given, no man will repent or turn to God. Here is where what theologians call "prevenient grace" comes into play—an act of God opening the mind and heart to the accusing and pleading influences of the Holy Spirit. As the old hymn, written by William Bengo Collyer, has it: "Those warm desires that in thee burn were kindled by reclaiming grace."

This grace "supplies light to the understanding, quickens the emotions, and so seals Divine Truth upon the consciousness that the sinner not only sees, but feels his spiritual danger. The motives to repentance have been furnished in the Word of God; opportunity to repent is afforded through the mercy and forbearance of God; and hope is found in the promises given to the pentitent and the contrite heart." (Simpson's *Cyclopaedia, in loc.*)

Repentance and CONVICTION are almost concomitant moves in the same category, though conviction is more an attitude of the mind bringing repentance, as repentance is more a move of the soul. (For an outline by Wesley on Methodist teaching see Sermon IX, *The Spirit of Bondage and of Adoption.*)

Methodists have always preached repentance, not as an intellectual or moral state, but as a necessary precondition of acceptance with God. As part of the conference COURSE OF STUDY in American Methodist Churches for some years, young ministers had to prepare a sermon on repentance as part of their examination for acceptance in the Conference. It should be stressed, however, that preaching repentance is not done to *explain* repentance as an intellectual concept, but to get people actually to *repent.*

It is "A hopeful determination to get right at any cost." . . . Dr. Olin Curtis puts it: "The whole feeling is this; 'God himself wants me to be right, then I can be right, then I will be right.' "

Olin Alfred Curtis, *The Christian Faith.* N. Y.: Eaton & Mains, 1905.
Schaff-Herzog. *Encyclopedia of Religious Knowledge, in loc.*
M. Simpson, *Cyclopaedia.* 1878.   N. B. H.

REPOSITORY OF RELIGION. A publication of the African Methodist Episcopal Church. (See AFRICAN METHODIST EPISCOPAL CHURCH, Publications.)

REPROBATION. This doctrine, which has been held of the more extreme among Calvinists, declares that the finally impenitent who go to eternal damnation, do so on account of the express and eternal predestinating decree of God. This admittedly fearsome doctrine is in general chiefly a matter of historical interest, for it is not

often voiced among responsible modern Calvinists. However, in the eighteenth century it was a matter of bitter controversy between the Wesleys and their detractors, and the controversy left marks upon later Methodism. It is in the interests of modern ecumenical understanding, therefore, to attempt a dispassionate judgment regarding this ancient stumbling-block.

Background to the Doctrine. Many modern Methodists may find it hard to understand why some perfectly sincere followers of our Lord should have affirmed this doctrine, which on the face of it seems so contrary to the concept of the universal love of God the Father. That self-righteous condemnation and controversy may be avoided, it is necessary to look behind this teaching, and to understand that there are reasons for it which, though firmly rejected by Methodists, are quite intelligible. In the first place, it is a dark mystery of life why some people who hear the Gospel accept it, and others do not. It is also a mystery of God's providential government of the world that some people should apparently have little or even no chance. The doctrine of Reprobation places this matter squarely upon the unfettered and unaccountable choice of the Sovereign Lord of all. This answer does not satisfy us, but as we reject it, we are aware that alternative answers are not free from difficulty.

For the general background to this matter in religious experience, Scripture exposition, and theological speculation, the reader is referred to the article ELECTION, especially to the note on the doctrine of Particular Election. The Augustinian would affirm that this stern predestinarian doctrine is in keeping with the justice and goodness of God, because the whole human race collectively, and every man in it, has sinned, and merits damnation. Therefore those whom God does not elect to save are justly lost, while His goodness is displayed in His will to save some who do not deserve to be saved. Many Calvinists have, wisely we feel, carried their speculation no further. They have affirmed the positive side of God's gracious action towards the Elect, and remained prudently silent regarding the dark mystery of the lost. However, the instinct to complete a speculative system is very strong in some minds. Therefore some have made themselves responsible for the doctrine of a double divine Predestination. Those who are finally damned will be lost because God has positively decreed that they shall be lost. This is the doctrine of Reprobation.

Scripture warrant has been sought for the doctrine of Reprobation, the leading passage being Romans 9:17-23. It is not possible here to expound the whole of this difficult passage, but the chief point is the reference to Exodus 9:12-16, with the phrase "and the Lord hardened the heart of Pharaoh." Scientific exegesis would observe that the ancient Hebrews were deficient in the means of expressing the idea of "indirect causation." It is natural for us to think of a "law of nature," for which the Creator is indeed ultimately responsible, which yet is self-acting within the sphere of nature. Thus it is possible, in an order perverted by sin, for God to *allow* things to happen according to natural law which are not His direct will. For ultimately good moral reasons God for a time permits human rebellion. The Hebrews did not find it easy either to grasp or to express this notion of indirect divine operation. They spoke as though everything which happened in God's world came straight from God. Thus the *intention* of the phrase "God hardened Pharaoh's heart" would be expressed in our speech by "Pharaoh's heart became hardened" (according to the working of a moral law, but not excluding Pharaoh's own choice of evil). Thus understood, the force of such a passage as Romans 9:17-23 is greatly reduced. It does not mean that God arbitrarily damned Pharaoh, but that his obstinacy, for which he was truly responsible, was over-ruled by God for a good purpose which ultimately extends to all men (cf. Romans 11:11-12).

Wesleyan Controversy Regarding Reprobation. JOHN WESLEY was hotly attacked by some Calvinist opponents as disloyal to the evangelical doctrine of salvation by grace, because he strongly affirmed the position more characteristic of catholic Christianity. This is that saving GRACE is in principle available to all men, because the effectual means of grace are open to all who will use them, and the universally loving God will by His *prevenient grace* enable all men who desire Christian salvation to use these means of grace. However, we may claim that Wesley's attitude as a practical and common-sense teacher is in accord with the intention of the Anglican Article X (VIII in the Methodist Articles), and XVII (see ARTICLES OF RELIGION for text of these particular Articles). He can most strongly affirm the positive spiritual values implicit in the strong doctrine of grace taught by the Calvinists (see *Minutes of Several Conversations* for 1745, August 2, Q. 22 and 23, *Works* VIII, 284-5). In this sense he is "within a hairbreadth of Calvinism." Yet he was splendidly free from their often arid and entangling speculations regarding God's government of the race. In particular, he totally repudiated the extreme, dreadful, and erroneous doctrine of Reprobation.

JOHN LAWSON

REPUBLICAN METHODIST CHURCH was formed in 1792 by the followers of JAMES O'KELLY, who had strongly contested the appointive power of Bishop ASBURY at the 1792 GENERAL CONFERENCE. O'Kelly had earlier participated in the schismatic Fluvanna Conference (1779) and as a presiding elder in the southern district, had been a strong advocate of democratizing the conferences. The church he founded showed an immediate success in VIRGINIA and gained several thousand members in the first few years. Its major characteristics were its democratic ideals. It gave laymen more rights and put all ministers on an equal basis. As a corollary, it was strongly anti-slavery.

In 1801, following a decline in the original growth, O'Kelly reorganized the church; he abolished all regulations and discipline, except the scripture, and renamed the body the Christian Church. After several years of co-operative activity, a union was effected with two other "Christian Churches" to form the American Christian Convention. This body in turn united with the Congregational Church to form the Congregational Christian Church. This later body is currently a part of the United Church of Christ.

E. S. Bucke, *History of American Methodism*, 1964.
Frank A. Kostyn, "A History of the United Church" in *United Church—History and Program*.
Vincent L. Milner, *Religious Denominations of the World*. 1872.   J. GORDON MELTON

REPUBLICAN UNITED BRETHREN CHURCH was a pro-war schismatic group formed by members of the White River

Conference of the UNITED BRETHREN IN CHRIST, during the Mexican War. The church's origin can be traced to an informal meeting of ministers and members of the White River Conference at Dowell Meeting House, Franklin Circuit, Ind., on March 12, 1848. At the meeting, a resolution was passed protesting conference action concerning P. C. Parker. Parker had been expelled from the ministry for "immorality" because of his participation in the war. This resolution was refused publication; therefore, an appeal was made to GENERAL CONFERENCE. The 1853 General Conference, however, sustained Parker's expulsion and also passed a strong anti-war resolution as well as a resolution on total depravity. These three actions became the formal basis for withdrawal. At a meeting at Union Chapel, Decatur County, Ind., Sept. 8-12, 1853, the new church was organized.

The Republican United Brethren substantially followed the United Brethren in polity but objected to certain powers of the bishops, the presiding elders, and the stationing committee. They also dissented on the issues of war and peace and total hereditary depravity.

The church was small (the first conference listed only two charges) and existed for only a short time. In the 1860's they became part of the Christian Union.

Origin, Confession of Faith Constitution and General Rules of the Republican United Brethren Church, Nashville, Tenn., 1858.
A. C. Wilmore, *History of the White River Conference*.
                                                     J. GORDON MELTON

RESTRICTIVE RULES. (See GENERAL CONFERENCE of The Methodist Church.)

RESURRECTION: General. There is no distinctive Methodist doctrine of the General Resurrection. In common with the general body of the Church catholic the Methodist Church teaches that one of the events connected with the final stages of the history of this world will be the Resurrection of all men, as a prelude to the Last Judgment (John 5:28-29; Revelation 20:13). This belief is affirmed in the creeds commonly used among Methodists, the ecumenical NICENE CREED reading, "And I look for the resurrection of the dead, and the life of the world to come," and the APOSTLES' CREED reading, "I believe in the resurrection of the body, and the life everlasting." The universal Church has never found it necessary to make her dogmatic definition more precise than this. Thus there is allowable a substantial liberty of interpretation as to what is intended by this part of the Christian hope, dependent upon the interpretation which is given to those parts of Scripture which speak of it.

This doctrine is plainly presupposed in the authoritative *Standard Sermons* and *Notes on the New Testament* of JOHN WESLEY, as in his other writings, and in the Wesley hymns. Significantly, however, the Wesleys presuppose rather than argue the point, because this doctrine was not a matter of controversy in their time. They are content to rejoice in the greatness of Christian hope, and to warn men of the reality of judgment to come. In his exposition of Scripture John Wesley states it as his opinion that the Resurrection of the Body, though real, is not the resurrection of the present material body of flesh and blood, but of a glorious body suited to the conditions of the Heavenly Kingdom, and cites the ancient Greek Father Macarius in support of this exposition (*Notes* on

I Corinthians 15:51-2; II Corinthians 5:2,4; Philippians 3:21). It may perhaps be stated that since his day the general body of more reliable Methodist opinion has followed this line.

Origin of the Doctrine. This Christian doctrine is the heritage of the Hebrew roots of the Church. In earlier periods the Hebrews held a view of human destiny beyond the grave similar to that of many other ancient religions, and not unlike that revived by "Spiritualist" teaching in the modern world. The shades of the departed were supposed to continue in existence, though with a reduced and denatured vitality and identity (Isaiah 14:9-10). Their abode was Sheol, a kind of "grave of the race" under the ground. (This word is rendered "hell" in K. J. V., and "Hades" in the Greek Bible; the term is not to be confused with "Gehenna," the place of punishment of the wicked, also rendered "hell.") God had withdrawn His "spirit" or principle of animation from these shades (Job 34:14-15), and therefore they were excluded from communion with God (Psalm 6:5, 115:17), though this idea was to some extent later modified by the conviction that the sovereignty of God extended even to the abode of the departed (Psalm 139:8). This frame of thought was challenged by the experience of religious persecution, particularly under the Greek tyrant Antiochus Epiphanes, when many Jews suffered martyrdom rather than desert their faith. It then seemed an inconceivable denial of divine justice that those who most merited to see the vindication of God in the Day of the Lord should be denied their share in this triumph of the very martyrs' deaths which were the ground of their merit. Thus faith in God's justice clothed itself in the expectation that the righteous departed would be raised from the grave, so that they might have their part in the promised divine Kingdom (Daniel 12:1-3). This belief developed in the period between the Old and New Testaments, so that by the time of our Lord it was a widely-accepted doctrine that in the day of the Messianic Kingdom there would be a General Resurrection of all men, the good and the bad, to divine judgment. The more conservative Sadducees, however, rejected this and other late developments of Jewish Messianic belief (Matthew 22:23, Acts 23:8).

For St. Paul God both set His seal upon this doctrine of Resurrection as the mark of triumph over death, and modified in a spiritual direction the conception of Resurrection by the wonder of Christ's rising from the dead (Romans 6:9). The Resurrection narratives in the four gospels indicate both that Christ rose from the grave, and that this Resurrection was no mere re-vivification of the physical body which had died on the Cross. There was a mysterious "glory" about the Risen Christ which corresponded to a complete triumph over death. The doctrine of a General Resurrection to judgment of all men therefore naturally passed over into the Church, and very significantly when St. Paul seeks to expound this Resurrection hope he does so by applying to the Resurrection of the believer that which the Church had learned from the experience of Christ's own Resurrection. He thus argues that when Christians are raised from the dead it will not be with a mere body of flesh and blood like the present, but with a "glorious" or "spiritual" body adapted to the Kingdom of Christ's triumph (I Corinthians 15:35-54).

Significance of the Doctrine. This important Scriptural doctrine symbolizes for the Christian the confident hope that the believer who, in Christ, triumphs over death,

has before him a destiny much more blessed than the bare survival of a disembodied ghost, or the denatured shade of his former self. The whole man will be alive in Christ's heavenly Kingdom, with every faculty proper to the human personality quickened to an abundance of life. The "Resurrection of the Body" answers to the idea of the fulness of triumph over death. It also provides a particular example of the general principle of the religion of the Incarnation, namely, that God has created that which is material as the expression of a high spiritual purpose. This material world, and man's physical frame which is a part of it, is the precious handiwork of God, which He has created as the means of making Himself known to man, and the means through which He will redeem man by His incarnate Son. Thus the destiny of God's handiwork is not to be "cast as rubbish to the void," as though it were spiritually unprofitable. The material creation is to be redeemed, that God's glory may be seen in it (Romans 8:21-23). Thus to the Christian it is not the case that man's non-material soul is the only element of permanent spiritual value about him. The body is likewise "the temple of the Holy Ghost" (I Corinthians 6:19-20), and is to be redeemed in Christ. In this respect the Christian Faith largely accords with the findings of modern physiological and psychological investigation, which teaches that the development of the non-material mental and spiritual activities of man is closely linked with the activity of the physical nervous system. "Body" and "soul" are interdependent, and together form the complete man. The "Resurrection of the Body" is the traditional way of saying that the whole nature of this unitary "man" is to be saved to the uttermost, though that body which is the due partner of the soul will not always be this present lowly material body.

It is only candid to observe that in the modern period many of the more radical among New Testament critics have affirmed that the New Testament, if rightly understood, does not require acceptance of the traditional doctrine that Christ's Resurrection included the raising of His body from the tomb, and the mysterious divine transformation of the physical body which had died on the Cross into a glorious Resurrection-body. It would be taught that the Apostles received an immediate mental impression that their Lord was indeed spiritually present with them, triumphant over death, and that the believing mind of the early Church constructed the Gospel Resurrection narratives as a means of symbolizing this faith. Thus the critic would claim that he believes in a "resurrection," in the sense that Christ triumphed fully over the power of death, but that the resurrection narratives are not to be taken literally. This is not the place to argue the pros and cons of this transformation of the traditional Christian system, but only to observe that if accepted it involves a very drastic reduction of the traditional incarnational principle. This cannot fail in turn to affect the traditional doctrine of the General Resurrection, which, as we have seen, was argued in the early Church from what was believed regarding Christ's own Resurrection. If it be accepted that Christ's Resurrection was not a divine act performed within the sphere of this physical world, but only the continuance of a "spiritual" presence, then it would seem that the hope which is set before the believer in Christ is not that of the Resurrection of the Body, but only the continuance of a "spiritual" soul.

Other modern critics have, in somewhat striking contrast to this, made much of the distinction between the Biblical doctrine of Resurrection and the commonly-accepted belief in the Immortality of the Soul. It has been rightly observed that "resurrection" is an Hebraic idea, while "immortality" goes back to categories of Greek thought. The Immortality of the Soul as a symbol of the believer's triumph over death answers to the notion that the permanently valuable "real man" is the non-material "soul," while the destiny of the spiritually non-profitable body is to be cast aside in the grave. This, it is argued, is a system of thought very different from the Biblical and incarnational doctrine that God works the spiritual through the material. Though there is much of substance in this contrast, the antithesis between Hebraic "resurrection" and Hellenic "immortality" is nevertheless not absolute. The two ideas have to some extent been reconciled in traditional Roman Catholic and Protestant thought, with the sanction that the concept of "immortality" is found in the New Testament, as well as that of "resurrection" (I Corinthians 15:53-54). The doctrine of Immortality accords with the Christian faith that the departed in Christ, awaiting the General Resurrection, are certainly not in a state of suspended animation, or of a dim Sheol-like existence. The saints who have gone before are even now in a state of spiritual blessedness, and rejoice in the immediate presence of Christ (Luke 23:43; Philippians 1:23). Nevertheless, this happy destiny does not, in the Christian view, preclude the idea of development in the unseen world, or of growth in blessedness as the saints are changed "from glory to glory." The Resurrection of the righteous at the culmination of God's redeeming purpose for the world may be viewed as a stage in this. Thus present Immortality and future Resurrection are not inconsistent, but complementary.

The First and Second Resurrection. A word may perhaps be added regarding this theoretical disjunction which has at times been in the Church a matter of obscure and not always very edifying controversy. Those who insist that the symbolism of Revelation 20:4-13 is to be taken literally have taught that the Resurrection of all the dead is in two stages. The saints will first rise from the grave, and will reign in glory with Christ upon the earth for "a thousand years" in the Millennial Kingdom. After this the remainder of mankind will rise, good and bad, for the Last Judgment, and the final vindication of God's sovereignty. Those who hold this view are called "pre-millenarians," teaching that Christ's Second Advent will take place before the Millennium. Another view, commonly held in more characteristically ecclesiastical circles, is that the historic Church already in some sense represents Christ's earthly reign, so that no distinct period of "Millennial Kingdom" is to be looked for. In this case, the Christian expectation is that at the end of the Age Christ will come in glory. There will then take place immediately the one General Resurrection of all men, and the Last Judgment. Those who hold this doctrine are "post-millenarians." We would commend the view that the ultimate and perhaps very distant stages of God's government of the world are inevitably shrouded in mystery. Not being matters of empirical human experience they can only be spoken of in symbolical language, expressing general spiritual principles. We cannot be certain exactly how far if at all the admittedly symbolical language of Scripture is to be taken literally, though it is authoritative to establish general principles. Therefore, while the believer may rightly cling to a confident Christian hope, it is unfitting to seek to know the unknowable (Matthew 24:44; Acts 1:7), and to divide the Church by over-confident controversy in these matters.

K. Barth, *The Resurrection of the Dead*. English trans. by H. J. Stenning, New York, 1933.
O. Cullmann, *The Immortality of the Soul and the Resurrection of the Body*. New York, 1958.
M. E. Dahl, *The Resurrection of the Body: A Study of I Corinthians 15*. London, 1962.
V. McLeman, *Resurrection Then and Now*. London, 1965.
C. V. Pilcher, *The Hereafter in Jewish and Christian Thought*. London and New York, 1940.
W. P. Pope, *A Compendium of Christian Theology*. London, 1880.
G. E. Rupp, *Last Things First*. London, 1964.
C. R. Smith, *The Bible Doctrine of the Hereafter*. London, 1958.
K. Stendahl, ed., *Immortality and Resurrection: Four Essays*. New York, 1965.
R. Watson, *Theological Institutes*. London, 1832.
J. Wesley, *Sermons*. 1831

JOHN LAWSON

REVELS, HIRAM RHOADES (1822-1901), American A.M.E. and M.E. minister, and also U. S. Senator, was born to free parents in Fayetteville, N. C., Sept. 1, 1822. He was of mixed African and Croatan Indian descent. Forbidden by law to attend southern schools, he was educated at Quaker institutions in INDIANA and OHIO and at Knox College, Galesburg, Ill. In 1845 he entered the ministry of the A.M.E. CHURCH. During the next eight years he taught school, lectured and preached in several midwestern states. Following a local church dispute in ST. LOUIS, he became a Presbyterian preacher for several years.

During the Civil War, Revels helped to recruit Negro regiments for the Union Army in MARYLAND and MISSOURI. In 1864 he became CHAPLAIN of a black MISSISSIPPI regiment and served a short time as provost marshal of VICKSBURG. Returning to the A.M.E. Church, he organized several congregations for that denomination in JACKSON. In 1866 he settled at Natchez, and in 1868 he joined the M.E. Church. In the latter year he was elected alderman, though he entered politics reluctantly, fearing race friction and the possibility of conflict with his work as a minister. In politics he won the liking and respect of the white people of the state. Elected to the state senate from Adams County, he was elevated by the legislature in January 1870, to the U. S. Senate, filling the seat that had been occupied by Jefferson Davis prior to the Civil War. Revels was a Republican but not a Radical. He served in the Senate until March 4, 1871.

Upon his retirement from the Senate, Revels was elected president of Alcorn University, a newly established school for Negroes. He filled the position with credit. Following the sudden death of JAMES LYNCH, another Negro Methodist preacher-politician, Revels served a few months as secretary of state *ad interim* of Mississippi. When he dissented from the political activities of Mississippi Republicans, Revels lost his position at Alcorn. However, in 1875, he aligned himself with white Democrats to overthrow the Carpetbag government in the state, and as a result was again appointed president of Alcorn, serving until 1883.

In 1875 Revels was received "by transfer" into the MISSISSIPPI CONFERENCE (ME) and was appointed to Holly Springs. The next year he was placed on the Holly

Springs District. As a reserve delegate to the 1876 GEN-ERAL CONFERENCE, he was elected editor of the *South-western Christian Advocate* but declined to serve. Apparently he served the church and the district at Holly Springs without giving up the presidency of Alcorn. In 1877 he was appointed to the Jackson District which he served for three years while also president of the college. From 1880 to 1883 he gave full time to Alcorn. Beginning in 1884 and continuing until his death, he was a presiding elder in what became, in 1890, the UPPER MISSISSIPPI CONFERENCE (ME). He served the Aberdeen and Greenwood Districts six and two years, respectively, and was on the Holly Springs District three different times for a total of nine years. He died while attending the session of his annual conference at Aberdeen, Miss., Jan. 16, 1901.

General Minutes, MEC.
Dictionary of American Biography, Vol. 15.
Minutes of the Upper Mississippi Conference (ME), 1901.
ALBEA GODBOLD

REVEREND, British Methodist. JOHN WESLEY's helpers and assistants can be divided into those who had Anglican orders, who would be addressed by the traditional English title "the Reverend," and the unordained itinerants who would be addressed as plain "Mister." When Wesley began his own ordinations, first for America and then for SCOTLAND, curious anomalies crept in. Thus when JOHN PAWSON, THOMAS HANBY, and JOSEPH TAYLOR were ordained for Scotland in 1785, they were forbidden to wear clerical dress south of the border and were addressed as "Mister" when in England, and as "the Reverend" when in Scotland. Ronald Knox's comment is apt: "In short he had evolved a system of Gretna Green ordinations, which unlike Gretna Green marriages were not meant to have any effect south of the border." (*Enthusiasm*, London, 1950, pp. 506-7, 511.)

When writing to JOSEPH COWNLEY in Scotland, Wesley addressed him as "Rev. Mr. Cownley, Minister of the Methodist Church, Leith-Wind, Edinburgh." After John Wesley's death in 1791 a few ordinations of preachers took place; and some Methodist advocates of separation from the Church of England, like SAMUEL BRADBURN, used the title "the Reverend." Thus when Portland Chapel was opened in BRISTOL on Aug. 26, 1792, Bradburn and Samuel Roberts read the liturgy in full clerical attire, to the annoyance of the local Anglican incumbent. Bradburn's comment was: "In everything that relates to the office of minister of Jesus Christ I consider myself as standing on equal ground with you. Why shouldn't I wear a gown and put on the bands and call myself 'The Rev.'?"

The party which hankered after full unity with the Establishment prevailed, however. The Wesleyan Conference laid down in 1793 that "no gowns, cassocks, bands or surplices shall be worn" by any of the preachers, and that "the title of Reverend shall not be used by us toward each other in future." This greatly displeased men like Bradburn, who wrote to ALEXANDER KILHAM on Dec. 12, 1793: "I really believe that the little interruption we met with will do us good. Do not destroy your gown and bands, nor suppose they are for ever done with. You will know better soon, if the Lord will, we must have a Methodist constitution or plan of discipline explained, and we shall in due course." The moderate party came to accept the conference rules, and many understood reception into

FULL CONNEXION as being tantamount to ordination. Thus WILLIAM THOMPSON wrote to JOSEPH BENSON in 1795:

It is proposed that the Methodist preachers shall have nothing to do with ordination of any kind because their being four years on trial and the fruit of their labour in that time appearing in the conversion of sinners, and their being received at Conference by their senior brethren giving them the right hand of fellowship, is a full proof that they are called of God and man to the work of the ministry, which we believe to be scriptural ordination. We will have nothing to do with gowns, bands, surplices, reverends or any honourable title, because we wish to continue the same plain men which we were, when we set out in the work of the ministry, and to transmit to posterity the same simplicity and plainness.

But, as the Wesleyan Methodist ministry evolved from what could be called "lay agency" to the full status of an ordained body in 1836, so honorific titles came back into vogue. In 1818 the title "Reverend" was permitted again; it frequently appears in the *Minutes of Conference* after that date; and in the *Wesleyan Methodist Magazine* under the portraits of the itinerants, the suffix "Preacher of the Gospel" is replaced by "the Reverend." This rapidly became the norm in all the branches of Methodism, though the first meeting of the Wesleyan Methodist Association in 1836 resolved that "it was inexpedient that the term 'Reverend' should be used in connexion with the name of any preacher of the Association." This was rescinded nine years later. As late as 1876 WILLIAM GRIFFITH introduced a motion in the annual assembly of the UNITED METHODIST FREE CHURCHES to discountenance the use of a term which he refused to use himself—but the motion was later withdrawn. It should be noted that the title was not overly popular in some sections of the Free Churches in Britain in the mid-nineteenth century, and that Charles Haddon Spurgeon, the famous Baptist preacher, always refused to use it. In 1874 the Wesleyan Methodist Conference, which had once forbidden the use of the title, was involved in a lawsuit through the refusal of an incumbent and his bishop (Christopher Wordsworth of Lincoln) to allow the title "the Reverend" on a tombstone (see OWSTON FERRY CASE).

In **American Methodism** the validity of the title "reverend" applied by the ordained elders to one another shortly after the organization of the M.E. Church, was the cause of much comment and some criticism. The marks of a society were still deeply engrained in the new church, and to many the title of *reverend* possibly more often applied to those who had been ordained and not simply licensed to preach, seemed an affectation and an imitation of English church formality. The title was thought by some at that time to "savor more of pride," as JOHN EMORY tells us, and was made the subject of a minute question in 1787, though not "exposed to print." After quite a discussion it was advised by the conference that everyone might use his own choice in the matter and be reverend, or deacon, or elder, or bishop, as he chose.

The issue really came to a head over the name "bishop" which had been applied to the superintendents at that date much to Wesley's distaste. Soon, however, and by a sort of popular consent, the name reverend did come to be applied to Methodist minsters, ordained or unordained, everywhere.

On the Eastern seaboard, where the Protestant Episcopal Church has always been strong, our ministers, as well as the clergymen of that church, are often addressed simply as "Mr."—an old formal English method of speaking of any minister—as "Mr. Wesley," we remember.

J. Emory, *Defence of Our Fathers.* 1827.
N. B. Harmon, *Rites and Ritual.* 1926.   JOHN KENT
                                                        N. B. H.

REVIVALS AND REVIVALISM. In various epochs of Church life and almost every country there have been seasons of remarkable religious interest accompanied with a great manifestation of divine power and grace in the "quickening of believers, the reclaiming of backsliders, and the awakening, conviction, and conversion of the unregenerate." (Schaff-Herzog, p. 2038.) During these great periods of *Revival*, as such times are called, the public mind as well as the Church mind has often been somewhat turned to spiritual subjects. Methodism itself was eminently revivalistic in its origin, and is sometimes spoken of as the "Methodist revival of the 18th and 19th Centuries." Previous to that there were great and unusual periods of spiritual awakening in the long history of the Church, the first being the great spreading out and conquest made by the Christian Church during the first three centuries of the Christian era. The Protestant Reformation itself has been called a revival, and there is reason to believe that periods of declension and even apostasy on the part of the church and people, are often followed by a great awakening of religion.

Before the time of Wesley, the Church of Scotland was born anew in the great revival under John Knox and his brethren. Before the Wesleyan revival had truly begun in Britain, Jonathan Edwards, in New England, began to preach with great earnestness the doctrine of JUSTIFICATION by faith alone. The result of his preaching was a significant revival of religion. Both in Britain and America the intense awakening of those who had been in sin, and their very real conversions were sometimes marked by unusual physical demonstrations.

Revival movements have affected all denominations though Methodism in all its branches has ever been in the front rank of those Christian communions which witness by changed lives and public testimony the spiritual strength of the Divine power in heart and life.

In America about the year 1800 a remarkable revival occurred in KENTUCKY and TENNESSEE which led to the formation of the Cumberland Presbyterian Church. Early Methodist circuit riders were involved in this, and such was the strength of the revival that there was a strong demand that the Methodist and Presbyterian bodies, especially those in the Tennessee and Kentucky sections of the United States, become one body. Differences in polity however, and perhaps certain doctrinal viewpoints also, kept this from coming about.

In a narrower sense, the word *revival* came to be the term by which Methodist preachers and people throughout the latter half of the nineteenth century—and the first half of the twentieth century—denominated those set periodic occasions during which sometimes for two weeks, sometimes a month, the gospel of regeneration and complete consecration was preached in the same place with fervor and earnestness day after day and sometimes night after night. In time, revivals as a sort of periodic professional technique established themselves in the Methodist, and indeed, in other churches, and the results were nearly always good. The appearance on the American scene of certain who became famous as great evangelists, and re-

vivalists, and who conducted greatly publicized periods of revival preaching, caused interest sometimes upon a nation-wide scale. In America, Charles Finney, SAM P. JONES, Billy Sunday, and in the present generation Billy Graham became noted as revivalists and huge crowds attended their meetings in many cities. D. L. Moody stirred London in his day with revival fires. In time there came about a class of men denominated as "evangelists" though indeed every preacher-in-charge was expected to be revivalistic.

In local Methodist churches during the latter part of the nineteenth century, times of revival were sometimes called "protracted meetings," and an annual revival period or protracted meeting was customarily scheduled in Methodist churches over American Methodism for many years. After a time many of these became perfunctory, attended by none but the faithful church people. Dr. CLOVIS CHAPPELL, well-known as an evangelist as well as a pastor and author, said that he had seen many protracted meetings which "did nothing but protract." But even so, experienced pastors insist that it is a good plan to have such hoped for revival periods again and again as these stir the people, and the cumulative effect of message after message has a striking gospel power.

Of late years, the influence of the church year, and of the church calendar as other Protestant bodies follow these rather closely has been more and more felt in Methodist churches. The Easter season (preceded by the Lenten period) has come to be taken as the time when successive nights of preaching are scheduled, though the term "revival services" is not heard as often as before.

It should be mentioned that revivals upon a gigantic scale as conducted by nationally known evangelists must be prepared for far in advance, and as these require, beside the evangelist, a huge party of helpers who attend to advance publicity, arrangements, management of the music, and organizations of big choirs, all entailing considerable expense, this mechanical and costly type of intensive crusading has in certain cases led to criticism. However, the general Church world usually concedes that with all their faults, such revivals do help greatly, for while many who profess conversion or reconsecration during such periods often fall away afterward, there remains in almost all cases a residue of a few cataclysmically changed and converted persons, who from then on are earnest Christians of the highest type. Meanwhile, if the pendulum does swing too far toward a forgotten church and a forgotten God, the Church will pray all the more earnestly that the revival fires will break out again from that One who will not leave Himself without witness anywhere in His universe.

T. Smith, *Revivalism and Social Reform.* 1957.
Ralph G. Turnbull, ed., *Baker's Dictionary of Practical Theology.* Grand Rapids, Mich.: Baker Book House, 1967.
Bernard A. Weisberger, *They Gathered at the River: The Story of the Great Revivalists and Their Impact upon Religion in America.* Boston: Little Brown, 1958.   N. B. H.

REYNOLDS, JOHN (1786-1857), Canadian Methodist bishop, was born near Hudson, N. Y., in 1786. He acquired "a fair education for the day and country" and soon became an animated, eloquent preacher. In 1808, he was taken on trial as assistant in the Augusta Circuit. Two years later, he was ordained deacon in the GENESEE CONFERENCE and stationed on Smith's Creek Circuit. For him, as for others, the War of 1812-14 proved a disrupting influence. He located, probably in 1814, taught school, traded in furs, and eventually became a successful merchant in Belleville. At the same time he was active as a local preacher, and was ordained as a local elder in 1824.

Evidently Reynolds became identified in the 1830's with those in the CANADA CONFERENCE who sought to maintain close connections with political radicalism. Presumably too he had a strong Canadian orientation and, more significantly, was intimately associated with the local preachers in his district. The union of 1833 with the Wesleyans appeared to threaten all these interests, and especially the rights of local preachers. Thus, it was not surprising that at the first General Conference of the revived M.E. Church, held in June, 1835, John Reynolds was elected bishop, and ordained on June 28.

Bishop Reynolds presided at the conferences and effectively directed the growth of his church until 1847, but because of age and infirmity he was unable to itinerate as had his predecessors. In 1847, Philander Smith was elected as his associate.

Bishop Reynolds died in 1857.

J. Carroll, *Case and His Cotemporaries.* 1867-77.
T. Webster, *M. E. Church in Canada.* 1870.   G. S. FRENCH

REYNOLDS, JOHN HUGH (1869-1954), college president, born at Enola, Ark., Jan. 3, 1869, was the son of Jesse M. and Eliza (Grimes) Reynolds. He received an A.B., HENDRIX COLLEGE, Conway, Ark., 1893; A.M., University of Chicago, 1897; special study, Oxford University, England, 1911-12; and was granted a number of honorary degrees. He became professor of History and Political Science at Hendrix College, 1897-1902; vice-president, Hendrix College, 1899-1902; professor of History and Political Science, University of Arkansas, 1902-12; acting-president, University of Arkansas, 1912-13; president of Hendrix College, Conway, Ark., 1913-45 (Hendrix College, Hendderson-Brown College, and Galloway Woman's College, consolidated in 1931). In 1903 he organized the Arkansas Historical Association and was its first secretary. He became director of the General Christian Education movement of the M.E. Church, South, in 1920-21 to raise $33,000,000 for colleges.

He was a member of the ARKANSAS Constitutional Convention, and of the commission on unification of American Methodism in 1924. He wrote *Makers of Arkansas History; Civil Government of Arkansas;* and, with D. Y. Thomas, *History of University of Arkansas.* He was editor of the publications of the Arkansas Historical Association (Vols. I, II, III, and IV).

His home until his retirement in 1945 was at Conway, Ark., and thereafter on Petit Jean Mountain near Morrilton, Ark., until his death in 1954. He was buried in Conway.

Hendrix College Bulletin, June 1954.
Who's Who in America, 1946-47.   KENNETH L. SPORE

RHEE, SYNGMAN (1875-1965), Korean independence leader and first president, was born in Pyung-San, Hwanghae Province, KOREA, March 26, 1875. He received a tutor's education in Confucian principles and Chinese classics. At the age of nineteen he entered a Methodist

SYNGMAN RHEE

Mission school (Seoul, Pai Chai) in SEOUL to study English.

Here he also imbibed democratic ideals and was soon campaigning for elimination of foreign influence in the Korean monarchy. He joined the Independence Club, and founded and edited *Maiyil Shinmun,* Korea's first daily newspaper.

By 1897 his efforts to reform Korea's weak government resulted in his arrest, six months torture in jail, and a sentence to life imprisonment. During the next seven years he embraced Christianity, organized fellow prisoners in classes in religion and English, translated English books and wrote his famous Korean work, *Spirit of Independence.*

Granted amnesty, he went to WASHINGTON to seek President Theodore Roosevelt's aid in protecting Korea's neutrality. Failing in this, he remained to secure a B.A. from Washington University in 1905, an M.A. from Harvard in 1908, and a Ph.D. at the hands of Woodrow Wilson at Princeton in 1910.

Rhee spent seventeen months in Korea as a YMCA secretary. Back in America as a delegate to the GENERAL CONFERENCE of the M.E. Church meeting in MINNEAPOLIS, April, 1912, he was warned not to return to Korea, whereupon he chose HAWAII as his base of activities.

For twenty-seven years he kept in close contact with the independence movement in Korea. When a Provisional Government of Korea was secretly formed in 1919, Rhee was elected president and continued to be elected until he gave up that assignment to establish the Korean Commission as the diplomatic agency of the government in exile in Washington, D. C.

While in Hawaii he organized a Korean Methodist Church, served as an educator in the Methodist Mission program and later established the Korean Christian Institute. In Washington he was a member of the Foundry Methodist Church and remained a close friend of the pastor, FREDERICK BROWN HARRIS.

At the close of World War II, Rhee was wildly received by his own people, somewhat less cordially by the American military authorities. Elected chairman of the first National Assembly he presided at the drafting of Korea's constitution and was elected president in 1948, 1952, 1956, and 1960. Taking advantage of his advanced age, party politicians brought his government into disfavor, and a student revolution resulted in his resignation and flight to Hawaii in 1960.

During his term of office no liquor was ever served at any government function and he was a constant Bible reader. He died in Honolulu, July 19, 1965. His funeral was held at Chung Dong Methodist Church, in Seoul, on July 27. An estimated one million fellow-citizens crowded the streets as the funeral procession moved to the National Cemetery.

Robert T. Oliver, *Syngman Rhee: The Man Behind the Myth.* N.d.

CHARLES A. SAUER

RHINEHART, WILLIAM (1800-1861), American United Brethren preacher and editor, was born in Rockingham County, Va., on Nov. 28, 1800. He was converted during a revival in a Lutheran Church at the age of twenty. Soon after, however, he joined the Church of the UNITED BRETHREN IN CHRIST. He was licensed as a minister in 1825 and ordained in 1829. He travelled as a preacher and presiding elder in the VIRGINIA CONFERENCE until 1834.

In that year Rhinehart became the first editor of the *Religious Telescope*, the denominational paper. Because the printing establishment was located at Circleville, Ohio, he transferred to the Miami Conference.

Presuming that the GENERAL CONFERENCE of 1837 would consider a constitution, he as a delegate prepared such a constitution for the publishing house beforehand. This was unanimously adopted. His literary gifts were further seen in his co-authoring a hymn-book in the English language in 1833.

In 1839 he resigned as editor and returned to preaching mostly in the Miami Conference, serving First Church in DAYTON from 1852 to 1854. He was a man of splendid physique and great physical strength, a powerful preacher and singer. He strongly opposed slavery and was a fervent advocate of temperance.

He died near Dayton, Ohio on May 19, 1861.

D. Berger, *History of U.B.* 1897.
W. A. Shuey, *U.B. Publishing House.* 1892.

ROY D. MILLER

RHODE ISLAND, U.S.A., the smallest of the fifty states is bounded by CONNECTICUT on the west, MASSACHUSETTS on the north and east, and the Atlantic Ocean on the south. The territory became known in 1636 as the refuge for Roger Williams and other liberal thinkers. Densely populated (922,461, estimated in 1970), the state is highly industrialized. It is known for its textile and jewelry industries, its naval installations, and its tourist resorts. There are sixteen colleges and universities in the state, including Brown (founded in 1764).

FREEBORN GARRETTSON delivered the first Methodist sermon in Rhode Island in 1787, and two years later JESSE LEE introduced regular services. Bishop ASBURY visited the state in 1791, preaching at PROVIDENCE and Warren. In 1794 the Warren and Greenwich Circuits were joined to include all of Rhode Island and some towns in southeast Massachusetts. ENOCH MUDGE, the first native Methodist preacher in New England, was appointed to the Warren Circuit. In 1796 there were two circuits in Rhode Island with 220 members, and in 1800 three circuits with 227 members.

The first Methodist church building in Rhode Island was erected at Warren in 1794 and was dedicated Sept. 24 that year. The church at NEWPORT dates from 1806, and it claims to be the first Methodist church in the world to have a steeple and a bell. Furthermore, it is one of the few church buildings still standing in which Bishop Asbury preached. The first Methodist church edifice in Providence was built and dedicated in 1816 when the congregation consisted of 111 members. A new and larger building was erected at Providence in 1822, and after 1846 the congregation was known as Chestnut Street Church. A second church was started at Providence in 1832, a third in 1840, and the present Mathewson Street Church in 1848. The latter has been known for its pulpit and radio ministry since 1936.

The growth of Methodism in Rhode Island was gradual and constant. In 1870 the denomination was the third largest in the state, ranking next to the Episcopalians and Baptists. At that time the M.E. Church had thirty-three congregations in the state to seventy-five for the Baptists and forty-two for the Episcopalians.

From the beginning down to 1840 the Rhode Island work was in the NEW ENGLAND CONFERENCE. It was in the Providence Conference, 1840 to 1880, and in the New England Southern Conference thereafter.

In 1841 the Providence Conference bought the Kent Academy which was founded at East Greenwich, Rhode Island in 1802, and made it the Conference Seminary. About 1880 the school's name was changed to East Greenwich Academy and as such it continued functioning until 1940. Eben Tourzee, a professor in the academy, established the New England Conservatory of Music. In its later years the East Greenwich Academy served partly as a high school for East Greenwich.

In 1900 the M.E. Church had about forty charges and some 6,000 members in Rhode Island. In 1970 The United Methodist Church reported about thirty-five charges and some 11,655 members in the state.

W. McDonald, *History of Methodism in Providence, Rhode Island, 1787 to 1867.* Boston: Phipps and Pride, 1868.
Minutes of the New England, New England Southern, and Providence Conference.
M. Simpson, *Cyclopaedia.* 1878.
General Minutes, MEC and MC.

DAVID CARTER

RHODES, BENJAMIN (1743-1816), English Methodist, was born at Mexborough, Yorkshire, where his father was a schoolmaster. He was converted in childhood and, on leaving school in 1759, went into the woolen industry. He became a CLASS LEADER at twenty-one and later a preacher. Called out in 1766, he was sent to the Norwich Circuit for two years and then traveled in widely scattered circuits from Dunbar and Newcastle to Sussex and Kent. He was "a man of great simplicity and integrity of mind, highly approved by his brethren and warmly attached to the whole economy of Methodism." He published a *Concise English Grammar*. His closing years were spent at Margate.

JOHN A. VICKERS

RHODES, JAMES MANLY (1850-1941), American minister and educator, president and owner of LITTLETON FEMALE COLLEGE, a private Methodist-related college which was located at Littleton, N. C. He was born in Four Oaks, Johnston Co., N. C., and received into the NORTH CAROLINA CONFERENCE of the M.E. Church, South, in December, 1875. He served the Fifth Street Methodist Church in Wilmington, N. C., prior to becoming, in January 1882, the first principal of Central Institute, which, after 1888, was known as Littleton Female College and after 1912 as Littleton College. Except for the years 1887-1888, when he was principal of the nearby Henderson Female College, Henderson, N. C., Rhodes served as president of Littleton College until it was destroyed by fire in January, 1919. In 1889 he purchased the college property from its stockholders and immediately began an extensive program of improvements.

He married first, Florence Simmons (1856-1888) of Virginia, and later, on Nov. 27, 1889, Lula Hester (1868-1937), daughter of Rev. and Mrs. W. S. Hester of Oxford, N. C., and a teacher of voice at Littleton College.

Described as "a man of convictions, who felt that he had a work to do," Rhodes dedicated his life to the training and development of young ladies "of real refinement and culture, with those principles that enter into the formation of noble character." Though small physically, Rhodes has been portrayed as a man "huge in determination, perservance, consecration." Around 1906 he founded Central Academy, a military school with a farm operated by self-help students.

Following the destruction of Littleton College, President and Mrs. Rhodes removed to FLORIDA in 1923 where he died in Bartow on July 2, 1941.

At the time of his death, President Rhodes was the oldest minister in the North Carolina Annual Conference. His body was returned to Littleton and buried in Sunset Hill Cemetery.

North Carolina Historical Review, July 1962.

RALPH HARDEE RIVES

RHODESIA, formerly known as Southern Rhodesia, is a landlocked, approximately circular country in southern central Africa. The designation derives from the name of Cecil John Rhodes (1853-1902), the British-born South African millionaire, colonialist and politician. The country is rich in natural mineral resources, including gold, uranium, chrome, zinc, tin, asbestos, coal and rare minerals. Tobacco, tea, cotton and cattle are its principal agricultural products.

Rhodesia is divided from ZAMBIA by the Zambesi River, flowing eastward from the Victoria Falls into MOZAMBIQUE (Portuguese East Africa). It is separated from the Republic of SOUTH AFRICA by the Limpopo River; the beautiful Chimanimani and Inyanga Mountains form its eastern boundary with Mozambique. Its area is 150,333 square miles, and its population was estimated in 1969 to be 5,090,000 including 4,835,500 Africans (95%) and 254,-500 persons of European descent. It is governed under an

electoral system which allows the African majority little voice. The government declared Rhodesia independent of Britain in 1965, and a republic in 1970, but this status has not won international recognition.

Human remains of extreme antiquity have been found in various parts of Rhodesia. Records of the tenth century A.D. indicate the existence of a substantial trade in gold and ivory, originating in the Rhodesian hinterland. At Zimbabwe, there are ruins of stone buildings erected between the 11th and the 15th centuries.

The first party of whites to settle in Rhodesia arrived in 1859. It was led by a British missionary of the London Missionary Society, Robert Moffat, and took up residence in the Nakolo country along the Zambesi. Moffat's son-in-law, David Livingstone, reached the Zambesi near Sesheke in June, 1851, and his later expeditions opened the interior of Rhodesia. The Portuguese showed interest in an east-west belt from Mozambique to Angola, but the British trader Thomas Baines secured from Lobengula the first concession to dig for gold in 1871.

Meanwhile, Cecil Rhodes was envisaging a "Cape to Cairo" railroad which would run for its entire length through British territory. In 1889, the British government delegated the function of government to Rhodes's British South Africa Company. The name "Southern Rhodesia" was officially adopted in 1898. The British South Africa Company's charter expired in 1923. The whites then chose by referendum to become a British colony rather than an additional province of South Africa. This new status gave a very large measure of self-government to the white electorate.

Methodism entered Rhodesia in 1891, when the British Wesleyan Methodist missionaries OWEN WATKINS and Isaac Shimmin reached Salisbury. Rhodes pledged £100 annually to the expenses of a British Wesleyan missionary in Rhodesia. Land grants were made by the Company at Epworth near Salisbury, and at Sinoia in the Lomagundi district. In 1892 stations were opened at Nengubo and Kwenda, then at Bulawayo after a rebellion among the Matabele. John White, a British Wesleyan Methodist minister who served in Rhodesia from 1894 until 1931, was outstanding in his defense of African interests against the abuses of colonial administration. He was responsible for several publications in the Shona language, and for the training, through the Waddilove Institute, of ministers, evangelists and teachers. The first three Africans were received into the Wesleyan ministry in 1904. In 1964 the district became a member of the newly-formed Christian Council of Rhodesia, which in the following year declared its opposition to the government's unilateral declaration of independence. A united college of education was opened in 1968 by seven denominations, including Methodists and also Roman Catholics. In the same year, statement on unity was issued by leaders of the Anglican, Congregational, Methodist and Presbyterian communities. At that time, the British-related Methodist District was responsible for over 700 places of worship, 285 primary schools with more than 60,000 pupils, four secondary schools, two teacher training colleges and an agricultural college. It had more than 30,000 full members and a total community of well over 60,000 under the pastoral care of thirty Rhodesian and twenty-six expatriate ministers.

The membership of the British-related District includes both Africans and Europeans, and although there are thus two distinct cultural traditions within the church, Africans and Europeans are welcome to each other's services and meetings. There is close cooperation with other denominations, for example in a united mission to the African townships of Bulawayo, and in the chaplaincy to university students in Salisbury.

In 1897-1898, the M.E. Church established work in the Umtali area of Rhodesia. In December 1897, Bishop JOSEPH C. HARTZELL conferred with Cecil Rhodes and Company officials and secured a grant to the proposed mission of 13,000 acres near Old Umtali, as well as the abandoned buildings there. The town had been moved from the old to a new site across the mountain, so that it could be situated on the line of the railroad being built at the time, from the Indian Ocean Port of Beira.

The first missionaries arrived in 1898, the Rev. & Mrs. Morris W. Ehnes, opening a school at Umtali in November. One of the Old Umtali buildings was assigned to the WOMEN'S FOREIGN MISSIONARY SOCIETY, Mrs. Helen Rasmussen (see SPRINGER, HELEN) arriving in 1901. She had served in the CONGO until 1895. In 1905 she became the wife of JOHN M. (later Bishop) SPRINGER. They pioneered new stations at Mrewa, Nyadiri and Mtoko, assisted by SAMUEL GURNEY. The southernmost station was opened at Mutambara in 1908. In 1954, a new station was opened at Nyamuzuwe. Parts of the original land grant at Old Umtali were exchanged for land grants at these new sites.

Rural education assumed early importance with emphasis on agricultural training, several large farms providing experience and demonstration. Virtually all of the primary education of the rural African people has been through mission-established schools. Evangelistic work was promoted, with gain in self-support of the village churches. A Church of 30,000 members and a school enrollment of 48,560 developed. In 1967, there were fifty-eight ordained African ministers, 1,620 African teachers, and eighty missionaries related to the work of the Rhodesia Annual Conference, with nearly all major administrative posts staffed by able African leaders.

By comity agreement, the Rhodesia District of the British Methodist Church works generally west and south of Salisbury, and the Americans in the east and south. Both branches of Methodism have churches in the major cities. The Epworth Theological College at Salisbury now trains the ordained ministry for both churches, as well as for other participating denominations. The Anglican, Congregational, Methodist and Presbyterian churches are seeking organic union.

The FREE METHODIST CHURCH established work in 1938 in the extreme southeastern corner of the country. Rev. and Mrs. Ralph Jacobs, already experienced in Mozambique, were the leaders. This mission is in a region of 10,000 square miles. Activity radiates from Lundi in the north of the area, near the Mutibi Reserve, Chikombedzi on the Nuentsi River at the center, and Dumisa at the southern angle near Mozambique. Each station received 100 acres from the government. The hospital at Chikombedzi is influential, and mobile clinics go into the villages. The Lundi Central School turns away many students for lack of space. African personnel is supported by the churches. The 1962 report showed 1,700 members with twenty-one outstation elementary schools enrolling 2,500.

The mission of the A.M.E. CHURCH (US) also has a small work in Rhodesia. The Zambesi Conference includes stations, and village evangelistic and educational work,

in both Zambia and Rhodesia, and there are scattered congregations in Malawi (Nyasaland).

Findlay and Holdsworth, *Wesleyan Meth. Miss. Soc.* 1922.
S. D. Gray, *Frontiers of the Kingdom in Rhodesia.* London: Cargate, 1923.
C. F. Andrews, *John White of Mashonaland.* London: Hodder & Stoughton, 1935.
H. I. James, *Rhodesia.* 1935.
B. S. Lamson, *Free Methodist Missions.* 1951.
M. W. Murphree, *Christianity Among the Shona.* London: Athlone Press, 1969.
E. W. Smith, *The Way of the White Fields in Rhodesia.* N.p., n.d.
C. Thorpe, *Limpopo to Zambezi.* London: Epworth Press, n.d.
World Methodist Council, *Handbook of Information,* 1966-71.
ARTHUR BRUCE MOSS
T. C. BAIRD

RICE, JOHN ANDREW (1862-1930), American preacher and educator, was born in Colleton County, S. C., Sept. 25, 1862, the son of Richard Blake and Rachel Jane (Liston) Rice. He won the A.B. (1885) and A.M. degrees at the University of South Carolina, and that school awarded him the honorary D.D. and LL.D. degrees in 1894 and 1905, respectively. The University of Alabama gave him the LL.D. in 1906. Rice did postgraduate study at, but did not win degrees from, Columbia Theological (Presbyterian) Seminary and the University of Chicago. He was married twice, first to Anna B. Smith on April 13, 1887, and after her death, to Laura Darnell, Aug. 7, 1902. He had three sons by the first marriage and a son and daughter by the second.

Rice was admitted to the SOUTH CAROLINA CONFERENCE (MES) in 1886. After two years on circuits, he served at Darlington four years, and in 1892 was appointed to the prestigious Washington Street Church, COLUMBIA. Beginning in 1894 he served six years as president of COLUMBIA (S.C.) COLLEGE for Women. He reorganized and rebuilt the college, raised its academic standards, and held the students to Victorian standards of conduct. Later he served as a trustee of the school.

In 1900, convinced that his understanding of the Bible was inadequate, Rice resigned as president of the college, took a nominal appointment as "conference secretary of missions," and did two years of study under William Rainey Harper, J. M. Powis Smith, and other Old Testament scholars at the University of Chicago.

In the fall of 1902, Rice transferred to the ALABAMA CONFERENCE and was appointed to Court Street Church, MONTGOMERY. It was the beginning of successive four-year pastorates in four of the leading churches of his denomination. The other three, in order, were Rayne Memorial, NEW ORLEANS; First Church, FORT WORTH, and St. John's Church, ST. LOUIS. While at Fort Worth, 1910-14, Rice served as a member of the inter-conference commission which selected DALLAS as the site for SOUTHERN METHODIST UNIVERSITY which opened in 1915. At the end of his four years in St. Louis (1918), the four-year limit on pastorates had been lifted and Rice desired to stay longer, but the St. John's congregation was not agreeable. He then returned to SOUTH CAROLINA and was appointed to Trinity Church, Sumter, where he remained two years.

An able and eloquent preacher, a liberal in theology and in his interpretation of the Bible, Rice had over the years become somewhat of a controversial figure in his denomination. Liberals had led in organizing the School of Theology at Southern Methodist University, and in 1920 Rice was invited to the chair of Old Testament there. He accepted and at the same time moved his ministerial membership to the LOUISIANA CONFERENCE which was known to be fairly liberal, as compared with some others.

Shortly before Rice went to Dallas, JOHN W. SHACK-FORD, superintendent of teacher training in the Board of EDUCATION at NASHVILLE, a liberal who was being criticized by conservatives in the church, asked Rice to write a book on the Old Testament for use in local church teacher training schools. When Rice submitted his manuscript, Shackford suggested eliding several statements which were likely to arouse the ire of the fundamentalists. Independent and unwilling to compromise, Rice refused, and the Board did not publish the book. Rice found another publisher and brought out the book after he arrived at Southern Methodist University. Soon there were demands from the "grass roots" of the church that Rice resign. Bishop EDWIN D. MOUZON, a liberal, defended Rice, saying his views were in line with all modern biblical scholarship, but it was to no avail. In the fall of 1921, Rice felt constrained to resign, and Bishop Mouzon appointed him to the church at Okmulgee, Okla. In 1922 Rice went to the Boston Avenue Church at TULSA, and in a successful five-year pastorate built the magnificent edifice for which that church is distinguished today. In 1927 he was appointed editor of the *Oklahoma Methodist,* and when it folded a year later, Rice, with the knowledge and consent of the bishop in charge, began supplying the First Congregational Church in Tulsa.

While Rice shocked conservatives by what they considered his irreverent views of the Bible, there could be no doubt about his honesty and integrity and his devotion to the truth and the church. He was an effective preacher, lecturer, and writer, and he exercised a liberalizing influence on the educational and religious thinking of his time. In the M.E. Church, South, rigidly conservative views of theology and the Bible began to wane soon after Rice resigned his professorship. He died in Tulsa, May 29, 1930.

Rice published four books; *The Old Testament in the Life of Today; The Primacy of Religion in Education; Why I Believe in the Bible;* and *Is Christ on Trial in Tennessee?* A volume entitled *Emotions Jesus Stirred,* which included six of Rice's sermons and a sketch of his life, was published in 1950.

General Minutes, MECS.
John A. Rice, *Emotions Jesus Stirred.* 1950.
Who Was Who in America, 1897-1942.   ALBEA GODBOLD

RICE, MERTON STACHER (1872-1943), American preacher and nationally known DETROIT pastor, was born in a KANSAS frontier parsonage on Sept. 5, 1872. His first pastoral appointment was to a five point circuit in Kansas, and his last appointment was to Metropolitan Methodist in Detroit where he served his closing thirty years. His formal education was received at BAKER UNIVERSITY. He earned his B.S. and his M.S. and was honored with the LL.D.

He served the First Church in Duluth, Minn. from 1904 to 1913 and after that went to the parish church that later came to be known as Metropolitan Methodist in Detroit. While he was there it grew from about 1,000 members to 7,000 members.

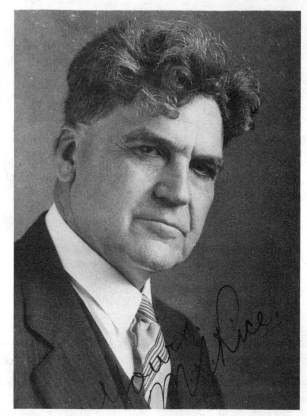

M. S. RICE

Rice insisted that his parish reach out in benevolent giving. He claimed that a people who could build a "cathedral" costing so much could give to others in like manner. Rice was a masterful preacher of Christ; a champion for righteous causes; and one who lives on in his fourteen published volumes.

He died in Detroit, March 7, 1943.

SCOTT D. MacDONALD

RICE, SAMUEL DWIGHT (1815-1884), Canadian minister and general superintendent, was born in MAINE in 1815. At an early age his family moved to Woodstock, New Brunswick, where he grew up in a strongly British environment. He received his undergraduate training at Bowdoin College, Maine, and then briefly went into business in 1837; however, he became a candidate for the Wesleyan ministry in the New Brunswick District.

After a very successful career as an itinerant in New Brunswick, Samuel Rice accompanied ENOCH WOOD to Canada West in 1847. He soon became involved in the Indian mission and was appointed head of the Mount Elgin Industrial School, a model training school for Indian youth. In 1850, however, he was transferred to Kingston, where his administrative skill resulted in the erection of an important church, and a substantial addition to the Victoria College endowment. This in turn ensured his appointment for three years (1854-57) as Moral and Domestic Governor of Victoria, an arrangement not calculated to strengthen the president's position.

From that time forward Rice took an extremely active interest in Methodist educational institutions. He believed that the church had an imperative duty to uphold the connection between knowledge and vital piety, not only

S. D. RICE

for its own children, but for society generally. To this end he worked manfully to build up the Methodist educational fund, and he gave much of his time and effort to the development of the Wesleyan Ladies' College in Hamilton.

Rice's administrative and ministerial abilities were regularly recognized by his communion. He was frequently a district chairman, and in 1873 and 1874 was president of the Wesleyan Conference in its final sessions. In 1882 he was elected president of the General Conference, and in 1883 the United General Conference elected him as one of the two general superintendents of the new Methodist Church.

Regrettably, ill health, the fruit of his past exertions, began to sap his energies at this crucial period for him and for Methodism and on Dec. 15, 1884, a few weeks after his election, he died.

To the editor of the *Canadian Methodist Magazine* (1885) Rice appeared to have inherited the "very best qualities" of the New England Puritans. "There was neither gall nor acid in his nature. Conscience, however, was with him an imperial power which reigned by Divine right, and from whose decisions there was absolutely no appeal . . . He was eminently a man of faith. He looked upon nothing as being too great or too difficult to be done or dared if it lay in the line of duty. . . . He had his frailities, perhaps his faults, but the prevailing impression which we get from the review of his whole life is, that he was a great and good man." (Vol. 22 (1885), 181).

G. H. Cornish, *Cyclopaedia of Methodism in Canada*. 1903.
T. W. Smith, *Eastern British America*. 1890. G. S. FRENCH

RICE, WILLIAM NORTH (1845-1928), was born in Marblehead, Mass., on Nov. 21, 1845, the son of William (a M.E. pastor) and Caroline Laura (North) Rice.

He received the A.B. (valedictorian) from WESLEYAN UNIVERSITY in 1865 and the A.M. in 1868; the Ph.D. from Yale University in 1867; and the LL.D. from SYRACUSE

UNIVERSITY in 1886 and Wesleyan University in 1915. He studied at the University of Berlin from 1867-68, 1892-93. His Ph.D. from Yale in 1867 was the first doctorate of philosophy in geology granted by Yale. His thesis subject was, "The Darwinian Theory of the Origin of Species."

He married Elizabeth Wing Crowell on April 12, 1870, and their children were Edward Loranus and Charles William.

Rice served at Wesleyan University (Connecticut) as professor of geology and natural history, 1867-84; professor of geology, 1884-1918; professor emeritus, 1918; acting president, 1907, 1908-09, 1918.

He was a member of many learned organizations, among them being: the Geological Society of America (v.p., 1911); and the American Academy of Arts and Sciences; a founding member, American Society of Naturalists (pres., 1891); member, Association of American Geographers.

William North Rice became a member of the NEW YORK EAST CONFERENCE, M.E. Church, in 1869, and was chairman of the Board of Examiners from 1896-1925. He was a member of the GENERAL CONFERENCE in 1884. He preached in Grace Church, BOSTON, for a time after graduation from Wesleyan. He was a member of the Council of Connecticut Federation of Churches (pres., 1910-11; secretary, 1913-19; pres., 1919-20; hon. pres., 1920).

He was the author of many works, such as: *Christian Faith in an Age of Science*, 1903; (with H. E. Gregory) *Return to Faith, and other Addresses*, 1916; *Through Darkness to Dawn*, 1917; *Poet of Science, and other Addresses*, 1919; *Science and Religion—Five Supposed Conflicts*, 1925; and was editor of the 5th edition of *Dana's Textbook of Geology*, 1897.

Rice, along with Caleb T. Winchester and their former professor at Wesleyan University, John M. VanVleck, became potent influences at Wesleyan University, in sympathy with the progressive leadership of President Eliot of Harvard. They liberalized the curriculum at Wesleyan in 1873, and were largely responsible for the combined emphasis on teaching and research there.

In his book, *Christian Faith in an Age of Science*, he wrote: "The scientific questions of our age and of all ages touch not the central truth of Christianity, 'that God was in Christ, reconciling the world unto himself'."

Within the field of geology he was most interested in the paleontological evidence for evolution. On Dec. 28, 1923, the Geological Society of America at its annual meeting at Washington, presented him with an engrossed testimonial, recognizing his services in the reconciliation of science and religion.

His grandson William A. Rice wrote: "I would guess that William North Rice contributed much more clarity and integrity, and 19th century liberal freedom of independent inquiry than he did fervor and emotional richness. There was a profound gentleness there . . . and a complete integrity which was inspirational."

For years Rice led religious classes of students; held Bible classes; conducted seminars; had personal conversations with groups of young ministers; and had confidential discussions with individuals who "in confusion of mind or depression of heart sought his counsel." He displayed personal fidelity to the practice as well as the theory of the Christian faith. He was a college professor for sixty years and a preacher of the Gospel for sixty-two years.

He died Nov. 13, 1928 in Delaware, Ohio, at the home

of his son, Edward L. Rice, then professor of zoology at OHIO WESLEYAN UNIVERSITY.

Alumni Record of Wesleyan University, Middletown, Conn., 1921.
Dictionary of American Biography.
Journal of the New York East Conference, 1929.
Who Was Who in America, Vol. I.
C. F. Price, *Who's Who in American Methodism.* 1916.

STEPHEN G. COBB

RICH, ISAAC (1801-1872), American layman, businessman, philanthropist, was born at Wellfleet on Cape Cod, Mass., U.S.A., on Oct. 24, 1801. His father was in the fish business and Isaac assisted therein. On his nineteenth birthday his father died, and Isaac became the chief support of his mother and ten children younger than he.

Isaac Rich started in the fish business in BOSTON, and by honesty and industry his progress was rapid and sure. In time, he became an extensive wharf and ship owner, with numerous places of business. By middle life, he was appointed United States representative on an international Fisheries Commission.

The Richs were Methodists. One evening in a REVIVAL meeting at his home church, the only acceptance of the pastor's altar call was Isaac. The pastor laid his hand on the lad's head, and offered a prayer that alluded to the boy who came to Jesus with loaves and fishes. Isaac Rich never forgot that hour of decision. He was a consecrated Christian and a loyal member of the Methodist Church for the rest of his life.

As his business and wealth increased he manifested a growing sensitiveness to his stewardship and helped every good cause; but his greatest work was the part he took in establishing BOSTON UNIVERSITY. His greatest philanthropy was his bequest to that institution, which was the largest sum ever given to an educational institution up to that time.

He died at Boston on Jan. 13, 1872.

Dictionary of American Biography
M. Simpson, *Cyclopaedia.* 1878.

DANIEL L. MARSH

RICHARDS, HERBERT EAST (1919-   ), American educator and minister, received his A.B. degree from DICKINSON COLLEGE; B.D. degree from DREW UNIVERSITY and THEOLOGICAL SEMINARY; M.A. degree from Columbia University and D.D. from College of Idaho. He taught Homiletics and the Christian Critisicm of Life at Drew University and Theological Seminary. He has also taught at Columbia University and is a member of the American Association of University Professors. Since 1951 he has been minister of the First Methodist Cathedral, Boise, Idaho.

In 1965 he received the Distinguished Citizen Award of the *Idaho Daily Statesman* newspaper. He is a charter member of the Board of Governors, the American Foundation of Religion and Psychiatry; chairman of the Board of Ministerial Training of Idaho and Television, Radio and Film Commission of the Idaho Methodist Conference. In 1965 he received the "Clergy Churchman of the Year" award given by Religious Heritage Foundation in Washington, D. C. He was cited by the Academy of Achievement receiving the Golden Plate award in 1966. For the past twelve years, his weekly radio and television broadcasts have had wide listening audiences.

Richards has been an exchange minister under the NATIONAL COUNCIL OF CHURCHES in England and has been a delegate to GENERAL and JURISDICTIONAL CONFERENCES of the Methodist Church in 1956 and 1960. He has served as CHAPLAIN of the Senate of State of Idaho for eight years. He has served also Presbyterian, Congregational and Baptist denominations as minister. His wife was Lois Marcey whom he married Jan. 1, 1941, and they have five sons.

Who's Who in the Methodist Church, 1966.

WENDELL L. COE

RICHARDS, THOMAS (1717-1798), British Methodist, was one of the earliest itinerants, being listed by JOHN WESLEY (*Minutes of the Methodist Conferences,* London, 1862, p. 60), along with THOMAS MAXFIELD and THOMAS WESTELL as his "sons in the Gospel" in 1760. For a time Richards was a master at KINGSWOOD SCHOOL. He attended the CONFERENCE in 1745. Selina Lady HUNTINGDON secured episcopal ordination for him and for thirty years he served as curate of St. Sepulchre's, Holborn.

A. SKEVINGTON WOOD

ERNEST G. RICHARDSON

RICHARDSON, ERNEST GLADSTONE (1874-1947), American bishop, was born at St. Vincent, British WEST INDIES, Feb. 24, 1874, the son of Jonathan C. and Dorothea Ann (Davison) Richardson. Jonathan was a Wesleyan Methodist preacher and missionary. Coming to the United States for higher education, Ernest won the A.B. degree at DICKINSON COLLEGE in 1896. He joined the NEW YORK EAST CONFERENCE that year, and while stationed at Wallingford, Conn., two years and at Seventh Street, NEW YORK CITY, one year, he pursued studies and won the A.M. degree at Yale in 1899. WESLEYAN UNIVERSITY awarded him the D.D. degree in 1913, and Dickinson conferred on him the LL.D. in 1920. He married Anna Isenberg, April 21, 1897, and they had one son and two daughters. Richardson's other appointments were: Olin Church, BROOKLYN, 1900-01; Fleet Street, Brooklyn, 1902-09; Bristol, Conn., 1910-12; Simpson, Brooklyn, 1913-16; and Brooklyn North District, 1917-20. He was a member of four GENERAL CONFERENCES, 1908-20.

Elevated to the episcopacy in 1920, he was resident bishop in ATLANTA, 1920-28, and PHILADELPHIA, 1928-44. He was in charge of the PUERTO RICO CONFERENCE, 1933-44. He served as president of the COUNCIL OF BISHOPS, 1941-42. After the accidental death of Bishop SCHUYLER E. GARTH in January 1947, Richardson was called out of retirement to administer the WISCONSIN AREA.

Richardson served on the Board of Home MISSIONS and Church Extension, 1910-44, and was president of it much of that time. For several years he was president of the Anti-Saloon League of America. The 1928, '32, and '36 General Conferences named him to the Commission on Interdenominational Relations, the group which officially dealt with plans and moves for the union of American Methodism, but he resigned before unification was effected in 1939 because his work in Puerto Rico, in which he was greatly interested, interfered with attendance at commission meetings on the mainland.

Richardson was a strong, legal-minded administrator. Always sure of himself, he was a splendid presiding officer. He established himself in the minds of ecclesiastical leaders as an interpreter of church law. It was almost universally agreed among those who knew him that he was the best parliamentarian in the church. He died at Philadelphia, Sept. 5, 1947.

Christian Advocate, Sept. 25, 1947.
General Minutes, MEC.
General Conference Journals, 1920ff.
C. T. Howell, *Prominent Personalities*. 1945.
Who Was Who in America, Vol. 2, 1943-50.   JESSE A. EARL
                                                     ALBEA GODBOLD

RICHARDSON, GLENN A. (1918-   ), American FREE METHODIST businessman and church leader was born at McPherson, Kan. He received the following degrees: A.B., GREENVILLE COLLEGE, 1940; M.B.A., University of Miami, Fla., 1958; LL.D., Greenville College, Ill., 1962. He married Mary E. Lowell in 1938. He was executive vice-president of Greenville College, 1958-62 and became president of that institution in 1962.

He is the author of *Oil Investment and Progressive Taxation* (1958). He has been a frequent delegate to the Central Illinois Annual Conference of his church and served as treasurer of the Conference. He has also been a delegate to General Conference, and president of the Association of Free Methodist Colleges and Secondary Schools.

                                             BYRON S. LAMSON

RICHARDSON, HARRY VAN BUREN (1901-   ), American church leader and president of the Interdenominational Theological Center, Atlanta, Ga., was born in Jacksonville, Fla., June 27, 1901, son of Martin V. and Bertha I. (Witsell) Richardson.

He received the A.B. degree from Western Reserve University, 1925; S.T.B., Harvard University, 1932; Ph.D., DREW UNIVERSITY, 1945; D.D., WILBERFORCE UNIVERSITY, 1941.

He served as chaplain of Tuskegee Institute, Alabama, 1932-48; president, GAMMON THEOLOGICAL SEMINARY, Atlanta, Ga., 1948-59, and president, Interdenominational Theological Center, Atlanta, 1959-   .

In 1949 he was a member of the Southeastern Advisory Committee of the NATIONAL COUNCIL OF THE CHURCHES

OF CHRIST in the U. S. A., and has been a member of the General Board of the Council since 1950. He is a member of the board of directors of the Southern Regional Council, Inc., and of the Atlanta Urban League. He is a member of the Council on Evangelism of The Methodist Church, of the citizens advisory committee on Urban Renewal; was chairman of the Negro division Community Services, 1958, co-chairman, 1959; he was treasurer of the Methodist Rural Life Fellowship from 1959 to 1962; he was field director of the program to train Negro rural ministers, under the auspices of the Home Missions Council of North America and the Phelps-Stokes Fund, 1945-50. He was president of the Georgia Council of Churches for two terms; he is a member of the Georgia committee of the Office of Economic Opportunity; he is a member of the Georgia Temperance League, of the Mental Retardation Planning Scientific and Advisory Committee; member of the executive board of the National Council of Christians and Jews; member of the board of directors of the Atlanta Tuberculosis Association, of the admissions committee of the Community Chest; he is a member of the Association of Methodist Theological Schools (member of the executive committee). He is the author of *Dark Glory*, 1947; contributor to the *Christian Way in Race Relations*, 1948; also of numerous articles in the field of race relations.

On June 22, 1927 he was married to Selma T. White. He resides in Atlanta, Ga.

Who's Who in the Methodist Church, 1966.   J. MARVIN RAST

RICHARDSON, JAMES (1791-1875), Canadian bishop, was born in Kingston, Upper Canada, Jan. 29, 1791. His father was a former naval officer, who had become an officer in the Provincial Marine, and a merchant as well. James Richardson was given a sound primary education, on which he built substantially in later life. As a boy he naturally became a sailor, and in 1812 received a commission in the Provincial Marine. He distinguished himself in combat, but suffered the grievous loss of one arm.

After the war Richardson left the navy and became a customs officer at Presque Isle, near Kingston. There he was converted and joined the Methodist Church. Here too, he was to meet his future colleague in the episcopate, PHILANDER SMITH. His own talents were quickly recognized and he was pressed into service as a local preacher. In 1824 after a severe struggle with himself, he decided to give up his comfortable secular position and to enter the itinerancy. Three years later he was taken into full connection and became a deacon.

From that time forward James Richardson rose rapidly in the estimation of his brethren. When EGERTON RYERSON gave up the *Christian Guardian* editorship in 1832, Richardson succeeded him. In his year as editor he continued the strong liberal orientation of the Methodist journal. Clearly, however, he was doubtful about the wisdom of the union of 1833, and he was regarded with suspicion by the Wesleyans. Thus, although he was appointed a district chairman in 1833, he became increasingly estranged from many of his former colleagues, especially the Ryerson brothers.

Rather than join the emerging M.E. Church, in 1836, Richardson took an appointment in Auburn, N. Y., but returned the following year. He was then admitted to the Episcopal Conference and stationed in TORONTO. Once again, in 1839, he was elected secretary of the Conference, but in 1840 he became agent of the BRITISH AND FOREIGN BIBLE SOCIETY.

Fortunately for the Episcopal Methodists, Richardson became a presiding elder again in 1852. By 1858 Bishop Smith's health had deteriorated and James Richardson was elected as his colleague. He continued as bishop until his death in 1875.

As minister and bishop Richardson was held in great esteem and affection by his brethren, by the other Methodist bodies, and by the people of his province. He earned the place which he was accorded, by the simplicity of his faith, the skill with which he carried out his episcopal duties, and the balanced way in which he sought to link the Church and society.

J. Carroll, *Case and His Cotemporaries.* 1867-77.
T. Webster, *James Richardson.* 1876.   G. S. FRENCH

RICHARDSON, JOHN (1734-1792), British minister, was the son of an alehouse keeper at Kirkleatham, Yorkshire. As curate of Ewhurst, Surrey, he was influenced by John Holman, a Methodist farmer. Richardson was converted under the ministry of THOMAS RANKIN in 1762. On being removed from his curacy because of his evangelical preaching, Richardson joined JOHN WESLEY. He first held an appointment at the Foundery and then became one of the readers at City Road Chapel (see LONDON, Wesley's Chapel). He conducted Wesley's funeral service.

A. SKEVINGTON WOOD

RICHARDSON, SIMON PETER (1818-1899), American itinerant who had a remarkable ministry covering nearly sixty years of Methodist history. He was considered one of the distinctive men of his generation and powerfully and effectively influenced the career of the noted evangelist and lecturer, SAM P. JONES.

He was born in the Dutch Fork, Newberry District, S. C., May 13, 1818. He was baptized in the Lutheran faith. In December 1840 he was received on trial into the GEORGIA CONFERENCE of the M.E. Church. When the FLORIDA CONFERENCE was organized in 1845 he transferred to that Conference, remaining in it until 1865 when he became general agent of the AMERICAN BIBLE SOCIETY for ALABAMA and west FLORIDA for eight years.

His ministry was for the most part divided between that of presiding elder and pastor in Georgia, Florida, and Alabama—in his latter years as a member of the NORTH GEORGIA CONFERENCE, M.E. Church, South. He was noted as church builder and as fiery CAMP MEETING preacher and evangelist. His unique style and manner gave peculiar emphasis and vitality to his message. Many stories are told of his unusual manner and ways.

He and his wife had ten children.

At the session of the North Georgia Conference which convened in Athens, Ga., Nov. 24, 1897, he was requested by the Conference to write his autobiography. This he did, entitling it *The Lights and Shadows of Itinerant Life.* He died June 15, 1899.

H. M. DuBose, *History.* 1916.
Simon Peter Richardson, *The Lights and Shadows of the Itinerant Life, An Autobiography of Rev. Simon Peter Richardson, D.D. of the North Georgia Conference.* Nashville: M. E. South Publishing House, 1900.   J. MARVIN RAST

RICHARDSON, TEXAS, U.S.A. **First Church** dominates the skyline of the city and can be seen from every approach. The church was formally organized in June of 1886 by a group of fifteen local Methodists. In 1898 a one-acre site was purchased and the first building was constructed at a total cost of $1,200.

The membership grew with the town, expanding rapidly in the period 1921 to 1924, and in 1924 the church completed a new brick building on the corner of Greenville and Polk Streets. An educational unit was added in 1951, and old army barracks from SOUTHERN METHODIST UNIVERSITY were used for additional church school rooms.

By 1953 First Church had a membership of 388. Richardson began to expand rapidly and the church purchased a new site in 1954. Groundbreaking services for a new fellowship hall, which was to serve as a sanctuary, were held on Sept. 22, 1957; and on April 13, 1958, open house was held in the new buildings. In over two years the membership grew to approximately 1,600 persons. A second educational unit became necessary.

Plans for a new sanctuary were inaugurated in 1962. Sept. 13, 1964, formal opening services were held in the new sanctuary. The sanctuary has a seating capacity of 1,050, is in the shape of a Greek cross, and has a unique round chancel.

Two church school sessions and two morning worship services are held each Sunday, and the average attendance in 1970 was 1,823 in church school and 1,366 in worship services. The membership is 4,005, and the church continues to grow in numbers and in spiritual influence in the community.

JOHN W. MORPHIS

MATTHEW RICHEY

RICHEY, MATTHEW (1803-1883), Canadian minister and educator was born 1803 in the County of Donegal, IRELAND, into a Calvinistic home. He was given a sound basic education with the view of entering the Presbyterian ministry. In his midteens he was invited to attend a Methodist prayer meeting. He was so impressed with the simple prayers of the little company that he was led to an awakening and conversion. Much against his parents' will, he joined the Methodist society and engaged in local preaching, in which he displayed unusual eloquence and passion. The strained relation at home and the call to adventure abroad combined with Providence to bring him to Saint John, New Brunswick, in 1820 at the age of seventeen. At first he found employment in a law office but soon became assistant master at Saint John Grammar School.

James Priestley realized at once that Richey had had some experience in preaching. At a district meeting held in Liverpool, Nova Scotia, he preached with such acceptability that he was invited to become an itinerant. He was received on trial in 1821 and into full connexion and ordained in 1825. For the first decade of his ministry he served circuits in the Atlantic provinces, growing quickly in stature, eloquence, and popularity. He had strong but narrow religious and political views with a deep reverence for the monarchy and the empire. He was more concerned for dignity and enlightenment than for the traditional enthusiasm of his fellow Methodists.

Matthew Richey came into prominence when, in 1835, he accompanied William Lord to Montreal. Although it was his first appearance in either of the Canadas, he won immediate recognition. John Carroll describes him in glowing terms:

For the power and pleasantness of his voice; ease and gracefulness of elocution; ready command of the most exuberant and elevated language, amounting almost to inflation of style; together with rich variety of theological lore, he scarcely ever had a superior, if an equal, in British North America. He was gentleman-like in his manners, Christian in his spirit and demeanor, and soundly Wesleyan in his teachings. (Carroll, *Case*, iv, 108)

With these characteristics he quickly won a foremost place in the pulpit and on the platform in Canada's largest city.

Undoubtedly his remarkable ministry in Montreal influenced Conference to appoint him as first principal of Upper Canada Academy. The fact that he had a classical education, used splendid diction, and expounded the truth with clarity and conviction, made him an excellent choice for this academic position. After he had been introduced at the opening ceremony, June 18, 1836, he delivered "an elegant address." The Royal Charter was granted Oct. 12, 1836; at the close of the first academic year there were 120 students enrolled. In the same year the Wesleyan University in Connecticut conferred upon Richey the M.A. degree. In 1847 the same institution granted him the D.D degree.

Not long after his dramatic installation as principal, administrative troubles arose both within the academy and without, in relation to the Conference. Richey, a member of the British Wesleyan group, was suspected by many in the Conference. Complaints were voiced against the principal. While the members of the Conference believed him to be sincere, well-intentioned, and noted for his facile speech, they agreed that he lacked tact and promoted inflated ideas which the Conference could not accept. John Ryerson, then prominent in the Conference, harshly criticized the principal:

Reichy (sic) flounces at some of our Rules for the Academy, especially that he is not to have the handling of the money and that there is no servant allowed him extra. I very much wish Reichey was out of the institution; if he is not, I am quite satisfied that he will ruin the institution or else ruin us. (Sissons, *Ryerson*, i, 383-384.)

It is evident that Principal Richey disliked the Canadian faction represented in the academy board and in the Conference. He apparently tried, however, to accommodate himself to their wishes. Anson Green was able to report a noticeable change in the attitude of the principal in 1838. He was doing well, and "had he done so from the commencement he would have saved us at least $1000." In 1839 the board named Jesse Hurlburt as acting principal, and in 1840 Egerton Ryerson became principal. In spite of Matthew Richey's difficulties with his board, he helped to establish higher education for Methodists in Upper Canada.

At the Conference in Hamilton June 12, 1839, Richey was stationed at Toronto. He played a major role in the controversy over the policy of *The Christian Guardian*, which at the time was under attack for taking sides in party politics. Outwardly the question was: Is *The Guardian* a religious journal, or has it a responsibility to become involved in political issues affecting the Methodist Church —such as the clergy reserves? Fundamentally the British and Canadian Methodists differed in their attitude to the relationship between Church and State. Alder, the British representative to the Canada Conference, was present to bring the "colonial church" into conformity with the mother church which recognized the established church in England.

Richey helped to precipitate the dissolution in 1840 of the union between the two conferences, and to fan the conflict of the years from 1840 to 1847. After the union was restored in 1847, he emerged again as a respected figure. He was co-delegate to the Conference in 1848 and president in 1849 and 1850.

On Oct. 13, 1849 he suffered a severe accident when his horse ran away. Because of this and doubtless because of his continuing antipathy to the Ryersons, he returned in 1850 to the eastern districts and was stationed at Halifax. He served a number of congregations in the three Atlantic provinces until he became superannuated in 1870. During those twenty years he is reported to have overcome his former prejudices and to have worked faithfully and harmoniously with the Canadian preachers. From 1856 to 1860 and again in 1867 he was President of the Eastern British America Conference.

Matthew Richey died in Halifax at the home of his son, then lieutenant-governor of Nova Scotia, Oct. 31, 1883. He had spent sixty-three of his eighty years in the ministry.

To his contemporaries Matthew Richey was an elegant, proud, gifted, but tactless man. Until his later years he was an uncompromising supporter of the traditions of British Methodism in America. An eloquent and dignified orator, he added a new note to Canadian Methodism.

J. Carroll, *Case and His Cotemporaries*. 1867-77.
D. W. Johnson, *Eastern British America*. 1924.
J. E. Sanderson, *First Century in Canada*. 1908, 1910.
T. W. Smith, *Eastern British America*. 1877-90.

Arthur E. Kewley

RICHMOND, JOHN P. (1811-1895), American preacher and publicist, was born in Middletown, Frederick Co., Md., Aug. 7, 1811. He graduated in medicine, in 1833. While practicing his profession in his home town, he was licensed to exhort. In 1835 he moved to Mississippi, where he was united in marriage (Oct. 14, 1831) to Mrs.

America Talley, widow of Alexander Talley, of MISSISSIPPI CONFERENCE. That year he was licensed to preach.

Richmond moved to Rushville, Ill., April 1836, supplied the Rushville Circuit until fall when received into the ILLINOIS CONFERENCE and appointed to Pulaski Circuit. In 1837 he served Macomb station and in 1838, Jacksonville. On invitation of JASON LEE, in 1839, he went to OREGON, became superintendent of the Indian Mission, Nisqually, on Puget Sound, the first Methodist work in the present state of WASHINGTON.

On Aug. 10, 1840 Richmond officiated at the marriage of his carpenter, WILLIAM HOLDEN WILLSON, and mission teacher, Miss Chloe Aurelia Clark, the first American marriage in what is now the state of Washington. On Feb. 28, 1842, his son, Francis, became the first American child born on Puget Sound. An elder son, Oregon, was born on shipboard before sailing for Oregon.

Richmond and his family left Oregon Sept. 4, 1842, for ILLINOIS. There he served churches at Petersburg, Springfield, Rushville, Quincy, and Mount Sterling. He located in 1848, having been elected to the State Senate. In 1852 he returned to Mississippi and served the Madison Circuit. His wife, America, died it is thought at Madison, Miss., in 1853. Richmond, on Oct. 18, 1859, married Kitty Grisby at Mount Sterling, Ill. Two years later he was back in Illinois where successively he served in the House of Representatives, as Presidential Elector, in the State Senate, in the Constitutional Convention, and superintendent of schools in Brown County. He went to Dakota in 1874, where he was in charge of the Bon Homme Mission for one year. He became postmaster at Tyndall, S. D., in 1884. He died at Oakdale, Neb., Aug. 28, 1895 (according to the *Pacific Christian Advocate* of Oct. 30, 1895).

A. Atwood, *Glimpses on Puget Sound*. 1903.
C. J. Brosnan, *Jason Lee*. 1932.
H. K. Hines, *Pacific Northwest*. 1899.
Ezra Meeker, *Pioneer Reminiscences of Puget Sound*. 1905.
ERLE HOWELL

RICHMOND, Natal, South Africa, **Indaleni Institution,** was originally founded by JAMES ALLISON who removed thither from Swaziland in 1847. He immediately started a small Industrial School for young men and women, but this venture did not long survive his resignation from the ministry in 1852. The present Institution was established by C. E. Dent (1899-1903), who erected a girls' dormitory and opened a girls' school. Under the governorship of A. W. Cragg (1913-1933) the Institution expanded considerably: a Spinning and Weaving School was equipped in 1920, a three-year course of industrial training in needlework, laundry, cookery, etc., was introduced, and the academic standard was gradually advanced from Standard IV to Standard VIII. Matriculation was offered and male students admitted during the term of S. le Grove Smith (1934-1941).

During 1946 the Nuttall Training College, which had been established at Allison's Edendale Mission, was amalgamated with the Indaleni Institution. A programme of expansion was carried out under the direction of J. Wesley Hunt (1942-1960) and included the erection of a Teacher Training College and a Men's Hostel.

The schools, which include the only Government Art School for Africans in SOUTH AFRICA, passed under the control of the government in 1956. The Methodist Church still controls the hostels which had an enrollment of 410 in 1966.

D. G. L. CRAGG

RICHMOND, VIRGINIA, U.S.A., (metropolitan population, 450,000) is the capital of the commonwealth of VIRGINIA and one of the historic cities of America. It was founded in 1742, but not until 1780 did it become the seat of the state government. Richmond is first mentioned in the annals of the M.E. Church for 1788 when Matthew Harris was preacher in charge and Richard Ivey was presiding elder.

Central Church, the first Methodist church in the Richmond area, formerly Manchester, was organized as a Methodist Society in 1786 at a private home located on Seventh Street between Perry and Porter Streets. The ninth session of the VIRGINIA ANNUAL CONFERENCE was held by Bishop FRANCIS ASBURY in Central Church in 1792. In the early days of the church (1797), the members constructed a frame chapel with the outside boards fastened up and down and this suggested the name "Old Plank Church." Later it was known as the Manchester Church, and finally as Central Church. It is now located at the corner of Porter and Thirteenth Streets (since 1900). Its Sunday school has been continuous since 1847. The 1970 membership was 697.

Trinity Church. This church had its beginnings in 1790 when a group of men and women formed a Sunday school. From 1790 to 1799 this group met in various places. Around 1799, a family named Parrott opened their home, located on Main Street, to the Sunday school workers. Their home was on Main Street near the old Market in the seventeen hundred block, East. In the rear of this home was a stable or warehouse which Mr. Parrott developed into a church. This building became known as the "Stable Church." When the congregation outgrew this, they were granted permission to meet in the Henrico County Court House. A church was built at the corner of Nineteenth and Franklin Streets in the year 1800 and this became known as the "First Church." Thomas Lyell was then appointed its pastor. Bishop Asbury preached the last sermon of his life in Trinity Church in 1816. In 1828 the congregation moved to Franklin Street between Fourteenth and Fifteenth Streets and the name was changed from "First Church" to "Trinity Church."

The congregation split in 1859 and built two churches on Broad Street—one at Tenth and Broad, which became known as "Broad Street Methodist Church," and one at Twentieth and Broad, which kept the name, Trinity. Trinity's congregation began to think about moving in the 1930's because of the shift in population, and finally moved to 903 Forest Avenue, Richmond, in the Fall of 1944. It had 1,928 members in 1970 and is one of the largest congregations of the Methodist churches of Richmond at the present time.

Centenary Church. This church was formed in 1810 in what was then the western section of Richmond—on Shockoe Hill. The congregation named their church "Shockoe Hill Methodist Church." It was located on Marshall Street between Fourth and Fifth Streets until 1841. The congregation then moved to Grace Street between Fourth and Fifth Streets and began a building, now standing as the oldest Methodist church structure in Richmond (1966). The suitable land for the church structure was difficult to purchase, since the property owners in the area said they did not want "shouting Methodists" in their neighborhood. Finally, through the offices of an intermediary, the congregation was able to purchase the present site for $3,926.50. The COKESBURY Book Store is located next to this church. At least two bishops have been elected from the pastors who served this church: Bishop JOHN C. GRANBERY and Bishop WALTER C. GUM. Present membership stands at 1,250.

River Road Church. Known from 1859 to 1960 as Broad Street Methodist Church, the congregation here was formed from Trinity Methodist Church in 1859. The cornerstone of the first church was laid at Tenth and Broad Streets on June 30, 1859. The church has been very prominent in the life of the city and state, and was located at Tenth and Broad only one block from the state capitol. When the "Merrimac" destroyed the "Congress" in the Civil War, DAVID SETH DOGGETT, who was the minister, opened in the church a meeting of the Ladies Defense Association for the purpose of raising funds to build "Ironclads." In 1888, the Woman's Missionary Union, Auxiliary to the Southern Baptist Convention, was organized in this church by delegates from ten states. In 1961, the congregation moved into the new church on River Road and changed the name from Broad Street to River Road Methodist Church. Its membership in 1970 was 632.

REVEILLE CHURCH, RICHMOND, VIRGINIA

Reveille Church. This great church, the largest in membership in Richmond (1970—2,008), is a merger of the former Monument Church and Union Station Church. On Nov. 26, 1950, Monument Church burned at 1800 Park Avenue, and Union Station had the need to move nearer to its membership. Selected leaders of the two churches met on March 28, 1951 at Union Station Church to consider the possibility of a union. A uniting service was held on June 21, 1951 at Thomas Jefferson High School, and the congregation continued to meet there until the present church was built at 4200 West Cary Street. The new church, with the most adequate facilities of any Meth-

odist Church in Richmond, opened on Oct. 31, 1954. One of the former pastors of this church was Bishop COSTEN J. HARRELL.

General Minutes.   A. PURNELL BAILEY

RICHMOND COLLEGE, Richmond, Surrey, England, one of the THEOLOGICAL COLLEGES of the Wesleyan Methodist Church, was opened in September 1843. In 1868 the college passed into the care of the WESLEYAN METHODIST MISSIONARY SOCIETY, and was used only for the training of prospective missionaries. This segregated system was given up in 1885, since which time students for both home and overseas work have been trained in each of the colleges. Nevertheless, among Richmond's proudest possessions are the Rolls of Honor, which record the high number of its sons who ended their lives in the foreign field. The library houses the major known part of the libraries of JOHN and CHARLES WESLEY and JOHN FLETCHER. Richmond College is a divinity school within the University of London, and the tutors serve as members of the theological faculty: the students take either the university internal degree in divinity or the diploma in theology.

Frank H. Cumbers, *Richmond College, 1843-1943.* London, The Epworth Press, 1943.   NORMAN P. GOLDHAWK

RICKETTS, ROBERT SCOTT (1843-1918), American educator, was born March 5, 1843, at Vicksburg, Miss., where his father, R. B. Ricketts, honored minister, was living. He graduated from CENTENARY COLLEGE at the beginning of the Civil War. The year before his death he received the degree of Doctor of Letters from MILLSAPS COLLEGE, the first honorary degree ever conferred by that institution. After service in the Confederate Army he began teaching school, the work to which he devoted his long and useful life. After a teaching association with the Collegiate Institute of BATON ROUGE, La., he taught at Port Gibson Female College, Port Gibson, Miss. In 1875, he went to Brookhaven, Miss., as a member of the faculty of Whitworth College. Appreciation of the charm of his personal character and admiration for his talents as a teacher led to his election as Head Master of the Preparatory Department of Millsaps College in 1894. In that position he served God and his fellow man with renowned success until two months before he died.

In 1877 he married Bertha Burnley. To them were born four sons and a daughter. The daughter, Cid Ricketts Sumner, became a novelist of distinction.

For fifty-two years Professor Ricketts taught with a gentle spirit and with peculiar success, with a great love of learning and a fine literary taste, exerting an indelible Christian influence upon the thousands of young men and women who loved and respected him. From his youth he occupied many official positions in the church and was a constant and regular attendant at its services.

He died on Feb. 25, 1918, in JACKSON, Miss., and was buried in Cedar Lawn Cemetery there.

Journal of the Mississippi Conference, 1918.
New Orleans Christian Advocate, 1918.   J. A. LINDSEY

RIDDELL, JOHN HENRY (1863-1952), Canadian and United Church of Canada minister and educator, was born near Bolton, Ontario, on Nov. 1, 1863, son of James and Anne Jane Riddell. He was educated at VICTORIA COLLEGE (B.A., 1890; B.D., 1892), and in 1898 was ordained in the Methodist Church. He married Florence Armstrong on June 12, 1894. There were two sons—Harold, killed in action in 1916, and Robert Gerald, a distinguished Canadian diplomat.

Riddell was posted to Manitoba in 1890, and in 1896 became professor of classics at WESLEY COLLEGE, WINNIPEG. Seven years later he moved to Edmonton where he founded ALBERTA COLLEGE (North) and became its first principal. In 1911 he founded Alberta College (South), later to become St. Stephen's College.

In 1917 Riddell returned to Winnipeg as principal of Wesley College. During these critical years his administrative skills and sound scholarship were of great value. He encouraged collaboration with Manitoba College and thus prepared for the ultimate union of the two institutions. Through his efforts, the college was placed on a much sounder financial footing.

Riddell was keenly interested in welfare legislation and in the history of religion in the West. In his latter years he wrote *Methodism in the Middle West,* a pioneering study. For his great services to church and society he was awarded honorary degrees by Victoria, Alberta, and Manitoba universities. He died at Carlton Place, Ontario, Nov. 9, 1952.

A. S. Cummings, "A History of Wesley College." Ms. 1938. W. Kirkconnell, *The Golden Jubilee of Wesley College, 1888-1938.* Winnipeg: Columbia Press, 1938.

F. W. ARMSTRONG

RIDGWAY, JOHN (1786-1860), British Methodist, was born in Hanley, Staffordshire, the son of Job Ridgway, one of the founders of the METHODIST NEW CONNEXION, and followed the family trade as a potter. He was by appointment "Potter to Her Majesty," the first mayor of Hanley, a county magistrate and deputy lieutenant; he refused a knighthood. He published an *Apology* for the New Connexion's principles, and helped to secure the legal settlement of the New Connexion. He died on Dec. 3, 1860.

OLIVER A. BECKERLEGGE

RIDPATH, JOHN CLARK (1840-1900), American educator and writer of popular historical works, the son of Abraham and Sally (Matthews) Ridpath, was born April 26, 1840, in Putnam County, Indiana. He graduated from Indiana Asbury University in 1863. He became a teacher; then principal of Thorntown Academy, a Methodist school, and in 1869 returned to Indiana Asbury as professor. In 1879 he became vice-president. He persuaded WASHINGTON C. DEPAUW, then one of the wealthiest citizens of INDIANA, to become a patron of Indiana Asbury. In 1884 he secured the change of name from Indiana Asbury to DEPAUW UNIVERSITY. He retired from teaching and was one of the most popular writers of historical works of his time.

Ridpath's *Cyclopedia of Universal History* was published in three large volumes at the time he was a professor in DePauw. It proved immensely popular and while historians mark it down for its inaccuracies and its sweeping treatment of men and events, its style was compelling and the writer knew how to emphasize the important and play down the less so. The writer was a genius at apt phraseology and description.

He married Hannah B. Smythe of Greencastle, Dec. 1, 1862. Five children blessed their home. For his publishing he moved to NEW YORK CITY. There he died July 31, 1900.

Dictionary of American Biography.
Who's Who in America.   W. D. ARCHIBALD

RIEMENSCHNEIDER, CARL (1844-1925), born May 14, 1844, was the son of Engelhardt Riemenschneider and served for fifty years as professor and president of German Wallace College (now BALDWIN-WALLACE COLLEGE) in Berea, Ohio. When his father was sent as missionary for Methodist work in GERMANY in 1850, young Carl received his education in German and Swiss institutions, notably Tübingen University, where he studied under conservative Tobias Beck. His university career was broken in the middle by two years service as instructor at the Martin Mission Institute, a Methodist ministerial training school in BREMEN.

In 1868 he came to Berea to teach classical languages, in which he excelled. Later he was professor of philosophy and theology. Elected vice-president in 1880 and president in 1893, he continued to teach regularly, even after his resignation of the presidency in 1908, until his retirement in 1917.

In 1870 he married Emily Smith, who bore him ten children, one of whom, Albert Riemenschneider, became director of the Baldwin-Wallace Conservatory of Music. He was long remembered for his leadership of student class meetings held Saturday nights. His deep speaking voice brought fame as public speaker and orator. Although he was not interested in church politics, he served as a delegate to the GENERAL CONFERENCE of 1900. He died in Berea, Nov. 8, 1925.

Der Christliche Apologete, Nov. 25, 1925.
Minutes of Central German Conference, 1926.

FREDERICK A. NORWOOD

RIEMENSCHNEIDER, ENGELHARDT (1815-1899), born April 9, 1815 in Eubach, Kurhessen, GERMANY, was one of the leading figures in the development of German Methodism in the OHIO valley of the United States and in his native country. He arrived in the United States in 1835 and proceeded to WHEELING, W. Va., and PITTSBURGH, Pa., where he was converted under the preaching of WILHELM NAST. He was received in full membership in the OHIO CONFERENCE in 1842.

In 1841 he was appointed to found the North Ohio Mission, a circuit of 400-500 miles in which he preached ten to twelve times per week. After two years in LOUISVILLE and a year in Pittsburgh he was appointed presiding elder of the North Ohio District in 1847. He married Katherine Nuhfer in 1843.

A new phase of his life began in 1850, when he was appointed to missionary work in Germany, where he spent the next twenty years, fostering missions already established and founding new ones. His work centered in FRANKFURT am Main, BREMEN, Bremerhaven, ZURICH, Ludwigsburg, and Basel. His wife died in Ludwigsburg. Frequently he encountered opposition from the authorities of the state churches.

After his return to the United States in 1870 he spent a year in Berea, Ohio, and another two in Allegheny, Pa., then four as presiding elder of the North Ohio District.

He retired in 1877, lived in Berea and Cleveland, and died Sept. 22, 1899, leaving two sons and four daughters.

Der Christliche Apologete.
Verhanglungen und Berichte of the Central Deutsche Konferenz, 1900.   FREDERICK A. NORWOOD

JAMES H. RIGG

RIGG, JAMES HARRISON (1821-1909), British minister, was born at Newcastle upon Tyne on Jan. 16, 1821. The son of a Wesleyan minister, he entered the Wesleyan Methodist ministry in 1845. As a circuit minister he was deeply interested in the ecclesiastical questions of the day: he published *Modern Anglican Theology* (1857) and *Essays of the Times* (1866). In 1868 he became principal of the Wesleyan Westminster Teachers' Training College, remaining there until retirement in 1903. In 1878 he was chosen president of the Wesleyan Conference; his name was associated with the admission of laymen into the Conference in that year, and with the Thanksgiving Fund, which raised £300,000 for Methodist work. He was one of the original members of the London School Board, and in 1886-88 was a member of the Royal Commission on Elementary Education. He founded the *London Quarterly Review* in 1853 and was closely associated with it until 1898, when it passed into the hands of the connection. Rigg was a life-long exponent of the side of the Wesleyan tradition which looked for inspiration to the Established Church, rather than to Nonconformity. Among his later writings were: *National Education* (1873); *The Churchmanship of John Wesley* (1878); *The Character and Life Work of Dr. Pusey* (1883); *A Comparative View of Church Organisation* (1887); *Oxford High Anglicanism* (1895); *Wesleyan Methodist Reminiscences* (1904); and a valuable short life of *Jabez Bunting* (1905). He lacked just the touch of creative ability which would have made him a great man.

JOHN KENT

RIGGIN, FRANCIS ASBURY (1848-1924), American minister, was born Sept. 7, 1848, in BALTIMORE, Md., the son of Israel and Emily Lee Riggin. He finished with honors at DICKINSON COLLEGE, Carlisle, Pa., with the A.B. and A.M. degrees. He joined the Methodist Church at age fifteen, was licensed to preach in his sophomore year in

F. A. RIGGIN

college, entered the PHILDELPHIA CONFERENCE in 1870, transferred to MINNESOTA CONFERENCE in 1871 and to ROCKY MOUNTAIN CONFERENCE in 1872, being stationed at Evanston, Wyo. In 1873 he was appointed to Beaverhead and Jefferson Circuit in MONTANA, with WILLIAM WESLEY VAN ORSDEL as junior preacher. Their charge extended from the Three Forks of the Missouri to Pocatello, Ida. Their headquarters were at Sheridan (Montana) where Hugh Duncan had built a church. At district conference in Helena, January 1874, they reported that each had traveled 4,000 miles on horseback and had together received nearly 100 new members. The next year they headquartered at Virginia City where they built a stone church and held revival services, assisted by T. C. ILIFF of Bozeman. Other appointments were: Beaverhead and Fish Creek 1875, presiding elder of Helena District 1876, presiding elder of Butte District 1877-80, superintendent of Montana Mission 1880-87, pastor at Fort Benton and Great Falls with Brother Van 1887-89, at Whitehall and Hope Circuit 1889-91. In November 1891, Riggin became superintendent of the Navajo Indian Mission; in 1893, presiding elder of Bozeman District; 1894, pastor at Great Falls; 1895, presiding elder of Great Falls District; 1896, pastor at Kalispell; 1897-99, superintendent of North Montana Mission; 1899-1912 superintendent of Epworth Piegan Indian Mission. He retired in 1912 and made his home on his son's farm at Barr, Mont., where he served surrounding rural appointments until his death April 16, 1924. Burial was at Glasgow, Mont., beside his wife, Ida Isabelle Jordan Riggin, who died June 21, 1919.

Mrs. Riggin was born Nov. 19, 1860, and was the sister of Walter Jordan, minister in the Christian Church. She was converted in a Riggin-Van Orsdel revival at Fish Creek in 1873, and married F. A. Riggin in 1876. They had three sons, Harrison Van Orsdel, Guy Asbury, and Kent Orville.

Francis Riggin's appeals in the *New York Christian Advocate* for ministers for Montana in the 1880's brought able men to the state, among them JACOB MILLS. In 1892 Riggin was delegate to GENERAL CONFERENCE and brought about the formation of North Montana Mission. He was an able administrator. Riggin and Van Orsdel were sometimes likened to Moody and Sanky, Van Orsdel the more famous for his singing, Riggin for his preaching. Both men largely shaped Montana Methodism.

E. L. Mills, *Plains, Peaks and Pioneers*. 1947.
Montana Christian Advocate.
ROBERTA BAUR WEST

RIGGIN, JOHN H. (1834-1913), an American minister, scholar, soldier and administrator, was born at Pittsville, Md., Oct. 7, 1834. Admitted to what is now the LITTLE ROCK CONFERENCE in 1865, for forty years rendered almost every type of service including twenty-one years as presiding elder, member of three GENERAL CONFERENCES and one of the founders of HENDRIX COLLEGE, of which he was a trustee for twenty years and from which he received the D.D. degree.

Considered remarkable in mental power, he had read the New Testament through before he was five years of age. He was self-educated, mastering higher mathematics and gaining a working knowledge of Latin, Greek and Hebrew. Eventually he became known as one of the scholarly and profound students of his day.

Licensed to preach at Glasgow, Mo., in June 1860, he intended to enter the itineracy the next year, but with the outbreak of the Civil War, he joined the Confederate Army, serving two years as a private and the remainder of the war as CHAPLAIN of an ARKANSAS regiment. This surrendered at Marshall, Texas at war's end, and a remnant of the soldiers accompanied their beloved chaplain back to Arkansas.

Abundant in many services, he was best known and remembered as a preacher. With his unusually retentive memory, his logical mind, his skilled use of the Scriptures, his chaste and expressive vocabulary, he was one of the most widely known preachers in that area of Methodism. He retired in 1909, making his home at Arkadelphia, Ark., until his death May 30, 1913. He had been given to Arkansas by the fortunes of war, and was one of the heroic men who gathered and reorganized and revitalized broken Methodism in this Conference (Little Rock) after the war.

ROY E. FAWCETT

RIGGLEMAN, LEONARD (1894-   ), American college president, was born at Blue Spring, W. Va., April 16, 1894, the son of Samuel C. and Harriet (Hamrick) Riggleman. He won the A.B. degree at MORRIS HARVEY COLLEGE in 1922, and the A.M. at SOUTHERN METHODIST UNIVERSITY in 1924. He did graduate study at Michigan and NORTHWESTERN UNIVERSITIES. The honorary degrees of D.D. and LL.D. were awarded in 1933 and 1944 by KENTUCKY WESLEYAN COLLEGE and Davis and Elkins College, respectively. He married Alice Pauline Steele, Aug. 16, 1922, and they have one daughter. Admitted on trial in 1918 in the WESTERN VIRGINIA CONFERENCE (MECS), Riggleman's appointments were: Omar, 1921-22; Milton, 1924-28; Rural Specialist at West Virginia University, 1928-30; professor of religion at Morris Harvey College, 1930-31; and president of the college, 1931-64. He was a delegate to the 1934, '38, '44, and '56 GENERAL CONFERENCES, and was a member of the General Board of EDUCATION (MECS), 1934-38. Retiring in 1964, he made his home at Huntington, W. Va.

Clark and Stafford, *Who's Who in Methodism*. 1952.
C. T. Howell, *Prominent Personalities*. 1945.
Minutes of the Western Virginia and West Virginia Conferences.
JESSE A. EARL
ALBEA GODBOLD

RIGOR, G. W. MILES (1831-1906), American United Brethren preacher, educator, writer and editor, crusader, and conference leader, was born Sept. 22, 1831, on a farm near Mount Pleasant in Westmoreland County, Pa. He joined the CHURCH OF THE UNITED BRETHREN IN CHRIST after a moving religious experience in 1850. Two years later he was licensed by the Mount Pleasant congregation and he entered Mount Pleasant College, Mount Pleasant, Pa. (no longer in existence) with the intention of entering the ministry. Before completing his education, he left college; but he continued his path to the ministry, being licensed by Allegheny Conference in 1854, ordained in 1860, and serving churches in the Allegheny Conference until 1862, when he transferred to the East Pennsylvania Conference.

He immediately threw himself into the work of his new conference relationships with great abandon. In 1863 he was elected English Secretary, a position he held for six years. In 1871 when there were no longer English and German secretaries, he was elected conference secretary and served through 1889. During nine of these years he also served as one of the presiding elders of the conference.

Regretting the fact that he had never completed his education at Mount Pleasant College, Rigor began to speak for establishing an educational institution under the auspices of the denomination in eastern PENNSYLVANIA. The opening of LEBANON VALLEY COLLEGE in 1866 was in large measure due to Rigor's labors. He and Thomas Rees Vickroy, a neighbor and a local preacher in the M.E. Church, held the lease for the operation of the college in the name of the conference from 1866 to 1871.

While serving as business manager and field representative for the college, Rigor involved himself in another project that engaged his interest—the founding of English-speaking congregations. He was the first pastor of the Trinity Church, Lebanon, Pa., when it was organized in 1866. Simultaneously, he was a participant in the preparation of articles of incorporation for the annual conference.

Rigor's interest in Christian education extended to the local church as he urged congregations to establish Sunday schools and expended his energies toward the establishing of a conference-wide Sunday school movement.

As a delegate to GENERAL CONFERENCE in 1873 and 1877, he was an outspoken critic on such issues as unequal representation and the secrecy law, both of which liberals in the church opposed. For the next twelve years, beginning in 1873, he expressed these liberal views. He became editor of two papers which arose in Pennsylvania to counter the conservative position of the *Religious Telescope* which was under the editorship of MILTON WRIGHT. These publications were the *United Brethren Tribune* and *The Monthly Itinerant*. During his editorship of the latter publication (1877-1885), Rigor continued to promote other causes with which he had become associated: Lebanon Valley College, the Sunday school movement, higher salaries for pastors, stronger denominational attachment, and campmeetings.

In the July 1876 issue of *The Monthly Itinerant*, Rigor described in glowing terms the observance of the Centennial of Independence at Philadelphia. In his diaries, he tells of his trip to Harrisburg to view the body of the slain President Lincoln. In his conference, he became a gadfly in the interest of the preservation of local church and pastoral records; and in 1866 and 1867, respectively, he presented for publication in the conference journal charts dealing with the bishops of the denomination and the time, place of meeting, and leadership of the annual sessions of the conference. In 1878 he challenged the Lancaster, Pa., *New Era* on its statement that MARTIN BOEHM had gone "over to the Methodists" after his United Brethren friends had "disowned him."

G. W. Miles Rigor died July 9, 1906 and is buried at the Stoverdale Church Cemetery, near Hummelstown, Pa., with his wife who followed him in death by a few days.

BRUCE C. SOUDERS

RIO GRANDE CONFERENCE, a conference for Spanish-speaking Americans, goes back to the work of the M.E. Church, South among Mexican-Americans in the last half of the nineteenth century. The Rio Grande Mission Conference (WEST TEXAS CONFERENCE after 1866), an English-speaking conference, was created by the 1858 GENERAL CONFERENCE. Its territory included west and southwest TEXAS. At its first session in 1859 the conference appointed Robert P. Thompson as a missionary to the Mexicans in the Rio Grande Valley. In time the work grew to two Mexican districts and there was a demand for a separate conference for the Mexican work.

In 1885 the Mexican work of the West Texas Conference, along with some churches in MEXICO, was organized as the Mexican Border Mission Conference. In 1891 the Northwest Mexican Mission Conference was formed to include Mexican work in west Texas and northwest Mexico. In 1914 some changes were made, and the Texas Mexican Mission was formed to include the Spanish-speaking work in Texas east of the Pecos River, while the Mexican Border Conference took in the work west of the Pecos, along with some churches in Mexico. In 1918 the Mexican Border Conference was merged with the Pacific Mexican Mission to form the Western Mexican Mission. In 1930 the Texas Mexican and the Western Mexican Missions became conferences and so continued until unification when they were merged to form the Southwest Mexican Conference of The Methodist Church. In 1948 the name of the latter body was changed to the Rio Grande Conference because though it was still a Spanish language conference and printed its minutes in Spanish, as time passed few of the ministers or church members had any direct ties with Mexico.

The Southwest Mexican Conference was organized at Dallas on Nov. 2, 1939 with Bishop A. FRANK SMITH presiding. It began with three districts—El Paso, Northern, and Southern—fifty-five pastoral charges, eighty-one societies, 6,364 members, forty-one women's societies with 814 members, property valued at $302,165, and $29,724 raised for all purposes during the year.

The Rio Grande Conference was organized at Corpus Christi on July 1, 1948 with Bishop Smith in the chair. It began with three districts—Northern, Southern, and Western—sixty-five pastoral charges, fifty-two ministers, 8,884 members including inactive ones, and property valued at $899,398.

Courage, evangelistic fervor, and devotion have characterized the Mexican-American work from the beginning. Alejo Hernandez, scion of a wealthy Mexican family who had been educated for the priesthood but who had become disillusioned with the Roman Catholic Church of that day, came to Corpus Christi, was converted, and in 1871 was admitted on trial in the West Texas Conference.

Hernandez had a brief but spectacular career as an evangelist among his people in both Mexico and Texas. He died in 1875 after accompanying Bishop JOHN C. KEENER on a trip to Mexico City to promote Methodism there. A. H. Sutherland and FRANK S. ONDERDONK stand high among the Anglo ministers who made a lasting contribution to the work. Sutherland was presiding elder of one of the Mexican districts in the West Texas Conference before the organization of the Mexican Border Mission Conference, and with his wife he established HOLDING INSTITUTE at Laredo. Onderdonk was superintendent of the Texas Mexican Mission from 1914 to 1929 and died in 1936 during his sixth year as a presiding elder in the Texas Mexican Conference. From 1938 to his retirement in 1960, Bishop A. Frank Smith was the guiding spirit of the Spanish-speaking work of The Methodist Church in the southwest. Clarence W. Lokey was effective as director of the Spanish language work of the Division of National Missions from 1948 to 1965.

Today there are active congregations of the Rio Grande Conference in all of the major cities and many of the smaller ones in Texas and New Mexico. El Paso and San Antonio have seven churches each, and there are four in Dallas. The conference has three schools: Harwood Girls' School at ALBUQUERQUE, Holding Institute at Laredo, and LYDIA PATTERSON INSTITUTE at El Paso. Lydia Patterson Institute has furnished a large proportion of the ministers for the conference, and for Spanish language work in other parts of the United States. Many of the ministers now in places of leadership in the conference are graduates of PERKINS SCHOOL OF THEOLOGY.

The record of the Rio Grande Conference is appreciated in The United Methodist Church. Church membership has nearly trebled since 1939. In 1946 the conference led American Methodism in proportionate giving to the Crusade for Christ. On a quota of $15,075 the conference paid $16,026. Between 1953 and 1956 the conference had a twenty-nine percent gain in membership, the largest increase for any conference in the church in the same period.

In 1968 the Rio Grande Conference reported four districts, 101 pastoral charges, seventy ministers, 17,488 members, and property valued at $5,532,120. The total amount raised for all purposes that year was $568,968.

General Minutes, MECS and MC.
Minutes of the Rio Grande Conference.
O. W. Nail, *Southwest Texas Conference.* 1958.

WILLIAM C. MARTIN

RIO DE JANEIRO, Brazil. The first steps to establish Methodism in BRAZIL were taken in 1835, when Bishop JAMES O. ANDREW sent FOUNTAIN E. PITTS of the TENNESSEE CONFERENCE to survey the possibilities of work in South America. Pitts sailed in July 1835, and shortly after arrival in Rio de Janeiro on August 19, organized a small Society of English-speaking Methodists in that city, promising to send them a missionary.

In 1836, upon his return to the United States, Pitts recommended entering the field and JUSTIN R. SPAULDING of the NEW ENGLAND CONFERENCE was sent to Brazil in March of that same year. In June he organized a Sunday school with thirty pupils, several of whom were Brazilians and were taught in Portuguese. He also organized a congregation of forty among the English-speaking persons.

In November 1837, other missionaries arrived—DANIEL

PARRISH KIDDER and his wife, Cynthia Harriet; a teacher, R. M. McMurdy, and a Miss Marcella Russell whom he soon married. Various severe illnesses, including yellow fever, soon struck at the little band. Cynthia Kidder died and was buried in the British (Protestant) Cemetery of Gamboa, Rio, where a tombstone marks her grave. Left with two infant children, Kidder returned to the United States at the end of 1840. Mr. and Mrs. McMurdy had first opened a little school, but discouraged and ill returned to the United States. Spaulding stayed on until the end of 1841, when he too left Brazil and the mission was closed by the home Board. Yet despite all, this early work in Rio had been effective enough to arouse the Roman Catholic hierarchy to rebuttal and strong opposition. Meanwhile, the home church was becoming bitterly involved in the dispute over slavery. No other missionaries were sent out, and thus Methodism's first efforts in Brazil closed without the establishment of any permanent work.

About twenty-five years later, in 1867, after the close of the Civil War, JUNIUS E. NEWMAN of ALABAMA went to Brazil as a Confederate emigrant, not as a missionary but properly accredited by Bishop W. M. WIGHTMAN to open Methodist work in the Empire. Deeply impressed with Brazil's need for the Gospel, Newman pled insistently with the Southern Methodist Church for missionaries.

The first to go was J. J. RANSOM of Tennessee, who arrived in Rio de Janeiro on Feb. 2, 1876. After some time studying the language and surveying the field, he held the first Methodist service in that city in a rented house on Jan. 13, 1878. With a congregation of around forty, none Brazilians, Ransom initiated permanent Methodist work in Rio de Janeiro, then capital of the Empire.

It was in March 1879 that the first Brazilians were received into the church—an ex-priest, Antonio Teixeira de Albuquerque, and a young lady, Francisca de Albuquerque. Four months later four other Brazilians joined the church.

Little notice was taken of the so-called "new religion" until the Catholic clergy began opposing it through its official organ, O Apostolo. Ransom invited them to attend his services but they did not accept. After a voyage to the United States, Ransom returned in May 1881 with two new missionaries—JAMES L. KENNEDY and J. W. KOGER—and MARTHA WATTS, a missionary teacher for a school in Piracicaba. Koger was sent to the latter place, and Kennedy stayed in Rio to assist Ransom.

That year a lot was bought for a church, and in 1881 they began building a pretty little chapel on what was then called Largo do Cattete, but is now the Praca Jose d'Alencar. This chapel still stands and adjoins the church which was built in 1886. Two other preaching points were established in the city, and by 1881 the Methodist Church in Rio had sixty foreign and six Brazilian members. One year later there were over thirty Brazilian members.

The construction of the temple itself had an interesting history. Under the Empire Catholicism was official and no other religion was allowed a structure that had the outward appearance of a church. Ransom and Kennedy began construction, but in March 1882 Ransom left for the United States on urgent matters, leaving the younger, inexperienced man with a tremendous responsibility. Catholic clergy and city councilmen under their pressure did everything to block the work. At one time Januzzi, the constructor, worked men all night in order to finish the task before fanatical clergy could induce the authorities

to rescind approval of a blueprint which they had approved and which included a more churchly facade and spirelets topping the side walls. Cattete Church was completed, however, and was ready for inauguration on Sept. 8, 1886, when Bishop J. C. GRANBERY arrived in Brazil for the first time. Here on Sept. 16, 1886, Bishop Granbery organized the smallest conference ever organized in Methodism. Its members were James L. Kennedy, J. W. TARBOUX, and HUGH C. TUCKER, who had just arrived with the Bishop. These men have been called the "Golden Trio of Brazilian Methodism."

The proclamation of the Republic supplanting the Empire in November 1889, brought official church-state separation, and from then on the work in the Federal District and surrounding area expanded constantly and solidly, not only along evangelical but along educational and social lines. Since the recent removal of the nation's capital to BRASILIA, the city of Rio de Janeiro and what was known as the Federal District is now called Guanabara State. There is also a state of Rio de Janeiro, and together they make up the First Ecclesiastical Region of the Methodist Church of Brazil. In 1966 it included thirty-five churches, fifteen parsonages, 6,173 members, two parochial schools, and three other outstanding institutions—COLEGIO BENNETT, INSTITUTO ANNA GONZAGA (Home for Children), and the INSTITUTO CENTRAL DO POVO (People's Central Institute for Social Service). A home for the aged, O Lar dos Anciaos, has been started on the property of the Anna Gonzaga Home.

J. L. Kennedy, *Metodismo no Brasil.* 1928.
Expositor Cristão, July 21, 1894.
World Outlook, May 1943.　　　　　EULA K. LONG

RIPLEY, DOROTHY (1769-1831), daughter of WILLIAM RIPLEY of Whitby, was born in Yorkshire. Deeply impressed in early years by Methodist preachers, she also came under Quaker influence, and in 1801 felt the call to cross the Atlantic to labor among Negro slaves. She went "without money in her purse putting her trust in the bank of faith." Securing an interview with President Thomas Jefferson, she received his approbation for her work, and for two years passed from city to city pleading the cause of the Negroes. Returning to England in 1805, she afterward returned to America and preached to the Indians. Emulating John Howard, the prison reformer, she visited American prisons. In 1806 by permission of the president she preached from the speaker's chair in Congress, with Jefferson and the senators present. From her center at Charleston, the stronghold of slavery, she preached the gospel of pity to slave owners and of patience to slaves. In an evangelistic tour in England she accompanied LORENZO DOW and in September, 1818, in Nottinghamshire met HUGH BOURNE. For thirty years she traveled on such errands of mercy, crossing the Atlantic eight or nine times. She would not permit any collection on her behalf. She published several tracts: *An Account of the Extraordinary Conversion and Religious Experience of Dorothy Ripley* (1817) and *The Bank of Faith* (1822). She died in Virginia, Dec. 23, 1831.

JOHN T. WILKINSON

RITCHIE, ELIZABETH, later Mrs. Mortimer, (1754- ?), British Methodist, born on Feb. 2, 1754, was the daughter of John Ritchie, a naval surgeon. JOHN WESLEY was a frequent visitor to her home in Otley; and, contrary to his rule of writing only in reply to letters he received, he sent her many letters of spiritual advice. She was a close friend of SARAH CROSBY. In 1790 Elizabeth went to live with the Rogers at City Road Chapel and left a detailed account of Wesley's last days.

JOHN A. VICKERS

RITSON, JOHN HOLLAND (1868-1953), English Methodist, was born at Bolton in 1868 and educated at Manchester Grammar School and Balliol College, Oxford, where he graduated with First Class Honors in Natural Science. He trained for the Wesleyan Methodist ministry at Wesley College, Headingley, and served as Assistant Tutor at Didsbury College 1891-94. After travelling in the Eccles and Blackheath circuits, he was appointed in 1900 one of the two general secretaries of the BRITISH AND FOREIGN BIBLE SOCIETY, where he remained until retirement. He travelled extensively and was "principally responsible for the reorganization of the work of the Society in Canada and Australia." At the first INTERNATIONAL MISSIONARY COUNCIL held in Edinburgh (1910), he was elected joint Recording Secretary and Chairman of the Literature Committee of the Continuation Committee. Mission and unity were central to his thinking, and he pleaded at the Fifth ECUMENICAL METHODIST CONFERENCE of 1921 for the twin priorities of "the growth of holiness in individual life" and for Christian cooperation and unity. His writings include *Christian Literature and the Mission Field* (1915). He also made a notable contribution to Ministerial Training, serving on its Committee from 1906. He helped raise £250,000 for this work, had a large part in the foundation of Wesley House, CAMBRIDGE (1925), and in the general re-equipment of the colleges after the First World War. He was president of the Wesleyan Conference in 1925, when Oxford conferred on him the degree of Doctor of Divinity. He retired in 1931, and died at Seaford in 1953.

Minutes of the Methodist Conference, 1954.   JOHN NEWTON

RITUAL, THE, is a name given to the several forms or offices which in The United Methodist Church in America guide the minister and direct him in the conduct of the formal rites of the Church. These offices came to American Methodism in the SUNDAY SERVICE or abridged *Prayer Book* which JOHN WESLEY sent over to America, and which was adopted by the M.E. Church at its organization in 1784. However, when the *Sunday Service* fell into desuetude in a very few years, and early Methodism turned away from an ordered *Prayer Book* as such, certain particular forms, namely, the Lord's Supper or Holy Communion; Infant Baptism; Adult Baptism; Matrimony; Burial of the Dead; and three forms for Ordination (for deacons, elders and bishops) which were in the *Sunday Service* were retained in the first edition of the *Discipline* of 1792, and these became known in American Methodism as the *Ritual.*

Every edition of the *Discipline* until 1968 has carried these eight forms, and while from time to time they have been amended and revised by respective GENERAL CONFERENCES, there have been no very great nor appreciable changes in these offices from their original adoption in 1784 until the present. The Baptismal offices perhaps provide the exception here, as the forms directing the

Rites of BAPTISM have, indeed, been greatly changed over what John Wesley originally sent. Also, many additional lessons or readings have been put into the BURIAL service, especially within recent years. However, the Sacrament of the LORD'S SUPPER, and the office for its celebration have been very little changed, and the forms for ORDINATION scarcely at all. Neither has the office for the Solemnization of Matrimony been altered appreciably since some rather sweeping deletions were made in this Service when it first went out of the *Sunday Service* into the 1792 *Discipline.* Ritualistic revision in the Methodist Churches in America has been greatly influenced by the revision of the like forms in the *Prayer Book* of the Protestant Episcopal Church in America, though not to an overwhelming extent.

The eight forms which were cited above as the original Ritual—Communion, the two Baptisms, Matrimony, Burial of the Dead, and the three forms of Ordination, remained with scarcely any revision and with no additions in American Methodism until 1864 in the M.E. Church, and in 1870 in the M.E. Church, South. At approximately that same time, both Churches added a service for the Reception of Members, largely following the office for Confirmation in the Protestant Episcopal Church. John Wesley did not send to American Methodism any office for Confirmation, and hence there was no formal rite whereby members were received into the M.E. Churches until the dates above mentioned, although thousands were meanwhile being received into Methodist churches everywhere due to the great growth of Methodism during the first half of the nineteenth century.

The 1864-1870 revisions of the two M.E. Churches also added a form for cornerstone laying, and one for the Dedication of Churches. In time quite a few other offices were added as the twentieth century progressed—for the dedication of a church, or of a memorial, or for commissioning church officers and the like. Other forms were added even after the unification of American Methodism. The Commission on WORSHIP of The Methodist Church, however, in revising the *Book of Worship,* and also the *Ritual* as directed by the 1960 General Conference, decided to keep in the *Book of Discipline,* itself, only the eight ancient forms sent over by Wesley, as they had been revised; together with two present and official formal orders of worship. The other offices of the *Ritual* may be found in the *Book of Worship,* but not in the present *Discipline* of the Church. However, in 1968 the *Discipline* appeared with no part of the *Ritual,* all of it being published in the *Book of Worship.*

The METHODIST PUBLISHING HOUSE, which is empowered to publish all books and literature of an official nature for The Methodist Church, holds the copyright on the offices of the *Ritual,* and from time to time brings out various editions of it in different sizes, types and bindings. Ministers quite often provide themselves with a copy of the *Ritual* entirely apart from the *Book of Discipline* or *Book of Worship.*

General Conferences have always felt competent to revise the *Ritual* and do revise it from time to time, usually through a commission or a committee, especially when there is a broader revision in view than the mere alteration of a word here and there. All such revisions must be formally adopted by the General Conference before they are in effect in the church.

A disciplinary regulation which for many years remained in the *Discipline* ordered, "Let our Ritual be invariably used." However, ministers have always and do now feel free to vary in certain slight degrees the offices of the *Ritual* when such variations seem to be called for by the needs of an immediate situation. In the service of Holy Communion, a rubric indicates what parts of the service may be used if the ministers be "straightened for time" or if it is to be used for the sick or in a home. Should a change in the *Ritual* be proposed which patently would seriously affect one of the doctrinal positions of Methodism, it could be challenged as a violation of the first RESTRICTIVE RULE binding on the General Conference. Such a challenge has never been given during any proposed ritualistic revision and possibly may never be.

R. J. Cooke, *History of the Ritual.* 1900.
N. B. Harmon, *Rites and Ritual.* 1926.
T. O. Summers, *Commentary on the Ritual.* 1873.   N. B. H.

RIVERSIDE, CALIFORNIA, U.S.A. **First Church** was formed by seven charter members Oct. 13, 1872. In November 1873 MARION M. BOVARD was appointed as the first pastor. He later became president of the UNIVERSITY OF SOUTHERN CALIFORNIA. In June 1876 a brick chapel was completed. A new frame church costing $6,000 was completed in June 1882. In 1893, thirteen members left to start the Arlington Church in Riverside. On Feb. 5, 1899 a $6,000 addition to the main building was dedicated. On Dec. 20, 1903 the Hicks Memorial Chapel costing $11,100 was dedicated. In 1907, 189 members withdrew in order to start the Grace Church in Riverside. In February 1945, the first $50,000 was realized toward building a new church. In November 1945 a thirteen-acre site on Brockton Avenue, the present location, was purchased. On Feb. 5, 1947 First Church was destroyed by fire. On Dec. 19, 1948 the first Sunday service was held in the new Fellowship Hall. In May 1949 the two-story educational building was completed and with Fellowship Hall was dedicated free of debt. On Sept. 11, 1955 the first Sunday service was held in the new sanctuary. In October 1957, a new organ was installed in the sanctuary and seventy-eight members left to start the Wesley Church in Riverside. First Church acted as sponsor by mortgaging its property for Wesley Church to obtain a loan to build. In May 1961, the memorial church tower was completed and the carillon installed. In October 1963 seventeen members withdrew to start the Rubidoux Church near Riverside. Again First Church sponsored the move by mortgaging its property for Rubidoux Church to obtain a loan to build.

Four of the church's former pastors became district superintendents and another a vice-president of the Southern California School of Theology. Three members have served as missionaries to INDIA and another in National Missions. The church has two full time ministers, with an assisting ministerial staff of six others. Church property was valued at approximately $1,250,000 and church membership was 2,312 in 1970.

General Minutes.   VIRGIL L. BATES

RIVINGTON, CHARLES (1688-1742), British publisher, was born at Chesterfield in 1688. Apprenticed to a LONDON bookseller, he soon set up on his own and became the best-known publisher of religious works in the early eighteenth century. He published GEORGE WHITEFIELD's *The*

Nature and Necessity of a New Birth in Christ (1737), and JOHN WESLEY's version of Thomas á Kempis, in 1735. Rivington also shared in the publication of Samuel Richardson's *Pamela* (1741-42). He died in London, Feb. 22, 1742.

JOHN KENT

RIZZI, DINA (1910-   ), Brazilian Methodist educator and leader in women's work, was born in Sertãozinho, State of São Paulo, of Roman Catholic parents. At the age of ten she was sent to the Methodist school in Ribeirão Preto, where for the first time she heard about the Bible. Through the influence of three missionaries—Lucy Wade, Rosalie Brown, and Mary McSwain, Dina was converted, joined the church, and became the only Protestant member of her family.

For three years she studied at the Methodist Colegio PIRACICABANO (now INSTITUTO EDUCACIONAL), receiving her degree as teacher in 1929. Later, she studied elementary education and social work at SCARRITT COLLEGE for Christian Workers and at Peabody College, both in NASHVILLE, Tenn. From 1930-41, Dina Rizzi served the Methodist School in Ribeirão Preto in several capacities. In January 1950 the religious education department of this school was moved to SÃO PAULO to become a training school for women Christian workers, the Instituto Metodista. In 1960 she was appointed principal (Reitora) of the institute.

She has been a member of the Legislative Committee of the Methodist Church of BRAZIL, a delegate to the General Conference of the Methodist Church of Brazil in 1960, and in 1962 Brazilian delegate to the celebration in South RHODESIA, of the seventy-fifth anniversary of the World Day of Prayer. This same year she was named to the Evangelical Latin American Consultation, which met in BUENOS AIRES, and in 1963, was a delegate to the Asian Consultation Committee which met in Port Dickson, MALAYA. On her return from this, she visited several countries in Europe to study the DEACONESS schools in GERMANY, SWITZERLAND, and England.

Besides being Reitora of the Methodist Institute in São Paulo, Dina Rizzi was also for ten years editor of the *Voz Missionaria,* official magazine of the Methodist women in Brazil. She is presently one of the vice presidents of the World Federation of Methodist Women, as president of the Latin American Evangelical Women's Federation.

EULA K. LONG

ROADMAN, EARL ALAN (1885-1967), American minister, educator, and president of two mid-western Methodist colleges, was born at Dike, Ia., Nov. 14, 1885. He attended country school and in 1899 entered Iowa State Normal College at Cedar Falls. He taught school for several years and in 1907 entered Upper Iowa University at Fayette, from which he graduated in 1909.

After completing his ministerial training at BOSTON SCHOOL OF THEOLOGY, he spent a year at Halle-Wittenberg University in GERMANY. Meanwhile he had married Irma Keen of Chicago, Sept. 5, 1910. To them were born six children.

Roadman served several pastorates in IOWA, then taught Bible and Rural Sociology at Upper Iowa University from 1919 to 1925. Returning to the pastorate at Grace Church,

Waterloo, Ia., he was called to the presidency of DAKOTA WESLEYAN UNIVERSITY, Mitchell, S. D., in 1927.

President Roadman guided the destinies of the college during nine of the most difficult years of her existence. The hardships which followed the financial panic of 1929 were greatly increased in this agricultural area by dust storms and crop failures. The question of college survival was a very real one. Roadman devised plans to aid students to pay tuition and continue in college. In lieu of cash, livestock and produce were accepted at premium prices. Faculty salaries were paid in credit vouchers accepted by local merchants, and the college was kept open and solvent.

In 1936 Roadman accepted the presidency of MORNINGSIDE COLLEGE, Sioux City, Ia., where he directed the destinies of that growing institution for the next twenty years. An indebtedness of $450,000 was liquidated by 1944 under his administration. Extensive campus improvements were made including a dormitory for women, Jones Hall of Science, and Allen Gymnasium. An old gymnasium was transformed into a well equipped library. By 1951 the endowment had been increased to over $1,000,000, over 1,500 students were on the campus, and the faculty had been enlarged accordingly.

Perhaps Roadman's greatest contribution was his monumental faith in the Christian colleges and his unique ability in administration. Upon retirement in 1956, he returned to his boyhood home at Dike to spend the last years of his life there. He died July 20, 1967.

C. T. Howell, *Prominent Personalities*. 1945.

MATTHEW D. SMITH

ROANOKE, VIRGINIA, U.S.A., a city of 90,955, is in the foothills of the Blue Ridge Mountains in the Roanoke River Valley. Until 1882, the settlement was known as "Big Lick" because of the salt deposits. It became an incorporated town in 1874. Prior to the coming of the early settlers, this section was a favorite spot for both the Indians and the fur bearing animals. As early as 1742, according to records, there was a settlement of sufficient size to have a local militia. The coming of the railroad—with the opening of the coal and iron fields in southwest VIRGINIA—transformed the tranquil town to one of bustling activity, growth and prosperity. In 1884 Roanoke became a city.

Among the early settlers in The Lick were the Methodist circuit riders. The first two Methodist Societies in the vicinity of Big Lick were in nearby Salem and what is now Vinton. Records show that the Salem Society dates back to 1803, and the date of the Vinton Society at about that time. In 1815 the Thrasher Chapel at Vinton was built.

Until 1866 it is assumed that the churches in the vicinity of present day Roanoke were a part of the Salem Circuit. In that year the Old Lick Charge was formed, consisting of Thrasher's Chapel (now Vinton), Cave Spring, Bethany, Mount Pleasant and Old Lick (northeast Roanoke). This latter group had been gathered together in 1859 under the ministry of JAMES E. ARMSTRONG. That same year, 1866, under the leadership of Isaac Canter, the Old Lick Society found a new meeting place—a school house which stood directly across the street from the present Greene Memorial Church, and was organized into the first official Methodist Church in Big Lick (Roanoke). In this same year the circuit name was changed from Old Lick to Big Lick Circuit, which was composed of Big Lick, Hollins, Salem, Vinton, Cave Spring and Mount Pleasant.

In 1873 the name of the Big Lick Circuit was changed to Roanoke Circuit and ten years later, 1883, Roanoke became a station appointment. By the year 1891 there were two stations organized in Roanoke City—Greene Memorial and Trinity. In the district conference records of 1892 and 1893 respectively, St. James and Grace appear as organized churches. In 1896 Belmont was organized and bracketed with Roanoke Circuit.

From five churches in 1896, Methodism grew as did the city, so that by 1917 there were seven churches; in 1934 ten churches. The new churches were built in suburban areas. At the present time there are eighteen churches within the city and its adjoining suburbs.

Through the years Greene Memorial has been the leading church, growing in membership (now 1,712) and responsibility to The Methodist Church. Raleigh Court, with 1,611 members, is second in membership. Huntington Court with 1,497 members is the third largest church. Trinity, Belmont, West End and Melrose have been, and still are. citadels of Methodism in Roanoke. The newer churches are also taking their place in the city. St. Paul, the only church of the former Central Jurisdiction in the city, is a leader among the Negro churches.

Today with a total membership of 13,163, the nineteen churches of the Roanoke Community find a challenge to better churchmanship in ministering to the people in the downtown, residential and the suburban areas. The churches are working together for the best solutions to the problems peculiar to each and are looking forward to making a better witness in the city.

Greene Memorial Church was able to celebrate in 1959 100 years of service at its downtown location. The congregation's move to that site is narrated in the Roanoke account just above. Isaac W. Canter who in 1866 found a meeting place for the congregation within Roanoke proper is credited with founding the church. I. W. Canter was the father of three distinguished sons: Dr. Hall Canter, dean of Randolph-Macon College; Noland Canter, M.D., distinguished lay leader; and Dr. Harry M. Canter, leading minister and long time secretary of the Old BALTIMORE CONFERENCE.

James E. Armstrong (later to be the historian of the Baltimore Conference) was the first assigned pastor in 1859. Until he came the Methodist Society had met in a Presbyterian church.

The church has had nice locations and three names in the conference listing: Old Lick, Roanoke, and Greene Memorial. The present name memorializes Leonidas Rosser Greene who was pastor for twenty months and who by devoted leadership gave the church a period of tremendous expansion 1885-86. His ministry was terminated by death of typhoid in the thirty-third year of his life.

Bishop COLLINS DENNY (1891) and Bishop NOLAN B. HARMON (1933-1940) served as pastors of Greene Memorial; Dr. J. MANNING POTTS, executive director of the "Crusade for Christ" and editor of the *Upper Room*, was pastor 1940-1944. Mr. and Mrs. FRANK LONG and their daughter and son-in-law, Mr. and Mrs. Schisler, represented this church in South America. Mrs. EULA KENNEDY LONG is the editor for BRAZIL for this *Encyclopedia*, and Mr. Schisler is author and editor of church school literature and magazines for the South American Church. Going into the ministry from this church have been a number of prominent preachers.

The Fishburn family has meant much to the church. T. T. Fishburn was a merchant, banker, industrialist, civic leader, lay preacher, and evangelist. He was one of the founders of the city, public school system, hospital, and Sunday school. R. H. Fishburn gave the tower chimes to the church. Junius B. and Blair J. Fishburn contributed parks to the city: Mill Mountain, Norwich, South Roanoke, Lakewood, and Fishburn Park; and J. B. gave to the State, Fairystone Park. The small prayer chapel, open at all times and visited by dozens of persons each day, is a Fishburn Memorial.

Greene Memorial has aided in the formation of Trinity, St. James, Grace, Belmont and other Methodist

GREENE MEMORIAL CHURCH, ROANOKE, VIRGINIA

churches. The tall clock tower of Greene Memorial "is as much a part of Roanoke as is Mill Mountain itself," *The Roanoke Times* once said.

Mildred R. Chapman, *Through Years of Grace*. Charlotte, N.C.: Observer Printing House, 1953.
J. W. Leggett, *What Hath God Wrought*. Progress Press, 1964.   GEORGE S. LIGHTNER

ROANOKE UNION SOCIETY, THE (1824-1828), organized in eastern NORTH CAROLINA, U.S.A., shared with the Baltimore Union Society, organized on May 21, 1824, a discussion as to need for reform in Methodist church government. The two societies were established following the meeting of the GENERAL CONFERENCE of the M.E. Church in BALTIMORE in 1828 when requests for the incorporation of democratic principles into the church government were refused. The Roanoke Union Society was organized at Sampson's Meeting House, Halifax County, N. C., on Nov. 6, 1824 with eleven members, seven local preachers and four laymen. Eli Benton Whitaker was chosen president of the society. Subsequent meetings of the society met at Bradford's Meeting House (see BRADFORD, HENRY) and at WHITAKER'S CHAPEL.

The Baltimore Union Society and the Roanoke Union Society became the models after which nearly all the reform societies in the United States were organized until the Conventional Articles of 1828 offered a set form. The members of the Roanoke Union Society did not originally intend to organize a new church; they merely sought reform within the established church government. In 1828 delegates from the various union societies assembled in Baltimore and adopted temporary "Articles of Association." At a call meeting of the members of the union societies in North Carolina, delegates gathered at Whitaker's Chapel on Dec. 19-20, 1828, and organized there the first annual conference of the M.P. CHURCH. Due to the short notice given, only the ministers, preachers and laymen from the Roanoke Union Society were present.

The twenty-six official members of this historic conference were: Ministers: JAMES HUNTER, WILLIAM BELLAMY, Miles Nash, William W. Hill, William Price, Eli Benton Whitaker, Albritton Jones, Henry B. Bradford, Thomas Moore; Local Preachers: Asa Steely, Aquilla Norman, Ira Norman, Thomas Steely, Israel Hutchins; Laymen: Arthur Pittman, Exum Lewis, Absalom B. Whitaker, William E. Bellamy, L. H. B. Whitaker, John F. Bellamy, David Barrow, Eli B. Whitaker, Jr., James C. Whitaker, Richard Jones, Wilson C. Whitaker, Richard H. Whitaker. Four circuits were established by the conference: Roanoke, Liberty (in and around Williamston), Warrenton and Oxford. In 1829 the Hillsboro and Guilford Circuits were added. William W. Hill was chosen as the first president of the Conference.

J. E. Carroll, *History of the North Carolina Conference of the Methodist Protestant Church*. Greensboro, 1939.
J. Paris, *History* (MP). 1849.   RALPH HARDEE RIVES

ROBB, WILLIAM NORMAN HADDEN (1894-   ), Irish layman, linen merchant, born in BELFAST, and holder of numerous lay offices in the Methodist Church in IRELAND. In particular he was the first, and so far the only person to hold both key offices of Connexional Lay Treasurer of Overseas Missions (1934-1946) and of Home Missions (1946-1964). He was also secretary of the WESLEY HIS-

W. N. H. ROBB

TORICAL SOCIETY (IRISH BRANCH) from 1942 to 1963, then vice-president, and, from 1965, president. He was a member of the WORLD METHODIST CONFERENCE, Oxford, 1951, and at LAKE JUNALUSKA, 1956.

F. JEFFERY

B. T. ROBERTS

ROBERTS, BENJAMIN TITUS (1823-1893), founder and first general superintendent of the FREE METHODIST CHURCH, was born at Cattaraugus, N. Y., in July, 1823. He had a remarkable conversion at the age of twenty-one and was a student at WESLEYAN UNIVERSITY, 1845-48, where he received B.A. and M.A. degrees. He was greatly influenced by STEPHEN OLIN, then president, and a classmate, DANIEL STEEL, who later became a HOLINESS theologian. A campus revival movement, led by JOHN WESLEY REDFIELD, helped shape Roberts' view of the mission of the church.

He joined the slavery-divided GENESEE CONFERENCE of the M.E. Church in 1848. He married Ellen L. Stowe, niece of George Lane, Book Agent of the M.E. Church, May 3, 1849 and thereafter served churches until his expulsion from the conference in Perry, N. Y., in 1858.

The charges against him were "insubordination and contumacy," based on articles published and statements made in his crusade to call Methodism back to JOHN WESLEY's teaching on holiness of heart and life. Fifty years later the Genesee Conference restored Roberts' parchments with this statement by Ray Allen, conference historian: "This heroic treatment might have seemed necessary at the time, but looked at half a century later it seems unjust and therefore exceedingly unwise." Free Methodists no longer dwell on these injustices; they do take comfort in this action.

Roberts edited his own paper, *The Earnest Christian,* and for a time he was also editor of *The Free Methodist.* He served as president of the Missionary Board, founded the first school at North Chili, N. Y., organized conferences, labored as an evangelist and pioneer church builder. His financial and organizational ability were remarkable. He sponsored the ordination of women, gave an address at the World Missions Conference in LONDON, 1888, and was author of *Fishers of Men, Holiness Teachings, First Lessons on Money, Why Another Sect, Ordaining Women.* He died at Cattaraugus, N. Y., where he was to hold a quarterly meeting, Feb. 27, 1893. The membership of the church he had reluctantly founded almost tripled in number during the last sixteen years of his life.

Roberts was a missionary at heart, an apostle of the underprivileged and weak. His administrative ability was unusual, his business sense uncanny. His writings are models of direct speech. He avoided the superfluous. His sermons, for his day, were brief—twenty to twenty-five minutes—but said more than many hour-long discourses. There was a strong social note in his preaching and writing. Like Wesley, he stressed the expression of Christian faith in practical service. For him, holiness was "love in action."

BYRON S. LAMSON

ROBERTS, COLIN AUGUSTUS (1886-   ), British Methodist, was born at Dawley, Shropshire, in 1886. He entered the Wesleyan Methodist ministry in 1909, having trained at Didsbury College, Manchester. He served as assistant to F. L. WISEMAN at the Birmingham Mission; as an army chaplain through the First World War; and as chairman of the London North and of the East Anglia Districts. In 1939 he was appointed to the Home Mission Department of the Methodist Church, becoming general secretary in 1948. In 1952 he was elected president of the Methodist Conference. After the Second World War he was the organizer and leader of the Christian Commando Campaigns, a renewed Methodist effort at urban evangelism. He edited *These Commando Campaigns* and *The Way We Have Been Led.* He married Dorothy, daughter of Irving Armstrong, and has one son and one daughter.

JOHN KENT

ROBERTS, GEORGE (1765-1827), American minister and physician, was born of English parents, probably in Talbot County, Md. He early had studious and spiritual leanings and embraced religion in 1783. After four years service in the local relation, he was assigned to Annamessex Circuit, 1789. Sent to New England to assist JESSE LEE the next year, he was presiding elder over CONNECTICUT circuits, 1793-95. He replied in print to Tolland Congregationist pastor Nathan Williams' defense of the standing order in 1793.

ASBURY stationed him at NEW YORK CITY for an unusual three-year term, 1796-98, during which time he built Duane Street Church. Asbury often sought his counsel, but while stationed at PHILADELPHIA he studied medicine, and, despite Asbury's pleadings, located and established himself at BALTIMORE in 1806 to practice "physic." Children by his second wife, who was Susannah LePage of New York, included GEORGE C. M. ROBERTS and a daughter who married HENRY SLICER.

George C. M. Roberts, *Centenary Pictorial Album.* Baltimore: J. W. Woods, 1866.
Strictures on a Sermon delivered by Mr. Nathan Williams, A.M. in Tolland on the Public Fast Day, April 17, 1793. N.p., Tuckniss, 1794.
EDWIN SCHELL

ROBERTS, GEORGE C. M. (1806-1870), American physician and local preacher, was born to George and Susannah (LePage) Roberts about the time his father left the ministry to study medicine. George C. M. Roberts was granted an M.D. in 1826 by the University of Maryland and then after serving 1826-29 in the traveling ministry, practiced and taught obstetrics, all the while maintaining unabated usefulness in the local ministry. He was co-editor of a pinoeering medical journal 1839-40, taught at Washington Medical University, was a founding member of the American Medical Association and headed the Medical and Chirurgical Faculty (of Maryland) 1859-70.

Besides Roberts' life-long leadership in Light Street Church, BALTIMORE (where his father's second pastorate had been concluded in his natal year), he was the principal founder of the American Methodist Historical Society in 1855. He also saw to erection of the Bishops' and STRAWBRIDGE monuments in Mount Olivet Cemetery, Baltimore, was a founder (1858) and president (1863) of the National Association of Local Preachers, besides giving impetus to the founding of the Home for the Aged of the M.E. Church, 1868. His attentions to bodies and souls did not go unnoticed. When he died after a long illness, 2,000 persons in deep respect passed the bier, while 2,000 more were denied admission.

Centennial Pictorial Album, 1866.
EDWIN SCHELL

ROBERTS, HAROLD (1896-   ), British Methodist scholar and statesman, was born at Ashley in Cheshire in 1896. He was educated at Hulme Grammar School, Manchester, and at University College, Bangor. He entered the Wesleyan Methodist ministry in 1919, and his theological college was Wesley House, CAMBRIDGE, to which he returned as assistant tutor in 1924-26. He then served on the Liverpool (Waterloo) circuit from 1926 to 1929, and from 1929 to 1934 was the CHAPLAIN to Methodist students at Oxford University, where he remained until 1940. In that year he was transferred to Richmond Theological College in LONDON, but the Second World War compelled the closure of the Methodist theological colleges, and so from 1941 to

1946 he served as the superintendent of the Ipswich (Museum Street) Circuit, in East Anglia.

He went back to teach theology at Richmond College in 1946, and in 1955 became the principal of the college, a post which he held until his retirement in 1968. He was elected president of the Nottingham Conference of the Methodist Church in 1957. In the course of his career he obtained an M.A. from the University of Wales, an honorary D.D. from Dublin, and a Ph.D. from the University of Cambridge. He took a large part in the ecumenical movement, in the fostering of closer relations between the British Methodist Church and the Church of England, and in the Methodist ecumenical movement. His publications include: *Belief in God* (1936), *The Holy Spirit and the Trinity* (1937), *The Sanctions of Christian Healing* (1950). He gave the Fernley-Hartley Lecture of 1954, and this was published in 1955 under the title *Jesus and the Kingdom of God*. A portrait of Roberts is in the World Methodist Building at LAKE JUNALUSKA, N. C., as he was an outstanding leader of the WORLD METHODIST COUNCIL for many years.

JOHN KENT

ROBERTS, JOHN CALVIN (1833-1909), prominent M.P. layman and benefactor of Kernersville, N. C. He was almost solely responsible for the impetus given to the efforts of J. F. McCULLOCH in the early twentieth century to establish a M.P. college in NORTH CAROLINA. At the NORTH CAROLINA ANNUAL CONFERENCE of 1901, Roberts offered $10,000 to be used for the establishment of a denominational college in the state and a special Ways and Means Committee of nine persons (including Mc-Culloch, A. M. Rankin, J. Norman Wills, J. Allen Holt), was appointed. Due to the economic conditions surrounding the panic of 1907, efforts to establish the school were temporarily postponed. When Roberts died on Aug. 12, 1909, he left the $10,000 bequest in his will, stipulating that it be used by the Conference Board of Education in the building or support of a college provided it should be opened by 1920, meanwhile loaning the interest to men who needed aid in preparation for the ministry. The will stipulated that if the college were not built by 1920 the entire bequest would become a permanent fund for the aid of ministerial students. A total of forty-eight young men had received assistance from this "Roberts Fund" by 1938. The cornerstone of the administration building at HIGH POINT COLLEGE was laid on June 29, 1922, and the building was named "Roberts Hall" in memory of the man whose generosity began the movement which culminated in the establishment of the college.

Journal of the North Carolina Conference, MP, 1901, 1908, 1909.
Our Church Record, June 23, 1898. RALPH HARDEE RIVES

ROBERTS, JOHN WRIGHT (1812-1875), second missionary bishop in LIBERIA, was born of free parents in PETERSBURG Va., Sept. 8, 1812. His father died while he was a boy. It was claimed that his mother, a woman of great force of character, had escaped from slavery. A chapter of the American Colonization Society which encouraged free Negroes to emigrate to Liberia, was established at Petersburg in 1825. "Aunty Roberts," as John's mother was called, resolved to go with her three sons—the other two were JOSEPH J. and HENRY J.—to Liberia, and they sailed in 1829. All three of the boys were converted and joined the M.E. Church before leaving the United States, and both Joseph and Henry served as local preachers in Liberia. Henry became a medical doctor. After entering business, Joseph became interested in politics, served as governor of Liberia, and in 1848 when the country became a republic, he was its first president and was re-elected to that office three times.

John Roberts joined the Liberia Mission Conference (ME) in 1838 and was elected to ELDER's orders in 1841. In 1851 he became presiding elder of the Monrovia District. The 1856 GENERAL CONFERENCE authorized the Liberia Mission Conference to elect a bishop to serve there, with the proviso that after his election he should present himself in the United States for consecration. Accordingly, FRANCIS BURNS, a fellow presiding elder with Roberts, was elected bishop in 1858, was duly consecrated, and served five years. Following Burns' death in 1863, Roberts became president of the conference. Then in 1864 the General Conference authorized the election of a successor to Burns, and in 1866 Roberts was elevated to the episcopacy. He came to New York and was consecrated by Bishops LEVI SCOTT and EDMUND JANES in St. Paul's M.E. Church, June 20, 1866.

Roberts was intelligent and somewhat reserved. As an administrator he was prudent and conciliatory, dignified and firm, treating his brethren with a degree of impartiality and kindness which won their respect and esteem. During his term as bishop, the mission in Liberia had unity and harmony and a fair degree of prosperity. By the time he was sixty years of age fever had weakened his body. He died at Monrovia, Liberia, Jan. 30, 1875.

Flood and Hamilton, *Lives of Methodist Bishops*. 1882.
Willis J. King, *History of The Methodist Church Mission in Liberia*. (Typescript). N.d.
F. D. Leete, *Methodist Bishops*. 1948.
National Cyclopedia of American Biography.
The National Magazine, March, 1854.
M. Simpson, *Cyclopaedia*. 1878.
JESSE A. EARL
ALBEA GODBOLD

ROBERTS, JOSEPH JENKINS (1809-1876), the first president of LIBERIA and loyal Methodist, as well as a leader of his people, was born of free parents in PETERSBURG, Va., U.S.A., on March 15, 1809. He migrated to Liberia in 1829 with his widowed mother and soon began to obtain leadership in that land. Having achieved importance in Liberia, after a time he came on a visit to the United States authorized to deal with matters of import duties and the like between his country and the United States. He was elected the first president of Liberia in 1849 and again in 1851 and 1853. Previous to his election white men had always served as presidents of the Liberian colony, but when the choice devolved upon the people, J. J. Roberts was elected for the terms as above stated.

Bishop Simpson states: "In 1844 a gentleman of Canandaigua sent a silver cup to the church in which Governor Roberts worshiped, and inquired if he was a member of any Christian denomination. The governor replied, 'I am happy to be able to inform you that I have long been a member of the M.E. Church—upwards of sixteen years—and have not failed to find support and consolation in the religion of Christ and the promises of the gospel.'"

His second wife was Jane Warren Roberts, whom he married in 1836, who was an educated woman and spoke excellent French. In Europe, which Roberts visited a number of times, he always received unusual attention. He signed a treaty with Great Britain in 1849 which recognized Liberia as an independent nation—a very important event for that colony in the time when the European nations were taking over large portions of Africa regardless of their claims to independence. Roberts visited Europe again in 1854 and 1862 and on his return from the latter visit became the Belgian consul in Liberia. In 1869 he again visited the United States. Then at the age of sixty-three, broken in health by his long service, he was again elected to the presidency of his country and was re-elected again, serving until January 1876, when he died in Monrovia in February.

Dictionary of American Biography.
M. Simpson, *Cyclopaedia.* 1878.   N. B. H.

ROBERTS, LELIA (1862-1950), American pioneer missionary to MEXICO, was born on Oct. 2, 1862, in Bell Mina, Okla. She came to Bonham, Texas, in early childhood and was educated at Carlton College and Sam Houston Normal. After teaching school in Palo Pinto, Texas, she volunteered to go as a missionary to Mexico. She was appointed in 1887 to the city of Saltillo at $25 a month. She served for forty-three years, and built a school of such quality and prestige that the president of Mexico and the governor of Coahuila gave her support. Many Mexican church leaders across the years have received their training under her guidance. She retired in 1930 and then gave twenty years of service to her local church, district, and conference before her death in 1950 at Bonham, Texas.

MRS. CLAUDE M. SIMPSON

ROBERT R. ROBERTS

ROBERTS, ROBERT RICHFORD (1778-1843), frontier American bishop, was born in Frederick County, Md., on Aug, 2, 1778. His father, Robert Morgan Roberts, was an Episcopalian and a Revolutionary soldier of Welsh descent.

In 1785 the family moved to Ligonier Valley in Westmoreland County, Pa. Pioneer conditions prevailed there and young Roberts' schooling practically ended at the age of seven years.

In 1796 he made an exploratory trip to the Shenango area in what is now Mercer County, Pa., where he homesteaded some land and built a rude log cabin. Here he lived for five years as a frontiersman, clearing his land, planting crops, hunting, fishing, and selling furs. Here he married Miss Elizabeth Oldham of York County.

In 1802 he became a CLASS LEADER, was licensed to preach, and admitted on trial into the BALTIMORE CONFERENCE. He was ordained in 1804 and 1806 by Bishops ASBURY and COKE. His first years in the ministry were spent on the hard Montgomery, Frederick, Erie, Pittsburgh and West Wheeling Circuits in MARYLAND, PENNSYLVANIA and VIRGINIA.

He built a mill on his land in Shenango and operated it to supplement his meager income, as a result of which he was rebuked by his conference in 1808 for neglecting his preaching appointments. He went to the general conference at BALTIMORE that year with only one dollar in his pocket and some bread, cheese and oats in his saddle bags.

At the request of some persons who heard him preach he was stationed in Baltimore in 1809, although he protested that he knew nothing about city ways. The next year he was sent to Fell's Point, in 1811 he was at Alexandria, and in 1813 he was appointed to PHILADELPHIA. In 1815 he was presiding elder of the Schuykill District, which included Philadelphia. When he was in Georgetown, Md., President James Madison asked Roberts to pray for him as president.

At the GENERAL CONFERENCE of 1816 at Baltimore, owing to the death of Asbury and the illness of Bishop McKENDREE, he was elected president of the conference. This was followed by his election as bishop. He had wide support because the East knew him from his service there and the West regarded him as a frontiersman.

His first episcopal residence was his log cabin at Shenango, but in 1819 he moved to a farm in Lawrence County, Ind., where he lived in another rude cabin built largely by himself. His episcopal labors took him from MAINE to MISSISSIPPI and to the Indian missions west of ARKANSAS. He died in INDIANA on March 26, 1843 and was buried in a cornfield on his farm, but his body was later moved to the campus of Indiana Asbury University (now DePauw), at Greencastle.

Dictionary of American Biography.
C. Elliott, *Robert R. Roberts.* 1844.
Flood and Hamilton, *Lives of Methodist Bishops.* 1882.
M. Simpson, *Cyclopaedia.* 1878.
W. B. Sprague, *Annals of the Pulpit.* 1861.
W. M. Tippy, *Robert Richford Roberts.* 1958.

ELMER T. CLARK

ROBERTS, WALTER N. (1898-1966), American E.U.B. minister, son of Alvadore and Hannah Roberts, Lewisburg, Ohio, was born Aug. 17, 1898. He graduated in 1921 from OTTERBEIN COLLEGE (B.A.) and in 1924 from UNITED (then Bonebrake) THEOLOGICAL SEMINARY (B.D.). Special studies were taken at Yale Divinity School and Union Theological Seminary in New York City and he received a Ph.D. degree from the Hartford Seminary Foundation School of Missions. Honorary degrees were received from Moravian Theological Seminary, LEBANON VALLEY COLLEGE, and Otterbein College.

He was married to a college classmate, Marjorie Miller, Aug. 22, 1922. Licensed by Miami Conference, CHURCH

OF THE UNITED BRETHREN IN CHRIST, in 1922, he was ordained by the same conference in 1924. He and his wife served a five-year term in the PHILIPPINE Islands, 1925-30, two years of which he also taught in UNION THEOLOGICAL SEMINARY, Manila. Upon their return to America, Roberts completed his graduate studies. Subsequently his dissertation was published under the title, *The Filipino Church*, a history of the Protestant Church in the Philippines.

Returning to his annual conference, he served a pastorate in DAYTON (Fort McKinley Church), where he also spent six years as an instructor in practical theology in the denomination's seminary. In 1938 he became president of that institution, now known as United Theological Seminary, and continued in that post until his retirement in 1965. He represented his denomination at the organizing session of the WORLD COUNCIL OF CHURCHES (Amsterdam, 1948) and the four subsequent sessions. In theological services he was a member of the Executive Committee of the American Association of Theological Schools for sixteen years and its accrediting commission for fourteen, visiting 122 theological schools in this capacity. He served a term as Executive Secretary of the Association, followed by a term as its president.

Death came suddenly to Walter Roberts, Feb. 20, 1966, a few hours following his return to Dayton from a four and a half month tour of AFRICA studying theological schools for the church's mission board in cooperation with British missionary societies. His wife took up residence at Otterbein Home in 1970 and died in October 1971.

Daily News, Dayton, Ohio, Feb. 21, 1966.
Minutes of the Ohio Miami Conference, EUB, 1966.
United News, quarterly bulletin, United Theological Seminary, March 1966, Vol. 65, No. 2.   JOHN H. NESS, JR.

WILLIAM ROBERTS

ROBERTS, WILLIAM (1812-1888), pioneer American clergyman in CALIFORNIA and OREGON, was born at Burlington, N. J., March 28, 1812. After admission to the PHILADELPHIA CONFERENCE in 1834, he filled various appointments before being selected in 1846 by the Board of Bishops of the M. E. Church to be superintendent of the OREGON MISSION which had been founded by JASON LEE in 1834. William Roberts and J. H. WILBUR, and families, left NEW YORK on the bark *Whiton,* celebrated in western Methodism because its skipper was Captain Gels-

ton, a devout Methodist who gave generous aid to missionaries. The *Whiton* took 148 days to reach the Golden Gate—a datum to be compared with the eighty-nine days and eight hours record of the clipper *Flying Cloud,* or the 130 days or more usually required by prairie schooners for their trip from Independence, Mo.

Roberts preached at Brown's Hotel, April 25, 1847, the day after he arrived in SAN FRANCISCO, the first Protestant services there since Sir Francis Drake's services at an unknown place nearby. "The bar was closed and the billiard room locked up until the service was over," Roberts reported, adding that he found his "very attentive congregation" to be composed mostly of homesick Americans. "The tearful eye and cheerful smile . . . made us feel like staying among them until others should be sent to furnish them with the gospel of peace." Aided by Wilbur, he organized a class meeting and a Sunday school in San Francisco and inspected Methodist prospects at San Jose, Monterey, and other settlements. But Oregon beckoned. Arriving there in June 1847, Roberts paid out $1,500 for lumber to send back and build San Francisco's first Methodist church, but was appalled to learn shipping would cost $1,100 more. Captain Gelston came to his rescue, not only carrying it to the Bay without cost, but contributing $1,000 to the project.

Roberts replaced GEORGE GARY as superintendent of the Oregon Mission. In 1849 he was directed by Bishop WAUGH to organize the Oregon and California Mission Conference which was under his superintendency until 1853 when the OREGON CONFERENCE was set up by Bishop AMES. In 1856 William Roberts was a delegate to the GENERAL CONFERENCE at INDIANAPOLIS, and had three years of service as agent of the AMERICAN BIBLE SOCIETY for Oregon and Washington. He was then stationed at PORTLAND and served as presiding elder of the Portland District. He died at Dayton, Ore., on Aug. 22, 1888.

Bishop WILLIAM TAYLOR, with whom he was associated in California, called him "a capable, noble brother, and a faithful minister of the gospel, one of God's noblemen."

L. L. Loofbourow, *In Search of God's Gold.* 1950.
M. Simpson, *Cyclopaedia.* 1881.   LELAND D. CASE

ROBERTS CHAPEL, Fayette County, western Pennsylvania, is said by some to have been the first Methodist meeting house to be built west of the mountains. This was in 1784 or 1785. It was located four and one-half miles south of Brownsville on the east side of the Monongahela River in Luzerne Township. Roger Roberts had settled there on a farm about 1770. ROBERT AYRES preached his first sermon on the REDSTONE CIRCUIT, which then embraced Roberts Chapel, in Roberts Chapel on Sunday, June 18, 1786, and preached there regularly each round of the circuit. Bishop ASBURY made a round of the Redstone Circuit in 1786 and said that he spoke to 300 or 400 persons at Roberts Chapel (on Luke 4:18) on Thursday, June 29. James Roberts, a son of Roger Roberts, became a Methodist preacher. It may be said that Roger Roberts' daughter, Cassandra, married William Hawkins who built Hawkins Chapel, another church on Redstone Circuit; and another daughter married a son of Edward Death who lived on an adjoining farm to the north, and at whose home Robert Ayres usually stopped when he made his rounds.

W. G. Smeltzer, *Headwaters of the Ohio.* 1951.   N. B. H.

ROBERTS WESLEYAN COLLEGE, North Chile, N. Y., a FREE METHODIST institution, was founded by Bishop BENJAMIN T. ROBERTS in 1866. It was first operated as a high school under the names of Chili and Chesbrough Seminary; then Roberts Junior College in 1921, and a senior college renamed Roberts Wesleyan College in 1949. Roberts is regionally accredited.

The college serves 600 students from twenty-two states and five foreign countries. Eighteen conferences of the church are represented in the student body. Primarily a liberal arts college, Roberts also offers programs in music, degree nursing, teaching education, religion and pre-professions. The forty-five full-time faculty are dedicated to teaching students and to giving individual counsel. An enrollment of 1,000 is presently looked for.

BYRON S. LAMSON

ROBERTSON, EDWARD PETER (1860-1941), American minister and educator, was born on Feb. 24, 1860, in a farm home near Cooksville, Wis., where his parents who had been married in Edinburgh, SCOTLAND, had for a time settled. They moved when young Edward was four years old to MINNESOTA, where his father died. His mother was left a widow with five children.

Edward Robertson attended country school until he was fifteen years of age, then worked for a time and in 1885 graduated from HAMLINE UNIVERSITY. That fall he was admitted into the MINNESTA CONFERENCE, ordained DEACON and began his active pastorate. Shortly thereafter he was married to Florence E. Jackson, a fellow student at Hamline.

In 1899, while serving as a presiding elder in Minnesota, he was elected as president of the Red River Valley University, a Methodist liberal arts college in Wahpeton, N. D.

Under President Robertson's leadership, the Red River Valley University was moved from Wahpeton to Grand Forks, N. D. in 1906 and operated as Wesley College, offering courses in religion, music and speech in affiliation with the University of North Dakota. Dormitories for men and women were built as well as a music conservatory, and in 1929 an administrative building was completed, being named Robertson Hall in honor of the president. Robertson (having received the honorary LL.D. degree in 1925 from the University of North Dakota) retired from his post in 1931.

During his long career Robertson became a leader in Methodist educational circles. He was a delegate to the GENERAL CONFERENCE of the M.E. Church five times. He died on Sept. 2, 1941 and was buried in Memorial Park Cemetery, Grand Forks.

WESLEY SHEFFIELD

ROBERTSON, LUCY HENDERSON OWEN (1850-1930), president of GREENSBORO COLLEGE, 1902-1913, was born at Warrenton, N. C., Sept. 15, 1850. She was married to D. A. Robertson on Nov. 1, 1869 and widowed by his death in January 1883. She taught in Greensboro Female College (now Greensboro College), 1878-1893. From 1893-1900 she taught history in the North Carolina State Normal and Industrial Institute (now University of North Carolina at Greensboro). Returning as teacher of Bible to Greensboro College in 1900, she was made president in 1902, a post she held until 1913.

Her influence spread far beyond the college. She was vitally interested in the causes of Temperance and Missions. She served as president of the Woman's Missionary Society of the WESTERN NORTH CAROLINA CONFERENCE for more than thirty years.

Five years before her death the alumnae of the college began soliciting funds for the establishment of the Lucy H. Robertson Chair of Religious Education in her honor. Mrs. Robertson died at Greensboro, May 28, 1930 and was buried in Green Hill Cemetery there. Few citizens of the state have had so profound an influence for good upon so many. Her successor, President S. B. TURRENTINE said of her that she held "before the vision of young womanhood ideals that promote not only the power to know, but the power to do."

Bulletin, Greensboro College, July 1930.

RAYMOND ALEXANDER SMITH

ROBINSON, ELLEN DOWNS (1824-1910), American lay woman, was born in 1824 in Hemingford, CANADA. She moved with her family to Champlain, N. Y. as a child. She taught school for eight years and then was invited in 1856 to teach Indian girls in Bloomfield Academy in Indian Territory. She taught there until the fall of 1866 when the war impoverished the school, and she moved to Paris, Texas. There she taught school again until 1872 when she married the Rev. J. C. Robinson. In 1882 she became president of the WOMAN'S FOREIGN MISSIONARY SOCIETY of the NORTH TEXAS CONFERENCE, in which office she served seven years.

MRS. CLAUDE M. SIMPSON

ROBINSON, FLORA LOIS (1884-1926), was the fourth principal of ISABELLA THOBURN COLLEGE. She was born in INDIA in a missionary home, daughter of JOHN EDWARD and Rhetta Terry ROBINSON. For higher education she went to GOUCHER COLLEGE where she established a reputation for brilliance, Christian leadership and winsomeness. Her roommate at Goucher, Jessie Wilson, daughter of Woodrow Wilson, in a memorial tribute, wrote of her blue-eyed, golden-haired loveliness, her humor, understanding smile and keen intelligence. This roommate who became Mrs. Francis B. Sayres paid her salary through the WOMAN'S FOREIGN MISSIONARY SOCIETY throughout her missionary service.

Later in 1909 she arrived at LUCKNOW to teach in the high school from which the Isabella Thoburn College had developed. Her sister, RUTH ROBINSON, was then principal of the college and her father a missionary bishop since 1904. Flora Robinson soon felt completely at home in India and quickly acquired recognition as an educator of great promise.

When her sister, Ruth, resigned on account of health difficulties, the board of governors asked the younger sister to accept the responsibilities of the principalship. The government of the United Provinces undertook to reorganize university education and to develop in Lucknow a teaching university, in contrast to the examining university which until then had dominated higher education in the province. After considerable discussion and plans that proved unpopular the government invited Isabella Thoburn College to become a special women's section of the university and a very choice site of thirty-two acres was obtained adjoining another department of the university.

Flora Robinson had acquired great influence with government officials and with the interested public. But after only eighteen months in office she resigned to marry Thomas J. Howells, an American businessman. In PITTS-BURGH, where she and her husband lived after their marriage, she spoke often in behalf of India. But after a very few years she died of pernicious anemia.

M. A. Dimmitt, *Isabella Thoburn College*. 1963.

J. WASKOM PICKETT

ROBINSON, HUBERT N. (1912-   ), American bishop of the A.M.E. CHURCH, was born in Urbana, Ohio on April 28, 1912. He was educated at Ohio State University where he received his A.B. degree. He attended also the Hamma Divinity School in Ohio. He also holds the honorary D.D. degree. Following ordination as deacon and elder, he was pastor of churches in OHIO and PENNSYLVANIA. He was elected to the episcopacy in 1964 from the pastorate of the Ebenezer Church in DETROIT, Mich. He resides in Detroit and supervises the work of the Eighteenth Episcopal Area District comprising four annual conferences in South Central Africa.

GRANT S. SHOCKLEY

JOHN E. ROBINSON

ROBINSON, JOHN EDWARD (1849-1922), missionary bishop for Southern Asia, elected by the M.E. GENERAL CONFERENCE in 1904, was born at Gort, County Galway, IRELAND, Feb. 12, 1849, of English parents. Left fatherless at six, he migrated to America in 1865 and was converted in NEW YORK. He married Rhetta Terry, joined the CEN-TRAL ILLINOIS CONFERENCE in 1874, and was assigned to INDIA "in the self-supporting work of WILLIAM TAYLOR." He was appointed to Rangoon as pastor, and thereby became the founder of the M.E. Church in BURMA, then administered as a province of British India. His appointments included several pastorates, the presiding eldership of several districts, and the editorship of *The Indian Witness*. His episcopal assignments were CALCUTTA, 1904; BOMBAY, 1908-1912; Bangalore, 1912-20.

Bishop Robinson was a handsome man, neat and poised, fluent and eloquent, but precise in speech. His only son became a distinguished surgeon. His five daughters all became missionaries in India. Two, RUTH and FLORA, served as principals of the ISABELLA THOBURN COLLEGE. Helen Robinson drowned when the ship on which she was returning to India was sunk by a submarine attack off the East Coast of Africa.

Bishop Robinson retired in 1920 and died in Bangalore, Feb. 15, 1922. He is buried there. It should be noted that there were two Robinson missionary bishops in India, John Edward and John Wesley, who for eight years served together as bishops in Southern Asia.

F. D. Leete, *Methodist Bishops*. 1948.
Mrs. J. E. Robinson and daughter, *In Memoriam*. 1923.

J. WASKOM PICKETT

ROBINSON, JOHN WESLEY (1866-1947), elected by the M.E. GENERAL CONFERENCE of 1912 as missionary bishop for Southern Asia, with residence in BOMBAY, supervising Bombay, Gujerat and Central Province Conferences. In 1916 after the accidental death of Bishop W. P. EVELAND, MALAYA, SARAWAK, Dutch East Indies and the PHILIP-PINES were added to the Bombay Area. In 1920 the General Conference elected Bishop Robinson a general superintendent and continued his assignment to Bombay. In 1924 he was shifted to the newly established Delhi Area.

He was born at Moulton, Ia., Jan. 6, 1866. His mother and one of his daughters had the same birthday anniversary. He worked as a printer before deciding to enter the ministry. He studied at GARRETT BIBLICAL INSTITUTE and was graduated in 1892. He had married Elizabeth Fisher of Harlan, Ia. in 1891.

J. W. Robinson was ordained DEACON and ELDER in the DES MOINES CONFERENCE and, after two years, was transferred to the NORTH INDIA CONFERENCE and appointed pastor of the Lal Bagh Methodist Church in LUCKNOW. His subsequent appointments were: superintendent, Lucknow District; agent, LUCKNOW PUBLISHING HOUSE; editor *Kaukab-i-Hind* (official Roman Urdu Weekly); secretary-treasurer, Famine Relief Fund; secretary, Bishop Thoburn Special Gift Fund; secretary, the Executive Board; secretary, Jubilee Movement; and superintendent, Allahabad District. Usually he held three or more such appointments simultaneously. Of him a colleague said, "He does everything better than any one else does. The secret is that he works in high gear sixteen hours a day and with absolute dedication."

From 1912 when the National Missionary Council was organized in India, until 1936 when he retired, he participated prominently in inter-church activities.

Bishop Robinson translated many popular hymns into Urdu. He was chairman of the governing boards of many educational and medical institutions. When there were no architects or construction engineers among missionaries he drew plans for buildings and personally supervised their construction. His skill in administration won the praise of churchmen, government officials and professional men, Christian and non-Christian alike.

After retiring he made his home in CALIFORNIA briefly, then returned to India and became the editor of *The Indian Witness*. On the death of Bishop JASHWANT R. CHITAMBAR in 1940, Bishop Robinson was asked by the COUNCIL OF BISHOPS of The Methodist Church to return to active service and administer the Lucknow and Hydera-bad conferences. When two new bishops were elected in 1941 and Bishop Robinson retired the second time, he returned to American but within a year departed again for India, where he served as superintendent of the Delhi District. Retiring a third time he made his home with his daughter and son-in-law in the episcopal residence in Delhi, which had been built under his direction twenty-five years earlier. Until the morning of the day of his death, May 30, 1947, in Naini Tal, India, he had never been a patient in a hospital or consulted a doctor except for a physical examination. His grave is in the Kaladungi Cemetery near Naini Tal, near the graves of his dear friend and predecessor, Bishop EDWIN W. PARKER and those of other early leaders of Indian Methodism.

J. WASKOM PICKETT

ROBINSON, MARK (?-c. 1840), British layman, who led a party of "Church Methodists" in Beverley, Hull, Yorkshire. He was a class leader and local preacher who was led in 1823 to examine the power of CONFERENCE when an action of Conference affected the Hull Circuit. He wanted to limit the powers of the preachers and to make the connexion into a sort of minor order in the Church of England, recognized by the episcopate, and subject to the local clergy. He persuaded an Irish Primitive Wesleyan minister to speak in Beverley in favor of his scheme and opened a chapel in a neighboring village, but the movement quickly dissipated. Several pamphlets by Robinson exist, including *Observations on the System of Wesleyan Methodism* (London 1825), and *The General Principles of the Church Methodist Constitution* (London 1826). He died between 1831 and 1840.

OLIVER A. BECKERLEGGE

ROBINSON, REUBEN D. (1815-1887), American physician and minister, was born Aug. 10, 1815, in Clark County, OHIO but moved with his parents to near LaFayette, Ind. at an early age. He graduated from Indiana Asbury University in 1843. After a brief medical practice he joined the NORTH INDIANA CONFERENCE in 1845. He married Mary K. Mahurin on Sept. 1, 1847. For a time he served as president of Fort Wayne College and was elected to lead his delegation to the GENERAL CONFERENCE of 1864. He died Aug. 18, 1887, in INDIANAPOLIS.

HAROLD THRASHER

ROBINSON, ROSWELL RAYMOND (1835-1923), American layman, businessman, philanthropist, was born in Taunton, Mass., on March 8, 1835. His formal education was in Taunton public schools and Bristol Academy. At the age of seventeen he started to work in a large store, first as clerk, then as cashier and bookkeeper, and then as one of the buyers. For two years he was treasurer of the Bay Screw Company of Taunton. At twenty-six he and his brother became interested in the manufacture of toilet soap. They established a plant and offices in Malden, Mass. The business prospered, first under the name "Robinson Brothers," and later as the "Potter Drug and Chemical Co." Roswell became connected with other very important financial and commerical enterprises.

His primary interest was in religion. He was a consecrated Christian, a loyal member of Center M.E. Church,

Malden; treasurer, Royal Arcanum; treasurer, Boston City Missionary and Church Extension Society; director, Y.M.C.A.

Robinson's chief philanthropy was BOSTON UNIVERSITY, of which he was a trustee for the last twenty-one years of his life. He was a tither, and his church and Boston University—especially its School of Theology—got the larger share of it. His gifts to Boston University were so great that the Trustees constituted him an Associate Founder eleven years before his death.

DANIEL L. MARSH

ROBINSON, RUTH EVELYN (1878-1954), was the third principal of the ISABELLA THOBURN COLLEGE (1908-18) and a Methodist missionary in INDIA from 1900 to her retirement in 1950. She was born in Bangalore, South India, June 15, 1878, the eldest child of JOHN EDWARD and Rhetta Terry ROBINSON. Her parents were Methodist missionaries and during her childhood they held appointments in Rangoon, BURMA, Simla (then India's summer capital), and Poona. Her father was elected missionary bishop for Southern Asia in 1904.

She graduated from GOUCHER COLLEGE in 1899 and a year later was appointed to India. She worked as an evangelist in BOMBAY for a year and was then appointed to LUCKNOW to assist ISABELLA THOBURN in her struggling woman's college. Except for a year of furlough in America, Miss Robinson remained there as a teacher until she was appointed principal in 1908. She was renowned for sympathy with and understanding of her girls and of the national longing for independence. The students regarded her as totally unselfish.

In 1918 following a break in her health, she resigned the college principalship and was appointed to Pauri, Garhwal, as principal of a junior high school for girls. In 1920 with health troubles continuing, she went to America. Two years later she returned to India and began a second career as an editor and author. She founded a monthly magazine, *The Treasure Chest,* in English for young Indians. She remained a Methodist missionary, but the magazine was sponsored and financed in part by an interdenominational woman's committee in America. The paper quickly won popular acclaim, and a demand for Indian language editions arose and several such editions were started. Eventually all editions were placed under Indian editors.

In 1938 she joined forces with E. STANLEY JONES in his Ashram at Lucknow and shortly thereafter established a rural center at Nigohan, Lucknow District, organizing and operating adult literacy classes with volunteer help.

At retirement age in 1943 she went to Bangalore, but almost immediately in an emergency she was asked to resume active work and return to the editorship of *The Treasure Chest*. She continued full time work until 1950.

Miss Robinson also edited *The Indian Temperance News* for two years, and was the author of five series of readers, extensively used in the teaching of English in India. She also wrote *An Introduction to English Prose and Verse*. She was the first woman member appointed to serve on the Bangalore Municipal Council, and was for six years president of the Woman's Christian Temperance Union of Madras. She died in Bangalore in 1954.

M. A. Dimmitt, *Isabella Thoburn College.* 1963.
J. N. Hollister, *Southern Asia.* 1956.   J. WASKOM PICKETT

ROBSON, EBENEZER (1835-1911), Canadian missionary, was born in Perth, Ontario, on Jan. 17, 1835 and died in Vancouver, B.C., on May 4, 1911.

He was educated at Victoria College, Cobourg, and was ordained in 1858. At this point the discovery of gold in the Fraser River brought to British Columbia a rush of adventurers from the United States and eastern CANADA. Among the newcomers were many Methodists. This situation led ENOCH WOOD, superintendent of Wesleyan Missions in Canada, to issue a call for volunteers for this new mission field. Four were selected, of whom one was Robson. The party left Toronto on Dec. 31, 1858, and, traveling via NEW YORK, the Isthmus of PANAMA, and by boat up the Pacific Coast, reached Victoria on Feb. 10, 1859. Soon four missionary charges were organized, one of which was Hope and Yale—some 100 miles up the Fraser—and to this new field Mr. and Mrs. Robson were sent.

While ministering to the spiritual needs of thousands of settlers, prospectors and miners, Robson observed (to quote his own words), "with grief and distress the ignorance and degradation of the Indians in the area." As a beginning, in 1859, he opened a school for Indian children in his own house; this was the start of Canadian Methodist missions among the Indians of British Columbia.

From Hope the Robsons went to Nanaimo on Vancouver Island in 1860 to work among the coal miners from England. Here Robson found many Flathead Indians living amid conditions similar to those at Hope. He began a school and preached to the Indians each Sunday. Within a year a chapel was built close to the Indian quarters, the first Indian church in British Columbia Methodism.

Mrs. Robson's failing health led them to return to Ontario in 1865, but fifteen years later they returned to British Columbia and were stationed at New Westminster. When the conference was organized in 1887 Robson was chosen as its first president. At that time he was pastor of Homer Street Church in Vancouver. Robson served a number of other fields in the province until, in 1900, after forty-two years in the ministry, he was superannuated. Even in retirement he continued to serve until 1910. He was known and loved in all parts of British Columbia.

Diary of Rev. Ebenezer Robson, Union College.
Mrs. F. C. Stephenson, *Canadian Methodist Missions*. 1925.
W. P. BUNT

ROCHA, ISNARD (1908-   ), Brazilian preacher, was born in Jahu, state of São Paulo, on Dec. 18, 1908. When he was three his parents moved to Santo Amaro, near SÃO PAULO. His parents were second-generation Presbyterians, but there was no evangelical church in the neighborhood.

When Isnard was five, a neighbor "stole" him from his parents to get him baptized in the Roman Catholic church, for they were scandalized that he had never received baptism. She first bought him a little sailor suit, white shoes and a hat; then, on a Sunday morning, invited him to visit her, saying that his mother had consented. She took him to her house, changed him into the new clothes and then—in a carriage pulled by two horses—took him to church. How his mother discovered what had happened is not told; but she followed them to the church, and, just as they were entering the sacristy, she struggled to get the boy back. The neighbor and her son, holding Isnard

tightly by his hands, would not give him up. The priest, angry at such a scene, excommunicated Isnard's mother then and there, and baptized the boy.

Isnard Rocha's own father became manager of a factory employing about 100 persons; and when the lad finished third grade, he began working there, but also attending school. In the meantime a Methodist church had been started in Santo Amaro. Isnard attended, and at sixteen made his profession of faith. At his side, among others, stood the godfather who had sponsored his baptism in the Catholic church.

Isnard continued studying, passed the preparatory examinations, and in 1928 entered GRANBERY INSTITUTO. There he spent eight years, completing both the course in the humanities and the theological course. He was planning to study for a doctorate in theology when the bishop urged him to postpone his studies and enter the ministry on trial. One year before graduation on Jan. 25, 1937, he married Esmeralda Barros, also a student at Granbery. Isnard was ordained DEACON in 1938, and ELDER in 1939, by Bishop DACORSO. Throughout the years since then he has served in many charges, both small and large, in the states of São Paulo and Minas Gerais, including six years as pastor of Central Church, São Paulo, the largest in Brazilian Methodism. He has been a district superintendent; director of youth work in São Paulo; regional secretary of Christian education for twelve years; editor of *Cruz de Malta*, the youth magazine, and of the *Expositor Cristão*, the official weekly. In February 1963, he was elected Reitor (dean) of the theological seminary in Rudge Ramos and served two years. Then he became pastor of Vila Mariana parish, which comprises three churches, in the suburb by that name in São Paulo.

During the past three years, the Methodist Press has published two historical books written by him in connection with the centennial of Brazilian Methodism. His wife, Esmeralda, has always been a leader in church work, and organist, choir director and president of the Methodist Women's Societies in that conference. She is presently secretary to an evangelical congressman in the state legislature of São Paulo.

They have three children, two sons, and a daughter, Isis, married to a young Methodist preacher, José Alaby, studying at Emory School of Theology. (1969)

EULA K. LONG

ROCHESTER, MINNESOTA, U.S.A., **Christ Church** (formerly First Church) is the modern church home of 3,402 Methodists. An outstanding feature of the church building is the great multicolored slab glass window portraying Christ, the Good Shepherd.

The birthplace of Methodism in Rochester was a log schoolhouse where in 1857, just two years after the first settlers arrived, seven persons met to organize a Methodist church. Later that year the first QUARTERLY CONFERENCE was held. Various buildings housed the church services until 1864, when the Methodists erected the first church in Rochester. The plot of land chosen was just one block from the world-renowned Mayo Clinic which was built some years later.

Subsequently two other frame buildings were erected on the original site, and in 1915 a fine brick structure was dedicated. In 1950 it became evident that due to the ever-increasing size of the congregation and the crowded conditions in the church school, a building program was again indicated. After much study a site six blocks south of the original plot was chosen, as it was still near enough to the Medical Center to allow the church to continue its ministry there.

Although a small city, Rochester, due to the Medical Center and a large manufacturing plant, probably has as many diverse elements in its populace as any city in the country. At Christ Church a large membership with a wide diversity of talented interests, education and training, has been merged so effectively that a vigorous and active congregation has emerged.

Due to several generous donors the church has an exceptionally fine organ, and the Minister of Music trains several Bell Choirs, as well as singing choirs. About 300 children, teenagers and adults actively participate in the music program.

Methodism in Rochester has had serving regular hospital chaplains and a parish visitor. The chaplain serving longest was John Mettam who took over the post in 1937. In 1937 Mrs. W. I. Kern became parish visitor and has continued in that capacity until the present time. She makes hundreds of family visits each year.

Among the ministers who have labored to make Christ Church a strong Christian force in the Rochester community have been: Frank Doran (1896), I. B. Wood (1914), H. G. Leonard (1920), R. J. Rice (1927), and Olin Jackson (1949).

Rochester Methodist Hospital is a 500-bed general hospital. The hospital is affiliated with the Mayo Clinic whose members compose its medical staff. This hospital as a Methodist related institution was started Jan. 1, 1954, when it was purchased from a private corporation. KARL P. MEISTER, former executive secretary of the Board of Hospitals and Homes of The Methodist Church; Ralph L. Jester of Des Moines, Ia., then a member of the Board; Judge H. A. Blackmun (now a Justice of the U. S. Supreme Court); and Bishop D. STANLEY COORS of the MINNESOTA CONFERENCE were the persons primarily responsible for the establishing of this organization as a nonprofit eleemosynary institution. The Kresge Foundation of DETROIT made funds available to meet certain early financial obligations. The hospital is fully accredited by the Joint Commission on Accreditation of Hospitals. In any given year patients are admitted to this hospital from almost every one of the United States and from many foreign countries.

In association with this hospital the Board of Directors also operates a fully accredited three-year diploma school of nursing, with a present enrollment of 215 students and graduating about seventy-five each year.

In October 1966 a new 571-bed hospital was opened. The hospital is so constructed that four future floors (about 450 beds) can be added vertically. Horizontal expansion of the lower four floors is also possible.

A new research department has been established and will be responsible for the investigation under controlled conditions of the design, arrangement, location, system and order of various hospital facilities, departments and methods which will improve care to the patient and help to more efficiently utilize personnel at all levels.

General Minutes.
A. H. Sanford, *The Rochester Methodist.* Published by the church, 1959,

ETHEL GIVENS
HAROLD C. MICKEY

ROCHESTER, NEW YORK, U.S.A. (population 293,695 in 1970), was incorporated as a village in 1817 and as a city in 1834. The first Methodist class there was formed in 1817 and First Methodist Church was organized in 1820 with Orren Miller as pastor. A brick building, occupied in 1825, was destroyed by fire in 1835. A new church erected at once housed the congregation until 1855 when it was sold. Another edifice built at that time served until 1901 when the congregation once again constructed a new sanctuary.

New congregations organized prior to 1860 drew some members from First Church. Asbury was established on the east side of the Genesee River in 1836. At midcentury a layman offered $10,000 to any denomination that would build ten new churches in the growing parts of Rochester. The Methodists persuaded him to reduce the number to four and soon started Corn Hill, Frank Street, North Street, and Alexander Street churches. A German-language church was established in 1848. The denomination had six churches in the city in 1876 with a total of 1,725 members. In 1912 the Italian Methodists occupied the North Street Church. Lakeview Church was built in 1913, Trinity in 1916, and Seneca in 1930. Asbury and First Churches merged in 1934 to form Asbury-First.

The FREE METHODISTS had one church in Rochester in 1876 and two in 1971. Their ROBERTS WESLEYAN COLLEGE, located in the suburbs of Rochester, had 665 students in 1970.

The Rochester United Methodist Home for the aging opened in 1956 with four residents. In 1971 it had about 110 persons in residence and a nursing home for forty patients.

In 1970, The United Methodist Church reported fourteen churches in greater Rochester with a total of 8,000 members, property valued at $7,450,232, and $716,851 raised for all purposes during the year.

Asbury First Church was formed in 1934 by the merger of First Church and Asbury Church. Both were old congregations, the one having been established in 1820 and the other in 1836. The First Church building was destroyed by fire in 1933, and the situation prompted the

ASBURY CHURCH, ROCHESTER, NEW YORK

members to accept Asbury's invitation to unite. At the time First Church had approximately 800 members to 1,275 for Asbury. Some ninety-five percent of the First Church members went into the merger. In 1934 the united congregation had 1,782 members.

Weldon F. Crossland, pastor 1932-58, led the congregation in a large building program, beginning in 1944. In June, 1955, the new sanctuary with a seating capacity of 1,000 was dedicated. An education building was added in 1961, and in November, 1964, the entire church plant, then valued at more than $2,000,000, became free of debt.

A memorial plaque from the former Asbury Church which now stands in the education wing of the new church shows that Clara Barton addressed a meeting in Asbury Church, Oct. 1, 1881, and that it led to the organization of the Rochester-Monroe County Chapter of the American National Red Cross, the second such chapter to be formed in America.

In 1970, Asbury First Church reported 2,316 members, property valued at $2,754,797, and $209,910 raised for all purposes during the year.

General Minutes, MEC, MC, and UMC.
E. W. Eanes, *Methodism in Rochester*. Rochester: University of Rochester, 1935.
M. Simpson, *Cyclopaedia*. 1878.

EDWARD W. EANES
RICHARD J. DAVEY
ALBEA GODBOLD

ROCK RIVER CONFERENCE, the historic name of what is today the NORTHERN ILLINOIS CONFERENCE.

ROCKEY, CLEMENT DANIEL (1889-   ), bishop of the Methodist Church of the Central Conference of Southern Asia, was born in Cawnpore, INDIA, Sept. 4, 1889, the son of Rev. and Mrs. NOBLE LEE ROCKEY. On Dec. 27, 1922 he married Helen Mary Cady, born in Chentu, CHINA, daughter of Rev. and Mrs. H. Olin Cady, missionaries in China. His degrees are: A.B., OHIO WESLEYAN UNIVERSITY, 1909, and honorary D.D., 1948; B.D., DREW THEOLOGICAL SEMINARY, 1912; M.A., NORTHWESTERN UNIVERSITY, 1921; Ph.D., Divinity School of University of Chicago, 1929.

He joined the NORTH INDIA CONFERENCE in January 1914. His appointments included: Bareilly Theological Seminary, professor of Bible, eight years, principal and professor, six years; district superintendent, BAREILLY, two years; Moradabad, four years; Kumaon, one year; Budaon, one year while principal of the Seminary; one year as pastor in Bareilly and Naini Tal for English services; services for non-conformists of the British troops stationed in Bareilly, over a ten-year period.

While living in Bareilly, Moradabad and Almora (Kumaon), he was manager of the local Methodist Boys' Middle or High School. During his first ten years of service he prepared Sunday school lesson notes in English, and in Urdu. He was one of the five-member committee for the Revision of the Urdu Old Testament, printed in 1930 in England, and now the translation in use. He was North India Conference delegate to GENERAL CONFERENCES of 1920, 1928, 1932, 1940.

He was elected bishop Jan. 1, 1941 by the Central Conference of the Methodist Church in Southern Asia, meeting in Delhi. He served the Lucknow Area, 1941-56; Burma Conference for 1941, after World War Two for 1940-50; and Indus River Conference, PAKISTAN, 1953-56.

He was retired by the Central Conference in session at Lucknow in November 1956, having come to the age of retirement. On the request of the Conference in West Pakistan he was appointed by the COUNCIL OF BISHOPS to serve as bishop of the Methodist Church in West Pakistan, December 1956 through September 1964. He moved from Lucknow, to Lahore, West Pakistan, in January 1957, and left for retirement in the United States on Oct. 1, 1964.

When *The Upper Room* could not get to India for three years, 1944-46, Bishop Rockey prepared devotional readings in English and in Urdu for use in India. In 1950 he prepared a translation of about twenty hymns in the *Git ki Kitab* (Song Book) in Urdu. During the eight years spent in Pakistan he helped in perfecting the translation into Urdu of some books prepared by the India Sunday School Union. These were published in English for use in India and permission was given to Pakistan to translate and make available in Urdu. He always preferred to preach in Urdu. He and his wife arrived in the United States in January 1965, and have retired in Eugene, Ore.

Who's Who in The Methodist Church, 1966.   N. B. H.

ROCKEY, NOBLE LEE (1857-1924), was born in Columbus, Ohio, June 7, 1857. Inflammatory rheumatism kept him crippled from his tenth to his twentieth year, but he finished the local school, and then taught a country school for three years. He worked his way through OHIO WESLEYAN UNIVERSITY and graduated in 1884. He was admitted to the COLORADO CONFERENCE and at once transferred to the NORTH INDIA CONFERENCE. He arrived in BOMBAY in December 1884, with his bride of three months, Mary Hadsell.

He was stationed first at Bijnor and then at Kanpur Memorial School. After that came appointments as district superintendent in Shahjahanpur, Dwarahat, BAREILLY, and Gonda. He went to Gonda in 1907 and gave that district eight years of consecutive administration. He had had much experience in evangelistic work. He was a versatile man and a tireless worker, exacting more from himself than he did from anyone else. He looked well to the property interests, and made himself acquainted with every person with whom he worked. His teaching spirit found scope in his summer schools and district conferences. His special interest in gardening made the mission compound yield new fruits, especially papayas.

For twenty-eight years he edited the widely read *Children's Friend* in both Urdu and Hindi. In conferring upon him the D.D. degree, Bishop HERBERT WELCH made special mention of the quality and quantity of Rockey's literary output, as well as his scholarly attainments. He sent out a constant stream of tracts in Hindustani and English. With his love of music he was a popular leader of congregational singing, and as a preacher he grew throughout his ministry. He was a much loved friend, especially by children.

He died in Bareilly on June 19, 1924. It was a joy to the parents that their son, CLEMENT, and daughter, Lois, returned to INDIA as missionaries and served for many years.

B. T. Badley, *Southern Asia*. 1931.
Minutes of the North India Conference, 1924.

JOHN N. HOLLISTER

ROCKFORD, ILLINOIS, U.S.A. In 1834 the first settlers came into northern ILLINOIS from Galena, to find a site for farm land and a town which would lie approximately half way between Galena and CHICAGO. A spot on the Rock River was chosen which was later to become Rockford. In 1835 a few settlers came to establish this community.

The Methodist Church was the first to begin work in the territory. In July of 1836 William Royal preached in a home of one of the settlers. Royal made several visits to the community that summer, and on Sept. 2, 1836, preached at Samuel Gregory's log house. At the close of the service he organized the first Methodist class with five members.

Methodism grew as the settlement flourished. In 1838 the first quarterly meeting was held in Rockford. The ROCK RIVER CONFERENCE was organized on Aug. 26, 1840, at Mount Morris, Ill., with the meetings being held in tents in a grove. In 1841 the Methodists had their first church home in Rockford. At the conference in Dubuque, Ia., in 1843, Rockford was made a station.

In 1848 the church site was moved and a new First M.E. Church was built at a cost of $7,000. By 1850 the congregation had outgrown the building and the pastor suggested formation of a second church on the west side of the river. Rock River, from which Rockford and the Rock River Conference get their names, runs right through the middle of the city of Rockford. In 1851 the Methodists on the west side of the river began holding their services in the home of one of their members. On Jan. 1, 1852, the group which was known at first as the Second M.E. Church, held an organizational meeting in the First M.E. Church, and the following year began work on a new building on Court Street. They subsequently became known as the Court Street M.E. Church. In September of 1853 the Conference redistricted the work and then formed the Rockford District.

For a long time there had been much dissatisfaction in the First M.E. Church over the matter of PEW RENTALS. The best solution seemed to be to divide the congregation. Eighty of the members moved out and organized the Third Street Church on Jan. 9, 1858. This division, however, was not a happy one. So, eighteen years later on May 18, 1876, the two congregations reunited. At reunion it seemed appropriate and desirable for the reunited church to take a new name. The name "Centennial," in honor of the national centennial year of the nation which was then being celebrated, was selected. Centennial Church therefore is the mother church of Methodism not only in Rockford but for all northern Illinois.

There are presently fourteen Methodist churches in Rockford with a membership of 9,282. Rockford is an industrial city surrounded by rich farm land with a present population of 144,707.

Court Street Church is the historic downtown church of Rockford, and is the second oldest Methodist church in the city. It was organized in January 1852, and was then called the Second M.E. Church. The first structure in which the new church was housed was located on the west side of Court Street, a half block south of the present location, and was dedicated in November 1854.

The present site on the corner of Mulberry and Court Streets was purchased on Sept. 5, 1883. On Aug. 11, 1884, a new building was started and was finally completed in the Spring of 1887. In 1911 two lots adjoining the church property to the north were purchased, and a new unit known as the Institutional and Educational

Building was begun. The new unit was dedicated on April 22, 1917. In 1927-29 the entire chancel was remodeled, and the church was dedicated by Bishop EDWIN HOLT HUGHES.

In 1960 plans were made for a new chapel to seat 300 and a three-story educational building. This new structure was in time consecrated by Bishop CHARLES WESLEY BRASHARES.

The Court Street Church has 2,891 members. It supports two missionaries in foreign fields, one in Africa and one in INDIA. It has sent many young men into the ministry, two of whom now serve in the NORTHERN ILLINOIS CONFERENCE. One of the distinctive phases of the program of the Court Street Church has always been its musical program. Over 300 voices comprise the six choirs which normally sing for its various services.

On March 18, 1969 the church sanctuary was burned almost completely, a confessed arsonist being arrested later and sentenced for this criminal act. The congregation meeting in the burned out shell of their church on Easter Sunday about three weeks after the fire made plans to rebuild, and the new sanctuary was occupied late in 1970. All the carved ornamentation in the former building was duplicated and the new building is as close a reproduction of the old (including the stained glass windows) as is possible. The total cost of rebuilding was a million and a half dollars.

General Minutes.   HAROLD McELVANY

ROCKVILLE, MARYLAND, U.S.A., the county seat of Montgomery County in that state, nine miles north of the District of Columbia line and today practically a part of WASHINGTON city, is a growing area where Methodism has been entrenched for a long time. The Montgomery Circuit came into being back around 1788 and was one of the circuits in the original BALTIMORE CONFERENCE. Washington, the nation's capital, was then but a small village itself, and BALTIMORE up until well into the twentieth century was always the dominant metropolitan influence over most of MARYLAND and certainly in Montgomery County. Hungerford Tavern seems to have been the original stopping place at what is now Rockville.

In 1844 the Rockville Circuit was taken from the Montgomery Circuit and made an entity of its own, and at the epochal division of the M.E. Church which came that very year, the Rockville circuit adhered strongly to the South. Visitors today marvel at finding the statue of a Confederate soldier across from the court house nine miles north of Washington city itself.

Losing the church building in a lawsuit by which the M.E. Church was given title to the property, four southern men of prominence in Rockville, two of them being E. E. Stonestreet and Elijah Barrett Prettyman, built the church now there, its adherence being of course to the M.E. Church, South.

The church has grown through the years with recent modern enlargements and improvements, and in 1969 celebrated its 125 years of Christian service with Bishop NOLAN B. HARMON, a former pastor, back for the anniversary sermon. The church is in the Washington West District of the Baltimore Conference (UMC) and with 1,723 members continues to grow. Other churches in Rockville are Faith, St. Marks, and the Millian Memorial.

Millian Memorial, begun in March 1952, has experienced a phenomenal growth from forty-three charter members to 2,435 by 1970. Located in a rapidly developing suburb of Washington, D.C., with a rather transient population, more than 3,300 members were recorded in its first sixteen years, about 1,000 transferring memberships upon moving from the area.

Early in 1952, John Curry Millian, an alert, capable religious leader and then district superintendent in the Washington area, motored along Viers Mill Road between Wheaton and Rockville, Md. At the halfway point he passed Viers Mill Village, a new community with a small shopping center and movie theater. The only other occupied homes he could see for two miles on either side were those in the first section of neighboring Wheaton Woods. As he was, among other duties, responsible for the establishment of mission churches in new communities, he considered the details of forming a new church in this locality. He began one in a short time by scheduling services in the Viers Mill Theater. Harold Bell Wright, with over ten years experience as a parish minister and Army chaplain, had just returned from KOREA and was available for appointment, and he was made its pastor. The Methodist Union of Washington and the Baltimore Conference Board of Missions and Church Extension both pledged support.

On March 2, 1952, twenty persons responded to the handbill announcement and attended the first worship service held in the Viers Mill Theater. By May 18, 1952, forty-three persons were recorded as charter members. Through cooperation of neighboring Methodist churches, much necessary furniture and equipment was donated or loaned. As more and more families came, classes were dispersed throughout the theater building. Class areas became known as Alphabet Room (where marquee letters were kept), the Pit (way down front), the Terrazzo Room (outer lobby), the Alley (hall back of projection booth), and the Teen Club (manager's office). Nearby records were efficiently kept by the secretary in his "office" at the popcorn stand.

In June 1954 Merrill W. Drennan was appointed pastor. Under his leadership the growth of Millian Church kept pace with the rapid development of the suburban community. The church school moved to the new Wheaton Woods Elementary School in September 1954. On land donated by the developer of Wheaton Woods, the first unit of Millian Church, which was a chapel seating 250 and a social hall, was built in 1955 and consecrated on November 27 of that year by Bishop G. BROMLEY OXNAM. An educational building was completed in February 1959, to accommodate the church school with two complete sessions each Sunday morning.

Three crowded worship services in the chapel each Sunday made it apparent that a larger sanctuary was essential. This was completed in 1964 and consecrated on Dec. 9, 1964, by Bishop JOHN WESLEY LORD.

In June 1965, Carroll A. Doggett, Jr. succeeded Drennan as pastor, and soon an educational assistant was added to the professional staff to give better coordination to a more comprehensive educational program. With building completed for the foreseeable future the congregation has been able to shift increased emphasis to its ministry with persons. This entire section of Maryland just north of the Capital city continues to grow as does Millian Memorial itself.

General Minutes.   N.B.H.
                                    CARROLL A. DOGGETT, JR.

ROCKY MOUNTAIN COLLEGE, Billings, MONTANA, is an interdenominational college under the sponsorship of the Methodist and Presbyterian churches and the United Church of Christ. The College of Montana (1878) and Montana Wesleyan (1889) merged in 1923 to form Intermountain Union College. After the partial destruction of its buildings in the earthquakes of 1935-36, this institution moved from Helena to the campus of Billings Polytechnic Institute, Billings, Montana, founded in 1903 with some connections to the Congregational Church. In 1947 these two institutions merged to form Rocky Mountain College.

Through its heritage it is the oldest institution of higher learning in the State of Montana, going back to the earliest movements for higher education in the Territory of Montana. It is the only Protestant senior college in the state. It offers the B.A. and B.S. degrees. The governing board of twenty-four members has six elected by the three supporting denominations (Methodist, Presbyterian, United Church of Christ), the balance at large by the board.

JOHN O. GROSS

ROCKY MOUNTAIN CONFERENCE was *first* organized on July 10, 1863 when eleven preachers, representing eight charges and 241 church members, gathered in DENVER City, COLORADO Territory, under the leadership of Bishop EDWARD R. AMES. At the time the conference boundaries included only Colorado.

After one year the name of the body was changed to the Colorado Conference, and it so continued until 1957 when it reverted to the original appellation. In the meanwhile, from 1872 to 1876, there was another Rocky Mountain Conference which had no relationship whatever to Colorado. It included the Territories of UTAH, IDAHO, MONTANA, and the western portion of WYOMING Territory. After its brief four-year existence, that Rocky Mountain Conference was divided to form the MONTANA and UTAH CONFERENCES.

On two occasions the territory of the Colorado Conference was enlarged. In 1948 the Utah Mission was dissolved and the Utah churches and those in White Pine County, NEVADA, became the Salt Lake District, later the Utah-Western Colorado District, of the Colorado Conference. The GENERAL CONFERENCE of 1956 authorized the Wyoming State Conference to merge with an adjacent conference. As a result the Wyoming work became the Wyoming District in the Colorado Conference. The new and enlarged body has since been called the Rocky Mountain Conference.

On two occasions the new Rocky Mountain Conference has taken in a few churches without enlarging its geographical boundaries. In 1963 the pastors and members of three CENTRAL WEST CONFERENCE churches, Central Jurisdiction, in Colorado were welcomed into the white conference. In 1964 the Simpson Methodist Church in Denver, a Japanese language congregation, with its two ministers, was incorporated in the Rocky Mountain Conference, because in that year the Japanese Provisional Conference was absorbed by the English-speaking Conferences of the Western Jurisdiction.

When first organized in 1863, the Rocky Mountain Conference though small proposed at once to start two institutions of higher learning, but only one, the Colorado Seminary which was the forerunner of the UNIVERSITY

OF DENVER, actually developed. Today Denver is one of the eight universities of The United Methodist Church.

In 1892, the ILIFF SCHOOL OF THEOLOGY was established at Denver to serve Methodism in the Rocky Mountain region. It was made possible by a gift by WILLIAM SEWARD ILIFF, a layman who was a leader in the political and economic development of the west.

In 1970, the Rocky Mountain Conference reported 405 ministers, 227 pastoral charges, 109,651 members, and churches, parsonages and other property valued at $50,-469,463.

E. S. Bucke, *History of American Methodism*. 1964.
Journals of the Colorado and Rocky Mountain Conferences.
K. E. Metcalf, *Beginnings of Methodism in Colorado*. 1948.
An unpublished Th.D. dissertation in Iliff School of Theology Library. WALTER J. BOIGEGRAIN

ROCKY MOUNTAIN CONFERENCE (1872-1876). (See UTAH.)

ROCKY MOUNTAIN CONFERENCE (EUB) was founded in 1951 and included one congregation in WYOMING in addition to churches in COLORADO and NEW MEXICO. The conference goes back to Oct. 19, 1869, when St. Clair Ross and his wife arrived in DENVER, Colo., looking forward to the establishing of a preaching appointment for the Church of the UNITED BRETHREN IN CHRIST. From Denver, they journeyed north or "down the Platte" to a village then known as Island Station, later known as Henderson, Colo. Here, in 1871, the first United Brethren Church building was erected and was dedicated on Jan. 21, 1872.

Under the authorization of the Board of Missions of the United Brethren Church, the work in Colorado was organized into a mission conference, April 15, 1872, by Bishop JOHN DICKSON. Three men who had brought their credentials with them made up the membership of this first Conference; they were St. Clair Ross, A. Hartzell, and W. H. McCormick. Shortly thereafter, the names of E. J. Lamb and L. S. Cornell were added to the list.

During this same period, the EVANGELICAL ASSOCIATION was developing work in the states of KANSAS and NEBRASKA and establishing work in Colorado. In 1885, a local preacher of the Kansas Conference attempted to organize a mission among the English-speaking people of the area of South Pueblo, Colo.; but this ministry failed for lack of interest in English services. In the year 1902, the Kansas Conference again tried to take up work in Colorado which resulted in the establishing of two missions, one in Ordway and the other in Colorado Springs.

About the same time, the Nebraska Conference of the Evangelical Association looked toward Colorado as a mission field and in 1887 established a mission in the vicinity of Yuma and Northeastern Colorado. Later, congregations were organized in Sterling, Denver, and Loveland.

Encouraged by the opening of new lands for homesteaders, the United Brethren Church organized a North Texas Mission Conference on Nov. 5, 1908, with small groups in north TEXAS, the "Strip" in OKLAHOMA, and New Mexico. This Conference finally became the New Mexico Mission Conference on Sept. 5, 1914; but the churches in the "Strip" in Oklahoma were transferred to the Oklahoma Conference and the churches in Texas went out of existence. In the development of this Conference

a special interest was being given to the Spanish-speaking population.

On June 2, 1920, the congregations organized by the Kansas and Nebraska Conferences of the Evangelical Association in Colorado were constituted as the churches of the newly organized Colorado Conference of the Evangelical Association (The EVANGELICAL CHURCH, following the merger of the Evangelical Association with the United Evangelical Church in 1922).

On Aug. 22, 1929, the Colorado Mission Conference and the New Mexico Mission Conference of the United Brethren Church were formally organized as the Colorado-New Mexico Conference of that church.

Following the merger of The Evangelical Church and the Church of the United Brethren in Christ in Johnstown, Pa., on Nov. 16, 1946, the Colorado Conference (Ev) and the Colorado-New Mexico Conference (UB), were merged in May 1951 as the Rocky Mountain Conference of The EVANGELICAL UNITED BRETHREN CHURCH. This conference united in 1969 with the conference of the same name in the former Methodist Church to form the Rocky Mountain Conference. At the same time the New Mexico congregations joined the New Mexico Conference in the SOUTH CENTRAL JURISDICTION of The United Methodist Church.

HAROLD H. MAXWELL

RODDA, MARTIN (dates unknown), British Methodist, eldest brother of RICHARD RODDA, was accepted as an itinerant preacher by JOHN WESLEY in 1763, but resigned in 1766 because of difficulties with a Welsh Methodist. He returned to the itinerancy in 1768, and in 1773 was stationed in East Cornwall under JAMES DEMPSTER, whom he accompanied to America in 1774. Rodda's strong loyalty to the British Crown caused trouble both for himself and for American Methodists in general, and he escaped with difficulty to England. After serving in three more English circuits (the last once more in his native Cornwall), in 1781 he retired permanently from the itinerancy.

E. S. Bucke, *History of American Methodism*. 1964.
T. Jackson, *Lives of Early Methodist Preachers*. 1871.
Minutes of the Methodist Conferences, 1862. FRANK BAKER

RODDA, RICHARD (1743-1815), British Methodist, was born at Sancreed, Cornwall, and converted at the age of thirteen. While working in the tin mines, he had several providential escapes. In 1769 he was appointed to the Glamorganshire Circuit and later was stationed several times in Wales and Cornwall. He was a pioneer of Sunday school work in CHESTER and one of the signatories of the HALIFAX CIRCULAR in 1791. In 1802 he settled in London.

JOHN A. VICKERS

RODRIGUEZ BORGES, ARMANDO ANDRES (1929-   ), bishop of the Methodist Church of CUBA, was born in Yaguaramas, Las Villas, Cuba, Nov. 30, 1929. His parents were Manuel Rodriguez and Elisa Borges. His early education was in his home town, but he later studied law and graduated from the University of Habana in 1954. He entered the Union Theological Seminary in Matanzas graduating in 1957. In 1956 he married Alida Barrios,

ARMANDO RODRIQUEZ

and to them were born five children, Alida, Elisa, Dorcas, Armando, and Otoniel. His ministry in the pastorate covered five different pastoral charges. Twice he was district superintendent serving the Oriente and Habana Districts. After the death of ANGEL FUSTER he became the administrative assistant of Bishop JAMES W. HENLEY. When Cuba was granted the status of an indigenous church, he was elected the first active bishop (Angel Fuster having been elected posthumously). He was consecrated to the office by Bishop ALEJANDRO RUIZ of MEXICO, Feb. 11, 1968.

GARFIELD EVANS

RODEHEAVER, HOMER ALVAN (1880-1955), noted American gospel singer, was born in Union Furnace, Ohio, Oct. 4, 1880. He was the son of Thurman Hall and Fanny (Armstrong) Rodeheaver.

He was for awhile a student in OHIO WESLEYAN UNIVERSITY. Bob Jones College, in TENNESSEE, awarded him the honorary degree of Doctor of Sacred Music in 1942.

He became widely known as musical director with William A. ("Billy") Sunday in his evangelistic campaigns, 1901-31, directing choruses in most of the leading cities of the United States, and he made a tour of the world with Evangelist W. E. Beiderwolf, 1923-24. In 1936 he made a tour of mission posts in the Belgian CONGO.

Rodeheaver was president of the Rodeheaver Hall-Mack Co., gospel music publishers, Winona Lake, Ind. He was founder of Rodeheaver's Boys Ranch, Inc., was trombone player with the Fourth Tennessee Regimental Band for four months in CUBA during the Spanish-American War in 1898, and was with the Y.M.C.A in FRANCE, August-December, 1918.

He was founder and promoter of the Summer School of Sacred Music, Winona Lake, Ind.; platform manager for large assemblies; conducted community song programs on National Broadcasting Company and Columbia Broadcasting System networks, and produced religious transcriptions.

He was the author of: *Song Stories of the Sawdust Trail,* 1917; *Twenty Years with Billy Sunday; Singing Black;* also various gospel songs and compilations.

Homer Rodeheaver never married. He was a lifelong Methodist. His residence and office were at Winona Lake,

Ind. He died Dec. 18, 1955, and his body rests in Oakwood Cemetery, Warsaw, Ind.

Who Was Who in America, Vol. 3.   J. MARVIN RAST

ROGERS, HENRY WADE (1853-1926), American jurist, educator, constitutional lawyer, and chairman of the powerful Committee on Judiciary of the GENERAL CONFERENCE of the M.E. Church for four quadrennia. He was born in Holland Patent, N. Y., on Oct. 10, 1853. At an early age he was adopted by an uncle for whom he was named. He received an A.B. degree from the University of Michigan in 1874, its A.M. in 1877. He took law at NORTHWESTERN UNIVERSITY, 1876-77. He was granted the LL.D. by WESLEYAN UNIVERSITY in CONNECTICUT in 1890 and by Northwestern University in 1915. He married Emma Ferdon Winner of Pennington, N. J., on June 22, 1876. Admitted to the bar in 1877, he came to be in great demand for his lectures upon law and jurisprudence, and was appointed U.S. Circuit Judge of the Second Judicial Circuit in September 1913.

Judge Rogers had served before that time as the chairman of the World Congress on Jurisprudence and Law Reform at the Chicago exposition in 1893.

The Dictionary of American Biography states that Rogers' greatest work was dean of the Yale School of Law at Yale University. The same account states that "besides the law, his chief interests were the Democratic Party and the Methodist Episcopal Church."

A strong Methodist, he was a lay representative from the M.E. Church to the M.E. Church, South, in 1894. Elected to his own GENERAL CONFERENCE and serving on the Committee of Judiciary in 1908, 1912, 1916, and 1920, he became chairman of that body, and the decisions of his committee were always adopted by the Conference in matters of ruling law. Judge Rogers also served on the committee to treat with the M.E. Church, South, regarding church union in the quadrennium between 1916 and 1920. He was chairman of the American Bar Association's Committee on Legal Education and Admission to the Bar from 1906 to 1917. He wrote *Illinois Citations,* 1881; *Expert Testimony,* 1883; and *Introduction to Constitutional History as seen in American Law,* 1889. For the Church he wrote the introduction to the reports of the Committee on Judiciary of the General Conference of the M.E. Church with rulings by the Board of Bishops, which publication was compiled under the authority of the General Conference. His introduction to these reports has been invaluable to students of Methodist Constitutional Law. (See *Reports of the Committee on Judiciary of the General Conference of the Methodist Episcopal Church,* by Arthur Benton Sanford. Introduction by Henry Wade Rogers, the Methodist Book Concern, New York-Cincinnati, 1924.)

He died at his summer house at Pennington, N. J., on Aug. 16, 1926.

National Cyclopedia of American Biography. New York: James T. White Co., 1896.
New York Times, August 17, 1926.
C. F. Price, *Who's Who in American Methodism,* 1916.
Who's Who in America. Vol. 14, 1926-27.   N. B. H.

ROGERS, HESTER ANN ROE (1756-1794), British Methodist, only daughter of the Rev. James Roe of Macclesfield, was born on Jan. 31, 1756. Her prejudices against

HESTER ANN ROGERS

Methodism were removed through the influence of DAVID SIMPSON, the Macclesfield curate after her father's death. She joined the society in spite of family opposition in 1774. The strain of nursing her mother in 1775 impaired her health, but her first meeting with WESLEY in 1776 encouraged her to become a devoted CLASS LEADER. Having nursed through final illness the first wife of JAMES ROGERS, one of Wesley's preachers, she married him on Aug. 19, 1784. She was with him during the DUBLIN revival and later at City Road, LONDON, where they witnessed Wesley's death. After prolonged suffering endured with cheerful piety, she died in BIRMINGHAM on Oct. 10, 1794, following the birth of her seventh child.

Besides keeping a diary from the time of her becoming a Methodist, Mrs. Rogers engaged in extensive correspondence about religious matters, contributed to the *Arminian Magazine*, and wrote some verse. Her *Experience* (1793), an autobiography including some selections from her diary, and her *Spiritual Letters* (1796) were combined with her *Funeral Sermon* by THOMAS COKE (1795) and an appendix by her husband, both quoting at length from her diary, to form a small volume which under several titles went through many reprintings on both sides of the Atlantic until early in the twentieth century. A further selection from her diary, under the title *The Life of Faith Exemplified* (1818), also gained considerable circulation.

The Experience and Spiritual Letters of Mrs. Hester Ann Rogers. London, 1833.
T. Jackson, *Lives of Early Methodist Preachers.* 1837-38.
JOHN A. VICKERS

ROGERS, JAMES (1749-1807), British Methodist itinerant, was born at Marsk, in Yorkshire, in 1749. He was justified in Whitby, Yorkshire, in February 1769, under the influence of William Ripley. He soon began to preach, and is reckoned as commencing his itinerancy in 1774. JOHN WESLEY had a high opinion of him, and in writing to Arthur Keene, July 23, 1784, described him as "an Israelite indeed" (*Letters*, vii, p. 226). He married Martha Knowlden in 1778. She died, however, in Macclesfield in 1782, and in 1784 he married Hester Anne Roe (see ROGERS, HESTER). They went to DUBLIN, where within a year Rogers saw 130 conversions and an increase of about 200 in the society. He was stationed at City Road Chapel after John Wesley's death. He retired from the itinerancy in 1806, and went to live in Guisborough, in North Yorkshire, not far from his native village, and there he died on Jan. 28, 1807.

T. Jackson. *Lives of Early Methodist Preachers.* 1846.
J. Wesley. *Letters*, references in vols. vi, vii, and viii.
W. L. DOUGHTY

ROGERS, ROBERT WILLIAM (1864-1930), American minister and scholar, was born in PHILADELPHIA, Pa., on Feb. 14, 1864, and was ordained by the PHILADELPHIA CONFERENCE in 1890. He received A.B. degrees from the University of Pennsylvania in 1886 and Johns Hopkins University in 1887. From 1887 to 1889, while working toward his doctorate from Haverford College, Rogers was an instructor in Greek and Hebrew. After receiving his doctorate in 1890, Rogers became professor of English Bible and Semitic History at DICKINSON COLLEGE. There he married Ida Virginia Ziegler on June 3, 1891.

In 1893, at the age of twenty-nine, Rogers was elected to the chair of Hebrew and Old Testament Exegesis at DREW THEOLOGICAL SEMINARY. Rogers remained at Drew for thirty-six years, specializing in the study of Semitic languages, the Old Testament, Greek, Hebrew, and the history of Babylon and Assyria. Rogers traveled to GERMANY and earned his doctorate at Leipzig in 1895. He also received the Doctor of Literature from the University of Dublin in 1914 and from Oxford in 1923. Rogers also lectured at Harvard, Columbia, and Princeton. He belonged to numerous learned societies, American and foreign, and was a life member of St. John's College, Oxford University. In 1929, he was forced to retire from his position at Drew because of illness, and died a year later at Chadds Ford, Pa., near Philadelphia in 1930.

Rogers was affectionately called the "Rabbi" while at Drew. His books, *The History of Babylon and Assyria* (1900) and the *Religion of Babylon and Assyria* (1909), attracted attention in America and abroad. Although he was an ordained minister, he never had a pastorate. It was said of Rogers that he made "the name of Drew known wherever pure learning was honored."

Christian Advocate (New York), Dec. 25, 1930.
Christian Century, Dec. 31, 1930.
J. R. Joy, *Teachers of Drew*. 1942.
W. P. Tolley, ed., *Alumni Record of Drew Theological Seminary, 1867-1925*. Madison, N. J.: Published by the Seminary, 1926.
WILLIAM H. GRAY

ROGERSON, J. J. (1820-1907), was born at Harbour Grace, Newfoundland. He was appointed to the Legislative Council of the colony in 1850, and to the Executive Council in 1858. He was elected a member of the House of Assembly in 1860, and was receiver-general from 1874 to 1882. An enthusiastic worker in the cause of temperance and moral reform, he was largely responsible for the establishment of the Fishermen and Seamen's Home in St. John's, and for the formation of the Protestant Industrial Society and the Native Society in that city. He was one of the founding trustees of George Street Methodist Church, St. John's, where with others he founded the Ragged Sunday School for poor children. For many years he was regarded as the leading Methodist layman in Newfoundland, and he gave generously to its support in many parts of the Island.

The Daily News, St. John's, Newfoundland, Oct. 18, 1907.
The Evening Telegram, St. John's, Newfoundland. Oct. 17, 1907.

N. WINSOR

ROMAINE, WILLIAM (1714-1795), Anglican Evangelical, was born at Hartlepool, England, Sept. 25, 1714. He was ordained an Anglican priest in 1738; and in 1748 he edited the Hebrew concordance of Marius de Calasso. At first attracted by JOHN WESLEY, Romaine went over to WHITEFIELD in 1755, and became the leading Anglican exponent of a rigid Calvinist theology. For the last thirty years of his life he was rector of St. Anne's, Blackfriars, London. His best known book was his *Treatise upon the Life of Faith* (1763). He died in London, July 26, 1795.

JOHN KENT

ROMAN CATHOLICISM AND JOHN WESLEY. The year 1745 brought the uprising under the Young Pretender, Bonnie Prince Charlie Stuart. The Pretender to the British throne was a Roman Catholic, and the fear engendered in Britain was part political, part religious. Catholicism was still associated with an atmosphere of intrigue such as it had possessed in the sixteenth and seventeenth centuries. It is against this background that JOHN WESLEY's reaction to Roman Catholicism must be understood. He, like other Methodists of his day, shared the fear of Roman Catholicism. In fact he was linked with it in the minds of many of his contemporaries. In 1739 he could write: "The report now current in Bristol was that I was a Papist, if not a Jesuit. Some added that I was born and bred in Rome, which many cordially believe!" (*Journal,* ii, 262.) In February 1744, a government order was issued "commanding all Papists and reputed Papists to depart from the cities of London and Westminster . . . by March 2." Wesley had intended to leave London on Monday, February 27, but "determined to stay another week, that I might cut off all occasion of reproach" (*Journal,* iii, 122).

In 1751 Wesley found it necessary to write a lengthy reply to Bishop GEORGE LAVINGTON of Exeter, who had charged the Methodists with popery (*Letters,* iii, 259); and misunderstanding of the Methodist position was not confined to educated circles. Wesley himself was prepared to allow Roman Catholics freedom in religious matters but not in political. In this he saw the Catholics as possible disturbers of the status quo. Wesley writes in January 1780: "Receiving more and more accounts of the increase of Popery, I believed it my duty to write a letter concerning it, which was afterwards inserted in the public papers. Many were grievously offended; but I cannot help it; I must follow my own conscience." He could insist that "with persecution I have nothing to do," but felt it necessary to go on: "No government . . . ought to tolerate men of the Roman Catholic persuasion . . . who cannot give any security to that government for their

allegiance and peaceable behaviour" (*Journal,* vi, 267). It was incumbent on Wesley's conscience to denounce what he believed to be the infidelity of Rome to the Christian gospel. "The most destructive" of all Roman errors he took to be justification by works "compared to which Transubstantiation and a hundred more are 'trifles light as air'" (*Journal* ii, 262). He lists ten things which the Romans "do add to those things which are written in the Book of Life": (1) Seven Sacraments. (2) Transubstantiation. (3) Communion in one kind only. (4) Purgatory, and praying for the dead therein. (5) Praying to saints. (6) Veneration of relics. (7) Worship of images. (8) Indulgences. (9) The priority and universality of the Roman Church. (10) The supremacy of the Bishop of Rome. (*Journal,* ii. 264.)

He had, further, a suspicion of Roman mystics, who "perpetually are talking of self-emptiness, self-inanition, self-annihilation" (*Letters,* v, 313). John Wesley also disliked what he called the inconsistency of the Roman Catholics. He accused them of misquotation of the Fathers: "I am no stranger to their skill in mending those authors who did not at first speak home to their purpose, and also purging them from those passages which contradicted their emendations." (*Journal,* ii, 262) He believed it to be their maxim that "no faith is to be kept with heretics" (*Letters,* vi, 271). He was also aware of Catholic intolerance (*Journal,* ii, 9). There is a certain note of cynicism in his remarking in 1765: "What wonder is it, that we have so many converts to Popery and so few to Protestantism, when the former are sure to want nothing, and the latter almost sure to starve?" (*Journal,* v, 151), and a corresponding delight in being able to note instances of converts from Rome (*Journal,* i, 357; iii, 427, 464; v, 151).

But Wesley's hostile criticism of Catholicism did not spring from or lead to an attitude of bigotry. He could allow himself to accept hospitality from a Roman Catholic (*Journal,* vii, 492); and in his sermon, "A Caution against Bigotry" (based on Mark 9:38-39, the incident of the man casting out devils), Wesley proceeds, after a criticism of the Catholic position, to acknowledge that still God may be using Papists in his work: "In every instance of this kind, acknowledge the finger of God. And not only acknowledge, but rejoice in His work" (Sermon, xxxiii). He could not "rail at or despise any man, much less those who profess to believe in the same Maker" (*Journal,* ii, 263).

In 1780 there took place the Lord Gordon Riots in LONDON. In the previous year an Act of Parliament had been passed which gave some legal relief to British Roman Catholics. Lord George Gordon presented to Parliament on behalf of his Protestant association a petition signed by some fifty thousand people demanding the repeal of this act. Vigorous rioting followed, and CHARLES WESLEY was concerned for the "trembling, persecuted Catholics" (*Letters,* vii, 20-21). Gordon requested John Wesley two or three times to visit him in the Tower of London where he had been imprisoned, and after receiving permission form the Secretary of State, Wesley acceded to this request on Dec. 19, 1780. A fortnight later he wrote of this visit:

I had no great desire to see Lord George Gordon, fearing he wanted to talk to me about political matters. . . . In our whole conversation I did not observe that he had the least anger or resentment to any one . . . Our conversation turned first upon

Popery, and then upon experimental religion . . . The theory of religion he certainly has. May God give him the living experience of it. (*Letters*, vii, 46)

Wesley's attitude is summed up in this experience: he could have no part in persecution of Catholics, and he believed that anyone with a vital knowledge of God would have to adopt the same attitude. Thus Wesley's complaint was not against Catholics as such, but against the lack of experimental religion which he deemed to be the state that so many of them were in.

His *Letter to a Roman Catholic* was written in 1749. It acknowledges the bitterness that has characterized both sides of the argument and seeks to set out plainly the Protestant faith in the Trinity and the Church. As practical measures Wesley suggests that both Catholic and Protestant should resolve "not to hurt one another . . . to speak nothing harsh or unkind of each other . . . to harbour no unkind thought, no unfriendly temper, towards each other . . . (and) to help each other on in whatever we are agreed leads to the Kingdom." (*Letters*, iii, 7-14) It therefore grieved him to have to write that Roman missionaries ("very few excepted") neither knew nor taught "true, genuine religion" (*Letters*, v, 121); and when his nephew SAMUEL became a Catholic in 1784, that his main concern was Sammy's lack of the knowledge of "Christ in you the hope of glory: . . . I care not a rush for your being called 'Papist or Protestant.' But I am grieved at your being a heathen." (J. Wesley, *Letters*, Vol. viii, p. 218, April 29, 1790; Vol. vii, p. 230-1, Aug. 19, 1784.) It has often been claimed that Methodism comes close to Catholic spirituality in its traditional insistence on CHRISTIAN PERFECTION; but, however that may be, the nineteenth century Methodist saw Rome as the true enemy of Christianity. There has grown gradually on both sides that attitude which leads to the present increasing acceptance of each other in sharing a common Lord and a largely common faith. This rapprochement more nearly reflects Wesley's own attitude than did nineteenth century Methodism's. One interesting if somewhat bizarre feature in this new relationship (at any rate in Methodist eyes) is the claim of John Todd, whose book *John Wesley and the Catholic Church* (London, 1958), has received the imprimatur. John Todd finds great inspiration in the life and teaching of John Wesley, and states that he has prayed to God—privately, though not publicly—through him.

BRIAN GALLIERS

ROME, ITALY. (See ITALY.)

ROMLEY, JOHN (1711-1751), English curate who would not let Wesley preach in the Epworth Church, was born at Burton, Lincolnshire, in 1711, the son of William Romley. During the latter years of SAMUEL WESLEY, he taught at the Charity School at Wroot, and served as amanuensis to the rector in compiling his commentary on *Job*. He matriculated at Magdalen Hall, Oxford, in 1735, and became curate of Epworth. A bitter anti-Methodist, he would not allow JOHN WESLEY to preach in the parish church (June 1742), and six months later refused him the sacrament. His action resulted in Wesley's practice of preaching either in Epworth churchyard (from his father's tomb), or at the market cross in the center of the village. On June 17, 1744, Wesley heard Romley preach two

"exquisitely bitter and totally false" sermons, and on April 21, 1745, commented: "Poor Mr. Romley's sermon . . . was another 'railing accusation.'" In October 1745, on the other hand, he heard Romley preach "an earnest affectionate sermon." Wesley's *Journal* for July 3, 1748 recorded: "I was quite surprised when I heard Mr. Romley preach. That soft, smooth, tuneful voice which he so often employed to blaspheme the work of God was lost, without hope of recovery." He did recover it in fact, shortly before his death in May 1751.

JOHN NEWTON

ROSARIO, Argentina, is the second largest city in ARGENTINA, with 761,300 people, and is in northern Argentina. It is connected with the capital by an excellent rail line and also air service.

First Church is the oldest Methodist church in Argentina outside of BUENOS AIRES. The church was founded in 1865, when Rosario was a city of 30,000, a promising river port just linked with the capital by rail.

A community of foreign business families—British, American, Swiss, and German—bought a cemetery and invited WILLIAM GOODFELLOW, Methodist mission superintendent, to come from Buenos Aires and dedicate it. From this contact it was decided to start a church for English-speaking Protestants. Thomas Carter was assigned and held his first service in a hotel in November of 1864. Within a year a building had been erected by subscription, without help from the Missionary Society in the United States. It was dedicated by Goodfellow in November of 1865. Carter founded the first Methodist paper in Latin America, the *South American Monthly,* published in English for two years.

THOMAS B. WOOD, noted missionary, was appointed to Rosario in 1870, and the following year began preaching in Spanish. A Spanish Sunday school was organized, its first pupils including four Indians and six criollos. The versatile Wood taught physics and astronomy in the National College, founded a Society for Prevention of Cruelty to Animals, which outlawed bullfighting, and started a temperance movement. He also served as U. S. consul in Rosario. A school begun in connection with the church became the COLEGIO AMERICANO.

While the central congregation remained English-speaking, it was the mother church for Methodism in the entire region. The church building was used for many years by a German congregation as well as by the Spanish Sunday school and for evangelistic work in Spanish, up to the present. Second Church (now called Resurrection Church), was established as a Spanish-speaking congregation. The entire area now numbers sixteen Methodist churches.

By the 1960's First Church included many bilingual families, second and third generation descendents of the original English families. Also in Rosario was a new community of North American business and technical people, attracted by growing industrialization of what was now Argentina's second city. In 1965 the first pastor who was not a missionary was appointed: Marcelo Perez Rivas, an Argentine. He held services in English on Sunday mornings and in Spanish on Sunday evenings.

Bishop SANTE UBERTO BARBIERI preached to large crowds at English and Spanish services upon the occasion of First Church's centenary on Nov. 7, 1965.

"The First Methodist Church of Rosario," unpublished ms., at First Methodist Church, Salta 2219, Rosario, Santa Fe Province, Argentina.
EDWIN H. MAYNARD

ROSEMONT, PENNSYLVANIA, U.S.A. **Radnor Church** is the oldest Methodist congregation meeting on the same site in Delaware County, Pa. The first Methodist preaching services were held at the home of Isaac Anderson and his wife, Lary Lane Anderson, and in 1778 meetings were held at the Mansion House owned by the James family. The Mansion House is still standing, although it has been greatly changed by alterations. Leader of these meetings was Adam Cloud. In 1780 a class was formed with George Gyger as the leader, a man who "hated rum, tobacco and the Devil." In the same year the first pastor was appointed: John Cooper with George Main as junior preacher. A meeting house was begun in 1783, being ready for occupancy in 1784. It was a log building twenty-five by thirty feet and was built on ground deeded to the congregation by Evan James. The ground had originally been part of the King's grant to William Penn. The first patent to the tract had been to David Meredith, a weaver of Radnorshire, England, from whom it had passed to the James family. When the Methodists were erecting their building, they were told the Methodists would soon be as "cold as cucumbers." Instead they became as "live coals from off the altar of God," and eventually became the mother church of the Bethesda Church, Merion Square and St. Luke's Church, Bryn Mawr. FRANCIS ASBURY visited the church July 2, 1787, when he "spoke to a few simple hearted souls," and again on July 7, 1792 when he stopped to dine on his way to PHILADELPHIA. On June 2, 1804 his mare, Jane, was lamed by a cow in Radnor, and on Wednesday, Aug. 7, 1805, he passed through the community, dining with Brother Gyger. On Tuesday, April 14, 1812, he preached again in the church. In 1833 the original church building was torn down, and a larger stone building was erected. A Sunday school was organized in 1843, and an educational building was added to the church in 1952.

F. Asbury, *Journal and Letters.* 1958.
G. M. Burlingame and W. A. MacLachlan, *Old Radnor Methodist Episcopal Church,* 1931.
FREDERICK E. MASER

ROSENBERGER, SILAS W. (1873-1950), American preacher, was born in Tiffin, Ohio, the son of Jacob and Sophia Rosenberger. After graduating from Heidelberg College, Tiffin, Ohio, he entered WESTMINSTER THEOLOGICAL SEMINARY, Westminster, Md. In 1902 he was ordained and became a member of the OHIO CONFERENCE of the M.P. Church, and that same year he married Miss Eva M. Ball. His first pastorates were in OHIO, and after a short period of service in the MARYLAND CONFERENCE he returned to Ohio for the remainder of his ministry.

During this period he was elected president of the Ohio Conference three times; elected to the GENERAL CONFERENCE six times; and was a member of the Uniting Conference of The Methodist Church in 1939. His most conspicuous service to the Church came in 1927 when he was elected executive secretary of the Board of Foreign Missions, and later when he became secretary of the combined four missionary Boards of Missions. In the administration of his office he was greatly assisted by his wife who had been prominent in the Women's Boards of Missions and who now was also a member of the General Board. Rosenberger returned to the pastorate in 1928, remaining in that capacity until his retirement in 1948. He died in Columbus, Ohio.

JAMES H. STRAUGHN

ROSS, ISAAC NELSON (1856-1927), American bishop of the A.M.E. CHURCH, was born in Hawkins County, Tenn., on Jan. 22, 1856. His education was self acquired. He was admitted to the Ohio Annual Conference in 1880, ordained deacon in 1882 and elder in 1883. He held pastorates in OHIO, PENNSYLVANIA, GEORGIA, WASHINGTON, D.C., and MARYLAND. He was elected bishop in 1916 from the pastorate of historic Ebenezer Church, BALTIMORE, Md., and served in West Africa and the southwestern United States. He died in 1927.

Bishop Ross in his pastorates was noted for construction and promotional ability. In COLUMBUS, Ohio, at St. Paul's Church, and at Big Bethel in ATLANTA, he did eminently constructive work. "He was one of the most popular pastors of the A.M.E. Church," Bishop Wright said of him.

R. R. Wright, *The Bishops.* 1963.
GRANT S. SHOCKLEY

ROSS, JOHN (1790-1866), principal chief of the Cherokee Indians from 1827 until his death and a staunch Methodist during the same period, was born Oct. 3, 1790. He was the son of David Ross, a Scotsman, and Mary McDonald Ross, one-fourth Cherokee; he was thus one-eighth Indian. He was called by one writer "a Scotchman with a dash of Cherokee blood," but nevertheless was completely identified with and accepted by the Cherokees. In 1809 he visited the Cherokees who had moved to the ARKANSAS territory, and he served in 1812 in a Cherokee regiment in the army of Andrew Jackson. He helped draft the Cherokee constitution in 1827. He was converted in 1828 under the preaching of JOHN B. McFERRIN and joined the M.E. Church. It was probably partly due to his influence over 1,000 fellow tribesmen enrolled in the Methodist societies among the Cherokees. His wife, Quatie (Elizabeth), was a very intelligent and devout Christian. His niece married Nicholas D. Scales, one of the Methodist missionaries to the Cherokees in east TENNESSEE.

The Ross home became a center of Methodist preaching and worship. Ross was strongly opposed to the removal of the Cherokees to the West and consistently refused to sign any treaty of removal. Other unauthorized Cherokees did sign such a treaty, however, and eventually (in 1838-39) Ross and his family had little choice but to move to what is now OKLAHOMA. On the way his wife, Quatie, died from exposure and was buried in LITTLE ROCK (the grave is now in Mount Holly Cemetery). In the Indian Territory he continued his loyal support of the church, being a close friend of JOHN HARRELL, one of the leaders in the INDIAN MISSION CONFERENCE. He married Mary Bryan Stapler, a Quaker, in WILMINGTON, Del. in 1845. Ross went to WASHINGTON, D.C. frequently to confer on Indian affairs, and was there when he died.

WALTER N. VERNON

ROSS, PETER (1821-1889), a superintendent of the A.M.E. ZION CHURCH, was born in November 1821, in Nova Scotia. He began his ministry in that part of the continent, joined the conference in June 1834, and was ordained a DEACON in December 1840, and an ELDER May 21, 1840. He was consecrated a Superintendent on May 24, 1856, and died April 10, 1889.

DAVID H. BRADLEY

ROSS, WILLIAM R. (1802-1885), pioneer physician and first IOWA class leader, was born Dec. 3, 1802, in Lexington, Ky., and began medical practice in INDIANAPOLIS, Ind., in September 1827. He migrated to Palmyra, Mo., in the spring of 1829 and from thence to Quincy, Ill. (1830), where his wife, Phebe, and two children died of cholera.

In August 1833 Ross removed to Flint Hills (now Burlington), Iowa, became the settlement's first doctor, druggist, storekeeper, postmaster, surveyor, and county clerk. He married Matilda Morgan on Dec. 3, 1833, recrossing the Mississippi River for the ceremony.

In 1833 Ross wrote PETER CARTWRIGHT, presiding elder at Quincy, asking for a preacher for Flint Hills. BARTON H. CARTWRIGHT was appointed and, in the Ross cabin, organized six people, with Ross as leader, into Iowa's first Methodist class on Sunday, April 27, 1834. Largely through his zeal as class leader, steward, and Sabbath school superintendent, Burlington became a station in 1837. After donating the two lots on which Old Zion was built (1838), Ross eventually sold his home to save the mortgaged church.

In later life, Ross lived at Eddyville, Albia, Hamilton, and Lovilia, where he was CLASS LEADER (1865-67). As class leader of Eddyville Mission (winter of 1844-45), he participated in Marion County's first QUARTERLY CONFERENCE, held near Attica, Ia. He died at Lovilia, Ia., on Oct. 12, 1885, and a boulder marks his Lovilia Cemetery grave.

A. W. Haines, *Makers of Iowa Methodism.* 1900.
Iowa Journal of History, April 1951.
E. H. Waring, *Iowa Conference.* 1910.
Yearbook of the Iowa Conference, 1866. MARTIN L. GREER

ROSSER, LEONIDAS (1815-1892), American presiding elder, evangelist, and author, was born July 31, 1815, in PETERSBURG, Va. Educated at WILBRAHAM ACADEMY and WESLEYAN UNIVERSITY (M.A., 1838), he was admitted on trial in the NEW YORK CONFERENCE in 1839. He transferred to the VIRGINIA CONFERENCE in 1840, and was ordained DEACON in 1841 and ELDER in 1843.

After three years at churches in RICHMOND, two years at Warrenton, and one in Bedford, Rosser, an intensely Southern partisan, was appointed to ALEXANDRIA (at that time it was still in the undivided BALTIMORE CONFERENCE, M.E. Church) where he helped to organize a Church South congregation. Two years later his conference appointed him to WASHINGTON, D.C. Beginning in 1852, he served the Fredericksburg District one year, the Norfolk District three years, and the Lynchburg District two years. Then he had two years as editor of the *Richmond Christian Advocate,* followed by one year as pastor of Union Church in the same city. Throughout the four years of the Civil War he served as chaplain or missionary to the Confederate forces in Virginia.

After four years on the Richmond District, 1865-69, Rosser had one year as conference missionary, three as Sunday school agent, one on the Randolph-Macon Dis-

trict, and then three more years as Sunday school agent. Beginning in 1877, he was appointed three years to the Randolph-Macon District and two to the Farmville District. The conference minutes say he was transferred to the DENVER CONFERENCE in 1882 and appointed to Denver, but apparently he did not go west. In 1883 he began a two-year pastorate at Central Church, PORTSMOUTH, followed by one year on the Pungoteague Circuit. Afterward he was supernumerary for three years and was superannuated in 1889.

Rosser was a trustee of RANDOLPH-MACON COLLEGE for thirty-six years, and since he was called "Doctor," presumably that school awarded him the D.D. degree. He was a delegate to four GENERAL CONFERENCES, 1850-66. In 1866 he strongly opposed lay representation in the General and annual conferences, and his vehement objection to permitting laymen to vote on ministerial qualifications resulted in the provision against such which remains in the *Discipline* to this day.

Throughout his ministry Rosser was known as an evangelistic preacher, and it is claimed that he won 20,000 converts. The last five years of his life were crowded with evangelistic work in his own and other states. He preached some 400 times in TEXAS the year before he died. Rosser's son, John C., followed him as a member of the Virginia Conference.

In addition to serving as editor of the conference paper, Rosser wrote reviews, pamphlets, and articles for the religious press. He wrote a book on *Baptism* which was in the conference course of study for a time. Other volumes from his pen were: *Experimental Religion, Recognition in Heaven, Class Meetings, Open Communion,* and *Initial Life.* He died in Ashland, Virginia, Jan. 24, 1892, and was buried there.

General Minutes, MEC and MECS.
Richmond Christian Advocate, Jan. 28, 1892.
Minutes of the Virginia Conference, 1892.   JESSE A. EARL
ALBEA GODBOLD

ROSWELL, NEW MEXICO, U.S.A. **First Church,** the first Protestant church in the Pecos Valley, had its beginnings in 1885 through the instigation of Mrs. Helen Johnson. She and her husband, Wiley, lived across the Pecos River some distance from Roswell. When one of the Johnson children died, Mrs. Johnson conducted the funeral services herself because there was no preacher in the vicinity. Feeling a great need for religious training for her remaining children and her friends, in 1885 Mrs. Johnson started a Sunday school on her land in a tent.

The Sunday school was moved to the schoolhouse located in the southeastern part of Roswell. Mother Johnson went from house to house in her light spring wagon carrying all her own children in it and inviting everyone to attend. As a "shouting Methodist," Mother Johnson could not rest until she could associate her group with the Methodist Church. The minutes of the QUARTERLY CONFERENCE, signed by secretary J. W. Sims, show that in 1887 the Roswell Mission was accepted as a Methodist church in the San Angelo District, WEST TEXAS CONFERENCE, Sims himself being appointed pastor in charge. There were eight charter members.

Permission was given the congregation to build a church by the Quarterly Conference of 1888 held at Seven Rivers, N. M. The adobe structure built at 311 North Pennsylvania Street was known as the M.E. Church, South. It was recently razed to make space for a parking lot. Members of other denominations cooperated in many ways: a friend, George Davis, gave the lot; the Board of Trustees included Capt. J. C. Lea, a Christian and leading Roswellite; also Steve Mendenhall, an Episcopalian; and William S. Prager, of the Jewish faith.

Before the building was completed, the mission acquired a new pastor in charge, William Gibbons. In February 1889, he reported that there were four teachers and thirty "scholars" in the Sunday school. Mrs. Mary Cobean was president of the LADIES' AID and also the first organist, using her own portable organ. By September 1889 the records show that membership had increased to twenty-six, Sunday school to fifty, and the pastor's salary to $150 per quarter (from original $27.50). The twenty-four by forty building, with walls nearly two feet thick, cost $408.85 (without roof).

When J. D. Bush became pastor in 1891, he was concerned with needed repairs for the church. Phelps White, Dave Howell, Bud Wilkerson and a friend were so touched when they saw women sitting on boards laid across beer kegs, and little children asleep on blankets on straw, they gave lumber for new benches. Bush constructed new seats and a pulpit.

The cowboys who came into town every Saturday night (sometimes from forty or fifty miles away) came largely for entertainment, but many of them found their way to church before they returned to their ranches. On one such occasion in 1895, a revival was being held in that adobe church. The church was crowded because a noted evangelist, Abe Mulkey, was the speaker. So impressed were the cowboys that they decided to make a contribution to the church. The bell they gave, now known as the "Cowboy Bell," was the first church bell to ring nearer than Las Cruces or EL PASO. The bell is now anchored on the corner of Pennsylvania and Second Streets.

The congregation rapidly outgrew the little church. John Stone gave two lots for a new building and a rock church was built where the present church now stands. It was dedicated on May 2, 1897 by the Rev. Mr. Eddington and Bishop JOSEPH S. KEY. During the period when the rock building was in use, the church was removed from the mission class and became self-supporting. The church also had the only lending library in town with about 1,000 books. At one period tubercular patients were cared for in the basement of the church.

After about twenty years the rock church became weakened and was torn down. The foundation of the present church was made of the rock from the old building, and its stained glass windows were carefully removed from the old to the new building. On May 17, 1936, Bishop H. A. BOAZ dedicated the church. It served as the annual meeting place on Homecoming Day for all veterans of the community regardless of church affiliation.

In the winter of 1956-57, the congregation again worshipped in the schoolhouse while the church was being repaired as the ceiling under the balcony had collapsed during a morning church service. Several buildings, including the old parsonage, were removed to make way for a new educational building and chapel. M. Buren Stewart and Austin H. Dillon dedicated it on Nov. 25, 1962. That same day, the seventy-fifth anniversary of the First Methodist Church of Roswell was observed.

First Church is not only the first church organized in Roswell, but literally the Mother Church of practically every church there. Out of her ranks have gone Chris-

tian, Episcopalian, Baptist, Northern Presbyterian and Southern Presbyterian men and women. Its membership in 1970 was 2,712.

General Minutes. MILDRED FITZGERALD

STEPHEN G. ROSZEL

ROSZELS, THE. Three American ministers, a father and two sons, each quite prominent, made their mark as leaders in the BALTIMORE CONFERENCE in the earlier half of the nineteenth century. **Stephen George Roszel** (1770-1841), the father, was born in Loudoun County, Va., on April 8, 1770, and was converted at the age of sixteen. Starting out from Loudoun County in 1789 under the immediate direction of Bishop ASBURY, he proved to be excellently endowed for the Methodist itinerancy, both physically and mentally. For the first five years he traveled "from the lowest point on the Chesapeake to the summit of the Alleghenies." (Armstrong, p. 450) Being the oldest son and the main dependence of a large family, he then felt impelled by duty to retire from the effective ranks for twelve years, but continued preaching in and near his native county. He turned out to be an ardent controversialist, and defender of Methodist doctrines and usages. He went back into the traveling connection again in 1807, and was stationed at various times in BALTIMORE, GEORGETOWN, Frederick, ALEXANDRIA and PHILADELPHIA, and was presiding elder over the Baltimore and Potomac districts. One year he served as an agent for DICKINSON COLLEGE. He was a strong preacher and ready debater, and had great influence on the floor of the GENERAL CONFERENCE. He was a member of the first delegated General Conference and every succeeding one until his death. He died in LEESBURG, Va., May 14, 1841.

Stephen Asbury Roszel (1811-1852), the son of S. G. Roszel, was born in Georgetown, D.C., Feb. 18, 1811. He was converted when he was sixteen years of age in Middleburg, Va., and for a time tried law, but soon closed his law office. Then while teaching in Dickinson College, he felt a strong call to preach. He entered the regular work of the ministry in 1838, and for fourteen years "gave full proof of his calling." He was elected reporter for the General Conference of 1840, and his published synopsis of the debates there showed his fitness for that type of work. He was himself elected a delegate to the 1848 General Conference which met at PITTSBURGH. It is said that he was greatly gifted in the pulpit, "Reason, imagination and eloquence pouring forth with a force of a rapid torrent." He died at an untimely age, having preached to a densely crowded audience at Fairfax Courthouse in northern VIRGINIA on Feb. 8, 1852, and then drove or tried to drive sixteen miles for an evening appointment. The day was cold and he was in an open buggy and his biographer tersely observes: "Pneumonia did its work."

S. Samuel Roszel (1812-1882), another son of S. G. Roszel, was born in Philadelphia, on Oct. 20, 1812. He graduated at AUGUSTA COLLEGE, then Methodism's strong college in what was considered the West. When Dickinson College was placed under the joint supervision of the Baltimore and PHILADELPHIA CONFERENCES, Samuel Roszel was elected as one of the instructors, but shortly yielded to the call of the ministry. Admitted to the Baltimore Conference in 1838, he was thereafter appointed to important and responsible fields on circuits and stations. He was presiding elder of the East Baltimore District for a time. He is said to have resembled his distinguished father, not only in the vigor of his intellect and powerful preaching, but in a commanding figure. "His tall, well-knit frame, his majestic head and handsome features, his well-modulated voice, engaging manner and felicity of expression, attracted multitudes in city churches and on camp-grounds." (Armstrong, p. 448.)

At the crucial session of the Conference at Staunton, Va., in 1861, when war had broken out and Virginia was invaded, the up-until-then-undivided Baltimore Conference faced its most critical moment. Roszel stood by the action of the Southern majority in the division that then came. After the Civil War was over, when the "Old Baltimore," as the Southern members proudly called themselves, petitioned to join the M.E. Church, South, Roszel was one of the men who went to NEW ORLEANS in 1866 and with Eldridge R. Veitch, LEONIDAS ROSSER, Samuel Regester, JOHN S. MARTIN, NORVAL WILSON, William G. Eggleston and John Poisal proudly took their Conference into the M.E. Church, South.

RANDOLPH-MACON COLLEGE and other institutions conferred upon S. Samuel Roszel the D.D. degree, and he was five times elected to his General Conference. He died in Fauquier County, Va., on April 27, 1882.

J. E. Armstrong, *Old Baltimore Conference.* 1907.
M. Simpson, *Cyclopaedia.* 1878.   N. B. H.

ROUND. JOHN WESLEY divided the country into extensive areas called "rounds," into each of which he sent his preachers to preach and to supervise Methodist activities generally. Their work entailed long journeys, sometimes extending to hundreds of miles and also long absences from home. As Methodism flourished, more preachers were needed, and the rounds were reduced in extent. Gradually the word "circuit" came to be substituted for "round."

W. L. DOUGHTY

ROUND CHURCH. (See ALBERT'S CHAPEL.)

ROUQUET, JAMES (1730-1776), British Anglican, converted as a schoolboy under WHITEFIELD, came up to OXFORD in 1748 and was introduced to CHARLES WESLEY. Rouquet was headmaster of KINGSWOOD SCHOOL for a period, probably from 1751 to 1754. As curate of St.

Werburgh's, BRISTOL, he was instrumental, along with his rector Richard Symes, in establishing Evangelicalism in that city. It was he who introduced Captain THOMAS WEBB to the Methodists. In his will of 1768 (later superseded) JOHN WESLEY appointed Rouquet as a trustee for his manuscripts.

A. SKEVINGTON WOOD

ROWE, GEORGE EDWARDS (1858-1926), Australian church leader and executive, was born in England, received his theological training at Richmond College there, and then left for South AUSTRALIA, where he served in four circuits.

In 1893 he was appointed to Wesley Church, PERTH, Western Australia District, where he assumed the responsibilities of a district which covered the whole of the vast state. It was a crucial time for the church. Substantial gold discoveries had been made in distant desert areas and miners were pouring into the country from the other states of Australia and from overseas. The church was ill-prepared to meet this crisis, but in Rowe it had a man who could match the hour. He managed to secure ministers, missionaries and agents and stationed them in strategic positions throughout the goldfields. When epidemics swept through the railway camps and mining fields, he organized the Order of "the Sisters of the People" and sent out trained nurses to share the hardships of the miners and to minister to them in temporary hospitals of hessian and canvas.

In 1896 he established a mission to the Chinese in Perth and brought the Rev. Paul Soon Quong to Australia to take charge of it. He directed the pioneering work of the church for three years as superintendent of Home Missions, and served for one year as superintendent minister of the great mining town of Kalgoorlie.

Rowe administered the church so successfully during this period of growth that it emerged strong enough to govern its own affairs and it was fitting that in 1900 he should be elected as president of the first WESTERN AUSTRALIA CONFERENCE. He visited England and America in 1902, and returned to Perth until 1906, when he was transferred to the QUEENSLAND CONFERENCE as minister of the famous Albert Street Church, BRISBANE. While minister of Wesley Church, Perth, he built for the Wesley Church Trust "Queen's Building," an impressive suite of buildings in the heart of the city. He died suddenly in Brisbane in 1926, some years after the honorary D.D. degree had been conferred upon him.

AUSTRALIAN EDITORIAL COMMITTEE

ROWE, GILBERT THEODORE (1875-1960), American minister, editor, and seminary professor, was born in Rowan County, N. C., Sept. 10, 1875. He was educated at Trinity College (DUKE UNIVERSITY), A.B., 1895; and Temple University, S.T.D., 1905. Honorary degrees were conferred upon him by Duke—D.D. in 1914, Litt.D. in 1925. Rowe joined the WESTERN NORTH CAROLINA CONFERENCE in 1896, and continued as a member of that conference all his life. For twenty years he was a distinguished pastor, holding the largest churches in his conference—Central, ASHEVILLE; Tryon Street (First), CHARLOTTE; Wesley Memorial, HIGH POINT; and Centenary, WINSTON-SALEM. His brethren elected him a delegate to the 1914 GENERAL CONFERENCE, and aside from

GILBERT T. ROWE

1918, sent him to every General Conference thereafter for the next thirty years, including the 1939 Uniting Conference. Usually he led his delegation, including 1944, the last time he was elected. In the 1930 General Conference at DALLAS, Rowe received ninety votes for bishop.

He was a delegate to the ECUMENICAL METHODIST CONFERENCE in 1921 and 1931. He served as fraternal delegate from his denomination to the 1928 General Conference of the M.P. Church. He was a prominent editor, having charge of the *North Carolina Christian Advocate* for two years, and serving as Book Editor of the M.E. Church, South and editor of the *Methodist Quarterly Review* in NASHVILLE for seven years.

He was a revered teacher, first as professor of Greek for one year at HENDRIX COLLEGE in ARKANSAS when a young man, next as an exchange professor at DREW UNIVERSITY for a year in his sixties, and finally he filled with distinction the chair of Christian Doctrine in DUKE DIVINITY SCHOOL from 1928 until his retirement in 1946.

Rowe was the author of two books, *The Meaning of Methodism* and *Reality in Religion.* Always interested in education, he was a member of his annual conference board of education for forty years, and served for a long period on the General Board of EDUCATION of the M.E. Church, South, and on the board of trustees of GREENSBORO COLLEGE. A diligent student, a clear thinker, a theological liberal when many contemporaries were conservatives, a popular preacher, a beloved teacher, a forceful personality combined with a tolerant and friendly spirit, Rowe was one of the ablest and most respected leaders of his time in NORTH CAROLINA and Southern Methodism. He died Feb. 10, 1960 and was buried at DURHAM, N. C.

ALBEA GODBOLD

ROWE, PHOEBE (c. 1855-1898), an Anglo-Indian lady of great influence in Indian Methodism, was born at Allahabad, United Province, INDIA, of an Indian mother and a Scots father. Her mother died before Phoebe was two years old. She and her father were dedicated church members. A Baptist minister visiting the home led her to "a conscious experience of sins forgiven." Three years later her father died. DENNIS OSBORNE recommended her to ISABELLA THOBURN, who employed her and guided her further education.

Bishop THOBURN paid her high tribute, calling her "the founder of our village evangelism, . . . the most peerless saint I have ever known, . . . destined to live in our history." In 1882 she was recognized as a missionary of the WOMAN'S FOREIGN MISSIONARY SOCIETY. When in 1887 it became necessary for one of the American missionaries, Miss Nickerson, to return to America, Miss Rowe was asked to accompany her. Miss Nickerson died en route.

Miss Rowe completed the voyage, addressed the annual meeting of the CINCINNATI Branch in a memorial service, and asked for someone to dedicate herself to take Miss Nickerson's place. Her appeal was answered by LUCY W. SULLIVAN, who became one of the great missionaries of her generation in India.

Miss Rowe was the first Indian woman elected to the Executive Board and was a charter member of the North West India Woman's Conference. She died of diphtheria in Naini Tal, on April 19, 1898.

B. T. Badley, *Southern Asia.* 1931.
J. N. Hollister, *Southern Asia.* 1956.
J. E. Scott, *Southern Asia.* 1906.   J. WASKOM PICKETT

ROWELL MINUTES. Jacob Rowell was one of JOHN WESLEY's preachers from 1749-84. In 1751, Wesley appointed him to IRELAND, where he remained for two years. Rowell was present at the first Irish Conference, held in Limerick on August 14 and 15, 1752, and took minutes of the proceedings. He did the same at the first Conference held in Leeds in May, 1753. These are known as the *Rowell Minutes* and are printed in the Appendix to Volume I of the *Minutes of Conference* published in 1862.

W. L. DOUGHTY

ROWLAND, JOSEPH MEDLEY (1880-1938), American pastor and ninth editor of what is now the *Virginia Methodist Advocate,* was a most versatile man. His talents brought him wide recognition as a strong preacher, a humorous lecturer, an author, a world-traveler, and an authority on the ways of life of mountain people. All this was in addition to his appreciated contributions during the seventeen years he edited the *Advocate.* So effective was he in so many directions, that it would be difficult to say in what specific area he made his greatest contribution. Unfortunately, his effective ministry came to a premature end on Aug. 17, 1938, when he was killed in an automobile accident while returning home from LAKE JUNALUSKA.

Rowland wrote three books, all widely read: *Travels in the Old World* provided helpful information about the Holy Land; and the other two volumes dealt with mountain people: *Blue Ridge Breezes* and *The Hill Billies.*

Journal of the Virginia Conference, 1939.
Richmond Christian Advocate, May 26, 1932.
GEORGE S. REAMEY

ROWLAND, THOMAS (c. 1790-1858), British Methodist, one of the leading WESLEYAN REFORMERS, became a Wesleyan itinerant in 1813. He was the only member of CONFERENCE to vote against the expulsion of SAMUEL WARREN in 1835, and himself ceased to be recognized as a Wesleyan minister in 1852. He later joined the ministry of the UNITED METHODIST FREE CHURCHES.

G. ERNEST LONG

ROWLANDS, DANIEL (1713-1790), Welsh Methodist, second son of the rector of Llangeitho, Cardiganshire, WALES, where he became curate to his brother John, who had succeeded to the living on their father's death in 1731. Rowlands was ordained deacon in 1733, priest in 1735. About 1735 a sermon by GRIFFITH JONES of Llanddowror made a deep impression upon him, and he became an eloquent evangelical preacher. In 1737 HOWELL HARRIS, who had himself begun preaching (as a layman) in 1735, heard him and sought his acquaintance. The clergyman Rowlands then followed the example of the layman Harris in founding religious societies, the beginning of the WELSH CALVINISTIC METHODISTS. At the first general assembly or "association" of these societies in 1743, Rowlands was appointed deputy-moderator to act in the absence of GEORGE WHITEFIELD. This in effect meant that he became the leader of the movement. Tension with Harris followed, and an incompletely healed rupture in 1751. Because of his Methodist activities Rowlands was suspended by his bishop in 1763 from the exercise of his functions as a clergyman of the Church of England. He continued to minister in a new building erected for him at Llangeitho, where he died Oct. 16, 1790.

Dictionary of National Biography.
Journal of the Calvinistic Methodist Historical Society, Vol. XII, pp. 41-64, June 1927.
W. Williams, *Welsh Calvinistic Methodism.* 1884.

FRANK BAKER

ROWSE, WILLIAM (1835-1899), NEW ZEALAND minister, was born in Cornwall, England. When twenty-three, he was accepted as a minister on probation, and at the end of the same year came to New Zealand.

After serving as a probationer in Canterbury and AUCKLAND he was appointed in 1863 to the Maori Mission. For fifteen years he served at Waima in North Auckland. By boat and by horseback he covered a wide circuit. During that time village schools were opened; teachers trained; churches built; young men sent out as local preachers; and a people sunk in the depths of degradation through liquor were won from its cruel bondage.

For the sake of his family, Rowse returned to circuit work in 1878 and died in Greytown on July 15, 1899. His was a devoted life, free from all self-advertisement, and many were the people he won to faith in goodness and in God.

W. Morley, *New Zealand.* 1900. WILLIAM T. BLIGHT

ROYAL OAK, MICHIGAN, U.S.A. **First Church,** begun as a "preaching place in a six-point circuit," is the parent of seven adjacent Methodist churches in the expanding suburbs of metropolitan DETROIT.

This church was organized in 1838, the town's first permanent church organization, although itinerant Methodist ministers had preached under the trees or in a vacant store room before that date. J. M. ARNOLD was one of the early ministers.

The first church building, of white frame with an attractive cupola, was completed in 1843 on the present site at a cost of $1,500. A parsonage was erected forty years later at a cost of $1,250, when Eugene Yager was the pastor.

In 1890 the first church was replaced by a brick structure at a cost of $5,000, plus much donated labor. The brick was donated by Edwin Starr, one of the members, from his own kiln. This served until the first unit of the present structure was built in 1918 at a cost of $90,000, under the pastorate of OSCAR THOMAS OLSON.

In 1928 the present church building was completed under the pastorate of Eugene Miles Moore, at a cost of $155,000. Since then, reconstruction and renovation have produced a plant valued at $1,346,090, with a sanctuary seating 875 and a four-level educational complex. The church presently underwrites a benevolence budget of $42,000.

The seven churches which First Church has sponsored are: St. John's and Campbell Memorial in Royal Oak; Berkley Church; Hazel Park Church; Ferndale Church; Faith Church in Oak Park; and Madison in Madison Heights.

The membership includes many prominent citizens, among whom are several professors at Wayne State University, a member of Congress, three judges, numerous industrialists and public school personnel. In 1970 the church reported a membership of 2,811.

General Minutes. MARSHALL A. WHEATLEY

RUBLE, JOHN H. (1811-1836), pioneer American circuit rider, was born in Washington County, Tenn. Converted under CAMP MEETING influences, he became a CLASS LEADER of the M.E. Church. Migrating to ILLINOIS, he received a preaching license Nov. 25, 1832, from Jacksonville Circuit, Sangamon District. Removing again to MISSOURI, Ruble was employed by William Ketron, Cape Girardeau District presiding elder, to travel Bellevue Circuit with Nathaniel Talbott. After three months he was sent to White River Circuit in ARKANSAS. He joined the MISSOURI CONFERENCE on trial, Sept. 4, 1833, and was sent back to the White River country. His next work was at Lexington, Mo. In 1835 he was admitted into full connection, ordained a deacon, and appointed to Burlington Circuit, ST. LOUIS District.

Ruble, the first Methodist preacher to be married in IOWA, took as his wife Diana Bowen in Burlington, in February 1836, and they began living in Mt. Pleasant, a hamlet of three houses, where he preached the first sermon. He was authorized to perform marriage rites by William R. Ross, Des Moines County Clerk, Michigan Territory, on Oct. 31, 1835.

Taken with a fever at Sullivan Ross's home in Burlington, Ia., Ruble died there April 14, 1836, the first Methodist itinerant to die in Iowa. The place of his burial at Mt. Pleasant is marked by a stone monument, erected about 1860 and restored in 1934.

Annals of Iowa, April 1936.
A. W. Haines, *Makers of Iowa Methodism.* 1900.

MARTIN L. GREER

RUDDLE, THOMAS (1839-1909), British educator, was born at Trowbridge, Wiltshire, Nov. 15, 1839. The son of a factory worker, he trained as a teacher, and in 1864 was appointed headmaster of the BIBLE CHRISTIAN School, SHEBBEAR COLLEGE, then very small. He had greatly raised the academic standing of the school by the time of his retirement in 1909. He died on Oct. 17, 1909.

JOHN KENT

RUDISILL, ABRAHAM WEHRLEY (1846-1889), was born in Hanover, Pa. He joined the BALTIMORE CONFERENCE in 1870 and held various appointments in MARYLAND, including presiding elder of the West Baltimore District. In 1884 he arrived in INDIA as a missionary of the M.E. Church.

As a layman, Rudisill had been a practical printer. As presiding elder of the Madras District, he felt the need of reading material for church members and for the unconverted. He obtained a boy's press which would print a leaflet four by six inches, and a small font of Tamil type. With this meager equipment, he began printing in a small room near the parsonage.

Mrs. Rudisill started a Tamil edition of *The Woman's Friend,* and her husband published it. In a few years Rudisill was superintendent of a publishing house which he then named for his wife, the Mary M. Rudisill Publishing House. Soon known as the Methodist Publishing House, it produced literature for the blind in Kanarese, Tamil, Telugu, and English. When publishing houses multiplied and competition became severe, the property was sold; and after accumulated debts had been paid, the remaining resources and responsibilities were transferred to the Methodist Publishing House of LUCKNOW.

Mrs. Rudisill died in 1889 and Rudisill went back to America in poor health. He died there a few months later.

J. WASKOM PICKETT

RUGG, EARLE MELVIN (1888-1952), American missionary to INDIA, was born at Farmington, N. Y., on April 15, 1888. He was educated at Rochester University (A.B., 1913); BOSTON UNIVERSITY SCHOOL OF THEOLOGY (S.T.B., 1916); SYRACUSE UNIVERSITY (M.Sc., in Education, 1940); and received an honorary D.D. from SOUTHWESTERN UNIVERSITY in 1948. He married Ellen Martha Foote on Sept. 7, 1915. She was born in Naini Tal, India, of missionary parents, and had graduated from Rochester University in 1913 with a B.A. in mathematics. Their children were Melvin, Jean, Grace (died, 1959, following an automobile accident), and Harold.

In 1916 Earle and Ellen Rugg arrived in India under appointment to Ajmere, Rajputana, for general mission work. Later he became principal of Boys High School, Ajmere. In 1926 he was principal of the Boys' School, Raiwind, Punjab. He faced difficulties of the depression with a restricted budget and necessary retrenchments. He also gave notable service as the director of Raiwind Christian Institute where he combined skill as a churchman and evangelist; also as educator with results recognized as valuable by the government officials, by church officers, and by humble neglected victims of an impoverished economy.

Rugg's methods of teaching trades and improving farm procedures were adopted as a model by many private and governmental schools. He assisted the Technical Services Association in devising better spinning wheels and pumps, and helped organize more remunerative employment for women. Both Earle and Ellen Rugg served as teachers.

High standards of scholarship and efficiency were developed.

His other services were as editor of the magazine *Christian Education* for several years; Methodist representative of the Round Table Conference Committee for Church Union; valued member of the Punjab Christian Council, which became the West Pakistan Christian Council after 1947 when PAKISTAN was formed. As chairman of the Committee on High Schools, he helped the schools through the difficulties of the first years of Pakistan independence. Rugg was a delegate to the M.E. GENERAL CONFERENCE of 1932; and to the CENTRAL CONFERENCE in 1928 and 1936.

He was elected president of the Christian Council in 1952, a short time before his tragic death in Lahore Hospital following a refrigerator explosion accident in Raiwind. The Ruggs served continuously in Raiwind except for their several furloughs from 1926 to 1952.

CLEMENT D. ROCKEY

ALEJANDRO RUIZ

RUIZ MUNOZ, ALEJANDRO (1921-   ), bishop of The Methodist Church of MEXICO, was born in San Luis Potosi, June 31, 1921. His early preparation was in the field of commerce. He graduated from the Union Theological Seminary in Mexico City and did postgraduate work for one year at SOUTHERN METHODIST UNIVERSITY School of Theology in Dallas, Tex. He married Ruth Guerra, the daughter of Bishop ELEAZAR GUERRA, and they are the parents of five children.

As a member of the intermediate department of the Gante Street Church in Mexico City, Alejandro Ruiz was sent by his pastor, Epigmenio Velasco, to help lead a small mission in a rural congregation. There he felt the call to the ministry, an experience which was strengthened later as he witnessed the faith and joy of his dying pastor in the hospital.

He entered the conference in 1943, was ordained DEACON in 1945, and ELDER in 1948 by Bishop Guerra. He held charges at Balderas, 1943-44, Peralvillo, 1945-46, Xalostoc, 1948-49, Aztecas, 1949-50, and Balderas, 1951-54. He was elected executive secretary of Christian Education, 1955-62.

He was first elected bishop (Iglesia Metodista de Mexico) for the period 1963-66; and subsequently at the General Conference held in Monterrey, September 1966, he was re-elected and again at the Mexico City General Conference, July 19-26, 1970 re-elected for the quadrennium beginning then.

Bishop Ruiz is a young, energetic and understanding leader. He is an excellent speaker, a good organizer, and a most efficient worker with young people. His aim is to help the church become self-supporting and to find the place in which each member of the conference can render the best service to the cause.

GUSTAVO A. VELASCO G.

RULE, WILLIAM HARRIS (1802-1890), British Methodist, born at Penrhyn, Cornwall, Nov. 15, 1802. After early experiments as a portrait painter and a school teacher, in 1826 he entered the Wesleyan Methodist ministry, and became an ardent student. He served the Wesleyan METHODIST MISSIONARY SOCIETY in Malta (1827), St. Vincent (1827-31), and GIBRALTAR (1832-1841), which latter place he used as a stepping-stone for enthusiastic and partially successful attempts at missionary work among Roman Catholics in SPAIN. The following twenty-six years of a vigorous active ministry in England included five years as CONNEXIONAL EDITOR (1851-57) and eight years in pioneer chaplaincy work among Wesleyan soldiers at Aldershot (1857-65). Rule is said to have mastered ten languages, and was a prolific writer, his chief work being a monumental *History of the Inquisition* (1868). His writings on Methodism included *A Memoir of a Mission to Gibraltar and Spain* (1844), *An Account of the Establishment of Wesleyan Methodism in the British Army* (1883), and *Recollections of my life and work at home and abroad in connection with the Wesleyan Methodist Conference* (1886). In 1854 he was awarded the D.D. by DICKINSON COLLEGE. He died Sept. 25, 1890.

Dictionary of National Biography.
Findlay and Holdsworth, *Wesleyan Meth. Miss. Soc.,* iv, 1922.
FRANK BAKER

RULES OF THE METHODISTS, in eighteenth-century England. On the founding of the early Methodist societies, JOHN WESLEY drew up his *Nature, Design and General Rules of the United Societies in London, Bristol, Kingswood and Newcastle upon Tyne* (first edition, John Gooding on the Side, Newcastle upon Tyne, 1743). He subsequently issued rules which are to be found as follows in Wesley's *Works* (T. Jackson's third edition): BANDS (viii, 272); CLASS LEADERS (viii, 301); HELPERS (viii, 309); STEWARDS (viii, 262); preachers and Preachers' Fund (viii, 326, 317); congregational singing (viii, 318; xiv, 346). For Rules of the FETTER LANE society (May 1, 1738), see Wesley's *Journal* (i, 458). (See also GENERAL RULES.)

JOHN BOWMER

RUNDLE, ROBERT TERRILL (1811-1896), English missionary to the Indians of the Hudson's Bay Territory, was born in Nylor, Cornwall, England, June 18, 1811, the third son of Robert and Grace Rundle, and grandson of the prominent Methodist lay evangelist, WILLIAM CARVOSSO.

In 1839, the Hudson's Bay Company reached an agreement with the WESLEYAN MISSIONARY SOCIETY in England to send the first party of missionaries into the area west of the Red River settlement of British North America. JAMES EVANS, an experienced missionary in Upper Canada, was chosen as the superintendent; and three young men, Rundle, Mason and Barnley, were recruited in England to serve with him.

After sailing to New York in April 1840, they journeyed to Montreal and were carried by the company canoes to their destinations, Barnley to Moose Factory, Mason to Lac la Pluie, and Rundle to Fort Edmonton. Since Evans failed to meet the brigade at Sault Ste. Marie, Rundle remained at Norway House, at the north end of Lake Winnipeg, until Evans' arrival. His first and highly successful missionary activity was among the Cree Indians of the Norway House region. It required from September 7 to October 17 for the company canoes to fight their way up the current of the North Saskatchewan to Fort Edmonton, the scene of eight years' arduous and often unrewarding labor.

While Rundle's room at the fort was constantly available, he travelled regularly to the forts at Rocky Mountain House in the south, Lesser Slave Lake to the north, Fort Pitt to the east, and to countless encampments of Indians —thousands of miles by horseback, cariole, canoe, and on foot. Perhaps the most impressive single experience began at Rocky Mountain House Fort in 1841. Having long dreaded an encounter with the famed Blackfoot tribe, he met them unexpectedly and was received with great warmth and affection. He went alone with them to their camps and was escorted back to Fort Edmonton by a Blackfoot warrior.

He introduced the Cree Syllabic recently invented by James Evans, taught singing, and conducted classes wherever he went. While evangelism was his primary purpose, he soon became oppressed by the recurrent starvation of the Indian peoples and their entire lack of agriculture. After repeated experiments with small gardens, he obtained the assistance of Benjamin Sinclair, a native Swamp Cree from Norway House, to assist in the formation of an agricultural settlement on the shore of Pigeon Lake in 1847, the first such attempt in the western region. Unfortunately his wrist was broken in a fall before Sinclair arrived, and in the summer of 1848 he was forced to return to England for medical care.

Rundle did not return, nor was he replaced from England. He married, served a succession of circuits until his superannuation in 1887; and died in 1896.

The importance of Rundle's work was obscured for many by the arrival of Roman Catholic missionaries in 1842 with consequent rivalry and confusion, by the disturbance surrounding the work of James Evans and Evans' death in 1846, by Rundle's misfortune and return to England in 1848, and by the transfer from English to Canadian control in 1854.

Recognition and honor were accorded to him as his work came to be seen in longer perspective. In the same year that David Livingstone was making his first African journey, Rundle was making the first missionary approach to the western tribes. He was accepted warmly by the Blackfoot and Stoney, Assiniboine and Cree, and they remembered him. Early travelers such as artist Paul Kane and the Earl of Southesk, saw the effects of his work and eulogized him in their writings. J. Hector of the Palliser Expedition was successful in having a mountain named in his honor. All succeeding missionaries found a door opened and a path prepared toward Christian understanding and a successful agriculture because Robert Terrill Rundle had been there before them.

Records of the Wesleyan Methodist Missionary Society. United Church of Canada, *Rundle in Alberta* (Toronto: U.C.P.H., 1940).   G. M HUTCHINSON

RUPERT, HOOVER. (See JUDICIAL COUNCIL.)

E. GORDON RUPP

RUPP, E. GORDON (1910-   ), British church historian, was born in London Jan. 7, 1910; he entered the ministry of the Methodist Church in 1934 and studied at Wesley House, CAMBRIDGE. After a period of circuit work at Chislehurst in Kent (1938-46), he returned to Wesley House as assistant to R. NEWTON FLEW, who was president in 1946-47. Rupp was appointed church history tutor at Richmond Theological College in 1947, and stayed there until 1952, when he went to Cambridge to lecture on Reformation history. In 1956 he was appointed the first professor in church history at Manchester University, where he remained until 1967, when he returned once more to Wesley House, Cambridge, this time as principal. He was president of the Methodist CONFERENCE in 1968.

Rupp holds a Doctorate of Divinity from Cambridge University, and an honorary D.D. from Aberdeen University. He is a Reformation scholar, having specialized in the life and writings of Martin Luther. He has taken a prominent part in the ecumenical movement, and has been one of the principal Methodist advocates of union between the Methodist Church in Britain and the Church of England.

Rupp's publications include *Martin Luther, Hitler's Cause or Cure?* (1945), a book written in reply to the assertion that Luther was Hitler's spiritual ancestor; *Studies in the Making of the English Protestant Tradition: Mainly in the Reign of Henry VIII* (1947); *Luther's Progress to the Diet of Worms* (1951); *Principalities and Powers* (1952); *The Righteousness of God* (1953), originally the Birkbeck lectures; *Thomas Jackson, Meth-*

odist Patriarch, the annual lecture of the WESLEYAN HISTORICAL SOCIETY for 1954; *Consideration Reconsidered* (1964), a contribution to the Anglican-Methodist debate. He has been the editor (with RUPERT E. DAVIS) of *A History of the Methodist Church in Great Britain*, the first volume of which was published in 1965, and for which he wrote a valuable introductory essay. An earlier work on the same subject, "Methodism in Relation to the Protestant Tradition," was delivered at the ECUMENICAL METHODIST CONFERENCE of 1951.

PETER STEPHENS

RUSBY, HELEN B., missionary to BOLIVIA, worked in the country from 1919 to 1956, returning for six months a few years later. She taught at the American Institute (now COLEGIO EVANGELICO METODISTA) in La Paz and was housemother to the smaller boys. Among them were a future president and vice-president of Bolivia and other prominent citizens. Among her dormitory boys were an ambassador to London, several prominent businessmen, a professor of Spanish, and some boys whom she indirectly influenced to go into the ministry. When Miss Rusby retired in 1956 the Bolivian government gave her the "Condor" award for her influence upon Bolivian boys. She is one of six or seven Methodist missionaries to receive this prize.

The Methodist Church in Bolivia, published in English and Spanish by the Historical Committee of The Methodist Church in Bolivia, 1961.   NATALIE BARBER

RUSH, CHRISTOPHER (1777-1873), the second superintendent of the A.M.E. ZION CHURCH, was born in Craven County, N. C., Feb. 4, 1777. He was converted at the age of sixteen. While it is not known whether he was "manumitted or purchased" through his own industry or the benevolence of friends, he himself states that he came to NEW YORK in 1798, joining the A.M.E. Zion Church in 1803. In 1815 he was licensed to preach. He was ordained DEACON and ELDER on the same day in 1822. In 1828 he was elected superintendent and is supposed to have served four years "with Varick in this position." It appears that he served the church twenty years following the death of Superintendent JAMES VARICK. There is a discrepancy here in that Varick is listed as the first superintendent from 1822-27. Bishop Singleton T. Jones gives the information listed above in which Rush is said to have served four years with Varick. This, too, is a little amiss for Rush is said to have lost his sight in 1852, which would mean that he served twenty-six years or twenty-eight in all. Bishop J. W. HOOD states that he served twenty-four years. Whether Varick failed of re-election in 1828 or died prior to the General Conference of that date is a moot question. Hood states that he died shortly before that Conference while Flood carried the account that Varick and Rush shared the superintendent's honors for four years.

Again there is a difference of opinion on the death of Superintendent Rush. Flood states that he died July 6, 1873 in his ninety-sixth year while the Official Directory issued by J. Harvey Anderson puts his death a year earlier. Supposing that he lost his eyesight in 1852, according to Flood the grand old man lived twenty-one years in darkness, part of the time confined to his room. He maintained a keen mind to the last. He is buried in Cypress Hill Cemetery in Brooklyn, N. Y.

One aspect of Father Rush's life which is mainly overlooked is his effort to further education. It was he who secured the property for the planned school in Essex County, N. Y. While this effort failed it early showed the interest of the church leaders in higher education.

D. H. Bradley, *A.M.E. Zion Church.* 1956.
J. W. Hood, *One Hundred Years.* 1895.
J. J. Moore, *History* (AMEZ). 1884.
C. Rush, *Short Account.* 1843.   DAVID H. BRADLEY

RUSLING, JOSEPH (1788-1839), American minister noted for his pulpit oratory and executive ability, was born near Epworth, England, May 12, 1788. He came to the United States with his parents in 1791, and joined the M.E. Church in 1808. In 1814 he joined the PHILADELPHIA CONFERENCE on trial, and leaping into almost immediate prominence, filled important appointments in TRENTON, PHILADELPHIA and WILMINGTON. He suffered from a pulmonary disorder, however, and leaving the pastorate, founded the first Methodist Book Store in Philadelphia in 1829, employing as a clerk ABEL STEVENS who later became the outstanding Methodist historian of the nineteenth century. Rusling wrote several small volumes of poetry, hymns and sermons. He died July 6, 1839.

Minutes of the Annual Conferences, Vol. III.
M. Simpson, *Cyclopaedia.* 1878.   FREDERICK E. MASER

RUSSEL, JOHN (1799-1870), American United Brethren circuit rider, pastor, administrator and bishop, was born March 18, 1799 in the Pipe Creek region of western MARYLAND. His parents were Jacob and Amelia (Smith) Russel. His paternal grandfather arrived in America from GERMANY on the ship *Patience*, Sept. 17, 1738.

PHILIP W. OTTERBEIN made occasional visits to the Pipe Creek settlement and rendered limited pastoral service. Through him the Russels became identified with the revival movement of the late 1700's and early 1800's. In 1818 John Russel was licensed as an exhorter in the Church of the UNITED BRETHREN IN CHRIST and traveled a Virginia circuit; in 1819 he was formally licensed and was sent to OHIO where he traveled a circuit spread over six counties. To prevent being lost in the forests he carried a hatchet in his saddlebags for the purpose of blazing trails. He was ordained in 1822 and in 1833, with Jonathan and George Dresbach, established the first printing plant of the United Brethren, and launched the *Religious Telescope*, the official organ of the denomination. When financial troubles beset the institution he loaned large sums of money at little or no interest to keep it from bankruptcy.

In 1838 John Russel was called to the pastorate of the OTTERBEIN CHURCH in BALTIMORE, serving 1838-41, and again 1851-54. In the interim between pastorates and afterward he served as presiding elder, publishing agent, and bishop. He was elected to serve in eight sessions of the GENERAL CONFERENCE. The General Conference of 1845 elected him bishop for four years. Not being re-elected in 1849, he returned to his conference. Then in 1857 he was re-elected for an additional four years.

Largely self-educated, Russel became an editor of German literature and the compiler of a German hymnal. As a pulpit orator and in public debate he had few equals.

In the days when his denomination had no theological seminary, after his retirement to his farm near Keedysville, Md., he conducted seminars for ministerial students. The student body, at one time numbering fourteen, worked on the farm in the mornings for room and board, and were taught by Russel in the afternoons. His spacious home was used as a hospital during the Civil War following the battle of Antietam.

Mrs. Russel, who was a Miss Harmon, entered fully into the life and labors of her minister husband. In addition to her family and church duties, she made the bishop's clothing. Russel himself made his own shoes. At his death Dec. 21, 1870, near Keedysville, it was found that he had willed large sums of money for the education of young ministers.

Paul E. Holdcraft, *History of the Pennsylvania Conference.* Fayetteville, Pa.: Craft Press, 1938.
Koontz and Roush, *The Bishops.* 1950. PAUL E. HOLDCRAFT

RUSSELL, CHARLES LEE (1886-1948), twenty-first bishop of the C.M.E. CHURCH, was born on Sept. 22, 1886, in Campbell, Clark County, Ala. He received an A.B. degree from Frelinghusen College, the Bachelor of Hebrew and S.T.B. degrees from Veshiva College, and an M.A. degree from Dropsie University for Hebrew and Cognate Learnings in PHILADELPHIA. He served as parish minister and presiding elder in ALABAMA, FLORIDA, GEORGIA, KENTUCKY, and WASHINGTON, D.C. He was the author of several periodicals, books, and pamphlets, especially *Light From the Talmud*. At the General Conference in 1938, he was elected to the office of bishop. As a bishop he made a significant contribution in beginning a rehabilitation and expansion campaign in his episcopal area. He died on Feb. 8, 1948, and was buried in Washington, D.C.

Harris and Patterson, *C.M.E. Church.* 1965. RALPH G. GAY

RUSSELL, ELIZABETH HENRY (1749-1825), or "Madam Russell," pioneer American Methodist in the Holston area of TENNESSEE and VIRGINIA, was born in Hanover County, Va., July 10, 1749. In 1776 she married Colonel William Campbell, a hero of the battle of King's Mountain, who died in 1781. In 1783 she married General William Russell of Aspenvale, Va., and soon thereafter they settled at Saltville, or "the Salt Lick," where he engaged in the manufacture of salt.

In 1788 Asbury held the first conference west of the Alleghenies at the home of Stephen Keywood near Saltville. During that conference both General and Mrs. Russell were converted, and she became "probably more eminent in the Methodist pioneer history of America than any other woman." The General died in 1793 and Madam Russell moved to a spacious log house near Abingdon, Va. There she had a "prophet's chamber" where preachers were entertained, and she kept in the house a movable pulpit for preaching services.

When James Madison was a candidate for president of the United States he visited General Francis Preston, son-in-law of Mrs. Russell, at Saltville. Madison called on Madam Russell and she prayed for him as the prospective head of the nation. He is reported to have said, "I have heard all the first orators of America, but I never heard any eloquence as great as that prayer of Mrs. Russell."

Madam Russell was a friend of ASBURY and entertained

him in her home on several occasions. She died March 18, 1825, and was buried at Aspenvale at her own request. The church at Saltville is called the Madam Russell Memorial Church.

Clyde E. Lundy, *Holston Horizons.* Bristol, Tenn.: Holston Conference Inter-Board Council, 1947.
I. P. Martin, *Holston.* 1945.
R. N. Price, *Holston.* 1903-13.

ELMER T. CLARK

RUSSELLVILLE, KENTUCKY, U.S.A. **The Methodist Temple** is one of the oldest and most revered churches of KENTUCKY, the sanctuary being widely known for its beautiful stained glass windows. REDFORD lists only nine cities in Kentucky in 1811 in which Methodist churches had then been organized and Russellville was one of them. The first society was organized there in 1808 with ten charter members. They met in a frame house on the corner of Spring and Fourth Streets for about ten years, and the Methodists were the first organized church in this city. In 1818 they erected a church building on the corner of Eighth and Summer Streets.

The congregation grew slowly, but under the spiritual leadership of John Johnson, one of the more forceful early preachers, it grew to twenty-one members. His successor was Edward Stevenson, later president of Logan College. Under his ministry Russellville was detached from a circuit and became a station.

In 1854 the present building was erected under the pastorate of Thomas Bottomly. Of red brick, this building was remodeled in 1917. In 1962 the Inez Carr Crawford Educational Building was erected under the pastorate of Robert G. Shaver.

One of the noted windows of the church is "The Good Shepherd," given by the General Board of Church Extension of the M.E. Church, South in loving memory of DAVID MORTON, a native of Russellville and the founder and first secretary of the Church Extension Program of that denomination. Two of the Temples' former pastors, H. H. KAVANAUGH and HENRY C. MORRISON were elected to the episcopacy.

On Aug. 3, 1958, the Temple observed its Sesquicentennial with Bishop W. T. WATKINS as the speaker. On Oct. 31, 1965, another special celebration took place commemorating the life of JOHN LITTLEJOHN, pioneer preacher in VIRGINIA and Kentucky, who lies buried in a little cemetery on Second Street in Russellville. Bishop ROY H. SHORT unveiled a marker to Littlejohn in the town square.

The 1970 church membership was 577 and the total value of the church property was approximately $400,000.

General Minutes, UMC, 1970.
A. H. Redford, *Kentucky.* 1868-70.

ROBERT G. SHAVER

RUSSIA. When men from FINLAND let their Macedonian cry be heard in the Swedish Conference in session in STOCKHOLM in 1874, the presiding bishop, WILLIAM L. HARRIS, said that he "saw the finger of God point towards Finland and Russia." Ten years later B. A. CARLSON was appointed to HELSINKI, the capital of Finland. As soon as possible he also visited St. Petersburg, then the capital of the Russian Empire, of which Finland was a part. After the annual conference in 1889 Bishop C. H. FOWLER and Carlson visited the Russian capital and rented a house at Vasili Ostroff. In November of that year the first Meth-

odist congregation in St. Petersburg was organized with seven members. The work was carried on by preachers and laymen from Finland—one of them, Hjalmar Salmi, mastered three languages: Finnish, Russian, and Swedish. He became the best helper GEORGE A. SIMONS could get. Simons was sent from the United States by Bishop WILLIAM BURT and appointed superintendent for Finland and Russia, with special direction to carry on and develop the work among the Russians and throughout the whole of that vast empire, which at that time numbered 116,000,-000 inhabitants. These were "widening horizons" indeed.

During the following ten years, however, the Methodist work in Russia was concentrated in St. Petersburg, the district of Ingria (Ingermanland) west of that city, where the people were Finnish-speaking, and the BALTIC STATES—besides two congregations in far-off Siberia. When the work in Finland was organized as an annual conference in 1911, Russia became a "mission," and so was the work in the Baltic States until the Baltic and Slavic Missions Conference was organized in 1924.

In 1911 there were nineteen places mentioned in the appointments, eight however "to be supplied." In 1920 there were only six pastors in the Russia Mission. The First World War had claimed its victims, and so did the Russian Revolution, which began in 1917.

In the beginning the Russian Revolution was hailed as the dawn of liberty, but soon it changed its face. In October 1918, Simons was compelled to leave Russia. ANNA EKLUND, "Sister Anna of Petrograd," a Finnish DEACONESS, stayed as long as possible. She watched over the church property and the pastors' home. She was all to the little fighting congregation until she herself had to leave and take her refuge in ESTONIA and then in Finland. She had come to St. Petersburg in 1907 and organized a deaconess institution, instructed a group of young women to be nurses, and was the leader of a very great and important help work during the First World War and the hard years following.

In 1922 and 1923 Bishop JOHN L. NUELSEN paid short visits to Russia. His presence caused some sensation and great expectations, reflected in the volume of *World Service* of the M.E. Church, published in 1923. As a consequence some of the bishops and leading men were invited to Moscow by a reform movement within the Russian Orthodox Church, asking them to help in organizing a democratic living church. Out of it however came nothing.

After many difficulties RAYMOND J. WADE, in 1928 had been assigned as Bishop of Northern Europe, got a visa to Russia, and there held what appeared to be the last annual conference of the Russian Mission. This was in 1939 Bishop Wade writes. "It lasted all night. I baptized four children and married two couples. No one dared act as Secretary," states the bishop in a letter. The situation was such that the bishop advised the few remaining Methodists to join the Baptists or other evangelical group, "which they did. So Methodism as such went out of existence in Russia."

R. E. Diffendorfer, *World Service.* 1923.
B. A. Carlson, "The Rising and Extension of the M.E. Church in Finland." Ms., Stockholm, 1909.
K. J. Hurtig, *Metodismen i Finland.* 1925.
Journal of the European Central Conference, ME, 1922.
L. A. Marshall, *American Pioneer in Russia.* 1928.
Minutes of the Central Conference of Europe, ME, 1911.

Minutes of Finland Conference, 1908-23.
Minutes of the Finland and St. Petersburg Mission Conference, 1908.   MANSFIELD HURTIG

RUST COLLEGE, Holly Springs, Mississippi, was founded in 1866 by the FREEDMAN'S AID SOCIETY of the M. E. Church. From its founding until the late 1930's, work was offered in elementary, secondary, and higher education. Then elementary and secondary education was discontinued in order to obtain provisional approval by the regional accrediting association. Chartered in 1870 as Shaw University, the college changed its name in 1890 to honor Richard S. Rust, secretary of the Freedman's Aid Society.

The education of Negro teachers for the public schools of MISSISSIPPI has received continuing special attention at Rust College. Its alumni include some of the church's ablest leaders. The institution is accredited by the Mississippi State Department of Education. Degrees offered are the B.A. and B.S. The governing board has twenty-one members elected by the board, and three ex officio. The ownership of the college is vested with the Board of Education of The United Methodist Church.

JOHN O. GROSS

RUSTIN, JOHN WALLACE (1899-   ), American preacher and city pastor, was born at Glenville, Ga., on Sept. 3, 1899. His father was James Miller Rustin and his mother Tallulah Augusta (Sasser) Rustin. He was educated at EMORY UNIVERSITY, receiving his A.M. at Columbia in 1932, an honorary D.D. degree from Emory in 1940 and LL.D. from Norfolk College in 1936. His wife was Jessie Colt Watts and they have a son and two daughters.

He was ordained in the Methodist ministry at the VIRGINIA CONFERENCE of 1922, and after serving in Danville, 1922-27; Trinity Church, Salisbury, 1928-31; and Ghent Church, NORFOLK, 1931-36, he was stationed at Mount Vernon Place, WASHINGTON, D.C., where he served from 1936-50. He transferred to the TENNESSEE CONFERENCE and was stationed at Belmont Church, NASHVILLE, 1950-59, and then at Broad Street, Kingsport, 1959-64. He was a member of the Board of Directors of the Chinese Community Church in Washington, the Department of Social Relations, president of the Washington Federation of Churches, vice-president of the Committee of the Religious Life of the Nation's Capital, and served on the National Christian Mission, on the Department of Church and Economic Life of the FEDERAL COUNCIL OF CHURCHES, and is a trustee of SCARRITT COLLEGE, Nashville, Tenn. He retired in 1964 and is a visiting professor at the CANDLER SCHOOL OF THEOLOGY, Emory University, Atlanta, Ga.

Clark and Stafford, *Who's Who in Methodism.* 1952. N. B. H.

RUTER, CALVIN (1794-1859), American preacher, was born in Bradford, Orange Co., Vt., on March 15, 1794. He emigrated with his parents to OHIO. In 1817 he was received into the OHIO CONFERENCE of the M.E. Church. In 1820 he transferred to the MISSOURI CONFERENCE, which then embraced nearly all of INDIANA and the states of ILLINOIS and MISSOURI. In 1832 the INDIANA CONFERENCE was organized and Calvin Ruter was elected secretary. He was re-elected to this office for six consecutive years. At this conference he was appointed with ALLEN WILEY and James Armstrong to a committee to consider the building of a conference seminary. He was a founder of Indiana Asbury (later to be DePAUW UNIVERSITY) and served as a trustee for many years. He was elected five times as a delegate to GENERAL CONFERENCE. He died at Patriot, Ind., on June 11, 1859.

F. C. Holliday, *Indiana.* 1873.   ROBERT S. CHAFEE

MARTIN RUTER

RUTER, MARTIN (1785-1838), versatile and active American educator and pioneer missionary to Texas, was born at Charlton, Mass., on April 3, 1785. From boyhood he manifested an unusual thirst for knowledge and this marked him all his life. He was converted and united with the M. E. Church in 1799, and in 1801 was admitted into the NEW YORK CONFERENCE, having traveled a portion of the previous year in New England under JOHN BRODHEAD. In 1804 he was stationed in Montreal, CANADA, as this was before the War of 1812, which effactually, —but by amicable mutual agreement—later divided American Methodism on the Canadian-United States border.

The following year Ruter returned to New England and in 1809 was appointed to the NEW HAMPSHIRE district where he filled a number of prominent appointments. In 1818, his educational ability being recognized, he was put in charge of the New Market Wesleyan Academy, and this subsequently was removed to WILBRAHAM, Mass. In 1820 the GENERAL CONFERENCE elected him BOOK AGENT to found and conduct the book business at Cincinnati, just at that time becoming the western center of the BOOK CONCERN. He was reelected BOOK AGENT again in 1824, but before his term of service expired, he was appointed president of AUGUSTA COLLEGE, in KENTUCKY, which position he accepted in 1828, and remained in charge of that college until August 1832. Wishing to get back into the itinerant ranks, he was transferred and stationed as pastor in the city of PITTSBURGH. However, when ALLEGHENY COLLEGE at Meadville, Pa., was accepted by the Conference in 1833, Ruter was unanimously selected as its president.

At the General Conference of the M. E. Church in Cincinnati in May 1836, the news of the decisive battle of

San Jacinto, where TEXAS won its independence, came while the Conference was in session. The appeal which had been growing in insistency from the Methodists in Texas that ministers be sent them was felt by Ruter, who offered himself on the spot as a missionary to Texas. A good deal of discussion ensued among the leaders of the Church about the advisability of sending someone there, but when they became convinced that the freedom of Texas, then a republic under its Lone Star flag, was "measurably secure" and that they were not invading a forbidden land, Ruter obtained his commission to go—not, however, until the next year when Bishop HEDDING appointed him "superintendent of the Texas Mission." ROBERT ALEXANDER of the MISSISSIPPI CONFERENCE and LITTLETON FOWLER of the TENNESSEE CONFERENCE were selected to go with Ruter to "the foreign field," as Texas was then called. The vast Texas Methodism of today cherishes the names of Ruter, Alexander and Fowler as their founding fathers.

Ruter left his family, whom he was destined never to see again, at New Albany, Ind., and fearful of yellow fever then raging in NEW ORLEANS, felt compelled to wait until late in the year to begin his journey. Then he came down the Mississippi by steamboat, landing at Rodney, La., and rode on horseback across LOUISIANA to Texas.

Arrived there, it is said that Ruter "rode more than two thousand miles on horseback, swam or forded rivers; preached almost daily, and not unfrequently three times a day; shrank from no fatigue; avoided no hardships and no danger. . . . lived upon the rough fare, and slept in the still rougher lodgings of that wild and sparsely-populated region." (Simpson, p. 770.) He did such work during the one year he was destined to serve there that he ever after left a deep impress on Texas and its Methodism. He formed societies, secured the building of churches, made arrangements for the founding of a college, and laid out the greater part of the state into circuits. The following Spring he started homeward to get his family and make his report to the mission authorities, but after riding about fifty miles was taken seriously ill, and died in Washington, Texas, May 16, 1838.

The versatility as well as energy of Martin Ruter can be seen in the fact that among his other accomplishments he published a *Hebrew Grammar*, a *History of Martyrs*, and an *Ecclesiastical History*, as well as numerous sermons and letters on various subjects. Martin Ruter kept a personal *Journal* which reflects the enormous work he did while he was traveling about in Texas. The *Journal* is especially moving when he neared his end and realized his condition and noted that no physicians were immediately available. Friends and physicians were with him, however, in his last moments in Washington, Texas, May 16, 1838.

John O. Gross, *Martin Ruter, Pioneer in Methodist Education*. Nashville: Board of Education, 1956.
M. Phelan, *Texas*. 1924.
E. A. Smith, Martin Ruter. 1915.   N. B. H.

RUTLEDGE, WOOLLS WILLIAM (1849-1921), Australian minister, was the son of James Rutledge who had accepted the position of a teacher at Castlereagh, NEW SOUTH WALES in 1840 and subsequently joined the staff of a boys' school at Parramatta, founded by William Woolls.

Woolls Rutlege attended the University of Sydney and was a journalist on the SYDNEY newspapers *Harbinger*

and *The Empire* until he became editor of the *Newcastle Chronicle*. In 1875 he entered the ministry and was appointed to Orange, and from 1877 to 1880 served in Sydney at Waverley and Newtown. The following twelve years were spent in country appointments and in 1893 he ministered again in Sydney at Ashfield. In 1896 he followed W. G. Taylor as superintendent of the Central City Mission, Sydney.

The effect of the economic depression in 1893 was still severely felt and the Mission had to find $50,000. Rutledge, recognized as an eloquent preacher and a renowned singer, with extraordinary administrative gifts, succeeded in not only overcoming the financial difficulties, but also in extending the work by establishing a rehabilitation center for alcoholics.

He also commenced the "Pleasant Sunday Afternoon" programme which has continued through the years. In order to promote the spirit of Church Union he was appointed to Newcastle in 1901.

His outstanding contribution to Church Union was recognized when he was elected as the first president of the Conference of United Methodism.

In 1910-15 he organized the Centenary Thanksgiving Fund of which today WESLEY COLLEGE within the University of Sydney and LEIGH THEOLOGICAL COLLEGE, Enfield, New South Wales, are the fruits of his labors.

AUSTRALIAN EDITORIAL COMMITTEE

RWANDA, Africa, lies north of BURUNDI, and borders the eastern shore of Lake Kivu. This "Pearl of Africa" high altitude country has an area of 10,166 square miles and the same physical characteristics as Burundi. It was formerly a German colony, and was mandated to Belgium by the League of Nations after World War I. Later it became a trustee of the United Nations (1942). There is a president and forty-four member elected assembly. The population in 1969 was 3,500,000.

Until 1962 Rwanda and Burundi formed one mission field of the FREE METHODIST CHURCH. When two independent nations were established in 1962, separate conferences were organized. There is a new hospital at Kibogora, and a Bible School was opened in 1965.

As in Burundi, education has traditionally received generous government aid. Missionaries have been encouraged to organize and administer the educational program. Bible study is a regular part of the curriculum. The mission-administered schools reach the populated areas of the country. School buildings serve as churches on Sunday. Great congregations assemble for the district and conference meetings. There has been a genuine revival in this fast-growing field. In 1969 there were 7,000 Free Methodist members and 8,000 students.

BYRON S. LAMSON

RYAN, HENRY (1775-1833), Canadian preacher, was born April 22, 1775. He was converted at the age of sixteen; and after being turned out by his father, he acted as a local preacher in Dutchess County. Received on trial in 1800, for the next three years he served circuits in VERMONT. In 1802 he was ordained DEACON and in 1804 ELDER. While attending Conference at ASHGROVE, N.Y., in 1805, he responded to a call for volunteers to go to Upper Canada, and was appointed superintendent of the Bay of Quinte circuit; WILLIAM CASE was appointed as his assistant. For the next twenty-five years he led the Methodists of Upper Canada successfully through three great struggles, only to fail dismally in the fourth, causing the first tragic schism in Canadian Methodism.

F. Reid described Henry Ryan in an article which appeared in *The Northern Christian Journal*.

He was well nigh six feet in height, of large, symmetrical proportions, with prodigious muscular developments, and without doubt one of the strongest men in his age . . . His voice excelled, for power and compass, all that I ever heard from human organs. When occasion required, and it gave its full power, it was "as when a lion roareth."

The first contribution to Canadian Methodism by Henry Ryan was the initiation of the CAMP MEETING movement, so significant in the life of the people of Upper Canada. NATHAN BANGS, who attended the initial meeting at HAY BAY, Sept. 27-30, 1805, paid tribute to Ryan, who, though helped by William Case, planned, promoted, and carried through this evangelistic effort and thereby established the utility of this technique. The converts and the awakened souls were nurtured in the CLASS MEETINGS, the PRAYER MEETINGS, and the preaching services.

During these first five years in Upper Canada, Ryan served with energy and spirit in several circuits. He proved to be a man of great activity—bold to a fault, pious and practical, adventurous and aggressive. As an itinerant, he was a powerful preacher and a mighty man of prayer. His courage, his fighting spirit, his enthusiasm and his ready wit, combined to make him one of the most vivid and striking personalities among the preachers of Upper Canada before 1830.

In 1810, Ryan was appointed presiding elder for the Upper Canada District. When the War of 1812 began, Ryan, in spite of his American connections remained loyal to Canada and Britain. Although many of the American preachers left, he stood at his post holding the work together in those days of bitter conflict. Especially he brought hope, encouragement, and a sense of purpose to a perplexed people. Nothing can dim Ryan's achievement during the War of 1812-14.

The next phase of his career was marked by a struggle of another kind in which his character and devotion were illuminated. The Wesleyan Methodist Conference, which had to date shown little interest in the Canadas, now sent missionaries first to Lower Canada and later to Upper Canada. As early as 1815 Ryan, then presiding elder of Lower Canada, came into collision with the Wesleyan missionary and his supporters, in MONTREAL. Ryan refused to tolerate the presence of the latter, believing that in so doing he was carrying out his responsibility.

Immediately there was a sharp division. Ryan reported the situation to FRANCIS ASBURY, who laid the matter before the missionary society. At its 1816 session the Methodist GENERAL CONFERENCE, with Ryan present to plead his cause, affirmed that it could not relinquish its work in Lower Canada.

During the next four years the problem became increasingly acute. British immigrants poured into the colonies and anti-American sentiment grew. The removal of Ryan to Upper Canada did not help, for the British Wesleyans were there too, in smaller numbers. In 1820 agreement was finally reached. The British Wesleyans were to concentrate on Lower Canada, and the M.E. Church was to

minister to Upper Canada, a solution that Ryan reluctantly accepted.

The final issue, which resulted in Ryan's disgrace, developed in 1823 when he failed to secure election as a delegate to the General Conference. As a presiding elder he claimed this position as a right and was humiliated when his subordinate was chosen over him. Accompanied by a local preacher, he attended the Conference (May 1824) unofficially and secured the right to address the court, pleading for the independence of the CANADA CONFERENCE. While permitted to speak, he could not mistake the coolness shown to him.

So much dissension resulted from Ryan's subsequent agitation that the new Canada Conference meeting at Hallowell, Aug. 25, 1824, had to declare itself. Separation from the M.E. Church (which Ryan demanded at once) was said to be inevitable but had to be worked out legally and in a brotherly fashion. Ryan's attitudes and actions rendered him undesirable as a presiding elder; hence he was stationed at Chippewa, a mission where he had a farm. He accepted these decisions but was never able to rise above the defeat and discipline meted out to him.

In 1825 he became superannuated and gave full time to agitation for the independence of the Canada Conference. Since he knew that the next General Conference would probably grant his wish, his trouble-making was probably malicious. He could not grasp the fact that independence would come in spite of his actions. By this time he was accusing his fellow preachers of corruption and was distributing literature containing allegations against the Conference.

Hence at the Conference of 1827, presided over by Bishop HEDDING, Ryan was charged with circulating scurrilous printed material, and with disturbing the peace and unity of the church. After a careful investigation, he was judged guilty. Though the bishop reproved him in the kindest spirit, Ryan was deeply angered and was located. Subsequently he traveled through the church making inflammatory speeches and disquieting the people.

Eventually Ryan organized the Canadian Wesleyan Methodist Church. But, at the Conference of 1828 the independence for which Ryan had fought was accepted. This limited his followers to personal friends and disgruntled society members. With his death the impetus went out of the splinter group—which continued until 1841 when the 1,951 members voted to unite with the New Connexion.

Henry Ryan's last years were bitter and unhappy. The cause for which he had sacrificed triumphed in spite of him and without him. His unfortunate schism proved neither popular nor dangerous. The unrest and strife which he generated militated as much against his new denomination as it did against the regular church. History has punished him by largely ignoring his useful life. Ryan is a pathetic example of a mighty man who fell, carrying down with him the glory of his earlier achievements.

He died on Aug. 14, 1833 at Gainsborough, Upper Canada, and is buried in Grimsby Township.

J. Carroll, *Case and His Cotemporaries*. 1867-77.
Centennial of Canadian Methodism, 1891.
G. F. Playter, *Canada*. 1862.
E. Ryerson, *My Life*. 1883.
A. Stevens, *Nathan Bangs*. 1863.   ARTHUR E. KEWLEY

RYAN, SARAH (1724-1768), British Methodist, one of WESLEY's most intimate correspondents, was born of poor parents on Oct. 20, 1724. At the age of seventeen she was stirred by WHITEFIELD's preaching. Later she heard Wesley at the Foundry and joined the society there. She was three times married, but with Wesley's encouragement refused to join her second husband when he settled in America. She lived for a time with Mary Clark and SARAH CROSBY in Moorfields. In 1757 Wesley made her housekeeper at BRISTOL, where she incurred the jealous wrath of his wife. From 1762, she was a close companion of MARY Bosanquet (FLETCHER) at Leytonstone and later in Yorkshire, where she died on Aug. 17, 1768.

JOHN A. VICKERS

J. S. RYANG

RYANG, JU SAM (1879-1950?), first Korean bishop of the autonomous Korean Methodist Church, was born in Kong-Moon-Ri, South Pyeng-Ahn Province, Korea, Jan. 25, 1879. He studied Chinese classics in KOREA, and later completed the work in a Southern Methodist high school in Shanghai, where he was baptized. In 1906 he established a Korean church in SAN FRANCISCO, and this he served for three years.

After graduating from VANDERBILT UNIVERSITY and the Divinity School of Yale University, he returned to Korea to be one of the first Korean elders ordained by his denomination. His first appointments were characteristic of his career—teaching in the Methodist Union Theological Seminary in SEOUL; editing a church magazine, *The Theological World,* and serving a pastorate.

In 1918 he became Centenary Secretary and Literature Secretary for his annual conference, and in a four-year campaign in which his team visited every circuit, he opened 150 new churches and enrolled 16,000 new adherents. At the close of the campaign he became Conference Missionary Secretary, which position he held until 1940. In 1921 he took charge of the Siberia-Manchuria Mission and continued a life-long contact with this work.

He was the first Korean district superintendent of the M.E. Church, South's mission work and in that capacity served four years. When not acting as district superintendent he taught in the seminary.

In 1928-30 he led the campaign for union of the two branches of Methodism in Korea, and became the first general superintendent when the Korean Methodist Church was organized in 1930. He was re-elected in 1934, as the Korean Church provides for term episcopacy. Being restricted by the constitution of his church to two terms only, he gave full time again to editorial work and the supervision of the Manchurian Mission.

During World War II, Ryang acted as trustee for all Methodist Mission Board property in Korea. For his management during this difficult time he has been highly commended. In 1945 he was elected President of the Korean Red Cross. It was this "crime" for which he was abducted by the communists when they occupied Seoul in the summer of 1950. His whereabouts since then have remained unknown and he is presumed dead.

Bishop Ryang held honorary degrees from two American universities. Chief among his many publications was a bilingual work, *Southern Methodism in Korea,* published in 1929.

CHARLES A. SAUER

RYCKMAN, HAROLD H. (1902-   ), American mission executive of the FREE METHODIST CHURCH and an ordained elder in the Pacific Coast Latin America Conference, was born at Dale, N. D. He was educated at GREENVILLE COLLEGE, A.B., 1927; graduate studies, Whittier College, California; honorary D.D. degree, Los Angeles Pacific College, 1963. He married Evelyn A. Bartholomew in 1927 (deceased 1964); married Lucile Damon in 1966. His pastoral service has been in Southern California Conference, 1929-45; Missionary Superintendent, Paraguay, 1946-52; Brazil, 1952-62; architect and builder for BRAZIL seminary complex; Area Secretary for Latin America since 1962. He was Executive Secretary for Free Methodist World Fellowship, 1964-65.

BYRON S. LAMSON

RYERSON, ADOLPHUS EGERTON (1803-1882), Canadian minister and educator, was born near Vittoria, Norfolk County, Upper Canada, on March 24, 1803, to Joseph and Mehetabel Ryerson. Colonel Joseph Ryerson served as a Loyalist officer in the American Revolution, and subsequently migrated first to New Brunswick and thence to Upper Canada, where he farmed for the remainder of his long life.

As a member of a prominent family, Egerton Ryerson attended the local grammar school where he laid the foundations of a sound classical education. In these same years too he witnessed the War of 1812-14, in which his father and three elder brothers participated. After the war, perhaps owing to their mother who had been one of WILLIAM BLACK's attentive auditors in New Brunswick, Egerton, along with his brothers, George, William, and John, was converted in the Methodist fold. Although he joined the church, he was not attracted immediately to the ministry; rather in 1824 he entered the Gore District Grammar School in Hamilton, as a prelude to legal training.

Intent though he was upon academic pursuits, Ryerson

was still deeply concerned about his spiritual condition. Possibly this acounted in part for a critical illness in 1824-25, during which he had another profound religious experience. He gave his first sermon on Easter Sunday,

EGERTON RYERSON

1825; at the conference held in September 1825, he was taken on trial and posted to the York and Yonge Street circuit. JAMES RICHARDSON, the future Methodist Episcopal bishop, was his superintendent.

Although he was ordained at the appropriate times (1827-29) and was a vigorous preacher throughout his career, Egerton Ryerson's life was not played out in the itineracy. Within a year he challenged the existing political and religious establishment in a massive letter published on May 11, 1826. Abruptly the unknown junior minister became a celebrity in Upper Canada. From that time forward he grew in stature both to his friends and to his enemies, a development which was facilitated by his appointment as first editor of *The Christian Guardian* in 1829. He held this post until 1832, from 1833 to 1835, and from 1838 to 1840.

As an editor and controversialist Egerton Ryerson had few outstanding rivals in his generation. A subtle, if prolix stylist, writing in an age addicted to partisanship and misrepresentation, he was often misunderstood.

Fundamentally, Ryerson's views epitomized those of Canadian Methodism at its best. Politically he was a liberal-conservative, one who sought to maintain British North America's monarchical institutions and relationships. He was unsympathetic toward radical political changes; he was more concerned with the spirit in which the political system functioned than with its outward forms. The spirit he hoped and strove for was to be characterized by every action. Second, he was convinced that the state must treat all social and religious groups equitably. Undoubtedly he preferred that church and state should be kept separate and that all religious denominations should provide for their own needs in their own ways. If state support was afforded for religious ends, it should be distributed impartially. Third, Ryerson approached secular issues as a Canadian. What was best for any group in Canada could never be determined in the light of extra-

neous or foreign conditions. On the contrary all had to put aside their inherited or transmitted prejudices and to consider all issues in the light of Canadian circumstances and needs. Holding to these views, Ryerson contributed greatly to the liberalization of Canadian politics and to the satisfactory readjustment of the church-state relationship.

Before he gave up *The Guardian*, Ryerson was deeply involved in the third of his great interests—education. In his first years as editor, he commented frequently on this subject and especially on the necessity of breaking the Anglican monopoly on university education. His unceasing efforts secured a charter for Upper Canada Academy. After it became VICTORIA COLLEGE, Ryerson became its first principal in 1841, a post which he held until 1847. During his remaining years, Ryerson was continuously active in the resolution of the university question and in the maintenance of Victoria University as an institution in which higher education was provided in a Christian context.

In 1844 Egerton Ryerson accepted office as superintendent of education in Canada West (Ontario), a position which he retained until 1876. During these years, filled with incessant administrative and political labors and often with acrimonious battles, he laid the foundations of the Ontario educational system. His purpose, throughout, was to build a system in which a useful and relevant body of knowledge would be imparted to all children, and to maintain an intimate connection between the moral ideals shared by all Christians and the subjects taught in the schools. To this end he resisted the introduction of denominational elementary schools, but, when obliged to accept them, tried to regulate them fairly and generously. When he retired, Ontario had a primary school system which could bear favorable comparison with those of other western countries.

Despite his preoccupation with educational and political issues, Ryerson's concern for his own spiritual condition and for the Methodism to which he was so devoted never diminished. In many ways not easily traced he contributed to the Canadianization of Wesleyan Methodism and to the liberalization of the outlook of his brethren. His election in 1874 as the first president of the General Conference of The Methodist Church of Canada was a fitting and symbolic climax to his career as a Methodist itinerant.

In his latter years Ryerson worked happily and vigorously on three books that were dear to his heart: *The Loyalists of America and Their Times* (1880), *Canadian Methodism, Its Epochs and Characteristics* (1882), and *The Story of My Life* (1883). He died full of honors, at peace with his church, his neighbors, and his opponents, in Toronto, Feb. 19, 1882.

The enormous throng who crowded the great Metropolitan Church in Toronto for his funeral testified to the esteem and affection in which Ryerson was held.

E. Ryerson, *My Life*. 1883.
———, *Canadian Methodism*. 1882.
C. B. Sissons, *Egerton Ryerson*. 1937, 1947. G. S. FRENCH

RYERSON, JOHN (1799-1878), Canadian minister, wise administrator, one whose aim was to preserve the institution and dignity of the Methodist Church, was born at Long Point, Upper Canada, the third son of Colonel Joseph Ryerson, a staunch Anglican Loyalist. To his dismay, five of his six sons became Methodist preachers,

John being the first to itinerate. With his two older brothers, George and William, John had a deep religious experience in 1815, probably at a Methodist CAMP MEETING. In spite of his father's opposition, he began to travel as a preacher on the Long Point circuit in 1820. The next year he was received on trial, "aged twenty-one, single, and not in debt." In 1823 he was ordained a DEACON and in 1825, an ELDER.

In spite of his studious ways and his ability to preach great sermons, he was destined to be an ecclesiastical statesman rather than a preacher or a pastor. His long list of high offices, heavy responsibilities, and honors begins in 1827 with his appointment as presiding elder of the Niagara district. In 1832 he was presiding elder of the Bay of Quinte district, and subsequently he was many times chairman of district. In 1843 he was elected president of Conference. He was chosen co-delegate from 1850 to 1858, the representative to the British Wesleyan Conference in 1846 and 1849: and representative to the GENERAL CONFERENCE of the M.E. Church in the United States twice.

He was elected to the important post of BOOK STEWARD in 1837 and held this office until 1841. With his brother's support, EGERTON RYERSON was re-elected in 1838 editor of *The Guardian*. The two brothers were key figures in determining the Methodist response to the Rebellion of 1837, in the removal of Principal MATTHEW RICHEY from Upper Canada Academy, and in the clash between the British and Canadian Wesleyans, leading to the disruption of 1840. The resolution and determination of John Ryerson, coupled with the debating and journalistic skills of his brother Egerton, were closely related to the Canadian Methodists' successful defence of their cause.

While attending the British Wesleyan Conference in 1846, John Ryerson entered into negotiations with ROBERT ALDER—negotiations that brought the reunion of the two Conferences in 1847. The new basis of union was so well-constructed that the two Conferences were able to collaborate effectively until other events suggested a new basis of separation. It was appropriate that John Ryerson became for several years the Canadian vice-president of Conference.

As a senior statesman, he was asked in 1854 to visit the territories of the Hudson's Bay Company, to investigate and reorganize the missionary work begun earlier by the Wesleyan Missionary Society. Upon completion of his long and arduous inspection tour he made his report, which was printed in 1855 under the title, *Hudson's Bay: or a Missionary Tour in the Territory of the Honorable Hudson's Bay Company*. He stressed that only eighteen Protestant missionaries served the vast area—thirteen Anglicans, four Methodists, and one Presbyterian. His journal provided invaluable information about the social and religious life of the Northwest at the middle of the nineteenth century.

Faced by declining health, John Ryerson became a superannuated preacher in 1860. He continued, however, to take an active interest in his church. Much of the material in Egerton Ryerson's *Canadian Methodism: Its Epochs and Characteristics*, a work which threw much light on the history of Canadian Methodism, was supplied by him. It reflected his awareness of the changing character of Methodism and of its changing role in Canadian society.

To his contemporaries he must have appeared austere, and deficient in the emotional fervor which Methodists were expected to display. He was in fact an ecclesiastical statesman, who labored mightily and effectively for the welfare of the Methodist Church in Canada. Aged, lonely, and almost forgotten, he died near Simcoe, Ontario, Oct. 8, 1878, and was buried in the Ryerson Cemetery.

Nathanael Burwash, *Egerton Ryerson*. Toronto: Oxford University Press, 1926.
J. Carroll, *Case and His Cotemporaries*. 1867-77.
A. Green, *Life and Times*. 1877.
C. B. Sissons, *Egerton Ryerson*. 1937, 1947.   A. E. KEWLEY

RYERSON, JOSEPH WILLIAM (1797-1872), Canadian minister, was born in New Brunswick, into an Anglican and Loyalist family. As a boy he took part in the War of 1812-14 and subsequently became a farmer and local preacher in Oxford County (Upper Canada). Received on trial in 1823, at the last session of the GENESEE CONFERENCE, in which Canadian Methodists participated, he was ordained in 1825.

Although he had little formal education, William Ryerson rapidly attained an outstanding reputation as an eloquent and fearless orator, one who could move masses of people "like forest trees swayed to and fro by the wind." His energy and ability brought prompt recognition among his brethren. He became a presiding elder in 1828 and a district chairman after the union of 1833. In 1840 he accompanied his brother, EGERTON RYERSON, to the fateful session of the British Conference which resulted in the severance of the 1833 union. As an outspoken defender of Canadian interests, he was elected president of the CANADA CONFERENCE in 1841 and again in 1847.

Superannuated in 1858, Ryerson returned to a farm near Brantford (Canada West). As he had long been interested in politics and closely identified with the liberally minded among his brethren, it was natural for him to seek election to the provincial legislature in 1861. He was returned, and kept his seat through two sessions. Increasingly infirm in his later years, he died at his farm in 1872, and was buried in the cemetery of the Sour Springs Church.

J. Carroll, *Case and His Cotemporaries*. 1867-77.
Christian Guardian, June 11, 1873.
C. B. Sissons, *Egerton Ryerson*. 1937, 1947.   G. S. FRENCH

RYFF, JULES (1874-1961), American FREE METHODIST pioneer missionary to Africa, was born in SWITZERLAND Dec. 21, 1874. He came to the United States at the age of sixteen, and worked in lumber mills and on farms. Converted in young manhood, he entered SEATTLE PACIFIC COLLEGE (then a Seminary) to prepare for full-time Christian service. He taught school for several years, served as pastor in the Washington Conference, then felt called to Africa. He married Elisabeth Ellen Eva, Oct. 8, 1902. In 1903 he and his wife went to SOUTH AFRICA, served two years at Fairview, Natal, and then transferred to Germiston. He superintended mission work at the compounds of the mines.

In his early years of missionary service, his wife died. A few years later, he married Ethel Davey. His children were: Lois, Ruth, Helen, and Frederic, the latter a Free Methodist missionary in the Transvaal.

Jules Ryff was a superior linguist, a master of German, English, French, Latin, Greek, as well as Sheetswa, Zula and other African dialects. He was adept in handling affairs with the nationals, government officials, and mine superintendents. He was truly a missionary statesman. He gave in all fifty years of missionary service, and died in Germiston, Dec. 15, 1961.

The Free Methodist, January 1962.
B. S. Lamson, *Free Methodist Missions.* 1951.

BYRON S. LAMSON

RYLAND, WILLIAM (c. 1770-1846), American minister who became chaplain of both Houses of the Congress of the United States, was born in IRELAND and migrated to MARYLAND in 1788. J. E. ARMSTRONG said that this was when he was eighteen years of age and that he first settled in Harford County, Md., where he was converted.

He came to BALTIMORE and entered the BALTIMORE CONFERENCE in 1802 and for twenty-seven years was in the itinerant ranks. He was a delegate to four GENERAL CONFERENCES of his Church. He served as CHAPLAIN both of the House of Representatives and the U.S. Senate and during that time acted as pastor to President Andrew Jackson and his family. After his superannuation, he acted as chaplain in the U.S. Navy, being stationed at the Marine Barracks in WASHINGTON where he spent the remainder of his life. He died Jan. 19, 1846. His papers are preserved in the Methodist Historical Society, Baltimore.

J. E. Armstrong, *Old Baltimore Conference.* 1907.

EDWIN SCHELL

Julio Sabanes

SABANES, JULIO MANUEL (1897-1963), bishop, was born in Montevideo, Uruguay, July 2, 1897, the son of Methodist parents. After attending primary school, he secured gainful employment and in time became a bank clerk. Joining the church, he rose to leadership in the Methodist Youth Movement, and was one of the founders of *La Idea*, the organization's periodical in Uruguay. Also, he engaged in open air evangelistic preaching. He married Juana Puch, the daughter of a Methodist minister, March 10, 1923, and they had three children, Julio Ruben who is a pastor and district superintendent in Argentina, and Charlos, and Miriam.

Sabanes joined the River Plate Annual Conference on trial in 1923 and was ordained elder in 1927. He was appointed traveling evangelist for Uruguay. In 1926 he served two small churches near Montevideo, and later became assistant pastor of Central Church in the city. In 1929 he was appointed to Central Church, Rosario, Argentina's second largest city where he served eighteen years. During part of that time he was also district superintendent in Rosario and editor of *El Estandarte Evangelico*, the conference magazine. He was a delegate to five Central Conference sessions and to the 1940 General Conference, Atlantic City, New Jersey.

In 1947, Sabanes was appointed to Central Church, Buenos Aires, and district superintendent in that city. During the next five years he engaged in many civic and community activities along with his church work. In September 1952, the dictatorial regime of President Juan Peron banned him from his pulpit and forbade him to engage in pastoral work.

In November 1952, the Latin American Central Conference elected Sabanes bishop, and in 1956 he was reelected for four more years. He was assigned to the Santiago Area (later Pacific Area) which included Chile, Peru, Panama, and Costa Rica. With his episcopal headquarters in Santiago, Chile, Sabanes traveled and superintended his area for the next seven years. Also, he attended several meetings of the Council of Bishops and the 1956 General Conference in Minneapolis. Because of poor health, Sabanes retired at the session of the Latin America Central Conference at Lima, Peru, in 1960. Known as a "gentle person" who was "greatly beloved," he spent his remaining days at his home in Buenos Aires, where he died after a long illness, Aug. 29, 1963.

World Outlook, October, 1963.
JESSE A. EARL
ALBEA GODBOLD

SACKETT, ALFRED BARRETT (1895-   ), British Methodist, born at Strood, Kent, England, the only son of A. B. Sackett, Wesleyan minister. He was educated at Kingswood School and Merton College, Oxford. During the Great War of 1914-18 he served with the Northumberland Fusiliers, winning the Military Cross. After six years as housemaster at Christ's Hospital (transferred from London to Horsham, Sussex, in 1902), in 1928 he began an eminently successful headmastership, lasting thirty-one years, at his old school, John Wesley's foundation, Kingswood School. He has served on many Methodist committees, including the World Methodist Council.

FRANK BAKER

SACO, MAINE, U.S.A. **School Street Church.** Jesse Lee, sometimes called the apostle to New England, preached the first Methodist sermon ever heard in Saco village, Maine, on Sept. 10, 1793. His text was "Behold ye despisers and wonder and perish" (Acts 13:41). After passing the night at the home of Dr. Josiah Fairfield, he left on his further travels in the province of Maine.

The first Methodist church in Saco was dedicated in 1828, and was known as Wesleyan Hall and "the Corn Crib." Four years later a larger building was needed. The church continued to grow and many members were added to the Kingdom of Christ. In 1847, the Methodist society had grown enough to warrant being host to the Maine Annual Conference. In 1943 on the one hundred and fiftieth anniversary of Jesse Lee's visit, Bishop G. Bromley Oxnam gave the anniversary address on "The Crusade for a New World Order." Through the years the loyalty, faithfulness, and charity of the School Street members and pastors has been marked.

JOHN H. JORDAN

SACRAMENT OF HOLY COMMUNION. (See Communion, The Holy.)

SACRAMENTAL FELLOWSHIP, METHODIST (British), is a devotional society of some 400 ministers and laymen pledged to pray daily for corporate Christian unity, seeking to foster the churchmanship and catholic inheritance of British Methodism. Originating in the 1920's among a group of Wesleyan ministers led by T. S. Gregory, it was inaugurated as a society in 1935 on a three-fold basis of doctrine, sacramental worship, and reunion. Its presidents have been Alfred E. Whitham (1935); J. E. Rattenbury (1938), and Donald Soper (1950). Annual conferences have maintained a high level of ecumenical understanding, and the society continues to exercise an influence largely disproportionate to its numerical strength. In association with certain other groups it publishes a bulletin, and it maintains contact with parallel movements in other communions.

A. S. Gregory

SACRAMENTO, CALIFORNIA, U.S.A., seat of Sutter's Fort, mecca of overland immigrants to California. Dr. William Grove Deal, physician and local preacher, began a Methodist ministry in the open air and aboard a ship. William Roberts organized a Methodist church in July 1849, on the foundation laid by Deal, and left the work in Deal's care.

John Sutter donated to the M.E. Church a lot on the southeast corner at Seventh and L Streets, and on this was erected a chapel shipped from Baltimore, the first church building in Sacramento. Isaac Owen arrived to serve as pastor on Oct. 23, 1849. On October 28 he received seventy-two persons into the church, and one week later held the first services in the new church edifice. Owen, who was thereafter to serve as presiding elder, was followed as pastor in 1850 by M. C. Briggs for the first of three pastorates in that city. Influential in opposing intemperance and slavery, he also led the California delegation to the convention which nominated Lincoln for the presidency in 1864.

One Methodist layman, J. H. Ralston, a brother of the prominent Methodist theologian, T. N. Ralston, wrote to his sister, Mrs. James B. Dodd of Kentucky, from Sacramento in 1850 as follows: ". . . There is much Drinking, gambling, etc in all this country. Say to Neely [T. N. Ralston], a vast field is open for Preachers. Why does not the church send them out here. . . . Preaching is Kneeded here as much as any where. . . ."

In 1852 a larger church was built, but soon was destroyed by fire. Rebuilt on the same site the new building was a few years later sold to the Jewish congregation to be the first synagogue on the Pacific coast. The fourth building was erected on Sixth Street in 1859-60 and completed in 1870. A historical marker indicates the site of the pioneer Methodist church.

The work of the M.E. Church, South was begun in Sacramento in April 1850, and a chapel was erected in August of that year on Seventh Street between J and K Streets. D. W. Pollock was the pioneer leader, but his health soon failed and he was succeeded by local preacher Penmann. In 1851 W. R. Gober assumed the work and also organized a school, Asbury Institute. Gober was capable and influential, and served two pastorates in Sacramento.

Perhaps the outstanding lay Methodist in Sacramento was Mrs. Lizzie Glide, who worked ardently in city mission work and gave generously, providing for the building of residence halls for girls in two cities and at Asbury College in Kentucky. The Glide Foundation which she established has had a deep and valued influence in California. C. M. and Mary Glide Goethe provided financial backing for city and state councils of churches and many other good works. Goethe has been widely honored for leadership in appreciation of nature and in guidance of youth.

Most noted among Sacramento Methodist preachers in this century was A. Raymond Grant, elected bishop while pastor at First Church. In 1970 there were seventeen United Methodist churches in Sacramento in addition to a ministry to students at Sacramento State College. There are eighteen ministers, and 7,431 members.

The Sacramento Methodist Union serves as a church extension society, and has been instrumental in securing sites on which a number of churches have been built.

First Church, organized in 1849, was a contemporary and not a child of the "gold-rush." There was no "god-rush" in the "gold-rush." But even before prospectors came seeking gold for men, pioneer preachers came seeking men for God.

William Taylor and Isaac Owen were sent by authority of the M.E. Church to California. Bishop Taylor came by way of "the Horn" at the tip of South America. Isaac Owen came by ox-team across the plains and mountains. When he arrived, he found Taylor already working in San Francisco, so he came on to Sacramento. Before leaving the east Taylor's friends in Baltimore framed and furnished a chapel 24 by 36 feet intended for San Francisco. It was shipped around Cape Horn and because Sacramento had a stronger society in need of a building, it was shipped on to Sacramento.

Since 1849, the original "Baltimore-California" Chapel and other church buildings have been replaced and congregations have risen and combined until in 1924 First Church became the latest successor, growing to be the second largest church in the California-Nevada Conference. Now a modern, multiple-staff institution of 2,060 members, it carries in stone over its main entrance, the figure of the Circuit Rider and the words: "To the pioneers of the Cross through whose heroism and self sacrifice we owe our present Methodism in this the Capital City of California."

Like them, First Church is still pioneering its program geared to serving from within the heart of a great and growing Capital City.

C. V. Anthony, *Fifty Years.* 1901.
California Christian Advocate.
L. L. Loofbourow, *In Search of God's Gold.* 1950.
J. C. Simmons, *Pacific Coast.* 1886.
Don M. Chase
Robert A. Panzer

SACRAMENT, THE. "Sacraments," states Article of Religion XVI (number XXV of the XXXIX of the Church of England), "ordained of Christ are not only badges or tokens of Christian men's profession, but rather they are certain signs of grace, and God's good will toward us, by which he doth work invisibly in us, and doth not only quicken, but also strengthen and confirm, our faith in Him. There are two Sacraments ordained of Christ our Lord in the Gospel; that is to say, Baptism and the Supper of the Lord."

This affirmation explains itself and denominates the two Sacraments which Methodism with the Protestant world accepts as such. *Sacrament* is from the Latin *sacramentum*. "The Romans used the word for their military oath and in that sense it has great significance, as in this ordinance, as well as in Baptism, we swear allegiance to the captain of our salvation," so stated Thomas O. Summers, an authority in this field. For a further explanation of these two sacraments, see Baptism and Communion, The Holy.

Article of Religion XVI, the first part of which is quoted above, goes on to mention five other rites "commonly called sacraments, that is to say, confirmation, penance, orders, matrimony, and extreme unction." The Article holds that these are "not to be counted for Sacraments of the Gospel; being such as have grown out of the corrupt following of the apostles, and partly are states of life allowed in the Scriptures, but yet have not the like nature of Baptism and the Lord's Supper, because they have not any visible sign or ceremony ordained of God." (See also Doctrinal Standards of Methodism.)

J. C. Bowmer, *Lord's Supper*, 1961.
————, *Sacrament*. 1951.
Robert W. Goodloe, *The Sacraments in Methodism*. Nashville: Methodist Publishing House, 1943.
N. B. Harmon, *Rites and Ritual*. 1926.   N. B. H.

SAHAI, GEORGE SYLVESTER (1908-1966), Indian minister and educator, was a third-generation Christian. His father was an ordained Methodist minister. Lucknow University conferred upon him the B.A., B.Ed.Sc., M.A., and Ph.D. degrees. He studied for a time in the Union Theological Seminary, New York. He married Lois Tika in 1934.

After seventeen years on the faculty of the Lucknow Christian College teaching history, he was appointed pastor of one of Indian Methodism's greatest churches, Central Church in Lucknow. In 1957 he became the first Indian principal of Leonard Theological College. Sahai's Ph.D. dissertation was on the subject, "Christian Missions and Indian Education." He set forth impressively the contribution of Christian missions to the development of modern education in India.

Sahai represented the Lucknow Annual Conference in the 1960 General Conference, and was a delegate to the tenth World Methodist Conference in Oslo, where he read a paper on Methodist beliefs. He represented the Methodist Church of Southern Asia in the World Council of Churches Assembly in New Delhi. He lectured in the United States on the theology of missions, conducted Bible study classes for the interdenominational missionary conference at Lake George, N. Y., and twice taught classes on missions at Garrett Seminary summer sessions.

He died in 1966 at Jabalpur from a heart attack, and is buried there.

The Indian Witness, 1966.   J. Waskom Pickett

SAINT, CHARLES (1764-1840), was born in England and came to Bonavista, Newfoundland, where he was converted under the ministry of George Smith, first Methodist missionary to Bonavista. After Smith's departure in 1796, Bonavista had no missionary for fourteen years, and during this period Charles Saint served as class leader and local preacher, and kept alive Methodism. He gave faithful and devoted service and strong leadership throughout his life.

Bonavista became—and still is—one of the largest pastoral charges in the Newfoundland Conference.

T. W. Smith, *Eastern British America*. 1877.   N. Winsor

ST. GEORGE'S CHURCH edifice, located at 235 North Fourth Street, Philadelphia, Pa., is the oldest Methodist meeting house in continuous use in America and one of the shrines of The United Methodist Church. Its claim to be the world's oldest Methodist Church edifice in continuous service has been challenged by the British Methodists.

The edifice was purchased by the Methodists in 1769 under the leadership of Joseph Pilmore from William Branson Hockley, whose mentally deficient son had purchased it at auction from a splinter group of the Dutch Reformed Church currently located at Fourth and Race Streets. The building as purchased consisted of four brick walls, a roof and a dirt floor. It was sold when the splinter group, who had over-extended themselves in borrowing money for the building, were unable to borrow further funds although they appealed both to the Anglican and the Dutch Reformed churches. The Trustees of the original project were arrested for the indebtedness on the building, and the auction was contrived to secure funds to pay the indebtedness and secure the release of the trustees from jail.

The St. George's Society, itself, was organized two years previously, in 1767, by Captain Thomas Webb who, on coming to Philadelphia from New York, had found a small group of the converts of George Whitefield meeting irregularly in a sail loft on Dock Creek (now Dock Street) at Front Street. Their leaders were Edward Evans, a cordwainer, maker of fine shoes for ladies, and James Emerson, an Irishman, a seller of Orange Lemon Shrub. These men, converted under Whitefield in 1741, had formed a group of "Methides," as they were then called, and held it together for twenty-six years until the coming of Webb who organized the group into "The Religious Society of Protestants called Methodists." Under Webb's inspired preaching and leadership the Society grew and in 1768 sought larger quarters in a house located at 8 Loxley Court. Prayer meetings were held on the first floor of the house and public preaching services were conducted in the courtyard in front of the building, with the preacher proclaiming his message through the window on the second floor, to the group gathered below in the yard. When Joseph Pilmore and Richard Boardman, Wesley's first Missionaries to America, arrived in Philadelphia in 1769 the Society had grown to about 100 members. Under Pilmore's prodding the Society again sought larger quarters and subsequently purchased the present structure. The building had been named St. George's Church by the Dutch Reformed splinter group when they were seeking financial aid from the Anglicans, and the Methodists continued the name. Asbury is purported to have referred to the building as the "Cathedral of Methodism."

Although St. George's is not the oldest Society in America, its building is the oldest in continuous use and its history is marked by a distinguished list of "firsts" and other important events.

All Wesley's itinerants visited St. George's first on coming to America, Philadelphia being at that time the port of entry to the new world. On Oct. 7, 1769, the first hymns published by an American Society were printed for St.

ST. GEORGE'S CHURCH, PHILADELPHIA, PENNSYLVANIA

George's. On Dec. 3, 1769, Joseph Pilmore here made the first public statement in America of the faith and the body of Principles of Methodism. On Dec. 8, 1769 he held at St. George's the first PRAYER MEETING in America, called "Intercession." The first Wesleyan itinerant licensed to preach by an American Society, JOHN KING, was licensed by Pilmore at Old St. George's Aug. 31, 1770. The first WATCH NIGHT held in America was held in St. George's Nov. 1, 1770, and on October 28 of the following year Francis Asbury preached his first sermon in America. The first three Conferences of American Methodism were held at Old St. George's in 1773, 1774, and 1775, and on Nov. 7, 1784, THOMAS COKE first publicly proclaimed and explained Wesley's new plan of church government for the American Methodists.

In 1784 RICHARD ALLEN, the first Negro licensed to preach by the Methodists in America, was licensed by St. George's and in the same year the church licensed Absalom Jones, the second Negro licensed to preach by the Methodists in America. In 1789 the Methodist Book Concern, now the METHODIST PUBLISHING HOUSE, was organized here by JOHN DICKINS, the pastor of St. George's. He lies buried in the churchyard behind the church, and EZEKIEL COOPER, his successor as "Book agent," lies buried at the front entrance. This is only a partial list of the distinctions of the Church.

It is informative also to note that John Adams of MASSACHUSETTS, representative to the first Continental Congress and later second President of the United States, worshipped here at times, and that THOMAS RANKIN records in his Journal that some of the Continental Congress worshipped at Old St. George's. According to a former

pastor of the church, FRANCIS TEES, St. George's through its history has financially aided in organizing or in preserving over 100 churches along the eastern seaboard. Tees also stated that numerous revivals have marked the history of the church, the most noted being 1836 when 1,281 persons were converted and fifty-three young men entered the ministry.

In 1920 when the Delaware River (now the Benjamin Franklin) Bridge was built, the church was threatened with destruction since the plans for the bridge placed one abutment where the church still stands. Through the influence and leadership of Bishop THOMAS NEELY the plans of the bridge were changed, the church was saved, and the roadbed of the bridge moved further south.

During the pastorate of Albert W. Cliffe guides for tourists visiting the building were added to the staff. During the pastorate of FREDERICK E. MASER (1958-1967) group visitations were encouraged, with groups coming from as far away as CHINA and AUSTRALIA, and the pastor made several preaching tours in the United States, Europe, and the South Pacific in the interest of the church. During this pastorate also the trustees instituted the St. George's Gold Medal Award presented annually to at least one layman and one minister for "distinguished service to The Methodist Church." The medal is patterned after the seal of Old St. George's, a dove carrying an olive branch in its bill surrounded by the words, "Let brotherly love continue." Among the first recipients were CHARLES C. PARLIN, Bishop FRED PIERCE CORSON, JAMES T. BUCKLEY and George Ruck. Subsequent recipients have constituted a Who's Who in American Methodism.

In 1967 under the leadership of the present pastor, Dr. John H. Barnes, an additional award was instituted, "The John Wesley Ecumenical Award." It commemorates both John Wesley's sermon, "The Catholic Spirit," and the Second Vatican Council. Among the first recipients was John Cardinal Krol of Philadelphia.

In its Historical Center adjoining the sanctuary, the Church houses the possessions of the Historical Society of the EASTERN PENNSYLVANIA CONFERENCE, including nearly 10,000 volumes of Methodistica and memorabilia of early Methodism. Among these are Asbury's Bible, spectacles and razor, Pilmore's *Journal*, the desk over which THOMAS RANKIN presided at the first conference of Methodist preachers in America, early LOVE FEAST cups, and letters of Asbury, Wesley, Whitefield and other early Methodists.

With the rehabilitation of the neighborhood near old St. George's and the establishment near the church of a residential area known as "Society Hill," it is hoped that a larger membership will result and that the past glories of Old St. George's will become present and future possibilities.

A. W. Cliffe, *Our Methodist Heritage*. 1957.
F. H. Tees, *Ancient Landmark of American Methodism or Historic Old St. George's*. Philadelphia: Message Publishing Co., 1951.
————, *Beginnings of Methodism*. 1940.

FREDERICK E. MASER

ST. JOHN'S RIVER CONFERENCE was organized Jan. 25, 1886, in Jacksonville, Fla., with Bishop E. G. AN-DREWS presiding. Composed of white ministers and churches, it was formed by dividing the denomination's FLORIDA CONFERENCE on racial lines. After 1886, the latter conference continued as a Negro conference.

The boundaries of the St. John's River Conference included FLORIDA east of the Appalachicola River and a small fraction of south GEORGIA. At the outset it had fifteen preachers, one probationer, five available supplies, and 657 members. By 1900 it had grown to twenty-eight appointments and 1,160 members.

For a few years, beginning in 1887, the conference published a paper called the *Florida Methodist*. The St. John's River Conference College was launched at Orange City in 1887, but for lack of financial resources it failed in five years. Thereafter some support was given to Cookman Institute at Jacksonville, a school for Negroes founded in 1874 by the FREEDMEN'S AID SOCIETY. Cookman merged with a school for Negro girls in 1922 to become BE-THUNE-COOKMAN COLLEGE at Daytona Beach. In 1928, the conference began patronizing TENNESSEE WESLEYAN COLLEGE, Athens, Tenn., and was given representation on that school's board of trustees.

The St. John's River Conference grew rapidly in the 1920's when large numbers of people from the North, many of them members of the M. E. Church, moved to Florida.

There was little fellowship or cooperation between the conferences of the two Episcopal Methodisms in Florida until the 1920's. In 1936, the St. John's River Conference joined the FLORIDA CONFERENCE (MES) in supporting the Methodist Children's Home at Enterprise. Voting unanimously for Methodist union, the St. John's River Conference came to the merger in 1939 with fifty-two pastoral charges and 14,085 members. SCHUYLER E. GARTH, who served as superintendent of the MIAMI Dis-

trict in the 1920's and was elected bishop in 1944 from the NORTH CENTRAL JURISDICTION, was one of several able leaders developed in this relatively small conference.

General Minutes.
C. T. Thrift, Jr., *The Trail of the Florida Circuit Rider*. 1944.

JESSE A. EARL

ST. LOUIS, MISSOURI, U.S.A. (population 607,718 in 1970), was founded in 1764 as a fur trading post in the wilderness. Prior to 1804 only the Roman Catholic religion was permitted in the city. However, beginning in 1798, JOHN CLARK, a Methodist preacher in ILLINOIS, secretly crossed over to MISSOURI and preached several times in the environs of St. Louis.

For a decade after St. Louis became a part of the United States, the Protestant preachers left it "to the Catholics and the infidels" and went to the rural areas which were then regarded as the more promising missionary fields.

Presbyterian, Baptist and Episcopalian missionaries began preaching in St. Louis in 1816, 1817, and 1819, respectively. Officially the Methodists began work in Missouri in 1806 when the WESTERN CONFERENCE appointed John Travis to the Missouri Circuit which extended some 300 miles up and down the Mississippi River and some fifty miles west. In the next decade several strong circuits were established in the rural areas. In 1817 JOHN SCRIPPS, who had been appointed to the Cold Water Circuit north and west of St. Louis, decided to make St. Louis a preaching point on his work. Learning that Joseph Charles, editor of the *Missouri Gazette*, had a Methodist background, Scripps asked his help. As a result, the paper announced Scripps' first preaching appointment in St. Louis for Sunday, April 23, 1817. The service was held in a log house which served the town as a theater. Later the Presbyterians allowed Scripps to use their little frame house, and he regularly preached there once every three weeks until the end of the conference year. Scripps saw "no visible results" but he believed good could be done in St. Louis. The preachers who followed Scripps in the next three years made no effort to establish work in St. Louis. One said he had no building in which to hold services, and another, according to Scripps, found work on the circuit more congenial.

JESSE WALKER, the "Daniel Boone of Methodism," a man of practical ability and marked determination, established Methodism in St. Louis. From 1807 to 1819 Walker rode circuits and served as PRESIDING ELDER in Illinois and Missouri. For reasons which are not clear, the MISSOURI CONFERENCE appointed him "missionary" in 1819 and 1820. This of course allowed him to work where he pleased in the conference. Walker and Scripps were friends, and since both had St. Louis on their hearts, Scripps encouraged Walker to try to establish a Methodist church in the city. Knowing the undertaking would be difficult, Walker laid his plans carefully. Leaving his family on his farm in Illinois, he rented an old two-room log structure in St. Louis, and lived in one room and fitted up the other as a chapel and a school room. He brought provisions from his farm. In the late fall of 1820, he announced his first preaching appointment in St. Louis. About a dozen came. Walker then visited throughout the town, making acquaintances and inviting people to church. As time passed, he won more adherents by his simple goodness than by his sermons, for he was not an impressive preacher.

In January 1821, Walker organized a class of six. His congregation soon outgrew the log house and even the courthouse nearby. Though he had no money, Walker determined to build a church. A man in Illinois gave him timber. He then begged money and had the logs cut and brought across the river. With the help of three men, he cut the lumber with a whipsaw, and in 1822 built a frame church thirty-five by forty-five feet at Fourth and Myrtle Streets, now Fourth and Clark. Thus was erected the first Protestant church building in St. Louis.

The Missouri Conference met in the St. Louis church, Oct. 24, 1822, and WILLIAM BEAUCHAMP, an eloquent preacher, was appointed there. Walker moved on and later established Methodism in CHICAGO. In 1830 the St. Louis congregation moved into a new brick church at Fourth and Washington.

Methodism grew slowly in St. Louis. In 1822 there were eighty-seven members; in 1839 there was still only one congregation with 365 white and 148 colored members. However, in that year, stirred by the celebration of the centennial of world Methodism, St. Louis Methodists raised $3,000 and started two new churches—Centenary and Mounds (now St. Paul's). Both have survived and still serve near their original locations.

The division of 1844 was keenly felt in St. Louis Methodism. In 1845 all of the congregations adhered South, but some members, insisting on adhering North, formed Ebenezer M.E. Church in that year. Three years later it reported 130 members. Though the M.E. Church organized a MISSOURI CONFERENCE in 1848 and started a second and third congregation in St. Louis in 1852 and 1857, through the years it was not as strong in the city as the Church South. However, the Church North was dominant in St. Louis during the Civil War. Editor D. R. McANALLY of the St. Louis Christian Advocate (MES) was imprisoned, and ENOCH M. MARVIN (later bishop), pastor of Centenary Church, went South to avoid arrest. Union Church (ME), organized in 1862, flourished under the pastor, Henry Cox, who required persons joining the church to swear allegiance to the United States with the stars and stripes floating over their heads.

The METHODIST PROTESTANT CHURCH had no constituency in St. Louis. The FREE METHODIST CHURCH had three congregations and 129 members in the city in 1968.

In 1858 some seventy-five Negroes in M.E. Church congregations withdrew and organized Wesley Chapel. As late as 1883 it was the only Negro M.E. Church in the city. In 1938 the CENTRAL WEST CONFERENCE (ME) had seven congregations and some 3,500 members in St. Louis.

The A.M.E. CHURCH organized St. Paul's Church in St. Louis in 1841 and established the Missouri Conference in 1855. In 1967 the denomination reported sixteen churches and 7,471 members in greater St. Louis. The A.M.E. ZION CHURCH began work in St. Louis in 1864. In 1967 it reported four congregations and 2,234 members. Shortly after its organization in 1870, the C.M.E. CHURCH began work in St. Louis, but in 1899 it still had only one congregation. In 1967 the denomination reported eleven churches and 6,340 members in greater St. Louis.

Considering the age and size of the City of St. Louis, Methodism has not established many institutions in or near it. The M.E. Church, South published the St. Louis Christian Advocate there, 1852-1931, and in 1865 that de-

nomination founded an orphanage in the city now known as the Methodist Children's Home. The St. Louis Mission and Church Extension Society and Kingdom House, inaugurated in 1885 and 1903 by the Church South, are still functioning. Barnes Hospital, established in 1914, was closely related to but not owned by the Church South, and today the bishop of the St. Louis Area has the responsibility of appointing its trustees. The MISSOURI EAST CONFERENCE appoints the chaplain at Barnes Hospital. In 1853 representatives of the M.E. Church started the Central Christian Advocate which later moved to Kansas City. In 1970 the two Missouri Conferences allocated apportionments to the churches with the promise that when enough funds are in hand a Methodist home for the aged will be built in the vicinity of St. Louis.

In 1970, The United Methodist Church reported twenty-five churches in the City of St. Louis with 11,329 members, property valued at $11,180,857, and $1,320,149 raised for all purposes during the year. The two St. Louis Districts which include the city and the suburbs to a distance of forty miles north, south, and west, reported 113 congregations and 50,062 members in 1970.

General Minutes, MEC, MECS, MC, and UMC.
Minutes of the St. Louis Conference (MECS).
Minutes of the Missouri East Conference.
Almer Pennewell, A Voice in the Wilderness. Nashville: Parthenon Press, [n. d., circa 1962].
St. Louis Christian Advocate files, St. Louis Public Library.
ALBEA GODBOLD

Barnes Hospital was established in 1914, as a trusteeship under the terms of the will of Robert A. Barnes, a St. Louis merchant who died in 1892. Barnes left $940,000 and directed the trustees to use $100,000 of it for a building. Convinced that an adequate plant could not be constructed for that amount, the trustees delayed building and invested the corpus. Twenty years later when it had grown to $2,000,000, they spent about half of it for a building and used the rest as endowment.

At the time Barnes Hospital was established Washington University Medical School was being reorganized. The two institutions affiliated, and through the years Barnes has been the teaching hospital of the Medical School.

Because of the friendship of Robert Barnes with Adam Hendrix, a banker in Fayette, Mo., who was a Methodist layman, Barnes Hospital from the beginning was related to the M.E. Church, South. Hendrix's son, Bishop EUGENE R. HENDRIX (MES), delivered the address at the laying of the cornerstone of the hospital, Oct. 11, 1912. In his speech the bishop said that Barnes "deemed the Methodists were best calculated to carry out his large plans" for a hospital for sick and injured persons without distinction of creed or color. Therefore Barnes provided in his will that the hospital trustees should be appointed by the Methodist bishop in charge in St. Louis, a practice that has continued to this day. Also, the Methodist Annual Conference which includes St. Louis appoints the hospital chaplain.

Barnes Hospital opened with twenty-six patients, Dec. 7, 1914. Today the hospital complex includes nine separate physical institutions which are owned or operated by the trustees. Among them are Children's, McMillan, Maternity, Wohl, Barnard Free Skin and Cancer, and Renard Psychiatric Hospitals. In 1970 these hospital units with over 1,200 beds reported some 350,000 in-patient days and 135,000 out-patients. With able medical men on its staff, Barnes is recognized as one of the outstanding private hospitals in America and indeed in the world. It keeps abreast of and contributes to the medical advances of our time. The late Evarts A. Graham organized the hospital's department of chest surgery, and he himself was the first surgeon in the world to remove an entire lung of a patient suffering from lung cancer.

Barnes Hospital is approved by the Joint Commission on Accreditation of Hospitals, and holds membership in the American Hospital Association, the Missouri Hospital Association, the Metropolitan Hospital Association of St. Louis, and the Association of American Medical Colleges.

The 1971 Agency Directory and Certification Manual of the Board of Health and Welfare Ministries, The United Methodist Church.
F. C. Tucker, *Missouri.* 1966.   NANCY CRAIG

Centenary Church. The trustees of Fourth Street (later First) Church resolved on March 2, 1838 that it was "expedient to build a new Methodist church in St. Louis." It was organized in 1839, and the pastor at Fourth Street served both congregations for three years. The cornerstone of Centenary Church was laid at Fifth and Pine Streets, May 10, 1842, and in October John H. Linn came from the KENTUCKY CONFERENCE to be the pastor. In 1843 the church reported 200 members, and in 1850 the Second GENERAL CONFERENCE (MES) was held at Centenary.

In 1867 Centenary Church decided to move farther west and bought a lot at the southeast corner of Sixteenth and Pine Streets for $36,000. The cornerstone of the new building was laid May 10, 1869, while the bishops of the denomination were in session in St. Louis, and Bishops J. O. ANDREW, H. N. McTYEIRE, and W. M. WIGHTMAN participated in the ceremony. In a crypt back of the chancel were placed the ashes of Thomas Drummond (1806-1835), the first Methodist preacher to die in St. Louis. Born in England, Drummond had come from the PITTS-BURGH CONFERENCE as a missionary to the frontier.

From the time of its founding to the unification of Methodism in 1939, Centenary was a strong and prominent church in Southern Methodism. Under the long ministry of CHARLES W. TADLOCK, 1913-17 and 1919-37, its membership rose to 3,600. Three of Centenary's pastors were elevated to the episcopacy—ENOCH M. MARVIN (1854-56 and 1859-61), WILLIAM F. McMURRY (1902-05), and SAM R. HAY (1906). The 1890 General Conference convened at Centenary.

Some thought that the rapid changes in downtown St. Louis before and after World War II would compel Centenary to relocate or die. But Centenary has stayed put, the only non-liturgical Protestant church to survive in the St. Louis downtown area. Not only has it remained downtown, it has also continued as a fairly strong church, and in recent years has experienced modest growth in membership. The entire church plant was renovated about 1960 at a cost of $250,000. Urban renewal with high rise and split-level apartments has brought residents back to the neighborhood and many have joined Centenary. The church continues to draw members from over the city, the suburbs, and even from across the Mississippi River in Illinois. Since all new expressways in the region enter downtown St. Louis within a few blocks of Centenary, the church is easily accessible from all sections of the metropolitan area.

The resident bishop, the two St. Louis district superin-

tendents, and the St. Louis Mission and Church Extension Society maintain offices in Centenary's education building.

In 1970 Centenary Church reported 790 members, property valued at $1,351,762, and $98,733 raised for all purposes during the year.

General Minutes, MEC, MECS, MC, and UMC.
Minutes of the Missouri East Conference.
Francis E. Williams, *Centenary Methodist Church of St. Louis.* St. Louis: Mound City Press, 1939.   J. LESTER McGEE

Grace Church began in 1892 as Lindell Avenue Church (ME) at Lindell and Newstead. The charter members came from Union Church which was then located near Grand and Washington. The new church reported 110 members in 1893. Within a few years the congregation had built and paid for a stately English Gothic church valued at $165,000.

In 1913 when Lindell Avenue had 372 members the Roman Catholics completed a tremendous new cathedral just across the street on Lindell. The Methodist congregation then moved approximately three miles west to Skinker and Waterman just off the northwest corner of Forest Park and two blocks from the northeast corner of the Washington University campus. Lindell Church not only relocated, it literally moved its impressive Gothic church building stone by stone to its new site, an unusual engineering feat for that day which was written up in several journals. Thereafter it was called Grace Church.

In the new location the church membership doubled by 1931 and Grace became the premier church of the denomination in St. Louis. At unification in 1939 the church had 1,235 members. Through the years Grace has had strong lay leadership, and several of its members have served on the general boards of the denomination. In 1961 Grace reached a peak membership of 1,691 and thereafter with the movement of people to St. Louis County it declined slowly.

About 1955 the entire church plant was modernized and a chapel was added. Under the leadership of Wesley H. Hager, pastor, 1949-70, Grace Church led St. Louis Methodism in contributions to world service and some other benevolent causes, participated in the ecumenical movement, and began working with neighboring Protestant and Roman Catholic churches in developing a ministry adequate for the changing metropolitan scene.

In 1970 Grace Church reported 1,197 members, property valued at $1,946,344 and $156,396 raised for all purposes during the year.

General Minutes, MEC, MC, and UMC.   WESLEY H. HAGER
ALBEA GODBOLD

Methodist Children's Home of Missouri began in 1865 as the Methodist Orphan Home (MES). In 1937 the name was changed to Methodist Children's Home, and at unification in 1939 when it began receiving modest financial support from all of Missouri Methodism, the words "of Missouri" were added.

In 1939 Central Wesleyan Orphan Asylum, Warrenton, Mo., was merged with the home in St. Louis. The former was founded in 1864 by German-speaking Methodists, and after their conference (ST. LOUIS GERMAN) was merged in 1925, the M.E. Church continued to maintain the orphanage. The St. Louis home received thirty-two children from Warrenton in 1939.

The Methodist Orphan Home was located on Maryland Avenue in St. Louis, not far from St. John's Church, and through the years that congregation took a special interest in it, giving both leadership and financial support. The children from the home regularly attended Sunday school and church at St. John's. From 1922 to 1939 the names of the trustees of the home were printed in the ST. LOUIS CONFERENCE *Minutes*, and prior to 1936 all of the trustees were members of St. John's Church.

In 1920 the St. Louis Conference voted to ask the churches to take a free will offering for the home on the Sunday before Thanksgiving. In 1923 the statistical tables in the conference minutes began to include a column showing the amount contributed by each charge for the orphanage. The first year St. John's Church gave $15,000, four other churches gave a total of $110, while the rest contributed nothing. The next year the St. John's members members reverted to giving directly to the orphanage, and the gifts of the other churches in the conference gradually increased until they reached a total of $1,230 in 1938. In 1941 all the churches in Missouri gave $6,051. In 1955 the amount was $35,895, and in 1970 it was $40,432.

In 1928 the home in St. Louis employed a professionally trained social worker as administrator, one of the first in the area to do so. Also, it became the first church-related children's home in Missouri to qualify for membership in the Child Welfare League of America.

In the years following the founding of the Orphan Home, interested persons bequeathed money to it and an endowment was built up. The home's financial report to the conferences in 1941 showed that about $20,000 of its total income of some $39,000 for the year was interest from its endowment.

In 1951 the home was relocated in two new buildings on a five-acre campus at 3715 Jamieson Avenue, St. Louis. The residence with four apartments for nine children each attracted wide attention, because it meant that with house parents in each apartment the children would be living in a family. In addition, the home maintained a staff of social workers.

Most of the children in the home come from homes broken by neglect, desertion, disease, and divorce, and they are referred to the institution by ministers, circuit courts, clinics, health departments, and welfare offices. Most of them need to stay in the home less than two years. Including the children who are served in its foster home program, the Children's Home ministers to 150 to 200 children each year.

Minutes of the St. Louis, Missouri, Southwest Missouri, Missouri East, and Missouri West Conferences.

DONALD L. GOUWENS
ALBEA GODBOLD

St. John's Church was established in 1868 partly as the result of dislocations caused by the Civil War. Asbury and Christy Chapels (MES) sold their properties and joined in launching St. John's Church in the Stoddard Addition, a fast growing suburb two and one-half miles west of the Mississippi River. With liberal financial assistance from First and Centenary Churches, a rather impressive building, which still stands, was erected at 29th and Locust Streets. The new congregation was organized, October 18, with eighty charter members. Francis A. Morris was the first pastor. St. John's quickly became one of the strong churches of the connection.

In 1901 the congregation erected at a cost of $220,000

ST. JOHN'S CHURCH, ST. LOUIS, MISSOURI

a magnificent Italian Renaissance edifice at Kingshighway and Washington five miles west of the river. The church then had 888 members. James W. Lee, who served three four-year terms as pastor between 1893 and 1914, led in relocating the church and almost singlehandedly raised the money for the new building.

About 1925 the congregation considered relocating again still farther west, but convinced that their architectural monument at the intersection of the two thoroughfares which traversed the city east and west and north and south would always draw people for worship, they decided to stay. In 1928 an education building and a chapel costing $300,000 were added to the church, and in 1949 the chancel was rebuilt and other improvements made at a cost of more than $100,000.

Believing that an endowment fund would be an asset if not a necessity for the long pull, the church officials inaugurated one in 1925. It grew slowly at first, totaling $75,000 in twenty years, but after another score of years it was eight times that amount. For many years income from the endowment was added to the corpus, but more recently it has been used to keep the large plant in first class condition and to buy parking space adjoining the church.

Prior to unification in 1939 St. John's was financially one of the strongest churches in the connection. In its first fifty years it raised for all purposes about $2,000,000 or an average of $40,000 per year, an impressive figure for a Southern Methodist congregation in that period. Probably one-half the money raised by the church in its first half century was given for causes outside its own walls. Some $150,000 went to help establish or build eight other churches of the denomination in St. Louis between 1879 and 1910. Between 1909 and 1938 substantial sums were donated to build "St. John's" Churches in Soochow, CHINA; RIO DE JANEIRO, BRAZIL; and Okayama, JAPAN. The Soochow church was said to be the largest and strongest of Southern Methodism in the Orient.

During its first seventy years St. John's was closely related to three service institutions in St. Louis—the Methodist Children's Home, Kingdom House, and Barnes Hospital—which were established in 1865, 1903, and 1914. Through the years the church raised large sums for the Children's Home and Kingdom House, while at the same time undergirding their annual budgets. In addition, many members of St. John's served on their boards of managers and trustees. For many years all of the trustees of the Children's Home and Barnes Hospital were members of St. John's.

Two St. John's pastors were elevated to the episcopacy, JOHN M. MOORE (1909) and IVAN LEE HOLT (1918-37).

Since World War II many churches of various denominations in the environs of Kingshighway and Washington have relocated farther west or have passed out of existence. For thirty-five years after deciding against moving farther west St. John's was able to hold its own and even grow a little in membership; it had 1,425 members in 1925 and 1,554 in 1960. But since the latter date its membership has declined—1,120 in 1965 and 569 in 1970.

It remains to be seen whether St. John's and many other churches similarly situated, that is, with loyal members, an impressive and well-equipped plant, an ample endowment, and a strategic location, can survive and continue to serve in our cities.

In 1971 St. John's Church reported 550 members, property valued at $1,848,000 and $86,102 raised for all purposes during the year.

Thomas M. Finney, *Life and Labors of Enoch M. Marvin.* St. Louis: James H. Chambers, 1880.
General Minutes, MECS.
Albea Godbold, *A Unique Church, Centennial Address,* St. John's Church, St. Louis. Typescript, 10 pp. 1968.
Minutes of the St. Louis and Missouri East Conferences.
St. Louis Christian Advocate files. St. Louis Public Library.
ALBEA GODBOLD

St. Paul A.M.E. Church, the oldest church of the denomination west of the Mississippi River, was established in 1841 by WILLIAM PAUL QUINN who had been commissioned by the General Conference to extend the boundaries of the denomination westward. Forbidden to preach in St. Louis because it was slave territory, Quinn, it is claimed, stood on the Illinois side of the river and preached across to people on the Missouri side. The result was the formation in May, 1841, of Little Bethel Church, later named St. Paul, in the home of Priscilla Baltimore in East St. Louis, Ill. John Anderson was the first pastor.

Coming across the river to St. Louis, the small congregation met in homes and blacksmith shops for at least two years. In time a church that cost $5,000 was built at Eleventh and Lucas Streets. In 1872 a new brick church was dedicated on an adjoining lot. Four years later the church reported 572 members.

In 1891 St. Paul relocated at Leffingwell and Lawton, dedicating there a church that cost $90,000. Because of an extensive urban renewal program, the congregation was compelled to move again in 1962, locating at Hamilton and Julian Avenues where it was able to build a church, an education building, a community center, and a parsonage.

As the mother church of the denomination in St. Louis, St. Paul established a mission at Enright and Pendleton Streets in 1925 which grew into St. John Church, a strong congregation.

Three St. Paul pastors have become bishops, NOAH W. WILLIAMS (1924-32), FRANK MADISON REID (1936-40), and G. WAYMAN BLAKELY (1953-64). Through the years St. Paul Church has entertained the A.M.E. General Conference several times. In 1969 the membership of the church was approximately 2,000.

Minnie Ross Sims, *History of St. Paul A.M.E. Church.* Pamphlet. 1965.
M. Simpson, *Cyclopaedia.* 1878.   GRANT S. SHOCKLEY

Union Memorial Church is the oldest continuing Negro congregation in St. Louis, and was recognized and honored in 1966 during the celebration of American Methodism's bicentennial. The church was organized in 1840 and in 1846 was served by a local preacher, James Farrar. The congregation worshipped at Broadway between Morgan Street (now Delmar) and Franklin Avenue. Adolphus Foshee succeeded Farrar, and the church was guided by various dedicated white preachers until 1865, when E. W. S. Peck of Baltimore, Md. became the first Negro pastor of the church. In 1873 under the pastorate of F. H. Small, the congregation bought the building on Wash Street (now Cole) for $10,000, and moved to the new location on Aug. 21, 1873. On Oct. 26, 1884 the edifice was dedicated, then called Wesley Chapel, with Bishop BOWMAN and E. W. S. Peck officiating.

In 1899 Wesley Chapel and Elliot Avenue congregations consolidated and sold Wesley Chapel for $10,000. The merged church was named Centennial. In April 1900, Bishop FITZGERALD, presiding over the annual session of the Central Missouri Conference at Marshall, Mo., appointed R. E. Gillum to Centennial, and soon thereafter the name was changed to Union Memorial M.E. Church.

By 1904 Union Memorial's membership had outgrown the building's capacity, and a committee contracted for the purchase of Temple Israel on the corner of Leffingwell Avenue and Pine Street. On July 28, 1907 the congregation moved to the new location, having purchased the building for $41,500.

The following churches were started by Union Memorial: First M. E. Church in Kinloch Park, 1907; Wesley Chapel, East St. Louis, Mo., 1908; Webster Groves, 1908; Cosby Chapel, 1914; Asbury, 1915; Samaritan, 1917; LaSalle Street, 1920, the last three located in St. Louis.

E. W. KELLEY served as pastor from 1939 to 1944, when he was elected to the episcopacy. He left a new parsonage as one of his contributions. Although each minister shared greatly in the growth of the church, J. J. Hicks brought outstanding recognition to Union Memorial. Under his leadership the property at Belt and Bartmer was purchased for $51,000 and an ultramodern building constructed. During the pastorate of John N. Doggett, Jr., a new parsonage has been purchased and a plan is proceeding to liquidate the outstanding debt. In 1970 the church reported 1,067 members.

Grace Bumbry, internationally famed Metropolitan Opera star, is a product of Union Memorial. She donated her talent in 1965 to aid her church in assisting promising young students.

JOHN N. DOGGETT, JR.

ST. LOUIS CHRISTIAN ADVOCATE, THE, was published weekly, barring a few interruptions, for or by the MISSOURI Conferences (MES) from 1850 to 1931. The organ was suppressed for a time during the Civil War because of the alleged seditious utterances of the editor David R. McAnally and he himself was imprisoned for some weeks.

McAnally served a total of thirty years between 1851 and his death in 1892. Controversy involving both ministers and laymen continually swirled around him, but even so he was a capable editor. He established policies which endured throughout the life of the paper—serious articles, sermons, and addresses dealing with contemporary religious, social and economic issues, together with extensive coverage of local, district, annual conference, and church-wide events. His high literary standards won subscribers outside church circles. Displaced by THOMAS M. FINNEY as editor in 1869, McAnally was recalled three years later, an indication that even his detractors recognized his superior journalistic ability.

Prior to 1891 responsibility for the paper was handled in various ways. At first a committee published it for the conferences. Then in 1870 a joint stock company called the Southwestern Book and Publishing Company bought and operated it. Two years later Logan Dameron, president of the company, bought up the stock and published the paper for the benefit of the conferences. In 1881 he tried to give the paper to the conferences but the ST. LOUIS CONFERENCE, influenced by a quarrel then in progress between McAnally and some ministers and laymen, would not agree. In 1886 Dameron deeded the paper to the conferences, retaining a life interest. Four years later he sold his interest, and in 1891 WILLIAM B. PALMORE bought the paper and gave it to the conferences. Thereafter it was wholly owned by them and was controlled through a joint conference publication committee.

McAnally died in 1892 and Palmore then became editor, serving until his own death in 1914. During Palmore's time the paid circulation rose to more than 20,000. He wrote good editorials and extensively covered local church news. Numerous anti-liquor and anti-tobacco articles marked him as a reform leader in Missouri. Travelogues covering his visits to mission stations and places of interest throughout the world gave readers fresh impressions of missions and world affairs.

Several editors followed Palmore in quick succession: Charles C. Woods, ALFRED FRANKLIN SMITH (later editor of the Nashville *Christian Advocate*), George B. Winton, and Charles O. Ransford. The latter took office in 1923 and though widely known in Missouri, he was unable to arrest the steady decline in circulation. With the onset of the economic depression, the conferences were unwilling to subsidize the paper and it ceased publication in October, 1931.

St. Louis Christian Advocate files, St. Louis Public Library.
F. C. Tucker, *Missouri.* 1966.   FRANK C. TUCKER

ST. LOUIS CONFERENCE ('ME). See MISSOURI CONFERENCE (ME).

ST. LOUIS CONFERENCE (MES) was organized at Boonville, Mo., in October 1846 with Bishop ROBERT PAINE presiding. Formed by dividing the MISSOURI CONFERENCE, its territory included the part of the state below the Missouri River. At the beginning the Conference had six districts, St. Louis, Boonville, Cape Girardeau, Lexington, Springfield, and Steelville. It had 12,567 white and 1,304 colored members.

In 1850 the *St. Louis Christian Advocate* was established as an official organ of the M.E. Church, South. With DAVID R. MCANALLY, an able writer and administrator, as editor, the paper achieved a wide circulation beyond MISSOURI, and it strengthened Southern Methodism in the state. The organ continued publication until 1931.

In 1855 the St. Louis Conference joined the Missouri Conference in launching CENTRAL COLLEGE at Fayette, the one Methodist college in the state which has survived to the present time. In 1869 the conference, interested in projecting a college in southeast Missouri, became affili-

ated with Bellevue Collegiate Institute at Caledonia which the citizens there had launched in 1867. Becoming convinced in time that there was no future for a school in Caledonia which was twelve miles from a railroad, the conference severed its connections with Bellevue in 1893 and three years later accepted Marvin College at Fredericktown which continued operation until 1924.

In 1877 the St. Louis District of the conference adopted as a church institution the Methodist Orphans Home which was begun two years before by a conference member, W. W. Prottsman, and a layman named W. H. Markham. In 1941 this institution, which had rendered outstanding service, received the children from the Central Wesleyan Orphanage at Warrenton, Mo., which was founded and maintained for many years by the ST. LOUIS GERMAN CONFERENCE (MEC). The name was then changed to the Methodist Children's Home of Missouri. Housed in new buildings in St. Louis, the home continues to render notable service to children.

Kingdom House in St. Louis grew out of a mission Sunday school which was started by St. John's Church in 1904. The WOMAN'S HOME MISSIONARY SOCIETY of the denomination soon took responsibility for "social work activities" at Kingdom House. Today the institution has an adequate building, and it receives financial support both from the conference and from the united fund of the city.

The conference established a summer assembly known as Epworth Among the Hills at Arcadia in 1908. In the 1950's a large camp called Blue Mountain was developed nearby as an added feature.

In 1892 Robert A. Barnes gave $1,000,000 for a hospital in St. Louis and stipulated that its trustees should be appointed by the presiding bishop of the Methodist Church. Barnes Hospital opened in 1914 and today it is the nucleus of one of the great medical centers of the world. While the hospital is neither owned nor operated by the church, the conference has maintained the chaplaincy from the beginning, and its Golden Cross offering is directed annually to the hospital.

In 1870 the St. Louis Conference was divided to form the Southwest Missouri Conference. (The new body was called the West St. Louis Conference until 1874.) Before the division the St. Louis Conference had nine districts, ninety-seven charges, and 20,304 white and 243 colored members. The next year the statistics were four districts, forty-six charges and 9,942 white and twelve colored members. In 1900 there were five districts and 26,791 members. At unification in 1939 the St. Louis Conference brought 268 ministers, 124 charges, 259 churches, and 46,379 members into The Methodist Church. In 1941 there were 62,949 members.

Three members of the St. Louis Conference were elected bishops in the M.E. Church, South, ENOCH M. MARVIN (1866), WILLIAM F. McMURRY (1918), and IVAN LEE HOLT (1938).

The Board of Finance (Pensions) of the Southern Church was domiciled in St. Louis from the time of its organization in 1922. LUTHER E. TODD, a member of the St. Louis Conference, was the first general secretary.

By authority of the 1960 SOUTH CENTRAL JURISDICTIONAL CONFERENCE, the three Missouri conferences were consolidated into two in 1961. All of the St. Louis Conference became a part of the new MISSOURI EAST CONFERENCE. At its last session in 1961, the St. Louis Conference reported six districts, Cape Girardeau, Farmington, Jefferson City, Poplar Bluff, Rolla and St. Louis. There were 243 ministers, 358 churches, 233 charges, and 89,199 members. The property was valued at $29,891,712.

General Minutes, MECS and MC.
Minutes of the St. Louis Conference.
Frank C. Tucker, *The Methodist Church in Missouri*. 1966.
F. E. MASER

ST. LOUIS GERMAN CONFERENCE (ME) was organized in St. Louis, Sept. 3, 1879 with Bishop THOMAS BOWMAN presiding. It was formed by dividing the SOUTHWEST GERMAN CONFERENCE. The latter (called Southwestern German Conference until 1868) was one of the original German language conferences created by the GENERAL CONFERENCE of 1864. The territory of the St. Louis German Conference included east MISSOURI, southern ILLINOIS, and southeast IOWA. At the beginning the conference had four districts, St. Louis, Belleville, Quincy, and Burlington. There were eighty-four charges and 7,564 members.

Methodist work among the Germans in Missouri began in 1844. (See MISSOURI.) A German mission district with eleven charges was formed in the MISSOURI CONFERENCE in 1844. But in 1845 the German preachers and churches opposed to slavery and unwilling to adhere South with the Missouri Conference, were attached to the ILLINOIS CONFERENCE, an arrangement which continued until the formation of the Southwestern German Conference in 1864.

The German Methodists established a college and an orphanage in Missouri which did notable work so long as the German language conferences continued. The Germans started what was called the German and English College in Quincy, Ill., in 1854, but it failed during the Civil War. Determined to establish a self-supporting school and to care for children orphaned by the war, the German Methodists then bought 932 acres of land at Warrenton, Mo. (1864). In 1869 they secured a charter for Central Wesleyan College and Orphan Asylum. Three years later a separate charter was issued for the college. Adequate buildings were erected, an endowment of $170,000 was built up, accreditation was achieved, and enrollment exceeded 350. The German Methodist College, Mt. Pleasant, Iowa, was merged with Central Wesleyan in 1908, bringing a theological department with it. The future seemed promising. But the first world war created difficulties for the school. Then in the 1920's the German language conferences disappeared, a turn of events which drastically curtailed financial support and the number of prospective students. The college closed in 1941.

Central Wesleyan Orphanage operated a 300-acre farm and cared for up to 100 children. It was one of the first orphanages in the nation to place children in cottages with house parents, thus simulating normal family life. At unification in 1939 the orphanage was merged with the Methodist Children's Home in St. Louis.

Partly due to German immigration into the region, the St. Louis German Conference grew and reached its peak strength about 1900. In that year it reported ninety-three charges and 11,134 members. In the years following the membership continued at about 10,000. As time passed some ministers and churches transferred to the English-speaking conferences. In 1925 when the St. Louis German Conference was absorbed by the overlying conferences

of the M.E. Church, it reported two districts, Peoria and St. Louis, sixty-two charges, 9,982 members, and property valued at $1,106,600.

General Minutes, MEC.
Frank C. Tucker, *The Methodist Church in Missouri*. 1966.
F. E. MASER

ST. PAUL, MINNESOTA, U.S.A., the capital city of MINNESOTA, is regarded as a strategic railroad center. St. Paul and MINNEAPOLIS are referred to as The Twin Cities. Only the Mississippi River divides them.

Methodism in St. Paul had its beginning in a series of small missions that were built along the Mississippi River. South St. Paul was the first mission, beginning in 1837. This was an Indian settlement and was called Kaposia. Two years later, RED ROCK, now Newport, another Indian settlement, established another mission. The first Methodist church in St. Paul was organized in 1848, and in 1849 the Market Street Church was built, the first Protestant and Methodist church building in Minnesota. Out of this first church came the Jackson Street Church in 1856; and out of this church came the present Central Park Church. Out of the old Market Street Church of St. Paul came the First Church, which recently has been united with the Trinity Church and is called First-Trinity. First-Trinity has a membership of 592 members. Central Park Church has a membership of 629.

Hamline Church is the most beautiful cathedral-like church building in St. Paul. It has a membership of 992 as of 1970. In former years, this church had a much larger one. This is likewise true of First and Trinity Churches. Hamline Church is the host to the MINNESOTA ANNUAL CONFERENCE each year, along with HAMLINE UNIVERSITY, named for Bishop LEONIDAS HAMLINE. This Methodist related university had its beginning in Redwing in 1854, even before Minnesota became a state. In 1880 it was moved to St. Paul where it has grown on its original site to one of the finest schools of higher learning in Minnesota. There are more than 1,200 students enrolled in Hamline University each year. Hamline was the first institution of higher learning in Minnesota, one of the first twelve Methodist colleges in the United States, and the fourth Methodist college to open as a coeducational college.

St. Anthony Park Church has another beautiful site and an up-to-date building containing a beautiful worship sanctuary, an adequately equipped educational unit and social hall, fine office facilities and a beautiful chapel. It has a membership of 578 members. It is located near the agricultural college of the State University and serves the student body in a very fine way as well as their resident membership. Centennial is a new suburban Methodist church located a block off from North Snelling Avenue. In fifteen years of its existence, this congregation that began with a chartered membership of sixty-seven has grown to a membership of 1,066. In this short period of time, they have built three units and have adequately furnished them. Fairmount Avenue Church began in 1852 and is located directly across the campus from MacCalester College on South Snelling Avenue. It has a remodeled church edifice .that Methodism in St. Paul is likewise proud of. It has a sanctuary "in the round," an adequate educational unit, offices, social hall and a beautiful church parlor. Its membership (1970) was 553. Arlington Hills Church has a membership of 548, and is located in the northeast part of St. Paul. St. Paul's Church is another beautifully located church, with a membership of 556.

In the twenty-five St. Paul United Methodist churches, there is a membership of 11,062 (1970). It should be added that St. Paul has been and is a strong Catholic city, claiming about forty percent of its total population. The Lutheran church is another strong group in St. Paul, as it is throughout Minnesota.

Hamline Church is the college church of Minnesota Methodism. It is located across Englewood Avenue from Hamline University, Methodism's only college in Minnesota, and has been closely associated with the University throughout the eighty-five years of its history. The church was literally born on the campus of the University. On Sept. 12, 1880, Hamline Church held its first service of worship in the auditorium of "Old Main," conducted by Charles F. Bradley of the University faculty. Services continued in "Old Main" for three years, until the first church building was erected on the site of the present building; and Hamline professors continued to serve the church as ministers until 1886 when the first full-time minister was appointed. The church continues its ministry to the campus. Many of the Hamline faculty are active members. Approximately half of the student body attend its services. The University frequently uses its facilities for chapel services, choir concerts and other special programs. Former presidents and faculty members are memorialized in its magnificent stained-windows.

After a destructive fire on Dec. 26, 1925, the present beautiful structure was erected. The exterior is of Bedford limestone in accurate Gothic detail, and the walls are laid in random ashlar.

Hamline Church has not only served Methodism's university, but it has also served the Minnesota Conference. Since the merger of the Minnesota Conference with the NORTHERN MINNESOTA CONFERENCE in 1948, all conference sessions have been held on the Hamline campus, with both the church and the university acting as hosts. Most of the ministers ordained in the past eighteen years have been ordained in Hamline Church.

E. F. Baumhofer, *Trails in Minnesota.* 1966.
Journals of the Minnesota Conference. ORVAL CLAY DITTES
PAUL O. METZGER

SAINT PAUL SCHOOL OF THEOLOGY (METHODIST),

Kansas City, Missouri, was one of the two schools authorized by the General Conference of 1956. The bishops of the Kansas, Missouri, Nebraska, and St. Louis areas appointed provisional trustees, and the school was chartered as the National Methodist Theological Seminary, March 3, 1958. The present name was assumed in 1961. Conversations concerning the school's use of the campus and facilities of NATIONAL COLLEGE culminated in the deeding of this property, valued at $2,500,000, to the seminary in 1964. The seminary opened on the former campus of National College in September, 1965, with an enlarged and expanded program in church vocations, including special emphasis on preparation for the pastoral ministry and the training of women for Christian vocations. It gives the B.D. and M.R.E. (Religious Education) degrees. The governing board is seventy-five trustees, nine of whom are chosen from the six jurisdictions plus three extra from the South Central Jurisdiction, twenty-six from the annual conferences, fifteen from the

Woman's Division of Christian Service, two from the Board of Education, four from alumni, nine at large, six bishops and the president ex officio.

JOHN O. GROSS

ST. PETERSBURG, FLORIDA, U.S.A., a resort city in Pinellas County with a population of 213,189 in 1970, was founded in 1888 and incorporated in 1903. Methodism was brought to the county by settlers from GEORGIA and north FLORIDA; in 1869 they built a church at Curlew, the oldest community in the county. What is now First Church, St. Petersburg, was established in 1889 by Southern Methodists when the town had a population of thirty. The church began with seven members. In 1891 the M.E. Church started what is now Christ Church. For many years afterward the two congregations were known as "Southern" and "Northern" churches.

At unification in 1939, the M.E. Church had five churches in St. Petersburg with 2,160 members to four for the M.E. Church, South with 1,833 members.

In 1970 The United Methodist Church had twenty churches in St. Petersburg with 22,332 members. The property of those congregations was valued at $8,454,367, and they raised for all purposes during the year $976,877.

First Church was founded in 1889 with seven members when the population of the village was 30. At the time the Congregationalists in the community were worshiping in a railroad car, and there was a small Episcopal church two miles away. The village was officially named St. Petersburg in 1890.

In 1895, citrus growers came to the St. Petersburg area seeking frost-free land. By 1900 the town had 1,575 people and First Church reported 134 members. In that year the congregation's frame building was moved to the present church site. In 1910 it gave way to a brick structure which in turn was replaced in 1924 by what is still one of the largest church edifices in Florida Methodism.

First Church had 1,137 members in 1924, and the number rose to 1,850 by 1927. The collapse of the Florida boom in 1928 and the national economic depression which began in 1929 caused a drop in membership to 966 by 1934. Beginning in 1924, First Church carried a debt which at times approached $300,000. Loss of the building valued at $600,000 was a constant threat. However, a strong sermon by O. E. Rice moved a winter visitor to offer a loan to the church. Three members added to the amount, and the financial crisis was eased. The building was finally dedicated debt free in April, 1936. In succeeding years improvements and innovations, including an eight-story carillon bell tower, were made. After 1934, the membership rose steadily; it reached 1,503 in 1939, 2,566 by 1950, and during the 1960's it was close to 3,000.

In 1970, First Church reported 2,899 members, property valued at $1,530,638, and $149,747 raised for all purposes during the year.

Christ Church was organized as a Methodist Episcopal congregation, St. John's River Conference, in 1891. Called "St. Petersburg" in the conference journal from the beginning, the name was changed to First Avenue in 1925 and to Christ Church in 1953.

At first the church grew slowly; five years after its founding it had only twenty members, and only 208 after 25 years. However, with the influx of people from the north after the first world war, the membership steadily increased, growing to 870 in 1925, 1,422 in 1939, 2,396 in 1950, and 3,726 in 1960.

During the pastorate of Schuyler E. Garth, 1929-33, later bishop, First Avenue began holding two morning services to seat the crowds, one of the first if not the very first church in the nation to do that. The church's seating capacity was then 1,039, but it drew large crowds because of its popularity with winter tourists and permanent residents alike.

A radio station in the church tower, the first in the city, was awarded a broadcasting license in the mid-1920's. Though the city now owns the WSUN radio station, the church sends its worship services, including Holy Communion, to some 250 shut-in members and others by means of radio. The church loses about 120 members by death each year, due to the fact that so many are retirees.

Medical Forums, now conducted in over 50 cities, originated in St. Petersburg and are held in Christ Church. Also, the church sponsors a Saturday night concert series by American college and school choirs.

Paul R. Hortin was appointed associate pastor of the church in 1931, became senior minister in 1933, and in 1970 was still serving in that capacity. In 1952 a new sanctuary with a seating capacity of 1,844 was erected and was soon debt free. In recent years 15 men from the congregation have gone into the ministry.

In 1970, Christ Church reported 4,332 members, 1,763 enrolled in the Church school, property valued at $1,405,571, and $147,319 raised for all purposes during the year.

PASADENA CHURCH, ST. PETERSBURG, FLORIDA

Pasadena Community Church was started in 1924 and organized in 1925 in the sparsely settled section of Pasadena seven miles from St. Petersburg. Sponsored by the M.E. Church, South, it was projected as a church for the whole community, and from the beginning it has drawn members from many different denominations. Its first building, erected in 1925, was of Spanish architecture.

Prior to 1929, the congregation was served for brief periods by three different ministers. In December, 1928, three laymen from the church attending a district conference, heard a sermon by a young minister named J. Wallace Hamilton. They asked for Hamilton as their pastor, and in May, 1929, he was appointed to the Pasadena Church. He served it continuously thereafter for 39 years until his death in 1968. During his long

ministry there Hamilton became widely known as one of the ablest preachers in the United States.

For many years the membership of the church grew slowly. It did not permanently pass the 100 mark until 1935. Beginning in 1941 when the membership was 360, Hamilton was given an associate pastor, but not until 10 years later did the number of members exceed 1,000. Thereafter the church grew rapidly, increasing from 1,283 members in 1952 to 1,668 in 1953. In 1956 there were 2,100 and in 1964 more than 3,000.

As a young minister apparently Hamilton worked harder at preparing sermons which would draw people to the services than at enlisting them as church members. Within a few years after he assumed the pastorate there were overflowing congregations and amplifiers were installed so people seated on benches outside the church could hear the services. Later additional ground was purchased so that people could sit in their cars while participating in worship. It is claimed that on Easter Sunday in 1951, there were 3,450 automobiles with 10,000 people listening to the service in what the church calls its Garden Sanctuary.

Between 1937 and 1957 Pasadena Church conducted four campaigns for funds and built two wings, two education buildings, and a chapel. Also, it acquired 18 acres for the Garden Sanctuary. In 1960, a new church edifice with a seating capacity of 2,000 was completed at a cost of $850,000, and a 50-rank organ valued at $150,000 was installed. Through the years the church has kept itself practically free of debt.

In 1970, Pasadena Church reported 3,510 members, 1,055 enrolled in church school, property valued at $2,402,152, and $132,825 raised for all purposes during the year.

W. E. Brooks, *Florida Methodism*. 1965.
A Brief Portrayal of Pasadena Community Church. Pamphlet, n.d.
General Minutes, UMC, 1970.
Minutes of the Florida Conference.
F. S. Mead, *Seven Miles Out*. Pamphlet, n.d.
James M. Smith, "History of the St. Petersburg District." Ms., 1966.
JESSE A. EARL
ALBEA GODBOLD
N. B. H.
FRANK M. SLEEPER

ST. SIMON'S ISLAND is some sixty miles south of SAVANNAH, Ga. While in America, JOHN and CHARLES WESLEY were associated with the island as well as with Savannah. General OGLETHORPE built a fort and a garrison town, both called Frederica, on St. Simon's Island and stationed a British regiment with a number of its families there. As chaplain to the colony, John Wesley ministered to the people on the island. Ruins of the fort and foundations of the houses may be seen today at the Fort Frederica National Monument at the northwest corner of St. Simon's Island. In the 1920's a causeway was built connecting the island with the city of Brunswick, Ga., and in succeeding years the island has been developed as a resort and residence area.

In 1947 the SOUTH GEORGIA CONFERENCE established a church on St. Simon's Island, and about the same time it purchased the Hamilton Plantation on the west side some miles south of Frederica. There under the guidance of Bishop ARTHUR J. MOORE, the South Georgia Conference Center, **Epworth-by-the-Sea,** was developed. The

LOVELY LANE CHAPEL, ST. SIMONS ISLAND

old Hamilton family chapel was renamed Lovely Lane Chapel, honoring the memory of the BALTIMORE edifice in which the CHRISTMAS CONFERENCE was held in 1784.

In the 1950's South Georgia Methodism built at Epworth-by-the-Sea a dining room, auditorium, youth building, and lodges which throughout the year accommodate numerous gatherings of young people and adults, some groups coming from outside the conference. Several annual sessions of the South Georgia Conference have been held at Epworth-by-the-Sea. The Winter Camp Meeting held in February has been a high point at the Center in recent years. The Arthur J. Moore Memorial Building at the Center was completed in June 1960, when Bishop Moore was presiding over the South Georgia Conference for the last time before his retirement.

Epworth Acres, just north of Epworth-by-the-Sea, is a section of privately owned homes on lots made available by the Conference Center. A number of the South Georgia Conference superannuate homes are there. By the mid-1960's the conference had erected an office building at the Center to house its Boards of Education and Missions. Thus, within a quarter of a century South Georgia Methodism transformed an old cotton plantation into a productive center of Christian influence, and gave it a name widely known in Methodism, Epworth-by-the-Sea.

Minutes of the South Georgia Conference, 1945-67.

WALTER S. McCLESKEY

ST. STEPHEN'S COLLEGE, formerly ALBERTA COLLEGE (South), former Methodist theological College in Edmonton, Alberta.

Originating as the theological department of Alberta College in 1909, Alberta College (South) took advantage, in 1910, of the offer of the University of Alberta of a free site on the campus of the new university. The building

then erected was known until the formation of The United Church of Canada in 1925 as Alberta College South, the theological college of the Methodist Church in Alberta.

J. H. RIDDELL was the first principal, and continued in office until 1917, when D. E. THOMAS became acting principal. In 1919 A. S. TUTTLE was elected principal and professor of philosophy of religion. Until 1925 the college provided high school matriculation subjects as well as theological courses, and also a men's residence for students. Since 1925 the college has provided theological courses exclusively. From 1911 until 1925 Alberta College South graduated ninety-four candidates for the ministry.

With church union in 1925, Alberta College (South) merged with Robertson College, the Presbyterian seminary in Edmonton, the premises used being those of the former Methodist institution. At first called United Theological College, in the spring of 1927 the two college boards became one under the new name of St. Stephen's College, incorporated by the provincial legislature. Until the death of J. M. Millar, former principal of Robertson College, Tuttle and Millar were joint principals, Tuttle becoming principal in January, 1930.

With the retirement of Tuttle, A. D. Miller, professor of Old Testament language and literature, was elected principal in October 1943, retiring from this office in 1946 after thirty-five years' service. E. J. Thompson became principal in October, 1946. Under Thompson's leadership, funds were raised for the erection of a new unit for classrooms, offices, and library, which was opened February 25, 1953. On Thompson's retirement in June, 1966, G. M. TUTTLE was appointed to succeed him as principal.

J. Macdonald, *The History of the University of Alberta.* Edmonton: University of Alberta, 1958.
J. H. Riddell, *Methodism in the Middle West.* Toronto: Ryerson, 1946.   J. E. NIX

ST. STITHIANS COLLEGE, Johannesburg, SOUTH AFRICA, is the newest connexional school for boys. It is set in 250 acres some ten miles north of Johannesburg and has an enrollment of 625 boys from the ages of five to seventeen. The school follows an academic course and seeks to prepare for University entrance. The first headmaster was Walter Mears, who was succeeded in 1962 by M. T. S. Krige. The foundation of St. Stithians in 1953 was the result of generous donations from two Cornishmen, Albert Charles Collins and William Mountstephens, in order to provide a liberal education with Christian teaching.

H. F. KIRKBY

SALAKO, NATHANAEL ODUYEBO (1903-   ), president of the Conference of the Methodist Church of NIGERIA, was born at Ikenne in the Ijebu Remo Division of the Western State on Dec. 12, 1903. He was educated at the Methodist schools of Ikenne and Iperu from 1912 to 1922 and then went to Wesley College, Ibadan, from 1923 to December 1927. He started as a sub-pastor at the Imo Methodist Church in 1928 where he taught. In 1929 he went to the Oyo Methodist Circuit as sub-pastor in charge of the circuit, as well as being headmaster of the Methodist school at Oyo. In 1930, however, he felt a definite call to go into the Methodist ministry and re-entered Wesley College in 1932 as a divinity student. He served Osu in Ilesha Circuit in 1933, returned to Wesley

College and then in 1935 was stationed as circuit minister to the Imesi-Ile Methodist Church. From 1936 to 1938 he was in charge of Oshogbo Methodist Church and in 1939 was at Igbo-Ora in Ibadan Circuit.

He was ordained as a minister in full connection with the British Methodist Conference in 1939. He served about within his own country and in September 1949, became the first African superintendent of Ilesha Circuit. The church advanced under his superintendency, two high schools being founded during that time.

His first wife was Mrs. Marry O. Salako whom he married on June 30, 1932, and to them were born two daughters. His first wife died on Aug. 7, 1942. On Dec. 21, 1944, he married Mrs. Comfort O. Salako. To them were born three daughters and three sons. His leadership of work in his country continued and the Methodist Church Conference which met at Yaba Methodist Church, Lagos, Jan. 22-24, 1968, appointed him as the president of the Methodist Church in Nigeria.

N. B. H.

SALAZAR, MARIO (1918-   ), Bolivian educator, is a native of COCHABAMBA. He received his normal school degree and law degree at the university there. In the United States he received a M.A. from Peabody, later taking other studies at GARRETT THEOLOGICAL SEMINARY and NORTHWESTERN UNIVERSITY. He married Julia Albricias, a teacher, and they have three children.

In 1954 he became director of American Institute (COLEGIO EVANGELICO METODISTA) in LA PAZ, and in 1964, director of the American Institute in Cochabamba. In the church Salazar was secretary of the annual conference, executive secretary of the Commission on Missions and Finance, a delegate to several international conferences, and in 1966 executive secretary of social action.

NATALIE BARBER

SALEM, NEW JERSEY, U.S.A. In 1774 Daniel Ruff visited Salem and preached in the court house. Among his hearers was THOMAS WARE, then a youth, but who became a distinguished minister. The first Methodist church in Salem was built in 1784. Both Thomas Ware and BENJAMIN ABBOTT were present at the dedication of this church. Later, Benjamin Abbott was baptized in the church. Both Ware and Abbott are buried in the cemetery of the church.

Until 1826 the Methodist Church in Salem belonged to the Salem Circuit. In 1789 it was a "six weeks circuit" embracing all of West Jersey south of BURLINGTON. During the same year an effective spiritual revival, resulting in a significant increase in church membership, took place within the bounds of the present Salem County. In 1790 Salem Circuit was sub-divided into the old Bethel Circuit, which included Gloucester County and north to Burlington. In 1804-05 Salem Circuit included the three counties of Salem, Cumberland, and Cape May. By 1809 Salem Circuit was limited to the counties of Salem and Cumberland.

In 1826 Salem Town became a preaching station with 105 members. JOHN LEDNUM was the first pastor. Thomas Ware was a supernumerary there.

Around 1850 some members withdrew from old Walnut Street Church, now known as First Church, to form the Broadway Church. These two churches now serve the Methodists of Salem.

Six sessions of the NEW JERSEY ANNUAL CONFERENCE have been held in Salem (1847, 1860, 1871, 1881, 1889, 1902).

G. A. Raybold, *Reminiscences of Methodism in West Jersey.* New York: Lane & Scott, 1849.
Joseph S. Sickler, *The History of Salem County, New Jersey.* Salem: Sunbeam Publishing Co., 1937.
F. B. Stanger, *New Jersey.* 1961.   FRANK BATEMAN STANGER

SALEM, OREGON, U.S.A. **First Church** dates from the arrival of the Methodist missionaries in 1840. That year JASON LEE began the removal of the Methodist Mission to Chemeketa, now North Salem. The first building erected on Mill Creek houses a sawmill and gristmill. In 1841 the Indian Manual Labor School was constructed and the First Methodist Church organized. DAVID LESLIE is credited with laying the foundations for Methodist work at Salem.

In 1848 JAMES HARVEY WILBUR and ALVIN F. WALLER were appointed to the Salem Circuit which included all Methodist work east of the Willamette River south of OREGON CITY. Membership of the circuit was 115 and that of Salem, 105. Initial services were held at the Oregon Institute which had acquired the building of the Indian Manual Training School from GEORGE GARY.

In 1849 William Helm and J. O. Raynor were appointed to the Salem Circuit with David Leslie, superintendent. In 1850 Alvin F. Waller became pastor at Salem and William Helm, superintendent. In 1852 WILLIAM ROBERTS, superintendent of the Oregon Mission Conference, reported a church building under construction at Salem. The edifice, 40 by 60 feet and costing $8,000, was dedicated Jan. 23, 1853.

A new building was projected in the summer of 1870, when C. C. Stratton was pastor. Construction began in August 1871, and the cornerstone was laid October 9. The building was completed and dedicated March 17, 1878, costing $45,000. In 1938 the membership was 1,342; in 1948 it was 1,647, and in 1970 the membership was 1,426. Property was valued at $1,011,283 in 1970.

Lee House. The first frame house built in the capital city of OREGON was built by the Methodist missionaries under the direction of Jason Lee in 1841. Mission headquarters were moved from their original location on the banks of the Willamette River some ten miles from the present city of Salem. The move was motivated by unhealthful conditions created by the winter floods, and also because the new site offered water power for a small saw and grist mill which was greatly needed by the mission in the undeveloped Oregon country.

The house, which was the home of Jason Lee, superintendent of the mission, was shared with three other mission families although it was only an eighteen by forty two-story house. The first meeting which led to the organization of the Oregon Institute, which became WILLAMETTE UNIVERSITY, was held in this house. Also important meetings concerning both the M.E. Church and a government for Oregon were held here.

After the close of the Indian Mission the house was sold by the church, and in private ownership it was used to house the second store operated in Salem, and the first post office. For over a century the house was used as a private residence, but it has now been moved to the

Thomas Kay Historical Park near Willamette University. With all the additions of over a century removed, it is being restored to the original structure and will be maintained as a historic shrine.

Lee Mission Cemetery is the burial place of Jason Lee, the first missionary to the Pacific Northwest. When Lee established his mission for the Indians of Oregon in 1834, the sovereignty of the Pacific Northwest was still in dispute between Great Britain and the United States. In this pioneer burial ground, near the grave of the missionary leader, are those of his two wives and infant son, and of Cyrus Shepard, the first teacher of the mission school. Nearby are the graves of many other early Methodist missionaries, including Alvan F. Waller, GUSTAVUS HINES, JOSIAH L. PARRISH, Alanson Beers, William Roberts, James H. Wilbur, Nehemiah Doane, and others. It is also the burial place of many of the Methodist circuit riders of pioneer Oregon including John Roork, Daniel Rader, George M. Booth and many others. The cemetery is in contemporary use and is under the direction of a board of trustees responsible to the OREGON CONFERENCE of The Methodist Church.

The **Old Parsonage** which housed a generation of Methodist missionaries and circuit riders of pioneer Oregon days was the second house built in what is now the capital city of Oregon. Built in 1841-42, directly after the Lee House was finished, it was first occupied by Gustavus Hines when he was in charge of the Indian Mission Manual Labor School.

When the Indian Mission was closed, the "Old Parsonage" as it became known in later years, was given by the Mission Board as a parsonage for the M.E. Church in Salem, and later for the circuit riders whose circuit included all the Willamette Valley south of Salem. In the "Old Parsonage" were held many meetings pertaining to the organization of the Oregon Institute, which became Willamette University, and meetings of the M.E. Church in pioneer Oregon.

For over a century the "Old Parsonage" was used as a private residence, but now it has been moved back near its original site, where it is being restored to its original structure. With the Lee House it will be a part of the Thomas Kay Historical Park.

C. J. Brosnan, *Jason Lee*. 1932.
General Minutes.
H. K. Hines, *Pacific Northwest*. 1899.
T. D. Yarnes, *Oregon*. 1958.

ERLE HOWELL
ROBERT MOULTON GATKE

SALINA, KANSAS, U.S.A. **First Church** looks back to May 2, 1860, when the first meeting was held in Salina. The church did not organize until 1863, but a Sunday school had been organized earlier and many of the meetings were held during the intervening months.

During the church's history, there have been two building locations within half a block of each other, and three sanctuary buildings. In 1965 an educational wing was added to the present building. The entire property, including three ministerial residences, is presently valued at over $1,000,000.

The church in 1962 accepted the responsibility for assisting in the organization and support of Trinity, a new Methodist church in Salina, and contributed $24,000 over a three-year period for such support, as well as releasing 150 members to go into the new church. At present the

church supports a missionary to the CONGO in Africa. In 1970 membership was 1,834, and the church had a staff of thirteen members with a total of six choirs.

General Minutes.

BASIL L. JOHNSON

SALISBURY, FRANK OWEN (1874-1962), British artist, was born on Dec. 18, 1874, at Harpenden, England, was educated privately and at Heatherly's and the Royal Academy Schools and studied also in Italy, Germany, and France. He received honorary doctorates from British and American institutions and was awarded the Victorian Order by the British Crown, and Cavaliere of the Order of the Crown of Italy.

Salisbury was a prolific painter of portraits and historical scenes. His subjects included most of the members of the Royal Family, six presidents of the United States, and numerous notable personages on both sides of the Atlantic. He received more official commissions than any other man, and he accompanied Queen Elizabeth to America on the occasion of the presentation of his portrait of King George.

Reared as a devout Methodist, Salisbury painted three portraits of JOHN WESLEY and also portraits of CHARLES and SUSANNA WESLEY, THOMAS COKE, FRANCIS ASBURY, and the five first officers of the WORLD METHODIST COUNCIL after its reorganization with permanent officials in 1951. Ten Salisbury portraits are in the World Methodist Building at LAKE JUNALUSKA, N. C., U.S.A., and three of these have been reproduced and sold widely.

Salisbury died at his home in LONDON on Aug. 31, 1962. He bequeathed his palatial home, Sarum Chase, to the BRITISH COUNCIL OF CHURCHES.

JOHN KENT

SALISBURY, NORTH CAROLINA, U.S.A., the Rowan County seat since 1753, lies west of the Yadkin River on historic Trading Path. It was the most important town in western NORTH CAROLINA for a century, and supply depot to surrounding states. Salisbury was encompassed by the Yadkin Circuit of the M.E. Church in 1780. Salisbury Society and Circuit were organized by BEVERLY ALLEN in 1783, served by JESSE LEE in 1784, HOPE HULL in 1785, and William Lambeth in 1796. The Circuit covered counties along Yadkin River south from Salisbury to the SOUTH CAROLINA line. Salisbury was host to the annual conference of Feb. 21, 1786. The Salisbury District, covering the Piedmont and much of the mountains of western North Carolina in 1801 (covering Rowan and Cabarrus Counties today), was originally in the VIRGINIA CONFERENCE. Then it went into the NORTH CAROLINA CONFERENCE from 1837-1890; and since 1890 has been in the WESTERN NORTH CAROLINA CONFERENCE.

From the Society of 1783 has grown the 1,740 member First Church of Salisbury. It has been on the present site since 1831, though the congregation rebuilt in 1857, again in 1917, and since 1960 has erected a $1,200,000 plant. Coburn Memorial Church was organized in 1888; Main Street and Park Avenue after 1899, and Milford Hills after 1950.

Among other Methodist denominations in Salisbury, the A.M.E. ZION CHURCH established its denominational school, LIVINGSTONE COLLEGE, in 1879, and has important Moore's Chapel and Soldier's Memorial Churches. The college presently has 900 students. The denomination's Hood Theological Seminary is on the same campus.

The C.M.E. CHURCH has Craige Street Church. The WESLEYAN METHODIST CHURCH has a mission in Salisbury. The United Methodist Church continues to station its district superintendent in Salisbury and the Salisbury district presently reports 20,164 members.

F. Asbury, *Journal and Letters.* 1958.
W. L. Grissom, *North Carolina.* 1905.
Journals of the Virginia, North Carolina, and Western North Carolina Conferences.
Jethro Rumple, *A History of Rowan County, North Carolina.*
N.p., n.d.   G. W. BUMGARNER

QUEEN SALOTE

SALOTE, TUPOU, QUEEN OF TONGA (1900-1965),

was born on March 13, 1900, at Nukualofa, TONGA, and was educated in AUCKLAND, NEW ZEALAND. She was the daughter of King George Tupou II and great-great-grand-daughter of King George Tupou I, a member of the world's oldest dynasty, the kings of which have been Christians and Methodists since the beginning of the nineteenth century.

Queen Salote became the leader of three Methodist classes and her son, Crown Prince Tunge, was licensed as a LOCAL PREACHER. The Queen is regarded as the head of the Methodist Church, which is related to Australasian Methodism; and in Tonga is the nearest approach of Methodism to the position of a state church in the world. She attended the coronation of Queen Elizabeth II in LONDON in 1952 and Her Majesty attended the Methodist Church when she visited Tonga; it was said to be the only instance when a reigning British sovereign worshipped in a Methodist service.

Queen Salote received three decorations from the British Government.

She died Dec. 16, 1965.

AUSTRALIAN EDITORIAL COMMITTEE

SALT LAKE CITY, UTAH,

U.S.A., was founded in 1847 by Mormon pioneers led by Brigham Young. From a population of 1,500 in 1848, the city had grown to 176,793 by 1970. It is located in the bed of pre-historic Lake Bonneville, in the shadow of the Wasatch mountains, about fifteen miles east of the Great Salt Lake. Salt Lake City has become the business, industrial, medical, transportation, communication and cultural heart of a vast agricultural-mining region. It has always been the international headquarters for the Church of Jesus Christ of the Latter Day Saints. The community has fostered numerous educational institutions, including WESTMINSTER COLLEGE, supported by Presbyterian (U.S.A.), Methodist, and United Church of Christ denominations. In 1970 there were three United Methodist congregations and one A.M.E.

Salt Lake City existed for seventeen years before Norman McLeod, a Congregational minister from DENVER, Colo., established the first Protestant church in 1864. By 1871 the Presbyterians, Methodists, Roman Catholics and Baptists had arrived.

Methodists A. N. Fisher and Bishop CALVIN KINGSLEY had preached in the Latter Day Saints' Tabernacle at the invitation of Church President (and one-time Methodist) Brigham Young in 1868 and 1869 respectively. In November 1869, Bishop MATTHEW SIMPSON urged the Methodist Missionary Board to create a UTAH mission. By December 1869, LEWIS HARTSOUGH was in Salt Lake City as the state's first Methodist mission superintendent. From the CENTRAL NEW YORK CONFERENCE, Gustavus Marshall Pierce was sent to be the pastor-organizer of Salt Lake City's First Methodist Church. Pierce arrived on May 8, 1870, preached his first sermon on May 15, and on the next day organized the congregation. By 1875, a $72,000 church had been erected, $52,000 of which was raised across the nation through the efforts of C. C. McCABE, then with the CHURCH EXTENSION SOCIETY. In 1905, First Church was relocated and a new building erected. This still serves the congregation.

Salt Lake City has five other Methodist churches. One, organized in 1892 in an abandoned Congregational chapel, received help from the CENTENARY FUND in 1921 to relocate and build a new church, and this continues today as Centenary Methodist Church. A west side project started by the Utah Mission Conference in 1894 was also rebuilt in 1922 with gifts from the Centenary Fund, and today serves a difficult neighborhood as Grace Methodist Church.

Liberty Park Church, organized and built in 1892, was relocated and rebuilt in 1904, only to be relocated and renamed Christ Methodist Church in the early 1950's.

The Community Methodist Church at Midvale, a suburb, was organized in 1907, and still continues its program in a building erected in 1924. Trinity Methodist Church was organized in 1956, in a new housing development southwest of the city which was built on the site of a World War II Air Force Recruit Replacement Center. In 1970, these six churches reported 2,763 members, combined budgets of $209,849, and properties valued at $1,563,881. Cooperative studies were instituted by the Salt Lake City Methodist Churches in 1967 to determine more effective patterns for carrying out their mission.

The WOMAN'S HOME MISSIONARY SOCIETY of the M.E. Church became interested in Utah in the early 1880's. DEACONESS work was established in Salt Lake City in 1894, and a pleasant home was erected in 1905. In 1937, new modes of operation transformed this building into a boarding residence for young women who had come to the city. Still another transition was effected in 1966 when the residence was renamed Crossroads Urban Center and a program of service to inner city youth was initiated by the Woman's Division of the Board of Missions of The Methodist Church.

General Minutes, UMC.

H. M. Merkel, *Utah.* 1938.

Thomas F. O'Dea, *The Mormons.* Chicago: University of Chicago Press, 1957.   WILLIAM R. PERSONS

SALTER, MOSES BUCKINGHAM (1841-1913), American bishop of the A.M.E. CHURCH, was born in CHARLESTON, S. C., on Feb. 13, 1841. He was educated at WILBERFORCE UNIVERSITY. In 1866, he was admitted to the South Carolina Annual Conference. He was ordained DEACON and ELDER in 1866 and held pastorates in SOUTH CAROLINA and GEORGIA. He was a presiding elder in South Carolina during 1868-70. He was elected bishop in 1892 from the pastorate of Emmanuel Church, Charleston. Bishop Salter served in South Carolina, KENTUCKY and TENNESSEE, TEXAS and OKLAHOMA, MISSISSIPPI and LOUISIANA and FLORIDA. He was elected to the ECUMENICAL METHODIST CONFERENCE of 1901. He retired in 1912.

R. R. Wright, *The Bishops.* 1963.   GRANT S. SHOCKLEY

SALTVILLE, VIRGINIA, U.S.A. **Madame Russell Church.** (See RUSSELL, ELIZABETH HENRY; KEYWOOD, VA.)

SALVADOR, Brazil. In 1880 Bishop WILLIAM TAYLOR made the attempt to plant Methodism in Salvador, capital of the State of Baia. Due to lack of workers, this effort proved unsuccessful and was soon given up. Thereafter, for many decades Methodist work in Brazil—except for that of GEORGE B. NIND in Recife, Pernambuco (1880-92), and that of JUSTUS NELSON in Belém and Manáus, Amazonas (1880-96)—was confined to the Southern third of the nation.

A second, and this time successful, effort resulted when the 1946 General Conference of the Methodist Church of Brazil, appointed Benedito Natal Quintanilha as the first "missionary" to that city, capital of the state. The financing of the plan was carried out by a fourth Sunday offering in all Sunday schools. By 1950, a house had been acquired, large enough for a congregation of forty, Sunday school, clinic, and pastoral residence. In 1955, Salvador became a regular pastoral charge; and in 1960, the Salvador District was organized with two pastoral charges and 117 members. The growth has been consistent since that date.

W. C. Barclay, *History of Missions.* 1957.

Journals of General Conference and Annual Conferences, Brazil, 1946, 1950, 1955, 1960.   D. A. REILY

SALVATION. Salvation has been defined as a right relation to God, fellowship with God being both the highest and noblest of human experiences, and also that which sets him free from bondage to sinful habit. The Bible opens with a graphic representation of the dreadful fact that man is a fallen and disobedient creature, spiritually alienated from God (Genesis i:26, 31; iii:23). However, the heavenly Father has done everything possible to lead back His children into a right relation with Himself. Without this salvation man is as a sheep which has gone astray, not knowing where he is, or in what direction he should go. Yet in every normal human being there is a God-implanted instinctive hunger for more than our pres-

ent life realizes. We feel in at least some dim way our contact with a world of spiritual reality, and we begin to appreciate it and to seek after it. So Wesley writes: "Whether this is natural, or superadded by the grace of God, it is found at least in some small degree in every child of man . . . not only in all Christians, but in all Mohammedans, all pagans. . . ."

We see the development of this conception in the Old Testament. In earlier days a right relation to Jehovah was considered as possible through membership of the People of Israel. Not until after the Exile, perhaps, did the pious Jew commonly think of himself as an individual in God's sight. In the Church the New Testament conception of God as "Father," and of man as His "child," was during ages of barbarism sometimes obscured, or even lost. Nevertheless, the promise of Jesus, "And if I go I will send you the Comforter, who will guide you into all truth," proved to be a reality. In times of spiritual renewal in the Church the race recovered the truly Christian idea of God as "Father," and came to believe in the possibility that men may become "sons of God."

Salvation requires a right relation to man as well as to God. In His summary of "all the law and the prophets" Jesus linked the love of neighbor with the love of God. Furthermore, the experience of modern industrial societies has led Christians back to the ancient conviction that the right relationship of man to man must include what we may call "social" situations. God requires a wholesome community as well as upright individuals.

How then is this right relation to God, this salvation, to be brought into human experience? The essential Christian answer is: "By grace are ye saved through faith." (Ephesians ii:8.) Being a real "Father," God was concerned for the lost son, and set out to help man to come once again into the family. This divine attitude, act, or initiative, is called "grace." Grace, then, is a personal influence brought to bear upon the spirit of man by the Spirit of God. In the gospel this grace of God is expressed in Jesus, in His coming to man as man, the loving invitation of His teaching, His delivering acts of healing, and His death and resurrection. His name was called "Jesus" because He came to save His People from their sins. (Matthew i:21.)

Thus Jesus is found to be not only the bringer of God's grace, but also the means whereby that divine concern is able to move out savingly to those who believe in Him. If we who are indwelt and empowered with His Spirit of grace follow His example of love, service, and forgiveness, then "Believe on the Lord Jesus Christ and thou shalt be saved" (Acts xvi:31) is fulfilled in us. The Good Samaritan of the parable is therefore an illustration of the grace of God going out through man.

"By grace are ye saved *through faith*." (Ephesians ii:8.) It remains for man to respond to the divine initiative of forgiveness and power. So St. Paul writes: "Work out your own salvation . . . for it is God which worketh in you." (Philippians ii:12, 13.) As sin involves personal choice and action, so also does salvation. The faith of man must cooperate with the grace of God. As Dr. Rufus Jones has said, "Something comes down from above, but something must also go up from below."

Faith in Christ occasions an eager desire to be like Him. It inspires the will to do God's will, as Jesus reveals and interprets it. "No spiritual good can be ours until we desire it; nor will any be withheld from us which through appreciation and preference we are capable of receiving." Faith therefore fulfills itself in "good works." As Wesley constantly urged: "To those who attentively consider the thirteenth chapter of the first epistle to the Corinthians, it will be undeniably plain that what St. Paul there describes as the highest of all Christian graces, is properly and directly the love of our neighbour. And to him who attentively considers the whole tenor both of the Old and the New Testaments, it will be equally plain that good works springing from this love are the highest part of the religion therein revealed."

What then, we ask, is the state of mind of the one who has come into a right relation with God? the one who possesses salvation? The thought of being "saved" lifts one's heart toward God, and hence brings a sense of joy. When a man honestly says "Our Father who art in heaven" he rises to strength, to assurance. Humbly, yet with certainty, he may with the Apostle Paul say: "I have fought a good fight, I have finished my course, I have kept the faith; henceforth there is laid up for me a crown of righteousness, which the Lord, the righteous judge, shall give to me at that day; and not to me only, but to all them also that love His appearing." (2 Timothy iv: 7-8.) So salvation culminates in life with God for ever.

W. N. Clarke, *An Outline of Christian Theology.*
Wm. Adams Brown, *Christian Theology in Outline.*
A. C. Knudson, *Present Tendencies in Religious Thought.*
W. L. Sperry, *What We Mean by Religion.*

ROBERT W. GOOOLOE

SALVATION ARMY, Br. (See BOOTH, WILLIAM.)

SAMOA is the name by which the Samoan Islands are usually referred to, and its eastern section—which is smaller than western Samoa—is a possession of the United States. American Samoa comprises seven eastern islands of the Samoan group—Tutuila, Aunuu, Manua Islands (Tau, Olosega, and Ofu) and Rose Island, which is a coral atoll. Western Samoa is now independent, but for awhile was under a NEW ZEALAND mandate. Population (1970): American Samoa, 27,769; Western Samoa, 141,000.

Samoans are an outstanding section of the Polynesian race, dignified and skilled in oratory, "the aristocrats of the Pacific." Samoans and Tongans have a racial affinity, with similarity in language. The comparative proximity of the two groups has led to frequent intermingling.

In 1828 a visiting Samoan chief professed conversion in TONGA very soon after missionary work began there. On returning to Samoa he began to persuade many of his neighbors to renounce heathenism and to accept the "Tongan religion," as Christianity was called. Samoan Methodists regard 1828 as the year when Christianity first reached their land.

PETER TURNER was the first resident European missionary. He came in 1835, accompanied by enthusiastic Tongan pastors, and found 2,000 already claiming to be Methodists. Revival scenes, like those in Tonga in the previous year, followed Peter Turner's ministry and in four years the number of adherents had grown to 13,000.

Unfortunately, Samoa was to provide a disturbing example of two evangelical Protestant missions operating in the same group. John Williams, the redoubtable pioneer of the London Missionary Society in many South Sea

Islands groups, visited Samoa in 1830 and left eight teachers from Tahiti. Shortly afterwards he discussed the position with the Methodist missionaries in Tonga and a definite policy of limiting areas of operations was agreed upon by the parent bodies of the Methodist and London Missionary Societies in Britain. The London Missionary Society, it was decided, should work in Samoa and the Methodists in Tonga and FIJI.

When, in 1836, London Missionary Society representatives arrived in Samoa they resented the presence of Peter Turner. He received instructions to vacate the field only after they had arrived. At that time communication was irregular and infrequent in the Pacific. The Samoan Methodists were in genuine distress; they were attached to Turner and the "Tongan religion"; they said they "heard of the 'Tahitian religion' only last night."

From 1839 to 1857 there was no official Methodist Church in Samoa but thousands of the Samoan converts refused to join the London Missionary Society. As the years went by many of them relapsed into heathenism.

When British Methodism created an independent Australasian Conference responsible for the Pacific Islands in 1855, it was decided to resume work in Samoa. This happened through the advocacy of JOHN THOMAS, the veteran Chairman in Tonga, who believed that those who still claimed to be Methodists in Samoa needed missionary oversight. He also contended that the Australasian Conference was not bound by the agreement made in 1839 between the London Missionary Society and the British Conference—a rather flimsy argument.

It is generally agreed that the decision to return was a blunder. When Martin Dyson arrived in 1857, he found fewer than 3,000 nominal Methodist adherents and religious life at a very low ebb. The main influence in the division was tribal feeling and a spirit of faction. Although he believed that the Samoan Methodists should be induced to join the London Missionary Society, Dyson finally accepted the situation. His work was followed by that of GEORGE BROWN, who became the most successful Methodist missionary in the history of the Pacific Islands. Both of these men maintained friendly relations with the missionaries of the London Missionary Society which their people were resolved not to join.

The later years of the century were marked by civil wars, the entry of foreign powers, and the division of Samoa between GERMANY and the U.S.A. in 1899. The residence of the famous writer, Robert Louis Stevenson, was in Western Samoa during this period.

When Germany was defeated in the 1914-18 war, the mandate for Western Samoa from the League of Nations was given to New Zealand. In 1919 pneumonic influenza caused the death of more than twenty percent of the population of Western Samoa in a few weeks; in Eastern Samoa not a life was lost through careful American quarantine.

Educational progress, church-building, happier relations with the London Missionary Society have marked recent years. Always the comparatively small Methodist Church in Samoa has been distinguished by its willingness to send workers to pioneer fields. In 1964 Samoan Methodism became an independent conference associated with the General Conference of the Methodist Church of Australasia.

Since 1962 Western Samoa has been an independent nation, with its motto, "Samoa founded upon God," a tribute to the effect of Christian missions and the ideal for Samoa's future.

G. Brown, *Autobiography*. 1908.
J. W. Burton, *Call of the Pacific*. 1912.
J. Colwell, *Century in the Pacific*. 1914.
M. Dyson, *Samoan Methodism*. 1875.
Findlay and Holdsworth, *Wesleyan Miss. Soc.* 1921.
S. Masterman, *Outline of Samoan History*. 1958.

HAROLD WOOD

JOHN VICTOR SAMUEL

SAMUEL, JOHN VICTOR (1930-   ), bishop of The United Methodist Church of PAKISTAN, was elected to this position on Oct. 15, 1968, in Multan, West Pakistan. He had previously been an ecumenical executive, a district superintendent, and a former staff member of the Methodist Board of Missions. A Pakistani, he is the first bishop to be chosen by the Methodists of Pakistan, and the first of his nationality to be elected to the Methodist episcopacy. Bishop Samuel is one of the youngest men ever elected to the episcopacy. His election came on the first ballot at the first meeting of the newly constituted Pakistan United Methodist Central Conference in Multan. His area includes the Indus River Annual Conference and the Karachi Provisional Annual Conference with approximately 40,794 members.

N. B. H.

SAN ANGELO, TEXAS, U.S.A. **First Church** is almost as old as the city in which it has witnessed for eighty-four years. The "fighting parson," A. J. Potter, a circuit rider, began preaching in the new county seat town in 1882. Preaching at times with a pistol on his hip and a Winchester in his pulpit, work was begun which resulted in the organization of First Church one year later. The first building was a white frame structure, the only Methodist church in a five-hundred mile area, and was used for all other Protestant services for several years. By 1906 the growing membership of 750 met its demands for additional facilities by moving to a new building at the present location on Beauregard and Oakes. This sanctuary served well until a membership of 1,919 necessitated expansion and remodeling by 1928. Destroyed by a fire in 1945, plans for a new and larger building were begun. In 1950 the present Gothic sanctuary was completed.

The education ministry of the church was first aided by the construction of Massie Memorial Education Building in 1924. Dedicated in honor of Mrs. Massie, a tireless, influential laywoman, the building was used by all divisions of the church school until growth in the classes demanded further expansion. The present four-story education building, completed in 1962, once again provides space for all classes in the same building.

The church's 1970 membership of 1,876 is guided by the pastor and a staff of eight full-time and three part-time employees, including three ministers, a director of education, and an organist-director of music.

The history of the growth and development of First Church closely parallels that of its home city. Through the years it has sought to meet the demands and challenges of San Angelo as the downtown church in a growing city.

GLENN D. WEIMER

SAN ANTONIO, TEXAS, U.S.A., an old historic city which combines the historic Texas-Mexican past with the forward looking impetus of a growing and great city, is situated in southwest TEXAS and has long been a dominant metropolis of that section of the state. Methodism was first introduced into San Antonio in April 1844 by circuit rider JOHN WESLEY DeVILBISS, missionary from OHIO, who in company with a Presbyterian minister, John McCollough, rode into the city from Seguin under an escort obtained from Captain Hay's Texas Rangers. On Sunday he preached in the County Clerk's office to a congregation of fifteen people. A year later, while serving as pastor of the Gonzales Circuit, he returned to San Antonio and established a regular appointment, preaching in the parlor of the Veramendi Hotel.

On Feb. 4, 1846, at the meeting of the TEXAS CONFERENCE in Houston, he was appointed to "The San Antonio Mission" with a missionary appropriation of $200. Moving to San Antonio, DeVilbiss became the first resident Protestant minister in the city. He taught a small school to supplement his salary allowance, and obtained the use of the court house for regular preaching services. At this time San Antonio was in the Rutersville District, and in May the district superintendent, Mordecai Yell, accompanied by two other Methodist ministers, visited the city, their unexpected appearance moving the lonely pastor to tears. In June 1846 the organization of a church was effected with eleven members enrolled. In 1853 a tract of land was purchased on Soledad Street, and a building was erected which was called Paine Chapel. The membership was by that time thirty-five whites and fifteen "colored." This building housed the growing church for some thirty years when the membership, then above 300 souls, purchased lots on the corner of Travis and Navarro Streets. The relocated church was thenceforth called Travis Park Methodist Church.

The influx of German people into the city, following their migration to Texas at and after mid-nineteenth century, led to the organization of a German Methodist Church. Their building, erected in 1876, still stands as a shrine in La Villita (Little Town), a typical mid-eighteenth century Spanish settlement in the heart of historic San Antonio. As the language barrier gave way, this and other German-speaking Methodist congregations merged with the English-speaking churches.

Immediately following the Civil War and the abolition

of slavery separate organizations of Negro Methodists began to appear, both the M.E. and the A.M.E. churches dating their origins as of 1867. The M.E. group recognized modern St. Paul's as their mother church. In 1970 there were eight churches of the former Central Jurisdiction with a membership of 2,327. The A.M.E. work was begun by Richard Haywood, who spent some four years in the organizational effort, preaching most of this time in an old stone building called "the Soap Factory" which was rented for $15 per month. This branch of Methodism now has ten churches in San Antonio with a membership of 2,600.

From the beginning of organized Methodism in San Antonio a "Mexican Mission" was maintained, this appointment later becoming part of a Mexican Mission District covering all of south Texas. In 1874 La Trinidad Church was organized by missionary A. H. Sutherland, and became the center of Methodist work among Spanish-speaking people. In 1878 the pastor reported 100 members and three Sunday schools. There are now in the city seven Spanish-speaking United Methodist churches, holding membership in the RIO GRANDE CONFERENCE which covers most of Texas and NEW MEXICO. The Wesley Community House, originally operated by the WOMAN'S SOCIETY OF CHRISTIAN SERVICE, offers playground facilities, fellowship, and religious training for hundreds of the underprivileged.

In old San Antonio, predominantly Latin and Catholic, Methodism made a slow beginning. The *Journals* of 1900 show only seven churches with less than 1,500 members, but with the turn of the century and the growth of the city Methodism grew apace. The several branches of Methodism now number fifty-seven churches with a total membership of over 35,000.

The institutional life of San Antonio Methodism began with the first meeting of the Rio Grande (Southwest Texas) Conference in Goliad in 1859. A San Antonio Female College was projected and fifty-five trustees were elected. After a few difficult years it disappears from record, but was opened again in 1894. In 1918 it was made coeducational and the name was changed to Westmoreland—later to the University of San Antonio. In 1942 it was deeded outright to the Presbyterian Church and became Trinity University.

For many years San Antonio has been the established center of Methodism in the SOUTHWEST TEXAS CONFERENCE. A Methodist Building is maintained with offices for the white, Negro and Latin superintendents, the conference treasurer, and for all conference secretaries. The annual conference meetings are regularly held in Travis Park Church.

Alamo Heights Church is one of the largest and finest churches in San Antonio. Started in 1910 as a struggling mission and connected with Travis Park Church for a while, it has grown into one of the major churches of the Southwest Texas Conference.

At one time, the church was on the outer rim of the city, but that same location today is in the heart of one of the great and rapidly expanding areas. It is now the second largest United Methodist Church in San Antonio, with a membership of 2,369.

Situated in one of San Antonio's most beautiful areas, the church has a plant valued in excess of $1,400,000.

Jefferson Church is part of a master plan development in south Texas following World War II. Projected by the San Antonio City Mission Board on the basis of sociological

and industrial surveys, its institutional functions have been related to three stages of development.

The first congregation met in surplus army tents in an undeveloped residential area, with the expected residential saturation the basis for all projections. From sixty-six members on March 10, 1946, membership grew to 1,000 in six years and 2,000 in fourteen years. It reported 1,711 members in 1970.

In the first phase, the church served as a social and recreational center for all of the people in the community. Its first buildings were therefore a chapel and a community recreation hall. A lighted sports area, food service facilities for large community gatherings, and a meeting hall for public forums made possible community service to the developing neighborhood. A week-day school was founded during the first phases.

The second planned phase took into account the organization of other churches and schools as well as the rise of service clubs and recreation centers. During this phase, the church turned to its denominational responsibilities and built facilities designed to serve its congregational needs: church school units and a large sanctuary. Organizationally, it undertook to become an effective institutional church for the northwest quadrant of the city.

The church entered its third planned phase after twenty years. It has sought to become an institutional center from which members will participate in the social and political life of the city. Its membership includes leaders of numerous educational, business, governmental, and industrial enterprises. The church houses a Child Care Development Center in cooperation with the national economic opportunity program, and undertakes social service projects especially related to poverty groups of the city.

Jefferson Church has from its inception been a center for experimentation and innovation in church life, both in worship and education, and in its approach to community service work. The existing plant consists of a sanctuary, a chapel, a community hall, and three educational buildings, all on ground level on a site comprising a city block. Architecture is a contemporary adaptation of Spanish Mission Colonial by the ecclesiastical architect Henry J. Steinbomer. Properties are valued in excess of $900,000.

Laurel Heights Church was organized in 1909 when San Antonio had a population of only 96,000. The nearest Methodist churches, Travis Park and West End, were each about two miles away. Among the leaders in promoting the new church were Judge and Mrs. J. O. Terrell and Allen K. Ragsdale. A small tabernacle was first built to serve as a temporary meeting-place. An English Gothic sanctuary was ready for use on Easter Sunday, 1912. The charter roll contained 178 names. An indebtedness of $30,000 had been incurred in the building program.

Six years later the debt was liquidated, and on Sept. 29, 1918, Bishop EDWIN D. MOUZON formally dedicated the church. In succeeding years two important building-expansion programs—in 1928 and 1958—have greatly increased the capacity and facilities of the church plant.

Throughout the span of its history Laurel Heights has been served by capable and dedicated ministers. Two pastors, A. FRANK SMITH and H. BASCOM WATTS, later became bishops.

In 1946 the Laurel Heights Church financed the building of a Methodist bishops' residence in Mexico City. Since the 1940's it has supported a missionary couple in South America, first in CHILE and in recent years in BOLIVIA. It gives fifteen scholarships annually to needy young people who are attending Texas Methodist colleges. Its members have accepted leadership roles, served on boards of directors, and engaged in a continuing program of volunteer services, all related to the Methodist institutions which serve the local community—the Methodist Hospital, the Wesley Community Centers, the Methodist Mission Home, and the Morningside Retirement Home. The church is presently moving toward a wider service to its own immediate neighborhood, which now possesses many aspects of the "inner city" with sub-standard housing and deprived families. Plans made in collaboration with a nearby Roman Catholic church call for a summer activities program for children, as a first step in an ecumenical program of social service. It is hoped that this "unity in mission" will expand in the years to come.

Methodist Mission Home of Texas. About the year 1890 Mrs. M. L. Volino, who operated a brothel in the "Red Light" district of San Antonio, was soundly converted to the Christian faith under the ministry of W. W. PINSON, pastor of Travis Park Church. She immediately converted her home into a place of refuge for her own and such other girls as wished to escape from a life of prostitution. Her word was, "I will give you a home and God will give you bread." The support of this "Rescue Home," as it was called, was taken over by Travis Park Church and later, in 1901, by the West Texas (Southwest Texas) Conference. By degrees it became a refuge for expectant, unwed mothers. This involved a new name, a new location, and eventually the support of six conferences of Texas Methodism. It now provides medical care, personal counselling, and rehabilitation training for hundreds of unfortunate girls and is a licensed adoption agency for their babies. During the seventy years of its existence it has served over 5,000 residents and has placed over 2,000 babies in Christian homes. A new twenty-acre site has been purchased for the home, and building plans involving more than a million dollars are under way.

Morningside Manor is a home for older adults, owned by the San Antonio District, situated on a twenty-acre campus in northwest San Antonio. Established in 1961 at a cost of $1,250,000, it has a capacity for 144 people.

Oak Island Church, located fifteen miles south of Bexar County courthouse, is on a site that has been under flags of six nations—France, Spain, Mexico, Republic of Texas, U.S.A., and Confederate States of America. Oak Island people today reflect something of this varied background. Huguenots fleeing religious persecution in FRANCE as early as 1684 settled in the English colony of MARYLAND, and they have descendents in Oak Island. In 1691 SPAIN, fearing French aggression in Texas, established a government in the present Bexar County area, though Spanish colonization did not begin there until 1718, when San Antonio was founded. A trickle of American colonists ventured into Texas in the 1820's. Some Oak Islanders today can trace back to Spanish land grants of the period. After Texas won independence from MEXICO by revolution in 1836, and during Republic of Texas days (1836-1846), tides of English-speaking and other immigrants poured into Texas. Among Oak Island settlers many German immigrants added to the mosaic of culture.

The first link of Oak Island with Methodism goes back to early eighteenth century and its indefinite boundaries when Spain claimed a large part of North America, including the new English colony of GEORGIA, when JOHN WESLEY ministered to colonists in 1736-1737. Wesley found Spanish-speaking settlers and immediately learned the Spanish language to minister to them. More than a century later, 1858-1859, John Wesley DeVilbiss continued Wesley's precedent in west and southwest Texas, including Bexar County. In 1867-1868 DeVilbiss organized a congregation in Oak Island. In 1871 the present building was begun with volunteer help from the community, including Comanche Indian contribution. When finished the building was used for the Oak Island public school on week days. Architecture is the simple classic type found in pioneer churches from New England to the Rio Grande. DeVilbiss and his son made by hand pews, pulpit, and lampstands, still in use. Oak Island cemetery holds graves of pioneers, circuit riders, soldiers of several wars, grave of Mrs. CHLOE STEVENS, Negro heroine of the Battle of San Jacinto, and many others whose lives contributed to building church and nation.

Oak Island Church, in the shadow of creeping urbanization, maintains its identity as a small church by the side of a road, continuing a Christian witness to all with warmth, friendliness, loyalty, and patriotism. An official Texas Historical Marker sponsored by the Texas State Historical Survey Committee and Texas Historical Foundation marks the site.

St. Andrew's Church, located in the northeast section of the city, was organized in 1952 by a small group of faithful people who first met on Wednesday evenings making preliminary plans for the new church. The first worship service was held in the Woodmen of the World Chapel, with the Alamo Heights Church providing hymnals and church school literature. Seventy-four members, representing thirty or more different families, were the first charter members. The church had expanded to 150 by September 14.

Sam L. Fore was the first pastor of St. Andrew's, and he served until June 1, 1957. Two units of a master plan of six buildings were completed in September 1954. This included a Fellowship Hall, which served the church as a sanctuary, and a Children's Building, designed to accommodate 300 children. Two other buildings were completed soon afterward, providing facilities for a kindergarten, week day school, library, Scout activities, church offices, and storage rooms.

Darrel D. Gray was pastor from 1957 through 1962, and under his leadership a new sanctuary was completed in April 1960.

An additional education building was completed during the pastorate of J. Barcus Moore.

Church membership in 1970 was 2,057.

Southwest Texas Methodist Hospital. This property of the Southwest Texas Conference is situated on seventy-four acres of land in the Oak Hills area of west San Antonio, and is part of a 750-acre medical complex which includes the South Texas State Medical School, Bexar County Teaching Hospital, Community Guidance Center, United Cerebral Palsy Treatment Center and Santa Rosa (Catholic) 300-bed Psychiatric and Rehabilitation Center. The hospital was projected in 1955, ground was broken for the first building on May 23, 1960, and the first patients were admitted Sept. 23, 1963. Still in the building process, it aims at a $20,000,000 project with 750 beds. It is modern in every respect including an underground survival complex with all vital facilities capable of accommodating 1,800 people for two weeks. It is fully accredited and at present has a professional staff of 402 physicians and an auxiliary of 940 women rendering free service.

Travis Park Church is known as "The Friendly Church in the Heart of the City." The battle of the Alamo had not yet begun when William B. Travis, a devout Methodist, in the fall of 1835 made a desperate appeal for religious instruction to Texas colonists. A few months later Travis was killed at the Alamo, but his plea for missionaries was answered by his denomination when the Methodists sent additional pioneer ministers to Texas. By 1842 John Wesley DeVilbiss, father of Travis Park Church and San Antonio Methodism, was sent to Texas to preach in several counties.

In 1846 DeVilbiss received his appointment to San Antonio where he was to organize a church. He and a Presbyterian minister made arrangements to preach in the court house on alternate Sundays and sometimes held joint services. From this humble beginning sprang one of the largest churches in the Alamo City, Travis Park Church.

In 1847 a lot was purchased on Villita Street. DeVilbiss began gathering funds to build a church. In 1853 the Methodists built a church situated on Soledad Street, on the muddy banks of the San Antonio River and named it "Paine Chapel." By 1883 the congregation was outgrowing its structure on Soledad Street and two lots were given on the corner of Travis and Navarro Streets to build a new church. In 1885 when the church had been built the name was changed to Travis Park. An education building was built next to the church on Navarro Street in 1910.

In 1921 Travis Park was enlarged to meet the requirements of its membership of 3,000. In subsequent years this great old church underwent three face-liftings. In later years the property on Travis Street next door to the church was purchased with funds left by the late Mrs. Ida Stephenson, and the Stephenson Memorial Building was erected. Ravaged by fire in October 1955, the church building was made useless and for the next three years morning services were held in the Texas Theatre.

Spearheaded by its faithful members, Travis Park Church, after considering many alternate proposals, began its rebuilding plans. The reopening of the church sanctuary took place on Sunday, Sept. 7, 1958. The properties of Travis Park are now worth $2,666,000, with a sanctuary seating capacity of approximately 2,000 and with adequate facilities for all activities.

Five of the former pastors were elected to the episcopacy: JOHN M. MOORE, EDWIN D. MOUZON, PAUL B. KERN, ARTHUR J. MOORE, and KENNETH W. COPELAND.

In 1970 the church membership was 3,221, and a very full and active program is being carried on for all age groups. One of the church's newest and most rewarding ministries is that of the Ichthus Coffee House each Saturday night, which affords San Antonio's many servicemen an opportunity for recreation in a religious atmosphere.

The WESLEY FOUNDATION, organized in 1953, is situated across the street from the main buildings of San Antonio College. It has improvements valued at $75,000, and ministers to some 500 Methodist students.

C. Stanley Banks and Pat Ireland Nixon, *Laurel Heights Methodist Church*. San Antonio: the church, 1949.
R. F. Curl, *Southwest Texas*. 1951.
Journals of the West Texas, Southwest Texas and Rio Grande Conferences.
General Minutes, UMC, 1970.
O. W. Nail, *Southwest Texas Conference*. 1958.
———, *Texas Methodism*. 1961.

M. Phelan, *Texas*. 1924.
H. Yoakum, *History of Texas*. New York: Redfield, 1855.

LOUIS UHLAND SPELLMAN
STERLING F. WHEELER
LUCY BANKS
RUTH G. JACKSON
WILMA DAVIS
EMMA GERDES

SANCHEZ Y BONET, SILVANO (1894-1967), a Cuban pastor, was born in Holguin, Orte., CUBA, Feb. 6, 1894, in the home of José Angel Sanchez Gomez and Lorenza Bonet Cedeño. His education was in the public schools of Holguin and later in CANDLER COLLEGE, Havana.

When only a youth he learned the printers' trade in which he worked until entering the ministry in 1921. Early in life he came under the influence of a Friends (Quaker) missionary who conducted a Sunday afternoon mission and was converted under the influence of Prospero Guerra.

It was unique that his first and last pastoral charge was Santiago de las Vegas, Havana. In addition he served seven other pastorates and was four times district superintendent.

Frequently he was called on to hold revivals, and in many issues of the conference paper were found gems of his writing. He was the author of the Conference hymn, *Cuba for Christ*.

His ministry was noted for faithfulness to all details, hard work, a friendly and jovial spirit, and a smile for every one.

Anuario Cubano de la Iglesia Metodista.   GARFIELD EVANS

SANCTIFICATION. (See CHRISTIAN PERFECTION and DOCTRINAL STANDARDS OF METHODISM.)

SANDERS, ARTHUR MACMILLAN (1886-1960), missionary to AUSTRALIA and TONGA, was born in Bloxwich, England. His grandfather, Kirkpatrick MacMillan, was the inventor of the bicycle. He trained as a teacher under the aegis of the University of Birmingham. In 1913 he was accepted as a candidate for the ministry in NEW SOUTH WALES and was immediately stationed at Murrurundi. In 1914 he was sent to Vavau, Tonga where he spent one third of his active ministry. Returning to New South Wales he served again with distinction in Strathfield, Gordon, Manly, and Concord Wesley. In 1942 he was appointed superintendent of the Newcastle General Mission. In 1949 he was elected Secretary of the Conference and President in 1951. He is affectionately remembered for the charm of his personality, his magnificent bass-baritone voice, the readiness of his wit, and his devoted service.

AUSTRALIAN EDITORIAL COMMITTEE

SAN DIEGO, CALIFORNIA, U.S.A. Methodism serves an area that is rapidly becoming a mecca for tourists in winter and summer because of its mild sub-tropical weather, and its accessibility from LOS ANGELES to the north and to MEXICO (Tijuana) twenty miles south. The University of California is expanding with four new colleges and a medical school. The Scripps Institution of Oceanography is located at a site most favorable for oceanographic exploration and research on the west coast. There are also San Diego State College, two private universities, five community colleges (junior), the Salk Institute for Biological Studies, and the Western Behavioral Sciences Institute.

San Diego and its excellent bay was first discovered in 1542 by the Spanish explorer, Juan Rodriguez Cabrillo. The first religious life was organized July 16, 1796 by Roman Catholic priests from the first CALIFORNIA mission, named San Diego de Alcala.

JEDEDIAH SMITH, a fervent Methodist nicknamed "Bible-toter Jed," came to San Diego, Dec. 12, 1826 as the first American to cross the deserts into California.

The first Methodists in San Diego held prayer meetings in homes and the bare upper room of the Army Barracks. Seventeen persons attended a meeting recorded as Feb. 6, 1869. The first QUARTERLY CONFERENCE met May 12, 1869; the first regular minister was appointed in October 1869, and the first building was dedicated Feb. 17, 1870.

The gold rush brought people to northern California over the routes of Jed Smith. Driving the gold spike on the Union Pacific Railroad on May 10, 1869 started people toward southern California and a land boom in the 1880's. Six churches were started during this period but only two of these continue today. Three churches were organized during the depression starting in 1892: La Mesa First, Nestor Community, and Otay M. E., which closed after the Otay Dam broke as a result of the 1916 flood.

Population quadrupled from 17,700 in 1900 to 74,638 in 1920, so eight new churches were built in the eight years between 1907 and 1915. Although the population doubled to 147,897 in 1930 only two churches were started in the 20's when the CENTENARY Movement was launched. The Depression stopped all new church extension except for the work of GOODWILL INDUSTRIES which began operations in San Diego Jan. 1, 1930. Myron Insko, as Executive Director, reported they started in a rented building with equipment worth about $5,000 and paid about $5,400 wages during that first year. There are now six branch stores and equipment worth about $650,000. They provide employment to 500 persons who receive wages of about $600,000.

The war years, 1940-45, brought into being five new churches to care for the military, their families, and the war industry workers. The post-war boom, 1947-58, saw the need for nine new churches to be built for young families seeking new homes in new tract areas, and increased the need for facilities in higher education. For ten years, 1956-66, Methodists sponsored the only Protestant university in San Diego. A million dollars was raised through the church for expansion, in addition to large amounts given through gifts and bequests from individuals and local churches. The University, however, at the 1966 annual conference requested to be released from the control and liabilities of the church. Thus they could feel free to apply for financial support from other sources.

A new pattern for starting new churches was developed in 1960. Rather than holding meetings in homes or public buildings, a demountable "A-frame" building was designed as a temporary building on the church site to serve all the needs of the people until they could organize and build their own first permanent unit. North Clairemont was started with this "A-frame" in 1960. It was dismantled and re-erected to start San Carlos in 1962. Later it was moved to start Park Hill in Chula Vista.

A vital organization in the development and support of Methodism in San Diego has been the San Diego Method-ist Church Union, which was organized Feb. 22, 1926. About two-thirds of the present churches have been aided at some time by cooperative effort through the Union in the form of a gift, guaranteeing a church loan, or holding a deed. They have been instrumental in stabilizing support for the work of WESLEY FOUNDATION at San Diego State College, and in encouraging and assisting local churches to support the development of Bethel Mission in Tijuana, Mexico. CHAPLAIN service for Methodists, primarily at the County General Hospital, was started in 1952. It has also become the coordinating agency for chaplain service at the Edgmoor Geriatric (county) Hospital.

In the nearly 100 years since Methodism started in San Diego at a prayer meeting with seventeen persons present (the lots, building, and parsonage for First Church costing $3,150), Methodism has grown to thirty-two churches belonging to the above Union. In 1970 twenty United Methodist churches reported a total membership of 12,229 and property valued at over $10,000,000.

Other Methodist churches in San Diego include one A.M.E. CHURCH, one C.M.E., one Evangelical, two FREE METHODISTS and one Free Methodist Latin American.

Meeting challenges of urbanization. Metro was organized early in 1967 as a department of the Union to involve and release the latent energies of Methodists in San Diego: (1) to serve the needs of people in contemporary metropolitan living; (2) to create better understanding and active concern among people of different economic, ethnic, racial, and creedal backgrounds, and (3) to enable these people to implement their concern through effective action, including cooperation with other denominations and community welfare agencies.

Specific Metro programs in operation are: (1) Good Neighbor Center, where volunteers provide a variety of emergency help for people living near the Center; (2) Servicemen's Center, providing a downtown lounge with a homelike atmosphere; (3) Summer Camps for more than 500 underprivileged children, being a cooperative ministry of Metro and Presbyterians utilizing the concern and talents of twenty-seven college student volunteers; (4) Operation Adventure craft classes on Saturdays with nearly 400 children enrolled; (5) an inter-racial vacation church school known as Operation Crosstown; (6) providing facilities for Woodlawn Park Community Library in an isolated semirural area; (7) established Metro Blood Bank for members of churches contributing blood, and (8) Seminars and Leadership Training for what Metro ought and can do in San Diego.

Plans for a Methodist Home in San Diego originated in 1946. In 1953 the San Diego Methodist Home Corporation took the responsibility of operating the Fredericka Home which had been organized in 1908. Pacific Homes Corporation, a benevolent, non-profit corporation of the conference, started operation of Casa de Manana in 1953, and developed Wesley Palms for occupancy in 1961. These three homes can now care for 720 persons, plus 115 in two convalescent hospitals, also operated by Pacific Homes Corporation.

"Work With Senior Citizens" is a pilot project to design and demonstrate ways of meeting needs of older adults to serve and be served through a local parish. The Women's Division of the National Board of MISSIONS started this project in 1960 with income from the Estate Trust Fund of Frank and Georgia A. Lynch, former members of

First Church. The work has expanded now to include five United Methodist Church parishes.

The latest creative attempt to meet the changing needs of people in a growing megalopolis is an ecumenical program, the New Adult Community. This project, initiated in 1967, was also made possible by funds from the Lynch Estate Trust Fund. A sincere effort is exerted to provide an ecumenical experimental ministry which can: (1) facilitate dialogue among "straight" young adults, the churches, and the new adult generation; (2) provide counsel, catalytic, therapeutic, or facilitative service for new adult groups or individuals; (3) collaborate with other community ministries and agencies in planning to meet the needs of the new adult generation, and (4) develop community comprehension groups which try to make churches sensitive and capable of meeting the needs of young adults, to have "authentic" adults whom they accept as their models, and to participate in the shaping of society.

Methodists have generally been "where the action is." Since 1939 they are increasingly ecumenical and cooperative. As United Methodists they have the added strength of two former E.U.B. churches to meet the needs of people in San Diego, "a city in motion."

First Church is the oldest Protestant church in San Diego. It began in an army barracks in February 1869, with seventeen members; it now lists a membership of 2,857. After several successive moves were made the First Church building was erected and dedicated in 1870, while D. A. Dryden was pastor. This building served the congregation for seventeen years until the second church, called the Brick Square, was built. When hard times fell upon San Diego in the 1890's it required a supreme effort by all concerned to save the church from foreclosure. In 1905, with good times restored, the Brick Square was sold to U. S. Grant, Jr. and the cornerstone laid for a new First Church at Ninth and C Streets, dedicated in 1906.

Chimes, weighing 9,600 pounds, proved to be a feature of the building. First Church became widely known through the Second World War years as a friendly church where service personnel and others, made mobile by circumstances, could find inspiration, help, food, housing, or whatever was needed. San Diegans spoke of it as "the Church of the Cross, the Chimes and the Crowds," as its lounges and offices over flowed. A new site was thereafter purchased under the ministry of Stan McKee.

The new Cathedral Church, seating 1,200 people, was built under the administration of Noel LeRoque and consecrated in November 1963. It is located at 2111 Camino Del Rio overlooking Mission Valley where over 85,000 people pass daily. A new period of growth promises continuing vitality and service to a vast city population. The church celebrated its centennial in 1969.

Edward J. P. Davis, *Historical San Diego: The Birthplace of California*. San Diego: the author, 1953.
Samuel D. Erwine, comp., *History of the First Methodist Church, 1869-1957*. San Diego, 1957.
General Minutes, UMC, 1970.
Robert F. Green, "Protestant Churches in San Diego." Unpublished thesis, on file with San Diego Historical Society Research Library at Serra Museum, San Diego, 1952.
Geraldine K. Haynes, *Fifty Years of Trinity Methodist Church, 1915-1965*. San Diego, 1965.
E. D. Jervey, *Southern California and Arizona*. 1960.
Journal of the Southern California-Arizona Conference.
The Methodist Woman, May 1965.

San Diego Historical Society Quarterly, April 1955.
San Diego Methodist Church Union *Minutes*.
William E. Smythe, *History of San Diego, 1542-1907*. San Diego: The Historical Company, 1907. HARRY E. SHIERSON

SANFORD, ALBERT MORRIS (1871-1952), Canadian Methodist and United Church of Canada minister, was born in Center Burlington, Hants County, Nova Scotia, on Dec. 23, 1871. In 1895 he graduated from MOUNT ALLISON UNIVERSITY, Sackville, New Brunswick. Upon completion of his arts course he became a probationer for the ministry, and served for two years as assistant pastor in Truro, Nova Scotia. In 1895 he came to Vancouver, British Columbia and was ordained at the annual session of Conference.

Then followed sixteen years in the pastorate. In 1913 he was appointed principal of Columbian College in New Westminster, the first degree-conferring institution in British Columbia. After Union in 1925, he became professor of Christian education and librarian in Union Theological College of British Columbia.

In the first decade of this century, when the city of Vancouver was experiencing a boom with a corresponding need for new churches, Sanford took on the responsibility of raising funds for church extension. Many a situation was saved by his borrowing from a bank solely on the strength of his own signature. In 1907, and again in 1925, he was elected President of British Columbia Methodist Conference. Not only was he the last President of this Conference, but he was also the first President of the United Church Conference of British Columbia. He played an important part in the life of the Methodist Church during its maturing years, and in the United Church in its formative decades. His place in the community was recognized by his election as the city's "Good Citizen" for 1952. After a brief illness he died on July 30 of that year.

Records of the British Columbia Conference.
E. G. Turnbull, *The Church in the Kootenays*. Trail: Trail Times, 1965.   W. P. BUNT

SAN FRANCISCO, CALIFORNIA, U.S.A. Methodism was begun by WILLIAM ROBERTS, who was appointed late in 1846 to superintend the OREGON and CALIFORNIA mission. He arrived at San Francisco on April 24, 1847, and the following day his colleague, JAMES WILBUR, preached on shipboard and Roberts preached in J. H. Brown's hotel, situated facing Portsmouth Square. This was the first Protestant service in the village of some 100 homes.

Shortly afterward Wilbur organized both a class and a Sunday school. In the late autumn Elihu Anthony visited San Francisco from San Jose and preached a few times in California's first schoolhouse and on shipboard. The class and Sunday school were still active.

Gold discovery disrupted life in San Francisco in the spring of 1848. In the winter of 1848-49, local preacher C. O. Hosford reorganized the class and preached regularly.

William Roberts returned to San Francisco early in 1849. He met with the class, but Presbyterian Timothy D. Hunt was conducting worship for all Protestants at that time.

Asa White, local preacher with his famous "blue tent," arrived at San Francisco May 10, 1849, and led Methodist work until the arrival of WILLIAM TAYLOR, Sept. 21, 1849. Taylor carried on his famous street preaching until 1856, when he left San Francisco. He and Isaac Owens established the Book Concern of the Pacific in 1850, first bookstore in California. S. D. Simonds was appointed pastor in San Francisco in 1852, and M. C. Briggs followed him in 1853.

The M.E. Church, South began work in San Francisco in May 1850, with Jesse Boring as superintendent. A. M. Wynn assisted for a few weeks. The outstanding minister of the Southern Church in San Francisco was O. P. Fitzgerald, who also served for four years as State Superintendent of Public Instruction, and was later elected bishop. The Glide Memorial Church has been the most successful church of the Southern Church tradition.

Three Methodist congregations established in the 1850's eventually grew to include German, Norwegian-Danish, Swedish, Chinese, Japanese, Korean, Filipino and Negro churches, as well as numerous undifferentiated congregations. In the late 1920's four congregations united to form Temple Church, and to build the William Taylor Hotel, with the Temple Church on the lower floors. Conceived as a scheme to produce revenues for mission, it was a casualty of the 1929 depression and was lost to Methodism. Great preachers in San Francisco after the pioneer period include Elbert R. Dille, William Stidger, and Walter John Sherman.

The Woman's Home Missionary Society's National Training School in San Francisco for a generation trained women as deaconesses and for pastoral work. Miss Katherine Maurer, most noted of its graduates, served at the U. S. immigration station at Angel Island for thirty-nine years. The Mary Elizabeth Inn, a home for working girls; Gum Moon Hall, a residence hall for Chinese girls; and the Goodwill Industries are Methodist institutions in San Francisco.

At present there are eighteen United Methodist churches in San Francisco, in addition to a ministry to students at San Francisco State College. There are nineteen ministers and 4,926 members. The episcopal and conference headquarters, and a branch of the Methodist Publishing House, are in San Francisco.

First A.M.E. Zion Church was one of the first Negro churches established in San Francisco—a very modest one, located on Stockton Street between Broadway and Pacific. The first pastor of the church was J. J. Moore. Like many of our leaders, he also assumed civic leadership and made many friends who proved to be "friends indeed in our time of need." One such friend was Thomas Starr King, the leader of the anti-slavery movement in California, and pastor of the first Unitarian Church on Stockton Street.

Church membership was growing rapidly. In 1864, King and his members sold their Stockton Street building and property to the Zion Church. It was a friendly transaction. For many years the Zion Church was known as the "Starr King Methodist Church."

By 1864 Moore had not only established himself as a religious leader, but also as the first Negro teacher in the whole state. He was elected bishop in 1868.

In 1872 Hillary was appointed pastor. He legally changed the title of the church to A.M.E. Zion Church of San Francisco.

From 1870 to 1906 little material is available on the history of the church because of the 1906 earthquake and fire. There was nothing to be salvaged from the ashes— not even a record. During the following three years there was no building and no pastor.

A new building was erected but was heavily mortgaged. The holder of the second mortgage wanted to foreclose, but Mayor James Rolph, Jr. aided the church by loaning sufficient monies to cover the mortgage. Many times the people became discouraged, but they persevered until, at last, success was in sight.

In 1919 W. J. J. Byers was again appointed to the Church, and under his leadership a Sunday school, Christian Endeavor, and evening service were started. The membership began to grow.

In 1926 Edward J. Magruder began a fifteen-year pastorate. During this time First A.M.E. Zion Church became the most famous and prosperous on the West Coast.

L. Roy Bennett came as pastor in 1956, from Montgomery, Ala. Under his pastorate the members have erected a beautiful $200,000 edifice.

Glide Memorial Church is an evangelistic center composed of several congregations which reflect the pluralistic nature of the city. These congregations are action-oriented and gather around various issues which confront persons involved with urban living. Not all members of the congregations identify themselves as Christians or as churchmen but do share a concern for the religious or "meanings" dimension of urban living. Those members of the several congregations who do identify themselves as Methodists constitute the worshipping congregation.

The sanctuary of Glide Church is the scene of Youth A-Go-Go rock 'n roll concerts, political education sessions, and meetings of homophile groups, as well as a center of worship. Simultaneously, in other rooms, an interviewer may be recording the story of a person who alleges that he was beaten by police; a committee of professionals and troubled young adults may be seeking a viable program to enable them to become self-determining and productive citizens; a group of laymen and clergy may be struggling to articulate their theological position on an issue facing the city; an inter-cultural group may be disagreeing strongly about political strategy and the tension between self-interest and corporate responsibility. Senior citizens may be discussing international events, or a distraught unwed mother may be considering with her counselor whether or not she will have an abortion.

In 1929 Elizabeth Glide established a trust in memory of her husband for the development of an evangelistic center in downtown San Francisco. Between 1929 and 1948 the life of the church centered around a pulpit ministry under the leadership of Julian C. McPheeters. In 1962 Bishop Donald H. Tippett appointed Lewis E. Durham to create an experimental center to discover new ways for the church to relate itself to urban culture. In the same year he called John V. Moore as pastor of Glide Memorial Church. From 1962 Glide Church, in cooperation with the Glide Urban Center, concentrated on meeting the needs of the residents of its neighborhood and on opening its facility to community concerns. From 1962 until 1966 Glide Church maintained a small, permanent congregation, while a large number of transients attended worship services. The present congregations function under the program of Glide Urban Center for the purpose of helping persons and groups to discover responsible ways of interacting and relating to the culture in which they live.

C. V. Anthony, *Fifty Years*. 1901.
California Christian Advocate.
Journal of the California-Nevada Conference.

General Mniutes, UMC, 1970.
L. L. Loofbourow, *In Search of God's Gold.* 1950.
J. C. Simmons, *Pacific Coast.* 1886.
DON M. CHASE
DAVID H. BRADLEY
LEWIS E. DURHAM

SANGRAMPUR, Bihar (Bengal Conference) is a village in INDIA in which there is a Methodist church with most of its members from a Moslem background. It started in 1884 as a result of family prayers conducted by a British official, E. McLeod Smith, subdivisional officer at Pakaur. On Sunday mornings, he was accustomed to gather together his staff of servants and office assistants for a worship service. Among them was a Muslim clerk, and his conversion attracted much attention. A school was opened in his village, and eight persons confessed Christian faith and were baptized.

In 1886 nineteen new converts were enrolled. In 1888 the headquarters of government was changed and the Bengal Conference purchased the government buildings and twenty-one acres of land. Two orphanages were moved there from CALCUTTA. By 1891, the church had 130 local members, mostly from among Muslims. A number of Methodist ministers and teachers have come from among the children and grandchildren of these former Muslims. In 1897 an earthquake severely damaged the buildings which had been bought from the government.

In this general section of Bengal, along the borders of the line that now divides India and PAKISTAN, there are several villages in which Christian congregations consist mostly of converts from Islam. But Sangrampur has the only Methodist congregation in the region consisting mainly of converts from Islam or descendants of such converts.

J. WASKOM PICKETT

W. E. SANGSTER

SANGSTER, WILLIAM EDWIN (1900-1960), British Methodist, was born in London on June 5, 1900. He entered the Wesleyan ministry in 1922 and soon made his mark as a preacher. In 1939 he was appointed to the Westminster Central Hall in LONDON, where he became nationally known. He was elected president of the Methodist Conference in 1950, and in 1955 he took charge of the Home Mission Department; his many evangelistic schemes were cut short by illness; he had to retire in 1959, and died on May 24, 1960. He wrote much: *Methodism Can Be Born Again* (1938) and *Methodism's Unfinished Task* (1947);

The Path to Perfection (1943), which also obtained him a Ph.D. at London University; and a series of books on preaching: *The Craft of Sermon Illustration* (1946); *The Craft of Sermon Construction* (1949); and *The Approach to Preaching* (1951). His sermons and lectures proved very popular in the United States.

P. E. Sangster, *Doctor Sangster.* 1962. JOHN KENT

SAN JOSE, CALIFORNIA, U.S.A. Methodism has served this area for over 120 years. The city is now one of the fastest growing of the state and nation. It is the county seat of Santa Clara County, which has close to a million people, and is located fifty miles south of SAN FRANCISCO. A Methodist society was first organized in San Jose in 1847 by the missionaries and is now the First United Methodist Church.

At the time of the organization of the CALIFORNIA CONFERENCE in 1851 San Jose reported 117 members. In 1857 it had become a station with seventy-five members and church property valued at $4,500. The Germans also organized an M.E. church which later merged with existing Methodist churches. The M.E. Church, South introduced services at an early period and in 1876 there were 796 members in the three churches.

In the great San Francisco earthquake of April 18, 1906 the First M.E. Church was so badly damaged that it had to be declared unsafe for use. GEORGE A. MILLER, who later became a bishop of Central America, was the pastor when the present edifice was constructed and dedicated in 1911. Distinguished pastors of this historic church, besides Bishop Miller, include WILLIAM L. "BILL" STIDGER, Frank Linder, Channing A. Richardson and C. B. Sylvester.

Methodism in San Jose has grown with the population. New churches have been built in the suburbs and outlying areas. Today there are ten churches in San Jose with a membership of 5,332. Recent mergers of the Latin American and Japanese Methodist churches have brought two Latin American and two Japanese churches into The United Methodist Church. Another new church was started in San Jose in 1968 in an area where a planned community is developing.

There is one FREE METHODIST CHURCH in San Jose, which recently deserted the downtown area for a suburban site and one small A.M.E. church located in the downtown area. The largest minority in San Jose is the Latin American people with 70,000 in the city and well over 100,000 in the county. The Negro population at present is less than one percent but growing.

Bishop DONALD H. TIPPETT, who retired in 1968 after twenty years of service in the San Francisco area, gave leadership to the development of The Methodist Church in San Jose and the Santa Clara Valley. San Jose District is one of the strongest districts of the Conference in numbers and financial strength. San Jose, First, has been a "mother" church in this growth.

DONALD A. GETTY

SANKEY, IRA DAVID (1840-1908), American evangelist and hymnologist, was born at Edinburg, Pa. As president of the Y.M.C.A. of New Castle, Pa., he attended the international convention of that body at Indianapolis, Ind., in 1870. There he met the noted evangelist, Dwight L. Moody, and began an association which lasted for many years.

As song leader Sankey traveled extensively with Moody through North America and Great Britain, conducting revival meetings. In later years he conducted such meetings by himself until stricken by blindness in 1903.

Many hymns of his own composition appeared in his compilations: *Sacred Songs and Solos* (1873); *Gospel Hymns* (1875) and *Young People's Songs of Praise* (1902). In 1906 there was published his autobiography, *My Life and the Story of the Gospel Hymns*.

Wheeler Preston, *American Biographies*. New York: Harper & Brothers, 1940.　　　　　　　　　　J. MARVIN RAST

SANTA ANA, CALIFORNIA, U.S.A. Methodism began in 1869, when W. H. Spurgeon bought land from the Spanish and established Santa Ana. Within months afterwards postwar soldiers drifted into the area. Some of them met one evening in the home of W. H. Titchenal and organized the M.E. Church, South. Four years later the M.E. Church began with eight members to establish their fellowship. For the next two years these two groups met in a school building, alternating Sundays for worship. In 1876 both purchased property and both put up white frame buildings. It was in one of these buildings later that Glen Martin built its first airplane.

By 1906 the Spurgeon Methodist Church had a red brick building in the center of town, while three blocks away the First Church (ME) members met in a red sandstone construction. Today these two churches are located about two miles apart, in new edifices less than ten years old, and are numbered among the strong Christian fellowships of the city. The red brick building of the Southern church is now a court room. One sits in the pew, still with its hymnal racks, wondering whether he shall receive grace from the pulpit on the left, or judgment from the bench on the right.

From these two mother groups have come other Methodist churches and causes. St. Luke Church, located in south Santa Ana, began as Richland Avenue in 1915, a mission church of First Methodist. A Latin American Church, named Gethsemane, also began as a mission church under the protective wing of First Church. Five other Methodist churches have sprung up adjacent to Santa Ana, mainly under the missionary zeal of these two original fellowships. And if you extend the radius ten miles, you would now find twenty growing Methodist churches in the area. There is also a strong GOODWILL INDUSTRIES organization in Santa Ana begun by the Methodists in 1924, and a thriving Salvation Army, with several FREE METHODIST fellowships, and an African Methodist.

Orange County, of which Santa Ana is the county seat town, has 40,000 Methodists. Within this number is a heavy concentration of the political and educational leadership of the cities. In this very rapidly growing part of southern California, Methodism is expanding and continuing to exert leadership.

First Church is located in the county seat of rapidly growing Orange County. Because of a long history of moral and spiritual leadership in the county, the congregation elected to remain in the center-city, near the civic center area, rather than relocate in the suburbs. Having completed in 1966 a ten-year building program, including the construction of a new sanctuary, the church is now concentrating on service projects in the inner city and is seeking to become an ever more vital laboratory for Christian life and mission.

In 1873 Will A. Knighten founded First Church, four years after the city of Santa Ana was established. On November 11 he wrote in his diary, "Went to Santa Ana for food. At night we had a class meeting. Six present. Prospects good." On November 29 he organized the First M.E. Church with eight charter members. At first the congregation met in a school building, in homes, and in Lattimer Hall. Then in September 1878, during the pastorate of F. D. Bovard, the first property was purchased on the corner of Second and Main Street.

C. W. Tarr led the congregation in building the first church structure on the Main Street site in 1880. The church was incorporated in 1884, while A. L. Dearing was pastor. By 1899 the congregation had outgrown the first buildings on Second and Main, so the property on the corner of Sixth and Spurgeon Streets was purchased, during the pastorate of J. B. Green. He remained to guide the congregation in building a new sanctuary, which was dedicated by Bishop J. W. HAMILTON on Jan. 6, 1901.

First Church, which had earlier commenced ministries to the Mexican American population in the city, purchased property at the corner of First and Garfield in 1912, for the erection of a "Methodist Mexican Church" with a Spanish speaking ministry. This has continued close ties ever since with the sister church, ultimately named Gethsemane Methodist Church. In 1916 the Annual Conference met in Santa Ana, during the ministry of E. J. Inwood.

In 1929 the Asbury Building, a major educational unit, was constructed during the pastorate of George A. Warmer, Sr., whose ministry during the depression years deepened the social conscience of the congregation. In 1941 the debt was paid off, with a prominent layman, W. A. Taylor, leading the mortgage burning ceremony. Alec G. Nichols was pastor in 1948, when the seventy-fifth anniversary of the church was celebrated. In 1966 the construction of a new sanctuary was completed, on the site where the former church structure had stood. This climaxed the building program carried on during the twelve-year pastorate of Bob Shuler, Jr.

Galal Gough was appointed pastor of First Church in 1967, together with G. Edward Garner. First Church continues developing special ministries to the inner city and among the ethnic minorities in Santa Ana. In 1970 it reported 1,868 members.

General Minutes, UMC, 1970.　　　　　　　GALAL GOUGH

SANTA CLARA VALLEY, CALIFORNIA, U.S.A. When the Spanish decided to occupy Alta (Upper) CALIFORNIA they established in SAN JOSE their first pueblo, a civilian community as distinguished from a military post (presidio) or a mission. Two missions, San Jose and Santa Clara, were near by.

When immigrants from the United States began to penetrate California, this valley was one of the first to attract them. In 1846 a Methodist exhorter, Adna Hecox, arrived and began to hold services, followed the next year by a local preacher, Elihu Anthony. The group they gathered was, with SAN FRANCISCO, the earliest continuing Protestant congregation in the state. In the next few years the churches at Santa Clara and San Jose became among the strongest of Methodist organizations. The UNIVERSITY OF THE PACIFIC was located here in 1850.

Santa Clara Valley has the highest concentration of United Methodist churches and membership in the CALIFORNIA-NEVADA CONFERENCE. First Church, Palo Alto, with its new 1-1/3 million dollar plant and 3,000 members, leads, but a dozen of the stronger churches in the Conference are near at hand. There are thirty Methodist churches in the Santa Clara Valley, with some 20,000 members.

LEON L. LOOFBOUROW

SANTA MARIA, Rio Grande do Sul, Brazil. **Lar Metodista** (Methodist Home) is a Methodist home for orphans and needy children. It was founded on June 24, 1939, under the inspiration and leadership of ADOLFO UNGARETTI and his wife, Dona Luiza Vurlod, who were its first directors.

The funds were mostly provided by the Methodist Women's Societies of the Second (Southern) Region. The original residence had a capacity for thirty children.

In 1955 a modern building was completed with capacity for seventy children and the supervisors. Two DEACONESSES and several other workers were appointed to care for the home. Attached to it is a primary school accredited by the state, which furnishes and pays for the teachers. The children help with the housework and care for their own farm vegetable gardens. Future plans include a trade school, the first unit of which—a printing shop—already operates and serves the home, the church, and the community.

World Outlook, May 1966.

EULA K. LONG

SANTA MONICA, CALIFORNIA, U.S.A. **First Church** was founded in 1876 in what was a small seaside resort near the not-then exploded metropolis of LOS ANGELES. It has grown into one of the five largest churches of the SOUTHERN CALIFORNIA-ARIZONA CONFERENCE and one of the three largest United Methodist congregations on the Pacific Coast. Sharing in the tremendous growth of the metropolitan area, the Santa Monica Church has become an urban church ministering to a community which has all the problems of expanding population, heavy scientific industrial concentration, high proportion of advanced level educational attainment, as well as "pockets of poverty," minority group ghettos, and political conservatism.

The University of California at Los Angeles is within walking distance. One aircraft concern has its main plant and headquarters here, with many members working also for two other aircraft plants in the community. The city is surrounded on three sides by Los Angeles, with the Pacific Ocean to the west.

A primary interest of the church is in the field of missions. In addition, the interest of young people has been enlisted for Christian service, with three of its young men being ordained at a recent annual conference session, while four other young people (including one young woman) were at the same time pursuing studies in Methodist theological schools. Their education has been helped in nearly every case by a "scholarship aid program" which has been in effect for a number of years in the church.

The church buildings include a sanctuary seating 900, church school facilities adequate for a splendid educational program, a dining room and social hall, plus a lovely chapel accommodating ninety persons. The slender spire, rising about 140 feet above the street, is a landmark in the entire community.

In 1970 the church reported 3,134 members, property valued at $1,407,731, and $240,844 raised for all purposes.

General Minutes, UMC, 1970.

NOEL C. LEROQUE

SANTA FE, NEW MEXICO, U.S.A. **St. John's Church** offers an impressive sight to visitors approaching on the LAS VEGAS highway especially at night. A tall lighted figure of Christ the Shepherd gleams in full stained-glass colors—an appropriate beacon for visitors to this city named in Spanish for the Holy Faith.

St. John's excellent plant, constructed in 1951 and 1965 of brick in contemporary architecture at a cost of nearly one million dollars, speaks eloquently of Methodism's growth in NEW MEXICO's capital city. It began in 1850, four years after the bloodless takeover from MEXICO by General S. W. Kearny's forces, when E. G. Nicholson, of Independence, Mo., preached from I Corinthians 2:1-2 to a small congregation of Americans, most of them connected with the Army. The service was held in the oldest governmental building in the United States, the adobe Palace of the Governors, erected in 1609 by the Spanish conquerors. Three years later Nicholson briefly returned with Walter Hansen, a Spanish-speaking Swedish Methodist, and Benigno Cardenas. Nicholson and Hansen viewed prospects dimly, but Señor Cardenas, though vested by illness, stayed and on Nov. 20, 1853, preached in the plaza and surrendered his Roman Catholic credentials. But Methodist work lagged. In 1865 when the newly organized COLORADO CONFERENCE sent "Father" JOHN L. DYER, "the Snowshoe Itinerant," formerly a missionary in South America, the Santa Fe congregation largely consisted of Governor W. A. Pile, who had been a Methodist minister, his family and staff.

THOMAS HARWOOD of DENVER was appointed to "New Mexico" in 1870, but when Governor Pile and family left, Harwood was loathe to press missionary work because he thought to do so "would result in a denominational struggle for existence, for I found the Presbyterians had a hard struggle to maintain their work." Later in 1873 after a vain effort to locate a key to the locked Presbyterian church, he preached in the Army Chapel to sixteen persons. An insight into his beliefs and methods is given by his impressions of Santa Fe: "This old town, noted for her age and homeliness, still squats in her filth and the people in their sins. She may have a brighter day, but it must be when the dim candlelight of her Romish altars shall be removed and the bright sun of Protestant Christianity shall rise." Statistics for the New Mexico Mission of the Colorado Annual Conference in 1876 list Cimarron, Elizabethtown, Las Cruces, Manzana, Palomas, Peralta, Silver City, Socorro, Valverde, and Vermejo—but not Sante Fe. Perhaps the capital city was without a regular pastor till appointment in 1880 of H. H. Hall, who raised an adobe church on San Francisco Street.

It served until, after financial vicissitudes, a new structure was dedicated in 1906 on Don Gaspar. Growth in membership and support led to groundbreaking March 4, 1951, under pastorship of Earl M. Nowlin for the present structure on Las Vegas Highway and Cordova Road. It was completed and opened Feb. 7, 1954 with the pastor, Howard Bush, noting 402 in Sunday school, 750 at morning service giving an offering of $1,012, with 374 cars parked on church grounds. A place of honor is given to a large bell which hung in the 1880 edifice, and which bears the inscription: "Come When I Call—To Serve God All." At formal dedication ceremonies led by Bishop W. ANGIE SMITH, Oct. 27, 1963, Roy L. Ward, the minister, could report 1,657 full members and 342 in preparation. In 1970 the church reported 1,800 members.

John L. Carpenter, *St. John's Methodist Church*, Founder's Day Program, Nov. 24, 1957. Reprinted in Service of Dedication, Oct. 27, 1963.
T. Harwood, *New Mexico*. 1908, 1910.
M. Simpson, *Cyclopaedia*. 1881.   LELAND D. CASE

SANTI, RICCARDO (1871-1961), and his sons **EMANUELE** (1904-   ), **FABIO** (1911-1956), and **TEOFILO** (1909-   ), were and are members of a remarkable family in ITALY, closely connected in the public interest with CASA MATERNA ORPHANAGE, which Riccardo Santi founded and which other members of the family have carried on.

RICCARDO SANTI

Riccardo Santi was orphaned at six years of age, and reared in a Methodist orphanage at Venice. As a boy he studied printing and later graduated from the Methodist theological seminary which had been established in Rome. He was ordained to the ministry in 1894. In 1900 he was married to Ersilia Bragaglia (1880-1956). She was a graduate of the Bologna Conservatory of Music. Riccardo held pastorates in Foggia, 1897; Bari, 1898-1899; Palermo, 1900-1902; Naples, 1903. Having occasion, as the son tells the story, to take two homeless children who were begging on the corner to his home, he became interested in this type of work from then on. Casa Materna under his leadership grew to become world-wide in its fame and through his sons it has continued to exert an enormously helpful influence in present day Italy.

Riccardo and his wife, Ersilia, were delegates to the M.E. GENERAL CONFERENCE in Springfield, Mass., U.S.A., in 1924; and also to that in Columbus, Ohio, in 1936. They were recommended to be selected as the European family of the year in 1951 by the *Christian Advocate* (Chicago).

Emanuele Santi became a minister, a teacher and a musician. For a time he was violinist for the Naples Symphony and he also had worked with his violin in Switzerland. On coming to America, he became director of the Conservatory of Music in Newburgh, N. Y. In 1935 he graduated from the Union Theological Seminary. He obtained his Ph.D. degree from Columbia University. Then he became a pastor in NEW YORK, serving a bilingual Methodist church in Yonkers for fifteen years; the Castle Heights Methodist at White Plains for five years. In 1956 he returned to Italy and became a co-director of Casa Materna and to this institution he has subsequently devoted his life. He has made frequent trips to interest the outside world in Casa Materna and visits America from time to time.

Fabio Santi, a lawyer, was a graduate of the University of Naples. He became a champion of the Methodists against Rome and Mussolini in the days of fascism. He served as director of Casa Materna from 1945 to 1956. His other activities and achievements included acting as mayor of Catholic Portici, and as leader in post-war reconstruction including the erection of a hospital. He also established a Scientific Lyseum (preparatory college), and was founder of a newspaper, *Il Vesuvio*. He was also president of Portici, a National Counselor, and a member of the Liberal Party of Italy.

TEOFILO SANTI

Teofilo Santi received the M.D. degree from the University of Naples, and was a graduate student at Padua in Berlin. He married Livia Lari (the daughter of a Baptist minister). Teofilo and Livia became co-directors of the Casa Materna in 1956. He served as Director, as well as Medical Director, of Casa Mia, and worked with the WORLD COUNCIL OF CHURCHES in caring for Protestant and Orthodox people in refugee camps in Naples during the war months. Casa Mia is the only Protestant day center in Naples for the care of families living in the slums.

Besides Casa Materna and Casa Mia, Teofilo is responsible for the new Evangelical Hospital in Ponticelli. Before this hospital came into operation, there was a staff of Protestant doctors working in clinics located in Protestant Churches in Naples.

Riccardo Santi also had a daughter, Luisa, who graduated from Columbia University in New York. She is now an American citizen and lives in New York City.

The Christian Advocate (Chicago), Oct. 18, 1951.
Christian Science Monitor, July 22, 1955.
Cyril Davey, *The Santi Story*. London: Epworth Press, n.d.
Le Protestant, Sept. 15, 1958.
Michigan Christian Advocate, Sept. 12, 1963.
Voce Metodista, July 1951, July 15, 1953; July 15, 1956.
World Outlook, July 1949, April 1955, March 1964.

SANTIAGO, Chile, is the capital and largest city in CHILE, and the fourth largest in South America. It is 116 miles from Valparaiso, its seaport. It stands on a wide plain at an altitude of 1,796 feet, and is backed by the chain of the Andes. The city is served by international as well as national airlines.

There are fifteen Methodist churches and preaching points in the city, including an English-speaking church which has often been served by a Methodist pastor. (See also SANTIAGO COLLEGE and SWEET MEMORIAL INSTITUTE.)

SANTIAGO COLLEGE is an elementary and secondary school for girls in SANTIAGO, CHILE, founded by Methodists and one that enjoys high prestige over Chile. It was established in 1880 by IRA LAFETRA, one of the missionaries brought by Bishop WILLIAM TAYLOR to start a self-supporting school as a means of introducing the Methodist Church.

LaFetra arrived in Chile with a letter of presentation from the secretary of state of the United States for the president of Chile. He explained to the president and the secretary of state of Chile why he had come and asked their advice. Their reaction was favorable to such a degree that they decided to enroll their own daughters in the school when it began. Soon after this interview the doors of Santiago College were opened to girls of every creed and social level.

From its beginning the school was a success. In a letter written in 1880 LaFetra explained the philosophy of Santiago College: "No professor should teach a specific religious creed or dogma. Nevertheless, this should not be interpreted to exclude the inculcating of the virtues of piety, devotion, reverence, obedience and honesty."

In 1924, upon the visit of Señora Elisa de Migel, an ex-student residing in the United States, the school had outgrown its locale and was in serious need of repairs to the buildings. Señora Migel left Santiago with the firm purpose of building a new Santiago College. The money she gave for this purpose was matched in 1924 by the M.E. Church in the United States, making possible relocation of the school in 1928. By 1932 the new classrooms were ready for use on a commodious new campus, enclosed and guarded with walls as are all such schools in Latin America.

While it had been started as a mission enterprise, the school in 1928 was incorporated independently from the Board of MISSIONS and became registered with the Board of Regents of the State of NEW YORK. In 1966 it received its own juridical personality from the Chilean government, and the board of trustees was organized in a way that gave more authority for decisions to be made locally.

From 1932 until 1959 the school was directed by Elizabeth Mason and grew from fewer than 300 students to 800. In 1966 there were 1,200 students enrolled from kindergarten through the secondary level.

Larry Jackson, "History of Santiago College." Unpublished ms. in custody of school, 1959.   JOYCE HILL

SANTOS, ALMIR DOS SANTOS (1912-   ), bishop of the Methodist Church of Brazil, was born in Cabo Frio, state of Rio de Janeiro, on April 23, 1912. He received his B.A. degree from the INSTITUTO GRANBERY and his B.D. from its theological school. Later, he studied at EMORY UNIVERSITY in the United States, specializing in the rural church and the church and community courses. He also took special courses in clinical pastoral training at the State Hospital in Elgin, Ill.

On April 23, 1938, he married Laura Jesus dos Santos, and they had three sons—Edson, Carlos Alberto, and Carlos Wesley. He was ordained DEACON that year, and ELDER in 1941. His activities have included pastorates in the state of Minas Gerais, teaching practical theology at the Methodist seminary in Rudge Ramos, São Paulo, conducting pastoral clinics, editing a magazine for pastors, and pioneering in industrial evangelization in the city of São Paulo. He has written a book on Christian stewardship, *Mordomía Cristâ*.

In 1963, he was elected general secretary of the Board of Social Action of the Methodist Church of Brazil, and led the church to a new consciousness of the importance of Christian witness in social concerns. This same interest raised him to the presidency of the Church and Society Commission of Latin American Churches, and to high office in the field of social action in the Confederation of Evangelical Churches of Brazil.

He was elected bishop in July 1965, by the General Conference of the Methodist Church of Brazil. His episcopal area comprises the states of Minas Gerais, Espirito Santo, Bahia, and supervision of the work in BRASILIA. His present episcopal headquarters are at Belo Horizonte, Minas Gerais.

EULA K. LONG

SAÕ PAULO, Brazil, is the largest city in BRAZIL, with a population of 4,098,000. It is an enterprising, modern metropolis in every way. The first Methodist church in São Paulo was organized on Feb. 10, 1884, by the American missionary, JAMES WILLIAM KOGER. The founding members were Giovanni and Clementina Bernini (Italians), a Mr. Bellinger (British), and BERNARDO DE MIRANDA, the Brazilian who became one of the country's first national preachers. The little congregation met first in the house of a Lutheran family, above a store on the Largo do Mercadinho (Square of the Little Market). They afterward met in several different places until Oct. 22, 1892, when the congregation established itself at Numbers 12 and 14, Largo do Arouche, the first property of the Methodist church in the city of São Paulo. There it remained for years.

In 1894, a new congregation started holding services on Rua Esperança, 15-B, the same location where the Methodist publishing house (IMPRENSA METODISTA) was founded by J. W. WOLLING, and where the official organ was edited and printed. This group became, eventually, **Central Methodist Church** of São Paulo, whose beautiful sanctuary stands at 659 Rua da Liberdade. The church was built in 1920, under the pastorate of MICHAEL DICKIE, with donations raised in the city, matching an equal sum from a church in the United States. In 1920, the publishing house was installed behind the church on the grounds, and remained there until 1957, when it was moved to new quarters in suburban São Bernardo do Campo.

In 1960, Central Church, under Brazilian leadership, began an extensive building project—a five-storied structure to meet the needs of the church school, with a primary and high school educational unit, and offices for the accommodation of the various Church Boards. Presently, there are about eighty organized churches in this great city, and seventy Sunday schools with more than 6,000 pupils. Many churches have parsonages and full-time pastors; others are served by supply pastors and students from the near-by Seminary at Rudge Ramos. The three Methodist Boards—Evangelism, Christian Education, and Social Concerns—have their headquarters in a building adjoining the church. There are more than twenty chapels and halls for worship located in the suburbs. Many churches carry on parochial schools and adult literacy classes in their buildings, conduct clinics, and perform social services of various types. There is also a weekly program on television, supported by the church.

In Santo Amaro, located on one of the finest physical properties of the Methodist Church, is the INSTITUTO METODISTA, and also the Theological Seminary, FACULDADE DE TEOLOGIA.

Instituto Metodista Educacional, formerly the Escola Metodista, was founded in Ribeirão Preto, São Paulo, on Sept. 5, 1899, by Leonora Smith, with Mamie Fenley as assistant, both of the WOMEN'S FOREIGN MISSIONARY SOCIETY (MES). Miss Smith had to finance the school out of her own meager salary, as Bishop EUGENE HENDRIX had warned that there would be no appropriation for it. This entailed a tremendous personal sacrifice. The school began in one room in the preacher's house, and was bitterly opposed by Catholics from the start.

In 1902-03, a severe yellow fever epidemic struck the city. Schools were closed and some public buildings transformed into hospitals. At this time, Misses Ada Parker and Willie Bowman of the school offered their services as nurses, and this so greatly impressed the public that a climate of admiration began to be manifested for the school. Rapid growth took place, and in 1914, the school was moved into a comfortable building in a good location. In 1949 religious education courses were offered, and with the sanction of the General Conference, this department was moved to Santo Amaro, São Paulo. The local church took charge of the school in Ribeirão Preto, and today it belongs to the Conference, and the principal is a Brazilian. It offers primary, high school, normal ond business courses, and its enrollment is over 900.

J. L. Kennedy, *Metodismo no Brasil.* 1928.   ISNARD ROCHA
EULA K. LONG

SARASOTA, FLORIDA, U.S.A. **First Church** was organized in October 1891, by William Tresca, a young man who had recently graduated from EMORY UNIVERSITY. At that time Sarasota was only a small village, and a store room on Main Street was secured as a meeting place for the twelve charter members. Within a year the church members made plans to build a church, and found a lot costing $40 on the corner of Main Street and Pineapple Street.

This lot was bought by one of the members and deeded to the church, and upon it a very plain building was built. In 1894 additional funds were raised and a vestibule and steeple were added to the plain building.

Tresca served as pastor of this church three different times over a period of several years. Other pastors came and went about every two years, until Watt Smith came in 1921 and stayed six years.

In 1911 the church was offered $1600 for their lot, so they agreed to sell it and moved the church building a short distance down Pineapple Street; this place has remained the site of the church through the years. In 1913 a new church was built at a cost of $10,000, and this building remained the church sanctuary until 1955. Then it became the chapel.

The church membership steadily increased through the years; by 1950 nearly 1,000 people belonged to this church, and it became necessary to build a much larger sanctuary. Over a period of three years enough money was raised or pledged for the building of a $500,000 sanctuary. It was completed and the first service was held in the new sanctuary on Christmas Day, 1955. Five years later all indebtedness had been paid and the mortgage-burning ceremony took place. In 1970 the membership was 2,119.

ELIZABETH GARRETT BRAREN

METHODIST CHURCH IN SARAWAK

SARAWAK, formerly a British Colony on the north coast of Borneo, is now an integral part of independent MALAYSIA, a member of the United Nations. It has a coastline of about 400 miles, and an area of approximately 50,000 square miles. The capital is Kuching in the western corner. The population approaches 900,000, consisting chiefly of Sea Dyaks (Ibans), Chinese and Malays.

Two missionaries of the M.E. Church in Malaya, Benjamin F. West and H. L. E. Leuring, explored the Dyak (Iban) country of Sarawak in 1890. However, no formal Methodist approach was made before the turn of the century. In 1901 a large company of Christian Chinese, forced from their homes in CHINA by the Boxer Revolt and persecution, was permitted to settle in Sarawak. Bishop FRANK W. WARNE of INDIA, learning of the venture, changed his itinerary so as to accompany them. Many of the migrant Chinese were Methodists, their preachers leading them. Going with them from HONG KONG to Sarawak, Bishop Warne greatly aided in the settlement and the establishment of Methodist congregations in the new habitat. The following year Benjamin West visited them for a period. On his return and report, JAMES M. HOOVER was transferred from Penang, Malaya, in 1903, as the first Methodist missionary directly appointed to Sarawak. With Mrs. Hoover he headed the mission for over thirty years, until his death in 1935.

The work first developed among the Chinese. Hoover extended it to the Malays, whose language he spoke. In recent years the approach to the Dyaks (Ibans) has met with extraordinary success. The Woman's Division of the Board of MISSIONS of The Methodist Church (U.S.A.) joined the effort in 1951. The present church membership is over 13,000, with an equal number of probationers, and a very large constituency. Evangelistic work is vigorous among the Hakka-speaking Chinese, and in the coastal towns from Bintulu eastward for 200 miles to the Brunei border.

Centers of work are: Kuching (the capital); Sibu (where the Hoover Memorial stands); Kapit (site of the important Christ Hospital serving over 20,000 patients annually); Bukit Lan (where a 400-acre farm provides agricultural training). Recently the Sarawak Iban Provisional Conference was formed, to give integrity to the great work among the Dyak peoples.

Ecumenical Methodism renders definite aid. The British Methodist Church supports several missionaries. The church in India provides an instructor in the theological seminary. A doctor and several nurses at Christ Hospital are from the PHILIPPINES, supported by Methodism there. Batak pastors from Sumatra (INDONESIA) work with the Bataks and Dyaks.

Barbara H. Lewis, *Methodist Overseas Missions.* 1960.
World Methodist Council, *Handbook of Information,* 1966-71.
World Parish, April 1966.   ARTHUR BRUCE MOSS

THE FIRST METHODIST CHURCH IN NORWAY

SARPSBORG, Norway, has the distinction of being the place where the first Methodist congregation in Norway

was organized by Ole P. Petersen on Sept. 11, 1856. The first Methodist church was built there and consecrated on November 1, 1857.

Shortly after the New Year of 1854, Petersen, whose remarkable life is narrated elsewhere (see NORWAY), made a journey to revisit a prominent layman in the Norwegian state church, whom he had visited formerly when he had been home in Norway. The following conversation took place: "Are you the O.P. Petersen who was here about four years ago?" "Yes, I am." "Welcome home, I am happy to see you again. But now I have to ask you a question: I have heard that many requests were made for you to return to Norway, and that the Methodist Church in America has now sent you here to preach God's word to us. Is that really true?" Telling him that it was, the man then said, with tears in his eyes, "May God bless the Methodist Church in America!"

Up to then Petersen had resided in his native town of Fredrikstad when he was in Norway, and had from there visited many other places. On one of his visits to the neighboring town of Sarpsborg, a revival movement came into being there, and in view of the prevailing conditions, it became necessary for him to settle in Sarpsborg. He took over a house that was being built, and adapted it into a chapel. That was the first Methodist chapel in Norway.

EILERT BERNHARDT

SASNETT, WILLIAM JEREMIAH (1820-1865), American minister and educator of GEORGIA and ALABAMA, was born in Hancock County, Ga., on April 29, 1820. He graduated at Oglethorpe University in 1839, and studied law for a while, but abandoned law for the work of the ministry. In 1843 he was appointed to the first church built by Daniel Pratt in what is now Prattsville, Ala., the church itself being a two-story frame building, the upper floor being used as a church, and the ground floor as a store. Sasnett was severely affected with rheumatism and found it impracticable to travel as a preacher, so in 1849 accepted the chair of English Literature in EMORY COLLEGE near Oxford, Ga. In 1858 he went to LA GRANGE Female College in Georgia, but the following year accepted the presidency of East Alabama College, then called the East Alabama Male College, at Auburn, Ala.— now an Alabama state institution widely known over the South as Auburn. Sasnett opened the college with the brightest of prospects, but within two years the Civil War broke out and the young men of the college were soon in military encampment. Being without students, the college closed with Sasnett remaining nominally its head. He "spent his time at his farm in Georgia 'superintending his large temporal interests, preaching the gospel and ministering to the needy in his neighborhood' until his last illness." "Keen of intellect, a great preacher, kind in heart, he was respected and beloved," states Marion Lazenby of him. Sasnett's scholarship was quite extensive as in 1853 he published a work on *Progress*; in 1860 a work on *Discussions in Literature.* Simpson says of him, "He was a powerful preacher, a great debater, and a devout Christian."

M. L. Lazenby, *Alabama and West Florida,* p. 344.
M. Simpson, *Cyclopaedia.* 1878.   N. B. H.

SASPORTAS, JOSEPH A. (? -1898), SOUTH CAROLINA minister and education leader of the M.E. Church. As butcher and commission merchant of CHARLESTON, S. C., he was a member of the Negro aristocracy in that city. He had been successful in business before emancipation and enjoyed a position of prestige. Along with Samuel Weston, of similar situation, he was influential in establishing Baker Theological Institute in Charleston in 1866. This institution was subsequently merged with CLAFLIN UNIVERSITY in 1871.

Sasportas, who was educated in the French private schools in Charleston, was influential in the establishing of Claflin University at Orangeburg, S. C., and served as trustee from its founding in 1869 until 1897.

In the brochure, *The Role of Claflin College in Negro Life*, appears this note regarding Sasportas: "A butcher and commission merchant; paid taxes on $6,700 worth of real estate, and 5 slaves before Emancipation (1861), a minister; preached to white and Negro congregations; served as Presiding Elder."

E. Horace Fitchett, "The Role of Claflin College in Negro Life in South Carolina," *Journal of Negro Education*, Winter 1943.
J. MARVIN RAST

SATTERFIELD, JOHN CREIGHTON (1904-   ), American lawyer, was born at Port Gibson, Miss., on July 25, 1904. He was the son of Milling Marion and Laura Stevenson (Drake) Satterfield. He graduated at the Port Gibson Junior College, 1924, received the A.B. degree from MILLSAPS COLLEGE, 1926; the LL.B. from the University of Mississippi in 1929; and Montana State University gave him the LL.D. degree in 1961, as did Dalhousie University the next year; and also the S.J.D. from Suffolk University in 1962.

He was admitted to the MISSISSIPPI Bar in 1929, and since that time has practiced in JACKSON, and serves in that city on the official board of Galloway Memorial Church. He now has an office in Yazoo City, Miss., and is also in First Methodist Church there. He was a delegate to the SOUTHEASTERN JURISDICTIONAL CONFERENCE of 1952, '56, '60, '64, and '68, where he took an active part in the deliberations of the body, frequently speaking upon matters at issue. He also was a member of the GENERAL CONFERENCE of 1952, '60, '64, '66, '68, and '70, and took the floor repeatedly, especially in defense of the Jurisdictional system. He served the General Board of Social and Economic Relations from 1952-60, and upon the important Interjurisdictional Study Commission of 1960-64. He has always taken an active part in Mississippi public life, serving as a member of the House of Representatives of that state, 1928-32, chairman of its Constitutional Committee, and secretary of the Judiciary and Ways and Means Committees of the state. He was a member of the Board of Governors of the American Bar Association, 1956-59, and president, 1961-62, the only Mississippian ever to head this national organization. Previous to that he had been president of the Mississippi Bar. He resides in Yazoo City, keeping an office there, as well as in Jackson—the state capital.

Who's Who in America, Vol. 34.
Who's Who in the Methodist Church, 1966.   N. B. H.

SAUER, CHARLES AUGUST (1891-1972), American pastor, missionary and author of German and French ancestry, was born on June 27, 1891, near Wheelersburg, Ohio, the son of Christian August and Anna (Miller) Sauer. He attended OHIO WESLEYAN UNIVERSITY, B.A., 1919; D.D.,

1958; and Ohio State University College of Education, M.A., 1928. He married the former Marguerite Suttles of Albion, Pa., on Aug. 17, 1920, and they had three sons.

Dr. Sauer, who was first engaged in the field of education, served during the first World War in the American Expeditionary Forces until February 1919. During the years 1921-32 he lived in Yeng Byen, KOREA, serving as missionary principal of the Mission High School there. From 1932-35 he was an instructor of farm engineering at the Konju Mission School. He was treasurer of the Korean Methodist Church in SEOUL, Korea, 1936-41, and again in 1946-50. During the interim of the second World War, 1942-46, he served as minister in the West Unity, Ohio, Methodist Church. He was treasurer for the National Christian Council Union Projects in Korea in 1950-62. In 1949-58 he returned to the field of education and his position of principal, working in the Korean Language School. From 1949 until 1962 he served as editor for the Korean edition of *The Upper Room*. Dr. Sauer wrote *Korean Language for Beginners*, 1925, and he revised it in 1950 and 1954; *Chinese Characters for Beginners*, 1930; *A Pocket Story of John Wesley*, 1967; and *Beginner's Lessons in the Book of Genesis*, written in the Korean language in 1938. During the year 1962 he was cited by the Minister of Defense in the Republic of Korea, and later that year he was awarded a Cultural Merit, which is the National Medal, by the President of the Republic of Korea. Dr. Sauer was a member of the OHIO ANNUAL CONFERENCE. He participated in the General Conference of the Korean Methodist Church in 1951, '54, '58, and '60, and served as a delegate to the GENERAL CONFERENCE of The Methodist Church in 1956. He acted as the editor for Korea in the *Encyclopedia of World Methodism*.

He died Sept. 13, 1972, at Ashley, Ohio.

Clyde Hissong, ed., *Ohio Lives*. Hopkinsville, Ky.: Historical Records Association, 1968.   N. B. H.

SAULT STE. MARIE, MICHIGAN, U.S.A., located on the rapids of the Saint Mary's River in the Upper Peninsula of MICHIGAN, is the seat of Chippewa County government. The city is the third oldest settlement in the United States. A new International Bridge finished in November 1962, links the twin cities of Sault Ste. Marie and Ontario, CANADA.

Methodism began in Sault Ste. Marie in the summer of 1832, when five Indian missionaries led by John Sunday, came up from Canada. John Clarke was appointed as a missionary to the Indians and to soldiers at Fort Brady at the May 8, 1833 session of the NEW YORK CONFERENCE. By 1834 thirteen log homes, a log schoolhouse, and a missionary's home was constructed on a site now known as the Mission Creek area two miles below the Rapids. Methodism had little impact on the white population of Sault Ste. Marie until Isaac Johnstone was appointed there by the DETROIT CONFERENCE in 1873. The congregation grew rapidly, outgrowing two church buildings. The present stone building of Central Church was erected in 1893-94. The membership in 1970 was 800. The Algonquin Methodist Church was organized in 1900 and now has a membership of over 100. Central Church entertained the Detroit Conference in 1894 and in 1928.

Mary Casler, *History of Methodism in Sault Ste. Marie*. N.d.
Minutes of the Detroit Conference.
J. H. Pitezel, *Lights and Shades*. 1883.   VERLE J. CARSON

SAUNDERS, JOHN ROUZIE (1890-1956), American preacher and missionary to BRAZIL, was born in Middlesex County, Va., on Aug. 31, 1890. He received his B.A. from RANDOLPH-MACON COLLEGE in 1915, his M.S. from Princeton, and his B.D. from Princeton Theological Seminary in 1920. During the summer of 1918, he worked in Saskatchewan under the auspices of the United Church of Canada. In 1920 he was ordained by Bishop EUGENE R. HENDRIX and in 1921 sailed for Brazil. Bishop JOHN M. MOORE, then in charge of the work in Brazil, named him principal of the forthcoming PORTO ALEGRE college, a position he held from its start in rented quarters to the completion in 1925 of its two main buildings.

In July of that year, Saunders began definite pastoral work. In the same year, he married Sara Stout, who had come from Clarksville, Tenn., as a missionary of the M.E. Church, South. Saunders served both in the South and in the Central Brazil Conferences. In 1939, he was appointed to Curitiba, capital of the state of Paraná, where he founded the church with two members, and left it eight years later with a flourishing congregation and a fine property on which an adequate church was later built. He also served as district superintendent, as professor at the Methodist seminary then at Porto Alegre, and lastly in Campo Grande, Federal District, where he supervised the building of a fine parsonage.

Outside the ministry, Saunders made a valuable and unusual contribution to the state of Rio Grande do Sul, introducing at his own expense several pecan trees (hitherto unknown to the region). These he gave to the State Agricultural School and to a few private individuals. They have proved a new source of wealth to that state.

In 1945 Randolph-Macon College conferred on him the D.D. degree. After retirement in June 1956, Saunders served briefly as pastor of churches in Yorktown and Denbigh, Va. He died suddenly of a heart attack on Oct. 28, 1956. He was survived by his widow and by a son, John Van Dyke Saunders, who became director of Latin American Languages and Area Development Program at the University of Florida.

John Saunders was known and personally loved for his humble, kindly, and self-effacing spirit.

EULA K. LONG

SAUQUOIT, NEW YORK, U.S.A. The Sauquoit Church on the Willowvale charge, Mohawk District, is the oldest Methodist church building in continuous use in the present NORTHERN NEW YORK CONFERENCE.

FREEBORN GARRETTSON held the first Methodist service in the community, then called Bethelville, in 1788, and the society was organized in 1792 by Jonathan Newman, the preacher in charge on the Otsego Circuit. A church building costing $950 was completed in July, 1801, and Bishop RICHARD WHATCOAT preached there, August 6. Bishop ASBURY preached in a grove near the church, June 21, 1807, and in 1811 the first annual conference within the bounds of the present Northern New York Conference was conducted in the church by Bishop McKENDREE. Bishop ENOCH GEORGE preached during a second conference in the church in 1816. In 1826, the church had 399 members, its largest enrolment ever.

During the pastorate of Benajah Mason in 1842, the present brick church was erected, the membership then standing at 240. The building, constructed on the original lot and boasting the first bell in the region, was dedicated Dec. 21, 1842 with fifteen preachers present. Beginning in 1884, several bequests totaling $4,200 were made to a trust fund which has been helpful to the church. Bishop JOHN P. NEWMAN, grandson of the first pastor, spoke at the one hundredth anniversary of the church in 1892.

The church building was redecorated in 1872, and in 1959 an addition was constructed. On May 18, 1963, a historical pageant was presented with addresses by Bishops W. RALPH WARD and HERBERT WELCH, the latter then being 100 years old. In 1967, improvements costing over $10,000 were made and a legacy and gifts totaling nearly $12,000 were received.

In 1970, the Sauquoit Church reported 220 members, property valued at $105,000, and $9,308 raised for all purposes during the year.

General Minutes, MEC and UMC.
Edith M. Jones, *History of Sauquoit Methodist Church* (Typescript, 9 pp.).   JESSE A. EARL

SAVANNAH, GEORGIA, U.S.A. Methodism in Savannah has the heritage of the early work of JOHN and CHARLES WESLEY and GEORGE WHITEFIELD, though the Methodist movement was not established until some time later. The town was founded by General OGLETHORPE on Feb. 12, 1733. The plan of the settlement was carefully laid out by Oglethorpe, and the streets and squares in the old part of the city today follow the original plan. In 1736 John Wesley came to Savannah as pastor of the Anglican Church. He was succeeded in this office in 1738 by George Whitefield, who proceeded to found BETHESDA ORPHAN HOUSE. With Wesley came his brother, Charles, later famous as a hymn writer, and BENJAMIN INGHAM and CHARLES DELAMOTTE. Ingham is considered the founder of the first school in Savannah. Whitefield's great concern at Bethesda was for education. He later failed in his attempt to have the institution chartered as a college. While in Savannah John Wesley prepared what is considered to be one of the earliest English hymnals, *Collection of Psalms and Hymns*. This book was published in 1737 in CHARLESTON, S.C., for there were no printing facilities in GEORGIA at the time. Perhaps Savannah's greatest claim to fame is the fact that it is the only place in the New World where all three of early Methodism's greatest leaders, the Wesley brothers and Whitefield, lived and labored. A second claim to fame for Savannah is that it was on a nearby plantation in 1793 that Eli Whitney invented the cotton gin, an event that was to have tremendous effect on the development of the Southern life and economy.

Even though the great Methodist founders had lived in Savannah before Methodism became established as an effective movement, the Methodist Church had a difficult time getting established there. In 1790 HOPE HULL was appointed to the church but was driven away by a mob, as were other preachers later. JESSE LEE was able to form a class with four members in Savannah in 1807, but by this date AUGUSTA, Ga., already had a Methodist church almost ten years old. The first Methodist church building was erected in 1812 and was dedicated by Bishop ASBURY.

On his first visit to Savannah in 1793 Asbury made the following observations in his journal: "Tuesday, January 29, 1793. We reach Savannah. Next day I rode

JOHN WESLEY STATUE, SAVANNAH, GEORGIA

twelve miles along a fine, sandy road to view the ruins of Mr. Whitefield's Orphan House."

A nine-foot bronze statue was unveiled in Savannah, Georgia, on Aug. 3, 1969, commemorating the ministry of John Wesley in Georgia. He was a missionary from the Church of England to Georgia, 1736-37. The monument was sponsored and paid for by local church subscriptions and support from historical and civic groups with the Savannah city officials giving great encouragement and support.

The statue depicts Wesley as a young clergyman of thirty-three years of age, as he was when he came to Georgia. The likeness was modeled after early portraits of Wesley. It stands in Reynolds Square on Abercorn Street near the Savannah River. It is directly adjacent to the spot where John Wesley had his house and garden after he came to America in 1736 with Oglethorpe. The chairman of the committee which sponsored the monument was James R. Webb, Jr., presently serving as pastor of St. Paul United Methodist Church in Columbus, Ga. The sculptor for the project was Marshall Daugherty of Macon, Ga.

Christ Church (Protestant Episcopal) had its beginning when General James Edward Oglethorpe landed at Savannah on Feb. 12, 1733, with 125 "sober, industrious, and moral persons" to found the colony of Georgia, for there accompanied them a minister of the Church of England, Henry Herbert. He had been chosen and sent out by the Society for the Propagation of the Gospel in Foreign Parts. This society was responsible for the sending, and in large part for the support, of the ministers of the Church of England in Georgia throughout the colonial period. Thus Christ Church began with the founding of the colony. In laying out the town a church lot was set apart, and Christ Church still stands on that spot.

Herbert left after a few months, and was followed by Samuel Quincy of BOSTON. In 1735 the Society appointed John Wesley as minister to Savannah. The church had not then been built and services were held in the General Building. A marker on the site commemorates Wesley's first service. In 1737 Wesley published his first hymnal for use here; this was also the first hymnal used anywhere in the Anglican Church. Also he anticipated the work of ROBERT RAIKES by fifty years in the founding of a SUNDAY SCHOOL. But his time in Savannah was not happy, for at that time he was a stickler for rules, and could not unbend for the needs of a pioneer congregation. He left almost in despair, but it was out of that despair that there came to him, as to Elijah at Mt. Horeb, the great experience at ALDERSGATE.

Wesley was followed in 1738 by George Whitefield, who founded in Savannah, Bethesda, the oldest orphanage in the United States. Whitefield began the building of a church building which was completed under his successor in 1750. This church burned in 1796, a second church was pulled down in 1837, and the present building in Greek Revival style erected in 1838. On either side of the entrance is a bronze tablet, one to Wesley and one to Whitefield.

Christ Church took a leading part in the formation of the Diocese of Georgia in 1823, in the securing of a bishop, and in the establishing of churches throughout the state. The first two bishops were also, for part of their episcopate, rectors of Christ Church. Until 1956 the bishop's office was in Christ Church, which is still outstanding in the life of the community and the diocese. The church is open to visitors every day, and is especially glad to welcome visiting Methodists.

Trinity Church. It was 1790 before the name "Savannah Town" appeared for the first time in the minutes of the M.E. Church. Hope Hull was assigned as its first preacher, but he met with such violence and opposition that he soon left.

Savannah's lingering prejudice against Wesley and the strong anti-slavery stand taken by the GENERAL CONFERENCE made conditions so unfavorable for Methodism until, in 1806, Bishop Asbury refused to make an appointment for Savannah. Instead, he called for a volunteer and young SAMUEL DUNWOODY accepted the challenge. Dunwoody was determined to stay at any cost, so he taught school for his support.

In 1807 Dunwoody's work began to show a little life and at conference time he could report five white and seven colored members. James Russell was appointed to Savannah in 1812 and began building a house of worship known as Wesley Chapel. The building was completed in 1813 and could boast a congregation of thirty white and thirty-five colored members. From this beginning, Wesley Chapel rapidly became one of the best appointments in the state. The membership outgrew the original building twenty-five years after its completion, and plans were made for a new building. This first Wesley Chapel brought many Methodist immortals to Savannah to conduct their ministry. Among these were WILLIAM CAPERS, JAMES O. ANDREW, IGNATIUS A. FEW, and GEORGE FOSTER PIERCE.

In the *Daily Georgian of Savannah*, Feb. 11, 1848, there appeared the following article: "The corner stone of the new Methodist Church to be erected in St. James Square, will be laid on Monday next and an address delivered by the Reverend Preston, D.D. of the Independent Presbyterian Church."

The cornerstone was laid on Feb. 14, 1848, and the minutes show a congregation of 331 members, but the name Trinity does not appear until later. The third QUARTERLY CONFERENCE for the Savannah Station of the M.E. Church, South, was held at Trinity Church on Aug. 10, 1850. It can be assumed that the building had been completed and named by this time, two and a half years after the laying of the cornerstone. The building follows the Corinthian style of architecture and both interior and exterior remain essentially unchanged to this day.

Trinity was the site of the first meeting of the SOUTH GEORGIA ANNUAL CONFERENCE in 1867 after the decision was made to divide the state into two conferences, North and South. This historic church has been host to many annual conferences since that date.

Even during times of tragedy, Trinity continued to hold fast. Great yellow fever epidemics in 1854 and 1876 took a large number of her members. During the epidemic of 1876, Edward H. Myers, pastor of Trinity, was in BALTIMORE, Md., representing the M.E. Church, South, at a joint meeting with the M.E. Church, trying to adjust claims of the church over property issues. When news of the sickness in Savannah reached him, he rushed home to minister to the sick and dying. His unselfish service to his flock cost him his life one week after his return, when Myers and 193 others fell victim. During the War Between the States many of Trinity's sons left for the battlefield and in 1862 the minutes of the third quarterly conference show that only six members were present; the others were with the Confederate Army.

Trinity boasts the oldest continuous Sunday school in

Savannah, being organized in 1822. The *Savannah Morning News* reported the sixty-seventh anniversary of the Trinity Sunday School in 1889 as follows:

It is older by five years than either the Presbyterian or the Baptist Sunday schools. Eighty-seven years ago these three denominations formed a Union Sunday School which was continued for twenty years. Trinity then withdrew and established a Sunday School of its own. Five years later the Baptists withdrew, and it was not until then that the Presbyterians and Baptists established Sunday Schools of their own.

Trinity is known as "The Mother Church of Savannah Methodism," having been instrumental in the establishment of ten other Methodist churches in the city of Savannah. The first of these "spiritual children " was born in 1866, and was adopted by the South Georgia Conference in 1868 as a project to build a church as a monument to John and Charles Wesley. Today this church is known as Wesley Monumental Church.

In 1921 Trinity numbered 1,044 members and by 1948, the membership had grown to almost 2,100. On Jan. 24 and 25, 1948, Trinity celebrated its Centennial Year with a special program led by ARTHUR J. MOORE, then presiding bishop of the ATLANTA, Ga. area; and W. E. SANGSTER, one of the outstanding leaders of the British Methodist Church. In 1970 Trinity reported 1,015 members.

Warren A. Candler Hospital was chartered by the Georgia Legislature in 1808 as the Savannah Poor House and Hospital, making it the second oldest institution of its kind in the United States. It was moved to its present site on Huntingdon Street in downtown Savannah in 1819.

The Savannah Hospital was deeded to the South Georgia Conference by the City of Savannah in 1931 and has been governed by a Board of Trustees approved by the Conference since then. It was renamed in honor of Bishop WARREN A. CANDLER, one of Methodism's and Georgia's most revered bishops.

Wesley Monumental Church is a monument to John and Charles Wesley. In 1849 Wesley Chapel was incorporated by an act of the Senate and House of Representatives of the State of Georgia, along with Trinity Church and Andrew Chapel for Colored People (both in Savannah), with the same trustees for all three. Wesley Chapel faltered but was reorganized on Jan. 19, 1868, with fifty-four members. The first regular church meeting was held on Feb. 23, 1868, with Daniel D. Cox, junior preacher of Trinity Church, being the first pastor.

The South Georgia Annual Conference, meeting on Dec. 16-21, 1868, recognized the need for this church and turned the project over to the Board of Domestic Missions. It was in 1868 that the decision was made to make of this church a monument to the Wesleys, as was stated in the Annual Conference Minutes of that year:

Trinity Church purchased with the cash (from the Board of Domestic Missions) an unfinished edifice belonging to the Lutherans, completed handsomely the building, and it was dedicated to God . . . bearing as its title the honored and revered name of Wesley. This was a proper tribute of respect to that apostolic man whose early ministry was in this city. As the amazed spectator surveys the splendid Cathedral of St. Paul's, in London, his eyes read as follows: "Here lies the body of Sir Christopher Wren, the architect of this house. Do you ask for his monument, look around you." So, if you ask for the monument of Wesley, look around you.

WESLEY MEMORIAL CHURCH, SAVANNAH, GEORGIA

The idea of constructing a large church building did not come until 1875 when, under the pastoral leadership of A. A. Wynn, the name was officially changed from Wesley Church to Wesley Monumental Church. The 1875 session of the South Georgia Annual Conference approved the plans and adopted Wesley Monumental as a project for world Methodism. J. O. A. Clark was appointed in 1875 to the special task of raising funds for Wesley Monumental.

The cornerstone was laid in 1875 and the first services were held on March 31, 1890. It is a Gothic structure, patterned after Queen's Kirk in Amsterdam, Holland. Each one of the strained glass windows is dedicated to one of Methodism's historic personalities: FRANCIS ASBURY, THOMAS COKE, JOHN FLETCHER, SUSANNA WESLEY, JOSHUA SOULE, WILLIAM CAPERS, JAMES O. ANDREW, and others. The Wesley Window, in the rear of the sanctuary facing the pulpit, contains life sized busts of John and Charles Wesley. In the large circle at the top of the window is a globe representing the world, and across it is written Wesley's famous utterance, "The World is my Parish." Although the membership of the church in December of 1875 was only 283, the sanctuary was planned and built to seat well over 1,000, a true venture of faith.

Wesley Monumental has been the victim of two fires, the first in 1945 and the second in 1953; both were believed to have been caused by lightning. Following each fire, the Jewish congregation of Mickve Israel Temple (the oldest Reformed Jewish congregation in America), located across the street from Wesley Monumental, graciously allowed her fire-stricken neighbors to use the Temple's facilities. In 1927, the Mickve Israel Temple had caught fire and the congregation used Wesley Monumental for their services.

Several annual conference sessions have been held in this church. Notably, the South Georgia Annual Conference chose Wesley Monumental as the site of its 100th session in June of 1965. Other events of importance which took place here were the Aldersgate Bi-Centennial Celebration in May 1938 and the Mid-Century Convocation of the Southeastern Jurisdiction in 1950. Perhaps her most notable pastor was W. N. AINSWORTH (serving from 1906 to 1909, and from 1916 to 1918), who was elected to the episcopacy in 1918 and served for twenty years as a bishop.

In 1970 the church reported 1,601 members, property valued at almost $1,000,000, and $104,566 raised for all purposes.

General Minutes, UMC, 1970.
Wesleyan Christian Advocate, July 24, 1969.

GEORGE E. CLARY, JR.
FRANCIS BLAND TUCKER
W. ROBERT BOROM
WARREN UPTON CLARY, M.D.

SAVANNAH CONFERENCE (CJ). (See GEORGIA CONFERENCE (CJ)).

SBAFFI, EMANUELE (1883-1965), Italian leader, was born in ROME, ITALY, Jan. 17, 1883, the son of one of the first converts in the Wesleyan Mission there. He entered the ministry in 1905, and served as pastor in Calabria, Ticino (Swiss), Lucania, Lombardy, Naples, Florence, and Rome. He also directed the Theological School, and edited *L'Evangelista.* He served as Synod secretary, and on the outbreak of war in 1940, assumed the position of "Vice-Presidente" of the Wesleyan Church in Italy, as the English Chairman had to leave the country.

It was chiefly due to Emanuele Sbaffi's astuteness, courage and selfless leadership (at one stage he sold the house he had inherited from his father to pay the stipends of the ministers) that the Church survived the war. At the union of the Wesleyan and Episcopal Methodist work in 1946, he was elected the first "Presidente, Sovraintendente Generale" of the "Chiesa Evangelica Metodista d'Italia," continuing by annual election in that office until he retired in 1958. He made an early study of John Henry Newman's theory of the evolution of dogma, and was a pioneer in the ecumenical movement in Italy.

R. KISSACK

THE PASTORS OF THE SBAFFI FAMILY
MARIO, PAOLO (SON OF MARIO),
EMANUELE, AURELIO, AND ALDO

SBAFFI, MARIO (1909-   ), Italian minister, was born Jan. 1, 1909, at Omegna, ITALY, the son of EMANUELE

SBAFFI. Trained under his father at Rome, he was accepted for the ministry in 1933. Fascist authorities cancelled his clerical immunity from military service because of his pacifist messages. He then served as medical orderly in the Italian navy. After the war he returned to La Spezia to rebuild with the labour of his congregation the war-destroyed church. In 1947 he moved to Rome, as minister of Via Firenze. He founded the *Voce Metodista* newspaper, and instituted the construction of "Ecumene," the Methodist Conference and Retreat centre at Velletri, with international student labour camps. In 1958 he was elected Chairman of the Italy District. He succeeded in making the Church capable of a life independent of the Methodist Conference of Great Britain, and when it was raised to the status of an autonomous conference on Oct. 4, 1962, he was elected the first President of the Italy Conference.

R. KISSACK

SCARRITT, NATHAN (1821-1890), American preacher and philantropist for whom SCARRITT COLLEGE was named, was born near Edwardsville, Ill., April 14, 1821. He worked his way through McKENDREE COLLEGE, and graduated valedictorian of his class in 1842. Later he received the M.A. degree from the University of Missouri and the D.D. degree from McKendree College.

After teaching school in ILLINOIS, Scarritt moved to Fayette, Mo., in 1845 to join his brother-in-law, William T. Lucky, in Howard High School. He was admitted to the MISSOURI CONFERENCE, M. E. Church, South, in 1846. From then until 1851 he was in the Indian Mission on MISSOURI's western border. He was principal of the Indian Manual Labor School at SHAWNEE MISSION from 1848 to 1851. Between the latter date and the outbreak of the Civil War he served pastorates in western Missouri. He was strongly opposed to secession, and stood forthrightly for the Union. After the War he discontinued ministerial work because of unsteady health and the demands of business ventures.

While at Shawnee Mission, Scarritt bought 200 acres of land near the new village of KANSAS CITY, Mo. This land became the site of present-day "down-town" Kansas City. The increase of land values as the village swiftly grew into a city made him a very wealthy man. He gave generously of his wealth to schools, churches and missions. He was a founder, benefactor and first president of CENTRAL METHODIST COLLEGE. To many churches and missions in western Missouri, particularly in and around Kansas City, he gave undetermined sums. His gift of $30,000 established Melrose Church, his family's church, and that of his son-in-law, Bishop EUGENE R. HENDRIX.

Nathan Scarritt was an early and consistent advocate of the reunion of the separated Methodist Churches. Thirty-six years after division he published a plan of union in the *St. Louis Christian Advocate* (Jan. 25, 1881), which in some respects was similar to the PLAN OF UNION ratified in 1939. He proposed three jurisdictions, North, South and West, each with its own GENERAL CONFERENCE, the election of its own bishops of equal status, the Church to be united in a General Council composed of all the bishops, general secretaries, clerical and lay delegates proportionately. Scarritt's plan did not contemplate the segregation of Negro conferences or churches. It was, however, too early for plans of union to materialize.

In 1888-90, when Miss BELLE BENNETT was urging the

establishment of a training school for DEACONESSES, Scarritt proposed to give two large lots in Kansas City valued at $25,000 and $25,000 in cash if she would raise $50,000 in the churches of Southern Methodism. The offer was accepted. He died before the project was begun. His children honored his pledge and aided the enterprise. The school was named Scarritt Bible and Training School and was opened Sept. 14, 1892. To better serve the M.E. Church, South, and to meet raised educational and academic standards, the school was moved to NASHVILLE, Tenn., in 1924 and named Scarritt College.

Nathan Scarritt was a delegate to nearly every General Conference after 1870. He died while attending the session of 1890. The *Journal* of that session records the extent of his influence.

M. L. Gray, *Missouri Methodism.* 1907.   FRANK C. TUCKER

SCARRITT COLLEGE TOWER

SCARRITT COLLEGE, Nashville, Tennessee, was established in Kansas City in 1892 as a training school for Christian workers. It was moved to NASHVILLE in 1924, and accepted the alumni of the Methodist Training School which operated in Nashville from 1907 to 1915. While the school honors a donor, NATHAN SCARRITT, MISS BELLE H. BENNETT is remembered as the one who secured the support of the Woman's Missionary Society of the M. E. Church, South. Through that organization Scarritt was able to erect the present campus.

The institution is part of the University Center where students may elect courses in VANDERBILT UNIVERSITY and Peabody College and utilize the Joint Universities

Library System. Ownership is vested in the GENERAL CONFERENCE.

Degrees offered are the B.A. and M.A. The governing board has fifty-six members nominated by the board of trustees and elected by the Board of MISSIONS.

JOHN O. GROSS

FRANZ SCHAEFER

SCHAEFER, FRANZ WERNER (1921-   ), bishop of The United Methodist Church, Geneva Area, was born March 10, 1921, in Birsfelden, Basel, SWITZERLAND. He attended schools in his home town and studied at the Theological Seminary of the Basel Mission in Basel. In 1945 he was received on trial in the Switzerland Annual Conference. From 1947 to 1953 he served as Secretary of Scout work for the Swiss Conference and President of Methodist Men from 1958 to 1962. He was a member of the Board of Directors of the FRANKFURT Seminary from 1960 to 1966 and has been president of the Bethany Deaconess Order in ZURICH since 1962. He served as district superintendent of the West District of Switzerland from 1958 to 1966. In 1960 he attended the GENERAL CONFERENCE of The Methodist Church (U.S.A.) in DENVER, Colo. In 1961 he took part in the OSLO, Norway, and in 1966 in the LONDON, England, WORLD METHODIST CONFERENCE. During the special session of the CENTRAL AND SOUTHERN EUROPE CENTRAL CONFERENCE he was elected bishop of the GENEVA Area in Lausanne, Switzerland, on Sept. 2, 1966. He resides in Zurich. Bishop Schaefer married Heidi Niederhauser in 1951. They have five children, three boys and two girls.

N. B. H.

SCHAEFER, JOHN F. (1909-   ), American E.U.B. minister, was educated at NORTH CENTRAL COLLEGE, received the B.D. degree from EVANGELICAL THEOLOGICAL SEMINARY, and continued graduate study at Union Theological Seminary, New York, where he was granted the S.T.M. degree. He enjoyed one year's fellowship study at the University of Tübingen, Germany, followed by pastorates in the ILLINOIS CONFERENCE for twenty years. He served four years as Professor of Practical Theology, Evangelical Theological Seminary. In 1959 he was elected to serve with the Board of MISSIONS as associate secretary, then became executive secretary of the World Division, before becoming the general secretary of the Board of Missions. He has made numerous visits to mission work in Asia, Africa and Latin America. He was a delegate to WORLD COUNCIL OF CHURCHES, Fourth Assembly, at UPPSALA, Sweden in 1968. Mrs. Schaefer is the former Marian Lang, whose father served in the Illinois Conference for many years. The Schaefers have three sons: John, Paul and Mark.

In The United Methodist Church, Dr. Schaefer was elected Associate General Secretary, World Division of the Board of Missions. His membership is with the NORTHERN ILLINOIS CONFERENCE.

MINNIE WOLGEMATHE

SCHARER, CHARLES WESLEY (1875-1954), was a missionary of the M.E. Church in INDIA, 1904-26. During all but two years of that time he served in the Belgaum District, which was then in BOMBAY Province but is now in the linguistically aligned, Kanarese-speaking Mysore State. His missionary career was brought to an abrupt end by an accident in which his back was broken. He recovered sufficiently to serve churches in the SOUTHERN CALIFORNIA-ARIZONA CONFERENCE until 1946. Although he could not return to India, he retained his membership in the SOUTH INDIA CONFERENCE, and worked continuously to win support of American Christians in prayer, personnel, and finance for service projects in India.

Scharer was born in Toledo, Ohio, May 13, 1875. His wife, Elizabeth, was born in Spring Mountain, Ohio, Sept. 16, 1879. Both were graduates of Taylor University, Upland, Ind., an institution named for Bishop WILLIAM TAYLOR and established by his admirers to train missionaries. Throughout his years in India, Scharer was fervent in EVANGELISM, making contact with many groups not previously reached, and bringing many of them to the avowal of Christian faith and purpose. Mr. and Mrs. Scharer both died in Pasadena, Calif., in 1954, he on May 16, and she on August 24.

Journal of the South India Conference.   J. WASKOM PICKETT

SCHAUB, FRIEDRICH (1855-1937), German-American minister and educator, was born at Lancaster, Wis., on June 21, 1855. He was graduated from the German-English College of Galena, Ill., in 1878 and received an M.A. in 1881. He was admitted to the Northwest German Annual Conference of the M.E. Church in 1878 and served churches in IOWA and ILLINOIS until 1883, when he became an instructor and a professor in 1887 at the German-English College. He was president of the college until 1893. After the college was moved to Charles City, Iowa, with its name changed, he again served as president (1898-1902). From 1902-1907 he was Superintendent of Schools for Floyd County, Iowa; then acting president of Charles City College (1911-1912) and professor of education (1907-1914). He received an honorary D.D. from Central Wesleyan College in 1907. When the Charles City College was merged with MORNINGSIDE COLLEGE, Sioux City, Iowa, in 1914, he became professor of biblical literature until his retirement in 1921. In 1922 he became principal of the Dorcas Institute, a training school for German Methodist DEACONESSES in CINCINNATI. He was the author of *George Roth* (1881), a biography of an early graduate of the Galena college.

P. F. Douglass, *German Methodism.* 1939.
Geschichte der Nordwest Deutschen Konferenz; Minutes of the Annual Conferences 1878-1937.   LOUIS A. HASELMAYER

SCHELL, EDWIN AUSTIN (1923-   ), American clergyman and historian, was born in St. Louis, Mo., on Jan. 10, 1923. He was converted in 1945 and entered the BALTIMORE CONFERENCE (TMC) in 1951. He became president of the Conference Historical Society in 1958 and served until 1962, at which time he became the executive secretary of the society, having in charge the Lovely Lane Museum in BALTIMORE. He was the local chairman of the Methodist BICENTENNIAL celebration in Baltimore in 1966 and is a contributing editor of this encyclopedia.

Who's Who in The Methodist Church, 1966.   N. B. H.

SCHELLHAMMER, EMIL (1904-   ), a minister and leader of German Methodism, was born April 5, 1904, at Friburg. He studied at Tübingen University and the Frankfurt Theological Seminary (PREDIGERSEMINAR) and was ordained ELDER in 1930. He served various circuits from 1926-38. In 1938 he went to Nuremberg, where he became second director of the Martha-Maria deaconess motherhouse and hospital, serving until 1951. He was on the Schwabach circuit from 1951-55, and then was district superintendent of Nuremberg District, 1955-58. He has been first director of Martha-Maria since 1958 and secretary of the South Germany Annual Conference sixteen times between 1935 and 1963. He was editor of the Methodist family magazine *Der Evangelist* (1951-59) and of a magazine for deaconesses, as well as contributor to several other periodicals. He was a delegate to the GENERAL CONFERENCE of 1960, author of books and booklets, teacher of ethics, psychology, and Old Testament at Nuremberg nursing school, president of the association of Methodist deaconess motherhouses in GERMANY and SWITZERLAND.

DIETER SACHMANN

SCHIELE, RUDOLF (1917-   ), German lay leader and businessman, was born Sept. 14, 1917, in BERLIN. Under Bishop J. W. E. SOMMER he organized the relief work of the Methodist Church in Germany in 1945 and served as its managing director until 1949. The "brother pfennig" (one pfennig a day from each member of the German Methodist Church) to serve certain relief projects was initiated by him. He was chiefly responsible for the founding of the Methodist *Maennerdienst* (men's service, i.e., lay activities) in Germany and the periodical for training church workers (*Der Mitarbeiter*). He is the lay leader of the Southwest Germany Annual Conference, delegate to the GENERAL CONFERENCE of the Church, a member of the executive committee of the Methodist Church in Germany, and served on the board of trustees of the theological seminary in Frankfurt (Prediger-seminar). He was chairman of the subcommittee for church institutions (schools, book concern, deaconess motherhouses), of the Joint Committee of the Methodist Church and the EVANGELISCHE GEMEINSCHAFT (E.U.B.

RUDOLF SCHIELE

Church) in Germany and Switzerland. He is also lay delegate to the Council of Methodist Central Conferences in Europe. He is an ordained lay preacher and resides in the Black Forest.

ALFRED KAELBLE

SCHILLING, SYLVESTER PAUL (1904-   ), American scholar and educator, was born at Cumberland, Md., on Feb. 7, 1904, the son of Sylvester and Ida (Weber) Schilling. He received the B.S. degree from St. John's College in 1923; an A.M. from BOSTON UNIVERSITY, 1927; S.T.B. there in 1929, and Ph.D. in 1934. He did postgraduate work at Harvard in 1929-30, and at the University of Berlin, 1930-31. His wife was Mary Elizabeth Albright, and they were married on June 18, 1930. Their children are Robert A. and Paula C.

Dr. Schilling joined the BALTIMORE CONFERENCE (ME) in 1928 and was pastor in Vienna-Oakton, Va., 1932-33; in BALTIMORE, 1933-36; Prince Frederick, Md., 1936-40; and Brookland Church, WASHINGTON, D. C., 1940-45. At this time he became professor of Systematic Theology and Philosophy of Religion at WESTMINSTER THEOLOGICAL SEMINARY, serving there from 1945-53, at which time he went to Boston University and became professor of Systematic Theology in the School of Theology there, becoming in 1954 also chairman of the Division of Theological Studies of the Graduate School. He has been visiting lecturer in a number of schools, and is a fellow of the Society for Religion in Higher Education; a member of the American Theological Society (president 1968-69); of the American Philosophical Association; and of the American Academy of Religion.

He spent 1959-60 in research at the University of Heidelberg, supported by a Faculty Fellowship of the American Association of Theological Schools, and carried out further research at the University of Tübingen in 1966-67. He gave the Lowell Institute Lectures in theology in Boston in 1968. Following his retirement from Boston University, he served as visiting professor of Systematic Theology at Union Theological Seminary, MANILA, Philippines, in 1969-70. He has written *Isaiah*

Speaks, 1958; *Methodism and Society in Theological Perspective,* 1960—this done for the Board of Social and Economic Relations of The Methodist Church as part of a four volume series issued at that time; *Contemporary Continental Theologians,* 1966 (paperback, 1969); *God in an Age of Atheism,* 1969. He has contributed significant articles to the *Encyclopedia of World Methodism.*

Who's Who in America, Vol. 34.
Who's Who in The Methodist Church, 1966.   N. B. H.

SCHISLER, JOHN QUINCY (1885-1967), American clergyman and educator, was born in Bono, Ark., on Oct. 15, 1885. He received the A.B. degree from HENDRIX COLLEGE and the B.D. from EMORY UNIVERSITY. He married Mary Irene Dodsan in 1914, whom he survived by a number of years. He served as a pastor in the NORTH ARKANSAS CONFERENCE for several years and as conference Sunday School Secretary from 1918 to 1920. In 1920 he joined the staff of the General Sunday School Board, M. E. Church, South. For six years he was assistant superintendent of Teacher Training, and for four years superintendent of the Department of Leadership Training. In 1930 he became Secretary, Department of the Local Church in a newly organized General Board of Christian Education. In 1940 at the Union of American Methodism he became Executive Secretary, Division of the Local Church, General Board of EDUCATION where he served until retirement in 1955. He was the author of several books and booklets; among the best known were *The Educational Work of the Small Church* and *Christian Teaching in the Churches.* "No man in the history of American Methodism has had more influence on the educational program of the church than John Schisler. He was diligent and devoted; he was creative and imaginative; he was wise and incisive; he was broad and he was deep. He was a pioneer in many areas of Christian education, establishing programs in church recreation, in church camping, in family life, in audiovisuals, in volunteer service projects, in theological education cooperative enterprises, and many more. He was an early leader in the ecumenical movement, and helped to shape the International Council of Religious Education and to create the NATIONAL COUNCIL OF CHURCHES of Christ in the U.S.A." (Bishop W. McFerrin Stowe). In 1958 he married Miss Freddie Henry. He died April 18, 1967.

WALTER N. VERNON

SCHISLER, WILLIAM RICHARD (1889-   ), American educator and lay missionary to BRAZIL, was born in Bono, Ark., on May 19, 1889. He graduated from HENDRIX COLLEGE in 1919; and in June 1920, married Frances Purcell, also a graduate of Hendrix. After teaching in the United States for a short period, Schisler was accepted by the Methodist Board of MISSIONS for Brazil. He arrived there in July 1921.

As a layman and educator, his work was always with Methodist schools in the state of Rio Grande do Sul. His first appointment was as teacher to Instituto União, URUGUAIANA, then as principal through 1929. In 1930, he was appointed to the Passo Fundo Educational Institute, and was named its principal in 1933. This position he held until retirement in 1958, with the exception of one year when an emergency at União forced him to return there. During all these years, Frances Schisler served tirelessly in the local church, and in the school as teacher, dietitian, and manager of the boarding department.

The two outstanding characteristics of Schisler's administration were his close personal relationship with his students, and the intimate relationship he established between the faculty and students and the local church.

Schisler's long tenure and his influence on the students resulted in strong support of the school by alumni, city, and state officials. Today its graduates occupy important posts in the Methodist ministry and educational establishments, in government, professional, business, and industrial fields.

The Schislers retired in July 1958, to NASHVILLE, Tenn. Two years later, upon the earnest invitation of former students and friends of the institute, he returned for a visit, during which he was conspicuously honored by Roman Catholics, as well as Protestants, by Rotary and other civic groups, and named Honorary Citizen of Passo Fundo. The Schislers have three children, of whom two are in missionary work in Brazil—WILLIAM, JR., a pastor and for nineteen years editor of Methodist church publications; Nancy (Mrs. James E. Tims); and George. The Schislers presently live in ATLANTA, Ga.

EULA K. LONG

SCHISLER, WILLIAM RICHARD, JR. (1924-), missionary in BRAZIL of the Methodist Board of MISSIONS, NEW YORK, was born in URUGUAIANA, Rio Grande do Sul, on May 5, 1924, hence his Brazilian citizenship. He graduated from the Instituto Educacional in Passo Fundo, then directed by his father; from VANDERBILT UNIVERSITY in 1947, with a B.A. degree; and from Yale Divinity School in 1952 with a B.D.

At a quadrennial Student Conference in 1950, at the University of Illinois, he met Edith Hume Long, daughter and granddaughter of missionaries in Brazil, and they were married on Aug. 25, 1951. Edith Long Schisler thus became the first third-generation missionary in that country. In 1952, they traveled to Brazil via Europe, where Schisler represented Brazil at the Faith and Order Conference in Lund, Norway.

In Brazil, Schisler was named editor of *Cruz de Malta*, the youth publication of the Methodist Church; and in 1955, editor-in-chief of all seven of the Church publications, a position he held until 1969. Throughout the years, he has been a speaker and counsellor at Youth Assemblies, and pastor and organizer of new congregations in the city of SÃO PAULO. While president of the Board of Trustees of the INSTITUTO METODISTA, he planned its modern chapel and developed its recent change into an Ecumenical Lay Institute.

During 1964 and 1965, Schisler worked closely with Dr. JOEL DE MELO, a prominent Methodist layman, in promoting an Evangelical radio station in São Paulo. He served a term as one of the presidents of the Christian-Jewish Fraternity, and worked closely with the Roman Catholics, speaking often in their churches.

At the 1965 General Conference of the Methodist Church of Brazil, he was one of four designated to prepare the new Liturgy Manual for use of the church in Brazil. He was also for a term on the Laity Commission of the WORLD COUNCIL OF CHURCHES, which he represented in Rochester and NIGERIA. In 1969 Schisler asked for transfer to his home conference—the Second Region

in South Brazil—and now serves as pastor in Passo Fundo, Rio Grande do Sul, and as district superintendent. The Schislers have four children.

EULA K. LONG

SCHNACKENBERG, CORT HENRY (1812-1880), NEW ZEALAND Methodist minister, was born at Wilmstedt, Hanover, GERMANY, in 1812. He came to New Zealand in 1839 and was engaged for some time as an agent for a SYDNEY firm to purchase flax and timber from the Maori people. At Kawhia, he came under the influence of JOHN WHITELEY. He was received as a catechist in 1844, and was sent to reestablish the Mokau Mission, where his influence spread among the Ngati-Maniapoto people, among whom he gathered congregations and established schools.

From 1857, when he was ordained after four years probation, until twenty-three years later, he labored among the Maoris and Europeans in the Kawhia, Aotea, and Raglan Circuits. This period included the tumultuous years of the Maori Wars.

Of a quiet, sincere, and earnest disposition, Cort Schnackenberg declined several offers to enter government service in order to fulfill his calling. Worn out with toil in an area embracing Raglan, Aotea, Waikato, Waipa, and Te Kopua, he died on the way to AUCKLAND seeking medical attention, on Aug. 10, 1880.

W. Morley, *New Zealand*. 1900. WESLEY A. CHAMBERS

SCHOENHALS, LAWRENCE R. (1912-), vice-president of SEATTLE PACIFIC COLLEGE, was born at Brown City, Mich. He holds a diploma from the Fort Wayne Bible College, 1932. His degrees are: B.A., GREENVILLE COLLEGE, 1935; M.A., University of Michigan, 1938; Ph.D., University of Washington, 1955; Greenville College conferred the Mus.D. in 1962. He was director of the Music Departments at Central College, Kansas; Huntington College, Indiana, and Seattle Pacific College, Seattle, Washington for a total of twenty-nine years. He also served as Registrar and Dean of Administration at Seattle Pacific, where he has been Vice-President since 1964. Dr. Schoenhals was the Musical Director, FREE METHODIST world-wide broadcast, Light and Life Hour, 1945-66. He holds membership in Phi Delta Kappa, College Music Society, National Church Music Fellowship, and American Musicological Society. Dr. and Mrs. Schoenhals live in Seattle, Wash.

BYRON S. LAMSON

SCHOFIELD, CHARLES EDWIN (1894-1951), American minister and educator, was born on April 18, 1894 in Geneva, Neb. He received the A.B. degree from the University of Nebraska, and the S.T.B. from BOSTON UNIVERSITY. He married Nora Fullerton in 1919. He served as a pastor in NEBRASKA, COLORADO, and WYOMING before going to ILIFF SCHOOL OF THEOLOGY as president in 1934. In 1942 he became president of SOUTHWESTERN COLLEGE, Winfield, Kan. and in 1944 was appointed Editor of Adult Publications, Editorial Division, General Board of EDUCATION of The Methodist Church. He was the author of several books, best known of which were *Aldersgate and After*, *We Methodists*, and *The Methodist Church*. At the SOUTH CENTRAL JURISDICTIONAL CONFERENCE in 1944 he received 102 votes for bishop (with 175 necessary to elect). He died in Nashville, Tenn.

WALTER N. VERNON

SCHOLZ, ERNST (1894-   ), German pastor, editor and free church leader, was born July 1, 1894, in BERLIN. After his studies at the Frankfurt Methodist Theological Seminary and at Vienna University, he became pastor in the Methodist Church in GERMANY, and for several years of the German Mission in LONDON, and of a circuit in Vienna. He was seven times a delegate to the GENERAL CONFERENCE of his church. For several times also he was a delegate to the WORLD METHODIST CONFERENCE meeting. In 1953 he was the recipient of the D.D. degree by UNION COLLEGE, Barbourville, W. Va., U.S.A. He became editor of a Christian education periodical and from 1959 to 1967 of the German Methodist weekly, *Der Evangelist*. He is well known as a member of the Evangelical Alliance and as a free-church ecumenical leader in Berlin. For two terms he served as district superintendent of West District, Northeast Germany Annual Conference. Now retired, he lives in Berlin.

KARL BEISIEGEL

SCHOLZ, LUISE E. (1890-   ), the wife of ERNST SCHOLZ, has been national president of the WOMAN'S SOCIETY OF CHRISTIAN SERVICE in AUSTRIA, 1924-33; president of W.S.C.S., Northeast Germany Annual Conference, 1934-48; treasurer of W.S.C.S. in GERMANY, 1936-46; president of W.S.C.S. in Germany 1946-69; president of the WORLD FEDERATION OF METHODIST WOMEN, 1956-61. She was a delegate to the World Assembly of the World Federation of Methodist Women, 1948-66, and also a delegate to seven European Methodist Consultative Conferences, 1939-66. She has been a member of the WORLD METHODIST COUNCIL, 1951-61. She was editor of the German Methodist Women's Magazine, 1949-68. She received the honorary L.H.D. degree in 1964.

KARL BEISIEGEL

SCHOOI. OF THEOLOGY AT CLAREMONT, California, is a continuation of the Maclay College of Theology, founded in 1885 by the M.E. Church. In 1894, it was moved to the campus of the UNIVERSITY OF SOUTHERN CALIFORNIA, then a Methodist-related university, and in 1922 it became an integral part of the university. In 1946, it was accredited by the UNIVERSITY SENATE as a graduate and professional school for the education of ministers. A study of ministerial education made by the Division of Higher Education, Board of Education of The Methodist Church, recommended that the school be strenthened and prepared for larger service. In 1952, the university severed what fragile ties it had with The Methodist Church, but nevertheless, an effort was made to continue the school of theology at the university. When this became impossible, there was a move to a new site at Claremont, where a fifteen-acre campus had been secured. In 1960, buildings were completed; funds had been provided by a campaign in the SOUTHERN CALIFORNIA-ARIZONA CONFERENCE. Additional buildings have been constructed, and this school now possesses an excellent plant in an established educational center. It offers the degrees of Th.M. and Ph.D. in Religion. The gov-

erning board consists of thirty trustees, elected on nomination of the executive committee by a corporation responsible to the SOUTHERN CALIFORNIA-ARIZONA ANNUAL CONFERENCE.

JOHN O. GROSS

KARL SCHOU

SCHOU, KARL ("CARL") JENSEN (1841-1889), Danish Methodist pioneer, was born at Holstebro, DENMARK, on May 22, 1841. His parents were a watchmaker, Jens Christian Schou, and Christine Lund Schou. He became a watchmaker like his father, and a very skillful one. Carl Schou left Denmark in 1861 to go to America. Coming from a Christian home, in the new world he at once found his way to the Methodist Episcopal Church. In the beginning of his stay in the United States he went first to Perth Amboy, N.J., and a little later to the town of Lafayette, Ind. By now he had decided to give his whole life to God and the Church. The so-called CAMP MEETINGS were of great significance to him.

Carl Schou started his training at GARRETT BIBLICAL INSTITUTE in Evanston, Ill., in 1868. Two years later he married Ane Marie Moller from Kolding, Denmark, to whom he had become engaged before he left Denmark. In order to make both ends meet, he had to start a workshop for repairing watches, and this later grew to a real watch shop.

Having ended his training at Garrett, he was attached to NORTHWESTERN UNIVERSITY in Evanston as a teacher. In 1872 his young wife died, and in the same year he was appointed superintendent of the church in Denmark to replace CHRISTIAN WILLERUP.

Carl Schou arrived at COPENHAGEN on Jan. 31, 1873. For sixteen years thereafter he was at work in his own country, and they were very successful years for the young Methodist Church. Several church buildings were erected, and the number of congregations grew to sixteen. It has been said of Carl Schou that he was the real founder of the church in Denmark. He reduced the work to a system.

Carl Schou married once more in 1878, this time to Louise Ulrikke Eneman from Kalmar, SWEDEN. He died in Aarhus on an official visit on July 31, 1889.

Svend Johansen, *Karl Schou, Superintendent i Metodistkirken.* 1934.

NIELS MANN

SCHRECKENGAST, ISAAC BUTLER (1864-1935), American preacher, college president and administrator, was born Oct. 5, 1864 near Danville, Iowa. His early education was received in the public schools of that community.

He enrolled at Iowa State College, Ames, Iowa in 1880, receiving the A.B. degree with honors in 1885. Feeling the call to the ministry, he joined the Iowa Conference and was ordained elder in 1887. In 1891 he entered Boston University School of Theology, receiving the S.T.B. degree in 1894.

In 1906 he received the Ph.M. degree from Iowa State College, and in 1908 he was awarded the honorary D.D. from Simpson College. Final academic honors came to him from Nebraska Wesleyan University in 1932 when, upon retiring he received the Lit.D. degree.

Following graduation from seminary, Schreckengast served Methodist Churches in West Liberty, Washington and Burlington, Iowa with great distinction. His last pastorate was at First Church, University Place, Lincoln, Neb., from which he was elected vice-chancellor and treasurer of Nebraska Wesleyan University in 1913, becoming Chancellor in 1917. During his first ten years of leadership, he raised $100,000 to pay off the school's indebtedness and led in a victorious campaign for a $1,000,000 endowment. During his years of leadership the Rachel Ann Lucas Library, Van Fleet Teacher's College and Magee Stadium were built.

He was a great preacher, beloved of his students for many years, having the largest weekly college prayer meeting in the world. He led four delegations of Nebraska Methodists to General Conference and was often called "the second bishop of Nebraska," as he frequently took the bishop's place in church dedications and ceremonies. Schreckengast died Sept. 11, 1935 after a long illness and was buried in Lincoln, Neb.

Minutes of the Nebraska Conference, 1935.
Nebraska Wesleyan *Alumni News.*   Everett E. Jackman

SCHULZ, EMIL (1905-   ), German Methodist, entered the ministry in 1930. After four years of theological training, he served circuit work mainly in Berlin as a member of the Northeast Germany Annual Conference. After the Second World War he transferred to the Northwest Annual Conference. In 1945 he started his work at the Methodist deaconess motherhouse, Bethanien, in Hamburg. Besides pastoral and administrative work at the Hamburg Methodist Hospital he was four years district superintendent of the Hamburg District. He is presently director of the motherhouse Bethanien, including five hospitals with a total capacity of 410 beds; also he is engaged in organizing social work as carried on by 312 deaconesses in hospital work, in circuits, Methodist old-people's homes, and in two Methodist recreation homes; also he is involved in directing educational work in a training school for girls which leads up to various possibilities of occupational choices for women, though emphasizing the preparation for hospital work.

Erich Baass

SCHUTZ, WALTER (1893-1961), American E.U.B. missionary, was born to Sarah Bixler and Albert Schutz on a farm near Pandora, Ohio, Aug. 9, 1893. To finish his high school education he enrolled at Martin Boehm Academy, Otterbein College. After high school he stayed on and obtained his B.A. degree from Otterbein

College in 1921. From there he took graduate work in economics at Ohio State University, but feeling the need to enter church service he left these studies.

His educational program was interrupted with nearly two years military service in the Field Medical Supply Depot, Camp Sherman, Chillicothe, Ohio during World War I. On July 3, 1922 he was married to Edna Isabel Hooper of Bradford, Pa., a college classmate.

Together they were appointed by the United Brethren in Christ for service in Sierra Leone, sailing in May 1923. Although a layman he was often called upon to preach to the natives. His major task was to supervise the schools of the Temne tribe. On his first return to America he spent some months studying at Bonebrake (now United) Theological Seminary, Dayton, Ohio. On his second furlough he spent three years in study at the same school, graduating with the B.D. degree. Miami Conference, Church of the United Brethren in Christ, licensed him in 1926 and ordained him in 1929. In subsequent service in Sierra Leone he served as head of Albert Academy, supervising the schools supported by the Mission, and General Superintendent of United Brethren work. After twenty-eight years and because of his wife's health, they returned to the United States in 1951, when he became Director of Public Relations at United Seminary, Dayton, and later Treasurer. In this institution he served for ten years until his death.

In Sierra Leone Walter Schutz was editor of the Sierra Leone *Outlook,* a member of the Fourah Bay College Council, chairman of the United Christian Council, a member of the national Board of Education, and organized the Bo Conference (an ecumenical movement that had great influence upon the nation and the church). He believed that the missionary was not sent to Sierra Leone to hold jobs but to train the natives to take that responsibility. Much of the current indigenous nature of this mission may be traced to Walter Schutz.

Death came suddenly Jan. 28, 1961. His remains were placed in a cemetery at Pandora, Ohio, Feb. 2, 1961.

Donald W. Keller, "The Life of Dr. Walter Schutz." Ms. in Commission on Archives and History.
United News, United Theological Seminary, Dayton, O., March 1966.   John H. Ness, Jr.

SCHWOPE (SCHWAB), BENEDICT (1730?-1810), a German Reformed minister who was probably born in Germany. The first real record of his life shows that in 1754 he was a member of the German Reformed Church, York, Pa. Later he moved to the Pipe Creek community near Westminster, Md., where in 1763, he was one of the elders of St. Benjamin's Church (Reformed). In 1771, the Reformed Coetus of ministers approved him for ordination.

In 1770-71, Schwope became involved in a congregational dispute among the members of the German Reformed church in Baltimore. John Christopher Faber, who also served St. Benjamin's Church, was the pastor. The members who were alienated from Faber turned to Schwope for leadership. They purchased land on Howard's Hill in Baltimore and organized an independent Reformed congregation with Schwope as pastor.

In 1772, Joseph Pilmore arrived in Baltimore to organize Methodist congregations. Pilmore lodged at the home of George Dagan, a vestryman in Schwope's church.

Schwope loaned his church for Pilmore's meetings, and the LOVELY LANE congregation, frequently referred to as the Mother Church of American Methodism, was organized.

The next year, wishing to follow the western migration, Schwope urged his friend PHILLIP WILLIAM OTTERBEIN, pastor in YORK, Pa., to succeed him in Baltimore. Otterbein refused on the ground that the congregation was guilty of several irregularities against the Coetus. During the succeeding year the invitation was repeated. This time Schwope asked another friend, FRANCIS ASBURY, to intercede, and in 1774 Otterbein accepted and assumed the pastorate.

Because of some delay in undertaking his western venture, Schwope continued for a time at St. Benjamin's Church. He and Otterbein were greatly influenced by the Methodist class meeting idea (*ecclesiola in ecclesia*), and under the influence of Asbury introduced it into the German Reformed churches of MARYLAND. There was a dearth of regular pastors among the German Reformed churches in Maryland, and the CLASS MEETINGS under CLASS LEADERS served to promote devotion and to maintain spiritual discipline in the church. Schwope served as the secretary, with Otterbein as chairman, of a small conference of Reformed ministers. In the semiannual meetings reports were received concerning the spiritual condition of the various classes. (A record of these conferences was written in the St. Benjamin's Church record for May 1774 to June 1776, while Schwope served as secretary.)

In 1792 Schwope helped to organize a German church in LEXINGTON, Ky., and during the same year he represented Lincoln County in the KENTUCKY Constitutional Convention.

Schwope married Susanna Welcker, date unknown, to which union eleven children were born. He died March 30, 1810 at the home of his son Jacob in Lincoln County, Ky.

There has been an unverified tradition in the BALTIMORE CONFERENCE of The Methodist Church that Benedict Schwope ordained ROBERT STRAWBRIDGE to the ministry.

Commission on Archives and History, Schwope File.
Joseph Henry Dubbs, *Historic Manual of the Reformed Church in the United States*. Lancaster, Pa., 1885.
Minutes and Letters of the Coetus of the German Reformed Congregation in Pennsylvania, 1749-1792. Philadelphia: Reformed Church Publication, 1903.
Paul E. Holdcraft, *The Old Otterbein Church Story*. Mimeo, 1960.   JOHN H. NESS, JR.

SCORE, JOHN NELSON RUSSELL (1896-1949), American preacher and college president, was born in a Methodist parsonage in White Church, Mo., on April 21, 1896. The name was originally "Scaar" or "Scarr," as his grandparents were from Scandinavia.

In preparation for the ministry his schooling included an A.B. degree from Scarritt-Morrisville College; B.D. from EMORY UNIVERSITY; and a Th.D. from the Pacific School of Religion in 1925. In recognition of his achievements, CENTENARY COLLEGE OF LOUISIANA conferred upon him the D.D. in 1931, and CENTRAL COLLEGE and SOUTHERN METHODIST UNIVERSITY conferred on him the LL.D. in 1943 and 1945 respectively.

Upon entering the ministry of the M.E. Church, South,

he was ordained in 1917, and became an Army CHAPLAIN in World War I, with overseas assignment. He returned to pastoral duties at the close of the War, and served with marked effectiveness the following widely scattered congregations: Wynne, Ark.; Epworth University Church, BERKELEY, Calif.; St. Paul's Methodist Church, HOUSTON, Texas; First Methodist Church, FORT WORTH. From Fort Worth he moved to the presidency of SOUTHWESTERN UNIVERSITY in Texas, where he labored until his death in 1949.

A strong and colorful character, he was a born leader of men, and had the capacity for making strong friendships. He received a significant vote for bishop at the GENERAL CONFERENCE of his Church in 1938, the last General Conference of the Church, South, before union. At the UNITING CONFERENCE at Kansas City, Score was chosen to preach to the Conference on Sunday night at its great worship service, and preached a sermon in keeping with the occasion to an enormous audience.

Under special appointment in 1936, he was the Annual Conference preacher for CZECHOSLOVAKIA, POLAND, and BELGIUM, and on Exchange Commission the same year in Great Britain. He was a member of the General Conferences of his church in 1934, 1938; the Uniting Conference in 1939; and a delegate to the General Conferences of 1940 and 1944. He held the honor of Scholia in the American Academy of Political and Social Science.

Though wide awake and concerned in many areas, surely it was EDUCATION—in its broad sense—which claimed his chief interest and effort. During his day the Methodist Church was becoming so insistent upon a "trained ministry" that seminary graduation was all but required for Annual Conference membership. Neither he nor the Church pushed quite that far; but the ministry of The United Methodist Church today shows the influence of such an ideal.

Score is survived by his widow and one son, the son now serving as teacher in Southwestern University, Georgetown, Texas.

C. T. Howell, *Prominent Personalities*. 1945.
Journals, of the Central Texas Conference, 1950; of the Little Rock Conference, MES, 1913.
Who's Who in America. 1946-1947.
Who's Who in the Clergy. 1935-1936.   N. B. H.

SCOTLAND. Methodism in Scotland goes back to the earliest years of WESLEY's ministry, when in 1741 GEORGE WHITEFIELD visited the country. His preaching was in part responsible for the revival at Kilsyth and Cambuslang, which in turn helped to pave the way for Wesley's first visit in 1751 when, accompanied by CHRISTOPHER HOPPER, he paid a two-day visit to Edinburgh at the invitation of Captain Gallatin. Thereafter for the next forty years Wesley visited Scotland approximately every alternate spring, making in all twenty-two visits, and in that time there was hardly a town which did not see him more than once. Sporadic preaching was supplied by the Newcastle circuit; the first determined effort was made in 1759 by Hopper; and Scotland first appears in the stations in 1765, with four circuits, Aberdeen, Glasgow, Edinburgh, and Dundee. In that or the previous year the first chapel was erected in Scotland at Aberdeen, and in the next sixty years societies were founded and chapels built throughout the land, from Campbeltown in the southwest to Wick in the north. There was work in the Orkneys and Caithness from about 1824 to 1840. Most of these chapels were later closed, so that Scotland is littered with the remains of lost Methodist causes.

In the early years Wesley was involved in controversy with a leading Scots minister, John Erskine, who republished in 1765 one of Hervey's attacks on Wesley, *Aspasio Vindicated*. This led to the loss of many members, including some of the most influential, such as Lady WILLIELMA GLENORCHY, and Methodism in Scotland did not recover from the blow for twenty years. It was this plight which, among other reasons, led to Wesley's ordaining men for Scotland—eleven in all—between 1785 and 1788.

At Wesley's death there were 1,179 members of society in Scotland, and these rose to a peak of 3,786 in 1819; after that they declined until they reached 2,143 in 1856. A number of causes contributed to the decline—the scattered nature of the circuits, whose members saw the minister irregularly in a land where a settled ministry was accepted as the norm; and the building program of VALENTINE WARD, who was chairman of one or other of the Scottish districts for thirteen years and left Scottish Methodism with a legacy of debt which crippled or killed many societies. Ward was sanguine to a degree, so that, in one case, he bought for a society of thirty members a chapel holding thirteen hundred.

The work was often hard and unrewarding, many of the early preachers suffering almost unbelievable privations. Those who were most at home were naturally Scotsmen themselves, and Scottish Methodism produced a number of able men. Such were THOMAS RANKIN, ALEXANDER MATHER, DUNCAN McALLUM and DUNCAN WRIGHT (both of whom preached in Gaelic as well as English) and Robert Dall, and the Moray Firth gave Methodism the scholarly GEORGE and JAMES FINDLAY.

All the other main branches of Methodism were represented in Scotland. The PRIMITIVE METHODISTS went to Edinburgh and the east from the Sunderland district, and from Carlisle to Glasgow, both in 1826. The METHODIST NEW CONNEXION had a society and chapel in Glasgow from 1814 for twenty years. The WESLEYAN METHODIST ASSOCIATION (and in due course the UNITED METHODIST FREE CHURCHES) were represented there from 1836. They were strengthened in 1857 by the accession of WESLEYAN REFORM SOCIETIES and lasted until 1884. The BIBLE CHRISTIANS had a society in Ayrshire for a short time from 1876.

The 1962 schedule of membership showed sixty-eight societies in Scotland with 12,809 members. Scottish Methodism is peculiar in that most of the stations are pastorates, and the church life reflects in many ways the Presbyterianism with which it is surrounded.

The SHETLAND ISLANDS, though geographically a part of Scotland, constitute a separate district.

W. F. Swift, *Scotland*. 1947.   OLIVER A. BECKERLEGGE

SCOTT, ISAIAH BENJAMIN (1854-1931), American bishop, was born at Midway, Woodford County, Ky., Sept. 30, 1854, the son of Benjamin and Polly (Anderson) Scott. His father was of free African descent and was identified with the "underground railroad" before the Civil War. He attended private schools in Frankfort, Ky., CLARK COLLEGE in Atlanta, and won the A.B. (1880) and A.M. (1883) at Central Tennessee College in NASHVILLE. New Orleans University conferred on him the D.D. degree in

1893. He married Mattie J. Evans in May, 1881, and they had six children.

Scott was admitted on trial in the TENNESSEE CONFERENCE (ME) in 1880, was transferred to the TEXAS CONFERENCE in 1881, and was ordained DEACON in 1882 and ELDER in 1884. His appointments were: 1880, Nashville Circuit; 1881-82, Trinity, Houston; 1883, St. Paul's, Galveston; 1884-85, supernumerary, during which time he apparently taught at Prairie View State Normal and Industrial College; 1886, Ebenezer, Marshall; 1887-90, Marshall District; 1891-92, Houston District; 1893-96, president of WILEY COLLEGE; and 1896-1904, editor, *Southwestern Christian Advocate*.

During his presidency, Scott freed Wiley College of debt. A writer of force, he increased the circulation and influence of the *Advocate*. He was a delegate to five GENERAL CONFERENCES, 1888-1904, and a member of three ECUMENICAL CONFERENCES, 1891-1911. In 1904, he was elected missionary bishop for Africa and was assigned to Monrovia, LIBERIA. Well informed on the church and its work, he proved to be a skilful administrator. Retiring in 1916, he moved to Nashville, Tenn., where he died July 4, 1931. Interment was in Nashville.

F. D. Leete, *Methodist Bishops*. 1948.
National Cyclopedia of American Biography.
Who's Who in America, Vol. 16.   JESSE A. EARL

SCOTT, JAMES (1835-1911), Wesleyan Methodist minister in SOUTH AFRICA, was the son of George Scott, a Methodist missionary in SWEDEN. He was born in STOCKHOLM on Sept. 14, 1835 and married Miss Helen Walker of Arbroath, SCOTLAND, on his twenty-fourth birthday.

Entering the ministry in 1859, he was immediately sent to King William's Town, South Africa. From 1861 to 1871 he labored at Thaba 'Nchu where he won the confidence of the African people and acquired a mastery of Tswana which later enabled him to serve on the Bible Translation Committee. Apart from eight years in England (1879-87) and short terms in Durban (1896-99) and Kimberley (1899-1903), he spent the remainder of his ministry in Bloemfontein, the capital of the Orange Free State (1871-79, 1887-96, 1903-09).

Scott was an important connexional figure: he served as Chairman of the Kimberley and Bloemfontein District (1888-96; 1899-1907) and Natal (1896-99); Secretary of Conference (1889-91); Ministerial Treasurer of the Supernumerary and Ministers' Widows Fund (1896-1909); and President of Conference (1892, 1897, and acting in 1898). But his greatest work was as pastor and administrator in Bloemfontein where he was father-in-God to the Methodist people and earned the respect of all sections of the community. He died on Nov. 18, 1911 and the pallbearers at his funeral included a Roman Catholic priest and a Jewish Rabbi.

Dictionary of South African Biography.
Minutes of the South African Conference, 1912.

D. G. L. CRAGG

SCOTT, JOHN (1792-1868), British Methodist, was born at Copmanthorpe, Nov. 16, 1792. He was the leading Wesleyan Methodist educationalist of the nineteenth century, having entered the ministry in 1811. As president of the Conference in 1843 he inspired the attempt to establish a Wesleyan day-school system; by the time of his death 671 Wesleyan day schools had been started. His

JOHN SCOTT

influence was largely responsible for the refusal of the Wesleyan Church to join in the voluntary education movement between 1846-70. He did much to secure the building of the Wesleyan WESTMINSTER Teachers Training COLLEGE, 1849-51; he became principal of the college in 1851, holding the post until his death. He was again chosen president of the Conference in 1852: only four others were elected twice in the next eighty years. He died at Blackheath, on Jan. 10, 1868.

JOHN KENT

SCOTT, JOHN, JR. (1820-?), distinguished American M.P. minister, was a member of the PITTSBURGH ANNUAL CONFERENCE, a writer, able debater and presiding officer. He was born in Washington County, Pa., on Oct. 12, 1820, and united with the Pittsburgh M.P. Conference in 1842. He was the son of John Scott (1783-1833), an Irishman who was a Wesleyan Methodist. John Scott emigrated to America in 1819 and settled in Washington County, Pa. He became an active "reformer" in the Methodist Church and a subscriber to *The Mutual Rights*. John Scott, Jr., published *The Missionary and Sunday School Journal* from 1851 until 1854 and he edited *The Methodist Recorder* and Sunday school papers from 1864 until 1870. He was elected editor of *The Recorder* again around 1879 and held the position for many years. *The Missionary and Sunday School Journal* was published by the Board of Foreign Missions at Pittsburgh with Scott as editor. In 1858, he recommended to the Pittsburgh Conference that a M.P. school be opened at Sharpsburg; this school, known as the "Allegheny Seminary," was opened about 1860-1861 and was maintained until the establishment of ADRIAN COLLEGE.

Scott served as president of the GENERAL CONFERENCE of the Methodist Church (the northern and western conferences of the M.P. Church which had split in 1858 over slavery) in 1866. He was president of the Pittsburgh Conference in 1858 and 1870. For a number of years beginning in 1854 he was a member of nearly all the conventions and general conferences of his denomination. At the Convention of 1858 he was made chairman of the Board of Missions and the Commission on the Book Department. He advised the compilation of a new hymnal for the church. Among his published works are *Fifty Years' Recollections in the Ministry* and *The Catechism of the History, Doctrine and Polity of the Methodist Protestant Church*. The latter was referred to as "thoroughly evan-

gelical, and written in the plain, easy and logical style of this eminent and venerable writer" by a committee of the General Conference of 1896. Scott published *Pulpit Echoes* (1870) and *The Land of Sojourn; or, Sketches of Patriarchal Life and Times* (1880). He received the D.D. degree from Washington College in Pennsylvania, in September 1860.

A. H. Bassett, *Concise History*. 1887.
T. H. Colhouer, *Sketches of the Founders*. 1880.
E. J. Drinkhouse, *History of Methodist Reform*. 1899.
Journal of the General Confernnce, MP, 1896.
The Methodist Protestant, May 16, 1928.

RALPH HARDEE RIVES

SCOTT, LEVI (1802-1882), American bishop, was born near Cantwell's Bridge, later Odessa, Del., on Oct. 11, 1802, of Methodist parentage; his father was for one year a member of the PHILADELPHIA CONFERENCE.

Levi Scott worked on a farm and in mechanical pursuits until 1822, when he was converted and determined to enter the ministry. He was licensed to preach in 1825 and was admitted into the Philadelphia Conference the following year. His appointments were successively Talbot, Dover, ST. GEORGE'S CHURCH in Philadelphia, and West Chester.

In 1832 his health made it necessary to take the supernumerary relation for one year, and then he resumed his work and served Kent, two years as presiding elder of the Delaware District, Franklin Street Church in Newark, two years at Ebeneezer in Philadelphia, and St. Paul's in the same city. In 1840 he became principal of the Grammar School at DICKINSON COLLEGE and in 1843 he assumed the presidency of the college.

He was a member of all the GENERAL CONFERENCES from 1836 to 1852. In 1848 he became assistant BOOK AGENT in NEW YORK and was elected a bishop in 1852.

His episcopal assignments took him into all, or nearly all, of the states and territories in America. Soon after his election he went to Africa and visited all the missions there and presided at the conference in LIBERIA. In 1876 he preached the funeral of Bishop EDMUND S. JANES and his sermon on that occasion was published in a booklet.

Bishop Scott suffered a paralytic stroke at the close of the General Conference of 1880, after which he could do little work. He died on July 13, 1882, at Odessa, Del., and was buried in the Old Union church yard there.

F. D. Leete, *Methodist Bishops*. 1948.
James Mitchell, *The Life and Times of Levi Scott, D.D.* New York: Phillips & Hunt, 1885.
M. Simpson, *Cyclopaedia*. 1878.　　ELMER T. CLARK

SCOTT, ORANGE (1800-1847), American minister, abolitionist, and founder of the WESLEYAN METHODIST CHURCH, was born in Brookfield, Vt., on Feb. 13, 1800, the youngest of the eight children of Samuel and Lucy (Whitney) Scott. At twenty-one years of age he had only thirteen months of schooling. After a CAMP MEETING conversion at Barre, Vt., in September 1820, he joined the M.E. Church. Within a year he was made a CLASS LEADER and licensed exhorter. In 1822 he was received on trial in the NEW ENGLAND CONFERENCE.

Revivals marked his work in NEW HAMPSHIRE and MASSACHUSETTS churches. As presiding elder he served the Springfield District (1830-1834) and the Providence District (1834-1835). His reputation became so great that in 1832 the most influential Congregational Church in RHODE ISLAND asked him to accept its pastorate but he declined. Shortly afterwards public sentiment turned against him because of his public advocacy of the anti-slavery movement. Scott circulated 100 copies of Garrison's "Liberator" and worked for church action to destroy slavery. Although a delegate to the GENERAL CONFERENCE of 1832, it was not until 1836 that Scott, chairman of the New England delegation, revealed himself the champion of the anti-slavery forces. Undeterred by General Conference opposition to abolition he spent 1837 lecturing for the American Anti-Slavery Society; in 1838, finding other journals closed to "radicals," he published *The Wesleyan Quarterly Review*. At the General Conference of 1840 Scott and delegates from the New England and New Hampshire Conferences sought to restore to the *Discipline* the early Wesleyan doctrine concerning slavery; i.e. to hold or trade slaves is sinful. Failing, Scott and LUCIUS MATLOCK convened an anti-slavery convention in NEW YORK, criticizing the ineptness of the General Conference and organizing the American Wesleyan Anti-Slavery Society.

From 1836 to 1842, because of poor health and intense abolitionist activity, Scott was intermittently in the active and supernumerary relationship of the New England Conference. After transferring to the NEW HAMPSHIRE CONFERENCE in 1842, Scott withdrew from the M.E. Church to become the founder and first president of the Wesleyan Methodist Church, which opposed slavery and the authority of the episcopacy.

His wife, Amy Fletcher, died in 1835. On Oct. 6, 1835, he married Eliza Dearborn of Plymouth, N. H. Scott died of tuberculosis on July 31, 1847, in Newark, N. J. He is buried in Springfield, Mass.

R. M. Cameron, *Methodism and Society*. 1961.
J. Mudge, *New England Conference*. 1910.
M. Simpson, *Cyclopaedia*. 1878.
W. B. Sprague, *Annals of the Pulpit*. 1861.   ERNEST R. CASE

SCOTT, ROLAND W. (1906-   ), is a graduate of AS-BURY COLLEGE (B.A., 1927), ASBURY SEMINARY (B.D., 1930), and DREW SEMINARY (M.A., 1938). He served as a missionary in INDIA, 1930-56. He was first a pastor at Taylor Church in BOMBAY, and then for one year was superintendent of Bombay District. In 1932, he was married to Geraldine Lacy. They had become engaged while he was a seminary student. Geraldine died in Bombay in 1941, leaving her husband with two sons, the elder, David, now a missionary in India.

In 1944 Scott was elected principal of Woodstock School at Landour, Mussoorie, in North India. He served there with distinction until returning to America on furlough. During his furlough he earned the Ph.D. degree from Columbia University. In 1967 he was awarded an honorary D.D. degree by Asbury College.

Returning to India in 1948, he joined the staff of the National Christian Council as secretary for evangelism and theological education. He was popular with his colleagues and was heard with respect by all church and mission representatives.

In 1956, he began a new career as a home-base secretary, becoming secretary for Southern Asia and the Near East for the NATIONAL COUNCIL OF THE CHURCHES OF CHRIST in the U.S.A. In 1958 he was made executive secretary for Southern Asia, North Africa, and Europe for the Division of World Missions, Board of MISSIONS (TMC). In 1960, he was promoted to the post of secretary for General Administration in the same division of the Methodist Board.

In response to a request from the WORLD COUNCIL OF CHURCHES in 1962, he went to Geneva as secretary of the Division of World Missions and Evangelism, and two years later he became assistant to the General Secretary of the World Council of Churches. In the middle of 1965 he resigned to become professor of World Christianity at GARRETT THEOLOGICAL SEMINARY.

The Indian Witness.
The National Christian Council Review.

J. WASKOM PICKETT

SCOTT, SOLOMON T. (1790-1862), bishop of the A.M.E. ZION CHURCH, was born Aug. 20, 1790, in Smyrna, Del. He was converted there in 1830 and was licensed to preach the following year, beginning his ministry in his birthplace. He joined the conference June 25, 1834, and was ordained a DEACON evidently prior to this time, May 22, 1834. The only explanation which we can give to this strange state of affairs is that he was evidently used as a pastor prior to the convening of the annual conference and was therefore ordained a deacon so that he could be of greater service. He waited ten years, May 20, 1844, before he was given ELDER's orders. He was elected a bishop in May 1856. He died Jan. 4, 1862.

DAVID H. BRADLEY

SCOTT, THOMAS (1772-1856), pioneer American preacher, attorney and judge, was born of Scotch-Irish ancestry at Skypton, Allegany County, Md., Oct. 31, 1772. He married Catherine Wood of Lexington, Ky., May 10, 1796.

Scott joined the church before he was fourteen, was admitted on trial in the conference at Leesburg, Va., in April 1789, and was ordained DEACON in 1791 and ELDER in 1793. His appointments were: 1789, Gloucester Circuit assistant; 1790, Berkeley Circuit assistant; 1791, Stafford Circuit; 1792, Frederick Circuit; 1793, Ohio Circuit; and 1794, Danville (Ky.) Circuit. In the spring of 1795 he located because, as he later said, of dire necessity. However, because of the illness of the preacher assigned to the Lexington Circuit, Scott, at the request of the presiding elder, supplied that charge most of the succeeding year.

After his marriage, Scott clerked in a store for a time and then ran a tailor shop, his wife reading law to him while he worked. Then he studied law in Lexington and became prosecuting attorney in Fleming County. In 1801 he settled in Chillicothe, OHIO, at the suggestion of ED-WARD TIFFIN, the first governor of the state (1803), who had been converted and joined the church under Scott's ministry in VIRGINIA eleven years before. Scott served as clerk for the Territorial legislature and in the same capacity for the state constitutional convention in 1802. At the first session of the state legislature, he was elected secretary of the senate, serving until 1809 when he was named as one of the judges on the state supreme court. In 1810 he became chief justice, serving until 1815 when he resigned because the pay was too low, the same reason for which he had left the Methodist itineracy twenty years before. He resumed the practice of law, and was for sixteen years, 1829-45, the register of the United States Land Office at Chillicothe.

While an itinerant Scott kept a journal which has been preserved. Also, he compiled "Memoirs" which were published in the *Western Christian Advocate*, 1851-54. He said that if the M.E. Church had provided adequate financial support for its itinerants, he would have remained in the traveling connection all his life.

Scott was a man of intelligence, ability, and integrity. His contemporaries felt that he had superior qualifications for the bar, but some believed that his fitness for the ministry was possibly greater and they were confident that had he remained in the traveling connection he might have risen to high office in the church.

F. Asbury, *Journal and Letters*. 1958.
J. B. Finley, *Sketches of Western Methodism*. 1854.
National Cyclopedia of American Biography.
J. S. Payton, *Our Fathers Have Told Us*. 1938. JESSE A. EARL

SCOTT, THOMAS J. (1835-1920) was a distinguished early Methodist missionary in INDIA. Born in New Alexandria, Ohio, graduate of OHIO WESLEYAN UNIVERSITY, he first arrived in India, Jan. 20, 1863. He served at Budaun, United Provinces, for six years, and in BAREILLY for thirty-four years. After a few years of teaching in the theological seminary there he became principal. He was an Urdu scholar, and served on the BRITISH AND FOREIGN BIBLE SOCIETY Committee for the revision of the Urdu translation of the New Testament.

For many years he maintained, at little cost to himself, an offer to reward his students with a gift of one rupee for every mistake they noted in his use of Urdu.

He was the founder of the Indian Sunday School Union, and a prolific writer for evangelism and religious education. His published works included a book on logic, for which he was awarded a prize by the government of the Uttar Pradesh; a book on natural theology for which Christian publishing societies awarded him a prize; two volumes on Biblical theology written in English and Hindustani, and five volumes of a commentary on the Bible in Hindustani.

A list compiled after his death mentions twenty-one books he wrote. He was a Fellow of Allahabad University, a member of several learned societies, and of two committees appointed by the government of the United Provinces. He was twice elected a delegate to the GENERAL CONFERENCE and twice a reserve delegate.

J. WASKOM PICKETT

SCRANTON, WILLIAM BENTON (1856-1922), American missionary to KOREA, was born in New Haven, Conn., on May 29, 1856. He graduated from the New York College of Physicians and Surgeons (Columbia University) in 1882, married Loulie Wyeth Arms, and took up private practice in Cleveland, Ohio.

Late in 1884 he answered a call for a doctor to go to Korea and was ordained by Bishop C. N. FOWLER under the missionary rule, and admitted to the NEW YORK EAST CONFERENCE. He sailed from SAN FRANCISCO, Feb. 3, 1885, with his wife, his two-year-old daughter and his mother, Mrs. Mary F. Scranton, the first missionary appointed by the WOMEN'S FOREIGN MISSIONARY SOCIETY to Korea. Also in the party were Dr. and Mrs. HENRY G. APPENZELLER.

Scranton reached SEOUL on May 4, 1885, and soon purchased a site for the Methodist mission adjoining the American Legation and the Duk-Soo Palace and began medical work. Later he opened two other medical centers in Seoul and during his missionary career acted as supervisor of the medical work of his mission in the capital city.

He was a versatile and vigorous administrator. He acted as secretary of the mission until his first furlough in 1891, and thereafter was superintendent of his mission except for furlough years until 1907. He was also active in Bible translation.

Administrative tasks became too strenuous and he resigned in June 1907 to take up private practice in Seoul, acting as medical adviser to the Chiksan and other mining companies. In 1917 he secured a medical practice in Kobe, JAPAN, where he died in March 1922. Inurnment was at Kasugano Cemetery in Kobe.

CHARLES A. SAUER

SCRANTON, PENNSYLVANIA, U.S.A., renowned in the past as the anthracite capital of the world, situated in the Pocono Mountains, is a city with a population of 102,294. It has long been the largest and most important urban area in northeastern PENNSYLVANIA. In 1818 a young Methodist itinerant, GEORGE PECK, was appointed to the Wyoming Circuit which included some twelve preaching appointments covering what is now Luzerne and Lackawanna Counties. It required riding the circuit in two weeks, or 136 miles on horseback. The only appointment apparently then within what is now the city of Scranton was at the home of Preserved Taylor, on the west bank of the Lackawanna River. In this early circuit, services were held in three churches, three school houses and six private homes. In 1820 Peck was appointed to the Canaan Circuit which included what is now Wayne County, a two weeks circuit with 223 members, twelve preaching places, but no church building anywhere. In 1831 Providence Chapel became one of the appointments on this circuit. This is now the Providence Church, the oldest Methodist organization in the city. As one of the classes of this appointment, there was organized in 1839 a class in Slocum Hollow, later known as Harrison. This was destined to become one of Methodism's outstanding congregations, now the Elm Park Church.

The Slocum Hollow class seems to have had good lay leadership and soon proposed that a church building be erected. The church building known as the "Village Chapel" was begun in 1841 upon a quarter of an acre plot of ground donated by the firm of Scranton, Grant and Co. With the erection of the "Village Chapel," the Slocum Hollow class became a station attached, along with Hyde Park, Dunmore and Blakely, to the Providence Circuit It was continued in this manner until 1854 when it appears as a separate appointment in the minutes of the Annual Conference under the name "Scranton."

The Village Chapel soon became too small to accommodate the growing society and was donated to the German Methodists. Although the construction of a new building was commenced in the fall of 1855, by the summer of 1856 the basement had been sufficiently completed so that the congregation moved in. In 1856 George Peck, after serving many important appointments including a term as Editor of *The Christian Advocate*, and presiding elder of the Wyoming District, was appointed as pastor to the Scranton charge. The years that followed were plagued with financial difficulties for the slowly growing congregation.

It is difficult to ascertain the exact number of members in the early days, but apparently in 1855 there were 125 full members, and by 1864 only 144. The QUARTERLY CONFERENCE records show that church membership began to grow slowly after 1860, but by 1879 the membership numbered around 400. After 1872 the church grew more rapidly. The appointment then appeared in Conference Minutes as the "Adams Avenue" Church.

During the decade after 1880 the city of Scranton grew rapidly and became the third city in Pennsylvania. The Adams Avenue congregation kept pace with the growth of this city. At the Quarterly Conference held in 1887, the pastor, J. E. Price, reported that due to the large attendance in the Sunday school and the crowds that thronged the church services, a new church edifice should be constructed. The Quarterly Conference acted favorably and a committee was appointed to select a suitable site for the new church. On April 13, 1891 the lots of the Elm Park triangle were purchased from W. W. Scranton. Ground was broken for the new church on Sept. 8, 1891 by William Connell, who was president of the Board of Trustees, W. H. Pearce being pastor. The cornerstone of Elm Park Church was laid on April 23, 1892 with impressive services. The dedication of the new church was to commence Monday, Dec. 12, but on Saturday morning, Dec. 3, 1892 the church was completely destroyed by fire. An Official Board Meeting was immediately called the very same morning under the leadership of the presiding elder, M. S. Hard, and it was resolved to rebuild at once. Within a few days subscriptions were received for over $12,000. The work of rebuilding was pushed rapidly, but again on March 22, 1893 a second fire completely destroyed the walls of the building, leaving only the tower and the chimes uninjured. However, the determination of the congregation prevailed, and the present structure was completed and an elaborate ten-day program of services was arranged for Dec. 7, 1893. The church building has continued to serve the Elm Park congregation to the present time.

For over a century Elm Park Church has occupied a unique position in northeastern Pennsylvania. For many years it had the largest membership of any Methodist Church in the WYOMING CONFERENCE. Since 1893 it has had the largest and most completely equipped church facilities of any church in the Conference, or of any other Protestant church in northeastern Pennsylvania. By reason of its large membership and adequate equipment and its able clerical and lay leadership, it has held a high place in religious circles throughout this region. During the period 1900-35, there was a consistent gain in membership. In 1935 the membership reported to Annual Conference was 2,512, and this number remained nearly constant until 1942 when a decline set in coincident with the decline of population in northeastern Pennsylvania. At the present time church membership numbers 1,319.

Included among its outstanding pastors have been such leaders as Joseph M. M. Gray, HENRY HITT CRANE, HAROLD C. CASE, and Benjamin L. Duval. Among its outstanding laymen the most prominent was the Honorable HENRY REED VAN DEUSEN, distinguished lawyer, who served as a member of the JUDICIAL COUNCIL of The Methodist Church during the first years of the Council. Elm Park Church continues to offer outstanding leadership to the Methodist churches of Wyoming Conference and the surrounding areas.

L. E. Bugbee, *Wyoming Conference.* 1952.
Henry Reed Van Deusen, *Elm Park Historical Sketches.* Scranton: Haddon Craftsmen, Inc., 1955.   GEORGE R. AKERS

SCRIPPS, JOHN (1785-1865), American minister, was born in Bridewell Parish, England, Aug. 26, 1785. He arrived in BALTIMORE, Md., with his father's family on July 4, 1791. The family went to CAPE GIRARDEAU, Mo., then a village, in May 1809.

JESSE WALKER, the Methodist circuit rider, visited the Scripps family in 1810 and took the young man with him across the Big Swamp to NEW MADRID, where they established a church, the oldest operating society west of the Mississippi River. Scripps was licensed to preach, and in 1814 he was sent to supply the ILLINOIS circuit of the TENNESSEE CONFERENCE. He was admitted to the conference the following year and appointed to that circuit. He formed another circuit, called the Okaw, and served both, or extended his "three weeks circuit" to a "six weeks circuit."

In 1815 Scripps preached in Kaskasia, Ill., and ST. LOUIS, Mo., both almost wholly Roman Catholic. At the close of the year the conference met at Shiloh on Scripp's circuit, and he went to Vincennes, Ind., to accompany the bishop to Shiloh and made entertainment arrangements for the conference members.

At the new MISSOURI CONFERENCE in 1816 he was sent to the Coldwater Circuit. He established an appointment in St. Louis and sold $300 worth of books on the circuit. His other appointments were: 1817-18, Boonslick Circuit in Central Missouri; 1818-19, Cape Girardeau; 1819-20, Boonslick; 1820-21, Blue River, Ind.; 1821-22, presiding elder of the Arkansas District; 1823, St. Louis; 1824, presiding elder of the Missouri District.

Scripps left the itineracy in 1825. When the conference was divided into Illinois and Missouri, he would not adhere to the Missouri Conference because of its stand on slavery. After this he married and went into business in Missouri. He removed to Rushville, Ill., in 1845. Here he owned and edited a local paper, engaged in business, lectured, preached, wrote, and was active in the local church. He died July 26, 1865.

Elmer T. Clark, *One Hundred Years of New Madrid Methodism.* New Madrid, the author, 1912.
A. M. Pennewell, *Jesse Walker.* 1958.   ALMER PENNEWELL

SCRIPTURE PLAYING CARDS, or **DRAW CARDS,** were packs of printed or handwritten cards, with a scripture text on one side and on the other a verse or two of a hymn. They were advertised "for Divine amusement" by James Kenton in 1786, and were in use among Methodists, Moravians, and others, in the late eighteenth and nineteenth centuries. CHARLES WESLEY apparently encouraged their use, and specimens have survived in his handwriting. There is no evidence that JOHN WESLEY used them, though they were advertised as to be "had of Mr. Wesley's booksellers in Town and Country." RICHARD GREEN conjectures as to their use:

The cards were shuffled, and either the whole or part of the pack was dealt out to the assembled company. The trump, or turn-up card, in all probability, was first used. . . . It would be a starting point for conversation. Persons holding cards having passages of Scripture relating to the first would probably speak of them . . . ; the singing of verses of the hymns would vary the proceedings and give additional interest to them; and prayer would naturally follow. (*Proc.* W.H.S., i, 15-25).

There is evidence, however, that such cards were used for the less-edifying purpose of SORTILEGE. ADAM CLARKE roundly denounced the cards as "the drivellings of religious nonage, of piety in superannuation," dismissing them as a variant of "bibliomancy," or divination by "dipping into the Bible, taking passages of Scripture at hazard, and drawing indications thence concerning the present and future state of the soul." He added: "Thank God, these have never been very common among us, and are certainly not of Methodist growth."

Among the Moravians such cards were "drawn for purpose of guidance," and also used to convey good wishes on a birthday or other anniversary. It is possible that the cards originated with the Moravians, from whom Wesley derived his habit of selecting passages of Scripture at random and of deciding matters by lot.

Wesley Historical Society, *Proceedings*, i, iv, vii.

JOHN NEWTON

SEABRA, MERCÊDES COIMBRA DE (1893-   ), Brazilian leader, outstanding in the work of the Methodist women of BRAZIL, was born in RIO DE JANEIRO, Sept. 4, 1893, and reared as a strict Roman Catholic. At the age of nineteen she married Lauro Seabra, a devout Presbyterian businessman whose influence and Christian example led her to accepting the evangelical faith in January 1917, in the Presbyterian church in SÃO PAULO. They had one son, Newton.

When her husband was transferred to PORTO ALEGRE in the state of Rio Grande do Sul, they found no Presbyterian church, so in 1923 both joined the Methodist Church and became loyal, hard-working members. Both served in many capacities—Dona Mercêdes taught a young woman's class in the church school, and was active both in the local and the regional women's societies, and as president of the local society promoted the founding of a home for aged Methodist women, and a clinic for children in Porto Alegre. In the regional conference, she acted as corresponding secretary, treasurer, vice-president and president, during a period of almost forty years. In 1930 she was on the committee that founded *Voz Missionaria*, the Methodist women's magazine. She has given marked leadership to women in the Southern region of Brazil. She continues to reside in Porto Alegre.

Eula K. Long, *Historico das Sociedades de Senhoras do Rio Grande do Sul*. Porto Alegre: Typografia Esperanca, 1933.

EULA K. LONG

SEAGER, LAWRENCE HOOVER (1860-1937), bishop of the EVANGELICAL CHURCH in the United States, was born on a farm near Fremont, Ohio, on April 19, 1860. He received his college degree at North Western College (NORTH CENTRAL) in Naperville, Ill., in 1887, and his seminary degree at EVANGELICAL THEOLOGICAL SEMINARY the following year. From 1888 until 1897 he served pastorates in the OHIO CONFERENCE of the EVANGELICAL ASSOCIATION. Beyond brief service as a presiding elder, Seager served his denomination as Assistant Editor of

Sunday School Literature and Editor of *The Evangelical Herald* (1901-1911), President of North Western College (1911-1915), and bishop (1915-1934). A man of large physical proportions and a unique capacity for friendship and leadership, Seager made his greatest contribution through his outstanding preaching ability. He died on Aug. 30, 1937, in LeMars, Iowa, survived by his widow (Mary Good Twigg, whom he married in 1896), and one son, Charles.

R. W. Albright, *Evangelical Church*. 1942.
The Evangelical Messenger, Sept. 11 and 18, 1937.
David Koss, "Bishops of the Evangelical Association, United Evangelical Church, and Evangelical Church." Ms.

K. JAMES STEIN

SEAMANDS, EARL ARNETT (1891-   ), came to INDIA as a missionary of the M.E. Church in 1919. He was a graduate of the college of civil engineering, University of Cincinnati. His appointments included the pastorate of the Richmond Town Church in Bangalore, the principalship of Industrial School at Kolar, the superintendency of five districts in the SOUTH INDIA CONFERENCE, and the executive secretaryship of the HYDERABAD Area.

Seamands was born in LEXINGTON, Ky., lived as a boy in ARIZONA, married Yvonne Shields of PITTSBURGH, Pa., and was soundly converted in OHIO. His training as an engineer combined with his fervent evangelism and his skill in dealing with people to make him outstanding in his generation as a builder of churches and church members. Tireless in touring the villages and visiting in their homes those who showed a desire to learn what Jesus taught about, and loving God with all his mind, he established schools, gave personal attention to hundreds of church members, and fired many of them with zeal to win others to Christ. He promoted schools and hospitals, called for doctors and nurses, teachers and clerks, and above all for ministers of the Gospel. He drew plans for all kinds of buildings, engaged contractors, and supervised construction. Also he collected money in India and in America for these buildings and to maintain the institutions which they housed.

He helped 135 Indian congregations build churches. He made a number of shuttle trips to India, to collaborate with bishops, district superintendents, pastors, and local congregations in planning for new churches, parsonages, and schools.

His sons, John and David, became missionaries in India and, with impressive fluency in several languages and ability and zeal to match their father's, were notably successful. Because of family health problems, both have had to resign as missionaries. John is now professor of missions in ASBURY SEMINARY and David is a pastor.

J. WASKOM PICKETT

SEAMEN'S MISSION, British Methodist, was started by the Wesleyan Methodist Church in the LONDON docks in 1843. It was originally local in character, but in 1885 the Seamen's Chapel Circuit was formed; the Seamen's Rest was built, which is still used by seamen in the port of London. The mission started homes in other ports, such as Chatham, Devonport, and Pembroke docks, as well as at naval stations abroad.

K. Heasman, *Evangelicals in Action*. London, 1962.

NORMAN BURNS

SEARCH, GEORGE LEWIS (1871-1936), American minister and home missions executive, was born Dec. 7, 1871, at Cedarville, N. J. In 1881 the family moved to Merrill, Iowa. He was converted at age eleven. After attending business college he had several years successful experience in business. He then entered MORNINGSIDE COLLEGE, Sioux City, Iowa, to prepare for the ministry. He joined the NORTHWEST IOWA CONFERENCE in 1905.

He superintended the Wall Street Mission in Sioux City from 1903 to 1905. In 1906 he opened the Helping Hand Mission in downtown Sioux City. This grew rapidly into an effective rescue institution. It included a unique hotel erected to shelter farm laborers who travelled through the city while following the annual wheat harvest northward across the nation. This hotel became a hostel for all unattached needy men. The Mission continued to operate until 1960.

In 1920 Search became Auditor of the Board of Home MISSIONS at PHILADELPHIA, Pa., and in 1922 became its Comptroller. His administration of the home mission funds was competent and effective. In 1933 he was incapacitated by a stroke and retired. He died July 15, 1936, and was buried at Monroeville, N. J.

Northwest Iowa Conference *Minutes*, 1936.   FRANK G. BEAN

SEARCY, HUBERT FLOYD (1908-1971), American college president, was born at Skipperville, Ala., on July 2, 1908, the son of Duncan Alexander and Susan Elizabeth (Hulon) Searcy. He was educated at BIRMINGHAM-SOUTHERN COLLEGE, A.B., 1929; LL.D., 1942; DUKE UNIVERSITY, A.M., 1933; Ph.D., 1937. His wife was Christine Mason Quillian (daughter of W. F. QUILLIAN, SR.), whom he married on Dec. 22, 1934, and their children are Jane Quillian, Susan Elizabeth, and Hubert Floyd, Jr. He was the assistant registrar of the Birmingham-Southern College, 1929-30; alumni secretary, 1930-32; occupied various positions in that college until in 1938 he was elected president of HUNTINGDON COLLEGE, Montgomery, Ala. He was a lay representative of the ALABAMA CONFERENCE of the M.E. Church, South, to the Uniting Conference in 1939; to the SOUTHEASTERN JURISDICTIONAL CONFERENCE, 1940, '44, '48, '52, '56; to the GENERAL CONFERENCE of The Methodist Church, 1944 and 1956. He served as a member of the UNIVERSITY SENATE of The Methodist Church, 1940-65; and the chairman of the Alabama Committee on the selection of Rhodes Scholars, 1962-63. He retired from the presidency of Huntingdon College in 1968 and was elected chancellor for life.

He died April 14, 1971.

Who's Who in America, Vol. 34.
Who's Who in The Methodist Church, 1966.   N. B. H.

SEASHORE METHODIST ASSEMBLY (formerly Seashore Camp Ground), assembly grounds of the MISSISSIPPI CONFERENCE, is located on the beach at Biloxi, Miss. It was established in 1870 by Methodists of the NEW ORLEANS District of the LOUISIANA CONFERENCE as a site for CAMP MEETINGS. The idea originated with William H. Foster, a lawyer and member of Felicity Street Church of New Orleans. He was assisted in the original plans by his pastor, John Matthews. The original property was purchased from J. H. Kellar, wealthy soap manufacturer of New Orleans. Adjoining acreage on the west was added later. It was dedicated as a camp meeting site in March

1872. From 1878-1921 the property was owned jointly by the New Orleans District of the Louisiana Conference, the Seashore District of the Mississippi Conference, and the Mobile District of the ALABAMA CONFERENCE. Title rested in the three above named Annual Conferences from 1921-1963. Since 1963 it has been owned solely by the Mississippi Conference. The original tract included land now occupied by Keesler Air Force Base.

This was the site of annual camp meetings for many years, the first one being held in June 1872. Among the great preachers who led the meetings from year to year were SAM JONES, Bishops McTYEIRE, MARVIN, and KEENER. It was also the site of Seashore Divinity School, established in 1907, which after 1931 became known as the Mississippi Conference Pastors' School. The Tri-State EPWORTH LEAGUE Assembly met here annually from 1904-1922. A preparatory school for boys was operated on the grounds from 1912-1926. The present annual program includes the Mississippi Conference Pastors' School, WOMEN'S SOCIETY OF CHRISTIAN SERVICE School of Missions, and other church conferences of various purposes.

The Assembly now consists of two units: the Spiritual Center which includes Leggett Memorial Church, Frazer Hall, Arlean Hall, Stevens Cafeteria, Recreation Hall, Van Hook Hall, and the superintendent's home. Frazer Hall and Arlean Hall together provide accommodations for 165 visitors. Arlean Hall is owned by the Mississippi Conference W.S.C.S. The second unit is known as Seashore Manor, which contains 125 apartments for retired couples, opened in 1965. The entire tract now includes twenty-three acres.

J. A. LINDSEY

SEATON, JOHN LAWRENCE (1873-1961), American minister and college president, was born in Manchester, IOWA, on Jan. 25, 1873. He received an A.B. degree in 1898 from Upper Iowa University, and S.T.B. and Ph.D. degrees from BOSTON UNIVERSITY in 1901 and 1905 respectively. While a student he preached in churches in Iowa and MASSACHUSETTS. He was pastor of churches in Norwood, Mass., and Dubuque, Iowa, after receiving his theological degree and until 1904. It was that year that he became professor of psychology and Bible at DAKOTA WESLEYAN UNIVERSITY, a post he held for ten years.

In 1914, Seaton became president of the College of the Pacific, San Jose, Calif.; in 1919 he became college secretary of the Board of EDUCATION, M.E. Church, and on May 15, 1924, he became the seventh president of ALBION COLLEGE, and held this position until June 30, 1945.

During Seaton's administration Albion College first attained national accreditation by the most significant accreditation bodies. Seaton was almost solely responsible in 1940 for obtaining Beta chapter of Michigan of Phi Beta Kappa for the college. College endowment rose from about $1,700,000 in 1924 to about $2,500,000 in 1945, and several buildings were constructed on the campus during the same period.

Seaton and Jessie Evans Davis of Maynard, Iowa, were married Aug. 27, 1900. They had one daughter, Mary (Mrs. John W. McDonald), at whose home Seaton died Jan. 28, 1961. Burial was in Riverside Cemetery, Albion, Mich.

R. Gildart, *Albion College, 1835-1960, A History*. N.p., n.d.
ROBERT GILDART

SEATTLE, WASHINGTON, U.S.A., is the metropolis of the Pacific Northwest and owes its founding largely to Methodist pioneers, as its first settlers, so far as can be ascertained, were all Methodists. Departing ILLINOIS in the early spring of 1851 by covered wagons, they traveled over the famous OREGON trail arriving in the Willamette Valley of western Oregon in August. Soon thereafter, three of their number went up into the Puget Sound country, then sparsely settled as compared with the Willamette Valley, to seek a likely place for the party to locate. Traveling north by canoe on Puget Sound, they went ashore on September 25 at what is now West Seattle. A tribe of Indians nearby was busily engaged in catching and smoking salmon. Its chief strode up the beach to bid them welcome. His name, Seattle!

Six weeks later, at dawn on November 13, in a pouring winter rain, the rest of the party, having come by schooner from Portland, were put ashore. All told they numbered twenty-four, twelve adults and twelve children. The children ranged in age from nine years to two months. The oldest man in the party was thirty-four. From them Seattle was born.

The first church established was a Methodist church. Its founder and first pastor was DAVID BLAINE who with his bride, Catherine, arrived in the late fall of 1853, having traveled from NEW YORK by way of PANAMA. Seattle was then a small settlement of thirty cabins and shacks rising amidst a straggling assemblage of stumps adjacent to the mud flats of the waterfront. Beyond stretched the primeval forest. On the first Sunday following his arrival, David Blaine conducted services in a boarding house at the corner of First and Cherry, and on that day, Dec. 4, 1853, established the First Methodist Church of Seattle with four charter members, one of them his wife Catherine. They rented the only quarters available for shelter, a two-room shack, one room on the ground floor and the other on the second floor, each 13 by 14 feet. Cracks between the boards were so wide—Catherine wrote to her well-to-do parents in upper New York State —that no windows were needed. Within two months after her arrival Catherine Blaine established the first school and became Seattle's first teacher. Housed in the "parsonage," the school enrolled fourteen children who attended five days a week.

Largely by his own efforts, David Blaine cleared the land and built the first church edifice and parsonage in Seattle. The parsonage was completed in 1854, the church dedicated in May 1855. A small incident reveals his character and ecclesiology. Paint was expensive and hard to get. No building in Seattle was painted. But Blaine believed that a building which carried the name of the Methodist Church should be representative of the best. So he painted the church white. For years it was known as the "White Church." He painted the parsonage to match. They were the only painted buildings in Seattle.

During the intervening years the church has built two new edifices, on each occasion moving a block or two up the hill from the waterfront. It grew and for several generations now it has ranked among the foremost. Its present membership of 3,366 ranks it with the First Methodist Church of GLENDALE, California, as one of the two largest Methodist churches on the West Coast. Two on its roll of distinguished pastors have been elected to the episcopacy: ADNA W. LEONARD in 1916 and J. RALPH MAGEE in 1932.

In 1853 David Denny and Dexter Horton, two Methodist laymen, established the first merchandise firm in Seattle. In the shipment of goods from SAN FRANCISCO with which they opened business was a small safe which previously had suffered the misfortune of having its back removed by dynamite. However, since no one knew this but Denny and Horton, it served as a place of deposit for much of Seattle's currency. They issued deposit slips to all depositors, and ere long from that safe began Seattle's first financial institution, Seattle First National Bank, presently one of the nation's great banks with 118 branches in the Pacific Northwest.

The second Methodist minister to arrive in Seattle was DANIEL BAGLEY, a Methodist Protestant. He with his wife and family in 1860 drove into town with Seattle's first buggy. Following the Indian War of 1856 Seattle's population declined and only twenty families remained. Daniel Bagley resurrected the dreams and hopes of the first settlers and imbued the community with a new spirit of confidence.

Shortly after his arrival he led in the establishment of the University of Washington. The Territorial Legislature in 1861, wearied under repeated petitions from Seattle for the establishment of a university there, stipulated a series of conditions which Seattle would have to meet to get a university—conditions which neither the Legislature (nor the Seattle people for awhile) thought were possible. They had all reckoned without Daniel Bagley. He believed the Territory should have a university and that it should be in Seattle.

He persuaded three Methodist laymen to give ten acres for the university—one of the requirements; hired men to clear the land, paying them in land, two acres a day at $1.50 per acre; and then recruited saw mill operator Herman Yesler, Seattle's first industrialist, to saw the logs, taking his pay also in land. In short he met all conditions and was able to announce the opening of the Territorial University in Seattle on Nov. 4, 1861. The astonished Legislature traveled en masse to Seattle. There they found the campus and buildings ready, and surmounting all, a tall fir tree stripped of its boughs and bark, flying the Stars and Stripes.

The University now enrolls 30,000 students. The ten acres which were its first campus now are Seattle's most valuable business property, yielding the University more than $2,000,000 income annually.

Next, knowing the need for coal, Bagley led in the development of the Newcastle coal field near Seattle, a profitable venture which was most important for the economic development of Seattle. But first and last, Daniel Bagley was a minister of the Gospel and servant of his Lord. He gave nearly forty-five years of enterprise and dedicated life for and through the Methodist Church in Seattle.

Three M.P. churches were organized in Seattle. The first, known after the 1939 reunion as "Capitol Hill Methodist Church," was organized in 1865 by Daniel Bagley, who as told above later became the first president of the University of Washington. The PUGET SOUND CONFERENCE was separated from the OREGON CONFERENCE in 1884, and its first session held in Seattle, August 21-25 of that year. Bishop C. H. FOWLER presided.

The founding of the second M.E. Church in Seattle, the Battery Street Church, was announced at the 1884 session of the conference. Its first pastor was L. A. Banks, and its forty-five charter members formerly had been in First Church. At that time, A. Farrell was appointed to open Scandinavian work in the area. A Swedish congregation was organized that year, and in 1889 a Norwegian-Danish church was established.

Other Methodisms in Seattle and the outlying regions are: A.M.E. Church, with three churches, having a total membership of 1,717 members, one church having 1,500; A.M.E. Zion has one congregation; C.M.E. has two churches with approximately 450 members; the Evangelical Methodists have one church with approximately eighty members and two other churches in nearby communities whose statistics could not be obtained.

The Free Methodists have thirteen churches—eight in Seattle proper and five in suburban areas, having a total membership of 2,168. They also have Seattle Pacific College having approximately a 2,000 enrollment; the Wesleyan Methodists have one church but have recently voted, it appears, to merge with other Wesleyan groups.

The United Methodist Church has twenty-five churches in Seattle with big Blaine Memorial among them, and the district itself listed 25,664 members in 1970.

First Church was the religious body in the city, being organized on Dec. 4, 1853 by David E. Blaine. The first membership consisted of four people: Mr. and Mrs. A. A. Denny, J. H. Nagle, and Catherine Blaine, the wife of the minister. The Blaines built their own home in 1854 and used it for services until the first building could be erected at Second and Columbia Streets in 1855.

In 1862, Daniel Bagley, a M.P. minister, filled the pulpit. He later became the founding Father of the University of Washington. In 1863, Nehemiah Doane was appointed to the pulpit and found a membership of six. In 1889, under the leadership of D. D. Campbell, the church moved to a new location at Third and Marion and erected a new building. In 1908 it made its third move to Fifth and Marion and erected the present building under the leadership of W. H. Reese.

Two pastors of this Church have been elected to the episcopacy: Adna Wright Leonard and J. Ralph Magee. E. Newton Moats started the plans for an expanded educational building in 1948-49, which was completed under the ministry of Cyrus E. Albertson. In 1960 a 250-apartment Retirement Home named Bayview Manor was erected by the Church on land given by the Charles Kinnear family. It is operated as one of the ministries of the Church. The Church has expanded its missionary giving to more than $70,000 per year, including specialized ministries in the Congo and in India. Located in the heart of the downtown portion of the city, First Church carries on programs of unusual evangelism with special ministries for the elderly, the broken family, the mentally retarded and the dispossessed. The Church owns and operates its own camp and provides a year-round program for all ages. In 1970 it reported 3,307 members.

University Temple Church stands adjacent to the campus of the University of Washington. It was organized in 1901 by Rial Benjamin, of the Methodist Evangelistic Union. The first Methodist sermon in the area was delivered in Payee's Hall, on Lake Union in 1892. A Ladies Aid Society was organized in 1901. The first building was erected in 1903 by W. H. Leech, City Missionary. The edifice was valued at $25,000 and dedicated April 28, 1907, by H. C. Jennings. The parsonage was erected under the leadership of John M. Canse in 1910-14. The building was enlarged and rebuilt under the pastorate of A. H. Lathrop in 1918. A sanctuary costing $350,000 was dedicated Oct. 16, 1927 under the ministry of J. E. Crowther. Debt was removed in 1947. An educational unit costing $500,000 was erected in 1956 under the pastorate of Cecil Ristow. A new parsonage was acquired in 1961 under the pastorate of Lynn Corson.

This congregation cooperates with the Wesley Foundation, located on an adjoining lot, in ministering to more than 2,000 Methodist students enrolled in the Uni-

UNIVERSITY TEMPLE, SEATTLE, WASHINGTON

versity of Washington. In 1970 University Temple membership was 1,998. The W.S.C.S. had 350 members and contributed $2,952. Value of land and buildings, including parsonage, was $1,320,731. Total giving was $198,301.

Blaine letters in Methodist Archives, University of Puget Sound, Tacoma, Wash.
E. Howell, *Northwest*. 1966.
Journals of the Oregon, Puget Sound, and Pacific Northwest Conferences.
T. D. Yarnes, *Oregon*. 1957.

EVERETT W. PALMER
ERLE HOWELL

WETER MEMORIAL LIBRARY,
SEATTLE PACIFIC COLLEGE, SEATTLE, WASHINGTON

SEATTLE PACIFIC COLLEGE, Seattle, Washington, was founded in 1891 as Seattle Seminary under the auspices of the FREE METHODIST CHURCH. College courses were introduced in 1910. The first baccalaureate degrees were conferred in 1915, and a graduate school was added in 1951. Full regional accreditation was received in 1936 and national accreditation at both the graduate and undergraduate levels in 1965. The main campus with nineteen major buildings is on the north slope of Queen Anne Hill in SEATTLE. The marine campus of more than 100 acres and thirty-two buildings is on Whidbey Island.

Seattle Pacific College affirms its position within the historical stream of Christian thought and practice. It maintains that education should lead to the transformation of the individual through faith in Jesus Christ, fulfilling the purpose of God in the fullest development of the individual personality. It contends that piety is no substitute for academic excellence but that excellence should advance equally on both levels.

Enrollment is about 3,000.

BYRON S. LAMSON

SECRETARIES, COUNCIL OF, was brought into existence in 1940 at the first meeting of the GENERAL CONFERENCE of The Methodist Church following the Uniting Conference. Its chief responsibility was to "promote the education and enlistment of the whole Church in its program of General Benevolences" (*Discipline,* 1940, Paragraph 843). The Secretaries in question were the executives of the general boards and AGENCIES of The Methodist Church, with special reference to those whose entire support depended upon the general benevolences of the Church. This Council of Secretaries as organized was directed to meet, to educate, and to enlist the Church

in its total benevolence giving. The Secretaries were also to "coordinate their educational and promotional activities in order to avoid duplication" (*Ibid.*, Paragraph 844).

As time went on, the Council of Secretaries itself found that in order to correlate better the work of the various agencies, there should be a careful study made of all the responsibilities in this field held by the several agencies, and also of their relation to each other. As a result of this, a study commission was appointed by the 1948 General Conference which reported at the 1952 General Conference and made many recommendations for the better organization—in some cases a rather thorough reorganization—of the boards and agencies of the Church. The 1952 Conference removed from the Council of Secretaries the responsibility for promoting World Service, and created a new Commission on Promotion and Cultivation to take this over. This represented a change from what had been during the first twelve years of the life of the Council of Secretaries, for the Promotion of World Service then was its major theme. Beginning in 1952, however, the emphasis upon the task of the Council of Secretaries as outlined by the *Discipline* was "to consider matters of common interest and cooperation among the several general boards and agencies of the church." It was to "report annually to the Council of Bishops and to the Council on World Service and Finance" (*Discipline,* 1952, Paragraph 1598).

Pursuant to this, the Council of Secretaries during the last years of The Methodist Church, became a strong executive body. It had much to do with planning ahead the general program of the Church, and was thought by many to exert more power than the COUNCIL OF BISHOPS in directing such ongoing program. Men of commanding leadership were usually elected to be executives in the different boards and agencies, and these men together exerted great influence, especially when their collective will and judgment was expressed in matters having to do with the ongoing of the Church.

In The United Methodist Church, the Council of Secretaries was continued by the Uniting Conference of 1968, but as was the case with other promotional agencies of the former Methodist Church, these in The United Methodist Church were largely pulled into the orbit of the PROGRAM COUNCIL, which itself is a new organization in American Methodism. The exact function of the Council of Secretaries under and in the work of the Program Council in The United Methodist Church has not as yet been clearly defined. The general purpose, however, of this organization remains what it has been all along—a general supervisory relationship to the program of each agency and board, and their cooperation in the life of the general church itself.

Disciplines, TMC, 1940-'64; UMC, 1968. Paragraph 1413

N. B. H.

SEDER, CHRISTIAN LEWIS (1830-1862), American Evangelical minister and casualty of an Indian massacre, was born July 29, 1830, in Hanover, GERMANY. At age sixteen he migrated to WISCONSIN in the United States and joined the Fox River Mission in 1854. The spirit of the founders in planting the EVANGELICAL ASSOCIATION from east to west, was still remarkably evident. Lewis Seder caught this spirit when he traveled with the Wisconsin circuit riders to the ILLINOIS CONFERENCE in 1856, received his license to preach, witnessed the organization of the Wisconsin Conference, and immediate action to establish a mission in MINNESOTA.

When the move was made in 1860 to form a conference out of the growing fields in Minnesota and those in IOWA, Seder volunteered for service among the frontiersmen of this new venture. In 1862 he was appointed to New Ulm, a newly established mission along the Minnesota River. Sunday, August 17, was a joyous day with his congregations near Redwood Falls beyond the Sioux Agency. However a warning reached them of an impending outbreak of the Sioux, whose savage instinct had been aroused by the laxity of government agents in fulfilling agreements. "Monday morning, August 18, massacres were begun at the Sioux Agency, murdering and destroying everything as they went." Seder headed a "mournful procession" of his congregation toward Ft. Ridgely to find refuge.

That day, homeward bound, Seder was fired upon by an Indian rebel, his dying body thrown out and his conveyance driven away. So he died Aug. 18, 1862 and became much more famous in the church as a martyr than he had been as a circuit rider.

The Evangelical Messenger, Vol. 15, 1862.
G. Fritsche, *Die Evangelische Gemeinschaft in Wisconsin, 1840-1920.* Published by Wisconsin Conference, n.d.
A. Stapleton, *Evangelical Association.* 1896.
————, *Flashlights.* 1908.
Albert H. Utzinger, *History of the Minnesota Conference, Evangelical Association.* Cleveland, O.: Evangelical Press, 1922.

ROY B. LEEDY

SEDDON, NATHAN RICHARD (1901-1950), NEW ZEALAND layman, was born and educated in Wellington. As a young man he entered the hardware trade and in 1932 purchased a hardware business of his own. He stood unsuccessfully for the Wellington mayoralty (1947) and as a Labour candidate for Parliament (1949). He became a member of the Wellington Education Board, and after a time, its chairman. He was also a member of the boards of governors of both Wellington College and Wellington Technical College.

An enthusiastic Bible class leader, he served for a number of years on the national executive of the Bible Class Movement, for a time serving as secretary, then as president. He was a regular representative to the annual Methodist conference and was frequently consulted about policy matters. He was also deeply interested in Y.M.C.A. work.

The New Zealand Methodist Times, July 1, 1950.

L. R. M. GILMORE

SEE, A. N. (1840-1925), American pioneer preacher and one of the presiding elders at the beginning of the NORTHWEST KANSAS CONFERENCE in 1882, was born in Chautauqua County, N. Y., on June 28, 1840. His higher education consisted of rather brief periods at ALLEGHENY COLLEGE and CORNELL COLLEGE. He served in the Union Army and later taught school under the Freedmen's Bureau when he joined the GEORGIA CONFERENCE (ME) in 1867.

He married Cynthia Northrup on Nov. 18, 1863. They had one son, James N. See. His first wife died in 1902 and he remarried in 1913.

This colorful figure served in the UPPER IOWA CONFERENCE and in the KANSAS CONFERENCE before the founding of the Northwest Kansas Conference. Thrice a presiding elder, he wrote, printed and bound his *Autobiography* as he neared the end of his long life. This salty account gives the flavor of an era as well as insight into its author. He sums up his travels on the Ellsworth District (1901-07) as 100,000 miles in six years—75,000 by rails and 25,000 by private conveyance.

He died at Ransom, Kan., and was buried in Salina.

Minutes of the Northwest Kansas Conference. 1925.
Oakley Graphic, Jan. 12, 1967.
A. N. See, *Autobiography.* N.p., 1919-21. INA TURNER GRAY

SEIDENSPINNER, CLARENCE ALFRED (1904-1967), American pastor, lecturer, and authority upon worship, was born on Feb. 15, 1904, at Kiel, Wis., the son of Alfred and Elsie (Shultz) Seidenspinner. He married Dorothy Benallack on June 11, 1927, and their children were Gilbert and Roberta. He received the B.S. degree from NORTHWESTERN UNIVERSITY in 1925, the B.D. from GARRETT BIBLICAL INSTITUTE in 1928, and the D.D. from LAWRENCE COLLEGE in 1943.

Joining the WISCONSIN CONFERENCE, he served at Oconomowoc, 1929; Ripon, 1937; and then went to the First Church, Racine, Wis., where he continued as pastor from 1940 until his death in 1967. He was a member of the Committee on Ministerial Qualifications and of the Board of Education of his Conference. His special field was literature and worship, and he was a special lecturer in contemporary literature and worship at Garrett Theological Seminary. He was called into consultative service by the Commission on WORSHIP of The Methodist Church a number of times, and wrote *Form and Freedom in Worship,* 1940; *Our Dwelling Place,* 1940; *Great Protestant Festivals,* 1952; *Give God a Chance,* 1953; *Progress Through Prayer,* 1955; and *A Protestant Primer,* 1947. He served for twelve years as chairman of the Commission on WORLD SERVICE AND FINANCE for his conference. He contributed to *The Christian Century, The Christian Advocate,* and various religious publications and became quite well known as an authority on church worship. He died in Racine, Wis. on Sept. 15, 1967.

C. T. Howell, *Prominent Personalities.* 1945.   N. B. H.

SELBY, JAMES ALFRED (1865-1940), American minister, was born near Easton, W. Va., the son of William and Sophia Selby. He was graduated from WESTMINSTER THEOLOGICAL SEMINARY in 1889 and was ordained a minister of the WEST VIRGINIA CONFERENCE of the M.P. Church. Greenville College in Tennessee conferred on him the D.D. degree in 1904.

He served for sixteen years as pastor in the Muskingum Conference in OHIO, having successively served Wellsville, Cambridge and Mt. Vernon, Ohio. While pastor at Mt. Vernon he was elected president of the Conference. At the close of this term he returned to the West Virginia Conference and served Bethany Church, Parkersburg, until he was again elected president of the Conference. He was elected to ten sessions of the GENERAL CONFERENCE of the M.P. Church, was a member of the Board of Home Missions, and a member of the Executive Committee of the General Conference. He remained in the active ministry until 1939 and died in Parkersburg, W. Va., Dec. 2, 1940.

FRANK L. SHAFFER

C. C. SELECMAN

SELECMAN, CHARLES CLAUDE (1874-1958), American bishop and author, was born Oct. 13, 1874, in Savannah, Mo., and died March 27, 1958, in DALLAS, TEXAS, where he was buried. He was the son of Isaac Henry and Josephine Smith Selecman. His educational training was at CENTRAL COLLEGE, Fayette, Mo., from which he also held honorary degrees, as well as from the University of Southern California and KENTUCKY WESLEYAN. The LL.D. degree was conferred upon him by Austin College, Sherman, Texas (1924), CENTENARY COLLEGE in Shreveport, La. (1923); Baylor University at Waco, Texas (1933); SOUTHERN METHODIST UNIVERSITY (1939).

Upon entering the ministry he was on rural charges for four years, including social service work at Kingdom House in ST. LOUIS, Mo., and later in NEW ORLEANS. He was pastor of Trinity Auditorium, an institutional church in LOS ANGELES, Calif. (1913-1920), First Methodist, Dallas, Texas (1920-1923). In 1918 he served with the Y.M.C.A. in the United States, England, and France, during World War I. In 1923 he became President of Southern Methodist University, which place he held until he was elected bishop in 1938.

On April 27, 1899, he was married to Bessie Kyle Beckner, who died in 1944. To that union were born two children, Francis A. Selecman and Sarah Josephine (Mrs. D. W. Forbes). He later married Mrs. Mabel White Mason of California.

The GENERAL CONFERENCE of 1922 established a General Board of HOSPITALS AND HOMES, and elected Selecman secretary. Soon afterwards he founded the Golden Cross Society, a church-wide movement for work of the church's healing ministry. The Methodist Hospital in Dallas was the birthplace of that society.

For the first six years of his service in the episcopacy, Bishop Selecman was in charge of the work of OKLAHOMA and ARKANSAS, and later in North Texas. In addition to the oversight of his episcopal area, he served as president of the General Board of EVANGELISM of The Methodist Church, to which he gave wide and creative leadership.

Bishop Selecman was Field Secretary of the War Work Commission of the M.E. Church, South (1918); a delegate to the World Conference on Faith and Order at Lausanne, Switzerland (1927), and in Edinburgh, Scotland (1937). In 1933 he was elected by the five Texas Conferences to plan for the 100th anniversary of Texas Methodism (1936). He was a member of Sigma Alpha Epsilon fraternity; a 33d degree Mason and Red Crown of Constantine.

He was author of the following volumes: *Christ or Chaos* (1923); *The Challenge of Citizenship* (1933); *Methodist Primer* (1947, revised in 1953); *Christian Nurture in the Home* (1948); *The Methodist First Reader* (1956).

C. T. Howell, *Prominent Personalities*. 1945.
Journal of the North Texas Conference, 1958.
Who's Who in America.   MRS. JOHN H. WARNICK

SELF, DAVID WILSON (1919-   ), American layman and educator, was born in Leighton, Ala., Oct. 10, 1919, to James T. and Lucy (Childers) Self. He received the B.S. (1942) and M.A. (1946) degrees from the University of Alabama and the Ed.D. degree (1965) from Columbia University. He was married to Helen Frances Huckabee, March 15, 1944.

For a year Mr. Self served as teacher and athletic coach, Brookwood, Ala. He was assistant principal, Greenville (Ala.) High School, 1947-49; principal, Frisco City (Ala.) High School, 1949-50; principal, Greenville High School, 1950-55; superintendent, Butler County (Ala.) Schools, 1955-58; superintendent, Phoenix City (Ala.) Schools, 1958-65, and Associate Professor of School Administration, University of Alabama, 1965-69. He has continued as General Secretary of the General Board of the LAITY, United Methodist Church, since 1969.

Mr. Self served as Conference Director, METHODIST MEN, 1957-64; member, General BOARD OF EDUCATION, 1962-68 and secretary of the Division of Local Church, 1964-68; chairman, ALABAMA-WEST FLORIDA CONFERENCE Board of Education, 1964-68; delegate to GENERAL and JURISDICTIONAL CONFERENCES, 1964.

Who's Who in The Methodist Church, 1966.
JOHN H. NESS, JR.

SELINA, COUNTESS OF HUNTINGDON. (See HUNTINGDON, COUNTESS OF.)

SELLEW, WALTER ASHBELL (1844-1929), American pastor, educator and bishop of the FREE METHODIST CHURCH, was born of Quaker parentage, at Gowanda, N. Y. He spent two years in Oberlin College when Charles G. Finney was president, and was graduated at Dartmouth, A.B., 1866; M.A. 1869. Converted in his senior year, he joined the Presbyterian Church, and later the Free Methodist Church. After studying law a year, he entered the ministry. He was principal of SPRING ARBOR SEMINARY in MICHIGAN. He founded Gerry Seminary, GERRY, N.Y., in 1884, serving as its principal. He spent ten years as pastor and district elder in New York and Pennsylvania.

In 1898 he was elected bishop and served eight consecutive terms until his death in 1929. He was instrumental in founding the Old People's Home in Gerry, N. Y., and served as president of the General Missionary

Board for many years. He was the author of *Clara Leffingwell, A Missionary*, and *The Obligations of Civilization to Christianity*. He was an able administrator and preacher extraordinary, and one of the best known and loved leaders of his church.

BYRON S. LAMSON

SELLON, WALTER (1715-1792), British Anglican, a protégé of the COUNTESS OF HUNTINGDON, and for a time vicar of Ashby-de-la-Zouch, was one of JOHN WESLEY's principal supporters in the Calvinistic controversy of 1770 onward, along with JOHN FLETCHER and THOMAS OLIVERS. He had made a special study of John Goodwin's Arminian writings, and answered both AUGUSTUS TOPLADY and Elisha Coles. His last parish was at Ledsham, Yorkshire.

A. SKEVINGTON WOOD

SELLS, JAMES WILLIAM (1897-   ), American minister and church official, was born at Atchison, Kan., June 27, 1897, son of James LeGrande and Clara (Hull) Sells.

He was graduated with the A.B. degree from MILLSAPS COLLEGE in 1929. LaGRANGE COLLEGE awarded him the LL.D. degree in 1955, and EMORY UNIVERSITY awarded him the D.D. degree in 1964.

In 1925 he was admitted on trial into the MISSISSIPPI CONFERENCE, M.E. Church, South. He was received in full connection and ordained DEACON in 1927, and was ordained ELDER in 1929.

He served as supply pastor in Taylorsville, 1920-21; Georgetown, 1921-23; Pascagoula, 1925-29; Summit, 1929-30; Ocean Springs, 1930-32; Forest, 1932-36; Court Street Church, Hattiesburg, 1936-40; Crystal Springs, 1940-44 (all in MISSISSIPPI).

He was field secretary of Whitworth-Millsaps College, 1930; executive secretary, SEASHORE METHODIST ASSEMBLY, Biloxi, Miss., 1930-32, and of Mississippi Rural Life Council, JACKSON, 1945. In the period 1945-52, he was extension secretary of the SOUTHEASTERN JURISDICTIONAL Council, ATLANTA, Ga., and in 1952 was made executive secretary of that Council.

In 1945 he became director of the Joint Radio Committee and director and producer of the Methodist Series, the Protestant Hour, Atlanta. In 1947 he was secretary of the National Methodist Rural Life Conference, Lincoln, Nebr. He has since 1959 been executive director of the Institute of Communicative Arts, Atlanta. He served as director of the Protestant Radio and Television Center, Atlanta, and of the Hinton Rural Life Center, Inc., Hayesville, N. C. He served with the United States Navy, 1917-18. Since 1944 he has been Rural Church Editor of the *Progressive Farmer* Magazine.

On Jan. 21, 1921, he was married to Vera Maude Britt. They had a daughter, Shirley Jeanne (Mrs. Robert Adams), deceased 1955.

A luncheon was given by the Southeastern Jurisdictional Council on Oct. 20, 1970 honoring Dr. and Mrs. Sells for "a quarter of a century of service" with all the episcopal leaders of the Southern Conferences and many others present.

Who's Who in The Methodist Church, 1966.   J. MARVIN RAST

SELMA, ALABAMA, U.S.A. **Methodist Children's Home,** a multiple service agency of the NORTH ALABAMA AND ALABAMA-WEST FLORIDA CONFERENCES of The United Methodist Church, is a home for orphans which was authorized by resolutions passed in regular sessions of the North Alabama and Alabama Conferences of the then M.E. Church, South, in 1889. Alabama Methodist Orphanage was in consequence opened in Summerfield, Ala., and the first child was admitted in September 1890. The orphanage was chartered and its board of directors incorporated by act of the ALABAMA legislature in February 1891.

To expand its facilities, the orphanage moved to Selma in 1911, having purchased the building and grounds of Selma Military Institute. Additional property was purchased in the 1920's to permit further expansion.

As the years passed, changing concepts in child welfare revealed the needs of neglected children from homes broken by desertion, crime, illness, and poverty. Responding to changing needs the orphanage in 1939 became the Methodist Children's Home, and directors and staff envisioned a broader concept of care for homeless children.

From this vision came the first Methodist Children's Village in the South—ten handsome, commodious, brick cottages constructed from 1948-51. Each cottage is "home" to ten or twelve children who live there with a housemother. Life in the cottages is as nearly like normal family life as possible. To become involved in community life, the children attend the Selma schools where they participate in campus activities. They also attend Sunday school and worship services in Selma United Methodist churches.

The Home's multiple service program encompasses group care of the Children's Village; foster homes which accommodate pre-school age children, and youngsters with special needs; Family Aid which provides limited financial assistance in special cases; and scholarships (made possible by a Living Memorial Fund) for worthy students to attend college or vocational schools.

Max E. Livingston, *The Methodist Children's Home—Pioneer and Leader in Services to Children.* Pamphlet, 1955.

RICHARD I. KIRKLAND

SEMINARIO CESAR DACORSO FILHO, Rio de Janeiro, Brazil. This recently founded Bible school is located on the campus of COLEGIO BENNETT, and its purpose is to prepare lay preachers of the First Region of the Methodist Church of BRAZIL. Originally called the "Asbury Institute," and founded in 1960, the name was changed in 1966 to honor the first Brazilian bishop by that name, who died that year. The director is Fred Maitland.

WILLIAM R. SCHISLER, JR.

SENEY, GEORGE INGRAHAM (1826-1893), American banker and philanthropist, son of Robert and Jane (Ingraham) Seney, was born May 12, 1826, at Astoria, N.Y. He was educated at WESLEYAN and New York Universities, graduating from the latter. His father, a Methodist preacher who had graduated at Columbia College, desired a college education for his son and sent him to Wesleyan University, but financial circumstances compelled a change to a local university. Seney's first position was that of paying teller in the Metropolitan Bank, NEW YORK. His ability was quickly recognized and he soon rose to its presidency. He took an important part in railroad financing, particularly of the Nickel Plate and the East Tennessee, Virginia and Georgia lines. During the

Grant-Ward episode in Wall Street in 1884, the bank was forced to close its doors. Seney turned over to the bank his personal fortune, costly residence and art collection so that the bank's depositors were paid in full. He later retrieved the larger part of his fortune.

JAMES M. BUCKLEY said that Seney's philanthropies began long before he was wealthy, for as a young man with an income of less than $5,000 a year, he then gave away more than one-fifth of it annually. Among his larger gifts were the following: Wesleyan University, $500,000; EMORY COLLEGE, $100,000; WESLEYAN Female COLLEGE of Macon, Ga., $250,000 for its main building and for the LOVICK PIERCE Professorship; BROOKLYN METHODIST HOSPITAL, $410,000 toward its founding; Long Island Historical Society, $100,000; Mamaroneck Methodist Church, $75,000; Metropolitan Art Museum, numerous paintings and art treasures under the guidance of Samuel Putnam Avery. During his lifetime, his gifts are estimated at more than $2,000,000.

Seney was a trustee of the Metropolitan Art Museum, of Wesleyan University, and was one of the Managers of the M.E. Board of MISSIONS. In 1890, he headed the subscription list for erection of the Washington Memorial Arch. In 1849, he was married to Phoebe Moser, of a well known Brooklyn family. To them were born three sons and six daughters.

Seney died April 7, 1893 in New York City.

Dictionary of American Biography.   HENRY L. LAMBDIN

SEOUL, Korea, a city of over 4,000,000, is the capital and largest city in South KOREA. It is the intellectual, political, commercial, and social center of the country.

Methodists cooperate with other agencies in the Christian Literature Society, which publishes and distributes much of the literature used in Protestant churches and schools in Korea; in the Korean National Christian Coun-

cil, and in the Committee on Mass Communications, as well as the Korea Bible Society.

Among the Methodist institutions in Seoul are the Tai Wha Christian Community Center, which was organized in 1919; Wyatt Baby Fold, which was opened in 1953; Home of Peaceful Rest, for retired women Christian workers, which was established in 1948; Jensen Memorial Student Center, opened in 1960; and Angels Haven, a home for 138 boys picked up off the streets of Seoul.

Ewha Girls' Junior and Senior High School was established in 1886 as the first school for girls in Korea. The present enrolment is 3,680. EWHA UNIVERSITY grew from this school and is now on a separate campus.

Pai Chai High School, Korea's pioneer school in modern education, had its beginning in a class in English started by HENRY G. APPENZELLER in August 1885. In June 1886, the King of Korea recognized the school by naming it Pai Chai Hak Dang, or Hall for Training Useful Men. Being the first attempt to teach the common branches of learning instead of Chinese classics, it is recognized as the beginning of modern education in Korea. In 1887 Pai Chai Hall, a one-story brick building, became the first foreign style school building in Korea. Pai Chai's English language trained students were in such great demand in the government and business world as interpreters, teachers, and writers, that it was not until 1908 that a class was graduated. Among the many outstanding leaders to come from the school was Syngman Rhee, first President of the Republic of Korea. Among successors to Appenzeller were D. A. Bunker, Hugh H. Cynn, and Henry D. Appenzeller, son of the founder. Ranking among the foremost of Korea's high schools, the junior and senior schools enroll nearly 3,000 boys.

Pai Wha Girls' High School was founded in 1898 by the Woman's Missionary Council of the M.E. Church, South. The present enrolment is 2,386.

Methodist Theological Seminary resulted as a merger in 1929 of the Union Methodist Theological Seminary and the Union Methodist Bible Training School, projects

BISHOP HERBERT WELCH MEMORIAL CHAPEL,
THEOLOGICAL SEMINARY, SEOUL, KOREA

METHODIST CHURCH,
WEST DISTRICT, SEOUL, KOREA

of both the M.E. and M.E. Church, South. The seminary received its charter as a four-year college in the spring of 1959. Present enrollment is 163.

YONSEI UNIVERSITY is supported by The United Methodist Church in cooperation with other Boards. SEVERANCE HOSPITAL, recognized in 1905, has been rebuilt on the Yonsei University campus with funds from The United Methodist Church and other cooperating agencies.

Among the new outreaches of the church in Seoul is that of providing two full-time Christian women workers and a half-time minister to work with patients in the government hospital which is affiliated with Seoul National University. Another area is concern for Christian witness among prisoners in the police stations and in government reformatories. Another outreach is the Service Men's Center.

Project Handbook: Overseas Missions, 1969.

CHARLES A. SAUER

SESQUICENTENNIAL OF AMERICAN METHODISM.

Definite plans for the Sesquicentennial Celebration of 1934 began officially as early as 1928. At this time Methodist branches elected Commissions to plan for the observance. A joint Commission was then formed, made up of representatives of the M.P., M.E., South, and M.E. Churches.

The officers of the Joint Commission which developed the program for the Celebration in BALTIMORE, Md., Oct. 10-14, 1934, as published in the souvenir booklet were: Chairman—Bishop EDWIN H. HUGHES, Washington, D.C. (M.E.); First Vice President—Hon. D. C. Roper, Washington, D.C. (M.E., South); Second Vice President—John H. Baker, Baltimore, Md. (M.P.); Secretary—Alfred H. Backus, Indianapolis, Ind. (M.E.); Assistant Secretary—NOLAN B. HARMON, Jr., Baltimore, Md. (M.E., South); and Treasurer—John H. Race, New York, N.Y. (M.E.). There were also various Commission members representing the M.E., the PRIMITIVE METHODIST, the M.E., South, the M.P., and the FREE METHODIST Churches.

The Celebration in Baltimore brought a multitude of delegates and visitors together for a five-day observance. This was not only significant in recognizing 150 years of American Methodism, but was also unique in the bearing which the observance had upon the proposed union of three branches of Methodism. In addition to the central celebration at Baltimore, annual conferences and local churches observed the Sesquicentennial. All through the churches there were indications of hope that in the plan and program of the observances, there might be, as a practical result, a union of American Methodists by at least the year 1944. Was it a matter of coincidence that the Sesquicentennial observance occurred as the Commissioners of three branches of American Methodism were developing a PLAN OF UNION?

The 150th anniversary celebration began in Baltimore, Md., on Wednesday morning, Oct. 10, 1934, with a Communion Service in the Scottish Rite Temple. Addresses of welcome were given by Albert C. Ritchie, Governor of Maryland; Howard W. Jackson, Mayor of Baltimore; and Ross W. Sanderson, Federation of Churches of Baltimore.

Thursday was designated as "One Day Union" with Bishop WILLIAM F. McDOWELL, presiding. Addresses were given by Bishops JOHN M. MOORE and FREDERICK D. LEETE. A union meeting was held of the Boards of Bishops and GENERAL CONFERENCE Executives of the M.P. Church with Bishop EDWIN H. HUGHES presiding. T. Albert Moore from the United Church of Canada was present. Others who participated in this historic day of observance included JOHN C. BROOMFIELD, T. FERRIER HULME of England, JOHN R. MOTT, Bishop EDWIN D. MOUZON, and S. PARKES CADMAN, who gave the evening address entitled "United Methodism in Protestantism."

Friday saw a three-fold program in separate sessions for delegates, women, and young people. The delegates' meeting saw Hon. Daniel C. Roper presiding in the morning and Bishop John M. Moore in the afternoon. Various areas of Methodist interest and influence were presented by outstanding personalities. Areas such as journalism, education, social contributions, and theology were subjects of addresses. The evening was climaxed by the historical pageant entitled "The Spreading Flame," written and directed by Harold A. Ehrensperger. The pageant was repeated on Saturday afternoon and evening.

Saturday morning the delegates met for an "Evangelistic Session" with Bishop Frederick D. Leete, presiding. Addresses were given by CLOVIS G. CHAPPELL and MERTON S. RICE. Probably one of the most significant presentations of the Celebration was the summary by Bishop Edwin H. Hughes, entitled "The Past and Future of Methodism."

Saturday afternoon a pilgrimage was conducted to Sam's Creek, Carroll County, Md., made famous by the early ministry of ROBERT STRAWBRIDGE. Here a dedicatory service was held, addressed by T. Ferrier Hulme. A memorial was unveiled at this historic site by Mrs. Laura Dempster Gronmeyer, great-granddaughter of Robert Strawbridge, commemorating the 150th anniversary of the organization of the M.E. Church in America.

The closing day, Sunday, found "preaching in all churches (Methodist) by bishops and delegates at both morning and evening services." A nation-wide broadcast at 3:00 p.m. was a truly historic climax.

Before the Celebration closed, a resolution was adopted by the delegates which read, "We desire to say to the Methodists of our land that the time has fully come for us to move forward in one body. Only so shall we keep faith with our fathers, and only so can we keep faith with our children." The Sesquicentennial was more than an observance of past history. It forecast the future!

JOHN HOON

SESSIONS, CLEO CARL (1909-   ), American pastor, educator, and administrator, was born at Altus, Okla., May 23, 1909, the son of Don E. and Ada (Harvey) Sessions. He was educated at SOUTHERN METHODIST UNIVERSITY receiving the B.S., B.D. and J.D. degrees, and TEXAS WESLEYAN COLLEGE gave him the D.D. degree in 1954. His wife was Maurine Doughty, whom he married on June 5, 1932. He joined the CENTRAL TEXAS CONFERENCE in 1936 and for the next few years served a number of pastorates, including Herring Avenue Church, Waco, 1944-48; Central Church, Brownwood, 1948-51; and then for six years was superintendent of the Gatesville District. He became pastor of the Central Church, FORT WORTH, 1957-60, and then the superintendent of the Cleburne District in the Central Texas Conference in 1960. He has been a member of the GENERAL CONFERENCES of 1956 and 1964 and of the JURISDICTIONAL CONFERENCE, 1956, '60, and '64. He was appointed a trustee

of Harris Hospital, Fort Worth in 1964 and of Southern Methodist University in 1960. In 1966 he was sent to the large Polytechnic Methodist Church, which has a close relationship to Texas Wesleyan College nearby.

Who's Who in The Methodist Church, 1966.

SEVEN GOLDEN CANDLESTICKS is a name in China mission work that originated in 1869 following a dramatic ordination service in Foochow, conducted by Bishop CALVIN KINGSLEY. Various annual conferences in the United States had then agreed to accept seven qualified Chinese pastors of the Foochow area as "ministers in absentia" and had authorized their ordination, four as both DEACONS and ELDERS, and three as deacons.

Mrs. Stephen L. Baldwin, in describing them in *The Missionary Advocate* of September 1870, called them the "Seven Golden Candlesticks," and that name stuck. In 1877 Bishop ISAAC W. WILEY organized the Foochow Annual Conference, and six of them were all transferred in, to become charter members of the new conference. (Lin Ching-ting had died the preceding May.)

The four elders were the Confucian scholar **Sia Sek-ong,** the two Hu brothers, **Hu Yong-mi** and **Hu Bo-mi,** and **Lin Ching-ting.** Sia became the leading preacher of the Conference and was the delegate to the 1880 GENERAL CONFERENCE. He refused to take any mission subsidy on his salary, so that non-Christians could not accuse him of "preaching for rice." Hu Yong-mi had already suffered much for his faith, when as pastor of the East Street Church in 1864, a mob had torn down the building, beaten him, insulted his wife and sister, and destroyed all their furniture. Mrs. Baldwin said of him, "His sermons, especially since his ordination, when he seemed to receive a fresh baptism of the Spirit, have been full of power." Lin, the only Hinghwa-speaking man of the seven, had been an opium smoker and "a partaker in every kind of sin." Mrs. Baldwin wrote, "Bold, eloquent, and full of zeal, yet hasty, impulsive and determined, we have been wont to call him our Peter, as we have termed Hu Yong-mi and Sia Sek-ong our beloved Johns." He, too, had seen persecution; at one time he received a thousand stripes on his bare back.

The three deacons were **Li Yu-mi,** a converted blacksmith, who used to keep his Bible open beside his anvil and study it between strokes; **Hu Sing-mi,** a younger brother of the two Hus who had already had an opportunity to study in America; and **Yeh Ing-guang,** who as a poor boy, almost a beggar, had been admitted to the mission boarding school, and after graduation had become a preacher.

The children and grandchildren of these seven continued the ministry handed down to them. Hu King-eng, daughter of Hu Yong-mi, became the first woman doctor in the Foochow area, serving in the mission hospital for women until the Nationalist riots of 1927. Other members of the Hu family to serve the church were Hu Sie-guang, for many years the treasurer and bookkeeper of the mission, and Dr. Doris Hsu, professor in Hwanan College and more recently in NEBRASKA WESLEYAN UNIVERSITY. Lin T'ien-ho, grandson of Lin Ching-ting, has been for forty years field secretary of the AMERICAN BIBLE SOCIETY and the China Bible House.

W. C. Barclay, *History of Missions.* 1957.
W. N. Lacy, *China.* 1948.　　　　　FRANCIS P. JONES

SEVERANCE UNION MEDICAL COLLEGE and **HOSPITAL,** Seoul, Korea, derived its name from the L. H. Severance family of Cleveland, Ohio, as they donated funds to erect the first modern hospital in KOREA under the direction of a Presbyterian missionary, O. R. Avison. This hospital (1904) and the medical college (1906) has gained the support of all Presbyterian and Methodist mission bodies working in Korea.

During the Korean War, buildings and equipment were more than eighty percent destroyed. Some of the buildings were rehabilitated under grants from the United Board of Christian Higher Education in Asia, and from various mission boards. However the need for a larger site led to the development of a new medical center on the Yonsei University campus. (See YONSEI UNIVERSITY.)

CHARLES A. SAUER

SEWARD, WILLIAM (1702-1740), the first Methodist preacher to die at the hands of a mob, came from a wealthy family from Badsey, Worcestershire. One brother, Thomas, was an Anglican clergyman; another, Benjamin, became a Methodist. After ten years' work for LONDON charity schools, in 1738 William was converted by the preaching of CHARLES WESLEY, from whom he was later estranged by his zeal for Calvinism. William accompanied GEORGE WHITEFIELD to GEORGIA in 1739, returning to Britain in 1740 to raise funds for the Orphan House. While on a tour of South Wales with HOWELL HARRIS, he was roughly handled by mobs at Newport, Carleon and Monmouth, and was partially blinded. On Oct. 22, 1740, while preaching at Hay, he received a fatal blow on the head from a large stone. He is buried at Cusop, close by.

Wesley Historical Society, *Proceedings,* xvii.

JOHN A. VICKERS

SEWARD, ALASKA, U.S.A. **Jesse Lee Home.** The WOMAN'S HOME MISSIONARY SOCIETY of the M.E. Church acquired land and contracted with Sheldon Jackson, the Government Agent for Education in ALASKA, to build an Industrial Home and School as early as 1890, but the GENERAL CONFERENCE of 1892 closed all Methodist work in Alaska.

Jesse Lee Home had its real beginning in Unalaska, Alaska in 1895, when Agnes Louisa Soule, a granddaughter of Bishop JOSHUA SOULE, arrived there, the first woman missionary to be sent to Alaska by the Woman's Home Missionary Society.

Miss Soule was to teach in the government school but immediately found need to make a home for some fifteen girls. The next year upon her appeal the Society in VERMONT sent her a helper and they made a home for thirty girls.

In 1898 she returned to Vermont on furlough and was married to A. W. NEWHALL. Together they returned to Unalaska and their life work. A new building was erected, boys were admitted, and a hospital provided.

The Methodist women of Vermont named the mission "Jesse Lee Home" to honor the early New England minister and evangelist.

Due to the influenza epidemic in Nome in 1919, many homeless children became the responsibility of the Methodist Church. New buildings were necessary. The Woman's Home Missionary Society decided to build a complete new home in Seward and bring all the children there. Newhall finished twenty-seven years of work and went on to Point Barrow in 1925.

R. V. B. Dunlap supervised building the new home and was the first Superintendent at Seward. The two buildings were only partially completed when the children and staff from Unalaska arrived there in 1925.

Charles T. Hatten became Superintendent in 1926. The children attended public school and community activities, and in 1931 the first Jesse Lee children graduated from high school in Alaska; before this they had gone to the states for high school and further education.

Harold Newton became Superintendent in 1938. War came soon after and the children were evacuated. The army took over the buildings. After the war the home was reopened and continues to serve Alaska children.

"I lived in Jesse Lee Home," is a proud statement of Alaskans from Ketchikan to the Arctic.

Seattle Times, April 12, 1959.　　CHARLES T. HATTEN

SEWELL, W. E. (1869-1941), an American missionary to CUBA, was born in Gadsden, Crockett County, Tenn., Jan. 23, 1869. His parents were Robert Allen and Nannie L. Folis Sewell. In his youth he was converted and attended HENDRIX COLLEGE in ARKANSAS. In 1890 he joined the MEMPHIS CONFERENCE and after teaching for two years in JACKSON, Tenn., he married one of his pupils, Lula Smith, 1896.

After transferring to the ARKANSAS CONFERENCE and serving there at Perryville for two years, he and his wife were accepted for missionary work in Cuba in 1898, being one of the first American missionaries at the close of the Spanish-American War. For the thirteen years that he served in Cuba he was supported by a loyal layman, a lumberman, from Hattiesburg, Miss., W. S. F. Tatum.

For health reasons he retired from Cuba and from 1913 to 1919 served three pastorates in the Memphis Conference. From 1919 to 1925 he was superintendent of Latin work in TAMPA. Transferring to FLORIDA, he served four pastorates in the FLORIDA CONFERENCE until his retirement in 1936. He died Feb. 12, 1941.

In Cuba he was noted for his personal interest in others and his name was always mentioned with devotion. It was said of him, "he always looked for the good in others."

GARFIELD EVANS

SEXSMITH, EDGAR ADGATE (1875-1959), American M.P. minister, was born in Clark County, Mo., Feb. 19, 1875. He was the son of John and Mary B. Sexsmith. After high school he attended a business college in Kahoka, Mo., and received his training for the ministry at WESTMINSTER THEOLOGICAL SEMINARY.

He joined the North Missouri Conference after his graduation from the Seminary in 1900 and was ordained the following year. In 1907 he was transferred to the MARYLAND CONFERENCE of the M.P. Church, where he served until his retirement in 1947.

In 1923 he became secretary of the Board of Young People's Work. He was Church Extension Superintendent of the Maryland Conference, 1926-28. His pastorate at Chestertown, Md., spanned six years, 1928-34. In 1934 he was elected president of the Maryland Conference, serving until unification in 1939. He was a member of three GENERAL CONFERENCES of the M.P. Church, and

was a delegate at the historic UNITING CONFERENCE held at KANSAS CITY, Mo., in 1939.

Sexsmith died in Baltimore, Md., Nov. 2, 1959.

Minutes of the Baltimore Conference, 1960.　PAUL E. KEEDY

SEXTON, GEORGE SAMUEL (1867-1937), American preacher and educator, was born in Middleburg, Tenn., June 10, 1867. He was convinced at an early age that he must be a preacher, so he worked his way through college and joined the LITTLE ROCK CONFERENCE in 1887. For ten years he served churches in the Little Rock Conference; and in 1897, for reasons of health, he transferred to the NORTH TEXAS CONFERENCE, where he served with distinction for seven years. In 1904, he was transferred to the TEXAS CONFERENCE and stationed at Central Church, Galveston. In 1906, he was sent to HOUSTON, Texas, where he was instrumental in building St. Paul's Church which, in its day, was one of the finest church buildings in Methodism.

During 1910 he served as Assistant Secretary of the Board of Church Extension of the M.E. Church South. He was called from this job to act as Field Secretary of the Washington City Church Commission, which was responsible for erecting a representative Methodist church in our nation's capital. He succeeded in a wonderful way in this task, and today the great Mt. Vernon Place Church in WASHINGTON, D. C., is a monument to his labors. In 1915 Sexton transferred to the LOUISIANA CONFERENCE, where he was to achieve his greatest distinction. For five years he was pastor of the great First Church of SHREVE-PORT, La., and then he was elected President of CENTE-NARY COLLEGE OF LOUISIANA, where he served for eleven years. When he became President of Centenary, it was a struggling little college with a student body of only forty-three students. Eleven years later it had a student body of more than 1,000, and the endowment had grown from $90,000 to nearly $2,000,000. His wide service received the recognition it merited in honorary degrees conferred by a number of colleges, among them being a D.D. from KENTUCKY WESLEYAN COLLEGE and the LL.D. from Centenary College and from SOUTHWESTERN UNIVERSITY of Georgetown, Texas.

After eleven very fruitful years at Centenary College, he was appointed the presiding elder of the Shreveport District of Louisiana Conference, in which office he served four years. He never lost his love for Centenary College, so after years in the presiding eldership, he was appointed Director of Public Relations for Centenary but he did not live long after this appointment. He died on July 4, 1937, before he achieved all of his dreams for Centenary College.

J. HENRY BOWDON, SR.

SEYBERT, JOHN (1791-1860), American minister and pioneer bishop of the EVANGELICAL ASSOCIATION, was born near Manheim, Pa., July 7, 1791. In 1804 his parents joined the followers of JACOB ALBRIGHT, founder of the Evangelical Association. After a remarkable conversion on June 21, 1810, John Seybert united with the Albright People at Manheim. He entered the ministry in 1820 and became an ardent builder and first bishop of the church Albright founded.

Seybert's diaries (eighteen volumes) yield these amazing figures: 175,000 miles (horseback, 1820-1842;

JOHN SEYBERT

one-horse wagon, 1843-1860); and 46,000 pastoral visits. He saw the church grow from one to eight conferences. On the eve of an epochal era of expansion in the late 1830's, he as a bachelor minister declared his desire to be found at the front. In 1838, organized missionary societies arose through his inspiration. He was president of the parent society when elected bishop in 1839. Forthwith he directed the attention of his workers to the German settlements of the Northwest Territory. With the dearth of German reading material in the west, Bishop Seybert in 1842 loaded his wagon at the publishing house in New Berlin, Pa., with an order of 23,725 volumes, charged to his account, and delivered these books to ministers in OHIO and westward.

The fruitage of Seybert's labor was in evidence throughout the church in his time. From NEW YORK to IOWA his wagon carried him and his books. His journeys ended at a revival meeting appointment at a church near Flat Rock, Ohio, Jan. 4, 1860, and he was buried in the church cemetery.

R. B. Leedy, *Evangelical Church in Ohio.* 1959.
W. W. Orwig, *Evangelical Association.* 1858.
S. P. Spreng, *John Seybert.* 1888.   ROY B. LEEDY

SEYMOUR, CONNECTICUT, U.S.A. **Seymour Church** is one of the oldest congregations in America. JESSE LEE, the "Methodist Apostle to New England," received his appointment to that region at the Conference in 1789. As an itinerant, he made several stops in the town of Derby, Conn. His first visit there occurred on March 19, 1791. John and Ruth Coe of the Chusetown section of the Derby township (later to be separated from Derby and called Seymour) were eager listeners, and asked Lee to preach in their community. This he did nearly three months later on June 9, 1791, in the Coe home. A class was formed, and it was organized as a Society in 1797. Bishop FRANCIS ASBURY records his visit to Derby on Aug. 19, 1793.

The little society met in various homes, the Bell School, and the Congregational Church. FREEBORN GARRETTSON presided over the first QUARTERLY CONFERENCE in the Congregational Church in 1803.

After paying the sum of forty dollars, the Methodist Society took possession of the Congregational Church property in September 1818. The building was small and

poorly constructed, and a new structure was erected in 1847. It was in the basement of that wooden Gothic structure that the first town meeting of Seymour, formerly Chusetown, was held on June 24, 1850. The bill in the state legislature to create Seymour as a separate town from Derby was submitted by Sylvester Smith (1807-1893). He was a local preacher and a paper manufacturer who later served as pastor of several churches in the NEW YORK EAST CONFERENCE.

Continued growth in the town and the church created the need for more space. In 1892 a large sanctuary was added to the building in the form of a modified Akron style plant. This arrangement served well, with several changes in the interior, until 1960 when an extensive renovation was undertaken. W. C. Sharpe, a member of the church and the editor of the *Seymour Record*, compiled the history of the church in the latter part of the nineteenth century.

W. C. Sharpe, *Annals of the Seymour M. E. Church.* 1885.
LOWELL B. JOHNSON

JOHN SHACKFORD

SHACKFORD, JOHN WALTER (1878-1969), American minister and General Secretary of the SUNDAY SCHOOL Board, M. E. Church, South, was born Jan. 10, 1878 at Walkerton, Va. Educated at RANDOLPH-MACON COLLEGE (A.B. with Phi Beta Kappa, 1900), and VANDERBILT (B.D., 1903), he was awarded the honorary D.D. by the former institution in 1912. After working three years with the Board of MISSIONS in NASHVILLE, Shackford served nine years as a pastor in VIRGINIA, including Broad Street Church, RICHMOND (1913-15). In 1915 he became superintendent of teacher training in the General Sunday School Board at Nashville, and at the 1922 GENERAL CONFERENCE was elected General Secretary of that Board. In 1930 when the General Conference largely on his recommendation merged the EPWORTH LEAGUE, EDUCATION, and Sunday School Boards to form the General Board of Education with three divisions, Shackford, believing the top offices should go to new men, returned to the pastorate.

During the next fifteen years he served two pastorates in NORTH CAROLINA and two in SOUTH CAROLINA and had a five-year term on the Rock Hill (S. C.) District. In 1945 he transferred to Virginia, served five years as pastor of Chestnut Avenue Church, NEWPORT NEWS, and retired in 1950 at the age of seventy-two.

Shackford was a pioneer and builder in the field of religious education. As secretary of the young people's department of the Board of Missions (1903-06), he developed a plan for a department of missionary education in that Board which was adopted by the 1906 General Conference. Soon after entering the pastorate, Shackford saw the need of a denominational program for promoting effective adult Bible study. Encouraged by the General Sunday School Board at Nashville, he drafted a plan which was adopted by the 1910 General Conference, thus creating the Wesley Bible Class movement in the church.

In his fifteen years with the General Sunday School Board Shackford furnished creative leadership when the time was ripe for noteworthy advances in the field of religious education. His intensely promoted teacher training program was widely regarded as the best in American Protestantism. He created a new set of text materials for use in the training schools, organized children's, youth, and adult divisions in the General Board at Nashville, and persuaded church colleges to establish chairs of religious education. Also, he was influential in the founding of the International Council of Religious Education.

For several years in the 1920's Shackford drew the fire of the fundamentalists from within and without his denomination. They correctly perceived that under his leadership the literature published by the General Sunday School Board was slanted away from what Shackford called "biblicism" and toward a more liberal interpretation of the Bible. Some annual conferences adopted resolutions demanding Shackford's resignation. Contrary to the advice of some church leaders who supported him, Shackford declined to try to appease his opponents. When he was re-elected General Secretary of the Sunday School Board by the 1926 General Conference, the opposition gradually faded.

Shackford's hymn, "O Thou Who Art the Shepherd," is included in the 1964 edition of *The Methodist Hymnal*. He published three books: *The Program of the Christian Religion,* 1917; *Education in the Christian Religion,* 1931; and *Jesus and Social Redemption,* 1940. He died Oct. 15, 1969, and was buried at Waynesville, N. C.

Elmore Brown, *The Struggle for Trained Leaders, the Story of John W. Shackford's Early Efforts to Provide Trained Teachers in the Church.* Nashville: Parthenon Press, 1966.

ALBEA GODBOLD

SHADFORD, GEORGE (1739-1816), was born near Kirton in Lindsey, Lincolnshire, on Jan. 19, 1739. He was the son of a shopkeeper, and as a youth joined the militia. Brought up an Anglican, he was much troubled about his spiritual life, was impressed by Methodist preaching, and converted in a farmhouse service in May 1762. He began to preach in the Epworth Circuit, and JOHN WESLEY asked him to become an itinerant in 1768. At the LEEDS Conference of 1772 he heard Captain THOMAS WEBB exhort the preachers to volunteer for service in America;

GEORGE SHADFORD

he and THOMAS RANKIN were impressed and offered to go. At the end of March 1773, John Wesley wrote to him: "The time is arrived for you to embark for America. You must go down to Bristol, where you will meet with Thomas Rankin, Captain Webb, and his wife. I let you loose, George, on the great continent of America. Publish your message in the open face of the sun, and do all the good you can." (*Letters,* vol. vi, p. 23.)

He travelled widely in America, preaching in NEW YORK, PHILADELPHIA and the southern states. When the War of Independence began, he decided that he must return to England, saying to Asbury, "I may have a call to go, and you to stay." He had done a great work in America, and on his return was sent to Epworth in 1778. John Wesley admired him, and he was one of the preachers named in the DEED OF DECLARATION. He superannuated in 1791, and lived for many years in Frome, in Somerset, where he died on March 11, 1816.

G. E. LONG

SHAFFER, CORNELIUS THADDEUS (1847-1919), American bishop of the A.M.E. CHURCH, was born in Troy, Ohio, on Jan. 3, 1847. He was a graduate of Berea College in KENTUCKY and held an M.D. from Jefferson Medical College in PHILADELPHIA, Pa. Shaffer was converted in 1860, licensed to preach in 1867, admitted into the Kentucky Annual Conference in 1870, ordained a DEACON in 1872 and an ELDER in 1874. He was a pastor and presiding elder in Kentucky, OHIO, NEW YORK and PENNSYLVANIA, and a General Officer (First Secretary-Treasurer of the Church Extension Society) during 1892-1900, before being elected bishop in 1900. He served in LIBERIA, West Africa, and in the western and southwestern United States. In his day he was the only bishop in the denomination who was also a practicing physician.

R. R. Wright, *The Bishops.* 1963.   GRANT SHOCKLEY

SHAFI, ELIJAH DANIEL MOHAMMAD (1906-1965) and **WINNIE M. JOHN** (1906-1965). Shafi was born Aug. 14, 1906, at Ludhiana (now East Punjab, INDIA) in a Muslim Sunni family. His mother was a close friend of Edith Brown, a greatly loved missionary in the Ludhiana Christian Medical College. An earnest search for peace led him to Daniel, a Christian "Sadhu" (an itinerant evangelist). Elijah added Daniel to his own name, and wandered far and wide in India till Daniel died. Then Shafi went to the United Presbyterian Seminary in Gujranwala, Punjab (now Pakistan), graduating in 1929. He was ordained in 1932, and married Winnie M. John on Oct. 3, 1933.

From 1932 to 1942 he was in charge of the home for Muslim converts in Lahore, known as St. Andrews Brotherhood, supported by a group of Lahore Christians. From 1942 to 1962 he was pastor of Lahore Central Methodist Church, during six years of which time he was also Superintendent of Lahore District. In 1962 he was sent to Drigh Road Church, Karachi, as pastor of the Church and for part of the time also Superintendent of the Karachi District; for the last two years he was made full-time Superintendent. On Dec. 22, 1965, returning to Karachi in a car, a motor truck wrecked the car in a head-on collision, killing four of the occupants—Elijah, Winnie and her two relatives.

Elijah was scrupulously honest, courageous in upholding the right, candid in expressing his opinions. He was ministerial delegate to the GENERAL CONFERENCE of 1956. That year he had one semester study time in Union Seminary, New York City. In 1961-2 a year's study in the London College of Bible and Missions, CANADA, earned for him the degree of B.R.E.

Winnie M. John, born Jan. 22, 1906, taught in Queen Mary's School, Lahore, for thirty-two years, being head of the Primary Department the last few years. She retired before he was transferred, and accompanied him to Karachi. They had five sons. Although having a full teaching load in Queen Mary's and supervising home activities, she was indefatigable in church activities, superintending district village schools, teaching a Sunday school class, pushing the adult literacy program, and president of the W.S.C.S. Both Elijah and Winnie were delegates to the CENTRAL CONFERENCE of 1956 in LUCKNOW. Both were also representatives of the Karachi Conference to the Methodist Consultation in Port Dickson, MALAYA in 1963. She was expecting to attend the Assembly in London in 1966 of the WORLD FEDERATION OF METHODIST WOMEN. Her keen, active mind made her a leader in group discussions. Her winsome, clear speaking was persuasive. She was a devoted wife, a faithful efficient mother, an ardent worker for the Church, a devoted servant of her Lord.

CLEMENT D. ROCKEY

SHAH, YAQUB, an early minister in INDIA, was converted at Shahjahanpur at the age of eighteen. He was then totally illiterate, and almost every conceivable external obstacle to progress was piled up on the road before him. But he had a good mind and a strong body and, overcoming all obstacles, became a minister of the Methodist Church and an unusually successful pastor and evangelist. Two of his sons became ministers, one being a college graduate. A grandson, ALFRED J. SHAW, became a bishop of The United Methodist Church.

J. WASKOM PICKETT

SHANGHAI, China. **Moore Memorial Methodist Church,** the largest church of the denomination in CHINA, was named for a little girl whose parents gave as a memorial to her the first contribution of funds. It was for many years the center of M.E. Church, South, ministry in Shanghai.

In 1946, when SIDNEY R. ANDERSON was its last missionary director, Moore Church had 1,500 members; and the Sunday school enrolled 700 pupils in seven departments. It had a day school of 200 from the poorest sections of the city; and its seven-day-a-week program included a nursery school, a Tuesday evening Bible class, a Thursday evening Mandarin class, a summer vacation Bible school, a school for teaching literacy, summer camps and conferences, a young women's volunteer band, physical education classes, and other educational and service organizations. Built "like a Gothic church of an American city," Moore Church was considered the largest and most diversified church in the Far East. When Shanghai was taken over by the Japanese in 1941, most of the church's ministries were continued under Chinese leadership. After 1949, when the Communist government was established, the church was able to maintain some of its activities, at least until the Red Guard "cultural revolution" in 1966, when according to reports all religious activities were banned.

W. W. REID

SHANGLE, H. S. (1856-1951), American preacher of the M.E. Church, South and noted leader in the state of OREGON, was born in VIRGINIA. He grew up in east Tennessee, was educated in private schools and VANDERBILT UNIVERSITY. He joined the SOUTHWEST MISSOURI CONFERENCE of his denomination in 1882. He was married to the youngest daughter of Rev. F. M. Paine at Altus, Ark., in 1884 and transferred to Oregon in 1890, being stationed at Albany.

In the Northwest, Shangle served churches in PORTLAND, SPOKANE, and Walla Walla, was twenty-five years a presiding elder and eight years a college president. He served as conference secretary of education, and conference missionary secretary.

Shangle was five times elected to GENERAL CONFERENCE. After his retirement in 1938 he wrote a short history of the M.E. Church, South, in Oregon.

With Methodist Union in 1939, Shangle became a member of the OREGON CONFERENCE of The Methodist Church. He died in Portland, Aug. 6, 1951.

Minutes of the Oregon Conference.
H. S. Shangle, *Historical Sketch of the Methodist Episcopal Church, South in Oregon: 1858-1939* N.p., n.d.

ERLE HOWELL

SHANNON, MARY ESTELLE (1880-   ), was principal of the ISABELLA THOBURN COLLEGE in LUCKNOW, 1925-39. She was born April 6, 1880, in Winfield, Iowa, was educated through high school in the academy of Cooper College, Moundsville, Mo., and to the B.A. degree level at BAKER UNIVERSITY, Baldwin, Kan. She taught for six years in Cooper Academy, and for two years in public schools in MISSOURI.

In 1909, she went to BURMA as a missionary of the Methodist WOMAN'S FOREIGN MISSIONARY SOCIETY. There she served as principal of the Methodist Girls' High School until 1923, when she proceeded on furlough. In 1924, she obtained a Master's degree from BOSTON UNIVERSITY and was elected principal of the Woman's College, Lucknow. She was the fifth successive American Methodist to hold that office, and had it longer than any previous incumbent. Throughout her administration the college moved forward steadily, acquiring new buildings and equipment, strengthening its faculty, developing new service programs, and training Indian women. She was tall, handsome, dignified, and reserved, but gracious.

Baker University granted her the honorary LL.D. degree, and the government of India awarded her the Kaiser-i-Hind gold medal for distinguished public service. She retired from the college principalship in 1939 and from work as a Methodist missionary in 1941, but from her home in TOPEKA, Kan., she continued to serve the church in many capacities for a decade and a half. She now lives in the home for retired missionaries at Robincroft, PASADENA, Calif.

M. A. Dimmitt, *Isabella Thoburn College.* 1933.
J. N. Hollister, *Southern Asia.* 1956.   J. WASKOM PICKETT

SHANNON, PAUL E. V. (1898-1957), American pastor, conference superintendent, and bishop of the E.U.B. Church, was born March 25, 1898, in Mountville, Pa., to Rev. and Mrs. A. L. Shannon, both of whom died when Paul was a young boy. After graduating from LEBANON VALLEY COLLEGE (A.B. 1918), he continued his studies in Bonebrake (now UNITED) THEOLOGICAL SEMINARY, graduating with the B.D. degree. In 1937 he was honored with the D.D. degree by Lebanon Valley College.

He was married in 1919 to Josephine S. Mathias (1896-1931), and they became the parents of two children. Shannon's second marriage was to Katherine Higgins in 1932. Two children were born to this union.

Pastorates served by Shannon included: Hillsdale-Falmouth, Pa.; Veedersburg, Ind.; Fairview, Dayton, O.; Liberty Heights, BALTIMORE, Md.; Dallastown, Pa.; and First Church, YORK, Pa. Between pastorates he served as Field Representative of Bonebrake (United) Theological Seminary. From his York pastorate (1935-1948) he was elected to the superintendency of the E.U.B. PENNSYLVANIA CONFERENCE, a position he held with distinction. In connection with his pastorates and administrative positions he served on many denominational and interdenominational boards, as well as with civic groups. Fraternally he was a Royal Arch and Knight Templar Mason.

Upon the death of Bishop DAVID T. GREGORY in 1957, Shannon was chosen by mail ballot to the office of bishop, with the East Central District as his diocese.

Following his presiding over the sessions of WESTERN PENNSYLVANIA CONFERENCE in 1957, Bishop Shannon returned to his home in York, Pa., to prepare for moving to the center of his new assignment. While conducting a dedicatory service during this interim he was fatally stricken, his death occurring several days later, May 23, 1957. Interment was in the Home Cemetery, Dallastown, Pa.

Journal of the General Conference, EUB, 1958.
Minutes of the Pennsylvania Conference, EUB, 1957.
PAUL E. HOLDCRAFT

SHAPLAND, RICHARD HENRY BOWDEN (1877-1937), British Methodist minister, entered the ministry of the UNITED METHODIST FREE CHURCHES in 1900, a few years before the denomination became part of the amalgamated UNITED METHODIST CHURCH of Britain. He gained a great reputation as a pastor and a deeply thoughtful preacher, especially during fourteen years at Burton-on-Trent, and in 1929 was elected President of the United Methodist Church. He was much admired in the wider church after METHODIST UNION in 1932, but failing health compelled

his retirement in 1935, followed by his death in his sixtieth year.

FRANK BAKER

SHARON, MISSISSIPPI, U.S.A., the county seat of Madison County, was in early days one of the most influential small communities in the State so far as Methodism was concerned. The Sharon Methodist Church, which gave its name to the community, was established in 1835, when Orsamus L. Nash was presiding elder of the Choctaw District and John Ira Ellis Byrd was pastor of the Madison Circuit. Dr. Birdsong Minter, a physician and local preacher, deeded to the church sixty-two acres of land for a church, cemetery, parsonage and district parsonage. This was the second Methodist parsonage in MISSISSIPPI and the first district parsonage. The town was incorporated in 1838.

Sharon Female College was established in 1837 as a union enterprise of several denominations, but by 1854 it had become a Methodist institution. Madison College was established as a school for boys in 1851 by Thomas C. Thornton, who was in his early ministry pastor of LOVELY LANE in BALTIMORE, MARYLAND. Both schools continued until some years after the Civil War. JAMES W. LAMBUTH and Bishop CHARLES B. GALLOWAY both taught in Madison College, the former shortly before going to CHINA as a missionary in 1854.

Many eminent Methodists are buried in the Sharon cemetery, including Dr. Thornton and the parents of Dr. J. M. Sullivan of MILLSAPS COLLEGE, who was for twenty-five years lay leader of the MISSISSIPPI CONFERENCE.

The present Sharon church was dedicated on May 15, 1892, by Warren C. Black. Church school rooms were added in 1951. The membership is small but the workers carry on the tradition of their fathers.

Early Methodist preachers at Sharon, in addition to J. I. E. Byrd, include WILLIAM H. WATKINS, Andrew T. M. Fly, Washington Ford, P. B. Bailey, Bradford Frazee, James Maclennan, Asbury Davidson, Frances H. McShann, J. B. Daughtry, James H. Laney, JOHN P. RICHMOND, Henderson H. Montgomery, George C. Light, James H. Merrill, Josiah M. Pugh, William M. Curtiss, and Samuel W. Speer, all these before the Civil War.

W. B. Jones, *Mississippi Conference.* 1951.   J. B. CAIN

SHAW, ALEXANDER PRESTON (1879-1966), was born in Abbeville, Miss., the fourth child among seven. Both his father, Duncan Preston Shaw, and his mother, Maria Petty Shaw, were former slaves and fully grown at the time of Emancipation. He was reared in a Christian home and was taught to observe the Christian virtues of honesty, truth and self-reliance and to be trustworthy at all times.

He attended, in his early boyhood, classes taught in church buildings. The equipment and instruction were both inadequate but by diligent study, under the most difficult circumstances, he obtained a primary and some grammar school training. In 1893 he entered RUST COLLEGE in the fifth grade, Rust having departments from the fifth grade through college, and here he received his A.B. degree in 1902. His professional training was received at GAMMON THEOLOGICAL SEMINARY in ATLANTA, where he received his B.D. degree in 1906. He did further study in theology at BOSTON UNIVERSITY SCHOOL OF THEOLOGY. Later in his career, Boston University gave him the honorary D.D. degree. Gammon Seminary also conferred an honorary degree upon him.

It was while at Gammon that he met Lottye B. Simon, a member of an outstanding Atlanta family, whom he married. From this union there were three sons and three daughters.

Young Shaw early felt the call to preach but hesitated to answer the call, feeling that a father and brother, Beverly, in the ministry sufficed, especially as both seemed unusually gifted. But the death of his favorite sister set him to thinking seriously about this call. He often talked about the experience that brought about his decision to preach. It seemed that this song came into his mind during the night, "Tell It Out Among the People That the Lord Is King." "He felt," he said, "that he must be a part of that telling." He was ordained a deacon at Boston University School of Theology in 1907 by Bishop GOOD-SELL and an elder at Warren Methodist Church, PITTS-BURGH, 1910, by Bishop WARREN.

He began his public career as pastor in the WASHING-TON ANNUAL CONFERENCE. He became a full member in 1908 and served several appointments, one of which was at Winchester, Va., where the parsonage was a one and a half story building. Shaw, being six feet four inches tall, was unable to stand erect in any room on the second floor. He was transferred, after a few years, to the LITTLE ROCK CONFERENCE and served for two years as the minister of Wesley Church, LITTLE ROCK, where much of his congregation was made up of students of PHILANDER SMITH COLLEGE. After two very successful years, he was transferred to the CALIFORNIA CONFERENCE and stationed at Wesley Church, LOS ANGELES, where he had a glorious pastorate for fourteen years. In 1928 he was elected editor of the *Southwestern Advocate* with office in NEW OR-LEANS. He served very successfully in this office for eight years. In 1936 he was elected a bishop in the M. E. Church at GENERAL CONFERENCE meeting at Columbus, Ohio. He was assigned to New Orleans area where he served for one quadrennium. In 1940 he was transferred to the BALTIMORE area where he served in an outstanding way, particularly in the field of evangelism and liquidation of mortgages on churches. He retired in 1952 but was called back into service in 1953 at the death of Bishop R. N. BROOKS and served the New Orleans area until 1956.

He wrote frequently and helpfully. Among his writings are: *Christianizing Race Relations*, 1928; *Thy Kingdom Come*—four sermons published in a brochure in 1944; a sermon, *Strength Measured by Weakness* in the *American Pulpit Series*, published by Abingdon, 1946; and two brochures, *The Spirit of Abraham Lincoln* and *What Must the Negro Do To Be Saved*. In the latter brochure he emphasized the fact that he must himself achieve and prove himself taking advantage of available opportunities; and not to depend upon special concessions. His position in this article was much commented upon. This last was published as an article in *Religion In Life*.

He was a man filled with "the milk of human kindness." He could sense the hurt in the human heart and there was always the sympathetic response. In the College of Bishops, as well as in the COUNCIL OF BISHOPS, he was one of the Nestors. Bishop Shaw died March 7, 1966, was buried March 12, 1966, following services in Holman Church, Los Angeles.

EDGAR A. LOVE

A. J. SHAW

SHAW, ALFRED JACOB (1906-   ), is the eighth bishop elected by the CENTRAL CONFERENCE OF SOUTHERN ASIA. His election took place on January 1, 1965. He is a third-generation Christian and a third-generation Methodist minister.

Bishop Shaw was born at Unao, Uttar Pradesh, INDIA, Oct. 1, 1906. His father, Samuel Jacob Shaw, was the preacher-in-charge of the Unao Circuit near North India's industrial metropolis of Kanpur; his mother was Halina (Solomon). His undergraduate studies were in the LUCK-NOW CHRISTIAN COLLEGE. He obtained the M.A. degree from Lucknow University and was made a Licentiate of Teaching by the University of Allahabad. He was ordained DEACON in 1944 and ELDER in 1947 in the LUCKNOW ANNUAL CONFERENCE.

He married Evelyn Michael on April 27, 1934, and their children were Alfred Inderkumar, Renuka Evelyn (dec. 1959), and Samuel Ajitkumar.

He was an instructor in Lucknow Christian College and warden of the largest hostel (1932-1948) and principal of the Centennial Higher Secondary School (associated with the Lucknow Christian College) from 1949 to 1957. From 1946 to 1948, and from 1950 to 1962, he edited the *Indian Witness*, official English language weekly of the Methodist Church in India. In 1957 he became pastor of Central Methodist Church in Lucknow, one of the most influential Methodist churches in India. In 1962 he was made secretary of the Central Conference Council of Christian Education. Like three previous bishops elected from positions in Lucknow, he was assigned to the BOM-BAY area.

Journals of the Lucknow Conference and the Central Conference of Southern Asia.
Who's Who in the Methodist Church, 1966.

J. WASKOM PICKETT

SHAW, ANNA HOWARD (1847-1919), ordained American M.P. minister, lecturer for the Woman's Christian Temperance Union, physician, and vigorous national leader in the woman suffrage movement, was born in Newcastle-on-Tyne, England, on Feb. 14, 1847. She came to the United States as a child and spent her early years on the MICHIGAN frontier. At the age of twenty-four she was converted to Methodism, and despite family opposition decided to become a minister, an almost unheard of vocation for women in that period. She worked her way through ALBION COLLEGE, where she graduated in 1875, and through BOSTON UNIVERSITY THEOLOGICAL SEMINARY where she was the only woman in her class, and where, although a licensed preacher, she was denied the financial exemptions accorded male students who also were licensed preachers. She then served as pastor of two MASSACHUSETTS parishes in the M.E. Church, but when that denomination refused to ordain her, Anna Shaw sought ordination in the M.P. Church, and on Oct. 12, 1880, became the first woman to be ordained in that denomination. Appalled by the sickness she observed in the BOSTON slums, she studied medicine at BOSTON UNIVERSITY and received an M.D. degree in 1885. She became a devoted friend of Susan B. Anthony and an active supporter of the woman's suffrage movement, to which cause she devoted her great oratorical powers. Her enthusiasm for this cause may be seen in the fact that during a two-week period in 1892 she traveled 7,000 miles and gave twenty lectures. In 1902 she succeeded Carrie Chapman Catt as president of the National American Woman Suffrage Association. She retired from this position in 1915, and during World War I served as chairman of the Women's Committee of the Council of National Defense.

Dr. Shaw was noted for her keen sense of humor. In a speech given in RALEIGH, N. C., in 1915, she declared: "God had to make some women foolish to match the men." Her speeches stressed the democracy of Christianity and argued that woman's "highest glory was not motherhood but womanhood." She was considered by Mrs. Catt and Nettie Rogers Shuler as a "master orator" who "stood unchallenged throughout her career as the greatest orator among women the world has ever known." She was the author of *The Story of a Pioneer* which was published in 1915.

When, in 1919, the Nineteenth Amendment to the American Constitution was passed, and women were urged to register and vote in the forthcoming elections, much of the credit for the successful completion of the woman suffrage movement could be traced to the dynamic influence of Dr. Shaw.

William N. Brigance and Marie Hochmuth, *History and Criticism of American Public Address*. New York, 1955-60.
Carrie Chapman Catt and Nettie R. Shuler, *Woman Suffrage and Politics*. New York, 1926.
Aileen S. Kraditor, *The Ideas of the Woman Suffrage Movement, 1890-1920*. New York, 1965.
National Cyclopaedia of American Biography. New York, 1917.
Elizabeth Taylor, "The Woman Suffrage Movement in North Carolina," *The North Carolina Historical Review*, January and April 1961.   RALPH HARDEE RIVES

SHAW, BARNABAS (1788-1857), pioneer Wesleyan Methodist missionary in southern Africa, was born near HULL in Yorkshire, England, on April 12, 1788, and was the son of a yeoman farmer, Thomas Shaw. The Missionary Committee sent Barnabas Shaw to the Cape of Good Hope in 1816, in response to an appeal from Methodist soldiers stationed in the colony. Earlier attempts to place a minister at the Cape had been thwarted by opposition from the authorities and Shaw was forbidden to preach. He also met with opposition from the clergy of the Anglican and Dutch Reformed Churches. But his own vocation was always primarily a missionary one and he determined to go northwards, beyond the boundaries of the colony, into Namaqualand. Leaving the Cape in September 1816, he and his wife established the first Methodist mission

BARNABAS SHAW

station in southern Africa at Leliefontein (Lilyfountain) in Namaqualand.

The Namaquas were a Hottentot people, primitive and simple. The mission station was cut off from Cape Town by mountains and rough, wild country. Shaw and his wife were both seriously ill soon after their arrival and one of their children died. But in spite of the hardships and with the help of a "native assistant," Jacob Links, the mission was soon firmly established.

Shaw became, as the number of Methodist ministers and missionaries increased, virtually a general superintendent or elder statesman of South African missions. He encouraged and directed the expansion of missionary work. He was for a long period chairman of the district. He was constantly advising the Missionary Committee in England on policy, strategy and stationing. He was a firm believer in discipline, critical of London Missionary Society men because they seemed to him too casual and undisciplined, and was often criticized himself by other Methodist missionaries as something of a tyrant.

So ardent was Shaw for the expansion of missions in the West that there was considerable tension, at one time, between himself and his namesake, WILLIAM SHAW, in the eastern Cape. Barnabas Shaw maintained that his colleague was an impractical visionary, expanding missions in the East at a foolish and improvident rate, and using men and money that might have been better employed in extending the Namaqua mission.

On his removal to the Cape in 1826 Shaw ministered chiefly in the village of Wynberg, now a suburb of Cape Town. He continued to concern himself with the colored people and with missions to the heathen. His heart was, perhaps, still in the north and with the frontier missions and he continued to advise the "home" committee on planning and expansion. Administrative and financial matters, nevertheless, occupied a good deal of his time.

In 1837 Shaw returned to England on account of his health and the education of his children, but in 1843 he was again back at the Cape, bringing with him his son, B. J. Shaw, to join him in the work. This time he was stationed at Stellenbosch, some little way inland from Cape Town. He seems rapidly to have become ill and infirm, but he retained much of his vigor of mind and was still full of plans for extending the work of the Church. In emergencies Shaw returned to Cape Town, took over control of the district, and showed himself able still to display a remarkable grasp of affairs. But his powers were plainly failing. He retired in 1854 and died on June 21, 1857.

Dictionary of South African Biography.
L. A. Hewson, *South Africa.* 1950.
J. Du Plessis, *A History of Christian Missions in South Africa.* London, 1911 (reprint, Cape Town, 1965).
B. Shaw, *South Africa.* 1841.
J. Whiteside, *South Africa.* 1906.
Celia Sadler, ed., *Never a Young Man—Extracts from the Letters and Journals of the Rev. William Shaw.* Cape Town, 1967.   P. B. HINCHLIFF

SHAW, HARRY (1872-1952), American layman, was born Feb. 15, 1872, the son of Joshua and Emily West Shaw. He attended Fairmont State College and West Virginia University, where he received B.A. and LL.B. degrees. Admitted to the bar in Marion County, W. Va., he was appointed Judge of the Circuit Court from 1928-1937. He served as president of the Board of Education of his district, as a member of the City Council of Fairmont, as member of the House of Delegates of WEST VIRGINIA, and as a member of the Draft Board in both World Wars.

As a churchman he was elected to the GENERAL CONFERENCE of the M. P. Church from 1912-1936, the UNITING CONFERENCE of 1939, and the General Conference of The Methodist Church in 1940. He was trustee of the WEST VIRGINIA CONFERENCE, served on the Legal Committee of the Uniting Conference, was a delegate to, and member of the Executive Committee of the ECUMENICAL METHODIST CONFERENCE, 1921 and 1931, and a member of the Ecumenical Methodist Council, Western Section. Shaw died in October, 1952, and was buried in Fairmont, W. Va.

FRANK L. SHAFFER

HERBERT BELL SHAW

SHAW, HERBERT BELL (1908-   ), American bishop of the A.M.E. ZION CHURCH, born at Wilmington, N.C., the son of John Henry and Lummie Virginia (Hodges) Shaw.

He was converted at St. Luke Church, Wilmington, N. C., June 13, 1920. He preached his trial sermon on July 12, 1927, was ordained DEACON, May 10, 1928, in Washington, D. C. and an ELDER, Nov. 15, 1930. He served the following churches: Bowen's Chapel, St. Andrews, Price Memorial in NORTH CAROLINA. He was elected and consecrated a bishop by the General Conference of his church, May 1952, at BROOKLYN, N. Y., and since has had charge of the eastern North Carolina area and SOUTH CAROLINA, as well as the Bahamas.

He holds the B.A., B.D., and D.D. degrees. He married Sept. 1, 1931. He has two children: John Herbert and Maria A. He has served as chairman of the Committee on Social Service and Harriet Tubman Foundation; Vice President, WORLD METHODIST COUNCIL, and was a delegate to the World Methodist Conference, OSLO, Norway; LAKE JUNALUSKA, N. C.; and LONDON, England.

Minutes of the General Conference, AMEZ, 1952.

DAVID H. BRADLEY

SHAW, JAMES, an Englishman who came to INDIA with the army and was serving as a Scripture reader when he met and heard WILLIAM TAYLOR. He decided promptly to become a Methodist. At the first QUARTERLY CONFERENCE in BOMBAY he applied for and was given a local preacher's license. He resigned his army appointment to become a full-time itinerant minister. He was ordained on Jan. 30, 1874, both as DEACON and ELDER, by Bishop M. C. HARRIS, who had been deputed by the COUNCIL OF BISHOPS as official visitor to India that year. Shaw served churches in Bangalore, HYDERABAD, Lahore, and Quetta, and assisted many of his fellow ministers in revival services.

J. N. Hollister, *Southern Asia.* 1956.
J. E. Scott, *Southern Asia.* 1906.   J. WASKOM PICKETT

SHAW, JOHN KNOX (1800-1858), American preacher and founder of the PENNINGTON SCHOOL (Seminary) at Pennington, N. J., was born in the town of Newton-Hamilton in the south of County Armagh, IRELAND, April 10, 1800. His parents were Presbyterian.

John was brought to America in his mother's arms. After a six week's voyage they landed in Portsmouth, N. H., and went to Washington, Cambridge Co., N. Y., where the elder Shaw purchased a farm to care for his wife and five children. The children studied in country schools which were supplemented by private tutors. They seem to have been specially solicitous on behalf of John for whom they hoped for a college education, but this did not come to pass.

In his sixteenth year he left home "to seek his fortune." He was modestly successful at selling books but in seven months returned home where an attack of remittent fever brought him to death's door. Shaw always believed that his life was prolonged in answer to the "fervent, effectual prayer" of his mother.

In a little while he accepted the position of teacher at White Plains, N. Y., where he came in contact with the Methodists and joined the church. When he finished his engagement he went to Bloomfield, N. J., to take a like position. He united with the Methodist society in nearby Belleville and soon moved from CLASS LEADER to EXHORTER and in 1824 to LOCAL PREACHER. On April 14, 1925, at the PHILADELPHIA CONFERENCE, he was received on trial and was appointed to Hamburg (N.J.) Circuit. In succeeding years he served the following charges: Asbury Circuit, Paterson, Essex Circuit, Staten Island Circuit, New Providence Circuit, Long Branch Circuit, Pennington, Swedesboro Circuit, Camden, Mount Holly and Burlington. He was presiding elder of the Camden District, 1845-48 and of the Trenton District, 1849-52. Other churches that followed were: Franklin Street, Newark, Morristown and Warren Street, Newark.

It was while John Knox Shaw was serving the church at Pennington that the Annual Conference took action to found an academy. The committee proposed that the locality successful in raising the most money for the enterprise should receive the school. Shaw took this as a great challenge and canvassed the state, gathering together a sum of $5,000. The conference voted to found the school and it was incorporated as the Pennington Seminary in 1839. John Knox Shaw was in fact the real founder, though he never served officially at the school. His good works are memorialized in the beautiful Shaw Memorial Chapel at what is now The Pennington School.

In 1857 he went to Warren Street Church, Newark, where he found a new society of seventy members and a church edifice in the process of erection. The funds of the trustees were exhausted; the congregation had already given liberally. So day by day he plodded the streets soliciting funds. The drain on his strength brought back his old malady and he died on Oct. 4, 1858. His funeral was the first service in that sacred edifice which had cost him his life to erect. He was laid to rest in Evergreen Cemetery, Morristown, N. J.

CHARLES R. SMYTH

WILLIAM SHAW

SHAW, WILLIAM (1798-1872), Wesleyan missionary in SOUTH AFRICA, was born in Glasgow, SCOTLAND, on Dec. 8, 1798. In 1819 he was appointed chaplain to the Sephton Party of British Settlers and accepted as a missionary by the Wesleyan METHODIST MISSIONARY SOCIETY. He settled at Salem, near Grahamstown, Cape Colony, in July 1820. Although his official responsibility was limited to his own party, Shaw became pastor to the entire settlement which was almost without clergymen. He travelled widely establishing societies and Sunday schools, recruiting LOCAL PREACHERS and caring impartially for members of all denominations. Under his supervision, an increasing

staff of Wesleyan ministers established societies in nearly every village in the Eastern Province. By 1860 there were twenty-two ministers and forty-four European chapels, besides a considerable work among the Cape Colored and Africans.

Within a year of his arrival at Salem, Shaw was planning a chain of missions among the tribes between the colonial frontier and Natal. His aim was to establish stations about thirty miles apart, so that assistance and companionship would be near at hand, and to place missionaries with all the major chiefs. The main features of the scheme were realized within a decade: Wesleyville was established in 1823; by 1830 there were six missions; and in subsequent years the number was further increased. As a result of warfare, financial stringency, a shortage of manpower and the iron grip of tribalism, immediate results were less grandiose than the vision. But strategically the scheme was a great success and laid the foundations of the strong Methodist work which later developed in the Transkei.

Less successful were Shaw's plans for education. His proposal for a teacher training center—the Watson Institution—was approved in 1834. However, instead of concentrating upon a central school, it was decided in 1838 to open branches on every mission. This decentralization combined with the lack of funds and trained staff to doom the venture, and many years were to pass before the Wesleyans had an efficient educational programme. Nevertheless, Shaw encouraged the Colonial Government to provide for African education, and cooperated fully with Governor Sir George Grey who established four industrial schools on Wesleyan stations in 1855.

After a visit to England between 1833 and 1837, Shaw returned as General Superintendent of Wesleyan Missions in South East Africa. This brought him added responsibilities in the Bechuana District (Orange Free State) and, after 1842, in Natal. Constant travel and the burden of oversight and administration eventually undermined his health.

A missionary of Shaw's stature could not avoid a measure of political involvement. His relationships with successive governors and local officials were generally cordial, and he often approached them about policy on the frontier and beyond. He occupied a unique position in that he was a highly-respected member of the settler community and the friend and adviser of several African chiefs. This gave him a breadth of outlook and sympathy which was denied either the humanitarian or the settler extremists. His views are open to criticism in detail but were generally characterized by a desire to be just to all parties. The exact extent of his influence in government circles is difficult to assess but it was not inconsiderable.

After the death of his first wife (Ann Maw—married Dec. 31, 1817; died July 6, 1854), Shaw was taken seriously ill. He returned to England in 1856 and married a widow, Mrs. Ogle, on March 12, 1857. It was his desire to return in 1860 and to inaugurate a South African Conference, but the missionary committee rejected his proposals. He therefore settled in England where he served as Chairman of the Bristol and York Districts and was elected President of CONFERENCE in 1865. After his retirement in 1869 he edited The Watchman and served on the missionary and education committees of the Conference. He died in London on Dec. 4, 1872.

Vision, ability and evangelical zeal blended in William

Shaw to produce a man who has every right to be termed the Father of South African Methodism.

W. B. Boyce, *Memoir of the Rev. W. Shaw.* London, 1874.
Dictionary of South African Biography.
Journal of the Methodist Historical Society of South Africa, August 1954, March 1955, October 1960, April 1961.
W. Shaw, *Story of My Mission.* 1872.
J. Whiteside, *South Africa.* 1906.   D. G. L. CRAGG

SHAW, WILLIAM E. (1869-1947), American pastor, missions executive and college president, was born at Preston, Minn. He was educated for his life work at Moore's Hill College, Indiana, and at GARRETT BIBLICAL INSTITUTE. From 1889 to 1896 he was an instructor at UNION COLLEGE, Kentucky, serving also for a time as vice-president. Joining the CENTRAL ILLINOIS CONFERENCE, he served pastorates until 1932, when he became PEORIA district superintendent. He had been pastor for twenty-two years of First Church, Peoria, the largest in membership in the conference and in the NORTH CENTRAL JURISDICTION, leading the church in building their large new edifice.

Shaw was a member of the commission which organized the Korean Methodist Church in 1930. The 1936 GENERAL CONFERENCE (ME) elected him Executive Secretary of the Board of Foreign MISSIONS. He was a delegate to each General Conference from 1916 to 1940. He was a valued member of the boards of Methodist Hospital, Peoria; WESLEY FOUNDATION, University of Illinois; and ILLINOIS WESLEYAN UNIVERSITY, serving over thirty years on each. Wesleyan called him to be its president in 1940 when it launched a ten-year expansion program. His ability to lead and inspire others helped overcome an emergency caused by destruction of the main building by fire in 1943. The new academic building bears his name. Shaw died on the way to the train, coming home from an alumni meeting in Chicago, the only president to die while in office.

Journal of the Illinois Conference, 1947.
Elmo Scott Watson, *The Illinois Wesleyan Story, 1850-1950.* Bloomington, 1950.   HENRY G. NYLIN

SHAW, WILLIAM EARL (1890-1967), missionary and U.S. Army CHAPLAIN in KOREA, was born in CHICAGO, Ill., Aug. 22, 1890. He graduated from OHIO WESLEYAN, 1916, Columbia University, M.A. 1921, BOSTON UNIVERSITY SCHOOL OF THEOLOGY, 1927. He was awarded the honorary D.D. degree by Ohio Wesleyan in 1950. He served as a U.S. Army chaplain in Europe in 1918.

As missionary in Korea 1921-1941, he served as district superintendent and for a time concurrently as mission treasurer. He was Director of Religious Activities, Ohio Wesleyan University, 1942-1945, missionary to the PHILIPPINES, 1945-1947, and missionary to Korea 1947-1961, where he served in administration, and as director of the Methodist Preachers Refresher Institute at Taejon and as Professor of New Testament in the Taejon Methodist Seminary.

After the Communist invasion of June 1950, he served for one year as U.S. Army Chaplain, acting as liaison with the Republic of Korea Armed Forces and was instrumental in organizing the Korean Chaplain's Corps. An only son William Hamilton Shaw, USNR, who also volunteered for service in Korea, was a member of the MacArthur landing party at Inchon, and was killed near SEOUL, September

1950. Shaw retired in 1961, and died on Oct. 5, 1967, in Los Altos, Calif. Inurnment was beside the grave of his son in the Foreign Cemetery, Seoul, Korea.

CHARLES A. SAUER

SHAWBURY INSTITUTION, in the Tsitsa River Valley, Transkei, SOUTH AFRICA, forms part of a mission which was located on its present site by W. H. Garner in 1843. The first step was taken in its development as an educational center when C. White built a school room in 1858. In 1878 W. S. Davis opened a Training Institution for girls, while a day school for boys also developed gradually. The work suffered a great setback as a result of the Mpondomise Rebellion in 1880 but the years that followed witnessed encouraging progress. William Mears, who was governor of the Institution from 1906 to 1935, combined enthusiasm for education with a practical knowledge of carpentry and building and was responsible for impressive developments at the Institution and in the surrounding Circuit. He was ably assisted by Mrs. E. C. Hobden who was principal of the school for a great part of this period. Male students were admitted after the introduction of secondary education at the close of Mr. Mears' governorship, and new teacher-training courses were initiated in the time of A. H. Briggs (1939-46). The schools were taken over by the Government in 1956 in terms of the Bantu Education Act (1953) but the church has hitherto retained control of the hostels.

J. Whiteside, *South Africa.* 1906.
David Wilson, *Shawbury, the Story of a Mission, 1843-1943.* N.p., n.d.   G. MEARS

SHEAT, LAURA LOUISA BLANCHE (?-1954), NEW ZEALAND laywoman, spent her early years in Nelson, where her father, Alfred Sheat, was a local preacher and circuit official. She graduated, M.A. with honors, at Auckland University College and had a distinguished career as a secondary school teacher. She achieved her widest influence during her twenty-five years at Auckland Girls' Grammar School.

She was actively associated with the Student Christian Movement and was an honored member of the Methodist Church at Mount Albert (Auckland), to which district she retired to care for her aged mother. She died on Oct. 18, 1954.

New Zealand Methodist Times, Nov. 13, 1954.
L. R. M. GILMORE

SHEBBEAR COLLEGE, British BIBLE CHRISTIAN school, now Methodist, was founded at Prospect House, Shebbear, North Devon, by SAMUEL and MARY O'BRYAN THORNE, 1829, and adopted by the connection in 1841 to provide education for ministerial candidates and sons of itinerant preachers. Under the governorship of JAMES THORNE (1844-70) and headmastership of THOMAS RUDDLE (1864-1909), the school gained a high reputation throughout the West and produced many missionaries and men of distinction. Ruddle's Christian education was continued by John Rounsefel (1909-33), a classical scholar, greatly loved by the people. The school is still linked with circuit life through Lake Chapel services.

Richard Pyke, *The Story of Shebbear College.* London, 1953.
ALYN W. G. COURT

SHEETS (SCHUTZ), HERMAN J. (1883-1936), was one of many American missionaries from German-speaking Methodist churches who have served with zeal and devotion in INDIA. His first appointment was to Terhoot (Juzaggarpur) in Bihar in 1906. He married Grace Bills, Dec. 2, 1908. His appointments included superintendent of Ballia District (LUCKNOW CONFERENCE), 1916-18, and Bijnor District (North India Conference), 1919-22, professor of New Testament and vice-principal of Bareilly Theological Seminary, 1923-34; and professor of New Testament Interpretation in Leonard Theological College, 1934-35. He was elected principal of Leonard and installed on Nov. 5, 1935. The following August he died at Mussoorie, India. During the First World War he changed his surname from Schutz to Sheets.

He was editor of a supplement to the Methodist *Discipline* for Southern Asia and joint editor of a Bible dictionary in Hindi. He was a popular preacher in English, Hindi, Urdu, and German.

B. T. Badley, *Southern Asia.* 1931. J. WASKOM PICKETT

SHEFFEY, ROBERT AYERS (1820-1902), American evangelist and prophet of prayer, was born in Ivanhoe, Wythe County, Va. He was the son of Henry and Margaret (White) Sheffey, of a highly respected Presbyterian family.

Converted Jan. 9, 1839, in a revival meeting at Abington, Va., he joined the M.E. Church. Sheffey studied at EMORY AND HENRY COLLEGE, 1839-40. He lost no time in taking up the duties of an itinerant Methodist preacher. However, his biographer never refers to any license to preach, ordination, conference relation, or pastorate. Somewhat like John the Baptist and the eccentric LORENZO DOW, Brother Sheffey traveled as a local evangelist over fourteen counties of southwestern VIRGINIA and southern WEST VIRGINIA, known and loved by the people. He lived in the saddle and carried a sheepskin on which he knelt to pray in the woods, and almost everywhere else.

Honest, sincere, courteous, childlike, Brother Sheffey was odd, peculiar, eccentric, and unique. His success in the conversion of thousands was due to his character, love for people, and his power in prayer rather than through his sermons. However, he had a thorough knowledge of the Bible. One of his common expressions was: "If you keep the heart right and the skin clean, you won't have need for lawyers, doctors, and penitentiaries."

Several doctors once gave a young man up to die of typhoid fever. Brother Sheffey immediately began to pray for his recovery. He went to the boy's mother and advised her not to worry; the son would recover. In a very brief time the lad was well and became a leading lawyer in southwest Virginia.

Robert A. Sheffey was at home in revivals and CAMP MEETINGS, singing and praying. He hated sham. On one occasion he was present at a revival meeting with several dignified preachers where no enthusiasm had been aroused. Finally Sheffey was called on to pray. He prayed: "Lord, I am sure that the devil is here, and I want you to take him by the nape of the neck, and take him to the edge of the cliff out here and kick him off." The brethren wilted but the meeting soon became a revival with power.

Mercer County *History* says: "The Rev. Robert Sheffey, a noted divine of that time (when Athens had the first saloon in Mercer County, West Virginia), prayed that the saloon be closed and a shoe and harness shop take its place and that really happened." In 1957 Athens did not have even a beer joint but more than a majority of the adult population had college degrees.

Sheffey lived among the people and these gave him what he needed. After the death of his first wife, Elizabeth Swecker, he married Eliza W. Stafford and they had one son, Edward, who became a prominent businessman and Methodist in Lynchburg, Va. Often Brother Sheffey would be away from home a month at a time, leaving the care of his wife and son to Providence. Mrs. Sheffey never murmured at her husband's absences. Sometimes he would ride home and talk to her as in their courting days and leave for an appointment without dismounting. Edward said once: "Uncle John thinks you ought to stay home more." Father Sheffey said: "Son, Uncle John doesn't know which way the rats run."

He died in Staffordsville, Va., Aug. 30, 1902. The presiding elder said to a full house at his funeral: "No one has so projected his life on the hearts of the masses as Sheffey has in southwestern Virginia and southern West Virginia."

W. S. Barbery, *Brother Sheffey.* Privately published, Barbery, Bluefield, W. Va., n.d.
McCormick, *The Story of Mercer County.* Charleston Printing Co., 1957. JESSE A. EARL

SHEFFIELD, England. Horace Walpole once described Sheffield as "one of the foulest towns in England in the most charming situation." An appropriate description at the time, but a libel now. Sheffield, built in the valleys, where four small rivers flow into the Don (thus providing the power for the early cutlers and grinders), is the center of the English steel and cutlery industry and has always been a famous stronghold of radicalism in religion and politics.

Methodism was introduced to Sheffield in 1738 through David Taylor, who had been converted by BENJAMIN INGHAM of the Oxford HOLY CLUB. One of Taylor's early converts was JOHN BENNET, who married GRACE MURRAY. Early meetinghouses (the first was opened in Cheney Square in 1741) were wrecked by the mob, who in 1745 suspected the Methodists of Jacobite sympathies. The famous Conference hymn, "And are we yet alive," derives from one riot when CHARLES WESLEY nearly lost his life. The home of Mr. and Mrs. Woodhouse for a time had two licenses, one for the sale of drink and the other for dissenting worship. When the preacher arrived, Mrs. Woodhouse used to summon the flock by suspending a white sheet from a tree.

The early society was torn by controversy between Arminian and Calvinist, which EDWARD PERRONET, the first superintendent, appointed in 1749, failed to control. However, as his circuit reached from Huddersfield to Leicester this is not surprising. The society was subsequently placed under THOMAS OLIVERS, and he secured in 1757 the erection of the Mulberry Street Meeting House, which served as headquarters of the small society for twenty-five years. Sarah Moore was one of the early members of a chapel still torn by dissensions, which were exacerbated by Thomas Bryant, an itinerant who claimed ordination from the wandering Greek bishop ERASMUS. Bryant took half the society with him to Scotland Street in 1764, which later had ALEXANDER KILHAM as one of its ministers and became the headquarters of the METHODIST NEW CONNEXION in Sheffield.

JOHN WESLEY himself visited Sheffield over forty times. Once on July 15, 1779, he preached in Paradise Square "to the largest congregation I ever saw on a week day." (*Journal*, vol. vi, p. 244.) The early Sheffield society was not wealthy, though James Bonnet, its benefactor, was a man of some means; Thomas Boulsover, the inventor of the famous old Sheffield plate, was an adherent; and James Vickers, who patented "Britannia Metal," also joined, and once had a tub of bullock blood tipped over him to cool his enthusiasm.

The first notable chapel was opened in 1780 in Norfolk Street, which was a hallowed center for more than a century; Carver Street, a fine example of early Methodist architecture, followed it in 1805. One of the circuit's itinerants, William Jenkins, was its architect. Laymen like Henry Longden, Thomas Holy, and James Vickers were active in the circuit, which numbered among its itinerants such notables as ALEXANDER MATHER, JOSEPH BENSON, ROBERT NEWTON, JABEZ BUNTING, THOMAS JACKSON, and, later, W. M. PUNSHON. All the three leaders of the Reform agitation of the 1850's, SAMUEL DUNN, WILLIAM GRIFFITH, and JAMES EVERETT, were at some time stationed in Sheffield. The town was in fact a notable center of liberal Methodism; the Protestant Methodists (see WESLEYAN METHODIST ASSOCIATION) had a chapel in Surrey Street (1831), which was the venue of the first Wesleyan Association Assembly. The Reformers later in 1861 built Hanover Chapel, which soon gathered a congregation of energetic shopkeepers, manufacturers, and artisans. In 1859 the WESLEYAN REFORM UNION was created, centered on Sheffield. PRIMITIVE METHODISM grew only slowly; the first minister was Jeremiah Gilbert, who came in 1819. His first plan was headed "The Sheffield Circuit of the People called Primitive Methodists, known also by the name of Ranters." This connection boomed after 1851 and reached further down into the social strata than any other group; its large chapels were Bethel (1835), and Petre (sic) Street (1869). Meanwhile the Wesleyans expanded, building the large Park (1831) and Brunswick (1834) Chapels. However it is noteworthy that only one more chapel was built between 1835 and 1865—a measure of havoc wrought by the internal divisions of Methodism.

Wesleyanism revived, however, and between 1867 and 1900 erected twenty-eight chapels, mostly sizable. An observer in 1875 stated that

Carver Street had an excellent congregation, both in quality and quantity, particularly the former; . . . last season it had the Mayor and the Master Cutler within a few pews of each other. In the main the congregation consists of members of the middle classes, with merchants, manufacturers and professional gentlemen. (Graham)

Of Brunswick Chapel similar observations are made, with the footnote,

There was a considerable admixture of the working classes and the poor were also present, though not in great numbers. I noticed several uncushioned benches for the poor. There were very few of them and none at all in the free, attic gallery. (*Ibid.*)

Continually the middle classes moved into the growing suburban areas of western and northern Sheffield; and chapels like the Park, in the older areas, were left denuded of leadership when other more select, Gothic-type churches, like Victoria (1861) were built for the people in the suburban villas.

In education, Sheffield Wesleyanism was notable for the opening in 1838 of the Wesleyan Proprietary Grammar School (later to be called Wesley College) of which SAMUEL D. WADDY was the most famous governor. In 1904 this college became the King Edward VII Grammar School, and passed into the hands of the local secular education authority.

Although the membership of all the Methodist groups increased, it hardly kept pace with the increase in population from 14,000 in 1736 to 135,000 in 1851 and 381,000 in 1901. New churches built after 1900 have tended to be in the areas of residential growth on the west and north of the city. The FORWARD MOVEMENT, however, influenced Sheffield greatly. Norfolk Street was replaced in 1908 by the Victoria Hall, which still has one of the largest congregations in Yorkshire, and its ministers have included E. BENSON PERKINS and William Wallace. In an effort to penetrate the world of industrial man in the east end of Sheffield, Attercliffe Hall was opened in 1927, but the experiment failed and the hall is now defunct. At Methodist Union (1932) some attempt was made to rationalize the untidy congeries of churches left as a Victorian legacy. Each circuit was given a segment of urban, suburban, and rural Sheffield. In 1965 the seven circuits in the city had 10,535 members. Strong and vigorous churches are to be found in the suburban areas, and a renovation scheme is in progress at the Victoria Hall, but it must be admitted that the gulf between the church and the mass of the population is greater than at any time since the days of John Wesley.

J. Everett, *Wesleyan Methodism in Sheffield*, 1823.
J. J. Graham, *A History of Wesleyan Methodism in Sheffield Park*. 1914.
Methodist Conference Handbook, 1940, 1951.
W. Parkes, *Thomas Bryant*. 1965.
T. A. Seed, *Norfolk Street Wesleyan Chapel, Sheffield*. 1907.
M. Walton, *Sheffield—Its Story and Its Achievement*. 1952.
Wesleyan Conference Handbook, 1922.
E. R. Wickham, *Church and People in an Industrial City*. 1957.   J. M. TURNER

SHELDON, HENRY CLAY (1845-1928), American church historian, theologian, and teacher, who for forty-six years was Professor of Church History and Systematic Theology in BOSTON UNIVERSITY SCHOOL OF THEOLOGY. He was born in Martinsburg, N. Y., on March 12, 1845, and graduated from Yale University in 1867. At the Boston University School of Theology, he was graduated in 1871, and spent a short time in the Methodist pastorate (1871-74). After a brief study in Europe, he assumed the chair above mentioned in the Boston University School of Theology, and from 1875 until his retirement in 1921, he earned for himself wide renown as an instructor, philosopher, and author. His *History of Christian Doctrine* (2 volumes, 1886), gained wide use in important circles and was translated into other languages, including Japanese. His five-volume *History of the Christian Church* (1894) established itself as a work of authoritative reference in ecclesiastical circles. He also wrote *A History of Unbelief in the Nineteenth Century*, 1907; *A Fourfold Test of Mormonism*, 1914; *Studies in Recent Adventism*, 1915; *Theosophy and New Thought*, 1916; *The Mystery Religions and the New Testament*, 1918; *Pantheistic Dilem-*

mas and Other Essays in Philosophy and Religion, 1920; and *The Essentials of Christianity,* 1922.

His students remember his classroom lectures as both formal, and informal, and it was said that no question was ever asked in class, but that he gave an answer.

Sheldon died on Aug. 4, 1928, and was buried in Newton Cemetery, Mass.

DANIEL MARSH

SHELDON, MARTHA A. (1860-1912), was a medical missionary to INDIA, appointed by the WOMAN'S FOREIGN MISSIONARY SOCIETY of the M. E. Church. Daughter of a Congregational pastor, she graduated from the University of Minnesota and the School of Medicine of BOSTON UNIVERSITY. She arrived in India in 1889, and was assigned to evangelistic work in Moradabad.

In 1893 she was transferred to Pithoragarh in Eastern Kumaun. Ever eager to live sacrificially and to serve those in most need, she moved on to Bhot, and established an outpost among the nomadic Bhotiya people. There she lived in very primitive conditions, far removed from the comforts of her girlhood, and from the rewards generally available to physicians and surgeons.

With British women, Annie Budden, at first, and Eva Browne, later, she lived in Dharchula during the winter and in Sirkha in the summer. These were not so much homes as they were bases from which these intrepid women moved into more remote areas, searching out needy people to whom they could bear witness of the love of God by word and deed. Among the converts were Hindus, Shokas, Humlis, and at least one Tibetan woman. Dr. Sheldon made a number of trips into Tibet, and established cordial relations with officials and the general public.

Her service to health and evangelism included healing by medicine and surgery, and the prevention of disease by improving sanitation and enriching diet. She planted fruit trees, grew her own vegetables, distributed vegetable seeds, and planted Kentucky bluegrass on mountain slopes. She lived as nearly as she could like the people about her, eager to set an example of frugality combined with proper diet.

She learned something of the language of that part of Tibet, said to differ considerably from the language around Lhasa. Her journeys into Tibet from India were made against the advice of India's officials and with no escort or protection from human sources. She died at Dharchula, Oct. 18, 1912, and is buried there.

Eva C. M. Browne, *The Life of Dr. Martha A. Sheldon.* N.d.
J. N. Hollister, *Southern Asia.* 1956.   J. WASKOM PICKETT

SHELLABEAR, NAOMI RUTH (-   ), went to JAVA as a missionary under the WOMEN'S FOREIGN MISSIONARY SOCIETY of the M.E. Church in 1909. She was first stationed in Batavia (Djakarta) and later transferred to Tuitenzorg (Bogor). There she served as principal of the Bible Woman's Training School. This school was later known as "Baitany" and continued to do effective work in the training of Bible Women for work in the church centers in Java until the Methodist Mission withdrew from that island in 1927.

While home on furlough in 1922-23 she studied in DREW THEOLOGICAL SEMINARY in Madison, N. J. While in that school she was married to William G. Shellabear,

a former missionary in MALAYA, then serving as a professor of missions in Drew Seminary. Mrs. Shellabear, being an able student in the Malay language, was able to give her husband valued assistance in teaching that language to missionaries both in Drew Seminary and also in the Kennedy School of Missions in Hartford Theological Seminary where he served as professor of Missions and Oriental Languages for several years prior to his retirement.

Since the death of her husband, Mrs. Shellabear has continued to live in a retirement home in Hartford, Conn.

SHELTON, CHARLES ELDRED (1859-1940), American educator and college president, was born in Mt. Pleasant, Iowa on June 16, 1859, the son of Orville Clarkson Shelton of the IOWA ANNUAL CONFERENCE of the M.E. Church. He was graduated from IOWA WESLEYAN UNIVERSITY in 1879 and received an M.A. in 1881. Admitted to the bar in 1880, he entered upon educational missionary work in BRAZIL under Bishop WILLIAM TAYLOR from 1880 to 1882, establishing schools at Bernambuce and Bahia. Upon his return to IOWA, he was a school principal in Agency, 1882-84 and DeWitt, 1885-89, with a period of law practice in Mt. Pleasant, 1884-85. He served on the faculty of the Western Normal College, Shenandoah, Iowa, 1889-92 and of Lincoln Normal University, Nebraska, 1892-93. After a term as superintendent of schools in Burlington, Iowa, 1893-99, he became president of SIMPSON COLLEGE, Indianola, Iowa, an institution of the DES MOINES ANNUAL CONFERENCE, from 1899-1910. Shelton's administration put special emphasis upon the Normal Program and Jubilee Financial Campaign (1905-10). His leadership was recognized by his presidency of the Iowa State Education Association in 1902 and by his receiving an honorary LL.D. from Iowa Wesleyan in the same year. He was the author of several textbooks on physical culture and mathematics and served as a local preacher of the Des Moines Conference.

Shelton married Julia Woodward and later Fannie Rosemond. Upon his retirement from Simpson College, he became supply for the Mt. Lake Park Summer Resort and Assemblies, MARYLAND, as well as engaging in European travel and study. He died in Mt. Lake Park on May 13, 1940.

Iowa Wesleyan College Archives.
Minutes of the Des Moines Annual Conference, 1899-1910.
Who Was Who in America 1897-1942.

LOUIS A. HASELMAYER

SHENANDOAH COLLEGE and **SHENANDOAH CONSERVATORY OF MUSIC,** Winchester, Virginia, are, respectively, a junior college and a four-year, degree-granting institution specializing in music. Although they share the same academic and residence facilities, they are governed by two separately incorporated boards of trustees and administered by one president and his administrative staff.

Founded by A. P. Funkhouser as a private school in Dayton, Va., in 1875, and chartered in 1876, Shenandoah Seminary was taken over by the CHURCH OF THE UNITED BRETHREN IN CHRIST in 1887. It became two separate institutions in 1937, the same year that the Conservatory was admitted to the accredited list of the National Association of Schools of Music.

In 1947, the College was accredited by the Southern

Association of Colleges and Schools; and in 1960, both institutions moved to their present location as a consequence of close and fruitful relationships between leaders of the VIRGINIA CONFERENCE of The Evangelical United Brethren Church and leaders of Winchester and Frederick County, Va. Since that move, both institutions have grown in size, fiscal stability, and academic quality.

The Governing Body consists of forty-one trustees elected by the Virginia Conference. Present statistics are: Library, 15,000 volumes; total enrollment, 600; administrative staff, four, College faculty members, forty, The Conservatory, seventeen; campus acreage, forty-two; number of buildings, seven; value of physical plant, $2,404,713; endowment, $125,000; current income, $949,519.

Clarence H. Connor, "A Study of the Functions of Shenandoah College and Shenandoah Conservatory of Music." Unpublished dissertation, University of Virginia, 1955.
Abram Paul Funkhouser and Oren F. Morton, *History of the Church of the United Brethren in Christ of the Virginia Conference.* Dayton, Va.: the conference, 1921.
David F. Glovier, *Pictorial History of the Virginia Conference.* 1965.
Yearbook of the E.U.B. Church, 1967.   BRUCE C. SOUDERS

SHENT, WILLIAM (?-1787), British barber and wig-maker, was the first to welcome the Methodist preachers to LEEDS. He became a leader of the society that met at his shop in Briggate and took the initiative in the building of the "Old Boggart House" chapel in 1751. From 1745 he traveled as a "half-itinerant," chiefly in Yorkshire and Lincolnshire; but the effect on his business caused him to locate in 1753. Later he succumbed to intemperance and was expelled from membership. Though restored through the championship of WESLEY, who employed him for a time at the BOOK ROOM in LONDON, he died in 1787, "a melancholy instance of human instability," says JOHN PAWSON.

Wesley's Letter Concerning William Shent. A notable letter written by John Wesley was responsible for the restoration of William Shent, as is noted above. This letter, Bishop EDWIN D. MOUZON of American Methodism once said, was "the best thing I think Wesley ever wrote." Here follows the letter:

London, January 11, 1779.

I have a few questions which I desire may be proposed to the Society at Keighley.

Who was the occasion of the Methodist preachers first setting foot in Leeds? William Shent.

Who received John Nelson into his house at his first coming thither? William Shent.

Who was it that invited me and received me when I came? William Shent.

Who was it that stood by me while I preached in the street with stones flying on every side? William Shent.

Who was it that bore the storm of persecution for the whole town and stemmed it at the peril of his life? William Shent.

Whose word did God bless for many years in an eminent manner? William Shent's.

By whom were many children now in paradise begotten in the Lord and many now alive? William Shent.

Who is he that is ready now to be broken up and turned into the street? William Shent.

And does nobody care for this? William Shent fell into sin and was publicly expelled the Society; but must he be also starved? Must he with his grey hairs and all his children be without a place to lay his head? Can you suffer this? O

tell it not in Gath! Where is gratitude? Where is compassion? Where is Christianity? Where is humanity? Where is concern for the cause of God? Who is a wise man among you? Who is concerned for the gospel? Who has put on bowels of mercy? Let him arise and exert himself in this matter. You here all arise as one man and roll away the reproach. Let us set him on his feet once more. It may save both him and his family. But what we do, let it be done quickly.—I am, dear brethren,
Your affectionate brother
J. Wesley

CHARLES WESLEY wrote to his brother on April 23, this year, "I shall be happy to hear you have saved poor William Shent."

J. W. Laycock, *Methodist Heroes.* 1909.   JOHN A. VICKERS

SHEPARD, WILLIAM ORVILLE (1862-1931), American bishop, was born at Sterling (near Rock Falls), Ill., April 11, 1862. His ancestors were early pioneers who struggled with the wilderness from the NEW YORK and PENNSYLVANIA line to INDIANA and ILLINOIS. He became self-supporting from the age of seventeen. His parents were connected with the Christian Church, and when he was converted his father refused to aid him in preparing to preach. It was a struggle, but Shepard was graduated from Jennings Seminary (Aurora, Ill.), DEPAUW UNIVERSITY, A.B., 1885; S.T.B., 1886; then A.M., 1888; D.D., 1896; LL.D., 1912; SYRACUSE UNIVERSITY, Ph.D., 1895 (hon. D.D. and LL.D.).

Shepard was ordained and joined the ROCK RIVER CONFERENCE in 1886, and his pastorates were: Blue Island, Elgin (First Church), Rockford (Court Street), Chicago (Oakland), Evanston, and Englewood (Chicago), all in Illinois, 1886-1909; district superintendent of the Chicago Northern District, 1909-12. Elected bishop in 1912, his episcopal areas were: Kansas City, Kansas, 1912-16; Wichita, Kansas, 1916-20; and Portland, Oregon, 1920-28, which Area included Washington, Oregon, Idaho, and Alaska. In 1928 Bishop Shepard was assigned to Paris, France, his area embracing France, Spain, Italy, Yugoslavia, Bulgaria, North Africa, Madeira Islands and Liberia. He made trips to South America, 1916, to Europe, 1920, to make a post-war survey of conditions and needs; and to South Africa, 1924. Twice he penetrated the Congo region by ox cart and on foot.

He married Emily Odell Aug. 15, 1883. They had four sons, William Odell, Chester Orville, Warren Vincent, and Mark. His book, *Oakland Sermons,* had charm, humor, and spiritual food.

Bishop Shepard had exceptional forensic talent. He was quick on the trigger on moral questions and a loyal and tireless worker. A successful preacher and effective missionary, he had a pleasing personality and made and held friends. A wide reader in the field of theology, philosophy, and science, he was interested in music and the arts. Bishop Shepard died in Paris, Nov. 30, 1931, and was buried in Mt. Hope, Chicago.

F. D. Leete, *Methodist Bishops.* 1948.
National Cyclopedia of American Biography.
Who's Who in America.   JESSE A. EARL

SHEPHERDSON, HAROLD URQUHART (1903-   ), Australian minister, was born in Bunbury, Western AUSTRALIA, a member of a dedicated Christian family. He was appointed as a missionary in 1927. He married Isabella Gray and was accepted to Milingimbi, North

HAROLD SHEPHERDSON

Australia to work among the Aborigines of Arnhem Land. For fifteen years he served there and then founded the Elcho Island Mission in 1942. This is situated about 300 air miles from Darwin. He early recognized the need for the mobility which air travel provides in the vast area of Arnhem Land covering 37,000 square miles, so in May 1936, he flew his first plane from Adelaide to Darwin. He is known affectionately as "Sheppie," but among the Aborigines he is "Bapa" or Father.

It was early realized that Elcho needed an industry to provide an occupation and income for its residents. Three areas have been developed: (a) agriculture, producing food for the mission; (b) timber, cypress logs cut on the mainland are towed to Elcho to be milled; (c) fishing, fish not needed on Elcho are frozen and flown to Darwin for sale.

Sheppie regularly leaves the established missions for the nine lonely outposts where he is the only known white man. He gathers groups together for worship after the preliminaries of exchange trading have been transacted.

For the fifty years of their married life, the Shepherdsons have dedicated themselves to their unique ministry.

AUSTRALIAN EDITORIAL COMMITTEE

SHERIDAN, JARRETT MITCHELL (1851-1929), American METHODIST PROTESTANT minister, was born near Lutherville, Md., Sept. 20, 1851. He taught school for four years and was admitted into the MARYLAND CONFERENCE in 1875. He was married in 1881 to Matilda Warfield Ridgely.

He served in the pastorate until 1907, when he became President of the Maryland Conference, serving in that office for five years. He was elected Superintendent of Church Extension of the Maryland Conference and then became Executive Secretary of the denominational Board of Home MISSIONS. In 1928 the Boards of Foreign Missions and Home Missions were merged into one Board of Missions, whereupon he returned to the church extension work of the Maryland Conference. On his death, Jan. 17, 1929, he was buried at Union Chapel, Md.

JAMES H. STRAUGHN

SHERLOCK, HUGH BRAHAM (1905-), president of the METHODIST CHURCH OF THE CARIBBEAN AND THE AMERICAS, is the son of Terrence Manderson and Adina

HUGH SHERLOCK

Trotter Sherlock, and was born in JAMAICA on March 21, 1905. He was educated at the Calabar High School, and at Caenwood (Methodist) Theological College, graduating there in 1932.

He married Thelma Coole on Dec. 18, 1942, and they have two children. Dr. Sherlock was with the Jamaica Civil Service, 1923-29, and then became a minister and was ordained in the Methodist Church in 1937. He served as minister in Turks Island in the Jamaica District, 1932-37, minister of the Ocho Rios Circuit, 1937-40; founder and director of Boys' Town, Kingston, 1940-56; chairman of the Jamaica Methodist District, 1956-66; chairman of the Board of Management of the St. Andrew High School; also the Excelsior High School, Morant Bay High School, York Castle High School. He was also chairman of the Board of Management of the Jamaica Youth Corps, 1955-65, and served as a Justice of the Peace in Jamaica. He has been honored with the decoration of Officer of the Most Excellent Order of the British Empire, 1954; and the recipient of the Freedom of the City of Kingston, 1955; and a United Nations Fellowship, 1954. He composed the Jamaica National Anthem in 1962.

He was vice president of the WORLD METHODIST COUNCIL, 1966-71, and acted as host for the Jamaica Methodists when the executive committee of the World Methodist Council met there in October 1964. He has been awarded Jamaica's Highest Citizen's Award, a Badge of Honour and Certificate of Merit, 1967.

Since his induction as President of the Methodist Church in the Caribbean and the Americas in 1967, he has resided in ANTIGUA, where that Church's headquarters are located.

EDWIN TAYLOR

SHERMAN, IRA EDICK (1914-), a missionary to CUBA and ARGENTINA, was born to Ira and Bessie Edick Sherman in Westville (Westford), N. Y., Feb. 1, 1914. After graduating from high school he obtained the A.B. degree from Hartwick College, Oneonta, N. Y., 1935. He obtained the B.D. degree from BOSTON UNIVERSITY in

1938 and the same year joined the WYOMING ANNUAL CONFERENCE. After serving pastorates in that Conference, he transferred to ROCK RIVER CONFERENCE and obtained the M.A. degree from NORTHWESTERN UNIVERSITY, 1947.

In 1938 he was married to Edith Elizabeth Batty, of Ware, Mass. Their three children are Arnold, a missionary in PERU, Catherine Elizabeth and Harold Dean.

Sherman and his wife were accepted as missionaries in Cuba in 1950 and served churches in the Isle of Pines, Guantanamo, and Cardenas. In 1960, because of communism in Cuba, they were transferred to Argentina where he has served pastoral charges in ROSARIO and BUENOS AIRES. He is also editor of *Pampa Breezes.*

GARFIELD EVANS

O. L. SHERMAN

SHERMAN, ODIE LEE (1897-   ), American bishop of the A.M.E. CHURCH, was born in Jacksonville, Texas. He received the A.B. degree from SHORTER COLLEGE in ARKANSAS. Later he was awarded honorary degrees from both Shorter College and WILBERFORCE UNIVERSITY. He was ordained DEACON in 1923 and ELDER in 1925, pastored in Arkansas and served as a presiding elder for almost twenty-seven years before being elected to the episcopacy in 1956. He resides at Waco, Texas and presides over the work of the Tenth Episcopal Area District comprising seven annual conferences in the state of Texas.

R. R. Wright, *The Bishops.* 1963.   GRANT S. SHOCKLEY

SHETLAND ISLES. The first Shetland Methodist was John Nicolson (1790-1828). In his teens he left his home near Aith, serving in the Napoleonic Wars in the Royal Artillery. While stationed at the Tower of London in 1810, he was won for Christ by a Methodist fellow soldier. Nicolson became an EXHORTER in the London East Circuit. His wife's unfaithfulness and his own ill health led him to return to the Shetlands in about 1820. He traveled from place to place, mostly in the West Mainland, found shelter and support where he could, and gathered a

Methodist society of about twenty members, with many more hearers. The Gruting Manse was built in 1922 as his memorial.

Nicolson in time wrote to the president of the Wesleyan Conference and the Missionary Committee asking that regular preachers be appointed to the Shetlands. After a personal investigation in June and July, 1822, Daniel McAllum reported on the destitute religious state of many of the 22,000 islanders, whose needs could not be met by the 12 ministers of the Established Church, each with several parishes and faced with difficult terrain; an aged Independent minister with a scattered flock of 150; and a Baptist lay preacher with a congregation of about 45.

In September, 1822, the first Methodist preachers arrived. John Raby, a Lancastrian, had served seven years in the West Indies; his two-year ministry was concentrated on the North Isles. The younger man, SAMUEL DUNN, was in his fourth year on trial. A fervent Cornishman, a typical revivalist and controversialist, later prolific in producing books and pamphlets, Dunn accepted great hardship as he traveled the Shetland mainland and nearby islands. He won support for Methodism but gained himself several enemies. Just before his three-year term in Shetland ended, a small-scale pamphlet war broke out, with Dunn at the center of the dispute. "Methodism will never thrive in Shetland," wrote *A Calm Observer:* "The reflecting portion of the people looks upon Methodism as a combination of arrogance, fanaticism, and unscriptural self-righteousness. Their chapels will soon be exposed for sale, and Messrs. Dunn, Lewis and Co. be released from their protracted and self-created martyrdom."

Despite such anonymous criticism, despite an aggrieved ex-Wesleyan, and Presbyterian and Baptist suspicion, and despite Dunn's turbulence, these were times of optimism and expansion. By 1832, membership rose to fourteen hundred, with fourteen chapels and several other preaching places, and six ministers. A highly respectable Shetlander named his child after Dunn. This success came not simply because Methodist theology and ethos were more attractive; it was the fact that the preachers were not Scots, and that their confident, vigorous activity was guided by ADAM CLARKE, who raised funds for the support of the preachers and the chapels, and ensured that many destitute people received practical aid. "The clothing I send, you are to divide with the most necessitous," urged Dr. Clarke in 1827, "whether they be Methodists or not. In this, let there be no respect of persons." Clarke took a personal interest in the Shetland Mission from the start, visiting the islands in 1826 and 1828; the Adam Clarke Memorial Church, Lerwick, built in 1870, replaced a chapel built there in 1824. "Since Dr. Clarke's death the mission has rather drooped," admitted James Catton, appointed chairman that very year, 1832. In seven years the membership fell by half. It seemed possible that, like the shortlived work in ORKNEY (1834-41, with never more than 200 members), Shetland Methodism would collapse. By 1845, however, the former level was regained, the Presbyterian disruption of 1843 adding 250 members to the Walls Circuit for a few years. The highest peak was reached in 1866, when there were over 2,000 members, 22 chapels, 5 circuits; and here an important factor was the guidance of John Stephenson, father of THOMAS B. STEPHENSON, who from 1849 revived the role of Clarke. He was followed by James Loutit and various Home Mission secretaries: the work still relies on Home Mission grants. The virtual isolation of this smallest British Methodist District and difficulties of travel encouraged, until recent years, distinctive features which modern pressures have not wholly removed.

In some communities a total indifference to denominational ties can be seen to have led the way to a more widespread interchurch activity. The only Methodist day school was in North Roe (1858-72), but Sunday schools, Bible classes, and more recently youth clubs and fellowships have made valuable contributions to community life. Family traditions are strong. In Fair Isles, for instance, the Wilson family, which pioneered the work, has provided three generations of LOCAL PREACHERS to maintain it. Shetland-born ministers include William Goudie (1857-1922) and his brother James (1861-1934). Sons of a Channerwick local preacher, both were missionaries in India, the former being secretary of the Wesleyan Missionary Society at the time of its centenary, and president-elect at the time of his death. From 1870 onward, the decline from emigration and other causes was countered by revivalist tactics; gains were conserved by a locally recruited lay agency. This held the membership at around sixteen hundred until 1910, followed by a steady drop to about eight hundred in 1966. Even so, despite social factors which in Shetland as much as elsewhere in Britain work against the Church, one Shetlander in twenty is still a Methodist member.

HAROLD R. BOWES

SHETTLES, ELIJAH LEROY (1852-1940), American minister, editor, author, and book-collector, was born in Pontotoc County, Miss., March 22, 1852. His parents, Abner and Caroline Browning Shettles, were natives of SOUTH CAROLINA.

His parents had very little of material things, and it became necessary for the son to work on a farm, and at times in a store. He later taught school, although endowed with little formal training at that time. In his account, *Recollections of a Long Life* (1935), the details of his life are graphically related. When he was almost forty years of age, he united with the Methodist Church; the QUARTERLY CONFERENCE granted him LOCAL PREACHER's license, and the TEXAS CONFERENCE admitted him on trial and assigned him to a circuit. In the seventeen years spent in the pastorate, there was a period of four years at Bryan, Texas, and later at Pittsburg, Texas, in each of which places he erected churches.

During his pastorate at Galveston, Texas, he married Mrs. Lillie Letts.

His Conference appointments were: Alum Creek (1892); Galveston West End (1893-1894); McKee Street, Houston (1895); 24th Street, Austin (1896 and 1899); Hempstead and Waller in 1897; Eagle Lake (1898); Bryan Station (1900-1903); Pittsburg Station (1904-1905); San Augustine District (1906); Calvert-Marlin District (1908-1910); Cameron Station (1911); Houston (1912); Navasota (1913-1916); Richmond Station (1917); Brenham District (1918-1921), all in Texas. He retired from the ministry in 1921, and devoted the rest of his life to collecting volumes on Methodist history, which books were placed at SOUTHERN METHODIST UNIVERSITY and Texas University at Austin.

When MACUM PHELAN prepared to write a history of Texas Methodism, he conferred with Shettles, who gave him much historical material for the proposed history. Shettles was the Associate Editor of *The Texas Methodist Historical Quarterly* (published from July 1909 through January 1911).

He died on May 28, 1940, in Austin, Texas, and was buried in that city.

Journal of the Texas Conference, 1940.
O. W. Nail, *Southwest Texas Conference.* 1958.
E. L. Shettles, *The Recollections of a Long Life.* Austin, 1935.
Southwestern Christian Advocate, June 6, 1940.

MRS. JOHN H. WARNICK

SHILLINGTON, THOMAS AVERELL (1800-1874), Irish layman, followed his father, Thomas Shillington, Sr., in the commercial life of Portadown in the north of IRELAND. He was CLASS LEADER, circuit STEWARD, served on district committees, and was in the forefront of the movement to increase lay responsibility in connexional affairs. For many years he was treasurer of the Chapel Fund, and was active in the foundation both of the Wesleyan Connexional School at Dublin (see WESLEY COLLEGE, Dublin), and METHODIST COLLEGE, Belfast.

In all this he followed and developed his father's tradition of lay service to Methodism. The father had been Chairman of the Dungannon Committee, a group of dedicated laymen who preserved the legal control over connexional property for the official Methodist Conference at the time of the secession of the PRIMITIVE Wesleyan METHODISTS. This attitude was taken despite Shillington's friendship for ADAM AVERELL.

Thomas Averell Shillington also had a tradition of service to the local community. In local government he had a position equivalent to that of Mayor today, and in 1865 became a member of the Senate of the then Queen's University of Ireland. So admired and trusted was his personal integrity and fairness, that he was often called upon to act as a mediator by those in dispute.

John Dwyer, *Christian Thoroughness: A Memorial Sketch of Thomas Averell Shillington.* 1875. FREDERICK JEFFERY

SHILOH CHURCH, near Pittsburg Landing, Hardin County, Tenn., is located in Shiloh National Park. According to a deed dated Oct. 29, 1852, John J. Ellis donated four acres of land to the M. E. Church, South. A one-room log church twenty-four by thirty feet was soon erected under the leadership of Jack Wolfe, a Methodist preacher.

The Civil War Battle of Shiloh was fought in the vicinity of the church, April 6-7, 1862, with Generals U. S. GRANT and Albert Sidney Johnston as the opposing commanders. Following the battle the Union soldiers either burned the church or used its timbers to repair roads heavily damaged by rain.

During the 1870's a sort of arbor with puncheon seats covered with boards was constructed on the church site and used for worship services. In 1881 a frame church somewhat larger than the original building was erected on the old rock foundation. In 1929 the basement of a new rock and brick church was constructed; because of the economic depression the building was not completed until 1949. It was dedicated, Aug. 31, 1952.

In 1971 Shiloh and Christ Church formed the Christ Church charge in the Cookeville District, TENNESSEE CONFERENCE. Shiloh reported sixty-six members, property valued at $21,300, and $1,893 raised for all purposes during the year.

Church History, McNairy-Hardin Group Ministry. (Pamphlet). March, 1968.
M. A. Milligan, Seeing Shiloh, 1862 and Today. (Leaflet from Library of Congress.)
Minutes of the Tennessee Conference, 1971. ALBEA GODBOLD

SHINKLE, AMOS (1818-1892), American layman of great influence in KENTUCKY Methodism, was born Aug. 18, 1818, in Brown County, Ohio. In 1846 he moved from OHIO to Covington, Ky., and was a leading citizen of that city until his death in 1892. His influence was greatly felt in both Covington and CINCINNATI, Ohio. His chief contribution to these two cities was the building of the suspension bridge across the Ohio River to connect them.

For many years Shinkle was the best-known layman of the M.E. Church in Kentucky. After the formation of the KENTUCKY CONFERENCE of the M.E. Church in 1866, he became an aggressive leader and helped to build churches and further the work of the conference. For many years Union M.E. Church in Covington, his home church, was one of the outstanding churches of Methodism and was served by many distinguished ministers. Shinkle, through his gifts toward the building of new churches on a matching basis, expedited the church extension program of the M.E. Church in Kentucky.

Shinkle's chief interest, however, was the establishment of a pension fund for retired ministers. Through his initial gifts, this was made possible, and he was named the first treasurer of the fund and was its largest benefactor. He was a delegate to the GENERAL CONFERENCE of 1872—the first one to which lay members were admitted—and was elected to membership in each of the five successive General Conferences.

The home he built for himself and his family was the largest and most elaborate in all northern Kentucky. Some years after his death in 1892, his family donated it to the SALVATION ARMY, and it now forms the nucleus for the institution known as Booth Hospital of Covington, Ky.

JOHN O. GROSS

SHINN, ASA (1781-1853), American preacher, was the chief polemical writer for the liberals in the constitutional controversy that raged in the M.E. Church in the 1820's. After the rupture of the Church, in 1828, Shinn went with the METHODIST PROTESTANTS where he gave large leadership to that new denomination during its initial years.

This son of Quaker parents was born in NEW JERSEY and brought as a child to the mountain wilds of western VIRGINIA, where, by 1795, we find the family residing in Harrison County on the west fork of the Monongahela River. Asa was converted in a Methodist meeting in 1799, the year of the organization of the Little Kanawha Circuit in that region, and in 1801 was admitted as a preacher in the BALTIMORE CONFERENCE.

He spent his ministry in the territory of the PITTSBURGH CONFERENCE. When the Conference was organized in 1825, he was named presiding elder on the Pittsburgh District. Though he never had the opportunity of attending school, by self-education he made himself a master of English. He was the chief contributor to the Mutual Rights, the organ of the "reformers" in the constitutional

controversy in the M.E. Church, where he wrote under the pen name of Bartimeus. In 1813 he published his Essay on the Plan of Salvation, and in 1840 a work on The Benevolence and Rectitude of the Supreme Being. It was Asa Shinn who argued the appeal of the expelled preachers Dorsey and Pool before the GENERAL CONFERENCE of 1828. Withdrawing from the M.E. Church after the rejection of that appeal, he led in the organizing of the Methodist Protestant Church. He was President of the first western Conference of the "Reformers" at CINCINNATI in 1829, the first President of the Pittsburgh Conference of the M.P. Church in 1833, and in 1838 and 1842 he served as President of the General Conference of the M.P. Church. The lingering effects of a kick in the head by a horse in his youth caused him to lapse into insanity four times in 1813, 1819, 1828, and 1843 until his death.

T. H. Colhouer, Sketches of the Founders. 1880.
The Mutual Rights.
M. Simpson, Cyclopaedia. 1878.
W. G. Smeltzer, Headwaters of the Ohio. 1951.
W. GUY SMELTZER

SHIPLEY, DAVID CLARK (1907-   ), American educator, theologian and professor of historical theology at the METHODIST THEOLOGICAL SCHOOL at Delaware, Ohio, was born at McKeesport, Pa., on March 26, 1907, and was educated at ASBURY COLLEGE, the UNIVERSITY OF SOUTHERN CALIFORNIA, and received the Ph.D. degree from Yale in 1942. He did post graduate work in Cambridge, England. Dr. Shipley joined the SOUTHERN CALIFORNIA-ARIZONA CONFERENCE in 1929, and served as pastor for four years. He then went to the University of California at Los Angeles (1933-36) and then to Yale, 1936-37. He became professor of historical theology at GARRETT THEOLOGICAL SEMINARY, 1945-55; professor of Christian ethics and historical theology at SOUTHERN METHODIST UNIVERSITY, Dallas, 1955-60; and the professor of theology at the Methodist Theological School in Ohio at Delaware in 1960.

Dr. Shipley has delivered several series of lectures at various universities and colleges, has served on the Commission on Ecumenical Consultation for the Methodist Church, is a consultant on the editorial board of the Library of Protestant Thought, Oxford University Press; a member of the American Theological Society; of the American Society of Church History, and other learned bodies. He has contributed to the Encyclopaedia Britannica, the Westminster Dictionary of Christian Education, The History of American Methodism, and articles to various professional journals. He continues to teach in the Methodist Theological School, Delaware, Ohio.

Who's Who in The Methodist Church, 1966.   N. B. H.

SHIPLEY, RICHARD LARKIN (1879-1947), American minister and editor of the M.P. CHURCH, was born at BALTIMORE, Md., June 10, 1879. In 1903 he graduated from the WESTMINSTER THEOLOGICAL SEMINARY and united with the MARYLAND CONFERENCE. He married Cora Belle Roberts.

Until 1932 he served important pastorates and in that year was elected editor of The Methodist Protestant-Recorder at Baltimore. This periodical was discontinued on the Union of American Methodism in 1939. Shipley then became pastor of the West Baltimore Church, which he served until his sudden death on Nov. 25, 1947. He was interred in Woodlawn Cemetery at Baltimore.

JAMES H. STRAUGHN

SHIPP, ALBERT MICAJAH (1819-1887), American minister, university professor, college president, Seminary dean, church historian, was born in Stokes County, N. C., Jan. 15, 1819.

He was graduated from the University of North Carolina, A.B., 1840; subsequently that institution conferred upon him the LL.D. degree. He was awarded the D.D. degree by RANDOLPH-MACON COLLEGE.

The SOUTH CAROLINA CONFERENCE of 1851 elected him to the first regular Board of Trustees of WOFFORD COLLEGE. At the first meeting of the Board in 1853, he was absent but was elected to the chair of English Literature. He declined acceptance, choosing to remain as Professor of History in the University of North Carolina.

At the Wofford College commencement of 1859, the first president, WILLIAM M. WIGHTMAN, resigned, and Shipp was elected president. In this position he served with distinction for the ensuing sixteen years—through the dark days of the Civil War until 1875. He succeeded in increasing the endowment of the College to $200,000 before the ill fortunes of the War virtually dissolved the holdings. A commencement program of 1868 notes that President Shipp, who was known for his scholarly attainments, delivered in Latin the farewell address to the graduating class.

Before coming to Wofford College, during the years 1840-49, Shipp had served as an itinerant Methodist minister, serving on circuits, on stations, as presiding elder, and for two and a half years as President of GREENSBORO FEMALE COLLEGE; and from 1849 to 1859 he was Professor of French, History, and Literature at the University of North Carolina.

Leaving Wofford in 1875, he went to VANDERBILT UNIVERSITY, Nashville, Tenn., where for ten years he was Professor of Exegetical Theology (three years Dean of the Theological Faculty, and three years Vice Chancellor of Vanderbilt University). He resigned in 1885 and retired to his home, Rose Hill, near Cheraw, S. C.

In December 1876, the South Carolina Conference requested Shipp to write the history of Methodism in South Carolina. This he did, stipulating that any profits from the work, *Methodism in South Carolina*, go to the benefit of aged preachers. He was a delegate from the South Carolina Conference to the GENERAL CONFERENCES of the M.E. Church, South, 1848-1886.

Shipp and his wife, who was Mary Gillespie of Rose Hill Plantation, Marlboro County, are buried in the Gillespie Cemetery near Wallace, S. C.

An elegant, modern dormitory, Shipp Hall, was formally opened in his memory on the Wofford College Campus on Oct. 26, 1963.

D. D. Wallace, *Wofford College*. 1951.   J. MARVIN RAST

SHIPSTONE, EVA (1915-   ), is the ninth principal, and the fourth Indian, to head ISABELLA THOBURN COLLEGE. She is a product of Methodism in INDIA, being a member of the British Methodist Church. She was educated in the Lal Bagh Girls' School and Isabella Thoburn College, both founded by the Methodist Episcopal pioneer ISABELLA THOBURN. Dr. Shipstone earned a Master's degree at BOSTON UNIVERSITY and a Ph.D. degree at Harvard University.

She was born in LUCKNOW on Dec. 23, 1915. Her father was on the faculty of LUCKNOW CHRISTIAN COLLEGE, of which he was a graduate. In the principalship she succeeded Dr. Evangeline M. Thillyampalam, an Anglican born in Ceylon, although Methodism in India contributed heavily to her education.

She came to Isabella Thoburn as a freshman, graduated with an excellent record and returned as a teacher of biology. She took a Master of Science degree from Allahabad University and a Ph.D. degree from Columbia, and, after fifteen years as principal of colleges in CEYLON and five years in North India, she returned to Isabella Thoburn as principal in 1955 following the death of Dr. SARAH CHAKKO.

Like all her predecessors except for Miss Thoburn herself, Dr. Shipstone had been a member of the faculty of the college before she became principal. But she was the first principal born in Uttar Pradesh, the large state of which Lucknow is the capital. Two of her sisters are also graduates of Isabella Thoburn College, and both have served as teachers in girls' high schools.

In 1966 Dr. Shipstone was awarded honorary degrees by GOUCHER and RANDOLPH-MACON COLLEGES.

M. A. Dimmitt, *Isabella Thoburn College*. 1963.

J. WASKOM PICKETT

SHIRKEY, ALBERT PATTERSON (1904-   ), American minister and city pastor, was born at Staunton, Va., on Jan. 8, 1904. He was educated at RANDOLPH-MACON COLLEGE and at the Theological Seminary at Richmond, Va. Trinity University granted him the D.D. degree in 1943 and AMERICAN UNIVERSITY in 1954, ASBURY the LL.D. in 1966. He married Leona Lauck on June 21, 1929, and they have three sons. He first joined the VIRGINIA CONFERENCE in 1928, and served for a time as pastor of Branch Memorial Church in RICHMOND, 1927-31; Pace Memorial in the same city, 1931-35; and then transferred to the BALTIMORE CONFERENCE where he was sent to Asbury Church in WASHINGTON, D.C., 1935-38. He was then transferred to the great Travis Park Church in SAN ANTONIO, Texas, where he served from 1938-49; then to St. Paul's Church, HOUSTON, Texas, 1949-50. He then came back to the Baltimore Conference and was stationed at the Mount Vernon Place Church in Washington, where he served from 1950 until his retirement in June 1969. Dr. Shirkey has been president of the Board of Christian SOCIAL CONCERNS of his conference; of its Board of EVANGELISM, 1956-64; was a delegate to the WORLD METHODIST CONFERENCE in Oslo in 1961; the president of the Greater Washington Ministerial Union, 1952-54, and of the Greater Washington Area Council of Churches, 1955-57; a member of the executive council of the Methodist Commission on CHAPLAINS, 1956-64, and also a member of the National Council of Chaplains; and was a delegate to the GENERAL CONFERENCES of 1940, '44, '48, and '60. He was a member of the President's Committee on Juvenile Delinquency and also a member of the President's Inaugural Committee, 1957; the Commission on Alcohol Studies; the co-chairman of the National Conference of Christians and Jews in Washington, and a director of the GOODWILL INDUSTRIES in the same city. He has also served as vice-president of the Board of Sibley Memorial Hospital; trustee of American University and of Asbury College, and upon the Board of Governors of WESLEY THEOLOGICAL SEMINARY. He has also been an organizer and director of World Brotherhood through the Church, Strasbourg, France and Hattenheim, Germany, 1950-51. He has written *The Lord is My Shepherd*, 1963, and *Meditations on the Lord's Prayer*, 1964. Other publications include *Wings for the Soul* (Poems, 1966) and *Love Never Fails* (meditations, 1967). He continues to reside in Washington, D.C.

Who's Who in America, Vol. 34.
Who's Who in The Methodist Church, 1966.   N. B. H.

SHIRLEY, FRANCES (1702-1778), Anglican Evangelical, an aunt of Lady SELINA HUNTINGDON, was one of the court beauties in the reign of George I. From 1749 she actively supported the work of the revival and opened her house at Twickenham for preaching. She was the patroness of JAMES HERVEY and a correspondent of GEORGE WHITEFIELD.

A. SKEVINGTON WOOD

SHIRLEY, WALTER (1726-1786), British Evangelical Anglican of the eighteenth century, was brother of the cruel Earl of Ferrers. Cousin to SELINA LADY HUNTINGDON, he had been a typical hunting parson, but appears to have changed his ways. He was converted under HENRY VENN, though HENRY MOORE claimed that part of the influence came from JOHN WESLEY. Shirley became rector of Loughrea, in Galway, IRELAND, and was an evangelical preacher who had to face opposition from the Bishop of Clonfert.

Shirley's chief historical significance is in connection with the controversy to which he gave his name. The 1770 Methodist CONFERENCE had taken stock of its relation to Calvinism, and had sought to define more closely the statement made at the 1744 Conference that "we have leaned too much towards Calvinism." It was emphasized that there was a place for faithfulness in Christian living: "We ought steadily to assert . . . that if a man is not faithful in the unrighteous mammon, God will not give him the true riches." Further, the maxim that "a man is to do nothing in order to justification" was labeled as being false; it being shown that loving obedience to God must be the characteristic of the Christian.

The attack on these propositions from the Calvinistic side was led by Shirley, who wrote a circular letter proposing that at the time of Wesley's 1771 Conference, which was to be held at BRISTOL, a rival meeting should be held. The plan was that the members of this rival meeting should then demand from Wesley's Conference the recantation of the 1770 Minutes. The 1771 Conference was, Wesley wryly remarked, better attended than usual because of the excitement. On Thursday, Aug. 8, 1771, Shirley attended with nine or ten others. After two hours of discussion it was Wesley's belief that "they were satisfied that we were not so dreadful heretics as they imagined, but were tolerably sound in the faith." An account supposed to be from Shirley's own hand acknowledged that he had been too hasty in his judgment of Wesley's sentiments. The controversy continued for some time longer, however, being taken up by such writers as AUGUSTUS TOPLADY, and while it reflected a genuine disagreement between Calvinist and Arminian, it pointed

also to the extreme difficulty of drawing up a formulation of belief in the area of theology.

B. J. N. GALLIERS

SHOEMAKER, ESTHER (1901-   ), a missionary of The Methodist Church, served in INDIA from 1927 to 1966. She was born in Norristown, Pa., Aug. 25, 1901. She was nurtured in the Friends' Church. She holds the B.A. degree from Wilson College at Chambersburg, Pa., the M.D. degree from Indiana University, and the diploma from the National Board of Medical Examiners. She had many contacts with Methodism during her years of study, and in 1926 she joined the M.E. Church in Chambersburg. She went to India as a missionary in 1927 and was appointed to the Ellen Thoburn Cowan Hospital in Kolar, Mysore State, South India.

This hospital was established in memory of Ellen Thoburn Cowan's work as a home-base secretary of the WOMAN'S FOREIGN MISSIONARY SOCIETY. Mrs. Cowan was a sister of Bishop JAMES THOBURN and of ISABELLA THOBURN. The hospital became Dr. Shoemaker's home and work center, and remained so throughout her forty years of notable service.

She was soon recognized as an able hospital administrator. In 1928, she was named as a Methodist representative on the managing committee of the Christian Medical College at Vellore, and except during furloughs, she served in that position until 1963. For some years she was on the executive committee of the college council.

She was active in her local church and in the SOUTH INDIA ANNUAL CONFERENCE. She was official correspondent of the South India Woman's Conference for twenty-five years, was on the executive board and interim committee for many years, was once delegate to the CENTRAL CONFERENCE, and frequently represented the Methodist Church in interdenominational gatherings including the triennial meeting of the National Christian Council of India. She was secretary of the Central Conference Council on Medical Work for twenty years, and for more than half of that time was also secretary of the medical scholarship committee. Her influence helped many able young people to commit themselves to the healing ministry and to prepare for it.

J. N. Hollister, *Southern Asia*. 1956.   J. WASKOM PICKETT

SHOEMAKER COLLEGE, Scott County, Virginia, was established in 1844 with funds left by James L. Shumaker, a businessman of Estelville, the present Gate City, Va. After many years the buildings were transferred to the county and became a public school. The endowment funds were given to EMORY AND HENRY COLLEGE.

SHOOK, JACOB (1749-1832), early American layman, was born in PENNSYLVANIA and went with his father to Burke County, N. C. After serving in the Revolution he settled in 1786 at the present town of Clyde in Haywood County, N. C., where he is said to have built the first frame house in the county. The house still stands, considerably enlarged, and a road marker has been erected there. The attic room where the first Methodist society in the county met has been preserved with pulpit and chair.

On Nov. 30, 1810, Bishop ASBURY, Bishop MCKENDREE, John McGee and HENRY BOEHM crossed the aboriginal

Cataloochee Trail from east TENNESSEE to western NORTH CAROLINA and stayed all night at "Vater Shuck's."

To commemorate this trip road markers have been erected by the State, the route has been designated and marked as the ASBURY TRAIL, and the Boy Scouts of America have established the Asbury Trail Award and confer a medal on Scouts who hike the rugged way followed by Bishop Asbury.

Jacob Shook died about 1832 and bequeathed a tract of land at Clyde for a CAMP MEETING site. The appointment was long called Camp Ground. It is now Louisa Chapel, named for Shook's unmarried granddaughter. It is the successor of the society organized by SAMUEL EDNEY in the Shook home and bears the date of 1798. There are numerous Shook descendants in the area today.

F. Asbury, *Journal and Letters.* 1958.
W. L. Grissom, *North Carolina.* 1905.   LOUISE L. QUEEN

ROY H. SHORT

SHORT, ROY HUNTER (1902-   ), American clergyman and bishop, was born in LOUISVILLE, Ky., on Oct. 19, 1902, the son of Jesse Peters and Minnie (Badders) Short.

He received the following degrees: University of Louisville, A.B., 1924; Louisville Presbyterian Seminary, B.D., 1927, and Th.M., 1929; KENTUCKY WESLEYAN (Winchester, Ky., now located at Owensboro), D.D., 1939; FLORIDA SOUTHERN COLLEGE, LL.D., 1949; TENNESSEE WESLEYAN, Litt.D., 1957; EMORY UNIVERSITY, D.D., 1957; EMORY AND HENRY COLLEGE, D.Cn.L., 1957.

Roy Hunter Short married Louise Clay Baird of Jeffersonville, Ind. on Sept. 1, 1926. They have three children, Hunter Baird, Murray Malcolm, and Riley Phillips.

He was ordained to the ministry in 1921 and joined the LOUISVILLE CONFERENCE. His KENTUCKY pastorates included Jefferson Circuit, 1921-22; Mt. Holly and Mill Creek, 1922-26; Oakdale Church, Louisville, 1926-28; Marcus Lindsey Church, Louisville, 1928-30; Greenville, 1930-35; superintendent, Elizabethtown (Kentucky) Dis-

trict, 1935-37; superintendent, Louisville (Kentucky) District, 1937-41; pastor, St. Paul Church, Louisville, 1941-44.

He was chairman of the denomination's 1956-60 emphasis on the local church. This was a program to strengthen and expand the more than 39,000 Methodist churches in the United States. He was a member of the Bishops Committee of Nine on 1960-64 quadrennial program.

Bishop Short was secretary of the COUNCIL OF BISHOPS of The Methodist Church, 1956-68; president, College of Bishops of the Methodist Southeastern Jurisdiction, 1957-58; chairman, Joint Committee on Christian Education in Foreign Fields, 1956-64; chairman, Methodist Interboard Commission on the Local Church, 1956-64; member, Methodist Co-ordinating Council, president of the Board of Missions, 1964-68, and has been a member of the Board of Publication. He was a member of the GENERAL CONFERENCES of 1938, '40, '44, and '48, and of the Uniting Conference of 1939.

He is a trustee of LAKE JUNALUSKA (North Carolina) Methodist Assembly; Emory University; and was president of the Board of Trustees, SCARRITT COLLEGE, 1953-64. He was made a Kentucky Colonel by Governor Lawrence Wetherby in 1951.

Bishop Short was the editor of *The Upper Room*, an interdenominational devotional guide published by the Methodist General Board of Evangelism, 1944-48. He is the author of *Your Church and You* (a membership manual for Methodist boys and girls), 1943; *Evangelistic Preaching; Evangelism Through the Local Church*, September, 1956; *My Great Redeemer's Praise*, 1957; and *One Witness in One World*, the study book for the 1964-68 quadrennium.

He was elected bishop in June 1948, and assigned to the JACKSONVILLE (Florida) Area. From 1952 to 1964, he served the NASHVILLE (Tennessee) Area, and in 1964 he was appointed to the Louisville (Kentucky) Area where he administers the work of the Louisville and Kentucky Annual Conferences, comprising more than 1,000 churches with a total membership of approximately 200,-000.

Who's Who in America, Vol. 34.
Who's Who in The Methodist Church, 1966.   N. B. H.

SHORT CREEK CHURCH, located two miles southwest of West Liberty, is the oldest church in Ohio County, W. Va. From around 1785 to 1807, the society met in the home of John Spahr, who settled in the area about 1770. Wilson Lee, a member of the Christmas Conference and a flame of fire, was pastor in 1785. Members were obliged to carry their arms to worship to protect them from a sudden onset of the savages who yet prowled the country.

Bishop FRANCIS ASBURY preached "to a crowd at John Spahr's in 1803," and on Aug. 23, 1807, Asbury wrote: "I preached in an excellent stone meeting house on Short Creek to about one thousand souls." In 1809 WILLIAM MCKENDREE, the first native bishop, dedicated the church, whose building had galleries and port holes resembling a fort.

RICHARD WHATCOAT, later bishop, was presiding elder over the Ohio Circuit in 1788. Henry Willis, the first man ordained by Asbury, was presiding elder in 1789. He was the traveling companion of Francis Asbury and JESSE LEE. Thomas Scott was pastor in 1793. After his marriage the salary was only $128 and Scott left the ministry and became the first Chief Justice of the Supreme Court of Ohio.

A wonder of the early ministry, VALENTINE COOK, the most distinguished alumnus of COKESBURY COLLEGE, was presiding elder in 1796 and 1797. He is credited with introducing the mourner's bench in CAMP MEETINGS.

John Spahr's son-in-law, gifted Jacob Young, was pastor in 1810 (and in 1830-31). One camp meeting had about fifty tents and forty wagons. The meeting was annoyed by rowdies selling liquor. When they would not listen to reason, Young took a strong man and a hammer with him, and knocked the heads out of the casks and spilled the whiskey.

GEORGE BROWN, one of the founders of the M.P. Church, was pastor in 1820. His predecessor, the eloquent John Waterman, was driven out of Wheeling by a pro-slavery mob headed by one Noah Zane. One of Brown's sermons converted Zane, and he had Brown to sign the emancipation papers of two of his slaves.

L. L. HAMLINE (later bishop) was pastor in 1830. The circuit's membership was 602. Alexander Campbell heard Hamline preach and agreed with his doctrine.

The present two-story brick church, valued at $50,500, was built under L. H. Jordan, in 1872. Jordan was one of the founders of WEST VIRGINIA WESLEYAN COLLEGE. With 162 members in 1965, Short Creek, probably, has been the best open-country church in the State for more than a century and a half.

F. Asbury, *Journal and Letters.* 1958.
George Brown, *Recollections of an Itinerant Life.* Cincinnati: R. W. Carrol and Co., 1866.
Journal of the West Virginia Conference.
J. Young, *Autobiography.* 1857.

JESSE A. EARL

SHORTER, JAMES ALEXANDER (1817-1887), American pioneer missionary to the Southwest, was born in WASHINGTON, D.C., on Feb. 14, 1817. After becoming a barber in PHILADELPHIA, Pa., he went west to Galena, Ill., to practice his trade. He was converted in 1839 and united with the M.E. Church there and after that year he returned to the east, became an A.M.E. in Bethel Church, Philadelphia, returned to Washington, D.C., was admitted to the Baltimore Conference in 1846, ordained deacon in 1848 and elder in 1850. Following an itinerancy of twenty-two years, Shorter was elected to the bishopric. While in this office he organized African Methodism in the southwest into the following annual conferences: Tennessee (September 1878), Mississippi (October 1868), Texas (October 1868), Kansas (1876).

R. R. Wright, *The Bishops.* 1963.   GRANT S. SHOCKLEY

SHORTER COLLEGE, North Little Rock, Arkansas, was founded by the Arkansas Annual Conference in the Bethel A.M.E. Church, LITTLE ROCK, in 1886, and called Bethel University. In 1887 the name was changed to Bethel Institute and in 1892 it was again renamed Shorter University and chartered in that name on May 18, 1894, at its present location in North Little Rock.

In 1903 its charter was amended to rename it Shorter College as it is now known. Flipper College, an A.M.E. school founded in 1917 at Talihina, Okla., was merged with Shorter in 1942. The Thomas H. Jackson Theological Seminary is located on the campus of Shorter College.

GRANT S. SHOCKLEY

SHOWERS, JOHN BALMER (1879-1962), American E.U.B. bishop, publisher, editor, seminary professor, and pastor, was born Sept. 29, 1879, near Paris, Ontario, CANADA. The son of Joseph Smith and Margaret (Morrow) Showers, he was reared in a devout home and first preached as a high school boy when his minister father became ill. After his early education in Canada, Balmer graduated from LEBANON VALLEY COLLEGE (A.B., 1907), and Bonebrake (later UNITED) THEOLOGICAL SEMINARY (B.D., 1910). Licensed to preach by his local church in 1898 and by Ontario Conference, CHURCH OF THE UNITED BRETHREN IN CHRIST, in 1899, he was ordained by Erie Conference, Sept. 7, 1902. He filled several pastorates: Dechard Circuit (1900-3) and Bradford Station (1903-4) in Pennsylvania, Westfield College (1906-7) in ILLINOIS, and Belmont Mission in OHIO (1908-10). On April 11, 1911, he married Justina Lorenz.

From 1910-26 Showers served as professor of New Testament Literature and Interpretation at Bonebrake Theological Seminary. Post-graduate study was carried out at Chicago (1910-11) and Berlin (1911-12) Universities and on a research venture to the Near East (1922). Beginning in 1926 he turned to denominational publishing interests, serving as associate editor of the *Religious Telescope* (1926-33), associate publishing agent (1931-33), and finally as publisher of *The Otterbein Press* (1933-45). The GENERAL CONFERENCE of 1945 elected him to the episcopacy and he was assigned to be bishop first of the Eastern Area and then of the North Central Area. From 1954-62, he lived as bishop emeritus in Dayton, Ohio, where he died on Sept. 25, 1962.

Dayton Daily News, Sept. 26, 1962.
Dayton Journal Herald, Sept. 26, 1962.
Koontz and Roush, *The Bishops.* 1950.   DONALD K. GORRELL

SHOWERS, JUSTINA LORENZ (1885-   ), American E.U.B. church woman, was born Jan. 4, 1885 in DAYTON, Ohio, the daughter of Dr. and Mrs. E. S. LORENZ, best known as the founder of the Lorenz Publishing Company, publishers of church music.

Following her graduation from Bryn Mawr College, Bryn Mawr, Pa., she served briefly as the secretary of Young Women's Work of the Women's Missionary Association, UNITED BRETHREN IN CHRIST. On April 11, 1911, she married J. BALMER SHOWERS, professor at Bonebrake (now UNITED) THEOLOGICAL SEMINARY in Dayton, Ohio, later publisher of *The Otterbein Press,* and then bishop of the Church.

Mrs. Showers is known best for her capable leadership in the women's work of the conference and the General Church (Trustee, WMA, 1921-46; President, WMA, 1941-46; President, Women's Society of World Service, 1947-55; President Emeritus, WSWS); also for her leadership in the YWCA, having served as president of the Dayton YWCA for a number of years, and for her gracious hospitality. Their home was always "a home away from home" to missionaries and their children, a number of the latter living in the home during high school and college days. Many conferences and general meetings have been held in this home. In recent years their home has become Mission Manor for missionaries on furlough, Mrs. Showers maintaining only her apartment.

MARY McLANACHAN

SHREVEPORT, LOUISIANA, U.S.A., is the strongest Methodist center in Louisiana. In 1839 Shreveport was incorporated under a charter granted by the Louisiana Legislature; and on March 24 of that same year Bishop Leonidas K. Polk, Missionary Bishop of the Protestant Episcopal Church, came by boat from Ft. Smith, Ark., to conduct the first recorded religious service in English in the Shreveport area. This was the beginning of Protestantism in northern Louisiana. In 1845 the M.E. Church, South began in Shreveport. Since there were not enough Methodist men to form a board of STEWARDS, a Baptist layman was borrowed to complete the organization. At a cost of $1,000, a Methodist building was erected. It was a small frame structure about thirty-five by forty feet on Market and Fannin Streets. For the next thirty-nine years, this was the only building of the Methodist denomination. It was enlarged from time to time.

In 1847 Robert J. Harp was appointed as the first regular Methodist pastor in Shreveport. This minister is remembered by a beautiful memorial window in First Church, now one of the ten largest churches of the entire denomination. Not much progress followed for the next twenty years because of the tension preceding and during the War Between the States.

After the war disappointment, sorrow, and poverty were the mood for the next five years, climaxed by the ravages of yellow fever which in 1874 took some twenty percent of the members of the struggling group. At no time were there more than 100 members. By 1881, however, the enrollment had climbed to 250, and the need for expansion was felt. To this end, lots were purchased at the head of Texas Street, and a building estimated at $30,000 was planned and built. On this same location, First Church now serves its vast membership.

The Lakeview Church, which has had numerous locations, is the second church in point of history, but it has never been as strong as either Noel Memorial or Mangum Memorial, the latter named for a young pastor who died of pneumonia contracted in an effort to drain the leaking basement of the church. Another early church bears the name of a distinguished minister of the Louisiana Conference, Wynn Memorial, for Robert H. Wynn. In 1970 there were 15,589 Methodists in fifteen churches in Shreveport, and the growth is steady.

The only M.E. Churches ever in the area were Negro bodies. Three very fine groups have existed for many years—St. Paul's, St. James, and Fairfield. They have had to move their locations more than once because of the pressure of an expanding city, but they came out well in the transactions.

Outstanding in Shreveport is Methodism's great college, CENTENARY, which has the distinction of being the oldest college west of the Mississippi River. It was moved from Jackson, La., to the present site in 1908, where it continues to grow and expand.

In this community the influence of the Methodist Church far exceeds its numerical strength, and one can easily detect the work of early and late leaders in its life and spirit.

Broadmoor Church is a family church of suburbia with one of the largest church school attendances of Louisiana Methodism.

The church began Sept. 12, 1939, meeting first on the campus of Centenary College in its old chapel. After several years there, the "triangle" where the present buildings reside became the site of the first building, a two-story fellowship hall and classrooms. A sanctuary was later added and then a three-story educational unit.

Construction now anticipated will double the present education square-footage, providing a multi-use building to seat and serve 780 persons at a meal and a complete youth facility. Four lots for parking have recently been concreted and constructed.

In 1970 Broadmoor Church reported 2,760 members, and property valued at $1,423,148.

First Church has had its origin and general development told in the above account. Its location at the head of Texas Street gives it a unique and commanding position. In 1881, the congregation having increased in membership to 250, purchased its present site for $2,700, and set about building a new church. This was completed in 1889. By 1913 this building proved inadequate and was replaced by the structure now standing.

As the city expanded, Methodism kept pace. The parent church, growing steadily stronger, assisted small congregations in outlying sections. Dedicated ministers, three of whom became bishops—LINUS PARKER, W. ANGIE SMITH and DANA DAWSON—have served First Church. With the assistance of three associates and staff, the church continues to progress. Television and radio broadcasts help to extend its influence. World Service giving far exceeds askings and special missionary projects are sponsored each year at home and abroad. A plan of voluntary proportionate giving, initiated in 1955, has been adopted as the permanent stewardship plan, replacing former canvassing of the membership. Greatly increased facilities have become necessary in recent years in order to serve a 1970 membership of 4,506. With the purchase and gift of surrounding property for parking areas and additional buildings, including the Dana Dawson Educational Building, completed in 1940; and Couch Chapel and the Activities Building in 1964, the value of the complete physical plant is in excess of $3,250,000.

Noel Memorial Church started in 1906 with thirteen charter members, and was the third Methodist church to be established in the fast growing city. The thirteen members met in a small cottage which was owned by J. S. Noel, Sr., located in a section of town where many homes were being built and the population was increasing. The membership grew rapidly. Bishop SETH WARD appointed R. J. Harp as the first minister to the church, which was then usually called "Shreveport City Mission," or sometimes Creswell Street Church. Mr. Noel, being a dedicated Christian and having faith in the growth of the church, decided to build a church which would be adequate for years to come. In 1911 he and his wife had the building started as a memorial to their son, J. S. Noel, Jr., who had met an untimely death.

In February 1913, approximately 300 members moved from the little frame house, which was only a block away, to the new brick building typical of the architecture of that day. The community and the membership of the church continued to grow until in 1924 there were over 1,000 members. In 1925 a fire of unknown origin completely destroyed the interior of the building. Although it was a sad time for the congregation, the loyal members by sacrificial giving, in addition to the insurance carried on the church, made possible the restoration of the building exactly as it had been in the beginning.

Expansion continued until more facilities became a necessity. A building for children's classes was completed in 1941. Before many years this was still inadequate and an activities building, with space for the youth department, offices, a large recreation area and a dining hall to seat some 600 persons was built. The C. W. Lane family, descendants of J. S. Noel, built a memorial chapel to Addie Noel Lane. The chapel completed the attractive appearance of the additions to the original church building. In 1943 Noel Memorial Methodist Church Library was established, and was the first church library in Shreveport. Mrs. Annie T. Munday, who was responsible in cooperation with the WOMAN'S SOCIETY OF CHRISTIAN SERVICE in establishing the library, helped other Methodist churches to establish their own. At this writing there are more than 7,000 volumes on the library shelves. Today the church has more than tripled its missionary efforts within the past few years, making its outreach felt in many parts of the world. The membership of the church at this time is 2,643.

Robert Cashman, *A History of the First Methodist Church in Shreveport, Louisiana (1845-1961)*. N.d.
R. H. Harper, *Louisiana*. 1949.
W. W. Holmes, *A Brief History of the Methodist Church in Shreveport up to 1926*. N.d.
Mrs. John L. Scales, Jr., *A Short History of First Methodist Church, Shreveport, Louisiana, 1939*. N.d.

JOLLY B. HARPER
MRS. T. HALLER JACKSON
SAM NADER

SHREWSBURY, WILLIAM J. (1795-1866), British missionary pioneer, was born at Deal, England. In 1815 he offered for overseas work, being appointed to the WEST INDIES. During pre-emancipation period he served in Tortola, Grenada, and Barbados for nine years, facing great difficulty and suffering constant persecution. In Barbados his house and church were both pulled down, and he narrowly escaped martyrdom. Returning to Britain in 1826 he was immediately appointed to South America, where he did pioneer work until 1836. He began new work in Southeast Africa and founded the Butterworth Station in Kaffirland. He died at Manchester in February, 1866.

R. Shrewsbury, *Memorials of Rev. W. J. Shrewsbury*. London, 1856.

CYRIL J. DAVEY

SHRINES, LANDMARKS, and **SITES** of The United Methodist Church, U.S.A. A Methodist **Historic Shrine** is a site or a structure which has been officially designated as a "Historic Shrine" by the GENERAL CONFERENCE. To qualify for this recognition the site or structure must have been so linked with significant events or outstanding personalities in the origin and development of The United Methodist Church or its antecedents, as to have distinctive historical interest and value for the denomination as a whole, as contrasted with local and regional historical significance, and it must have features which invite and justify pilgrimages.

At the time of union in 1968, The Methodist Church had twelve official Historic Shrines: JOHN STREET CHURCH, New York City; ST. GEORGE'S CHURCH, Philadelphia; BARRATT'S CHAPEL, near Frederica, Del.; ROBERT STRAWBRIDGE'S LOG HOUSE, near New Windsor, Md.; GREEN HILL HOUSE, Louisburg, N. C.; ST. SIMON'S ISLAND, Brunswick, Ga.; EDWARD COX HOUSE, Bluff City, Tenn.; WYANDOT INDIAN MISSION, Upper Sandusky, Ohio; REHOBETH CHURCH, near Union, W. Va.; Old MCKENDREE CHAPEL, Jackson, Mo.; ACUFF'S CHAPEL, Highway 11-W between

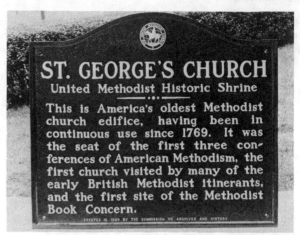

SHRINE MARKER ERECTED AT ST. GEORGE'S
IS SIMILAR TO MARKER ERECTED AT ALL SHRINES

Blountville and Kingsport, Tenn.; and the OLD STONE CHURCH Site and Cemetery, Leesburg, Va. The E.U.B. Church had two historic shrines: OTTERBEIN CHURCH, Baltimore; and ALBRIGHT MEMORIAL CHAPEL, Kleinfeltersville, Pa. The 1970 General Conference named WHITAKER'S CHAPEL, near Enfield, N. C., as the fifteenth Historic Shrine.

The *Discipline* of The United Methodist Church provides that before a site or a structure can be designated as a Historic Shrine by the General Conference, it must first have been officially named a **Historic Site** by a Jurisdictional or an Annual Conference, and its claims for meriting the status of a Historic Shrine must have been reviewed by the General COMMISSION ON ARCHIVES AND HISTORY with such recommendation as that Commission deems proper to the General Conference.

Historic Landmarks: A Methodist Historic Landmark is a site or a structure which has been officially designated as a "Historic Landmark" by the General Conference. The qualifications for a Historic Landmark are the same as those for Historic Shrines in every particular, *except* that this term is applied to important sites and structures *which have little remaining in the way of monuments to invite pilgrimage*. Prior to union in 1968, no sites or structures had been designated as Historic Landmarks. The 1970 General Conference named MCMAHAN'S CHAPEL in Texas, METHODIST HOSPITAL in Brooklyn, N. Y., and the site of LOVELY LANE CHAPEL, Baltimore, as the first Historic Landmarks.

Historic Sites. Jurisdictional and Annual Conferences may designate as Historic Sites any sites or structures within their boundaries which have been related to significant events and important personalities in the origin and development of The United Methodist Church or its antecedents. The president of the Commission on Archives and History of the conference making such a designation is required to advise the General Commission on Archives and History which keeps a register of all Historic Sites and supplies numbered markers for them.

Discipline, UMC, 1968.

ALBEA GODBOLD

SHUCK, DANIEL (1827-1900), American United Brethren bishop, was born Jan. 16, 1827. His father, John Shuck, was a devout Lutheran and good Bible student; his mother, born in GERMANY, migrated to America and early in life joined the UNITED BRETHREN Church in Harrison County, Ind.

Educated in the county schools, Daniel Shuck entered Indiana University for one year. Friends and even the bishop of his area discouraged further education preparatory to entering the ministry, an unfortunate trend of the church in that day.

At the age of seventeen he joined the INDIANA CONFERENCE, Church of the United Brethren in Christ, and for fifteen years, except for the one year in the university, he served circuits in INDIANA and KENTUCKY. He married Harriet B. Cannady, March 11, 1847.

His major interests were in education and missions. In 1858 he was sent to Missouri where the controversies on slavery and secret orders were rife. He served with distinction until 1861, when the GENERAL CONFERENCE elected him bishop and assigned him to the new episcopal district being opened on the Pacific Coast. A. W. DRURY, historian, wrote, "Bishop Shuck was missionary, circuit preacher, presiding elder and bishop all together or one after another." After two quadrenniums the General Conference discontinued this area as an episcopal district. He took up work again in Indiana Conference, but soon returned to the Pacific Coast to assist in promoting the work there. He played a large part in establishing San Joaquin Valley College at Woodbridge, Calif., becoming in 1879 its first president and a trustee for the institution over many years.

Although he signed the minority report on secret orders in the 1889 General Conference, he was one of two who refused to leave the denomination in the subsequent division. He died Nov. 2, 1900, and was buried in the cemetery at Woodbridge, Calif.

A. W. Drury, *History of the UB.* 1924.
Koontz and Roush, *The Bishops.* 1950.
H. A. Thompson, *Our Bishops.* 1889.   JOHN H. NESS, SR.

SHUEY, WILLIAM J. (1827-1920), American United Brethren leader, missionary and administrator, was born in Miamisburg, Ohio, Feb. 9, 1827, to Adam and Hannah (Alley) Shuey. After pursuing his studies in the common schools of Montgomery and Clark Counties (OHIO), he entered the Ohio Conference high school, a Methodist institution in Springfield, Ohio. Converted at the age of sixteen, he soon thereafter set his mind and heart to the Christian ministry which service began at nineteen years of age, serving as a junior preacher on a large circuit embracing DAYTON, Ohio. He joined Miami Conference of the UNITED BRETHREN IN CHRIST in 1848, serving the following appointments: Lewisburg Circuit; First Church, Cincinnati; and First Church, Dayton. For three years he also was presiding elder.

In 1855 he, along with D. K. FLICKINGER and D. C. KUMLER, became the first United Brethren missionaries to SIERRA LEONE. When Kumler became ill, Shuey returned with him to America. He became assistant Publishing Agent in 1864 and two years later the sole Agent, which position he served with distinction until his retirement in 1897. Following this he served four years as business manager of the Union Biblical Seminary (now UNITED THEOLOGICAL SEMINARY). It had been largely through the instrumentality of Shuey that this seminary was founded in 1871 and located in Dayton, Ohio. Bishop MATHEWS said of Shuey: "His commanding leadership was conspicuous. He possessed rare mental power and a self-

reliance that made him a formidable and successful leader. He had few peers, if any, in our church." During the period of litigation, when the Church faced division by the withdrawal of the UNITED BRETHREN IN CHRIST (Old CONSTITUTION), Shuey's management of the Publishing House and its finances enabled the Church to come through the period with little adverse effect. Legal assistance was made available to local churches, annual conferences, and general church agencies.

William J. Shuey died Feb. 21, 1920, and was buried in Dayton, Ohio.

The Evangel, May 1920.
Religious Telescope, March 6, 1920.
D. B. Shuey, *History of the Shuey Family in America.* Galion, O.: the author, 1919.   JOHN H. NESS, SR.

SHULER, ROBERT P. ("Bob") (1880-1965), American preacher and evangelist, and crusader for public and private morality, was born in Grayson County, Va., on Aug. 4, 1880, and was educated at EMORY AND HENRY, which later gave him the D.D. degree in 1932, as ASBURY COLLEGE had done in 1928. He married Nelle Reeves, and they had eight children.

He began his ministry at Pocahontas, Va., in 1902, and entered the HOLSTON CONFERENCE on trial in 1903. After serving churches in VIRGINIA and TENNESSEE, in 1906 he went to TEXAS, where he held pastorates in four of the conferences of the M.E. Church, South. In 1920 he transferred to the PACIFIC CONFERENCE and began a ministry at Trinity Church in LOS ANGELES, serving there until his retirement in 1953. Under Shuler's leadership Trinity Church became the largest church in Southern Methodism on the Pacific Coast, and its men's organization the largest in the denomination. Before unification Shuler was a strong leader of Southern Methodism.

He was a member of the GENERAL CONFERENCE (MES) of 1918, '22, '26, '34, '38, taking a strong part in each of these where the issue of unification was debated, as he was heavily against it. He spoke strongly against the admission of women to the traveling ministry, especially in a notable debate in the General Conference of 1934.

"Bob" Shuler was one of the most powerful voices for fundamentalism in Methodism, both before and after unification. His magazine abounded with attacks on modernism, especially during the climactic days of the Scopes Trial in 1925 in Dayton, Tenn. He likewise was engaged in many struggles in the realm of social action. He periodically attacked the low state of morals in the movie colony in Hollywood, Calif., and, particularly in the 1920's and 1930's sought better municipal government for Los Angeles. He was a leader in the Prohibition movement, and in 1932 polled 564,000 votes in CALIFORNIA for U. S. Senator on the Prohibition ticket. For several years in Los Angeles he operated his own radio station, KGEF, which served as a major vehicle to express his views.

Shuler opposed unification in 1924-1925, mainly because of the jurisdictional proposal, but in 1939 when union came, he supported it wholeheartedly. After unification he continued to be in opposition to many of the actions of the reorganized SOUTHERN CALIFORNIA CONFERENCE because of his increasing conservatism on social issues. He declared in 1957 that "personal heart-warming salvation has too much been swallowed up in the Social Gospel."

He edited *Bob Shuler's Magazine,* and the *Fundamen-*

talist, besides *The Methodist Challenge*, and was the author of a number of books and pamphlets, including *What New Doctrine Is This?* and *Some Dogs I Have Known*.

He died Sept. 11, 1965.

C. T. Howell, *Prominent Personalities*. 1945.
E. D. Jervey, *Southern California and Arizona*. 1960.
Thacker, "The Methodist Church in Southern California in Relation to the 'Social Gospel,' 1928-1941." Unpublished dissertation, University of Southern California.
EDWARD D. JERVEY

SHUMAKER, EDWARD S. (1867-1929), American preacher and reformer, the son of David W. and Sarah Ann (Seitz) Shumaker, was born July 20, 1867, at Greenville, Ohio. Later the family moved to Effingham County, Ill. He was a local preacher when he enrolled at DePauw University in 1889. He was admitted into the Northwest Indiana Conference in 1890. His leadership against the liquor traffic in Williamsport attracted national attention. In 1903 he became field agent for the Indiana Anti-saloon League. In 1907 he became its superintendent. His leadership helped to outlaw beverage alcohol in Indiana. Indiana's organization became a national figure. DePauw University gave him a D.D. degree. After national prohibition was adopted political persecution arose and he was a martyr to the cause for which he gave his life. He married Lena Truax in 1895. She died two years later. In 1900 he married Flora Hollinger. Five children blessed their home. He died Oct. 25, 1929, at his Indianapolis home.

J. J. Detzler, *Northwest Indiana Conference*. 1953.
Who Was Who in America.
W. D. ARCHIBALD

JOHN WESLEY SHUNGU

SHUNGU, JOHN WESLEY (1917-), African bishop of The United Methodist Church, was born in Onalua, Congo, on Oct. 8, 1917, the eldest of sixteen children, and the son of Ndjadiyu Utshudiangandu and Kama (Elena) Shungu. He received his primary schooling at Tunda Methodist School and became a student teacher until 1935. He also attended the Wembo Nyama Bible School, 1938, and until 1943 he served as a local preacher at Tunda, Methodist mission district and station. In that year, 1943, he entered the Old Umtali Schooling and Theological School which he attended for five years. On

June 7, 1936, he was united in marriage to Louise Lutshumba and their children are Henriette (Mrs. Daniel Kikumba), Denise (Mrs. Dimandja), Daniel, Catherine, John, Philipp, Davis, Armand, Mathias, Christine, Christophe, Cyrille, and Louise.

John Wesley Shungu was admitted on trial into the Central Congo Conference, 1942; ordained deacon, 1948; and elder in 1952. His pastorates have included in the Congo: Matapa, 1939-42; Tunda, 1942-43; professor of Old Testament and New Testament, Wembo Nyama Bible School, 1949-54; superintendent of Wembo Nyama District, 1954-60; director of the Lodja Bible School, and also pastor in Lodja, 1960-64. He was elected bishop by the Central Conference, Mulungwishi, Katanga, Congo, on Sept. 1, 1964, and has served the Congo Area, Luluabourg since that time and was included as a member of the Council of Bishops.

Bishop Shungu has been the delegate to the Africa Central Conference in 1948, '52, '56, '60, and '64; to the General Conferences of 1952 and '56; to the International Missionary Conference in Germany, 1952; to the World Council of Churches, New Delhi, India, 1961; to the consultation Board of Missions, 1952; to the Latin American consultations, 1962; Asian Consultation, 1963; member of the Evangelist Mission to America, 1959; legal representative (since 1960) and treasurer of the Women's Division of Christian Service as field treasurer, 1961-64. He received the D.D. from Asbury Theological Seminary in 1964.

He is the author of *New Testament Otetela Bible Concordance*, 1940; translator and compiler: *How to Pray*, 1949; *Temperance*, 1951; and *History of Christian Church*, 1952.

Who's Who in the Methodist Church, 1966.
N. B. H.

SHY, PETER RANDOLPH (1898-), thirtieth bishop of the C.M.E. Church, was born on May 10, 1898, at Kelly, Ga. He holds a B.A. degree from Paine College, and M.A. degrees from Fisk University and Columbia University. He was ordained deacon in 1921 and elder in 1925. For ten years he was a professor at Miles College, and from 1940 to 1948 was academic dean of Lane College. He has served churches in Alabama and Tennessee. In 1958, he was elected to the office of bishop in the C.M.E. Church.

Harris and Patterson, *C.M.E. Church*. 1965.
Ethel L. Williams, *Biographical Directory of Negro Ministers*. New York: Scarecrow Press, 1965.
RALPH G. GAY

SIERRA LEONE is a West African state, with an area of 27,925 square miles and a population (1968 estimate) of 2,475,000, belonging to some fourteen main ethnic groups. The capital, Freetown, has one of the finest natural harbors in Africa. Land for a settlement of free Negroes (the so-called "Black Poor") was purchased in 1787 on behalf of some British philanthropists. The settlement did not prosper, but was re-formed in 1792 on the basis of some 1,100 Negroes who had fought for Britain in the American War of Independence and had subsequently been unsuccessfully transplanted to Nova Scotia. In 1800 the population was augmented by "Maroons" captured in the Slave Wars in Jamaica. In 1808 the London Directors of this "Province of Freedom" (who included William Wilberforce and other members of the Clapham Evangelical circle) ceded the colony to the British Crown. In the same year the act abolishing the Slave Trade came into force, and thereafter British warships intercepted vessels carrying slaves. These "recaptives" were brought into Freetown, and they and their descendants became the principal element in the colony, marked by western education and dress, earnest Christian profession, and a "Creole" (more precisely "Krio") culture fusing western and African elements. They travelled widely as traders and missionaries throughout West Africa and were responsible for the first introduction of many areas to Christianity. The Colony acquired additional territory on several occasions in the nineteenth century, and in 1896 a British Protectorate brought the frontiers to approximately their present position. One result was the gradual movement of large numbers of hinterland peoples to Freetown and the old Colony villages. Sierra Leone became independent in 1961.

The settlers of 1792 were Christians, mostly of evangelical outlook, and they included Methodists who formed their own society, 200 strong. They corresponded with the British CONFERENCE asking for an itinerant, but not until 1811, when THOMAS COKE sent out GEORGE WARREN and three schoolmasters, was the request granted. Warren found the whole apparatus of Methodist organization and discipline already in progress. He died within eight months, and his successors quarrelled with the Freetown society, until in 1821 the superintendent declared it dissolved. Thereafter it maintained a separate existence until 1861, bringing many Maroons and recaptives under Christian influence. The Maroons formed a separate congregation and leased it to the Wesleyan mission, but this relationship was severed by 1835. Recaptives, feeling themselves treated as inferiors in the Settler chapel, formed their own West African Methodist Church, under the leadership of a notable preacher, Anthony O'Connor, in 1844.

By mid-century, therefore, the Colony had four separate Methodist connexions. The Settler and Maroon churches, representing small communities, were eventually subsumed, but the mission-supported Wesleyan Methodists, and the entirely independent West African Methodists, each spread in Freetown and the Colony villages. In 1859 the West African Methodists amalgamated with the (English) UNITED METHODIST FREE CHURCHES, and accepted a missionary superintendent. New work begun in the Mende area of the hinterland showed encouraging results, but never recovered from the so-called "Hut Tax War" of 1898. The union of Methodist churches in Britain in 1932 brought the two Methodist churches in Sierra Leone together for a short time, but by 1934 the West African Methodist Church reemerged under its old name. It now has about 2,000 full members.

The Wesleyan Mission formed a base for the mission in GAMBIA, and Wesleyan emigrants were the point of contact for the Yoruba mission in NIGERIA and many other places of Christian expansion. Attempts in the hinterland, however, did not prosper until the operations in Mende country began in the 1930's. These accelerated work on a Mende Bible (published 1959) and include a well-known hospital at Segbwema. The Wesleyans early had an educated indigenous ministry (a Sierra Leonean, Charles Knight, was Chairman in the 1870's). An autonomous Sierra Leone Conference, with two districts, was established in 1967. The membership in 1968 was 8,163,

with a total community something more than twice that number and some 400 places of worship.

The WESLEYAN METHODIST CHURCH of America sent missionaries to the northwest part of the hinterland, its first overseas field, in 1889. Its work (in Limba, Temne and Loko country) has remained small, but influential. An autonomous conference was established in 1940: membership is about 2,300.

Part of the COUNTESS OF HUNTINGDON's Connexion in the Colony affiliated to the A.M.E. CHURCH U.S.A. in 1887, and expanded under a series of colorful leaders. Its present constituency, however, is probably less than 1,000.

The United Methodist Conference represents a work which goes back to 1841 when the Mendi Mission was established in Sherbro, following public interest in the United States in the *Amistad* incident. In 1846 the work was subsumed into that of the American Missionary Association, and in 1883 handed to the UNITED BRETHREN IN CHRIST. With over 11,000 full members, mostly in the Mende, Sherbro and Kono areas, the United Methodists are now the largest Christian body in the country.

The Church of the United Brethren in Christ, which in time became a component part of The United Methodist Church in America, early showed a concern for Africa. On Jan. 1, 1854, the Mission Board of that Church voted "to establish a mission station on the Big Boom River in the interior of Africa at an early period."

W. J. SHUEY, D. K. FLICKINGER and D. C. KUMLER, M.D.—all of them ministers of the Miami Conference (UB)—set sail from New York, Jan. 23, 1855 and after a tedious thirty-four day voyage the vessel put in at Freetown, Sierra Leone, Africa. A mission site was selected at Mo Kelli, 120 miles south of Freetown, but the selection was unfortunate and three years later the work was relocated at Shenge, sixty miles southeast of Freetown. During the first decade seven missionaries were sent to Africa: at the close of seven years the only fruit of the mission were two Negro youths.

From 1855 to 1869 the mission confronted crisis after crisis. Two of the first three missionaries soon returned to America: the third remained for fourteen months before he returned. Upon his departure the new mission was served by J. A. Williams, a Negro from Freetown. As the toll in terms of broken health and lives lost mounted, there was a question of keeping on, but it was resolved that the work should be continued with renewed efforts.

In December 1870, the Board sent to Sierra Leone, JOSEPH GOMER and his wife, Negroes from DAYTON, Ohio. Their service in the mission covering twenty-two years was most fruitful. Others came to aid them. In 1877 Miss Emily Beeken, the first missionary sent out by the Women's Missionary Association, arrived at Rotifunk. The episcopal address to GENERAL CONFERENCE in 1897 conveyed a note of victory: "After more than forty years of toil and trial, our missionaries are beginning to see the dawn of a glorious day in Africa." But the British colonial government in endeavoring to suppress slavery, cannibalism and witchcraft had aroused the deep anger of some of the natives. The latter in 1898 rose without warning to exterminate the white men. More than a thousand persons died before this mob madness subsided and among the dead were seven of the missionaries supported by the Women's Missionary Association.

However new missionaries volunteered to return to the places of despolation and United Brethren in America gave generously to rebuild what had been so wantonly destroyed. Education programs have played a great role in this mission. In addition to the numerous congregational schools, the Albert Academy (for boys) and Harford School for Girls have had a distinguished career. The medical program of the mission, operating through dispensaries, a hospital, and a new eye clinic, has achieved signal results. However, as always evangelistic work is the fundamental concern of the mission. In 1967 thirty-six missionary personnel helped to forward the mission of the church in this area.

L. L. Berry, *Century of Missions*. 1942.
G. H. and M. L. Clarke, *The American Wesleyan Mission of Sierra Leone*. Marion, Ind., 1940.
G. J. Cuming, ed., *Studies in Church History*. Cambridge, 1970.
Findlay and Holdsworth, *Wesleyan Meth. Miss. Soc.* 1922.
D. K. Flickinger, *History of the . . . Missions among the Shesbso and Mendi Tribes*. Dayton, O.: 1885.
C. Fyfe, *A History of Sierra Leone*. London: Oxford University Press, 1962.
Journal of Religion in Africa, No. 3, 1970.
C. Marke, *The Orgins of Wesleyan Methodism in Sierra Leone*. London, 1913.
Sierra Leone Bulletin of Religion. 1961.
W. Vivian, *Mendiland Memories*. London, n.d.   A. F. WALLS
                                                   LOIS MILLER

FERDINAND SIGG

SIGG, FERDINAND (1902-1965), Swiss publisher, bishop and distinguished ecumenist, was born on March 22, 1902, the son of a carpenter in Thalwil near ZURICH, SWITZERLAND. He was initially trained a banker and administrator. Then he was called to the ministry and trained in Frankfurt Methodist Theological Seminary (1924-27). After one year in the pastorate, chiefly amongst laborers, Bishop JOHN L. NUELSEN appointed him his secretary. This proved providential, for the Bishop opened his eyes to ecumenical life as well as to church administration. Sigg was elected general manager of the Methodist Publishing House in Zurich and served in this new capacity from 1936-55. Up to his last day he was a member both of the Swiss Association of Publishers and of the Federation of Swiss Protestant Publishers.

When Sigg took over, the publishing house was in bad shape. He completely reorganized the publishing depart-

ment and the printing shop and proved an outstanding businessman and publisher. Within one year he took over a second publishing house, to serve particularly in the field of ecumenical life. He was a man of vision. As editor he was responsible for the Swiss Methodist periodical on missionary life and affairs (1933-53) and the weekly *Schweizer Evangelist* (1940-65).

As a Christian businessman he belonged to that leading group of Boldern Academy (near Zurich) which devoted itself to businessmen's retreats. But it would be a grave mistake to think of him only in such a capacity. He was a good theologian, and—in every sphere of life —a pastor of men and women. His intensive study in the fields of psychology and sociology enabled him to communicate in the thoughtforms of modern man. He was a superb speaker and writer. But he knew the danger of a merely verbal message, and that is why he joined emphatically in more than one relief project, such as the Swiss protestant action "Bread for Brothers."

On Oct. 17, 1954, Ferdinand Sigg was consecrated bishop of the Central and Southern Europe Central Conference at BRUSSELS, BELGIUM. During the war he had already shouldered responsible tasks when Bishop Nuelsen retired. He was president of the Swiss Annual Conference and later fellow worker of Bishops PAUL N. GARBER and ARTHUR J. MOORE. The GENEVA Area is in itself an "ecumenical compendium," including territories with Protestant or prevailing Roman Catholic church life, reaching into East European countries with the official ideology of dialectical materialism and Moslem North Africa. A Swiss state churchman said of him that "the world was his parish." Often a delegate to GENERAL CONFERENCE before becoming a bishop, he was, after 1955, a member of the Executive Committee of the WORLD METHODIST COUNCIL.

Strangely enough, Ferdinand Sigg had learned little about the ecumenical movement in Seminary. As secretary to John L. Neulsen he not only found literature about Stockholm and Lausanne, but he also shared in the work of the European Relief Center and met Adolf Keller, to whom he became deeply devoted as a friend. Nuelsen undoubtedly introduced his secretary to ecumenical involvement but with the advice of keeping true to the Methodist heritage and of sharing its contribution in ecumenical conferences.

In 1933 he became a member of the Swiss Protestant Youth Conference, which he represented in 1936 at the Geneva International Youth Conference. In 1944, as the President of the Swiss Methodist Mission Board, he became a delegate to the newly founded Swiss Protestant Missionary Council whose President he was from 1957 onward. He represented this Council both at Willingen (IMC, 1952) and at GHANA (1959). He attended the World Conferences at Amsterdam, Evanston and New Delhi and was one of the founders and presidents of the new European Conference of Churches.

In 1953 his wife Alice, his equal in devotion and as a leader, died. Bishop Sigg died Oct. 27, 1965, and was buried in Fluntern Cemetery, Zurich, on Nov. 1. Following burial, a memorial service was held in the Fraumunster in Zurich.

C. ERNST SOMMER

SILVA, ALFREDO HENRIQUE DA (1872-1950), Portuguese minister and educator, was born at Oporto, Jan.

18, 1872, the son of an Army officer who died while Alfredo was a baby. Brought up by widowed mother as a strict Roman Catholic, he received his early education at a Primary School run by Jesuits, where he gained a prize for memorizing the "Cathechism against Protestantism," which later he saw to be so full of lies and perversions that it furthered his conversion, which took place in the Methodist church of Mirante, Oporto, built by R. H. Moreton.

Against much maternal opposition, sometimes physical, da Silva persisted in his adherence to the Methodists, and in his late teens was appointed teacher in the Day School opened by Moreton. Some little time later he entered the Methodist ministry, being the first Methodist to be ordained, in November 1898, in the Iberian Peninsula. In due course he succeeded Robert H. Moreton as superintendent of the Portuguese Methodist Church, which office he held till his retirement in 1948. He was a teacher, and later, until 1942, Director, of the Oporto Industrial and Commercial Institute.

Alfredo da Silva was the founder in Portugal of the Y.M.C.A.; he inaugurated the Oporto Y.M.C.A. in a dependency of the Mirante Methodist Church in 1894, and was its President, both there and later in its own building in Oporto, for twenty-five years, as well as its President Emeritus until his death. One of this organization's first activities was to set up evening classes for laboring and office workers; in this, as in many other fields, Alfredo da Silva pioneered the way later followed by others. He helped organize Y.M.C.A. activity for Portuguese troops in France and elsewhere during the first World War. As a member of the Oporto City Council he helped reorganize the sanitation of the city and also organize the remodelling of its electric tramway system. For his efforts in organizing food distribution in the difficult days which came at the end of World War I, he was awarded the "Ordem de Cristo" by the Portuguese Government. He also presided over the Commission which received the visit of gratitude of the French Government to Oporto headed by Marechal Joffre.

To help further the reform of Technical School teaching in Portugal, he visited, for study purpose, Rio de Janeiro and other foreign cities. He worked and travelled much in the cause of peace and reconciliation, being representative for Portugal to the Churches International Alliance for Peace and Brotherhood. For thirty-seven years he edited the weekly *Amigos da Infancia*. He left little published material, aside from some articles, some hymns and translations, and some pamphlets, including one on the slave traffic against which he labored effectively —"The Monster of Slavery"—a collection of articles which appeared in the Lisbon newspaper *O Seculo*. He was editor for some years of the Methodist monthly *O Portugal Evangelico*, on which he also worked with his ministerial colleague and friend, J. Antonio Fernandes. He is buried in the Agramonte Cemetery, Oporto.

ALBERT ASPEY

SILVA, JOÃO PARAHYBA DARONCH DA (1931-),
Brazilian Protestant leader, was born in Carazinho, state of Rio Grande do Sul, on Jan. 8, 1931. After graduation from the Instituto Educacional de Passo Fundo (Methodist), he attended the theological seminary in Rudge Ramos, São Paulo, from which he received the B.D. de-

gree in 1953. He was ordained deacon in 1954 and elder in 1956.

Silva married Neyde Terezinha on May 23, 1959. They have two children, João Marcos and Susana Denise.

After serving several pastorates, including Piracicaba and Ribeirão Preto, he was elected Executive Secretary for Social Action in 1964 at the General Conference of the Methodist Church of Brazil. In this capacity, he was sent in 1965 as Brazil's delegate to El Tabo, Chile, to the Latin American Conference on Theological Studies. He has since been made president of the Brazilian branch of I.S.A.L (Church and State in Latin America), and a member of the Centro Dom Vital (a Catholic lay movement). He has published one book, *The Church, Body of Christ*.

Parahyba Silva is frequently interviewed by newspapers and secular magazines as interpreter of the Protestant point of view on social questions affecting the nation.

EULA K. LONG

SILVA, JUVENAL ERNESTO DA (1907-), Brazilian preacher and chaplain in the armed forces of Brazil, was born in São Roque, state of São Paulo, on June 20, 1907. His mother was a faithful member of the Baptist Church, but the father was not an evangelical and strongly opposed his wife's religion and her attendance at services.

When Silva was sixteen, the family moved to Santo Amaro, now a part of the city of São Paulo. There he worked in a factory by the side of Isnard Rocha, who later also became a Methodist preacher. He began attending services in the Methodist church, which he joined on Dec. 24, 1924, on profession of faith. Feeling called to the ministry, he studied and prepared himself for entrance to Instituto Granbery, though he had to continue work at the factory.

His mother, very ill before dying, asked her husband to help Silva in his studies as she wanted him to become a preacher. This he promised; and her Christian witness at death so impressed the unbelieving husband that he turned from his violent opposition to the church, yet remained indifferent to its mission. Years later, when Silva became a preacher, he had the joy of receiving into the church his own father.

Silva entered Granbery in 1927, and graduated both in the scientific and theological courses in 1935. In 1936, he married Carmen de Oliveira, by whom he had one son. He was ordained both deacon and elder by Bishop Cesar Dacorso. In 1937, in addition to pastorates, he was Secretary of Christian Education for the Second Region of the church. In 1941, he received a scholarship to study in the United States, but was forced to return in 1942 because of the outbreak of the Second World War. For the next two years, he served as chaplain at Granbery Instituto and later he became chaplain to the Brazilian Armed Services, then acting in Italy. Near the front, he had more than one narrow escape from death.

Returning to Brazil, he remained in the military chaplaincy, where he was promoted to captain. He settled in Rio de Janeiro, and did excellent work among military men and in the surrounding Protestant churches. His wife Carmen died in 1963. After her death, Silva returned to his native state, São Paulo, to live in Sirocaba near his son's family.

ISNARD ROCHA

OSWALDO DA SILVA

SILVA, OSWALDO DIAS DA (1922-   ), bishop of the Methodist Church of BRAZIL, was born in Biriguí, state of São Paulo, on May 31, 1922. He came of a Methodist family, his grandfather, Etéocle Afini, having been a preacher. Bishop Silva received his primary and high school education in Biriguí, after which he graduated from the Methodist theological seminary in Rudge Ramos, São Paulo. He married Maria da Penha and they have five children—Poliana, Lígia, Osvaldo, Hélio, and Rosa Helena.

He was ordained DEACON in 1946 and ELDER in 1948. He has held pastorates in various cities in the states of Rio Grande do Sul and São Paulo; has served as a District Superintendent and as secretary of the Regional (area) Board of Missions. While pastor of Central Church in PORTO ALEGRE, Rio Grande do Sul, he helped the Woman's Society found the Lar da Velhice, a Methodist home for the aged in that city.

He was elected bishop by the ninth General Conference of the Methodist Church in Brazil, in July 1965. His field, the Fifth Region, comprises the states of Goiás, Mato Grosso, and Western São Paulo. The present episcopal residence is in Campinas, São Paulo.

EULA K. LONG

SILVEIRA, GUARACY (1893-1953), Brazilian preacher and writer, descendant of a family distinguished in law and politics, was born in Franca, state of São Paulo, on Sept. 27, 1893. After studying in Catholic primary schools (he was reared a traditional Catholic), he went to INSTITUTO GRANBERY, from which he received his B.S. degree in Science and Letters. He was converted while there, and joined the Methodist church, and decided to enter the ministry. In 1920, he was ordained DEACON, and in 1921 ordained ELDER by Bishop JOHN M. MOORE. From 1915 to 1938, he served as pastor of both rural and large city churches, including Piracicaba and Central Methodist Church in SÃO PAULO. At various times, he served as presiding elder.

Guaracy Silveira was editor of the official Methodist weekly, *Expositor Cristão*, for two terms (1930-34 and 1938-42); and in 1937 was presiding officer of the Central Brazil Annual Conference, in the absence of a bishop. He was a leading figure in the movement for autonomy of the Methodist church in BRAZIL; a member of the committee which drew up its constitution, and presiding officer of the first session of its first General Conference. He was also the first General Secretary of the Board of Missions; the first Protestant army CHAPLAIN, serving with the São Paulo troops during the 1932 revolution; and the first Protestant congressman in the legislature of Brazil, to which he was elected in 1933. During his 1945-50 term, he signed two Brazilian constitutions.

A writer, a poet, and teacher, Guaracy Silveira was the author of numerous articles in both religious and secular papers; and of several books, religious, fictional, and political in nature. Among these were *Lutero, Loyola e o Totalitarismo*, and *O Evangelho, Patrologia e Rasao* (The Gospel, Patristics, and Reasoning).

He married Etelvina Crem, a descendant of German immigrants to Brazil, who had been converted by early Methodist missionaries. All their children have distinguished themselves professionally, and are active in the Methodist Church.

Guaracy Silveira died on Aug. 5, 1953.

PAULO GUARACY SILVEIRA

SILVER, MABEL IRENE (1902-1972), American E.U.B. medical missionary to SIERRA LEONE, WEST Africa, was born in BALTIMORE, Md., March 23, 1902. She graduated from LEBANON VALLEY COLLEGE in 1925 with a B.S. degree, and from the University of Maryland School of Medicine in 1929, the only woman in the class.

She received the Diploma in Tropical Medicine and Hygiene from the University of London in the spring of 1932, and from there went to Sierra Leone to serve as a medical missionary of the UNITED BRETHREN IN CHRIST. All but two years (1933-35), when she served in Taiama, were spent in Rotifunk. During her thirty years of service the dispensary developed into a small hospital, known as the Hatfield-Archer Hospital. Thousands of patients were treated, and dozens of young men and women trained to serve as medical assistants.

She received in June 1953 the high honor of being included in the Queen's Coronation Honor List as a Member of the British Empire.

Returning to the United States in 1962, she became a staff physician at the Rosewood State Hospital, Baltimore, until final retirement in 1970.

In 1971, at a special ceremony to honor her at the Sierra Leone Embassy in Washington, she was presented a citation from Sierra Leone's Prime Minister Siaka P. Stevens. In making the presentation Ambassador to the United States Dr. John Akar said, "She cared for the bodies of our countrymen and their souls with a judicious blend of medicine and prayer."

She died April 2, 1972.

ESTHER L. MEGILL

SILVER SPRING, MARYLAND, U.S.A. **Marvin Memorial Church** is located in a suburban community which affords little comparison to the rural atmosphere of ninety-six years ago, when in September 1872 a small group of devoted Christians founded the first church at Four Corners.

The very early history of organization could not be located, but both members and non-members had the desire to have a house of God in the area where people might come to worship. The land for the new church was donated by Mr. and Mrs. Oliver Clark and Mr. and Mrs.

George N. Beale, none of whom was a member of the Methodist faith.

While the church was being built, services were held in an old barn which was situated across the Intersection from the present church site. The men of the community provided the foundation by hauling logs. Carpenters were hired to build above ground, and the little white church, recently torn down, was completed in October 1872.

The church was first known as Wesley Chapel M.E. Church, South, and Paul Haddaway was the first pastor. Members walked, rode horseback, or drove in horse and buggy to get to church. Sometimes they passed through toll gates located at Georgia Avenue, Dale Drive, White Oak and Ednor. The toll charge was one cent per mile for one trip to church, and toll was required for the return trip also.

In 1941 it became necessary to disband the Marvin Church at Independence Avenue and Tenth Street S.E., WASHINGTON, D.C. Four Corners Church received the principal cash gift, the altar rail, pulpit furniture, pews, pipe organ and other supplies. A new location adjacent to the old property was bought for $30,000.

Four Corners Church was on a circuit with Lay Hill and Colesville, Md. Divine worship was so arranged that on one Sunday services were held in the morning and the next Sunday services were held in the afternoon. Four Corners became a station church in 1942.

The ground breaking for the new sanctuary was held Nov. 4, 1945 at which time the membership had grown to approximately 500 members. In 1970 Marvin Memorial reported a total full membership of 1,592.

Maryland Living, August 18, 1968.   MRS. MARY MILSTEAD

SIMMONDS, JOSEPH HENRY

SIMMONDS, JOSEPH HENRY (1845-1936), NEW ZEALAND Methodist minister, was the second minister of that church to be born there in Nelson. He entered the ministry in 1869 and served the church with distinction and ability for fifty-four years. Three years were spent as a missionary in FIJI, then twenty-one years in important New Zealand circuits, where in a fresh and scholarly presentation of the Gospel, he influenced many young men toward the Christian ministry.

For fifteen years (1896-1911) he was governor of the theological college, and for twenty-eight years principal of Wesley College (Paerata), in which position he secured the present splendid site and formulated the scheme to blend Maori, Pacific island, and European boys in a secondary school. In 1895 he was president of the Wesleyan Methodist Conference.

He was a member, for several years, of the AUCKLAND University Council. He made valuable contributions to afforestation. His book, *Trees From Other Lands: Eucalypts in New Zealand,* has become a standard work. He contributed many articles to the *Journal of Agriculture* and to other periodicals.

He was a man of kindly spirit and of the highest ideals.

New Zealand Methodist Conference Minutes, 1937.
                                                    WILLIAM T. BLIGHT

SIMMONS, JAMES

SIMMONS, JAMES (1792-1873), a bishop of the A.M.E. ZION CHURCH, was born Dec. 3, 1792, in Accomac County, Va. He was converted in early life and joined the conference May 19, 1832. A year later he was ordained a DEACON, May 18, 1833, and on the same day

was given ELDER's orders. He was elected bishop May 24, 1856, and died Nov. 25, 1873.

                                                    DAVID H. BRADLEY

SIMMONS, JOHN C.

SIMMONS, JOHN C. (1827-1906), American pioneer minister and writer, was born at Jackson, Butts County, Ga., May 26, 1827. He and ALEXANDER WYNN, his co-worker in CALIFORNIA, were licensed to preach in August 1848, in a log church built by Simmons' father on their farm. He was educated at EMORY COLLEGE, Oxford, Ga. He and his brother, William A., answered the missionary call to California, arriving at SAN FRANCISCO in February 1852. On June 28, 1853, he married Margaret Campbell, daughter of Judge Charles Campbell. His appointments included: Grass Valley, 1852; Stockton, 1853; Mariposa, 1856; SAN JOSE, 1858; presiding elder, San Francisco District, 1859; SACRAMENTO, 1861; Professor, English Literature, Pacific Methodist College, 1866-1869; Conference Sunday School Agent, 1870; presiding elder, San Francisco District, 1871; Santa Clara District, 1873; Agent, Pacific Methodist College, 1877; Dixon, 1878; San Francisco, 1881; organized a church at Oakland, 1882; Chico, 1883; Colusa, 1887; President, Pacific Methodist College, 1890; Salinas, 1891; Lincoln, 1895; presiding elder, Merced District, 1896; Modesto, 1898. He was a delegate to the ECUMENICAL METHODIST CONFERENCE in London, England, 1901. He was superannuated in 1902 and then served Salinas, 1903-1906.

He was the author of: *Southern Methodism on the Pacific Coast,* 1886; *The Kingdom and Coming of Christ,* 1891; *The Saint and His Savior,* 1896; *My Trip to the Orient,* 1902.

Simmons died April 21, 1906, after hearing that the earthquake and fire had destroyed many churches and left hundreds of friends homeless.

H. M. DuBose, *History.* 1916.
Minutes of the Pacific Conference.
J. C. Simmons, *Pacific Coast.* 1886.   PEARL S. SWEET

SIMON, JOHN SMITH

SIMON, JOHN SMITH (1843-1933), British Methodist historian, was born at Glasgow on June 25, 1843. He entered the Wesleyan ministry in 1863; was elected to the LEGAL HUNDRED in 1895, and president of the Wesleyan CONFERENCE in 1907. He was principal of Didsbury Theological College from 1901-13. Trained originally as a lawyer, he was an authority on Methodist law and discipline as well as on Methodist history in the eighteenth century. The extraordinary fruit of his retirement was his learned biography of JOHN WESLEY, published in five volumes between 1921 and 1934. He had laid the foundation for this work in his Fernley Lecture of 1907, *The Revival of Religion in England in the Eighteenth Century.* The later works were: *John Wesley, and the Religious Societies* (1921); *John Wesley and the Methodist Societies* (1923); *John Wesley and the Advance of Methodism* (1925); *John Wesley, the Master Builder* (1927); and *John Wesley, the Last Phase* (1934) completed by his son-in-law A. W. HARRISON. Simon died in his sleep on June 28, 1933.

                                                    JOHN KENT

SIMONS, GEORGE ALBERT

SIMONS, GEORGE ALBERT (1874-1952), American minister and superintendent, was born at Laporte, Ind., on March 19, 1874, the son of George Henry and Ottilie

GEORGE A. SIMONS

Schultz Simons. He was a graduate of BALDWIN-WALLACE COLLEGE, of New York University, and DREW THEOLOGICAL SEMINARY, with an A.B., B.D., A.M., and D.D. degrees. He entered the ministry in 1899, and served several charges in his own land until he was appointed as superintendent of the FINLAND and St. Petersburg Mission Conference in 1907-11. He was superintendent-treasurer of the RUSSIA Mission, 1911-21; the Russia Mission Conference and Baltic Mission, 1921-24; the Baltic and Slavic Mission Conference, 1924-28.

He became director of the Ministers' Training Institute in Riga, Latvia, in 1923-27. He was a delegate to the M.E. GENERAL CONFERENCES in 1912 and 1920. He became editor and publisher of *Christiansky Pobornik* (Russia *Christian Advocate*) and of the Baltic and Slavic *Bulletin*. During the First World War he was chairman of the American Red Cross Committee in Russia, and a member of the board of the American Hospital for Wounded Russian Soldiers in Petrograd. He had to leave Petrograd in October of 1918 following the revolution there.

He accompanied a commission of the M.E. Church during the summer of 1919, visiting various European countries, and supervised distribution of relief supplies sent by the M.E. Church to Finland, Russia, etc., during the winter of 1920.

Simons was decorated by the Finnish Government, the Russian Red Cross, Estonian Red Cross, and the Latvian government. He wrote many Methodist books, pamphlets, and tracts in Russian while he lived in Europe. Unmarried, his sister Ottilie accompanied him to Russia. His mother died in their home in St. Petersburg (now Leningrad), and was buried there in 1913. Simons returned to the United States where he served several charges, even until his death in Glendale, N. Y. in 1952.

L. A. Marshall, *American Pioneer in Russia*. 1928.
Nya Budbäraren (Finland), Sept. 1, 1952.

MANSFIELD HURTIG

SIMPSON, DAVID (1745-1799), English clergyman, was born Oct. 12, 1745, near Northallerton, Yorkshire, and educated at St. John's College, CAMBRIDGE. He was converted about 1767 by means of the unitarian Theophilus Lindsey. Ordained deacon (1769) and priest (1771) in the Church of England, after two brief curacies in the

south of England he came to Macclesfield. The earnestness of his preaching at St. Michael's Church there earned him the title of "Methodist," and his opponents succeeded in having him deprived of his curacy. In 1779 he was appointed the first incumbent of the newly-consecrated Christ Church, Macclesfield, where he remained for twenty years. Christ Church was founded by Charles Roe (1715-81), who had strong Methodist sympathies. (His niece, HESTER ANN ROE, married Wesley's preacher JAMES ROGERS.) WESLEY was welcomed to the pulpit and behind the communion rail of Simpson's church, and Simpson in his turn preached for Wesley and on at least one occasion (in 1784) attended the Methodist CONFERENCE. Another of Wesley's colleagues, BRIAN BURY COLLINS, obtained his title as curate to Simpson, and thus was enabled to secure ordination as a clergyman. Wesley had a strong Methodist cause at Macclesfield, and Simpson's presence there secured close cooperation between church and society. Simpson was a prolific writer, whose publications included the following: *A Collection of Psalms and Hymns and Spiritual Songs: for the use of Christians of every denomination* (1776); *The Happiness of Dying in the Lord: with an Apology for the Methodists* (1784: a sermon on the death of James Rogers' first wife, with a lengthy defence of Methodism); *A Discourse on Beneficence, and the wonderful remunerations of Divine Providence to charitable men: with a great variety of examples* (1789: the examples include John Wesley); and his most frequently reprinted work, first published in 1797, *A Plea for Religion and the Sacred Writings*. Simpson died March 24, 1799, and was buried at Christ Church, Macclesfield.

Dictionary of National Biography.
FRANK BAKER

SIMPSON, JAMES (1873-1938), Canadian local preacher and temperance lecturer, leading labor figure, and first socialist mayor of Toronto, was born in Lancashire, England, Dec. 14, 1873, and came to Canada at the age of fourteen. He shortly became a "printer's devil," but with the formation of *The Toronto Daily Star*, joined its staff and for many years was its city hall reporter. Maintaining his membership in the typographical union, he rose from presidency of the local union to presidency of the Toronto Trades and Labor Council, finally becoming vice-president of the Trades and Labour Congress of Canada.

Familiarity with city politics led to a similar ascent from membership in the Toronto Board of Education in 1905 to its chairmanship in 1910. He was elected a controller on the city council in 1914 by the highest vote ever given a candidate up to that time. A socialist from his early years, he first contested the mayoralty of Toronto as a socialist candidate in 1908, and was prominent thereafter in efforts to organize a labour-socialist party in Canada, especially the Independent Labour Party in Ontario (1916), the Canadian Labour Party (1921), and the Co-operative Commonwealth Federation (1933). The breadth of his activities did not always endear him to some of his early fellow-socialists. In 1910 he was expelled from the Social Democratic Party for refusing to divulge confidential material of the Royal Commission on Industrial Training and Technical Education, of which he was a member. He not only led several strikes, but he also participated in numerous arbitrations of major labor disputes. He represented Canadian labor at several international gatherings, perhaps the most dramatic being the International Socialist Congress in Vienna, in the first days of the war of 1914-18. He toured Europe as a government appointee on various labor and education commissions, and lectured internationally on behalf of Prohibition. From 1916-22 he promoted these causes through a newspaper, *The Industrial Banner,* of which he was editor and publisher.

Simpson maintained throughout an active life within the Methodist and United Churches, and in interdenominational organizations such as Christian Endeavor, the Lord's Day Alliance, the Dominion Prohibition Alliance, and the Social Service Council of Canada, of which he was for some time a vice-president. He was approached by the Methodist General Superintendent, S. D. CHOWN, to take on a post as interpreter of church to labor and labor to church; and although Chown's plan was blocked, Simpson remained the most accessible labor leader of his time to the members of the Department of Evangelism and Social Service, a fact which, in particular, cut some of the losses of the church in the printers' strike of 1921, in which the large Methodist Publishing House was deeply involved. It was out of this long history of activities in social reform on a broad front that he gathered the support which brought him regular election to the Toronto Board of Control after 1930 and in election as mayor of Toronto in 1935. He was defeated, however, in 1936; and two years later, recovering from a lengthy illness, died in a motor accident.

Canadian Forum, November, 1938.
H. J. Morgan, *Canadian Men and Women of the Time.* Toronto, 1912.
Toronto Globe, January 2, 1935.   A. R. ALLEN

SIMPSON, JOHN DIXON (1858-1921), American minister, was born in Bradford, Coosa County, Ala., April 22, 1858. His parents moved to Prattville, Ala., where he received his elementary and high school education. He was licensed to preach in 1877. In 1878 he was admitted on trial into the ALABAMA CONFERENCE, and appointed to the Rimbert Hill charge. In 1879 he was married to Hortense Wilson of Mobile, Ala., to which union were born two children, John and Hortense. He was ordained DEACON by Bishop McTYEIRE at Pensacola, Fla., in 1880, and two years later, at Troy, Ala., he was ordained ELDER. He transferred to the NORTH ALABAMA CONFERENCE in 1883. Later he attended Southern University, at Greensboro, Ala., where he graduated in 1887. In the North Alabama Conference he served as pastor, presiding elder, and college president with distinction, serving the Florence, Decatur, Tuscaloosa, and Birmingham Districts.

Simpson was called to the presidency of BIRMINGHAM-SOUTHERN COLLEGE in 1910, where he served until 1916. In 1911, a vacancy having occurred on the Birmingham District, he was appointed to serve the district until Conference, in connection with the presidency of the college. In 1916 he was appointed as pastor of First Church of Athens. In November 1918, he became pastor of First Church, Woodlawn, in the Birmingham District.

He died June 18, 1921, and was buried in the Oak Hill Cemetery, Birmingham, Ala.

G. FRED COOPER

SIMPSON, JOHN FISHER (1887-1963), American educational leader and editor of the *Texas Christian Advocate,* was born at Utopia, Texas, March 24, 1887, son of John Harper and Fannie (Fisher) Simpson. He married Grace Willard, Dec. 21, 1910, and they had one daughter, Catherine (Mrs. William T. Meyers). He was educated at SOUTHWESTERN UNIVERSITY, A.B., 1909; D.D., 1933; University of Texas, M.A., 1930; VANDERBILT, B.D., 1924; graduate study, University of Chicago and Union Seminary, New York. He was received in the TEXAS CONFERENCE in 1909, and transferred to the SOUTHWEST TEXAS CONFERENCE in 1911. His appointments included: Giddings, Texas, 1909-10; student, Vanderbilt, 1911-12; Miles, Texas, 1912; Sherwood Circuit, Texas, 1913; Poteet Circuit, Texas, 1914; San Benito, Texas, 1915; Cuero district, 1922; executive secretary, Board of Education, Southwest Texas Conference, 1924-30; Director, Leadership Education, General Board of EDUCATION (MES), 1930-39, and The Methodist Church, 1939-48; Minister of Education, Travis Park Church, SAN ANTONIO, Texas, 1948-49; Editor of the *Texas Christian Advocate,* 1949-59, when he retired with fifty years of service. He was a member of GENERAL CONFERENCES of 1930, 1938, and UNITING CONFERENCE, 1939. He was the author of *The Workers Conference,* 1943. He died July 19, 1963, and is buried in Rose Hill Cemetery, Ft. Worth, Texas.

C. T. Howell, *Prominent Personalities.* 1945.
Journal of the Southwest Texas Conference, 1964.
O. W. Nail, *Texas Methodism.* 1961.   J. DANIEL BARRON

MATTHEW SIMPSON

SIMPSON, MATTHEW (1811-1884), a strong and commanding American bishop, was born at Cadiz, Ohio, on June 2, 1811. He spent two months at MADISON COLLEGE in Unionville, Pa., and then studied medicine under Dr. James McBean of Cadiz and qualified as a practitioner.

In 1834 he joined the PITTSBURGH CONFERENCE of the M.E. Church on trial and was sent to the Cadiz circuit, then to PITTSBURGH, and then to Williamsport. In 1837 he became Professor of Natural Science in ALLEGHENY COLLEGE and in 1839 he was elected President of Indiana Asbury University (later DEPAUW UNIVERSITY). Here he remained for nine years, declining during the period the presidency of NORTHWESTERN, DICKINSON and WESLEYAN UNIVERSITY.

He was a member of the GENERAL CONFERENCE of

1844 which adopted the PLAN OF SEPARATION resulting in the formation of the M.E. Church, South. He was an outstanding anti-slavery advocate. At the General Conference of 1848 he spoke against receiving LOVICK PIERCE as a fraternal delegate from the southern Church and was the author of the resolution which repudiated the Plan of Separation. The adoption of this resolution led to an appeal to law and the U. S. Supreme Court upheld the southern position.

In 1848 Simpson became editor of the *Western Christian Advocate* and through its columns he carried on an energetic anti-slavery crusade. He was elected a bishop in 1852.

In 1857 he was fraternal delegate to the British and Irish Conferences and to the Evangelical Alliance in BERLIN. From Europe he proceeded to the Holy Land. He was elected president of GARRETT THEOLOGICAL SEMINARY in 1859, and while he moved from Pittsburgh to EVANSTON, Ill., he devoted little time to the affairs of the Seminary.

Simpson knew Abraham Lincoln and when the latter became President the bishop plunged deeply into politics. He attempted to secure the appointment of Methodists to national offices and was successful to a considerable degree. Then he took up another project.

He and his colleague, Bishop AMES, secured from Secretary of War Stanton an order instructing the Union Generals to place at Simpson's disposal all of the conquered churches of the M.E. Church, South. The bishop seized McKendree Church in NASHVILLE, Tenn., the present Church Street Church in KNOXVILLE, and others in TENNESSEE, LOUISIANA and elsewhere. It seems that Lincoln was not aware of this action and apparently did not approve of it, since he countermanded an order to turn over a Southern Presbyterian Church in ST. LOUIS to the northern branch of that denomination. On the death of Lincoln the bishop visited President Andrew Johnson, and while disliking the new President, he thought Johnson would "be harder on the South" than his predecessor. In this he was mistaken, for Johnson demanded that Simpson return McKendree Church to its owners. The bishop delayed two months but finally complied. Simpson warmly favored the impeachment of the President.

In 1863 Simpson moved to PHILADELPHIA where some laymen gave him a home. During the whole course of the war he delivered addresses favorable to the Northern cause. He attended the opening of the Sanitary Fair at Philadelphia in 1864 at the request of Lincoln, and his speech on that occasion denounced the Southern leaders. On the death of Lincoln the bishop preached his funeral at the White House and also at Springfield where the slain President was buried.

Simpson was the author of *A Hundred Years of Methodism, Lectures on Preaching,* and *Cyclopaedia of Methodism.* He died at Philadelphia on June 18, 1884.

R. D. Clark, *Matthew Simpson.* 1956.
G. R. Crooks, *Matthew Simpson.* 1890.
Dictionary of American Biography.
Simpson Manuscripts in the Library of Congress.
E. M. Wood, *Matthew Simpson.* 1909.   ELMER T. CLARK

SIMPSON, WILLIAM (1812-1864), American circuit rider, was born Jan. 22, 1812, in Huntingdon County, Pa., and joined the M.E. Church in 1832. Emigrating to Centerville, St. Joseph Co., Mich. (1833), he served as

CLASS LEADER and received an EXHORTER's license in 1836, soon after removing to Hennepin, Ill., where Presiding Elder John Sinclair employed him to travel Bureau Circuit. Transferred to Bloomington Circuit on April 2, 1837, he received a preacher's license and, joining the ILLINOIS CONFERENCE (Sept. 27, 1837), was assigned to Helena Circuit, Wisconsin Territory. He served Belleview Circuit in 1838 and Prairie Du Chien, Wis., in 1839.

When the Illinois Conference was divided (1840), Simpson became a ROCK RIVER CONFERENCE itinerant, assigned successively to Lancaster (1840), Hamilton Grove (1841), Ft. Madison (1842), and West Point (1843). He married Nancy Range on Feb. 22, 1842.

An original member of the IOWA CONFERENCE, this pioneer Iowa preacher served Mt. Pleasant (1844-45), Pleasant Valley (1846-47), and Cedar (1848-49), before traveling as Council Bluffs missionary in 1850 and 1851, organizing a circuit and forming several societies. Leaving the Council Bluffs Mission with 240 members, Simpson, after preaching at Brighton (1852) and Ft. Madison (1853), was presiding elder of Montezuma District in 1854 and of Oskaloosa District in 1855-58. He was reserve delegate to GENERAL CONFERENCE, 1856 and 1860. After serving New London and Agency City, he was assigned to Marshall (now Wayland), Iowa, where he died Feb. 22, 1864.

A. W. Haines, *Makers of Iowa Methodism.* 1900.
Minutes of the Annual Conferences of the M.E. Church, 1837-1864.
E. H. Waring, *Iowa Conference.* 1910.
Yearbook of the Iowa Conference, 1844-1864.
                                    MARTIN L. GREER

SIMPSON COLLEGE, Indianola, Iowa, was established as Indianola Male and Female Seminary in 1860. The name was changed to Simpson Centenary College in 1867, honoring Bishop MATTHEW SIMPSON of the M.E. Church. The present name was taken in 1884. A gift of $100,000 from Mrs. HENRY PFEIFFER in 1942 sparked a building program for the college which has resulted in the erection of fifteen new buildings. The Gardner Cowles Foundation gave $176,000 for the Carver Science Hall, and $200,000 for the million-dollar Dunn Library. Carver Science Hall is perhaps the only building erected on a preponderantly white campus to honor a Negro.

George Washington Carver, the distinguished Negro scientist, had his first two years of college work at Simpson College. Degrees offered are the B.A. and B.M. (Music). The governing board has forty-three members, seven ex officio, three elected by alumni, all confirmed by the South Iowa Annual Conference.

                                    JOHN O. GROSS

SIMS, DAVID HENRY (1886-1965), American bishop of the A.M.E. CHURCH, was born in Alabama, on July 18, 1886. He received the A.B. degrees from Georgia State and Oberlin College (Ohio); the B.D. degree from the Oberlin Graduate School of Theology; and the A.M. degree from the University of Chicago. He was later awarded honorary degrees by MORRIS BROWN COLLEGE in Georgia, Allen University in South Carolina and WILBERFORCE UNIVERSITY in Ohio. Following his ordination as DEACON and ELDER, he served as pastor in OHIO, RHODE ISLAND and SOUTH CAROLINA. In 1924 he was elected to the presidency of Allen University, in which position he remained until his elevation to the episcopacy in 1932. The author of several books and articles, he resided at PHILADELPHIA, Pa., and was assigned to the writing of Methodist history and polity until the time of his death in 1965.

R. R. Wright, *The Bishops.* 1963.   GRANT S. SHOCKLEY

SINGAPORE is an island with an area of 225 square miles, linked to the mainland (Malay Peninsula) by a railroad and automotive causeway, separated from Sumatra and Bat (INDONESIA) by a narrow strait. Having been an integral part of MALAYSIA (constituted in September 1963), Singapore became an independent nation in September 1965, and at that time was admitted to the United Nations as a sovereign state. Population is 1,987,900 (1968 estimate), of which Chinese are seventy-five percent, Malays twelve percent, with smaller groups from INDIA and PAKISTAN, together with Eurasians and Europeans. The city of Singapore sprawls around and behind a very important harbor, the world's fifth port and the largest trans-shipping center in Southeast Asia.

The name Singapore is an Anglicised form of the Sanskrit term meaning "Lion City." Tradition has it that during the early Moslem invasions of India, a group of Sikhs of the Singh (lion) clan fled by sea, around CEYLON, down the Straits of Malacca, to the tiny island at the southern extremity of the Malay Peninsula, a scant forty miles above the Equator. There they landed, building a small settlement which they called Singapore. However that may be, the island and its fishing community had been known by that name for centuries before British influence became dominant in the early 1800's.

Decades of contention with Dutch, French and Portuguese colonial interests had passed when Sir Stamford Raffles secured a treaty in 1819 from the Sultan of Johore (Malay peninsula) in favor of the East India Company of Great Britain. This instrument assured to Britain free access for shipping, with rights of development and other significant political and commercial privileges. The subsequent history of Singapore until World War II paralleled that of the Malay States on the peninsula. Singapore became a Crown Colony, while the States gained the status of Protectorates under the hereditary Sultans.

Singapore's superb harbor and the narrow strait between it and Sumatra to the southwest, is a veritable nexus of the oceans. Any ship bound from Europe or Africa for a port on the east coast of Asia, or in the adjacent island groups, or vice versa, must pass through Singapore.

After Pearl Harbor and the destruction of all Allied naval power and merchant shipping between India, AUSTRALIA and the Western Pacific, Japanese ground and air forces swarmed southward along the Malay Peninsula. Resources of tin, rubber, grain producing areas, fell to them. But the ultimate objective was Singapore, for, with that strategic central port in hand, India might be attacked by a pincers—by sea around Ceylon, by land across northern BURMA. Singapore fell without a siege, its strong defenses having been constructed against naval and not land attack. After the defeat of Japan, British sovereignty was restored, the Federation of Malaysia was established and autonomy achieved. A wearisome and costly struggle against communist infiltration and sabotage has practically eliminated that menace.

As a national entity, Singapore is geographically one of the smallest of independent states. However, the wealth is very great, and the strategic position for commerce and either peace or war, is almost unparalleled. The viability of the new nation will rest primarily upon its internal strength in terms of racial harmony, political leadership and success in development.

Methodist mission work was instituted at Singapore on Feb. 7, 1885, upon the arrival of WILLIAM F. OLDHAM and JAMES M. THOBURN, under appointment of the SOUTH INDIA ANNUAL CONFERENCE. In later years these two were to become bishops, outstanding leaders of the missionary enterprise of the M.E. Church. Oldham promptly established a congregation, at first including Chinese, Tamils, Eurasians and English. The QUARTERLY CONFERENCE was formally organized in a few weeks. The first church building was erected before the end of the year on land granted by the municipality. The Chinese colony, deeply interested in education, provided several thousand dollars for a school. The Tamils quickly developed their own congregation and school. Miss Sophia Blackmore of Australia, destined to give forty years of service in Malaya, was sent by the Minneapolis Branch of the WOMAN's FOREIGN MISSIONARY SOCIETY, arriving in July 1887. Record of the development of the work throughout Malaya, with Singapore as the center, will be found in articles entitled, INDONESIA, MALAYSIA, SARAWAK.

Methodism has made an outstanding contribution to education in Singapore. An Anglo-Chinese school was founded in 1886, with Bishop William F. Oldham as its first principal, and two other schools had been opened by 1888. By 1963, there were thirteen Methodist schools with a total enrollment of 9,759. These schools use English as a medium of instruction. They are, in principle, inter-racial, but over ninety percent of the students are Chinese. The church is also responsible for one Tamil-language and two Chinese-language schools. All Methodist schools in Singapore receive government grants.

A small printing-plant was established at Singapore in the early years of the mission. Across the decades it has grown until the Singapore Methodist Publishing House of today is the most influential Christian press in the entire island world. Wide-ranging and immense quantities of material have been issued, not alone for Methodist institutions, but equally for the uses of many other civic, cultural and denominational agencies. The impact of the printed pages, bearing this imprint, is incalculable.

The recent rapid political shifts in no way alter the central strategic, determinative role of Singapore for all Southeast Asia.

A new organizational alignment in world Methodism occurred when the autonomous Methodist Church in Malaysia and Singapore was organized on Aug. 9, 1968. Singapore is of dominant influence in the new Church. Singapore is involved in the Singapore-Malaya Annual Conference, the Malaya Chinese Annual Conference and the Tamil Provisional Annual Conference. Bishop YAP KIM HAO, the first bishop of the new autonomous Church, presides over the Church with his headquarters in Singapore. There are twenty-four Methodist congregations at the last reporting in the two districts of the two annual conferences, largely in Singapore, and these have a total of 6,440 members. Services are held in nine different languages: English, eleven; Tamil, four; Malay, three; Hokkien, four; Punjabi, Hinghwa, Foochow, Cantonese, Hakka, one each. These churches are served by sixteen ordained ministers and six supply pastors. A number of new churches have been built in recent years including Christ, Trinity, Pentecost and Barker Road.

Trinity College, 7 Mount Sophia, Singapore is operated by the Methodists in cooperation with the Anglicans, English, Presbyterians, and since 1962, with the Lutherans. This is a four-year theological college for both English and Chinese-speaking candidates for Christian work. Students come from all over Southeast Asia: HONG KONG (Chinese), PHILIPPINES (Filipinos), INDONESIA (Indonesians and Chinese), PAKISTAN (Pakistanis), Singapore/MALAYSIA (Chinese Indians). The majority of students are Methodist but four other churches are represented: Presbyterian, Congregational, Anglican, Lutheran (both American and Swedish branches). Dr. Timothy Chow, principal since 1968, came from the Chinese mainland to Hong Kong and was District Superintendent of the Methodist Church, Hong Kong (British Methodist).

Headquarters for the new Church are on Coleman Street, Singapore, where the bishop is housed, also the treasurer of the Church, and other officers of the general Church. There is also a Book Room established there.

Ho Seng Ong, *Methodist Schools in Malaysia.* Petaling Jaya, Malaysia: Board of Education, Malaya Conference, 1964.

ARTHUR BRUCE MOSS

SINGH, ASHOKE B. (1904-   ), lay leader of Southern Asia, was named after the famous Indian King Asoka, who reigned 272-232 B.C. He was born in Bengal, and became an A.B. of Calcutta University about 1925, where he also received the M.A. degree. His special interests have been education and social concerns. For almost twenty years he taught in various high schools, some of which he organized. In 1945 he married Dolly Burge.

In 1949 Singh became principal of Collins Institute, a Methodist institution, a Bengali high school in Calcutta. He continues as principal of Collins, and is also the secretary of its board of governors. He is chairman of the board of governors of Mount Hermon High School in Darjeeling, and also of Champahati Bengali Girls' High School. He is secretary of the managing committees of Kutipara Rural High School, and of Ushagram High School, Asansol, another Methodist institution.

Singh serves the Methodist Church in Southern Asia as vice-president of the Board of Lay Activities; member of its all-India committees, interim committee, and of the executive board. In the BENGAL CONFERENCE he is lay leader. He was a lay delegate to the GENERAL CONFERENCE of 1952, 1956, 1960, 1966, and to the CENTRAL CONFERENCES of INDIA in 1952, 1956, 1960, and 1964.

He is a member of the Christian Burial Board of Calcutta and of several other groups interested in social service. He is a staunch nationalist but is quoted as saying, "I am a great admirer of the American way of life."

CLEMENT D. ROCKEY

SINGH, LILAVATI 1867-1909), an Indian Methodist, was principal-elect of the ISABELLA THOBURN COLLEGE when she died in Chicago in May 1909. For thirty years she was connected with ISABELLA THOBURN, and her school and college.

Coming to the school as a small girl, Ethel Raphael (as she was then known) was at first indifferent, but later she became extraordinarily responsive to Miss Thoburn's efforts.

Under the influence of Miss Thoburn's school, she came to the conviction that her father had made a mistake when he changed his name at the time of his conversion. She adopted the surname that he had renounced, and for her personal name she chose Lilavati, a popular Indian name which she thought suitable for an Indian Christian.

Within a year of completing high school, she found that her father had selected a husband for her. She insisted that she was not ready to marry and must continue her education. Her father insisted that he would spend no more money for her study. An aunt provided some help, but met misfortune and could not continue. Lilavati sold some jewelry that relatives had given her. Miss Thoburn wanted her to stay on, and promised that she personally would obtain the necessary funds.

Lilavati, with a Mrs. Chakerbutty and her daughter Shorat, was the first of Miss Thoburn's girls to complete the high school course. All were devout Christians, and all made notable contributions to the education of women in North INDIA.

Four years later Miss Singh graduated from the University of Calcutta and began teaching Persian and English in the college. In 1896, she stood second in Allahabad University among candidates for the M.A. degree.

In March 1899, Miss Thoburn went to America in search of funds for the college and soon cabled for Miss Singh to join her. This she did in August. She proved to be a very capable public speaker. She addressed the Ecumenical Missionary Conference in New York in April 1900. After hearing that address, former president Benjamin Harrison remarked, "If I had given a million dollars to foreign missions I should count it wisely invested, if it had led only to the conversion of that woman."

The two ladies returned to India in June and entered a year of recurring crises and perpetual strain. Bishop E. W. PARKER died in June 1901, after a long illness. In September Miss Thoburn died of cholera after less than twenty-four hours of illness. Miss Singh took over many of Miss Thoburn's responsibilities and was a tower of strength to the new principal. In 1903 Miss Singh was elected vice-principal of the college.

In 1908 she went again to America to represent the college in church gatherings and for advance study. Following her plea to the general executive of the WOMAN's FOREIGN MISSIONARY SOCIETY, money was appropriated for a much-needed classroom building. In that year, for health reasons, FLORENCE NICHOLS resigned as principal and Miss Singh was elected as her successor. RUTH ROBINSON was asked to serve until Miss Singh could finish her duties in America and return to India.

Then tragedy struck. Miss Singh died in Chicago in 1909. Thus ended an era. The case for the education of Indian women had been proved and the Methodist Church, through a succession of heroic women, had made a historic record.

M. A. Dimmitt, *Isabella Thoburn College.* 1963.
J. N. Hollister, *Southern Asia.* 1956.
J. M. Thoburn, *Isabella Thoburn.* 1903. J. WASKOM PICKETT

SINGH, MANGAL (1902-   ), Indian bishop, was the fourth citizen of INDIA elected to the Methodist episcopacy, and the first Methodist bishop born in the Himalayan mountain area. He was elected by the CENTRAL CONFERENCE of Southern Asia at LUCKNOW in October 1956, and was assigned to the BOMBAY Area. In 1964, on the retirement of SHOT KUMAR MONDOL, he was assigned to the Delhi area.

Bishop Singh was born on Dec. 31, 1902, in the remote village of Thalisain in the District of Garhwal, accessible then only by walking or on a sure-footed mountain pony. During the lifetime of his great-grandparents the district was a part of NEPAL. It was ceded to the East India Company in 1816. The Methodist Church began work in Garhwal in 1865 with JAMES MILLS THOBURN as the first missionary. Another Methodist pioneer, JAMES H. MESSMORE, baptized the young lad and PRESTON S. HYDE sponsored his education in the Mission School at Pauri. He was influenced strongly by two other missionaries, both of Scandinavian origin, HARRY HANSON WEEKS and HARRY A. HANSON.

His father, Chandar Singh, is remembered as a devout man, opposed to idolatry and favorable to the Church but not a member thereof. He was called "an unbaptized Christian." Mangal Singh was not the first convert of the village but was the first to leave the village to study in the Boarding School, and the first local resident to conduct public worship services, and to bear witness to Christ Jesus as Lord and Saviour.

The future bishop made rapid progress in school, several times receiving double promotion. After two years in College he became a teacher in a Mission School, took training as a teacher, and was invited to join the Government Educational Service, but chose instead to work through the Church and to become a minister of the Word and the Sacraments. He won a Bachelor's degree from Agra University, and then passed the course of study for the ministry in the NORTH INDIA CONFERENCE. His appointments included Supervisor of Hostels in Ramsey High School at Almora; Superintendent, BAREILLY District; Delhi Area Promotional Secretary for the Advance for Christ; and Pastor of Christ Church, Delhi. In 1948 he represented North India Annual Conference in the GENERAL CONFERENCE of The Methodist Church. He then received a Crusade for Christ scholarship for advanced study and the next year received a Master's degree in Education from the UNIVERSITY OF DENVER. In 1956 he represented the Delhi Annual Conference in the General Conference and his election as bishop took place in the Central Conference of that year. In 1933 he married Violet Thomson, daughter of George B. Thomson, a fellow Garhwali minister. They have two sons and two daughters. A daughter is married to a son of Bishop A. J. SHAW of the Bombay Area.

The Indian Witness files.
Who's Who in The Methodist Church, 1966.

J. WASKOM PICKETT

SINGH, MASIH CHARAN (1884-1964), was a highly respected, hardworking minister of the Methodist Church in INDIA. He was born in Moradabad, Dec. 26, 1884, the elder of two sons of Ram Singh, an ordained local preacher. He was a student in the Methodist Boys' School at Cawnpore (now Kanpur), and passed the Allahabad University matriculation examination in the first division in 1907. He went to the United States and studied at Moore's Hill College, Indiana, where he was graduated with a B.A. degree. Returning to India, he served as

manager of the boys' hostel of the Cawnpore school for a year, and then joined the faculty of LUCKNOW CHRISTIAN COLLEGE.

He did much preaching and was invited to become pastor of the Central Methodist Church at LUCKNOW, then the premier Indian-language Methodist Church in India. He joined the LUCKNOW ANNUAL CONFERENCE and was ordained DEACON and ELDER Dec. 19, 1921.

After four years in the pastorate he began a long career as district superintendent, serving in the Arrah, Cawnpore, Ballia, Lucknow, and Gonda districts. For sixteen years he was simultaneously superintendent of a district and pastor of Central Church, where he preached to a congregation that included members of the faculties of Lucknow University and of the Lucknow Christian and ISABELLA THOBURN COLLEGES.

Twice he represented his Annual Conference in the GENERAL CONFERENCE, and ten times in the CENTRAL CONFERENCE. He was conference treasurer for ten years and chairman of his Conference relations committee for twelve years. For fifteen months he edited *Kaukab-i-Hind,* the official Methodist weekly periodical in Urdu. He served on the Lucknow Christian College, Isabella Thoburn College, and Leonard Theological College boards of trustees and on the United Provinces Christian Council and the North India Christian Book and Tract Society. He was in demand as a preacher in interdenominational conventions. Despite his many exacting tasks, he translated a number of English hymns into Urdu, and, most surprisingly, prepared a monumental concordance of the Bible in Urdu. When he had worked on the Old Testament for nearly four years, he learned that a new translation was soon to be published. That made a completely fresh start necessary. He turned to work on the New Testament, and when a comprehensive concordance had been completed, went back to work on the Old Testament with the new translation. For over seventeen years he devoted many hours of every week to this self-imposed task, for which he received no monetary payment. But he was rewarded with the gratitude of the Indian Church and a sense of duty faithfully done. The 1,331-page work was published in 1959 by the LUCKNOW PUBLISHING HOUSE.

He was awarded an honorary D.D. degree by EVANSVILLE COLLEGE in 1948. He was married to Daisy Lilavati Childs, June 12, 1916. She was a lay delegate to the General Conference of 1936. Singh died at his home in Lucknow, Feb. 27, 1964, and is buried there.

Minutes of the Northwest India Conference, 1912-20; and of the Lucknow Conference, 1921-49.
Minutes of the Central Conference of Southern Asia.

J. WASKOM PICKETT

SIOUX FALLS, SOUTH DAKOTA, U.S.A., now the largest city in the state, was founded in 1856 and incorporated as a city in 1883.

Sioux Falls has three colleges: Augustana, Sioux Falls, and Nettleton. There is also the North American Baptist Seminary and Pettigrew Museum.

Thomas Cuthbert, a local Methodist preacher, was the first appointed pastor in Sioux Falls and organized the First Methodist Church in 1871. An Englishman, he settled across Sioux River southeast of the city. His circuit included Canton, Beloit, and Hudson. Cuthbert continued to serve smaller circuits in the Sioux Valley until his death in 1905. First Church was built in 1873 under J. W. Rigby.

It served also as a parsonage. A second building was erected in 1878 under William Fielder and dedicated in 1881 by Lewis Hartsough. The third building was erected in 1890. In 1913 the present building was dedicated. An educational building and chapel were added in 1957.

Wesley Church was organized in 1890. In 1950 Asbury Church was founded. The youngest church, Hilltop Heights, was organized in 1958 with thirty-five charter members and had 226 members in 1969.

Early records state: "There were no cliques or factions . . . There were only three churches in Sioux Falls, the Congregational, Methodist, and Episcopal . . . All were called upon to contribute to each other's welfare . . . The first church bell was secured by the Methodist church people, aided by the members of other churches and by citizens generally. By mutual agreement of the churches, services were held by each at the same hour, and it was distinctly understood by the donors of this bell that it should ring out not only for the benefit of all the churches, but on other important occasions."

In January of 1964, forty-two churches cooperated in the National Christian Teaching Mission, which was highlighted by a city-wide religious census. First Methodist Church led out in this effort.

There is a Free Methodist Church and a Wesleyan Methodist Church in Sioux Falls.

Sioux Falls had five United Methodist Churches (1970) with a combined membership of 5,006. First Church is the oldest and largest—3,026 members—with the most impressive building.

First Church was organized in 1871. Its first meeting place was an old government barracks. From this inauspicious beginning the church has grown to a membership in 1970 of 3,026. Not only has the church had a history of continued growth in membership, but it has been instrumental in establishing two other congregations in the city of Sioux Falls. It has also demonstrated a vital sense of missionary interest and in recent years it has consistently ranked among the first twenty churches in the United States in Advance Special giving. In 1963 it ranked tenth. One of the Advance Special projects was the erection of the high school building at the American Institute in La Paz, Bolivia. Other Advance Special projects include the support of a missionary couple in India. The church has also contributed seven young men to the ministry. Over 1,300 students are enrolled in the Church School. Additional Methodist churches are being planned in Sioux Falls.

General Minutes, UM, 1970.
M. D. Smith, *South Dakota*. 1965.

Jesse A. Earl
Arnold Herbst

SIOUX INDIAN MISSION. In the spring of 1837 Methodism came to Minnesota under the leadership of Alfred Brunson of Prairie du Chien. Arriving at Fort Snelling with the purpose of establishing missions among Indians, it was learned that Chief Little Crow of Kaposia, a Sioux (Dakota) band of twelve lodges and consisting of about 200 souls, located about eight miles below the fort on the west side of the Mississippi on what is now South St. Paul, was willing to have a mission established in his village.

Perhaps Little Crow was following his father's philosophy, who, on his deathbed appointed his son his successor as Chief and admonished him, "Teach your people to be honest and laborious, and adopt such of the habits of the whites as will be fitted for their change of circumstances, and above all be industrious and sober and make yourself beloved and respected by the white people."

David King, who had come to Minnesota with Brunson, organized the first class at Kaposia consisting of John Holton, leader, and wife, Sarah, Jacob and Margaret Fahlstrom, Taylor and Eliz Randolph, and Martha and William Brown. This mission was strengthened in October by the addition of T. W. Pope and James G. Whiteford as teachers and preachers and the Hiram DeLap family as farmer and housekeeper. A successful school was operated by King, except that the migratory habits of the Indians were a decided drawback. When in school, however, the children showed capacity for learning.

Due to illness, Brunson was succeeded in 1839 by Benjamin T. Kavanaugh, who brought his brother William with him. Upon arrival at Kaposia he found the mission in confusion due to difficulty between missionaries, subsequently including himself, and Indian Chiefs. Kaposia was left by Kavanaugh in the hands of David King as he moved across the river to Red Rock.

In 1840 the first Methodist church in Minnesota was organized at Kaposia with whites, half-bloods and Indians as members: David King, preacher, John Holton, class leader, Mary Holton, J. W. Simpson, James Thompson (interpreter), Mrs. Thompson, Jacob and Margaret Fahlstrom and children Nancy, Jane and Sally, Hep-per, Ha-pa, Chah-tee-k-kah, Hanah Taliaferro, Elizabeth Wiliams, Mr. and Mrs. Randolph, Mary McClaire, Susan Bassett, Tah-she-nah-sah-pak, We-no-nan-zhee, Anna Prevost, Mux-zah-ton-kah. Mak-cah-pee-wee, Chasta, We-oh-wasta, Hap-pah Baldwin, Eliza Gonwell, Susan Mozho, Angeline Ozhee, Edmund Brizett, Mary Taliaferro, and Mr. Bush.

Kaposia Mission was closed in 1852 when the Sioux were moved by treaty to a reservation along the upper Minnesota River.

E. F. Baumhofer, *Trails in Minnesota*. 1966.
Doane Robinson, *History of Dakota or Sioux Indians*. State Department of History, South Dakota, 1904.

LeRoy H. Klaus

SIPPRELL, WILFORD JAMES (1866-1952), Canadian Methodist and United Church of Canada minister and educator, was born in Oxford County, Ontario, on Sept. 12, 1866. In 1888 he was licensed as a local preacher; in 1890 he was accepted as a probationer for the ministry. Ordained in 1895, he was stationed at Norwich Avenue Church in Woodstock, Ontario.

In 1897 he was appointed to the principalship of Columbia Methodist College in New Westminster, the first degree-conferring institution in British Columbia. He filled this office with distinction until 1911. The next two years were given to travel and study in Europe and Britain. Returning to Canada, he served Mount Pleasant Church in Vancouver for seven years and Metropolitan Church in Victoria for ten. Then he spent another year in Europe and the Holy Land.

Sipprell represented British Columbia at the Ecumenical Methodist Conference in Toronto in 1911, and at a similar gathering in 1921 in London, England. He was a member of each of the Canadian Methodist General Conferences from 1906 until the inaugural council of The United Church of Canada in 1925, and of all succeeding General Councils until 1934, the year of his retirement. For fourteen years thereafter he was active in preaching, traveling, and fundraising, especially for the pension fund of the church. He died on Dec. 28, 1952, in Victoria.

G. H. Cornish, *Cyclopaedia of Methodism*. 1903.
Records of British Columbia Conference.　W. P. BUNT

SITES, NATHAN (1830-1895), pioneer CHINA missionary, was born near Belleville, Ohio. He became a carpenter and worked his way through OHIO WESLEYAN UNIVERSITY, graduating in 1859. That same year he was admitted on trial in the NORTH OHIO CONFERENCE, and in the following year, after hearing R. S. MACLAY tell of the work in Foochow, volunteered for appointment to China. He arrived in Foochow in September 1861, to begin a ministry of thirty-four years.

His first language teacher was a Confucian scholar, a Sia Sek-ong, who was converted and became one of Foochow's outstanding preachers (see SEVEN GOLD CANDLESTICKS).

He was the most indefatigable of the missionaries in constant travel from city to city, preaching the gospel. Mintsing, Futsing, Hinghwa, Yenping—these were only a few of the populous centers in which he laid firm foundations for the Christian church. In 1879 he was mobbed and severely beaten in Yenping, but after his wounds were healed he continued his work with unabated zeal. As STEPHEN BALDWIN said of him, "He delighted to go into new places to preach the Gospel where it had never before been preached."

Nathan Sites died in 1895, just after completing a series of New Year meetings in Liutu.

W. C. Barclay, *History of Missions*. 1957.
W. N. Lacy, *China*. 1948.
S. Moore Sites, *Nathan Sites, an Epic of the East*. New York: Revell, 1912.　FRANCIS P. JONES

SKEVINGTON, JOHN (1814-1845), NEW ZEALAND Methodist minister, was born at Sherwood, Nottingham, England. With other Wesleyan Mission reinforcements he came out to join the New Zealand Mission staff in the ship "Triton" in 1840. Staying in Hobart, Tasmania, he worked with the Bush Mission among the Aborigines, and later assisted at Wesleydale, Geelong, until directed by the Wesleyan Missionary Society to proceed to New Zealand.

There he was set the task of commencing the mission at Waingongoro (later known as Taranaki South), where his territory stretched from Oeo to Waitotara on the west coast of the North Island. Among a people recently released from slavery, he labored effectively for three years. Visiting Auckland for the district meeting, he died suddenly during the evening service in the old High Street Church on Sept. 21, 1845. His ministry in New Zealand lasted but three years.

W. Morley, *New Zealand*. 1900.　WESLEY A. CHAMBERS

SKILLINGTON, JAMES EDGAR (1878-1965), American minister and parliamentarian, was born in Breezewood, Pa., Dec. 2, 1878. He was educated at Williamsport Dickinson Seminary, DICKINSON COLLEGE (A.B. 1905, M.A. 1910, D.D. 1922) and DREW THEOLOGICAL SEMINARY.

He was admitted into the CENTRAL PENNSYLVANIA CONFERENCE of the M.E. Church in 1901 and spent his entire ministerial career of sixty-four years in its membership. Sixty of these years were spent as supply pastor, pastor and district superintendent. For decades he filled the leading pulpits with distinction and gained universal recognition, not only for his eloquence, but also as the outstanding ministerial leader of the Conference. His memberships on conference boards were numerous and important, including those of the Home for Children, Home for the Aged, LYCOMING COLLEGE, Board of Education, Board of Ministerial Training and Trustees of the Annual Conference, of which he was president for almost twenty-five years.

Skillington was a member of each GENERAL CONFERENCE of the M.E. Church and The Methodist Church from 1924 to 1952, and headed his conference delegation at each of these from 1928 to 1948, including the UNITING CONFERENCE and the related JURISDICTIONAL CONFERENCES. He was universally recognized as a skilled parliamentarian and was a member of the Committee on Rules of the respective General Conferences from 1936 to 1952. His judgments and interpretations of the *Discipline*, or on parliamentary situations, were usually accepted by the officers of General and Annual Conferences as authoritative. He was a member of the World Service Commission of the M.E. Church from 1924 to 1940, and of the COUNCIL ON WORLD SERVICE AND FINANCE of The Methodist Church from 1940 to 1952.

The *Discipline* required his retirement at age seventy-two but he continued to serve as a supply pastor on a circuit near his home for six more years. He died at Roaring Spring, Pa., on May 1, 1965.

The Altoona Mirror, Altoona, Pa., May 2, 1965.
C. T. Howell, *Prominent Personalities*. 1945.
Journal of the Central Pennsylvania Conference, 1965.
CHARLES F. BERKHEIMER

SLADE, EDMOND B. (1839-1919), American United Brethren minister, was born Oct. 1, 1839, the sixth of eleven children, near DAYTON, Ohio. His father was a woolen manufacturer, and Edmond assisted him in this work until his fourteenth year, when the family moved to a farm near Troy, Ohio. Soon thereafter the mother died. Young Slade was converted in 1856 and felt called to preach. Since he had promised to stay with the family until his twenty-first birthday, he delayed the answer to his call. During the Civil War he was sergeant in Company G, Tenth Indiana Infantry, the family having moved to Fountain County, Ind.

In 1863 Slade married a young widow, Mrs. Deborah Johnson, and together they raised three children. In 1869 the family moved to Potawatomie County, Kan., and joined the UNITED BRETHREN IN CHRIST. Slade still felt a call to the ministry, but imagined that he couldn't measure up to the requirements without suitable education. He promised God however that his first son would enter the ministry. When death took the elder boy Slade yielded himself unconditionally to God.

Edmond joined the Northeast Kansas Conference, Church of the United Brethren in Christ. He remained a member until his death. After serving several pastorates he was elected presiding elder in 1881, living in Lecompton, Kan., seat of Lane University. The Slades soon became good friends of college youth, opening their home for lodging. Among their circle of friends were Ida Elizabeth Stover and David J. Eisenhower, students at Lane, married on Sept. 23, 1885. One of their sons, Dwight, became the thirty-fourth president of the United States.

In prayer, Edmond Slade would lose himself completely in ecstasy and wander all over the church on his knees, stopping to lay his hands on some particular person's head while praying. If preaching and someone entered the church late, as much as fifteen minutes, he would stop and begin again.

After twelve years as presiding elder, Slade became field agent for Lane University and later served seven years as local agent for Campbell College, another United Brethren school. When Campbell College merged with Kansas City University in 1913, Slade and his wife moved to the Baker Home for ministers near Puente, Calif., where they lived together until his death, Sept. 23, 1919. He was buried at Pomona, Calif.

Religious Telescope, Nov. 8 and Dec. 13, 1919.

JOHN H. NESS, JR.

SLADE, JOHN (1790-1854), American preacher, was born in SOUTH CAROLINA. He has been called the "Father of Florida Methodism." However, he was not the first minister to be appointed to the FLORIDA frontier after it was taken over from Spain. His name and that of his brother, Frederick Slade, appear on a petition dated Jan. 25, 1814, signed by 105 patriots, asking that the "Republic of East Florida" be admitted into the United States. It is quite possible that he may have been a "local preacher" and worked among the "patriots" of East Florida before Florida became a territory of the United States.

In 1822 he travelled as a supply in the SOUTH CAROLINA CONFERENCE. He was admitted into that Conference in 1823, and appointed with John I. Triggs to the Chattahoochee Mission. He was admitted into full connection and ordained a DEACON in 1825; and in 1828 was ordained an ELDER.

His appointments included: 1823, Chattahoochee Mission, Oconee District; 1824, Early Mission, Oconee District; 1825, Appling, Savannah District; 1826, Tallahassee Mission, Tallahassee District; 1827, Ohoopee, Savannah District. In 1829 he was superannuated and in 1830 he located on a farm in Thomas County, Ga., because of failing health.

In 1845, when the FLORIDA CONFERENCE was organized, John Slade was readmitted into the Florida Conference and served for nine years in the travelling connection. His appointments then were: 1845, Bainbridge, Ga., Quincy District; 1846, Blakely, Ga., Quincy District; 1847, Troupville, Ga., Tallahassee District; 1848, Warrior, Ga., Tallahassee District; 1849, Bainbridge, Ga., Tallahassee District; 1850, Irwin, St. Marys District; 1851, Holmesville Mission, St. Marys District; 1852, Wakulla, Tallahassee District; 1853, Troupville, Ga., Madison District; 1854, Thomasville Circuit, Ga., Madison District.

W. E. Brooks, *Florida Methodism.* 1965.
C. T. Thrift, *Florida.* 1944.　　WILLIAM E. BROOKS

SLATER, OLIVER EUGENE (1906-　　), American bishop, was born in Sibley, La., on Sept. 10, 1906, the son of Oliver Thornwell and Mattie (Kennon) Slater.

EUGENE SLATER

He received the B.A. degree from SOUTHERN METHODIST UNIVERSITY in 1930; B.D from PERKINS SCHOOL OF THEOLOGY, 1932. Honorary degrees included D.D. from McMURRY COLLEGE, 1951; L.H.D. from SOUTHWESTERN COLLEGE, Winfield, Kan., 1961; LL.D. from BAKER UNIVERSITY, 1962; LL.D. from Southern Methodist University, 1964.

On Nov. 25, 1931, he was united in marriage to Eva B. Richardson of Dallas, Texas, an S.M.U. graduate. They have two children: Susan (Mrs. H. Kipling Edenborough, Dallas, Texas) and Stewart Eugene, San Antonio, Texas.

Eugene Slater joined the WEST TEXAS CONFERENCE of the M.E. Church, South in October 1932. He served pastorates at Rochelle, Texas, 1932-33; Menard, Texas, 1933-36; Ozona, Texas, 1936-42; Woodlawn, SAN ANTONIO, 1942-44; Bering Memorial, HOUSTON (TEXAS CONFERENCE), 1944-50; Polk Street, Amarillo (NORTHWEST TEXAS CONFERENCE), 1950-60. He was elected bishop at the SOUTH CENTRAL JURISDICTIONAL CONFERENCE, San Antonio, Texas, June 1960, and assigned to the KANSAS Area with headquarters in TOPEKA, Kan. He was assigned to San Antonio-Northwest Texas Area, June 1964, with headquarters in San Antonio.

In August of 1952 he was one of sixteen guests of the U.S. Navy on a cruise to Pearl Harbor, Hawaii. In 1954 he was an accredited visitor to the Evanston Assembly of the WORLD COUNCIL OF CHURCHES. Bishop and Mrs. Slater visited Methodist missions in six countries of South America during November and December 1956. He was delegate to the South Central Jurisdictional Conference, 1948, 1956, 1960, and a delegate to the GENERAL CONFERENCE, 1956, 1960. He attended the WORLD METHODIST CONFERENCE, Oslo, 1961, and visited Methodist churches and institutions in Europe and North Africa; attended the World Methodist Conference, LONDON, England, 1966, and made episcopal visitation to JAPAN, KOREA and the PHILIPPINES.

He has been a member of the General Board of EDUCATION, General Board of LAY ACTIVITIES, and the General COMMISSION ON ARCHIVES AND HISTORY. He was chairman of the Committee to Study the Employed Lay Career Worker in The Methodist Church.

He is a member of the Board of Trustees of Southern Methodist University, McMurry College, Southwestern University, Southwest Texas Methodist Hospital, San Antonio and Methodist Hospital, Lubbock.

Who's Who in America, Vol. 34.
Who's Who in The Methodist Church, 1966.   N. B. H.

SLAVERY AND AMERICAN METHODISM.
Slavery was already firmly embedded in the life of the nation into which the M.E. Church was born in 1784. The church's tradition, on the other hand, included a strong antislavery strain, inherited from JOHN WESLEY and the English Methodist CONFERENCE (see SLAVERY AND BRITISH METHODISM). Several of the early American Conferences over which Asbury presided, made antislavery statements or recommendations. The legislation of the constitutive CHRISTMAS CONFERENCE of 1784 is famous because it was more uncompromising than any that had gone before or was to come thereafter. "We view it as contrary to the Golden Law of God . . . and the unalienable Rights of Mankind, as well as every Principle of the Revolution, to hold in the deepest debasement . . . so many souls that are all capable of the Image of God" (*Discipline*, 1785, p. 14). This lofty pronouncement was followed by legislation according to which Methodists were to have a year to begin emancipating their slaves, and five years in which to finish it. The alternatives were voluntary withdrawal or expulsion. These rules, however, were already marked by the portentous exception exempting those states in which the civil laws forbade emancipation.

We have also to note, in this consideration of beginnings, in 1789, when the GENERAL RULES were first introduced into the formulae of the new Church (by a process which is more obscure than we might like, but which was doubtless initiated by the General Superintendents, COKE and ASBURY), that a new Rule on slavery, which had not been deemed necessary in England, was included. It forbade (as one of the long list of specifications under the general heading of "doing no harm"), "the buying and selling the bodies and souls of men, women and children, with an intention to enslave them" (*Discipline*, 1789, p. 48). It should be noted that this forbade not the holding, but only trading in, slaves. In fact the high ground taken by the Christmas Conference could not be maintained, and before six months were up, began that long process which was to leave the Church not only enmeshed in compromise, made for the sake of unity, but with shattered unity as well.

The concessions were not made without opposition from a small but zealous minority. Soon after the Christmas Conference, FREEBORN GARRETTSON and PHILIP GATCH, two of the leading early itinerants, and certain others who are not named for us, emancipated their slaves. But the opposition met by those (especially Coke and Asbury) who preached emancipation, from mobs who muttered threats and brandished clubs induced a feeling of hopelessness. The GENERAL CONFERENCE of 1816 admitted alike the duty and the impossibility of reform when it reported that "little can be done to abolish a practise so contrary to the principles of moral justice" (*Journals of the General Conference*, I, 169-70). The *trading* in slaves forbidden by the General Rule likewise defied not only prohibition, but even restriction. In 1796 expulsion was still the penalty for selling a slave.

Buying one was permitted under the supervision of local church committees who were to operate under certain elaborate provisions. By 1808 the General Conference gave up attempting to regulate either the buying or the selling of slaves, leaving the matter to each Annual Conference (*Journals of the General Conference*, I, 93). This obviously allowed a great deal of latitude, and many Conferences, while retaining the Rule in print, acted pretty much as though it didn't exist. The General Conference never really regained the control it had thus relinquished; and it is not unfair to say that its actual legislation in the matter was of monumental unimportance. At one time the General Conference was greatly exercised over the phrasing of the General Rule on slavery. Should it read "the buying or selling" or "the buying *and* selling" etc.? In 1840, only a quadrennium before the separation of Episcopal Methodism, the General Conference confirmed the decision of an Annual Conference which excluded the testimony of Negroes from the records of Church trials.

The growing power of the North in the General Conference is reflected in the Episcopal elections of 1836. Though four new Bishops were elected, not one of them was a slaveholder. WILLIAM CAPERS was passed over (in spite of the fact that he was most obviously of Episcopal stature) because he was a slave owner. The southerners resented this slight most strongly—saying that it amounted to proscription.

In this matter the northern Conferences were joined by the "border Conferences." Among these the BALTIMORE CONFERENCE, particularly, made every effort to keep its ministers clear of entanglement with slavery. The feeling there was very strong that the "Itinerancy" belonged to the whole Church, and that nothing which made it unacceptable to the northerners ought to be allowed. From another point of view, it may be regarded as one more instance of the unfortunate tendency among Methodists to adopt a double standard of conduct—one for its laymen and quite a different one for its ministers. Nevertheless, it has been estimated that by 1843, 200 travelling preachers and 1,000 local preachers held nearly 1,200 slaves.

It was at this same General Conference of 1836 that the fraternal delegate of the English Conference thought it appropriate to remind the Americans to maintain at the least the antislavery principle in the abstract, and said so in his address. Whereupon the American Conference bristled defensively, said they always had done so, and that if the English brethren had understood the American situation more thoroughly, their delegate would not have found it necessary to intervene as he did.

Speaking of the South and North generally, we may say that in the former, the intensity of the effort to defend slavery grew *pari passu* with the intensity of the Abolitionist movement in the North—which took its rise in the 1830's. Speaking of Methodism especially, and for the time being of that in the South, we discover that they always denied, in spite of their practice, being "proslavery." So far as this writer has been able to discover, of the leading apologies for slavery which appeared in the region, and which made it out to be a divinely ordained blessing for white and black alike, none was written by a Methodist. This does not mean that the Southern Methodist point of view was not presented ably and in lively fashion in the Southern Methodist periodicals, for it was. SAMUEL DUNWOODY, a member of the

South Carolina Conference, preached a sermon, which may be regarded as typical. On the one hand, he insisted that he was "no advocate for slavery," on the other, that Scripture sanction indicates that slavery is not a moral evil, and in principle is justifiable in certain instances. Henry B. Bascom was perhaps the most voluminous, but by no means the only writer in the field.

The Rev. Dr. Smith, President and Professor of Moral and Intellectual philosphy of Randolph-Macon College, published his *Lectures on the Philosophy and Practise of Slavery* in 1856. Abel Stevens, writing in the *Methodist Quarterly Review*, says Smith begins with the statement "Slavery is right *per se*" (39 [1857]: 274). A reviewer of this book in the *Quarterly Review of the M.E. Church, South* goes on to state Smith's further argument, which, to be sure, goes over pretty familiar ground: all men are *not* created equal; the inferior race has no *right* to equality; the slaves are daily brought into contact with civilizing influences; the South is much better off socially and religiously with slavery than the North is without it; reason and the Bible are *for* it, while against it is *sentiment;* but the God of the Bible must be vindicated. (April, 1857, pp. 242 ff.)

Slavery was not, however, defended in principle in any major work by a Methodist. The "Radical Abolitionism" of the North was always there, a good target for attack, and the Southern Methodists, like many of those in the North, supported the operations of the Colonization Society, which was regarded as a safe channel for the expression of concern for the Negro's welfare, and which was more impressive for size and bustle than for solid achievement. Furthermore, many leading Southern Methodists, especially William Capers and James O. Andrew, gave much thought and energy to the evangelization of the slaves. This activity was regarded as the "crowning glory of the Church." Many Methodists (and neither North nor South had a monopoly on these) were apparently sincere in believing that the Church's main, indeed its sole, business was evangelization. Consequently whatever hindered success in that endeavor was *ipso facto* outside the church's legitimate field of endeavor.

Blacks had been the object of Methodist evangelism from the beginning. Bishop Coke was convinced that he had a special gift for speaking effectively to them. Bishop Asbury speaks of being much affected at seeing them crowd to the Communion table. Beginning as early as 1786 they had a special column in the statistical summaries of the Annual Conferences.

The planters often objected to the activities of the evangelists among their slaves as tending to make them restive and insubordinate; and of course teaching them to read was taboo, which makes it seem a very truncated sort of evangelism in a Protestant communion. And, for obvious reasons, it was considered better to have them attend the meetings of the whites than to hold assemblies of their own, except under very special circumstances and then only under strict supervision of white authorities. In the whites' meetinghouses they were usually required to sit in a special gallery or a restricted place on the floor. Usually too, they had to wait till all the whites had communed before they could take their places at the Table. Transgressors of these limitations were sometimes violently dealt with. It was just such an incident which led to withdrawal of the Negro section of the congregation of St. George's Church in Philadelphia, and the formation, in 1816, under the leadership of Richard

Allen, of the African Methodist Episcopal Church. Allen was the first of the few Negroes to be fully ordained, though a considerable number were made local deacons, and more still were useful preachers. Four years later the African Methodist Episcopal Zion Church was formed as the result of a similar succession of events in the John Street Church in New York City.

Northern Methodism furnished no Abolitionist leader of national stature, but La Roy Sunderland, Lucius Matlack and especially Orange Scott, all of them members of the New England Conference, became notable leaders among the Methodists. They refused to be discouraged by the fact that the officiary and most of the church press was opposed to them. They had not been silent in the General Conference, but they agitated with much more success in the Annual Conferences, especially those of the Northeast. Their tactics were not always dignified, and it is to be feared that they made great nuisances of themselves in many instances. For instance, while the roll-call at the beginning of a Conference session was being gone through to "pass the character" of the members, they would challenge each other with having gone to Abolitionist meetings etc. This would give rise to discussions in which the cause was aired, and lengthy delays were imposed. Finally, the Bishop out of sheer weariness, would rule that being an Abolitionist was not an obstacle to "passing the character" of the Conference members. This was not such a small victory as it may seem, for Lucius Matlack had been barred from full membership in the Philadelphia Conference for years because of his Abolitionist sympathies, and finally succeeded in gaining admittance only by transferring to the New England Conference, where a post was found for him alongside Orange Scott at Lowell, Mass. These same men put Abolitionist resolutions before quarterly and annual conferences. Sometimes the bishop or presiding elder would refuse to put the question, on the grounds that it was not a part of the proper business of the session. The officials would thereupon be charged with oppressive and high-handed abuse of power; to this the reply was often a charge of slander. It must be admitted that both sides were at times guilty of departure from brotherly charity in both word and action.

The Abolitionists founded Societies which at first used the name Methodist but when that was denied them, changed to "Wesleyan." When they were refused access to the Church's official *Advocates* they started their own periodicals. They were greatly disheartened by the lack of action in the General Conference of 1840. In that year Scott, Matlack and others called an antislavery convention which met in New York. Out of this convention grew the American Wesleyan Antislavery Society. By 1841 Orange Scott was saying of the M.E. Church, "There is . . . no alternative but to submit to things as they are or secede." In 1843 out of the Wesleyan Antislavery Society and sundry other disaffected groups grew The Wesleyan Methodist Connection of America, which became actually a church of considerable proportions, and constituted an ominous forerunner of the still greater split which was only a year away. (See Wesleyan Methodist Church of America.)

The fateful General Conference of 1844 awoke to a shocked awareness that the Abolition movement had grown up within the Church to proportions that would no longer be denied. The vote in "the Harding affair" of the Baltimore Conference (one hundred and seventeen to fifty-six) showed that the so-called border Conferences were prepared to continue voting with the North to maintain their historic policy of keeping the ministry free from entanglement with slavery; and there had been enough talk about slaveholding being a sin to indicate that the days of accommodation over lines geographical or otherwise were about over. So when, by a vote of 110 to 68, the Conference voted to ask Bishop Andrew (who had inherited a slave-girl from one wife, and become legally the owner of another by marrying again a woman who owned one) to "desist from the exercise of his office so long as this impediment remains," the slave-holding Conferences resolved that the action rendered "a continuance of the jurisdiction of this General Conference over these conferences inconsistent with the success of the ministry in the slaveholding states" (*Journals of the General Conference*, II, [1844] 109). (See also PLAN OF SEPARATION.) No matter how much each side might allege juridical grounds for its action (the North maintained the amenability of the bishops to the General Conference, while the South would allow nothing of the sort) everybody knew that the split was fundamentally a question of slavery in the Church. The division might conceivably have been carried out in such a way as to minimize frictions; but instead, mutual provocations multiplied, and the Plan of Separation which was intended to assuage the strife only increased it. Thus began the long separation of the M.E. Church, South, and the M.E. Church (north), which was to be until 1939—or nearly a century—in healing.

Though the delegates on the spot worked out a fairly equitable division of the property (consisting mostly of the assets of the BOOK CONCERN) there was a revulsion of feeling in the North during the next quadrennium. Many of those delegates who, in 1844, had agreed to the separation were not returned to the General Conference of the Northern Church in 1848. Their successors repudiated the agreement. The Southern Church brought suit in two States, NEW YORK and OHIO. The case in New York was decided in favor of the Southern Church. It declared the General Conference competent to divide the Church and the property. The decision of the Ohio Court, though not rendered till after the other had been handed down, was in direct contradiction to it: the General Conference was not competent to divide the Church. Members, of course, had freedom to leave in any numbers they wished, but they had no right to the property of the Church which they had left. The decision of the New York Court was not appealed by the Northern Church, but that of the Ohio Court was appealed by the Southern Church. In both cases the losers in the lower court may have assessed the situation keenly enough to know what they were about, for the Supreme Court decided unanimously in favor of the Southern Church. The monetary value of the settlement is put at $80,000; but the Southern Church felt that, in addition, the unanimity of the decision gave them the status of a co-ordinate division of the Church, on an equal footing of legitimacy with the Northerners.

After the separation was an accomplished fact, the rest of the story may be subsumed under two heads: first, the way the two Churches brought their respective Disciplinary statements into harmony with the new situation in which each found itself in the matter of slavery; and, second, the melancholy matter of the rivalries and animosities which characterized the relations of the two Churches to each other. The two stories run concurrently, so far as time is concerned, but we shall for the sake of clarity deal with them topically, though it means going over the same time-period (1848-1864) more than once. Actually, what I have here designated as the second of my two topics—the rivalries and animosities of the two Churches—continued to subsist long after 1864; but this date seems the most fitting terminus for a treatment which regards them as effects of slavery; for it was in that year that the Emancipation Proclamation of President Lincoln began to take effect, and slavery came to an end.

We shall begin with the treatment accorded the Disciplinary statements on slavery by the M.E. Church, South. The Southern Church in its first General Conferences (1846, 1850 and 1854) was well occupied in getting its ecclesiastical machinery running. It was not till 1858 that it got rid of the rule on slavery, which it had taken over, along with the rest of the *Discipline* from pre-separation days. But doubtless a desire not to alienate the "border Conferences" during the critical period when they might, in whole or in part, join either Church, played its part in the delay. The matter was considered briefly in their General Conference of 1846, more seriously in those of 1850 and 1854; but the General Rule on Slavery was not actually dropped till 1858.

The Northern Church did not adopt new and more stringent antislavery provisions until two years later, that is in the General Conference of 1860. The same motives prompted the delay as had operated in the South—that is to say, a desire not to alienate the border Conferences. When finally the "new chapter" was adopted for the *Discipline*, it read, "We believe that the buying, selling or holding of human beings, to be used as chattels is . . . inconsistent with . . . that Rule in our Discipline which requires . . . us to do no harm" (*History of American Methodism*, II, 209). This was the strongest statement the radical Abolitionists could get at the time. Even so, it excited the fears of the border Conferences, and to allay them it was still further weakened by an explicit declaration that it was advisory and admonitory in character. Indeed it was not till 1864 that the holding of slaves was made an unqualified impediment to membership in the (Northern) M.E. Church. Before this, ironically, the slaves had been emancipated by the civil power as a military measure. Caesar in the service of Mars had accomplished what the spirit of John Wesley in the service of Christ had been unable to bring about. But indubitably Caesar, using the methods of Mars, left for generations yet unborn an entail of bitterness and alienation.

The border Conferences whose favor was so assiduously courted by both North and South were six in number: Baltimore, Baltimore East, Philadelphia, Western Virginia (soon to become simply West Virginia), Kentucky and Missouri. In these the struggle was particularly envenomed. In the General Conference of 1844 the Northern Church had promised not to try to set up churches in the territory of the Southern Church. But there was room for honest doubt where the lines lay. The ecclesiastical issue was clouded by the political one as Secession became a burning question—the border States adhered to the Union. So though neither Church erred on the side of modesty in estimating the limits of its missionary activity, there is no ground for charging the

Northern Church with violating its promise in seeking the adherence of the border Conferences.

That part of the Baltimore Conference which lay in Virginia adhered with the rest of that state to the Confederacy, and the Methodists therein met by themselves till after the Civil War when the whole Baltimore Conference joined the Southern Church. On the other hand, some of the preachers of the KENTUCKY CONFERENCE of the Southern Church, having proclaimed their loyalty to the Union, refused to go to appointments in the Confederacy. After the War, eighteen of them withdrew and threw in their lot with the Northern Church. Roughly fifteen percent of the membership of the Northern Church was in the border Conferences in 1861. They had the preponderance in West Virginia; but in Kentucky and Missouri, the majority were in the Southern Church.

At times, as we shall see, the hostility boiled up in violence (see BORDER WAR); even when it did not, strong language was used on both sides, the vehement expression of the zeal with which each Church threw itself into the cause of the section in which it lay. Early in the war one northern preacher said, "Let Davis and Beauregard be captured, to meet the fate of Haman. Hang them up on Mason and Dixon's line, that traitors . . . may be warned. Let them hang until vultures shall eat their rotten flesh from their bones; let them hang until the crows shall build their filthy nests in their skeletons: let them hang until the rope rots, and let their dismembered bones fall so deep into the earth that God Almighty can't find them in the day of resurrection." Over against that bit of eloquence, we may put this description by a Southern preacher of the emissaries of the Northern Church, who came into the South "as enemies of the people and institutions of the slave states, rank, rotten with the foul virus of an incurable disease, foes of God and man, spies and traitors of their country and their kind, let them stay where they belong!" (Posey, p. 363.)

CALIFORNIA was another place where both churches were at work—but there was room for both in that spacious country. MISSOURI, however, was another story. The tradition of violence spilled over from the long struggle between Free-soil and slavery factions into the ecclesiastical realm. And because the lines between Southern and Northern Methodism corresponded closely with those already drawn, the tactics employed in both struggles were pretty much the same. In June of 1855, in Andrew County, Missouri, a preacher of the Northern Church attempted to conduct a protracted meeting in spite of threats. When he arrived he was met by a mob which tarred and feathered him. Perhaps the most celebrated clash of all was the one over ANTHONY BEWLEY, who moved from TENNESSEE to Missouri, but decided to remain in the Northern Church. In 1860 he and a companion were charged with poisoning wells and burning towns in TEXAS. He decided to return to Missouri, but on the way he was hanged by a mob near Fort Worth. "Before the separation was generally accepted, clashes along the border between the Churches became frequent, disturbing, even destructive. . . . It was not rare for services conducted by one side of the controversy to be broken up by the other" (Posey, ibid., p. 361).

The Southern Church seems to have been the more aggressive in the disputed territories before the outbreak of the War. It must be said, however, that the Northern Church, once the Union Armies had begun to occupy portions of the Confederate States, made indefensible use of the occupying forces as a screen behind which a campaign of ecclesiastical advancement was carried on. Bishop AMES was the principal promoter of this scheme, which involved securing the collaboration of military commanders to secure the use of churches and pulpits in occupied territory for ministers and chaplains of the Northern Methodist Church. In fairness it must be said that the Methodists were not alone in this sort of activity. Indeed probably the most famous case (made so by the protest of the ousted minister himself) was Presbyterian. President Lincoln himself was finally drawn into the discussion, and made it quite clear that he did not approve the replacement of one minister by another, except for open expressions of hostility to the cause of the Union. But after the President thought the Presbyterian difficulty had been solved by his intervention, he had to intervene to keep the commanders in "certain Southern military departments" from doing the same thing with Methodist churches for Bishop Ames.

So it went during the war years, each hostile act evoking a response still more hostile. The limits of our task as sketched earlier make it unnecessary to follow the melancholy story through the years of the Reconstruction. But just after the War's end, occurred an expression of opinion so refreshingly at variance with the prevailing temper that it may stand as the expression of a happier "might-have-been."

In 1865, John H. Caldwell preached two sermons in the Methodist Church in Newman, Georgia. They were published later, and bore a message of moderation which, as the event was to prove, went unheeded in the violent post-bellum atmosphere. These sermons gave vent to convictions "long pent up in his heart." Antislavery sentiments were stifled before the war, though they existed. God, Mr. Caldwell continued, has put an end to slavery, which shows that though the relationship involved was not wrong, at least the Southern practice of it was: the law punished the black man more severely than the white; the slaves were improperly fed, clothed and housed. Our contention that the Southern Church was not proslavery after the separation makes no sense— "if it was not pro-slavery, what was it?" Our children have been trained up to cherish the bitterest sentiments toward the North, but we shall shake hands with our late foes and cooperate with the Union.

In sum, we may say that though Methodism furnished neither defenders of slavery nor Abolitionist leaders of national stature, they furnished the matrix out of which great numbers of the rank-and-file of both parties were drawn. In this, as in so many other matters, Methodism was a representative cross section of the nation. At the present writing, the question of chattel slavery is a matter of historic interest only in the United States. Nevertheless, the prohibition against both the holding of and trading in slaves, still stands in our General Rules, a monument to a struggle now happily long past. All other declarations on the subject have, as might be expected, disappeared from the Discipline.

E. S. Bucke, History of American Methodism. 1964.
John H. Caldwell, Slavery and Southern Methodism: Two Sermons Preached in the Methodist Church in Newman, Georgia. 1865.
R. M. Cameron, Methodism and Society. 1961.
Journals of the General Conferences.
D. G. Mathews, Slavery and Methodism. 1965.

Walter B. Posey, *Frontier Mission: A History of Religion West of the Southern Appalachians to 1861.* Lexington, Ky.: University of Kentucky Press, 1966.

W. W. Sweet, *The Story of Religion in America.* New York: Harper, 1950.   RICHARD M. CAMERON

SLAVERY AND BRITISH METHODISM. The right to sell slaves to the Spanish colonies brought great prosperity to the eighteenth-century English slave trade. About three million slaves were carried in English ships during the eighteenth century; in 1768 alone, English ships carried 53,000 out of about 100,000 slaves. They were bought for about £20-25 in West Africa and shipped to Jamaica, the main American market, where they were sold for about £40-50 each. Slaves made a great contribution to British wealth, making the trade highly respectable and creating a formidable vested interest with many able political defenders.

The Wesley brothers had met slavery as far back as 1736, and they never forgot its cruelties. Years later, on reading the book of "an honest quaker," Anthony Benezet, John Wesley branded the trade as "that execrable sum of all the villainies" (*Journal,* Feb. 12, 1772). Benezet's book shaped his own *Thoughts on Slavery* (1774). The "grand idol" of slavery was "the god of gain"; slavers were "petty tyrants over human freedom"; their excuses were "empty and hypocritical," and their methods inhuman. "I deny that villainy is ever necessary. A man can be of no necessity of degrading himself into a wolf." Wesley pleaded, "Give liberty to whom liberty is due, that is, to every child of man, to every partaker of human nature. Let none serve you except by his own act and deed, by his own voluntary choice. Away with all whips, all chains, all compulsion. Be gentle toward all men." He underlined these arguments in his *Serious Address* of 1777, and poured scorn on those who lamented the temporary loss of the trade in the American Revolutionary War. When the Committee for the Abolition of the Slave Trade was formed in 1787, Wesley wrote letters of support to Thomas Clarkson and Granville Sharp. He promised Clarkson to republish his pamphlet of 1774, with a recommendation of the committee (*Works,* xiii, 113). He preached on slavery at Bristol, a great center of the trade; the next day the society spent a day of fasting and prayer "for those poor outcasts of men" (*Journal,* March 6-7, 1788). The last book he read was the autobiography of an African slave, Gustavus Vasa; his last and most famous letter, written on Feb. 24, 1791, was to encourage WILLIAM WILBERFORCE: "Go on, in the name of God and the power of his might, till even American slavery, the vilest that ever saw the sun, shall vanish away before it."

The abolition of slavery was the only major social concern of John Wesley that was convincingly and wholeheartedly continued by early nineteenth-century Methodism. This was partly because the slavery issue was increasingly bound up with the rapid expansion of Wesleyan overseas missions. West Indian planters soon realized the danger of allowing Methodist instruction of their slaves, and they incited the colonial authorities to persecute Methodist missionaries and societies. Methodism was thus identified with the abolitionist cause; Wilberforce persuaded the 1791 Conference to support abolitionist petitions, while his own followers were soon dubbed "a set of Methodists" (*Eclectic Review,* August, 1810). The Conference of 1807 greeted the abolition

of the English slave trade by forbidding missionaries to marry anyone without the emancipation of their slaves. It was an apt decision, as abolitionist effort was now concentrated on the destruction of slavery itself. From 1807 to 1833 there was a prolonged battle between Methodism and the West Indian interests. The Jamaican legislature prohibited Methodist instruction of slaves in 1807; the Wesleyan COMMITTEE OF PRIVILEGES persuaded the British government to annul the law in 1809. The creation of the WESLEYAN METHODIST MISSIONARY SOCIETY proper in 1814 gave Methodists a new focal point of opposition. RICHARD WATSON, one of its secretaries from 1821, published a convincing answer to charges that Methodism taught sedition, disobedience, and rebellion to West Indian slaves. He was strongly supported by JABEZ BUNTING, who published full details of the Demerara and Barbadoes persecutions in the *Wesleyan Methodist Magazine.* Watson and Bunting warmly supported the newly started Anti-Slavery Society and rallied Methodism to the abolitionist cause.

There was a strong reply to those Jamaican missionaries who denounced emancipation in 1824; the Missionary Committee declared it an irregular meeting;

and they hold it to be the duty of every Christian government to bring the practice of slavery to an end, . . . and that the degradation of men merely on account of their colour, and the holding of human beings in interminable bondage, are wholly inconsistent with Christianity. . . . They will not compromise the principles of Christianity . . . to obtain favour. (*Wesleyan Methodist Magazine,* 1825, pp. 117-19.)

Watson remained firm despite the disapproval of the colonial secretary. Conference recommended antislavery petitions in 1829 and 1830, and in 1830 and 1831 urged Methodist voters to support abolitionist candidates at Parliamentary elections. When the Jamaican slave insurrection of 1831 was blamed on missionary teaching and made the pretext for further wholesale persecution, the Conference of 1832 defended the "peaceable conduct" of Methodist slaves, and the "prudent conduct" of their missionaries. It denounced the destruction of five chapels by Jamaican white mobs, noting that slavery corrupted the owners and their agents even more than the slaves. It repeated its condemnation of the Jamaican resolutions of 1824 and thanked the government for its promised protection (*Minutes of the Wesleyan Methodist Conference,* 1832).

In December, 1832, T. F. Buxton wrote to the dying Richard Watson to tell him that the government would introduce an emancipation bill and wanted their advice. The 1833 Emancipation Act was hailed by the Conference of 1834 in its "Annual Address to the Societies": "We congratulate you on this happy accomplishment of your ardent desires. . . . God hath made of one blood all nations of men for to dwell on the face of the earth; and we anticipate the time when, by the admission and triumph of this great truth, all civil distinctions arising from colour and complexion shall be abolished" (*Minutes of the Wesleyan Methodist Conference,* 1834). Over 130 years later, that time has still not arrived. Slavery was by no means dead. Other nations abolished slavery in time, but the trade to the Americas survived until 1865. There was even controversy over the terms of the 1833 act; the compensation of £20,000,000 to the former slave owners was not welcomed by all Methodists, though the

Wesleyan Methodist Magazine accepted it as an act of national repentance.

In 1840, the Conference recommended a new Society for the Extinction of the Slave Trade and the Civilisation of Africa (*Minutes of the Wesleyan Methodist Conference, 1840*). British Methodism occasionally clashed with American Methodism on the subject of slavery, and ROBERT NEWTON on his return from a visit to America in 1840 said,

If I were a coloured person I scarcely know what fate I should prefer, to be a slave in the South, or a reputed freeman in the North, and yet to have my manhood trodden down, and my feelings lacerated every hour, by the cruel ban under which those of African blood in every degree are doomed to suffer. (G. Smith, *History of Wesleyan Methodism* (1872) iii, 406).

Wesley, J. *Thoughts on Slavery*. London. 1774.

MICHAEL S. EDWARDS

SLEDD, ANDREW (1870-1939), American educator and teacher of New Testament Language and Literature, was born on Nov. 7, 1870, at Lynchburg, Va., the son of Robert Newton and Frances Carey (Greene) Sledd. His father was a prominent member of the VIRGINIA CONFERENCE. He received his A.M. and A.B. degree from RANDOLPH-MACON COLLEGE, took a Master's in Greek at Harvard, and later received the Ph.D. in Latin at Yale, 1903. He was, as he would have said, a Latinist, and took the chair of Latin at EMORY COLLEGE at Oxford, Ga., in 1898, serving there until 1902. On March 14, 1899, he married Annie Florence Candler, the daughter of Bishop WARREN A. CANDLER, who was at that time president of Emory at Oxford. Sledd became the professor of Greek in Southern University at Greensboro, Ala., for one year, and then he was made president of the University of Florida during the early days of that institution. The Florida University named a building in his honor long afterward.

At the founding of the School of Theology at EMORY UNIVERSITY in 1914, his father-in-law, Bishop Candler, acting as president and chancellor of the newly founded seminary, called Sledd to that institution and for a quarter of a century he served as professor of New Testament, Languages and Literature at Emory.

A. Sledd, as he usually signed his name, started as a layman, but while teaching at Oxford he was licensed to preach in 1898. Twelve years later he was admitted on trial in the FLORIDA CONFERENCE in 1910. He moved his Conference membership to ALABAMA, however, when he taught in that state, and kept his membership in the ALABAMA CONFERENCE for the rest of his life. He was never in the regular pastorate, but did serve churches for brief periods. He was "known to his pupils for the exactness of his thinking and his abhorence of shoddyness." His classroom insights in the interpretation of the Greek New Testament will never be forgotten by those whom he taught.

Sledd wrote *The Bibles of the Churches*, Cokesbury, 1930; *His Witnesses—A Study of the Book of Acts*, with C. A. Bowen, the general church school editor, 1935; *St. Mark's Life of Jesus*, Cokesbury, 1930. He was considered somewhat liberal for his day in Scriptural interpretation, but publicly opposed the unification of the Episcopal Methodist Churches when this forward looking move came about in the mid-twenties and thirties.

Sledd's first child, Andrew, born in 1903, died in 1919, but seven other of his eight children, as well as his wife, survived him. He died on March 16, 1939.

Raymond H. Firth, "The Life of Andrew Sledd." Unpublished ms., Emory University.
Journal of the Alabama Conference, 1940.
C. F. Price, *Who's Who in American Methodism*. 1916.

N. B. H.

SLEEPER, JACOB (1802-1889), American layman and philanthropist, was born in New Castle, MAINE, on Nov. 21, 1802. His parents died when he was fourteen years old and the rest of his youth was spent under the care of his uncle in Belfast, Maine. After attending Lincoln Academy for a period, he went to work. By the time he was twenty-one he had a store in Belfast. In his early twenties he moved to BOSTON and in real estate and wholesale clothing he amassed a considerable fortune.

Sleeper yielded to public pressure and became a member of the Aldermanic Council of Boston, then a member of the State Legislature, and later served two terms in the Governor's Council. He was twice appointed by the Commonwealth an Overseer of Harvard University.

Sleeper was described by those who knew him well as handsome, having remarkably penetrating and sympathetic eyes. He was wise, cheerful, tactful, winsome, and modest. One of his mottoes was, "Do as much good as you can, and don't make a fuss about it."

Jacob Sleeper gave his heart to God in his youth and joined the M.E. Church. He gave to his church the first fifty dollars he ever earned by his own exertions and was always a generous supporter of every Methodist cause. He belonged to Bromfield Street Church, Boston, and was a longtime CLASS LEADER, for fifty-nine years Sunday school superintendent, and forty-six years treasurer of the Trustees.

Jacob Sleeper joined LEE CLAFLIN and ISAAC RICH in securing a Charter for BOSTON UNIVERSITY and in helping to start it in its progressive course of educational service. He died on March 31, 1889.

Dictionary of American Biography. DANIEL L. MARSH

SLICER, HENRY (1804-1874), American minister, was born in Annapolis, Md., March 27, 1801. While serving an apprenticeship in BALTIMORE he was converted and licensed to preach, and in 1822 began his fifty-two year ministry in the BALTIMORE CONFERENCE. Besides pastorates in every important station in WASHINGTON and Baltimore, he presided fifteen years over districts, was CHAPLAIN of the U. S. Senate for seven terms, and served two years as agent for the Metropolitan Church project at Washington.

Eight GENERAL CONFERENCES between 1832 and 1872 heard the voice of the old "war horse" lifted in debate, and in that of 1860 he led the unsuccessful struggle to defeat the "new chapter." That same year DICKINSON COLLEGE honored him with a D.D. degree. While he was on Potomac District in 1832 a remarkable revival took place, as well as a tussle with the Baptists. The latter called forth his treatise on BAPTISM. He later in 1838 published an influential sermon against dueling and led the BOOK COMMITTEE minority, 1868-72, against the "era of fraud." The temperance cause found him an able and widely sought advocate.

Colleagues remembered him as one who loved the Master and the Methodist Church and defended both with vigor. Rheumatism pained and slowed his steps, but he remained in effective relation until near April 23, 1874 when he closely followed his wife, Elizabeth, in death. They are buried in Greenmount Cemetery, Baltimore.

J. E. Armstrong, *Old Baltimore Conference*. 1907.

EDWIN SCHELL

SLOAN, HAROLD PAUL (1881-1961), American minister and editor, was born in Westfield, N. J., Dec. 12, 1881, the son of Theodore Reber and Miriam B. Hickman Sloan, who was herself the daughter of a Methodist clergyman. He studied at the University of Pennsylvania, Crozer Theological Seminary and DREW THEOLOGICAL SEMINARY, where he received his B.D. degree in 1908. He married Ethel Beatrice Buckwalter, April 3, 1909. They had two children, Ruth B. and Harold Paul, Jr.

He joined the NEW JERSEY CONFERENCE (ME) in full connection in 1906. He served in various churches and as District Superintendent of the Camden District from 1934 to 1936. He was elected a delegate to the GENERAL CONFERENCE in 1920, and to every subsequent General Conference until his election as Editor of the (New York) *Christian Advocate* in 1936.

Sloan was conservative in his theological position and became an ardent fundamentalist in the modernist-fundamentalist controversies of the 1920's. Feeling that modernism was entering Methodism mostly by way of the Conference COURSE OF STUDIES, he headed a drive culminating in 1920 when thirty annual conferences sent memorials to the General Conference demanding an investigation of, and appropriate changes in, the Course of Study. The General Conference voted that the new studies were to be in "full and hearty accord with those doctrines and that outline of faith established in the constitution of the church; and that the *Discipline*, with some special emphasis upon the ARTICLES OF RELIGION, and the standard sermons of JOHN WESLEY, fifty-two in number, recognized as standards in American Methodism, shall be included in the conference course."

Sloan continued his fundamentalist campaign through a publication, *Call to Colors*, which later merged with a magazine called *The Bible Champion*, later to become *The Essentialist*. He was unable, however, to influence the General Conference further by his fundamentalist position, although in 1928 he addressed that body charging "flagrant disloyalty to the Methodist doctrinal standards in seminaries, pulpits, and Sunday school literature."

He was a delegate to the ECUMENICAL METHODIST CONFERENCE in LONDON in 1921, and he received an honorary doctorate from the University of Pennsylvania in 1940.

As Editor of the *Advocate*, he stated in his first issue his "basic loyalty . . . to the historic Christian faith itself," and during his four-year tenure many of his editorials centered in theological presentations of his own strongly held religious viewpoint. He took no steps to update the format of the paper or to make it more attractive to the average layman.

Sloan was a prolific writer, being the author of nine books. He also taught for a time at Temple Theological Seminary, and became a Trustee of Drew Theological Seminary and of ASBURY COLLEGE, Kentucky. After leaving the office of Editor, he became pastor of the Wharton Memorial Church in PHILADELPHIA, where he also conducted a radio ministry, "The Living Christ Hour," and began likewise to speak out strongly against communism. He was tall, powerfully built, with a friendly face topped by a mass of white hair. He possessed a clarion voice and demonstrated great skill in debate.

He died in 1961. A memorial service was held for him on May 25 in the Haddonfield Methodist Church, Haddonfield, N. J.

C. T. Howell, *Prominent Personalities*. 1945.

FREDERICK E. MASER

SLOANE, ISRAEL (1825-1863), American United Brethren missionary martyr, was born in MARYLAND, June 18, 1825. At about eighteen years of age he was converted. In the same year he enrolled at Oberlin College, where he remained for two years. During this period he decided upon entering the ministry. He transferred to OTTERBEIN COLLEGE and joined the Scioto Conference, CHURCH OF THE UNITED BRETHREN IN CHRIST.

In 1854 he was sent to CANADA as the first missionary of the United Brethren in Christ to that country, having served a number of appointments previously in Scioto Conference. Although he remained in Canada only four years he succeeded in establishing the Ontario Mission Conference in 1856. Feeling impelled to go to CALIFORNIA as a missionary he went there in 1858 and succeeded in forming a mission conference. The rigors of this life were quite strenuous. He served Humboldt Bay while Indians were on the warpath. Injured by an unmanageable horse in the Cache Creek Mountains, he died Aug. 26, 1863, having established more than a score of congregations and organized two mission conferences. Twice married, his second wife survived him.

Religious Telescope, Dec. 21, 1864.
Weekley and Fout, *Our Heroes*. 1908. ROBERT R. MacCANON

SLUTZ, FRANK DURWARD (1882-1956), American lay leader and educator, was born in Mt. Hope, Ohio, on Nov. 27, 1882. He received the A.B. and A.M. degrees from MT. UNION COLLEGE, and the A.M. from Harvard. He taught in several elementary schools in OHIO and COLORADO and was superintendent of schools in Pueblo, Colo., from 1912 to 1917. For the next ten years he was director of Moraine Park School, DAYTON, Ohio, and from 1927 to 1932 was educational adviser at Chicago Teachers College. Slutz held various positions in The Methodist Church at the local, annual conference, and national levels. From 1948 to 1952 he was a member of the General Board of EDUCATION, and from 1948 to 1956 he was a member of the Curriculum Committee. He served the General Board of LAY ACTIVITIES and the Young Men's Christian Association in numerous capacities, and he gave many lectures to industrial managers and to labor unions. He was twice a delegate to the GENERAL CONFERENCE. For thirty-five years he conducted a summer boys' camp at Cass Lake, Minn. Slutz died on Dec. 16, 1956.

Clark and Stafford, *Who's Who in Methodism*. 1952.

WALTER N. VERNON

SLUTZ, LEONARD DOERING (1913-   ), American layman, prominent in GENERAL CONFERENCE and general Church work, was born on April 7, 1913, in CINCINNATI,

Ohio, his father and grandfather being Methodist ministers, Earl R. and William Leonard Slutz respectively. His mother was Edna Lee Davis. He was educated at OHIO WESLEYAN UNIVERSITY, B.A., 1934; and the University of Cincinnati, LL.B., 1937. He has since practiced law as partner in a well known legal firm in Cincinnati.

Mr. Slutz was a member of the Commission on Inter-jurisdictional Relations (1956-68), and Chairman of that important body (1964-68). He was the chairman of the Committee on Judicial Administration at the 1956 General Conference, the vice-chairman of the Committee on Conferences in 1966, and secretary of the Committee on Conferences of the General Conference of 1968. He has been a member of the General Conference (TMC), 1952, '56, '60, '64, '66, and '68. He is also a member of the WORLD METHODIST COUNCIL, serving on its executive committee, and was a member of the General Assembly of the NATIONAL COUNCIL OF CHURCHES, 1960-64.

He has served as president of the Board of Alumni Directors of Ohio Wesleyan; on the Governing Board of the White Cross Hospital in Columbus, Ohio; the Bethesda Hospital and Bethesda Home for the Aged; Wesley Hall and Emanuel Community Center in Cincinnati. During the second World War, he was the commanding officer of the USS LSM 301. In Ohio he has been a member of the Board of Trustees of the Cincinnati Human Relations Commission, of the Ohio Civil Rights Commission, and has served as an instructor in speech at the University of Cincinnati, and also as an instructor in the College of Law, 1957-59. His reports at the General Conference of 1966 and '68 upon the matter of the dissolution of the Central Jurisdiction and matters pertaining thereto were received with great appreciation by the Conference as matters of high import.

Who's Who in Methodism, 1952.   N. B. H.

SLUYTER, EUNICE (1916-   ), arrived in INDIA in August 1939, as a missionary of the Reformed Church of America. She served as the treasurer and a teacher in Sherman Girls' High School of the Arcot Mission in Chittoor (then in Madras Presidency, now in Andhra State). When she met SARAH CHAKKO in 1943, Miss Sluyter became eager to work with her in ISABELLA THOBURN COLLEGE. On furlough in America next year, she obtained permission from authorities of the Reformed Church to transfer to the Board of MISSIONS of The Methodist Church. In 1945 she joined the staff of the college as a Methodist missionary.

When it seemed that the government of Uttar Pradesh would insist on Hindi for all instruction in the college, Miss Sluyter accepted an invitation from the LUCKNOW PUBLISHING HOUSE to develop a program of publishing and organizing book clubs and reading courses. A year later she was appointed director of literature for the Methodist Church in Southern Asia.

The next CENTRAL CONFERENCE (1956) appointed a Commission on Literature with representatives of all Annual Conferences in India. She was made secretary of the commission. The Board of Missions provided funds to assist in the program which included Bible correspondence courses, "Tin-Trunk" libraries for villages, reading rooms, book clubs, and training for would-be writers. She encouraged conference committees to produce and sell the literature needed within their boundaries. In March 1965,

she was elected publisher for the Methodist Church in Southern Asia.

M. A. Dimmitt, *Isabella Thoburn College*. 1963.
J. N. Hollister, *Southern Asia*. 1956. J. WASKOM PICKETT

SMALES, GIDEON (1817-1894), NEW ZEALAND Wesleyan minister, was born at Whitby, Yorkshire, England, and was received on probation by the LIVERPOOL Conference in 1837. He arrived in New Zealand on the mission vessel "Triton" in May 1840. On Dec. 29, 1840, he married Mary Anna Bumby (1811-62), sister of John Hewgill Bumby, General Superintendent of the New Zealand Mission, who had been drowned in tragic circumstances in the previous June.

Smales was stationed at Newark for two years, and was transferred to Porirua near Wellington in 1842. In September of the following year, he was appointed to Aotea, where work had been begun by H. Hanson Turton in 1841. After three months of fundraising, Smales arrived at Rauraukauere on the Aotea Harbor, in January 1844, where he supervised the building of a station which he named "Beechamdale." There he served with great devotion until 1856.

Wishing to make provision for his family of seven, Smales left the service of the Mission (which forbade its agents to own land) and bought a farm which he called "Hampton Park" at East Tamaki, near Auckland. In 1860 he built a stone church (St. John's) on his farm and it has been used ever since by both Anglicans and Methodists.

While they were visiting England in 1862, Mrs. Smales died, and later he married Mary Anne Baxter (1845-69). She bore him three children, all of whom died in infancy. Smales returned to New Zealand in 1868 as an accredited supernumerary minister of the British Conference. In the following year his second wife died.

Possessing private means, Smales generously built a "Home Institute" on the Thames gold-fields in 1868, as a social center for miners and citizens. This venture involved him in severe financial loss.

He visited the U. S. A. and England on a lecture tour in 1871-72, and about this time remarried. This third wife, Elizabeth Tayler, bore him seven children. All ten children of the first two marriages predeceased Smales. Of the third family C. G. Hunt wrote in 1957, "a son and three daughters are still living in New Zealand." Smales died on Oct. 5, 1894, and is buried in the crypt of St. John's Church, East Tamaki.

C. G. Hunt, *Some Notes on the Wesleyan Mission at Aotea* (typescript, Waikato Historical Society, Hamilton, New Zealand, 1957).
Gideon Smales, *Opinions and Testimonials*. Whitby, England; Horne & Son, 1872.

SMALL, JOHN BRYAN (1845-1915), Zion Methodism's first bishop to Africa, was born March 14, 1845 at Frazer, St. Joseph's Parish, Barbadoes, British WEST INDIES. Educated for the priesthood of the Anglican Church, he early persuaded his father to permit him to visit JAMAICA and other islands in the area. Later he proceeded to Africa and there remained more than three years, learning some of the native dialects while in residence. He joined the A.M.E. ZION CHURCH intentionally that he might bring to the African continent the Negro Church.

On coming to America, he served several churches in the New England area and then transferred to the PHILADELPHIA and BALTIMORE area, becoming a presiding elder in that Conference. He was elected a bishop of the Church in 1896. Bishop Small died on Jan. 15, 1915.

Bishop Small will be remembered for his significant work in the Gold Coast and LIBERIA and for his plan of bringing to America promising young African men to be trained in the denominational and other Church-supported schools for work in their home areas. Several of these young men gave a good account of themselves, such as Osam Pinanko and J. E. K. Aggrey.

J. W. Hood, *One Hundred Years.* 1895.   DAVID H. BRADLEY

SMART, JAMES S. (1825-1892), American preacher, was born in Searsport, MAINE, on March 31, 1825. His father, Ephraim, was a local preacher, a selectman, and member of the state legislature. James left home at seven due to his father's death, and went to sea for a time. A tragedy on the vessel led to his conversion at sixteen.

He moved to MICHIGAN and was licensed to preach at Dexter; in 1848 he joined the MICHIGAN CONFERENCE on trial. He served continuously for forty-four years, rising to prominence in the DETROIT CONFERENCE. Twice was the presiding elder of the Flint District, and he was elected seven times as delegate to the GENERAL CONFERENCE.

In the Civil War he raised a company of men for the U. S. Army and served as chaplain of the 23rd Michigan Infantry, mostly in KENTUCKY and TENNESSEE. He wrote many reports of the war for the *Northwestern Christian Advocate.*

Smart was a trustee of ALBION COLLEGE twenty-four years, and by it was given an honorary D.D. degree. He served as Financial Agent for GARRETT BIBLICAL INSTITUTE two years; his work gave existence to Heck Hall. He also served as Financial Agent for Albion College. He was notable as a fundraiser for church indebtedness; perhaps no minister in his time dedicated more churches than he.

He was married to Elmira Carter in 1850, who with seven children survived him. One of his sons, Frederick A., followed his father as a minister in the Detroit Conference. Smart was prominent in conference causes; a member of the Centenary Committee in 1866; a promoter of reforms, including the election of presiding elders, a leader in the temperance movement. He had a commanding presence and was a vigorous and effective speaker.

He died at Flint, Mich., March 2, 1892.

M. B. Macmillan, *Michigan.* 1967.
Minutes of the Detroit Conference, 1892.
                                                      RONALD A. BRUNGER

SMART, WYATT AIKEN (1883-1961), American theologian, preacher, author, and teacher, was born in Newberry, S. C., on Oct. 22, 1883. His father was Richard Davis Smart, a distinguished minister of the M. E. Church, South; his mother was Ella Aiken. He was educated at the Webb School at Bell Buckle, Tenn., did undergraduate work at VANDERBILT UNIVERSITY (A.B., 1904), and pursued further studies at Union Theological Seminary in New York (B.D., 1907) and at the University of Chicago. He was awarded the D.D. degree in 1919 by SOUTHERN METHODIST UNIVERSITY and in 1930 by OHIO WESLEYAN.

Joining the VIRGINIA CONFERENCE in 1907, he served

Trinity, Lynchburg, 1907-09; Park View Church, PORTSMOUTH, 1909-13; First Church, Charlottesville, 1913-14 (all in Virginia). On Dec. 30, 1909, he married Ethel Bradshaw Chappell, and they had one daughter, Helen, who became Mrs. Millard Rewis of the Virginia Conference. In 1914, Smart was called to the newly founded School of Theology at EMORY UNIVERSITY, and for the next forty years he remained there as a professor of Biblical Theology and Chaplain of Emory from 1943. He retired in 1952, but continued to teach for some time thereafter. He was much in demand as a speaker and lecturer, having a positive incisive approach both in preaching and speaking, and he greatly influenced college students. He delivered the Fondren Lectures at Southern Methodist University; the Cole Lectures at Vanderbilt; and the Quillian Lectures at Emory. For many years he wrote expository notes upon the Sunday school lessons, as these were published in various magazines of his Church, and these were much read.

He was the author of *The Spiritual Gospel,* Abingdon-Cokesbury, 1946 (the Quillian Lectures, 1945); *Still the Bible Speaks,* 1961, based on the Cole Lectures; and *The Contemporary Christ,* the Fondren Lectures of 1942.

Smart was a delegate to the third World Conference on Faith and Order at Stockholm, and was four times a delegate to the GENERAL CONFERENCE of his Church, being elected from the Virginia Conference in which he maintained a life-long membership. He was put in strong nomination for the episcopacy at the SOUTHEASTERN JURISDICTION CONFERENCES of 1944 and 1948, and while twice he received a majority of the votes cast, he did not receive the sixty percent required for election.

The so-called fundamentalist controversy broke on the Church early in his career, and he spoke out in candor "not so much for a cause as for the sake of truth," as J. Calloway Robertson stated it. His students, after his retirement, put his portrait in the School of Theology at Emory. He died on April 8, 1961, and was buried in the cemetery at Decatur, Ga., not far from Emory.

C. T. Howell, *Prominent Personalities.* 1945.
Minutes of the Virginia Conference, 1961.
Who's Who in Methodism, 1952.   N. B. H.

SMETHAM, JAMES (1821-1889), British Methodist painter, was born at Pateley Bridge in Yorkshire on Sept. 9, 1821. He was the son of a Wesleyan Methodist minister; he attended the school for Wesleyan preachers' sons at Woodhouse Grove. Leaving there in 1836, he was articled to an architect, E. J. Willson, of Lincoln, who was an associate of Pugin. Smetham decided, however, to become a painter, and for some time supported himself as a portrait painter. His father's death in 1847 led to his conversion, and from then on he turned more and more to religious subjects. From 1851 to 1877 he taught drawing at the Wesleyan Normal School, or teachers' training college, at Westminster (see WESTMINSTER COLLEGE). As a painter, however, he never succeeded; his biographer says that he was defeated by "Photography, Pre-Raphaelism, and Ruskinism," for he clung to an older, less fashionable style. His highest point was the exhibition of "The Hymn of the Last Supper" at the Royal Academy in 1869, but later attempts, such as "The Women of the Crucifixion," were rejected. He suffered much from depression in his later years and died in London on Feb. 5, 1889. There is a memoir, by William Davies, which serves as an introduction to *Letters of James Smetham* (first edition, 1891); there was a second edition in 1892, reprinted in 1902. The letters were edited by Sarah Smetham and William Davies.

W. Davies, *Letters of James Smetham.* London, 1891.

JOHN KENT

SMITH, ALEXANDER COKE (1849-1906), American bishop, was born near Lynchburg, Sumter County, S. C., on Sept. 16, 1849. The son of W. H. and Asabella (McLeod) Smith, he was the fourth generation of native Americans. His father and mother were both devoted Christians.

Converted early in life, Coke Smith was graduated from WOFFORD COLLEGE in 1872, and the same year he joined the SOUTH CAROLINA CONFERENCE. He was appointed to Cheraw charge, 1872; Washington Street Church, COLUMBIA, three years; Greenville, four; Trinity, CHARLESTON, two; presiding elder, Columbia District, three.

He was professor of Mental and Moral Philosophy of Wofford College, 1886-90; and that year he headed the delegation to the GENERAL CONFERENCE; professor of Practical Theology in VANDERBILT UNIVERSITY, Nashville, Tenn., 1890-92. Appointed pastor of Granby Street Church, NORFOLK, Va., three and a half years; Court Street Church, Lynchburg, Va., four years; returned to Granby Street Church, Norfolk, now Epworth. He attended the ECUMENICAL METHODIST CONFERENCES, 1891, and 1901. At the former he gave an address, "Christian Co-operation," which was followed by the most remarkable debate of the Conference, said one who was present. He was a fraternal delegate to the Methodist Church of CANADA, 1898.

On Dec. 22, 1875, he married Kate Kinard, daughter of General H. H. Kinard of Newberry, S. C., and they had eight children—one of whom became a member of the VIRGINIA CONFERENCE. He was elected bishop by the M.E. South General Conference of 1902. He died in Asheville, N. C., Dec. 27, 1906, and was buried in Norfolk, Va.

A sincere Christian, he shone more brightly as a pastor-preacher than anywhere else. He combined the gift of adaptability with pathos and could hold the interest and attention of the learned and the ignorant. A friend who called upon Bishop Smith about three months before his death said: "As he talked, I felt as if Jesus Christ was in the room."

COLLINS DENNY (later bishop) said, "Bishop Smith was a man of rare versatility and adaptability, and charmed every circle and community into which he entered . . . Coke Smith can truly be called 'a great man.'"

F. D. Leete, *Methodist Bishops.* 1948.
National Cyclopedia of American Biography.
South Carolina Conference *Minutes*, MES, 1907.

JESSE A. EARL

SMITH, ALFRED FRANKLIN (1869-1962), American clergyman, editor and publisher, was born at Charleston, Mo., on March 28, 1869. He was educated at CENTRAL COLLEGE and VANDERBILT UNIVERSITY and received two honorary degrees.

He joined the MISSOURI CONFERENCE of the M.E. Church, South, in 1892, and was appointed to Centralia.

ALFRED F. SMITH

His other pastoral appointments were Maberly, Hannibal, Inlso, Oklahoma, Galloway Memorial Church in JACKSON, Miss., St. Paul's Church and Centenary Church in ST. LOUIS.

He was President of Central College for Women, 1903-08; editor of the *St. Louis Christian Advocate*, 1918-21; CHAPLAIN of Barnes Hospital in St. Louis, 1921-23; Editor of the *Christian Advocate* at Nashville, Tenn., 1923-32, and BOOK EDITOR and PUBLISHING AGENT, 1932-40. He retired in 1940.

Smith was a member of the Executive Committee of the FEDERAL COUNCIL OF CHURCHES, the GENERAL CONFERENCE of 1930, the ECUMENICAL METHODIST CONFERENCE of 1931, the Conference on Life and Work at Oxford, England, in 1937, and the Conference on Faith and Order at Edinburgh in 1937. He died on March 7, 1962, at Cairo, Ill., and was buried at St. Louis, Mo.

Christian Advocate, April 12, 1962.
Who's Who in America.

ELMER T. CLARK

SMITH, ANGIE FRANK (1889-1962), American bishop, was born at Elgin, Texas, on Nov. 1, 1889, and educated at SOUTHWESTERN and VANDERBILT UNIVERSITIES, receiving honorary doctorates from Southwestern and MCMURRY COLLEGE. He entered the ministry of the M.E. Church, South, in 1912 and joined the NORTH TEXAS CONFERENCE in 1914. He served pastorates at Detroit, Dallas, Austin, San Antonio, and Houston.

Elected a bishop in 1930, he was assigned to OKLAHOMA, the Indian Mission and MISSOURI, then to the three conferences in Missouri, and spent the rest of his episcopal career in TEXAS. He retired in 1960.

Bishop Smith was a member of the GENERAL CONFERENCES of 1926 and 1930, the Commission on Constitution and the Hymnal Commission. He was delegate to the ECUMENICAL METHODIST CONFERENCE in 1931 and fraternal delegate to the United Church of CANADA in 1934. He was director of the Aldersgate Commemoration in 1937 and 1938 and a member of the Commission on the Unification of American Methodism in 1938 and 1939. In 1940 he became president of the Division of National MISSIONS of the united Church and occupied that post until his retirement. He also served as a member

A. FRANK SMITH

of the Methodist Commission on Army and Navy CHAP-LAINS. He was a member of the Board of Trustees of five Methodist institutions of learning and held numerous other positions of distinction. He died at his home in Houston, Texas, on Oct. 6, 1962.

F. D. Leete, *Methodist Bishops.* 1948.
Who's Who in America. ELMER T. CLARK

SMITH, ANNA CHURCHILL (1876-1963), American missionary to Africa and to the home church, was born into a Wesleyan Methodist parsonage family in New England. Growing up in a devout home, she early had a concern for her own salvation and that of people everywhere. As a student in Houghton College, she dedicated her life for service in Africa.

As the young wife of the Rev. Willard Boardman they went to Africa in 1902. Twenty days after their arrival her husband died of African fever. She remained to serve there.

Four years later she married the Rev. J. Hal Smith and in 1910 they were assigned by the Mission Board of the UNITED BRETHREN IN CHRIST as the first missionaries to the Kono Country in SIERRA LEONE. Mrs. Smith was the first white woman to enter this area of Sierra Leone.

For five years they served together, Mrs. Smith compiling a dictionary of Kono words which greatly facilitated learning the language.

Ill health forced Mrs. Smith's return to the States; her husband remained but met accidental death in 1915.

After regaining her health, she was appointed Special Support Secretary in 1916, a position she filled for more than twenty-five years.

Death came to her March 4, 1963 at Corry, Pa., where she made her home following retirement in 1942. From 1942-1945 she served as pastor of the Wayne Valley Church near her home.

Mrs. Smith was the author of several books: *Glimpses into African Mission Life* (1911), *Mendi-English Dictionary* (1910), and *The Radiant Life of Vera B. Blinn* (1921).

She was constantly presenting the cause of missions overseas. She was also a monthly contributor to the

Woman's Evangel; prepared "mission newsletters" for the supporting constituency; and cared for all correspondence related to special support.

Four characteristics sum up her life: her dedication to one purpose; her prayer life; her generosity, and her simple faith and trust in God.

World Evangel, June-July, 1963. MARY McLANACHAN

SMITH, BENJAMIN JULIAN (1899-   ), twenty-seventh bishop of the C.M.E. CHURCH, was born on Dec. 27, 1899, at Barnesville, Ga. He received an A.B. degree from Howard University in 1924, B.D. from GARRETT BIBLICAL INSTITUTE in 1927, and an honorary D.D. degree from LANE COLLEGE in 1944. He held pastorates in WASHINGTON, D.C., ILLINOIS, NEW YORK, and MISSOURI. From 1935 to 1954, he served as general secretary of the Board of Religious Education of the C.M.E. Church and was a delegate to the first assembly of the WORLD COUNCIL OF CHURCHES in Amsterdam. At the General Conference in 1954, he was elected to the office of bishop and presently serves as president of the Board of Christian Education of his denomination in addition to his episcopal area.

Harris and Patterson, *C.M.E. Church.* 1965.
Ethel L. Williams, *Biographical Directory of Negro Ministers.* New York: Scarecrow Press, 1965. RALPH G. GAY

SMITH, CHARLES RYDER (1873-1956), British Methodist scholar, was born at Mansfield. He entered the Wesleyan ministry in 1895. He served in Bombay 1903-08, then in English circuits; in 1920 he was appointed theology tutor at Richmond College, London, and he was college principal from 1929 to 1940. He gave the FERNLEY LECTURE in 1927, *The Sacramental Society.* He was professor of theology in London University, 1932-40. He was elected president of the Wesleyan Conference in 1931. Characteristic of his many later scholarly works was *The Bible Doctrine of Salvation* (1941).

JOHN KENT

SMITH, CHARLES SPENCER (1852-1922), American bishop of the A.M.E. CHURCH, was born in Colbourne, Canada on March 16, 1852. He was educated at Central Tennessee College and Walden University (Tennessee), receiving the M.D. degree from the latter institution in 1880. Honorary degrees were later bestowed upon him by WILBERFORCE UNIVERSITY, Ohio (LL.D.) and VICTORIA COLLEGE, Canada (D.D.). Smith, who was ordained DEACON in 1873 and ELDER in 1876, held pastorates in ALABAMA, TENNESSEE, PENNSYLVANIA and ILLINOIS. While in Alabama he was elected to the State Legislature (1874-1876). He was the founder and organizer of the Sunday School Union of the A.M.E. Church; he was its first Corresponding Secretary-Treasurer, a position which he held and developed until his election to the episcopacy in 1900. He also had the distinction of having produced and edited the first Sunday school literature published by Negroes in America. A church historian of note, he wrote the sequel to Daniel A. Payne's *History of the A.M.E. Church* in 1922. Bishop Smith supervised the work of the Twelfth, Thirteenth, Sixth, Tenth and Fourth Episcopal District Areas. He retired in 1920 and died in 1922.

R. R. Wright, *The Bishops.* 1963. GRANT S. SHOCKLEY

SMITH, CHARLES WILLIAM (1840-1914), American bishop, was born in Fayette County, Pa., on Jan. 30, 1840. He was the son and grandson of Methodist preachers. His father, Wesley Smith, was a distinguished Methodist minister for nearly fifty years, who was serving a WEST VIRGINIA circuit when Charles was born. Charles Smith was educated in the schools of western PENNSYLVANIA and West Virginia; he attended ALLEGHENY COLLEGE, Pennsylvania (not a graduate). He received the honorary degree of A.M., D.D., and LL.D.

Converted in his eighteenth year, he was ordained and joined the PITTSBURGH CONFERENCE in 1859. He married Caroline L. Lindley of Connellsville, Pa., on Dec. 5, 1865. His pastoral appointments in and near Pittsburgh successively, 1859-79, were: Centerville, Carmichael's, Brownsville, Pittsburgh, Uniontown, Allegheny, Canton, Pittsburgh (again) and McKeesport; presiding elder of the Pittsburgh District, 1880-84; editor of the *Pittsburgh Christian Advocate* twenty-four years, 1884-1908. Smith was one of the most powerful editorial writers in the M. E. Church.

Elected bishop in 1908, Bishop Smith was assigned to ST. LOUIS, Mo.

Bishop C. W. Smith was a member of the CENTENNIAL Conference in Baltimore, Md., 1884; a delegate to eight GENERAL CONFERENCES; to the ECUMENICAL CONFERENCE at Washington, D.C., 1891; London, England, 1901; and Toronto, Canada, 1911.

Eminently successful in every office, Bishop Smith became a leader of men by attractive kindness. That spirit expressed in his editorial chair made his paper strong and helpful and his work as editor and bishop inspiring. He was a trustee of Woman's College, Baltimore, and of the UNIVERSITY OF PUGET SOUND, Washington.

He was on the commission which compiled the first joint hymnal of the M. E. Church and the M. E. Church, South, in 1905.

Bishop Smith presided over the WEST VIRGINIA ANNUAL CONFERENCE which opened in Fairmont on Oct. 7, 1914. He died in Washington, D.C., on Oct. 31, 1914, and was buried in Homewood, Pittsburgh.

F. D. Leete, *Methodist Bishops.* 1948.
National Cyclopedia of American Biography.
M. Simpson, *Cyclopaedia.* 1878.   JESSE A. EARL

SMITH, CHESTER A. (1884-1972), American layman, widely known as the well-nigh perennial delegate to GENERAL CONFERENCES, was born in Peekskill, N. Y., on Nov. 15, 1884, in which city he continued to live.

His father, Louis H. Smith, was a descendant of John Howland, a signer of the Mayflower Compact in 1620. His mother, Abbie E. Lent, was a descendant of Isaac Lent who fought in the Revolutionary War in the Continental Army.

Mr. Smith served in World War I as a Field Clerk in the Army. Later he entered Columbia College, receiving an A.B. (1923) and M.A. from Columbia University in 1924. For fifty-four years he served as a court stenographer. Then upon retirement in 1954, he decided to become a lawyer so that he might earn enough money to pay off a debt of $43,000 owed by a bankrupt school of which he had been a trustee. He was graduated from the New York Law School in 1959 with a LL.B. degree. Although he had not practiced law, he had paid off $13,000 of the debt by 1966.

Active in the educational, civic, political, and cultural life of Peekskill, he was honored for his contribution to the community by a Citizens' Committee which erected a portrait tablet of him in the rotunda of the Municipal Building.

In the First Methodist Church of Peekskill, Chester Smith was the lay representative to the NEW YORK ANNUAL CONFERENCE for thirty-four years. Elected by that annual Conference as a lay delegate, he attended General Conference of the M. E. Church from 1916-36; the Uniting Conference, 1939; and General Conferences of The Methodist Church from 1940-64. In all (counting the Uniting Conferences), he was a member of fourteen General Conferences—a record unexcelled by anyone in Methodism, lay or clerical. He also was a member of the Northeastern Jurisdictional Conferences from 1940-64. He was a prolific writer, having written over seventy-five brochures on Peekskill and other historical subjects; contributed to the *Christian Advocate, Zion's Herald,* and the *Upper Room.*

Over the years, Mr. Smith was an outstanding foe of the liquor traffic. He several times urged the General Conference to substitute the word "cup" for "wine" in the Communion Ritual. Opposed to the use of tobacco, he fought every effort to remove the restriction against the use of tobacco by ministers. He felt the Methodist Church was wrong in accepting money from the JAMES B. DUKE Foundation—calling it "blood money". Advocate of peace, he refused to serve as a trustee of the Peekskill Military Academy, and urged the General Conference to delete the hymn, "Onward Christian Soldiers," from the Hymnal. Staunch opponent of racial segregation, he worked for over thirty years to get the CENTRAL JURISDICTION abolished from the organizational set-up of The Methodist Church.

While many of his positions have not prevailed in Annual, Jurisdictional, or General Conferences, he was respected for his convictions and for the able way in which he presented them. At the General Conference of 1964, held in Pittsburgh, Roy Turnage of North Carolina, offered the following resolution as a testimony to Mr. Smith's Christian witness and dedication:

I move we stand in respect to Chester A. Smith, who has livened this Conference and really put it on a high level when we may have taken it too lightly. Could we honor him in that respect?

He was given a standing ovation!
Chester Smith died Sept. 29, 1972.

Daily Christian Advocate, General Conferences, 1916-1964.
Chester Smith of Peekskill. Published by the New York Conference Historical Society, n.d.   C. WESLEY CHRISTMAN, JR.

SMITH, DAVID MORTON (1854-1931), publishing agent, Southern layman, the son of Jeremiah R. and Thurza (Young) Smith, was born on Oct. 14, 1854, near KNOXVILLE, Tenn. Educated in the public schools and a commercial college, Smith became cashier and general office man for a leading firm in Nashville, Tenn., for twelve years. In 1886 he was made business manager of the Southern METHODIST PUBLISHING HOUSE. Named assistant agent by the GENERAL CONFERENCE in 1890, he was elected senior publishing agent in 1902, the first layman to fill this post. He was reelected each quadrennium until his retirement in 1922, and was agent *emeritus* until his death.

The payment of $288,000 by the government for Civil War damages to the NASHVILLE publishing plant, despite a demand by the General Conference of 1902 that the church "retire from the printing business as speedily as possible," was the beginning of a new era in Publishing House history. This came about after 1902 when David M. Smith, who knew the House thoroughly, and A. J. LAMAR, a minister who knew the church, both became publishing agents ("Smith and Lamar"). In 1906 a new building was erected in Nashville. Annual sales increased from less than $500,000 in 1900, to more than $2,100,000 in 1922.

The *Nashville Christian Advocate* said of him in announcing his death Aug. 14, 1931: "Smith was conservative in times of financial panic; he was progressive when indications warranted advances." He laid a solid foundation for the enormous future growth of the Publishing House of the M. E. Church, South, and this contributed greatly to the strength of the united Methodist Publishing House after unification.

He organized the Men's Bible Class in historic McKendree Church in NASHVILLE, TENN., and for thirty years was treasurer of that church. For twenty years Smith was treasurer of the General Board of EDUCATION of the General Sunday School Board. He was also treasurer of the General Conference Delegate Fund.

David Morton Smith married Virginia Cunnyngham on Dec. 9, 1879. She was the daughter of W. G. E. Cunnyngham, a former Sunday School editor. They had six children: Melville, Jessie, Robert, Mildred, Virginia, and William. He died on Aug. 14, 1931.

E. S. Bucke, *History of American Methodism.* 1964.
History of McKendree Methodist Church, Nashville, 1933.
C. F. Price, *Who's Who in American Methodism.* 1916.

JESSE A. EARL

EARL M. SMITH

SMITH, EARL M. (1895-), American missionary to URUGUAY, was born in Ionia, Neb., but grew up in CALIFORNIA. He was educated at Stanford University, graduating in 1920, and at GARRETT BIBLICAL INSTITUTE (1922). He was married to Bessie Marie Archer and they went as missionaries to the River Plate region in October 1922.

For two years he worked in ARGENTINA at Ward College (COLEGIO WARD) in BUENOS AIRES and the Union Theological Seminary (FACULTAD EVANGELICA DE TEOLOGIA). In 1924 they moved to Uruguay, assigned to Friendship

House in the stockyards district of MONTEVIDEO. There the Smiths lived and worked for thirty-seven years, making Friendship House a well-known institution with a Methodist church at its center and social work for the region around it. In 1925 Smith founded in Montevideo the first GOODWILL INDUSTRIES in Latin America.

For twenty years he was treasurer of the M.E. Mission for Uruguay. At sixty-five he was appointed to Melvin Church and helped to establish social work in connection with it. Although retired in 1965, he was asked to continue in service as superintendent of the Montevideo District of the Uruguay Annual Conference.

He helped found and keep active the Fellowship of Reconciliation in South America, and proposed the Consultation on Nonviolence in Latin America which was held in Montevideo in 1966, with delegates and visitors from nineteen countries.

Earl Smith is considered an authority on social work. He has written eight books in Spanish on topics from the Holy Spirit to the essentials of Christianity. One of his books, *Treasured in Her Heart,* is published in English (1966).

Barbara H. Lewis, *Methodist Overseas Missions.* 1960.

BESSIE ARCHER SMITH

SMITH, EARNEST ANDREW (1913-), American minister, was born Aug. 25, 1913 at MACON, Ga. He obtained an A.B. degree from RUST COLLEGE, 1937; an A.M. from Oberlin University, 1938; an honorary D.D. from GAMMON THEOLOGICAL SEMINARY, 1958, and took doctoral studies at Hartford Seminary Foundation, 1948-50. He was married to Milverta Alice Gooden, Sept. 28, 1939.

Mr. Smith was ordained DEACON in 1939 and two years later ELDER. He preached at Alexander City, 1939-41, and Marion, 1941-43, both in ALABAMA. After a two-year period as a public school teacher, he became CHAPLAIN and professor at Rust College, 1945-51; pastor in San Antonio, Texas, 1951-57; and then president of Rust College, 1957-66. He was then elected Associate General Secretary, General Board of Christian SOCIAL CONCERNS, where he has continued in The United Methodist Church.

Dr. Smith has been a member of the COMMISSION ON STRUCTURE OF METHODISM OVERSEAS, 1964-66; BOARD OF EDUCATION, 1964-66; board of directors, Camp Fire Girls; Phi Beta Sigma. He has written *Is It Ever Right to Break a Law?* which was issued in 1969.

JOHN H. NESS, JR.

SMITH, EDWARD (1797-1856), American WESLEYAN METHODIST CHURCH leader and minister in the Allegheny Conference, one of the six original conferences in the Wesleyan Methodist denomination, was born in Rockbridge County, Va., in 1797. He was a member of the Utica, N. Y. organizing convention and was elected vice president of the body. A contemporary, ORANGE SCOTT, describes him as "being of Irish ancestry, southern born, a man of noble appearance, more than six feet in height, a ready debater, a good theologian, a warm advocate of Methodist doctrine, a staunch reformer."

Smith was an outstanding leader in the denomination from its beginning. He called the meeting to order at the First General Conference in Cleveland, Ohio in 1844. He was strongly opposed to secret societies. He was president of his home conference, the Allegheny, the largest in the connection. He did a good volume of business for the Book Concern and raised much money for missions. Scott says, "As a missionary beggar I never saw his equal." The Allegheny Conference had a net increase of 775 members for 1845. The Wesleyan Missionary Society was organized in 1846 and Smith was made General Superintendent of Missions. His first project proposed the employment of evangelists and pioneer church workers among the people of Ontario, Canada, mainly the 20,000 freedmen who had escaped from slavery in America. He moved to Troy, Ohio from PITTSBURGH to direct the operation from there.

Smith's notable anti-slavery address, "Love Worketh No Ill to His Neighbor," came into the hands of the Friends people who had 2,000 copies printed and circulated in NORTH CAROLINA among the Friends there. This able lecture refuted the arguments advanced by those who attempted to defend slavery from the religious standpoint. This led to the breaking-away from the M.E. Church, South, of a group who called for a Wesleyan minister to come as their leader.

Edward Smith died in Morrow County, Ohio, June 6, 1856.

I. F. McLeister, *Wesleyan Methodist Church of America*. 1934.
M. Simpson, *Cyclopaedia*. 1878.   GEORGE E. FAILING

SMITH, EDWIN WILLIAM (1876-1957), British pioneer missionary, was born in 1876 at Aliwal North, SOUTH AFRICA, the son of a PRIMITIVE METHODIST missionary. He was educated in England and entered the Primitive Methodist ministry in 1897, returning as a missionary to Basutoland in 1898. In 1902 he led the pioneer mission to the Bal-Ila, in Northern Rhodesia: he reduced their language to writing, made a grammar and dictionary, translated most of the New Testament, and produced an important anthropological study of the tribe. In 1916 he was seconded to the British and Foreign Bible Society, where he ended as editorial (translations) superintendent. His HARTLEY LECTURE, *The Golden Stool* (1926), influenced colonial administration. He was a president of the Royal Anthropological Institution, and received the Pitt-Rivers Memorial Medal in 1931, the first missionary to do so. He died on Dec. 23, 1957.

JOHN KENT

SMITH, EUGENE LEWIS (1912-   ), American minister and a mission/ecumenical leader, was born at Rockwell City, Iowa, on April 13, 1912, the son of Roy Leslie and Lois (Lewis) Smith. He received the A.B. degree from WILLAMETTE UNIVERSITY in 1934, the B.D. from DREW UNIVERSITY in 1937, and the D.D. from Willamette in 1958 and from Payne Theological Seminary in 1964. He was awarded the Ph.D. degree by New York University, 1945, the Litt.D. by AMERICAN UNIVERSITY, 1959, and the L.H.D. by MacMURRAY COLLEGE in 1966.

Dr. Smith served a number of pastorates and upon the retirement of RALPH DIFFENDORFER, he was elected general secretary of the Division of World MISSIONS of the Board of Missions of The Methodist Church. In this capacity he served until 1964, when he became executive secretary of the New York office of the WORLD COUNCIL OF CHURCHES. Dr. Smith's lectureships include SOUTHERN METHODIST UNIVERSITY, SCARRITT COLLEGE, and OHIO WESLEYAN UNIVERSITY (all in 1956); SOUTH-

WESTERN UNIVERSITY, 1963; Union Theological Seminary, the PHILIPPINES, in 1968; and Austin Theological Seminary in 1969. He has taught on the faculties of New York University and DREW THEOLOGICAL SEMINARY. He was a vice-president of the NATIONAL COUNCIL OF CHURCHES, 1955-58; was a member of its Commission on Religion and Race; a member of the Theological Education Fund Committee and of the Commission of the Churches on International Affairs, a member of the executive committee of the WORLD METHODIST COUNCIL and is a past president of the COUNCIL OF SECRETARIES of The Methodist Church. He wrote *The Power Within Us*, 1948; *They Gird the Earth for Christ*, 1952; *God's Mission and Ours*, 1961; and *Mandate for Mission*, 1968. He has been a frequent contributor to church publications, and his articles have been translated for publication in Swedish, German, French, Spanish and Japanese. In his present position, he resides in NEW JERSEY with an office in the Interchurch Center in NEW YORK CITY. He was a member of the GENERAL CONFERENCES in 1960, 1964, 1968, and 1970.

Contemporary Authors, Vols. 23-24. Detroit: Gale Research Company.
Dictionary of International Biography, 1969-70.
Who's Who in America, Vol. 34.
Who's Who in the Methodist Church, 1966.   N. B. H.

SMITH, GEORGE (1800-1868), British historian, was born at Condurrow, Cornwall, England, on August 31, 1800, the son of a small farmer. He received an elementary education and was employed at first in farm work and carpentry. He then entered the building trade and eventually acquired considerable wealth. He became a Wesleyan LOCAL PREACHER in 1823 and, along with an enterprising business career, found time for study, writing, and lecturing. In 1859 he was awarded the degree of LL.D. by the University of New York. Of his many biblical and historical works the most important is his *History of Wesleyan Methodism* in three volumes (1857). He died at Camborne, Cornwall, on Aug. 30, 1868.

G. ERNEST LONG

SMITH, GEORGE GILMAN (1836-1913), American minister and author, the historian of GEORGIA Methodism, was born on Dec. 24, 1836, at Sheffield, in what is now Rockdale County, Ga. His parents were George G. and Susan Howard Smith. His father was a physician who was also postmaster of Atlanta, Ga., 1851-55.

Smith received his elementary education in a school taught by his mother, and from 1853 to 1855 he studied classics with J. T. McGinty of Atlanta, and J. W. Rudisill of Sandersville, Ga. He spent a term and a half at EMORY COLLEGE, Oxford, Ga. For a while he was a clerk in the post office at Augusta, Ga.

In 1857 Smith was admitted on trial in the GEORGIA CONFERENCE, M.E. Church, South; in 1859 he was ordained DEACON and entered full connection. On Sept. 28, 1859, he married Sarah J. Ousley, and after her death he married Nannie L. Lipps.

When the War Between the States began Smith became a CHAPLAIN in Phillip's Legion. He was severely wounded in 1862, and even though he survived with a withered arm and a lame leg, his health was permanently impaired. In spite of his handicaps, and in addition to his pastoral appointments, he wrote by hand six major works and several lesser volumes. He was the biographer of Bishops Asbury, Pierce, and Andrew. Also of great importance are his *History of Methodism in Georgia and Florida,* and *History of Georgia Methodism, 1786-1866.* He preserved much of Georgia history from oblivion, for no other history of Methodism in Georgia was attempted until the middle of the twentieth century. He drew upon such primary sources as the veteran Lovick Pierce, and during his long life he was intimately acquainted with the men who made Methodist history in the South.

After the war he served at Valdosta and Quitman, Ga., then a part of the Florida Conference. He was transferred to the Baltimore Conference, then to West Virginia, and then back to North Georgia in 1879. Smith was superannuated in 1888 and spent his last years in Vineville near Macon, Ga.

Emory College conferred upon him both the M.A. and D.D. degrees. In recognition of his contribution to Methodist history he was elected one of the vice-presidents of the Methodist Historical Society of New England—which was a unique honor then for a Georgian. He died in 1913 in Macon, Ga.

Minutes of the Annual Conferences of the M.E. Church, South, 1858-1865.
A. M. Pierce, *Georgia.* 1956.   Donald J. West

SMITH, GERVASE (1821-1882), British Wesleyan Methodist, was born at Langley, Derbyshire, on June 27, 1821. He entered the Wesleyan ministry in 1844, and, having spent twenty-five years as an itinerant, was, in 1879, appointed secretary of the Metropolitan Chapel Building Fund along with Francis Lycett. In 1866 Smith was elected to the Legal Hundred; in 1873 he became secretary of Conference, and in 1875 president. His appointment as secretary of Richmond College illustrated his interest in the Wesleyan Theological Institution, and visits to Canada, 1874, and Australasia, 1877, his interest in overseas work. In 1880 he became treasurer of the Auxiliary Fund. He died on April 22, 1882.

B. Gregory, *Recollections of Dr. Gervase Smith.* London.
                                                   H. M. Rattenbury

SMITH, HARRY LESTER (1876-1951), American bishop, was born at Indiana, Pa., on April 15, 1876. The son of George W. and Lucy (Shepherd) Smith, Harry Lester married Ida L. Martin on June 29, 1899, a youth worker in one of his churches, and to them was born one son who died at the age of thirty-five.

Working with his father in the oil fields, Smith gave up an industrial career in the oil industry when he received a call to preach in an evangelistic meeting near Armagh, Pa. Beginning to preach at twenty, he joined the Pittsburgh Conference in 1906. He was educated at Allegheny College (A.B., 1904; A.M., 1906); Drew Seminary (B.D., 1905), and Columbia University, New York. He was later given the honorary D.D. and LL.D.

His appointments were Pitcairn, Pa., 1897-1900; assistant pastor Meadville, 1900-01; Congregational Church, Cory, 1901-03; Leonia, N. J., 1903-05; assistant and then pastor at Bellevue Church, Allegheny, 1905-09; Delaware Avenue, Buffalo, N. Y., 1909-12; Central Church, Detroit, Mich., 1912-20.

He was elected bishop in 1920, and assigned to the following areas: Bangalore, India, where he "had the reputation of being a tiger hunter," 1920-24; then to

Helena, Mont., 1924-28; Chattanooga, 1928-32; Cincinnati, 1932-44; and the Ohio Area, as it became after Church Union and in 1944.

Bishop Smith was a member of the Hymnal Commission of 1930-34; secretary of the (M.E.) Board of Bishops and President of the Council of Bishops after 1939. "A fine looking man," Bishop H. Lester Smith was, "a genius in parliamentary procedure," and a remarkable administrator. He was often seen sitting beside the presiding bishop in the General Conference giving counsel in administering the business.

Aggressive, athletic and strong, Bishop Smith nevertheless suffered from heart trouble for years. Once he said he was never up to par until 11:00 A.M. He had a number of severe heart attacks. Two days before his death, after talking about many things, a friend on leaving said, "The Lord be with you, Bishop," and he rejoined in clear tones, "And with you and your wife." His death occurred at 6:00 on Sunday morning, Oct. 6, 1951, and he entered his Sabbath rest. A "churchman extraordinary," Bishop H. Lester Smith was companionable, patient, approachable, democratic in spirit and a "Christian human being" with a sense of humor.

F. D. Leete, *Methodist Bishops.* 1948.
Ohio Annual Conference *Journal,* 1952.
Who's Who in Methodism.   Jesse A. Earl

SMITH, HENRY (1877-1924), American missionary to Cuba, was born in Cincinnati, Ark., March 23, 1877. His bride was Beulah Jackson Vann of Collinsville, Ala., and a few weeks after their marriage in 1907 they went to Cuba as missionaries. Their first appointment was Mayari, Oriente, and their last one was at Cienfuegos, while Smith was also superintendent of the Central District.

They had two daughters, and their home which was characterized by an unusual congeniality and their love for music, attracted many of the Cuban youth.

Smith's deep concern for the need of training a national ministry led him to make unusual personal sacrifices. A visitor from the North remarked to a friend, "Why does Smith in such an important church position dress so shabbily . . . ." "You don't understand," replied the friend. "That man is keeping at least ten young men in school in training for the ministry . . . No sacrifice is too great for him."

Illness which the doctors could not diagnose caused his retirement in 1923, and he died the following year.

                                                   Garfield Evans

SMITH, HENRY WESTON (1827-1876), first American Methodist clergyman in the Black Hills of South Dakota, was killed by Indians en route from Deadwood to preach at Crook City.

He was born at Ellington, Conn., and at age twenty-three was licensed as an Exhorter in the M.E. Church. He preached in various New England communities including Worcester, Holyoke and Bloody Brooks, Mass., and Tolland and Summers, Conn. His first wife, Ruth Yeomans of Franklin, Conn., lived but a year after marriage. In 1857 he married Lydia Ann Joslin, of Tolland, Conn. They had four children: Gerald, Edna, Elmer and Gertrude.

An ardent unionist, he enlisted in 1861 in Company H, 52nd Massachusetts Infantry and participated in several engagements. In 1867 he studied medicine at Louisville Ky., but apparently preached more than he practiced. In 1876 he joined the gold rush to the Black Hills of Dakota.

Six feet tall, heavily bearded, soft spoken, Smith moved unobtrusively among the immigrants surging across the prairies to the cluster of mountains where in 1874 General George A. Custer's expedition had discovered gold. At the boom village of Custer he preached on May 7 in a log cabin with a sawdust floor. The diary of George V. Ayres, a merchant, records that thirty men and five women attended, and "the congregation paid strict attention to the sermon except when there was a dog fight outside."

The town of Custer was deserted overnight when word came of a strike in Deadwood Gulch, and Smith moved to the new center in the wagon train of Capt. C. V. Gardner, a Methodist layman.

Deadwood of that day was rough—but "dear, delightful and dev'lish," one pioneer later recalled. Miners and bullwhackers often filled its one main street and Smith, supporting himself by manual labor, preached to them, often in front of Bent & Deetkin's Drug Store. One contemporary noted that "the shout of the gamblers and sports calling for trade" could be heard above his exhortations.

Sunday, Aug. 20, 1876, after his usual service he tacked on his cabin door a note, said to have been written on a leaf torn from a hymnal, "Gone to Crook City and if God willing, be back at 2 P.M." A few hours later at Crook City, now a forgotten ghost town nine miles away in the foothills, a horseman told of seeing a body at a place about halfway called "The Rest." It was Smith, a bullet hole in his breast, his Bible at his feet. Smith's body was taken to Deadwood on a load of hay. A public welfare committee chose Seth Bullock, first Black Hills' sheriff, to conduct a religious service. A professional gambler provided an Episcopal prayer book and Bullock commenced, considerably embarrassed. To his aid came one Deacon C. E. Hawley, who carried on with evangelical fervor.

Smith's remains now lie in Mt. Moriah Cemetery, overlooking Deadwood, with graves of Wild Bill Hickok, Calamity Jane, and Potato Creek Johnny nearby. Nothing of Smith's original sandstone statue remains but the feet. A white stone shaft on the Deadwood-Spearfish Highway (U.S. 14) is near the place he was murdered, and here memorial services have been regularly held since 1924 on the Sunday nearest August 20. A Preacher Smith Memorial has been set up at DAKOTA WESLEYAN UNIVERSITY, Mitchell, S. D., where may be seen the memorabilia—including the bloodstained notes of his undelivered sermon.

Leland D. Case, *Preacher Smith, Martyr*. Published by Hot Springs, S. D., *Star*, 1929.   LELAND D. CASE

SMITH, HORACE GREELEY (1881-1968), American minister and president of GARRETT THEOLOGICAL SEMINARY, was born March 28, 1881, near Ransom, Ill. After attendance at local schools, he was graduated in 1905 with a B.A. from NORTHWESTERN UNIVERSITY. Later degrees included an S.T.B. (1910) from Garrett, and honorary doctorates from SIMPSON COLLEGE, Northwestern, DePauw, and BOSTON UNIVERSITIES.

In 1909 Smith married Edith Gorsuch of Clarence, Ill., and to them were born three daughters.

In 1910 Smith became a member of the ROCK RIVER

CONFERENCE. After serving as Y.M.C.A. Secretary at Northwestern University he became pastor of the North Shore Church, Glencoe (1912-17); Hemenway Church, EVANSTON (1917-24); and Wilmette Parish Church (1926-32). New church buildings were constructed during each of these pastorates. Between the Hemenway and Wilmette pastorates he served as superintendent of the CHICAGO Western District.

While minister in Wilmette, Smith was called to the presidency of Garrett Theological Seminary (then known as Garrett Biblical Institute), where he had been a trustee and part-time teacher for eight years. As president he served with distinction and dedication from 1932 until 1953. Drastically affected by the depression, the seminary had been on the verge of closing when Smith became its head, but by the time he retired in 1953 it was on a sound financial footing with a large student body and growing faculty of highly trained scholars. On May 22, 1961 the seminary renamed its Gothic tower in Smith's honor.

Smith also served on the World Service Commission (1928-32) and Board of EDUCATION (1932-54) of The Methodist Church, and was for a term president of the Association of Methodist Theological Schools. He was a delegate from the Rock River Conference to the GENERAL CONFERENCE of 1928, '36, '40, '44, and '52, as well as the UNITING CONFERENCE of 1939.

Horace Smith published more than 150 articles and was the author of two books: *The World's Greatest Story* (1964) and *Don't Retire From Life* (1965), both published by Rand, McNally. After retirement he continued to live in Evanston, though he spent some time each winter in FLORIDA. He died in St. Petersburg, Fla., Feb. 20, 1968.

Clark and Stafford, *Who's Who in Methodism*. 1952.
                                    ELEANOR DARNALL WALLACE

SMITH, ISAAC (1758-1834), American preacher, was born in New Kent County, Va., on Aug. 17, 1758, and was received on trial in the VIRGINIA CONFERENCE in 1784. He served the Salisbury and Tar River Circuits in NORTH CAROLINA and in 1786 was appointed to CHARLESTON, S. C. with Henry Willis, becoming one of the founders of Methodism in that state. He filled prominent appointments until 1796, when he located and entered the mercantile business in Camden. He married Ann Gilman, a cousin of James Rembert, and they had several children.

In 1820 Smith was readmitted to the Conference and sent to COLUMBIA, and the following year he was PRESIDING ELDER of the Athens District in Georgia, then a part of the South Carolina Conference. In 1822 he was sent as a missionary to the Creek Indians, in charge of a school to be established among them. He continued in this capacity until 1827, when he became superannuated. He died of cancer in Marion County, Ga., on July 20, 1834 at the home of his daughter Jane, wife of Rev. Whitman C. Hill.

Isaac Smith was called "the Saint John of the South Carolina Conference." His sons, Isaac Henry and James Rembert Smith, were local preachers and several grandsons were in the itinerary. One of the latter was the historian GEORGE G. SMITH.

A. D. Betts, *South Carolina*. 1952.
C. F. Deems, *Annals*. 1856, 1857, 1858.
A. M. Shipp, *South Carolina*. 1883.   LOUISE L. QUEEN

SMITH, JEDEDIAH STRONG (1799-1831), leader of Mountain Men and first American to cross overland to CALIFORNIA, was born at Jericho (now Bainbridge) in the Susquehanna Valley of southern New York, Jan. 9, 1799, to Jedediah and Sally (Strong) Smith. His parents became Methodist converts in 1813 at Northeast Township, Pa., and later in life he, himself, was a member and supporter of the Methodist Church at ST. LOUIS. In 1821 Jedediah, having moved west with his parents, hunted in ILLINOIS, and in 1822 became one of the "enterprising young men" recruited by General William H. Ashley at St. Louis for exploring, trapping, and trading in the northern Rocky Mountains and plains. In the next nine years he became familiar with almost every part of America's West.

He is credited with many firsts in annals of the West. He was the first white man to penetrate the Black Hills of SOUTH DAKOTA; first to make "an effective discovery" of the South Pass in WYOMING which made possible an overland trek from the MISSISSIPPI to OREGON or California in one season; in 1826-27 he was the first American to break through the Rocky Mountain barrier to Spanish-settled California; and the first person to explore the coast from MEXICO to CANADA, and to crisscross NEVADA, north-south, east-west.

Jedediah Smith's most remarkable quality was his personal character. It was backed by a six-foot physique which enabled him to tangle with a grizzly bear in the Black Hills and live. The Mountain Men, whose hardihood and uncouth ways are legend, admired and respected him. He is said always to have carried in his pack a Bible and a Wesleyan hymn book. Few of Jedediah's letters are preserved, but one dated Christmas Eve, 1829, from "Wind River, East Side of the Rocky Mountains," tells of his "need of the watch and care of a Christian Church" and asks "our society" to bear him up "before a Throne of Grace."

A state redwoods park in northern California bears his name and the Jedediah Smith Society was established in 1957 at the UNIVERSITY OF THE PACIFIC at Stockton to pursue research and disseminate information on the man and his era.

Forever Beginning, 1766-1966. Lake Junaluska, N.C.: Association of Methodist Historical Societies, 1967.
Dale L. Morgan, *Jedediah Smith and the Opening of the West.* Indianapolis: Bobbs-Merrill, 1953.
The Pacific Historian, 1968.
Alson J. Smith, *Men Against the Mountains: Jedediah Smith and the South West Expedition of 1826-29.* New York: John Day, 1965.
Maurice S. Sullivan, *The Travels of Jedediah Smith.* Santa Ana, Calif.: Fine Arts Press, 1934.
————, *Jedediah Smith, Trader and Trailbreaker.* New York: Press of the Pioneers, 1936.   LELAND D. CASE

SMITH, JOHN (1758-1812), American pioneer circuit rider and journalist, was born in Kent County, Md., on March 10, 1758. He was converted June 9, 1779, was received on trial as a traveling Methodist preacher in 1784 when American Methodism was organized. Stevens wrote: "Smith labored faithfully, notwithstanding the infirmities of a feeble constitution, for ten or twelve years in the East and the West." Dr. Lawrence Sherwood says he traveled ten circuits, but he and *The History of American Methodism* name only three, REDSTONE, 1786-87 (Pennsylvania and West Virginia); Greenbrier (West Vir-

ginia), 1787-88, and Holston, 1788. His valuable *Journal* covered only the two years of preaching on Redstone and Greenbrier circuits. He was the first circuit rider on the Greenbrier circuit. The manuscripts were written in pain and weariness while riding on horseback over the West Virginia hills or by camp-fires or fireplaces. They had been in existence for more than 165 years when they were rediscovered by Sherwood in GARRETT SEMINARY'S Library (Greenbrier Ct.), and he made the original discovery of some other of Smith's writing on the Redstone Circuit.

Smith's spelling was unique, but his education was far above the average then: "Crost the Blue Ridge which is Said to run round the World . . . Rode thro Shepherdstown where I saw two saw Mills and two grist Mills watered by a Small Stream . . . on June 26, 1786— Crost the great Ohio over into the Indian Country in company with Mr. Asbury, Henry and several others . . . Rode to A Little Town in the Wilderness called Clarksburg. (Next day). Rode near 30 miles higher to A small settlement call'd Buckhannon . . . Was at Fort Wheelan (Wheeling)."

Clarksburg Circuit formed in 1787 was the first one whose entire bounds were within the state of WEST VIRGINIA. The Greenbrier manuscript is of a more descriptive nature.

In 1787 Redstone Circuit was divided into three circuits, Redstone, Ohio, and Clarksburg. This is evidence of amazing progress, and John Smith had a major part in it. He was in company with the first Methodist preachers to enter the state of OHIO, June 26, 1786. This is the first record of Asbury going into Ohio.

After his abundant labors, John Smith's death was remarkably triumphant as he said, "I long to see the face of God." He died at Chestertown, Kent County, Md., May 10, 1812, and "rests at Hinson's Chapel near the great and good Wm. Gill."

E. S. Bucke, *History of American Methodism,* 1964.
A. Stevens, *History of The M.E. Church.* 1864.
                                    JESSE A. EARL

SMITH, JOHN L. (1811-1899), American preacher and administrator, the son of Bowlin and Lovewell (Owens) Smith, was born in Brunswick County, Va., May 24, 1811. In 1826 the family moved to Green County, Ohio. In 1837 he was licensed to preach. In 1840 he was admitted into the INDIANA CONFERENCE. In 1844-45 he built ROBERTS CHAPEL in INDIANAPOLIS. For thirty-two of his fifty-one years of ministerial life he served as presiding elder. Six times he was elected to GENERAL CONFERENCE. He was on the BOOK COMMITTEE for thirteen years. For twenty-five years he was officially related to Indiana Asbury University. He helped establish schools at Thorntown, Stockwell, and Valparaiso. He married Louisa J. Kline, Dec. 1, 1840, and they had two sons. He retired from Valparaiso District in 1891 and lived there until his death March 11, 1899.

J. J. Detzler, *Northwest Indiana Conference.* 1953.
John Lewis Smith, *Indiana Methodism: A Series of Sketches and Incidents, Grave and Humorous, Concerning Preachers and People of the West.* Valparaiso, Ind.: n.p., 1892.
                                    W. D. ARCHIBALD

SMITH, JOHN OWEN (1902-   ), American bishop, was born Sept. 21, 1902, at Johnston, S. C., the son

JOHN O. SMITH

of Walter Hill and Annie Elizabeth (Long) Smith. He received the A.B. degree from WOFFORD COLLEGE in 1922; a B.D. from Yale University, 1925; a D.D. from WOFFORD College, 1947; and a D.D. from EMORY UNIVERSITY, 1963. On Dec. 27, 1924, he was united in marriage to Mildred Brown and their children are Mildred Adela (Mrs. John G. Lepingwell) and Betty Jean (Mrs. William G. Katzenmeyer).

He was admitted on trial in the SOUTH CAROLINA CONFERENCE in 1925 at Abbeville, S. C.; full connection, 1927; ordained DEACON, 1927; ordained ELDER, 1929. After serving a number of pastorates, he became superintendent of the Spartanburg District, 1954-60, and in 1960 was appointed pastor of Bethel Church, CHARLESTON. He served at Bethel Church for only five days when he was elected bishop at the SOUTHEASTERN JURISDICTIONAL CONFERENCE in 1960.

John Owen Smith was a delegate to every GENERAL and Jurisdictional CONFERENCE from 1948. He was an accredited visitor to the WORLD COUNCIL OF CHURCHES in Amsterdam in 1948 and a voting delegate to the World Council of Churches, Evanston, Ill., 1954. He is the past secretary of the Southeastern Jurisdictional Council; was a member of the General Board of EDUCATION, 1952-64, and is now a member of the General Board of SOCIAL CONCERNS and PROGRAM COUNCIL. He has also been a member of the WORLD METHODIST COUNCIL.

Bishop Smith administers the work of The United Methodist Church in the NORTH and SOUTH GEORGIA CONFERENCES, comprising some 1,600 churches with a total membership of approximately 360,000 members. He resides in Atlanta, Ga.

Who's Who in America, Vol. 34.
Who's Who in The Methodist Church, 1966.   N. B. H.

SMITH, LEGRAND B. (1900-   ), missionary to BOLIVIA, was born in Poughkeepsie, N. Y., and received his Th.B. degree from Gordon College, Ph.B. from Brown University, B.D. from Drew University, and M.A. from Peabody College. He was married to Mildren Sarah Faily in 1924, and has two sons and a daughter.

Smith worked at Iquique English College in CHILE for five years and in Bolivia from 1934 to the present. During this time he was director of both American Institutes (La Paz—COLEGIO EVANGELICO METODISTA—and Cochabam-

ba). He has also served as a pastor, executive secretary of the conference, executive secretary of evangelism and Christian education, conference treasurer, and treasurer of the mission. He was superintendent of the Southern District and presently is superintendent of the Central District. As senior Methodist missionary serving in Bolivia, he received one of the highest awards the Bolivian government can bestow. In a ceremony in La Paz, Bolivia's capital, the "Grand Order of Bolivian Education" was presented to Colegio Evangelico Metodista, formerly the American Institute of La Paz, and to Smith.

Highland Echoes, October 1959.
The Methodist Church in Bolivia. Published in English and Spanish by the Historical Committee of The Methodist Church in Bolivia, 1961.   N. B. H.

SMITH, MARION LOFTON (1889-   ), American educator and college president, was born on Jan. 26, 1889, in Chambers County, Ala. He was educated at Kingswood College and at EMORY UNIVERSITY where he received an M.A. and B.D. in 1921 and a Ph.D. from Yale in 1929. He served as President of the Board of Education of the MISSISSIPPI CONFERENCE from 1944-48; he was elected President of MILLSAPS COLLEGE in 1938 and while there was president of the Association of Methodist Colleges from 1945-46. His wife was Bertha Elizabeth Wallace, whom he married on Aug. 11, 1907, and to them were born three daughters. Dr. Smith married a second time Mary Elizabeth Hanes on June 2, 1938. Following his retirement, he resided at Moss Point, Miss.

C. T. Howell, *Prominent Personalities.* 1945.   N. B. H.

SMITH, MATTHEW DINSDALE (1891-   ), American missionary and educator, was born at Montfort, Wis., Feb. 1, 1891, and reared in northeast IOWA and SOUTH DAKOTA. During his school years the family resided in Alpena where the father, Albert Francis Smith, was engaged in the mercantile business.

Mr. Smith received the A.B. degree in 1912 from DAKOTA WESLEYAN, and in 1914 the M.A. degree from Columbia University. He taught history and mathematics in the public high schools of South Dakota for four years.

In 1917 he offered his services as a foreign missionary of the M.E. Church and was sent to Callao, PERU, as principal of the Mission High School. Here he married a fellow missionary, Loretta Fern Sage, of Grand Rapids, Mich., Dec. 29, 1920.

After a year's furlough they were transferred to Puebla, MEXICO, where Mr. Smith became president of the Mexican Methodist Institute. Three buildings were added to the plant during the eleven years of their labors there. During the furloughs he completed work in 1930 for the Ed.D. degree at the University of California.

Upon returning to the United States in 1933, Dr. Smith served three years as dean of KANSAS WESLEYAN UNIVERSITY at Salina and accepted a similar position at his Alma Mater, Dakota Wesleyan University, where he remained eight years.

An urgent call from the Board of MISSIONS in 1944 persuaded Dr. Smith and his wife to go to PANAMA as director of the strong Methodist school there, The Pan American Institute. Three new buildings on a new campus were added to the school plant during their eight years of service.

In 1952 Dr. Smith responded to a pressing invitation to return to his alma mater as president. Here he guided the institution through a financial crisis and then a disastrous fire in 1955. Within one year College Hall was rebuilt on a larger scale and Dayton Hall, a woman's residence, was added.

At the age of sixty-seven, Dr. Smith retired, and for two years (1958-60) he became the executive secretary of the South Dakota Foundation of Private Colleges.

He served as a member of the General Board of EDUCATION of The Methodist Church for twelve years (1940-44, 1952-60) and from 1952 to 1968, he was chairman of the South Dakota Conference Historical Committee. Under his editorship the *Circuit Riders of the Middle Border*, a history of the Conference, was published in 1965. At present he has charge of the archives of the SOUTH DAKOTA ANNUAL CONFERENCE, located in the Conference Center at Mitchell, S. D.

Clark and Stafford, *Who's Who in Methodism.* 1952.
C. T. Howell, *Prominent Personalities.* 1945.
Who's Who in America, Vol. 32.
Who's Who in American Education, 1950.   JOHN V. MADISON

SMITH, MERLIN G. (1894-   ), FREE METHODIST educator, was born at Delta, Ohio. His degrees are: A.B., GREENVILLE COLLEGE, 1911; A.M., University of Illinois, 1916 and Ph.D., 1918. He was professor of mathematics and physics, Greenville College, 1919-1926; president of SPRING ARBOR JUNIOR COLLEGE, 1926-1933; and president, ROBERTS WESLEYAN COLLEGE, 1933-1957. He is a member of the Rochester Astronomy Club (N.Y.) and the National Education Association. He is author of "Why I Believe In God," in *Presbyterian Life* and of various articles in *The Free Methodist*. He retired in 1959. Dr. and Mrs. Smith now reside at Bradenton, Fla.

BYRON S. LAMSON

SMITH, PHILANDER (1796-1870), Canadian Methodist bishop, was born in Schoharie County, N. Y. At an early age he came to Brockville, Upper CANADA, with his parents. He was converted during the great revival of 1817, and in 1820 was taken on trial by the GENESEE CONFERENCE. Ordained ELDER at the Conference of 1824, he became a presiding elder in 1826. Unfortunately, within a few years his health deteriorated and he was superannuated. During the conference year, he was able to take a small station again.

In 1834 Smith once more was superannuated, probably because he objected, as did many others, to the union of 1833. Three years later he asked for a recommendation to the BLACK RIVER CONFERENCE in the United States, but within a short time JAMES RICHARDSON and he joined the Methodist Episcopal Conference.

According to JOHN CARROLL, Smith subsequently was involved in financial and possibly other difficulties. These, however, did not weaken his devotion to the Episcopal Methodists or his determination to preach as he was able. Thus, when Bishop JOHN ALLEY died unexpectedly in 1847, Philander Smith was elected bishop to assist his aging friend, Bishop JOHN REYNOLDS.

Bishop Smith held office in the Canadian M. E. Church until his death, which occurred in Brooklin, Ontario, March 29, 1870. Doubtless he was regarded by that date as a rather old-fashioned preacher. In any

event, he served his church as minister and administrator as faithfully as his health would permit. It was a goodly heritage which he bequeathed to his colleague, Bishop James Richardson and to the latter's successor, Bishop ALBERT CARMAN.

J. Carroll, *Case and His Cotemporaries.* 1867-77.
T. Webster, *James Richardson.* 1876.   G. S. FRENCH

SMITH, ROCKWELL CARTER (1908-   ), Seminary dean and authority on rural church work and rural sociology, was born on March 6, 1908, in Holyoke, Mass. His parents were Stephen G. and Ethel (Carter) Smith, and he received his education at DePAUW UNIVERSITY, BOSTON UNIVERSITY (S.T.B., 1931), and the University of Wisconsin from which he received the Ph.D. degree in 1942. He received the honorary D.D. from DePauw in 1949. His wife is Frances Dyer Eckardt, and they married on Aug. 27, 1931. He joined the NEW ENGLAND CONFERENCE in 1929, and after serving a number of pastoral charges in MASSACHUSETTS, went to Belleville, Wis., in 1938, where he was research assistant at the University of Wisconsin, 1937-40. He became a Professor of Rural Church Administration and Sociology at GARRETT THEOLOGICAL SEMINARY, 1940, and thereafter devoted his life to that institution. He became dean of students in 1957.

He is a member of the American Sociological Association and the Rural Sociological Society, of the European Rural Sociology Society, the World Association of Agricultural Economists, and the American Association of University Professors. He is the author of *Rural Church Administration,* 1953; *People, Land and Churches,* 1959; *The Church in Our Town,* 1945, and *The Role of Rural Social Science in Theological Education.*

"Rocky" Smith, as he is often called, has been in demand over American Methodism for lectures, addresses and direction in many of the conferences held for the benefit of ministers in rural appointments. In 1969 he relinquished the deanship and became the occupant of a newly established chair in Sociology of Religion. He and his wife reside in Evanston, Ill.

Who's Who in The Methodist Church, 1966.   N. B. H.

SMITH, RODNEY ("GIPSY") (1860-1947), British revivalist, was born on March 31, 1860, of Gypsy stock. He was the son of Cornelius Smith, and he was born in the parish of Wanstead, near Epping Forest, Essex. He experienced conversion at a service in the PRIMITIVE METHODIST Chapel in Fitzroy Street, Cambridge, on Nov. 17, 1876. The following year he became an evangelist under the direction of WILLIAM BOOTH—later General Booth of the Salvation Army—and began work in Whitechapel, London, under the auspices of the Christian Mission, the title at that time of Booth's organization. Smith ran further successful missions in Whitby, Sheffield, and Bolton. In 1879, as the Christian Mission was being transformed into the Salvation Army, Smith was promoted to the rank of captain. For some years he made his center at Hanley, in Staffordshire, where he was highly regarded and received a testimonial from the people. This was against the regulations of the Salvation Army, however, and he had to resign his post. He became an independent revivalist and in 1889 made the first of five visits to the United States; in 1894 he went to Australia. In England he carried through great missions in London, Manchester,

Birmingham, and in 1897 became a missionary under the control of the National Free Church Council. During the First World War he preached to the British troops in France, and was awarded the M.B.E. He never lost touch with Methodism, and was associated with the Wesleyan Methodist Church in revival campaigns in the 1920's. He died on Aug. 14, 1947.

Gipsy Smith, *His Life and Work, written by Himself*. London. 1902.   JOHN T. WILKINSON

ROY L. SMITH

SMITH, ROY L. (1887-1963), American preacher, writer, editor and publisher, was born in the midst of a blizzard in a tarpaper house at Nickerson, Kan., on Jan. 28, 1887. His parents were poor and in 1905 his father was killed in an accident in the mill where he was employed. In spite of his financial handicaps Smith graduated from SOUTHWESTERN COLLEGE, Winfield, Kan., in 1908, received his A.M. at NORTHWESTERN UNIVERSITY in 1915, and was granted the B.D. degree from GARRETT BIBLICAL INSTITUTE that same year. During his life, twelve colleges and universities awarded him honorary degrees. He filled lectureships at many colleges and was a member of the graduate faculties of three institutions. He married Mabel Conley on April 6, 1908, and they had two children.

Smith was ordained in 1908, serving pastorates in KANSAS, ILLINOIS, MINNESOTA, and CALIFORNIA. During the time he was pastor of First Church, LOS ANGELES (1932-40), it was the largest Methodist church in the world. In 1936 he was chosen as one of the six "most representative Methodist preachers in America" and in 1942 as one of the ten "most effective Protestant preachers in America."

He was first employed as a writer when he was eleven years old and this employment continued with some newspaper or magazine until the time of his death. He published his first book in 1920. Since that time more than forty books have come from his pen. In 1940 he was elected editor of *The Christian Advocate,* official newsmagazine of The Methodist Church, and served until 1948. From 1948-52 he was one of the two general managers of The METHODIST PUBLISHING HOUSE.

Smith was elected delegate to three GENERAL CONFERENCES, four JURISDICTIONAL CONFERENCES, the UNITING CONFERENCE in 1939, two ECUMENICAL METHODIST CONFERENCES, and the WORLD COUNCIL OF CHURCHES meeting in Amsterdam. He was a member of the Boards of Temperance and of EVANGELISM of The Methodist Church. His alma mater, Southwestern College, named a lectureship for him as well as a college and student center.

He died on his way to a preaching appointment on April 20, 1963, and was buried in Wildmead Cemetery at Nickerson, Kan., on April 25.

Who's Who in America.   C. ORVILLE STROHL

SMITH, THOMAS WATSON (1836-1902), Canadian minister and author, was born in Windsor, Nova Scotia, in 1836, the son of a clergyman. Educated in Windsor, he was received on probation in 1857 for the Methodist ministry. Before his ordination in 1861 he served in Aylesford, Woodstock, and Andover; subsequently he preached in Nashwaak, Gagetown, Shelburne, Wallace, and Bermuda. Returning from the south with impaired health in 1875, he spent the next five years as a supernumerary in Windsor and Halifax.

In 1880, Smith was appointed editor of *The Wesleyan,* a post he held until ill health again forced him into retirement in 1886. His biographer tells us that:

For editorial work he had unique qualifications. He caught with ease the salient and critical points of public and passing events. There was a judicious reticence when that seemed a desirable policy, but a fearless and uncompromising attitude in regard to moral issues, . . . and the paper was made a power through the length and breadth of the land. (Johnson, p. 395.)

In 1877 Smith published the first volume of *The History of Methodism . . . in the Late Conference of Eastern British America,* the second of which followed in 1890. In these, Methodism is traced from the arrival of the first disciples of JOHN WESLEY in the Atlantic Provinces to the setting up of the Eastern British American Conference in 1855, with special attention to local congregations and workers. Smith was a member of the Nova Scotia Historical Society, and contributed many papers, including a notable one on *Slavery in Nova Scotia.* He was also a member of the Historical Society of MASSACHUSETTS.

He was President of the Nova Scotia Conference in 1890, and was delegate to the General Conferences of 1882, 1883, and 1890. MOUNT ALLISON and Dalhousie Universities conferred honorary degrees on him.

He died in Halifax, March 8, 1902.

G. H. Cornish, *Cyclopaedia of Methodism in Canada.* 1903.
D. Johnston, *Eastern British America.* 1924.

E. ARTHUR BETTS

SMITH, WILBUR KIRKWOOD (1913-   ), American bishop of the Methodist Church of BRAZIL, was born on June 21, 1913, in PORTO ALEGRE, State of Rio Grande do Sul, of missionary parents. After finishing the high school course at Porto Alegre Institute (Methodist), he came to the United States, where he received his A.B. degree from ASBURY COLLEGE in 1935; his B.D. from the CANDLER SCHOOL OF THEOLOGY at EMORY in 1936; and M.A. from the University of Kentucky in 1938. He also studied at the Kent School of Social Work connected with the University of Louisville.

WILBUR K. SMITH

He married Grace Buyers, also of missionary parents, and they have six children. In 1938, he was ordained deacon at the KENTUCKY CONFERENCE, and sailed for Brazil, where in 1940, he was ordained elder. Throughout the years, until 1965, Wilbur Smith served in the States of Rio Grande do Sul and Paraná, as pastor, district superintendent; Reitor (Principal) for eleven years of the Instituto União in URUGUAIANA; and as Secretary of the Board of Social Action of the Methodist Church of Brazil (1950-55).

In July 1965 he was elected bishop by the General Conference of that Church—the first second-generation missionary to be so honored. His area comprises the States of Santa Catarina and Paraná. One of Bishop Smith's announced plans is to use the new lay order of deacon which was created at the 1965 General Conference of the Church in Brazil. "I think the Church has opened its doors wide to the laymen in a way . . . that will affect the advancement of the Church," he stated.

His episcopal headquarters are at Curitiba, Paraná, Brazil.

EULA K. LONG

SMITH, WILLIAM ANDREWS (1802-1869), American church leader and college president, was born in Fredericksburg, Va., on Nov. 29, 1802. His parents died when he was very young, and he was adopted by Russell Hill of PETERSBURG, Va. When seventeen years old he was converted and joined the M.E. Church. He received a good elementary education and read the classics, but not being able to attend college, studied in the home of his uncle, Mr. Porter, in Orange County, Va., and afterward taught school in Madison County. In 1824 he traveled the Gloucester Circuit in the VIRGINIA CONFERENCE and in February 1825, was admitted on trial in that Conference where he served several pastorates. In 1833, while agent for RANDOLPH-MACON COLLEGE, the carriage which he was driving upset and fell on him breaking his right thigh and laming him for life.

W. A. Smith was a delegate to every GENERAL CONFERENCE from 1832 to 1844. He was active in the General Conference of 1844 and defended Bishop J. O. Andrew against the Northern majority which deposed him. He was noted for his deliberative and forensic eloquence, and was the most prominent advocate of the Southern point of view. The next year Smith was a member of the LOUISVILLE CONVENTION which organized the M.E. Church, South, and subsequently of all the General Conferences of that church from 1846 to 1866. In 1846 he was called from his pastorate in VIRGINIA to the presidency of Randolph-Macon College where he served for twenty years. Randolph-Macon, then located at Boydton, Va., steadily grew through the efforts of Smith and the agents of the college. An endowment of $100,000 was raised which was the largest amount of money raised by a church college up to that time. During the Civil War the college lost both its students and its funds, but scores of ministers by then had entered the ministry under Smith's care.

In 1866 Smith became the pastor of Centenary Church in St. LOUIS, where he served for two years. From there he was called to be president of CENTRAL COLLEGE in MISSOURI.

Smith is best known to Methodist historians for his preparation and sponsorship of a measure in the 1854 General Conference of the M.E. Church, South, giving the bishops of that Church the power to declare unconstitutional any rule or regulation adopted by a General Conference which in their view was unconstitutional. This measure, formally adopted by that Conference, gave the Southern bishops the power, not to veto, but to "check" any legislation they deemed unconstitutional until it could be referred back to the Conference, which then might by two-thirds majority adopt the measure again and send it to the Annual Conferences for constitutional approval.

This measure when adopted was given a place in the *Discipline* in the chapter on the General Conference, "and was thus incorporated as a part of the RESTRICTIVE RULES of the Constitution" (DuBose, p. 113). It was, however, clearly seen by W. A. Smith in 1854 that this statutory action was not itself constitutional and he was preparing at a later date to have this measure adopted by a constitutional vote of the Church. However, Smith died before this matter could be finally settled as it was destined to be in 1870 by his disciple LEROY M. LEE, who by a statesmanlike paper and enabling motion put into effect what W. A. Smith had been aiming at in 1854. Southerners credit Smith with the sponsorship of this measure which gave to the bishops of the Church, South, an enormous power in establishing them as the judges and guardians of constitutional law. (See JUDICIAL COUNCIL.)

Smith died March 1, 1869, while on a visit to RICHMOND.

H. M. DuBose, *History*. 1916.
W. W. Sweet, *Virginia*. 1955.
F. C. Tucker, *Missouri*. 1966.   J. MANNING POTTS

SMITH, WILLIAM ANGIE (1894-   ), American bishop, was born in Elgin, Texas, on Dec. 21, 1894, the son of William Angie and Mary Elizabeth (Marrs) Smith. He received the A.B. degree in 1917 and the D.D. in 1937 from SOUTHWESTERN UNIVERSITY and the A.M. degree in 1924 from Columbia University. He was also a student at PERKINS SCHOOL OF THEOLOGY, VANDERBILT UNIVERSITY School of Religion, and Union Theological Seminary. The following institutions conferred on him an honorary D.D. degree: McMURRY COLLEGE, 1927; CENTENARY COLLEGE, 1934; CENTRAL COLLEGE, 1946; and Southwestern University. He received the LL.D. from SOUTHERN METHODIST UNIVERSITY, 1945; Litt.D. from OKLAHOMA CITY UNIVERSITY, 1945 and the S.T.D. in 1958.

W. ANGIE SMITH

On July 20, 1920, he married Bess Owens of Fort Worth, Texas. They have three children, William Angie III, Bryant Wesley and Shelby Lee. William Angie Smith is the brother of the late Methodist Bishop ANGIE FRANK SMITH of HOUSTON, Texas, and his wife, Mrs. Bess Smith, was president of the world organization of Bishop's Wives, 1964-68.

Smith was ordained to the ministry of the M.E. Church, South, in 1921. He served a number of pastorates including Mt. Vernon Place Church, WASHINGTON, D. C., 1934-36; First Church, BIRMINGHAM, Ala., 1936-38; and First Church, DALLAS, Texas, 1938-44. In 1944 he became the first bishop elected by the SOUTH CENTRAL JURISDICTION of The Methodist Church and was assigned to the OKLAHOMA-NEW MEXICO Area. Bishop Smith was president of the General Board of EVANGELISM of The Methodist Church from 1952-64 and of the Board of Trustees of Centenary College, 1932-33. He served a one-year term as president of the COUNCIL OF BISHOPS of The Methodist Church, 1957-58, and had the responsibility of the Pacific Area of the Latin America Central Conference, 1960. He also had responsibility for visitation to Latin America from 1944-60; and now has visitation responsibility for MEXICO. He was assigned as Methodist bishop of HONG KONG and FORMOSA for a one-year term expiring Aug. 1, 1961.

Bishop Smith was a vice-president of the Methodist Board of MISSIONS, and president of Division of Education and Cultivation of that Board from 1952 until 1964. He was a chairman of the COMMITTEE ON STRUCTURE OF METHODISM OVERSEAS, 1948-64 and of the Four-Year Study Program of the Board of Missions. He is president of the CHAPLAIN'S Commission and Commission on Interjurisdictional Relations. Since 1938 he has been a trustee of Southwestern University and since 1944 of Southern Methodist University. He has been an honorary president of McMurry College Board of Trustees since 1944; and president of the Oklahoma City University Board of Trustees since 1944. He is an adopted member of twenty-two Indian tribes, with official title of Chief Tissoya, meaning in English, "Dependable." He is a member of the Oklahoma Hall of Fame and was appointed by Gov. Henry Billman as an Ambassador for Oklahoma. During the twenty-four years he presided over the Oklahoma-New Mexico Area, every year each Conference showed a

net increase in membership. At the end of the twenty-four years, the membership of the Area was more than doubled.

Who's Who in The Methodist Church, 1966.   N. B. H.

SMITH, WILLIAM MILTON (1915-   ), a bishop of the A.M.E. ZION CHURCH, was born on Dec. 18, 1915 to George and Elizabeth Smith in Baldwin County, Ala. He was educated at Lomax-Hannon High School and later received a B.S. degree from Alabama State College, Montgomery, Ala.; an A.M. from Tuskegee Institute, Tuskegee, Ala.; and a B.D. from Hood Theological Seminary, SALISBURY, N. C. He also did work at PERKINS SCHOOL OF THEOLOGY, SOUTHERN METHODIST UNIVERSITY, Dallas, Texas.

His pastorates included Ebenezer, MONTGOMERY, Ala., and Big Zion, MOBILE, Ala. He is a member of the Board of Directors of numerous institutions, including Mobile General Hospital and the Mobile Chamber of Commerce. He was elected to the episcopacy in 1960.

DAVID H. BRADLEY

SMITH ISLAND, MARYLAND, U.S.A., is part of a group of small islands with many Methodist people (proportionately) in the Chesapeake Bay off the eastern shore of MARYLAND at Tangier Sound just above the line dividing Maryland from VIRGINIA. First reference to the island is in the account of Captain John Smith, who as early as 1607 crossed the Bay from his settlement at Jamestown, Va., to the Eastern Shore of what is now Maryland, noting certain "isles, rivers, straits, and places for harbors and habitations." These have since been identified as Smith's, Holland's, Deal's and Tangier Islands and the straits and sounds within this area. Settlement did not proceed rapidly, but by 1666 reports concerning the section had been so favorable that considerable settlement had occurred and Somerset County itself had been formed.

The beginning of organized Methodism on Smith's Island is vague, but it is generally thought that Methodism was fostered through the ministry of Joshua Thomas, called "The Parson of the Islands." Born Aug. 30, 1776, he was first influenced by the Episcopalians but later became a Methodist and spent his life as a preacher among the island people. He died Oct. 8, 1853 and was buried on Deal's Island where his grave bears an appropriate marker and inscription.

There is no extant record of an organized church on Smith's Island until 1855, although Methodist revivals were previously held for many years throughout the islands. The first church was built in 1854 but was burned the following year; but from that date a clearer record is available. Churches were built in 1855 and 1866. In 1896 Calvary Church was built at Rhodes Point, and in the following year chapels were built at North End and at Drum Point and a new church was erected at Tylerton. In 1938 a disastrous fire made it necessary to rebuild the church that had been built at Ewell. Today churches are located at Rhodes Point, Tylerton and Ewell.

The chief industry of the Island is oyster and crab fishing. The Island has no hotels, taverns, theatres or crime, and policemen are unnecessary. Pastors of the Island have been called "Water Circuit Riders."

No Methodist bishop ever visited the Island until 1959 when Bishop G. BROMLEY OXNAM preached at Ewell. Since then the Island has been regularly visited by his successor, Bishop JOHN WESLEY LORD.

The isolated, clannish islanders have been termed a living link with the England of 300 years ago, and in 1959, when a *Together* magazine writer accompanied Bishop Oxnam to the Island, he spoke of their speech as a "charming tongue that hints of their Elizabethan ancestors." Access to the Island can be had through the mail-produce boat which departs each day from Crisfield, Md.

Together Magazine, August 1959.
Adam Wallace, *The Parson of the Islands or the Life of Joshua Thomas.* Philadelphia, 1872. FREDERICK E. MASER

SMITHIES, JOHN (1802-1872), one of the early missionaries to AUSTRALIA, was born in Yorkshire, England. He was the first Wesleyan Methodist minister to take up an appointment in Western Australia. He arrived in the Swan River Colony in 1840 as a missionary sent out by the Wesleyan Missionary Society. He had had nine years experience in Newfoundland and two years in a Circuit in England, and was well equipped for his new task. He was charged with the conversion and welfare of the aborigines and the pastoral care of the colonists, of whom there were then only 2,311 in the colony after twelve years of colonization.

Smithies' first task was an extremely difficult one because of the nomadic character of the aborigines and the second, that of finding a place for the church in the daily lives of people who were dominated by the sheer struggle for survival in an arid and harsh land. He faced his tasks, however, with courage, determination and ability.

Within a matter of weeks he had laid the foundation stone for a commodious Chapel at Fremantle, the port of PERTH, and went on to establish a school for the native children at Perth and later, a flourishing Mission at Wanneroo, a few miles to the northwest of Perth. He built a Chapel at Perth costing £1200, a mission residence, and a school room and, very soon, he had the second largest primary school in the Colony.

For twelve years he carried on alone, the only Methodist minister in a state covering almost one million square miles, and in all that time he was unable to meet and have fellowship with another Methodist minister. In 1852 he was joined by William Lowe. This enabled him to move the aboriginal mission from Wanneroo to York into the rich wheat growing country to the East that was being opened up in the Avon Valley. Here he re-established the mission, established Wesleyan Methodism and speedily built a mission house, church and school. In 1855 he was transferred from Western Australia to TASMANIA where he served in several circuits. He died at Barrington, Tasmania, in 1872.

AUSTRALIAN EDITORIAL COMMITTEE

SMUGGLING was widely regarded in eighteenth-century England as an unconventional but legitimate form of free trade. Rich and poor alike benefitted; the gentry had duty-free luxuries, while fishermen found a profitable and exciting sideline. By 1770, 470,000 gallons of brandy and 350,000 pounds of tea were smuggled into Cornwall alone in a single year, at a cost of £150,000 to the Exchequer.

JOHN WESLEY consistently opposed smuggling and tried to stamp it out in the Methodist societies. On July 26, 1753, he examined the St. Ives society. "I found an accursed thing among them; well nigh one and all bought or sold uncustomed goods." (*Journal.*) He told them, "either they must put this abomination away, or they would see my face no more." Later, he thought—wrongly—that Cornish Methodism had reformed. "That detestable practice of cheating the King is no more found in our societies." (*Journal,* Sept. 21, 1762.) In fact, both Richard Trewavas of Mousehole in 1770 and Henry Carter of Breage (1749-1829) were both Methodist sympathizers and smugglers; Carter's smuggling survived his conversion and his call to preach, though he afterward prohibited swearing on his ship, and conducted Sunday services for English smugglers at Roscoff in Brittany. Nor was smuggling confined to Cornwall. Wesley denounced it at Sunderland (*Journal,* June 16, 1757; June 23, 1759), at Dover (Dec. 3, 1765), and at Rye, in Sussex (Dec. 23, 1773). He raised the subject in a Bristol Pastoral Address in 1764, and in letters to JOSEPH BENSON and Zechariah Yewdall. He wrote his famous tract, *A Word to a Smuggler,* in 1767. In it, he defined the practice as "a general robbery. It is, in effect, not only robbing the King, but robbing every honest man in the nation." A smuggler is "no honester than a pickpocket." It was agreed at the Conference of 1767 that members who persisted in smuggling should be expelled. Wesley's total opposition may have helped to convince Methodists that smuggling was a sin rather than a harmless misdemeanor, but the practice survived well into the nineteenth century. RICHARD TREFFRY conducted a service at the Lizard in the Helston Circuit in Cornwall in 1802; he had seen a smuggler land his goods before the service, and so he had few hearers. On the whole, public approval of smuggling died through changes in fiscal policy rather than through religious pressure.

J. B. Cornish, *Autobiography of a Cornish Smuggler.* London, 1894.
J. Pearce, *Wesleys in Cornwall.* 1964. MICHAEL S. EDWARDS

SMYTH, WILLIAM HENRY (1864-1949), Irish minister, was born in Newtownards, County Down, and entered the ministry in 1886. He was a skilled debater and an able administrator, and connexional offices were soon opened to him. In these he served with distinction, particularly as Secretary of Religious Education and a representative of the Irish Methodist Church at ecumenical conferences. After the establishment of the Parliament of Northern IRELAND, he became one of the CHAPLAINS to the House of Commons. In 1921 he was elected to the highest office of the church, and was the first to receive the official title of President of the Methodist Church in Ireland, in addition to the previous title of Vice-President of the Conference. He was again elected to this office in 1927.

FREDERICK JEFFERY

SNAITH, NORMAN HENRY (1898-   ), distinguished British Old Testament scholar, was born at Chipping Norton, near Oxford, the son of John A. Snaith, PRIMITIVE METHODIST minister, himself also the son of a Primitive Methodist minister. He was educated at the Paston School, North Walsham; the Duke's School, Alnwick; and the Manchester Grammar School, of which he was school captain. He went to Corpus Christi College, Oxford, on an open scholarship, and took a B.A. in mathematics in 1920. Accepted for the Primitive Methodist ministry in 1921, he studied at Mansfield College, Oxford, 1922-25. He rapidly established himself as an Old Testament scholar, and after serving in several circuits was stationed at Wesley College, Headingley, LEEDS in 1936 as Old Testament tutor; he was principal of the college from 1953 to his retirement in 1961.

He was elected president of the Methodist CONFERENCE in 1958. He acted as visiting professor at SOUTHERN METHODIST UNIVERSITY, Dallas, Texas, 1949, and at United College, Bangalore, in 1957-58. He was awarded the D.D. of Oxford University, as well as the honorary D.D. of Glasgow and the honorary D.Litt. of Leeds University, where he was an associate lecturer from 1936-62. He gave the Speaker's Lectures at Oxford, 1961-65. Perhaps his best-known book was *The Distinctive Ideas of the Old Testament* (1944; 9th English ed., 1962; American ed., 1946). He published commentaries on many parts of the Old Testament; *The Jewish New Year Festival* (1948); and contributed to both *The Interpreter's Bible* (1954) and the *New Peake Commentary* (1962). In 1958 he published an edition of the Hebrew text of the Old Testament for the BRITISH AND FOREIGN BIBLE SOCIETY, an important culmination to his life's work.

JOHN KENT

SNAVELY, GUY EVERETT (1881-   ), American college president and educator, was born at Antietam, Md., on Oct. 26, 1881, the son of Charles Granville and Emma (Rohrer) Snavely. He received the A.B. degree from Johns Hopkins University, 1901, and the Ph.D. in 1908; also the *Alliance Francaise* in Paris in the summer of 1905. He holds honorary degrees from twenty-three universities and for many years has taken part in the activities of learned societies and academic organizations throughout the United States.

Dr. Snavely served as teacher of Romance Languages and Literature in various colleges, and held an executive position in ALLEGHENY COLLEGE, before going to Converse College in Spartanburg, S.C., in 1919 to be dean. In 1921 he was elected president of BIRMINGHAM-SOUTHERN COLLEGE and served until 1938. He was the executive director of the Association of American Colleges, 1937-54; a trustee of MILES COLLEGE, Hood College, and AMERICAN UNIVERSITY.

Dr. Snavely was a lay member of the Joint Hymnal Commission, 1930-34, from the M.E. Church, South. He has been a delegate to the GENERAL CONFERENCE of his Church and has served actively in the Association of American Colleges of which he was president, 1929-30. He is an officer of the French Legion of Honor, 1947; has written *Choose and Use Your College, History of the Southern College Association; The Church and the Four Year College,* 1955; *A Search for Excellence: Memoirs of a College Administrator,* 1964; and has been chancellor of Birmingham Southern College since 1955.

Who's Who in America, Vol. 34.
Who's Who in The Methodist Church, 1966.   N. B. H.

SNEAD COLLEGE, Boaz, Alabama, was established in 1899 by the M.E. Church as Boaz Academy, a mission school. Reorganized as a high school in 1906, it was named for John H. Snead, one of the early settlers of Boaz, a member of the M.E. Church. In the early years

of the institution, Snead paid off an indebtedness on the school, and out of gratitude the name was changed to The John H. Snead Seminary. It became a junior college in 1935. The governing board has twenty-five members elected by the NORTH ALABAMA CONFERENCE.

JOHN O. GROSS

NICHOLAS SNETHEN

SNETHEN, NICHOLAS (1769-1845), American preacher and reformer known as "Francis Asbury's Silver Trumpet," was born on Long Island, N. Y., Nov. 15, 1769. He entered the itinerary of the M.E. Church in 1794 and was sent to New England, where he served successively the Fairfield and Tolland circuits in CONNECTICUT, Vershire circuit in VERMONT, and the Portland circuit in MAINE.

In 1798 he was appointed to CHARLESTON, S. C., and in 1800 he was chosen to travel with Bishop ASBURY. He was assigned to this post again in 1801. He was also stationed in BALTIMORE, PHILADELPHIA, GEORGETOWN, ALEXANDRIA, and FREDERICK.

While at Georgetown in 1811 he was elected CHAPLAIN of the House of Representatives. In 1816 he was a candidate of the Federalist Party for a seat in the National House but was defeated. He was also defeated when he ran for the MARYLAND House of Delegates.

Snethen was secretary of the GENERAL CONFERENCE in 1800 and a member of that body in 1804 and 1812.

In 1803 he married Susannah Hood Worthington. She owned land at Linganore in Maryland where in 1814 Snethen located and settled. He later suffered reverses and moved westward to a farm near Merom, Ind.

Snethen was interested in the causes which gave rise to the M.P. CHURCH: opposition to episcopacy and the presiding eldership and support of lay representation in all the councils of the Church. He presided at the General Conference which organized the Associated Methodist Churches and when in 1830 the name of that body was changed to the Methodist Protestant Church he affiliated with it. He was a contributor to *The Wesleyan*

Repository, begun in 1821, and to its successor, *The Mutual Rights.* In 1834 he became one of the editors of *The Methodist Protestant*, published in Baltimore.

After the death of his wife and daughter in 1830, he united with the OHIO CONFERENCE of the M.P. Church and served in CINCINNATI, LOUISVILLE, Ky., and Zanesville, Ohio, later retiring because of age.

Snethen was interested in education under religious auspices, and in 1836 he became president of Dearborn College, a new institution established near Lawrenceburg, Ind. The venture failed when in 1839 a fire destroyed the building. He accepted an invitation to become president of a seminary to train ministers in 1843. It was to be called Snethen Seminary and was to be located at Iowa City, Iowa, but his death on May 10, 1845 at Princeton, Ind., prevented any active service. He was buried at Princeton.

F. Asbury, *Journal and Letters*. 1958.
T. H. Colhouer, *Sketches of the Founders*. 1880.
E. J. Drinkhouse, *History of Methodist Reform*. 1899.
H. L. Feeman, *Asbury's Silver Trumpet*. 1950.
M. Simpson, *Cyclopaedia*. 1878.   ELMER T. CLARK

SNOW CREEK CHURCH in Iredell County, North Carolina, was organized during the great revival of 1801-02 in central NORTH CAROLINA. PHILIP BRUCE said he organized it in the fall of 1801, but according to tradition it was formed by Peter Claywell in 1802. The first deed calls it King's Meetinghouse, after Richard Hugg King who at the time was a licensed Methodist preacher. However, he was originally a Presbyterian and later he returned to that church and became a noted preacher in it. The meetinghouse was built next to what was known as Snow Creek Cemetery, and in time it took that name. During much of the nineteenth century, Snow Creek was the dominant church of its region. It continues as a work on the Friendship Charge, Statesville District. In 1969 it reported sixty-three members and property valued at $58,000.

Iredell County Deeds.
M. H. Moore, *Sketches of the Pioneers of Methodism in North Carolina and Virginia*. Nashville: Southern Methodist Publishing House, 1884.   HOMER KEEVER

SNOWDEN, RITA FRANCES (1907-   ), NEW ZEALAND deaconess, was born at Hope, Nelson, and brought up at Brightwater. Feeling the call to full-time service in the church—following six years at business—she trained at Methodist Deaconess House, CHRISTCHURCH. She was later appointed home missionary supply in a rugged country area in the middle of the King Country. Here she established a reputation for hard work and originality. She was next moved to Otorohanga, to be the first full-time agent of the Methodist Church.

During the depression years the church moved her to the AUCKLAND Central Mission. Here she picked up a germ on the lining of her heart, and was for two years totally incapacitated. Following recovery, which many deemed miraculous, she commenced a writing ministry. She wrote forty-three books, published by EPWORTH PRESS and ABINGDON PRESS, and widespread contributions to religious publications in New Zealand, England, SCOTLAND, United States, CANADA, and AUSTRALIA. For almost five years—on recovery—she was in charge of the Church Book Caravan, covering New Zealand from end to end.

When the Second World War brought this to an end, she served the church in the Epworth Bookroom for some years. Later, she served the wider church as lecturer and guest speaker in several countries, including a time as guest of QUEEN SALOTE in TONGA. In 1957-58, Miss Snowden was elected first woman vice-president of the New Zealand Methodist Conference. In 1960 she was made a fellow of the International Institute of Arts and Letters. She long served as a devotional broadcaster. In 1966 she made her home at "West Hills," Titirangi, Auckland.

Journal of the Auckland Methodist Synod. L. R. M. GILMORE

SNYDER, HENRY NELSON (1865-1949), American educator and college president, was born in MACON, Ga., on Jan. 14, 1865. He was educated at VANDERBILT UNIVERSITY, and at Gottingen University, GERMANY. In 1890 he became professor of English in WOFFORD COLLEGE, and in 1902 he was elected president of the college, serving in this capacity until his retirement in 1942.

Snyder served in a number of the GENERAL CONFERENCES of his church, and was an active leader in the Commission on Unification, the General Board of EDUCATION, and the joint Hymnal Commission. He scarcely ever attended a General Conference as a lay representative without receiving votes for the office of bishop by members of the conference who were unaware that he was not a minister.

His keen perception of literary values made him a helpful member of the Hymnal Commission. Once when a bishop objected to too many deletions of CHARLES WESLEY's "not-too-wonderful" hymns, Snyder remarked, "Bishop, we are greatly improving Charles Wesley's reputation as a hymn writer."

As president of Wofford College, Snyder added several distinguished scholars to the faculty, substantially increased the endowment, expanded the physical plant, and placed a major emphasis on scholarship. During his administration, Wofford came to be numbered among the strong liberal arts colleges of the East. Snyder died in Spartanburg on Sept. 18, 1949.

A. D. Betts, *South Carolina*. 1952.
Henry Nelson Snyder, *An Educational Odyssey*. Nashville: Abingdon-Cokesbury Press, 1947.
D. D. Wallace, *Wofford College*. 1951.

CLARENCE CLIFFORD NORTON

SNYDER, SAMUEL S. (?-1863), American United Brethren home missionary martyr, was sent by the Home Missionary Board of KANSAS in 1854 to assist W. A. Cardwell, later becoming first presiding elder of the Kansas Conference, CHURCH OF THE UNITED BRETHREN IN CHRIST. His life was threatened almost daily, but he was fearless. As a lieutenant of colored troops, he was among 150 citizens shot by the blood-thirsty mob called Quantrill's Raiders at Lawrence, Kan., in August 1863. Later the United Brethren church in Lawrence was renamed in his memory.

Nothing is known of the life of Samuel S. Snyder until he was received into the ministry of the Allegheny Conference (western PENNSYLVANIA) in 1845 and was ordained in 1847. For several years he served this conference as presiding elder before going to Kansas.

Weekley and Fout, *Our Heroes.* 1908-11.

ROBERT R. MacCANON

SOCIAL CONCERNS, BOARD OF CHRISTIAN, an administrative agency of The United Methodist Church (U.S.A.) with headquarters in WASHINGTON, D. C. This Board is responsible for pursuing the task of Christianizing society through a program of study and action in relationship to pressing community, national and world problems. Officially established by the 1960 GENERAL CONFERENCE of The Methodist Church, the Board was formed through the union of three former Methodist agencies: the Board of Temperance, the Board of World Peace and the Board of Social and Economic Relations. It had been felt for some time that many of the issues dealt with by the separate agencies were interrelated and, in some cases, overlapped; therefore, it seemed best, from the standpoint of effectiveness of program and efficiency of administration, to combine these boards for a united approach. The Board was located in Washington largely because of the desirability of having representation at the national center of influence.

The purpose of the Board as stated in the *Discipline* of The United Methodist Church is "to relate the gospel of Jesus Christ to the members of the Church and to the persons and structures of the communities and world in which they live . . . seek to bring the whole life of man, his activities, possessions, and community and world relationships, into conformity with the will of God . . . [and] show the members of the Church and the society that the reconciliation which God effected through Christ involves personal, social, and civic righteousness."

The Board, since its establishment, has grown to be a major Board of The United Methodist Church, with a large membership—presently about ninety members—from a great variety of occupations. The staff is composed of a General Secretary and three Associate General Secretaries as well as a number of department heads and administrative personnel. Responsible for the co-ordination of the total program, the General Secretary serves as the chief administrative officer of the Board. The three Associate General Secretaries are primarily responsible for programming matters in their assigned areas.

The Board carries on its work through three divisions: the Division of Peace and World Order, the Division of Human Relations and Economic Affairs, and the Division of Alcohol Problems and General Welfare. These divisions are each engaged in a program of research, education and action with respect to certain assigned issues. Among those issues for which the General Welfare Division is responsible are: alcohol problems, gambling, crime, sex and moral values, and community welfare policies and practices. Some of the concerns under the purview of the Human Relations Division include: race relations, civil liberties, church and state relations, labor-management relations, unemployment and housing. Other issues are dealt with by the Peace Division, such as: American foreign policy, the United Nations, disarmament, foreign aid, immigration, conscientious objectors and the draft. The Board attempts to bring these concerns to the attention of the churches, their members, and the communities they serve.

There are certain specific and traditional functions of the Board. The Board attempts to train leadership in the field of Christian social concerns through national, regional, and annual conference assemblies. In addition, the General Board produces dozens of pieces of literature each year dealing with the specific program areas assigned. The Board's fortnightly publication, *Concern,* seeks to keep its subscribers well-informed on current pressing social issues and to look at these from a Christian perspective. Certain special days receive encouragement for observance by the churches, through the production of helpful resource materials. These presently include: Labor Sunday, Commitment Day, World Order Sunday, Race Relations Sunday, and Social Creed Sunday.

Where the General Conference has taken action on a specific matter, the Board of Christian Social Concerns may occasionally testify before a Congressional Committee using the General Conference resolution as the basic document for such testimony. As legislative matters related to social concerns come before the United States Congress periodically, the Board attempts to keep leadership throughout the Church informed of the issues involved, and of opportunities for appropriate and effective action. The Board does not engage in lobbying, seeking only to stimulate the Christian citizenship responsibilities of Methodist people. Of no small advantage, however, is the strategic location of the Methodist Building, just a block from the Capitol and directly across from the Supreme Court.

The Board has played a significant role in response to the great tension in recent years over race relations. This role has focused upon awakening the conscience of the Church, building an inclusive Church in an inclusive society, and supporting the enactment of specific national legislation guaranteeing the civil rights of all people without discrimination.

Further, the Board cooperates with annual conferences, districts and local churches in arranging Washington Study Programs, through which Methodist groups visit the Washington scene and examine government policies from the vantage point of the Christian faith. Also, thousands of Methodists annually visit the United Nations in New York studying that international organization through the facilities of the Methodist Office and the Woman's Division of the Board of Missions. The Church Center for the United Nations, which houses the Methodist Office for the U.N., was completed in 1963. This twelve-story structure, across the street from the United Nations, was a project initiated by the General Board of Christian Social Concerns. Both in purpose and function the Church Center for the United Nations is ecumenically oriented. A number of denominational offices as well as the International Affairs Commission of the National Council of Churches operate U.N.-related programs at the Church Center.

J. ELLIOTT CORBETT

SOCIAL CONCERNS, BRITISH. Declarations on social matters have been made from time to time by the British Conference. It has thereby approved declarations on social questions whose social judgments may be said to carry the explicit approval of the Methodist Church. Among such declarations are the *Christian Significance and Use of Leisure* (1935), which emphasized the need for the Church to set a positive example; *The Gambling Problem* (1936), which asserted that gambling is contrary to an acceptance of the divine will and providence; and *The Christian Observance of Sunday* (1939), which said that in the general interest of the community, public legislation should be based on the principle that the character of Sunday as a day of rest and recreation and worship should be preserved, that any change should be at the instance of the community, and not for the benefit of an interested group.

There have also been two important statements on family life. *Marriage and the Family* (1939, revised in 1961) said that

provided that the means employed are acceptable to both husband and wife, and that, according to the best evidence available, they do neither physical nor emotional harm, for the purpose of conception-control there is no moral distinction between the practice of continence and the use of estimated periods of infertility, or of artificial barriers to the meeting of sperm and ovum, or indeed of drugs which would, if effective and safe, inhibit or control ovulation in a calculable way.

The statements on *Divorce* (1946, 1948 and 1967) reaffirmed the Methodist view that the norm and standard of Christian marriage is the lifelong and exclusive union of one man with one woman. But the Conference also recognized that there are courses of conduct which so violate the pledges and obligations of marriage that they destroy it; and therefore divorce is possible for Christians, though it should only be granted when a marriage has broken down beyond the possibility of restoration. Another important declaration on a traditionally Methodist topic was *Total Abstinence and Temperance Reform* (1951), which said that teetotalism was not a condition of membership of the British Methodist Church, but that our obligations to our neighbors and the call to complete personal dedication fully justified the refusal to compromise with the habit of drinking intoxicants.

Peace and War (1957) said that war was contrary to the spirit, teaching, and purpose of Christ. Some Methodists were pacifist; others believed that war was sometimes the lesser of two evils: the Methodist Church would uphold the liberty of conscience of both groups. "The Christian pacifist contends that no war can be justified. The non-pacifist contends that the use of nuclear weapons of mass destruction cannot be justified."

In 1961, the Conference issued another declaration, *The Church in Multi-Racial Communities*, which identified Methodism with the declaration of the second Assembly of the World Council of Churches, holding that "any form of segregation based on race, colour, or ethnic origin is incompatible with the Christian doctrine of man and the nature of the Church of Christ."

In 1963 a declaration of *The Treatment of Animals* condemned all sports that inevitably caused suffering to animals, or harmed the character of those either taking part in or watching them.

In 1960, the *Christian View of Industry in Relation to the Social Order* said that the Christian ought not to put individual, sectional, or class interests before the interests of the community. The primary function of industry is to provide by cooperative effort the goods and services needed by the community; acquisitiveness as such is not Christian. No form of contemporary social organization perfectly reflects the mind of God. (See *Declarations of Conference on Social Questions;* official publication.)

John Kent

SOCIAL CREED, THE METHODIST, is a series of affirmations which were drawn up first in 1908 within the M. E. Church and published in the *Discipline* of that year as "The Church and Social Problems" (p. 479). This early statement on social problems was limited largely to the economic situation. It was prepared and presented to the General Conference by the unofficial Methodist Federation for Social Service, with Bishop Herbert Welch as its first president. Having no other official body charged with the responsibility for Christian leadership in this field, the M. E. Church gave its official approval to the Federation and adopted its corpus of social principles. The Federation further called upon the Church to "continue and increase its work of social service," and urged its ministry to "the fearless but judicious preaching of the teachings of Jesus in their significance for the moral interests of modern society." (*Discipline*, 1908, p. 481.)

The United Methodist *Discipline*, 1968, par. 96, aptly states that "The interest of The Methodist Church in social welfare springs from the gospel, and from the labors of John Wesley, who ministered to the physical, intellectual, and social needs of the people to whom he preached the gospel of personal redemption." Methodism affirms that the Spirit of Christ in the New Testament is the solution to all social evils.

The factual formulation of the Creedal statements in 1908 in the M. E. Church resulted from the swelling impetus of the "social gospel," as it was beginning to be called, and in the midst of an industrial and economic life characterized by a great deal of tension and injustice. The exploitation of workers was common and was marked by long hours in hot, ill-equipped factories. An inefficient industrial commercial system, moreover, resulted in undue fluctuation in employment, poor relationship between wages paid and profit earned, and bad working conditions for women and children. A call had already been made for the amelioration of such conditions, and, along with the Church, other concerned organizations were arising in the interest of this cause: "trade unions, farmers' organizations, institutions for aid and support of the homeless, and groups concerned about the immigrants flooding the nation." (Ward, p. 20.)

With a few changes and additions the M. E. statement on the Church and social problems was adopted in December 1908, by the Federal Council of Churches of Christ in America at their first meeting, and in 1912 the M. E. Church adopted the changes and additions made by the Federal Council. One item among the additions and changes had to do with the liquor traffic. In December 1912, the Federal Council added two more principles, both pertaining to economic life, and in 1916 the M. E. Church in turn included these two principles in its own statement.

The M. E. Church, South, in 1914, endorsed the Social Creed, and in 1916 the M. P. Church in its General Conference made the action of the three great bodies of Methodism unanimous. From that time, this creed or its revisions and expansions have been published in all Methodist *Disciplines* of the three churches. When they came together in 1939 as The Methodist Church, they, of course, continued the Creed in the *Discipline* of 1940 and succeeding quadrennia.

Within the present *Discipline* the original material has been greatly amplified. In place of the few terse statements in the 1908 *Discipline,* there are now whole paragraphs dealing with the family, economic life, responsible use of power, poverty and unemployment, wealth, social benefits for workers, the right to organize for collective bargaining, town and country life, urban life, Christian vocation, the Church and general welfare, alcohol problems, crime and rehabilitation, gambling, mental health and medical care, drug abuse, sex in Christian life, social welfare, human rights, civil liberties and civil rights, peace and world order, international organizations, the Christian and military service. The Creed concludes with a "mandate" to read, study and apply these principles. (See also ETHICAL TRADITIONS IN AMERICAN METHODISM.)

In parallel with the compilation and endorsement of the Social Creed, there came about within the respective Churches certain agencies charged with responsibilities in this whole field. In 1904 a Temperance Society was organized, which became in 1912 the Board of Temperance of the M. E. Church. It evolved by 1916 into the Board of Temperance, Prohibition and Public Morals. In 1918 the M. E. Church, South, organized a Board of Temperance and Social Service. The Commission on World Peace was established in the M. E. Church in 1924, and after union of the Churches there came into existence in 1952 a Board of World Peace, and a Board of Social and Economic Relations. In 1960, at a reorganization of these interests, there was created a Board of Christian SOCIAL CONCERNS, with a Division of Temperance and General Welfare, a Division of Human Relations and Economic Affairs, and a Division of Peace and World Order. The Division of Temperance and General Welfare (1960) became in 1964 the Division of Alcohol Problems and General Welfare. At the Uniting Conference of 1968, The United Methodist Church continued the Board of Christian Social Concerns, with a general committee appointed to study and recommend any needed modifications in its structure or mission.

General Conferences are competent to modify the Creed and change its language from time to time and do so. Methodists differ in interpreting the import of various items of the Social Creed, and especially in their application. Such differences will appear in the future as in the past. It may confidently be expected, however, that future General Conferences will honor the request of the earlier ones and continue to publish in the *Book of Discipline* the, or a, Social Creed.

The Social Creed is not considered binding Methodist law, as are statutory enactments in the *Discipline,* but as it does have behind it the force of General Conference acceptance, and full promulgation, and is the result of the thinking of representatives of the whole Church upon practical situations of everyday life, it will always be held in the highest regard by Methodist people everywhere. It is usually referred to in current terminology as the Methodist Social Creed, rather than as the Social Creed of the Churches as it was formerly called.

Discipline, TMC, 1964.
Samuel D. Lewis, "The Historical Development of the Social Creed of The Methodist Church." Unpublished ms., Candler School of Theology.
W. G. Muelder, *Methodism and Society.* 1961.
A. D. Ward, *Social Creed.* 1965.   SAMUEL D. LEWIS

SOCIETY, METHODIST USE OF THE TERM. *Society* commonly means "a collection or aggregate of persons usually thought of as forming a more or less cohesive, collective group." But in Methodist terminology, it early came to have a technical sense in that WESLEY began to speak of his followers in their different meetings as "societies," and in the GENERAL RULES, which he wrote, he spoke of "the rise of the United Society first in London and then in other places." He never intended to found a Church, and religious "societies" of various sorts were well known and often found all over Protestantism when Wesley lived.

Again and again we find him speaking of "meeting the society" in such and such a place; and in America the term persisted for years, so that in many stories of the origin of churches in this *Encyclopedia* it will be found that the original organization is spoken of as "a society which was formed." Indeed it took some time for the societies in America, even in the M. E. Church, to begin to recognize themselves as local churches, rather than societal groups, and there are those today who hold that the great organized Methodist churches of the present still have about them many of the marks of the early Societies.

Wesley gave rules for admission to his Societies. In a letter to VINCENT PERRONET in the year 1748, *A Plain Account of the People Called Methodists,* he told how the original societies began by certain persons, who wished to be guided in Christian understanding and living, coming to his brother CHARLES and to himself for help. Wesley said, "But I soon found they were too many for me to talk with severally so often as they wanted it. So I told them, 'If you will all of you come together every Thursday, in the evening, I will gladly spend some time with you in prayer, and give you the best advice I can.' . . . Thus arose, without any previous design on either side, what was afterward called *a Society;* a very innocent name, and very common in London, for any number of people associating themselves together." (*Letters,* II, p. 294.)

Thus the name came to be used in a technical sense in early Methodism. The different groups because of their organization became something of a church within a Church. Not until 1784 in America and some years after Wesley's death in England, did the "Societies" decide to become a Church—or Churches, as finally happened over the world.

Dow Kirkpatrick, *The Doctrine of the Church.* Nashville: Abingdon, 1964.
E. W. Thompson, *Doctrine of the Church.* 1939.   N. B. H.

SOCIETY MEETING. Unlike churches with a congregational polity, in Methodism a gathering of all the local members possessed no authority at all in Wesley's time, and has achieved only very little during this present century. Early Society Meetings were occasions when the members of the various CLASS MEETINGS in each society came together for worship or fellowship, but not for business. This was transacted by Wesley's TRAVELING PREACHERS in conjunction with the LEADERS' MEETING and the TRUSTEES. It was customary for preachers to hold a Society Meeting after a preaching service in the smaller rural societies, either on Sunday afternoons or on weekday evenings. These were occasions for exhortations specifically aimed at committed Methodists rather than at the general public often present at the preaching services, and frequently some aspect of the GENERAL RULES was "explained and enforced." From 1821 onwards the preachers were "peremptorily required to read the pastoral address of the Conference to all the societies in their respective circuits." The periodical LOVE FEAST often constituted a form of Society Meeting, though frequently several societies joined together for this exercise. In the twentieth century the annual Society Meeting became the occasion for introducing new members and officers, and for reporting on the statistics and spiritual health of the society. At METHODIST UNION in Britain in 1932 an annual society meeting was made mandatory, and its gradual improvement in status was recognized by charging the members with electing their own representatives to the Leaders' Meeting in the proportion of one for each thirty members. (See also BRITISH METHODISM, ORGANIZATION OF.)

W. Peirce, *Ecclesiastical Principles*. 1873.
Spencer and Finch, *Constitutional Practice*. 1958.

FRANK BAKER

SOCIETY FOR THE PROPAGATION OF THE GOSPEL IN FOREIGN PARTS (S.P.G.) is an Anglican society

formed in 1701, ninety years before the publication of William Carey's famous tract, *An Enquiry into the Obligations of Christians to use Means for the Conversion of the Heathen* (1792). The Society was formed to assist in the missionary work initiated by the Society for the Promotion of Christian Knowledge (S.P.C.K.), founded by Thomas Bray and four laymen in 1698. The work of the S.P.C.K. was essentially literary and educational; the S.P.G. was intended to provide the ministrations of the Church of England for British people overseas, and also to evangelize the non-Christian races of the world. In the eighteenth century the S.P.G. chiefly concerned itself with the first of these aims, finding and financing for example CHAPLAINS for British soldiers and settlers in INDIA and North America. Nevertheless, it is worth remembering that when JOHN and CHARLES WESLEY set out for the new American colony of GEORGIA in 1735, John clearly envisaged the evangelization of American Indians among his plans, and the conflict between the role of chaplain and evangelist characteristic of the Society in its earlier years was illustrated by the frustration of his Indian work. John had been a member of the S.P.C.K. since 1732. In the nineteenth century the S.P.G. joined in the expansion of missionary work common to all the Churches, and now has financial responsibility for more than sixty Anglican missionary dioceses, for nearly a thousand European missionaries, and many non-European workers.

JOHN KENT

SOCKMAN, RALPH WASHINGTON (1889-1970), Ameri-

can pastor and radio preacher of national note, was born at Mount Vernon, Ohio, Oct. 1, 1889, son of Rigdon Potter and Harriet O. (Ash) Sockman. He was graduated from OHIO WESLEYAN UNIVERSITY in 1911 with the B.A. degree; M.A., Columbia University, 1913; Ph.D., 1917. The D.D. degree was conferred upon him by Ohio Wesleyan in 1923, and subsequently he was recipient of honorary degrees from a number of educational institutions.

Sockman's ministry was unique in that he served but one church and that for a period remarkably long in the Methodist connection, forty-four years and eight months. He began his pastorate at Madison Avenue Methodist Church, NEW YORK CITY, in 1916 as associate pastor, and became pastor in 1917, serving continuously until his retirement in 1961, at which time he became minister emeritus. During his pastorate the church became Christ Church, and Sockman led the building program for the present church edifice on Park Avenue.

The clergyman is probably best known for his preaching during thirty-six years on the National Radio Pulpit, and he has also had a television series. "The sermons delivered in a highly personal way," observed The New York *Times*, "brought in an average of 30,000 letters a year."

In a poll conducted by the *Christian Century* Sockman was named one of the six foremost clergymen of all denominations in the United States. *Look* magazine described him as "the most widely known of the nation's Methodist ministers." *Time* magazine called him one of the most noted preachers of our time. He participated in many interdenominational church councils and conferences and delivered numerous lectures. He served as visiting professor at Union Theological Seminary, New York, and at Yale University—also after his retirement as director of the Hall of Fame for Great Americans, New York City. He could easily have been elected a bishop, but rejected the suggestion saying that he preferred the pastorate.

He served as president of the Carnegie Foundation's Church Peace Union; president of the Methodist Board of World Peace; and a member of the Central Committee, WORLD COUNCIL OF CHURCHES.

Sockman was the author of numerous books, with three being selections of the Religious Book Club: *The Higher Happiness, How to Believe*, and *The Whole Armor of God*, with *Man's First Love* being a Pulpit Book Club selection.

On June 15, 1916, he was married to Zellah Widmer Endly. They have a daughter, Elizabeth Ash.

After retiring in 1961 Sockman continued to forward a ministry of preaching and writing. His death after a brief illness came on Aug. 29, 1970, in his New York home.

Who's Who in America, Vol. 34.
Who's Who in The Methodist Church, 1966.

J. MARVIN RAST

SOLOMON, ABRAHAM (1836-1903), was born in Je-

rusalem, Feb. 11, 1836. He studied under Rabbi Ezra Hasometh and received a diploma. His father set him up in business, and he went to Persia, and after that, in 1857, to INDIA, CHINA, AUSTRALIA, the PHILIPPINES, and back to India. In BAREILLY, he met another Jew who had come under Christian influence, and he was given a copy of the New Testament. He read it with strong interest and was almost persuaded to become a Christian.

Later he visited Peshawar and met a Presbyterian minister who had been born a Jew, Isador Lowenthal. Under Lowenthal's influence Solomon was again strongly drawn toward Christ. Business took him to Balkh and Bokhara. In 1864, he returned once more to India. In Moradabad he met EDWIN W. PARKER who urged him to accept Christ at once. He did so and was baptized on June 3, 1864. After his conversion, Solomon lost all interest in trade and wealth and became a teacher in a Methodist school. At a CAMP MEETING two years later, there came to him a transforming experience. He became a full-time minister, and in 1879 was admitted to membership in the NORTH INDIA CONFERENCE. Eleven years later he was made presiding elder and continued in that office until in 1900, at the age of sixty-four he was retired. The number of Christians in his district had increased year by year, until when he retired they numbered almost 6,000. His successor, H. A. Cutting, said that Solomon knew the district like a farmer knows his fields or a shepherd his flock. He died on July 24, 1903.

Abraham's son, Joshua, served as a minister in the North India Conference, and Joshua's son, Samuel, has served the church as a layman in many ways, including supervision of the construction of a large church. Samuel's daughter is president of the National W.C.T.U. in India, and her husband is the Delhi Area Executive Secretary. Their son, Jagdish, has been selected for admission to the India administrative service.

J. N. Hollister, *Southern Asia*. 1956.   J. WASKOM PICKETT

SOLOMON ISLANDS form a chain of islands, generally large and of volcanic origin, 900 miles in length, to the southeast of New Guinea.

In 1902, through the initiative of GEORGE BROWN, Methodist missionary work began in an area of the Solomons untouched by any other missionary society. The pioneer party was led by JOHN FRANCIS GOLDIE, a man of restless energy, who had the astonishing record of forty-nine years service in the Solomons. He retired at the age of eighty-one in 1951, knowing that every island in the Methodist area had received the Gospel.

The lives of Goldie and other early missionaries were frequently in jeopardy in a district of inveterate head-hunters. The South Sea Islands teachers showed an intrepidity and devotion equal to that of their white leaders.

From 1922 the New Zealand Methodist Church became responsible for the work in the Solomons. NEW ZEALAND had become a separate Conference in 1913 and desired its own missionary sphere.

During World War II the Japanese occupied the Solomons. Fierce fighting in which American troops were conspicuous followed. Some missionaries were evacuated by the Government; two stayed with the natives in the interior of islands, one of these for the duration of the war.

The Solomon Islands mission, with its dramatic record of evangelistic success since 1902, became part of the United Church in 1968 (see UNITED CHURCH OF PAPUA, NEW GUINEA AND THE SOLOMON ISLANDS). In recent years it has sent teachers to the pioneer district, the Highlands Region (see NEW GUINEA, HIGHLANDS CHALLENGE).

G. Brown, *Autobiography*. 1908.
Clarence T. J. Luxton, *Isles of Solomon: A Tale of Missionary Adventure*. Auckland: Methodist Foreign Missionary Society, 1955.
R. C. Nicholson, *Son of a Savage*. N.p., 1924.

A. HAROLD WOOD

SOMEILLÁN, ENRIQUE BENITO (1856-1928), first Methodist minister to CUBA, was born in Caibarién, Cuba, but had to leave the country for political reasons, at thirteen years of age. He went to St. Augustine, Fla., and from there to a Presbyterian school in Chattanooga, where he was converted. On a voyage to Key West he met a Methodist preacher and became interested in a mission

to the Cuban exiles in Key West. Eventually he became pastor of the newly formed congregation.

While in Key West he visited the tomb of VANDUZAR, who had died several years previously, and read the inscription of the last words of Vanduzar, "Don't give up the Cuban Mission." There Someillán resolved to dedicate his life to his own people in Cuba. In 1883 he led a mission to Cuba, and left there the beginnings of a congregation.

In 1888 the members of the Church in Habana petitioned the FLORIDA CONFERENCE, of which Someillán was a member, to return Someillán to Cuba. In 1899 Someillán, with his family, returned to Cuba and was appointed to Santiago de Cuba.

In 1901, through a misunderstanding, he joined the Congregational Church which later was absorbed into the USA Presbyterian Church.

He was instrumental in the conversion and call to the ministry of most of the early Methodist Cuban pastors, such as MANUEL DEULOFEU and Clemente Moya.

Always he maintained a broad concept of spiritual unity and in almost all interdenominational meetings he was a valued member. His fifty years of ministerial service gave leadership to the ecumenical spirit and the discovery and training of younger leaders.

S. A. Neblett, *Methodism in Cuba*. 1966. JUSTO L. GONZÁLEZ

SOMMER, C. ERNST (1911-   ), bishop, German Methodist leader and former dean of the Frankfurt Theological Seminary (PREDIGERSEMINAR), was born Dec. 2, 1911, in Turkey, the son of J. W. ERNST SOMMER. He was educated in high school, college, and university in FRANKFURT, where he received the Ph.D. in 1935, M.A. in 1936, M.Ed. in 1938. He taught in high school and junior college from 1938 onward. He was with the German army in France and Northern Africa (from 1941). After the war in 1950 he was elected professor of Christian education and church history in the Frankfurt Methodist Theological Seminary. He was appointed its dean in 1953. The GERMANY CENTRAL CONFERENCE of The United Methodist Church elected him bishop on May 27, 1968. He was the first bishop to be elected anywhere by the newly organized United Methodist Church.

Sommer has been active in educational work as a member of German Methodist Board of Education, of the Free Church Sunday School Association and Curriculum Committee, chairman of European Committee and member of Board of Managers of the World Council of Christian Education, president of the German Methodist Historical Society, member of the executive committee of the Methodist Church in Germany, and of Council of Methodist Central Conferences in Europe. He was a delegate to the GENERAL CONFERENCES of The Methodist Church (U.S.) of 1964, 1966 and 1968. He is a member of the WORLD METHODIST COUNCIL. He has edited various publications, e.g., *Dienst am Kinde* (1949-54), Bible and church history study material (1952-65). He is author of *Matthias Claudius* (1935) and *Christ Calling Young People Today* (1965).

He presides over the conferences of Germany, the Frankfurt area.

ERNST SCHOLZ

SOMMER, J. W. ERNST (1881-1952), German bishop and distinguished scholar and church leader, was born on

J. W. E. SOMMER

March 31, 1881, the son of a then Wesleyan Methodist German minister and his British wife in Stuttgart, GERMANY. He was educated at KINGSWOOD, and then Cambridge University, England, and later at Lausanne, SWITZERLAND. After a brief period of assistant professorship in LONDON (where he married Beatrice Dibben; they had three daughters and one son, C. ERNST SOMMER), he became missionary in Turkey (1906-12) serving as dean of teacher training college, then dean of missionary training college near BERLIN (1913-20). He was professor of Old Testament and Ethics at Frankfurt Methodist Theological Seminary from 1920, becoming its president from 1936 until 1946, when he was elected bishop by the Germany Central Conference.

He had been district superintendent (part time) for eleven years (1926-37), and this gave him much help in understanding church administration and practical church affairs. During the war—before he was elected bishop —(1941-45), he was in charge of a circuit in addition to his Seminary work.

Bishop Sommer was recognized as a magnificent scholar, brilliant in debate, and of painstaking interest in the men whom he taught. For many years he was a leader in German Sunday school work through lectures and publications of various types. His dynamic personality loved encounter and lived through dialogue. He had great affection for young people. Significantly, enough, the last service he rendered a day before his death was a lecture to young leaders in Switzerland.

A member of the "World Alliance for Promoting International Friendship through the Churches," he took part in the noteworthy "Faith and Order Conference," in Lausanne in 1927. His contacts during these years necessarily took him also to the Amsterdam Conference of 1948. He wrote a significant preparatory article for this Conference: "Ecumenicity in one's home country." His confréres regarded him as a bishop of theological vision, of ecumenical range; added to this there was a deep sense of social responsibility. This was realized in his ethical teachings and in a slender but important volume on the social question and JOHN WESLEY, and evidenced also in his approach to the diaconate concerning man's body and mind and social life.

Bishop Sommer founded the Methodist Relief Work after World War II, which he co-ordinated with the Evangelical Relief Work of all Protestant Churches in Germany. With Pastor Niemoeller he was responsible for the founding of the "Co-operative Fellowship of Christian Churches in Germany." All the while he remained mis-

sionary minded. After six years of serving as a bishop he had, with the help especially of Bishop RICHARD C. RAINES and the INDIANA Area, U.S.A., put German Methodism on its feet again following that dreadful period of evil in general, and war in particular. Sommer was a great leader of men and a devout Biblical scholar. He left a deep impress on his people and Church.

F. D. Leete, *Methodist Bishops*. 1948.
C. E. Sommer, *Bischof Dr. J. W. E. Sommer in memoriam.* Der Evangelist, Anker-Verlag, Frankfurt a.M., 1952. N. B. H.

SOONG, CHARLES JONES (1864-1918), Chinese layman, was born in Hainan, Kwantung province, CHINA, on Sept. 10, 1864. When only nine years old, he was sent with his brother to East INDIA, and in 1877 he was an apprentice in his uncle's tea and silk shop in BOSTON, Mass. In some way he became a member of the U.S. Coast Guard and sailed to Wilmington, N. C. There he was converted and joined the Fifth Street M.E. Church, South. His Chinese name was Soon Chiao-chun, but when he was baptized he took the name of Charles Jones Soong, for Captain Charles Jones of the vessel on which he reached Wilmington.

Young Soong became a protégé of General JULIAN S. CARR, a wealthy manufacturer of DURHAM, N. C., who sent him to Trinity College (later DUKE UNIVERSITY) and VANDERBILT UNIVERSITY. From the latter institution he graduated in theology in 1885.

He returned to China as a missionary appointed by Bishop HOLLAND N. McTYEIRE, travelling with W. H. PARK, a medical missionary. In China he added a "g" to his name and became a pastor. He married Miss Ni Kwei-tseng, who became a Methodist and one of the most notable women leaders of the Church in China.

As a missionary and preacher, Soong encountered difficulties, and he eventually left the pastorate to become a publisher of Bibles. Unitl his death, he remained an outstanding Methodist layman.

Six children were born to the Soongs, and at least four of them became famous. His eldest daughter married Dr. Sun Yat-sen, called the George Washington of China. Another married Dr. H. H. Kung, descendant of Confucius, finance minister of China, and a man of great wealth. A son, T. V. Soong, was both finance and foreign minister and an international financial statesman. The youngest daughter, Mayling, became internationally famous as the wife of Generalissimo CHIANG KAI-SHEK.

Charles Soong died on May 4, 1918.

Elmer T. Clark, *The Chiangs of China.* Nashville, n.d.

ELMER T. CLARK

SOOTHILL, WILLIAM EDWARD (1861-1935), British UNITED METHODIST missionary in CHINA. Born in Halifax, England, he entered the ministry of the UNITED METHODIST FREE CHURCHES (from 1907 a part of the United Methodist Church of Britain), and spent twenty-nine years as a missionary in Wenchow, China. Not only did he engage in pioneering tasks such as founding a hospital, a training college, schools, and two hundred preaching places, he also wrote many books interpreting the Chinese people, and became one of the world's greatest authorities upon the Chinese language. He served as President of the Imperial University of Shansi, was president-designate of the proposed Christian University at

Hankow, designed to serve the whole of China—a plan brought to nothing by war and revolution—and in 1920 was appointed Professor of Chinese at Oxford University.

FRANK BAKER

SOPER, DONALD (1903-   ), British Methodist minister and Life Peer, distinguished as preacher, open-air speaker, Christian socialist and pacifist, and writer, was born in LONDON. He was educated at Aske's School, Hatcham; St. Catherine's College, CAMBRIDGE; and at the London School of Economics. He trained for the Methodist ministry at Wesley House, Cambridge, and was first stationed at the South London Mission, 1926-29. He was then at the Central London Mission, 1929-36, and since 1936 he has been minister of the Kingsway Hall, London, and superintendent of the West London Mission, originally founded by HUGH PRICE HUGHES. Soper is a past alderman of the London County Council, and also of the Greater London Council which replaced it.

He was elected president of the Methodist CONFERENCE in 1953. A well-known open-air speaker on religious subjects, he has for many years held an open-air meeting on Tower Hill in London every Wednesday lunchtime, and in Hyde Park every Sunday afternoon. He is the chairman of the Christian Socialist Movement, and his Christian contribution to English politics was recognized when he was made a Life Peer in 1964. He has also been prominent in the SACRAMENTAL FELLOWSHIP and in the PEACE FELLOWSHIP. He has sought to encourage Methodist EVANGELISM through the Order of Christian Witness, an association of laymen and ministers who devote some part of each year to concentrated evangelistic work in a specific area. He has published many books, including *Christ and Tower Hill; All His Grace* (the Methodist Lent Book for 1957); *Practical Christianity Today;* and *Aflame with Faith.*

JOHN KENT

SOPER, EDMUND DAVISON (1876-1961), American teacher, administrator and author, was born in Tokyo, JAPAN, July 18, 1876. His parents, Julius and Mary Frances (Davison) Soper, were among the first Methodist missionaries to Japan. Soper's deep personal interest in the missionary movement led colleagues and students to refer to him as "Mr. Missions." He was also consistently committed to the values in church related colleges and devoted the greater part of his professional life to teaching and administration in such institutions.

On June 15, 1905, he married Miriam Alice Belt. Twin boys were born of this marriage: Robert Wells and Herbert Davison. Following Mrs. Soper's death in 1938, he was married on Nov. 10, 1939 to Moneta Troxel, a missionary-teacher on furlough from KOREA who survives him.

Soper held A.B. (1898), D.D. (1913), and LL.D. (1927) degrees from DICKINSON COLLEGE; B.D. (1905) and LL.D. (1935) degrees from DREW THEOLOGICAL SEMINARY; and was granted honorary doctorates from SYRACUSE (1931), OHIO NORTHERN and DEPAUW UNIVERSITIES (both in 1935). He was a member of Phi Beta Kappa, Omicron Delta Kappa and Kappa Delta Pi.

His service included five years as Field Secretary for the Missionary Education Movement; Professor of Missions and Religion, OHIO WESLEYAN (1910-14) and Drew

Seminary (1914-19); Professor of the History of Religion, NORTHWESTERN UNIVERSITY, (1919-25); Vice President and Dean, Divinity School, DUKE UNIVERSITY (1925-28); President, Ohio Wesleyan (1928-38); and Professor of the History of Religion, GARRETT THEOLOGICAL SEMINARY (1938-48). After retirement in 1948 he lectured for three years under the Board of MISSIONS at Leonard Theological College, Jabalpur, INDIA, and elsewhere in the Orient.

In 1932-33, Soper was president of the Methodist Education Association and in 1934 was president of the Association of American Colleges. He was a member of the Edinburgh Missionary Conference (1910); the Faith and Order Conferences in Lausanne (1927), Edinburgh Conference (1937); and the Oxford Conference on Life and Work (1937). His far-reaching commitment to the ecumenical movement since its inception, to the modern missionary movement, to amicable race relations as an integral part of Christian world relations, and to an understanding of comparative religion is indicated by the titles of his books: *The Faiths of Mankind* (1918 and 1931); *The Religions of Mankind* (1921, 1938 and 1951 and still in print); *What May I Believe?* (1927); *Lausanne: The Will to Understand* (1928); *The Philosophy of the Christian World Mission* (1943); *Racism: A World Issue* (1947); *The Inevitable Choice* (1957).

Soper died Oct. 23, 1961 in Evanston, Ill.

ELEANOR DARNALL WALLACE

SORTILEGE in early Methodism. JOHN WESLEY learned from the MORAVIANS and resorted to sortilege when making important decisions—e.g., whether to marry Miss SOPHIA HOPKEY in GEORGIA; before printing his sermon on Free GRACE; before going to BRISTOL (*Journal*, ii, 158). The early Methodist society at FETTER LANE fixed the BANDS by lot, and appeal to lots was always accompanied by the prayer that "God would give the perfect lot." Wesley defended his practice in *The Principles of a Methodist Farther Explained* (*Letters*, ii, 245 ff). As Moravian influence decreased in early Methodism, so did the use of lots; and after Wesley's separation from the Fetter Lane Society (1740), it largely dropped out of the customs of Methodism, though not so completely that the Conference could not revive its use during the Sacramental Controversy after John Wesley's death.

JOHN C. BOWMER

SOSA, ADAM F. (1902-   ), pastor in the River Plate region of South America, was born in Asunción, PARAGUAY, son of Florentino and Ida Maldini Sosa. His parents had been sent to Paraguay from BUENOS AIRES, his father as lay preacher in charge of the Methodist Church in Paraguay and his mother to teach in the Asunción school. The father later was ordained and in 1916 became the first native district superintendent in the River Plate Annual Conference.

Adam, eldest of eight children, studied in the public schools of Argentina and, after ten years of commercial work, entered the Buenos Aires Union Seminary in 1932. He has served several pastoral charges in ARGENTINA; has been a district superintendent; has taught church history in the FACULTAD EVANGELICA DE TEOLOGIA in Buenos Aires; has been for several years president of the River Plate Confederation of Evangelical Churches and the Argentine Federation of Evangelical Churches; has been

ADAM F. SOSA

co-president of the Argentine Fellowship of Christians and Jews and is now one of its honorary presidents.

Since 1932, Mr. Sosa has been involved in the work of Christian literature through the River Plate Commission on Christian Literature, of which he has been editorial secretary to the present time. His main work is the translation of books into Spanish from English, French, Italian and Portuguese. He has been chief editor of *El Predicador Evangelico* and *Cuadernos Teologicos,* two interdenominational magazines for preachers. Original works are: *Breve historia del Apostol San Pablo* and *Vivir sin religion.*

EDWIN H. MAYNARD

SOTO, ASENSI MIGUEL (1892-1961), a minister and educator, was born in Valencia, SPAIN, Oct. 17, 1892. After his education in the Los Escolapios (monks) schools in Spain and FRANCE he became a resident in Paris for five years during World War I, where he was engaged as a representative of a French banking firm. His business required frequent trips to LONDON, South America, the United States, and at times, CUBA. In Cuba he became interested in the Methodist Church and after receiving a license to preach in 1923 he joined the Cuban Annual Conference (MES) and served the following charges: Holguin, Habana Central, Matanzas, Santiago de las Vegas, Pinar del Rio, Herradura, Camagüey, Cardenas, Jovellanos, Cienfuegos, and Iglesia Universitaria, Havana. He married Rosa Ana Nonell, and they had three children.

In 1960 he retired but continued to be active in translating Christian literature. For a number of years he served as District Superintendent of the Central District, as Editor of *Revista Trimestral,* as Director de la Cruz Aurea, and as Secretary of Lay Activites. His outstanding contribution was director-administrator of El Evangelista Cubano (1944-60) and Publications' Agent (1956-60). In 1960 until his death he was editor of *Accion Metodista,* the Spanish interpretation of *The Methodist Story.*

With his wife he published *El Himnario Metodista,* and wrote the book *La Mayordomia o el Cristianismo Práctico.* He published Bishop Paul B. Kern's *La Biblia en Esta Era de Desorientación;* he prepared for printing *The Interpretation of Methodism (Understanding The*

Methodist Church) by Bishop Nolan B. Harmon, and *Jesus of Nazareth* by Alejandro Westphal.

He was a Rotarian and always active in civic affairs. Although often racked by weakness and pain he continued to work and write prodigiously. His amiable and ever unselfish spirit made him an outstanding leader and never to be forgotten friend.

GARFIELD EVANS

JOSHUA SOULE

SOULE, JOSHUA (1781-1867), American bishop and author of the Constitution of the M.E. Church, was born at Bristol, MAINE, on Aug. 1, 1781. He was a lineal descendant of George Soule who came to America on the *Mayflower.* His parents, who were Presbyterians, were Joshua and Mary (Cushman) Soule.

He united with the M.E. Church in 1797 and joined the NEW ENGLAND CONFERENCE on trial in 1799. He served as a pioneer preacher, was presiding elder of the Maine District in 1804, and was later stationed in NEW YORK and BALTIMORE.

In 1816 he was elected BOOK EDITOR of the Church and in 1818 he became editor of the *Methodist Magazine,* a revival of the *Arminian Magazine,* which was published in 1789 and 1790. Between 1816 and 1820 he was active in the work of the AMERICAN BIBLE SOCIETY and treasurer of the newly organized Missionary and Bible Society of the Church.

At the GENERAL CONFERENCE of 1808 there was dissatisfaction with the administration of the Church. The General Conference, which had no restrictions on its powers, was a meeting of all the Methodist preachers who had served four years or more. Since the General Conference was usually held near a few of the large cities and conferences, preachers from more distant communities found it difficult to attend. Without any assistance, Soule prepared the draft of a Constitution, which was adopted at the 1808 General Conference with few changes. He was then only twenty-six years old. The Constitution provided for a delegated General Conference with six RESTRICTIVE RULES on its authority. This has continued with practically no changes until the present time.

In 1820 Soule was elected a bishop, but he declined the office because legislation was enacted providing for the election of presiding elders by the annual conferences, which Soule regarded as a violation of the Constitution which he had written. After serving in New York and Baltimore during the ensuing quadrennium he was again elected bishop in 1824. He accepted the office because the offending legislation had been rescinded.

As a bishop he resided for several years at Lebanon, OHIO. He was a fraternal delegate to the British and Irish Conferences in 1842.

When the PLAN OF SEPARATION, which set up two General Conferences, one in the North and one in the South, was adopted and the Church was divided over legal issues arising out of slavery, Soule adhered to the M.E. Church, South, although he had never lived in the South. He held that the action of the General Conference in virtually deposing a bishop who had violated no rule of the Church and who had not been charged or tried, was a violation of the Constitution.

He thus became the senior bishop of the M.E. Church, South, and was accepted as such by its first General Conference. He moved to NASHVILLE, Tenn., and later built a home on a farm near that city. He was active bishop in the various Southern Conferences for ten years, though enfeebled by the end of that time.

He died on March 6, 1867, and was buried at the old City Cemetery in Nashville. His body was later disinterred and buried on the campus of VANDERBILT UNIVERSITY by the side of Bishops McKENDREE and McTYEIRE.

Dictionary of American Biography.
H. M. DuBose, *Joshua Soule.* 1911.
J. F. Hurst, *History of Methodism.* 1901-04.
History of the Organization of the MES. 1845.
H. N. McTyeire, *History of Methodism.* 1884.
J. Mudge, *New England Conference.* 1910.
M. Simpson, *Cyclopaedia.* 1878.
J. J. Tigert, *Constitutional History.* 1894.   ELMER T. CLARK

SOUTH AFRICA. The Methodist Church of South Africa owes its foundation to British soldiers. Although there is evidence of Methodism among the troops during the first British occupation of the Cape (1795-1803), its origin is usually traced to the second occupation in 1806. A Society was formed under the leadership of George Middlemiss of the 72nd Regiment and later of Sergeant JOHN KENDRICK, whose requests led eventually to the appointment of BARNABAS SHAW as Wesleyan minister at the Cape. Shaw felt called to mission work among the heathen and found little scope for this at Cape Town. He therefore trekked to the Kamiesberg, some 250 miles due north of Cape Town, and founded the Leliefontein mission among the Namaqua. This became the base from which missionaries advanced northward into Great Namaqualand and Damaraland (present South West Africa).

The difficulties were immense: the people were semi-nomadic, the distances great and the country barren and thinly populated. JACOB LINKS, Johannes Jager, WILLIAM THRELFALL and EDWARD COOK gave their lives in the work and the health of other missionaries was undermined. Money was chronically short and by 1867 the stations in South West Africa had been handed over to Rhenish missionaries. The territory was entered again during World War I. The Leliefontein mission was retained and is still an isolated and difficult outpost. The work in Cape Town (interrupted by Shaw's departure) was recommenced in 1820 and made good progress among the Cape Colored people and the whites, whose numbers were swollen by immigration.

Leliefontein was also the base from which SAMUEL BROADBENT set out on his first unsuccessful attempt to establish a mission in Bechuanaland. On a second journey he made contact with the Barolong, and eventually settled with JAMES ARCHBELL at Thaba 'Nchu, which was annexed to the Orange Free State in 1884 and is now the site of the MOROKA INSTITUTION.

In the second half of the century Wesleyan Methodism was established in Bloemfontein and several other white towns in the Orange Free State, at that time an independent Boer Republic. After the discovery of diamonds at Kimberley in 1867, work was undertaken among the white diggers and the thousands of African laborers who flocked thither from all parts of Southern Africa.

In 1820 settlers from Great Britain were located in Albany, on the disturbed frontier between the Cape Colony and the Xhosa tribes. This brought young WILLIAM SHAW to South Africa as CHAPLAIN to one of the parties, and he soon made the settlement a second and more important base for missionary advance in South Africa. Shaw rapidly organized the WESLEYAN METHODIST CHURCH among the settlers and supervised its establishment in most towns of the Eastern Cape. He also conceived and carried out a plan for a chain of stations from the Eastern Frontier to Port Natal (now Durban). This venture appeared more hazardous than the Namaqua Mission, for it involved settling with tribes which were periodically at war with the Colony. However, although mission stations were destroyed on several occasions, only J. S. THOMAS was murdered—and that by mistake. In other respects conditions were easier than in the west: the country was more fertile, the distances less and the people more settled. But once again the resources in men and money were too slender and the missionaries evoked little response from the strongly tribalized Africans. For the greater part of the nineteenth century these missions were not numerically large, but firm foundations were laid for the considerable Methodist witness in the modern Transkei.

The first Wesleyan minister in Natal was James Archbell, who travelled with the British occupation force in 1842. Between 1849 and 1851 there was considerable immigration from England as a result of which the work among whites was firmly established. In 1862 Ralph Scott, an ex-INDIA missionary, began work among Indians imported as laborers on the sugar plantations. (The Indian Mission has never been large and numbered 1,074 full members in 1966.) A large African work also developed within the colony and in the early years of the twentieth century a mission was established in Zululand. A remarkable development took place in 1874 when African Methodists in Natal decided that they should take a more active part in the evangelization of their own people. Led by Daniel Msimang (later a pioneer in Swaziland), they formed a movement known as Nzondelelo which collected funds and began to appoint evangelists in heathen areas. The white missionaries were suspicious but the misunderstanding was cleared up in 1877. Nzondelelo has continued to work in association with the Church for nearly a century.

Wesleyan ministers were stationed in the Transvaal from 1871, but only after the First War of Independence (1881) was this area given special attention. This was partly on the initiative of the Natal Synod which offered to release a man, give up part of its grant and raise additional funds for a Transvaal mission. OWEN WATKINS was accordingly appointed Chairman and General Superintendent and was ably assisted by GEORGE WEAVIND. Societies had already been formed by untrained African laymen (see Transvaal African Pioneers) in several rural areas. These were brought into formal association with the Church and new stations were opened up. Gold was discovered on the Witwatersrand in 1885 and Wesleyan local preachers soon began services in Johannesburg and other mining camps. Watkins sent in a resident minister in April 1887 and by 1889 a staff of four was caring for whites and Africans. In 1966 there were close to sixty Methodist ministers in the Witwatersrand conurbation.

When RHODESIA was opened to white colonists in 1890, Watkins and Isaac Shimmin were not far behind the Pioneer Column and obtained several grants of land from Cecil Rhodes.

Methods of Work. In many towns Methodism was the first English denomination to make its appearance and members of other Churches found a ready welcome in its fellowship. This led to some departures from the strict British Methodist system, but the life of the white circuits generally resembled that of the mother church.

Where tribalism was strong, African converts settled on mission stations under the patriarchal government of the missionary, but the circuit system has now become general. Much emphasis has always been laid on EVANGELISM and discipline and African circuits retain the class system to the present day.

The evangelization of Africans demanded a knowledge of the vernacular, and Methodists were prominent in the study of Bantu languages. W. B. BOYCE produced the first Xhosa Grammar, and W. J. Davis, J. APPLEYARD and H. H. DUGMORE made important contributions to Xhosa grammar and literature. Archbell was a pioneer Tswana grammarian.

From the beginning education went hand in hand with the gospel. After the foundation of HEALDTOWN in 1855, this aspect became increasingly important. Prominent among the educational institutions were those established at Bensonvale, CLARKEBURY and SHAWBURY in the Cape, Indaleni in Natal, Kilnerton in the Transvaal and Moroka in the Orange Free State. This advance was largely dependent upon government financial assistance and for many years the Church cooperated closely with the Provincial Education Departments. In 1956 the Bantu Education Act of 1953 came into operation and the central government assumed control of African education and placed it under a special department. The Methodist Church objected to the policy and the philosophy behind it, but decided to lease school buildings to the state and to retain control of hostels at boarding establishments. This uneasy partnership is still in operation.

Methodist Connexional Schools for white children are now four in number. Their flourishing condition is a pleasing contrast to a history of false starts and broken hopes.

Shaw College, Grahamstown, was opened in 1861 under the inspiration of George Wood and the Rev. W. Impey, Chairman of the Albany District. The headmaster was Peter MacOwen who was assisted by Theo, brother of the famous South African novelist Olive Screiner. The venture was wrecked by financial depression and was abandoned in 1863.

The Wesleyan High School for Girls, Grahamstown, was founded by John Walton in 1880 under the principalship of his daughter. It provided a sound Christian education for nearly fifty years, and many former pupils became prominent in the Women's Work of the Church. The financial depression of the late 1920's made it impossible to carry on after 1928.

The depression also wrecked Methodist educational work in Queenstown. A Wesleyan Collegiate School for the sons of colonists and ministers was commenced at Lesseyton, near Queenstown, in 1870 under the headmastership of Josiah Slater, who was succeeded by T. Chubb. The institution was moved to Queenstown in 1878 and a girls' school was established in 1882. The pupils of The Wesleyan Grammar School for Boys were transferred to a government school in 1902. The High School for Girls, which came to be known as Queenswood, was discontinued in 1932.

See also EPWORTH SCHOOL, KEARSNEY COLLEGE, KINGSWOOD COLLEGE, and ST. STITHIANS COLLEGE, present-day thriving connexional schools.

Medical Missions. In the past thirty years the Church has entered the field of medical missions, again with financial assistance from the State. There are at present four mission hospitals. The Mount Coke Hospital (143 beds in 1966), near East London, was founded in 1933 under the superintendence of Dr. H. M. Bennett, who was ordained in 1937 and retired in 1961. The Moroka Hospital (134 beds in 1966), at Thaba 'Nchu, Orange Free State, was established in 1938 and has been a first class training school for nurses since 1948. (See also MOROKA INSTITUTION.) Bethesda Hospital (149 beds in 1966), Ubombo, Zululand, was opened in 1940 with assistance from Lord Maclay of Glasgow. It is a training school for nurses and midwives and owes much to the services of Dr. R. Turner, medical superintendent in 1940-43 and from 1953 to the present day. Manguzi Hospital (63 beds and presently expanding), near Kosi Bay in Maputaland is the most isolated of the institutions and is normally approached by air. Founded in 1948, it passed through a critical period in 1961-65 when it was without a resident doctor and had to be served by doctors who flew in from hospitals up to 100 miles away. Dr. W. E. Laufer, who was the first medical superintendent, returned to this post in 1965. The Methodist Church also operates fifteen mission clinics in various parts of South Africa.

The financing of the work is a major problem. The Provincial authorities pay approximately eighty-five percent of the total cost of maintenance in certain cases, while the Central Government meets ninety-five percent to 100 percent of maintenance costs for infections and venereal diseases. Even with this generous assistance, the maintenance and development of the work has been a considerable strain upon the financial resources of the church. The State is prepared to provide capital for the expansion of hospitals situated on land owned by the South African Bantu Trust, and the church may soon be compelled to sell its hospital sites in order to carry on its work.

Another grave problem is the shortage of staff, which is common to mission hospitals of all denominations. In 1966 six doctors were urgently required in the four Methodist hospitals and there was little prospect of the vacancies being filled. A legacy of the late Dr. Elsie Clubb was providing medical training for two ministers, but this scheme, which will supply two doctors every six years, only partially meets the need.

Beyond the boundaries of the Republic, a hospital was operated at Mahamba, Swaziland, between 1926-34 and 1950-63. The chief reason for its discontinuance was the total inadequacy of the grants from the British administration. The government has now taken over the buildings as a tuberculosis hospital, while the Methodist Church maintains a mission clinic.

Constitutional Development. For over fifty years Methodist missions in South Africa were completely subject to the Missionary Committee of the British Conference which paid the piper and therefore called the tune. The Cape of Good Hope (in the west) and Albany (in the east) were constituted separate districts in 1823. While William Shaw remained in charge (1820-56) the work in the east remained a unity, for he was Chairman and General Superintendent of Albany, the Bechuana Mission (Orange Free State), the Transkei and Natal. After his departure fragmentation took place: Natal had already become a separate district in 1853; and in 1863 Albany was divided into the Grahamstown, Queenstown and Bechuana (later known as Kimberley and Bloemfontein) Districts. The Clarkebury District (Transkei) was separated from Natal and Queenstown in 1880.

A multiplicity of districts subject to a committee in London and without opportunity for mutual consultation left much to be desired. William Shaw saw the need for a South African Conference as early as 1860 but his proposals were rejected by the Missionary Committee. The first step to independence was the introduction of Triennial Meetings which took place in 1873, 1876 and 1880 and made possible a certain amount of cooperation between the districts. After the visit in 1880 of John Kilner, representing the Missionary Committee, the six districts were formed into an Affiliated Conference which held its first meeting in 1883. Grants from overseas were progressively reduced and disappeared completely by 1902. Legislation and the election of the President had to be confirmed by the British Conference until 1927, when the Wesleyan Methodist Church of South Africa became autonomous. The Transvaal remained a missionary district of the British Conference until 1932 when it united with the Primitive Methodist Mission (a small body with two circuits) and the South African Conference to form the present Methodist Church of South Africa.

The constitution of South African Methodism is based upon that of the British Church. Three hundred and seventy-three circuits (usually serving a single race) are grouped into eight districts (the Transvaal was divided into Northern and Southern Districts in 1956) whose multiracial synods meet annually. The Annual Conference, which is also multi-racial, has about one hundred and twenty members, over half of whom are the elected representatives of the district synods. The President, who holds office for one year, is elected at the previous conference, and there is a full-time secretary.

The Ministry. The Church is served by an itinerant ministry presently numbering 650. The first ordained native of South Africa was Jacob Links, who was martyred with William Threlfall in 1825. His successors among the Cape Colored people have been relatively few in number. African catechists were employed at an early stage in the Albany District but it was 1865 before the first African candidates for the ministry were accepted. Most famous of the pioneers was Charles Pamla. The real growth of the African ministry dates from 1880 when Kilner criticised the "timid if not at times jealous hands" which had held back suitable candidates, and insisted on over fifty being accepted by the Triennial Meeting. There

are now over 300 African ministers in the active work and they provided their first President in the person of Seth Mokitimi, who presided at the 1964 Conference.

For many years South Africa leaned heavily upon Great Britain for its supply of white ministers, but the reliance was never complete: a number of British settlers entered the ordained ministry in the time of William Shaw, and the steady trickle of South African candidates became a great majority in the 1950's.

Theological Training has a history of slightly over a century. In the early days missionaries were recruited and trained in England, or served their full probation in the field. In 1866, however, the first African candidates for the ministry were received, and in 1867 Healdtown Institution became a training school for both native teachers and ministers. In 1883 theological training was transferred to Lesseyton Institution near Queenstown, where it continued till 1921. In the Transvaal theological training was provided at Kilnerton (see Kilnerton Training Institution, Pretoria, Transvaal).

In 1916 the Wesleyan Methodist Church cooperated with other churches, missions, and state bodies in founding the South African Native College at Fort Hare, Alice (near East London), for the higher education of Africans. This later became the University College of Fort Hare. Wesley House was opened in 1921 at Fort Hare as a residence for Methodist students at the College, and it became the training center also for Methodist theological students. At first separately, then in cooperation with the Presbyterian and Congregational churches, African, Cape Colored and Indian candidates for the ministry were trained at Fort Hare till 1959. From 1948, first in affiliation with the University of South Africa, then with Rhodes University, Grahamstown, a Department of Divinity was established at Fort Hare, and theological degrees and diplomas were available for selected theological students. The majority of candidates continued to follow the less advanced two-year course provided by the churches.

When in 1960 the South African government took over Fort Hare, the churches' theological training there came to an end and in 1963 the Federal Theological Seminary of Southern Africa was opened at Alice in the Eastern Cape. John Wesley College is a constituent college of this Seminary, joined on a federal basis with the colleges of the Anglican, Presbyterian and Congregational churches, and the American Board of Missions. The Seminary provides three-year courses at different standards to meet the varying educational qualifications of candidates, and the Colleges join in lectures and the provision of staff.

South African Methodism did not possess its own theological training center for white candidates for the ministry till 1930 when a small college was opened at Mowbray, Cape Town, which provided a two-year theological course. This continued till 1940 when the war dried up the supply of candidates and brought training to an end. After the war the Methodist Church joined with the Anglican, Presbyterian and Congregational churches in setting up and endowing a Faculty of Divinity at Rhodes University, Grahamstown, in the Eastern Cape, and in 1947 Livingstone House was opened at the University as a residence for theological students of the three non-Anglican churches. Degrees and diplomas in arts and divinity are provided at the University for white theological students of any church wishing to avail themselves of them, lectures (apart from some denominational subjects) are shared by students of all the churches, and the staff of the Faculty of Divinity is appointed by the University in consultation with the cooperating churches.

In 1966 the Methodist Church opened the Clifton Pastoral Center at Johannesburg to provide short post-collegiate training in practical and pastoral work for white probationers as a supplement to the academic courses provided at Rhodes University.

Students of all races are expected to gain practical experience in circuit work during the vacations, and all candidates for the ministry serve for three or four years as probationers before or after their college training. During this period of probation they are engaged in full-time circuit work and complete additional courses of study and reading in theology, the Bible and other subjects.

Division and Reunion. One of the most disturbing features of contemporary South African Christianity is the proliferation of African Independent Churches, which now number approximately 3,000 and account for more than twenty percent of the total African population. Methodism has had her share of secessions: Nehemiah Tile founded the Tembu National Church in 1884; James Dwane seceded in 1895 and was responsible successively for the African Methodist Episcopal Church (in association with the American Church of that name) and the Order of Ethiopia (in association with the Anglican Church). A considerable secession in 1932-33 led to the establishment of the Bantu Methodist Church. Unfortunately there is little contact between the Methodist Church of South Africa and the bodies which have seceded.

Ecumenism is a tender plant in South Africa. Although the Methodist Church is fully involved, the movement is regarded with misgivings in certain quarters. The Methodist Church is a member of the World Council of Churches and the Christian Council of South Africa, of which Seth Mokitimi was elected President in 1966, the first African to hold this office. African Methodists have played a prominent role in the Inter-Denominational African Ministers' Association of South Africa (IDAMASA) and provided the first full-time General Secretary, A. L. Mncube. Union conversations with Presbyterians and Congregationalists broke down soon after World War II. In the early 1960's the Church of the Province of South Africa (Anglican) initiated separate conversations with the Presbyterians (later joined by the Congregationalists) and Methodists. These have led to the formation of a Unity Commission involving all four denominations, which started work in 1968.

Church and State. Relations between the Methodist Church and the various governments have usually been good. During the nineteenth century Wesleyan missionaries such as Thomas Jenkins and PETER HARGREAVES played an important role in relations between the Transkeian tribes and the colonial authorities. William Shaw was highly regarded by successive Governors of the Cape and was able occasionally to shape official policy on important matters. Such direct influence was rare in the Boer Republics (Orange Free State and Transvaal) and after the Cape and Natal attained self-government. Much was achieved, however, by personal contacts with government officials both before and after the formation of the Union of South Africa in 1910. An unsettling feature of the present situation is the increasing breakdown of such relationships and the growing suspicion between Church and State.

This breakdown is a result of the implementation of *apartheid* by the Nationalist Government which has ruled South Africa since 1948. The Methodist Church has been less vocal on this subject than some other denominations, but its official opposition to the ideology and the injustices that result has been made clear by statements of Conference, Synods and individual leaders. Many white members do not support their Church's official stand on race relations although the majority probably oppose the Government.

Race in the Church. The racial situation understandably causes tensions and difficulties within the Church. From time to time there has been talk of separation on racial lines, but the Conference of 1958 resolved that the Methodist Church should remain "one and undivided." There have been renewed efforts since then to express this unity more fully but there are no grounds for complacency as segregation is almost complete at the local level. The increasingly strict application of *apartheid* will make the situation progressively more difficult.

Membership. After a century-and-a-half the Methodist Church of South Africa is established in every part of the country and includes a good cross-section of the various population grups. The official return of full members presented to the 1966 Conference was 343,658 (African 251,492; white 67,584; Cape Colored 23,508; Indian 1,074). According to the 1960 Census the number of Methodist adherents was as follows:

	Adherents	Total Population	Methodist Percentage
African	1,319,672	10,927,922	12.1
White	269,825	3,088,492	8.7
Colored	117,903	1,509,258	7.8
Asiatic	2,019	477,125	0.4
TOTAL	1,709,419	16,002,797	10.7

These figures indicate that Methodism is second to the Dutch Reformed Church in total membership; has the largest number of adherents among the Africans; and ranks third among the whites (D.R.C. 42.9%; Anglican 12.6%).

Free Methodist Church (U.S.A.). Missionaries originally serving in LIBERIA and MOZAMBIQUE transferred to Natal and established the first station on a 2,300-acre farm at Fairview on the Indian Ocean, seventy-five miles south of Durban. Other stations, each located on large farms, are at Itemba and Edwaleni. The latter is the conference center. At Greenville, Cape Province, there is a flourishing hospital and nurses training school, supported largely by government subsidy. A new tuberculosis sanitarium has been established. The capital expenditure and annual operating expenses are provided by the government. There is a regularly organized conference. In recent years several new churches have been erected in the new African cities of the Durban area. A Bible Institute for laymen has been established at the Edwaleni Conference Center. Ministerial training is received at Union Bible School, Sweetwaters. In 1969 there were about 1,850 members in the Natal area.

Pioneer missionary G. Harry Agnew, founder of the Mozambique mission, followed his new converts to the gold mines of the Transvaal in 1895. He established a Bible school at Witbank and cooperated with independent missionary, A. W. Baker, in establishing schools and churches at the mines. The entire work was later put under Free Methodist supervision. This part of the work is for the men from Mozambique who are on contract with the mines for periods of one to two years. At the mine schools, the men learn to read. They receive instruction in Biblical and related subjects. The Christians are conserved and some become leaders of the churches when they return home. Also there are new converts regularly reported.

There is a great demand for Bibles and Christian literature. Colportage work is an important part of mission work in this area. A Bible school, located on a dairy farm campus, Eastern Transvaal, prepared African evangelists for work in the new locations developing so rapidly around the Transvaal cities. Generous grants of land by government and cooperative financing by Africans and the mission have resulted in the erection of many churches in recent years. The Transvaal district is part of the Mozambique Conference. This district makes generous contributions to the home conference budget from their above-average earnings. There are about 2,000 members in this district.

L. A. Hewson, *South Africa*. 1950.
South African Methodism—Her Missionary Witness. Cape Town: Methodist Publishing House, 1966.
J. Whiteside, *South Africa*. 1906.　　D. G. L. Cragg
　　　　　　　　　　　　　　　　　　E. Lynn Cragg
　　　　　　　　　　　　　　　　　　Byron S. Lamson

SOUTH AUSTRALIA CONFERENCE. British settlement in what is now the Australian State of South Australia dates from 1836. The colonizing body was the South Australian Company the chairman of whom sought as settlers "those who fear God" and expressed the hope that "the present movement will lay the foundation of a new kingdom in truth and righteousness." This idealism was shared by a number of Methodists who arrived in the first ships or came shortly afterwards. The first Wesleyan CLASS MEETINGS were organized within six months of the proclamation of the colony. In the sixty-four years between 1836 and Methodist Union in 1900, four Methodist bodies worked in the State. The WESLEYAN METHODISTS were present from the beginning and their work expanded as the population grew and settlement was extended. In 1838 the first minister, William Longbottom, arrived unexpectedly, being shipwrecked near the South Australian coast while en route to his appointment in West Australia. By 1876, forty years after the colony's beginning, they had 179 churches.

The PRIMITIVE METHODISTS date from 1840, the first two ministers arriving from England in 1845. Their growth was also rapid and by 1876 this body had 106 churches.

The BIBLE CHRISTIAN denomination owed its origin in South Australia to an invitation sent by Cornish immigrants to the Conference in England. Two ministers arrived in 1850 and began work among the mining community most of whom had come from Cornwall and other areas in England's South-West. 1876 returns put the number of Bible Christian churches at 87.

The fourth Methodist group, the METHODIST NEW CONNEXION, dates from 1863, when James Maughan formed a society with ten members, the parent congregation of ADELAIDE's present-day Central Methodist Mission. Two churches were built but there was little growth after Maughan's death in 1871. After twenty years the membership was only eighty-two and in 1888 the Connexion merged with the Bible Christian Church.

An Annual Conference or Assembly within a nationally organized church with full or partial autonomy was established in all three bodies with the Primitive Methodists leading the way in 1856. South Australia Wesleyans were initially responsible for the work in West Australia and at Port Darwin in the Northern Territory. One of the last acts of the Wesleyan General Conference prior to union was to constitute West Australia a separate Conference, the first State meeting taking place in 1900.

Methodist Union. The movement towards Methodist Union in South Australia is part of the wider story of union throughout the country as a whole. A distinctive feature of the South Australian situation, however, was the greater relative strength of the Primitive Methodists and Bible Christians vis-a-vis the Wesleyans compared with what prevailed in other States. The "Minor Methodists" (as the non-Wesleyan bodies were termed) were convinced of the desirability of union as early as 1887 and from then until the inauguration of the united Church on Aug. 14, 1899, they never wavered in their commitment to union. The first United Conference was held in February 1900.

The *Minutes* of the 1900 Conference give the following figures for Methodism at the time of union: Churches, 457; Ministers (including probationers), 132; Church Members, 15,426. The population of the State was then 370,000.

Church and Society. As has already been mentioned South Australia had a higher percentage of non-Wesleyans among its Methodists than was found in the other Australian states. It also had a higher number of non-Anglican Protestants than was usual in British colonies. A well-known history of early South Australia bears the title "Paradise of Dissent" and this points to the strength and influence of the non-Anglican churches during the State's formative years. Some of the leading pioneers were Congregationalists. Methodists increased rapidly, especially with the influx of Cornish miners following the discovery of copper in the 1840's. The State's Lutheran population has always been relatively high, the first settlers from the Continent arriving as early as 1839.

The number of Anglican adherents has always been about thirty percent of the population. Two significant results of the high Non-Anglican element in the population was the successful resistance to early proposals to establish the Church of England as the official church, and the growth in the nineteenth century of a secular system of State education. The debate over the latter raged through the 1850's and 1860's. Opposition to State finance for Church schools was *de facto* opposition to the Church of England and the consequence was a public educational system from which all forms of religion were excluded. Not until 1943 was legislation passed to allow Church representatives to enter the schools for a half-hour period of religious instruction each week.

Another result of the religious composition of the State's population was that until recently there has been an identifiable Church influence on social legislation, particularly with regard to gambling and the sale of alcoholic liquor.

Since World War II immigration from Europe has steadily altered the State's denominational picture. The population is now approximately 1,200,000 and in the last census Anglican adherents numbered 29%, Roman Catholics 21% and Methodists 22%.

Methodist Growth. In almost all towns and districts in South Australia there is (or in the past has been) a Methodist church. Prior to union it was not unusual to find all three Methodist denominatons even in small towns. The growth of Methodism kept pace with the opening up of the country in the last half of the nineteenth century. The pioneer missionaries often travelled long distances by horseback or bicycle, visiting farmhouses and settlements, and gathering together in homes, halls and churches the first congregations.

The mining communities from 1850's to the early years of this century were predominantly Methodist and each body erected numerous churches and halls many of which became redundant when the work of the mines ceased.

Recent years have seen a decrease in the rural population. This together with the development of good roads and the automobile has meant the closing of a number of small churches. At the same time the metropolitan area around Adelaide has expanded rapidly since the end of World War II. The metropolis now includes nearly seventy percent of the total State population. The Church's Home Mission Department is continually engaged in establishing new causes, some of them being joint charges with the Presbyterian and Congregational churches. Statistics for the South Australian Conference as of May 1969, are as follows: Number of ministers in active work, 153; number of churches, 452; number of members, 35,850.

Conference Institutions. Prince Alfred College, Methodist Ladies' College, Wesley Theological College, Lincoln College, Westminster School, Resthaven Homes for the Aged, Memorial Hospital, Kate Cocks Babies Home, Epworth Book Depot, Annesley Deaconess College. (See also ADELAIDE.)

AUSTRALIAN EDITORIAL COMMITTEE

SOUTH BEND, INDIANA, U.S.A., is the former home of the Miami, Iroquois, Pottawattomi and Mound Builder Indians. The city takes its name from a large bend in the Saint Joseph River. The river flows south from MICHIGAN into INDIANA and then bends back north to empty into Lake Michigan. The Indians and early missionaries enjoyed the excellent transportation it afforded. Father Jacques Marquette, renowned Jesuit missionary explorer, used the river for his work.

N. B. Griffith, a Methodist minister, was the first Protestant clergyman to come to South Bend. He preached his first sermon on Jan. 31, 1831. During the next four years, a budding congregation met in private homes and in an old log school. In 1835 and 1836, temporary church structures were built. First Church of South Bend descends from this earliest Methodism.

Saint Paul's Church was organized in 1883. The present building, erected in 1903, witnesses to the generosity of the Studebaker family. The architecture represents a pre-Renaissance revival of antique and Byzantine art. An ancient baptismal font, claimed by some to be the oldest in use in the United States, graces the sanctuary. Studies indicate that the font was made by "The Cosmati," a group of Roman marble workers in the 12th and 13th centuries. It is believed that the marble was quarried from the ruins of ancient Rome. Mayer and Company of Munich, Germany, made and installed the heavily insured art glass windows.

The Board of Home Missions and Church Extension of the former M.E. Church regularly granted funds to help with the growth of Methodism in South Bend. From 1902

to 1926, the larger churches sponsored societies in many new communities and in new neighborhoods in old towns. Grace Church helped to inaugurate Methodist services in the Lowell Heights and River Park settlements. In 1912, three local churches gave birth to new mission congregations: First Church initiated Trinity; Epworth came into existence as a mission of St. Paul's; Stull was dedicated through the efforts of Grace Church. The great Roman Catholic university, Notre Dame, has received deserved praise for "its helpful boost to grass roots ecumenism when on March 6, 1966, the (newly formed) Clay Methodist Church held its first worship services in the engineering building on the Notre Dame campus. This has continued weekly ever since and will, until the Clay Church, now under construction, is completed." (*South Bend Tribune*, May 6, 1968.) The sole stipulation of the president of Notre Dame was that the arrangement must be free. Methodist Bishop RICHARD C. RAINES gratefully noted the above agreement and said, "With Methodists worshipping on the Notre Dame campus, we are manifesting today a united witness to Christ that cuts across ancient historical boundaries." (*Ibid.*)

John A. O'Brien, noted author and theologian at Notre Dame, quoted Father Theodore M. Hesburgh, Notre Dame's president, as saying, "It is to the good of Notre Dame, its faculty and students that Methodists are praying on her campus. The world is no longer divided between Christian bodies but between those who believe in God and those who do not. Christians are drawing closer together, praying together, and working together for the good of all" (*Together* Magazine, March, 1968).

In 1970 there were seventeen United Methodist churches in South Bend, with a total membership of 8,571. Grace Church is the largest of these with a membership of 1,706. South Bend is in the North Indiana Conference of The United Methodist Church.

First Church. Rev. N. B. Griffith was appointed to Fort Wayne Mission in 1831, and arrived with his family in South Bend, Jan. 24, 1831. Early in April Griffin preached in the barroom of a small tavern kept by Benjamin Coquillard, a Roman Catholic, and organized a Methodist class with eight members. The class consisted of Samuel Martin and wife, Benjamin Potter and wife, Benjamin Ross and wife, Rebecca Stull, and Simeon Mason. Martin and Ross were appointed class leaders. From June to autumn, 1831, the following were added by certificate: William Stanfield and wife, Samuel Newman and wife, Samuel Good and wife, and Jacob Hardman, M.D., later a trustee. Several Baptists, Presbyterians, and United Brethren, residing in town, put their membership in the Methodist Church with the understanding that when their denominations organized they would join them.

In 1832 the Conference Minutes reported South Bend Mission, N. B. Griffith, pastor. Worship was held in a log schoolhouse.

First Church in reality goes back to 1833 when the South Bend Circuit was formed. The first church edifice was erected in the fall of 1836, a small frame building. During J. B. DeMotte's pastorate, 1845-46, the Methodists and Presbyterians united in a protracted meeting which resulted in about 150 conversions.

About 1849, a small frame church was replaced by a brick church. This was dedicated Aug. 17, 1851, by L. Berry, president of Asbury (now DEPAUW University) and J. L. Smith. During 1869-70, First Church was enlarged and rebuilt under John Thrush. By 1876 First

Church reported 389 members and property valued at $33,000. First Church contributed to the growth of other churches through the years in South Bend, and a mission started by First Church became an independent church, Milburn Memorial Chapel, erected by Mrs. Clem Studebaker as a memorial to her father, George Milburn. The chapel was dedicated by H. A. Gobin, April 1, 1883. This cost around $10,000.

Edythe J. Brown, *The Story of South Bend*. South Bend, Ind.: South Bend Vocational School Press, 1920.
J. J. Detzler, *Northwest Indiana Conference*. 1953.
General Minutes, UMC, 1970.
M. Simpson, *Cyclopaedia*. 1882.
South Bend Daily Times, Aug. 31, 1894.
South Bend Tribune, May 5, 1968.

JESSE A. EARL
DONALD F. MCMAHAN

SOUTH CAROLINA, U.S.A., is an Atlantic Coast state and one of the original thirteen. Containing 31,055 square miles, it is the fortieth state in size. Its population in 1970 was about 2,600,000. Its coastal plain is called the low country, and the piedmont and mountainous section the upcountry. The first permanent English settlement was in 1670, and CHARLESTON was founded in 1680. The colony had proprietary rule (1670-1719), royal rule (1720-1775), and statehood beginning in 1776. The earliest provisions for proprietary rule made possible the large plantations and the slaveholding aristocracy which prevailed until the Civil War. The upcountry has become industrialized, and the low country, known for its agrarian economy of cotton and tobacco, is now developing industry.

Methodism came early to South Carolina. JOHN and CHARLES WESLEY visited the colony in 1736-37, and GEORGE WHITEFIELD was in Charleston fourteen times during his American evangelistic tours (1737-1770). John Wesley's seventy-four page *Collection of Psalms and Hymns*, printed at Charleston in 1737, was "the first collection of hymns published for use in the Church of England."

JOSEPH PILMORE, who came to America in 1769 as one of Wesley's first official missionaries, visited Charleston in January 1773. He soon had a revival under way. Proceeding to GEORGIA, he later returned and delivered his last sermon in Charleston, March 8, 1773. Pilmore did not organize a Methodist society because he could not remain in South Carolina and there was no other Methodist preacher to take charge.

After Pilmore's departure, there was no more Methodist preaching in Charleston until the arrival of FRANCIS ASBURY. Accompanied by three preachers—Woolman Hickson, JESSE LEE, and Henry Willis—Asbury appeared on Feb. 24, 1785. En route he and his party visited Cheraw, and Asbury preached at Georgetown. Remaining in Charleston three weeks, they laid the foundation for organized Methodism. The bishop appointed Willis as preacher in charge, and he soon organized a Methodist society. In 1786 the church had thirty-five white and twenty-three colored members.

James Foster who, beginning in 1776, served two years as a traveling preacher in VIRGINIA, located and moved to South Carolina. He ministered in the state and won some members before Asbury's arrival in 1785. Foster's work made possible the Broad River Circuit which covered parts of Newberry, Fairfield, Union, and Chester counties. In 1786 it had 210 members.

Asbury immediately linked South Carolina Methodism with the conference he held at Louisburg, N. C. in April 1785. At that gathering John Tunnell was appointed to Charleston and Woolman Hickson to Georgetown. Jesse Lee says the conference "took in" the Broad River Circuit that year, but it does not appear in the appointments until 1786. The conference in 1786 was held at SALISBURY, N. C.

The first Methodist conference in South Carolina met at Charleston, March 22, 1787, with Bishops Asbury and COKE in charge. The sessions were held in a new church building, the first to be erected by the Methodists in the city. A wooden structure sixty by forty feet with balconies for Negroes, it came to be known as the Cumberland Street Church. The SOUTH CAROLINA CONFERENCE dates from the 1787 session. At that time it had work in Georgia, and in 1822 work in FLORIDA was added. In 1824 northwestern South Carolina became a part of the HOLSTON CONFERENCE, but the territory was returned to the South Carolina Conference in 1844. In 1830 Georgia and Florida were set off as the GEORGIA CONFERENCE. In 1850 a part of the North Carolina territory was given to the NORTH CAROLINA (MES) CONFERENCE and the remainder went to it in 1870. Thereafter the South Carolina Conference was limited to its own state boundaries.

In 1791 Charleston Methodism suffered a schism led by WILLIAM HAMMETT, a British Methodist preacher who had served as a missionary in the WEST INDIES. Though not a member of the South Carolina Conference, he desired, and the laymen wanted him, to be appointed to Charleston. Unable to have his way, Hammett called Asbury a tyrant, and said he himself was being persecuted. Leading what he called the "Primitive Methodist" movement, Hammett developed a large following and built several churches. He died in 1803, and most of his followers returned to the Methodist fold.

In 1833 a small group of laymen tried to get legal control of all Methodist property in Charleston so as to transfer it to the M.P. CHURCH. Their plan thwarted, they organized a M.P. church in the city, but it did not prosper. However, there was a SOUTH CAROLINA CONFERENCE (MP) from 1839 to 1939. At the time of unification it brought five ministers, four charges, and some 400 members into The Methodist Church. The Charleston Colored Mission (MP) was formed in 1892, changing its name to South Carolina Colored Mission in 1924. In 1939 it brought twelve ministers, eleven charges, and about 1,200 members in the SOUTH CAROLINA CONFERENCE (CJ).

Negroes were admitted as members of Methodist churches in South Carolina from the beginning. At the first conference in 1787, the preachers were enjoined to minister to the colored people and enroll them in the societies. WILLIAM CAPERS (later bishop) was called the founder of missions to the slaves. In 1861 the South Carolina Conference had 48,600 colored and 37,986 white members.

Following the division in 1844, the South Carolina Conference of course adhered South, and this left the M.E. Church with no work in the state until after the Civil War. In 1866, however, it organized the colored South Carolina Conference. Many Negroes then transferred from the Southern to the Northern Church, while others joined the independent Negro Methodist denominations. By 1869 the Negro membership of the South Carolina Conference (MES) had dropped to 2,411, while in the same year the

South Carolina Conference (ME) reported 22,489 members.

After unification in 1939 the South Carolina Conference (Negro) was the strongest in the Central Jurisdiction. It reported 47,066 members in 1968. In that year the CENTRAL JURISDICTION was abolished, and the conference was received into the SOUTHEASTERN JURISDICTION pending merger with the South Carolina Conference which had been organized in 1787.

The Negroes who remained in the M.E. Church, South, after the Civil War formed the C.M.E. CHURCH in 1870. In 1966 that denomination had about three dozen pastoral charges in South Carolina. The A.M.E. CHURCH organized a conference in South Carolina in 1865. In 1966 it had 71,000 members in the state. It founded Payne Institute at Cokesbury, moved it to COLUMBIA in 1880, and changed its name to Allen University. The A.M.E. ZION CHURCH organized a South Carolina Conference in 1893. In 1966 it had about fifty ministers and seventy churches. Its Central Wesley College, Central, S. C., was chartered in 1909. Some South Carolina members of the M.E. Church, South who declined to enter The Methodist Church in 1939 formed the SOUTHERN METHODIST CHURCH. In 1966 it had fifty-two pastoral charges in the state. In 1962 it established Southern Methodist College at Orangeburg.

In 1915 the South Carolina Conference (MES) was divided to form the UPPER SOUTH CAROLINA CONFERENCE. Differences among conference leaders over management of the *Southern Christian Advocate* and some other matters caused the division. In 1947 the two bodies merged to form again the South Carolina Conference which covered the whole state. The consolidated conference then had 317 pastoral charges and 170,313 members.

The outstanding Methodist institutions in South Carolina are: *South Carolina Methodist Advocate* (formerly *Southern Christian Advocate*), Epworth Children's Home at Columbia, the Methodist Homes at Greenwood and Orangeburg, Claflin College at Orangeburg, COLUMBIA COLLEGE for women in Columbia, WOFFORD COLLEGE at Spartanburg, and SPARTANBURG JUNIOR COLLEGE.

Through the years the following native South Carolina Methodists have been elevated to the episcopacy: William Capers, WILLIAM M. WIGHTMAN, H. N. McTYEIRE, WILLIAM W. DUNCAN, A. COKE SMITH, JOHN C. KILGO, EDWIN D. MOUZON, PAUL HARDIN, JR., JOHN O. SMITH, EDWARD J. PENDERGRASS, and JAMES S. THOMAS. Two others, J. W. TARBOUX and CYRUS B. DAWSEY, became bishops in the Methodist Church of BRAZIL.

In 1970 the two South Carolina Conferences of The United Methodist Church reported 786 ministers, 598 total charges, 239,458 members, and property valued at $120,441,362.

F. Asbury, *Journal and Letters*. 1958.
W. C. Barclay, *History of Missions*. 1950.
A. H. Bassett, *Concise History*. 1882.
A. D. Betts, *South Carolina*. 1952.
W. M. Jenkins, *Steps Along the Way*. 1967.
General Minutes, UMC.
Minutes of the South Carolina Conferences.
A. M. Shipp, *South Carolina*. 1884.   J. MARVIN RAST
                                           ALBEA GODBOLD

SOUTH CAROLINA CONFERENCE was organized in CHARLESTON, March 22, 1787, with Bishops FRANCIS ASBURY and THOMAS COKE in charge. The sessions were

in what came to be known as the Cumberland Street Church, the first to be built by the Methodists in the city. (See SOUTH CAROLINA for account of early Methodism in the state.) At the outset there were twelve preachers, six circuits, and 2,070 white and 141 colored members. In 1796 the GENERAL CONFERENCE designated six conferences with boundaries, and South Carolina was one of the six. It included South Carolina, GEORGIA, and part of NORTH CAROLINA. In 1822 FLORIDA became a part of the conference.

Northwestern South Carolina became a part of the HOLSTON CONFERENCE when it was formed in 1824, but the region was returned to the South Carolina Conference in 1844. In 1830 Georgia and Florida were set off as the GEORGIA CONFERENCE. Part of the North Carolina territory was given to that conference in 1850 and the remainder in 1870. Thus after eighty-three years, the South Carolina Conference was limited to the boundaries of its own state. In 1871 it reported 35,532 members. In 1915 the conference was divided to form the Upper South Carolina Conference, but the two merged into one conference again in 1947 which then had eleven districts, 317 pastoral charges, 771 local churches, and 170,313 pastoral charges, 771 local churches, and 170,313 members.

The M.E. Church launched the *Wesleyan Journal* at Charleston in 1825, but the next year the paper was merged with the *Christian Advocate* in NEW YORK which was then called the *Christian Advocate and Journal*. Sectional differences over slavery made necessary a southern paper, and in 1837 the *Southern Christian Advocate* began in Charleston with the understanding that it would serve several conferences. In 1858 the paper became the official organ of the South Carolina, Georgia, and Florida conferences, and for a time it was published in AUGUSTA and MACON. In 1877 it came back to Charleston as the organ of the South Carolina Conference alone. It moved several times within the state, and in 1917 was permanently located at COLUMBIA. Today it is called the SOUTH CAROLINA METHODIST ADVOCATE.

The South Carolina Conference always demonstrated a missionary spirit. It sent TOBIAS GIBSON to Natchez in 1800, and MATTHEW P. STURDIVANT to the TOMBIGBEE CIRCUIT in ALABAMA in 1808. Following the organization of the conference missionary society in 1821, WILLIAM CAPERS (later bishop) was appointed superintendent of Indian Missions. A mission school and church were maintained among the Creek Indians in Georgia and Alabama until 1830 when the Indians were moved west to Indian Territory. The conference did not condemn slavery, but it did regard the slaves as souls to be saved. By 1828 nearly one-third of the Negro membership of the M.E. Church was in the South Carolina Conference. In 1828 with William Capers leading, the conference began the "Plantation Missions," a mission to the thousands of unreached slaves on the great plantations. The work grew rapidly. In 1855 there were twenty-six missionary stations in the conference served by thirty-two preachers, and the missionary collections were about $25,000 per year. In 1861 there were 48,600 Negro and 37,986 white members in the conference. Prior to the organization of the C.M.E. Church in 1870, the South Carolina Conference had a "Cokesbury Colored District" directed by a Negro presiding elder. After the entry of the M.E. Church into South Carolina following the Civil War, many of the Negroes transferred to that Church.

The first foreign missionaries sent out by the M.E. Church, South—CHARLES TAYLOR and BENJAMIN JENKINS—went from the South Carolina Conference to CHINA in 1848. The South Carolina Conference has sent more missionaries to BRAZIL than any other conference in Methodism.

The South Carolina Conference has promoted EDUCATION. The conference met at the home of Edward Finch in Newberry County in 1794, and the next year Asbury dedicated there the MT. BETHEL ACADEMY, a 40 by 20-foot building. The school continued until 1820. In 1834 the conference established the Dougherty Manual Labor School, soon called COKESBURY INSTITUTE, in the Mt. Ariel Community, Abbeville County. A strong institution, Cokesbury continued until 1918 when the plant was sold to Greenwood County for a public high school. In 1859 some forty-seven of the effective preachers of the conference had been educated at Cokesbury.

In 1850 BENJAMIN WOFFORD, a local preacher, died and left $100,000 for the establishment of a Methodist college in Spartanburg. WOFFORD COLLEGE opened in 1854 and continues as a strong and influential Methodist school. In 1869 Wofford tried to inaugurate a divinity school or department with a faculty of three. Wofford has had two presidents of regional if not national stature—JAMES H. CARLISLE (1875-1902) and HENRY N. SNYDER (1902-1942). COLUMBIA COLLEGE for women, established in 1859, has become a first-rate institution. LANDER COLLEGE, started as Williamston Female College in 1872, was moved to Greenwood in 1904 and became a conference college in 1906. In 1948 the conference gave the school to the community of Greenwood. SPARTANBURG JUNIOR COLLEGE, an accredited institution which is related to both the board of education and the board of missions of the general church, began as the Textile Industrial Institute in 1911. The Boylan-Haven-Mather Academy, begun at Camden in 1887, is under the direction of the board of missions.

Other institutions related to the conference are: Epworth Children's Home, Columbia, which began as Epworth Orphanage in 1896; the Methodist Home, ORANGEBURG, which was founded in 1953; the Methodist Home at Greenwood, started in 1968; the South Carolina Methodist Camp, Cleveland, which began in 1963; the Killingsworth Home for business women at Columbia which began in 1947; and Bethlehem Community Centers at Columbia (1945) and Spartanburg (1930).

In 1970 the South Carolina Conference reported 644 ministers, 475 pastoral charges, 194,104 members, and property valued at $108,886,901. In 1968 the conference anticipated and began preparations for merger in due time with the South Carolina Conference (1866).

A. D. Betts, *South Carolina*. 1952.
General Minutes.
Journal of the South Carolina Conference.   ALBEA GODBOLD

SOUTH CAROLINA CONFERENCE (1866) was organized in CHARLESTON, April 2, 1866, with Bishop OSMAN C. BAKER presiding. It was a Negro conference of the M.E. Church, though it had a few white members when it began. At the beginning its boundaries included SOUTH CAROLINA, FLORIDA, and GEORGIA. In 1968 when the conference became a part of the Southeastern Jurisdiction, the year of organization was added to its name to distinguish it from the South Carolina Conference which dates from 1787.

Missionary work preceded the formation of the conference. In 1862 Bishop Baker sent T. Willard Lewis, a white minister who was a graduate of New York College, to work in Beaufort, S. C., and Florida. Going to Charleston in 1865, Lewis won the confidence of the Negro members of Trinity Church (MES), and declaring that the M.E. Church made no distinction between the races, persuaded them to walk out en masse while two preachers were begging them to stay. The group formed Centenary Church (ME). Old Bethel and Wesley, Negro M.E. churches in Charleston, were also constituted in 1865.

With the help of two Negroes, Samuel Weston and JOSEPH A. SASPORTAS, who had been successful in business before emancipation and who later became ministers in the conference, Lewis soon established Baker Theological Institute in Charleston and served as its president. The organizing session of the conference was held in the institute.

In December 1865, Bishop BAKER sent Alonzo Webster of the VERMONT CONFERENCE to Charleston to help Lewis. With Webster working in Charleston and Lewis in the surrounding territory, they organized a number of Negro Methodist congregations. V. H. Bulkly and J. R. Rosemond, Negro preachers, assisted the white ministers. Rosemond founded some eighty preaching places along the NORTH CAROLINA line.

When organized the conference had two districts, Charleston and Florida. The one district included South Carolina and the other Florida and Georgia. The conference had fourteen ministers, twelve charges, and 3,137 members including 346 probationers. The conference grew rapidly, reporting about 28,000 members in 1870.

In 1872, the FLORIDA and GEORGIA CONFERENCES were established, thereby limiting the South Carolina Conference to its own state.

There were unsuccessful efforts to start a conference paper in 1866 and 1875. In 1881 the *Methodist Messenger* was established at Charleston; it soon moved to Orangeburg and continued publication until 1887. Later, support was given to the general church publications.

In 1881 the conference noted that there were some white congregations of the M.E. Church within its boundaries which it could not serve, and it voted over the objection of at least two of its members, to ask the BLUE RIDGE (Atlantic) CONFERENCE (North Carolina) to supply the white churches with pastors.

As Methodist unification approached, the conference debated the issues and voted for it eighty-two to forty. In 1939 the conference received twelve ministers, eleven pastoral charges, and 1,236 members from the South Carolina Colored Mission of the M.P. Church. The eleven charges became the Berkeley District which continued fifteen years before it was absorbed by the conference. Reporting 40,461 members in 1940, South Carolina was the largest conference in the CENTRAL JURISDICTION.

Through the years education was a prime concern of the conference. Fortunately there was help from the north with the educational endeavors. In 1969, LEE CLAFLIN, a prominent layman, and his son WILLIAM CLAFLIN who was governor of MASSACHUSETTS, offered financial assistance for the establishment of a college for Negroes in South Carolina. The property of a defunct women's college at Orangeburg was purchased, the school was opened in October, and on Dec. 18, 1869 it was chartered as

Claflin University. In 1871 Baker Theological Institute was merged with the new school. In 1924 the name of the institution was changed to CLAFLIN COLLEGE. L. M. DUNTON, a white man, rendered outstanding service as president of Claflin from 1885 to 1922.

Claflin furnished trained leadership for the conference, and the conference in turn supported the school. The preachers raised money for the college, including scholarship funds for students. It was estimated that 17,000 students enrolled at Claflin during its first half century. Today it is a strong Methodist college.

In 1968 when The United Methodist Church was organized and the Central Jurisdiction was abolished, the South Carolina Conference (1866) became a part of the SOUTHEASTERN JURISDICTION, pending merger with the SOUTH CAROLINA CONFERENCE which dates from 1787.

In 1970 the conference had 142 pastors, 123 pastoral charges, 45,354 members, and property valued at $11,554,461.

A. D. Betts, *South Carolina*. 1952.
General Minutes.
W. M. Jenkins, *Steps Along the Way*. 1967.   ALBEA GODBOLD

SOUTH CAROLINA METHODIST ADVOCATE is the official organ of the SOUTH CAROLINA CONFERENCE of The United Methodist Church, Southeastern Jurisdiction. It is owned and controlled by that Conference—which embraces the whole state of SOUTH CAROLINA—under the direction of trustees elected by the Conference. The present *Advocate* continues the *Southern Christian Advocate* founded in 1837. The pages of this church weekly mirror the growth of church and culture in interaction in ways that point to the positive relationship between the Christian faith and the secular order.

The *Southern Christian Advocate* itself was born June 24, 1837 in the midst of the sacred-secular debate over slavery. Earlier, in 1825, the South Carolina Conference in Charleston published for nearly two years *The Wesleyan Journal*, edited by WILLIAM CAPERS. The only other American Methodist journal then in existence was *Zions Herald*, an unofficial church paper published in BOSTON. In 1826, the *Christian Advocate*, published in NEW YORK, appeared. In 1827, the New York and Charleston ventures were combined into a single publication named, *The Christian Advocate and Journal*, to which was added in 1828, *Zion's Herald*. In 1833, *Zion's Herald* withdrew.

Largely because the southern regions of Methodism felt they were not free enough to express their views on certain "domestic institutions" (slavery), the GENERAL CONFERENCE of 1836, in CINCINNATI, authorized the establishment of three regional papers on a par with the New York *Advocate*: one in NASHVILLE (already in print); another in RICHMOND (not to begin till later); and another in Charleston. William Capers was appointed editor of the Charleston paper and its first issue appeared June 24, 1837, designed for readers in the South Carolina Conference (which then included large sections of eastern NORTH CAROLINA) and the GEORGIA CONFERENCE (which then included northern FLORIDA). Many subscribers were from as far away as ALABAMA, TENNESSEE, and VIRGINIA, making appropriate its founding name, *Southern Christian Advocate*.

From its beginning the *Southern Christian Advocate* was a paper of personal journalism reflecting the intimate relationship of Christianity and the secular world.

Despite its founding editor's claim that slavery was a "civic and political matter," the direction of his editorship and his founding of "missions to the slaves" confirmed the intimate relationship of the gospel to the world. His claim to fame today rests, not so much on the fact that he was later a bishop of the M. E. Church, South, but rather on his ministry to the Negro slaves.

Other secular interests of concern to the sacred were represented in the *Advocate*. It was the *Progressive Farmer* of its days, with columns of advice on raising poultry, when to dig sweet potatoes, how to preserve grapes, how to candle eggs. As late as 1866, when the *Advocate* was published then in MACON, Ga., because of the Civil War, its editor proposed that the weekly "adapt itself more fully to the wants and interests of the present time," and became a "double paper—one half devoted, as heretofore, to Religion and the Church; and one half to Literature, Science, Art, the News, the Markets, Advertisements, etc. etc." In short, the *Advocate* sought to become a family newspaper-journal, "being all that a family that takes but one Newspaper can need."

Theological and ecclesiastical issues were not, however, forgotten. From its earliest days, the *Southern Christian Advocate* was an open forum where ministers and laymen debated contemporary issues. In 1843, one such issue was what sort of coat a minister should wear. The editor proposed that the issue be ventilated in the pages of the *Advocate*, and promised "to publish whatever the brethren have to say, pro and con." He urged "writers on either side" to "avoid all personalities and keep to the matter in hand in a perfectly good humor, until the subject shall be thoroughly sifted." (*SCA*, Jan. 6, 1843.) The same debate continues in our day in the use of the pulpit robe, and/or the clerical collar as appropriate ministerial garb.

Recent editors of the *Advocate* (now called the *South Carolina Methodist Advocate* after Virginia, North Carolina, Georgia, Alabama, Florida, ARKANSAS and MISSISSIPPI established their own Conference journals, and the use of the more inclusive title *Southern Christian Advocate* seemed inappropriate) have continued the open policy of debate on current issues. Under the editorship of J. MARVIN RAST, debate during the nineteen-thirties on the union of the three branches of Methodism was fully covered. The debate over segregation in church and society produced its share of "pros and cons" during the editorship of this writer and his successor, Adlai C. Holler. Presently under the capable leadership of A. McKay Brabham, Jr., the *Advocate* is giving full coverage to such issues as the ecumenical debate over the NATIONAL and WORLD COUNCIL OF CHURCHES. The secret of the *Advocate's* power lies here. It has never been simply a trade journal of the church, but has been a pulpit where responsible editors have been able to enlist the laity in creative dialogue on the relation of the gospel to the world.

Advocate editors have been: William Capers, 1837-1840 (later bishop); WILLIAM MAY WIGHTMAN, 1840-1854 (later bishop); E. H. Myers, 1854-1871; F. Milton Kennedy, 1871-1878; Samuel A. Weber, 1878-1885; W. D. Kirkland, 1885-1894; John O. Willson, 1894-1902; W. R. Richardson, 1902-1904; G. H. Waddell, 1905; S. A. Nettles, 1906-1914; William C. Kirkland, 1915-1920; R. E. Stackhouse, 1921-1926; Emory Olin Watson, 1927-1933; Robert O. Lawton, 1933-1936; JOHN MARVIN RAST, 1936-1941; D. D. Peele, 1941-1948; John L. Sandlin, 1949; D. D. Peele, 1950-1952; J. Claude Evans, 1952-1957;

Adlai C. Holler, 1957-1961; and A. McKay Brabham, Jr., 1961 to date.

A. D. Betts, *South Carolina.* 1952.
Mason Crum, *The Southern Christian Advocate, An Historical Sketch.* N.p., 1945.
Southern Christian Advocate, June 23, 1887; June 24, 1937.

J. CLAUDE EVANS

SOUTH DAKOTA, U.S.A., population 661,406 in 1970, is in the north central part of the country. It is bounded by NORTH DAKOTA on the north, MINNESOTA and IOWA on the east, NEBRASKA on the south, and WYOMING and MONTANA on the west. A rolling plain, the state's area of 77,047 square miles is divided by the Missouri River into eastern and western parts of nearly equal size. A chain of large lakes is formed behind dams on the river. Semi-arid, the east produces farm crops and the west grows wheat and cattle. The badlands with their sharp erosional sculpture are intriguing. A part of the Louisiana Purchase in 1803, Dakota (including North and South Dakota) became a territory in 1862. South Dakota was admitted to the Union in 1889. Fur trading was important in the early days, but no attempts were made to settle the region until 1856 when pioneers from Minnesota and Iowa located at Sioux Falls and Medary. Railroads and the discovery of gold in the Black Hills in 1875 brought many people. South Dakota has led the nation in the production of gold for the last 20 years.

Methodism entered South Dakota almost with the first settlers. In 1860 Bishop O. C. BAKER, presiding over the UPPER IOWA CONFERENCE, appointed S. W. INGHAM as a missionary to all the territory between the Big Sioux and Missouri Rivers. Ingham preached his first sermon in South Dakota at Vermillion on Oct. 14, 1860. He served two years in the region, traveling some 7,000 miles on horseback, and organized a Methodist class at Vermillion. Other missionaries followed Ingham. In 1870 the first Methodist church in South Dakota was built at Elk Point by Fred Harris. A church was erected at Sioux Falls in 1873.

In 1880 the Black Hills Mission and the Dakota Mission were organized, the one covering the part of South Dakota west of the 101st meridian and parts of Wyoming and Montana, and the other the part of South Dakota east of the meridian. In 1885 the Dakota Mission became the Dakota Conference, and in 1891 the Black Hills Mission was designated as the Black Hills Mission Conference. Due to prolonged drouth and other discouraging factors, the latter was reduced to the status of a mission again in 1901, and in 1913 it was absorbed by the Dakota Conference. At its peak strength the Black Hills body had no more than twenty-two charges and about 1,100 members. However, it was adventurous, establishing Black Hills College at Hot Springs and Methodist Deaconess Hospital at Rapid City. The college operated from 1890 to 1900, and the hospital from 1912 to 1939.

The name of the Dakota Conference, organized in 1885, was changed to South Dakota Conference in 1892 and back to Dakota Conference again in 1896.

Some German, Swedish, and Norwegian-Danish churches were organized in South Dakota, but they were members of foreign language conferences each of which covered several states. (See NORTHWEST GERMAN CON-FERENCE, NORTHWEST SWEDISH CONFERENCE, and NORWEGIAN-DANISH CONFERENCE.)

South Dakota was adversely affected by drouth and economic depression in the 1920's and 1930's. Dust storms which were disastrous for agriculture beggar description. Pastors became distributors of the relief provided by the Red Cross and county welfare departments. Some college professors were paid mostly in kind. Church membership declined. Between 1927 and 1931 the Dakota Conference membership dropped from 28,835 to 23,306, a decline of about twenty per cent. Not until 1937 did the conference membership equal or surpass the 1927 figure. Eventually the economy of the state was strengthened by the huge dams constructed by the Federal government on the Missouri River.

At unification in 1939 the Dakota Conference was continued in The Methodist Church. At that time it was a part of the Des Moines Area. In 1952 the NORTH CENTRAL JURISDICTIONAL CONFERENCE changed the name of the Dakota Conference to South Dakota Conference, and it made the two Dakotas an episcopal area with the bishop's residence at Aberdeen, S. D.

The South Dakota Conference supports DAKOTA WESLEYAN COLLEGE at Mitchell, WESLEY FOUNDATIONS at three state schools, the Methodist Hospital at Mitchell, homes for the aged at Watertown, Gettysburg, and Mitchell, and three youth camps. In 1970 the conference reported three districts, 112 charges, 177 ministers, 44,147 members, and property valued at $19,099,512.

M. D. Smith, *Circuit Riders of the Middle Border,* 1965.
General Minutes, MEC and MC.
Minutes of the Dakota and South Dakota Conferences.

JOHN V. MADISON

SOUTH DAKOTA CONFERENCE succeeded the Dakota Conference in 1953. The Dakota Conference in its early years superseded or absorbed the missions projected by the M.E. Church in South Dakota. (See SOUTH DAKOTA for beginnings of Methodism in the state.)

The Black Hills and Dakota Missions, divided by the 101st meridian, were organized in South Dakota in 1880. The Dakota Mission went on to become the Dakota Conference in 1885 (it was called the South Dakota Conference from 1892 to 1896), and it absorbed the Black Hills Mission in 1913. Thereafter the Dakota Conference covered the entire state.

Though the work was called the Dakota Conference, it was a mission field for many years. In 1885 only four churches in the conference were self-supporting, and as late as 1922 the denominational board of missions appropriated some $35,000 to supplement pastors' salaries. It was not until 1937 that the churches of the conference were on a completely self-supporting basis.

At the beginning the Dakota Conference had ninety-five churches and approximately 5,000 members. In 1914, after absorbing the Black Hills Mission, the conference reported 171 charges and 18,810 members.

The Dakota Conference was strongly interested in education from the beginning, voting unanimously in 1886 to accept DAKOTA WESLEYAN UNIVERSITY which was launched at Mitchell the year before. Through the years the school had difficulties, but today with an endowment of more than $1,000,000, a plant valued at $3,500,000, and a student body of 900 it is one of Methodism's accredited senior colleges.

The Dakota Conference accepted Methodist Deaconess Hospital which was started in Rapid City by the Black Hills Mission in 1912. The institution continued operation until 1939. Dakota Deaconess Hospital at Brookings was operated from 1912 to 1930. The Methodist Hospital in Mitchell began in 1916. A fine institution, it is today the only Methodist hospital in the two Dakotas.

At unification in 1939 the Dakota Conference reported 125 charges, 29,643 members, and property valued at $2,333,190. By 1953, when the name was changed to the South Dakota Conference, the number of charges had dropped to 115, but the membership had risen to 39,354.

The South Dakota Conference was organized at Aberdeen on June 2, 1953 with Bishop EDWIN E. VOIGT presiding.

In 1949 the Dakota Conference authorized the organization of Methodist Homes, Inc. for the purpose of building homes for the aged. Jenkins Memorial Nursing Home was opened at Watertown in 1954. In 1964 Wesley Acres at Mitchell and Oahe Manor at Gettysburg (retirement homes) were dedicated.

The conference supports WESLEY FOUNDATIONS at three state institutions of higher learning, and it maintains three youth camps.

In 1952 the two Dakota Conferences requested that they be constituted as an episcopal area. The NORTH CENTRAL JURISDICTIONAL CONFERENCE concurred, and since that time the bishop of the Dakota area has lived in Aberdeen, S. D.

In 1970 the South Dakota Conference reported three districts, Northern, Southern, and Western, with 112 charges, 177 ministers, 44,147 members, and property valued at $19,099,512.

General Minutes, MEC and MC.
Minutes of the Dakota and South Dakota Conferences.
M. D. Smith, Circuit Riders of the Middle Border, 1965.

JOHN V. MADISON

SOUTH GEORGIA CONFERENCE (MES) was formed during the session of the GEORGIA CONFERENCE at Americus, Nov. 28 to Dec. 5, 1866, with Bishop HOLLAND N. McTYEIRE presiding. Under authority granted by the 1866 GENERAL CONFERENCE the GEORGIA preachers voted for two conferences in the state, the dividing line to run generally east and west a little north of MACON. In the division the South Georgia Conference received more territory but only about half as many members as the NORTH GEORGIA CONFERENCE. In the realignment of boundaries, the South Georgia Conference received also the Bainbridge and Brunswick Districts which had been in the FLORIDA CONFERENCE since its establishment in 1845. At the close of the 1866 session of the Georgia Conference, Bishop McTyeire read out the appointments of the South Georgia and North Georgia Conferences. In 1867 the South Georgia Conference met in SAVANNAH, while the North Georgia body convened in ATLANTA. (See GEORGIA for beginnings of Methodism in the state and an account of the Georgia Conference.)

The South Georgia Conference's increase in church membership between 1867 and 1939 was impressive. Beginning with 19,626 members in 1867, church membership trebled by 1900, and was about six times the original figure by 1939.

From the beginning the South Georgia Conference joined the North Georgia Conference in supporting EMORY and WESLEYAN COLLEGES. Wesleyan at Macon, founded in 1836, is the oldest permanent college for women in the United States. From the beginning the conference owned and supported Andrew College which was founded at Cuthbert in 1852 and was named for Bishop JAMES O. ANDREW. In time it became an accredited junior college. At different times the conference sponsored other colleges which did not live long. In 1916 the churches of the conference were assessed $16,000 for higher education, and the money was distributed to seven colleges and the General Board of EDUCATION at Nashville.

The Methodist Children's Home was established at Macon in 1873, and the Vashti School for Girls was started at Thomasville in 1903. Today the latter is a secondary school related to the National Division of the Board of Missions. The conference gives support to the Warren Candler Hospital which was founded at Savannah in 1903.

The South Georgia Conference came to unification in 1939 with eight districts, 213 charges, and 117,100 members. Its churches and parsonages at that time were valued at $6,247,400. Merged with parts of the Georgia Conferences of the M.E. and M.P. Churches, the new body became the South Georgia Conference of The Methodist Church.

Beginning in 1949 the South Georgia Conference developed Epworth-by-the-Sea on ST. SIMON'S ISLAND. It serves not only as a summer assembly but also as a year round facility for the conference and its organizations and groups. The archives of the conference historical society are housed there. Because of the ministry of JOHN and CHARLES WESLEY on St. Simon's during their sojourn in America, Epworth-by-the-Sea has been designated as a national Methodist Historic Shrine.

The South Georgia Conference raised $116,686 for higher education in 1968. The conference joins the North Georgia Conference in supporting nine Wesley Foundations in the state. The Wesleyan Christian Advocate, supported by both Georgia conferences, had a circulation of 49,000 in 1968. Institutions developed and supported in more recent years by the South Georgia Conference are: the South Georgia Methodist Home for the Aging at Americus, and the Hotel Ware for retirement at Waycross.

In 1970 the South Georgia Conference reported nine districts, 352 charges, 454 ministers, 143,579 members, and property valued at $75,878,595.

General Minutes, MECS and MC.
Minutes of the South Georgia Conference.
A. M. Pierce, Georgia. 1956.

ALBEA GODBOLD

SOUTH INDIA ANNUAL CONFERENCE includes portions of Madras and Mysore states, and embraces a territory covering 88,371 miles with a population of over 10,000,000. Work is mostly among the Hindus and with the Christian constituency. Outside of Bangalore, which is one of the principal cities, Belgaum, and Kolar, its work is largely carried on among rural people. The conference has nine districts, and at last reporting there were 98,036 members. Evangelistic work in the conference is fifty percent self-supporting, and ninety percent of the leadership is carried on by Indian pastors.

Bangalore is the largest and most important district in

the conference, as Bangalore itself is second to Madras among the cities of South INDIA. Mysore is the official capital, but Bangalore is the seat of the state government.

Madras is the third city in Indian population, and is an ancient and historic seaport founded in 1640. It is the capital of Madras State, the third city in India in population last reported as 1,900,000. There is a tradition that the Apostle Thomas suffered martyrdom there. Protestant worship dates from 1680, coming in with the East India Company. Methodist work was begun in 1874. There are two self-supporting Methodist churches in the city—the Tamil and Emmanuel Methodist Churches. There is also the St. Christopher Teachers Training College, which the Division of World Missions has assisted in sponsoring with other denominational agencies since 1945; and the Woman's Christian College, which likewise is an interdenominational enterprise with the Woman's Divison of Christian Service of The Methodist Church cooperating. Founded in 1915, the college is now affiliated with the University of Madras.

The Belgaum District in this conference is situated about a city of 127,885 inhabitants, 305 miles south of BOMBAY, and at a rather high altitude. The London Missionary Society began work in the city in 1820, which work was transferred in 1904 to the M. E. Church. There are two Methodist congregations in the city. There are boys' and girls' Methodist high schools and self-supporting churches in Belgaum, Gulbarga, and Raichur.

The Bidar, Chidaguppa, Gokak, Gulbarga, Raichur, Shorapur, and Yadgiri Districts are the other districts of the conference. Evangelistic work is carried on in each of these, and there are other Protestant agencies at work in this particular region.

Discipline, UMC, 1968.
Project Handbook Overseas Missions, United Methodist Church. New York: Board of Missions, 1969.   J. WASKOM PICKETT

SOUTH IOWA CONFERENCE (MC) was organized at Ames, June 26, 1958 with Bishop F. GERALD ENSLEY presiding. It was formed by changing the name of the IOWA-DES MOINES CONFERENCE which included approximately the south half of the state. The Iowa-Des Moines body had been created in 1932 by merging the Iowa and DES MOINES CONFERENCES.

The Des Moines Conference dated from 1864 and when formed it included the west half of the state, but half of its territory was taken in 1872 to form the Northwest Iowa Conference (see NORTH IOWA CONFERENCE). The Iowa Conference dated from 1844, and when formed it included the whole state, but after the organization of the UPPER IOWA CONFERENCE in 1856 and the Des Moines Conference in 1864, the IOWA body was limited to the southeast quarter of the state. Under the circumstances the South Iowa Conference when organized, like the Des Moines Conference before it, felt justified in claiming historical continuity from 1844.

At its beginning in 1958, the South Iowa Conference had 350 ministers, 277 pastoral charges, and 136,362 members. There were six districts—Boone, Burlington, Council Bluffs, Creston, Des Moines, and Ottumwa. In 1960 a seventh district, Newton, was formed.

The South Iowa Conference supported two colleges, IOWA WESLEYAN at Mt. Pleasant founded in 1842, and SIMPSON at Indianola dating from 1867. Iowa Methodist

Hospital at DES MOINES was founded in 1901; beginning with thirty beds, its plant expanded several times during the years; Blank Memorial Children's Hospital was added in 1943, and Yonkers Memorial Rehabilitation Center in 1959.

The conference supported three retirement homes, Wesley Acres at Des Moines, Heritage House at Atlantic, and Halcyon House at Washington. It sponsored the GOODWILL INDUSTRIES at Council Bluffs and at Des Moines.

The South Iowa and North Iowa Conferences jointly supported WESLEY FOUNDATIONS at Drake University and at the three state universities. They also cooperated in the work of the Hillcrest Children's Services at Cedar Rapids and the Iowa Methodist Services to Youth at Des Moines.

In 1968 the South Iowa Conference had 308 ministers, 216 pastoral charges, 142,918 members, and property valued at $80,979,676. In that year the NORTH CENTRAL JURISDICTIONAL CONFERENCE voted that in June, 1969, the conferences in Iowa should merge into one body to be called the Iowa Conference.

R. A. Gallaher, *Methodism in Iowa.* 1944.
Minutes of the South Iowa Conference.   JOHN A. NYE

SOUTH KANSAS CONFERENCE of the M. E. Church was organized March 11, 1874 at Fort Scott with Bishop JESSE T. PECK presiding. It was formed by dividing the KANSAS CONFERENCE. Its territory included the south half of the state. The conference had four districts—Fort Scott, Humboldt, Emporia, and Wichita. It reported ninety-three charges, forty-three churches, and 9,226 members.

In 1882 the South Kansas Conference was divided to form the SOUTHWEST KANSAS CONFERENCE. This limited the South Kansas body to the eastern third of the south half of the state.

In 1914 the South Kansas Conference was absorbed by the Kansas Conference. The new and enlarged body then covered the eastern third of the state. In the year prior to the merger the South Kansas Conference reported four districts—Emporia, Fort Scott, Independence, and Ottawa—33,006 members, and 297 churches valued at $1,178,225.

D. W. Holter, *Fire on the Prairie.* 1969.
Minutes of the South Kansas Conference.   F. E. MASER

SOUTH LEIGH, England, a village near Witney, in Oxfordshire, at whose parish church JOHN WESLEY preached his first sermon on Sunday, Sept. 26, 1725. He made no mention of the fact in his diary, though the manuscript of the sermon survives. The sermon was on "Seek ye first the Kingdom of God and his righteousness." He preached there again on Oct. 16, 1771, and noted in his *Journal* (v, p. 432) that "one man was in my present audience who heard" the sermon he had given forty-six years before. The man was called Winter. In the south Midlands, where the name Leigh is frequently found, it is pronounced as though it was spelled "Lye," the way in which Wesley originally wrote it. In the first volume of the Standard Edition of John Wesley's *Journal* there is a reproduction of an old print of the South Leigh Church.

V. H. H. Green, *Young Mr. Wesley.* 1961.   JOHN KENT

SOUTH MERRITT ISLAND, FLORIDA, U.S.A. **Georgiana Church** is one of the oldest churches in FLORIDA Methodism. Called "The Little Church in the Wildwood," it was founded in 1885 and Franklin Allen, Sr. homesteaded the land where the church now stands. He donated the ground for the church and the old part of the cemetery. One year later the church building was started and lumber for the church was brought down from St. Augustine, Fla. in sailboats. Volunteer labor and donated materials made it possible to conduct services on Thanksgiving Day, Nov. 25, 1886. A Rev. White was the first Methodist minister. Mr. and Mrs. Frank Munson, charter members and founders of the Georgiana Church, took an active interest in the growth and development of the church and carried on faithfully until their demise in 1950. For lack of leadership, the church was permitted to close for six years, but on Jan. 15, 1956, Mr. and Mrs. R. E. Gillette and Mr. and Mrs. C. K. Hall invited local Methodists to the first service to be held since the church had been closed. The refurbishing of the building and the growth in membership has been consistent because of the devoted interest of those who want "The Little Church in the Wildwood" to continue its role as "The Mother of Methodism" on the east coast of Florida.

SOUTHERLAND, SILAS BRUCE (1817-?), American M. P. minister, was a member of the MARYLAND CONFERENCE, and actively participated in the affairs of his denomination on a General Conference level. He was born in Prince George's County, Md., on May 21, 1817. Following the death of his parents he moved to Harper's Ferry, Va., and engaged in the apothecary business. He read and studied continuously, especially in the field of law. When he was converted in February 1839, his purposes were changed from the law to the ministry. He was licensed to preach by the M. P. Church and in 1841 was received into the Maryland Conference. He filled most of the prominent appointments of this conference, including a term as its president. He was repeatedly chosen to represent the conference in the GENERAL CONFERENCES. He was a member of the committee appointed by the General Conference of 1880 to prepare the hymnal, *The Tribute of Praise.* At a semi-centennial celebration at Old St. John's Church in BALTIMORE in 1878, he gave an address "of great force and beauty." He was one of five representatives from the M. P. denomination at the first ECUMENICAL METHODIST CONFERENCE held in London in 1881. He presided one day during this conference and also presented an address on "Non-Episcopal Methodism in America." He was a representative of his denomination at the General Conference of the M. E. Church which met in Baltimore in May, 1876. He was a member of the historic uniting convention of 1877. He received the honorary D.D. degree from the University of Georgia.

A. H. Bassett, *Concise History.* 1887.
E. J. Drinkhouse, *History of Methodist Reform.* 1899.
M. Simpson, *Cyclopaedia.* 1882.   RALPH HARDEE RIVES

SOUTHERN ASIA CENTRAL CONFERENCE in the M. E. Church developed on the initiative of annual conferences in INDIA. The earliest record on the subject is a letter from JAMES MILLS THOBURN to JAMES H. MESSMORE, saying,

In 1879 I became impressed that we needed an organization in which all parts of our scattered work in India would be represented to look after the general interests, and to keep us from drifting apart. . . . I wrote to Brother [EDWIN WALLACE] PARKER giving an outline of what I thought was needed. . . . My letter crossed one from him to me of practically the same import.

These letters led to the holding of a two-day joint session of the North India and South India Conferences. No bishop was present. George Bowen of Bombay was elected to preside. Both Annual Conferences had called for a joint session. They voted to hold a delegated conference in July 1881, and to ask the General Conference to recognize and to commit to it "all those interests of the church in India which are included in Part IV of the *Discipline* entitled 'Educational and Benevolent Institutions.' "

The proposition was opposed by the Board of Bishops and by the Board of MISSIONS, and although approved by the Committee on Missions in the GENERAL CONFERENCE of 1880, the measure was defeated by the vote of the Conference. Nevertheless, the delegated conference as planned in India was held in July 1881, and assumed authority to act on its own initiative in many areas. It addressed no request to the 1884 General Conference, but the subject was prominent in the discussions there, and Edwin W. Parker and WILLIAM TAYLOR presented a memorial asking for "a sub-ordinate General Conference in India," and their memorial was viewed favorably. The Conference already organized in India was recognized under the name Central Conference, and a Central Conference was also authorized for JAPAN.

As Methodism had by then spread from India into other countries, eventually including BURMA, SINGAPORE, MALAYA, the Dutch East Indies, SARAWAK, and the PHILIPPINE ISLANDS, the Central Conference of India was renamed the Central Conference of Southern Asia. Its powers were extended. In 1920 a Commission was appointed which under the chairmanship of J. WASKOM PICKETT prepared a Constitution for the Central Conference of Southern Asia. In 1928 this Central Conference was given authority to elect its bishops, the number predetermined by the General Conference.

In the PLAN OF UNION by which the M. E., M. E. South, and M. P. Churches were united in 1939, Central Conferences were continued, and Jurisdictional Conferences in the United States were set up, modeled somewhat on the plan that had proved so valuable in Central Conferences.

The title of this Conference as listed in the *Discipline* of The United Methodist Church (1968) is Southern Asia Central Conference. It comprises the following Annual Conferences: AGRA, BENGAL, BOMBAY, DELHI, GUJARAT, HYDERABAD, LUCKNOW, MADHYA PRADESH, MORADABAD, NORTH INDIA, SOUTH INDIA, and NEPAL Mission. These conferences are administered through four episcopal areas, namely, Bombay, Delhi, Hyderabad, and Lucknow.

J. WASKOM PICKETT

SOUTHERN CALIFORNIA CONFERENCE. (See SOUTHERN CALIFORNIA-ARIZONA CONFERENCE, and CALIFORNIA.)

SOUTHERN CALIFORNIA-ARIZONA CONFERENCE. The SOUTHERN CALIFORNIA CONFERENCE (ME) was formed in 1876 by dividing the CALIFORNIA CONFER-

ENCE. (See CALIFORNIA CONFERENCE, and CALIFORNIA.) At first the conference included only the south half of the state, but in 1917 it was expanded to include the southern part of NEVADA, and in 1920 it took in the state of ARIZONA. At unification in 1939, the Southern California Conference absorbed part of the PACIFIC CONFERENCE and all of the ARIZONA CONFERENCE (both MES). In 1940, the name was changed to the Southern California-Arizona Conference. (See ARIZONA, and PACIFIC CONFERENCE.)

In 1853, the California Conference sent Adam Bland as a "missionary" to LOS ANGELES, then a town of a few more than 1,600 people. He was told there were no Methodists in the town. He wrote of the place that "of all the society I ever saw here is the worst." But impressed with the country, he predicted that it was "destined . . . to be the big end of CALIFORNIA." A Los Angeles District was soon formed, but because of pro-slavery sentiment, the Methodist Episcopal Church made little progress in Southern California until after the Civil War. In 1875 the population of Los Angeles was 8,450 and the surrounding county had over 24,000. By that time the Northern Methodists had grown stronger, thus making possible the organization of the Southern California Conference the next year. When organized the new conference had 27 preachers and 1,257 members.

The coming of the railroads in the late 1880's brought thousands of people into southern California, and the conference experienced rapid growth. Between 1886 and 1889 the number of preaching appointments jumped from 80 to 130, the conference membership rose from 3,909 to 5,173, and two new districts were created. As time passed a strong Los Angeles Missionary and Church Extension Society was organized which solicited financial assistance from over the conference as well as from within the city for building new churches. The Northern Methodists grew much more rapidly in southern California than the southern branch of the church. The Southern California Conference came to Methodist unification in 1939 with 106,522 members, while the southern California part of the Pacific Conference brought only 8,509.

At its first session in 1876, the Southern California Conference looked toward the establishment of a school in Los Angeles. In 1880, the UNIVERSITY of SOUTHERN CALIFORNIA was launched with M. M. BOVARD, a member of the conference, as president. Several other schools were started soon afterward, but due to economic reverses in the region they closed or merged after a few years. In 1885, a substantial gift made possible the establishment of a theological seminary in connection with the university. The conference failed to take all legal steps necessary to insure ownership and control of either the university or the seminary, and ultimately it lost both institutions.

In 1955, the conference authorized a new but continuing seminary to be called the Southern California School of Theology. Retaining the faculty of the School of Religion of the University of Southern California, the new seminary operated in temporary quarters until it could be housed in 1960 in excellent new buildings at Claremont.

In 1957, after several years of negotiations, the conference accepted the Balboa University in San Diego, and changed its name to California Western University. CALIFORNIA WESTERN UNIVERSITY stands as the only Protestant affiliated institution of higher learning in its county.

The conference voted in 1918 to require seminary training of all new ministers entering on trial, the first conference in Methodism to set so high a standard. In 1957, at heavy expense, the conference enrolled all of its preachers in the ministers' reserve pension plan, the first conference in the connection to achieve that distinction.

Through the years the Southern California Conference ministered to various language groups within its bounds —Chinese, Japanese, Korean, Italian, Portuguese, Filipino, Hawaiian, Latin American, German, Scandinavian, and American Indian.

A Negro church was organized in the conference in 1888. At the time of unification in 1939, there were five Negro congregations, and since the CENTRAL JURISDICTION did not include the WESTERN JURISDICTION, they remained as integral parts of the Southern California Conference. Twenty years later there were ten Negro churches with a total of 6,128 members. There were no integrated churches in the conference prior to 1939, but in recent years the conference has appointed some Negro pastors to all white churches.

Several institutions in the Los Angeles area, such as the Frances DePauw Home, the Spanish American Institute, the Plaza Community Center, and the Church of All Nations, are notable for the special services they render to particular groups. In addition, the conference maintains a home for children, a home for girls, several homes for the aged, and the Methodist Hospital in Los Angeles.

An epochal event occurred in the conference's life when the HAWAII Mission became a district of the conference. This action came pursuant to an enactment of the 1964 General Conference giving the Hawaiian Mission the right to become a provisional annual conference or to merge with the Southern California-Arizona one. Hawaii, which had been under the supervision of Bishop GERALD KENNEDY, the resident bishop in Los Angeles, voted to join the Southern California-Arizona, and this was done. In June 1967, it became the Hawaiian District of that conference. It brought into the conference (1968 report) twenty-seven pastoral appointments, 6,893 members, and churches, parsonages and other property valued at $9,286,541. The 1968 session of the Western Jurisdictional Conference was held in Honolulu.

In 1970 the Conference reported 934 ministers, 495 charges, 260,047 members, and property valued at $180,637,498.

General Minutes, ME, MES, UMC.
Minutes of the Southern California-Arizona Conference.
E. D. Jervey, Southern California and Arizona. 1960.

ALBEA GODBOLD

SOUTHERN CHRISTIAN ADVOCATE. (See SOUTH CAROLINA METHODIST ADVOCATE.)

SOUTHERN CHRISTIAN RECORDER. A publication of the African Methodist Episcopal Church. (See AFRICAN METHODIST EPISCOPAL CHURCH, Publications.)

SOUTHERN CONFERENCE (ME) was organized at NEW ORLEANS, La., Oct. 29, 1924, with Bishop CHARLES L. MEAD presiding. It superseded the SOUTHERN GERMAN CONFERENCE. Its territory was TEXAS and LOUISIANA, and at the outset it included the work which had been in the Southern German Conference. It began with two districts—Brenham and San Antonio—thirty-three charges, 4,518 members, and property valued at $358,035.

In 1926 the Southern Conference absorbed both the Southern Swedish Mission Conference and the GULF CONFERENCE. This brought all of the white work of the M.E. Church in Texas, Louisiana, and MISSISSIPPI into one conference, and it so continued until unification in 1939.

The Southern Swedish Mission Conference was organized at Austin, Texas, Dec. 5, 1912 with Bishop ROBERT McINTYRE presiding. It had eleven charges and 1,057 members. Methodist work among Swedish immigrants in Texas had begun much earlier. The Austin Conference (ME) organized a Scandinavian District in 1885 and continued it until the formation of the Southern Swedish Mission Conference. It is claimed that between 1838 and 1910 some 7,000 Swedes settled in Texas, mostly around Austin. Conscious of the need of native trained leadership, the Swedish Mission Conference established Wesleyan Academy at Austin and maintained it until 1926 when the property was sold for $100,000 and the money given to TEXAS WESLEYAN COLLEGE at Fort Worth. When the Swedish Mission Conference was absorbed by the Southern Conference in 1926 it had thirteen charges, 1,804 members, and churches and parsonages valued at $93,200.

The Gulf Mission (ME) was organized at Jennings, La., Jan. 20, 1893 with Bishop EDWARD G. ANDREWS presiding. Composed of white ministers and churches, it was formed by dividing the LOUISIANA CONFERENCE along racial lines. In 1896 its territory was extended to include east Texas, and in 1900 it took in the white work of the denomination in Mississippi. At the beginning the mission had only seven charges and 354 members. In 1897 it became the Gulf Mission Conference and in 1904 the Gulf Conference. In the latter year it had forty-two charges and 2,859 members. Since some Northern Methodists were moving South, and since the Gulf Conference did not face the language limitations of Swedish and German Methodism, it was believed that the new conference would grow. But many northerners who came south soon became southern in their sympathies and tended to unite with the stronger Southern Church. Moreover, ministerial students going north of necessity for training failed to return. The merger with the Southern Conference in 1926 was necessary for economy and efficiency. In its last year the Gulf Conference reported three districts, thirty-nine charges, nineteen ministers, 5,327 members, and property valued at $423,150. Bishop W. RALPH WARD was admitted on trial in the Southern Conference in 1929.

In 1927 the Southern Conference reported seventy-eight charges and 11,896 members. The final session of the conference was held at SAN ANTONIO, Oct. 17-18, 1939 with Bishop Mead presiding. It brought into The Methodist Church seventy-five charges, 14,110 members, and property valued at $972,952.

General Minutes, MEC.
O. W. Nail, *Texas Methodism*. 1961.
C. G. Wallenius and E. D. Olson, *A Short Story of the Swedish Methodism in America*, reprint from Vol. 2, *The Swedish Element in America*. Chicago, 1931.

FREDERICK E. MASER

SOUTHERN GERMAN CONFERENCE (ME) was organized at Industry, Texas, Jan. 15, 1874 with Bishop THOMAS BOWMAN presiding.

Methodist work among the Germans in LOUISIANA and TEXAS began in the 1840's. In the spring of 1842, some Germans who had moved from CINCINNATI to NEW ORLEANS invited Peter Schmucker to come down and preach to them. Schmucker organized a class and entrusted it to Karl Bremer, a young man who had been converted in Germany and was licensed as a local preacher in America. When the MISSISSIPPI CONFERENCE met in November (it included Louisiana at that time), the appointments listed a German mission in New Orleans, and the next year Bremer was appointed preacher in charge. When the LOUISIANA CONFERENCE (MES) was organized in 1847 it had three German mission appointments in New Orleans. Because of upheavals in Europe, many Germans emigrated to Texas between 1845 and 1850. The Texas Conference (MES) first listed a German appointment in 1848.

The M. E. Church on reentering the South following the Civil War quickly developed work among the Germans in Texas and Louisiana. The TEXAS CONFERENCE (ME) was organized in 1867, and though primarily a conference of Negro ministers and churches, it reported a German district of three charges the first year. The 1870 minutes of the Northern Church's Louisiana Conference (organized in 1869) show a German mission in New Orleans.

When the Southern German Conference began in 1874 it included all of the German preachers and churches which had been in the TEXAS CONFERENCE, and beginning in 1880 the conference also took in the German work of the denomination in Louisiana. In 1880 the conference reported four districts—Austin, Dallas, New Orleans, and San Antonio—twenty-five charges, and 1,251 members.

The Southern German Conference felt the need of native trained leadership and endeavored to establish Immanuel Institute at Rutersville. It was short-lived, and five years later the conference started Mission Institute at Brenham. In a few years it was called Blinn Memorial College in honor of the man who gave it $20,000. About the turn of the century Blinn was a fairly strong institution. Then financial and other problems beset it, the interest of the conference became lukewarm, and in 1934 the school became a municipal junior college.

The last session of the Southern German Conference was held in New Orleans, Oct. 31 to Nov. 4, 1923. To avoid embarrassment the word "German" was deleted from the name, and it became the Southern Conference. In 1923 the Southern German Conference reported two districts, thirty-three charges, 4,445 members, and property valued at $392,275.

E. S. Bucke, *History of American Methodism*. 1964.
P. F. Douglass, *German Methodism*. 1939.
General Minutes, ME, MES.   FREDERICK E. MASER

SOUTHERN ILLINOIS CONFERENCE of The United Methodist Church is located in the southern third of the state of ILLINOIS. Methodism entered this territory in the person of Joseph Lillard, a Methodist local preacher, who preached there a short while in 1793. In 1797 Hosea Rigg established Methodism in St. Clair County.

Illinois was in the WESTERN CONFERENCE, 1803-12; in the TENNESSEE CONFERENCE, 1812-16; and in the MISSOURI CONFERENCE, 1816-24. The Southern Illinois Conference was separated from the ILLINOIS CONFER-

ENCE in 1852. The first session of the new conference was at Belleville, October 27, with Bishop E. R. AMES presiding. There were forty-six pastoral charges with 14,948 members and sixty-five traveling preachers.

The early years were not entirely peaceful ones. In 1864 Southern sympathizers among the Methodists were forced to withdraw and organize separate bodies which were called (in various places) the Illinois Christian Association, the Christian Union of Illinois, and the Christian Union Church. These bodies came together to form the Southern Illinois Conference of the M.E. Church, South. At a convention on June 8, 1867, Bishop DAVID S. DOGGETT welcomed them into Southern Church. The first conference was Oct. 16, 1867, at Nashville, Ill., with Bishop Doggett presiding.

Large numbers of German-speaking immigrants settled in Southern Illinois prior to the Civil War. In 1857 two German language Districts were created in Southern Illinois. In 1864 these became part of the ST. LOUIS GERMAN CONFERENCE where they remained until 1924 when merger brought them back into the Southern Illinois Conference. Thirteen charges and ten pastors were received at that time.

At unification in 1939, the ILLINOIS CONFERENCE of the M.E. CHURCH, SOUTH, and the ILLINOIS CONFERENCE of the M.P CHURCH came into the Southern Illinois Conference of The Methodist Church. In 1968 the ILLINOIS CONFERENCE of the E.U.B. CHURCH was merged into the larger body.

Benevolent institutions of the conference include MCKENDREE COLLEGE, the oldest college in the Midwest founded at Lebanon in 1828; Holden Hospital (Carbondale); the Children's Home (Mt. Vernon); Alton Memorial Hospital; the Old Folk's Home (Lawrenceville); and a number of small educational institutions which have passed out of existence.

In 1970 the conference reported 76,125 members in 240 charges served by 325 ministers.

J. C. Evers, *Southern Illinois Conference.* 1964.
Journal of the Southern Illinois Conference.

J. GORDON MELTON

SOUTHERN METHODIST CHURCH was formed in 1934 by members of several congregations of the M.E. Church, South, who did not wish to participate in the merger with the M.E. Church. They felt that the M.E. Church was apostate and full of heresy and infidelity and also that merger would eventuate in the racial integration of the annual conferences and churches.

The withdrawing members, meeting in convocation at Columbia, S. C., set up plans to perpetuate what they considered to be the M.E. Church, South. In attempting to retain local church property and the name "Methodist Episcopal Church, South," the group became the center of a series of landmark court decisions culminating in the mandate of Judge George Bell Timmerman on March 12, 1945. The bishops of The Methodist Church were legally established as representatives of the membership of The Methodist Church with control over its property; and the name, "Methodist Episcopal Church, South," was established as the property of its legal successor, The Methodist Church. The name Southern Methodist Church was then adopted by the withdrawing group.

The church claims to be Arminian-Wesleyan in doctrine and has added statements of belief on prevenient GRACE, the WITNESS OF THE SPIRIT, CHRISTIAN PERFECTION, and the evangelization of the world. It has also added statements on the creation account of Genesis, premillennialism, and Satan. It is somewhat unique among American denominations, for it has placed a statement favoring racial segregation among the doctrinal beliefs.

Departing from its episcopal heritage, the new body is congregational in polity. It retains the annual and general conference but has dropped the office of district superintendent and replaced the bishop with a quadrennially elected president.

The church grew very little for the first twenty years but experienced a large growth in the 1960's concurrent with the national racial crisis. Its present membership approximates 10,000 in two conferences in over forty local congregations. The church operates a school, Southern Methodist College, at Orangeburg, S. C. Also at Orangeburg is the headquarters and Foundry Press, which publishes the *Discipline* and the monthly *Southern Methodist,* the two official publications of the church.

The Southern Methodist Church is a member of both the American and International Councils of Christian Churches and is associated with the FUNDAMENTAL METHODIST CHURCH, EVANGELICAL METHODIST CHURCH IN AMERICA, and the METHODIST PROTESTANT CHURCH in the International Fellowship of Bible Methodists. Missions are supported in NIGERIA, Tanganyika, and Ethiopia; and other independent missions are partially supported.

Discipline of the Southern Methodist Church, 1960.
Issues of the *Southern Methodist.*
Walter McElreath, *Methodist Union in the Courts.* 1946.
J. GORDON MELTON

SOUTHERN METHODIST UNIVERSITY, Dallas, Texas, was established by the educational commission appointed in 1910 by the five annual conferences of the M.E. Church, South, in Texas. These annual conferences confirmed the work of their commission which resulted in the university's being chartered by the State of Texas on April 17, 1911. The university was designated as the connectional institution for all conferences west of the Mississippi River by action of the General Conference of the M.E. Church, South, in 1914.

Classes began in the university on September 22, 1915. Its first-year class of 706 students was at that time the largest first-year enrollment of any university in this country's history. At its opening it had two buildings and thirty-five faculty members. In 1964 it had seventy buildings, fifty of which were erected after the Second World War. (Combined assets of the two universities founded in 1914, EMORY and Southern Methodist, had grown to $153,558,628 in forty-eight years.)

The properties of the university in 1914 were vested with trustees elected by the General Conference of the M.E. Church, South. At the uniting conference in 1939 this responsibility was shifted to the South Central Jurisdiction of The Methodist Church. A Phi Beta Kappa chapter was established in 1949.

Schools are the University College, the schools of Humanities and Sciences, Business, Engineering, Arts, Law, and Theology, the Graduate School, and Dallas College.

The governing board has sixty-three trustees: eight bishops, twenty-five members at large elected by the South Central Jurisdiction, and thirty from the annual conferences of the jurisdiction. The Board of Governors has twenty members, of whom eleven are trustees.

JOHN O. GROSS

SOUTHERN NEW JERSEY CONFERENCE (MC) was authorized by the 1964 NORTHEASTERN JURISDICTIONAL CONFERENCE when NEW JERSEY was designated as an episcopal area. The Jurisdictional Conference recommended that the two New Jersey annual conferences change their names to NORTHERN NEW JERSEY and Southern New Jersey. Both conferences concurred. Bishop PRINCE A. TAYLOR presided at the session of the New Jersey Conference at Ocean City when it voted on June 10, 1965 to change its name to the Southern New Jersey Conference, effective July 1 of that year. At that time the conference had four districts, 316 charges, 105,450 members, and property valued at $60,848,949.

The New Jersey Conference (ME) was created by the 1836 GENERAL CONFERENCE. It was formed by dividing the Philadelphia Conference to which New Jersey Methodism had been attached from the beginning. (See New Jersey for the beginning of Methodism in the state.) The New Jersey Conference was organized at Newark, April 26, 1837 with Bishop BEVERLY WAUGH presiding. It began with four districts, Camden, Newark, Paterson, and Trenton, 71 charges, and, 18,060 members. The Rahway and Burlington Districts were added in 1842, and the Newton District in 1852. Twenty years after it was created, the New Jersey Conference membership had doubled, and in 1856 the General Conference divided it to form the NEWARK CONFERENCE. Thereafter the New Jersey Conference included a little more than the southern half of the state.

After the Newark Conference was set off, the New Jersey Conference had 119 preachers and 20,457 members. Because of the Civil War growth of the New Jersey Conference was negligible until 1867 when it reported 24,117 members. Thereafter the membership increased steadily, and in 1900 it was 50,470. The conference came to unification in 1939 with four districts, 298 charges, and 80,214 members. A part of the Eastern Conference (MP) was merged with the New Jersey Conference at that time.

The New Jersey Conference supported the PENNINGTON SCHOOL and DICKINSON COLLEGE from the beginning. Pennington has continued and is today a strong Methodist secondary school with an endowment of $2,-000,000, a plant valued at $2,500,000, and 250 students. The conference has sustained a close relationship with Dickinson College though the school is in PENNSYLVANIA. Following the Civil War the conference approved the FREEDMEN'S AID SOCIETY and raised money for its work. Also, it gave support to DREW THEOLOGICAL SEMINARY and DREW UNIVERSITY when they appeared.

Beginning about 1900, the New Jersey Conference developed a close relationship with the Methodist Hospital at PHILADELPHIA. It gave support to the Methodist Home for the aged, established at Collingswood in 1888, and to the Methodist Deaconess Center, started at Camden in 1913. In later years the New Jersey Conference joined the NEWARK CONFERENCE in establishing homes for the aged at OCEAN GROVE, OCEAN CITY, Branchville, and Collingswood. The conference maintains a youth camp called the Conference Center at Brown's

Mill. The two conferences cooperate in WESLEY FOUNDATIONS at Princeton and Rutgers, and they maintain campus ministries at nine state colleges.

In 1940, one year after unification, the New Jersey Conference reported four districts, 299 charges, and 81,944 members.

In 1965 the New Jersey Conference received twenty-two ministers and twenty charges from the DELAWARE CONFERENCE of the CENTRAL JURISDICTION as that conference was merged with the overlying conferences of the Northeastern Jurisdiction. These ministers and churches represented about fifteen percent of the strength of the Delaware Conference.

In 1970 the Southern New Jersey Conference reported six districts, Camden-Metropolitan, Central, Northeast, Southeast, Northwest, and Southwest, 311 charges, about 322 preachers, 109,671 members, property valued at $78,894,195, and $5,482,679 raised for all purposes during the year.

J. Atkinson, *Memorials in New Jersey.* 1860.
General Minutes, ME, TMC, UMC.
Minutes of the New Jersey and Southern New Jersey Conferences.
F. B. Stanger, *New Jersey.* 1961. FRANK BATEMAN STANGER

SOUTHGATE, THOMAS SUMMERVILLE (1868-1928), American financier and lay leader in the Southern Methodist Church, was born in Richmond, Va., in 1868, the son of Thomas M. and Mary E. (Portlock) Southgate. He established the T. S. Southgate and Company Wholesale Provisions at NORFOLK, Va., in 1892 and also became a prominent director in various important companies in VIRGINIA and over the South. He saw that Hampton Roads would be an important factor in the nation's commerce, and developed at that gateway a vast center of distribution of manufactured products to all southern markets. The business grew enormously. It was later incorporated as T. S. Southgate and Company and of this he was president until his death when it had become one of the largest of its kind in America.

He married Nettie Duncan Norsworthy of Norfolk on Oct. 6, 1891, and to them were born five children. T. S. Southgate was the first conference lay leader of the VIRGINIA CONFERENCE of the M.E. CHURCH, SOUTH, and one of the first to be aware of the possibilities of laymen as an organized force in the Methodist Church. He was known far and wide as an ardent supporter of missions and had great influence among the laymen in the Church. He was a member of the Norfolk City Council for eight years, a director of the Norfolk and Western Railway, and the vice-president of the American Commission to Europe in 1913 which was to study rural credits. Out of this Commission's report grew the present farm Loan Bank System.

Thomas Southgate was a life-long tither and was repeatedly elected president of the Southern Methodist LAYMEN'S ASSOCIATION. He was state chairman of the organization that raised $3,500,000 in Virginia for missions, and $1,250,000 for Christian education—an unusually large amount for that day. It was said of him, "Although multitudinous enterprises drew heavily upon his time and energy, he did not permit them to shut him out of a full life as a citizen nor as an alert and understanding participant in the larger affairs of the nation." He had a great interest in the peculiar economic and social problems of the Negro people of his state, and he worked and befriended that race helping in its development, "and by its individuals he was beloved." (*The National Cyclopaedia of American Biography*) Southgate died in Philadelphia, Pa., on Sept. 27, 1928.

National Cyclopaedia of American Biography.
Norfolk Ledger-Dispatch, Sept. 28, 1928.
Richmond Christian Advocate, May 26, 1932.
Who's Who in America, 1928-29.   N. B. H.

SOUTHLANDS TRAINING SCHOOL

SOUTHLANDS TRAINING COLLEGE, British teachers' training college for women, was founded by the Wesleyan (now Methodist) Education Committee in Battersea, London, in 1872 to train teachers to work first and foremost in the Methodist day schools. To it were transferred a small group of women students from WESTMINSTER COLLEGE—which has begun as a mixed college twenty years earlier. These formed the nucleus of the new college at a time when it was a most unusual thing for a woman to leave her home in order to train for a career of her own. The college grew in size and reputation for fifty years when the committee decided to move it to a more open site permitting further developments and offering better facilities for study and recreation.

The magnificent site on Wimbledon Parkside (formerly owned by the Royal House of France) was purchased, and the college was transferred to its present premises in 1929.

From 1949 to the present day it has been constantly enlarged, so that in ideal conditions and a rural setting six miles from the center of London, five hundred women students train for service in the secondary/modern and primary schools of England and go out to teach all over the world.

The religious life of the college is conducted in accordance with the tenets and usage of the Methodist Church directed by the principal and Methodist chaplain of the college. Daily worship is an integral part of the corporate life of the college, and special attention is given to the systematic instruction of the Bible and in the preparation of the students for giving Bible lessons.

Southlands today is a constituent college of the University of London Institute of Education, and its large tutorial staff are lecturers of the institute. It continues to be directed by its own governing body which is responsible to the Methodist Education Committee, and which owes many of its beautiful buildings to the generosity of Methodist benefactors both great and small.

M. S. JOHNSON

SOUTHWEST CONFERENCE began as a conference of the M. E. Church. It was organized at Muskogee, Okla., on Dec. 4, 1929 with Bishop CHARLES L. MEAD presiding. Its territory was ARKANSAS and OKLAHOMA, and it was formed by merging the LITTLE ROCK CONFERENCE with the Oklahoma part of the Lincoln Conference. At its beginning the Southwest Conference had four districts—Fort Smith, Hot Springs, Little Rock, and Oklahoma—eighty-eight charges, 7,156 members, and property valued at $608,766.

In 1848 the M. E. Church reentered MISSOURI, Arkansas, and the territory to the west. Following the Civil War the denomination had an Arkansas Conference composed of both white and Negro churches and ministers. In 1878 the Negro work of the Arkansas Conference was set off as the Little Rock Conference. The new conference began with two districts and twenty-nine charges. At the end of the first year it reported 1,443 members. In 1900 there were four districts and 4,502 members. At its last session in 1928 the Little Rock Conference reported three districts, seventy-one charges, 5,915 members, and property valued at $480,615.

In 1902 the M. E. Church organized the Okaneb Conference. It was formed by merging the Negro work of the Oklahoma Conference with the western part of the Central Missouri Conference, a Negro conference. The territory of the Okaneb Conference was Oklahoma, KANSAS, NEBRASKA, and western Missouri. The next year the name was changed to the Lincoln Conference. The Lincoln Conference began with two districts—Oklahoma and Topeka—forty-seven charges, 1,878 members, and property valued at $67,215. At its last session in 1928 it reported four districts, sixty-seven charges, 3,665 members, and property valued at $612,256. Some 1,250 of the members were in Oklahoma.

At unification in 1939 the Southwest Conference became a part of the CENTRAL JURISDICTION. It reported that year three districts—Fort Smith, Little Rock, and Oklahoma—eighty-one charges, 6,361 members, and property valued at $373,420. After the Second World War the number of church members in the conference steadily declined, particularly in Arkansas. The report of the district superintendents in 1967 declared that at one time the Little Rock District had strong rural churches with families that owned their homes and farmed their own land. But as time passed the older generation died, the people left the farms, and the churches had become only skeletons of what they had been in former days. The conference reported 4,853 members in 1953, a twenty-four per cent decline from the 1939 figure.

The Southwest Conference and its predecessor bodies have supported PHILANDER SMITH COLLEGE. Founded in 1877, Philander Smith has become a strong Methodist senior college. It has a plant valued at $3,000,000, an endowment of about $600,000, and an enrolment of more than 800.

On the abolition of the Central Jurisdiction in 1968, the Southwest Conference became a part of the Little Rock Area of the SOUTH CENTRAL JURISDICTION pending merger.

In 1970 the Southwest Conference reported two districts—Little Rock and Oklahoma—forty-one charges, about forty-three ministers, 3,095 members, and property valued at $1,363,279.

General Minutes, MEC and MC.
Minutes of the Southwest Conference.   ALBEA GODBOLD

SOUTHWEST KANSAS CONFERENCE (ME) was organized at Burlington, March 1, 1882 with Bishop H. W. WARREN presiding. It was formed by dividing the SOUTH KANSAS CONFERENCE and it included "all territory west of the east line of Cowley, Butler and Marion Counties and south of the north line of Marion, McPherson, Rice and Barton Counties and of this line continuing directly west to the west line of the state." This meant that the conference was comprised of approximately the west two-thirds of the south half of the state.

At its organization the conference had three districts— Wichita, Newton, and Larned—and fifty-two ministers, sixty-seven charges, and 6,370 members. During the first ten years there was rapid growth; in 1892 the conference had 129 charges and 19,166 members. Southwest Kansas was the first conference in the connection to require each candidate for admission to pledge that he would refrain from the use of tobacco.

The conference established a number of institutions. SOUTHWESTERN COLLEGE (called Southwest Kansas College until 1908) was founded at Winfield in 1885. Wesley Hospital was established at Hutchinson in 1912; it moved to Wichita in 1917. In 1915 Stewart Hospital at Hutchinson was acquired; its name was changed to Grace Hospital in 1922. In 1924 Epworth Hospital at Liberal was purchased for $50,000. The conference joined other conferences in the state in building a home for the aged at Topeka in 1904 and in launching a children's home at Newton in 1927.

At the time of unification in 1939, the Southwest Kansas Conference merged with the Northwest Kansas Conference to form the CENTRAL KANSAS CONFERENCE. The Southwest Conference brought to the merger 213 pastoral charges and 66,457 members.

Herbert, Barton and Ward, *Southwest Kansas Conference.* 1932.
D. W. Holter, *Fire on the Prairie.* 1969.
Minutes of the Southwest Kansas Conference.
FREDERICK E. MASER

SOUTHWEST MISSOURI CONFERENCE was organized at Lexington, Mo., Sept. 30, 1874 with Bishop JOHN C. KEENER presiding. It superseded the West St. Louis Conference which had been formed by dividing the ST. LOUIS CONFERENCE in 1870. The territory of these two conferences was the same, the southwest quarter of the state. At the end of its first year in 1871 the West St. Louis Conference reported six districts and 12,529 members.

In 1905 the Southwest Missouri Conference absorbed the WESTERN CONFERENCE which included all Southern Methodist work in Kansas, and designated it as the Western District. At the time there were nineteen charges and over 2,300 members in Kansas. After 1914 the Western District was abolished and the Kansas work was incorporated in the Kansas City District of the Southwest Missouri Conference.

The Southwest Missouri Conference grew steadily. In 1900 it had 31,780 members, and in 1939 it brought into The Methodist Church 125 charges and 41,516 members. In 1941 it had 65,918 members.

From its beginning the Southwest Missouri Conference joined the Missouri and St. Louis Conferences in supporting CENTRAL COLLEGE at Fayette. The Southwest Missouri Conference was also more or less affiliated with several other schools. In 1872 the Springfield District of the conference projected Morrisville Institute which continued under varying names and with tenuous conference affiliation as an academy or a college until 1924. Cottey College at Nevada began in 1884 and was under the auspices of the conference for a long period. In 1927 the institution was acquired by the P. E. O. SCARRITT COLLEGE, now in Nashville, Tenn., began as a Bible and Training School in KANSAS CITY in 1892 and was operated there until 1924.

The names of Bishop EUGENE R. HENDRIX and NATHAN SCARRITT are associated with the early history of the Southwest Missouri Conference. While never a member of the conference, Hendrix lived in Kansas City from 1886 till his death in 1927. Because of Scarritt's generosity when Scarritt College was founded, the school was named for him.

All of the Southwest Missouri Conference territory became a part of the MISSOURI WEST CONFERENCE in 1961. At its final session in 1961 the Southwest Missouri Conference had six districts, Joplin, Kansas City, Marshall, Nevada, Sedalia, and Springfield. It reported 251 charges, 405 churches, 93,878 members, and property valued at $25,988,328.

General Minutes, MECS and MC.
Minutes of the Southwest Missouri Conference.
F. C. Tucker, *Missouri*. 1966.   FREDERICK E. MASER

SOUTHWEST TEXAS CONFERENCE (MC) goes back to the Rio Grande Mission Conference created by the GENERAL CONFERENCE of 1858. The Mission Conference was organized at Goliad, Texas, Nov. 9, 1859 with JESSE BORING presiding in the absence of Bishop GEORGE F. PIERCE. It was formed by dividing the TEXAS CONFERENCE. At the beginning the Rio Grande Mission Conference included west, southwest, and a part of northwest TEXAS. This meant that it had within its bounds not only the territory of the present Southwest Texas Conference, but also parts of the territory of the present CENTRAL TEXAS, NORTHWEST TEXAS, and NEW MEXICO CONFERENCES.

In 1862 the Rio Grande Mission Conference was designated as the RIO GRANDE CONFERENCE. In 1866 the name was changed to the West Texas Conference, and on Oct. 17, 1939 at SAN ANTONIO, with Bishop A. FRANK SMITH presiding, the West Texas Conference became the Southwest Texas Conference of The Methodist Church.

The Rio Grande Mission Conference began with twenty-five charges, twelve preachers, and 1,257 white and 138 colored members. Among early conference leaders was "Fighting Parson" ANDREW JACKSON POTTER who organized more than a dozen churches. Others prominent in the early days were H. G. Horton who preached in the Indian territory around Uvalde, JOHN WESLEY DE VILBISS who delivered the first Protestant sermon in San Antonio in 1844, and organized a Methodist class there in June, 1846, and HOMER S. THRALL who later wrote *A Brief History of Methodism in Texas.* Among the twelve preachers at the beginning were three Germans, an indication of the strong German element in southwest Texas.

The first Methodist society in southwest Texas was organized at Bastrop in 1833 by James Gilleland, a layman. He conducted a service in an unfinished warehouse, using a barrel for a pulpit, and then formed the society with eleven charter members, one of whom was a Negro slave woman, Celia Craft. The next year DAVID AYERS organized the first SUNDAY SCHOOL in Texas at old San Patricion. Because he proved zealous in distributing Spanish New Testaments, Ayers was driven out of the colony by an irate priest.

In the early years the West Texas Conference established a number of academies and colleges. At one time or another the following towns and cities had a Methodist school or college: Rutersville, San Angelo, San Saba, Cherokee, Lampasas, Fredericksburg, Austin, Bastrop, San Marcos, Seguin, San Antonio, and Goliad. Some of the institutions failed during the Civil War; others gave way to an advancing state program of high school and college training. Rutersville College was one of the four that preceded SOUTHWESTERN UNIVERSITY at Georgetown, which now has the support of all the Texas conferences and which is the oldest Protestant college in Texas.

At its first session in 1859 the Rio Grande Mission Conference appointed Robert P. Thompson as a missionary to the Mexicans of the Rio Grande Valley. In 1874 the West Texas Conference set up the Mexican Border Mission District with six charges, and by 1881 there were two Mexican districts with 732 members. This work led to the formation of the Mexican Border Mission Conference in 1885. (See RIO GRANDE CONFERENCE.)

In 1874 the German work in Texas and LOUISIANA was organized as the German Mission Conference. In 1917 the name was changed to the Southwest Texas Conference, but the next year the conference was abolished and the German churches and ministers were received into the overlying English-speaking conferences. The merger brought about 1,300 members into the West Texas Conference. For the next three years the West Texas Conference maintained a separate district for the German churches.

The West Texas Conference came to unification in 1939 with eight districts, 179 pastoral charges, 64,958 members, and property valued at $5,409,396. As the Southwest Texas Conference of The Methodist Church, its membership increased eighty per cent between 1939 and 1968.

The Southwest Texas Conference has four retirement homes which can accommodate 700 guests: Hilltop Village at Kerrville, the Golden Age Home at Lockhart, Morningside Manor at San Antonio, and Wesley Manor at Weslaco. There are two hospitals: Knapp Memorial at Weslaco, and Southwest Texas Methodist at San Antonio. The conference maintains a Methodist Building at San Antonio, and the Methodist Kerrville Association, a recreational and educational camping facility at Kerrville. It joins the other Texas Conferences in supporting the Methodist Children's Home at Waco and the WESLEY FOUNDATIONS at the state institutions of higher learning. The conference contributed in 1968 for Methodist colleges, seminaries, and Wesley Foundations $187,473.

In 1970 the Southwest Texas Conference had six districts, 272 charges, 469 ministers, 114,971 members, and property valued at $57,348,400. The total amount raised for all purposes that year was $8,534,573.

R. F. Curl, Southwest Texas. 1951.
General Minutes, MES, TMC, UMC.
Minutes of the Southwest Texas Conference.
O. W. Nail, Texas Methodism. 1961.
M. Phelan, Methodism in Texas. 1924.   L. U. SPELLMAN

SOUTHWESTERN CHRISTIAN RECORDER. A publication of the African Methodist Episcopal Church. (See AFRICAN METHODIST EPISCOPAL CHURCH, Publications.)

SOUTHWESTERN COLLEGE, Winfield, Kansas, was founded by the M. E. Church as Southwest Kansas Conference College in 1885. The name was changed to the present one in 1908.

In 1950, Richardson Hall, the main building of the institution, was totally destroyed by fire. Previously North Hall, the original building, had been condemned by the state fire marshal. The loss of these two buildings precipitated a crisis in the life of the college. A special session of the Central Kansas Conference was called, and it was voted to proceed with a million-dollar building program on the campus at Winfield. This initiated a plan that has made it possible for the college to have a new and modern educational plant. It offers the B.A. and B.M. (Music) degrees. The governing board has thirty-five members, elected by the Central Kansas Annual Conference.

JOHN O. GROSS

SOUTHWESTERN UNIVERSITY, Georgetown, Texas, was chartered in 1840 as Rutersville College honoring MARTIN RUTER, the founder of the Methodist Church in Texas. News of the decisive battle of San Jacinto, which freed Texas from Mexico, was received while the General Conference was in session at Cincinnati, Ohio. Ruter, then president of ALLEGHENY COLLEGE, volunteered to go to Texas and must be considered a founder of that state along with Sam Houston and the Austins, Moses and Stephen.

Under the leadership of FRANCIS ASBURY MOOD, president of Soule University, the rights and assets of Ruterville College and those of three other Methodist colleges— Wesleyan, founded in 1844, McKenzie, 1848, and Soule University, 1856—were transferred to project a central university at Georgetown. This institution opened as Texas University in 1873, and in 1875 the name was changed to Southwestern University. Degrees offered are the B.A., B.S., B.S. in Education, B.M. (Music), B.S. in Business, B.F.A. (Fine Arts). The governing board has twenty-six members, plus four ex officio; nineteen elected by the annual conferences of TEXAS and NEW MEXICO, seven elected at large.

JOHN O. GROSS

SPAIN. It could well be said that Spanish Methodism began in GIBRALTAR, where, as happened in so many other places, British soldiers, here as early as 1792, began to hold services among themselves under the leadership of ANDREW ARMOUR, a Glasgow Scot who had been converted in a Wesleyan chapel in Ireland while on military service there. The Wesleyan METHODIST MISSIONARY SOCIETY took an early interest in this work, seeing Gibraltar as a possible *pied à terre* for an advance into the Iberian Peninsula, as well as into countries of the eastern Mediterranean region. The first missionaries sent fell early victims of yellow fever, but in 1832 WILLIAM H. RULE came to Gibraltar from service in Malta and St. Vincent, and soon began a determined effort to evangelize Spain, especially through the circulation of the Scriptures. Rule was a man of intellectual gifts above the average, full of energy and zeal, and of clear mind and determined will. He succeeded in initiating class meetings in Cadiz and tried to establish evangelical churches and schools in various places. His enthusiasm infected the Committee of the Society to the point of their coming to envisage Gibraltar as a potential nursery for Spanish work, not only in Spain itself but in Spanish America. This dream, however, did not materialize. Even so fearless a man as Rule, before the all-powerful Roman Church, was forced to retire from direct activity in Spain, and in 1839 this first chapter was brought to a close. Nevertheless, the pamphlets and booklets published by Rule, together with his collection of hymns and his Bible commentaries, have greatly helped many and various generations of Spanish evangelicals down the years. A larger work of his, a well documented study of the Inquisition, was probably also inspired by his experience at this time.

The continuing history of Spanish Methodism began some quarter of a century later, when in 1868 the September Revolution, led by General Prim, opened the doors of Spain to the preaching of the Gospel. The temporary breakdown of the monarchy, though not leading to the establishment of democratic government as many hoped, brought a greater measure of toleration, and the Wesleyan Missionary Society, in common with other evangelical churches, was quick to take advantage of this new opportunity. George Alton, then missionary in Gibraltar, sent a number of agents to work in Barcelona and the Balearic Islands, with the injunction, as he said to one, "to act as a good man and a Methodist among his friends, while pursuing his own (secular) calling." These colporteurs met with an encouraging response.

The first missionary to be sent from Britain directly to Spain was a layman, W. T. Brown, who had learned Spanish in order to work among Spanish sailors in the Port of London. He opened a school in Barcelona, and by 1876 there were three preaching places there, with an aggregate membership of twenty-three. Brown was later ordained in 1879, and served for a number of years after in the Balearic Islands. The first Methodist church in Spain, later moved to its present situation in the Calle de Tallers 26, Barcelona, was constituted in September of 1871, with a membership of ten. Soon the work was extended to various outskirts of Barcelona, churches and schools being set up in Pueblo Nuevo, Clot, Rubí, San Cugat, and in the Balearic Islands. In this latter place rapid progress was made, the membership there in 1876 reaching 118. The work in the Balearics has always remained relatively strong, down to the present day, when many tourists visit the churches there.

Among the missionaries who worked in Spain may be noted: Robert Simpson (1876-1889), marked by a saintliness which transfigured his human quality of friendship, and of whom Romanist and Protestant alike used to say "Don Roberto is a saint"; J. G. Wheatcroft Brown (1883-1896), who became Chairman of the District in succession to Simpson in 1889; Franklyn G. Smith (1884-1916), whose tenacity and sanguine activity secured the continued existence of the Church through highly critical periods, and whose thirty-two years of ministry, first in the Balearic Islands for eight years, and then in Barcelona, probably constituted the most significant missionary contribution made to Spanish Methodism; and J. W. Lord (1916-1924), and Samuel H. G. Saunders (1924-1933), these latter consolidating the extension work done by Franklyn G. Smith.

These missionaries were splendidly supported by various Spanish workers, among whom may be mentioned:

D. Esteban Cirera, who labored meritoriously in Minorca and Barcelona; D. Miguel Longas, former Roman Catholic Missionary in Africa, Chile and Spain, professor of philosophy at Tiers, and one of the most popular and eloquent of Spanish priests, who, from his conversion in 1899, to the time of his death in 1918, like the Apostle Paul, preached with great effect the faith of which he once made havoc; and Juan Bibiloni, first a colporteur and later a lay-pastor in Majorca. The first Spanish superintendent of the Mission was D. José Capo (1920-1953), who, with his two brothers, D. Juan and D. Samuel, carried the work forward. Each of these three brothers gave also a son to the ministry, D. Alfred, D. Humberto and D. Enrique respectively, the two latter now occupying important positions in the United Spanish Evangelical Church, of which D. Humberto is First Secretary.

Parallel with this activity there arose in other parts of Spain work which came under the auspices of the M. E. Church. The founder of this work was Pastor Francisco Albricias, a convert from Roman Catholicism, who had worked in Catalunia, and who, for health reasons, set up home in Alicante, where he began to hold evangelical meetings; in January of 1897 he opened a day school to which, not being able to use the name "Protestant," he gave the title of "Escuela Modelo" ("Model School"), which grew considerably from its beginnings in a tent, until it came to be housed in a large and handsome building. In 1919 realizing the need for greater material resources than those he could personally command, Albricias offered the school and church of Alicante, together with those in Seville, to the M.E. Church, which in 1920 organized its SPANISH METHODIST MISSION.

The onward march of the Methodist Missions in Spain was interrupted by the Revolution of 1936 and the Civil War which lasted until 1939. The principal workers, both in the British related work in Catalunia, as in the Andulacian churches of the M. E. Church, had to flee the country, and from 1939 on the churches were closed, surviving only in private houses, where meetings continued to be held. Thus, clandestinely, the Church survived. It was not until 1945, with the publication of the "Fuero (Constitution) de los Españoles" which permitted Protestants to hold worship services "provided they are held within buildings and with no public manifestations," that the churches could begin to reorganize themselves. The churches of the Spanish Episcopal Methodist Mission had suffered very great damage, and what was left of them was integrated in the Spanish Evangelical Church, which for a long time had been a kind of Federation linking the different Missions which were working in Spain, and which from 1945 onwards began to emerge as an embryonic national church made up of the various Missions.

The Catalunian Methodists in 1945 reorganized their churches and their circuits, with the help of George Bell (1948-1955), of the Methodist Missionary Society of Great Britain, and in 1955 the Mission was integrated into the new Evangelical Church of Spain ("Iglesia Evangelica Española"), made up of Lutheran, Reformed and Methodist elements, and of whose total membership Methodists represented about a quarter part. In 1969 this Church continued to progress, and owed much to the Methodist contribution which it received a decade and a half ago.

ALBERT ASPEY

AUGUST G. SPANGENBERG

SPANGENBERG, AUGUST GOTTLIEB (1704-1792), MORAVIAN, was born at Klettenberg on July 15, 1704, the son of a Lutheran pastor. He was influenced by Count NICOLAUS ZINZENDORF and the Moravians and became deeply interested in missionary work. Spangenberg was much impressed by the Moravian settlement at Herrnhut, declined a chair of theology at Halle University, and became a Moravian. John Wesley was convinced of his lack of faith by Spangenberg, who shared with PETER BÖHLER the honor of bringing the two Wesley brothers to their historic experience in 1738. Spangenberg organized Moravian missionary work in England, and set up headquarters at Lightcliffe in 1742, a few months later organizing the first London Moravian congregation at FETTER LANE. He died at Berthelsdorf in September, 1792.

C. W. TOWLSON

SPANN, JOHN RICHARD (1891-   ), American pastor, theological teacher and secretary of the Commission of Ministerial Education of The Methodist Church, was born near Valley View, Tex., Oct. 2, 1891, the son of Frank White and Mary Ussery Spann. He received the A.B. degree from RANDOLPH-MACON COLLEGE, 1915, the D.D. in 1932; the M.A. from SOUTHERN METHODIST UNIVERSITY, 1916; the B.D. from DREW UNIVERSITY SCHOOL OF THEOLOGY, 1918; he did post graduate work for a year at Union Theological Seminary and Columbia University, before becoming a navy chaplain in June of 1918. He served in that capacity until the end of the war. On July 12, 1918, he married Julia Mouzon (deceased Oct. 31, 1932). The Rev. Edwin Spann of the VIRGINIA CONFERENCE is their son. June 4, 1949 he married Cecile Clark (deceased Oct. 13, 1963).

Dr. Spann served a number of churches in TEXAS and MISSOURI before becoming a teacher in the School of Theology of Southern Methodist University, 1923-27. He later became the pastor of other churches in Texas and LOUISIANA, including First Church, BATON ROUGE, La., 1933-41, and Laurel Heights Church, SAN ANTONIO, Tex., 1941-46. Following a year of service on the San Antonio District he was elected to the Secretaryship of the Com-

mission on Ministerial Training of The Methodist Church, with headquarters in NASHVILLE, Tenn. Here he united and expanded the correspondence work and the short term training schools for pastors. He also helped in the unification of ministerial education of the ministers under the Board of EDUCATION. He retired in 1961.

N. B. H.

SPARKS, W. MAYNARD (1906-   ), American E.U.B. bishop, was born in Rockwood, Pa., Dec. 16, 1906, a son of the Rev. and Mrs. George A. Sparks. He was graduated from LEBANON VALLEY COLLEGE in 1927; from UNITED THEOLOGICAL SEMINARY in 1930; and from University of Pittsburgh in 1936.

He was licensed as a Quarterly Conference minister, Nov. 1, 1919; granted license by ALLEGHENY CONFERENCE, CHURCH OF UNITED BRETHREN IN CHRIST, 1923; and ordained in the same conference by Bishop GRANT D. BATDORF, 1930.

On Oct. 27, 1931 he was married to Blanche M. Frank, and they have three sons.

Following sixteen years of pastoral service in western PENNSYLVANIA, Dr. Sparks was elected Superintendent of Allegheny Conference of The E.U.B. Church, 1946-50. In 1950 he was elected to the faculty of Lebanon Valley College to serve as Assistant Professor of Religion. In 1953 he assumed the office of Chaplain in addition to his teaching duties. In 1958 he was elected a bishop of The E.U.B. Church and assigned to the Western Area with residence in SACRAMENTO, Calif. At the GENERAL CONFERENCES of 1954 and 1958 he served as Recording Secretary. In 1963 and 1967 he was a co-editor of the *Book of Discipline*. In The United Methodist Church Bishop Sparks was assigned to the SEATTLE Area.

Overseas assignments were as follows: SIERRA LEONE, West Africa, 1961 and 1967; GERMANY and SWITZERLAND, 1965; BRAZIL, 1967.

Beginning with the 1954-58 quadrennium he was a member of the COMMISSION ON CHURCH UNION, which in cooperation with a similar Commission from The Methodist Church formed a PLAN OF UNION that made possible the advent of The United Methodist Church, Dallas, Tex., April 23, 1968. The Seattle Area over which he presides comprises the CALIFORNIA, NORTHWEST CANADA, and PACIFIC NORTHWEST CONFERENCES formerly of the E.U.B. CHURCH and the PACIFIC NORTHWEST CONFERENCE of the former Methodist Church.

J. S. Fulton, *History of the Allegheny Conference*. Otterbein Press, 1931.
Minutes of the Western Pennsylvania Conference, EUB, 1966.
United Seminary *Bulletin*, January 1959.   A. BYRON FULTON

SPARLING, JOSEPH WALTER (1843-1912), Canadian minister and educationist, was born at Blanshard, Perth County, Ontario, on Feb. 14, 1843, the son of John and Mary (Williams) Sparling. He was educated at St. Mary's High School, VICTORIA UNIVERSITY, and NORTHWESTERN UNIVERSITY. Ordained in the Methodist ministry in 1871, he served various charges in Ontario from 1874 to 1883. In 1888 he was elected President of the Montreal Conference.

In 1889 he assumed the principalship of WESLEY COLLEGE in WINNIPEG. By 1906 he had a permanent staff of six professors; had removed the mortgage indebtedness, and had established a small endowment fund. A crowning achievement was the opening of Sparling Hall, a ladies' residence, in 1912. He died in Winnipeg on June 16, 1912.

Sparling was a genial and lovable person, who had a remarkable talent for raising and utilizing money effectively. He was recognized as a major figure in his conference and in Canadian Methodism as a whole. He used his gifts for the benefit of Manitoba and his church.

R. S. Cummings, "History of Wesley College." Ms., 1938.
J. H. Riddell, *Middle West.* 1946.
W. S. Wallace, ed., *Macmillan Dictionary of Canadian Biography.* London: Macmillan, 1963.   F. W. Armstrong

SPARTANBURG JUNIOR COLLEGE, Spartanburg, S. C.,

began as the Textile Industrial Institute in 1911. Its founder was David English Camak, who started with one pupil and $100. The institution was founded to serve persons in the textile industry, and for many years its educational offerings were limited to elementary and secondary education for both adults and children. In 1927 it became a junior college with special emphasis upon combining part-time employment with academic work.

At the time of union of the three branches of Methodism, the college became the property of the Board of Missions of The Methodist Church. It is now operated jointly by this board and the South Carolina Conference. R. B. Burgess served as president from 1923 to 1962. In 1942 the present name was assumed. The governing board has twenty-three members: fifteen elected by the South Carolina Annual Conference, six by the Division of National Missions, and the general director and the treasurer of the Division of National Missions.

John O. Gross

SPAUGY, L. DORSEY. (See Judicial Council.)

SPAULDING, JUSTIN (1802-1865), American preacher

and pioneer missionary to Brazil, was born in Vermont in 1802, and was received on trial in the New England Conference in 1825. He was pastor in Augusta, Maine, when Fountain E. Pitts appealed to the Missionary Society of the church for a permanent missionary in Rio de Janeiro. Bishop Elijah Hedding appointed Spaulding to Rio de Janeiro to initiate what became known in Brazil as the "Spaulding-Kidder Mission." With a wife and a "domestic," he sailed from New York on March 23, 1836. Arriving April 29, he began to room with a German Lutheran family, and that same night preached to some thirty or forty persons—"a small society of pious persons" —which Pitts had organized while in Rio.

In June he moved to larger quarters where he could house a congregation and start a Sunday school. In July 1836, urged by the English-speaking people in Rio, he opened a school for their children. He also distributed Bibles and thousands of tracts in English and Portuguese. In answer to his appeals for help, Daniel P. Kidder was sent out as an evangelistic missionary, R. J. McMurdy as a local preacher, and Marcella Russell as teacher for the school. They sailed from Boston on Nov. 12, 1837. The last two mentioned married soon after arrival.

A series of unfortunate circumstances brought about the closing of the mission. The discouraged McMurdys left very soon. Then on April 16, 1840, Kidder's wife, only twenty-two, died and was buried in the British Gambôa

Cemetery, where a large tombstone still marks her grave. Kidder, left with two infant children, returned to the States before the end of the year. Only Justin Spaulding remained.

The financial straits of the infant Missionary Society, however, and the conviction that religious liberty was too precarious in Brazil, as there had been so much persecution, led the home Society to recall Spaulding at the end of 1841. One of the members of his congregation, a Mrs. Martha Walker, lived long enough to constitute a continuing link with the Methodism of later years, when J. J. Ransom arrived and organized a church. At home Justin Spaulding transferred to the New Hampshire Conference.

J. L. Kennedy, *Metodismo no Brasil.* 1928.   D. A. Reily

SPAULDING, WESLEY J. (1828-1909), American minister

and educator, was born in Newark, N. Y., on April 18, 1828, but moved to La Grange County, Ind., where his father was a businessman and banker. He was graduated from Indiana Asbury (DePauw) in 1854 and later received an M.A. and an honorary Ph.D.

Admitted to the Indiana Annual Conference of the M.E. Church, he transferred to the Iowa Annual Conference in 1855 to become Professor of Latin and Greek at Iowa Wesleyan University, an institution to which he would devote most of his life. In 1860-61 he was stationed at Ottumwa, Iowa, but returned to the University as vice president and acting president 1861-63. He was assigned in Indiana for one year at Mount Vernon but then accepted a retired relationship because of ill health 1865-69 when he acted as superintendent of schools in Sturgis, Mich. Returning to Iowa in 1870, he served churches in Wapello, Keosauqua, Washington and Fairfield. In 1875 he became vice president of Iowa Wesleyan and was president in 1876.

Spaulding initiated important curricular revisions, expanded the Normal Program and in 1877 effected the affiliation of the University with the Iowa Conservatory of Music which under its founder, Alexander Rommel, made Iowa Wesleyan an effective leader in music education throughout the area.

In 1884 Spaulding resigned the presidency to accept a retired relationship in the Iowa Annual Conference. He continued to reside in Mount Pleasant as an active supply preacher, giving much time to civic and banking affairs.

Spaulding was granted an honorary Litt.D. by Iowa Wesleyan in 1905. His wife, Martha Berry Spaulding, who received an honorary M.A. in 1867, taught occasionally at Iowa Wesleyan. He moved to Denver, Colo., in 1907 and died there on Feb. 22, 1909.

Louis A. Haselmayer, *The Presidents of Iowa Wesleyan.* Mount Pleasant, 1968.
Iowa Wesleyan Archives.
Minutes of the Iowa Annual Conferences.
Louis A. Haselmayer

SPAYTH, HENRY G. (1788-1873), German-born American

United Brethren itinerant preacher and church historian, was born in Wurtenberg, Germany. He was brought to America by his parents at the age of three. His first work as a minister in the Church of the United Brethren in Christ was serving as an itinerant preacher in 1812 in the Original Conference in Maryland and Virginia.

Later he moved to Mount Pleasant, Pa., where he both taught school and preached.

He located in OHIO and became presiding elder in the Muskingum Conference during its early years. Then in 1835 he joined the Sandusky Conference, when it was formed, and resided at Tiffin, Ohio for the remainder of his life.

The GENERAL CONFERENCE of 1845 appointed him chairman of a committee to revise the church hymnbook which was published in 1848. The same General Conference requested him to write a denominational history which he did jointly with WILLIAM HANBY, published in 1851. Much of that history was gleaned from personal interviews with early church leaders or the experiences of the two writers.

He died at his home, Sept. 2, 1873. His body was placed to rest in the family vault in the Tiffin Cemetery near the main entrance.

A. W. Drury, *History of the U.B.* 1924.
Eberly, Albright and Brane, *History of the U. B. Church.* 1911.
Religious Telescope, Sept. 10, 1873. C. DAVID WRIGHT

SPEARE, ALDEN (1825-1902), American layman, businessman, and philanthropist, was born in Chelsea, Vt. Both his father and grandfather were physicians. His formal education was received in the public schools and in the Newbury Seminary.

Speare moved to BOSTON when he was nineteen and began his business career as a clerk in a drygoods store. Seven years later he established the "Alden Speare & Sons Co.," a firm dealing in oil and laundry supplies. He became one of the leading businessmen of Boston, a charter member and president of the Boston Chamber of Commerce, president of the Associated Boards of Trade, vice-president of the Merchants Association, incorporator and president of Penny Savings Bank, director of the Atchison, Topeka & Santa Fe Railroad, and a director of seven other railroads.

Speare was a life-long member of the M.E. Church, which he generously supported. As his wealth increased his liberality grew until he was giving forty percent and finally nearly all his income. He lived in Newton, a suburb of Boston, and was the chief force in building the Newton Center Methodist Church. He had many philanthropic and civic interests, Newton Library, Mayor of Boston among them, but his deepest interest, after his Church, was BOSTON UNIVERSITY. He was a trustee of the University and supported it so generously that the Corporation made him an Associate Founder.

DANIEL L. MARSH

SPEED, FANNY HENNING (1820-1902), was born on Sept. 12, 1820, in Jefferson County, Ky., near LOUISVILLE. Originally from VIRGINIA, the Hennings were wealthy and of high social standing. Fanny Henning attended the academy at Science Hill.

When twenty-two years of age, Miss Henning married Joshua Speed, an intimate personal friend of Abraham Lincoln. Lincoln visited their home in Louisville, and on many matters Speed served as an advisor to the future President. He was offered a place in Lincoln's cabinet but declined. His brother, James, accepted in his stead.

In early life Mrs. Speed became a Christian. Her parents were Virginia Episcopalians. But when she became old enough to choose for herself, she united with the M.E. Church, South. When the M. E. Church was organized in Louisville in 1865, she became a member of the new society. A few years later when the church secured its permanent home at Third and Guthrie Streets, the name "Trinity," which she proposed, was accepted.

Mrs. Speed's interests were not limited to Trinity. The KENTUCKY CONFERENCE, struggling with poverty and the peculiar problems growing out of its location, was heartened and helped by her. Her biographers called her the "LADY HUNTINGDON of American Methodism." Certainly she was to the preachers of the Kentucky Conference all that the early friend of WHITEFIELD and the WESLEYS was to them.

Mrs. Speed was generous in her support of all the general benevolences of Methodism. Her special interests, however, centered around the Kentucky mountain districts and Negroes. To help the former, she was chiefly instrumental in founding UNION COLLEGE at Barbourville, Ky. To help the Negroes, she gave freely to the industrial and educational schools of the FREEDMEN'S AID SOCIETY.

Fanny Henning Speed died in Louisville, Ky., Aug. 10, 1902.

JOHN O. GROSS

SPEIGHT, JOHN F. (1804-1860), American M.P. minister and official, was born on Nov. 18, 1804, in Greene County, N.C. On Sept. 29, 1840, he married Emma Lewis, daughter of Exum Lewis of Mount Prospect, N. C.

Speight entered the NORTH CAROLINA CONFERENCE of the M.P. CHURCH as an itinerant preacher in March 1831, and was made Superintendent of the Roanoke Circuit. For his ministerial labors that year he received $70.80. In addition to the Roanoke Circuit, Speight also served the Guilford, Orange, Granville, Albemarle, and Tar River Circuits and the Tabernacle Mission. In November 1850 he was made the Superintendent of the newly-formed Halifax Circuit. He served as secretary of the North Carolina Conference in 1838 and 1839, and was president in 1851, 1855 and 1859. He was a delegate to the GENERAL CONFERENCES of 1854 and 1858. In 1854 he was appointed to serve as agent to solicit funds for MADISON COLLEGE in Pennsylvania. Later he took an active part in organizing JAMESTOWN FEMALE COLLEGE and was elected one of its trustees. In 1859 he was made general agent for the college. His pledge of $400 was the largest individual gift made to the ill-fated college.

Speight died on June 29, 1860. His widow gave the land on which in 1877 was built Speight's Chapel, named in his honor. This church, located between Whitakers and Tarboro, N. C., was dedicated by WILLIAM H. WILLS. After being closed for some years, Speight's Chapel was reopened in May 1956, and now has an active congregation of 110 members.

J. Elwood Carroll, *History of the North Carolina Conference* (MP). Greensboro, 1939.
Journals of the North Carolina Conference, MP.
Our Church Record, June 23, Sept. 29, 1898.
RALPH HARDEE RIVES

SPELLMEYER, HENRY (1847-1910), American bishop, was born in New York City. After graduating from New York University, he pursued theological studies at Union Theological Seminary, and entered the NEWARK CON-

FERENCE in 1869, being ordained DEACON in 1871. Serving this Conference with distinction during his entire ministry of thirty-five years, his pastorates included St. James, Elizabeth; Calvary, East Orange; and Central, Roseville and Centenary of NEWARK.

In 1896 he was elected to GENERAL CONFERENCE and was placed on the BOOK CONCERN committee and also on the BOOK COMMITTEE. He became a member of the Committee on the Entertainment of the General Conference, and was made its first chairman. The 1900 General Conference continued him in these offices. The General Conference of 1904 gave him 612 votes out of 691 to elect him bishop with the largest vote ever cast, up to that time, for that high office.

Bishop Spellmeyer died March 14, 1910, and was buried in Evergreen Cemetery, Elizabeth, after services held in Centenary Church, Newark, N. J.

FREDERICK G. HUBACH

SPENCE, ROBERT (1748-1824), British Methodist bookseller and publisher was born March 8, 1748, at Stillington near YORK. Spence's blacksmith father died when he was a child, and he was educated at a dame school in the village and by a curate supplied by the absentee incumbent, the famous Laurence Sterne. At thirteen Spence went into service as a postilion in a local family, who greatly resented his serious ways after joining the Methodists in 1763. His brother John was a Methodist LOCAL PREACHER in York, and managed to secure his apprenticeship to a bookbinder at Pontefrace, whence he returned to York and launched his own business—a secondhand bookstall in the Thursday Market. Later he removed to a small shop on the old Ouse Bridge, and then to a larger building in High Ousegate. It was from this latter address that he ventured into the publishing business, printing many books and pamphlets for Methodists.

Spence's *Collection of Hymns from Various Authors,* published in 1781, borrowed so heavily from Wesley's much larger and much more famous *Collection* issued the previous year that he encountered severe criticism, and for a time pondered leaving the Methodists. He decided against it, saying: "The loss of Robert Spence will be of no consequence to them whatever; they can do better without me than I can without them." Eventually the tables were somewhat turned, however, for his shilling hymn book, subsequently entitled *A Pocket Hymn Book, designed as a constant companion for the pious,* caused Wesley in his turn to issue a *Pocket Hymn Book* in 1784, and another in 1785, which went through many editions. Spence's *Pocket Hymn Book* seems to have outsold Wesley's, and became the standard work in the U.S.A., where it went through at least sixteen editions before 1899. This was probably due largely to the advocacy of THOMAS COKE. Spence's *Pocket Hymn Book,* in fact, was the chief ancestor of the American *Methodist Hymnal.* Nevertheless Robert Spence retained a genuine love for Wesley's *Collection,* as for Wesley himself and the Methodists in general. At his death in York on Aug. 4, 1824 he had been a member of the Methodist society for sixty-three years and a local preacher for fifty-seven.

Frank Baker, *Union Catalogue of the Publications of John and Charles Wesley,* Durham, N. C., 1966, item 396.
Richard Burdekin, *Memoirs of the Life and Character of Mr. Robert Spence, of York,* York, 1827.
R. G. McCutchan, *Our Hymnody,* 1937.   FRANK BAKER

SPENCE, WILLIAM H. (1875-1935), American minister, central figure of the book, *One Foot in Heaven,* was born in Huron County, Ontario, Canada, April 4, 1875. He was licensed to preach in the Canadian Methodist Church in 1899. He graduated from the University of Toronto in 1904, married Hope M. Morris of Stratford, Ontario, and moved the same year to the United States, where he joined the NORTHWEST IOWA CONFERENCE. After pastorates at Lake Mills and Clarion in IOWA he was appointed in 1909 to Fort Dodge, where a large new church was built and many of the incidents recounted in *One Foot In Heaven* occurred.

In 1917 he served a year at Hanscom Park Church, OMAHA, Neb., in the NEBRASKA CONFERENCE, later returned to Northwest Iowa Conference for two years at Grace Church, Sioux City, Iowa, and in 1920 transferred to the COLORADO CONFERENCE to Park Hill Church, DENVER, Colo. In 1923 he served at Burlington in the IOWA CONFERENCE. His last charge was Mason City, Iowa, in the UPPER IOWA CONFERENCE, where he served from 1929 to 1935. He retired for health reasons in 1935 and died December 1 of that year. He is buried at Mason City.

In 1916 he was named a member of the General Board of EPWORTH LEAGUE and was one of the founders of the Epworth League Institute at Lake Okoboji in Iowa, serving as its dean for three years. He was a member of the GENERAL CONFERENCE in 1916 and 1928.

In 1940 his son, Hartzell, published the book, *One Foot In Heaven.* It is in general his father's biography. The book was widely read and was made into a motion picture which was viewed by millions of people.

Minutes of the Upper Iowa Conference, 1936.

FRANK G. BEAN

SPENCER, HARRY CHADWICK (1905-   ), American minister, was born April 10, 1905 in Chicago, Ill., to John Carroll and Jessie Grace (Chadwick) Spencer. He attended Albany College, 1921-22, and received his B.A. degree from WILLAMETTE UNIVERSITY, 1925. The same school honored him with the D.D. degree in 1935. He studied at University of Chicago Divinity School, 1926-28 and received the B.D. degree from GARRETT BIBLICAL INSTITUTE, 1929. Harvard University conferred an M.A. degree, 1931. He was married to Mary Louise Wakefield, May 26, 1935.

Dr. Spencer was ordained by ROCK RIVER CONFERENCE as DEACON, 1931, and ELDER, 1933. He served for two years each at Washington Heights and Portage Park Churches, CHICAGO, before becoming Recording Secretary to the Board of Missions, 1935-40. He was Assistant Executive Secretary, BOARD OF MISSIONS, 1940-45 and Secretary, Department of Visual Education of the Board, 1945-52. Since 1952 he has been the executive leader of the TELEVISION, RADIO AND FILM COMMISSION (TRAFCO).

In his professional service Dr. Spencer served one year as president, COUNCIL OF SECRETARIES, The Methodist Church; chairman of RAVEMCO (Radio, Visual Education and Mass Communication Committee), Division of Foreign Missions, NATIONAL COUNCIL OF CHURCHES, 1948-53; chairman, Broadcast and Film Commission, National Council, 1961-63; chairman, World Association for Christian Broadcasting, 1961-63; and representative of RAVEMCO to Asia Conference on Mass Communication, Bangkok, 1955, and TOKYO, 1958. Dr. Spencer has written many magazine articles on mass communications, produced a large number of motion pictures, television and radio series, and was the author of a mission study book on Latin America.

Who's Who in America, 1970-71.
Who's Who in The Methodist Church, 1966.

JOHN H. NESS, JR.

SPENCER, PETER (ca. 1779-1843), American Negro and founder of the AFRICAN UNION METHODIST PROTESTANT CHURCH, was born about 1779 in Kent County, Md., living his early life as a slave. Upon the death of his master he moved to WILMINGTON, Del., where he became a member of Asbury M.E. Church.

In 1805 Peter Spencer led a number of Negroes out of Asbury M.E. Church who requested permission to build a church of their own. The Asbury trustees granted this wish and Spencer began to hold outdoor meetings with his small group. Later a house was used for their services. In 1812 they erected their first church edifice, Ezion M.E. Church. In 1813 Spencer and about fifty Negroes formally withdrew from the M.E. Church and established their own denomination which they called The Union Church of Africans. This never became a denomination, but it did eventually establish churches and elementary schools in several eastern states and Canada. In 1816 Spencer and other leaders accepted RICHARD ALLEN's invitation to attend the organization convention of the AFRICAN METHODIST EPISCOPAL CHURCH in PHILADELPHIA but never united with Allen's group. Little else is known about the personal life of Spencer. In 1865 a schism occurred in the First Colored Methodist Protestant Church at BALTIMORE, MD. A large group from this body united with the Union Church of Africans which in 1866 changed its name to African Union First Colored Methodist Protestant Church. Later this designation was changed to the African Union Methodist Protestant Church (AUMP).

D. J. Russell, *History of the African Union Methodist Protestant Church.* Philadelphia: Union Star Book and Job Printing and Publishing House, 1920. GRANT S. SHOCKLEY

SPENCER, WILLIAM ANSON (1840-1901), American minister, was born Sept. 6, 1840, at Rock Island, Ill., the son of Judge and Mrs. J. W. Spencer. Spencer was educated at Rock River Seminary and NORTHWESTERN UNIVERSITY where he graduated in 1861, later becoming a Trustee of the University. He enlisted in the Eighth Illinois Cavalry in September 1861 and served as chaplain 1863-65. He graduated from Garrett Biblical Institute (now GARRETT THEOLOGICAL SEMINARY) in 1867, entered CENTRAL ILLINOIS CONFERENCE, served the Camden Mills Circuit, Hale Chapel, and Moline, transferred to ROCK RIVER CONFERENCE, and became pastor at State Street Church and later First Church in CHICAGO.

He toured the world and the Far East missions with Bishop WILLIAM L. HARRIS in 1873-74. In 1881 he became presiding elder of the Dixon District, and in 1885 assistant secretary of the CHURCH EXTENSION SOCIETY. In this capacity he traveled widely, was especially concerned with the development of work in the Northwest and solicited $250 in gifts with which to start churches on the frontier. He became ill at the ERIE CONFERENCE in 1901, developed pneumonia a few days later at his home in PHILADELPHIA, and died Sept. 25, 1901. His

wife, four sons, and a daughter, Miss Clarissa Spencer, a missionary in JAPAN, survived him. He was the author of the song "Harvest Time," and was renowned for his singing and evangelistic preaching.

Minutes of the Rock River Conference, 1901.

ROBERTA BAUR WEST

SPIVEY, LUDD MYRL (1886-1962), American educator, was born at Eclectic, Ala., on Dec. 5, 1886, and was educated at Epworth University in Oklahoma, VANDERBILT UNIVERSITY, and the University of Chicago. He received the LL.D. degree from BIRMINGHAM-SOUTHERN COLLEGE and Miami University, Ed.D. from Stetson University, and Doctor of Humanities from Philathea College in Canada. He was a member of six scholastic fraternities.

He entered the ministry of the M.E. Church, South, in 1912 and joined the ST. LOUIS CONFERENCE, serving pastorates at Valley Park, Mo., and Scruggs Memorial and Grand Avenue Churches in St. Louis.

In 1922 Spivey became Dean and Professor of Sociology at Birmingham-Southern College. In 1925 he was elected President of FLORIDA SOUTHERN COLLEGE at Lakeland, Fla., where he remained for thirty-two years. At the beginning of his administration, the institution had only two buildings and 200 students and an indebtedness of about half a million dollars. Spivey paid the debt, erected a dozen new buildings, and increased the enrollment to 2,000 students. When he retired the college gave him a home at Palm Beach and a liberal pension.

Spivey died in the Good Samaritan Hospital at West Palm Beach on Dec. 27, 1962. His funeral was conducted in the chapel he had erected at Florida Southern College and he was buried in Oak Hill Cemetery at Lakeland.

He traveled widely in Europe and elsewhere, and was nationally known as an educator and financial administrator for the institution he served.

Who's Who in America.
Who's Who in Methodism, 1952. ELMER T. CLARK

SPOKANE, WASHINGTON, U.S.A. The first preaching service in the small village of Spokane Falls was held by S. H. Havermale, presiding elder of the Walla Walla District in 1875. Havermale was on his way to Colville, WASHINGTON Territory, to establish a church there. On returning to Spokane Falls a year later, he again held preaching services and appointed J. H. Laird, who organized the first Methodist Church in 1878 with a charter membership of ten. This was eleven years before Washington became a state.

The Congregational Church had organized six months prior to Laird's coming. Over the years, Spokane Methodism has grown until now there are ten churches in this city of 170,000 people.

Spokane Methodism has always been active in institutional life. The largest concentration of Methodist related institutions in the Pacific Northwest is found within the city. The Spokane Deaconess Hospital, a multi-million dollar institution, was established in 1892 and is now in its seventy-fifth year of service. In 1939 Spokane Goodwill Industries was organized under Methodist auspices. Today its net worth is one third of a million dollars with employees numbering 160—all but six of whom were handicapped when they came. Its annual pay roll is $360,000.

Spokane Methodist Homes, Inc. opened Rockwood Manor, a retirement home for the elderly, on Nov. 1, 1960 with space for 250 residents. This is one of the best operated retirement homes on the west coast.

District youth camp, Twinlow, received its initial impetus from Spokane pastors in the early 1930's and is now one of the youth centers in the PACIFIC NORTHWEST ANNUAL CONFERENCE.

The present day Central Church, successor to First Church, is closest to the mid-city of any Protestant congregation. It has taken the leadership in bringing together other Protestant congregations and the Roman Catholics in an organization, "Mid City Concerns," to help solve the core-area problems of the city.

A new building was recently completed by this church and will be used extensively by the congregation and the new organization.

General Minutes, UMC.

SPOTTSWOOD, STEPHEN GILL (1897-   ), American bishop in the A.M.E. ZION CHURCH, was born July 18, 1897 to Abraham Lincoln and Mary Elizabeth (Gray) Spottswood. A graduate of ALBRIGHT COLLEGE and Gordon Divinity School, Massachusetts, he did graduate work at Yale University. He married Viola Estelle Booker (deceased), and is the father of five children. He spent thirty-four years in the pastorate, serving the following points: PORTLAND, MAINE; West Newton and Lowell, Mass.; NEW HAVEN, Conn.; INDIANAPOLIS, Ind. (Jones Tabernacle); WINSTON SALEM, N.C. (Goler Memorial); St. Luke, BUFFALO, N. Y., and John Wesley Church, WASHINGTON, D.C. He has been closely identified with the National Association for the Advancement of Colored People and the WORLD METHODIST COUNCIL. He serves as Chairman of the Board of Finance of the denomination and is a Trustee of LIVINGSTONE COLLEGE, SALISBURY, N. C. Bishop Spottswood was elected and consecrated a bishop in May 1952.

DAVID H. BRADLEY

SPRAGUE, LEVI L. (1844-1936), American preacher and educator, was born at Beekman, N. Y., on Dec. 23, 1844. His father, Nelson Sprague, a carpenter and "joiner," after practicing his trade in various places, finally settled on a farm near LeRaysville, Pa. Because of his family's frequent moves, much of Levi's early education was under private teachers. At LeRaysville, when he was fourteen years of age, he studied for three years in a private academy of which Chester P. Hodge was the principal.

After two years of teaching in the ungraded public schools, he entered Eastman College of business at Poughkeepsie, N. Y. On graduating from Eastman he came to WYOMING SEMINARY, Kingston, Pa., as a teacher in the business department and in 1867 was made head of the department. At this time he was interested in the legal profession, and in his extracurricular time he studied law in the office of a prominent law firm. However, under the influence of REUBEN NELSON and David Copeland, presidents of Wyoming Seminary, he began the study of theology and in 1876 was admitted to the WYOMING CONFERENCE. On Dec. 22, 1869 he was married to Jennie Russell, an art teacher at Wyoming and niece of Mrs. Nelson.

After fifteen years as head of the business department of Wyoming Seminary, he was elected in 1882 as president of Wyoming Seminary, which position he held for fifty-four years. His death terminated seventy-one years of uninterrupted service to this school.

L. E. Bugbee, *Wyoming Conference*. 1952.
Minutes of the Wyoming Conference.   WILBUR H. FLECK

SPRENG, MINERVA STRAWMAN (1863-1924), American missionary leader, was born Minerva Strawman, near Lindsey, Ohio, March 10, 1863, the daughter of the Rev. and Mrs. Daniel Strawman.

In early girlhood she heard the call to missionary service through her church, the EVANGELICAL ASSOCIATION, and its importance never wavered for her to the end of her life. Her father encouraged her interest in missions from the very beginning and guided her with his kindly and wise direction. Her marriage to E. M. Spreng lasted only nineteen months, when he died suddenly in 1887.

In 1892 she was elected president of the Woman's Missionary Society of the Evangelical Association, an office which she held for thirty-two years. This organization was her very life and nothing was too hard for her to attempt. Its very inception in 1884 can be traced to a letter in 1880 which she and two others prepared which was signed by fifty petitioners requesting permission of the Board of MISSIONS to organize women's missionary societies.

She had a deep concern for the training of the children of the Church and gave strong support to the Mission Band, an auxiliary organization for the children. She was a missionary statesman, a good administrator, a valuable member of the Board of Missions, and a world Christian. Death came April 5, 1924 at CLEVELAND, OHIO with burial in Lindsey, Ohio.

During her presidency the sum of $52,702.52 was raised for the establishment of a Chair of Missions in the EVANGELICAL THEOLOGICAL SEMINARY at Naperville, Ill. This was named in 1940 as the Mrs. E. M. Spreng Memorial Chair of Missions, given in her memory who gave thirty-two years of distinguished leadership as president of the Woman's Missionary Society of The Evangelical Church.

Evangelical Missionary World, May 1924. L. ETHEL SPRENG

SPRENG, SAMUEL P. (1853-1946), American EVANGELICAL ASSOCIATION bishop, was born in Wayne County, Ohio, Feb. 11, 1853. Educated at North Western College (now NORTH CENTRAL COLLEGE), Naperville, Ill., he was licensed by the OHIO CONFERENCE, Evangelical Association, in 1876. Spreng served several pastorates and a term as presiding elder before he was elected in 1887 as editor of the *Evangelical Messenger*, official English paper of his church. After serving twenty years in this capacity, Samuel Spreng was elected bishop in 1907 and filled the office continuously until 1930. He made seven episcopal visits to Europe and one to CHINA and JAPAN. As an editor he strongly supported a union of the Wesley bodies in America.

He was married to Miss Margaret A. Beck, Sept. 18, 1878. He died April 18, 1946 at his home in Naperville, and was buried in the Naperville Cemetery.

In addition to denominational offices Bishop Spreng was vice-president of the National Anti-Saloon League for twenty years, a member of the Administration Board of the Federal Council of Churches, and author of a number of books. Some of these were: *History of the Evangelical Association, History of the Evangelical Church, What Evangelicals Believe, The Life and Labors of John Seybert,* and the *Life of Charles Spurgeon in Messages of Hope and Faith.*

Evangelical Messenger, May 11, 1946.
David Koss, *Bishops of the Evangelical Association.* Unpublished ms., 1959.
R. M. Veh, *Evangelical Bishops.* 1939. JOHN H. NESS, JR.

SPRING ARBOR COLLEGE, Spring Arbor, Michigan, founded in 1873 as Spring Arbor Seminary, is now accredited as a four-year liberal arts college of the FREE METHODIST CHURCH. A large campus development and building program has been loyally supported by the alumni and the denomination. Large gifts from private donors and foundations have made possible a pay-as-you-go building program of unusual proportions. The faculty has a high percentage of doctorates and master's degrees. Present enrollment is about 600.

BYRON S. LAMSON

SPRINGER, CORNELIUS (1790-1875), American minister and editor, was born of Swedish parentage near Wilmington, Del., on Dec. 29, 1790. He became a member of the M.E. Church at the age of eighteen. He was teaching school when he enlisted in the War of 1812, serving as lieutenant of a company. He resumed teaching at the close of the war but in 1816 left his position in the Putnam Academy to enter the ministry in the OHIO CONFERENCE of the M.E. Church, where he served for fourteen years.

He was among the earliest of those who sought a change in the government of the church and became one of the founders of the M.P. CHURCH. He was elected president of the Conference in 1830 and in 1831 he was appointed editor of the *Methodist Correspondent,* serving four years. In 1837 he was elected president of the PITTSBURGH CONFERENCE. He became editor of the *Western Recorder* in 1839, resigning after six years because of failing eyesight. He retired to private life and acted as supernumerary assistant on the Zanesville circuit. In 1856 and 1857 he represented Muskingum County in the OHIO Legislature.

He married Mary A. McDowell of Chillicothe, Ohio in 1820 and after her death he married Catharine B. Monday in 1849. He married Elizabeth Trapp in 1857. He died on Aug. 17, 1875, after serving fifty-nine years in the ministry.

T. H. Colhouer, *Sketches of the Founders.* 1880.
M. Simpson, *Cyclopaedia.* 1878.   ANN G. SILER

SPRINGER, HELEN EMILY (1868-1949), pioneer missionary in RHODESIA and the CONGO, Africa, was born in New Sharon, Maine, April 2, 1868, and died in the Belgian Congo, Aug. 23, 1949. She was graduated from Holyoke (Mass.) High School, and Woman's Medical College, PHILADELPHIA. She first went to Africa in 1901. On arrival in Rhodesia she married a young missionary, William Rasmussen, who died in 1895. Later she married a fellow-missionary, JOHN M. SPRINGER, who was elected missionary bishop of Africa in 1936. Together they shared

the early pioneering life of the interior of Africa. They traveled thousands of miles on foot, at other times using hammocks, donkeys, mules, and bicycles. In 1907, to dramatize the need of "the dark continent," Dr. and Mrs. Springer trekked through the heart of the continent from the Indian Ocean to the Atlantic Ocean, accompanied by native carriers. One of Mrs. Springer's major missionary accomplishments was in translating Christian literature and scriptures into several native tongues. She helped to reduce three languages to writing and produced textbooks for schools in the various languages, as well as in English. She wrote a number of hymns and translated other hymns as well as several Books of the Bible into various languages. She witnessed and was a part of the great transformation of Central Africa, which has seen the rapid introduction and extension of motor roads, railroads and airplane routes. After the election of Dr. Springer to the missionary episcopacy, she helped him carry on his heavy administrative responsibilities throughout Central and South Africa. Wherever possible, she accompanied him on episcopal travels and was a great inspiration both to the missionaries and the African Christians. One of her major concerns was the welfare of the African women and children. She wrote *Snapshots from Sunny Africa.*

W. W. REID

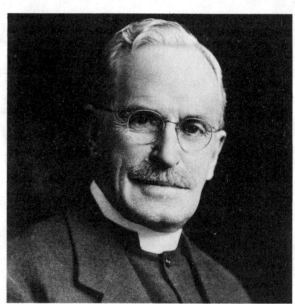

JOHN M. SPRINGER

SPRINGER, JOHN McKENDREE (1873-1963), missionary bishop, was born in Cataract, Wis., Sept. 7, 1873 and died in Penney Farms, Fla., Dec. 2, 1963. He was educated at NORTHWESTERN UNIVERSITY, and at GARRETT BIBLICAL INSTITUTE. Appointed for missionary service to AFRICA in 1901, he arrived there only three years after the RHODESIA mission had been established. Ten years later he battled with primitive conditions in opening work in the Republic of CONGO, then the Belgian Congo. With his first wife, he trekked across the continent from the Indian Ocean to the Atlantic in 1907, and helped dramatize to American Methodists the needs of the African people. In 1913 he established a mission station at Kambove, overlooking a valley that was called Livingstone's Spruit, gateway to the copper mines, one of the objective points toward which Livingstone was striving at the time of his death in 1873. For some twenty-eight years Springer was stationed not more than 300 miles from where the great explorer died, and in 1938 he was able at last to visit the place of Livingstone's death, where his heart was buried. Springer saw missionary work develop from its very inception to the place where annual conferences are constituted mainly by Africans. In 1936 he was elected missionary bishop for Africa, and finally retired in 1944. After retirement he spent fifteen more years in Africa. In 1935 Bishop Springer was decorated with the Order of the Lion, by the Belgian Government. Springer Institute in Mulungwishi, the Congo, was named in his honor. He wrote *Campfires in the Congo* and *I Love the Trail*.

W. W. REID

SPRINGFIELD, ILLINOIS, U.S.A., the capital of ILLINOIS and Sangamon County, was settled in 1818 by a SOUTH CAROLINA family and became the county seat in 1823. Largely through the efforts of Abraham Lincoln, it became the state capital in 1837. Incorporated as a city in 1840, Springfield is the center of a rich agricultural region which raises corn, grain, and livestock. Its diversified industries produce farm implements, shoes, food mixes, electronic and automatic equipment. The city has six railroads and is the seat of Concordia Theological Seminary and Springfield Junior College. Famous for fine buildings and parks, Springfield has an impressive state capitol in the form of a Greek cross. Abraham Lincoln's home and monument here are owned and maintained by the state. Lincoln, his wife, and three sons are buried here.

The Sangamon Circuit was created in 1820 as a part of the Illinois District in the MISSOURI CONFERENCE. That year James Simms, who had just been received into the Conference, was sent to Sangamon Circuit and preached the first Methodist sermon in Springfield. After itinerating one year, he left the work, became a local preacher, and established a business in Springfield. He was the first member of the lower house of the legislature from Sangamon County.

In 1821 John Glanville was appointed to the circuit and a small society was formed in Springfield. PETER CARTWRIGHT, the unique circuit rider, was sent to this circuit in 1824. His first year, with a wife and six children, he received a salary of forty dollars. The second year he received sixty dollars.

Simpson says, "In 1825-26 the first M.E. Church, a plain structure, was erected under the superintendence of Peter Cartwright, and was for many years the only house of worship." (*Cyclopaedia.*)

In his *First Methodist Church History*, Piersel says, "A small schoolhouse was erected in '28, and used for religious services on Sunday. Preachers of various denominations made their appointments, which often clashed, and the result was not satisfactory." Pascal P. Enos gave the church two lots, deed dated Oct. 10, 1831. "Very soon thereafter the Methodist chapel was erected." It was probably erected in 1833, the year given as the 100th anniversary date, being 1833-1933.

Smith W. Robinson directed the first revival in the Methodist Church in 1833. So many members were received that Springfield was made a new station in 1834, with Joseph Edmundson the first preacher.

In 1839 the upper house of the Legislature sat in the Methodist Church and appropriated $150 for rent. By 1854 the old church was sold and a new brick building, costing $10,000 and seating 500, was erected. In 1858 the church subscribed $200 for the Illinois Conference Female College at Jacksonville.

The war governor of Illinois, Richard Yates, during the early 1860's, seems to have been the first Methodist governor. Richard Yates, Jr., was governor forty years later and a member of his church's Board of Stewards.

In 1876 Springfield had four churches: First Church with 345 members and $30,000 worth of property; Second Church, 181, and $10,000 in property; German M.E. Church, 38, and building valued at $4,000; and an A.M.E. Church with 218 members and building estimated at $7,000.

First Church erected a new stone edifice in 1885. This was dedicated on October 25, seating nearly 700. A great revival was held in the new church for seventeen weeks in 1886. Thomas Harrison was the preacher, 2,000 were converted and First Church gained 500 new members.

Kumler Church was built and dedicated April 15, 1888. First Church made large contributions to the development of this church. In March 1892, the West Mission had a Sunday school, and First Church led in buying a lot for the West End Mission, where the people built a church and called it Douglas Avenue. In 1970 this church had 1,068 members.

By 1898 First Church made arrangements for raising money for a South End Church to take the place of the former mission. Within a short time Laurel Church came into being. In 1970 it had 1,153 members.

Elaborate remodeling of First Church began in 1922. Before it was completed it cost approximately $100,000. By 1946 the membership of First Church reached 2,204. In 1970 it reported 2,899 members.

In 1970 Springfield had ten United Methodist Churches, and Springfield District reported a membership of 24,850.

General Minutes, UMC, 1970.
W. G. Piersel, *First Methodist Church, Springfield, Illinois, 125 Years*. Published by the church, 1947.
M. Simpson, *Cyclopaedia*. 1878.   JESSE A. EARL

SPRINGFIELD, MASSACHUSETTS, U.S.A., situated on the Connecticut River ninety-two miles southwest of BOSTON, and only three miles from the state boundary, is the third largest city in the commonwealth with a population (1970) of 162,078. Settled in 1636 the area has been known since the colonial period as a leading center for the manufacture of arms.

Bishop FRANCIS ASBURY made three visits to Springfield, the first being on July 15, 1791 when he made this entry in his journal, "At six o'clock I delivered a discourse in Mr. C---'s house on the text, 'Tis time to seek the Lord, till he come and rain righteousness upon you.' The people were a little moved, and one person was under deep conviction. This place is a haunt of soldiery, the armory being moved here. There appears to be very little religion among the inhabitants."

At nearby WILBRAHAM the first session of the NEW ENGLAND CONFERENCE was held in September 1797. In 1819 Springfield Methodism was separated from the Tolland, Conn. circuit. Daniel Dorchester was appointed first resident pastor. The first Methodist building in the city was called Asbury Chapel. From this congregation was formed the 1844 Pynchon Street Church. Eventually the Pynchon Street Church divided, forming Trinity Church on Bridge Street, and Grace Church on South Main Street. These groups reunited May 8, 1922 to form the influential Trinity Church housed in a cathedral edifice adjoining Forest Park and completed May 19, 1929 after seven years of construction under the leadership of Fred Winslow Adams. Here in 1947 the Seventh ECUMENICAL METHODIST CONFERENCE was held.

There are three Methodist churches in Springfield: Liberty, Trinity, and Wesley with a total membership (1970) of 3,183.

Trinity Church is one of the most beautiful and imposing religious edifices in America. Seven years in the building, it was dedicated in 1929, a granite quadrangle of fourteenth century English gothic design, set deep within spacious lawns and against the sylvan background of historic Forest Park.

Dominating the complex of buildings is the Singing Tower with its carillon of sixty-one bells yielding forty-eight tones, one of the largest ever cast by the famous Bellfounders, John Taylor and Company of Lough-borough, England.

Flanking the Sanctuary are Grace Chapel, credited as being "as impressive and beautiful a gem of its size as can be found in America"; the Educational wing, and the Community House. The latter contains a modern, regulation-size swimming pool with adjacent lockers and shower facilities, a gymnasium, small game room, and assembly hall.

The seven-day-a-week institutional program of Trinity serves the entire community and averages a cumulative

TRINITY CHURCH, SPRINGFIELD, MASSACHUSETTS

total of 100,000 people a year, including over 8,000 individual participants. The active membership of the church in 1970 was 1,890.

One of the notable stained glass windows in the Sanctuary pictures the famous aviator, Charles Lindbergh, and during World War II his representation "among the saints" elicited considerable national controversy. The memorabilia in the history cabinet include an authentic water pitcher once owned and used by JOHN WESLEY; the original draft of Angela Morgan's well-known poem "Sanctuary," which she wrote after visiting Grace Chapel; and a personal letter to the church in the handwriting of Mahatma Ghandi, expressing appreciation that his likeness appears in one of the aisle windows.

This is the fourth structure of the society, which was organized as the Pynchon Street Church on Feb. 9, 1844. Trinity was host to Methodism's quadrennial GENERAL CONFERENCE in 1924, and in 1947 entertained the Ecumenical Methodist Conference in its first session following World War II.

General Minutes, UMC.
Minutes of the New England Conference.
M. Simpson, *Cyclopaedia.* 1878.
ERNEST R. CASE

SPRINGFIELD, PENNSYLVANIA, U.S.A. **Covenant Church** is a comparatively recent church, being organized on Christmas afternoon in 1921. Springfield is located on the outskirts of Philadelphia, and the church was begun by a group of Christian people, among whom Methodists were discovered in the majority. During March of 1922, a Board of Trustees was chosen to serve the Springfield Community Church, Methodist Episcopal. By December of 1924, with more than 200 members, buildings were dedicated and the three-year-old congregation was housed.

From 1928 Springfield was served by appointed ordained ministers of the PHILADELPHIA CONFERENCE, and while struggling through the depression years, membership increased steadily, with temporary building additions being made.

In 1953 a new sanctuary was completed, and the name of the congregation was officially changed to Covenant Methodist, honoring a substantial gift from the sale of a Covenant Church in PHILADELPHIA. Membership had grown in some thirty-one years to 1,300 persons. An educational facility was added in 1961, featuring a never closed private prayer room, opening to the street. Only six ministers had served the steadily enlarging congregation in this period.

The congregation in 1970 numbered 2,020 members with a church school enrollment of 1,089. It is served by a staff of four ministers, an organist, three secretaries, and three sextons. In April of 1968 the original building used for worship was demolished to make way for a new unit consisting of a fellowship hall, kitchen, music ministry rooms and youth ministry facilities. The Church is characterized by its lay committee program, volunteer choir ministry, its involvement in the changing suburban patterns of churchmanship, and its emphasis on worship as a centrality in the life of seeking Christians.

KENNETH G. FANSLER

SPRINGFIELD, VIRGINIA, U.S.A. **Springfield Church** is located on the growing edge of mushrooming Fairfax County, in the metropolitan area of WASHINGTON, D.C.

The church has had a phenomenal growth. Starting in an elementary school auditorium in January 1954, with thirty-three members, it has grown to be the third largest Methodist church in the VIRGINIA CONFERENCE, with 2,808 members in 1970.

Two units of a beautiful and functional edifice were erected in 1955 and 1960. A third unit provides adequate room for all church activities. A tall steeple, with tower chimes, dominates a busy shopping area. The church building, valued at more than $700,000, provides a beautiful sanctuary seating 750 worshippers, twenty-eight class rooms, offices, library and social hall. The social hall has served as the main community center for the young city and has been used by numerous civic, fraternal and business organizations. In one typical month, more than fifty different organizations held meetings in the church building.

The church library contains more than 2,500 volumes covering various phases of religion, philosophy and related subjects. The collection of pictures, film strips, tapes and records, to augment the regular curriculum materials, is one of the most significant in Northern Virginia.

One outstanding characteristic of this congregation is the comparative youthfulness of the membership. The estimated average age of the adult membership is less than forty years. This is due to the large proportion of the membership which comes from families of men and women on active duty with the Armed Forces or serving with one of the Federal establishments located in the Washington metropolitan area. These members bring unusual talents and a rich background of experience to enhance the religious life of the church.

The church supports a well-rounded program of religious and community action and service under the leadership of two ministers, a Director of Christian Education and a competent church staff. While concerned with enormous problems of providing church facilities and staff, the church has always been interested in Christian outreach. Partial support is being given to missionaries in CHILE and RHODESIA as well as to church extension projects with the District.

George W. Harrison was the first pastor assigned to the new congregation in January 1954, and served for eleven and one-half years.

ESDRAS S. GRUVER

SPURLOCK, BURWELL (1790-1879), American pioneer circuit rider, Confederate chaplain, statesman, was born in Montgomery County, Va. Although self-educated, he was unique, a great orator.

From Dec. 5, 1810, to March 15, 1815, he was Captain of Militia. Ordained a DEACON by Bishop ASBURY, he was admitted to the OHIO CONFERENCE and was appointed to the Guyandotte Circuit, WEST VIRGINIA, which included what is now CHARLESTON and Huntington, 1818-1821, and again in 1823. His circuit activities covered eastern KENTUCKY and southern West Virginia, an area 300 miles long. In 1851 he was appointed to the Wayne (M.E. Church, South) Circuit.

In 1842 Spurlock was one of the commissioners to fix the bounds of Wayne County, setting it off from Cabell. When the division of the M.E. Church came, he joined the WESTERN VIRGINIA M.E. Church, South, CONFERENCE. Elected to the Secession Convention in Richmond, Va.—West Virginia was then part of VIRGINIA—he voted against secession. During the Civil War, he remained in old Virginia, but returned to Wayne County after peace came. He was a Confederate chaplain with 131 men in his Cavalry detachment, and prayed for all of the 131 to be returned home alive. Although sixty-four of them were wounded, all 131 returned home and every one of the 131, it is said, were converted under Spurlock shortly before he died.

Judge James H. Ferguson declared Burwell Spurlock "the greatest man he had ever known," and further said that if he had had a technical education he "would have been made a bishop."

Spurlock's first wife was Sallie Morrison and they had four children. His second wife was Nancy Garrett and they had eight children.

Burwell Spurlock died in Wayne County, W. Va., on Aug. 5, 1879, on the farm where his father, Jesse Spurlock, had lived.

George S. Wallace, *Cabell County Annals and Families*. Richmond: Garrett and Massie Publishers, 1935.
Wayne County News, Wayne, W. Va., April 4, 1958.
JESSE A. EARL

SPYWOOD, GEORGE A. (1798-1876), superintendent of the A.M.E. ZION CHURCH, was born Jan. 5, 1798, in PROVIDENCE, R. I. where on March 7, 1818 he was converted. He was licensed to preach in the same city in 1831. He joined the traveling connection June 20, 1842, was ordained a DEACON May 18, 1843, an ELDER, eleven years later, and was consecrated a superintendent May 24, 1852. He died March 9, 1876.

DAVID H. BRADLEY

SQUANCE, THOMAS H. (1790-1868), pioneer British missionary to CEYLON, was born at Exeter on Feb. 3, 1790, became a local preacher in 1807, was accepted for the ministry in 1812 and appointed to Liskeard. At the LIVERPOOL Conference of 1813, he volunteered to join THOMAS COKE'S "mission to the East" and was one of the five missionaries who landed in Ceylon after Coke's death in 1814. Squance served usefully, first at Jaffa, then in other stations, and finally in Negapatam, INDIA, until 1823. He died on April 21, 1868.

W. M. Harvard, *Ceylon and India*. 1823. CYRIL J. DAVEY

STACEY, JAMES (1818-1891), British Methodist, was born in Sheffield on Feb. 28, 1818, was helped by JOSEPH BARKER, and studied under THOMAS ALLIN. He entered the METHODIST NEW CONNEXION ministry in 1839 and became one of its most able and cultured ministers. He served as Missions Secretary for four years and from 1863 as resident tutor and governor of Ranmoor College, becoming principal from 1865-76. He served as president in 1860 and 1881. He wrote biographies of JOHN RIDGWAY and W. N. HALL, the CHINA missionary. He died at Ranmoor, Sheffield, on May 11, 1891.

W. J. Townsend, *James Stacey, D.D.* London, 1891.
OLIVER A. BECKERLEGGE

STACK, JAMES (1801-1883), NEW ZEALAND Methodist lay missionary, was born at Portsmouth, England. He came to AUSTRALIA and there offered for Wesleyan mission work in New Zealand as a lay agent. He was one of the original party at Wesleydale (Whangaroa) in 1823, and when the station was destroyed by hostile Maoris in 1827, he assisted with the reestablishment of the work at Mangungu in the Hokianga District. In 1831, he visited England, and owing to some differences of opinion with the missionary committee, he entered the ministry of the Church of England.

Returning to New Zealand he worked with the Church Missionary Society until 1847. After a failure in health, he returned to England and spent his retirement in his native town.

C. H. Laws, *Toil and Adversity at Whangaroa*. Wesley Historical Society, New Zealand, 1945. L. R. M. GILMORE

STAEBLER, CHRISTIAN (1852-1927), American EVANGELICAL ASSOCIATION minister, was born Sept. 24, 1852, in Oxford County, Ontario, Canada of Swabian and Swiss ancestry. He completed a German course at NORTH CENTRAL COLLEGE and was a member of the first graduating class (1878) of the EVANGELICAL THEOLOGICAL SEMINARY, Naperville, Ill.

After twenty-seven years of fruitful pastoral service in the CANADA and NEW YORK CONFERENCES, Evangelical Association, he was elected editor of *Das Evangelische Magazin* and German Sunday school literature. Holding this position to the end of his career (1903-26) he became prominent in the official circles of the Evangelical Association.

"He was a man of distinguished and notable talent," said his biographer, Editor Frye of the *Evangelical Messenger*. Yet, "he was constantly employed in adding to his resources by study and by using his talents to the full in those tasks to which he was called. His authorship of a wide variety of promotional material, manuals, books, etc. on Sunday school and young people's work; his ministry at conventions, and as a member of various denominational boards and commissions; his outstanding membership on the Lesson Committee of the International Sunday School Association—all gave him a wide outlook and enabled him to exercise a powerful influence in the life of the Church."

In his memorial service message in CLEVELAND, OHIO, June 16, 1927, with burial in the same city, Bishop S. P. SPRENG declared, "Above all he was a man of deep religious life, and high moral purpose . . . His name is written high in the records of the Church."

The Evangelical Messenger, Nov. 14, 1925; Oct. 23 and Nov. 20, 1926; June 25, 1927. ROY B. LEEDY

STAFFORD, CHARLES LEWIS (1844-1930), American minister and college president, was born on Sept. 26, 1844 in Clark County, OHIO, but moved to IOWA at an early age. Educated at the Denmark Academy, he was graduated from IOWA WESLEYAN UNIVERSITY in 1871. Admitted to the IOWA ANNUAL CONFERENCE of the M.E. Church in 1870, he served churches for twenty years at Fairfield, Oskaloosa, Burlington, Albia, Keokuk, and Washington; was PRESIDING ELDER of the Muscatine District, 1884-88; and was stationed at the First Church, Ottumwa, 1889-90. He received an honorary D.D. from Upper Iowa University in 1889.

Elected president of Iowa Wesleyan University in 1891, he launched a vigorous financial campaign, completed the Chapel and Hall of Science in 1893 and the Elizabeth J. Hershey Hall for Women in 1897. He revised the Academy course and the Normal Program and introduced the Commercial and Art courses.

Stafford returned to the pastoral ministry in 1899 at Muscatine and Bloomfield; was district superintendent at Oskaloosa, 1908-13, and held two-year appointments in West Liberty and Wilton before retirement in 1918.

He was a delegate to the GENERAL CONFERENCES of 1892, 1896, 1900, 1912 and to the ECUMENICAL METHODIST CONFERENCE in London, 1901. Iowa Wesleyan granted him an honorary LL.D. in 1905. Stafford married Mary Allen, Iowa Wesleyan, in 1869, one of the Seven Founders of The P.E.O. Sisterhood. He died on Sept. 1, 1930 in Oak Park, Ill.

Louis A. Haselmayer, *The Presidents of Iowa Wesleyan*. Mount Pleasant, 1968.
Iowa Wesleyan Archives.
Minutes of the Iowa Annual Conferences.

LOUIS A. HASELMAYER

STAFFORD, MARGARET V. (1892-1962), missionary and deaconess administrator, served as superintendent of Grant Hall (a dormitory for girls) and Elmore Home for the Aging, MILWAUKEE, Wis., from 1934 until her retirement in 1959. Through her aggressive leadership Methodist Manor, a commodious home for the aging, was established in West Allis, a Milwaukee suburb.

Miss Stafford was born in Rutland, Vt., July 28, 1892. Her parents were Ora E. and Libbie J. Kelley Stafford. Two of her ancestors, Stephen Hopkins and Richard Henry Lee, signed the Declaration of Independence.

She was trained as a deaconess in the Chicago Training School (now consolidated with GARRETT THEOLOGICAL SEMINARY). In 1920 she went to Nanping, CHINA, where she served as mission secretary and business manager of Alden Spears Memorial Hospital.

Called back to America by illness in her family, she served with ARTHUR W. HEWITT at Plainfield and Adamant, Vt., and then went to the midwest to work in Jennings Seminary, Aurora, Ill. From that post she went to Milwaukee to superintend Grant Hall and Elmore Home (now Methodist Manor). After retirement she lived in the retirement home, which had been established largely through her efforts, until her death July 16, 1962.

WILLIAM BLAKE

STAFFORD, THOMAS ALBERT (1885-1969), American clergyman, and church official, was born April 23, 1885, at Enniskillen, North Ireland. He was educated at Lincoln-Jefferson University, the University of Chicago (where he studied business administration) and GARRETT THEOLOGICAL SEMINARY, which later conferred on him an honorary D.D. degree. He came to the United States from Canada in 1906, and in 1907 married Mary Anna Fullerton. They had a daughter Grace, who is Mrs. Chester H. Lunde.

Stafford joined the NORTHERN MINNESOTA CONFERENCE of the M.E. Church in 1911 and served churches until 1917, when he became assistant treasurer of the Board of PENSIONS, Chicago. He advanced to treasurer in 1929 and served in this post until 1938, when he was made executive secretary. He held this position until 1952 when he retired. He was responsible for much of the progress in pensions' legislation and administration

made in The Methodist Church following unification. In retirement he served as CHAPLAIN in the new Methodist Building in Evanston, Ill., until 1966.

He wrote a number of books of prose and poetry, and a book in the area of church finance, *Pension Administration in the Methodist Episcopal Church*. His three books of verse are: *Peace of Mind, The Stars Are Always Shining* and *The Mind of Christ. Guide Marks on the Christian Way* and *The Practice of the Presence* are books of devotional material. *Christian Symbolism in the Evangelical Churches* and *Within the Chancel* are specialized but standard works which come from his lifelong interest in symbolism.

On his eighty-fourth birthday in 1969 the United Methodist Board of Pensions paid tribute to him and named the chapel of the Methodist Building in Evanston in his honor. He died in Chicago, Nov. 10, 1969.

Who's Who in The Methodist Church, 1966.   T. OTTO NALL

STALKER, ARTHUR W. (1860-1930), American minister, was born Nov. 6, 1860, in Commerce, Mich., two years after his father, Thomas Stalker, had come from England to preach in America. The son received his first academic degree in 1884. He married Mary Hendrickson. He served pastorates in Dixboro, Clinton, DETROIT, SAULT STE. MARIE, in MICHIGAN, and MADISON, Wis., where LAWRENCE COLLEGE conferred on him a D.D. degree. He was called to Ann Arbor, Mich., to preach in this University city, and for twenty-five years charmed people with his personality, and preached to vast numbers of students and townspeople.

Perhaps his greatest contribution to Methodism came through his creative efforts toward the formation of the local and international WESLEY FOUNDATION movement. As early as 1882 a petition had been presented from the Ann Arbor Quarterly Conference to the Committee on Education of the DETROIT CONFERENCE suggesting the formation of a boarding and lodging home for Methodist students attending the University of Michigan. The building would have been called Haven Hall. In 1884 Ann Arbor instituted the first recorded Methodist organization for students aside from the Sunday school. In 1885, since there were more Methodist students in the University of Michigan than students of any other denomination, a Wesleyan Guild was incorporated under the laws of Michigan with a Methodist Board of Trustees, an executive council, and an advisory board of twenty-five. By 1894 the Methodists outside of Ann Arbor had begun to help pay the bills.

In his volume, *The Church Follows Its Students*, Dr. Shedd informs us that magnificent experiments in student work in three universities took place in the decade 1910 to 1920. The leaders of these movements were: James Baker at Illinois University, who had created a Wesley Foundation at Urbana; A. W. Stalker at the University of Michigan; and Edward Blakeman, who led a student movement at Wisconsin University. These three men were blazing new trails in Methodist student work.

In *The Christian Advocate* of Feb. 23, 1895, James T. Buckley called the Ann Arbor church "the most important pulpit in Methodism." Doubtless this was partly because of the large number of students from overseas attending this church. Stalker realized the challenge of preaching the gospel to all the world. Within a year after his arrival in Ann Arbor, Carolyn Owens had begun classes for

Chinese students who met on Sunday afternoons, and Stalker himself taught a bi-weekly Bible class for Chinese students. Indemnity due the United States from the Boxer Uprising was used to send Chinese students to the United States, many of whom came to Ann Arbor to study at the University of Michigan. The list of American students who went as missionaries to CHINA, INDIA, and South America lengthened under Stalker's pastorate. Seven missionaries went from the Ann Arbor student group in the year 1920. In 1921 the Wesleyan Guild Corporation purchased a student building next to the church and named it Wesley Hall. The name was later changed to Stalker Hall.

Besides a growing student work, marking Stalker's twenty-five year ministry in Ann Arbor, membership in the local church grew from 634 in 1905 to 1,692 in 1930. Stalker was a superbly practical religious thinker. "He did not dwell on the sins of the world so much as on the opportunity for doing good . . . the sane enjoyment of life."

Arthur W. Stalker preached his last sermon in the Ann Arbor Church Nov. 6, 1930, on his seventieth birthday. He died Nov. 19, 1930. The Memorial Service was led by the new pastor, FREDERICK B. FISHER, on Nov. 30, 1930.

CHARLES W. BRASHARES

JOHN S. STAMM

STAMM, JOHN S. (1878-1956), American E.U.B. bishop and educator, was born March 23, 1878. His parents were charter members of the congregation at Elida, Kan. As a youth he gave marked evidence of a religious bent. This was developed and strengthened through his years of undergraduate study at NORTH CENTRAL COLLEGE and his theological study at EVANGELICAL THEOLOGICAL SEMINARY. He was ordained by and became a member of the KANSAS CONFERENCE of the EVANGELICAL ASSOCIA-

TION. After serving two parishes in KANSAS, he transferred to the ILLINOIS CONFERENCE where he continued in the parish ministry. He was married in 1912 to Priscilla Marie Wahl.

In 1919 he became professor of Systematic Theology in Evangelical Theological Seminary. In this position he continued until 1926 when the general conference of the Evangelical Church elected him to the episcopacy. Quadrennially thereafter he was reelected until 1950 when the GENERAL CONFERENCE of The E.U.B. Church granted him retirement. As bishop, he was stationed for eight years in KANSAS CITY, Mo., and for sixteen in Harrisburg, Pa.

As pastor, professor and bishop, two concerns dominated his activities. In preaching and in writing, he vigorously promoted the cause of evangelism. With equal zeal he espoused the growing ecumenical movement. He gave wise and strong leadership to the program which eventuated in the creation of The E.U.B. Church in 1946. In 1948 he was a denominational delegate to the Amsterdam organization meeting of the WORLD COUNCIL OF CHURCHES. He served as consultant to the programs which produced the Revised Standard Version of the Scriptures and *The Interpreter's Bible*.

The Telescope-Messenger, March 31, 1956. PAUL H. ELLER

STAMM, PRISCILLA MARIE WAHL (1884-1965), American E.U.B. mission leader, was born Feb. 2, 1884, in Glasgow, Mo. Active in her home church, she was married in 1912 to JOHN S. STAMM, who served as bishop, 1926-50.

Her name early became identified with missions. In the KANSAS CONFERENCE, EVANGELICAL ASSOCIATION, she was Branch secretary of Mission Bands. In ILLINOIS she was secretary of Little Heralds, and later Branch president. In 1919 she was elected denominational Woman's Missionary Society vice-president. Her special assignment was Missionary Candidates' Secretary.

She was general president of the Woman's Missionary Society of The Evangelical Church, 1926-44, residing first in KANSAS CITY, Mo., and then in HARRISBURG, Pa. In 1944 she was made honorary president of the Board of Missions, having completed twenty-five years of service to the Board. Upon the formation of The E.U.B. Church in 1946, she was named to the WOMEN'S SOCIETY OF WORLD SERVICE Council, and in 1950 she was voted president emeritus relationship. She was active in effecting union of the Woman's Board with the General Board of Missions of The Evangelical Church in 1930; in raising $50,000 for a Chair of Missions at EVANGELICAL THEOLOGICAL SEMINARY; and in laying the basis of union for The E.U.B. Church women's work.

She died at Friendly Acres Home, Newton, Kan., Dec. 19, 1965, with burial in Kansas City, Mo.

The Telescope Messenger, March 1, 1966.
World Evangel, March 1966.   MRS. RAYMOND M. VEH

STAMP OF SHORTLANDS, BARON (1880-1941), British Methodist, was born at Bexley, Kent. This most distinguished and loyal Methodist became a Methodist on his marriage. He was an outstanding economist whose public service in the academic and business worlds was as great as that of any Methodist in this century. He became chairman of the London, Midland, and Scottish Railway and a director of the Bank of England before those two bodies were nationalized. In 1939 his work on the Economic Advisory Council was recognized by his appointment to the wartime post of Adviser on Economic Coordination to prepare the nation for the changes needed to win the war. He was killed in an air raid in 1941.

H. J. Jones, *Life of Lord Stamp*. London, n.d.   E. R. TAYLOR

STANDARD SERMONS. The sermons contained in "the first four volumes of Wesley's sermons" constitute, together with his *Notes on the New Testament*, the doctrinal standard of the Methodist Church in Great Britain. Counsel ruled in 1914 that "the first four volumes of Wesley's sermons" means Vols. 1-4 of those published in eight volumes in 1787-88, forty-four in all. (These four volumes were originally published separately in 1746, 1748, 1750, and 1760.) Local preachers and candidates for the ministry must assent to the doctrines contained in these sermons. The model deed (DEEDS, TRUST) declares that "no person shall be permitted to preach who shall teach any doctrine which is contrary to what is contained in these Standard Sermons." In the Deed of Union, however, the Clause on Doctrine adds that the sermons "are not intended to impose a system of formal and speculative theology on Methodist preachers, but to set up standards of preaching and belief which should secure loyalty to the fundamental truths of the gospel of redemption." These words originated in the Wesleyan Methodist Conference of 1919, and their ultimate background was the Fundamentalist controversy.

J. Wesley, *Standard Sermons*. 1921.   JOHN C. BOWMER

STANFORD, WESLEY MATTHIAS (1846-1923), American Evangelical clergyman, editor, reformer and bishop, was born in the farm home of his parents in Rockland Township, Venago County, Pa., on May 15, 1846. Coming from a devout family, he experienced a change of heart when still a young boy, and he united with the church. His education was in the common schools of his county. When he was eighteen years of age, he began to teach school in the winter and attend college during the summer. Although the PITTSBURGH CONFERENCE, EVANGELICAL ASSOCIATION, licensed him to preach in the spring of 1871, he was not assigned a charge until the next year since he wished to finish his college education. His ministry was blessed by an annual average of seventy-five conversions for the next ten years.

After these years in the pastorate he was chosen assistant editor of *The Evangelical Messenger* in the spring of 1882. He continued in this office until the fall of 1887. Owing to difficulties involving the church press, he resigned and returned to the pastorate in 1888 where he served for eighteen months, aiding in bringing over 100 souls to conversion.

On Oct. 1, 1890 he was elected editor-in-chief of *The Evangelical*, continuing only until the fall of 1891, when he was elevated to the episcopacy by the GENERAL CONFERENCE meeting in PHILADELPHIA.

He served as bishop for eleven years, when his tenure lapsed according to the reservations imposed by The United Evangelical Church. In 1902 he returned to the editorship of *The Evangelical*, which he served for eight years. He then became editor-in-chief of the United Evangelical Sunday school literature. He remained in this office until the union of the two branches of The Evangelical Church in 1922.

Bishop Stanford was married twice. His first wife was Rose A. Weimar, who died Oct. 27, 1919. His second wife was Mrs. Amelia Kichline of Allentown, Pa.

Bishop Stanford was of large physical frame and strong in endurance. He placed emphasis upon use of the Bible and urged memorization of Scripture. This he himself did, memorizing at least one verse each day until the time of his death. He died in his home in Harrisburg, Pa., April 8, 1923.

The Evangelical, Dec. 20, 1893.
Evangelical Messenger, April 23, 1923.
David Koss, *Bishops of the Evangelical Association, United Evangelical Church, Evangelical Church*. Unpublished thesis, Evangelical School of Theology, 1959.
R. M. Veh, *Evangelical Bishops*. 1939.

ALFRED JOHN THOMAS

STANGER, FRANK BATEMAN (1914-   ), American minister, historian and seminary president, was born at Cedarville, N. J., on Aug. 31, 1914, the son of Francis Albert, Jr. and Sarah Rush Bateman Stanger. He was educated at ASBURY COLLEGE, graduating *magna cum laude* in 1934. He attended ASBURY THEOLOGICAL SEMINARY 1934-35. He received his Th.B. at Princeton Theological Seminary in 1937; an S.T.M. in 1940 and an S.T.D. in 1942 from Temple University; a D.D. from Philathea College in 1953 and an LL.D. from Houghton College in 1962. On June 2, 1937 he was married to Mardelle Amstutz and they have three children, Marilyn, Frank Jr., and Jane.

Stanger joined the NEW JERSEY CONFERENCE in 1936 and served a number of pastorates including First, Collingswood, 1951-59. He served as Secretary and Vice-President of the New Jersey Conference Educational Society; Secretary of the Board of Directors of the Wesley Foundation at Princeton; as a member of the Conference Sustentation Fund Commission; the Conference Board of Education; as President of the Conference Historical Society, 1948-59, and as co-chairman of the special committee to celebrate the 125th anniversary of the Conference. He was a member of the Area Committee to celebrate the bicentennial of the arrival of PILMORE and BOARDMAN in America. He served as President of the Northeastern Jurisdictional Methodist Historical Society and as a member of the Executive Committee of the American Association of Methodist Historical Societies. He has been a delegate to JURISDICTIONAL CONFERENCES, the GENERAL CONFERENCE, and WORLD METHODIST CONFERENCES.

In 1959 he became Executive Vice President of Asbury Theological Seminary and Professor of Preaching and Pastoral Work. Since 1962 he has served as President of the Seminary. He was the recipient of the Distinguished Alumni Award by Asbury College in 1961. He is a member of The Evangelical Theological Society, The Wesleyan Theological Society, The Association of Seminary Professors in the Practical Fields, and Theta Phi.

He has written *The Pauline Doctrine of Conscience*, 1940; *The Life and Work of the Rev. Joseph Pilmore*, 1942; *A Workman That Needeth Not to be Ashamed*, 1958; and was editor of *The Methodist Trail in New Jersey*, 1961.

Who's Who in America, Vol. 35.
Who's Who in The Methodist Church, 1966.   N. B. H.

STANIFORTH, SAMPSON (1720-1799), British Methodist soldier, was born at SHEFFIELD, December 1720. Uneducated, without religion, he learned to bake, but enlisted as a soldier (1739); he fought in Flanders, FRANCE. Under Methodist influence he renounced swearing, drinking, gaming, and plundering. Purchasing his discharge, he settled in Deptford in 1748, prospered, becoming constable and overseer of the poor. Never formally itinerant, after 1763 he preached widely and frequently in LONDON, did much pastoral work, sponsoring the Deptford and Rotherhithe Chapels. Ordained in 1764 by the Greek bishop Erasmus, and "called" by dissenting congregations, he would not forsake Wesley's connection. His *Autobiography* is vivid and moving. He died in March 1799.

N. Dews, *History of Deptford.* Deptford, 1884.
T. Jackson, *Lives of Early Methodist Preachers.* 1846.

GEORGE LAWTON

STANLEY, HERBERT HAVILL (1888-1965), prominent minister of the BELGIUM CONFERENCE, was born in Semley (England) on April 2, 1888. He studied architecture and theology in LONDON, and went to Brussels in 1921, entering the Methodist Mission in BRUSSELS in 1922. The same year he married Ruth Thonger. He served both as architect and pastor, and Belgian Methodism is grateful for his architectural ability. The most admired churches he built are Brussels Central (1924), Liege (1929), GHLIN (1933), HERSTAL (1947). He was pastor in charge of Ghlin (French), 1923-25; ECAUSSINNES (French), 1929-32; Brussels Wesley Church (American), 1933-40, and again from 1945-56. During Nazi occupation, he was kept in an internment camp, 1941-44. He retired in 1956 at Granges lez Valence, France. He died there on Nov. 30, 1965.

WILLIAM G. THONGER

JACOB STANLEY

STANLEY, JACOB (1776-1850), British Methodist, a noted preacher, was born at Alnwick, Northumberland, England, on Jan. 14, 1776. He joined the Methodist society at the age of eleven, became a Wesleyan itinerant in 1797, and was president of the CONFERENCE in 1845. He was regarded as one of the leaders in Conference of those opposed to the dominance of JABEZ BUNTING. He died on Sept. 8, 1850.

GEORGE LAWTON

STANNARD, GEORGE (1803-1888), NEW ZEALAND Methodist minister, was born in Yorkshire on March 13, 1803, and spent his early years in Ireland. Through the representations of Dr. Day, tutor to NATHANIEL TURNER's children at Mangungu, he left England in 1841 with three other Irish families to emigrate to New Zealand. Leaving the vessel at the Bay of Islands to walk overland to meet it at its destination, he arrived to learn that the ship, *Sophia Pate,* had been wrecked with all passengers lost, on the bar at the entrance of the Kaipara Harbor.

In 1844, George Stannard was received into the Wesleyan Mission, and subsequently labored at Newark, Ihipuku, Waitotara, Kai Iwi (where he began the native institution), Waikouaiti, Wesley Three Kings, and Raglan. In 1866 he retired from the active ministry, but from his home in Wanganui continued to work among Maoris and Europeans until his death on Dec. 8, 1888.

Minutes of the New Zealand Methodist Conference, 1889.

WESLEY A. CHAMBERS

STANSBURY, WALTER A. (See JUDICIAL COUNCIL.)

STANSTEAD WESLEYAN COLLEGE was founded in 1873, in the Eastern Townships of Quebec, an area then largely inhabited by English-speaking persons. The objective of its founders was to provide a broad secondary education "under wholesome Christian influences" for young men and women. To this end, extensive facilities were provided; an experienced staff was appointed; and the Methodist Church was asked to take the responsibility for the college's spiritual welfare.

Since its inception, Stanstead has remained a responsibility of the Methodist Church and later of The United Church of CANADA. Its facilities have been enlarged and improved continuously. Above all, it has sought to provide a sound education in a religious, but nonsectarian context.

G. H. Cornish, *Cyclopaedia of Methodism.* 1881, 1903.
Centennial of Canadian Methodism. Toronto, 1891.

G. S. FRENCH

STANTS, NELSON E. (1921-   ), American E.U.B. minister, was born at Ruffsdale, Westmoreland County, Pa., April 21, 1921. He worked for three years as lathe operator for United States Steel, McKeesport, Pa. This was followed with three years in the Army Air Corps during World War II. He graduated from NORTH CENTRAL COLLEGE and EVANGELICAL THEOLOGICAL SEMINARY, and completed residence work for the Ph.D. at BOSTON UNIVERSITY. Stants was ordained by the WESTERN PENNSYLVANIA CONFERENCE of The E.U.B. CHURCH, May 1953 and served pastorates in Naperville, Ill.; Pawtucket, R.I.; Oil City and Youngwood, Pa. Elected Assistant Director of Stewardship, June 1, 1965, he became Executive Secretary, Jan. 1, 1967. He was a member of the following E.U.B. agencies and committees: The General Council of ADMINISTRATION, General PROGRAM COUNCIL, General Board of CHRISTIAN EDUCATION, Department of Communication, the Adult, Youth, and Children's Councils, General Church CURRICULUM COMMITTEE, and the Council of Executive Officers. He has also served as a member of the NATIONAL COUNCIL OF CHURCHES, Division of Christian Life and Mission Program Board, as well as on the National Council Section on Stewardship and Benevolence. He is married to the former Alice Marie Dyer of Yukon, Pa., and they have two children. In The United Methodist Church Nelson Stants is the Assistant Secretary for Field Cultivation, Division of Interpretation of the Program Council. His membership is with the Western Pennsylvania Conference.

CAWLEY H. STINE

STAPLETON, AMMON (1850-1916), American Evangelical churchman and historian, was born in Oley, Pa., Jan. 15, 1850 to William and Elizabeth Stapleton. He received his formal education at CENTRAL PENNSYLVANIA COLLEGE (A.B., 1871; M.S., 1888; A.M., 1895) and was awarded the D.D. degree by Ursinus College in 1907. His marriage to Sarah E. Crandall took place March 11, 1875.

During forty-five years of ministry, he was a pastor, presiding elder and prolific writer. Ordained in 1875 in the CENTRAL PENNSYLVANIA CONFERENCE, EVANGELICAL ASSOCIATION, his life was invested in that area. As a writer he earned the reputation of being an expert historian. His particular genius lay in his tireless persistence in unearthing significant details. His works have been of worth to later historians. Books which enriched his own church were: *Natural History of the Bible*, 1885; *Annals of the Evangelical Association of North America* and *History of the Evangelical Church*, 1896; *Flashlights of Evangelical History* and *Evangelical Daughters of Song*, 1908; *A Wonderful Story of Old Time Evangelical Evangelism*, published posthumously, 1917. His more general works included *Compend of Church History*, 1885; "German Printing in Pennsylvania," article in Pennsylvania German Magazine, Vol. 5, p. 87 ff.; *Memorials of Hugenots in America*, 1901.

He was a life member of the Pennsylvania Historical Society and a member of the Pennsylvania German Society.

After having preached at both Sunday morning and evening services in St. Paul's Church at Williamsport, Pa., he died on Sept. 18, 1916.

R. W. Albright, *Evangelical Church*. 1942.
Shortess and Gramley, *Central Pennsylvania Conference* (EC). 1940.
Who Was Who in America, Vol. I.   ARTHUR C. CORE

STAR OF ZION. (See AFRICAN METHODIST EPISCOPAL ZION CHURCH.)

STARKVILLE, MISSISSIPPI, U.S.A. **First Church** has the largest congregation in the NORTH MISSISSIPPI CONFERENCE. Before the removal of the Indians from this area, one of the favorite spots of the Choctaw Indians was a spring which they called "Hicashabaha" which, according to tradition, means "sweet gum leaves on the water." Following the Indian removal in 1832, a settlement called Starkville grew up near this source of water. In 1834 Starkville was visited by a Methodist circuit rider, Jacob Matthews, who preached to a small group of people in the sweet gum grove. The people were seated on rails, and he used a stump for his pulpit. A Methodist society was formed in 1835 and the first church was built in 1839. The sweet gum grove has been the site of four Methodist church buildings. The second was built in the 1850's, the third in 1885, and the fourth in 1925. This church has a unique ministry since Starkville is the site of Mississippi State University. An educational annex was

built in 1963-1964 which is one of the finest in the conference.

In 1970 First Church reported 1,592 members, property valued at $775,000, and $87,412 raised for all purposes.

General Minutes, UMC, 1970.   GENE RAMSEY MILLER

STARR, LEE ANNA (1853-1937), noted advocate of women's rights and temperance, was one of the few women to be ordained into the ministry of the METHODIST PROTESTANT denomination. She was the daughter of David L. and Sarah Harper Starr and was born at Point Pleasant, W. Va. Dr. Starr was educated in the public schools at Athens, Ohio, and did further study at the University of Chicago, Augustana Theological Seminary, and NORTHWESTERN UNIVERSITY. KANSAS CITY UNIVERSITY conferred the D.D. degree on her and ADRIAN COLLEGE gave her the LL.D. degree. She was ordained at Princeton, Ill., on Sept. 5, 1895, and became a member of the ILLINOIS CONFERENCE of the M.P. CHURCH. She served a number of churches and charges in the Illinois Conference, including: Ohio, Canton, Paris, and Avalon Park, CHICAGO. She also served Plymouth Church in ADRIAN, Mich. Dr. Starr was a clear, logical and forceful speaker. For six years she was a national representative of the Woman's Christian Temperance Union; she also took an active role in the work of the National Temperance Alliance. In addition to numerous articles in denominational and temperance publications, she was the author of the booklet, *The Ministry of Women*, and the book, *The Bible Status of Women*. LYMAN E. DAVIS said of Dr. Starr: ". . . she occupies a place among the elect ladies of her denomination second only to that of Dr. Anna Shaw." Dr. Starr died in Pittsburgh.

L. E. Davis, *Democratic Methodism*. 1921.
Minutes of the Illinois Conference, MP.

FRANK W. STEPHENSON

STATE COLLEGE, PENNSYLVANIA, U.S.A. **St. Paul's Church** is rooted in the Methodist church which once flourished at Centre Furnace, about two miles from State College. This one room wooden structure with a seating capacity of about 100 was built on the side of the hill opposite the old charcoal-iron furnace, whose stone stack still serves as an historical landmark at the eastern approach to the town.

In 1888 a new church was built in the town proper. It was a one-story frame structure costing $3,500. Its most notable exterior feature was its red and white striped "barber pole" steeple, which served as a landmark of that day.

The present stone edifice, built at a cost of $45,000, was dedicated in 1912. Common contemporary comment was, "The Methodists will never get that church paid for, let alone fill it." Since that time the church has undergone various renovations, alterations, and enlargements, and the 1970 membership was 2,382. Two morning services have been conducted for the past ten years in order to accommodate the attendance.

A new education building was dedicated in 1958, and a further addition in 1965.

The WESLEY FOUNDATION was instituted in 1920, with Harry F. Babcock serving as the first student pastor. (Dr. Babcock is now minister emeritus of St. Paul's Church.)

The Wesley Foundation was formed in order to provide students of Methodist preference living on the campus of the Penn State University with "a church home away from home." It was first housed in a wing of the main church, but in 1957 a new building was consecrated for the use of the students. At that time the Wesley Foundation became separated from St. Paul's Church. It became an independent entity, supported by the CENTRAL PENNSYLVANIA CONFERENCE. At present there are about 2,000 students of Methodist preference attending the University.

MRS. J. R. DOTY

MRS. STATELER

L. B. STATELER

STATELER, LEARNER BLACKMAN (1811-1896), American minister, was born of German parentage July 7, 1811, near Hartford, Ky., the youngest of the six children of Steven and Rhoda Pigman Stateler. His grandfather, Ignatius Pigman, was elected deacon by the CHRISTMAS CONFERENCE, and became a pioneer preacher in MARYLAND. L. B. Stateler joined the church at seven years of age, was licensed as an EXHORTER in 1829, admitted on trial into the KENTUCKY CONFERENCE in 1831 and ordained ELDER in 1835 in MISSOURI CONFERENCE. There he served the Cedar Creek, Bowling Green, Canton, and CAPE GIRARDEAU Circuits and organized work at Fort Madison and Burlington, Iowa. He married Melinda, daughter of Elijah Purdom, on Jan. 26, 1836. They had one adopted daughter, Eliza, who married A. D. Weaver.

Stateler responded to the Nez Perce-Flathead appeal for the Bible, but was not accepted. He was appointed teacher and preacher among the Creek Nation, Delaware, Shawnee, Wyandotte and Choctaw Indians for twelve years, becoming in 1844 a charter member of the INDIAN MISSION CONFERENCE, which adhered to the South in the 1844 Separation. In 1854 he became a charter member of the KANSAS MISSION CONFERENCE (MES), and served Wakarusha, Leavenworth City Mission, and Grasshopper Mission. In 1862 he was sent to DENVER, but found his church in Episcopalian hands. While there, his Kansas home was burned in the Civil War border warfare, and Mrs. Stateler set out for Denver, driving a team of mares and accompanied by one hired man driving an ox team

and another driving the loose stock. Stateler met them at Fort Kearney. The 700-mile trip was made in midwinter.

In 1864 they went to MONTANA with the famous frontiersman Jim Bridger's sixty-two-wagon train. Stateler preached his first Montana sermon July 3, 1864. They subsisted on the sale of butter from the cows which they had driven through to Montana. On Christmas Eve 1864 he organized the church of Willow Creek.

In Montana Mrs. Stateler prudently hid her Southern sympathies, but on one occasion relieved her feelings by retiring to a deep canyon and shouting, "Hurrah for Jeff Davis!"—and was surprised and pleased to hear her words repeated by echo. Some twenty years later when Jefferson Davis, late president of the Confederacy, heard of the incident through Bishop JOHN C. KEENER, he sent from his home at Beauvoir, Miss., a cabinet-sized photograph inscribed "with grateful affection and admiration both for herself and her husband, whose devoted service in the cause of Christianity is meet for a monument higher than man could build."

In 1866 the Statelers went to OREGON where he was assigned the Albany Circuit by Bishop KAVANAUGH. But the climate affected his health, and in April 1867 he started back to Montana, having learned that Bishop ENOCH MARVIN of the Missouri Conference had appointed him "Superintendent of Missions in Montana and Colorado." He was presiding elder of Montana (Helena) District, 1867-74; and again presiding elder, 1880-89. He served Willow Creek, Gallatin City, Virginia City and Bozeman. He built Stateler Chapel at Willow Creek in 1873. He retired in 1892, and died at Corvallis, Mont., at the E. J. Stanley home, May 1, 1896. His funeral was May 4 at Stateler Chapel, Willow Creek, and burial was there beside his wife who died April 13, 1889.

Stateler served the church sixty-five years in eight Conferences, and never lived in a parsonage. He was twice delegate to GENERAL CONFERENCE, and attended the

ECUMENICAL METHODIST CONFERENCE in 1891. Though the Statelers lived frugally, their gifts to the church totalled $25,000, and they contributed to the building of every Southern Methodist church and parsonage built in Montana during their lifetime. L. B. Stateler planted Southern Methodism in Montana and nourished it for thirty years.

E. L. Mills, *Plains, Peaks and Pionéers*. 1947.
E. J. Stanley, *L. B. Stateler*. 1916.   LELAND D. CASE
                                              ROBERTA BAUR WEST

STATEN ISLAND, NEW YORK, U.S.A., is a fifty-seven square mile island in Richmond County at the gateway of NEW YORK Harbor. It early became the scene of Methodist preaching and Bishop FRANCIS ASBURY visited it on several occasions. His first visit was in November 1771, when he preached at the home of PETER VAN PELT November 9, twelve days after his arrival in America. On this trip he preached also at the home of Justice Hezekiah Wright in Rossville. By 1773 a circuit had been formed which has been called "Francis Asbury's first circuit in America."

The first CLASS MEETING was organized in 1771, with Israel Disosway as leader; from this developed Woodrow Church near Van Pelt's home, erected in 1787 under THOMAS MORRELL's ministry.

During the Revolutionary War, the island was occupied by British troops, and there is no record of Methodist services. Asbury resumed his visits after the war and preached at Woodrow Church on numerous later occasions. A pulpit Bible, still preserved, was presented to the church by Nancy Disosway in 1795, used by Bishop Asbury after that date. At Nicholas Crocheron's on May 24, 1802, after preaching at the new North End Church Asbury recorded in his *Journal*: "Several came forward and joined the society. I have visited upon the island for thirty-one years; and I am pleased to find there is a revival of religion."

Staten Island became part of the New Jersey Circuit in the PHILADELPHIA CONFERENCE in 1773; in 1792 it was a circuit alone, but from 1794 to 1809 it was in the Elizabethtown and Staten Island Circuit. HENRY BOEHM, who had been Asbury's traveling companion, was appointed to Staten Island and Woodrow in 1835. The NEW JERSEY CONFERENCE was formed that year and the island was included in that Conference. When the NEWARK CONFERENCE was organized in 1857 Staten Island was included therein. Growth of Methodism was steady. By 1850 there were five churches in the county, and a hundred years later there were a dozen.

F. Asbury, *Journal and Letters*. 1958.
V. B. Hampton, *Francis Asbury on Staten Island*. Staten Island Historical Society, 1948.
———, *Newark Conference*. 1957.
A. Y. Hubbell et al., *History of Methodism and the Methodist Churches of Staten Island*. New York: Richmond Publishing Co., 1898.
World Outlook, November 1954.   VERNON B. HAMPTON

STATION. In the colonial period all traveling preachers were appointed to CIRCUITS. NEW YORK, PHILADELPHIA and BALTIMORE were vast circuits. Some circuits required five or six weeks of constant travel for the itinerant in making his rounds.

Simpson says: "This term [Station] is used in Meth-

odism and signifies a single church supplied by a pastor. It is used in distinction from circuits, where a number of appointments are united in one pastoral charge. In British Methodism the pastoral work is generally arranged in circuits, which embrace several important churches; but in the United States the larger churches are generally separated from each other, and are known in the appointments as stations."

It is not clear when the word station was first used.

At present in The United Methodist Church "a pastoral charge shall consist of one or more churches . . . to which a minister is or may be duly appointed or appointable as preacher in charge. . . . A pastoral charge of two or more churches is a circuit."

E. S. Bucke, *History of American Methodism*. 1964.
Discipline, 1964, 1968.
M. Simpson, *Cyclopaedia*. 1882.   JESSE A. EARL

STATIONING OF PREACHERS. During JOHN WESLEY's lifetime he determined to which CIRCUIT the TRAVELING PREACHERS should be assigned, and announced his decisions at the annual Conference, though he did in fact consider requests and solicit advice beforehand. In the early years a preacher's length of stay in any circuit was only a few months, but the normal period soon came to be one year, which occasionally might be extended to two, but might never exceed three. The "three-year-rule" was written into Wesley's 1784 DEED OF DECLARATION, and continued to be observed by many Wesleyan circuits well into this century, even after METHODIST UNION had rendered it obsolete.

With the establishing of the M.E. Church in America in 1784, it was acknowledged that the elected bishops should exercise Wesley's prerogative of stationing the preachers, and this has been true of most of the offshoots and divisions of this church, in both America and elsewhere. The refusal in 1792 of JAMES O'KELLY's plea for liberty of appeal against an appointment by a bishop led to the first major schism, and similar rebellion against hierarchical authority brought about the organization of the METHODIST PROTESTANT CHURCH nearly forty years later. Mainstream American Methodism, however, continued to regard the episcopal stationing of preachers as a key element in the Methodist system. Increasingly during this present century, however, Methodist bishops have taken others into their confidence, considering requests from the laymen and ministers concerned, and seeking advice from the DISTRICT SUPERINTENDENTS, though the final decision is episcopal. One of the major events at each annual conference is the bishop's reading of the appointments.

Matters took a very different course in Britain. At the first conference after Wesley's death a Stationing Committee was formed, consisting of one representative from each of the Districts into which that same 1791 Conference divided the country. A similar procedure was devised for Irish Methodism. The Stationing Committee met for three days during the week preceding the Conference in order to draw up a plan of the stations for the forthcoming connexional year. This was presented to the Conference itself, which accepted the majority of the recommendations, but usually altered a few, either because of peculiar circumstances unknown to the committee or because of special pleading.

Although many refinements have taken place over 180

years, this has remained the basic procedure for stationing British Methodist ministers. Circuits extend invitations to the ministers of their choice each year, and report those which have been accepted to the minister representing their District on the Stationing Committee—normally the CHAIRMAN OF THE DISTRICT. In their turn the representatives supply the Secretary of the Conference with these provisional arrangements, and he embodies them in a "Preliminary Draft of the Stations of the Ministers." This, together with a list of ministers who are expected to move and for whom no provisional arrangements have been made, is furnished to each member of the Stationing Committee, which meets to prepare a "First Draft" of the Stations for despatch to every minister in advance of the annual Conference. At the Conference in its Ministerial Session any appeals against this First Draft are considered, and occasional adjustments or emergency alterations are made. At the final (third) reading of the Stations no change may be made unless all parties are agreed upon it, but the President and the General Purposes Committee have the power to fill vacancies arising between one annual Conference and another.

Spencer and Finch, *Constitutional Practice and Discipline*. 1958.

FRANK BAKER

Stationing Committee, American. The non-Episcopal Methodist Churches which continue the itinerant system usually have their appointments worked out, as the British do, by a Stationing Committee. The Methodist Protestant Church so managed it, as that Church had no bishops and no district superintendents. Each Conference (M.P.) elected a Stationing Committee upon which in many Conferences there were laymen sometimes in equal numbers with the ministerial members. The MARYLAND CONFERENCE of the M.P. Church empowered the president of the Conference himself to be its Stationing Committee.

The appointments in Methodist Protestant life were announced or placarded publicly sometime in advance of their final reading in order to allow for any appeals which might be made by ministers affected to be brought before the entire body. The Conference had the right to overrule its Stationing Committee when such an appeal came about, but as it turned out, it was almost unheard of for a minister's appeal against his appointment to be allowed. This was because the allowance of one such appeal would unsettle all other appointments—or threaten to unsettle them—and it was felt that after the Stationing Committee had worked out the entire pattern of appointments for the Conference, this pattern should stand unless there were very good reasons for overruling it in favor of one person. Usually in Methodist Protestant life, there was a second reading of the proposed appointments, then eventually a third and final one against which there was no appeal.

Other non-Episcopal Methodisms manage their appointment making in much the same way as did the Methodist Protestants. In Episcopal Methodism, of course, the bishop makes the appointments and his decision is final.

N. B. H.

STATISTICS, DEPARTMENT OF, formerly the Statistical Office (The Methodist Church, U.S.A.). An office with

a director empowered to collect and publish the general statistics of The Methodist Church (see General Minutes) was formally set up in 1941 with Thomas P. Potter as editor. Previously the GENERAL CONFERENCE ordered the BOOK EDITOR to collect and publish the statistics of the church. In 1952 in the general reorganization of The Methodist Church, the office was placed under the direction of the COUNCIL ON WORLD SERVICE AND FINANCE. It was supported by the General Administration Fund of the Church.

Its duties were to distribute and collect the forms prepared by the Committee on Official Forms and Records for the Pastors Report to the Annual Conference. These were then processed by computer for the *General Minutes*, which is published by the METHODIST PUBLISHING HOUSE.

Those who were in charge of the office for The Methodist Church are: Thomas P. Potter, 1941-42; Albert C. Hoover, 1943-59; Frank Shuler and Warren Erwin, 1960; Frank Shuler and Douglas Crozier, 1961; Murray Leiffer and Douglas Crozier, 1962; Roy A. Sturm and Douglas Crozier, 1963-65; Roy A. Sturm and Lois B. Hart, 1966-68.

The office is continued in The United Methodist Church and is presently located in the Headquarters of the Council on World Service and Finance at 1200 Davis Street, Evanston, Ill. Vernon Sidler is now in charge of the Department.

ROY A. STURM

STATTON, ARTHUR BIGGS (1870-1937), American United Brethren teacher, pastor, conference superintendent, and bishop, was born March 27, 1870, in the parsonage of the church of which his father was pastor near Sycamore, Ill. His father, Isaac K. Statton, was one of four brothers who were ministers, all natives of WEST VIRGINIA. His mother was Hester Wallahan, also of West Virginia.

Arthur Biggs Statton was educated in San Joaquin Valley College, Woodbridge, Calif., and Western College, Toledo, Iowa (A.B. and A.M.). LEBANON VALLEY COLLEGE conferred the D.D. degree upon him in 1909.

While teaching Natural Sciences and Languages at YORK COLLEGE, York, Neb., Statton was married to a former classmate, Lola B. Brown, of Harvey, Ill. To their union two children were born, Philo A., and Madeline (Mrs. Edward Oswald).

Statton received his license to preach in 1892, and in 1893 he was received into the membership of EAST NEBRASKA CONFERENCE, CHURCH OF THE UNITED BRETHREN IN CHRIST. He was ordained in 1896. Following brief pastorates in IOWA, he served the St. Paul's U.B. Church, HAGERSTOWN, Md., 1897-1917, with much success and distinction. From 1917 to 1925 he was a district superintendent in his conference. His spectacular success both as a pastor and administrator led inevitably to his being chosen as a bishop of the denomination, his assignment being the South West District, with headquarters in KANSAS CITY. From 1925 to the time of his death in 1937 his labors in the episcopacy were rewarded with continuous success. His administrative ability, his eloquence on the platform, his keen sense of humor, and his unfeigned piety left their impress upon the former United Brethren Church.

Bishop Statton died Dec. 8, 1937. Interment was in Rose Hill cemetery, Hagerstown, Md.

Paul E. Holdcraft, *The Life of Bishop Arthur Biggs Statton.* Chambersburg, Pa.: The Craft Press, 1948.
Koontz and Roush, *The Bishops.* 1950.
Minutes of the Pennsylvania Conference, 1938.

PAUL E. HOLDCRAFT

STAUFFACHER, CHARLES A. (1879-1956), American E.U.B. bishop, was born in an Iowa parsonage home, Oct. 29, 1879. Like his father, he became an ordained minister in the UNITED EVANGELICAL CHURCH, serving successively in five parishes. In these years, he was an enthusiastic promoter of the Christian Endeavor and for four years was president of this state-wide interdenominational Christian youth movement.

In 1921 he began his denominational administrative service with one year as Associate Missionary Secretary. In 1922 when the United Evangelical Church and The EVANGELICAL ASSOCIATION joined to become The EVANGELICAL CHURCH, he became the Executive Secretary of the Forward Campaign. For four years he gave himself to this cause which, seeking evangelistic and financial goals, strove to strengthen the denomination and its programs. From 1926 to 1934 he was Field Secretary of the Missionary Society. The GENERAL CONFERENCE in 1934 elected him to the episcopacy, and he was stationed in KANSAS CITY, Mo. He was quadrennially reelected, continuing in Kansas City until ill health compelled his retirement from the episcopacy of The E.U.B Church in 1954. He died in Cedar Falls, Iowa, Nov. 14, 1956.

The missionary operations of the denomination elicited his deepest concerns. In this cause he visited the Orient three times. In 1937 he presided over the meeting which brought into being the CHINA Conference of The EVANGELICAL CHURCH.

The Telescope-Messenger, Vol. 122, p. 14.   PAUL H. ELLER

STAUNTON, VIRGINIA, U.S.A. Central Church is the oldest continuous Methodist church in the Staunton District of what is now the VIRGINIA CONFERENCE. It was founded in the 1790's in the blacksmith shop of Sampson Eagon with prayer meetings, which gave the name "Gospel Hill" to this area. The first church was built in 1797, although the deed was not recorded until 1806 when the congregation officially became a member of the BALTIMORE CONFERENCE. The church outgrew two buildings by 1860 and the present building, the fourth on the same location, was built in 1896. Educational buildings were added in 1927 and 1964.

In 1846 the congregation founded the Wesleyan Female Institute in a nearby building. An addition adjoining the church was erected in 1850. The Institute continued operation under difficulties during the Civil War years, later becoming a prominent college for young ladies, with a progressive curriculum and civic responsibility. In 1870 it was moved to new buildings, where it grew in student body, faculty and in its modern curricula, offering calisthenics, bookkeeping, typing and stenography, an early school to offer these to young ladies. Due to financial difficulties, it closed in 1896.

Central Church, which had both white and Negro members, has given birth to seven churches in the present Staunton urban area. In so doing, it has maintained its

leadership in program, size, and benevolent giving while remaining a downtown church.

Meeting in Central Church in 1861, the Baltimore Conference voted to unite with the M.E. Church, South. One of the last meetings of the Baltimore Conference, M.E. Church, South was held in Central, which then became a part of the Virginia Conference of The Methodist Church.

RICHARD M. HAMRICK, JR.

STEBBINS, GEORGE COLES (1846-1945), American hymn writer and churchman, was born Feb. 26, 1846, in a rural community near Albion in Orleans County, N. Y. The boy had the privilege of growing up in a Christian home. The example of his parents formed and guided his interests and concerns throughout his life. At the age of twelve, shortly after the death of his father, George participated in a "Singing School," and came under the influence of Dexter Manly, the vocal instructor of the group. This experience awakened his interest in music and was, in fact, the beginning of his musical career. In later years he traveled to Buffalo and then to Rochester to study singing. While at Rochester, Stebbins met and married Elma Miller, the daughter of a local preacher.

In 1869 the family moved to CHICAGO. There Stebbins became a charter member of the Apollo Club and directed the choir of the First Baptist Church. He later moved to BOSTON and, while there, was invited to meet Dwight L. Moody, who asked him to join him in evangelistic work. Stebbins did so, and travelled to many countries and cities directing the music. During his travels with Moody, he began to write gospel hymn tunes. Among the better known tunes he wrote for hymns are: *Saviour Breathe An Evening Blessing, Saved By Grace, There Is A Green Hill Far Away,* and *True Hearted, Whole Hearted.* A collection of his hymn tunes, manuscripts, letters, etc., collected by his long time friend, J. B. Clay, is preserved in the National Cathedral in Washington, D.C. It is known as "The George Coles Stebbins' Deposit of Gospel Hymns."

After the death of his wife and only son, Waring, Stebbins moved to Catskill, N. Y., where he lived with his sister, Mrs. Ella Miller. There he spent his last years editing his music, carrying on a large correspondence, reading and praying for those engaged in evangelistic work around the world. Though deaf, and unable to hear the music or the sermon, he went faithfully to the worship of God at the Methodist Church in Catskill as long as he was able.

In appreciation of his life's work, and in recognition of his contribution to Christian hymnody, the people of Catskill, assisted by friends across the land, raised a memorial fund to install a set of electronic bells in the steeple of the Methodist Church. Through them his music still proclaims the Good News of Jesus Christ, as it also does in the singing of congregations around the world. George Coles Stebbins died Oct. 6, 1945, having lived and served his God for nearly 100 years. Interment took place on Oct. 8, 1945, in the Maple Grove Cemetery, Kew Gardens, N. Y.

History of the Methodist Chuch, Catskill, N. Y. 1946.
George C. Stebbins, *Reminiscences And Gospel Hymn Stories.* New York: George H. Doran Co., 1924.

C. WESLEY CHRISTMAN, JR.

STECKEL, KARL (1913-   ), is a member of NORTH-WEST GERMANY ANNUAL CONFERENCE, formerly WEST GERMANY CONFERENCE of the E.U.B. CHURCH since 1936. He was born Jan. 27, 1913, the son of Richard Steckel, superintendent of the West Germany Conference (EUB), and Lydia Herrmann. He married Ruth Schneidereit in 1939. He was educated at the Universities of Munster i. Westfalen and Tuebingen; Theological Seminary (EUB) in Reutlingen, 1932-36. His appointment to circuits have been Bebra, 1936-37; Tabarz, 1937-39; HAMBURG, 1939-50; Boehum, 1950-52. In 1940-45 he saw military service during the war at the East and West front. He then became professor of Old Testament and Systematic Theology at the Theological Seminary in Reutlingen, 1952, and has been president since 1966. He was made president of the united THEOLOGICAL SEMINARY in FRANK-FURT/Main at the union in 1968. He was vice-president of E.U.B. Church Council in GERMANY, 1966-68, and a delegate to the GENERAL CONFERENCE (EUB) in HARRIS-BURG, Pa., 1958. He was a member of the Working Association of Evangelical Youth in Germany, 1947-52; member of the GERMANY CENTRAL CONFERENCE since 1952; and a member of "Deutscher Ökumenischer Studienausschuss" since 1958. He was co-editor of a Christian education periodical, 1946-52; editor of the German E.U.B. Church weekly, *Der Botschafter*, 1965-67; contributor to *Calwer Bibellexikon*, 1961-63; editor *Die Evangelisch-methodistische Kirche—Was sie glaubt*, 1968.

STEDEFORD, CHARLES (1864-1953), was born in Bristol, England, and entered the BIBLE CHRISTIAN ministry in 1883. After twenty-six years in circuit work, gaining a reputation for fervent evangelism, he served continuously as Foreign Missions Secretary of the UNITED METHODIST CHURCH (BR.) from 1910 until Methodist Union in 1932. He traveled twice to CHINA and once to AFRICA in search of first-hand knowledge of missions in these countries. In 1928 he became president of the United Methodist Church Conference. He continued to preach into his eighty-eighth year and died at Wylde Green, BIRMINGHAM, on April 7, 1953.

H. Smith, *United Methodist Church*. 1933.   A. W. G. COURT

STEEL, EDWARD ROBERT (1865-1933), American minister, was born in Lockesburg, Ark., on July 25, 1865, the youngest son of Thomas George Tucker and Phoebe Turrentine Steel. In September of 1887 he enrolled in Central Collegiate Institute at Altus, Ark. This school became HENDRIX COLLEGE, and was moved to Conway, Ark. in 1890. Because of the death of his father, he was forced to drop out of college in the middle of his senior year and did not complete his formal education. In 1893 he was admitted into the LITTLE ROCK CONFER-ENCE. He served the Peytonville Circuit, the Center Point Circuit, and then Asbury Church in Little Rock. Later he became chaplain of the State Penitentiary, where he served for two years.

In 1899 he married Katherine Tyler, the oldest daughter of Joseph K. Tyler and Harriet Marsh. They became the parents of four sons, Richard Tucker, Samuel Tyler, MARSHALL TURRENTINE, and David McIntosh.

In 1900 Steel was transferred to Bentonville in the ARKANSAS CONFERENCE. He served churches at Benton-ville, Fayetteville, and Fort Smith, later becoming presiding elder of the Fort Smith District. From here he was sent to Conway, Ark. In all of these pastorates except the one in Fort Smith, new church buildings were started under his ministry. In 1914 he was transferred once more to the Little Rock Conference, where he served First Church in Pine Bluff. Here another church building was constructed. On leaving Pine Bluff he served as presiding elder of the LITTLE ROCK District, later the Monticello District, and then the Pine Bluff District. In 1917 Hendrix College conferred an honorary D.D. degree upon him.

Edward Steel died in Camden, Ark., on Sept. 24, 1933 and was buried in Pine Bluff.

Journal of the Little Rock Conference, 1933.

MARSHALL T. STEEL

STEEL, MARSHALL TURRENTINE (1906-   ), American pastor and college president, was born at Fort Smith, Ark., on Jan. 2, 1906, the son of E. R. and Kate (Tyler) Steel. He was educated at HENDRIX COLLEGE, B.A., 1927; D.D., 1939; Union Theological Seminary, B.D., 1931; and SOUTHERN METHODIST UNIVERSITY, LL.D. (*causa honoris*), 1948. He married Ouita Burroughs on Sept. 4, 1930, and their children are William E., Robert T., and Sarah (Mrs. Norwood O. Hill). Dr. Steel joined the LITTLE ROCK CONFERENCE (MES) in 1927 and served in Bauxite, Ark., 1931-32; Monticello, Ark., 1932-33; LITTLE ROCK, 1933-36, at which time he became pastor of the large Highland Park Church, DALLAS, TEXAS, serving there as pastor from 1936 to 1957. The following year he became president of Hendrix College, Conway, Ark. He was a delegate to the JURISDICTIONAL and General Conferences of 1948, '52, '56, '60, and '64; and a member of the Board of Publication of The Methodist Church, 1944-61. He has also served upon the general Board of EDUCATION since 1961. He was a speaker at the Methodist Men's Broadcast, 1952-59, and was named the outstanding Man of the Year by the Dallas Junior Chamber of Commerce, 1939; also named Man of the Year in ARKANSAS, 1962.

Who's Who in America, Vol. 34.
Who's Who in the Methodist Church, 1966.   N. B. H.

STEEL, SAMUEL AUGUSTUS (1849-1934), American preacher, editor, and author, was born near Grenada, Miss., on Oct. 5, 1849, the son of Ferdinand Lawrence and Amanda Fitzgerald (Hankins) Steel. His parents educated him at the isolated MISSISSIPPI farm on which they lived during and after the Civil War. Licensed to preach at seventeen, he held a pastorate in Hickman, Ky., before entering EMORY AND HENRY COLLEGE in Abingdon, Va., where he also served as a pastor. In 1873 he was chosen CHAPLAIN of the University of Virginia, and he was able to continue his education there. He was later awarded the M.A. degree by Emory and Henry College and the D.D. by EMORY COLLEGE in GEORGIA.

Between 1875 and 1918, S. A. Steel served many of the principal urban pastorates of the M.E. Church, South, in VIRGINIA, SOUTH CAROLINA, Mississippi, TENNESSEE, KENTUCKY, MISSOURI, TEXAS, and LOUISIANA. He was named a fraternal delegate to the 1888 GENERAL CONFER-ENCE of the M.E. Church. His pastoral duties were interrupted by appointment as the first secretary of the EP-

WORTH LEAGUE and editor of the *Epworth Era* (1894-18-98); by extensive travel as a CHAUTAUQUA lecturer, and by the presidencies of the Manual Labor School at Lumberton, Miss., the Logan (Kentucky) Female College, and the Memphis Conference Female Institute.

Besides contributing widely to the church press, he wrote *The Modern Theory of the Bible; En Route; Fraternity and other Addresses;* the autobiographical *The Sunny Road;* and other books and pamphlets. In his years of retirement he prepared a weekly column, "Creole Gumbo," for the Memphis *Commercial Appeal.*

Grandson, son, and father of Methodist preachers, S. A. Steel exemplified in his career the vitality of the Methodist tradition in the American South in the era following the Civil War.

Journal of Louisiana Conference, MES, 1934.

EDWARD MARVIN STEEL, JR.

STEELE, DANIEL (1824-1914), American college president, theologian, and writer of holiness literature, was born on Oct. 5, 1824 in Windham, N. Y. He joined the NEW ENGLAND CONFERENCE in 1849, after he had graduated from WESLEYAN UNIVERSITY the previous year with high honors. In 1850 he married Harriet Binney, the daughter of Amos Binney, another Methodist theologian. He served pastorates in Boston, Lynn, Syracuse, and Springfield from 1850-61 and 1878-87. He spent twenty-five years as a teacher at such colleges as SYRACUSE UNIVERSITY, Wesleyan University, Genesee College, BOSTON UNIVERSITY and New England Deaconess Training School. In 1872 Daniel Steele became the first president of Syracuse University.

In 1870 Steele received what he affirmed to be the second blessing and immediately put his intellectual abilities to work on behalf of the rising HOLINESS MOVEMENT, of which he became the leading literary exponent. Several of his books became classics in this field. In 1875 *Love Enthroned,* his first book, was widely received. This was followed by *Milestone Papers, Binney's Theological Compend Improved,* and *A Defense of Christian Perfection.* All of these are still in print nearly 100 years later. The last mentioned book was written specifically against the idea of gradual perfection as expounded in a book by Steele's colleague JAMES MUDGE. Other books from this prolific writer include *Half Hours with St. Paul, Half Hours with St. John's Epistles, The Gospel of the Comforter, Jesus Exultant, Commentary on Joshua, Commentary on Leviticus and Numbers,* and a *Substitute for Holiness.* Steele died on Sept. 2, 1914, and it is the finest commentary on his life that the above mentioned James Mudge wrote Steele's obituary which appeared in the *Minutes of the New England Conference.*

Minutes of the New England Conference, 1915.
M. Simpson, *Cyclopaedia.* 1878. J. GORDON MELTON

STEELE, GEORGE McKENDREE (1823-1902), American pastor and educator, was born in Strafford, Vt., April 13, 1823. The son of an itinerant with eleven children, he graduated from WESLEYAN UNIVERSITY in 1850, and the same year taught Mathematics and Latin at Wesleyan Academy, WILBRAHAM, Mass.

Joining the NEW ENGLAND CONFERENCE in 1853, Steele was engaged in pastoral work until 1865 at which time he was chosen president of LAWRENCE UNIVERSITY,

Appleton, Wis., and held that position for fourteen years. He was an inspiring teacher and resourceful administrator, earnest, sympathetic, and full of humor.

Subsequently he was head of WILBRAHAM WESLEYAN ACADEMY for thirteen years. He was a member of the Board of Visitors to the U. S. Naval Academy in 1871, and a member of two General Conferences, 1868 and 1872.

A frequent and much appreciated contributor to Zion's *Herald,* he wrote at least twenty-five carefully prepared papers between 1855 and 1873 dealing with literary, biographical, scientific, metaphysical, theological, social, historical, and educational subjects. These were published in such magazines as the *Atlantic, Boston Review, Christian Examiner,* and theological quarterlies of different denominations.

George McKendree Steele died Jan. 14, 1902.

M. Simpson, *Cyclopaedia.* 1882.
W. F. Warren, *George McKendree Steele, A Memoir.* Chicago: privately published, 1902. JESSE A. EARL

STEELE, MARIANNE SHIRLEY TRABUE (1865-1961), an outstanding laywoman in the M.E. Church, South, and leader in the church's mission program, was born in NASHVILLE, Tenn., on Dec. 1, 1865, and was educated in Nashville schools and at Ward's Seminary, Nashville.

In 1889 she was married to Hume Steele, a prominent attorney of Pulaski, Tenn., and they had four children. Upon the death of her husband in 1906, Mrs. Steele became identified with the woman's missionary work of the M.E. Church, South. Because of this new relationship, it became necessary to change her residence from Pulaski to Nashville.

Mrs. Steele became one of the most distinguished women in the Southern church. From 1910-14, she was president of the TENNESSEE CONFERENCE Woman's Missionary Society; from 1917-19 she was president of the Federated Boards of the Women's Missionary Society of North America; and from 1914-33 she was educational and candidate secretary of the Women's Section of the BOARD of MISSIONS of the M.E. Church, South. In connection with her work, Mrs. Steele taught classes in missionary education in pastors' schools and training schools all over the United States.

She died on Sept. 4, 1961.

The Nashville Banner, Nov. 4, 1928.
Pacific Methodist Advocate, Aug. 5, 1926.
World Outlook, January 1934. CULLEN T. CARTER

STEINHAUER, HENRY BIRD (c.1820-1884), Canadian missionary, was born about 1820 near Rama, Ontario, into an Ojibway family. From 1829 to 1832 he attended school at the Indian mission on Grape Island in the Bay of Quinte, and subsequently spent some time at Cazenovia Seminary in NEW YORK state. He studied at Upper Canada Academy in Cobourg in 1837, and in 1836 helped WILLIAM CASE at the Alderville Indian Mission. In 1840 he went to Rainy Lake, in what became northwestern Ontario, to assist William Mason, a Wesleyan missionary. He was soon called, however, to act as interpreter, teacher, and translator in collaboration with JAMES EVANS at Norway House.

Steinhauer was received on trial in 1851 and ordained

by the Wesleyan Methodist Conference, which met in London, Canada West, in 1854. In company with THOMAS WOOLSEY, who was ordained at the same Conference, Steinhauer went again to the northwest territories and took up the work begun by ROBERT RUNDLE at Lac la Biche. With the help of Benjamin Sinclair, Rundle's lay assistant, he established a new mission at White Fish Lake. Here Steinhauer remained, with the exception of one year, until his death on Dec. 30, 1884.

He taught the Indians how to grow crops and livestock in order to make possible a settled economy. His congregation numbered four hundred; it employed two local preachers. There were regular class meetings, a Sunday school and two day schools at the mission. Among his family of ten, one daughter married JOHN MC-DOUGALL; Egerton and Robert became Methodist ministers. Steinhauer maintained his scholarly interests, and in 1865 helped to revise the hymnary and catechism in Cree syllabics. He was a man of great charm and energy who was revered by his fellows.

J. Carroll, *Case and His Cotemporaries.* 1867-77.
G. H. Cornish, *Cyclopaedia of Methodism.* 1881.
J. Maclean, *Henry B. Steinhauer.* Toronto: Methodist Publishing House, n.d.   J. E. NIX

STEPHENS, DAVID S. (1847-1921), American minister and educator, was born May 12, 1847, in Springfield, Ohio, the son of Rev. and Mrs. O. P. Stephens. He was educated in the public schools, attended Wittenberg College, entered ADRIAN COLLEGE in his senior year and graduated in 1869. He secured his M.A. degree in Edinburgh, Scotland, and completed further graduate work at Harvard University. In 1870 he became a member of the Adrian College faculty, teaching Philosophy and Ethics. From 1882-88 he was president of the College, resigning to become editor of the *Methodist Recorder.* After eight years he was elected Chancellor of KANSAS CITY UNIVERSITY. He held this position for fifteen years, when ill health compelled him to resign. Stephens was ordained by the OHIO CONFERENCE of the M.P. CHURCH, representing that Conference at three GENERAL CONFERENCES. He was also a denominational representative to the ECUMENICAL METHODIST CONFERENCE in LONDON. Besides granting him his earned Ph.D. degree, WESTERN MARYLAND COLLEGE conferred on him the honorary D.D. degree. He served four years as president of the General Conference.

FRANK W. STEPHENSON

STEPHENS, GRACE (1863?-1936), a saintly Anglo-Indian Methodist evangelist, was born in Fort St. George, Madras, INDIA, in 1863 or 1864. Converted while in her teens under the ministry of Bishop WILLIAM TAYLOR, she joined the Methodist Church and began a ministry of witness, visitation, and service that extended to many parts of Madras city. She began her church work in 1886 and was appointed a missionary of the WOMAN'S FOREIGN MISSIONARY SOCIETY of the M.E. Church in 1891. She taught and preached; she fed the hungry, comforted the bereaved, warned the sinful, healed the sick, and took loving care of little children. She was known and loved by multitudes in Madras, and her influence was felt in all sections of India. After meeting her, an American businessman said, "One can't be in her presence without

realizing that she has lived long with Christ Jesus." She died May 30, 1936.

J. WASKOM PICKETT

JOHN STEPHENS

STEPHENS, JOHN (1772-1827), British Methodist, was born in Cornwall, Feb. 8, 1772. He entered the WESLEYAN METHODIST ministry in 1792. He was elected president of the Wesleyan CONFERENCE in 1827, and warmly supported Protestant Methodists. He was strongly conservative in religion and politics, and was deeply distressed by the behavior of his son, JOSEPH R. STEPHENS, in 1834. He superannuated in 1834, and died at Brixton Hill, on Jan. 29, 1841.

B. Gregory, *Sidelights.* 1898.   JOHN KENT

STEPHENS, JOSEPH RAYNER (1805-1879), British Methodist, was the son of JOHN STEPHENS, president of the Wesleyan CONFERENCE, but he was expelled from the ministry in 1834. All his active life he was a stormy petrel, unwilling to temper enthusiasm for the causes he took up with tact or conformity. He called himself a Tory Radical and attacked the Poor Law Amendment Act of 1834; at the same time he was secretary of a liberation society, working for the disestablishment of the Church of England. It was his refusal to give up this work that led to his suspension by the Wesleyan Conference, which was anxious not to alienate Anglicanism. When Stephens joined the Chartists he became one of their outstanding orators, and so inflammatory was some of his eloquence that he was imprisoned for subversion, and the Methodist WILLIAM LOVETT denounced him in his newspaper. After release from prison in 1839, Stephens concentrated more on preaching and pamphleteering; it was too dangerous for a man on 'five-years' bail to go on making political speeches.

G. J. Holyoake, *Joseph Rayner Stephens.* 1881. E. R. TAYLOR

STEPHENS, MATTHEW (?-1928), was a beloved early pastor in North INDIA. A convert from Islam, he was noted for the dignity of his manner, the reverence of his services, the neatness of his dress, his respectful treatment of everyone with whom he dealt, and his instructive and inspiring preaching. He was pastor of Central Methodist Church in LUCKNOW for an aggregate of twenty-six years. He died on Oct. 24, 1928.

J. WASKOM PICKETT

STEPHENS, WILLIAM HENRY (1856-1941), missionary to INDIA, was born in Pennsgrove, N. J., and was educated at Collegiate Institute. As a young man he had studied architectural engineering. One day, when he was studying the blueprint of a building, he was deeply impressed by the thought that life too ought to have a plan. He decided to give up planning buildings and began to build a life. This resolve led him to prepare for Christian service, and found him ready to respond when WILLIAM TAYLOR sought recruits for India. Bishop Taylor himself took the young man to the boat, put him on board, gave his blessing, and assigned him to Bombay.

When the BOMBAY CONFERENCE was formed in 1892, with the division of the SOUTH INDIA CONFERENCE, the name of William Henry Stephens was read out as one of the original members. His chief field of service was Bombay and the Marathi area of western India, with residence sometimes in Bombay and sometimes in Poona. Several years of his life were spent in the Central Provinces, building congregations of Anglo-Indian and Marathi people around Kampti. His willingness to help also took him to distant Karachi and Quetta.

After retirement he stayed on in India, so his lifetime of work extended over sixty years. He was always among those who do with their might what their hands find to do. In the words of Bishop B. H. BADLEY, "For Methodists to say *Poona* is to think *Stephens.*" Over the door of his home in CAMDEN, N. J. was this motto: "Without Him, not over the threshold: with Him, anywhere." He died on June 25, 1941, and was buried beside his wife in Poona.

B. H. Badley, *Indian Missionary Directory.* 1892.
B. T. Badley, ed., *Stephens, Missionary Extraordinary.* Lucknow Publishing House, 1941. JOHN N. HOLLISTER

STEPHENS, GEORGIA, U.S.A. **Center Church,** a very old church in Oglethorpe County, vested its authority at first in the following commissioners: David McLaughlin, David Patrick, George Williamson, George Moore and John Beasley.

On Oct. 13, 1813, one acre of land was purchased from Silas and Savannah Griffin, and on May 7, 1814, one-half acre of land was purchased from David McLaughlin on which was to be placed a "meeting house" where the various groups of Methodists, Baptists and Presbyterians would have a common center to worship Christ as Lord of all.

The Meeting House was named Center for three reasons: it was on the watershed between the Oconee and Savannah Rivers; it was on or near the central point between the six nearest churches, two each of the three denominations using it; and it was a place where the various groups could have a common center to worship Christ as Lord of all. This was indeed a unique and worthy aim, and "Center Meeting House," later to become Center Methodist Church, reflected both this brotherly spirit and adaptability.

The original house was built of hand hewn logs. In 1852 the log building was replaced by a frame structure, and dedication services were conducted by H. H. Parks in July of the same year.

Descendants of the original subscribers have contributed largely to the leadership of the church, J. Robert Campbell entering the ministry while a member there. The contribution of the women of the church has been considerable. The mothers of Joseph A. Thomas and J. Osgood Grogan, who served many years in the NORTH GEORGIA CONFERENCE, were members of Center Church in their girlhood. Two other members, descendants of the McLaughlin family, married ministers who served many years in the North Georgia Conference, George K. Quillian and O. B. Quillian.

The first Woman's Society was organized in 1894.

Today, Center Church has seventy-four members, is well-organized and manifests a fine spirit of devotion and loyalty.

ELIZABETH QUILLIAN WATTERS

STEPHENSON, FRANKLIN WILLIAM (1882-   ), American administrator, minister, educator, author and historian, was a leader in the work of the M.P. CHURCH on the GENERAL CONFERENCE level for sixteen years prior to Methodist unification. He is the son of Chandler Worth Stephenson, a M.P. minister who served pastorates in the MICHIGAN and OHIO ANNUAL CONFERENCES, and L. Alice Hathaway Stephenson. Dr. Stephenson received his bachelor's degree from ADRIAN COLLEGE in 1906, and graduated from WESTMINSTER THEOLOGICAL SEMINARY (now Wesley Theological Seminary) in 1913. The D.D. degree was conferred upon him in 1926 by Adrian College.

Dr. Stephenson served pastorates in MICHIGAN and PENNSYLVANIA and from 1921-24 was the pastor of the M.P. Church in Muncie, Ind. From 1924 until 1940 he served as Executive Secretary, Department of Educational Institutions of the Board of EDUCATION of the M.P. Church, with headquarters in PITTSBURGH, Pa. He held the office of president of WESTMINSTER JUNIOR COLLEGE, Tehuacana, Texas, for six years. He served as president of the Council of Church Boards of Education for one term and after unification served for one year on the Board of Education of The Methodist Church in Nashville, Tenn. Following his official retirement in 1955, he continued in charge of several churches in western Pennsylvania and Michigan. In 1967 he published the book *For Such a Time,* described as "a brief account of Bishop [JAMES H.] STRAUGHN's life and part in bringing the M.P. Church into The Methodist Church." Since 1965 Dr. Stephenson has been Curator of the DETROIT CONFERENCE Historical Society. In 1968 he was elected to membership in "The John Wesley Society" at Wesley Theological Seminary. The Adrian College Alumni Headquarters on the grounds of the College has been named in his honor.

Dr. Stephenson has been married three times: in 1910 to J. Mabel Darling; in 1959 to Elsie Bradshaw; and, in 1967, to Mrs. Walter Mallan. He resides in Adrian, Mich.

F. W. Stephenson, *For Such a Time.* 1967.

RALPH HARDEE RIVES

STEPHENSON, THOMAS BOWMAN (1839-1912), British Methodist, was born at Newcastle upon Tyne in

T. BOWMAN STEPHENSON

1839. He was educated at Wesley College, Sheffield, and trained for the ministry of the WESLEYAN METHODIST CHURCH, which he entered in 1860, at RICHMOND THEOLOGICAL COLLEGE. His ministry was devoted to the twin aims of evangelism and social service, which for him were two sides of the same coin. His pioneering work among deprived children in Lambeth led the Wesleyan Conference of 1871 to recognize his Children's Home (now the NATIONAL CHILDREN'S HOME AND ORPHANAGE), of which he was appointed full-time principal in 1873, and at which he spent the greater part of his ministry.

His work among children led him on to consider the training of women for the service of the church and community. He published a short book, *Sisterhoods*, in 1890, and in 1900 he began the organization of the Wesley Deaconess Institute, modeling it largely on the German Protestant Deaconess Home at Kaiserswerth. He was elected president of the Wesleyan Conference in 1891, and on resigning as principal of the National Children's Home, became superintendent of the Ilkley Circuit. Here he secured the college which is now the training center of the Methodist Deaconess Order, and from 1903 to his retirement in 1907 he was warden of the Deaconess Institute. In 1907 he published a short life of WILLIAM ARTHUR.

Stephenson was deeply interested in church music and hymnody, and was the author of the hymn, "Lord grant us like the watching five." A life of Stephenson, by Bradfield, was published in 1913. He died in 1912, and was carried to his grave in the Children's Home Cemetery in LONDON by twenty-four old boys of his home. He was one of a group of men who, entering the Wesleyan ministry after about 1860, found it impossible to accept the traditional Wesleyan circuit system, with its rigid itinerancy and its emphasis on the absolute authority of the superintendent. The FORWARD MOVEMENT, of which Stephenson's work among deprived children was one of the more positive aspects, resulted in part from this recognition that the great cities of the late nineteenth

century required more varied methods of evangelism than those inherited from the past. Stephenson was also one of the first Wesleyan Methodist ministers not in a department to be exempted from the requirements of the itinerancy; the same policy was followed in the case of the superintendents of the new Central Halls.

JOHN NEWTON

STERLING, JAMES (1742-1818), American layman, preeminent merchant, and lay evangelist, was born in Coleraine, Northern Ireland, on Jan. 6, 1742 (some descendants give date of Feb. 14, 1743), the son of Archibald and Jane (Hunter) Sterling, subsequently of Caln Township, Chester County, Pa., U.S.A., where they are buried in the Brandywine Manor Presbyterian Churchyard.

At twelve years of age Sterling came to America, working with his uncle as a peddlar and later in a store in PHILADELPHIA. About 1762 he opened a general store in BURLINGTON, N. J., where because of his imports and wealth he was called "New Jersey's first merchant-prince." Said John Jay Smith, "In early times no other like concern in Philadelphia could compete with his store."

By his two marriages, first with Mary Shaw (1748-85) and second with Rebecca Budd (1760-1841), he had eighteen children. Of these, John W. was a local preacher, and Mrs. Rebecca B. Cowperthwaite, founder of the church school in Burlington, became the wife of John D. Porter of the NEWARK CONFERENCE.

Major Sterling distinguished himself in public offices, principally as Burlington's third mayor (1801-06). According to family tradition he began his service in the New Jersey Militia (1775-77) by fitting out at his own expense the company he captained.

Brought up a Presbyterian, Sterling heard ASBURY preach about 1771 and became a fervent Methodist, providing the materials for the first meeting house (c.1787). His home in Burlington was a hostel for all Methodist itinerants, especially at Conference time. He was a close friend of Asbury, EZEKIEL COOPER, who wrote his obituary, and all Methodist leaders of his day.

His most abiding influence is seen in the many Methodist societies which he and BENJAMIN ABBOTT together, in their travels as evangelists, established on the eastern seaboard, especially in NEW JERSEY. JOHN ATKINSON wrote, "Probably no layman in the State ever did more to advance the cause of religion and Methodism than Mr. Sterling."

He died on Jan. 6, 1818 and is buried with his second wife in the Methodist Graveyard on Lawrence Street, Burlington. A portrait, given by the writer, hangs in OLD ST. GEORGE'S, PHILADELPHIA.

American Daily Advertiser, Philadelphia, Jan. 19, 1818.
F. Asbury, *Journal and Letters*. 1958.
J. Atkinson, *Memorials in New Jersey*. 1860.
J. Ffirth, *Benjamin Abbott*. 1825.
A. M. Sterling, *The Sterling Genealogy*. New York, 1909.

F. ELWOOD PERKINS

STETLER, ROY HERBEN (1890-   ), American E.U.B. publisher, was born in Salem Township, Luzerne County, Pa., on May 10, 1890, to Samuel N. and M. Eudora (Pollock) Stetler. Following graduation from Berwick (Pennsylvania) High School in 1909, he worked one year as a clerk for the American Car and Foundry Company. In 1911 he moved to HARRISBURG, Pa., as assistant to the manager of THE EVANGELICAL PRESS, the printing arm of The EVANGELICAL CHURCH. That same year he married Dora E. Lohr, and to them were born three children. In 1922 Stetler was elected Publishing Agent of The Evangelical Church, and later was named a Publisher of the merged E.U.B. Church, in which capacity he served until his retirement in 1958.

Stetler, long active in community affairs, is a past president of the following: Harrisburg Kiwanis Club, Harrisburg Chamber of Commerce, Pennsylvania State Y.M.C.A., Harrisburg Central Branch Y.M.C.A., and he is a director of the Harrisburg Polyclinic Hospital and Harrisburg National Bank and Trust Company. AL-BRIGHT COLLEGE conferred upon him an honorary Litt.D. degree in 1948.

He has been an active layman and teacher in Harrisburg's Harris Street E.U.B. Church for over fifty years, and he has preached in countless pulpits throughout the United States. He began writing for the official church paper of his denomination in 1931, and has published five books of his writings: *Just Chats* (1948), *Seeing God In Little Things* (1951), *In The Strangest Places— God* (1953), *God Was There* (1956), and *With God We Can* (1958). In retirement he and his wife live in Harrisburg.

EDWIN L. STETLER

ABEL STEVENS

STEVENS, ABEL (1815-1897), American church editor and leader and one who exerted enormous influence during the controversies and turmoil of the mid-nineteenth century in American Methodism, was born in PHILADEL-PHIA, Pa., on Jan. 19, 1815. He entered the NEW ENGLAND CONFERENCE in 1834, and after serving one year as agent of WESLEYAN UNIVERSITY, Middletown, Conn., was the following year stationed in BOSTON. In 1837 he made a European tour. In 1848 he became editor of *Zion's Herald,* and in this position remained

for twelve years, becoming known throughout the Church for the strong positions he took, and his great ability in the editorial field.

Stevens was counted as a moderate in opposition to the abolitionist party then growing in the M.E. Church, and as editor of *Zion's Herald* opposed strongly the attitude of ORANGE SCOTT and LUCIUS MATLACK for their actions and statements in furtherance of the American Anti-Slavery Society. It was partly because of such opposition that when in 1848 he was elected editor of *The Christian Advocate,* he declined to accept. However, in 1852 when *The National Magazine* was commenced, he was appointed editor. He was considered by the Southerners a somewhat balancing influence while he had charge of these papers, and he took the side of the M.E. Church, South following its organization under the PLAN OF SEPARATION, feeling that the GENERAL CONFERENCE of 1844 had been competent to produce such a plan, and the Southerners empowered to act under it.

In 1860, Stevens became corresponding editor of *The Methodist* and retained this position until 1874. His writings were voluminous and widely circulated during his lifetime. These included *The Memorials of the Introduction of Methodism into New England; Memorials of the Progress of Methodism in the Eastern States: Church Polity; The Preaching Required by the Times; Sketches and Incidents: A Budget from the Saddle-Bags of an Itinerant; Tales from the Parsonage; The Great Reform; Systematic Benevolence;* and his enduring *History of Methodism;* and *History of the Methodist Episcopal Church* (four volumes, New York, Carleton and Porter, 1864-67). This monumental work has long been considered an authority regarding the overall life and sweep of Methodism at that period. Stevens also wrote *Centenary of American Methodism; The Women of Methodism;* and the *Life and Times of Nathan Bangs.*

Abel Stevens died at the Hotel Vendome, San Jose, Calif. on Sept. 11, 1897.

E. S. Bucke, *History of American Methodism.* 1964.
M. Simpson, *Cyclopaedia.* 1881. N. B. H.

STEVENSON, DANIEL (1823-1897), American minister, was born at Versailles, Ky., on Nov. 12, 1823. He came from a long line of Methodist ancestry reaching back to the first days of Methodist work in MARYLAND under ROBERT STRAWBRIDGE. His grandparents were among the first settlers to come to Kentucky—migrating to Mason County on the Ohio River. Stevenson graduated from Transylvania College in 1847. He joined the KENTUCKY CONFERENCE on trial in 1850. In 1849 he married Sarah Hitt Corwine, the daughter of Richard and Sarah Hitt Corwine. A son, Richard Corwine Stevenson, was for many years professor of history at OHIO WESLEYAN UNIVERSITY.

Although Stevenson held a number of titles and served one term as a presiding elder in the Kentucky Conference, he is best known for his work as an educator. He was one of the founders of KENTUCKY WESLEYAN COLLEGE. Its charter was secured in 1858, but because of the war the school did not open until later. Stevenson served two years as a field agent for the institution. He was superintendent of public instruction in KENTUCKY from 1863 to 1867, being the first person to give full-time work to this office.

Stevenson will be remembered because of his connection with the founding in 1865 of the Kentucky Conference of the M.E. Church in COVINGTON. For some years there had been agitation on the part of a number of people in Kentucky asking for the Kentucky Conference to transfer to the M.E. Church. The records show several meetings between Bishop H. H. KAVANAUGH and Stevenson on this matter. However, when the conference refused to vote favorably on a majority report requesting such action, Stevenson along with seventeen other members relocated. In 1865, Bishop D. W. CLARK of CINCINNATI, OHIO, met with these eighteen and fourteen others making thirty-two assembled in Covington, Ky., for the formation of the Kentucky Conference.

While Stevenson was pastor of Trinity Church, LOUISVILLE, KY., he formed an acquaintance with Joshua and FANNIE SPEED. In later years the large bequest that came from Mrs. Fannie Speed made possible a substantial endowment for UNION COLLEGE at BARBOURVILLE, KY.

In 1879 Stevenson undertook to reestablish AUGUSTA COLLEGE which had been closed in 1850. He labored there until 1887 when Union College was taken over by the Kentucky Conference of the M.E. Church. He served from 1887-97 as Union College's first president under Methodist auspices. He died in Barbourville on Jan. 2, 1897.

JOHN O. GROSS

STEVENSON, GEORGE JOHN (1818-1888), British Methodist, was an expert on Methodist hymns. Originally a schoolmaster, he was a LONDON bookseller from 1855. He also edited the *Wesleyan Times* (1861-1867). He published *City Road Chapel, London* (1872); *The Methodist Hymn Book and its Associations* (1869), enlarged as *The Methodist Hymn Book Illustrated* (1883); *Memorials of the Wesley Family* (1876); *Methodist Worthies* (7 vols., 1884-86). He died in London, Aug. 16, 1888.

W. L. DOUGHTY

STEVENSON, WILLIAM (1768-1857), American preacher, was born near Ninety-Six, S.C., on Oct. 4, 1768. He was nurtured as a Methodist class leader and local preacher, 1800-09, under WILLIAM MCKENDREE and Bishop ASBURY in Smith County, Tenn. Moving to Bellevue, Mo., in 1809, he joined the TENNESSEE CONFERENCE in 1815. In the fall of the same year he preached the first Protestant sermon on TEXAS soil at Pecan Point, on Red River, northeast of present Clarksville. About the same time he preached the first Protestant sermon in what is now OKLAHOMA. In 1816 he moved to Mound Prairie, Ark., and in 1818 was named presiding elder of a new district named Arkansas in the recently created MISSOURI CONFERENCE. He pioneered the laying of Methodist foundations throughout the state for the next half-dozen years.

During these years he sent several of his preachers into east Texas unofficially to see if they would be permitted to preach, even though Roman Catholicism was the state religion there; he also carried on correspondence on the same topic with Stephen F. Austin, Texas political leader whom he had known in MISSOURI and ARKANSAS.

In 1826 he moved to Claiborne Parish, La., where he continued to establish churches and districts. He created a new Natchitoches District, and was made presiding elder, and later did the same for the Monroe District. He retired in 1832 but lived until 1857.

Stevenson's contribution lies in his strategy and courage in establishing outposts on the wilderness frontier of Arkansas, Oklahoma, LOUISIANA, and Texas. Horace Jewell wrote: "The history of Methodism west of the Mississippi is more bound up in his life and labors than perhaps any other man's." In 1970 the NORTH TEXAS CONFERENCE completed plans to have an official Texas State Historical Marker erected in honor of Stevenson on Interstate 30 some miles south of the site of the 1815 preaching.

New Orleans Christian Advocate, 1858.
W. N. Vernon, *William Stevenson*. 1964. WALTER N. VERNON

STEWARD (in American Methodism) was the designation of a lay officer of the Methodist Church who had official responsibility for managing many matters connected with the temporal well-being of his local church. The name came from an appointment by JOHN WESLEY in the early days of the Methodist movement who found it necessary to select men to receive, account for, and disburse the collections which had then begun to be taken in the societies.

Wesley tells in his *Plain Account of the People Called Methodists* that feeling the weight of the care of temporal things, especially the matter of distributing the collections, he "chose out first one, then four, then after a time, seven, as prudent men as I knew, and desired them to take charge of these things upon themselves, that I might have no incumbrance of this kind" (p. 185, Vol. V, *Wesley's Works*). He added that the business of these "stewards" is "to manage the temporal things of the society. To receive the subscriptions and contributions. To expend what is needful from time to time. To send relief to the poor. To keep an exact record of all receipts and expenses. To inform the minister if any of the rules of the society are not punctually observed. To tell the preachers in love if they think any thing amiss, either in their doctrine or life." (*Ibid.*)

It was a happy choice which led Wesley to choose the word "steward" for these lay administrators, and from that day to this the steward has played a prominent part in the ongoing of the whole Methodist movement. In American Methodism at its beginning the pastor in charge was empowered to appoint the stewards for each charge as Wesley had at first done. Bishop ASBURY defended this practice on the ground that the pastor would know better than anyone else who might serve acceptably in this position. The revolt against the strongly centralized administration of early Methodism brought about a change here so that eventually the stewards were elected by the quarterly conferences in each charge, but on nomination of the pastor.

The number of stewards allowed each charge differed from time to time as the General Conference has seen fit to determine.

History of The Office 1784-1968. Stewards in the Methodist Church were in time nominated by a nominating committee and elected at the last QUARTERLY CONFERENCE of the year for the year yet to come. They took their office at the beginning of the Conference year following their election. However, if a steward was elected to fill a vacancy in the Board of Stewards, he took office immediately after his election. Vacancies were filled by the quarterly conference in regular or special sessions, for the OFFICIAL BOARD of the Church could not elect stewards as this was the privilege of the quarterly conference only.

Stewards held office for one year, subject to reelection by the quarterly conference year after year, as is often done. The *Discipline* carefully outlined the duties of stewards, and these duties have, of course, grown enormously with the great growth of the organizational pattern and work of each local church. The stewards in each charge were organized as a Board of Stewards, or as was usually the case, as the nucleus and preponderant majority of the Official Board.

The "recording steward" in each local church was the secretary of the Quarterly (now Charge) Conference, and kept the records of each session of that Conference. These records or minutes were signed by the DISTRICT SUPERINTENDENT—or whoever acted as president—as he closed each Conference session and approved the minutes. The recording steward was elected such by the Quarterly Conference itself.

Another steward, known as the district steward which office is yet called for, represents in the District Stewards' Meetings the interest of his particular church. His especial duty is to meet with the other district stewards as each fiscal year opens, and see that the money, which must be raised during the year by the respective churches of the District, is allotted equitably to the different charges of the District. The district steward is said to be the only church officer in American Methodism for whom no rules of guidance whatever are outlined in the *Book of Discipline,* nor is there any specific delineation of his duties. Former *Disciplines* provided that stewards be "men of solid piety, who both know and love the Methodist doctrine and discipline, and of good natural and acquired abilities to transact the temporal business." (*Discipline* 1788, *et sg.*) The 1964 *Discipline* altered this to "stewards shall be persons of genuine Christian character who love the church and are competent to administer its affairs." All stewards had to be members of the local Methodist church except in certain situations in the Central Conferences in lands outside the United States.

Ex officio stewards known in the later years of The Methodist Church were those who served as stewards by virtue of their particular church office—the church lay leader, the church business manager, the director of Christian education or the educational assistant, the church-school superintendent, the chairmen of all commissions, the secretary of stewardship, the lay member and first reserve lay member of the Annual Conference, the president of the WOMEN'S SOCIETY OF CHRISTIAN SERVICE, the president of METHODIST MEN, the church treasurer or treasurers, the financial secretary, the membership secretary, the president of the Youth Adult Fellowship, and the president of the Methodist Youth Fellowship, or the president of the Youth Council if more than one fellowship is organized. These persons by virtue of their office enjoyed all the privileges of stewards in the meetings of the Board of Stewards. As most of these were and are elected to their respective church positions by the quarterly (now charge) conference, to that extent they too are elected persons.

In The United Methodist Church. In the reorganization of The Methodist Church when it became The United Methodist Church in 1968, the name steward largely disappeared from the *Discipline* of that year except in the case of the district steward. Those who were formerly called stewards were to be called members of the "Administrative Board" and certain specified persons, as the chairmen of various local committees, were specifically named rather than being called stewards as such. The other Methodisms, aside from The United Methodist Church, of course keep the name and in common parlance the officers of each local church and members of the administrative board will no doubt continue to be called stewards for some time to come.

The finances of the local church have traditionally provided the great work and care of the Board of Stewards. That Board's relationship to the Official Board in the local church will be described under that organization.

Disciplines.
R. Emory, *History of the Discipline.* 1844.
N. B. Harmon, *Organization.* 1962.
J. Wesley, *Works.* 1829-31.   N. B. H.

STEWARD (in British Methodism). This title JOHN WESLEY may have borrowed from the old RELIGIOUS SOCIETIES, and he began to use it almost as soon as the first truly Methodist society was organised at the Foundery, LONDON, in 1739. The original duty of the stewards he appointed for the London society was to collect and disburse money for paying off the debt on the Foundery and for keeping it in good repair. Shortly afterwards Wesley added the responsibility for distributing the money collected for the poor, so that they also functioned like the modern "Stewards of the Poor Fund," except that in that capacity they did not make the physical arrangements for the administration of the Lord's Supper. Soon all the financial affairs of most Methodist societies throughout England were in the hands of similar officers. They were really what are now known as "Society Stewards," but carried out also the duties which, after Methodism grew in size and complexity, were delegated to chapel and poor stewards. The CIRCUIT QUARTERLY MEETING was in effect a meeting of all the stewards and all the class leaders of the societies in each circuit, together with the preachers stationed there, and at the first such Quarterly Meeting (Oct. 18, 1748) from among the "particular stewards" serving the different societies two were appointed as "general stewards" to look after the finances of the circuit as a whole. This office underwent many developments, and after Wesley's death became that of "Circuit Steward." In 1753 two of the Foundery stewards, William Briggs and THOMAS BUTTS, were asked to take care of Wesley's bookselling business in London. They thus became the first of a long series of BOOK STEWARDS, this office also in origin being an extension of the work of a regular society steward, although it soon became a highly specialised responsibility. Although some division of the duties of the stewards came gradually to be accepted, during Wesley's lifetime the situation remained somewhat amorphous, and stewards at different times and in different places carried out varying duties or combinations of duties, and were accorded varying degrees of prestige and authority, although Wesley made it quite clear that they were superior in status to the class leaders. In 1794 the trustees of a society were empowered to choose their own steward to oversee the building or buildings for which they were responsible, but neither his title nor duties were fully defined, and several variants have remained, the most common titles being chapel steward and property steward. Only in the nineteenth century was the office of poor steward clearly separated from that of society steward, and not until 1867 was the title "circuit steward" officially accepted in Wesleyan Methodism in place of "general steward."

Davies and Rupp, *Methodist Church in Great Britain*. 1965.
W. Peirce, *Ecclesiastical Principles*. 1873.
Spencer and Finch, *Constitutional Practice*. 1951.

Frank Baker

STEWARDSHIP has come to be the term in present-day Methodist use and in that of other Christian bodies for a general attitude toward personal property as this is held by the Christian individual. It denominates an attitude toward earthly possessions, such possessions being considered not solely as private, personal holdings, but as values held in trust for God who is the Giver of all goods, as well as of life itself. Since the soul of each Christian admittedly belongs to God, so also he feels his possessions should also belong to God with he himself, of course, to administer and manage these in line with what he feels to be the will of God in property values, as in all the relationships of life.

Stewardship, as so denominated, occupies a position apart from the two prevalent driving forces in the realm of economics which the world has known for many centuries. One of these driving forces is the "profit motive" wherein each individual feels the need to acquire for himself—not always for selfish reasons—whatever he may gain in the way of goods of this world, in order first to support himself and family, and possibly to acquire the power and prestige which comes through the acquisition of money or other riches.

The other system is communism in which all theoretically share equally in all goods and values. In its pure form communism has always been quite intriguing to idealistic and Christian people. Indeed, the early Christians, as the Book of Acts tells us (4:32), for a time had "all things in common" with no one to have a claim more than another, and all to share equally "as each had necessity." This pattern of procedure, however, did not work out with such good people as the early Christians, nor is it believed that it will work any better today unless it be enforced by a ruthless police power which sooner or later comes to be the very breath of life to the communistic systems as the world now knows them. Many Christian groups through the ages and from time to time have endeavored to live as communistic colonies, but, while it seems to be quite noble in theory, in actual practice the system breaks down, as it broke down in the Book of Acts when the Greek Christians thought they were mitigated against by the Apostles (who were Jews) in the distribution of the daily goods and values (Acts 6:1).

However, again and again the communistic ideal has been before the Church, and at the time of the Reformation it was found necessary to formulate for the Church of England an Article of Religion—"The riches and goods of Christians are not common, as touching the right, title, and possession of the same, as some do falsely boast. Notwithstanding, every man ought, of such things as he possesseth, liberally to give alms to the poor, according to his ability." (*Article XXIV*—UMC). John Wesley passed this article on to American Methodism with no change at all and it is now Article XXIV of The United Methodist Church.

Our Christian forebears in England considered this Article necessary as an affirmation that each Christian does have a right to his own possessions. Our Church, therefore, teaches that the title to one's private property is inherent in the individual, and this has been a fundamental precept among the Anglo-Saxon people, and among other peoples who are outside present-day communistic lands. The above Article of Religion does however guard against a rapacious capitalism—the "profit motive"—by affirming that every man out of his own private possessions must give to the poor according to his ability—and this means that there is a Christian obligation to share with others.

Stewardship for most Christians seems to be the answer to both these conflicting economic systems. The individual Christian truly and rightfully owns his own goods and values, and no one else may rightfully claim them; but in this world he holds all such in trust for God and for his fellow man. He is a steward keeping in trust his own share of this world's goods.

There is enormous literature on stewardship put out by the Methodist Churches, especially by the Board of the Laity, and other lay organizations in the different large Methodist Churches. Many Christian men of means sincerely feel their obligation to fulfill the ideal which Christian stewardship imposes upon them. Just as our wills are ours to make them God's, so our goods likewise are ours to use for God.

N. B. H.

STEWARDSHIP, CHRISTIAN. Br. (See Christian Stewardship Organization; Ethical Traditions, Br.; Lay Movement in Methodism.)

STEWARDSHIP, DEPARTMENT OF, E.U.B. Church, was established by the 1958 General Conference. Although the operations of the department were directed by a full-time Secretary of Stewardship, it was amenable to the Council of Administration until 1966.

This late emergence of a Department of Stewardship was the culmination of a variety of stewardship interests within other organizations of both the Church of the United Brethren in Christ and The Evangelical Church. Interestingly, in both bodies, the original stewardship emphasis came from the youth who in the early 1890's formed the Young People's Christian Union of the United Brethren Church and the Young People's Alliance of The Evangelical Church.

By 1901, the stewardship attainments of the Young People's Christian Union attracted so much attention that the General Conference of the United Brethren Church formed a Christian Stewardship Commission. It continued to function until 1913, when it became the Commission on Stewardship and Finance and assumed responsibility for shaping and promoting the general budget. In 1917 General Conference formed the Board of Administration and assigned the duties of the Commission to the new Board.

In 1922 when the Evangelical Association and The United Evangelical Church, which had separated in the 1890's, came together again, they formed a Commission on Finance similar to that which had been founded by the Association in 1915. The Commission was instructed to "emphasize the unity of the various departments and promote Christian stewardship and the principle of tithing." In 1938 the Commission was abolished and its responsibilities turned over to the newly formed Administrative Council of the General Conference; and in 1942, the promotion of Stewardship became the responsibility of the Executive Secretary-Treasurer of the Council. When the Church of the United Brethren in Christ merged with The Evangelical Church in 1946, the E.U.B. Church followed the stewardship policies of its predecessor.

BRUCE C. SOUDERS

STEWART, ANDREW (1851-1925), Canadian minister and educator, was born in Albion township, Peel county, Ontario, the son of John Stewart and Mary (Jamieson) Stewart. He was educated at Victoria College (B.D., 1879), and was ordained in 1879.

In the same year he was appointed to Rock Lake circuit in Manitoba. Subsequently he served at Crystal City, Killarney, and other points. In 1889, Stewart became a lecturer at Wesley College, which he served in various capacities until 1921. He was president of his Conference in 1887 and 1900 and a delegate to the fifth ECUMENICAL METHODIST CONFERENCE (1921). He died in Winnipeg, March 25, 1925.

Andrew Stewart was given honorary degrees by Wesley College and the University of Manitoba. This was a small recompense for his work as a Methodist pioneer in northwestern Manitoba and as a teacher and member of the governing body of Wesley College.

G. H. Cornish, *Cyclopaedia of Methodism*. 1903.
T. G. McKitrick, *Andrew Stewart of the Prairie Homesteads*. Crystal City: Author, 1950.
J. H. Riddell, *Middle West*. 1946.   F. W. ARMSTRONG

CARL D. STEWART

STEWART, CARL DEVOE (1902-   ), American minister and missionary to Mexico and Cuba, was born at Sylvania, Ga., on Oct. 26, 1902. He was educated at EMORY UNIVERSITY, where he received the Ph.B. degree in 1928; the B.D. in 1929; the M.A. at the University of Denver in 1938; and the Th.D. from the ILIFF SCHOOL OF THEOLOGY in that same year. He was given the honorary degree of LL.D. by ASBURY COLLEGE in 1954. On Dec. 15, 1928, he married Miriam Sarah Thacker, and their children are Barbara Joanne (Mrs. Hubert E. Floyd) and Joseph Thacker.

He was received on trial in the NORTH GEORGIA CONFERENCE in 1929 and appointed to the Moultrie circuit, 1926-27. He was then sent as a missionary to MEXICO

to teach Bible in the LYDIA PATTERSON INSTITUTE, 1929-31. Later he was transferred to CUBA where he served as pastor of five congregations. As District Superintendent he served the Havana and the Oriente Districts. He was president of the Board of Directors of CANDLER UNIVERSITY, 1959-61 and an instructor in the UNION SEMINARY, 1946-48. After leaving Cuba in 1960 he was director of Methodist Cuban Relief in Miami, Fla. for two years and later pastor in Lakeview, CHICAGO.

He was related to the General Board of MISSIONS by being its treasurer in Cuba and having its power of attorney.

After the death of his first wife (1963), he married Lavetta E. Serott (1967).

Who's Who in the Methodist Church, 1966.   N. B. H.

STEWART, GEORGE WASHINGTON (1858-1915), tenth bishop of the C.M.E. Church, was born on Feb. 3, 1858, near Lynchburg, Va. He joined the church, and he was licensed to preach in 1880. Bishop Stewart attended Central Tennessee College in Nashville and GAMMON THEOLOGICAL SEMINARY in Atlanta. In 1882, he joined the Kentucky Conference and was transferred to the Indian Territory where he was an organizer of missions. In 1884, he was transferred to the Tennessee Conference where he served as pastor and PRESIDING ELDER. At the General Conference in 1910, he was elected to the office of bishop and presided over the state of ALABAMA. Bishop Stewart died on Sept. 20, 1915, at Birmingham, Ala.

Harris and Patterson, *C.M.E. Church*. 1965.
The Mirror, General Conference, C.M.E., 1958.
RALPH G. GAY

STEWART, JOHN (? -1823), made the first sustained effort by Methodists to evangelize the American Indians in 1815 or 1816. Dr. Wade Crawford Barclay has written a concise account of Stewart's work:

At the Ohio Conference held in September, 1814, Marcus Lindsey was appointed to the Marietta Circuit. Sometime later, at a camp meeting which he held near Marietta, one of his converts was John Stewart, a free-born mulatto—part Indian. He was living at the time—drunken and poverty-stricken—with a tavern keeper and was intent on suicide. But by his conversion he was set upon his feet and soon thereafter started upon a career so filled at once with romance and far-reaching influence that it has won a prominent place in Methodist history.

Following his conversion Stewart managed to rent a house for himself and set himself up in his trade—that of a dyer. He united with the Methodist Church in Marietta and soon thereafter was licensed as an EXHORTER. He was a man "of no learning," but "a melodious singer." Believing that he had a call from God, "his mind became much exercised about preaching." Following a severe illness, he went one day into the fields to pray:

It seemed to me that I heard a voice, like the voice of a woman praising God; and then another, as the voice of a man, saying to me, "You must declare my counsel faithfully." . . . They seemed to come from a northwest direction.

Much impressed, Stewart set off with his knapsack to the northwest. At "the old Moravian establishment among the Delawares" at "Goshen, on the Tuscarawas river," he heard of Indians living on a reservation farther north. Continuing his journey he finally arrived at the house of William Walker, Sr., at Upper Sandusky, a government Indian sub-agent and interpreter. Encouraged by Mrs. Walker, "a most amiable woman, of good education and half Wyandotte," Stewart began religious work among the Wyandotte tribespeople. He induced Jonathan Pointer, a Negro, to become his interpreter. Freely mixing songs with his exhortations and prayers, he succeeded in awakening considerable religious interest and, in time, won a number of converts—among others Pointer, his interpreter, and several of the Indian chiefs. He continued his labors, with two intervals for trips to Tennessee and to Marietta, until the spring of 1818. About this time objections arose because Stewart, though not ordained, had both administered baptism and performed the marriage ceremony. Learning that a QUARTERLY CONFERENCE was to be held near Urbana, he determined to attend and apply for license as a LOCAL PREACHER. Attestation of the granting of license is contained in a letter written to JAMES B. FINLEY some years later by Moses Crume, who in 1818 was PRESIDING ELDER of the Miami District, Ohio Conference:

John met me in the town of Urbana; from which place I went to the quarterly meeting, accompanied by that man of God, Rev. Bishop George. Here we found Stewart, with several of his red brethren, the Wyandotts, with a recommendation from the chiefs that had been converted, earnestly desiring to have him licensed to preach the Gospel, according to the rule and order of our church. At the proper time, and by the advice of the venerable Bishop George, his case was brought before the quarterly meeting conference, his recommendation read, and his brethren heard, who gave a good account of his life and labors in the conversion of many of their nation: those present testifying for themselves what God had done for them, through his instrumentality; and I think it was with the unanimous vote of that respectable body of men, that he was licensed: all believing that they acted in conformity to the will of God.

The report of his work and the licensing of Stewart created so much interest that several of the Local Preachers present volunteered to go in turn to assist him "until the ensuing session of the Ohio Annual Conference"—it apparently being agreed that when Conference came provision for permanent assistance should be made. Stewart continued to labor among the Wyandot, in association with the missionaries placed in charge, though with increasing ill health, until his death of consumption on December 17, 1823.

Reprinted from Wade Crawford Barclay: *History of Methodist Missions*, Vol. I, pp. 203-205. Methodist Board of Missions. 1949. Used by permission.

STEWART, LUTHER CALDWELL (1893-1962), twenty-second bishop of the C.M.E. Church, was born on June 26, 1893, at Pleasant Hill, Ala. He received an A.B. degree from PAINE COLLEGE in 1914 and was licensed to preach the same year. In 1916, he was ordained a deacon and in 1917 an elder. From 1917 to 1919, he served as a chaplain in the United States Army. He served churches in Florida, Kentucky, and Alabama. The General Conference elected him editor of *The Christian Index*, the official publication of the denomination, in 1938. Here, he served until 1946 when

he was elected to the office of bishop. He died on Nov. 16, 1962.

Clark and Stafford, *Who's Who in Methodism*. 1952.
Harris and Patterson, *C.M.E. Church*. 1965. RALPH G. GAY

STEWART, WILLIAM ANDREW (1894-), bishop of the A.M.E. ZION CHURCH, was born to Eli and Allie Stewart in Evergreen, Ala. He attended public school in Conecuh County. He is a graduate of Phelps Hall Training School and Tuskegee. He also did undergraduate study at Howard University in Washington, D.C. Upon graduation from Tuskegee, he taught school in Macon County and Tuskegee, Ala.

He transferred to the Western North Carolina Conference (AMEZ) and became a pastor under Bishop Lynwood Westinghouse Kyles. During his pastorate he graduated from LIVINGSTONE COLLEGE and Hood Theological Seminary. He married Miss Sula Cunningham and to this union seven children were born.

His subsequent ministry proved successful, and he built churches and parsonages and paid debts wherever he was sent.

He was elected to the episcopacy on May 15, 1952. While pastor of Old Ship A.M.E. Zion Church in MONTGOMERY, Ala., he had been active in civic work and had brought about many transformations in the community; namely, the reforms of the attitudes and services of the L. and N. Railroad Company and the Western Railroad Company. His episcopal residence has recently been in WASHINGTON, D. C.

DAVID H. BRADLEY

STIDGER, WILLIAM LEROY (1885-1949), American preacher and professor of homiletics, was born March 16, 1885, at Moundsville, W. Va., the son of Leroy L. and Etta B. (Robinson) Stidger. He studied three years at ALLEGHENY COLLEGE and one at BOSTON UNIVERSITY SCHOOL OF THEOLOGY, and won the Ph.B. degree at Brown University in 1912. His honorary degrees were: D.D., Litt.D., and L.H.D. from Allegheny, KANSAS WESLEYAN, and Salem (Oregon) Colleges. He married Iva Berkey, June 7, 1910, and they had one daughter.

Stidger was admitted on trial in the NEW ENGLAND SOUTHERN CONFERENCE in 1911, was ordained DEACON in 1913 and transferred that year to the CALIFORNIA CONFERENCE where he was ordained ELDER in 1915. His appointments were: 1911-12, instructor, East Greenwich Academy; 1913-15, Calvary, SAN FRANCISCO; 1916-18, First, SAN JOSE; 1919, publicity agent, Centenary Campaign; 1920-24, St. Mark's, DETROIT; 1925-27, Linwood, KANSAS CITY, Mo.; and 1928-49, professor of homiletics, Boston University School of Theology. He served, 1929-37, as morning preacher first at Copley Church and then at the Church of All Nations in BOSTON.

As a pastor, Stidger had a flair for publicity. In San Francisco he installed a revolving cross on his church, perhaps the first one ever so used. He knew how to make news; it was said that he made the front page of the newspapers about once a week.

He demonstrated originality in preaching, introducing the dramatic book sermon, the dramatic art sermon, the hymn sermon, and what he called the symphonic sermon. The latter employed besides a text a rhyming couplet frequently repeated throughout like a symphonic theme. In 1938 he offered the first course ever taught on Radio Preaching. The National Federation of Press Women gave him a citation for producing a radio program of excellence and public service.

An omnivorous reader, Stidger began early in his ministry the practice of reading a book a day and kept it up. A facile writer, he conducted for years a newspaper column entitled, "Getting the Most Out of Life." He exceeded his aim of publishing one book a year, bringing out in all some fifty-three volumes. Some were books of sermons and poems while others dealt with preaching, church administration, and biography. Some of the titles were: *Standing Room Only*, 1921; *There Are Sermons in Books*, 1922; *The Symphonic Sermon*, 1923; *Henry Ford —The Man and His Motives*, 1923; *God Is at the Organ*, 1927; *Preaching Out of the Overflow*, 1929; *Edwin Markham, A Biography*, 1932; *Those Amazing Roosevelts*, 1938; *Rainbow Born Is Beauty* (poems), 1941; and *Immortals of the Christian Ministry*, 1947.

Stidger had a large capacity for friendship, knowing and making friends of people in all walks of life, and at times he quietly used that endowment to help persons who needed a friend. Bishop F. J. McConnell said Stidger was capable of getting men who had made bad breaks back on their feet and helping them to a new start; he helped some criminals to an honest life and found new chances for youths who had made fools of themselves. McConnell added that while Stidger was a great advertiser he was also the most secretly working helper of men on the edge of ruin he ever knew.

Stidger died suddenly in Boston, Sunday, Aug. 7, 1949, after having dressed in preparation for filling a preaching engagement.

Christian Advocate, Aug. 25, 1949.
General Minutes, MEC.
F. J. McConnell, *By The Way*. 1952.
Minutes of the New England Conference, 1950.
Who Was Who in America, 1943-1950.
Who's Who in the Clergy.

JESSE A. EARL
ALBEA GODBOLD

STIEFEL, KARL (1867-1948), German-American minister and college professor, was born at Hall, Württemberg, GERMANY on May 21, 1867 and emigrated to Burlington, Iowa. He enrolled at the MOUNT PLEASANT GERMAN COLLEGE from which he received a diploma in 1893 and an M.A. in 1904. In 1893 he was admitted to the ST. LOUIS GERMAN CONFERENCE of the M.E. Church and served a pastorate at St. Charles, Mo. (1893-1895). He was professor of Biblical Exegesis and Historical Theology at the Mount Pleasant German College (1895-1908). From 1908 to 1913 he was at the Eden German Methodist Church, ST. LOUIS where he gained prestige as a writer and preacher. In 1913 he accepted a professorship of Exegesis and Ancient Languages at GERMAN WALLACE COLLEGE, Berea, Ohio, but upon his arrival he found that this college and its affiliate, Baldwin University, were being combined into BALDWIN-WALLACE COLLEGE with the emphasis on the English language. He became Professor of Bible here until his retirement in 1937. He wrote many articles in *Der Christliche Apologete* and *Der Bibelforscher*, leading journals of German-American Methodism, as well as a historical survey of German-American Methodist writings. CENTRAL WESLEYAN COLLEGE con-

ferred an honorary D.D. upon him in 1909. He died in Berea on June 26, 1948.

Haselmayer, *The History and Alumni List of the Mt. Pleasant German College; Jubiläumsbuch der St. Louis Deutschen Konferenz; Minutes of the Annual Conferences 1893-1948; Baldwin-Wallace Alumnus*, August 1948; Z. F. Meyer Collection of German-American Methodism (Iowa Wesleyan).

LOUIS A. HASELMAYER

STILES, LOREN, JR. (? -1863), was a co-founder of the FREE METHODIST CHURCH. He was a pastor and PRESIDING ELDER in the Genesee Conference of the M.E. Church, and co-founder with B. T. ROBERTS, of the Free Methodist Church in 1860. He was pastor of the independent "free church" at Albion, N. Y., prior to organization of the new "Free" church. He and his congregation joined the new denomination. He was a gifted preacher of superior culture. He died May 7, 1863.

BYRON S. LAMSON

STILLINGFLEET, EDWARD (1635-1699), some of whose writings influenced JOHN WESLEY, was born at Cranborne in Dorset and educated at St. John's College, CAMBRIDGE. He became Dean of St. Paul's in 1678, and although out of favor in the brief reign of James II, was made Bishop of Worcester after the Revolution of 1689. He was a Latitudinarian theologian whose *Irenicon* (1659) sought to reconcile Episcopalians and Presbyterians by showing that forms of Church government were not of the essence of Christianity. Jesus did not institute a particular Church order; the New Testament references to Church order were ambiguous; the form of the Church might be decided by what was best for its spiritual welfare, unity and peace in any particular age. He envisaged the possibility of presbyterian ordination taking place within the framework of an episcopal Church in cases of necessity. This was what attracted John Wesley to his writings: in July 1756, for instance, he wrote to James Clark, an Anglican parson who had preached against Methodism, that he thought that Stillingfleet had unanswerably proved "that neither Christ nor his apostles prescribed any particular form of Church government, and that the plea for the divine right of Episcopacy was never heard of in the primitive Church" (*Letters*, iii, p. 182). There is no evidence as to when Wesley first read Stillingfleet's *Irenicon*. This letter is the first trace of his influence as such, though his name is mentioned in a letter to CHARLES WESLEY written in July 1755 (*Letters*, iii, 136). Opinions differ as to whether Stillingfleet or Lord Peter King had more influence on Wesley's opinions on ordination, but in the decisive Letter to the American Brethren (Sept. 10, 1784), he quoted King's *Account of the Primitive Church*, not the *Irenicon*.

J. H. S. Kent, *Age of Disunity*. 1966.
A. B. Lawson, *John Wesley*. 1963.
E. W. Thompson, *Wesley: Apostolic Man*. 1957. HENRY RACK

STILLWATER, OKLAHOMA, U.S.A. **First Church** ministers to students at Oklahoma State University and was the first union of northern and southern Methodist churches in OKLAHOMA. At times 1,000 students attend its two morning worship services. It has a membership of 3,060, plus 3,500 Methodist students at OSU.

First M.E. and First M.E., South, were both organized

in 1890 and united in 1939 with pastors of both churches, John A. Callan and blind Wilmore Kendall, serving as co-pastors the first year. Joe E. Bowers became the first pastor of the new First Church, November 1940.

J. W. Hubbard, appointed to the First M.E. Church in February 1890, was the first minister of any church in Stillwater. In 1891 the church organized the first Epworth League in Oklahoma, with F. E. Miller as president. In 1892 the First M.E. Church erected a building, followed in 1893 by the First M.E. Church, South, a building rented in 1893 to the Agricultural and Mechanical College for school purposes. The southern church erected a new building in 1917 which was later sold to the Church of Christ. The northern church built the present sanctuary in 1923. A new educational unit was added in 1958 with a sunken court as a distinctive feature.

Bishops W. McFerrin Stowe and Kenneth Copeland are former pastors. In 1960 First Church was one of a number of churches with two lay delegates to the General Conference; they were M. A. Beeson and W. H. Wilcox.

Irving L. Smith

STILLWELL, SAMUEL, (1763- ?), and his nephew, **WILLIAM M. STILLWELL** (? -1851), were leaders of a schism in New York Methodism early in the nineteenth century. Samuel Stillwell was born in Jamaica, Long Island, Oct. 22, 1763, moved to New York in 1783, and became prominent in municipal affairs. In 1799 he was elected a member of the state assembly and four years later was city surveyor and had much to do with laying out the city of New York. It is not known when he became a Methodist, but by 1791 he was the leader of a class of Negroes. He was a strongminded, fearless man and became spokesman for some of the trustees of John Street Church in opposition to what they thought to be the dictatorship of the M.E. Church.

His nephew, William M. Stillwell, joined the New York Conference on trial in 1814, and, becoming a pastor of two Negro churches in the city, was influential in getting them to leave the M.E. Church. He is said to have been an attractive man, of middle height, with a ruddy complexion, blue eyes and auburn hair. He was much influenced by his uncle.

As a result of the opposition of the Stillwells to what they thought was the arbitrary government of the conference over their property, between three and four hundred persons were led by the Stillwells to leave the M.E. Church. This group for a time grew quite strong numerically. The Stillwellites, as they came to be called, drew up formal Articles of Association making the Bible their rule of discipline. They established a completely democratic organization in which decisions were made by both male and female members of the congregation. For a time William Stillwell preached in a schoolroom on Chrystie Street until a new building was erected on the same street and occupied on Dec. 31, 1820. The group after a time approved a book of *Discipline* which followed the doctrine of the M.E. Church.

After a time William Stillwell revolted against the organization which he had helped found, and in 1826 the church in Chrystie Street declared its independence from the larger body. William Stillwell died in Astoria, Long Island, Aug. 8, 1851, and his church did not long survive his death. Meanwhile, the larger part of those who had withdrawn from the M.E. Church joined the Methodist Protestant movement which also was in revolt against the highly centralized M.E. organization. It is commonly assumed that most of the Stillwellites in time became Methodist Protestants, or certainly dropped out entirely from M.E. records. (See also the African Methodist Episcopal Zion Church.)

E. S. Bucke, *History of American Methodism.* 1964. N. B. H.

STILZ, EARL BAUER (1892-1960), American missionary to the Congo, was born Oct. 8, 1892.

He was educated at Vanderbilt University, and then was ordained a local preacher. Together with Rev. and Mrs. H. P. Anker and T. E. Reeve, he was with the second group of missionaries to arrive in the Central Congo in 1917, after a long journey starting Aug. 29, 1916.

He retired in 1954. His outstanding contribution was in linguistic work, doing the major part of translating the New Testament into Otetela, as well as translating numerous other books, such as H. E. Fosdick's *Manhood of the Master,* Bunyan's *Pilgrim's Progress,* as well as many hymns. He was in charge of the press and construction work mostly at Wembo Nyama but also at Tunda and Lodja. He also was actively engaged in agricultural work. He died on Sept. 4, 1960.

Inman Townsley

STINSON, JOSEPH (1801-1862), Canadian minister, was born in Leicestershire, England. He came of a Methodist family and naturally gravitated to the ministry. After a period as a local preacher, he volunteered as a missionary and in 1823 was sent to Melbourne, Lower Canada. He was received into full connection in 1827.

After a few years at Gibraltar, Stinson returned to Upper Canada in 1833 as general superintendent of missions. In 1839 he was, in addition, president of Conference. As missions superintendent he imparted new vigor to the development of the Indian work, and faithfully defended the Indians' interests with the local authorities.

In common with many of his Wesleyan brethren he was caught up in the disputes accompanying the dissolution of the union in 1840. He returned to Britain in 1842 and held circuits there until 1857. In the interval he was one of the first to regain his balance and to promote the reunion of the English and Canadian Conferences that took place in 1847.

When he came back to Canada in 1857 as president of the Conference, he was welcomed as a long-lost brother. He held office as president until 1861, during which time he labored unceasingly to fulfill the duties of his office.

Stinson (D.D., Victoria, 1856) gave his last public lecture on his favorite theme, "The Aborigines of Canada." After a short illness, he died on Aug. 26, 1862. He was remembered with affectionate warmth by his brethren.

J. Carrol, *Case and His Cotemporaries.* 1867-77.
Minutes of Conference of the Wesleyan Methodist Church in Canada, 1863. G. S. French

STOCKHAM, WILLIAM HENRY (1861-1923), American manufacturer and layman of the M.E. Church, South, was born at Lafayette, Ind., on Sept. 15, 1861, and received a degree in mechanical engineering at the University of Illinois. He was superintendent and secretary of the Illinois Malleable Iron Company in CHICAGO from 1887 to 1892 and then became president of the Stockham Manufacturing Company. In 1903 he went to BIRMINGHAM, Ala., as president of Stockham Pipe and Fittings Company.

Active in Methodist affairs, Stockham was Chairman of the Board of Trustees of the International SUNDAY SCHOOL ASSOCIATION, a member of the Executive Committee of the World's Sunday School Association, President of the Birmingham Sunday School Association, member of the Executive Committee of the Alabama State Y.M.C.A., and Trustee of BIRMINGHAM-SOUTHERN and ATHENS COLLEGES.

Stockham was one of the early supporters of the Southern Assembly at LAKE JUNALUSKA, serving as Vice President and one of the Commissioners or Trustees. He was Superintendent of the Assembly in 1919 and a few years thereafter. He died in Birmingham on Nov. 16, 1923.

Who's Who In America.   ELMER T. CLARK

STOCKHOLM, the capital of SWEDEN, lists 790,000 inhabitants (1965). It is the residence of the bishop of the Northern Europe Central Conference of The United Methodist Church.

Remarkable was the work of George Scott, an English Methodist minister in Stockholm from 1830-42 (see SWEDEN). His influence on the free-church movement in Sweden proved most astonishing, but for the organized Methodist Church in Sweden it became only incidental.

In the 1860's Methodism was founded anew through Swedish men converted on the BETHEL SHIP, "John Wesley," in NEW YORK harbor. When American Methodism celebrated its hundredth anniversary in 1866, Scandinavian immigrants there decided to start a college and a theological school in CHICAGO, and they decided to send Albert Ericson to Stockholm to prepare himself for his task as teacher in Swedish literature. He was asked to preach while in Sweden, and did so, and his friends rented a house in Benikebrinken in Stockholm. He felt himself, however, obliged to return to America.

Then came Victor Witting from America on a private visit to his homeland, and he was besought and consented to remain. With Bishop CALVIN KINGSLEY he paid a first visit to Stockholm. Bishop Kingsley preached, and the people asked him earnestly to send a missionary to Stockholm. They were later disappointed when A. J. Anderson, of the CENTRAL ILLINOIS CONFERENCE, was nominated but could not accept the invitation.

These Methodist friends had rented a house in the south part of Stockholm, at Wollmar Yxkullsgatan; and Johan Kihlström, who some years earlier had been converted by Carl Olof Rosenius, a friend and helper of George Scott, consented to take care of the little flock of Methodists. Later Kihlström served as pastor in charge in several places, became the district superintendent of the Stockholm District in 1880, but was killed suddenly in a railway accident, April 29, 1882. He was a very gifted and earnest man and was much lamented.

On January 8, 1868, St. Paul, the first Methodist congregation in Sweden, was organized in Stockholm. It proved a worthy church, its architecture reminding one of an English chapel.

Soon it was deemed necessary to reach out to other parts of Stockholm. In 1879 a hall was rented in Rorstrandsgatan (later Wallingatan) in northern Stockholm, and a congregation was organized there in 1882. In the east section of Stockholm, Carl Hultgren in 1886 was named to begin work. Meetings were held in very uncomfortable rooms, but great crowds flocked around the gifted preacher, and a congregation was organized in 1890. Since this was the third in Stockholm, it was called Trinity.

Next year came a young man, Karl Edvard Norstrom (1859-1918), and he saw it as his first task to build a church. Among his hearers was a Mrs. Emma Benedicks, widow of a bank manager of a wealthy, very social-minded family, who did much for the poor. When the pastor visited her to get a gift for the new church, he secured the amazing sum of 100,000 Swedish kroner ($20,000), and was encouraged at once to start the build-

TRINITY CHURCH, STOCKHOLM, SWEDEN

INTERIOR, TRINITY

ing of the Trinity Church—still looked upon as one of the finest of the free churches built at that time. Mrs. Benedicks later offered the pastor another gift, 50,000 kroner, but the people decided to give the money to St. Peter's Church. The act proved an inspiration for this congregation, and they were enabled to complete their church building in 1901. Trinity Church was dedicated October 7, 1894. The 1894 Annual Conference had been held there the previous August. Mrs. Benedicks died the year after, age sixty-nine.

Other churches were organized and buildings erected: St. Marcus, 1890—its present chapel dedicated in 1904 —and several smaller chapels in other parts of Stockholm. At present there is consideration of concentrating the work, as has been done in GOTHENBURG.

A Central Mission started in 1914 is still at work though under different conditions. A children's home was for some years maintained. Three of the congregations have had homes for the aged, two still at work. The Bethany Deaconess Institution has its headquarters and its hospital in Stockholm.

The Publishing House has been located in Stockholm ever since 1878, and a building was bought in 1924 to become the headquarters of the church.

The rapid growth of Stockholm brought on the need for reorganization and new planning for the future work in both city and suburbs. There has been a kind of community agreement among the different free churches, and in consequence the Methodists have undertaken to care for an ecumenical congregation in Bollmora in the southeast section.

MANSFIELD HURTIG

STOCKTON, THOMAS HEWLINGS (1808-1868), was born in Mount Holly, Burlington County, N. J., on June 4, 1808. His father, WILLIAM S. STOCKTON, was a noted preacher in the M. P. Church. The parents later moved to TRENTON, then to Easton, Pa., and later to PHILADELPHIA.

In 1826 Thomas H. Stockton joined ST. GEORGE'S CHURCH in Philadelphia. He was a printer and a student of medicine, but in 1829 he united with the Associated Methodist Church, which became the M. P. Church the following year, and entered its ministry. He was placed on a circuit and in 1830 was sent to Baltimore. Then he was appointed to Georgetown in the District of Columbia and became CHAPLAIN of Congress, holding that position for three sessions. He was elected again in 1862.

While in Philadelphia he erected a church at Eleventh and Wood Streets. He moved to CINCINNATI in 1847, and while there he was elected president of Miami University but declined the position.

He was noted as an editor. In 1837 he compiled a hymn book, and in 1839 he established at Philadelphia a periodical called the *Methodist Protestant Letter Press*. His other publications included *The Christian World* (1840-1845), *The Monthly Reporter* (1846), *The Bible Alliance* (1850), and *The Bible Times* (1856-1858). He also wrote and published thirteen books, one of which appeared in print after his death. He received the D.D. degree from Gettysburg College.

In 1863 as Chaplain of Congress he participated in the dedication of the National Cemetery at Gettysburg at which Abraham Lincoln delivered the address.

He died on Oct. 9, 1868, and was buried in Mount Moriah Cemetery in Philadelphia.

T. H. Colhouer, *Sketches of the Founders.* 1880.
E. J. Drinkhouse, *History of Methodist Reform.* 1899.
M. Simpson, *Cyclopaedia.* 1878.

ELMER T. CLARK

WILLIAM S. STOCKTON

STOCKTON, WILLIAM SMITH (1785-1860), Methodist layman and editor and one of the founders of the M.P. CHURCH, was born at Burlington, N. J. on April 8, 1785. In 1822 he moved to PHILADELPHIA, where he lived for nearly the rest of his life.

He was identified with the controversy which gave rise to the M.P. Church in 1829-30. In 1822 he published a book entitled *Truth Versus a Wesleyan Methodist* in reply to a work entitled *Methodist Error*. In 1821 he founded *The Wesleyan Respository*, a periodical which became *Mutual Rights* and was the leading exponent of the position of the Reformers who organized the M.P. Church. He was invited to become the editor of *Mutual Rights* but declined. He was the author of *Seven Nights*, a book against alcohol. He was connected with a political paper called *The People's Advocate*, and also with the publication of the works of JOHN WESLEY.

In Philadelphia he was active in movements for the alleviation of poverty. He was in charge of the large institution in the suburbs called the Blockely Alms House and the old Alms House on Spruce Street which was immortalized by Longfellow in his *Evangeline*.

Stockton was twice married. His first wife was Elizabeth S. Hewlings of Burlington, whom he married in 1807, and in 1828 he married Emily H. Dream of Leesburg, Va.

In 1860 he returned to Burlington, where he died on Nov. 20, 1860. He was buried there near the grave of his father.

T. H. Colhouer, *Sketches of the Founders.* 1880.
E. J. Drinkhouse, *History of Methodist Reform.* 1899.

ELMER T. CLARK

STOCKTON, CALIFORNIA, U.S.A., population 102,663, was in early days considered the gateway to Southern Gold Mines. Beginning in 1849, a NEW YORK layman named James Westbay and a Rev. Hopkins of TENNESSEE held regular prayer services in Westbay's tent on the main channel of the San Joaquin River. On March 16, 1850, **Central M.E. Church** was organized from this nucleus by James Corwin who had driven oxen across the plains with ISAAC OWEN. CALIFORNIA was then a part of the Oregon-California Mission Conference. Central Methodists organized the city's first "classical" school. After various locations and buildings, Central Church is now located on Pacific Avenue across the street from the UNIVERSITY OF THE PACIFIC. Pioneer preacher Isaac Owen organized the University of the Pacific in Santa Clara, Calif., in 1851, the first chartered institution of higher learning in California. It moved soon thereafter to San Jose where the campus remained until 1924, when it moved to its present site on Pacific Avenue in Stockton.

The German M.E. Church was organized in 1855 by August Kellner and was discontinued in 1935. The original building for this work was said to be the first German Protestant church building in the State. A Chinese Mission was organized in 1870. This work became the Chinese Christian Center in downtown Stockton and was served by GEORGE H. COLLIVER of the University of the Pacific, 1938-48. At its peak the Center operated ten student clubs. In 1957 the Chinese Center was merged with Clay Street Church to become St. Marks. Wilbur Choy, a product of the Mission, was St. Mark's first pastor. Epworth Chapel was organized in 1892 by adults and Epworth Leaguers of Central Church and in 1923 became known as the Mexican M.E. Church. The name was changed to La Trinidad in 1957. Visher M.E. Church was begun as a mission Sunday School of Central Church in 1882. It was organized as Clay Street M.E. Church in 1886. In 1923 a Filipino Church was organized. It became St. Peter's in 1956.

In 1939 Monroe Hess, Sr., Executive Director for GOODWILL INDUSTRIES in SAN FRANCISCO, assisted by some of his board members, organized Goodwill Industries of Stockton. They were assisted in this project by Methodist laymen of Stockton.

St. Paul's Church was organized in 1950 when Methodist Men of the city canvassed the area west of the University. W. D. Nietman, Professor of Philosophy at the University, was the first pastor. The Hammer Lane Project was organized in 1957 through cooperative efforts of several churches in Stockton. The name was later changed to Holy Cross.

Missionaries of the M.E. Church, South, were appointed to a California Mission in 1849. They travelled by way of PANAMA and arrived in California in 1850. The Mission Superintendent was JESSE BORING and ALEXANDER WYNN was appointed first pastor in Stockton. Grace Church was organized in August of 1850. Under the California Oriental Mission of the Southern Church, a Korean Mission was organized in Stockton in 1922. It was discontinued in 1938.

E.U.B. Work. A San Jose pastor, Michael Guhl, organized a small Evangelical mission in Stockton in February of 1866, but it was discontinued later that year when Guhl transferred to work with the German M.E. Church in Stockton. No further Evangelical work was attempted here. A layman, W. W. Lucas, began a United Brethren Sunday school in the following year and L. S. Woodruff was appointed to serve the congregation. In 1927 a new building was dedicated and the church was named Woodruff Memorial. The membership grew to include several hundred members, but after World War II the members began to move to other parts of the city, the membership declined, and a new freeway was routed through the church property. The church was closed in June of 1968 by action of the California Conference, and the property was sold to the State of California.

In 1946 a mission was begun in north Stockton by the Woodruff Memorial congregation. At first it was known as the Vail Mansion E.U.B. Church, but was later renamed Grace E.U.B. Church. From 1946 until 1959 the congregation worshipped at Vail Mansion on Monroe Street. Ten acres were then purchased on Rose Marie Lane and a new structure built. After the Methodist-E.U.B. merger, the name was changed to Faith United Methodist Church.

In 1850, when California became a State and Stockton a city, the Ebenezer A.M.E. Church was organized with "Father" Peter Green as pastor. In 1860 a school for Negro children was opened in the A.M.E. Church, and soon property was given by a Captain Weber for a new school building. The first teacher was the pastor of the A.M.E. Church. Emmanuel Quivers, a son of a former slave, attended this school and the District School at Waterloo, but was rejected at Stockton High School by vote of the Board of Trustees. Superintendent George Ladd, who had supported his application, then was able to get young Quivers into Mission High School in San Francisco. It was through this episode and its aftermath that Negro schools were discontinued in Stockton and open enrollment established in the city's schools in 1879. The first enrollees were two Negro girls in that same year.

St. Matthews C.M.E. Church was organized by an Oakland pastor, Webster West, in 1947 under the California Conference of that denomination.

C. V. Anthony, *Fifty Years*. 1901.
Journals of the California-Nevada Conference and its predecessors.   A. MYRON HERRELL

B. FOSTER STOCKWELL

STOCKWELL, BOWMAN FOSTER (1899-1961), American bishop, theologian and writer, was born in Shawnee, Okla., on Sept. 17, 1899. Son of a Methodist minister of the OKLAHOMA CONFERENCE, he studied at OHIO WESLEYAN UNIVERSITY and BOSTON UNIVERSITY, majoring in theology at the Universities of Stuttgart and Heidelberg. He also served for two years as secretary to JOHN R. MOTT, traveling with him through the Orient.

Stockwell married Vera Loudon, an Ohio-born prospect for missionary work, and then served a short period as pastor in MASSACHUSETTS. In 1926 under the M.E. Board of Foreign MISSIONS, he was sent to BUENOS AIRES, to teach in the Union Seminary (now FACULTAD EVANGE-LICA DE TEOLOGIA), a joint enterprise of Methodists, Disciples of Christ, and Waldensians. In 1927 he was elected principal of that seminary, which he was to direct—with short interruptions—until in May 1960, he was elected by the Latin America Central Conference to be a bishop of The Methodist Church. Assigned to the Pacific area, he made his residence in LIMA, PERU. Shortly after his inception in the charge, he was asked by the Latin America Central Conference to participate in a survey of the state of theological education throughout Latin America. In Buenos Aires while making this study, he became ill and after several weeks passed away on June 5, 1961.

Stockwell's two major concerns were theological education and Christian literature. He brought the Union Seminary of Buenos Aires to its present situation as a school of university level, and launched a program of publication of Christian literature that continues through the River Plate Commission on Christian literature, and has provided hundreds of Christian and theological books to the whole Spanish-speaking world. He founded two magazines for preachers, *El Predicador Evangélico* and *Cuadernos Teológicos*.

Bishop Stockwell was also a champion of ecumenism. He was instrumental in the founding of the River Plate Confederation of Evangelical Churches, was a delegate to the Tambaram Conference (1938), and attended the WORLD COUNCIL OF CHURCHES assemblies at Amsterdam, 1948, and Evanston, 1954. His hobby was the study of old Spanish Protestant literature of the sixteenth century and the history of that interesting period in church history. He did great and systematic work for truth and enlightenment through his entire career. A son, Eugene L. Stockwell, is assistant general secretary of the World Division of the Board of Missions of The United Methodist Church in New York. Bishop Stockwell wrote ¿*Que podemos creer?* (What may we believe?); ¿*Que es el protestantismo?* (What is Protestantism?); and *Nuestro mundo y la cruz* (Our World and the Cross).

ADAM F. SOSA

STOKES, ELWOOD H. (1815-1897), American minister, was born of Quaker parents, Oct. 10, 1815 at Medford, N.J. He attended public school up to the age of thirteen and was then apprenticed to a book-binder in PHILADEL-PHIA. He rose to the position of foreman within a few years. To his experience in the book-bindery he attributed his knowledge and love of literature. He was married to a Miss Neff on July 31, 1838 who died four years later. On Jan. 6, 1847 he was married to Sarah Anne Stout, who served with him throughout a long ministry.

Converted in 1834 in Union Church, Philadelphia under the ministry of the famous CHARLES PITMAN, young Stokes became a CLASS LEADER. Licensed to preach in 1843, he was at once appointed to the Salem (N.J.) Circuit. He joined the NEW JERSEY CONFERENCE in 1844 and spent fifty-three years in its service.

He was president of the Ocean Grove Association, 1875-97, guiding its development toward the erection of the great auditorium. He broke ground for this remarkable structure in 1893; four years later his funeral was held there. Bishops JAMES N. FITZGERALD and JOHN P. NEW-

MAN conducted the service, which was attended by 7,000 people. Despite his limited formal schooling, Stokes was no mean scholar. His preaching was pictorial and marked by literary allusions and quotations. He published six books of verse. His many friends memorialized him by erecting a statue in bronze which stands between the great auditorium and the ocean.

Journal of the New Jersey Conference, 1894.
Newark *Evening News,* July 17, 1897.
New Jersey Tercentenary Almanac, p. 497.

HENRY L. LAMBDIN

STOKES, MARION BOYD (1882-1968), missionary to KOREA and to CUBA, was born in COLUMBIA, S. C., Dec. 12, 1882. He graduated from WOFFORD COLLEGE in 1903, and received the M.A. degree from EMORY UNIVERSITY in 1923, and the D.D. degree from ASBURY COLLEGE in 1933.

After two years teaching in the public schools at Jordan, S.C., and two years in the pastorate at ASHEVILLE, N. C., he went to Korea in 1907. He served as district missionary and district superintendent in assignments to Songdo, Wonsan, Choonchun and Seoul stations. In the latter station he also acted and was founder and superintendent of the Seoul City Mission. He was an able speaker in the Korean language and wrote a text for new missionaries, *Korean by the Clause Method.*

In 1941 he was appointed to the Isle of Pines in Cuba, where he was evangelist and pastor until his retirement in 1948. He then served as a supply pastor in NORTH and SOUTH CAROLINA. In 1952-53, as a civilian with the U.S. Armed Forces in Japan, he was a Korean translator.

Stokes was a member of the Korea and the WESTERN NORTH CAROLINA CONFERENCES. Son of a minister, he was the father of four Methodist ministers: Dr. Mack Stokes, associate dean at the CANDLER SCHOOL OF THE-OLOGY, EMORY UNIVERSITY; Dr. James Stokes, editor of the *North Carolina Christian Advocate;* Dr. Lem Stokes, director of the quadrennial emphasis of The United Methoditst Church, 1968-72, and Charles Stokes who serves as a missionary in Korea.

Stokes died in Charlotte, N. C., July 4, 1968.

CHARLES A. SAUER

STONE, FRED DENTON (1875-1956), American pastor, district superintendent, publishing agent, was born in Rock Falls, Ill., Jan. 18, 1875, the son of Daniel Delavan and Nancy (Bean) Stone. He graduated from the Normal School at Dixon, Ill., 1896, and studied at GARRETT BIBICAL INSTITUTE, 1896-97 (hon. D.D., LL.D.). On Oct. 19, 1898, he married Dora May Ashby and they had one son, Fred Denton, Jr. Ordained to the ministry of the M.E. Church, 1897, Stone joined the ROCK RIVER CON-FERENCE and gave fifty-nine years of service to the Methodist Church, holding successively the following appointments in ILLINOIS: Erie; Mendota; Dixon; First Church, Elgin; and Irving Park, CHICAGO, 1924-36; superintendent of the Chicago Western District, 1918-24; Publishing Agent of the M.E. Church (1936-1940) and then of The Methodist Church, 1940 to 1948, when he retired. He served with distinction as a delegate in six GENERAL CONFERENCES, 1924-44, and at the Uniting Conference, 1939.

Stone gave valuable assistance to many committees and boards aiding greatly in the merger of the Chicago

Training School with Garrett Seminary. A life member of the Chicago Methodist Social Union, he served it for thirty-five years. His influence was felt in the helpful merger of the German, Swedish, and Norwegian-Danish Conferences into the Rock River Conference. While serving the general Church, he was always "a Methodist preacher," and his interests went out to the local church, to the annual conference, as well as the general Church, and world. Endowed with a remarkably alert mind, he frequently pointed out the way to solve problems and improve conditions. Serving as Publishing Agent before and after unification, he helped reorganize the former publishing corporations of the Uniting Churches into one Publishing House. The BOARD OF PUBLICATION of The Methodist Church formally declared: "He will always be remembered with affection and held in high esteem for his vital contribution to the very difficult task of bringing order out of chaos."

Bishop HARMON, then BOOK EDITOR, who was intimately associated with Stone, said of him: "He was a man short in stature but unusually sagacious and he and Mr. Whitmore (the other agent) ably saw the Publishing House through these early combining years, and through the troubles incident to the second World War."

After retirement in 1948 Stone lived in Evanston, Ill., the last years of his life. He died in Chicago on Oct. 4, 1956, and was buried in Memorial Park, Evanston.

Journal of the Rock River Conference, 1957.
Clark and Stafford, *Who's Who in Methodism*. 1952.

JESSE A. EARL

STONE, MARY (1872-1954), noted Chinese medical doctor, and one of the first two Chinese women to receive an M.D. degree in the United States, was born in Kiukiang, CHINA, in 1872, and died in CALIFORNIA on Dec. 29, 1954. Her Chinese name was Shih Mai-yu.

Her father was a Christian preacher, the first convert in the Yangtze Valley; her mother was principal of a mission school. She was educated in Methodist mission schools in Kiukiang, and received her medical degree from the University of Michigan in 1896. Returning to China, she founded the Elizabeth Denton Danforth Hospital under the auspices of the WOMAN'S FOREIGN MISSIONARY SOCIETY. For twenty-five years she headed this institution, personally training more than 500 young Chinese women as nurses. Many of these continued their medical training in America and Europe. For some years she was national president of the Woman's Christian Temperance Union of China. In 1920, with financial help of American friends, she withdrew from Methodist work and founded the Bethel Mission in Shanghai; it included high school, four orphanages, a nurse training school, and a theological seminary. At the time of her death, it was reported that the mission had graduated more than 2,500 nurses. The mission buildings were badly damaged by bombs during the Sino-Japanese war.

W. W. REID

STONEHOUSE, GEORGE (1714-1793), British friend of JOHN WESLEY, was born at Hungerford Park, Berkshire, and was educated at Pembroke College, CAMBRIDGE. He became vicar of Islington in 1736, but influenced by a society at Islington which had been founded by JAMES HUTTON, he developed leanings toward Moravianism, resigned his vicarage, and retired to Woodstock, near Ox-

ford, where THOMAS JACKSON, in his *Life of the Rev. Charles Wesley*, says that he "appears to have spent the residue of his days in inglorious 'stillness'." He disbelieved in the doctrine of eternal punishment.

John Wesley had many meetings with Stonehouse, and wrote in 1781: "He is all original still, like no man in the world, . . . but perhaps if I had his immense fortune I might be as great an oddity as he." The suggestion that CHARLES WESLEY was at one time his curate (see Tyerman's *Life of John Wesley*, i, 305), has been disproved by an examination of the Islington vestry records (*Proceedings of Wesley Historical Society*, v, 238-39). John Wesley's *Journal* reveals the deep affection which Stonehouse had for the Wesleys. He died at Bristol in 1793.

JOHN T. WILKINSON

STONEHOUSE, W. J. (1909-   ), Canadian ordained elder of the East Ontario Conference of the FREE METHODIST CHURCH, was born at Bracebridge, Ontario. He attended public schools in D'Arcy, Saskatchewan area; was a student at McCord Bible School, Sask.; and received a B.Th. degree from Central School of Religion, Indianapolis, Ind. An honorary D.D. degree was conferred on him by GREENVILLE COLLEGE in 1960.

He served pastorates for twelve years in Alberta, British Columbia and Manitoba, becoming Conference Superintendent for twenty-four years in Ontario. He was a leader in the movement that resulted in the merger of Holiness Movement of Canada and Free Methodist churches in 1958. Later, he became General Missionary Board representative in overseas visitation with areas including IRELAND, EGYPT, HONG KONG, PHILIPPINES, TAIWAN and JAPAN. In 1960 he was official delegate to the Asia Fellowship Conference. He has been Superintendent of the East Ontario Conference since 1959.

BYRON S. LAMSON

STOODY, RALPH WAINMAN (1896-   ), American minister and long-time director and general secretary of the Commission on Public Relations and METHODIST INFORMATION (TMC), was born in Rochester, N. Y., on April 19, 1896. His parents were John Henry and Fannie (Wainman) Stoody. He was educated at OHIO WESLEYAN UNIVERSITY, receiving in 1917 a B.A. degree; was a student at GARRETT BIBLICAL INSTITUTE, 1917-18; and received the S.T.B. degree from BOSTON UNIVERSITY SCHOOL OF THEOLOGY in 1920. He studied further at Columbia University in the summer of 1930, and at Harvard in the summer of 1938. He was awarded the S.T.D. by Gordon College in 1939; the honorary D.D. degree by Ohio Wesleyan in 1947, and the Litt.D. by AMERICAN UNIVERSITY in 1958. He married Lucile Bennett on March 5, 1918, and they have one daughter.

For a time he was connected with the former *Epworth Herald* in CHICAGO, 1917-18; and then was ordained in the ministry of the M.E. Church in 1920. His pastoral record included South Walpole, Mass., 1919-20; St. Alban's, Vt., 1920-23; St. Johnsbury, Vt., 1923-26; Chestnut Street, Portland, Maine, 1926-34; and Union Methodist Church, Fall River, Mass., 1934-40. In 1940, upon the organization of the Commission on Public Relations and Methodist Information of The Methodist Church, Dr. Stoody was made its general secretary and director, and

RALPH STOODY

the West Riding of Yorkshire. He was trained early in a bookseller's shop, and at eighteen was managing a printing office with the responsibility for printing a weekly paper and oversight of the staff. He was an insatiable reader: "I frequently read until eleven at night and began again at four in the morning," he said of himself as a young man. "Nor had I patience to eat my meat unless I had a book before me." His conversion was a long process, which is described by him in the autobiographical statement included in the *Lives of Early Methodist Preachers*. He began to itinerate in February 1763, and after serving on many circuits was appointed by the Wesleyan CONFERENCE corrector of the press (1793-94). He then became editor, from 1794 to 1804, when he was succeeded by JOSEPH BENSON. From 1804 Story undertook the oversight of the printing works. He died on May 22, 1818.

JOHN KENT

W. McFERRIN STOWE

in this position he served in NEW YORK for the next twenty-four years until his retirement in 1964.

In connection with his work, he was a member of the Department of International Justice and Goodwill, and the Department of Religious Radio of the NATIONAL COUNCIL OF CHURCHES; was a Methodist representative and consultant of the Church of the Air program of the Columbia Broadcasting System; a member of the WORLD METHODIST COUNCIL, 1947, '51, '56, and '61; and the president of the COUNCIL OF SECRETARIES of The Methodist Church, 1956. During the first World War he served as a sergeant with the American Expeditionary Forces in France, 1918-19. He was briefly a war correspondent in the Mediterranean and North African theatres in 1945, and again in Japan and Korea in 1953. He was a press official at the organizing assembly of the WORLD COUNCIL OF CHURCHES in Amsterdam, Holland, in 1948, and again in New Delhi, India, in 1961. He headed the press room of the WORLD METHODIST CONFERENCE in 1947, '51, '56, '61, and '66. He was also a member of the executive committee of the WORLD METHODIST COUNCIL, and of various organizations (Methodist, interdenominational and secular), having to do with public relations. He broadcast a series of religious addresses over radio through the American Broadcasting Company and the National Broadcasting Company networks during the second World War. His dissertation was a history of the United States, Religious Journalism (1939). In 1959 he published *Handbook of Church Public Relations* (Abingdon). Since retiring in 1964 he has divided his time between Cape Cod and Florida.

Who's Who in The Methodist Church, 1966.   N. B. H.

STORY, GEORGE (1738-1818), British Methodist, was one of JOHN WESLEY's itinerants. He was born at Harthill, in

STOWE, WILLIAM McFERRIN (1913-   ), American bishop, was born on Jan. 28, 1913, in Franklin, Tenn., the son of John Joel and Myra Anderson McFerrin Stowe. He received his B.A. degree from HENDRIX COLLEGE in 1932; the B.D. from DUKE UNIVERSITY in 1935; the Ph.D. from BOSTON UNIVERSITY SCHOOL OF THEOLOGY in 1938. He has received honorary D.D. degrees from OKLAHOMA CITY UNIVERSITY, 1955, and Hendrix College, 1956. On July 28, 1943, he was united in marriage to Twila Farrell. They have three children, William McFerrin, Jr., Twila Gayle, and Martha Elizabeth.

McFerrin Stowe, as he is usually referred to, was ordained to the ministry of The Methodist Church in 1940. He has served the following pastorates: Alta Loma, Texas, 1938-40; Garden Villas Church, HOUSTON, Texas, 1940-44; First Church, STILLWATER, Okla., 1949-51; St. Luke's Church, OKLAHOMA CITY, 1951-64. He was a staff member of the General Board of EDUCATION of The Methodist Church in Nashville, Tenn., 1944-49. He was elected bishop of the SOUTH CENTRAL JURISDICTIONAL CONFERENCE in DALLAS, Texas in 1964, and assigned to the KANSAS Area.

He is past president of the Oklahoma City Council of Churches and the president of the Oklahoma Conference Methodist Board of Education. He was a member of the GENERAL and JURISDICTIONAL CONFERENCES of The

Methodist Church of 1956, '60, and '64. In 1958 and 1962 he was a delegate to the World Methodist Theological Institute held in Oxford, England. He is a member of the Oklahoma City's Mayor's Committee on Human Relations; Board of Directors of the Urban League of Oklahoma City; Board of Trustees of Oklahoma City University; Executive Committee of the Board of Trustees of Oklahoma City University; Board of Trustees of Scarritt College; COORDINATING COUNCIL of The Methodist Church; Board of Opera Association of Oklahoma City; Commission on Ecumenical Consultation (created by the COUNCIL OF BISHOPS of The Methodist Church, merged with another group in 1964); Executive Committee of Oklahoma Methodist Conference Council; and Board of Trustees of the Methodist Manor in Tulsa, Okla. He is president of the Oklahoma Conference of The Methodist Commission on Higher Christian Education and the dean of the Oklahoma Methodist Pastors' School. He has been a visiting professor at the following: ILIFF SCHOOL OF THEOLOGY, SCARRITT COLLEGE, special lecturer at Boston University School of Theology, PERKINS SCHOOL OF THEOLOGY, WESTMINSTER THEOLOGICAL SEMINARY, Graduate School of Religion, UNIVERSITY OF SOUTHERN CALIFORNIA and GAMMON SCHOOL OF THEOLOGY. He has been a lecturer in Pastor's Schools and speaker at Religious Emphasis Weeks throughout the nation. His counseling areas include religious, vocational and personal problems, as well as general pastoral counseling. He is the author of two books, *The Characteristics of Jesus*, published in 1962 by Abingdon Press, and *The Power of Paul*, 1963, Abingdon Press. For the 1968-72 quadrennium he was reassigned to the TOPEKA (Kansas) Area.

Who's Who in America, Vol. 34.
Who's Who in The Methodist Church, 1966.   N. B. H.

STRANGERS' FRIEND SOCIETY, a British Methodist relief organization, was started in the eighteenth century and intended to look after the "destitute sick poor, without distinction of sect or country, at their own habitations." The original founder was John Gardner, of Smithfield, LONDON, who in December 1785, wrote to JOHN WESLEY to say that "a few of us are subscribing a penny a week each, which is to be carried on the Sabbath by one of ourselves, who read and pray with the afflicted . . . Our benevolent plan is opposed by my class-leader; therefore we are constrained to seek your approbation before we proceed." In his reply, dated December 31, 1785, John Wesley immediately offered to subscribe threepence a week; similar societies were founded in other parts of the country, and in 1790 Wesley drew up their rules (see the entry in his *Journal* for March 14, 1790). Gardner became a doctor, and his tomb bears the inscription, "Dr. John Gardner, Last and Best Bedroom, 1807." The Strangers' Friend Society did much good work in the nineteenth century, and a few of the societies still exist.

L. Tyerman, *John Wesley*. 1890.   JOHN KENT

STRAUGHN, JAMES HENRY (1877-   ), American bishop and METHODIST PROTESTANT President, was born at Centreville, Md., on June 1, 1877, the son of James Henry and Laura Maria (Simmons) Straughn. In 1895 he entered WESTERN MARYLAND COLLEGE, receiving the A.B. degree in 1899, and from that same college the A.M. in 1902, D.D. in 1922, and LL.D. in 1949. From WESTMIN-

STER THEOLOGICAL SEMINARY he received the B.D. in 1901; ADRIAN COLLEGE, LL.D., 1937; WEST VIRGINIA WESLEYAN COLLEGE, LL.D., 1941; ALLEGHENY COLLEGE, LL.D., 1941.

On June 1, 1904, he was united in marriage to Clara Bellamy Morgan of Cumberland, Md., and they had one child, Laurlene (Mrs. Robert W. Pratt). Mrs. Straughn died July 27, 1965.

James Henry Straughn was admitted on trial to the MARYLAND CONFERENCE, M. P. Church, in 1901, full connection and ELDER in 1903. His pastorates included Mount Tabor Church, WASHINGTON, D. C., 1901-04; First Church, Lynchburg, Va., 1904-06; Broadway Church, BALTIMORE, Md., 1910-12; Christ Church, Laurel, Del., 1912-19; St. John's Church, Baltimore, Md., 1919-20; Rhode Island Avenue Church, Washington, D. C., 1923-26; and North Baltimore Church, Baltimore, 1932-36. He was president of West Lafayette College (Ohio), 1906-10; president of the Maryland Conference, 1920-23; treasurer and promotion secretary of the GENERAL CONFERENCE of the M.P. Church, 1928-32; and president of this Conference, 1936-39.

Straughn became chairman of the Methodist Protestant Commission upon the death of ALBERT NORMAN WARD, and in that capacity, according to Bishop JOHN M. MOORE, represented his Commission in preparing for and conducting the Uniting Conference "with remarkable ability, adaptability, geniality, and cooperative insight." At the Uniting Conference itself under the direction of the PLAN of UNION, which allowed the M.P. delegates to elect two bishops for The Methodist Church, James H. Straughn was elected a bishop, as was J. C. BROOMFIELD, and both these men were consecrated as bishops of The Methodist Church. This was an impressive ceremony participated in by bishops of the two Episcopal Methodisms. The famous photograph of the three leaders of the respective Commissions on Church Union, Bishop E. H. HUGHES for the M.E. Church, Bishop John M. Moore for the M.E. Church, South, and Bishop-elect James H. Straughn for the M.P. Church, has become well known over Methodism, and these three men standing together became a symbol of reunited Methodism.

Bishop Straughn at the UNITING CONFERENCE was assigned to the NORTHEASTERN JURISDICTION, whose College of Bishops and Jurisdictional Conference in turn assigned him to the PITTSBURGH Area. In this Area he served as bishop until his retirement in 1948.

Bishop Straughn is a trustee of Western Maryland College, a member of the Board of Governors of Wesley Theological Seminary in Washington, D. C. He is the author of *Methodism*, 1946, and *Inside Methodist Union*, 1958.

Since retirement, Bishop Straughn has lived in Baltimore. He was active in the decision to bring Westminster Theological Seminary to the campus of AMERICAN UNIVERSITY in Washington, D.C.

J. M. Moore, *Long Road to Union*. 1943.
J. H. Straughn, *Inside Methodist Union*. 1958.
Who's Who in The Methodist Church, 1966.   N. B. H.

STRAWBRIDGE HOUSE near New Windsor, Carroll County, Md., was designated as a Methodist historic SHRINE by the 1940 GENERAL CONFERENCE. ROBERT STRAWBRIDGE, the local preacher from IRELAND who, according to Asbury's *Journal* for April 30, 1801, "formed the first

ROBERT STRAWBRIDGE HOUSE,
NEW WINDSOR, MARYLAND

[Methodist] society in Maryland—and America," lived with his wife Elizabeth in the log cabin from 1760 to 1776. The house, constructed of logs and later enlarged and clapboarded, was the meeting place for Strawbridge's first class until 1768. Lost sight of for many years, the Strawbridge house was rediscovered in 1915 by Mrs. Arthur Bibbins, a Maryland Methodist historian. In 1924 the American Methodist Historical Society placed on the front porch of the house a plaque recounting the work of Strawbridge and listing the names of the first class and society members. A Strawbridge Shrine Association was formed in 1934 to purchase and preserve the house, a goal thus far not achieved.

A state historical marker on Maryland Route 31 south of New Windsor directs tourists to the Strawbridge house, while a marker on Route 407, another mile south, points to the site of the Strawbridge Log Meetinghouse which was built in 1764. A concrete monument installed on the latter site in 1914 was enlarged in 1934. The BALTIMORE CONFERENCE has owned the log meetinghouse site since 1909.

EDWIN SCHELL

STRAWBRIDGE, ROBERT (? -1781), one of the earliest Methodist preachers in America, was probably born at Drumsna not far from Carrick-on-Shannon, County Leitrim, IRELAND. His date of birth is unknown, but it is believed that he may have been converted through the influence of LAWRENCE COUGHLAN who, previous to his own conversion, had been a zealous Roman Catholic. Strawbridge began preaching at once, but his straightforward message aroused opposition which drove him to Sligo, where his efforts were more favorably received. In time he made Terryhugan his headquarters, and from here he itinerated throughout the neighborhood. He married Elizabeth Piper, a Methodist, and with her emigrated to America, settling on Sam's Creek, Frederick County, Md.

The date of Strawbridge's arrival in America has been a center of controversy. Court records in Frederick County show that there was as early as 1753 a grand jury presentment against a Robert Strawbridge for stealing a pig, but whether this is the same Strawbridge is debatable. Most Methodist historians believe that he arrived in America between 1760 and 1766. Shortly after his arrival, however, he began preaching in his own home to his neighbors. He is thought to have baptized Henry Maynard

ROBERT STRAWBRIDGE

in 1761, '62 or '63 and to have begun organizing Methodist Societies in 1763 or 1764. His first class, consisting of seven or eight persons, met at his home. A second class was formed at JOHN EVANS' house on Pipe Creek. These were among the earliest Methodist classes formed in America.

Around this time also Strawbridge built a log meeting house on Sam's Creek about a mile southwest of his home. A subsequent owner of the property dismantled it and used the logs to build a barn.

Strawbridge soon began to preach out-of-doors beneath what came to be called the "Strawbridge Oak." He also began itinerating in a wider and wider circle, leaving the care of his farm to his neighbors. He established Societies in many places, and he is the first Methodist to have preached on the Eastern shore of Maryland. Assisted by one of his spiritual sons, Richard Owen (or Owings), he also planted Methodism in Georgetown on the Potomac River and in several places in Fairfax County, Va. Through him or his followers several chapels were erected in the region of Aberdeen, Md., before the arrival in 1769 of JOSEPH PILMORE and RICHARD BOARDMAN, WESLEY's first missionaries to America. Among the men influenced directly or indirectly by Strawbridge for the Methodist work were FREEBORN GARRETTSON, Richard Owen (or Owings), Sater Stephenson, Nathan Perigau, Daniel Ruff, Richard Webster, Joseph Presbury, and JOHN HAGERTY. These influenced others, including PHILIP GATCH and WILLIAM WATTERS, the first native born American to join the itinerary.

With little regard for church order Strawbridge had assumed the right to administer the sacraments. This was contrary to Methodist discipline and at the first conference of the Methodist preachers in America in 1773 at ST. GEORGE's, PHILADELPHIA, the practice was condemned. For some unknown reason Strawbridge was not present. ASBURY in his Journal says that Strawbridge was made an exception to the rule, but it was resolved that he would be permitted to administer the sacraments only under the direction of an assistant. Strawbridge generally ignored the action of the conference. (See COMMUNION, THE HOLY and ORDINATION.) Asbury, in particular, was displeased by this "irregularity," and the comments in his *Journal* about Strawbridge are seldom favorable.

Strawbridge's popularity, however, was tremendous, and in the early days of Methodism and for long afterward, in the region where Robert Strawbridge labored, more converts were won for the Societies, and more young men were inspired to become itinerant preachers, than in any other section of the country.

Strawbridge's name was dropped from the Conference *Minutes* in 1774, but was printed again in the *Minutes* of 1775. That was the last time his name appeared. Strawbridge, however, continued his work as a permanent pastor of the Sam's Creek and Bush Forest Societies until his death.

He spent the last five years of his life on a farm not far from BALTIMORE, the use of which was presented to him during his life by Captain Charles Ridgely, its generous owner. Originally buried on the farm of Joseph Wheeler, where he had died in the summer of 1781, Strawbridge's ashes and those of his wife were later removed and reinterred near the grave of FRANCIS ASBURY in Mount Olivet Cemetery, Baltimore.

The old Strawbridge home with an addition, both covered with clapboard, still stands near Windsor, Maryland. A tablet commemorates its importance for Methodism. The house was designated as a historical shrine by the GENERAL CONFERENCE of 1940.

R. M. Bibbins, *How Methodism Came.* 1945.
W. Crook, *Ireland and American Methodism.* 1866.
Frederick E. Maser, "Robert Strawbridge, Founder of Methodism in Maryland," *Methodist History,* January 1966.
M. Simpson, *Cyclopaedia.* 1878.　　　　JAMES H. STRAUGHN

STRAWMAN, DANIEL (1830-1900), American Evangelical minister, preacher, counselor, and leader, was born Oct. 17, 1830, near Denmark, Morrow Co., OHIO, where his father and grandparents, Swiss immigrants, had settled in 1825. They were among the first fruits of the Sandusky Circuit of the EVANGELICAL ASSOCIATION founded a year later. After a penitential struggle of six years Strawman was converted on Feb. 17, 1848. The next day while meditating on the preaching of God's servants he sensed his own inescapable call.

His biographer said he was a man of pronounced personality, sterling integrity, and sound judgment. He was an acknowledged authority on church government and wielded great influence as a member of the Board of Missions and General Conference in shaping the policy of the church in all her enterprises. . . . He insisted on the necessity of the new birth and Christlikeness. . . ." (*Evangelical Messenger,* 1900, p. 314.)

He was a member of every GENERAL CONFERENCE from 1863 to 1887. Of him Editor S. P. SPRENG, said: "His advice was often sought by the highest officials of the Church. In General Conference his counsel was highly respected. In the Ohio Conference he towered above all others for years. . . . He preached with overwhelming power and swept everything before him by the flood-tide of mingled spiritual power, logic, and pathos." (*Ibid.,* p. 296.)

The Ohio Conference, Evangelical Association, licensed him in 1850, ordained him DEACON in 1852, and ELDER IN 1854. His wife Sarah was a daughter of David and Margaret Houser. Minerva Strawman, one of his daughters, at the age of seventeen, initiated the founding of the Woman's Missionary Society of the Evangelical Association. From 1885-88, Daniel Strawman was superintendent of the Orphan Home at Flat Rock, Ohio and contributed much to the modernization of that institution during that period. He died in 1900 at his home in Lindsey, Ohio and was buried in the family burial ground nearby.

Evangelical Messenger, 1900, p. 296.
R. B. Leedy, *Evangelical Church in Ohio.* 1959.
　　　　　　　　　　　　　　ROY B. LEEDY

STRETTON, JOHN, a local preacher from Limerick, IRELAND, arrived in Newfoundland in 1770 and established a fish business at Harbour Grace. He became one of the chief helpers of LAWRENCE COUGHLAN, who introduced Methodism into Newfoundland. After Coughlan's departure from the island in 1772, thirteen years passed before a Methodist missionary was sent. John Stretton, together with Arthur Thomey, another Irish merchant at Harbour Grace, conducted services, met the classes, visited the sick, and held prayer meetings. Stretton built at Harbour Grace a chapel which he gave to the connection. He appealed to WESLEY for a Methodist preacher, but his request was not granted until 1785 when John McGeary was stationed in Newfoundland.

T. W. Smith, *Eastern British America.* 1877.
William Wilson, *Newfoundland and Its Missionaries.* Cambridge: Dakin and Metcalf, 1866.　　　　N. WINSOR

WILLIAM P. STRICKLAND

STRICKLAND, WILLIAM PETER (1809-1884), American editor and author, was born at Pittsburgh, Pa., Aug.

17, 1809. He was the son of Peter and Mary W. Shepperd Strickland. He was a minister of the M.E. Church, 1833-67; assistant editor New York *Christian Advocate and Journal*, 1856-60; a prominent and prolific author of books and periodical articles of Methodist significance; and in later years a Presbyterian minister, 1870-84.

Reared in the Presbyterian tradition, William Peter Strickland became a Methodist in 1830. He entered the Methodist ministry in OHIO in 1833, after receiving his education at the University of Ohio, at Athens. For several years he was stationed in CINCINNATI and for four years was an agent for the AMERICAN BIBLE SOCIETY. In 1856 he was transferred to the NEW YORK CONFERENCE, where he served both in the pastoral ministry, and from 1856-60 as assistant editor of the *Christian Advocate and Journal*. In 1861, at the outbreak of the Civil War, he joined the 48th New York Regiment as CHAPLAIN and until 1863 was stationed at Port Royal, S. C. From this point he wrote a series of articles for the *Christian Advocate and Journal*, colorfully documenting and describing the early phase of the Civil War (and the beginnings of Reconstruction) in this area.

Although returning to New York in 1863 upon the death of his first wife, Elizabeth Talbott Strickland, he continued until 1864 as a chaplain and as a writer for the New York *Christian Advocate*. In 1867 he assumed the supernumerary relationship with the M.E. Church, and by 1870 was a member of the Long Island Presbytery of the Presbyterian Church in the U.S.A. Until 1878 he was pastor of the Presbyterian Church of Bridgehampton, Long Island, resigning in 1878 following the death of his second wife. In that year he was dismissed to the New York Presbytery and served until his death as an evangelist.

Awarded the D.D. degree by the University of Ohio, Strickland throughout his career was consistently literary. In 1849 his *History of the American Bible Society* was published. This was followed by many other books, among them the *History of the Missions of the Methodist Episcopal Church* (1850); the *Genius and Mission of Methodism* (1851); *Pioneers of the West* (1856); and *The Pioneer Bishop, or the Life and Times of Francis Asbury* (1858). In 1856 the autobiography of PETER CARTWRIGHT, *The Backwoods Preacher*, edited by Strickland, was published. In his early career Strickland was editor of the *Literary Casket* and associate editor of the *Western American Review*. He was also a contributor to many other publications, among them the *Methodist Quarterly Review* and *Harper's Magazine*.

Strickland died at Ocean Grove, N. J., July 15, 1884, and was buried in Greenwood Cemetery there.

S. Austin Allibone, *A Critical Dictionary of English Literature and British and American Authors*, Vol. II. Philadelphia: J. B. Lippincott Co., 1891.
Appleton's Cyclopedia of American Biography.
Christian Advocate (New York), 1861-63; July 24, 1884; Sept. 9, 1926.
Journal of the New York Conference, 1856-1867.
Methodist Centennial Yearbook, 1884.
J. P. Pilkington, *Methodist Publishing House.* 1968.

JAMES P. PILKINGTON

STRINGFIELD, THOMAS (1796-1858), American minister and editor, was born in Barren County, Ky., on Feb. 13, 1796, the son of John and Sarah Stringfield. His parents came from NORTH CAROLINA to TENNESSEE, removed to KENTUCKY and then to ALABAMA.

Thomas Stringfield served under Andrew Jackson in the War of 1812 and received a forehead wound which left a scar for life. He joined the TENNESSEE CONFERENCE in 1816 and served the Elk River, Tennessee Valley, Cahawba, Limestone and Flint Circuits, and the Nashville and Huntsville Stations. In 1824 he became a charter member of the HOLSTON CONFERENCE and was appointed Presiding Elder of the Knoxville District. He subsequently served circuits, districts and stations in various parts of east Tennessee and southwest VIRGINIA.

Around 1825 when Stringfield was on the French Broad District the so-called Gallagher controversy over CALVINISM VS. ARMINIANISM swept the region and he became the leading defender of the Methodist position.

In 1836 he became the first editor of the *Southwestern Christian Advocate* published at Nashville, Tenn., and remained in this position until 1841, becoming well known throughout the country for his editorial abilities.

On Oct. 10, 1824, he married Sarah Williams of Strawberry Plains, Tenn. She died on April 5, 1842, and the following year he married Mrs. H. Cockville of Alabama. He was the father of four children.

Stringfield was a member of the GENERAL CONFERENCES of 1824, 1828, 1832, and 1844. He was a member of the LOUISVILLE CONVENTION of 1845 which accepted the Plan of Separation. He with the Holston Conference adhered to the M.E. Church, South, and he was a member of the General Conference of that Church in 1846 and 1850. He became an agent of the AMERICAN BIBLE SOCIETY in 1844 and in 1849 he was appointed to the Greenville District. His following appointments were the Knox Circuit, agent for Strawberry Plains College, Dandridge Circuit, and Loudon Circuit. He died on June 12, 1858, at Strawberry Plains.

Journal of the Holston Conference, 1858.
I. P. Martin, *Holston.* 1945.
R. N. Price, *Holston.* 1903-13.   L. W. PIERCE

STROH, BYRON FREEMAN (1909-   ), American minister and executive, was born in Akron, Ohio, on Dec. 20, 1909, the son of Freeman Wesley and Alice McIntosh Stroh. He received his collegiate training at ASBURY COLLEGE, A.B., 1935; DUKE UNIVERSITY, M.A., 1936; Yale University, B.D., 1939; and did post graduate work at the University of Chicago, 1943-45. Asbury College awarded him the D.D. degree in 1955. His wife was Mary Jean Newby, whom he married on July 23, 1941, and their children are John Alan, James Freeman, and Mary Gregory. He joined the NORTH INDIANA CONFERENCE in 1940, going into full connection and being ordained ELDER in 1942. His appointments were Daleville, Cambridge City, Main Street Church in Kokomo (all Indiana), and in 1955 he became superintendent of the Fort Wayne District where he served for five years. In 1960 he became the executive assistant of the INDIANA Area, INDIANAPOLIS, in which position he served for five years. In 1965 he became the pastor of the North Church in Indianapolis.

Dr. Stroh was a delegate to the GENERAL CONFERENCES of 1956, '60, '64 and '66; to the WORLD METHODIST CONFERENCE, 1956, '61, and '66; has been the chairman of his Conference's Continuing Educational Committee; a member of the Indiana Governor's Commission on Youth; and serves as a trustee of DePauw University, Taylor University, and the Methodist Theological School in Ohio; and also of the Methodist Hospital in Indianapolis and Parkview Hospital in Fort Wayne, Indiana. He served twelve years on the Board of Publication, and in 1968 he was appointed to the General Council on World Service and Finance.

Who's Who in The Methodist Church, 1966.   N. B.H.

STROHL, C. ORVILLE (1908-   ), American minister and college president, was born Sept. 18, 1908 in Meade County, Kan., the son of Clarence Elmer and Ida Rebecca Haywood Strohl. He graduated from Southwestern College in 1931, having served as a student supply pastor while attending college. He received the Th.M. degree from Iliff School of Theology and the D.D. degree from Iowa Wesleyan College.

He was received into the Iowa-Des Moines Conference in 1933 and transferred to the Central Kansas Conference in 1954. He was pastor of the following churches in Iowa: Carlisle, Madrid and New London. He was an instructor at Iowa Wesleyan College, 1943-45. In 1945 he became Executive Secretary of the Des Moines Area Commission on Christian Education and continued in this position until 1954 when he was elected President of Southwestern College.

Under his administration the institution has made decided advancement in buildings, endowment, faculty changes and enrollment. The faculty has grown, with a greater percent holding doctorates; enrollment increased from 325 to 749; endowment increased from $580,761 to $3,150,000; and eight new buildings at a cost of $3,123,573.

Dr. Strohl is an officer of the Association of Colleges for Inter-cultural-International Study; Chairman of the Committee on Tuition Grants for the State of Kansas; member of the Winfield Planning Commission; Educational Council, Kansas State Chamber of Commerce; American Association of Colleges; National Association of Schools and Colleges of The Methodist Church; and North Central Association of Colleges and Secondary Schools.

Dr. Strohl has contributed to numerous religious publications.

Journal of the Central Kansas Conference, 1955, 1967.

WILLIAM F. RAMSDALE

STRONG, JAMES (1822-1894), American biblical scholar, was born in New York City, Aug. 14, 1822. His parents died when he was very young, and he was reared by an aunt and his maternal grandmother under Protestant Episcopal influences. He studied at Lowville Academy in New York, and then entered Wesleyan University, Middletown, Conn., from which he received in due course three degrees. He taught for two years in the Troy Conference Academy at Poultney, Vt.

In 1847 he moved to Flushing, Long Island, where he projected and built the Flushing Railroad, of which he became president in 1852. Three years later he relinquished this post and became president of the Corporation of Flushing.

In 1858 he became professor of biblical literature in Troy University, where he served until 1863, part of this period as acting president. He became professor of exegetical theology in Drew Theological Seminary, Madison, N. J., in 1868, and served in this post until his death.

At the 1872 General Conference of the M.E. Church he was largely responsible for securing legislation which admitted laymen to membership in the General Conference, and he himself was elected as the first lay delegate by the Newark Conference.

Strong is best known for his *Exhaustive Concordance of the Bible*, published in 1890, and his *Cyclopedia of Biblical, Theological and Ecclesiastical Literature* in ten volumes, which he edited with John McClintock. He was the author or editor of at least a dozen other important works in the field of biblical literature.

He was a member of the Anglo-American Bible Revision Committee for ten years and of the Palestine Exploration Society in 1872. In connection with the latter, he traveled extensively through Palestine and the Far East as the chairman of the Archaeological Council of the Oriental Topographical Society.

He died at Round Lake, N. Y., Aug. 7, 1894, and was buried at Flushing, Long Island.

Dictionary of American Biography.
V. B. Hampton, *Newark Conference*. 1957.
M. Simpson, *Cyclopaedia*. 1878.   M. W. GREEN

STROTHERS MEETING HOUSE, in Sumner County, Tenn., was erected about 1800 near Cottontown.

The General Conference which met at Baltimore, Md., May 1, 1800, made provision for the organization of the Western Conference. It was organized by Bishops Asbury and Whatcoat at Bethel Academy in Kentucky, Oct. 6, 1800, and was formed from districts in Ohio, Kentucky, Tennessee, and Mississippi.

The log building, twenty by twenty-four feet, known as Strothers Meeting House, was an appointment in the newly organized Western Conference. In it Bishop Asbury conducted the third session of the Western Conference, Oct. 2, 1802, which was the second Methodist Conference conducted in the State of Tennessee.

This building was moved from its original location to the Red River Pike and used continuously as a church until 1857, when it was supplanted by a new frame building, and its name was changed to Bethel.

Under an inspiring address delivered by Bishop Horace M. DuBose at the Annual Conference in Gallatin, Tenn., Oct. 22-26, 1930, the Historical Society decided to preserve this historic building. Therefore, it was moved from near Cottontown to Scarritt College campus in Nashville. It was formally opened as a Methodist Museum by Bishop DuBose, May 10, 1931.

CULLEN T. CARTER

STROUD, JOHN EDGAR (1905-   ), American missionary who with his wife, Hazel Hogan Stroud, has served in several mission fields and is now the pastor of the St. Croix Methodist Church in Frederiksted, St. Croix, Virgin Islands. John Stroud was born at Mooresville, Tenn. and was married on May 31, 1928.

John Stroud was student pastor at the University of Virginia one year and then went to China in 1930. There he worked in the Institutional Church in Soochow, returning on furlough in 1935 to his homeland. From 1936 to 1943 the Strouds did mission work in the Ten-

NESSEE CONFERENCE, but in 1943 went to CUBA to help develop a rural church there. They founded an Agricultural School, developed the Churchwell Clinic in Mayari, and built two camps (one of these being the first "church camp" which had been built in Cuba). They organized twenty-three churches in the seventeen years they spent in the island. Their service was terminated when they had to flee to escape arrest as spies after the Castro revolution. For three years they worked with Cuban refugees in MIAMI, Fla., and then John Stroud was assigned a pastorate at Cherokee, N. C., 1963-65. The Mission Board, however, requested him to go to St. Croix in the Virgin Islands to work in Spanish with the Puerto Ricans and others who had come there and to organize new work with English-speaking people coming to St. Croix from the mainland. An English-speaking church was organized in 1966 and a second one is at present underway.

N. B. H.

STUART, CHARLES MACAULAY (1853-1932), American clergyman, editor, and educator, was born in Glasgow, SCOTLAND, Aug. 20, 1853. He was educated at Kalamazoo College (Michigan), receiving an A.B., 1880 and an M.A. in 1883. He received a B.D. from GARRETT in 1885 and an A.M. from NORTHWESTERN the same year. He married Emma R. Littlefield on Oct. 10, 1883.

After a pastorate in ILLINOIS and another in MICHIGAN, he became associate editor of the *Northwestern Christian Advocate* in 1886 and continued in that post until 1896. In that year Garrett Biblical Institute called him to the chair of Sacred Rhetoric (sometimes called Homiletics and now often entitled Preaching). In 1909 Professor Stuart returned to the *Northwestern Christian Advocate* as Editor and continued at that task until 1912, at which time he was elected President of Garrett Biblical Institute, in which position he served until retirement in 1924.

His presidency at Garrett was marked by several distinct items of progressive achievement. The graduate work of the Institute was set apart as a separate school, with a larger and greatly strengthened faculty. It was at the beginning of this administration that the distinguished theologian, HARRIS FRANKLIN RALL, joined the faculty. Special attention was given to the rural and the urban church by the selection of specialists in those fields.

In 1914, Heck Hall, the school's only dormitory, burned to the ground and thus precipitated financial problems which overshadowed all others for years. The erection of new buildings on another sector of the campus of Northwestern University plus the increased cost of the expanded educational program called for more financial support than was forthcoming from the church of that day. The accumulation of these obligations became an oppressive burden which, when the depression came in 1929, precipitated a serious crisis for the school.

Stuart's work as a teacher, as indeed that as an editor or administrator, was characterized by distinctive personal factors. Frequently in the classroom, he left the rostrum and standing by the desk of a particular student, carried on a dialogue with him. His teaching, as was true of most of his work, was illuminated by a subtle humor.

His permanent literary output was not very large unless one includes his editorial work. He edited some of the papers of his colleague, Francis Hemenway, and more especially those of Charles Joseph Little. He was secretary of the Joint Hymnal Commission of the two M.E. Churches which brought out the issue of 1905. Stuart was a member of the Society of Biblical Research and a member of the Religious Education Association, a member of the Northwestern University Settlement Board, and a trustee of several other institutions. The widespread esteem in which he was held may be gauged in part by the honorary degrees awarded him—D.D., Garrett, 1885; LL.D., Northwestern, 1909; D.D., WESLEYAN, 1906; Litt.D., SYRACUSE, 1904; Litt.D., OHIO WESLEYAN, 1909; LL.D., NEBRASKA WESLEYAN, 1909.

Charles Macaulay Stuart served the church as a member of the DETROIT and the ROCK RIVER CONFERENCES. He retired as president of Garrett Biblical Institute in 1924 because of ill health and died Jan. 26, 1932.

HORACE GREELEY SMITH

STUART, GEORGE RUTLEDGE (1857-1926), American minister, evangelist and crusader, was born Dec. 14, 1857 in Talbott, Tenn., the son of Caswell and Maria M. Stuart, who had been prosperous but were stripped of all their possessions by the Civil War. They took up farming at which they were not successful and Stuart's father turned to drinking, increasing the family's problems. At fourteen years of age, living in New Market, Tenn., George Stuart was converted in a revival meeting. He brought his father to Christ and the whole family joined the Presbyterian Church. At a very early age he felt the call to preach, and began his education for that purpose. In 1880 he decided to join the M.E. Church, South, and to become a preacher. He entered EMORY AND HENRY COLLEGE, and in the Spring of 1882 he received his diploma. On Sept. 6, he married Zellie Sullins, daughter of the college president, DAVID SULLINS.

Stuart joined the HOLSTON CONFERENCE in 1884. His first appointment was Cleveland, Tenn. While pastor there he undertook the task of raising money for the building of CENTENARY COLLEGE, with marvelous success. He accepted the chair of English and Natural Science in the college, where he taught for five years.

Evangelist SAM JONES invited George Stuart to join him in his evangelistic work. They were most successful for a number of years. Bishop JOHN C. KEENER then appointed Stuart as pastor of Centenary Church, CHATTANOOGA, in 1892. However, he felt the call to evangelistic work so strongly that when the authorities would not appoint him as an evangelist, he asked to be located, and then joined Sam Jones in campaigns throughout the nation. No greater voices were heard against sin and liquor than those of George Stuart and Sam Jones. After the death of Sam Jones, Stuart divided his time between revivals and the Chautauqua platform, for he was a great public platform man also, being a colorful, dynamic personality who was a natural master of assemblies.

In 1912, he was appointed pastor of Church Street Church, KNOXVILLE, by Bishop Keener. In 1916 he was transferred to First Church, BIRMINGHAM, Ala. For eleven years he filled this great Church to its capacity from Sunday to Sunday, and increased its membership to one of the largest in the denomination.

Stuart was largely responsible for establishing the Eva Comer Cooperative Home for young business women in Birmingham. While at First Church, he took the lead in establishing, with the help of some of his friends among both preachers and laymen, the Assembly grounds at LAKE JUNALUSKA, N. C. George Stuart was one of the original thirteen cottage owners on "The Lake" in 1913. His father-in-law, David Sullins, relates in his diary that in 1916, Stuart took public subscriptions for stock in the assembly and raised $106,000. The auditorium at Lake Junaluska, in which the WESTERN NORTH CAROLINA CONFERENCE usually holds its sessions, was named Stuart Auditorium in his honor.

He published a volume of sermons, *The Saloon Under the Search Light, What Every Methodist Should Know,* and *Methodist Evangelism*—the last being the Sam Jones lectures at EMORY UNIVERSITY in 1923. In 1927 W. W. PINSON published a biography, *George R. Stuart, His Life and Work.*

He died in Birmingham, Ala., on May 11, 1926, when the GENERAL CONFERENCE of the M.E. Church, South, was in session at MEMPHIS, and that body paused to pay tribute to his memory. His body was carried by special train to Cleveland, Tenn., for interment.

C. F. Price, *Who's Who in American Methodism.* 1916.

ELMER T. CLARK
GEORGE F. COOPER

STUART, ROBERT MARVIN (1909-), American bishop, was born on Nov. 22, 1909 at Paullina, Iowa. He received the A.B. degree from Taylor University (Upland, Ind.) in 1931; the S.T.B. from BOSTON UNIVERSITY in 1934 and S.T.M. in 1935; and the D.D. from Taylor. On June 8, 1933, he was united in marriage to Mary Ella Rose. They have one son, Robert Lee.

Robert Marvin Stuart was ordained a DEACON in 1933 and an ELDER in 1934. His pastorates include Shideler, Ind., 1931; Woods Hole, Mass., 1932; El Cerrito, Calif., 1935; Trinity Church, SAN FRANCISCO, 1938; First Church, Palo Alto, Calif., 1942-64. He was elected a bishop of The Methodist Church at the WESTERN JURISDICTIONAL CONFERENCE in PORTLAND, Ore., in July, 1964, and was assigned to the DENVER Area. In 1968 he was reassigned to the same area.

He was a delegate to the Jurisdictional Conferences of 1944, '48, '52, '56, '60, and '64; to the GENERAL CONFERENCES of 1948 (reserve), '52, '56, '60, and '64; to the WORLD METHODIST CONFERENCE at OXFORD, England in 1951 and at LAKE JUNALUSKA, N. C., in 1956.

He is a member of the Board of EDUCATION; the Interboard Committee on Christian Vocations; and the Interboard Committee on Town and Country Work. He is a trustee of the ALASKA METHODIST UNIVERSITY, the ILIFF SCHOOL OF THEOLOGY, and the UNIVERSITY OF DENVER.

Who's Who in America, Vol. 34.
Who's Who in The Methodist Church, 1966.   N. B. H.

STUART, WILSON (1873-1934), British Methodist, was a prominent temperance advocate. Born at Leek, Staffordshire, in 1873, he had a distinguished career at the Leeds Branch of the Victoria University, which he entered in 1892. He studied philosophy at St. John's College, Cambridge, 1898-1901. He entered the Wesleyan Methodist ministry in 1899. A passionate teetotaller, he was one of the English advocates of prohibition. In 1919 he became organizing secretary of the United Kingdom Al-

liance and spent the rest of his ministry entirely in total abstinence work. He died on Aug. 9, 1934.

J. Malins, *Wilson Stuart.* London, 1935.   JOHN KENT

STUBBINS, ROLAND CLINTON (1885-1967), American M.P. minister and historian, was born on Jan. 28, 1885, the son of George P. and Margaret A. Williams Stubbins of Hillsborough, N. C. He studied at Orange Grove Academy, Liberty Normal School, Trinity Park (now DUKE UNIVERSITY), Hoffman University, and the University of Chicago, and conducted research at the University of North Carolina at Chapel Hill and Raleigh. He joined the NORTH CAROLINA CONFERENCE of the M.P. Church in 1908 and was ordained an ELDER in 1911. He was a member of the GENERAL CONFERENCE in 1924, 1928 and 1932, where he held several important positions. He served as president of the Young People's Conference of the North Carolina Conference, as well as president of the Pastors' Summer Conference, member of the conference faculty and the conference Board of Trustees. He served a number of churches and circuits in NORTH CAROLINA.

Among Stubbins's special interests was the history of Methodism and, as a result of his interest, WHITAKER'S CHAPEL was restored in 1965. He was a member of the Historic Hillsborough Association and, because of his great love of nature, was a member of the Audubon Society and was responsible for several towns and cities, including Greensboro, being designated as "Bird Sanctuaries." He was also active in Boy Scout work. Stubbins was possessed of a deep spiritual quality, a warm, vibrant, friendly disposition and a keen sense of humor that had endeared him to a host of friends throughout North Carolina.

On Dec. 22, 1908, he married Vera Williams, daughter of Cary and Maria Pinchbeck Williams of Ringwood, N. C. To this union was born one daughter. Stubbins died in DURHAM, N. C., on Feb. 17, 1967, and was buried in the Hillsborough Cemetery.

Clark and Stafford, *Who's Who in Methodism.* 1952.
Durham (N.C.) *Herald,* Feb. 19, 1967.
North Carolina Christian Advocate, Feb. 23, May 18, 1967.

RALPH HARDEE RIVES

STUBBS, JOSEPH EDWARD (1845-1914), American minister and educator, earned two degrees at OHIO WESLEYAN UNIVERSITY and studied in Berlin. He was school superintendent in Ashland, Ohio, and for eight years was president of Baldwin College in that state. He was president of the University of Nevada for twenty years.

Through his experience and ability Stubbs became the dominant force in shaping education in NEVADA. He secured the cooperation of the estate of Comstock millionaire John W. Mackay in building and endowment programs, and raised educational standards in the state. He was a member of the CALIFORNIA CONFERENCE of the M.E. Church. He was possibly the most constructive Protestant churchman in the first half century of Nevada's life as a state.

Governor Tasker L. Oddie said of Stubbs:

He was our greatest citizen. His monument for all time to come will be the University of Nevada, destined to become, as he had planned, more and more as the years go by, the center and source of Nevada's true development and awakening. He laid the foundations broad and deep.

Samuel B. Doten, *An Illustrated History of the University of Nevada.* Carson City: State Printing Office, 1924.
L. L. Loofbourow, *Steeples Among the Sage.* 1964.

LEON L. LOOFBOUROW

STUDEBAKER, CLEMENT (1831-1901), American industrialist, philanthropist, and churchman, the son of John and Rebecca (Mohler) Studebaker, was born March 12, 1831, near Gettysburg, Pa. In 1835 the family moved to Ashland County, OHIO. Here he learned blacksmithing and wagon making from his father. In 1850 he came to SOUTH BEND, Ind. In 1868 the Studebaker Brothers Manufacturing Company was organized, with Clement Studebaker as its first president. It soon was the largest manufacturer of horse-drawn vehicles in the world. His home was one of culture and refinement. In 1878 he represented INDIANA at the Paris Exposition. He was a trustee and president of the Chautauqua Association. For twenty-one years he was trustee of DEPAUW UNIVERSITY. Twice he was a delegate to GENERAL CONFERENCE. He promoted Epworth Hospital in South Bend, and gave St. Paul's Church a new building. His first wife was Charity M. Bratt who died in 1863. In 1864 he married Anna Milburn Harper. Three children blessed their home. He died Nov. 27, 1901.

Dictionary of American Biography.
Who's Who in America, 1897-1902.   W. D. ARCHIBALD

STUDENT VOLUNTEER MOVEMENT, an interdenominational organization, was formed during the years 1886-89 in the United States under the influence of Robert G. Wilder, Luther D. Wishard, and Dwight L. Moody. JOHN R. MOTT served as the first chairman of this organization, which became the channel for the overseas missionary concern of American students for more than sixty years. In 1959 the Student Volunteer Movement became the Commission on World Missions of the National Student Christian Federation.

W. R. Hogg, *Ecumenical Foundations.* New York: Harper, 1952.
John R. Mott, *Addresses and Papers,* Vol. I. New York: Association Press, 1946.
C. P. Shedd, *Two Centuries of Student Christian Movements.* New York: Association Press, 1934.   PAUL F. BLANKENSHIP

STULL, JOHN (1825-1894), American Evangelical minister, was born Nov. 20, 1825, in Bedford County, Pa. His parents located near Belleville, Ohio, in 1832. Deprived of an opportunity to attend any higher institution of learning, he unsuccessfully turned to farming, but found peace only when he yielded to his conviction of a call to the ministry.

Thirty-eight successful years followed, twenty-four as PRESIDING ELDER. On his influence and ability J. B. Kanaga wrote: "All admit his pulpit power which defies description or analysis. There was in his best pulpit efforts a might and majesty that bore all before it. His prayers often seemed to bring down the very hush of heaven and the solemnity of eternity." (*Evangelical Messenger,* 1895, p. 433.)

E. D. Paulin related that he witnessed the power of

Stull's prayer at the Sunday morning service of one of his quarterly meetings. For fifteen minutes he prayed with such remarkable ferver and intercession that the whole congregation was wondrously stirred.

John Stull was licensed by the OHIO CONFERENCE in 1855. He was ordained DEACON by the same conference in 1857 and ordained ELDER two years later. He was living in Marion, Ohio at the time of his death and was placed in the family burial plot nearby.

Evangelical Messenger, 1895.
R. B. Leedy, *Evangelical Church in Ohio.* 1959.

ROY B. LEEDY

STUNTZ, CLYDE BRONSON (1886-1965), older son of HOMER CLYDE STUNTZ and Estelle Clark Stuntz, was born at La Grande, Iowa, Oct. 8, 1886, and three months later accompanied his parents to INDIA. He returned to Mt. Vernon, Iowa, with his parents in 1895 and completed high school there in 1902. He studied shorthand and typing during that summer, and in the fall went to Manila to become his father's secretary for three years. He returned to Mt. Vernon in 1905 to enter CORNELL UNIVERSITY, and a year later transferred to Middletown, Conn., to enter WESLEYAN UNIVERSITY. There he received his A.B. in English (1910) and D.D. (1945). Other degrees: M.A. Sanskrit from Columbia University (1913), and B.D. (1913) DREW THEOLOGICAL SEMINARY.

Stuntz joined the NORTH IOWA CONFERENCE in September 1913. His first and only appointment in the United States was Farley, Iowa, a two-point circuit. On Nov. 20, 1915, he sailed for CALCUTTA, India under appointment to be pastor of Thoburn Church in that city.

On Nov. 25, 1913, he married Florence Ada Watters, daughter of Dr. and Mrs. P. M. Watters of the NEW YORK EAST CONFERENCE, and they had five children. Florence was known as Sally by her college friends and kept that name.

Fearing that his German surname might bring suspicion on his loyalty to the Allies then fighting Germany, the official Board of that church asked the bishop in charge to transfer the Stuntzes elsewhere. Sent to Lahore, now in PAKISTAN, he soon showed ability in using the language, fluently speaking Urdu, the generally spoken language of north-west India; and Punjabi, prevalent in the Punjab; and Gurmukhi, the language of the Sikhs.

The Outcastes, who had become Christians a few years earlier, now needed education because of their general illiteracy. They also needed homes, with land of their own to cultivate, instead of continuing as tenant farmers. Clyde attacked both of these problems. In Lahore he was given supervision of a primary school for boys. He soon had it moved to a rural area twenty-five miles from Lahore, a small town named RAIWIND. The school developed into a high school, and now also has a teacher training department to train teachers for Rural Primary Schools. Clyde Stuntz served as the principal interchangeably with EARLE RUGG, a fellow missionary of similar age and training.

Stuntz also had responsibility for serving the church in the villages. With a ready memory for names he soon had the reputation of being able to call by name several thousand of the village Christians. Watching the efforts of the government of India to secure more arable lands, by providing canals to irrigate land where the average rainfall was about ten to twelve inches a year, Stuntz found it possible to secure some village sites for Christians who wished to become farmers. Each village was called chak (chuck) and had its own number. He settled many Christian families in other neighboring chaks also. The grateful Christians decided to give the first chak, which he secured for their settlement, the name Stuntzabad (more euphonious than its English equivalent— Stuntz-town). Stuntzabad has a well equipped rural high school, an excellent health center to provide for its medical needs, and a post office, thus giving it great importance.

In August 1947, Pakistan, as an independent nation, separated from India. Millions of the population moved, Muslims from the India side setting their goal in Pakistan, while Hindus and Sikhs left Pakistan to enter into the new bounds of India. Confusion and frequent dangerous clashes between the two sets of refugees created problems. Many Christians wished to move into the neighborhood of their relatives and had to cross the new dividing line. Stuntz and his wife operated free bus transportation for families who had urgent need for making such a change. Later the Pakistan government decorated Clyde Stuntz for service to the refugees during the disturbances.

The final term, 1951-56, consisted of one year in Karachi helping organize the developing Methodist work in Karachi, and the last four years in Lahore, where he served the West Pakistan Christian Council in developing the stability and efficiency of the expanding settlement program for Christians. He also served as hostel superintendent of the men's hostel for post graduates of Forman Christian College in Lahore.

In November 1956, even while the Centenary of Indian Methodism was being observed in LUCKNOW, Stuntz returned to the States to settle in Monroe, La. He died in December 1965, following a heart attack.

CLEMENT D. ROCKEY

STUNTZ, HOMER CLYDE (1858-1924), American bishop and outstanding missionary teacher, administrator and evangelist, was born at Albion, Pa., on Jan. 29, 1858. He was in the line of succession of several generations of Methodist preachers.

His education came mostly from his own efforts and self discipline. When a boy he worked on farms and in a blacksmith shop. As an older man, his rugged body and his dynamic preaching gave evidence of this early physical training. His ambition was to be an attorney at law, but he had an urgent call to the ministry, following an overwhelming conversion experience.

He joined the UPPER IOWA CONFERENCE in 1884. Shortly afterwards he married Estelle Clark of Chelsea, Iowa, and on Oct. 8, 1886 at La Grande, Iowa, their son, Clyde Bronson Stuntz, was born. Three months later the family started for INDIA. He served in that country for almost eight years, returning to the States in 1895.

H. C. Stuntz was evangelist, teacher, administrator and director of Methodist publications. He was transferred to the SOUTH INDIA CONFERENCE and stationed in BOMBAY, pastor of Grant Road Church. He also served on the *Bombay Guardian,* a Christian weekly published there. Two years later he was transferred to the NORTH INDIA CONFERENCE, and placed in charge of the English work in Naini Tal, in the Himalayas. For two years, during 1891-93, he was Editor of the *Indian Witness,* the official

weekly of the Methodist Church in India. In 1893 he was sent to CALCUTTA and transferred to the BENGAL CONFERENCE, staying there until the family returned to the States in 1895. When the Board of the EPWORTH LEAGUE in India was organized in 1894, he was made General Secretary.

On the invitation of Bishop FRANCIS WARNE he went to MANILA in April 1901, and was made PRESIDING ELDER of the PHILIPPINES District of the MALAYSIA Mission Conference. He returned to the States in 1908.

In 1908 he was elected to be Associate Secretary of the Board of MISSIONS of which ADNA B. LEONARD was General Secretary. His main work during the quadrennium was to visit the churches in the interest of the work on the foreign field. His popularity and effectiveness as a preacher and orator brought him to the attention of many persons, and he was elected bishop at the GENERAL CONFERENCE of 1912, and at his own request was assigned to South America, with his residence in BUENOS AIRES, ARGENTINA. He served this area with able dedication, and in 1916 was appointed to the OMAHA Area with jurisdiction over churches of IOWA and NEBRASKA.

Bishop and Mrs. Stuntz had three children, Clyde, Hugh and Clara. Clara died in early womanhood within the first two years of her marriage. HUGH STUNTZ was a missionary to South America, and later president of SCARRITT COLLEGE for several years.

During his days in the Omaha Area, Bishop Stuntz gave stimulating and inspiring leadership, not only to his churches, but in financial campaigns for hospitals, homes and colleges. During his days in Omaha, the old building of Brownell Hall, an Episcopal school for girls, was purchased and made into a home for working girls of Omaha, and was known as Stuntz Hall. He personally guaranteed a note for $10,000 to start the West Nebraska Methodist Hospital in Scottsbluff. He made so many pledges to colleges, hospitals and homes, that on his death, they equalled three years of the amount of his entire salary. These pledges were paid in full by the members of his family over a period of years.

During the First World War, 1917-18, Bishop Stuntz was also Administrator of War Work for the M.E. Church.

In January 1924, Bishop Stuntz was stricken with a cerebral hemorrhage, and he died on June 3, 1924. He was laid to rest in Forest Lawn Cemetery in Omaha, Neb., the only bishop to be buried in Nebraska.

B. T. Badley, *Southern Asia.* 1931.
W. C. Barclay, *History of Missions.* 1957.
J. N. Hollister, *Southern Asia.* 1956.
F. D. Leete, *Methodist Bishops.* 1948.
Minutes of the Nebraska and Northwest Iowa Conferences, 1924.
EVERETT E. JACKMAN

STUNTZ, HUGH CLARK (1891-   ), American missionary and college president, was born in Naini Tal, INDIA, June 29, 1891, the son of HOMER CLYDE and Estelle May Clark STUNTZ. Hugh Stuntz spent part of his boyhood in India and the PHILIPPINES. During the first World War he served as CHAPLAIN with the Rainbow Division of the A.E.F. He received his college education from WESLEYAN UNIVERSITY, Middletown, Conn., A.B., 1914; B.D., GARRETT BIBLICAL INSTITUTE, 1920; and M.A., Columbia University, New York, 1926. The D.D. degree was conferred by Garrett in 1939. He was married to Florence Wolford, Nov. 28, 1917. They have three children, William W., Richard C., and Jane A.

He was admitted on trial to the ROCK RIVER CONFERENCE in 1918, and into full connection, 1920. He then transferred to the River Plate Conference. He served as field secretary of the Board of Foreign MISSIONS of the M.E. Church, 1919-20. For twenty years he served in religious and educational work in CHILE, ARGENTINA, and BOLIVIA. He was appointed to the staff of interpreter-translators for the American delegation to the Peace Conference in BUENOS AIRES in 1936.

From 1940 to 1943, Dr. Stuntz served as Public Relations Director, and from 1943 to 1956, as president of SCARRITT COLLEGE for Christian Workers in NASHVILLE, Tenn. Upon retirement from this position, he served for five years as pastor of Emmanuel Methodist Church in MONTEVIDEO, URUGUAY, and later in public relations and as platform manager at the LAKE JUNALUSKA Assembly in North Carolina. He and his wife now live at 1338 Alcazer Avenue, Ft. Myers, Florida.

Dr. Stuntz published *The United Nations, A Challenge to the Church*, Abingdon Press, 1948, and *A Cup of Kindness*, Abingdon, 1968.

Clark and Stafford, *Who's Who in Methodism*. 1952.

D. D. HOLT

STUNTZABAD, a town of PAKISTAN, was named in gratitude for the efforts of CLYDE B. STUNTZ to secure land for Christian settlers. It is 165 miles southwest of Lahore, and is a focal center of rural work of the Methodist Church in this area. It was made possible through an elaborate system of canals providing irrigation for growth of wheat and cotton despite the low rainfall of ten to fifteen inches of rain a year. Stuntzabad provides leadership for five important projects usefully serving Christian farmers in a rural area of a twenty to twenty-five mile radius.

Central Methodist High School was founded as a village primary school almost thirty years earlier but was made a High School in 1953. Present enrollment, beginning with Kindergarten and through the High School, approximates 600. One-fourth are girls, and for these a girl's section is being organized and a hostel set up, so that there will soon be two High Schools, one for boys—the other for girls. P. R. Michael is the capable Pakistani headmaster. His wife, Mrs. Molly Michael, has been serving on the staff and is organizing the Girl's High School. The School has also sponsored within a fifteen mile radius the organization and development of ten or more Village Primary Schools.

Adult Literacy Center: An effective agency for development of the adult literacy program in Stuntzabad, producing and hand-printing literature for those just becoming literate. The program is effectively prepared and supervised by an American, Miss Helen Fehr, who had many years of experience in this type of work in India.

Stuntzabad Clinic: This is an excellent and effective Dispensary and Clinic with a modicum of hospital work. It is supervised by Miss Greta Wiseman, an American, who is aided by a well selected and trained group of Pakistani helpers. Emergency cases are handled as it is over fifteen miles to the nearest medical base. Serious hospital cases are motored to the nearest mission hospitals fifty to sixty miles distant.

Area Extension Service: This has been established to help in agricultural experiments and give assistance to farmers so that they may improve their farming and marketing of produce. There is also a Co-operative Grain Shop which provides cash advances to farmers for purchasing seed, for purchasing farm implements (including bullocks), and that they may purchase and store the new crop for resale to the farmers at prices below the market price.

CLEMENT ROCKEY

STURDIVANT, MATTHEW PARHAM (1776, *circa*-1850-52), the first Methodist minister ever sent into what is now ALABAMA, was born about 1776 somewhere in NORTH CAROLINA, and died after Aug. 30, 1850, and before 1852 in Nelson County, Va. He was buried at Massie's Mill (no tombstone). He married Agnes Kent, daughter of William, on Nov. 24, 1813, in Halifax County, Va. She died after 1860. There were six sons and five daughters to live to maturity.

Sturdivant joined the VIRGINIA CONFERENCE on March 1, 1805, and on Jan. 2, 1808, was assigned from the SOUTH CAROLINA CONFERENCE by Bishop ASBURY to the "Tombigbee River Settlements"—appointment, "Tombigbee," then being in MISSISSIPPI Territory, now in Alabama. It took him thirteen days to get to his charge through many hundreds of miles of new and uncharted wilderness. He reported no members the first year but was reappointed on Jan. 1, 1809 to Tombigbee, with Michael Burdge as his helper, and at the Dec. 30, 1809, Conference, reported seventy-one white and fifteen colored members. Thus began Methodism in what is now part of the ALABAMA-WEST FLORIDA CONFERENCE.

Sturdivant was assigned in 1810 to Fayetteville, N. C., and in 1811 to Sparta, Ga., and located in December of 1811. He joined the Virginia Conference again in 1813 and was sent to Franklin, N. C. He located finally on Feb. 20, 1814, and lived in Pittsylvania, Bedford, Amherst and Nelson Counties, Virginia. Lazenby's *History of Methodism in Alabama and West Florida* says of him: "He had complete self-abnegation, perfect consecration and dauntless courage" (p. 36).

M. E. Lazenby, *Alabama and West Florida*. 1960.
A. West, *Alabama*. 1893.   FRANKLIN S. MOSELEY

STUTTGART, in the South GERMANY Annual Conference, is the capital of Baden-Württemberg (650,000 inhabitants). It is the only city with the closest net of United Methodist local churches in West Germany. It is also the residence of the district superintendent of the Stuttgart District, and of fifteen pastors in twelve circuits. There are two hospitals—Bethesda (Motherhouse Elberfeld) and Staatsrat von Fetzer-Klinik (Martha-Maria Nuremberg)—offices of a radio and open-air mission, and broadcasting via Radio Luxembourg and through WTEL, Philadelphia, Pa., U.S.A., in German. Stuttgart also has the only German Methodist publishing house, Christliches Verlagshaus and Druckhaus West.

For more than one reason Stuttgart is historical ground for Methodism. It was the place where the Evangelical United Brethren (EVANGELISCHE GEMEINSCHAFT) had their first conference in Europe (1865), and now have about the same number of members in the city as the former Methodist Church. It was the first city where British Wesleyan Methodists founded a church. General super-

E. U. B. PUBLISHING HOUSE,
STUTTGART, GERMANY

intendent J. C. Barratt started a meeting there in 1867. M. Class was the first pastor. The first Wesleyan Methodist communion service was held on Jan. 6, 1873, after forty years of society work within the Lutheran State Church. In 1873 came the dedication of the "English" chapel at Stuttgart-Bad Cannstatt, along with the residence of the general superintendent and the first Wesleyan training college for ministers. In 1879 came the dedication of the Sophienkirche (now Auferstehungskirche), the first Wesleyan city church, with much support

AUFERSTEHUNGSKIRCHE, STUTTGART, GERMANY

by the missionary society in London. This was bombed in 1944, and rededicated by Bishop J. W. E. SOMMER in 1950, constructed with financial help from Great Britain.

Episcopal Methodists from the United States have worked in a suburb of the city since 1875. In Stuttgart the Church Union Conference took place, uniting the Wesleyan Methodists and the M.E. Church in Germany in 1897. That union was a great help; by 1906 the first church had grown to 561 members. Again in 1969 Stuttgart was the place of a Church Union Conference, that of South German United Methodism. The new church has about 10,000 people there. Therefore a new strengthening can be expected that will help to work more effectively in the growing new suburbs.

DIETER SACKMANN

JOHN A. SUBHAN

SUBHAN, JOHN ABDUS (1899-   ), Methodist bishop of INDIA, was born in CALCUTTA, India, on Aug. 8, 1899, the son of Hafiz Allah and Mariam (Chiragh Ali Bakhsh). He was born in a Moslem home, brought up in strict Islamic tradition, but was converted from Islam to Christianity and baptized in an Anglican Church in Calcutta on July 7, 1912. He was a member of the Church of England from that date to 1921, when he joined the Church of Rome. He studied for a time for the Roman Catholic priesthood, but returned to the Evangelical Church in 1924.

He united with the M. E. Church in 1926 and was received into full membership of the NORTH INDIA CONFERENCE and ordained as a DEACON in BAREILLY on Feb. 8, 1931, and as an ELDER on Jan. 8, 1933. Bishop J. R. CHITAMBAR ordained him a deacon, and Bishop J. W. ROBINSON, an elder.

His academic career included the B.A. degree from Allahabad University in 1923, where he majored in English literature, philosophy and Arabic; and the B.D. from Serampore College in 1931, where he majored in the Old Testament, New Testament in Greek, Arabic and

Urdu literature. In 1952 Asbury Theological Seminary in Kentucky gave him the D.D. degree, and in 1962 the same degree was awarded him by Serampore College, Serampore, Bengal.

Bishop Subhan is an accomplished linguist, being conversant with Urdu, Bengali, Hindi, Persian, Arabic, Greek (New Testament), as well as English, of course, and French to an extent. He has some knowledge of Gujarati and Marathi, the two among the major languages in India which are spoken in the States of Bombay and Gujarat, where he was appointed to serve during the first twelve years of his episcopacy.

He founded the St. John's Christian Union in St. John's High School, Agra, forming a band of preachers, mostly senior students, who were to evangelize the non-Christians in surrounding villages. He became the secretary of the Student Christian Movement in the same college.

He was a delegate of the Methodist Church to the International Missionary Council at Tambaram, India, 1939; member of a Goodwill Mission organized by the National Christian Council of India to the United States and Canada, 1947; delegate to the International Missionary Council, Whitby, Ontario, Canada, 1947; chairman of the Board of Governors, Henry Martyn Institute of Islamic Studies, Jabalpur, M. P.; and chairman of the Board of Governors, Leonard Theological College, Jabalpur, M.P. In the Central Conference of the Methodist Church in Southern Asia, he has been chairman of Evangelism and Church Extension; of that on the Commission on the Course of Study; of that on the Commission of Church Union. He has been a visiting professor of World Religions, 1966-67, at Boston University School of Theology at Boston, Mass. (U.S.A.); and has also been the lecturer in the Henry Martyn Institute of Islamic Studies, Lahore, which was an interdenominational institute for Islamic Research. He was offered its principalship in 1944, but his bishop appointed him to be the principal of the Methodist Seminary in Bareilly. He was, however, elected to the episcopacy in the Methodist Church by the Central Conference of Southern Asia in 1945 and served as bishop until his retirement in 1968.

He married on Oct. 21, 1926, Dorothy Sinclair Day of a well-known Anglo-Indian family in North India. They have three children, Malcolm (now living in Belgium); Stanley (an engineer in London, England); and Tara, the youngest, who married an American citizen and became Mrs. Ralph Vargas and now lives in the United States.

Bishop Subhan has written a number of books in English and a large number of books in Urdu. Among these are *Sufism: Its Saints and Shrines, Islam: Its Beliefs and Practices, How a Sufi Found His Lord* (his own autobiography which has been reprinted several times), *The Episcopacy in the Church of England* (as viewed by a Methodist), *God in Islam and Christianity* (Henry F. Nau Memorial Lecture at Concordia Theological Seminary, Nagercoil, South India).

Bishop Subhan retired in 1968, and is presently working in the rehabilitation of ex-convicts and the prevention of crime within the area of the entire state of Andhra Pradesh—a work partly supported by the Government of India and also largely by public subscription. He also supervises a teaching institution for destitute children.

How a Sufi Found His Lord. (Autobiography).
Who's Who in The Methodist Church, 1966.   N. B. H.

SUCASAS, ISAIAS FERNANDES (1896-   ), Brazilian bishop emeritus of the Methodist Church of Brazil, was born in Cataguazes, State of Minas Gerais, on Aug. 9, 1896, the fourth of thirteen children of devout Methodist parents (see José Sucasas). He studied at Granbery Institute in Juiz de Fora, Minas Gerais, receiving a Bachelor's degree in Science and Letters, and a degree in Theology. He was ordained deacon in 1927, elder in 1929, and was elected as bishop in 1946.

Much of his activity was in his native state, where he served both as District Superintendent and as pastor. He was pastor of Catete Church in Rio de Janeiro, when elected bishop in 1946, and put in charge of the Second Region, which he administered for nine years. Following this, he presided for a period of ten years over the Third and Fifth Regions. He pioneered in the organization of two night Sunday schools; the celebration of dawn services for laborers; the use of a loudspeaker in church; and the printing of a weekly church bulletin.

In recalling his experiences, Bishop Sucasas stressed three: 1) his evangelistic activities in what was then virgin territory along the Doce River in Minas Gerais; 2) the severe persecutions he and his family underwent in three different towns of the state, and 3) the founding of Methodist work in Brasilia, at the time when the new capital was being built, and when he acquired for the Methodist Church 8,800 square meters of land. Almost alone, working with his bare hands, Bishop Sucasas cleared and fenced in one of the properties, drilled two wells, built two septic tanks and two frame houses—one to serve for Church and Sunday school, and the other a nine-room residence for pastor and teachers.

He held the first Methodist service in Brasilia on May 5, 1957, in a frame shed. The Methodists were the first group to raise the Brazilian flag in the new Federal District, and the solemn occasion was attended by the city's Mayor. (At this time, the capital had not been officially inaugurated.)

His great helper and co-laborer has always been his wife, Jacíra Corrêa, who was the niece of a priest and had come from a staunch Roman Catholic family that had at first strongly opposed the marriage but relented when they came to know Isaias. She has become an outstanding leader among Methodist women of Brazil. At the time of Brasilia's official inauguration, "Dona" Jacíra was present, her arms full of Methodist magazines, hymn books and leaflets which she freely distributed to all, even to the Cardinal and priests and nuns.

Bishop and Mrs. Sucasas have five sons and one daughter—Leslie, Wesley, Solon, Livingstone, Isaias Jr. and Magda-Luz. In July 1965, at the General Conference of the Methodist Church of Brazil, he retired and was given the title of bishop emeritus. He lives now in São Paulo.

Eula K. Long

SUCASAS, JOSÉ FERNANDES (1862-1952), naturalized Brazilian lay evangelist and outstanding religious leader, was born in Pontevedra, Spain, on March 19, 1862. His father was a rustic, nearly illiterate farmer and wine-maker.

Eager to have a son in the priesthood the family turned him over early in life to the care of priests, under whom he served as sacristan during fourteen years. Dissatisfied with what he experienced, he left them and apprenticed himself out to become a tailor, in which trade he excelled. After completing military duty, José left Spain and went to Paris, from where he eventually traveled to ARGENTINA and BRAZIL, where he became a naturalized citizen.

One Sunday afternoon in one of Rio's parks, he saw a young girl with her parents. She immediately appealed to him, and he found that they too had come from Spain, and were evangelicals, though not yet professing church members. Later, when he visited in their home, and when Sucasas let them know he was a Catholic, the father—Ezequiel del Riego—gave him a New Testament, telling him not to return until he had read it through. Sucasas read it with moderate interest, and with this done the girl's parents allowed him to visit the home once a week.

Before long, Riego was commissioned to do some fine sculpturing in the city of Cataguazes, state of Minas Gerais. Young Sucasas, deeply in love with Maria da Encarnacão del Riego, followed, and before long they were married. They were the parents of thirteen children, ten of whom lived to maturity. Sucasas wanted to learn more of the Gospel, but there was no evangelical pastor in Cataguazes to whom he could turn for enlightenment. One day, as he worked in his tailorshop, he met a young man in the street offering books for sale. Curious, Sucasas spoke to him. The man was FELIPE DE CARVALHO, a Methodist preacher selling Bibles and New Testaments. José bought two and began reading. Some time later Felipe returned to the city looking for a hall in which to preach, and Sucasas, now living in a comfortable and fairly large house, offered him the use of his front room. Thus Methodist work was born in Cataguazes.

One Sunday a mob of fanatics armed with sickles, knives and guns attacked the house, screaming "Death to the Protestants!" They dragged out the preacher and his wife, then heavy with child, and kicked them through the streets. Though José Sucasas had not yet experienced a real conversion, he defended the couple as best he could until the police arrived. When the mob had finally dispersed, the policemen asked Carvalho what he wanted done to his attackers. "Nothing," he replied, "only see that order is maintained. Free them—for they do not know what they are doing." Then, torn and bleeding, Carvalho and his wife knelt on the dusty street and prayed to God for their persecutors. At that moment, Sucasas was truly converted, and from then on, he became a strong pillar of Brazilian Methodism. Everywhere he preached the Gospel he brought many to Christ. A distinguished lawyer was so impressed with his earnestness that he too was converted and later became a Presbyterian preacher.

In the local church Sucasas served in all capacities, even as preacher when needed. He was bitterly persecuted at times, once almost thrown into a hot furnace by an ignorant fanatical baker who wanted to stop his preaching. Yet he remained firm and unshaken. Maria died on Dec. 31, 1951, and José lived only a few months longer, until Aug. 5, 1952.

Two of the sons became outstanding ministers: ISAIAS, who became a bishop of the Methodist Church of Brazil, and José, outstanding in the Methodist ministry for some years and editor of the official church weekly, *Expositor Cristão*.

Voz Missionaria, 1953.   EULA K. LONG

SUCRE, Bolivia, is the former political and cultural center of BOLIVIA. It is legally the capital of Bolivia, though actually LA PAZ has taken over this function. Sucre has a university older than Harvard. In this old city, which is the center of the Southern District of the conference, there was a church organized in 1957 which includes university as well as professional and working people. A missionary from the Division of World MISSIONS of The United Methodist Church is usually appointed as pastor.

Sucre also has a Student Center and a Student Hostel, both of which are aimed at providing Christian influence for university and normal school pupils.

Barbara H. Lewis, *Methodist Overseas Missions*. 1960.

N. B. H.

SUE BENNETT COLLEGE, London, Kentucky, was opened in 1897 as a missionary school for youth of the Kentucky mountains and was named for Sue Bennett of Richmond, Ky. Her sister, Miss BELLE H. BENNETT, was a pioneer leader in promoting missionary work among the women of the Church, South. The school continues as a project of the Woman's Division of Christian Service.

For years it functioned as an elementary, secondary, and normal school. In 1922 it began work as a junior college, and has been accredited by the Southern Association since 1932.

The governing board has a maximum of twenty-five members elected by the Board of MISSIONS, one half of whom must represent the Woman's Division of Christian Service of the Board of Missions.

JOHN O. GROSS

SUGDEN, EDWARD HOLDSWORTH (1874-1935), an English Wesleyan who became an influential leader in Australian Methodism, was the son of James Sugden, of Yorkshire, who had been for seven years assistant tutor at Headingly College, Leeds, and six years circuit minister in Bradford. Edward Sugden was appointed the first Master of Queen's College, Melbourne.

Sugden with his wife and family arrived to take charge of the College in January 1888. He was a comparatively young man when he became Master of the infant college, but he grew with it, and it with him.

A genial, broadminded, scholarly man, and withal a most devout evangelical Christian, he was essentially a young man's man. From the outset he won not only the respect but also the affection and admiration of his students in all the faculties. He was a man of catholic tastes and of great versatility.

While being an arrestive theological teacher he was at the same time an expert in music, a master of English literature, especially of English drama, and of the literature associated with JOHN WESLEY, the founder of Methodism. Many of Sugden's works were published.

In 1906 he was elected president of the VICTORIA AND TASMANIA CONFERENCE and President-General of Australasian Methodism during 1923-26. For many years he had committed to him the charge of the theological training of students for the Methodist ministry. The gracious Christian character of his wife contributed to the inner life of the college.

His clear and scholarly expositions of Scripture, his large sympathy, charming simplicity of manner and manifestly evangelical zeal won him a ready welcome in the pulpits not only of his own but of other churches.

Outside his activities as a minister of his own Church and in addition to his publications, he did useful service as a member of the MELBOURNE University Council and as president, up to the time of his death, of the Trustees of the Public Library, Art Gallery and Museum.

After forty years of splendid service as Master of Queen's, Sugden retired in February 1928. He died on July 22, 1935.

AUSTRALIAN EDITORIAL COMMITTEE

SUKH, EMMANUEL (c1886-1929), was a member of the LUCKNOW CONFERENCE of the Methodist Church in INDIA. He came from among the Mazhabi Sikhs, as did many of the prominent Methodists of Northern India. He was educated in the Methodist Boys' School at Sitapur, the Centennial High School, LUCKNOW, and the School of Commerce of LUCKNOW CHRISTIAN COLLEGE. His wife Polly, from the same background, was a licentiate of medical practice, trained in the government medical college at AGRA. Both held coveted posts in government employ in Agra, she in the woman's hospital, and he as confidential clerk to the district magistrate, when they decided that God was calling them to full-time Christian service. Bishop FRANCIS W. WARNE asked them to go to an unoccupied area in Bihar, Raghunathpur in Shahabad District, where some years before several families of Dhusiya Chamars had petitioned that someone be sent to teach them of Christ.

When the couple arrived, they learned that the long delay in the church's response had destroyed the interest of those who had petitioned. Instead of the welcome he had expected, Sukh was greeted with curses, and in several villages he was stoned. But the patient persistence of the preacher and the physician slowly brought results. First a few Chamars declared their faith and were baptized. Land was bought, and a small hospital and staff buildings were constructed. Thereupon, the combination of preaching and healing, supported by fervent witnessing by local converts, produced a mass movement in which thousands showed a desire to follow Christ.

Sukh acquired much influence both with the public and with officials. He was appointed an honorary magistrate; and a year or two later the governor of the state, Lord Sinha, a Hindu and the only Indian ever raised to the British peerage, appointed him to membership in the legislative council. When the council was first permitted to elect its presiding officer, and a deadlock developed after many ballots, the leading candidates withdrew their names and proposed that the council proceed to elect Sukh. This was done.

In 1923 he was appointed district superintendent. The unavailability of trained personnel and a severe shortage of money led to a policy of retrenchment at a time when thousands were calling for instruction and baptism. When Mr. and Mrs. Sukh were appointed to another district, and the hospital in Raghunathpur was transferred to government ownership and management, the Church was seriously hurt.

Sukh died in 1929 after a short illness. On his deathbed he gave a triumphant witness and urged his family and his associates to make greater efforts to bring India to Christ.

Journals of the Lucknow Conference.   J. WASKOM PICKETT

SULLINS, DAVID (1827-1918), American preacher and educator, was born on July 28, 1827, near Athens, Tenn. He graduated from EMORY AND HENRY COLLEGE in 1850 and became a member of the HOLSTON CONFERENCE the same year. His appointments were Burnsville, ASHEVILLE, N. C., Jonesboro, CHATTANOOGA, KNOXVILLE, Wytheville, Bristol and other leading charges.

He married Ann Rebecca Blair in 1855 and was the father of two sons and two daughters.

At Jonesboro he was pastor and also principal of the school from 1852 to 1857; at Blountville he was in war and educational work from 1859 to 1865, and at Wytheville he was school principal as well as pastor from 1865 to 1868.

He became president of Sullins College in Bristol in 1868 and served in that capacity until 1885. He was one of the founders and president of Centenary College at Cleveland, Tenn., from 1885 until his retirement.

He died in the home of his daughter, Mrs. GEORGE R. STUART, in Birmingham, Ala., and was buried at Cleveland, Tenn.

Journal of the Holston Conference, 1918.
I. P. Martin, *Holston.* 1945.   L. W. PIERCE

SULLINS, TIMOTHY (1812-1885), American minister and brother of DAVID SULLINS, was born on Dec. 4, 1812, in Blount County, Tenn. He joined the HOLSTON CONFERENCE in 1833 and served as pastor, presiding elder, and agent for EMORY AND HENRY COLLEGE until 1846, when he suffered a stroke of paralysis.

On Jan. 28, 1858, he was married to Virginia Rogers of KNOXVILLE, Tenn., to whom he had been engaged before his stroke. He was an invalid during the last thirty-eight years of his life.

Sullins was a delegate to the GENERAL CONFERENCE in 1844, which adopted the PLAN OF SEPARATION providing for the division of the Church into Northern and Southern branches, the LOUISVILLE CONVENTION which provided for the organization of the M. E. Church, South, and the Southern General Conferences of 1846 and 1854.

He died at Knoxville on Feb. 18, 1885, and was buried in the Old Gray Cemetery.

Journals of Holston Conference.
I. P. Martin, *Holston.* 1945.   L. W. PIERCE

SULLIVAN, LUCY W. (1854-1943), was born at DAYTON, Ohio, Feb. 19, 1854. At the age of sixteen, she was converted and began a life of witness and service that continued until her death in INDIA on Dec. 2, 1943.

Miss Sullivan studied for two years in Cincinnati Wesleyan College. Illness forced her to discontinue her college studies, but even in illness she was persistent in good works, teaching children, and exhorting people of all ages to be disciples of Jesus Christ. ISABELLA THOBURN and PHOEBE ROWE led her to an interest in missions in India, and when her health was fully restored, she volunteered for service there.

In 1888 she was appointed to LUCKNOW as a DEACONESS. Her next appointment in 1895 was to the Women's Training School at Muttra (Mathura now), and in 1902 she went to Pithoragarh in isolated Eastern Kumaun where she soon sensed that she had begun the work for which God had been preparing her from her childhood. She and two of her associates, the British Annie Budden and the American MARTHA SHELDON, acquired immense influence with all classes of the population. To Indian and British officials, to priests, landowners, merchants, artisans, and even to nomadic tribesmen from NEPAL and Tibet—these women became legendary, honored for their kindness and goodness and suspected of having unlimited power with God and man.

Perhaps nowhere in India do Brahmans compose a larger majority in the population than in Pithoragarh and its environs. A few of these Brahmans became avowed believers in Christ, but the overwhelming majority remained Hindus. Nevertheless most of them made many adjustments to the social ethics and religious practices advocated and demonstrated by Miss Sullivan and her associates.

An influential Brahman, wishing to adopt for himself the Hindu life of renunciation and asceticism but convinced that for others the Christian way of life is best, made over his two sons to Miss Sullivan. She adopted them and successfully transmitted to them her faith and conviction. They are today distinguished Christian educators, the elder Jai Datt Patial as principal of the Allahabad Christian College, the other Mani Datt Patial as vice-principal of the United Theological College at BAREILLY.

B. T. Badley, *Southern Asia*. 1931.
J. N. Hollister, *Southern Asia*. 1956.   J. WASKOM PICKETT

SUMATRA. (See INDONESIA.)

SUMMERFIELD, JOHN (1798-1825), like many of the early preachers who guided the American Methodist Church in its first steps of organization and growth, was a native of England. Although born in Preston, Lancashire, England, on Jan. 31, 1798, he spent most of his life on Irish soil. Summerfield, much to the disappointment of his hard-working and religiously zealous father. William Summerfield, spent his teenage years in rebellion and waywardness. But in 1817, at the age of nineteen, he came under the spell of evangelical Methodism, and was converted. Immediately following his conversion, Summerfield began public preaching. He was boyish looking, delicate and pale due to physical weaknesses, but always eloquent and persuasive in delivery.

In 1821 he arrived in NEW YORK CITY, accompanied by his father, brother and two sisters. There he began a short but influential ministry. The youthful Summerfield was recognized immediately for his preaching ability. A sermon before the fifth anniversary of the AMERICAN BIBLE SOCIETY propelled him into national prominence. He was received into the TROY CONFERENCE in 1821, and was first appointed to New York City under the supervision of JOSHUA SOULE.

Summerfield's pulpit eloquence opened many doors to him, and invitations to preach came from TRENTON, PHILADELPHIA, BALTIMORE, and WASHINGTON. In the spring of 1821, the young minister preached at the Foundry Chapel in the capital, and John Quincy Adams and John C. Calhoun were in the congregation. The following Sunday, Summerfield preached to a vast number congregated on the steps of the Capitol Building and was compared to GEORGE WHITEFIELD by one of the Washington newspapers. Following an illness, and a trip to Paris as the American representative to an international Bible Society Congress, Summerfield returned to the United States and received his elder's orders at the 1824 GENERAL CONFERENCE in Baltimore.

He was later appointed a "missionary within the bounds of the Baltimore Conference." His life-long weakness and failing health did not permit him to serve actively for very long. John Summerfield died while visiting his father in New York City on June 18, 1825, being only twenty-seven years of age at the time. Bishop Joshua Soule composed the tribute which appeared on the cenotaph honoring Summerfield, which was erected not far from the JOHN STREET CHURCH, the site of his first American sermon:

The learned and the illiterate attended his ministry with admiration, and felt his preaching was in the demonstration of the Spirit and of the power.

M. Simpson, *Cyclopaedia*. 1880.
William M. Willett, *A New Life of Summerfield*. New York: J. B. Lippincott and Co., 1857.   L. CARROLL YINGLING, JR.

SUMMERS, HENRY (1801-1883), pioneer American preacher, was born in VIRGINIA, was converted (1820) and licensed to preach in INDIANA in 1822. After serving as a LOCAL PREACHER for ten years, in 1832 he united with the ILLINOIS CONFERENCE, M.E. Church, and preached under PETER CARTWRIGHT's supervision. In 1836 Summers became presiding elder of Rock Island District, consisting of circuits in Illinois and in southern IOWA. After he traveled this district until 1839, BISHOP MORRIS assigned him to the newly formed Iowa District, composed of Fort Madison, Burlington, Rockingham, Dubuque, and missions at Manchester, Bellevue, Richland, and on the Fox and Iowa rivers.

With the division of the Iowa District (1840), he was presiding elder of Burlington District, ROCK RIVER CONFERENCE, and of Des Moines District in 1843, made up of scattered appointments in the Iowa interior along the Des Moines River.

For eight successive years Summers superintended the planting of Methodism in Iowa as a presiding elder. Revivals followed his work; it was reported that he had as many as a hundred conversions at a single quarterly meeting. In 1844 Summers, an original member of the IOWA CONFERENCE, transferred to the Rock River Conference and continued his ministry in Rock River, WISCONSIN, Peoria, and CENTRAL ILLINOIS conferences until 1868, when he superannuated. He was a delegate to GENERAL CONFERENCE from the Wisconsin Conference in 1852.

S. N. Fellows, *Upper Iowa Conference*. 1907.
A. W. Haines, *Makers of Iowa Methodism*. 1900.
E. H. Waring, *Iowa Conference*. 1910.
Yearbook of the Iowa Conference, 1844. MARTIN L. GREER

SUMMERS, THOMAS OSMOND (1812-1882), American minister, author, editor, preacher, teacher, and theologian, was born Oct. 11, 1812 at Purbeck, Dorset, England, the son of James and Sarah Summers. He came to New York in 1830, sought admission to the Methodist Church in 1832, was converted in 1833, preached his first sermon at Bells' Meeting House in MARYLAND on Nov. 9, 1834, and was admitted on trial in the BALTIMORE CONFERENCE at Winchester, Va., in March 1835. He was ordained a DEACON at the 1837 session of the Baltimore Conference, in which he served until appointed a missionary to BUENOS AIRES in 1839. He was appointed to GALVESTON, TEXAS about the same time, and actually went to Texas in 1840,

T. O. SUMMERS

where he later also served HOUSTON. He toured much of the United States in 1842 seeking funds for the work in Texas. In 1844 he was appointed to Tuscaloosa, Ala., and there married Miss N. B. Sexton. In 1845 he was appointed to Livingston, Ala., and in 1846 to MOBILE, but about that time he was made assistant editor of the *Southern Christian Advocate* and moved to CHARLESTON, S. C. He was appointed chairman of the committee to revise the hymnbook for the newly organized M.E. Church, South, and under his leadership, many hymns were restored to their original form. Summers in this did the church a great service, despite the fact he impaired his health in pushing the work through the printers in NEW YORK in six weeks. His endeavors then and later in hymnology left the church richer in its music and worship. In 1855 he moved to NASHVILLE, Tenn., where he lived the rest of his life.

Known to have little formal education, nevertheless, his capacity and accomplishment was such that he was early awarded the D.D. degree by Ruter College in Texas. Never strong in body, he suffered from poor eyesight and was permanently impaired in health as the result of a fall from a second story window in sleepwalking.

Summers possessed a catholic spirit, and he was equally at home in Methodist, Baptist, or Presbyterian churches, the penitentiary, insane asylum, or VANDERBILT Chapel, which he helped found and where he lived and taught during his last years. A partial catalogue of his various duties includes: Secretary of TEXAS CONFERENCE, 1840; permanent Secretary of the LOUISVILLE CONFERENCE, 1845; Assistant Secretary, GENERAL CONFERENCE of the M.E. Church South, 1846; and Secretary 1850-82. He was the BOOK EDITOR of the M.E. Church, South, 1850-82. He also served as editor of the following: Nashville *Christian Advocate*, 1866-78; *Southern Quarterly Review*, 1858-61, and 1880-82; all Sunday School publications, 1846-70; *General Conference Minutes*, 1858-78; *Minutes of Annual Conference*, 1858-81. He wrote, edited, and revised over 500 works of various sizes on such diverse subjects as theology, prayer, Commentaries, the Book of Worship, Disciplines, Hymnbooks, etc.

Summers was keenly interested in hymnology, worship, liturgy, and theology. He was a genius for literature and work, a gatherer rather than a creator. His was not an original mind. Editing suited his taste.

Having helped in the establishment of Vanderbilt University in 1874, he was made professor of Systematic Theology and Dean of the Theology Faculty in 1875, a position he held until his death. He was again elected Secretary of the General Conference in 1882, but served only one day. He died at his home in Nashville on May 6, 1882. His funeral was preached in the Chapel at Vanderbilt, and he was buried on the campus he loved so much.

O. P. Fitzgerald, *Dr. Summers.* 1885.   N. B. H.

SUNDARAM, GABRIEL (1900-   ), bishop of The Methodist Church, was elected by the CENTRAL CONFERENCE OF SOUTHERN ASIA in 1956. He was born in Hanumakonda, Andhra Pradesh, on Oct. 13, 1900. His high-school studies were in Wesley Boys High School, Secunderabad; his undergraduate college work in the Nizam College, Hyderabad; and his post-graduate studies in LUCKNOW. He was awarded the D.D. degree by BALDWIN-WALLACE College, U.S.A.

He joined the staff of Hyderabad Boys School in 1922 and became principal in 1932, when its student enrollment was 250. During his sixteen years as principal the enrollment grew to more than 1,000. It now has more than 4,000 students. Prior to his election as bishop, he was Executive Secretary of the Council of Christian Education of the Southern Asia Central Conference.

At different times, Bishop Sundaram has been president of the Hyderabad, Andhra and Uttar Pradesh Christian Councils and has represented Indian Methodism in many international organizations, including the INTERNATIONAL MISSIONARY CONFERENCE in Madras, India; the WORLD COUNCIL OF CHURCHES General Assembly in Delhi; the EAST ASIA CHRISTIAN CONFERENCE in Singapore and Bangkok; and the WORLD METHODIST COUNCIL in Oxford. He has been president of the Boards of Governors of LUCKNOW CHRISTIAN COLLEGE, ISABELLA THOBURN COLLEGE, Allahabad Christian Institute, and the Henry Martyn Institute of Islamics.

He married Caroline John in 1923. She died in 1930 and subsequently in 1932 he married Pajabai Peter. His son, Ernest Sundaram, made a distinguished record as a medical student and is a fellow of the Royal College of Surgeons. The son is now superintendent of the Clara Swain Hospital at BAREILLY, India's first modern hospital established for women and children, now a general hospital. The bishop's daughter and son-in-law are also graduates of medical colleges and serve in Christian institutions.

Journals of the Hyderabad, Lucknow, Bengal and South India Annual Conferences.
Minutes of the Southern Asia Central Conference and Executive Board.   J. WASKOM PICKETT

SUNDAY SCHOOLS, CHURCH SCHOOLS, American Methodist. As early as 1737 while in Georgia, JOHN WESLEY taught the catechism to children on Sunday afternoon before the evening service (*Journal*, January 31, 1737). At the first Methodist CONFERENCE in 1744 the question was raised as to what and how to teach persons, including children. In 1748 the conference asked, "Might not the children in every place be formed into a little society?" and the answer given was, "Let the preachers try by meeting them apart, and giving them suitable exhortations."

In 1769 Miss HANNAH BALL gathered children together on Saturday and Sunday in a parish house at Wycombe, near LONDON, and taught them the Bible. She reported her activities to John Wesley. There were a few other such early efforts, and in 1780 ROBERT RAIKES started an experiment in instructing poor children in "the rudiments of learning and in religion" on Sundays. The children attended from 10 A.M. until 5:30 P.M. with an hour for lunch and time also for a church service in the afternoon.

John Wesley quickly saw possibilities in the new movement and encouraged it. In his *Journal* as early as 1784 he refers to visiting a Sunday school.

Gradually the Sunday school became a regular institution in the Methodist movement, not only in England but also in many areas overseas, including the United States. FRANCIS ASBURY is generally credited with starting the first Sunday school in America at Thomas Crenshaw's in Hanover County, Virginia, possibly in 1783 or 1784, with some accounts saying 1786. However, another claim for priority is a Sunday school started in 1785 by William Elliott, a Methodist, at his plantation home in Accomac County, Virginia.

Growth was slow in America in the beginning. Interdenominational efforts were widespread at first, through the American Sunday School Union. In 1827 the Sunday School Union of the M.E. Church was launched and it gave impetus to the work. The catechism was used as a teaching tool and, of course, the Bible. Large use was made of Sunday school libraries; many books were printed especially for them. In 1830 the American Sunday School Union had its imprint on two hundred such volumes.

The Methodist GENERAL CONFERENCE of 1840 created a Committee on Sunday Schools, and provided for the appointment of an editor for the "Youth's Magazine and Sabbath-Schools books." In succeeding years many teaching materials were provided, both magazines and books. Membership increased rapidly, and the whole movement gained strength.

From 1850 to 1900 American Methodists improved their teaching materials, cooperating in the planning of Uniform Lessons, and also moving toward graded materials. JOHN H. VINCENT, superintendent of Sunday School Instruction until elected bishop, introduced in 1870 a Berean Series of uniform lessons for the M.E. Church that were strongly biblical and changed subjects each quarter to provide variety. They encouraged daily Bible reading in the home, and the aim of each lesson was to point to Christ. These materials were instrumental in moving the emphasis away from the exclusive use of the catechism. They were also an important development in the move in 1871 toward producing descriptions of lessons interdenominationally, and these eventually became what is now called by Methodists the International Lesson Series. Both Northern and Southern Methodism used the International Uniform Lessons almost as soon as available.

Launched in April, 1873, in the M.E. Church was *Sunday School Classmate*, the oldest magazine now being issued with the original title by The Methodist Church as a church school publication. In the Southern Church, ATTICUS G. HAYGOOD, A. G. E. Cunnyngham, and JAMES ATKINS were pioneer leaders.

Graded lessons were adopted in 1910 in the two larger Methodisms in the United States, and there was joint publication for some years between these two groups and the Congregational Churches. This example of coopera-

tion was only one of many indicating the way in which Methodist groups have participated in all the major ecumenical Christian education movements. Among these movements were such as the American Sunday School Union (Methodists belonged from 1824 to 1827), International Lesson Committee (1871-   ), International Sunday School Convention(s) (1872-1958), Sunday School Council of Evangelical Denominations (1910-1922), Leadership Training Publishing Association (now Cooperative Publication Association) (1932-   ), International Sunday School Association (1905-1922), International Council of Religious Education (1922-1950), and, at present, the Division of Christian Education of the NATIONAL COUNCIL OF CHURCHES of Christ in the United States of America (1950-   ).

Methodist educators have been influenced by significant studies across the years, such as *Christian Nurture*, by Horace Bushnell; *The Varieties of Religious Experience*, by William James; *A Social Theory of Religious Education* and *What Is Christian Education?* by George Albert Coe; *A Project Curriculum for Young People*, by Erwin L. Shaver; *Can Religious Education Be Christian?* by Harrison S. Elliott; *Christ and Christian Education*, by William C. Bower; *Faith and Nurture*, by H. Shelton Smith; *The Clue to Christian Education*, by Randolph Crump Miller; *The Teaching Ministry of the Church*, by James D. Smart; *The Gift of Power*, by Lewis J. Sherrill; *The Gospel and Christian Education*, by D. Campbell Wyckoff; *The Church Redemptive*, by Howard Grimes. Among influential Methodist leaders from 1915 to 1950 have been ARLO A. BROWN, E. B. CHAPPELL, C. A. BOWEN, JOHN Q. SCHISLER, CLARENCE TUCKER CRAIG, WADE CRAWFORD BARCLAY, and Donald M. Maynard.

A significant feature of the Sunday school movement has been that it is essentially a lay enterprise. It has enlisted hundreds and thousands of lay men and women as its leaders—teachers and administrators. This factor, in turn, has called for a strong leadership education system through which these lay persons could be trained for their tasks. In the 1860's Sunday school institutes were launched for training teachers, and under John H. Vincent's guidance courses of study were prepared, examinations conducted, and diplomas issued. A CHAUTAUQUA Sunday-School Assembly was organized at the Chautauqua Lake Camp-Ground Assembly (New York state) in 1874 and it became a center for teacher training. Subsequently, scores of Chautauqua-type assemblies were set up throughout the United States. In 1901 the author of a book on *Sunday-School Movements in America* said, "The most prominent people in Sunday-school work are the Methodists." This was perhaps largely because of the great emphasis on training leaders.

The emphasis on leadership has continued. In the 1920's and 1930's in the Southern Church, it had a fresh impetus under the leadership of JOHN W. SHACKFORD and John Q. Schisler. This involved an effort to help teachers gain an understanding of how children, youth, and adults learn at various ages, with great attention to method. Large district schools for leadership training were held annually during these years in most of the major cities of the South.

Since about the 1930's the term *church school* has been used as a concept somewhat larger than Sunday school, for it embraces not only the Sunday school but also vacation church school, Sunday evening sessions, weekday—or night—meetings, and outdoor sessions.

One aspect of the Christian nurture of youth for some

fifty years (before being merged in the Sunday school/church school) was the EPWORTH LEAGUE. Organized in 1890 in the M.E. Church and a few years later in the Southern Church, it was a powerful force in recruiting and training youth as Christian churchmen. It provided more of an opportunity for youth (and older children) to develop on their own initiative than was generally true in the Sunday school. Meetings were usually held on Sunday afternoon or night, preceding the evening worship service. The League developed yearly summer assemblies on an annual conference basis, combining study, inspiration, and challenge to full-time church-related work. It developed strong concern and support for the overseas mission program, and, in its later years, for social issues. *Epworth Herald* was the League magazine in the Methodist Episcopal Church, and *Epworth Era* in M.E. Church, South. The Epworth League was made a part of the church school in the Southern Church in 1930, and at Union in 1939 it was replaced by the Methodist Youth Fellowship (also a part of the church school).

Sunday school/church school leaders have always considered that the enlisting of new disciples—as well as their nurture—has been among their most important tasks. Thus the Sunday school/church school has in every era been the channel through which many new persons, especially children and youth, came into discipleship and into church membership. In 1964 about 200,000 church school members joined the church on profession of faith. The organization of new Sunday schools has often served as the means of starting new churches.

The educational ministry of the church has in the twentieth century made large use of several new forms of ministry. One of these has been the daily vacation church school. This type enterprise has been a graded school operating usually in the summer for a half day and for one to three weeks in a local church. Sometimes such schools are carried on jointly by two or more churches. Many children are reached through these schools who do not attend the Sunday church school sessions. About one and a half million pupils attended these schools in 1964.

Another new type ministry has been graded classes in Bible and religion during the week for public school pupils, often for one or more hours that are released (or made available) by the public school. This was for some years called weekday religious education, but is now being referred to as Through-the-Week Religious Education. It has gained new importance since the Supreme Court rulings regarding Bible reading or prayers in public schools.

A concern for the mission program of the church has always been an integral part of the Sunday school/church school. In the last twenty-five years especially there has been regular giving to mission work by church school classes. In 1964 church schools gave almost $4,000,000 for World Service and Conference Benevolences. This was about one-eighth of the total amount given for World Service by the whole church. There have also been regular curriculum studies of the mission work of the church, at home and abroad.

The Sunday school/church school has been a helpful movement in regard to the recruiting of persons for full-time church-related work. A high percentage of persons going into such work has come through the church school.

In recent years printed resources for teaching have been supplemented by frequent use of drama, music, and projected films. Wide use is also being made of such resources as maps, charts, models, recordings, flat pictures, murals, and puppets. All such resources are considered as tools to assist in the teaching-learning process. The teacher's basic task is conceived as essentially that of guiding persons in a group process of learning so as to encourage them to make such changes in attitude and behavior as will lead toward the purpose of Christian education (see below for a statement of purpose).

With the great increase in the number of people living in cities, there has come an expansion of facilities for conferences and retreats in rural areas, usually related to the program of Christian education. Almost every annual conference has a conference assembly ground, and the facilities of these are usually filled throughout the summer with older children, youth, adults, and family groups. The enterprises conducted in such centers are carefully structured to include worship, study, discussion, and recreation, often making particular use of the outdoor setting.

Special attention has been given since about 1950 to the religious needs of older adults, and efforts made to minister to their specialized situation. The magazine *Mature Years* is issued to appeal to this constituency.

The ministry to youth is now focused exclusively on teen-agers, with all those beyond high school considered young adults. A special ministry is being launched to these young adults (many of whom have difficulty adjusting to modern city life and contemporary culture) to whom conventional church programs seem to offer little appeal.

In view of the impact of changing cultural patterns, theological views, and educational methods, The Methodist Church is in the midst of the most sweeping reconstruction of its church school curriculum that has been made for some fifty years. In cooperation with other denominations, through the Cooperative Curriculum Project, Methodist Christian education leaders (Division of the Local Church and Editorial Division) helped to prepare a Design for the Curriculum of the Church's Educational Ministry which, with certain variations, was adopted and issued in 1965 as the *Design for Methodist Curriculum*. An earlier document, *Foundations of Christian Teaching in Methodist Churches* (1960), produced through the General Board of Education's Curriculum Committee, provided a basic statement on the nature and work of the church, the gospel the church teaches, the nature of Christian education, and the curriculum of Christian education. These two documents have provided theological and educational guidelines for the church's educational ministry, for new curriculum, and subsequently for a series of publications for children issued in 1964; new resources for adults issued in 1967 (and 1969); and new resources for youth issued in 1968.

Christian Advocate, Feb. 16, 1961.
Classmate, Dec. 8, 1917.
Frank G. Lankard, *A History of the American Sunday School Curriculum*. New York: Abingdon Press, 1927.
M. Simpson, *Cyclopaedia*. 1882.   WALTER N. VERNON

SUNDAY SCHOOLS, British Methodist. There have been four stages in the development of British Methodist Sunday schools. These cannot be distinguished by specific dates, but have tended to overlap, reflecting the degree of understanding and concern for the teaching and training of children felt within Methodism.

Concern for children's welfare. One fruit of the evangelical revival was a new sense of responsibility for others, especially those neglected by the society as a whole. The Industrial Revolution was accompanied by a rapid increase in the population, and children were often employed in the mills for twelve or more hours a day every weekday. So Sunday schools were opened to care for children on their one free day, Sunday, and so to occupy their time to prevent their running wild and committing crimes. Often these schools were promoted by Methodists and other Christians together, so gaining the widest possible support from society. This cooperation continued until the disturbances of the French Revolution led Anglicans to fear that Jacobite influences motivated schools conducted by Dissenters. Records suggest that HANNAH BALL, who opened a Sunday school at High Wycombe in 1769 (eleven years earlier than ROBERT RAIKES' first venture) deserves the title of Methodist pioneer in this field. John Wesley encouraged her and others, commending Sunday schools as "that blessed work," and terming them "nurseries for Christians." (Journal, vii, p. 3, July 18, 1784.) At first every school was experimental; the pioneers defined their own aim. If a Methodist church building existed, the school was erected as near as possible, so that the children could be taken to worship easily. These early schools were financed and maintained mainly by voluntary contributions. In contrast to other Sunday school workers, those in Methodism seldom received any payment, though they devoted several hours every Sunday to their teaching.

Concern to teach. Teachers were encouraged by their pupils' eagerness to learn. The first curriculums included writing, spelling, arithmetic, and other subjects as well as reading, the Bible being the only textbook. Many schools divided their pupils into four groups, namely, infants (up to age seven), ignorant (those of seven plus those unable to read well), instructed (those from seven to fifteen who could read), and adults (those of fifteen plus). School lasted for four hours or more, and provided the only education many children and adults received. The educational pioneer J. K. Shuttleworth believed a well-run Sunday school bore "its natural fruit" in a well-attended day school. So the early nineteenth century saw Methodists, in common with other Christians, opening day schools, often conducted in the same building as the Sunday school. In 1838 the Wesleyans appointed an Education Comittee with oversight of both, though a quarter of Wesleyan preaching places still have no Sunday school.

Concern to teach the Bible. The growing concern on the part of society that day-school education should be provided for all children led Methodists to revise the aims of their Sunday schools. They realized there was no longer any need to teach secular subjects on Sunday. Opposition grew to teaching these until the practice ceased. Teachers rejoiced they could concentrate on teaching the Bible, for, as William Cocker (1816-1902), a METHODIST NEW CONNEXION educationalist, put it, "polished intellects might not be unconnected with polluted hearts." Biblical lesson courses were introduced and magazines started both for the help of teachers and for the edification of children. In 1874 WESLEYAN METHODISTS appointed a minister to promote day and Sunday school work and the following year to concentrate on Sunday schools. Other branches of Methodism made similar appointments later, and by the time of the Methodist Union, in 1932, each had well organized Sunday school headquarters, with full-time ministerial and lay leaders serving their constituencies.

Concern for Christian discipleship. Throughout the history of the movement many Sunday school teachers had done more than teach facts, whether the ABC's or the life of Jesus. They brought children into a personal knowledge of Christ as Savior, and Methodism owes an incalculable debt to their witness and work. But the philanthropic motive dominant in the eighteenth century continued, and many were content if they could give children a knowledge of Christ. Church leaders allowed devoted enthusiasts to manage their Sunday schools, and even permitted the presentation in some areas of "going away" Bibles to children of fourteen.

Since Methodist Union, and especially since the establishment of the Youth Department in 1943, the concern has been to regard Sunday school teaching as the church doing its essential work of teaching and training its young disciples. Many attempts have been made to abolish the gap between Sunday school and church, the most promising being the transferring of the main teaching session to Sunday morning, so that more children can become active participants in morning worship. Teaching involves much more than talking. Methodist lesson notes, based on agreed courses prepared by Methodists and other Christian educationalists, seek to bring children into personal relationship with Christ, and to guide them to make ever fuller responses to him within the life of his church. A high percentage of new church members received is the justification for maintaining "this blessed work."

E. H. Hayes, J. K. Meir, *The Child in the Midst*. London, n.d.

J. K. MEIR

SUNDAY SCHOOL/CHURCH SCHOOL PUBLICATIONS. The Methodists in America inherited John Wesley's commitment to the necessity for Christians to read, study, write, and publish. Wesley once said, "It cannot be that the people should grow in grace unless they give themselves to reading. A reading people will be a knowing people."

In January, 1823, *The Youth's Instructor and Guardian* was launched, designed for "all lovers of youth, as well as children and young people themselves . . . those who have superintendence of Sabbath-schools . . . and secretaries of Juvenile Missionary Societies." Send us, the readers were urged, "accounts of the Christian experiences and happy deaths of children and young persons."

By 1828 there was also a *Child's Magazine* being produced, and many Sunday school books and tracts. In May, 1838, *The Youth's Magazine* appeared. The first few issues contained features entitled "Sunday School Teachers Love Feast," "Anecdotes of Rev. John Wesley," "Education of Females," "Description of a Camp-Meeting" (a poem), "Hints to Sunday School Teachers," and "Grave-Yard Flowers."

The Sunday School Advocate was the next periodical to appear; it was issued for the Methodist Sunday School Union in October, 1841. It contained eight pages, appeared twice a month, and referred to itself as "this Sunday School friend." It carried articles, poetry, illustrations, stories, hymns, short sermons, book reviews, and Sunday school statistics.

Methodist Episcopal Church After 1845. After Episcopal Methodism divided in 1844-45, *The Sunday School Advocate* continued in the Methodist Episcopal Church, and was referred to as the only official Sunday school periodical of the denomination. In 1860 the General Conference authorized the issuing of a journal for teachers, and the publishing of "graduated lesson books for classes." This is presumably the beginning of graded materials for Methodists. Later there appeared the *Sunday School Journal for Teachers and Young People*. JOHN H. VINCENT started the *Sunday School Teachers Quarterly* which later was called *The Sunday School Teacher*. In 1869 *Golden Hours* was started for young people; it ran until 1880 when it was discontinued for lack of support.

In April, 1873, *The Sunday School Classmate* began as a weekly Sunday school paper; it is still being issued as *Classmate* on a monthly basis. In 1892 the *Epworth Herald* was issued to care for the concerns of the Epworth League. By 1902 there were study periodicals for younger children, older children, early teen-agers, older teen-agers, young people, the home department; as well as periodicals for teachers of primary and beginner children. Most of the lessons presented were based on the Uniform Lessons.

Methodist Episcopal Church, South. Meanwhile, the M.E. Church, South had launched a *Sunday School Journal* following the 1850 General Conference, and in 1851 the *Sunday School Visitor* appeared. In 1858 *Home Circle* began, but it and other publications were disrupted by the Civil War; the Publishing House in Nashville was taken over by Federal troops. But by 1871 the *Sunday School Visitor* was back in circulation, and new titles issued that year were *Our Little People, Sunday School Magazine,* and *Lesson Papers*.

By 1906 there was a special lesson periodical for younger and older children, early teen-agers, older teen-agers, and home department. Soon there were added *Primary Teacher, Boys and Girls,* and *Adult Student*. Most of the lesson treatments were based on the Uniform Lessons. As in the Northern Church, the Epworth League movement called for its own publication, the *Epworth Era*.

In 1910 the Methodist Episcopal Church, the Methodist Episcopal Church, South, and the Congregational-Christian Churches cooperated in setting up the Graded Lesson Syndicate, producing jointly the first series of closely graded lessons. By 1915 the series was in use with children and youth. Some shifts were made in publications of the Southern Church in 1930, when the Sunday school and the Epworth League were merged.

The Methodist Church. The next major adjustment came in 1940 following Union in 1939. Publications of the three uniting churches were brought together as the publishing interests of all three were unified. They included a closely graded series, a group graded series, a uniform lesson series (for adults only, after the first few years), and, within a few years, a series for small churches. Best known titles of periodicals since Union have been *Child Guidance in Christian Living, The Church School, The Christian Home, Highroad, Adult Student, Adult Teacher, Home Quarterly, Wesley Quarterly*. Some new titles added since 1940 have been *Mature Years, Studies in Christian Living, Roundtable, Christian Action,*

Music Ministry, Epworth Notes, Adult Bible Course, and *Lecciones Cristianas*, an adult quarterly in Spanish.

In the early 1960's the Methodists joined other Protestant groups in creating a Cooperative Curriculum Project, through which a basic curriculum plan or design for a Protestant curriculum for the teaching ministry of the church was developed. Out of this grew a new beginning in creating a Methodist curriculum plan, and, subsequently, new curriculum resources. In the fall of 1964 a completely new series for children was ready, under the title of Christian Studies for Methodist Children. It was immediately successful, having the widest acceptance that any Methodist curriculum for children has ever received. As these lines are written further plans are being made to enlarge and advance this whole program.

Methodist church school publications have shown a capacity for adaptability across the years. New approaches—sometimes radically new—have been made in almost every generation—both in pupil's and teacher's materials. A wide range of book publications for the educational ministry have been issued to serve church libraries, leadership education enterprises, vacation church schools, weekday religious education, camping situations, conferences, and assemblies.

Originally, editors of church school publications were on the staffs of the publishing houses or Book Concerns. By 1930 in the Southern Church and since 1939 in The Methodist Church, they have been staff members of the denominational boards of education, but having a working relationship to their publishing houses. Circulation of publications has followed rather closely the enrollment of the Sunday school/church school. In 1965 it reached its highest peak ever, at 7,888,868.

Since Union in 1939 the CURRICULUM COMMITTEE of The Methodist Church has studied its task and its field of operations a number of times. The result of the first study was a document called *Some Points of Needed Emphasis in Making the Curriculum of Christian Education,* issued in 1947. The second study resulted in a longer document called *Educational Principles in the Curriculum.* It contained four sections: Educational Principles Implied in Basic Christian Beliefs, Understanding the Nature of Christian Education, Christian Education and the Protestant Witness, and Implications for Methodist Curriculum Construction. *Foundations of Christian Teaching in Methodist Churches,* issued in 1960, dealt with The Nature and Work of the Church, The Gospel the Church Teaches, The Nature of Christian Education, and The Curriculum of Christian Education. The latest document, *Design for Methodist Curriculum* (1965), deals with The Objective of Christian Education, The Scope of the Curriculum for Christian Education, The Context of the Curriculum for Christian Education, and Learning and Learning Tasks in Christian Education.

The present base for curriculum planning for the educational ministry of the church is well expressed in the following statement:

"The objective of the church as manifested through its educational ministry is that all persons be aware of and grow in their understanding of God, especially of his redeeming love as revealed in Jesus Christ, and that they respond in faith and love—to the end that they may know who they are and what their human situation means, increasingly identify themselves as sons of God and members of the Christian community, live in the spirit of God in every relationship, fulfill their common discipleship in the world, and abide in the Christian hope."

WALTER N. VERNON

SUNDAY SCHOOL UNIONS or **ASSOCIATIONS** were—and are—organizations for the encouragement of the formation of Sunday schools in connection with the church life of America. On Jan. 11, 1791 the first Inter-denominational Sunday School Association was organized in PHILADELPHIA under the name of "A Society for the Institution and Support of First Day or Sunday Schools in the City of Philadelphia." The meeting had been advertised in Dunlap's *American Daily Advertiser* and representatives attended from several churches including ST. GEORGE'S METHODIST CHURCH. A constitution was drawn by which the Society met every three months. Three schools were opened: one for girls under the care of a John Ely, the other two for boys, one under the leadership of John Poor and a second under Thaddeus Brown. As time went on some of the schools that were opened met during the week, and it is thought by some that these were the forerunners of the nationwide public school system. Among the more prominent persons in the movement were Benjamin Rush, a signer of the Declaration of Independence, Matthew Carey, a liberal Roman Catholic and Bishop William White of the Episcopal Church who for forty-six years held the position of President. Spelling, writing and reading were taught besides the Bible, and the students came, for the most part from families of the poor and illiterate. The success of the enterprise was measured partly by how ably the schools kept young hoodlums and possible delinquents off the streets and gave them a useful occupation. One of the schools housed in the New Street building of Old St. George's continued to grow until by 1841 St. George's was responsible for three First Day Schools.

During the years following the War of 1812 with England, Sunday School Unions or Associations began to spring up in most of the states, the most notable one being the New York Sunday School Union established February 26, 1816. The following year a meeting was held in Philadelphia to draw together various Sunday and Adult School Associations that had come into existence. Eleven organizations united in 1817 under the name, "Sunday and Adult School Union." The growth of Sunday Schools under the new organization was phenomenal, and its work spread throughout the country. On May 25, 1824 a new name and constitution were approved to reflect this national character when the American Sunday School Union was organized. It is still a strong organization (1968).

During the year 1824 also a Committee on Education of the Methodist Episcopal Church urged the General Conference to give greater attention to the religious instruction of its youth, and three years later the Sunday School Union of the Methodist Episcopal Church was organized with the purpose not merely of instructing the poor and illiterate but with the broader purpose of establishing Sunday Schools in connection with every Methodist Episcopal Church in the country and of distributing tracts and books to assist toward this end.

In 1833 the Union was united with the Tract Society of the Methodist Church, becoming The Sunday School Union and Tract Society. The organization purchased its materials at cost from the Publishing House of the Methodist Church, and with the destruction of the Publishing House by fire in 1836 it became practically defunct. The Sunday School Union, however, was separately re-organized in 1840 and began another era of vigorous leadership in the establishing and support of Sunday Schools.

With the bisection of the Church in 1844 the Northern Church continued the activities of the Sunday School Union which by 1875 had accomplished one of its purposes in that every Church now had a Sunday School in connection with its work.

The Southern Church had always been a strong supporter of Sunday Schools and also formed a Sunday School Association. This organization performed its task effectively, and in the chaotic post war years was one of the means of providing many southern children with the only formal education they would know. Unfortunately, the rather loose affiliation which these schools, sponsored by the Sunday School Association, had with the local church gave rise often to friction between the pastor of the church and the Sunday School Superintendent. In 1866 the General Conference of the Southern Church removed the schools from the domination of the Association and made them an integral part of the church.

At the time of the union of the three branches of Methodism in 1939 all Sunday School work came under the Board of Education. In 1964 "Church Schools" as they came to be called, were placed under the Board of Education who "may" co-operate through the Inter-board Committee on Christian Education and such agencies as the National Council of Churches, the World Council of Christian Education and Sunday School Association and the World Council of Churches." (*Discipline*, 1964, P. 1426)

E. S. Bucke, *History of American Methodism*. 1964.
Edwin Wilbur Rice, *The Sunday School Movement and the American Sunday School Union*. Philadelphia, 1927.

FREDERICK E. MASER

SUNDAY SERVICE, THE, was the name which John Wesley gave to the edition of the *Book of Common Prayer* of the Church of England which he prepared for the American Methodists when he sent to them THOMAS COKE, RICHARD WHATCOAT, and THOMAS VASEY, as ordained men for the purpose, as American Methodists insist, of starting a Church in America. This was in 1784, and the gathering of the American Methodist preachers in Baltimore at the CHRISTMAS CONFERENCE with Thomas Coke, Whatcoat and Vasey, and the presentation of the *Sunday Service* and their acceptance of it was an important move in the formation of the Methodist Episcopal Church in America.

Mr. Wesley explained the *Liturgy*, as it was often called, as being an edition of the *Book of Common Prayer*. His preface to the book is as follows:

I believe there is no Liturgy in the world, either in ancient or modern language, which breathes more of solid, Scriptural, rational piety than the Common Prayer of the Church of England; and though the main of it was compiled considerably more than two hundred years ago, yet is the language of it not only pure, but strong and elegant in the highest degree.

Little alteration is made in the following edition of it, except in the following instances:

1. Most of the holy days (so called) are omitted, as at present answering no valuable end.

2. The service of the Lord's day, the length of which has often been complained of, is considerably shortened.
3. Some sentences in the offices of baptism and for the burial of the dead are omitted; and
4. Many Psalms left out, and many parts of the others, as being highly improper for the mouths of a Christian congregation.

John Wesley

Bristol, September 9, 1784

The exact name of the Liturgy as can be seen upon the title page was "*The Sunday Service of the Methodists in North America, with Other Occasional Services;* London, printed in the year of 1784." Coke and his attending presbyters brought the *Sunday Service* to America in loose sheets to avoid payment of the much heavier duty on bound books, and after its adoption by the Christmas Conference, JOHN DICKINS, who subsequently came to be the first BOOK STEWARD in America, took these unbound copies and had them bound together with a collection of *Minutes* of the Christmas Conference in most of the respective copies. Certain of them seem to have been bound also with some of the hymns which were recommended for use of the Methodists in America.

The *Sunday Service* was an abridgement of the *Book of Common Prayer* and beside its ordering of worship and psalms, contained 24 of the 39 Articles of the Church of England. These Mr. Wesley selected and edited somewhat and as it came about these Articles forthwith were adopted by American Methodists as Standards of Doctrine. (See ARTICLES OF RELIGION for Mr. Wesley's changes and amendments.)

In editing the *Prayer Book*, Mr. Wesley changed the word *Priest* to *Elder* throughout; the word *Bishop* he always changed to *Superintendent;* he left out all directions for singing or chanting when these were found in the Rubrics of the *Prayer Book;* and he left out the entire Office for Confirmation, so that American Methodism had no form for the reception of members, save baptism, until 1864 in the Methodist Episcopal Church, and 1870 in the Methodist Episcopal Church, South.

The Christmas Conference adopted the *Sunday Service* formally, agreeing that its members would "form themselves into an Episcopal Church under the direction of superintendents, elders, deacons and helpers according to the forms of Ordination annexed to our Liturgy, and the form of discipline set forth in these Minutes." This became the plan of Church government which American Methodism was destined to adhere to. Richard Whatcoat in his memoirs, as quoted by Bishop TIGERT, states, "We agreed to form a Methodist Episcopal Church, in which the Liturgy, as presented by the Reverend John Wesley should be read and the Sacraments be administered by a superintendent, elders and deacons, who shall be ordained by a presbytery using the episcopal form as prescribed in the rear of Mr. Wesley's Prayer Book" (p. 44). A second edition of the *Sunday Service* came out in 1786, which edition was printed in London at the press of Frys and Couchman. It had 25 Articles, as by this time the American Methodists had inserted an Article of their own having to do with the obligation of the Methodist Church to the Civil ruler in America, since Mr. Wesley had naturally omitted the comparable Article which affirmed allegiance to the King.

There has been some confusion over the first editions of the *Sunday Service*, Bishop Tigert holding in the *Making of Methodism* that the editions of 1784 and 1786 are both American Methodist; but that in 1788 there was a third edition of the *Sunday Service* for the British Wesleyan Connexion, and in 1792 both an American and British edition. Whatever be the case for the Wesleyan Connexion in England, for America there appear to have been only two editions, and these were of 1784 and of 1786. The 1786 edition was destined to be the last, for the *Sunday Service* never proved popular and, indeed, was little used in early America. JESSE LEE said that the preachers tried for awhile to read prayers on the Lord's Day, and to read part of the morning service on Wednesdays and Fridays; but the same author said that the preachers were satisfied they could pray better and with more devotion with their eyes shut than they could with their eyes open. So the *Prayer Book*—as it is often referred to—was soon laid aside and has never been used since in public worship, though some of its material has been reprinted from time to time.

As can be seen clearly today no more incongruous idea presents itself in the history of Churches than that of expecting American Methodism in 1784 to be guided and directed by Book of Prayer forms. Methodism itself was a revolt against formalism, and the age in America was one of immense freedom in all departments of life. That the early Methodists should soon get rid of the stately forms of the English Church is not surprising. There were saved, however, out of the *Sunday Service* eight forms, or offices—now called the RITUAL—which to this day have been kept in those Methodist Churches claiming descent from the Christmas Conference. These forms are the Service of Holy Communion; the Infant and Adult Baptismal Offices; Matrimony; Burial of the Dead; and three forms for Ordination—of Bishops (as superintendents soon came to be called); of Elders; and of Deacons.

In discarding the *Sunday Service,* American Methodism was in the process of creating a book of its own, and one which embodies its own genius much more definitely than did the *Book of Common Prayer*—a book which American Methodism not inaptly named the DISCIPLINE. Not ordered worship, but ordered life and activity came to be the genius of American Methodism on its side of the ocean.

In connection with the first edition of the *Sunday Service*, it is interesting to note that the printed pages of the book were brought to America in loose sheets, and this gave American Methodists a chance to revise in certain instances Mr. Wesley's own edition of the *Prayer Book*. Making the sign of the cross upon the forehead of a child being baptised (the *signation* so called) was kept by Mr. Wesley, but the page containing that was reprinted in America so that that ceremony was done away and does not appear in the books John Dickins put out; likewise, the "manual acts" in Communion whereby the priest was told to take the patten containing bread in his hand, and again to take the vessel containing the wine in his hand during the Prayer of Consecration—these two ceremonies were left out by the American brethren. Also a great many sweeping changes were made in the Offices of the *Ritual* when these were taken from the *Sunday Service* and put in the *Discipline* of 1792. Most of these were in the interest of brevity, but some for reasons clearly which agreed more with American thinking along particular lines. Bishop Asbury was accused of destroying a large invoice of the *Prayer Book* which Wesley had sent to America, but this cannot possibly be believed. (*The Times and the Teachings of John Wesley* by Arthur W. Little, D.D.; Second Edition, The Young Churchman Co., Milwaukee, Wisconsin, 1905, quoting a *Methodist in Search of the Church*, p. 104. This reference states that a few copies escaped, and one is preserved in the Library of the General Theological Seminary in New York.)

While very scarce, several copies of the *Sunday Service* have been carefully preserved in various places. The Book Room at the Publishing House in London has a 1786 copy; and 1784 copies are in the Library of DREW THEOLOGICAL SEMINARY, Madison, New Jersey; one in EMORY UNIVERSITY, Atlanta, Georgia; in the Public Library, New York; and in the Library of Congress in Washington, D. C.—kept in their Rare Book Room.

F. Baker, *John Wesley*. 1970.
R. J. Cooke, *History of the Ritual*. 1900.
N. B. Harmon, *Rites and Ritual*. 1926.
T. O. Summers, *Commentary on the Ritual*. 1874.   N. B. H.

SUNDERLAND THEOLOGICAL INSTITUTION was a PRIMITIVE METHODIST theological college in England for the training of ministers which functioned between 1868 and 1881. The Primitive Methodist Conference of 1865 had decided to use the secondary school opened at Elmfield House, York, in 1864, as a venue for the introduction of ministerial training under JOHN PETTY. This was an interim measure, and in 1868 the Connexion bought what had been an infirmary in Chester Road, Sunderland, for £1,500, and spent a further £1,836 on adapting the building to its new purpose. Part of the money which was used for this came from the fund which had been raised to celebrate the jubilee of the Connexion. WILLIAM ANTLIFF was the first principal and tutor, remaining there until 1881. When HARTLEY COLLEGE was opened in MANCHESTER in 1881, it was found that there was not any need for two institutions and the work of ministerial training was concentrated in Manchester, which had the advantage of being a university center. The Sunderland building was sold; it still exists as a Roman Catholic school.

Wesley Historical Society *Proceedings*, xxx.

JOHN T. WILKINSON

SUNG, JOHN (Sung Shang-chieh, 1901-1944), evangelist in CHINA, was born Sept. 27, 1901 in a Methodist parsonage in the Hinghwa Conference. After graduation from the Methodist high school there he attended OHIO WESLEYAN UNIVERSITY, where he graduated in three years with honors. By this time his earlier dedication of himself to the ministry had faded and he went to Ohio State University for a Ph.D. in chemistry. He decided to study a year at Union Theological Seminary in New York, with the hope that he might become an intelligent layman.

On Feb. 10, 1927, he had a nerve-shattering religious experience which overturned his plan of life. After six months in a mental hospital, and the intercession of his college teacher, Rollin Walker, he returned to China where for fifteen years he was a blazing evangelist. His first three years were spent in his home area, and during that time he joined the Hinghwa Annual Conference. But he soon asked for an appointment as evangelist-at-large and began systematic campaigns in other parts of China. For three or four years he worked in conjunction with the Bethel Evangelistic Band in Shanghai, and after

that on his own. He visited almost every province in China and everywhere left behind him a revitalized church.

Outside the mainland he made at least six visits to SINGAPORE and MALAYSIA, and preached also in INDONESIA, Siam, Indochina, TAIWAN and MANILA. The Bible societies had no difficulty in following his trail, for the sale of Bibles and Testaments always doubled and tripled wherever he went.

In January 1940, he returned to Shanghai seriously ill. He was able to do a little more work the following year, but by June 1943 he had to stop public speaking altogether. He died Aug. 18, 1944.

Many found fault with his preaching: He was inclined to allegorical exegesis; especially in his earlier years, he was too censorious of others; for a time he overstressed faith healing. But, with it all, there was unquestionably a power of God to touch the conscience of his hearers. He made no attempt to gather his thousands of converts into Methodist churches. But all the churches of eastern Asia have felt the influence of his impassioned preaching.

Leslie T. Lyall, *John Sung*. London: China Inland Mission, 1954; Chicago: Moody Press, 1964.   FRANCIS P. JONES

SUPERINTENDENT, American Methodist. The title and office of superintendent came over to American Methodism as part of the Connexional plan devised by JOHN WESLEY. THOMAS RANKIN and FRANCIS ASBURY were sent to America to be "general superintendents" of the work, and Wesley preferred that name to the title "bishop" for the office of general superintendent as this developed in the M.E. Church after 1784.

In the *Sunday Service*, or Prayer Book, which Wesley sent to American Methodism, he invariably changed the name "bishop" to "superintendent" in those offices where a bishop is called upon to ordain, or to be ordained. However in 1786—certainly by 1794—COKE and Asbury adopted "bishop" in place of "superintendent"— much to Wesley's distaste, and to the objection of many Methodist ministers who had begun complaining at the arbitrary overlordship of Asbury. The title "bishop," however, became established, but with it also there has come down through the years a parallel definition of a bishop as "a general superintendent," and his work is called in the Constitution of The United Methodist Church "general superintendency." The third RESTRICTIVE RULE of the present United Methodist Church prevents the general conference from "destroying episcopacy or doing away with our plan of itinerant general superintendency." Each bishop today considers himself a general superintendent of the whole Church. (See EPISCOPACY.)

British Methodist. In English Methodist usage the CIRCUIT superintendent minister is the spiritual and administrative leader of the circuit to which he is appointed. He is chairman of all official meetings, including the circuit quarterly meeting; in consultation with his colleagues he makes the preaching plan; he is responsible for the working of Methodist discipline in the circuit; he is usually responsible for the care of candidates for the ministry in his circuit. The superintendent's authority is guarded against that of the Chairman of District, inasmuch as the Chairman of District may only enter a circuit officially either at the invitation of, or after consultation with, the superintendent minister. In modern English Methodist usage the word "superintendent" has no episcopal overtone; this belongs to the title of "Chairman of District."

District Superintendents—formerly called presiding elders in American Methodism—supervise and care for a district within their respective annual conferences. The change of name from presiding elder to district superintendent was done first in the M.E. Church in 1908, and then by the Uniting Conference in Kansas City for The Methodist Church in 1939. The name and functions of the District Suprintendents were continued in The United Methodist Church, about as they had been in The Methodist Church.

Development of the Presiding Eldership. On Oct. 24, 1769, Wesley sent RICHARD BOARDMAN to America as his "assistant" in order to superintend the work in America. Methodism in America was growing and becoming more complicated, so in 1771 Wesley sent one who turned out to be a more capable man in the person of Francis Asbury, with the explicit instructions to give strict attention to discipline (keeping all parts connected to the whole).

Asbury set about diligently to fulfill these plans, becoming Wesley's equal as a traveler on horseback. All the country districts, towns, and plantations became his parish. "But while he was thus engaged in visiting the plantations and villages, an undue eagerness to extend the work in the towns had unhappily led to a comparative neglect of discipline." (Tigert, p. 57.) When news of the neglect reached Wesley, he immediately set out to remedy the situation by sending Thomas Rankin, June 3, 1773, to America to serve as General Assistant or Superintendent with powers superior to any which had been vested in his predecessors in office. Rankin, a strict disciplinarian, with the aid of Asbury, did much to bring about the effective organization of connectionalism in American Methodism.

The first American Conference in 1773 did much to enlarge the superintending power for the General Assistant. The sixth rule of that conference was: "Every preacher who acts as an assistant (i.e., has charge of a circuit) to send an account of the work once in six months to the General Assistant." (Ibid., p. 69.) This provided a continuing touch with the spread and growth of Methodism.

There are hints of the beginning of the office of presiding elder in this desire for a connection with all the work. By the time the M.E. Church was organized in 1784 the office was virtually created, although the title was not explicitly given to it. "It came with the first Superintendents, the first ordinations, the first formal provision for the administration of the sacraments, and is, therefore, coeval with the organization of the Church," said Bishop Tigert (p. 213).

The twelve elected and ordained elders at the CHRISTMAS CONFERENCE, Dec. 24, 1784, were in reality "presiding elders," although the title does not appear in the *Discipline* until 1792. The title in fact does not appear regularly in the *Minutes* until as late as 1797. These twelve men were assigned to districts, or rather to groups of circuits. The Methodist system was determined by all organizational moves to remain connected.,

During the period from 1784 to 1792 the "presiding elders" relieved the General Assistant of many duties. Yet, the bishop, as he now was, had no "cabinet," as such. The cabinet in a sense had its origin in the COUNCIL

that Asbury formed in 1789, by which he hoped to avoid the necessity of a GENERAL CONFERENCE. The Council itself could only act in an advisory manner and soon vanished from the scene.

From the beginning the "presiding elder" could not act contrary to an express order of the superintendents. The elder acted as an advisor, a link in the connectional system. In 1786 this restriction was made definite in the *Discipline,* in answer to what the duties are of an ELDER: "To exercise within his own district, during the absence of the superintendents, all the powers vested in them for the government of our Church. Provided, that he never acts contrary to an express order of the superintendents."

The General Conference of 1792. It was in this conference the office and title of presiding elder was defined. The General Conference determined that there should be presiding elders, and that they should be chosen, stationed, and changed by the bishop, provided no elder should preside in the same district more than four years successively. The presiding elder was thus formally created to be in effect a sub-bishop, and an arm of the Church's disciplinary administration. The following section was framed by the General Conference of 1792:

Quest. 1. By whom are the presiding elders to be chosen?
Ans. By the bishop.
Quest. 2. What are the duties of the presiding elder?
Ans. 1. To travel through his appointed district. 2. In the absence of a bishop to take charge of all the elders, deacons, traveling and local preachers, and exhorters in his district. 3. To change, receive, or suspend preachers in his district during the intervals of the conferences, and in the absence of the bishop. 4. In the absence of a bishop to preside in the conferences of his district. 5. To be present, as far as practicable, at all the quarterly meetings; and to call together, at each quarterly meeting, all the traveling and local preachers, exhorters, stewards, and leaders of the circuit, to hear complaints, and to receive appeals. 6. To oversee the spiritual and temporal business of the societies in his district. 7. To take care that every part of our Discipline be enforced in his district. 8. To attend the bishop when present in his district; and to give him when absent all necessary information, by letter, of the state of his district.
Quest. 3. By whom are the presiding elders to be stationed and changed?
Ans. By the bishop.
Quest. 4. How long may the bishops allow an elder to preside in the same district?
Ans. For any term not exceeding four years successively.
Quest. 5. How shall the presiding elder be supported?
Ans. If there be a surplus of the public money in one or more circuits in his district, he shall receive such surplus, provided he does not receive more than his annual salary, after such surplus is paid him, or if there be no surplus, he shall share with the preachers of his district, in proportion with what they have respectively received, so that he receives no more than the amount of his salary upon the whole.

Tension immediately came about over the bishop's power to choose presiding elders. JAMES O'KELLY and WILLIAM McKENDREE wanted the presiding elders to be elected by the annual conferences. The move failed in 1792 and O'Kelly withdrew from the Church. McKendree stayed on to become in time a bishop himself and next to Asbury the greatest champion of the Asburian episcopacy.

Coke and Asbury in their *Notes* to the *Discipline* of

1796 made reference to the office and duty of presiding elder as created in 1792:

And we believe we can venture to assert, that there never has been an episcopal church of any great extent which has not had *ruling* or *presiding* elders, either expressly by name, as in the apostolic churches, or otherwise in *effect* . . . The Conference clearly saw that the bishops wanted assistants; that it was impossible for one or two bishops so to superintend the vast work on this continent, as to keep everything in order in the intervals of the conference, without other official men to act under them and assist them: and as these would be only the agents of the bishops in every respect, the authority of appointing them, and of changing them, ought, from the nature of things, to be in the episcopacy. (*Discipline,* 1796; 1808.)

Asbury's great policy was to establish itinerancy in the new American Church, and to do this he saw that an episcopacy strong enough to command the appointments, both of all preachers and of all local congregations, must be had. The revolt against the episcopacy was destined to be fought out for several decades over the bishops' right to appoint the presiding elders. For should they be elected by vote of a conference, they would be beholden to the conference and controlled by it, not by the bishop. The episcopacy would be greatly minimized, the bishop himself becoming no more than a moderator.

Meanwhile the CABINET composed then—and now—of all presiding elders (district superintendents) had come about. In 1812 William McKendree, having become a bishop in 1808, summoned the presiding elders to meet with him to help make the appointments. Thus for the first time came the cabinet.

The question of electing the presiding elders was debated, but not settled in 1812 nor in 1816, but a more epochal move came at the General Conference of 1820. A resolution was passed ordering that when the appointment of one or more presiding elders should be required, the bishop must nominate three times the number out of which the Conference itself should elect the needed elders.

NICHOLAS SNETHEN had introduced this resolution back in 1812. It seemed to be a workable solution, until a few days later in the 1820 Conference JOSHUA SOULE was elected bishop. Soule refused the office saying that the episcopacy would be such a different entity under this mandate that he would not and could not consent to be ordained. Soule's move, coupled with a powerful protest by Bishop McKendree, caused the resolutions to be suspended for four years until the mind of the annual conferences upon them might be obtained. They became known as the "suspended resolutions." As it turned out, when the annual conferences discussed and voted upon this matter, the resolutions were in effect killed.

When the General Conference of 1824 convened, "the Reformers," as they were being called, met defeat, and moves for lay representation also seemed lost in the M.E. Church. Soule was again elected and consecrated bishop, he himself being destined to be a tremendous bulwark of the Asburian episcopacy in the great division coming later in 1844.

The M.P. CHURCH, composed largely of the reforming elements, then organized in 1828-30. This Church had no bishops at all and no presiding elders, but strongly incorporated laymen into all the conferences and councils of the Church.

This seemingly ended the struggle to make the elder-ship elective in episcopal Methodism; for while the Church divided in 1844 over the slavery issue, and the power of a General Conference to depose a bishop for holding slaves, there was no division over the presiding eldership continuing to be an arm of the episcopacy either South or North. True, in the M.E. General Conference of 1876, the elective presiding eldership was again brought up, and rather strongly supported, but again the move failed to pass.

From 1844-1939. Within both Episcopal Churches there was a continual struggle over the term a presiding elder might serve upon one district. Once in 1904, in the M.E. Church, J. W. Lambert presented a memorial to the General Conference to remove the time limit from the office altogether. This failed. In time in the M.E. Churches, limitation of six years was put upon the length of time a district superintendent might serve on any one district. This provision was continued in The Methodist Church and in The United Methodist Church. This measure effectually prevents a "self-perpetuating cabinet" in which the district superintendents were moved—or moved themselves!—from one district to another, year after year as was formerly the case, especially in the Southern Church.

The big change during this period was the change in title. In the General Conference of the M.E. Church of 1908, J. M. BUCKLEY presented the following resolution, which was referred to the Committee on Revision:

Whereas, the name "Presiding Elder" was attached to the office now known by it in part for a reason that no longer exists; and,

Whereas, In many parts of this country the name and the office are confounded with the uses of the word "elder," and,

Whereas, The functions of the office are not suggested to other denominations and the public by the word "presiding elder," and,

Whereas, The proper dignity of the office is no longer conserved by its retention; therefore,

Resolved, That the title of this office be changed to "district superintendent."

Subsequently, its committee having acted favorably, the General Conference adopted the new title.

The Office Since 1939. The plan of union in 1939 preserved this historic ministerial office keeping it under the term "district superintendent." An attempt to adopt the name "district elder" at the Uniting Conference was rather weakly made, but this failed, and "the D.S." has come to be the presiding elder's name in modern American Methodism.

The duties of the office were increased by disciplinary direction in 1939. There were then sixteen expressed duties of the district superintendent; whereas, the *Discipline* of the M.E. Church, South listed only eleven in 1938 (it had nine in 1846); and the M.E. Church listed only twelve. In The United Methodist Church there are twelve listed duties, but these are very important. All of them may be summed up in the first item, "to travel through his district in order to preach and oversee the spiritual and temporal affairs of the Church." Duties of presiding, administering, supervising, and counseling pastors, and seeing that all the provisions of the *Discipline* are carried out, are all outlined in a quite definite way.

In negotiations leading to the PLAN OF UNION between The Methodist Church and the E.U.B. Church, the latter were found to have elective district superintendents, a move which had been made in that Church quite a few years before in answer to the same type of argument which had strongly been expressed in the earlier days of the M.E. Church. The Methodist negotiators, however, did not feel that the elective presiding eldership was wise for the enlarged Methodist Church nor that a plan of union which embraced it would be accepted by the Church as a provision of the plan of union. The E.U.B. brethren gave way on this, as they did upon the matter of term episcopacy.

Present regulations in The United Methodist Church are: "He [the bishop] shall choose and appoint district superintendents annually, but within the Jurisdictional Conferences of the United States he shall not appoint any minister or district superintendent for more than six years in any consecutive nine years." (*Discipline*, 1968, Paragraph 391.3.) The present Church, therefore, maintains the office of the district superintendents—formerly the presiding elder—pretty much as it has been through the long years of Methodist development in America.

The district superintendent is in effect a sub-bishop. He can do everything which a bishop does under certain conditions except ordain. Wise bishops state that a good cabinet is a key to successful administration in any annual conference. In spite of other organizations which are empowered to take over large divisions of the administrative work in an annual conference, the bishop with his cabinet are still the responsible parties for overseeing the spiritual and temporal affairs of the whole Church. They, and not a program committee, or any conference board or organization are to be praised or blamed accordingly as success and good administration is carried out.

A. H. Bassett, *Concise History*. 1877.
Disciplines.
R. Emory, *History of the Discipline*. 1844.
N. B. Harmon, *Organization*. 1962.
Journals of the General Conferences.
Powers McLeod, "A D.S. Speaks: We Ask the Wrong Questions," *Christian Advocate*, Oct. 5, 1967.
J. J. Tigert, *Constitutional History*. 1894.
N. B. H.
JOHN KENT

SUPERNUMERARY, British Methodist. In English Methodist usage a supernumerary is a minister who has retired, or "superannuated." He is not normally put in charge of a society or circuit, but there are a few "active supernumeraries," as they are called, who take charge of a society. A supernumerary minister will preach, however, as long as he is physically able. Permission to retire is normally given after forty years in the active ministry.

JOHN KENT

SUPERNUMERARY FUND, at Christchurch, New Zealand, deals with pensions and allowances for retired ministers.

Prior to the separation of the NEW ZEALAND Conference from the Australasian Conference in 1913, New Zealand ministers were members of the Australasian Supernumerary Fund. After the separation, the first balance sheet presented to the New Zealand Conference showed accumulated funds of £69,713, of which £52,770 had been transferred from the Australasian Fund. At the same time the Wesleyan and Primitive Methodist Churches in

New Zealand having united, £8,752 was transferred from the Primitive Methodist Supernumerary Fund.

The 1966 capital fund stood at over £170,000. There were 46 supernumerary ministers and 43 widows of ministers who were annuitants, with 249 ministers who were contributing members. The personal payment of each minister was and is subsidized by his circuit or department. Substantial increases in the rate of contribution have been instituted to offset rising costs.

A supernumerary minister on his retirement may receive his benefits from the fund as an annuity, or he may commute a large portion of his interest in the fund. This latter provision enables him to benefit also from the social security benefits offered by the government, and it helps him very materially in setting up his own home.

In 1928, a subsidiary fund was established called the Ministers' Home Acquirement Fund, personal payments into which were subsidized by a grant from the Connexional Fire Insurance Fund. In addition there is the Supernumerary Benevolent Fund, which as its name implies exists to make *exgratia* payments to annuitants under circumstances of special need.

In 1916, a retiring fund was established for home missionaries, and in 1921, a similar fund for deaconesses. The personal payments of members are subsidized in each of these funds by the home or overseas mission department, as the case may be, or by the circuit concerned. Because the basis of service is different here from that of the ministers, contributors receive their benefits in the form of a cash payment on retirement.

H. L. Fiebig: *Inheritance*. Wesley Historical Society, New Zealand, 1967.
HERBERT L. FIEBIG

SUPPLY PASTOR. (See MINISTRY, American Methodist.)

SURINAM (Dutch Guiana) is a Dutch territory on the Atlantic coast of northeast South America. Under the Charter of the Kingdom of The Netherlands, promulgated Dec. 29, 1954, Surinam became a partner with The Netherlands rather than a colonial possession. The capital is Paramaribo. The area is 55,198 square miles and the population approximates 265,000, including 100,000 creoles, 125,000 orientals, 35,000 Negroes and aborigines, and 5,000 Europeans.

The British made the first settlement in the early 1630's, a colony being founded in 1651. The Dutch captured it in February 1667, the Treaty of Breda confirming the tenure in exchange for NEW YORK (U.S.A.) to the British. Alternate control between The Netherlands and Great Britain persisted with several shifts. The Treaty of Paris in 1815 finally confirmed Dutch sovereignty. Under the Charter of 1954, Surinam is an autonomous and integral element within the Kingdom of The Netherlands.

Methodism is represented in Surinam by the small mission of the A.M.E. Church. The work is administratively connected with the larger field in adjacent British Guiana. The membership is quite small.

World Methodist Council, *Handbook of Information*, 1966-71.
ARTHUR BRUCE MOSS

SUSQUEHANNA CONFERENCE (EUB) traced its beginnings back to the mother conferences of both the CHURCH OF THE UNITED BRETHREN IN CHRIST and of the EVANGELICAL ASSOCIATION.

Conference meetings of OTTERBEIN and his associates were held as early as 1774. It was from the 1789 conference, however, that Pennsylvania Conference of the United Brethren in Christ dated its history. This conference was held in the parsonage of Philip William Otterbein in BALTIMORE. On Sept. 25, 1800, in Kemp's farm house just a few miles west of Frederick, Md., the conference was formally organized: a name for the new church was chosen (United Brethren in Christ) and two bishops were elected—Philip William Otterbein and MARTIN BOEHM.

The work spread westward across the mountains into western PENNSYLVANIA and MARYLAND and into VIRGINIA and OHIO. The GENERAL CONFERENCE of 1830 divided this original conference into the Hagerstown Conference (later known as the Pennsylvania Conference).

Again in 1846, Pennsylvania Conference was divided. All territory east of the Susquehanna River became the East Pennsylvania Conference while the remainder was known as the West Pennsylvania Conference. (In time the "West" was dropped and only "Pennsylvania" was used.)

The Maryland Conference was formed in 1887 with the withdrawal of nineteen ministers and twelve charges from the Virginia Conference.

In 1901, the Maryland Conference merged with the Pennsylvania Conference. From that time until 1964, the boundary of Pennsylvania Conference extended from the mouth of the Susquehanna River northward to the mouth of the Juniata River, from this point westward along the Juniata to the Tuscarora Mountain, thence southward along the summit of the mountain to the Potomac River, thence southeastward along the Potomac to the District of Columbia and northeastward to the mouth of the Susquehanna River including the cities of Washington and Baltimore.

The first annual conference of the Evangelical Association was held Nov. 15, 1807 in the home of Samuel Becker near Kleinfeltersville, Pennsylvania. This conference chose "The Newly Formed Methodist Conference" as the name of the new church and elected JACOB ALBRIGHT bishop and GEORGE MILLER elder.

At the General Conference held in New Berlin, Pa., in 1826, the church was divided into two conferences. The territory in Ohio and the west formed the Western Conference, while the churches of Pennsylvania, NEW YORK, Maryland, and Virginia formed the Eastern Conference.

The Eastern Conference was again divided in 1839, when "the territory west of the Susquehanna (and the north branch of the same), Carroll County, Maryland, and Washington County in the western part of the State, the Shenandoah Valley in Virginia, as far south as Woodstock, and several of the counties in (now) West Virginia, along the Potomac River" formed the West Pennsylvania Conference. The Western Conference was re-named Ohio Conference.

A further division was made in 1851 when the western districts of West Pennsylvania Conference were transferred to the newly formed Pittsburg Conference. The name of West Pennsylvania Conference was changed to Central Pennsylvania Conference in 1859.

A minor change in boundary occurred in 1950 when the Western Pennsylvania Conference of The Evangelical United Brethren Church was formed. Churches of the former Allegheny Conference (UB) within the territory of the Central Pennsylvania Conference were exchanged for churches in Altoona. This had the effect of excluding Blair County from the Central Pennsylvania Conference territory.

On Jan. 1, 1965, the Pennsylvania and the Central Pennsylvania Conferences merged to form the Susquehanna Conference. The boundary of Susquehanna Conference was as follows: the territory west of the Susquehanna River from its mouth in Maryland up along the north branch of the same to the Wyoming County line in the northern part of Pennsylvania, thence westward to the juncture of the Tioga, Lycoming, and Potter County lines, thence southward to the juncture of the Centre, Blair and Mifflin County lines, thence eastward to the Juniata River at Lewistown, eastward to the Tuscarora Mountain, thence southward along the Tuscarora summit to the Potomac River, thence eastward along the Potomac to the District of Columbia, thence northeastward to the mouth of the Susquehanna River, including the cities of Washington and Baltimore. In 1967, there were 380 ministers in all classes with a total of 95,179 church members. In 1969, approximately sixty churches entered union with the BALTIMORE CONFERENCE while the remaining congregations joined with the CENTRAL PENNSYLVANIA CONFERENCE of the former Methodist Church and a number of congregations from the Eastern and Western Pennsylvania Conferences of the former E.U.B. Church to compose the present Central Pennsylvania Conference.

A. W. Drury, *History of the U.B.* 1924.
P. E. Holdcraft, *Pennsylvania Conference*. 1938.
A. Stapleton, *Evangelical Association*. 1900.

CHARLES R. MILLER

SUTCLIFFE, JOSEPH (1762-1856), British Methodist, was born at Baildon, Yorkshire. He is named fifth in the list of preachers at the BRISTOL Conference of 1790. In 1786 he was appointed by JOHN WESLEY to Redruth Circuit. A man of scholarly attainments, he published the following works: *An Introduction to Christianity; A Grammar of the English Language; a Commentary on the Holy Scripture;* a volume of sermons on regeneration; together with many pamphlets. He was also the author of a "History of Methodism to the Death of Dr. Coke," in four volumes, the manuscript of which has never been published and is in the Methodist Archives at City Road, LONDON. He composed "Lines on the Erection of a Statue to the Memory of John Wesley in the Wesleyan College, Richmond, June 14, 1849." He died in 1856 at the advanced age of ninety-four.

J. T. WILKINSON

SUTHERLAND, ALEXANDER (1833-1910), Canadian minister and historian, was born in Guelph Township, Upper Canada, Sept. 13, 1833. Educated at Victoria College, he was taken on trial in 1856 and ordained in 1859.

A man of great scholarly and intellectual ability, Sutherland soon became an outstanding preacher. He held a number of important charges, including St. James Methodist Church in Montreal, prior to his appointment in 1874 as Missionary Secretary of the Methodist Church, a post which he held until his death.

As Missionary Secretary, Sutherland presided over one of the most fruitful periods in the development of Cana-

ALEXANDER SUTHERLAND

dian Methodist missions. During his years in office, the Northwest was opened effectively to the church, and missions were established in Japan and China. His vision, foresight, and tireless advocacy contributed much to this process of expansion and consolidation.

Alexander Sutherland was one of the first to realize that the Methodist Churches and, especially his own branch, would be unable to meet singly the missionary challenge of an expanding and changing Canada. Within the Methodist Church of Canada he fought vigorously and skillfully for acceptance of the general superintendency, which in turn opened the way for union with the Methodist Episcopal Church.

Despite his heavy burdens as preacher and administrator, he contributed to the volume entitled *Centennial of Canadian Methodism* (1891); he also wrote *Methodism in Canada: Its Work and Its Story* (1903) and *The Methodist Church and Missions in Canada and Newfoundland* (1906). These works present important aspects of Canadian Methodist history in a thoughtful and intelligible form.

Sutherland was a member of all general conferences from 1874 to 1906, fraternal delegate to the British Conference in 1903, and president of Toronto Conference in 1882 and 1884. He was given a D.D. by Victoria University in 1879, and in 1891 he was offered the principalship of MOUNT ALLISON UNIVERSITY. His greatest reward was the knowledge of the growth of Methodist missions under his responsibility.

He died in Toronto, June 30, 1910.

G. H. Cornish, *Cyclopaedia of Methodism in Canada*. 1881. *Minutes* of the Toronto Methodist Conference, 1911.

G. S. FRENCH

SWAIN, CLARA (1834-1910), was the first qualified woman medical practitioner in INDIA and established the first modern hospital for women and children in Asia. She was born in Elmira, N. Y., on July 18, 1834. A graduate of a woman's medical college in PHILADELPHIA, Pa., she left for India as a missionary of the WOMAN'S FOREIGN MISSIONARY SOCIETY in November 1869.,

Miss Swain taught school in western NEW YORK near her birthplace and childhood home. When a woman phy-

sician became very ill and wrote of the need for women doctors, Clara Swain considered this matter and prayed about it. She soon decided that God called her to qualify for and practice medicine. While studying in Philadelphia, she began to think of missionary service to India. She was informed that the Woman's Union Missionary Society was planning to send a woman doctor to India. Just then Miss Swain learned of the organization in BOSTON of the Woman's Foreign Missionary Society of the M.E. Church, and on inquiry, she found that the society wanted to send her to India.

She and ISABELLA THOBURN were the first missionaries of the society, and they traveled to India together, arriving in BAREILLY, Jan. 20, 1870, during the session of the India Mission Conference.

While Dr. Swain was the first woman doctor in India and represented the newly established Woman's Foreign Missionary Society, the way had been prepared for her by the missionary men and women of the Board of MISSIONS. In 1864 the board had reluctantly appropriated $100 for medicines to be used by Dr. J. S. Johnson, but in doing so explained that they did not intend to encourage the practice of medicine and declared that "the preaching of the Gospel to the heathen is the primary work of the mission."

Another ordained missionary, DR. JAMES L. HUMPHREY, had studied medicine while on furlough, and on his return had organized classes of Indian women to be trained as medical assistants. The first trainees were recruited from the girls' orphanage in Bareilly.

In her book, *A Glimpse of India,* Dr. Swain wrote, "My medical work began the day of my arrival. As I had no medicines with me, I procured a few simple remedies from Mrs. Thomas who had been obliged to care for the sick in the mission compounds."

Her boxes containing books, medicines, charts, and skeleton came to Bareilly one month after her arrival, and ten days later she began a medical class with fourteen girls from the orphanage and three married women. So extraordinary did this seem that within a few weeks the lieutenant-governor of the provinces, Sir William Muir, and Lady Muir came to see what was being done and how the people were taking it. Soon Rajahs, nawabs, and leaders in many walks of life were excited about this new thing, a foreign woman possessing knowledge of medicine and eager to help sick women and the children, and to train Indian women. In her first year she treated over 1,300 patients.

In six years after Dr. Swain's arrival in India, three more Methodist women missionary doctors arrived in India. All three married Methodist missionaries. Miss N. Monelle became Mrs. HENRY MANSELL, Julia Lore became Mrs. George Harrison McGrew, and Lucille H. Green became Mrs. Nathan G. Cheney. Except during a health furlough from 1876 to 1880, Dr. Swain continued her work in Bareilly until 1884, when she went to Khetri State in Rajputana to treat the Rani Saheba. Her treatment was so successful that she was asked to become physician to the Rani and the women of the court. She was given permission to open a clinic for women and a girls' school. She decided that this was a God-given opportunity to develop, without expense to the mission, a new center for Christian witness. She was appointed to Khetri and continued her Christian service from that vantage point until March 1896, when poor health dictated that she should give way to some younger and stronger woman, and she returned to America. The Rani and the entire court pled with her to remain and assured her that she and her Lord would be loved and honored by them all to the end of their lives.

Late in 1906, she returned to India for the celebration of the Jubilee (the fiftieth anniversary) of the beginning of the M.E. missions in India. She was received with acclaim and affection everywhere she went, and especially in Bareilly and Khetri. She remained in India until the second week of January 1908. She died in Castile, N. Y., on Christmas morning in 1910, and is buried in a cemetery near her childhood home in Canandaigua, N. Y.

In the ninety-six years since she began her work for India's women, hundreds of dedicated Christian women from India and other countries have followed her example, and two great Christian medical colleges are now training hundreds of both men and women to heal millions without discrimination on account of creed, caste, or sex.

J. N. Hollister, *Southern Asia.* 1956.
J. E. Scott, *Southern Asia.* 1906.
C. A. Swain, *India.* 1909.   J. Waskom Pickett

SWALLOW, SILAS COMFORT (1839-1930), American preacher, editor and reformer, was born March 9, 1839 near Wilkes Barre, Pa., educated in the public schools, Wyoming Seminary (of which his father was a trustee), and in Susquehanna Seminary, Binghamton, N. Y. Before entering the ministry he taught school, studied law and served as a Lieutenant in the Civil War.

He entered the Baltimore Conference of the M.E. Church in 1863, transferring to the Central Pennsylvania Conference upon its organization in 1869, and in that conference served as pastor in a number of charges. He was eminently successful as a church builder, presiding elder and church financier. He was an eloquent and forceful preacher and revivalist, but also a vigorous and unrelenting foe of all types of evil. He opposed keeping open camp meetings on the Lord's Day because this required transportation facilities, and the selling of food on the grounds. To him the "arch enemy" was the traffic in spirituous liquors, and he fought this with every weapon he knew, sparing no one who supported the evil, or refused to join the Prohibition movement.

In 1892 he became Superintendent of the Methodist Book Room in Harrisburg and Editor of *The Central Pennsylvania Methodist.* Through this medium he supported the connectional interests of Methodism, but likewise wielded a cutting blade against all unrighteousness, as he saw it. He published an unrestrained exposé of graft on the part of Pennsylvania politicians in the state government and for this he was prosecuted and convicted, but later acquitted when the State Superior Court reversed the verdict. He was the Prohibition Party's candidate for mayor of Harrisburg, for the state legislature, for State Treasurer, for Governor and, in 1904, for President of the United States.

While he had no equal as a controversial figure in the Central Pennsylvania Conference, most of its members found him to be friendly and brotherly to them. He and his wife were very generous to the church, leaving to the Conference a home for retired ministers and other bequests.

Taylor University granted him the D.D. degree.

He represented his conference in the General Conferences of 1880 and 1896.

Christian Advocate (New York), Nov. 3, 1904; Aug. 28, 1930.
Journal of the Central Pennsylvania Conference, 1931.
Patriot-News, Harrisburg, Pa., March 7, 1965.
Who's Who in America, 1906, 1912-13.
     Charles F. Berkheimer

SWAN FAMILY, Americans of Swedish origin, made important contributions to the development of Indian Methodism in the State of Bengal.

Hilda Marie (1880-1957) was the first of the family to arrive in India. Her mother's sister, Hilda Larson, had long been a missionary in the Congo and in Angola, Africa. Hilda Swan was born in a parsonage near Sutton, Neb., June 23, 1880. She prepared for missionary service at the Chicago Training School and, reaching India in 1904, was appointed to Pakaur. Her appointments were varied and her accomplishments numerous. She died in America, Sept. 30, 1957.

Henry Marcus (1876-1963), four years older than Hilda, followed her to India. He was born in New Sweden, Iowa, March 12, 1876, and was educated at Northwestern University (Ph. B.), Garrett Biblical Institute (B.D.), and Chicago University (M.A.). He was highly trained in vocal and instrumental music.

He, too, was first appointed to Pakaur. Later appointments included the superintendency of three districts. He supervised the construction of many church and school buildings. At one time he was simultaneously manager of the Mount Hermon School estate, pastor of the Union Church, Darjeeling, and superintendent of the Pakaur District. He was editor-in-chief of the Bengali Methodist Hymnal. He returned to the United States on furlough in 1937, and because of his wife's ill health was unable to return to India. His wife, the former Edna Pauline Lundeen, was the mother of five sons and two daughters. She died April 4, 1948. He survived until June 3, 1963.

Beulah Marie Blomberg (1898-   ), a niece of Henry and Hilda, was born in Kansas City, Mo., Nov. 21, 1898. Her father was also a Methodist minister. She was graduated from Northwestern University (B.Sc.), and went to India as a missionary in 1923. Like her uncle and aunt, she began her work at Pakaur. Her appointments included the principalship of the Santali Boarding School, the supervision of buildings for the school, the management of village schools, and a hospital and district evangelism.

Charles Lundeen (1909-   ) is a son of Edna Lundeen and Henry Swan. He was born in Calcutta, India, Aug. 8, 1909, completed high school in India and continued his education in Chicago University (Ph.B.), Garrett Biblical Institute (B.D.), and Northwestern University (Ph.D.). He returned to India as a missionary in 1930 and was admitted to the Bengal Conference in 1932 and ordained there. In 1933 he married Kathleen Doucette, a missionary of the Canadian Baptist Mission in South India. His appointments have included teaching in the Mount Hermon School at Darjeeling in the Bengal Conference, and district superintendent of Sironcha and Hyderabad Districts, both now in the Hyderabad Conference. Since 1942 he has been in the United States and is now professor of sociology in Albion College.

     J. Waskom Pickett

SWANSEA, Wales. Those readers of the *Journals* who are acquainted with the geography of Swansea will remember the visits paid by John Wesley to "Oxwych" and will need no reminder that Methodism in and around Swansea had its birth not in the town itself but on the Gower peninsula. Of Gower, Wesley wrote, "Here all the people talk English and are, in general, the most plain, loving people in Wales." (*Journal,* vol. 5, p. 90. July 31, 1764.) Of Swansea, however, it is on record that "a man had need to be all fire who comes into these parts, where almost everyone is cold as ice." (*Journal,* vol. 5, August 27, 1763, p. 28.) As early as 1758 Wesley had touched on the borders of Gower while traveling from West Wales to Cardiff. He remembered the place, and at the Conference of 1760 proposed that the Yorkshireman THOMAS TAYLOR, subsequently president in 1796 and 1809, should explore possibilities of establishing the work in that area. This was done by Taylor in the winter of 1761-62—at his own expense, with no fixed abode and no circuit appointment. The work progressed slowly but surely until, at the Conference of 1795, Swansea appears as the head of a circuit consisting probably of Gower, Swansea, and Neath.

Our forefathers in the first decades of the nineteenth century are not famous for their written records. They were too busy living their Methodism amid the complex social changes of their time—but we have the record in the lives of those who have descended in almost unbroken sequence from the early pioneers. In Gower, for instance, Beynons, Bevans, Tuckers, and Jenkins have maintained a connection with Methodism over seven or more generations. The Wesleyan societies of Gower, having existed for nearly fifty years on cottage meetings, finally began to build their own chapels in the first years of the nineteenth century (Oxwich, 1808; Horton, 1813; and Pitton, 1833), and the first phase of Swansea Methodism was complete.

By this time, however, in Swansea itself, the Industrial Revolution was beginning to make its mark, and large numbers of Devonians and Cornishmen crossed the Bristol channel in search of employment. Soon after their arrival from the West Country the BIBLE CHRISTIANS of their number began to look for ways of practicing their faith in the English language, and in 1844 the mother church, Oxford Street, was built. The Vivian family, whose industrial enterprise begun in 1810 had drawn so many from over the water, began to expand their industry in Landore and Hafod, and from house meetings the Hafod society was born. The Vivians allowed land for the chapel, and Oxford Street gave generous support; and from the stone laying in 1873, the work and witness at Hafod began to consolidate. The Bible Christians' attempt to found a society on the east side of the Tawe in Delhi Street met with little success, and after about forty years it had to close for lack of support.

The earliest years of PRIMITIVE METHODISM in Swansea are not recorded, but it is known that in 1833-34, Henry Higginson, popularly known as "the roving ranter" or "six feet of eccentricity," tramped across from Blaenavon to mission Swansea. Within two months he had founded two societies, one in Swansea, the other at Mumbles. The Swansea society eventually grew into Pell Street, which in turn became the head of the "Prim" Circuit along with the West Country foundations of Pentrepoeth (1859), Plasmarl (1885), and Gorseinon (c. 1910). Of the Mumbles society there is no trace, except possibly that the

first Methodists in Murton, two miles away, were attached to the Primitive Methodist connection about 1840. The independent spirit of the "Prims" was so marked that even after Methodist Union they maintained their separate existence as the "Pell Street Circuit" until 1951.

The history of the WESLEYAN METHODIST movement in Swansea follows a pattern only slightly different from that of the other Methodist traditions which were almost wholly an "immigrant culture."

It was natural that Wesleyan Methodism should keep a strong hold in Gower, where Wesley himself had appeared—so strong in fact that in 1864 Gower became a separate circuit in the Wesleyan connection.

In the town of Swansea, the West-Country Wesleyans moving in were joined and strengthened by an indigenous Methodism as folk from Gower moved into the town, and they too began to work up their denominational causes. Almost simultaneously in the 1840's a little Wesleyan society at Sketty and Wesley, which became the circuit church, appear—and in Morriston, still the most Welsh area of Swansea, Glantawe Street (1840) had a society which was the center of the English-speaking community. At this time the Anglican Church was Welsh speaking, and a change of denomination meant a complete change of language and community.

As the second half of the nineteenth century began, the smaller Wesleyan societies which had now outgrown their meetings in houses and hired rooms committed themselves to a phase of building, and the older larger societies set their minds to rebuilding. And so there arose Landore (1861), missions at Greenhill and Sandfields, Murton (c. 1870), and Brunswick (1873); Sketty was rebuilt in 1876 and Mumbles, where HUGH PRICE HUGHES was converted, in 1877. At this point a tribute must go to the ministries of the Rawlings father and son, who guided the circuit through this massive expansion program. After this comprehensive plan, the Wesleyans built only three more chapels before METHODIST UNION in 1932, in Clydach, Brynmill, and Brynhyfryd.

At Union, Swansea found itself with two circuits. The Primitive Methodists showed the independence of the Welsh, and though they came into the connection they kept their (Pell Street) circuit. The United Methodists, the Wesleyans of Swansea, and the Wesleyans of Gower joined to form a "Swansea and Gower Circuit." This later arrangement, however, proved unsatisfactory, and in 1940 Gower received Synod's permission to resume the status of a separate circuit with a resident minister.

The Second World War and its aftermath caused some drastic reshaping of the circuits, for enemy action destroyed the Wesley, Pell Street, and Oxford Street chapels. The War Damage Commission made possible the erection of replacement chapels on the Townhill and Penlan Housing Estates, but the destructive effects of the war were deeper than damage to buildings only. The men who left the land in Gower, when they returned, returned neither to the land nor to the Gower chapels, and a considerably weakened Gower Circuit joined the town circuit again in 1962. The former Primitive Methodists, without their circuit church, had meanwhile joined the main Swansea Circuit in 1951.

The reshaping is still taking place. As a result of population shifts, old and proud chapels are becoming redundant. In contrast, on the housing estates the circuit has new buildings and the slow painstaking work of building up societies from the thousands of residents.

The circuit, though only too conscious of its weak points, is now unaware of its strength. Two hundred years of Methodism in continuous work and witness cannot easily be forgotten, and the same spirit of adventure and consecration that saw our fathers over the water and settled in the Land of Promise—the same Spirit guides their children.

PETER JENNINGS

SWARTZ, MORRIS EMORY (1868-1944), named after two bishops, was born in Pine Grove Mills, Pa. on Feb. 7, 1868. He was graduated from DICKINSON COLLEGE and DREW THEOLOGICAL SEMINARY with the A.B. and B.D. degrees respectively. Dickinson College honored him with a D.D. degree in 1910. Swartz served as pastor of a number of outstanding churches in the CENTRAL PENNSYLVANIA CONFERENCE and as Superintendent of the Harrisburg and Sunbury Districts. From 1919 to 1925 he was Secretary of the Washington Area and from 1925 to 1927, Editor of the *Washington Christian Advocate*. During the Centenary Movement he served as Director of the Speakers Bureau. He was a delegate to the GENERAL CONFERENCE of 1928 and 1932. He was also a member of the UNITING CONFERENCE of 1939 by virtue of his membership on the Commission on Union which drafted the PLAN OF UNION which united the three branches of Methodism.

He died on Easter Sunday, April 9, 1944, in York, Pa.

LESTER A. WELLIVER

SWEDEN. The Kingdom of Sweden comprises the greater part of the Scandinavian Peninsula in Northern Europe and has an area of 449,793 square kilometers, or 173,378 square miles, and a population of 7,978,000 (1969). The Lutheran Church is the state church. Several free churches count together 322,400 members, or 4.5 percent of the population. If they included youth members and Sunday school scholars, it would be 733,796 or 9.1 percent of the population.

JOHN WESLEY early had some positive connections with Sweden. Visitors from Sweden saw him and exchanged letters with him. Carl Magnus Wrangel, who had worked in the Swedish churches in America (1759-68), was returning home when he met John Wesley in LONDON and, inspired by him, organized a society for tracts and religious literature, *Pro fide et Christianismo*. There were also the learned professor Johan Henrik Lidén of Linköping and others.

In 1804 an English mechanical engineer, Samuel Owen (1774-1854), was invited by Swedish authorities to come to Sweden. He built and organized a workshop and a foundry and became "the father of the Swedish steam-fleet." He was a Methodist, as were several of his workers. For their benefit he asked the Wesleyan Missionary Society in London for a missionary to be sent to STOCKHOLM, and they sent J. R. STEPHENS from 1826-30 and then George Scott. During his time in Stockholm (1830-42) Scott played a most remarkable part in the free-church movement in Sweden. This is fully documented in the academic treatise by Gunnar Westin, a Baptist, who later became professor of church history at the University of Uppsala. Scott learned quite soon to preach in Swedish. His evangelistic fervor and zeal won many people, who gathered around his pulpit. By extensive traveling throughout the whole country Scott came into contact with many people. He made many friends, even among the nobility and the Swedish clergy. He influenced many who became leading men in the Swedish free-church movement: Carl Olof Rosenius (1816-68); F. O. Nilsson and Anders Wiberg, the first Baptist leaders; Carl Tellström, a missionary to the Laplanders and others. Scott was also one of the leading men in organizing a Swedish Tract Society, the Swedish Missionary Society (1835), and the Swedish Temperance Society in 1837.

He built a church in Stockholm, dedicated in 1840, first called the "English Church," later called *Betlehemskyrkan,* the Bethlehem Church. This became the headquarters of *Evangeliska Fosterlands Stiftelsen* (the "evangelical National Society for Home and Foreign Missions"), a historic religious shrine in Stockholm, unfortunately pulled down in 1953 to give room for modern skyscrapers. Traveling in England and America in order to collect money for this church and other evangelical enterprises, Scott painted a somewhat dark picture of the religious situation in Sweden, and this irritated the Swedes. The liberal press and some of the Lutheran clergy cooperated in making him and his work suspect and raised an outcry against him. A mob assaulted his church during a service on Palm Sunday in 1842. Scott himself escaped, but was compelled to leave Stockholm and his promising work. He died in Glasgow in 1874.

For the Methodist Church in Sweden, the work of George Scott became only an episode. The next visitation of Methodism to Sweden was through seamen and immigrants who were converted on the BETHEL SHIP, "John Wesley," in New York harbor. The leader of this important mission (1845-75) was a Swede, OLOF GUSTAF HEDSTROM (1803-77) from Småland. (See BETHEL SHIP.) During his leadership many Scandinavians were converted. Returning home to DENMARK, NORWAY, FINLAND, and Sweden, these began to witness about their personal experience of salvation in Jesus Christ, and gathered around them some groups of people. They used an American-Swedish Methodist hymnal edited in Chicago in 1862 by Jacob Bredberg, and in time asked for help from the Methodist Episcopal Church in America for the work thus begun in their homeland.

Johan Peter Larsson (1825-1915) was among the first Methodists to come in. Already in 1852-54 he had worked in Kalmar and other places on the east coast of Sweden. But he was sent to Norway and Denmark as one of the Methodist pioneers. He returned in 1866 and began work in GOTHENBURG. C. Levander and John Lindqvist worked in Gotland, in the Baltic Sea, and after many endeavors they persuaded the Methodist superintendent, CHRISTIAN WILLERUP, in COPENHAGEN to send them a helper in Adolf Cederholm. He, however, died early, only forty-five years of age, in 1867. At the same time Albert Ericson studied in Stockholm, preparing himself for a position as teacher and master of a Scandinavian educational institution in CHICAGO. He began to preach in a small hall in Benikebrinken, in Stockholm. Great crowds assembled to hear him, but he had to return to America.,

On the very day when the friends in Stockholm "with weeping tears" bade Ericson farewell, a pastor in Chicago, and a leading man in the Swedish-American Methodist work and editor of its organ, *Sändebudet* ("Åmbassador"), was invited to make a trip to his homeland. Victor Witting (1825-1906) came, preached to great crowds, saw the situation and the opportunity, and consented to stay. He returned to America to get his family and bring them with him to Stockholm. The Wittings arrived in November, 1867. In April, 1868, Victor Witting was appointed superintendent for the Methodist work in Sweden, which had before been under the superintendency of Christian Willerup in Copenhagen.

Born in Malmö in 1825, Witting became the organizer and founder of the Methodist Church in Sweden until it became an organized Annual Conference in 1876. Witting then returned to America, working there as one of the leaders of the Swedish-American Methodist work until his death in 1906.

New Year's Eve, 1867, the first Methodist WATCH-NIGHT service was held in Stockholm; and on Jan. 8, 1868, the first Methodist congregation was organized. This was St. Paul's, with fifty-seven members. A week later came the Emanuel Methodist Episcopal Church in Gothenburg with thirty-five members.

At a meeting in Stockholm, Sept. 17-24, 1868, seven men organized themselves and the Methodist work as *Svenska Metodistmissionärsföreningen*, the Swedish Methodist Missionary Society. Five places were mentioned in the proceedings: Stockholm, Gothenburg, Wallda, Wisby, and Kalmar. In Kalmar an old preaching house was bought in 1868. In Karlskrona the first Methodist chapel was built in 1869-70 and dedicated on Feb. 27, 1870. The word "missionary" was fortunately dropped. The first printed *Minutes of the Annual Meeting* reported about the Swedish preachers of the Methodist Episcopal Church (1874). That year there were already seventy-five places on the appointment list, divided among three districts.

Methodism spread like wildfire. It prompted, however, unrest and persecution. A preacher was sent to prison for some days. Another Methodist was killed. Numerous were the attempts by the Lutheran parish boards to hinder the Methodists and other free-church workers by forbidding them to preach and hold meetings. All kinds of conventicles (assemblies) were prohibited by the Edict against Conventicles (*Konventikelplakatet*) of 1726, and this edict was not cancelled until 1858 and 1860. It ordered even prison and expatriation for violators. In 1873 a new law about "confessors of foreign doctrines" was enacted, whereby dissenters were allowed to leave the state church, if they entered another Christian church. Only the Methodists, the Roman Catholics, and a few Baptist groups used this opportunity. There is a vivid description of an audience with the king by seventy-five Methodists from all over Sweden in February, 1875, when they presented a petition asking for the Methodists the right to be allowed to establish an independent denomination. The king was very gracious, but the permission was not given until March, 1876.

That same year, in August, 1876, in St. John's Church in UPPSALA, the Sweden Annual Conference was constituted, Bishop EDWARD G. ANDREWS presiding. Eight ELDERS, eighteen DEACONS, and twenty-three probationers were listed as charter members. Nine preachers were admitted on trial. Victor Witting returned to America. His task as superintendent was completed. He himself sums up later the results of the work during this period thus:

Less than nine years ago there had not been even one Class or Chapel, not one congregation or Sunday School. Now there were fifty-five traveling preachers, of whom twenty-six

were ordained. There were fifty-nine local preachers, who labour without salary or compensation. Out of their combined efforts during this brief period had come a membership of 5,563 persons and 4,931 children in 125 Sunday Schools. There were thirty-one churches and chapels. (Victor Witting, *Memoirs from My Life.*)

He also started in 1869 a church magazine, *Lilla Sändebudet*, a monthly which in 1882 was enlarged to a weekly periodical, *Svenska Sändebudet*, and, from 1873, *Söndagsskolklockan* for the SUNDAY SCHOOLS.

In 1873 a theological school was started in Örebro. It was moved to Stockholm in 1876 and to Uppsala in 1883, where it stayed until January, 1924, when the Union Scandinavian Theological School, Överas, in Gothenburg began its work.

The latter half of the nineteenth century was marked by great revivals throughout Sweden. Some of those reclaimed by these revivals stayed within the state church; others went into separate organizations. In 1848 the first Baptist congregation was organized; in 1856 came *Evangeliska Fosterlandsstiftelsen*, which, within the boundaries of the state church, desired to work for home missions and foreign missions; and then in 1878 came *Svenska Missionsförbundet* (the Swedish Covenant Church, Congregationalist).

But these decades were also years of unrest and dispute, and brothers in Christ exchanged not-too-kind pamphlets about dissenting doctrines and church orders. In 1905 the revival in WALES was felt as a wave of blessing and a new life all over the Scandinavian countries. Some years later the Pentecostal movement, in Scandinavia, introduced and prompted by a Norwegian Methodist minister, T. B. Barratt (1862-1940), awakened interest and hopes, but also caused serious divisions, especially among the Baptist groups. Under the strong leadership of Lewi Pethrus (1884-   ), however, it has grown to be the second in size among the Swedish free churches.

Through the decision in 1876 Sweden was incorporated as a full member in the world-wide Methodist Episcopal Church. American bishops presided at the annual conferences. Sweden was represented by delegates at succeeding GENERAL CONFERENCES. In Sweden as in all other lands it was always recognized as a great honor to be elected a delegate. A few were elected several times. THEODOR ARVIDSON, for instance, was six times a delegate, until he himself became a bishop in 1946. One of the lay delegates, Harold Lindström, has become widely known through his work, *Wesley and Sanctification* (London: Epworth Press, 1946). Representing only a small minority, the Swedish delegation could scarcely expect to exert too important an influence—except perhaps in one point: the influence and status of the laymen in the annual conferences, to which they were thoroughly committed.

More than thirty American bishops have visited Sweden in presiding at the annual conferences, most of them coming only once. The conference always found it interesting and inspiring to meet all these different and revered personalities.

In 1904 Europe got its first resident bishop in WILLIAM BURT, who lived in ZÜRICH; followed by the learned and greatly respected Bishop JOHN L. NUELSEN. In 1920 the first Scandinavian was elected bishop by the General Conference of that year—ANTON BAST from Copenhagen

—whose evangelistic fervor and extensive social work inspired many. He had to withdraw some years later after a legal judgment, which by many is still looked upon as a great mistake. Bishop RAYMOND J. WADE then took over episcopal responsibility in 1928 and made Stockholm his residence. The Second World War prevented the bishop's visit to Scandinavia; and during the war years in 1942 Theodor Arvidson by a formal decision of the COUNCIL OF BISHOPS of The Methodist Church was entrusted with the right to represent the resident bishop, and even to ordain. In consequence of his superintendency, after the war was over he was elected bishop at the CENTRAL CONFERENCE held in Gothenburg in April, 1946.

Ninety-nine years after the first annual conference there are, as these lines are written, 188 churches (144 charges); 90 active ministers, 36 retired, 142 local preachers. Members including probationers are 9,977. There are 156 Sunday schools with 4,712 children. During the period from 1899 until 1920 the total membership reached a high point in 1920 of 17,000 or more. Sunday schools reached their highest point in 1918 with 22,485 scholars.

The last decade has been a decline period for all Sunday schools. Most of the free churches have experienced a more or less continuing decrease. The state church recognizes all people born within the boundaries of Sweden as its adherents, if they have not formally and explicitly withdrawn from the church. Even free-church members have to pay sixty percent of the church taxes to the state church under the pretext that their pastors are keeping the register for all citizens. There is a growing opinion calling for a more complete religious freedom. The status of the free church is now regulated by the Law of Religious Freedom passed in 1951.

There has also been a remarkable renewal within the Lutheran State Church from about 1910. There has come about a new activity, inspired by the watchword: the Church of our Fathers. There is also a strong High-Church movement. But on the other side, Sweden is seeing a strong trend toward a blatant atheism; there are endeavors from a political standpoint which would exert an undue influence on the Church; and all this may lead to a separation between Church and state. On the other hand these trends are working in favor of the ecumenical movement, and deepening the feeling among the several churches that all must stay together. Methodism has always been open to and for such discussions.

In 1905 the first free-church meeting was held, with the intention that it should be repeated every fifth year. In 1918 Baptists, Methodists, and Congregationalists (Svenska Missionsförbundet) organized a Free Church Cooperation Committee. Some years later this was enlarged to embrace eight of eleven Swedish free churches, as a Free Church Council. A suggestion that this council should form a free-church confederation has so far not won approbation.

Social work has played an important part in Swedish Methodism. The Bethany DEACONESS Institution has attracted the most public attention and acknowledgment. It dates back to 1900, when a society of eighty-five persons was formed in Gothenburg. They appointed Anna Kaijser as their first deaconess. By an agreement with the Methodist Hospitals and Deaconess Institutions in Hamburg and Frankfurt am Main in GERMANY, Swedish girls were trained as nurses there until 1920, when a new law for health service in Sweden came into force. In cooperation with state institutions, the Methodist deaconesses now prepare for an examination approved by the state. Since 1946 young women from all the evangelical churches of Sweden have been received for a three-year course of study. The School of Nurses has about one hundred students; 340 registered nurses are now working within the foundation in many parts of Sweden, as well as in the mission field. For nearly fifty years Louise Erikson, a daughter of the manse, was the inspiring leader of the whole institution. A hospital in Stockholm is the center of the work.

Göte Bergsten (1896-1954) inspired the organization of a special work, where surgeons and pastors cooperate in helping people. The "Society of Saint Luke" works on an ecumenical basis, also training pastors in this special type of soul curing.

For the work among destitute children, an organization, F.V.B.U. (the Society for Care and Training of Children and Youth) was started in 1903. The first children's home was opened in 1905. Five homes and two day nurseries are now administered by the institution. State and community now pay a great part of the expenses.

So-called "Central Missions" worked in Stockholm, Gothenburg, and Malmö for several years, but the greater social responsibility now devolving on the state and communities has made such missions more or less unnecessary. In Stockholm the Central Mission is still at work.

Homes for aged people are provided by several churches and meet a real need in the present situation.

During the World Wars and afterward, a very extensive relief work was done, especially among children, in AUSTRIA and Germany as well as in Sweden's neighbor countries—Norway and Finland. Thousands of children and other refugees were taken care of, and the Methodists took their part. Gideon Henriksson and Theodor Arvidson were the leaders of that work.

Both evangelistic and social has been the work by the missionaries in foreign fields. The Conference in Norrköping in 1907 was an important starting point. Bishop J. C. HARTZELL, who had just returned from Africa, awakened a great enthusiasm. Two young men volunteered to go to Africa. One died after only two years' work, but the other, JOSEF A. PERSSON (1888-1964), gave over fifty years of his life to a very important and greatly blessed work in Mozambique and South Africa. Other Swedish men and women have worked as pastors and nurses in different parts of the world under the auspices of the Board of Missions in New York. In North Africa, LIBERIA, CONGO, ANGOLA, ZAMBIA, RHODESIA, MOZAMBIQUE, and the Union of SOUTH AFRICA, in INDIA, MALAYSIA, and SUMATRA, Swedish men and women have given their lives in a useful and meaningful service. Egon Aström (1903-45) became a martyr in Sumatra in 1945. His companion, Ragnar Alm, has now returned home after more than thirty years in the same field. The last years he has been acting as professor at the ecumenical Nommensen University.

Swedish Methodism has always felt a special obligation to help the Swedish-speaking Methodists in Finland in their shortage of ministers. More than seventy-five members of the Sweden Annual Conference have worked in Finland for several years, for two to twenty, or even thirty. Some have stayed there for the rest of their lives.

A Home Mission Society was started in 1896. It has been a very important organization, helping financially small congregations throughout the land. At Borås in the west and several places in the far north are churches which have been under the special care of the Home Mission. Karl Karlsson (1887-1962) was called the "Evangelist of Norrland," and one of his sons is the present leader of this important financial agency.

Recent years have been noteworthy for the erection of many church buildings. Towns and cities are growing rapidly. New housing areas need strategy even in directing the work of the churches. In the last quadrennium five new churches have been dedicated: in Sandviken, Filipstad, Östersund, Eskilstuna, Gävle. In Gothenburg four congregations are united in the Trinity Church, and a great church edifice is to be built. In Stockholm also some reorganization has been made necessary. In one of the suburbs, Bollmora, Methodists are taking the responsibility for a congregation on an ecumenical basis. Associate Membership is practiced in several places in a progressive degree.

Negotiations have recently been made with the Svenska Frälsningsarmen (Swedish SALVATION ARMY), a national branch or outgrowth, dating from 1905, from the International Salvation Army, about a closer practical cooperation between them and the Methodists. It is a comparatively small group of fifteen hundred members (soldiers) with thirty-five officers and twenty-two halls.

Youth work has been well organized ever since 1892. For many years it operated in Sweden as in America under the name of the EPWORTH LEAGUE. Methodists have been pioneers in Sweden for a special work among the teenagers, "Juniors." Two laymen, Ernst Börjesson, a manager, and Paul Rosell, a teacher, have been the great and suggestive leaders in that work.

Swedish Methodism has fostered a great many personalities not mentioned above, leaders as K. A. Jansson (1854-1933), K. E. Norström (1859-1918), Axel Engström (1863-1944), Aug. V. Norman (1866-1952), J. M. Erikson (1848-1915), Gustaf Wagnsson (1857-1929), G. A. Gustafson (1865-1922), August Strömstedt (1880-1944), Simon Lindberg (1899-   ), Henry Atterling (1901-   ); great preachers as Gustaf Lindstrom (1850-1931), MAGNUS FREDRIK ÅHGREN (1851-1937), Eric Schutz (1852-1915), Herbert Lihndaker (1885-1955), David Sandberg (1895-   ), and Gosta Rosenqvist (1908-   ), and many others. The work of Methodism in Sweden proceeds.

J. M. Erikson, *Metodismen i Sverige.* 1895.
Odd Hagen, *Methodism in Northern Europe.* 1961.
J. Julen, *Metodistkyrkan i Sverige.* 1923.
Minutes of the Annual Meetings of Swedish Preachers of the Methodist Episcopal Church, 1868-75. Ms.
Kyrkor och samfund i Sverige, omfattning och verksamhet (Official Statement about Churches and Religious Societies in Sweden), Stockholm, 1963.
Minutes of Sweden Conference, 1874-1965.
Svenska Folkrörelser, ii. Stockholm, 1937.
Gunnar Westin, *Den kristna friförsamlingen i Norden.* Stockholm, 1956.
—————, *George Scott.* 1928, 1929.
Victor Witting, *Minnen frön mitt lifå* (*Memoirs from My Life*).
                                        MANSFIELD HURTIG

SWEDESBORO, NEW JERSEY, U.S.A. **Old Stone Church** is one of the oldest Methodist preaching places in NEW JERSEY. It is located at the crossing of Bridgeport and Hendrickson Mill Roads near Swedesboro. The

section was known in the eighteenth century as the Adams Neighborhood, or Oak Grove. Methodist preaching began in Oak Grove through the work of visiting local preachers, and by 1793 it had become one of the first regularly established preaching places in New Jersey. In that year "Old Stone, Oak Grove" was built. The ground was donated by the Adams Family who resided in the vicinity. The indenture reads: "John Adams of the Township of Woolwich, county of Gloucester, State of New Jersey and Francis Asbury and Thomas Coke, Superintendents of the Methodist Episcopal Church in America . . . under articles in or of Doctrine, contained in or of discipline, revised and approved of by the General Conference held at Baltimore in November Anno Dom. one thousand seven hundred ninety three." It was signed before Joseph Blackwood, "one of the Judges of the Inferior Court of Common Please for Gloucester County." It was recorded in the Clerk's office of the above named county.

As time went on changes came to the community and, for many years, the church was not used except by the members of one of Old Stone's children, Bethesda Church, Swedesboro, who held a yearly anniversary service in the stone structure. Still more recently the SOUTHERN NEW JERSEY CONFERENCE of The United Methodist Church purchased some land adjacent to the church in anticipation of a building development. "Old Stone" at "Oak Grove" which has stood for so long a time as a memorial to early Methodism in New Jersey may soon again become an active church witnessing for Christ.

                                        FREDERICK E. MASER

SWEDISH METHODISM IN AMERICA. Methodist work among Swedish sailors and immigrants began aboard the "BETHELSHIP John Wesley" in NEW YORK harbor with the first sermon May 25, 1845 by OLOF G. HEDSTROM. He came from SWEDEN in 1825, married, was converted, and joined the Methodist ministry, 1835, NEW YORK CONFERENCE. His assignment to "Bethelship" was made because of an appeal to Methodists by Peter Bergner, converted sailor, for aid in his work among his countrymen. Hedstrom's work expanded, and soon (July 7, 1845) led to organization of Immanuel Church, Brooklyn, the first Swedish M.E. Church in the world.

Hedstrom's younger brother, Jonas, coming from Sweden in 1833, was also converted in New York. In 1838 he was a blacksmith in Victoria, Ill. Swedish immigrants were sent there by brother Olof, and Jonas was called upon to preach to them. This led to organization of Victoria Church, Dec. 15, 1846, and later other churches including Chicago, 1852.

Churches were founded in other midwestern states, in New England, along the Pacific coast, and in TEXAS. Greatest immigration from Sweden was in the 1880s. Census figures of 1920 showed Minnesota with over 112,000 foreign-born Swedes, Illinois over 105,000, New York over 53,000. Methodist work among them increased rapidly, especially in Chicago area. Churches were grouped as "Swede" districts in English-speaking conferences. A convention at Chicago, 1866, proposed Swedish conferences, and a theological seminary. The Northwest Swedish Conference was organized, 1877, for the north-central states. Rapid growth caused division in 1893 into the Central, Northern, and Western conferences.

EASTERN SWEDISH CONFERENCE, organized 1901, continued until merger 1941 with contiguous conferences. Pacific Coast Mission Conference organized 1908, merged 1928. Southern Mission Conference (Texas) existed from 1912 to 1926, and continued as a Swedish district several years, as did Pacific, before final absorption.

Peak of interest and action in the work and churches was reached about 1913-18. Statistics (1924) showed 208 churches in 179 charges, 20,622 members, 177 active pastors and 105 local preachers. Decreased immigration, disuse of Swedish language, and long distances in conferences were factors in the final dissolution of churches and conferences. Amalgamation into English-speaking conferences was facilitated by the 1924 General Conference Foreign-language Report, a result of anti-German feeling generated by World War I.

The Central, Northern, and Western conferences reunited in 1928 to strengthen their position. But their 1942 session, Chicago, was the final one, after 97 years as a language church. Theirs had been a vital mission among an immigrant people and their children. The parent church, which had mothered them, received them again. They had also been instrumental in founding Methodism in their native Sweden, also in supplying men and women for the ministry, and mission fields, especially INDIA and KOREA. An aggressive Woman's Foreign Missionary Society furnished funds and workers.

Education and benevolences were not forgotten. The Swedish Theological Seminary began in Galesburg (Illinois), 1870, moved to Galva 1872, Evanston 1875. First building was on NORTHWESTERN UNIVERSITY campus (1883), the second on Orrington Avenue, 1907. Seminary graduates numbered 366 by 1934, when the academy and theological programs ceased, and the resources were combined with those of the Norwegian-Danish Seminary, also in Evanston, to found a two-year Liberal Arts college. The new institution, Evanston Collegiate Institute, became KENDALL COLLEGE in 1950, which by 1967 had over 700 enrollment with quadrupled facilities. At Austin, Texas, Texas Wesleyan College functioned from 1912 to 1931, with High School and Junior College status.

Bethany Home and Hospital, CHICAGO, and Bethany Terrace, in nearby Morton Grove, continue the work begun in EVANSTON, 1890, relocated in Chicago, 1892. First building erected 1893, added to in 1920, with hospital addition, 1927. Two large apartment buildings for the aged were also erected, and Bethany Terrace in 1965. Susanna Home for Young Women ministered from 1907 until merged with Bethany in 1929. Emmanuel Home, Clay Center, Kansas, organized 1900, merged in 1929. Total Bethany facilities are: 850 beds and rooms, staff of 615, assets $13,000,000, budget $3,500,000. The Home, and Kendall College, are affiliated with Rock River Conference. In New York State, Bethel Home, begun in Brooklyn in 1911, moved to Ossining 1920, cared for 40 aged in 1941.

City Mission work among immigrants was conducted in Chicago 1904-23. Scandinavian Seamen's Missions at New York City and Galveston, Texas, continue the work of Hedstrom's Bethelship. An insurance society, with peak membership of 5,400, served its members from 1878 to 1928. Camp meetings and revivals were the meat and drink of Swedish Methodists. Their Book Concern published a Christmas annual, *Vinter-Rosor*, and other journals and literature, including a weekly, *Sändebudet* (The Messenger), founded 1862, now published monthly. Central Northwest Fellowship meets annually in Chicago, the center of activities over the years.

It would be difficult to list outstanding leaders, but these should be mentioned: Olof and Jonas Hedstrom, Victor Witting, N. O. Westergreen, Albert Ericson, C. G. Nelson, William Henschen, James T. Wigren, D. S. Sorlin, Alfred Anderson, Carl G. Wallenius, Leonard Stromberg, Winnie M. Gabrielson, O. E. Olander.

HENRY G. NYLIN

SWEET, EVANDER McIVER, SR. (1837-1932), American minister, educator and writer, was born in Quincy, Fla., Oct. 27, 1837. On June 9, 1862, Evander McIver Sweet married Cornelia Anna Brown, musician and artist, daughter of Col. James E. Brown, State Senator, and granddaughter of Rev. John Brown, second president of Franklin College (University of Georgia). Though an invalid twenty years, she organized thirty-eight WOMAN'S FOREIGN MISSIONARY SOCIETIES and related groups.

On May 28, 1873, Sweet, a school-teacher of eight years in Hemphill, TEXAS, was licensed to preach in Sabine County. Also the Beaumont District Conference elected him president of their school in Jasper County. This was the only church school in East Texas, founded eight years after the Civil War ended, when all schools had been disbanded.

In 1880-81, Sweet was president of Jefferson District Conference School at Daingerfield. Among his pupils were Senator Morris Shepherd, Governor O. B. Colquitt, and W. D. Bradfield.

Sweet was transferred, in 1885, to CENTRAL TEXAS CONFERENCE, serving as pastor at Waxahachie, Arlington Circuit, and Manfield Circuit. Appointed president of Granbury College (Weatherford College) 1890-92, he also edited the Granbury *Collegian*. Church publications printed both his prose and poetry. He was superannuated in 1895. He died at the age of ninety-four, and is buried in Oakwood Cemetery, Forth Worth, Texas.

Granbury *Collegian*, October 1890.
Journal of the Northwest Texas Conference, 1909.
Journal of the Central Texas Conference, 1914, 1916, 1936.
O. W. Nail, *Texas Centennial Yearbook*. 1934.

PEARL S. SWEET

SWEET, WILLIAM HENRY (1843-1919), a pioneer KANSAS educator and minister, was born in Brown County, Ohio, on July 14, 1843, the son of Benjamin F. and Jane (Robinson) Sweet. He served briefly in the Union army, finished normal school, taught school a year and then graduated from OHIO WESLEYAN with an A.B. in 1872 and an M.A. in 1875. In 1885 Chaddock College, Quincy, Ill., awarded him an honorary doctorate. On Sept. 7, 1875, he married Rose A. Williams. Their children were Paul, WILLIAM WARREN, Emma, Ruth, and Ralph.

From 1872-77 Sweet was professor of mathematics at BAKER UNIVERSITY, and he served there as president from 1879-86. He accepted the presidency of Baker University at Baldwin City when it was at a low ebb with only forty students. During his term as president Century Hall was built, and in six years time the student body grew to

475—four more than were enrolled at Kansas University that year.

His pastorates in the KANSAS CONFERENCE were Centralia and Holton. In 1886 he joined the new KANSAS WESLEYAN UNIVERSITY faculty as professor of psychology and ethics. He taught there for two years, was field secretary for Wesleyan in 1909-10, and served as a trustee of that institution from 1889-1914. His NORTHWEST KANSAS CONFERENCE pastorates were: First Church, Salina; Minneapolis; Beloit; Downs; Lincoln; Marquette; University Church, Salina and Mentor. He served six years as PRESIDING ELDER of the Salina District. He was a member of the 1892 and 1896 GENERAL CONFERENCES.

In 1915 the Sweets retired to Centralia, Wash., where he died on Jan. 5, 1919, and she died nineteen days later on January 24. During his retirement, Sweet compiled and wrote *A History of Methodism in Northwest Kansas,* which his children published posthumously.

Alumni Record of Baker University, 1917.
Minutes of the Kansas and Northwest Kansas Conferences.
C. F. Price, *Who's Who in American Methodism.* 1916.
W. H. Sweet, *Northwest Kansas.* 1920.   INA TURNER GRAY

SWEET, WILLIAM WARREN (1881-1959), American minister and noted historian, was born at Baldwin, Kan., Feb. 15, 1881. He graduated from OHIO WESLEYAN UNIVERSITY in 1902 and from DREW THEOLOGICAL SEMINARY in 1906. He earned the degrees of A.M. and Th.M. from Crozier Theological Seminary in 1907, Ph.D. from the University of Pennsylvania in 1912. He received a D.D. from CORNELL COLLEGE in 1922 and L.H.D. from DePAUW UNIVERSITY in 1956. Most of his life was spent as a professor of history. He taught at Ohio Wesleyan, 1911-13; at DePauw, 1913-27; University of Chicago, 1927-46; GARRETT THEOLOGICAL SEMINARY, 1946-48, and PERKINS SCHOOL OF THEOLOGY, 1948-52. He was the author of numerous historical books including *History of the North Indiana Conference; Rise of Methodism in the West; Circuit Rider Days Along the Ohio; Indiana Asbury-DePauw University; Methodism In American History; A History Of Latin America,* and others. He died at Dallas, Texas, Jan. 3, 1959, remembered as one of Methodism's outstanding historians.

                                            HAROLD THRASHER

SWEET MEMORIAL INSTITUTE is a complex of Methodist institutions and services in SANTIAGO, CHILE, that has provided, from time to time, training for other Christian vocations; training for ministers; services to the community in the form of a day nursery, club work, and recreation; and training for workers in child care.

The institute began as a training school for pastors, but theological education has now been turned over to an interdenominational center, and Sweet Memorial Institute works entirely in the field of child care and the training of workers for child care.

In June 1914, a biblical seminary was organized in Santiago under leadership of GOODSIL F. ARMS. His purpose was to provide a more thorough preparation for Chilean pastors than could be achieved through the conference course of study. It was begun as a joint project of the Methodist and Presbyterian churches, but almost always included students from other denominations. In 1938 the Presbyterian Church withdrew and, since the

Methodist Church did not have financial resources to maintain the seminary, it was closed. Students who made preliminary studies as prescribed by the conference were referred to the Union Theological Seminary (FACULTAD EVANGELICA DE TEOLOGIA) in BUENOS AIRES, ARGENTINA.

In 1924 a donation by the Sweet family of TOPEKA, Kan., U.S.A., made it possible to organize the Sweet Memorial Institute in honor of Timothy and Annie B. Sweet. Its purpose was to prepare young women for various phases of local church activity. Emphasis was given to social service since the institute was located in a lower-income section of Santiago.

In April 1926, the first class of seven young women entered the school under direction of ARTHUR WESLEY. In June of that year a dispensary was opened, with emphasis upon the preventive aspect of medical care. The following year, under leadership of Mrs. Scott Hauser, a day nursery was established to care for the children of working mothers. The dispensary and day nursery gave students the opportunity to practice theories that were discussed in formal classes.

In 1928 the program was amplified to include club work with the neighborhood children, a library, and an organized recreation program. This development took place under the direction of Mrs. WALTER CARHART.

The medical work and day nursery were reorganized in August 1940, under leadership of Florence Prouty. The Sweet Memorial Day Nursery has become one of the outstanding pioneers in child care, not only in Chile but throughout Latin America.

The day nursery also is an observation and practice center and a postgraduate study center for the schools of nursing of the University of Chile and Catholic University, the National Health Service, and the schools of medicine of the two universities. The courses are attended by nursery school teachers, social workers, pediatricians, and midwives from all over Latin America.

In 1945 the training school aspect of Sweet Memorial Institute was reorganized as the Training School for Christian Workers. The course of study was revised to include the needs of young men who were preparing for the ministry. Thus the biblical seminary was reopened and formed a pre-seminary for those young men and young women who would complete their formal theological preparation in Buenos Aires.

In 1962 the training school was closed, to be incorporated into the new Theological Community. Sweet Memorial Institute continues to serve through the day nursery and the club program for the neighborhood.

Barbara H. Lewis, *Methodist Overseas Missions.* 1960.
                                                 JOYCE HILL

SWENGEL, URIAH FRANTZ (1846-1921), American Evangelical minister and bishop, was born on a farm near Middleburg, Pa., Oct. 28, 1846. The Christian atmosphere of this home is attested by the fact that not only he, but his three brothers, entered the ministry. In the latter years of the Civil War he joined the Union Army, and was present at the surrender of General Lee at Appomattox. Following a brief tenure as a teacher and a short period of time in college, at the age of twenty-one he sought and was granted a license to preach in 1867 by the Central Pennsylvania Conference of the EVANGELICAL ASSOCIATION. He was ordained DEACON in 1869, and ELDER in 1871. For a period of thirty years he was the pastor of churches in central PENNSYLVANIA. Three times he was pastor of Trinity Church, YORK. He was then elevated to the office of PRESIDING ELDER, in which capacity he served for twelve years in what was then The UNITED EVANGELICAL CHURCH. He was finally granted the highest office of the church, and served with faithfulness and distinction as a bishop for the eight year maximum permitted by the church.

Uriah Swengel was intensely interested in the work of the SUNDAY SCHOOL and Christian Endeavor. For the church's Leadership Training program he wrote a book, *Modes and Methods of Work.* He also served for a time as editor of Sunday school literature for his denomination. His interest in temperance is indicated by his active leadership in the work of the Anti-Saloon League.

He was one of the chairmen of the joint commission on union, which led, the year following his death, to the union of The United Evangelical Church and the Evangelical Association to form the EVANGELICAL CHURCH.

He was the author of several books and was awarded the honorary M.A. and D.D. degrees.

Swengel was married three times: to Mary Hipple, Lottie Antony, and Beulah Buck. The third union was blessed with two children, Clark and Ada.

After a lengthy and often painful illness he died at his home at HARRISBURG, Pa., March 8, 1921. He was buried at York with the funeral address being given by Bishop W. H. FOUKE.

Yearbook of the United Evangelical Church, 1922.

HOWARD L. ORIANS

SWITZERLAND is a federal republic of southwestern central Europe, bordered in the north by GERMANY, west by FRANCE, south by ITALY, and east by AUSTRIA and Liechtenstein. It contains 15,962 square miles, and in its habitable sections is densely populated by 5,700,000 (1966) inhabitants.

There are four national languages: in the north and east, German (69%); in the west, French (20%); in the south, Italian (9.5%); and in some sections of the east Retoroman (1.2%). Formerly a federation of independent states, the Swiss Confederation is organized as a federal state, including twenty-five cantons (states). In 1291 the first three cantons signed their first covenant. It has had its present extension since 1815. Bern is the federal capital. Other important cities are Zürich, Basel, Geneva, Lausanne, St. Gallen, Lucerne, Winterthur, and Biel.

Because of its political neutrality Switzerland is not a member of the United Nations organization, but it is involved in all its humanitarian, cultural, and administrative institutions. GENEVA is of course the European site of the United Nations and the center of many of the above-mentioned institutions. Geneva is also the place where the Red Cross movement was initiated and still is its world center.

More than half of the population are Protestants (of the calvinistic type); forty-five percent are Roman Catholics; and about one percent are Old or Christian Catholics.

Protestantism. Switzerland, in the sixteenth century, was one of the most important centers of the Reformation on the European continent. The movement started in ZÜRICH through the labors of Huldrych Zwingli. His successor, Heinrich Bullinger, was the author of the *Confessio Helvetica Posterior,* the official confession of faith in a number of Protestant countries. Under the influence of John Calvin, Geneva became the center of the French-speaking and other reformed churches. Calvin's influence was so important that Geneva was called the "Rome of Protestantism."

The more industrial cantons, as Zürich, Basel, Berne, Geneva, Vaud, accepted the Reformation movement, while the so-called primitive cantons stayed Roman Catholic. For a long time, until the middle of the nineteenth century, there were serious tensions between the respective cantonal governments because of confessional questions.

Methodism. JOHN WILLIAM FLETCHER (Jean Guillaume de la Fléchère), a native of Nyon on the Lake of Geneva and a close friend of JOHN WESLEY, is considered to be the first Swiss Methodist. From 1777 to 1781, paying a visit from England to his home country, he preached there and organized SUNDAY SCHOOL classes for about 100 children.

In this French-speaking section of Switzerland, the influence of Robert Haldane, a Methodist from Scotland, was even greater. In Geneva leading church men, as Gaussen, Frédéric Monod, Merle d'Aubigné, and César Malan, were deeply influenced by his preaching. Expelled from the Geneva national Protestant Church, these "Methodists" organized what is still known as the Geneva Free Evangelical Church. Their influence reached Bern and its vicinity, where the "Evangelical Society" was formed. This organization still exists as a part of the Bernese national Protestant Church.

In 1839 Henri Olivier, of St. Peter's Church in Lausanne, was influenced by John Wesley's and John William Fletcher's writings. Because of his new views he had to leave the church. In 1840 CHARLES COOK, a Wesleyan minister, was sent from England to Lausanne and a church organized. The work prospered for a certain time. In Lausanne the John William Fletcher Memorial Church, now called Chapelle du Valentin, was built and a theological seminary for the French-speaking work on the European continent established. In 1901 after a rapid decline in membership the last Methodist sermon in the French-speaking WESLEYAN METHODIST CHURCH was preached, and the beautiful building was sold to the German-speaking M.E. Church.

Methodist Episcopal Church. The year 1856 marks the beginning of the work of Methodism in Switzerland as it exists today. Ernst Mann, a young convert from the Palatinate (Germany) went to Geneva and Lausanne, having heard that Germans and German-speaking Swiss people were almost without spiritual care in these French-speaking cities. In the same year Hermann zur Jakobsmuhlen was sent to Zürich and began to hold services there. The work grew rapidly, circuits were formed, and QUARTERLY CONFERENCES were organized. The whole work then was a part of the Germany and Switzerland Mission of the M.E. Church, later of the Germany and Switzerland Annual Conference. Its very able leader was LUDWIG SIGISMUND JACOBY.

In 1887 the Switzerland Annual Conference was organized with thirty ministers and 5,634 members. The first session was held in Bern, Bishop W. X. NINDE being the presiding bishop. The conference territory was divided into two, sometimes three, districts. For nearly thirty years Bishop JOHN L. NUELSEN, who was born in Zürich but was an American citizen, was the able and much loved leader of Methodism in Switzerland. He resigned with honor his responsibilities at the UNITING CONFERENCE in May 1939, in KANSAS CITY.

The Methodist Church. During the Second World War, when no bishop could reach Switzerland, FERDINAND SIGG was regularly elected as the president of the conference. After the war Bishop PAUL N. GARBER and Bishop ARTHUR J. MOORE had oversight of the work. When the CENTRAL AND SOUTHERN EUROPE CENTRAL CONFERENCE (Geneva Area) was formed under the leadership of Bishop Arthur J. Moore, Ferdinand Sigg was elected as its first bishop. After his death in 1965, Bishop FRANZ SCHAFER, also a member of the Switzerland Annual Conference and a DISTRICT SUPERINTENDENT, was elected in his place.

In 1965 there were two districts, with sixty-three circuits, ninety-three ministers and 10,898 members. Twenty of these ministers are retired. The theological training of Swiss Methodist ministers takes place at the seminary maintained by the German and Swiss Conferences together at FRANKFURT, Germany, an institution that has been distinguished by the services of such teachers as J. W. E. Sommer, Paulus Scharpf, Theophil Spoerri, and FRIEDRICH WUNDERLICH. These men and others have formed and molded an entire generation of preachers. It is usual that one of the teaching staff is a member of the Switzerland Annual Conference. During the two world wars the border between Switzerland and Germany was closed, so it was necessary for Swiss Methodism to send its students to the theological seminary of the Basel Mission in BASEL.

Swiss Methodism shows a vital interest in missions. In connection with the Board of MISSIONS and the Women's Society of Foreign Missions in the United States, missionaries were sent especially to CHINA, MALAYA, and the Indies. In 1966 Swiss missionaries worked in connection with Methodist churches in North Africa, in the CONGO, and in ARGENTINA. Many Methodists work with interdenominational missions, as the Philafrican Missionary Society in ANGOLA (Africa), and the Swiss Missionary Society in SOUTH AFRICA. Some also went to PERU for the Swiss Mission to the Latin American Indians.

During the last few decades Swiss Methodists have developed a remarkable system of social concern. The Switzerland Annual Conference runs three Homes for the Aged in Horgen, Eschlikon, and Basel-Hammerstrasse. Local Methodist churches own smaller homes for the aged in Geneva and Basel-Allschwilerplatz. In Degersheim a fine orphanage is the home of about twenty-five children, who mostly come from broken families. "Viktoria," a former hotel, was purchased in 1933. It is a most beautiful vacation place at Teuti-Hasliberg, in the Bernese Oberland. By and by it became the important center of a most useful training of lay people.

The DEACONESS motherhouse "Bethany" (*Diakonissenhaus Bethanien*) is an organization of its own, but strongly related to the Methodist conference. The 256 sisters, most of them trained and registered nurses, are all members of the Methodist Church, and the two directors are ministerial members of the conference. Its center is at Zürich. It runs two hospitals and a number of homes for the Aged.

One of the most important arms of Swiss Methodism is its publishing house, the CHRISTLICHE VEREINSBUCHHANDLUNG. Founded very early as a branch of the German Methodist publishing firm in BREMEN, it now has its own important printing facilities, a book shop with branches in several towns, and a publishing firm, the Gotthelf-Verlag. In its buildings at the Badenerstrasse 69, in Zürich, are located the offices of the administration of the Swiss Methodist Church.

In spite of the fact that the Methodist Church is a minority church among the state-related Protestant, Roman Catholic, and Old Catholic Churches in Switzerland, its influence in the religious life of the country is greater than statistics indicate. Its voice is heard in the ecumenical organizations and groups. After union with the E.U.B. Church, the Evangelische Gemeinschaft, which body was only a little smaller, it became the largest free church in Switzerland.

Evangelische Gemeinschaft began its work in Switzerland when EVANGELICAL ASSOCIATION ministers from America entered in 1865, following the sessions of the Germany Conference, seeking an opening for work in this country. When American missionaries were not accepted favorably, the Germany Conference (Evangelical Association) sent Jacob Schmidli, a native Swiss minister. His work was concentrated in the vicinity of Bern, which eventually became the center of denominational life in Switzerland. A district of the Germany Conference was formed in 1868, and in 1879 the Switzerland Conference was organized.

In 1868 the Germany Conference sent J. P. Schnatz as missionary to Alsace, France. It wasn't until Conrad Zwingli, a Swiss, assumed the work that it began to grow. The relationship with the Swiss conference continued in both Alsace and Lorraine, and today this area still remains an integral part of the Switzerland Conference.

A branch publishing house was opened by the Stuttgart plant of the Germany Conference in Bern in 1895. It soon developed into an independent enterprise under the auspices of the Switzerland Conference. Although it did not operate presses, it served as a center for editorial and publication work.

A Deaconess Society was established in Strassburg, France, by the Bethesda motherhouse in Germany in 1889. It became the center for deaconess work in France, just as later Basel was to serve for Switzerland. The earliest work of this society in Switzerland was begun in 1896 at Zürich. In 1923, the French and Swiss work became autonomous, although friendly relations have continued with the society in Germany. In 1966, there were 108 deaconesses in Switzerland, with two hospitals and several homes under their care, while in France there were forty-four deaconesses with a hospital and home to supervise.

Since there was no theological seminary established by the Swiss conference, ministerial students enrolled at the Reutlingen, Germany institution. The Switzerland Conference assisted in the control of this school along with the three conferences in Germany.

The Switzerland Conference (E.U.B.) in 1966 had 101 organized congregations and 128 unorganized appointments. There were seventy-one ministers on the roll, 6,219 members, and an additional 9,091 persons who were considered "friends of the church."

The Switzerland Conference met annually, but quadrennially it became a part of the European Central Conference of the church for the purpose of integrating the total work in Europe. It also sent representation to the quadrennial sessions of the GENERAL CONFERENCE of the denomination in America.

R. E. Grob, *Bischofliche Methodistenkirche in der Schweiz.* 1931.
Minutes of the Switzerland Annual Conference.
John L. Nuelsen, *Kurzgefasste Geschichte des Methodismus.* Bremen, 1929.   HERMANN SCHAAD

SWORMSTEDT, LEROY (1798-1863), American minister and BOOK AGENT of the Western BOOK CONCERN from 1844 to 1860. He was the person named as defendant in the suit brought by the M.E. Church, South, to recover its share of the proceeds of the Book Concern following the division of the M.E. Church in 1844. He was born in MARYLAND in October 1798, converted at the age of eighteen, and later was admitted into the OHIO CONFERENCE. He filled a number of prominent stations and was presiding elder on the Lancaster, Zanesville, and CINCINNATI districts. In 1836 he was elected assistant agent of the Western Book Concern then located at Cincinnati, and in 1844 he was elected by the GENERAL CONFERENCE to be its principal agent. He became Book Agent at the time of the bisection of the M.E. Church and when in 1868 the General Conference of the Northern Church repudiated the PLAN OF SEPARATION, the Southern Church sued to recover their equity in the Book Concern. Swormstedt was necessarily named as defendant. The suit was eventually decided in favor of the South in 1857 by the Supreme Court of the United States. Swormstedt, however, continued to travel through the South representing the Book Concern while the Southern Conferences were organizing into a new connection. His presence was noted at the 1844 session of the MISSISSIPPI CONFERENCE by its historian, John G. Jones, who in that era of bitter partisanship rather tartly observed that Swormstedt was one to whom "he would not like to owe anything but love, unless he could have the money ready as soon as called for" (Jones, Vol. 2, p. 504). Swormstedt, however, was a faithful servant of the Church and Bishop SIMPSON says of him that "he had systematic habits, fine business qualifications, and labored earnestly for the success of the Church in every department which he filled." He died on Aug. 27, 1863, after he had superannuated in 1860.

M. Simpson, *Cyclopaedia.* 1878.   N. B. H.

SYDNEY, Australia, capital of NEW SOUTH WALES, is the site of the first British settlement in AUSTRALIA which began under Governor Phillip in 1788. The first community consisted, in the main, of a convict colony. From such humble beginnings, Sydney has grown into a city of three million people.

Methodism began in Sydney under the leadership of devout Methodist laymen, who, sensing the spiritual needs of the colony, requested the British CONFERENCE by letter in 1812 to appoint a minister. (For his coming and the development of work in Sydney see NEW SOUTH WALES CONFERENCE.)

Special present day institutions in Sydney here follow:

Central Methodist Mission. In 1884 the historic York Street Methodist Church in downtown Sydney became the Central Methodist Mission. In outward appearance the stately old building remained unchanged, despite the new name, but the change represented a change in strategy and in emphasis. The church continued its preaching ministry but it added a new dimension of a practical down-to-earth service to the needy of Sydney. It became identified with the unemployed, the prostitutes, the orphans and unwanted children, the down trodden and the defeated, the deserted and the destitute.

Since 1884, the Mission has continued to serve the needs of all kinds of people, adapting its programme to meet changing circumstances. At present 730 people are cared for in the fourteen homes, hostels and hospitals controlled by the Mission. Their ages range from six months to the late nineties. Their needs cover a wide spectrum of human need.

A series of attractive buildings in delightful surroundings scattered throughout 100 miles of the Sydney metropolitan area provide a network of compassion for them.

The homes are: *Frank Vickery Village, Sylvania.* A self-contained village for the aged with accommodation for eighty people in single and double units and flats, together with a chapel and recreation area. Named in honor of Frank Vickery, a Mission benefactor and a descendant of the Hon. Ebenezer Vickery, M.L.C., who purchased the Lyceum property in 1906 and gave it to the Mission for its headquarters. *Hoban House, Maroubra,* a former private hotel providing accommodation in individual rooms for fifty aged men and women. Named in honor of S. J. Hoban, Superintendent of the Mission, from 1915 to 1921. *Sunset Lodge, Enfield.* A home providing accommodation and some nursing care for fifty aged ladies. *W. G. Taylor Home, Narrabeen,* provides single room accommodation for 100 aged men and women. Named in honor of the founder and first Superintendent of the Central Methodist Mission, W. G. TAYLOR.

Hospitals include *Lottie Stewart Hospital, Dundas.* A 114-bed geriatric hospital now financed by the State Government, but controlled by a board appointed by the Central Methodist Mission. *Waddell House, Ashfield.* A 35-bed private hospital specializing in psychiatric care and treatment. Australia's first Christian psychiatric hospital.

Children's Homes are *Bernard-Smith Children's Home, Pymble.* A large two-story residence providing accommodation and long term care for twenty-one children whose family life has been disrupted by social tragedy. *Dalmar Children's Home, Carlingford.* A settlement of cottages providing accommodation and long term care for 100 children in family style living. Most children are the victims of social tragedy; very few are orphans. One of the two features of the Mission's programme of institutional care that traces its origin back to the early days of the Mission. Although the Dalmar home has been located at three different sites it has provided an unbroken record of service for needy children for almost eighty years. *Gateway Children's Home, Lewisham.* The newest addition to the Mission's child care programme, this home, open in 1964, provides short term care for children whose family life is disrupted by sudden emergencies. It accommodates up to fifteen children and occasionally one or two mothers for up to three weeks while social workers arrange a long term solution to the problem which brings each child into the home.

Hostels are *Evangelists' Training Institute.* An Institute established by W. G. Taylor in the early days of the Mission to train young men in evangelism to prepare them for entry to the Christian ministry. The Institute offers practical experience, a formal lecture programme and study facilities for young men and women to gain entry to the theological course leading to the Methodist ministry in New South Wales. *Men's Hostel, Francis Street, East Sydney.* A Hostel offering cubicle type accommodation for thirty men who are being rehabilitated from "skid row." *Night Refuge, Francis Street, East Sydney.* A night refuge offering overnight accommodation for thirty derelict men. *Youth Hostel, Francis Street, East Sydney.* A Hostel for thirty-five Australian and overseas students living temporarily in Sydney for university and technical college training at a tertiary level. *Margaret Hallstrom Home, Leichhardt.* A home for unmarried mothers offering accommodation for up to twelve girls at any one time.

The headquarters of the Mission are now located in the two million dollar Wesley Centre, a nine floor office building in the heart of the city. The building includes three floors of community facilities where an extensive group dynamics programme is undertaken, a restaurant and dining room, a chapel and the Lyceum Theatre, used by the Mission as a church on Sunday evenings.

Life Line is the name given to a twenty-four-hour telephone counselling service established originally in Sydney by the Central Methodist Mission in March 1963, and now in existence throughout the world. The Life Line concept is based on a telephone manned by trained volunteers twenty-four hours a day with a well publicized number, "trouble team" facilities providing instant mobility in relation to suicide emergencies and an extensive follow up counselling programme staffed by professionals.

Other centers based on the Sydney pattern are now in existence in Adelaide, South Australia; Brisbane, Queensland; Morwell, Victoria; Broken Hill, Newcastle and Wollongong, New South Wales. Overseas there are centers in Canada, New Zealand, South Africa and the United States of America.

In the United States the centers are known by the name "Contact." All of the centers are affiliated with Life Line International, an organization set up in 1966 to promote the establishment of new centers, to act as a means of exchange for ideas, experience and know-how among existing centers and to coordinate standards of operation and training.

Newtown Methodist Mission. Newtown circuit was formed in 1855 by division from the Sydney South Circuit. As the suburbs of Sydney developed so it was found necessary to divide the circuit as in 1866 to form Ashfield, in 1884 Stanmore, and in 1886 Rockdale. Newtown itself became a Mission in 1928 under the leadership of A. E. Walker.

Population shifts have to a large degree determined its activities. Apart from normal circuit activities it is noted for its, social work. It provides a specialized nursing service for Aged People and fellowship amenities for pensioners. It maintains two hostels which provide accommodation for country youth employed in Sydney.

Newtown Church was built in 1860 and is often spoken of as a Cathedral church together with Waverley. Well attended Youth Groups and Senior Citizens Societies are in its membership but with the exodus of young families there are very few indigenous couples within the 30-45 age group.

Wayside Chapel, King's Cross, has come to be a special institution in Sydney's religious life. The former William Street Methodist Church, built in 1871, was one of the landmarks of the city and located strategically where the main thoroughfare carried the traffic of the city to Kings Cross and beyond to the Eastern Suburbs. For many years, in common with many other noble religious monuments in the changing inner city, its decline in strength, both congregationally and in terms of influential witness, was a source of concern to the New South Wales Methodist Conference.

Baffled as to what to do, the Methodist Church sold the property in 1955. The final services in this grand old church edifice were held on July 24 of that year. A portion of the sale price was used to purchase another property (to be used as a hostel) on the eastern side of Kings Cross. This venture also failed, and in 1961 still another property was bought. The new property, comprising two two-story flats, was located at 27-29 Hughes Street, Kings Cross.

Here Ted Noffs and his wife, Margaret, began their work in the heart of a population of 100,000 people on Sunday, Jan. 12, 1964, with a congregation of twelve people sitting in two rooms on the ground floor of one of the flats. Noffs had been sent there by the Methodist Church "to conduct an experiment." There was no staff and, with the exception of the flats, no plant and equipment with which to work. Mr. and Mrs. Noffs and the small core of people who gathered around them—most of them were unchurched people—declared that they were prepared to "wander in faith" to seek God's will for this massively populated area of the city. The doors of the church were opened to the world.

Since that day the Wayside Chapel has developed into one of the major experiments in the Christian world.

A full-time staff of thirteen ably assisted by voluntary teams numbering some 250 people serve the needs of humanity in this complex area. Australia's first drug referral center was opened by the Chapel in 1967. A mobile unit, aimed at meeting the needs of migrant people in the inner-city, began operating in 1968. By the end of 1970 over 3,000 couples had been married at the Chapel and hundreds of children baptized.

Mr. Noffs' book, *The Wayside Chapel,* was published by Collins in London in December 1969. Newspaper accounts of this experiment have appeared across the world, including one which appeared in *The New York Times* on Jan. 18, 1970.

Leigh College, Enfield. During the early years of Methodism in Australia, the men for the ministry came from the British Conference and it was not until 1862 that the Australian church began to think in terms of training its own ministry. In 1863 "Newington House" on the Parramatta River became the "Provisional Theological Institution" with J. A. Manton as its first Principal. In 1883 theological students were moved to "The Hermitage" within Newington College, Stanmore.

It is interesting to read in the Minutes of Conference in the years between 1900 and 1914 the constant protests about the inadequacy of the training and the accommodation given to theological students. It was not until 1915 that major changes were made when about ten acres situated on Liverpool Road, Enfield, were purchased "for the purpose of establishing a Theological College, to be called Leigh College, this perpetuating the name of the noble Methodist Missionary, SAMUEL LEIGH." The first Principal was William E. Bennett, who was succeeded on his retirement in 1942 by S. R. Bowyer-

Hayward, who came from England to take up the appointment.

In 1919 a system of co-operative training for theological students of the Methodist, Presbyterian and Congregational Churches was introduced. Students from the three churches come together for lectures in St. Andrews College within Sydney University, teachers being appointed by each of the three churches. This system of united classes in the basic areas of theological training has continued up to the present time and has proved exceedingly valuable.

Many lectures are still given at Leigh College in areas not covered by the United Faculty and in specific subjects required by the Methodist Conference and, of course, the College is still the residential center for all men in training for the New South Wales Conference of the Methodist Church of Australasia.

The Methodist Ladies' College, eight miles west of Sydney, owes its origin to the annual Church Conference of 1883, but it was not until 1886 that the school was opened for day girls and boarders.

From the time of the erection of the "Towers" building, under Principal H. Kelynack, the school has steadily progressed. Today it provides education from Kindergarten to University Entrance level. The total enrollment is 840 of whom 145 are boarders.

Newington College, Stanmore, is the senior college of the Methodist Church in this State. It celebrated its centenary on Saturday, October 27th, 1962. Newington is situated on a twenty acre site and incorporates several splendid ovals, gymnasium and Olympic swimming pool.

Recognized as one of the great Public Schools, it has through the years produced leaders who have figured prominently in the political, judicial, medical, commercial and ecclesiastical disciplines of Australia.

Associated with it are the Preparatory Schools, Wyvern and Lindfield.

The College Council consists of ten clergy and fifteen laymen and is supported by the strong membership of the Old Boys' Union.

The 1968 enrollment: Senior School, 835; Preparatory Schools, 280 (including 220 boarders).

The present Headmaster is Douglas Trathen.

Ravenswood School for Girls was acquired and established as a Methodist School in 1924 and is on the Northern Shore suburban line about ten miles from Sydney. Up to the year 1949 the School had ministerial control, but since that date a Headmistress has been in charge. The School possesses a complete range of modern buildings, and provides a full course from Kindergarten to University Entrance.

The present total enrollment is 574 of whom 102 are boarders.

Wesley College within the University of Sydney. In 1855 the New South Wales University Act provided for assisting the four leading religious denominations of New South Wales to establish colleges at the University and offered about fifteen acres to each with a £1 for £1 subsidy towards buildings. The Wesleyans could not raise the cash and their fifteen acres went to the Prince Alfred Hospital.

In 1907 the New South Wales Conference decided to celebrate the Centenary of Wesleyanism in Australia by endeavouring to obtain about two acres from the University to build its Wesley College. The foundation stones were laid on Dec. 2, 1916 by GEORGE BROWN, President, Hon. William Robson, M.L.C. and Mr. Fred Cull. The College was opened in 1917 with eight resident students. Today the College, in large, impressive buildings, has 150 students.

AUSTRALIAN EDITORIAL COMMITTEE

SYMAYS, MAURICE A. (1879-   ), is a prominent lay member of the Belgium Conference of The Methodist Church, his home church being the Central Church, Brussels. He was born in Ghent, Belgium, August 2, 1879, and in time became a Doctor of Law and of Political Science. In the First World War in 1917 he won the Military Cross for distinguished service. He entered the Belgian Ministry of Finance in 1919, and was a director of that ministry at the time of his retirement in 1946.

Symays was an agnostic who was brought to Christ through reading a Bible which he purchased in the Methodist Building in Brussels. He joined the Church in 1924 and became a local preacher, and for some time was the Conference Lay Leader. In 1945 he was elected administrator and counsellor of the Belgian Methodist Mission Legal Corporation (A.S.B.L.). He has been the Methodist lay representative in a great many interdenominational activities. Since retirement he continues to reside in his home in Brussels.

WILLIAM G. THONGER

SYRACUSE, NEW YORK, U.S.A., in 1970 had a population of 192,529. It is centrally located in the state which may account for its being a hub of religious activities. The new Church Center building completed in 1967 houses more different denominations under one roof than any other building in the world (N. Y. State Council of Churches, Church Women United, Syracuse Area Council of Churches, Baptist State Convention, Seventh Day Baptist, United Church of Christ, United Presbyterian Synod and Presbytery, Methodist Area, Conference, and District, and Lutheran Upper New York Synod).

Syracuse is both an educational and industrial center. It is the home of SYRACUSE UNIVERSITY, Le Moyne (Roman Catholic) College, Onondagua Community College, the State University College of Forestry, and the Upstate Medical Center for the State University.

Historically Syracuse is of interest as the seat of the Iroquois Indian Confederacy. Ephriam Webster, the first permanent white settler in the city, opened a trading post in the area in 1786. Syracuse was incorporated as a village in 1825 and as a city in 1845.

The first Methodist church in what is now the City of Syracuse was the First Ward Church founded in 1807. This Society was begun in what is now the North Side of the city but was then known as the town of Salina. In 1816 St. Paul's Church was founded on what is now the far South Side of the city. First Church, now located in the heart of the city, was the first Methodist church in the actual village of Syracuse. It began in the year 1824 with a class of nine members in a village that had a population of less than 400. In May of 1835 People's A.M.E. ZION CHURCH was organized, the first Negro Methodist church in Syracuse. It grew out of a class meeting in a small house on South Crouse Avenue. In 1849 some members from First Church broke with the institution on the question of HOLINESS. This group formed a church known as Hemlock Church until they later took the name of FREE METHODIST.

The second half of the nineteenth century saw further development in Syracuse Methodism. In 1852 another group left First Church; this time the division was over the question of abolition of slavery. The group leaving First Church founded a WESLEYAN METHODIST CHURCH. The first Methodist church on the west side of Syracuse was West Genesee formed in 1854. In 1868 a group from First Church founded Centenary Methodist, on the near west side of Syracuse. The following year (1869) another group from First Church founded University Methodist, which stands in the University section on the near east side of the City. During 1869 and 1870 Furman Methodist was organized on what is now the near south side of the City. In 1876 Brown Memorial was organized on the west side. Furman, Brown, and Hopps Memorial (a C.M.E. CHURCH, organized sometime later) are now yoked in the Syracuse Methodist Inner-City Project (M.I.P.). Bellvue Heights Church was organized on the West Side in 1888. Three years later (1891) another church was founded in what is now the University section —Erwin Methodist. In 1893 Lafayette Avenue Church was organized some ten blocks south of Furman Methodist. A year later (1894) Rockefeller Methodist was founded on the far east side of the city, and this is still an area of rapid development. Woodlawn Methodist was organized sometime during this decade on the far north side of the city.

During the twentieth century few societies have been organized in the city, but much expansion, new building, relocation, and some consolidation has taken place. The Church of the Redeemer, an Italian language church, was organized in the north side in 1905. James Street Methodist, located in the Eastwood section of the City, was formed in 1911. The summer of 1967 witnessed the organizing of Bright Memorial Chapel, an A.M.E. CHURCH.

All of the churches mentioned in this article are still in existence with the exception of Centenary, which united with First Church when the latter rebuilt in 1961 after a spectacular fire which totally destroyed the church building in 1957, and the Church of the Redeemer, which closed its doors due to the decline of Italian-speaking residents in Syracuse.

SYRACUSE UNIVERSITY, Syracuse, New York, was founded in 1870 by the Methodist Episcopal Church with financial assistance from the city of Syracuse. Classes began on September 4, 1871. The first permanent building, the Hall of Languages, was dedicated in 1873 and is still the home of the College of Liberal Arts.

A cosmopolitan institution, the university has attracted, within the space of one year, 1964, such speakers as the president of the United States, the vice-president, a Supreme Court justice, many other government officials, scholars, artists, novelists, and poets. Students are drawn from every state in the Union and more than eighty foreign countries. Nearly eight hundred international students are registered each academic year in undergraduate or graduate programs.

Unusual academic offerings include: a comprehensive program in continuing education, utilizing the resources of all colleges and divisions of the university. Included are professional and general education programs for adults in the Syracuse metropolitan area; a conference program for national and international groups at three Adirondack residential centers; four institutional branches with programs leading to a master's degree in engineering and science and business administration; a foreign studies program for undergraduates in other countries; an expanded theater program in downtown Syracuse, and a wide range of courses for teachers in the Central New York State; several programs in the Maxwell Graduate School of Citizenship and Public Affairs offering the student on-the-scene training in Africa and Asia; a joint university-community program carried out through the Youth Development Center and studying the causes of and exploring different methods for dealing with juvenile delinquency; semester and summer programs conducted by University College and the College of Liberal Arts for American students in France, Italy, and Japan.

The university is fully accredited by the Middle States Association of Colleges and Secondary Schools and by the Board of Regents of the State of New York. It has schools of Architecture, Art, College of Business Administration, Maxwell Graduate School of Citizenship and Public Affairs, Education, L. C. Smith College of Engineering, State University College of Forestry at Syracuse University, Graduate School, College of Home Economics, Journalism, College of Law, College of Liberal Arts, Library, Music, Nursing, Social Work, Speech and Dramatic Art, University College, Utica College, and Division of the Summer Sessions. The assets of this internationally known education center total well over $125,000,000 and include some forty new buildings erected since the Second World War. The governing board has fifty-eight members, fourteen nominated by the annual conferences in New York and elected by the board.

JOHN O. GROSS

JOSEPH SZCZEPKOWSKI

SZCZEPKOWSKI, JOSEPH (1890-   ), Polish Methodist preacher, was born in Brooklyn, N. Y., Dec. 12, 1890. He joined St. Paul's Methodist Church, Jersey City, N. J., at the age of sixteen and later entered the ministry. He served as pastor of St. Paul's Church, Hamtramck, Mich., and West Warren Church in MASSACHUSETTS.

In 1929 he moved to POLAND, where he became a teacher of English. He established the Department of

English Philology at Copernicus University in Torun, Poland, and is still connected with this institution as a visiting deputy professor. During the Second World War he returned to the active ministry and served as pastor of several Methodist churches in Poland. He was the first principal of the Biblical Seminary in Klarysew, near Warsaw, and in 1957 he was appointed director of the English Language School in Warsaw. In that same year he was elected general superintendent of the Methodist Church in Poland. Later he was reelected twice, each time for an additional four-year term. He retired in 1969.

Szczepkowski graduated from Cazenovia Seminary, Cazenovia, N. Y., and SYRACUSE UNIVERSITY. He also studied at Michigan University Teachers' College, DREW UNIVERSITY, GARRETT BIBLICAL INSTITUTE, Union Theological Seminary in New York City, and Cambridge University in England.

Early in life he married Zofja Makowska. There were two children, a son Jan and a daughter Stefania (Bieniak).

GAITHER P. WARFIELD

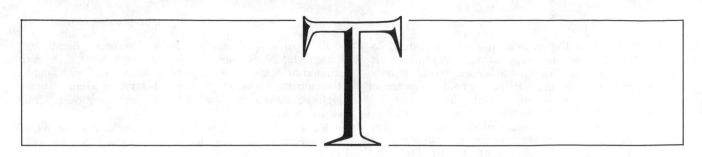

TABERNACLE CAMP GROUND, an Alabama CAMP MEETING site which was established in 1828, has had great influence on the Methodism of that state. It was the result of a conversation between two hunters who accidentally made each other's acquaintance as they were separately hunting one day in the woods that then covered the state. The names of these two hunters were Henry and Joyner. They discovered that they were both Methodists and their conversation soon turned to building a meeting house for their respective families.

A meeting house was duly built just above the spring that now supplies water for the camp ground. The annual camp meeting sprang from this early meeting house, and has continued with only a few omissions to this day.

The early cabins where the camp meeting attendants stayed were called tents, and to many they are "tents" today, though they are now wooden or concrete block structures.

A camp meeting continues to be held here in August of each year, and so far as can be ascertained it has always been held in August. W. G. HENRY, SR., whose ancestor was the Henry mentioned above, said: "No one factor had done as much as this camp meeting to keep God and religion keenly in the minds and hearts of the people of this community."

Many of the great preachers of Methodism have been heard during these camp meetings. The writer of this note has seen as many as one hundred converted and join the Church at one of these camp meetings. In 1898 there were sixty or more cabins on the ground. The buildings were all burned in 1916, and again in 1962, but there now are about fifteen cabins on the ground. The descendants of these early campers still return for camping on the grounds.

EBENEZER HEARN was the first presiding elder of this area. The following are some of the early families to camp on these grounds—names that will be recognized as prominent for many years in Alabama Methodism: Henry, Joyner, Randall, Miller, Woods, Eubanks, McReynolds, Duncan, Leech, Ervin, Storey, Lavender, Bell, Lawrence, Franks, Wharton, Murrah, Ellis and many other families. Tabernacle is among the oldest camp grounds in American Methodism.

M. E. Lazenby, *Alabama and West Florida.* 1960.

R. B. LAVENDER

TABLE OF METHODIST ANNUAL CONFERENCES. (See Appendix.)

TACKABERRY, FOSSEY (1796-1847), Irish preacher, was born in the County of Wexford. He was converted in 1815 under the preaching of Andrew Taylor, one of the General Missionaries sent into south-east IRELAND by the Irish Conference. Even as a local preacher, still with farming as his livelihood, Fossey Tackaberry was more like an itinerant in his work of spreading the Gospel message. So he offered for the ministry and was accepted as a candidate in 1822. He then gave himself fully to preaching, in which he excelled, and had a wide circuit ministry covering all the main centers in Ireland. So much was he beloved of the people that Conference sent him to the BELFAST North Circuit in 1843, and there he healed disputes and misunderstandings that had occurred among Methodists in that city. His last circuit was Sligo, to which he was appointed in 1846 in the midst of the baneful effects of the Irish Famine. He threw himself wholeheartedly into the relief of distress, never forgetting the preaching of the Gospel as well. He rescued an orphan boy of ten years of age, after the death of the only surviving relative to care for him, an elder brother of fourteen. From this boy whom he rescued, Fossey Tackaberry caught typhus fever, and within a month was dead.

C. H. Crookshank, *Methodism in Ireland.* 1885-88.
Robert Huston, *Life and Labours of the Rev. Fossey Tackaberry.* N.p., n.d. FREDERICK JEFFERY

TACOMA, WASHINGTON, U.S.A., a city of 151,061 (1970), is located on the east shore of Puget Sound.

Work of The United Methodist Church in Tacoma inheres in seventeen congregations with 8,508 members (1970); the Tacoma Community House, founded in 1910 to serve less fortunate children and families, and carried on by the Woman's Division of the Board of MISSIONS in cooperation with local supporting agencies; and the UNIVERSITY OF PUGET SOUND. The University was founded in 1888 by the Puget Sound Conference of the M.E. Church. It continues a vital relationship with the PACIFIC NORTHWEST CONFERENCE.

Methodist work in the Tacoma area began in Steilacoom, five miles to the south, in 1853. In 1874 C. N. Hoxie was appointed to both Steilacoom and to a new preaching point—Tacoma. The Steilacoom work soon closed, as Tacoma boomed with its selection as the western terminus of the Northern Pacific Railroad. Services were held in a tent until the first building of **First Church,** a store building, was acquired. In 1878 Tacoma's first church building was erected by the new congregation. In the ensuing years five other congregations shared the use of the building during their formative life; hence Baptist, Catholic, Congregational, Presbyterian, and Episcopalian work in Tacoma began in the building of the hospitable Methodists.

During the pastorate of George C. Wilding, 1888-91, Methodism spread throughout the pioneer city. He persuaded his people that First Church should inaugurate an ambitious missionary program, and projected a plan for four additional Methodist churches. He located the churches and assigned to the proposed churches members of First Church who lived in those areas. The people responded and the churches were established. By 1910, most of the present day Methodist churches of Tacoma had been founded. One former Swedish Methodist congregation and one former Japanese Methodist church are among the present congregations.

Methodists founded the GOODWILL INDUSTRIES of Tacoma, an institution which continues today under an independent board. No work of the M.P. Church or M.E. Church, South, existed in Tacoma at the time of unification, nor has there been any predominantly Negro congregation of The Methodist Church. Other Methodist denominations are represented by one A.M.E. CHURCH, one C.M.E. CHURCH, and two FREE METHODIST Churches.

Mason Church was established in 1891 and bore from the beginning the name of the land developer who gave the land for the original building. Mason and three other churches came into being through the missionary vision of the pastor of the First Church, George C. Wilding, who sent colonies of members from that church to establish new suburban congregations.

Mason Church's history parallels that of the University of Puget Sound, which is located in the same north-end community. The church has had close association through the years with this Methodist-related university. The congregation's several buildings were constructed in 1891, 1911, 1944, and 1960.

During the 1950's Mason Church became the largest Methodist church in Tacoma. The longest pastorate in the history of the church, that of J. Henry Ernst, was a period of remarkable growth, culminating in the construction of a large and substantial sanctuary-social building. A notable feature of this building is an eighty-foot long faceted-glass portrayal of The Lord's Prayer by glass artist Gabriel Loire, of Chartres, France.

John Martin Canse, *Pilgrim and Pioneer: Dawn in the Northwest.* New York: Abingdon Press, 1930.
Erle Howell, *Northwest.* 1966.
JOHN C. SOLTMAN

TADLOCK, CHARLES WILLIAM (1874-1942), American minister and church leader, was born on a farm near St. Joseph, Mo., Feb. 11, 1874. He was educated at CENTRAL COLLEGE, Missouri, receiving the Ph.B. degree in 1901. Central conferred on him the D.D. degree in 1915. Tadlock was admitted on trial in the MISSOURI CONFERENCE, M.E. Church, South, in 1900; was received into full connection in 1902, and was ordained elder in 1904. His appointments in the Missouri Conference were: 1900, Lebanon Circuit; 1901-02, Warrenton Circuit; 1903, Vandalia and New Harmony; 1904-07, Olive Street Church, St. Joseph; 1908-11, Fayette; 1912, Columbia.

In 1913 Tadlock was transferred to the ST. JOSEPH CONFERENCE, and thereafter his appointments were in the City of St. Louis as follows: 1913-16, Centenary; 1917, Cabanne; 1918, St. Louis District; 1919-36, Centenary; 1937, St. Louis District; 1938-42, General Secretary, Board of Finance (Board of Pensions, Missouri Corporation, after 1940).

At different times Tadlock served as president of the St. Louis Conference boards of education and missions. He was a member of the board of curators of Central College. He was elected president of the Metropolitan Church Federation in St. Louis. The M.E. Church, South sent Tadlock as its fraternal messenger to the GENERAL CONFERENCE of the M.E. Church at DES MOINES in 1920. He was a delegate to the General Conference in 1926,

1934, and 1938, and to the Uniting Conference in 1939.

During Tadlock's second pastorate of eighteen years at Centenary Church, St. Louis, he became widely and favorably known in the M.E. Church, South. The period between the two world wars was the heyday of the "downtown" church in American Methodism. As such a congregation, Centenary grew in the 1920's to more than 3,500 members under Tadlock's able leadership. His pastoral and pulpit ministry inspired and won the loyalty of his people. The writer of Tadlock's memoir in the conference journal declared that from his youth the man "had the capacity to excel—and did excel." However, he was "devoid of desire for popular applause or acclaim or for mere honors." Always he devoted himself to doing well and honestly the work which fell to him. "The word which fit his character was sterling." He died on May 9, 1942 and was buried in Oak Grove Cemetery, St. Louis.

Journal of the St. Louis Conference, 1942.
C. F. Price, *Who's Who in American Methodism.* 1916.
ALBEA GODBOLD

TAFT, MARY BARRITT (1772-1851), British Methodist, a noted woman evangelist, exercised a wide influence over the North of England as a traveling preacher until her marriage to a Wesleyan minister, ZECHARIAH TAFT, confined her to circuit work. Among those who were converted through her preaching was THOMAS JACKSON. She died at Sandiacre, Derbyshire, England, on March 26, 1851.

Memoir of Mary Taft, By herself. London, 1827. G. E. LONG

TAFT, ZECHARIAH (1772-1848), British Methodist, protagonist of women preachers, entered the Wesleyan ministry in 1801. In 1803 he published *Thoughts on Female Preaching* "for the comfort and encouragement of an eminently pious female who thought it her duty to call sinners to repentance." (*Scripture Doctrine,* 1820, dedication.) In 1809 he published a Reply to an anonymous article in the *Methodist Magazine* which claimed that preaching by women was unscriptural. A revised and enlarged version of his *Thoughts* appeared in 1820, entitled *The Scripture Doctrine of Women's Preaching,* dedicated to his own wife, MARY BARRITT TAFT, one of the best examples of the practice which he was defending. This went through a second edition in 1826. His major work was *Biographical Sketches of the lives and public ministry of various holy women,* in two volumes (1825, 1828), a useful collection of the lives of nearly fifty women preachers in Methodism, beginning with SUSANNA WESLEY. Taft became a SUPERNUMERARY in 1828. He was arraigned before the Wesleyan CONFERENCE in 1835 for his sympathies with the WESLEYAN METHODIST ASSOCIATION, but the matter was dropped. He died Jan. 7, 1848.

FRANK BAKER

TAGG, FRANCIS THOMAS (1845-1923), American minister, was born June 2, 1845, in Union Mills, Md. He was educated at Carroll Academy, Union Mills, received his M.A. from WESTERN MARYLAND COLLEGE in 1915, and also received an honorary D.D. degree from ADRIAN COLLEGE in 1893.

Prior to entering the ministry, Tagg was a teacher

and principal of Carroll Academy from 1863 to 1870. In 1870 he was ordained and received into the MARYLAND CONFERENCE of the M.P. CHURCH. He served pastorates in VIRGINIA, MARYLAND, and WASHINGTON, D. C. between 1870 and 1884.

He became Secretary of the M.P. Church's Board of Foreign MISSIONS in 1884 when the JAPAN mission work was being organized and in need of experienced leadership. He continued in this position until 1892, when he returned to the pastorate for a short period.

In 1892 he was named editor of *The Methodist Protestant,* remaining in this post until his retirement. He was elected President of the GENERAL CONFERENCE of the M.P. Church in 1904 and in 1908.

He was a delegate to some of the most important conventions held in his time: the World's Sunday School Convention, held in 1879 in TORONTO, CANADA; the World's Missionary Congress held in LONDON in 1888; and the ECUMENICAL METHODIST CONFERENCE, in London in 1901.

Tagg was honored by his Conference as it elected him a delegate to all General Conferences from 1884 to 1916.

He died in BALTIMORE, Md., June 18, 1923. Interment was in Chester Cemetery, Centreville, Md.

Who Was Who in America, 1897-1942. JAMES H. STRAUGHN

TAHLEQUAH, OKLAHOMA, U.S.A., **Oklahoma Methodist Home** was opened for the reception of children on Jan. 1, 1918, in Britton, Okla. J. E. McKee and his wife were elected superintendent and matron. They served until June 1919. In 1920 it was reported that the frequency of the changing of superintendents and matrons in the Home had been a source of disturbance, and on Sept. 29, 1920, Mr. and Mrs. J. S. Hively were employed as superintendent and matron and put in charge of the Home and farm. They came from the state home at Pryor. At this time there were fifty children in the Home.

By 1938 an oil well had been drilled on the land at Britton, and because of the unsuitability and run down condition of the buildings there, it was decided that the Home should be moved to a new location just as soon as a suitable site could be secured. At the session of the Conference held in OKLAHOMA CITY in 1939, it was reported that 220 acres of land located at Tahlequah, Okla., had been purchased, through the efforts of W. B. Hubbell, who was superintendent at that time. Under his leadership plans were completed and the buildings started. Before these buildings could be completed the work was stopped by war conditions.

In October of 1941, H. H. Allen replaced Hubbell as superintendent, and on March 25, 1942, the old Home at Britton was closed and the sixty boys and girls were transported to the new Home at Tahlequah. This new Home was dedicated on Sunday, July 5, 1942 by Bishop CHARLES C. SELECMAN.

In November of 1945, E. C. Webb was appointed to be superintendent of the Home, and a five year expansion program was set in motion.

W. C. Mathes was appointed to follow Webb and during his administration and that of Virgil Alexander, who followed him in 1961, the Home continued to build and grow. In 1964 Howard Davis was appointed to be superintendent.

Rather extended services are now being offered to the young people of the Methodist Home. Among these is the expanded vocational program. A serious effort is being made to offer some vocational training to every boy and girl at the Home.

Clegg and Oden, *Oklahoma.* 1968.
Journal of the Oklahoma Conference.
Together, Oklahoma Area News Edition, December 1970.
HOWARD DAVIS

TAI TAPU, a small village twelve miles from Christchurch, NEW ZEALAND, contains a well-appointed Methodist church, on one wall of which is a plaque with this inscription:

The site on which this Church stands was formerly owned by the brothers William, Robert and George Rhodes, one of whose ancestors rescued John Wesley from the flames at Epworth Rectory, Lincolnshire, on 9th February, 1709.

This tablet was presented by their kinsman, Colonel the Honourable Sir R. Heaton Rhodes, K.C.V.O., K.B.E., M.L.C.

WILLIAM T. BLIGHT

TAIWAN (Formosa) is an island lying one hundred miles off the Fukien coast of CHINA. The name, Taiwan, means "Terraced Cove." It is separated from mainland China by the Formosa Strait, and from the PHILIPPINE ISLANDS by the Bashi Strait to the southeast. Sixty small islands nearby are known as the Penghu (Pescadores).

Taiwan is 250 miles north-south, and eighty miles wide, with an area of 13,885 square miles. The population is 10,661,000, including several hundred thousand aborigines of Polynesian origin living in secluded mountains, 7,000,000 Formosans or descendants of the fourteenth century migration from Fukien, 3,000,000 Mandarin-speaking Chinese who fled the mainland in 1948-49 during the Communist take-over, and 20,000 Americans, Europeans and others in diplomatic, military, business and missionary work.

Since 1949 Taiwan has been the "exile" seat of government of Nationalist China, a charter member of the United Nations, and one of the five permanent members of the Security Council. The capital is Taipei near the northern tip of the island.

The aboriginal Polynesians have been inhabitants since the beginning of history. Spanish and Portuguese navigators attempted settlements, calling the island "Formosa" because of its beauty. The Dutch held control for a time, but they were finally expelled by the Chinese. French footholds lasted only briefly. Chinese control was factual until the conclusion of the Sino-Japanese War in 1895, the Japanese ruling Taiwan for the next fifty years.

Taiwan served JAPAN as a major springboard for attacks to the south and east in the first phase of the second World War. The island was restored to China as a province after the Japanese collapse in 1945. Retreating from the Communist offensives until 1949, the Nationalist Government succeeded in escaping to Taiwan, and has maintained control there.

The complete autonomy and integrity of Nationalist China was guaranteed by the United States, and its Seventh Fleet has constituted a barrier in the adjacent waters. Despite continuous shelling and other harassment, Nationalist China has held certain off-shore islands along the mainland coast, notably Quemoy in Amoy harbor, and Matsu farther to the north. Generalissimo CHIANG KAI-SHEK continues as first president of the National Republic of China. He and MADAME CHIANG are Methodists.

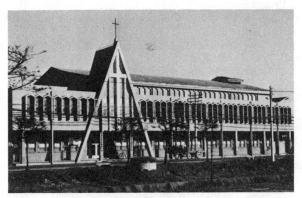

WESLEY CHURCH, TAIPEI, TAIWAN

Among the Chinese who fled to Taiwan (1948-49), were Methodists and others related to Methodist institutions. Early in 1953, the Methodist Board of MISSIONS sent missionaries to Taiwan to restore the church for the refugees under the leadership of Bishop RALPH A. WARD, who served until his death in HONG KONG. What was begun as "an interim ministry to the evacuees from Communist oppression" developed into an indigenous church.

The work centers in Taipei (north), in Taichung (center), and Tainan (south). Evangelistic efforts move out into the villages. At Taipei there is an important medical unit—the Water of Life Clinic—personally financed and founded by Dr. and Mrs. Edward Perkins, and named for the notable hospital they had maintained for many years at Kiukiang, China, prior to the Communist advance. The Law School of historic Soochow University was reactivated by its alumni in 1951 at Taipei. It developed five departments, and enrolled 1,500 students. The work was organized as the Taiwan Provisional Annual Conference, a commission of three bishops from America exercising presidency in rotation until 1964.

In 1952 the FREE METHODIST CHURCH of the United States began work in Taiwan at Kaohsiung, a port city thirty miles south of Tainan. The founders were experienced China missionaries, Miss Geneva Sayre, evangelist and administrator, and Miss Kate Leininger, a nurse. Miss Sayre had been United Nations Children's Fund director for the Honan Province, where she "risked her life after the political turmoil to establish the Bible School on a firm basis," before yielding to house arrest, from which she was permitted to be released in 1951.

Success attended the work. The first church was dedicated at Kaohsiung in 1953, and the average was one a year for a decade. A second center was established at Pingtung, fifteen miles inland. The Bible school was organized in 1955. The 1962 Annual Report of the Free Methodist Board of Missions indicates 1,212 members of the church and several thousand in the community.

Statistics of The United Methodist Church in Taiwan: Membership in 1968 was reported as 3,255; ministers, twenty-three elders (three retired), three deacons, four on trial, four theological students, and ten supply pastors. Churches reported were fourteen local churches, four chapels and two preaching points. Villages where work was being carried on consisted of two refugee villages,

a Good News village, Kaohsiung, and Peace Village in Taipei.

Encyclopaedia Britannica.
Knettler, *Methodism in Taiwan.* N.d.
B. S. Lamson, *Venture.* 1960.
Barbara H. Lewis, *Methodist Overseas Missions.* 1960.
L. R. Marston, *From Age to Age.* 1960.
World Methodist Council, *Handbook of Information,* 1966-71.
ARTHUR BRUCE MOSS
HAZEN G. WERNER

TALBOT, SAMSON D. (1819-1872), a bishop of the A.M.E. ZION CHURCH, was born in West Bridgewater, Mass. He married Sarah De Groat of Onondaga, N. Y. in 1844. Following her death, he married Sarah Gassaway in December 1865. He was converted and called to preach in 1841, joining the New York Conference in 1844, at which time he was ordained a deacon by Superintendent CHRISTOPHER RUSH. The following year he was ordained an elder. His pastorates included NEW YORK, BOSTON, NEWARK, N. J., ROCHESTER, SYRACUSE, WASHINGTON, and Troy. For some time he was treasurer of the Book Concern. He was elected to the bishopric in 1864.

DAVID H. BRADLEY

TALLAHASSEE, FLORIDA, U.S.A. **Trinity Church** is the oldest of the larger churches of the FLORIDA CONFERENCE, having been first established as a Methodist Society in 1824 by missionaries and appointees of the SOUTH CAROLINA CONFERENCE. The Tallahassee District of this Conference was created in 1825, and included three charges: Chattahoochee Mission, Early Mission and Tallahassee Mission. The Florida Conference, having been authorized by the GENERAL CONFERENCE in 1844, was organized in the Tallahassee Methodist Church in 1845. Trinity Church now numbers 2,613 members, and serves a constituency made up of business and professional people of the community, government officials and employees, and university faculty and students.

GEORGE A. FOSTER

TALLEY, NICHOLAS (1791-1873), American pioneer preacher of SOUTH CAROLINA, was born near RICHMOND, Va., on May 2, 1791, and died on May 10, 1873. He was converted in Green County, Ga., in 1810, under the preaching of HOPE HULL, and was received on trial in the SOUTH CAROLINA CONFERENCE, 1812, and sent to the Little Peedee Circuit. This was then more than 100 miles in extent and contained twenty-eight preaching appointments. In his ministry, he was twenty-two years on districts, twelve on stations, nine on circuits, and fourteen on missions. For many successive sessions he was elected a delegate to the GENERAL CONFERENCE. Chreitzberg states that he had the longest record of effective service in the South Carolina Conference of any man with the exception of one other who had received fifty-four appointments and had been a superannuate for five years. "Mr. Talley was above common height and of great physical endurance; his face was expressive of intelligence and benevolence; his voice was not musical, but rather nasal, and his delivery somewhat monotonous; yet in all his ministry, he was self-possessed, dignified, and refined. His preaching was hortatory in character and often powerful in effect, his ministry popular and successful. He lived to the age of 82 years. . . ." (Chreitzberg, p. 234.) According to Simpson, "The last entry in his diary was May 2, 1873, as follows: 'My birthday. Eighty-two years I have lived on the bounty and goodness of God. I feel grateful, and hope to believe he doeth all things well.'" He was buried in the Washington Street Cemetery in COLUMBIA, S. C.

A. M. Chreitzberg, *Methodism in the Carolinas*. 1897.
M. Simpson, *Cyclopaedia*. 1878.   N. B. H.

TAMPA, FLORIDA, U.S.A., on FLORIDA's west coast, is the State's third largest city, and dates back to a place of settlement at the time of the first Spanish occupation or before 1763. Tampa became incorporated in 1855 in the newly established and growing State of Florida.

In January 1843, Andrew J. Deavers was appointed to the "Chickichaty and Tampa Bay" Circuit. In 1844 it became known as the "Hillsboro," but the following year when the FLORIDA CONFERENCE was organized, it was left out as an appointment because of a shortage of preachers. The next year the Hillsborough Circuit reappeared. In January, 1852, a new frontier district was begun and named the Tampa District. Tampa has remained through the years as a conference district.

The first Methodist services were held in Tampa in the Palmer House, perhaps as early as 1843. A society was finally formed there in July 1846, by John C. Ley, who was pastor of the Ocean Pond Circuit. The society met in the homes of its members and then later in the court house. In 1850, under the leadership of John R. Comer, the first church building was begun in Tampa; it was completed in 1852. This church, which was used by a number of other denominations, was known affectionately as "The Little White Church." This building, which stood on the corner of Lafayette and Morgan was used as the Methodist Church until a new structure was built in 1890. It is said that Andrew Jackson gave a contribution of a five dollar gold piece toward the construction of this church. Franklin Stewart, the first presiding elder of the Tampa District, was the first Methodist preacher to preach in the "Little White Church." In 1891 the appointment to Tampa began to read, "Tampa and Mission." In 1891 the membership was reported to be 439 members and two local preachers.

As the town spread out it became difficult for everyone who was a Methodist to come to the First Church. Some families in the Hyde Park Section became concerned that their children were unable to go to SUNDAY SCHOOL. On Sunday, March 12, 1899, thirty persons met to form the first Sunday school in a two-room red school house, located at what is now Platt and Magnolia. Two Sundays later John Dodwell of Port Tampa, newly established appointment, preached in Hyde Park both morning and evening, but regular preaching services were not scheduled.

The following year Henry Hice was appointed pastor of Hyde Park Church as it had become, and regular church meetings were held at a furniture store on Hyde Park Avenue at Cleveland. A little frame church building was erected that year, 1900, on the present site of the church. The present church was built in 1907 by generous gifts from members, at a total cost of $30,000.

Other churches began to organize as the city grew in population until by 1926 there were thirteen Methodist churches in Tampa. The number had increased to fifteen by the time of unification.

The M.E. Church never had a church in Tampa. They were very successful on the other side of Tampa Bay in St. Petersburg where they had five churches. Today, there are thirty United Methodist churches within the greater Tampa Area.

First Church of Tampa was established on July 26, 1846 under the leadership of John C. Ley with seventeen members present. This was ten years before the city of Tampa was established. The community at that time was known as Fort Brooke. The first church services were held in the Palmer House, the leading hotel of the community. Services were held later in the residences of some of the people and in the court house.

The first church building was begun in 1850 and completed in 1853. It was known as "The Little White Church" and was located at the intersection of Lafayette and Morgan Streets. The first pastor was Franklin Stewart. In 1890 a new sanctuary was erected under the leadership of J. C. Sale. This building was torn down in 1967 to make room for the construction of a new sanctuary and administration building.

The First Church of Tampa is the first Protestant church to be built on the West Coast of Florida and is the Mother of Methodism on the West Coast. Two pastors from this church have been elected to the episcopacy, the late JOHN BRANSCOMB in 1952; and EDWARD J. PENDERGRASS, in 1964.

The church reported 1,181 members in 1970.

Hyde Park Church was established in 1900. It has been instrumental in establishing several neighborhood churches and in providing young people for Christian ministry. It serves the west-end of Tampa, including the University of Tampa, and in 1970 reported 1,255 members.

Palma Ceia Church is a relatively young church. In April 1946 thirteen people met in a home in southwest Tampa, a rapidly growing area, to consider establishing a Methodist Church to serve the people there. Easter Sunday, April 16, 1946, the Church found its birthplace in the Palma Ceia Theatre, where it continued to meet for worship during the next two years. In 1948 the first unit of the church building was completed on the present Dale Mabry location. By this time there were 400 members of the congregation. In January 1949, Bishop ROY SHORT dedicated the first unit of the church, which was a fellowship hall and classroom area.

In January 1951, ground was broken for the Spanish-inspired modern masonry sanctuary. It was completed in time for Christmas services 1952. Additional educational space was provided in 1957 by the construction of two units that tied the existing building together.

Palma Ceia church has been active in serving the community, and it continues to grow and serve. At the present the church is building a new fellowship hall, recreation area, and administrative complex, the total cost to be $450,000. The membership of Palma Ceia Church was 2,581 in 1970, and it is expected to grow even larger.

Though a relatively young church, Palma Ceia has worked for purposes, goals, and desires, in line with the Christian faith of the ages. It is the firm conviction of the people of this church, that Palma Ceia will be able to continue to give dynamic leadership for Christian living in Tampa, and in the world.

A significant part of the church plant is the colorful stained glass rose window which crowns the altar of the nave at Palma Ceia and portrays the Old and New Testaments. The window was created and fashioned in Munich, Germany, shipped to Tampa and placed in the church. It was given in memory of one of the charter members by his wife and children. The huge window, designed in brilliant hues, creates an inspiring focal point in the church sanctuary. It gives a vivid picture of the foundations of Christian faith, and is a continual inspiration to all who worship in the sanctuary.

Seminole Heights Church is an influential church which followed the growth of this expanding city. The vision and foresight of First Church, Tampa, gave birth to a meeting place on the edge of the city. W. A. Meyers, presiding elder, and W. A. Cooper, pastor of First Church, as well as several other preachers, brought the vision to fulfillment. W. F. Dunkle preached the first sermon on June 19, 1921, and J. W. Windham, Jr., was put in direct charge. The Sunday school grew rapidly and in three months the attendance passed 200.

The annual conference met in ORLANDO on Dec. 17, 1921, and appointed R. L. Allen pastor in charge. He, with the presiding elder, organized the church with 112 charter members.

In March 1922, John B. Culpepper, Sr., and J. B. Culpepper, Jr., held a tent revival meeting for the church and new members made necessary a new building for worship. The new church seated 400, but in three years it was overcrowded and people were turned away. Sunday school classes met under the trees and in the school house. Ground was broken for a new sanctuary on June 16, 1926. Bishop HOYT M. DOBBS laid the cornerstone in the spring of 1927. The first service was held by R. L. Allen in the new sanctuary on March 11, 1928.

From the membership of Seminole Heights, thirteen young people have gone into full time Christian service. One of the former ministers, E. J. Pendergrass, is now a bishop of the Church.

The Alpha Auxiliary was organized in 1925 for the purpose of buying a pipe organ, a project that was completed in December 1934, after raising $10,000. The church labored for many years to pay out of debt and finally by devoted service and hard work of preachers and laymen alike, the church was dedicated by Bishop ARTHUR J. MOORE on January 14, 1945. It presently has a membership of 1,830 (1970).

Ybor City is situated in the heart of the city of Tampa. In its early history the population was basically Cuban, Italian, and Spanish. The Home Missionary Society of the UNITED BRETHREN IN CHRIST, in cooperation with their Florida Conference, opened a mission in 1942. The Rev. and Mrs. Plutarco Roa, who had served as missionaries in South America, were appointed as the first missionaries. After a long period of visitation in the homes of the community, a church of seventeen members was organized on Easter Sunday, 1945. In addition to the church a kindergarten and elementary school were added to meet the needs of the community. In 1965 approximately 330 children were enrolled in the schools. With a mission staff of thirteen and with the change in the community, the entire ministry has been under study, with a possible change in the area of mission.

In The United Methodist Church several former Methodist projects were united administratively to this work under the supervision of Hector Navas, successor to Plutarco Roa.

General Minutes, UMC, 1970.
Mrs. Paul Lake, *History of Hyde Park Methodist Church.* 1944.

WILLIAM E. BROOKS
THOMAS G. MITCHELL
HAROLD E. BUELL
MRS. S. J. OZBURN
ROY BEN RIDLEY
LOIS MILLER

TAMPERE, Finland (Tammerfors), is the second largest city in FINLAND, located about one hundred miles north of HELSINKI. Methodist work began under great difficulties in this city since the Methodist Church is a minority church in Finland, which has a state church. Only within comparatively recent years have people been permitted to join the Methodist Church without court procedures. Bishop ODD HAGEN, administering Finland as part of the Stockholm Area, encouraged the people to buy an old three story house in Tampere about 1957, and a sanctuary was arranged for on the third floor, while shops, offices, and apartments were in the lower stories of this building. The pastor and his family also lived in it.

Following a visit of Bishop HARMON in 1962, the WESTERN NORTH CAROLINA CONFERENCE undertook to assist the Tampere congregation, then of about 100 members, to build a new church which would more adequately do the work of the church in this large and growing city. The Western North Carolina Conference assumed a $50,000 special for the Tampere church, and a new building was erected and the church consecrated on May 23, 1968. The church has a SUNDAY SCHOOL, a woman's society, and an organized men's group, and at present gives promise of growth and strength. The old building was taken care of by the Finnish Conference and was remodeled and the rent from its various offices presently assists in supporting the program of the church.

William Stokes of Reidsville, N. C., made a personal visit to Tampere while the rebuilding project was in a formative stage, and his representation before the Western North Carolina Conference, as well as the leadership of Bishop EARL G. HUNT, materially assisted in the raising of the $50,000 mission special within the allotted time.

N. B. H.

TANGITERORIA, Northland, NEW ZEALAND, was the site of a mission station in the Northern Wairoa district founded by JAMES WALLIS in 1836. He was succeeded by JAMES BULLER in 1840. Buller labored there for fourteen years, preaching in many villages round the Kaipara Harbor and on the Northern Wairoa River, and even crossing from time to time to preach in villages near Whangarei, on the east coast. While resident at Tangiteroria, Buller visited Auckland and conducted the first Methodist services there in September 1841.

The site of the station is marked by a simple cairn which stands about two chains (Ed. Note: a chain measures twenty-two yards) back in a farmer's paddock from the Whangarei—Dargaville Road.

W. Morley, *New Zealand.* 1900.   L. R. M. GILMORE

TANNER, BENJAMIN TUCKER (1835-1915), American bishop of the A.M.E. CHURCH, was born in PITTSBURGH,

Pa., on Dec. 25, 1835. He was educated at Avery College and Western Theological Seminary, both located in PENNSYLVANIA. He was converted in 1856 and ordained DEACON and ELDER in 1860. He was pastor of a Presbyterian Church in WASHINGTON, D. C. from 1860-68. Following this pastorate he embarked upon a distinguished literary career as editor of *The Christian Recorder* (1868-1884) and founder-editor of the *A.M.E. Review* (1884-1888). In 1888 Tanner was elected to the episcopacy. After supervising the work of the Eleventh, First, Fifth and Ninth Episcopal Districts, he retired in 1908 and died in PHILADELPHIA in 1915. Bishop Tanner, the author of a standard work, *Outline of A.M.E. Church History* (1884) and other books, was the head of one of Philadelphia's most distinguished Negro families, including his son, the world acclaimed artist, Henry O. Tanner.

R. R. Wright, *The Bishops.* 1963.   GRANT S. SHOCKLEY

TAPPAN, JOHN (1799-1862), American bishop of the A.M.E. ZION CHURCH, was born June 20, 1799, in NORTH CAROLINA, later evidently moving to NEW YORK where (after his conversion, Sept. 5, 1830), he began preaching in 1832. He joined the conference June 18, 1833, and was made a DEACON May 20, 1834, and an ELDER May 20, 1844. The date given for his elevation to the superintendency appears as being June 4, 1854, which evidently means that he was elected in a special General Conference of that year. He died in December, 1862.

DAVID H. BRADLEY

TARBELL, MARTHA (1862-1948), American writer and author of *Tarbell's Teachers' Guide* for forty-two years, was born in 1862 in INDIANA. The daughter of Horace Sumner and Martha (Treat) Tarbell, she graduated from DEPAUW UNIVERSITY, A.B., 1884; A.M., 1887; D.Litt, 1933. Her father was a teacher and public school administrator. She collaborated with her father in the preparation of a series of school geographies in 1896, and various textbooks in language from 1891 to 1903. In 1907 she published *The Geography of Palestine*, and in 1910 *In the Master's Country*. In 1906 the first issue of *Tarbell's Teachers' Guide* appeared. This annual publication was destined to have great influence with Church School teachers. She continued as author of the *Guide* until her death, Oct. 27, 1948.

For many years Miss Tarbell taught a Bible class in Calvary Methodist Church in EAST ORANGE, N. J. A member of Phi Beta Kappa and the Garden Club and Woman's Club of the Oranges, she was active in both church and community work. Throughout her long life her devotion and service toward the Methodist Church never wavered.

Newark (New Jersey) *Evening News*, October 28, 1948.
    HENRY L. LAMBDIN

TARBILL, ELMER ELLSWORTH (1861-1903), American scholar and clergyman, carried forward the tradition of hardy circuit-riding on the open range cattle country and mountains of WYOMING. He was born on a farm in OHIO, Dec. 23, 1861. OHIO WESLEYAN UNIVERSITY conferred his A.B. in 1887, A.M. in 1893, and Ph.D. in 1899; in 1889 he was given the S.T.B. degree by BOSTON UNIVERSITY. Ordained in 1886 by Bishop CYRUS

D. Foss, he was admitted on trial at Horton, Kan., and ordained as elder in 1894 at Abilene, Kan., by Bishop JOHN H. VINCENT.

After serving several charges in KANSAS, he was appointed superintendent of the Wyoming Mission on Nov. 18, 1896, at the age of thirty-five. Applying himself with ardor to the challenge of the unchurched cattle empire, in six years he traveled 10,500 miles by stage and 125,000 miles by rail. In one Wyoming town he was received with frontier hospitality and broadmindedness reflected in a sign over a saloon: "Tonight. Preaching at 7:30, Dance at 9. After Dance, Big Poker Game." His achievement of having all indebtedness paid on every church in Wyoming brought about a facetious threat of E. M. Mills, secretary of the Twentieth Century Thank-Offering Commission: "This is so contrary to Methodist practice that Brother Tarbill deserves to be arraigned for heresy!"

Tarbill's health broke under the strain and in 1903 he was stationed at Fort Collins, Colo., where he was stricken in the pulpit. A few weeks later he died in Kansas City, Kan., on Aug. 13, 1903, aged forty-one, leaving a widow and three children.

Central Christian Advocate, Sept. 9, 1903.   LELAND D. CASE

J. W. TARBOUX

TARBOUX, JOHN WILLIAM (1858-1940), American preacher, missionary to BRAZIL, and first bishop of the autonomous Methodist Church in that country, was born in Georgetown, S. C., on Sept. 13, 1858. He graduated from WOFFORD COLLEGE, was ordained in December 1877, and soon afterwards married Susan Frances Kirkland. After a few years of pastoral work in the U.S.A, he went to Brazil with his wife and baby son, arriving in RIO DE JANEIRO in July 1883. He was one of the three preachers (JAMES KENNEDY, J. W. Tarboux and H. C. TUCKER), who in 1886 constituted the first Annual Conference of the Methodist Church in Brazil—the smallest conference ever to be organized in Methodism.

While in Brazil, Tarboux served as pastor, presiding elder, church organizer and educator. He was best-known and best-loved for his twelve years of service as President (Reitor) of Granbery College (INSTITUTO GRANBERY) in JUIZ DE FORA, State of Minas Gerais. His dream was to make it a Methodist University, and he founded Schools of Dentistry, Pharmacy and Law, which became well-known over Brazil. In this work, Mrs. Tarboux, called the "Mother of the Granbery Boys," was his invaluable helper.

Upon superannuation in 1921, he retired to MIAMI, Fla., where for seven years he engaged actively in the development of a church which was named later, in his honor, the Tarboux Memorial.

When the organizing General Conference of the autonomous Methodist Church in Brazil met in São PAULO, on Sept. 4, 1930, Tarboux, though long absent, was elected its first bishop. He sailed for Brazil immediately and was consecrated in Catete Church, Rio de Janeiro. He was re-elected in January 1934, since at that time bishops were elected for five years and not for life-tenure. On this occasion, he ordained CESAR DACORSO as the first Brazilian bishop. He thus ended thirty-seven years of service in Brazil. Broken in health, Bishop Tarboux returned to Miami where he died on May 2, 1940.

Tributes to his life of service were countless. One of Brazil's most famous journalists, the Catholic Austregésilo de Atayde, wrote in a Rio paper, "Never in the eyes of a foreigner, have I seen such tender remembrance of our country." Bishop Tarboux was survived by his wife, three daughters, and two sons.

Expositor Cristao, May 28 and July 9, 1940.
J. L. Kennedy, *Metodismo no Brasil*. 1928.
O Granberyense, May 31, 1940.
World Outlook, October 1940.   EPAMINONDAS MOURA

TASMANIA. (See VICTORIA AND TASMANIA CONFERENCE.)

TATE, WILLIS McDONALD (1911-   ), American educator and university president, was born in DENVER, Colo., on May 18, 1911. He spent his boyhood in SAN ANTONIO, Texas, graduating from the old Main Avenue High School. He then went to SOUTHERN METHODIST UNIVERSITY, where he received the A.B. degree in 1932, M.A. (in sociology) in 1935, and did further graduate work at the University of Texas and at the University of Chicago. He holds honorary degrees from TEXAS WESLEYAN COLLEGE, CENTENARY COLLEGE (Louisiana), the UNIVERSITY OF DENVER, OKLAHOMA CITY UNIVERSITY, and the University of Tulsa. As an athlete he was a member of Southern Methodist's championship football team of 1931, receiving strong nomination for the All-American football team.

Dr. Tate entered the teaching profession and for a time was principal of the Alamo Heights Elementary and Junior High Schools in San Antonio. In April 1943, he went to HOUSTON, Texas, where he became executive assistant to the pastor of the First Methodist Church there.

He married, in 1932, Joel Estes of Cleburne, Texas, a classmate at S.M.U. They have two children, a son, Willis, Jr. of Dallas; and a daughter, Mrs. John Withers of the same city, and three grandchildren. Dr. Tate's brother, Robert S. Tate, Jr., is pastor of the First Methodist Church in Austin, Texas.

In September 1945, Dr. Tate went to Southern Methodist University as assistant dean of students; on July 1, 1948, he was appointed dean of students. He was elected fifth president of Southern Methodist on May 6, 1954, succeeding UMPHREY LEE.

Dr. Tate is active in church and public affairs, being past chairman of the Council of Protestant Colleges and Universities; past president of the Texas Association of Colleges and Universities; past chairman of the Inter-University Council of the Dallas and Fort Worth Metropolitan Areas, and vice president of the UNIVERSITY SENATE of The Methodist Church. He was a member of the GENERAL CONFERENCE of The Methodist Church of 1964 and '66, and being elected chairman of chairmen by the other committee chairmen, it was his duty to remain upon the platform to introduce properly and keep in order the reports of the various legislative and standing committees of the Conference. He is co-author with A. Q. Sartain and W. W. Finlay, of *Human Behavior in Industry* (McGraw-Hill, 1954).

Journal of the 1964 General Conference, TMC.
Who's Who in America. Marquis Co.   J. DANIEL BARRON

TAUROA, MATARAE (1896-1956), NEW ZEALAND Methodist Maori minister, was born in Te Patunga, Whangaroa, and was educated at St. Stephen's Maori Boys' School (Anglican) and Wesley College, Three Kings. He trained for the ministry at the theological college at Dunholme, AUCKLAND.

He was a fluent preacher in both English and Maori and held a number of important circuit appointments. He retired to his birthplace, where he became a recognized elder of the people. He died at Kaeo, Northland, on Dec. 17, 1956.

New Zealand Methodist Times, April 27, 1957.
L. R. M. GILMORE

TAVARES, JOÃO EVANGELISTA (1869-1939), Brazilian Methodist preacher, was born Dec. 27, 1869, in the state of Minas Gerais. Though from a poor home, he managed to study at GRANBERY COLLEGE (now INSTITUTO) in JUIZ DE FÓRA; he graduated from the school of pharmacy in Ouro Preto, Minas Gerais, in 1907, and from the law school in RIO DE JANIERO in 1915.

In 1890 he became an exhorter and local preacher, was ordained DEACON in 1892 and ELDER in 1895. He was pastor of more than ten charges in the Federal District (then Rio de Janeiro) and interior; for a term he was editor of the weekly *Expositor Cristão*, and was secretary of the Conference Board of Missions. In this post, he pioneered the cause of self-support for the Brazilian Methodist ministry, making the first motion to this effect at the Annual Conference in 1919.

Twice, in 1916 and in 1917, because of the absence of a bishop (the bishops then were North Americans), he was elected to preside over annual conferences. In 1930 he received an honorary diploma from the Y.M.C.A. in Rio de Janeiro, commemorating thirty years as member and worker for the same. He was known as a Latin scholar and proficient writer, was a good preacher, counselor, and friend. He retired in 1930, after forty years in the service of the Methodist Church. His wife was Cristina Bouças Tavares, by whom he had several children. He and his wife lived to celebrate their fiftieth wedding anniversary. He died in Todos os Santos, near Rio, Sept. 16, 1939.

J. L. Kennedy, *Metodismo no Brasil*. 1928.
ANTONIO DE CAMPOS GONÇALVES

TAWA, HIKA (? -1831), was the first convert of the NEW ZEALAND Wesleyan Maori Mission. He was a native of rank who had received instruction from SAMUEL LEIGH at Wesleydale in 1823. When the mission was reestablished at Mangungu, he came for further teaching. He was baptized on Feb. 16, 1831, but died shortly afterward.

W. Morley, *New Zealand*. 1900.   L. R. M. GILMORE

CHARLES TAYLOR

TAYLOR, CHARLES (1819-1897), an American minister and physician who went to CHINA in 1848 as one of the very first missionaries of the M.E. Church, South. He was born in BOSTON, Mass., on Sept. 15, 1819, and was graduated from the University of New York with highest honors in 1840.

He went to SOUTH CAROLINA early in 1841, taught in a private school in Aiken, and then for three years taught in the COKESBURY CONFERENCE SCHOOL. At the close of 1844 he was admitted on trial into the SOUTH CAROLINA CONFERENCE, Bishop JAMES O. ANDREW presiding. He was appointed as junior preacher on the Darlington Circuit, and it was while serving that large circuit that a conversation with WILLIAM CAPERS led Taylor to volunteer to be a missionary. In 1845 he was pastor at Camden, S. C.

In 1846 he was married to Charlotte Jane Gamewell, daughter of JOHN GAMEWELL, who had been ordained by Bishop ASBURY. The newly-wedded couple went to PHILADELPHIA, where Taylor studied medicine and received his medical doctorate.

Meanwhile various attempts were made to find another missionary to go to China with Taylor. BENJAMIN JENKINS, printer of *The Southern Christian Advocate*, volunteered in response to an editorial appeal by WILLIAM M. WIGHTMAN, editor. Jenkins was ordained DEACON and he and Taylor were ordained ELDERS the same day in Norfolk, Va. They sailed for China from Boston in April 1848. In China both men studied Chinese and began preaching. Taylor also served and witnessed through his medical ministry.

Ill health led Mrs. Taylor to return home in 1852, and Taylor rejoined her in 1854. Back home he spent much time traveling, telling the needs of the China mission and stimulating missionary interest. In 1856 he became a professor in Spartanburg Female College, and president in 1857. The GENERAL CONFERENCE made him the first

SUNDAY SCHOOL secretary of the M.E. Church, South. In the straitened days of the Civil War, he returned to the Conference and was for four years presiding elder of the Wadesboro District, and in 1866 pastor of Sumter Circuit. That year he was elected president of KENTUCKY WESLEYAN COLLEGE. His last years were spent in ALABAMA. He died at Courtland on Feb. 1, 1897.

While in China he published a work on *Harmony of the Gospels*, as well as several tracts in Chinese. He also wrote *Five Years in China*, and *Baptism in a Nutshell*. Of Taylor's ministry in China, Bishop H. M. DuBose said "few had made footprints before him." DuBose classed Taylor with JOHN W. LAMBUTH and YOUNG J. ALLEN as constituting a trio of "master missionaries" preeminent in the history of connectional missions.

A. D. Betts, *South Carolina*. 1952.
H. M. DuBose, *History of Methodism*. 1916.
M. Simpson, *Cyclopaedia*. 1881.   N. B. H.

TAYLOR, CHARLES E. (? -1950), was a NEW ZEALAND Methodist layman. Badly crippled in childhood, he became by sheer courage, ability and faith a leading figure in legal and civic affairs and an outstanding layman of the Methodist Church of New Zealand. Following several years as mayor of Feilding, he declined nomination as candidate for a "safe" seat in Parliament. He was head of a well-known legal firm in the Manawatu district. But nearest to Charles Taylor's heart was the work of the Kingdom of God. He occupied, with conspicuous ability, nearly every office open to a layman of the Methodist Church, and was a valued member of numerous boards and committees. His greatest concern was overseas missions, and his able advocacy of this work was a constant challenge to the whole church.

ARTHUR H. SCRIVIN

TAYLOR, DEAN (1878-1943), American newspaper editor-owner and writer, and prominent layman, was born at Warren, Ohio, on Oct. 8, 1878, the son of Benjamin J. and Gertrude T. Taylor and grandson of Matthew B. Taylor and Adaline Adams Hapgood, all prominent Warren Methodists. Following in the footsteps of his maternal grandfather and his father, Taylor was a delegate to the GENERAL CONFERENCES of the M.E. Church in 1928, 1932, 1936, the Uniting Conference in 1939, and 1940. He was a member of the Board of Home MISSIONS and CHURCH EXTENSION, 1928-43, Commission on EVANGELISM, 1932-1943, and Chairman of the General Conference sub-committee on LAY ACTIVITIES in 1932, 1936.

He graduated from MT. UNION COLLEGE, Alliance, Ohio, in 1902 and from Harvard University in 1903. He married Jessie I. Minneley of Meadville, Pa., in 1906. Their two sons, Ben J. Taylor of Fairfield, Iowa, and James S. Taylor, Bedford, Iowa, became newspapermen and served on the Board of Lay Activities of the SOUTH IOWA CONFERENCE. Ben J. was a delegate to the General Conference in 1948.

Dean Taylor was the author of *The Aldersgate Call And The New Day* and *Centennial of Fairfield Methodism*. He was a trustee of IOWA WESLEYAN COLLEGE at Mt. Pleasant, Iowa, and a member of the Sigma Alpha Epsilon fraternity and other organizations. After working on several OHIO daily newspapers, he with his father and brother, Alfred W. Taylor, purchased the *Daily Journal* at Fairfield, Iowa, in 1906; this was consolidated with the *Weekly Ledger* in 1920. He was postmaster at Fairfield from 1921 to 1930. He then repurchased the interest in the *Daily Ledger*. He died on Sept. 23, 1943, at Rochester, Minn., and was buried in Evergreen cemetery at Fairfield, Iowa.

Who's Who in Iowa, 1940.
Who's Who in Pan-Methodism, 1940.   BEN J. TAYLOR

TAYLOR, EDWARD THOMPSON (FATHER) (1793-1871), colorful American sailor preacher, was born of unknown parents near RICHMOND, Va. Leaving a foster home, he ran away at the age of seven to go to sea. For ten years he shared the common life of a sailor of his time. On a night in 1811 young Taylor was attracted by the interest surrounding religious services which were being conducted in BOSTON by ELIJAH HEDDING, a powerful Methodist evangelist, who later became the eighth bishop of the M.E. Church. Failing to gain entrance by the door of the building in which the services were being held, Taylor climbed through a window. The revivalist's message persuaded the young sailor to become a Christian in general and a Methodist in particular. Thereafter, he listed his birthdate as the date of his conversion.

Following his religious experience, Taylor returned to sea. During the War of 1812, he served on an American privateer, the Black Hawk, and was captured by the British. While he was imprisoned at Halifax, Nova Scotia, his fellow prisoners, tiring of the English chaplains, received permission from their captors to choose one of their own number to pray and to preach for them. Taylor was chosen. This chance to preach must have nurtured in him a fascination for the pulpit, but immediately after his release from the captivity of the British, he became a peddler of tin and iron ware in the small coast towns of MASSACHUSETTS. He stopped his selling anytime he had a chance to win a convert to his new-found faith, and yet he did not meet the minimum standards for entrance into the ranks of the Methodist itinerary; he could not read the Bible or the hymnbook. However, he often created his own opportunities to preach as a layman, expounding upon a Biblical text which another read for him.

Taylor's tremendous determination was exemplified by his efforts to learn to read. Around 1815 he became a farm worker for a woman in exchange for his lodging and for instruction in reading. As soon as he was able to read, he was sent by Amos Binney to Newmarket Seminary, but six weeks of formal education was all that Taylor could endure while studying with youngsters who were half his own age.

"Father" Taylor was admitted to the Methodist conference of his area after he had learned to read, and he was assigned to a regular circuit in 1819. He rode the circuit for about ten years until he was commissioned to start a campaign which would bring some redeeming influence to the sailors of Boston. He started his work in 1828 in a small Methodist chapel, and by 1833 he was preaching in the newly-built, nonsectarian Seamen's Bethel which was located in the North Square. From his pulpit there, he preached for nearly forty years.

Taylor toured Europe in 1832, and took a trip to the Holy Land in 1842. He was chaplain of the *Macedonia* when it sailed from America to IRELAND in 1846 to carry food to the Irish who were suffering the pains of a potato famine.

The work of Father Taylor brought him into contact with numerous famous people of his time. While he was seeking funds for Seamen's Bethel, the minister met Ralph Waldo Emerson—then pastor of the Second Church (Unitarian) of Boston—and a life-long friendship ensued. Emerson was impressed by the realism and vividness of the converted seaman's sermons. The famous poet and essayist declared that Taylor was made by the same hand that had made Shakespeare, Demosthenes, and Burns. Of the five sermons that Emerson wrote after leaving the ministry, one of them was delivered for his friend, Father Taylor, at Seamen's Bethel.

Walt Whitman wrote a newspaper article about Taylor. Charles Dickens devoted a whole chapter to him in his *American Notes,* and Herman Melville probably used the vibrant minister as his pattern for "Father Mapple" in the novel *Moby Dick.* Other notables who took advantage of opportunities to hear Father Taylor preach included: Daniel Webster, Richard Henry Dana, Jenny Lind, William Ellery Channing, and Horace Mann.

The Seamen's Bethel was run without sectarianism and without deference to the wealthy and influential people who came to hear Father Taylor preach. Well-dressed Bostonians had to stand or sit around the wall of the church, the pews being reserved for the sailors. Declaring that "the world is just large enough for the people. There is no room for a partition wall," Taylor often prayed: "O Lord, deliver us from bad rum and bigotry." His sermons were considered to be among the best of the times, but no complete one survives because he always spoke extemporaneously.

Edward Thompson Taylor was successful in accomplishing the task for which Seamen's Bethel was built—to bring a Christlike influence to bear upon the sailors of the area. One of Boston's mayors said about the ex-seaman, "He is worth a hundred policemen."

Dictionary of American Biography.
Gilbert Haven and Thomas Russell, *Father Taylor, the Sailor Preacher.* New York: Hunt and Eaton, 1871.

JOHN W. YEATES

TAYLOR, EDWIN LLEWELLYN (1924-   ), secretary of the Conference of the METHODIST CHURCH IN THE CARIBBEAN AND THE AMERICAS, was born on May 3, 1924, at St. Michael, Barbados, son of Edwin Hilton Taylor and Miriam (Kirton) Taylor. He married Marguerite Elaine Rogers of St. Andrew, JAMAICA, on April 29, 1953. She was Sister in charge of the Public Health Service of the Bahamas, 1959-65. They have one daughter, Jennifer Marguerite.

Edwin L. Taylor was educated at Harrison College, Barbados, 1936-1941; at Caenwood Theological College, Jamaica, 1946-50; and at RICHMOND COLLEGE, University of London, B.D., 1957-58. He served as circuit minister, Kingstown, St. Vincent, 1950-51; Tunapuna, Port-of-Spain Circuit, Trinidad, 1951-52; Bahamas District, June, 1952, to February, 1967; Andros and Windward Mission Circuit, 1952-57; superintendent of Circuit, 1955-57, residing at Orange Creek, Cat Island. He became minister in charge of Wesley Church, Nassau, 1958-67, and also 1964-67 at St. Michael's Methodist Church, Nassau, which was built in 1964. He became secretary of the Bahamas District Synod, 1962-64.

In 1958 and 1964, E. L. Taylor attended courses of study at the Ecumenical Institute, Bossey near GENEVA, SWITZERLAND. He attended the WORLD METHODIST COUNCIL Executive Committee in Jamaica, October 1964, and also as a member of the Council attended the WORLD METHODIST CONFERENCE, London, in August 1966. He has been a member since 1964 of the Methodist Committee in consultation with the Anglican Church of the Province of the WEST INDIES. He was secretary of the Provincial Synod of the Methodist Church, Western Area, 1962-67. Designated secretary of the newly organized Methodist Church in the Caribbean and the Americas in 1964, he took up that appointment in May 1967, and resides in ANTIGUA where that Church's headquarters are located.

HUGH B. SHERLOCK

TAYLOR, HERBERT JOHN (1893-), American manufacturer and leader of religious youth movements, was born at Pickford, Mich., April 18, 1893, son of Frank and Nellie (Salkeld) Taylor. After graduation from NORTHWESTERN UNIVERSITY in 1917, he served in World War I as lieutenant (j.g.) U.S.N.R.F.; then engaged in insurance and real estate business at Pauls Valley, Okla. Joining the Jewel Tea Company, in 1924, he rose rapidly to assistant to the presidency, then became vice president and in 1931 president of the Club Aluminum Company.

Associated with religious activities since college days, he for many years was chairman of the Board of Trustees of the First United Methodist Church of Park Ridge, Ill. He also has been chairman of the board of the Young Life Campaign of Dallas, the Christian Workers Foundation, Christian Service Brigade, Inter-Varsity Christian Fellowship, the Christian Camps Foundation, National Boys and Girls Week, and other groups relating laymen, particularly young people, to Christianity. He served on the Price Adjustment Board of the War Department, seeking to renegotiate World War II contracts for reduction of excessive profits.

Rising rapidly in Rotary International, he became its 1954-55 president. Seeking to translate the Sermon on the Mount into modern terms as a code for businessmen, he devised *"The Four Way Test of the Things We Think, Say or Do."* It asks "1. Is it the *truth?* 2. Is it *fair* to all concerned? 3. Will it build *goodwill* and *better friendships?* and 4. Will it be *beneficial* to all concerned?" *The Four Way Test* was copyrighted in 1946 by Rotary International, and now is routinely used as vocational service indoctrination of new members of Rotary Clubs.

Herbert Taylor and Gloria Forbrich were married June 21, 1919, and they have two children, Gloria Beverly and Ramona Estelline.

The Rotarian Magazine, Sept. 1957, pp. 26 ff.
Who's Who in America. LELAND D. CASE

TAYLOR, ISAAC (1787-18 ?), British writer on philosophical and religious subjects, was born in 1787 at Lavenham, one of the most beautiful villages in Suffolk, and was the son of Isaac Taylor (1759-1829), an Independent minister at Colchester. He settled at Ongar in Essex, and wrote a score of works. As early as 1818 he was on the staff of the *Eclectic Review,* and he later contributed to *Good Words.* His writings include: *Natural*

History of Enthusiasm (1829); *Fanaticism* (1833); *Spiritual Despotism* (1835); *Physical Theory of Another Life* (1836); *Home Education* (1838); *Logic in Theology and Other Essays* (1859); *Ultimate Civilisation* (1860); and *The Restoration of Belief* (1864). His connection with Methodism lies in his book, *Wesley and Methodism* (1851), which gives an independent approach to the subject, but is not of the first importance.

JOHN T. WILKINSON

TAYLOR, ISABEL ANNIE (? -1961), NEW ZEALAND Methodist laywoman, was born in Marton, but after her marriage to Charles E. Taylor, lived in Feilding for over forty years. She was a devoted worker in the Feilding Methodist Church—a Bible class leader for about thirty years, a local preacher, and an effective lay pastor. She served a term as national president of the Methodist Women's Missionary Union, and was for several years a member of the standing committee of the Conference on Spiritual Advance.

In addition to her work in the local church, she was vitally interested in the BRITISH AND FOREIGN BIBLE SOCIETY and the Women's Christian Temperance Union. As mayoress, during her husband's term as mayor of Feilding from 1929 to 1935, Mrs. Taylor gave herself unsparingly in organizing relief work for needy people during the depression. She died at Feilding on Sept. 18, 1961.

New Zealand Methodist Times, Dec. 2, 1961.
L. R. M. GILMORE

J. PAUL TAYLOR

TAYLOR, J. PAUL (1895-), American minister and an ordained elder of the Genesee Conference, FREE METHODIST CHURCH, is now bishop-emeritus of that denomination. GREENVILLE COLLEGE conferred upon him the D.D. degree in 1949, and Houghton College, N. Y., the Litt.D. degree in 1958. He served in the Central Illinois and Genesee Conferences of the Free Methodist Church, a total of fifty years—twenty-five as pastor, one as evangelist, seven as superintendent, and bishop seventeen. He was elected bishop in 1947. He is the author of *The Music of Pentecost; Holiness, the Finished Foundation,* and *Goodly Heritage.* Bishop and Mrs. Taylor live in Winona Lake, Ind.

BYRON S. LAMSON

TAYLOR, JAMES (1823-1913), was a NEW ZEALAND Methodist layman who was born in Tunbridge Wells, Kent, England, on Aug. 17, 1823, and arrived in New Zealand on Nov. 13, 1840.

Robust in mind and body, he proved an ideal pioneer. During the Maori disturbances in the Hutt Valley, he joined the militia, receiving his commission as captain in 1846. Settled in Tawa Flat, he followed farming pursuits and was appointed a justice of the peace. He established a SUNDAY SCHOOL of which he was superintendent for sixty years. One room in his hospitable home was known as "the prophets' chamber," and was almost exclusively used by visiting preachers. For many years treasurer of the Primitive Methodist connection in New Zealand, he died in 1913.

ARCHER O. HARRIS

TAYLOR, JOSEPH (1752-1830), British Methodist, was born at Duffield near Derby in 1752. He became a Wesleyan itinerant in 1777, and overwork during a revival in West Cornwall, in which it is said that there was an increase of six hundred members, left him with a permanently weakened constitution. He was one of the three preachers whom JOHN WESLEY ordained for SCOTLAND; the ordinations (as DEACON and ELDER) took place on Aug. 1 and 2, 1785; the certificates have disappeared. Taylor had already been included in the LEGAL HUNDRED under John Wesley's DEED OF DECLARATION, 1784, and was one of the seven trustees appointed to be John Wesley's literary executors under a deed of 1790. He was elected president of the Wesleyan CONFERENCE in 1802. For the last nine years of his life he was a *supernumerary* at Derby, where he practiced the strictest frugality, that he might be the more charitable. He died on June 22, 1830.

JOHN NEWTON

TAYLOR, LANDON (1813- ?), American pioneer preacher in IOWA, was born in NEW YORK state in 1813. As a young man he emigrated to OHIO in 1834. Converted three years later, he was licensed to preach in 1842. He went to Iowa in 1845 and was received into the IOWA CONFERENCE at the session held in Old Zion Church, Burlington, that year. Mount Pleasant circuit was his first appointment in Iowa.

The following year, 1846, with a co-pastor, John Jay, he was appointed to the Montezuma Mission, the first work in Poweshiek County. Upon coming to Montezuma, they found nearly everybody afflicted with the "chills." Many families had moved together in order to have enough well persons to care for the sick. Taylor himself was seized with the ailment and although severely afflicted, continued his preaching.

Taylor was one of five men received into the Conference in 1845, who became prominent workers in Methodism. The others: L. B. Dennis, M. H. Hare, John Norris and Michael See. With the division of the Conference

in 1856, he became a member of the newly established UPPER IOWA CONFERENCE.

In the latter part of his life, he became the author of a book, *The Battlefield Reserves.* It was a portrayal of pioneer Methodism in Iowa. He is remembered and revered, not only by Methodism but in circles of other faiths, for his deep consecration and consuming zeal.

RUSSELL G. NYE

PRINCE A. TAYLOR

TAYLOR, PRINCE ALBERT, JR. (1907-   ), American editor and bishop, was born at Hennessey, Okla., on Jan. 27, 1907, the son of Prince Albert and Bertha Ann (Littles) Taylor. He attended Samuel Huston College in AUSTIN, Texas, where he received his A.B. degree in 1931. Further degrees have been: B.D. from GAMMON THEOLOGICAL SEMINARY; M.A. from Union Theological Seminary and Columbia University in New York City in 1940; Ed.D. from New York University in 1948; D.D. from RUST COLLEGE in 1949, Gammon Seminary in 1950, and DICKINSON COLLEGE in 1967; the LL.D. from PHILANDER SMITH COLLEGE; and Litt.D., UNIVERSITY OF PUGET SOUND. On July 18, 1929, he was united in marriage to Annie Belle Thaxton. They have one daughter, Isabella Taylor Butts of Atlanta, Ga.

Prince A. Taylor was ordained elder in 1931 at the NORTH CAROLINA (ME) CONFERENCE. He held pastorates at Kernersville, N. C., 1931; Northwest Greensboro Charge, 1931-34; St. Thomas, Thomasville, N. C., 1934-37; East Calvary, New York City, 1937-40. He was the summer pastor at St. Mark's Church, New York City, 1940-42, 1945-48.

At the CENTRAL JURISDICTIONAL CONFERENCE in NEW ORLEANS, La., he was elected a bishop of The Methodist Church on June 16, 1956, and assigned to the Monrovia, LIBERIA Area where he spent eight years. In 1964 he was assigned to the NEW JERSEY Area.

Further work and positions have included teaching

in BENNETT COLLEGE, 1940-43; Gammon Seminary, 1943-48; exchange teacher at CLARK COLLEGE, 1943-48; adult counselor for the Central Jurisdiction National Methodist Student Commission, 1944-48; director of the Correspondence School for Commission on Ministerial Training, Central Jurisdiction, 1945-48; editor of the *Central Christian Advocate*, New Orleans, 1948-56; president of the COUNCIL OF BISHOPS, 1965-66; chairman of the Board of Directors of Religion In American Life since 1967. He is chairman of the COMMISSION ON THE STRUCTURE OF METHODISM OVERSEAS; chairman of the executive committee of the WORLD METHODIST COUNCIL; a member of the General Board of MISSIONS; vice-president of the New Jersey Council of Churches; a member of the Commission on Ecumenical Affairs; General Board, NATIONAL COUNCIL OF CHURCHES. He is a trustee of several educational institutions, including Union Theological Seminary, WESLEY THEOLOGICAL SEMINARY, AMERICAN UNIVERSITY, and DREW UNIVERSITY. He served on Gov. Richard J. Hughes' select Commission on Civil Disorder, State of New Jersey, 1967-68; is a member of the New Jersey Youth Commission, and the Pennsylvania/New Jersey/Delaware Committee on Regional Development.

Bishop Taylor was decorated twice by the Government of Liberia, and in 1964 received the St. George's Award Medal for distinguished service in The Methodist Church.

His episcopal residence is at Princeton, N. J., and he presides over the New Jersey Area which includes the NORTHERN NEW JERSEY (formerly the Newark) and the SOUTHERN NEW JERSEY Conferences.

Who's Who in America, Vol. 34.
Who's Who in The Methodist Church, 1966.   N. B. H.

TAYLOR, SAMUEL (1711-1772), British Anglican, the vicar of Quinton in Gloucestershire, was one of the six clergymen who were members of the first Methodist conference held in 1744; he was third on the list at the Conference of 1746. He was the son of Abdias Taylor, incumbent of St. John's, Worcester, the town where he was born. He entered Merton College, Oxford, in 1728; his first appointment was at St. Clement's, Worcester, and his second at Quinton, near Evesham (not to be confused with another Quinton, near Birmingham), where he stayed until his death in 1772. His association with the WESLEYS extended from 1743 to May 1746. CHARLES ATMORE, in his *Methodist Memorial,* says that Taylor "went out into the highways and hedges, into the streets and lanes of the city, in order to compel sinners to come to the marriage supper of the Lamb" (p. 221), and adds that he suffered greatly in the Methodist persecutions in the Wednesbury and Darlaston area in Staffordshire. In March 1772, John Wesley preached in Quinton Church. RICHARD WHATCOAT was under Taylor's ministry in his early years.

JOHN T. WILKINSON

TAYLOR, THOMAS (1738-1816), British Methodist, was born at Rothwell, near LEEDS, on Nov. 11, 1738, and after a careless youth was converted by the Methodists. He became one of JOHN WESLEY's preachers in 1761, and saw hard service, with privations and persecutions, in WALES, IRELAND, SCOTLAND (where he pioneered Methodist work in Glasgow), and England. His account of these experiences may be found in *Lives of Early Meth-*

THOMAS TAYLOR

odist Preachers. He had little formal education, but by hard study mastered Latin, Greek, and Hebrew, and published numerous sermons, tracts of a controversial nature (including *An Answer to Paine's "Age of Reason"* in 1796), and a full scale *History of the Waldenses and Albigenses.*

Taylor was one of the inner group of preachers on whom John Wesley relied in the last decade of his life. In the controversy over the administration of the SACRAMENTS after Wesley's death in 1791, Taylor strongly favored their administration by the Methodist preachers. He was chosen president of the Wesleyan CONFERENCE in 1796, and in this capacity he pronounced sentence of expulsion upon ALEXANDER KILHAM, the final act of the drama which led to the formation of the METHODIST NEW CONNEXION. Taylor was elected president a second time in 1809, and died at Birch House, near Bolton, in Lancashire, on Oct. 13, 1816, after an itinerancy of fifty-five years. In the words of THOMAS JACKSON, "Next to Mr. Wesley, he filled the place of an effective man considerably longer than any other Methodist preacher." His desire, expressed in his last sermon shortly before his death, "to die, like an old soldier, sword in hand," was granted, and James Montgomery's ode, written in his memory, effectively conveys his indomitable spirit:

> Servant of God; well done,
> Rest from thy lov'd employ.

T. Jackson, *Lives of Early Methodist Preachers.* 1846.
JOHN NEWTON

TAYLOR, VINCENT (1887-1968), British Methodist biblical scholar, was born on Jan. 1, 1887, and was educated at Accrington Grammar School and at the University of London. He entered the Wesleyan Methodist ministry in 1909 and spent many years in circuit ministry before being appointed as New Testament tutor (and later principal) of WESLEY COLLEGE, Headingley, in 1930. He remained there until his retirement in 1953.

His early interest in New Testament scholarship lay in the literary and historical criticism of the Gospels; his writings in this period included *The Historical Evidence for the Virgin Birth* (1920); *Behind the Third Gospel* (1926), which was concerned with the Proto-Luke hypothesis; and *The Formation of the Gospel Tradition* (1933), which dealt with form criticism. His great commentary on *Saint Mark's Gospel* (1952) shared the same interest. In these works his conclusions were usually less radical than those of continental scholars like Rudolf Bultmann. His later writings on the Person and Work of Christ reveal a stronger theological interest. His work on the atonement appeared as a trilogy: *Jesus and His Sacrifice* (1937), *The Atonement in New Testament Teaching* (which was the FERNLEY-HARTLEY LECTURE for 1940), and *Forgiveness and Reconciliation* (1941). His trilogy on the Person of Christ was given as the Speaker's Lectures at Oxford (1951-56) and published as *The Names of Jesus* (1953); *The Life and Ministry of Jesus* (1954); and *The Person of Christ in New Testament Teaching* (1958). He also contributed to *The Interpreter's Bible*. He received a number of honorary doctorates; was elected a Fellow of the British Academy in 1954, and given the academy award of the Burkitt Medal for Biblical Studies in 1960. He died on Nov. 28, 1968.

PETER STEPHENS

WILLIAM TAYLOR

TAYLOR, WILLIAM (1821-1902), American missionary and bishop, whose "mission field" embraced six continents, was born on May 2, 1821, in Rockbridge County, Va. Although a church member for some years previously, he was "converted" at Panther Gap Camp Meeting in 1841. Before the CAMP MEETING closed he had entered upon that ministry of personal evangelism and "street preaching" which was to carry him to the far corners of the earth. In 1842 he received his first appointment, as "junior preacher" on the Franklin Circuit of the BALTIMORE CONFERENCE. The Conference received him on trial in 1843, and appointed him to the Deerfield Circuit.

At the session of the Conference in 1845 he was received into full membership, ordained a DEACON, and appointed to the Sweet Springs Circuit. His marriage to Annie Kimberlin occurred in 1846. Further appointments included GEORGETOWN, D. C. (1846) and North Baltimore Station (1848).

Taylor began his long and illustrious career as a missionary with his appointment to the CALIFORNIA Mission in 1849, by Bishop BEVERLY WAUGH. There a bar-room was often his chapel and a whiskey keg his pulpit, but much of his preaching was done out of doors in the streets of California's rapidly growing towns. Hundreds responded to his messages during his seven years among the adventurers and outcastes who had been led to California by the lure of gold. The years from 1857 to 1862 were spent in evangelistic tours through New England, the Midwest and CANADA. The first of his many missionary journeys overseas took him to AUSTRALIA, NEW ZEALAND and Tasmania, where he labored with great success until 1866. His plans to open evangelistic work in INDIA, to which he felt called at this time, were interrupted by the illness of his son, Stuart. At the advice of his doctor, Taylor, with his family, sailed to SOUTH AFRICA instead, where the climate was said to be more favorable.

An invitation to preach in a Wesleyan Methodist Church led to a two-year mission in South Africa (1866-1868), where Taylor began the program of preaching in English to the European settlers, a program that was to prove very effective during the many years of his ministry overseas. Welcomed by ministers and congregations of the Wesleyan Church (this had been true in Australia also), Taylor was able to preach to large audiences. But his heart was drawn to the non-whites, the Kaffirs and others, and he began the ministry through interpreters which would lead to the conversion of thousands in Africa, India and South America.

The years from 1868 to 1870 were spent in evangelistic campaigns in England and the WEST INDIES and again in Australia and in CEYLON. Having heard of the evangelistic successes of Taylor's preaching in Australia and South Africa, JAMES MILLS THOBURN, afterwards a bishop of the M.E. Church in India, invited William Taylor to conduct evangelistic campaigns in India as well. Taylor arrived in BOMBAY in November 1870, and began a ministry which was to reach thousands in the principal cities of India. He soon discovered that many of the Europeans and Anglo-Indians, though members of established churches, were only nominal Christians. These became the center of his attention, first in LUCKNOW, the headquarters of Methodist work in India, and later in other cities outside the area of the Methodist field. This incursion into areas already "occupied" by other denominations led to much misunderstanding. Small evangelistic bands, somewhat after the manner of the Methodist "CLASS MEETINGS," were formed of those who were converted under Taylor's preaching. In February 1872, in response to the request of some members of these bands, Taylor organized a Methodist congregation in Bombay. In quick succession similar congregations were formed in the larger cities of India. The various cities in which Taylor preached and established churches in India, and later in South America and Africa, are too numerous to list here.

In the larger cities of India, Taylor developed what he called a "Pauline Method of Missions." Counting on the fact that in every large town and city there were colonies of English-speaking people, he determined to form fellowship bands, which if requested might be organized into churches. These would voluntarily undertake the support of their own pastors, and would become centers for the evangelization of other English-speaking people, and eventually, of the masses of India. It was proposed that the churches would neither ask nor accept any funds from the Missionary Society of the Church in America, beyond the passage of missionaries to India. The ministers would have no stated salary, but would live on a subsistence allowance as near the level of the native Indians as health and efficiency allowed. An adequate development of Indian resources would make it unnecessary to depend on the Missionary Society. Appropriations in advance, he believed, might hinder a healthy development of the churches. New churches were organized so rapidly, however, that it was found difficult to supply them with pastors raised up in India; hence it was deemed legitimate to call missionaries from America, whose transit, in most cases, would be paid by the Missionary Society, but whose salaries would be paid in India by the churches to which they ministered.

The "Pauline Method" proved so effective in the beginning that it was soon possible to organize an independent Mission with Taylor as Superintendent. In 1874 this Mission became the Bombay and Bengal Mission of the M.E. Church and two years later became the SOUTH INDIA CONFERENCE. Taylor's effort to carry on a self-supporting mission in India, and later in South America, in the name of the M.E. Church, but not under the direction of its Missionary Society, led to heated debate with officials of that Society. Also, the bishops of the M.E. Church felt unable to ordain and appoint ministers to work in areas outside the control of the Missionary Society. This led Taylor to request that he be "located" by the South India Conference. Eventually, responsibility for all of the work established by Taylor was assumed by the Missionary Society because of growing difficulties in finding support within the Mission itself.

Taylor left India in 1875, at the request of Dwight L. Moody, to engage in an evangelistic campaign in LONDON, and to visit his family in California, whom he had not seen for over seven years. He had intended to return to India, but became convinced that God was calling him to plant missions on the West Coast of South America also. He arrived in Callao, PERU, in 1877. For the next seven years he was engaged in establishing a self-supporting Mission in Peru, CHILE, and BRAZIL. Finding that the European settlers were more interested in education than in evangelism, he recruited teacher-preachers to man his mission centers. The support for this work was to be given entirely by local residents. Some of the self-supporting centers became permanent, others did not.

Elected as a lay delegate by the South India Conference, Taylor attended the GENERAL CONFERENCE (ME) of 1884. In an unprecedented action, he was nominated, elected a missionary bishop, ordained, and assigned to Africa within the space of twenty-four hours. He was to supervise the work of the Missionary Society in LIBERIA, but was free to establish self-supporting centers outside that country. Soon a chain of mission stations was established in the valley of the CONGO and its tributaries, stretching inland from ANGOLA to Luluabourg. Centers were also opened in MOZAMBIQUE on the East Coast.

The General Conference of 1896 retired Bishop Taylor, then seventy-five years of age. He lived at Palo Alto, Calif., until his death in 1902.

While many evidences of the self-supporting missions of Bishop Taylor remain in Africa and South America, the well-established churches spread across India are to this day the principal monument to the vision and zeal of this great missionary statesman. Few men have traveled more widely, raised more money, or recruited more missionary workers for the cause of Methodist missions than did William Taylor.

W. C. Barclay, *History of Missions*. 1957.
M. H. Harper, *India*. 1936.
W. Taylor, *Darkest Africa*. 1898.
————, *India*. 1875.
————, *South Africa*. 1867.
————, *Story of My Life*. 1895.
————, *Ten Years in India*. 1882.   MARVIN H. HARPER

TAYLOR, WILLIAM GEORGE (1845-1934), was born at Knayton, Yorkshire, England, of Wesleyan Methodist stock. He was accepted for the ministry in England and sent to RICHMOND COLLEGE for training. Answering a call for men to go to AUSTRALIA, he was appointed to BRISBANE in 1870, later serving in several other QUEENSLAND circuits. In 1879 he transferred to the NEW SOUTH WALES CONFERENCE for the remainder of his ministry.

He was instrumental in promoting revivals of religion in several places, and throughout his years of service was in demand for the leadership of evangelistic missions. His gospel singing was a feature of his work.

In 1884 he was appointed to the Central SYDNEY CIRCUIT and he soon founded the Central Methodist Mission. It is authoritatively claimed that this was the first Central Mission, the English counterparts soon following.

He was a pioneer of the field of social service institutions, establishing eleven of these.

He also founded a Christian journal called *The Weekly Greeting*.

He was instrumental in establishing open air services in the heart of Sydney, for which he organized brass bands to provide the music and to lead the processions which were a feature of this work. He was later called to England to conduct missions there and in the U.S.A.

He served in the Central Mission for a period of twenty-five years during which he became President of the New South Wales Conference. He wrote his autobiography, entitled *The Life Story of an Australian Evangelist*. The English edition was called *Taylor of Down Under*. He became a supernumerary in 1913.

AUSTRALIAN EDITORIAL COMMITTEE

TEAS, GEORGE W. (1808-1864), American pioneer circuit rider, was born in 1808 at Sparta, Tenn. Entering the ministry of the M.E. Church, he served in ARKANSAS and MISSOURI before removing to BURLINGTON, Iowa, where he practiced law. When the Black Hawk Purchase became a part of MICHIGAN Territory (1834), Teas, failing to gain a seat in the Territorial Council, blamed the Methodists and withdrew from the Church, announcing:

Let all men know from shore to shore,
That G. W. Teas is a Methodist no more.

Afterwards he repented, returning to his church, and someone wrote:

> Let all men know from California to Maine,
> That G. W. Teas is a Methodist again.

In 1844 BARTHOLOMEW WEED, with a certificate of Teas' restoration to the Church, recommended that his credentials be restored, but the IOWA CONFERENCE restored Teas' parchments to him only after he personally renewed his request in 1846. He was appointed to Three Rivers Mission in 1849, having previously traveled six years in the itinerant ministry. Henceforth, the name of George W. Teas, listed as an effective elder (1850), appears frequently in the annals of early Iowa Methodism. He worked in Burlington, Oskaloosa (1850-1852), Keosauqua (1852-1853), Winchester (1853-1854), Wapello (1854-1855), Washington (1855-1857), DES MOINES, and Indianola, where he was the first to preach. Granted a "worn-out" preacher's superannuate status from 1857 to 1861, he located then, making his home at Washington, Iowa, until his death in 1864.

R. A. Gallaher, *Methodism in Iowa*. 1944.
A. W. Haines, *Makers of Iowa Methodism*. 1900.
E. H. Waring, *Iowa Conference*. 1910.
Yearbook of the Iowa Conference.   MARTIN L. GREER

TE AWATAIA, WIREMU NEERA (c. 1800-1866), NEW ZEALAND Methodist Maori layman, was in young manhood a noted warrior. He became chief of the tribes in the Aotea, Waipa, and Raglan districts. He was one of the first converts after JAMES WALLIS established a mission station at Raglan in 1835, when he took the name of Wiremu Neera (William Naylor).

In 1839, he felt constrained to preach the Gospel to the Maoris of Taranaki, an area which he had formerly assisted in laying waste. On his return home, he publicly released all the prisoner slaves his war parties had captured in their former campaigns.

He was among the first signatories of the Treaty of Waitangi, and remained loyal to the British Crown during the Maori Wars of the 1860's. Greatly honored both by Maoris and Europeans, he spent his closing years in Raglan. After his death in 1866, a monument was erected to his memory by the government on a centrally situated site in Raglan Township—a grateful acknowledgement of his many public services.

E. H. Schnackenberg, "Romance of a Rangatira" (manuscript).
                                        L. R. M. GILMORE

TECUMSEH, MICHIGAN, U.S.A., was settled in May 1824, and named for the famous Indian chief. Methodism came to Tecumseh in the fall of 1826 when JOHN BAUGHMAN made Tecumseh a regular preaching point on the Monroe Circuit, a three-weeks circuit covering parts of MICHIGAN and OHIO. In January 1828, a Society was organized with eleven charter members. One of these, Margarette Cross, had been converted in IRELAND in her youth; her husband was a local preacher in Ireland under JOHN WESLEY and they had entertained him in their home. Later in 1828 came Joseph Bangs, brother of NATHAN BANGS; Joseph was a local preacher and a strong pillar of early Methodism in this area.

In 1831 Tecumseh was made head of a large four-weeks circuit covering six counties, and 400 miles in length. By 1836 the circuit had 483 members, the largest in Michigan. The circuit continued to have a large membership, though it was steadily cut down in geographical area. In 1851 Tecumseh was made a station.

In 1842 the first wooden church was built. Luther Whitney, senior preacher on the circuit, did manual labor that year and raised funds for four new churches at one time. In 1863-64 a large brick church was built at a cost of $10,376, and was dedicated on Aug. 11, 1864. It survived two fires and stood over a century only one block from the center of town. In 1905 a kitchen addition was built as a memorial to Lemon Barnes, a former member of the conference. In 1965-66 a new church costing $350,000 was built west of the Red Mill Pond.

In 1855 the LADIES AID SOCIETY was organized, one of the earliest such organizations. The first PARSONAGE was acquired in 1853; a second parsonage was built in 1860; the third in 1890.

Through the nineteenth century, Tecumseh was a place of Methodistic importance; it was served by prominent ministers and was a favorite place for ministerial retirement. Several men have gone into the ministry from Tecumseh, including Donald Benedict, one of the founders of the East Harlem Protestant Parish.

E. H. Pilcher, *Michigan*. 1878.   RONALD A. BRUNGER

TEES, FRANCIS HARRISON (1875-1951), a well known American historian and pastor, was born in PHILADELPHIA in 1875. He was educated at Dickinson Preparatory School and DICKINSON COLLEGE and joined the PHILADELPHIA CONFERENCE in 1900. His greatest work was as pastor for sixteen years (1931-47) of historic Old ST. GEORGE'S CHURCH in Philadelphia. His constant research about Methodism and particularly about early Methodism in Philadelphia resulted in the publication of a number of books on Methodist history: *The Beginnings of Methodism in England and America; The Story of Old St. George's; Whitefield, the Methodist; Methodist Origins;* and *The Ancient Landmark of American Methodism.*

His small stature, his pince nez glasses and his neat conservative dress became a familiar sight to historians and librarians in and about Philadelphia. He died Oct. 4, 1951 and was buried in Mt. Vernon Cemetery, Philadelphia.

A. W. Cliffe, *Our Methodist Heritage*. 1957.
Minutes of the Philadelphia Conference, 1952.
                                        FREDRICK E. MASER

TEETOTAL METHODISTS. In 1837 teetotalism reached St. Ives, Cornwall, by advocacy from Shropshire, and by the following year had become well-established. By 1840 it claimed a membership of more than half the population, but found some opposition from the circuit ministers. In 1841 the MANCHESTER Conference voted against teetotalism, and this view was shared by Jonathan Turner, the newly appointed superintendent of the St. Ives Circuit. Early in September came a severe clash, and about 250 members of teetotal conviction broke away from the St. Ives Society, and about 150 from other societies. Organizing themselves as a Methodist society, they adopted Wesley's *Rules*, with the addition of a rule on abstinence, and took the name of *Teetotal Methodists*. By 1842 the number had reached some 600 members with twenty-four local preachers; a new circuit

was formed. In St. Ives the group met in the room of a linen draper until the completion of the chapel in 1842; other chapels were erected later elsewhere, and class tickets and preaching plans were issued. After some years the large circuit was divided; each new circuit seems to have been largely independent, and there does not appear to have been any annual conference. The denomination was confined to West Cornwall and does not seem to have had a regular ministry, the desire for which ultimately became the cause of disintegration. In 1848 some societies passed over into the WESLEYAN METHODIST ASSOCIATION, on condition that abstaining preachers should be appointed to them; at St. Ives the crisis came in 1860, some societies joining the METHODIST NEW CONNEXION, and, from areas further west, others joining the UNITED METHODIST FREE CHURCHES. Probably by 1865 the separate denomination had ceased to exist. The unifying force had been the conviction of teetotalism, but probably the actual separation would not have occurred if there had not been the pressure of ministerial demand.

Wesley Historical Society *Proceedings*, xxxiii.

JOHN T. WILKINSON

TE KOPUA, Waipa, NEW ZEALAND, was the site of an early Wesleyan mission station founded by THOMAS BUDDLE in 1841, where he served a four-year term. Buddle had chosen an early site in the Waipa area during the previous year, but had been prevented from occupying it because it was a Maori sacred place. JOHN WHITELEY, who supervised the area, upheld the Maori objection, and the site at Te Kopua was chosen instead. Later George Buttle served at Te Kopua for many years, making the station almost self-supporting by keeping a flock of sheep. This was a European missionary's appointment until the Maori Wars in 1860, and a Maori minister's appointment from 1891 to 1921. The site is marked by a memorial erected in 1962.

W. Morley, *New Zealand*. 1900.
New Zealand Methodist Home and Maori Mission Records.

L. R. M. GILMORE

TELEVISION, RADIO AND FILM COMMUNICATION, an agency of The United Methodist Church, originated as and is an extension of the Television, Radio and Film Commission of The Methodist Church. It is an agency created by the GENERAL CONFERENCE to produce, distribute, research and in general supervise the church's efforts to communicate the Christian message through electronic and photographic mass media.

TRAFCO, as the Commission is commonly called, began in the work of the COUNCIL OF SECRETARIES of the church. For a number of years H. G. Conger had served the Council in the former M.E. Church in the preparation and distribution of missionary promotion materials (mostly slide lectures). After unification in 1940, these functions were transferred in part to the Board of Missions. At the close of the second World War, the increased availability of 16mm sound motion picture projectors and the newly developed filmstrip with recording made possible a wider utilization of audiovisuals in the churches. As a result, the Council appointed an interboard committee under the chairmanship of N. F. Forsyth to produce additional materials for the entire church. It was finally decided that an inter-agency and church-wide organization was needed.

Following an action by the General Conference in 1948, representatives of the agencies met and drew up a constitution which provided for a board of managers appointed partly by the agencies and partly by the bishops of the church. Bishop DONALD H. TIPPETT was elected the first president of the Commission.

The General Conference of 1952 approved the Commission as one of the agencies to be included in World Service funds. Approximately $100,000 were made available the first year. The Commission voted to establish an office in NASHVILLE, Tenn., and elected HARRY C. SPENCER executive secretary. The staff then consisted of four or five persons—now nearly fifty.

An important factor in the early development of the Commission was the interest of Bishop CHARLES C. SELECMAN in sponsoring a film on the life of JOHN WESLEY. With the funds which he was able to raise and money in the World Service budget, the film was produced by J. ARTHUR RANK in London in 1953.

In 1953, also, the bishops asked that TRAFCO make a study of the possible use of television by the church. As a result of this study, the TV-Radio Ministry was established with funds raised by a special appeal to the churches. It has been continued during the years since as a World Service Special fund, with the income averaging between $200,000 and $300,000 per year. Three significant TV series were produced, but unfortunately, the income was not sufficient to maintain a continuous production schedule in the expensive TV spectrum. TRAFCO has been forced in recent months, therefore, to concentrate on radio, a less expensive medium.

TRAFCO has maintained strong ties internationally through a special relationship with the World Division of the Board of Missions, through Radio Visual Education and Mass Communications Committee (RAVEMCCO) of the NATIONAL COUNCIL, and through the World Association for Christian Communications.

Certain main points seem evident:

1. The increased use of a wide variety of audiovisuals and teaching machines in the schools will require the church to use similar methods to have an effective influence on young people and children in the church school.

2. The lack of trained teachers in the churches will make it necessary that the material be conveniently packaged. At the same time, the content of the film must be especially designed to be used by volunteer (frequently untrained) teachers.

3. To use radio and television effectively is demanding. Broadcasters commonly believe that they must sell products and they do it by entertaining audiences, and thus with them an educational approach is not appropriate. Yet the church was not founded to provide amusement and entertainment for the multitudes. Its purpose is the proclamation of the gospel of Christ. Some hearers —unbelievers—at first resent and reject this message. The Commission has always taken as its task to present the Christian position in such a way as to gain a hearing from an audience that at the beginning at least may be partly antagonistic. Minds and attitudes must be changed not by manipulation but within the context of the Christian faith and its emphasis on human worth—an assignment more difficult and complex than preaching to a "captive" audience of friendly hearers in church on

Sunday morning. Yet it is felt that unless the church undertakes seriously to meet the world where the people live, it cannot hope to present its faith to the millions who never darken the church door.

In June 1968 and 1969, TRAFCO produced Night Call, a radio program which was in the nature of a nationwide telephone call-in, broadcast late at night. A guest and host in the studio would be open by long distance telephone calls to answer questions of import to anyone in the nationwide audience who wished to ask such questions. Night Call received numerous awards.

An office of TRAFCO has been established in New York due to the importance of that city in mass media. The original headquarters continue to be in Nashville, Tenn.

Disciplines, TMC, 1952, 1956, 1960, 1964; UMC, 1968, Paragraph 834, 835.　　　　　　　　　　　　HARRY SPENCER

TELFORD, JOHN (1851-1936), British Methodist and renowned editor, was born in Wigton in 1851, trained at DIDSBURY COLLEGE; thence to WESTMINSTER COLLEGE and to many circuits. He was Wesleyan CONNEXIONAL EDITOR for twenty-eight years from 1905 (with one year as book steward after Robert Culley's death in 1910). Telford had a life-long interest in the Wesleys and the Methodist revival, and his biography of JOHN WESLEY (London, 1886) became the standard work. He also edited Wesley's *Letters* (8 vols., London, 1931) and produced the volumes of Wesley's *Veterans* (7 vols., n.d.) compiled from *Lives of Early Methodist Preachers*. He died July 25, 1936.

FRANK CUMBERS

TELFORD BEQUEST. JOHN TELFORD'S career is briefly described above. As a long-term result of his interest in the WESLEY family, he bequeathed 23,000 pounds towards the establishment of a Methodist ministerial training seminary in OXFORD, a place intimately connected with the Wesleys themselves. This college was never built, chiefly because the expansion of Methodism, which it was hoped would follow Methodist Union, did not take place. After consultation with the Charity Commissioners, however, it was agreed that the money should be held in trust and used to provide bursaries for ministerial training students, and to further specific schemes, such as libraries, at the existing colleges.

JOHN C. BOWMER

TE MAHOE, early NEW ZEALAND Wesleyan mission station, was situated on the banks of the Mokau River about two miles from the sea. It was opened by George Buttle in 1841, "there having been urgent and repeated applications to be favored with the services of a resident Missionary" (Wesleyan *Methodist Missionary Report*, 1842, p. 59). He was succeeded there by CORT HENRY SCHNACKENBERG, who served there as a catechist from 1844 until his ordination in 1857. A Maori catechist—Hone Eketone—then superintended the station from 1858 until his death in 1862. Shortly after this the station was closed because population had moved from the area. The site was marked by a memorial cairn in 1966.

Cort H. Schnackenberg, "Unpublished Diaries" (held by Wesley Historical Society, New Zealand).　　L. R. M. GILMORE

TEMPERANCE IN AMERICAN METHODISM. (See ETHICAL TRADITIONS IN AMERICAN METHODISM.)

TEMPERANCE MOVEMENT IN BRITAIN. "Are you a man? God made you a man; but you make yourself a beast." These words are part of JOHN WESLEY's appeal in "A Word to a Drunkard" (*Works*, xi, 169-71). This powerful tract sought to show its readers that by succumbing to the power of liquor they were throwing away their reason and understanding and preparing themselves for every work of the devil. Wesley called for repentance from a habit which, he claimed, made a man an enemy to his king, his country, his fellows who saw him in such a state, and his God. The temperance movement as such had not begun in the eighteenth century, but Wesley's observations of his fellows left him only too aware of the danger into which many could fall through drink. There were times when he felt it necessary to reprove those who were drunk. He lodged at an inn on a journey westward in 1744:

there was a company of men exceeding drunk. Nature suggested, "Why should you speak to them? It will be, at best, labour lost; for you may be well assured none of them will mind one word you say." However, we spoke a few words to them: one of them immediately rose up and said it was all true, followed us as well as he could into our room, and appeared deeply convinced and strongly desirous to serve a better Master. (*Journal*, iii, 1953-54.)

Wesley's personal attitude seems to have varied from time to time as regards the taking of wine. As a young man he had for a while, under the influence of the famous Dr. Cheyne, drunk only water (*Journal*, v, 373). But in 1771, after reading Dr. Cadogan's book on *Chronic Distempers*, he said: "Why should he condemn wine *toto genere*, which is one of the noblest cordials in nature?" (*Journal*, v, 430.) Wesley could see that in the whole pattern of nature there was a use for alcohol, but its abuse brought him to say that it was best avoided. The sermon, "The Use of Money," contains a passage which discusses the kinds of work in which a Christian may properly engage:

Neither may we gain by hurting our neighbour *in his body*. Therefore we may not sell anything which tends to impair health. Such is, eminently, all that liquid fire, commonly called drams, or spirituous liquors. It is true, these may have a place in medicine. . . . But all who sell them in the common way, to any that will buy, are poisoners general. (Sermon, xliv.)

By 1787 Wesley was clear in his judgment on the matter of liquor: "Distilled liquors have their use, but are infinitely overbalanced by the abuse of them; therefore, were it in my power, I would banish them out of the world." (*Letters*, viii, 26.) It was left to the nineteenth century to produce what we now understand as temperance movements. The "Pledge of the Seven Men of Preston" was made in 1832, written by Joseph Livesey (1794-1884). On the history of this subject one may consult *The English Temperance Movement*, by HENRY CARTER (London, 1933); the movement received much stimulus from its American equivalent. In Britain, the national drinking habits had been altered by the Beerhouse Act of 1830, which allowed any retailer to sell beer, and rapidly nearly doubled the number of places where beer could be sold. Livesey was concerned about the human tragedy involved in drunkenness. Confronted by someone who said, "I hate a drunkard," his response was, "On the contrary, I love a drunkard, and pity him from my heart" (quoted by Carter, *op.cit.*, p. 24). Livesey's method of advocating abstinence was that of moral suasion: such a presentation of the facts of alcohol's effect on the physical and moral welfare as would appeal to men to abstain from it and join him in his crusade. His popular lectures were full of dramatic appeal. Setting fire to the spirit taken from a quart of ale he would argue:

The effect of the alcohol, which you now see burning on the plate, is to destroy the coats of the stomach and to injure the livers of those who drink it, and to produce externally a red-hot face and a nose covered with brandy blossoms. . . . I remember, when lecturing at Burnley, a man observed, when he saw the spirit on fire, "I have drunk as much of that as would have lit all the lamps in Manchester." There is, my drinking friends, one consolation on this subject for you, that if from your ale you do not get much food, you get plenty of fire. (Quoted by Carter, *op.cit.*, p. 41.)

Alongside Livesey's efforts at moral suasion came another approach, that of the United Kingdom Alliance, which was formed in 1853. The aim of the alliance was to press for legislative reform, and unlike Livesey's work, it appealed for support even to those who were not abstainers themselves but who could see the necessity of some reform.

We can now attempt to glimpse how these movements affected the Methodism of the nineteenth century. The non-Wesleyan bodies were more attracted to temperance (and especially to teetotalism) than were the Wesleyans. The PRIMITIVE METHODIST Conference rejected in 1827 the intriguing suggestion that trustees should provide wine for the use of the preachers before or after service; HUGH BOURNE often spoke on the issue, with a result that part of the connectional magazine was set aside to deal regularly with the question; and in 1832 the question was formally asked: "What is the opinion of Conference in regard to Temperance Societies?" (*Primitive Methodist Conference Minutes*, 1832) and the answer was given, "We highly approve of them, and recommend them to the attention of our people in general." After Hugh Bourne became a SUPERNUMERARY in 1842, he devoted his attention largely to teetotal preaching (cf. H. B. Kendall, *Origin and History of the Primitive Methodist Church*, London, n.d., i, 470). The first Primitive Methodist Connexional Temperance Secretary was appointed in 1897 (Kendall, *op.cit.*, ii, 531). There even arose a group who called themselves the "TEETOTAL Wesleyan METHODISTS"; this body sprang up at St. Ives, in Cornwall, in 1841, as a reaction against the views of the parent body. Few Wesleyans, however, seem to have been initially attracted to the temperance and teetotal movement. The Conference of 1841 forbade the use of unfermented sacramental wine, and declared that preachers were not allowed to advocate total abstinence in a circuit other than their own without the permission of its superintendent. JABEZ BUNTING spoke of the "annoyances arising from teetotalism (cf. B. Gregory, *Sidelights on the Conflicts of Methodism*, London, 1898, p. 318). Cornwall was spoken of as being in a state of "fermentation" on the subject, and teetotal tracts in that county could arouse high passions (Gregory, *op.cit.*, pp. 318, 514-15). In 1873 the Wesleyan Conference ap-

pointed a committee on the question of intemperance; in 1875 the Temperance Committee was formed; HUGH PRICE HUGHES, whose practical work among victims of alcohol provides a stirring chapter in the history of the West London Mission, was appointed secretary of the Temperance Committee in 1882; the mood of the connection changed in the last quarter of the nineteenth century, and by 1911 this committee could rejoice in its report to Conference that so many churches used unfermented wine, hoping that all would follow (*Wesleyan Methodist Conference Minutes*, 1911, p. 521). In 1918 the name of the committee was significantly changed to that of Temperance and Social Welfare. This brings us to the period of Methodist temperance thought which was dominated by HENRY CARTER. Carter was appointed secretary of the Wesleyan Temperance Committee in 1911, and continued this work into the united church until 1942. MALDWYN EDWARDS sees four significant parts to Carter's contribution to temperance work: he promoted effective temperance work within the Methodist Church; he communicated his enthusiasm to other churches; he was adept at employing the approach of moral suasion in conjunction with that of practical legislative reform; and he refused to isolate alcoholism from other evils (*Methodism and England*, London, 1943, p. 115). A result of the last emphasis is that the British Methodist Church now has a Department of CHRISTIAN CITIZENSHIP, which is able to consider temperance work in the context of wider social issues. The 1935 Methodist Conference passed a standing order on the use of unfermented wine in Communion Services, and in 1942 it was laid down that intoxicants should not be supplied, sold, or used on Methodist trust premises. But total abstinence is not a condition of membership of the British Methodist Church, although it is commended to members by a Conference Declaration and is one of the requirements for membership of the Order of Christian Citizenship, which is connected with the department of that name. There is evidence, however, that the feeling of Methodists in general is by no means as strongly in favor of total abstinence now as it has been in the past: the change in drinking habits and the decrease in open drunkenness as compared with conditions at certain times in the nineteenth century have a great deal to do with this. The question of the use of unfermented communion wine also arises in the context of Anglican-Methodist relations in Britain, and is one of the practical problems which would have to be solved in order to make organic union possible. (See also ETHICAL TRADITIONS, BR.)

B. GALLIERS

TEMPLIN, LESLIE G. (1894-   ), was a missionary in INDIA from 1921 to 1944. His appointments were all in the GUJARAT CONFERENCE.

He was born in Salina, Kan., Sept. 26, 1894. His uncle, Fred M. Perrill, and his aunt, Mary Louise Perrill, were missionaries in India. His younger brother, Ralph, also served the church in India, while a twin brother, Lester, and another brother were Methodist ministers in America. In 1940, he and his twin brother were both delegates to the GENERAL CONFERENCE, and being identical twins, were subjects of much confusion. It is claimed that even long-time friends and close relatives had difficulty in telling them apart.

Leslie made lasting contributions to the church in Gujarat by a distinguished service as principal of the Methodist Boys High School at Baroda, 1921-26, 1928-34, and 1937-39, and as founder and first director of the Village Educational Service. He was superintendent of the Godhra District from 1929 to 1931 and of the Ahmedabad District from 1939 to 1944. He was secretary of the Gujarat Annual Conference for fifteen years and treasurer for four years. He represented his conference in the General Conference in 1940 and 1944. On retirement from the staff of the Board of Missions in 1946, he became a professor at SOUTHWESTERN COLLEGE in Winfield, Kan.

Gujarat Annual Conference *Minutes.*   J. WASKOM PICKETT

TENNANT, THOMAS (1741-1793), British Methodist preacher, was born in LONDON in 1741 of East Anglican parents. He first preached in St. George's Fields, and after accompanying WESLEY from March to August, 1770, was received on trial and appointed to the Newcastle Circuit. For many years he suffered from nervous debility, but as "a man of a meek and quiet spirit" (*Minutes* of Wesleyan Methodist Conference, 1793), he was widely accepted as a preacher. A member of the original LEGAL HUNDRED, he was one of the signatories of the HALIFAX CIRCULAR in 1791.

T. Jackson, *Lives of Early Methodist Preachers.* 1846.

J. A. VICKERS

TENNANT, THOMAS HARDESTER (1772-1886), pioneer American preacher and centenarian, was born in VIRGINIA in 1772 and died in Washington County, Ark., 114 years later, in 1886. He was admitted on trial in the MISSOURI CONFERENCE in 1818 and assigned to the ARKANSAS circuit. This vast wilderness stretched from Fort Smith, Ark., down the valley of the Arkansas River to Arkansas Post on the Mississippi. He was appointed in 1819 to the Pecan Point circuit, a swamp-and-cane-brake section of eastern Arkansas, based at Pecan Point, a river port fifty miles up-river from MEMPHIS, the circuit ranging across the valleys of the St. Francis, Black and the White rivers to LITTLE ROCK.

In this second year of his ministry he was married to Christine Haek and by the dowry of his bride he became responsible for ownership of several slaves. The M.E. Church had interpreted such ownership as morally wrong and barred slave owners from official position. Despite a plea that legal conditions, particularly the requirement that an owner liberating a slave must give bond for the conduct of the freedman, made it impossible for him to meet the requirements of the church, Tennant was discontinued in the traveling connection—in effect his actual dismissal.

Thomas Tennant's long life furnishes a frame for the image of the church in sharing and shaping the direction of the infant American nation. In 1844 the same charge against Bishop JAMES O. ANDREW had led to a division of the church; Tennant's case provided a parallel incident which points up clearly the struggle for dominance in the interpretation of the gospel. Here, even in the south, at the lower levels of official power, the law of the church prevailed.

Because slavery was an accepted factor in this wild and raw society, Tennant's influence was but slightly impaired by his forced location. He continued to the end of his strength to preach in CAMP MEETINGS and REVIVALS and his family grew into the leadership and usefulness of the local church.

BENJAMIN C. FEW

TENNESSEE, sometimes called the "Volunteer State" because of the number of Tennesseans who volunteered for the Mexican War, is in the south central part of the United States. It is bounded by KENTUCKY and VIRGINIA on the north, by NORTH CAROLINA on the east, by GEORGIA, ALABAMA, and MISSISSIPPI on the south, and by the Mississippi River on the west. Because of its length and the nature of its terrain, it has three distinct sections, east, middle, and west. The Cumberland Mountains divide east and middle Tennessee, and the Tennessee River separates middle from west Tennessee.

The first white men to visit Tennessee were Spanish and French explorers and missionaries. The territory was granted to Sir Walter Raleigh in 1584, and to the Proprietors of Carolina in 1663. England, France, and Spain claimed the region until the Treaty of Paris in 1763 gave England full possession. In 1776 the territory was united with North Carolina at the request of its inhabitants, and it continued as a part of that commonwealth until it was admitted to the Union in 1796 as the State of Tennessee. Casting its lot with the South in the Civil War, Tennessee, like Virginia, was the scene of many conflicts, some 454 skirmishes and battles occurring within its boundaries.

Tennessee's agricultural products include tobacco, corn, cotton, hay, dairying, and cattle. Among its manufactures are chemicals, cement, coal, copper, textiles, lumber, and metal products. Water power developed under the Tennessee Valley Authority produces electricity, assures flood control, and helps to maintain navigable channels.

Organized Methodism entered Tennessee in 1783 when JEREMIAH LAMBERT was appointed to the Holston Circuit which included southwest Virginia and east Tennessee. Among preachers who followed Lambert to the region were Henry Willis, Mark Whittaker, Mark Moore, and Reuben Ellis. In 1786 the Nolichucky Circuit was formed. A year later BENJAMIN OGDEN crossed into Tennessee from Kentucky to organize the Cumberland Circuit. In 1788 two more circuits, the French Broad and the New River, were set up in east Tennessee, and a year later the Holston District was established.

In 1802, the year that annual conferences were first listed in the *Discipline*, the Tennessee work was a part of the WESTERN CONFERENCE. In 1812 that conference was divided to form the OHIO and TENNESSEE CONFERENCES. The Holston, Cumberland, Nashville, Wabash, Mississippi, and Illinois Districts then fell within the Tennessee Conference. In 1824 the HOLSTON CONFERENCE was set off from the Tennessee Conference. The new body included east Tennessee, southwest Virginia, western North Carolina, and northeast South Carolina. In 1840 the Tennessee Conference was again partitioned to form the MEMPHIS CONFERENCE which included west Tennessee, west Kentucky, and north Mississippi.

When the M.E. Church was divided in 1844, all of the Tennessee conferences adhered South and kept their same boundaries. Since many people in east Tennessee favored the North in the Civil War, the M.E. Church had no difficulty in organizing a Holston Conference of its own at Athens, Tenn., on June 1, 1865, the boundaries of which were the same as the Holston Conference of the

Southern Church, except that it did not include any Virginia or Georgia territory. At the outset the new conference included both white and Negro ministers and churches, but in 1880 the Negro work was set off as the East Tennessee Conference. In 1866 the Tennessee Mission Conference (ME) was organized. Including middle and west Tennessee, it became the Tennessee Conference in 1868. In 1877 the white work of this conference was set off as the Central Tennessee Conference which continued until unification. It brought about 9,500 members into The Methodist Church in 1939.

In 1829 the M.P. Church organized a Tennessee Conference with eight ministers. In its first decade the conference sent missionaries to ARKANSAS and TEXAS. In 1870 the Holston Conference (MP) was formed, but four years later it was absorbed by the VIRGINIA CONFERENCE (MP). In 1858 a West Tennessee Conference was created; it continued twenty years and was then absorbed by the Tennessee Conference (MP). A Spring Creek Colored Mission Conference was set up in west Tennessee in 1884; it dissolved in 1920. In 1938 at its last session prior to unification, the Tennessee Conference had seven ministers, six pastoral charges, and 860 members.

Other Methodist bodies have work in Tennessee. The A.M.E. CHURCH has one conference embracing the entire state. The C.M.E. CHURCH has headquarters at Jackson and maintains LANE COLLEGE in that city. A few circuits of the Tennessee-Kentucky Conference of the FREE METHODIST CHURCH are in Tennessee. The WESLEYAN, CUMBERLAND, EVANGELICAL, INDEPENDENT, and SOUTHERN METHODIST CHURCHES have small memberships in the state.

At unification in 1939, the three merging denominations had a total of eight conferences in Tennessee. Six of the eight included some territory in adjoining states. The conferences of the M.E. Church, South brought 323,523 members into The Methodist Church, the M.E. Church 75,987, and the M.P. Church 860 for a grand total of 400,370.

As The Methodist Church began in 1939, the number of conferences in Tennessee was reduced to five. Three—Holston, Memphis, and Tennessee—were in the SOUTHEASTERN JURISDICTION, and two—East Tennessee and Tennessee—in the CENTRAL JURISDICTION. In 1964 the two Central Jurisdiction conferences merged with part of the LEXINGTON CONFERENCE to form the Tennessee-Kentucky Conference. In 1968 when The United Methodist Church was organized, the Central Jurisdiction was abolished and the Tennessee-Kentucky Conference was absorbed, its ministers and churches being placed in the conferences of the Southeastern Jurisdiction in which they happened to be located.

NASHVILLE was the headquarters of the M. E. Church, South from 1846 to 1939, and it has continued as an important center for Methodism as well as for several other denominations. Agencies of The United Methodist Church located in Nashville include the BOARD OF PUBLICATION and the Publishing House, the ABINGDON PRESS and the Parthenon Press, the Board of EVANGELISM, the UPPER ROOM, the BOARD OF EDUCATION, and the TELEVISION, RADIO AND FILM COMMISSION.

Tennessee Methodists support three junior colleges, HIWASSEE at Madisonville, MARTIN at Pulaski, and Morristown Normal and Industrial College at Morristown. They have three senior colleges, LAMBUTH at Jackson, TENNESSEE WESLEYAN at Athens, and SCARRITT at Nashville.

The Holston Conference also supports EMORY AND HENRY COLLEGE at Emory, Va., which is in its territory. The church maintains WESLEYAN FOUNDATIONS and campus ministries at the state higher institutions of learning. VANDERBILT UNIVERSITY at Nashville and the UNIVERSITY OF CHATTANOOGA, once Methodist related schools, have long since passed from church control.

Other Methodist institutions in Tennessee include Methodist hospitals at MEMPHIS and Oak Ridge, a children's home at Greenville, and McKendree Manor at Nashville and several other homes for the aged.

In 1968 the membership of The United Methodist Church in Tennessee was about 375,000, some 10.5 per cent of the 1960 population of the state. The four conferences had a total membership of 465,200 and property valued at $187,818,682.

J. B. McFerrin, *Tennessee.* 1895.
Minutes of all the Tennessee Conferences, ME, MES, MP, TMC
Outline of Development of Methodism in Tennessee. Nashville: Tennessee Historical Records Survey, 1940.
H. T. FOWLER
JAMES R. COX

TENNESSEE CONFERENCE was organized Nov. 12, 1812 at Fountain Head, near present day Portland, Tenn., in the home of a man named House, with Bishops ASBURY and McKENDREE in charge. At the time it was the largest conference geographically in America, embracing the states of TENNESSEE, southern KENTUCKY, INDIANA, ILLINOIS, MISSOURI, ARKANSAS, LOUISIANA, MISSISSIPPI, and ALABAMA. At the beginning its membership was 22,699. During the first session seventeen men were admitted on trial. (See TENNESSEE for history of early Methodism in the state.)

In 1813 the MISSISSIPPI CONFERENCE was carved from the Tennessee Conference, and in 1816 the MISSOURI CONFERENCE, composed of Illinois, Missouri, Arkansas, and part of Indiana, was taken from it. The Tennessee Conference was further reduced in size by the creation of the KENTUCKY CONFERENCE in 1820 and the HOLSTON CONFERENCE in 1824. This limited the Tennessee Conference to four districts, Nashville, Forked Deer, Caney Fork, and Huntsville (north Alabama). The conference then had thirty-four charges and 13,537 members. In 1840 the MEMPHIS CONFERENCE was organized, three of its districts being taken from the Tennessee Conference.

Outstanding leaders in the Tennessee Conference in the period before and after the Civil War were A. L. P. GREEN and JOHN B. McFERRIN. Green was elected to the GENERAL CONFERENCE eleven times, and McFerrin wrote a three-volume *History of Methodism in Tennessee.*

On the division of the M.E. Church in 1844, the three Tennessee Conferences adhered South. Recognizing the strategic importance of middle Tennessee, the M.E. Church, South made NASHVILLE its headquarters. Throughout most of their history the Nashville *Christian Advocate* (1832-1940) and the *Methodist Quarterly Review* (1847-1930) of the Southern Church were published in Nashville.

In 1850 the Tennessee Conference (MES) reported some 43,300 members. During the next six years there was no growth; indeed the total dropped to about 41,000. The conference was then divided into twelve well-manned districts, emphasis was placed on deepening the spiritual life of the people, and by 1860 the membership had risen to nearly 49,000.

The Civil War was disastrous for the Tennessee Conference due partly to the fact that beginning in 1862 a large portion of middle Tennessee was in the hands of the Union army. In 1865 the conference reported a total membership of about 33,000. The plant of the Publishing House in Nashville was badly damaged by the Union forces. After the war the Southern Church sought reparations from Congress, and in 1898 that body granted $288,000. While negotiations were in progress it was charged in the church papers that the publishing agents had acted unethically, that some individuals were receiving unduly large commissions for their services in pressing the claims of the church on the federal government (see PUBLISHING HOUSE CONTROVERSY).

After the war the Tennessee Conference (MES) recuperated slowly at first and then more rapidly. In 1870 it reported about 34,000 members, in 1875 about 41,000 and in 1885 some 53,000. At unification in 1939 the conference had eight districts, 625 churches, 98,970 members, and property valued at $5,621,255.

Today the conference supports a Methodist chair at VANDERBILT UNIVERSITY, and it maintains MARTIN JUNIOR COLLEGE at Pulaski, a series of WESLEY FOUNDATIONS and campus ministries, a number of camps and youth projects, and McKendree Manor for the aged at Nashville. SCARRITT COLLEGE and a number of the general boards and agencies of The United Methodist Church are located in Nashville.

In 1970 the Tennessee Conference had six districts, 365 ministers, 730 churches, 133,358 members, and property valued at $52,259,716.

C. T. Carter, *Tennessee Conference.* 1948.
General Minutes, ME, MES, TMC, UMC.
J. B. McFerrin, *Tennessee.* 1888.
Minutes of the Tennessee Conference.   CULLEN T. CARTER

TENNESSEE CONFERENCE (EUB) traces its beginning to April, 1856, when the VIRGINIA CONFERENCE appointed John Ruebush as a missionary to upper East Tennessee. Ruebush preached in schoolhouses, homes, and churches of several denominations. On recommendation of the BOARD OF MISSIONS, the Virginia Conference appropriated funds for the erection of church buildings in TENNESSEE; and the first structure, Otterbein Chapel, was dedicated in 1859. The first annual conference session, with Bishop GLOSSBRENNER presiding, was held in 1866.

Active in the early years of the conference were R. J. Bishop and Enos Keezel, both of whom came from Virginia. In 1865, Andrew Elliot Evans from the White River Conference (Indiana) and Daniel Beauchamp of the Upper Wabash Conference (Indiana) were sent by their respective conferences to aid in the mission work in Tennessee. The first annual conference elected Ruebush as presiding elder and recognized Keezel, Bishop, Beauchamp, and Evans as members.

During the years following the Civil War the church grew steadily and began to move westward across the state. On November 26, 1896, the Tennessee River Conference (later known as West Tennessee Conference) was organized at Parsons, Tenn., with W. M. Bell, Missionary Secretary, presiding. The original conference then became known as the East Tennessee Conference. In 1918, the two conferences were merged to form the Tennessee Conference.

In 1896, the Chickamauga Conference was organized at CHATTANOOGA. The conference was under the auspices of the Board of Missions and was organized for the purpose of ministering to Negro groups in that portion of the state. The conference was dissolved in 1913, because, in the words of A. W. DRURY, the Chickamauga Conference was "more a hope than a realization."

The Tennessee Conference reached from Johnson City, the eastern terminal, to the Tennessee River, 100 miles west of Nashville. In 1966, it had twenty-five charges with thirty-three churches, thirty-two ministers including four probationers, and a membership of 4,825. The conference owned a church camp, Trinity Hills, located forty miles south of Knoxville, which accommodated eighty campers and workers and where the entire camping program of the conference was conducted. In 1970, it was united with the Holston and Tennessee Conferences of the former Methodist Church.

A. W. Drury, *History of the U.B.* 1924.   J. CASTRO SMITH

TENNESSEE-KENTUCKY CONFERENCE was organized in Nashville, Tenn., Aug. 18-19, 1964 with Bishop CHARLES F. GOLDEN presiding. It was formed by merging the Tennessee and East Tennessee Conferences (see Tennessee) and a part of the LEXINGTON CONFERENCE, all of the CENTRAL JURISDICTION. Its boundaries included the states of KENTUCKY and Tennessee and southwestern VIRGINIA. The conference began with five districts but reduced the number to three the next year. In 1965 it reported 105 ministers, 118 pastoral charges, and 16,531 members.

The conference supported Morristown College at Morristown, Tennessee, an accredited Methodist junior college which in 1968 had an enrollment of about 350, an endowment of over $200,000, and a plant valued at more than $1,000,000.

On the abolition of the Central Jurisdiction in 1968, the Tennessee-Kentucky Conference was absorbed by the several conferences of the Southeastern Jurisdiction in Kentucky and Tennessee.

In its last year the Tennessee-Kentucky Conference reported three districts, Knoxville, Lexington, and Nashville; 115 pastoral charges, 16,042 members, and property valued at $6,710,778.

General Minutes, MEC, and MC.
Minutes of the Tennessee-Kentucky Conference.
Discipline, MC.   ALBEA GODBOLD

TENNESSEE WESLEYAN COLLEGE, Athens, Tennessee, was established as Athens Female College in 1857 under the sponsorship of the M.E. Church, South. During 1866-68 it was transferred to the HOLSTON CONFERENCE of the M.E. Church, made coeducational, and renamed East Tennessee Wesleyan University. Following the death of General and President ULYSSES S. GRANT, the name was changed in 1886 to Grant Memorial University. This same year the FREEDMEN'S SOCIETY, broadening its educational program to include Southern white people, opened a university in CHATTANOOGA, Tenn. In 1889 the two institutions were merged, with the plan that the Athens campus would be used for a college of liberal arts and a secondary school while graduate professional schools would be developed at Chattanooga. The new name of the older school was continued for the combination, and in 1892 was changed to U. S. Grant University. During

1904-6 the college was moved to Chattanooga; and in 1907 the name became UNIVERSITY OF CHATTANOOGA, with the branch at Athens called the Athens School of the university—a secondary school with some junior college courses.

In 1925 the Athens School was separated from the university and became a junior college and secondary school with its present name. Since 1954 it has been a senior college, offering the B.A. and B.S. degrees. Its governing board has fifty-five members, plus a maximum of five honorary and six *ex officio*, who are elected by the Holston Conference of The United Methodist Church on nomination of its Board of Education.

Gilbert E. Govan and James W. Livingood, *The University of Chattanooga: Sixty Years.* Chattanooga, Tenn.: the university, 1947.
LeRoy A. Martin, *A History of Tennessee Wesleyan College, 1857-1957.* N.p., 1957.

JOHN O. GROSS

TENNEY, MARY ALICE (1889-   ), American FREE METHODIST author, scholar, and teacher, was born at Nora Springs, Iowa. Her baccalaureate degrees are: A.B., GREENVILLE COLLEGE; A.M., University of California; Ph.D., University of Wisconsin; later Greenville College conferred the Litt.D. She has been professor of English at Los Angeles Pacific College, at Houghton College and Greenville College. Dr. Tenney is a member of the Modern Language Association and the Conference on Christianity and Literature. She is author of *Still Abides the Memory,* 1942; *Blueprint for a Christian World,* 1953 (translated into Japanese and Chinese); *Adventures in Christian Love,* 1964; and she collaborated in writing *Spiritual Renewal for Methodism.* She is a special writer of Sunday school materials and of articles for religious periodicals. Now retired, she resides at Greenville, Ill.

Directory of American Scholars.
Who's Who in American Women.

BYRON S. LAMSON

TENT METHODISTS. In 1814 two LOCAL PREACHERS of the Methodist society in BRISTOL who had found it difficult to procure village rooms for preaching conceived the idea of a traveling tent to be used during the summer months. The first was erected at Whitchurch, near Bristol, on April 24, 1814. Among those who conducted the service was John Pyer (1790-1859). In 1815 the work spread to Bedminster; and in April, 1816, on the occasion of a public hanging, the tent was pitched in Gallows Field, Bristol, and a nightly service was held, some thousands attending. In July, 1818, following a mission to Southampton and the Isle of Wight, it was deemed necessary to appoint a regular missionary, and Pyer was chosen. In the same year a tent mission at Dursley, in Gloucestershire, added some 450 members to the Wesleyan society in a few months. This was followed two years later by the building of a new chapel. About this time charges of irregularity developed and regulations were set up: a tent should only be used in any circuit by consent of the superintendent, and should be under his direction; only accredited local preachers should serve; all persons converted should be brought into the Methodist society. Eventually the leaders of the movement were expelled; and converts who gathered around them formed themselves into a distinct community, taking the name of Tent Methodists. The mission work continued in Bristol;

in 1820 Pyer was invited to LONDON and had large success. Coming to MANCHESTER in 1821, he remained nine years and built the Canal Street Chapel in Ancoats. In 1830 he was engaged in London as a missionary of the Christian Instruction Society. Four years later he became the settled pastor of a Congregational Church at South Molton, in North Devon; in July, 1839, he came to Davenport, where he remained for twenty years until his death on April 7, 1859. The Tent Methodists labored in Salford, Lancashire; and one, Peter Arrive, a local preacher, was expelled in 1822 because of his "association with tent-folk." By this time the new society numbered nearly three hundred; two tents and one large chapel were in continual use in different parts of Salford.

Christian Reformer, 1822.
London Christian Instructor, 1822.
K. P. Russell, *Memoir of the Rev. John Pyer.* London, 1865.

JOHN T. WILKINSON

TERRELL, JAMES MILAS (1868-1943), American preacher and missionary to BRAZIL, was born in Pigeon Valley, near Waynesville, N. C., on Oct. 1, 1868. His father, Capt. William Terrell, was a strict Presbyterian, his mother a devout and loyal Methodist. Their home nevertheless was a haven for traveling Methodist preachers; and it was there, at the age of twelve, that James came to know and admire a young circuit rider, JAMES L. KENNEDY, who a few years later went to Brazil as a missionary. Kennedy's life, Terrell later testified, influenced him into missionary work.

His education was first at EMORY AND HENRY COLLEGE in southwest VIRGINIA, and then at VANDERBILT, from which he graduated in three years, in 1897. He was ordained by Bishop ALPHEUS WILSON, served three charges in NORTH CAROLINA, and left for Brazil in June, 1900. His first appointment was to an English-speaking congregation in Petropolis, state of Rio de Janeiro. There he met May Umberger, a missionary heading the Methodist Woman's Board school in that town, and they were married on July 18, 1901.

Few missionaries have served in more capacities, lived more sacrificially, or influenced more Brazilians into the ministry than James Terrell. During forty-three years in Brazil, he was circuit rider, pastor, presiding elder; editor of a church periodical (*O Testemunho,* organ of the Rio Grande do Sul Conference); professor of Greek, Hebrew, and ecclesiastical history in Methodist seminaries; builder of churches and parsonages. Wherever they lived, the Terrells opened their home to young Brazilian students and many of these have been—and are still—prominent Methodist preachers. Among them was CESAR DACORSO, who lived with six others in the Terrell home while attending COLEGIO (now Instituto) UNIAO. Dacorso became the first Brazilian bishop of the Methodist Church in that country.

Always aware of the need in interior points of the state, Terrell opened new trails and preaching points, skimping and sacrificing, using his own salary for the building of a church or parsonage, or for the upkeep of needy students. Once in a small city of Santo Angelo, after several Methodists had been arrested for holding services and were being held in the basement of a hotel, Terrell dared to stand up against the mayor, claiming support from the laws of the land and of God. Then he preached in the hall of this hotel while grains of corn were being pelted in his face, and sang loudly so those in the basement could be cheered and encouraged to stand firm. Often when no money had been allotted to start work in a new place, Terrell himself paid the rent for a small hall, built some benches, and when Sunday night came, would attract passersby, by singing solos or duets with his wife. Because of the personal debts Terrell often incurred for these projects, Bishop WALTER LAMBUTH threatened to recall him to the United States. Today several churches and parsonages stand as monuments to his devotion and sacrificial spirit.

In 1907-08, while pastor of Central Church, PORTO ALEGRE, he acquired the property on which a fine church now stands. Terrell was a founding member of the South Brazil Conference, now called the Second Region. This was organized by Bishop Lambuth in the Terrells' home in Santa Maria. He was also founder of the seminary in connection with Porto Alegre College, and had as his first pupil, SANTE UBERTO BARBIERI (later bishop of The Methodist Church).

Ill health due to overwork, a sunstroke, and minor accidents forced Terrell to return with his family to the United States several times. But once well, Terrell was back working hard in Brazil. James Terrell died Sunday morning, January 3, 1943, after running to catch a bus for Ipiranga Church of which he was pastor. He died in the bus. He was buried in the Protestant Cemetery of the Redeemer, near the grave of his long-time friend and inspirer, J. L. Kennedy.

Expositor Cristão, Jan. 12, 19, and 23, 1943.
E. M. B. Jaime, *Metodismo no Rio Grande do Sul.* 1963.

EULA K. LONG

TESTIMONY was a term that came into its greatest use in nineteenth century Methodism. It referred to the custom of persons, at CLASS MEETINGS, PRAYER MEETINGS or REVIVAL meetings, arising, at the invitation of the leader, to tell the group how they came to be saved, or what special blessings God had given them. It was believed a person was not "walking with God" if he were not ready to stand up and testify in this way concerning his faith. "Testimony Meetings," frankly so called, were often held.

As time went on the "testimonies" became stereotyped rehearsals of former statements, and they lost their power to influence others who had heard them repeatedly at the meetings. During the last half century various attempts have been made to revive the custom but without much success. The first testimony or fresh testimony of any sincere Christian always has great effect.

FREDERICK E. MASER

TETER, EBER (1846-1928), American Wesleyan minister, was born near Boxley, Ind., Jan. 28, 1846, the son of Eber Teter, Sr., a devout Methodist who had led in the organization of a WESLEYAN METHODIST CHURCH in Boxley in 1844. The younger Teter's childhood home was a station on the Underground Railroad.

Eber Teter, Jr. was converted as a child. Although quite young, he served in the Union Army during the Civil War. At the war's end, he answered the call to preach and studied at Wheaton and ADRIAN Colleges. In 1870 he served six months as an assistant on the Westfield Circuit, and was ordained. His leadership ability was recognized immediately. But for the next seventeen years

he vacillated between the ministry and a business career, apparently because of inadequate pastoral salaries.

In 1887 Eber Teter proposed a new type of Wesleyan conference government—a full-time president with superintending authority. The Indiana Conference of his church adopted the proposal and permanently ended his inactive status by electing him its first full-time president. He served for fourteen years with great effectiveness. Organized churches increased by forty-two percent, membership by thirty-one percent, church buildings by eighty-seven percent.

In 1889 Eber Teter was elected General Conference President, which position he held longer than any other man—until 1927. From 1901-19, he served as General Missionary Secretary, responsible for denominational missions at home and abroad. Churches multiplied, conferences were organized, new foreign fields were added, two Wesleyan colleges were founded. He became the theologian of the church and stamped indelibly upon it his beliefs and principles. In 1927 a grateful church elected him General Conference President Emeritus. He died June 29, 1928, known already as the "Grand Old Man of the Church."

LEE HAINES

TETER, ISAAC PEARL (1829-1900), Iowa preacher, was born in Lewis County, Va. (now W. Va.), May 11, 1829. He joined the M.E. Church at the age of sixteen and was granted a preacher's license in 1851. Removing to IOWA, he was admitted in 1855 into the IOWA CONFERENCE on trial, ordained DEACON in 1855, and was received into the Conference in full connection. He was ordained ELDER by Bishop AMES in 1857.

Teter spent forty-seven years in the active ministry, all in the Iowa Conference, serving Troy, 1853-54; Montrose, 1854-55; Winchester, 1855-56; Ft. Madison, 1856-57; Drakeville, 1857-58; Albia, 1858-59 and 1883-84; East Des Moines, 1859-60; Sigourney, 1860-62; Oskaloosa, Simpson, 1862-63 and 1888-93; Keosauqua, 1865-68; Mt. Pleasant Circuit, 1872-75; Danville, 1875-76; Main Street, Ottumwa, 1876-79; Kirkville, 1879-80; Centerville, 1880-83; South Ottumwa, Willard Street, 1893-97; and New Sharon, 1897-1900. He was PRESIDING ELDER of Burlington District, 1868-72, and of Ottumwa District, 1884-88.

Isaac Pearl Teter was commissioned a CHAPLAIN of the Seventh Iowa Infantry during the Civil War, as a member of Oskaloosa Quarterly Conference. Returning to Iowa in 1864, as a member of Chatham Square, Keokuk, QUARTERLY CONFERENCE, he was appointed Chaplain in the U. S. Post Hospital, Keokuk, Iowa, by President Lincoln and remained in that position until the close of the war. While he was pastor at Sigourney, in the fall of 1861, Teter was elected to the Iowa Senate. In 1896 he was a delegate to GENERAL CONFERENCE. He died in New Sharon, Iowa, March 6, 1900, and was buried at Ottumwa, Iowa.

A. W. Haines, *Makers of Iowa Methodism.* 1900.
Minutes of the Iowa Conference, 1853-1900.
E. H. Waring, *Iowa Conference.* 1910.   MARTIN L. GREER

TEVIS, MRS. JULIA A. (1799-1880), American educator, was born in Clarke County, Ky., Dec. 5, 1799. The daughter of Pendleton and Mary Heironymus, she was chiefly educated in WASHINGTON City and GEORGETOWN, D. C.

In 1820 she became governess in the family of General Smythe of Wytheville and later in the family of Captain Frank Smith of Abingdon, Va.

She married John Tevis, presiding elder of the Holston District, in 1824, and the same year moved to Shelbyville, Ky., a small town about twenty miles from Frankfort, where on March 25, 1825 they founded Science Hill Female Academy.

Through this institution Mrs. Tevis became widely known over the South and West. She presided over the Academy until near her death. Through the years more than 3,000 young ladies were under her care.

Mrs. Tevis was the mother of Benjamin P. Tevis, M.D., who was associated for a long time with his mother in conducting Science Hill Academy. In 1876 he was elected a lay delegate to the GENERAL CONFERENCE of the M.E. Church. Mrs. Tevis died in June 1880.

M. Simpson, Cyclopaedia. 1882.
JESSE A. EARL

TEWARSON, SUBARNO BIDYOTTAM (1897-   ), is a layman from the Garhwal District of the Indian Himalayas. He has achieved distinction as an educator and as a manager of church and mission finances. He was born in Pauri, Garhwal, Sept. 16, 1897. His parents were early converts from the Kohli caste of Hindus. He completed high school studies in the Methodist High School at Pauri, which was then the only high school in Garhwal. The distinguished missionaries JAMES H. MESSMORE and PRESTON S. HYDE were his teachers of English and Bible, and profoundly influenced him. The school now is known as the Messmore Intermediate College.

Tewarson earned the B.S. degree in 1918, the Licentiate of Teaching in 1927, and the M.A. degree in 1930. He began teaching in the LUCKNOW CHRISTIAN COLLEGE, continued in the Messmore High School at Pauri, and in 1923 became the headmaster of Ramsey High School at Almora. In 1947 he was appointed principal of the Parker Intermediate College at Moradabad.

On reaching retirement age in 1956, he became the first Indian associate treasurer of the Methodist Church in Southern Asia and a secretary of the Inter-Mission Business Office in Bombay.

This new career was opened to him because he had served efficiently as unpaid treasurer of the North India Conference for ten years. His work in Bombay was so much appreciated that he was made branch treasurer and directed all financial operations of the Board of Missions throughout the area of the CENTRAL CONFERENCE OF SOUTHERN ASIA.

For nine years he was a government-nominated commissioner of the Municipality of Almora.

Journals, The North India Conference, 1923, 1927, 1956.
Minutes of the Executive Board of the Methodist Church in Southern Asia, 1956-64.
J. WASKOM PICKETT

TEXARKANA, ARKANSAS, U.S.A., **First Church.** On Dec. 2, 1902, JAMES THOMAS arrived in Texarkana to be pastor of the First Methodist Church. All he had was a name for the church, no members and no real estate. On December 14, he organized the church with forty-eight members.

On Dec. 7-12, 1904, two years later, the LITTLE ROCK

ANNUAL CONFERENCE met in what remains today as a churchly sanctuary, debt free.

The first year of its existence this church paid the second highest amount of benevolences of any church in the Conference, and has continued to be a leader in all phases of the Church program. First Church, Texarkana, boasts some of the most beautiful windows in the world, with their great expanse of superb Belgian glass, valued at over $100,000. There are over 600 different tints and hues in these windows. The roster of pastors include some well known names in American Methodism, James Thomas, Phillip Cone Fletcher, FORNEY HUTCHINSON, and Bishop AUBREY G. WALTON.

The membership of 1,275 in 1970 includes prominent people of all walks of life in the city, and at the same time, the largest percentage of laboring people of any of the eight Methodist churches in these twin cities. The church, while located in ARKANSAS, near the State Line between TEXAS and Arkansas, draws forty percent of her members from the Texas side of the line. Dr. Robert H. Chappell, son of CLOVIS G. CHAPPELL, went from this church as a medical missionary to INDIA.

TEXAS, U.S.A., population 10,989,123 in 1970, is in the southwest. It is bounded by OKLAHOMA on the north, ARKANSAS and LOUISIANA on the east, the Gulf of Mexico on the southeast, MEXICO on the southwest, and NEW MEXICO on the west. With an area of 267,339 square miles, it is by far the largest of the forty-eight contiguous states. Its terrain rises slowly from the Gulf of Mexico to 4,000-foot mountains in the north and west, and its climate ranges from subtropical to mid-temperate. Texas leads the nation in the production of oil, cattle, sheep, cotton, rice, and some other categories. Manufacturing is now an even greater contributor to the state's economy than minerals and agriculture. Successively under Spain, France, and Mexico, the Texans won their independence in 1836 and formed a republic which was admitted to the Union in 1845. Counting the Confederacy, 1861-1865, six flags have flown over Texas.

Methodism first entered Texas in the fall of 1815 when WILLIAM STEVENSON, a member of the TENNESSEE CONFERENCE, traveled from Bellevue (Caledonia), Missouri, through Arkansas as far as Pecan Point, Texas on the south side of the Red River. Stevenson preached to American settlers there and formed a society. Pecan Point became a preaching place for the circuit riders. In 1816 the MISSOURI CONFERENCE was formed, and it appointed Stevenson to the Hot Springs Circuit in Arkansas. In 1818 he was appointed to "Mt. Prairie (Ark.) and Pecan Point"; it was the first time any place in Texas was included in a list of Methodist appointments. THOMAS HARDESTER TENNANT was the second preacher appointed to Pecan Point, and the circuit was eventually enlarged to include DeKalb, Clarksville, Paris, Bonham, Honey Grove, and other places.

In 1833 James P. Stevenson, son of William, went into east Texas from the Sabine Circuit in Louisiana which he was traveling. He preached near present day Milam and organized a society at the home of Samuel McMahan. In 1834 MCMAHAN'S CHAPEL, recognized today not only as the oldest continuing Methodist but also the oldest continuing Protestant congregation in Texas, was organized. In 1837 Bishop ELIJAH HEDDING appointed MARTIN

RUTER, president of ALLEGHENY COLLEGE at Meadville, Pa.; LITTLETON FOWLER at LaGRANGE COLLEGE, Ala.; and ROBERT ALEXANDER, pastor at NATCHEZ, Miss., as missionaries to Texas. They were attached to the MISSISSIPPI CONFERENCE, and east and south Texas became a part of the ARKANSAS CONFERENCE which was formed in 1836 by dividing the MISSOURI CONFERENCE.

In 1840 the Texas Conference (ME) was formed to include all of the state except the northeast. Between 1840 and 1968 the M.E. Church, the M.E. Church, South, the M.P. Church, and The Methodist Church organized a total of fifty annual conferences, missions, and mission conferences in Texas (see Table of Methodist Conferences), far more than in any other one state. In 1844 the GENERAL CONFERENCE authorized the division of the Texas Conference to form the Eastern and Western Texas Conferences, both of which adhered South. In 1846 Western Texas changed its name to the Texas Conference, and in 1847 Eastern Texas became the East Texas Conference.

In 1859 the Rio Grande Mission Conference, covering west and southwest Texas, was carved out of the Texas Conference. Three years later it was designated as the RIO GRANDE CONFERENCE, and in 1866 it became the WEST TEXAS CONFERENCE. In 1866 the NORTHWEST TEXAS CONFERENCE was formed by merging the northern parts of both the Texas and Rio Grande Conferences. In 1867 the East Texas Conference was divided to form the Trinity Conference in northeast Texas. Trinity changed its name to NORTH TEXAS CONFERENCE in 1874. Then in 1910 the Northwest Texas Conference was divided to form the CENTRAL TEXAS CONFERENCE. No other significant changes were made in the names or boundaries of the five Southern Methodist conferences which served Anglo-Saxons in Texas between 1910 and unification in 1939. Moreover, after unification the names and boundaries of the five conferences continued essentially the same, except that the name of the West Texas Conference was changed to SOUTHWEST TEXAS CONFERENCE.

The M.E. Church, South had work among the German- and Spanish-speaking people in Texas. In 1874 the German Mission Conference was organized to include work in Texas and Louisiana. The name was changed to Southwest Texas Conference in 1918, and the next year the conference disappeared and the German work was absorbed by the overlying English-speaking conferences. In 1885 a Mexican Border Mission Conference was formed which included work in Texas and over the border in Mexico, and in 1891 a Northwest Mexican Mission Conference was organized to include work in the southwestern United States and part of Mexico. In 1914 conference lines were redrawn and the Mexican Border Conference included the Mexican work in Texas west of the Pecos River, NEW MEXICO, and part of MEXICO, while the Texas Mexican Mission (Texas Mexican Conference after 1929) included all Mexican work east of the Pecos River. Then in 1918 the Pacific Mexican Mission which had included the Mexican work in ARIZONA and CALIFORNIA, was merged with the Mexican Border Conference to form the Western Mexican Mission (Western Mexican Conference after 1929). Thus at the time of unification in 1939 the Southern Church had two conferences for Mexican work —the Texas Mexican Conference and the Western Mexican Conference.

Following the Civil War, the M.E. Church organized work in Texas, as it did in all of the southern states. In 1867 it formed the Texas Mission Conference (Texas Conference after 1868) by dividing the Mississippi Mission Conference which had been organized at New Orleans in 1865. The Texas work included both white and Negro ministers and churches. In 1874 the SOUTHERN GERMAN CONFERENCE was established in Texas, and in the same year the West Texas Conference was set off from the Texas body. In 1877 the white ministers and churches in the West Texas Conference were organized as the Austin Conference. The Austin Conference continued until 1911 when part of it went with the Gulf Conference which for some years had included the denomination's white work in Louisiana and Mississippi. The remainder of the Austin Conference went with the newly formed Southern Swedish Mission Conference in Texas. Both the Gulf Conference and the Southern Swedish Mission Conference were absorbed in 1926 by the Southern Conference which continued until unification in 1939. Thus the M.E. Church came to unification with three conferences in Texas—Southern, Texas, and West Texas.

The M.P. Church organized the Texas Conference in 1848, setting it off from the Louisiana Conference. Though the denomination organized twelve other conferences and mission conferences in Texas between 1848 and 1920, the Texas body was the basic conference in the state, most of the others being formed from it and a number of them being absorbed by it as the years passed. The more important ancillary conferences of the denomination in the state were Central Texas (1878-1912), Colorado (1860-1880), Colorado Texas (1880-1912), and the Colorado Texas Colored Mission Conference (1920-1939). Thus the M.P. Church came to unification in 1939 with two conferences in Texas—Texas and Colorado Texas Colored Mission Conferences.

Other Methodist denominations have work in Texas. The A.M.E. CHURCH has several conferences in Texas along with PAUL QUINN COLLEGE at Waco, founded in 1872. The C.M.E. CHURCH has four conferences in the state and TEXAS COLLEGE at Tyler, founded in 1894, while the A.M.E. ZION CHURCH has one conference. The FREE METHODISTS also have one conference in Texas.

The M.E. Church, South was of course the largest of the merging denominations in Texas in 1939. Its five Anglo-Saxon conferences had 445,159 members and its two Mexican conferences 5,993 for a total membership of 451,152. The M.E. Church had 14,760 members in its Southern Conference, not all of whom resided in Texas, plus 33,791 members in its two Negro conferences. The M.P. Church brought about 75 churches and some 4,000 members into The Methodist Church.

Sixteen members of Texas conferences have been elevated to the episcopacy: SETH WARD (1906), EDWIN D. MOUZON (1910), JOHN M. MOORE (1918), HIRAM A. BOAZ and SAMUEL R. HAY (1922), PAUL B. KERN and A. FRANK SMITH (1930), WILLIAM C. MARTIN and CHARLES C. SELECMAN (1938), PAUL E. MARTIN, WILLIS J. KING, and W. ANGIE SMITH (1944), KENNETH W. COPELAND, W. KENNETH POPE, and O. EUGENE SLATER (1960), and ALSIE H. CARLETON (1968). Six other bishops were at some time members of Texas conferences before their election: HOYT M. DOBBS (1922), ARTHUR J. MOORE (1930), H. BASCOM WATTS (1952), W. RALPH WARD (1960), and LANCE WEBB (1964). In addition, two bishops though never members of any Texas conference, served Methodism in the state before their election: Enoch M. Marvin (1866), and Ivan Lee Holt (1938).

Since unification in 1939 Methodism has grown in Texas. The Highland Park Church, Dallas, and First Church, Houston, are probably the largest Methodist churches in the world, the one reporting over 9,182 members in 1969, and the other 9,280. In Texas The United Methodist Church owns and operates one university, six colleges, and two training schools, and it supports seven hospitals, 13 retirement and nursing homes, one children's home, one home for unmarried mothers, and one church paper, *The Texas Methodist* (see *Texas Christian Advocate*).

In 1968 the eight annual conferences in Texas reported 782,088 members and property valued at $350,811,673. Add 30,000 members and property valued at $9,575,000 from the part of the New Mexico Conference which is in the state of Texas, and the 1968 figures for Texas are approximately 812,000 church members and property valued at $360,386,000.

General Minutes, ME, MES, TMC.
Minutes of all Texas annual conferences.
O. W. Nail, *Texas Centennial Yearbook*. 1934.
————, *Texas Methodism*. 1961.
————, *Southwest Texas Conference*. 1958.
M. Phelan, *Methodism in Texas*. 1924.
W. N. Vernon, *North Texas*. 1967.   Olin W. Nail

TEXAS CHRISTIAN ADVOCATE. The Methodists of Texas had a paper as early as 1847 when Robert B. Wells started in the town of Brenham the *Texas Christian Advocate and Brenham Advertiser*. It was partly a church paper and partly a regular weekly newspaper, as its name suggests. At the end of the first year the paper was moved to Houston and Orceneth Fisher edited it under the name of *The Texas Christian Advocate*. About a year later Chauncey Richardson became editor, and he renamed it the *Texas Wesleyan Banner*. The General Conference of 1850 gave it official recognition. It carried much general news, and was not exclusively a religious paper. The editor claimed for it the largest circulation in Texas—1,500. But it had financial troubles, and when the salary was reduced Richardson resigned. A loyal layman, Charles Shearn, helped to steady the paper financially, as did David Ayres a few years later. Various preachers served as editors, and it was moved to Galveston in 1854 and renamed the *Texas Christian Advocate*. When Galveston was blockaded during the Civil War the paper was moved back to Houston, but soon suspended publication, not to resume until December 1864.

In 1866, I. G. John was elected editor and served for eighteen years. In the same year a youth started working for the printers who eventually became the publisher and an outstanding Methodist churchman—Louis Blaylock. Blaylock and his partner, William A. Shaw, as publishers, and John as editor made the paper strong and popular. It was militant against gambling and saloons. By 1884 it had 10,500 subscribers and was the outstanding religious paper in the state.

In 1887 the paper was moved to Dallas, with Blaylock still the publisher and with a circulation of 18,000. In 1898 George C. Rankin was chosen editor and became the most popular editor in the paper's history. During his seventeen-year tenure he fought gambling, prostitution,

dancing, liquor, and Sabbath disrespect, and rallied Methodists and others in favor of prohibition laws.

After Rankin's death in 1915, editors included W. D. Bradfield, A. J. Weeks, and E. A. Hunter. During these years (until 1924) Louis Blaylock as publisher provided a stable base for the finances of the paper, and is remembered with gratitude for his loyalty and integrity.

In 1932 the name was changed to *The Southwestern Advocate*, serving for a time Oklahoma and New Mexico as well as Texas Methodism. Twenty years later it was again named the *Texas Christian Advocate*. In 1960 it became *The Texas Methodist* and assumed newspaper format and size, under the editorship of Carl E. Keightley. By arranging for a large number of local church editions of the paper, the circulation during the next five or six years reached over 60,000. In 1965 a Rio Grande Conference edition in Spanish was begun, and the paper set up its own printing plant. In 1967 the first layman was chosen editor in the person of Jon Kinslow, a former newspaperman.

O. W. Nail, *Texas Methodism*. 1960.   Walter N. Vernon

TEXAS COLLEGE, Tyler, Texas, was founded in 1894 by a group of ministers of the C.M.E. Church. Instruction began in 1895 with O. T. Womack as the first president. The name of the institution was changed to Phillips University in 1909, but resumed the name of Texas College in 1912. The institution has a four-year undergraduate liberal arts program. It has a governing board of twenty-four regular members, not including ex-officio members and advisory members. Members of the governing board are nominated by the five annual conferences of the C.M.E. Church in the state of Texas and confirmed by the board of trustees.

Library, 32,583 volumes; total enrollment, 500; number of foreign students, one; total faculty, forty; campus acreage, sixty-six; number of buildings, twenty-five (two buildings are now under construction); value of physical plant, $1,455,000; endowment, book value, $408,000; market value, $457,000; current income, $955,000; current expenditures, $936,000.

TEXAS CONFERENCE goes back to the organization of Methodism in Texas. (See Texas for beginnings of Methodism in the state.) The Texas Conference (ME) was organized at Rutersville, Texas on Dec. 25, 1840 with Bishop Beverly Waugh presiding. The conference territory included all of Texas except the northeast which was then in the Arkansas Conference. The Texas Conference began with three districts—Galveston, Rutersville, and San Augustine. It had sixteen charges, and 1,623 white and 230 colored members.

The Texas Conference was divided in 1845 to form the Eastern Texas and Western Texas Conferences. In 1846 the Western body changed its name to the Texas Conference (MES). Both Texas conferences adhered South. In 1859 and 1866 more conferences were carved from the Texas Conference territory, and in 1902 the East Texas Conference, which had given up part of its territory in 1874 to form the Trinity (North Texas) Conference, was absorbed by the Texas Conference. There has been little change in the boundaries of the Texas Conference since that time. Its territory is east Texas.

In 1902 the Texas Conference had 171 charges, 54,107 members, and churches and parsonages valued at about

$850,000. By 1920 there were 230 pastoral charges, 82,477 members, and property valued at $3,792,903. The conference came to unification in 1939 with 274 pastoral charges, 123,658 members, and property valued at $8,938,642.

The Texas Conference (MC) was organized at First Church, Houston, on Nov. 8, 1939, with Bishop A. FRANK SMITH presiding. After the second world war the population of Texas grew rapidly. In 1940 the population of the state was 6,414,000. By 1967 the estimated population was nearly 11,000,000. The Texas Conference grew with the population, its membership nearly doubling in the same period of time.

McMAHAN'S CHAPEL near San Augustine is both the oldest continuing Protestant and Methodist congregation in Texas. Bishop A. Frank Smith presided over the Texas Conference from 1934 to 1960, a record of continuous supervision of one conference by one bishop.

LON MORRIS, a Methodist junior college at Jacksonville, is within the bounds of the Texas Conference. In 1968 the conference contributed $187,707 to the Texas Methodist College Association. The conference supports the Methodist Hospital and the San Jacinto Hospital at Houston. It has three retirement homes, Crestview at Bryan, Moody House at Galveston, and Happy Harbour at La Porte. In cooperation with other conferences, the Texas Conference supports eight WESLEY FOUNDATIONS in the state, the Methodist Home for Children at Waco, the Methodist Mission Home for unmarried mothers at San Antonio, and *The Texas Methodist* at Dallas.

In 1970 the Texas Conference reported eleven districts, 527 pastoral charges, 718 ministers, 232,517 members, and property valued at $123,318,432. During that year the conference raised for all purposes $17,827,840.

General Minutes, ME, MES, TMC, UMC.
Minutes of the Texas Conference.
O. W. Nail, *Texas Methodism.* 1961.　　ALBEA GODBOLD

TEXAS CONFERENCE (CJ) began as the Texas Mission Conference (ME) which was organized at HOUSTON, Jan. 18, 1867 with Bishop MATTHEW SIMPSON presiding. It was formed by dividing the Mississippi Mission Conference, and the territory was the state of TEXAS. At the outset the body was composed of both white and Negro ministers and churches. The mission conference began with fourteen charges and 491 members, but in the first session it created three districts, one of which was German, and listed a total of nineteen charges. On Jan. 25, 1869 the mission conference became the Texas Conference with Bishop Simpson again presiding. At the time it had five districts, forty-four charges, and 3,547 members.

In 1874 the Texas Conference was divided to form the WEST TEXAS CONFERENCE and at the same time the SOUTHERN GERMAN CONFERENCE was organized to include all the German work of the denomination in Texas and LOUISIANA. Thereafter the Texas Conference was a Negro conference and its territory was east Texas.

In 1873 WILEY COLLEGE, named for Bishop ISAAC W. WILEY, was founded at Marshall. Wiley is the second oldest college for Negroes west of the Mississippi River, the first school west of the river to receive a Carnegie Library, and the first Negro college west of the river to be granted "A" rating. It has an endowment of $1,000,000 and an enrollment of about 700.

The Texas Conference came to unification in 1939 with five districts, 102 charges, 22,356 members including in-active ones, and property valued at $698,400. As a conference in the CENTRAL JURISDICTION of The Methodist Church it had in 1968 four districts—Beaumont, Houston, Marshall, and Navasota—102 charges, 106 ministers, 19,421 members, and property valued at $5,360,319.

One member of the Texas Conference was elected bishop, WILLIS J. KING (1944).

In 1968 the name of the Texas Conference was changed to Gulf Coast Conference, and it was placed in the Houston Area of the South Central Jurisdiction pending merger with the Texas Conference of that Jurisdiction.

General Minutes, MEC and MC.
Minutes of the Texas Conference.
O. W. Nail, *Texas Methodism.* 1961.　　F. E. MASER

TEXAS WESLEYAN COLLEGE, Fort Worth, Texas, had its beginning as coeducational Polytechnic College, established in 1891. The name was changed to Texas Woman's College in 1914. Then in 1935, it returned to coeducational status as Texas Wesleyan College.

This institution passed through several periods of change, and its future was uncertain for a time because of the founding of SOUTHERN METHODIST UNIVERSITY, as well as a heavy debt incurred during the depressed 1930's. In 1935 the resources of Texas Wesleyan Academy in Austin were transferred to Texas Wesleyan College.

Credit for the survival and ultimate progress of Texas Wesleyan College is due to the leadership of Law Sone, who served as president from 1935 to 1968. Degrees offered are the B.A., B.S., B.M. (Music), B.S. in Business, and Master of Education. The governing board has twenty-five trustees elected by five annual conferences in Texas.

JOHN O. GROSS

THACORE, CYRIL MADHAVLAL (1905-　　), president of LUCKNOW CHRISTIAN COLLEGE, was born at Nadiad in Gujarat, May 1, 1905. His father, Madhavlal N. Thacore, was a pioneer Methodist minister serving both rural and city churches in Gujarat. Two of Thacore's uncles have also been pastors, and two of his sisters are married to Methodist ministers.

His academic career is replete with honors. He earned the B.A. honors degree from Bombay University in 1928, was made Dakshina Fellow of Gujarat College in Bombay University (1928-29), and was awarded the M.A. degree in 1930. In 1933 he won a teacher's diploma from London University, and in 1948 obtained the Ph.D. from Lucknow University. In 1951 he was awarded an honorary LL.D. degree by OKLAHOMA CITY UNIVERSITY. He joined the faculty of Lucknow Christian College in 1930 as a lecturer in English and three years later became head of the department. In 1937 he was elected vice-principal and in 1949, president, the designation being changed from principal that year.

During his presidency various departments of the college have been upgraded and expanded. Bachelor of Arts courses, which had been closed in the reorganization that set up Lucknow University, were reopened in 1954 with the full approval of the university. The college of Physical Education inaugurated a postgraduate diploma course in 1955. Facilities for science courses have been strengthened by the addition of much new equipment. The University Grants Commission of the government of

INDIA and the Kresge Foundation of DETROIT have joined the State government and the Methodist Board of MISSIONS in providing the necessary funds. A beautiful chapel has been constructed as a memorial to Bishop J. W. CHITAMBAR. The hostels have been reconstructed and enlarged.

Thacore was married in 1934 to Josephine Desai of Nadiad, Gujarat. Their three children have made distinguished records in universities in India and abroad.

Dr. Thacore has been president of the Uttar Pradesh Christian Council, chairman of the North India Board of Christian Education, member of the Uttar Pradesh Board of High School and Intermediate Education and of both the academic and executive councils of Lucknow University, and of the executive board of the Methodist Church in Southern Asia. He was the lay delegate of GUJARAT CONFERENCE to the GENERAL CONFERENCE of 1932.

J. N. Hollister, *Southern Asia.* 1956.   J. WASKOM PICKETT

THAKUR, NARAIN SINGH, a landowner in Budaun District of the United Provinces, was converted in 1864. He lived in a village near Budaun City where he was a recognized leader. He embraced Christian teaching eagerly and became a zealous nonprofessional evangelist. There was persecution from the time of his baptism but his courage never wavered. He built a small chapel near his house and invited people to it for worship and study. After years of devoted service he was attacked one night. The next morning he was discovered with his head almost severed from his body. The identity of his assailants was never discovered.

J. WASKOM PICKETT

THEOLOGICAL COLLEGES, British. The Methodist Church in Great Britain owns and maintains several residential colleges for the training of its ministers for home and overseas service. The WESLEYAN METHODIST CONFERENCE allocated grants from the CENTENARY FUND of 1839 for the erection of two theological institutions, one in the vicinity of LONDON and the other in the neighborhood of MANCHESTER, to replace the centers of ministerial training then in existence in rented properties at Hoxton and Abney House, both in London. Estates were acquired near the two large cities, and buildings were added to the existing houses, with accommodations for between sixty and seventy students and houses for tutors in each place—DIDSBURY COLLEGE, Manchester, opened in 1842, and RICHMOND COLLEGE, Surrey, opened in 1843. In 1868 the denomination opened another such institution, WESLEY COLLEGE, Headingley, LEEDS, to which in 1881 was added HANDSWORTH COLLEGE, BIRMINGHAM. In 1926 they added another for postgraduate ministerial training, Wesley House, CAMBRIDGE.

The METHODIST NEW CONNEXION opened a theological institution at Ranmoor, SHEFFIELD, in 1862, and the UNITED METHODIST FREE CHURCHES at Manchester in 1872. With their incorporation into the UNITED METHODIST CHURCH in 1907 these institutions were amalgamated in Victoria Park College, Manchester. After years of cooperation between this institution and Hartley College, Manchester, which in 1881 took over the ministerial training of the PRIMITIVE METHODISTS, the two colleges joined forces in 1934 as HARTLEY-VICTORIA COLLEGE.

The curricula of the larger colleges are similar. Students normally stay for three or four years, under the guidance of a principal, three or four tutors, and an assistant tutor. Each college works in close cooperation with the local university. When places are available, it is common for men from overseas or non-ministerial university students to live in the colleges and to share in their life. In the interests of economy and efficiency The Methodist Church decided that it must reduce the number of six theological colleges which it took over at METHODIST UNION in 1932. In 1968 Wesley College, Headingley, was amalgamated with Didsbury College, and renamed Wesley College, Bristol. In that same year Handsworth College was closed, joining forces with The Queen's College, Birmingham, an Anglican institution, to form the first English ecumenical theological college.

NORMAN P. GOLDHAWK

THEUER, DONALD A. (1927-   ), American E.U.B. layman, was born in Cleveland, Ohio, on Jan. 20, 1927. His grandfather, CARL HAUSER, was publisher for the EVANGELICAL ASSOCIATION and his father, Charles J. Theuer, was manager of the Cleveland publishing house for THE EVANGELICAL CHURCH. Elected publisher by the 1966 GENERAL CONFERENCE of The E.U.B. Church, Donald Theuer served in that position until the formation of The United Methodist Church in 1968, when he was elected by the BOARD OF PUBLICATION as Vice President and Assistant General Manager for Administration.

In 1950 Theuer received the A.B. degree from NORTH CENTRAL COLLEGE. In 1952 he received the M.B.A. degree from the School of Business, University of Chicago. He served with the U.S. Air Force occupation forces in Germany in 1945-46. Theuer held positions at Ford Motor Company, Detroit, in the divisional controller's office (1952-1956) and with the marketing staff (1962-65). From 1956 to 1962, he served the BOARD OF MISSIONS of The E.U.B. Church as treasurer and business agent for the West Africa Mission, SIERRA LEONE. Sharing this missionary service with him was his wife, Lilburne Ruth Kaiser. They are the parents of three children: Marlynn, Marc and Jon.

Theuer joined the staff of the E.U.B. Board of Publication in 1965 as director of literature and periodicals. In 1966 he became assistant publisher and on Jan. 15, 1967 he assumed the office of publisher. Other responsibilities include: trustee of EVANGELICAL THEOLOGICAL SEMINARY, delegate to the Consultation on Church Union, member of the executive committee and program board of the Division of Christian Education of the NATIONAL COUNCIL OF CHURCHES of Christ in the U.S.A.

CURTIS CHAMBERS

THIRKIELD, WILBUR PATTERSON (1854-1936), American educator, FREEDMEN'S AID SECRETARY, and bishop, was born at Franklin, Ohio, on Sept. 25, 1854, his family of Norse origin coming from England to America. The son of Eden Burrowes and Amanda Thirkield, he was educated at OHIO WESLEYAN UNIVERSITY (A.B., 1876; A.M., 1879), BOSTON UNIVERSITY SCHOOL OF THEOLOGY (S.T.B., 1881; later honorary D.D., LL.D). On Oct. 27, 1881, he married Mary Haven of Malden, Mass. She was the daughter of Bishop GILBERT HAVEN and they had five children.

After a pastorate in CINCINNATI, he was called to CLARK UNIVERSITY, a Negro school at Atlanta, Ga., to organize, help establish and serve as dean of GAMMON THEOLOGICAL SCHOOL, the first theological school in the South open to Negroes. The school opened with only two students, and for two years Thirkield was the only professor. During the first year Gammon Hall was erected, and in the second year the enrollment reached twenty-nine.

In 1888 Elijah H. Gammon gave the school $200,000 for endowment and it became independent of Clark with Thirkield as first president, serving 1883-1900, and securing an endowment and equipment totaling $700,000. Upon making Gammon the leading institution of its kind in the South, Thirkield resigned, but remained chairman of its board of trustees until his death. He was elected General Secretary of the EPWORTH LEAGUE, November 1899, and General Secretary of the Freedmen's Aid and Southern Education Society, 1900-06.

At the solicitation of President Theodore Roosevelt and others he became president of Howard University, WASHINGTON, D.C., 1906-12. Here he enlarged the endowment, doubled its annual income, increased enrollment from 936 to 1,409 and faculty from 90 to 132 and added to the plant additions valued at $500,000.

He was elected bishop in 1912 with his residence in NEW ORLEANS, where, of course, the M.E. Church, South, was the dominant Methodism. Thirkield gave himself largely to uniting and to guiding Negro Methodists in the South.

He made many official visits to Latin America and MEXICO and founded several farm schools to prepare peons for land ownership, and centers for training in the care of children.

A member of the Phi Beta Kappa and Beta Theta Pi fraternities, Bishop Thirkield wrote seven books and published several addresses, including: *The Higher Education of the Negro; The Personality and Message of the Preacher*, 1914; and the *Book of Common Worship for the Several Communions*. This last as well as a book, *Service and Prayers for Church and Home*, gave him something of a reputation as a liturgist, a field of interest then in its incipiency in Methodism.

He was a trustee of a number of colleges. Bishop Thirkield died in Brooklyn, N. Y., on Nov. 7, 1936, and was buried in Franklin, Ohio.

He was an energetic, progressive educator, an eloquent public speaker and a man of great force of character, broad scholarship and high ideals.

Clergy Who's Who.
F. D. Leete. *Methodist Bishops.* 1948.
National Cyclopedia of American Biography, The.

JESSE A. EARL

THOBURN, C. STANLEY (1902-   ), is president of the North India Theological College at BAREILLY, INDIA. This college was established in 1964 by action of the Methodist Church in Southern Asia, the Punjab and North India Synods and the Malwa Church Council of the United Church of North India, and the Church of India, Burma, and Ceylon. It continues the work of the Bareilly Theological Seminary, founded in 1872 and of theological schools previously serving the other cooperating churches. The property of the Bareilly Theological Seminary is now used by this college.

Thoburn is the younger son of the late Rev. and Mrs. Lyle Thoburn. The father came to India as a missionary of the M.E. Board of Foreign MISSIONS in 1893, and the mother came as an appointee of the WOMAN'S FOREIGN MISSIONARY SOCIETY in 1894. They were married in 1899. Stanley was born in Almora, India, in 1902. An older brother was born in LUCKNOW in 1900. The father died of cholera in Lucknow in 1905 while serving as agent of the Methodist PUBLISHING HOUSE. The widow remained in mission work, and the sons completed high school in India. The brothers both returned to India as missionaries. Their father was a nephew of Bishop JAMES MILLS THOBURN and of ISABELLA THOBURN, founder of the college that bears her name.

Stanley Thoburn holds the following degrees: B.A. from ALLEGHENY COLLEGE; S.T.B., M.A., and Th.D. from BOSTON UNIVERSITY; and D.D. from Serampur University. He returned to India as a missionary in 1928. His appointments in India have included: professor, Bareilly Seminary; pastor, Naini Tal English Church; superintendent, Naini Tal District; district missionary, Sitapur; and Leonard Theological College professor for twenty years.

His brother, Wilbur Thoburn, served as a lay missionary in India and in PAKISTAN, at LUCKNOW CHRISTIAN and Forman Christian Colleges, and since 1961 has been a professor at Iowa State University.

J. WASKOM PICKETT

ISABELLA THOBURN

THOBURN, ISABELLA (1840-1901), was the first missionary appointed by the WOMAN'S FOREIGN MISSIONARY SOCIETY of the M.E. Church. Her eagerness to go to INDIA and her obvious qualifications for missionary service contributed largely to the organization of the society. Accompanied by Dr. CLARA SWAIN, the second appointee of the society, she arrived at BAREILLY on Jan. 20, 1870. The Annual Meeting of the India Mission was then in session. These extraordinary women were joyfully received by the mission and especially by Miss Thoburn's brother, JAMES, whose letters from India to the family at home had first awakened her interest in missionary service.

Isabella was the ninth child in a family of five boys and five girls. The parents emigrated from the North of IRELAND to America and settled on a sixty-acre farm near St. Clairsville, Ohio. After reaching the top in local schools, she entered Wheeling Seminary in VIRGINIA. Her brother David wrote to their brother James that "Bella is the genius of the family. She excels in painting and as a writer." After Wheeling, she studied for a year in the Cincinnati Academy of Design. These were the tragic years of America's Civil War, and she spent much time caring for the wounded. But after leaving school, she gave most of her time to teaching, and in that found her vocation.

In 1866 her brother James, by then the recognized leader of Methodism in India, wrote Isabella a personal letter in which he expressed the conviction that there could not be a vigorous church in India so long as the women remained untaught. He asked if she would like to come and help educate Indian girls. She replied promptly that she would come when the way opened. Immediately she began to pray and work for opening. Others also prayed and worked, with the result that the Woman's Foreign Missionary Society of the M.E. Church was organized on March 30, 1869.

On her arrival and that of Clara Swain in 1870, Miss Thoburn was appointed to LUCKNOW. Nothing was said as to the nature of work expected of her. She started to Lucknow immediately. Within a month she had settled, learned a little Hindustani, and decided to give first place to the education of girls, second place to evangelistic work with women secluded in their homes. On April 18, 1870 she opened a school for girls in a tiny, dark room on a crowded, dusty and noisy street. "It seemed a great mistake to start a school there," her brother wrote later, "but the venture was made on the principle that the best possible is always the right thing to do." On the first day there were but six girls enrolled. Within six months, after two moves to better locations, the six had grown to twenty-five. The next year the house of the treasurer of the last King of Oudh was purchased. With it came nine acres of land. By the end of 1872, the school had twenty boarders and forty-five day students. The school was then named Lal Bagh Girls' School.

From these humble beginnings two great institutions have developed—the ISABELLA THOBURN COLLEGE on property known as Chand Bagh (Moon Garden), and the Lal Bagh Higher Secondary School.

Miss Thoburn's creative personality is also reflected in other institutions in India and in America. She assisted in the founding of Wellesley Girl's School in Naini Tal and Cawnpore Girls' High School, now the co-educational Methodist High School of Kanpur. During a four-year health leave in the United States she made massive contributions to deaconess work in CHICAGO and CINCINNATI. When a hospital grew up out of the deaconess work in Cincinnati, she became its first superintendent.

Miss Thoburn started holding college classes in India in 1886. Progress was slow. Ten years later she wrote, "seventeen girls have passed the entrance examination and ten the intermediate examination. The first B.A. candidate will appear [in the university examination] this year. Eleven college students are now in attendance."

Miss Thoburn died of cholera in Lucknow, Sept. 11, 1901. She had called her college the "Lucknow Woman's College," but after her death the authorities quickly and unanimously decided that it should be known as the "Isabella Thoburn College."

M. A. Dimmitt, *Isabella Thoburn College.* 1963.
J. N. Hollister, *Southern Asia.* 1956.   J. WASKOM PICKETT

JAMES M. THOBURN

THOBURN, JAMES MILLS (1836-1922), was the first bishop of the Methodist Church to reside in INDIA. He was elected missionary bishop for India and MALAYSIA by the M.E. GENERAL CONFERENCE of 1888.

Thoburn's parents migrated to America from IRELAND early in the nineteenth century and settled on a farm near St. Clairsville, Ohio. James was born there March 7, 1836. When he was fourteen years old his father died, leaving his wife with ten children and a mortgaged farm. A year later James enrolled at ALLEGHENY COLLEGE. He was converted through the preaching of Bishop CALVIN KINGSLEY. A book on early piety awakened his interest in missions. He joined the PITTSBURGH CONFERENCE and was ordained in 1858.

The next year he arrived in India with four new missionary couples. One of the men, J. R. Downey, died eleven days after reaching Lucknow. Mrs. Downey remained in India and later married Thoburn. She died in 1864 and Thoburn returned to America to place his son with relatives. He attended the GENERAL CONFERENCE of 1864, and there began to develop remarkable influence as a spokesman for missions.

After returning to India in 1866, he soon became a recognized leader of Methodist missionaries. He helped to start *The Indian Witness,* and was its first editor. He and WILLIAM TAYLOR joined forces and became an influential team for evangelism and church growth. Coming home several times, he acquired wide recognition in America.

When the General Conference decided to elect a missionary bishop for India and Malaysia, there was quick agreement that Thoburn was the man. His election on the first ballot was acclaimed throughout Southern Asia, but the Methodists there objected to the limitations placed upon the authority of missionary bishops.

Of his influence in America it was said that "Thoburn put India on America's heart." JOHN R. MOTT called him "possibly the greatest ecclesiastic of the nineteenth century." Twelve years after his election as bishop, the General Conference decided that India should have three bishops and elected E. W. PARKER and F. W. WARNE.

Parker died without holding a Conference session. Thoburn suffered a serious break in health but remained in office until 1908. He died at Meadville, Pa., on Nov. 28, 1922.

A letter to his sister, ISABELLA THOBURN, was in part responsible for her coming to India. She there founded the college known by her name.

Bishop Thoburn's many writings included *My Missionary Apprentice*, 1886; *The Deaconess and her Vocation*, 1893; *Christless Nations*, 1894; *The Church of Pentecost*, 1899; *Life of Isabella Thoburn*, 1903; *The Christian Conquest of India*, 1906; *India and Southern Asia*, 1907; *God's Heroes Our Examples*, 1914.

William Henry Crawford, ed., *Thoburn and India: Semicentennial Sermon and Addresses Delivered at the Thoburn Jubilee*. New York: Eaton & Mains, 1909.
J. N. Hollister, *Southern Asia*. 1956.
F. D. Leete, *Methodist Bishops*. 1948.
William Fraser McDowell, *Creative Men: Our Fathers and Brethren*. New York: Abingdon Press, 1934.
W. F. Oldham, *Thoburn*. 1918.   J. WASKOM PICKETT

THOM, WILLIAM (1751-1811), British Methodist, was the first president of the METHODIST NEW CONNEXION. He was born at Aberdeen, SCOTLAND, in September, 1751, had a good education, and was brought up in the Church of Scotland, but early joined the Methodists. Wesley took him out to travel in 1774, and in his circuits he often saw real revivals. Wesley appointed him as one of the first LEGAL HUNDRED in the Deed Poll. In the disputes after Wesley's death about the observance of the Sacraments, Thom was a reformer, and joined with ALEXANDER KILHAM in founding the Methodist New Connexion, of which he was an early statesman. Altogether he served as president of conference six times, and as BOOK STEWARD from 1803 to his death. He died at Shooter's Hill, Hanley, Staffordshire, on Dec. 16, 1811.

O. A. BECKERLEGGE

THOMAS DAVID W. (1833- ?), was a pioneer Methodist missionary in North INDIA. He and Mrs. Thomas arrived in January 1862, along with H. D. Brown and W. W. Hicks and their wives. Mr. and Mrs. Brown and Mr. and Mrs. Hicks served only a few years, but Mr. and Mrs. Thomas gave long and distinguished service. In 1865, the India Mission was organized as the first Methodist Annual Conference in Asia. Bishop EDWARD THOMSON appointed Thomas principal of the girls' orphanage in BAREILLY. As in many other missions, the care of orphans quickly became a major concern. The need was compelling, and the church had an unmistakable duty to meet the need. But Thomas was one of the first to recognize the limitations the work had in evangelism because the orphanage children were separated from their countrymen.

In 1868 Thomas made another effort to help needy people when he founded an industrial institution to give employment. It was abandoned a few years later as unsuccessful. Mrs. Thomas took an active part in the effort that led to the appointment of Dr. CLARA SWAIN as the first woman missionary doctor sent to India, and when Dr. Swain organized her first class for medical training fourteen of the seventeen in it were girls from the orphanage. Thomas led a deputation, which included Dr. Swain, to ask the Nawab of Rampur for a hospital site. The Nawab gave his entire estate of forty-two acres and two buildings in Bareilly.

Thomas took the lead in organizing the theological seminary at Bareilly (now North India Theological College). He gave $20,000 to purchase land and construct buildings and the Board of Foreign MISSIONS gave the same amount. He then served as the first principal.

He wrote a commentary on Genesis, a book on the Trinity, and a pamphlet in Roman Urdu on miracles.

B. H. Badley, *Indian Missionary Directory*. 1892.
B. T. Badley, *Southern Asia*. 1931.
J. N. Hollister, *Southern Asia*. 1956.
J. E. Scott, *Southern Asia*. 1906.   J. WASKOM PICKETT

THOMAS, FRANK MOREHEAD (1868-1921), American preacher and editor, was born in Bowling Green, Ky., July 3, 1868, the son of R. C. and Elizabeth Thomas. At an early age he consecrated his life to Christ and joined the M.E. Church, South. He attended the public schools of Bowling Green and at the age of eighteen graduated from Ogden College. He received the M.A. degree from VANDERBILT UNIVERSITY in 1892 and the B.D. degree the next year. In 1906, at the age of thirty-eight, KENTUCKY WESLEYAN COLLEGE conferred upon him the D.D. degree.

Thomas was admitted to the LOUISVILLE CONFERENCE of the M.E. Church, South, in 1893. As CHAPLAIN of the 3rd Regiment, Kentucky National Guards, he served with his company in the Spanish American War in CUBA in 1898. He held the leading appointments of his conference, including the Louisville District, 1910-14. He was a delegate to four GENERAL CONFERENCES and was fraternal delegate of the Southern Church to the General Conference of the M.E. Church in MINNEAPOLIS in 1912. He was a member of the FEDERAL COUNCIL OF CHURCHES of Christ in America, a member and in certain meetings secretary of the Joint Commission then dealing with church union, and had served longer than any other man on that commission at the time of his death. In 1918 he was elected by the General Conference as BOOK EDITOR and Editor of the *Quarterly Review*, which position he held with distinction until his death in 1921.

He wrote many articles for religious publications and in 1915 published one volume entitled *The Coming Presence*. He was a man of outstanding intellectual endowments and attainments, a philosopher and a theologian of deep consecration and unusual spiritual insight.

Journal of the Louisville Conference, 1921. HARRY R. SHORT

THOMAS, JAMES (1860-1943), American preacher, was born in Chambers County, Ala., April 8, 1860. He went to ARKANSAS in 1887 and conducted a private school in the mountains west of Hot Springs. He engaged in the practice of law during that time, having been admitted to the bar in the circuit court at Hot Springs. He was licensed to preach in 1890 and was admitted on trial into the LITTLE ROCK CONFERENCE (MES) in 1891. He served pastorates at Hot Springs, LITTLE ROCK, TEXARKANA and Pine Bluff. He was the founder of First Church at Texarkana and served it as pastor for two quadrennia. He served fourteen years as a PRESIDING ELDER; two years as Centenary Secretary and nine years as Commissioner of HENDRIX COLLEGE.

Thomas raised the first permanent endowment for

Hendrix College and for seventeen years was Chairman of its Board of Trustees. For meritorious service in the field of education Hendrix conferred upon him the D.D. degree.

James Thomas was one of the founders of the Arkansas Methodist Orphanage (now children's home) and served that institution as superintendent for twenty years, most of that time in connection with other positions of responsibility. He was Secretary of the Little Rock Conference Board of Trustees from its organization in 1899 until his death. For more than twenty years he was Secretary of the Conference Board of Missions. For many years he was one of the commissioners in charge of the publication of *The Arkansas Methodist*.

He represented his conference in five GENERAL CONFERENCES: 1906, 1922, 1926, 1930, 1934, in the special session of 1924, and several times as an alternate delegate. He was a member of the General Board of CHURCH EXTENSION from 1910 to 1943. He twice represented his conference at ECUMENICAL METHODIST CONFERENCES at LONDON in 1901 and at ATLANTA in 1931.

He died at his home in Little Rock, Ark., July 10, 1943, and is buried in Oakland Cemetery in that city.

Journal of the Little Rock Conference, 1943.

HAROLD DAVIS SADLER

JAMES S. THOMAS

THOMAS, JAMES SAMUEL (1919-   ), American bishop, was born at Orangeburg, S. C., on April 8, 1919, the son of a Methodist minister, the late James S. Thomas, Sr.

He received the following degrees: B.A. from CLAFLIN COLLEGE, in 1939; D.D., 1953; B.D. from GAMMON THEOLOGICAL SEMINARY, in 1943; M.A. from DREW UNIVERSITY, in 1944; Ph.D. from Cornell University, New York, in 1953; and LL.D. from BETHUNE-COOKMAN, in 1963.

On July 7, 1945, he was united in marriage to Ruth Naomi Wilson. They have four daughters: Claudia, Gloria, Margaret, and Patricia.

In 1939-40, James Thomas was a rural school principal in Florence County, S.C. He was ordained an elder of

The Methodist Church in 1944, and became a member of the SOUTH CAROLINA CONFERENCE of the CENTRAL JURISDICTION. From 1942 until 1947 he was a pastor in the South Carolina Conference, Central Jurisdiction. At Gammon Theological Seminary, he was a professor of Rural Church, director of field work, and head of the practical studies division (1947-53). In the summers of 1948 and 1952 he acted as president of Gammon. From 1953 until 1964 he was associate director of the Department of Educational Institutions of the BOARD OF EDUCATION of The Methodist Church, NASHVILLE, working with Methodism's thirteen Negro colleges.

He was chairman of the Committee of Five created by the Central Jurisdiction in 1961 to look after and make recommendations concerning the moves being made to integrate the Conferences, churches, and membership of the Central (Negro) Jurisdiction with the five geographic Jurisdictions of The Methodist Church. He was elected a delegate to the GENERAL CONFERENCE of 1964 and subsequently in June 1964, was elected bishop by the Central Jurisdiction at its meeting in Daytona Beach, Fla., after a record-breaking seventeen ballots. He was assigned to the DES MOINES Area in July 1964, and became the second Negro Methodist bishop to lead a predominantly white area of 300,000 Methodists and 916 churches. Methodism is Iowa's oldest and largest denomination. The episcopal residence is in Des Moines.

Who's Who in America, Vol. 34.
Who's Who in The Methodist Church, 1966.   N. B. H.

THOMAS, JOHN (1796-1881), was a pioneer British missionary to the Friendly Islands. Born at Worcester, England, he was converted under Wesleyan preaching and offered for missionary work after reading the life of Henry Martyn. Both the London Missionary Society and the Wesleyan, WALTER LAWRY, had failed to establish work in the Friendly Islands, and Thomas was sent to begin again. With a Tasmanian, James Hutchinson, and their wives, they landed at TONGA in June, 1826. Persevering and tactful, quickly learning the language, he established happy relations with islanders and chiefs. For twenty-five years he was "the father of the mission," witnessing a remarkable change from intertribal warfare to settled government, and from paganism to Christian faith. A decisive event was the baptism of King Taufaahau and his wife, in 1831, as King George and Queen Charlotte (Salote). After four years of missionary deputation in England, Thomas returned to Tonga in 1854, when the South Seas were handed over to the new Australasian Conference until 1860. He was a true "father of God" to Tonga, and his influence is still felt in the Christian basis of the Tongan constitution and laws. He died on Jan. 29, 1881.

G. S. Rowe, *A Memoir of J. Thomas*. London, n.d.

CYRIL J. DAVEY

THOMAS, JOHN SAUNDERS LADD (1875-1959), American preacher, educator, was born at Pembrokeshire, South Wales, May 1, 1875. He was educated in WALES, LONDON and America, studying also in the graduate school of Chicago Theological Seminary. He was ordained deacon in the ROCK RIVER CONFERENCE in 1902, received into full membership in 1905, and ordained an ELDER in 1906. In 1922 he was called to First Church, GERMANTOWN,

PHILADELPHIA, then one of the commanding Methodist churches in the East, remaining there until 1942 when he became Dean of the School of Theology of Temple University, Philadelphia. He served in this last capacity for ten years. He was elected to four GENERAL CONFERENCES, and was also active in the Faith and Order Movement, attending the World Conferences of Faith and Order in 1927 and again in 1937. He was also a delegate to the ECUMENICAL METHODIST CONFERENCE in London in 1921, and that in Atlanta, Ga., in 1931. He served with distinction on the Commission on Ritual and Orders of WORSHIP of The Methodist Church, 1940-44. He was also a trustee of both DREW UNIVERSITY and of DREW THEOLOGICAL SEMINARY, as well as of Temple University, and the Methodist Hospital in Philadelphia.

Thomas received many honors including the Conwell Award from Temple University in 1957. His chief contribution to Methodism was as a pulpit orator. His forthright, picturesque language, his challenging message, and his warm spirit evoked an appreciative response from hearers who filled the churches wherever he preached. He died July 14, 1959.

Minutes of the Philadelphia Annual Conference, 1960,

FREDERICK E. MASER

THOMAS, T. GEORGE (1909-   ), British Methodist Member of Parliament, was born of devoted Methodist parents in Port Talbot in 1909. After education at Tonypandy Grammar School and the University College of Southampton, he became a school teacher, first in LONDON, then in Cardiff, where he was elected President of the Cardiff Association of the National Union of Teachers. For five years he served on the National Executive of the N.U.T., which proved a stepping-stone to a fruitful political career. He was elected Labour Member of Parliament for Central Cardiff (1945-50), and from 1950 to the present time has been the Member for West Cardiff. From 1951 he has served as Chairman of the Welsh Parliamentary Labour Party and in various government positions. In 1951 he was appointed Parliamentary Secretary to the Minister of Civil Aviation, and in more recent years has been Joint Parliamentary Under Secretary of State, first at the Home Office (1964-6), next at the Welsh Office (1966-7), and then at the Commonwealth Office (1967-8). In 1968 he was made a Privy Councillor and became the Secretary of State for Wales.

For over forty years he has served Methodism in various offices, including that of LOCAL PREACHER. He was elected Vice President of the Methodist CONFERENCE in 1960. He has also served as President of the National Brotherhood Movement, and has been active in the work of the WORLD METHODIST COUNCIL. In 1959 he delivered the BECKLY LECTURE at the British Methodist Conference, on the subject of *The Christian Heritage in Politics*.

FRANK BAKER

THOMAS, WILLIAM (1889-   ), a minister of the Belgian Conference of The Methodist Church, was born in Mezieres (Switzerland) on March 20, 1889, the son of a prominent pastor of Geneva, Frank Thomas. He graduated in Letters and in Theologie at universities both in Geneva and Berlin. He studied in America and obtained the Ph.D. degree from DREW UNIVERSITY in 1948. He

was assistant to his father in his ministry from 1914 to 1919, and was then appointed a missionary of the M.E. Church, South, in Belgium in 1922.

He was thereafter pastor of the Antwerp (French) Methodist Church (1922-47), and again in 1949-53. He became district superintendent of the Flemish work, 1925-50, and has been professor in the Brussels Protestant Theological School since 1950. He became president of that school in 1952, and served in that capacity until 1958. He married Adrienne Blauben in Antwerp in 1922. He was honorably retired by and in the Belgian Conference of the Methodist Church in 1961.

WILLIAM G. THONGER

THOMAS, WILLIAM NATHANIEL (1892-1971), Rear Admiral and Chief of CHAPLAINS, United States Navy, was born in Rankin County, Miss., March 21, 1892, the son of John C. and Annie Laura (Thompson) Thomas. He won the B.A. degree with honors at MILLSAPS COLLEGE in 1912. In 1935, Millsaps awarded him the D.D. degree, and in 1941 AMERICAN UNIVERSITY so honored him. He married Martha Ellen Fondren, Feb. 18, 1913, and they had two sons, William N. and John E.

Thomas began his ministerial career in the MISSISSIPPI CONFERENCE in 1911, serving several pastorates, including Summit, 1914-17. He was commissioned a chaplain in the United States Navy in January, 1918, and in succeeding years served at a Navy hospital, a naval station, on battleships, and at the Naval Academy, Annapolis. He was chaplain at Annapolis, 1924-27, and again 1933-45. His ministry to the midshipmen was so highly esteemed that the rule limiting chaplains to three years at any one post was set aside and his second tour of duty ran twelve years. Moreover, he was elected an honorary alumnus of the Naval Academy, a distinction accorded few non-graduates.

In 1945, Thomas became the first chaplain ever elevated to the rank of Rear Admiral, and in that capacity he served four years as Chief of Chaplains. In recognition of his service in the navy he was given the victory medal, the legion of merit, and other important citations.

On retiring from the navy in 1949 at fifty-seven years of age, Thomas was offered but declined the presidency of several institutions of higher learning. He was a trustee of American University, an advisory member of the Methodist Commission on Chaplains, an advisory member of the Naval Council of the Service Men's Christian League, and was on the board of control of the United States Naval Institute. He moved to LAKE JUNALUSKA, N. C., and was for twenty years a member of the board of trustees of the Lake Junaluska Methodist Assembly. He assisted in raising funds for that institution, and served as Dean of the Memorial Chapel. In the latter capacity he conducted the early morning communion services. While in retirement he served several interim pastorates in churches of different denominations in NORTH CAROLINA and MISSISSIPPI. He died at Lake Junaluska, April 27, 1971, and after funeral services in the Naval Academy Chapel at Annapolis, was buried with military honors in the Chaplains' Lot, Arlington National Cemetery.

Who's Who in America, 1946-47.
Waynesville Mountaineer, Waynesville, N. C., Apr. 28, 1971.

ALBEA GODBOLD

THOMPSON, PETER (1847-1909), British Methodist, was born at Esprick, Lancashire, in 1847. Converted at the age of eighteen, he entered the ministry of the WESLEYAN METHODIST CHURCH in 1871. After successful work at Broughton-in-Furness, in 1885 he was sent by Conference to East London, where in response to *The Bitter Cry of Outcast London* (1883), the East End Mission was born. With St. George's Chapel as his headquarters, he founded, organized, and developed the mission, and, concerned with all social problems, served on the local Board of Guardians (who were concerned with the administration of poor relief). He became the first promoter of the Anti-Sweating League (which wanted to improve conditions of work in London). Amid a scene of incredible depravity he established social services: soup kitchens to provide cheap nourishment for those on the verge of starvation, outings in the country for children and their mothers, gospel temperance propaganda to combat drunkenness; and under his influence two notorious gin palaces and music halls were purchased and turned into mission centers. He died in 1909.

R. G. Burnett, *Story of the East London Mission.* London, 1946.   JOHN T. WILKINSON

THOMPSON, ROBERT FRANKLIN (1908-   ), American minister and university president, was born at Primrose, Neb., on May 30, 1908, the son of John F. and Sophia (Maxwell) Thompson. He was educated at NEBRASKA WESLEYAN UNIVERSITY (A.B., 1930; LL.D., 1947); and received his B.D. at DREW UNIVERSITY in 1931, M.A. there in 1934, and Ph.D. in 1940. He took post-graduate work at OXFORD, England, and at the University of Zürich, SWITZERLAND, and received the honorary L.H.D. degree from the AMERICAN UNIVERSITY in 1960, a D.P.S. from the UNIVERSITY OF THE PACIFIC, and a D.H. from WILLAMETTE UNIVERSITY, both in 1967. His wife was Lucille Burtner, whom he married on June 30, 1931. They have two daughters.

Dr. Thompson joined the NEW YORK EAST CONFERENCE for a time, but became a professor of Willamette University in OREGON, 1937-42, and then the president of the UNIVERSITY OF PUGET SOUND, Tacoma, Wash., in 1942.

He was a dean at the Pacific Northwest Pastors' School; a member of the executive committee of the General Conference COUNCIL ON WORLD SERVICE AND FINANCE, (1952-64, and 1968-   ); a general secretary of the National BOARD OF EDUCATION of The Methodist Church, 1964; a member of the executive committee of the WORLD METHODIST COUNCIL; chairman of the Finance Committee of the American Section of the World Methodist Council, 1968; president of the World Affairs Council, 1945-46; and on the Board of Directors of Pacific First Federal, Nebraska Wesleyan University, and Tacoma General Hospital, the Washington State Historical Association, and the National Association of Methodist Colleges and Universities. He resides in TACOMA, Wash.

Who's Who in America, Vol. 34.
Who's Who in The Methodist Church, 1966.   N. B. H.

THOMPSON, THOMAS (c.1755-1828), British layman, was born near HULL, Yorkshire, England, the son of a farmer. Employed at first in the household of WILLIAM WILBERFORCE, he became a wealthy banker and also a

Member of Parliament, where he used his influence to defend the interests and promote the aims of Methodism. In 1795 he presided over the meeting of Methodist trustees named to draw up the PLAN OF PACIFICATION. He was also chairman of the public meeting at LEEDS in 1813 that led to the founding of the Wesleyan Methodist Missionary Association, of which he became the first lay treasurer in 1815. He was the author of *French Philosophy,* a work of Christian apologetic. He died in Paris on Sept. 14, 1828.

                           G. E. LONG

WILLIAM THOMPSON

THOMPSON, WILLIAM (1733-1799), first President of the British CONFERENCE after the death of JOHN WESLEY in 1791, was born at Fermanagh in IRELAND and became a Methodist preacher in 1757.

He went to England prior to 1765 and entered the itinerancy there, being appointed to DUBLIN. He underwent persecution in common with many other Methodists of the period and on one occasion was imprisoned and several of his hearers were impressed into the King's navy; their release was secured by the COUNTESS OF HUNGTINGDON.

For more than thirty years Thompson served circuits in the British Conference. In 1766 he was appointed to Athlone and then recrossed the Channel to serve in succession Edinburgh, Glasgow, Newcastle, LEEDS, YORK, MANCHESTER, Birstal and Halifax. He served six years at Edinburgh, five each at Newcastle, and Leeds, and two each at Manchester, Birstal and Halifax.

On the death of John Wesley, March 2, 1791, Thompson dispatched from his Halifax Circuit a circular (The HALIFAX CIRCULAR), signed by himself and several others, which was intended to prepare the preachers for the problems that would face them at the approaching Conference. It was proposed that offices be filled according to seniority for one-year terms, that one be designated to preside annually at the Irish Conference, and that committees be set up to direct the affairs of the districts between Conferences. This circular led to various meetings of preachers, at some of which the Halifax proposals were repudiated, but the discussions served to fix the general administrative pattern.

Thompson was elected President at the Conference in 1791, the Conference passing over THOMAS COKE and ALEXANDER MATHER to so elect him. At the same Conference he was assigned to the Wakefield Circuit.

William Thompson was a well-known and successful preacher, fitted to occupy the post. But he was not one of the notables of Methodism such as Thomas Coke, JOSEPH BENSON, Alexander Mather, or JOHN PAWSON. There has been speculation as to why the Conference passed over men like these, and especially Coke and the others who had been ordained by the Founder himself. Perhaps Thompson's leadership in the affair of the Halifax Circular had an influence. Some have thought that an administration less autocratic than that of Wesley was desired. "The chief reason which determined the choice," according to George Smith, "was Thompson's peculiar genius for ecclesiastical polity. Brought up in the north of Ireland, he had closely studied the system of the Presbyterian Church government and was probably far ahead of his compeers in acquaintance with ecclesiastical questions."

Thompson was largely responsible for the preparation of the PLAN OF PACIFICATION of 1795. This prevented the dispute regarding the liberty of Wesleyan itinerants to administer the SACRAMENTS from becoming totally destructive of Methodist Societies.

After his presidential year, Thompson preached three years (1792-94) in LONDON and three in BIRMINGHAM, where he was also Chairman of the District. He died on May 1, 1799, and was buried in St. Mary's Church, Birmingham.

Minutes of the Conference.
W. Myles, Chronological History. 1799.
G. Smith, Wesleyan Methodism. 1857-61.
A. Stevens, History of Religious Movement. 1858-61.
Wesley and His Successors. 1891.   ELMER T. CLARK

THOMPSON, WILLIAM ERNEST MORLEY (1894-1969), Irish minister, was born in BELFAST, and entered the ministry in 1917. Much of his early ministry was as a missionary in British Guiana, and he returned to the home work in 1935. From 1941 to 1947 he was Secretary of the Methodist Church in IRELAND, and in 1948 became President of the Church. In 1959 he retired from the active ministry, but continued to play a leading part in the Conference and in connexional affairs generally. His experience as Secretary of the Church during the difficult years of the Second World War has been the foundation of much valuable guidance since. He died in June 1969.

FREDERICK JEFFERY

THOMSON, EDWARD (1810-1870), American educator, editor, and bishop, was born at Portsea, England, on Oct. 12, 1810. His parents emigrated to America when he was about nine. Taking the medical degree at the University of Pennsylvania, he settled in Wooster, Ohio. At nineteen he became infected with skepticism by his

EDWARD THOMSON

teachers. However, while practicing medicine, his agnosticism was shaken by a sermon by Russell Bigelow. He experienced conversion but was bitterly opposed by his Calvinistic father especially as to joining the Methodist Church. However, in 1832 he did join the OHIO CONFERENCE.

At his first sermon in a grove meeting, it is said sixty-five penitents came to the altar, and forty-six united with the church. He is said to have combined eloquence and great spiritual power in his sermons. Bishop GILBERT HAVEN refers to Thomson's absorption in thought and concentration. The story is that after his first marriage, his Detroit congregation had a party for him and his new wife. At the party he did not recognize his wife but told her "that he believed he had seen her somewhere but could not recall where."

After filling appointments in OHIO at Norwalk, Sandusky City, CINCINNATI and Wooster, Edward Thomson transferred to the MICHIGAN CONFERENCE, serving in DETROIT. He became principal of the Norwalk Seminary, Ohio, 1838-43; editor of the Ladies' Repository, 1844-46; first president of OHIO WESLEYAN, 1846-60; editor of the Christian Advocate and Journal, New York, 1860-64; and was elected bishop in 1864.

Bishop Thomson traveled extensively as bishop and everywhere elicited the respect and confidence of the people. He made the first episcopal visit to INDIA. Author of several books and published addresses, he was more of an essayist than editor. He said, "A minister's success, so far as salvation is concerned, depends not in part upon literary attainments and in part upon the power of God, but wholly upon the latter."

While en route after attending Conference in CHARLESTON, W. Va., Bishop Thomson died of pneumonia in a hotel in WHEELING, W. Va., on March 22, 1870. He was buried in Delaware, Ohio. Thomson Church in Wheeling was named for Bishop Thomson.

In his day Bishop Edward Thomson was called by some "the most accomplished of all the bishops of the M.E. Church." He was remarkably successful in all the positions he held.

Christian Advocate, Sept. 9, 1926.
F. D. Leete, Methodist Bishops. 1948.
M. Simpson, Cyclopaedia. 1882.   JESSE A. EARL

THOMSON, GEORGE (1698-1782), a leading Anglican evangelical, was "from the first a hearty friend of the Oxford Methodists," says Tyerman. As early as 1732 or 1733 Thomson was preaching evangelical doctrines in his parish of St. Gennys, Cornwall. JOHN WESLEY visited St. Gennys on several occasions, until in 1753 Thomson's insistence on Calvinism caused a separation. On his deathbed, however, Thomson sent for Wesley and received Communion from him.

A. SKEVINGTON WOOD

JOHN F. THOMSON

THOMSON, JOHN FRANCIS (1843-1933), was the first M.E. minister ordained in ARGENTINA and possibly in all Latin America. He was born in SCOTLAND and came to BUENOS AIRES with his parents as a lad of eight in 1851. He learned Spanish and spoke it as fluently as any Argentine.

At the age of thirteen he had a conversion experience at the English-speaking M.E. church, established in Buenos Aires in 1836. The pastor, WILLIAM GOODFELLOW, who "had a special genius for the discovery of men, God's men, for the work of the church," made him study, and afterward sent him to the United States to be trained for the ministry at OHIO WESLEYAN UNIVERSITY. Upon graduation Thomson returned as an ordained minister and a missionary of the church, ready to begin the Spanish-speaking work that Goodfellow and the M.E. Board of MISSIONS had in mind. Thomson married Helen Goodfellow, a niece of William Goodfellow.

Thomson began his regular Spanish work with a SUNDAY SCHOOL in the home of Doña Fermina Leon de Aldeber in the Boca section of Buenos Aires.

Appointed in 1868 to open the Methodist work in MONTEVIDEO, URUGUAY, for a year he commuted so as to preach one Sunday in Montevideo and one in Argentina. The following year he established himself in Montevideo,

staying until 1878, when he was again appointed to the Buenos Aires church.

He was charged then with the organization of the Province of Buenos Aires District, and started churches in Mercedes, Chivilcoy, Balcarce, Lomas de Zamora, La Plata, and other cities. His work in Buenos Aires culminated with the formal opening (1896) of the building of the Second Methodist Church (Spanish-speaking).

In 1898 he returned to Montevideo, where, as he said of himself, "the missionary in charge was pastor of both the English and the Spanish speaking churches, superintendent of both Sunday schools, official interpreter to the United States Embassy, chairman of the University Club and editor of its magazine." This public work was a great asset for Thomson's work among students and unchurched people. It was a time of controversy in all the fields of thinking. Thomson excelled in polemics and debate with the Roman Catholic clergy—debate which was natural, given the circumstances of the country's religious life.

He died in Buenos Aires on Feb. 2, 1933.

Juan C. Varetto, *El Apostol del Plata, Juan F. Thomson.* Buenos Aires, 1943. DANIEL P. MONTI

THONGER, WILLIAM G. (1889-   ), minister of the BELGIUM Conference of The Methodist Church and longtime leader in Belgian Methodism, was born in Paris, on Oct. 27, 1889. He studied and graduated in the French State Colleges, Sorbonne University, and the Protestant Theological Seminary in Paris. In 1926 he received the honorary D.D. degree from RANDOLPH-MACON COLLEGE in Ashland, Va.

After serving a pastorate at Les Ollieres (Southern France) from 1914-19, Thonger entered the service of Methodist Relief in Belgium in 1920. He married Renee Brunnarius in Paris on Jan. 17, 1920. In 1922 the Thongers were appointed missionaries of the M.E. Church, South, in the Belgian Methodist Mission as it was then. After withdrawal of American support in consequence of the depression of 1929-34, Thonger was left in charge of the Belgium Conference, as it had become in 1932. Appointed as superintendent he served as such until his retirement in 1961.

Besides the acknowledged leadership he has given to Methodism in Belgium, Thonger has served many general Protestant enterprises. He has been in the Belgian Federation of Protestant Churches—of which he was president for a number of years—and the Belgian Bible Society, where he served as president from its origin in 1946 until 1963. He remains the honorary president of this organization. Thonger has been a clerical delegate to eight GENERAL CONFERENCES of his church and is a member of the executive committee of the CENTRAL CONFERENCE of CENTRAL AND SOUTHERN EUROPE. He has taken a part in a great many other world-wide and European religious gatherings. He has three daughters and three grandchildren. He resides in BRUSSELS where he has served so long and continues to act in many helpful capacities. He is the editor of the Belgium section of the *Encyclopedia of World Methodism.*

N. B. H.

THORNBURG, AMOS ADDISON (1900-1967), American pastor, district superintendent and lecturer, was born in Huntington, W. Va., Nov. 11, 1900, the son of Joseph Soule Thornburg, a minister in the M.E. Church.

Amos Thornburg graduated from WEST VIRGINIA WESLEYAN COLLEGE, 1921, A.B.; GARRETT SEMINARY, 1925, B.D.; NORTHWESTERN, 1926, A.M.; and later received the honorary D.D. and L.H.D. He married Alice Elizabeth Sutherland on Sept. 2, 1926, and they had three children. Both Amos Thornburg and his son Richard were delegates to the GENERAL CONFERENCE in 1964.

Thornburg was admitted to the WEST VIRGINIA CONFERENCE in 1919 on trial. After serving as assistant pastor, and pastor of the Belington, W. Va., Circuit, he received the following appointments: Normal Park, CHICAGO, 1926-29; Sterling, 1929-32; Aurora, 1932-34; Wilmette Parish, 1934-38 (all in ILLINOIS); Mathewson Street, PROVIDENCE, R. I., 1934-44; Grace Church, ST. LOUIS, Mo., 1944-48; First Church, Hollywood, Calif., 1948-56; Trinity, Chicago, 1956-61; superintendent Chicago Northern District, 1963-65; Arlington Heights Church, Arlington Heights, Ill., 1965-67.

At Wilmette Thornburg's Sunday school and youth work attracted national attention and missionary activity reached new prominence at First Church, Hollywood. He succeeded GLENN R. PHILLIPS when the latter became a bishop.

Thornburg was a member of the COMMISSION ON WORSHIP, 1944-64, and Hymnal Commission, 1960-67, and lectured on these subjects. He was also a trustee of Northwestern University. In June 1967, he was electrocuted in a tragic accident in the flooded cellar of his parsonage.

Christian Education Bulletin, January 1949.
Who's Who in The Methodist Church, 1966.   JESSE A. EARL

THORNE, JAMES (1795-1872), British BIBLE CHRISTIAN minister, was born near Shebbear, North Devon, Sept. 21, 1795. In 1816 he became WILLIAM O'BRYAN's first itinerant, and many revivals marked his ministry. In 1821 Thorne evangelized Kent. He succeeded O'Bryan as virtual leader of the connection in 1829, and was five times president of Conference. He ably edited the connectional magazine for thirty-eight years and governed the connectional school for twenty. Wise and humane, with extraordinarily broad sympathies, he supported Catholic emancipation, the Evangelical Alliance, total abstinence and—inevitably—Liberalism and free trade, and promoted Methodist union. He died on Jan. 28, 1872, and was buried at Lake.

F. W. Bourne, *James Thorne.* 1895.   GLYN COURT

THORNE, MARY EVANS, who is reputed to be the first female Methodist CLASS LEADER in PHILADELPHIA, if not in America, was born of Welsh parents in Bristol, Bucks County, Pa. Her maiden name was Evans. Later her family settled in Newbern, N. C., where she was converted, joined the Baptists and married a Mr. Thorne. After the death of her husband, she with her parents and their family returned to Philadelphia. She united with the Baptists in Philadelphia, but feeling they were not sufficiently spiritual she prayed for guidance, and walking through the streets of Philadelphia, came upon the Methodists who were holding a meeting led by JOSEPH PILMORE. She felt that in the Methodists she had found what she wanted, and she joined the Methodist Society, retaining also for the time being her Baptist membership. Pilmore quickly

recognized her gifts and appointed her as the first female class leader in the city.

Her mother and brother attended some of the Methodist meetings with her, but they were unimpressed. Her parents decided to return to Newbern to get away from the Methodist influence. Mary Thorne, however, remained in Philadelphia, making her living as a school teacher.

In letters in the archives of Old ST. GEORGE's, Philadelphia, she describes how during the British occupation of Philadelphia in the Revolutionary War, the British Army commandeered St. George's building for a cavalry school, and how the Methodist Society met for a time in her home. She also states that when she was leader of three Methodist Classes she was jeered at in the streets, called "Mother Confessor," stoned in effigy and finally dismissed from the Baptist Church.

Before the close of the Revolution she married a Captain Parker and the couple returned to England in 1778 on the same ship as THOMAS RANKIN. They landed at Cork, and here she met JOHN WESLEY through RICHARD BOARDMAN whom she had known in Philadelphia. She and her husband were soon on terms of particular intimacy with John Wesley, who appointed Captain Parker a steward of the Gravel Lane Chapel, LONDON. Captain Parker had a large interest in several ships, but these were lost at sea, and, in their old age, the couple was reduced to poverty. They had one son who helped them greatly. They also appealed to the British Methodists for assistance.

The dates of Mary Thorne's birth and death are not known, but Lednum, the Philadelphia Methodist historian, says that her son taught for a time at Woodhouse Grove among the Wesleyans of England, later emigrating to Philadelphia where he died leaving a widow and a daughter.

She had corresponded with both Joseph Pilmore and Richard Boardman and was a close friend of FRANCIS ASBURY. Many of her letters are in the archives of Old St. George's Church, Philadelphia.

J. ATKINSON, *Wesleyan Movement in America.* 1896.
J. Lednum, *Rise of Methodism.* 1859.   FREDERICK E. MASER

THORNE, SAMUEL THOMAS (1860-1891), was born on Oct. 15, 1860, at Norton Barton, Launcells, Cornwall. He was educated at SHEBBEAR COLLEGE where he was also converted, and at Bradford Gammar School in Yorkshire. Elected a CIRCUIT STEWARD at eighteen, he entered the BIBLE CHRISTIAN ministry and in 1886, with THOMAS VANSTONE opened the Yunnan mission in CHINA. Settling at Chaotong Fu, he traveled extensively, preaching and curing cases of opium poisoning; he was helped by his wife, Lois Malpas. His labors, recurrent fevers, privations and journals broke even his robust physique, and he died at Chaotong Fu on Sept. 23, 1891.

T. Ruddle, *Samuel Thomas Thorne.* 1893.   GLYN COURT

THRALL, HOMER S. (1819-1894), American minister and author, was born in Underhill, Vt., Dec. 19, 1819.

He was trained for the ministry at OHIO WESLEYAN UNIVERSITY, which school conferred on him a M.A. degree in 1850. SOUTHWESTERN UNIVERSITY at Georgetown, Texas, conferred a D.D. degree in 1884. After being received on trial in the OHIO ANNUAL CONFERENCE in

1840, he spent fifty-four years in the itinerant ministry, a period which, in many respects, was eventful and interesting in the world's history. It was a period of great inventions and developments, social, political, and religious, all of which influenced him to write important volumes on the history of TEXAS and of Texas Methodism.

His pastoral charge was Little Kanawha, Ohio, in 1840; then Summerville, Ohio, in 1841. The next year he was admitted into full connection in the Conference and was transferred to Texas as a missionary. All of the later years were spent in Texas.

After the Battle of San Jacinto in 1836, when DAVID AYERS and Miss Lydia McKenry, daughter of a famous KENTUCKY preacher, wrote letters to the New York *Christian Advocate* concerning the importance of more missionaries being sent to Texas, those letters reached Homer Thrall, who then determined to make Texas his future home. In 1842 the Ohio Conference met, and LITTLETON FOWLER of Texas arrived there and called for volunteers. The *Minutes* of that conference show that Homer S. Thrall then took up his work as missionary in Texas.

Soon after the War Between the States (1866), Thrall became President of Rutersville College, a school organized from the concept of MARTIN RUTER in 1840, and one which lasted as a Methodist school for about thirty years.

Other appointments of Homer S. Thrall were: Bastrop, Texas (1845); AUSTIN (1846-1847), where he built the first Methodist Church in that city; Washington, Texas (1848); GALVESTON (1849-1850); Victoria and Lavaca (1851-1852); in 1853 he was Bible Agent; Rutersville, Texas (1854); Galveston District (1855-1857); Austin District (1858); Columbus District (1860-1861); Victoria District (1862-1864). Later he went to SAN ANTONIO, Texas, at which place he was superannuated in 1891, and resided there until his death Oct. 12, 1894.

Thrall was twice married, first to Miss Amanda J. Kerr, June 27, 1847, who lived but a few years. Later he married Mrs. Amelia L. West, July 21, 1852. He was sent to Texas when the state was comparatively a wilderness, the people few and scattered. He knew the fathers of the Republic of Texas, Generals Houston, Rusk, President Mirabeau Lamar, and others, including every Governor of the state. He was on intimate terms of friendship with them all.

His books included: *A History of Methodism in Texas* (1872); *History of Texas* (1876); *A Pictorial History of Texas* (1879); *The People's Illustrated Almanac, Texas Handbook* (1880); *Brief History of Methodism in Texas* (1889).

MRS. JOHN H. WARNICK

THRAPP, JOEL SMITH (1820-1896), American M.P. minister and editor, was a member of the Muskingum Conference in OHIO, and was active in the work of the GENERAL CONFERENCE and Conventions of the M.P. CHURCH. He was also actively associated with ADRIAN COLLEGE. He was born on April 9, 1820, the son of Joseph Thrapp (Oct. 16, 1776-May 12, 1866), who was active in early Methodist endeavors in the Muskingum Valley. Two other members of Joel Smith Thrapp's family, his brother, Israel Thrapp, and J. A. Thrapp, were also members of the Muskingum Conference of the M.P. Church.

Joel Smith Thrapp was converted and received into the M.P. Church on Sept. 1, 1839. He was licensed to preach in May 1842, and was received into the traveling connection in September of that year. He was elected a representative to the General Conference of 1858 and was a member of the Free State Conferences held at CINCINNATI in November 1857. He was also a member of the convention held in Springfield, Ohio, in 1858, the convention of 1860 which met in PITTSBURGH, and the Non-Episcopal Convention held in Cleveland in June 1865. He was a member of the sub-committee of the joint Methodist Protestant and Wesleyan Convention held in Union Chapel, Cincinnati, in May 1866; and of the General Conference of 1867 which was held in Cleveland. He served as book agent and publisher of *The Western Methodist Protestant* (later *The Methodist Recorder*) from December 1864, until December 1866. He was a member of the General Conference of the Methodist Church in 1871 which met in Pittsburgh. He represented the Muskingum Conference at the famous Uniting Conference of the M.P. Church in 1877. Beginning in 1866 he served for many years as the general agent for Adrian College and traveled extensively among the various annual conferences of his denomination in its interest.

T. H. Colhouer, *Sketches of the Founders.* 1880.
E. J. Drinkhouse, *History of Methodist Reform.* 1899.
M. Simpson, *Cyclopaedia.* 1882.   RALPH HARDEE RIVES

WILLIAM THRELFALL

THRELFALL, WILLIAM (1799-1825), South African missionary martyr, was born at Hollowforth, Lancashire, England on June 6, 1799, and entered the WESLEYAN METHODIST ministry in 1821. He was appointed to labor with WILLIAM SHAW among the British settlers in Albany but his strong missionary vocation made him restless and he soon accepted the offer of a passage to Delagoa Bay. However, repeated attacks of malaria compelled him to return to the Cape on a passing whaler. After convalescing with BARNABAS SHAW at Leliefontein (Lily Fountain) he volunteered to establish a mission in Great Namaqualand (now South West Africa). He set out in June 1825 with JACOB LINKS (the first Namaqua received into the Wesleyan ministry) and Johannes Jager. During August 1825 they were murdered by their Bushman guides who coveted their oxen and possessions. Threlfall's concrete achievements were negligible but his heroic endeavors and martyr's death have earned him an honored place in Methodist history.

N. A. Birtwhistle, *William Threlfall*. London, 1966.
Dictionary of South African Biography.
B. Shaw, *South Africa*. 1841.   D. G. L. CRAGG

THROCKMORTON, J. RUSSELL. (See JUDICIAL COUNCIL.)

TIFFIN, EDWARD (1766-1829), first governor of OHIO (1803-07), was among prominent Methodists in early Ohio history. Born in Carlisle, England, on June 19, 1766, he was reared in the established Church of England. He came to the United States at eighteen, finished his education in medicine at the University of Pennsylvania at twenty-one and immediately thereafter established a practice in Berkeley County, then in VIRGINIA. There, in 1790, he became a Methodist and two years later was ordained a LOCAL PREACHER by FRANCIS ASBURY.

Tiffin and his brother-in-law, Thomas Worthington, both men of means, freed their slaves when they decided to settle in Ohio territory. They located in Chillicothe, Ohio, in the spring of 1798.

Practicing medicine and preaching to Methodist societies in the valleys of the Scioto River and Paint Creek in Ross County, Tiffin became one of the region's best-known and respected citizens. Ross Countians sent him to the Legislature, where he was elected speaker in 1799. He also became a member of the Constitutional Convention organized Nov. 1, 1802, which established statehood for Ohio. He was the unanimous choice for first governor of Ohio and was reelected without opposition in 1805.

A man with Jeffersonian ideals, Tiffin continued in politics, being elected to the U. S. Senate before the end of his second term as governor, succeeding Thomas Worthington who was to become Ohio's sixth governor. In 1812, President Madison named Tiffin to the new post of Commissioner of the General Land Office.

While others sought safety from the British who were sacking Washington in 1812, Tiffin arranged to move the precious land office records to safety ten miles away. These records were among the few saved from the stampede and fire that engulfed the nation's capitol.

In 1814, at his request, he was named surveyor-general of the Northwest in order that he might return to his beloved Ohio home. He spent the next fifteen years, almost to his death, in that position, with headquarters in Chillicothe, serving under three presidents.

During those last years he also resumed two other of his early professions—the practice of medicine and preaching. He died Aug. 9, 1829. Historians have described Edward Tiffin as a man of "magnetic personality . . . versatile . . . of great ability."

                    JOHN F. YOUNG

TIGERT, JOHN JAMES, III (1856-1906), American bishop, editor, and teacher, was born in LOUISVILLE, Ky., Nov. 25, 1856. He attended the public schools of his city. In order to make his way, he clerked in the grocery store of Daniel Montz who took great interest in him and helped with his education. He entered VANDERBILT UNIVERSITY Theological Department and graduated in 1877. The same year he joined the LOUISVILLE CONFERENCE of the M.E. Church, South, and was appointed to a small church in his home city. While there he continued his studies under John A. Broadus in the Baptist Seminary. In 1881 he went to Vanderbilt University as an instructor and continued his studies for the M.A. degree, which he received in 1884. On graduation he became Professor of Philosophy in the University. In 1890 he was sent to KANSAS CITY, Mo., for four years as pastor of a large church. At the GENERAL CONFERENCE of 1894 he was elected as BOOK EDITOR of the church and Editor of the Methodist *Quarterly Review*, and in 1906 was elected to the episcopacy. He married Amelia McTyeire, daughter of Bishop HOLLAND N. MCTYEIRE, in 1878. Their son, John J. Tigert, IV, became Commissioner of Education of the United States and President of the University of Florida. EMORY AND HENRY COLLEGE and the University of Missouri conferred upon Bishop Tigert the degrees of D.D. and LL.D.

Bishop Tigert wrote many articles for religious publications and was the author of a number of important books on Methodism. Among them are *The Constitutional History of American Episcopal Methodism*, which has long been considered authoritative in its field; *The Making of Methodism, The Life of Thomas Coke, The Doctrine of the Methodist Church in America,* and a volume on theism, *A Survey of Paths that Lead to God*. He was a member of each General Conference from 1882 to the time of his election to the episcopacy.

Bishop Tigert was privileged to preside over only one annual conference. While at lunch on his way to his next conference in Indian Territory a small bone lodged in his throat, blood poisoning developed and in a few days, on Nov. 21, 1906, he died in Tulsa, Okla. He is buried in Nashville, Tenn.

Louisville *Courier Journal*, Nov. 22, 1906.   HARRY R. SHORT

TILLETT, JOHN (1812-1890), American preacher, called in his biography, "The Iron Duke of the Methodist Itinerancy," was born in Camden County, N. C., on Nov. 23, 1812. In 1833 he entered RANDOLPH-MACON COLLEGE in VIRGINIA. There his teachers had a deep influence on his life, and he was converted in a college revival in 1834, changed his vocation from law to the ministry, and was graduated A.B. in 1837 and M.A. in 1840. He served in the NORTH CAROLINA CONFERENCE from 1839 until 1886. On Oct. 6, 1841, he was married to Elizabeth Jenkins Wyche.

John Tillett was a man of deep spiritual powers and advocated by his life, and by his preaching "not a new doctrine, but a new life." His evangelistic preaching was of unusual power. Of one such revival led by him in Oxford, N. C., it was said that "it revolutionized Oxford; it revolutionized the country around about." He was a man who rigidly enforced the discipline of the Methodist Church, requiring his members to live up to its moral precepts. As their pastor, John Tillett had a vital influence on WASHINGTON DUKE and his sons, "Buck and Ben" (J. B. DUKE and BENJAMIN N. DUKE). He fought fearlessly against alcohol, gambling, and other personal and social sins of his day. Many times he made enemies, but his converts became men and women of great character and faith. When his own son, away at school, signed a note for a dishonest laborer for $85 and the laborer disappeared, John Tillett required the boy to pay the $85 and the interest. This son, Henry Augustus Tillett, became an outstanding lawyer and always emphasized the sacredness of a contract. Another son, W. F. TILLETT, noted Dean of VANDERBILT UNIVERSITY, reflected the great strength and moral character of his father.

After twenty-one years of serving with her husband, the first Mrs. Tillett, the mother of his nine children, died in 1862, and he was married again in 1863 to a sister of his first wife, a widow, Mrs. Louisa Yancey Speed. John Tillett died on July 17, 1890 and was laid to rest in Elmwood Cemetery, Charlotte, N. C.

A. W. Plyler, *The Iron Duke of the Methodist Itinerancy.* Nashville: Cokesbury Press, 1925.   R. G. TUTTLE

TILLETT, WILBUR FISK (1854-1936), American theologian, author, hymnologist, and dean of the VANDERBILT School of Religion, was born on Aug. 25, 1854, in Henderson, N. C. He was the son of JOHN TILLETT, known as the "Iron Duke of American Methodism." Brought up in the severe years in the South following the Civil War, young Tillett managed to pursue studies through books, college and seminary, and to graduate from RANDOLPH-MACON COLLEGE in 1877, and from Princeton Seminary in 1880. He married first in 1888, Kate O. Schoolfield, who died the following year; and he married again on Jan. 25, 1894, Laura McCloud. He became the professor of systematic theology at Vanderbilt University in 1886, and from that date took a leading part in the activities of his conference and in the theological and church work of the entire South. He was elected a member of the GENERAL CONFERENCE (MES) in 1902, 1906, and 1910. At the 1906 Conference, he was one of the leaders calling for a "re-statement of the faith"—a move which was warmly greeted by certain liberal elements of that day, but was frowned upon by the bishops and conservative forces. Tillett's speech carried the conference but opponents managed to attach a proviso that no restatement of faith be made unless the other Methodist Churches (chiefly the Methodist Episcopal) would join in the effort. As they never did, nothing came of this effort.

Heading the Vanderbilt Divinity School in 1886 and later at the time of the "Vanderbilt Controversy," he found himself strangely divided between the opposing forces. Charges that the Theological School was allowing, if not disseminating, heresy among young ministers, impelled the M.E. Church, South, to move to see that the whole institution should fully reflect its own ideals. A lawsuit over University ownership resulted. The decision in the courts went against the Church, and a self-perpetuating Board of Trustees continued to carry on the work of the University. The Church turned then from the Vanderbilt Theological School for a time, building and supporting SOUTHERN METHODIST UNIVERSITY in Texas and EMORY UNIVERSITY in Atlanta, with their divinity schools.

Tillett felt very keenly this whole issue and used to say so in private to those who knew him best. However, he remained in Vanderbilt spending in all fifty-four years of his life there.

Perhaps the crowning work of his life was service upon the Joint Hymnal Commission, which was composed of representatives of the M.E. Church, the M.E. Church, South, and of the M.P. Church. This commission met and compiled a new Methodist Hymnal during the 1930-34 quadrennium. Tillett's vast knowledge in the field of hymnody was of great use to the Commission. He and EARL E. HARPER on the sub-committee of "New Hymns" personally read 8,000 new manuscripts of hymnic material submitted for inclusion in the Hymnal. Tillett's own hymn, "Oh Son of God Incarnate," in the Methodist Hymnal and elsewhere, has come to be in the beloved hymnody of the Church. The tune "Incarnation" was written for this hymn by Alfred Wooler at the request of Dean Tillett himself.

A classicist in his likes and dislikes, he was found by other members of the Hymnal Commission to be on the side of the ancient, time-tested expressions of devotion rather than the newer hymns. His fellows on the Commission never forgot a defense he made of the old classic hymn "*Dies Irae*," although it was admitted by all that no one ever sang it in a present-day church. The Commission, however, voted against Tillett and excluded the "*Dies Irae*," following the argument of J. M. M. GRAY that "we are not building a museum for the perpetuation of Christian antiquities, but a hymn-book out of which people can sing." Tillett took his defeats as he took his victories, in his sure, steady way, and never lost the admiration of both friends and those who opposed him. He died in Nashville, Tenn., full of honors and years, at his home on the campus at Vanderbilt on June 4, 1936.

Tennessee Conference Journal, 1936.
C. F. Price, *Who's Who in American Methodism.*   N. B. H.

TILLMAN, SADIE WILSON (1896-   ), American lay church worker and president of the Woman's Division of Christian Service, was born at Allisona, Tenn., April 30, 1896, daughter of Lemuel Ransom and Janie (Swan) Wilson.

She received the diploma of Harris Teachers College in 1918. She was graduated from Peabody College, B.S., 1923; M.A., New York University, 1924. ILLINOIS WESLEYAN UNIVERSITY conferred upon her the degree of L.H.D. in 1963. She married J. Fount Tillman on Aug. 23, 1934.

She was a teacher in Davidson County, Tenn., 1915-16, 1921, and in ST. LOUIS, 1919-20. She was director of religious education, Laura Haygood Normal, Soochow, CHINA, 1924-27. She then went to the BOARD OF EDUCATION of the M.E. Church, South, where she was associate secretary of missionary education, 1927-34.

Among her other positions of leadership in the church she was president of the Tennessee Conference WOMAN'S SOCIETY OF CHRISTIAN SERVICE, The Methodist Church, 1950-53; national vice-president, Methodist Woman's Division Christian Service, 1952-56, and president, 1956-64; member of the executive committee, WORLD METHODIST COUNCIL, 1956-65; member, General Board of the NATIONAL COUNCIL OF CHURCHES, 1956-64; member of the administrative committee, United Church Women, 1957-63; member of the executive committee, United States Conference, and of the Central Committee, WORLD COUNCIL OF CHURCHES 1961-68; member of COMMISSION ON STRUCTURE OF METHODISM OVERSEAS, 1964-68; member of Commission on Ecumenical Affairs, 1964-68. She was a delegate to the GENERAL CONFERENCE in 1952, 1960 and 1966.

The chapel of the Church Center at the United Nations plaza was furnished and named "Tillman Chapel" in her honor as the outgoing president of the Woman's Division in 1964.

She was a member of the board of the Marshall County Library, 1950-55. She served as a trustee of MARTIN JUNIOR COLLEGE, 1953-58, and since 1954 has been a trustee of SCARRITT COLLEGE. She was a trustee of NATIONAL COLLEGE, 1956-64, and of BENNETT COLLEGE, 1956-64. She was state president of the National Association American Pen Women, 1938-40. She is the author of *What Do You Know About China*, 1929, also of children's stories, programs, plays. She resides at Palmetto Farm, Lewisburg, Tenn.

Who's Who in America, Vol. 34.
Who's Who in The Methodist Church, 1966.   J. MARVIN RAST

TILLY, EDMUND A. (1864-1916), American preacher and missionary to BRAZIL, was born Sept. 24, 1864, in Bristol, Tenn. After graduation from King College, a Presbyterian school in that city, he spent a year at VANDERBILT school of theology. He joined HOLSTON CONFERENCE in 1885, and was appointed first to Pocohontas, Va. In 1888 he went to Brazil, where he was ordained elder by Bishop J. C. GRANBERY. In November 1890, he married Ella Virginia Porter whose father had freed his slaves in ALABAMA and sailed for Brazil in August 1868. Like several other early missionaries in Brazil, Tilly suffered indignities and opposition. One time, while preaching at Catete Church, Rio, a man threw a large stone at him through an open window. Tilly, who had been an agile baseball player in his youth, caught it and threw it back toward the attacker, much to the latter's surprise and discomfiture. After this, Catete Church protected its windows with heavy screens.

During his service in Brazil, Tilly was pastor, presiding elder, teacher in the theological department of INSTITUTO GRANBERY, and editor for a term of the Methodist weekly organ, *Expositor Cristão*. He also published a book of sermons on Christian doctrines.

In 1907 he suffered a slight stroke. Returning to the United States, he settled in Ashland, Va., and taught for a while in the theological department of RANDOLPH-MACON COLLEGE. In 1913, after his wife's death, and seemingly completely recovered, Tilly went back to Brazil but was unable to continue work for more than two years. He returned to the United States and died Nov. 27, 1916, in Bristol, Va. He was survived by four daughters—Margaret Carson, Ella, Laura Sale, and Katherine Cole.

I. P. Martin, *Holston*. 1945.
World Outlook, May 1943.   EULA K. LONG

TILTON, NEW HAMPSHIRE, U.S.A., is situated on the Winnipesaukee River, and is the home of TILTON SCHOOL. Historically it is tied in with neighboring Northfield and Sanbornton since Northfield first included the complete area. Consequently Methodism in Tilton, taking root in interdenominational effort, began as early as 1804 when Lewis Bates and Caleb Dustin, pastors on the Bridgewater Circuit, preached in a barn owned by a Baptist, Deacon Jonathan Clough, located in that part of Sanbornton which is now Northfield. In 1805 a permanent Methodist society was formed with an eight member "Class." That year MARTIN RUTER, one of the most scholarly men of early American Methodism, baptized nine persons in the school house on Bay Hill. When the NEW ENGLAND CONFERENCE met in Canaan, N. H. the following year, Northfield, mem-

tioned for the first time in the minutes, already had thirty-one members. Meetings continued alternately in the Northfield meeting house, on the Tilton Fair Grounds, and in the school house on Bay Hill. In Northfield on Sept. 8, 1828, a new brick church owned by the town was dedicated and made available for worship until it was no longer needed, when it became the "Town House." George Storrs, a member of the NEW HAMPSHIRE CONFERENCE, who located in 1836, was first to occupy the town-owned parsonage by the bridge on the Sanbornton side of the river. The town voted Storrs permission to cut wood on the parsonage lot for his own use "provided he leaves the fences in good order." It was considered necessary to sell part of the parsonage land in order to make the final payment on the minister's home.

East Tilton Methodist Church near Union Bridge was built around 1835 and was last repaired through the exertions of D. W. Davis, 1879. James B. H. Norris appears on the records of Northfield as one of their preachers who in 1834 was residing at Union Bridge. The steward's record commences September 1838, at Union Bridge or East Sanbornton on the Gilford Circuit with L. H. Gordon preacher in charge. Twenty-nine other preachers were appointed here during this church's life.

As a way of avoiding controversy in 1855, a committee from out-of-town was engaged to recommend a location for a new church nearer the rapidly expanding Conference-owned seminary in what is now the town of Tilton. Thereupon the First Methodist Church was built, where it now stands on the Main Street at a cost of $10,000, in spite of financial depression. It was dedicated Feb. 4, 1857 by Bishop OSMAN C. BAKER, who preached the dedicatory sermon, John Currier, pastor, assisting.

Since 1884 many improvements have been made resulting in an attractive, well-equipped church, and a parsonage on Main Street was bought in 1916. The New Hampshire Conference was held here in 1888, 1910, and 1918. Faced with the need for additional space, the church voted in 1967 to build a new church, to buy nearly five acres of land near the Tilton-Franklin line, and to sell the present church building and land.

Cole and Baketel, *New Hampshire Conference*. 1929.
Lucy R. H. Cross, *History of Northfield*. Concord, N. H.: Rumford Printing Co., 1905.
Journals of the New England and New Hampshire Conferences.
M. T. Runnels, *History of the Town of Sanbornton*, Vol. I. Boston: Alfred Mudge & Son, 1882.   WILLIAM J. DAVIS

TILTON SCHOOL, Tilton, New Hampshire, now a boys' boarding and day school, was founded in 1845 as the New Hampshire Conference Seminary. Originally co-educational, in 1939 it limited admission to boys. From 1852 to 1903 it operated as a college. In 1859 the name was changed to New Hampshire Conference Seminary and Female College. After 1903, when college work was discontinued, the name was changed to Tilton Seminary. The present name was adopted in 1923. The governing board has twenty-six members; five elected by the NEW HAMPSHIRE CONFERENCE, five by the alumni, fifteen by the board, and the headmaster ex officio.

JOHN O. GROSS

TIME CAPSULE. During the BICENTENNIAL celebrations of The Methodist Church in 1966 a Time Capsule was buried

TIME CAPSULE MARKER

on April 24, at 4:30 p.m., in Mount Olivet Cemetery in BALTIMORE. It is proposed to be raised during the Tercentenary Celebration of American Methodism.

The cylindrical shaped stainless steel receptacle, three and one-half feet long and ten inches wide with tapered ends was designed by H. Stanley Coates of Belmont, Mass., and was manufactured by Louis Sack Company, Somerville, Mass., under the guidance of the Chairman of the Committee, Ernest R. Case, then pastor of Belmont Church, Belmont, Mass.

Eight categories of items were placed in the capsule containing in all fifty-six items.

1. A bound historical notebook of documents, letters, clippings etc.

2. Audio-visual materials including taped messages to Methodists in 2066 from 57 Bishops, 18 General Secretaries, and one sister church (AFRICAN METHODIST EPISCOPAL ZION), and a filmstrip "Live or Die, I Must Ride."

3. Books and Pamphlets including the Revised Standard Version of the Holy Bible (presented by AMERICAN BIBLE SOCIETY on this its 150th Anniversary); *Young Reader's Bible*; *Discipline*, 1964; *Hymnal*; *Report of Hymnal Committee*, 1964; *Book of Worship*; *General Minutes*, 1964; *Decisions of the Judicial Council*, 1960-1964; *Fact Book*, 1964; *History of American Methodism* (3 Volumes) Emory S. Bucke, Editor; *The Dramatic Story of American Methodism* by Frederick E. Maser; *Methodist Evangel*; *Endless Line of Splendor* by H. Luccock and Paul Hutchinson; *Methodist Story Book*; Church Related Vocations and Service Projects, 1966; *Tourist Guidebook* by George Jones.

4. Magazine and Journals: *Christian Advocate* (4/7/66); *Christian Home* (3/66); *Methodist History* (1/66); *Together* (11/59 and 5/66); *Upper Room* (Mar to April, 1966); *Zions Herald* (1/66).

5. Church School Literature: *Learners and Literature*; *Methodist Student* (Spring 1966); *Methodist Teacher* (Spring 1966); *Methodist Student* (1-11); *Methodist Teacher* (1-11); *Adult Student* (Mar. 1966); *Adult Teacher* (Mar. 1966); *Studies in Christian Living* (Spring 1966); *Class Mate* (Mar. 1966).

6. Stamps: 1 special album containing 24 U.S.A. postage stamps relating to Methodists or Methodist influence.

7. Coins and Medals: Mint Sets: Philadelphia and Denver 1964; "Clad" Quarter—1965; Carver-Washington Commemorative Half Dollar; Medal received from Pope Paul VI commemorating the closing of the Vatican Council, Dec. 8, 1965; Bicentennial Medal.

8. Miscellaneous Items: World Methodist Flag; Pencil (Commemorating the World Methodist Conference, Aug. 18-26, 1966, London, England); "Rubbing" of bronze plaque noting the burial place of the capsule.

ERNEST R. CASE

TIME LIMIT is a term constantly used by American Methodists with reference to the number of years a pastor or DISTRICT SUPERINTENDENT may be allowed to stay in one appointment. At the beginning of the Methodist movement, changes in appointments made both by JOHN WESLEY in England, and by FRANCIS ASBURY in America were quite frequent. It was not uncommon for men to be changed annually, or even after a few months, in certain instances, or whenever a move seemed needed. On the other hand, Bishop Asbury felt competent to continue appointing a person to the same church, or to a nearby church, as he did with JOHN DICKINS whom he wished to keep in PHILADELPHIA to manage the BOOK CONCERN, and so continued to move Dickins about in the Philadelphia churches to keep him where he could run the publishing business. This caused much criticism among the other brethren who were usually moved much more sweepingly, and it is said that the Philadelphia preachers, and perhaps some of the other Methodists there, in order to force Dickins to itinerate as they were forced to do, asked that the Book Concern be moved from Philadelphia. So it went to NEW YORK.

The fixing of the time limit by the GENERAL CONFERENCE came about in 1804. There was in Albany in 1800 a pastor by the name of Stebbins, who was very popular with the people but whose reappointment for that special place, Asbury felt, would be a mistake. The Bishop, however, yielded to local pressure and reappointed Stebbins, causing discussion among the other preachers. AARON HUNT suggested to Asbury that in order to take care of this situation the General Conference should pass a measure forbidding the reappointment of any minister for a term longer than two years. Asbury saw at once that this would comprimit his power. "So then you would restrict the appointive power?", he asked, but not unpleasantly. "Nay, sir," was Hunt's reply, "we would aid in its execution for in the present instance it seems deficient." (Harmon, p. 28.)

Abury's failure to object encouraged Hunt, and he with Totten of the PHILADELPHIA CONFERENCE presented the resolution asking for a three-year time limit and it was passed in the 1804 General Conference. Thus, when 1808 came and the delegated General Conference was set up and given all powers not denied it, but forbidden to do anything to destroy "our plan of itinerant general superintendency," in that plan already was the time limit fixed by General Conference action and respected by Asbury.

Subsequent General Conferences from time to time have changed the time limit. Through the greater part of the nineteenth century the time limit held, but with longer and longer terms (1836 made it two; 1864 changed it to three years; 1888 made it five). Later on, first in the M.E. Church and then in the M.E. Church, South, the time limit, after being much modified, was eventually removed entirely. (See Sherman, pp. 184-85.) For a time in the latter years of the M.E. Church, South, a bishop could not reappoint a man to his same station after four years had passed without the consent of a majority of the presiding elders, as they were then. (The M.E. Church, South changed the two year limit of 1836 to four years in 1866.) In The Methodist Church, however, all restrictions had been removed by the time of union and there are none now in The United Methodist Church (except district superintendents). However the influence of the four-year term which was standard in the South is still felt psychologically in many conferences though a bishop may now reappoint a man continuously to one position.

District Superintendents. Until well in the twentieth century, bishops could reappoint presiding elders or district superintendents (as they became), to the superintendency of successive districts, though the four-year time limit, as it was then, prevented the presiding elder from being given charge of any one district for longer than four years. It was possible, however, to keep a man in the district superintendency by moving him from district to district at the end of each four year term, and thus the "self-perpetuating cabinet," as it was called, with the cabinet members themselves heavily influential in seeing that each other were kept in cabinet positions, came to be known over both Episcopal Methodisms. In order to obviate this, the General Conference first in the M.E. Church, then in the M.E. Church, South, passed a measure which after union in 1939 held that "within the Jurisdictional Conferences of the United States" no bishop could appoint a minister as district superintendent "for more than six consecutive years nor for more than six years in any consecutive nine years" (*Discipline*, 1964, Paragraph 432.3). This regulation is continued in The United Methodist Church (*Discipline* 1968, Paragraph 391.3). Thus there is a six-year time limit in The United Methodist Church *in re* the district superintendency.

N. B. Harmon, *Organization*. 1962.
P. A. Peterson, *Revisions of the Discipline*. 1889.
D. Sherman, *Revisions of the Discipline*. 1874.   N. B. H.

TINDALL, JOSEPH (1807-1861), pioneer Wesleyan Methodist missionary in Great Namaqualand (later South West Africa) was born at Gringley-on-the-Hill, Nottingham, England, on June 15, 1807, and married Sarah Goodyer on April 18, 1830. Under the influence of T. L. Hodgson he sold his business and emigrated to the Cape Colony, arriving in Cape Town on Jan. 16, 1836. He re-established himself in business in Cape Town and engaged actively in religious work. In 1839 he went to Great Namaqualand as catechist-assistant to EDWARD B. COOK and in 1843 was accepted for the ministry. Until 1855 he continued to minister at isolated mission stations in Great Namaqualand and Damaraland. Tribal warfare resulted in constant insecurity, while recurring fever and harsh conditions undermined his health. He was subsequently transferred to the relatively settled circuit of Somerset West. But the privations of earlier years carried both him

and his wife to an early grave. Mrs. Tindall died in 1860 and he on Nov. 25, 1861, at the age of fifty-four.

B. A. Tindall: *The Journal of Joseph Tindall, Missionary in South West Africa*. Van Riebeeck Society No. 40, Cape Town 1959.
G. MEARS

TINDLEY, CHARLES ALBERT (1851-1933), founder of Tindley Temple in PHILADELPHIA, was born about July 7, 1851 in Berlin, Md., to Charles and Esther Tindley. His mother died during his infancy, and he, a Negro boy, was bound out into virtual slavery and treated with such unkindness and cruelty that "he often vied with the dogs for crumbs that fell from his master's table." A friend taught him to read after he had discovered some scraps of printed pages and inquired as to their meaning. He developed an unquenchable thirst for knowledge and continued his self-education through private study and later correspondence courses. Coming to Philadelphia, he was for a time a hod carrier, then became sexton of the church of which he later became pastor.

In 1885 he joined the DELAWARE CONFERENCE, serving several churches and eventually becoming the DISTRICT SUPERINTENDENT of the Wilmington District. In 1902 he was appointed to the church which today bears his name. Originally located on Bainbridge Street, the church at the time of his appointment had 130 members and a property valued at $10,000. During his ministry of thirty-one years the church was moved to its present site, its name being changed to Tindley Temple. At one point it numbered more than 12,000 members and was the largest Methodist church in the world, and at his death in 1933 numbered 7,109 members, 2,666 preparatory members, and owned a property valued at $400,000. Tindley was elected seven times to the GENERAL CONFERENCE, leading the delegation four times. An honorary D.D. degree was conferred upon him by BENNETT COLLEGE and an honorary Ph.D. by the Brandywin School. He was twice married and had six children by his first wife.

As an orator he was without peer in his day. "His towering physique, his commanding voice, his majestic eloquence, his cogent reasoning, and his inimitable style combined to render him the most popular preacher of his time." One of his most successful sermons was "Heaven's Christmas Tree." The first time he preached this sermon, which he repeated many times, over 100 persons professed conversion.

He died July 26, 1933, and his death was as dramatic as his life. Three times he whispered to his wife, "I have told you I was going to Heaven." Then, with his last breath he added, "I am going now."

Journal of the Delaware Conference, 1934.
FREDERICK E. MASER

TIPLADY, THOMAS (1882-1967), British Methodist, was born of Methodist parents in Wensleydale and early dedicated to Christian service. After training at RICHMOND COLLEGE for the Wesleyan Methodist ministry he served as an army chaplain during the first World War. The books and a lengthy lecture tour describing his experiences brought him to attention in the United States. In 1922 he began a noteworthy ministry in Lambeth, where in face of much criticism he transformed the Methodist church into a cinema known as "The Ideal." This work he supported by the writing of some 250 hymns, several of which became widely known in the U.S.A. and CANADA. Dr. Erik Routley thus assesses his hymns: "His language was never very original and the thought forms were wholly traditional, but he managed always to avoid awkward or recondite images, and at his best he is very good indeed." (*Hymns Today and Tomorrow*, Nashville, Abingdon Press, 1964, p. 157.) The Lambeth Mission was destroyed by bombing in 1945, but was rebuilt, and Tiplady maintained an interest in the work throughout many years of retirement.

Thomas Tiplady's hymn "Above the Hills of Time the Cross is Gleaming" became very popular in America when set to the Londonderry air and published in the *Methodist Hymnal* of 1934. It was however omitted from the *Methodist Hymnal* of 1964 due to the great opposition of the musicians on the Hymnal Commission to the use of the Londonderry air in a hymnal.

Tiplady, following the second World War, sent his entire collection of hymns and poetry in manuscript form to the BOOK EDITOR of The Methodist Church in America requesting that the collection be kept in the United States and that it should be opened for use by those who might desire any of the material with no copyright charge to be made. NOLAN B. HARMON, who was then Book Editor, put the collection in the library of the METHODIST PUBLISHING HOUSE in NASHVILLE, Tenn., where it remains.

Thomas Tiplady died on Jan. 7, 1967.

FRANK BAKER
N. B. H.

TIPPETT, CHARLES B. (1801-1867), American minister, was born in Prince Georges County, Md., Dec. 19, 1801. At the age of eighteen he began a long and useful career in the BALTIMORE CONFERENCE, including sixteen years as a presiding elder and a quadrennium as assistant BOOK AGENT at NEW YORK, besides a nineteen-year membership on the general book committee.

He led the EAST BALTIMORE CONFERENCE delegation in 1860 and was also a member of the 1832, '44, '52, and '64 GENERAL CONFERENCES. A soul winner, he also "possessed many elements of true greatness and power," together with the wisdom of honest purpose and intuitive discernment in both ministerial and family life. Suddenly stricken, he died Feb. 25, 1867 and was buried at Mt. Olivet Cemetery, BALTIMORE.

J. E. Armstrong, *Old Baltimore Conference.* 1907.

EDWIN SCHELL

TIPPETT, DONALD HARVEY (1896-   ), American bishop, was born in Central City, Colo., on March 15, 1896, the son of William and Louise Eugenia (Magor) Tippett. He received the A.B. (1920) and the D.D. (1930) degrees from the University of Colorado; the B.D. degree from the ILIFF SCHOOL OF THEOLOGY in 1924; the M.A. from New York University in 1932; L.H.D. from the UNIVERSITY OF SOUTHERN CALIFORNIA in 1943; the LL.D. from the College of Surgeons and Physicians in 1944, and the UNIVERSITY OF THE PACIFIC, 1949; Litt.D. from Samuel Houston College, 1944; S.T.D. from WESTMINSTER THEOLOGICAL SEMINARY, 1956; D. Sacred Litt. from ILLINOIS WESLEYAN UNIVERSITY, 1959; D.D. from the Pacific School of Religion, 1962; and Arts D. from WILLAMETTE UNIVERSITY, 1963. In 1922 he and Ruth Underwood were married and she and Bishop Tippett have two sons, Donald Mead and Philip Auman.

Donald Harvey Tippett was admitted on trial at the COLORADO CONFERENCE, 1919, ordained DEACON, 1921, full connection and ELDER in 1922. His pastorates have included: Longmont (1919); Johnstown (1920-22); Christ Church, DENVER (1922-25); and Gunnison (1926-27)—all in Colorado; The Church of All Nations, NEW YORK CITY (1928-31); Bexley Methodist Church, COLUMBUS, Ohio (1931-40); First Church, LOS ANGELES (1940-48). It was while serving the Church of All Nations that he suffered a "brass knuckles" attack from members of the notorious Jack "Legs" Diamond gang and sustained permanent damage to one eye.

In Seattle in 1948 Donald H. Tippett was elected bishop at the Western JURISDICTIONAL CONFERENCE and assigned to the SAN FRANCISCO AREA, which included presidential supervision of the CALIFORNIA-NEVADA, the PACIFIC JAPANESE PROVISIONAL, and the CALIFORNIA ORIENTAL PROVISIONAL CONFERENCES.

During these pastoral years he was a member of the Jurisdictional Conferences of 1940, '44, and '48, and the GENERAL CONFERENCES of 1944 and '48. These were also teaching years when he was instructor at the University of Colorado, Western State College of Colorado, Teachers' College of Columbia University, and lecturer in homiletics at the University of Southern California and Visiting Professor of Homiletics at Iliff in Denver.

He has been president of the TELEVISION, RADIO AND FILM COMMISSION (1948-64); chairman of the Commission on CHAPLAINS (1952-64); and chairman of the Department of Ministerial Education (1952-64); and 1964-68 chairman of the Commission on Promotion and Cultivation; president of the Northern California-Nevada Council of Churches (1966-67); and president of the COUNCIL OF BISHOPS of The Methodist Church, 1967-68.

Bishop Tippett is trustee of the Iliff School of Theology (since 1945), and was a trustee of the Pacific School of Religion (1948-58); and has been on the Board of Regents of the University of the Pacific since 1948. He is the recipient of the Norlin medal, University of Colorado (1949); Distinguished Citizen Award, City and County of Denver (1958); and received a citation for distinguished service in the U. S. Air Force (1958). He received the Rock Award (Youth for Service) in 1966; and an Award of Honor from Iliff in 1967. He is the author of *Desires of a Religious Man* (1942).

Bishop Tippett delivered the following lectures and learned papers: For the GLIDE FOUNDATION in 1956, *The Doctrine of Suffering;* The Fondren lectures at SOUTHERN METHODIST UNIVERSITY in 1960, *Toward a Responsible Ministry;* Willson lectures at Vanderbilt in 1961, *The Role of the Church in Educating for Christian Citizenship;* Jarrell lectures at EMORY UNIVERSITY, 1962, *The Church in the Life of Yesterday and of Today;* the Danforth Associates, 1962, *The Place of the Christian Educator in a Democratic Society;* Fondren lectures at SCARRITT COLLEGE, 1968, *Evangelism: Anachronism or Challenge?*

In 1950 Bishop Tippett was assigned to travel to South East Asia, Malaya, and Sarawak. He and Mrs. Tippett returned via the Holy Land and Western Europe. The trip was climaxed by a preaching mission in England and in the American Church in Paris. Two years later the bishop and his wife took their four-month missionary tour as an African safari, penetrating that continent deeply to visit mission stations, and to lecture and preside at annual conferences. Bishop Tippett was one of three bishops to represent the Church at the Centennial of Methodism in HAWAII, and one of a delegation to represent the United States in Jerusalem for the seventh anniversary of Israel's statehood. In 1957 Bishop Tippett was assigned to visit KOREA, JAPAN, OKINAWA, TAIWAN, and HONG KONG. It was at the United States government's request that they returned to Okinawa, for Bishop Tippett to serve as Protestant chaplain for the Armed Forces there during the Christmas season. The next year the Bishop was invited by the Secretary of the Navy and the State Department to go on a good will tour of duty to South America, a part of President Eisenhower's "People to People" program. Bishop Tippett retired at the Western Jurisdictional Conference, July 1968.

Who's Who in America, Vol. 34.
Who's Who in The Methodist Church, 1966.   N. B. H.

TIPPLE, BERTRAND MARTIN (1868- ?), American minister and missionary to ITALY, was born at Camden, N. Y., on Dec. 1, 1868, the son of Martin and Sarah Elizabeth (Squier) Tipple. He was educated at Cazenovia Seminary and at SYRACUSE UNIVERSITY where he received the A.B. degree in 1894, and the D.D. in 1904; he also attended DREW THEOLOGICAL SEMINARY, receiving the B.D. there in 1897. On June 2, 1897, he married Jane Baldwin Downs and their children were Silva, Elizabeth and Bertrand S. He joined the NEW YORK EAST CONFERENCE and was appointed to Epworth, at New Haven, Conn., in 1897; to Embury Memorial, BROOKLYN, 1900; First Church, Stamford, Conn., 1906. From that point he was transferred to the Italy Conference in 1909, and was at the American Church in Rome. He was there made the president of Reeder College Seminary in 1910; the Methodist College in Rome in 1911; and soon obtained recognition as an outstanding Protestant leader. He was one of the officers of the Seventh World's SUNDAY SCHOOL ASSOCIATION Convocation in SWITZERLAND in 1913; a member of the Edinburgh Missionary Conference of 1910; the ECUMENICAL METHODIST CONFERENCE of 1911. He was received by the Queen of Italy in 1910.

Tipple wrote several books dealing with Italian Methodism. Among them *Italy of the Italians*, published by the Methodist Publishing House in Rome in 1911; *Methodism in Italy*, by the same publisher in 1912. He translated in 1910 *Papal and Italian Rome*, done by Ernesto Nathan, the mayor of Rome. Tipple also contributed to the *Forum Methodist Review* and other church periodicals.

C. F. Price, *Who's Who in American Methodism*. 1916.
    N. B. H.

TIPPLE, EZRA SQUIER (1861-1936), American historian and seminary president, was born in Camden, N. J., on Jan. 23, 1861, the son of Bertrand Martin and Sarah E. (Squier) Tipple. He was educated at SYRACUSE UNIVERSITY, receiving an A.B. in 1884 and A.M. in 1885, a Ph.D. in 1886, a D.D. in 1899, and an LL.D. in 1913. He also attended DREW THEOLOGICAL SEMINARY, receiving the B.D. in 1887. He married Edna E. White on June 24, 1897. He served pastorates as follows: St. Luke's, Grace Church, and St. James, NEW YORK CITY, and in 1905 went to Drew Theological Seminary as a Professor of Practical Theology. He became president of Drew Seminary in 1912-28; president of DREW UNIVERSITY, 1928-29;

honorary president, 1929-36. Tipple was a member of every M.E. GENERAL CONFERENCE, 1904-36; a trustee of Syracuse University, and of Drew Seminary for Young Women. He made quite a contribution to Methodist history with his *Life of Freeborn Garrettson*, published by the Methodist BOOK CONCERN in 1910; and even more by *Francis Asbury: the Prophet of the Long Road*, 1916; and *The Drew Theological Seminary*, 1867-1917. He was also the editor of *The Heart of Asbury's Journal*, Methodist Book Concern, 1905. He died Oct. 17, 1936.

Minutes of the New York Conference, 1937.
C. F. Price, *Who's Who in American Methodism*. 1916.
    N. B. H.

TIPPY, WORTH MARION (1866-1961), American preacher, was born near Walkerton, Ind., Nov. 8, 1866. He was a graduate student and Sage scholar at the Sage School of Philosophy at Cornell University 1891-1893. He received the D.D. degree from both DePauw and Baldwin Universities in 1907. He served churches in INDIANA, OHIO, and NEW YORK. From 1917 to 1937 he was the Executive Secretary of the Church and Social Service Commission of the FEDERAL COUNCIL OF CHURCHES of Christ in America. He founded the Methodist Church Conference on Social Work in 1929. He served as its Executive Secretary for eight years and then became its President. He organized the selection and nomination of CHAPLAINS for the U. S. Army and Navy in 1917, worked for the religious care of interned aliens and prisoners of war, and for the cooperation of churches nationally with the Public Health Service. He was married to Zella B. Ward, May 16, 1895. She preceded him in death in 1948.

Tippy was the founder and first director of the DePauw Archives (now the Joint Archives of DePauw University and Indiana Methodism). He was the author of *The Church, A Community Force*, 1914; *A Methodist Church and Its Work*, 1919; *The Church and the Great War* and *Pioneer Bishop* (the biography of Bishop ROBERT RICHFORD ROBERTS).

He died Oct. 2, 1961, at Laurel, Miss., and was buried at Vevay, Ind.

C. F. Price, *Who's Who in American Methodism*. 1916.
    ROBERT S. CHAFEE

TITTLE, ERNEST FREMONT (1885-1949), American preacher, author and church leader, was born on Oct. 21, 1885, in Springfield, Ohio. He was the son of Clayton Darius and Elizabeth (Henry) Tittle. He received his A.B. from OHIO WESLEYAN UNIVERSITY in 1906, the B.D. from DREW THEOLOGICAL SEMINARY in 1908. Honorary doctorates were later conferred upon him by Ohio Wesleyan, GARRETT BIBLICAL INSTITUTE, Wittenberg College and Yale University.

He was ordained in 1908 and on June 11 married Glenna Myers. The Tittles became the parents of three children: John Myers, Elizabeth Ann (Mrs. David Poston) and William Myers.

After two years in a rural OHIO charge, Ernest F. Tittle became greatly taken by Walter Rauschenbusch and his "social gospel." It was this emphasis which he brought to his preaching in later Ohio pastorates at Riverdale in DAYTON (1910-13); University Church in Delaware (1913-16); and Broad Street Church in Columbus (1916-18).

In 1918 at the age of thirty-three he was called to the First Church of Evanston, Ill., where he remained until his death. Toward the close of World War I, between his Columbus and Evanston pastorates, he served for eight months with the Y.M.C.A.—two months in the United States and six months in the front lines in France. These experiences led him to become a firm pacifist, and he never wavered from this point of view. War seemed to him a defiance of God's will and the consummation of unreason. It was an appeal to reason which colored much of his preaching in his early years in Evanston.

In a poll taken by *The Christian Century* six years after his coming to that city and while he was still under forty, Tittle was named one of Protestantism's twenty-five outstanding preachers. His distinguished preaching, dedicated pastoral ministry, keen intelligence and appealing personality attracted increasing numbers to his congregation. At the same time his pacifist views and liberal attitudes toward race relations and international affairs evoked violent opposition from local veterans' organizations and several Chicago newspapers. Though criticism of his progressive views was never completely stilled during his lifetime, it was rendered largely ineffective by the support he received from leading laymen in his church. On March 6, 1933, thirty-seven of them issued a ringing declaration of a "free pulpit." This not only assured Tittle of the support of his own congregation, but helped historically to insure the liberty of preachers everywhere to speak according to their consciences.

Tittle lectured annually at numerous colleges and universities. Named lectureships included: The Lyman Beecher at Yale; Earl at the Pacific School of Religion; Ayer at Colgate-Rochester; Merrick at OHIO WESLEYAN; Gates at Grinnell; Russell at Auburn; Wilkin at Illinois; Mendenhall at DePauw; and Shaffer at NORTHWESTERN.

The First Methodist Church (Evanston) membership, which stood at 1,000 when he came in 1918, increased almost three and a half times during his thirty-one-year ministry. To meet the needs of this growing congregation, enlargements and remodeling of the church plant costing some $750,000 were undertaken in the late '20s and completed in 1930. This made the church proper one of Methodism's most impressive religious structures and gave it a Gothic chapel of unusual grace and beauty. In 1966 this chapel was rededicated in Tittle's memory as "The Ernest Fremont Tittle Chapel."

Though an indefatigable pastor and preacher and active in Evanston community life, Tittle's contributions to the denomination at large and to the ecumenical movement are suggested by the following activities:

He was a delegate to the GENERAL CONFERENCES of 1928, '32, '36, '40, and '44, and to the JURISDICTIONAL CONFERENCES of 1940 and '44. He attended the Oxford World Conference on Church, Community and State in England; was a member of three major commissions of the former FEDERAL COUNCIL OF CHURCHES, and of the Crusade for a New World Order sponsored by the Methodist COUNCIL OF BISHOPS. He was president of the Chicago Council Against Racial and Religious Discrimination, and was a longtime member and finally chairman of the WORLD PEACE COMMISSION of The Methodist Church. At the General Conference of The Methodist

Church in 1944, during the progress of World War II, Tittle, as Chairman of the important committee on the State of the Church, presented a majority report from that Committee whose effect was to refuse to sanction prayer for victory during the great conflict. A minority report asking that the Church pray for victory presented by CHARLES PARLIN was adopted by the General Conference on a "vote by orders"—by only one clerical vote. A report reconciling the two sides was subsequently worked out a day or two later.

In 1937 Tittle suffered a serious heart attack, but continued with only slightly curtailed energies his many activities at both the local and national levels. As he grew older his preaching was based more and more on those central truths relating to the nature of God and Christ and their relevance to man's place in the universe. A special emphasis in his services of worship, which were always dignified and liturgical, was his pastoral prayer. To the preparation of these prayers he gave almost as much time and prayerful thought as to his carefully organized sermons. He wrote a book of *Pastoral Prayers* in his later life and in this book made much of his helpful thought along this line available to other ministers.

His sermons were delivered with only an occasional written memorandum and upon their preparation he once stated to the editor of this *Encyclopedia* that he put "six hours a day, six days a week." Without the help of a public address system his voice easily reached to the farthest pew in a church which seated 1300 people.

Tittle was a prolific writer and ten of his books were published before his death and three in the years immediately following. Among these were *What Must the Church Do to Be Saved?*, 1921; *The Foolishness of Preaching*, 1930; *Christians in an Unchristian Society*, 1939; *A Mighty Fortress*, 1949-1950 (which contained a biographical introduction by Paul Hutchinson, entitled "Portrait of a Preacher"); and *A Book of Pastoral Prayers*, as mentioned above, 1951.

Dr. Tittle was at work upon the exposition of St. Luke's gospel for the INTERPRETER'S BIBLE when he died leaving his work uncompleted. The part of the writing he had completed was subsequently brought out by another publisher in a book entitled *The Gospel According to Luke*, 1951. A sudden heart attack took his life on Aug. 3, 1949.

C. T. Howell, *Prominent Personalities.* 1945.
E. F. Tittle, *A Mighty Fortress.* New York: Harper & Brothers, 1949. See foreword by Paul Hutchinson.
Who Was Who in America. Vol. II

ELEANOR DARNALL WALLACE

TITUS, MURRAY THURSTON (1885-1964), American missionary to INDIA, considered one of the foremost authorities on Mohammedanism, was born on Nov. 5, 1885, in Batavia, Ohio. He was educated at OHIO WESLEYAN, Chicago University, and the Kennedy School of Missions, receiving in time the degrees of Ph.D. and D.D. On July 6, 1910, he was married to the former Olive Glasgow, and they went to India that same year. He first served as an instructor in English in LUCKNOW CHRISTIAN COLLEGE. Subsequent appointments in India included: DISTRICT SUPERINTENDENT, Bijnor, Budaun, and Moradabad Districts; principal, Lucknow Christian College; and secretary of National Christian Council. He served for many years as honorary treasurer of the executive board of the M.E. Church in Southern Asia.

A careful student of Mohammedanism, and especially its place in the life of India, he wrote *The Religious Quest of India* (Oxford Press), *Islam in India, The Young Moslem Looks at Life,* and *A Primer of Islam.* He was widely acclaimed by Christians and Moslems for the breadth and depth of his understanding and the accuracy and fairness of his writings.

He retired from missionary service on Nov. 1, 1951, and subsequently became professor of missions at WESTMINSTER SEMINARY (now Wesley Seminary) at Washington, D.C. He died on Oct. 31, 1964. The executive committee of the Board of Missions paying its tribute to him quoted him as saying, "The enduring values are not ended by life's earthly span."

The Indian Witness, Dec. 10, 1964.   N. B. H.

TOASE, WILLIAM (1782-1863), British Wesleyan pioneer in the CHANNEL ISLANDS and FRANCE, was born Aug. 23, 1782, at Kilton, near Guisborough, Yorkshire, and entered the Wesleyan ministry in 1804. He spoke French, and after early home missionary service he worked among French prisoners of war in England, 1810-15. From 1815-22 he was appointed as general superintendent of the Channel Islands societies. From 1836-47, he did much to organize Wesleyan work in France. Superannuating in 1848, he returned to the Channel Islands, but in 1852 he was appointed to take charge of the work in Boulogne. He died there on Sept. 20, 1863.

Memorials of the Rev. W. Toase, by a Friend. London, 1874.
H. M. RATTENBURY

TOBAGO. (See TRINIDAD AND TOBAGO.)

TOCKER, ANNIE CONSTANCE (1889-   ), NEW ZEALAND deaconess, was born and brought up at Greytown in the Wairaparapa district. She served the Greytown Borough Council, first as librarian (1910) and later as assistant town clerk (1912). In 1914, she enrolled at Methodist Deaconess House, CHRISTCHURCH, and on completion of her training, became deaconess at Wesley Church, East Belt, Christchurch, from 1916 to 1918. She undertook training as a nurse at Christchurch in 1918, and in the following years, occupied important positions in that field.

In 1926, she joined the child welfare department at WELLINGTON as acting manager, and spent the rest of her active working years in that service. She worked for three years as district child welfare officer at Hawera from 1937 to 1940, after which she was recalled to Wellington as district manager. During these years she maintained a vital interest in many church and community organizations. She was a foundation member of the Public Health Committee (1928-49) and a member of the mayor of Wellington's Metropolitan Relief Committee (1940-49).

When ill health forced her retirement in 1949, she settled in Wellington.

L. R. M. GILMORE

TODD, EDWARD H. (1863-1951), American preacher and educator, was born in Council Bluffs, Iowa on April 2, 1863. He was received on trial in the DES MOINES CONFERENCE in 1886. The following year he was married to Florence Ann Moore. In 1893 he moved to the State of WASHINGTON and served at Oaksdale; Colfax; Montesano; VANCOUVER; Epworth Church, TACOMA; and Grace, SEATTLE.

He became corresponding secretary of the College of Puget Sound (later University) in 1905, later becoming vice-president of WILLAMETTE UNIVERSITY. He was elected president of the UNIVERSITY OF PUGET SOUND in 1913, a position he held until he became president emeritus in 1942. He was designated official historian of College of Puget Sound in 1944 and wrote *A History of the College of Puget Sound.* His other published work was *A Practical Mystic.* While president of the College of Puget Sound, Todd increased enrollment, strengthened financial resources, changed the location and erected more substantial buildings.

The following colleges conferred upon him honorary degrees: SIMPSON COLLEGE, D.D.; Gooding College, LL.D., L.H.D.; and BOSTON UNIVERSITY, D.Sc. in Education.

Minutes of the Puget Sound, Oregon, and Pacific Northwest Conferences.
ERLE HOWELL

TODD, LUTHER EDWARD (1874-1937), American minister, was born at New Franklin, Mo., Sept. 16, 1874, and died in ST. LOUIS, Nov. 25, 1937. He was a graduate of CENTRAL METHODIST COLLEGE, and studied at VANDERBILT. In 1912 Central College conferred on him the D.D. degree.

Todd joined the MISSOURI CONFERENCE (MES) and was ordained elder in 1899. His appointments in that conference were: Fulton Circuit, 1897; Macon, 1898; Hundley Church, St. Joseph, 1899-1902; Macon, 1903. In 1904 he was transferred to the ST. LOUIS CONFERENCE, and from that time forward all of his appointments were in the City of ST. LOUIS. He served First Church, 1904-05; Lafayette Park, 1906-08; Centenary, 1909-12; Wagoner Place, 1913-15; St. Louis District, 1916-17.

In 1918 Todd was elected General Secretary of the newly created General Board of Finance (PENSIONS) of the M.E. Church, South, with headquarters in St. Louis. He served in that capacity until his death.

Under Todd's leadership, the M.E. Church, South, launched a church-wide campaign for a Superannuate Endowment Fund in 1924, the first major effort of the denomination to provide adequate pensions for its retired preachers. The QUARTERLY CONFERENCES of 6,400 pastoral charges accepted quotas aggregating $10,500,000 to be paid over a period of five years. Approximately $4,500,000 was realized on the pledges, the shrinkage being due in part to the economic depression which was casting its shadow over the land soon after the project got under way.

Todd was praised for splendid service rendered the church under trying circumstances. He was almost unanimously reelected as General Secretary of the Board of Finance at each succeeding GENERAL CONFERENCE. When he took office in 1918, the assets of the Board were about $500,000. At the time of his death in 1937, the figure was about $6,000,000.

Todd was the author of *Evangelism Exemplified—or Pulpit and Pew in United Action,* 1914; *The One-to-Win-One Helper,* 1915; and *The Child Church Member,* 1917. In addition, he wrote several pamphlets on evangelism, and one pamphlet on the superannuated preacher entitled *The Forgotten Man.*

C. F. Price, *Who's Who in American Methodism.* 1916.

ALBEA GODBOLD

TOGO is a small country in West Central Africa on the Gulf of Guinea, a member of the United Nations since 1960. The area is 22,000 square miles with a population of 1,815,000. The capital is Lomé.

For decades Togo was a long, narrow, north-south strip, lying as a sort of buffer between the British Gold Coast and French Dahomey. The African chiefs of Togo ruled in a quasi-independence, owing direct allegiance to no one as actual overlord. This acceptable state of things continued until an International Council was held in BERLIN in 1884 to determine the colonial fate of Central Africa. GERMANY then received a "share" in possessions at various points. Her commissioner for West Africa, Gustav Nachtigal, came from Togo, and proposed that Germany assume sovereignty over this "no man's land." The Powers agreed, and Nachtigal signed a treaty with a king of Togo in 1884.

In World War I, British and French forces executed a simple "pincers" and erased German Togo. The area was divided, Britain receiving a League of Nations Mandate to the western third and France accepting a mandate to the eastern two-thirds. When the surge for independence developed rapidly in Africa after World War II, British Togo joined with Gold Coast to form GHANA. Instead of merging with Dahomey, French Togo preferred to remain autonomous, becoming a member of the United Nations in its own right.

Early in 1843 the noted British Wesleyan missionary, THOMAS BIRCH FREEMAN, visited Togo. He possessed rare ability in gaining friendship with the local chiefs. When the king of Anécho granted permission for preaching and for schools, the work developed in an area radiating from the coastal towns, Anécho and Grand Popo. Following Freeman came John Milum, stationed as chairman at Lagos, E. J. Williams, and J. F. T. Halligey, who all built in the Togo field as zealously as in Dahomey and Lagos (NIGERIA). Since 1957 this work has been included in the Dahomey-Togo District. Methodist influence has been a definite factor in the affairs of independent Togo, though subordinate to that of the main Protestant Church of Togo, the Eglise Evangélique du Togo (formerly the Ewe Presbyterian Church). In 1968 the Church had five primary schools, with 1,140 pupils, and one secondary school with eighty-four students.

R. Cornevin, *Histoire du Togo.* Paris: Berger-Levrault, 1969.
H. W. Debrunner, *A Church between Colonial Powers: Church in Togo.* London: Lutterworth Press, 1965.
Findlay and Holdsworth, *Wesleyan Meth. Miss. Soc.* 1922.
World Methodist Council, *Handbook of Information,* 1966-71.

ARTHUR BRUCE MOSS

TOKYO, Japan, is the largest city in the world. Though a large part of the city was destroyed by the bombs of the Second World War, it has made a remarkable recovery, and it is hard to find any traces of the terrible destruction. The visitor who lands at the airport is whisked into the heart of the city by the monorail, completed shortly before the Olympic Games of 1964. The Imperial Palace is in the center of the city, near the Tokyo railway station, and not far away stands the beautiful Diet Build-

ing, symbol of the democracy of modern JAPAN. Wide avenues have been constructed, great buildings erected, and there is a netway of subways taking one very quickly to various parts of the city, but it is still possible to find narrow little streets which give the flavor of old Japan. Railroads run out in all directions. On the new line to Osaka, the fastest trains in the world set out every thirty minutes during the day.

Tokyo is the center of the Christian work of the land. In the early days Tokyo became the headquarters of the missionary work of both the Methodist Episcopal and the Canadian Methodist Churches. They both worked here, though they spread out in different directions into the hinter-land, the M.E. work toward the north, the Canadian work across the island and to the west. Many of the churches in Tokyo were begun by these missions, for example, the Ginza Church in the heart of downtown Tokyo, founded by the M.E. Church; and the Chuo Kaido ("Central Tabernacle") begun by the Canadians and carrying on a special program of work for the university students. There are great churches founded by other denominations, too; Reinanzaka (Congregational), near the American Embassy, served by the famous Kozakis, father and son, for two generations; or Fujimi Cho (Presbyterian), the church of the famous Dr. Uemura. All of these are now included in the United Church of Christ in Japan. The Wesley Foundation is prominent among the organizations ministering to the tens of thousands of university students in the city.

In the very center of the city on a prominent corner of the Ginza, the famous shopping and business street of the city, stands the nine story building of the Kyobun Kan (Christian Literature Society), and adjoining it, really a part of it, is the building of the Bible Society. This building stands on the site of the former Methodist Publishing House. It was erected before the war, when S. H. WAINRIGHT of the Southern Methodist Church was the Executive Secretary of the Society. Besides the bookrooms and offices of the Society, this building houses the offices of the National Christian Council and of the United Church of Christ in Japan with various missionary and other organizations cooperating with it. Plans are under way, however, for the church to erect its own building.

Tokyo is the educational center of the nation. There are great government institutions, beginning with Tokyo University, the most highly regarded university in the land. There are a number of Christian schools of high grade, Protestant and Catholic. Probably the largest is AOYAMA GAKUIN UNIVERSITY, founded by the M.E. Church. It is a co-educational institution, and can carry the child all the way from kindergarten through university. Of its more than 12,000 students the great majority are in college and university departments. Other Methodist-related institutions dating from the pre-war period are Tokyo Eiwa College and High School for girls, founded by the Canadians, and the Tokyo Women's Christian College, a union institution with which Methodists have cooperated since its founding.

The International Christian University is located in Mitaka, a suburb of Tokyo. Methodists took a prominent part in the planning and establishment of this great union institution, which began work in 1953. It has an extensive campus and a number of modern and beautiful buildings. The number of students is strictly limited (about 1,000) and emphasis has been maintained on holding up high standards. Already the school and its graduates enjoy an enviable reputation. Not far away (and soon to move to part of the I.C.U. campus) is the Tokyo Union Theological Seminary, where ministers for the United Church are trained. Recently the American School, the school for English-speaking children which many missionary children attend, purchased land from I.C.U. and built a very up-to-date school plant there. A number of missionary residences have been built in the neighborhood.

There are a number of Christian Social Service Institutions in Tokyo. Aikei Gakuen, projected by Methodist women, Airindan and Kyoai Kan, supported by the Canadians, and the newer Bott Memorial, named in honor of a Canadian missionary, are among those giving important service to the poor of the great city. It is evident that Christians are seeking to minister to the physical, the intellectual, and the spiritual needs of the largest city on earth!

JOHN B. COBB, SR.

TOLAND, REBECCA (1859-1947), one of the first missionaries of the M.E. Church, South, was born in Artesia, Miss., December 1859. During her early childhood, the family moved to Chapel Hill, TEXAS, where she grew up and was educated. She belonged to an aristocratic Southern family that had migrated from SOUTH CAROLINA, although her maternal ancestors were from SCOTLAND.

She was among the early missionary women sent to foreign fields by the WOMAN'S FOREIGN MISSIONARY SOCIETY (MES). Her first appointment to MEXICO was as teacher in Laredo Seminary, now Holding Institute, where she worked for nine years. Then for twelve years she worked at Colegio Ingles at San Luis Potosi. She was its founder and became its principal.

In 1902 she was transferred to CUBA, but previously (1898) her sister, Doctor Irene Toland, had volunteered to assist the American soldiers during the Spanish-American War as a trained nurse. Doctor Toland had had yellow fever in Texas in 1867 and was therefore immune from its repetition, hence her services were in great demand. Stationed on the hospital ship "Los Angeles" in Santiago de Cuba, she fell a victim to typhoid fever, and it was recorded that her funeral was the first Protestant one ever held in Santiago de Cuba. Later her remains were taken to the United States and interred with military honors.

The Woman's Board of Foreign Missions considered opening a boarding school for girls in Santiago de Cuba as a memorial to Doctor Toland, but instead the school was started in Habana. Under the leadership of Rebecca Toland, the school was relocated in Matanzas with the purchase of a beautiful old palatial home situated on a high hill overlooking the city and bay, and the Yumuri River.

Not long after, the Board helped her purchase more land and erect adequate buildings for dormitories and class rooms. Because of friendship with a wealthy family, there was included in their will an adjoining tract of land and a large dwelling known as the "Quinta Tosca." Later this was to become the site of the present UNION SEMINARY in Matanzas.

Through Rebecca Toland's able administration the school grew until it became one of the foremost boarding

schools for girls in the island, and almost always there was a waiting list of applications. Although she was a stern disciplinarian her students and teachers revered her, knowing that they could always count on her as a friend. Her motto was, "Trust in the Lord with all thine heart," and often she was heard to say, "This is the Lord's work, not mine."

S. A. Neblett, *Methodism in Cuba.* 1966.   GARFIELD EVANS

TOLD, SILAS (1711-1778), English Methodist schoolmaster and philanthropist, was born in Bristol on April 3, 1711, the son of a well-born but impoverished doctor. He was educated at Colston School. At fourteen he was apprenticed as a sailor and spent eleven adventurous years at sea. In December 1734, he married Mary Verney and two years later settled in LONDON as a clerk. Introduced to the Methodists by Charles Caspar Greaves in 1740, in 1744 he took charge of the Foundery Charity School. For over twenty years he administered in Newgate and other prisons, especially to those condemned to death, accompanying them to Tyburn and assisting their families. He died in December 1778.

S. Told, *Life.* 1786.   JOHN A. VICKERS

TOLEDO, OHIO, U.S.A., a city of approximately 400,000 in 1970, at the northwest corner of the state and situated at the mouth of the Maumee River on Lake Erie, is the Lucas County seat. It is the only Great Lake's port with a foreign trade zone, which gives the city international interests. It also is the third largest soft coal port in the world and is known as the "glass capital."

Methodist preaching began in what was then Tremainsville (now the western part of the city) in 1825. Shortly after this two classes were formed and from one of these the present Collingwood Church developed. The second class later led to the establishment of Monroe Street Church. In 1836 the first building to house a Methodist congregation within the then city limits was erected on Huron Street; a larger one took its place in 1851 on a fine downtown lot and in 1865 this was replaced by a large Gothic structure which was named St. Paul's. These three early churches—Collingwood, Monroe Street, and St. Paul's—sent out missions over the years and these founded other churches. Following are the churches established from 1844 to 1907: Bethany (1844), Broadway (1859), Third Street Church (now Euclid Avenue since it moved to a new location; 1866), Asbury and St. Johns's (1872), Clark Street (1890), Spring Street (1891; which became Wesley Church in a new location in 1925), Epworth and Western Avenue (1894), Central (1896), St. James (1898). In 1904 Hamilton Memorial Church was started but no longer exists.

Ironville Church, begun in 1907, was closed recently when the entire neighborhood was taken over for an urban renewal plan. There were four German Methodist churches in Toledo, two of which no longer exist, and two which came into the OHIO CONFERENCE at the time of the merger in 1933. They are Emanuel, which started as a "house church" in 1848, and Zion (1858). In 1969 Emanuel merged its membership with neighboring churches and the building was sold. Zion Church has relocated on Anthony Wayne Trail, and carries on an energetic program in South Toledo.

As the city expanded and people moved out to suburban

areas, two churches, Asbury and Epworth, relocated and built new buildings to extend a growing service to their communities. Three new churches have also been built in locations of strategic need: Aldersgate, Ottawa River and Church of the Cross. Trilby Church, once suburban, is now part of Toledo, and the immediately surrounding towns which are a part of the greater Toledo area have very active Methodist churches. Two churches, Epworth and Collingwood, have over a thousand members; and Monroe Street with more than three thousand is the third largest church in the Conference, and leads the Conference in its giving to Advance Specials.

In 1958, Dr. W. Arthur Milne, the district superintendent, led Toledo Methodists into a new venture: the establishment of an Inner-City Parish. Five churches in a changing area of the city, with membership declining, formed the nucleus of this parish: St. Paul's, for so long the leading downtown church which had struggled for years to serve the immediate neighborhood as it declined; Wesley; and three churches in the "North Corridor," Emanuel, St. John's and St. James.

In 1959 one of the pastors was designated as part-time director of the parish. Support came from the district through the Methodist Union and the Board of Missions. Shortly after the Central Jurisdiction's churches merged with the Ohio Conference, Braden Church, one of the largest Negro churches, became a part of the Inner-City Ministry, as it is now called. East of the river, Clark Street also joined this newer work. Toledo was one of the pioneers in the Inner-City movement. In 1969, in a complete restructuring, this work became the Toledo United Methodist Central City Ministry. A full-time director was assigned and it now comprises the North Parish: St. James and St. John's, Wesley, St. Paul's, Braden, Clark Street, Bancroft (formerly an E.U.B. church) and Broadway.

In 1905 the WOMAN'S HOME MISSIONARY SOCIETY leased a private hospital on Robinwood Avenue and called it Deaconess Hospital. From there deaconesses went out to work in the needy part of the city, and their early work started three Methodist agencies busily serving the city. In 1908 Steven W. Flower willed his home and land to the new hospital, and so there came Flower Hospital and Flower Esther Hall—the latter a residence for girls coming to the city for business or technical schooling. Flower Hospital has grown steadily since moving to new quarters in 1924 and has sponsored, since 1955, a new development in nearby Sylvania, known as Crestview Center. This consists of Crestview Apartments for Retired People; and Lake Park, a long-term nursing care hospital with modern facilities.

Friendly Center Community House is the result of a building campaign undertaken in 1940 by the WOMAN'S SOCIETY OF CHRISTIAN SERVICE of the Ohio Conference. A new building was begun in 1948, completed in 1949, and this houses a busy center working with the changing minority groups in this area.

It became necessary to divide the Toledo District when in 1968 the E.U.B. and Methodist Churches joined. The Toledo District is made up largely of churches in the greater Toledo area and nearby towns extending only as far south as Bowling Green. In 1969 the Toledo District had the distinction of raising the largest amount of money and the largest proportion above its asking of any district in the country for the Fund for Reconciliation. This is to

be taken as a symbol of its growing concern for a relevant ministry not only at home but around the world.

M. Simpson, *Cyclopaedia.* 1878.
Successive *Journals* of the Ohio and antecedent Conferences in which Toledo has been.   MARTHA LEACH TURNER

TOLLAND, CONNECTICUT, U.S.A., is a small farming and residential community in the northeastern part of the state with approximately 2,000 inhabitants. Methodism came with JESSE LEE, the apostle to New England, when he preached there on April 2, 1790. The society became a part of the Hartford Circuit and on Aug. 11, 1793, was host to the first Methodist Annual Conference ever held in CONNECTICUT, and the second held in New England. Twelve preachers attended and Bishop ASBURY himself was present and presided. Nathaniel B. Mills was appointed the first preacher to Tolland in 1790. LORENZO Dow, whose home town was in neighboring South Coventry, was influenced by the Methodist preaching in Tolland.

The first church was erected in Tolland in 1793, and in 1807 a lease for land was given for 999 years. Tolland became a separate station in 1839 and the building being used in 1966 was erected in 1880. However, there was a federation with the Congregational Church in 1921 and Methodist work was disbanded there in 1959.

R. C. Miller, *New England Southern Conference.* 1898.
A. Stevens, *Memorials of Early Progress.* 1852.

                                        DAVID CARTER

TOLLEY, WILLIAM PEARSON (1900-   ), American minister and university chancellor, was born at Honesdale, Pa., on Sept. 13, 1900, the son of Adolphus Charles and Emma Grace (Sumner) Tolley. He was educated at SYRACUSE UNIVERSITY, A.B., 1922; A.M., 1924; DREW UNIVERSITY, B.D., 1925; Columbia University, A.M., 1927; Ph.D., 1930; LL.D., 1955. He is the recipient of about thirty-five honorary degrees from universities of the United States, and in other lands, including state universities as well as those connected with the Church. On July 3, 1925, he married Ruth Canfield, and their children are William Pearson, Nelda Ruth (Mrs. Richard Preston Price, Jr.), and Katryn Diane (Mrs. Arthur J. Fritz, Jr.).

Dr. Tolley was received on trial and ordained a DEACON in the NEW YORK EAST CONFERENCE in 1924 and came into full connection the next year. He was the alumni secretary of DREW THEOLOGICAL SEMINARY in 1925-27; instructor there in Systematic Theology, 1926-28; assistant to the president, 1927-28; acting dean of Brothers College (of Drew University), and instructor in philosophy, 1928-29; dean, 1929-31; professor of philosophy, 1930-31. In that year he became president of ALLEGHENY COLLEGE in Meadville, Pa., but in 1942 was elected chancellor of Syracuse University, retiring Sept. 1, 1969.

He was a member of the UNIVERSITY SENATE of the Methodist Church, 1932-36, its vice-president, 1956-60, and was president after 1960. He holds a number of positions with business companies. Chancellor Tolley was decorated chevalier of the Legion of Honor in France and is a member of various honor societies in universities of the nation. In 1930 he published *The Idea of God in the Philosophy of St. Augustine,* was the editor with others of a *Preface to Philosophy* in 1946, and the author of *The Transcendent Aim* (1967). He has written rather extensively in the field of philosophy. He has been in demand as a speaker upon many university occasions.

Who's Who in America, Vol. 34.
Who's Who in The Methodist Church, 1966.　　N. B. H.

TOLLS. The Turnpike Trust Act (1706) created bodies of trustees who were empowered to levy tolls on specified lengths of road. By 1838 there were over 1,100 trusts covering 23,000 miles of road in Great Britain. Unless they took byroads, Wesley and his preachers must have paid heavily in tolls (see Wesley's *Journal*, June 15, 1770). Conditions varied from county to county, but in general, people going to church were exempt; much depending on the interpretation given locally to "proper" or "usual" place of worship. Preachers gained exemption by producing their plan. Legal opinion, requested by the Wesleyan Conference in 1829, pronounced in favor of the preachers' claims. In 1870 a test case came before the High Court. The last toll was taken on Nov. 1, 1895.

Wesley Historical Society *Proceedings*, xxii, 91-94.
　　　　　　　　　　　　　　　JOHN C. BOWMER

TOLPUDDLE MARTYRS, Br. (See TRADE UNION MOVEMENT, Br.)

TOMBIGBEE CIRCUIT, located in the southwestern part of what is now ALABAMA, was the first organized work of the M.E. Church in that state. When the SOUTH CAROLINA CONFERENCE met at CHARLESTON, Dec. 28, 1807, Bishop ASBURY, aware that white people were moving into the "Tombeckbee" (it was so listed in the *General Minutes* until 1839) region, called for volunteers to go there as missionaries. MATTHEW PARHAM STURDIVANT, a young man who had joined the VIRGINIA CONFERENCE in 1805, accepted the challenge, and traveled over 400 miles from the seat of the conference to reach his appointment. He organized the circuit.

So far as is known, Sturdivant did not record his experiences in a diary, but apparently he made the people of the region aware that a Methodist preacher was working in their midst. During the first year he did not organize any Methodist societies or enroll any members. However, at the session of the South Carolina Conference, Liberty Chapel, GEORGIA, in December 1808, he gave such a stirring report of his year in Alabama that the conference, impressed with the possibilities of the new circuit, reappointed him for a second year and gave him an assistant, Michael Burdge. A year later they reported seventy-one white and fifteen colored members on the Tombigbee Circuit.

As new annual conferences were formed in the west and south, the Tombigbee Circuit fell successively in several of them as follows: WESTERN CONFERENCE (1811), TENNESSEE CONFERENCE (1812), MISSISSIPPI CONFERENCE (1813-32), and ALABAMA CONFERENCE (beginning in 1832). For the first ten years, due primarily to Indian troubles, the Tombigbee was the only Methodist circuit in Alabama. At that time the circuit covered at least 1,000 square miles. It began below the converging of the Alabama and Tombigbee Rivers and extended up the latter into what is now Choctaw County, Ala., and westward a short distance into MISSISSIPPI.

Bethel Church, organized in 1809 about two miles south of the present town of Leaksville, Miss., was the first church on the Tombigbee Circuit to erect a building (1811). The location and name of the first church building on the Alabama part of the Tombigbee Circuit is not known.

By 1817 the Tombigbee Circuit had grown to 517 white and 100 colored members, and the next year the Mississippi Conference formed the Alabama District with two additional circuits, Whitesand Creek and Chickasawhay. Also, at that time the Tennessee Conference began work in the northern part of Alabama. In its last year, 1847, the Tombigbee Circuit, much smaller geographically than in earlier times, reported 288 white and 119 colored members.

A. D. Betts, *South Carolina*. 1952.
General Minutes, MEC, and MECS.
M. E. Lazenby, *Alabama and West Florida*. 1960.
A. West, *Methodism in Alabama*. 1893.　　J. GORDON MELTON
　　　　　　　　　　　　　　　ALBEA GODBOLD

TONGA, or Friendly Islands, are in the South Pacific, and enjoy the status of being an independent Polynesian kingdom, with a Treaty of Friendship with Great Britain. They have an area of 269 square miles, and the principal export is copra. The population (1969) is 83,000.

The missionary spirit implicit in the Evangelical Revival impelled the British Conference to send preachers to the South Seas. Captain Cook's fascinating descriptions of the Pacific Islands influenced the choice of Tonga.

Tonga has had a very strange missionary history: first initial failures, then resounding success, followed by an almost fatal disruption in 1885, incomplete reunion in 1924, and now the evils attending a multiplicity of sects. The Tongans are pure Polynesians, proud of their history of independence. Courteous, enthusiastic but often fickle, they were at first satisfied with their own heathen religion and treated missionaries with scorn.

The London Missionary Society left a number of unordained artisan-missionaries in 1797. The Tongans were interested only in stealing their tools. When three of these unfortunate missionaries were killed during tribal fighting, the rest of the party left Tonga without having won a convert.

WALTER LAWRY, Methodist missionary, was designated by the British Conference for Tonga. He was so eager that he did not wait for a colleague. He sailed from SYDNEY and landed in Tonga in 1822. He stayed only fourteen months. The "Friendly Islands" (as Captain Cook had named the group) proved distinctly unfriendly to Lawry.

In 1826 JOHN THOMAS and John Hutchinson resumed the mission. The opposition towards them gave them so much discouragement that Thomas sent his goods off to Sydney in a passing ship and asked for leave to retire. Fortunately the Committee in Sydney, instead of granting his request, sent NATHANIEL TURNER and WILLIAM CROSS, most capable reinforcements.

In Ha'apai, the central group, the ruling chief had become skeptical of his gods and interested in the new teachings. He was Taufa'ahau, afterwards to become King of Tonga under the name of George Tupou I, ultimately respected far beyond the bounds of Tonga as "The Grand Old Man of the Pacific." He quickly accepted Christianity and began to destroy idol-houses. In a crusading spirit he persuaded many people in all parts of Tonga to forsake heathenism.

In 1834 an extraordinary revival burst out in a northern island of the Tongan group during a service conducted by a Tongan preacher. It spread in a few weeks throughout Tonga. To the missionaries it seemed a veritable modern Pentecost. The greatest proof of the genuineness of the revival was the offer of many Tongan converts to accompany European missionaries to FIJI and SAMOA.

Taufa'ahau made the communion rail of the first church out of the spears he had used. He became a local preacher. The King (as he became in 1845) strongly encouraged education. In 1866 a new missionary, James Egan Moulton, founded Tupou College, named after the King. It was an ambitious project but Moulton was a syndicate of talents—classical scholar, skilled musician, writer of some of the most beautiful and inspiring hymns in any language. His success as a teacher swept the Tongans almost off their feet.

For two years before 1880 Moulton was absent in England working on the revision of the New Testament with his brother, W. FIDDIAN MOULTON, at CAMBRIDGE. During his absence troubles in Tonga began to fall thick and fast.

The Chairman of the Mission was Shirley Baker, an able and astute person. There had been unfortunate personal jealousies on the staff and Baker was criticized also because of his political activities and his personal influence with the King. This was a period when various Pacific Island groups were being annexed by foreign powers. It was to Baker's credit that he supported the Tongans' determination to remain independent, but he himself resigned from the Mission to become the Premier of Tonga.

Baker used his position as Premier to support a plan for ecclesiastical self-government which the King particularly desired. One can understand the belief in the Australasian Conference that Tonga, barely fifty years after Christianity first appeared in the land, was not mature enough to handle its own affairs. It was the same story as with the American Colonies' claim for independence, this time in a missionary setting, both in cause and effect.

In 1885 the King, at Baker's instigation, formed an independent church, generally called the "Free Church," that is free from any link with AUSTRALIA. A missionary, Jabez Watkin, was induced to become its President. Pressure soon becoming persecution developed against the loyal church members who supported Moulton. What had been a resplendent jewel in the crown of Methodist Missions was being virtually destroyed. Assaults, destruction of gardens, and finally the exile to Fiji of about 200 loyal Wesleyans followed.

The confused history of this sad period led to the deportation of Baker through the intervention of the British High Commissioner from Fiji. However, the division of the churches remained, although calmer feelings prevailed before long.

Forty years passed before reunion was effected. This had been the aim of Rodger Page who labored from 1908 with patience and an abiding love for the Tongan people. When reunion took place in 1924 it was, unfortunately, incomplete. Nearly one-third of the "Free Church" remained outside union, and they have divided into two churches since then. All three of the churches are Methodist in doctrine and polity, but the two dissenting churches have no connection with Australia, whereas the parent body is now an Independent Conference associated with the General Conference of the Methodist Church of Australasia. One reflects that if this status had been granted forty years before, the sad divisions would have been prevented.

Queen Tupou SALOTE who became ruler of Tonga in 1918, at the age of eighteen, was an influence behind the union movement. Her sagacity and her consistent Christian leadership won her the respect of her people. Yet, even with her advocacy of union, local quarrels and family disputes worked against the complete restoration of harmony and unity.

The Mormons and other sects who have entered Tonga in recent years have added to the sorry spectacle of disunity. The Mormons have now made Tonga the headquarters of their missions in the South Seas, and have spent great sums in educational institutions which attract many Tongans. The desire for better education has risen to feverish heights among Pacific Islanders, and this is readily exploited by proselytizers.

Before the fatal division in 1885, the Methodist Church had the allegiance of ninety percent of the Tongans, the rest being Roman Catholics. In a population of over 80,000 today, fifty percent belong to the Methodist Church.

CENTENARY CHURCH, NUKU'ALOFA, TONGA

King Taufa'ahau Tupou IV, who succeeded his mother in 1965, and his brother, the Premier, are both local preachers. They continue the support which their mother gave to Methodism.

In 1952 the Tongans built in the capital, Nuku'alofa, their magnificent church which seats over 2,000. It is the largest Methodist church building in the Southern Hemisphere.

The Chairman of the recently-formed Pacific Council of Churches is a Tongan leader, the Rev. Dr. John Havea.

Tonga has sent many of its best ministers to pioneer mission fields in other parts of the Pacific. Among the Methodist people there is a high quality of devotion and a strong determination to resist the encroachments of materialism by loyalty to the truths of evangelical religion.

J. W. Burton, *Call of the Pacific*. 1912.
——————, *Missionary Survey of the Pacific Islands*. 1930.
G. Brown, *Autobiography*. 1908.
J. Colwell, *Century in the Pacific*. 1914.
S. Farmer, *Tonga and the Friendly Islands*. 1855.
Findlay and Holdsworth, *Wesleyan Meth. Miss. Soc.* 1921.
W. Lawry, *Friendly and Feejee Islands*. 1850.
W. Mariner, *Account of the Tonga Islands*. 1818.
J. E. Moulton, *Moulton of Tonga*. 1921.

B. Thompson, *Diversions of a Prime Minister*. 1894.
J. G. Turner, *Pioneer Missionary to Tonga, Nathaniel Turner*. 1872.
T. West, *Ten Years in South-Central Polynesia*. 1865.
A. H. Wood, *History and Geography of Tonga*. 1932.

A. HAROLD WOOD

TOOKES, HENRY YOUNG (1882-1948), American bishop of the A.M.E. CHURCH, was born in Madison, Fla. His education was received at Florida Memorial College and EDWARD WATERS COLLEGE. Conferred upon him were the honorary degrees of D.D., LL.D. and S.T.D. He was converted in 1897, licensed to preach in 1901, admitted to the Florida Conference in 1904, ordained a deacon in 1906 and an elder in 1909. He held pastorates in FLORIDA and ILLINOIS, and was a presiding elder in Florida. He was elected bishop in 1932. He served in West Africa and the southwestern United States. Bishop Tookes was an outstanding money raiser for Edward Waters College. He died June 8, 1948.

R. R. Wright, *The Bishops*. 1963.   GRANT S. SHOCKLEY

TOPEKA, KANSAS, U.S.A., is the capital of the state of KANSAS. It was staked off Dec. 18, 1854 and incorporated in 1857. It was settled by anti-slavery men in the days of the Kansas-Nebraska struggles. The city was formerly a great railroad center, and by air travel and otherwise is yet dominant in its region.

Topeka Methodism started with the historic CLASS MEETING in the first settlers' cabin Dec. 23, 1854. The first church was organized March 21, 1855. It was first named in the M.E. Church records in 1855 as a mission connected with the MISSOURI CONFERENCE. J. S. Griffing was the pastor. In 1856 sixty members were reported. There were eighty-two members in 1861 and church property valued at $4,000.

As Topeka grew so did local Methodism. The North Topeka Church was organized in 1869 and became the Kansas Avenue Church in 1880. A decade later the East Topeka congregation was established, and in 1887 the Oakland Church came into being with JOSEPH DENISON, a former president of BAKER UNIVERSITY, as its pastor. The Lowman Memorial Church was chartered in 1885 and Euclid Church in 1888. Trinity, which began life as the Walnut Grove Sunday School in 1887, emerged with its new name in 1919 and is now combined with Euclid as the University Church. In 1915 the Highland Park Church was born and in 1953 two new churches, Crestview and Countryside, were organized to serve growing residential areas. The Sullivan Chapel, which opened in 1961 as the Topeka Methodist Indian mission, is one of the newest of the city's Methodist organizations and serves a unique parish.

Topekans also support a FREE METHODIST CHURCH and four WESLEYAN METHODIST congregations. The first of these was organized in 1876 following a six-week evangelistic meeting. The oldest Negro congregation is St. John A.M.E., organized in 1868 as a mission church. It assumed the name of St. John in 1878 and became one of the largest and strongest Negro church communities in Kansas. Other Negro congregations include Brown Chapel A.M.E. (1887); St. Mark A.M.E.; Lane Chapel; Mt. Olive, and Asbury.

During and following the great Kansas River floods of 1903 and 1951, and the devastating tornado of June 8,

1966, Topeka Methodist churches and their members, along with other denominational organizations, offered aid and shelter to thousands of Topekans.

Two former Topeka pastors are: HAROLD C. CASE, who has served as president of BOSTON UNIVERSITY for fifteen years; and Bishop EUGENE M. FRANK, a native of Kansas, in Topeka when elected bishop in 1956.

First Church is the historic downtown church in this capital city. Starting with a class meeting in the first settlers' cabin on the banks of the Kaw River on Dec. 23, 1854, the church was officially organized March 21, 1855, with J. F. Griffing as pastor. The church is probably best known for its long and continuous radio ministry which started when Harold C. Case was pastor in 1934, and has continued to the present without interruption, bringing the Sunday morning service to listeners in a five state area. In recent years First Church's Advent and Lenten services have also been televised.

The congregation has met in three different locations. Its first permanent building was a stone building at the intersection of Sixth and Quincy Streets, which was begun Oct. 16, 1860. Its completion was delayed by a famine, and by the Civil War. At one point the unfinished building was rented to the House of Representatives for the Legislative Session, and the rent paid for plastering of the interior.

In 1882 the congregation moved to a new stone building of Gothic design with two steeples, located at Sixth and Harrison. This building was destroyed by fire Aug. 9, 1921. It was replaced by another and more modern Gothic stone structure in 1922. The lighted tower of this building is now a distinctive feature of Topeka's downtown area. Since 1960 the facilities of the church have been expanded to include a two-store youth activities building, a street-level chapel seating 265 persons, a modern administration building, and a paved parking lot for ninety automobiles. For a number of years, the church has maintained a membership of more than 3,000.

Among the distinguished pastors of this church, have been two who had served as college presidents (Joshua Lippincott and JOHN T. MCFARLAND); one who became President of Boston University (Harold C. Case); and one who was elected a Bishop (Eugene M. Frank). The church has had three unusually long pastorates: Edmund Kulp (1916-26); Ormal L. Miller (1938-48), and Ewart G. Watts (1956-   ).

Known for its missionary outreach, the congregation has helped organize and given substantial financial support to three other Methodist churches in Topeka. It has consistently been the leader of its Conference, and among the leaders of the nation in World Service and Advance Special giving. One of its special projects was the purchase of a Methodist Student Center building adjacent to The University of La Paz in BOLIVIA.

General Minutes.
M. Simpson, *Cyclopaedia*. 1882.   JESSE A. EARL
EWART G. WATTS

TOPLADY, AUGUSTUS MONTAGUE (1740-1778), Anglican Evangelical, was the son of an army major and a graduate of Trinity College, DUBLIN. He was born at Farnham, England, Nov. 4, 1740. He was converted under James Morris, one of the Methodist preachers. After ordination to the ministry of the Anglican Church (1764), Toplady settled in the parish of Broadhembury, Devon

(1768). He was the leading protagonist against JOHN WESLEY in the Calvinistic controversy of 1770 onward. Toplady was steeped in the learning of the Reformers and Puritans. His *Historic Proof of the Doctrinal Calvinism of the Church of England* (1774) is now widely assessed as one of the weightier statements to emerge from the debate. His hymn "Rock of Ages" is a priceless possession of the Church Universal. He died in London, Aug. 11, 1778.

A. Toplady, *Works.* 6 vols. London, 1794; new ed., 1825.
Wright, *Life of Augustus Toplady.* London, 1911.

A. SKEVINGTON WOOD

TORONTO, Canada. In 1805 the Yonge Street circuit, which included the village of York, capital of Upper Canada, was organized by the M.E. Church. From that date services were held regularly in and around York, but the first chapel was not built until 1818. A frame building, about thirty by forty feet, it stood near the corner of King and Bay streets, on land now occupied by the massive headquarters of the Canadian Imperial Bank of Commerce. It was one of the many monuments of HENRY RYAN's untiring zeal as PRESIDING ELDER in Upper Canada.

The first services were held in November 1818, the preacher being David Culp. Among those who succeeded him in the early years were the future bishop JAMES RICHARDSON, EGERTON, WILLIAM, and JOHN RYERSON, and Franklin Metcalf. By 1832, however, the Society had grown so that a new church became necessary. The Adelaide Street Church, at the corner of Tornoto and Adelaide streets, was opened in 1833. Regrettably, the old church became a theatre.

At this point, York, which was to become Toronto in 1834, was growing rapidly. Among the new settlers were many Wesleyan Methodists, who opened their first church in July 1832, on George Street. After the Union of 1833, the two buildings were used by the Canadian church as a whole. Rented temporarily to the Congregationalists in 1837, the George Street Church was reopened by the Wesleyans after the dissolution of the Union in 1840. It became the center of a highly influential congregation, including many merchants, and Richard Woodsworth, the father and grandfather of JAMES and J. S. WOODSWORTH respectively. So great was the increase of people that in 1844 a new chapel was erected on Richmond Street West.

With the reunion of 1847, two circuits were established in Toronto; the Richmond Street and Adelaide Street churches continued as the principal city congregations in the Canada Conference. Each church drew the ablest ministers in the Connection among whom were JOHN CARROLL, S. D. RICE, GEORGE DOUGLAS, ALEXANDER SUTHERLAND and JOHN POTTS. Each led in founding new churches in the expanding city and suburbs, including Yorkville, Davenport, Elm, Sherbourne and Gerrard Street churches. Richmond Street itself was closed in 1882.

Again, by the 1860's, the Adelaide Street Church was becoming obsolete. At the instigation of W. M. PUNSHON, president of Conference from 1868 until 1872, of Egerton Ryerson and ANSON GREEN, a block of land at the corner of Queen and Church Streets was purchased in 1870. On it was erected the Metropolitan Methodist Church, a handsome Gothic structure, modeled on Doncaster Parish Church (Yorkshire), Punshon's native city. Completed in 1872, the Metropolitan quickly became one of

METROPOLITAN CHURCH, TORONTO, CANADA

the principal churches in Canadian Methodism. To its pulpit came John Potts, WILLIAM BRIGGS, S. P. Rose, R. P. BOWLES, and in it were held many great Methodist events.

By the end of the century Toronto Methodism boasted a multitude of great and small churches, of which possibly the most influential were the Metropolitan, Sherbourne Street, Carlton Street and Trinity churches. Some of these have ceased to exist since the Union of 1925; others such as the Metropolitan have continued. The latter, especially, is now a great downtown church, serving not so much a congregation as the varied needs of the homeless and the transient in the commercial heart of the city. It remains, nonetheless, a visible embodiment of a century of Methodism in Toronto.

T. E. Champion, *Churches of Toronto.* 1899.
A. Green, *Life and Times.* 1877.

G. S. FRENCH

TORRANCE, CALIFORNIA, U.S.A., is an industrial city (population 136,000) with the vast majority of the people industrial workers. The churches are active and the Methodist population has grown with the city.

First Church was built in 1923 with twenty-seven charter members. The original building is today used for a recreational center. The new sanctuary was built in 1961. The membership of the church in 1970 was 1,462.

Walteria Church was organized in 1951 with forty-two members. In 1970 it had a membership of 314.

Riveria Church was organized Sept. 1, 1956. It has grown to 806 members. **Central Church** has 296 members, and **Hope Church** had 167 in 1970.

General Minutes, UMC, 1970.

TORSEY, HENRY P. (1819-1892), American educator and preacher, was born in Monmouth, Maine, Aug. 7, 1819.

At age seventeen, while a student at Monmouth Academy, he joined the M.E. Church and was licensed to preach at nineteen.

Spending four years in Maine Wesleyan Seminary, he taught at East Greenwich Academy. Two years later he was assistant teacher at Kent's Hill. In 1844 Torsey was elected president of Maine Wesleyan Seminary, joining the MAINE CONFERENCE in 1848.

When Torsey took over the academy, it was financially embarrassed and ready to surrender its charter. During the thirty-eight years under the presidency of Torsey, students increased and the school became very successful. Resigning on account of poor health, President Torsey was retained on the faculty as professor *emeritus* until his death.

Torsey was honored with D.D. and LL.D. degrees. He was elected to three GENERAL CONFERENCES, 1860, 1868, and 1876. With a little time off during his presidency, he was twice a member of the State Senate. He was with the treasury department in the south for one year, and overseer of the Freedmen's interests in SOUTH CAROLINA for part of 1865. For health reasons he declined President Lincoln's appointment as Secretary of the MONTANA Territory.

His heavy educational load kept him from much preaching. However, his message was strong and clear on the great themes. For fifty-two years, he was a member of Kent's Hill Church near the Seminary, and was a liberal contributor and effective official.

He married a minister's daughter, Emma Jane Robinson, in 1845. She was a preceptress of the Seminary for several years.

Torsey had original and effective methods as a teacher and administrator. The Maine Conference obituary describes his teaching ability in these words: "He could win the confidence of the timid and retiring, cordially appreciate the faithful efforts of those not brilliant, keenly expose the slothfulness of the indolent, and effectually counteract them and at the same time make every student feel that he was the special friend of the president."

Henry P. Torsey died at Kent's Hill, Sept. 16, 1892.

Maine Conference *Journal*, obituary.
M. Simpson, *Cyclopaedia*. 1882.   JESSE A. EARL

TOTTEN, WILLIAM T. (1862-1936), American M.P. minister and educator, President of Yadkin Collegiate Institute (see YADKIN COLLEGE) for twenty-six years, was the eldest son of John Henry and Margaret Frances Smith Totten. He was born in Rockingham County, N.C., on Feb. 13, 1862.

William T. Totten attended local schools and Oak Ridge Institute, from which he graduated in 1881. Afterward, he graduated from Yadkin College and taught at Pilot Mountain, Yadkin College and at other places in NORTH CAROLINA. He was the last M.P. minister to obtain a degree from Yadkin College.

He was admitted into the NORTH CAROLINA CONFERENCE of the M.P. CHURCH in 1885 and ordained in 1888. He served the following charges: Albemarle, Spring Church, Halifax, LaGrange, Mecklenburg, Greenville, Shiloh, Catawba, Mocksville, Union Grove and Draper. In 1898 he personally assumed the responsibility for the indebtedness of Yadkin College and for the next twenty-six years conducted this institution as "Yadkin Collegiate Institute." Following the closing of Yadkin

Collegiate Institute in 1924 (it was consolidated into HIGH POINT COLLEGE), Totten was again given ministerial assignments in the North Carolina Conference.

He married Mrs. Jeannettie Barham Daniel of Pleasant Hill, N.C., in 1891; from this union there were three children. Following his wife's death in July 1923, Totten married Callie Tarkington of Chowan County, N.C., on Sept. 1, 1925. She died on April 7, 1929, and he married Mrs. Ellen Norman Cobb of Halifax, Va., in 1931. She died in 1938.

William T. Totten died on Nov. 26, 1936, at Yadkin College and was buried there.

Journal of the North Carolina Conference, MP, 1937.
Olin B. Michael, *Yadkin College, 1856-1924: A Historic Sketch*.
Salisbury, 1939.   RALPH HARDEE RIVES

TOWNSEND, ALONZO G. (1854?-1937), American minister and educator, was born in CHARLESTON, S.C., and educated in the private schools of Charleston and later entered the University of South Carolina from which he graduated. He was received into the SOUTH CAROLINA CONFERENCE of the M.E. Church on trial in 1878, coming into full membership in 1880 and ordained an ELDER in 1882. He served from some of the smallest to some of the largest appointments in the conference, including Centenary Church, Charleston, 1899-1901. He taught at CLAFLIN COLLEGE, Orangeburg, S.C., 1883-1891. Townsend served as presiding elder of the Florence District in the 1890's and as district superintendent of the Sumter District, 1921-27. He was first married to Emma L. Harleston of Charleston. To this union three children were born, two girls and one boy. This wife preceded him in death in the late twenties. His second wife was Mrs. Ocala Blume Trescot of Charleston.

Townsend was one of the leading scholars of his day, a true and loyal servant of God. After several years of retirement, he died in Sumter, S.C., in 1937.

A. R. HOWARD

TOWNSEND, WILLIAM JOHN (1835-1915), British Methodist historian, was born in Newcastle upon Tyne on Jan. 20, 1835, studied under JAMES STACEY, and entered the METHODIST NEW CONNEXION ministry in 1860. Townsend was elected president in 1886 and was president of the UNITED METHODIST Conference in 1908; he was president of the Free Church Council in 1902. He had a distinguished circuit ministry, but was most famous as a historian, writing the lives of ALEXANDER KILHAM and of James Stacey, *The Story of Methodist Union, a Handbook of the Methodist New Connexion,* and many other works, besides taking a large share in the production of the *New History of Methodism* (1909). He was editor of the Connexional Magazine for four years and missionary secretary for five. He died at Newcastle upon Tyne on March 7, 1915.

O. A. BECKERLEGGE

TOWSON, MARYLAND, U.S.A., is located a few miles north of downtown BALTIMORE. In 1839 the citizens of Towson town erected a building known as Epsom Chapel, to be used as a place of worship for any religious group in the community. A Methodist Society was promptly formed and the Chapel was dedicated on Sunday, Nov.

10, 1839, under Methodist Episcopal auspices. The church then became a part of the Summerfield Circuit.

Methodism grew rapidly in Baltimore County. The circuit was divided in 1854, and the Towson congregation became a part of the North Baltimore Circuit. A parsonage was built on Joppa Road in 1856 and served as the home of ministers' families until 1958.

A society of the M.P. Church was formed in 1861 and met in the Odd Fellows Hall in Towson. This group later moved to the Epsom Chapel and worshipped there until its own building was erected in 1909, at Allegheny and Bosley Avenues.

Towson Church was made a station appointment at the BALTIMORE CONFERENCE (ME) of 1869, with a membership of eighty-six persons. A new brick building was erected at 622 York Road and was dedicated on Oct. 26, 1871. Two committees were formed in 1951 to consider merger of First and Second Churches, so that the Methodists of Towson might become "one people." As a result the present Towson United Methodist Church was organized in May 1952. Worship was held in both churches until Easter Day, April 18, 1954.

With the construction of the Baltimore Beltway, land became available from GOUCHER COLLEGE and was purchased as a site for relocation of the merged congregations. In October 1957 a new church school building was consecrated and on May 11, 1958, Bishop G. BROMLEY OXNAM led the service of consecration for the new sanctuary. During the period of merger and relocation, Lewis F. Ransom was minister.

In 1970 Towson reported 2,507 members, property valued at $1,125,000, and $172,250 raised for all purposes.

General Minutes, UMC, 1970.　　　JOHN BAYLEY JONES

TOY, JOSEPH (1748-1826), early American class leader, educator, and preacher in NEW JERSEY and MARYLAND, was born on his father's plantation, which fronted on Delaware River near the mouth of the Rancocas Creek, Burlington County, N. J., April 24, 1748. He came from a devout Swedish background, and was a cousin to Bishop White of the Church of England. He attended Thomas Powell's boarding school in BURLINGTON, N. J., until he was twenty years of age.

In 1770 Toy came under the influence of Captain THOMAS WEBB, who was preaching in Burlington. Webb induced Toy to form and lead a Methodist class in Burlington. The following year Toy moved to TRENTON, N. J., formed a new Methodist class in his house, and later led in the erection of a frame meetinghouse for the Methodist Society. Toy is also listed as a trustee of the Methodist Society in New Mills (Pemberton), N. J.

In 1776 Toy moved from Trenton to Maryland. In 1779 he sponsored a Methodist Society in Abingdon, Md., and was instrumental in building a meetinghouse there.

When COKESBURY COLLEGE was built in Abingdon in 1786, Bishops ASBURY and COKE requested Toy to become instructor in mathematics and English literature. When Cokesbury was destroyed by fire a few years later, Toy moved to BALTIMORE and continued his teaching in a substitute building. This, likewise, burned later.

As early as 1789 Toy began to preach regularly. Relieved of his duties as instructor, he was ordained a DEACON in 1797 and entered the "traveling connection" in 1801. He was admitted into "full connection" in 1804.

All of his itinerant ministry, except one year (VIRGINIA CONFERENCE, 1803-1804) was served in the BALTIMORE CONFERENCE. J. E. ARMSTRONG reports that at the age of seventy Toy was heard to say that he had not disappointed a congregation in twenty years.

He retired in 1819 and died on Jan. 28, 1826.

J. E. Armstrong, *Old Baltimore Conference*. 1907.
J. Atkinson, *Memorials in New Jersey*. 1860.
R. M. Bibbins, *How Methodism Came*. 1945.
Methodist Magazine, 1826.
Minutes of the Methodist Conferences, 1773-1813.
E. M. Woodward and J. F. Hageman, *History of Burlington and Mercer Counties*. Philadelphia: Everts & Peck, 1883.

　　　　　　　　　　　FRANK BATEMAN STANGER

TRACTS AND TRACT SOCIETIES. JOHN WESLEY was a pioneer in spreading challenging religious literature written in such a way that ordinary people could understand and respond, and this was published at prices which they could afford. Many of his publications, indeed, occupied only four pages or so, and were advertised for sale at two or three shillings a hundred, so that they could be bought for free distribution. The first such tract was entitled *A Word in Season: or, Advice to a Soldier*; this was published early in 1743, and continued in print until Wesley's death. Because such ephemeral items were usually issued without the name of author or printer, and with no indication of the edition or the date, it is exceedingly difficult to secure precise facts about them. The most frequently reproduced appear to have been *Swear not at all*, of which at least twenty-seven distinct editions were published between 1744 and the end of the century; and *Remember the Sabbath Day*, of which twenty-nine are known. It is almost certain, however, that there were several more editions of each, for a number of those so far discovered are known only by a single survivor out of a complete edition of two thousand or more copies. On Dec. 18, 1745 Wesley recorded in his *Journal* that the London Methodists "had within a short time given away some thousands of little tracts among the common people." Some of the tracts were in fact printed on posters to be pasted up in public places (as is known from the ledgers of one of Wesley's printers, William Strahan), though in the nature of the situation it is unlikely that one of these will ever be discovered.

In January 1782, John Wesley issued proposals for establishing what appears to have been the first Tract Society known, and began canvassing donations towards it. Subscribers to the Society's funds were supplied with an appropriate quantity of tracts of their own choice, at cost. In commending this scheme, which may well have originated with THOMAS COKE, Wesley wrote:

I cannot but earnestly recommend this to all those who desire to see true, scriptural Christianity spread throughout these nations. Men wholly unawakened will not take the pains to read the Bible. They have no relish for it. But a small tract may engage their attention for half an hour, and may, by the blessing of God, prepare them for going forward.

The first "tracts" issued by this Society were much larger works than *Swear not at all* and its companions—skillful abridgments of JOSEPH ALLEINE's *Alarm to Unconverted Sinners*, and Richard Baxter's *Call to the Unconverted*, to which was soon added WILLIAM LAW's *Serious Call to a Holy Life*. These three works, however, although they contained a total of over 400 pages, each bore on its title page the words: "This book is not to be sold, but given away." Reissues of Wesley's earlier tiny tracts and of many of his sermons helped redress the financial balance a little, and furnished a more realistic hope that the recipient would read his gift. The first catalogue of this first Tract Society, issued in 1784, listed thirty publications thus available for free distribution. Maintaining stocks of these tracts continued to be one of the important tasks of Wesley's BOOK STEWARDS.

This was an idea which was suited to the times, and inspired imitators. In 1795 HANNAH MORE began to issue her "Cheap Repository Tracts," supported by subscribers all over the country. Her private efforts led to the formation in 1799 of the Religious Tract Society. Behind this new form of EVANGELISM lay both directly and indirectly the Methodist Revival, and speaking of her project to John Newton, Hannah More confessed that "my great and *worldly* friends are terribly afraid I shall be too methodistical (a term now applied to all vital Christianity)."

Although soon far outstripped by the activities of the Religious Tract Society, Wesley's followers continued to expand their own efforts, and even broaden their purpose from specific evangelism to general uplift. Once again impetus for a new approach was supplied by Thomas Coke. In 1806, possibly earlier, he began publishing tracts independently of the Conference, employing his own printer and book agent, and setting up his own Tract Repository. Wesley's four-page tracts were by-passed for somewhat more substantial items, especially the Wesleys' sermons. Coke also went farther afield than the Wesleys' own publications, and probably wrote at least one tract himself—*A Plain Catechism . . . for Children.* Spurred to action by Coke's initiative, in 1808 the Conference officially accepted tract-distribution as a connectional responsibility, taking over Coke's work. By that time he had forty separate tracts in his catalogue. The early "official" publications bore the imprint: "For the Methodist Tract Society, for Promoting Religious Knowledge," but this was later dropped. The 1811 Conference recommended the formation of auxiliary tract societies in the circuits, and the 1812 Conference authorized the appointment of a Wesleyan Tract Committee. The Society was reformed by direction of the Conference in 1828, and within ten years had published 410 tracts. Between 1825 and 1838 no fewer than 36,787,111 copies were issued, and by 1871 there were 1,250 separate titles. Tract libraries were established in the circuits, and the itinerancies of both local preachers and ministers greatly helped in the tract distribution.

In the smaller branches of British Methodism the book rooms were also responsible for the issue of tracts. The PRIMITIVE METHODISTS established tract societies in the areas of Cheshire under WILLIAM CLOWES, and in Derbyshire under HUGH BOURNE. In the early days of Anglican Tractarianism the Wesleyan Methodists produced their own "Tracts for the Times" in defense of the Methodist position. Also tracts were prolific in the internal Methodist controversies of the first half of the nineteenth century, but these so-called "tracts" were of a quite different *genre* from the inexpensive homilies distributed by the tract societies.

The same kind of thing happened in America. James P. Pilkington writes: "The tract—brief, pointed, anecdotal, and lively—could well be called the foundation of The METHODIST PUBLISHING HOUSE, since it was for the publication of such as these that the BOOK CONCERN was called into being in 1789. The Methodists were among the first in the field with these 'books for the poor,' which were the nearest thing to mass media the early nineteenth century had to offer, and 'covered the land like the leaves of autumn'" (*The Methodist Publishing House: a History,* Vol. I, p. 194). At first the works were sold as cheaply as possible. In 1808 the GENERAL CONFERENCE ordered the Book Concern to appropriate $1,000 for the free distribution of books, and in 1817 an official Methodist Episcopal Tract Society was begun on similar principles to those in England, mainly under the auspices of the Book Concern in New York. The *Address, Constitution, and By-laws of the New York Methodist Tract Society* was published in 1818, and local branches varying in size and influence seem to have sprung up throughout the country. The text of many of the tracts was taken from their British predecessors, and the publishing houses in both countries offered special discounts to SUNDAY SCHOOLS, which thus served as among the more efficient and prolific tract-distributors. The most powerful organization rivalling the Methodists in this field was the interdenominational American Tract Society, founded in 1825, mainly from an amalgamation of the American Tract Society instituted in BOSTON in 1814, with a similar New York Society. The M.E. Church declined to affiliate with this body (as later with the American Sunday School Union) on the grounds that it was dominated by Calvinists.

In both Britain and America the tract societies experienced an ebb and flow in usefulness, the highest tide probably being during the 1820's, and another after the halfway mark of the century. Simpson's *Cyclopaedia of Methodism* notes that at the General Conference of 1876 it was reported that during the previous year almost 36 million pages of Methodist tracts had circulated in the United States, and a further 36 million in foreign missions.

From Wesley's small beginnings the publication and distribution of helpful pamphlet literature at low cost or none at all has never dried up. Sometimes this has been due to private enterprise, as in the case of Wesley himself and of Thomas Coke. During the century following Wesley's death the official publishing house was usually the sponsor. During the present century this function has largely been taken over by connectional organizations, sometimes independently, sometimes in collaboration with the Methodist Publishing House. Noteworthy in this respect have been the HOME MISSION DEPARTMENT in Britain and the General BOARD OF EVANGELISM in America, but many other bodies might be named in this fruitful enterprise which continues to follow Wesley's lead in adjusting a tried method to the needs and tastes of the changing generations.

F. Cumbers, *Book Room.* 1956.
J. P. Pilkington, *Methodist Publishing House.* 1968.
M. Simpson, *Cyclopaedia.* 1883.   FRANK BAKER
                                                    JOHN T. WILKINSON

TRADE UNIONISM and British Methodism. Continental labor movements owed their inspiration largely to Proudhon and Marx, but in England, in the words of Morgan Phillips, the debt was "more to Methodism than to Marx." When organized labor movements began to appear in Industrial Revolution England, Methodism was sweeping through the working classes, and it was natural that the two movements should interact upon each other. The more sober and responsible Methodism made English workingmen, the more likely they were to be trusted by their fellows with the organization of their unions and the administration of their funds.

It was not only that many of the early trade union leaders were Methodists; the constitution of many of the unions was modeled upon the CLASS MEETINGS and BAND meetings and CIRCUITS of Methodism. Men who had seen how effective could be such organization for the spreading of the gospel and the control of the members adapted it to the needs of men who had to find some means of giving expression to their corporate voice in dealing with their employers and government. Particularly in the Durham coal fields was the parallel close, and here many of the most effective and prominent leaders were PRIMITIVE METHODIST local preachers, many of whom spread trade union membership among their congregations as they traveled round the Methodist chapels in the mining villages.

One major consequence of this phenomenon was that, although many of the Methodist trade unionists were vigorous and militant in pursuit of their social and economic aims, there has been a tradition of conciliation machinery in industrial disputes in England, and a respect for negotiated agreements on the part of the men that may owe more than a little to the recognition that both masters and men might belong to the same church or even class meeting, or at any rate that both sides were Christian.

E. R. TAYLOR

TRANSPORTATION OFFICE of The United Methodist Church, U.S.A., is an agency of that Church which is directed "to represent the Church in its relation with responsible persons or concerns operating all modes of transportation." The office is under the supervision of the Council on World Service and Finance and is supported by the general administration fund of the Church.

Prior to unification, in 1939, the M.E. Church had established a Transportation Committee to serve the needs of the traveling minister. In 1912, E. K. Copper, a District Superintendent from the Northern Minnesota Conference, opened the Transportation office in Chicago. In 1916, this office was under the jurisdiction of the Council of Secretaries headed by THOMAS STAFFORD. E. K. Copper was assisted in his office by his daughter, Joyce.

The M.E. Church, South, also had a Transportation Committee headed by William Cassetty. Cassetty was a layman and had offices in Nashville. At the time of union, in 1939, and when E. K. Copper retired, Cassetty became the travel representative for the United Church, and maintained his offices at The Methodist Building on Rush Street in Chicago until his retirement in 1952. In that year in the general reorganization of almost all church agencies by the General Conference, the Transportation Committee experienced a redefining of its work. The functions of the former Committee were given to the COUNCIL ON WORLD SERVICE AND FINANCE, with the Transportation Office becoming a department of the Council.

In carrying out its work, the Transportation Office

endeavors to be skilled in the routing, shipping, and rate structure of both passenger and freight costs. Personnel specializing in the field of air transportation and rail transportation are employed.

The railroads, in addition to granting passes through this office, also issue clergy certificates which allow special rates for ministers. The office processes the major portion of clergy applications. With the reduction and consolidation of rail passenger transportation, the office is being increasingly concerned with all forms of air transportation—that of the individual minister on official duty, giving assistance in securing charter flights, as well as for tours both domestic and foreign. The office also processes bus clergy certificate applications which allows a reduced rate for motor coach travel.

In 1963 the Transportation Office developed a service presently called the *Convention Bureau,* which concerns itself with the seeking out and publishing of a list of hotels that grant clergy rates. Another facet of the Convention Bureau is assistance rendered various church agencies, boards, commissions, and committees in planning and successfully conducting a large meeting.

For the Church to maintain a helpful mutual relationship with hotels, clergy bureaus, passenger associations, airlines, etc., an aggressive public relation program is continually maintained. In May 1966, the Transportation Office opened a branch in Nashville, which serves the general agencies of the Church located there in expediting their travel.

James Hoge succeeded Mr. Cassetty as director in 1952. The present director is Harlan E. Lance. Headquarters offices are in Evanston, Ill., and a branch office in Nashville.

HARLAN E. LANCE

TRANSVAAL AFRICAN PIONEERS toiled for years among the heathen before the Transvaal District was formed by the British Conference in 1880. See KLASS DHOBA, HANS AAPJIE, SAMUEL MATHABATHE, MEYI LOTHI, ROBERT MASHABA, DAVID MAGATA, and MOLEMA.

TRAVELING PREACHER. In English usage this was an eighteenth century full-time preacher of the Gospel who had been taken into the "Connexion" by JOHN WESLEY and worked and preached as Wesley directed. The term "travelling preacher" helped to distinguish such a person from the "LOCAL PREACHER," who preached in a single locality in his spare time.

In America, pretty much the same usage prevailed. The present definition in the glossary of terms, published in the appendix of the *Discipline* of The Methodist Church (1944-1964) was: "Preacher, traveling. One who is on trial or in full connection in an Annual Conference." A note is appended to this definition stating that it has an interesting historical background; that the minister in early Methodism who devoted his full time to the work of the ministry and was therefore subject to appointment in first one place and then another, was called a "travelling preacher" in contradistinction from the local preacher, who because he served only part-time and earned his livelihood by other means, was tied to local communities and unable to travel or itinerate. A good definition of a traveling preacher may be that such a one is "under appointment in the itinerancy." This will probably be true in any special branch of the world-wide Methodist Connection.

Discipline. 1964. (Glossary of terms).
M. Simpson, *Cyclopaedia.* 1878. N. B. H.

TRAVIS, JAMES (1840-1919), British Methodist, was born March 6, 1840. He entered the PRIMITIVE METHODIST ministry in 1859, and eventually became one of its foremost administrators. Deeply concerned for ministerial education, he was one of the founders of HARTLEY THEOLOGICAL COLLEGE, MANCHESTER, and, as a trustee, raised large sums for its erection. He was a pioneer (with JOHN ATKINSON) in missionary legislation at the LIVERPOOL CONFERENCE of 1888 and creator of the Missionary Committee. At the Reading Conference of 1885 Travis became the architect of the CHAPEL AID ASSOCIATION. In 1892 he was elected president of the Primitive Methodist Conference. An exponent of Free Church principles, he was the first Primitive Methodist to become president of the National Free Church Council. He was an eloquent and informed preacher. A portrait in oils hangs in the library, Hartley Victoria College, Manchester.

J. T. WILKINSON

TREFFRY, RICHARD, JUNIOR (1804-1838), British Methodist, was born at Camelford, Cornwall, England, on Nov. 30, 1804, the son of a minister, and also RICHARD TREFFRY. He was educated at KINGSWOOD SCHOOL, and entered the Wesleyan Methodist ministry in 1824. Owing to ill health he retired from CIRCUIT work in 1830; and during his retirement he published, among other writings, *An Enquiry into the Doctrine of the Eternal Sonship of Our Lord Jesus Christ*, which was a reply to the criticism of this doctrine by ADAM CLARKE. He died at the age of thirty-three, in Penzance, Cornwall, on Jan. 20, 1838.

R. Treffry, *Memoirs.* 1838. G. E. LONG

TREFFRY, RICHARD, SENIOR (1771-1842), British Methodist, was born at Newton, near St. Austell, in Cornwall, on Nov. 25, 1771, and became a Wesleyan itinerant in 1792. Largely self-taught, he acquired considerable theological knowledge, and published numerous sermons, tracts, and biographical studies, including the standard life of JOSEPH BENSON. Treffry often served as a Chairman of District, was elected president of the Wesleyan Methodist CONFERENCE in 1833, and in 1838 was appointed house governor of the new theological institution which was being established for the training of the ministry at Hoxton, in London. He resigned this office, the conferring of which was a mark of great confidence on the part of his brethren (1841), and died at Maidenhead on Sept. 19, 1842.

JOHN NEWTON

TREMBATH, JOHN (? -c. 1793), British Methodist, became one of WESLEY's assistants in 1743. In 1747 he accompanied Wesley on his first visit to Ireland and was left in charge of the DUBLIN society. Trembath's eloquence and zeal won him great popularity, but he was also vain and untrustworthy. He later married a wealthy and accomplished wife, left the itinerancy, and took up farming. After his wife deserted him, he sank into poverty. Wesley met him in Cork in 1756, and again in Cornwall in 1782. He died of paralysis in Cork around 1793.

J. A. VEVERS

TRENTON, NEW JERSEY, U.S.A., county seat of Mercer County and the capital of the state, situated on the Delaware River, thirty miles north of PHILADELPHIA, was founded about 1720 by Colonel William Trent, formerly of Philadelphia.

On Nov. 21, 1739, GEORGE WHITEFIELD preached in the courthouse in Trent-town. He did not, however, establish either classes or a Society. Methodism was introduced into Trenton by Captain THOMAS WEBB in 1766. He preached to the people in a stable located near what is now the corner of Broad and Academy Streets.

In 1768 a Methodist Society was formed and a frame chapel erected. JOSEPH TOY served as the first class leader. This original chapel was taken down in 1772 and a frame chapel was erected on the same site. The Trenton Society, consisting of nineteen members, among whom was John Fitch, the inventor of the steamboat, secured subscriptions from some 122 persons for the erection of this "meeting house." Bishop ASBURY laid the cornerstone on April 22, 1773. The building was known as the "Plank Church" because of the material used in its construction. Many historians believe this building to be the third Methodist church built in North America and the first in NEW JERSEY. Through the years it has been known as the "Mother Church of Trenton Methodism." By 1894 eleven Methodist churches had grown from it.

The first Annual Conference held in New Jersey met in the "preaching house" in Trenton on May 23, 1789. Eleven other sessions of the Annual Conference have met in the city of Trenton (1839, 1844, 1852, 1857, 1865, 1872, 1877, 1891, 1897, 1904).

The 1970 *General Minutes* show eight United Methodist churches in Trenton (Asbury, Broad Street, Cadwalader Heights, First, Greenwood Avenue, Hamilton Avenue, St. Pauls, and Wesley).

Daily True American, Sept. 17, 1894.
190th Anniversary Booklet of the First Methodist Church of New Jersey. Trenton, N. J., 1962.
F. B. Stanger, *New Jersey.* 1961. FRANK BATEMAN STANGER

TRIBOU, DAVID HOWARD (1848-1922), was an outstanding figure of New England Methodism and distinguished CHAPLAIN of the U.S. Navy. He was born at Hampden, Maine, Sept. 16, 1848, died in PHILADELPHIA, May 31, 1922, and was buried in Hampden. His education was at Hampden Academy, the East Maine Conference Seminary, Bucksport, Maine, and BOSTON UNIVERSITY SCHOOL OF THEOLOGY. He received the honorary D.D. degree from WESLEYAN UNIVERSITY in 1901. He married Katherine Davis of Ellsworth, Maine, March 6, 1873, and they had one child, Frances, who was married to H. S. Tinsman.

He was a descendent of Thomas Tribou, a Frenchman, who appeared in MASSACHUSETTS early in the eighteenth century. Through his paternal grandmother he was descended from Elder Brewster of Mayflower fame, and also from Stephen Hopkins, another Mayflower passenger.

He joined the EAST MAINE CONFERENCE in 1872 and was admitted into full membership in 1876. During the period of his retirement, 1909-1917, while living in Bucksport, Maine, Chaplain Tribou was Secretary of the Conference, Conference Historian, and served on numerous boards and committees. He was a member of the GENERAL CONFERENCE of 1908. In the years when he was stationed in or near Boston, he was a staff member of *Zion's Herald* and a regular contributor to its columns. He was a delegate to the second ECUMENICAL METHODIST CONFERENCE, held in Washington in 1891, and also to the fourth, held in Toronto in 1911. At the beginning of World War I, Chaplain Tribou was called back to active duty by the U.S. Navy, at his own request, though he was then sixty-nine years of age.

His appointment to the chaplaincy, Feb. 5, 1872, was on the recommendation of Senator Hannibal Hamlin. He was appointed by President Grant and the appointment was confirmed by the Senate. He served as chaplain on ten ships in home, European and South American waters. The Navy Department consulted him on matters other than those concerning the work of a chaplain. In addition to his regular work he was a member of the Board of Medals of Honor for World War I, meeting in Washington 1919-1921.

Chaplain Tribou was known as a powerful preacher. His language was rich in descriptive phraseology, rugged and convincing, virile with all the virility of the sea. Among his ministerial friends he sometimes startled those who did not know him well, by his natural brusqueness and abruptness of speech. In *The History of the Chaplains Corps* we find this evaluation of him:

"The loving nickname by which he is known among his friends is 'Roaring Bill Tribou', a name gained by his habit of bursting forth in thunderous denunciation or approbation when stirred. . . . The Corps knows him as its 'Grand Old Man' and honors him as one whose years of labor and accomplishment have won for him an imperishable place. But the Corps loves him for the splendid catholic humanity and tender sweetness of his personality."

One of the Chaplain's much quoted words of advice to young chaplains was, "Go right on and bring things to pass. Never mind who is for you or against you, and especially never care who gets the credit."

On the occasion of the seventy-fifth and final session of the East Maine Conference, which was also the fiftieth year of the Chaplain's membership, he delivered a remarkable historical address, *Seventy-Five Years of Methodism in East Maine*. Following the address he returned to his duty as Chaplain at the Naval Home in Philadelphia and died a month later.

ALFRED G. HEMPSTEAD

TRIMBLE, HENRY BURTON (1885-1962), American pastor and theological dean, was born at Hot Springs, Va., on Dec. 26, 1885, the son of Stephen and Matilda Jane (Rucker) Trimble. He attended Roanoke College at Salem, Va., where he received the A.B. degree in 1907, and the same institution awarded him the D.D. degree in 1923. He was a B.D. of VANDERBILT UNIVERSITY in 1909, an A.M. of Columbia in 1913, and a B.D. of Union Theological Seminary in 1913. Other honorary degrees were awarded by HENDRIX COLLEGE in 1922 (D.D.); and by BOSTON UNIVERSITY in 1939 (LL.D.).

He married Mattie Lorena Cargille in 1914. To them were born three daughters and a son. Trimble was ordained in 1909, and served at Heber Springs, Ark., 1909-11, Clarendon, 1911-12; Central Church, Hot Springs, 1914-15; First Church, Fort Smith, 1915-17; Lakeside Church, Pine Bluff, 1918-22; McKendree Church, NASHVILLE, Tenn., 1922-28; Central Church, ASHEVILLE, N. C., 1928-31; Professor of Homiletics, 1931-37. In 1937 he became Dean of the CANDLER SCHOOL OF THEOLOGY at EMORY UNIVERSITY. He served in World War I as CHAPLAIN in the U.S. Army, and was the Chairman of the General Conference Budget Commission (MES), 1926-28. Among his books are *Motive and Method in Stewardship*, 1938; *Methodists at Work*, 1935; *To Every Creature*, 1940.

His outstanding work was as Dean of the Theological School at Emory University where he became known as an able administrator, a wise counselor to the students, and the scholarly director of the various functions of that school. He retired in 1954 and died in Atlanta in 1962.

T. H. English, *Emory University*. 1966.
C. T. Howell, *Prominent Personalities*. 1945. N. B. H.

TRIMBLE, (MRS.) JANE (1755-1839), distinguished American pioneer, was born in Augusta County, Va., March 15, 1755. A Presbyterian in early life, she moved to KENTUCKY and in 1790 joined the M.E. Church whose doctrines pleased her better. At age fifteen she had memorized the four Gospels and though living in the backwoods this pioneer mother was familiar with the great English poets.

An extraordinary woman, she was familiar from childhood with the warwhoop of the Indian, and several of her family perished in the Revolutionary and Indian wars. In 1784, she emigrated to Kentucky (her husband having gone ahead to build a log-cabin), traveling on horseback, carrying her oldest child behind her, and Allen, eleven months old and a future governor of OHIO, in her lap. She crossed the dangerous swollen Clinch River amid the shouts and prayers of those who watched her. She and her husband freed their slaves. Her husband purchased land in Ohio but died before the family started for their new home there. She took her eight children to Ohio.

In Highland County, Ohio, she organized one of the first Sunday schools in the state. Instrumental in organizing a Methodist Church, she visited the poor, the prisoners, and had preaching in her own house. "Elect lady of the church in the wilderness," she adorned her church and country as few women of her day did.

Mrs. Trimble possessed a vigorous mind and was one of the ablest and best women in Methodism for almost fifty years. She was the mother of Governor Allen Trimble of Ohio and grandmother of J. M. Trimble of the OHIO CONFERENCE. She died in 1839 in the home of her son, Ex-Governor Trimble.

M. Simpson, *Cyclopaedia*. 1882.
A. Stevens, *Compendious History*. 1867. JESSE A. EARL

TRIMBLE, JOHN BROWNLEE (1850-1929), American minister, missionary executive and church builder, was born at Malakoff, Ontario, CANADA, Jan. 30, 1850. At age eleven he was converted and felt called to preach. He attended Victoria College, Cobourg, Ontario, and entered the ministry of the Canadian Methodist Church. He married Mrs. Catherine Donaghue. In 1881 he joined the NORTHWEST IOWA CONFERENCE, where he served successively at Rockwell City, Galva and Odebolt. In 1893 he became PRESIDING ELDER of the Sheldon District with such success that this district was conspicuous over the entire Church in missionary giving. In 1898 he was assigned to the Sioux City District. In this and a subsequent term on this district five new churches were founded and four houses of worship built, all in Sioux City. One church bears his name.

In 1903 he was chosen Field Secretary of the Board of Foreign MISSIONS with offices at New York City. He was a capable speaker on the urgency of world evangelism but his greatest strength lay in the field of management. He was a member of the GENERAL CONFERENCE in 1896, 1900, 1904, 1908 and 1912. In 1913 he was made Executive Secretary of the General Conference Commission on Finance.

In 1916 he returned for a second term as Superintendent of the Sioux City District. In 1922 he became Executive Secretary of the Methodist Hospital in Sioux City. He retired in 1924. His death occurred June 27, 1929. He is buried in Graceland Cemetery, Sioux City, Iowa. His sister, Lydia Trimble, was head of the Hwa Nan missionary school at Foochow, CHINA, under the WOMEN'S FOREIGN MISSIONARY SOCIETY.

Minutes of the Northwest Iowa Conference, 1929.
B. Mitchell, *Northwest Iowa Conference.* 1904.

FRANK G. BEAN

TRINIDAD and TOBAGO—a two island unit—is an independent member of the British Commonwealth occupying islands located seventy-five miles south of Grenada at the southern limit of the Caribbean Windward Islands, and ten miles from the northeast coast of VENEZUELA. The capital is Port-of-Spain. The area of Trinidad is 1,864 square miles and Tobago has 116 square miles. Several other islets are in the group. The total population is over a million, of which over ninety percent reside on Trinidad.

The economy has been based on tropical fruits, sugar, and molasses. The pitch lake at La Brea is said to be the world's chief source of supply for natural asphalt.

Trinidad was visited by Christopher Columbus on July 31, 1498, and the islands were held by Spain for decades. The competition of the European powers brought about the capture and recapture of the islands by Spanish, Dutch, French and British forces. Progress toward responsible self-government accelerated after 1900, the first parliamentary elections being held in 1924. The two-island unit achieved autonomy and membership in the United Nations in 1962. Trinidad maintains an Allied strategic military position, providing naval and air bases commanding the open passage between the Caribbean Sea and the South Atlantic Ocean.

It was not until 1809 that a British Wesleyan Methodist minister, Thomas Talboys, was stationed in Trinidad. He found there a few Methodists at scattered points. Upon receiving his report, THOMAS COKE agreed that he might remain and establish work. By 1812 he had built a chapel for a congregation of about 140 members, practically all Negroes. John Dace succeeded him, enlarging the membership to over 200 by 1814.

In 1811 Trinidad was included in a new Methodist District of St. Vincent. During the period of the autonomous West Indian Conference (1883-1903), Trinidad became a separate district. When these West Indian districts reverted to the control of the British Wesleyan Methodist Conference, a Barbados and Trinidad District (which for a time included British Guiana) was set up. This was renamed the South Caribbean District in 1967, when the autonomous METHODIST CHURCH IN THE CARIBBEAN AND THE AMERICAS was inaugurated.

In early years there was a language barrier among the French-speaking Negroes, and there had been a strong Roman Catholic tradition since the days of French and Spanish control. The British governors were frequently changed, and the license and privileges granted by one governor for the missionary were often revoked by his successor. Opposition to Methodism reached a peak in 1818-20, and it was not until 1827 that the first permanent Methodist church was opened in Hanover Street (now Abercromby Street), Port of Spain. By 1839 the Circuit had three ministers, but after 1845 there was some retrenchment, and membership stagnated or declined. It was not until 1870 that a new period of expansion began, with the opening of new churches in Port of Spain and San Fernando. In 1874, a minister was stationed at Savannah Grande, where work among East Indians had recently begun. (This area was later handed over to a Canadian Presbyterian mission.)

In 1919 a Methodist Oilfields Mission was opened to help in giving pastoral care to those who were coming into La Brea from other parts of the West Indies to find work.

The first West Indian chairman of the district was a Barbadian, Errol S. M. Pilgrim. He was appointed in 1942.

The first British Methodist preacher to visit Tobago was WILLIAM TURTON. Son of a Barbados planter and a local preacher, he landed in 1795, finding the only other Christian leader to be a Moravian preacher named Montgomery, whose son, James, was to be the noted hymn writer. Turton organized a small society but he suffered exposure and illness during a French raid and was compelled to abandon the work. Early in 1817, John Brown and James Catts touched at Tobago en route to HAITI. There was interest in their preaching. In 1818 the first British Wesleyan minister, Jonathan Raynar, was stationed on the island for a few months, several planters having pledged their support. A church was built in Scarborough in 1824-26, almost entirely from local funds, including a grant from the Legislative Council. By 1833, however, there were still only seventy-four members. The Wesleyan schools were the first on the island, and in 1854, Gilbert Irvine, the first Tobagonian minister, began work.

In 1967 the year of autonomy within the Methodist Church in the Caribbean and the Americas, there were 18,300 full members in Trinidad and Tobago. The church was responsible for twelve schools.

Since before 1916 the American based A.M.E. CHURCH has been at work in Trinidad. Another strand of the Methodist tradition is woven into the UNITED CHURCH OF CANADA. Methodism is the third largest denomination after the Roman Catholic and Anglican churches.

Cyril Davey, *Under My Skin.* London: Cargate Press, 1967.
J. Merle Davis, *The East Indian Church in Trinidad.* New York: International Missionary Council, 1942.
Findlay and Holdsworth, *Wesleyan Meth. Miss. Soc.* 1921.

C. B. Franklin, *A Century and a Quarter of Hanover Methodist Church History, 1809-1934.* Port of Spain, Trinidad, 1934.

Kindling of the Flame, British Guiana, 1960.

World Methodist Council *Handbook of Information,* 1966-71.

ARTHUR BRUCE MOSS
PAUL ELLINGWORTH

TRINITY, THE HOLY. The Methodist Church joins with the general body of the universal Church in proclaiming this doctrine as a cardinal article of the Christian faith. There is thus no distinctive Methodist doctrine of God. The first Article of the American United Methodist Church set forth this belief. See ARTICLES OF RELIGION.

God has three ways of being God—the Father, the Son and the Holy Spirit. This doctrine is a mystery of revelation disclosed in the experience of the Church, and witnessed to by scripture and tradition. Though a reality disclosed to us from beyond man's rational calculation, yet the triune nature of God is not foreign to the rational appraisal of man's mind or to his religious experience.

The formulation of the doctrine arose out of the religious experience of the early Christian community. The first Christians shared the faith of Israel in a Creator God in covenant with his people (I Chronicles 29:10-19). They knew him as the holy one far *beyond* them, the mysterious source of all things, visible and invisible. The greatness and grandeur of His nature was reflected in "the starry heavens above and the moral law within" (Psalm 19). God disclosed himself to them as the personal Father of all, the Creator (Isaiah 64:8; John 14:6-11; II Corinthians 1:3-4).

God was not only *beyond.* He also came to confront them in Jesus Christ. The disciples of Jesus, all Jews convinced of the oneness of God, came to the conviction that the God they had known through Israel was uniquely present in their master of Galilee. In Jesus of Nazareth they were challenged and claimed for discipleship by and with a new covenant by this same Father God (Ephesians 1:3-8). The authority, nature, and work of God were manifest in Jesus. His patience under suffering, his compassionate forgiveness to those who crucified him were no less than the love of God. The assurance of his living presence with them after the death and entombment were enough to convince them *he was God.* "God was in Christ reconciling the world unto himself" (II Corinthians 5:19), they said. He was the Son of the Father, the concrete example of the mysterious beyond. They called this manner of his nature, Redeemer, Saviour.

Beyond and *before,* God was also *within* them. After Jesus' physical departure, they experienced a continuing sense of his abiding presence in their fellowship, the Christlike presence of God bringing a faith in Christ and a love of the Father, bringing pardon and power for moral transformation in their personal and corporate life. The creation stories of Genesis (Gen. 2:7) spoke of God breathing his breath into the creatures he had made and thereby giving them life. The Hebrew word for spirit is *ruah* which also means breath or wind. Ancient man knew that where there is breath in man there is life. When the breath goes, so does the life. God was understood to be present in all men as the animating principle of life. That presence was called the Spirit. Later the Nicene Creed was to speak of the Holy Spirit as the Lifegiver,

the activating, personal Spirit by whom and in whom we live, move, and have our being.

But as the Spirit was present in all men by birth, he was understood to be uniquely present in some men to direct and complete their lives. His personal inspiration and direction of the prophets enabled them to speak forth the judging and renewing message of God to their day and its needs. The Spirit was present in the kings of Israel to assist them in the ruling of the nation. The High Priest was led by the Spirit in his offering of the people's worship to God. The tragedy of the prophets, priests and kings of Israel was that they never fully knew who it was who was so working in them. God the Creator beyond, and the Spirit within, was clouded in a mystery, a mystery which would be illumined in Jesus of Nazareth. Yet the prophets spoke of a day in the future when God would pour out his personal spirit upon everyone. Not simply upon prophets, kings and priests; "your sons and daughters shall prophesy, your young men shall see visions and your old men shall dream dreams" (Joel 2:28f). Another prophet of Israel, the great Jeremiah, anticipated a new covenant written on the human heart (Jeremiah 31:31). Men would no longer live by the outer direction of the law; they would have the inner direction of the Spirit of God. With the clarification that Jesus Christ gave to the nature of God, the Holy Spirit could come to all men in a fuller way. Men could open themselves to his inspiration with greater understanding and cooperation. The prophet's dream of a universal outpouring of God's Spirit into the hearts of men could be fulfilled. This is the promise of the Spirit we read of in the Gospels and in the Acts of the Apostles. The early church believed it came to this fuller awareness of the Holy Spirit at Pentecost. This personal presence of God called and equipped leaders, converted sinners, and established fellowship in the church.

In its own experience the church knew God in three ways—God *beyond,* God *before,* God *within.* It gave expression to this as it invoked the blessing of Father, Son, and Holy Spirit upon one another (II Corinthians 13:14). How was it to explain this experience of knowing God in three ways? This threefold nature of God was not simply limited to man's experience, three modes of revelation for the convenience of his own understanding. The church insisted that *God himself had three ways of being God,* that the threeness was intrinsic in His very nature. So the biblical record points to the presence of the Holy Spirit in man prior to Pentecost, even at the dawn of creation. And the redemptive, revealing Christ of God was present before the foundation of the world, and "all things were made through him" (John 1:3, Col. 1:16, Heb. 1:2). Now how were the early Christians to hold their Jewish inheritance of monotheism, and yet give honest expression to their conviction that Jesus was divine? How were they to express their experience of God's presence *within* while maintaining that he was *beyond* and *before* them as well? After many attempts to solve the doctrinal problem by compromising the testimony of experience, the Church formulated the theological definition we know as the doctrine of the Trinity.

At first the church affirmed its faith by and in doxologies and such confessions as the Apostle's Creed without regard to the theological problems involved. Many of the early attempts to define the trinitarian doctrine suffered from one extreme or another. At the Council of Nicaea

(A.D. 325) and at Constantinople (A.D. 381) the doctrine was defined in its simplest outlines in the face of pressing extremes or heresies. The real distinction, yet the co-equality and co-eternity of the three divine Persons was there affirmed. The eastern Church tended to interpret the doctrine from the standpoint of the *difference* of the three Persons. In the West, however, the unity of the Divine Substance, safeguarding the co-equality of the persons, was strongly stressed. With different emphasis, the universal Church has thus taught the unity and the trinity of God.

Methodist teaching has historically followed the traditions of the Western church. John Wesley used every instance possible to stress the doctrine of a triune God, and its immediate importance for religious experience. This is clearly demonstrated in his *Explanatory Notes on the New Testament* and in his *Sermons*. Wesley's sermon, "On the Trinity," insists it is the fact of the Trinity given by revelation which is the object of belief. We are not expected to believe a mystery, how "these Three are One," but rather, the *fact* that they are one. This fact of the Trinity is verified in genuine Christian experience and is vital for man's salvation. According to Wesley, salvation means acceptance by God the Father on the basis of the Son's merits. This divine acceptance is communicated to man by the Holy Spirit. The Holy Spirit within brings us to acknowledge Jesus as the Christ, and the Son shows us the Father. Wesley acknowledges that the words "trinity" and "person" are not to be found in scripture; hence he will not insist on these words as necessary to orthodoxy. But if one will use the direct words and experiences as witnessed to in scripture, he will necessarily come to an understanding and experience of the God who has three ways of being God. Like Luther, Wesley declined to speculate about the metaphysical constitution of the inner triunity of God. His stress was upon the revealing and redeeming work of the triune God.

This trinitarian heritage was passed by Wesley to the American Methodists. The *Notes on the New Testament* and the *Sermons* of John Wesley were considered the doctrinal standards of American Methodism. Alongside the *Articles of Religion* revised from the Church of England these standards are referred to as permanent doctrinal foundations in the first RESTRICTIVE RULE of the Constitution of The United Methodist Church in America. The first four *Articles of Religion* affirm Methodist belief in the doctrine of the Holy Trinity, and creeds used in the worship services of contemporary Methodists affirm the same. The "Foundations of Christian Teaching in Methodist Churches" affirm the same trinitarian doctrine—God as Creator, Redeemer, and Life-giving Spirit.

Today the trinitarian language of the 4th century—three Persons and one Substance—is by some considered inadequate. Our concept of personhood has changed radically. It is perhaps better to speak of a threefold eternal determination of the divine Being, of the God who has three ways of being God. Though Methodism has been concerned primarily with the revealed and redemptive Trinity, the latter must never be separated from the inner reality of the transcendent God. The doctrine of the Trinity contains within it the most crucial affirmations of the Christian faith—the sovereignty and self-revelation of God; the redemption of sinful man through the divine Saviour, Jesus Christ; the living presence of God in his creation and in his Church. Compromise at any point, as do the Unitarians, the Divine Science groups, the

Mormons and others, and the whole theological edifice of the Christian faith begins to crumble. The doctrine of the Trinity is a safeguard against false deistic conceptions of a "supreme being," far removed and now uninvolved in his creation and church. Against pantheism the doctrine insists upon the transcendence as well as the immanence of God.

R. Garrigou-Lagrange, *The Trinity and God the Creator* (on St. Thomas Aquinas), trans. Eckhoff. St. Louis, Mo., 1952.
A. C. Headlam, *Christian Theology: The Doctrine of God.* Oxford, 1934.
L. Hodgson, *The Doctrine of the Trinity.* London and New York, 1944.
J. R. Illingworth, *The Doctrine of the Trinity.* London, 1907.
J. N. D. Kelly, *The Athanasian Creed.* London and New York, 1964.
G. A. F. Knight, *A Biblical Approach to the Doctrine of the Trinity* (Old Testament doctrine). London, 1957.
J. Lawson, *The Biblical Theology of St. Irenaeus.* London, 1948.
C. W. Lowry, *The Trinity and Christian Devotion.* London and New York, 1946.
W. K. McDonough, *The Divine Family: the Trinity and Our Life in God.* New York, 1963.
J. E. L. Newbigin, *Trinitarian Faith and Today's Mission.* London, 1963.
One Lord, One Baptism. London: Commission on Faith and Order of the World Council of Churches, 1960.
J. Pohle and A. Preuss, *The Divine Trinity: A Dogmatic Treatise.* London and St. Louis, Mo., 1943.
Dom Mark Pontifex, *Belief in the Trinity.* London and New York, 1954.
G. L. Prestige, *God in Patristic Thought.* London, 1952.
A. E. J. Rawlinson, ed., *Essays on the Trinity and the Incarnation.* London, 1928.
C. C. Richardson, *The Doctrine of the Trinity.* New York, 1958.
St. Augustine, *On the Trinity* (trans. by S. McKenna). 1963.
St. Hilary of Poitiers, *On the Trinity* (trans. by S. McKenna). New York, 1954.
H. P. Van Dusen, *Spirit, Son and Father.* New York, 1958.
A. W. Wainwright, *The Trinity in the New Testament.* London, 1962.
J. Wesley, *Standard Sermons*, LV.   LYCURGUS M. STARKEY, JR.

TRINITY HALL SCHOOL, British Methodist. One of the first references to Trinity Hall School, is to be found in the *City Road Magazine* of 1872. In an article on "The Education of Wesleyan Ministers' Daughters," T. P. BUNTING speaks of the opening of "the beautiful house in Southport, provided by Mr. Fernley's far-seeing and wide embracing bounty." John Fernley (see FERNLEY-HARTLEY LECTURES) did, in fact, meet the entire cost of the building, about 8,000 pounds, and was conspicuous in organizing the appeal for 2,500 pounds needed for the furnishings and equipment. The school opened with its full complement of fifty pupils, on Oct. 1, 1872, though the "official" opening was celebrated on November 7, with a special service in Trinity Church, and a dinner at the school.

The school within recent years catered to about 260 girls, of whom about one-fifth were the daughters of ministers. It occupied about five acres in the pleasant, residential area of Birkdale, and had twelve acres of playing fields close by. The primary function was always the provision of a grammar-school education, leading up to the General Certificate of Education and university entrance—and its first concern was for the daughters of ministers and missionaries. However, the Conference regretfully decided by official action that the school, because it was too small and financially unviable, would have to be closed as from 1969-70.

MARJORIE LONSDALE

TROMMER, KARL SIEGFRIED (1920-   ), missionary to South America and one of the founders of the Patagonia Provisional Annual Conference, was born in Netzschkau, Vogtland, GERMANY. He was first educated in the art of bookbinding. Then, deciding for the ministry, he became an assistant minister in the Methodist Church of Germany in 1939. During the Second World War, he was a member of the German army, serving with Rommel's Afrika Corps. During the years 1943-46 he was a prisoner of war, and was called to be a CHAPLAIN to prisoners in the United States.

After release and repatriation, he undertook theological studies at the Methodist theological seminary (PREDIGER-SEMINAR der Methodisten Kirche) in Frankfurt, Germany, and at GARRETT THEOLOGICAL SEMINARY, Evanston, Ill., where he was a CRUSADE SCHOLAR. He also studied at SCARRITT COLLEGE and VANDERBILT UNIVERSITY in Nashville, Tenn., and was trained in counseling at Ohio State University Hospital.

Siegfried Trommer held two pastoral appointments in Germany, 1949-54. He had been accepted as a missionary by the Board of MISSIONS of The Methodist Church (New York) in 1949, but political conditions delayed his assignment until 1954, when he was appointed to ARGENTINA. In 1955 he became pastor of the trilingual church (Spanish, German, English) at San Carlos de BARILOCHE in Rio Negro Province, at the northern edge of the region known as Patagonia. Under his direction a new, well-appointed church building was erected and opened in 1964, in Bariloche.

He was also named to the Field Committee for Argentina. In 1961, while continuing as pastor at Bariloche, he was also made superintendent of the Patagonia District. Upon formation of the Patagonia Provisional Annual Conference in 1963, he became general secretary of the conference and superintendent of its southern district, while still serving as pastor at Bariloche. He is vice-president of its Coordinating Committee. He was a delegate to the GENERAL CONFERENCE of 1964 and its adjourned session in 1966.

Who's Who in The Methodist Church, 1966.

EDWIN H. MAYNARD

TROTT, NORMAN LIEBMAN (1901-   ), American minister and president emeritus of WESLEY THEOLOGICAL SEMINARY, was born in BALTIMORE, Md., Sept. 25, 1901, son of Frank Boyd and Margaret (Tatum) Trott.

He was graduated with the B.S. degree from Johns Hopkins University in 1931 and did post-graduate study there. He held the Baltimore Rauschenbusch Fellowship for research in social attitudes, 1935-38. WESTERN MARYLAND COLLEGE conferred upon him the D.D. degree in 1955, and the AMERICAN UNIVERSITY conferred upon him the LL.D. degree in 1961.

He was admitted on trial into the BALTIMORE CONFERENCE in 1930, was ordained DEACON in 1933 and was received in full connection and ordained ELDER in 1935. His pastorates were in Arbutus, 1926-33; Baltimore, 1933-39; Brunswick, 1939-47; Hagerstown, 1947-50—all in

MARYLAND. He was district superintendent in Baltimore, 1950-55. In 1955 he became president of Wesley Theological Seminary, and served there until his retirement in 1967.

In 1952 he became a trustee of Wesley Theological Seminary. He was a member of the GENERAL CONFERENCES, 1952 through 1966. He was a member of the General BOARD OF EVANGELISM, 1956-64, and of the General BOARD OF CHRISTIAN SOCIAL CONCERNS, 1960-64. Also he was a member of the Commission on Ecumenical Consultation, 1956-64, Commission on Ecumenical Affairs, 1964-68, and of the *ad hoc* committee on union of The Methodist Church and The E.U.B. Church established in 1964; he holds membership in the United States conference, WORLD COUNCIL OF CHURCHES; consultant on church union since 1960. He has served as a member of the board of trustees of GOUCHER COLLEGE, the American University, Eye Research Foundation of Bethesda, Maryland General Hospital; also he has served as a member of the board of the Church Executive Development Board, Inc., and Asbury Home for the Aged. In 1918 he served with the U.S. Army.

He is a member of the Association of Methodist Theological Schools (past president). He is the author of *What Church People Think,* 1937; *Teen Agers Tell,* 1948, and is contributor of articles and verse to church periodicals.

On Sept. 2, 1930, he was married to Lillian Durfee. He continues to reside in Washington, D. C.

Who's Who in America, Vol. 34.
Who's Who in The Methodist Church, 1966.   J. MARVIN RAST

TROUNSON BENEVOLENT TRUST BOARD, was set up by the NEW ZEALAND Methodist Conference of 1929 to administer a gift of £11,000 of New Zealand Inscribed Stock given by James and Martha Trounson, Auckland Methodists, as a benevolent fund for the following categories of Methodists: (1) widows or children of deceased Methodist ministers; (2) supernumerary ministers or retired home missionaries; and (3) lay people. While ministers in active work are excluded, grants can be made under exceptional circumstances to deaconesses, home missionaries, and divinity students.

Both Mr. and Mrs. Trounson have died since their original gift was made. The secretary of the trust in 1966 was E. E. Sage.

ERNEST E. SAGE

TROUSDALE, SAMUEL WHITNEY (1853-1909), American minister, was born in Fayette, Wis., on Nov. 12, 1853. He grew up in a home of devout Christian parents. He graduated from the University of Wisconsin in 1877, taught Greek and Elocution there for one year and graduated from BOSTON UNIVERSITY SCHOOL OF THEOLOGY in 1882. He received the B.A. and M.A. degrees from the University of Wisconsin; a D.D. from LAWRENCE UNIVERSITY, and the Ph.D. degree from OHIO WESLEYAN UNIVERSITY. He was a half-brother of Bishop BASHFORD.

His ministerial life was spent in the WEST WISCONSIN CONFERENCE which he joined in 1882. His pastorates were at Delton; Hudson; First Church, Eau Claire; Platteville; First Church, LaCrosse; presiding elder of Platteville District, 1898-1903, and PRESIDING ELDER of Madison District, 1903 until his death. He was head of his conference delegation to GENERAL CONFERENCE in 1896, 1900, 1904, and 1908.

Trousdale was greatly interested in the SUNDAY SCHOOL and worked in General Conference toward the formation of the Sunday School Board. Also chief among his interests were the superannuated ministers and their support. He was for many years a leader in his conference. He passed away at Wesley Hospital in Chicago, Ill., on June 4, 1909. The funeral was held in Madison, Wis., and Bishop WILLIAM FRASER McDOWELL preached the funeral sermon.

Year Book of the West Wisconsin Conference, 1909.

JOHN W. HARRIS

TROY CONFERENCE was carved from the NEW YORK CONFERENCE by the 1832 GENERAL CONFERENCE. The new conference held its first session in connection with the New York Conference which convened in NEW YORK CITY, June 7, 1832 with Bishop ROBERT R. ROBERTS presiding. The next session of the Troy Conference was at Troy, N.Y., Aug. 28, 1833 with Bishop ELIJAH HEDDING presiding. The territory of the conference was northeastern NEW YORK and western VERMONT. In 1833 it had four districts, fifty charges, sixty-six preachers, and 18,492 members.

PHILIP EMBURY organized the first Methodist society within the bounds of what came to be the Troy Conference. He formed the society at ASHGROVE in 1770 and served as its leader until his death in 1775. A church was built there in 1788, the first to be erected in the conference. FREEBORN GARRETTSON was appointed presiding elder in 1788, and, with other preachers to help him, he brought Methodism from New York City up the Hudson and Champlain valleys as far as CANADA. Garrettson rode a one-thousand mile circuit four times a year to visit the work.

By 1860 the Troy Conference had grown to seven districts and about 32,000 members including probationers. At that time the Burlington and St. Albans Districts in northwestern Vermont were taken from the Troy Conference and attached to the VERMONT CONFERENCE which had been formed in 1844 and which desired to have all of Vermont within its bounds, though the preachers and churches west of the Green Mountains seemed to prefer alignment with the Troy Conference. Part of the Vermont territory passed back and forth between the two conferences several times. In 1868 the Burlington District came back to the Troy Conference, was transferred to the Vermont Conference again in 1880, and back to the Troy Conference once more in 1884. Thereafter there was little change in the boundaries of the Troy Conference until 1940 when the Vermont Conference, which then embraced the Vermont work east of the Green Mountains, merged and became a part of the Troy body. In 1964 a few churches in extreme northwestern MASSACHUSETTS which had been in the Troy Conference were transferred to the NEW ENGLAND CONFERENCE. In 1941 the Troy Conference reported about 69,000 members.

In the early years the Troy Conference supported a number of schools and academies. In 1853 the conference decided to establish Troy University, secured subscriptions of $200,000, and soon opened the school. It continued four years and was forced to close for lack of money. Today the conference supports GREEN MOUNTAIN and VERMONT (junior) COLLEGES, strong Methodist re-

lated schools with adequate plants, modest endowment, and good enrolments. In addition, the conference helps to maintain campus ministries at state institutions of higher learning.

Service institutions supported by the conference include the Saratoga Retirement Center, and the Charlton Home for teenage girls. The conference joins other conferences in supporting Gateway which is the Methodist Home for Children at Williamsville, N. Y. and the Methodist Hospital in BROOKLYN.

In 1970 the Troy Conference reported four districts, 232 charges, 279 ministers, 87,452 members, property valued at $53,733,284, and $5,416,834 raised for all purposes during the year.

General Minutes, MEC and MC.
Minutes of the Troy Conference.
Henry Graham, *Troy Conference.* 1908.

LAWRENCE R. CURTIS

TRUEMAN, GEORGE JOHNSTONE (1872-1949), Canadian educator, was born on Jan. 31, 1872, in Point de Bute, a small village near the New Brunswick town of Sackville. He was a descendant of that valiant band of Yorkshire Methodists who settled in the area in 1774.

George Trueman attended local schools and subsequently the normal school in Fredericton to prepare for teaching, his chosen profession. He then taught at Upper Sackville (1891-94), after which he was principal of St. Martin's Superior School (1895-1900). Then he entered MOUNT ALLISON UNIVERSITY, graduating with the B.A. in 1902 and the M.A. in 1904. He served as principal of Charlotte County Grammar School, 1904-5, and Riverside Consolidated School, 1905-8, before accepting a call to the principalship of STANSTEAD WESLEYAN COLLEGE in the province of Quebec where he remained until 1920. While there he spent vacations at the Universities of Berlin and Heidelberg in Germany, and at Columbia in New York, obtaining the Ph.D. degree from Columbia in 1919, his thesis being "School Funds in the Province of Quebec." For the next three years he was associate secretary of the Board of Education of the Methodist Church in Canada, and traveled from coast to coast visiting schools and colleges.

In 1923 he was invited to be president of MOUNT ALLISON UNIVERSITY, with which he was associated until his death in 1949, the last three years being in retirement. His years in the college on the hill by the Tantramar were not easy ones. He had barely assumed office when the United Church of Canada came into being, bringing administrative changes to all its institutions. One of these was the union of the Mount Allison Faculty of Theology with the Presbyterian College in Halifax to form Pine Hill Divinity Hall in that city. Soon the depression began to make itself felt, and financing became most difficult. For years no buildings of any size had been erected to meet the needs of the growing enrollment, and when the Memorial Library was erected in 1926-27, a very heavy burden was laid upon the president because of building difficulties. Three bad fires resulted in the destruction of four buildings, the last being the "fireproof" Men's Residence, with the loss of several lives. These buildings were replaced with better ones. During his presidency the Ladies' College, which in some departments ran parallel with the university, was incorporated in the latter institution.

Despite his heavy load at the college, Trueman took a leading part in educational advances in the Maritime Provinces and across CANADA. He helped to set up, and for years was chairman of, the Common Examining Board of the Maritime Provinces and Newfoundland. He was president of the Mental Hygiene Council of New Brunswick, chairman of the Maritime Religious Education Council, and a member of the executive of the New Brunswick Museum, to mention but a few of the many agencies to which he gave leadership. He often attended General Council and served on its boards and committees. Immediately before his death he was elected mayor of Sackville by acclamation. His hobbies included gardening and golf.

He was a true man in the best sense. Though strict and severe at times, his students respected him and grew to love him. In 1897 he married Agnes Fawcett of Upper Sackville, who survived him. He died on Feb. 18, 1949, after a short illness, and was buried in Sackville.

E. A. BETTS

TRUSCOTT, THOMAS A. (1870-1941), missionary to South America, was born in Devon, England. Truscott arrived in BUENOS AIRES, ARGENTINA, in April of 1906. Within a week he was asked to supply the First Church (English-speaking) of Rosario. He built up the church and erected the present building.

In MONTEVIDEO, URUGUAY, in 1920 he was appointed to Emmanuel Church—at the time not known by that name, but as the English-speaking congregation of Central Church. In April of 1921 four lots were purchased at auction across the street from the administration building of the University of Montevideo. No money was in hand, but Truscott proved a good money-raiser. Plans were made, and on April 5, 1925, the cornerstone was laid by Bishop WILLIAM F. OLDHAM. In 1927 funds were exhausted but the big basement was finished and the congregation moved in. Truscott kept up his money-raising, and in 1933 the present building—a large stone structure with four magnificent stained-glass windows—was ready for full occupancy. It was dedicated in the presence of the U.S. Secretary of State, Cordell Hull, who was then attending the Pan-American Congress in Montevideo.

Aside from the building, which Methodists owe largely to him, Truscott laid enduring spiritual foundations. He was minister of the church until 1940, when he retired. He died in Lomas de Zamorra, Argentina.

EARL M. SMITH

TRUST CLAUSE. (See DEEDS OF TRUST.)

TRUSTEES are, as the name indicates, persons who are empowered to hold in trust property for the benefit of other persons or corporations—for instance, for a church, annual conference, circuit, district, or general Church, as the case may be. In American Methodism, trustees are church officers appointed for the purposes of holding the legal specific title to church property, of taking care of it, and of following out certain duties and responsibilities outlined for such trusteeship in the *Discipline*. In the different branches of world Methodism, there are some differences in provisions regarding trustees, but in a general way these provisions are much the same in all the Churches.

Trustees of a local charge or church in The United Methodist Church are elected by the charge conference (formerly the QUARTERLY CONFERENCE) or by a "church conference" if the charge conference wishes it. From earliest days the quarterly (now the charge) conference, has exercised this elective power. In all cases where the law of the state, or in some instances of a Territory, directs the mode of election, that mode must be strictly followed out. It is presently the law in The United Methodist Church that the Board of Trustees of a local church shall consist of not fewer than three nor more than nine persons, each of whom shall be over twenty-one years of age and at least two-thirds of each Board must be Methodists. Such Board is divided into three classes. Each year the term of one of these classes expires and an election is held to elect trustees for the next three years in place of those whose terms have expired. Trustees, however, may be reelected to succeed themselves. By keeping two-thirds of the Board over for each new year, a more stable Board of Trust is obtained. (*Discipline*, 1968, Paragraph 1528-29.)

Trustees of a local church are directed by the *Discipline* to make an annual report. As the Deed of Trust ("trust clause") is very important, information regarding this, the amount and value of the property, the title by which it is held, the expenditures and liabilities, and the amount of monies which have been raised during the year for building or improvement are all usually a part of the trustees' formal reports.

Trustees are held amenable to the charge conference for the manner in which they perform their official duty. Before the trustees may make any sale either to pay debts or for reinvestment, they must be authorized to do so by the charge conference. In certain instances the preacher-in-charge and district superintendent must consent to financial or important moves.

Disciplinary regulations have been carefully drawn up as to what is to be done with Church property when it is abandoned or can no longer be used for the purpose originally planned.

Trustees who are members of a local church and have been elected by the charge conference are recognized as members of that body, and as such usually serve upon the Administrative Board. Trustees of parsonage property may be appointed, or elected, in the same way, and perform the same general duties as those of church building property. Disciplinary regulations regarding all these matters vary from time to time in any one church and vary somewhat in the different branches of Methodism, so the current *Discipline* of these bodies is to be referred to for exact information upon all points.

Trustees in the M.E. Church previous to Church union in 1939 seemed to have been more dominant in managing the affairs of the local church than were the STEWARDS. The contrary was the case in the M.E. Church, South, the trustees acting more as passive custodians of property. It was noticed at the UNITING CONFERENCE in 1939 that it was always "trustees and stewards" when a delegate from the north was reporting; always "stewards and trustees" when a southerner reported.

Trustees of the Annual Conference must be elected by each respective Conference and will hold the property devised to them. They must be incorporated unless the Conference itself is incorporated. The *Discipline* gives rather complete directions regarding their qualifications and duties.

There are also District trustees, which have obligations and duties with reference to District property, such as the District parsonage, or property left to a District. Present regulations call for these to be nominated by the District Superintendent and elected by the District Conference, and where there is no District Conference, they may be elected by the District Board of Stewards or by the Annual Conference on nomination of the District Superintendents. (Paragraph 716.2.)

For the church itself there is a general Board of Trustees which must be incorporated under the name of the Board of Trustees of The United Methodist Church. Regulations are outlined as to how they may be elected by the GENERAL CONFERENCE, the extent of their terms, how the personnel of the Board is to be divided between lay and clerical, with provisions and empowerment similar to that having to do with trustees of the Annual Conference and local church.

Since Church union in 1939, the Board of Trustees of The Methodist Church, now The United Methodist Church, has been the successor in trust of the Trustees of the M.E. Church, of the Board of Trustees of the M.E. Church, South, and of the Board of Trustees of the M.P. Church. For fear that certain rights and entrustments might lapse, successive General Conferences have been continuing to elect Boards of Trustees of the three Churches above named. These meet in a *pro forma* manner from time to time and make what moves are necessary to perpetuate their trust. However, insofar as is possible, the trustees of the general Church take over these former responsibilities where they may.

In the organization of The United Methodist Church in 1968, trustees of The Methodist Church were continued as were also trustees of The E.U.B. Church for the purpose described above—that is, to continue to hold property devised to these institutions, as there may be a fear that the taking of a new name, or merging into another church or control may jeopardize such holding. General trustees of The Methodist Church were nominated by the COUNCIL OF BISHOPS of that Church and elected by the Uniting Conference in 1968.

See successive *Disciplines* and General Conference *Journals.*
N. B. H.

TRUSTEES FOR METHODIST CHURCH PURPOSES, British, is an incorporated board established under the provisions of the Methodist Church Act, 1939. It holds in perpetuity, generally as custodian trustee, such special Methodist property as colleges, schools, homes for the aged, hostels, and the like, which are not settled on the ordinary Model Deed Trust (see DEED, TRUST). The main work of the board is the custody of many thousands of invested funds arising from gifts, bequests, proceeds of sale and accumulations, including recovery of income tax on behalf of local trustees, committees, and institutions.

E. BENSON PERKINS

TSUCHIYAMA, TETSUJI (1885-1946), a Japanese elder of the FREE METHODIST CHURCH, Japan Conference. His secondary education was in Kumamoto, JAPAN, and he graduated from a United States high school in 1911. He attended college in TOKYO and also Pasadena University

and received the B.D. from DREW THEOLOGICAL SEMINARY in 1918. He received the M.Th. from Princeton University, where he was also awarded the honorary D.D. degree, and did special studies in Israel.

Tsuchiyama secured a new campus and buildings for Osaka Seminary (now Osaka Christian College), of which he was president, 1918-38. He was pastor of Third Free Methodist Church in Osaka for four years; a delegate to the North America General Conference, 1935. He made an extended speaking tour in the United States including Japanese churches on the Pacific Coast. His college campus was destroyed during the second World War. Tsuchiyama, paralyzed and near death, was located by Free Methodist Chaplains and given medical assistance. After his death, funds were raised and the college rebuilt. A thorough scholar, he was an able administrator, and an unusually effective gospel preacher. He is the author of *From Darkness to Light,* 1927; *Victory of the Cross,* 1945; and contributed a section to *Heroes of Other Lands* by H. F. Johnson.

Johnson, *Heroes of Other Lands.*
Lamson, *Lights in the World.*   BYRON S. LAMSON

TSUI, H. H. (Ts'ui Hsien-hsiang) (1895-   ), CHINA church administrator, was born in Shantung province and studied at Yenching University in Peking, where he received the baccalaureate degrees in arts and divinity; and then at DREW UNIVERSITY, where he received the Th.D. He joined the Shantung Annual Conference, and was appointed associate professor of systematic theology at Cheloo University in Tsinan, Shantung. From 1931 to 1935 he was secretary of the National Christian Council, Shanghai. In 1935 he became executive secretary of the Church of Christ in China and has continued. (A hint of Chinese attitudes toward denominations is offered by the fact that he could hold this top administrative position in a sister denomination for over thirty years without giving up his membership in the Shantung Conference.)

He was an active participant in the Three Self Movement (see article on CHINA) since its organization, and thus has been able to continue work under the Communist regime. In 1962, at a reorganization of the Board of Managers of Nanking Union Theological Seminary, he was made vice chairman of the board. That is the last definite word that has been heard of him by 1967.

China Christian Yearbook, 1936-37 (Shanghai).
F. P. Jones, *The Church in Communist China* (N.Y.: Friendship Press, 1962).
Documents of the Three Self Movement (N.Y.: Asia Dep't., National Council of Churches, 1963).   FRANCIS P. JONES

TUBMAN, WILLIAM VACANARAT SHADRACH (1895-1971), president of the Republic of LIBERIA, was born Nov. 29, 1895, the son of Rev. Alexander Tubman and Elizabeth Barnes Tubman. His grandfather, William Shadrach I, had migrated to Liberia in 1834 from Augusta, Ga. The Tubman family were very strict Christians, and the day began with prayers at 4:00 a.m. The boys tended their own gardens, and were not allowed to sleep on mattresses because their father believed it made a person soft and lazy!

William Tubman finished his high school education in 1913 and continued to study privately until he passed his bar examination in 1916 and was admitted to the bar in 1917. In 1923 he was elected to the Senate; at the age of twenty-eight he was the youngest senator in Liberian history.

In 1937 he was appointed Associate Justice of the Supreme Court. The conservative element in the True Whig party were afraid of his liberal ideas and his tremendous popularity. However, he was astute enough to use this time to secure support from the tribal leaders in the party, and in 1943 he was asked to stand for election to the presidency.

Since that time he served as a national leader, famous for his "Unification Policy" which made progress in overcoming the century-old animosity between U.S. settlers and the indigenous African peoples; and for the "Open Door Policy" which encourages foreign capital and investment. This has made possible the development of Liberia's huge iron ore deposits. He was re-elected president six terms. His story was featured in a special section of the *New York Times*, Nov. 27, 1966, the section terming President Tubman "pace-setter for a democratic and stable government in Africa." This was upon his seventy-first birthday and was material underwritten by certain international advertisers. He was serving his sixth term as president when he died suddenly in London on July 23, 1971, following a severe surgical operation.

Lawrence A. Marinelli, *The New Liberia*. Africa Service Institute, 1964.
New York *Times*. July 24, 1971.   N. B. H.

TUCKER, CHARLES EUBANK (1896-   ), American bishop of the A.M.E. Zion Church, was born in Baltimore, Md., Jan. 12, 1896, the son of William A. and Elivia (Clark) Tucker. In 1922 he married Amelia Moore. One daughter was born to this union, Bernice. He was educated at Beckford and Smith College, Jamaica, B.W.I., completing this work in 1913. He attended Lincoln University in Pennsylvania, completing his work here in 1917, after which he attended Temple University for the next two years. He studied law under the Hon. Charles Gogg at Point Pleasant, Va. He began the practice of Criminal Law in Louisville, Ky., in 1929 and was a candidate for the Assembly of that state in 1933. He began pastoral work early in life serving the following churches: Middletown, Delta and Williamsport, Pa.; Hilliard Chapel, Montgomery, Ala.; Sharon, Miss.; Augusta, Ga.; Key West, Fla.; Stoner Memorial, Louisville, Ky.; Jones Temple, New Albany, Ind.; and as presiding elder in the Philadelphia and Baltimore Conference, the Kentucky Conference and the Indiana Conference. From this last assignment he was elected to the bishopric at Pittsburgh in 1956.

DAVID H. BRADLEY

TUCKER, FRANK CORNELIUS (1892-   ), American historian and one of the leaders in Missouri Methodism, who has served important churches and districts in his conference including Francis Street, St. Joseph; Centenary, St. Louis; the St. Louis District; and the Cape Girardeau District. He was a member of eight General Conferences (1930-1956), and of the General Board of Education (1934-1956). He was a determined advocate of the unification of the Methodist Churches from 1920 onward; and his wider ecumenical efforts brought him to the presidency of the Missouri State Council of Churches, and the Metropolitan Federation of Churches

of St. Louis. A curator of Central Methodist College, he is presently Chairman of the Board.

Frank Tucker was born in Farmington, Mo., and was educated in Central Methodist College (A.B., D.D.) and the Divinity School of Yale University (B.D.). He married Elnora Lamar Cunningham and has two children, Frank C., Jr., and Elnora Elizabeth. He retired in 1960 and is the author of three histories: *Old McKendree Chapel; The Methodist Church in Missouri, 1798-1939*; and *Central Methodist College, 110 Years*. He has contributed several articles to this *Encyclopedia*. He resides in Cape Girardeau, Mo.

H. C. TUCKER

TUCKER, HUGH CLARENCE (1857-1956), American preacher and missionary to Brazil, was born in a two-room farmhouse near Nashville, Tenn., on Oct. 4, 1857, the fourth of eleven children of deeply religious parents. Hugh Tucker joined the church at the age of thirteen. Eager for an education, he worked on his father's farm and on those of neighbors, did odd jobs, and one summer made a survey for the American Bible Society. The day finally came when he rode horseback to Nashville to live with an older brother while he studied in the academic and Bible departments of Vanderbilt University, where he graduated in 1879. He was received at once on trial in the Tennessee Conference and for several years served as circuit rider. By 1885, however, he had decided that he wanted to be a missionary.

As if in answer to this desire, he received a letter one day from the Board of Missions of the M.E. Church, South, saying that an English-speaking congregation in Rio de Janeiro, Brazil, was looking for a pastor. He must be single, as they could not afford a married man. Tucker gladly responded and with Bishop J. C. Granbery and daughter Ella, he sailed for Brazil, arriving there after twenty-six days, on July 4, 1886. When Bishop Granbery organized the Conference, Tucker was one of the three charter members. Thus began a long, varied, fruitful, and extraordinary career of service in Brazil.

A year or so later, Tucker accepted an additional position with the American Bible Society, which position he held for forty-seven years. He traveled to Brazil's cities, villages, and hinterland—on muleback, in oxcart, by canoe or steamboat up its rivers, by ship or train, and finally by plane. He trained colporteurs, preached the Gospel to thousands who had never heard the Word of God; distributed over the years, through the Bible Society, 2,500,000 copies of the Scriptures; prayed and begged until at last he secured funds for the building of a splendid nine-story Bible House in Rio de Janeiro. Though often in danger from accidents, wild animals, tropical diseases, and enemies of the Gospel, he was always miraculously saved.

His record of service for the Bible Society was matched by an amazing list of other activities. Tucker founded a mission for American and other seamen and was one of the founders of both the Evangelical and Strangers' Hospitals in Rio, was a member of the board of trustees of several Methodist colleges and other institutions. Tucker founded in Rio the INSTITUTO CENTRAL DO POVO (Peoples' Central Institute) in 1906—the first social service project of its kind in Brazil; and he also started the first public playground for children in Rio de Janeiro. He worked with the Federation of Evangelical Churches; with the Society for Combating Leprosy, and was the negotiator in the purchase of the COLEGIO BENNETT property in Rio.

Tucker was a delegate to the INTERNATIONAL MISSIONARY CONFERENCES of Edinburgh and Jerusalem, and to the Panama Conference on Christian Work in 1916. Four times he was a delegate to World SUNDAY SCHOOL Conventions. Nonofficially, he aided the Brazilian government in its campaigns against yellow fever and for the control of flies and mosquitoes. With all these multiple activities, Tucker found time to write numberless articles, a biography of the prominent Brazilian newspaper editor, José C. de Rodrigues, and in 1902 a book, *The Bible in Brazil*.

From SOUTHWESTERN UNIVERSITY in Texas, he received a D.D. degree in 1920; and later an LL.D. from RANDOLPH-MACON COLLEGE, Virginia. Helping him tirelessly in church and community activities was his wife, Ella, (known as Dona Elvira in Brazil), whom he had met aboard ship on his first trip to Brazil. They had two children, Elvira and Clarence. The latter died as a little boy, of yellow fever. Mrs. Tucker would meet incoming ships to welcome and help new missionaries and visitors to Brazil; she was a gracious hostess both to the distinguished and the humble. Hers was an unforgettable life of serving and blessing others. She died on Jan. 11, 1953, and was buried in the family plot in Petersburg, Va.

When Tucker was to retire to the United States in 1934, the government of Brazil honored him with the Order of the Southern Cross. After retirement he continued active, writing and speaking on Brazil. In November, 1953, at the age of ninety-six, he was given a trip to Brazil to attend the formal inauguration of a new building at the Peoples' Institute to be named in his honor. This service was attended by high dignitaries both of Brazil and the United States.

Hugh C. Tucker died on Nov. 4, 1956, at the age of ninety-nine in Media, Pa., at the home of his daughter. Survivors included this daughter, Mrs. L. A. Estes, and three grandsons. He was a world citizen, a true and worthy ambassador for Christ.

J. L. Kennedy, *Metodismo no Brazil*. 1928.

ANTONIO CAMPOS DE GONÇALVES

TUCSON, ARIZONA, U.S.A., population 265,000 is a popular health and winter resort. "Tucson" is the Spanish form of Papago name, Tuqui Son, meaning "black base" or "water at foot of black mountain." It was acquired by the United States in the Gadsen Purchase of 1853. Tucson is the home of the University of Arizona and the Davis-Monthan Air Force Base.

Arizona became a Territory in 1863. Tucson served as the capital from 1867 to 1877. The first Protestant ministers arrived in 1870, representing the M.E. Church. One was Chaplain Alexander Gilmore of the NEW JERSEY CONFERENCE assigned to Fort Whipple near Prescott. The other was Charles H. Cook of the ROCK RIVER CONFERENCE who, inspired by a series of magazine articles, reached Fort Bowie on his way to Pima Village to preach to the Indians. In 1872 Glezen Asbury Reeder of the NORTH OHIO CONFERENCE was appointed first superintendent of the Mission. In 1875 Rev. and Mrs. D. B. Wright arrived from NEW YORK and the first CAMP MEETING in the Territory was held in a mesquite grove near Tempe (thirty conversions reported). In 1877 Rev. and Mrs. J. J. Wingar and family came by covered wagon from KANSAS.

The appointment (1879) of George H. Adams of the COLORADO CONFERENCE to serve as superintendent brought about the organization of the ARIZONA Mission at a meeting in Tucson on July 8, 1881. Soon a four page quarterly, *The Arizona Methodist,* was being published. This was followed by an abortive attempt to establish Arizona Wesleyan University. In 1880 land was purchased in Tucson for the start of First Church. The second pastor appointed was JOSEPH F. BERRY who, for reasons of health, arrived on Sept. 30, 1882. Later elected to the episcopacy, Berry was for many years the senior bishop of the M.E. Church. Another pioneer Arizona pastor was M. M. BOVARD, named superintendent (1890-96), who later became the first president of the UNIVERSITY OF SOUTHERN CALIFORNIA.

The M.E. Church, South responded to the challenge of the new Territory when the Los Angeles Conference met in 1871 and appointed Alexander Groves as missionary to Arizona. Among the pioneer preachers was a school teacher from Missouri, L. J. Hedgpeth, whose grandson, Herschel, was to serve as district superintendent for Arizona (1955-61), and who is currently on the staff of the National Division of the BOARD OF MISSIONS. Not until 1921, one year before Arizona became an Annual Conference, was any effort made to organize work in Tucson. J. C. McPHEETERS (later pastor of Glide Church, SAN FRANCISCO, and president of ASBURY THEOLOGICAL SEMINARY) came from MONTANA (1922) to be the first pastor of what is now Catalina Church (see below), which is currently the largest church in the SOUTHERN CALIFORNIA-ARIZONA CONFERENCE. From the college department Margaret Billingsley went as a missionary to KOREA, later to serve as an executive secretary of the Board of Missions. Among the ministerial leadership of this day were J. E. Harrison, W. J. Sims, J. L. Lyons, S. Douglass Walters and E. Clyde Smith. Pioneer lay families of Southern Methodism have given two governors to the State, Sidney Osborn and Paul Fannin, the latter becoming a U.S. Senator.

The unification of Methodism greatly strengthened the work in Arizona. Abandoned appointments recall Methodism's march with the people in developing a vast and difficult Territory. Men like Paul F. Huebner, Frank S. Williams and Frank M. Toothaker maintained the tradition. In 1961 the State was divided into two administrative units. The Tucson District of the Southern California-Arizona Conference extends south from the city limits of PHOENIX. Chilton C. McPheeters was in time appointed superintendent and returned to his childhood home. Expansion continued with the acquisition of ten church sites, the start of seven new churches, and plant construction valued at over three million dollars. The twelve churches in Tucson reported in 1970 a membership of 8,985. The forty-seven churches in the District reported a total membership of 21,293. Tucson also has two C.M.E. CHURCHES, one A.M.E. CHURCH and one EVANGELICAL METHODIST congregation.

Catalina Church is the largest Methodist church in Arizona, numbering 3,681 members. It has become known for sponsoring a Sunday Evening Forum which is the largest in the nation. Originally it was known as University Church. Organized April 16, 1922, near the University of Arizona, it is now in its second location in Tucson functioning under its present name.

Prior to the organization of the University Church, W. J. Sims was appointed to open up work in Tucson and to serve as presiding elder of the Safford District. Property near the University of Arizona campus was purchased in 1921 for the development of the church. A charter membership of fifty persons constituted the church at its organization.

A Woman's Missionary Society was organized Sept. 14, 1922 with Mrs. L. E. Wyatt as president. George B. Pottorff, a layman with preaching experience, assisted Sims in the early days of the church. The first unit of the church was completed and occupied by the congregation on Feb. 1, 1924. A few months prior to this Julian C. McPheeters was appointed pastor, and led the congregation in a period of great growth and activity until 1930.

Catalina has proved missionary-minded from the very beginning. Miss Margaret Billingsley and Miss Grace Thatcher were among the first young people to commit themselves to full-time missionary service. Within two and a half years of its organization, the church had over 400 members and by the time it was five years old the number had grown to 735. During the first six years of its life, University Church licensed six young men for the ministry, led seven men to enter the Conference for full-time service and two others for missionary work.

Moffett Rhodes was appointed pastor in 1930, followed by Donald Householder in 1932 and R. C. Cantrell in 1936.

In 1942 the Fellowship Class of the church developed a discussion group which first met in the living room of the parsonage, outgrew that and then moved to the sanctuary, outgrew that and then moved to the high school auditorium, and finally to the auditorium at the University of Arizona. This activity came to be known as the Sunday Evening Forum and is now the largest forum of its kind in the United States, averaging more than 1,800 persons in attendance during the twenty-week season each year. Mary Jeffries Burt has been its director since its inception. The Sunday Evening Forum celebrated its twenty-fifth anniversary in 1967.

The missionary interest of the church inevitably led to the sponsorship and development of a community center in Tucson which has continued throughout the years. Maurice G. Ballenger was appointed pastor in 1942. During his ministry University Church established an outpost mission and moved to its present location at 2700 East Speedway Boulevard. The church assumed the name Catalina Church after moving to its new location. A complex of new buildings began to take shape at this site, first a barracks building, then the Fellowship Hall and administration unit, followed by the youth building, the sanctuary and the music building.

The city of Tucson grew rapidly during the decade of 1950 to 1960 and Catalina Church grew with it. Hayden S. Sears was appointed pastor in 1953 and during his tenure the church grew to more than 4,000 members, with a church school average attendance of more than 1,300 and a full choir program of twelve choirs, including more than 600 voices.

CHILTON C. McPHEETERS

TUILOVONI, SETAREKI (1916-   ), was the first president of the autonomous Methodist Church in Fiji within the fellowship of the Methodist Church of Australasia. He was born on Matuku, an island in the Lau Group of Fiji and was trained as a school teacher, but after war conditions had kept him in NEW ZEALAND where he endeavored to study, he suffered for a time tuberculosis in an advanced form. After his recovery, he commenced serious work in the ministry, and had larger and larger involvements in the general work of the Christian churches. The American Methodist Church offered him a scholarship so that he might study at DREW THEOLOGICAL SEMINARY in NEW JERSEY, and he returned to Fiji with a B.D. degree and in 1951 was appointed director of the Methodist Young People's Department. He had married in his home village during the period following his illness and his wife, Sera, has greatly helped him in his career. They have six children. In 1960 Queen Elizabeth II honored him by creating him a Member of the Order of the British Empire. In 1961 he was appointed a member of the executive committee of the Department of World Mission and Evangelism of the WORLD COUNCIL OF CHURCHES. For the past five years, Setareki Tuilovoni has been executive secretary of the Pacific Conference of Churches, traveling throughout the entire Pacific area and exercising a progressive and stimulating influence on churches of all denominations. He represented the Pacific Churches at the INTERNATIONAL MISSIONARY COUNCIL at GHANA and at the Assembly of the World Council of Churches at UPPSALA.

The Missionary Review, Sydney, Australia, July-August 1967.
N. B. H.

TULLIS, EDWARD LEWIS (1917-   ), American minister and mission leader, was born in CINCINNATI, Ohio, March 9, 1917, the son of Ashar Spence and Priscilla Daugherty Tullis. He was educated at KENTUCKY WESLEYAN COLLEGE, receiving the A.B. in 1939; a B.D. at the Louisville Presbyterian Theological Seminary, 1947; and the D.D. from UNION COLLEGE in 1954. His wife was Mary Jane Talley, whom he married on Sept. 25, 1937, and they have a son and daughter.

He was admitted on trial in the KENTUCKY CONFERENCE, M.E. Church, South, in 1939, and has served as pastor in Frenchburg, 1937-39; Lawrenceburg, 1939-44; associate pastor, Fourth Avenue Church, LOUISVILLE, 1944-47; Irvine, 1947-49; Frankfort, 1952-61; and First Church, Ashland, since 1961. He became associate secretary of the Division of National MISSIONS in the Board of Missions of The Methodist Church, 1949-52. He is a trustee of Kentucky Wesleyan College, The Methodist Home at Versailles, Ky.; the METHODIST THEOLOGICAL SEMINARY IN OHIO; the LAKE JUNALUSKA ASSEMBLY in North Carolina; the ALASKA METHODIST UNIVERSITY; and the SUE BENNETT COLLEGE in London, Ky. He has been a delegate to the GENERAL CONFERENCE of The Methodist Church, 1956, '60, '64 and '68; a member of the WORLD METHODIST COUNCIL; the Methodist Commission on Appalachian Development; the Board of Managers of the Board of Missions of The United Methodist Church and the Interboard Committee on Town and Country Work. He was also chairman of the Kentucky Conference Board of Missions and the Southeastern Jurisdiction's Committee on Missions (1960-68).

Who's Who in the Methodist Church, 1966.   N. B. H.

TULSA, OKLAHOMA, U.S.A., a city of over 328,000 inhabitants and a metropolis of the South Central region of the United States. Over half a hundred churches and

BOSTON AVENUE CHURCH, TULSA, OKLAHOMA

Methodist institutions serve its Metropolitan area. The first Methodist Church there was the second religious organization founded in the city—in 1889. The present building is one of the finest examples of pure Gothic architecture in America.

The Boston Avenue Church, erected in 1925, was one of the first adaptations of modern architecture to church building. The edifice has drawn the admiration of architects from all over the world. Tourists go through the building daily.

The Tulsa churches are among the foremost in evangelistic endeavor and benevolent giving in the entire denomination. Four Methodist institutions are presently located in Tulsa; Methodist Manor for the Aged; Frances Willard Home for young women; WESLEY FOUNDATION at Tulsa University, and the GOODWILL INDUSTRY for the Handicapped.

Boston Avenue Church is one of the six largest churches in world Methodism, with a membership of 6,756. It is located in the heart of the city of Tulsa, sometimes called "The Oil Capital of the World," where sixteen percent of the population affirms a Methodist preference and where there are more college graduates, in proportion to the general population, than in any other city in the United States with a population of more than 200,000. Boston Avenue is one of fifty churches in the Wesleyan tradition in this city. Its unique architecture is said to be the first attempt on a major scale at unconventional or non-traditional design in the twentieth century. The entire building was designed by Adah Robinson, an art teacher at the University of Tulsa, who was assisted by a nineteen-year-old student who later became a famous architect. Atop the seventeen story spire is a tower chapel of prayer, but in the main sanctuary where all of the symbolism is indigenous (except the cross) one finds color, form, and other appointments blended in a circular room, affording a place of worship both unique and practical. The Italian glass mosaic behind the choir stalls contains over 700,000 individual pieces of Byzantine and Venetian tile. These, pointing to the cross through Osage Indian symbolism, speak a word of faith and strength. The church plant is valued at more than $6,000,000. Visitors find points of interest in the circuit rider statuary, the court to the Irish Methodist pioneers, the History and Archives Room depicting early Indian days with accompanying church history, and the Rose Chapel. There are two pipe organs in the building. The educational unit is said to be the second largest cantilevered building in the country at this time. Dr. FINIS A. CRUTCHFIELD, Jr. is presently senior minister and leads a staff of twenty-three full-time members, of whom four are ordained clergymen.

First Church is noted for its architectural excellence, as well as the strength and vigor of the congregation. In 1924 Bishop ERNEST L. WALDORF appointed Charles Drake Skinner of New York as pastor of First M.E. Church, Tulsa, to further a building program. He was the youngest clergyman to receive the D.D. degree from SYRACUSE UNIVERSITY except S. PARKES CADMAN. He sought advice from Bishop CHARLES H. FOWLER on building plans. Bishop Fowler said, "Only stone is suitable material from which to build a church to God." Bishop Waldorf and Skinner envisioned at that time for Tulsa the largest Gothic Cathedral in the Southwest, wishing it to be artistic, beautiful and useful. This was to be the third church of stone for Skinner to sponsor. This

church was dedicated in 1928. The type of masonry is known as Range Ashlar. Masons hammered the rough, hard, variegated stone into shape for the two-foot thick walls. This stone does not absorb stains and is cleaned by weather action. Trim is of Indiana Limestone. The body of the church is cruciform and so appears both from interior and exterior views. Entering the sanctuary the eye is led by a procession of stone arches and traceried windows to the vaulted room and massive trusses of solid oak, then downward to the chancel of tile and marble to the great rich multi-colored window in the background. The stained glass windows, combined with the especially designed lighting fixtures with coronas of metal and open tracery work, is in keeping with ancient churches and the lighting effect is pure Gothic. A handsome chapel with seating capacity of 200 opens off the south transept. Adjoining the sanctuary is the four-story educational building which contains five auditoriums; it also houses the library and offices. The community hall on the lower level seats 1,200 and has facilities for seating and serving 400 people. The little formal garden in the courtyard is landscaped with shrubs of Bible nomenclature. When S. Parkes Cadman preached in the pulpit of the sanctuary he told the congregation, "This is the most beautiful church in the world but one, and I know them all."

Bishop W. ANGIE SMITH and Bishop PAUL E. MARTIN were consecrated at this church's altar in June 1944. A plaque commemorates the occasion. Heritage Hall, a two story masonry building acquired recently with twenty rooms now in use for Sunday school classes, brings the number of rooms in the church complex to over 100. The landscaped parking area with a foundation located across the Avenue is enclosed with a low rock wall from the same quarry as was used for the Cathedral.

The forerunner of this great church was an Indian Mission organized in Tulsa, Creek Nation, Indian Territory, in December 1886 by Wiley F. Bowden of the ARKANSAS CONFERENCE, under James Murray in KANSAS, Superintendent of Indian Missions. In 1887 a note was signed to the CHURCH EXTENSION Society by a Delaware Indian and a Creek Indian woman and others for $500, one-half a gift. Services were held in the summer of 1887 under a brush arbor while church building progressed. This church was the first formally dedicated M.E. Church in the Indian Territory (Nov. 27, 1887). Population of the settlement then was about 100 Indians and whites. This little church had the honor of being the seat for the ninth and last session of the Indian Mission and the first session of the INDIAN MISSION CONFERENCE, with Bishop JOHN M. WALDEN presiding, March 21-23, 1889. This congregation built a larger structure of brick to keep up with this fast growing southwest frontier town, and this was dedicated on May 20, 1906, about one year before statehood.

First Church offers a variety of services to the traveling public, as well as to its own congregation and the large city. The 1970 membership was 3,531.

Frances E. Willard Home. This home for underprivileged girls has been a Methodist institution since 1958 when Mrs. Josephine M. Buhl, the founder and president of its Board of Directors, presented the forty acre tract and buildings of the Home to the OKLAHOMA CONFERENCE of The Methodist Church. Bishop W. Angie Smith formally accepted this property, valued at $350,000 for the Conference. It is located in the hill region of the old

Osage Nation. The complex includes Willard House—the original residence—Buhl House, Mabee House, Lyons House and a superintendent's residence. The girls are from various areas and range in age from ten years through high school. They attend Tulsa public schools.

The start of this Home was in 1917 when Mrs. Buhl called a Woman's Christian Temperance Union meeting on Feb. 17, the birthday of FRANCES E. WILLARD, to found a home for needy girls (not delinquent). The first home was soon outgrown; a forty-acre tract was purchased southcast of town with brick and concrete buildings. Care of livestock and gardening was routine for the girls in addition to schooling. In 1955 this property, now encroached upon by the city, was sold to the Conference for a Methodist Manor, and the present Willard Home for girls was purchased. The Oklahoma Conference has carried forward a building program at the Manor, including a fifty-bed infirmary, nine cottages, and the new Lyons building housing 160 residents in all. These come from many parts of the country.

Wesley Foundation Student Center, adjacent to the campus of the University of Tulsa, serves out of town students primarily. A full time director offers counseling, Bible study, and communion services.

Memorial Drive Church began as a non-denominational Sunday school which met at 8310 East 15th Street in the Memorial Drive Community Center. In this non-denominational fellowship more than 400 attended Sunday school. The group did not have a minister; no worship services were held in the morning. A Vesper Service was held in the evening with approximately fifty-five persons in attendance.

Through the influence and encouragement of L. C. Clark, Chairman of the Tulsa District Board of Missions, land was purchased at 15th and 79th East Avenue for the purpose of organizing a Methodist church. Memorial Drive was the first project of the Tulsa District Board of Missions. Bishop W. Angie Smith appointed E. E. Holmberg to this situation on Sept. 28, 1950.

Twenty-six persons attended a first service in the pastor's home on April 19, 1951. On May 6, 1951 the first membership and organizational service was held at Will Rogers Church with forty-four persons as full members and twelve as preparatory members. The WOMAN'S SOCIETY OF CHRISTIAN SERVICE was organized May 3, 1951 with Mrs. W. E. Diron as president.

In April 1951 the Tulsa District Board of Missions pledged $20,000 to erect a new building. The opening service in the new building was on Sept. 23, 1951, with 164 in the Sunday school and 170 in the worship service.

On Sunday evening, June 24, 1951, the Community Sunday Evening Vesper Service, at which E. E. Holmberg had been presiding and preaching, was discontinued. Funds belonging to the Vesper Service congregation were divided equally between the Community Center and the Methodist church. The new church met on the parsonage lawn the first Sunday evening of July.

The first QUARTERLY CONFERENCE was held June 25, 1951, with H. BASCOM WATTS as district superintendent. E. E. Holmberg named the church, The Memorial Drive Methodist Church. Roger Prim was the treasurer. The Chairman of the Board, Joe Daugherty, was elected at an OFFICIAL BOARD meeting following the Quarterly Conference. Additional buildings have been constructed as needed. To date, total evaluation of all church property is in excess of $750,000. The church has continued to

grow and in 1970 there was a membership of 2,046.

Oklahoma Methodist Home For The Aged, Inc. was established in 1956 on forty acres of land near the residential center of the city of Tulsa. The Home is owned and operated by the Oklahoma Conference of The United Methodist Church.

At the date of March 15, 1968, the Home had served a total of 334 members, with a present family of 152, its total capacity. There are cottages for completely independent living, apartments for semi-dependent living, private rooms for semi-dependent living, and fifty beds for the care of bed patients in the Health Center.

University Church is adjacent to the University of Tulsa. In March 1922, a broken down car and a muddy road prompted two families to hold Sunday school for their children in their own home. There the Johnsons and the Henrys began what is now University Church. Fourteen years later in 1936, having used first a tent, then a roughly constructed tabernacle, the congregation moved into the first unit of the present structure located at 5th and South College. Over a period of eleven years, 1933-44, the men of the church acquired a stone quarry, dug the stone, hauled them to the site, and, in many instances, put them in place to build a Gothic structure of rustic stone. After the first unit was built the men labored for two years building the seventy foot tower which they completed as "a testimony of faith" before beginning the sanctuary. The first two units and the tower were constructed and then a third unit consisting of a basement and three floors was completed on Dec. 17, 1950, and was dedicated by Bishop W. Angie Smith.

The original congregation was known as Kendall Methodist Church, which was then the name of the University of Tulsa. In 1929 the Grace Church sold its property and united with the Kendall Church to constitute what is now the University Church. The membership in 1970 was 2,507.

Will Rogers Church is named after the famous Will Rogers of Oklahoma and is located in the area of Tulsa that is now called the Will Rogers Area. The litany of its consecration service was led by Will Rogers, Jr., when the church was consecrated.

In the fall of 1943, eight dedicated Methodists, with no place to meet but a family home, took the first preliminary steps toward organizing this church. Its charter was given on Easter Sunday, 1944, with fifty-two members uniting with the church. Within a period of fifteen years, two fine educational buildings, a chapel, and sanctuary seating over 900 people, had been constructed. In the past ten years, four additional plots of real estate have been added to the church, including two new parsonages, and two houses that are being used for church school classes. Three of these plots of property are adjacent to the present church property.

Will Rogers Church has been a church of service both inside and outside the church building itself, and has been unusually blessed with an exceptional number of able laymen and women. During its short history, eight persons have gone into full-time work of the church.

In 1970 the church had a membership of 2,672, property valued at over $700,000, two well attended services on Sunday morning, ten choirs, four bell choirs, and over 300 young people participating in the youth program.

General Minutes, UMC, 1970.
Fannie B. Misch, *Methodist Trails to First Methodist Church*.

Tulsa: Chamber of Commerce, 1961. OSCAR L. FONTAINE
FINIS A. CRUTCHFIELD, JR.
FANNIE BROWNLEE MISCH
QUITMAN MCCRORY
JOHN R. WEBB
BONNER E. TEETER

TUNNICLIFFE, JOHN (-1948), Methodist layman in CALIFORNIA. An orphan in County Sligo, IRELAND, he was apprenticed to the keeper of a general store. He came to SAN FRANCISCO empty-handed. By hard work and careful management he built up a successful grocery chain in that city. Then his physicians called a halt. He must play golf. Instead he began to walk the streets of Grace Church parish in the Mission District for his church. Increasing his activity year by year, he walked into the councils of the Annual and the GENERAL CONFERENCES. In 1924 he was appointed Western Representative of the Board of Foreign MISSIONS (ME). For twenty years he gave full time volunteer service. He met steamers, secured and forwarded supplies, and raised three-quarters of a million dollars for the Board. Having no children, his estate was divided between home and foreign missions and the retired ministers. He lavished a gracious personality on Kingdom goals.

L. L. Loofbourow, *In Search of God's Gold*, pp. 229-230.
LEON L. LOOFBOUROW

TUNSTALL, England, is the most northern of the former six towns of the potteries, Staffordshire, England, now united as the city of Stoke on Trent. In the early nineteenth century Tunstall was the center of the PRIMITIVE METHODIST revival movement associated with the name of WILLIAM CLOWES, who was himself born there, and who was the leader of a group which was at first called the Clowesites, but soon became one of the formative elements in Primitive Methodism itself. The first written plan of the new Primitive Methodist denomination was issued from Tunstall in 1811, as the head of a circuit extending into four counties, Staffordshire, Cheshire, Derbyshire, and Lancashire. The first Primitive Methodist chapel was set up at Tunstall in 1811 and consisted of two cottages transformed into a meetinghouse. The second Conference of the METHODIST NEW CONNEXION was held there in 1821 and so was the Jubilee Conference of 1860.

JOHN T. WILKINSON

TURNER, GEORGE ALLEN (1908-   ), ordained elder of the Kentucky-Tennessee Conference of the FREE METHODIST CHURCH and professor of English Bible, ASBURY THEOLOGICAL SEMINARY, was born in Willsboro, N. Y. He holds the A.B. degree from GREENVILLE COLLEGE, the S.T.B. degree from New York Theological Seminary, and the S.T.M. and Ph.D. degrees from Harvard University Divinity School. Greenville College conferred upon him the Litt.D. degree. He has served as pastor of Free Methodist churches in SOUTH DAKOTA, ILLINOIS, MASSACHUSETTS, and OHIO and as pastor of Congregational Churches in South Dakota and Ohio. He was superintendent of the Kentucky-Tennessee conference of the Free Methodist Church, 1936-38. He was Lecturer at mission educational institutions in Japan, Taiwan, India and Egypt, 1961. He is the author of *Portals to Bible Books*, 1958; *The More Excellent Way*, 1952; *The Vision Which Transforms*, 1964. He is editor, *The Evangelical Bible Commentary* and is now associate editor of *The Asbury Seminarian*. Dr. Turner and his family reside at Wilmore, Ky.

BYRON S. LAMSON

TURNER, HENRY McNEAL (1834-1915), American founder and organizer of the A.M.E. CHURCH in the state of GEORGIA, and in West and South Africa, was born near Newberry, S. C. on Feb. 1, 1834, of free parents. He was educated at Trinity College, BALTIMORE, Md. Turner was licensed to preach in 1853 by the M.E. Church, South. In 1858 he was admitted to the Missouri Conference, ordained DEACON in 1860 and ELDER in 1862. Following a brief career in the pastorate he received an appointment from President Abraham Lincoln as U. S. Army CHAPLAIN. He served as presiding elder in Georgia and as founder-editor of *Southern Recorder*, 1882.

Turner was a leader of considerable influence in both church and state. Beginning with his bishopric (1880-1915), there was a shift of power in his Connection from North to South. An advocate of African colonization for the Negro, his position of influence greatly aided that ill-fated movement. He rightly deserves the title of Father of the church of Africa, as he organized it in SIERRA LEONE, LIBERIA and SOUTH AFRICA. Bishop Turner died at Windsor, Canada, on May 9, 1915.

R. R. Wright, *The Bishops*. 1963.   GRANT S. SHOCKLEY

NATHANIEL TURNER

TURNER, NATHANIEL (1793-1864), New Zealand Methodist minister, was born at Wednesbury, England, and entered the ministry in 1821. He was appointed to NEW ZEALAND and arrived at Wesleydale (Whangaroa) in 1823 with his wife, just as Samuel Leigh was forced to leave through ill health. Work proved difficult, and the Maoris were unresponsive. Early in 1827, the station was destroyed by hostile Maoris, and the Turners, along with other missionaries, were forced to flee for their lives. Turner was next appointed to the Friendly Islands

(Tonga) and after that to Hobart. From there he returned to New Zealand as chairman in 1836, until succeeded by John H. Bumby. After terms in Tasmania and NEW SOUTH WALES, he died in Brisbane on Dec. 5, 1864.

C. H. Laws, *Toil and Adversity at Whangaroa*. Wesley Historical Society, New Zealand, 1945.
J. G. Turner, *The Pioneer Missionary—Life of the Rev. Nathaniel Turner*. Melbourne: George Robertson, 1872.

L. R. M. GILMORE

TURNER, PETER (18? -1873), British Methodist missionary pioneer to the South Seas, was born in MANCHESTER, England, about the beginning of the nineteenth century and entered the Wesleyan ministry in 1829, leaving for Polynesia the following year. His twenty-three years of service were outstanding in length and quality. From 1830-36 and, again, 1841-54, he spent in the FRIENDLY ISLANDS, during the last period sharing in the great revival which swept the islands. In 1836-41 he pioneered Wesleyan missionary work in SAMOA, at the request of Friendly Islanders who were at work there, but after considerable inter-mission difficulties, the Wesleyan work was in part handed over to the London Missionary Society, and in part recommenced by the Australian Methodist Conference. In 1854 Turner returned to NEW SOUTH WALES, and died at Windsor, AUSTRALIA, Nov. 2, 1873.

M. Dyson, *My Story of Samoan Methodism*. London, 1875.
CYRIL J. DAVEY

TURNPIKES, Br. (See TOLLS, Br.)

TURRENTINE, SAMUEL BRYANT (1861-1949), American minister and educator, was born in Chatham County, N. C. Nov. 15, 1861. Educated at the University of North Carolina, VANDERBILT UNIVERSITY and Columbia, he served as principal of Union Literary Academy in Chatham County, taught at Cartersville Institute, Cartersville, Ga., and was professor of Hebrew and New Testament Greek at Trinity College (now Duke University). Trinity College honored him with the D.D. degree.

He was admitted into the NORTH CAROLINA CONFERENCE in 1888 and at the division of this Conference in 1890 became a member of the newly organized WESTERN NORTH CAROLINA CONFERENCE, in which he served throughout his ministry. Ordained a DEACON in 1890 and an ELDER in 1892 he served pastorates in Kings Mountain, Morganton, WINSTON-SALEM (Centenary), Charlotte (Trinity), GREENSBORO (West Market Street) and Salisbury (First). He also served as presiding elder of the CHARLOTTE, Greensboro and Shelby Districts.

In 1913 he returned to his first love, the education of young women, and became the president of GREENSBORO COLLEGE. There he remained until 1935, after which he became president emeritus and professor of Bible and special lecturer in Bible.

He was a member of the Board of Trustees of what is now DUKE UNIVERSITY from 1893 until his death on April 12, 1949. He was a charter member of the North Carolina College Conference and served as its vice-president; chairman of the Conferences' committee on high school relations and was vice-president of the Southern Association of Colleges for Women. He was the author of a historical volume, *A Romance of Education*, giving much source material related to Greensboro College.

His wife, the former Sallie Lenora Atwater, to whom he was married Jan. 4, 1888, preceded him in death on the fifty-fifth anniversary of their marriage.

Journal of the Western North Carolina Conference, 1949.
Samuel Bryant Turrentine, *A Romance of Education: A Narrative including recollections and other facts connected with Greensboro College*. Greensboro, N. C., 1946.

CHARLES D. WHITE

TURTON, H. HANSON (1818-1887), New Zealand minister, was born at Bradford, England, where his father, Isaac Turton, was a Wesleyan minister. He was ordained in 1839, and arrived in NEW ZEALAND on the mission vessel "Triton" on May 8, 1840. After some months spent at Mangungu, Turton went in 1841 to open the Aotea station. In 1844, he was appointed to Ngamotu, New Plymouth, where he stayed ten years. While travelling along the coast to take up work at Ngamotu, the whole Turton family almost lost their lives, when cut off by the tide.

Turton founded a Maori training center at Ngamotu, which was named the Grey Institute (in honour of Governor George Grey). "He distinguished himself subsequently," writes Morley (p. 83), "by a public controversy with Bishop Selwyn (first Anglican bishop of New Zealand) on 'Sacerdotal Assumptions,' and had not the worst of the argument." Short appointments followed at Kawhia (1857) and Manukau (1858).

In 1858, Turton retired from the ministry and commenced business as a house and general agent. Later he became an interpreter in government service. He represented New Plymouth in Parliament during 1863 and 1864, and then resigned in order to act as commissioner to investigate Maori land titles under the New Zealand settlements act. He worked for the Native Department in Wellington from 1874 to 1883, and died on Sept. 18, 1887.

Dictionary of New Zealand Biography, ed. G. H. Scholefield. Department of Internal Affairs, 1940.
W. Morley, *New Zealand*. 1900.
W. J. Williams, *New Zealand*. 1922.

L. R. M. GILMORE

TURTON, WILLIAM (1761-1818), British Methodist pioneer missionary in the WEST INDIES, was born in Barbados, and converted under THOMAS COKE, 1788, becoming a Methodist preacher. Apart from a brief visit to America, when he preached in Long Island churches, Turton's whole distinguished career was in his own islands. In 1795 he pioneered in TOBAGO; in 1796 he worked in the Swedish island of St. Bartholomew; in 1799 he became the first pioneer in the Bahamas at Turks Island and Nassau. When James Rutledge was appointed his colleague, he spent his time in the "out-islands." Turton was appointed chairman and general superintendent of the Bahamas District and found additional opportunity of pioneering in Rock Sound, Eleuthera, Abaco, etc. He died, after twenty years of hard service, much of it in new areas, on May 7, 1818, at Nassau.

W. Moister, *Heralds of Salvation*. London, 1878.   C. DAVEY

TUSCALOOSA, ALABAMA, U.S.A. **First Church** was founded in 1818 by EBENEZER HEARN. Tuscaloosa was the focal point of the CIRCUIT which then covered an area from forty to sixty miles wide and roughly 200 miles long. The time of its founding was very significant—ALABAMA was just becoming a state. LAZENBY gives three reasons for the rapid growth and the fine type of Methodism produced within the bounds of this circuit. First, "the circuit was served by far-seeing and consecrated men"; second, "this section was settled by men of high character"; and third, Tuscaloosa early became the locale of culture and the home of Sims Female Academy, and of the University of Alabama. In January 1826, the legislature moved the capital of the state to Tuscaloosa, which was already the seat of Tuscaloosa County.

Tuscaloosa became a station in 1824. It was at that time an appointment of the MISSISSIPPI CONFERENCE as was much of western Alabama. John Kesterson was its first station pastor. The ALABAMA CONFERENCE was organized later in Tuscaloosa in 1832. In 1870 First Church became a member of the newly organized NORTH ALABAMA CONFERENCE. Under the leadership of some of the ablest men of Methodism, both laymen and preachers, the Tuscaloosa church has played a vital part in the progress of Methodism and the Kingdom throughout the years. The record shows that four men who later became bishops had served First Church, Tuscaloosa; ROBERT PAINE, 1820-21; JOHN C. KEENER, 1845-46; J. H. McCOY, 1895-97; CLARE PURCELL, 1924-26. Two laymen of the church have served as governor of the State of Alabama, Henry W. Collier and William W. Brandon. J. H. CHITWOOD had a long and distinguished pastorate in this church, and was a member of the JUDICIAL COUNCIL, as well as its pastor when he died in 1966.

In 1824, as it became a station, Bishop SOULE held the Mississippi Conference in Tuscaloosa. This was the second Annual Conference held in Alabama. Tuscaloosa First Church is presently, with its 1,594 members (1970), the center of a metropolitan area of twelve Methodist churches having an enrollment of over 6,000 members. The Tuscaloosa District is one of the twelve districts of the North Alabama Annual Conference.

General Minutes, UMC, 1970.
M. E. Lazenby, *Alabama and West Florida*. 1961.

GEORGE F. COOPER

TUSKEGEE, ALABAMA, U.S.A. **Butler Chapel.** In the year 1865 when the Negro slaves were freed, some were anxious to own their homes. In the ALABAMA community now known as Zion Hill were a few scattered houses which had been occupied by former slave holders. These were purchased by Negroes. There was also a one-room log cabin that had been used as a schoolhouse. This was used as a meeting place and schoolhouse by Zion Hill's new residents. They were taught by white teachers. With the settling of the Negro families, the whites began to move out. The most of the homes bought by Negroes were sold to them by a man named Phelps.

It was in this settlement that Butler Chapel A.M.E. ZION CHURCH was organized during the fall of 1865 by Rev. J. M. Butler. Butler had been sent to Tuskegee by Bishop JOSEPH J. CLINTON from the First Alabama (AMEZ) Conference, held in MOBILE. The first church was built in 1867. It was renovated and extended in 1869 and 1875. The plans were made in 1887 for a new edifice. Improvements to this church have been made during various administrations.

J. M. Butler was succeeded by Solomon Derry, who was also Macon County's first Negro teacher.

R. F. Thweatt was the first superintendent of Butler Chapel's Sunday school. He was succeeded by Lewis Adams who held this position until his death, April 30, 1905. Adams' death came suddenly on Sunday morning near the end of the Sunday school when he collapsed at the altar.

During these early years, Adams operated a shop where tin utensils were made. He was a skilled craftsman in metals. He never had any formal training, but his owners had taught him to read and write. His training as a mechanic was also learned while in slavery. Later, he opened a shop in the town of Tuskegee where he made shoes, harness and tinware. Lewis Adams was not only resourceful, but was interested in improving his church and community. He dreamed of industrial education for his people, and was alert to every opportunity to translate his dreams into reality. He was the leader of his people. During this period Negroes in the vicinity were voting without restriction. Adams was approached by one Colonel Foster, and A. L. Brooks. Both sought the support of the Negro voters during their campaign. Adams pledged to them his support with the understanding that if elected they would use their influence to help establish a normal school for Negroes in Tuskegee. Both men were elected; Colonel Foster to the State Senate and Brooks to the House of Representatives. At the request of Senator Foster, Brooks introduced a bill asking for an appropriation of $2,000 to pay the salaries of teachers for a Normal School for Colored to be located at Tuskegee. No provision was made, however, for land, building, or equipment. These were to be furnished by persons who would benefit from the school. After the bill was passed, the next step was to secure a teacher. Adams was appointed to the committee that would make this selection. Requests were sent to Talladega and Selma, Ala., and to Atlanta, Ga., and Hampton, Va., for recommendations. Booker T. Washington, having been recommended by General Armstrong of Hampton, was agreed upon, and was destined to earn world renown in what he did in Tuskegee during the subsequent years.

When Washington arrived at Tuskegee, he went first to the office of George Campbell, the chairman of the committee that had made selection of him. Campbell sent Washington to Adams, who arranged for his lodging and the use of Butler Chapel's facilities for the beginning of his work. So it was that on July 4, 1881, the Tuskegee Normal School was established.

The membership of Butler Chapel and the community were proud of the contribution that it had been able to make toward the establishment of this institution. And during its formative years they assisted the school by sponsoring suppers, festivals and making contributions of money as far as they were able.

As the school grew, the demand for skilled labor was in evidence. Adams closed his business to become a part of the school where he taught his trades.

Among its many contributions, Butler Chapel entertained the first meeting of the Bishop's Council of the A.M.E. Zion Church ever to be held in the South. The pews that are now in use in the church were built at Tuskegee Institute, and installed for this meeting.

Butler Chapel has always enjoyed a creditable ministry. J. T. McMillan was the first pastor to serve for an entire quadrennium. He was followed by such noble clergymen as C. W. Turns, D. C. Pope, William A. Stewart and many others. Two of these former pastors are now bishops: D. C. Pope and WILLIAM A. STEWART.

During the year of 1939, William E. Carson was appointed to this charge. His ministry, lasting over a seventeen-year period, was a most constructive one. Many improvements were made to the church, and the membership grew to the point that Butler Chapel is now the first appointment in the Alabama Conference. Also during Carson's administration an Alabama marble marker was placed on the spot where Washington taught his first classes. The church has continued to make progress and with the cooperation of the membership has grown to even greater proportions. K. L. Buford succeeded W. E. Carson in 1956.

In honor of the work of Booker T. Washington, who from such an humble beginning gave to the world Tuskegee Institute, and Lewis Adams, whose love for his church, his community, and his people, helped to make Washington's work in Tuskegee possible, The Booker T. Washington-Lewis Adams Memorial Building has been erected.

Tuskegee United Methodist Church was organized in 1835 at Tuskegee. The town itself was named in honor of Creek Chief, Tuskegee. General Thomas Woodward, whose wife was a Methodist, built the first house at Tuskegee. The first court house, made of logs, was used in 1835 as a preaching place. Later a schoolhouse was used by the Methodists and others for religious worship. In 1841 the Methodists completed a house of worship and through the years the church has been kept up and supported by the white families living in Tuskegee. At present the congregation worships in a churchly building and the last reported membership was 343.

M. E. Lazenby, *Alabama and West Florida.* 1960.

DAVID H. BRADLEY
N. B. H.

TUTTLE, AUBREY STEPHEN (1874-1949), Canadian Methodist and United Church of Canada minister and educator, was born in Pugwash, Nova Scotia, Oct. 2, 1874. He was educated at MOUNT ALLISON UNIVERSITY. Received on trial in 1897, he served on circuits in Nova Scotia, and was ordained in 1902.

Coming to Alberta in 1905, he took up pastorates in Calgary (Wesley), Medicine Hat (Fifth Avenue), and Edmonton (McDougall and Grace). In 1919 he became principal of Alberta College South, which position he retained for twenty-four years.

Following Union, the college became St. Stephen's College, a theological college of the United Church. Tuttle was president of conference in 1918 and 1932, and from 1940 to 1942 was Moderator of The United Church of Canada. He retired in 1943 and was buried on October 20, 1949, in Victoria, British Columbia.

For his distinguished services Tuttle was given honorary degrees by Mount Allison University and the University of Alberta. Tuttle was a man of keen mind and strong character who greatly stimulated the intellectual and spiritual development of those with whom he worked.

G. H. Cornish, *Cyclopaedia of Methodism*, ii. 1903.
The United Church Observer, Nov. 15, 1949. J. M. FAWCETT

TUTTLE, LEE FOY (1905-   ), American minister, secretary of the WORLD METHODIST COUNCIL, and editor of *World Parish*, was born on Jan. 21, 1905, the son of John Mark and Nancy (Quarles) Tuttle. He was educated at DUKE UNIVERSITY where he received the A.B. in 1927, and did postgraduate work in the Divinity School there, 1931-32. He also studied at Yale where he received the B.D. degree in 1934, with postgraduate work in 1934-35. He was awarded the D.D. degree by Elon College in 1955. On Nov. 12, 1930, he married Lula Mae Simpson, and their children are Marcia Lee and Diane (Mrs. Glen B. Hardymon).

Dr. Tuttle was received on trial in the WESTERN NORTH CAROLINA CONFERENCE (MES) in 1929, and into full connection in 1931, receiving his ordination as ELDER in 1936. For a time he was youth director of the Western North Carolina Conference and then became the director of Christian Education at Wesley Memorial Church at HIGH POINT, 1929-32. He was the pastor of the Humphrey Street Congregational Church, New Haven, Conn., 1932-35, while he was a student at Yale. He was appointed to the old Brevard Street Church in CHARLOTTE, N. C. in 1935-37; the Forest Hill Church, Concord, 1937-39; Main Street Church, Thomasville, 1939-44; Central Church, ASHEVILLE, 1944-49; and First Church, Charlotte, 1949-56 (all in NORTH CAROLINA). He was superintendent of the WINSTON-SALEM District in 1956-61, at which time he was elected secretary of the World Methodist Council with headquarters at LAKE JUNALUSKA, N. C. The John Wesley Ecumenical Award of the Old ST. GEORGE'S CHURCH in PHILADELPHIA was awarded him in 1968.

In addition to editing the *World Parish*, he is chairman of the Ministerial Exchange Commission between British and American Churches. He was a delegate to the SOUTHEASTERN JURISDICTIONAL CONFERENCE, 1948, '52, '56, '60, and '64; a delegate to the GENERAL CONFERENCE of 1952, '56, '60, and '64; a member of the METHODIST COMMISSION ON OVERSEAS RELIEF, 1952-64; of the BOARD OF PUBLICATION of The Methodist Church, 1956-68; a member of the executive committee of the Methodist Commission on Ecumenical Consultation, 1960-64; and a trustee of Lake Junaluska Assembly since 1955. He was a delegate to the Tenth WORLD METHODIST CONFERENCE, 1961; a delegate to the Third and Fourth Assemblies of the WORLD COUNCIL OF CHURCHES, 1961 and 1968; and an official observer of the Second Vatican Council, 1963-64. He has also been a managing director of the Epworth (England) Old Rectory since 1962; a trustee of BREVARD COLLEGE since 1942, of the Children's Home, Winston-Salem, N. C., since 1945, and is on the executive committee of the COMMISSION ON ARCHIVES AND HISTORY. In connection with his responsibility as general secretary of the World Methodist Council, he has become well known to the Methodism of various lands and Methodist leadership over the world. He represents the World Methodist Council in the general supervision of editorial and promotional work for the *Encyclopedia of World Methodism*.

Who's Who in America, Vol. 34.
Who's Who in The Methodist Church, 1966.   N. B. H.

TWENTIETH CENTURY FUND. A scheme inaugurated at the British Wesleyan CONFERENCE of 1898 to raise "one million guineas from one million Methodists" by the beginning of the new century. It was to be allocated as follows: 300,000 pounds for general building developments, 250,000 pounds for building Westminster central buildings, 200,000 pounds for education, 100,000 pounds for home missions, 100,000 for overseas missions, and 50,000 pounds for the National Children's Home. It was completed by 1902, and the historic roll of a million signatures is deposited at the Westminster Central Hall.

E. BENSON PERKINS

TYERMAN, LUKE (1820-1889), British Wesleyan Methodist, was a notable Methodist historian. He was born on Feb. 26, 1820, at Osmotherley, near Thirsk, Yorkshire, and entered the Wesleyan Ministry in 1844. A Methodist preacher of the old school, he was particularly intense in his attacks on popery. Ill health forced him to superannuate in 1864, and he devoted the rest of his life to his scholarship.

Although much had been written about eighteenth-century Methodism before his time, Tyerman was the first historian to produce serious, scholarly biographies of JOHN WESLEY, GEORGE WHITEFIELD, and JOHN FLETCHER (the "designated successor"). Tyerman's life of John Wesley has only been superseded in recent years, and there is still no other important study of Fletcher. He might properly be called the father of modern historical studies. His publications included: *Life and Times of the Rev. Samuel Wesley*, 1866; *Life and Times of the Rev. John Wesley*, 1871; *The Oxford Methodists*, 1873; *Life of the Rev. George Whitefield*, 1876-77; *Wesley's Designated Successor*, 1882. He died on March 30, 1889.

H. MORLEY RATTENBURY

TYLER, JAMES (1877-1952), prominent Methodist layman of AUCKLAND, New Zealand, was connected as a young man with the Helping Hand Mission. Later he joined Pitt Street Church and, after serving for some years as Sunday school superintendent, he transferred to the Mount Eden Church where he occupied a similar position. Altogether he served fifty years as a Sunday school superintendent.

As a young man he joined the engineering staff of the Auckland City Council and supervised the construction of such major works as Grafton Bridge and the Waitakere Dam. He rose to the position of city engineer, where he served fifteen years.

During retirement he was a most valued member of many official boards, and gave special service to the Overseas Mission Department. He was elected vice-president of Conference in 1946.

L. R. M. GILMORE

TYLER, TEXAS, U.S.A. **Marvin Church** is the historic downtown church and a famous landmark of the city. The church was first organized in 1845 as First Methodist and located on a lot not far from the present site.

The cornerstone of the present building was laid in 1890 and inscribed "M.E. Church South, Erected 1890," indicating the church fathers were contemplating a new name for the church. In 1891 the church was named Marvin Methodist Church in honor of Bishop ENOCH MARVIN, then presiding bishop over the EAST TEXAS CONFERENCE. Marvin Church was completed and first occupied in early 1892. It was then known as the cathedral church west of the Mississippi and is still an imposing structure with its steeples, tall roof lines and spires. The handsome colored glass picture windows are the originals depicting many biblical scenes, characters and Christian symbols.

In June 1898 the church was sold to satisfy a mortgage. Mrs. John Douglas bought the property and rented it to the congregation for twelve months and it was then bought back by the congregation in 1899. The sanctuary was remodeled in 1950, making it more useful for present day worship; but none of the original structural lines were changed. The auditorium now seats 986 persons comfortably. A beautiful chapel and educational building were added at this time. Also several additional city lots were purchased and a youth center was built to add to facilities and activities of the church. In 1970 Marvin Church had a membership of 2,530 persons.

GEORGE W. JONES

TYREE, EVANS (1854-1921), American bishop of the A.M.E. CHURCH, was born in DeKalb County, Tenn., on Aug. 19, 1854, as a slave. He received the A.B. degree from Centenary Tennessee College and the M.D. degree from MEHARRY MEDICAL COLLEGE. He was converted in 1866, licensed to preach in 1869 and admitted to the Tennessee Annual Conference in 1872. He was ordained a DEACON in 1875 and an ELDER in 1876. He held all of his pastorates in TENNESSEE. He was elected bishop in 1900 from the pastorate of St. John's, NASHVILLE. He served in the southwestern part of the United States. Bishop Tyree was one of three A.M.E. bishops holding medical degrees in his generation.

C. F. Price, *Who's Who in American Methodism.* 1916.
R. R. Wright, *The Bishops.* 1963.   GRANT S. SHOCKLEY

U BA OHN (1918-   ), president of the Conference of the Methodist Church in Upper BURMA, was born July 6, 1918, in Magyo village, Chaungu Township, Monywa District of Upper Burma. His father was a converted Muslim and after a time became head of a Methodist elementary school.

U Ba Ohn's early years were spent in this school at the Ma-u-ale-ywa village in the Pakokku District. At the age of ten he went into the Wesley Anglo-Vernacular High School at Monywa as a hostel student. His father died when he was fourteen years old, and he went into the employment of the Burma Oil Company to support his widowed mother and family. He married at the age of twenty while in the employ of the Burma Oil Company, but later became interested in the studies of the Bible and became a local preacher. During the second World War, he and his wife moved to his wife's village to take refuge and there under the Japanese occupation endeavored to hold together the scattered groups of Christians and also hold services of worship. After the war, on May 30, 1947, he resigned from the Burma Oil Company and went into the Theological Training Institution of the Methodist Church in Mandalay. He was accepted in 1950 as a probationary minister and sent to Pakokku. He later went into full connection and was ordained in January, 1954. In 1964 he became chairman of the Mandalay District. When the Methodist Church in Upper Burma became an autonomous body, he was elected as the first president of the Methodist Conference. His term as president ended in November, 1970, but he continues at work in Upper Burma.

N. B. H.

UDGIR, a town in the Osmanabad Civil District in Maharashtra, INDIA, is the headquarters of an ecclesiastical district of the same name in the BOMBAY ANNUAL CONFERENCE. Methodist work in and around the town was started in 1932 as a home missionary project by the churches of the Bombay Conference. The area was selected because of its proximity to the Bidar District of the SOUTH INDIA CONFERENCE, in which a strong movement had produced many converts and a vigorous upsurge of Christian worship and witness. The group that was turning to Christ was known as Madigas, and their language was Kanarese. But their relatives in Osmanabad District were called Mahars, and their language was Marathi. They were essentially the same people, with a common origin, common social institutions, and a depressed position in the social system and economy of their villages.

In 1942 Udgir was made a district headquarters. The total Methodist community was 301, but there were many seekers. The district now reports more than 5,000 Methodists, including baptized children. The revival movement conquered the barriers of language.

Education and healing are emphasized among these people. The literacy rate among Christians was only two percent in 1942. In 1966 it was thirty-one percent, despite the fact that almost all converts are illiterate until they make contact with the church. A coeducational boarding school, with the Hindi name Prakashalaya (Place of Light), has produced twenty-one teachers, nine pastors, two doctors, eight nurses, two laboratory technicians, a pharmacist, a secretary, a paramedical organizer of leprosy treatment, eleven machinists, five motor mechanics, and many who are profitably employed in other useful work. More slowly, a medical service is being developed. Five centers for medical service have been opened. A survey has revealed a larger incidence of leprosy than had been estimated, as high as five percent in some villages.

A self-help program is digging new wells, improving housing, and introducing smokeless chimneys, ventilation, and sanitation, and is constructing roads.

J. WASKOM PICKETT

UMBREIT, SAMUEL J. (1871-1945), American Evangelical missionary, bishop, editor, was born Feb. 22, 1871 in Manchester, Wis. He studied at NORTH CENTRAL COLLEGE where he received the Ph.B. and Ph.M. degrees. He was licensed to preach in the Illinois Conference of the EVANGELICAL ASSOCIATION in 1895, and ordained ELDER in 1905. He served several pastorates in WISCONSIN before being appointed missionary to JAPAN in 1905. He was district superintendent in the Japanese Conference for fifteen years and Mission Superintendent for thirteen. In the later office he also served as Superintendent for three years of the newly established CHINA Mission.

In 1926 the GENERAL CONFERENCE elected him bishop with residence in Europe. He served eight years at this post until the European bishopric was discontinued. The GENERAL CONFERENCE then elected him editor of the German periodical, *Der Christliche Botschafter,* the oldest publication in the denomination and the oldest German religious weekly paper in the United States. Although he retired in 1942, he continued to edit this paper by special arrangement until his death in Harrisburg, Pa., Jan. 27, 1945.

While serving in Japan, Umbreit was a member for several years of the faculty of the Aoyama Gakuin Theological Seminary, a Methodist institution. EVANGELICAL SEMINARY conferred upon him the D.D. degree. In addition to editorial duties Umbreit wrote several books. Two of these in Japanese were *From Darkness to Light* and *Three Conversions.* One book was written in German, *Twenty Years in Japan.*

June 29, 1899, he married Miss Amanda Bauernfeind, sister of the well-known Evangelical missionary, Dr. SUSAN BAUERNFEIND. Following her death in 1937 he married Mrs. Anna M. Kolb. He was acquainted with outstanding religious leaders of the Orient and Europe and had come to possess a global-minded spirit that lifted him above anything partisan and sectarian.

The Evangelical Crusader, Feb. 10, 1945.
The Evangelical-Messenger, Feb. 10, 1945.
R. M. Veh, *Evangelical Bishops*. 1939.   JOHN H. NESS, JR.

UMPQUA ACADEMY, Wilbur, Oregon, was established in 1854. It was sometimes referred to as Wilbur Academy. At the organizing session of the OREGON CONFERENCE of 1853, Bishop E. R. AMES appointed JAMES H. WILBUR to the Umpqua Mission, as superintendent of the work in southern OREGON. He established his headquarters by taking a land claim, building a residence, and erecting a log schoolhouse.

In 1854 J. H. B. Royal was appointed the first principal. About that time the school moved to a new and more imposing building, high above the surrounding valley where it could be seen for several miles. Incorporation was in 1857, and for many years this was the only school of its grade between SACRAMENTO, Calif., and SALEM, Ore.

The building burned in 1873. The trustees decided to locate at a new site a half mile from the center of the village, and there a commodious building was erected. In 1881 the enrollment was 130. There was no further report to the conference until 1884. Only two terms had been taught during that year, and there was no principal. In 1887, the last year in which reports were made, the institution was free of debt, but the enrollment was only ninety-nine. The work of the academy was being superseded by the public schools. It was voted June 30, 1888, to lease the premises to the public school district for ten years for $500.

On Oct. 30, 1900, a resolution was adopted to sell to the district for $400. The building no longer remains.

JOHN O. GROSS

UNGARETTI, ADOLFO MELCHIOR (1885-1943), Brazilian preacher, was born in Cachoeira do Sul, state of Rio Grande do Sul (then a province), on Jan. 6, 1885. He was the son of Italian parents who had emigrated to BRAZIL when quite young. His name appears first in Methodist annals in 1904, when he was licensed to exhort and named assistant to Mateo Donatt, for work among Italian colonists in Rio Grande do Sul.

In 1906 he entered INSTITUTO GRANBERY as a ministerial candidate. After returning to his native state in 1910, he taught briefly at a school in Uruguaiana, founded by Aleixo Vurlod, an evangelical Frenchman. This school was soon acquired by the Methodist church and renamed Colegio União, now INSTITUTO UNIÃO. There Ungaretti met and in 1912 married Luiza Vurlod, daughter of the school's founder; and they had seven children, of whom Erasmo, the youngest and only son, became a distinguished Methodist minister. The eldest daughter married JOSÉ PEDRO PINHEIRO, a Methodist preacher who in 1955 was elected bishop of the church. The other daughters became active in Christian work.

Ungaretti was admitted on trial in 1913; received his first appointment that year to Cruz Alta; and in 1915 was ordained ELDER. While pastor in Cruz Alta, he visited many adjacent areas, founding churches in Palmeira das

Missões, São Gabriel (on the border with URUGUAY), and Caxias do Sul—a region populated by Italian colonists, where he suffered severe persecution at the hands of the fanatics and Roman Catholic clergy. He also served in important city charges—Alegrete, Uruguaiana, the Institutional Church in PORTO ALEGRE, and in SANTA MARIA.

While pastor in Santa Maria, he founded in 1939 the Lar Metodista (Methodist Home) for orphans and abandoned children. In this project his wife, Dona Luiza, gave great assistance. He died in 1943, while pastor of Gloria Church in Porto Alegre, at the age of fifty-nine; thirty years of these he had given to the Master's cause in South Brazil.

JOSÉ P. PINHEIRO

UNIFICATION OF AMERICAN METHODISM. The Protestant Reformation's emphasis on the priesthood of all believers and the right of the individual to think for himself has resulted in a process of division and subdivision in Protestant history. Both in England and in North America the Methodist people followed this usual Protestant pattern. Within fifty years after the death of JOHN WESLEY there were several Methodist churches in the British Isles. These separate churches sent organizers to areas of the British Empire, and in the colonies in time were to be found the same churches as in the home land. The WESLEYAN METHODIST CHURCH, and the PRIMITIVE METHODIST CHURCH, planted in the United States by their mother churches in Great Britain, are still in existence in the United States, in spite of union movements on both sides of the Atlantic.

Several divisions took place in the M.E. Church previous to the great one of 1844. These are described in the article on the M.E. Church. A different issue presented itself in 1844. Then the SLAVERY issue was agitating the whole country. When the GENERAL CONFERENCE of the M.E. Church met, it had before it two cases involving this issue. Francis A. Harding of the BALTIMORE CONFERENCE had been suspended without trial, by a vote of his Conference, for holding slaves. He had married a young woman who owned five slaves, and the laws of MARYLAND forbade the freeing of these or any slaves. He appealed his case to the General Conference, and that body voted two to one to sustain the Baltimore Conference in its suspension of Harding.

The other case attracted far more attention because it involved a bishop. Bishop JAMES O. ANDREW of GEORGIA had been willed a slave whom he was to send to LIBERIA when she became of age. She refused to go and the laws of Georgia did not permit the freeing of slaves. Also Bishop Andrew had married a woman who owned slaves. He followed every legal way to make these slaves solely his wife's, and not his own property. This was to no avail, and since a Methodist bishop was a slave holder, what was to be done? Bishop Andrew was popular throughout the Church, admittedly a gentle, good, kind man. The General Conference after long and heated debate voted by a vote of two to one that Bishop Andrew should "desist" from the exercise of his office. The debate was acrimonious, and finally a committee was appointed which recommended a PLAN OF SEPARATION. This Plan was adopted, and the M.E. Church, South, subsequently organized.

It was decided a few years later that both bodies (the M.E. and M.E. South) came from the same Church and that each was as much entitled as the other to claim that it was a continuation of the mother church. Since the United States was soon involved in war between the North and the South, it seems to have been a wise decision that was made by the General Conference of 1844. The M.E. Church could better serve the North, and the M.E. Church, South, the South in the years of strife. It was to be almost 100 years before the two main currents of American Methodism came together again under a PLAN OF UNION adopted by a constitutional vote in both Churches and their UNITING CONFERENCE convened in KANSAS CITY in 1939.

The Southern delegates at the General Conference of 1844 called a Convention in LOUISVILLE, May 1, 1845, and that Convention set the first General Conference for May 1, 1846 at PETERSBURG, Va. This was the beginning of the M.E. Church, South. As the Civil War came, there was a growing tendency in the North to refer to the Plan of Separation as a document of secession, and the M.E. Church, South, as a secession church. From the day of the setting up of the Southern Church, there were very decided differences between the two sections in their understanding of the authority of the General Conference.

In 1848, four years after the separation, a representative of the M.E. Church, South, the distinguished LOVICK PIERCE of Georgia, went to the General Conference of the M.E. Church at PITTSBURGH as a fraternal messenger, but that Conference refused to receive him. The southern General Conference of 1850 therefore passed a resolution that no fraternal gesture would be made again from their side until the M.E. Church should take the initiative in asking for one. That initiative was taken in 1869.

The bishops of the M.E. Church, South, were in session in ST. LOUIS during May of 1869 when Bishops E. S. JANES and MATTHEW SIMPSON appeared before them with a communication from the bishops of the M.E. Church. The message contained these sentences: "It is fitting that the Methodist Church which began with disunion should not be the last to achieve the reunion which the providence of God seems to render inevitable at no distant date." The bishops, who came as messengers of good will, had been instructed to discuss with their Southern brethren, "propriety, practicality and methods of reunion."

The bishops of the M.E. Church, South, in their reply, expressed their deep satisfaction in receiving the overture, but called attention to some of the controversies and disputes over boundaries that had arisen in preceding years. The General Conference of the M.E. Church in 1868 had authorized the appointment of a Commission to negotiate for union with other Methodist bodies. The year 1872 saw the renewal—or beginning—of the exchange of fraternal messages, and to the General Conference of the Southern Church in Louisville in 1874 came three fraternal messengers from the M.E. Church. Their addresses stirred enthusiasm and warmed hearts. Fraternal delegates were thereupon sent from the South to the Northern General Conference of 1876. The most important action of that General Conference was the appointment of a Commission of Five to meet with a similar commission, authorized by the previous session of the Southern Conference in 1874. The two Commissions were authorized to do what they could to remove obstacles to union. These two Commissions met in Cape May, N. J., Aug. 17-23, 1876. A tablet unveiled at Cape May within

quite recent years serves to emphasize for today's Methodists the importance of the CAPE MAY COMMISSION.

At the Cape May meeting the first business was the passing of this resolution: "Each of said churches is a legitimate branch of Episcopal Methodism in the United States, having a common origin in the Methodist Episcopal Church organized in 1784." The Commission then considered many conflicting claims and made certain adjustments. Before adjournment it adopted rules for the settlement of claims in the future.

Later action by the two General Conferences made final the conclusion in the resolution adopted by the Cape May meeting, and there was removed the stigma of secession from the M.E. Church, South.

In 1888 the General Conference of the M.E. Church, South passed a historic motion that a Commission on Federation of Methodism be appointed, composed of three bishops, three other ministers and three laymen, to act with a like Commission of the M.E. Church, with a "view to abating hurtful competitions, and the waste of men and money in home and foreign fields." The Joint Commission met in WASHINGTON, D.C., Jan. 7-8, 1898. This meeting decided on the preparation of "a common catechism, a common hymn-book, and a common order of worship." Both General Conferences approved. Joint Commissions were appointed.

The mission work in BRAZIL and CUBA was allocated to the Southern Church, and that in PUERTO RICO and the PHILIPPINES to the Northern Church. A common publishing house was established in CHINA.

In 1907 the two Churches and the Methodist Church of CANADA united in the setting up of the Methodist Church of JAPAN. The Joint Commission in its meeting at BALTIMORE, April 18, 1906 decided to organize the Federal Council of Methodism. Both General Conferences approved this decision. One of the phrases which disturbed the Church, South, was "reunion of the churches." Reunion seemed to imply the coming back, or return to a former status. Union could come only in the organization of a new governmental structure.

In 1908 the General Conference of the M.E. Church authorized the appointment of a fraternal deputation to visit the General Conference of the METHODIST PROTESTANT CHURCH, inviting consultations with them on union. The M.P. General Conference responded cordially but proposed that the M.E. Church, South be invited to the discussions. THOMAS H. LEWIS, President of the M.P. General Conference, visited the Southern Methodist General Conference in 1910, and created great enthusiasm for union. The Commission of the M.E. Church then issued a statement "tendering a brotherly invitation to the Commissions of the other two churches to consider with us at this time the desirability and practicability of organic union." That action really started the negotiations that never ceased until union was consummated.

Each Commission representing one of the three Methodist Churches decided on a joint Committee of Nine, three from each Commission, to prepare a suggested plan for discussion. This Committee met in Cincinnati, Jan. 18-20, 1911. Each member of the Committee set forth in a paper or address his conclusions regarding plans for a united Church. The Committee of Nine suggested two names for this church—the "Methodist Episcopal Church in America," or the "Methodist Church in America." This and other proposals were considered by the Joint Commission. This approved the report of the

Committee of Nine with two important additions: "We suggest that the colored membership of the Methodist Episcopal Church, the Methodist Protestant Church, and such organizations of colored Methodists as may enter into agreement with them, may be constituted and recognized as one of the Quadrennial or Jurisdictional Conferences of the proposed organization." The other item was this: "We suggest that the Quadrennial Conferences shall be composed of an equal number of ministerial and lay delegates to be chosen by the Annual Conferences within their several jurisdictions according to some equitable plan to be provided for."

The General Conferences of the M.E. and the M.P. Churches met in May 1912. The General Conference of the M.E. Church declared: "We heartily approve the action of our Commission on Federation in proposing the question of organic union to the Commissions in joint session in Baltimore, believing that the membership of the Methodist Episcopal Church would welcome a corporate reunion of the Methodisms of America." However the General Conference did not press for the creation of a definite plan, probably because there was a feeling that the M.E. Church, South, was not yet ready to proceed.

The General Conference of the M.E. Church, South, met in OKLAHOMA CITY in May 1914. After an address by Bishop E. E. Hoss on "Unification," the General Conference enthusiastically and unanimously approved a move to continue negotiations for union by reorganization. It continued to place members on the Federal Council of Methodism, and authorized them, in case the General Conference of the M.E. Church in 1916 should appoint a Commission on Unification, to increase their number to twenty-five and to act as a Commission on Unification. This was done.

One of the most important efforts to get the mind of the two Churches was the presentation of thirty-four papers by Methodist leaders from over the country at a "Working Conference on the Union of American Methodism," held in Evanston, Ill., Feb. 15-17, 1916. This was under the auspices of the John Richard Lindgren Foundation for the promotion of International Peace and Christian Unity.

The General Conference of the M.E. Church in 1916, with Bishop EARL CRANSTON of the M.E. Church and Bishop E. R. HENDRIX of the M.E. Church, South, clasping hands, declared itself in favor of unification of the two churches in accordance with a "general plan of reorganization"—the idea of union by reunion was laid aside.

The Joint Commission on Unification met Dec. 29, 1916 to Jan. 2, 1917 in Baltimore. It was a historic place for such a meeting, and the ablest leaders of Methodism were there. Visits to the graves of early Methodist leaders, services in the church which was the successor of LOVELY LANE CHAPEL, and a traditional WATCH NIGHT Service created an atmosphere never to be forgotten. After fruitful days of discussion the Joint Commission adjourned to meet June 27, 1917 in Traverse City, Mich.

The Traverse City meeting concerned itself with discussions of the nature and responsibility of Conferences. These questions were faced: (1) What powers shall the General Conference have? (2) What powers shall be assigned to the Jurisdictional Conferences? 3) How can there be a general superintendency which may be jurisdictionally elected? A broad substantial basis of agreement was reached, though no one thought of the agreement as setting forth final conclusions. The Joint Commission

adjourned July 3 to meet Jan. 28, 1918 in Savannah, Ga. The Savannah meeting lasted two weeks—the longest ever held.

A JUDICIAL COUNCIL—new in Methodism—was approved as the body to pass finally on constitutional and legal matters. The status of the Negro membership in the United Church was discussed under these headings: (1) Should the Negro membership be given an Associate Regional Conference such as was proposed for foreign countries? (2) Should it be given an Associate General Conference of its own, with some representation in the larger General Conference? (3) Should the Negro membership be given a full Regional or Jurisdictional Conference such as was proposed for the several sections of the white membership? Eight days were given to a discussion of those plans. Then the Joint Commission adjourned to meet in ST. LOUIS, June 10, 1918. After four great meetings and twenty-eight days of discussion a plan was worked out. It was not entirely acceptable, but a way to union had been found. The Joint Commission recommended to the General Conferences that their Commissions be continued.

The General Conference of the M.E. Church, South, met in Atlanta in May 1918, expressed its appreciation of the work of its Commission and voted to continue the Commission.

The Joint Commission met in Cleveland, Ohio, July 7-10, 1919. The meeting concerned itself with the status of Negro membership in the reorganized church. The Northern members proposed "that the colored membership of the Church shall be constituted and recognized as a Quadrennial or Regional Conference, with proportionate representation in the General Conference." A Committee was appointed to work out a plan for union. The Committee met in Richmond, Va., Nov. 7, 1919. The plan worked out by the Committee was presented to the Joint Commission at a meeting in Louisville, Ky., Jan. 15, 1920. On insistence of the Southern group, the Negro membership was set up as a Regional Conference, but this proposal proved a divisive influence in the Northern Church. Largely for that reason the Plan was rejected at the General Conference of the M.E. Church at DES MOINES in 1920.

It must be said that many in the Southern Church were also dissatisfied with the Plan. The Northern General Conference proposed a joint Convention with 200 to 400 members from each Church. What would the Southern General Conference do? Many Southerners who were opposed to union said, "We had a plan. The Northern General Conference turned it down. Let us forget the whole thing." The Committee dealing with unification had sixty percent for union and forty percent against union, and a Committee of Nine was appointed to recommend the action to be taken by the larger Committee and the General Conference. IVAN LEE HOLT was Chairman of that Committee of Nine, and there were meetings each night for a week. The real turning point in the unification discussion in the South came when the Chairman of the Committee of Nine persuaded Judge John Candler of Atlanta, and the three other antiunificationists on the Committee, to vote for a proposal to recommend the creation of a new Commission on Unification. That recommendation was approved and the General Conference named a new Commission. This was in 1922. It voted also that the bishops be empowered to call a special session of the Southern General Conference, in case a plan should be worked out, and the General Conference of the M.E. Church in 1924 should approve that plan.

The General Conference of the M.E. Church met in Springfield, Mass., in May 1924, and voted 802 to 13 for the Plan of Union. A majority of the bishops in the Southern Church (nine to five) thereupon called a special session of the General Conference of the M.E. Church, South, to meet in Chattanooga July 2, 1924.

At Chattanooga the minority group of five bishops presented to the General Conference a protest against the legality of the call for a special session. In conformity with their argument, a resolution was introduced to call a session of the General Conference in 1925 to consider the Plan of Union. This in effect became a minority report and was voted down.

Then the Plan approved by the Northern General Conference was overwhelmingly approved. Since this was a constitutional change it had to go to the Annual Conferences for their approval. A church-wide debate and widespread agitation resulted, and the Plan did not receive the constitutional majority required in the Annual Conferences—especially those of the deep South.

Years of acrimonious dissension then ensued in the South. When the General Conference of the Southern Church met in Memphis in 1926, many of the delegates had been elected on the strength of their attitudes, pro or con, on unfication. Feeling ran high. While the unificationists were in majority, it seemed best at the time to recommend no new Commission. Instead a Committee was appointed to write and publish the history of the unification movement. FRANKLIN N. PARKER, of EMORY UNIVERSITY, was made Chairman, and the report was written by Ivan Lee Holt and V. C. Curtis, of Mississippi. It contained a full history of proceedings to date and was published.

When the General Conference of the M.E. Church, South, met in Dallas in 1930, a resolution was adopted creating a Committee of Fifteen on Interdenominational Relations. Similar action had been taken by the General Conference of the M.E. Church and by the General Conference of the M.P. Church in 1928. On July 1, 1930 the Committees of the M.E. Church and the M.P. Church held a joint meeting, but they did not care to go too far with discussions until the Southern Church could enter the meetings. When the General Conference of the Southern Church met in 1934 it authorized the appointment of a Commission on Unification to negotiate with Commissions of the other two Churches appointed by their respective General Conferences in 1932. In 1935 the Joint Commission held meetings—at Louisville in March, and at Evanston in August. A Plan of Union was adopted and recommended to the General Conferences. The Plan of 1920 had never been adopted by the Joint Commission, but simply recommended to the General Conferences for their consideration.

The General Conferences of the M.E. Church and the M.P. Church gave overwhelming approval to the Plan, and their Annual Conferences in voting gave the constitutional majorities. Twenty-five of the thirty-eight Annual Conferences of the M.E. Church, South, asked the bishops of the church to submit the Plan to the Annual Conferences in 1937. This was done, and the vote in the Annual Conferences was 7650 for and 1247 against the adoption of the Plan. So the Plan had the constitutional majorities in the Annual Conferences before the General

Conference met in Birmingham in 1938. There the Plan was finally approved though its constitutionality was challenged. The Judicial Council of the M.E. Church, South, just established, in one of the great documents in American Methodist history, held the Plan to be constitutional and constitutionally adopted. All was now in readiness for the Uniting Conference.

This was held under the direction of the Plan of Union itself in the heart of the nation, at Kansas City, in May 1939. Committees had been set up before to harmonize the respective disciplines, and to work out an organization for the General Conference and the Boards of the United Church.

The Chairmen of their Commissions in the closing months had been Bishop EDWIN HOLT HUGHES for the M.E. Church; Bishop JOHN W. MOORE for the M.E. Church, South; and Dr. JAMES H. STRAUGHN of the M.P. Church. They were the three presiding officers. Bishop John M. Moore had a genius for working out details, and of his work Bishop Hughes said, "He is the real author of the Plan."

At the Uniting Conference the Holy Communion was celebrated at the Cathedral of the Protestant Episcopal Church, as the conference began. The final and climactic act of this Uniting Conference was the adoption of the Declaration of Union. It brought into being The Methodist Church. Fourteen thousand people were crowded into Convention Hall for the final service. Bishop John M. Moore presided. OSCAR T. OLSON led the worship service, prepared by him and by Bishop Holt. Bishop Holt announced the first hymn, "The Church's One Foundation," Bishop E. G. RICHARDSON gave the invocation and the collect, Bishop ROBERT E. JONES announced the hymn, "O For a Thousand Tongues to Sing," Bishop ARTHUR J. MOORE led in prayer, and Bishop FREDERICK D. LEETE led in the Canticle of the Church. Bishop PAUL B. KERN read the Scripture lesson, the Seventeenth Chapter of John, and Bishop JOHN C. BROOMFIELD, just elected bishop by the M.P. delegates, announced the litany hymn, "Jesus With Thy Church Abide." Bishop EDGAR BLAKE gave the profoundly impressive commemoration of the faithful.

Many men deserve credit through the years for their work looking toward this Methodist Union, but Bishop Blake chose these six for special recognition: ALBERT NORMAN WARD and THOMAS HAMILTON LEWIS of the M.P. Church; EUGENE RUSSELL HENDRIX and EDWIN D. MOUZON of the M.E. Church, South; EARL CRANSTON and WILLIAM F. McDOWELL of the M.E. Church. Bishop Edwin H. Hughes made an impassioned and eloquent address with the moving refrain, "The Methodists are One People."

The Declaration of Union was thereupon read by Bishop John M. Moore, the 900 delegates standing and repeating after each of the five declarations, "We do so declare." Bishop A. FRANK SMITH led a liturgical prayer of thanksgiving, the formal vote was taken and Bishop Moore declared, "The Methodist Church now is! Long live The Methodist Church!" It was 8:59 P.M., May 10, 1939. The benediction was pronounced by Bishop JOHN L. NUELSEN, the senior bishop of the M.E. Church.

No one who was fortunate enough to be present can ever forget the inspiration of that hour. It will go down in Methodist history with the Uniting Services of the Methodist Churches of Great Britain at City Road Chapel and Albert Hall in 1932. The Methodist Church from these services went forth in majesty and power.

J. M. Moore, *Long Road to Union.* 1943.   IVAN LEE HOLT

UNION, BRITISH METHODIST. The first sixty years after the death of JOHN WESLEY in 1791 were marked by divisions which resulted in there being five main branches of British Methodism during the second half of the nineteenth century. These were Wesleyan Methodism, the unbroken stream from the days of Wesley; METHODIST NEW CONNEXION, 1797, in opposition to Conference authority; PRIMITIVE METHODISM, 1812, organized from aggressive revivalism; BIBLE CHRISTIAN, 1819, from evangelism in the West Country; and the UNITED METHODIST FREE CHURCHES, formed from the incorporation in 1857 of the LEEDS PROTESTANT METHODISTS, started in 1827, the WESLEYAN METHODIST ASSOCIATION, started in 1837 (both opposed to Conference authority), and the WESLEYAN REFORM CHURCHES, which dated from 1849, a large secession due to public criticism of alleged bureaucracy.

The idea of a fuller union of British Methodism gained ground, encouraged by the ECUMENICAL METHODIST CONFERENCES, the first of which was held in Wesley's Chapel, LONDON, in 1881. The union of the three smaller branches, the Methodist New Connexion, the Bible Christian Methodists and the United Methodist Free Churches, in 1907 created the UNITED METHODIST CHURCH.

At the invitation of the Wesleyan Methodist CONFERENCE in 1918, the remaining two conferences (Primitive and United Methodists) joined in appointing representatives to a large committee to work out a scheme of union. During ten years of committee work the respective conferences discussed the broad policy of union. The final votes of the different conferences approving of union were taken in 1927 and 1928.

The first necessary step was the securing of an act of Parliament, under the powers of which a united body could take over the propertied trusts and funds of the three separate churches. The Methodist Church Union Act of 1929 was an enabling act. It did not itself secure union, but gave power to a uniting conference, if and when it so determined, to bring together the three churches into a unity by creating a new church to be named The Methodist Church.

The Uniting Conference was held in the Albert Hall, London, on Sept. 20, 1932. The three churches were represented by their respective conferences. The numbers approximated to their membership relationships in the ratio of: Wesleyan, 10; Primitive 4; United, 3; the total slightly exceeding 1,600. Methodist and other visitors crowded the Albert Hall to its full capacity of 12,000. When constituted, the Uniting Conference elected JOHN SCOTT LIDGETT the first president and ROBERT W. PERKS the first vice-president. The voting for union was unanimous, first by the separate votes of each conference and the Wesleyan LEGAL HUNDRED, and then by a solemn standing vote of the Uniting Conference as a whole. The resolution thus passed under the act of Parliament created one united church "under the name of 'The Methodist Church'." The Deed of Union which had been prepared, setting up the constitution, forms of government, doctrinal standards, and basis of membership of the united church was then adopted. The MODEL DEED for the trust property was likewise presented and adopted.

After the completion of the formal and legal acts and the signing of the related documents, a message from King George V was presented by the Duke of York, who also spoke for himself. Messages were presented from all the Protestant churches, including personal words from the two archbishops of the Church of England, and from the prime minister and other political leaders.

In accordance with the Constitution the united Conference assembled in the Central Hall, Westminster, to confirm the stationing of the ministers, appoint the Chairmen of Districts and departmental and other committees, and to transact all other necessary business for the first year of The Methodist Church.

[Editor's Note: The historical study of the subject was shifted to a new level by the publication of *The Age of Disunity,* by John Kent (1965) and *Methodism Divided,* by Robert Currie (1968). Both books were based on sociological analysis rather than on conflicts of personalities, and endeavor to set Methodist union in a wider historical perspective. They should be consulted.]   E. BENSON PERKINS

UNION AMERICAN METHODIST EPISCOPAL CHURCH was formed in 1850 by members of the Union Church of Africans who withdrew to form a church with an episcopal polity. Their doctrine is Wesleyan, although they require their ministers to give assent to the APOSTLES CREED only as a doctrinal standard. The chief difference in polity from the rest of Methodism is that a general conference is not called except to deal with proposed changes in polity or name.

There are two schools: the Local Preachers' Training School in Camden, N. J., and the Union College and Seminary, Philadelphia. Foreign work is carried on in CANADA.

The last year for which statistics are available was 1957, when the church reported 27,560 members and 256 churches.

Census of Religious Bodies, 1936.
Yearbook of American Churches, 1971. J. GORDON MELTON

UNION CATALOG OF METHODIST HISTORICAL MATERIALS is a compilation of Methodist historical materials prepared by librarians in Methodist theological seminaries, the UPPER ROOM library, and the library of the METHODIST PUBLISHING HOUSE in cooperation with the American Association of Methodist HISTORICAL SOCIETIES. Preparation of this catalog consisted of microfilming thousands of library shelf list cards and the filing of these for reference and publication. The preliminary edition, published in 1967, is to be kept up-to-date in its card file. A second edition, under the direction of Kenneth Rowe of DREW UNIVERSITY, is planned for late 1972. Information concerning the publication, or materials located in its file, is available from the COMMISSION ON ARCHIVES AND HISTORY, Lake Junaluska, N. C., and from Rose Memorial Library, Drew University, Madison, N.J.

ELIZABETH HUGHEY

UNION COLLEGE, Barbourville, Kentucky, was founded by citizens of Barbourville in 1879. The name was chosen to indicate its spirit and purpose—a school brought into being by the united efforts of local citizens, to be open to all, without regard to religious creed or political affiliation. In 1886 the property was purchased by the Board of Education of the KENTUCKY CONFERENCE of the M.E. Church. Its first president under Methodist auspices was DANIEL STEVENSON, a distinguished educational leader of the Kentucky Conference. While the school was operated as a college from the beginning, it did for many years include elementary and secondary work. Since 1930 its academic offerings have been limited to those of a senior college. In 1932 it became the first fully accredited Methodist college in Kentucky.

After unification in 1939 it was related to both the Kentucky and LOUISVILLE Conferences of The Methodist Church. A fully accredited graduate program in teacher education was instituted in 1960. Degrees offered are the B.A., B.S., B.M. (Music), M.A. in Education. The governing board has twenty-seven trustees, eighteen elected by the Kentucky and Louisville Conferences, three by alumni, six by the board.

JOHN O. GROSS

UNION COLLEGE OF BRITISH COLUMBIA (Vancouver).

The territory which is now British Columbia was first entered from the northwest by fur traders at the end of the eighteenth century, when forts and trading posts were established in the interior. In the mid-nineteenth century the south, and particularly the southwest (Vancouver Island and the Lower Fraser Valley, where today the bulk of the population resides), was opened up, chiefly because of the discovery of the Fraser River and Cariboo gold fields. The story of the territory throughout these years is a romantic one of prospectors and explorers, pack trains, wagon roads, and riverboats, culminating in the completion of the transcontinental Canadian Pacific Railroad in 1885. The territory became a unified Crown colony in 1866 and a province of the Dominion of CANADA in 1871.

Settlers in British Columbia were early provided with the services of the churches to which they were accustomed by ministers from eastern Canada and the British Isles. It was soon decided, however, that the new province should provide and train its own ministry. The Methodists founded Columbian College in New Westminster in 1892, providing a full program in arts in affiliation with the University of Toronto, and the full bachelor of divinity program in theology. Columbian College was the first institution of higher education in British Columbia, and the only such institution west of Winnipeg.

In 1906 the Presbyterians established Westminster Hall in Vancouver for the teaching of theology. By holding its classes in the summertime, Westminster was able to attract as visiting lecturers, eminent scholars who could not otherwise have been available—such as George Adam Smith, Shailer Matthews, James Moffatt and many outstanding Canadian theological professors.

The University of British Columbia was founded in 1908 and began work in Vancouver. To be near the university, the theological department of Columbian College moved to Vancouver and became Ryerson College. Ryerson, Westminster and the Anglican Theological College entered into affiliation with the university, an affiliation which continues to this day. Shortly after the first war the three colleges began to teach some subjects in cooperation; this association has continued to be an important factor in the strength of theological education.

In 1925 church union occurred. In the same year the University of British Columbia moved to a new campus at Point Grey. Hence, in 1927 Union College of British Columbia came into being in a new building situated on the new university campus. The Anglican Theological College also moved, and the earlier cooperation continued.

The additions to the original building have been principally these: tower section with offices and chapel, 1934; married students' apartments and principal's residence, 1959; new academic wing, 1962. The buildings are now complete and modern, containing all the facilities necessary for operation of a theological college, including residence accommodation for ninety students. being its leader. Three years later this was moved to

Union College, one of eight theological colleges of The United Church of Canada, provides for students the training necessary prior to ordination by the church. It grants a testamur in theology at the conclusion of three years' study, and, after appropriate additional work, grants the degrees of bachelor of theology, bachelor of divinity, and master of sacred theology. It is an associate member of the American Association of Theological Schools.

G. H. Cornish, *Cyclopaedia of Methodism in Canada*. 1903. M. Ormsby, *British Columbia: A History*. Toronto: Macmillan, 1958.   E. M. NICHOLS

UNION SCANDINAVIAN THEOLOGICAL SCHOOL, GOTHENBURG, SWEDEN

UNION SCANDINAVIAN THEOLOGICAL SCHOOL

(Överas), Gothenburg, Sweden. As early as 1881, J. M. Reid, the missionary secretary, on a visit to Scandinavia pleaded for a Union Scandinavian Theological School in Gothenburg. The SWEDEN Conference had already in 1873 started a theological school in Örebro, A. H. Berg being its leader. Three years later this was moved to STOCKHOLM with Gustaf Fredengren and then, from 1881, John E. Edman as its directors. The latter gave more than thirty years of his life to the school as teacher and director. In 1883 it was moved to UPPSALA and remained there for forty years under the leadership of able men. Besides Edman there were Albert Hallen (born in 1858, he had been in America several years, and was rector in Uppsala, 1892-95); K. A. Jansson (1854-1933); August Strömstedt (1880-1944); and Jonathan Julen (1887-1963). John Edman was both a learned and very modest man.

During all these years the scheme of a Union Scandinavian School was much discussed. Economic difficulties hindered the accomplishment, as perhaps did also the disruption of the political union between Sweden and NORWAY. In 1920 Scandinavia got its first native bishop, a Dane, ANTON BAST, and a closer cooperation between the Scandinavian countries began to prevail. The church in America favored the school plan and promised considerable help. A special committee found a suitable building in Gothenburg. "Overås" had been built by the family of James Dickson, originally from SCOTLAND, in 1864. Now in possession of the city, it was sold to the Methodists for the considerable sum of 250,000 Swedish kronor ($50,000). Another 100,000 kronor were spent on rebuilding and renovation. The world-wide depression in the 1930's made difficulties. The American mission board could not for several years do anything. Discussions were meanwhile going on about the apportionment of the purchase money and the current expenses among the Scandinavian conferences. In 1939, however, a considerable sum was sent from America, and in 1946 about 200,000 Swedish kronor, thus clearing the heavy burden of the debt, and making it possible to buy an estate, the income of which helped the finances of the school. In 1965 an ultimate and equitable decision and agreement concerning the ownership and apportionment as between the different Scandinavian conferences was concluded.

In January 1924 the Union School started its work at Överås under the leadership of Jonathan Julen, who served until 1940; then Josef E. Ruther from 1940-46; Axel Lager, 1946-47 and 1953-56; ODD HAGEN, 1947-53, elected bishop in 1953; Alf Lier from 1957-63; and from 1963, Thorvald Källstad. Odd Hagen and Alf Lier were Norwegians, so also is E. Anker Nilsen, now one of the teachers. The other members of the present faculty are Gunnar Larson and Arne Widegård.

The students are associated with the several Methodist churches in Gothenburg, thus participating in practical church work. The courses of study have been revised from time to time. Special courses have been carried through for those preparing for missionary work. More than fifty young men and women have already gone from Överås as missionaries in faraway lands. "A School of Prophets" is the aim and ideal of Överås according to the late rector, Josef E. Ruther.

Metodistkyrkauns Teologiska Skola Överås, 1874-1924-1949. Gothenburg, 1949.

AXEL LAGER
MANSFIELD HURTIG

UNION THEOLOGICAL SEMINARY, MANILA, PHILIPPINES

UNION THEOLOGICAL SEMINARY, Manila, Philippines. In 1905, George E. Nicholson of Iola, Kansas, gave $10,000 for the erection of the seminary. In 1907, Rev. Harry Farmer was put in charge of the Florence B.

Nicholson Seminary which was opened in July. The Presbyterians furnished class and dormitory rooms and gave valuable help with the teaching force. In 1908 the school opened in the Ellinwood Seminary in Malate and transferred on August 15 to the new Florence B. Nicholson Seminary at Caloocan. On October 15, 1912, the school moved back to the Ellinwood Seminary in MANILA. In June 1926, the school moved into a new building of reinforced concrete, three stories high on Taft Avenue. By this time the work was supported jointly by the Methodists, Prebyterians, United Brethren, Disciples, and Congregationalists. Students from other groups have always been welcome. In June, 1962, the seminary moved to its present location at Dasmariñas, Cavite, twenty miles south of Manila.

In the beginning years all the instruction was given in Spanish, but due to the rapid changes brought about by the public schools, English was introduced in 1912. In 1919, the standard of the school was raised until only high school graduates were admitted. At the present time two years of liberal arts are required for the B.Th. and B.R.E. degrees and four years of liberal arts are required for the B.D. degree. Graduate courses are also available under the Southeast Asia Theological Association.

The late Bishop BENJAMIN I. GUANSING was the first Filipino president of the seminary and he was succeeded by President Jacob Quiambao. There is an average of about eight-five students in the seminary.

BYRON W. CLARK

UNION THEOLOGICAL SEMINARY, Matanzas, Cuba, an interdenominational institution of theological education, founded in October, 1946 under the joint auspices of the Methodist and Presbyterian Churches of CUBA. Five years later the Protestant Episcopal Church became the third body supporting the enterprise. During the years prior to the revolution of 1959, and under the leadership of Alfonso Rodriguez Hidalgo, the Seminary grew rapidly. It enrolled students not only from Cuba, but also from Venezuela, Guatemala, Colombia, the Dominican Republic, Mexico, Puerto Rico, Chile, and other Spanish speaking countries. Its location high on a hill overlooking Matanzas Bay became the center of Cuban Protestantism. The number of its students was often doubled from one year to the next.

The plan of training men for the ministry had its beginning at Candler College in the early twenties when special courses were taught by the Rev. B. F. Gilbert. Later, students who wanted to prepare for the ministry were boarded in one of the mission buildings under the guidance of E. E. CLEMENTS and assigned to various local congregations. After several years they were transferred to the third floor of the Central Methodist Church in down town Havana and local pastors did the teaching. None of these methods was entirely satisfactory for lack of library facilities and a trained teaching staff. Under the leadership of Bishop PAUL B. KERN, and A. W. WASSON, Secretary for Latin America of the Methodist Board of Missions, overtures were made to the Presbyterian Church to establish a Union Seminary. Prior to this W. G. FLETCHER, a retired missionary to Cuba, had promised to raise $50,000 if and when a Union Seminary might be organized.

In 1956, when the Seminary celebrated its tenth anniversary, it was recognized as one of the best institutions of theological education in Latin America. However, after 1959, and progressively as the Castro regime became more and more oppressive, the growth of the Seminary was limited, especially since it became increasingly difficult to receive foreign students. Actually (1967) it is the only major educational institution which remains in the hands of the Church. It continues to serve the three churches which support it, and in every way possible to adapt its program and curriculum to the new circumstances of the country.

Files of the *Board of Missions of the Methodist Church*.

JUSTO L. GONZALEZ

UNIONTOWN, PENNSYLVANIA, U.S.A. **Asbury Church** was founded by FRANCIS ASBURY in the year of 1784, and is the second oldest congregation in the WESTERN PENNSYLVANIA CONFERENCE. The original church was a log structure thirty-five feet square, located on Peter Street, begun in the fall of 1785 and completed in the spring of 1786. Both Bishop Asbury and ROBERT AYRES preached in it for the first time in the summer of 1786. Eighteen of the twenty times that Asbury passed through the PITTSBURGH CONFERENCE, he preached at the church in Uniontown. The group Conferences of this area were held in the church in 1788, 1790 and 1792. The Union School was begun by Bishop Asbury in this church, and later carried on in an addition to the original log church. The Widow ANN MURPHY, famous woman of Methodism, was an early leader in the Church.

In 1833 a larger church building of brick was constructed on the same site. The church continued to grow and in 1878 a new structure was built on Morgantown Street to house the congregation. This structure still stands and is now an apartment house. On June 14, 1914 the cornerstone of the fourth church was laid and in February 1919, the congregation moved into its present brownstone structure.

The Annual Conference session of the former Pittsburgh Conference was held in Asbury Church many times. Through the years many able preachers have served the church, and it has had one pastor who became a bishop, FRANCIS E. KEARNS. The church is the leading Methodist church of the Uniontown area, and has a membership of over 1,100 people, with a large constituency. The church has property valued at $1,600,000, with PARSONAGE and adequate parking area. Four choirs serve the church. Asbury Church, now 174 years old, faces a favorable future in an area that has just recently begun to grow industrially, after suffering a severe depression coincident with the loss of its coal resources.

Uniontown School (1792-97), an early Methodist educational institution. In the early 1790's Bishop Francis Asbury envisioned the establishment of an Academy of Learning in each of his presiding elder's districts. This was one of the three or four that were actually established. It was located in Uniontown, which was the main center of early Methodism west of the Appalachian Mountains. Its manager and guiding leader was Charles Conaway, the presiding elder of the district. Its first principal was a Mr. Sheppee, and after a short time he was succeeded by John Hooker Reynolds. Reynolds, who later became an Episcopal rector, and William Wilson were the teachers in the school. Several later leaders in the region were among its students. The school closed because of financial difficulties and lack of leadership when Charles Conaway located from the ministry in 1797.

F. Asbury, *Journal and Letters*. 1958.
Raymond Bell, "Methodism Comes to Uniontown." Ms.
W. G. Smeltzer, *Headwaters of the Ohio*. 1951.

J. ROBERT GRAY
W. GUY SMELTZER

UNITED BRETHREN IN CHRIST, CHURCH OF THE. Organized originally among German-speaking people in MARYLAND, PENNSYLVANIA, and VIRGINIA about 1800, it moved westward following the migration of persons from these sectors. In 1946 it was united with The EVANGELICAL CHURCH to form The EVANGELICAL UNITED BRETHREN CHURCH.

PHILIP WILLIAM OTTERBEIN, trained in the German Reformed tradition and sponsored in America by the Dutch Reformed Church, arrived in the New World in 1752 and was called to the Lancaster, Pa., congregation, second largest Dutch Reformed congregation in America at that time. He gradually gathered around himself a group of lay persons who contributed to a modest spiritual awakening among the Germans in the Middle Atlantic states. About 1767 he heard a German Mennonite, MARTIN BOEHM, share his faith at a "great meeting" held on the farm of ISAAC LONG in Lancaster County, Pa. Following that service Otterbein hurried forward, embraced the bearded speaker, and exclaimed, "Wir sind brüder" (we are brethren). These two became fast friends and worked together over the years as human founders of the United Brethren in Christ.

In a conference (1789) at his parsonage in BALTIMORE, Md., Otterbein and his lay ministers gave simple organization to the fellowship which had been holding sporadic conferences since 1774. It wasn't until Sept. 25, 1800 that formal organization took place in a two-day session at the home of PETER KEMP, a mile west of Frederick, Md. At that time Martin Boehm and Philip William Otterbein were elected bishops, a name "Church of the United Brethren in Christ" was selected, examination of the brethren was conducted, and other business transacted. From this date conferences were held annually.

Both Otterbein and Boehm soon withdrew from active responsibility as their health declined. CHRISTIAN NEWCOMER and GEORGE ADAM GEETING, two of their followers, became leaders and continued the progress of the movement. On August 13, 1810 Christian Newcomer convened a conference at the home of Michael Kreider in Ross County, Ohio. With the organization of this western conference, later named the Miami Conference, problems of communication arose between the two groups. The western group requested a delegated conference with their eastern brethren. This became the first GENERAL CONFERENCE of the denomination and was convened June 6, 1815 near Mount Pleasant, Pa., midway between the two areas. At that time a Discipline and CONFESSION OF FAITH were approved and a form of church government instituted.

For two years the Church experimented with the new Confession of Faith, the Discipline and church government. Then a second General Conference was held at Mount Pleasant, June 2, 1817. It improved the Discipline, elected two bishops, formed a third annual conference, and arranged for quadrennial sessions of the General Conference.

In 1834, under authority of the General Conference, a Printing Establishment was formed at Circleville, Ohio. It was moved by vote of the General Conference in 1853 to DAYTON, Ohio, where it continued through the remainder of the Church's life. Other general church agencies were established in conjunction with the Printing Establishment so that Dayton became the general church's headquarters.

The English language quickly replaced the German, so that by 1834 when the first periodical was issued, *The Religious Telescope*, it was an English-language paper. Sunday school training began as early as 1820, in Corydon, Ind. OTTERBEIN COLLEGE, at Westerville, Ohio, became in 1847 the first educational institution of the Church. It was also the first coeducational school in OHIO.

United Brethren had very little work in the south in mid-nineteenth century. When the Civil War broke out, the Church was not seriously affected by a threat of division. It was not until late in the century that division resulted over the secrecy issue.

A small minority, led by Bishop MILTON WRIGHT, father of Orville and Wilbur Wright of aviation fame, walked out of the 1889 General Conference, meeting in York, Pa., and formed their own General Conference. They claimed to represent the Church holding to the original intent of the Discipline of 1841, especially in reference to its opposition to secret societies. Courts of law during the 1890's gave favorable decisions to the majority body (Liberals) and required that the minority (Radicals) take a new church name. They assumed that of Church of the United Brethren in Christ (Old Constitution) and continue today as a small church body of less than 30,000 members.

Over the years the Church of the United Brethren in Christ engaged in conversations with other church bodies relative to organic church union. Some of these negotiations were with the following: 1809-17, METHODIST EPISCOPAL; 1813-17, EVANGELICAL ASSOCIATION; 1829-33, METHODIST PROTESTANTS; 1855, WESLEYAN METHODISTS; 1902-09, Methodist Protestant and Congregationalists; 1909-17, Methodist Protestants; 1926-30, Evangelical Synod of North America and the Reformed Church in the United States; and 1933-46, The EVANGELICAL CHURCH. In the last instance only did union take place.

At the sessions of the FEDERAL COUNCIL OF CHURCHES in 1933, overtures were made and active negotiations were begun soon thereafter between the Evangelicals and the United Brethren. After thirteen years of careful deliberations a Plan of Union was approved and at Johnstown, Pa., Nov. 16, 1946, it was consummated. With the formation of The EVANGELICAL UNITED BRETHREN CHURCH not a single congregation was lost from either former denomination, probably the first time such had occurred in American church union negotiations.

The Church of the United Brethren in Christ did not originate from schism, but it came out of the revival of religion of the late eighteenth century in America. Its doctrine was evangelical and Arminian. In government it held in balance the episcopal, presbyterial, and congregational elements. Bishops were the superintendents of the Church, elected every four years by the General Conference and eligible for reelection. Ministerial elders and laity were elected in equal numbers to the General Conference by vote of the entire membership. The General Conference was the supreme legislative body of the Church, meeting quadrennially. Only one ordination was recognized, that of an elder, and pastors were appointed according to the itinerant plan.

Baptism and the Lord's Supper were recognized as sacraments but the mode of baptism and the manner of observing the supper were left to be determined by the individual. Anti-slavery legislation was first approved in 1821 and temperance legislation in 1841.

Mission fields were operated in SIERRA LEONE (West Africa), JAPAN, CHINA, the PHILIPPINE Islands, and the WEST INDIES. One seminary, Bonebrake Theological Seminary, Dayton, Ohio, and five colleges were operated by the Church.

At the time of union in 1946 there were in the United States 2,740 organized churches with 441,566 members and 1,328 itinerant elders. Church property was valued at more than $40,000,000, while funds received for all purposes during the year amounted to $9,051,239.

A. W. Drury, *History of the U.B.* 1924.
J. H. Ness, *History of Publishing.* 1966.
Yearbook of the E.U.B. Church, 1947.   JOHN H. NESS, JR.

UNITED BRETHREN IN CHRIST, THE (Old Constitution) was formed by members of the UNITED BRETHREN IN CHRIST who objected to legislation adopted at the GENERAL CONFERENCE of 1889. These were primarily revisions of the Confession of Faith and the Constitution. They were particularly disturbed by the modification of the rule on secret societies. Following the vote and proclamation of the new Confession and Constitution, Bishop MILTON WRIGHT led fifteen delegates who walked out motivated by a desire to form the dissenters into a continuing body. About 20,000 members were lost to the parent body within a few years.

Four bishops were elected to carry on the work of the church under the "old constitution": Milton Wright, H. T. BARNABY, Hallack Floyd, and HENRY J. BECKER. Immediate efforts were made to take over the denominational property by court action. The court ruled against the seceders. A publishing house was set up in DAYTON, Ohio. The *Christian Conservator*, the organ of the conservative party in the parent body, was adopted as the official organ of the new church. In 1897 the publishing interests and church headquarters were moved to Huntington, Ind., where a projected college was to be established. Central College, later Huntington College, opened its doors that same year.

This church, like its parent, moved basically Wesleyan. The differences with other branches of the United Brethren were mainly over the interpretation of the Constitution.

The church retained the episcopal polity and the systems of quarterly, annual and general conferences. It differs from most Methodist and United Brethren denominations in allowing only ministers and church officials to attend the quadrennial general conference. Both men and women are eligible for the ministry of which there is only one order, that of ELDER.

Mission work was begun very soon after the denomination was stabilized. The first work was established in Danville, SOUTH AFRICA, and in CHINA. At present, work is being carried on in SIERRA LEONE, West Africa, JAMAICA, China, Honduras.

In 1967 the church reported 310 churches with 22,586 members.

A. W. Drury, *History of the U.B.* 1924.
W. E. Musgrave, *The Church of the United Brethren in Christ Teachings and Progress*, rev. R. W. Rash. Dept. of Christian Education, Church of the United Brethren in Christ, 1956.
Origin, Doctrine, Constitution and Discipline of the United Brethren in Christ, 1965-1969. Huntington, Ind.: U. B. Publishing Establishment.
R. W. Rash, J. L. Towne, M. I. Burkholder, *What United Brethren Believe.* Dept. of Christian Education, Church of the United Brethren in Christ, 1951.   J. GORDON MELTON

UNITED CHRISTIAN CHURCH. The organization of what became the United Christian Church can be traced to a series of meetings in late 1868 and 1869. As early as the Civil War period, ministers and laymen of the UNITED BRETHREN IN CHRIST began holding meetings of their own because of disagreement with stated United Brethren doctrines and practices concerning infant baptism, bearing arms, and membership in secret societies. In 1869 George W. Hoffman was elected preacher, and a declaration of principles was adopted. The organization remained loose until 1877 when a Confession of Faith was adopted, the name "United Christian Church" was selected, and classes were organized. The church existed until 1889 without a constitution, when the 1841 *Discipline* of the United Brethren in Christ was adopted as stating its polity.

The doctrine of the church is in general Wesleyan, though the doctrine of total depravity is emphasized. Three ordinances are practiced: Baptism, the Lord's Supper, and Footwashing. Membership in oath-bound secret societies is forbidden, as is participation in war. Music in the church service is limited to congregational singing, without instrumental accompaniment.

The highest authority in the church is the annual conference, which has the power to revise the *Discipline*. The district conference has direct oversight over the local church. Each congregation is organized into classes. An official board oversees the church's temporal affairs. Women are ineligible for membership on it.

The mission work of the church is carried on by the Mission Board. Work is currently being carried on in Africa and INDIA. A campmeeting association also is functioning. The church has always been small and all of the congregations are located in and around HARRISBURG, Pa. In 1967 there were 600 members in twelve churches.

Frank S. Mead, *Handbook of Denominations in the United States.* New York: Abingdon, 1968.
Origin, Doctrine, Constitution and Discipline of the United Christian Church. Myerstown, Pa.: Church Center Press, 1950.
Yearbook of American Churches, 1971. J. GORDON MELTON

UNITED CHURCH OF CANADA. (See CANADA.)

UNITED CHURCH OF PAPUA, NEW GUINEA, AND THE SOLOMON ISLANDS was formed in 1968, the inaugural service being held at Port Moresby, the administrative center, on Jan. 19, 1968.

The following Methodist districts were included in the United Church: New Guinea Island Region, Papuan Islands Region, Solomon Islands, and Highlands Region.

(The beginning and development of mission work in these districts are dealt with in separate articles as Australian Overseas Missions, NEW GUINEA, PAPUA and SOLOMON ISLANDS.)

These four districts had for some time been advancing towards their own union and the status of a self-governing Conference. Their own United Synod had been created. At this juncture it was realized that more than this was desirable. Negotiations began in March 1964, with the Papua Ekalesia (i.e. Papuan Church) which was the former London Missionary Society in Papua. This was a notable mission established in 1871, but recently given its independence by the parent Society. (The work of the Papua Ekalesia is now continued in the United Church in two regions, Papuan Mainland Region and the Urban Region.) A European congregation in Port Moresby, called the United Church, Port Moresby, also entered into the union.

The United Church was born through the conviction that evangelizing a vast territory could be done effectively only through the amalgamation of Christian forces. As far as Methodists and the London Missionary Society were concerned there had never been any overlapping in their areas, but the pooling of resources greatly aided progressive evangelistic and educational work.

The United Church has 250,000 members and adherents in a territory which extends a distance of about 1,500 miles, from the borders of West Irian (formerly Dutch New Guinea) through the mainland of Papua and New Guinea, the islands (New Britain and others) and the Solomon Islands.

Politically, Papua, New Guinea and the northern section of the Solomon Islands, which have been a Trust Territory under the United Nations, are moving toward independence. (The southern section of the Solomon Islands is a British Protectorate.) It is opportune that at a time of political development, the United Church has been formed as an independent, self-governing church, incorporating Methodist and London Missionary Society traditions, and with the prospect of including other Missionary Churches working in these regions.

The United Church has appointed six bishops for the various sections of the vast territory. Four of these six are indigenous leaders, three of them being ex-Methodists; the two other bishops are European missionaries. One of the indigenous bishops, a brilliant student, is the son of a former savage in the Solomon Islands; his leadership is an indication of the progress Methodist missions have made in recent years in this territory.

The administrative headquarters of the United Church is at Port Moresby, the center of government and trade for the whole region.

Statistics for the four Methodist districts at the time of the formation of the United Church:

	Members	Adherents	Total of Average Congregations
New Guinea Island Region	17,895	26,969	39,698
Papuan Islands Region	12,758	9,895	29,025
Solomon Islands	8,306	14,650	—
Highlands Region	11,277	7,650	16,984

G. Brown, *Autobiography.* 1908.
J. W. Burton, *Call of the Pacific.* 1912.
Benjamin Danks, *In Wild New Britain.* 1933.
                                        A. HAROLD WOOD

UNITED EVANGELICAL CHURCH, THE. Although the formal organization of The United Evangelical Church was not effected until Nov. 30, 1894, it was evident in early 1891 that the division of the Evangelical Association was coming. A keen personal rivalry had developed among several prominent leaders. Some of this centered in an effort to place rather strict limitations upon the episcopacy of the church. During the 1880's so much ill will had been created on both sides of the church that compromise seemed impossible.

The Evangelical Association General Conference of 1887 delegated the decision of indicating the place for the 1891 session to the Board of Publication, which named Indianapolis, Ind., as the location. A minority disputed this right of the General Conference to delegate this authority and insisted that this prerogative belonged to the oldest annual conference, the East Pennsylvania Conference. (General Conference locations had been named by this conference in the earliest years of the church.) The East Pennsylvania Conference named Philadelphia, Pa., as the place for the 1891 session. The minority met in the latter location with Bishop Rudolph Dubs in attendance, while the majority group with Bishops J. J. Esher and Thomas Bowman, who were inter-related through marriage of their children, met in Indianapolis. Each group organized and carried out its work as though it were the official body of the denomination. During the quadrennium there were literally two churches within the Evangelical Association, each with its own set of officers claiming to be the church. Court cases were held to determine property rights. In most instances the majority group was favored.

Toward the end of the quadrennium the minority group met in Naperville, Ill., Nov. 30, 1894, and organized itself as The United Evangelical Church. There were 61,120 members and 415 itinerant ministers. It arranged for the purchase of a publishing house that had been privately formed several years earlier in Harrisburg, Pa., and reaffirmed much of the organization that had previously been approved by the 1891 General Conference at Philadelphia. One of the major innovations was the place given to laity, not only in the General Conference but the other levels of church government. In the 1894 General Conference laity were accorded an equal ratio with ministers as members of the body.

Two colleges were supported by the church, Albright College, Myerstown, Pa., and Central Pennsylvania College, New Berlin, Pa. Bishops were limited to two consecutive terms of service or a total of eight years. In 1900 mission work was initiated in China, while in 1921 a home missions area was opened in the Red Bird section of the Kentucky mountains.

In 1907 youth of the two denominations resulting from the division began efforts toward reunion. Four years later members of a Joint Commission on union met in Chicago and began the negotiations which eventually led to reunion, Oct. 14, 1922, in the Mack Avenue Church, Detroit, Mich. The reunited denomination became known as The Evangelical Church, which had a membership of 259,417 persons and 1,856 ministers.

A large number of the East Pennsylvania Conference would not participate in the reunion. They withdrew to form The Evangelical Congregational Church, a small body that continues to exist today with its church headquarters located at Myerstown, Pa.

The United Evangelical Church was Methodistic with no distinctive doctrine other than those it had espoused previously within the fellowship of the Evangelical Association. (See Evangelical Association and The Evangelical Church.)

R. W. Albright, *Evangelical Church.* 1942.
J. H. Ness, *History of Publishing.* 1966.　　John H. Ness, Jr.

UNITED METHODIST CHURCH was a British Methodist denomination formed in 1907 by the union of the Bible Christians, the Methodist New Connexion, and the United Methodist Free Churches. The new body existed until Methodist union in Britain took place in 1932, when it joined the Primitive Methodist and Wesleyan Methodist Churches, and the long chapter of Methodist disunity came almost to an end. In 1907 the membership of the three uniting bodies totaled 149,159 in England, together with about 16,000 members overseas, in Jamaica, Africa, and China; these figures had not altered very much by 1932, when the home membership stood at 132,019, together with an overseas membership of slightly less than 16,000.

The constitution of the United Methodist Church derived largely from that of the Methodist New Connexion, and differed from the contemporaneous constitution of Wesleyan Methodism. There was, for example, no ministerial session of the Annual Conference; the secretary of Conference was often a layman; the laity had more freedom of action in the local societies. Instead of the Wesleyan ministerial Legal Hundred, there were twenty-four Guardian Representatives, twelve laymen and twelve ministers, appointed for six years at a time, who were the legal guardians of the rights and privileges of the United Methodist Church. It was held that the doctrines of the body were based on the revelation in Holy Scripture, but no reference was made to the Standard Sermons or other writings of John Wesley in the official definition. At first the new body kept open the New Connexion theological college at Ranmoor, Sheffield, and the college of the United Methodist Free Churches at Victoria Park, Manchester; in 1919, however, Ranmoor finally closed, and from then on Victoria Park was linked with the Primitive Methodist College in Manchester, Hartley: this was part of the movement toward Methodist union; in 1932 Victoria Park also closed. The new body also inherited three boarding schools: Shebbear College, adopted by the Bible Christians in 1841; Ashville College, Harrogate, opened by the United Methodist Free Churches in 1876; and Edgehill Girls' College, North Devon, opened by the Bible Christians in 1884; all three schools continued after Methodist union in 1932.

Throughout the 1920's the chief event in the history of the Church was the progress of the negotiations toward complete Methodist union. The chief points of discussion were the Doctrinal Statement, which it was finally agreed should include a guarded reference to John Wesley's *Standard Sermons* and *Notes on the New Testament;* the proposal to have a ministerial session in the Conference and District Synods, which aroused the traditional Free Methodist suspicion of the Wesleyan doctrine of ministerial authority, but was finally accepted when it was made clear that the Wesleyan Church did not regard the ordained ministry as a kind of exclusive priesthood; and the question as to whether laymen could administer the Holy Communion, a problem settled by a compromise which allowed the continuance of the Free Methodist tradition of lay administration at least for the time being. The last was the most important question: if the Wesleyan Methodist negotiators had been obliged to insist on their own tradition of ministerial administration, Methodist union would not have taken place. The United Methodist Church voted very heavily in favor of union in all its church courts, and the whole body was carried into the new denomination successfully.

The Conference of 1907 decided to publish a *United Methodist Magazine*, and a weekly journal, *The United Methodist:* these survived until 1932, when they were discontinued. The United Methodist Church was formed at a time when all the British Free Churches were beginning to suffer a decline in membership; it also had to face the strains of the First World War very soon after its foundation; once that war had ended, Methodist union became the center of Methodist historical development. It therefore lived as a bridge church between one period and another. Among its most distinguished servants were W. J. TOWNSEND; CHARLES STEDEFORD, who was overseas mission secretary from 1910 to 1929; and DAVID BROOK, an able scholar who played an important part in the union negotiations of 1907, and who also did more than anyone else to lead the United Methodist Church into the union of 1932: he was chairman of the interdenominational Methodist Union Committee from 1922 to 1932.

H. Smith, *United Methodist Church.* 1933.   JOHN KENT

UNITED METHODIST CHURCH, THE, U.S.A., is the organization which came into being by the union of The Methodist Church and The EVANGELICAL UNITED BRETHREN CHURCH in a Uniting Conference at DALLAS, Texas, April 22—May 5, 1968. The United Methodist Church, whose history under that name is in its early years, represents the confluence of the larger branches of all past Methodism in America, and is one of the largest organized Church connections on earth. For the moves that brought The United Methodist Church into being in 1968, see METHODISM IN THE UNITED STATES; and also ECUMENICITY AND THE METHODIST CHURCH; and EVANGELICAL UNITED BRETHREN CHURCH.

N. B. H.

UNITED METHODIST COMMITTEE FOR OVERSEAS RELIEF (formerly Methodist Committee for Overseas Relief, commonly referred to as MCOR). An Agency of The United Methodist Church created by the GENERAL CONFERENCE of 1940 for the purpose of providing emergency relief to persons in overseas countries, especially CHINA and Europe, who had suffered from war and of coordinating relief appeals from many lands and many agencies. Bishop HERBERT WELCH, then retired, was made its chairman and director; Miss SALLIE LOU MACKINNON, secretary. Other outstanding Methodists who were chosen to serve on it included RALPH E. DIFFENDORFER, Bishop ARTHUR J. MOORE, JOHN R. MOTT, Harry N. Holmes, James V. Claypool and EUGENE E. BARNETT.

The work of this Committee was found so necessary and important that it was continued by the General Conference of 1944 and every succeeding General Conference. In 1944 it was authorized "to be the representative of the Methodist Church in the field of overseas relief; also in the field of rehabilitation" in consultation with the overseas units of the BOARD OF MISSIONS. (Paragraph 2020, *Discipline* 1944).

Support for the Committee was to come from voluntary gifts and participation in the communion offerings (Fellowship of Suffering and Service), including the offering on World-wide Communion Sunday. When General Advance Specials were established by the General Conference of 1952, this Committee became one of the three participating agencies (Paragraph 759, *Discipline* 1952). The same General Conference set up the Week of Dedication and designated the Methodist Committee for Overseas Relief as one of the church bodies to receive a share of the annual offering (Paragraph 761.2, *Discipline* 1952). Any church-wide appeals for war emergencies or post-war work were also to be shared in by the Committee.

The Committee was at first expected to be temporary but its help has been so frequently and consistently needed, that it has been continued in The United Methodist Church.

Chairmen of the Committee have been Bishop Herbert Welch (1940-48), Bishop W. W. PEELE (1948-52), Bishop FREDERICK B. NEWELL (1952-60), Bishop JAMES K. MATHEWS (1960-64), and Bishop RALPH T. ALTON (1964-   ). The executive heads of the agency have been Bishop Herbert Welch (1940-48), Bishop TITUS LOWE (1948-52), Dr. GAITHER P. WARFIELD (1952-66), and Dr. J. HARRY HAINES (1966-   ).

The responsibilities of the Committee have grown since its inception. In 1944 it was empowered to act "also in the field of rehabilitation" (Paragraph 2020, *Discipline* 1944). The next General Conference ordered the Committee "to give special attention and assistance to national workers and the people of our Methodist churches overseas" and "to cooperate with Church World Service and other interdenominational relief agencies" (Paragraph 2009.3, c and d, *Discipline* 1948). At the General Conference of 1964 the authorization was widened "to be the representative of the Methodist Church in the field of overseas relief, and rehabilitation for victims of disaster and of endemic circumstance; and service to refugees" (Paragraph 1312.1, *Discipline* 1964). One should keep in mind that assistance to refugees was prominent in the original mandate (Paragraph 1738.1, *Discipline* 1940). The 1964 General Conference also mentioned specifically "the Division of Interchurch Aid, Refugee and World Service of the World Council of Churches" as one of the cooperating interdenominational relief agencies (Paragraph 1312.3, *Discipline* 1964).

At the General Conference of 1968 the Commitee came under the umbrella of the Board of Missions of The United Methodist Church and it became known as United Methodist Committee for Overseas Relief. Its various responsibilities were continued, as well as its independence as an administrative agency and its authority to receive and allocate funds, to acknowledge gifts by its own vouchers and to participate in all church-wide offerings.

The work of the Committee is now recognized as a vital part of the life of the Church. Its program comprises —*Relief*: helping the stricken with food, clothing, initial shelter, and medical supplies; *Rehabilitation*: the longer road of helping people to help themselves; *Resettlement*: moving refugees and others from a place of no opportunity to a place where they can "belong" again; *Renewal*: helping downtrodden people in endemic need "to realize their own inherent strength and to exercise that strength for making their own destiny."

Dr. J. Harry Haines, the present director, reports that UMCOR in the first half of 1970 received an emergency appeal on the average of every eleven days from around the world, and that to each such appeal the Committee "has been able to answer responsibly within seventy-two hours."

Methodist Compassion for a World in Need. New York: MCOR, 1960.
INASMUCH, Twenty-five Years of Service through MCOR. New York: MCOR, 1965.   GAITHER P. WARFIELD

UNITED METHODIST FREE CHURCHES was a British Methodist denomination which existed from 1857 to 1907, when it became part of the UNITED METHODIST CHURCH, which in turn became part of the Methodist Church in 1932. When the body was formed in May, 1857, it consisted of the WESLEYAN METHODIST ASSOCIATION, people who had seceded from the Wesleyan Methodist connection in 1837 as a result of the SAMUEL WARREN controversy, and who numbered about twenty thousand; and many WESLEYAN REFORMERS (about five hundred societies with about nineteen thousand members), who had seceded from or been expelled from the Wesleyan connection in the course of the FLY SHEETS controversy in 1849. These reformers held that the ministry should represent, not rule, the laity, that the laity should have full rights in the Annual Assembly, and that laymen should control admission to or expulsion from the local societies. They also wanted to relax the connectional bond, giving the local societies considerable autonomy and weakening the power of any central institutions. They emphasized a rather revivalistic approach to religion, and inherited a strong suspicion of the value of training men for the ordained ministry. In the early days of the new body ministers were often seen as potential dictators and treated as though they were the hired servants of the laity. Among the early leaders were the Wesleyan ministers who had been expelled in 1849, WILLIAM GRIFFITH and JAMES EVERETT, and MATTHEW BAXTER. More important was RICHARD CHEW, who possessed the constructive ability which the older leaders of the community had lacked. The new denomination prospered: a Foreign Mission Fund was started in 1858, and between 1859 and 1862 mission fields were started in both West and East Africa, and a missionary was sent out to Tasmania. Gradually the anti-ministerial feeling of the laity relaxed: ministers came to form a large majority of the Annual Assembly, and as early as 1876 a theological college was projected at Victoria Park, Manchester, which was to remain open until Methodist union in 1932. The first principal was Thomas Hacking (1814-93).

A school for the education of the sons of ministers and laymen, Ashville College, was founded in 1877, and still exists. The denomination had a reputation both for teetotalism and for a radical attitude in politics. The United Methodist Free Churches grew more rapidly than the other liberal Methodist denominations in England, and in 1907 there were 79,948 members; there were 438 ministers, 2,983 LOCAL PREACHERS, and about 189,000 Sunday school scholars. The decision to unite with the BIBLE CHRISTIANS and the METHODIST NEW CONNEXION came about slowly but surely; the groups were divided by history rather than by deep-seated ecclesiastical principles, and the three bodies became the United Methodist Church in 1907.

O. A. Beckerlegge, *United Methodist Free Churches.* 1957.
                                        JOHN KENT

UNITED METHODIST MEN is the "authorized organization of the men of the church." (*Discipline*, UMC, 1968, paragraph 1220.) Methodist Men was the name of its predecessor organization in The Methodist Church designed to give specific work to those laymen in each Church who were not otherwise called into service on the Official Board, or in other departments of local church activity. At the reorganization which came about in 1968 (at union of the E.U.B. Church with The Methodist Church), the Uniting Conference made several changes in the specifications regarding what it decided to call United Methodist Men. This is listed as a Section in the Division of Lay Life and Work of the General Board of the Laity of the Church under the present system of administration. In the local church, United Methodist Men are to be organized under the OFFICIAL BOARD of the church, and local organizations of United Methodist Men are designated as "local fellowships."

The purposes of this organization are to encourage its members to define and interpret the purposes of United Methodist Men; to apply the findings and utilize the resources of the Section on Lay Ministries for improvement of the quality of the men's fellowship and for the increased effectiveness of the ministry of Christian men in the world; to anticipate the nature of the ministry which the church must provide for its men who are called to be servants of Christ in the world; and to engage in projects which will challenge United Methodist Men. Other purposes are stated in the Disciplinary directives regarding work of this organization and these may be summed up in saying that it is an endeavor to utilize the power of men in each local church toward fulfilling more deeply all the purposes of a lay Christian in the present day United Methodist Church.

Strong efforts have been made and are being made through the proper officers of the General Board of the Laity to encourage the organization of more groups of United Methodist Men, and to provide printed materials from time to time to assist them in planning their work and enlarging their own opportunities. (See also LAY MOVEMENT IN AMERICAN METHODISM.)

Disciplines, TMC, UMC.   N. B. H.

UNITED THEOLOGICAL SEMINARY, Dayton, Ohio, was formed July 1, 1954 by uniting Bonebrake Theological Seminary (founded 1871) and the Evangelical School of Theology (founded 1905). The merger followed the union of the United Brethren Church and the Evangelical Church in 1946.

During the U.B. GENERAL CONFERENCE in 1869, MILTON WRIGHT, later bishop, and the father of Orville and Wilbur Wright of aviation fame, urged the establishment of a theological seminary. As a result the Union Biblical Seminary was launched in 1871. In 1910 the name of the school was changed to Bonebrake, because John Bonebrake, a layman, gave it 3,840 acres of land in honor of six great uncles who had been pioneer ministers in the church.

The EVANGELICAL CHURCH introduced a department of theology in the curriculum of its Schuylkill Seminary in Reading, Pa., in 1905. The first class in theology was graduated in 1907. The Reading school merged with ALBRIGHT COLLEGE, Myerstown, Pa., in 1928, and its theology department was then separately organized as the Evangelical School of Theology.

The United Theological Seminary campus is a wooded and landscaped area of thirty-five acres. It has six buildings, including a chapel built in 1961. The plant is valued at about $2,500,000, and there is an endowment of about $1,500,000.

During the 1969-70 school year the seminary had 239 students representing twelve denominations, twenty-one states, and two foreign countries. There were seventeen full-time faculty members and three instructors. The school grants the degrees of Master of Divinity, Master of Sacred Theology, and Master of Religious Education. The library contains about 62,000 volumes.

JOHN R. KNECHT

**UNITED WESLEYAN METHODIST CHURCH OF AMER-
ICA, THE,** was formed in 1905 by Methodists who immigrated to the United States from the WEST INDIES and wished to carry on the tradition of the British Methodist Church. They are a small body and have experienced little growth.

Their doctrine is Wesleyan and their polity is that of the British Methodist Church. A general conference meets biennially. A periodical, *The Herald*, is published.

The last available report of 1966 listed five churches and 550 members.

Yearbook of American Churches, 1971.   J. GORDON MELTON

UNITED (WESLEYAN) THEOLOGICAL COLLEGE was founded in Montreal, CANADA, in 1872, and began work in 1873 with GEORGE DOUGLAS as principal. The object of the college was to provide theological training for ministers and missionaries, especially within the province of Quebec. At the General Conference of 1878, the college became affiliated with VICTORIA UNIVERSITY.

Following the union of 1883-84, the college was constituted as a connectional institution of the Methodist Church and in 1887, the Quebec legislature amended the charter to allow the college to confer degrees in divinity. Since then, under a succession of distinguished principals, the college has continued to provide a scholarly training for prospective ministers.

The college, now known as United Theological College, is a constituent part of the Faculty of Divinity, McGill University, in which capacity it fulfills not only its traditional function, but also shares in the provision of graduate theological education on an ecumenical basis.

Centennial of Canadian Methodism, 1891.
G. H. Cornish, *Cyclpaedia of Methodism in Canada*. 1881.
                                        G. S. FRENCH

UNITING CONFERENCE, U.S.A., a name given to the Conference in Kansas City, Missouri, in 1939, at which the M.E. Church, M.E. Church South, and the M.P. Church united to become The Methodist Church (see UNIFICATION OF AMERICAN METHODISM); and also after used as the name of the Conference in DALLAS, Texas, 1968, at which The Methodist Church and the E.U.B. CHURCH united to form The United Methodist Church (see METHODISM IN THE UNITED STATES, The United Methodist Church).

N. B. H.

UNIVERSITY OF CHATTANOOGA, Chattanooga, Tennessee, was a Methodist institution sold in 1969 by its trustees to the state of TENNESSEE to become the Chattanooga Branch of the University of Tennessee. Chattanooga University was founded in 1886 by the FREEDMEN'S AID SOCIETY of the M.E. Church, which at that time was extending its program to include education of poor white Southerners. After three years the school was merged with Grant Memorial University of Athens, Tenn. In 1892 the name was changed to U. S. Grant University, and in 1907 to University of Chattanooga. The following year, after a successful endowment campaign, the Freedmen's Aid Society transferred the property to a self-perpetuating board of trust, with the restriction, removed in 1935, that two-thirds of the trustees must be members of the M.E. Church. At that time the university consisted of schools of law, medicine, and theology and a college of liberal arts at Chattanooga and a preparatory school and two-year normal college at Athens. In 1925 the Athens branch became a separate institution, TENNESSEE WESLEYAN COLLEGE, while the Chattanooga branch continued as a liberal arts college.

On the transfer to the University of Tennessee, since The United Methodist Church through its trustees had an equity in the property because of a reversionary clause, the state agreed to keep the chapel intact for religious worship and to place on it a plaque stating that the institution was founded by the M.E. Church. The state further agreed that courses in religion would be included in the curriculum and that, when necessary, the costs for this work would be supplemented by a foundation made up from the endowment of the University of Chattanooga, now held in trust by a separate board of trustees, who must include a member of the Board of Education of The United Methodist Church.

Gilbert E. Govan and James W. Livingood, *The University of Chattanooga: Sixty Years*. Chattanooga, Tenn.: the university, 1947.
LeRoy A. Martin, *A History of Tennessee Wesleyan College, 1857-1957*. N.p., 1957.   JOHN O. GROSS

UNIVERSITY OF DENVER, Denver, Colorado, was chartered as Colorado Seminary in 1864 by the Territory of COLORADO. The leader in the movement to start an educational institution when DENVER was a frontier town of 3,200 inhabitants was JOHN EVANS, who had been appointed by President Lincoln as the territorial governor. Evans was also one of the founders of NORTHWESTERN UNIVERSITY, and his name is perpetuated in the one given to the city of Evanston, Illinois.

The early life of the university was intimately tied to the development of both the state and the church. Its first chancellors were distinguished clergymen, including DAVID H. MOORE and WILLIAM F. McDOWELL, later bishops in the M.E. Church.

The institution became known as the University of Denver in 1880, but Colorado Seminary continues as the name of the property holding corporation. The Social Science Foundation was established in 1926. The university has a chapter of Phi Beta Kappa. It has the following schools: College of Liberal Arts and Sciences, Graduate College (1891), Law (1892), Business Administration (1908), Engineering (1919), Librarianship (1931), Social Work (1931), Music (1941), Education (1942), Speech and Theatre (1943), Art (1946), Hotel and Restaurant Management (1946), Communication Arts (1952), International Studies (1965). The governing board has twenty-eight trustees nominated by the board and confirmed by the ROCKY MOUNTAIN CONFERENCE.

JOHN O. GROSS

UNIVERSITY OF THE PACIFIC, Stockton, California, was chartered by the Supreme Court of the territory in 1851, during the gold rush days, as California Wesleyan University. Since there was no statutory provision for a university, the first name chosen was California Wesleyan College. In 1852 the name was changed to the University of the Pacific; to College of the Pacific in 1911; and back to the original one, University of the Pacific, in 1961.

Prominent among those who took part in the founding of the college were four ministers intimately connected with the beginnings of California: WILLIAM TAYLOR, ISAAC OWEN, MARTIN C. BRIGGS, and Edward Bannister. The college was located in Santa Clara until 1870 when it moved to San José. In 1924 the college was relocated in Stockton.

The university includes schools of liberal arts, music, pharmacy, engineering, and dentistry. In 1960 the Board of Regents approved a plan to allow the university to grow in size by organizing small colleges, thereby enabling it to have the advantages which inhere in a smaller school. Since 1962 Raymond College and Covell College, enrolling 250 students each, have been started, and a third, Callison College, opened in 1967. They follow the pattern created at Oxford and Cambridge, with special emphasis on individual initiative on the part of students. Covell College is a Spanish-speaking liberal arts college.

Degrees offered are the B.A., B.S., M.A., M.S., M.M. (Music), Ed.D. (Doctor of Education), Ph.D., M.S.C.S. (Clinical Sciences), and D.D.S. The governing board is made up of thirty-six members, thirty elected by the CALIFORNIA-NEVADA CONFERENCE and six by the SOUTHERN CALIFORNIA-ARIZONA CONFERENCE.

JOHN O. GROSS

UNIVERSITY OF PUGET SOUND, Tacoma, Washington, was established as Puget Sound University in 1888; the name was changed to University of Puget Sound in 1903, to the College of Puget Sound in 1914, and in 1960 back to the University of Puget Sound, to accord with the diversity of educational programs offered. The university now has six schools: arts and sciences, graduate, business, education, music, and occupational therapy. The institution was founded by the Puget Sound Annual Conference (now PACIFIC NORTHWEST) one year before Washington achieved statehood, and was the second church-related college in Washington. It has grown along with the development of the northwestern corner of the United States. Since 1914 it has been served by only two presidents. This long continuity in leadership has proven most advantageous to the development of the institution. It offers the B.A., B.S., B.M. (Music), B.M.E. (Music Education), B.S. in Business, B.S. in Education, B.A. in Physical Education, B.S. in Occupational Therapy, B.Ed. (Education), M.A., M.A. in Business Administration, M.A. in Education, M.Ed. (Education), M.F.A. (Fine Arts), M.M. (Music), M.S., and M.S.T. (Teaching) degrees. The governing board is made up of thirty-six trustees, thirty elected by the board, six by the alumni association, subject to confirmation by the Pacific Northwest Conference.

JOHN O. GROSS

UNIVERSITY SENATE, an agency of The United Methodist Church, which fixes and evaluates educational standards for the educational institutions of the Church. The University Senate originated under this name in the M.E. Church in 1892, when there was clearly a need for an arbiter to evaluate the worth and grade of institutions and educational processes which were being patronized by the Annual Conferences of the Church, or by other church-wide groups. The University Senate of the M.E. Church was the first standardizing agency of its type in the United States, antedating by about three years the powerful North Central Association of Colleges and Secondary Schools.

The *Discipline* of the Church provided then, and provides now, that the members of the Senate are to be "practical educators" and they are directed by the *Discipline* how they may report and how function. From 1892 to 1939, the University Senate grew in prestige in the M.E. Church, and in order to assure it complete independence the General Conference of 1926 specified that the members of the Senate should not be members of the Board of Education of the Church. The Senate, however, worked largely under the Board of Education and its support devolved upon that Board.

At Church Union in 1939, the University Senate of the M.E. Church was carried over and adopted by the new Church. Its support was provided for by the BOARD OF EDUCATION, but it was independent of that Board in making its evaluation, in providing educational standards for the Church, and in announcing the schools, colleges and universities of the Church which are in accord with its standards.

The University Senate has been perpetuated in The United Methodist Church with little change. The *Discipline* fixes the number of members who shall be upon the Senate, gives it certain standards and directions, and empowers it to investigate the personnel, scholastic requirements, and so forth, of any designated educational institution claiming to be, or adjudged to be related to The United Methodist Church. The Senate is also to act as a consultant and counselor on all educational matters having to do with the educational institutions related to the Church.

The University Senate has great accrediting and evaluating power as the educational institutions related to the Church are anxious to obtain its favor and approval. The executives of church-related institutions are glad to conform to requests of the Senate to furnish it such information as it may need in exercising its powers.

The sweeping powers of the University Senate are outlined in the paragraph which declares that "no educational institution or foundation of The United Methodist Church shall hereafter be established or reopened until its plans and organization shall have been approved by the University Senate." It also forbids any annual conference or provisional annual conference to acquire or affiliate with any school, college, university or other educational institution unless the Educational Division of the Board of Education shall certify that it has reasonable assurance of financial support and the Senate shall then approve its affiliation. Leading educators usually compose the

Senate and its value is recognized in many ways over The United Methodist Church. (Also see EDUCATION, Higher, in the U.S.)

Discipline, UMC, 1968.
N. B. Harmon, *Organization*. 1962.   N. B. H.

UNIVERSITY OF SOUTHERN CALIFORNIA was founded in 1880 by the M.E. Church at LOS ANGELES. It expanded with the growth of the city and in addition to its college of liberal arts has 13 professional schools. Enrollment in 1962 was 14,899, of which 6,721 were undergraduates. Until 1928 it was closely related to the SOUTHERN CALIFORNIA-ARIZONA CONFERENCE. In the session held that year, the conference gave permission to the board of trustees to elect members without respect to Methodist membership. The university, however, continued to be classified by the UNIVERSITY SENATE as a Methodist-related institution until 1952. In that year the charter was amended and all references to The Methodist Church were deleted. For further information on the church relationships with the University of Southern California see SCHOOL OF THEOLOGY AT CLAREMONT.

JOHN O. GROSS

UPHAM, SAMUEL FOSTER (1834-1904), American preacher and educator, was born in Duxbury, Mass. on May 19, 1834, the son of Samuel Frederick and Deborah (Bourne) Upham. His father was a Methodist minister who served churches in the NEW ENGLAND and PROVIDENCE CONFERENCES for seventy years.

Samuel Foster Upham was educated at East Greenwich Academy and WESLEYAN UNIVERSITY, graduating from the latter institution in 1856. The same year he joined the Providence Conference. In 1864 he transferred to the New England Conference, where for the next seventeen years he occupied significant pulpits in Lowell, Boston, Lynn, and Springfield. In 1881 Upham became professor of Practical Theology at DREW THEOLOGICAL SEMINARY. He held this position until his death. Fourteen hundred students were instructed by him during the course of his professorship.

Like his father he was repeatedly elected a delegate to the GENERAL CONFERENCE. Of the five times he served in this capacity, three times he was elected Chairman of the Committee on Itinerancy. He also served on the General Missionary Committee, the Hymnal Commission, and the Committee to revise the Constitution of the Church. He was a trustee of Wesleyan Academy and Wesleyan University. In 1872 MT. UNION COLLEGE granted him a D.D. degree.

Upham married Lucy G. Smith of Middletown, Conn. on April 15, 1857. Five sons were born of this union; two died in infancy. The other three became Methodist ministers. On Oct. 5, 1904, he died in Madison, N. J.

J. M. Buckley, *History of Methodists*. 1896.
Minutes of the New England Conference, 1904, 1905.
M. Simpson, *Cyclopaedia*. 1878.   ERNEST R. CASE

UPPER IOWA CONFERENCE (ME) was organized Aug. 27, 1856 at Maquoketa, IOWA, with Bishop EDMUND S. JANES presiding. It was formed by dividing the IOWA CONFERENCE, and its territory included the north half of the state. At the beginning the conference had seven districts—Davenport, Dubuque, Iowa City, Janesville, Marshall, Sioux City, and Upper Iowa. There were fifty-eight preachers, seventy-two charges, and 8,320 members.

At its first session the conference passed a resolution that the Upper Iowa Conference adopt CORNELL COLLEGE, located at Mt. Vernon, as their college and they pledged themselves to its patronage and support. The school began in 1853 as Iowa Conference Seminary, was chartered in 1854, and the name changed to Cornell in 1855. From the beginning Cornell granted women equal privileges with men in the student body and on the faculty.

In 1864 the Upper Iowa Conference was divided and its western half became a part of the newly formed DES MOINES CONFERENCE. In a new alignment eight years later that same territory became the NORTHWEST IOWA CONFERENCE. Then in 1948 the Northwest Iowa and the Upper Iowa Conferences merged to form the NORTH IOWA CONFERENCE.

In its last year the Upper Iowa Conference had 223 churches, 62,845 members, and property valued at $7,484,079.

S. N. Fellows, *Upper Iowa Conference*. 1907.
R. A. Gallaher, *Methodism in Iowa*. 1944.
Minutes of the Upper Iowa Conference. FREDERICK E. MASER

UPPER MISSISSIPPI CONFERENCE (ME) was organized at Holly Springs, Miss., Feb. 5, 1891 with Bishop EDWARD G. ANDREWS presiding. The conference was formed by dividing the MISSISSIPPI CONFERENCE (ME, 1868). At the outset the conference had five districts—Aberdeen, Corinth, Greenville, Holly Springs, and Yazoo. There were eighty-eight charges and approximately 15,200 members.

RUST COLLEGE, one of the ten surviving Negro institutions of higher learning developed in the South by the M.E. Church following the Civil War, is within the bounds of the Upper Mississippi Conference. Launched in 1866, Rust was among the first schools for Negroes in MISSISSIPPI. Chartered as Shaw University in 1868, the name was changed to Rust University in 1890, in honor of Richard S. Rust of CINCINNATI, who as secretary of the FREEDMEN'S AID and Southern Educational Society was greatly interested in and helpful to the institution. In 1914 the name was changed again to Rust College. The Upper Mississippi Conference supports the college, designating a special day each year when the churches receive offerings for the school. ALEXANDER P. SHAW, born at Abbeville, Miss., graduated from Rust in 1902, and was elected a bishop in the M.E. Church in 1936 and served until retirement in 1952.

In 1939 the Upper Mississippi Conference became a part of the CENTRAL JURISDICTION of The Methodist Church. On the abolition of that Jurisdiction in 1968, the conference became temporarily a part of the Jackson Area of The United Methodist Church, pending merger with the NORTH MISSISSIPPI CONFERENCE of the SOUTHEASTERN JURISDICTION.

In 1967 the Upper Mississippi Conference reported 56 ministers, 67 charges, 14,428 members, and property valued at $2,749,457.

General Minutes, MEC and MC.
Minutes of the Upper Mississippi Conference.
G. R. Miller, *North Mississippi*. 1966.   FREDERICK E. MASER

UPPER ROOM, THE, published by the BOARD OF EVAN-
GELISM of The United Methodist Church, U.S.A., is the
world's most widely used daily devotional guide. It was
first issued in April, 1935, with GROVER C. EMMONS as
editor. A group of devout Christian people in SAN AN-
TONIO, Texas, had been concerned and in prayer over
the lack of daily devotions in Christian homes. This concern with suggestions for some sort of prayer guide was
brought to the attention of the Board of MISSIONS of
the M.E. Church, South, which met in NASHVILLE, Tenn.,
on Dec. 13, 1934. The Board accepted the recommendation to publish a devotional guide.

Grover C. Emmons, then with the Board at Nashville,
was assigned the task and he developed a booklet with a
Scripture reading, a text, a short meditation, a prayer,
and a devotional "thought for the day" all on one page.
The first copy of the issue had been sent to the press with-
out a name. At a conference in RICHMOND, Va., he heard
J. W. Smith, a minister and pastor of Virginia, speak on
Pentecost, and decided on the name, *The Upper Room.*
Emmons wired the printer his decision. Dr. J. MANNING
POTTS, later the editor, was chairman of the meeting,
and vouches for this story.

From the beginning in 1935 until 1948, *The Upper
Room* was issued as a quarterly. Since 1948 it has been
bi-monthly. The first printing was for only 100,000 copies,
the second 160,000, and the third 211,000 copies. Circulation has grown steadily and is presently a record breaking
3,000,000 copies per issue. From 1935 until 1940 when
the Board of Missions of the newly formed The Methodist
Church moved to New York, *The Upper Room* was
produced by the Committee on Evangelism, Hospitals,
and Homes (MES). In 1940 it was transferred to the
Commission on Evangelism, which later became the General Board of Evangelism of The Methodist Church. With
this transfer, Emmons became Coordinate Executive Secretary and Managing Editor, a position he held until his
unexpected and untimely death in 1944.

ROY H. SHORT succeeded Grover Emmons as Editor
of *The Upper Room* in 1944, and served four years until
elected bishop in 1948. Dr. J. Manning Potts was then
elected editor (in 1948), and served until his retirement.
Dr. WILSON O. WELDON of the WESTERN NORTH CARO-
LINA CONFERENCE succeeded him as present editor.

The Book of Discipline provides that no monies from
World Service may be used in producing *The Upper
Room,* or other devotional literature, and that no money
from such literature may be used by the Board, since the
Board is a World Service Agency. A reserve fund is, how-
ever, allowed to be created, and the headquarters build-
ing occupied by the Board of Evangelism (1908 Grand
Avenue, Nashville, Tenn.) was constructed with Upper
Room funds.

During more than thirty years of service to the Church
there has been little change in the managing staff. There
have been only four editors, but great changes have
taken place in all other phases of *The Upper Room.* One
of the most important has been in the multiplicity of
languages in which publication takes place. In answer
to requests the following language editions came about:
Hindustani in 1937; Spanish and Korean in 1938; Braille
and Portuguese, 1940; Chinese, 1947; Armenian, 1949;
Ilocano, Tagalog, Australasia, Swedish, and Norwegian,
1950; Japanese and India (English), 1951; Greek, Italian,
Hindi, and Urdu, 1952; Telugu, Arabic, and Thai, 1953;
British Isles, Persian, Hungarian, Finnish, and Russian,

1954; Cebuano, Gujarati, and Tamil, 1955; French, 1956;
Burmese and Talking Book, 1957; Burma (English,
Marathi, Sinhalese), 1958; Kannada, 1959; Malayalam,
1960; Danish, 1961; Bengali, Santhali, and Pampango,
1962; and German, 1965.

The devotional life is stressed in many ways. *The
Upper Room* organization has a department by this name,
with responsibility for the production and distribution of
books and booklets. Beginning with *A Pocket Prayer
Book* by Bishop RALPH S. CUSHMAN—which has sold
over 1,800,000 copies—*The Upper Room* now has published over 200 different devotional titles and has sold
more than 14,000,000 copies.

In 1946 *The Upper Room* began producing radio
programs. These are furnished to stations free for broadcast as a public service. The programs are of such nature
in music, message, quality, and without denominational
bias, that they have had wide acceptance by and in over
2,000 stations, Armed Services Radio, etc.

In the headquarters building at Nashville, there is a
lovely Upper Room Chapel featuring a Pentecost stained-
glass window, and a life-sized wood carving of Leonardo
da Vinci's painting of *The Last Supper.* Regular services
for the Board of Evangelism are held there each Wednesday, special services for the public from time to time, and
many worship services by visiting groups. More than
50,000 people visited the Chapel and Museum in 1965.
In addition to the museum with more than six hundred
items, there is a devotional library of about 10,000 volumes, many of which are quite rare.

The department of Family WORSHIP promotes family
worship, not only throughout Methodism, but throughout
the world. The Fellowship of *The Upper Room* holds a
prayer vigil each morning in the Grover C. Emmons
Prayer Room, called appropriately, after a volume of his
prayers, *Alone With God.* This is for people throughout
the world who have requested prayer and also for the
staff and the work of the Board. The Fellowship also
distributes literature, helps with the work of Chaplains,
and other language editions. Recently a Chaplain's Service
Department has been added.

Since 1949 *The Upper Room* has given an annual and
widely publicized citation for outstanding work in world-
wide Christian Fellowship. Persons receiving this honor
have been: JOHN R. MOTT, Frank C. Laubach, RALPH
S. CUSHMAN, Jesse M. Bader, John Mackay, Margaret
Applegarth, IVAN LEE HOLT, Warner Sallman, Samuel
McCrea Cavert, G. BROMLEY OXNAM, Theodore F.
Adams, RALPH W. SOCKMAN, James R. Mutchmor, HELEN
KIM, Billy Graham, and HARRY DENMAN.

The Upper Room is endorsed and sponsored by many
groups and denominations. Most foreign editions are
produced by other groups. It is truly an interdenominational, interracial, and international publication of great
scope and wide influence.

Charles M. Laymon, *Thy Kingdom Come, Twenty-five Years
of Evangelism.* Nashville: General Board of Evangelism, The
Methodist Church, 1964.
Lief Sevre, *The Romance of The Upper Room.* Nashville: The
Upper Room, 1964.   BROOKS B. LITTLE

UPPSALA, Sweden, has a population of 85,000 plus
16,000 students at its world-famed university. It is
SWEDEN's most important university city (the university
was founded in 1477) and the Lutheran archbishop's
seat.

ST. JOHN'S CHURCH, UPPSALA, SWEDEN

In 1871 the first Methodist minister, Nils Peter Sandell (1832-1910), was sent to Uppsala, and a congregation was organized the same year. In 1875 St. Johannis (St. John's) Church was dedicated by Bishop MATTHEW SIMPSON, several prominent members of the Community Council and of the university being present. In 1876, Bishop E. G. ANDREWS presiding, the Sweden Annual Conference was organized at a session in Uppsala at St. John's.

In 1882 the church building was enlarged to become the largest church in Sweden. In connection with this enlargement St. John's was enabled to offer suitable accommodations for the nascent Union Scandinavian Theological School. For forty years, 1883-1923, this important institution was situated in Uppsala. Many generations of Swedish Methodist ministers had their training there. It meant also a good deal for the congregation that these groups of young, enthusiastic, and ardent men, preparing for the ministry, should take an important part in the life and work of the church, preaching and witnessing in the choir and SUNDAY SCHOOL and in the work among young people. They were also called to preach in the many small chapels and meetinghouses in the countryside, around the city. Most of these chapels and groups of religious people belonged however to another free church, which thus greatly profited by these theological students. Occasionally such local churches became too dependent on these young men—which made some difficulties when the theological school in January, 1924, was moved to GOTHENBURG.

Especially was the Sunday school in St. John's led by able laymen. There were times around 1900 when the Sunday school numbered more than a thousand pupils.

Great preachers have gathered crowds around the pulpit in St. John's and exerted no mean influence on many generations of students of the university: FREDRIK ÅHGREN in 1882-84 and 1906-10; C. P. Carlsson in 1884-87; Eric Schütz, 1890-95; Gustaf Lindström, 1895-98; Carl Hult-

gren, 1901-04; K. E. Norström, 1913-18; Martin Martling, 1924-28; David Sandberg, 1936-39, and others.

In 1944-45 a building was erected in connection with the church, containing, among other accommodations, quarters for a parsonage and an old people's home.

Methodist students from all over the country during their years at the university have found a spiritual home in St. John's and have made a noteworthy contribution to the life of the church, besides their activities in the Free Church Student Movement.

MANSFIELD HURTIG

URBAN MINISTRIES IN AMERICAN METHODISM. The enormous growth of huge metropolitan centers in world Methodism and the urbanization of life in many lands has called for a different technique in carrying on Methodist Church work from that which was needed in earlier days among an agrarian population and in rural life. In the United States, where urban population has increased ten fold since 1850, an early move toward meeting this expanding challenge is observed in the creative, large-scale efforts of Foreign Language Churches, City Missionary Societies, Institutional Church Movement, Goodwill Industries, Mass Revivals, Settlement Houses, Association Movements (YMCA & YWCA), Rescue Missions, and a broad range of eleemosynary services. Methodist concern for urban residents has expressed itself constantly yet in manifold forms. These gigantic projects supplemented the ministry of thousands of regular city Methodist congregations. Indeed most of the aforementioned special work was regarded as evangelical outreach of the urban church despite its dominant social service nature. The denomination supported both religious and social work.

The earliest churches of the denomination began in the colonial cities along the eastern seaboard. Somewhat later, following the Civil War, as the industrial and commericial communities boomed, Methodism expanded its local work and launched many new congregations. By 1950, more American Methodists resided under urban circumstances than rural. The task has grown larger and more complicated. Thus the denomination's effort to serve city dwellers during the past one hundred years has really been the joint undertaking of both regular city churches and special experimental programs. Here follows an outline of some of these:

Foreign Language Churches proved to be a major Protestant phenomenon. Following the 1860's, industrial cities grew rapidly. During the period between the Civil War and World War I, millions of people emigrated from Europe and Asia. Most immigrants settled in the cities, converting the territory into polyglot neighborhoods. Wherever they took up residence, the territory was inundated with major social change. During this period of industrial expansion, there emerged the various branches of Methodism in America: German, Italian, Swedish, Norwegian, Danish, Negro, Spanish, Chinese, Japanese and Korean. Moreover, additional missions were extended among Poles and Czecks. The majority of every minority ethnic group resided in the city. A relevant ministry began via the group's language and culture. Remnants of the denomination's linguistic work persist today. At its peak, Methodism carried on its urban ethnic ministry in more than twenty foreign languages. Spanish-speaking Americans, whether of Mexican or Puerto Rican lineage, have great numerical significance in contemporary American cities.

City Missionary Societies within Methodism constitute another program aimed at the solution of a ministry to the urban poor in cities of 75,000 population and above. Community-wide local missionary societies were organized among churches in order to procure funds and to pool leadership in behalf of weak urban churches. The fuller mobilization of the denomination's local resources to meet the special problems of ethnic groups and slum residents was an objective but partly realized.

The Institutional Church Movement thrived during the latter half of the nineteenth century and the early decades of the twentieth century. It reached its zenith about 1900 with approximately two hundred Institutional Churches located in the larger U.S. cities. Methodism's work of this type was established in BOSTON, NEW YORK, LOS ANGELES, and elsewhere. Such projects were located chiefly in polyglot slums. Each constituted an evangelical arm of the church. Religious ministry was combined with professional social services. The Institutional Church provided all of the ministries (social, material, familial, cultural, medical and spiritual) required by urban man, making them available under a single roof. Here the multiple staff included minister, social worker, doctor, teacher and kindred workers. The annual budget was enormous, requiring large subsidies from the denomination. A great host of urban residents were served through this comprehensive ministry.

Goodwill Industries. Another type of ministry was launched in 1910 by Methodism at Boston. Designed primarily to aid physically handicapped persons (deaf, blind, amputees, elderly, etc.) who needed gainful employment, it aimed at the practical fulfillment of the slogan, "Not charity but a chance." The Boston project marked the beginning of GOODWILL INDUSTRIES which has now spread to several hundred cities throughout the English speaking world. The program is practical. Used furniture, clothing, shoes, and other household goods are donated locally to Goodwill. Handicapped persons (who are taught the requisite skills) earn wages by making necessary repairs. This chance to learn and earn enabled the worker to participate in his own rehabilitation. Renewed merchandise is sold in a local Goodwill store at a reasonable price. Thousands of handicapped urban poor have been helped by Goodwill Industry. The program is still expanding.

When great numbers of rural young men and women emigrated to cities in the middle and latter part of the nineteenth century and continued into the twentieth century, Protestant leaders were quick to see that these single youth merited a special ministry not available from the regular churches. This concern led to the founding of the *Association Movement.* Hence the YMCA as an evangelical arm of the city church was established in Boston (1851) and spread from city to city. The work focussed attention upon rural Protestants (including many Methodists) who needed spiritual guidance under urban conditions. The city was regarded as a sinful place. People said that God made the country but the Devil made the city. Later, the YWCA was begun in New York (1858) in order to provide a parallel ministry among the many young women who had migrated cityward. Association activities included not only Bible Study groups and evangelical witnessing on street corners but also the care of the sick in hotels, fund-raising to aid the destitute, and

personal work in rescue missions. Thus newcomer rural youth became involved in a practical concern for the city, one which was already espoused by indigenous Methodism. Young adults received a special ministry in behalf of the church.

Other types of special ministries rounded out the creative experiments. To cite a few—*Settlement Houses, Mass Revivals, Rescue Missions, Councils of Cities, Negro Church Centers,* and numerous Eleemosynary Projects— is to omit many other worthy undertakings. Suffice it to report that Methodism has wrestled with American city problems for more than a century. *Evidently the momentum for nearly all of these movements had run down by the 1940's.* The city began to hurt desperately and it became a wilderness of neglected ministries. Just then a new burst of social concern appeared. It is largely a post World War II happening.

On the contemporary scene, many experiments are groping toward a relevant ministry. These efforts focus largely in three spheres: among the urban poor, among middle class residents and with respect to special problems (dope addiction, prostitution, sex deviation, delinquency, etc.). Geographically speaking, the projects extend from Bangor to San Diego, from Seattle to Miami. A desperate search for adequate ministries presses on. Most of the experiments are regarded as an evangelical outreach of the urban Methodist church. Financial subsidies continue to be made on this basis. Both the secular and religious worlds are familiar with some of the contemporary forms: Coffeehouse, Ecumenical Dialogue, Lay Interneship, Teen Forum, Teen Challenge, Koinonia Group, Store Front, Night Ministry, Senior Citizen, Racial Cause Advocate, Neighborhood Meeting, Religious Art Festival, High-rise Apartment Ministry, Interracial Neighbor Program, Industrial Chaplaincy, and so on. Such terms reveal new and old directions taken by the urban ministry in this lively period of church renewal. Great seriousness invests the manifold efforts to provide relevant ministries in contemporary urban society.

Even a brief account of Methodism's ministry to urban residents must embrace both humanitarian and religious elements. The denomination's dual concern has persisted for many decades. Methodism has remained aware of the problems and concerned about the needs of the changing urban populations. The denomination has expended its funds, utilized its facilities and deployed its personnel to meet the needs in language, out-patient clinics, job training, employment, homemaking, alcoholism, drug addiction, youth work, recreation, social services, education— indeed pioneering in nearly every form of eleemosynary and religious work. Sentiment, piety and ignorance have rarely marked the dominant response of Methodism. Rather the complex, sophisticated approach through experimental programs coupled with the unheralded current work of approximately 3,000 inner city churches and kindred efforts, have brought hope and succor to millions of urban residents in the United States during the past one hundred years. That the totality of these efforts (past or present) falls short of the full urban task is acknowledged. This, even today, is due to a critical shortage of well-trained, dedicated young clergy and capable young social workers. The American task is larger than the work of a single denomination or that of all of the denominations.

A. I. Abell, *The Urban Impact Upon American Protestantism.* Cambridge: Harvard University Press, 1943.

W. C. Barclay, *History of Missions.* 1957.

W. E. Clark, et al, *The Church Creative.* New York: Abingdon Press, 1967.

Dwight W. Culver, *Negro Segregation in the Methodist Church.* New Haven: Yale University Press, 1953.

Charles H. Hopkins, *The Rise of the Social Gospel in American Protestantism.* New Haven: Yale University Press, 1940.

Winthrop S. Hudson, *The Great Tradition of the American Churches.* New York: Harper & Brothers, 1953.

—————, *Religion in America.* New York: Charles Scribner's Sons, 1965.

Henry F. May, *Protestant Churches in Industrial America.* New York: Harper & Brothers, 1949.

H. Richard Niebuhr, *The Social Sources of Denominationalism.* New York: Henry Holt Co., 1929.

—————, *The Kingdom of God in America.* Chicago: Willett, Clark & Co., 1937.

Liston Pope, *Millhands and Preachers.* New Haven: Yale University Press, 1942.

Richard A. Raines, *New Life in the Church.* New York: Harper & Brothers, 1961.

Ross W. Sanderson, *The Church Serves the Changing City.* New York: Harper & Brothers, 1955.

Frederick A. Shippey, *Protestantism in Suburban Life.* New York: Abingdon Press, 1964.

J. W. Smith & A. L. Jamison, eds., *The Shaping of American Religion.* Princeton: Princeton University Press, 1961.

J. W. Smith & A. L. Jamison, eds., *Religious Perspectives in American Culture.* Princeton: Princeton University Press, 1961.

W. W. Sweet, *Methodism in American History.* 1954.

George W. Webber, *God's Colony in Man's World.* New York: Abingdon Press, 1960.   FREDERICK A. SHIPPEY

URBANA, ILLINOIS, U.S.A. **First Church** was the first organized church in the twin cities of Urbana-Champaign in the heart of the central ILLINOIS prairie, and now the home of the University of Illinois. The first services were held in 1836 by James Holmes, a mill-wright, while Indians camped nearby. The Society was organized in 1839 and services were held in the courthouse. In 1840 the first church, thirty by forty feet, was built. The pastor and congregation cut, scored, and hewed the frame out of timber on Nancy Webber's woods nearby. They hauled logs to Colonel Busey's Crystal Lake Creek saw mill for siding. It was white-washed with a mixture some of the women made which evidently had too much salt. The cows that pastured in the church yard discovered this and licked at it—especially at church time. Boys were stationed at the church during services to keep the cows away. Fifteen years later this first church building was sold for $350 and converted into a livery stable.

In 1856 a new brick church with a tall white frame steeple was built. It was dedicated by the famous circuit rider and presiding elder of central Illinois, PETER CARTWRIGHT, who also, as a member of the State Legislature, was one of a small group of its members who was responsible for the establishment of the University of Illinois in 1867.

A third church building was erected in 1892-93 and given to the congregation as a gift by one of its devout members, Jairus C. Sheldon, in memory of his son, Clarence.

The present building is of Indiana limestone and in Gothic style with a bell tower. It was dedicated by Bishop EDWIN HOLT HUGHES in 1927.

There were two famous preachers of this church: ROBERT McINTYRE, who preached to overflow crowds while he was pastor here, and who was later elected bishop; and FRANK CRANE, who was pastor in 1889 and became famous for his metropolitan "newspaper sermons." Paul Burt, prominent in the general work of the Methodist Church, especially on the Commission on WORSHIP, served as pastor of Wesley Church in Urbana and at the same time as director of the University of Illinois WESLEY FOUNDATION from 1928-62.

Wesley Church reported a membership of 1,059 in 1970 and First Church, located in the heart of a new uptown business section, reported 1,863 members in this same year. First Church was chiefly responsible for the establishing of Grace Church (418 members), now in the southeast section of the city.

General Minutes, 1970.

URMY, RALPH BRAINERD (1867-1947), American preacher and editor, was born at SAN FRANCISCO, Calif., on Feb. 28, 1867. He was educated at the UNIVERSITY OF THE PACIFIC, GARRETT BIBLICAL INSTITUTE and DREW THEOLOGICAL SEMINARY. ALLEGHENY COLLEGE awarded him a D.D. degree in 1908. Urmy was received on trial into the NEWARK CONFERENCE in 1896 and served churches in East Orange, Mendham, Morristown and NEWARK. In 1921 he transferred to PITTSBURGH CONFERENCE, and was appointed to Bellvue church, which he served until he became editor of the *Pittsburgh Christian Advocate* in 1928. He served as editor of the *Pittsburgh Christian Advocate* until 1931, then returned to the pastorate of Bellvue. In 1934 he returned to Newark Conference, served the Westfield and Lyndhurst churches, and retired in 1940. He was a member of four GENERAL CONFERENCES, and was for fourteen years a member of the Board of Foreign MISSIONS. As a member of the Executive Committee of the METHODIST FEDERATION FOR SOCIAL ACTION, he took a leading part in determining its policies. His stand upon social issues brought him into prominence during the period when the nation was still little concerned over hours and working conditions in the steel and coal industries. During the First World War he served as a Y.M.C.A. secretary in France. He married Marion F. Saxe in 1897. To them were born four sons and a daughter. Urmy died on Feb. 1, 1947 and was buried in Evergreen Cemetery, Morristown, N. J.

HENRY L. LAMBDIN

URUGUAY, a republic on the east coast of South America at the mouth of the Rio de la Plata, is bounded by ARGENTINA and BRAZIL. It is the smallest country of South America in area, but not in population. The respective figures are 72,172 square miles and 2,852,000 persons (1969 census). A traditionally prosperous economy has given Uruguay a comparatively high standard of living, and in 1961 it ranked third of all Latin American countries in per capita income. There is freedom of worship, with a preponderance of Roman Catholics and an Evangelical (Protestant) minority of 42,772 (1960)— approximately 1.6 percent of the population. While the population is concentrated in the metropolitan area of MONTEVIDEO, the economy is essentially agricultural, being based upon livestock. Major industries are derived from agriculture, such as packing houses for meat, mills to process cereal grains, a wool industry and textiles.

The Spanish explorer, Juan Diaz de Solis, discovered the Rio de la Plata in 1515, going ashore near the site of Montevideo. Possessing neither silver nor gold, the area was slow in being developed. In 1680 the Portuguese from BRAZIL founded Colonia as a rival to the Spanish at BUENOS AIRES. The Spanish founded Montevideo in 1726, and the city changed hands several times.

After becoming free from their European mother countries, Argentina and Brazil contended for the area that is now Uruguay. Great Britain interceded between them in 1827, and both relinquished their claims in the treaty of Aug. 27, 1828. Uruguay had declared its independence in 1825, but even after 1827 it was beset by rival forces without and within. Ruined by civil wars, dictatorships, and intrigue, Uruguay did not achieve full freedom until the early years of the twentieth century, under the several terms of Jose Batlle y Ordonez as president.

Uruguay has been governed by a series of constitutions, the present one having been adopted in 1934 and amended in 1952. It gives the country a unique executive, replacing the office of president with a nine-man executive council, but return to a single president was voted on in November 1966.

Uruguay is known as a leader in social reforms, including universal suffrage, medical service, old-age and service pensions, free and compulsory education, and the abolition of capital punishment. At the same time, it has gone further in state ownership of business and industry than other countries of the hemisphere. Principles of socialism have been applied in nationalization of public facilities and banking, control of distribution of primary necessities, and of government ownership of businesses as varied as meat packing and insurance.

Separation of church and state was first provided in the 1919 constitution, and in a now-secular society the dominant tone borders on a practical agnosticism. Holy Week is called "Tourist Week," and Christmas is called "Family Day."

Methodist history is traced to the brief visits of the American, FOUNTAIN E. PITTS (in 1835 while on a survey tour of South America) and JOHN DEMPSTER (in 1838 while stationed at Buenos Aires, Argentina). Dempster requested the Board of Managers of the Missionary Society in the United States to send a permanent missionary, since he judged conditions to be favorable. The board sent WILLIAM H. NORRIS, who arrived in 1839, and who worked in Argentina also. He obtained permission from the government to build a church, but found his work difficult because of war between Uruguay and Argentina. In 1842 Norris was transferred to Argentina, ending the first chapter of the work in Uruguay.

In 1870, JOHN F. THOMSON was sent from Argentina to reopen the work. Of his many accomplishments, perhaps the most far-reaching was his conversion of FRANCISCO G. PENZOTTI, an Italian immigrant whom Thomson trained in Argentina as an evangelist, and who for twenty years was an effective preacher all over Latin America and an agent of the AMERICAN BIBLE SOCIETY for South America.

The arrival of THOMAS B. WOOD from Argentina in 1876 marked the firm establishment of Methodist work, especially in the field of education. During this period other Uruguayans joined Penzotti as evangelists to their own people. Notable among them were Juan Correa and Carlos Lastrico. They suffered frequent persecution and were imprisoned. By 1880 Wood listed six centers of Methodist work in addition to the capital city. The following year William Tallon came from Buenos Aires to be pastor of the American Church in Montevideo. He was effective in defense of Protestantism from the pulpit

and in public discussions in the university. His influence brought into the church a number of young men of superior education. In 1884 an Italian immigrant, Daniel Armand Ugon, opened a theological school used jointly by Methodists and Waldensians—an early example of close cooperation between the two denominations that has continued through the years.

Throughout its early years, Methodist work in Uruguay was a part of the mission headquartered in Buenos Aires. When the South America Conference was organized in 1893, Uruguay became a district. This was a time of expansion into towns in the interior. For a time the Uruguay District also included appointments in Entre Rios Province of Argentina and Rio Grande do Sul Province of Brazil.

Educational work was established early, with day schools for girls being organized by the WOMEN'S FOREIGN MISSIONARY SOCIETY of the M.E. Church and for boys by the mission. Today the outstanding educational institution is CRANDON INSTITUTE, founded at Montevideo in 1879 and now having coeducational work from kindergarten to junior college. In addition to its Montevideo campus, there is a branch in Salto.

Subsequent years have seen growth both in churches and institutions. Among notable institutions in Uruguay today are Friendship House, a social service center, and GOODWILL INDUSTRIES, the first of its kind to be set up outside the United States. Methodists played a major role in establishing the interdenominational Evangelical Hospital in Montevideo.

Methodism in Uruguay is small. In 1965 there were twenty-one organized churches and twenty-three preaching places, with 2,056 full members of The Methodist Church and nearly 600 preparatory members. Some growth has taken place since then as later figures will show. The church has enjoyed cordial relations with the Waldensian Church, a Protestant denomination brought from ITALY by immigrants. In the 1960s the church was engaged in negotiations for possible merger of the Methodist and Waldensian Churches and the Disciples of Christ in Uruguay, PARAGUAY, and Argentina.

The proposed regional merger reflected a "Rio de la Plata spirit" that already exists within Methodism. The easy exchange of ideas and personnel between Montevideo and Buenos Aires has led to many cooperative projects. Much of the initiative and support for such work as the Church and Society Board and the Latin American Board for Evangelical Missions have come from Methodists of Uruguay and Argentina. The world-renowned Union Theological Seminary (FACULTAD EVANGELICA DE TEOLOGIA) in Buenos Aires traces its history to a little training school begun in Montevideo and later transferred across the river.

In the mid-1960s Uruguayan Methodism felt the pinch of a let-down in the country's accustomed prosperity. Within the church there was tension between traditional forms and an impulse for change. The intellectual freedom of Uruguayan culture encouraged liberals within the church to experiment with ways to make the influence of Christianity felt in the social order, and a number of churchmen became active politically. A restlessness with old forms led to a revolutionary experimental plan voted by the 1965 annual conference, whereby pastors of Montevideo District were assigned to specific churches only for purposes of residence, making the entire district a single parish divided into three circuits. The experiment was watched with interest by Methodists elsewhere.

Uruguay Annual Conference (until it became an autonomous church in 1969) comprises all the Methodist work in Uruguay. As has been narrated, Uruguay became a district of the South America Annual Conference of the M.E. Church when that conference organized in 1893. The 1952 GENERAL CONFERENCE separated Argentina and Uruguay, which were then together in the River Plate Conference (Discipline, 1948, ¶ 1866), into the Argentina Annual Conference and the Uruguay Provisional Annual Conference. In 1960 the General Conference gave authority to the Uruguay Provisional Annual Conference—as well as to the PERU Provisional and the BOLIVIA Provisional Annual Conferences—to become organized into regular annual conferences during the quadrennium ending in 1964, provided they should have a minimum of twenty-five ministerial members. Uruguayan Methodism fulfilled this requirement, and became officially recognized as an Annual Conference in 1964 (Discipline, 1948, ¶ 1866; 1960, ¶ 2007-1; 1964, ¶ 1846). Chief Conference offices were of course in Montevideo, and the Conference itself was in the LATIN AMERICA CENTRAL CONFERENCE and in the Buenos Aires Episcopal Area.

However, in 1968 the Uruguay Conference asked for and received from the General Conference of The United Methodist Church authorization to become an autonomous Methodist Church. The authorization was granted subject to certain conditions being met. They were duly met and the autonomous Methodist Church of Uruguay (Iglesia Evangélica Metodista en el Uruguay) was organized at a constituting conference on Dec. 5-8, 1969, in Montevideo. The Rev. EMILIO CASTRO, forty-two years of age, a former district superintendent, ecumenist and Christian social action leader, was elected on the third ballot as president of the new Church. This is formed as is indicated above from the former Uruguay Annual Conference of The United Methodist Church and has 2,730 members (full and preparatory), with nineteen organized congregations, twenty-eight preaching places and 1,620 Sunday school students. The ordained and lay ministers number twelve. Montevideo, of course, will be the headquarters of the new Church which will maintain the close relationship with The United Methodist Church in the United States.

In the Methodist Church of Uruguay, districts have been eliminated and an executive committee of twelve—six ministers and six laymen—exercise the supervision of the entire church.

W. C. Barclay, *History of Missions.* 1957.
El Estandarte Evangelico de Sud America. 1911.
Carlos T. Gattinoni, "La Iglesia Metodista en la costa oriental de America del Sud." Unpublished thesis, 1929.
Barbara H. Lewis, *Methodist Overseas Missions,* 1960.
W. Stanley Rycroft and Myrtle M. Clemmer, *A Factual Study of Latin America.* New York: Commission on Ecumenical Mission and Relations, United Presbyterian Church, 1963.
Alberto G. Tallon, *Historia del Metodismo en el Rio de la Plata.* Buenos Aires: Imprensa Metodista, 1936.

EDWIN H. MAYNARD
ARTHUR BRUCE MOSS

UTAH, U.S.A. (population 1,060,631 in 1970), is in the Rocky Mountains. It is bounded on the north by IDAHO and WYOMING, on the east by COLORADO, on the south by ARIZONA, and on the west by NEVADA. The region was ceded by MEXICO to the United States in 1848. The state's 84,916 square mile area is broken by fertile irrigated valleys. Utah is noted for the Great Salt Lake in the north and Lake Powell on the Colorado River in the south. In recent years manufacturing has become the state's major industry, moving ahead of mining, agriculture, and tourism. In 1847 some 2,000 Mormons entered the Salt Lake Valley, and according to the 1970 census, seventy-two per cent of the state's population were Latter Day Saints. Organized as a territory in 1850, Utah was admitted to the Union in 1896 after the Mormons agreed to outlaw polygamy.

JEDEDIAH SMITH, trapper and explorer, crossed the region in 1826 and may have been the first Methodist to set foot in what is now Utah. The first Methodist sermon in Utah was delivered in the Mormon Tabernacle, Salt Lake City, in 1868 by A. N. Fisher at the invitation of President Brigham Young. Soon after the completion of the Union Pacific Railroad in 1869, more Methodists entered Salt Lake City and the territory. LEWIS HARTSOUGH, a Methodist preacher, held regular services in the home of the Episcopal Bishop in Salt Lake City. Coming from Laramie, Wyo., on a prospecting tour, Hartsough did some preaching at Wasatch, Ogden, and Corinne, as well as at Salt Lake City. C. C. Nichols, local Methodist preacher and railroad employee, moved to Salt Lake City in the fall of 1869, and found time to do some preaching while serving as agent at the railroad station.

First Methodist Church at Salt Lake City was organized on May 22, 1870, and it continues as one of the most important Methodist congregations in the state. In the same year churches were built at Corinne and Ogden. Methodist churches were erected at Tooele in 1871, at Bingham Canyon and Copperton in 1874, and at Park City in 1884. By 1900 there were about ten Methodist churches in Utah. For the next fifty years growth was slow because of the dominance of the Mormons and the lack of immigration. With the heavy movement of population westward after the second world war, Methodist membership in Utah increased.

The 1872 GENERAL CONFERENCE of the M.E. Church created the ROCKY MOUNTAIN CONFERENCE which included Utah, Idaho, Montana, and the part of Wyoming north of Utah. Organized at Salt Lake City, Aug. 8, 1872 with Bishop RANDOLPH S. FOSTER presiding, the conference began with three districts, seven preachers, and 201 members. In 1877 the conference was divided to form the Utah and MONTANA CONFERENCES. The Utah Conference included Utah, eastern Idaho, and the part of Wyoming north of Utah up to the 43rd parallel. Organized at Salt Lake City, Aug. 10, 1877 with Bishop ISAAC W. WILEY presiding, the Utah Conference began with one district and 143 members. The conference did not grow, and in 1880 the General Conference designated it as the Utah Mission. The mission began with 142 members. After 1891 the territory of the mission was limited to Utah. In 1892 it reported 1,076 members. Thereafter it grew slowly, achieving a total of some 2,000 members by 1930 and 2,554 by 1948. In the latter year the Utah Mission was absorbed, becoming a part of the Utah-Western District of the COLORADO CONFERENCE. Three years later there were 2,862 members in the Utah part of the district, and in 1951 some 4,337.

In 1957 the Colorado Conference absorbed the WYOMING STATE CONFERENCE and the name was changed to the ROCKY MOUNTAIN CONFERENCE. Thus eighty-one years after the Rocky Mountain Conference of which Utah had been a part was divided to form the Utah and Montana Conferences, Utah was again included in a conference called Rocky Mountain.

In the last quarter of the nineteenth century the Utah Methodists started several schools, one of which, Rocky Mountain Seminary at Salt Lake City, had an enrollment of 135. WESTMINSTER COLLEGE at Salt Lake City (an outgrowth of Rocky Mountain Seminary), was founded in 1875, and is supported by the Methodists. Presbyterians, and the United Church of Christ, with a present enrollment of 800 students. With help from the Women's Division of the denomination, the women's societies in the Utah Mission established Esther Halls for business and professional girls at Salt Lake City and Ogden, as well as the Highland Boy Community House at Bingham Canyon. Esther Hall in Salt Lake City has now become the Crossroads Urban Center serving the Negro and Spanish-American population.

In 1970 the Utah-Western District of the Rocky Mountain Conference reported twelve charges in the state of Utah with a total of 4,598 members. First Church and Christ Church, Salt Lake City had some 983 and 1,142 members, respectively, and First Church, Ogden had nearly 1,000. The property in the Utah part of the district was valued at $2,535,496.

General Minutes, ME, TMC, UMC.
Minutes of the Utah Mission and the Rocky Mountain Conference.
H. M. Merkel, *Utah.* 1938.   WARREN S. BAINBRIDGE

UTICA, NEW YORK, U.S.A. (population 90,000 in 1970), was settled about 1786 on the site of Fort Schuyler, and it was incorporated in 1832. FREEBORN GARRETTSON, who became presiding elder in New York State in 1788, traveled and preached over a wide area. It is believed that he preached in a home about two miles from Utica. In any event, it is known that Methodism reached Utica by 1791. WILLIAM COLBERT, presiding elder of the Genesee District, passed through Utica in 1803 and dined with Robert Stewart. In July, 1809, Bishop ASBURY passed through and wrote, "This is a flourishing place and we shall soon have a meetinghouse here."

Originally Utica was a point on the Oneida Circuit. In 1812 it became the head of a circuit in the Oneida District, GENESEE CONFERENCE, with Seth Mattison as the preacher in charge. The next year there were 423 members. As a station in 1819, Utica reported eighty-two members; Elias Bowen was appointed pastor that year.

In 1843 Utica reported 308 members. About that time the community became agitated over the question of slavery, and in a convention held there, May 31, 1843, the WESLEYAN METHODIST CHURCH was organized. The membership of the M.E. Church in the city showed a slight drop the next year, but by 1848 it had increased twenty per cent and a mission congregation with 102 members had been formed. By 1876 there were three churches with a total of 731 members, and in 1900 there were six with 1,282 members.

The A.M.E. ZION CHURCH in Utica is the oldest Negro congregation in the Mohawk Valley. In 1862, the pastor of that denomination in SYRACUSE visited Utica and, following services in homes and vacant stores, organized a mission. In 1873 the little congregation purchased the building of the Corn Hill M.E. Church, and five years later secured a structure near the courthouse which it used until 1916 when a new edifice called the Hope

Chapel A.M.E. Zion Church was erected. Displaced by urban redevelopment in recent years, the congregation purchased the Trinity Moravian Church, 751 South Street. For more than sixty years, Hope Chapel was the only Negro church in Utica.

In 1970, The United Methodist Church had three churches in Utica—Asbury, Central, and Dryer Memorial. They reported respectively 263, 737, and 452 members, with property valued at $146,000, $558,000, and $135,000, and they raised for all purposes during the year $13,000, $47,000, and $22,000.

Collier's Encyclopedia. Crowell-Collier Publishing Co., 1965.
General Minutes, MEC and UMC.
E. S. Bucke, *History of American Methodism,* Vol. 1. 1964.
M. Simpson, *Cyclopaedia.* 1878.   JESSE A. EARL
W. C. WOOD

KOGORO UZAKI

UZAKI, KOGORO (1870-1930), bishop of the JAPAN Methodist Church, was born in Himeji, March 17, 1870. He went to Kobe in 1886 to study western learning, and there met the LAMBUTHS, pioneer Methodist missionaries, who taught him English. He thus became one of the first students at Palmore Institute. He became a Christian and was baptized in 1887. In 1888 he entered the Theological Department of Aoyama Gakuin in TOKYO, but when Kwansei Gakuin was established in Kobe the next year, he transferred to the new school, and so was one of the first graduates from its Theological Department. Some years later he studied at VANDERBILT UNIVERSITY.

He was ordained in 1893, the first Japanese elder in the Southern Methodist Conference. He served churches in Kobe, Hiroshima, Osaka, and Kyoto. In Kyoto, in addition to his church work, he was professor in the Third Government University. When the Japan Methodist Church was organized in 1907, he was made editor of the *Advocate,* and later became secretary of the Board of Missions. In 1913 he was elected President of Chinzei

Gakuin, Methodist Boys School in Nagasaki, at the same time serving as PRESIDING ELDER of the Kyushu District. In 1919, he was elected as the third bishop of the Japan Methodist Church. He was re-elected twice, serving until his death in 1930.

Bishop Uzaki was recognized as a leader of outstanding ability, not only in his own church and in all Christian circles in Japan, but even in non-Christian circles. He served as Chairman of the National Christian Council of Japan and on its Executive Committee; he represented Japan at the ECUMENICAL METHODIST CONFERENCE in LONDON; he was the head of the delegation from Japan at the Missionary Conference at Jerusalem. In 1926 when the Japanese Government created a committee of Buddhist, Shinto, and Christian leaders to investigate the institutions of religion in Japan, he was appointed as the Christian representative. After his death he was awarded the Sixth Order of Merit by special Imperial order because of the value of his service to Japan.

JOHN B. COBB, SR.

UZAKI, TAKESABURO (1900-   ), Japanese FREE METHODIST and ordained elder of JAPAN General Confer-

ence, and bishop of the same. He attended Japanese elementary and middle schools, and studied at Osaka Seminary, taking advanced studies in Pauline literature, New Testament theology, Life of Christ, philosophy, zoology, church history. He was contributing editor for *Japan Sunday School Commentary* for five years, and was the author of booklets on *Japanese Customs, The Christian Faith, Stewardship* (The Blessing of Giving) and others. He was pastor of Nippon Bashi Free Methodist Church (largest Free Methodist Church in Japan) for twenty-six years. His reinforced-concrete church was the only building of the area to survive the incendiary bombing of World War II. Uzaki continued here as pastor during the war years. He has been bishop of Japan General Conference since 1962. He has served as a member of the Board of Directors and Vice-president, Free Methodist World Fellowship; professor, Osaka Christian College; "Incho" (chancellor), Osaka Christian College and Seminary. His foreign travels include deputational and executive visits to North and South America. His residence is in Osaka, Japan.

BYRON S. LAMSON

V

VALDOSTA, GEORGIA, U.S.A. **First Church** was organized in 1859, and continues its ministry only two blocks from where it began. Its membership in 1970 numbered 2,174.

The vaulted mellow wooden ceiling of the sanctuary is emblematic of the naturally endowed forest land in which this community is set, as well as the spirit of the congregation which worships beneath it. A sanctuary constructed in 1896 was destroyed by fire in 1904, and was replaced by the present structure. This was renovated in 1952 and a great organ installed. The Strickland Memorial Building was constructed in 1941 and this expanded the educational facilities. Another educational unit was added in 1960. Resolving to retain its downtown location, land has been purchased to make the position secure.

First Church has given leadership in the establishing of five other Methodist churches in the area. This congregation has provided the last five mayors of the city, and this fact will indicate something of the church's position and influence in the community. Its gifts in leadership and stewardship to the wider church have been significant.

Sessions of the SOUTH GEORGIA ANNUAL CONFERENCE were held in this church in 1896, 1906, 1918, 1927, 1941, 1958, and 1969. Six young men have gone into the ministry from this church.

Pastors since 1930 include: J. P. Dell, A. W. Rees, C. M. Meeks, L. A. Harrell, L. H. Cochran, Albert S. Trulock, Mack Anthony, T. A. Whiting, A. Jason Shirah, and Frank Robertson.

JOSE L. VALENCIA

VALENCIA, JOSE LABARRETTE, SR. (1898-　　　), Filipino bishop, was born in Tagudin, Ilocos Sur, PHILIPPINES,

on Aug. 25, 1898, the son of Victor M. and Juana (Labarrete) Valencia. He spent his school years in the United States, receiving an A.B. from CORNELL COLLEGE, Mount Vernon, Iowa, in 1925; did post graduate summer work at GARRETT THEOLOGICAL SEMINARY in 1925, '27, and '28; and regular post graduate work at DREW UNIVERSITY SCHOOL OF THEOLOGY. He received the B.D. degree from Drew University in 1929; M.A. from Silliman University, 1947; and D.D. from Cornell College in 1948. It was while a student at Cornell College that he was converted from Roman Catholicism to Protestantism. On April 10, 1930, he married Manuela L. Lardizabal—their children are Jose L., Jr. (Methodist minister, WYOMING CONFERENCE), Ressureccion Florence (Mrs. Novin D. Schuman).

Jose L. Valencia was admitted on trial and ordained deacon in the UPPER IOWA CONFERENCE in 1928; full connection, elder in the Philippine Islands Annual Conference, 1930. His pastorates include: Methodist Church, Vigan, Ilocos Sur, 1929-31; United Evangelical Church, Tagudin, 1931-32; Methodist Church, Tuguegarao, Cagayan, Philippine Islands, 1932-41, 1943-48. He was superintendent of the Cagayan-North Isabela District at the time of his election to the episcopacy in 1948. His Area now includes the Northern and Northwest Philippines Annual Conferences on Luzon Island and the Mindanao Annual Conference on Mindanao Island.

He was secretary of the Philippine Islands Annual Conference, 1935-36, and the Philippine Islands North Annual Conference, 1936-38; a delegate to the Tambaram Missionary Conference; to the World Council of the WORLD COUNCIL OF CHURCHES; EAST ASIA CHRISTIAN CONFERENCE; delegate to the GENERAL CONFERENCE of 1948. He has been a trustee of the Union Theological Seminary, Manila since 1936 and chairman of the Board of Trustees (1948-52); trustee of Harris Memorial College, 1948-50; trustee of Mary Johnston Hospital, Manila, and chairman of the Board since 1960; trustee of Mary Johnston School of Nursing since 1950, Philippine Christian College, MANILA (1949-1967). He served with the U.S. Navy, 1918-19. He is also a Mason (33°). His present address is Baguio City, Philippines.

Who's Who in The Methodist Church. 1966.　　　N. B. H.

VALENZUELA, RAIMUNDO ARMS (1916-　　　), bishop of the Methodist Church of CHILE, and missionary to that land, was born in Temuco, Chile. He was the son of J. Samuel Valenzuela, a minister of the Chile Annual Conference, and Olive Arms Valenzuela, daughter of the Rev. and Mrs. GOODSIL F. ARMS, pioneer Methodist missionaries in Chile. The Valenzuela family immigrated to the United States in 1927, settling in KANSAS.

His education consisted of an A.B. degree from the College of Emporia, Kansas, 1936; B.D. from DREW THEOLOGICAL SEMINARY, 1940; and Ph.D. from DREW

UNIVERSITY, 1955. He married Dorothy D. Bowie of Rochester, N. Y., in 1940, and they have five children.

Valenzuela became a member on trial of NEW YORK ANNUAL CONFERENCE and served Warren Street Church, BROOKLYN, 1940-42. He transferred to the Chile Conference in 1943 and was admitted in full in 1945. First he did student work, then was pastor of First Church, Concepcion, 1945-60, and again in 1963. He was conference secretary of Christian education in 1956 and 1960-62. After 1963 he was co-editor with Mrs. Valenzuela of the *New Life in Christ Curriculum* for the LATIN AMERICAN EVANGELICAL CHRISTIAN EDUCATION COMMISSION (CELADEC). He was a delegate to the LATIN AMERICA CENTRAL CONFERENCES of 1944, 1952, 1956, 1960, and 1964, and to the GENERAL CONFERENCES of 1964 and 1966.

Valenzuela's other activities were as organizer and general secretary of the Student Christian Movement of Chile, 1944-54; delegate to the General Committee of the WORLD'S STUDENT CHRISTIAN FEDERATION, 1946 and 1949; and chairman of CELADEC, 1962-66.

At the last Latin America Central Conference in SANTIAGO, Chile, in January 1969, Dr. Valenzuela was elected a bishop for a four-year term; and at the concomitant organization of the Methodist Church of Chile (which took place in connection with the Central Conference meeting), he was elected bishop for that new autonomous church. He was forthwith consecrated as such and assumed the superintendency with his residence to be in Santiago.

N. B. H.

VALLEY STREAM, LONG ISLAND, NEW YORK, U.S.A.

Grace Church is the largest Methodist church in the Metropolitan area. It is located on the outskirts of NEW YORK CITY in a typical suburban community. A handsome sanctuary of colonial structure and the corresponding educational building are the result of a sixty-year culmination of effort on the part of faithful members and some eleven pastors.

In the beginning, services were held in the Valley Stream firehouse. Then, in 1905, $2,000 was raised—$1,000 of the money coming from The Board of CHURCH EXTENSION of the M.E. Church—and the first church building was erected on what is now the site of the educational building. Sponsors of these first services were the "Sinner's Hope Chapel," which had been founded by the mother church, St. John's Methodist in Elmont. At that time Valley Stream was mostly farm land, and as the village grew, Grace Church grew with it, realizing most of its growth in the last ten or twelve years.

The membership has more than doubled in a twelve-year period and the SUNDAY SCHOOL is run on double session. Five choirs (including a Bell choir), three youth groups, eight women's groups, two couples' clubs, and a men's group, make for a well-rounded church-church school program. The 2,719 church members, as well as the inhabitants of this largest village in New York State, look to Grace Church for leadership in this community.

PAUL L. SARTORIO

VALTON, JOHN (1740-1794), British preacher of French Catholic origin, was born in LONDON on Nov. 23, 1740. Educated partly in FRANCE, he became an Anglican and, after working in the Ordnance Office, served for eighteen years in the army. Coming under Methodist influence at Burfleet, he became a CLASS LEADER and began to exhort, but did not feel ready to enter the ministry until 1775. A member of the original LEGAL HUNDRED, he had a diffident pulpit manner. Ill health caused him to locate, though he continued to preach. In 1792, he wrote a pamphlet supporting the campaign against West Indian slavery. He died on March 23, 1794.

J. Sutcliffe, *Life and Labours of J. Valton*. London, 1830.

JOHN A. VICKERS

VAN CORTLAND, PIERRE (1721-1814), American lieutenant-governor of NEW YORK in the early days of the Republic and a prominent Methodist layman, was born in New York City on Jan. 10, 1721. He possessed a large manor, originally consisting of 83,000 acres. He was an ardent friend of the republic during the Revolutionary War, and such men as George Washington, Benjamin Franklin, and Governor George Clinton were frequent visitors at his home. His daughter, Catharine, afterwards Mrs. Van Wyck, was converted under a sermon by WOOLMAN HICKSON, and uniting with the church, introduced Methodism into the family.

Governor Van Cortland early identified himself with Methodist interests and his house was a preaching-place until he gave land for a church building and erected a house of worship upon it. It turned out to be one of the best sites for a church in America. From the piazza of his house GEORGE WHITEFIELD had preached to listening hundreds, and Bishop ASBURY, FREEBORN GARRETTSON, and other early preachers found a hearty welcome in this hospitable abode.

In 1804 the first CAMP-MEETING east of the Hudson was held in Carmel, Putnam County, N. Y. Governor Van Cortland and his family attended it, and the presiding elder having applied for a grove on his land, he readily offered it, saying, "I have seen all this grove grow up, and have been solicited to cut down the trees because of the goodness of the soil, yet I have never consented to it, nor could I tell why till your application for it solved the mystery. It seems as if it is from the Lord." In this grove, camp-meetings were held annually until 1831. While the governor lived, he and his family were constant attendants, and remarkable spiritual influences accompanied many of the meetings. He died calmly and triumphantly May 1, 1814.

National Cyclopedia of American Biography.
M. Simpson, *Cyclopaedia*. 1881. N. B. H.

VAN COTT, MARGARET NEWTON (1830-1914), American woman who became one of the first women EVANGELISTS in the M.E. Church, was born in NEW YORK, March 25, 1830, as Margaret Newton, the daughter of William K. Newton, an Englishman and a member of the Protestant Episcopal Church. At the age of eleven years, she was confirmed at the Church of the Epiphany. During her girlhood, her home for a time was so near the M.E. Church at the corner of McEwen and Grand Streets in the Williamsburg section of New York, that she could hear the singing and the prayers. Her mother would not allow her to attend the Methodist services, although she longed to do so. She married Peter Van Cott in 1847. They had two daughters, although the

MARGARET VAN COTT

first child died when quite young. Her husband's failing health caused her to endeavor to carry on the business by which he had supported his family, and following the death of her daughter, Mrs. Van Cott lost her father and husband in rapid succession. Out of her sorrows, she made a surrender of herself to God, began to attend the prayer meetings of the Duane Street M.E. Church, and agreed to attend CLASS MEETINGS to aid in the singing, but only on the promise that she would not be asked to speak. However, she there found herself compelled to testify, and began to hold meetings over the city. At first these were for Negro people but then she began to accept wider invitations holding what we should call today revival services. Her preaching resulted in many conversions, and she began a public work which extended, it is said, to almost every state in the Union.

In 1868 she gave up all of her business and devoted herself entirely to the winning of souls. In her first year as an itinerant evangelist, she was able to count 500 persons received into various churches. She understood how to conduct promise and praise meetings, prayer and fasting meetings, mothers' meetings, and so forth, beside preaching nightly and twice on Sunday wherever she happened to be. In an age which frowned upon women taking the leadership in public affairs and preaching from the pulpit, she was a pioneer in activities which many women of a later generation began to emulate. She died on Aug. 29, 1914.

M. Simpson, *Cyclopaedia*. 1881.   N. B. H.

VANCOUVER, WASHINGTON, U.S.A. The first Protestant religious service held on the Pacific Coast was conducted by JASON LEE at Fort Vancouver Sept. 28, 1834, by invitation of John McLoughlin, chief factor of the Hudson's Bay Company. WILLIAM ROBERTS came to Fort Vancouver 1847-48, held services in private homes, and formed a class.

Chauncy O. Hosford was the first regular pastor appointed to the Vancouver Circuit in 1854. Since then Vancouver First Methodist Church has had a continual succession of ministers. In 1962 the appointments were

listing seven churches and nine ministers in the area of the first Vancouver circuit.

The first church building in Vancouver was erected in 1858. The second building to house this congregation was built in 1883, which building was later completely remodeled and a pipe organ added in 1910. The first unit of the present building was opened in 1950 and completed in 1960, its total value being $593,000.

The tenth session of the OREGON CONFERENCE (ME) was held in Vancouver in 1862, with Bishop MATTHEW SIMPSON presiding. There were forty-three members and five probationers. The thirty-first session of the Oregon Conference met there in 1883 with Bishop HENRY W. WARREN presiding. There were sixty-eight elders and thirty local preachers. The Puget Sound Conference (see PACIFIC NORTHWEST CONFERENCE), which was organized in 1884, held its sixth session in Vancouver in 1889. Bishop THOMAS BOWMAN presided. There were forty-two members, fourteen undergraduates, and twenty-two local preachers.

The membership of First Church has steadily grown. Beginning in 1854 with eighty-five members, it reported 1,784 in 1970. Other churches have likewise grown. There are in the present Vancouver district of the Pacific Northwest Conference of The United Methodist Church 11,517 members.

A. Atwood, *Conquerors*. 1907.
General Minutes, 1970.
H. K. Hines, *Pacific Northwest*. 1899.
Journals of the Oregon and Puget Sound Conference.
Carl Landerholm, *A History of the First Methodist Church of Vancouver, Washington*. N.d.   C. T. HATTEN

VANCURA, VACLAV (1883-   ), Methodist superintendent in CZECHOSLOVAKIA, was born on April 19, 1883, in Čermna, Bohemia. He studied in the schools of Bohemia (the public school, the high school, and one year at the Prague University as a special student), and in 1905 left to do missionary work in Surinam, Dutch Guiana. Later he studied in Oberlin, Ohio, and six years at Moravian College, Bethlehem, Pa., in the United States, where in 1963 he received the Th.D. degree. He also attended seminars at VANDERBILT UNIVERSITY, BOSTON UNIVERSITY, and Peabody in NASHVILLE. In PITTSBURGH he served a Czeck congregation (1915-18) and was secretary for the Y.M.C.A. in Siberia during the First World War (1918-20). Since 1922 he has acted as district superintendent of the Methodist Church and founder of several congregations in Czechoslovakia. From 1941 to his retirement in 1960, he was the leading superintendent.

N. B. H.

VAN DEUSEN, HENRY R. (See JUDICIAL COUNCIL.)

VANDERBILT UNIVERSITY, Nashville, Tennessee, traces its origin to a need sensed in the M.E. Church, South, for a central university. The first action looking toward such an institution was taken in the 1858 General Conference of that church. The Civil War which opened in 1861, prevented the consummation of the plan until 1872. Then representatives from seven annual conferences of the M.E. Church, South, meeting in what is known as the "Memphis Convention," completed plans for a university to be known as the Central University of the M.E.

Church, South. Bishop HOLLAND N. McTYEIRE participated in this convention, and it was largely due to his leadership that the university idea became a reality.

The convention set $1,000,000 as the amount needed to found the university but concluded that if one half was raised by the date set for opening it could proceed. Although the effort was praiseworthy, in view of the depleted economic conditions of the South, it was destined to fail. The year of solicitation of funds did not yield enough to pay for the expenses of the agents.

It was at this point that Bishop McTyeire's leadership proved most strategic. Through his personal connections with Cornelius Vanderbilt (Mrs. Vanderbilt was a first cousin to Mrs. McTyeire), the bishop secured a gift of $1,000,000 for the establishment of the university. This generous grant, made on March 27, 1873, prompted the board of trust to change the name from Central University to Vanderbilt University. In making his gift, Vanderbilt stipulated that Bishop McTyeire was to be president of the board of trust, and should be empowered to carry out plans for the university to purchase the needed land, erect the first buildings, and select the faculty. He was to have the right to veto any "injudicious appropriations or measures"; and all of his decisions were to be final, unless reversed by three fourths of the board of trust. The bishop faithfully discharged the heavy obligations placed upon him; and at the time of his death in 1889, Vanderbilt University had become established as the most influential educational institution in southern Methodism.

In 1893, James H. Kirkland succeeded LANDON C. GARLAND who had served as the university's first chancellor under Bishop McTyeire. Kirkland, a layman, while a loyal churchman, naturally did not combine the interests of both the university and church in the same fashion as Bishop McTyeire. Some of the bishops of the M.E. Church, South, who during Bishop McTyeire's life had left the university in his hands, after his death became active in the board of trust. Grasping the provision in the MEMPHIS Convention which requested the bishops to become a board of supervisors, they openly challenged the administrative practices of the new chancellor and held that these would alienate the university from the church. In a short time, there developed a power struggle between some of the bishops (not all, for the COLLEGE OF BISHOPS was divided in its loyalties) and the chancellor for control of the university.

The final test was to center about a self-perpetuating board of trust and the election of its members. The board of trust held that the charter secured by Bishop McTyeire made it a self-perpetuating body. He had insisted that the board should select its own members in order to prevent ill-considered choices. A commission authorized by the GENERAL CONFERENCE of the M.E. Church, South, of 1906 concluded otherwise, that the General Conference alone could fill vacancies on the board. The commission went further and held that, since the church founded the university, the COLLEGE OF BISHOPS possessed the power to take it over, if in their judgment it was not being administered in harmony with the church's directions.

The commission's decisions were resisted by the board of trust. When the GENERAL CONFERENCE of 1910 elected three trustees to the board of trust, the board refused to seat them and proceeded to fill the existing vacancies. Court proceedings were instituted by the bishops to enforce mandates of the General Conference in the Chancery Court of TENNESSEE. This court ruled in favor of the bishops, holding that the General Conference could fill the vacancies on the board of trust. The university appealed this decision to the Tennessee Supreme Court, and the decision of the Chancery Court was overruled. This ruling not only vested the control of the university with the board of trust, but recognized Cornelius Vanderbilt as the founder, thus depriving the bishops of the right of veto power that they claimed was derived because the church was the founder of the university. The court, however, did uphold the right of the General Conference or its authorized agent to confirm the nominations made by the board of trust to fill vacancies on that board.

The court's decision pleased neither side. Bishop ELIJAH HOSS, leader of the opposition, declared, "We lost everything. We did not get the shadow of a shade." Kirkland is reported as saying to the university's attorneys, "Well, gentlemen, you lost your case. We get no relief. The cudgel of the General Conference is still there in its right to confirm or reject any trustee-elect." (Moore, p. 124.)

At the General Conference of 1914, the future of Vanderbilt as a Methodist university depended upon that body's accepting the interpretation of the charter made by Tennessee's Supreme Court. The conference itself was almost evenly divided, as may be seen in the final vote. After several days of heated discussion, 151 members voted to sever all relations with the university, and 140 voted to keep the university.

It should be noted here that the question of the university's affiliation with the church was not the one the court was asked to decide. The question was, "What are the legal rights of the church?" The General Conference in refusing to accept the only relationship that it had ever possessed, namely, the right to determine the membership on the board of trust, permitted the university to pass into the hands of a private corporation.

The aforementioned vote justifies the conclusion that the historic controversy should not be solely construed as an encounter between the church and Vanderbilt. Rather it was a struggle between two factions, each led by powerful leaders holding different points of view on the operation of a church-related university. Because of the nature of the issues involved, the church was destined to be hurt regardless of which side won. In the end Methodism lost Vanderbilt, but a dispassionate review of the controversy has convinced many church leaders that had the form of control advocated by those who led the attack upon Vanderbilt become fixed, the church's future leadership in higher education would have been seriously limited.

The General Conference of 1914 committed to a commission of sixteen the closing of the Vanderbilt chapter and the beginning of plans for two new universities.

Between 1872 and 1914 Vanderbilt University was the most potent educational factor not only in southern Methodism but in the South. Its theological school had supplied almost all of the professionally trained ministers and missionaries. Most of the South's colleges had been enriched with teachers educated at Vanderbilt, and through the Southern Association of Schools and Colleges (the South's accrediting agency), Vanderbilt helped to set qualitative standards for all higher education.

After the break, Vanderbilt continued the development which had been started previously. Its professional schools are rated among the nation's best, and its divinity school has approximately fifty per cent of its enrollment from The United Methodist Church.

John O. Gross, "The Bishops vs. Vanderbilt University," *Tennessee Historical Quarterly*, March 1963, and *Methodist History*, April 1964.
E. Mims, *Vanderbilt University*. 1946.
J. M. Moore, *Life and I*. 1948.
J. J. Tigert, *Holland Nimmons McTyeire*. 1955.
Tennessee Supreme Court *Reports* 129, ii, 279ff.

JOHN O. GROSS

VANDERHORST, RICHARD H. (1813-1872), second bishop of the C.M.E. CHURCH, was born on Dec. 15, 1813, at Georgetown, S. C. He was a slave owned by the Wragg sisters and learned the trade of a carpenter. In 1835 he joined the M.E. Church and was made a CLASS LEADER. Later, he was given a license to preach. From 1868 to 1870, Richard Vanderhorst was a presiding elder in a Negro annual conference. When the first GENERAL CONFERENCE met in 1870 to establish the new C.M.E Church, he was the second to be elected to the office of bishop. He was consecrated by Bishops McTYEIRE and PAINE of the "mother" denomination. Bishop Vanderhorst served only eighteen months; he died on July 17, 1872.

Harris and Patterson, *C.M.E. Church*. 1965.
I. Lane, *Autobiography*. 1916.

RALPH G. GAY

VANDUZAR, J. E. A. (1852-1875), first Methodist missionary to the Cubans, appeared in GEORGIA at some unknown date and at Tallahassee, Fla., in 1873, was licensed to preach. The same year he joined the FLORIDA CONFERENCE and was appointed in 1874 to Cuban mission work in Key West, where CHARLES A. FULWOOD was pastor of Stone Church. On the boat trip to Key West he became acquainted with the youthful HENRY B. (Enrique Benito) SOMEILLAN, who was destined later to carry out Vanduzar's mission to Cuba.

He was described as "amiable, magnetic and dynamic," which gave him an easy approach to his Cuban friends. He was devoted to his work and in a letter to the BOARD OF MISSIONS' Secretary said, "this is an important mission. It is an entrance-gate through which the island of Cuba, so beautiful, can be entered."

In 1875 a terrible epidemic of yellow fever broke out in Key West. He was advised to leave the island with the hordes of those escaping to the mainland. His reply was, "The Lord placed me among the Cubans and among them I will live or die." Soon he succumbed and his dying whisper to Doctor Fulwood was, "Don't give up the Cuban Mission." These words are inscribed on his tomb in the Key West cemetery.

S. A. Neblett, *Methodism in Cuba*. 1966.   GARFIELD EVANS

VANDYKE, EDWARD HOWARD (1863-1921), American minister and missionary, was born May 20, 1863, in Odessa, Del. As a child he lived with his parents on a farm on Wye Island in Queen Anne's County, Md., and was a member of the M.P. church there. VanDyke was converted in 1875. He prepared for the ministry through study at WESTMINSTER THEOLOGICAL SEMINARY, graduating in 1887. That same year he joined the MARYLAND CONFERENCE of the M.P. Church.

For three years he served pastorates in MARYLAND, then feeling the need to serve the Church in the field

of foreign missions, he offered his services as a missionary to JAPAN. VanDyke arrived in Japan with his wife, Carrie, on Jan. 25, 1890.

During the more than twenty-five years that followed, VanDyke became a highly respected figure in Japan. He had a natural gift for the Japanese language, and he shared with the Japanese a love of architecture and music. He served as President of the Japan Mission Conference and later was President of Nagoya College. His dynamic leadership caused the college to grow steadily and soundly. Enrollment grew to 400 under his administration. His interest in the Japanese language and culture prompted him to write a book explaining a system of simplified Japanese characters. The plan had merit, but was not generally supported.

His selfless devotion to the development of Methodism in Japan was recognized by ADRIAN COLLEGE, Adrian, Mich., when it bestowed its D.D. degree on VanDyke in 1911.

In 1916 Van Dyke attended the GENERAL CONFERENCE held in Zanesville, Ohio, representing the Japan Mission Conference. At that time he reluctantly gave up his work in Japan to become pastor of several Maryland Conference churches which he served from 1917 to 1921.

VanDyke died very suddenly May 24, 1921, while on his way to Centreville, Md., for interment services for his father who had died a few days before. They are both buried in Chester Cemetery in Centreville, Md.

Minutes of the Maryland Conference, MP, 1922.

JAMES H. STRAUGHN

ANNIE VAN GRONINGEN

VAN GRONINGEN, ANNIE J. M. (1901-1961), was a lay member of the Belgium Conference who was born in BRUSSELS on Aug. 22, 1901, the daughter of a Dutch Reformed pastor, and was blessed with an excellent education and remarkable linguistic qualifications. She entered the service of the Methodist Mission in Brussels as secretary in 1921 and became assistant treasurer in

1935. During the Nazi occupation (1940-44) under trying circumstances she gave evidence of unusual gifts in administration. She was elected conference treasurer in 1960, lay delegate to the European Methodist Uniting Conference in 1939, also to three GENERAL CONFERENCES of The Methodist Church, 1952, 1956, 1960. She was a member of Executive Committee of the CENTRAL AND SOUTHERN EUROPE CENTRAL CONFERENCE. She died in Brussels on Oct. 8, 1961. A tablet placed at the entrance of Susanna Wesley Residence in Brussels commemorates the part taken by Annie van Groningen in preparation and erection of this institution for the aged.

WILLIAM G. THONGER

W. W. VAN ORSDEL

VAN ORSDEL, WILLIAM WESLEY ("Brother Van") (1850-1919), American legendary Methodist EVANGELIST who, with a mellow baritone voice, sang and preached his way into hearts of listeners during forty-seven years on the frontier, winning the sobriquet of "Best Loved Man in Montana." He started life on a farm near Gettysburg, Pa., in March 1850, youngest of seven children born to William and Mary Van Orsdel, both of whom died before he was twelve. Impressionable "Willie" watched fearfully as Union and Confederate forces swayed in the great blood-letting, July 1-3, 1863. There, after the Gettysburg Address, Nov. 16, 1865, President Abraham Lincoln shook the boy's hand and patted his head—an experience never forgotten.

Acting upon what he called "a sound conversion to the Lord's side of human affairs," Will became a member of the Gettysburg Methodist church at age twelve. Later he joined his brothers, Samuel and Fletcher, in protracted meetings, then did freelance evangelism while employed near Oil City, Pa., as an operator of a stationary engine. By arrangement with his boss, he avoided working Sundays by pumping more oil in six days than others did in seven.

Drawn westward to CHICAGO, Will was thrilled by the famed lecture, "The Bright Side of Life in Libby Prison," of CHARLES C. McCABE, "the singing CHAPLAIN" who afterwards became a Methodist bishop. When young Van Orsdel asked if he should return east, McCabe advised: "Go away out West and you will realize what Paul meant when he said that he rejoiced he did not build on another

man's foundation." Van Orsdel took the advice, and at age twenty-two, at Fort Benton, Mont., he stepped from the Missouri River Steamer *Far West*, penniless and still owing $50 on his passage, but happy. With a carpetbag in one hand, a Bible under his arm, he stalked the streets for a place to preach. Tradition supported by old timers' recollections says he delivered his first sermon in a saloon called The Four Deuces. The rough crowd was delighted with his singing, especially a song which he later made known throughout MONTANA, *Diamonds in the Rough*, a ballad of a converted circus clown.

His passion to evangelize the Blackfeet Indians soon cooled, but not before they invited him to join a buffalo hunt with the privilege of shooting the lead buffalo. Charlie Russell, Brother Van's warm friend who was later to achieve fame as "the cowboy artist" and whose canvases are now valued at fabulous figures, painted the scene— Van Orsdel wearing a Prince Albert coat and plug hat with a six shooter, astride a plunging horse. The canvas is on display in a Great Falls museum.

Completely gregarious, Brother Van loved people. He went by ox team to the new diggings at HELENA, singing and preaching. There a bearded miner put $50 in the collection plate, explaining "I'm way ahead. If I ain't got it, I can't lose it." Brother Van rode circuit, covering 4,000 miles, with his big-boned chestnut horse. Once he walked from Bozeman to a mining camp where he was mistaken for a horsethief. His hasty captors were for hanging him, but he demurred eloquently. "If he's Brother Van like he says," yelled one of them, "make him sing!" Never did he do *Diamonds in the Rough* more feelingly. "Saved a life with that song," he afterwards quipped. "My own!"

As Indian scares subsided the gold camps flared and ranchers came, then homesteaders and townspeople. Van had started as a lay evangelist but was ordained and in time became PRESIDING ELDER of the Great Falls, North Montana Mission, and Helena districts. At first he teamed with scholarly FRANCIS ASBURY RIGGIN, but soon found another evangelistic partner, THOMAS C. ILIFF, and the two became known as "The Heavenly Twins." At 1874 meetings in Helena, it was said that Iliff "would dangle the sinners over the brimstone pit, and then Brother Van would sing and pray them back again."

Roving Montana from border to border, Brother Van went horseback or by stagecoaches, then graduated to freight and passenger trains, and finally to a Model T Ford. Many Methodists kept a room ready for him, and there still are spare bedrooms in some Montana homes known as "Brother Van's room." He was everybody's friend, and equally at home with bullwhacker or soldier, sheep man or cowman, miner or merchant. All the love which had gone into a romance with Jennie Johnson, blighted by her death due to tuberculosis, he poured into Montana Methodism. He was instrumental in building a hundred churches, fifty parsonages, six hospitals, and two institutions of learning.

He died Dec. 19, 1919 at Great Falls and is buried in Prickly Pear Valley at Forestvale Cemetery, near Helena, in a plot marked by a large boulder, similar to the one over the grave of his friend, Charlie Russell. It is graven with two words: "Brother Van."

Paul Adams, *When Wagon Trails Were Dim*. Montana Conference Commission on Education, 1956.
Ramon F. Adams and Homer E. Britzman, *Charles M. Russell,*

The Cowboy Artist, A Biography. Pasadena: Trails End Publishing Co., 1948.

Stella W. Brummitt, *Brother Van.* New York: Missionary Education Movement, 1919.

The Epworth Herald, Jan. 3, 1920.

Floyd E. Green, "Brother Van: The Story of William Wesley Van Orsdel." Ms., Montana State College, 1955.

Robert W. Lind, *From the Ground Up, The Story of "Brother Van" Orsdel.* Missoula: Robert W. Lind, 1961.

George Logan, *History of North Montana Mission.* N.p., n.d. circa 1909.

E. L. Mills, *Plains, Peaks and Pioneers.* 1947.

Alson Jesse Smith, *Brother Van, A Biography of the Rev. William Wesley Van Orsdel.* Nashville and New York: Abingdon-Cokesbury, 1948.

Together Magazine, July 1958.   LELAND D. CASE

VAN PELT, PETER (1717-1783), American layman, born on Staten Island, N.Y., was baptized "Petrus" as an infant on April 16, 1717, by a minister of the Reformed Protestant Dutch Church. He came of Dutch ancestry long established on the Island, his father being Johannes Van Pelt. In spite of opposition to Methodists by the Reformed Dutch, Van Pelt welcomed FRANCIS ASBURY in 1771. Asbury preached in Van Pelt's house on Wood Row, near Rossville.

Van Pelt was a farmer and civic leader who served in the French and Indian War. Town meetings were held in his home. In November 1771, he was in PHILADELPHIA and heard Asbury who had arrived in America a few days before. On his journey by stage from Philadelphia to NEW YORK, he met Van Pelt and was invited to his home and to preach to the people of Staten Island. In Van Pelt's house Asbury preached his first sermon in the province of New York, on Saturday, Nov. 9, 1771. He preached twice more at Van Pelt's on this occasion and also at the home of Justice Hezekiah Wright in Rossville. Among those who heard Asbury was Peter's brother, Benjamin Van Pelt, who later went to the west where Asbury met him and where he became a leader of Methodism on the frontier.

From the early Methodist preaching in Peter Van Pelt's home the influence spread and the homes of other prominent men were opened. Van Pelt died in February 1783. In 1947 the Methodist churches of Staten Island dedicated a bronze marker in honor of Francis Asbury and Peter Van Pelt on the grounds of Woodrow Church, the "Mother Church of Staten Island Methodism."

V. B. Hampton, *Newark Conference.* 1957.

VERNON B. HAMPTON

VANSTONE, THOMAS GRILLS (1851-1898), British BIBLE CHRISTIAN pioneer missionary, was born at Putford, Devon, March 16, 1851. He found employment in London at nineteen, but was remarkably directed into the ministry. Appointed to the Kingsbrompton Circuit, Somerset, he lodged with Robert and Elizabeth Burston of Venn, Upton, who aroused his enthusiasm for missionary work, and in 1885 with S. T. THORNE he pioneered the connectional mission to Yunnan. Fever and unremitting toil however broke his health, and he was invalided home in 1892, thereafter serving in the Chagford Circuit, which flourished under his care. He died at Whiddon Down on May 13, 1898, and was buried at Providence, Throwleigh.

L. H. Court, *Dartmoor Saints.* 1927.   GLYN COURT

VAN VALIN, CLYDE E. (1929-   ), American FREE METHODIST, ordained elder, of the Kentucky-Tennessee Conference, was born at Windham, N. Y. He married Beatrice Roushey in 1950. His education included the A.B., ROBERTS WESLEYAN COLLEGE, 1951; B.D., ASBURY THEOLOGICAL SEMINARY, 1954. He has served as pastor, Allentown, Pa., 1954-58; Eastern Regional Director of Free Methodist Youth, 1958-59; General Representative, F.M.Y., 1960; Director-Chaplain, John Wesley Seminary Foundation and pastor Free Methodist Church, Wilmore, Ky.

BYRON S. LAMSON

VARICK, JAMES (dates uncertain), a Negro minister of early NEW YORK who was selected as the first bishop, or as it is commonly called, the first superintendent of the A.M.E. ZION CHURCH.

Little is known about Superintendent Varick and all that does appear of the record is confusing. Bishop JONES states that the date of his birth has been certified as being 1781. J. W. HOOD and JOHN JAMISON MOORE declare that Varick was one of the members who first began meeting separately in 1770. Still another account states that he was licensed to preach at the age of seventeen in 1813. To have been a leader in 1780 makes it appear that something must have been wrong with his calculation as well as prevailing custom. It is not at all unreasonable to suppose that only older people were accorded the privilege of leadership. Some educational attainment may have allowed for greater participation but in no account can we find a record of this educational attainment. Comparing him with CHRISTOPHER RUSH, the latter was at least thirty-eight years old before he was licensed to preach.

It is concluded that Varick was born in Newburg, N. Y., anywhere between 1750 and 1796. Somewhere between these two dates seems more reasonable. We call attention to the fact that Rush speaks of Abraham Thompson as being old, but nowhere states such of Varick. If the latter, as Hood states, was born in 1750, by 1820 he would have been seventy years old, an advanced age even in these days of longevity. Certainly Thompson could not have been much older. Father Thompson was passed over because of his age and his earlier stand. Certainly Varick had to be younger.

Wheeler states that James Varick was the son of Richard Varick, a man of Dutch descent. Richard is supposed to have been born in Hackensack, N. J. He moved, with his parents, to New York City. James Varick's mother was of Dutch-Indian-Negro lineage. He is supposed to have been born in Newburg, N. Y. (according to Wheeler in 1750) while his mother was in that city visiting. It is unknown whether his mother was free or slave. The family was very influential in New York and it may have been that James was sent to school, there being two or three available at the time. James Varick became a shoemaker and maintained a shop in Orange, now Baxter Street. He must have been a boy of sixteen when PHILLIP EMBURY and Captain THOMAS WEBB began their preaching mission in New York.

According to some calculations, James Varick was married to Aurelia Jones in 1798, when he was approximately forty-eight years of age. (This again would make him rather old by the time the first yearly conference was held.) To this union were born four children: Daniel,

Andrew, Emeline and Mary. No member of Varick's family ever became a member of Zion Church. While this is also true of the family of PETER WILLIAMS, yet Peter never left the Mother Church as such, and when he died he was buried in an Episcopal Church yard.

The record is not clear as to when James Varick began to preach. It appears that he was not among the early ministers of the period (1800) for his name as a preacher does not appear in any of the early writings. His relationship to the African Chapel (later called Zion) had to be that of a layman. In the period, 1800-1820, the name of Varick appeared more and more frequently however.

Because of the peculiar circumstances under which the Zion Church was laboring, it was decided to appoint a District Elder or Superintendent in 1821. It was the Superintendent's task to supervise the work in all the churches. While Rush states that there was no real precedent for such a move, yet the office which the chief elder held in the City of New York may have given the ministers the idea. Abraham Thompson, from all custom, should have been chosen the District Elder, but possibly because of his early actions in the church he was passed over and the position given to James Varick. Bishop Moore uses the term "District Chairman" instead of Elder or Superintendent. He may be right in taking this stand since ordinations to this office had not been accomplished. It appears, however, that seniority played a part in the election as would naturally be the custom among the group. It is this writer's opinion that background and custom would have dictated this.

Varick, one of the two original elders, was elected first by the members of Zion Church.

From the ministerial angle certainly Abraham Thompson appeared to insist on his viewpoint more frequently than any other of this group. One cannot overlook the shadow of Peter Williams behind every action of the Negro group in New York. While we have only Rush to whom to turn (and all writers, John Jamison Moore and J. W. Hood included, have had only his records for this early period), all other accounts which can be located have brought no other interpretation.

In 1822, according to the Disciplinary provisions, James Varick was elected the first Superintendent of the new denomination. He was re-elected in 1826. Some writers state that he died in his second term, "shortly before the conference in 1828," early in 1828. Bishop John J. Moore who was very close to the period and was enough of a student to be at one time one of the secretaries for the General Conference, has him presiding in 1828. Bishop Singleton T. Jones states that he was Superintendent for four years while Christopher Rush apparently assisted him. Bishop E. D. W. Jones states that he had passed away by the conference of 1828. The difference of opinion is too divergent to allow for a decision as many of these accounts and statements are based on reminiscences and are not wholly reliable. When the conference met in New York in 1828, Leven Smith was urged for the position of Superintendent. He declined, and Christopher Rush was selected. At this conference James Anderson came from New Haven and George Tredwell from Long Island. Jacob Matthews succeeded Christopher Rush as pastor of the Mother Church.

D. H. Bradlay, *AMEZ Church*. 1956.
C. Rush, *Short Account*. 1843.

DAVID H. BRADLEY

THOMAS VASEY

VASEY, THOMAS (c. 1746-1826), was a British clergyman-itinerant whose birthplace and origins are unknown. It is said that he lost his wealth for espousing Methodism. His chief claim to fame lies in the fact that he was one of the two elders whom JOHN WESLEY ordained and sent to America with THOMAS COKE when the Methodist Episcopal Church was organized in 1784. It is said that Wesley first employed Vasey in 1775 as one of his preachers, and perhaps he was one whom Wesley would have liked to have the Bishop of London ordain for America. At any rate, Wesley did ordain him a DEACON and then an ELDER, in BRISTOL on Sept. 1 and 2, 1784. He thereupon sent Vasey to America with Coke and RICHARD WHATCOAT, and there he labored for two years. However, Vasey apparently did not feel that John Wesley's ordination was sufficient, for he was reordained a priest by Bishop White of the newly organized Protestant Episcopal Church in America, who himself had just been ordained to the episcopacy by the bishops in England.

Bishop Simpson states that Vasey was a great sufferer, that he preached not "about Christianity, but Christ." After a short while in America, Vasey went back to Britain, where he had a curacy for a short while, but then rejoined Wesley in 1789. He traveled mainly in northern England until 1811, but was involved in SACRAMENT and trustee controversies (Bristol, 1794). He was a Reader (resident clergyman) at Wesley's Chapel, LONDON, 1811-25, with a large class. He was named in Wesley's DEED OF DECLARATION. He died on retirement at LEEDS on Dec. 27, 1826.

J. G. Stevenson, *City Road Chapel*. 1872.   G. LAWTON

VAZEILLE, MRS. MARY (1710-1781), sometimes listed as Mary Wesley, was born Mary Goldhawk, married Anthony Vazeille, and after his death married JOHN WESLEY. On that occasion the *Gentleman's Magazine*, which gave the date as Feb. 18, 1751, spoke of her as a merchant's widow with an income of £300 per annum. John Wesley refused to touch any of her money, which was wholly secured for her and for her four children. CHARLES WESLEY was very unhappy about the match both before and after the event, and his forebodings proved justified. Although at first she made an attempt to accompany John Wesley on his preaching travels, this proved too exhausting a task. Remaining at the Foundery, she served as a kind of secretary for John Wesley, but soon became very jealous as she read the many letters from women Methodists to him, especially those from SARAH RYAN. In 1758 she left him, vowing to see him no more, yet continued to dog his footsteps. From time to time she returned, and he did not turn her away, although for thirty years (to use his own words) she had "torn the flesh off my bones by her fretting and murmuring."

Granted that he could give no woman that all-absorbing attention that had already been given to God, the springs of his genuine affection were dried up by his wife's perverseness, which was probably worsened by a streak of mental unsoundness, and it remained for him only to show what infinite stores of fortitude and forbearance he possessed. She died on Oct. 8, 1781, aged seventy-one, but Wesley was not informed of the event until after his return to LONDON from a preaching journey on the day of her burial.

G. E. Harrison, *Son to Susanna.* 1937.
J. A. Leger, *Wesley's Last Love.* 1910.

MALDWYN L. EDWARDS

VEH, RAYMOND M. (1901-   ), American E.U.B. minister, editor, youth leader and preacher, was born June 26, 1901 at Gibsonburg, Ohio. Degrees were received from the following schools: B.A., NORTH CENTRAL COLLEGE; M.A., University of Illinois; D.D. and Litt.D., WESTMAR COLLEGE.

He was licensed by the Ohio Conference, EVANGELICAL CHURCH, in 1928 and was ordained two years later. Raymond M. Veh was married to Helen Zimmermann, Nov. 17, 1928.

He served as Director of Student Activities, Pilgrim Foundation, University of Illinois, 1924-25; Professor of Sociology and Assistant Dean of Men, EVANSVILLE COLLEGE, Evansville, Ind., 1925-27. In October 1927, he was elected Adult Counsellor for the Youth Fellowship and editor of the *Evangelical Crusader.* He continued in the editorship and with the union of his church and the UNITED BRETHREN IN CHRIST in 1946, he became editor of the E.U.B. youth publication, *Builders.* He also edited the denominational *Year Book.*

Raymond Veh served in a number of interdenominational activities: Editorial Advisor, Protestant Committee on Scouting; Committee on Youth Work, NATIONAL COUNCIL OF CHURCHES of Christ in America; Vice President, Cooperative Publishing Association; denominational representative for the AMERICAN BIBLE SOCIETY since 1937; representative at the first World Conference of Christian Youth, Amsterdam, Holland, 1939; WORLD COUNCIL OF CHURCHES, Amsterdam, 1948, and Evanston, Ill., 1954.

He is the author of a number of denominational publications: *Thumbnail Sketches of Evangelical Bishops; The Evangelical Church at Work; My Church Faces Union; Life as an Achievement; Evangelical United Brethren Church Calendar;* and *Interesting Evangelical Churches.*

Although retired and living in a Milwaukee, Wis., suburb, he retains his membership in the OHIO WEST CONFERENCE of The United Methodist Church.

CLINTON L. ALLEN

VELASCO URDA, EPIGMENIO (1880-1940), Mexican minister, was born in Cuicatlán, Oaxaca, MÉXICO, on March 24, 1880. Through contact with a missionary he studied in Puebla where he decided to enter the ministry. He finished his theological training there, and entered the Conference on trial in 1906, was ordained DEACON in 1908, and ELDER in 1910.

Velasco made something of a record by being pastor in the "Cathedral of Methodism" (Gante Church, México City) for twenty-five years in two terms, 1907-22, and 1930-40. From 1922-30 he was pastor of Central Church, Puebla, and under his leadership a beautiful church was built to replace the old one burned by accident just three days after he preached his first sermon there. His name, with those of JOHN WESLEY BUTLER, J P HAUSER and Mrs. Gould C. Hauser, will long be remembered with the history of Gante Street Church, "La Santísima Trinidad." He has been known and remembered as a true pastor, a real shepherd to his flock. Always active, he noted those not present at regular church services and looked for them immediately. He was an excellent organizer. With the shake of his hand and a smile on his face, he transmitted to others the joy of the Gospel. He could find a task for everybody and obtained their consent to do it. Convincing and moving in his preaching, he was strong and evangelistic.

Epigmenio Velasco was a lover of music from childhood. He had a good tenor voice and loved to sing, especially "The Holy City." His church was never without a choir. He organized mixed groups and men's choirs. He translated choir music and hymns; made arrangements and composed a few hymns, both words and music. He was professor of music at the National Preparatory School of México City; also of the Methodist boys school in Puebla, 1922-30. It was his joy to lead congregational singing, large choirs, and large assemblies and conventions. He organized concerts of sacred music with the best elements of selected music. He was the first to direct Handel's "Messiah" in Spanish.

He was a champion in brotherliness. He represented the Church at international conferences at PANAMÁ, Edinburgh, LONDON and several in the U.S.A. Doña Josefina Guevara de Velasco, his wife, was most active in denominational women's work and was president of the Interdenominational Women's Association. This couple was blessed with seven children, all active in church work. He died on March 19, 1940.

GUSTAVO A. VELASCO G.

VENEZUELA is an oil-producing, mining, and stock raising country on the northern coast of South America, which boasts one of the highest per capita incomes in South America and has one of the lowest percentages of Protestants. Venezuela has an area of 352,150 square miles and a population of 10,035,000 (1969). The location is tropical, but climate is moderated by altitude in its mountain areas.

Columbus first set foot on the South American continent in what is now Venezuela in 1498. After early explorations, Spanish power was established, and the region was a colony of Spain until 1821. Under leadership of Simon Bolivar a state known as Gran Colombia was established, a confederation of what are now Venezuela, COLOMBIA, and ECUADOR. Secession of Venezuela in 1830 broke up the confederation, and it has been an independent republic ever since. The 1961 constitution guarantees religious freedom, but there have been interreligious tensions even in modern times.

Venezuela has never had a substantial Methodist mission, though some of the earliest Protestant contacts were by Methodists. The two great Bible colporteurs, ANDREW M. MILNE and FRANCIS PENZOTTI, visited Venezuela early in 1886 from ARGENTINA as part of a tour that took them through the northern and westcoast countries of South America. Beginning at the port city of La Guayra, they visited many of the cities of Venezuela. As a result of the interest generated by that visit, a group of families petitioned the South American Mission, headquartered in BUENOS AIRES, to send Penzotti to them as a permanent missionary. Penzotti was sent instead to Peru, and no missionary was available for Venezuela. However, a colporteur, H. D. Osuna, organized a Methodist SUNDAY SCHOOL in the capital city of Caracas in 1888. It lasted only five months.

Other Protestant groups then established work in Venezuela and, under comity agreements, the Methodist Church has since not undertaken to reestablish work there.

W. C. Barclay, *History of Missions.* 1957.
W. Stanley Rycroft and Myrtle M. Clemmer, *A Factual Study of Latin America.* New York: Commission on Ecumenical Mission and Relations, United Presbyterian Church. U.S.A., 1963.

EDWIN H. MAYNARD

VENN, HENRY (1724-1797), was one of several Evangelical Anglican clergy connected with eighteenth-century Methodism and JOHN WESLEY. He was born in Barnes, Surrey, March, 1724, of a line of Anglican clergy, was educated in LONDON and BRISTOL and entered St. John's College, Cambridge, in 1742. Ordained deacon in 1747, he was fellow of Queen's College from 1749 to 1757. His spiritual life was deepened by reading the *Serious Call* of WILLIAM LAW. Venn served two curacies: to Mr. Langley, of St. Matthew's, Friday Street, London, from 1750; and Clapham, Surrey, from 1754.

In 1759 he began his most famous work as vicar of Huddersfield in Yorkshire. His preaching drew large crowds, and he made a point of visiting out-lying hamlets and preaching in houses. His work attracted the mistaken criticism that he preached faith alone and not Christian works. Declining health prompted him to remove to Yelling, Huntingdonshire, in 1771, where he was noted for his insistence on Sabbath observance. Besides the publication of various sermons his works were: *Fourteen Sermons* (1759); the *Complete Duty of Man* (1763), a work in which he criticized the doctrine of Christian perfection as John Wesley taught it; *Examination of Dr. Priestley's Free Address on the Lord's Supper* (1769); *Mistakes in Religion Exposed* (1774); and *Memoirs of Sir John Barnard, M.P. for the City of London* (1786).

In July, 1761, Venn was forced to discuss with John Wesley the preaching of the Methodists within his parish, a "tender point." Where a "gospel ministry" was already performed, Wesley did not wish the Methodists to begin, but whether they should cease such preaching when it had been begun before such a gospel ministry commenced was another matter. By the following month a compromise was reached: "Venn was well pleased that the preachers should come once a month." Wesley preached for him at Huddersfield in 1765 and at Yelling in 1776. Venn gave up Arminianism for moderate Calvinism. His liberal ec-

clesiastical views may be seen in the support that he gave to an Independent chapel in Huddersfield, and in his preaching in a barn in Huntingdonshire.

H. Venn, *Life and Letters of H. Venn.* London, 1839.

B. GALLIERS

VERMILLION, SOUTH DAKOTA, U.S.A. SOUTH DAKOTA Methodism had its beginnings at Vermillion. Bishop O. C. BAKER, presiding over the UPPER IOWA CONFERENCE at Dubuque, appointed SEPTIMUS WATSON INGHAM missionary to "all that territory between the Missouri and Big Sioux Rivers." He started from Sioux City, IOWA on Oct. 12, 1860 and arrived at Vermillion at Sundown. He delivered the first sermon to be preached by a Methodist in the dining room of Mulholand's Tavern on Sunday, October 14, to twenty persons not one of whom was a Methodist.

He only preached as he made the rounds of his vast circuit so did not organize a class until Jan. 13, 1861. This group has the distinction of being the first Dakota group to participate in the Sacrament of the LORD'S SUPPER, quarterly meeting and LOVE FEAST.

Following "The Great Stampede" of Indians in September 1862, all Vermillion residents retreated across the rivers for protection. Among others, three Methodists returned and the church was reactivated in November by Jason L. Paine. Meetings were held in various business places and homes, as well as the log school house after it was built in 1864.

A PARSONAGE was erected in 1869 on top of the bluff overlooking the town and the Vermillion and Missouri River valleys. Four years later, on August 21, a chapel was dedicated. A great flood nearly destroyed the city in 1881. It was rebuilt on higher ground, and when the church outgrew its chapel it built a new church at Main and Dakota Streets in 1895. This served a growing congregation for thirty-two years.

The University of South Dakota was started, and Vermillion was chosen as its location. The church sought to serve the Methodist students and found many supporters among the faculty and administration.

On Nov. 20, 1927 the church was seriously damaged by fire. Because of the WESLEY FOUNDATION work, it was decided to build a new and larger building nearer to the campus. A called session of the Annual Conference assumed approximately one third of the cost of a new building, $30,000. The new building provided space for student activity and a new, attached parsonage. It was dedicated on Sept. 15, 1929, while Lorne A. McDonald was the pastor.

Clair E. Mitchell was appointed pastor in 1964, and under his leadership a new parsonage was secured, a separate building and site for the Wesley Foundation acquired, and the old building remodelled.

VERMONT, U.S.A., is one of the six New England states, and it was the first state to be admitted to the Union (March 4, 1791) after the Union was formed by the thirteen original states. Vermont is bounded on the north by CANADA, on the east by NEW HAMPSHIRE, on the south by MASSACHUSETTS, and on the west by NEW YORK. In 1970 its population was 437,744. Vermont's chief topographical feature is the Green Mountain chain down the middle of the state. The state ranks high in the mining of marble, granite, talc, and asbestos; it has a great dairying business; and its winter sports attract many people. It produces maple syrup, puts out stone and clay products, and manufactures machinery, furniture, paper, and other wood' products. Vermonters are traditionally a sturdy, self-supporting, independent people.

It is claimed that Methodism began in Vermont with a certain Mary Appleton Peckett who had been a housekeeper in JOHN WESLEY's home in England for three years prior to her marriage to Giles Peckett. In 1774 the Pecketts came to New England, and eventually to Bradford, Vt. There in 1780, in her own home, "Mother Peckett," as she was known, started the first Methodist meetings. Some of the famous itinerant preachers of that day—LABAN CLARK, MARTIN RUTER, and LORENZO DOW—were among those who shared her hospitality.

Samuel Wighton did some preaching on what was called the Lake Champlain Circuit in 1788. In that year FREEBORN GARRETTSON was the presiding elder of a district extending from New Rochelle, N.Y. to Lake Champlain, and it is believed that he made a visit to Vermont. JESSE LEE preached in Windham County, Vt., on Sunday, April 18, 1790.

In 1793, THOMAS WARE succeeded Garrettson as presiding elder, and his work embraced much of Vermont. In 1794, Methodism came into Vermont from New Hampshire, and also from Massachusetts with Joshua Hall. Hall was sent as a missionary under GEORGE ROBERTS who was then presiding elder in Massachusetts. In 1795, THOMAS COOPER was appointed to the Orange Circuit, known the following year as Vershire. In 1795 Vermont appears for the first time in the statistical report of the conferences with Vershire as its only appointment. Jesse Lee says that Vershire was the first Methodist circuit in Vermont, and that while there was some preaching about, no real societies were organized before that time. The Vershire Circuit, according to Lee, extended from the towns near the Connecticut River to Montpelier, and to the mouth of Onion River which runs into Lake Champlain. Lee says, "Many of the places where we preached in that circuit were quite new settlements; the houses were very small and but scattering through the country. The preachers had to encounter many difficulties and endure many hardships; but one thing which made up for all the difficulties was this: the people were fond of attending meetings by day or night and were very kind to the preachers."

There was a widespread revival in Vermont in 1798-99. Hundreds were converted and nearly 500 joined the societies. By 1804 the Vermont District had 2,529 members, making it the largest district in the NEW ENGLAND CONFERENCE.

The Methodist society at Barnard, Vt., had a long and colorful history. Today a bronze tablet standing outside Barnard village says that the New England Conference met there twice, with Bishop ASBURY himself presiding over at least one of the sessions. Asbury was entertained in a rambling farm house which still stands. He is said to have preached on that occasion to 3,000 people who gathered in a grove nearby.

Important early Methodist leaders who traveled through or lived in Vermont include WILBUR FISKE, ELIJAH HEDDING, and OSMON C. BAKER. Hedding and Baker became bishops. JASON LEE, famous as the father of Methodism in OREGON, though born in Canada, became more of a Vermonter than a Canadian before going west. Following the death of his first wife Anna Marie in Oregon, Lee returned east and married Lucy

Thompson, a member of the Methodist church in Barre, Vt.

The VERMONT CONFERENCE was created in 1844. Several Methodist academies were started in the state, the most important being Newbury Seminary at Newbury in 1834. VERMONT (junior) COLLEGE at Montpelier today is the descendant of Newbury Seminary.

The first Methodist theological school in America was established in Vermont. Though there was strong opposition in the denomination to theological schools, in 1839 the New England Conference called a convention to consider the establishment of such an institution. Osmon C. Baker, principal of Newbury Seminary mentioned above, began giving theological instruction to a class of ministerial students in the same year, and in 1841 the Newbury Biblical Institute was constituted under Baker. In 1844 JOHN DEMPSTER became head of the institute. He moved it to Concord, N. H., in 1846, and the next year it was incorporated as The Methodist General Biblical Institute. In 1867 the institute was moved to BOSTON UNIVERSITY SCHOOL OF THEOLOGY.

The Vermont Conference of the M. P. Church was organized at Shelburne in February 1830 with five ministers and five lay delegates. L. Chamberlain was elected president and Chandler Walker secretary. The conference was never strong. Though listed in the *Discipline* as a separate conference until about 1864, the work in Vermont was allied with that in New York after about 1850. The roster of delegates to the 1854 GENERAL CONFERENCE includes one clerical and one lay delegate from the "New York and Vermont Conference." In 1877 eastern Vermont was a part of the Boston Conference (MP), while the western part of the state was included in the New York Conference. In 1854 the New York and Vermont Conference had twenty-five appointments, twenty-eight itinerant and thirty-three unstationed preachers, and 1,609 members. After about 1900 the M. P. Church had little or no organized work in the New England states.

In 1941 the Vermont Conference of The Methodist Church was absorbed by the TROY CONFERENCE. At the time the Vermont Conference had eighty-eight appointments and 11,685 members. In 1968 The Methodist Church had about 22,000 members in Vermont.

General Minutes, MEC and MC.
Eldon H. Martin, *Vermont History,* an article published by the Vermont Historical Society, July, 1954.
M. Simpson, *Cyclopaedia.* 1881.   N. B. H.

VERMONT COLLEGE, Montpelier, Vermont, a junior college for women, traces its origin to Newbury Seminary, founded at Newbury, Vermont, in 1834. It was moved to its present location in 1865, became a junior college in 1936, and in 1953 was reorganized as a junior college for women. The present name was assumed in 1958.

Newbury Seminary is remembered as one of the creative educational centers of early Methodism. It claims among its former students two presidents of NORTHWESTERN UNIVERSITY, the founder of theological education in The Methodist Church, JOHN DEMPSTER, and some of the ministers who opened educational institutions for Negroes following the Civil War. Outstanding among these were Richard S. Rust and Alonzo Webster. Newbury's theological department ultimately became the theological school of BOSTON UNIVERSITY. The governing board has twenty trustees: twelve are self-perpetuating and elected by the board, four by the TROY ANNUAL CONFERENCE, four by the alumni association.

JOHN O. GROSS

VERMONT CONFERENCE (ME) was created by the GENERAL CONFERENCE of 1844. It was formed by dividing the NEW HAMPSHIRE and Vermont Conference. Its first session was held at Rochester, Vt., beginning June 18, 1845. At that time it had three districts, Danville, Montpelier, and Springfield; forty-five pastoral appointments; and 9,076 members. Its territory was eastern Vermont; the western part of the state which comprised the Burlington District was in the TROY CONFERENCE.

Vermont Methodism existed many years before there was a Vermont Conference. (See VERMONT.) NICHOLAS SNETHEN, the first Methodist preacher to receive an appointment to Vermont, was sent there from a conference held in CONNECTICUT. The NEW ENGLAND CONFERENCE, organized in 1797, included NEW YORK and the New England states. In 1800 the NEW YORK CONFERENCE was set off from the New England body. The New York Conference included all of Connecticut and parts of MASSACHUSETTS, Vermont, and NEW YORK. In 1804 Vermont and New Hampshire were returned to the New England Conference. Western Vermont was placed in the New York Conference in 1812 where it remained until 1833 when it became a part of the Troy Conference. Meantime, eastern Vermont went with the New Hampshire and Vermont Conference when it was created in 1829, an arrangement which continued until 1844 when the Vermont Conference was formed.

From 1847 to 1888 Vermont Methodism had a paper called the *Vermont Christian Messenger*. It was published part if not all of the time at Montpelier. Several academies were started, the strongest being Newbury Seminary founded at Newbury in 1834. In 1849 the Female Collegiate Institute was added to the seminary. Springfield Wesleyan Seminary was opened at Springfield in 1847. Bakersfield North Academy was launched at Bakersfield in 1844. In 1868, under the vigorous leadership of Amasa G. Button, a member of the conference who was long president of the board of trustees of Newbury Seminary, the school was moved to Montpelier, and the remnants of the other academies were consolidated with it. The name was changed to Montpelier Seminary. In the 1930's the institution almost failed, but on becoming a junior college in 1936 it took on new life and changed its name to VERMONT COLLEGE. In 1968 it had an enrollment of more than 500 with a plant valued at $3,000,000.

The first Methodist theological school in America was established at Newbury, Vt., in connection with Newbury Seminary in 1841.

Arriving at the best or most desirable conference alignment for the work in Vermont proved difficult. As indicated above, the work in western Vermont continued in the Troy Conference after the Vermont Conference was created in 1844. But the record shows that from 1860 to 1868, and again from 1880 to 1884, the Burlington District made up of the churches on the west side of the Green Mountains, was transferred to the Vermont Conference in serious attempts to unify the work in the state. Apparently the arrangement did not work well, for at the end of each period the Burlington District went back to the Troy Conference.

In 1856 the General Conference voted that Vermont east of the Green Mountains should become a part of the NEW HAMPSHIRE CONFERENCE, provided a majority of both conferences agreed to the merger. The consolidation did not take place, and indeed nothing was done about it until eighty-four years later. The 1940 NORTHEASTERN JURISDICTIONAL CONFERENCE directed the Vermont Conference to merge with the Troy Conference by June, 1942. The union was effected in 1941. Since that time all Methodist work in Vermont, except Canaan and Beecher Falls in the extreme northeastern part of the state, has continued in the Troy Conference.

The three Vermont districts of earlier years had been reduced to one in 1941. In the first year after the merger the Burlington District included the whole state. Subsequently the churches in southern Vermont were grouped with some New York congregations to form the Troy, later the Bennington-Troy, District, with the rest of Vermont continuing as the Burlington District.

First Church, Burlington, with about 1,300 members is the strongest Methodist congregation in the state. Rutland and St. Johnsbury have about 1,000 members each.

In 1941 the Vermont Conference had eighty-eight appointments, 11,685 members, and property valued at $1,276,710. In 1968 there were about 22,000 members of The Methodist Church in Vermont.

General Minutes, MEC and MC.
Eldon H. Martin, *Vermont College.* Nashville: Parthenon Press, 1962.   ALBEA GODBOLD

VERNON, M. LEROY (1838-1896), American missionary to ITALY, was born at Crawfordsville, Ind., on April 23, 1838. He was educated and converted at IOWA WESLEYAN UNIVERSITY. He married the daughter of CHARLES ELLIOT, who had advocated M.E. Church work in Italy since 1832. When the Board of Missions of that Church had accepted the principle of missions in Catholic lands (on Sept. 20, 1870, the very day that Rome fell to Victor Emmanuel), Vernon was appointed on March 14, 1871 to be missionary and superintendent of the Mission work of the M.E. Church in Italy. He based his mission first on Bologna, then (after 1874) on Rome. He left Italy in 1888, when the mission numbered 1,159 members. He died on Aug. 10, 1896.

J. F. Hurst, *History of Methodism.* 1904.   REGINALD KISSACK

VERNON, WALTER N., JR. (1907-   ), American minister, church school editor and historian, was born in Verdun, Okla., on March 24, 1907, the son of Rev. and Mrs. W. N. Vernon. His father, a Methodist minister, served in TEXAS and OKLAHOMA for forty years. Graduated from Paris (Texas) Junior College, and SOUTHERN METHODIST UNIVERSITY (B.A., M.A., B.D.), he was admitted on trial in the NORTH TEXAS ANNUAL CONFERENCE in 1929, and ordained an ELDER in 1933. After serving pastorates in and near DALLAS for ten years, he joined the editorial staff of the Methodist Board of Christian Education (MES) in Nashville, Tenn., in 1938, as editor of youth publications. In 1944 he was appointed Editor of General Publications and Administrative Associate in the Editorial Division of the BOARD OF EDUCATION of The Methodist Church, a position he held until he retired.

He has acted as special news correspondent at Methodist GENERAL CONFERENCES for the Dallas *Morning News* since 1934; has edited the *Daily Christian Advocate* for the SOUTH CENTRAL JURISDICTION since 1940. He is author of numerous articles for the church press, as well as of *Methodist Profile, William Stevenson—Riding Preacher;* and *Methodism Moves Across North Texas,* a history of North Texas Methodism. He is author of the hymn, "God of All, Who Art Our Father," a hymn published in 1961 by the Hymn Society of America, and is the author of an article on The Methodist Church in the latest publication of *The Westminster Dictionary of Christian Education.* In 1962, he delivered the Fair Lectures at Southwestern Audio-Visual Workshop.

In 1953 an agency of the NATIONAL COUNCIL OF CHURCHES sent him to ten countries in Africa to aid churches there in their use of audio-visual materials. In 1958 he attended the World Convention on Christian Education, TOKYO, JAPAN. In 1963 he was given the honorary degree of Doctor of Letters by WEST VIRGINIA WESLEYAN COLLEGE. For his book, *Methodism Moves Across North Texas,* an Award of Merit was given in 1968 by the American Association for State and Local History.

His wife is the former Ruth Mason of Paris, Texas; their children are Walter N. Vernon, III, of Dallas, Texas, and Kathy, the wife of Rev. Stanley P. Clark, a member of the NORTH ALABAMA CONFERENCE.

The Dallas Morning News, Dec. 7, 1968.
C. T. Howell, *Prominent Personalities.* 1948.

J. DANIEL BARRON

VERNON, WILLIAM TECUMSEH (1871-1944), American A.M.E. clergyman and bishop, was born near Lebanon, Mo., on July 11, 1871. His father was the Rev. Adam Vernon, a slave of Colonel Miles Vernon of TENNESSEE and MISSOURI. The son attended the Old Town School in Lebanon until he was fifteen, when he entered Lincoln Institute, Jefferson City, from which he graduated in 1890. He taught school at Bonne Terre, and was school principal at Lebanon. He studied for a time in WILBERFORCE UNIVERSITY in OHIO. He was ordained in the Missouri Conference, A.M.E. Church, in 1899, and was appointed president of Western University at Kansas City, Kan. He began with one building and ten students; ten years later there were four large buildings and 400 students. He became prominent as an orator and public speaker. His fame spread, and President Theodore Roosevelt appointed him Registrar of the U. S. Treasury, one of the highest offices held by a Negro up to that time. In 1912 he was elected president of Campbell College, Jackson, Miss., where he served for four years.

In 1916 he became pastor of Avery Chapel, MEMPHIS, and became one of the most popular preachers in the city. A fervent sermon on missions at the General Conference in St. Louis in 1920 is said to be a chief factor in his election there as bishop. He was assigned to supervise A.M.E. work in SOUTH AFRICA, and went reluctantly, but found the work interesting. He established the Emily Vernon Institute in Basutoland, named in honor of his wife. He encouraged a young student, Hastings Banda, who became a protégé of his, and later a prominent political leader in Africa.

In 1924 he was assigned to the conferences in Bermuda, Nova Scotia, Ontario, MICHIGAN, ILLINOIS, and INDIANA, and in 1928 he was appointed to the six conferences in ARKANSAS. In 1932 he was suspended by the General Conference; according to Bishop R. R. WRIGHT, JR.,

the suspension was a political move and undeserved. But the succeeding General Conference did not restore him, and he returned to Western University to serve. He held the degrees of M.A., D.D., and LL.D., and was a thirty-third degree Mason. At least five churches are named for him. He died in July 1944, at Kansas City, Kan.

G. A. Singleton, *African Methodism.* 1952.
C. S. Smith, *History* (AME). 1922.
R. R. Wright, *The Bishops.* 1963.
————, *Encyclopedia* (AME). 1916.

WALTER N. VERNON

VERSAILLES, INDIANA, U.S.A. **Tyson Temple** is an unusual church which has been the beneficiary of an unusual benefactor. There has been a Methodist congregation in Versailles since its organization in 1834, but it achieved distinction in 1937 with the dedication of Tyson Temple, the gift of James Tyson who was born at Versailles and baptized in the Methodist Church. He learned the printer's trade, left home as a young man, and later joined with Charles R. Walgreen in the organization of the Walgreen Drug Company. Tyson, or "Uncle Jim" as he was more familiarly known, became the chief benefactor of his home town with the creation of the Tyson Trust Fund. The Trust Fund consisted of 18,000 shares of common capital stock of the Walgreen Drug Company.

Benefits received by the community from the Tyson Fund include: fifty-five percent of a $225,000 water and sewer system for the town, fifty percent of a $140,000 school which is a memorial to his father, a $50,000 library, and the $150,000 Tyson Temple which was built as a memorial to his mother, Eliza Adams Tyson. The annual income from the Tyson Trust Fund is received by and distributed by the trustees of the Tyson Versailles Fund, who are also the trustees of the Methodist church. The trustees of the church also elect three of their number to serve as the trustees of the library.

The architecture combines "Uncle Jim's" preferences in architectural styles. It has now wood in its basic construction but is built entirely of glazed brick, terra cotta, glass bricks, steel, granite, aluminum, lead and copper. The building is surmounted by a cast aluminum tower that is tipped with an aluminum cross. This cross stands 100 feet from the ground. In this tower is the bell which hung in the original church used by the congregation. James Tyson's mother had been a charter member of this first church.

Columns flank the entrance of the church and other columns stand at either side of the chancel. The dome over the chancel is covered with gold leaf and the archway with silver leaf. The ceiling of the church is painted a light blue and is studded with silver stars. These stars are said to be representative of the sky around Versailles in October at the time of Uncle Jim's mother's death. Although offerings are received as normally in a church, this was not Uncle Jim's intention. Instead he had a hollow metal post with a slot in the top installed in the vestibule of the church to receive any offerings that worshippers cared to make.

The Tyson Fund also provides for the maintenance of the church and the library.

ROBERT S. CHAFEE

VEVERS, WILLIAM (1791-1850), British preacher and writer, was born in 1791, became a Wesleyan itinerant in 1813, and governor of the Wesleyan Collegiate Institution, Taunton, in 1849. He was the author of a number of books and pamphlets, including *The National Importance of Methodism,* a vindication of Methodist loyalty and patriotism; and *A Defence of the Discipline of Methodism,* in reply to the criticisms of SAMUEL WARREN. Vevers died at Taunton, Somerset, England, on Sept. 8, 1850.

G. E. LONG

VICK, NEWIT (1766-1819), American Methodist pioneer and local preacher who founded VICKSBURG, Miss. The more "Norman-English" surname of Le Vieke lives on in our American surname of "Vicks" and "Viek." From the Robert and Nicholas Le Vieke line of Huguenots came the founder of Vicksburg, who was born March 17, 1766, in Southampton County, Va., and died Aug. 5, 1819 in MISSISSIPPI.

His father was William Vick the second, and his mother was Martha Boykin—both of early colonial families—and they had nine children, all born in Southampton County, Va. One of these was Newit Vick, born in 1766.

In 1791 Newit Vick married Elizabeth Clarke, born in 1772 in Northampton County, N. C., the daughter of James Clarke. They lived for several years in VIRGINIA where four of their children were born. Late in 1799 Newit Vick moved with his family down into NORTH CAROLINA with the idea of eventually establishing a permanent residence in the great southwest, the Mississippi Territory. For more than five years he lived in North Carolina. Three of his children were born in that state.

Before 1806 he left North Carolina, going overland until reaching Muscle Shoals, Ala. There he purchased a keel boat and with his family, slaves and material possessions floated down the Tennessee River into the Mississippi and landed at the mouth of Coles Creek on the line of Jefferson and Adams Counties, in southern Mississippi. After a short time of prospecting there, he settled on a valuable tract of land twenty miles from NATCHEZ and five miles west of the present town of Fayette. He named this place "Spring Hill."

In November 1813, the first Methodist Conference for the Mississippi area was held there in Vick's home, his commodious two-story brick residence being suitable for the lodging of the ten ministers who were to attend. Members of his family have often pointed with pride to the large mahogany dining table around which these God-fearing men then conferred in their plans to spread the Gospel of Christ. N. Vick Robbins, a great-grandson, in the 1920's marked this spot with a marble shaft to commemorate this conference, and the site of his ancestor's home.

To the Mississippi Territory Newit Vick brought the same zeal and fervor for historic Christianity that he had shown in Virginia for sixteen years before coming to Mississippi. There he had labored for the advancement of Christianity as a Methodist, and this he continued to do to the time of his death. He was known as a "LOCAL PREACHER" and was called Reverend Newit Vick, though apparently he was never regularly ordained. Certainly he was not a "circuit rider," as some have written, nor was he a "poor Methodist preacher," as others have stated. Legal records in Virginia and Mississippi document this.

At his "Spring Hill" home, five of his children were born, John Wesley Vick being the first, born March 1806.

By the year 1814, Newit Vick made the decision to move up the Mississippi to higher ground, for the land near Natchez had been subject to the periodic overflows of the Mississippi River. There were no steamboats then and so overland by Indian trails they journeyed until they reached the northeastern part of what is now Warren County. There they settled upon a tract of land that Vick called "Openwoods" because of the sparse growth of timber and canebrake. The ground was high above the Mississippi River.

Accompanying Vick and his family was his wife's nephew, Foster Cook, who had also lived in the vicinity of "Spring Hill." Foster Cook's widow in time married Judge James Bland, who was the great-grandfather of Bishop NOLAN B. HARMON. The Vicks and Cooks located on fine tracts of land and soon around them several families of relatives came from Virginia. Other Virginians likewise came to remain there for their entire lives.

Vick was the first "local preacher" to come to the MISSISSIPPI CONFERENCE, and he was also the first minister to proclaim the Gospel in the northern half of Warren County. Before this time the settlements had been made south and southeast of "Walnut Hills." The way being fairly well open now into this heretofore wilderness, other settlers came to the area near the lower Yazoo bluffs.

Newit Vick possessed real leadership. He had the mind of a statesman who realized his responsibility to the Triune God. Mature, practical judgment was his and he acquired other tracts of land besides "Openwoods," including that upon which Vicksburg now largely stands. He laid off several streets near the river, and elsewhere, sold some lots for commercial use, and in his will provided land for Vicksburg to have a "commons" on the riverfront for the use of its citizens.

He himself gave the name of "Vicksburg" to this budding town in honor of his ancient family name. The city block where the old court house now stands was chosen as the site for his town home. Although busily engaged in this project, he was always diligent in the cause of Methodism and he and other settlers built a log church on the old Benton road as a place of worship.

In August of 1819, Vick and his wife were stricken with yellow fever. They both died the same day, Aug. 5, 1819, and are buried in their private cemetery on the "Openwoods" tract.

Newit Vick left a lengthy will, dated Aug. 2, 1819, making provision for all his family and other bequests. Unfortunately the will was contested by some members of the family and in the final decision the City of Vicksburg was deprived of his bequest of the tract of land that was to be a "Commons" on the riverfront "forever."

This man of God had received a priceless heritage from his forebears and now his mantle was to fall upon the shoulders of his descendants, among whom this writer rejoices to have a place.

Chancery Court Records, Warren County, Miss.
J. G. Jones, *Mississippi Conference.* 1908.
Dunbar Rowland, *Mississippi.* Atlanta, 1907.

MRS. N. VICK ROBBINS

VICKSBURG, MISSISSIPPI, U.S.A, is an old, historic city, occupying a commanding situation on the Mississippi River, and one of great importance in the earlier history of the United States. This was due to its key position in river travel, which was the only important travel in that earlier day.

Methodism in Vicksburg antedated the naming of the city. Tobias Gibson, after arriving in the Mississippi Territory via flatboat, organized a church at Warrenton (about four miles from what is now the center of Vicksburg), and named it "Hopewell." There services were held until 1822. At a slightly earlier date, in 1814, the "Redbone" church was built about twelve or fourteen miles below Vicksburg, and inland from the river. The records call this church "Bethel" but the local people have always known it as "the Redbone church." About the year 1854 a brick edifice was built by two brothers, Joel and Benjamin Sellers Hullum, the former a Presbyterian and the latter a Methodist. Benjamin Sellers donated three bricks to one by his brother Joel, the agreement being that the church was to be used three Sundays for the Methodists and one for the Presbyterians. It was built by slaves and was used by Union soldiers during the siege of Vicksburg in 1863 as a hospital for their wounded and sick.

Tobias Gibson was emphatically the father of Methodism in Mississippi, arriving there in 1799. In 1814 Newit Vick and Foster Cook, his nephew, having migrated to Warren County, erected a neat church in the "Openwoods" settlement, seven miles from the present city of Vicksburg. The Methodist Church in Vicksburg proper may be said to have commenced in 1820, when John Lane, a Methodist preacher, laid off the town. Services were held in a blacksmith shop, and also in the private residences of Newit Vick and John Lane. In 1825 Vicksburg was included in the appointments of the Mississippi Conference as the Warren Circuit. In 1830 it was left "to be supplied." The first church of which we have any record in Vicksburg proper stood at the corner of Grove and Cherry Streets, the deed being dated July 27, 1837. In 1846 the Grove and Cherry Streets Church was given to the colored Methodists (then slaves) as a place of worship.

April 7, 1846, John Wesley Vick and wife, Catherine Ann Barber, conveyed to the M.E. Church, South, just organized, the lot at the corner of Crawford and Cherry Streets. A stately brick church was erected there which the congregation occupied for more than a half century. It was dedicated in 1850 by the noted William Winans, and has long been known as "Crawford Street." During the historic siege of Vicksburg a cannonball from the Union gunboats was embedded in the back of this building and remained there after the surrender until the building was torn down in 1899. The church was held by the U.S. Army from 1863 to 1865. The cannonball is said to be in the Archives of the State of Mississippi, at Jackson.

Among the distinguished pastors who served Vicksburg were Charles K. Marshall, who made his home there in his latter years, and Charles B. Galloway, who was elected bishop shortly after he left Vicksburg to become editor of the New Orleans Christian Advocate. When Charles B. Galloway became pastor in 1877, he was only twenty-eight and Crawford Street was then perhaps the strongest Methodist church in Mississippi. In the summer of 1878, yellow fever became epidemic in Vicksburg, and both the young pastor and his wife came near dying of the dread disease.

During the pastorate of A. F. Watkins, 1896-1900, the historic old church structure was replaced by a stately building in keeping with the growth of the congregation.

Bishop Galloway dedicated this church May 27, 1902. This building was destroyed by fire April 5, 1925, during the pastorate of G. H. Thompson. The edifice now standing is the result of the work and constructive activities of the loyal members and the able building committee of Crawford Street.

On May 9, 1887, the trustees of Crawford Street Church bought a lot on Shorter Mulberry Street, during the pastorate of R. J. Jones, and a small church was there erected. It was known as the South Vicksburg Church. Nolan B. Harmon, Sr. was the first pastor assigned to this mission church. It grew rapidly and in 1902 a new church was built on Washington Street. During the pastorate of W. H. Saunders in 1914 the present Gibson Memorial Church was completed. The work of enlarging the auditorium and building a substantial Sunday school annex was done in 1948.

T. O. Prewitt, when Superintendent of the Vicksburg District in 1951, was instrumental in beginning Hawkins Church on Halls Ferry Road. A number of faithful Methodists from Crawford Street Church, W. A. Tyson then being pastor, formed the nucleus of this new church. It has grown rapidly and a Sunday school annex has been added to the main building.

In 1951 T. O. Prewitt was also instrumental in the beginning of the Northview Church on Sky Farm Avenue. The Church was first located on Openwood Street and called "Springfield," but in 1954 a large plot of ground was secured on Sky Farm, where a neat church and Sunday school annex now stand.

Representing the Negro Methodists in Vicksburg, the A.M.E. Church is perhaps the oldest. In 1846 its congregation occupied the building at the corner of Cherry and Grove Streets, which had been given to them by the founders of Crawford Street. At the present time they have a membership of about 300. The Wesley Church, formerly in the Central Jurisdiction of The Methodist Church, has a membership presently of 100. It dates its history back to 1859, and celebrated its 111th anniversary, with Bishop E. J. Pendergrass and other ministers taking part in the ceremonies on Nov. 5, 1970.

J. G. Jones, Mississippi Conference. 1908.
Mississippi Methodist Advocate, Nov. 4, 1970.
Vicksburg Evening Post, centennial edition, 1925.

A. Peale Harmon

Metropolitan Church, Victoria, British Columbia

VICTORIA, Canada, **Metropolitan Church.** In February 1859, a team of missionaries from the Canada Confer-

ENCE, led by that indomitable veteran, EPHRAIM EVANS, reached Victoria, capital of British Columbia. At that time Victoria was a town of 3,000 people, but it had no Protestant churches. Within a month of his arrival, Evans began to make plans for a church. With the help of Governor Sir James Douglas, land was secured and in May 1860, the new church was opened. Thirty years later a new Metropolitan was built at the corner of Pandora and Quadra streets; a stone Gothic structure, it would accommodate 1,800 people.

From 1890 onward, under the leadership of men such as Solomon Cleaver, C. T. Scott, H. S. Osborne, and W. J. SIPPRELL, the Metropolitan Church played an effective role in establishing Methodism firmly in Victoria. Its people would encourage the foundation of several other Methodist churches, such as Centennial, Wesley, James Bay, and Victoria. With Union it became Metropolitan United Church, and in this new form has continued to keep alive the Methodist tradition in the flourishing capital of British Columbia.

Victoria *Daily Times*, May 28, 1927.   G. S. FRENCH

VICTORIA PARK COLLEGE, Manchester. (See HARTLEY VICTORIA COLLEGE, Manchester.)

VICTORIA AND TASMANIA CONFERENCE. Tasmania.
The first Methodist service was held in Hobart, Tasmania in 1820, when a Cornish minister, BENJAMIN CARVOSSO, preached on the steps of the court house from the text, "Awake thou that sleepest, arise from the dead, and Christ shall give thee light." His wife stood beside him and led the singing. In his four days' visit before proceeding to SYDNEY, New South Wales, Carvosso included a service for the prisoners who were numerous in those early convict days. A few Methodist laymen afterwards organized CLASS MEETINGS in Hobart.

In 1821, SAMUEL LEIGH, the pioneer missionary in Sydney, called at Hobart on his return from furlough in England. He appointed William Horton and NATHANIEL TURNER to establish preaching places in the town and inland districts also. By 1832 Methodism had spread to the north of the island and a minister was appointed to Launceston where the leading layman was Henry Reed. Reed was not only a devoted LOCAL PREACHER but a merchant of substance and a foundation director of the Bank of Australasia. JOSEPH ORTON became chairman of the new district of Tasmania (then called Van Diemen's Land) in 1835.

Wesley Church, Hobart, was built in the style of Wesley's Chapel, City Road, LONDON, in the early days of the settlement and is still the center of worship in southern Tasmania. Paterson Street Church, Launceston, with its lofty spire, has a commanding place in the northern city.

Victoria. The first settlers in Victoria crossed Bass Strait from Launceston in 1835. One of the first party was Henry Reed of Launceston. Evidently he preached the first sermon, in the open air, in the future city of Melbourne.

Henry Reed's effort was followed by the visit of Joseph Orton in 1836. He was the first ordained minister of any denomination to preach in MELBOURNE. Among the early settlers in Melbourne were William Witton, local preacher, and John Peers, musician and choirmaster. Two others were James Dredge and Edward Stone Parker,

Methodists who were sent by the Government to be Protectors of the Aborigines. WILLIAM WITTON was the first class leader; afterwards he became a home missionary and travelled extensively in the western district and Gippsland in the east.

Francis Tuckfield established missionary work among the Aborigines in the Geelong-Colac area where the Government made a grant of 64,000 acres for the purpose. It was called Buntingdale, after JABEZ BUNTING, the renowned Methodist leader in England. Tuckfield found it impossible to induce the nomadic Aborigines to settle to farming or to give him an opportunity for evangelism and education. After some years, covetous squatters persuaded the Government to withdraw the grant of land. It was not through any slackness on Tuckfield's part that this effort failed.

After using a temporary church in 1840, the Methodists erected a solid building in the main thoroughfare of Melbourne, Collins Street, in 1841. It was largely the work of John Peers, who obtained a pipe organ also. Not long afterwards Joseph Orton, worn out by his exertions, was obliged to return to England but died when the ship was rounding Cape Horn. The first resident superintendent of the Melbourne circuit was Samuel Wilkinson. The earnestness of the preachers and the zeal of their congregations led to conversions and the spread of the Methodist witness throughout Victoria.

Discovery of Gold. The gold rush which began in 1851 brought a great change to Victoria. Golddiggers poured in from all parts of the world. Many settlers left their farms and workers in the towns gave up their employment. All flocked to the diggings in Ballarat, Bendigo and other places. The arrivals from overseas averaged 1,800 weekly, this continuing for some years.

The influx of migrants led to the establishment of the Wesleyan Immigrants Home on two acres in Carlton, a Melbourne suburb, given by the Government. Migrants were met on shipboard and any without shelter, money or friends received accommodation and assistance.

Victoria became a separate colony from New South Wales in 1851. The first District Meeting or Synod for Victoria was held the same year, with William Butters as Chairman. He proved a wise and energetic administrator in the unusual conditions. Butters appealed to England for more ministers because of the swollen population. Methodism provided the first resident minister on the goldfields at this time.

Many of the miners were from Cornwall, the English county conspicuous in Methodist history from the time of JOHN WESLEY. Some of these Cornishmen were local preachers and they began prayer meetings and services. Passersby were attracted very often by the Cornish miners' singing of hymns in their tents.

A noted visitor to Victoria at this time was Robert Young, commissioned by the British Conference to report on the work in AUSTRALIA and the South Seas. The result of his visit was the separation of Australasian Methodism from Britain in 1855. Young was instrumental also in securing for Victoria a considerable increase in the number of ministers from England.

The first Conference in 1855 appointed DANIEL DRAPER to be Chairman in Victoria. Draper was not only a zealous preacher and an indefatigable organizer but also a builder of churches.

Draper's most notable building was the fine Gothic structure, Wesley Church, Melbourne, the cathedral church of the denomination in Victoria ever since it was erected in 1858. Many stately churches in Victoria and other States bear witness to Draper's enterprise. He was lost in the S. S. *London,* in the Bay of Biscay in January 1866, while returning from a visit to England; he conducted prayer meetings with the passengers until the ship sank.

The visit of WILLIAM TAYLOR, the American evangelist, in 1863 brought revival scenes to Tasmania and Victoria, with lasting effects.

Home Missions and Development. After the gold rush had subsided more attention was given to agriculture and the subdividing of land enabled more families to develop the country. Wherever settlements arose Methodist preachers accompanied the people. Methodist causes spread through the forests of Gippsland and the' wheat areas of the Wimmera. In some districts there were no other preachers but the Methodists who almost lived in the saddle, like John Wesley and his preachers and the circuit-riders in America. Many services were held in farm houses, wool sheds and the open air.

In 1875 the Conference established the Home Mission Society to cope with the extension of this work through country districts. The first General Secretary was JOHN WATSFORD, who had been a missionary in FIJI and whose venerable appearance earned him the name of "Father" Watsford. As a fervent evangelist he stamped the imprint of his personality upon the life of Methodism in Victoria.

Five local preachers were recruited and sent out as Home Missionaries in 1875, and within fifteen years there were sixty agents supported by the Home Mission Society. Some of these remained in the work for the rest of their active years; others prepared for the ordained ministry. In many cases Home Mission stations progressed to reach the status of circuits. Since the decline in population in some rural areas in the middle of the twentieth century, there have been amalgamations.

Since 1953 the work has been under the direction of the Department of Home Missions and Church Extension (including the Church Building Committee). New housing estates have 'been provided for and consolidation of the work everywhere has been planned and achieved, often in consultation with other denominations to avoid overlapping.

Hospital and prison chaplaincy work has been faithfully directed. Victorian DEACONESSES sponsored by the Home Mission Department have been growing in numbers and effectiveness.

The Victoria and Tasmania Conference in recent years has adopted the policy of separating some Chairmen of Districts from circuit responsibility. More of these "pastors of pastors" would have been appointed if finance permitted.

In 1967 a Department of Lay Training, affiliated with Home Missions, was established to raise standards of theological knowledge among Methodist laymen.

Notable service has been given to the Home Mission Department over the years by its leaders, including E. S. Bickford, A. T. HOLDEN, T. C. Rentoul and A. W. Pederick. Holden was in charge of this work from 1904 until his death in 1935. Pederick retired in 1967 after twenty-one years' leadership in the Department. While maintaining vigilant supervision of the work of Home Missions in Victoria, Holden, Rentoul and Pederick, in succession, have directed the work of the Federal Inland

Mission through the remote areas of the north and center of the continent.

City Missions and Immigration. As with all large cities throughout the world, Melbourne has had special needs in its inner areas. Wesley Church, in the heart of the city, became a Mission in 1893, with A. R. Edgar as Superintendent. Other Superintendents included S. J. Hoban, A. McCallum and Sir Irving Benson. A striking statue of John Wesley in front of Wesley Church typifies the spirit of the Mission; Wesley is shown with riding boots and preaching gown.

Sir Irving Benson, the only Methodist minister in the world who has been knighted, retired in 1967 after a ministry of forty-two years at Wesley Church and the Mission. Not only in length but in widespread influence his ministry was unique.

The Central Mission includes the Boys' Training Farm at Tally-ho, Princess Mary Club and Moreland Hostels for girls, old people's home, a friendless men's refuge, and a home for unmarried mothers. Similar work of Christian service has been done in other inner areas—Collingwood, Fitzroy, Carlton, Prahran, North Melbourne, South Melbourne. In connection with all these Missions most devoted work has been accomplished by the Sisterhood.

Work among needy children began in 1891 with the Children's Home at Cheltenham. This developed into "Orana" Peace Memorial Homes, Burwood, after the 1939-45 war, a model institution visited by child care experts from far afield, with its cottages and chapel. The family of the late Fred J. Cato was prominent in supporting this work. Keith Mathieson has been the superintendent for the past twenty years in the Department of Child Care.

The Babies' Home owed its inspiration to young laymen in 1929; Oswald Barnett and Douglas Thomas were among the leaders. Epworth Hospital was established in 1920. The church has developed homes for the aged in various parts of Victoria and Tasmania, under the Department of Adult Care directed by W. J. Johnson. Especially in the last twenty years these have multiplied and are filling a strong-felt need.

Immigration. The Immigrants' Home did not long survive the influx of golddiggers in the middle of the last century. After serving thousands of needy migrants it was closed in 1860.

In the post-war period, with large-scale European migration, the Methodist Church has revived its concern for migrants. T. C. Rentoul, Superintendent of Home Missions and Chaplain-General of the Military Forces, drew up a plan in 1945 just before he died. The first migrant chaplain to England in 1949 was A. W. Pederick, Superintendent of Home Missions. The work is now attached to the Department of Adult Care, under the leadership of W. J. Johnson. Much has been done to provide homes for British migrants through the indefatigable efforts of Howard Dunn and others. Similar work has been done amongst non-British migrants; many scores of these, particularly White Russians at Dandenong, have been provided with homes through the earnest efforts of Mr. and Mrs. A. R. Williams of that city.

W. J. Trewin, who speaks Italian and Spanish, went to Italy for two years to become better acquainted with the needs of migrants from Italy, and he now has a special mission for these people in Melbourne. Through the use of the simultaneous translation system at the Church of All Nations at Carlton, N. C. Lowe has been able to bring the message of the Gospel and offer Christian help to large numbers of non-English-speaking migrants.

Overseas Missions. In 1839 a missionary meeting was held, the first, it is believed, of any denomination in Melbourne. The inspiration came from Francis Tuckfield, the devoted pioneer to the Aborigines at Buntingdale.

Methodist pioneers were determined to support the outreach of their denomination everywhere. This infant society, the Port Phillip Branch Methodist Missionary Society, was the forerunner of Methodist Overseas Missions. Not only gifts but workers, as time went on, were sent to the South Seas.

Early missionaries from Victoria included John Whewell to Tonga in 1859, and Martin Dyson to SAMOA in 1857. Fiji, notorious for cannibalism, received notable Victorians such as Frederick Langham (1858-95), translator of the Fijian Bible; Lorimer Fison, missionary-anthropologist; C. O. Lelean (1902-38); R. L. McDonald (1908-36).

The work in North INDIA was served by such Victorians as T. Clement Carne (from 1915), Austin James (1925-58), and S. I. Weeks.

The pioneer of our work in PAPUA in 1891 was a Victorian, W. E. BROMILOW, known for his translation work; another, in later years, was A. W. Guy (twenty-three years). In New Britain, Victoria was represented by a pioneer, Benjamin Danks, and the veteran W. H. Cox (thirty years). Malaria and other tropical diseases made service in Papua and New Britain more hazardous.

Revived work for the Aborigines in North Australia, soundly based on anthropological research, has been done in this century by our Church; a prominent Victorian was Arthur Ellemor.

Medical missions have been devotedly served by Victorians including Dr. H. G. Judkins in Papua, Drs. Edward, Edna and Adelaide Gault in India, and Dr. Olive Long in Fiji.

No States in Australia have done more than Victoria and Tasmania for educational as well as evangelistic work overseas; Leslie Thompson, Arthur Adamson, Dr. Cyril Cato, Harold Chambers, Miss Olive Morrissey, Miss F. J. Pearce are only a few who gave educational leadership in various fields.

In "Shangri-la," the vast Papua-New Guinea Highlands, unknown until thirty years ago, pioneer work, rightly regarded as romantic, has been done by Methodists. A large primitive population is being reached. A Victorian, John Hutton, has been one of those used by God for the conversion of thousands since our work began in the Highlands in 1950.

The Women's Auxiliary, Laymen's Missionary Movement and Young Women's Missionary Movement have loyally supported Overseas Mission work with prayer, gifts and service.

Young People's Work. Sunday school work began immediately after the first Methodist services were held in 1835, as early records give witness.

Great advances in teaching methods have been used in the present century. With the secularization of Sunday and increasing materialism in the community more difficulties have been encountered in maintaining attendances and interest. In spite of this, Methodist Sunday school and general youth work has been actively and successfully promoted.

The Sunday School Department began in 1873. Its name has been changed several times and is now the Department of Christian Education. A new programme envisaging education for adults as well as those of younger ages was introduced in 1970. All these efforts have been effectively directed by a succession of able ministers set apart by Conference, some of whom received inspiration from their studies in America, these including Dr. Clifford Wright.

The Christian Endeavour Society has been a vital part of youth work but in some places has been replaced by new activities. The Methodist Youth Fellowship, for general youth work, has become popular. Summer Camps have been most profitable for leadership training as well as physical and spiritual recreation.

Cooperation with the Presbyterian Church has developed in various fields, and in none has this been more fruitful than in the production of Graded Lessons for Sunday Schools through the Joint Board established over forty years ago. In recent years these Lessons have been adopted by the Congregational Church also and accepted in New Zealand and other places outside Australia. The Headquarters of this work has been in Melbourne.

Religious instruction in state schools has been an interdenominational enterprise in Victoria. The Council of Christian Education in Schools, supported by seven denominations, has provided an agreed syllabus for the use of ministers and other accredited agents. Since 1950 the subject of Religious Instruction has been recognized as part of the school curriculum by the State Education Department. Several of the Directors of the Council have been Methodist ministers.

Social Witness. Through its Department of Christian Citizenship (formerly called the Social Service Department) and the forum offered every week by Wesley Church, Melbourne, in its broadcast, *Pleasant Sunday Afternoon*, our Church has been able to exercise a positive influence towards the solution of social problems.

Liquor, gambling, the sweating evil in industry, have been some of the questions dealt with. Flagrant evils, such as backyard totalisator betting, have been trenchantly exposed. Governments have been influenced by the work of the Department and the publicity given through Wesley Church P.S.A. Leadership has been given also in the discussion of international affairs.

From 1900 to the present day the Methodist Church in Victoria has given a clear witness for social righteousness through the utterances of such leaders as T. S. B. Woodfull, G. A. Judkins, H. Palmer Phillips, J. W. R. Westerman, and an outstanding layman in the early years of this century, W. H. Judkins.

Methodist Union. After the Wesleyans had begun work in 1835, a few members of the other Methodist bodies gradually came to Victoria and, in loyalty to their upbringing in the Homeland, they determined that they must have a separate Methodist existence in the new land.

PRIMITIVE METHODISTS established a society in 1849. Characteristically, they began operations in the open air at Flagstaff Hill where a mob of hooligans attacked them. A minister, John Ride, came in 1850. Through the days of the gold rush the Primitives carried on aggressive and successful evangelistic work including camp meetings in country districts.

Small causes from the UNITED METHODIST FREE CHURCHES began in Victoria in 1851.

The BIBLE CHRISTIANS, whose strongholds were in Cornwall and Devon, were represented in Victoria from 1856 onwards. It was chiefly in the goldfields that Bible Christians were found although, even there, they were not as numerous as their fellow-denominationalists in the copper mines of South Australia.

The last was the METHODIST NEW CONNEXION in 1865, with only one church, at North Richmond. In 1888 it was accepted into the Wesleyan Methodist Church.

For some years it had been apparent to many members of the smaller bodies that union was both desirable and inevitable. On the Wesleyan side there was some reluctance. By 1884 the Wesleyan Conference in Victoria had decided to open negotiations for a Basis of Union but progress was slow.

W. H. FITCHETT was the leader of the Union movement in Victoria and in the Australasian General Conference. It was actually in Victoria that more opposition came from the strongly-entrenched and somewhat conservative Wesleyans. There was much distress when, in 1897, the Victorian Wesleyan Conference failed to get a two-thirds majority in the voting for union. Very quickly this position was reversed in 1898. As the other denominations had agreed upon union no obstacles were left; and a Methodist Union Bill was passed by the Victorian Parliament to give property rights to the united church.

In 1902 the united Conference was held in Wesley Church, Melbourne. The Methodist Church of Australasia came into being with great acclamations and high hopes. (The name "Australasia" was retained even after NEW ZEALAND became independent in 1913; it was felt that the work in the Pacific Islands justified the continued use of the full geographical title.)

Membership since 1902 has not kept pace with the growth of population. The growing secularist spirit has not been adequately met, even by a united Methodist Church. Yet it would have been unthinkable for the followers of John Wesley to have remained divided.

Statistics for the Victoria and Tasmania Conference as of May 1969, are as follows: Number of ministers in active work, 321; Number of churches, 848; Number of members, 55,586.

C. I. Benson, *Victorian Methodism*. 1935.
Blamires and Smith, *Wes. Meth. Church in Victoria*. 1886.
J. C. Symons, *Daniel James Draper*. 1870.
Victoria and Tasmania Conference minutes and reports.

A. HAROLD WOOD
TED NOFFS

VICTORIA UNIVERSITY, Canada (and Canadian moves in higher education). In 1829, less than a year after the M.E. Church in CANADA became independent of its mother church in the United States, it launched two major projects: a newspaper to advance its views and a seminary to educate its young people. The paper, *The Christian Guardian*, was in operation within three months of the Conference's decision to publish it, under the editorship of EGERTON RYERSON. The seminary took longer to establish.

Education in Upper Canada was, in Ryerson's words, largely for "a wealthy few of a particular creed." The governor and ruling clique assumed that the Church of England was the established church of the young colony and intended that higher education in Upper Canada should be under the control of that church and supported by a state endowment. A royal charter had been granted in 1827 for the establishment of King's College in York (now TORONTO) under the control of the Church of England and requiring that its professors subscribe to the Thirty-nine ARTICLES OF RELIGION. The college was to

have the support of a large endowment provided by the Crown for education in Upper Canada. It was even stated by Archdeacon John Strachan, the president-designate, that the college was to be a missionary institution to bring as many as possible of the people of the province into communion with the Church of England. But in a province where less than a quarter of the population were Anglicans, the venture was so unpopular that the opening of the college was delayed until 1843, after the charter had been modified along more liberal lines.

The Methodists were not disposed to acquiesce in the preservation of aristocratic privilege in education. Many of them were United Empire Loyalists, but they had come under the influence of American democratic ideals. Contrary to the belief of many of the ruling class that a university under Anglican control was necessary to train citizens who would be loyal to Britain and British institutions, the Methodists refused to acknowledge that they needed lessons in loyalty and that the Church of England had any right to monopolize education in the province. And they believed, with the Colonial Secretary, that the country must make the university and not the university the country.

As it was, scores of young Canadian Methodists were students at American institutions, and since the active and thriving Methodists were derisively labeled "Yankee republicans" and "disloyal levelers," it was clearly advisable that they should have their own college in Canada. They therefore sought and obtained a royal charter in 1836—the first ever granted to a non-Anglican institution —and in June of that year the Upper Canada Academy was opened in the town of Cobourg. Although the Charter gave university powers, it was thought wise to begin at a subcollege level and as a coeducational institution.

By the time Upper and Lower Canada were united in 1841, the academy had achieved considerable success. But already there were three other church colleges in the planning stage, and the Methodists were agreed that it was time they undertook teaching at the university level. An act was proclaimed in August, 1841, incorporating the academy as "Victoria College" (so named for Queen Victoria), and in October teaching began on the college level. The college was no longer coeducational. Young

VICTORIA COLLEGE, TORONTO, ONTARIO

men requiring secondary education were provided for in a preparatory department, and the young women were taken care of in private schools in Cobourg.

The Conference had resolved in 1830 that its "seminary of learning" should be "purely a literary institution" where "no system of theology shall be taught . . . , but all students shall be free to embrace and pursue any religious creed, and attend any place of worship, their parents or guardians may direct." (Sissons, p. 6.) This resolution must be interpreted in the light of the royal charter, where it is expressly stated that the purpose of the academy is "for the general Education of Youth, in the various branches of Literature and Science on Christian principles." By "system of theology" the founding fathers appear to have meant a denominational theology imposed willy-nilly on staff and students. The Canadian Methodists had two convictions: first, that education must not be purely secular, or, as expressed by Ryerson in his inaugural address as principal in 1841, that "the fundamental principles of Christian theology be taught to all students"; and, second, that adherence to any particular theology and attendance at worship should not be required of teachers or students. The establishment of Upper Canada Academy along these lines was one of the first effective blows struck in the province for the cause of religious liberty.

It has often been assumed that the Methodist Church founded Victoria University chiefly for the training of Methodist ministers, but this was not the case. To begin with, for the Methodists of that time, sound conversion mattered more than formal education. Fitness for the ministry meant the preaching ability and fervor of the converted, and it was the view of many that education could do little to improve it. But in addition, it was precisely those who had this ability whom the Conference wanted to keep on circuits. The church was deeply involved in winning the frontier; it was committed to the evangelization of a nation that was in the building. There were some who doubted the need of an educated ministry, but the church as a whole was primarily concerned to organize itself to meet the pressing claims of its nation-wide task.

It was not until 1842 that probationers were appointed to attend college, and then only at their own request, and only one or two attended each year until 1854. Those who did attend took the regular arts course. From the beginning such subjects as Christian evidences and apologetics, with the reading of the Greek New Testament and the Hebrew Bible, were part of the arts course. As time went on, special courses in divinity were given, but the faculty of divinity was the last of the four faculties to be established at Victoria.

The faculty of arts made steady progress over the years, depending on such development of the curriculum as finances and the supply of teachers permitted. Teachers were seldom imported. The usual method was to place a young graduate under appointment and send him away to study for a year or two. Thus, in 1892, Victoria had eleven professors, all Canadian-born, and departments of classics, oriental (Near-Eastern) languages, mathematics, science, English, modern languages, and ethics. Other subjects such as Christian evidences, church history, and biblical introduction were taught in arts by the faculty of theology. Federation (see below) brought the transfer of mathematics and science to the University of Toronto, and at the same time the department of religious knowledge was added to the faculty of arts. In recent years there has been some expansion of the subjects taught in arts at Victoria by a system of "cross appointments" with the University of Toronto, so that now some modern history, Spanish, and philosophy are also taught there.

Another faculty was added to Victoria when the Toronto School of Medicine was disjoined from the University of Toronto in 1854. Similarly, the Montreal School of Medicine and Surgery came under the wing of Victoria in 1866. The teaching continued to be carried on in Toronto and Montreal, and almost the only function of Victoria University was to confer the degrees. A more indigenous development took place when a faculty of law was instituted in 1860. Victoria continued to give the degrees of bachelor and doctor of laws until federation with the University of Toronto, when it handed over its students in both medicine and law to that university.

The teaching of science had progressed to such an extent that a chair of natural science was established in 1849, and in 1887 a faculty of science was set up and the degree of bachelor of science was offered.

Theology became a department of the faculty of arts in 1871, and in 1872 a two-year course for probationers and a four-year course leading to the bachelor of divinity degree were announced. Finally, the faculty of theology was formed in 1873, with NATHANAEL BURWASH as dean and professor of theology. In 1892 there were seventy-nine students in theology; in 1893, 121; and by 1915, 226. In 1874 only one professor gave his full time to teaching in the faculty of theology, the others being professors in arts doing part-time teaching in theology. But by 1916 the faculty of theology had five professors and three lecturers, with five others giving about one-half of their time to theological teaching.

Victoria College had scarcely received university powers when an attempt was made by the government to consolidate the institutions of higher learning in the province, of which there were now four, each belonging to a major denomination. Three of these were in financial difficulties. The other, King's College, was endowed by lands intended for grammar schools and seminaries of higher learning. In the view of their supporters the other colleges had as much right as King's to government grants and endowments. But when the government proposed to create one university comprising the four colleges, no one was happy about the terms. King's objected to any partnership, especially if it involved sharing its monopoly of government support. Victoria and Queen's objected that they were to lose their autonomy, probably also the teaching of arts, and all this with no clear provision of government support. Fortunately the government resigned before the bill came to its final reading.

Victoria's position was clear. The Methodist Church had a deep interest in higher education; it claimed to have an inalienable responsibility for the education of its youth. It believed also that higher education should not be separated from nurture in Christian faith, although it rejected the idea of religious tests or indoctrination. On these premises, along with its belief in religious equality, it fought consistently for fifty years before a satisfactory provincial scheme of university consolidation and support was worked out.

The second major attempt, which involved the secularization of King's College, again pleased no one and led to the foundation by Strachan of a new Anglican college. The proposal was rejected by Victoria as a "godless" measure.

The third attempt, the University Act of 1853, had much in its favor, but the affiliated colleges, which were to share "any surplus of the . . . University Income Fund," did not receive such support because a surplus was in fact never allowed to exist. Dissatisfaction with the administration of this act smoldered for years and broke out in increasingly insistent demands for the establishment of one university with control of the curriculum and examinations and with authority to confer degrees, in which the colleges would be equal partners equally supported by public funds. The situation became even more serious when, with confederation of the provinces in 1867, education was turned over to provincial jurisdiction, and the government of Ontario declined to continue the grants to denominational colleges which had been made annually for some years. In the following year, representatives of the colleges drew up a petition to the Legislature requesting "that effect be given to the intention of the University Act of 1853," and including a much-improved scheme for the organization of the university. But the Legislature refused to act on the petition, and fifteen more years passed before another strong move was made to form a federated university.

Meanwhile, in spite of financial troubles which required a campaign to retire a debt of $30,000 and build an endowment of $100,000, Victoria took advantage of the flowing tide of scientific progress and increased its staff and facilities for the teaching of science. In 1877 it opened Faraday Hall as the center of its studies in science, which was at that time the only building in the province devoted exclusively to scientific work. Very soon all the universities in the province began to realize that the desired progress in teaching and research in science would require vastly increased support by the government. Under this impulse, several prominent university administrators, of whom it may be said that President Burwash of Victoria was the foremost, began to think of the "provincial university" as a federation of colleges based on a division of the curriculum so that the costly work in science and in other subjects might be borne by the university proper with increased provincial support, while the denominational colleges would enjoy the full tuition fee and their students would have free tuition in university subjects. This was the essence of the scheme that came into effect in 1890, when Victoria entered into federation with the University of Toronto. Two other colleges—Trinity (Anglican) and St. Michael's (Roman Catholic)—entered later. It is this scheme, somewhat improved but substantially the same, that still obtains in the University of Toronto.

Victoria was not put on easy street by federation. In fact a campaign for $450,000 by the Methodist Church was necessary in order to provide buildings in Toronto and increase Victoria's endowment. Campaigns for funds have been required since, too, but Victoria has prospered because it has refused to depart from the sound principles in which it was founded. It consistently refused to give up its arts program and become a theological satellite of a provincial university, because it continued to believe that freedom to pursue truth need not and should not be divorced from the Christian life and faith, that arts, science, and theology belong together. Its wise administrators from the beginning to the present have made this concern their settled policy.

The relation between Victoria and the church is seen in part in its constitution. From the beginning until the present the church has controlled the university through the appointment of its governing board. The Charter of 1836 provided for the government of the college by nine trustees and five visitors, who together made up the board, elected by the ministers of the Annual Conference of the Wesleyan Methodist Church of Canada. The situation has not changed appreciably since then. The most significant change was made in 1915 in order to bring the constitution of the board of regents into line with the requirements of the pension scheme of the Carnegie Foundation.

After Church Union in 1925, when the faculty and most of the students of Knox College entered The United Church of Canada, another act was passed in 1928 creating two colleges—Victoria and Emmanuel—instead of two faculties in Victoria University.

According to this act, the board of regents was to have forty-two members, of whom twenty-two were to be elected by the General Council of the church. Five members were to be elected by the graduates of Emmanuel College, this being interpreted to include any person who had studied theology for one year or more in Knox College or in the faculty of theology of Victoria. Seven other persons were to be co-opted. For the first time, the board was to choose its chairman. Three other persons were members of the board ex officio—the chancellor and president and the two principals. The appointment of the principal and professors of Emmanuel College was to be subject to confirmation by the General Council.

While the church gave birth to Victoria University and has controlled it through the board of regents, it has never interfered directly to determine its policy, except on two occasions when academic freedom became the basic issue in controversies concerning higher criticism. From about 1883 there were repeated attempts to give the General Conference of the Methodist Church control over appointments to theological faculties in church universities, although, strangely enough, no attempt seems to have been made to discipline pastors who had been influenced by higher criticism.

After much bitter dispute the matter was settled in 1910. In that year the General Conference accepted two principles already laid down by the Victoria staff; that the teaching in the church's colleges must conform to the church's doctrinal standards, and that the teachers in the colleges must be protected "in the free and proper discharge of their duty." Since that time there has been no interference on theological grounds with professors in the church's college, and much of the credit for this happy state must go to Victoria University and its great president, Nathanael Burwash.

Church union was followed by a reorganization of Victoria University into two colleges, Victoria and Emmanuel, constituted as noted above. Since more space was needed, a separate building for Emmanual College was erected in 1931, and five new houses were added to Burwash Hall, the men's residence.

The union on the campus between the Victoria and a former staff of Knox College (Presbyterian) was accomplished peacefully and Victoria University has enjoyed the utmost harmony between its colleges. The last sentence of C. B. Sissons' *History of Victoria University* is this: "As the two colleges work side by side they will continue to represent that fusion of the sacred and the secular which is the tradition of the founders and the spirit of the evangel." (p. 330)

The partnership of the colleges is not to be judged by the disparity in their size. (Victoria College has about 2,400 students and Emmanuel about 100.) Emmanuel is the largest of the eight theological colleges of The United Church of Canada. Besides the bachelor of divinity degree it offers the degree of bachelor of religious education. About one third of the students are enrolled in graduate studies. In 1944 it joined with the Anglican and Presbyterian theological colleges on the Toronto campus to form the Toronto Graduate School of Theological Studies. Master's and doctor's degrees are given by the individual colleges, the chief function of the school being to facilitate co-operation in teaching. Recently the school was incorporated, and more recently still it was strengthened by the addition of the graduate departments of the Roman Catholic University of St. Michael's College, whose arts faculty, like Victoria's, is federated in the University of Toronto.

Victoria University has been strengthened recently in both arts and theology by the development of its Centre for Reformation and Renaissance Studies. This is at present largely a specialized library being built around a fine collection of Erasmiana. Undoubtedly it will soon be a strong center of research in the graduate field.

From its humble beginning in one small building in a small town, Victoria University has prospered and grown in Toronto. Its 1967 enrolment was about 2,500 students, and it had a teaching staff of 134. It has ten major buildings, assets valued at $15,000,000, an endowment of more than $6,000,000, and an operating budget of $2,500,000.

A History of Victoria University. Toronto: University of Toronto Press, 1952.
C. B. Sissons, *Egerton Ryerson*. 1937, 1947.   A. G. REYNOLDS

VILVORDE, Belgium. The Methodist Church (Flemish) was organized in 1928 following a revival under a Gospel tent erected on the city square next to the William Tyndale monument. This monument was erected in memory of the martyrdom of the translator of the Bible into English (burned at the stake in Vilvorde, Oct. 6, 1536). In 1934 a large dancing hall was secured and made a sanctuary. In 1956 a new Tyndale Memorial Church was built. Pastors have been P. Mietes, 1928-32; A. Parmentier, 1933-47; M. Vannieuwenhuyse, 1948-50; A. Pieters, 1951-59; W. Toormans since 1960.

WILLIAM G. THONGER

VINCENT, BURTON JONES (1877-1931), American bishop of the FREE METHODIST CHURCH, was born in a Free Methodist parsonage at Ypsilanti, Mich., Aug. 15, 1877. Converted when a child, he joined that Church. He was a student at SPRING ARBOR Seminary in MICHIGAN, and Marion College, Indiana, granted him the A.B. Called into the ministry, he joined the Northern Indiana Conference in 1899. He served as pastor and district elder in INDIANA, WISCONSIN, CALIFORNIA and WASHINGTON. He spent nine years in church schools: as assistant principal Evansville Seminary; principal of Spring Arbor Seminary, Mich.; Los Angeles Seminary, Calif.; and of Wessington Springs Seminary, South Dakota. He was Editor of the church's Sunday school literature, 1923-31; and bishop, 1931. He died at Evanston, Ill., in August 1931, having held only four conferences.

Vincent was a leader of youth, a lover of men. He had a genius for administration. He was an excellent writer, gifted preacher, equally at home founding new churches on the frontier or in serving as pastor of large college congregations.

BYRON S. LAMSON

JOHN H. VINCENT

VINCENT, JOHN HEYL (1832-1920), American bishop, author, educator, lecturer, and organizer, was born in Tuscaloosa, Ala., on Feb. 28, 1832, the son of John Himrod and Mary (Raser) Vincent. His father, a farmer, trader, miller, postmaster, and Methodist Sunday-school superintendent, was a descendant of Levi Vincent, French Huguenot, who fled France in 1685 and settled at New Rochelle, N. Y. In 1837, the family returned north to the vicinity of Lewisburg, Pa.

At eighteen he was licensed to "exhort" and as a Methodist LOCAL PREACHER was appointed to Luzerne (Pa.) Circuit. After attending academies at Milton and Lewisburg, Pa., he studied briefly at the Wesleyan Institute, Newark, N. J., and in 1857 completed the course of study prescribed by the Conference. During this time he worked in a store and served as principal of an academy. From time to time he studied Greek, Hebrew, French and physical science under special teachers. As part of his education he visited Egypt, Palestine, Greece, and Italy in 1862.

Ordained a DEACON in 1855, he served churches in northern NEW JERSEY. In 1857 he was ordained an ELDER and transferred to the ROCK RIVER CONFERENCE, where he held pastorates at Joliet, Mt. Morris, Galena, Rockford and Trinity Church, Chicago. U. S. GRANT, later General and President of the United States, attended his church at Galena and they became lifelong friends.

In 1866 he was made general agent of the M.E. SUNDAY SCHOOL Union in New York City and in 1868 was elected corresponding secretary of the Sunday School Union and TRACT SOCIETY with headquarters in the same place. He had previously seen the vital need for trained teachers, and in 1855 he had organized the "Palestine Class" for study of Biblical history and geography. In 1857 at Joliet, Ill., he started a church normal class (interdenominational) to provide trained teachers. The work rapidly spread beyond the limits of his own parish and in 1861 he held the first Sunday School Teacher's Institute in America. In that year he prepared a manual, *Little Footprints in Bible Lands*, the first of a large quantity of

Sunday school literature which the new idea demanded.

In 1865 Vincent established the *Northwestern Sunday School Quarterly* in Chicago and in 1866 *The Sunday School Teacher*. In these he introduced the system of Sunday school lessons with lesson leaves. As Corresponding Secretary of the Sunday School Union, he was also editor of all M.E. Sunday school publications. Under his management the circulation of the *Sunday-School Journal* increased tenfold, while his lesson leaves had a circulation of nearly 2,500,000 copies.

The complete series of his books form an encyclopedia of the beginning of the modern Sunday school movement. All his work was preliminary to the ultimate development of the Chautauqua Sunday-School Teachers Assembly, founded jointly by Vincent and Lewis Miller of Akron, Ohio. This was in 1874 when an institute, interdenominational in character, met for two weeks at Fair Point, Chautauqua, N. Y., for the preparation of Sunday school teachers. The organization grew from year to year. The time session was extended to eight weeks and came to include a complete summer school with classes, lectures, concerts and entertainments. Chautauqua became a meeting place for various Christian groups while still retaining its early aim of training teachers for all Protestant Sunday schools. The Chautauqua Literary and Scientific Circle, founded by Vincent in 1878, marked the beginning of guided home study and correspondence courses, and within a few years had 100,000 students enrolled. The Chautauqua summer courses were the forerunners of college summer sessions. Vincent's pioneering went far beyond denominational limits and eventually the Chautauqua idea grew into one of the most extensive movements for popular education in the United States.

In 1888, John Vincent was elected a bishop of the M.E. Church and was stationed first at Buffalo, N. Y., and then at TOPEKA, Kan. From 1901-04 he had charge of the church's work in Europe from headquarters in ZÜRICH, SWITZERLAND. In 1904 he retired from the episcopacy. In demand as a college preacher, he was the first Methodist minister invited to Harvard University as University preacher. Harvard, OHIO WESLEYAN and Washington and Jefferson College all granted him honorary degrees. During the Civil War he served as a member of the Christian Commission.

Later writings include *The Home Book* (1886); *The Modern Sunday-School,* and *Better Not* (1887); *Studies in Young Life* (1889); *Our Own Church* (1890); *Family Worship For Every Day in the Year* (1905); *To Old Bethlehem* and *The Church at Home.*

He was married on Nov. 10, 1858 to Elizabeth Dusenberry of Portville, N. Y. They had one son, George Edgar Vincent, who was president of the University of Minnesota, 1911-17, and president of the Rockefeller Foundation, 1917-29. Bishop Vincent died in Chicago, Ill., on May 9, 1920.

Dictionary of American Biography.
John H. Vincent, *The Chautauqua Movement.* N.p.: the author, 1886.
Leon H. Vincent, *John Heyl Vincent.* New York: Macmillan Company, 1925.   WILLIAM M. TWIDDY

VINELAND, NEW JERSEY, U.S.A., **First Church.** On April 12, 1863, a Methodist class and church were organized in Vineland, N. J., which came to be known as the First Methodist Church. A building was begun in 1864 and completed in 1867. In December 1932, fire destroyed the original building, which was then replaced by a Gothic stone structure.

The practice of using bottled, unfermented grape juice for communion originated in this church. T. B. Welch, one of the founders of the Welch Grape Juice Company, was elected communion steward in First Church in 1869. He agreed to serve provided that he would be permitted to use the pure juice of grapes, pasteurized through a new method developed by his company. The same practice was subsequently widely adopted throughout American Methodism.

F. B. Stanger, *New Jersey.* 1961.   HENRY L. LAMBDIN

VINEY, RICHARD (Fl. 1740), a British tailor who accompanied JOHN WESLEY to GERMANY, became an original member of the society at FETTER LANE in LONDON. Viney was attracted by Count ZINZENDORF and joined the MORAVIANS, but afterward criticized them and was expelled in 1743. He translated some of PETER BÖHLER's sermons at OXFORD, where he became a Moravian minister. Afterward, Viney rejoined the Methodists and assisted John Wesley at the Orphan House, Newcastle, but proved to be a disturbing influence and "quite perverted" JOHN NELSON's society at Birstall.

J. Wesley, *Journal,* iii, May 16, 1744, p. 139. C. W. TOWLSON

VIRGINIA, U.S.A., is one of the original thirteen colonies with an area of 40,817 square miles, and a population of 4,543,249 (1970). Since 1950 the population has grown more than 1,200,000, increasing especially along the Potomac across from Washington, and in the big cities—NORFOLK, PORTSMOUTH, NEWPORT NEWS, and RICHMOND.

Topographically the state is divided into the tidewater section where the colonial settlers first made their homes; the Piedmont region running back to the Blue Ridge Mountains; and the area across the Blue Ridge, the great Valley of Virginia, the Shenandoah, which has become famous in history and noted for the beauty of its scenery. The Commonwealth, as its people insist on calling their state, is also famous for its colonial culture, its statesmen who led the nation in its formative period, its historic estates, and its many battlefields on which the fate of the nation was decided in both the American Revolution and the Civil War. Virginia furnished four of the first five presidents of the United States, and it has been to date the birthplace of eight—Washington, Jefferson, Monroe, Madison, Tyler, William H. Harrison, Taylor, and Wilson, the last three being elected from other states.

The first permanent settlement in the Commonwealth was made at Jamestown on May 13, 1607, the colonists bringing with them the forms and ceremonies of the Church of England. Civil and ecclesiastical history are closely interwoven in early Virginia, and the Church of England was traditionally more at home there than in any other colony. Stringent laws passed by the legislative Assembly of Virginia and a copy of the Act of Uniformity in Britain adopted by the colony, drove the Puritans away, and greatly discouraged the Quakers, Congregationalists, and all non-episcopal groups.

GEORGE WHITEFIELD preached a few sermons in Virginia about 1740, but Methodism proper was planted there by ROBERT WILLIAMS who became a local preacher in England, and arrived in New York in 1769. Williams came to Virginia in 1772, and preached his first sermon in Norfolk at the door of the courthouse. He also visited Portsmouth, where a prominent businessman, Isaac Luke, was converted. After Williams came RICHARD BOARDMAN, JOSEPH PILMORE, FRANCIS ASBURY, and other Methodist pioneers. Pilmore and WILLIAM WATTERS, the first native itinerant preacher, crossed the Potomac at Alexandria, and preached where opportunity afforded on their way to Norfolk. DEVEREAUX JARRATT, a clergyman of the Church of England, in the tidewater region, was friendly to the Methodist preachers and allowed them to hold services in his parish. He also administered the sacraments to the Methodists.

When the Revolution began, most of the Anglican preachers returned to England, and since the Methodist preachers were not ordained, the Methodists generally were without the sacraments. Yet due to the flaming evangelistic work of Williams both in Virginia and NORTH CAROLINA, the Methodist societies increased rapidly, and the matter of the sacraments became urgent. The Virginia preachers then differed sharply with Asbury regarding their right to administer the sacraments. A historic meeting was held at the Broken Back Church, Fluvanna County, beginning May 18, 1779, in which the Virginians, led by ROBERT STRAWBRIDGE from MARYLAND, decided they would ordain each other, and proceed to administer the sacraments regardless of anything Asbury or Wesley himself might do or say. After a year Asbury succeeded in getting the action of the preachers at the Fluvanna County Conference annulled, and in due time John Wesley himself sent over ordained men—THOMAS COKE, RICHARD WHATCOAT, and THOMAS VASEY—with a liturgy which he had prepared, and bestowed his blessing upon whatever the American Methodists would do, telling them to "stand fast in the liberty in which God had so strangely made them free."

JAMES O'KELLY went into Virginia after he withdrew from the Methodist Episcopal Church in opposition to Asbury, and organized the REPUBLICAN METHODIST (later called the Christian) CHURCH, which after more than a century united with the Congregational Church. However, remarkable revivals continued in Virginia through the first half of the nineteenth century and Methodism grew rapidly.

When the 1796 GENERAL CONFERENCE formed annual conferences with geographical boundaries, the northern and western counties of Virginia (that part of Virginia which was north of the Rappahannock and west of the Blue Ridge) were assigned to the BALTIMORE CONFERENCE, whose preachers had been manning the stations. The Baltimore Conference extended down to the Holston Conference in Southwest Virginia. Fredericksburg, on the south side of the Rappahannock, was however kept as a Baltimore Conference appointment. The HOLSTON CONFERENCE extended up from Tennessee as far as the New River, or thereabouts, and this portion of the Commonwealth yet remains in the Holston Conference.

When the M.E. Church, South was organized in 1845, the Virginia Conference, of course, adhered South. The Baltimore Conference, holding northern and western Virginia, endeavored to act as a "bridge Conference" between the South and North and continued its adherence to the M.E. Church until the outbreak of the Civil War. Then the Baltimore, a border conference, split and two conferences were created, as no bridge could possibly span the tragic gap that then opened between the sections of the nation. The Shenandoah Valley and northern Virginia and the churches in Maryland that adhered South became, as they called themselves, the Old Baltimore Conference, and in 1866 this conference, which had remained independent during the Civil War, formally joined the Southern Church.

For some years after the 1844 division, strained relations existed between the Methodists in the Virginia Conference proper and the Baltimore Conference Methodists across the Blue Ridge because the Virginia Conference felt that all Methodists in the Commonwealth should have declared themselves Southern. For some years after the Civil War there was some antipathy between the Virginia Conference and the Baltimore Conference, although both were then in the M.E. Church, South.

At Methodist unification in 1939, the Jurisdictional line was drawn along the Potomac and the West Virginia state line, and all of the state of Virginia, except the Holston section, was included in the new and enlarged Virginia Conference. At the Uniting Conference in Kansas City in 1939, since it was known that the Virginia Conference would be unusually large if the Virginia part of the Baltimore Conference should be added to it, an effort was made to unite the four Virginia districts of the Baltimore Conference with the Virginia districts of the Holston Conference to form a new annual conference. This, of course, would have created a long and narrow conference extending from Bristol on the Tennessee line up to Alexandria across from Washington. The move failed because the Holston people did not wish to see their conference divided, even though they, too, knew that the Holston Conference would be greatly enlarged by merger with the Holston Conference (ME) as a result of unification. The four Virginia districts of the Old Baltimore Conference had to go into the Virginia Conference because of the way the Jurisdictional line was drawn.

The Holston Conference delegation (MES) to the Uniting Conference had agreed in advance with the Baltimore Conference delegation that they would jointly ask at Kansas City that the Virginia districts of the Holston and Baltimore Conferences be merged to form a new conference, and an agreement to that effect was signed in advance of the Uniting Conference (the signed agreement is in the possession of the writer of this article). However, since no annual conference ever wishes to be divided, the Holston Conference delegation disregarded the advance agreement when they arrived at Kansas City, and then the SOUTHEASTERN JURISDICTIONAL CONFERENCE delegates, acting for the Jurisdiction, placed the four Virginia districts of the Baltimore Conference in the Virginia Conference of The Methodist Church.

In retrospect all agree that what was done was more statesmanlike than the creation of a narrow, five-hundred-mile-long "shoe string" conference on the western boundary of Virginia. Subsequently, Bishop W. W. PEELE, who was called upon to administer the new Virginia Conference for twelve years, made such good appointments and supervised the work so ably that the different sections of Virginia Methodism were well woven into the present powerful Virginia Conference.

The M.E. Church had a Virginia Conference from 1869 to 1906. Never strong, it was absorbed in time by the Baltimore, Holston, and WEST VIRGINIA CONFERENCES. At the time of unification parts of the Northern Church's Baltimore Conference and the WASHINGTON CONFERENCE of Negro Methodists were included within the Commonwealth. The METHODIST PROTESTANT CHURCH also had a Virginia Conference which was organized in 1829. In 1870 more than half its ministers and churches went into the M.E. Church, South, and thereafter the M.P. conference was not strong though it continued until 1939. The Virginia Conference of the A.M.E. CHURCH included the entire state, along with a portion of West Virginia. The C.M.E. and A.M.E. ZION denominations also had many Virginia churches. The merger of the E.U.B. VIRGINIA CONFERENCE in 1968 did not appreciably enlarge the Virginia Conference, though the UNITED BRETHREN were traditionally strong in the Shenandoah Valley.

Other accounts in this *Encyclopedia* tell of the growth of Methodism in the cities of the Commonwealth, and of early shrines and preaching places. In 1968 the Virginia Conference had 381,458 members, making it one of the largest conferences. When the statistics for the Virginia districts of the Holston Conference and the Virginia part of the North Carolina-Virginia Conference (CJ) are added, The United Methodist Church had in Virginia in 1970 approximately 820 pastoral charges, 398,273 members, and property valued at $175,000,000.

W. W. Bennett, *Virginia.* 1871.
L. M. Lee, *Jesse Lee.* 1848.
Richmond Christian Advocate files.
W. W. Sweet, *Virginia.* 1955.   N. B. H.

VIRGINIA CITY, MONTANA, U.S.A., along with Bannack, represents the earliest Methodist work among the unsettled mining population of pioneer MONTANA. Gold was discovered in Bannack (Grasshopper Creek) in 1862, in Virginia City (Alder Gulch) in 1863, and in Helena (Last Chance) in 1864. A Methodist class was formed by laymen in Virginia City in winter, 1863-64, and a LOCAL PREACHER, Hugh Duncan, preached there. The first regularly appointed minister, A. M. Hough, arrived in 1864 and dedicated a log cabin chapel on November 6.

Methodist work languished after the miners wandered on to other diggings, especially Helena.

E. L. Mills, *Plains, Peaks and Pioneers.* 1947.
                                    FREDERICK A. NORWOOD

VIRGINIA CONFERENCE dates its sessions officially from the first conference held in the state after the CHRISTMAS CONFERENCE. This was in May, 1785, at Mason's Chapel in Brunswick County, with Bishop ASBURY presiding. However, six sessions of American Methodist conferences had been held in VIRGINIA prior to the 1785 gathering.

In 1773 there were 100 members in the Virginia Methodist societies. By the time the great spiritual awakening under GEORGE SHADFORD reached its peak in 1776, five circuits had been formed with 2,456 members. By 1779 there were twelve Virginia circuits, with twenty-three preachers and 4,507 members. At Asbury's death in 1816, the membership totaled 24,361. Evangelistic concern has ever marked Virginia Conference churches.

Many persons prominent in American Methodism have been associated with the Virginia Conference. ROBERT WILLIAMS, a "rousing evangelist," first appeared at NORFOLK in 1769. WILLIAM WATTERS, the first American-born itinerant, and RICHARD OWINGS, first LOCAL PREACHER, were active in the Virginia societies. Four of Wesley's eight official missionaries to America—JOSEPH PILMORE, THOMAS RANKIN, George Shadford, and Francis Asbury —participated in the planting of Virginia Methodism. The

feet of Asbury literally tracked the state. His first appointment to Virginia was in 1775. He preached his last sermon in RICHMOND, and died a few days later, March 31, 1816, at George Arnold's home in Spotsylvania County.

ROBERT STRAWBRIDGE brought Methodism to northern Virginia, probably established the LEESBURG CHURCH in 1766, and organized societies in Fairfax County. Other familiar Methodist names connected with Virginia Methodism are: PHILIP GATCH, preacher on the Hanover and Sussex Circuits; JESSE LEE, native Virginian and Methodist historian; JOHN DICKINS and NOLAN B. HARMON, book editors of the church, the latter being elected bishop while a member of the Virginia Conference; JOHN EARLY, bishop and one of the founders of RANDOLPH-MACON COLLEGE; JAMES DUNCAN, ROBERT BLACKWELL, and J. EARL MORELAND, presidents of the college; STITH MEAD, of CAMP MEETING fame; LORENZO DOW, free lance evangelist; J. MANNING POTTS, editor of *The Upper Room* and noted historian of the church; and GAITHER P. WARFIELD, director of METHODIST COMMITTEE FOR OVERSEAS RELIEF.

Virginia has given thirteen native sons to the Methodist episcopacy: WILLIAM McKENDREE (1808); ENOCH GEORGE (1816); BEVERLY WAUGH (1836); John Early (1854); DAVID S. DOGGETT (1866); JOHN C. GRANBERY (1882); WILLIAM TAYLOR (1884); WILLIAM W. DUNCAN (1886); COLLINS DENNY (1910); WILLIAM B. BEAUCHAMP (1922); PAUL B. KERN 1930); PAUL N. GARBER (1944); and WALTER C. GUM (1960). Two other bishops, members of the Virginia Conference when elected, were born elsewhere—JAMES CANNON, JR. (1918) and Nolan B. Harmon (1956).

Virginia Methodism has had close relationships with the divisions and reunions within American Methodism. The threatened breach over the ordinances in 1778-1779 troubled the conferences held at Leesburg and at Broken Back Church in Fluvanna County. The first serious division in American Methodism was led by the enigmatic JAMES O'KELLY, Virginia preacher who, objecting to Asbury's episcopal power, marched out in 1792, taking many with him. Because of the schism, the conference suffered a net loss of 4,317 members between 1794 and 1800. The formation of the METHODIST PROTESTANT CHURCH later left its mark on the conference. There was a heavy representation from Virginia in the convention which brought the METHODIST PROTESTANT CHURCH into being.

The Virginia Conference was of course greatly involved in the division of the church over the problem of slavery. Virginia Methodism included more slaveholding members than in any other state. When the issue reached its peak in the GENERAL CONFERENCE of 1844, Virginia had four delegates, two of whom—John Early and WILLIAM A. SMITH—took active parts in the debates. The delegation stood firmly against the northern-backed resolution asking Bishop JAMES O. ANDREW to resign. Subsequently, following the north-south division, the first General Conference of the new Methodist Episcopal Church, South convened in a Virginia city—PETERSBURG, and selected a Virginia delegate as president pro tem.

Three-quarters of a century after it began, American Methodism, born in the American Revolution, knew the throes of the Civil War. Southern Methodism, though devoted to the cause of the Confederacy, knew much heartsearching because of slavery. Much of the war centered in Virginia. Incredibly the church lived and carried on its work amid the tragedy and confusion which military campaigns brought to Virginia. The conference, in its membership, felt the ravages of war. By 1863 there was a decline of 11,150 in white membership, and a loss of 5,000 Negro members during the war years. Nine ministers of the conference were ordinary soldiers or officers in the Confederate Army. Twenty-two served as CHAPLAINS and two as army missionaries. The end of the war launched a period of intense evangelistic fervor, resulting in an increase of 27,000 members by 1880, as compared with 1865.

When union came to American Methodism in 1939, the Virginia Conference had 171,964 members. A new conference was then organized consisting of the ten districts of the former Virginia Conference, and two districts and parts of four others from the former BALTIMORE CONFERENCE (MES). In addition, the new conference received sixteen charges from the MARYLAND CONFERENCE (MP) and two from the NORTH CAROLINA CONFERENCE (MP), while from the M.E. Church came the following numbers of charges: BALTIMORE CONFERENCE, seven; WILMINGTON CONFERENCE, five; BLUE RIDGE-ATLANTIC CONFERENCE, one; HOLSTON CONFERENCE, six; and WEST VIRGINIA CONFERENCE, five. The new Virginia Conference was organized with fourteen districts, and in 1941 it reported 207,677 members.

In 1965 the Virginia Conference extended invitations to the charges of the Virginia District of the NORTH CAROLINA-VIRGINIA CONFERENCE (CJ) to merge with it. The merger was effected in 1968.

Virginia Methodism has always had an interest in education. EBENEZER ACADEMY appears to have been the first Methodist school in Virginia. Established in 1784, it passed out of Methodist hands about 1800. Harrisonburg School, in Rockingham County, was opened by Asbury in 1794, but had brief duration. Randolph-Macon College, chartered in 1830, is the oldest permanent Methodist college in America. It opened at Boydton in 1832, and after the Civil War moved to Ashland. In 1968 the school reported an enrollment of nearly 900, an endowment of over $3,000,000, and a plant valued at nearly $9,000,000. RANDOLPH-MACON WOMEN'S COLLEGE, located at Lynchburg, opened in 1893, a dream of William Waugh Smith. He became its first acting president. The school holds a top position among American colleges for women. VIRGINIA WESLEYAN COLLEGE at Norfolk, sponsored by the conference, opened in 1966 with the promise of becoming a strong church college.

FERRUM JUNIOR COLLEGE at Ferrum was founded in 1913. It was originally established as Ferrum Training School to serve mountain children. RANDOLPH-MACON ACADEMY, founded at Front Royal in the 1890's, had merged with it another school in 1933. Other educational ventures included: Blackstone College for girls (originally Blackstone Female Institute, opened in 1894 and now closed); and Randolph-Macon Female Institute at Danville, opened in 1897, and later passed from Methodist control.

The conference has participated in the METHODIST STUDENT MOVEMENT. Virginia Methodism sponsors WESLEY FOUNDATIONS at the various state schools, and has units of the Student Movement at the colleges related to the church.

Virginia Methodism seems to have claim for establishing the SUNDAY SCHOOL Movement in America. In the 1780's Thomas Crenshaw began a Sunday school in Hanover County, Virginia, and William Elliott started one on the Eastern Shore. Christian education has long been a vital part of Methodism's life and progress, and the conference has pride in these modest beginnings in Virginia.

The first foreign missionary of American Methodism, MELVILLE COX, although a New Englander, was a member of the Virginia Conference for a short time and later sailed for LIBERIA from Norfolk in 1832. Virginia Conference churches have increasingly supported the mission enterprise across the years. Today the conference journal lists thirty-nine missionaries from Virginia, and a large number of others are being supported by Virginia Conference churches. The Advance Special program of the Methodist BOARD OF MISSIONS, so vital a part of mission support in recent years, was largely the outgrowth of a plan formulated by a member of the Virginia Conference, William Archer Wright. The WOMEN'S SOCIETY OF CHRISTIAN SERVICE of the conference (49,581 members in 1968) has been an integral and vigorous part of the mission interest. The conference ranks high in The Methodist Church in support of missionaries. Church extension is also a robust movement in the conference, and in the growing population centers, especially in northern Virginia and Norfolk-Portsmouth, it has kept pace by establishing many new churches. The Alexandria and Arlington Districts reported a total of 73,153 members in 1968.

The conference has had its own paper since 1832, beginning under the name of *Virginia Conference Sentinel*. Later names were, *Baltimore and Richmond Christian Advocate*, *Richmond Christian Advocate*, and presently *Virginia Methodist Advocate*, the name adopted in 1939 when it merged with the *Baltimore Southern Methodist*. There have been ten editors, beginning with Ethelbert Drake and continuing to George S. Reamey, who has served since 1939.

A powerful social awakening came in Virginia Methodism, as in other Protestant churches, in the years following the Civil War. It evidenced great zeal for temperance under the leadership of Bishop James Cannon, Jr. Important forward strides came in 1908 through the leadership of William Francis Drewry, physician, and Joseph T. Mastin, minister of the conference, who infused the whole Commonwealth with a new concern for social welfare, and started welfare organizations. The conference today is vitally associated with the Alcohol Education Council, and kindred interdenominational groups. Within the conference there are the Virginia Methodist Children's Home at Richmond, and six homes for the aged in different parts of the state.

Laymen were active from the earliest days of the Conference. GABRIEL P. DISOSWAY, a Methodist citizen of Petersburg, took part in the founding of Randolph-Macon College. In 1870, when lay delegates were first seated in the General Conference, the Virginia Conference delegation included seven laymen. Laymen were more active in the conference from that time forward. Lay representation in conference bodies has tended to provide greater business efficiency, organization and administration. Virginia Methodism developed a lay organization of unusual strength, promoting stewardship, trained lay speakers, organized groups of Methodist Men, and encouraging greater use of laymen in the life and leadership of both the conference and the local churches.

In 1970, the Virginia Conference reported 16 districts, 768 charges, 383,176 members, property valued at $169,-

449,606, and a total amount of $24,568,069 raised for all purposes during the year. At that time it had the largest membership of any conference in the connection.

W. W. Bennett, *Virginia.* 1871.
General Minutes, ME, MES, TMC, UMC.
Minutes of the Virginia Conference.
W. W. Sweet, *Virginia.* 1955.   HAROLD H. HUGHES

VIRGINIA CONFERENCE (EUB), which included counties both in WEST VIRGINIA and MARYLAND, dated its annual sessions from the Original Conference of 1800. In addition to Henry Baker, Christian and Henry Crum and Simon Herr, who were native to this section, OTTERBEIN, GEETING, BOEHM, and NEWCOMER preached in this area.

The first session of the Original Conference to meet within the bounds of the later Virginia Conference was held at Abraham Niswander's home, May 25, 1808. At this conference some procedures were outlined for authorizing men to preach and assignments were made to circuits.

Early classes grew up around Mt. Jackson, Harrisonburg, Winchester, along the Potomac River at Sleepy Creek, and in Augusta and Loudon Counties. Among those who supplied homes for the preachers and places in which to meet were the Ambrose, Stickley, Senseny, Niswander, and Funkhouser families.

The Original Conference, also called the Hagerstown Conference, was divided in 1830 to form the Hagerstown (later Virginia) and Harrisburg (later Pennsylvania) Conferences. The first session of the Virginia Conference was assembled at Hinckel's Schoolhouse, Shenandoah County, Virginia, April 27, 1831, with Bishop HENRY KUMLER presiding.

Little effort was made to build meeting houses in the early years, so that the Whitsel Church, built about 1824, is believed to be the oldest church in the conference.

In 1833, the conference authorized the printing of a Hymnal in English. They were joined in the project by the Pennsylvania Conference. This book was used for many years in the church.

The first foreign mission offering received in an annual conference session was taken by Bishop GLOSSBRENNER at the Bethlehem Church, Augusta County, in 1851.

The denominational stand on SLAVERY adopted by the General Conference of 1817, although approved by members of the Virginia Conference, created many difficulties in local situations. United Brethren in Virginia were often looked upon with suspicion by their neighbors. Bishop MARKWOOD, who had been raised in Virginia, had a price of $500 placed on his head by the Confederate States of America. During the war period from 1862 to 1865, it was necessary to hold two annual sessions of conference, one north of the Potomac River and the other in the Shenandoah Valley.

In 1875, the Rev. A. P. Funkhouser and Professor J. N. Fries started a school at Dayton, Virginia. It was later purchased by the conference; and in 1960, the institution was moved to a new campus in Winchester, Va. It is known as SHENANDOAH COLLEGE, a junior college, and Shenandoah Conservatory of Music, a four-year, degree granting institution.

In 1966, there were ninety-two ministers in all classes with 147 organized congregations and 22,049 members.

The churches of the conference were placed in the West Virginia, Baltimore, and Virginia Conferences at the time of conference union in 1970.

A. W. Drury, *History of the U.B.* 1924.
Abram Paul Funkhouser and Oren F. Morton, *History of the Church of the United Brethren in Christ of the Virginia Conference.* Dayton, Va.: the conference, 1921.
D. F. Glovier, *Pictorial History of Virginia Conference.* Staunton, Va.: McClure Printing Co., 1965.
J. Lawrence, *History of the U.B.* 1860.
H. A. Thompson, *Our Bishops.* 1889.   H. FRED EDGE

VIRGINIA METHODIST ADVOCATE, formerly the historic *Richmond Christian Advocate,* is published in RICHMOND, Va., and is the official organ of the VIRGINIA CONFERENCE of The United Methodist Church. It dates from the spring of 1832, and is the oldest Methodist paper in continual service in one place in the Southland.

This weekly periodical was first named the *Virginia Conference Sentinel,* but within a few years the name was changed to the *Richmond Christian Advocate.* Immediately following Methodist UNIFICATION in 1939, this paper was merged with the *Baltimore Southern Methodist,* then published in Salem, Va., and became the *Virginia Methodist Advocate,* the name it still has.

The first ten editors of the Virginia Methodist Advocate (and its predecessor publications) were: Ethelbert Drake, 1832-36; LEROY M. LEE, 1836-58; LEONIDAS ROSSER, 1858-60; JAMES A. DUNCAN, 1860-66; W. W. BENNETT, 1866-77; JOHN J. LAFFERTY, 1877-1904; JAMES CANNON, JR., 1904-18; Graham H. Lambeth, 1918-21; JOSEPH M. ROWLAND, 1921-38; George S. Reamey, 1939-.

Drake first began the publication because he recognized the need for it, and financed it at his own expense as a service to the church. Four years later he turned it over to the Virginia Conference, and sought "more peaceful work," and a more inviting opportunity to provide financially for his family. Later on this paper passed again into private hands for a while, but for many years now it has been owned and published by the Virginia Conference.

For about the first fifty years of publication, the *Sentinel* and the *Richmond Christian Advocate* served one rather unique function for a church periodical. They provided frequent treatments of national and international news, presumably because readers often did not have other sources of reliable information as to world happenings. Of course in those former days the news was usually several weeks old when published.

Principal emphases of this church paper, however, were not in the secular but in the religious realm. Local church news had not then gotten into the columns of the church press as is now the case, but there was a need definitely felt for religious instruction over and beyond what went on at church. When it is borne in mind that "Uniform Lessons" in the SUNDAY SCHOOL did not come into being until 1872, and Graded Lessons much later (1908), it will be recognized that religious teaching at best was unsystematized and fragmentary. So the church paper gave prominence to some of the great doctrines of the church; to treatments of various kinds of important Scripture passages, and there were scattered paragraphs each dealing with some aspect of religious truth.

As denominationalism was strong in those days, and for some time thereafter, debates were occasionally carried on in the *Advocate* between Methodists and spokesmen of other denominations. In 1847, for example, there was quite a little controversy with the Presbyterians, though this time it was not predestination. It seems that a Calvinist magazine had claimed, of all things, that JOHN WESLEY was no Republican! The Methodist editor was appropriately indignant, of course, but apparently unable to answer this specific charge. He retorted by saying, "Suppose John Wesley was not a Republican. He was still a faithful minister of Christ." Seemingly, that ended this particular argument!

These early Methodist papers were not without occasional touches of both sarcasm and humor. In an *Advocate* article (Sept. 21, 1876), written by a bachelor minister who obviously did not like the way some pastoral appointments were made, it was stated that "in these progressive days" the minister with a large family to support is adapted to do the most good in the highest-paying churches, while "bachelors are peculiarly fitted to small and poor appointments." The article added that in earlier years, a minister's training, character and general competence were influential factors in the appointment system, but now this was quite properly out-moded. Only the size of one's family merited any consideration! While the writer was obviously disturbed about the situation, he wrote in a light and humorous vein.

With the advent of the twentieth century, the Advocate began to devote increasing attention to various social issues and related matters of serious import. As early as 1926 this paper dealt with the question of race, pleading for fair-play for all persons of whatever color. Even before that, under the editorship of James Cannon, Jr., later bishop, much was said on *Advocate* pages about the Temperance movement, with special reference to the Prohibition law the "drys" had been successful in getting the State Legislature to enact. (This law was later rescinded.) Bishop Cannon at one time was an extremely influential factor in Virginia state politics, as well as influential in his Church, and he was responsible, more than any other person, for the passage of Prohibition legislation.

J. M. Rowland, as editor, wielded a mighty pen against the liquor traffic. Also in his day there was quite a discussion of the proposed unification of the three largest branches of Methodism, the merger which was consummated in 1939.

Rowland and the *Advocate* took a strong stand for Unification, and successfully withstood charges brought by Collins Denny, Jr., a Richmond attorney and son of Bishop COLLINS DENNY, that the *Advocate* had presented only the pro-union side of the controversy. Denny, as spokesman for the "Laymen's Organization for the Preservation of the Southern Methodist Church," had tried without success to get the *Advocate* to carry certain material opposed to Unification. He finally took his case against the *Advocate* to the Richmond District Conference, but was voted down fifty to eight. Although Bishop Denny unquestionably had some basis for his grievance, nothing came of it. Sentiment for Unification was too strong for him to carry his point.

George S. Reamey assumed the editorship shortly after the tragic death of Dr. Rowland (August 1938) in an automobile accident. He continued the policy of supporting Unification and during the Uniting Conference itself, the editor wired daily stories from KANSAS CITY to a Richmond newspaper covering discussions and debates.

In the years since then, the *Advocate* has continued to carry timely editorials and articles interpreting to its readers important news of the denomination, and giving a religious interpretation of world news. Many controversial articles have, from time to time, found their way to its pages. Under present editorship the *Advocate* has consistently followed the policy of carrying both sides of controversial matters, the better to enable its readers to formulate their own opinions.

Files of the *Richmond Christian Advocate* and *Virginia Methodist Advocate*.
W. W. Sweet, *Virginia*. 1955.   CEORGE S. REAMEY

VIRGINIA WESLEYAN COLLEGE, Norfolk, Virginia, was approved June 15, 1961, by vote of the VIRGINIA ANNUAL CONFERENCE to be a residential coeducational liberal arts college located on the boundary between Norfolk and Virginia Beach, Va. The conference also contributed $1,500,000 toward the purchase of land and the initial building program. A charter was granted July 27, 1961, by the Commonwealth of VIRGINIA; construction was begun in July, 1965; and the college opened with 125 students on Sept. 12, 1966. The governing board has from twenty-two (minimum) to thirty-six (maximum) trustees, elected by the Virginia Annual Conference upon nomination of its Board of Education. The charter requires that at least seventy-five percent of the trustees be members of The United Methodist Church.

The campus includes three hundred acres and one "student village," a complex of buildings in contemporary architectural style, combining facilities for living and learning. Other villages will be added, each providing study, lounge, dining, and living quarters as well as classrooms and libraries.

JOHN O. GROSS

VOEGELEIN, FREDERICH WILLIAM (1849-1920), American Evangelical preacher and missionary, was born Dec. 24, 1849, in Knielingen, Germany. At the age of two he came with his parents to SYRACUSE, N. Y. In 1869 he joined the Kansas Conference of the EVANGELICAL ASSOCIATION, was ordained DEACON in 1872, ELDER in 1874 and served churches in MISSOURI and KANSAS. In 1873 he was married to Kate E. Henneck and became pastor at Leavenworth for the next three years.

From 1876 to 1884 Voegelein was under appointment by the Board of Missions as pastor at SAN FRANCISCO and SAN JOSE, Calif., and most of the time presiding elder of the CALIFORNIA District of the Pacific Conference. His energy, vision, and strength as a preacher and administrator enabled him to lead in the expansion of the District and prepare it to become a separate conference.

Next the Board sent him and his wife to TOKYO, Japan, where he served variously as pastor, presiding elder, Director of Training School, and prospector for a mission location in CHINA. For his wife's health they returned to California in 1906, but he continued to direct and work for the overseas missions.

In 1908 Voegelein rejoined California Conference and was appointed PRESIDING ELDER. Under his leadership the conference achieved self-support. He retired in 1919 after fifty fruitful years in the ministry. Death came at Los Angeles, Aug. 19, 1920, after he had arranged for his wife to give their estate to open a church home for the aged in the city of Burbank. From further contributions the Pacific Evangelical Home for Aged People was established, bringing to fruition the dream of the Voegeleins.

J. Russell Davis, *From Saddlebags to Satellites: A History of the E.U.B. Church in California, 1849-1962.* N.p.: California Conference, 1963.
Proceedings of the California Conference, EA, 1921.

FLOYD B. LA FAVRE

ERWIN VOGT

EDWIN E. VOIGT

VOGT, A. ERWIN (1907-   ), Australian preacher, entered the ministry in 1931 in South AUSTRALIA. He was given the direction of the Thanksgiving Memorial Crusade in his State, 1946-48, and was Federal Director of the Crusade for Christ throughout Australia, 1948-51.

He was appointed to the Central Mission, ADELAIDE, in 1949, where many social enterprises and the use of the Mission's own radio network for preaching and publicity have given him unique influence. He was President of the SOUTH AUSTRALIA CONFERENCE in 1957.

A. HAROLD WOOD

VOICE OF MISSIONS. A publication of the A.M.E. Church. (See AFRICAN METHODIST EPISCOPAL CHURCH, Publications.)

VOIGT, EDWIN EDGAR (1892-   ), American bishop and college president, was born Feb. 13, 1892, near Kankakee, Ill., son of Theodore G. and Dorothea (Kukuck) Voigt. He married Eleanor Hemsted Dodge, Aug. 27, 1921 (deceased 1965). Their children are Paul Stuart, Nancy (Mrs. John R. Mahoney).

During World War I, Bishop Voigt was Y.M.C.A. Secretary on Great Lakes Naval Training Station, 1917-18; then a second lieutenant and pilot in the Army Air Service, 1918-19.

He received the following educational degrees: a B.S. from NORTHWESTERN UNIVERSITY in 1917; A.M., 1922; B.D. from GARRETT BIBLICAL INSTITUTE in 1921; D.D. in 1942; Ph.D. from Yale University in 1924; LL.D. from SIMPSON COLLEGE in 1954; Litt.D. from DAKOTA WESLEYAN UNIVERSITY in 1960; L.H.D., ILLINOIS WESLEYAN UNIVERSITY, 1961, MCKENDREE COLLEGE, 1961. He was a Thayer Fellow, American School of Oriental Research in Jerusalem, 1922-23; and a Fellow of the National Council of Religion in Higher Education.

He was ordained a DEACON in 1920 and an ELDER in 1924, in the ROCK RIVER CONFERENCE. He was an instructor of Biblical Literature at Northwestern University, 1920-21; an assistant professor at Garrett Biblical Institute, 1924-28; an associate professor, Garrett Biblical Institute, 1928-32; associate pastor, First Church, Evanston, Ill., 1932-36; pastor of First Church and Director of the WESLEY FOUNDATION, Iowa City, Iowa, 1936-42; president of Simpson College, Indianola, Iowa, 1942-52. He was elected a bishop of The Methodist Church by the NORTH CENTRAL JURISDICTIONAL CONFERENCE at Milwaukee, Wis., in July 1952. He was assigned the Dakotas Area of The Methodist Church from 1952-60; and in 1960 the newly created Illinois Area.

He was a member of the North Central Jurisdictional Conference, 1948-52; of the General Conference, 1952; of the Society of Biblical Literature; as bishop he was chairman of the Inter-board Committee on Christian Vocations; and chairman of the Commission on Worship.

During the quadrennium, 1960-64, *The Methodist Hymnal* and *Book of Worship* were revised under the direction of the Commission on Worship. Bishop Voigt presided over all the sessions and matters connected with revision of *The Hymnal* and *Book of Worship*, and he presented to the General Conference of 1964 these two revised books for official adoption. This was done and Bishop Voigt and his fellow commissioners were thanked and applauded by the conference.

Bishop Voigt is the author of *Latin Verses of Judith*, 1925; and of *Hebrew for Beginners*, 1939. He was a contributor to the *Abingdon Bible Commentary, Church School Journal, Adult Student, Christian Home.*

He retired from the active episcopacy in 1964, and assumed the presidency of McKendree College in Lebanon, Ill., through June, 1968.

Who's Who in America, Vol. 34.
Who's Who in The Methodist Church. 1966.   N. B. H.

VOLLER, ELLWOOD A. (1916-   ), American FREE METHODIST educator, was born at Bay City, Mich. He attended SPRING ARBOR (Junior) COLLEGE, Western State, Kalamazoo, Mich. (B.S.); Michigan State, Lansing, Mich. (M.A. and Ph.D.). He received the honorary LL.D. from Eastern Nazarene College, Wollaston, Mass. He married Bethavery Smith in 1938.

Dr. Voller served in various educational capacities including the assistant dean of Students, Michigan State; president, ROBERTS WESLEYAN COLLEGE, 1957-68; president, Spring Arbor College, where he has been since 1968. His memberships include: Association of Higher Education; American College Public Relations Association; National Education Assocation; Michigan Counsellors Association; American Association of Higher Education; Council for the Advancement of Small Colleges (Executive Board 1967-69); Land O'Lakes Boy Scouts Council (Chairman Explorer Com.); and Central Board of Ministerial Training, Free Methodist Church. He resides in Spring Arbor, Mich.

BYRON S. LAMSON

VORDENBAUMEN, FREDERICK (1824-1899), American German Methodist leader, was born in Bergholzhausen, GERMANY, on July 17, 1824, but came in early life to America. He had been brought up as a member of the Lutheran Church, but in 1849 he was, according to Bishop H. M. DuBose, "soundly converted." At this time he lived in Galveston, Texas. Four years later he became a minister, joining the Texas Conference in 1854. He was one of the leaders in organizing the GERMAN MISSION CONFERENCE in the then southwest and became its father in the Gospel in many ways. "His singular piety and his loyalty to the standards of the Church helped to give character to the devotion and faithfulness of the German Methodists which has distinguished them through many years." He died in 1899, and the German Conference itself within a score of years was subsequently dissolved and its members went into the component TEXAS and LOUISIANA CONFERENCES of the M.E. Church, South.

H. M. DuBose, *History of Methodism*. 1916.   N. B. H.

VOZ MISSIONARIA (*Missionary Voice*), the official quarterly magazine of the Methodist Women's Societies in Brazil, was founded Sept. 18, 1929. Its founders were MERCÊDES SEABRA and EULA KENNEDY LONG, OTTILIA DE OLIVEIRA CHAVES and Nair G. Martins, Lydia W. da Silva and Glaucia W. Duarte, respectively presidents and corresponding secretaries of the three Regional Conferences of the Brazilian Methodist Church at that time. They were assisted by Leila Epps of the Woman's Board of Foreign Missions of the M.E. Church, South, who had been designated by it to help develop literature for the Brazilian Methodist women, and she was afterward named its first editor.

Meeting in São Paulo in September 1929, this group decided upon three steps to unify and promote women's work—to organize them into a "Confederation"; to adopt a pin with the motto, *Viver para Servir* (Live to Serve), suggested by Eula K. Long; and to publish a quarterly magazine with programs for their meetings and articles stressing the Christian home and evangelism.

Starting with 1,000 copies only, the magazine's growth has been phenomenal, outdistancing in circulation any Protestant magazine in South America, and with a sub-scription list that surpasses the membership of the Brazilian Methodist Church. This amazing growth is due to the efforts of conference and local agents—women like Zaida Guerra and Fafa Castagnino—who have generated tremendous enthusiasm and have alone secured hundreds of subscribers, placing the magazine in the hands of Roman Catholics, in doctors' and dentists' offices, and with women of other Protestant denominations. The *Voz* not only covers Brazil but goes to Portuguese-speaking people in Portugal, the Madeira Islands, and Angola.

OTTILIA CHAVES

VRINDABAN, India, is the traditional birthplace of the Hindu god Krishna, with whom is associated a doctrine of grace. The population in 1961 was 22,199. During British rule the name was anglicized as Brindaban, but with independence the official spelling was changed to the present form.

To Hindus of the Vaishnavite school, Vrindaban is a sacred city comparable to Banaras. Every year for many centuries pilgrims in great numbers have visited Vrindaban and other locations in the vicinity because Hindu mythology associates them with episodes in the life of Krishna. The town has scores of temples, some large, ornate, and expensive. Under temple auspices accommodation is provided for hundreds of Hindu widows who have dedicated themselves to the temple, and to a life of service in poverty and debasement. They cut their hair and sometimes shave their heads and wear a very simple garb. The temple authorities are supposed to take care of them, and each day give them a very small dole of food. In return many of these widows spend from six to ten hours a day chanting the name of Krishna or honorifics which are applied to Krishna in common parlance in Vaishnavite Hinduism.

Dr. Emma Scott, a Methodist Episcopal missionary, opened a dispensary in Vrindaban in 1897 and became the first foreigner to live in the city. She was so moved by the spectacle of these widows that she determined to buy land and build a hospital for women. After much searching, she found a suitable location and purchased it from a Moslem. Some Hindus protested and went to court to prevent the opening of any Christian mission in the town. Dr. Scott won the case in the local court, but successive appeals prevented the use of the land until the last appeal was decided in the Privy Council in London. With that final court victory, Dr. Scott proceeded to open a clinic, and she slowly acquired the grateful backing of the local population. Other doctors and nurses representing the Woman's Foreign Missionary Society (ME) served for varying periods. In 1950 the Division of World Missions of the Methodist Board of Missions joined to support and enlarge the venture.

It is now the Creighton-Freeman Christian Hospital and School of Nursing, with 125 beds. Student nurses number approximately forty. The present superintendent is Dr. Charles V. Perrill. His wife, Wilma, is the able assistant superintendent. The names of Dr. Mary Burchard, Eunice Porter, a registered nurse, and Elda Mae Barry are held in the highest repute in the town and surrounding territory, and the Christian Gospel has penetrated deeply into the mind and heart of residents of Vrindaban.

J. N. Hollister, *Southern Asia*. 1956.
J. E. Scott, *Southern Asia*. 1906.   J. WASKOM PICKETT

WACO, TEXAS, U.S.A. **Austin Avenue Church** for sixty-six years has held its place as the largest Methodist church in Central Texas. On Dec. 31, 1900, the Fifth Street Methodist charge in Waco authorized a Board of Trustees to receive and hold the property of a newly established congregation. Three lots on the corner of Austin and Twelfth Streets in Waco became the location of the new church. Very soon an imposing structure was completed at a cost of $25,000, with an auditorium which would seat 600 persons and Sunday school facilities for an enrollment of 300. For twenty-five years the church worshipped in this location, and as the congregation grew in membership it became the center of Methodism in Central Texas. In keeping with the Methodist tradition of four-year pastorates, six pastors served during the first twenty-four years.

In 1925 the membership had so outgrown the original building that a new location was acquired, still downtown in Waco, only one block from the original site. A new sanctuary seating 1,200 people and educational facilities to care for 1,000 persons were erected. This building costing over $300,000, miraculously escaped the devastation of a tornado in 1953, but the next year fire destroyed the interior of the edifice.

Immediately a building program was undertaken and in one year the church was completely rebuilt, more adequately furnished than before the tragedy. The $600,000 cost of restoration was immediately underwritten by the congregation and was paid in full within three years. Although Waco has shown a tremendous growth and now has twenty United Methodist churches in the city, the Austin Avenue Church, with a membership of 2,574, continues to lead in the ministry to which it was called seventy years ago.

Methodist Home is a home for children owned and operated by The United Methodist Church in Texas and New Mexico. In November 1890 Bishop Joseph S. Key and Horace Bishop, pastor of the historic First Church in Waco, challenged the Northwest Texas Conference (M.E. Church, South) to provide a decent home for orphan children. Today the resulting Methodist Home is owned and operated by five Annual Conferences of Texas, and the New Mexico Conference.

The city of Waco bid successfully for the new orphanage by making a gift of cash, and by donating the then Miller residence with its surrounding ten acres of farm land.

W. H. Vaugh, John H. McLean, W. F. ("Dad") Barnett, and Abe Mulkey, a traveling evangelist, and his wife, Louisa, were instrumental in the early development of the Home. Mulky would devote one night out of each revival meeting to tell about the Methodist Home and its work, and then would take an offering. The original Administration Building bore an inscription on the cornerstone, "Preached, prayed, and sung up by Reverend Abe and Louisa Mulkey." A burst of construction in the 1920's helped the Home bring its physical plant more closely in line with the needs of the children.

In 1938 the first cottage, the Lois Perkins Home, was started, and some of the older dormitories on the campus were remodeled to conform with the cottage plan for housing children. This marked the beginning of the transition from dormitories and institutionalized custodial care. Today there are twenty cottages on the campus, which covers an area of 114 acres. In addition to this, the Home carries on a farm and ranch program with these facilities being located in the Waco area.

In 1969 the Home was caring for about 400 children on its campus with an additional seventy-five pre-school children being cared for in its foster home program. It is a multiple-service agency and has programs for group care, foster home care, and adoption when children are eligible to be placed. The Home is an associate member of the Child Welfare League of America.

The Chapel on the campus is the Harrell Memorial Chapel, a gift of Dr. T. M. Harrell of Corpus Christi, Texas.

The present administrator of the Methodist Home is Kennard B. Copeland. Hubert Johnson, administrator for thirty-two years, is now the executive director of the Methodist Home Foundation.

The Waco home is the largest Children's Home associated with the Methodist Association of Hospitals and Homes. It is supported by free-will offerings taken in the Methodist churches of Texas and New Mexico. The Home has served over 8,700 boys and girls in its seventy-five years.

EDWARD R. BARCUS
JACK KYLE DANIELS

WADDY, RICHARD (1769-1853), British Wesleyan Methodist itinerant, was born at Bilton, Yorkshire, Nov. 24, 1769. He began to itinerate at Berwick in 1793. He was the father of SAMUEL DOUSLAND WADDY. He wrote *A Vindication of the Methodists in a Letter to the Rev. T. Y. Derby* (1804), and *The Christian Soldier's Manual* (Leeds, 1815). He died at Southampton, Oct. 4, 1853.

JOHN KENT

WADDY, SAMUEL DOUSLAND (1804-1876), British Wesleyan Methodist, was born at Burton on Trent, Aug. 5, 1804. The son of RICHARD WADDY, he entered the Wesleyan Methodist ministry in 1825. He was the chief founder of Wesley College, SHEFFIELD, one of the earliest Wesleyan schools, which opened in 1838; he was governor and chaplain from 1844 to 1862; for the controversy which surrounded his appointment see *Sidelights on the Conflicts of Methodism*, by BENJAMIN GREGORY (1898). Waddy was elected president of the Wesleyan Methodist Conference in 1859. He returned to circuit work in 1862, retiring to BRISTOL in 1870, where he died on Nov. 7, 1876.

JOHN KENT

WADE, ALEXANDER LUARK (1832-1904), American educator, was born Feb. 1, 1832, near Rushville, Ind., the son of George and Anna (Luark) Wade. The family moved to Monongalia County, W. Va., when Alexander was seven. Seven years later his father died and the boy worked on the farm to help support his mother. He was educated in a log school house. Joining the M.E. Church, he became a LOCAL PREACHER, and was ordained ELDER. He was a lay delegate to the 1884 GENERAL CONFERENCE.

During his career, Wade taught twelve years in rural schools; served for some years as clerk and recorder of Monongalia County; was principal of the Morgantown, W. Va. public schools, 1871-73; assistant county superintendent of schools, 1873-75; and county superintendent, 1875-79. While in the latter office he effected reforms in rural teaching and administration which made him favorably known in this country and abroad. He began lecturing and writing on the subject of education in 1871.

Prior to Wade's day, pupils in rural schools wasted much time because there was no planned program or objective for them. One writer claims that students in academies accomplished more in one year than the average rural school pupil did in fifteen. Wade insisted that there should be an objective for each pupil. He was appointed principal of the Negro school in Morgantown where he tested his plan and later he published the results.

John Rhey Thompson, president of the University of West Virginia, himself a Methodist minister, made addresses along with other preachers advocating Wade's proposed reform. The WEST VIRGINIA superintendent of education approved the plan, and the state of MASSACHUSETTS adopted it. The editor of the *National Journal of Education* declared that Wade's contribution to education was greater than that made by New England.

Wade became popular in many states as a lecturer. In 1881 he published his famous work, *A Graduating System for Country Schools.* He died May 2, 1904 in Richmond, Va.

Ambler, *West Virginia Stories and Biographies.* New York: Rand McNally, 1942.
W. S. John, "The Origin of the Graded School System" in the *West Virginia Review,* May, 1932.
Lambert, *Pioneer Leaders of Western Virginia.* Parkersburg, West Virginia: Scholl Printing Company, 1935.

JESSE A. EARL
ALBEA GODBOLD

WADE, CYRUS ULYSSES (1849-1937), American minister, was born March 16, 1849, at LaGrange, Ind. He trained as a lawyer and was a successful attorney when he felt called to the ministry. He married Mary Will on March 27, 1873. Among their children was RAYMOND J. WADE, who later was elected bishop. Mrs. Wade died in 1891, and he married Elizabeth Welborn in 1893. He joined the NORTH INDIANA CONFERENCE in 1881 and had an outstanding record as pastor, presiding elder and secretary of the Preacher's Aid Society. He was elected to three GENERAL CONFERENCES in 1900, 1904 and 1908. He died Feb. 6, 1937.

C. F. Price, *Who's Who in American Methodism.* 1916.

HAROLD THRASHER

WADE, RAYMOND J. (no middle name) (1875-1970), American bishop, was born in LaGrange, Ind., on May

RAYMOND J. WADE

29, 1875, the son of CYRUS U. and Mary Will Wade. He received his education at DEPAUW UNIVERSITY and was later given an honorary degree by DePauw. He also held honorary degrees from Taylor University and ALBION COLLEGE. On Dec. 4, 1904 he was united in marriage to Ella L. Yarian (deceased 1909) of Nappanee, Ind. They had one son, Paul Raymond, and two daughters, Elizabeth E. and Mary Elouise. On Aug. 6, 1913, he married Myrtle L. Mudge (deceased March 3, 1969) of Elkhart, Ind.

Raymond J. Wade joined the NORTH INDIANA CONFERENCE in 1894. His pastorates included FORT WAYNE, INDIANAPOLIS, Arcadia, Nappanee, Kendallville, First Church at Richmond, and Trinity at Elkhart—all in INDIANA. He was district superintendent of the Goshen District, North Indiana Conference, 1915-20; corresponding secretary of the Commission on Conservation and Advance, 1920-24; executive secretary of WORLD SERVICE COMMISSION, 1924-28. He was secretary of the M.E. GENERAL CONFERENCE, 1920-28. While serving in Europe from 1928-39, he was president of the University of Scandinavia's School of Theology at Gothenburg, SWEDEN.

Raymond Wade was elected bishop by the General Conference of the M.E. Church in 1928 and assigned to the STOCKHOLM Area in Northern Europe. He did an outstanding work there. The Norwegians, Swedes and Danes paid him a spontaneous tribute of affection and regard when at the Oslo Conference of World Methodism he stood to be recognized. The ovation he received was unforgettable.

He also supervised the work of the Methodist Church in the Madeira Islands (PORTUGAL), SPAIN, FRANCE, ALGERIA, TUNISIA, DENMARK, NORWAY, SWEDEN, FINLAND, ESTONIA, LATVIA, LITHUANIA, RUSSIA, and Siberia. He was assigned to the Detroit Area in 1940-48, retiring from the active episcopacy in the latter year.

Bishop Wade was president emeritus of the Board of HOSPITALS AND HOMES of The Methodist Church and for twenty-five years was president of the Bay View Association at Bay View, Mich. Because of his extensive travels in Europe by means of the airplane—then something of an innovation in episcopal travel—he was known as "The Flying Bishop." His official address during the last months of his life was the Methodist Home for the Aged, Sunny Shores Villas, in ST. PETERSBURG, FLA. He died in that city Jan. 24, 1970. Services were held in Christ Church there and the interment was in Petoskey, Mich.

F. D. Leete, *Methodist Bishops*. 1948.
Who's Who in the Methodist Church, 1966.   N. B. H.

WADE, THOMAS SMITH (1838-1911), is generally acknowledged to have been the outstanding figure in Southern Methodism in WEST VIRGINIA during the last half of the nineteenth century. Born Aug. 5, 1838, in Highland County, Va., he and his family moved to what is now West Virginia where he grew up on a farm in Wood County near PARKERSBURG. His education was received in the poorly equipped schools of that day but being of a superior intellect he became a great student and an educated man.

At the age of twenty he was admitted on trial into the WESTERN VIRGINIA CONFERENCE, M.E. CHURCH, SOUTH. His ministry spanned fifty years, of which twenty were spent as a presiding elder. He was for four years a CHAPLAIN in the Confederate Army, the Nineteenth Virginia Cavalry. He was a delegate to six GENERAL CONFERENCES and for twelve years was a member of the BOOK COMMITTEE. He was also a delegate to two ECUMENICAL METHODIST CONFERENCES and to the first great Conference on Church Federation. He was for twelve years editor of the *Methodist Advocate* of his Conference in connection with other duties as pastor or presiding elder.

He wrote the history of the Western Virginia Conference, a work which was never published in book form, although running serially in the Methodist *Layman's Herald*. In 1888, while presiding elder of the Charleston District, with residence at Barboursville, he established a college in buildings left vacant by the moving of the Cabell County Courthouse to Huntington, and served as its first president. First called Barboursville Seminary, it later became MORRIS HARVEY COLLEGE.

He was married in 1871 to Ella Hursey and to this union were born two children, Harry Marvin Wade and Fanny Isabel (Wallace). He died on July 7, 1911 and is buried in Clarksburg, W. Va.

Journal of the Western Virginia Conference, MES, 1911.
                                        J. B. F. YOAK, JR.

WAGNER, ELLASUE CANTER (1881-1957), versatile American missionary to KOREA, was born in Huntersville, W. Va., on Aug. 8, 1881. She graduated from Marion Junior College and Martha Washington College (later going into EMORY AND HENRY COLLEGE), and subsequently received the M.A. degree from SCARRITT COLLEGE.

She went to Korea in 1904 from the HOLSTON CONFERENCE Area, and began work in Songdo where a wide variety of educational, social, and evangelistic activities occupied most of her life in Korea. She established Holston Institute, a school for Korean girls, in 1904, and acted as principal for many years. She also served for several years as superintendent of the Songdo social community center.

From 1926 to 1934 she was assigned to Seoul where she was superintendent of the Social Evangelistic Center, in which Northern Methodists and Northern Presbyterian missionaries cooperated with the Southern Methodists. During this time she was editor of *The Korea Mission Field*, a monthly interdenominational missionary magazine. She was chairman of the committee celebrating the fiftieth anniversary of Methodism in Korea in 1934, and wrote a pageant *At the Hermit's Gate*, depicting events leading to the opening of the work. She was a member of the commission on union which organized the Korean Methodist Church and a member of the organizing General Conference. She was one of fourteen missionary women ordained by Bishop JU SAM RYANG in 1931. It was said of her that she "loved the Old Korea and watched the rise of the New Korea with pride."

Miss Wagner was author of *Korea: The Old and The New; Korea Calls;* and *The Dawn of Tomorrow*. In 1921-23 she served in the Literature Department of the BOARD OF MISSIONS (MES) in NASHVILLE. She died on Nov. 22, 1957 at Bristol, Tenn. and was buried in the Holston Conference Cemetery in Emory, Va. She did not close her work in Korea until forced to leave by the forced missionary withdrawal in 1940 with the Second World War impending.

                                        CHARLES A. SAUER

WAHL, PRISCILLA MARIE. (See STAMM, PRISCILLA MARIE WAHL.)

WAIKOUAITI (now named Karitane), Otago, New Zealand, was the site of the first Methodist mission station in the South Island, a few miles from Dunedin. It was established by JAMES WATKIN on May 16, 1840. Earlier, Watkin had served in Tonga and had removed to Australia for health reasons. Requests from Maori leaders, backed up by John Jones, whose whaling station was at Waikouaiti led to Watkin's appointment there.

Watkin was succeeded in June, 1844, by CHARLES CREED, during whose term the first Christian European service was conducted by him in Dunedin. Creed was on hand to meet the first Scottish settlers when they arrived at Port Chalmers on March 23, 1848.

D. J. D. Hickman, *Before 1848 and After*. Wesley Historical Society, New Zealand, 1948.   L. R. M. GILMORE

WAIMA, Hokianga, NEW ZEALAND, was the site of an important mission station twenty miles from MANGUNGU, founded in 1839. The first resident missionary was JOHN WARREN. The site is marked by New Zealand's largest oak tree, which has a spread of branches 130 feet in diameter. This historic tree was grown from an acorn brought from England by Mrs. Warren, and had first been planted in a pot at Mangungu.

"The Waima Mission House," writes WILLIAM MORLEY, "was the longest occupied of any in the Hokianga, and continued to be the residence of a European missionary until 1894." (p. 77) For some thirty years after that it was the residence of the Maori minister of the district, until the erection of a new home at Upper Waima.

Waima village, some miles away, remains the center of Maori mission work in the Hokianga District to this day, having its own resident Maori minister.

W. Morley, *New Zealand*. 1900.   L. R. M. GILMORE

WAINGAROA, early Wesleyan Mission Station, near Raglan, New Zealand, was founded by JAMES WALLIS at the end of 1834. When boundary disputes with the Church Missionary Society arose in 1836, Wallis was temporarily withdrawn and appointed to Tangiteroria. Later he was reappointed to Waingaroa and labored there until 1862.

His work in the area is commemorated by a memorial seat which was erected on the foreshore of Raglan township by his descendants. Recently, in 1959, a brick cairn and bronze memorial tablet was erected and dedicated on the site of the work reestablished by Wallis after his temporary withdrawal.

C. H. Laws, *First Years at Hokianga*. Wesley Historical Society, New Zealand, 1945.
W. Morley, *New Zealand*. 1900.   L. R. M GILMORE

SAMUEL H. WAINRIGHT

WAINRIGHT, SAMUEL H. (1863-1950), missionary educator and executive of Japan Christian Literature Society, was born in the state of Missouri. Not long after graduating from Missouri Medical College, he felt God's call to join the newly established Southern Methodist Mission in JAPAN. On May 21, 1888, he and Mrs. Wainright arrived in KOBE. That very night he was called on to teach a class at Palmore Institute.

The Wainrights spent their first two years at Oita on the island of Kyushu, where he taught English in the government middle school while diligently studying the Japanese language. Here he was instrumental in leading a group of young men to Christ. At a time of great crisis, the Mission superintendent, W. R. LAMBUTH (later bishop), accompanied by two Japanese Christians from Kobe, visited Oita. There on the afternoon of Dec. 31, 1889 and in the WATCH NIGHT Service following, there was such an outpouring of the HOLY SPIRIT that it can truly be described as a real Pentecost. From the little "Oita Band" came a number of men who gave their lives to Christian service. One of them, T. KUGIMIYA, many years later became bishop of the JAPAN METHODIST CHURCH.

From 1890 to 1906 the Wainrights were working at Kwansei Gakuin (now a university) in Kobe, where Wainright was principal of the Academic Department. From 1906 to 1912 he was in the United States serving as pastor and district superintendent in ST. LOUIS, Mo.

In 1910 the Japan Christian Literature Society was organized with most of the missions cooperating. It was decided to invite Dr. Wainright to return to Japan to become executive secretary of the Society. His ability in the Japanese language, his scholarship and interest in Christian literature, and his executive ability all together made him the ideal man for the position. He returned to Japan in 1912 to devote the rest of his active life to this challenging task.

In the great earthquake of 1923 the building of the society in TOKYO and also that of the Methodist Publishing House were destroyed. This proved a blessing in disguise for it led to the union of these two institutions, the sale of the Society's land, and eventually to the erection of a great new building on the site of the former Methodist Publishing House on the Ginza in downtown Tokyo. This building, which escaped the bombs of the Second World War, stands today as a memorial to Wainright's great work for Christian literature.

Dr. and Mrs. Wainright retired in 1940, fifty-two years after their arrival in Japan. Wainright died in Oakland, Calif., on Dec. 7, 1950. In the summer of 1963, the Kye Bun Kan (Christian Literature Society) held a great memorial service, 100 years after Wainright's birth. His daughter, Mrs. Elizabeth Wainright Grant, was invited back to Japan especially for this impressive ceremony.

JOHN B. COBB, SR.

WAKELEY, JOSEPH BEAUMONT (1804-1876), American pastor, ecclesiastical antiquarian and historian, was born in Danbury, Conn. He joined the M.E. Church when he was about sixteen years old and then in 1833 went into the NEW YORK CONFERENCE on trial. In 1844 he transferred to the NEW JERSEY CONFERENCE, and in 1852 to the NEW YORK EAST, and then back to the New York Conference again. He served seven years as a presiding elder. His cast of mind was said to be practical rather than logical. Interested in church history, he studied the early annals of the Church and wrote several books, some copies yet referred to even today. Among them were: *Lost Chapters in the History of American Methodism; Heroes of Methodism; The Prince of Pulpit Orators—a portraiture of the Rev. George Whitefield, M.A.; The Patriarch of One Hundred Years, or Reminiscences of the Rev. Henry Boehm; The Bold Frontier Preacher—a portraiture of the Rev. William Craven; Anecdotes of the Wesleys; The Temperance Cyclopedia;* and *The Wesleyan Demosthenes: Joseph Beaumont.* His love of the classics and of the Church's past caused him to revolt against any innovations, and one of his last messages was, "Preach the old gospel. We want no new one. The old gospel is to save the world; it cannot be improved. One might as well attempt to improve a ray of sunshine while revivifying a flower. The grand old gospel forever!" He died in New York, April 27, 1876.

Encyclopedia Americana. New York: American Book-Stratford Press, Inc., 1950.   N. B. H.

WALDEN, JOHN MORGAN (1831-1914), American bishop, was born at Lebanon, Ohio, Feb. 11, 1831, the son of Jesse and Matilda (Morgan) Walden. Two years later his mother died, and he lived with relatives near Cincinnati, attending a local school. In 1844 he was on his own and became a wanderer. He worked briefly at carpentering, clerking, and other jobs. Somehow he managed to graduate from Farmers' College, College Hill, Ohio, in 1852 and taught there the next two years. While in college he wrote romantic stories for a newspaper under an assumed name. He pursued newspaper work in ILLINOIS and OHIO for two years. Becoming deeply interested in the KANSAS troubles, he went there in 1856 and published a paper and served as a delegate in several state conventions. He married Martha Young of Knox County, Ohio, July 3, 1859, and they had two sons and three daughters.

In 1858, Walden was admitted on trial in the CINCINNATI CONFERENCE and was ordained DEACON in 1860 and ELDER in 1862. His first appointments were: 1858, North Bend assistant; and 1859, Lynchburgh assistant. His remaining assignments were in Cincinnati: 1860, York Street; 1861, York Street and Ludlow; 1862-63, Ladies Home Mission; 1864-66, Corresponding Secretary, Western FREEDMEN'S AID SOCIETY; 1867, East Cincinnati District; 1868-71, Assistant Agent, Western BOOK CONCERN; and 1872-83, Agent. An able businessman, he made the Book Concern a financial success.

Walden was active during the Civil War, raising two regiments to defend Cincinnati against threatening attack. He was one of the founders of the Republican Party, and was the chief founder and for many years the president of the Freedmen's Aid Society which began in Cincinnati in 1866. He was a delegate to five GENERAL CONFERENCES, 1868-84, and to the first three ECUMENICAL CONFERENCES, 1881-1901.

Elected bishop in 1884, during his career Walden presided at least once over every annual conference and mission of his church in the United States and inspected Methodist missionary work in Europe, MEXICO, South America, CHINA, and JAPAN. A close student with a retentive mind, he had an enormous fund of exact knowledge concerning church law and the details of the work committed to his hands. Bishop EDWIN H. HUGHES said he was the best informed bishop in the church while others referred to him as a walking encyclopedia. Though he stood with the North in the Civil War, he was one of the earliest leaders in his denomination to speak out and work for the unification of American Methodism. He died at Daytona Beach, Fla., Jan. 21, 1914, and was buried in Cincinnati.

General Conference Journal, 1916.
E. S. Bucke, *History of American Methodism*. 1964.
F. D. Leete, *Methodist Bishops*. 1948.
National Cyclopedia of American Biography, Vol. 19.
JESSE A. EARL
ALBEA GODBOLD

WALDORF, ERNEST LYNN (1876-1943), American bishop, was born in South Valley, Otsego, N. Y., May 14, 1876. He was educated at SYRACUSE UNIVERSITY, A.B. and D.D.; KANSAS WESLEYAN and ALBION COLLEGES gave him the LL.D. He married Flora Janette Irish in 1902, and they had four sons and one daughter. He was ordained in the ministry of the M.E. Church in 1902, and held the following pastorates: Shortsville, N. Y.; Union Springs; Phelps; Clyde; Centenary Church, SYRACUSE 1907-11; Plymouth Church, BUFFALO, 1911-15; First Church, CLEVELAND, Ohio, 1915 until elected bishop in 1920.

ERNEST L. WALDORF

Meanwhile he served as president of the WORLD SERVICE Commission and was chairman of the committee to direct the Million Unit Fellowship Movement. He became trustee of NORTHWESTERN UNIVERSITY at EVANSTON, ILL.; president, WESLEY FOUNDATION Corporation at the University of Illinois in Urbana; vice-president, Board of HOSPITALS, HOMES and Deaconess Work; bishop of WICHITA Area, 1920-24; KANSAS CITY Area, 1924-32; CHICAGO Area, 1932, and died in 1943 and was buried at Morningside Cemetery, Syracuse, in the plot next to that of his good friend, Bishop WALLACE E. BROWN.

Bishop Waldorf was a large man of genial disposition. He had an amazing genius for accomplishing things with Christian diplomacy. One could never be certain whether the Bishop arranged events or whether events themselves just happened to fall in the order the Bishop felt best for the Kingdom. No wonder his sons became noted athletic coaches!

A real part of the Bishop's success came from the fact that Mrs. Waldorf also had unbounded energy and devotion. She drove the family car thousands of miles to get her husband to his various meetings. She died at the age of eighty-seven sitting at the telephone. Waldorf is a noted name around Chicago and through all Methodism which the Waldorfs so jubilantly served.

CHARLES W. BRASHARES

WALES. Welsh-speaking Methodism dates its official existence from August, 1800, when the Methodist Conference, largely through the influence of THOMAS COKE, authorized two of its ministers, OWEN DAVIES and JOHN HUGHES to take up missionary work in Wales. But there were already in existence English-speaking circuits in the border areas of Flintshire and Denbighshire and in South Wales. A few Welsh-speaking LOCAL PREACHERS had already preached in Welsh before 1800. With their help the two conference missionaries pioneered a movement which was to spread Wesleyan Methodism through the length and breadth of the principality.

The first period of Welsh Wesleyan Methodist history, 1800-1816, is a record of amazing and continuous progress. The earlier CALVINISTIC METHODISM had lost much of its original evangelical zeal. Many were dissatisfied with the prevailing Calvinism of the period. So the new Arminian Evangelical movement which offered salvation for all was welcomed in every part of Wales.

Davies and Hughes began their mission in Wrexham, Ruthin, and Denleigh, forming in October, 1800, their first circuit—Ruthin. By 1803 there were 3 more, Caernarvon, Wrexham, and Welshpool, with 6 ministers, 57 societies, and a membership of 1,344. This progress was recognized by Conference in 1803, when the North Wales District was formed, with Owen Davies as the first chairman. In 1805 work began in South Wales with the appointment of three Welsh-speaking ministers to "English" circuits in South Wales with authority to open up new places among Welsh-speaking people. There were many of these in the older "English" societies, who warmly welcomed the new Welsh preachers. By 1810 there were five Welsh-speaking circuits in South Wales, Neath, Carmarthen, Merthyr Tydfil, Brecon, and Cardigan.

In 1810 there were in Wales 20 circuits, 49 ministers, and 5,649 members, representing continuous progress despite constant opposition from other Christian bodies who resented the Wesleyan "intruders" because of their Arminian theology. The early preachers were constantly engaged in theological controversy. To make known their distinctive beliefs they established their own book room in 1809 and began to publish their periodical, *Yr Eurgrawn*.

The years following 1816 were very difficult owing to decreased membership, administrative changes, and financial hardship largely caused by economies forced upon the connection in the post-Napoleonic period. Circuit amalgamations, especially in South Wales, hindered and sometimes crippled the progress of the Welsh-speaking societies. This period, preceded by the death of Thomas Coke, the great friend and advocate of the mission to his native Wales marked the loss to Wales of several of the early leaders, notably Owen Davies, the first chairman. By the end of the second decade the number of ministers had fallen to 29 and the membership had not progressed beyond 5,338. Recovery came slowly, and one encouraging new aspect was the founding of Sunday schools, which numbered 178 by 1824, and which were attended by adult scholars as well as children. This slow but uninterrupted progress was recognized by the 1828 Conference, which divided the territory into two—the North Wales District and the Second South Wales District. This provision was to last until 1903, when North Wales was further divided into the two present districts.

The decade 1830-40 brought further increases of membership and the erection of many new chapels. There were 25 circuits, 49 ministers, and 11,926 members in the Welsh districts in 1840. In 1831 a serious constitutional dispute began in Anglesey and Caernarvonshire which led to the secession of a group which became known as the Wesleyan Methodists Minor (*Y Wesle Bach*). This dispute originated in the dissatisfaction of certain local preachers with authority entrusted to the ministers by Conference. They argued for greater elasticity in the planning of preaching appointments and a larger share for the laity in the governing of the Church. The Wesleyans Minor became a part of INDEPENDENT METHODISM in 1832, but in 1838 transferred their allegiance to the WESLEYAN METHODIST ASSOCIATION. But neither of these were able to provide sufficient help for the Welsh seceders in their extremely difficult task of keeping together their scattered societies.

In 1838 many of the Wesleyan Methodists Minor returned to their original fold, and several of the chapels were received back into the North Wales District. When the Wesleyan Methodist Association became part of the UNITED METHODIST FREE CHURCHES in 1857, there were only six Welsh societies to share in that union. These eventually either returned to the Wesleyan Methodists or joined other denominations. It cannot be said that the Wesleyans Minor made any new *theological* contribution, for they adhered to Wesleyan doctrines. But many of their constitutional principles were eventually accepted by the Wesleyan Methodist connection.

At the time of the WESLEYAN REFORM agitations of the middle period of the nineteenth century, a number of Reform societies were established in Wales. These made very little progress after 1853, for the cause of Conference was championed by able leaders, notably THOMAS AUBREY and Rowland Hughes. Spared from dispute and schism, the Welsh districts had to face difficulties caused by crippling debts—the result of a too-adventurous policy of chapel building in former years. But in 1850 the Jubilee of the connection in Wales was celebrated with a new determination to tackle financial problems. Thomas Aubrey (1808-67), who became the chairman of the North Wales District in 1854, realized that it wasn't enough to clear existing debts. To place his district's economy on sure foundations the District Home Mission Fund (1855) and the District Chapel Fund (1856) were established. Similar steps were taken in South Wales. Aubrey also pioneered mission schemes to expand as well as consolidate the work.

This strenuous period of reconstruction was followed by the great religious revival of 1859, which began with the evangelical labor in Cardiganshire of Humphrey Jones of Tre'rddol, a Wesleyan LOCAL PREACHER. Connectional statistics indicate the substantial gains of those momentous years. Before the revival the Wesleyan Methodists comprised 11,702 members, 54 ministers, and 30 circuits (1857), but four years later, 16,766 members, 68 ministers, and 37 circuits (1861).

The latter part of the nineteenth century was marked by growing confidence and advance. It was an age of great preachers: men like the well-beloved JOHN EVANS (1840-97), Eglwys-bach. Theology, literature, and poetry, especially hymn writing flourished. The new Welsh book room was opened at Bangor in 1887, and connectional publications enjoyed a constant increase in circulation. The resurgent national concern for better education found a ready response; and in 1897, through the advocacy of Thomas Hughes (1854-1928), the Welsh Training of Candidates Fund came into being, to enable young Welsh candidates for the ministry to enter the colleges of the University of Wales.

The aspirations of Welsh Methodism found new expression in the Welsh Assembly, which met for the first time at Machynlleth in 1899 under the presidency of Edward Humphreys (1846-1913). The Synods continued to have the same relationship to Conference; but the Assembly was allowed to deliberate policy for the Welsh Districts.

During the present century many adverse factors have militated against the work of the Christian Churches in Wales. Despite many setbacks Welsh Methodism has striven to fulfill its historic mission. Interest in the study of the history and literature of early Methodism in Wales has been renewed by the Historical Society of the Methodist Church in Wales (founded, 1945). In 1957 the Standing Committee for Methodism in Wales was set up by Conference to review problems and opportunities and to link together all Districts, both English and Welsh-speaking, in a new strategy for the work of the principality.

Welsh Methodism has enriched the life of Wales in many ways, notably in the nineteenth century, through its broader theology, its closely knit organization, and courageous policy of chapel building. It has also enriched the Church in other lands. Ever since 1814 when the first missionary, William Davies (1785-1851), went out to Sierra Leone, Welsh Methodism has in each generation provided men for the work overseas. Many Welshmen have also served in England, and a number of them have been elected to the chair of Conference. Three of these, at least, were Welsh-speaking: RICHARD ROBERTS, HENRY MALDWYN HUGHES and HAROLD ROBERTS. (See also SWANSEA.)

A. H. Williams, *Welsh Wesleyan Methodism.* 1935.
D. Young, *Wales and the Borders.* 1893.   M. PENNANT LEWIS

ALAN WALKER

WALKER, ALAN (1911-   ), Australian preacher and evangelist, was born in SYDNEY, AUSTRALIA, June 1911, the son of the late Rev. A. E. Walker, a former president of the NEW SOUTH WALES CONFERENCE. He was educated at the Fort Street Boys' High School and graduated at the University of Sydney in 1936 and awarded his Mastership in 1943. He entered Leigh Theological College in 1929 and was ordained in 1934.

In 1936-38 he was the associate director of the Young People's Department of the New South Wales Conference. In 1939-44 he was stationed in the coal mining district of Cessnock and for the ten following years was superintendent of the WAVERLEY Methodist Mission where he established a community center and hostel.

In 1945 he was a delegate to the First Assembly of the WORLD COUNCIL OF CHURCHES at Amsterdam and the following year was appointed as an advisor to the Australian delegation at the United Nations. In 1953-56 he was director of the Mission to the Nation for the Methodist Church in Australasia and in 1956-58 conducted missions in America and Canada.

He was awarded the Order of the British Empire for his leadership of the Mission to the Nation and in 1956 was awarded the honorary D.D. degree by Bethany Biblical Seminary of CHICAGO, U.S.A.

In 1958 he succeeded F. H. Rayward as superintendent of the Central Methodist Mission, Sydney.

His nation-wide television program, "I Challenge the Minister," which ran for seven years, had an estimated viewing audience of half a million.

His publications include *Coaltown,* a sociological survey of Cessnock, New South Wales; *Heritage Without End,* a history of the Methodist Church in Australia; *The Whole Gospel for the Whole World* and *A Ringing Call to Mission* (1966); *The Many-Sided Cross of Jesus* (1962); *The Life-Line Story* (1967).

Dr. Walker has conducted missions in various parts of the world and in varying capacities has attended all assemblies of the World Council of Churches since the first in 1948. In 1963 he founded the Life-Line Center in Sydney and since then has worked to build Life-Line International of which organization he is world president. The New South Wales Conference elected him secretary in 1969-70 and president-elect for 1970-71.

AUSTRALIAN EDITORIAL COMMITTEE

WALKER, DOUGAL ORMONDE BEACONSFIELD (1890-1955), American bishop of the A.M.E. CHURCH, was born in Layou, St. Vincent, British West Indies, on Jan. 5, 1890. He received the A.B. degree from BOSTON UNIVERSITY, S.T.B. from Harvard University, and the M.A. from Western Reserve University. Later he received the honorary degrees of D.D. and LL.D. He was admitted into the ANNUAL CONFERENCE in 1913, ordained a DEACON in 1913 and an ELDER in 1915. He held pastorates in MASSACHUSETTS, NORTH CAROLINA, PENNSYLVANIA, OHIO and NEW YORK. He was president of WILBERFORCE UNIVERSITY, 1936-41, and was elected bishop in 1948 from the pastorate of Bethel Church in BUFFALO, N. Y. He was assigned to the Fifth Episcopal District. Bishop Walker was one of the first Negro Democrats and political leaders in the state of Ohio. Bishop WRIGHT says that he "was regarded as one of the best thinkers of the Church. He was outspoken, could not be diplomatic but gained his objectives by aggressive action." He was such an opponent of Governor John W. Bricker of Ohio that the governor threatened to hold up the state's appropriation to Wilberforce University and refused to accept an honorary degree on the same platform with Bishop Walker. Named for him are Walker Temple, LOS ANGELES and ST. LOUIS; Walker Church at LONG BEACH, CALIF. and St. Vincent's Island.

R. R. Wright, *The Bishops.* 1963.   GRANT S. SHOCKLEY

WALKER, GEORGE WILLIAMS (1848-1911), American educator and minister, was born Feb. 11, 1848. His father was Rev. Hugh A. C. Walker, and his mother a sister of Bishop WILLIAM M. WIGHTMAN. The son graduated from WOFFORD COLLEGE in 1869, and then taught school for four years. He joined the SOUTH CAROLINA CONFER-

ENCE in December 1873. He served as a pastor for eleven years (one year of which was at Lexington, Mo.), and in 1884 went to PAINE COLLEGE, Augusta, Ga., as a teacher when the school was two years old. In 1885 he succeeded Morgan Callaway as president at a critical time in the school's history. His conference memoir declared that he "did a monumental work at Paine." He died May 28, 1911.

General Minutes, MES, 1911.　　　GEORGE E. CLARY, JR.
WALTER N. VERNON

WALKER, JESSE (1766-1835), American pioneer preacher, was born June 9, 1766 in Buckingham County, Va., the son of Elmore and Mary LeSelle Walker. He was converted and joined the Methodist Church in 1786. About two years later he married Susanna Webley, daughter of a prominent family. About 1789 Walker and his family migrated to North Carolina and in 1796 moved to Tennessee, locating near Nashville.

Soon after his conversion he became a local preacher and in 1802, moved by the sudden death of two children, he united with the WESTERN CONFERENCE. He served three circuits: Red River, Livingston, and Hartford in KENTUCKY and TENNESSEE.

In 1805 presiding elder WILLIAM McKENDREE sent Walker and LEWIS GARRETT to MISSOURI, in the territory recently purchased by the United States. In 1806 Walker accompanied McKendree on a trip through Southern ILLINOIS. As a result of this tour Walker was appointed to Illinois in the Autumn of 1806.

In 1807 Walker was appointed to the Missouri Circuit and the following year he was returned to the Illinois Circuit. He served the CAPE GIRARDEAU Circuit in Missouri during 1809 and 1810, and in the latter year he, with young JOHN SCRIPPS, established Methodism in NEW MADRID. In 1811 he returned to the Illinois Circuit and in 1812 he became presiding elder of the Illinois District and served in this capacity four years. In 1816 he was transferred, as presiding elder, to the Missouri District.

In 1819 and 1820 he was missionary-at-large in Missouri. He opened work in ST. LOUIS and in 1821 was appointed there and organized a class, built a church, and entertained the conference in 1822. Again appointed missionary, he went north to contact the Pottowatomie Indians, then returned and went as delegate to the GENERAL CONFERENCE.

While attending the General Conference at BALTIMORE in 1824, he went to WASHINGTON and secured permission from the Government to establish a mission school for Indians in Northern Illinois; this he opened in 1825 a few miles north of the present city of Ottawa. From his school he scouted the wilderness of Northern Illinois for new settlers. One of these excursions took him to CHICAGO, then a village around Ft. Dearborn. He continued occasional visits to Chicago, and on Nov. 25, 1830, reporting to Bishop R. R. ROBERTS, he closed his report with these words: "I still have hopes that Chicago will some day receive the gospel." His hopes were fulfilled. In June 1831, Walker, assisted by Stephen R. Beggs, organized the first church in Chicago, with eight members. In 1834 he built a church house twenty-eight by thirty-eight feet in size at a cost of $580. This class became the Chicago Temple (First Church, Chicago).

In 1834 Jesse Walker retired from active work, but he continued to preach. He died on Oct. 4, 1835. He was

first buried on his farm on the Des Plaines River, ten miles west of Chicago, but later was interred at Plainfield, Ill., his former home. It was said of him, "When we sought to find Brother Walker, he was always farther on." Governor John Reynolds called him "a kind of Martin Luther of the church of the west, and bore the standard of the cross triumphantly throughout the wilderness country."

Elmer T. Clark, *One Hundred Years of New Madrid Methodism.* New Madrid, Mo.: the author, 1912.
A. M. Pennewell, *Jesse Walker.* 1958.　ALMER PENNEWELL

WALKER, SAMUEL (1714-1761), Anglican Evangelical, was curate of Truro, Cornwall, from 1746. Converted through George Conon, a Scottish schoolmaster, Walker's preaching filled the church and purged the town. He set up classes in order to conserve the gains of revival and in 1750 founded a Clerical Club. In Cornwall JOHN WESLEY regarded Walker as the sole exception to his somewhat arbitrary rule that no clergyman in a settled parish could do work of lasting worth. Wesley was in considerable correspondence with Walker over the question of separation from the Church of England.

G. C. B. Davies, *Early Cornish Evangelicals.* 1957.
E. Sidney, *Life of S. Walker.* London, 1838.
A. SKEVINGTON WOOD

WALLBRIDGE, ELIZABETH (1770-1801), British Methodist, was born at Arreton, Isle of Wight, in 1770. She was converted in 1797 by a Wesleyan Methodist itinerant, and lived an intensely pietistic life until her death at Arreton on May 30, 1801. Legh Richmond (1772-1827), an Anglican parson, made of her life story one of the most successful tracts of the nineteenth century: she is remembered by its title *The Dairyman's Daughter* (1811).

T. Grimshawe, *A Memoir of the Rev. L. Richmond.* London, 1828.　　　JOHN KENT

WALLER, ALVAN (1808-1873), American missionary, minister and university financial agent in the Pacific Northwest. He was a member of the GENESSEE CONFERENCE in NEW YORK, when in 1839 he was appointed a member of the OREGON mission. He was a member of a large reinforcement of the mission recruited by JASON LEE, who had made a long trip across country to seek the added workers. Lee brought the new missionaries, not across the plains, but by the long sea voyage around Cape Horn, reaching Oregon in June 1840. When the Indian mission was closed in 1846, Waller remained in Oregon to help build the church among the pioneers who were settling the Oregon country.

His conference memoir states: "For the space of thirty-two years Bro. Waller has been identified with every vital interest of Oregon Methodism. He has labored among the Indians; has been in pastoral work on our circuits and districts; took an active part in establishing the *Pacific Christian Advocate;* has toiled for years to build up the WILLAMETTE UNIVERSITY; . . . and perhaps more than any other one man has circulated Methodist books among the people."

Overshadowing all other work of this devoted minister was his work for Willamette University, a Methodist university and the oldest in the Pacific Northwest. He served many years as its "Agent," a position which involved raising money to support the school, and of having full charge of all the business of the school. Many years he returned his full salary to the University, and supported his family by selling his land claim, a few acres at a time. In 1860 he launched a campaign for a new building; it required a decade of sacrificial labor to raise the money, and almost as long to build, as Waller sought to pay as he built. He personally supervised the building operations from burning the bricks to the point where the four-story college hall waas ready for use in the fall of 1867. It was fittingly named "Waller Hall."

R. M. Gatke, *Willamette University*. 1943.

ROBERT MOULTON GATKE

WALLIS, JAMES (1809-1895), NEW ZEALAND Methodist minister, was born at Blackwell, London, England. He was received into the ministry in 1833, and came to New Zealand, arriving at Hokianga in December, 1834, where he was appointed to Waingaroa (Raglan). In 1836, when arguments with the Church Missionary Society about spheres of influence arose, he was withdrawn for a period, but returned in 1839, and labored there until 1862. Several Maori chiefs of high rank were converted under his fruitful preaching. In his later years, Wallis entered the European work and served at Onehunga and Pitt Street, AUCKLAND. He became a supernumerary in 1868, and spent a long retirement in Auckland until his death on July 5, 1895.

Wallis imbued his family with missionary zeal to such effect that two daughters, a son, and a grandson became missionaries to the South Seas.

C. H. Laws, *First Years at Hokianga*. Wesley Historical Society, New Zealand, 1945.
C. T. J. Luxton, *The Rev. James Wallis of the Wesleyan Missionary Society*. Wesley Historical Society, New Zealand, 1965.
L. R. M. GILMORE

WALLS, WILLIAM JACOB (1885-   ), a bishop of the A.M.E. ZION CHURCH, a son of Edward and Harriet (Edgerton) Walls, was born at Chimney Rock, N. C., May 8, 1885. He graduated from LIVINGSTONE COLLEGE, Salisbury, N. C., in 1908, and from the Hood Theological Seminary in 1913. He received the M.A. degree from the University of Chicago in 1941. He married Dorothy Louise Jordan. He was pastor of the following churches: Cleveland, Lincolnton, and SALISBURY in NORTH CAROLINA, and Broadway, Louisville, Ky. He became editor of the *Star of Zion* in 1920, serving as such for four years, at which time he was elected to the episcopacy in Indianapolis, Ind. (1924). For a number of years he was secretary of the Board of BISHOPS of the Zion Methodist Church, and for a like period chairman of the Board of Trustees of Livingstone College. From 1921 on he has been identified with the WORLD METHODIST COUNCIL. He has also been identified with the WORLD COUNCIL OF CHURCHES, the World Council of Religious Education, and the NATIONAL COUNCIL OF CHURCHES. At present he is also the chairman of the Board of Christian Education, Home and Church Division, of the denomination.

E. L. Williams, *Biographical Directory of Negro Ministers*. 1966.
ETHEL L. WILLIAMS

WALSH, THOMAS (1730-1759), one of the earliest Irish Methodist preachers, was born in Ballylinn, County Lim-

erick, and brought up as a practicing and sincere Roman Catholic. He became increasingly dissatisfied with his faith, and was advised by an elder brother, who had abandoned the Church of Rome, and by Philip Guier, a notable member of the IRISH PALATINES, to read the Bible. This led to a firm belief in Jesus Christ as the one mediator between God and man, and he abjured the Church of his fathers for that of the Protestant Established Church (Anglican).

He was then nineteen years old, and in that same year he heard for the first time Methodist open air preachers. He noted that their message was in full accord with the Articles and Homilies of the CHURCH OF ENGLAND, and he joined the Methodist Society formed in the town of Newmarket. In Methodism, and particularly as expressed in the hymns of CHARLES WESLEY, he found that full joy in salvation which he sought. He consulted JOHN WESLEY as to whether he should preach. Wesley sent him to Shronil, County Tipperary, in July 1750, and advised him to preach in Irish (his mother tongue) as well as in English.

Thomas Walsh proved a most successful preacher. His zeal triumphed over bitter opposition from mobs. When thrown into prison in Bandon, he continued to preach through the window of his cell. His preaching in the Irish language won many souls in the south and west of the country. His great appeal led Wesley to bring him to England in 1753, and a considerable part of his remaining short ministry was spent in that country. John Wesley said on one occasion, "Give me half-a-dozen men like Tommy Walsh, and I'll turn the kingdom upside down."

He threw himself into Biblical study in the original Hebrew and Greek, and became a recognized expert therein. Wesley said that he was the best Hebrew scholar he had ever met, for he knew the meaning of every word every time it occurred in the Old Testament. In all his activity, his radiant Christian character shone clearly, and no one could doubt but that he deserved to be called a true saint.

All this time, Thomas Walsh never had a whole day free from pain or weakness. His life was described as a lingering death, for he suffered from that scourge of Ireland, consumption or tuberculosis. He accentuated this weakness by failing to take enough rest. He studied late and rose by four every morning. When with Wesley on the latter's first visit to the north of IRELAND in 1756, he was chased by a mob from Newtownards, and received a severe wetting in crossing open fields to escape. This made his health even worse, and his last illness began at BRISTOL in February 1758. He was moved to DUBLIN where he died in one of the rooms of the Whitefriar Street chapel, April 8, 1759, when still only twenty-eight years of age. His remains lie in an old Dublin graveyard called the "Cabbage Garden" from the Capuchin Order which formerly owned the land. He is commemorated by a tablet in Ballingrane Methodist Church, County Limerick.

C. H. Crookshank, *Methodism in Ireland*. 1885-88.
Richard Green, *Thomas Walsh, Wesley's Typical Helper*. London: Charles H. Kelly, 1906.
J. Morgan, *Thomas Walsh*. 1762.
FREDERICK JEFFERY

WALTER, JOHN (1781-1819), American Evangelical Association minister, was born Aug. 21, 1781 near Quakertown. His parents were too poor for him to receive an education, but he did learn the trade of a tailor and the art of basketmaking. He was converted through the preaching of JACOB ALBRIGHT and became Albright's first assistant in 1802. Although John Walter was often required to *spell* his texts, he was one of the finest orators that the early EVANGELICAL ASSOCIATION produced.

He was married Aug. 8, 1808 to Miss Christiana Becker, from which union three children were born. In 1810 he published at his own expense the first hymnbook of the denomination, *Eine Kleine Sammlung alter und neuer Geistreicher Lieder.* It contained fifty-six hymns, a number of which Walter had written himself. The two most popular German camp meeting songs, based on their use in various songbooks, were composed by John Walter and entitled, "Kommt, Bruder, Kommt, wir eilen fort" (Come, Brother, Come, we'll journey on) and "Wer will mit uns nach Zion gehn?" (Who will go with us to Zion?). His itinerating ceased abruptly in 1813 due to tuberculosis. He then did a little farming and tried to support his family, but it became necessary for friends to supply him with the necessities. Death came to him Dec. 3, 1818 at his home in Lebanon County, PA. His body was laid to rest in a private cemetery where for 112 years the grave was poorly kept. In 1930 the remains were moved to the Evangelical church cemetery at Ono, Pa., and a proper marker was erected.

R. W. Albright, *Evangelical Church.* 1942.
Evangelical Messenger, Sept. 27, 1930.
J. H. Ness, *History of Publishing.* 1966.
R. Yeakel, *Jacob Albright.* 1883.   JOHN H. NESS, JR.

WALTERS, HAROLD CRAWFORD (1886-1958), British Methodist, was born at Highgate in 1886. Entering the Wesleyan ministry in 1909, he went to BURMA almost immediately, and served there for about twenty years. Returning to England, he served with distinction as a circuit minister and District Chairman, and was elected president of the Methodist Conference in 1956. He was the first president to visit two other continents, AFRICA and North America, in his year in office. He died Feb. 24, 1958.

JOHN KENT

WALTERS, ORVILLE SELKIRK (1903-   ), American minister, physician, educator and an ordained elder of the FREE METHODIST CHURCH, is director of health services and professor of psychiatry, University of Illinois. He was born at Enid, Okla. He was a student at CENTRAL COLLEGE, MCPHERSON, KAN., the University of Kansas and St. Louis University. He holds the degrees A.B., A.M., Ph.D., and M.D. He is a graduate of the Menninger School of Psychiatry, 1956; and is a Diplomate, American Board of Psychiatry and Neurology; Fellow, American College of Physicians. Dr. Walters is the author of *Christian Education in the Local Church* and *You Can Win Others.* He served as editor of *Recent Books,* 1958-63. He is author of twenty papers published in scientific and medical journals besides numerous published articles in the field of psychiatry and religion. His service record includes: general director of Service Training, 1937-60; president, Central College, McPherson, Kan., 1939-44; director, Free Methodist Foundation, University of Illinois, 1958-   ; presently, director of Health Services and professor of psychiatry, University of Illinois. Dr. and Mrs. Walters make their home at Urbana, Ill.

BYRON S. LAMSON

WALTHAM, MASSACHUSETTS, U.S.A., nine miles west of Boston on the Charles River and known as the home of the Waltham Watch Company from 1854 to 1950, is now the center of 250 diverse industries; here are located Bentley College and Brandeis University. Still standing on Winter Street, across the Cambridge Reservoir from Route 128, and now owned by the Polaroid Corporation, is the house occupied the latter part of the eighteenth century by Abraham Bemis, prominent Methodist layman, whose only daughter Mary married George Pickering, Maryland-born New England Methodist itinerant. Here, in "the Bemis-Pickering homestead," Francis Asbury was entertained on many of his New England travels from 1791 through 1813; he mentions this home at least twenty times in his *Journal.*

Entertained here over the years were nine bishops and 400 preachers. A Methodist society which took up its location in the adjoining community of Weston and continues until the present was organized in this historic house in 1792. From the Weston society, the first Methodist church in Waltham itself was organized in 1837. Waltham Methodism grew into two churches. The older of these, Asbury Temple, gave up its identity and merged with Immanuel Methodist Church in 1939. This 911-member congregation (1970) is influential in city and conference affairs. Immanuel Church building contains a unique rose window, executed by the Connick Studios of Boston, depicting the life of Christ through plant symbols. Located in Waltham is Grove Hill Cemetery where Pickering, oldest effective Methodist minister at the time of his death in 1846, lies buried.

Polaroid Farmhouse on Winter Street, one mile from Route 128, originally built in 1710, occupied for about a century and a half by the Bemis-Pickering families, then owned for almost another century by the Stewart family, and now the property of the Polaroid Corporation, was, according to tradition, a haven for nine Methodist bishops and 400 itinerants from 1790 to 1850.

GEORGE PICKERING, born in Maryland and converted at OLD ST. GEORGE'S in Philadelphia, itinerated throughout New England and married Mary Bemis (1777-1859), daughter of Abraham, owner of "the farmhouse." Here in this rural setting Methodism found a headquarters for the entire region surrounding Boston. Bishop ASBURY, a frequent sojourner at the farmhouse, wrote in his Journal: "O! a solitary house, and social family; a comfortable table, pure air, and good water, are blessings at Waltham." Other notables definitely known to have tarried here include Jesse Lee, Bishops George, Hedding, Roberts, and Whatcoat.

The four rooms and fireplaces in the front of the building with broad floorboards and rough-hewn basement beams were added in 1793; in 1910 sections constructed prior to 1793 were torn down and certain alterations were made in the structure. Although not open to the public, between 80,000 to 90,000 scientists, engineers, and salesmen from around the world annually spend time in this home-like setting deliberately preserved by the Polaroid Corporation for small, informal, creative meetings. Dr. Edwin Land and his associates, under the banner of science, are endeavoring to enrich life through the projected results of small group meetings in this farmhouse, just as Bishop Asbury and his associates endeavored to do under the banner of religion. The furnishings of the house are eighteenth century reproductions; and on the walls hang engravings and memorabilia of early Methodist leaders.

Christian Science Monitor, July 20, 1960.
J. M'Clintock, *Sketches*. 1854.
Methodism in Waltham, 1887. ERNEST R. CASE

WALTON, AUBREY GREY (1901-   ), American bishop, was born in Clarksdale, Miss., on June 20, 1901, the son of Charles Barron and Carrie Mae (Eddins) Walton.

From HENDRIX COLLEGE he received his B.A. degree in 1928 and D.D. in 1946; from DUKE UNIVERSITY, B.D., in 1931, and D.D. in 1962; from CENTENARY COLLEGE, LL.D., 1963; and from SOUTHERN METHODIST UNIVERSITY, LL.D., 1966.

On Sept. 17, 1930 he was united in marriage to Mildred Henry of Helena, Ark. They have two children, Mildred (Mrs. Robert Ziegler) and James Macon.

Aubrey Walton was admitted on trial, NORTH ARKANSAS CONFERENCE, in 1931; ordained DEACON in 1933, and ELDER in 1935. His pastorates, all in ARKANSAS, include: Calico Rock, 1931; Eureka Springs, 1932; Siloam Springs, 1933-34; Searcy, 1935-39; First Church, TEXARKANA, 1939-44; First Church, LITTLE ROCK, 1944-60. He was elected bishop of The Methodist Church in June 1960, and assigned to the LOUISIANA Area.

Bishop Walton was a delegate to the ECUMENICAL METHODIST CONFERENCE in SPRINGFIELD, MASS., 1947; Oxford, England, 1951; LAKE JUNALUSKA, N. C., 1956; delegate to the SOUTH CENTRAL JURISDICTIONAL CONFERENCE, 1948, '52, '56, and '60; GENERAL CONFERENCES of 1952, and '56. He was the chairman of the South Central Jurisdictional Council, 1956-60. He is a member of the WORLD METHODIST COUNCIL (since 1951) and of the General BOARD OF MISSIONS of The Methodist Church. He had the responsibility for visitation in South and Central America, 1960-68.

He was trustee of Hendrix College from 1944-60. At present he is a trustee of Southern Methodist University, Centenary College, DILLARD UNIVERSITY, ST. PAUL SCHOOL OF THEOLOGY, and the Methodist Home Hospital in NEW ORLEANS, La. He is a member of the Board of Visitors, The Divinity School, DUKE UNIVERSITY, and is presently president of the TELEVISION, RADIO AND FILM COMMISSION, The United Methodist Church.

Bishop Walton administers the work in the LOUISIANA ANNUAL CONFERENCE, comprising about 460 churches with a total membership of about 125,000 and resides in New Orleans, La.

Who's Who in America, Vol. 34.
Who's Who in The Methodist Church, 1966. N. B. H.

WALTON, VIOLA (1911-   ), American FREE METHODIST and president of the Woman's Missionary Society (international), was born in Marquette, Kan., and studied at McPherson College, Kan., receiving there a teacher's certificate. She taught in elementary schools in KANSAS, 1932-35. She occupied secretarial positions of importance in Elgin, Ill., and in CHICAGO for about twenty years thereafter. She served on the Education Committee, Church Council of the Free Methodist Church in Elgin and was denomination representative on the Winona Committee. She served also as a member of the Christian Business and Professional Women, Warsaw, Ind.; Literary Club, Winona Lake, Ind.; officer of Woman's Missionary

Society in West Kansas and Illinois; and became a General W.M.S. officer in 1955. She has been president of Woman's Missionary Society (international) since June 1969. She is also a member of the Church's Commission on Missions. She resides in Winona Lake, Ind.

BYRON S. LAMSON

WANG, CHIH PING (1878-1964), Methodist bishop, was born in Peking, CHINA, the son of an official in the old Chinese government. He studied in an old fashioned native school, a mission school and Peking University. In 1900 he joined the NORTH CHINA CONFERENCE. He became a pastor and a teacher in Shan Hai Kwan and other small districts in North China, and from 1907 to 1913 he taught in the Methodist Academy (Hui Wen Academy) in Peking.

In the latter years he went to the United States and earned the Ph.D. degree at SYRACUSE UNIVERSITY. This institution awarded him the honorary D.D. degree in 1932.

When he returned to China in 1917 he became a teacher in Peking University and then to Tientsin as the general secretary of the Y.M.C.A. From 1926 to 1930 he was pastor of Asbury Methodist Church, Peking. He was elected bishop in 1930 and assigned to the North China, Shantung and West China (for a time West China was divided into two conferences) Annual Conferences. He was the first bishop elected by the CHINA CENTRAL CONFERENCE, but found the work uncongenial and resigned a few years later. During and after World War II, he continued active in the work of the Church, but little information has been obtained since the rise of the Communist regime. He died on Feb. 22, 1964.

F. D. Leete, *Methodist Bishops*. 1948. PHOEBE W. LEE

WANG, LUCY (Wang Shih-ching) (1899-   ), college president, was born in Fukien province and after study at Hwanan College in Foochow she studied in the United States and received her B.A. degree from MORNINGSIDE COLLEGE and her M.A. degree from the University of Michigan. After returning to CHINA in 1923 she taught for one year in Amoy University and then returned to her Foochow alma mater as professor of chemistry and dean. In 1930, after another period of study in the United States, she became president of Hwanan College, a position she retained until the Communist confiscation of all Christian schools in 1950. Dr. Wang continued to teach in the reorganized school system, first in the normal college that took over the Hwanan campus, and then in Foochow University. She is now retired.

China Christian Yearbook, 1936-37.
Who's Who in Modern China. Hong Kong, 1954.
FRANCIS P. JONES

WAR DAMAGE. The bombing of Great Britain during the Second World War resulted in some three thousand recorded cases of damage to Methodist church buildings. These varied in extent, some being relatively slight and capable of repair, while nearly a thousand involved substantial destruction. This damage was fairly widespread over England, with some in Scotland, but it was most concentrated in the large cities. Government policy, which applied equally to all churches, was that of an *ex gratia* payment for the repair, reinstatement, or replacement of the fabric of damaged churches, while property generally was dealt with through a contributory fund. A feature of the policy toward churches which was of great importance was known as "portability." This meant that, because of the displacement and rehousing of the population, an assessed church war-damaged payment could be used on another site where there was need. A fund of over £600,000 was raised to supplement government payments, of which half was used for Methodist war damage overseas.

E. BENSON PERKINS

WARD, ALBERT NORMAN (1871-1935), American minister and educator, was born in Harford County, Md., Nov. 27, 1871.

He received his B.A. degree from WESTERN MARYLAND COLLEGE in 1895. His M.A. degree was earned at George Washington University in 1902.

In 1895 Ward entered the MARYLAND CONFERENCE of the M.P. CHURCH. He served churches in BALTIMORE, Md.; WASHINGTON, D.C.; and SEATTLE, Wash. He began his career as an educator in 1913, when he became vice-president of Western Maryland College, serving until 1916.

He then resumed the pastorate until 1919, when KANSAS CITY UNIVERSITY named him its chancellor. In 1920 he returned to his Alma Mater, Western Maryland College, as president. He remained there for fifteen years.

He earned a permanent place of honor at this fine small institution as he guided the college through an era of expansion and development. In 1929 he inaugurated and served two years as chairman of the Liberal Arts Movement for smaller colleges, an association designed to attract nationwide financial assistance for colleges. Western Maryland College's trustees named a boys' dormitory for Ward and a girls' dormitory for his wife.

Several outstanding colleges and universities honored him with honorary doctorates for his work in the field of education. ADRIAN COLLEGE and OTTERBEIN COLLEGE presented him D.D. degrees in 1920; he received LL.D. degrees from Kansas City University (1921) and George Washington University (1932). He died Sept. 22, 1935 in Westminster, Md.

Who Was Who in America, 1897-1942.   JAMES H. STRAUGHN

WARD, ALFRED DUDLEY (1914-   ), American minister and Church executive, was born at Toronto, Ontario, Canada, on Aug. 9, 1914. His parents were Alfred and Alice J. (Adams) Ward. He received the A.B. degree from the University of Delaware in 1944, and M.A. in 1947; the B.D. from Union Theological Seminary, New York, in 1950. TENNESSEE WESLEYAN awarded him the D.D. degree in 1965. His wife was Alice L. M. Armstrong, whom he married on Sept. 26, 1942, and they had three children—Alice, Beverly Lynne, and John.

Dr. Ward came to the United States in 1942 and was naturalized in 1951, for a time serving as assistant to the president of a business company. He was ordained to the ministry of The Methodist Church in 1950, NEW YORK EAST CONFERENCE. He then became widely known as the director of a series of studies in economics sponsored by the FEDERAL COUNCIL OF CHURCHES and the NATIONAL COUNCIL OF CHURCHES during the years

1949-53—which studies were published in twelve volumes during that and subsequent years.

He was elected the general secretary of the Board of Social and Economic Relations of The Methodist Church, 1953-60, and when this Board was merged into the Board of CHRISTIAN SOCIAL CONCERNS, he became the associate general secretary of its division of Human Relations and Economic Affairs. In 1963, he was elected general secretary of the Board itself which position he continues to occupy in The United Methodist Church.

Dr. Ward is a member of the Institute of Chartered Accountants, Ontario; the National Council of Churches, serving on its General Board, as a member of its Assembly, and on the executive committee of the Division of Christian Life and Work and the chairman of its Budget Committee 1960-63; he was a member of the Board of Managers of Church World Service, 1961-64. He has written *American Economy-Attitudes and Opinions*, 1953; *Social Creed of the Methodist Church*, 1956, revised, 1964; *Secular Man in Sacred Missions*, 1968; the editor of *Goals of Economic Life*, 1952, and the director of a series, *The Ethics and Economics of Society*, 1952-54 and of the four volume series, *Methodism in Social Thought and Action*, 1958-62.,

Who's Who in America, Vol. 34.
Who's Who in The Methodist Church, 1966.   N. B. H.

WARD, ERNEST F. (1850-1937), the first Free Methodist foreign missionary, was born in Elgin, Ill., April 25, 1850. He arrived in INDIA in January 1881, as a "faith" missionary, as the FREE METHODISTS had no mission board at this time. Mrs. Ward's savings from her school teaching paid the transportation costs. Their home conference in ILLINOIS recognized the call, gave approval, special ordination, and the promise of prayer!

Ernest Ward reported his work regularly in the denominational paper. Meager support was given. The denominational Mission Board was organized in 1882. Ward accepted it as his "advisory committee." He continued independent planning and financing of his work until 1904, when he asked for missionary appointment under the Board.

Three daughters were born to the Wards while they were in India. Mrs. Phoebe Ward died in 1910 in Seattle. The oldest daughter, Ethel, returned with Ward to India. He was able to speak and write several languages. He retired in 1927 and resided in Los Angeles, Calif., where he died Nov. 3, 1937.

BYRON S. LAMSON

WARD, HARRY FREDERICK (1873-1966), American minister, professor, and social reform leader, was born in LONDON, England, Oct. 15, 1873, the son of Harry and Fanny (Jeffery) Ward. Coming to America in 1891, he studied at the UNIVERSITY OF SOUTHERN CALIFORNIA and won the A.B. degree at NORTHWESTERN (1897) and the A.M. at Harvard (1898). He achieved Phi Beta Kappa, and was awarded the LL.D. by the University of Wisconsin (1931).

Ward was admitted on trial in the SOUTHERN CALIFORNIA CONFERENCE in 1893 and was left without appointment to attend school each year until 1899 when he transferred to the ROCK RIVER CONFERENCE. He was head resident, Northwestern University Settlement, 1898-1900, and served successively as pastor of Wabash Avenue and Union Avenue Churches in CHICAGO and Euclid Avenue Church in Oak Park, 1899-1912. He was professor of social service, BOSTON UNIVERSITY SCHOOL OF THEOLOGY, 1913-18, and professor of Christian ethics, Union Theological Seminary, New York, 1918-41, when he retired. He continued as a member of the Rock River Conference until his death.

Throughout his life Ward was widely recognized as a social crusader. His colorful personality was a combination of high intelligence, high-strung intensity, and deep commitment. He was instrumental in writing the SOCIAL CREED adopted by the 1908 GENERAL CONFERENCE, and was chairman of the American Civil Liberties Union, 1920-40, and chairman of the American League for Peace and Democracy, 1934-40. He led in founding the METHODIST FEDERATION FOR SOCIAL SERVICE, served as its editorial secretary, 1907-11, and then as general secretary until 1944. Under his vigorous leadership, the Federation was for many years an effective although unofficial social conscience for American Methodism. Prior to unification in 1939, it championed the eight hour day, minimum wage laws, social security, the right of labor to organize, and other causes, and was the most influential organization of its kind in American Protestantism.

Unfortunately as time passed, Ward's blinding vision seemed to blur his good judgment. Under his leadership the Federation for Social Service tacked sharply to the left. Always critical of the abuses of capitalism, the organization began attacking the system itself and embraced the socialist vision of a classless society. Both Ward and the Federation then lost much of the respect which socially conscious Methodists had accorded them. The 1952 General Conference emphatically dissociated The Methodist Church from the Federation and set up its own Board of Social and Economic Relations.

Among Ward's books were: *Social Creed of the Churches*, 1913; *Social Evangelism*, 1915; *The New Social Order—Principles and Programs*, 1919; *Our Economic Morality*, 1929; *Which Way Religion?* 1931; *In Place of Profit*, 1933; and *The Soviet Spirit*, 1945. He died at Palisade, N. J., Dec. 9, 1966, and was buried at North Bergen, N. J.

General Minutes, MEC and MC.
E. S. Bucke, *History of American Methodism*, Vol. 3.
Minutes of the Rock River Conference, 1967.
Who's Who in America, 1940-41.
Who's Who in the Clergy.   LOUISE L. QUEEN

WARD, JAMES THOMAS (1820-1897), American minister and M.P. president, was born at Georgetown, D. C., on Aug. 21, 1820, the eldest son of Ulysses and Susan V. (Beall) Ward. He received his education at Columbian Academy, WASHINGTON, D. C. and at Brookeville Academy, Montgomery County, Md. He was licensed to preach in 1840, and after a year of theological studies under Augustus Webster and Andrew A. Lipscomb was received as a ministerial member of the MARYLAND CONFERENCE of the M.P. CHURCH. For twenty-five years Ward served pastorates in MARYLAND, WEST VIRGINIA, PHILADELPHIA and Washington, D. C. In 1886 he moved to Westminster, Md., and assumed teaching duties for a year in the WESTMINSTER SEMINARY (a Literary and Classical School). In 1867 he became traveling agent for WESTERN MARYLAND COLLEGE (opened 1867) and

in 1868 its principal. This title was changed to president in 1873. After eighteen years he resigned the College presidency and in 1886 was elected president of the Westminster Theological Seminary (opened 1882), a position he held until his death, March 11, 1897.

Ward received the D.D. degree from ADRIAN COLLEGE in 1871, and that of F.S.Sc.A. from the Society of Science and Art, LONDON, ENGLAND in 1887. His sermons and articles appeared frequently in the periodicals of his denomination and his *A Daily Manual for Bible Readers* was published in Baltimore in 1894.

T. H. Lewis, *Maryland Conference* (MP). 1879.
The Methodist Protestant, April 7, 1897.
Minutes of the Maryland Conference, MP, 1897.
                              DOUGLAS R. CHANDLER

RALPH A. WARD

WARD, RALPH ANSEL (1882-1958), American bishop, was born at Leroy, Ohio, June 26, 1882, the son of Fletcher D. and Harriet G. (Walker) Ward. He held the A.B. (1903) and A.M. (1906) from OHIO WESLEYAN UNIVERSITY, the S.T.B. (1906) from BOSTON UNIVERSITY SCHOOL OF THEOLOGY, and the D.D. (1919) from BALDWIN-WALLACE COLLEGE. He married Mildred M. Worley, Sept. 7, 1905, and they had two daughters. His wife died in 1947, and in 1948 he married Katherine Boeye, a former missionary to CHINA.

Ward was admitted in the NEW ENGLAND CONFERENCE in 1907, ordained DEACON under the missionary rule, and transferred at once to the NORTH OHIO CONFERENCE. He served supply pastorates in MASSACHUSETTS, 1906-09. He transferred to the Foochow China Conference in 1909 and was ordained ELDER in 1910. Devoting one year to language study in China, he was appointed to the Foochow District, 1910-15.

Returning to the United States on furlough in 1916, Ward served three years as associate secretary of the Centenary Campaign, and then was associate secretary of the Board of MISSIONS for Eastern China, 1919-24. He was president of Anglo-Chinese College, Foochow, 1925-27, and then came to America to serve as executive secretary of the Committee on Conservation and Advance, 1928-32. Returning to the mission field, he transferred to the Central China Conference and was appointed city missionary in Nanking, 1933-37. The East Asia Central Conference elevated him to the episcopacy in 1937 and assigned him to the Chengtu Area which included west China. In 1940 he was sent to Shanghai with responsibility for the work in the lower Yantze River valley.

The Japanese imprisoned Ward, Nov. 5, 1942, besieged him with questions, and finally resorted to torture trying to make him confess that he was an American spy. As the ordeal progressed he said, "You can keep this up until you kill me, but remember—I follow a Master who died on a cross!" He was released from prison Sept. 20, 1945, but though he was suffering from malnutrition and though he had not seen his family and had not even been allowed to write to his wife while incarcerated, he declined to return to America and started at once on a 600-mile tour of his episcopal area so that, as he said, he could take to the people of America a story of the bravery and persistence on the part of the Chinese Christians in the face of persecution and destruction of church property.

Following a year of rest in America, Ward returned to China in 1947 and stayed on even after the communists took control. But in 1951, at the urging of Chinese friends and associates, he left mainland China and went to HONG KONG to work among refugees from the interior. Though he retired in 1953, the COUNCIL OF BISHOPS continued to assign him to administer the work in Hong Kong and TAIWAN. He led in strengthening Methodism in both places, including the relocating of Soochow University on Taiwan. During his last illness Bishop Ward ordained three young Chinese men who knelt at his bedside. Moments after telling them in a weak voice to go and preach, he passed into a coma. He died in Hong Kong, Dec. 10, 1958, and the funeral was held there four days later.

F. D. Leete, *Methodist Bishops*. 1948.
J. C. Schwarz, *Who's Who in the Clergy*. New York, 1936.
World Outlook, April, 1946 and February, 1959.
General Minutes, MEC.
ALBEA GODBOLD
JESSE A. EARL

WARD, ROBERT (1816-1876), New Zealand PRIMITIVE METHODIST minister, to whom belongs the distinction of establishing the connection in New Zealand, was born in Sporle, Norfolk, England, in 1816. He entered the ministry in 1835, where he served for nine years in English circuits, proving his gifts as a preacher and winning more than four hundred people to Christ. Selected by the missionary committee to go to New Zealand, he and his family arrived in New Plymouth in the latter part of August, 1844.

While ministering to a European congregation, he also sought to evangelize the Maori people. In this latter work he had some success, but the scattered nature of the Maori work made this very arduous, so that reluctantly he relinquished his efforts and concentrated on building up the European congregations. At the same time his interest in the Maori people never wavered, as is evident in his published work, *Life among the Maori People in New Zealand*. During his term of ministry in New Plymouth of nearly nine years, he visited Wellington in 1847. He spent nine years in Auckland, which was followed by a second term in New Plymouth of nine years. In 1868, he was transferred to Wellington, where he remained until his death on Oct. 13, 1876. His ministry of forty

years, of which over thirty were spent in New Zealand, was a marvel of sustained and divinely blessed activity.

Guy and Potter, *Primitive Methodism in New Zealand*. 1893.
ARCHER O. HARRIS

SETH WARD

WARD, SETH (1858-1909), American bishop, was born in Leon County, Texas, Nov. 15, 1858, the son of Samuel Goode and Sarah Ann (Wyche) Ward. Samuel, a native of Lynchburg, Va., left the University of Virginia in 1837 without graduating and went to TEXAS. A soldier in the Mexican War, he was wounded at San Jacinto and was present at the fall of Mexico City.

Seth Ward lived and worked on a farm until he entered the ministry at twenty-three. His formal education was limited to five months in a country school. However, his father instructed him, and in time he became an assiduous reader, mastered good books, and acquired a personal library which included the best volumes. He was gifted as a poet and had an interest in geology. SOUTHWESTERN UNIVERSITY awarded him the D.D. degree in 1900. He married Margaret E. South, Jan. 5, 1886, and they had two sons and one daughter.

Ward was converted at thirteen, and, influenced by his mother, joined the NORTHWEST TEXAS CONFERENCE in 1881. He was ordained deacon in 1883 and elder in 1885. In 1882 he transferred to the TEXAS CONFERENCE. His appointments were: 1881, West Corsicana Circuit; 1882, Centerville Circuit junior preacher; 1883, Kosse Circuit; 1884-85, Calvert and Hearne; 1886-89, St. James, Galveston; 1890-93, Huntsville; 1894-95, HOUSTON District; 1896-98, Shearne, Houston; 1899, commissioner of education for Texas Methodism; 1900-01, Central Church, Galveston; and 1902-05, assistant secretary, General Board of MISSIONS.

Ward rose rapidly in the conference, filling strong appointments and being accorded positions of leadership. He was elected to four GENERAL CONFERENCES, 1894-1906, leading his conference delegation each time. He was chosen a delegate to the 1901 ECUMENICAL CONFERENCE in LONDON but did not go because he felt obligated to stay in Galveston which had not recovered from the 1900 hurricane which devastated the city and killed 6,000 people. Deeply interested in education, he organized a theological department at Southwestern University and served as a trustee of both that institution and VANDERBILT. Serious and yet amiable and cheerful, he was regarded as a man of sound judgment, an able preacher, and a good executive.

Elected bishop in 1906, Ward was assigned to supervise the mission work in CHINA, JAPAN, KOREA, and MEXICO. He soon won the admiration of workers on the mission fields. Though ill in the summer of 1909 with what was later believed to be a brain tumor, he sailed for the Orient and died in Kobe, Japan, on Sept. 20. Interment was in Houston, Texas, where he lived after his elevation to the episcopacy.

Christian Advocate (Nashville), Sept. 24, 1909.
General Conference Journal, 1910.
General Minutes, MES.
National Cyclopedia of American Biography.
Who Was Who in America, 1897-1942.

ALBEA GODBOLD
JESSE A. EARL

WARD, THOMAS (1823-1894), bishop of the A.M.E. CHURCH and organizer of African Methodism in the far west, was born in Hanover, Pa., Sept. 28, 1823. Admitted into the New England Conference in 1846, he was ordained deacon in 1847 and elder in 1849. His effective work as Missionary Superintendent of the Pacific Coast in 1856 resulted in the organization of the California Conference (AME) in 1865, extending the denomination's boundaries from coast to coast. Following his election to the bishopric in 1868, Ward further developed the work of the church in the west and southwest by organizing Oklahoma (Indian Territory Mission) Conference in 1879; the Iowa Conference in 1883; and the Rocky Mountain Conference in 1892. Bishop Ward was awarded the honorary D.D degree by WILBERFORCE UNIVERSITY later in his ministry. He died at Washington, D. C., on June 10, 1894.

GRANT S. SHOCKLEY

WARD, VALENTINE (1781-1835), British Methodist, was born at Madeley, Shropshire, on Jan. 4, 1781. He became a Wesleyan itinerant in 1801. He played an important role in the development, or misdevelopment, of Wesleyan Methodism in SCOTLAND, where he was chairman of one or other of the Scottish districts for about thirteen years. He was stationed in Glasgow, for example, 1811-13, 1820-22, and again in 1827-28, while he was in Edinburgh, 1814-16, and in 1823; from 1817-19 he served in Aberdeen. His building program was an important factor in the numerical decline of Scottish Wesleyanism between 1819 and 1856: the legacy of debt which resulted crippled the societies. In one case it is said that he bought for a society of thirty members a chapel holding 1,300 people. Ward's reputation did not suffer in his own lifetime, however, and in 1834, when a dispute broke out in Jamaican Methodism, he was appointed as General Superintendent of West Indian Missions and sent out to effect a settlement. He was having some success when his health broke down and he died at Montego Bay, JAMAICA, on March 26, 1835.

G. E. LONG

WARD, WALTER WILLIAM (1887-   ), American clergyman and church hospital sponsor, was born June 7, 1887, near Hillsboro, Texas. In early manhood he became a registered pharmacist. He attended Polytechnic Prep School and College before receiving the A.B. degree from SOUTHWESTERN UNIVERSITY; he later attended the School of Theology at SOUTHERN METHODIST UNIVERSITY. The

D.D. degree was conferred on him in 1935 by Southwestern University, and the LL.D. degree in 1969 by Texas Christian University. He joined the Central Texas Conference in 1918; he has served several pastorates and was twice district superintendent. Since 1950 he has served in various capacities with Harris (Methodist) Hospital in Fort Worth; for nine years he was commissioner-chaplain; for two years he handled public relations; and since 1960 has been field representative. He was a delegate to General Conferences in 1934, 1938, 1939, and 1944, and to jurisdictional conferences in 1940, 1944, and 1948. He served as conference secretary from 1938 to 1951, and delivered the 75th anniversary address of Central Texas Conference in 1941. He was a member of the Texas Methodist Historical Commission, 1950-60; and of the Texas Methodist Planning Commission for several years. He has served as a trustee of Southern Methodist University, 1932-59; of WESTERN METHODIST ASSEMBLY, 1929-30; of Texas Christian University's Harris College of Nursing since 1947. He has directed a program of scholarships for nurses in training, which has assisted nearly 500 during the last ten years, and has secured $300,000 for a scholarship endowment.

Schwarz, J. C., Editor, *Who's Who in the Clergy, 1935-36*. New York, 1936.
O. W. Nail, *Texas Methodism*. 1961.   WALTER N. VERNON

W. RALPH WARD, JR.

WARD, WILLIAM RALPH, JR. (1908-   ), American bishop, was born in Boston, Mass., on Oct. 16, 1908, the son of William Ralph and Janie (Johnston) Ward. He received the A.B. from BAKER UNIVERSITY in 1930 and the D.D. in 1951; BOSTON UNIVERSITY, S.T.B., 1932, S.T.M. in 1935, and D.D. in 1963; from MOUNT UNION COLLEGE, the LL.D. in 1960; the S.T.D. from SYRACUSE UNIVERSITY in 1961; and the L.H.D. from Keuka College in 1963. On June 3, 1933, he married Arleen Burdick. Their children are Ralph A., David B., and Gerald W. R.

W. Ralph Ward, Jr. was ordained to the ministry of

the M.E. Church in 1932. His pastorates included Waldoboro, MAINE, 1931; Porter Church, East Weymouth, MASS., 1932-33; Hingham, Mass., 1933-34; First Church, East Weymouth, 1934-40; NEWPORT, R.I., 1940-41; Manchester, CONN., 1941-48; and Mt. Lebanon Church, PITTSBURGH, 1948-60. He was elected bishop in 1960 and has been the bishop of the SYRACUSE Area since that time.

He has been a member of the General Board of CHRISTIAN SOCIAL CONCERNS; vice-president of the General Board of MISSIONS; president, Division of National Missions; honorary life member, W.S.C.S.; president of the Pittsburgh Area Council of Churches, 1957-58; chairman of the Denominational and Interdenominational Staff Conference, 1964; director of the New York State Council of Churches: a delegate to the Oxford Institute on Methodist Theological Studies, London, 1958; member of the WORLD METHODIST COUNCIL; member of the Commission on Promotion and Cultivation, and president of the denomination's PROGRAM COUNCIL, 1968-72. In 1970 he was also a member of the Quadrennial Emphasis Committee, of the Social Principles Study Commission, of the Interboard Committee on Town and Country Work, of the International Methodist Historical Society, and of the General Assembly of the NATIONAL COUNCIL OF CHURCHES.

He was an Edmund Beebe Fellow at Boston University, a trustee of Hartford Seminary Foundation, 1944-49; present trustee of Syracuse University; Bethune-Cookman College; Folts Home for the Aged; Methodist Home for Children, Williamsville; Clifton Springs Sanatarium; Blocher Homes. He is the recipient of the Freedom Foundation award, 1951; man of the year award, B'nai B'rith, Pittsburgh, 1954. He is a member of the Newcomen Society in North America, Zeta Chi, Theta Chi Beta. Bishop Ward has contributed articles to *The Upper Room*, *Prayers for Today, Christian Advocate*, and to other publications. He is the author of *Authentic Man Encounters God's World*.

Who's Who in America, Vol. 34.
Who's Who in The Methodist Church, 1966.   N. B. H.

WARDLE, WILLIAM LANSDELL (1877-1946), British Methodist, was educated at the Perse School, Cambridge. From there he went as a scholar to Gonville and Caius College, Cambridge. He entered the PRIMITIVE METHODIST ministry in 1901. In 1903 he became tutor in Old Testament studies at Hartley College, Manchester, and remained in this post until 1946, apart from the years 1916-18, when he served as a chaplain to the forces in the First World War. In 1928 he was made principal of the college, and in 1938 was chosen as president of the Methodist Conference. His works included: *Israel and Babylon* (this was the HARTLEY LECTURE for 1925, for which he was awarded the D.D. of Dublin University); *History and Religion of Israel; Ezekiel* (in the Abingdon Bible Commentary); and articles in Peake's *Commentary on the Bible*. In 1933 he was president of the Society for Old Testament Study; he was a lecturer—and later reader —in the Old Testament at Manchester University. He died in 1946.

J. T. WILKINSON

WARE, THOMAS (1758-1842), American pioneer preacher, member of the CHRISTMAS CONFERENCE, and a

historian of its sessions, was born in Greenwich, N. J., Dec. 19, 1758. He united with a Methodist society and at FRANCIS ASBURY's solicitation commenced a public ministry. Ware was present at the Christmas Conference in 1784 when the M.E. Church was organized, though he seems to have been more of an interested observer than a participant in all that took place—possibly because he was then quite young. In 1785 he received a regular appointment and in 1787 volunteered to go to east Tennessee where he traveled extensively through both Tennessee and North Carolina. He was instrumental in the conversion of General Russell and his wife, MADAME RUSSELL (nee Elizabeth Henry), who was a sister of Patrick Henry. Ware returned to the east in 1791 and after other appointments was placed in charge of a district on the Peninsula (Delaware and Maryland). At the General Conference of 1812, he was elected Book Agent and after holding this office for four years, returned to the pastorate and continued in the itinerancy until 1825.

Thomas Ware wrote an article on the Christmas Conference published in the *Methodist Magazine and Quarterly Review* for January 1832, and this article has often been cited by historians of early Methodism in its analysis of men and events at that important organizing Conference. He was a great champion of Coke and Asbury, and defended the positions they took at the Christmas Conference and subsequently. Methodist constitutional historians rely greatly on Ware for their judgment on these and kindred matters. He died at Salem, N. J., March 11, 1842.

Methodist Magazine and Quarterly Review, January 1832, p. 98.
M. Simpson, *Cyclopaedia*. 1878.   N. B. H.

WARFIELD, GAITHER POSTLEY (1896-   ), American minister and missionary to POLAND, was born in Rockville, Md., on Feb. 13, 1896. He was the son of Robert Clarence and Maggie (Webb) Warfield, and was educated at DICKINSON COLLEGE (A.B. in 1917, M.A. in 1923, and the honorary D.D. in 1942). He also became a B.D. of DREW UNIVERSITY and studied later at Union Theological Seminary in New York. He joined the BALTIMORE CONFERENCE of the M.E. Church, South in 1922, and was transferred to the WEST VIRGINIA CONFERENCE (MES) in 1924, in which Conference he was ordained DEACON and ELDER and came into full connection in 1926. He served in the first World War, 1918-20, as a second lieutenant, and was decorated with the Officer's Cross of Order of Merit First Class (Germany).

In 1924 he went as a missionary to Poland, then being opened up by the activity of the Centenary Commission (CENTENARY FUND) of the M.E. Church, South. He served in various capacities in Poland and while there married Hania Maria Dropiowski, the daughter of Dr. Peter Z. Wladyslaw Dropiowski. The second World War broke, Poland was invaded, and Warfield was taken prisoner by the Russians and kept as a prisoner of war for sometime, finally obtaining his release since he was an American citizen, and going back to Warsaw. He remained in Poland until Germany declared war upon the United States and as Warsaw was occupied by the German army, he then was put in a German prison camp, where he was kept until the summer of 1942, finally obtaining release as a non-combatant and sailing with his wife and daughter, Monica (Mrs. Charles M. Kulp), to NEW YORK.

Following these experiences and narrating them, he and his wife published a book, *Call Us to Witness*, in 1944.

While granted the status of "a missionary on furlough," 1942-46, he was drawn into relief work on the staff of the recently organized METHODIST COMMITTEE FOR OVERSEAS RELIEF. He served for six years as executive officer for this organization. In 1952 he was elected General Secretary of this organization, in which capacity he served until his retirement in 1966, his work taking him over the world in assisting and directing in the expenditure of vast funds for the needy in various lands. He kept a residence in his native town of ROCKVILLE, where his father-in-law came to live after the Communist take-over in Poland. Dr. Warfield holds membership in the VIRGINIA CONFERENCE of The United Methodist Church and continues to reside in Rockville.

Who's Who in The Methodist Church, 1966.   N. B. H.

WARING, EDMUND H. (1826-1916), American minister and historian, was born on Oct. 17, 1826 at Brienton, Herefordshire, England and attended school there. He came to the United States in 1842, attended school for a year and became a cabinet maker apprentice in Bellefonte, Pa. He began local preaching in the Erie Conference of the M.E. Church in 1849 and filled an exhausting circuit of 277 miles in six counties. In 1850 he transferred to the Baltimore Conference as a circuit rider and was ordained deacon in 1852 and elder in 1855. He transferred to the Iowa Conference in 1857 and served a succession of charges at Kossuth, Des Moines, Oskaloosa, Burlington, Keokuk, Ottumwa, Fairfield and Knoxville and was presiding elder of the Mt. Pleasant District. Stricken with severe bronchitis, he retired from pastoral work in 1876, although he continued active in other areas of church life. He had been an official reporter for the General Conferences of 1860 and 1864 and served as official delegate from Iowa in 1868 and 1872. In retirement he acted as a Court Reporter in his Judicial District and devoted himself to historical studies. At his death on Oct. 5, 1916, he was senior minister of the Iowa Conference.

Waring was a trustee of Iowa Wesleyan University 1864-67. His long service as Secretary of the Conference (1859-75) aroused his historical interests. He delivered sermons and addresses for many anniversary observances of Iowa Methodism and of Iowa Wesleyan University, some of which were published. These studies culminated in 1910 with his *History of the Iowa Annual Conference of the Methodist Episcopal Church*, which covered in considerable detail the period from 1833 to 1909. The book is based upon a study of all published histories of Methodism for the middle west and upon a firsthand examination of Iowa Conference records. It is the most important contribution to the Iowa Conference history written to the present time. Iowa Wesleyan granted him an honorary D.D. in 1910.

Iowa Wesleyan College Archives.
Minutes of the Iowa Conference, 1857-1917.
E. H. Waring, *Iowa Conference*. 1910.

LOUIS A. HASELMAYER

WARNE, FRANCIS WESLEY (1854-1932), American bishop, was born at Erin, Ontario, Canada, Dec. 30, 1854, the son of Francis and Agnes (McCutcheon) Warne. The elder Warne was a local Methodist preacher for sixty years. Young Francis was converted as a boy of thirteen in a revival, and one critic then complained that the meeting was a failure because it won only one lad. He was educated at George Town Academy and Albert College in Ontario, and GARRETT BIBLICAL INSTITUTE (B.D., 1884). The D.D. degree was awarded him by NORTHWESTERN UNIVERSITY (1900) and Toronto University (1924). He married Margarette E. Jefferis, May 15, 1879, and they had one daughter.

Deciding for the ministry at seventeen during the funeral of his elder sister. Warne joined the Toronto Conference in 1874 and was ordained in 1876. After serving circuits in Toronto, he volunteered for missionary work in the wilds of Manitoba in 1879 and established five churches in three years. After graduating from Garrett, he was received on credentials in the ROCK RIVER CONFERENCE in 1884, and was appointed to Pullman, Ill., that year, and to Austin, 1885-87.

On hearing Bishop JAMES M. THOBURN tell of the need for missionaries in INDIA, Warne offered himself for service there. He transferred to the BENGAL CONFERENCE, arrived in CALCUTTA in January 1888, and was immediately appointed pastor of the Thoburn (English-speaking) Church. From 1890 to 1900 he served both the church and the Calcutta District.

The 1900 GENERAL CONFERENCE elected Warne and E. W. PARKER missionary bishops for Southern Asia. Due to the death of Parker and the failing health of Bishop Thoburn, for most of the quadrennium Warne superintended all the work in India, BURMA, MALAYSIA, and the PHILIPPINES. He organized the M.E. Church in the Philippines in 1903, ordained the first Filipino Protestant minister, and dedicated the first Filipino Protestant church at Pandacan near MANILA. In 1904 Warne was assigned to LUCKNOW. There in North India in the next twenty years he did his greatest work, becoming the leader of the Mass Mission Movement which won 30,000 converts a year for twenty years. In 1924 he was assigned to Bangalore and supervised the work in South India and Burma. He retired in 1928. Meantime, the 1920 General Conference elected him a bishop or general superintendent of the M.E. Church.

A man of ability characterized by evangelistic zeal, Warne became an acknowledged leader in the work in Southern Asia soon after arriving in India. As a bishop in the region he rendered distinguished service to the church. A prolific writer, some of his works were: *The Darjeeling Disaster, Its Bright Side*, 1900; *The India Mass Mission Movement*, 1915; *A Tribute to the Triumphant, Mrs. L. S. Parker*, 1915; and *The Lord's Supper*, 1924.

Warne was unusually active during retirement. His platform ability, wide experience, and evangelistic and missionary zeal kept him in great demand for sermons and addresses at CAMP MEETINGS, youth gatherings, and retreats. He died Feb. 29, 1932, at the Methodist Hospital, BROOKLYN, N. Y., and was buried at his own request at Ballinaford, Ontario, Canada, in the little country churchyard adjoining the church where he preached his first sermon sixty years before.

General Conference Journal, 1930.
General Minutes, MEC.
F. D. Leete, *Methodist Bishops*. 1948.
National Cyclopedia of American Biography.
Who's Who in America.   JESSE A. EARL
ALBEA GODBOLD

WARNER, ARIEL NATHANIEL (1885-1951), was a missionary to INDIA for thirty years in the M.E. Church and, after Union, of The Methodist Church. After withdrawal for health reasons in 1940, he served in the BALTIMORE CONFERENCE. For several years he was associate pastor of the Mount Vernon Place Church, WASHINGTON, D.C.

He was born in Hamilton, Va., Oct. 28, 1885, and was educated in RANDOLPH-MACON and ASBURY COLLEGES, graduating from Asbury in 1908. On Aug. 9, 1910, he married Helen Gertrude Leggett of Mississippi, also a graduate of Asbury, and they departed for India a few weeks later. Their first appointment was to Basim, Berar, where their work was of a quality that attracted attention and evoked strong expectations. A year later he was appointed to the pastorate of Bowen Church, Bombay.

Later appointments included the superintendency of Nagpur and Bombay Districts. He and Mrs. Warner formed a hard-working and effective partnership in service. Their influence was felt in a wide circle and at all levels of society. They corresponded with many congregations, church organizations, and individuals in America and stimulated their participation in missionary work.

Warner was awarded the honorary D.D. degree by his Alma Mater. His Annual Conference elected him to GENERAL CONFERENCE, and he was a familiar and influential member of several sessions of the CENTRAL CONFERENCE and executive board of the Methodist Church in Southern Asia.

Mrs. Warner was responsibile for compiling and editing the book, *Moving Millions,* published by the Central Comittee on the United Study of Foreign Missions. She wrote the first chapter, entitled "The Miracle of Modern India."

Robert E. Speer, in an introduction to the book, wrote "Nowhere else in condensed and yet adequate form can any such account of present-day India be found as is presented in this book."

J. N. Hollister, *Southern Asia.* 1956.
The Missionary Education Movement of the United States and Canada. Boston, Mass., 1938.   J. WASKOM PICKETT

WARNER, DAVID SNETHEN (1857-1928), Free Methodist, was born in Livingston County, N. Y. At fourteen years of age he entered A. M. Chesbrough Seminary, N. Y., and graduated in 1875. His further education was at the University of Rochester (A.B., 1879; M.A. 1888). He was a professor at SPRING ARBOR Seminary, Mich., 1879-83; and at Gerry Seminary, N. Y., 1883-87. He was principal of Spring Arbor Seminary, 1893-1905, and of A. M. Chesbrough Seminary, 1906-08.

Elected assistant editor of Sunday school literature in 1907, he was made editor in 1908, serving until 1919 when he was elected bishop. During his editorship he traveled in Palestine and EGYPT. He wrote: *Glimpses of Palestine and Egypt; The Holy Spirit; The Book We Study.* He died at Spring Arbor, Mich., May 13, 1928. D. S. Warner was a gifted writer, a scholar, and inspiring teacher and preacher of the gospel.

BYRON S. LAMSON

WARNER, IRA DAVID (1886-1964), American United Brethren bishop, was born Sept. 4, 1886, at Clayton, Ohio, twelve miles from Dayton. Following high school at Brookville, Ohio, he taught two years in public schools before entering college. He graduated from OTTERBEIN COLLEGE, Westerville, Ohio, 1911; in 1921 Otterbein conferred the D.D. degree. He attended Biblical Seminary, New York, 1919-20. He married Edna May Landis, June 28, 1911, from which union there were two children.

He served successively in the Church of the UNITED BRETHREN IN CHRIST, First Church, CHATTANOOGA, 1911-13; Oak Street, DAYTON, 1913-17; First Church, CANTON, Ohio, 1923-29, from which pastorate he was elected to the episcopacy by the 1929 GENERAL CONFERENCE. His assignment was to the Pacific Coast, where he continued until his retirement in 1958.

During his first quadrennium on the Pacific District, Mrs. Warner died on July 8, 1934. Three years later he married Ada May Visick, a school teacher and public speaker of Laverne, Calif.

Bishop Warner's twenty-nine years in the episcopacy were notable for his emphasis on evangelism, establishing new churches, and lifting the educational standards of the ministry. He made five episcopal visits to SIERRA LEONE, West Africa.

He wrote several books, of which the most noted is *Building the Body of Christ.* He passed away July 1, 1964 with burial in Rose Hill Gardens of Reflection, Whittier, Calif.

Church and Home, Sept. 1, 1964.
Koontz and Roush, *The Bishops.* 1950.
H. A. Thompson, *Our Bishops.* 1889.   JOHN H. NESS, SR.

WARREN, GEORGE (17?-1812), first Wesleyan Methodist missionary to Africa, was born at Helston, Cornwall, England, and became an itinerant preacher in 1808. In 1811 he volunteered for missionary work and was sent, in answer to an appeal from freed slaves who had been sent to colonize the area, to SIERRE LEONE. After a fifty-two day journey, he landed at the newly named Freetown. With help and welcome from the chaplain and the governor, he worked effectively for eight months, doing some village touring in addition to work in Freetown. He died of fever July 23, 1812, the first Methodist missionary martyr in West Africa.

CYRIL J. DAVEY

WARREN, HENRY WHITE (1831-1912), American bishop, was born at Williamsburg, Mass., on Jan. 4, 1831. He was educated at WESLEYAN UNIVERSITY and received honorary degrees from DICKINSON COLLEGE and OHIO WESLEYAN UNIVERSITY.

He taught natural science at America Seminary and ancient languages at WILBRAHAM ACADEMY and entered the ministry of the M.E. Church in 1855. His appointments were at WORCESTER, BOSTON, LYNN, Westfield, CAMBRIDGE and Charlestown in Massachusetts; and at PHILADELPHIA, then BROOKLYN, N. Y., and again at Philadelphia. He was a member of the Massachusetts House of Representatives in 1863 and was elected a bishop in 1880.

He was assigned to ATLANTA, Ga., where he interested himself in the Negro Methodists and GAMMON THEOLOGICAL SEMINARY. He then served several other conferences and practically all the foreign mission fields; made two trips around the world in visiting the missions, and went to South America as episcopal supervisor twice in one quadrennium. His last assignment was to DENVER, where he devoted himself and his funds largely to the

University of Denver and the Iliff School of Theology. He died at University Park, Colo., on July 22, 1912, shortly after his retirement.

Journal of the General Conference, 1914.
Who's Who in America.   Elmer T. Clark

WARREN, JOHN (1814-1883), New Zealand Methodist minister, was born in Norfolk, England. In 1836 he became a probationer and served in the Ipswich Circuit. Designated for missionary work in New Zealand, he served temporarily in Tasmania, and arrived in New Zealand in 1840. One of his first tasks was to accompany Samuel Ironside and some of the Hokianga chiefs to the Bay of Islands for the signing of the Treaty of Waitangi. Some time was spent at Mangungu, learning to speak Maori, and then Warren was appointed to open a new station at Waima, where he served for sixteen years. While there, his wife planted a young oak tree grown from an acorn which she had brought from England. This resulted in the growth of the largest oak tree in New Zealand, with a spread of branches reaching 130 feet.

Transferring to the European work in 1855, Warren filled appointments in Nelson, Wellington (1860), Auckland (1865), and Onehunga (1866), retiring in 1869. He died in Auckland on Nov. 23, 1883.

Dictionary of New Zealand Biography. New Zealand Department of Internal Affairs, 1940.   L. R. M. Gilmore

WARREN, ORRIS H. (1835-1901), American pastor, editor and author, was born at Stockbridge, N. Y., Jan. 3, 1835. He attended the Oneida Conference Seminary for two terms, beginning in 1851, and completed his studies at Oberlin, Ohio. His health gave way and he had to leave college for a time, but later joined the Oneida Conference in 1862, and filled appointments at Waterville, Utica, Cazenovia, Ithaca and Baldwinsville. At the latter place he took a supernumerary relation because of the illness of his wife, and began to engage more definitely in literary work. After a time he became assistant editor of the *Northern Christian Advocate* and upon the death of its editor, Dr. Lore, in 1875, conducted this paper as acting editor until the General Conference of 1876, which unanimously elected him editor for the succeeding four years. His writings include a book, *The American Episcopal Church.* Orris H. Warren died at Syracuse, N. Y., on Nov. 23, 1901.

M. Simpson. *Cyclopaedia.* 1881.   N. B. H.

WARREN, RALPH BARCLAY (1908-   ), ordained elder of the East Ontario Conference of the Free Methodist Church, is pastor at Kingston, Ontario and Editor of the *Canadian Free Methodist Herald.* He was born at Eganville, Ontario. He holds the degrees B.A., Queen's University, Kingston, Ontario; and the B.D., Emmanuel College, Victoria University, Toronto, Ontario. He was a teacher six years at Annesley College, Ottawa, Ontario, and was for ten years at Lorne Park College, Port Credit, Ontario. He has served as pastor of churches in Ontario twenty-three years. He is author of *Spiritual Strength for Today* and *You Can Gain Spiritual Strength.* Since 1950 he has been the editor of *The Canadian Free Methodist Herald.* He is the writer of a weekly column now used by nineteen newspapers. He is pastor of Polson Park

Free Methodist Church, Ingston, Ontario. Rev. and Mrs. Warren reside at Kingston, Ontario.

Bryon S. Lamson

WARREN, ROBERT HOPKINS (1876-1938), Free Methodist bishop, was born in Glenwood, N. Y., March 7, 1876. Largely self-educated, he was a wide reader and became one of the denomination's most gifted pulpiteers. He was called to the ministry at eighteen years of age, and gave forty-four years of service to the Church. He served as pastor in Colorado, Wisconsin, Kansas, New York, Washington and California. In the last three conferences he served also as district elder. He was elected bishop in 1935, but served only three years before he died Sept. 6, 1938. For three years he was Chairman of the Commission on Christian Education.

Byron S. Lamson

WARREN, SAMUEL (1781-1862), British preacher, helped to found the Wesleyan Methodist Association. He became a Wesleyan itinerant in 1802 but was suspended in 1834 for conducting a public agitation against the decision to establish the theological institution. He then began a lawsuit, contesting the connectional control of the Oldham Street Chapel, Manchester, in the circuit of which he was Superintendent. Judgment was given against him, and thus the legal validity of the Deed of Declaration was confirmed. Expelled by the Conference of 1835, he took with him about eight thousand members to form the Wesleyan Methodist Association, which was joined in 1836 by the Leeds Protestant Methodists. He soon left the association, received Anglican orders in 1838, and became rector of All Souls, Manchester, where he died on May 23, 1862.

G. E. Long

WARREN, WILLIAM FAIRFIELD (1833-1929), American minister, scholar, educator and university president, was born at Williamsburg, Mass., on March 13, 1833. He graduated with the A.B. degree from Wesleyan University in Connecticut, and pursued advanced studies in Halle and Berlin Universities in Germany. He served as pastor of Methodist churches in Andover, Wilbraham and Boston, Mass. He taught in the Methodist Mission Institute at Bremen, Germany. This Institute was later moved to Frankfort-on-Main, and still exists.

In 1867, when what is now Boston University School of Theology was moved from Concord, N. H., to Boston, Warren was appointed president. He assisted Methodist laymen in securing from the Great and General Court of Massachusetts a Charter for Boston University with which was to be merged the School of Theology. Warren was formally elected president of Boston University in 1873, and served thirty years until 1903.

Warren was a truly great educational statesman. He was always progressive, never radical. He gave Boston University its character, and made it intellectually respectable anywhere. Even before the University had achieved fame, he assembled a faculty which included such notables as Alexander Graham Bell, who invented the telephone while at Boston University; Borden Parker Bowne, who was regarded as one of America's greatest philosophers; Dallas Lore Sharpe, one of the greatest nature writers of his generation; and Henry Clay Sheldon, a universal scholar. Warren was the author of numerous books, which showed thorough scholarship within his chosen field—the history and philosophy of religions. His hymn "I Worship Thee O Holy Ghost" was one of the most beloved hymns in the 1932-1964 Methodist Hymnal. He died on Dec. 6, 1924.

Dictionary of American Biography.
M. Simpson, *Cyclopaedia.* 1878.
Who's Who in America.   DANIEL L. MARSH

WARREN, OHIO, U.S.A. First Church is the largest Protestant church in the city, and the largest Methodist church in the Youngstown District. It is located downtown in the heart of the city, and architecturally is an excellent example of classic Greek design.

The church was organized in 1819, just twenty-one years after the city had been settled. The first church structure was located on the banks of the Mahoning River. In 1837 a downtown location was purchased for the building of a new church. In 1917 the present edifice was constructed on North Park Avenue, under the leadership of J. C. Smith. From this time membership grew considerably, and during the past fifteen years has averaged around 2,700.

Former pastors have included CHARLES BURGESS KETCHAM (later president of MT. UNION COLLEGE) and Harold Mohn (later General Secretary of the Advance Program of the Methodist Church). In 1969 the church observed its sesquicentennial.

The church recently sponsored the establishment of a new church in the suburb of Howland, Ohio.

In 1970 First Church reported 2,340 members and property valued at over $1,250,000.

General Minutes, 1970.
First Church News, Nov. 3, 1939.
Harriet Taylor Upton, *20th Century History of Trumbull County, Ohio.* Chicago: Lewis Publishing Co., 1909.
                                    ROBERT B. HIBBARD

WARRENER, WILLIAM (1750-1825), British Methodist, was the first missionary appointed by the Wesleyan Conference. Born in 1750, he became a preacher in 1779 and volunteered for America in 1786. With WILLIAM HAMMETT, ADAM CLARKE, and THOMAS COKE, he landed after being driven off course at St. John's, ANTIGUA, on Christmas morning 1786, where the preachers found JOHN BAXTER's slave congregation. Coke left Warrener in charge of the work in Antigua, and the appointment was confirmed by the 1787 Conference. In 1790 he was transferred to St. Christopher and remained in the WEST INDIES until 1797. He remained active in Britain until 1818, and was a speaker at JABEZ BUNTING's inaugural meeting of the WESLEYAN METHODIST MISSIONARY SOCIETY at LEEDS, at the Old Boggard House, on Oct. 6, 1813. Warrener died at Leeds, Nov. 27, 1825.

                                    CYRIL J. DAVEY

WARRENITE CONTROVERSY. An agitation led by SAMUEL WARREN against a proposal of the WESLEYAN METHODIST CHURCH to found a theological institution for the training of its ministers (see Theological Colleges). For this he was expelled by the Conference of 1835, founding the WESLEYAN METHODIST ASSOCIATION. The

controversy resulted in a huge mass of pamphlet literature and newspaper publicity.

                                    FRANK BAKER

PAUL A. WASHBURN

WASHBURN, PAUL ARTHUR (1911-   ), American bishop and former E.U.B. minister, and executive secretary of the COMMISSION ON CHURCH UNION of the E.U.B. Church, was born at Aurora, Ill., on March 31, 1911, the son of Eliot Arthur and Lena (Burhnsen) Washburn. He is a graduate of NORTH CENTRAL COLLEGE and of EVANGELICAL SEMINARY. Ordained by the Illinois Conference of The Evangelical Church, he served as pastor of congregations in Eppards Point Township, ROCKFORD and NAPERVILLE, ILL.

He has served on the following General Boards and Agencies of the former E.U.B. Church: The General Program Council, Council of Administration, Council of Executive Officers, and the COMMISSION ON CHURCH UNION, of which last he was the executive secretary.

Bishop Washburn was a delegate to every GENERAL CONFERENCE of his Church from 1946 to 1962. He was a member of his Church's Commission on Federation and Church Union since 1958, and a representative of the denomination to the CONSULTATION ON CHURCH UNION. He is a trustee of North Central College and of Evangelical Theological Seminary. He also served as Guest Lecturer in Religion and Pastoral Theology at Rockford College, Rockford, Ill.; North Central College; and Evangelical Theological Seminary. In 1959 and again in 1960 he served as Lecturer in Homiletics at the Rural Leadership School of Michigan State University.

He is married to Kathryn Fischer and they are the parents of four children, Mary (Mrs. Ronald Lee Smith), Jane (Mrs. Edwin Eigenbroot), Frederick and John.

At the UNITING CONFERENCE of the Methodist and E.U.B. Churches, held in DALLAS, Texas in 1968, Dr. Washburn was elected a bishop on the first ballot in an election held at the last session of the General Conference of the E.U.B. Church on Monday, April 22, 1968. He was solemnly set apart that same day for the duties of the episcopacy by the bishops of the E.U.B. Church, with Bishop ROY H. SHORT of the former Methodist Church participating at the invitation of the E.U.B. bishops. Bishop Washburn was assigned to the NORTH CENTRAL JURISDICTION of The United Methodist Church and at the Jurisdictional Conference held at PEORIA, Ill., was assigned to the MINNEAPOLIS Area.

Daily Christian Advocate. Dallas, Texas, April 23, 1968.

REUBEN P. JOB

WASHINGER, WILLIAM H. (1862-1928), American United Brethren minister and bishop, was born at Jacksonville, Pa., on Sept. 9, 1862. He was converted Jan. 3, 1881, and joined the Church of the UNITED BRETHREN IN CHRIST. He prepared himself for teaching in the public schools, and devoted five years to this service. In 1885 he married Miss Romaine E. Funkhouser.

In 1889 Washinger was granted an annual conference license and became a member of the PENNSYLVANIA CONFERENCE. He received his ordination in 1894. He graduated from LEBANON VALLEY COLLEGE in 1891.

He served pastorates at the Otterbein Church, HARRISBURG, Pa., and Chambersburg, Pa., and also organized the Derry Street mission in Harrisburg. He served fifteen years as superintendent of the Pennsylvania Conference.

He was elected bishop in 1917 and became supervisor of the Pacific Area, which included CALIFORNIA, OREGON, COLUMBIA RIVER, and MONTANA CONFERENCES. After making a thorough survey of this field he adopted a program of evangelism and one of finance. Bishop Castle, who once served this field, wrote of him, "No such report ever has been made of work on the Pacific District."

He served a period of time as a member of the board of trustees of Lebanon Valley College and also of Baker Home. In the midst of public duty, after a brief illness, Bishop Washinger died at Dayton, Ohio, May 18, 1928.

A. W. Drury, *History of the U.B.* 1931.
Koontz and Roush, *The Bishops.* 1950. CLAYTON G. LEHMAN

WASHINGTON, U.S.A, population 3,352,892 in 1970, is in the Pacific northwest. It is bounded by CANADA on the north, IDAHO on the east, OREGON on the south, and the Pacific Ocean on the west. The Cascade Mountains divide the state into east and west Washington. With one-half of its 68,192 square mile area in forests, the state has one-sixth of the standing saw timber in the land. The Grand Coulee and other dams on the Columbia River furnish low-cost electric power. Manufacturing includes aircraft and other products. With heavy crops of fruits and berries, the state leads the nation in the production of apples. Washington was organized as a territory in 1853, and it was admitted to the Union in 1889.

Following the Snake and Columbia Rivers, the Lewis and Clark Expedition in 1805 touched what is now Washington. The first white settlement in the region was made in 1810 by David Thompson of the British Northwest Company. In 1811 Americans under John Jacob Astor erected a fort in north central Washington. In 1846 Britain ceded all territory below the forty-ninth parallel to the United States. In 1863 Idaho Territory was carved from Washington Territory.

Methodism first touched Washington on Sept. 2, 1834 when JASON LEE and his party arrived at Fort Walla

Walla. The earliest Methodist work in the area was the Indian Mission which Lee established July 10, 1834 at Nisqually near Olympia. In 1836 Marcus Whitman and his wife started a mission at Waiilatpu near present Walla Walla. On Aug. 23, 1853 JOHN F. DeVORE organized a Methodist society at Steilacoom and built there that year the first Methodist church in the territory. In December 1853, First Methodist Church, SEATTLE was organized. Within two more years there were Methodist societies at Vancouver, Olympia, and several other places.

All Methodist work in Washington was a part of the OREGON CONFERENCE until 1873 when the East Oregon and Washington Conference (called COLUMBIA RIVER CONFERENCE after 1876) was formed; it included the churches in east Washington. The work in west Washington continued with the Oregon Conference until 1884 when the Puget Sound Conference was organized. The division of the Washington work between two conferences continued until 1929 when the Puget Sound Conference merged with the Columbia River Conference to form the PACIFIC NORTHWEST CONFERENCE. The Oregon part of the Columbia River Conference was placed in the Oregon Conference in 1922. Since 1929 all of Washington Methodism has been in the Pacific Northwest Conference.

The M.E. Church had foreign language work in the northwest. The North Pacific German and Northwest Norwegian-Danish Missions were organized in 1888 and the Pacific Swedish Mission Conference was started in 1908. The German mission became a mission conference in 1892 and was designated as the Pacific German Conference in 1905. The Norwegian-Danish work became the Western Norwegian-Danish Mission in 1892 and was made the Western Norwegian-Danish Conference in 1896. All of these foreign language bodies covered Washington, Oregon, Idaho, and Montana, and in the case of the Swedish conference, all states west of the Rocky Mountains. Since each body had more churches in Washington than in any other one Northwestern state they are mentioned in this article. The German and Swedish work was merged with the English-speaking conferences in 1928, but the Norwegian-Danish body continued and was absorbed in 1939.

A METHODIST PROTESTANT church was founded in Seattle in 1864. Some work of the denomination continued in the state until unification in 1939 when three Methodist Protestant churches with a total of about 800 members entered the Pacific Northwest Conference of The Methodist Church.

The M.E. Church, South, through its Columbia, East Columbia, and Northwest Conferences (see OREGON), maintained a few churches in the state of Washington from about 1866 to 1939. At the time of unification it had only two churches in the state with a total of 394 members.

In 1970 the Pacific Northwest Conference had in the state of Washington 236 pastoral charges, 101,718 members, and property valued at $52,416,524.

General Minutes, MEC and MECS.
Minutes of the Pacific Northwest Conference.
E. Howell, *Northwest.* 1966.   ERLE HOWELL

WASHINGTON, ARKANSAS, U.S.A., is historically significant because ARKANSAS Methodism began three miles from the town, and because it was the gateway through which Methodism entered northeastern Texas, southeastern Oklahoma, and portions of northern Louisiana; and also because the present church building, a well preserved colonial style edifice, dates from 1860.

In 1814 WILLIAM STEVENSON, a Methodist preacher from MISSOURI, visited and preached in the vicinity of what is now Washington. In 1816 the newly organized MISSOURI CONFERENCE appointed Stevenson to the Hot Springs Circuit in Arkansas. Stevenson preached at Pecan Point on the Red River in Texas, and as presiding elder in Arkansas, 1819-21, the Pecan Point Circuit was in his district.

Stevenson's family and other Methodist families from Bellevue Valley, Mo., moved to Mound Prairie, Hempstead County, Ark., in 1816. In 1817 they built Mount Moriah Church at Mound Prairie, the first Methodist church to be erected in Arkansas. The next year the congregation rebuilt a mile away and called it Henry's Chapel, the name it bore for half a century. The LITTLE ROCK CONFERENCE has now placed a marker on the chapel site which is some three miles from Washington.

Hempstead County was organized in 1818, and Washington was laid out as the county seat in 1820. The Methodist Church at Washington was organized in 1822. The Washington District of the Arkansas Conference was formed in 1842 and it continued until 1896. The Arkansas Conference met in Washington in 1838 and 1847. The Ouachita Conference was there for its first session in 1854, and the Little Rock Conference convened there in 1870. Washington was the capital of Arkansas, 1863-65 (during the Civil War), and it claimed a population of about 40,000 at that time. A school called the Washington Male and Female Academy was operated in Washington for about fifteen years prior to the Civil War.

Washington began to decline after the railroad from Little Rock to Texarkana passed it by in favor of Hope ten miles to the southeast. In time Hope became the county seat as well as the head of the Methodist district. In 1970 the Washington church had eleven members, and it was one of five churches on the Washington Circuit.

General Minutes, MEC, and MECS.
S. T. Baugh and Robert B. Moore, Jr., *Methodism's Gateway to the Southwest* (pamphlet). Little Rock: Epworth Press, 1966.
W. A. Vernon, *William Stevenson*. 1964.   ALBEA GODBOLD

WASHINGTON, D. C. (population 746,169), is the capital of the United States, situated on the Potomac River, and was named after George Washington. It has been the seat of government since 1800, and has grown rapidly until today it is one of the great cities and the prime showplace of the nation. GEORGETOWN was situated on the bluffs of the Potomac above the site selected for the Capitol, and while now considered the northwest section of Washington, D. C., Georgetown was a sedate and conservative old MARYLAND town before Washington City ever began to grow up around it.

This section of the country was within the bounds of the old Frederick Circuit and was visited by ASBURY as early as 1772. In 1797 he speaks of visiting a famous bridge above Georgetown—no doubt the well-known "chain bridge" as it has been known since that time—and of finding WILLIAM WATTERS in charge of Georgetown circuit. In 1802 Washington is mentioned in connection with Georgetown, William Watters being pastor. In 1805 Washington appears as a separate appointment and reported in the following year sixty-one white and twenty-five

colored members. The church grew rather slowly in Washington, having in 1812 only ninety-one white and fifty-one colored members. This was about the time of the commencement of the second war with England. During that war, Washington itself was burned, including the Capitol and official buildings.

After the war HENRY FOXALL—some say in gratitude for his foundry being spared by the British—gave a gift of ground and building, and a second appointment in Washington was added, called thenceforth, Foundry Church—now on Sixteenth Street. To this Thomas Burch was appointed pastor, and from that time the church grew rapidly. With the increase of the population other charges were added and in due time a separate Negro church was formed.

The A.M.E. and the A.M.E. ZION CHURCHES also established congregations in Washington, where at present there is an enormous Negro population, making up at present almost half the population of the District.

In 1853 a lot was secured and steps were taken toward the building of a Metropolitan Church, but the agitations that shortly followed concerning slavery, and the excitement in the public mind, and then the Civil War, held up the building of this church. At the close of the war, however, another effort was made to erect a church, and under the labors of F. S. DeHass a large and impressive building was erected (see Metropolitan Church). Metropolitan was sometimes called the "Church of the Presidents" because of the attendance there of Presidents Grant and McKinley and its nearness to the Capitol.

The BALTIMORE CONFERENCE, within whose territory Washington has always been situated, divided in its allegiance between the South and the North at the time of the Civil War. Following the war, there were two Baltimore Conferences each having churches in Washington. Also, the MARYLAND CONFERENCE of the M.P. CHURCH had certain strong churches there. Washington being a border city, rivalry between the three Methodisms was somewhat more intense there than in other cities of the border. The M.E. Church, South in 1850 began a congregation which in 1917 built Mount Vernon Place Church to be the "representative church of Southern Methodism" in the capital.

Memberships in the various Methodisms grew as the city itself grew, and this growth has been enormous within the years since the first World War, and even more since the second. Southern Methodism was never quite as strong within Washington City as was the M.E. Church, and the drawing of the Jurisdictional line by the PLAN OF UNION—the Potomac River—put all Methodists on the southern side of the Potomac within the VIRGINIA CONFERENCE, and all those north of the Potomac within the Baltimore. Union was in due time agreed to by all, and the Methodist Church and churches have grown greatly in the metropolitan area of Washington since that time.

The establishment of AMERICAN UNIVERSITY and the bringing in upon its grounds the WESLEY THEOLOGICAL SEMINARY from Westminster, Md., and the support of the entire church for American University as promoted and in a large measure obtained by Bishop G. BROMLEY OXNAM, has greatly helped Methodist influence in the capital city in the educational aspects of its work.

As is well known, Washington has come to be more and more dominant not only as the capital of the nation, but as a major influence of all world affairs. The residence of the M.E. bishop of the area was moved from Baltimore to Washington following the death of Bishop AMES in 1879 and has since been located there.

Administratively, Washington is presently divided into three districts: Washington Central; Washington East; and Washington West, with each of these districts reaching out into contiguous Maryland territory in their respective directions. Latest statistics indicate that something like 90,000 Methodists are in the metropolitan Washington area north of the Potomac. The Alexandria and Washington Districts of the Virginia Conference across the River have also grown enormously of late years, and many Methodists, of course, live in those districts and work in Washington. Since 1940 Bishops ADNA LEONARD, EDWIN H. HUGHES, CHARLES W. FLINT, G. Bromley Oxnam, and JOHN WESLEY LORD have administered the Washington area with the Baltimore Conference, the overarching conference containing the District of Columbia.

Asbury Church for 132 years has stood at the corner of Eleventh and K Streets, Northwest, in Washington city. Asbury has sometimes been referred to as the "daughter" of Foundry Church, since in the years between 1814 when Foundry was organized and 1836 when Asbury Church began, there was a felt need for a separate church for the Negro membership in the city. Eli Neugent, Benjamin McCoy, and others sensed this need and had much to do with the selection of the site at the K Street corner. This came about in 1836, and Asbury began its development there in a frame building. An increasing membership came because the location was accessible to the many Negro people to whom it was expected to minister. In the same year the QUARTERLY CONFERENCE met and gave to the church its official name—Asbury Methodist Church —in honor of Francis Asbury. In 1845 membership had increased so greatly that a brick church was erected on the original site, and then in 1916 the present church was erected there.

From 1836 to 1863 the Board of Trustees was composed of both whites and Negroes. Only white pastors were at that time appointed to the church, and local Negro preachers were called on to assist them. In 1864, however, Negro trustees were elected to succeed the white trustees.

The Washington Annual Conference, which was a Conference of Negro churches and members, was organized on Oct. 27, 1864, in the Sharp Street Methodist Church in Baltimore, Md., and Asbury Church took its place in that. At that time Elisha P. Phelps was serving as pastor of both Foundry and Asbury. After the Washington Annual Conference organized, Asbury was continuously served by ministers of its own group. Among those were: J. M. Peck; JAMES THOMAS; E. W. S. Peck; N. M. CARROLL; J. H. Dailey; J. W. E. BOWEN—later a bishop; D. W. Hayes; I. L. Thomas; MATTHEW W. CLAIR, SR.— later a bishop; Julius S. Carroll; James U. King; J. H. Jenkins; Robert Moten Williams; and James D. Foy.

With the absorption of the Washington Conference in the surrounding Baltimore Conference, Asbury with other churches of that Conference in Maryland and the District of Columbia went into the Baltimore Conference—now of The United Methodist Church. The present membership of Asbury is 2,130.

Capitol Hill Church, completed and consecrated in June 1967, now stands five blocks from the United States Capitol, Washington, D. C., an imposing new church building. Its history is as follows:

After some groundwork by two district superintendents,

four Quarterly Conferences of Methodist churches within eleven blocks of the United States Capitol voted to combine in a city parish with one pastor and assistant. The plan was for the parish to give a united ministry to the area which was then starting a renaissance in remodeled homes, as it was then becoming fashionable to buy and remodel a house on Capitol Hill. Edward B. Lewis, then pastor of a large suburban church of Washington, was asked to come to Capitol Hill and help start the project. Thomas C. Starnes was the first assistant during the parish days. J. H. Searls followed him as assistant through the uniting and building days.

After three months as minister of the parish, the pastor presented to the four Official Boards a plan to unite the four churches into one within that conference year (1960-61). He challenged them to make a great Christian witness by uniting as one effective congregation on Capitol Hill. The vote was almost unanimous—only seven against out of more than 100 officials who were thus challenged.

The congregations continued to meet in their respective churches during that conference year until May 1961. The fifth Sunday of each month was a united morning worship. Advent and Lenten services were held together. Following disciplinary requirements, the congregations were united as one on April 30, 1961, using one building, Old Trinity, selected by a conference committee, for the site of the new building. Bishop John Wesley Lord presided in the uniting service with the District Superintendent Orris G. Robinson. The name selected was The Capitol Hill Methodist Church.

Plans then began for the new church. The three abandoned churches and parsonages were sold over a period of time to obtain money. The united congregation began growing with new spirit, and pledged enough over the following three years to make it possible to borrow the further needed funds. Fifth and Pennsylvania Avenue, S.E., at 421 Seward Square proved a good location. During the construction of the church building, the united congregation worshipped in the Methodist Building across the street from the Capitol, and beside The Supreme Court building. Three and four services were held in the little Methodist Building chapel with the large lobby also holding people listening through the public address system broadcast in each area. The congregation grew in numbers and popularity during these years. The Capitol Hill Community continued to attract new families and career people from the government, as well as students and professional people.

The new Capitol Hill Church enjoys large congregations with leading members of government attending the services. Its membership includes different races and national backgrounds. It serves all economic classes through education, community programs and Christian opportunities. Its program is attracting youth and young couples. Waugh, Trinity, North Carolina Avenue (M.P.), and Wilson Memorial were the four churches which united in this effective and promising way.

Dumbarton Avenue Church. In October 1772, the first Methodist sermon preached in Georgetown was delivered by ROBERT WILLIAMS, an Englishman who was an itinerant preacher, according to an account published in 1806 by William Watters, the first native American itinerant. Watters accompanied Williams on the occasion of his preaching in Georgetown, and the first meetings were held in a cooper's shop near N and 31st Streets.

Bishop Asbury's first visit appears to have been in the

DUMBARTON AVENUE CHURCH, WASHINGTON, D.C.

late fall of 1772 when he preached to a large number of slaves who were collected to hear him. From Asbury's *Journal* there is this notation about Georgetown, dated March 8, 1773: "I was also much comforted by a letter, which I lately received from RICHARD OWINGS part of which was as follows, 'I know not what it will come to. Almost every person seems to be under a religious concern. There are about twenty-two persons already joined in society at Seneca. At George-town, four have been lately enabled to rejoice in God; and one at Rock-creek. Blessed be GOD, who hath not forgotten to be gracious'."

On Dec. 24, 1772, ROBERT STRAWBRIDGE and Richard Owings were sent by Francis Asbury to build up the cause of Christ in Frederick County.

On Nov. 2, 1795, Bishop Asbury recorded in his *Journal* that he had come to Georgetown and "found a congregation waiting at the new chapel." This building was located on Montgomery (28th) Street near Bridge (M) Street. The "new chapel" was a simple brick building, thirty by forty feet, on a lot fifty-six by 120 feet. In 1806 this meeting house was enlarged to forty by sixty feet, and two stories high.

In subsequent years, Bishop Asbury made frequent journeys to Georgetown to visit the congregation and Henry Foxall. Foxall and Asbury were boyhood friends in Birmingham, England. Before becoming a Methodist minister, Asbury worked in Foxall's father's foundry in England.

In 1801 Thomas Lyle was appointed to Georgetown, which appears for the first time in the minutes, and which includes, also, the city of Washington. The Georgetown Church became a separate station in 1805 and reported the following year 202 members.

The church school has had a most interesting history.

In 1819 Samuel McKenny and John Dickinson, with other zealous Methodists, started a small school for the religious instruction of the young. Records of the church school from 1819, as well as records of the church from 1800, are in the archives of the Dumbarton Avenue Church.

In 1849 the building was sold to the municipal corporation of the town for $1,200 for use as a public school and a new church was built at 3133 Dumbarton Avenue. HENRY SLICER, then the pastor, visited many of the larger cities in the East, at the request of the official board, to solicit subscriptions, and he received many liberal contributions. The new church was dedicated July 3, 1850, when the pastor was JOHN LANAHAN.

During the years 1862-63 the church was used by the federal government as a hospital, and the congregation met in rooms of the old customs house over the post office on 31st Street. Soon after the building was reopened for worship the Baltimore Conference was in session there. The Washington *Star* of March 10, 1863, reports that President Lincoln was a visitor at the service on Sunday, March 8, 1863, (during this Conference) and that Bishop MATTHEW SIMPSON preached the sermon on that occasion.

In 1897-98 the building was completely remodeled, enlarged, and redecorated. A modern facade was built, new stained glass windows were installed in memory of honored and deceased members, and the organ was rebuilt and improved. The first level was restored in 1961.

The Dumbarton Avenue Church has become known as the Mother Church of Washington Methodism. Other churches of Washington which have their heritage in Dumbarton are Foundry, St. Luke's, Eldbrooke, Mt. Zion and Capitol Hill.

Foundry Church was the first Methodist church to be started in the central section of the city. The land and the first building were the gift of Henry Foxall, iron founder, Methodist lay preacher, frequent contributor to Methodist activities, and friend of Francis Asbury, Thomas Jefferson and many other religious and political leaders. Traditionally, he provided the new church, a few blocks from the White House, in gratitude and thanksgiving when his foundry was spared during the British attack on Washington in August 1814. The first church building was dedicated Sept. 10, 1815, by NICHOLAS SNETHEN. Foundry's name is derived from two sources, JOHN WESLEY's "Old Foundery" in London and Foxall's foundry in the Georgetown section of the District of Columbia.

After nearly ninety years Foundry's first location became principally a business district, and the church moved in 1904 to a more residential area, its present site at 16th and P Streets, Northwest, approximately one-half mile north of the White House. The present church is Gothic in style. A modern educational building of matching stone and architecture was added in 1961. The McDowell Pulpit, whose design and beauty is much commented on, was the gift of Methodists throughout the United States in memory of Bishop WILLIAM F. McDOWELL. The lectern, symbolic of unification of the three branches of Methodism in 1939, is in memory of Bishop EDWIN HOLT HUGHES.

From the first, Foundry's congregation has included among its worshippers many who have worked for the Federal Government—from lowly clerks to cabinet officers—as well as many senators, congressmen and presidents. Most of the presidents since John Quincy Adams have attended Foundry one or more times. Abraham Lincoln became a life director of the Methodist Missionary

FOUNDRY CHURCH PULPIT, WASHINGTON, D.C.

Society on Jan. 18, 1863, after hearing a missionary sermon by Bishop Matthew Simpson. Lincoln's certificate of membership is on display in the church. Rutherford B. Hayes attended Foundry nearly every Sunday during his administration. Franklin D. Roosevelt and Winston Churchill attended a special Christmas day service in 1941. In addition many ambassadors, students and visitors from around the world have participated in the church's activities.

Among the ministers at Foundry, FREDERICK BROWN HARRIS served the longest, thirty-one years (1924-55). In addition he was Chaplain of the U.S. Senate for many years. Three other Foundry pastors have served as chaplains of the Senate and the House of Representatives for shorter periods of time. Theodore Henry Palmquist's ministry from 1955 to 1964 was the second longest. Three Foundry pastors have been elected bishops. These were JOHN EMORY, JESSE T. PECK and LUTHER B. WILSON, who were at Foundry in 1818-20, 1852-54 and 1900-03, respectively.

Pastors and members have had important roles in social problems at times. For instance, Henry Slicer's sermon on duelling in 1839 has been credited with passage of legislation which outlawed duels in the District of Columbia. After many decades of participation in various temperance movements, members of Foundry helped to establish the American Anti-Saloon League in 1896.

Foundry's varied programs have included a Sabbath school started in 1819, a missionary society in 1828, a drama group in 1934, an opportunity class for handicapped children in 1962, and a pastoral counseling service, since expanded into an area wide service, in 1961. Members of Foundry started or helped to form at least six new congregations in Washington—one M.P. and five M.E. churches—during the nineteenth century.

The neighborhood has changed where Foundry is located. Upper middle class, one-family residences have given way to rooming houses for government employees. Later they became homes for some of Washington's more impoverished citizens. Multiple story apartment buildings and headquarters for trade and professional organizations are following these. The Foundry membership of 1,723 (1970) is drawn not only from the immediate neighborhood but the more remote sections of the District of Columbia and suburban communities in Virginia and Maryland. The church has continued to be influential through its mission, concern and outreach.

Georgetown is a restored pre-Revolutionary town which has been engulfed but not lost in the nation's capital. The historic town lies approximately one mile and a quarter west-northwest of the White House. The old part of the town is nearly a mile square. On the west lies Georgetown University; to the north is famous Dumbarton Oaks; on the east are Rock Creek and The Potomac Parkway; and to the south are The National Monument Canal and The Potomac River.

Georgetown was settled late in the seventeenth century. It was laid out as a town in 1751, chartered as a city by the Maryland Assembly in 1789, merged into the District of Columbia in 1871, and annexed to the city of Washington in 1878.

To perpetuate the historic town, the eighty-first congress passed legislation in 1950 to preserve the character of this section of Washington, D. C. Hence it was to be known as "Old Georgetown." Furthermore, legislation was passed regulating the height, exterior design and construction of all private and semi-public buildings in the area to conform with the colonial and federal homes which are there.

For the beginning of Methodism in Georgetown, see Dumbarton Avenue Church above.

Methodism as has been indicated grew very slowly in Georgetown until the 1790's when the construction began on the site for the national government, Washington, D. C. Georgetown became the residence for the planners and many of the workers who were building the new city. During Asbury's visits to Georgetown he was usually entertained by Lloyd Beall and Henry Foxall, two very prominent members of the church. Foxall was mayor of Georgetown from 1821-23. A close friend and neighbor of Foxall was Francis Scott Key, who wrote the National Anthem in 1814.

Methodism continued to grow in Georgetown with the establishment of Mt. Zion in 1816, a Negro congregation; Congress Street M.P. Church, 1829; Mt. Tabor M.P., 1874; and Aldersgate M.E. South, 1914. Subsequently the Congress Street, Mt. Tabor and Aldersgate Churches merged to become in 1946 St. Luke's Church, which is located a few blocks northwest of "Old Georgetown." The mother church, Dumbarton Avenue, and Mt. Zion are the two remaining churches in the old Georgetown section.

Although Methodism continued to be strong in Georgetown up until 1945, the town became less significant from 1860 until the renovation of the old federal and colonial homes began in the 1930's. This restoration of the town continued until most of the city had been completely restored by 1960.

In addition to attracting some of the major leaders of our nation to reside in Georgetown during the 1960's, many young people began frequenting the town by 1964. The major ministry of Dumbarton Avenue Church in

Georgetown in the latter part of the 1960's was to the youth and young adults.

Methodism has had a significant role in one of America's oldest existing towns, "Old Georgetown."

Metropolitan Memorial has long been considered a church of connection-wide import. Old Washingtonians used to call it "the church of the Presidents" because Presidents U. S. Grant and William McKinley were wont to attend services there.

A movement to erect this church began in 1852 at the session of the GENERAL CONFERENCE of the M.E. Church with a memorial "touching the erection of a house of worship in Washington city." This memorial was approved and the members present voiced their intention to aid in its promotion. The Baltimore Conference meeting the next year, appointed one of their leaders, Henry Slicer, to solicit funds. On Oct. 23, 1854, the cornerstone was laid at the corner of John Marshall Place and C Street, Northwest. Bishop Matthew Simpson delivered the address. Due to the Civil War the building was not completed until 1869. The building then erected was a churchly one in every respect, large and imposing with a tall steeple. It was one of the landmarks of Washington during the last half of the nineteenth century. Not too far from the capitol, the building dominated the region at and around the lower end of Pennsylvania Avenue, and was frequently used for meetings of church-wide import.

On Feb. 28, 1869 Bishop Simpson dedicated the church in the presence of a large congregation from all parts of the country. On Easter Sunday, March 28, 1869, the church was formally declared organized with JOHN P. NEWMAN as minister. Ninety-four persons were received by letter and three on probation. In the congregation at this service were the President of the United States Ulysses S. Grant; the Vice-President Schuyler Colfax; the Chief Justice of the Supreme Court, Salmon P. Chase, and many members of Congress. President Grant was the first chairman of the Board of Trustees, and occupied the Presidential Pew for eight years.

Newman was three times appointed pastor of Metropolitan, and was elected bishop in 1888 while still its minister. Another minister of Metropolitan was later elected bishop, FRANK M. BRISTOL, who served the church ten years before being elevated to the episcopacy in 1908.

In "Old Metropolitan" Bishop JOHN F. HURST publicly presented the plan for American University on March 25, 1890. In October of 1891 the Second ECUMENICAL METHODIST CONFERENCE was held in the church with delegates from every quarter of the world in attendance. President Benjamin Harrison addressed the Conference. From 1897-1901 President William McKinley regularly attended the services of the church. He always stayed for communion and insisted on kneeling at the altar rail with others just as they happened to come from nearby pews.

In 1930 a shifting population made it desirable to relocate. The present site was selected in northwest Washington opposite American University, and on June 22 ground was broken for a new sanctuary. Bishop William Fraser McDowell presided over this building's dedication on Feb. 7, 1932. The then Vice-President of the United States, Charles Curtis, was the speaker. In 1951 the Parish Hall was constructed and dedicated by Bishop CHARLES WESLEY FLINT and Dr. EDWARD G. LATCH.

Increased membership and attendance at Sunday morning worship services soon made it imperative that the sanctuary be enlarged, and the church was extended forward four bays, making it possible to seat 900 to 1,000 persons at each service. The present sanctuary was dedicated Feb. 22, 1959, by Bishop G. Bromley Oxnam.

Wall tablets memorialize Presidents Grant and McKinley as well as many other prominent national figures. Worked into the chancel floor is a marble tile brought from the ruins of Solomon's Temple by Bishop Newman. A Keystone originally over the pulpit in Old Metropolitan was cut from a stone also brought from the ruins of Solomon's Temple. This Keystone is now on the east wall of the Baptistry. The present pulpit and altar rail were made in part from olive wood from the Garden of Gethsemane and Mount of Olives and cedar wood from Mt. Lebanon. This wood was brought from the Holy Land in rough logs.

In recent years Metropolitan, along with American University and Wesley Seminary, entertained the Northeastern JURISDICTIONAL CONFERENCE in 1960; and the Baltimore Conference held its annual sessions here in 1948, 1964, 1965, 1966 and 1969. In 1970 the membership was 2,648. There are four full-time ministers on the staff plus a part-time Seminary student. The annual budget is in excess of $280,000.

MOUNT VERNON PLACE CHURCH, WASHINGTON, D.C.

Mount Vernon Place Church was founded in 1850 as the "Representative Church" of the M.E. Church, South, in the Nation's Capital. William W. Bennett served a year as the pastor, later distinguishing himself in Southern Methodism as a minister and as a historian. During 1851 the forty-five member congregation organized a Sunday school, and purchased a building from another Protestant church, which bequeathed its communion service. Six years later the church sold the building and moved into temporary quarters until 1863, when it constructed its own edifice.

This Southern congregation worshipped as well as it could during the Civil War. In 1865 William V. Tudor, an urbane young bachelor, became the minister and revitalized the church. A new building was erected in 1869. The church named itself Mount Vernon Place in 1872.

Outstanding preachers filled the pulpit during the next several decades, among them ALPHEUS W. WILSON, later a bishop, and FORREST J. PRETTYMAN. Samuel W. Haddaway organized the first mission church.

The years 1858 and 1918 had a mutual significance. At its General Conference of 1858, the M.E. Church, South, passed a "memorial" that a Representative Church should be erected in Washington, D. C. This new edifice was occupied during 1918, and came to full power under the pastorate of CLOVIS G. CHAPPELL.

Six pastors served within the next two decades, including W. ANGIE SMITH (1934-36), one of four Mount Vernon ministers who later became bishops. During the Depression of the 1930's a Relief Committee was organized to help the homeless and the hungry.

Two pastors served between 1936 and 1966. Both advocated a full continuous program, and each added a new educational building. JOHN W. RUSTIN (1936-50) inspired government and military personnel to make Mount Vernon their church home while in Washington during World War II, and encouraged the creative use of drama in the Church through a group known as the Mount Vernon Players. Later ALBERT P. SHIRKEY (1950-69), led Mount Vernon Place Church in its ministry as a downtown church to meet the problems of the changing urban community, regardless of race. Mount Vernon is one of the outstanding churches of the National Capital Area and of Methodism.

J. E. Armstrong, *Old Baltimore Conference.* 1907.
Edison M. Amos, ed., *190th Anniversary of the Founding of Methodism in the Nation's Capital.* Washington, D.C.: Georgetown Printing, 1962.
Lillian Brooks Brown, *A Living Centennial Commemorating the One Hundredth Anniversary of Metropolitan Memorial United Methodist Church.* Washington, D.C.: Judd & Detweiler, 1969.
Homer L. Calkin, *Castings from the Foundry Mold: A History of Foundry Church, Washington, D.C., 1814-1964.* 1964.
Lloyd G. Davis, *A Brief History of the Founding of Methodism in Georgetown.* Washington, D.C.: Dumbarton Avenue Methodist Church, 1898.
James Ewin, *Foundry, 1814-1914.* Washington, 1914.
The Georgetowner, Vol. 7, No. 67.
General Minutes, 1970.
The Iron Worker, Vol. XXV, No. 1, Winter 1960-61. Lynchburg, Va.: Lynchburg Foundry Company, 1961.
Rosenberger, Francis Coleman, ed., *Records of The Columbia Historical Society of Washington, D.C., 1960-1962.* Washington, D.C.: The Society, 1963.
Souvenir Journal, 130th Anniversary, Asbury United Methodist Church.
N. B. H.
FRANK L. WILLIAMS
EDWARD BRADLEY LEWIS
EDISON M. AMOS
HOMER L. CALKIN
MILTON B. CRIST
ROYCE L. THOMPSON

WASHINGTON, MISSISSIPPI, U.S.A., in the southern part of the state six miles from the Mississippi River, was laid off by Andrew Ellicott near a spring known since that time as Ellicott Spring. Here in 1799 the first Methodist congregation was formed by TOBIAS GIBSON, missionary from SOUTH CAROLINA. This consisted of Randal Gibson and his wife, William Foster and his wife, Caleb Worley, and Sarah Bullen, with some others who joined before the organization was fully perfected in the spring of 1800. The Washington church organization, which is the oldest in Mississippi, has worshiped in three buildings, the first a union structure, built in 1805 and burned

in 1810; the second inside the campus of Jefferson College, in which the Mississippi constitutional convention of 1817 was held; and the present building, which was constructed in 1827-28. This last is now the second oldest Methodist building in Mississippi.

Jefferson College, later known as Jefferson Military Academy, was chartered in 1802 and opened for students in 1811. This school continued until 1962. Elizabeth Academy was opened for students in 1818, and was one of the first schools for the higher education of young women in the United States. It continued its useful career until around 1845.

Washington was the territorial capital at the time of the formation of the state government and was the capital of Mississippi for a number of years. The first station on the Natchez Trace out of Natchez was at Washington, and the building still stands just back of the Methodist church. The oldest Presbyterian church in Mississippi, now at Pine Ridge, was organized at Washington in 1807.

J. B. Cain, *The Cradle of Mississippi Methodism.* Natchez, Miss.: n.p., 1920.
J. G. Jones, *Mississippi Conference.* 1887, 1908.   J. B. CAIN

WASSON, ALFRED WASHINGTON (1880-1964), American missionary to Korea and Mission Board Secretary, was born near Fayetteville, Ark., May 7, 1880. He graduated from the University of Arkansas in 1902, and received his B.D. from VANDERBILT University in 1905, going to KOREA the same year.

He was admitted on trial in the China Annual Conference under the missionary rule—which waives certain normal training requirements. From 1905 to 1922 he served as head of the Songdo High School (originally Anglo-Korean School) and did evangelistic work in the Songdo area. From 1922 to 1926 he was president of the Union Methodist Theological Seminary in Seoul.

In 1926 he became Professor of Missions and comparative religion in the PERKINS SCHOOL OF THEOLOGY at Southern Methodist University. From 1934 to 1940 he was foreign secretary of the Board of MISSIONS of the M.E. Church, South, at Nashville. With the union of Methodism in 1939, he became Associate Secretary for missions in Latin America for the Board of Missions of The Methodist Church with headquarters in New York City.

Wasson was a delegate to the Madras Conference of the INTERNATIONAL MISSIONARY COUNCIL in 1938, and to the Foreign Missions Conference of North America, 1934-50; he was chairman of the Committee on Cooperation in Latin America, 1940-50; a member of the FEDERAL COUNCIL Committee on Religious Work in the Canal Zone, 1940-50, and was delegate to the General Conference (MES), 1926 and the UNITING CONFERENCE of Methodism in 1939.

Coming to New York as he did in 1940, when the mission work of the Southern Church had to be consolidated into the new world-wide empire of American Methodism, Wasson had considerable pioneering work to do in his new executive position. He was a quiet man of singular sweetness of spirit, consecrated to his work and unflagging in carrying out any task the church gave him.

He served as visiting professor during the summers of 1947-49, at GARRETT BIBLICAL INSTITUTE. Retiring in 1950 he returned to DALLAS, where he was visiting professor at Perkins School of Theology, 1950-52. He filled the same role at SCARRITT COLLEGE in Nashville in the spring quarters of 1951-53.

He was author of *Church Growth in Korea,* 1934; the *Invincible Advance,* 1938; and *Influence of Missionary Expansion Upon Methodist Organization,* 1948.

He held an LL.D. degree from the University of Arkansas, 1926, and a Ph.D. from the University of Chicago, 1931.

He died in Dallas, Texas, on Sept. 6, 1964, and was buried in Hillcrest Memorial Park.

Clark and Stafford, *Who's Who in Methodism.* 1952.
Who's Who in America, 1946-47.   CHARLES A. SAUER

WATCHMAN, THE, the first British Methodist newspaper, begun in 1834 to defend Wesleyan Methodism against the attacks of reformers, and continuing as a conservative weekly until 1885. (See MAGAZINES AND NEWSPAPERS OF BRITISH METHODISM.)

WATCH-NIGHT. The first watch-night service was held at Kingswood, England, sometime prior to April 1742. "The custom was begun at Kingswood by the colliers there, who, before their conversion, used to spend every Saturday night at the ale-house. After they were taught better, they spent that night in prayer. Mr. WESLEY hearing of it, ordered it first to be once a month, at the full of the moon, then once a quarter, and recommended it to all his Societies." (Myles, p. 17.)

John Wesley's account of Watch-night is: "I was informed, that several persons at Kingswood, frequently met together, at the school, and (when they could spare the time) spent the greater part of the night in prayer and praise and thanksgiving. Some advised me to put an end to this; but upon weighing the thing thoroughly, and comparing it with the practice of the ancient Christians, I could see no cause to forbid it. Rather, I believed, it might be made of more general use. So I sent them word, 'I designed to watch with them, on the Friday nearest the full of the moon, that we might have light thither and back again.' I gave public notice of this, the Sunday before, and withal, that I intended to preach, desiring they, and they only, would meet me there, who could do it without prejudice to their business or families. On Friday abundance of people came. I began preaching between eight and nine, and we continued until a little beyond the noon of night, singing, praying and praising God." (*Ibid.*)

Wesley explained his position more fully in a letter written at Limerick June 8, 1750 to the Rev. John Baily of Kilcully, Cork: "You charge me fourthly, with holding 'midnight assemblies.' Sir, did you never see the word Vigil in your Common Prayer Book? Do you know what it means? If not, permit me to tell you that it was customary with the ancient Christians to spend whole nights in prayer, and these nights were termed *Vigiliae* or Vigils. Therefore, for spending a part of some nights in this manner, in public and solemn prayer, we have not only the authority of our own national Church, but of the universal Church in the earliest ages." (*Letters,* Vol. III, 287.)

In his *Journal* Wesley writes under the date of April 9, 1742, "We had the first Watch-night in London." In 1789 it was stated that "every watch-night should be held until midnight."

Watch-Night in America. On Thursday, Nov. 1, 1770

the first watch-night service in America was held at Old ST. GEORGE'S, PHILADELPHIA by JOSEPH PILMORE. Another Watch-night Service was held in NEW YORK on November 5, and a third such service was held in Philadelphia on December 31, the first time that a watch-night was held on New Year's Eve in America. According to Asbury's *Journal* a watch-night service was held also at Old St. George's on Nov. 4, 1771. It was not until sometime later that the service began to be held exclusively on New Year's Eve.

Francis H. Tees records the following story about an historic watch-night service. In the year 1776 George Washington was hard pressed for funds to keep his struggling Revolutionary Army together at Valley Forge. "He wrote to his friend, Robert Morris, banker and merchant, of Philadelphia, beseeching him to send him $50,000 in cash . . . . on Wednesday morning, Jan. 1, 1777, long before daylight, Morris set out for the homes of his friends, roused them from their beds and finally got the money which he sent to Washington." (p. 149)

Tees claims there is sufficient circumstantial evidence to prove that Morris "told his friends that he had just come from an all night prayer meeting in St. George's Methodist Church where prayers were offered that God would open up the hearts of the people to furnish the money needed to pay the troops at Valley Forge that the Army might be saved." (p. 149)

Watch-night services have been held continuously at Old St. George's since that first service in 1770.

W. Myles, *Chronological History.* 1799.
F. H. Tees, *Methodist Origins.* 1948.
J. Wesley, *Letters.* 1931.
J. Wesley, *Works.* 1829-31.   FREDERICK E. MASER

WATERBURY, CONNECTICUT, U.S.A., is a city of 107,000 and is in the NEW YORK CONFERENCE of The United Methodist Church. It began as a plantation known as Mattatuck, established in the Naugatuck Valley by young men from the Farmington Colony, on land purchased from the Indians. Articles of agreement were signed on June 6, 1674 whereby each man agreed to live four years at Mattatuck, pay his taxes and build a mansion house of sufficient size, in return for eight acres of land on the town spot and a certain amount of meadow land.

In Bishop ASBURY's *Journal,* dated Sept. 23, 1796, he mentions preaching in the Separatist Meeting House located in that part of ancient Waterbury known as "Columbia." A Methodist class, numbering five persons, was formed in the Pine Hole District of Waterbury, in the summer of 1815, by Samuel Cochrane, preacher in charge of the Litchfield Circuit. This was the beginning of First Methodist Church. Mrs. Mary Peck, a member, invited those living in the center to hold their meetings in her small red house. When attendance increased, meetings were sometimes held in school houses. The first Methodist sermon in the center is said to have been preached in a hotel ballroom.

Following a revival in 1830, membership increased to about 100. School houses were no longer available for religious purposes and it became necessary to erect a house of worship. For a long time it was impossible to get anyone to sell a lot to the Methodists. It was argued that the Methodists wherever they gained a foothold "were like Canada thistles—they were sure to spread and could not be kept down." It was "easier to keep them out than to root them out when once in." Finally a lot was obtained and the first house of worship was built. In the spring of 1833, Davis Stocking was appointed as the first of a long line of stationed preachers.

In 1850 the congregation had grown so large that a lot had to be purchased and the second house of worship erected. In this new home the church enjoyed twenty-four years of marked activity and steady growth. Missions were started by consecrated laymen who went into outlying districts. The Waterville mission was started in 1872 and a chapel built there in 1875. In 1884 this mission was deeded to the trustees of the Grace Methodist Church, without encumbrance.

A Sunday school started in August 1886, in a vacant store, was the beginning of St. Paul's Church. In 1886 Timothy Church, a trustee in First Church, gave a lot on the west side of the Naugatuck River to the people of that section for a church. Services were first held in a vacant store about 1916. Timothy Church's lot was sold and a larger lot purchased. Work was begun in 1931 on the West Side Hill Church. Unavoidable circumstances delayed completion of the building and services could not be held there until 1941.

In 1876 Anson F. Abbott, a member of the First Church, offered a lot on the corner of North Main Street and Abbott Avenue as a free gift, without conditions except to build a church thereon. The offer was accepted and the present First Church edifice was dedicated in May 1878.

In 1970 there were two United Methodist churches with a total membership of 899 in a city which is more than seventy percent Roman Catholic. Representing the Negro Methodists is the Mount Olive A.M.E. Zion Church.

Difficult decisions must be made by the Methodist churches, but the Waterbury people, with the tradition that is behind them, expect to face and overcome contemporary obstacles.

Minutes of the New York East Conference.
M. Simpson, Cyclopaedia. 1882. Gratia Booth

WATERHOUSE, RICHARD GREEN (1855-1922), American

bishop of the M.E. Church, South, was born near Spring City, Tenn., on Dec. 4, 1855. He joined the Holston Conference in 1878 and served the Altamont and Spencer Mission, and Jonesboro. In 1881 he was junior preacher on the Abingdon Circuit and during his tenure there he attended Emory and Henry College, from which he graduated in 1885. Then he served Centenary and Church Street Churches in Knoxville and the Radford District.

In 1892 he became a professor in Emory and Henry and the following year he was elected president, occupying this position until 1910. He was a member of all the General Conferences from 1894 to 1910.

In 1910 he was elected a bishop and assigned to the Pacific Coast with headquarters at Los Angeles. Here he remained four years. Then he returned to the Holston Conference and presided over it in 1915 and 1916. Ill health forced his retirement in 1918.

Waterhouse married Miss Carrie Steele of Crystal Springs, Miss., on Feb. 3, 1887, and on her death he married Mrs. Mary Thomas Carriger of Morristown, Tenn., on Oct. 10, 1894. He was the father of a daughter and two sons. He died as the result of an automobile accident

at Knoxville on Dec. 8, 1922, and was buried at Jefferson City, Tenn.

Journal of the Holston Conference, 1923.
I. P. Martin, Holston. 1945. L. W. Pierce

WATERLOO, IOWA, U.S.A. First Church is a mid-city

church. Asbury Collins preached the first sermon there the fall of 1846 in a log cabin on the west bank of the Cedar River. Three emigrant wagons had arrived and the people owning them settled there.

The church was known as "Big Woods Mission" in 1853. This was one year before Waterloo was platted. In 1855 the church was moved from the log cabin to the Waterloo Seminary, corner of Eighth and Bluff Streets. In 1856 services were transferred to the newly built Benight's Hall, corner of Fourth and Commercial Streets. In 1861 the First Methodist parsonage was erected, valued at $1,650.

In 1863 the First Church was erected. Only the basement was finished. In 1864 the first Annual Conference was held here in the basement of the church. A new church was built in 1889 at the corner of Fifth and Jefferson Streets. Valuation of this church was $16,500. Crowded conditions made it necessary to build the present building at West Fourth and Randolph in 1911. The church was dedicated on March 5th of that year. On the night before the dedication the building caught fire near the organ, and about $20,000 damage was done. The dedication was thereupon held at the Syndicate Theater. The church was erected at a cost of $75,000, and had a seating capacity of 1,500 in the sanctuary. The present education building was dedicated May 4, 1951.

In 1970 First Church had 2,319 members and property valued at $1,000,000.

WATERS, EDWARD (1780-1847), American bishop of the

A.M.E. Church, was born near West River, Md., on March 15, 1780. A former slave, he was converted in 1798 and licensed to preach in 1810 by the M.E. Church. He was ordained a Deacon in 1818 and an Elder in 1820. He itinerated from 1820 to 1836, when he was elected bishop by the A.M.E. Church. He resigned in 1844 and died June 5, 1847.

Edward Waters was actually an "assistant" bishop. He never held an annual conference or ordained a minister. The first college for Negroes in the State of Florida, Edward Waters College, was named in his honor.

R. R. Wright, The Bishops. 1963. Grant S. Shockley

WATERS, FRANCIS B. (1792-1868), American minister

and educator, was born on Jan. 16, 1792, in Somerset, now Wicomico, County, Md. He graduated from Pennsylvania College at eighteen years of age. He gave up law for the ministry and was licensed to preach while yet a youth. At twenty-six years of age he was made president of Washington College, serving at this time for five years, and after an interim of connections with other institutions of learning and periods of preaching he accepted a second election to the presidency of Washington College. At the age of thirty he received the D.D. degree from Washington College.

Waters was also a contributor to religious periodicals and was one of the founders of the M.P. Church, being president of the Convention that gave the new church its

Constitution and Discipline in 1830. It was at his suggestion that the name Methodist Protestant Church was adopted. He was president of the GENERAL CONFERENCES of 1846 and 1862.

Waters was married twice, first to Margaret Chairs of Queen Anne's County, Md., in 1818; and in 1833 he married Elizabeth Chairs, sister of his former wife. He died on April 23, 1868, and is buried in Baltimore.

T. H. Colhouer, *Sketches of the Founders*. 1880.
M. Simpson, *Cyclopaedia*. 1878.   ANN G. SILER

WATERS, GEORGE STWIRE (1842-1924), American Indian minister, was born May 7, 1842, near Astoria, Ore. He was a full-blooded American Indian of the Klickitat Tribe, and was educated in the Fort Simcoe Indian School conducted by JAMES H. WILBUR and the Chemawa Indian School near SALEM, Ore. He returned home to Fort Simcoe where Wilbur gave him instruction in Bible and other subjects preparing him for the Christian ministry.

He was received on trial in the OREGON CONFERENCE of the M.E. Church in 1869 and became a full member of that Conference and was ordained DEACON by Bishop E. S. JANES in 1871. He was a charter member of the COLUMBIA RIVER CONFERENCE when it was organized in 1874. All his appointments were to the Simcoe Indian Mission or missionary at large.

Waters was a successful pastor and an efficient evangelist to the Indians of WASHINGTON, OREGON and IDAHO. He was especially remembered by the Nez Perce Indians among whom he, and his brother Joe Stwire (the noted Chief, White Swan), and THOMAS PEARNE held a revival meeting in which more than 300 were converted and added to the church.

His mother had heard the preaching of JASON LEE at The Dalles, Oregon, and was very glad to have her son go to school and be a minister.

He died May 13, 1924, and was buried in the White Swan Methodist Cemetery, a part of the land donated to the Methodist Church by Chief White Swan for church, camp meeting and cemetery.

Journals of the Oregon and Columbia River Conferences, 1855-1924.
Papers at Indian Agency, Toppenish, Wash.
                                        CHARLES T. HATTEN

WATKIN, JAMES (1805-1886), New Zealand Methodist minister, was born at Manchester, England. Entering the ministry in 1830 he served some years in Tonga and later in New South Wales. While in Tonga he wrote a pamphlet called *Pity Poor Fee-Jee*, which not only inspired many to offer for missionary work, but has been described as "one of the most precious and fruitful bits of missionary literature ever given to the world."

In 1840, he transferred to the New Zealand Mission and was appointed to Waikouaiti, where the presence of a missionary had been requested by the well-known whaler and storekeeper, John Jones. From this base, Watkin made extensive journeys throughout the area in his pastoral care, which, after the withdrawal of Samuel Ironside from CLOUDY BAY in 1843, stretched from the Seaward Kaikouras to Stewart Island. Under his influence J. F. H. Wohlers of the German Mission settled at Ruapuke Island in Foveaux Strait and labored there for forty years. Watkin was replaced at Waikouaiti by CHARLES CREED in 1844.

He later returned to Australia where he became president of the General Conference in 1862. In 1869 he became a supernumerary and spent his retirement near Sydney until his death on May 14, 1886. He was buried at Rookwood, New South Wales.

D. J. D. Hickman, *Before 1848 and After*. Wesley Historical Society, New Zealand, 1948.   L. R. M. GILMORE

WATKIN, WILLIAM JAMES (1833-1909), New Zealand Methodist minister, was the son of JAMES WATKIN, early Wesleyan missionary to both Tonga and New Zealand. Entering the ministry in 1857 he became much sought after as a preacher for special occasions. Though possessed of a ready wit, he was an excessively modest man and labored in many hard country circuits.

During the years 1882-84 he was principal of Wesley College and in 1889 was elected president of the New Zealand Wesleyan Conference. In 1893 he superannuated and spent his declining years as a most effective preacher in the Onehunga and adjoining circuits until his death on Sept. 28, 1909.

New Zealand Methodist Conference Minutes, 1910.
                                        WESLEY A. CHAMBERS

WATKINS, ALEXANDER FARRAR (1856-1929), American minister and educator, was born in Natchez, Miss., on Dec. 18, 1856, a son of W. H. and Elizabeth Jones WATKINS. He attended CENTENARY COLLEGE, then received the A.B. degree at VANDERBILT UNIVERSITY.

He was licensed to preach in 1880, was admitted to the MISSISSIPPI CONFERENCE where he served the following appointments; First Church, JACKSON; Crawford Street Church, VICKSBURG; president of Whitworth College (two years); Financial Secretary of the Superannuate Endowment Fund (a connectional appointment); presiding elder of Jackson District; First Church, Hattiesburg; president of MILLSAPS COLLEGE (twelve years); First Church, Yazoo City; Central, MERIDIAN; and Brookhaven.

Watkins was secretary of the Mississippi Conference for twenty-eight years. He was a member of the General BOARD OF MISSIONS (MES) from 1906 until his death. He was eight times a delegate to the GENERAL CONFERENCE, and was secretary of the General Conference from 1906 until his death. In 1908 he was named a delegate to the Federal Council of Churches. In 1911 he was a member of the ECUMENICAL METHODIST CONFERENCE in Toronto, Canada. He served on the Committee of Fifteen to draft a Constitution for the M.E. Church, South, which, however, failed of adoption.

In June 1892 he married Lula Gaulding of Arkadelphia, Ark. Seven children were born to them. Death came to him on July 26, 1929, at Brookhaven, Miss. He was buried at Jackson, Miss.

Journal of the Mississippi Conference, 1929.
New Orleans Christian Advocate, 1929.   J. A. LINDSEY

WATKINS, OWEN (1842-1915), Wesleyan Methodist minister, pioneer missionary and first chairman of the TRANSVAAL and SWAZILAND District, SOUTH AFRICA, was born at Worsley, near Manchester, England, on July 17, 1842, and was accepted for the Wesleyan ministry in 1863. He was sent to RICHMOND COLLEGE to be a missionary student but ill health compelled him to remain in England. However, after a later illness his doctors advised

OWEN WATKINS

removal to South Africa and his missionary vocation at last found fulfillment. He was sent to Pietermaritzburg, NATAL, in 1876 and served as secretary of the Natal Synod until his appointment as chairman and general superintendent of the newly constituted Transvaal and Swaziland District in 1880. Watkins adopted the strategy of WILLIAM SHAW and proposed to extend three chains of missions into Central Africa from Swaziland in the east, Pretoria in the center and Bechuanaland in the west. This plan was not fully carried out, but he travelled indefatigably throughout the Transvaal laying the foundations of a thriving work. Assisted by colleagues such as GEORGE WEAVIND he made contact with African evangelists who had independently begun Methodist work (see TRANSVAAL AFRICAN PIONEERS), purchased a number of mission farms such as Kilnerton and provided pastoral care for white communities, especially along the newly-discovered Witwatersrand gold reef. His address at the May Meetings in 1884 and his fascinating reports aroused much interest and enthusiasm in England.

In 1891 he was sent north with Isaac Shimmin to establish missions in Mashonaland (part of RHODESIA) which was being opened up by Cecil Rhodes and his Chartered Company. Rhodes had earlier promised assistance, and Watkins obtained three mission farms and stands in the new townships of Salisbury and Umtali. Leaving Shimmin at Umtali, he walked 200 miles to the east coast port of Beira, contracted fever en route, and arrived home in PRETORIA on the point of death.

Watkins was sent to England to recuperate and in 1892 was elected to the Legal Hundred. He hoped to return to Africa and to lead a Wesleyan advance across the Zambesi, but his wish was not granted and he spent the rest of his ministry in British circuits.

A man of strong personality, iron will and great ability to adapt himself to demanding situations, Watkins was one of the greatest missionaries to serve in South Africa. He died on Dec. 22, 1915 and was honored by a special resolution of the 1916 Conference.

L. A. Hewson, South Africa. 1950.
Journal of the Methodist Historical Society of South Africa, Vol. II, No. 7 (April 1957), III, No. 2 (October 1958), and III, No. 3 (February 1960).
Minutes of the British Wesleyan Conference, 1916.
J. Whiteside, South Africa. 1906.   D. G. L. CRAGG

WATKINS, WILLIAM HAMILTON (1815-1881), American minister and leader of MISSISSIPPI Methodism, was born in Jefferson County, Miss., April 11, 1815, one of several children of Asa and Sarah Watkins. He joined Cane Ridge Church in September 1831, and was soon after given a license to preach and recommended for admission into the MISSISSIPPI CONFERENCE, which came about in 1835. During his long ministry he served pastorates in NATCHEZ, VICKSBURG, JACKSON, Woodville, and NEW ORLEANS, as well as a term of service as presiding elder of the NATCHEZ District. He was for one year president of CENTENARY COLLEGE, then at Jackson, La., and also principal of the Woodville Female Seminary in connection with his pastorate at that place. Centenary College conferred upon him the honorary D.D. degree; he is said to have been the first native Mississippian ever to receive this degree. He was a member of the LOUISVILLE CONVENTION in 1845 that organized the M.E. CHURCH, SOUTH; and in 1866, 1870, and 1878 he was a member of the GENERAL CONFERENCE.

Watkins was married on Dec. 18, 1842 to Mrs. Elizabeth Johnson in New Orleans. Two of their sons became ministers, ALEXANDER F. WATKINS, for twelve years president of MILLSAPS COLLEGE, and Calvin C. Watkins. A grandson, Herbert B. Watkins, was a member of the Mississippi Conference, and a granddaughter, Janie Watkins, was a missionary to CHINA.

William H. Watkins died on Feb. 5, 1881, at his home in Jackson; his final resting place was in the historic Cane Ridge cemetery in Jefferson County.

J. G. Jones, Mississippi Conference. 1887, 1908.
Journal of the Mississippi Conference, 1881.
T. L. Mellen, In Memoriam: Life and Labors of the Rev. William Hamilton Watkins. 1886.   J. B. CAIN

WATKINS, WILLIAM TURNER (1895-1961), American editor, and bishop, was born at Maysville, Ga., May 26, 1895. Of Welsh origin, his family came to America in the eighteenth century. They settled first in Maryland and Virginia, one ancestor moving to GEORGIA about the time of the Revolution. Reared in a dedicated home, joining the country church in childhood, called to preach in early youth, he moved on to become a teacher of church history at EMORY UNIVERSITY, Atlanta, Ga.

He was educated at YOUNG HARRIS COLLEGE and Emory, Ph.B., 1926; D.D., 1939; student at Edinburgh University, Scotland, 1926-27; Yale Divinity School, New Haven, Conn., 1927-28. He was awarded the honorary D.D. by Union College, 1949. He married Frances Edith Hancock, Jan. 21, 1914, and they had five children.

Watkins joined the NORTH GEORGIA CONFERENCE in 1914, and served various appointments in it until 1930. His first assignment was Middleton Circuit, Elbert County, Ga. His last pastorate was Emory University Methodist Church, 1928-30. He then became professor of church history at Emory, 1930-38. While teaching he ably edited the *Wesleyan Christian Advocate*, 1932-36, official organ of Georgia Methodism. He was a delegate to the GENERAL CONFERENCE (MES) in 1934 and 1938, when he was elected bishop; he was the youngest of the bishops elected in 1938 by his denomination, and the last bishop consecrated by the Southern Church as Methodist union came the next year. His areas were COLUMBIA, S. C., 1940-44; LOUISVILLE, KY., 1944-56.

A liberal on the social aspects of the Gospel, Bishop Watkins was "supremely at home in the pulpit" and was in constant demand at notable gatherings.

He wrote *Out of Aldersgate* in 1938; and *The Christian Hope* in 1953.

For twenty years he took no vacation, and rose each day at 4 a.m. to begin his work. A mild heart attack in 1956 was followed two years later by physical and nervous exhaustion. He retired early (October 1959) but never regained full health, dying on Feb. 6, 1961. He was buried in Louisville, Ky.

C. T. Howell, *Prominent Personalities*. 1945.
F. D. Leete, *Methodist Bishops*. 1948.
Southeastern Jurisdictional Conference *Journal*, 1964.

WALTER N. VERNON

WATKINSON, JOSEPH (? -1950), New Zealand Methodist layman who arrived in Auckland in the ship "Suret" after a passage of 112 days from England. An active local preacher and Sunday school teacher, he also became treasurer of the children's fund and missionary treasurer. He was a man of rare personal charm and Christian grace. Only his excessive modesty kept him from reaching even higher places in the church.

ARCHER O. HARRIS

WILLIAM L. WATKINSON

WATKINSON, WILLIAM L. (1838-1925), British Methodist, was born at Hull in 1838, and entered the WESLEYAN METHODIST ministry in 1858, after a bare six-weeks' training at RICHMOND THEOLOGICAL COLLEGE, LONDON. He was sent as a supply to the Stratford upon Avon Circuit, and found himself in sole charge when the superintendent died. He rose rapidly to prominence as an outstanding preacher and as a popular religious writer and journalist. Numerous volumes of his sermons were published, including *The Blind Spot* (1899) and *The Shepherd of the Sea* (1920). Denied early educational opportunity, he was an omnivorous reader all his life, especially in the fields of theology, science, and philosophy. He delivered the FERNLEY LECTURE of 1886 at WESLEY's CHAPEL, LONDON, on the typically original subject, *The Influence of Scepticism on Character*. From 1893 to 1904 he was connectional editor; he introduced pictures into *Methodist Magazine*, and generally enhanced its popular character, "but the drudgery of the position was never," (F. CUMBERS, *The Book Room*, (London, 1956) p. 124.) it has been said, "congenial to him." He was elected president of the Wesleyan Methodist Conference in 1897. He died in 1925.

F. Cumbers, *Book Room*. 1956.
E. Watkinson, ed., *Correspondence of F. W. MacDonald and W. Watkinson, 1919-1925*. London, 1927. JOHN NEWTON

WATSFORD, JOHN J. (1822-1907), was the first Australian-born Methodist minister. His father, converted under SAMUEL LEIGH, was one of the original PARRAMATTA Methodists. He himself owed his awakening to DANIEL DRAPER in 1833—a period which he had thought peculiarly unproductive. His ministry stretched through sixty-six years. In his early years he played a great part in the heroic age of South Sea Missions.

Originally a pioneer missionary in FIJI, Watsford returned to proclaim the need of a strong Church in the homeland if ever the people there were to fulfill their obligations to the brown races of the Pacific. Strong in intellect and of powerful physique he possessed great spiritual capacity and power. The tremendous impetus given to sane evangelism by his personal example and advocacy has not spent itself but abides to this day. Victoria is a missionary spirited state to a large extent as a result of Watsford's impact upon it.

His active ministry extended to every part of AUSTRALIA, and everywhere there were hundreds who traced to him their spiritual birth. During his term in SOUTH AUSTRALIA he was largely responsible for the founding of Prince Alfred College, ADELAIDE.

In 1871 he was president of the Australasian Wesleyan Conference. Seven years later he became president of the first General Conference. In 1881 he was in LONDON as representative to the ECUMENICAL METHODIST CONFERENCE. To a remarkable degree he was representative of everything that is characteristic of Methodism. He was ardent, fearless and untiring.

In 1875 he was appointed general secretary of the Home Mission Society. When John Watsford was asked to undertake this work he at first hesitated because he loved circuit work, and because he loved his home and large family. But he was appointed general secretary, year by year for eight years. He travelled thousands of miles annually, preaching, lecturing, holding revival services, and in every way directing and helping the work.

In 1886 he became editor of the *Spectator* and was also appointed organizer of the Jubilee Thanksgiving Fund, when £30,968 was raised.

"Watsford," wrote Dr. FITCHETT, "would have been a man of mark in any calling. He has many of the qualities of an orator, and a natural faculty for leadership which is felt by everyone who comes within the range of his influence. A fearless man, who speaks the truth and does the right in scorn of consequence. Rich in a strong fibred, clear-eyed common sense, which sees the path to be trodden when subtler intellects often stumble and grope."

During sixteen years of retirement he was known and revered as "Father Watsford"—the saint and patriarch of the Church. For the last three or four years he felt that God had given him a ministry of intercession, and he lived in an atmosphere of prayer for the Church, for the unconverted, for Christ's Kingdom.

J. Colwell, *Century in the Pacific.* 1914.
————————, *Illustrated History.* 1904.

AUSTRALIAN EDITORIAL COMMITTEE

WATSON, C. HOYT (1888-1969), an ordained elder of the Pacific Northwest Conference of the FREE METHODIST CHURCH and president emeritus, Seattle Pacific College, was born at Endora, Kan. His degrees are: B.A., 1918 and M.A., 1923, University of Kansas; honorary doctorates have been conferred by Whitworth and GREENVILLE COLLEGES. He was professor at Orleans Seminary, Nebraska and CENTRAL COLLEGE, McPherson, Kan. He taught at the University of Kansas for five years and at the University of Washington, one year. He was president, Seattle Pacific College, for thirty-three years. He served as pastor of churches in KANSAS and WASHINGTON and was conference Sunday school secretary, Washington Conference, for ten years. He was also general educational secretary for four years.

Watson's crowning achievement was his presidency of Seattle Pacific College. For thirty-three years he guided the institution in the ways of evangelical ecumenism to serve the Seattle community and the nation as well as the Free Methodist Church. The School of Missions, The Department of Education and Teacher Training, with a special emphasis on physical education and the preparation of coaches and recreational leaders, are among his noteworthy accomplishments. He died on Aug. 17, 1969.

BYRON S. LAMSON

WATSON, CLAUDE A. (1885-   ), an ordained elder of the Arizona-Southern California conference of the FREE METHODIST CHURCH, chairman of the Investment Committee, was born in Antioch Township, Mich. He was a student at Alma College in Michigan and holds the degrees J.D. and LL.B. GREENVILLE COLLEGE conferred the LL.D. He was pastor of Free Methodist churches in MICHIGAN and CALIFORNIA and served as superintendent in the Southern California Conference. He is an attorney at law, a member of the California State Bar and Supreme Court Bar. He was nominee of the Prohibition Party for Vice-President, 1936, and for President in 1944 and 1948. He is the author of *Repeal Has Succeeded; God's Plan for Civil Government; Fifth Column in America; False Freedoms; Bloody Hands.* Dr. and Mrs. Watson live in Los Angeles, Calif.

BYRON S. LAMSON

WATSON, EDWARD L. (1861-1936), American minister, was born in BALTIMORE, Md., Feb. 6, 1861 of Roman Catholic parents. Converted in Jefferson Street M.E. Church at age fifteen, he became a traveling preacher at age nineteen ably filling eleven BALTIMORE CONFERENCE Stations and a presiding eldership besides Hennepin Avenue, MINNEAPOLIS. While assistant at First Church, Baltimore (LOVELY LANE), he completed undergraduate and graduate studies at Johns Hopkins University. His marriage to Edith Hann was blessed with five children.

Association with JOHN F. GOUCHER and the University fueled his zeal for history and led to service of forty years with the American Methodist HISTORICAL SOCIETY, the last fifteen as president. In 1925 he was elected the first president of the Association of Methodist Historical Societies, continuing until his death. He played a great part in getting the FRANCIS ASBURY equestrian statue erected in WASHINGTON, D.C. Appropriate marking of the SESQUICENTENNIAL of American Methodism was his concern from 1927; and as acting president of the Baltimore Sesquicentennial Commission, he led in bringing the great 1934 celebration to pass.

Although technically retired in 1932, he was on his way to broadcast a radio message when suddenly stricken Dec. 29, 1936.

EDWIN SCHELL

WATSON, ELLA B. (1863-1940), American lay woman and a native of Illinois, grew to young womanhood in that state, being a graduate of Hedding College. She went with her family to NEBRASKA and settled in LINCOLN, where she became a member of Trinity Church, remaining so until her death.

She was a school teacher for a short time and began her work as corresponding secretary of the NEBRASKA CONFERENCE, WOMAN'S FOREIGN MISSIONARY SOCIETY (MES), in 1885. In 1906 she was elected to the task of corresponding secretary of the Topeka Branch of the Society. She carried on a heavy correspondence with individuals and societies, much of it by longhand. She also wrote many articles for missionary publications.

In addition to her writing, Miss Watson spent much time in traveling, speaking at Women's Foreign Missionary gatherings, at annual conferences, and at other Methodist gatherings. On several occasions she traveled abroad.

Miss Watson was a lay delegate to several GENERAL CONFERENCES, and on her way to that of 1940, she became ill and died in the home of friends in Montclair, N. J., on April 24, 1940. Word came to the Nebraska Conference delegation shortly before the opening session. Bishop WILLIAM C. MARTIN announced her passing to that session, and a prayer was offered in her memory. Her body was returned to Lincoln, where she was buried. She left a great impression on Methodism of the midwest.

EVERETT E. JACKMAN

WATSON, RICHARD (1781-1833), British Methodist, was born on Feb. 22, 1781, at Barton-on-Humber, Lincolnshire. He entered the WESLEYAN ministry in 1796, but in 1800 withdrew on doctrinal grounds, becoming an itinerant in the METHODIST NEW CONNEXION in 1803. Partly through the influence of JABEZ BUNTING he returned to the Wesleyan ministry in 1812. He rapidly made a reputation as a writer, and in 1818 wrote a reply to ADAM CLARKE's unsound doctrine of the Eternal Sonship: this public disagreement with Clarke was the root of much later bitterness in Wesleyan Methodism, as it was never forgiven by JAMES EVERETT. In 1820 Watson published *Observations on Southey's Life of Wesley,* an official answer to Southey's book. Always interested in overseas missions, Watson was secretary to the WESLEYAN MISSIONARY SOCIETY from 1821-1825 and honorary secretary from 1827-1831. He was the leading Wesleyan opponent of slavery.

In 1823 Watson began to publish his *Theological Institutes,* which formed the Wesleyan theological mind until W. B. POPE replaced them. In 1829 at the time of the

RICHARD WATSON

LEEDS organ controversy (see Leeds Protestant Methodists), Watson wrote *An Affectionate Address to the Trustees, Stewards and Local Preachers of the South London Circuit;* this was the classic statement of the conservative Wesleyan view of Church government. In 1831 he wrote a *Life of John Wesley,* which remained standard for many years. Watson was president of the Wesleyan Methodist Conference of 1826. At the time of his death, on Jan. 8, 1833, he stood second only to Jabez Bunting in the estimation of the connection.

T. Jackson, *Richard Watson.* 1834.   JOHN KENT

WATT, ROLLA VERNON (1868-1925), American layman of the CALIFORNIA CONFERENCE and considered to be the leading Christian layman of the Pacific Coast, was born in Ohio. He came to SAN FRANCISCO when nineteen, and lived there for fifty years. He was an active member of the Central Methodist Church official board for forty-two years, superintendent of its Sunday school for thirty-three years, a director and/or president of the city Y.M.C.A. for twenty-nine years and for a like period as trustee of the UNIVERSITY OF THE PACIFIC.

He was the organizer in 1889 of the California Conference Lay Association, and one of its early presidents. When the GENERAL CONFERENCE adopted that organization as part of its denominational machinery he was its first vice-president and then its president. He was elected to the General Conference in 1900, and to each of the succeeding sessions until his death—seven times in all. He was long a member of the BOOK COMMITTEE which had supervision of the publishing interests of the church.

His business field was insurance, and he was the Pacific Coast agent for several of the larger companies. Developing a large earning capacity, he started as a tither, but in-creased his giving until it was the large part of his income. He continued in business in his later years that he might assist especially Central Church and the University.

Endowed with a large body and an attractive presence, Rolla Watt matched these in his gracious religious personality.

L. L. Loofbourow, *Cross in the Sunset.* 1961.
LEON L. LOOFBOUROW

WATTERS, WILLIAM (1751-1827), first native-born American to enter the Methodist itineracy, was born Oct. 16, 1771, in what is now Harford County, Md., the son of Godfrey and Sarah Watters. He was educated at a neighborhood school. Originally Anglican, the family was won to Methodism by ROBERT STRAWBRIDGE and others. William was converted in 1771.

In October 1772, he joined ROBERT WILLIAMS on a preaching tour to NORFOLK. Though not present at the first conference in PHILADELPHIA in 1773, that body appointed him to NEW JERSEY as junior preacher with JOHN KING. However, he continued at Norfolk until September, and then was sent by THOMAS RANKIN to the Kent Circuit. He attended the 1774 conference, was admitted on trial, and was appointed to Trenton, N. J. Thereafter he served circuits in MARYLAND and VIRGINIA until 1784 when he located. He was active again a few months in 1786, and during 1801-05, and was a local preacher the rest of his life.

Watters loved the itineracy and had good success, but marriage and poor health compelled location. He married Sarah Adams, June 6, 1779; they had no children.

Watters played an important role during the controversy over the administration of the sacraments. He presided at the 1778 conference, the first native-born American to function in that capacity, when the Virginia and NORTH CAROLINA preachers agreed to wait one year before deciding whether to proceed with administration of the sacraments. He was the only preacher to attend both conferences in 1779. Though not invited to attend the conference to be held by ASBURY in DELAWARE in April, he learned about it and determined to go with the aim of persuading Asbury to be present at the May conference in Virginia. He wanted Asbury's help in dissuading the preachers from taking a step that would mean schism. Asbury could not go to Virginia, but he did write letters to the leaders of that conference. Unmoved, the majority of the southern preachers proceeded to administer the sacraments.

At the conference in Baltimore in 1780, Asbury, Watters, and GARRETTSON were appointed a committee to attend the conference of the southern preachers in Virginia and try to dissuade them from their course, and in the end they succeeded; the sacraments were suspended until JOHN WESLEY could take action.

During the controversy some preachers on each side accused Watters of favoring their opponents, but on the whole he kept the good will of both groups; the pro-sacrament preachers said that Watters was the only man on the other side who treated them with affection. In his autobiography Watters declares that his one aim throughout the controversy was to prevent schism, that he could have conscientiously administered or not administered the sacraments, provided all the preachers would have agreed on the one or the other course.

Watters died at his farm home in Fairfax County, Va.,

March 29, 1827, and was buried there. In 1889 the VIR-GINIA CONFERENCE erected a monument over his grave.

General Minutes, MEC.
D. A. Watters, *First American Itinerant.* Cincinnati: Curt and Jennings, 1898.
William Watters, *A Short Account of the Christian Experience of William Watters.* Alexandria, Virginia: S. Snowden, 1806.
ALBEA GODBOLD

BASCOM WATTS

WATTS, HENRY BASCOM (1890-1959), American bishop, was born at Yellville, Ark., Nov. 6, 1890, the son of Joseph H. and Mary T. (Sims) Watts. His father, a pastor in the then Arkansas Conference, transferred to the NORTHWEST TEXAS CONFERENCE in 1896. Bascom Watts was educated at SOUTHWESTERN UNIVERSITY (A.B., 1813, D.D., 1932), and SOUTHERN METHODIST UNIVERSITY (B.D., 1918). He married Minne E. Keyser, Aug. 20, 1913, and they had two children. Their son Ewart is a member of the KANSAS EAST CONFERENCE.

Admitted on trial in the Northwest Texas Conference in 1914, Bascom Watts was ordained DEACON in 1916 and ELDER in 1918. His appointments in the Northwest Texas, CENTRAL TEXAS, WEST TEXAS, LITTLE ROCK, and East Oklahoma CONFERENCES were: 1914, Buchanan Street, Amarillo; 1915-16, Ochiltree; 1917-21, Lockney; 1922, First, Cisco; 1923-25, St. John's, Waco; 1926-29, University, AUSTIN; 1930-35, Laurel Heights, SAN ANTONIO; 1936-38, First, LITTLE ROCK; 1939-40, Boston Avenue, TULSA; and 1950-51, Tulsa District.

Though Watts was a "transfer" man who served in five annual conferences, he was also a conference minded man who willingly worked on boards and committees and was soon recognized as a conference leader wherever he was. In both the West Texas and Little Rock Conferences he was chairman of the board of education. In the East Oklahoma Conference he was chairman of the commission on world service and finance and chairman of the Oklahoma Methodist Foundation, and in addition he served on the board of trustees of Southern Methodist University and represented the Oklahoma-New Mexico Area on the Jurisdictional Council. He was a delegate to the 1934 GENERAL CONFERENCE from West Texas and he led the East Oklahoma General Conference delegation in 1948-52 and was a reserve delegate in 1944. He was elected bishop in 1952 and was assigned to the NEBRASKA Area which he superintended until his death, Nov. 3, 1959. Burial was in Tulsa, Okla., following a funeral service in Boston Avenue Church at which the church choir sang, in accordance with his request, "A Charge to Keep I Have" and the "Hallelujah Chorus."

General Conference Journals, 1930-52.
South Central Jurisdictional Conference Journal, 1939-52.
General Minutes, MECS and MC.
Minutes of the West Texas, Little Rock, and East Oklahoma Conferences.
Elmer T. Clark, *Who's Who in Methodism.* Chicago: Marquis, 1952.
Who's Who in America.
ALBEA GODBOLD

WATTS, ISAAC (1674-1748), **AND THE WESLEYS.** In their enthusiastic appreciation of the hymns of JOHN and CHARLES WESLEY some Methodist scholars have tended to overlook the important contribution both to the practice of hymn singing and to the corpus of Christian hymnody of Isaac Watts, and the Wesleys' acknowledged debt to him. Watts' *Hymns and Spiritual Songs* was published in 1707, shortly before the birth of Charles Wesley, and while John was a young child not yet old enough to begin those incomparable lessons at his mother's knee. It seems likely that at Epworth there was little singing apart from the New Version of metrical psalms by Tate and Brady—certainly John Wesley characterized the Old Version by Sternhold and Hopkins as arrant doggerel.

Watts was a different proposition altogether. His *Psalms of David* (1719) became firm favorites with both John and Charles, and were regularly sung by the members of the HOLY CLUB at Oxford both as a group and as individuals. To these and the New Version were gradually added some of the few samples of hymns written by the Wesleys' father and elder brother, especially "Behold the Saviour of mankind," by the rector of Epworth. On the voyage out to GEORGIA the treasures of German hymnody were introduced to the two brothers by the Moravians, and John speedily began learning German and translating some of these into English verse.

In 1737 John Wesley published America's first hymn book. (Earlier compilations from the *Bay Psalm Book* of 1740 onwards had been restricted to metrical psalms, and poems of human composition were frowned upon in divine worship.) He had varied material to hand, yet half of his Charleston *Collection of Psalms and Hymns*—thirty-four out of seventy items—came from Isaac Watts. It is true, however, that Wesley's editorial pen was just as active upon the hymns of Watts as on most other writings which he published, and his alterations tended to make Watts' hymns still more personal and evangelical.

The same was true in the following year of 1738, when Wesley published in London a second collection with the same title, begun in Georgia: of seventy items thirty-three were from Watts, including his "Our God, our help in ages past," altered by Wesley to what became its best known form, "O God, our help. . . ." In *Hymns and Sacred Poems,* which appeared the following year, the compositions of Charles Wesley first began to appear, and

John forsook his heavy dependence upon Watts, except for metrical psalms. But hymns and poems (and especially psalms) continued to appear in Methodist publications: in a third *Collection of Psalms and Hymns* (1741), in a three-volume *Collection of Moral and Sacred Poems* (1744), in the famous *Collection of Hymns for the use of the People called Methodists* (1780), and in the *Collection of Psalms and Hymns for the Lord's Day*, appended to the *Sunday Service* of the Methodists in 1784.

The Wesleys certainly gratefully acknowledged the important pioneer work of Isaac Watts, and enjoyed a session of walking and singing with him on 4 October 1738. John Wesley felt unhappy about some of Watts' later Arian tendencies, but gladly abridged a part of his *Ruin and Recovery of Mankind* to form *Serious Considerations concerning the doctrines of Election and Reprobation* (1740), and prepared a brief biography of Watts for inclusion in the *Arminian Magazine*. It is good to know that the admiration was mutual, and that before his death in 1748 Watts paid high tribute to Charles Wesley's verse, testifying that "that single poem 'Wrestling Jacob' [Come, O thou traveller unknown] was worth all the verses he himself had written."

Frank Baker and George Walton Williams (eds), *John Wesley's First Hymn-Book: a facsimile with additional material.* London and Charleston, S.C., 1964.

Frank Baker, *Representative Verse of Charles Wesley.* London, Epworth Press, and Nashville, Abingdon Press, 1962.

FRANK BAKER

WATTS, MARTHA HITE (1845-1909), American educator, first missionary sent to BRAZIL by the WOMAN'S FOREIGN MISSIONARY SOCIETY of the M.E. Church, South, was born in Bardstown, Ky., on Feb. 13, 1845. Her father was a prominent lawyer, and Martha grew up in an atmosphere of culture, social gaiety, and world interests. Grieved by the death of her fiancé in the Civil War, she decided to prepare herself for teaching, went to the Louisville Normal School, and then taught in the city schools.

Though nominally a Christian, Martha had never experienced a real conversion until she attended a revival at Broadway Methodist Church. Almost at once she began giving herself to Christian Service. She organized a missionary society for young girls before such a group had been authorized—as was then necessary—by the GENERAL CONFERENCE of 1878. From then on, close association with two outstanding Methodist women of that day, Mary Helm and Maria Gibson, led her into missionary work. She applied, was accepted, and appointed to Brazil by Bishop J. C. KEENER in February 1881; and went to that country in company of the early missionaries, J. J. RANSOM, J. L. KENNEDY, and J. W. KOGER. They arrived in RIO DE JANEIRO on May 16, 1881.

Martha Watts was sent at once to PIRACICABA, São Paulo, for the express purpose of establishing a school for girls. Its foundations had been laid a few years before by Annie and Mary Newman, daughters of J. E. NEWMAN, a Methodist preacher, one of the self-styled "Confederate exiles" who had come to Brazil in 1867. This was the first Methodist educational institution in Brazil and was named Colegio (later Instituto Educacional) Piracicabano. It opened officially on Sept. 13, 1881, with only one little pupil, Maria Escobar, but for three months Miss Watts kept the school going. She often told of conditions in those days when "respectable ladies" did not go alone on the streets; so to protect herself, she always carried books and an umbrella—badges of propriety.

Under her the school pioneered in the teaching of social sciences, for which there were not even any textbooks at the time; in languages; bookkeeping, for a short period in 1882; and kindergarten (1884). She introduced coeducation in the lower grades. There was strong persecution instigated by the Roman Catholic Church, but despite opposition the school's advanced curriculum, high standards, discipline and moral education, won the esteem of the most prominent families of the area. One of the local papers wrote: "The great importance of this school is not only in the instruction it affords, but in the moral education it imparts, which will lead to the regeneration of our customs."

Prudente de Morais Barros, who became governor of the state when the Republic was proclaimed in 1889, and was later elected first civil president of Brazil, held Miss Watts in such high esteem that he invited her to become his minister of education. This position she declined, as she had dedicated her life to the service of the Church.

Successful in this school, Miss Watts was appointed twice to found others—the Colegio Americano in Petropolis (which was the precursor of Colegio Bennett, Rio de Janeiro); and the COLEGIO IZABELA HENDRIX in BELO HORIZONTE, Minas Gerais. Undergirding all she did was a profound love for her "girls"—not just to see them "educated" but to instill love of truth, self-discipline, and the ideal of service.

Severe illness forced her retirement in 1909. She returned to Louisville, Ky., where she died on Dec. 30, 1909, and was buried in Cave Hill Cemetery. Former students in Brazil, led by Eugenia Smith Becker, placed a bronze plaque in Broadway Church as a "tribute of love and gratitude for the influence she had exerted in their lives by her beautiful service."

J. L. Kennedy, *Metodismo no Brasil.* 1928.

Eula K. Long, *Martha Watts of Brazil.* New York: Woman's Division of Christian Service, n.d.

EULA K. LONG

BEVERLY WAUGH

WAUGH, BEVERLY (1789-1858), American bishop, was born in Fairfax County, Va., on Oct. 25, 1789, the son of Captain James Waugh, a Revolutionary veteran. He received a secondary education and became the manager of a store in Middleburg, Va., in 1807. Two years later he joined the BALTIMORE CONFERENCE on trial and was appointed to the Stafford and Fredericksburg circuit. His other appointments were Greenbrier (now in WEST

VIRGINIA); Washington in 1811 and again in 1817; Stephenburg (Virginia); five times to BALTIMORE; presiding elder of the Potomac District, Montgomery, Berkeley, Pell's Point, GEORGETOWN and FREDERICK.

When the reform movement which resulted in the formation of the M.P. CHURCH arose, Waugh was favorable to the election of PRESIDING ELDERS and as a consequence he was not elected to the GENERAL CONFERENCE in 1824. However, he adhered to the M.E. CHURCH and eventually lost interest in the matter and championed the prevailing order.

In 1828 he was elected assistant BOOK AGENT with JOHN EMORY, and in 1832 he became Book Agent when Emory was elected a bishop. He was a member of the General Conferences of 1816, 1820, 1828, and 1836. As Book Agent he paid the indebtedness on the PUBLISHING HOUSE and erected a new building on Mulberry Street in NEW YORK. On Feb. 18, 1836 the Publishing House was burned, the manuscript journals of FRANCIS ASBURY and JESSE LEE being destroyed in the fire. The loss was estimated at $200,000. Waugh at once began raising funds for rebuilding and was engaged in this task when he was elected bishop on the first ballot at the General Conference of 1836.

His first episcopal assignment was to the TROY CONFERENCE. In the next twenty-two years he traveled 100,000 miles and made 12,000 appointments in all sections of the Church.

When the abolition agitation became acute in the Church he held to a neutral course. Although a Southerner he was opposed to SLAVERY, but he refused to allow the extremists to present their resolutions in his conferences. At the General Conference of 1844 he tried to avert a division of the Church by urging that the case of Bishop ANDREW be deferred. But when the division came he adhered to the northern branch of the Church.

Bishop Waugh died in Baltimore on Feb. 9, 1858, as the result of exposure at a camp meeting and was buried in Mount Olivet Cemetery near Bishops Asbury, GEORGE and Emory. His ruling that the annual conference year commences when the appointments are announced at an annual conference and continues until the announcing of appointments at the next annual conference has become authoritative Methodist law.

Dictionary of American Biography.
Flood and Hamilton, *Lives of Methodist Bishops.* 1880.
H. C. Jennings, *Book Concern.* 1924.
F. D. Leete, *Methodist Bishops.* 1948.   ELMER T. CLARK

WAUGH, JAMES WALTER (1832-1910), American missionary to INDIA, was born in Mercer, Pa., Feb. 27, 1932. He was graduated from ALLEGHENY COLLEGE in 1854, and in 1856 won his M.A. degree. In 1858 he was received on trial in the SOUTHERN ILLINOIS CONFERENCE, with permission to attend GARRETT BIBLICAL INSTITUTE as a "missionary student." He sailed for India in 1859, and received his B.D. degree from Garrett in absentia. Ten years later he was awarded the D.D. degree.

Waugh was a practical printer, and in 1860 was appointed to BAREILLY to establish the press which in 1866 was transferred to Lucknow. He was four times the agent of the Methodist Publishing House of India. He also served as superintendent of the Bareilly, LUCKNOW, and Kumaon districts. For three years he was principal of the Kanpur Memorial School, and was the first principal of

Oak Openings in Naini Tal, later named Philander Smith College. A former pupil of his said: "He was the best Christian I ever knew."

Waugh had a fluent use of Hindustani. He was also a gifted singer, and a number of the hymns he used were of his composition. He was a good translator, an excellent accountant and business man.

He died in Moradabad, India, Jan. 21, 1910, and was buried there. An Indian preacher said: "He loved us and in proof of it he left his body in our midst, buried here in India. He loved us, he worked for us, and died among us."

Journal of the North India Conference, 1911.
                                        JOHN N. HOLLISTER

WAUGH, THOMAS (1853-1932), British WESLEYAN METHODIST and connectional evangelist, was born on Sept. 3, 1853, in Cumberland, and was renowned in his youth as a wrestler. Converted in 1876, he entered Headingley College in 1880. In 1883 he joined Thomas Cook as a connectional evangelist, remaining in this work until 1910. This was part of an attempt to combine the revivalistic methods of Moody and Sankey with the circuit system. Even after his final superannuation, Waugh continued lecturing and preaching. He published *The Power of Pentecost.* He died Oct. 17, 1932.

T. Waugh, *Twenty-three Years a Missioner.* London, 1906.
                                        H. M. RATTENBURY

WAUKEGAN, ILLINOIS, U.S.A. **First Church** is located on the west shore of Lake Michigan in Lake County, Ill., in one of the fastest growing and most prosperous counties of the state. It is a downtown church, across the street from Waukegan's spacious new library. City Hall is a block south, and Y.M.C.A. a block east. Nine other churches are within four blocks.

In 1847 Waukegan was first listed in the ROCK RIVER (now Northern Illinois) Conference. At that time Waukegan was a part of Old Lake Circuit—changed in 1847 to Little Fort, the name Waukegan bore from early days until 1848. First Church's first official board meeting was Aug. 11, 1849, JOHN F. DEVORE, pastor. There were seventy-one members. On Oct. 10, 1849 the first church building was dedicated, with Hooper Crews, circuit rider of northern Illinois from an early date, preaching the dedicatory sermon. That building was replaced by the present sanctuary during the pastorate of J. W. Funston (1913-18). During the time of Harold McElvany (1955-59) an educational building, chapel, and other facilities were constructed. In 1966 the church was free of debt, and membership that year was over 2,200.

In 1956 First Church sponsored a new Methodist congregation (Faith), located on the west edge of Waukegan, about two miles from First Church. From 1945 to 1965 six young persons of First Church entered full-time Christian service. In 1963 the church for the first time had two full-time conference members as pastors: W. Gehl Devore (same last name as the first pastor in 1849), senior minister; Richard A. Brewer, associate; and a full-time Director of Christian Education. Membership in 1970 was 1,973.

In addition to serving Waukegan, First Church has many contacts with the Navy personnel at Great Lakes Naval Training Center, about four miles south.

                                        W. GEHL DEVORE

WAUSAU, WISCONSIN, U.S.A. **First Church** is the oldest congregation in Wausau, dating back to 1847 when a Methodist circuit rider arrived in Big Bull Falls (Wausau), when the population included but five women. Since that time the congregation has erected five buildings (one having been destroyed by fire in 1869, supposedly started by the Indians). The present unit, costing approximately a million dollars, was completed in 1966.

Located in downtown Wausau the church is community minded, as evidenced in its many concerns. A week-day class for retarded persons began in 1959, and was a pioneer project in the area; the early establishment (1957) of an "open door" policy holding that persons of all nationalities, races, or economic conditions should be included in the fellowship of First Church; exchange programs with Negro young persons and churches of the CHICAGO area to provide experiences in inter-racial living for persons in this "all-white" community; work with patients from the Marathon County Hospital by staff and college students; a growing educational concern for peace and world order; and continuous broadcasts of the Sunday morning services since 1958.

The educational ministry of the church holds itself to be creative and unique. Unusual interest is always taken in certain expressions of religious art to be seen in the church. Among these are the large painting, "If Thou Hast Known" in Memorial Chapel, painted in 1917 by Louis Amorosi (using Rib Mountain, near Wausau, as the setting for his sketch); the great facade stained-glass window on the south wall of the sanctuary, more than two stories high and entitled "Come Unto Me," featuring the figure of Christ surrounded by persons of all races; the large mosaic on the north wall behind the altar symbolizing Christ's last week; and the art work in the Wesleyan Room featuring important events and emphases of early Methodism, and the life of JOHN and CHARLES WESLEY.

First Church, one of three Methodist churches in the Wausau area, had a membership of 954 in 1970, a total raised for all purposes of over $100,000, and a paid staff totaling eight persons.

MARLIN E. SMITH

WAUWATOSA, WISCONSIN, U.S.A. **Wauwatosa Church,** the largest Methodist church in WISCONSIN, came into being in pioneer days. A circuit rider, J. Lackenbie, brought the small group of settlers together in various homes for several years before the church officially came into being in May of 1848, shortly before Wisconsin became a state. The ecumenical interests of this community were manifested early: the village schoolhouse was used by all Christians for their worship, including Roman Catholic and Protestants. On Sunday morning in May of 1919, the sanctuary was burned to the ground. The Masons offered the use of their Temple across the street for the services and meetings of the Methodists, an offer they gratefully accepted. A Gothic style church building of Lannon stone was created in 1923 and this was three times enlarged over the succeeding years.

Fifty-two ministers have served the people of Wauwatosa through this church, which was originally called "First Methodist," and then, later, simply, "Wauwatosa." Five young men have been trained for the ministry from this church and are now serving as ministers: Edwin Beers, James Collins, Charles T. Hein, Robert Kuhn, and James Scott. Two young men are missionaries: John

Frenck and James Newing, though each is now affiliated with other than the Methodist church. Five young men are currently studying in preparation for the Methodist ministry. One minister was elected an episcopal leader of the denomination from this church: FRANCIS E. KEARNS. Three ministers are currently serving this congregation of 2,139 members.

HAROLD R. WEAVER

WAVELAND, MISSISSIPPI, U.S.A., has been the site of a summer assembly and training center for what has been the CENTRAL JURISDICTION of The Methodist Church. Bishop ROBERT E. JONES of the M.E. Church, seeing the necessity for such a center for the Negro Conferences of his Church, became instrumental in establishing such a center at Waveland on the Mississippi Gulf Coast just west of Bay St. Louis. The center grew in influence and importance with several buildings being added to the original one and training programs of significance being held there, especially through the summer season. The devastating hurricane, Camille, of 1969 largely destroyed the Waveland buildings, but these have been put back and repaired to a great extent through the help of the general Church. Although the Central Jurisdiction is being dissolved, Waveland bids fair to continue its work in the foreseeable future. Several sessions of the MISSISSIPPI CONFERENCE (CJ) have been held at Waveland.

N. B. H.

WAVERLEY, New South Wales, Australia, was established to commemorate the end of World War I. The Rev. James Green (president) was set aside to visit the circuits and collect funds. On May 30, 1922 the family of the late EBENEZER VICKERY, Jr. offered to the Conference their large home, "Edina," and two acres. The hospital was opened on Feb. 5, 1919, with Matron Hunter, M.B.E., as matron. On Nov. 11, 1922, "Edina" was handed over to the church. Since then it has developed into a very well equipped private hospital with 102 surgical beds, thirty-two maternity beds, with three operating theater rooms and modern equipment. It deals with about 3,500 patients each year. There have been 320 nurses trained to become Registered Nursing Sisters. In 1933 a chapel to the memory of Jane Ellen Vickery was erected.

WAY, SAMUEL JAMES (1836-1916), was a distinguished citizen and churchman in SOUTH AUSTRALIA for over fifty years. His father, James Way, was a leading BIBLE CHRISTIAN minister who pioneered the denomination's work in South Australia. Samuel Way was born in England and educated at the Bible Christian college at Shebbear in Devon. He joined his family in South Australia in 1853.

Way's contribution to South Australia was a many-sided one. He was called to the Bar in 1861, was made a Queen's Counsel in 1871 and five years later, after a short time as Attorney General in the State legislature, was appointed Chief Justice. He later became Lieutenant Governor and on a number of occasions acted as the Queen's representative. He was made a baronet in 1899. In the legal sphere he achieved eminence and was the first Australian to be nominated to the Judicial Committee of the Privy Council.

Way gave his support to numerous philanthropic and

educational organizations, serving both as Vice Chancellor and Chancellor of the University of Adelaide. On his death it was said that "it will be impossible to write the history of many of our great institutions without taking his contribution into account."

Way came from a notable Bible Christian family but his ecclesiastical interests became increasingly catholic in character. He was a Bible Christian delegate to the ECUMENICAL METHODIST CONFERENCE held in WASHINGTON in 1891, the New York *Christian Advocate* describing him as "the most distinguished lay member of the Conference from abroad." He was one of the state's leading advocates of Methodist Union and spoke at the inaugural service of the new church in Adelaide on Aug. 14, 1899. At the time he was circuit steward of the Bible Christian Church in Franklin Street.

AUSTRALIAN EDITORIAL COMMITTEE

WAYLAND, EWING TATUM (1916-   ), American minister and Church editor, was born at Heber Springs, Ark., on Dec. 31, 1916, the son of Edward Theodore and Sue (Koontz) Wayland. He was educated at HENDRIX COLLEGE, A.B., 1938 and D.D., 1958; and at SOUTHERN METHODIST UNIVERSITY, B.D., 1941. He married Frances Susan Stewart on Sept. 5, 1940, and they have three sons, Ewing Tatum, Jr.; Fred Stewart; and George Burden. He entered the NORTH TEXAS CONFERENCE on trial in 1940, but transferred to the NORTH ARKANSAS CONFERENCE in 1941 and came into full connection in 1942. He served in Mintner, Texas, 1939-41; Prairie Grove, Ark., 1941-44; Batesville, Ark., 1944-45. He then became chaplain in the U.S. Navy, 1945-46. He was associate editor of *The Arkansas Methodist*, published in LITTLE ROCK, ARK., 1946-48, and became editor of this publication in 1948, serving until 1960. He was also the editor of *The Louisiana Methodist* from 1951 to 1960. He was then elected by the Board of PUBLICATION to be the editor of *The Christian Advocate*, the general organ of The Methodist Church published in Park Ridge, Ill. In 1963 he was named editorial director of *Together* and *The Christian Advocate* publications in that year.

Dr. Wayland was the secretary of the North Arkansas Conference, 1948-52; the chairman of its Conference Board of Social and Economic Relations, 1952-56; secretary of the Arkansas Inter-Board Council, 1957-59; and the treasurer of the South Central Jurisdiction's Historical Society, 1952-60. He was a trustee of PHILANDER SMITH COLLEGE, Little Rock, serving as vice-chairman of that Board. He belongs to the Methodist Press Association, of which he has been president, and the Associated Church Press, of which he is a director. He is a member of the Council of Secretaries (UMC) and of the Commission on History and Archives. He presently resides in Mount Prospect, Ill.

Who's Who in America, Vol. 34.
Who's Who in The Methodist Church, 1966.   N. B. H.

WAYMAN, ALEXANDER WASHINGTON (1821-1895), American bishop of the A.M.E. CHURCH, was born in Caroline County, Md., in September 1821. A meager education was self acquired and later in his life he was awarded the D.D. degree by Howard University. He was converted in 1835 and later united with the M.E. Church. After transferring his membership to the A.M.E Church

in 1840, he was ordained DEACON in 1845 and ELDER in 1847. Wayman was pastor of churches in NEW JERSEY, PENNSYLVANIA, WASHINGTON, D. C., MARYLAND and VIRGINIA. Elected to the EPISCOPACY in 1864, he served the Second, Fourth, Third, Seventh, Ninth and Tenth Episcopal District Areas. The organizer of six annual conferences and the author of several texts on A.M.E. polity and history, he died Nov. 30, 1895.

GRANT S. SHOCKLEY

WAYNESBORO, GEORGIA, U.S.A., is in Burke County and Methodism has been a part of Burke County history almost from the beginning, as revealed by Bishop ASBURY, who visited Methodist and other churches in the vicinity several times. An entry in Asbury's *Journal* indicates that he was not favorably impressed with Waynesboro: "Let preachers or people catch me in Waynesboro (again) until things are altered and bettered." (*Journal*, Feb. 25, 1792.)

Fortunately for posterity, conditions altered. BASCOM ANTHONY, pastor of the Waynesboro Methodist Church from 1888 to 1892, wrote in his delightful book, *Fifty Years in the Ministry:* "When I reached there a hundred years later, they had greatly changed, and that for the better . . . . it was in many ways the most delightful people I have ever lived among."

Few accurate church records are today available due to disastrous fires which twice have destroyed church buildings and twice the county courthouse. The Waynesboro church was established between 1812 and 1815, and since 1857 has occupied its present site. On this, four successive edifices have been built.

In 1970 there were 741 members on the church roll, and the congregation worships in a churchly sanctuary. There is on the wall a plaque noting that Bishop ARTHUR J. MOORE was admitted to the SOUTH GEORGIA CONFERENCE in this church. A modern education and recreation building has been added to the church plant in recent years.

LILLIAN POWELL

WEATHERBY, SAMUEL S. (1840-1924), was a Methodist missionary about whom little is known, but that little is enough to warrant inclusion of his name among significant Methodists. For three years he served in Gonda, United Provinces, INDIA, 1870-73, immediately following the pioneer, SAMUEL KNOWLES. He loyally followed the policies of his predecessor, touring extensively and inviting his hearers to confess their sins and declare their faith.

One young high-caste man, in his late teens, heard the preaching with joy and followed the missionary from place to place. At length, on the third or fourth day, he responded to the invitation and was baptized with the name of "Thomas." He accompanied Weatherby home to Gonda and later went with him to LUCKNOW, always eager to learn more about Christ. He was soon an established Christian, married to a Methodist, and became the father of three sons and two daughters who were educated in the colleges in Lucknow. One son became chief justice of the high court of Oudh and was knighted as Sir George Thomas. Two sons, Charles and Edward, entered the provincial civil service and rose to be district magistrates and collectors. A daughter became an inspectress of schools and married a distinguished surgeon. The other daughter became the wife of a convert from Islam who inherited a large estate and the title of Rajah. As Rani Sheba Nawab Ali, she was true to her Christian profession and is gratefully remembered for her philanthropies.

Weatherby supervised the building of a district parsonage in Gonda. From Gonda he went in 1873 to Pauri, GARHWAL, and during a stay of three months built and opened a dispensary which continued in valuable community service for over seventy years. He died on Sept. 2, 1924.

J. WASKOM PICKETT

WEATHERFORD COLLEGE, Weatherford, Texas, was founded by the Masonic Lodge at the close of the Civil War. In 1884 the Weatherford Masonic Institute was renamed Cleveland College in honor of President Grover Cleveland. In 1889, Granbury College was moved to Weatherford, merged with Cleveland College, and chartered as Weatherford College.

In 1913 the college became the property of the CENTRAL TEXAS CONFERENCE of the Methodist Church, and in 1944 was merged with SOUTHWESTERN UNIVERSITY (Texas). Because of inability to secure adequate financial support, Southwestern University in 1949 deeded the Weatherford College properties, endowment, and loan funds to the Parker County (Texas) Junior College District formed for the purpose of operating Weatherford College as a tax-supported institution. It operates now as a public junior college.

JOHN O. GROSS

WEATHERHEAD, LESLIE DIXON (1893-   ), British Methodist minister, son of a Scots Presbyterian, was born in London in 1893, and educated at Newton Secondary School, Leicester, RICHMOND Theological COLLEGE, Surrey, and London and Manchester Universities. During the first World War he served the British Armed Forces in India and Mesopotamia, first as an officer, then as a CHAPLAIN. In 1919 he was placed in charge of the English Methodist Church in Madras. Returning to England in 1922 he was stationed first at the Oxford Road Methodist Church, Manchester, whence he moved to an even more outstanding ministry at Leeds Brunswick (1925-36). Here he developed a clinic for psychotherapy by close cooperation between physicians, psychiatrists, and ministers of religion. The Methodist Conference then permitted him to serve the interdenominational City Temple, London (1936-60), of which he remains the Minister Emeritus. In 1955 he was elected President of the Methodist CONFERENCE. Through his teaching (especially in the field of psychology), preaching, and writing, he became one of the best known Methodists on the British scene, with an international reputation. Among many honors he was made a Freeman of the City of London, a Commander of the British Empire (1959), and President of the Institute of Religion and Medicine (1966). The best known of his many writings (of which thirty-five are listed in *Who's Who*) are probably *The Transforming Friendship* (1928), *Psychology in the Service of the Soul* (1929), *Psychology and Life* (1934), and *Psychology, Religion, and Healing* (1951).

FRANK BAKER

WEAVER, CHARLES ANDERSON (1880-1956), American educator and lay missionary to BRAZIL, was born in

Atlanta, Ga., on Oct. 13, 1880. Upon graduation from EMORY COLLEGE in 1900, he taught at WEAVERVILLE COLLEGE, and then at DAVENPORT COLLEGE, both in NORTH CAROLINA. There he met and married Margaret Umberger. Feeling the call to mission service, he applied to the Board of MISSIONS (MES) and was sent to Brazil in 1911. His first appointment was to Colegio Uniao in URUGUAIANA, state of Rio Grande do Sul. There he served as professor, and then as Reitor (principal). In 1918 Mrs. Weaver died from childbirth complications. Weaver came to the United States with his four small children, arranged with relatives for their care, and returned to Brazil at the end of the year.

He was next appointed to Instituto GRANBERY, JUIZ DE FÓRA, remaining there as professor, then as Reitor. In 1927 he married Dona Eunice Gabbi (see EUNICE G. WEAVER), a young Methodist woman who had been educated in Methodist and other schools, and this proved a most happy and fruitful union.

In 1928 Weaver was granted a leave of absence from Granbery in order to accept an invitation to teach on a so-called "Floating University" that visited forty countries. Eunice Weaver accompanied him as a student. At the end of his term at Granbery, in 1934, Weaver served as superintendent of the Peoples' Institute (Instituto Central do Povo) in RIO DE JANEIRO, until 1939. In this interim, the family had been reunited, as Eunice Weaver made a home for the children.

Forced to retire from active work because of a crippling disease, he was able to help his wife on the long trips she had to make in behalf of her work for children of leprous parents. Today—from the Amazon to Central and South Brazil—at least nine homes and libraries for these children are named in his honor.

Weaver died in Rio de Janeiro on Jan. 10, 1956. The city press honored him with splendid tributes. He was buried in the Gambôa (British) Cemetery.

J. L. Kennedy, *Metodismo no Brasil.* 1928. EULA K. LONG

WEAVER, CHARLES CLINTON (1875-1946), American minister, educator and Conference leader in Western NORTH CAROLINA, was born in Ashe County, N. C., June 21, 1875. His father, J. H. Weaver, had been a distinguished Methodist preacher and presiding elder.

He was received on trial in the WESTERN NORTH CAROLINA CONFERENCE in 1901. He received his education at Trinity College (now DUKE UNIVERSITY) and at Johns Hopkins (Ph.D.). Trinity College also bestowed a D.D. degree on him.

In 1901 he became president of Rutherford College, where he stayed until 1903 when he became president of DAVENPORT COLLEGE. In 1910 Weaver transferred to the HOLSTON CONFERENCE where he became president of EMORY AND HENRY COLLEGE until 1920.

Returning to his home Conference in 1920, he served pastorates at Monroe (Central), WINSTON-SALEM (Centenary), ASHEVILLE (Central), CHARLOTTE (First) and as presiding elder or district superintendent of the Greensboro and Winston-Salem Districts.

In 1944 he became superintendent of the Hugh Chatham Memorial Hospital in Elkin, N. C., where he remained until his death Feb. 19, 1946. He was a member of the General BOARD OF MISSIONS, trustee of many institutions and a member of every GENERAL CONFERENCE between 1918 and 1944 except in 1926; he was a member of the 1939 Uniting Conference and the Southeastern Jurisdictional Conference of 1940 and 1944.

On June 18, 1902 he was married to Florence Stacy, who became the first president of the Western North Carolina Conference Woman's Society of Christian Service. Their four sons and one daughter have assumed active roles in North Carolina education and church life.

Western North Carolina Conference Journal, 1946.

Charles D. White

Eunice Gabbi Weaver

WEAVER, EUNICE GABBI (1902-1969), Brazilian Methodist social worker, educator, organizer of national and international work in behalf of leprosy victims, was born on Sept. 20, 1902, in São Manuel (state of São Paulo). She received her education in Methodist schools in Buenos Aires, Argentina, where her parents then lived; at Colegio Uniao (Uruguaiana, Brazil); and in Piracicaba (São Paulo), where she graduated from the normal school, specializing in sanitation.

From earliest childhood, she had been shocked and grieved by the plight of begging lepers, and determined to give her life to their relief. In 1927 she married Charles Anderson Weaver, a missionary of the Methodist Church, whose wife had died nine years previously. This proved a happy union and one which encouraged her to continue with her ideals. In 1928 the couple toured the world on a so-called "Floating University," he as teacher, she as student. Everywhere the ship anchored, Eunice Weaver inquired as to what was being done or could be done for lepers.

When they returned, Weaver was appointed superintendent of the Peoples' Central Institute (Instituto Central do Povo) in Rio de Janeiro. Mindful of the lepers' plight, Mrs. Weaver began work by organizing Brazilian women, whatever their religious affiliation—Catholic, Protestant, or spiritualist—into local societies for aiding leprosy victims. Since the Vargas administration was then establishing needed colonies for the segregation and treatment of lepers, Eunice Weaver concentrated on helping the still uncontaminated children and the families broken up by the "colonization" of parents. Leprous mothers, knowing

of this service, turned over their newborn babies willingly to the care of the "homes." As this project expanded, it was aided financially by state and federal governments.

In 1935 Mrs. Weaver organized the locals into a National Federation of Societies, whose objective was caring for and educating the children for self-support, thus preventing them from becoming dangers to society as beggars, prostitutes, and criminals. She was director of the program from its inception. As knowledge of the work spread, she was invited by nine other Latin American countries to advise and help them organize the same type of work. In Brazil itself, there are now 168 societies in which some 18,000 women work as volunteers; and thirty homes that care for about 5,000 children.

In 1938 Brazil sent Eunice Weaver as its representative to the Cairo International Congress on Leprosy, where she was the only woman to read a paper before the scientists and missionaries. Later she was sent to a similar gathering in Havana, Cuba. In 1942 the Brazilian government sent her as its delegate to the Pan-American Child Congress in Washington. The U. S. Department of State invited her while there to speak before colleges and universities, and to observe social conditions in the States. This same year the government of Brazil listed her in its *Book of the National Order of Merit*, with the title of "Comendadora" given the first time to a woman. The radio program of Standard Oil also gave her its coveted "Honor to Merit" diploma and gold medal.

In 1956 she was the first woman not directly associated with the Brazilian Airforce (F.A.B.) to receive its Order of Aeronautical Merit. In 1963 she became the first Protestant to receive a bronze plaque with her name, from the Roman Catholic "Damien-Dutton" Society. And in July 1965, at the celebration of the fortieth anniversary of Rio de Janeiro's daily, *O Globo*, Eunice Weaver was one of forty outstanding citizens to be named as among the "notables" of the country.

In 1955 she lost her husband and great moral support, Anderson Weaver. She continued directing and expanding the work of the federation from its headquarters in Rio de Janeiro until her death from a heart attack Dec. 9, 1969, while supervising work in Porto Alegre. She was buried in the Gambôa Cemetery in Rio.

Eula K. Long

WEAVER, JAMES B. (1833-1912), American political reformer, was born June 12, 1833, at Dayton, Ohio. The family in 1835 removed to Cassopolis, Mich., and from thence in 1843 to a quarter section in Davis County, Iowa, where Weaver attended school. From 1847 to 1851 he carried mail between Bloomfield and Fairfield and later worked in a store. In 1856 he graduated from Ohio State Law School, Cincinnati, and practiced law in Bloomfield. He served with the Second Iowa Infantry during the Civil War, and was brevetted brigadier-general March 13, 1865. General Weaver, in 1866, became district attorney of the Second Iowa Judicial District and was a federal assessor of internal revenue, 1867-73.

"Calamity Jim" Weaver, whose reform views blocked his Republican political advancement, was a Methodist Sunday school superintendent. In 1871 he spoke at the first State Methodist Convention, held at Iowa City, and was a General Conference delegate, 1876. Turning to the Greenback Party, he served in the U.S. House of Representatives, 1878-81, and was Greenback Party presidential candidate in 1880. From 1885-89 he was again in Congress, backed by the Democratic and Greenback-Labor parties.

Becoming identified with Farmers' Alliance, an agrarian reform movement which became the Populist Party, General Weaver was a presidential candidate again in 1892. Although defeated he received twenty-two electoral votes. From 1904-06 he was mayor of Colfax, Iowa, and died Feb. 6, 1912, at Des Moines, Iowa.

Dictionary of American Biography.
A. W. Haines, *Makers of Iowa Methodism.* 1900.
Iowa Journal of History, October 1953. MARTIN L. GREER

WEAVER, JONATHAN (1824-1901), American UNITED BRETHREN bishop, was born Feb. 23, 1824, in Carroll County, Ohio. Although his parents were strict on such matters as the observance of the Sabbath and his mother was diligent in giving spiritual guidance, young Jonathan Weaver never attended a Sunday religious service until he was fourteen, as there were no churches in the vicinity of the Weaver's frontier home. Whenever Methodist or United Brethren ministers came to the area, they held meetings in private homes, usually on week nights.

At the age of seventeen, Jonathan was converted at a camp meeting; but he feared how his father might react since he was not a professing Christian. He was joyfully surprised when his father urged him to stick with his decision, and shortly thereafter he was influential in bringing his entire family to Christ. Several other members of his family later went into Christian service.

Jonathan had no sudden impulse to enter the ministry and when he started to give thought to the matter, he feared that his meager education would be a hindrance. The concern about his own lack of education prompted him to campaign in later years for an educated ministry and in support of the movement to establish colleges. He spent seven years as soliciting agent for OTTERBEIN UNIVERSITY (now Otterbein College), the first such institution of the Church of the United Brethren in Christ, founded at Westerville, Ohio, in 1847. He succeeded his older brother Solomon, who played a prominent role in the establishing of two other United Brethren colleges.

Ordained in 1848, Jonathan Weaver soon established himself as a strong and noted preacher, but he was so serious about his work that he was always disappointed with the results. He gained a reputation as a writer for the *Religious Telescope;* but in 1865, his supporters failed to have him elected as its editor. However, the same GENERAL CONFERENCE that failed to elect him editor turned about and elected him bishop, a position he held until 1893.

During his tenure as bishop, Jonathan Weaver was identified with the liberalizing tendencies within the denomination. Most significant of all was his gradual change from an anti-secret society position to the pro side of the debate. His numerous books and pamphlets helped to mold the organization and doctrinal position of the church. Death came to him Feb. 6, 1901, and he was buried in the Woodland Cemetery, Dayton, Ohio,

Koontz and Roush, *The Bishops.* 1950.
H. A. Thompson, *Biography of Jonathan Weaver, D.D.* Dayton, O.: U.B. Publishing House, 1901. BRUCE C. SOUDERS

WEAVER COLLEGE, Weaverville, N. C., known as "Weaverville College," "Weaverville Male College," and after

1912 as "Weaver College," was chartered as an independent co-educational college on Dec. 7, 1873, and deeded in 1883 to the WESTERN NORTH CAROLINA CONFERENCE of the M.E. CHURCH, SOUTH. A local academy in Weaverville had been destroyed by fire in 1873, and the citizens decided not only to rebuild it but to expand its program into a college. Montraville Weaver gave the ground on which the first building, the Administration Building, was located. A second tract of land was donated by R. W. Pickens. Eventually the campus covered fifty-five acres. For a number of years the college conferred the B.A., B.S., and M.A. degrees. However, the M.A. degree was not offered after 1896 and after the school became a junior college in 1912 no degrees were granted. From 1912-34 the academic program consisted of two years of high school and two years of college work. Membership in the various literary societies was compulsory. No tuition charges were made to itinerant preachers or their children. An Alumni Association was established in 1915.

J. A. Reagan, M.D., was the first of a number of men who served as president of Weaver College. In the summers of 1923 and 1924 the Board of Young People's Work of the NORTH CAROLINA CONFERENCE of the M.P. CHURCH held ten-day Young People's Conferences at Weaver College. In 1934 the Western North Carolina Conference of the M.E. Church, South, merged Weaver College, Rutherford College and Brevard Institute into the present-day BREVARD COLLEGE.

Nell Pickens, *Dry Ridge—Some of Its History, Some of Its People.* Weaverville, N.C., 1962. RALPH HARDEE RIVES

WEAVIND, GEORGE (1850-1916), WESLEYAN METHODIST missionary in the TRANSVAAL, SOUTH AFRICA, was born at Worcester, England, on April 13, 1850, and was sent to the 'Vaal River Mission' in 1873. He learned to speak Dutch, became a burgher (citizen) of the Republic and married Wilhelmina van Boeschoten, sister of the then secretary of the Transvaal Republic, on May 12, 1875. This gave him an understanding of and sympathy with the Boers which helped to establish good relations between the mission and the civil authorities.

Weavind erected the first Methodist church in PRETORIA and became secretary of Synod when the Transvaal and Swaziland district of the British Conference was constituted in 1881. When ill-health compelled OWEN WATKINS to relinquish the chairmanship in 1892, Weavind took his place and continued in office until 1901. He established a Training Institution at Potchefstroom. This was later moved to Kilnerton and Weavind served as Governor from 1892 to 1901. From 1889 to 1892 he superintended the rapidly developing work in Johannesburg and along the Witwatersrand. In addition he served at Mafeking (1902-03), Krugersdorp (1905-06), and among the African and Cape Colored people of Pretoria (1907-16). Weavind was dedicated to his work and combined a flair for administration with a simple piety. He died in Pretoria on May 16, 1916.

A. Burnet, *A Mission to the Transvaal.* 1909.
Dictionary of South African Biography, 1967.
Minutes of British Wesleyan Methodist Conference, 1916.
J. Whiteside, *South Africa.* 1906. D. C. VEYSIE

WEBB, JOSEPH BENJAMIN (1902-), South African Methodist minister, was born on Nov. 6, 1902, in Queenstown, Cape Province, of settler stock, with English, Scot-

J. B. WEBB

tish and Huguenot ancestry. His parents moved to the alluvial diamond diggings of the Western TRANSVAAL when he was eight years old, and here he met the Rev. Percy Whitehouse, who led him to accept Jesus Christ as Saviour. He graduated at the Transvaal University College (now Pretoria University) and subsequently went to WESLEY HOUSE, Cambridge, England, where he was awarded his M.A. degree. After serving in churches in Johannesburg and PRETORIA, he began his twenty-year ministry at the Methodist Central Hall, Johannesburg in 1942. He became the best-known clergyman in SOUTH AFRICA through his preaching, broadcasting, public speaking and writing, and was elected president of the Methodist Conference of South Africa in 1949, 1954 and 1961, the only minister ever to serve as president three times. He became vice-president of the WORLD METHODIST COUNCIL in 1951 and was awarded honorary doctorates in divinity by the University of Toronto and Rhodes University, Grahamstown, South Africa. Retiring from active work in 1964, he settled at St. Michael's-on-Sea, Natal.

S. P. Freeland, *J. B. Webb—An Appreciation.* Cape Town: Methodist Publishing House, 1961.   S. P. FREELAND

WEBB, LANCE (1909-   ), American bishop, was born in Boaz, N. M., on Dec. 10, 1909, the son of John Newton Shields and Delia (Lance) Webb. He received the B.A. degree from McMURRY COLLEGE, 1931; OHIO WESLEYAN UNIVERSITY, D.D., 1960; SOUTHERN METHODIST UNIVERSITY, LL.D., 1966; ILLINOIS WESLEYAN, L.H.D., 1965, and MacMURRAY COLLEGE, D.D., 1967.

On June 30, 1933 he was united in marriage to Mary Elizabeth Hunt. Their children are Gloria Jeanne (Mrs. David B. Davis) and twins, Mary Margaret (Mrs. Lee Edlund) and Ruth Elizabeth.

He was admitted on trial to the NORTHWEST TEXAS CONFERENCE in 1933. His pastorates include Shamrock, Pampa, Eastland, Texas, 1934-41; CHAPLAIN, professor of religion at McMURRY College, 1937-38; senior minister, University Park Church, DALLAS, 1941-52; North Broad-

way Church, COLUMBUS, OHIO, 1953-64. He was elected BISHOP at CHICAGO in 1964 and assigned to the ILLINOIS Area.

Bishop Webb has been chairman of the Commission on Worship since 1964. He was a delegate to the GENERAL and JURISDICTIONAL CONFERENCES 1956, '60, and '64; chairman, Ohio Area Council on Higher Education, 1960-64; chaplain, Ohio State Senate, 1961-64; chaplain, International Civitan Club, 1951-52.

He is a trustee of the Methodist School of Theology in Ohio; BALDWIN-WALLACE COLLEGE; McKENDREE COLLEGE; ILLINOIS WESLEYAN UNIVERSITY; and McMURRY COLLEGE. Bishop Webb is author of *Conquering the Seven Deadly Sins,* 1955; *Discovering Love,* 1959; *Point of Glad Return,* 1960; *The Art of Personal Prayer,* 1962; *On the Edge of the Absurd,* 1965; *When God Comes Alive,* 1968. Two of his books have been published in Korean and one in Spanish.

Who's Who in America, Vol. 34.
Who's Who in The Methodist Church, 1966.   N. B. H.

WEBB, PAULINE MARY (19 ?-   ), daughter of the Rev. and Mrs. Leonard F. Webb, British Methodist minister. After three years of teaching in the Thames Valley Grammar School, Twickenham, in 1952 she was appointed Youth Education Secretary of the METHODIST MISSIONARY SOCIETY, and in 1954 editor of *Kingdom Overseas.* Rapidly becoming well-known as a challenging speaker and writer, with a special appeal to young people, in 1965 she was elected the third woman vice-president of the British Methodist CONFERENCE, the youngest person ever to occupy that office.

FRANK BAKER

THOMAS WEBB

WEBB, ("CAPTAIN") THOMAS (1724-1796), was a lay pioneer of American Methodism. Enlisting in 1744 in the Forty-eighth Regiment of Foot, he went to America in 1755 and lost an eye in 1759, while serving with Wolfe in Quebec. Webb married Mary Arding of New York in 1760.

Captain Webb's life in America was not without colorful interest. He was sent to Albany, N. Y., about 1764 and put in charge of the barracks, and then hearing of a Methodist society being organized in NEW YORK paid it an early visit. The few persons assembled in Philip Embury's house were astonished and alarmed to see a British officer in uniform enter their room, but they were agreeably surprised when he made known to them that he was himself a Methodist, who had been converted in England, meeting Wesley in Bristol, and had been licensed to preach. He became for a time their most active preacher and was a leading spirit in obtaining the site for the John Street Church, heading the subscription with thirty pounds, which was then the largest amount contributed by any individual. During the building of the church, he visited Philadelphia where he organized a Methodist society and collected thirty-two pounds to aid the church building in New York. In 1769 he helped Joseph Pilmore and the society in Philadelphia to purchase St. George's Church, and contributed largely also to this. He extended his effort upon Long Island and to many places in New Jersey and Delaware and also visited Baltimore.

He began to preach, always with a drawn sword laid across the pulpit, and to form societies, particularly in New Jersey, Pennsylvania, and Delaware. During a second visit to England, 1772-3, he begged the Leeds Conference to succor the American work, and he married his second wife, Grace Gilbert of Antigua.

He endeavored to get Joseph Benson to come to America, but failing in this, he came back with Thomas Rankin and Mr. Yearby.

John Wesley said of him in writing to a friend in Limerick, "Captain Webb is now in Dublin—invite him to Limerick; he is a man of fire and the power of God constantly attends his word." Charles Wesley, always a bit more careful than John, did not regard the Captain so favorably, saying that "he is an inexperienced, honest, zealous, loving enthusiast." But in 1774, John Adams, the patriot of Massachusetts, heard him preach in St. George's, and gave this account, "In the evening I went to the Methodist meeting, and heard Mr. Webb, the old soldier, who first came to America in the character of a quartermaster under General Braddock. He is one of the most fluent, eloquent men I have ever heard." (Simpson, *Cyclopaedia*.) Although a prisoner of war as a Loyalist for a time early in the American Revolution, Webb managed to get back to England and built the Portland Chapel in Bristol at his own expense. He was not a thorough scholar, but was in the habit of using the Greek Testament, and before leaving America he gave his copy to a brother minister, and it subsequently came into the possession of Bishop Levi Scott. Matthew Simpson comments upon Webb, "He well deserved the title of the first Apostle of Methodism in America."

In 1783 he settled in Bristol, where he died on Dec. 20, 1796. He is buried in Portland Chapel, which he helped to build.

Frank Baker, "Captain Thomas Webb," *Religion In Life*, xxxiv, 406-21 (Summer, 1965).
Dictionary of American Biography.
Worthington C. Ford, *British Officers Serving in America*, 1754-1774. Boston: D. Clapp & Son, 1894.
A. J. Lambert, *The Chapel on the Hill.* Bristol: St. Stephen's Press, 1929.
Proc. W.H.S., XIX, 1665, XXIII, 152.
John Pritchard, *Sermon Occasioned by the Death of the Late Captain Webb.* Bristol: Edwards, 1797.
M. Simpson, *Cyclopaedia.* 1878.
J. B. Wakely, *Lost Chapters.* 1858.   J. A. Vickers

WEBB, WILLIAM ROBERT (1842-1926), American educator and for a time U. S. Senator from Tennessee, was born Nov. 11, 1842, in Person County, N. C., the son of Alex Smith and Cornelia Adelina Stanford Webb. He entered the University of North Carolina but his schooling was interrupted by the Civil War. After the war he received the B.A. degree in 1869. He married Emma Clary in 1873 and to them were born eleven children.

Young Webb enlisted in the Confederate Army in 1861 and took part in the battles of Seven Pines, Savage Station, Malvern Hill, where he was wounded, and on recovery became adjutant of Company K, North Carolina Cavalry. He fought at Spottsylvania Courthouse, Yellow Tavern, Five Forks. He was captured at Amelia Cross Roads, and for a time was a prisoner at Harts Island, N. Y.

Returning to Tennessee he organized the Webb School at Bell Buckle and in this school was destined to make for himself a national reputation. His service as a teacher really extended over a period of sixty years, the last fifty-six of which at Bell Buckle were spent within the bounds of the Tennessee Conference.

The Webb School at Bell Buckle became known at an early date for the strictness of its discipline, and the thoroughness of its scholastic training in all the disciplines of life. So strict was the discipline and so successful those who graduated from the school, that Bell Buckle for a time was considered a school for incorrigibles—which it was not—though many a difficult youth "found himself" there. Webb's discipline was strict but always just. The one thing he would never tolerate was falsehood or deceit—one who lied to him or his fellows, being dismissed at once. "What Thomas Arnold was to England, that William R. Webb was to the Southland," stated W. F. Tillett, in a formal memoir read to and published in the minutes of the Tennessee Conference at Webb's death.

Among the pupils and graduates of the Webb School were such church leaders as E. B. Chappell, W. W. Pinson, John E. Harrison, W. H. Hlyce, J. K. Lee, George L. Beals, George A. Morgan, W. K. Matthews, Berry J. Duncan, R. R. Paty, J. T. Currcy, Clovis Chappell, C. A. Waterfield, F. F. Shannon and Josiah Sibley.

For a time under gubernatorial appointment, Webb served as U. S. Senator from Tennessee, Jan. 24—March 4, 1931. A layman, he enjoyed enormous influence within the Tennessee Conference. He died in Bell Buckle on Dec. 19, 1926.

Minutes of the Tennessee Conference.
C. F. Price, *Who's Who in American Methodism.* 1916.

WEBSTER, THOMAS (1809-1901), Canadian minister, was born in Wicklow County, Ireland, Oct. 24, 1809. In 1812 he moved with his family, first to New York, and then to a pioneer farm near London, Upper Canada. There his family reestablished their Methodist connections, and his aspirations soon turned toward the ministry.

At this point (1838), the M.E. Church was being rebuilt in the wake of the 1833 union. Webster identified himself with that body, and in 1838 was taken on trial. He was ordained Elder in 1842 and preached thereafter on many circuits in Ontario.

As were his rivals, Egerton Ryerson and John Carroll, Thomas Webster was keenly interested in religious journalism. He was one of the founders of the *Canada Christian Advocate*, the newspaper of the M.E. Church, and its editor for several years. He is better known, however, for his *History of the Methodist Episcopal Church in Canada* (1870), and for his *Life of Reverend James Richardson* (1876). The history is a useful but scarcely impartial work. It reflects very accurately the animosities which bedeviled the Wesleyan-Methodist Episcopal relationship until shortly before the union of 1884. In contrast, the biography of Bishop RICHARDSON embodies the understanding and respect of one of his close associates.

Webster was a PRESIDING ELDER for many years, a senator of ALBERT COLLEGE, and regularly a delegate to the GENERAL CONFERENCES of his church. He received a D.D. from ILLINOIS WESLEYAN UNIVERSITY.

Shortly after the union, which he reluctantly accepted, Webster retired from the active ministry. He died in Newbury, Ontario, May 2, 1901. His brethren remembered him affectionately as a saintly man who had labored faithfully for the honor and welfare of his church.

G. H. Cornish, *Cyclopaedia of Methodism in Canada.* 1881.
Minutes of the London Methodist Conference, 1901.
G. S. FRENCH

WEDGWOOD, JOSIAH (1730-1795), famous British potter and creator of the Wedgwood china, was born in Burslem in Staffordshire; and his daughter Susannah was the mother of Charles Darwin, the naturalist. The Wedgwood potteries produced a valuable black basalt bust of JOHN WESLEY and the well-known teapot which is preserved in Wesley's house on City Road, London. The teapot has the Wesley graces written by John Cennick. The design is said to have been copied from Wedgwood's wife's apron and is called "calico" or "Wesley Wedgwood." It is still used by the company.

S. Smiles, *Josiah Wedgwood.* London, 1894.
ELMER T. CLARK

WEED, BARTHOLOMEW (1793-1879), American pioneer preacher, was born March 6, 1793, in Danbury, Conn. He was trained as a Calvinist, but joined the Methodists at the age of eighteen. During the early years of his ministry, it is recorded, he preached at a camp meeting on the Stony Ground, near Flemington, N. J. He was received into the PHILADELPHIA CONFERENCE in 1817.

Weed transferred to the ILLINOIS CONFERENCE in September 1837, and served Galena District (a work including the IOWA work north of the Iowa River) as PRESIDING ELDER in 1837 and 1838. He was assigned to be the pastor of the Iowa City work in 1839 and organized that church in 1840, after Joseph L. Kirkpatrick of Iowa River Mission held the first religious services in Iowa City in 1839.

When the Iowa District was divided in 1840, Weed became presiding elder of Dubuque District, ROCK RIVER CONFERENCE, and traveled that territory for three years. He became presiding elder of Burlington District in 1843, serving this work for two years. While still a member of Rock River Conference he was elected as delegate to the historic GENERAL CONFERENCE of 1844. Weed was one of the presiding elders at the organization of the IOWA CONFERENCE and an original member of its first session in 1844.

Weed transferred to the NEW JERSEY CONFERENCE in 1845. His last years were spent in the NEWARK CONFERENCE, where he superannuated in 1864. The last seven years of his life were spent as chaplain of the Essex County jail. He died in Newark, N. J., on Jan. 5, 1879.

S. N. Fellows, *Upper Iowa Conference.* 1907.
A. W. Haines, *Makers of Iowa Methodism.* 1900.
E. H. Waring, *Iowa Conference,* 1910.
Yearbook of the Iowa Conference, 1844-45.
MARTIN L. GREER

WEEKLEY, WILLIAM MARION (1851-1926), American United Brethren bishop, was born five miles from Centerville, Va. (now WEST VIRGINIA). His parental home was the stopping place for both preachers and worshippers. As a lad, he had major church responsibilities and felt the call to the ministry. Beginning in 1870 in the Parkersburg Conference, CHURCH OF THE UNITED BRETHREN IN CHRIST, he served as a circuit rider among scattered people over the rough, hilly roads of West Virginia. He married Rosa L. Wilson in 1875.

In 1878 he was elected presiding elder (later called Conference Superintendent). A walk of twenty-five miles to visit some of his churches was not unusual. He limited his service in "the eldership" to four years, as he believed that long terms for presiding elders were inadvisable.

From 1882-84, he was pastor of the church in Parkersburg, W. Va., during which time his wife died. In June 1885, he married Miss Emma Gibson. A few months later he was again elected presiding elder and served four years followed by a pastorate at Buckhannon, W. Va., for one year. Pressure from general church leaders led him to transfer to the Rock River Conference (U.B.) in northern ILLINOIS, where his assistance was needed to strengthen that conference as it had been severely weakened by the church schism of 1889. From 1892-95, he was presiding elder. Then in 1895 he became General Secretary of the Church Erection Board and had phenomenal success during his ten years in office.

He was elected bishop in 1905 at TOPEKA, Kan., and was assigned to the Western District of the United States, headquarters at DES MOINES, Iowa for a time and later at Kansas City, Mo.

Despite impaired health much of his life William Weekley had wide interests and whole-hearted commitment to the work of his Church. In 1913 he was transferred to the Eastern District. He requested retirement as bishop in 1917, but he did accept the office of Superintendent of Evangelism and traveled constantly until 1921.

Bishop Weekley wrote several books: *Twenty Years on Horseback; Getting and Giving,* and *From Life to Life.* With BISHOP H. H. FOUT he produced a two-volume set of biographies entitled *Our Heroes.*

A dynamic leader, he died June 8, 1926, at his home in Parkersburg, W. Va. Interment was in the Odd Fellows Mausoleum, Parkersburg.

Koontz and Roush, *The Bishops.* 1950. GALE L. BARKALOW

WEEKS, ANDREW JACKSON (1869-1939), American minister and editor, was born on May 31, 1869, at Walnut Hill, La., the son of Wiley F. and Laura (McNeely) Weeks. Educated in the TEXAS public schools, he joined the Methodist Church at Ryan's Chapel, Texas in 1881. He married Mattie Payne, March 19, 1893. Their children were Vivian (Mrs. Forest Dudley), Agnes, Marvin Wightman and Andrew Jackson, Jr. Licensed to preach at Homer, Texas in 1887, he joined the EAST TEXAS CONFERENCE in 1891, was ordained an ELDER and admitted into full connection in 1893. Change in conference boundaries made him a member of the TEXAS CONFERENCE, and by transfers he became a member of the WEST TEXAS CONFERENCE, 1904; the NORTHWEST TEXAS, 1915; the OKLAHOMA, 1926; and the NORTH TEXAS, 1928. Appointments were Augusta Circuit, 1891-93; Center Station, 1894-97; Rusk Station, 1898; First Church, Marshall, 1899; San Augustine district, 1900-02; Central Church, GALVESTON, 1903; Marlin, 1904; West End, SAN ANTONIO, 1905-06; San Antonio district, 1907-10; Superintendent, Home Missions for Texas and NEW MEXICO, 1911-12; First Church, SAN ANGELO, 1913-14; Yoakum, 1915; Clarendon, 1916-17; Stamford district, 1917-18; Editor, *Texas Christian Advocate*, 1919-22; Editor, Missionary Literature of General Board PUBLICATIONS, M.E. CHURCH, SOUTH, 1923-26; Oklahoma district, 1927-28; Sherman district, 1929-31; Editor, *Texas Christian Advocate* (second time), 1932 till his death, Dec. 12, 1939.

SOUTHWESTERN UNIVERSITY, Georgetown, Texas, conferred on him the D.D. degree. He was a delegate to the GENERAL CONFERENCE (MES) of 1902 and 1910; the ECUMENICAL METHODIST CONFERENCE, LONDON, England, 1921; the sixth Ecumenical Conference, 1931, being secretary of that conference till his death. He was also a delegate to the Universal Conference on Life and Work, STOCKHOLM, Sweden, 1925. He was a member of the JUDICIAL COUNCIL (MES) from 1934 to 1939.

Bishop H. A. BOAZ said of Weeks, "He was unlike anyone I ever knew, a man of unique personality, being in a class to himself. He had an unusual mind. He was a clear thinker, a close observer, and a student of human nature. He was a man of worldwide vision, interested in everything that concerned the Christian church over the world." His piercing sense of humor and his unstinted devotion to all good things in all areas of the human scene endeared him to all who knew him.

Journal of the North Texas Conference, 1940.
C. F. Price, *Who's Who in American Methodism*. 1916.
O. W. Nail, *Texas Methodism*. 1961.   J. DANIEL BARRON

WEEKS, HARRY HANSON (1877-1962), was a M.E. missionary in INDIA from 1907 until the achievement of union made him a minister of the Methodist Church in Southern Asia. He was born in the coastal village of Vik, in Helgeland, NORWAY, and was known as Harry Hanson. Migrating to the United States in 1893, he joined relatives in a part of SOUTH DAKOTA where Scandinavians predominated. There were so many Harry Hansons that he added his birthplace to his name, and Vik was soon changed to "Week." His school fellows called him "seven days." Another change made him "Weak," and the lads called him "strong man" (he was tall, big and strong). A fourth and last change made him Harry Hanson Weeks. Before that time another HARRY HANSON had joined his annual conference in India.

He graduated from DAKOTA WESLEYAN UNIVERSITY in 1907 and went to India. On furlough he earned the M.A. degree from NORTHWESTERN UNIVERSITY. In 1925 Dakota Wesleyan conferred on him the honorary D.D. degree.

His appointments included: principal, Boys' Vocational School, Lodhipur, Shahjahanpur; superintendent, BAREILLY, Shahjahanpur, GARHWAL, Bijnor, and Moradabad Districts; and principal and manager of the Messmore

High School at Pauri. For outstanding service in the Messmore School and to the public welfare he was honored by the British king with the coveted Kaiser-i-Hind Gold Medal. He retired in 1944 and died in 1962.

He was very active in the First Methodist Church of Redlands, CALIF., after retirement, and the church named its social hall in his honor. He began his work in India as a single man but Clara Hatheway came to India as his fiance and they were married in Bombay, Oct. 29, 1909.

Minutes of the North India Conference.   J. WASKOM PICKETT

WEEMS, CLARENCE NORWOOD (1875-1952), American missionary to KOREA, was born in Oostanaula, Gordon Co., Ga., on Feb. 18, 1875. He graduated from the University of Arkansas in 1899, and received the M.A. degree from EMORY UNIVERSITY in 1925. At an early age, Weems felt a call to religious work and after ten years of teaching in ARKANSAS and KENTUCKY entered missionary service.

He was appointed to Korea in 1909, where he served for thirty-two years. His first assignment was to Songo where he was in charge of educational work as well as serving either as district missionary or district superintendent. In 1933 he was transferred to Wonsan to continue the same activities, "a career district superintendent," until retirement. Especially active in the training of preachers in Korea as well as America, he had an unusual record in the number of promising young men sent to the United States for further study.

Weems was a member of both the Korea and NORTH GEORGIA CONFERENCE. He was a member of the Commission of Twenty appointed to draft plans for organization of the Korean Methodist Church in 1930. Three of his four sons served in Korea, with either the U. S. Armed Forces, or the U. S. State Department, and the fourth was a missionary to Korea until he retired for family health reasons.

Clarence N. Weems officially retired in 1941 and died in Decatur, Ga., Feb. 26, 1952.

CHARLES A. SAUER

WEIDLER, VICTOR OTTERBEIN (1887-1950), American E.U.B. bishop, son of Rev. and Mrs. Z. A. Weidler, was born at Highspire, Pa., Jan. 27, 1887. His paternal and maternal grandparents were ministers. He was converted during high school days and remained in that city in employ of the Hensel Clothing Company until he entered LEBANON VALLEY COLLEGE, from which institution he graduated in 1910. Following graduation he taught school three years in Waynesboro, Pa. The Waynesboro U.B. Church voted him quarterly conference license in 1913. He joined the ERIE CONFERENCE, Church of the UNITED BRETHREN IN CHRIST, and was ordained in 1916. A number of pastorates were served in this conference until 1926, when the Home MISSION BOARD of the denomination called him to assume the superintendency of the MINNESOTA CONFERENCE. During this time he also served the pastorate of the First U.B. Church in MINNEAPOLIS.

In 1934, following the sudden death of the General Secretary of the Board of Home Missions and Church Erection, Weidler was elected to this post. Then four years later, following the death of Bishop A. B. STATTON, he was elected by a mail ballot to the bishopric and assigned to the Southwest District. He served in this area until his death which occurred in Chatham, ONTARIO,

V. O. WEIDLER

Canada, Aug. 5, 1950, as he and his wife were en route to Kitchener, Ontario, to attend the General Board of Christian EDUCATION and the Commission on EVANGELISM.

On his birthday, 1920, he was married to Dora Housekeeper of Bowling Green, Ohio. Lebanon Valley College conferred on him the D.D. degree in 1935, and in 1942 YORK COLLEGE granted him the LL.D. degree. He was buried in Bowling Green, Ohio, Aug. 7, 1950.

The Telescope-Messenger, Sept. 9, 1950.   JOHN H. NESS, SR.

WEI LI KUNK HUI, the Chinese name of the unified Methodist church which was created by the unifying of separate Methodist Churches in China in 1941. (See CHINA.)

WELCH, EDGAR T. (1881-1963), American layman and food executive, was born in Vineland, N. J., Jan. 22, 1881, the son of Charles Edgar and Jennie (Ross) Welch. He was the grandson of Thomas Bramwell Welch who, as an 1869 Methodist communion steward, perfected sterilized, unfermented grape juice and founded the Welch Grape Juice Company. Edgar T. Welch studied at Williamsport Dickinson Seminary.

At the age of twelve he joined the Vineland Methodist Church. In 1898 he joined the Westfield, N. Y., Methodist Church, remaining active there throughout his life. He was a member of the executive committee of the General BOARD OF MISSIONS of the M.E. Church from 1924 to 1939. He served as president of the General Board of LAY ACTIVITIES from 1939 to 1944. He was a delegate to each GENERAL CONFERENCE from 1928 to 1944, as well as to the UNITING CONFERENCE of 1939.

By his first marriage to Grace Harris, July 23, 1902, he had four children: Charles E., Thomas H., Paul R., and Jean (Mrs. Donald C. Tiedemann). By his second marriage to Myrtie Warren he had one son, Ross Warren (deceased).

He died June 26, 1963 and was buried in Westfield Cemetery. On July 13, 1963 the WESTERN NEW YORK ANNUAL CONFERENCE posthumously awarded him a certificate of appreciation.

Time, September 3, 1956.
Who's Who in Methodism, 1952.
Westfield Republican, July 2, 1963.   ERNEST R. CASE

WELCH, HERBERT (1862-1969), American bishop and centenarian, was born on Nov. 7, 1862, in New York City, the son of Peter A. and Mary (Loveland) Welch. He received his early education at Public School 35, New York City, and the Brooklyn Collegiate and Polytechnic Institute in Brooklyn. He graduated from WESLEYAN UNIVERSITY, Middletown, Conn., in 1887 with an A.B. degree and from that same University received the following degrees: A.M., 1890; D.D., 1902; and LL.D. in 1906. He received the B.D. degree from DREW THEOLOGICAL SEMINARY in 1890, and attended Oxford University in England, 1902-03. He also received honorary degrees from NORTHWESTERN UNIVERSITY, LL.D., 1910; Western Reserve University and University of Vermont, LL.D., 1911; OHIO WESLEYAN UNIVERSITY, LL.D., 1924; WEST VIRGINIA WESLEYAN COLLEGE, Litt.D., 1928; ALLEGHENY COLLEGE, LL.D., 1932; and the D.D. degree from BOSTON UNIVERSITY in 1938, and Brooklyn Polytechnic Institute, LL.D., 1958. On June 3, 1890 he married Adelaide Frances McGee, and to them were born two daughters, Dorothy McGee (Mrs. Anthony F. Blanks) and Eleanor Loveland.

Herbert Welch entered the ministry of the M.E. Church in 1890; full connection, ordained DEACON, 1892, ELDER, 1894. He served several pastorates in the NEW YORK CONFERENCE, including St. Luke's Church, NEW YORK, 1892-93; Summerfield Church, BROOKLYN, 1893-98; First Church, Middletown, Conn., 1898-02; Chester Hill Church, Mount Vernon, N. Y., 1903-05. In 1905 he was elected president of Ohio Wesleyan University, serving in this capacity until 1916 as in May of that year he was elected to the EPISCOPACY of the M.E. Church. He was resident bishop of JAPAN and KOREA from 1916 to 1928; of the PITTSBURGH Area, 1928-32; and the Shanghai Area, 1932-36. Bishop Welch retired in 1936, but was appointed by his colleagues to administer the BOSTON Area in 1938-39 to fill a vacancy caused by the death of Bishop Burns.

Bishop Welch after retirement served as chairman and executive of the METHODIST COMMITTEE FOR OVERSEAS RELIEF (now UMCOR), 1940-48, during which time he supervised the raising and distribution of $7,500,000 for relief purposes abroad. His lectureships included the Fondren, SOUTHERN METHODIST UNIVERSITY, 1924; Merrick, OHIO WESLEYAN UNIVERSITY, 1937; Tipple, Drew University, 1937; and Carol Gardner, "Religion and Medicine," College of Physicians and Surgeons, Columbia University, 1962. He served on numerous boards of trustees including those of Wesleyan University, Ohio Wesleyan University, Drew University, and was chairman of the trustees of JOHN STREET CHURCH, New York, 1936-44. He was one of the five organizers and the first president of the Methodist Federation for Social Service, 1907-12. He was a member of the University Senate, 1908-16; of the Commission on Church and Social Service of the FEDERAL COUNCIL, 1908-17. He was a fraternal messenger from United States Methodism to the Methodist Church of CANADA, 1914; a delegate to the GENERAL CONFER-

ENCE of the M.E. Church, 1916, at which he was elected BISHOP. He was chairman of the Joint Commission which organized the Methodist Church of Korea, which united there the Korean conferences of the M.E. Church and the M.E. Church, South. He was vice-president of the National Christian Council, CHINA, 1935-36; and in the AMERICAN BIBLE SOCIETY, 1936-48, he was chairman of its Committee on Foreign Agencies. He was a member of the executive committee of the Federal Council, 1936-44. He was decorated in 1928 and given the third-class order of the Sacred Treasure (Japan); decorated with the medal of Republic of Korea by the Ambassador from Korea, 1952; received an honor citation from the Nationalist Republic of China, 1947 and 1952; an honor citizen, Republic of Korea, 1956; citation for public service, Ohio Wesleyan University, 1954, and the Poe medal from this University in 1957. He was named Methodist Man of the Year in *World Outlook* in 1958, and given an alumni citation, Golden Jubilee award, from Brooklyn Polytechnic Institute in 1960. In June 1947—in his eighty-fifth year —he delivered the baccalaureate sermon at Wesleyan University, his alma mater, on the occasion of his sixtieth anniversary when the College Chapel Altar was dedicated in his honor.

Herbert Welch was the author, with others, of *The Christian College*, 1916; *That One Face*, 1925; *College Lectures* (printed in Korean), 1935; *Men of the Outposts*, 1937; and a frequent contributor to the religious press; the Affirmation of Faith (commonly called The Korean Creed) is largely credited to him. (See CONFESSION OF FAITH.) He was the editor of *Selections from the Writings of John Wesley*, 1901, and his book, *As I Recall My Past Century*, released on Nov. 7, 1962, on the occasion of his 100th birthday was autobiographical. He resided in New York City until his death on April 4, 1969, in the 107th year of his age. He exerted as long as he lived enormous influence in the church he served.

Who's Who in America, Vol. 34.
Who's Who in The Methodist Church, 1966.   N. B. H.

WELDON, WILSON OSBOURNE (1911-   ), American minister and editor of the national and interdenominational devotional guide, *The Upper Room*, was born in Camden, S. C., on March 15, 1911, the son of John Wesley and Leila Mae (Wilson) Weldon. He was educated at the University of South Carolina (B.A. in 1931) and received a B.D. from DUKE in 1934, and the D.D. from HIGH POINT COLLEGE in 1952. He married Margaret Hammond Lyles on July 19, 1939, and they have two children—Wilson, Jr. and Alice Adelaide; an elder daughter, Nanci Leila, a Methodist missionary, died in 1965. Dr. Weldon was the professor of Bible at COLUMBIA COLLEGE in South Carolina, and director of the WESLEY FOUNDATION in 1934. He joined the WESTERN NORTH CAROLINA CONFERENCE in 1936 as the minister of education for Centenary Church in WINSTON-SALEM. Other pastorates have been China Grove; First Church, HIGH POINT; Memorial Church, Thomasville; First Church, Gastonia; Myers Park, CHARLOTTE and West Market Street, GREENSBORO. He was a delegate to the WORLD METHODIST CONFERENCE in 1956, and has been a member of the JURISDICTIONAL CONFERENCES of 1952, '56, '60, and '64, and of the GENERAL CONFERENCES of 1956, '60, and '64. He is a trustee of GREENSBORO COLLEGE, OF SCARRITT COLLEGE, and has written two books: *Facing Life Now*

and Then, 1959; and *The Thrill of Christian Living*, 1965. He is also the author of a *Pastoral Relations Committee Manual*, 1962. He was elected by the Board of EVANGELISM as editor of *The Upper Room* on April 5, 1967, and also is executive secretary of *The Upper Room* section of the Board of Evangelism. He completed his duties as pastor of the West Market Street Church on June 11, 1967, at which time he assumed the editorship of *The Upper Room* in NASHVILLE, TENN.

Who's Who in The Methodist Church, 1966.   N. B. H.

WELLINGTON, New Zealand. **Wesley Church,** Taranaki Street, has had an honored history. Methodism's witness in Wellington began among the Maoris who had settled there before the first immigrants arrived.

On the first immigrant ships there were many Methodists, and services were soon commenced: first probably in a cottage, and then in a large Maori meeting house. Here John Aldred, the first resident minister, met his congregations. Later the people met in a Maori church, but this was blown down in a gale. The congregation then gathered in "the Exchange" until a small weatherboard church, twenty-two by sixteen feet, was built. This building was enlarged to hold 130 people. In 1843 it was replaced by a brick church seating 300, but in 1848 it was destroyed in a tremendous earthquake. The new church was opened in February, 1850, and for eighteen years this was well filled. In 1868, a handsome church was opened in Manners Street, but eleven years later, a fire, originating in the opera house opposite, spread to the church which was destroyed. WILLIAM KIRK and his officials thereupon bought an acre of land nearby in Taranaki Street for £3,000; and in March, 1880, the new church, largest in NEW ZEALAND, was opened. It seated 1,200 people. An organ costing £600 was built, and the debt on the property was £6,000. Part of the Manners Street land was sold to help pay off this debt, and the rest of the land was leased. For many years the congregation filled the large church, which still houses a thriving work. A complete modernization of the church interior was undertaken in the early 1960's, and the site was greatly improved by the city's street-widening program.

In 1882, a schoolhouse with a large central hall and seventeen class rooms were built behind the church. The cost was £1,200, raised largely by the teachers themselves. In 1898 a large infant school to hold 250 children was built for £460. At this time the total school roll was about 800.

The first parsonage was built of raupo reed. A weatherboard house in Manners Street replaced it, and in 1865 a new two-story house was built on the same site. Ten years later a commodious house was bought on "The Terrace" and in 1882, it was sold to help build a large house next to the Taranaki Street Church. The cost was £1,100.

The present parsonage in Macfarlane Street was built in 1913 for £1,500, and the former parsonage was leased as a boarding house. Later still, it became a hostel, but was demolished in 1965.

Wesley Church Social Services Trust Board, Inc., was formed in 1949 to administer all social services undertaken by the central Wesley Church in the city on Taranaki Street. These include:

Wesleyhaven Eventide Homes Settlement. In 1949, Mr. and Mrs. W. T. Strand gave the Methodist church about 150 acres of land for the specific purpose of establishing an Eventide Homes Settlement. The first buildings erected were a block of service flats including eight self-contained private villas, nurses quarters and charge room, a superintendent's cottage, and a settlement kitchen. With the necessary road construction and other expenses, the cost was approximately £60,000, the state providing nearly half by way of subsidy. These buildings provide accommodation for thirty elderly people. In 1957 negotiations took place with the Deckston Hebrew Trust for a Jewish accommodation block as a unit within Wesleyhaven. Since then the ladies' auxiliary of the Associated Churches of Christ have also provided a villa on the same terms. Expansion of the settlement is still going on and provides a wonderful service for the elderly folk of Wellington.

Epworth House. This hostel was opened in February, 1959, for young women. It accommodates twenty-one boarders and a matron. Costing only £11,000, it is claimed as one of the finest hostels in the city.

Church House. In 1953, the old parsonage next door to Wesley Church, which for over thirty years had been leased as a boardinghouse, became available to a group of twelve young men of the church, who lived there on a community basis. The building was demolished in 1965.

In 1966 careful thought was being given to ways in which the work of the trust board might best be integrated into the general work of the Central Districts Methodist Social Services Association.

ROBERT THORNLEY

WELLINGTON (New Zealand) **CHARITABLE AND EDUCATIONAL ENDOWMENT** was originally a trust founded for educational purposes. After the Maori Wars, it was decided to establish four institutions in the North Island for the education of Maori children under the care of the Wesleyan Church. Three were actually opened near AUCKLAND, New Plymouth, and Wanganui. In 1852 George Grey, the governor, conveyed seventy-three acres of the town lands of Wellington to the Wesleyan Church "for the instruction of our subjects of all races, and of children of other poor and destitute persons being inhabitants of islands in the Pacific Ocean."

However, it was found impossible to begin a school in Wellington. The seventy-three acres produced no revenue. The Maori population near the city steadily declined. Land disputes led to unsettlement, and ultimately, in 1865, the government took seventy of the acres for botanical gardens and a recreation reserve. The remaining three acres were then let for residential purposes. About £4,228 was received, and some of it was used to buy land in the Manawatu area, and later near Wellington. In 1872 a day school was opened in Dixon Street, but in 1879 it burned down, and the work was carried on in a building rented from the Central Wesleyan Church.

In time the education work was centered in kindergarten schools, but first one and then another was closed because of decreased attendance. In 1921 an orphanage was opened at Masterton, called Homeleigh, and year by year the board of the endowment has assisted in its maintenance.

In 1940, the board began to make an annual grant toward the Rangiatea Maori Girls' Hostel at New Plymouth, of the Home and Maori Mission Department. The board's present policy is to divide its net revenue equally between the Masterton home and the New Plymouth

hostel. The assets of the board in 1966 exceeded £100,000.

WILLIAM T. BLIGHT

WELLIVER, LESTER ALLEN (1896-   ), American minister and educator, was born at Stockton, Pa., Feb. 2, 1896. He was educated at DICKINSON COLLEGE (A.B., 1918; M.A., 1922; D.D., 1940), and DREW THEOLOGICAL SEMINARY (B.D., 1920). WESTERN MARYLAND COLLEGE granted him the LL.D. degree in 1944.

He entered the ministry of the M.E. CHURCH in 1918, being admitted on trial in the ERIE CONFERENCE and transferring to the CENTRAL PENNSYLVANIA CONFERENCE in 1919. In 1918 he served in the chaplaincy of the U. S. Army. As a pastor he served five churches. A leader in Central Pennsylvania Methodism, he was superintendent of the HARRISBURG District (1936-42) and of the Williamsport District (1955-61). Elected president of WESTMINSTER THEOLOGICAL SEMINARY in 1943, he served until 1955. He was a member of the Board of Governors of the Seminary from 1940 to 1955. In 1954 he became a member of the JUDICIAL COUNCIL of The Methodist Church, serving as president from 1960 to 1964. He has been a member of the WORLD METHODIST COUNCIL and was a delegate to its Conferences at Oxford, England in 1951 and at LAKE JUNALUSKA, N. C. in 1956. He also served on the Board of EDUCATION of The Methodist Church from 1940 to 1954. He is a trustee of Dickinson College, Carlisle, Pa. He was a member of the GENERAL CONFERENCES of The Methodist Church in 1940, 1948 and 1952 and of the Northeastern JURISDICTIONAL CONFERENCES of 1940, 1944, 1948 and 1952. He was long a member of the Association of Methodist HISTORICAL SOCIETIES and is a past president of the Northeastern Jurisdictional Society. He was one of the Research Editors of *The Journal and Letters of Francis Asbury*, 1958.

Granted the retired relation in 1966, he presently resides in Harrisburg, Pa.

Journal of the Central Pennsylvania Conference, 1965.
Who's Who in America, Vol. 34.

WELLONS, RALPH D. (1890-   ), was a missionary in INDIA from 1918 to 1941; and president of Pembroke State College at Pembroke, N. C., from 1942 until he reached the retirement age.

He was born at Needmore, Ind., Jan. 28, 1890, and was educated at Indiana University (A.B., 1914; A.M., 1924) and Columbia University (Ph.D., 1927). He married Willafred Howe, Aug. 18, 1914. She also had graduated from Indiana University.

They went to India in 1916, and he became professor of English in LUCKNOW CHRISTIAN COLLEGE. A few years later he was elected vice-principal. In 1931 when JASHWANT R. CHITAMBAR, the principal, was elected bishop by the Central Conference of SOUTHERN ASIA, Wellons was chosen to succeed him. He served as principal for ten years in a critical period, and made a lasting contribution to education in the North of India and to the Christian church throughout the land. Retiring in 1941 because of family health problems, he was invited the next year to the presidency of Pembroke State College, which primarily served American Indians.

Wellons was ordained in the North India Conference and, when it was divided in 1920, he became a charter member of the Lucknow Annual Conference. He maintained his ministerial status and sense of vocation throughout his distinguished career as an educator. When he retired from the presidency of Pembroke College, he served as pastor of St. Paul Church, Winter Park, Fla., for a year, and as associate pastor of Winter Park Church for seven years.

Dr. and Mrs. Wellons are now living in the Methodist Retirement Home at Durham, N. C.

J. N. Hollister, *Southern Asia*. 1956.
Minutes of the North India and Lucknow Conferences, 1917-42.
J. WASKOM PICKETT

WELLS, ELIZABETH JEANNE (1877-1941), began in 1901 a notable career of missionary service in INDIA. She was born May 20, 1877, at Pleasant Hills, Iowa. Her father was a farmer. She was converted at the age of nine and joined the church the same year. With the hope of becoming a missionary, at home or abroad, she entered Missouri Wesleyan College at Cameron, Mo., and before her graduation decided for India. After receiving the B.S. degree, she went to the Chicago Training School. In March 1901, she was appointed to India by the Des Moines branch of the WOMAN'S FOREIGN MISSIONARY SOCIETY. Her first responsibility was as superintendent of the orphanage in the Methodist Girls' School at HYDERABAD. Later she served as principal of a girls' primary school at Vikarabad and lifted its boarding school enrollment from twelve to 100.

She was very versatile. One year she vaccinated 150 persons. She was a zealous evangelist, often going into villages to make friends with all classes of people and to bear witness about Christ. She studied the abilities of her girls and guided many of them into activities and studies in which they became highly proficient.

In her later years she started a school in rural surroundings near Hyderabad in the hope that it might help improve rural homes and farms. After some years the school was moved to Zahirabad, where it has become highly successful in her declared aims. She died July 15, 1941.

J. WASKOM PICKETT

WELLS, JACOB ELBERT (1873-1949), American pastor and district superintendent, was born in Marion County, W. Va., Nov. 27, 1873, the son of Richard D. and Mary J. (Atha) Wells. After teaching school nine years, he went to WEST VIRGINIA WESLEYAN COLLEGE (A.B., 1907, D.D., 1923) and BOSTON UNIVERSITY SCHOOL OF THEOLOGY (S.T.B., 1910). He married Daisie W. Furbee, June 29, 1910, and they had two daughters.

Admitted on trial in the WEST VIRGINIA CONFERENCE (ME) in 1904, Wells was ordained DEACON in 1910 and ELDER in 1912. He held student pastorates in WEST VIRGINIA and MASSACHUSETTS. After serving six charges in West Virginia, 1910-23, he was appointed to the Elkins District, 1924-28. Thereafter he had one charge in Parkersburg, two in Huntington, and the Buckhannon District, 1935-40.

Especially interested in young people, Wells served as conference president of the EPWORTH LEAGUE, 1912-22, and he emphasized Christian education and missions. A trustee of West Virginia Wesleyan College, 1916-46, he chaired the semi-centennial celebration in 1940. Wells

initiated the custom of an annual banquet for retired members of his conference. His brethren elected him a delegate to the 1928 GENERAL CONFERENCE and to the 1940 JURISDICTIONAL CONFERENCE. He died March 12, 1949, and was buried at Alma, W. Va.

Haught, *West Virginia Wesleyan College*, 1890-1940. Buckhannon, W. Va.: West Virginia Wesleyan College.
Pittsburgh Christian Advocate, September 23, 1926.
West Virginia Conference Journal, 1904-49.
J. C. Schwarz, *Who's Who In The Clergy*. New York: Schwarz, 1946.
ALBEA GODBOLD

WELLS, JOSEPH (1798-date of death uncertain), American M.P. layman of Wellsville, OHIO, served his church as trustee, class-leader, steward, delegate to numerous ANNUAL CONFERENCES, four GENERAL CONFERENCES and two conventions of his denomination. He was born on March 21, 1798, in Washington County, Pa., but he spent most of his life in Wellsville, Ohio, which was named for his family. A M.P. CHURCH was organized in his home by George Brown in 1829 and the church was thereafter affectionately known as "Uncle Josey's Church." For seven years prior to the establishment of this church he lived in the community but refused to unite with the M.E. CHURCH of which his relatives were members. He was liberal in his gifts to the church and its interests and is remembered as a pioneer layman in the M.P. Church.

T. H. Colhouer, *Sketches of the Founders*. 1880.
M. Simpson, *Cyclopaedia*. 1882. RALPH HARDEE RIVES

WELLS, JOSHUA (1764-1862), American minister, was born in Maryland, Dec. 6, 1764. He joined the M.E. CHURCH in 1787 and entered its BALTIMORE CONFERENCE in 1789. During the deistic decade and ministerial shortage after 1790, he became a trusted elder who was shifted by Bishop ASBURY to fill strategic stations at NEW YORK, BOSTON, BALTIMORE, PHILADELPHIA, and WILMINGTON, Del. From the latter place he was assigned to Wilmington, N. C., thence he came back to the Baltimore Conference where he married a widow, Mrs. Eve Reinicker, in 1812. He was superannuated in 1821, but continued to be a delegate to GENERAL CONFERENCES, serving altogether in nine of them—1800-32. During the 1820 General Conference, Wells, WILLIAM CAPERS, S. G. ROSZEL and Bishop ENOCH GEORGE attempted to work out a compromise over the question of the elective PRESIDING ELDERSHIP. After a prolonged debility, Wells died in Baltimore, Jan. 25, 1862.

J. E. Armstrong, *Old Baltimore Conference*. 1907.
EDWIN SCHELL

WELSH ASSEMBLY. (See Wales.)

WELSH CALVINISTIC METHODISM. Perhaps even more than England, Wales was spiritually dead at the beginning of the eighteenth century, in spite of an occasional exception like GRIFFITH JONES, rector of Llanddowror. A new warmth of evangelism was introduced by the conversion in 1735 of HOWELL HARRIS, a young layman of Trevecka, Brecknockshire, who soon began to exhort his neighbors to flee from the wrath to come, with rapidly increasing success. Simultaneously a young clergyman, DANIEL ROWLANDS, was converted, and began an evangelical ministry in Llangeitho, Cardiganshire. Under their ministry others were converted and began to preach in their own area and to itinerate in the surrounding countryside, especially HOWELL DAVIES in Pembrokeshire, WILLIAM WILLIAMS of Pantycelyn, Carmarthenshire (author of "Guide me, O thou great Jehovah"), and Peter Williams, also of Carmarthenshire.

In 1742 this group assembled at Watford for their first "Association," inviting GEORGE WHITEFIELD, who had already expressed his sympathy to Harris, to preside. National and regional Associations continued to be held both annually and quarterly, presaging the annual CONFERENCE and the QUARTERLY MEETING so important in Wesley's Methodism. In spite of the theological differences between them the Wesleys wished the Welsh Calvinistic Methodists well, and co-operated with them as far as possible, especially through their itinerant spokesman, Howell Harris. Like the Wesleys, they too were members of the Church of England, whose hope it was that they might bring about a spiritual awakening within that church; indeed they owed the title "Methodist" to this fact. They also formed local societies under the pastoral oversight of lay "overseers," "exhorters," and "stewards." These societies at first met in private houses, but later in special meeting places, in which the Lord's Supper was administered by Methodist clergy. Like the English Methodists they too were subjected to persecution by hooligans, mobs, and unfriendly clergy. In spite of the similarities, however, there was relatively very little contact with Wesley's Methodism, and no official connection.

A struggle for leadership between Rowlands and Harris, exacerbated by a period of mental instability through which the latter passed, brought about a temporary disruption in 1750. Harris himself retired to Trevecka, where he organized an experimental religious community known as the "Family," which secured the support of the COUNTESS OF HUNTINGDON, and by 1755 had grown to over a hundred members, with fifty more in neighbouring farms. By 1760 Harris had returned to his preaching itinerancy, but his "Family" survived him for almost seventy years, though their links with Welsh Calvinistic Methodism were. very slender. In 1763 Harris and Rowlands were reconciled, though Harris was not able to reconcile himself to the growing independence from the Church of England of Rowlands' supporters, no more than they took kindly to the monastic tendencies of Harris's "Family," nor of his friendliness with the Wesleys and the Moravians.

The reconciliation of Rowlands and Harris coincided with a new burst of revivalism after a dry decade, and Welsh Calvinistic Methodism continued to experience recurring waves of revival. Their great leader during the latter half of the eighteenth century was THOMAS CHARLES of Bala, again an Anglican clergyman who strove to keep the Methodists within the fold of the Church of England. In 1801, however, he drew up for them "The Rules and Purposes of the Special Societies among the People called Methodists in Wales," and a virtual separation took place in 1811 with his ordination of eight lay preachers, though like Wesley he continued to hope that declared separation might be avoided. In 1826 the pious fiction was dispelled by the enrolment in the High Court of Chancery of a "Constitutional Deed declaratory of the Objects and Regulations of the Welch Calvinistic Methodist Connexion."

In 1842 the Welsh Calvinistic Methodists were invited to consider union with the Presbyterian Church in England, as their polity was in fact presbyterian. A fraternal relationship developed which led to their eventually adopting the title "Presbyterian Church of Wales," even though they retained their autonomy and continued to use the older name as a kind of sub-title. Because of this affiliation they did not become linked with the ECUMENICAL METHODIST CONFERENCE as it was nor its successor the WORLD METHODIST COUNCIL.

In the closing decade of the eighteenth century Welsh emigrants brought the denomination to America, their first official church being "Penycaerau" in Oneida County, New York, organized in 1824. From this they spread to most areas in the nation, though their numbers remained comparatively small. Fraternal relations with Presbyterianism developed in America along similar lines to those in Wales, and in 1920 the Welsh Calvinistic Methodist Church was officially incorporated with the Presbyterian Church in the U.S.A.

From the beginning the Welsh Calvinistic Methodists supported the work of the London Missionary Society, and in 1840 sent their own missionaries to Assam and Brittany. Their Indian missions, which far surpassed the French in importance and permanence, though remaining small, are now incorporated in the United Church of North India.

The total community of the church in Wales is now approaching 200,000.

D. E. Jenkins, *Calvinistic Methodist Holy Orders.* 1911.
Journal of the Historical Society of the Presbyterian Church of Wales, formerly *Transactions of the Calvinistic Methodist Historical Society,* 1916 to the present time.
John Hughes Morris, *The Story of our Foreign Mission.* Liverpool: Evans, 1930.
D. J. Williams, *Welsh Calvinistic Methodism.* 1937.
W. Williams, *Welsh Calvinistic Methodism.* 1884.

FRANK BAKER

WEMBO-NYAMA, CHIEF (?-1940), a chief of the Atetela in the heart of the CONGO in Central Africa, who proved to be a friend and supporter of Methodist missions. The Congo Free State was established in 1876 and the Atetela helped the Belgians drive out the Arabs in 1893. Chief Wembo-Nyama was commissioned to enforce the rubber tax and took wives and slaves. The Free State became the Belgian Congo in 1910, cannibalism was outlawed, and the slaves returned home in 1912.

Bishop WALTER LAMBUTH of the M.E. CHURCH, SOUTH selected as a mission site Wembo-Nyama's village, and with JOHN GILBERT, an American Negro, visited there in 1912. Chief Wembo-Nyama seemed pleased to have a mission established among his people, and Bishop Lambuth explained that it would take him at least a year and a half to go back to America and obtain the necessary supplies and personnel and to return. As Lambuth was leaving the Chief took the Bishop to a certain tree in his village and said that he would cut a notch in that tree at each full moon, and that when eighteen notches had been cut, he would expect the Bishop back. Lambuth agreed, and in spite of difficulties, made it back in time to establish what continues today as a strong mission station.

Chief Wembo-Nyama was also instrumental in encouraging the missionaries in the development of a written language, and the missionaries in time saw that a dictionary and the Sunday school lessons were printed. By 1935 the New Testament had been translated.

The Wembo-Nyama mission celebrated its Silver Jubilee Year in 1939, at which time there were thirty-four missionaries, 192 native preachers, 290 churches, 5,760 members, 3,178 probationers, ninety-eight woman's societies, 186 schools, 7,561 students, 232 native teachers, 149 girls homes, three hospitals, 115,372 dispensary patients, 417 major operations, 548 lepers. Beside Wembo-Nyama there was Tunda, Minga and Lodja, comprising this part of the mission field. There were ninety-one Bible schools and twenty-one normal school graduates.

The bishops of the Southern Methodist Church greatly appreciated the help of Chief Wembo-Nyama, who lived to see the mission's Jubilee Year celebrated. Bishop JAMES CANNON gave the Chief a gold watch in 1922, Bishop ARTHUR MOORE a bicycle in 1936, and also an engraved bronze medal was presented him on behalf of the Board of MISSIONS of the M.E. Church, South, in 1939. Wembo-Nyama died in 1940, leaving twelve wives and twenty-three children. One of the young men of this mission, JOHN SHUNGU, was elected the first bishop of African descent in The United Methodist Church and continues to serve.

Harry P. Anker, *History of the Methodist Episcopal Congo Mission*. 1935.
Newell Booth, "We're Back in the Congo," *Together*, March 1961.
J. Cannon, *Southern Methodist Missions*. 1926.
The Missionary Voice, September 1927.
W. W. Pinson, *Walter Russell Lambuth*. 1925.

PEARL S. SWEET

WERNER, HAZEN G. (1895-　　), American bishop, was born on July 29, 1895, in Detroit, Mich, the son of Samuel E. and Emma E. (Graff) Werner. From ALBION COLLEGE he received the A.B. degree in 1920; from DREW THEOLOGICAL SEMINARY, B.D., 1923. He did graduate study at Columbia University. He has been awarded the following honorary degrees: Albion College, D.D., 1934; OHIO WESLEYAN UNIVERSITY, D.D., 1941; MOUNT UNION COLLEGE, LL.D., 1949; OHIO NORTHERN UNIVERSITY, LL.D., 1949; BALDWIN WALLACE COLLEGE, S.T.D., 1957; and Miami University, LL.D., 1960.

On May 22, 1924, he was united in marriage to Catherine Stewart of New York City. They have one son, Stewart Hazen, and one daughter, Joy Ann (Mrs. Wilfred Pollender).

Hazen Werner was admitted on trial in the MICHIGAN CONFERENCE in 1920; ordained DEACON, 1922, and ELDER in 1924. He was pastor of Westlawn Church, DETROIT, 1924-28; Cass Avenue Church, Detroit, 1928-31; Court Street Church, FLINT MICH., 1931-34; Grace Church, DAYTON, OHIO, 1934-45. He became professor of practical theology, Drew Theological Seminary, 1945-48. He was elected BISHOP of The Methodist Church in July 1948, by the North Central JURISDICTIONAL CONFERENCE and was appointed resident bishop of the OHIO Area. In 1964 he was assigned the presidency of the HONG KONG and TAIWAN AREA.

Bishop Werner was chairman of the National Methodist Family Life Conferences in Chicago, 1951; Cleveland, 1954; Chicago, 1958; and Chicago, 1962. In 1964 he became chairman of the World Family Life Committee, chairman of the General Committee on The Advance, and on One Great Hour of Sharing. He is a member of the Board of EDUCATION, Board of TRUSTEES of The United Methodist Church, and Commission on PROMOTION AND CULTIVATION. He is a liaison bishop to KOREA. In 1951 he was a delegate to the ECUMENICAL METHODIST CONFERENCE, Oxford, England. In 1956 he was a speaker at the ninth WORLD METHODIST CONFERENCE. He is in constant demand nationally as a lecturer in the field of Christian Family Living.

His travels have included: an extensive study trip to Europe in 1937; a preaching itinerary in England under direction of the British Council of Churches, 1949; four-month trip to INDIA and the Far East by assignment of the COUNCIL OF BISHOPS, 1951; visit to Korea on invitation of the Methodist Council of Korea and the Division of World MISSIONS of The Methodist Church, 1953; lecturer to Methodist CHAPLAINS in Armed Services in Europe, Berchtesgaden, GERMANY, 1955; three month visitation to countries of Southeast Asia by assignment of Council of Bishops, 1955-56; three-month visitation to AFRICA by assignment of Council of Bishops, 1959.

Bishop Werner is the author of the following books: *And We Are Whole Again*, 1945; *Real Living Takes Time*, 1948; *Live With Your Emotions*, 1951; *Christian Family Living*, 1958; *The Bible and the Family*, 1966. He is the author of the following booklets, *When the Family Prays, The Pastor and the Pre-Marriage Conference, Marks of a Christian Home, Is the Ministry for Me?, So You're Going to Join the Church*. He is a contributor to many religious magazines, frequently writing articles on family life or on counseling and personal problems.

Who's Who in America, Vol. 34.
Who's Who in The Methodist Church, 1966.　　N. B. H.

WERREY, MARY ANN (c. 1801-1825), was a British BIBLE CHRISTIAN itinerant preacher. Nothing is known of her origins, but she was received into connection in 1820, and in the next three years she evangelized the Isles of Scilly, Guernsey, and Jersey, establishing societies and winning many converts. In Jersey she was called in a remarkable dream to preach in Scotland. Taking ship to Blyth, she preached for some months in Northumberland, suffering greatly from starvation and incipient tuberculosis, but never sparing herself. She was finally given hospitality by the Barwick family, who took her to Scotland. She preached in Edinburgh in May, 1825, but her last days, like her first, are mystery.

F. W. Bourne, *The Bible Christians*. 1905.　　GLYN COURT

WERTZ, DAVID FREDERICK (1916-　　), American college president and bishop, was born at Lewistown, Pa., on Oct. 5, 1916, the son of Jesse Price and Ada (Barratt) Wertz. He received the A.B. degree from DICKINSON UNIVERSITY in 1937, and an S.T.B. in 1940. He married Betty Jean Rowe on Aug. 25, 1938, and their children are Robert Gary, Joan Rowe (Mrs. John J. Monoski, III), Donna Jean, and Elizabeth Barratt. Wertz joined the CENTRAL PENNSYLVANIA CONFERENCE in 1940 on trial and was ordained a DEACON, coming into full connection in 1942. His appointments were Hickorytown, PA., 1934-37; NEW BEDFORD, Mass., 1938-40; Doylesburg, Pa., 1940-43; Stewartstown, 1943-46; Camp Curtin Methodist Church, HARRISBURG, 1946-49; Allison Methodist Church, CARLISLE, 1949-53; and in that year became superintendent of the Williamsport District, on which he served until 1955. He was elected president of LYCOMING COLLEGE in Williamsport, in 1955. He was a delegate to the Northeastern JURISDICTIONAL CONFERENCES of 1956, '60,

'64, and '68, and to the GENERAL CONFERENCES of 1964, '66, and '68; a member of the Board of EDUCATION of The Methodist Church, 1960, and of the General Board of CHRISTIAN SOCIAL CONCERNS, 1960. He is a trustee of Central Pennsylvania Conference, a member of the executive committee of the West Branch Council of Boy Scouts of America, president, 1966-68; a member of the executive committee of the Foundation for Independent Colleges of Pennsylvania, 1955, serving as vice-chairman in 1965. He has occupied other prominent civic offices in his community. He was elected bishop on July 25, 1968, by the Northeastern Jurisdiction and assigned to the WEST VIRGINIA Area.

Who's Who in America, Vol. 34.
Who's Who in The Methodist Church, 1966.   N. B. H.

WESLEY, ANNE ("NANCY") (1702-1742), sister of JOHN and CHARLES WESLEY is less known than any other of the Epworth family, but she was somewhat unique among the sisters in enjoying a happy married life. John Lambert, whom she married in 1725, was a highly respected land surveyor, and her choice was approved both by her father and mother. Her brother Samuel was so pleased that he sent a poem, "To My Sister Lambert on Her Marriage." At least one son was born, and John Wesley stood sponsor at his baptism in 1726. The boy received a legacy of a hundred pounds under the will of Matthew Wesley, but it is probable that he died before reaching manhood, and that branch of the family became extinct.

John Wesley was on happy terms with Anne and her husband, and not only wrote from time to time but also looked upon her home "as a resting place" where he could look at "loving faces and be at ease." The familiarity of these visits is seen from the fact that he would call in the early morning or the afternoon or in the evening for dinner. On one occasion in January, 1742, John was ill and had numerous visitors, and the Foundery "bands" met around his bedside. He asked Anne, who was present, if she was not offended; "Offended," she said, "I wish I could always be with you. I thought I was in heaven." (*Journal*, Jan. 1, 1742) She had close connection with the work at the Foundery, and she was there when her mother died. The date of her death is unknown, but the absence of any reference to her by either John or Charles after 1742 suggests that she died shortly afterward.

There are indications that her husband drank too heavily. Charles Wesley wrote in his *Journal* on November, 1738.

This evening my brothers Lambert and Wright visited me. The latter has corrupted the former, after all the pains I had taken with him, and brought him back to drinking: I was full yet could not speak, prayed for meekness, and then set before Wright the things that he had done in the devil's name towards reconverting a soul to him. He left us abruptly, I encouraged poor Lambert to turn again to God.

Lambert was, however, a better character and far more intelligent than William Wright, and his drinking habits do not appear to have shadowed his married life.

MALDWYN L. EDWARDS

WESLEY, ARTHUR FREDERICK (1885-   ), American bishop and missionary, was born at North Branch, Mich., on Oct. 26, 1885, the son of Frederick Newton and Elizabeth Louise (Melvin) Wesley. From ALBION COLLEGE he received the A.B. degree in 1913, the D.D. in 1933, and did post graduate work at GARRETT THEOLOGICAL SEMINARY, 1914-15. From Northern Baptist Theological Seminary he received the S.T.B. degree in 1916, the Th.D. in 1921, and from the University of Michigan, the M.A., 1925.

On Aug. 20, 1908, he married Grace Margaret Shaw, and their children are Harriet Elizabeth (Mrs. Herbert G. Garland), Donald Charles, Louise Grace (Mrs. Ralph Belsa), and Robert N. His first wife died in 1944, and he married Luisa Teresa Bissio in 1945, and their children are Bernice Irene (Mrs. David Welch), Elizabeth Louise and Ruth Suzanna.

He was received on trial in the DETROIT CONFERENCE in 1908 and ordained DEACON and ELDER respectively in 1916 and 1920. He served in the Detroit Conference, 1908-10, then in the MICHIGAN CONFERENCE until 1913, then in Oak Park, Ill., Willard Memorial Church (ROCK RIVER) CONFERENCE, 1917-18. He went to ARGENTINA as a missionary in 1918 and served there for a year, going then to MONTEVIDEO, URUGUAY in 1919. There he began to show the talents which earned him the gratitude of other missionaries and of the Methodists of Argentina and Uruguay. He was the founder and the pastor of the Friendship House in Montevideo, and served various mission stations in these lands. For a time he came back to DETROIT serving the Fourteenth Avenue Church, 1957-58. He was professor of the Sweet Memorial Institute in SANTIAGO, 1927-28, and professor and treasurer of the Union Theological Seminary in Santiago, 1927-28, formerly known as Sweet Memorial Institute. He was the general treasurer of the Methodist Church in Argentina and Uruguay, 1929-44; superintendent of the Southern District of Argentina, 1940; and of the Central Chile District, 1928, 1952-53.

Wesley was elected bishop in 1944 by the LATIN AMERICA CENTRAL CONFERENCE and was assigned to the Atlantic Area which comprised Argentina, Uruguay, and BOLIVIA. There he served from 1944-49. He was the pastor for eight years, 1949-57, of the Union Church, Santiago (founded in 1885), and built three buildings there without salary—a labor of love. He retired in 1955.

Bishop Wesley's heart and most of his effort was put into Spanish work, but he was also pastor of English-speaking congregations for about ten years in the Latin American Countries. He edited and published thirty-five books of which five were his own, *The Gospel of the Holy Spirit*, 1922; *Vintage of the Years* (his autobiography, 1955; *La Magia Blanca; Material para Programas Misioneros;* and *Motivas y Metodos para la Observancia Dominical.* He translated and published quite a few other volumes. The total number of volumes of evangelical books published, 50,000; of magazines, 20,000. Over ninety percent of these were in Spanish. In Buenos Aires he fostered the work of the Boca Mission until it had a well rounded social program. This became Methodism's largest institutional church outside the United States. He built three buildings for the Boca Mission—including a lovely Gothic chapel.

After retirement and coming home, he took a charge in Detroit, and finally settled in Lakeland, Fla., where he continues to reside.

Arthur F. Wesley. *Vintage of the Years.* Argentina: Methodist Press, 1956.
Who's Who in The Methodist Church, 1966.   N. B. H.

WESLEY, BARTHOLOMEW (n.d.), great-grandfather of JOHN and CHARLES WESLEY was rector of Catherston and Charmouth in Dorset in 1650, but the dates of his birth and death are unknown. He was the son of Sir Herbert Wesley, or Westley, in the county of Devon. On Saint Bartholomew's Day, 1662, the feast day of the apostle whose name he bore, he was ejected from his livings.

At the university he studied medicine as well as divinity, and there is some evidence that while rector of Charmouth in Dorset, he was from time to time consulted as a physician. After his ejection he continued to preach as occasion permitted but gained his livelihood as a physician. His son, John Wesley, became the father of SAMUEL the rector of Epworth.

MALDWYN L. EDWARDS

WESLEY, CHARLES (1707-1788), famous hymn writer and partner with his brother JOHN in the Methodist revival, was born at Epworth on Dec. 18, 1707, and received his early education from his mother, SUSANNA. He entered Westminster School at London in 1716, at the insistence of his eldest brother, SAMUEL, who was a master, and who defrayed the cost of his education. He was made a king's scholar in 1721 and thenceforward his maintenance was provided by the school.

He became captain of the school, as much for his prowess as his studies. It seems that Garrett Wesley, an Irish relative, wanted to adopt Charles as heir and went in person to prevail upon Charles to succeed to his estates. Charles, according to tradition, declined because he preferred to remain in England, and so Garrett Wesley adopted Richard Colley on condition that he assume the arms and surname of Wesley. His heir became Lord Mornington in 1747, and the grandfather of the first Duke of Wellington.

In 1726 Charles entered Christ Church, Oxford, the largest and most distinguished of the colleges in that period, and one that John had only recently left. At first he was content to live the normal life of an undergraduate, enjoying the diversions of university life. However, his religious exercises occupied more and more of his time as the HOLY CLUB, which he had founded, began methodically to apportion time for devotion and reading and charitable works. In 1729, when John returned to the university as fellow of Lincoln, he took over the leadership of the club and still further enlarged its activities.

Chiefly because of John's insistence, Charles was ordained an Anglican priest in 1735; he left the university, where he had been a tutor, and in October, 1735, he sailed with his brother for the new colony of GEORGIA. John was a chaplain to the colonists and missionary to the Indians, but Charles was secretary to the management committee of the colony and private secretary to General JAMES OGLETHORPE. He had a miserable time in Georgia, partly because of ill health, partly because of the spitefulness of ill-natured women who caused misunderstanding between the general and himself, and partly because of his own inability to carry out secretarial duties.

He left Frederica, Georgia, in August, 1736, and arrived in Deal on December 3, ostensibly on leave with dispatches for the British committee for the colony. In 1737 Charles attended several meetings of the committee and expressed himself as ready to return as a missionary

THE "RUSSELL" PORTRAIT OF CHARLES WESLEY
ENGRAVED BY T. A. DEAN
FROM THE PORTRAIT BY JOHN RUSSELL, R.A.

THE "GUSH" PORTRAIT OF CHARLES WESLEY
ENGRAVED BY J. COCHRANE
FROM THE PORTRAIT BY WILLIAM GUSH

but not as a secretary. He also made several visits to Oxford and shared again the life of the Holy Club.

His return to Georgia was delayed by his mother's well-founded objections and by his own ill health. In February, 1738, an illness at Oxford brought him to death's door. Upon convalescence he began to teach English to PETER BÖHLER, a Moravian missionary on his way to America, and in return Böhler instructed him, as he was instructing John Wesley, in the meaning of salvation by faith. At the end of April the illness recurred, and he was tempted to believe that it was because of his want of faith. It was in the house of Mr. Bray, a brazier, "who knows nothing but Christ, yet, by knowing him, knows all things," that Charles Wesley came into an instantaneous experience of conversion on Whitsunday, May 21, 1738. On the following Wednesday night about ten o'clock John was brought to Mr. Bray's house by a troop of friends and declared to his brother, "I believe!" They sang what is now known as the "Conversion Hymn" and they parted after prayer. It was the true beginning of the revival.

During the remainder of the year Charles preached in the London churches that were open to him, gave himself to the visitation of prisoners at Newgate prison, and he often accompanied felons to their execution at Tyburn. In July 1738, he became a helper to his friend GEORGE STONEHOUSE, vicar of Islington; but his bold evangelical preaching infuriated the churchwardens, and they were supported by the Bishop of London. Stonehouse gave way, and Charles Wesley was barred from the pulpit in the spring of 1739.

However, his life's work was already beginning to take shape. On May 29 he was invited by Mr. Franklins, a farmer at Broadoaks in Essex, to preach in his field. About five hundred listened to his discourse on the text, "Repent for the Kingdom of Heaven is at hand." This and a few other country engagements prepared him for a beginning in London. On June 24, 1739, he spoke to nearly ten thousand people in Moorfields, on "Come unto me all ye that labour and are heavy laden and I will give you rest." Thus encouraged, he preached to great multitudes on Kennington Common. On Sundays his practice seems to have been to preach at Moorfields and then later on Kennington Common.

For the next ten years he was engaged with his brother in a constant itinerary throughout England, preaching the Gospel in the open air. Like his brother John he was often in danger of life, but his fearlessness and his refusal to show his back to the rioters gradually turned odium into unwilling admiration. On one notable occasion in St. Ives, Cornwall, on July 18, 1743, the mob ran on him, fortified by the beating of the drums, and cried out that he should not preach. Charles recorded in his *Journal*, "My soul was calm and fearless. . . . I walked leisurely through the thickest of them who followed like ramping and roaring lions but their mouth was shut."

The decade ended with the terrible riots at Cork in May, 1750, and by this time the Methodists had received nationwide publicity and their numbers and influence were steadily increasing.

In 1749 Charles married Sarah Gwynne, the daughter of Squire MARMADUKE GWYNNE of Garth near Builth Wells. It proved to be a happy union, and when they settled in BRISTOL Charles gradually ceased from itinerating. This was a great trial to John, who in the expanding work of Methodism needed his brother in the visitation of the societies. One must not forget, however, that although Charles remained in Bristol until 1771, he contrived periodically to make preaching tours in the West Country and gave oversight to the work in Bristol itself. Since NEWCASTLE UPON TYNE, LONDON, and Bristol were the three main centers of Methodism, he was rendering invaluable service from his Bristol home. It was shortly after his own marriage that he rode in great haste to Newcastle to prevent John from marrying GRACE MURRAY. He has been attacked for this precipitate action, since John Wesley loved Grace, and she was a convinced and ardent Methodist. In his defense, however, it might be argued that in those early years of the revival, to have chosen one woman of ordinary standing from the societies

might have caused jealousy, resentment and ill-natured gossip, which would have affected Methodism adversely.

In 1771 Charles moved to London, chiefly to help forward the career of his two musically gifted sons, and for the last seventeen years of his life superintended the societies during the long absences of John. In 1739 the Foundery had been the one center of London Methodism, but in 1743 another chapel was opened at West Street and preaching houses were later opened at Snowsfields, Southwark, and Spitalfields. These were all served by Charles Wesley, but when in 1778 the "New Chapel," now known as Wesley's Chapel, was opened, Charles gave the greater part of his time to its ministrations. One must remember also that since only ordained ministers were allowed to administer the Sacraments, Charles with a little clerical assistance had to serve all the numerous London Methodists who came to the Lord's Table.

During his stay in Bristol and London, Charles attended the Annual Conferences frequently and in later years strove to restrain his brother from any irregular ecclesiastical action which would hasten the separation from the Church of England. He was bitterly hurt and dismayed when John Wesley ordained preachers in 1784 for the work of Scotland and America, and especially by the ordination of COKE and ASBURY to be "superintendents" of the Methodist societies in America; he was not deceived by the term and knew they would in fact be bishops.

Nevertheless nothing was allowed to destroy the close friendship which existed between them. John was always, in his own words, his "first and last unalienable friend, . . . a brother, still as thy own soul beloved."

Charles Wesley's greatest contribution to the universal Church was in his hymns. It was inevitable that in so prolific an output the standard should be uneven; even so it is amazing that so high a proportion should be so good. The 1780 collection of hymns remains unsurpassed, and the majority were written by Charles. Bernard Manning said of this hymnbook that "in its own way it is perfect, unapproachable, elemental in its perfection. You cannot alter it except to mar it; it is a work of supreme devotional art by a religious genius." *The Hymns of Wesley and Watts*, p. 74 (Epworth 1942). Some of the greatest hymns used by all the historic churches in their observance of the great Christian festivals were written by Charles, and none has given finer or fuller expression to the evangelical content of the Christian faith.

Using with utmost facility an astonishing variety of meters, and with a masterly employment of Anglo-Saxon and words of Latin derivation as occasion required, Charles wrote hymns for believers in all aspects of their Christian living. Nor was he concerned only with the solitary pilgrim on his way from earth to heaven. No hymn writer has written with more delight on the fellowship of all believers. He wrote deathless hymns on the Church, and like his brother John, he taught the Methodist people that religion, though personally enjoyed, must be socially expressed.

In himself he was always prone to moods of exultation and despair, and like his father he was subject to gusty bouts of anger which fell as quickly as they arose. He was devoted to his wife and family and beloved by all his friends. The Wesley charm was his in full measure. He had neither the gifts nor inclination for leadership, and none had less ambition. All he desired was to be of service to God and man. He has his own unique place in the Methodist story, and the partnership of his brother and himself is without parallel in the whole history of the Church.

Charles Wesley died in London on March 29, 1788. So great was his attachment to the Anglican Church that he refused to be buried in the unconsecrated ground on City Road where both his brother and mother are buried, the former in the rear of Wesley's Chapel, City Road, and the latter across the road in the Dissenters' cemetery of Bunhill Fields. He rests in the garden of the parish church of Marylebone.

This love of the Anglican Church meant that his restraining hand on John steadied him when subject to the pressure of preachers and people alike. There was no precipitate withdrawal, and in consequence when Methodism almost insensibly became a separate Church, there survived a sense of the value of the historicity, liturgy, and Sacraments of the Church that gave her a spacious background against which to develop her own ethos in the nineteenth century.

MALDWYN L. EDWARDS

WESLEY, CHARLES, JUNIOR (1757-1834), eldest son of the poet and hymn writer, was born at Bristol on December 11, 1757, and from earliest years showed that talent for music which made him later well known throughout the country. His father recorded in his *Journal* that when young Charles was only two years and nine months old "he surprised me by playing a tune on the harpsichord readily and in just time. . . . When he played himself, she used to tie him up by his back string to the chair for fear of his falling. Whatever tune it was, he always put a true bass to it." Quoted by G. J. Stevenson, *Memorials of Wesley Family* (London, 1876), p. 447.

It was partly for his sons' sake that Charles, Senior, moved to London. There his son Charles was introduced to many leading musicians. Mr. Kelway, the famous organist at St. Martin-in-the Fields, gave him lessons, while another fine musician, Mr. Morgan, gave him tuition in "thorough base and composition." A gift from his uncle, John Wesley, of Dr. Boyce's three volumes of cathedral music, seems to have confirmed him in a particular predilection for church music. He knew the score of many oratorios by heart, as well as much of the music of Handel, and Corelli, Scarlatti, and Geminiani. When he was twenty years old his father wrote, "Charles has now been for some years under Dr. Boyce's tuition learning composition. . . . With two such masters as Mr. Kelway and Dr. Boyce he believes he has the two greatest masters of music in Christendom."

He played at numerous private concerts given by Lord Mornington and others, and went to Windsor to play before the king at least once each year for many years. Until his mental illness George III regarded Charles Wesley, Junior, as his favorite musician, and the prince regent continued to show royal favor by appointing him as his musician-ordinary and teacher of his daughter, the Princess Charlotte.

Charles, Junior, never identified himself with Methodism, though he was always on friendly terms with the leading preachers and laymen. As a church organist and the organist of St. Marylebone Church, Paddington, he could not attend the Sunday services. He did, however, regularly attend a Methodist class meeting. He was devoted to his mother and his sister and read to them daily from the Bible and the service of the Church of England.

When Mrs. Wesley was too old to attend church he brought her an outline of the sermons he had heard and also delighted her with organ performances at home.

He wrote many musical works which were admired and well received in his day, but have not survived. Thomas Jackson, who knew him well, said, "In music he was an angel, in everything else a child." Stevenson, p. 467.

MALDWYN L. EDWARDS

WESLEY, CHARLES (1793-1859), eldest son of SAMUEL WESLEY, the musician, and grandson of CHARLES WESLEY, SENIOR, brother of JOHN, was educated at home until the age of ten years when he was sent to a school near Maidstone and then to St. Paul's School, London. In 1818 he went to Christ's College, Cambridge, and partly from innate ability and partly because of his seniority he showed great skill in logic. In 1821 he was ordained priest at Salisbury Cathedral and was appointed to Pimlico and after one year to the staff of St. Mary's Chapel, Fulham. He served for a time at St. Paul's, Covent Garden. In 1833 he was made chaplain to the king's household at St. James, and later sub-dean of Her Majesty's Chapels Royal, and in 1847 chaplain in ordinary to Queen Victoria. He continued to be connected with St. James Palace for thirty years and was present at all national ceremonies, which included the confirmation, coronation, marriage, and first churching of the queen, and the baptism and marriage of the princess royal.

He was a staunch Anglican and deeply regretted the separation of Methodism from the Established Church and greatly longed for a reunion. In 1824 he married Eliza Skelton of Hammersmith, and there were four children of the marriage, two of whom survived infancy. He was a quiet, retiring man, and his daily duties at St. James Palace shut him off from the ordinary life of the Anglican Church, so that little is known of his labors save that he was the author of two books, one on logic and one on the church catechism.

MALDWYN L. EDWARDS

WESLEY, EMILY (1691-1771), sister of JOHN and CHARLES WESLEY, was born at South Ormsby on Dec. 31, 1691. Following the birth of her brother, SAMUEL, there was a daughter, Susanna, who died when only two years of age. Emily, as the eldest surviving daughter, played a major part in family relationships. Her mother's tuition was supplemented by instruction from her father, and she gained a reputation in the family as a good classical scholar. John Kirk, an early biographer of Mrs. Wesley, described Emily as one "who worked hard all day long, read some pleasant book at night, and though she had few diversions was contented and happy." She had an especial gift in music and poetry, and her brother John said she was the best reader of Milton he had ever heard.

She had no difficulty in securing a post as teacher in the boarding school of Mrs. Taylor in Lincoln. But she was "overworked and underpaid," and with surprising initiative for a young woman in those days, she not only left on her own account, but set up her own school in Gainsborough. While staying in London with her uncle, Matthew Wesley, she had met and fallen in love with an Oxford student named Leybourne. For three years she maintained a correspondence with him, and when it was broken off she said that nearly half a year she never slept half a night. In a letter to John she wrote, "Let

Emma's hapless case be told by the rash young, or the ill natured old."

One reason for going to Lincoln was to rescue herself from the gloom into which she had now fallen. At Gainsborough, however, when it seemed all prospects of marriage were over, a Quaker physician paid her some attention. John was adverse to the match, but Emily broke it off for reasons of her own. She disliked his habit of obstinately holding to his opinions; "An unmarried woman could never be wrong in an argument with a bachelor. So farewell George Fox and all thy tribe, for Rockwood and Ringwood, and Towler, and Tray."

A little later however, when forty-four years of age, she married Robert Harper, an apothecary of Epworth, and John Wesley performed the ceremony just before his departure for America. It proved to be an unfortunate and unhappy marriage, and it was quickly terminated. Harper used up all her savings and thought himself "very kind" if once a month he gave her ten shillings. She left him and went to live at the Foundery in London. Once the Foundery had been used for the casting of cannon, but since 1716 it had been unused. John Wesley purchased it cheaply, and it became the first headquarters of his work. In addition to a chapel and a house for lay preachers, he built a coach house and stable as well as apartment for his own use. His mother went there in 1739, and Emily followed her a year later.

When West Street Chapel was taken, she was accommodated in the Chapel House, and once again she lacked nothing. She passed her time in the services and week-night meetings, and her chief concern was the welfare of the society and the care of the people. When she was too ill to join in public worship, she followed the service by throwing open a window which opened on to the gallery behind the pulpit. She had reached her eightieth year when she died in 1771 in London; in the very year in which John Wesley lost Emily, Charles Wesley moved to London from Bristol and supplied the place his sister had left.

All the sisters were devoted to John, but Emily deserves to be remembered as the one who was with him for the longest period. For twenty years of his unhappy married life, she gave him the affection and sympathy which he needed. Perhaps it is true to say that in so far as he ever had a home it was in her West Street rooms. John was throughout her life the one constant object of her devotion. As early as 1725 we find her begging John to be the repository of her secrets; and when in 1729 she begged John to keep friendly with Leybourne, she said the request ought to weigh more with him than anybody's except his mother, and that while life remained she would be his most affectionate sister. In a later letter she described John as the one selected from "our numerous family" to be from childhood "my counsellor in difficulties, the dear partner of my joys and griefs." She concluded by saying that her only fault in regard to him was that she loved him too well. Her love was in fact possessive and therefore too demanding. For example, when instead of visiting her in Gainsborough he chose in the summer of 1738 to visit the Moravians in Germany, she was acutely disappointed and told him so in vigorous language. Even after she had come to live with him in London she could not restrain her desire to have more of his company and to reproach him for want of affection. But John not only provided for Emily, but also for her maid to whom she was greatly attached. Hetty Wesley has given us a picture of her in verse, which, allowing for eighteenth-century rhetorical exaggeration, still means that Emily was a singularly attractive woman.

> Thy virtues and thy graces all
> How simple, free and natural;
> Thy graceful form with pleasure to survey
> It charms the eye, the heart away.
> . . . .
> To all thy outward majesty and grace,
> To all the blooming features of thy face,
> To all the heavenly sweetness of thy mind,
> A noble, generous, equal soul is joined,
> By reason polished, and by arts refined.

MALDWYN L. EDWARDS

WESLEY (WESTLEY), JOHN (c. 1636-1678), grandfather of JOHN WESLEY and CHARLES WESLEY, was first trained for the ministry by his father, the Rev. Bartholomew Wesley. He graduated from New Inn Hall at Oxford University and then took a master's degree. His special aptitude (later to show itself in his son) was for oriental languages, but he chose the life of a preacher rather than the more settled life of the scholar.

In 1658, during the protectorate of Oliver Cromwell, Wesley was approved by a committee of triers and inducted as vicar of Winterborn, Whitchurch, in Dorset, England. He stayed here through four happy and useful years but on Bartholomew's Day, 1662, with two thousand other clergymen, he chose to be evicted from his living rather than use the "new Book" of Common Prayer. On August 17, 1662, he spoke to his people for the last time on the text: "And now brethren I commend you to God and the word of His Grace."

After a few years in which he and his ever increasing family moved from Melcombe, Ilminster, Bridgewater, Taunton, to Preston near Weymouth, his health deteriorated. This was due not only to the constant anxiety of preaching and the constant risk of discovery, but to a period of six-months' confinement in Poole prison and smaller sentences elsewhere. The passing of the Five Miles Act (1665), forbidding a clergyman to teach or come within five miles of a city or town unless he had taken the nonresistance oath, made his work more hazardous. In 1678 he died when, as Dr. Calamy, his biographer, said, "He had not been much longer an inhabitant here below than his blessed Master was, whom he had served with his whole heart, according to the best light he had."

A. Clarke, *Memoirs of the Wesley Family*. 1823.

MALDWYN L. EDWARDS

WESLEY, JOHN (1703-1791), founder of Methodism, was born on June 28, 1703, at EPWORTH in England, where his father was Anglican rector for nearly forty years. He was the fifteenth of the nineteen children of SAMUEL and SUSANNA WESLEY, both of whom have their own place in history.

Both the grandfathers of John Wesley were clergymen who were ejected from their pulpits in 1662, but his father broke that nonconformist tradition by becoming a Tory in politics and a High-Church Anglican.

The family life at Epworth was the first great influence in shaping the life of John Wesley. There was no "mother fixation," as some modern biographers have supposed, but certainly the early instruction in the Epworth Rectory, followed by his mother's later letters and her constant advice, gave her an influence on his upbringing which is difficult to exaggerate.

His father, the rector of Epworth, allowed him to become a communicant at eight years of age, and because of the sacrifice of both parents he became a foundation scholar at CHARTERHOUSE School, an ancient Carthusian monastery in LONDON, on Jan. 28, 1714. Despite the stern discipline of Dr. Walker, the headmaster, and the spartan conditions of living, no word of complaint has ever been recorded of the six years he studied there. He is remembered in a verse of the school song, since he was ever the loyal Carthusian and visited the school many times during the course of his long life.

On Jan. 24, 1720, he entered Christ Church at Oxford as an exhibitioner; this was the college where SAMUEL, his elder brother, had preceded him, and CHARLES, his younger brother, was to follow. Through these years he was in constant correspondence with his parents, and when in 1725 he decided to assume holy orders, both parents expressed their joy; the rector urged him to study the language which would give him mastery of the original text of the Bible, and Susanna advised him to read "practical divinity."

Thus John Wesley began to read the *Imitation of Christ* of Thomas á Kempis and Jeremy Taylor's *Holy Living and Dying.* This was the second factor which determined his later apostolate, for in Taylor he found a spur to holiness of living. It led him to read the great mystical writers and to follow their counsel in the culture of the inner life. From Taylor he was led on to William Law's *Serious Call to a Devout and Holy Life* and *Christian Perfection.* His mother advised him to read also Henry Scougal's *Life of God in the Soul of Man,* a book which later became a favorite with both John and Charles Wesley.

In 1726, when Charles Wesley went from Westminster to Christ Church, John was elected a fellow of Lincoln College, and in the interchange of letters between him and his father occurred the rector's memorable phrase: "What will be my own fate before the summer is over, God knows; but wherever I am, my Jack is Fellow of Lincoln." His mother said in a softer tone, "I think myself obliged to return great thanks to Almighty God for giving you good success at Lincoln."

In the summer of this year John went to Epworth and nearby WROOT, where he preached and assisted his father in the two parishes. In September 1726 he was back at Oxford, and his rising reputation was such that he was chosen Greek lecturer and moderator of the classes. In the first capacity he lectured weekly on the Greek New Testament, more to instruct the undergraduates in divinity than in Greek. As moderator he presided over the daily "Disputations" at Lincoln College and fully developed his talent for logic. When he took his Master of Arts degree on Feb. 14, 1727, his three lectures were in the fields of natural philosophy, moral philosophy, and religion.

The life of scholar and tutor, so entirely congenial to him, was rudely broken by the need to assist his father, who was becoming increasingly infirm. Between August 1727 and November 1729, John spent more time in Epworth and Wroot than in Oxford, and the rector wanted him to stay in the parish and in due time succeed him. This was not in accord with John's wishes, and when Dr. Morley, the rector of Lincoln College, told him in a letter (Oct. 21, 1729) that "the interests of the College and the obligation of the statutes" required his return,

he did not hesitate to resume once more his academic teaching and studies.

There was not only Charles to greet him, but also the famous HOLY CLUB which Charles had founded. The story can be told in Charles' words:

My first year at College I lost in diversions; the next I set myself to study. Diligence led me into serious thinking; I went to the weekly sacrament, persuaded two or three young students to accompany me and to observe the method of study prescribed by the Statutes of the University. This gained me the harmless name of Methodist. In half a year after this my brother left his curacy at Epworth and came to our assistance. We then proceeded regularly in our studies and in doing what good we could to the bodies and souls of men. (Charles Wesley as revealed in his *Letters,* p. 14, FRANK BAKER, Epworth, 1948.)

John, meanwhile, was continuing his reading of the mystics and coming to a clearer understanding of the supreme value of Holy Writ. In this very year of 1729 he said he had not only begun to read but to study the Bible: hence he said, "I saw the indispensable necessity of having the mind which was in Christ and of walking as He walked, not only in many or most respects, but in all things."

With these views he naturally became a member of the Holy Club and as naturally became its head. At first only William Morgan of Christ Church and Robert Kirkham met with the Wesley brothers for the reading of Greek and Latin classics and the study of the Greek New Testament. Others were added as the years went on, and the activities of the club increased. At first, at the suggestion of William Morgan, the brothers agreed to visit the prisoners at the "castle" or prison and the poor in those parishes where permission had been received.

Strangely premonitory of John Wesley's later interest in education was the school he started. He and his friends paid the mistress and, when necessary, clothed the children and supervised their work. Children in the workhouse were taught, and books were read to the old people. The ridicule and scorn excited in the university was principally directed against, not the devotional and ascetic practices, but these works of charity.

In time the difficulties of the Holy Club so multiplied that it began to disintegrate. The early death of William Morgan was unjustly supposed to be due to the fastings and austerities which he practiced and served to bring the rules into greater opprobrium. An article in *Fog's Journal* in December 1732 severely criticized John and the other members of the club, but later men who were to be so distinguished as Thomas Broughton, BENJAMIN INGHAM, GEORGE WHITEFIELD and JAMES HERVEY had joined. Wesley recorded in 1733 that the seven and twenty communicants at St. Mary's had shrunk to five, and his incessant travels of around a thousand miles had loosed his grasp on the discipline and practice of the club.

Perhaps the realization of this led to his compilation of forms of prayer for each day in the week. It was his first publication and was printed in 1733, to be followed in 1735 by *The Christian's Pattern,* an edition of the *Imitation of Christ* by Thomas á Kempis. Later in the club's history, six years after its inception, George Whitefield became a member and gladly adopted their ascetic mode of life.

The death of Samuel, the rector, on April 23, 1735, unsettled John, and the meeting between General JAMES

OGLETHORPE and himself caused him to accept the offer of a chaplaincy in the colony of GEORGIA. His father had been one of the first supporters of this new colony, named after George II, who granted the charter on June 9, 1732. Only his advanced age had prevented the rector from offering his own services, and he suggested that JOHN WHITELAMB, his curate, should be invited. Samuel Wesley, Jr., the eldest son, had written two poems with James Oglethorpe as the hero and a third poem had been inscribed to him.

Yet stronger than any liking of Oglethorpe, or interest in his scheme, was the fresh opportunity of leaping the wall between himself and God. All of Wesley's reading of the mystics and good works could not secure him the communion with God which steadfastly he set before him as a goal. He frankly confessed that a chief reason for going to Georgia was to save his own soul. "I hope to learn the true sense of the gospel of Christ by preaching it to the heathen."

WESLEY MARKER AT SAVANNAH, GEORGIA

In Georgia. Georgia marks a third stage in his spiritual pilgrimage. Whatever his motives, none could deny his apostolic zeal in his daily religious services and in the frequent celebration of Holy Communion. A plaque outside the Protestant Episcopal Church in SAVANNAH makes John Wesley the founder of SUNDAY schools in America, and certainly he gave much time to the instruction of the young. He ministered to French and German colonists by conversing with them in their own language, and he even attempted to conduct a service in Italian at the request of several immigrants. There were also Spanish Jews who sought out Wesley, and of whom he spoke so happily, declaring that some of them "seem nearer the mind that was in Christ than many of those who call Him Lord."

This necessity to learn German, French, and Spanish helped him when he came to his great work of translating hymns. His first hymnbook, entitled a *Collection of Psalms and Hymns,* was published at CHARLESTON in 1737. In it he included hymns of ISAAC WATTS, three of his father's and others of his brother, Samuel, in praise of the Trinity. But the outstanding feature of the book is John Wesley's superb translations from the German of such hymns as Lange's "O God, Thou Bottomless Abyss," Freyling-heusen's "O Jesus Source of Calm Repose," and Richter's "Thou Lamb of God, Thou Prince of Peace."

Finally, in Georgia was laid the foundation of the system of classes which later became a distinguishing mark of BRITISH METHODISM. Wesley said in his *Journal* that, since no doors had been opened for a mission to the Indians,

We agreed (1) to advise the more serious among them to form themselves into a little society and to meet once or twice a week in order to reprove, instruct and exhort one another; (2) to select out of these a smaller number for a more intimate union with each other which might be forwarded, partly by conversing singly with each other and partly by inviting them all together to one house, and this accordingly, we determined to do every Sunday in the afternoon.

It appears that the members were largely German, and while the society met once or twice in a week, the inner circle had its own Sunday afternoon gathering.

The Moravians. There were a number of Moravians on the ship "Simmonds" in which Wesley sailed to Georgia, and his contacts with these people constituted another important factor in his conversion and subsequent life. He was greatly impressed with the unperturbed behavior of the Moravians in a storm and learned that even their women and children were unafraid because of their faith. Later one of their leaders, AUGUST GOTTLIEB SPANGENBERG, asked him pointedly, "Do you know Jesus Christ?" Wesley replied, "I know that He is the Savior of the world." "But," persisted the Moravian, "do you know he has saved you?" Wesley replied in the affirmative, but he confessed in his *Journal,* "I fear they were vain words." (*Journal,* Vol. 1, P. 151.) This episode created a spiritual dissatisfaction in Wesley's heart which eventually, and under the tutorship of another Moravian, PETER BÖHLER, led to his evangelical awakening.

Wesley's mission in Georgia was not successful, and even he regarded it as a failure. George Whitefield, however, declared, "The good Mr. John Wesley has done in America is inexpressible. His name is very precious among the people and he has laid a foundation that I hope neither men nor devils will be able to shake. O that I may follow him as he has followed Christ."

Nevertheless, Wesley's usefulness in the colony was strictly limited, and his mission ended in a near fiasco. His rigid High Churchmanship divided the people and turned many against him. He had a mismanaged and unfortunate love affair with SOPHIA HOPKEY, and when he foolishly repelled her from communion after she married another man, it led to his indictment. In the end he was obliged to leave the colony under something like a cloud.

Aldersgate. Wesley returned to England in deep spiritual dejection, which our fathers would probably have called "conviction for sin," though he was certainly no sinner if the term implies moral wrongdoing. But he reproached himself over and over again, declaring that he was "carnal, sold under sin," in a "vile abject state of bondage to sin," and "altogether corrupt and abominable."

When he reached England he met Peter Böhler, who told him that salvation was by faith alone and finally convinced him of the truth of the doctrine. Wesley's first impulse was to cease preaching, but the Moravian told him to "preach faith until you have it, then because you have it you will preach it." Wesley followed that advice, and at once great success attended his ministry. This led on May 24, 1738 (*Journal,* Vol. 1, p. 475-76), to the experience about which he wrote what are perhaps his most famous words:

In the evening I went very unwillingly to a society in ALDERSGATE STREET, where one was reading Luther's preface to the Epistle to the Romans. About a quarter before nine, while he was describing the change which God works in the heart through faith in Christ, I felt my heart strangely warmed. I felt that I did trust in Christ, Christ alone for salvation, and an assurance was given me, that he had taken away *my* sins, even *mine,* and saved *me* from the law of sin and death.

The Belgian priest, Father Maximin Piette, in his book *John Wesley in the Evolution of Protestatism* (Sheed and Ward, London, 1937), has minimized this Aldersgate experience, but actually it was the source of Methodist teaching on salvation, assurance, and holiness. It was the watershed of Wesley's whole career, and it gave him charter and compass for a course from which he never deviated. Even more, it gave him the spiritual energy for his pilgrim's progress, so that never again was he Christian with a burden on his back. Until his dying day Wesley dated his experience, his message, and his doctrine back to this date of 1738.

At Oxford and in Georgia he had sought salvation through devotional exercises and by good works through unremitting service of his fellows. But neither had brought him peace with God. In his own way he came to know that neither righteousness nor merit can earn God's favor nor fit man for heaven. After years of travail he saw in a flash that salvation cannot be worked for nor merited, but can only be received by simple faith.

His first action after conversion was to help in drawing up orders for the religious society which he had been attending in FETTER LANE. Then he preached before the university at St. Mary's, Oxford, on "By grace are ye saved through faith." This was, as the university authorities were quick to realize, a new emphasis by a new voice in a new and disturbing fashion. It was the manifesto of the new revival.

Meanwhile in his restlessness of spirit he determined to go to the fountainhead of the Moravian movement, Count ZINZENDORF and the members of the Herrnhut settlement in GERMANY. Wesley stayed many days there, and whilst in their services and schools he saw much to admire, there were some niggling doubts which later were to grow in his mind. The Moravian reliance upon God's grace could lead to a passivity in which even the means of grace, known and used by the Church in all centuries, could be neglected.

The breach with the Church of England, which Wesley never acknowledged, led almost at once to the closing of London churches against his brother and himself. In the course of 1739 only four were open to him, but, at Newgate jail among condemned prisoners, both John and Charles discovered that if conventional means of proclaiming the Gospel were forbidden, unconventional opportunities were ready to hand.

Beginning of Field Preaching. In the spring of 1739, another event of large importance for the revival occurred. This was the beginning of field preaching, or preaching in the open air, which was forced on the leaders by the closing of the churches against them. George Whitefield began preaching in the field to the miners at Kingswood, near BRISTOL, and he attracted great throngs of spiritually neglected people. Leaving for America, he asked John Wesley to take over this work. The idea was repugnant to the correct and proper presbyter of the Church of England, who declared that he had been "so tenacious of every point relating to decency and order, that I should have thought the saving of souls almost a sin if it had not been done in a church." (*Journal*, March 31, 1739, Vol. 2, P. 167.)

Nevertheless, on April 2, 1739, he began the work. In words to become immortal he said, "At four in the afternoon I submitted to be more vile, and proclaimed in the highways the glad tidings of salvation, speaking from a little eminence in a ground adjoining to the city to about three thousand people." His life's work had begun. (*Journal*, Vol. 2, P. 172.)

He preached in the open air all over England. At GWENNAP PIT in CORNWALL he preached to crowds estimated at many thousands. One of the most famous episodes of his career was his sermon from his father's tomb at Epworth when he had been refused the pulpit and denounced by the curate.

Wesley became "the soul that over England flamed." For fifty years he rode over most roads in England and preached in every conceivable place. Twenty times he toured SCOTLAND, twenty-four times he was in WALES, twenty-one times in IRELAND. Reading and writing as he rode along, he traveled a quarter of a million miles and preached more than forty thousand times. Only FRANCIS ASBURY in America surpassed him as an itinerant.

Persecution and Attack. Wesley and his preachers encountered persecution and physical violence of the most bitter kind. The attacks came mainly from those in the Church of England, chiefly squires and parsons, who strongly disapproved of the practice of preaching in the open air and thus disregarding parish boundaries. They were repelled and disgusted by some of the emotional excesses which characterized the revival in the opening years. The fact that only a few people became hysterical and that the Wesleys did not countenance such behavior could not allay the suspicions of the enemies.

The opposition was strengthened by the fact that when Charles Stuart tried to gain the throne of England, the Methodists by their classes and "nocturnal meetings" seemed possible Papists and Jacobites in disguise, and therefore traitors. On numerous occasions rabbles egged on by parson and squire set upon Methodists and maltreated them. Even John and Charles Wesley, as well as some of their assistant preachers, were in danger of their lives. The brothers rode the storm triumphantly because they showed no fear; they never turned their backs to the rioters, and they always went unhesitantly to the leader of the mob. The decade of rioting ended with the frightful excesses in Cork where priest took the place of parson.

The fighting was done with pens as well as fists. William Warburton, Bishop of Gloucester, wrote his *Office and Operations of the Holy Spirit,* and Wesley replied in a devastating "letter" which effectively scotched his accusations. A more important literary opponent was GEORGE LAVINGTON, Bishop of Exeter, who published a work in three parts entitled *Enthusiasm of Methodists and Papists Compared.* He argued that John Wesley was a Papist in disguise. He reached this conclusion by comparing certain sayings from Roman Catholics with extracts from the *Journals* and writings of Wesley and Whitefield. Wesley not only refuted the charge, but convicted the bishop of woeful ignorance, and, in places, of downright dishonesty.

All these attacks gave the Wesleys wide publicity and sympathy from the general public, while stimulating the loyalty and devotion of their followers. The movement spread rapidly and societies were formed especially in the centers of population.

The First Chapels. In 1739 Wesley erected the first chapel for his societies. It was a small building at Bristol and was known as the NEW ROOM in the Horsefair. It had a preaching place, living quarters, a conference room on the second floor, and a stable for the preachers' horses. It is still in existence, the oldest Methodist shrine in the world.

In the same year, 1739, Wesley acquired a ruined cannon factory in London which he repaired and remodeled. This was the famous FOUNDERY, the second Methodist meetinghouse in the world, and was London headquarters of the Methodist movement for forty years. It was a chapel, residence, book-room and center for a wide variety of social activities.

The third center was a NEWCASTLE UPON TYNE, where Wesley established his noted ORPHAN HOUSE in 1742. It also housed many activities and was the headquarters in the north of England, but the original intention of developing a home for orphans was never realized.

It has been said that Methodism built a school before it built a church. At the Foundery in London, sixty children were taught. But the first great educational venture of the Methodists, also in 1739, was a school for miners' children at Kingswood, the cornerstone of which was laid by George Whitefield. In 1748 Wesley established at Kingswood a "New School," alongside the "Old School"; this was mainly for the sons of the preachers. Originally they were known as the "Old House" and the "New House." For a short time there was also a school at the New Room, Bristol, with four masters and a mistress. It was officially adopted by the Conference in 1756. In 1851 it was removed to Bath and is today one of the finest public schools in England.

Beginning of Lay Preaching. Almost coincident with the building of the first chapels, lay preaching began. This was to become one of the most potent instruments for the spread of Methodism, not only in England, but also in America and other parts of the world.

The first lay preachers were THOMAS MAXFIELD and JOHN CENNICK. Maxfield was a convert who was employed by Wesley at the Foundery "to pray and expound the Scriptures, but not to preach." However, in 1740 or 1741 he began to preach in earnest. This outraged Wesley, who rushed to London to bring an end to such irregularity. But his mother cautioned him to hear the young man before passing judgment; this Wesley did and immediately gave Maxfield permission to preach.

John Cennick was converted in 1737 and soon began preaching. There can be no doubt that he was one of Wesley's lay preachers before Maxfield was. He first preached at Kingswood June 14, 1739. Cennick became master of Kingswood School, but he embraced Calvinism and was disowned by Wesley and joined Whitefield and the CALVINISTIC METHODISTS, but left them for the Moravians.

Methodist Organization. By the 1740's the Methodist movement had become so strong that some kind of organization was needed. Thus emerged the class meeting, the first of which was at Bristol in 1742. In due course a threefold plan was adopted. The society consisted of all the members who met and worshiped together. The class was a dozen or more persons, under a leader, who made financial contributions and met weekly for testimony and discipline; later, tickets were required for admission, and

these quarterly tickets were proof of good standing. The band was a smaller group of the same sex and marital status; the band soon disappeared, but the class meeting continued as a main source of strength.

Then the most important of all Methodist organizations, the CONFERENCE, appeared. The first was held at the Foundery in London on June 25-30, 1744. In addition to the two Wesley brothers there were four clergymen of the Church of England. There were also four of Wesley's lay preachers, including Thomas Maxfield, but these were not admitted to all the sessions; of these only one, JOHN DOWNES, continued to the end as a Methodist preacher.

The subjects discussed were three: What to teach, how to teach, and what to do. The discussions were called "conversations," and to this day the procedure in British Methodism both in Conference and Synod is the asking and answering of questions. The *Minutes* of this first Conference are preserved. It was stated that all the Methodists regarded themselves as members of the Church of England, and that it was to be defended in preaching and life.

This conference published no statistics, which were slow in appearing. In 1746 the circuits were gathered into seven areas, with thirty sub areas. In 1748 there were nine divisions and sixty-seven circuits, and the numbers continued to increase year by year. In 1766 the first tabulation of membership was included; it showed ninety-seven preachers, not including the Wesleys themselves, appointed to forty circuits with 19,761 members, with some omissions. There was a complete report in 1767, when 25,911 members were listed.

The Calvinistic Controversy. In the 1770's the Calvinistic controversy reached its height. George Whitefield, the COUNTESS OF HUNTINGDON, Richard and ROWLAND HILL, and others were strongly biased toward the theology of Calvinism, the predestinarian aspect of which the Wesleys and their followers opposed. When the Conference met at Bristol in 1771 a rival conference was held of Calvinistic sympathizers, and Wesley was asked to receive a deputation representing them. They held a two-hour discussion and retired thoroughly discomfited, their leader acknowledging publicly that he had been mistaken.

Nevertheless it was a pyrrhic victory, because the offended Lady Huntingdon proceeded to regroup her forces. The attack came in two waves.

First was the written slanders of such bitter controversialists as AUGUSTUS TOPLADY and the Hills, mainly in the columns of the *Gospel Magazine* but also in pamphlets. Second, the Calvinistic preachers were sent to evangelize where Methodism was strong, in attempts to disrupt the societies. These were troubled days for Wesley, but his victory was complete, and in spite of the attacks, Methodism continued steadily to increase.

Lady Huntingdon built her own chapels in many places. She founded TREVECKA College as a training school for preachers and the main field of Calvinistic Methodist operations then as now was in Wales. But doctrinal controversy is only a memory.

Methodism Becomes a Church. Another important development was the virtual emergence of Methodism as a separate Church, although it did not become definite until after the death of Wesley. On Feb. 28, 1784, Wesley signed the historically significant DEED OF DECLARATION, making the ANNUAL CONFERENCE through the LEGAL HUNDRED preachers the heir of Wesley and establishing the principle of itineracy. Wesley, by the hard logic of facts, was providing for a Church which would continue after his death, distinct in form and ethos from the Anglican Church which gave it birth.

Perhaps of still greater importance was Wesley's ORDINATION in 1784. The Deed of Declaration made possible a British Church, but the ordinations led to a world Church. The action was taken after his fruitless attempt to persuade bishops to ordain men for America following the close of the Revolutionary War. The Methodists in America were demanding the ordinances at the hands of their own preachers.

Wesley had become convinced by reading King's book on the *Primitive Church* that presbyters and BISHOPS were of the same order. Therefore, in September 1784 at Bristol, he ordained Dr. THOMAS COKE as "SUPERINTENDENT" for America and sent him to the New World. There was convened the famous CHRISTMAS CONFERENCE at BALTIMORE, at which Francis Asbury was elected and consecrated superintendent, and the M.E. CHURCH was organized. Wesley's ordinations continued, in spite of vigorous protests from his brother Charles; he ordained a total of twenty-seven persons.

It is a remarkable instance of Wesley's invincible youthfulness that at the end of a long life he was still looking upon the whole world as his parish. Already the work in the WEST INDIES was spreading, since its inception by NATHANIEL GILBERT in 1760, and when violent storms drove Dr. Thomas Coke and three young missionaries nearly two thousand miles off their course to ANTIGUA in 1786, the labor of the local preacher, JOHN BAXTER, there found powerful reinforcement. Other islands were visited and evangelized. Before he died Wesley could see a fulfillment of his brother's lines:

> When he first the work begun,
> Small and feeble was His day;
> Now the world doth swiftly run,
> Now it wins its widening way.
> (Methodist hymnbook Great Britain, No. 263.)

The Spread of Methodism. When John Wesley died in 1791, Methodism had spread all over the United Kingdom and had nearly 75,000 "members in the Society" in 115 circuits. It did not greatly influence either the upper classes or the agricultural laborers. Success was chiefly in the northeast, the west country, and Cornwall. Wesley's greatest trophies were the miners of Kingswood, Cornwall, and Newcastle. The movement also found ready lodging with artisans, small tradesmen, and the workers flooding into the new industrial areas of Lancashire and Yorkshire.

There were reasons for the astonishing spread of the revival. In the early days the England that Wesley traveled on horseback was mainly pastoral and agricultural, and the woolen industry was in the Cotswolds rather than Yorkshire. There were faint indications of the coming industrialism, but the progress was not strongly marked until the later years of George II. Wesley dealt with a population considerably less than in modern London, and the absence of densely crowded towns, together with the open nature of the country, enabled him to address huge crowds in the open air in every part of England.

To evangelize industrial England would have been too great a task for any evangelist, but it was within the compass of a devoted and growing army of preachers and people, and by the end of the century the work could safely be entrusted to Wesley's spiritual children.

Methodist success was also due largely to the parochial and conservative habits, outlook, and machinery of the Church of England. Its strength lay in the south and it was unable to adapt itself to new conditions. In the eighteenth century the parochial system was still the same as at the Reformation. There was not a single bishop in Lancashire of the West Riding of Yorkshire until 1826, when the Bishop of Ripon was appointed. MANCHESTER did not have its bishop until 1847. LEEDS, which early became an important Methodist center, was one parish of 150,000 people until the middle of the century. Because Methodism was more mobile, adaptable, and freer from custom and prejudice, it was able to seize an opportunity which the Church of England lost.

Deeper than these immediate reasons for the growth of the revival was the man and his message. Wesley was a natural leader of men who excited their lively respect, obedience, and affection. The experience of JOHN NELSON, who on MOORFIELDS Commons heard Wesley for the first time must have been similar to that of many. "My heart beat like the pendulum of a clock and when he spoke I thought his whole discourse was aimed at me." When he talked with Wesley he declared that it had been a "blessed Conference . . . When we parted, he took hold of my hand, and looking me full in the face, bade me take care I did not quench the spirit." (Journal of John Nelson in *Lives of the Early Methodist Preachers*, Vol. 1, p. 36 (London, 1871).) All who met Wesley knew his effortless mastery of men and recognized that he was the undisputed father of his people.

With the man went the message. Wesley declared a Gospel which was an invitation to a more abundant life. He taught men they could accept it by faith; they could enjoy it; and they could possess it to the full. In an age when rationalism had cast a blight upon religion, when enthusiasm was frowned upon, and probability was the guide to life, it was small wonder that the sheep who had not been fed moved quickly to these lush pastures. The Christian faith was invested with color and gaiety because it acquired a new meaning.

In distinction from Charles, who had a quick and fiery temper, John Wesley retained remarkable composure and self-control even under the most serious provocation. His wife was a termagant who could rise to ungovernable fury, but there is no instance of his losing his temper and retorting to her in kind. This evenness of disposition was allied to a magnanimity that prevented him from using the same weapons as his traducers. It was said of his generosity that it knew no bounds except an empty pocket. When his own simple wants were provided he gave away all that he had.

The final impression of the man is the completeness of his dedication to God and the work God gave him to do. He was as frugal and abstemious in habit as he was neat and simple in appearance. As JOHN WHITEHEAD said, "a narrow pleated stock, a coat with a small upright collar, no buckles at his knees, no silk or velvet in any part of his apparel, and a head as white as snow, gave an idea of someting primitive and apostolic." (*Life of Rev. John Wesley*, Vol. 2, p. 485, John Whitehead (London 1796).) He rose early each morning and devoted many hours daily to praying and reading. In no life was the balance between the culture of the soul and the service of the people so exquisitely maintained.

"The Best of All is . . ." In the final decade of the century Wesley had little more than one full year to live, but to the end he made his ambitious itineraries, and he died striving to maintain his promise to serve the Methodist people in Leatherhead. It was fitting that the text of his last sermon should be, "Seek ye the Lord while He may be found, call ye upon Him while He is near."

The next day, feverish and ill, he stayed at Balham, and fought off his sickness sufficiently to write to WILLIAM WILBERFORCE one of the best known of his letters: "Go on in the name of God and in the power of His might, till even American SLAVERY (the vilest that ever saw the sun) shall vanish away before it." (*Letters*, Vol. 8, p. 265, Feb. 24, 1791.)

He returned to the CITY ROAD CHAPEL in London in growing bodily weakness. Like all the Wesleys he knew how to die well. At first he tried to sing Isaac Watts' hymn, "I'll praise my Maker while I've breath," and later, when singing had become impossible, he made a supreme effort and cried, "The best of all is God is with us."

MEMORIAL TABLET, WESTMINSTER ABBEY

Thus died John Wesley, on March 2, 1791. His life spanned practically the whole of the century.

The funeral took place a week later, and although it was at the very early hour of five o'clock in the morning, it was attended by thousands. When the officiating minister, JOHN RICHARDSON, in the prayer of committal, sub-

stituted for "brother" the word "father," the effect was immediate and overwhelming. A low wave of sobbing swept the crowd, because they realized that under God their father had been taken from them. It was a last spontaneous tribute.

Wesley rests in the graveyard of WESLEY's CHAPEL on City Road in London, which he had formally opened in 1778. Across the street, in the Non-conformist cemetery of BUNHILL FIELDS, is the tomb of his mother, Susanna Wesley. Both of these sacred spots for nearly two centuries have been visited by Methodists from all parts of the world. The life of John Wesley is a story without an ending.

MALDWYN L. EDWARDS

WESLEY, MRS. JOHN. (See Mrs. VAZIELLE.)

WESLEY, KEZIA (1709-1741), the nineteenth and last child of SAMUEL and SUSANNA WESLEY and sister of JOHN and CHARLES, was born at EPWORTH in March 1709. She was somewhat delicate in health, and it may have been for this reason that she developed mentally more slowly than the others. When she was eighteen she became a pupil-teacher at LINCOLN and gave and received instruction for her board only. In a letter to John on Jan. 26, 1729, she speaks of her "want of money and want of clothes." (Stevenson, p. 417) In a second letter six months later she speaks of "my own constant ill health these three years past."

She had a great love for her brothers and wrote in a letter to John on Jan. 20, 1731, of loving him with "more than a sister's love." She longed for him to come to Epworth but feared "the pain of parting if your stay be short will infinitely outweigh the pleasure of seeing you." This letter reveals the loneliness and frustration of a girl who had returned unwillingly to Epworth because she had not sufficient money in Lincoln for proper clothing, and so could not keep her place. Three years after returning home, her sister MARY was married to JOHN WHITELAMB; and "Kezzy," her pet name, was the only child remaining at the rectory.

At this juncture the unscrupulous WESTLEY HALL came to the rectory and made love to her. There is no doubt that he proposed marriage and she accepted him. On his return to LONDON, however, he courted and married her sister, MARTHA, who did not know of his attentions to her sister. In a later letter to John, Kezia professed resignation, but there are indications that she felt Hall's desertion keenly, and it may have further affected her health.

John Wesley made arrangements for her to lodge with HENRY PIERS, the friendly vicar of Bexley. She was happy in a household so well disposed to herself and on such excellent terms with her brothers. From here in March 1738, she went to London to care for Charles in his illness. He recovered but she became dangerously ill. It is said that she and Charles received the Holy Communion every day. As John and Martha were specially drawn to each other, so Charles and Kezzy were the other's favorite sister and brother. In the last two years of her life they met as frequently as Charles' work permitted.

She died in London on March 9, 1741. There is no indication of the nature of her death, but Charles in his *Journal* suggests that she died "without pain or trouble" and that she was full of thankfulness, resignation, and love. She was scarcely thirty years of age when she died, and only in the last few years of her life had she known any real anchorage from want and trouble.

MALDWYN L. EDWARDS

WESLEY, MARTHA (c. 1707-1791), sister of JOHN and CHARLES WESLEY, was born at EPWORTH in 1706 or 1707, and was the favorite of her mother. "What my sisters call partiality," she said, "was what they might all have enjoyed had they wished it, which was permission to sit in my mother's chamber when disengaged, to listen to her conversation with others, and to her remarks on books and things out of school hours." (Stevenson, p. 356) At the age of fourteen she went to the home of her uncle, MATTHEW WESLEY, brother of the rector, who practiced medicine in LONDON. For three years she enjoyed the advantages of his home and attended the services at St. Dunston's and St. Paul's Cathedral.

After a stay at Epworth, darkened by an unhappy friendship with JOHN ROMLEY, her father's curate, she returned to London. She was now beautiful, intelligent, and highly attractive, and her earlier disappointment in love made her more ready to return the affection of WESTLEY HALL. At this stage Hall was a friend and fellow student with her brothers at Oxford, and she married him in 1735.

Martha did not know that Westley Hall had already made love to her sister, KEZIA, at Epworth, and that the family were so much puzzled by his change of front that they supposed Martha must have beguiled him. SAMUEL, her brother, actually addressed a poem to her, in which he declared she had "loaded her conscience with her sister's blood." (*Family Circle*, p. 151)

But the family came to realize that the weakness lay in the husband. After a few years of married happiness he became successively a MORAVIAN, a Quietist, and a Deist. Despite the fact that his wife bore him ten children, of whom nine died in infancy, he had many illicit love affairs.

Because of his temper and his infidelities the Wesley brothers took the one child and provided for his education. He was showing great promise when at school he was smitten with smallpox; his mother rushed to his bedside but he was already dead. By that time Westley Hall had preached and practiced polygamy. He would leave his wife for months at a time and finally departed with a woman to the WEST INDIES. He returned to England, and there is evidence that before he died he was repentant, but he never lived with his wife again.

After being deserted Martha became increasingly attached to Mrs. Charles Wesley and took an almost maternal interest in her nieces and nephews. When Sally Wesley grew up she became Mrs. Hall's most loved and intimate companion. Among Martha's London friends was the famous Dr. Samuel Johnson, and she has her place in Boswell's *Life of Johnson*.

She was nearest to John Wesley in age and was especially devoted to him. For the greater part of her married life she was dependent upon an allowance which he made to her, and when he died he left her a small legacy from the sale of his books.

ADAM CLARKE, who knew them intimately, was struck by their similarity in habits and in cast of mind, and by the likeness of her handwriting to John's. Even in disposition they were alike. Both had complete self-control, poise, and generosity, and Charles once remarked, "It is

vain to give Patty anything to add to her comforts, for she always gives it away to some person poorer than herself." (Adam Clarke, Vol. 2, p. 350) She died on July 12, 1791, and was buried with her brother John in the vault at WESLEY'S CHAPEL in CITY ROAD, London.

MALDWYN L. EDWARDS

WESLEY, MARY (1696-1734), sister of JOHN and CHARLES WESLEY, grew up a cripple, owing to a fall in childhood due to the carelessness of her nurse. This caused the villagers of Epworth to pass unkind comments which she bore without resentment, although in one letter to Charles, she wrote, "I have been the ridicule of mankind and the reproach of my family." (Letter Jan. 30, 1726, Stevenson, p. 289)

She was the family favorite because of her even temper and her desire to be of service. She not only assisted her mother in the management of the home, but was an unpaid secretary to her father. She remained in the rectory until her marriage. When most of the family condemned her sister HETTY for her elopement, it was "Molly," to use her pet name, who remained faithful to Hetty, and when Molly died, Hetty described her in verse as "my tenderest, dearest, firmest friend." (*Family Circle*, p. 144)

She was one of the few sisters who found true happiness in marriage. JOHN WHITELAMB was a boy from WROOT who had been educated at the school of the village. When he came to the rectory to act as an amanuensis to the rector and to draw wretched illustrations for the *Dissertations*, the rector tutored him and later secured financial help to enable him to go to Oxford. At Lincoln College he applied himself diligently to his studies. In a letter to his father, John Wesley said,

John Whitelamb reads one English, one Latin, and one Greek book alternately and never meddles with a new one till he has ended the old one. If he goes on as he has begun, I dare take upon me to say that by the time he has been here four or five years, there will not be such a one of his standing in Lincoln College, perhaps not in the University of Oxford. (June 11, 1731)

After his ordination Whitelamb returned as the curate of the parish to declare his love for Molly. The rector was delighted and gave him the living at Wroot. In one year Molly died in childbirth at Wroot in November 1734, and her child was buried with her. For another thirty years he was the rector of Wroot, known for his faithful preaching and pastoral care. He never shared in the Methodist revival but fulfilled conscientiously the labors of a parish priest.

MALDWYN L. EDWARDS

WESLEY, MATTHEW (1661-1737), was the brother of SAMUEL WESLEY, SR., rector of EPWORTH, and the son of the Rev. JOHN WESLEY who died about 1678. From his father he received the rudiments of a classical education, and he may also have received a part of his education in one of the Dissenting academies. There is no record of his receiving a university education, though ADAM CLARKE, earliest biographer of the Wesley family, believed he studied abroad and received a degree at a foreign university. Mrs. Wesley, in a letter to John (1731) said that her brother-in-law, Matthew, "had tried all the spas in Europe, both in GERMANY and elsewhere." (Stevenson p. 37)

His qualifications were probably not high, because in his will he referred to himself as an apothecary. In verses to his memory in the *Gentleman's Magazine* he was not called a doctor or physician. Nevertheless he seems to have had an extensive practice in LONDON and to have been widely known and respected. He appears to have made a modest fortune, because when at the age of seventy years he determined to visit Epworth, he took a manservant with him, and on arrival was scandalized, in SUSANNA'S words, "at the poverty of our furniture and much more at the meanness of the children's habit." (*ibid.*, p. 38)

There is no evidence of any close friendship between the rector and Matthew, and this was due in part to the fact that Matthew remained a Dissenter, and had little sympathy with his brother's rigid Anglicanism. There may have been also differences of temperament. Matthew was a rich man and a "careful economist" who was much scandalized by what appeared to be the improvidence of his brother. When he returned to London he wrote accusing his brother of bad management and begetting offspring for which he could not provide. The rector answered the charges in full, and ending, "I can struggle with the world but not with Providence, nor can I resist sickness, fires and inundations." (Stevenson p. 44)

When the Epworth rectory burned in 1709 Matthew took HETTY and Susanna Wesley, and they stayed with him a considerable time. Hetty repaid his kindness later, not only by nursing him in sickness, but in a poem contributed to the *Gentleman's Magazine* after his death:

> Alas, the sovereign healing art,
> Which rescued thousands from the grave,
> Unaided left the gentlest heart,
> Nor could its skillful master save.

MARTHA WESLEY later lived with him for some years and was treated with great kindness. When she married WESTLEY HALL her uncle gave her four hundred pounds as a marriage portion. In his will nine hundred pounds was divided among some of the children of the Epworth household. Therefore, any coolness between his brother and himself did not disturb his care for those members of the Epworth family who came to stay with him. His London home was open to the three boys as well as the sisters, and he showed compassion to the brilliant but unhappy Hetty Wesley when she married WILLIAM WRIGHT and came to live in London.

MALDWYN L. EDWARDS

WESLEY, MEHETABEL ("HETTY") (1697-1750), sister of JOHN and CHARLES WESLEY, was born at Epworth in 1697. She has been immortalized in the novel by Arthur Quiller-Couch, and she was the most talented and loveliest of the Wesley sisters. As a child she was "gay and sprightly, full of mirth and good-humour and keen wit." It was she who, more than any other member of the family, was plagued by the poltergeist whom the family dubbed "old Jeffrey." During the ghostly disturbances in January, 1716, she trembled and turned uneasily in her sleep, and she found the noises followed her as though under her feet.

As she grew, Hetty was pursued by a number of young men, but they were judged unsuitable either by her parents or herself, though possibly John Romley, the curate, made a certain impression on her. There was found among John Wesley's papers a poetic letter from Hetty to her mother which ended with the words:

> Pray speak a word in time of need,
> And with my sour-looked parent plead
> For your distressed daughter.

This doubtless refers to the rector's disapproval of Romley. The rector's instinct was right, for Romley was a vain, unstable man who came to an early death through alcoholic poisoning.

By the time she was twenty-seven Hetty began to make clandestine appointments with a man whom her father called "an unprincipled lawyer" and eloped with him. He declared his readiness to marry her, but did not do so, and she returned in shame to Epworth rather than continue as his mistress. The rector, who had consistently denounced adultery and punished offenders in his own parish, was horrified at his daughter's conduct. He secured her consent to marry the first to come who sought her hand in marriage.

This proved to be William Wright, a traveling plumber and glazier, who was in every respect unsuited to be her husband, since he had no breeding, education, or good manners. Her sorrow was increased by the successive deaths of the babies born to her. One of her poems, "Mother's Address to a Dying Infant," had the despairing line: "And with the blossom blast the tree!"

These years were made worse by the stiff and uncompromising attitude of the rector and the family at Epworth. Hetty begged, in a long letter to her father on July 3, 1739, for his forgiveness and reconciliation, but the rector never really softened in the harshness of his attitude. Her lot became easier when her mother went to live at the Foundery in 1739, and she was present at her mother's bedside when she died in 1742. During these years Hetty became a Methodist and regularly attended services at the Foundery. Occasionally she received visits from both John and Charles Wesley, and with their help she was able to visit Bristol to seek relief from the curative springs at the Hot Wells. She was virtually an invalid, and in a letter to Charles on October 4, 1745, she spoke of "continuing exceeding weak, keeping my bed except when I rise to have it made, it is almost incredible what a skeleton I am grown, so that my bones are ready to come through my skin." She died on March 21, 1750, at London, and Charles Wesley recorded in his *Journal*, "I followed her to her quiet grave and wept with them that weep."

Hetty Wesley was a minor poet, and while some poems were printed in the *Gentleman's Magazine* and a contemporary anthology, others were printed at a later date in the *Poetical Register*, the *Christian Magazine*, and the *Arminian Magazine*. It is not in her poetry, however, but in the drama of her life, unforgettably told by Arthur Quiller-Couch, that Hetty remains as the most highly gifted and yet the most tragic figure in the Epworth family circle.

MALDWYN L. EDWARDS

WESLEY, SAMUEL, Rector of Epworth (1666-1735), father of John and Charles Wesley, was born at Winterborn Whitchurch, 1666 and after private education till the age of twelve was sent by his widowed mother to a Dissenting academy in London in 1678. From this academy of Mr. Veal's at Stepney he went to that of Charles Morton at Newington Green, and in both centers laid the foundations of an excellent classical education.

At a date and for a cause not known he decided to become an Anglican, and went to Oxford in 1683 with the intention of entering the Church as priest. He became a servitor at Exeter College, which meant that his maintenance was secured by waiting on other students. After five-years' residence in which he secured his degree and published a small book of poems, he was ordained priest on February 24, 1689, by the Bishop of London.

For a year he was chaplain of a man-of-war, but upon his marriage he resigned his position for a curacy in London. In this period he doubled his slender income of thirty pounds by his writings, and especially his share in the *Athenian Gazette*. In 1691 through the influence of the Marquis of Normanby he received the living at South Ormsby in Lincolnshire. In this village Wesley had the care of three hundred people. He continued his literary work, and in 1693 published *The Life of Our Blessed Lord and Saviour Jesus Christ: an Heroic Poem in Ten Books*.

When Samuel left South Ormsby to become rector of Epworth early in 1697, he remained for a time chaplain to the Marquis of Normanby, and in 1701 dedicated his *History of the Old and New Testament* to the nobleman. He stayed at Epworth until his death thirty-nine years later.

In the first period, until 1710, he had to contend with natural disasters such as the three fires of the rectory: in 1702 when two thirds of the building was destroyed; in 1704 when all his flax was lost; and the total destruction of the old rectory in 1709. The floods often destroyed his crops, and he had also to face the surly hostility of the villagers. With the building of the new rectory, however, the attitude of his parishioners changed, and although he was never free from poverty, nor from natural calamities, he was able to work more happily in the parish and with visible signs of success.

In addition to his poems and a printed discourse on the Sacrament of the Lord's Supper, with the shortened title of *The Pious Communicant Rightly Prepared*, Samuel Wesley wrote a commentary on the Book of Job in Latin (*Dissertationes in Librum Jobi*); in this the Hebrew text was collated with the Chaldee paraphrase and the Septuagint, and with other versions in Syriac, Arabic, Latin, and the English translations of Tyndale and the Authorized Version of 1611. It was extremely erudite, and orientalists such as ADAM CLARKE thought highly of it, but John Wesley's laconic comment was that it "contained immense learning but of a kind which I do not admire." Nothing will remain of all his literary work except his one great hymn on the death of Christ:

> Behold the Saviour of mankind
> Nailed to the shameful tree!
> How vast the love that him inclined
> To bleed and die for thee!

Wesley has been justly criticized for the severity of his conduct toward Hetty Wesley when she returned in disgrace after eloping with a faithless suitor. He bears responsibility for her ill-fated marriage, though it is fair

to remember that, apart from the three brothers and Mary, all the rest of the family shared his judgment. While he made what provision he could for his daughters, he never fully understood them, and none, apart from Mary, who acted as his secretary for long years, spoke of him with affection, but only with respect. It would be difficult, however, to estimate his influence over his sons.

His married life was happy, but the large family of nineteen children and the constant struggle against poverty, added to his own choleric disposition, often produced squalls. In one instance there was a famous and protracted quarrel over "the rightful sovereign" in which Susanna refused to waver in her loyalty to the exiled Stuarts, and Samuel left home, until the accession of Queen Anne. Despite surface disagreements, each spoke in devoted terms of the other, and in one of his letters to Samuel, Junior, in September, 1706, the rector described his wife as "one of the best of mothers" and urged him to love and reverence her "as much as you can." She in turn replied to her brother Samuel Annesley's criticism of the rector's business inefficiency by saying, "Where he lives, I will live, and where he dies, will I die and there will I be buried. God do so unto me and more also if ought but death part him and me."

Samuel Wesley died at Epworth on April 25, 1735. From his tomb by the side of the church, John Wesley preached on June 6, 1742, when the curate refused to allow him to participate in the service in the church and preached against him.

MALDWYN L. EDWARDS

WESLEY, SAMUEL, JUNIOR (1690-1739), the oldest son of SAMUEL, and the brother of JOHN and CHARLES WESLEY, was born in London on February 10, 1690. He was the only one of the Epworth brood to have private teaching as a child apart from his mother's instruction. For a year he was under the tuition of John Holland, a good but eccentric scholar who kept a private school in Epworth. In 1704 he went to Westminster School, and three years later became a king's scholar and ceased thenceforth to be a financial liability to his parents. The school had a reputation for classical learning, and Samuel quickly became an eager and outstanding student. In his last year he was singled out by Dr. Spratt, Bishop of Rochester, to read to him the classical authors and books of science. It was a striking tribute to Samuel's ability, but he did not appreciate the honor, and in a letter to his father in Latin in August, 1710, he said the bishop had taken him away from his studies and from school "not only without benefit but without pleasure."

However, his merits became known to Francis Atterbury, who succeeded Bishop Spratt the following year as Bishop of Rochester. Chiefly through his influence Samuel secured entrance to Christ Church, Oxford, in 1711. At once he became known among the university wits and scholars. Upon the completion of his degree and the taking of his ordination vows he returned as usher (a master) at Westminster School. He was now able to support the Epworth family, and the rector, his father, said in a letter written February 28, 1733,

You have been a father to your brothers and sisters, especially to the former, who have cost you great sums in your education, both before and since they went to the University. Neither have you stopped here, but have showed your pity to your mother and me in a very liberal manner, wherein your wife joined with you, when you did not overmuch abound yourselves, and have done even noble charities to my children's children. (*Family Circle*, p. 101.)

Apart from financial help the elder son maintained a regular correspondence with his father and his mother; the letters to the father made inquiries about study, since by this time the relations between them were not tutor and pupil but fellow students. Indeed Samuel, the son, gave his father considerable help in the preparation of the *Dissertations*. The rector would have liked Samuel to have succeeded him at Epworth, and only when he declined did he turn to John. Even then he enlisted his eldest son's aid in his appeal to John. Samuel took up the plea of his father, but after the interchange of letters, he had to confess himself worsted. As John was not slow to point out, he himself was in a similar position as a clerk in holy orders who was teaching, and yet unwilling to accept the Epworth living, even though his father wished it.

Samuel did not want his brothers to go to Georgia in 1735 and realized that Charles Wesley was totally unfitted to be secretary to General Oglethorpe, but he was unable to convince Charles, who learned from bitter experience that his elder brother had been right. Once back in England Charles and John lodged in turn with Mrs. Hutton, a well-meaning but temperamental family friend. She was puzzled and disturbed by their behavior before their evangelical conversion, and far more so in the days that followed. She communicated her fears to Samuel who did not wait to hear from John, but identified himself wholly with her point of view. She had wondered what might be the effect upon her own sons, but Samuel expressed an equal anxiety for his two brothers, whom he felt in some sense he could call his own sons. Mrs. Hutton then declared that in the new movement converts were expected to have an assurance of forgiveness and to know precisely the day and hour of their conversion. Samuel was alarmed because, as a child of his age, he abhorred "enthusiasm" and as a High Churchman he feared where these irregular practices, and manifestations of feeling, might lead.

John replied in a moderate and reasoned letter on October 30, 1738, but Samuel was not moved from a conviction that the new doctrines were potentially dangerous. John defended himself again, but without success, and the correspondence ceased with Samuel's sudden death in November, 1739. It must be made clear that Samuel praised when praise was possible, and in particular he was very pleased to hear that John had built a charity school, and he wanted a church to be built for the Kingswood colliers. Before he died John heard that Samuel had received "a calm and full assurance of his interest in Christ," and he was inclined to suppose that had he lived, the attitude of Samuel to the revival might have undergone a change.

But Samuel's wholehearted acceptance of High Church views, his detachment from any form of proselytizing, begotten of his chosen way of life, and his own disposition made him unfitted to judge the revival impartially. The disapproval of those first excesses expressed so eloquently by Robert Southey in his famous *Life of Wesley* would certainly reflect the views of Samuel. The later stages of the revival, involving further departures from established Anglican order, would have pained him even more.

There are four aspects of Samuel's life that are worthy of special mention. He was not only a fine classical scholar but an effective teacher. It was partly because of his tuition that Charles Wesley on coming to Westminster in 1716 became a king's scholar and later captain of the school. There seems little doubt that if he had not avowed Jacobite sympathies, and heroically stood by the banished Francis Atterbury, Samuel might legitimately have hoped for a higher preferment at Westminster instead of continuing as usher. When he lost the undermastership at his school he secured the headmastership of Tiverton Grammar School in 1732. He quickly showed himself a great headmaster, and in the last seven years of his life he added considerably to the numbers of the school.

When he died the whole town and countryside mourned his loss and in the long record of that school no name shines more brightly.

Secondly, tribute must be paid to him as a minor wit and poet of the Augustan age in English poetry. In his *Poems on Several Occasions* he revealed himself as master of the epigram and witty satire. Samuel Wesley, Junior, also revealed the family gift of hymn writing. None of his hymns survive in modern hymnbooks, but some enjoyed a long popularity. These included the moving hymn on the death of Christ:

> See streaming from the accursed tree
> His all-atoning blood.

Note his hymn on the worth of Sunday:

> The Lord of Sabbath let us praise
> In concord with the blest.

Perhaps his best known hymn is a commentary on Isaiah 40:6-8 beginning with the words:

> The morning flowers display their sweets,
> And gay, their silken leaves unfold;
> As careless of the noonday heats,
> And fearless of the evening cold.

This ends with the lines,

> Perish the grass, and fade the flower,
> If firm the word of God remains.

Thirdly, one must remark upon his happy married life. Of the nine children who married, it was only his brother Charles, and possibly Anne, who had similar unbroken happiness. Samuel's wife, Ursula Berry, was the granddaughter of one of the ministers ejected by the Act of Uniformity in 1662; and the daughter of John Berry, who in later life became vicar of Whatton. Samuel drew a sympathetic portrait of him in his poem, "Parish Priest." Many children were born to them, but apart from a son and daughter, they all died in infancy. The son grew to maturity and then died in June, 1731, to the almost inconsolable grief of his parents. The daughter married a Mr. Earle of Barnstaple, and Stevenson in his *Memorials of the Wesley Family* quotes a story to the effect that one of her many daughters crossed over to France and married the celebrated Marshal Ney. This hearsay story, however, has never been substantiated and must be dismissed as legend. Many of Samuel's poems were written in praise of his wife; on each of his birthdays, he wrote a poem to her. When he wrote a poem for his sister, Anne, on her marriage to John Lambert he asked only that the union would be as happy as his own.

Be he a husband blest as I,
And thou a wife as good as mine.

Lastly, Samuel inherited Jacobite views from his mother, and sustained his loyalty to the exiled Stuarts until his death. His sympathies were deepened by his friendship with Francis Atterbury, who became Bishop of Rochester in 1713. In 1722 Atterbury was sent to the Tower of London as one of those implicated in a plot to bring the Pretender, Charles Stuart, to the throne of England. Despite his spirited defense before the House of Lords, Atterbury was sentenced to perpetual banishment, and gradually his former friends fell away. But Samuel, who firmly believed in his innocence, not only maintained a correspondence with him, but defended him publicly on every occasion. This may easily have cost him preferment in his own profession, but he never wavered in his loyalty, and Atterbury said in a letter in 1730, "He has shown an invariable regard for me all along in all circumstances, and much more than some of his acquaintances who had ten times greater obligations." His Jacobitism was one more mark of that steadfastness of character which kept him faithful to his family and to his friends whatever the sacrifice involved. Perhaps in the epitaph he suggested for himself there is implicit the recognition of what his loyalties had cost:

Here Wesley lies in quiet rest.
Hated in earnest for his jest,
Here his worldly bustle ends,
Safe from his foes and from his friends.

Samuel Wesley, Junior, died at Tiverton on November 6, 1739.

MALDWYN L. EDWARDS

WESLEY, SAMUEL (1766-1837), son of CHARLES WESLEY, was born at BRISTOL on Feb. 24, 1766. Like his brother CHARLES, Samuel had the instincts of a musician. His father said that "his first attempts were picked up from street-organs . . . ; (Stevenson, p. 491) whilst his brother was playing he used to stand by with his childish fiddle scraping and beating time." By the time he was five years old it was said that Samuel knew all the airs, recitatives, and choruses of "Samson" and the "Messiah" by words and music. Although skilled as a violinist, the organ was his favorite instrument. In LONDON he excited the interest of Lords Barrington, Aylesford, and Dudley, and Sir Watkin Williams Wynne, who were all lovers of Handel's music. A contemporary described Samuel's skill in improvising upon a theme and said he had heard him "give more than fifty variations on a pleasing melody all of which were not only different from each other, but showed excellent taste and judgment." (ibid., p. 496) He was a good classical scholar, and in both Latin and Greek obtained proficiency, but his first and last love was music. In 1779, when he was only thirteen years of age, he gave private concerts and continued for nine years. Samuel played the violin and Charles played the organ.

Toward the end of his father's life Samuel became a convert to the Roman Catholic Church because he said "the Gregorian music had seduced him." Charles Wesley, Sr., however, would not hear of such an explanation. "The loaves and fishes, madam, the loaves and fishes," was his rejoinder to the Duchess of Norfolk, who told him of his son's defection from Protestantism.

There is little doubt that the news saddened the father and cast a shadow over his two remaining years. Samuel's uncle, JOHN WESLEY, wrote him a loving but frank letter in which he begged him as a first step to believe Jesus Christ to be his Savior, "and then I will talk to you of transubstantiation and purgatory." (Letter, Aug. 19, 1784) Shortly after the death of his father and then his uncle, Samuel wrote a pamphlet, *Vindex to Verax*, attacking doctrinal errors in the Roman Church, and then before he was thirty he renounced Romanism altogether.

In 1793 he married Charlotte Martin in an Anglican Church but later entered into a liaison with Sarah Suter, by whom he had several children, including SAMUEL SEBASTIAN WESLEY. His home in Barnet was frequently visited by Mrs. Charles Wesley, his mother, and by his sister. When he moved to London he continued to occupy an apartment in his mother's house. By this time he was known and admired for scholarship and wit as well as for his music. He gave concerts in many towns and cities, but in 1817 he became gravely ill and for two years was compelled to retire from public life. Upon recovery he became organist at Camden Town and in Ely Place. In 1826 he discovered in the library of the Fitzwilliam Museum three hymn tunes of Handel and set them to three of his father's hymns: "Sinners Obey the Gospel Word," "O, Love Divine how Sweet Thou Art," "Rejoice the Lord is King."

Despite contemporary praise for his musical compositions, he left no enduring music, but at his funeral on Oct. 11, 1837, his son, Samuel Sebastian Wesley, was present, and it was through him that his father gave his greatest gift to the world of music.

J. T. Lightwood, *Samuel Wesley, Musician.* 1937.

MALDWYN L. EDWARDS

WESLEY, SAMUEL SEBASTIAN (1810-1876), son of the musician SAMUEL by his mistress, Sarah Suter, and grandson of CHARLES WESLEY, was born in London on Aug. 14, 1810. He received instruction from his father, and in 1819 was chosen as one of the choristers at St. James' Chapel Royal, where he remained eight years. His musical education in singing and piano was enlarged by the duty of choristers to assist in special concerts.

In 1827 he was appointed organist at St. James, Hampstead Road, London, and in 1829 at St. Giles, Camberwell. Other preferments followed, until in 1832 he became organist at Hereford Cathedral. Here he married the sister of the dean and became the father of five sons and one daughter. In 1842 he accepted the post of organist in Leeds Parish Church during the incumbency of the celebrated Dr. Hook.

After seven years he went to Winchester Cathedral, and for fifteen years was organist there. More than any other musician he was called upon to give organ recitals at the opening of organs throughout the country. During his stay at Winchester two of his sons were ordained priests and two became doctors.

Finally in 1865 he became organist at Gloucester Cathedral, where he remained till his death. In 1872 he published some of his psalm tunes under the title *The European Psalmist*. Perhaps his best remembered published work is *Twelve Anthems*, which contains anthems in general use by cathedrals and parish churches. He died at Gloucester on April 19, 1876, and was buried at Exeter by the side of his only daughter. He ranks among the very greatest of English composers of church music.

MALDWYN L. EDWARDS

WESLEY, SARAH (1759-1828), daughter of Charles Wesley, was born at Bristol on April 1, 1759. It seems that like her mother she was very beautiful until an attack of smallpox marred her appearance. She had a great love for reading, and her brother Charles, Junior, said, "She devoured books from the age of six and taught herself to write an original print hand." Like her two brothers she had a good ear and a fine taste for music, but unlike them she was unwilling to give to musical practice what she could give to reading books. Indeed she shunned company "except for the good Methodist or Quakers," and when she went out a book was in her hand.

She was a great favorite of John Wesley, and he once refused to let his wife's ill conduct prevent him from taking Sally on an outing they had planned together. Charles wanted John to return to Bristol to prevent his wife from publishing injurious statements against him, but John replied, "Brother, when I devoted to God my ease, my time, my life, did I except my reputation? No. Tell Sally I will take her to Canterbury to-morrow." (*Journal*, Vol. 6, p. 89.) When John wrote to her following the death of Charles, whom she had watched over so long with such tender care, he signed himself, "Dear Sally, Yours invariably, J. Wesley."

Sally was also much loved by her aunt, MARTHA WESLEY, and in the last ten years of Martha's life, she and Sally were often in each other's company; and through her aunt, Sally was introduced to the great Dr. Samuel Johnson. She was encouraged to show him her poetry, and he said to her aunt, "Madam, she will do."

She was always attached to Bristol, and she and her brother Charles returned there in 1828 to refresh their memories and, on Sally's part, to recover her health. Unhappily, the malady developed, and it was in Bristol that she died on September 19, 1828. She was buried in St. James' Churchyard.

MALDWYN L. EDWARDS

WESLEY, SARAH GWYNNE (1726-1822), wife of CHARLES WESLEY, was born of wealthy parents in Garth, Breconshire. Her father was a magistrate and squire, and nine children and twenty servants comprised his household. In addition there were generally guests, and night and morning the domestic chaplain read prayers with family and friends. She had known JOHN and Charles WESLEY since August 1747, when they stayed five days with the family while Charles was on the way to IRELAND. He returned seven months later, and Sarah Gwynne helped to nurse him from his illness. She went with her father in June 1748 to see the Methodist work in BRISTOL after visiting Oxford.

On Saturday, April 8, 1749, Charles and she were married, and after much separation due to his preaching tours, they settled down in Bristol in September 1749. In 1753 she was attacked by smallpox which destroyed her beauty.

Eight children were born in Bristol, but five died in infancy and were buried in St. James' Churchyard in the Horsefair; the three who survived went with their parents to LONDON in 1771, and the two sons soon became known

in musical circles. The house at No. 1 Chesterfield Street, Marylebone, was the home of Mrs. Wesley for thirty years, and here she entertained the distinguished people who attended the musical concerts given by her two sons.

Generally on Sundays she worshiped at West Street Chapel, but when WESLEY CHAPEL on City Road was opened, she often attended there, despite the distance. In 1788 her husband died after a happy marriage of thirty-nine years. From that time until his own death, John Wesley not only wrote to her constantly but saw that she was well cared for. After John's death, WILLIAM WILBERFORCE, who felt himself under obligation to both Charles and John, made over to Mrs. Charles Wesley an annuity of sixty pounds annually for thirty years until her death at the advanced age of ninety-six years. Her son Charles and her daughter Sarah never married, and remained with her until the close of her life. She died in 1822 and was buried in the same vault as Charles Wesley in the old churchyard of St. Marylebone in London. Later her two sons were also buried there.

MALDWYN L. EDWARDS

SUSANNA WESLEY

WESLEY, SUSANNA (1669-1742), mother of JOHN and CHARLES WESLEY, was born in London on January 20, 1669, was the "Mother of Methodism" and one of the greatest women in the religious history of the British people. She was the twenty-fifth child of the learned and celebrated SAMUEL ANNESLEY, the leader of Dissenting ministers in London during the reign of Charles II. He was in charge of St. Helen's, Bishopsgate, when SAMUEL WESLEY married Susanna, his lively and beautiful daughter, in 1688, and there he continued in great peace and industry until his death in 1696.

Susanna's married life lasted about forty-six years, thirty-nine of which were spent at Epworth. Of her nineteen children, ten survived infancy, and all the seven girls and three sons were uncommonly gifted. This was due in part to her remarkable method of education. As soon as they could speak they were taught the Lord's Prayer and later some collects, a catechism, and portions of Scripture. Each day they had six hours of school, and in "a quarter of a year could read better than most women could do as long as they live." The fire of 1709 broke this strict regime, and when the children were dispersed into several families Susanna lamented that "they got knowledge of several songs and bad things," and also "a clownish accent and many rash ways." Not without difficulty she brought them back into the old paths and even added the singing of Psalms at the beginning and ending of school. After the general retirement at 5 P.M. the eldest took the youngest, and the second the next, for a reading of the Psalm and lesson for the day.

Not only did she teach her children collectively, but she set apart a period each week to instruct them individually. Later in life John referred to the Thursday she set apart for him and said in a letter, "If you can only spare me that little part of Thursday evening which you formerly bestowed upon me in another manner, I doubt not it would be as useful now for correcting my heart, as it was then for forming my judgment."

As they grew older she instructed them not only in letters to absent members of the family but in manuals designed for them all. The first essay, rewritten in 1712, was an argument for the existence of God and his essential nature and attributes. More important was her commentary on the Apostles' Creed; article by article, she made distinctive and penetrating remarks. This applies especially to her teaching on the Holy Spirit who "leads us into all the truth, helps our infirmities, assures us of our adoption, and will be with the Holy Catholic Church to the end of the world."

The last treatise she wrote was an exposition of the Ten Commandments, because she believed that the creed and the commandments contained "a summary of the moral law."

When her husband died she went to stay for a short time with her daughter, MARTHA, and her son-in-law, Westley Hall. It was while receiving the Sacrament at his hands that she received a full assurance that she was the child of God. "While my son Hall was pronouncing these words in delivering the cup to me, 'The blood of our Lord Jesus Christ which was given for thee,' the words struck through my heart and I knew God for Christ's sake had forgiven me all my sins."

This experience predisposed her to accept the strange and irregular ecclesiastical behavior of her sons in the first days of the revival, and after the death of Samuel, Junior, to live at the Foundery, which John Wesley in 1739 had purchased for his Methodist people in London. Here she was close to her daughter, Martha, and also to Hetty in Soho. Another daughter, Anne, was not far away at Hatfield, and Kezzy was in the family of the friendly vicar of Bexley. But chiefly she was now at the heart of the new Methodist movement and took her full part in the Foundery services. The woman who had once taken Sunday evening services in the rectory kitchen during the absence of her husband in convocation in London was the very person to stand as champion of THOMAS MAXFIELD, the first lay preacher. John Wesley took his mother's advice and listened to Maxfield and then threw away his prejudices. "It is the Lord; let Him do what seemeth Him good. What am I that I should withstand God?"

Susanna had argued better than she realized, for the revival could not have spread without its lay preachers. It was her greatest contribution to the Methodists. When she died on July 30, 1742, all her family in London was gathered around her. Just before she died she said, "Children, as soon as I am released sing a Psalm of praise to God." Until she actually lapsed into unconsciousness her last hours were in happy communion with God. The "innumerable company of people" who gathered for the burial service was an indication of the respect and affection in which she was held, and John Wesley recorded in his *Journal* that it was one of the most solemn assemblies he ever saw or expected to see. She was laid to rest fittingly in Bunhills Fields, City Road, close to the graves of John Bunyan and Isaac Watts, and only a stone's throw from the site where Wesley's Chapel was later to be built and John Wesley was buried.

Quite apart from the fact that she was the mother of John and Charles, she has her own imperishable place in the Methodist story because of her saintliness of character. The uninspired lines of Charles Wesley engraved on her tombstone must not be taken as the final reflection of the son upon his mother's life. It is in a funeral hymn written shortly after her death, and beginning

> What are these arrayed in white,
> Brighter than the noonday sun,

that he did justice to her memory, and two lines catch the essence of her timeless appeal:

> God resides among his own,
> God doth in His saints delight.

MALDWYN L. EDWARDS

WESLEY, SUSANNA "SUKEY" (1695-1764), sister of JOHN and CHARLES WESLEY, was born at South Ormsby in 1695. In her early days ADAM CLARKE found her to be "good natured, very facetious, and a little romantic." (Adam Clarke, Vol. 2, p. 271.) After the rectory fire at Epworth in 1709 the family was dispersed, and Sukey went to stay with her uncle MATTHEW WESLEY in London. Then she stayed with a maternal uncle, Samuel Annesley, before she sailed for India.

She made an unfortunate marriage with Richard Ellison. Mrs. Wesley declared that her son-in-law was "a gentleman of good family but a coarse, vulgar, immoral man." The father was even more scathing in condemnation; he said that Dick Ellison was the "wen" of his family, and his company was no more pleasant than all his physic. This seemed to be the general opinion of the Wesley family. Martha said, "He wanted all but riches," while Samuel, Junior, thought that he prided himself on the fact that he had neither religion, manners, nor good nature.

Ellison's wealth vanished, due partly to his own profligacy, and also due to the destruction of his house by fire and the flooding of his lands for two years because of the neglect of the commissioner of sewers. Sukey left him when his "harsh, despotic and coarse nature" made him quite intolerable, and because "under his unkindness she well nigh sank into the grave."

When he had been reduced to poverty, he came to

London to seek help from John Wesley. John, who never refused any appeal for help, secured assistance from the charitable Mr. Butterfield and showed him such kindness that he underwent a change of heart and attended the services at the Foundery. Charles Wesley, writing to his wife on April 11, 1760, said, "Yesterday evening I buried my brother Ellison. Sister Macdonald, whom he was always fond of, prayed with him in his last moments. He told her he was not afraid to die, and believed God, for Christ's sake, had forgiven him. I felt a most solemn awe overwhelming me whilst I committed his body to the earth." Sukey survived him four years, and it is probable that although they were never reunited as man and wife, they knew each other in a restored relationship as fellow Methodists. She divided her last years among her children, four of whom survived infancy. She died on Dec. 7, 1764, in London.

MALDWYN L. EDWARDS

WESLEY BANNER AND REVIVAL RECORD was a monthly British Methodist periodical of revival news for local preachers, leaders, and members, edited by a Wesleyan Methodist minister, SAMUEL DUNN (1797-1882). It commenced in the unpromising year of 1849. The *Papers on Wesleyan Matters,* a publication which supported the conservative element in Wesleyan Methodism, and the *Wesleyan Times,* a journal which supported the Wesleyan reforming party, had already appeared, and mutual recrimination over these publications and the Conference "test" declaration condemning the FLY SHEETS was growing. Dunn was critical of the Conference administration and could not refrain from comment in the *Wesley Banner.* The *Banner* at once incurred suspicion; revivalism as well as reform was held to be a disruptive influence in the 1840's. Dunn himself realized this when he himself wrote that he was accused of enmity to Methodism in polity. This was in the *Wesley Banner,* April 13, 1849. The fact that WILLIAM GRIFFITH was associated with Dunn in the *Wesley Banner* in no way allayed official suspicion. Dunn was charged at the 1849 Derby and Nottingham District Meeting with contravening Methodist law and disturbing the peace of the societies through the *Banner.* The District Meeting called for its discontinuance; Dunn refused and appealed to the Annual Conference. At the 1849 Conference, along with Griffith and JAMES EVERETT, Dunn was questioned by the president concerning the authorship of the Fly Sheets; and when he refused to give a simple, categorical answer, a special committee was set up to go into his whole case. The judgment of the District Meeting on the *Wesley Banner* was confirmed, the publication being described as "the organ of a small minority avowedly designed, by appeals to the public, to correct the administration of Methodism, thus attempting to supersede the authority of the District Meeting and of the Conference" (*Minutes of the Wesleyan Conference,* 1849). The end of the *Banner* was demanded as a condition of Dunn's continuance in the ministry; when he refused the Conference expelled him. It was not surprising that the *Banner* became more outspoken after Dunn's expulsion. It then described the 1835 declaratory laws as "steeped in apostasy and unbelief," and as "false in its statements and wicked in its principles." For a while, it became a typical publication of the Wesleyan reforming party, but after a few years

petered out altogether. It has been correctly stated that it is a remarkably dull book to read in its volume form.

M. S. EDWARDS

WESLEY COLLEGE, Bristol. (See DIDSBURY COLLEGE, Manchester.)

WESLEY COLLEGE, Dover, Delaware, was established by the Wilmington Conference in 1873 as Wilmington Conference Academy. In 1918, it was rechartered as Wesley Collegiate Institute, with junior college instruction beginning in 1922. The college was closed from 1939 to 1942, when it reopened as Wesley Junior College. The present name was assumed in 1958. The governing board has thirty-six members, nominated by the board and elected by the PENINSULA ANNUAL CONFERENCE.

JOHN O. GROSS

WESLEY COLLEGE, Dublin, Ireland. This school was originally founded in 1845 as the Wesleyan Methodist Connexional School at St. Stephen's Green, DUBLIN. Among its early pupils were Sir Robert Hart and George Bernard Shaw. In 1872 a new site was purchased; it was to the side and rear of the Methodist Centenary Church, St. Stephen's Green, Dublin, and there Wesley College was established in 1879. For many years the school was only for boys, but in 1911 girls were admitted, and it became one of the few coeducational secondary schools in the country, for even today the majority of such schools in the Republic of IRELAND are single-sex.

The main College building was designed for some 250 pupils, and the boys' boarding department was there. With the success of the school numbers grew. Two boarding houses for girls and another for junior boys were opened in more residential areas of the city, but easy of access to St. Stephen's Green.

In 1964 a new site of over fifty acres was obtained at Ludford Park, on the south side of the city, and about five miles from the center. A complete transfer of all departments came about in 1969. The school has become the largest Protestant secondary school in the Republic, with 533 pupils (272 boys and 261 girls); 352 of these are day pupils and 181 are boarders (1966-67).

The Connexional School was under the cumbersome dual control of a Governor (always a minister) and a Headmaster (usually, though not always, a layman). The first Governor was Robinson Scott. Perhaps the most important name from the early period is that of Robert Crook, who for a period (1856-62) held both offices. When the school was established as Wesley College, Thomas McKee was Governor and Maxwell McIntosh was Headmaster. As they both left in the same year, 1891, the opportunity was then taken to combine the two offices into one principal, viz.: Samuel Hollingsworth 1891-99; William Crawford 1899-1910; Thomas J. Irwin 1910-45; Mortimer Temple 1945-47; and Gerald G. Myles 1947- .

F. Jeffery, *Irish Methodism.* 1964.
R. Lee Cole, *Methodism in Ireland.* 1960. FREDERICK JEFFERY

WESLEY COLLEGE of Grand Forks, North Dakota, is the outgrowth of the Red River Valley University, a Methodist liberal arts college launched in Wahpeton, N. D., in

1892. From the beginning the Wahpeton venture was beset with financial difficulties.

In 1899, E. P. ROBERTSON became president of the institution, a post he was to fill until his retirement in 1931. In 1906 the school adopted the name of Wesley College and was relocated at Grand Forks. There it became affiliated with the University of North Dakota, and a campus was acquired directly adjacent to the university. The college discontinued all of its work except speech, music, and religion. Other courses necessary for a B.A. degree were taken at the university. For many years it continued to grant the B.A. degree.

The Wesley College program included dormitories for both men and women, a chapel and a WESLEY FOUNDATION for Methodist students, a dining hall, and other activities. In January, 1965, the trustees decided to sell their existing buildings to the university and to concentrate future efforts on offering religion courses within the university's department of religion and ministering to Methodist students at the university. Plans have been projected for a new Wesley Center of Religion to serve as the future Wesley College work.

JOHN O. GROSS

WESLEY COLLEGE, Greenville, Texas, originally opened in 1902 as an independent school in Terrell, Texas called Terrell University. It became a Methodist school in 1905 under the presidency of J. J. Morgan, with the name of North Texas University School. In 1909 it became a junior college and was renamed Wesley College; and in 1912 was relocated in Greenville, Texas on a twenty-acre campus. It carried on excellent work for some years, but competition by state schools and later the Great Depression of the 1930's caused its closing in 1934.

W. N. Vernon, *North Texas.*   WALTER N. VERNON

WESLEY COLLEGE, Headingley, LEEDS, one of the THEOLOGICAL COLLEGES of the Wesleyan Methodist Church, dates from September, 1868, and was the first of the Methodist theological institutions to be built entirely as a college. It served especially the special interests of Methodism in the northeast of England, but in the interests of economy and efficiency it was closed in 1968 and amalgamated with DIDSBURY COLLEGE, Bristol, and thereupon was renamed Wesley College.

NORMAN P. GOLDHAWK

WESLEY COLLEGE (Manitoba), the first liberal arts college of the Methodist Church in western CANADA, received its charter from the Manitoba legislature in 1877, the same year in which the University of Manitoba was incorporated and but seven years after the province itself was formed. Manitoba College had already been established in 1871 in the Red River Settlement by the Presbyterian Church. In June 1938, thirteen years after the formation of The UNITED CHURCH OF CANADA, these two institutions were joined by legislative enactment to form the present United College, Winnipeg.

The "special" conference in Manitoba, held in 1872, "drew the attention of the church to the desirableness of an early effort to establish a college at WINNIPEG." Following an appeal for aid at the Methodist Conference in London, Ontario, the next June, George Young was authorized to collect money in the East for such a college. With the $6,000 subscribed he was able to open on Nov. 3, 1873, the Manitoba Wesleyan Institute in a building adjacent to the first Grace Church at the corner of Main Street and Water Avenue.

Starting with an enrollment of forty-seven students in its three departments, primary, elementary, and secondary, the institute carried on for four years. Although in 1877 the enrollment was seventy-one, the shortage of students and funds brought the closing of the school in the spring of that year. The subsequent influx of new settlers, the growth of business, and the growing demand for better provisions for college training, led to the utilization of the 1877 charter. In 1886 the board of Wesley College met with a special committee of the Manitoba and Northwest Conference of the Methodist Church to consider "the establishment of a theological Institute." It was decided unanimously to proceed with the foundation of Wesley College, and in October 1888 affiliation with the University of Manitoba was approved by the University Council.

Meanwhile the board undertook to raise funds, obtain administrative and teaching staff, acquire facilities, and provide courses. J. W. SPARLING, of Kingston, ONTARIO, agreed to become principal; R. R. Cochrane was appointed professor of mathematics and classics, and G. J. Laird of science and modern languages. In October 1888 these two professors and seven students opened the first classes of Wesley College in Grace Church. A year later, in rented quarters at 12 Albert Street, Andrew Stewart introduced classes in theology, English, and history. From 1890 to 1895 the college was located in a brick building on Broadway at Edmonton Street. In 1892 J. H. RIDDELL was added to the staff in classics, and a year later W. F. Osborne in English and French. These six men formed the administrative and teaching staff during the college's formative years.

With an enrollment of eighty-three in the session of 1894-95, and with increasing demands on staff, it became obvious that a new and permanent home must be obtained. Foreseeing this need, the Conference of 1891 had recommended the purchase of a new site. In January 1896 the new four-story, residential college, built of Calgary sandstone on a five-acre site bounded by Portage and Ellice Avenues, was opened. This building, constructed for $75,000, still stands as a distinctive unit in the extensive complex of United College and is now called Wesley Hall. It was followed by Sparling Hall (women's residence), 1912, George Bryce Hall (library and theology department), 1951; Manitoba Hall (arts and science) and Ashdown Hall (reading room and offices), 1959; Graham Hall (men's residence) and Riddell Hall (gymnasium-auditorium and dining room), 1963. The names of these seven buildings, which accommodate about sixteen hundred students, commemorate the vision, idealism, and dedication of those pioneer Christians who helped found Wesley College, and symbolize the historic steps which led to the amalgamation of Wesley and Manitoba Colleges into a single institution, United College.

The first graduating class in 1890 consisted of two persons, Miss Berta Earle and John D. Hunt. This seems to have established Wesley College as a coeducational institution. Thus when a permanent women's residence was provided, the board named it Sparling Hall in tribute to J. W. Sparling, the competent and popular first principal who held office from 1888 to 1912.

Riddell Hall commemorates the work of two distinguished Canadians: John H. Riddell, professor of classics (1893-1903) at Wesley College, founder and first principal of ALBERTA COLLEGE in Edmonton, who was recalled to Wesley College as principal in 1917, at a time of great peril to both college and nation, and who would lead it through difficult times to the amalgamation with Manitoba College in 1938, and his son, R. G. Riddell, before his untimely death in 1951, a prominent diplomat.

Graham Hall, in recognition of W. C. GRAHAM, first principal (1938-55) of United College, was adopted as the name of the men's residence in Wesley Hall before being transferred to the new building erected during the regime of his successor, W. C. Lockhart.

Ashdown Hall bears a name to which the community during Wesley College's half-century and succeeding generations are greatly indebted. Probably no other family has contributed more generously than the three generations of Ashdowns. James H. Ashdown, Sr., prominent hardware merchant and former mayor of Winnipeg, served Wesley College from 1888 to 1924 successively as bursar, vice-chairman, and chairman of the board.

The bronze memorial plaque placed on the chapel of United College by the Historic Sites and Monuments Board of Canada honors the life and work of George Bryce teacher, administrator, and historian, who established Manitoba College and became its first professor. Manitoba Hall retains the honored name of Manitoba College itself.

From the outset, Wesley College included three areas of instruction: a preparatory or collegiate division, a faculty of theology, and a faculty of arts and science. Initially there was much individual tutoring and mutual interchange between these departments, but eventually they were separated into three distinct yet complementary units. The basic courses in the collegiate department have been those authorized by the Provincial Department of Education, chiefly for grades eleven and twelve. The faculty of theology provides courses leading to a diploma in theology, and the bachelor of divinity degree. While the college was affiliated with the University of Manitoba, the curriculum, examinations, and degrees in arts and science were those of the University.

From its inception Wesley College worked in fairly close collaboration with the university and with other affiliated colleges, particularly with its neighbor, Manitoba College. This involved, not only representation on the university council and on various special committees, but also an increasing interchange of instructors and classroom accommodation. Indeed for one year, 1913-14, Manitoba and Wesley Colleges submerged their identities in a working arrangement under which both faculties and student bodies operated as "United College." This experiment in cooperation coincided with the start of a period of crises and controversy in Manitoba's educational evolution precipitated by war, financial stringency, and conflicting ideas about university development in Manitoba. A measure of stability was achieved, however, by the amalgamation of Wesley and Manitoba Colleges in 1938.

United College, which by 1967 had an enrollment approaching two thousand and a staff of about ninety, continues to represent a cross-section of the community. Initially most Wesley College students were Anglo-Saxons whose parents came from Eastern Canada or the British Isles. The staff had similar backgrounds, with most members coming from such Eastern institutions as Victoria College, the University of Toronto, and Queen's University. Later, as new immigrants arrived, the pattern changed; both groups were enriched by the addition of Icelandic, Mennonite, Ukrainian, Oriental, and other new Canadian elements. There are over thirty ethnic groups and about as many religious faiths represented in the student enrollment.

When Wesley College emerged from its half-century of establishing roots, of planning the nature and direction of a growth commensurate with the demands of the new West, it brought into United College a rich tradition, a record of achievement, a liberal philosophy, and an ecumenical approach. These should be assets in this complex world in which to the usual areas of social concern at the local, national, and international level have been added new and often frustrating complications.

A listing of Wesley graduates who have distinguished themselves in various fields of interest would be impressive, but they would present no common mold or pattern. Within the church and its college in the West were undoubtedly represented from the outset as wide a variety of beliefs, attitudes, ideals, prejudices, hopes, fears, and frustrations as in any other community. In most classrooms, as in congregations and on busy streets, the types ranged from the quiet, conservative, conformist, and demonstrative idealists to the most skeptical, analytical, and socially minded realists. Indeed, SALEM G. BLAND, a member of the staff from 1904 to 1917 and a widely-known exponent of the social gospel, used to maintain that the Christian church should be big enough and discerning enough to cater to the essential needs of all such groups. That Wesley College encouraged this comprehensive perspective is symbolized most clearly in the career of J. S. WOODSWORTH, one of its most distinguished sons— a man who sought in his long career as preacher and reformer to explain the ultimate social implications of Christian love.

In 1967 United College became the University of Winnipeg.

A. B. Baird, *Manitoba Essays*. Toronto: Macmillan, 1937.
A. S. Cummings, "A History of Wesley College." Ms., Winnipeg, 1938.
W. Kirkconnell, *The Golden Jubilee of Wesley College, Winnipeg, 1888-1938*. Winnipeg: Columbia Press, 1935.
W. L. Morton, *One University*. Toronto: McClelland and Stewart, 1957.
J. H. Riddell, *Middle West*. 1946.   A. D. LONGMAN

WESLEY DAY. John Wesley recorded in his *Journal* that at 8:45 P.M. on Wednesday, May 24, 1738, in a society room in ALDERSGATE STREET, London, his "heart was strangely warmed." He went on: "I felt I did trust in Christ, Christ alone, for salvation; and an assurance was given me that He had taken away *my* sins, even *mine*, and saved *me* from the law of sin and death."

Although the interpretation of this experience (often known as Wesley's "evangelical conversion"), and even its importance to him, is still being debated by scholars, most Methodists have recognized it as an epochal event in his life, from which sprang successful evangelism if not the initial desire to evangelize. In order both to commemorate the event and to seek a renewal of the spirit of evangelism British Methodists during this century have held special services on this day, whether it fell on a Sunday or during the week. This observance was begun by the London Mission Committee in 1924 with a procession of witness and an open air evangelistic campaign in Hyde Park attended by many thousands. In following years observances on a smaller scale were encouraged by the British branch of the INTERNATIONAL METHODIST HISTORICAL SOCIETY, and were especially memorable in 1938, the bicentenary of the event.

At the WORLD METHODIST COUNCIL meeting in Oxford in 1951 the function of Wesley Day was extended to ALDERSGATE SUNDAY, "the Sunday falling upon or immediately preceding Wesley Day," which was endorsed by the Council as "an occasion for remembering the faith of our founders and for rededicating ourselves in universal fellowship to the spreading of scriptural holiness throughout the world."

FRANK BAKER

WESLEY DEACONESS ORDER owes its origin to the work of deaconesses in New Testament times, to the revival of that work within the Protestant Church in 1833 by Pastor Theodor Fliedner at Kaiserswerth on the Rhine, and to the need for the work of women in the big city missions begun in British Methodism in the 1880's.

In 1890 Thomas B. Stephenson founded the Wesley Deaconess Order within the WESLEYAN METHODIST CHURCH, with headquarters at Mewburn House, Bonner Road, LONDON. In the following year, THOMAS J. COPE founded a similar order with the UNITED METHODIST FREE CHURCHES with headquarters at Bowron House, Wandsworth Common. In 1895 J. Flanagan established a Sisters' Settlement linked with St. George's Hall in the Old Kent Road, London, to serve the PRIMITIVE METHODIST CHURCH. The course of the first two orders ran parallel; both met with initial suspicion and opposition, and both were eventually recognized by their respective Conferences in 1907.

In those days of widespread poverty, with no national health scheme, no old-age pensions, and no unemployment benefits, much of the work of the deaconesses was social, and they used to good effect their nursing and first-aid training. But from the first, their tasks were predominantly spiritual. From 1894 missionary service played an increasing part in their work, and by 1907 they were serving in SOUTH AFRICA, CEYLON, NEW ZEALAND, West Africa, CHINA, and INDIA.

In 1902 the Wesleyan order transferred its training center and administrative headquarters to Ilkley, Yorkshire, where students received a one-year course of training, extended to two years in 1928. After Methodist Union, twenty-five deaconesses from Primitive Methodism, fifty-seven from United Methodism, and 298 from Wesleyan Methodism joined to form one order with 380 members in 1935, and the college at Ilkley became its headquarters. In 1936 Conference accepted a Service for the Ordination of Deaconesses, and later conferences stressed the need to give deaconesses full opportunity for colleagueship with ministers and for initiative and leadership in the Church.

The provisions of the welfare state lessened the need for much of the social work previously undertaken by deaconesses, and they were given new and varied opportunities for service, in addition to the continuing work in City Missions and circuit chapels. Caravan Campaigns began in 1934; chaplaincies in the army and air force began in 1940; and many deaconesses have full pastoral charge of churches in rural areas and on new housing estates. Every active member of the order is a local preacher.

Candidates, who must intend life service, are accepted by the General Committee of the Order, which is appointed by and answerable to Conference, for the order is a department of the church. Training includes Old and New Testament study, theology, church history, psychology, homiletics, and deaconess work in theory and practice. In their third year after leaving college, probationers are ordained into the full membership of the order by the president of the Conference at the annual convocation of the order.

W. Bradfield, *Life of T. B. Stephenson*. London, 1913.
H. Smith, *Ministering Women*. London, 1912.   T. MORROW

WESLEY FAMILY. The family into which JOHN and CHARLES WESLEY were born was certainly both ancient and honorable, although the family tree furnished by GEORGE J. STEVENSON in his *Memorials of the Wesley Family* must be treated with great caution as highly speculative, especially in the earlier centuries. We are only on safe ground in the seventeenth century, with the Wesleys' Puritan ancestors, and even here many problems remain. John Wesley himself was nothing like as interested in his ancestry as we are, though he did wax enthusiastic about the thought of four generations of his family "preaching the gospel, nay, and the genuine gospel, in a line." (Wesley, *Letters*, V, 76.) He was referring to Charles and himself, their father, and their paternal grandfather and great-grandfather, both of whom were among the ejected ministers of 1662.

About the great-grandfather, Bartholomew Westley, very little is known for certain, except that he was the minister of the combined parishes of Charmouth and Catherston in Dorset at the time of King Charles II's narrow escape after the battle of Worcester, that in 1662 he was ejected from Allington, and that thereafter he made his living as a physician until his burial in Lyme Regis on Feb. 15, 1670/71. Much more is known about his son JOHN WESTLEY (c. 1636-1678?), especially from a lengthy account published by Edmund Calamy in his *Continuation of the Account of Ministers . . . ejected* (1727). He was arrested after "preaching at a meeting," and contracted a fatal illness "by lying on the cold earth" in prison. Conflicting evidence exists about the date of his death, which took place either in 1670 or 1678. John Westley had a large family, of whom MATTHEW (?1661-1737) became a London physician, and SAMUEL (1662-1735) the rector of Epworth.

In 1683 Samuel Wesley deserted the Dissenters to become a priest in the CHURCH OF ENGLAND, instilling in his own children a love of his adopted church. In 1688 he married SUSANNA (1669-1742), apparently the twenty-fifth child of Dr. SAMUEL ANNESLEY (c. 1620-96), one of the leading London Dissenters, though she herself (like her husband) was a convert from Dissent to the Church of England. Dr. Annesley's second wife was a daughter of the Puritan and Parliamentarian John White (1590-1645). John Wesley appears to have believed that another of his great-grandfathers (this time on the paternal side) shared the same name, being John White (1574-1648), the "Patriarch of Dorchester" and founder of Massachusetts, but this has been strongly contested by White's biographer, Frances Rose-Troup.

Samuel Wesley continued to spell his name with a "t" long after his marriage, and this spelling was also used for a time by at least some of his children, including the most famous, John. Samuel and Susanna Wesley appear to have had nineteen children, though biographical data have not been traced for all of these. Nine died in infancy. Ten survived—three boys and seven girls. The oldest was SAMUEL WESLEY, Jr. (1690-1739), like his brothers an Anglican clergyman and a poet, who was somewhat distressed at the furore created by John and Charles during the months immediately preceding his death. The following child, baptized Susanna after her mother on March 31, 1692, died just over a year later, shortly after the birth of Emilia Wesley, who was baptized Jan. 13, 1692/3. In her middle years EMILY married an EPWORTH tradesman, Robert Harper, but he did not treat her well, and she moved to London, making one of her brother's Foundery circle, and dying about 1771. After Emily came twin brothers, baptized Annesley and Jedidiah on Dec. 3, 1694, one of them dying a month later, the other a year and a month later. Then came SUSANNA, apparently born in 1695, whose marriage to Richard Ellison also turned out badly. She died in LONDON in 1764. The next child was MARY, apparently born in 1696, who on Dec. 21, 1733 married her father's protégé, JOHN WHITELAMB, died in childbirth, and on Nov. 1, 1734 was buried in her husband's church at WROOT. After Mary came MEHETABEL ("Hetty"), who was involved in a liaison with an anonymous lawyer, and gained a name for her unborn child by marrying William Wright, a plumber of Louth, on Oct. 13, 1725. Her tragic years ended with her burial in London on March 21, 1749/50.

After Hetty there is a serious gap in our knowledge of the Wesley children, due largely to the destruction both of the Epworth parish registers and of the contemporary transcripts made from them. There seems to have been at least one child born during each of the years 1698, 1699, and 1700, and according to family tradition two of them were boys named John and Benjamin. If the parents' belief that they had had nineteen children is correct, the first of these births was probably of twins who died in infancy. The one certain fact is that on May 16, 1701, Susanna Wesley bore twins once more, and the following day Samuel wrote to the Archbishop of York: "Last night my wife brought me a *few* children. There are but *two* yet, a boy and a girl, and I think they are all at present. We have had four in two years and a day, three of which are living." From this time we have the documentary evidence of the transcripts from his registers which Samuel Wesley prepared for the Bishop of Lincoln. These show that on May 31 the twins were baptized, the one John Benjamin (acccording to family tradition in perpetuation of the names of the two dead boys), the other ANNE. The boy died seven months later. Anne Wesley survived, to marry John Lambert, a local land surveyor. Like her sisters, Anne did not enjoy a happy marriage. Her son John had a daughter Anne who married John Jarvis, the sea captain son of James Jarvis, one of the first trustees of JOHN STREET Methodist Church in New York. Through them an enduring branch of the Wesley family was thus early planted in America, and one of John Wesley's letters addressed to Nancy Jarvis in PHILADELPHIA still survives. (Wesley Historical Society, *Proceedings*, XIX, 89-93.)

After the birth of these twins Susanna Wesley seems to have enjoyed her longest period of freedom from childbearing, no less than twenty-five months, mainly owing to an estrangement from her husband over their differing political views. (See W.H.S. *Proceedings*, XXIX, 50-57.)

The fruit of their reconciliation was John Wesley, born June 17, 1703 and baptized July 3. No child was born to them in 1704, and the baby boy born the following May was accidentally smothered by his nurse when a few weeks old. The next child was MARTHA, who was born in 1706, although no details are available, and married one of the less worthy members of the HOLY CLUB, WESTLEY HALL. He was unstable, became a polygamist, and deserted his legal wife. After Martha came Charles Wesley, born Dec. 18, 1707, and baptized on the 29th. Mrs. Wesley was pregnant with her last child when young Jackie was providentially rescued from the blazing Epworth rectory in February 1709. A few days later the father wrote: "I hope my wife will recover, and not miscarry, but God will give me my nineteenth child." (Thomas Jackson, *Life of Charles Wesley*, London, Mason, 1841, II. 497.) This "fire child" was baptized KEZIA, who died unmarried in 1741, having been jilted by Westley Hall in favor of her elder sister Martha.

Samuel Wesley, Jr. had several children, but all of them except one girl seem to have died young; four are buried in the cloisters of Westminster Abbey. John Wesley had no children of his own, though he proved a good stepfather to MARY VAZEILLE's children. Charles Wesley was the only one through whom the Epworth branch of the family name was continued. In 1749 he married Sarah (1726-1822), daughter of MARMADUKE GWYNNE, the squire of Garth near Builth Wells in Wales. Charles and Sarah Wesley had eight children, four boys and four girls, of whom three survived—CHARLES (1757-1834), SARAH (1759-1828), and SAMUEL (1766-1837). Neither Charles nor Sarah married, but Samuel redressed the balance by fathering two families, one by a legal marriage, and another (after separation from his wife) by his former housekeeper. Three children were born of the marriage, including the Rev. Charles Wesley, D.D., Dean of the Chapel Royal (1793-1866); and at least seven of the liaison with Sarah Suter, of whom the most famous was the well known composer of church music, SAMUEL SEBASTIAN WESLEY (1810-76). Many lines of the family appear to have survived into the present century through Samuel Wesley the musician, though those with the surname Wesley all stem from the illegitimate branch.

The classical work on this subject is by ADAM CLARKE, his *Memoirs of the Wesley Family*, first published in one volume in 1823, and in a greatly improved and enlarged edition in two volumes, which first appeared in 1836. Much broader in coverage, and fuller in some of its documentation, is George J. Stevenson's *Memorials of the Wesley Family* (London, Partridge, 1876), but some of his documents and conclusions must be treated with caution. A useful modern study is *Family Circle* (London, Epworth Press, 1949), by MALDWYN L. EDWARDS. Briefer monographs making use of unfamiliar documents and research into public records are the present writer's "John Wesley's Puritan Ancestry" (*London Quarterly Review*, CLXXXVII, 180-86, 1962), H. A. Beecham's "Samuel Wesley Senior: New Biographical Evidence" (*Renaissance and Modern Studies*, VII, 78-109, 1963), and "Wesley Family," by Malcolm Pinhorn (*Blackmansbury*, I, 36-51, 1964-65).

FRANK BAKER

WESLEY FOUNDATION, THE, is the educational ministry of The United Methodist Church in the United States on the campus of a state or independent college or university.

The first Wesley Foundation was established at the University of Illinois on Oct. 13, 1913, under the leadership of JAMES CHAMBERLAIN BAKER (later Bishop) and his then student assistant, ELMER A. LESLIE. From this beginning, growth was rapid and in 1966 there were 198 accredited Wesley Foundations throughout the United States. These formed part of the Methodist Student Movement, which included 646 other Methodist student groups called Wesley Clubs and Methodist Student Fellowships. Wesley Foundations in The Methodist Church were accredited by the Department of College and University Religious Life of the Board of Education.

Wesley Foundations also exist outside the United States. The first of these was founded in Tokyo in 1931.

Most Wesley Foundations have as director an ordained Methodist minister under the appointment of the bishop. The student activities are carried out by student leadership, usually in an elected council, and the whole program of each Wesley Foundation is under the supervision of a board of directors consisting of ministers, faculty, laymen, and students. Financial support comes from local churches, annual conferences, the Board of Education, and the WOMAN'S SOCIETY OF CHRISTIAN SERVICE.

Important areas of concern in the Wesley Foundations through the years have included the ministry to foreign and international students, work camps, social action in fields such as human rights, peace, and race relations, and the Faculty Christian Movement. The METHODIST STUDENT MOVEMENT has taken a primary role in ecumenical studies and conversations, and belongs to the University Christian Movement and the WORLD STUDENT CHRISTIAN FEDERATION. Many Wesley Foundations offer courses in religion, and some of these have been approved for credit by the colleges and universities.

No great change was made in the Wesley Foundation organization and work when The United Methodist Church came into being in 1968. Many Methodist ministers have been called to their life tasks through participation in the Wesley Foundation, as have missionaries and leaders in every phase of the church. The Wesley Foundations stand as an aid to the church in holding students for Christ and his church during their college years.

Discipline, TMC, Paragraphs 1366-1368 (1964); U.M.C., Paragraphs 1113—sq. (1968).
JOHN O. GROSS

WESLEY GUILD, the official youth movement of British Methodism from 1869 to 1943, was inspired by W. B. FITZGERALD. It was based on the principles of comradeship, culture, consecration, and Christian service. In 1901 a department was set up to promote the movement through the connection; and the secretaries were successively W. B. Fitzgerald, George Allen, and Alfred Robinson. Parallel movements were encouraged for children, and the guild accepted responsibility for hospital work at Ilesha, West Africa. In 1932 Methodist CHRISTIAN ENDEAVOURS came under the wing of the department, which was renamed the Methodist Guild Department. The Wesley Guild Holidays, Limited, controls twelve centers for family holidays and leadership training. In 1943 the department was incorporated into the Methodist Youth Department.

L. E. Ingram, *Fifty Years For Youth*. London, n.d.
D. S. HUBERY

WESLEY HISTORICAL SOCIETY, British, is a society whose objects are to promote the exact study of Methodist history and literature and to provide a medium of intercourse for all those interested in such subjects. The original idea of the society was suggested by George Stampe of Grimsby, who enlisted the help of RICHARD GREEN, who was then a tutor at Didsbury Wesleyan Methodist Theological College in Manchester. On June 20, 1893, Richard Green sent a letter to about twenty people whom he thought might be interested in the formation of a Methodist historical society. As a result of this, the first actual meeting was held in 1894, at the time of the Wesleyan Methodist Conference in Birmingham: the first resolution passed was that the society should be called the Wesley Historical Society. At first only working membership was contemplated, but in September, 1895, the society was reconstituted with an open membership. Richard Green was president from 1894 until his death in 1907; he was followed by JOHN S. SIMON from 1907 until his death in 1933. JOHN TELFORD was appointed in 1933, but he was then advanced in years and died in 1936; EDMUND LAMPLOUGH, who had been vice-president of the Methodist Conference in 1935, followed him, only to die in 1940. Francis Fletcher Bretherton was then president until his death in 1956. W. Lamplough Doughty succeeded him until 1963, when he broke with tradition and decided to retire in order that a younger man might take his place: the new president was MALDWYN EDWARDS, who has written many books on the history of Methodism.

The written work of the society began in the form of a manuscript journal which was circulated among the members; from 1897 the best of the material gathered in this way was published in the form of the *Proceedings of the Wesley Historical Society*, which appears as a quarterly, and has been of great value to the student of British Methodist history. There is in print a *General Index* to the first thirty volumes, 1897-1956; the present editor of the *Proceedings* is J. C. Bowmer of the Methodist Archives and Research Centre in London.

In 1934, when HENRY BETT lectured on "The Early Methodist Preachers," the experiment was first tried of holding a public lecture under the auspices of the society at the time of the annual Methodist Conference. In 1935 no formal lecture was given, but from 1936 the lecture has been given every year, and all have been published, apart from the lecture of 1943. (A list of the lectures down to 1959 will be found in the *Proceedings*, xxxii, part iv.) Another scheme for the encouragement of Methodist historical study was the setting up of a Wesley Historical Society Library in the crypt of Wesley's Chapel, London, in April, 1959; the nucleus of the library was the collection of Wesleyana bequeathed to the society by one of its former presidents, F. F. Bretherton. The society began to develop local branches as far back as 1926, when the Irish branch was formed; there are also branches in Yorkshire, the Northeast, East Anglia, South Wales, Plymouth and Exeter, Lincolnshire, Cornwall, Lancashire and Cheshire, London, and West Midlands. These local branches publish bulletins of their own, and are forming local collections of Methodist historical material.

JOHN C. BOWMER

WESLEY HISTORICAL SOCIETY (Irish Branch). The headquarters are in the Historical Room, Aldersgate

House, University Road, BELFAST 7, Northern IRELAND. Here are kept for consultation the records and Wesleyana of Irish Methodism.

WESLEY HISTORICAL SOCIETY of New Zealand was founded as a branch of the British Wesley Historical Society in 1931 by direction of Conference, with C. H. Laws, as president. Members received *Proceedings* of the parent body, with accompanying pamphlets of local historical interest.

A change of policy in 1943 led to the issuing of occasional Proceedings in the form of historical brochures dealing with topics of NEW ZEALAND Methodist interest. An order of "sustaining members" continue to receive the British *Proceedings*. It is the society's aim to preserve the early records of New Zealand Methodism and to publish material of historical and inspirational value.

L. R. M. GILMORE

WESLEY HOUSE, Cambridge, one of the Theological Colleges of the Wesleyan Methodist Church, after opening in rented premises in October, 1926, moved into its own buildings in Jesus Lane. Made possible largely through the generous gifts of two laymen, Wesley House is designed for postgraduate students in training for the ministry. It has accommodation for twenty men and two tutors. Its students become members of the university, and normally take the Theological Tripos.

NORMAN P. GOLDHAWK

WESLEY POETICAL WORKS. The major contribution of JOHN and CHARLES WESLEY in the realm of verse was their hymnody (see HYMNODY, British Methodist). It was not their only contribution, however. Speaking in general, Charles was the lavish creative artist, John the critic and compiler. It is widely recognized that John Wesley inherited a large share of the poetic genius of his family. At Oxford he dabbled in occasional verse, sometimes of a very light variety, such as the poem on Cloe's favourite flea, translated from the Latin on 16 June 1724 (*Letters* I.8-9). In Georgia he embarked on those admirable translations into English verse of some of the greatest devotional poems in the German language, and by these he is best known. They include Paul Gerhardt's "Jesu, thy boundless love to me," Tersteegen's "Thou hidden love of God," and Zinzendorf's "Jesu, thy blood and righteousness My beauty are, my glorious dress." John Wesley's heartbreak over the loss of GRACE MURRAY was poured out in a moving poem of thirty-one stanzas which proves that he had the makings of a true poet.

John Wesley was eager to help the Methodists in general to appreciate the inspiration of great verse, especially devotional verse, and to this end he prepared and published several anthologies, of which the best known is the three volume *Collection of Moral and Sacred Poems* (1744). He was one of the few who at that period appreciated the poetry of George Herbert, and therefore included his writings in many anthologies from the first *Collection of Psalms and Hymns* (1737) onwards. Wesley was also audacious enough to rewrite some of them (such as "Teach me, my God and King") so that they could more readily be used for public worship as well as private devotion. Some people may judge that he went far beyond audacity in his popularising of Milton's *Paradise Lost,*

which he greatly admired. Not only did he cut out much of the less interesting and more difficult sections, at the same time adding asterisks to denote the purple passages and notes to illuminate the obscurities that he felt compelled to retain; he himself bound the poem together by supplying connecting links in good Miltonic blank verse.

At the outset of their joint publishing career, the *Hymns and Sacred Poems* of 1739, John and Charles Wesley agreed not to identify their individual compositions, and this modesty has proved a source of frustration and speculation for scholars ever since. After careful study of the few poems known to be written by John one scholar, HENRY BETT, later followed by J. ERNEST RATTENBURY, devised canons by which he believed he could identify John's work from among their joint publications, but without being completely convincing. Many clues, however, including John Wesley's own evidence in the preface to his 1780 *Collection,* make it abundantly clear that by far the largest bulk of Wesley poetry is from the pen of Charles. Altogether Charles Wesley wrote some nine thousand hymns and poems, well over a million words of verse.

It is natural to wonder about the quality of this enormous output. Charles Wesley was often repetitive, sometimes feeble, but his verse maintains a much higher average of quality than all but the greatest poets have achieved at their best. Some of his hymns are gems, loved all over the world. Hundreds more are equally good, and as poetry far superior to most hymns by other writers which have nevertheless come into common use. But nobody wants to sing hymns by one man all the time, and even John Wesley met resistance from the loyal Methodists when he tried to encompass something like this. Thus it has happened that a few of Charles Wesley's hymns have become great favourites, while others have been almost forgotten, or from time to time "discovered" by curious and enthusiastic students.

There is no doubt that Charles Wesley was a poetic genius. In an age of somewhat stodgy couplets he experimented with lilting lyrics, and wrote with technical mastery in a hundred different metres, including some that no one had used before. Most of his best work displays a classic compactness, a skilful interweaving of carefully chosen words, and a dramatic or liturgical unfolding of his theme which proved him a master of the art of rhetoric. The results of this are usually more felt than clearly understood without painstaking analysis of the poems stanza by stanza, line by line, occasionally word by word. He was so steeped in the classics of both Rome and Jerusalem that his allusive quality (part of the charm of poetry) also proves elusive to most of us less well educated admirers from a distance. He brought to his writings personal warmth, a deep religious experience akin to passionate love, an eager spirit of evangelism and occasionally the imagination and impatience which is characteristic of the artistic temperament (this is seen especially in his unpublished satirical verse). He was a pioneer of the Romantic Revival in literature as well as of the Evangelical Revival in religion. His hymns reflect many moods, as we may see by naming a few of them, from the adoring wonder of "Love divine, all loves excelling" (based on Dryden's "Fairest Isle") to the martial vigour of "Soldiers of Christ, arise," and the wistfulness of "Jesu, lover of my soul." Above all, however, it is the note of joy that predominates, the joy that God has come down into human history and into the human heart;

the joy of the Easter triumph over sin and over death in "Christ the Lord is risen today!" and even more the joy of knowing that God has done all this for people like Charles Wesley, like you and me, the joy of the hymn written on the first anniversary of his conversion on Whitsunday 1738—"O for a thousand tongues to sing my great Redeemer's praise!"

Much of Charles Wesley's work remains unpublished, including almost all his satirical and political verse. In 1868 Dr. GEORGE OSBORN began the task of publishing the whole of the poetical works of the two brothers, but in fact he omitted not only much unpublished work of which he knew and (of course) that which had not then been discovered, but also a few items which had in fact been published. His thirteen volumes of *The Poetical Works of John and Charles Wesley* (London, Wesleyan-Methodist Conference Office, 1868-72) contain some 4600 items published by the brothers and a further 3000 left in manuscript by Charles. For *Representative Verse of Charles Wesley* (London and Nashville, 1962) the present writer read a further 1350 unpublished poems, some of which are presented in that volume, as is also a summary of the bibliography of the subject.

FRANK BAKER

WESLEY PORTRAITS, JOHN AND CHARLES. The first known but one of the least worthy of the many portraits of John Wesley is an engraving on copper made in 1741, probably by George Vertue. Later in life, John Wesley sat for many artists and many important portraits. The **Williams,** by John Michael Williams, painted in 1742, is generally regarded as the best likeness of Wesley in early life. The original is at Didsbury College, Bristol; there is a copy in the Board Room of the Methodist Publishing House in London. An engraving of this portrait, made by JOHN DOWNES, formed the frontispiece to the first edition of John Wesley's *Notes on the New Testament* (see his *Journal,* November 4, 1774, and *Proceedings of Wesley Historical Society,* iii, 186; iv, 121).

The **Hunter** portrait, painted by Robert Hunter, was engraved in dark mezzotint by James Watson. The original, for which Wesley sat on July 31, 1765, is in the World Methodist Building, Lake Junaluska, N. C., U.S.A. The **Hone** portrait, painted by Nathaniel Hone, was painted in 1765, and the original hangs in the National Portrait Gallery, London. The **Russell** portrait, by John Russell, was painted in 1773, but although the original is said to be the picture hanging in the dining room of Kingswood School, Bath, this is doubtful; there is a second copy at Wesley's Chapel, City Road, London (see *Proceedings,* viii, 1; x, 67).

The **Romney** portrait was painted by George Romney and is generally considered to be the best likeness of John Wesley in later life. Wesley says that he sat for Romney on January 5, 1789, and that he thought highly of the artist. The original is now in the United States (see *Proceedings,* xiii, 182). The most familiar portrait of Wesley, however, is the **Jackson,** done by John Jackson in 1827 "at the desire of an influential group of Wesleyans who wished to have a standard typical portrait of Wesley." This picture appeared as the frontispiece to *Wesley's Hymns.* The original hangs in the Board Room of the Methodist Publishing House in London, but it is not rated highly as a likeness. The **Horsley,** painted by Thomas Horsley of Sunderland in 1790, is now at Richmond Theological College, London, and a replica is in the

Sunderland Art Gallery. The **Hamilton,** painted by William Hamilton, presents John Wesley in his eighty-sixth year (see his *Journal,* December 22, 1787). The original is in the National Portrait Gallery in London. John Wesley is also known to have sat for Joshua Reynolds in 1755, but the original picture was probably lost in a fire at Dangan Castle, in Ireland, the home of the Duke of Mornington (see *Proceedings,* iii, 191; xxvii, 174).

There are many more portraits of varying degrees of merit; the most recent are the versions painted by FRANK SALISBURY, and which are now in the United States. JOHN TELFORD wrote a short book on the subject of the portraits of John Wesley, *Sayings and Portraits of John Wesley* (London, 1924). In addition to the references to the *Proceedings* given above, see ii, 49; iii, 185; and iv, 1.

As for Charles Wesley, eight portraits in all are known, of which the best are: the **Russell** portrait, done by John Russell, who was a personal friend of Charles Wesley and his family; the original, which shows Charles at the age of sixty-four, is in the Methodist Mission House, Marylebone, London. The **Gush,** painted by William Gush, is of uncertain date, but was probably done in the mid-nineteenth century; the original is at Kingswood School, Bath. The **Hudson,** painted by Thomas Hudson, shows Charles in early manhood; the original is in the Board Room of the Methodist Publishing House in London. The **Spilsbury** engraving was done by Jonathan Spilsbury, and is said to be "the finest portrait of the poet and the only one published during his lifetime" (see *Proceedings,* ix, 4). There are other portraits, one by F. J. JOBSON, which is now at the Methodist Publishing House in London, and one by J. W. L. Forster, which is now at Victoria University, Toronto. There is a portrait known as "Charles Wesley in Old Age," of which the whereabouts of the original is unknown as well as the name of the artist. The picture called "Charles Wesley preaching to the Indians" was painted by Robert Ronald McIan (1803-56). On the general subject see *Proceedings,* xxxi, 86.

J. Telford, *Sayings and Portraits.* 1924.
Wesley Historical Soc. *Proceedings,* ii, 49; iii, 185; iv, 1.

JOHN C. BOWMER

WESLEY POTTERY AND BUSTS. Few men have had as many carved and moulded effigies made of them as John Wesley. These range from the mid-eighteenth century caricature carved from the vertebra of a horse, to the superbly modeled late eighteenth century bust by Enoch Wood which is considered the best likeness of Wesley in later life. Wesley busts, plaques and figures were made of wax, wood, ivory, metals and other materials, but it is the ceramic items that are most numerous.

Though busts and creamware with Wesley transfers were produced at Leeds and other Yorkshire potteries as early as the late eighteenth century, and Wesley pottery was produced in Wales and Scotland as well as from Devon to Sunderland, England, in the nineteenth century, the earliest and the majority of them were produced in Burslem and other towns of the Staffordshire Pottery District.

On his first visit to Burslem in March of 1760 Wesley held services in the open air. His discourse was not disturbed by the continuous loud talking and laughing, or even by a lump of potters clay which was thrown at him

Portraits of John Wesley

Russell Portrait

Hunter Portrait

Jackson Portrait

Romney Portrait

Salisbury Portrait

Wesley Busts

HOLLOW BACK ENOCH WOOD
(CLARK COLLECTION)

SOLID BACK, FULL
GOWN ENOCH WOOD
(CROWDER COLLECTION)

PARIAN REPRODUCTION BY
JOHN ADAMS & CO. OF THE
BUST BY SILVESTER
(FORMERLY ATTRIBUTED
ERRONEOUSLY TO ROUBILIAC).
(CROWDER COLLECTION)

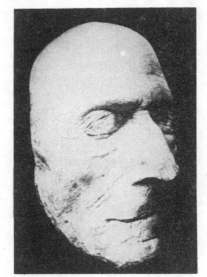

PLASTER CAST OF A
DEATH MASK OF WESLEY
(DREW SEMINARY)

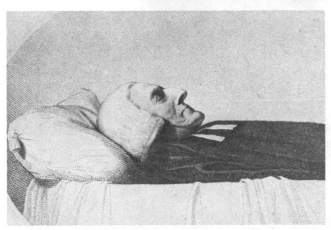

PHOTOGRAPH OF A PRINT OF RIDLEY'S
SKETCH OF WESLEY AS HE LAY IN STATE

COADE'S BUST OF WESLEY
(NEW ROOM, BRISTOL)

striking him on the face. He recorded: "I met a young man, JOSIAH WEDGWOOD, who had planted a flower garden adjacent to his pottery. He has his men wash their hands and faces and change their clothes after working in the clay. He is small and lame, but his soul is near God." An old advertisement for reproductions of the blue and white teapot in the museum at Wesley's House in London states that Wedgwood designed such a teapot for Wesley in creamware, and presented it to him in 1761. Mr. Joseph G. Wright pointed out certain features which cast doubt on this story. (*Proceedings* of the Wesley Historical Society, vii. 97-99.) He believed that the only kind of teapot made by Josiah Wedgwood with a Wesley connection was one made about 1772 or later on which Guy Green printed the portrait of Wesley after Nathaniel Hone. The Hone Portrait was painted about 1765; Green produced transfer wares with his name incorporated from 1770 to 1799; and the earliest teapot with this transfer was of the mould style popular between 1765 and 1775.

Though exact dating is impossible, undoubtedly transfer portraits on teapots, mugs and jugs were the earliest ceramic representations of Wesley. Possibly the earliest item was a mug with a transfer of Wesley similar to the "First Known Portrait" (*Sayings and Portraits of John Wesley*—JOHN TELFORD, p. 63). That Wesley pottery was being produced before 1774 is pointed out by Tyerman (*The Life and Times of John Wesley*, Vol. iii, p. 174). After mentioning the waxwork effigy taken by Mrs. Wright of New York in 1774 he states: "From the manuscript letters of Samuel Bardsley, we learn that already the potters of Staffordshire had printed his likeness on their crockery; and Mr. Voyes of Cobridge had had it engraved on the seals he sold." An engraving drawn and published by T. Holloway in 1776, and the portrait of Wesley published in the first issue of the *Arminian Magazine*, are other likenesses printed on eighteenth century jugs and teapots.

These items continued to be produced throughout the latter eighteenth and into the nineteenth centuries. At the time of the 1839 Centenary a large quantity of Wesley Pottery was manufactured which included busts, plaques, plates, mugs, jugs and general tea ware. Other transfers used were from the portraits painted by Romney in 1789, the Arnold and Barry miniatures, both painted about 1790, the Edridge Portrait painted in 1791 and that painted by Jackson in 1827.

Bas-relief plaques were produced in the eighteenth century by at least three potters. ENOCH WOOD produced a small one in 1780. Several examples are known including one given by him to Miss Anne Bourne which is illustrated in the book, *The Wood Family of Burslem*. A larger one produced by Enoch Wood is undated, but the bas-relief bust was used on small "Pratt-ware" flasks of a pottery style popular about 1790. The two known examples are in the Botteley Collection housed at the Methodist Archives and Research Center in London, and in the Crowder collection. Two lovely jasperware medallions were first produced about 1780 to 1790. They were by Turner, Lane End, Longton, and John Flaxman while he was modeling for Josiah Wedgwood between about 1775 and 1787. The Flaxman moulds are still used by the Wedgwood Factory, and through the years many plaques have been produced. As late as 1966 a small jasper plate with this bas-relief was sold at the World Methodist Conference in London.

Except for the finely modeled and detailed early nineteenth century Derby biscuit figure, the statuettes of Wesley are not of the quality of the bas-relief plaques. An almost exact but not quite as finely detailed copy of this figure was produced at the Minton Factory, and one marked and dated example was made in 1857. George Coker, who worked at the Derby Factory from 1825 to 1840 and was employed by the Minton Factory in 1853, probably produced the latter figure. A few figures were made in the late eighteenth and early nineteenth centuries but are more or less caricatures. Possibly a unique figure of this period is a 15½ inch tall figure of Wesley in a red pulpit in the Crowder collection. The majority of figures were produced at the time of the 1839 Centenary and later. Though not good Wesley portraits, these include the interesting sham clocks from the Sampson Smith Factory. The Kent Factory produced at least two figures as well as the 11½ inch tall copy of the Enoch Wood Bust. This unfortunately has been pictured in and attributed to Enoch Wood in at least one book on Staffordshire Pottery, and one highly regarded museum collection of Staffordshire busts and figures.

In 1781 Enoch Wood modeled from life a portrait bust of Wesley with such detailed accuracy of features, even to the facial veins and wrinkles, that it became the recognized prototype of most subsequent portraits and busts. FRANK O. SALISBURY, who painted the large portraits in the World Methodist Building at Lake Junaluska, North Carolina, was the latest prominent artist to use Wood's bust as the model for a Wesley Portrait. Prior to the rediscovery of the correspondence between Dr. ADAM CLARKE and Enoch Wood in which 1781 was definitely given by Wood as the date, there was a controversy among authorities as to when the modeling of this bust was done. Some accepted 1784 as the date of modeling as that would have been the 81st year of Wesley's life, and the earliest marked busts gave his age as 81. The library of the Garrett Biblical Institute owns Enoch Wood's original letter written to Dr. Adam Clarke in 1830. The following important excerpts from this letter document the date of modeling.

Burslem, October 6, 1830.

My Dear Sir: I am favored with your letter of the 2d instant, from which I am happy to learn that a whole length marble statue of Mr. Wesley is now in progress. The bust which I had the pleasure to present to you a few years since was taken out of the original mold cast upon the clay model, for which Mr. Wesley favored me with five separate sittings, at the last of which he did me the credit to say that there had been many attempts at his likeness by different artists, but he thought this was much the best. He, however, asked me if I thought it had not a more melancholy expression than himself, and I perceived I had fallen into that error, I think owing to his generally being engaged in writing while sitting to me, and from which I withdrew his attention with some difficulty. He therefore sat down again and in a few minutes after I had made the alteration he came behind me to look at it and immediately desired me not to touch it again, "lest" (as he said), I should "mar it," and again expressed himself quite satisfied with it.

I then told him he might consider the likeness finished, but that I should place it upon a pedestal, on the back of which I should place a medallion, with his name and age inscribed, as well as any remarkable occurrence of his life. He, without the smallest hesitation, related to me the circumstance of his father's house being on fire when he was a child, and that his life was then saved from the flames by his being taken out of an upper story through a window. This I fully then intended to model on a medallion on the pedestal. He seemed pleased with this idea and said: "You may write underneath or around it, 'Is not this a brand plucked out of the Fire?'" This I deferred doing because I was anxious to procure an exact drawing of his father's house, but to this day it has not fallen into my hands; and therefore it has not been carried into effect.

Mr. Wesley's companion, Joseph Brudford, was present at two or three of the last sittings and was so much pleased with the growing likeness of Mr. Wesley that I observed he threw all the impediments which he could with propriety do in the way of Mr. Wesley rising from the sittings, in order to give me a full opportunity of perfecting the resemblance. Your bust of Mr. Wesley was taken by me in the year 1781, with the greatest care and attention I was then capable of, in the twenty-second year of my age, having practiced the art from a very early age.

Mr. Manning may with confidence rely upon every line, wrinkle or vein marked upon your bust being a true and correct copy of nature.° ° °

My dear Sir, your obedient and obliged servant,

ENOCH WOOD.

Rev. Dr. Adam Clarke, Pinner, Middlesex.

No example of the 1781 edition is known to exist. Possibly there were only a few of these early busts all of which have perished, or possibly the early ones were without identifying plaques as Enoch Wood was not in business for himself until about 1784. It is apparently in this year that the first marked examples were produced, and there is in the Botteley Collection one of these busts marked "aged 81" known to have been made by Enoch Wood and given by him to his son. Most of these busts with hollow backs and gowns with flattened drapery were made during Wesley's lifetime, whereas most of those made by the Wood Factory after Wesley's death have a fuller gown and a solid back with a round, oval, square or rectangular plaque giving the date of Wesley's death and other information.

Following the issuance of Woods Bust a large number of copies appeared, probably from most of the potteries. These varied from good to inferior workmanship, and most were unmarked. Some of the marked or documented examples include busts produced by J. Dale, J. Meir, Leeds, Newbottle, Thomas Hawley, Wedgwood, Copeland, Charles Salt, Kent, Messr. Massey, Robinson and Leadbeater, W. R. Goss, Hewitt and Leadbeater and others.

Two large busts are considered to be good likenesses of Wesley. The life-size marble bust in the National Portrait Gallery, London, is attributed to the little known sculptor, Silvester. His bust of Wesley was listed in the 1788 catalogue of the Royal Academy of Art, and his address was given as Lyceum, Strand. Mr. Henry Graves, from whom the bust was purchased in 1868, proposed that the bust was sculptured by the famous French sculptor, Roubiliac, and this attribution was accepted by early authorities on Wesleyana but not by the National Portrait Gallery. Silvester was listed as the sculptor after the findings reported in a London newspaper (The Times, March 5, 1928).

Several pottery reproductions have been made of this bust. The first was made by Messrs. John Adams and Co. of Hanley and was available at the first North Staffordshire Conference in 1870. (The Methodist Magazine, July 1870, p. 650.) The Rev. Richard Green loaned his copy of the Adams bust to Harper and Co. of Burslem who produced a few smaller copies. Later the bust was reproduced by Messrs. Robinson and Leadbeater who incorporated the Roubiliac attribution into an inscription on the back of the bust.

The other large bust of which copies are to be seen at the library of the Wesley Historical Society in London and the New Room in Bristol is of a black material, and the facial features have a striking resemblance to the plaster cast of the reputed "death mask" pictured in The Story of Methodism by A. B. Hyde, 1888 edition. There is however another plaster cast of a "death mask" with less fullness to the lips and face which was formerly owned by the Rev. RICHARD GREEN and is now at Drew University. Comparison of photographs of the two plaster casts makes one wonder if the one in Hyde's book was actually from a life mask and if it could have been the model for this bust. Mr. Aldridge who gave the bust to the Wesley Historical Society furnished with it three typed pages of information. In these he stated that the bust had been in his family, that it was executed by Coade in 1793 at his Artificial Stone Manufactory and that it was probably taken from a cast of a life mask made while John Wesley was staying with one of Mr. Aldridge's ancestors, a Mr. Whitchurch of Salisbury, England. He further stated that Mr. and Mrs. Whitchurch were mentioned in John Wesley's Diary for August 8th, 1787, and October 5th, 1789. Possibly this bust represents Wesley at the age of 84 or 86 years. Except for more fullness of the lips and face the features of this bust closely resemble those of the sketch made by William Ridley as Wesley lay in State at City Road Chapel. Dr. Osborn considered this sketch to be the most accurate outline of Wesley's features.

Many varieties of Wesley pottery can be seen and studied in the Methodist Archives and Research Center in London, where the Botteley, Lamplough and other collections are housed, and at the World Methodist Building at Lake Junaluska, North Carolina, where the late Dr. Elmer T. Clark deposited his collection. There are smaller but interesting collections at Drew, Garrett and the New Room. Alderman Horace Hurd of Bradford, England, and Dr. T. H. Crowder of South Boston, Virginia, have large and representative private collections.

The Connoisseur, Vol. XIX, N. 13 (September 1907).
Arthur D. Cummings, A Portrait In Pottery, The Epworth Press, London, 1962.
Frank Faulkner, The Wood Family of Burslem, Chapman and Hall Limited, London, 1912.　　　　T. H. CROWDER

WESLEY SEMINARY is a training school for Methodist ministers at Montero, BOLIVIA. The seminary was founded in 1960. From a beginning class of six, it has grown to a student body of about forty men and women (1966). The seminary is responsible for producing the main body of the Spanish-speaking ministry of The United Methodist Church in Bolivia. It emphasizes theological subjects, social sciences and technical vocational subjects. The teaching staff numbers sixteen.

The goal of the seminary is to produce a nonprofessional ordained pastor for the frontier ministry—both geographical and social frontiers. This frontier pastor must be also a community leader to shepherd the people of God in the ministry of the total church.

The seminary year is divided into two semesters of four months each, with four days spent in class and two in practical work in rural areas, which includes preaching and helping with churches or new congregations. Some students bicycle on rough roads from thirty-four to seventy-eight miles each weekend and cover several preaching points in a circuit around Montero. Besides preaching, Sunday school, and youth work, students also help in Methodist cooperatives. One of the four years of preparation is spent as a practice year. James Pace was founder and directed the seminary up to July 1966. He was succeeded by Jose Carlos Diaz.

Highland Echoes, October 1963.
The Methodist Church in Bolivia. Historical Committee of the Methodist Church in Bolivia, 1961.   EDWIN H. MAYNARD

WESLEY SOCIETY, THE, is the name of an organization of Methodists in the United States which grew out of an informal meeting in NEW YORK City on Jan. 11, 1955. In its membership were represented Methodist ministers, professors, and students who shared a common concern for the present-day relevance of the thought of JOHN and CHARLES WESLEY. Its aim was the recovery of the Wesleyan tradition in contemporary Methodism. It was distinct from various historical societies in Methodism, and considered itself a movement rather than a party within the church. Its main purposes were to unite in conferences and retreats those who shared in its concerns, and to encourage research and publication in this area of interest. It had no official connection with The Methodist Church.

The founder and president of the Wesley Society was Dr. Franz Hildebrandt, then Professor of Theology at Drew University. During World War II Dr. Hildebrandt, a Lutheran pastor in GERMANY, went into voluntary exile in England, and served a German-speaking congregation in CAMBRIDGE. In England he came under the influence of the Wesleyan tradition, and in time joined the British Methodist Church as one of its ministers. It was in this capacity that he came to the United States to serve on the faculty of DREW.

Within the first seven or eight years of its existence under the leadership of Dr. Hildebrandt various national meetings and retreats of the Wesley Society were held, chiefly on the eastern seaboard. During these same years various state and regional societies were formed throughout the country. These societies carried on independent programs, and some of them were quite active, meeting regularly and publishing their own newsletters. At the same time on a rather irregular basis the national society published a newsletter which was distributed to the membership of the Wesley Society countrywide. The membership was always quite modest in size. The direction of the national Wesley Society was carried on under the continuous presidency of Dr. Hildebrandt and a small group predominantly composed of seminary professors known as the COUNCIL.

After the early 1960's it became increasingly difficult to maintain a national organization, although local and regional societies may still be in existence. Since the departure of Dr. Hildebrandt in 1968 from the United States to SCOTLAND, the national Wesley Society has not functioned.

Communications regarding the Wesley Society are still received by the secretary, Professor Robert S. Eccles, DE-PAUW UNIVERSITY, Greencastle, Ind. Funds of the society and the roster of members are in the hands of Professor E. Dale Dunlap, ST. PAUL SCHOOL OF THEOLOGY.

ROBERT S. ECCLES

WESLEY THEOLOGICAL SEMINARY, Washington, D.C., is a continuation of WESTMINSTER THEOLOGICAL SCHOOL founded by the MARYLAND CONFERENCE of the METHODIST PROTESTANT CHURCH in 1881 at Westminster, Md. In 1953, plans were adopted to move the seminary to Washington, to property given by the AMERICAN UNIVERSITY at the northwest corner of its campus. The name was changed to Wesley Theological Seminary in 1957, and first classes were held in 1958.

A complete educational plant has been constructed at a cost of $4,607,000, of which $1,500,000 was given by the S. S. Kresge Foundation and the balance by the seminary's constituency. Through the generosity of JOSEPH RANK of England, a second casting of the equestrian statute of John Wesley at the Horse Fair, BRISTOL, was made possible for the seminary's campus. The seminary chapel is named for Bishop G. BROMLEY OXNAM, chairman of the board of governors during the transition period. The Kresge academic quadrangle honors the donors of the gift that assured the success of the relocation plans.

Degrees offered are the S.T.B., Th.M., S.T.M., and M.R.E. Additional educational opportunities for advanced degrees are open to the students at The American University.

The governing board is made up of fifty-one members elected by the GENERAL CONFERENCE of The United Methodist Church.

JOHN O. GROSS

WESLEY'S CHAPEL, often called City Road Chapel. (See LONDON, Wesley's Chapel.)

WESLEY'S HOUSE. (See LONDON.)

WESLEY'S NOTES ON THE OLD AND NEW TESTAMENTS. John Wesley's *Explanatory Notes upon the New Testament* with his forty-four STANDARD SERMONS form part of the doctrinal standards of BRITISH METHODISM. The *Notes* were begun in January 1754 (*Journal*, iv, 91); published toward the end of 1755; revised, 1759 (*Journal*, iv, 361), and 1787 (*Journal*, viii, 345). In this work he was greatly helped by his brother CHARLES and also by J. A. Bengel's *Gnomon Novi Testamenti*. For the Greek text which Wesley used and his translation, see the *Proceedings of Wesley Historical Society* (ix, 105; xxvii; v; xxiv, 6). Wesley's *Notes on the Old Testament* were published in three volumes in 1765, but the work is "meagre and unsatisfactory," says Adam Clarke. (Cf. L. Tyerman, *Life and Times of Wesley*, ed. 1890, ii, 552.) Wesley used Matthew Henry's *Exposition* and Poole's *Annotations*.

JOHN C. BOWMER

WESLEY'S SHORTHAND. During his Oxford days John Wesley taught some of his pupils to use James Weston's system of shorthand, but there is no evidence that he used it himself. He seems to have preferred a combination of "his own scheme of abbreviation" and "a shorthand unknown to modern experts" (CURNOCK, Introduction to *Journal*, I, 4). In GEORGIA, however, under pressure from his brother CHARLES, who insisted on this form of privacy in their personal correspondence, Wesley learned to use the shorthand system of their friend, Dr.

John Byrom. Charles was already an expert in Byrom's shorthand, which was expounded in *The Universal English Shorthand* (Manchester, 1767). John began to use the system for his *Diary* on Dec. 20, 1736, and all his later diaries are written in it. His interest in the subject was no doubt further stimulated when, in 1748, he was given a copy of a recently published treatise on the teaching of shorthand, by the author, Mr. Macaulay, a tea-merchant of Manchester. (W.H.S. *Proceedings*, VI, 148.)

JOHN NEWTON

WESLEY'S WORKS. The publications of JOHN and CHARLES WESLEY were so voluminous that in their own lifetime there were two attempts to collect them. The first was in 1746, when they gathered together in fifteen volumes the current editions of some seventy items, both prose and verse, both original and edited. The second better known attempt was launched in 1771, and was limited to the prose publications of John Wesley, with a few exceptions, such as his *Notes* on the Bible, his *Natural Philosophy*, his *Christian Library* (comprising fifty volumes) and many of the texts prepared for KINGSWOOD SCHOOL. This first separately printed edition of his *Works* was issued in weekly numbers and gathered together in thirty-two volumes during the years 1771-74. For this edition Wesley did undertake a revision of his writings, but unfortunately they were very carelessly printed by William Pine of Bristol, and the incomplete errata which were issued were seldom bound up with the volumes concerned.

In any case this first edition was incomplete, insomuch as Wesley lived and continued to write until 1791. Not for almost twenty years after his death, however, did the Methodist Conference of 1808 sponsor a new edition of Wesley's Works. This second edition was prepared by the CONNEXIONAL EDITOR, JOSEPH BENSON, and appeared in seventeen volumes 1809-13 (Vol. 17 is an index, frequently bound with Vol. 16). Like most of its successors, this edition omitted most of Wesley's publications which were not thought to be completely original, as well as all the musical and poetical works, and some others. At least a few volumes of this edition were reprinted under the description of the "third edition," and another reprint was undertaken in the U.S.A. This "first American edition" was published in Philadelphia and New York in 1826-27, occupying ten volumes.

THOMAS JACKSON became connexional editor in 1824. He furnished a far more complete and scholarly edition of Wesley's Works in fourteen volumes (1829-31), in most instances using the latest text supplied by some of Wesley's personally annotated copies—though it can be shown that these annotations were frequently hurried emendations forced upon Wesley in his old age by printing errors which had arisen in previous editions, while the earliest editions (which he did not consult) frequently preserved a demonstrably purer text. Jackson's edition has remained the standard ever since, though it has undergone many minor changes from time to time, including the addition of a few newly discovered letters or pamphlets. The numbering of the many editions of Jackson's collection is quite chaotic, and because some were reset with a different size of type and paper, discrepancies sometimes arise in citations from it by different scholars, so that it is necessary to specify which of many editions is used. Occasionally Jackson's edition was issued in fifteen volumes, the last volume comprising Wesley's *Explanatory Notes upon the New Testament*. The "First American Complete and Standard Edition" edited by JOHN EMORY (first published in New York, 1831, in seven volumes) was in effect a reprint of Jackson, with some rearrangement of the material. The edition of Wesley's Works published in recent years by the Zondervan Publishing House was a lithographic reproduction of the 1872 English edition.

Students of the Wesleys have long desired a critical annotated edition of John Wesley's Works, and the demand has increased during this last twenty years or so with the intensified attention being given to Wesley's theology. This century has welcomed standard editions of his *Journal* (by NEHEMIAH CURNOCK, 8 volumes, 1909-16), his *Standard Sermons* (by E. H. SUGDEN, 2 vols., 1921), and of his *Letters* (by JOHN TELFORD, 8 vols., 1931). This still leaves some hundreds of his writings large and small, however, without any truly definitive edition, so that we remain dependent upon that prepared by Thomas Jackson in 1829-31. The need for such a definitive edition was pointed out by the present writer in the Jubilee Issue of the *Proceedings* of the WESLEY HISTORICAL SOCIETY in June 1943, although at the time it seemed a dream hardly likely of fulfilment.

Almost twenty years later, in 1960, a group of concerned scholars at four American universities took practical steps to fill this need, with what was at first known as the "Wesley's Works Editorial Project." They realized at the outset that it would be a long, complex, and costly enterprise, though they could not possibly imagine all the problems involved, many of them stemming from the peculiarities of Wesley's own literary methods. Already a decade has been spent in extensive researches and in debating the findings of preliminary studies. Happily most of the major problems thus revealed have now been resolved. The first few volumes are under way, and it is hoped that they will begin to appear at the rate of two or three a year by 1974.

Directing this enterprise are the deans of the theological faculties of Drew, Duke, Emory, and Southern Methodist Universities, to whom have been added more recently the Dean of Boston University School of Theology, together with the Director of the Department of the Ministry and the Executive Secretary of the Commission on Archives and History of the United Methodist Church. Supervising the editorial processes are three General Editors (WILLIAM R. CANNON, ROBERT E. CUSHMAN, and ERIC W. BAKER) and the Editor-in-Chief, FRANK BAKER, who together with other members form a consultative Editorial Committee. A large international and interdenominational team of scholars has been enlisted to edit the series of about thirty volumes of John Wesley's original prose works, which will be published by The Clarendon Press of Oxford, England.

The Oxford Edition of John Wesley's Works is intended to offer an accurate, annotated text of his writings for the use of scholars and general readers. Its editorial canons are those of modern historical scholarship as generally understood and practiced. The various texts will be based on critical examinations of all extant prototypes which may have received Wesley's personal attention in any way, and will provide a minimal textual apparatus enabling the reader to verify the copy text and to note significant variants. Each of the major categories of Wesley's writings will form a unit consisting of one or more volumes, and will be complete in itself. Each unit will have a concise introduction, each individual item a preface. To these will be added brief annotations on names, citations, sources, cross-references, etc. The aim throughout will be a maximum exhibition of Wesley himself and a minimum intrusion on the reader by the editors. An index will be supplied for each unit, and a general index for the whole edition. The first unit will provide a definitive bibliography of the Wesleys' publications, both prose and verse, both original and edited, which will serve for cross-reference throughout the new edition.

FRANK BAKER

WESLEYAN, THE. For some years prior to 1832 the Methodist leaders in the area known as Eastern British America (now the Atlantic Provinces of CANADA) had felt the pressing need of a regional periodical for the instruction and unification of their people. In March of that year the first number of *The Nova Scotia and New Brunswick Wesleyan Methodist Magazine*, a little quarterly, made its appearance. Only four issues were printed, because the Missionary Committee in London feared an injurious effect on the circulation of English Methodist publications and ordered its discontinuance, thus forcing its promoters to fall back on the use of such space as was afforded them in secular publications.

A second attempt was made in February 1838, when the first issue of *The Wesleyan* appeared, sponsored by the Nova Scotia district and published in Halifax. Continued pressure from London forced its discontinuance after a few issues. Then for a few months came *The Christian Herald;* and in 1840, *The British North American Wesleyan Methodist Magazine* began publication. This gained a measure of approval in London because it was sponsored by two districts, Nova Scotia and New Brunswick. Printed in Saint John, N.B., its somewhat intermittent course came to an end in 1847.

In April, 1849, appeared the first issue of the revived *Wesleyan*, which soon became a weekly paper and continued without interruption until 1925. In 1852 the name was changed to *The Provincial Wesleyan*, and in 1875, back to *The Wesleyan*. For most of the period it was published in Halifax, then Truro, N.S., then Sackville, N.B. It began with four large pages, then expanded to eight, and finally sixteen of magazine size.

Through its history, the journal maintained a remarkably broad and forward-looking approach to the varied problems with which it dealt. News of Christian groups and movements far removed from Methodism was featured. Moral reforms were fearlessly advocated, the temperance issue being given prominence. An attitude of friendliness toward other Maritime denominations, and a recognition of the universal brotherhood of man were stressed. An editorial of 1900 said: "To be a Christian means to let no artificial distinctions of society or wealth or colour or nationality limit your love."

The contribution of *The Wesleyan* to Methodism in the Maritime Provinces and beyond was great. Especially in the early days it provided a mouthpiece for the educational institutions known as Mount Allison, at Sackville, N.B. It did much to bring together the Methodists and to prepare them for the all-Canadian union consummated in 1884; and when this was accomplished, it worked toward the union with other denominations, bearing fruit when the whole church entered the union of 1925 without dissent.

From the time of continuous publications, the editors of *The Wesleyan* were: 1849-54, Alexander W. MacLeod; 1854-60, Matthew H. Richey (later lieutenant-governor of Nova Scotia); 1860-62, Charles Churchill; 1862-69, John McMurray; 1869-73, HUMPHREY PICKARD; 1873-79, Alexander W. Nicholson; 1879-80, Duncan D. Currie (the first not to hold the position of Book Steward, for the six earlier men held both offices); 1880-86, T. WATSON SMITH; 1886-95, JOHN LATHERN; 1895-1902, GEORGE J. BOND; 1902-07, JOHN MACLEAN (who was brought in from Western Canada); 1907-24, David W. Johnson; 1924-25, Herbert E. Thomas.

When The United Church of Canada came into being, its Maritime Conference decided unanimously to continue the publication of what had long become a Maritime paper, under the name *The United Churchman*. Through the years it has preserved the best features of *The Wesleyan*, to which much was added, and has exerted a powerful influence on the church life of these provinces. The editors have been: 1925-29, H. E. Thomas (as the *Wesleyan* editor); 1929-48, William F. Partridge; 1948-58, W. Fraser Munro; 1958-   , Evan D. Murray.

G. S. French, *Parsons and Politics*. 1962.
D. W. Johnson, *Eastern British America*.
T. W. Smith, *Eastern British America*. 1877, 1890.

W. FRASER MUNRO

WESLEYAN CHRISTIAN ADVOCATE is the official conference paper for the GEORGIA CONFERENCES of The United Methodist Church, begun in June 1837, as the *Southern Christian Advocate*, the official organ of the Georgia and SOUTH CAROLINA CONFERENCES. The *Southern Christian Advocate* was published in CHARLESTON, S. C., by a committee of the South Carolina Conference under the name of the *Wesleyan Journal*. The first number was issued on Oct. 1, 1825, edited by STEPHEN OLIN and WILLIAM CAPERS. The last issue appeared March 3, 1827, when it was united with the *Christian Advocate*, published by the M.E. CHURCH in NEW YORK.

During the nine years succeeding—from 1827 to 1836 —the increasing agitation of the SLAVERY question seriously threatened the harmony and unity of the Church, as well as the success of the missions among the Negroes in the southern states. The delegates from these states to the GENERAL CONFERENCE of 1836 felt the necessity for the establishment of a religious newspaper in the South to defend their interests and institutions. Accordingly, at the General Conference of 1836 resolutions were passed authorizing the publication of a weekly religious paper on the same footing with the *Christian Advocate and Journal* (New York), and the *Western Christian Advocate* (Cincinnati), and the *Christian Advocate* at RICHMOND, NASHVILLE, and CHARLESTON.

The *Southern Christian Advocate* was first published in Charleston on Saturday, June 24, 1837, and was particularly intended to represent the South Carolina and Georgia Conferences, the publishing committee being composed of ministers of those two conferences. It was under the editorship of William Capers, later elected bishop. Burgess and Jones of Charleston were the first publishers. This firm printed the paper from its beginning date to March of 1847, except for a short period—March 1843 to June 1843—during which time it was printed and published by B. B. Hussey of Charleston. After 1847, the *Advocate* purchased its own printing press and equipment necessary for independent publication.

William Capers served as editor from 1837 to 1840. Whiteford Smith served from May of 1840 to November of 1840 as editor *pro tem.* In November of 1840 WILLIAM M. WIGHTMAN accepted the editorship and served until 1854. E. H. Myers became editor in 1854 and continued in that post until 1872.

As the Civil War advanced and certain sections of the South became less secure because of the southward moving Federal armies, Charleston itself was in great danger of bombardment. And, because of the imminent danger confronting Charleston, the Georgia Conference started agitation late in the year of 1861 to move the office of the *Advocate* to AUGUSTA, GA., on April 10, 1862.

In 1865 it became evident that Augusta also would soon be taken by the Federal forces and that a move of the *Advocate* was again necessary. Hence, Myers began to make preparations for removal to a still safer position. After the issue of April 13, 1865, the *Southern Christian Advocate* was suspended and removed to MACON, where it resumed publication on June 19, 1865. This suspension and removal cut the *Advocate* off from its subscribers and correspondents for over two months. It also lost heavily because of the utter failure of the Confederate currency at this time. The move to Macon was made in order to give the paper greater security of publication, but a tragic and ironic fate attended this removal. Macon itself was in possession of United States forces, and the publishing house there was in ashes, but it was too late to change plans. Myers set out upon the tremendous task of putting the *Advocate* back on its original basis, a thing that could hardly be expected in the dying days of reconstruction.

F. Milton Kennedy served as editor from 1872 to 1878.

The Georgia and South Carolina Conferences had been expanding during these years and it became evident that the Georgia Conference needed its own paper. So on June 4, 1878, the *Wesleyan Christian Advocate,* under the editorship of ATTICUS G. HAYGOOD, made its first appearance. Haygood had been an official contributor to the *Southern Christian Advocate.* John W. Burke, head of the Macon company doing the printing of the *Advocate,* was the assistant editor. Haygood and Burke continued in office until June 3, 1882. At that time Weyman H. Potter became editor and continued through Nov. 5, 1890. W. C. Lovett assumed the editorship Nov. 12, 1890, and continued thus until Dec. 24, 1890, when the paper moved to ATLANTA. Burke held the assistant editorship during all these years. He resigned Dec. 24, 1890 after twenty-five years of service.

W. F. Glenn and T. T. Christian were editor and business manager of the *Advocate* after its move to Atlanta. They continued in office from Jan. 7, 1891, through 1899. In 1900 W. C. Lovett succeeded T. T. Christian as business manager, and BASCOM ANTHONY became a member of the staff. In 1901 Lovett was made editor and he continued as editor through Dec. 20, 1920. He had as assistant editors and business managers during these years J. W. HEIDT (1901-02), M. J. Cofer (1902-12), and R. F. Eakes (1912-20). WILLIAM P. KING became editor in 1920 and L. J. Ballard was the assistant editor and business manager. In 1923 A. M. Pierce became editor with Ballard continuing as assistant editor and business manager.

Elam F. Dempsey became editor and business manager on Dec. 5, 1930, and continued to Nov. 25, 1933, when W. T. WATKINS became editor. L. W. Neff became business manager at that time.

Financially, the outlook was so gloomy in 1932 that the NORTH GEORGIA CONFERENCE, early in its session, voted to discontinue the paper. But when it was learned that Watkins was willing to serve as editor without remuneration for one year, the Conference reconsidered its previous vote and the *Wesleyan* gained a new lease on life under his editorship. The length of his service without remuneration stretched to four years. Even so, in 1936, it became necessary to adopt a new plan of administration. Instead of one editor, a staff of editorial writers, on which both conferences were equally represented, was chosen and a general manager was elected to have overall direction of the paper. Under this arrangement subscriptions quickly increased and continued through the years. The *Advocate* was moved back to Macon from Atlanta on Dec. 1, 1936. The first issue of the publication to come from a Macon press in forty-six years appeared Dec. 18, 1936. The remarkable growth of the *Wesleyan* since 1936 has been led by the following general managers: Charles A. Britton, Jr., Frank Q. Echols, Florence M. Gaines, C. Hoke Sewell, and Dan H. Williams.

The format of the *Advocate* in time was changed, new printing and photographic equipment purchased, until at the present time the *Wesleyan Christian Advocate* is considered to be fulfilling its mission ably. It has always enjoyed a wide circulation and continues to give strong leadership in the field of church journalism.

A. M. Pierce, *Georgia.* 1956.
The Wesleyan Christian Advocate, Centennial Edition, June 24, 1937.   C. HOKE SEWELL

WESLEYAN CHURCH, THE, U.S.A., was formed by the merger of the WESLEYAN METHODIST CHURCH and the PILGRIM HOLINESS CHURCH on June 26, 1968, at Anderson, Ind.

The Wesleyan Methodist Church of the United States of America was founded in 1843. From the very beginning of the M.E. CHURCH in America, SLAVERY was an issue. Strong statements against slavery appeared in early editions of the Methodist *Discipline.* Before Methodism penetrated deeply and largely into the South, there had been little disagreement over such strong statements. By the middle 1830's, however, the slavery issue had become acute and there was great agitation.

It is fair to say that opposition to slavery was the common bond that drew together a great many Methodist ministers who on other issues also wanted to reform the church. A strong leader of these was ORANGE SCOTT. Such men, including the eminent LUTHER LEE, were zealous soul winners, great preachers, and effective writers. As reformers, however, they met with opposition from leaders of the M.E. Church. Some local quarterly conferences refused to grant LOCAL PREACHERS licenses to those who favored abolition of slavery. Some PRESIDING ELDERS and DISTRICT CONFERENCES refused credentials and appointments to the reformers. To climax it all, at the 1840 GENERAL CONFERENCE of the M. E. Church, J. O. ANDREW, a slave holder (by virtue of inheritance and by marriage) was elected to the bishopric. Presiding BISHOPS restrained debate on slavery in the General Conference sessions.

What appeared to be arbitrary restraint on the part of the bishops only added fuel to the fire of the reformers, and they turned out to be not only anti-slavery, but anti-episcopacy. Their opposition to episcopal government grew out of what they felt to be the arbitrary exercise of authority of certain leaders in the Church.

Some Methodists began to sever connections with the M.E. Church in 1841, and the first Wesleyan Methodist conference was established in the state of MICHIGAN that year. Later in 1842, Orange Scott, J. Horton, and L. R. Sunderland withdrew from the M.E. Church, and published in the first number of a weekly paper called *The True Wesleyan*, their reasons for withdrawal. These men, along with Luther Lee and L. C. MATLACK, met in February 1843, to formulate plans for a new denomination. This meeting resulted in the call for a general convention which was held at Utica, N. Y. commencing May 31, 1843. At this convention an overall organization was effected, a DISCIPLINE adopted, and a name chosen, The Wesleyan Methodist Church.

In 1843 it was believed that the ministers and lay delegates present at the organizing conference represented almost 15,000 people. These first Wesleyan Methodists forsook parsonages and churches—for they took no property with them—and then banded together to form their new connection.

The Church continued to grow and prosper. In 1948 the group of people known as the HEPHZIBAH FAITH MISSIONARY ASSOCIATION affiliated with the Wesleyans. In 1958 the MISSIONARY BANDS OF THE WORLD entered the fold. In 1966 a merger was worked out with the Reformed Baptist Church of CANADA.

A more important union and slight change of name came about in 1968 by union with The Pilgrim Holiness Church. This Church dates back to 1897 when the International Holiness Union and Prayer League was organized by Martin Wells Knapp and Seth C. Rees. Going through several name changes, this group emerged as the International Apostolic Holiness Church in 1913. A merger was effected in 1919 with the Holiness Christian Church which dated from 1882. The new body was called the International Holiness Church. In 1922 two bodies, the Pentecostal Rescue Mission and the Pilgrim Church, merged with the International Holiness Church to form The Pilgrim Holiness Church. In 1924 the Pentecostal Brethren in Christ united with the Pilgrim Holiness Church. The People's Mission Church joined in 1925. Over the ensuing years, the church grew, augmented in 1946 by the acceptance of the Holiness Church. Union with the Wesleyan Methodist Church came June 26, 1968, and the new church was called simply The Wesleyan Church.

The doctrinal position of The Wesleyan Church is, as its name implies, Wesleyan. They regard the ARTICLES OF RELIGION adopted by early American Methodism as their standard. They are, however, representative of that branch of Methodism termed "holiness." They place a great deal of emphasis on "entire SANCTIFICATION" and the holy life. They also hold to the literal second coming of Christ.

Church Government. The Wesleyan Church is committed to principles of representative government patterned after the national government. The entire church is governed by direct vote or by elected representatives. Each local church may call its own pastor and enjoys considerable autonomy. The annual conference, composed of an equal number of ministers and laymen, elects its own officers, orders the work of the churches in its district,

and ratifies the appointments of the pastors. The General Conference, generally meeting each four years, includes equal representation of lay and ministerial delegates elected by the annual conferences, and exercises final authority on all legislative matters of the denomination (except that constitutional changes must also be submitted for approval to the several annual conferences). General superintendents, elected for a quadrennial term, supervise the work of all the departments, institutions, and organizations of the Church; preside over sessions of the General Conference; and act as a board to render decisions on points of law between the sessions of the General Conference.

Education. Education was an early concern of both the Pilgrims and Wesleyans. Attempts were made to establish colleges as early as 1860 by the Wesleyan Methodists. They finally succeeded after several attempts with the establishment of Houghton College in 1883. Others founded over the years include Central College (South Carolina, 1916), Millonvale College (Kansas, 1908), Marion College (Indiana, 1923), Houghton Academy (New York, 1945) and the Wesleyan Methodist College of Melbourne (Australia, 1961). From the Pilgrim-Holiness tradition comes Owasso College (Michigan).

Missions. The Missionary Program of the Wesleyan Church dates back to 1889 when J. Augustus Cole landed in SIERRA LEONE. From this beginning the foreign mission program has grown until at present there is work on all the continents and in the islands of the Pacific, as well as an extensive home mission program.

Publishing. The comparatively new Wesleyan Church possesses two publishing houses as a result of the recent merger. The church school literature was merged before the denominations were. The three major periodicals of the former Wesleyan Methodist Church, *The Wesleyan Methodist, The Wesleyan Youth* and *The Wesleyan Missionary*, were merged with the major Pilgrim Holiness publications, the *Pilgrim Holiness Advocate* and *World Missions Bulletin*.

The membership of the Wesleyan Church is slightly over 100,000 located in about 2,500 local churches.

Discipline of the Wesleyan Church, 1964.
Manual of the Pilgrim Holiness Church, 1964.
I. F. McLeister, *Wesleyan Methodist Church of America*. 1959.
Wesleyan Methodist files.   J. GORDON MELTON

WESLEYAN COLLEGE, Macon, Georgia, was chartered as Georgia Female College in 1836, and the name was changed to Wesleyan Female College in 1843, when it became the property of the GEORGIA CONFERENCE. The present name was adopted in 1924, and the institution continues as a liberal and fine arts college for women. It was the first institution in the world to be chartered as a college for women. GEORGE F. PIERCE, later a bishop of the M.E. Church, South, was the first president of the college. In 1840 degrees were conferred upon eleven members of the first graduating class. When the Civil War began in 1861, Wesleyan was the largest college in GEORGIA with 173 students, followed by EMORY with 126.

Wesleyan College lists among its alumnae and former students the three Soong sisters who have had important roles in the life of CHINA, one as the wife of Sun Yat-Sen, and the youngest as the wife of CHIANG KAI-SHEK.

Degrees offered are the B.A., B.S., B.M. (Music), B.F.A. (Fine Arts). The governing board has thirty-six trustees, six elected from the NORTH GEORGIA CONFER-FERENCE, six from the SOUTH GEORGIA CONFERENCE, six from the FLORIDA CONFERENCE, six to eighteen at large, two bishops ex officio.

JOHN O. GROSS

WESLEYAN DELEGATE MEETINGS were meetings organized by the GRAND CENTRAL ASSOCIATION in 1835 in the course of the controversy over the plan to set up the first Wesleyan Methodist theological college in England. The first meeting was held in Manchester, April 20-23, 1835, and the second—with about one hundred delegates —was held at Sheffield, at the time of the Wesleyan Methodist Conference there, July 30–August 7, 1835. The association of reformers hoped to extract from the Conference greater powers for the laity in the Wesleyan Methodist constitution. The Conference refused to negotiate with the delegates, however, or to grant any of their demands. The delegates came chiefly from the north and midlands. Later in 1835 the beaten reformers seceded, to the number of about fifteen thousand, from Wesleyan Methodism, and set up the WESLEYAN METHODIST ASSOCIATION.

JOHN KENT

WESLEYAN FEMALE COLLEGE, Murfreesboro, N. C., originated in 1852 and was a college affiliated with the VIRGINIA CONFERENCE of the M.E. Church, South, until about 1881. Then eastern North Carolina became a part of the NORTH CAROLINA CONFERENCE, at which time the college passed into the control of the latter conference.

Wesleyan Female College exerted a significant influence in education in northeastern North Carolina and southeastern Virginia during the forty years of its existence. The College was used for barracks by the Confederate Army for a while during the War Between the States and later as a hospital. Due to the exigencies of the war the College was forced temporarily to send the students to their homes and to disband the faculty.

In 1877, during the administration of President William G. Starr, the College was destroyed by fire but it was rebuilt in 1881.

A wide course offering was available for the Wesleyan students including classes in French, German, Spanish, Italian, as well as Latin and Greek. The cost for a session in 1858 was $15 for the Academic Department and $18 for the Collegiate Department, plus additional fees for specific courses. Room and board cost $60 per session in 1857-58. There were two sessions per academic term. It is estimated that between the opening of the College and 1877, about 1,500 students had matriculated. In 1889 students at the College received board plus instruction in English, French, Latin, German and piano for a nine months term for $200.

Wesleyan Female College was not rebuilt following another and final destructive fire of 1893.

Annual Catalogue of Wesleyan Female College, Murfreesboro, North Carolina, 1857-58 (New York: 1858).
Biennial Report of the Superintendent of Public Instruction of North Carolina, 1887-1888 (Raleigh: 1889).
Branson's North Carolina Business Directory, 1890 (Raleigh: 1889).
Edgar V. McKnight and Oscar Creech, *A History of Chowan College* (Murfreesboro, N.C.: 1964).

William S. Powell, *Higher Education in North Carolina* (Raleigh: 1964).
Benjamin B. Winborne, *The Colonial and State Political History of Hertford County, North Carolina.*

RALPH HARDEE RIVES

WESLEYAN METHODISM, British, was the main channel of descent of Methodism from John Wesley's day. After Wesley's death in 1791 control of the Wesleyan Societies was taken over by the CONFERENCE of itinerants which he had set up. In 1795 the Conference for the first time authorized the itinerants to administer the Sacraments in societies which had no objection to their doing so, and this act is usually taken to mark the actual moment of separation of Wesleyanism from the Church of England. No attempt was made from the Anglican side to preserve the link between the two bodies; on the Wesleyan side an important tradition of friendliness toward the Establishment survived the separation, and for generations many Wesleyans did not regard themselves as Dissenters.

In 1796-97 there was an internal struggle over the Wesleyan constitution; in 1797 about one tenth of the membership withdrew to form the more democratic METHODIST NEW CONNEXION. No concessions were made, however; the Wesleyan itinerants continued to monopolize legislative authority; they alone attended the annual Conference; they alone could admit or expel from the local societies, which, it is important to remember, were never thought of as being independent local churches, in the style of the British Nonconformists. Membership continued to increase after 1800, but the connection had to survive the strains of the Napoleonic Wars, when the British government became suspicious of any kind of lower-class organization: hence the attack of Lord Sidmouth in 1811.

The dominant figure of post-Wesleyan Methodism was JABEZ BUNTING, the outstanding minister between 1815 and 1849. Bunting helped to start the WESLEYAN METHODIST MISSIONARY SOCIETY (1814); he did much to make the Wesleyan itinerants more conscious of their role as ministers of Christ's Church; he established the Theological Institution (1834) to help to train them for their work; he did his best to persuade the laity to accept a church order in which all final decisions remained in the hands of the ministry, and he firmly believed that in doing so he was maintaining Wesleyanism as John Wesley had conceived it. He was mentally arrogant; he had too little sympathy with opposition to know how to cope with it, but he, if anyone, molded the Wesleyan societies into a regular denomination.

Between about 1820 and 1857 Wesleyan history largely revolved around the constitutional issues and the personality of Bunting. The demand for a more democratic church order, especially for lay representation in the Conference, was repulsed again and again, in the Leeds organ controversy (see LEEDS PROTESTANT METHODISTS) of 1827-28; in the SAMUEL WARREN or theological college controversy of 1834-37; and in the FLY SHEETS controversy of 1849-57. In each case the result was a secession from Wesleyan Methodism, of the Leeds Protestant Methodists in 1828, the WESLEYAN METHODIST ASSOCIATION in 1837, and the UNITED METHODIST FREE CHURCHES in 1857. Many issues exacerbated the conflict, including the personal hatred of JAMES EVERETT for Jabez Bunting; the publication of the anonymous Fly Sheets, which were pamphlets attacking Jabez Bunting and his supporters;

and the education question, in which it seemed to many Wesleyans that their leaders ought not to support the policy of government involvement in education. These quarrels overshadowed the highly successful CENTENARY FUND Celebrations of 1839. Matters came to a head at the Conference of 1849, when James Everett, WILLIAM GRIFFITH, and SAMUEL DUNN were accused of having written the Fly Sheets; they refused to answer either yes or no to the direct question about authorship and were expelled for contumacy. The agitation in favor of the expelled ministers, which lasted from 1849-57, shook Wesleyan Methodism to its foundations; a third of the membership disappeared, and although these losses were made up in the 1860's and 1870's, a certain note of confidence and optimism vanished, never to return.

The lay representation which the seceders demanded in 1849 was granted in 1877-78, owing to the efforts of a new generation of Wesleyan Methodist ministers, among them WILLIAM BUNTING and MORLEY PUNSHON, who saw this as the minimum condition of permanent recovery. Other pressures also now began to act on the connection, which showed great resilience in the last quarter of the nineteenth century. The pressure of industrialization on the English churches first became apparent about 1860. The WESLEYAN HOME MISSION DEPARTMENT was created to try and organize the recovery of ground lost in the new urban areas. One result was the FORWARD MOVEMENT, which set up central missions in many of the larger towns between 1875 and 1900. The principle of itinerancy survived, but ministers tended to stay longer in the same circuit, and some central-mission appointments became virtually permanent, as in the cases of HUGH PRICE HUGHES at St. James Hall, London; J. S. LIDGETT at the Bermondsey Mission, London; and SAMUEL COLLIER, at the Central Mission in Manchester. The first results of the Forward Movement were good, but it seems that success here did not check the decline which had started in the circuits about 1880, though the full results of this decline did not show themselves until after the First World War.

Another important episode was the missionary controversy (1890), in which H. P. Hughes sharply criticized the policy of Wesleyan missions in INDIA; later history was to bear out the suspicion that there was more to be said for his point of view than was admitted by the official committee of inquiry which rejected it *in toto*. Hughes was more successful on the political level; he led the late nineteenth-century movement to identify Wesleyan Methodism politically with the Liberal Party. The alliance was symbolized in the career of the statesman, H. H. FOWLER, who became the first Wesleyan Methodist to hold cabinet rank when he became president of the Local Government Board in the Liberal government of 1892.

During the nineteenth century Wesleyan Methodism also moved steadily away from the Church of England. The rise of the Anglo-Catholic movement after 1833 made Wesleyans much more hesitant about the virtues of Establishment, and Anglo-Catholic attacks on the validity of Wesleyan ministerial orders made matters worse. Wesleyan Methodism, however, did not officially support the Free Church campaigns for Disestablishment, and this restraint played an important part in the survival of the Church of England. From about 1870 closer links were established with the other Free Churches, and this process reached its climax in the formation of the National Council of Evangelical Free Churches, whose first annual assembly met in 1896. The social and political influence of Wesleyan Methodism reached its peak about 1900, in the era of the Nonconformist conscience. The self-confidence of the period was symbolized in the TWENTIETH CENTURY FUND, a scheme started at the Conference of 1898 to raise a million guineas from a million Methodists. It was largely the idea of ROBERT PERKS, who drove the plan forward to success by 1902. Westminster Central Hall, London, the central office and church of the present Methodist Church, was one result of the raising of the fund.

In retrospect, the religious influence of the Wesleyan connection on Victorian England is seen as conservative; biblical criticism and scientific thought affected the Wesleyans more slowly than it did the Congregationalist and Presbyterian Churches; as late as 1904, J. A. BEET had to resign his post as the theological tutor at Richmond College, London, because he was determined to publish a book which rejected the doctrine of the eternal punishment of the wicked and substituted a version of the annihilation theory. The connection produced preachers rather than theologians, though RICHARD WATSON, W. B. POPE, and J. S. LIDGETT all made contributions of a limited kind to standard evangelical theology. The emphasis on experience rather than dogma led to warm support for forms of Christian action: between 1840 and 1870 the connection steadily became more teetotal, a movement which changed the nature of the English Free Churches in general. It was significant of the Wesleyan tendency not to commit the connection entirely to the Dissenting tradition, however, that the appropriate connectional department was styled the TEMPERANCE (not the Teetotal) Department. The terrible schism of 1849-57 perhaps made the Wesleyans unduly nervous of open controversy. On the other hand, the connection took a large share in the early nineteenth century efforts to educate the poorer children of the country; hundreds of connectional day schools were built between 1840 and 1870; these schools were slowly abandoned after the state took over elementary education in 1870, and today less than fifty of them survive.

The twentieth century was in some ways not a happy time for Wesleyan Methodism. The social and political influence of the connection began to diminish even under the sympathetic Liberal government of 1906-14. After the First World War, moreover, the Liberal Party declined rapidly with the decay of the social system which had given it and the Wesleyan connection prominence. The most important development in the twentieth century was the achievement of union with the two other important Methodist churches in 1932. This process may be traced back to the admission of laymen into the Wesleyan Conference in 1878, a change which greatly reduced the constitutional gap between Wesleyanism and the other Methodist denominations.

The Wesleyan connection took the initiative in seeking union, setting up an exploratory committee in 1913. The First World War then hindered progress, but in 1918 a joint committee of the three churches was empowered to draw up a draft scheme of union. In the negotiations which followed, the Wesleyan negotiators, led by ALDOM FRENCH, consented to the abolition of the LEGAL HUNDRED, and accepted the innovation of a lay vice-president, but persuaded the other Methodists to accept the idea of a two-session Conference, in which the ministry still sat by itself in the so-called pastoral session. There was more opposition to union in the Wesleyan connection than elsewhere, especially among the ministers; their leader was J. E. RATTENBURY. This opposition took a high view of the Church, the ministry, and the Sacraments, and was anxious to safeguard the long-term possibilities of union with the Church of England. As late as 1926 the vote in the Wesleyan Synods in favor of the scheme of union was only sixty-six percent in the representative sessions, and only fifty-seven percent in the pastoral sessions. In the Conference of 1926, however, the opposition vote was reduced to twenty-five percent, the lowest of the whole struggle. This made eventual union inevitable, and a compromise between the two sides in 1927 made the final consummation possible in 1932. But the degree of opposition in Wesleyan Methodism helps to explain the slow development of the united Methodist Church. At the time of METHODIST UNION the Wesleyan Methodist connection had about 500,000 members, and was larger than the two other Methodist bodies put together. Quite apart from this contribution to the ecumenical movement—no other large-scale union has taken place in England in the present century—Wesleyan Methodism also contributed to the theological reconstruction of Christianity. W. F. MOULTON played a large part in the preparation of the Revised Version; his elder son, J. H. MOULTON, became an authority on the Egyptian papyri and wrote a standard *Grammar of New Testament Greek;* with G. Milligan he also compiled a standard *Vocabulary of the New Testament.* Moulton was killed in the First World War. W. F. LOFTHOUSE, W. F. HOWARD, and VINCENT TAYLOR all wrote important works on the New Testament. One of the ablest British leaders of the ecumenical movement was R. NEWTON FLEW, who entered the Wesleyan ministry in 1910. Wesleyan Methodism preserved throughout its existence a memory of its origins within the Church of England; it never completely identified itself with Dissent or with Free Churchmanship. If Wesleyans slowly abandoned the attitude to the Bible which came naturally to the Wesleys, they continued to sing Charles Wesley's hymns, and so to be moved by the theology which enlivens them. If the eighteenth-century class meeting had largely ceased to exist by the end of the nineteenth century, it is also true that Wesleyanism had not forgotten Wesley's insistence on religion as a communal pursuit—this bore new fruit in the group movement among Methodists in British universities in the twentieth century. Nor did anything quite destroy in the Wesleyan mind the conviction implanted there by the Wesleys, that the Church exists to evangelize. This mood was the deepest contribution of Wesleyan Methodism to the modern ecumenical movement.

R. Currie, *Methodism Divided.* 1968.
R. E. Davies, *Methodism.* 1963.
Davies and Rupp, *A New History of Methodism,* vol. i. 1965.
M. L. Edwards, *After Wesley.* 1935.
J. H. S. Kent, *Age of Disunity.* 1965.
E. R. Taylor, *Methodism and Politics.* 1935. JOHN KENT

WESLEYAN METHODIST ASSOCIATION was a body of British Wesleyan Methodists who seceded from the old connection in 1835 and finally accepted a new constitution, as the Wesleyan Methodist Association, in 1837. The LEEDS PROTESTANT METHODISTS also formed part of the association, which represented an extreme reaction against the authoritarian traditions of the Wesleyan Methodist ministerial Conference. The association repudiated legislative authority in the Conference, which it renamed "An-

nual Assembly," dropped for the time being the title "Reverend," and asserted the constitutional independency of each local Methodist society—a radical departure from Wesleyan principle. The leader was ROBERT ECKETT. In 1848 the membership of the association was 20,775. There were 3 circuits with more than 1,000 members: Camelford (Devon), 1,534; Rochdale (Lancashire), 1,298; Leeds (Yorkshire), 1,266. There were 330 Sunday schools and 42,032 scholars. There were 96 pastors. After 1849 the association became involved in the agitation about the FLY SHEETS; in 1857 it merged its identity in the UNITED METHODIST FREE CHURCHES.

JOHN KENT

WESLEYAN METHODIST MISSIONARY SOCIETY. (See METHODIST MISSIONARY SOCIETY.)

WESLEYAN REFORM UNION is a British Methodist body which emerged at the time of the FLY SHEETS controversy, when the Wesleyan Methodist societies were divided by questions of church order. The four hundred Reformers who met in London in 1850 were a mixed body led by the alleged writers of the Fly Sheets, JAMES EVERETT, SAMUEL DUNN, and WILLIAM GRIFFITH. This group did not stay together, and William Griffith remained with the section which became the Wesleyan Reform Union, with a membership of about 17,000 and 250 preaching places. The principal centers were Yorkshire, Derbyshire, Lincolnshire, Northamptonshire, and Cornwall. Griffith was three times president of the Wesleyan Reform Union Conference. Although the union respects the memory of John Wesley and adheres substantially to the doctrines of Methodism, it did not become part of the Methodist Church in the Union of 1932. The essential differences between the Wesleyan Reform Union and the Methodist Church are:

1) Wesleyan Reform Union local churches are all separate entities, self-governing, not admitting outside interference.

2) The property of the Wesleyan Reform Churches is their own.

3) The Wesleyan Reform Union Conference, which meets annually, is a body of delegates from churches and circuits, from which a General Committee, including officials and secretaries of departments, is elected by vote of Conference, and this is the executive body.

4) The authority of the Wesleyan Reform Union ministry is more restricted than that of Methodist ministers. Local preachers may, when required, perform the same offices as the separated ministry. The Wesleyan Reform Union remained small, and in 1965 had about 5,600 members and 158 preaching places.

WILLIAM T. BURKITT

WESLEYAN REFORMERS (British). This term is often found in books and articles describing the agitation in WESLEYAN METHODISM during the middle of the nineteenth century. Unease at the lack of democracy in Methodist polity had already caused several controversies and divisions, notably the Leeds Protestant Methodists and the WESLEYAN METHODIST ASSOCIATION, but discontent remained, especially with the autocracy of JABEZ BUNTING. This found a focal point in the anonymous FLY SHEETS circulated to Wesleyan ministers in 1844, 1846, 1847, and 1848. A spate of pamphlets and articles in periodicals led to the tearing apart of the parent connection. This came to a head at the Wesleyan Conference of 1849, when JAMES EVERETT, SAMUEL DUNN, and WILLIAM GRIFFITH refused explicitly to deny their association with the Fly Sheets and were expelled. By means of mass meetings and press propaganda "The Three Expelled" aroused widespread public sympathy. They and their followers were popularly known as "Wesleyan Reformers" and their campaign as "The Wesleyan Reform Movement." Within a few years 100,000 members were lost to the Wesleyan Methodist Church. The Wesleyan Reformers as a whole did not constitute themselves into a separate denomination, however. After protracted discussions many joined forces with the Wesleyan Methodist Association in 1857 to form the UNITED METHODIST FREE CHURCHES. A smaller number became federated in 1859 as the Wesleyan Reform Union. Others drifted back to Wesleyan Methodism or to other denominations, or severed their Christian affiliations completely.

FRANK BAKER

WESLEYAN SERVICE GUILD, THE, is an organization of The United Methodist Church which is auxiliary to the WOMEN'S SOCIETY OF CHRISTIAN SERVICE. It was organized in the former Methodist Episcopal Church in 1921, and continued in The Methodist Church. It is composed of employed women who of necessity must set other times for their meetings than those which are held during normal business hours. This Guild uses the same program materials, magazines, and other literature as does the Women's Society, and through pledges and gifts aids in the support of the same type of mission to community local and general work. The Guild members, in part because of the diversity of their occupations, have been active in many phases of Christian Social Relations. Because there is a diversity of skills among the members of the Guild, it makes it possible to explore and assist in many specialized areas of work at home and abroad.

Disciplinary regulations outline the aim, duties and composition of the Wesleyan Service Guild, in its general, Conference and local church organization. Such regulations may be expected to be altered in minor particulars from quadrennium to quadrennium. Guild members pioneer in week-end gatherings for seminars on such subjects as mission study, spiritual development, and Christian Social relations. Membership of the Wesleyan Guild at last reporting was 122,700 and their gifts and pledges are proportionate to their membership. The Guild has played an influential part in the outreach of the Church to peoples in fifty-two countries and the United States; to the work with the United Nations, and to the local church.

Discipline U.M.C. 1968 ¶ 159.3; 1308.1; 1309.2.

MRS. JOHN M. PEARSON

WESLEYAN TAKINGS was an anonymous book which first appeared in 1840 in connection with the Centenary Celebrations of British Wesleyan Methodism. It was a collection of a hundred written sketches of WESLEYAN METHODIST ministers of the period, prefaced by the quotation, "Whose is this image? And they said _____'s; and they marvelled." Entertaining, sly, and cutting, the book

gave offense because it was disrespectful to the pastoral office. The portrait of JABEZ BUNTING revealed the subject and (for many) the author: "He is great in mind, and great in influence—too great to be forgiven; if he were less so, it might be borne." (*Takings*, p. 6) Bunting's career, it was said, was "a monotony of greatness." His real offense to the anonymous author was his great power as a ruler: "He has kept his eyes fixed on the working of the whole of the machinery, while others have attended to the rotatory motion of a single wheel." (p. 12) The third edition contained a further biting preface for the guidance of the "Wesleyan detective force" in hunting down the author. The book was attacked in the *Wesleyan Methodist Magazine,* and general suspicion fell on JAMES EVERETT, who was in fact the author. Jabez Bunting's London District recommended the Conference to discover the identity of the author; it sent letters to the suspects, including Everett and his colleague, RICHARD BURDSALL, who were stationed at YORK. These letters were simply ignored; similar letters from the Conference of 1841 were met with defiance. Everett refused to answer "because of the suspicious circumstances in which I have been placed by Dr. Bunting and his Committee, and subsequently the Conference." (*Takings*, vol. ii, p. xii) Although Jabez Bunting declared in the Conference that the book could not kill a flea, even the president, JAMES DIXON, was obliged to clear himself of suspicion before the Conference. The Conference condemned the book, especially the preface to the third edition, which it called "Unworthy of any person maintaining the Christian or ministerial character" (*Minutes of the Wesleyan Methodist Conference,* 1841). It also condemned the letters which Everett and Burdsall had written. In 1851, in the midst of the great crisis of Wesleyan Methodism, a second volume of *Takings* was published; this contained further violent attacks on Jabez Bunting reprinted from the *Wesleyan Times,* a journal which supported the reforming party in Wesleyanism.

Wesleyan Takings (Anonymous), 1840-57.

MALDWYN L. EDWARDS

WESLEYAN UNIVERSITY, Middletown, Connecticut, chartered in 1831, was the first of the permanent Methodist colleges to begin classroom work. (RANDOLPH-MACON was chartered in 1830 and opened classes in 1832.) Its founders were the NEW ENGLAND and NEW YORK ANNUAL CONFERENCES, and its charter stated it was to be managed "in behalf of the annual conferences or GENERAL CONFERENCE of the M.E. Church." While the control of the institution was thus vested with the M.E. Church, the charter stands as an example of tolerance in a time of intense denominational rivalry. It held that "subscribing to religious tenets shall never be a condition of admission to students or a cause of ineligibility to the president, professors, or other officers."

At the outset it demonstrated that church control was not inconsistent with a "nonsectarian" spirit. A charter granted in 1870 required that "at all times the majority of the trustees, the president, and a majority of the faculty shall be members of the Methodist Episcopal Church." These restrictions were removed by revision of the charter in 1907. The 1907 charter granted twelve conferences in the northeastern part of the United States the right to elect one trustee each. It did, however, leave with the board itself the conditions under which they were to be elected and the continuation of the right to elect. By 1937 election of trustees by the twelve annual conferences was discontinued.

The university, now a self-perpetuating institution, makes no claim of Methodist connection except a historical one. Efforts to change the name of the university have on two occasions failed.

Beginning with the first president, WILBUR FISK, all of the presidents from 1831 until 1924 were Methodist ministers, with one exception: the fourth president was a Methodist layman. Since 1924 the presidents have been laymen and members of other denominations.

By its charter, Wesleyan was given the rights for a university, but notwithstanding pressures for theological and law schools it never expanded beyond an arts and science college.

The college from its inception through the first quarter of the twentieth century was Methodist-oriented with its roots deeply imbedded in the life of the church. At least eighteen of its alumni were elected bishops in the M.E. Church (two in the M.E. Church, South). Until 1930, twenty percent of the graduates entered the ministry, the large majority in the M.E. Church. Its leadership was felt in every area of the church's life, particularly in education.

The name "Wesleyan" was adopted by fifteen or more institutions, and its graduates led in establishing the church's eduational program on the expanding frontier. Twenty-six percent of Wesleyan's graduates entered the teaching profession, and almost half of this number were connected with institutions of higher education. In the period when it had vital church connections it was never placed lower than fourth on the relative proportion of graduates of the colleges and universities who appeared in *Who's Who in America*.

Wesleyan's interest in being a church-related institution began to wane during the first quarter of the twentieth century. It no longer enjoyed the exclusive interest of Methodist conferences, and the conferences themselves did not possess the interest in education that existed in the founding conferences. This may have been foreseen by Wilbur Fisk, who gave to the New York Conference his "dying request" that it nurse Wesleyan University.

No one can estimate with accuracy the money received prior to 1930 by Wesleyan because of its Methodist connections. A check of the list of persons who helped to build Wesleyan's plant and endowment shows a preponderance of Methodist members. Its endowment during the administration of the last Methodist president, Shanklin (1908-24), increased from $1,540,632 to $4,392,019. The university participated in the financial development program of 1915-20 sponsored by the Board of EDUCATION of the M.E. Church.

The centennial of Wesleyan University was commemorated Oct. 10-12, 1931. The centennial sermon was preached by Bishop HERBERT WELCH, class of 1887, from the text, "Remove not the ancient landmark, which thy fathers have set."

The scholarship of Wesleyan under Methodist auspices gave it a reputation of being an educational institution of quality. Its Phi Beta Kappa chapter was installed in 1845. The roster of its professors included many excellent scholars who kept abreast of the developments of their fields, and who had an awareness of the relationship of religion to their work as teachers.

JOHN O. GROSS

WESLEYANA. Even during JOHN WESLEY's lifetime, and especially during his latter years, he was so venerated that engraved portraits and porcelain busts depicting him were in great demand, as were souvenirs of his visits to various homes or areas, or of his association with different people—chairs in which he sat, china which he used, articles of clothing which he had worn, coins which he had presented, locks clipped from his head (of which the writer has one). Personal letters from him were passed on as family heirlooms, and have increased enormously in value through the years. Examples of the five hundred or more items which he and his brother CHARLES published, which passed through two thousand editions during his lifetime, and many more since, continued to be read (or at least preserved) for sentimental if not always for devotional or theological reasons.

Wesley made it easier for treasure hunters in that he hoarded his correspondence and notebooks through the years, from time to time publishing extracts in his *Arminian Magazine*. By his will (1789) all his papers were bequeathed to THOMAS COKE, JOHN WHITEHEAD, and HENRY MOORE, "to be burnt or published as they should see good." At Wesley's death two years later Coke was in America, Moore stationed in BRISTOL, and Whitehead, then a LOCAL PREACHER living in LONDON, took charge of the manuscripts, agreeing to the request of the London preachers that he should prepare a biography of Wesley. He refused to allow his fellow literary executors to see Wesley's manuscripts until he had published the biography, which became a personal rather than a Methodist enterprise. Coke and Moore tried to forestall him by publishing a hasty life of Wesley, but they had to do so without much of the documentation enriching Whitehead's two volumes, which appeared in 1793 and 1796. After finishing volume two Whitehead handed the papers back to Methodism in the person of JOHN PAWSON, superintendent of the London circuit. Pawson proceeded to burn many items which he considered unedifying, including Wesley's annotated copy of Shakespeare, and probably many of the notebooks which contained his shorthand diary for the years 1742-81. It seems likely that other manuscripts were given away as souvenirs. When Henry Moore heard of this he protested, and the remaining books and papers were sent to him, to be used in his enlarged biography of Wesley, published in two volumes (1824-25) after the death of his fellow-executor Coke. Moore's collection was bequeathed to three literary executors, and from the last survivor, William Gandy, passed to J. J. Colman of Norwich, thence to his son Russell J. Colman, and eventually (as the Colman Collection) to the Methodist Church of Great Britain, which now houses it in the Methodist ARCHIVES and Research Centre in London.

Only the published material was available to Robert Southey when he compiled his biography of Wesley, though he did correspond with CHARLES WESLEY's daughter SARAH, obtaining from her some family traditions. Like his brother John, Charles Wesley also retained masses of correspondence and other papers, including many unpublished manuscript collections of hymns and poems. These were acquired for Methodism from his daughter Sarah Wesley by THOMAS JACKSON, and are similarly cared for in the Methodist Archives, which thus owns by far the best collection of Wesley manuscripts in the world. Many Wesley manuscripts of various kinds are to be found elsewhere, however, especially letters. Because in his later years Charles Wesley disagreed with his brother's increasing tendency to separate from the CHURCH OF ENGLAND he took a less active part in the life of the Methodist societies, and although highly regarded by many did not receive the mass veneration accorded his brother. One indication of this is that very few of his letters and other relics have been preserved apart from those kept by the family. G. J. STEVENSON secured some.

During the first half of the nineteenth century many Methodists tried to secure whatever they could which had been associated in any way with the Wesleys, especially John Wesley. Sometimes this was done with scholarly intent, more often with a purely sentimental or antiquarian interest, and usually with a mixture of the two. One of the earliest was WILLIAM MARRIOTT, one of the general executors of Wesley's will, who transmitted the fever to his son Thomas, who vividly remembered being taken when he was five to see Wesley lying in state in his coffin. Thomas Marriott (1786-1852) became a well known Methodist antiquary, enriching the pages of the *Wesleyan Methodist Magazine* with many articles based upon his collection of Wesleyana. Marriott's collection was bequeathed to GEORGE OSBORN. Much of Osborn's collection, including many bound volumes of pamphlets, was acquired by DREW UNIVERSITY in 1880, a decade before Osborn's death.

ADAM CLARKE is best known for his Bible commentary, but he was a deeply-read scholar in many fields, and it is largely to his enthusiasm for the Wesleys that we owe the survival of many early Methodist traditions and items of Wesleyana. For his *Wesley Family* Clarke utilized his own accumulations, those of Thomas Marriott, and (among others) those of JAMES EVERETT. Everett was notorious as a critic of the Methodist establishment as personified in JABEZ BUNTING, but he was also a great admirer of Wesley, a prolific writer on Methodist history, and an enthusiastic collector of Wesleyana and Methodistica. A large part of Everett's collection was bought by LUKE TYERMAN from the aged Everett, and he used it to good effect in his own works on the Wesleys and early Methodism. Many of the manuscripts in Tyerman's collection were purchased by George Stampe of Grimsby, co-founder with RICHARD GREEN of the WESLEY HISTORICAL SOCIETY, from whom they passed to EDMUND SYKES LAMPLOUGH, who will be discussed later. Tyerman's pamphlets were purchased about 1895 and found their way to Drew University—over 2,000 titles in 275 volumes. Many of these came originally from Everett, whose early start and business for several years as a practicing bookseller gave him more opportunities than most later collectors. Others of Everett's collected pamphlets are now in the British Museum. One of Everett's most prized treasures he retained until his death in 1872. Through his literary executors it came to the United Methodist Church, and thus to the present Methodist Archives in London. This was a bound volume of holograph letters by Wesley and his colleagues, which formed the backbone of George Eayrs' *Letters of John Wesley*.

The latter half of the nineteenth century was the high day of collectors of Wesleyana and Methodistica, with many public auctions at which Wesley items sold for moderate prices, with plenty of Wesley material still in private hands, and occasional large collections coming on the market, such as those of Samuel Romilly Hall and John Sundius Stamp, descendant of one of Wesley's stepdaughters. Much of this material, happily, gravitated towards institutions, where it was usually carefully pre-

served while remaining accessible to scholars. Thus G. A. K. HOBILL'S LIBRARY was presented to the METHODIST NEW CONNEXION CONFERENCE, whence it came to VICTORIA COLLEGE, and then to HARTLEY-VICTORIA COLLEGE. Similarly CHARLES PREST's pamphlets went to the Wesleyan Methodist Conference, Hall's to DIDSBURY COLLEGE, Stamp's (like Thomas Jackson's wonderful library) to RICHMOND COLLEGE. There were still pickings for the multiplying private collectors, however, among whom a few may be mentioned. Many private collections, large and small, eventually went to appease the rising desire of Methodist institutions overseas for relics of their founder.

Thomas E. Brigden was a true scholar-antiquarian, who wrote the British section of Bishop J. F. HURST's *History of Methodism*. Much of Brigden's collection was bought by W. H. FITCHETT and presented to Queen's College, MELBOURNE, which owns the best collection of Wesleyana outside the British Isles and the American continent. C. D. Hardcastle was a modest but eager collector who secured many of the rarer Irish editions of the Wesleys' publications, especially of their hymns; most of these are now in the Wesley Historical Society library in Belfast. E. Thursfield Smith of Whitchurch was able to accumulate a much more extensive collection, much of which came to EMORY UNIVERSITY, some to Rylands Library, MANCHESTER, some to Didsbury College, and some onto the open market. The varied holdings of Joseph G. Wright of Wolverhampton were sold by public auction after his death in 1910, though some portions have found their ways eventually to Methodist institutions. Richard Green's wonderful collection of the publications of the Wesleys (strongest in first editions) was bought after his death by Sir John Eaton, and presented to VICTORIA UNIVERSITY, Toronto. Marmaduke Riggall's Wesleyana were sold by auction in 1928.

One of the most resolute bidders at most of these auctions (under his pseudonym of "Smyth"), was E. S. Lamplough, who secured much of George Stampe's collection. So enthusiastic was Lamplough that he even managed to persuade the WESLEYAN METHODIST MISSIONARY SOCIETY to part with much of the material in their Museum of Methodist Antiquities in return for generous financial support, with the condition that upon his death this material would revert to the Methodist Church. Lamplough assembled one of the most voluminous and valuable collections of Wesleyana and Methodistica ever in private hands, and at his death in 1940 bequeathed the whole collection to Methodism. It now swells the rich resources of the Methodist Archives and Research Centre. More recently ISAAC FOOT's library has been purchased by the University of California, the valuable Wesleyana therein being allotted to the campus at Santa Barbara. The bulk of my own collection of Wesleyana and Methodistica has been purchased by DUKE UNIVERSITY, which now holds easily the second best collection in the world of eighteenth century editions of the Wesleys' writings, second only to that in the Methodist Archives, London.

Although a few Americans began collecting Wesleyana in the nineteenth century (like Curtis H. Cavender, who specialized in anti-Methodist literature and used the anagram "Decanver" as a pseudonym) the heyday of the American collection has been the twentieth century. Again the normal procedure has been for the holdings of the private collector to find a permanent home in some Methodist institution. Thus (to mention only a few of those who have died) Ezra Squier Tipple's Wesleyana went to Drew University, Bishop F. D. Leete's (after some migrations) to the Perkins School of Theology, Southern Methodist University, Bishop G. Bromley Oxnam's to Wesley Seminary, Washington, and Elmer T. Clark's to the World Methodist Building, Lake Junaluska. Elmer Clark also bought from J. Ernest Eagles of Cliff College the best collection of Wesley pottery then extant apart from that of James Botteley, presented to the Wesleyan Methodist Conference in 1912.

Many more names, both of individuals and of institutions, cry aloud for inclusion, but enough has been said to underline the fact that there has been and remains a great veneration for John Wesley and the Methodists of his day, a great enthusiasm to possess human artifacts associated with him, and (we believe) an increasing appreciation of his outstanding contribution under God to the spiritual development of the world. (See also Wesley Pottery and Busts.)

FRANK BAKER

WESLEYDALE, near Kaeo on the Whangaroa Harbor, was the name given to the first Wesleyan mission station in New Zealand, founded by Samuel Leigh in 1823. After only two months, when the mission staff suffered many indignities at the hands of unfriendly Maoris, Leigh's health broke down and he was forced to return to Australia, leaving Nathaniel Turner and John Hobbs (at that time a lay missionary) in charge.

With few encouragements and many disappointments, the missionaries faithfully carried on the work for several more years. Then early in January, 1827, a war party under Chief Hongi, attacked and destroyed the station, the missionaries escaping only with their lives. They returned temporarily to New South Wales and reestablished the mission later the same year in the Hokianga District.

In New Zealand Methodism's centenary year, 1922, a memorial cairn was erected to mark the site of Wesleydale, and in the main street of nearby Kaeo a beautiful church was built as a memorial to the pioneer missionaries and their families.

C. H. Laws, *Toil and Adversity at Whangaroa.* Wesley Historical Society, New Zealand, 1945.
R. F. Snowden, *The Ladies of Wesleydale.* London: Epworth Press, 1957.
L. R. M. GILMORE

WESSINGTON SPRINGS ACADEMY, Wessington Springs, South Dakota, was established as an elementary and secondary school in September 1886 by the South Dakota Conference of the Free Methodist Church. Largely through the influence of A. B. Smart, a Methodist minister of Wessington Springs, the location committee chose Wessington Springs as the most desirable location. The school was opened Nov. 15, 1887, Professor J. K. Freeland, principal. In 1916 the name was changed to Wessington Springs Junior College. After careful study the trustees in April 1964, decided to change to a four-year high school program to begin on Sept. 1, 1964. There are approximately 100 students.

BYRON S. LAMSON

WEST, ARTHUR (1910-   ), American minister and Executive Secretary of Methodist Information of The United Methodist Church, was born in Grant City, Mo.,

on Feb. 13, 1910. He was the son of Elmer E. and Maude (Younkin) West. His education was at Missouri Wesleyan, A.A., 1929; Baker University, A.B., 1931, and D.D., 1953; Boston University, M.A., 1934, and S.T.B., 1935. He specialized in journalism and public relations at Northwestern University, 1945-55, and at the University of Chicago, 1957. His wife is Vera Spreckelmeyer, whom he married on Sept. 27, 1931, and their children are Paul and David.

Arthur West was received on trial in the Missouri Conference in 1928 and into full connection in 1933. He received his elder's orders in 1935. He served as pastor in Civil Bend, 1928-29; Wesley Church, St. Joseph, 1929-31; Savannah, 1931-32, (all appointments in Missouri). He was then transferred to Massachusetts where he served at Whitman, 1933-35; then came back to Cuba, Mo., in 1936. He was then in Warren, R. I., 1936-42; and in Grace Church, Bangor, Maine, 1944-48. He was made the religion editor of the *Providence Journal* and *Evening Bulletin,* 1942-44, and that of the *Bangor* (Maine) *Daily News,* 1946-48. He then went into the work of the Commission on Public Relations and Methodist Information of The Methodist Church, being made associate director in charge of the Chicago office in 1948-64. On the retirement of Dr. Ralph Stoody, he was elected general secretary of Methodist Information, 1964 —the name of this organization being changed in 1968 to United Methodist Information.

Dr. West has also served as associate editor of the Northwestern Jurisdiction *Daily Christian Advocate,* 1948-52, and was a member of the press staff of the Second Assembly of the World Council of Churches, 1954, and of the World Methodist Conference, 1947, '51, '56, and '61. He serves upon several other church bodies having to do with Methodist publications and upon that of the National Council of Churches. He is the author of *Faith of the Family,* 1952. United Methodist Information has its headquarters offices in Dayton, Ohio. There are other national level offices in New York; Nashville; Washington, D.C.; and Evanston, Ill.

Who's Who in The Methodist Church, 1966.   N. B. H.

WEST, MILDRED (? -1959), New Zealand Methodist deaconess, was born in Taranaki, where she became a Sunday school teacher. After seven years in Wellington caring for a family of motherless children, she was appointed in 1920 to be deaconess at the Baring Square Methodist Church, Ashburton, Canterbury, where she served for many years.

She was deeply interested in the work of the Women's Christian Temperance Union, the Plunket Society (infant welfare), and the National Council of Women. In her retirement she lived at Te Awamutu and became a greatly loved member of the congregation there.

New Zealand Methodist Times, June 6, 1959.
L. R. M. GILMORE

WEST ALLIS, WISCONSIN, U.S.A., **Methodist Manor, Inc.,** is a church-operated home for the aging owned and operated by the East Wisconsin Conference of The United Methodist Church. Located on nineteen acres of land, it offers a home to 195 aging men and women. Construction was completed in 1960 at a total cost of $2,600,000, which included land, furnishings, and construction.

Methodist Manor has a Health Center of sixty-four beds licensed by the Boards of Health of the State of Wisconsin and the city of West Allis, and planned to give skilled nursing care to the residents. The Health Center is Medicare certified. Construction of an independent nursing home is imminent.

Methodist Manor is operated under a corporation of twenty-seven directors, elected by the East Wisconsin Conference of The United Methodist Church—nine ministers, nine laymen and nine laywomen. The functional operation of Methodist Manor has as its single aim the care of aging men and women and is an entirely non-profit organization. Adequate resident activities make home-life challenging. Methodist Manor allows no discrimination on the basis of race, color or national origin.

Methodist Manor is a member of the East Wisconsin Methodist Homes Association and is under the direction of the Executive Director, George H. Palmer.

WEST CHINA MISSION. In 1891, Szechwan, West CHINA, was selected by the Methodist Church of CANADA for its new mission field. It was situated at the head of China's central highway, the Yangtze River, in one of the most populous and inaccessible parts of the country.

The original party of missionaries consisted of Dr. and Mrs. VIRGIL C. HART, veterans of missionary work in China under the Methodist Episcopal Church, U.S.A., their daughter, Stella (afterward Mrs. Hare), Dr. and Mrs. Omar L. Kilborn, Rev. and Mrs. George E. Hartwell, and Dr. and Mrs. David W. Stevenson. The group landed at Shanghai on Nov. 3, 1891; in mid-February they left for the interior, arriving in Chengtu, the capital of Szechwan on May 21, 1892. At that time the China Inland Mission had six or seven workers in Chengtu, and the Methodist Episcopal Church had a single male missionary.

The first reinforcements, James Endicott and his wife, and Dr. H. Mather Hare, arrived in Chengtu in the spring of 1894. They were accompanied by Sara C. Brackbill and Dr. Retta Gifford (later the second Mrs. Kilborn), sent out by the Woman's Missionary Society. The latter were sent to replace Amelia Brown, who had been with the pioneer party, but had married Stevenson before they left Shanghai. In 1896 Dr. and Mrs. W. E. Smith joined the group in Chengtu.

The growth of the mission was slow at first. By 1901 there were only nineteen missionaries under the General Board and the Woman's Missionary Society. In 1917 the mission staff included seventy-five men, sixty-seven of whom were married, and thirty-five single women; in 1919 there were 155 under the General Board and thirty-two women under the W.M.S. At Union, there were 218 missionaries on the field, 177 under the board and forty-one under the W.M.S. By 1917 Szechwan had eight foreign missions with 443 missionaries, the Canadian Mission having thirty-six percent of this total.

As the number of missionaries increased, the territory of the mission expanded. In 1894 Kiating, 100 miles south of Chengtu, was opened; in 1905, Junghsien and Jenshow; in 1907, Penhsien and Tzeliutsing; in 1908, Luchow. In 1910 the mission took over the London Missionary Society field in West China, thus including Chungking in its territory. In 1911 Chungchow was opened; in 1913, Fowchow. By 1925 there were ten stations and a hundred outstations.

In 1892 a SUNDAY SCHOOL was started; in 1894 a church was built in Chengtu, the gift of Jairus Hart of Halifax. In 1893 the street chapel preaching began. Unfortunately the antiforeign riots of 1895 destroyed everything, but in 1896 the missionaries returned from Shanghai, and the work began again. In that year, churches were opened in Chengtu and Kiating, and the first convert was baptized, after a little less than five years work. By 1917 membership was 1,700; forty-three children were baptized members not as yet classed as communicants. There were nine native ordained preachers, twenty-eight probationers and evangelists, and eighteen Bible-women.

Steps were taken to make the Chinese church entirely indigenous and its Conference a separate, self-directing entity. The church was given a definite name (*Mei Dao Hwei*) as distinct from the mission. Also on recommendation of the Mission Council, the Mission Board made the whole grant for evangelistic or pastoral work directly to the Conference instead of through the medium of the Mission Council. The council also gave authority to Conference in all matters that had to do with regular pastoral work. Thus, the Conference had become virtually self-governing.

Emphasis was laid also on medical mission work. Two of the original four men sent out to China were doctors. Kilborn and Stevenson opened a dispensary in November 1892, but they had to close it after three months because the time was completely taken up and language study crowded out. During 1894 two hospital buildings were erected in Chengtu, and medical work began in 1895, but these structures were completely destroyed in the riots of that year. 1896-97 saw the second hospital built with a dispensary, waiting room and two wards for twenty-five patients. In 1907 a new modern hospital was begun under R. B. Ewan. By 1917 there were twenty-one doctors, fifteen men and six women, working in eleven hospitals in the ten central stations. A medical college was established in 1914, in connection with the university, to train native medical workers.

Dental hospitals were opened in Chengtu and Chungking, and in 1920 a faculty of dentistry was established in the university. In 1908 a pharmacist was sent to the field.

While small schools were opened soon after arrival in 1893, it was not until 1904 that special emphasis was laid on education, and J. L. Stewart was appointed solely to educational work. By 1907 the stated policy was to have an educational missionary in each central station. About 1903 an educational revolution swept the nation, creating a new demand for Western methods.

The new enthusiasm created by the national reform led the Canadian Mission and others to unite their efforts in the West China Christian Education Union, all the missions adopting similar grades, courses, and textbooks along with registration, certification, and inspection of schools. The aim was to develop "a complete and properly co-ordinated system of Christian education, parallel to the system of the Chinese Government, but with such deviations from it as from time to time seem necessary."

In March 1909, the Canadian School for Missionaries' Children was opened in temporary quarters with five pupils and one teacher, Lela A. Ker of the W.M.S. A new school building was begun in December 1916.

The greatest educational venture in West China was the establishment, in 1910, of the West China Union

University at Chengtu. This institution was formed by the united effort of the Friends' Foreign Mission Association of Great Britain and Ireland, the American Baptist Foreign Mission Society, the Board of Foreign Missions of the Methodist Episcopal Church, U.S.A., and the General Board of Missions of the Methodist Church, Canada. In 1910 only classes in arts and science were attempted. A medical faculty was added in 1914; a faculty of religion in 1915; education, in 1918; and dentistry, in 1920. To these faculties must be added pharmacy courses, an agricultural department, and the Union Middle School, the Union Normal School, the Union Bible Training School, the Union Training School for Missionaries, and a lower and higher primary school. The University was controlled by a board of governors in the homelands, and in 1922 it was incorporated under the board of regents of the university of the State of New York. The campus of over 150 acres contained some twenty-two teaching buildings and dormitories and thirty-four teachers' residences. The first class, two in number, was graduated in 1915. Girls were first admitted to university classes in 1924.

An important means of reaching the people was through the mission press. After the Boxer Rebellion in 1900, J. Endicott took charge of the press. The earliest business was with the West China Religious Tract Society and the AMERICAN BIBLE SOCIETY. In 1904 the whole plant was moved into new press buildings at Chengtu. In 1918 over 21,000,000 pages of literature were printed in Chinese, English, Tibetan, and Miao.

Three times prior to 1925 the Canadian missionaries were forced to give up their work and flee to the coast. The first outbreak was in 1895, when riots broke out in Chengtu, lasting for about a day and a half, in which all the foreign missionaries were thankful to escape with their lives. The missionaries returned within a year and were compensated for their losses.

The second exodus was in 1900, when the consuls ordered everyone to the coast, as the result of the Boxer upheavals in the northern provinces. When the missionaries returned in 1901 they found their property intact.

The third general exodus was in 1911, owing to the revolutionary disturbances which led to the overthrow of the empire and the establishment of the Republic of China. In September, 1911, all Chengtu missionaries were asked by the British consul to gather in the compounds of the Canadian Mission inside the city. After three months in the crowded quarters almost all were sent to the coast. In two or three months the missionaries were able to return to their stations. Despite the fact that government and rebel troops and brigands were everywhere, no missionary in West China received bodily harm, and there were only insignificant losses of property.

The missionaries returned in 1912, to enter upon a decade of continuous political unrest. The central government had little control. Ambitious politicians and their warlord allies sprang up everywhere. In Szechwan these fought the national forces from the nearby provinces, and each other. Yet there was no animus against the foreigner. Hospitals, churches, and schools were places of refuge, fairly well respected by all parties. In the midst of this turbulence and violence the mission was able to progress. From the early 1920's onward, however, the missionaries faced a new menace, a rising tide of antiforeign, anti-Christian feeling, aided and abetted by Communism which was beginning to acquire influence in China.

With the formation of The United Church of Canada in 1925 the mission passed to the new denomination.

J. H. Arnup, *A New Church Faces a New World*. Toronto: United Church, 1937.
K. J. Beaton, *West of the Gorges*. Toronto: United Church, 1948.
G. J. Bond, *Our Share in China*. Toronto: Methodist Missionary Society, 1909.
E. J. Hart, *Virgil C. Hart: Missionary Statesman*. Toronto: McClelland, 1917.
G. E. Hartwell, *Granary of Heaven*. Toronto: United Church Publishing House, 1939.
Our West China Mission. Toronto: Methodist Missionary Society, 1920.
United Church Archives, Manuscript material, Toronto.

G. A. HALLOWELL

WEST INDIES, THE, sometimes called The Antilles, is an archipelago of several hundred islands and cays separating the Caribbean Sea from the Atlantic Ocean. The largest island, CUBA, is only ninety miles south of Key West, Fla. The total population of all the islands approximates 19,650,000.

The larger islands are autonomous nations, members of the United Nations: Cuba (Spanish-speaking); Hispaniola, divided between HAITI (French-speaking) and the DOMINICAN REPUBLIC (Spanish-speaking); JAMAICA, TRINIDAD AND TOBAGO, and BARBADOS (English-speaking). PUERTO RICO (Spanish-speaking) is a self-governing commonwealth associated with the United States of which its people are citizens. The many lesser islands are associated in different ways with Great Britain, France, the Netherlands and the United States. To the east of Puerto Rico, the chain divides into two groups, the Leewards and the Windwards.

Methodism came to the West Indies in 1760, when NATHANIEL GILBERT, lawyer and planter, returned to ANTIGUA from a sojourn of a few years in England where he was converted by JOHN WESLEY. In a short time he organized a Methodist Society of over 200, almost all Negroes. Nathaniel's brother, FRANCIS GILBERT, and his wife Mary continued the work after Nathaniel's death until ill health forced Francis back to England.

In 1778 JOHN BAXTER, a local preacher, went to Antigua as a shipwright for duty at "Nelson's Dockyard," English Harbour, where the British fleet was based. The mission grew steadily under his leadership. After the organization of the M.E. Church (U.S.A.) in 1784, Baxter was ordained by THOMAS COKE at BALTIMORE, Md., in June 1785, FRANCIS ASBURY certifying the action in the *Minutes*. Coke visited the West Indies in late 1786-87, going to many of the islands, organizing Baxter's work into a regular circuit. Coke made four more visits to the West Indies in the following decade, visiting the growing work in many of the islands.

From 1885 to 1904, British Wesleyan work in the West Indies, with the exception of the Bahamas and Honduras, was transferred to an autonomous West Indian Conference. After 1894, the Conference met in two sections, concerned respectively with the Eastern and Western parts of the area. For financial and other reasons, the two sectional conferences invited the Wesleyan METHODIST MISSIONARY SOCIETY in 1903 to resume responsibility for the area. In 1967, the METHODIST CHURCH IN THE CARIBBEAN AND THE AMERICAS was inaugurated.

The Methodist Church (U.S.A.) inherited the work of

the M.E. Church and the M.E. Church, South in Cuba, Puerto Rico and the VIRGIN ISLANDS. Other Methodist Churches at work in the West Indies are the A.M.E. in BAHAMAS, Jamaica, Haiti, Dominican Republic, Trinidad, the Leewards; the A.M.E. ZION CHURCH in the Leewards; the WESLEYAN METHODIST CHURCH (U.S.A.) in Haiti and Puerto Rico; the FREE METHODIST in the Dominican Republic; the United Church of CANADA in Trinidad.

W. C. Barclay, *History of Missions.* 1957.
T. Coke, *History of the West Indies.* 1808-11.
———————, Journals (Extracts). 1793, 1816.
Cyril Davey, *Under My Skin.* London: Cargate Press, 1967.
W. Easton, *Western Windows.* London: Cargate Press, n.d.
Findlay and Holdsworth, *Wesleyan Meth. Miss. Soc.* 1921.
Forever Beginning. Jamaica, 1960.
J. E. Henderson, *A Visit to the West Indies.* London: Methodist Missionary Society, 1939.
Kindling of the Flame. British Guiana, 1960.
Barbara H. Lewis, *Methodist Overseas Missions.* 1960.
J. A. Vickers, *Thomas Coke.* 1969.
F. D. Walker, *West Indies.* N.d.
World Methodist Council, *Handbook of Information,* 1966-71.
PAUL ELLINGWORTH
ARTHUR BRUCE MOSS

WEST LAFAYETTE, OHIO, U.S.A. **Methodist Protestant Home for the Aged** was opened in March, 1917, in the buildings formerly used for the West Lafayette College and though located within the boundaries of the Muskingum (later Ohio) Annual Conference, it was open to elderly members from throughout the entire Methodist Protestant Church. *The Methodist Protestant-Recorder,* on June 7, 1935, noted that some forty-three persons had been received in the home since its opening. Reverend J. Sala Leland, E. R. Biggs and Mrs. C. A. Isner were among those who served as president or superintendent of the Home. Following the Methodist Union of 1939, the Home has been privately operated.

West Lafayette College was in existence between 1900 and 1916 and was one of the official colleges of the M.P. Church. It was established by the Muskingum Annual Conference and the Honorable Vincent Ferguson donated land valued at $20,000 about one mile east of West Lafayette, Ohio, on Route 16. The charter for the college was secured on April 16, 1900, and S. A. Fisher, W. L. Wells, Joseph Porteus, H. C. Ferguson and J. W. Cassingham were elected by the Conference to serve as the first Board of Trustees. A brick building was erected to accommodate the needs of the preparatory and commercial departments of the college and the institution opened in September 1900. By 1904, there was an average attendance of 100-125 students. West Lafayette College closed in the fall of 1916 and was united with ADRIAN COLLEGE. The college buildings were then used as a Home for the Aged for the M.P. Church. Since Methodist Union in 1939, the Home has been privately owned.

W. L. Richard, "History of West Lafayette College," unpublished history sent to the author in 1968 by Mr. Richard, a resident of West Lafayette, Ohio.
Scattered issues of the *Journal of the General Conference of the Methodist Protestant Church.* RALPH HARDEE RIVES

WEST NEBRASKA CONFERENCE (ME) was organized at Kearney, Neb., Sept. 10, 1885 with Bishop EDWARD G. ANDREWS presiding. The conference superseded the West Nebraska Mission which was formed in 1880 by dividing the Nebraska Conference. At the beginning the West Nebraska Conference included the western two-thirds of the state. It had three districts, Platte Valley, Niobrara Valley, and Republican Valley; sixty-six charges, and 3,366 members.

The Northwest Nebraska Conference was carved from the West Nebraska Conference in 1892. Then in 1913 West Nebraska was absorbed by the NEBRASKA CONFERENCE. At its final session in 1912 the West Nebraska Conference reported three districts, Holdredge, Kearney, and North Platte; 105 pastoral charges, and 13,975 members.

General Minutes, MEC.
E. E. Jackman, *Nebraska.* 1954.   E. E. JACKMAN

WEST OHIO CONFERENCE (ME) was organized at Urbana, Ohio, Sept. 9, 1913 with Bishop WILLIAM F. ANDERSON presiding. The conference was formed by merging the CENTRAL OHIO and CINCINNATI CONFERENCES pursuant to a specific enabling act passed by the 1912 GENERAL CONFERENCE. The territory of the West Ohio Conference was western Ohio. The conference began with ten districts, 351 charges, 464 preachers, 124,711 members, and 753 churches and 286 parsonages valued at $6,920,090.

The West Ohio Conference supported OHIO WESLEYAN and OHIO NORTHERN UNIVERSITIES and the Cincinnati Missionary Training School. Hillsboro College closed soon after the conference was formed. The conference was related to the Christ Hospital in CINCINNATI and the Flower Deaconess Hospital in Toledo, and it shared with the other Ohio conferences in the support of LAKESIDE, and the Methodist Children's Home near Columbus.

The West Ohio Conference continued in existence for fifteen years and experienced moderate growth during that time. In 1927 it had eight districts, 358 charges, 505 preachers, 136,849 members, and 664 churches and 323 parsonages valued at $14,123,683.

In 1927 the West Ohio Conference joined the OHIO CONFERENCE in asking the General Conference to merge the two bodies into one conference to be called the Ohio Conference. The General Conference so ordered, and in September, 1928 the Ohio Conference became the largest in the denomination; it then had 229,650 members.

General Minutes, MEC.
Minutes of the West Ohio Conference.
John M. Versteeg, *Methodism: Ohio Area, 1812-1962.* 1962.
ALBEA GODBOLD

WEST OKLAHOMA CONFERENCE. (See OKLAHOMA CONFERENCE, MES, and OKLAHOMA CONFERENCE, MC.)

WEST PALM BEACH, FLORIDA, U.S.A. **First Church** is the mother church of the Palm Beaches. Organized in 1892, the church recently celebrated seventy-five years of service to the greater Palm Beach area.

The first building was erected in 1898. Built largely with volunteer help, everyone in town, including the saloon keeper, made some contribution. In 1914 an impressive brick church was erected at a cost of $60,000. Within ten years it was apparent that the brick church could no longer meet the needs of a growing membership. In 1925 the present structure was erected with balcony on three sides, seating approximately 1,500. Almost before completion, the financial crash left the church with a colossal debt. In 1937-38, the congregation lost the building to the company holding the mortgage, and worshipped briefly in the high school auditorium, just a block away. A refinancing plan finally made it possible for the congregation to regain possession and eventually retire the debt.

A Program of Progress was inaugurated in 1966 to completely remodel the educational building and sanctuary, which resulted in what is said to be one of the most beautiful and serviceable plants in the southeast. In 1968 and 1969, ten new faceted glass windows were installed, depicting events in the life of Christ. In 1970 First Church reported 1,907 members.

General Minutes, 1970.   CLARENCE M. YATES

WEST TEXAS CONFERENCE began as the West Texas Conference of the M.E. Church. It was formed by dividing the TEXAS CONFERENCE. The conference was organized at Austin, Jan. 22, 1874 with Bishop THOMAS BOWMAN presiding. Composed of both white and Negro ministers and churches at the beginning, the conference reported in 1875, three districts, fifty-four charges, and 5,338 members.

In 1877 the white ministers and churches of the West Texas Conference were constituted as the Austin Conference. Organized at Dallas, Nov. 15, 1877, the Austin Conference had only eight charges and 400 members, but it immediately organized two districts—Dallas and Denison—with a total of nineteen charges. In 1910 there were thirty-three charges and 3,637 members. The next year the Austin Conference was dissolved and its ministers and churches were absorbed by the OKLAHOMA and GULF CONFERENCES and the Southern Swedish Mission Conference.

The West Texas Conference established Samuel Huston College in Austin in 1900. In 1952 it merged with Tillotson College which was started in the same city by the Congregational Church in 1876. Now HUSTON-TILLOTSON COLLEGE, it is related to both The United Methodist Church and the United Church of Christ. The college plant is valued at more than $3,000,000 and the enrolment is nearly 1,000.

After the formation of the Austin Conference the West Texas Conference continued as a Negro body. In 1900 it had five districts and 11,057 members. It came to unification in 1939 with six districts, 102 charges, 15,767 members, and property valued at $595,654. Continuing as a conference of the CENTRAL JURISDICTION in The Methodist Church, the West Texas Conference reported in 1968 four districts—Austin, Dallas, San Antonio, and Waco—ninety-four charges, 20,101 members, and property valued at $5,326,578. Following the abolition of the Central Jurisdiction in 1968 the West Texas Conference was united with the former Anglo conferences in TEXAS, primarily the SOUTHWEST TEXAS and the NORTH TEXAS.

General Minutes, ME, TMC.
Minutes of the West Texas Conference. FREDERICK E. MASER

WEST TEXAS CONFERENCE (MES). (See SOUTHWEST TEXAS CONFERENCE.)

WEST THOMPSON, CONNECTICUT, U.S.A. This Methodist church in the rural northeastern part of CONNECTICUT is the outgrowth of services conducted in the neighboring town of Pomfret in 1792 by John Allen. The move-

ment was nurtured by Noah Perrin, who was lay leader for the first sixty years. Services were held at the home of Jonathan Nichols, and for many years a bronze plaque on the house stated this. This plaque is now in the Methodist church in neighboring North Grosvenordale. The sixth NEW ENGLAND CONFERENCE met here in 1796 with Bishop ASBURY presiding, and thirty preachers were in attendance, some coming from MAINE. The first Methodist church building was erected in Thompson in 1797, and Bishops Asbury and WHATCOAT preached here on the same day in 1800. A second church, built in 1841, was used for worship until 1963. This simple colonial structure was dismantled in 1963, and moved piece by piece to the Belmont Hill School in Belmont, Mass., where it has been restored for chapel purposes. This church was the mother of thirteen neighboring churches including Putnam, Danielson, Eastford, East Woodstock, North Grosvenordale, East Thompson, Webster, and Attawaugan. West Thompson was included in the flood control area of the U.S. government project completed in 1965, and the few remaining members merged with the Methodists of North Grosvenordale.

R. C. Miller, *New England Southern Conference*. 1898.
                                                    DAVID CARTER

WEST VIRGINIA, U.S.A., is an eastern mountain state bounded on the north by PENNSYLVANIA and a fraction of MARYLAND, on the east and south by VIRGINIA, on the southwest by KENTUCKY, and on the northwest by OHIO. Its area is 24,181 square miles and its population is 1,793,000 (1967 estimate). West Virginia was a part of Virginia until Virginia seceded in 1861. West Virginia was admitted to the Union in 1863. The state produces thirty per cent of the nation's bituminous coal, and coal accounts for eighty per cent of its total annual income. West Virginia leads the eastern states in the production of natural gas, and it manufactures steel and iron, glass and pottery. The hilly terrain is not conducive to large scale agriculture. About sixty-five per cent of the state is in forests. The state has twenty-one institutions of higher learning.

The exact date of the beginning of Methodism in West Virginia is not known, although it was certainly not long after the movement began in America. ROBERT STRAWBRIDGE spread the seeds of Methodism over four states, and he may have been the first Methodist preacher to visit what is now West Virginia. Strawbridge raised up a number of young preachers, one of whom, RICHARD OWINGS, along with JOHN HAGERTY, is credited with having done "the first Methodist preaching" in the Shenandoah Valley. It is probable, but not certain, that these two were the first Methodists to preach in the eastern panhandle of West Virginia. Bishop ASBURY implies that there was preaching in Shepherdstown, W. Va., about 1772 when he refers in his journal for Aug. 17, 1802 to "thirty years' occasional preaching" there. Philip V. Fithian visited Berkeley Springs, W. Va. in August, 1775 and reported that "a Methodist preacher was haranguing the people." The next year Asbury was at Berkeley Springs for his health, and he did some preaching while there.

Prior to 1775 Methodist work in West Virginia was sporadic, but in 1775-76 Asbury reported in a letter to John Wesley that there was a "blessed outpouring of the Spirit in several counties bordering upon Maryland." The revival was largely the work of WILLIAM WATTERS, the first native Methodist preacher in America. In his autobiography Watters says that in Berkeley County "the work increased on every hand." FREEBORN GARRETTSON assisted in that first in-gathering. In the latter part of 1776 while on the Fairfax Circuit, "he extended his travels far up the Potomac to what was called New Virginia, where his labors were greatly successful."

As a result of the work of Watters, Garrettson, and others, the Berkeley Circuit, the first in West Virginia, was formed in May, 1778, and Edward Bailey was appointed to it.

Until about 1784 the penetration of Methodism into what was to become West Virginia was in the eastern panhandle to the base of the Allegheny Mountains. Then Methodism began to "spill over the mountains" to westward flowing waters, going into the Redstone and Greenbrier regions.

Methodism entered the north and north central portions of West Virginia by way of Pennsylvania from the old REDSTONE CIRCUIT which was formed in 1784. In 1787 the Ohio and Clarksburg Circuits were carved from the Redstone Circuit. The Ohio Circuit included the northern panhandle of West Virginia. Clarksburg was the first circuit wholly within present-day West Virginia.

The Greenbrier region, consisting of present-day Monroe, Greenbrier, and Pocahontas Counties in southeast West Virginia, was inhabited at the close of the Revolutionary War by several families who had been Methodists prior to settling there. A Methodist society was organized near Union, West Virginia late in the summer of 1784; at first it met in homes and later in a school house. REHOBOTH CHURCH, now one of the historic SHRINES of American Methodism, was completed in June, 1786. The manuscript journal of JOHN SMITH for 1787-88 tells of his trials in forming a circuit in this pioneer region.

In 1790 attempts were made to establish the Randolph and Kanawha Circuits in western West Virginia, but the region was too sparsely settled for continuous Methodist work at the time. The next appearance of Methodism in a new area was the formation of the Little Kanawha Circuit in 1799 after two local preachers, WILLIAM BEAUCHAMP and Reece Wolf, wrote letters asking for a circuit preacher. By 1803 there were seven circuits within the bounds of present West Virginia—Berkeley, Allegheny, Pendleton, Greenbrier, Ohio, Clarksburg, and Little Kanawha. The Allegheny Circuit was formed in 1783 by dividing the Berkeley Circuit, and the Pendleton Circuit was carved in 1794 from the Allegheny.

In 1803 Methodism penetrated a new region and it resulted in the formation of the Guyandotte Circuit the next year in southwest West Virginia. The first preacher assigned to the circuit was ASA SHINN, later one of the founders of the METHODIST PROTESTANT CHURCH.

During the first quarter of the nineteenth century the original circuits described above extended their bounds and subdivided to form more circuits. The new circuits, down to 1826, were: Monroe, 1805; Randolph, restored in 1806; Monongalia, 1806; New River, 1808; East Wheeling, 1810; Big Sandy, 1810; Hampshire, 1813; Harrison, 1816; South Branch, restored in 1819; Preston County, 1819-1822; Short Creek, 1819; Big Kanawha, restored in 1820; Jefferson, 1820; Middle Island, 1820; Lewis, 1821; Nicholas, 1823; Wheeling (town), 1825; Logan, 1825; and Charleston, 1825.

The M.P. Church began early in West Virginia and was relatively strong in the state. The first M.P. congregation in the state was organized in 1829 in a building that was erected in 1819 and is known as Old Harmony Church. The West Virginia work of the denomination was first attached to the Pittsburgh Conference (MP). The West Virginia Conference was created in 1854 by dividing the Pittsburgh Conference. At unification in 1939 the West Virginia Conference brought about 260 churches and some 20,000 members into the West Virginia Conference of The Methodist Church. (See West Virginia Conference (MP).)

Since West Virginia was border territory, following the division of the M.E. Church in 1844, it became a no-man's land with both the Northern and Southern branches of the church striving to occupy it. Perhaps the most controversial area was the Kanawha District to which in 1846 the OHIO CONFERENCE (ME) and the KENTUCKY CONFERENCE (MES) both made a complete list of appointments. The M.E. Church organized its WEST VIRGINIA CONFERENCE in 1848, and the M.E. Church, South formed its WESTERN VIRGINIA CONFERENCE in 1850. The preachers and laymen in the M.E. and M.P. conferences played a large part in the formation of the state of West Virginia during the Civil War. The work of the Southern Church in the state suffered during the war, but it recovered when the conflict was over and carried on until unification in 1939. In addition to the Western Virginia Conference, the Southern Church's HOLSTON CONFERENCE had work in the extreme southern edge of West Virginia, and its BALTIMORE CONFERENCE had work in the eastern panhandle of the state. The West Virginia part of the Western Virginia Conference (MES) brought nearly 45,000 members to unification in 1939, not to mention modest numbers which came from the Baltimore and Holston Conferences. The West Virginia (ME) had 89,782 members in 1939.

Before unification in 1939, no fewer than 17 annual conferences included a part, if not all, of West Virginia within their bounds. They were as follows: (1) M.E. Church conferences before the division of 1844: Baltimore, Western, Ohio, Pittsburgh, and Kentucky; (2) M.P. Church conferences: Ohio, Pittsburgh, and West Virginia; (3) M.E. Church conferences after 1844: Western Virginia (1848-1864), West Virginia, Baltimore, and Virginia; and (4) M.E. Church, South conferences: Kentucky, Western Virginia, Virginia, Baltimore, and Holston.

With such a background of varied and divided church loyalty, it was said, as Methodist unification approached, that if unification would work anywhere it would work in West Virginia. It has worked well. Though the state showed a six per cent decrease in population between 1940 and 1967, the West Virginia Conference had an increase of twenty-six per cent in membership between 1940 and 1968. About twelve per cent of the population of West Virginia were members of The Methodist Church in 1968, a higher percentage than Methodism could boast in any other state in that year. Other evidence of the success of unification is the marked growth of WEST VIRGINIA WESLEYAN COLLEGE (Buckhannon, W. Va.), the new hospital at Clarksburg, two child care centers, the home for the aging, an educational center. WESLEY FOUNDATIONS at the state institutions of higher learning, the designation of West Virginia as an episcopal area in 1960, and the reception of former CENTRAL JURISDICTION ministers and churches in the state into the West Virginia Conference in 1964.

In 1968 The Methodist Church had in West Virginia 587 charges, 200,084 members, and property valued at $87,168,520.

General Minutes, MEC and MC.
Minutes of the conferences in West Virginia.
Lawrence Sherwood, *Methodist Ministers of the West Virginia Conference.* Nashville: Methodist Publishing House, 1964.
LAWRENCE SHERWOOD

WEST VIRGINIA CONFERENCE (ME) was created by the 1848 GENERAL CONFERENCE. (It was called the Western Virginia Conference until after West Virginia was admitted to the Union in 1863.) The conference, formed by dividing the PITTSBURGH CONFERENCE, was organized at Wheeling, July 5, 1848 with Bishop LEONIDAS L. HAMLINE presiding. It began with three districts, thirty-seven charges, fifty-one preachers, and 13,899 members. This conference had more than twice as many members as the WESTERN VIRGINIA CONFERENCE (MES) which was organized two years later, and the relative strength of the two bodies continued somewhat the same until unification ninety-one years later.

For many years the West Virginia Conference was officially related to MT. UNION COLLEGE and OHIO WESLEYAN UNIVERSITY in OHIO, and ALLEGHENY COLLEGE in PENNSYLVANIA. In 1890 the conference started the co-educational school at Buckhannon which became WEST VIRGINIA WESLEYAN COLLEGE. The *Pittsburgh Christian Advocate* was the official paper for the conference.

By 1875 the membership of the West Virginia Conference had nearly doubled, and by 1900 it had doubled again. It came to unification in 1939 with five districts, 248 charges, 89,782 members, and property valued at $6,973,105.

General Minutes, MEC.
Minutes of the West Virginia Conference. ALBEA GODBOLD

WEST VIRGINIA CONFERENCE (MP) was formed by dividing the PITTSBURGH CONFERENCE, and it was organized at the session of that conference in Allegheny, Pa., Sept. 20, 1854. It was called the Western Virginia Conference until 1869. Peter T. Laishley was the first president. The conference began with twenty-four charges, fifty churches, twenty-four preachers, and 3,036 members. In the first twelve years the church membership increased thirty per cent.

The West Virginia Conference was torn by dissension when the northern and western conferences of the M.P. Church organized themselves as the "Methodist Church" in 1866. About one-fifth of the ministers and churches of the West Virginia Conference withdrew and were received into the Pittsburgh Conference which allied itself with the "Methodist Church". At the same time two circuits of the Muskingum Conference in OHIO withdrew and were received in the West Virginia Conference because they wished to remain in the Methodist Protestant Church. Following the reunion of the M.P. Church and the "Methodist Church" in 1877, conference boundaries were readjusted, and in 1878 the West Virginia Conference reported thirty-three charges and 8,571 members.

J. A. Selby, president of the West Virginia Conference in 1917, reported that in the 1880's "we began to see how great was our loss every year because so few of our towns and cities were occupied, [and] we began to make arrangements to remedy this defect." He then named ten

West Virginia cities and towns in which M.P. churches had been built, noted that more than one-third of the charges in the conference had been organized in the preceding thirty years, and pointed out that the total church membership of the conference had increased by one-third in that time.

As it came to unification in 1939, the West Virginia Conference (MP) reported seventy-three churches, seventy-six ministers, 19,454 members, and churches and parsonages valued at $1,304,050.

I. A. Barnes, *The Methodist Protestant Church in West Virginia.* Baltimore: Stockton Press, 1926.
Minutes of the West Virginia Conference.
Yearbook of the Methodist Protestant Church, 1918.
ALBEA GODBOLD

WEST VIRGINIA CONFERENCE (EUB) was originally part of the VIRGINIA CONFERENCE. In 1836 Jacob Rinehart, presiding elder of the Virginia Conference, and Moses Michael were sent by the conference across the Allegheny Mountains to the western part of VIRGINIA. On Aug. 20, 1836, in a little log church owned by the Lutherans about two miles from the Ohio River in Mason County, they organized the first UNITED BRETHREN class in this territory. This class is now known as the Union appointment. The first church building erected was the Sand Hill Church near Point Pleasant, Mason County, dedicated in 1847.

In 1840 a colony of Germans, members of OTTERBEIN'S CHURCH in BALTIMORE, Md., came to Braxton County, near the center of what is now WEST VIRGINIA, with Daniel Engle, a licensed preacher; and in 1841 they established a class on Steer Creek, Braxton County, later known as the Otterbein appointment. In 1846 Benjamin Stickley, the mountain evangelist, was sent by the Virginia Conference to Lewis Mission, a circuit covering 300 miles in Lewis, Braxton, Barbour, Gilmer, and Upshur Counties.

In the years following 1836 many new churches were established. Because of the problems of travel over the mountains, the Virginia Conference found it difficult to serve this section. The GENERAL CONFERENCE of 1857 agreed to incorporate the part of Virginia west of the mountains into a new Mission Conference to be called the Parkersburg Conference. The first session of this new conference was held at Centerville, in Tyler County, March 4, 1858, with Bishop J. J. GLOSSBRENNER presiding. There were eleven charter members. In 1863 the State of West Virginia was formed from the western part of the State of Virginia, thus placing all of the churches of the new conference in the State of West Virginia. Later Garrett County, Md., was added to this conference. In 1897 the name of the conference was changed to the West Virginia Conference.

Among the early pioneers of the Virginia Conference who crossed the mountains and helped to establish the work in this section were Jacob Bachtel, Zebedee Warner, J. W. Perry, J. W. Miles, H. R. Davis, Levi Hess, J. T. Hensley, Eli Martin, Samuel Martin, and G. W. Statton.

Bishop W. M. WEEKLEY was born within five miles of the spot where the West Virginia Conference was organized and served as an itinerant presiding elder in the conference for twenty years.

In 1967 there were ninety-six charges and 245 churches in the conference, with ninety-eight ordained ministers, twenty-two probationers, twenty-one lay preachers and sixteen ministerial students. The membership was 24,472; the total value of local church property, $7,045,959.

In 1965 the West Virginia Conference cooperated with the denomination in a program of assistance to Appalachia. The Heart and Hand House in Philippi and a branch in South Charleston were under the direction of the denominational Board of Missions.

The West Virginia Conference included all of the state of West Virginia except eight counties of the eastern panhandle. It also included Garrett County, Maryland.

In 1969, the conference united with the West Virginia Conference of the former Methodist Church, retaining the name common to both.

D. Berger, *History of U.B.* 1897.
C. H. Cox, "History of West Virginia Conference." Ms.
A. W. Drury, *History of the U.B.* 1924.
A. P. Funkhouser, *The History of the Church of the United Brethren in Christ, Virginia Conference.* 1921.
T. C. Parsons, *Sketches of History of the West Virginia Conference.* 1934.
Z. Warner, *Life and Labors of Jacob Bachtel.* United Brethren Publishing House, 1868.
W. M. Weekley, *Twenty Years.* 1924.
West Virginia Conference *Journals,* 1858-1967.

KENNETH J. SCOTT

WEST VIRGINIA CONFERENCE (MC) was organized at Fairmont on Sept. 8, 1939 with Bishop ADNA W. LEONARD presiding. The conference was formed by merging at unification the WEST VIRGINIA CONFERENCE (ME) with 90,000 members, a part of the WESTERN VIRGINIA CONFERENCE (MES) representing about 44,000 members, the WEST VIRGINIA CONFERENCE (MP) with 20,000 members, and small West Virginia segments of several other conferences. The territory of the West Virginia Conference at the beginning was the state of West Virginia, except three counties in the eastern panhandle and two in the northern panhandle which were assigned to the BALTIMORE and PITTSBURGH CONFERENCES, respectively. At the same time the West Virginia Conference included a part of Garrett County, Maryland. In 1940 the conference reported thirteen districts, 472 charges, 154,178 members, and property valued at $13,164,939.

No other conference (save the Baltimore) began unification with such a large admixture of members from the three uniting churches as did the West Virginia Conference. Unification proved helpful to Methodism in West Virginia. Between 1940 and 1968 there was a substantial increase in the membership of The Methodist Church notwithstanding a slight decrease in the population of the state during the same period. (See WEST VIRGINIA.)

At its 1940 session the West Virginia Conference noted that it was the largest in the Northeastern Jurisdiction and that it had no home or hospital though there was need for both in its territory. By 1950 the conference had established at Burlington, W. Va., the Children's Home. By 1955 the Union Protestant Hospital at Clarksburg was under way. The Beckley Child Care Center was established in 1962, and the next year the Glenwood Park Home for the Aged in Mercer County had begun.

The West Virginia Conference received MORRIS HARVEY COLLEGE at Barboursville (founded 1888) from the former Western Virginia Conference (MES) and WEST VIRGINIA WESLEYAN COLLEGE at Buckhannon (founded 1890) from the West Virginia Conference (ME). West Virginia Wesleyan now has an endowment of about

$1,500,000, a plant valued at nearly $7,000,000, and some 1,700 students. Morris Harvey College moved to Charleston in 1935 and became an independent institution in 1942. The conference maintains three WESLEY FOUNDATIONS at state institutions of higher learning, and has campus ministries at seven other schools. The conference owns one camp called Spring Hill Education Center.

In 1968 the West Virginia Conference reported eleven districts, 572 charges, 482 ministers, 194,452 members, property valued at $84,703,930, and a total of $10,048,780 raised for all purposes during the year.

General Minutes, MEC, MECS, and MC.
Minutes of the West Virginia Conference.
Lawrence Sherwood, *Methodist Ministers of the West Virginia Conference.* Nashville: Methodist Publishing House, 1964.

LAWRENCE SHERWOOD

WESLEY STATUE AT WEST VIRGINIA WESLEYAN

WEST VIRGINIA WESLEYAN COLLEGE, Buckhannon, West Virginia, was established as West Virginia Conference Seminary in 1890 by the M.E. Church. In 1904 the school attained college status, and the name was changed to West Virginia Wesleyan. When unification of the three branches of Methodism was completed, the West Virginia Conference had two colleges—MORRIS HARVEY and West Virginia Wesleyan. The UNIVERSITY SENATE recommended that the conference concentrate its interest upon West Virginia Wesleyan. Morris Harvey became an independent private college at Charleston, and West Virginia Wesleyan the sole college in the state owned by The Methodist Church.

At that time, as the nation was emerging from the depression years of the 1930's, both schools were struggling to survive. In 1939, West Virginia Wesleyan's total resources were listed at $674,509 and its indebtedness $209,674. Morris Harvey's resources were $303,220 and its indebtedness $33,065. Unification opened the way for West Virginia Wesleyan to increase its ability to draw students from the North Central JURISDICTION, and since then the enrollment has tripled. It was one of the first schools in the South to admit Negroes. In 1955 it enrolled more preministerial students than any other Methodist college in America. It offers the B.A., B.S., and B.M.E (Music Education). The governing board has forty members plus three ex officio, elected by the WEST VIRGINIA CONFERENCE; half of the board are laymen and half are ministers.

JOHN O. GROSS

WEST WISCONSIN CONFERENCE (ME) was organized at Madison, Wis., Aug. 20, 1856 with Bishop MATTHEW SIMPSON presiding. The conference was formed by dividing the Wisconsin Conference. (See WISCONSIN for beginnings of Methodism in the state.) Its territory was southwest Wisconsin; the northwestern part of the state was placed in the MINNESOTA CONFERENCE which was also created in 1856. Four years later the Northwest Wisconsin Conference was formed, but after eight years it was absorbed by the West Wisconsin Conference which then included the west half of the state. After 1868 there was little or no change in the boundaries of the West Wisconsin Conference.

The West Wisconsin Conference began in 1856 with five districts—Portage City, Madison, Platteville, Prairie du Chien, and La Crosse—sixty charges, and 5,962 members. After absorbing the Northwest Wisconsin Conference in 1868, it had 10,514 members. By 1900 the membership had grown to 20,763 and by 1939 to 38,633.

Realizing that they and the people needed learning, the pioneer circuit riders helped to provide and back up such attempts as Foster Institute, later known as Brunson, Mineral Point Seminary, Mount Hope, Tomah, and Kilbourn Institutes, Galesville Institute, later called University, and LAWRENCE UNIVERSITY. Youth camps were conducted from the early days. Summer camps were held on the Platteville Campgrounds, and there were camps at Wonewoc, Lake Chetek, and Lacrossette. In later years better sites were purchased at Pine Lake (1948), and Whispering Pines (1953).

In 1917 the Morrow Memorial Home for the Aged was dedicated at Sparta. The conference now has also the Schmitt Methodist Home at Richland Center. The Methodist Hospital was established at Madison in 1919, and later the Lakeside Methodist Hospital at Rice Lake. These four institutions continue to serve. Hospitals started at Richland Center and La Crosse have been given up.

The name of the WOMAN'S FOREIGN MISSIONARY SOCIETY appeared in the 1870 conference journal, and the WOMAN'S HOME MISSIONARY SOCIETY was organized in 1884. In 1968 the WOMEN'S SOCIETY OF CHRISTIAN SERVICE reported 11,120 members and $163,262 paid for local work.

In 1968 the West Wisconsin Conference reported 128 charges, 143 ministers, 53,172 members, property valued at $20,866,575, and a total of $3,008,422 raised for all purposes during the year.

P. S. Bennett, *History of Methodism in Wisconsin.* Cincinnati: Cranston & Stowe, 1890.
General Minutes, MEC and MC.
Minutes of the West Wisconsin Conference.   ALBEA GODBOLD

WESTELL, THOMAS (c. 1719-1794), British Methodist, a carpenter of BRISTOL, was one of the first four whom WESLEY joined in society there in April, 1739. Westell became the third of Wesley's assistants, traveling spasmodically as a "half-itinerant" in Cornwall (1769) and Sussex (1776), but usually living in Bristol. A memorial to him is found in Portland Chapel, where he was buried on April 24, 1794.

C. Atmore, *Methodist Memorial.* 1801.   JOHN A. VICKERS

WESTERN AUSTRALIA CONFERENCE began officially in 1840 as a missionary outpost under the control of the WESLEYAN MISSIONARY SOCIETY in England. It remained under the sole leadership of JOHN SMITHIES for twelve years when a second missionary was appointed. In 1855 the first Conference of the Australasian Wesleyan Methodist Church was held in SYDNEY and it took over the direction of the Church in Western AUSTRALIA. In 1866 the first meeting of ministers and laymen was held in Western Australia to discuss administrative problems and this became an annual meeting until 1873, when four Annual Conferences were established in Australia, NEW SOUTH WALES, VICTORIA, SOUTH AUSTRALIA and NEW ZEALAND. Western Australia then became a District under the control of the South Australia Conference and the Superintendent Minister of Wesley Church, PERTH, became the Chairman of that District.

The Wesleyans were the only Methodists to really establish themselves in the Colony and union presented no real problems. When it was consummated in 1897, some years earlier than in most of the other Australian States, there was only one PRIMITIVE METHODIST minister in the Colony and one BIBLE CHRISTIAN minister.

The growth of the Colony was painfully slow until the discovery of gold in the 1890's and the growth of the Wesleyan Methodist Church reflected that pattern. However, by 1900 it was ready to manage its own affairs. In that year the Western Australia Conference was established with three Districts. In 1965 there were six Districts with seventy-five ministers and probationers, four deaconesses and thirteen home missionaries. There were, in addition, four ministers working in the northern parts of the State under the Methodist Federal Inland Mission Board and a mission to the aborigines at Mogumber under the control of the Overseas Mission Board. The conference has Departments of Home Missions, and of Christian Education, both with full-time Directors, and a Department of Christian Citizenship and a State Secretary for Overseas Missions. The Conference now trains its own ministers at the Barclay Theological Hall which is part of KINGSWOOD COLLEGE, the Methodist residential College in the University of Western Australia. The 1965 membership returns revealed that there were 145 churches, 7,665 under instruction and 6,375 adherents in the State.

Aborigines in Western Australia. The Aborigines of Western Australia were from the beginning of the Colony the deep concern of the Wesleyan Missionary Society and when it sent out John Smithies to commence work in the Colony in 1840 he was expressly charged with responsibility for their evangelization and welfare. Immediately after his arrival he met the Government Superintendent of Aborigines and Interpreter, a Wesleyan layman named Francis Armstrong, and sought his assistance in establishing a native school in Perth. Later this was transferred to Wanneroo a few miles to the northwest of Perth where a mission station was established on land granted by the Government. This came to be considered the most successful mission in the Colony. In 1853 it was moved to more arable land at York in the Avon Valley. The move proved to be disastrous and within three years the mission was closed.

It was not until 1951 that the Methodist Church of Western Australia took up this work again. In that year it assumed responsibility, through the Overseas Mission Board, for a native settlement at Mogumber, on the Moore River, which had been conducted by the Department of Native Affairs.

After its failure to establish an Aboriginal settlement at Moore River, the Western Australian government approached the Methodist Church with the offer of the whole settlement, consisting of over 12,000 acres worth £100,000 with a yearly subsidy to assist its educational and agricultural work. There were only four old men and four small children left at the settlement, although it was estimated that there were 30,000 full-blood and part-Aborigines in the state. In the next five years the Board of Missions spent nearly $200,000 on developing the mission. The number of natives on the mission has steadily grown, the standard of education improved, the farm developed and a new sense of security and hope has come to the Aborigines.

In 1966 Mogumber became a training center. The emphasis is now placed on preparing the Aborigines to take their place as citizens in society. The chief architect of this progress, E. A. Clark, was subsequently decorated by the Queen for his outstanding work. Situated ninety miles from Perth, the area was slowly transformed and brought under cultivation. Children's homes have been built and staffed by missionary cottage mothers, caring for up to ten children, neglected, deserted or orphaned in Perth or surrounding areas. Up to 100 children altogether call Mogumber home, from babies to teenagers; they receive medical attention, schooling, domestic training and the opportunity to grow in a Christian home. An agriculture school trains boys to a standard where they are acceptable for employment on neighboring farms and high school opportunities are available for bright students. The agricultural school is now controlled by the Education Department while the mission is particularly responsible for the family, social and spiritual welfare of the children.

Methodism and the Goldfields. Gold was discovered in the north of Western Australia in 1886 and later in the east. In each case there was a tremendous desert barrier to be breached but despite that towns and cities grew up rapidly on the mines far beyond the reach of either road or railroad. One of the mining engineers living in an iron hut 100 miles north of Kalgoorlie was a young man named Herbert Hoover, later destined to live at the White House, Washington. The church was ill equipped to meet this situation. It was lamentably short of trained ministers and the church coffers were empty. It rose to the occasion, however, and soon its ministers and agents had penetrated to the furthest fields travelling on horseback, camel, bicycles and even on foot. Methodism flourished on the mining fields. The adventurous and freedom loving miners were attracted by the evangelical zeal of the Methodist preachers and the freedom of worship which they encouraged. In ten years the population of the State trebled and the membership of the Methodist Church grew fourfold. The number of Methodist

ministers in the Colony grew from eight to thirty and there were seventeen home missionaries in the fields as well. Forty-seven percent of the increased membership came from the goldfields and nearly half of the total ministerial force was stationed there.

The New Wheat-Belt Area presented the Church with a new problem and a new opportunity. As alluvial gold mining petered out and was replaced by deep mining hundreds of miners were forced to leave the goldfields. Almost overnight Methodism was faced with the challenge of a new frontier. Ministers released from the goldfields were transferred to the new wheat growing areas adjacent to the Eastern Goldfields Railway. In 1903 the Conference established the Great Southern Mission to cope with a similar problem which was developing in the South. New settlers were taking up land along the Great Southern Railway which linked Perth and Albany and which had been opened in 1889, and ministers and missionaries moved in with them. They had often to travel great distances and were called upon to conduct services in coffee palaces and pubs, private homes, schools or hay sheds. Towns sprang up quickly along the line and churches were built. This was a period of great progress for the church, perhaps its period of greatest growth. In twenty years the number of Methodist churches in the State nearly doubled and the church deployed over one-third of its work force over the wheat-belt area to cope with the demands of the expanding frontier.

As stated above, organizational work began in 1903, when T. Allen was secretary for Home Missions. He organized the appointments to Narrogin (Harley J. Morrell) and Katanning (T. Pollard James). In 1911 the Conference set A. J. BARCLAY apart to work as General Superintendent of Home Missions. He recruited men from Eastern Australia and England, demonstrating a capacity to read the prospects and possible population movements. In his term of office, many areas were under the pastoral care of the Methodist Church so effectively as to be the main circuits of the present Conference.

Industrial Development. The next phase of Western Australian development came after the 1939-45 war. When big complexes were established at Kwinana and elsewhere around Perth, the population increased from 490,000 to 825,000 in the years 1945-1965.

The Methodist denomination was charged with the responsibility of matching the resources of the Church with this growth. It was a question of finding men and buildings in areas that had been only bush.

This was successfully done in many areas, while in other such Timber Mill towns there was little success.

More recently L. L. Semple has led a move to minister to the rapidly growing industrial complexes in the North-West. This has happened because of the iron ore mining explosion which makes Western Australia the key state in Australia's future industrial progress. Statistics for the Western Australian Conference as of May 1969, are as follows: 63 active ministers, 145 churches, and 7,898 members.

J. Colwell, *Century in the Pacific*. 1914.
————. *Illustrated History*. 1904.
AUSTRALIAN EDITORIAL COMMITTEE

WESTERN CHRISTIAN RECORDER. A publication of the African Methodist Episcopal Church. (See AFRICAN METHODIST EPISCOPAL CHURCH, Publications.)

WESTERN CONFERENCE, the original conference in what was then called the west, was created by the GENERAL CONFERENCE at BALTIMORE in October 1796. At the beginning the territory of the Western Conference was somewhat indefinitely referred to as KENTUCKY and TENNESSEE. In 1804, however, it included "OHIO and the part of VIRGINIA which lies west of the great River Kanawha, with the ILLINOIS, and the NATCHEZ (circuits)." This vast region today has about twenty annual conferences, and in the past when conferences were smaller, it included even more.

Bishop ASBURY conducted conferences of preachers in Kentucky and Tennessee before the territory was formally designated as the Western Conference. He held a conference at Masterson's Station near LEXINGTON, Ky., April 15-16, 1790, stationing twelve preachers on six circuits, with FRANCIS POYTHRESS as PRESIDING ELDER. Five of the circuits were in Kentucky, and one, the Cumberland, was in Tennessee. Apparently there was no conference in the region in 1791, but in 1792 and again in 1793 Asbury met with the preachers at Masterson's. A conference was conducted at Lewis' Chapel near BETHEL ACADEMY in 1794, but Asbury missed it because of illness. In 1795 he met the preachers at Ebenezer in Greene County, Tenn., and in the spring of 1796 once again at Masterson's in Kentucky.

The 1796 General Conference divided the M.E. Church into six annual conferences with geographical boundaries. One of the six was the Western Conference which included "the states of Kentucky and Tennessee." In view of the General Conference action of 1796, one would expect the 1797 meeting of the Kentucky and Tennessee preachers to be called the Western Conference. But as a matter of fact the conference in that region was not referred to in the *General Minutes* as the Western Conference until 1802. Presumably Bishop Asbury was responsible for the failure to call the Western Conference by its proper name for six years.

Asbury did not attend the first session of the Western Conference which was held at Bethel Academy beginning May 1, 1797, but he sent a plan for stationing the preachers. That year the conference reported six charges in Kentucky and two in Tennessee with a total of 2,274 white and ninety colored members.

The Western Conference showed no appreciable growth from 1796 to 1800, a matter of real concern to Asbury. In 1797 he replaced Francis Poythress with JOHN KOBLER as presiding elder. Then in 1800 he moved most of the preachers to other conferences and brought in WILLIAM McKENDREE from VIRGINIA as presiding elder. Placing McKendree in charge of the Western Conference was one of the best and most strategic appointments Asbury ever made. McKendree had a remarkable capacity to lead in the work and to infuse the preachers with his own consecrated and aggressive spirit. He formed new circuits and found or developed preachers to man them. He soon extended the work of the Western Conference into Illinois, OHIO, MISSOURI, and other areas. In 1803 the conference reported three districts, fifteen charges, and 3,985 white and 186 colored members. Five years later, when the General Conference overwhelmingly elected McKendree a bishop, the Western Conference had five districts, thirty-six charges and some 16,000 members. In 1812 the Western Conference under that name disappeared, its territory being divided to form the OHIO

and TENNESSEE CONFERENCES. In its last year the Western Conference reported eight districts, sixty-nine charges, and 30,782 members.

W. E. Arnold, *Kentucky.* 1935-36.
General Minutes. N. B. H.

WESTERN CONFERENCE (MES) was organized by the GENERAL CONFERENCE of the Southern Church in 1870, and held its first session at Leavenworth, Kan., on September 8 of that year. Bishop McTYEIRE presided. It was organized out of those Methodists who adhered to the M.E. Church, South, or were in sympathy with the South, and who wished to be connected with that Church following the Civil War which had ended six years before. There were twenty-five traveling and eleven local preachers, 1,538 white, 133 colored, and thirty-seven Indian members reporting at the organizational meeting. The next General Conference—1874—defined the Western Conference so as to "include the states of KANSAS, NEBRASKA, and the territories of WYOMING and IDAHO and other territories east of the Rocky Mountains and West of the MISSOURI state line not included in other Conferences." With the growth of the Church, South, and of the M.E. Church, Annual Conferences in these states and territories were in due time organized. In 1890 the Western Conference was made to include "the states of Kansas and Nebraska." By that time other regions originally covered had been put into other Conferences. In 1906 the Western Conference was placed into the SOUTHWEST MISSOURI CONFERENCE.

Discipline, MES, 1870, 1874.
P. A. Peterson, *Revisions of the Discipline.* 1889. N. B. H.

WESTERN MARYLAND COLLEGE, Westminster, Maryland, opened in 1867 and was chartered in 1868 by the MARYLAND CONFERENCE as an institution of the METHODIST PROTESTANT CHURCH. Since Unification in 1939, Baltimore and Peninsula annual conferences have supported the college through their conference-wide budgets. Western Maryland College, along with other privately supported and church-related colleges in MARYLAND, has received scholarship grants from the state for students of Maryland preparing to teach in its public schools. Maryland has also made a grant toward the erection of a building. It is the only state to utilize and finance educational resources of private colleges and universities not directly under state control.

Degrees offered are the B.A., B.S., and M.Ed. (Education). The governing board is a self-perpetuating body, with all members elected for life or until resignation; one third plus one must be United Methodist ministers.

JOHN O. GROSS

WESTERN NEW YORK CONFERENCE superseded the GENESEE CONFERENCE. On June 5, 1964 the Genesee Conference voted to become the Western New York Conference, effective July 1, 1964, subject to the approval of the NORTHEASTERN JURISDICTIONAL CONFERENCE. Conference leaders pointed out that the new name would enable outsiders to understand more readily the geographical location of the conference, and it would obviate the error of printing "Tennessee" for "Genesee" in the GENERAL CONFERENCE *Daily Christian Advocate.* The

Jurisdictional Conference approved the change of name on June 25, 1964.

The first session of the Western New York Conference was held at Jamestown, N. Y., June 9-13, 1965 with Bishop W. RALPH WARD, JR. presiding. The conference began with five districts, 221 charges, 255 ministers, 83,-281 members, and property valued at $44,549,862. Its territory is western NEW YORK. It should be noted that the same region, though not with exactly the same boundaries, was designated as the Western New York Conference (ME) from 1872 to 1876.

The Genesee Conference (ME) had been formed in 1810 by Bishops ASBURY and McKENDREE in accordance with discretionary authority granted them by the 1808 General Conference. When created the Genesee Conference embraced territory taken from both the NEW YORK and PHILADELPHIA CONFERENCES—the Cayuga and Upper Canada Districts from the former, and the Susquehanna District from the latter. Thus at the outset the new conference included western New York, a part of PENNSYLVANIA, and a part of CANADA. Named for the Genesee River, the conference was organized at Lyons, N. Y., July 20, 1810 with Bishop McKendree presiding. At the beginning the conference had sixty-three preachers, twenty-eight charges, and 10,693 members.

The difficulties and tensions during and following the War of 1812, with England—and Canada—resulted in 1824 in the division of the Genesee Conference to form the CANADA CONFERENCE. Then in 1828 the General Conference authorized the bishops to divide the Genesee Conference again if it approved. The division was made in 1829, thereby forming the ONEIDA CONFERENCE with some 19,000 members and leaving about 13,000 in the Genesee Conference. In 1848 the EAST GENESEE CONFERENCE was carved from the Genesee body. The new conference had about 16,500 members, while some 10,500 remained in the Genesee Conference.

The 1872 General Conference consolidated the five conferences of central and western New York into four. In the process the East Genesee Conference disappeared; its territory was divided between the CENTRAL NEW YORK and the Genesee Conferences. As suggested above, the name of the enlarged Genesee Conference was then changed to Western New York, but in 1876 it reverted to Genesee. (See NEW YORK.) The new Genesee Conference embraced most of western New York and a small part of Pennsylvania, and it began with 29,116 members. In 1880 a part of the Genesee Conference territory was assigned to the Central New York Conference, thereby reducing the membership of the former to about 23,380. After 1880 there were no important changes in the boundaries of the Genesee Conference until 1962 when it gave up its work in Pennsylvania in exchange for the part of the ERIE CONFERENCE that extended into New York.

The Genesee Conference came to unification in 1939 with four districts, 259 charges, 63,752 members, and property valued at $10,195,012. The conference received a few ministers and churches from the Onandaga Conference of the Methodist Protestant Church at that time. The 1932 General Conference assigned the Negro work in Buffalo to the Genesee Conference, and that arrangement continued after unification in 1939.

For many years in the nineteenth century the Genesee Conference maintained or was related to a number of schools. The most important was the Genesee Wesleyan Seminary at Lima, New York, which opened in 1832,

was a strong and influential academy for a century, struggled for survival for the next 20 years, and finally expired in 1951 while trying to become a viable junior college. The conference now supports SYRACUSE UNIVERSITY. In 1968 the conference contributed over $70,000 for Christian higher education, much of it being used in an ecumenical approach to ministry to students in state supported schools.

The summer program at CHAUTAUQUA (see Chatauqua Institution) began in 1874 and continues with an average attendance of 50,000 each year. Within its boundaries the conference has Beechwood Retirement Homes owned and operated by the Niagara Frontier Methodist Homes, Inc., the Rochester Methodist Home, and three youth camps. The conference joins other conferences of the area in supporting the Folts Home in Herkimer, and the Gateway Methodist Home for Children.

In 1970 the Western New York Conference reported five districts, 227 charges, 310 ministers, 82,336 members, property valued at $56,067,338 and a total of $7,498,146 raised for all purposes during the year.

F. W. Conable, *History of the Genesee Annual Conference.* New York: Nelson and Phillips, 1876.
General Minutes, MEC and MC.
Minutes of the Genesee Conference.
Minutes of the Western New York Conference.

ALBEA GODBOLD

WESTERN NORWEGIAN-DANISH CONFERENCE (ME) grew out of mission work among Norwegian and Danish immigrants on the west coast. In 1878 CARL J. LARSEN, a wood carver, began a CLASS MEETING composed of Scandinavian people in his own home in Oakland, Calif. Larsen had been converted at a Norwegian-Danish Methodist church in CHICAGO. Soon Larsen's home was too small for the class meeting, and a Seventh Day Adventist church was rented for the gatherings. In 1880 Larsen and his group erected a church costing $1,100 at Market and 24th Streets, Oakland, the first Scandinavian Methodist Episcopal Church on the Pacific coast. Larsen then joined the CALIFORNIA CONFERENCE and gave full time to the ministry. Serving as a missionary among the Norwegians and Danes, Larsen transferred successively to other conferences and succeeded in organizing churches at PORTLAND, SEATTLE, TACOMA, and Spokane, and at Moscow, Idaho, and Kalispel, Butte, and Helena, Montana.

Until 1888 all Norwegian-Danish churches were linked with the English-speaking conferences, but in that year the Northwest Norwegian-Danish Mission was organized at Moscow, Idaho, with fourteen charges in WASHINGTON, OREGON, and IDAHO. The next year the mission reported 282 members. In 1892 the name was changed to Western Norwegian-Danish Mission, and in 1895 it became the Western Norwegian-Danish Conference. Its territory included CALIFORNIA, Oregon, Washington, Idaho, MONTANA, and UTAH. The organizing session was held at Astoria, Ore., on Sept. 19, 1895 with Bishop THOMAS BOWMAN presiding. The conference began with five districts, California, Montana, Oregon, Utah, and Washington; and thirty-three charges. Ten of the charges were in Washington. There were 621 members.

The Western Norwegian-Danish Conference continued until unification in 1939 when it was absorbed by the overlying English-speaking conferences. Various factors, including reduced Scandinavian immigration, caused its demise. The conference was never large, but the good it did cannot be fully measured by statistics. In its last year it had two districts, California and Pacific Northwest, and thirteen charges, thirty-five preaching places, twenty ministers, 1,323 members, and property valued at $307, 500.

General Minutes, MEC.
M. T. Larson, ed., *Memorial Journal of Western Norwegian-Danish Methodism*, 1944. F. E. MASER

WESTERN NORTH CAROLINA CONFERENCE was organized at Concord, Nov. 26, 1890 with Bishop JOHN C. KEENER presiding. It was formed by merging parts of the NORTH CAROLINA and HOLSTON CONFERENCES. Its territory included all of NORTH CAROLINA west of a north and south line a little east of CHARLOTTE and GREENSBORO. The new conference included most of the piedmont and all of the mountain section of the state, areas that were destined to grow in population because of industrialization and tourism. The conference began with nine districts, 134 charges, 56,232 members, and property valued at $678,380. At the beginning there were two Methodist colleges within the bounds of the conference, GREENSBORO COLLEGE for women, and Trinity College (later DUKE) which was then located near HIGH POINT. The conference grew steadily. In 1910 there were eleven districts, 227 charges, and 91,960 members. In addition to Trinity College which had moved to DURHAM, the conference then supported four colleges within its bounds, DAVENPORT, Greensboro, Rutherford, and WEAVERVILLE. By 1925 the conference had 294 charges, and 136,302 members. It came to unification in 1939 with nine districts, 310 charges, 167,110 members, and churches and parsonages valued at $14,768,373.

Following unification the Western North Carolina Conference of The Methodist Church was organized at Greensboro, Oct. 21, 1939 with Bishop CLARE PURCELL presiding. The boundaries of the conference remained the same after unification. But due to its own growth and to receiving some ministers and churches from both the BLUE RIDGE-ATLANTIC CONFERENCE (ME), and the NORTH CAROLINA CONFERENCE (MP), the Western North Carolina Conference immediately provided for two new districts, and in 1941 its membership had risen to 181,950.

Several church papers were being published in North Carolina when the Western North Carolina Conference began in 1890. Within a few years, however, only two remained, the *North Carolina Christian Advocate* at Greensboro and the *Raleigh Christian Advocate*, each serving its respective annual conference. In 1919 the two were consolidated under the name of the *North Carolina Christian Advocate* published at Greensboro, which since that time has been one of the strongest conference and area organs in the church.

The Western North Carolina Conference supports the Methodist Children's Home at WINSTON-SALEM; and the Methodist Home for the Aged at CHARLOTTE. The plant at Charlotte is valued at $5,000,000, and it has about 500 residents, some of whom are cared for without charge. In 1968 the conference contributed to its homes for children and the aged $477,673. The conference supports GOODWILL INDUSTRIES and Bethlehem Houses at Charlotte and Winston-Salem, as well as seven WESLEY FOUNDATIONS at state institutions of higher learning. The LAKE JUNALUSKA ASSEMBLY, owned by the SOUTHEASTERN JURISDICTION, and the Brooks-Howell Home for retired missionaries and deaconesses at ASHEVILLE, owned by the Women's Division of the BOARD OF MISSIONS, are within the bounds of the conference.

Four members of the Western North Carolina Conference have been elected bishops, JAMES ATKINS (1906), W. WALTER PEELE (1938), PAUL N. GARBER (1944), and W. KENNETH GOODSON (1964).

In 1968 the NORTH CAROLINA-VIRGINIA CONFERENCE (CJ) was merged with the overlying conferences of the Southeastern Jurisdiction, and the Western North Carolina Conference received from that body forty-eight charges, 102 churches, thirty-six ministers, and 10,398 members.

The Western North Carolina Conference owns BREVARD COLLEGE, and it shares the ownership of Greensboro and High Point Colleges with the North Carolina Conference. Two colleges within the bounds of the conference, BENNETT and PFEIFFER, are related to both the General BOARD OF EDUCATION and the Board of Missions as well as to the conference. The conference is related to Duke University, and makes an annual contribution to the DUKE DIVINITY SCHOOL. In 1968 the Western North Carolina Conference raised for its colleges and Wesley Foundations $780,531.

Measured by church membership, the Western North Carolina Conference was the second largest conference in the M.E. Church, South prior to 1939. It continued as one of the strongest conferences in The Methodist Church. In 1970 in The United Methodist Church the conference reported fourteen districts, 687 charges, 961 ministers, 283,005 members, and property valued at $174,721,064. It raised for all purposes that year $24,196,584.

E. T. Clark, *Western North Carolina*. 1966.
General Minutes, MES, TMC, UMC.
Minutes of the Western North Carolina Conference.

ALBEA GODBOLD

WESTERN PENNSYLVANIA CONFERENCE was organized at Grove City, Pa., June 20, 1962 with Bishop W. VERNON MIDDLETON presiding. It was formed by merging the PITTSBURGH and ERIE CONFERENCES. As its name indicates, its territory includes western PENNSYLVANIA. After boundaries were adjusted and transfers were made the new conference reported in 1963, 10 districts, 782 churches, and 233,452 members.

Since the Erie Conference was carved out of the Pittsburgh Conference in 1836, the merger of the two to form the Western Pennsylvania Conference was in a sense a return to the *status quo ante*. However, with some 41,000 members before it was divided in 1836, the original Pittsburgh Conference was only a little more than one-sixth as strong numerically as the newly formed Western Pennsylvania Conference in 1962.

The 1960 NORTHEASTERN JURISDICTIONAL CONFERENCE readjusted the boundaries of a number of conferences to make them conform as nearly as possible to state lines. This action was preliminary to the merger of the Pittsburgh and Erie Conferences. In 1962 the Jamestown District (N. Y.) of the Erie Conference went to the GENESEE CONFERENCE, while the Genesee Conference appointments in Pennsylvania were incorporated in the Western Pennsylvania Conference, and the Pittsburgh Conference churches in the northern panhandle of WEST VIRGINIA were given to the WEST VIRGINIA CONFERENCE.

The Western Pennsylvania Conference has ALLEGHENY COLLEGE at Meadville, and it has representation on the boards of trustees of MOUNT UNION COLLEGE and WEST VIRGINIA WESLEYAN. It maintains WESLEY FOUNDATIONS at Penn State, the University of Pittsburgh, and the state colleges at Edinboro and Indiana, Pennsylvania. The conference owns the Robert Boyd Ward Home for Children at Pittsburgh, and it is related to the following institutions: the Elizabeth A. Bradley Children's Home, Oakmont; the Ruth M. Smith Children's Home, Sheffield; and the Zoar Home for Girls, Allison Park. The conference supports three homes for the aged: the Methodist Home for the Aged, Meadville; the Methodist Home, Pittsburgh; and Arbutus Manor, Johnstown, which was projected in 1967.

In 1968 the Western Pennsylvania Conference reported 10 districts, 529 ministers, 519 pastoral charges, 226,876 members, and property valued at $138,361,727.

General Minutes, MC.
Minutes of the Western Pennsylvania Conference.

W. GUY SMELTZER

WESTERN PENNSYLVANIA CONFERENCE (EUB) covered the western third of the State of PENNSYLVANIA. Its northern boundary was an arc encompassing the lower two-thirds of the region and touching Greenville, Oil City, Clearfield, and Tyrone. The eastern boundary rested in the valley east of the Allegheny Mountains. With the exception of Ellerslie, MARYLAND, the southern and western boundaries followed the state line. The Conference was formed in 1951 through the merger of the Allegheny Conference of the former UNITED BRETHREN CHURCH and the Pittsburgh Conference of the former EVANGELICAL CHURCH.

The United Brethren witness began in 1795, when CHRISTIAN NEWCOMER conducted a preaching tour which brought him into the region. Beginning in 1800, these preaching places were under the supervision of the Original (Hagerstown) Conference. When the Original Conference was divided in 1830, the circuits were under the supervision of the Pennsylvania Conference. Continued growth caused the formation of the Allegheny Conference in 1838.

The first class was organized by the Evangelicals in 1806. From the beginning, the work was supervised by the Eastern Conference until 1839. In that year the circuits became one of three districts in the newly formed West Pennsylvania Conference. Twelve years later, the creation of the Pittsburgh Conference was authorized. In March, 1852, it held its first meeting in Pittsburgh.

In 1967 the Conference had a membership of 51,696. There were 298 organized congregations and 165 pastoral charges. Ministerial leadership in all classes was 229. The value of local church property exceeded $24,900,000. The churches gave for all purposes $3,587,000. The conference maintained an office at Johnstown, Pennsylvania.

There were two significant historical sites within the bounds of the Conference. The oldest was the BONNET SCHOOL HOUSE near Mt. Pleasant, Westmoreland County, Pennsylvania, where the first session of the General Conference of the United Brethren Church was held. The second site was First Church, Johnstown, Pennsylvania, where in 1946 the former Evangelical Church and the former United Brethren Church merged to create The Evangelical United Brethren Church.

In 1969, the conference united with the Western Pennsylvania Conference of the former Methodist Church to form a conference of the same name. A small group of churches in the eastern portion of the conference joined with the Central Pennsylvania Conference.

D. Berger, *History of U.B.* 1897.
J. S. Fulton, *History of the Allegheny Conference of the Church of the United Brethren in Christ*, 1931.
C. H. Keller, *A History of the Allegheny Conference of the Church of the United Brethren in Christ*, 1943.
A. Stapleton, *Annals of the Evangelical Association.* 1900.
R. Yeakel, *History of the Evangelical Association.* 1900.

WILLIAM C. BEAL, JR.

WESTERN VIRGINIA CONFERENCE (MES) was created by the 1850 GENERAL CONFERENCE and was organized Sept. 4 of that year at Parkersburg with Bishop JAMES O. ANDREW presiding. The conference was formed by dividing the KENTUCKY CONFERENCE. At the beginning it had three districts, Greenbrier, Parkersburg, and Guyandotte. The Guyandotte District was in KENTUCKY. There were twenty-four charges and 5,354 white and 149 colored members.

The work of the M.E. Church, South in WEST VIRGINIA suffered greatly during the Civil War. Between 1860 and 1866 no legal sessions of the Western Virginia Conference were held. There were two sessions of the conference in 1866, one in February at Greenup, Ky., and the other at Parkersburg in September. In 1860 the conference reported forty-seven charges, sixty-five preachers, and 10,045 full members, but in 1867, the first year for which statistics are available following the war, there were only forty-one charges, forty-six preachers, and 6,731 members. However, recovery was rapid; in 1870 the conference had 10,882 members, and the number had risen to about 13,000 by 1875. In 1900 there were 24,196 members.

The Western Virginia Conference launched MORRIS HARVEY COLLEGE at Barboursville, W. Va., in 1888, and many of its graduates became ministers in the conference. The school moved to Charleston in 1935, and at unification in 1939 it was accepted as one of the colleges of the WEST VIRGINIA CONFERENCE of The Methodist Church. However, in 1942 it became an independent college.

The Western Virginia Conference patronized two church papers, the *Central Methodist* and the *Methodist Advocate,* both of which were published independently under several different names for some years in Louisville, Ky. and Parkersburg and Moundsville, W. Va., respectively.

One member of the Western Virginia Conference, U. V. W. DARLINGTON, was elected bishop in 1918.

In 1920 the Western Virginia Conference reported 32,342 members, and in 1939 it brought to unification 51,680 members, some 44,733 of them in the state of West Virginia. In 1939 the conference also reported five districts, 132 charges, 130 preachers, and 409 churches and 133 parsonages valued at $4,040,109.

General Minutes, MES.
Minutes of the Western Virginia Conference.

ALBEA GODBOLD

WESTFIELD, NEW JERSEY, U.S.A., **First Church.** Methodism in Westfield has had a long and significant history. In 1849 a small and dedicated group met under a tree-canopy on the farm of one Cornelius Leveridge. For two years outdoors or in homes they met and planned and in 1851 elected trustees, prepared a certificate of incorporation and obtained Conference permission to become a mission station. A small building erected in 1852, soon outgrown, was followed by a larger edifice in 1876 and this by the present gray-stone building erected in 1910. An educational annex, a remodeled sanctuary and a renovated chapel wing have marked succeeding years.

In 1970 with a membership of 2,467, an Official Board of 100 members and a church school of over 1,000, Westfield is the largest church in Methodism's NORTHERN NEW JERSEY CONFERENCE. Property is valued at over $1,600,-000.

Involvement in missions is deep and meaningful. Benevolence giving for world, national and local projects totals $53,000, twenty-eight percent of the annual budget. Included is support of several missionary families, student and ministerial scholarships, schools, universities, church Conference projects. Special offerings represent concern for needs ranging from resettlement of Cuban refugees to summer camperships for inner city youth. A racially integrated congregation, this church has also been sensitive to the ecumenical emphasis, with growing dialogue and cooperative ventures with Roman Catholic and Jewish brethren.

JOHN WESLEY LORD, pastor here for ten years (1939-48), became a bishop in 1948. Another former pastor, GORDON E. MICHALSON, is President of the SCHOOL OF THEOLOGY AT CLAREMONT, Calif. One of the prominent laymen, Joe Mickle, was President of CENTENARY COLLEGE, Shreveport, La., for almost twenty years. Mrs. Franklin Reed of this church was four years the President of the WORLD FEDERATION OF METHODIST WOMEN.

In 1949 a significant centennial celebration was observed. This Westfield Church has been on the growing edge of the suburban expansion and has become a noteworthy congregation in Methodism.

V. B. Hampton, *Newark Conference.* 1957.

GERTRUDE W. BEATTYS

WESTMAR COLLEGE, Le Mars, Iowa, was the result of the union of two schools, York College and Westmar College. York College was established at York, Neb., in 1890 by the CHURCH OF THE UNITED BRETHREN IN CHRIST. Western Union College was founded at Le Mars, Iowa by The UNITED EVANGELICAL CHURCH in 1900. The first building of Western Union College burned only a few weeks before first classes were scheduled. This severe test for the new college was survived, and Thoren Hall, replacing the original strucure, was dedicated Sept. 18, 1901.

These two institutions are not the total ancestry of Westmar College. Other church-founded schools whose records and alumni, by various paths, have become the responsibility of the present institution include Western College (later Leander Clark); Avalon College of Avalon, Mo.; Gould College of Harlan, Kan.; Lane University of Lecompton, Kan.; Campbell College of Holton, Kan.; and Kansas City University of Kansas City, Kan. This indicates the difficulties of establishing and maintaining a college in the latter nineteenth and early twentieth centuries.

The depression of the thirties struck hard at both struggling institutions. They managed to survive through various student "work" programs and the great devotion and sacrifice of the faculty members. Relative prosperity returned with the flood of post-World War II "G. I.'s."

A final crisis struck York College in 1951. A fire destroyed the Administration Building. The sponsoring denominations had united in 1946, and the leaders felt that the maintenance of two colleges, constantly in financial difficulties, and located within 200 miles of each other, was not sound. Formal union was effected June 30, 1955, though students and faculty had transferred to Le Mars in the fall of 1954.

Degrees granted: B.A., B.S., B.Mus., B.Mus.Ed.

In the E.U.B. Church the governing board was comprised of thirty-four trustees, twenty of whom represented supporting conferences of the E.U.B. Church. In The United Methodist Church, the College will in time be related only to the IOWA CONFERENCE.

Library, 58,000 volumes; total enrollment, 1,200; total faculty, seventy-five; campus acreage, twenty-five; number of buildings, twenty-four; endowment, $725,000; current income, $1,858,740; current expenditures, $1,791,250; value of physical facilities, nearly $6,000,000.

C. J. ATTIG

WESTMINSTER, MARYLAND, U.S.A., is a small city, the county seat of Carroll County, located northwest of Baltimore about thirty miles. In Methodist annals it had always been one of the major centers of the METHODIST PROTESTANT CHURCH since from early days it maintained a close relationship to WESTERN MARYLAND COLLEGE located there. The College was founded and the first building erected in 1867 by F. R. Buell with the assistance of J. T. WARD, a M.P. minister. Buell sought the financial support of the MARYLAND ANNUAL CONFERENCE, but instead the Conference authorized the incorporation of a Board of Trustees which in August 1868, bought the College from Buell and elected J. T. Ward as the first president.

The influence of Western Maryland College and the strength of Methodist Protestantism in Maryland centering here served to strengthen and increase the influence of Westminster as the years went by. In time, on adjacent property given by the College, WESTMINSTER THEOLOGICAL SEMINARY was established and a great many of the ministers of that Church received their collegiate and theological training at the two institutions.

The Westminster M.P. local church grew in close connection with the College, but one city block away was Centenary M.E. Church. In 1941, two years after the 1939 unification of Methodism, these two churches merged becoming the Westminster Methodist Church, which now reports (1970) 1,681 members. Lowell S. Ensor of the former M.E. Church became pastor of the newly merged congregation and in 1947 was elected President of the College.

Also in the city is **Union Street Methodist Church,** formerly of the Washington Conference of the CENTRAL JURISDICTION, but now a part of the BALTIMORE CONFERENCE. These two churches became a single parish in 1969 with the same ministers serving both churches.

Three miles outside of Westminster is **Stone Chapel,** one of the earliest churches of Methodism, built in 1783. The original church still exists and reports in 1970 a membership of 220.

Home for the Aged (1895-1942), an institution for the care of needy aged and infirm of the Maryland Conference (MP), was located in Westminster. At the time of Methodist Union, the home was merged with two other

Homes of like nature. The merger was completed in 1942. These three homes were then consolidated under one roof and renamed "The Asbury Methodist Home for the Aged" in Gaithersburg, Md.

General Minutes, UMC, 1970.

LOWELL S. ENSOR
GEORGE K. MATHER

WESTMINSTER COLLEGE, British Methodist teachers' training college, was opened in central LONDON in 1851 for men and women teachers. From 1872 women students went to their own college in Battersea. In 1930 the college instituted a four-year course which produced a number of graduate teachers. In 1946 the original policy of two-year courses was started again, as with increased opportunities to enter universities, few desired a four-year course. The premises became increasingly unsuitable, and in 1954 it was decided to build new premises at North Hinksey, OXFORD. The new buildings for 220 resident students were opened in September, 1959. In response to a request by the Ministry of Education, numbers increased to 400 by 1962, and growth continued. In 1960 the college reverted to its original policy of training women as well as men, and the initial course of training was extended to three years. The University of Oxford gave permission for forty graduates to be trained at Westminster for the Oxford University Diploma in Education. Former students occupy distinguished positions in education at home and abroad in schools of all types, including those for the handicapped and underprivileged, and in administration.

H. T. HUGHES

WESTMINSTER COLLEGE, Salt Lake City, Utah, is related to the United Methodist and Presbyterian Churches and to the United Church of Christ. It was established as Salt Lake Collegiate Institute in 1875 by the Presbyterian Church; the name was changed to Sheldon Jackson (Junior) College in 1895. It became a senior college in 1944. In 1953 affiliation was effected with the ROCKY MOUNTAIN CONFERENCE of The Methodist Church. It is the only evangelical senior college in UTAH, where the population is preponderantly Mormon.

Degrees offered are the B.A. and B.S. The governing board consists of thirty-six members; it is a self-perpetuating body with each participating denomination entitled to nominate two members each per year for three-year terms.

JOHN O. GROSS

WESTMINSTER COLLEGE, Tehuacana, Texas, was founded at Westminster, Texas, in 1895. It was moved to Tehuacana in 1902. When Trinity College, then at Tehuacana, was moved to Waxahachie, Texas, the property was offered to the TEXAS ANNUAL CONFERENCE of the METHODIST PROTESTANT CHURCH on condition that this church maintain a college there for ten years. The conference complied with this agreement and in 1912 obtained title to the buildings and grounds. James L. Lawlis was president during the years of these undertakings.

For fourteen years it was operated as a four-year college. The demands for its accreditation as a senior college could not be met, and in 1916 it became a junior college, the first of its kind in Texas. It became a junior college of SOUTHWESTERN UNIVERSITY, Georgetown, Texas in

1942, but because of continued financial difficulties the university returned the college in 1949 to its previous trustees. In 1952 the properties were sold to the CONGREGATIONAL METHODIST CHURCH.

JOHN O. GROSS

WESTMINSTER THEOLOGICAL SEMINARY, Westminster, Maryland, an institution of the M.P. Church, opened in connection with WESTERN MARYLAND COLLEGE under the supervision of the MARYLAND CONFERENCE (MP). THOMAS HAMILTON LEWIS was principal. Before classes were started it was determined by the Board of Trustees of the College that a theological school was impractical within the college organization. Land was purchased adjacent to the college campus and a building was erected for an independent school which was incorporated as the Westminster Theological Seminary of the Methodist Protestant Church in 1884, and Thomas Hamilton Lewis was elected the first President. Under the presidency of HUGH LATIMER ELDERDICE (1897-1932) a new classroom-administration building and residences for the President and faculty members were erected.

In 1957 the name was changed to Wesley Theological Seminary and in September 1958, it was moved to Washington, D. C., where it operated in connection with American University. Up to that time the presidents were Thomas H. Lewis (1882-86), JAMES T. WARD (1886-97), Hugh L. Elderdice (1897-1932), FRED G. HOLLOWAY (1932-35), CHARLES E. FORLINES (1935-43), LESTER A. WELLIVER (1943-55), Norman L. Trott (1955-   ). (See WESLEY THEOLOGICAL SEMINARY.)

L. E. Davis, *Democratic Methodism.* 1921.
Methodist Protestant Recorder, Dec. 22, 1931. M. J. SHROYER

WHAKATUMUTUMU, near Te Kuiti, NEW ZEALAND, was the site of an early mission station on the banks of the Mokau River, established by Frederick Miller in 1840. Miller had been sent to New Zealand by the London Missionary Society, but through the influence of JOHN WHITELEY, he accepted employment under the Wesleyan mission, as a catechist. Miller worked faithfully at Whakatumutumu under the superintendency of Whiteley for eight years, and then died at his post of duty at the early age of thirty-two. The station was never reoccupied by European missionaries, but the site is marked by a memorial cairn, unveiled in May, 1959.

G. Elliott, *Sowing the Seed in Pioneer New Zealand.* Wesley Historical Society, New Zealand, 1959. L. R. M. GILMORE

WHATCOAT, RICHARD (1736-1806), second elected bishop of American Methodism, was born in Quinton parish, Gloucestershire, England, on Feb. 23, 1736, the son of Charles and Mary Whatcoat. At the age of eighteen he was apprenticed for eight years, at the conclusion of which he entered business at Wednesbury.

In 1758 he began attending Methodist meetings and entered the itinerancy in 1769. He traveled for fifteen years and then in 1784 he was ordained by JOHN WESLEY and selected to accompany THOMAS COKE and THOMAS VASEY to America where they organized the Methodists there into a Church. This was done at the famous CHRISTMAS CONFERENCE at Baltimore, Md.

Following the organization of the M.E. Church, Whatcoat continued in America taking his place in the itinerant

RICHARD WHATCOAT

ministry. Because he was one of the few ordained preachers who could administer the sacraments, he was nearly always appointed as elder over a number of circuits, in which capacity he traveled for fifteen years in the middle states. In 1790 he accompanied Bishop FRANCIS ASBURY on a tour of the South.

In 1786 John Wesley sent word by Coke that the Conference should elect Whatcoat a General Superintendent or Bishop, as was Asbury, but the preachers in the Conference of 1787 declined to so elect him, probably because they feared it would result in Asbury's recall to England. Also, they did not like to feel that Wesley could control their own elections. However, Whatcoat was elected bishop in 1800, winning over JESSE LEE by one vote; this led to an estrangement between Asbury and Lee, who accused Asbury of influencing the election.

As bishop, Whatcoat traveled over the whole eastern seaboard and inland as far as Kentucky and Tennessee. He usually traveled with Asbury but sometimes went alone. He was sixty-four years old when elected, and the hardships of the office were too much for his rather frail strength. He survived only six years after his election.

Whatcoat preached his last sermon at Milford, Del., on April 8, 1806. In failing health he made his way to the home of RICHARD BASSETT, a prominent Methodist who lived at Dover, Del., where he died on July 5, 1806. He was buried under the altar of Wesley Chapel in Dover. Nearly a year later, on March 30, 1807, Asbury preached his funeral there. Funeral sermons in the nature of memorials were preached at several other places also at the request of the conference. "A man so uniformly good I have not known in Europe or America," was Asbury's tribute to him.

F. Asbury, *Journal and Letters*. 1958.
H. Boehm, *Reminiscences*. 1875.
S. B. Bradley, *Richard Whatcoat*. 1936.
Dictionary of American Biography.
W. Phoebus, *Richard Whatcoat*. 1828.
P. P. Sandford, *Memoirs*. 1843.
W. B. Sprague, *Annals of the Pulpit*. 1861. ELMER T. CLARK

WHEDON, DANIEL DENISON

WHEDON, DANIEL DENISON (1808-1885), American preacher, theologian, author and editor, was born March 20, 1808, in Onondaga, N. Y. He graduated from Hamilton College in 1828 and took up the study of law, but abandoned this profession to go into teaching. He taught at Cazenovia Seminary, New York State, in 1830-31; was

a tutor at Hamilton College in 1832; and in 1833 was elected Professor of Ancient Languages and Literature at WESLEYAN UNIVERSITY, Middletown, Conn. In 1843, he became a minister of the M.E. Church and served churches at Pittsfield, Mass., and Jamaica, L.I., N. Y. In 1845 he was made Professor of Logic, Rhetoric and History at Michigan University and served there in that capacity until 1852. In 1853 he reentered the pastorate and served once more at Jamaica. The M.E. GENERAL CONFERENCE of 1856 elected him to be editor of *The Methodist Quarterly Review*—one of the influential magazines of the Church. He served as editor for twenty-eight years. Failing health forced his retirement in 1884.

Whedon was the author of many articles and books dealing with a wide variety of subjects. Some of his books are: *Public Addresses* (1856); *Commentary on Matthew and Mark* (1860); *Freedom of the Will* (1864); *Commentary on the New Testament*, 5 Vols. (1860-75); *Commentary on the Old Testament*, 7 Vols. (1880-86); and a posthumous volume, *Essays, Review and Discourses* (1889).

In the late 1850's, Whedon engaged in the debate going on in the Church over the question of whether or not the General Conference had a right to make any rule against slave holding. He supported the position that the General Conference had such a right. As early as January 1866, however, he wrote an editorial urging the northern Church to accept the overtures of the southern Church to heal the wounds caused by the Civil War, and to work for the reunification of the Church. His voice, and the appeal *in re* the Southern Church, unfortunately were not heeded.

Whedon's greatest contribution to Methodism, probably, was in the area of developing an indigenous Methodist theology. His book on *Freedom of the Will* and his article in *Bibliotheca Sacra* (1862) on "Doctrines of Methodism" are his best known contributions in this area.

EMORY AND HENRY COLLEGE in VIRGINIA gave him the D.D. degree and Wesleyan University gave him the LL.D.

After his retirement in 1884, Whedon resided at Atlantic Highlands, N. J. He died there on June 8, 1885.

E. S. Bucke, *History of American Methodism*. 1964.
Methodist Quarterly Review, 1856-1884.
National Cyclopedia.
M. Simpson, *Cyclopaedia*. 1878.   C. WESLEY CHRISTMAN, JR.

WHEELER, ALFRED

WHEELER, ALFRED (1824-1892), American preacher, physician, and editor, was born in New Haven, Huron County, Ohio, Sept. 14, 1824. He graduated with honors from OHIO WESLEYAN UNIVERSITY, and won the M.D. degree at Jefferson Medical College in 1852. Also, he held the D.D. degree. He married Lydia P. Curtis in 1850.

In 1853, after one year of medical practice, Wheeler joined the NORTH OHIO CONFERENCE and served several charges, including two years, 1866-67, on the Cleveland District. In 1862, he became an army CHAPLAIN, and a little later served six months without pay as surgeon to an Ohio battery. Returning to his conference in 1864, he became agent in 1865 for the centenary fund raised in connection with the CENTENNIAL celebration of American Methodism.

In 1869, Wheeler transferred to the ERIE CONFERENCE, and after several pastorates was elected editor in 1876 of the *Pittsburgh Christian Advocate*, serving two quadrennia. Then followed six years on the New Castle District and nearly two on the Erie District.

In his day Wheeler was regarded as an ecclesiastical statesman and was certainly one of the strongest leaders in the M.E. Church. Six times a delegate to the GENERAL CONFERENCE, 1868, 1876-92, he also went to the 1881 ECUMENICAL CONFERENCE. Alert to the interests of his church, a skillful debater, a trusted counselor of Bishops SIMPSON, AMES, and HARRIS, who themselves were church lawmakers, it was claimed that scarcely any important legislation was adopted by the General Conference without Wheeler's guidance or support. He was one of the first churchmen to suggest the idea of a Methodist university in WASHINGTON, D. C. He died July 7, 1892, on Staten Island, N. Y.

General Minutes, MEC.
M. Simpson, *Cyclopaedia*. 1878.
W. G. Smeltzer, *Headwaters of the Ohio*. 1951.

JESSE A. EARL

WHEELER, JOHN (1815-1881), American clergyman and educator, was born April 7, 1815, in Portsmouth, England. With his family he came to America in 1820, settling at Bellefontaine, Ohio. He was converted in 1824 and joined the M.E. Church. Wheeler studied in Norwalk Seminary of OHIO in 1835 and attended ALLEGHENY COLLEGE, 1837-39. Removing to INDIANA, he entered Indiana Asbury (now DePauw) UNIVERSITY, which had MATTHEW SIMPSON as its new president, and graduated in 1840. He was principal of Franklin Institute in INDIANAPOLIS, 1840-42, and, during these two years was married to Mary Yandes. Wheeler was Professor of Latin at Indiana Asbury from 1842-54, and edited *Asbury Notes*, a literary journal of the University.

In 1855 Wheeler entered the OHIO CONFERENCE ministry and became president of Baldwin Institute (Baldwin University), Berea, Ohio, in 1856. While at Berea he helped establish German Wallace College, the first American German college. He transferred to the IOWA CONFERENCE in 1870 and became President of IOWA WESLEYAN UNIVERSITY, Mt. Pleasant, where he labored for five years. Again, President Wheeler was instrumental in founding a German college (1873).

After retiring as President of Iowa Wesleyan in 1875, Wheeler became pastor of First Church, Keokuk, Iowa. Then, in succession, he became the PRESIDING ELDER of the Keokuk and the Mt. Pleasant districts, in 1876 and in 1877. This eminent Methodist scholar died June 18, 1881, at Mt. Pleasant, Iowa, where he was buried.

L. A. Haselmayer, "Das Deutsche Kollegium: Wesleyan's Teutonic Past," *Purple and White* of Iowa Wesleyan, Fall 1959.
M. Simpson, *Cyclopaedia*. 1878.
E. H. Waring, *Iowa Conference*. 1910.
Yearbook of the Iowa Conference, 1870-1881.

MARTIN L. GREER

WHEELING, WEST VIRGINIA, U.S.A. (population 46,854 in 1970), was founded in 1769 by Colonel Ebenezer Zane. It was then called Fort Henry, the location of the last battle of the Revolutionary War. Wheeling served as the first and third capital of the state.

Methodism was brought to Wheeling in 1785 by WILSON LEE, one of the preachers on the famous REDSTONE CIRCUIT.

A German Methodist Church, an offshoot of Fourth Street, was organized in 1839. It was the first German Methodist church in the world. Other Methodist churches formed in Wheeling prior to 1875 were: Chapline Street and North Street, 1848; Wesley Chapel, 1850; Thomson, 1855; Simpson (colored) and Zane, 1866; Benwood, 1870; and Steinrod, 1874. In 1876 the M.E. Church had seven congregations in the city with 1,336 members, and in 1900 the same seven reported a total of 5,640 members. The WESTERN VIRGINIA CONFERENCE (MES) had no organized work in Wheeling.

The Conference WOMEN'S SOCIETY OF CHRISTIAN SERVICE established the House of the Carpenter in Wheeling in 1964, an urban missionary project which promotes the work of all Methodist churches in the city.

In 1970 The United Methodist Church reported eleven churches in Wheeling—Aldersgate, Christ, Elm Grove, Fourth Street, Greggsville, Mount Olive, North Street, Simpson, Thomson, Triadelphia, and Warwood. The three largest congregations were: Christ, 1,348; Elm Grove, 907; and Fourth Street, 680. The smallest was Simpson Church with eighty-two members. The eleven churches reported a total of 6,302 members, property valued at $4,509,212, and $169,872 raised for all purposes during the year.

George Brown, *Recollections of Itinerant Life*. Cincinnati: Carroll and Company, 1868.
Methodist Story, June, 1965.
General Minutes, MEC and UMC.
M. Simpson, *Cyclopaedia*. 1878.

JESSE A. EARL
ALBEA GODBOLD

Fourth Street Church was organized by Wilson Lee, one of the preachers on the Redstone Circuit, in 1785. The group met in the home of Colonel Ebenezer Zane, the founder of Wheeling, and his wife Elizabeth became the first member of the society.

In 1819 when the population of the town was 1,200 and the church membership was thirty, a one-room brick church was erected on the fourth street from the Ohio River, the lot being donated by Noah Zane. In 1836 when the church had 273 members and the town 6,000 people, a new church edifice with a seating capacity of 2,000 was dedicated, and thereafter the building was used for secular as well as religious meetings. Jenny Lind sang in the church in 1851, people bidding up to $250 for choice seats for the event. The PITTSBURGH CONFERENCE met in the church, July 5, 1848, and on that occasion it divided to form the Western (later West) Virginia Conference. In 1870 Bishop EDMUND S. JANES dedicated Fourth Street's third church building.

In 1951 the Fourth Street congregation occupied its fourth edifice, the church facilities comprising one-half of the structure called the Methodist Building; the other half is rented for commercial office space.

During its history Fourth Street Church has been associated with some prominent church leaders. Bishop ASBURY preached in Wheeling in 1808, and RICHARD WHATCOAT, later bishop, was presiding elder in 1788. Among the pastors were: THOMAS SCOTT, later chief justice of OHIO; GEORGE BROWN, one of the founders of the M.P. Church; Wesley Smith, father of Bishop C. W. SMITH; GORDON BATTELLE, able educator before West Virginia became a state; and Alexander Martin, first president of West Virginia University.

In 1839 Fourth Street helped to establish a German Methodist Church in Wheeling, the first of its kind in the world. Since that time Fourth Street has assisted in launching several new congregations in the city. Some membership figures for the parent church are: 649 in 1900, 1,183 in 1920, 1,241 in 1939, and 850 in 1942.

In 1970 Fourth Street Church reported 680 members, property valued at $1,655,829, and $28,413 raised for all purposes during the year.

Christian Advocate, July, 1866.
Pittsburgh Christian Advocate, September 23, 1926.
General Minutes, MEC and UMC.
G. G. Nichols and A. G. Sprankle, *History of the Panhandle, West Virginia.* 1879.
McConnell and Liggett, *Wheeling's First 250 Years.* 1942.
MRS. R. B. CRAIG

WHELLER, HAROLD MANUEL (1882-   ), Australian minister, was President of the QUEENSLAND CONFERENCE in 1926, and President-General of the Methodist Church of Australasia in 1941-45. He was a member of the University Senate, 1946-56; the State President of the WORLD COUNCIL OF CHURCHES and Queensland Council of Churches; and Chairman of the Queensland Temperance League. For twenty-five years he was the Superintendent of the Central Mission when he officiated with dignity over a large and progressive church and directed extensive social agencies. He is known and esteemed publicly as the founder of a unique form of Aged People's Settlement, which he continues to administer, and is recognized throughout Australia as a wise leader in all major Church movements.

AUSTRALIAN EDITORIAL COMMITTEE

WHITAKER, CLIFTON LAWRENCE (1863-1926), American M.P. clergyman and educator, was born on May 9, 1863, the son of Lawrence B. and Alice P. Whitaker of near Enfield, N. C. Early in life he united with WHITAKER'S CHAPEL, one of the historic Methodist churches in America. He attended OAK RIDGE INSTITUTE and YADKIN COLLEGE, taught school for a while, and in 1888 was ordained as a Methodist Protestant minister in the NORTH CAROLINA CONFERENCE. While at Yadkin College he met Clara Peebles of Davie County, N. C., and on Nov. 17, 1892, they were married. To this union three children were born.

Whitaker's first pastoral charge was the Albemarle Circuit, Creswell, which was followed by appointments to the North Granville Circuit, Mocksville, Tar River Circuit, Winston Station (Winston-Salem), Granville Circuit, Roanoke Circuit, High Point, Asheboro, Mebane and North Davidson Circuit. He was President of the Annual Conference in 1901-02. He was a staunch supporter of the movement aimed toward the establishment of HIGH POINT COLLEGE, contributing liberally in a financial way, and making many speeches on behalf of the college. When the college opened in 1924 he was assigned to teach in the Preparatory Department, and later taught Bible and served as college librarian. He was given the D.D. degree by WESTERN MARYLAND COLLEGE.

His brother, Cary Hamilton Whitaker (Nov. 30, 1860-Aug. 18, 1935), was also an outstanding member of the North Carolina Conference of the M.P. Church. Clifton L. Whitaker died on Feb. 18, 1926, and was buried in Green Hill Cemetery, Greensboro, N. C.

Journal of the North Carolina Conference, MP, 1926.
RALPH HARDEE RIVES

WHITAKER, JAMES (1861-1940), British and American minister, was born in Cowling, Yorkshire, England, on Dec. 29, 1861, the third of five children of William and Ellen (Stowe) Whitaker. He attended school in Cowling and Skipton and was an active member of the UNITED METHODIST FREE CHURCH of Cowling. On July 10, 1866, he laid a memorial stone at the church and began his study for the ministry. He attended Hulme Cliff College until 1888. After graduation, Whitaker went to serve in the NEVADA MISSION CONFERENCE, U.S.A. He was admitted to the CALIFORNIA CONFERENCE (ME) on probation in 1888, and into full membership in 1890, while he was serving the Quincy, Calif., church.

On July 19, 1891, James Whitaker and Laura Drew, daughter of pioneer members of the Quincy Church, were married there. From this union there were two daughters and three sons—four became public school teachers and one a physician.

During the next ten years of his ministry, James Whitaker earned five academic degrees—Litt.B., Midland University; A.M. and Ph.D., Allegheny College; S.T.B., DENVER UNIVERSITY; and S.T.D., Taylor University.

While serving Central Church of Sacramento, he was appointed CHAPLAIN of the Assembly of the State of CALIFORNIA during the forty-first session of the State Legislature.

After serving eleven charges a total of thirty-eight years, he was appointed Pastor of Hospitals and Homes, which he served until retirement in 1938. Stricken while returning home from Conference, James Whitaker died in San Jose, Calif., on July 15, 1940, survived by his wife and four children.

Minutes of the California Conference, 1892, 1901, 1902, 1911-1941.
HARRY E. SHAFFER

WHITAKER, JOSEPH WALDO (1879-1966), American M.P. layman and Methodist benefactor, was born Oct. 18, 1879, the son of John Simmons and Emma Waldo Whitaker of "Strawberry Hill," near Enfield, N. C. In 1965 he personally financed the complete restoration of historic WHITAKER'S CHAPEL, located near his home. In recognition of his services, "Mr. Waldo," as he was called, was given a special "Certificate of Appreciation" by the NORTH CAROLINA CONFERENCE of The Methodist Church in June 1965.

He was a member of the Halifax County Board of Commissioners for forty years and president of the North Carolina Association of County Commissioners, 1932-33. He was mayor of Enfield, and held many positions of prominence in business and civic affairs. He was noted for his many philanthropic endeavors and interests. He died on April 16, 1966, and was buried at Whitaker's Chapel.

Journal of the North Carolina Conference, 1965.
The News and Observer (Raleigh, N.C.), April 18, 1966.
The Evening Telegram (Rocky Mount, N.C.), April 18, 1966.
RALPH HARDEE RIVES

WHITAKER'S CHAPEL, considered by Methodist Protestants prior to 1939 as the historic shrine of democratic Methodism in America, is located on NORTH CAROLINA Route 1001, six miles east of Enfield, Halifax County. The first Whitaker's Chapel, a log structure, was erected by Richard Whitaker soon after he settled on a grant of

WHITAKER'S CHAPEL, NORTH CAROLINA

land in Halifax County in 1740. Originally Anglican, the congregation joined the Methodists in 1776 or 1778. Asbury preached in the chapel at least three times—March 21, 1786; January 17-18, 1789; and March 2, 1804. Presumably Whitaker's Chapel was a preaching point on the North Carolina and Roanoke Circuits when JOHN DICKINS was appointed to them in 1777 and 1779, respectively. Also, it was probably the meetinghouse where Dickins and his family worshiped in 1781-82 when he was located (probably because of poor health) and lived in his own house near Halifax only a few miles from the chapel. In time the log chapel was torn down and an unceiled frame church was erected. In 1850 the latter edifice was moved some 500 yards away, presumably to be used as a dwelling, and a new frame church was erected. In 1880 the third structure was moved across the road to the spot where it now stands.

As the demand for democracy in American Methodism developed, the sentiment was strong in Halifax County, North Carolina. Then in 1828 a call went out to the members of the "Union Societies" in North Carolina, and nine itinerants, five local preachers, and twelve laymen gathered at Whitaker's Chapel on December 19. There in a two-day session they organized what came to be the NORTH CAROLINA CONFERENCE of the METHODIST PROTESTANT CHURCH. It was the first M.P. Conference to be formed anywhere, even antedating the organization of the denomination's General Conference. In succeeding years the North Carolina Conference (MP) met at Whitaker's Chapel five more times—in 1830, 1833, 1842, 1845, and 1849—and prior to 1939 the conference held its annual session nine additional times in churches in Halifax County.

Due to dwindling membership, services at Whitaker's Chapel were discontinued about 1948, and the building fell into disrepair. In 1964, J. WALDO WHITAKER, a descendant of Richard Whitaker, paid for restoring the chapel. Then on December 20, 1964, 136 years after the organization of the North Carolina Conference (MP), the North Carolina Conference (MC) Historical Society sponsored a commemorative service in the chapel. Bishop PAUL N. GARBER of the Raleigh Area delivered the sermon. So far as is known, Bishop Garber was the first Methodist bishop since Asbury to preach in Whitaker's Chapel. In 1965 the North Carolina Department of Archives and History erected an appropriate marker at Whitaker's Chapel.

The cemetery beside Whitaker's Chapel dates from the 1850's, and a still earlier one near the site of the first log structure is preserved. During its history Whitaker's Chapel furnished several men for the Methodist Protestant ministry, and a number of Methodist Protestant preachers are buried in its cemetery. An endowment of $5,000 now provides funds for the upkeep of the chapel and the cemetery.

Whitaker's Chapel was officially designated a historic SHRINE of The United Methodist Church at the special session of GENERAL CONFERENCE in 1970.

J. Elwood Carroll, *History of the North Carolina Conference of the Methodist Protestant Church*. Greensboro, 1939.
Our Church Record, June 23, 1898.
Methodist Protestant Memorial Collection, North Carolina Wesleyan College, Rocky Mount, N. C.
John Paris, *History of the Methodist Protestant Church*. Baltimore, 1849. LOUISE L. QUEEN

WHITE, EDWARD (1822-1872), Canadian Methodist minister, was born in PENNSYLVANIA, in November, 1822. With his parents he came to CANADA at an early age, and became a probationer for the Methodist ministry in 1848. Four years later he was ordained in Kingston, Ontario.

In 1858, while serving at Smithville, Ontario, he was one of four young ministers, chosen from several volunteers, to be sent to the far-western coast of Canada to establish Methodism in what was at that time the Crown Colony of British Columbia. Leaving TORONTO on Dec. 31, 1858, the missionary party travelled via New York, Panama, San Francisco, and arrived in Victoria on Feb. 10, 1859. In the evening of Sunday, February 13, White preached in an unfinished room in the court house, in which, earlier in the day, two services had been held by other members of the party. Thus began Methodism in British Columbia. Within a few weeks four missionary charges had been surveyed, one of which, New Westminster, was assigned to White. Soon a little frame chapel, in the midst of the dense forest, was dedicated, the first Methodist Church in the colony.

In 1863 White was stationed in Nanaimo, a busy coal-mining town about seventy-five miles north of Victoria. His pastoral responsibilities extended from the outskirts of Victoria to Comox, another seventy-five miles north of Nanaimo on the east coast of Vancouver Island. Owing to ill health, White returned to Ontario in 1871. Shortly thereafter he was sent to England to recruit ministers for Canadian Methodism. On his return journey he contracted smallpox and died in hospital in Montreal on June 16, 1872.

G. H. Cornish, *Cyclopaedia of Methodism*. 1881, 1903.
J. E. Sanderson, *Methodism in Canada*. 1908-10. W. P. BUNT

WHITE, GOODRICH COOK (1889-), American university chancellor and longtime president of EMORY UNIVERSITY, was born Nov. 13, 1889, the son of George Berry and Florence Richards (Cook) White. He was educated at Emory College, at Columbia University, and received a Ph.D. from the University of Chicago in 1927; an LL.D. from the UNIVERSITY OF CHATTANOOGA in 1947; and the same degree from HAMLINE UNIVERSITY, from the University of North Carolina, and from DICKINSON COLLEGE. He was the recipient of other honorary degrees from other institutions of learning in America.

On May 4, 1915, he married Helen Dean Chappell,

the daughter of EDWIN B. CHAPPELL. He taught for a time in KENTUCKY WESLEYAN COLLEGE, then at WESLEYAN COLLEGE at Macon, Ga.; became professor of mental and moral science at Emory, 1914-18; associate professor of psychology, 1919-20; professor, 1920-42 at Emory University. He also became dean of the College of Arts and Sciences and dean of the Graduate School in 1929-42. He was elected president of Emory in 1942, and served until 1957, becoming at that time chancellor.

Dr. White held memberships in many important educational commissions of various college associations of the nation. He was a member of the General BOARD OF EDUCATION, of the M.E. Church, South, 1934-40 (and then of the same Board in The Methodist Church), and a member of the UNIVERSITY SENATE of The Methodist Church, 1940-60. He was a member of the President's Commission on Higher Education, 1946-47; president of The Southern University Conference, 1949-50; member board of trustees of Wesleyan College and of CLARK COLLEGE; a member of the Georgia Academy of Science (President 1939); president of the United Chapters of Phi Beta Kappa, 1952-55.

Since retirement, Dr. White has lived in ATLANTA, not far from the University which he led for so many years.

Who's Who in America, Vol. 34.   N. B. H.

WHITE, HUGH A. (1901-   ), American Secretary of FREE METHODIST World Fellowship, was born at Evart, Mich. He studied at SPRING ARBOR COLLEGE, Western Michigan University and the University of Michigan. His degrees are: A.B., M.B.A., and C.P.A. Spring Arbor conferred the honorary LL.D. degree in 1967. Mr. White was Senior Partner of White, Bower and Prevo, Certified Public Accountants, and is now president of Allied Investments, Inc. He is a member of the Michigan Association of Certified Public Accountants and president of the board of trustees of Spring Arbor College. He is Secretary of the Free Methodist World Fellowship. He resides at Bloomfield Hills, Mich.

BYRON S. LAMSON

WHITE, JAMES HENRY (1855-1948), Canadian minister, was born on March 24, 1855, a son of EDWARD WHITE, who was one of the quartet of pioneer Methodist missionaries who arrived in Victoria, British Columbia, from eastern CANADA on Feb. 10, 1859. In 1871 his parents returned to Ontario. The son, James Henry, was received on probation for the ministry by the London and Niagara Conference in 1876, and was ordained on June 5, 1881. Following two pastorates in Ontario, he accepted an invitation from the congregation in New Westminster in 1887. Five other pastorates followed, namely, Victoria (Centennial), New Westminster, Vancouver (Mount Pleasant), Chilliwack, and Nelson. All of these were strategic congregations in the rapidly developing life of the province.

In 1902 the Methodist Board of Home Missions appointed White superintendent of missions for British Columbia and the Yukon Territory, which post he held until retirement in 1923. Sympathetic, understanding, and wise in counsel, he proved to be a helpful friend to pioneer congregations and their ministers. With a statesman's vision, he helped prepare the Methodists for union, in 1925, with the Congregationalists and Presbyterians.

White was sincere and fervent in his preaching, an advocate of temperance and social justice, and particularly a friend and counselor of young ministers. In 1892 he was President of British Columbia Conference. In 1904 VICTORIA UNIVERSITY, Toronto, conferred on him an honorary D.D. He died on May 26, 1948, and was buried in New Westminster.

G. H. Cornish, *Cyclopaedia of Methodism.* 1881, 1903.
Records of British Columbia Conference.   W. P. BUNT

WHITE, JOHN (1574-1648), may have been the maternal grandfather of SAMUEL WESLEY, rector of EPWORTH and father of JOHN and CHARLES WESLEY. The maternal grandfather of SUSANNA WESLEY, wife of Samuel, was also named JOHN WHITE.

The subject of this sketch was a contemporary of his namesake, and in several matters of public interest they were associated. From Winchester School White went to New College, Oxford, and became a fellow of that College in 1595. After ordination he preached frequently in and around Oxford and in 1606 became rector of Trinity Church, Dorchester. His sympathy with those being persecuted for their religious views led him and others to secure a patent for the colony of MASSACHUSETTS in New England as a refuge for those who suffered for their faith.

He himself was roughly treated by Archbishop Laud and for a time suffered imprisonment. During the British civil war his house was plundered by Prince Rupert's cavalry, and he lost his library. He fled to London and was appointed minister of the Savoy Chapel.

In 1640 he was made a member of the Committee of Religion appointed by the House of Lords, and in 1643 he was appointed to the Westminster Assembly of Divines. For a short time he was rector of Lambeth and during that period refused the wardenship of New College (1647).

Increasing physical weakness prompted his return to Dorchester, where for many years he had labored. He died at seventy-four years of age, respected and admired by his townsmen who spoke of him as the "Patriarch of Dorchester." John Wesley appears to have believed that White's daughter, Mrs. John Wesley, became the mother of Samuel Wesley, rector of Epworth, but Frances Rose-Troup (*John White, the Patriarch of Dorchester*, New York, 1930) shows that this is highly unlikely.

MALDWYN L. EDWARDS

WHITE, JOHN (1590-1644), the father of SUSANNA WESLEY's mother, son of Henry White from Pembrokeshire, entered Jesus College, Oxford about 1607 and on completing his studies was admitted to the Middle Temple and became a member of the bar and a bencher. As a convinced Puritan he was regularly employed by Puritans in law cases. In 1640 he became a Member of Parliament for the borough of Southwark, and threw himself into the opposition to the established Church. He was appointed chairman of the Committee for Religion and became a member of the Westminster Assembly of Divines. In one of his speeches (1641) he contended, as JOHN WESLEY did later, that bishops and presbyters were the same order, but he pushed matters to an extreme when he argued that the offices of deacons, curates, and vicars were human in origin and had no validity. He was prejudiced against bishops and could see no useful purpose even in that office. In his office as chairman of the Committee for Religion, it is recorded that in 1643 he received a list of a hundred "scandalous clergy," and later he published a book entitled *The First Century of Scandalous Malignant Priests*. A few months later, before he could publish his second volume, he died. John White may have been a learned lawyer, but he allowed his bitter animus against the Anglican Church to prejudice his mind. Even if one allows some of the cases he cited to be men of evil character, they were only a hundred out of eight thousand who were ejected from their livings during and after the British civil war. His attack lacks weight because he pushed it too far. He was buried in the Temple Church on January 29, 1644, and the inscription on the marble stone reads:

> Here lyeth a John, a burning shining light,
> His name, life, actions, were all White.

One must comment on the strange fact that the maternal grandfather of SAMUEL WESLEY and the maternal grandfather of Susanna Wesley were both named John White.

MALDWYN L. EDWARDS

WHITE, MOSES CLARK (1819-1900), a pioneer American missionary in Foochow, CHINA, opened what was probably the first dispensary in that nation. He was born in Paris, Oneida County, N. Y., on July 24, 1819, and was educated at WESLEYAN UNIVERSITY at Middletown, Conn., and at Yale Divinity School. He was ordained and joined the Methodist Conference in 1847. That same year he married Jane Isabel Atwater of Homer, N. Y., and together they sailed for China as missionaries. She died at Foochow the following year, but Moses White remained there until 1853. During this period he conducted the dispensary in Foochow. He also translated and published *The Gospel of Matthew* in the Foochow dialect— the first Christian work in that language. Returning to the United States in 1853, he received his medical degree from Yale, practiced medicine in New Haven, and served on the faculties of Yale and Wesleyan until his retirement. He died on Oct. 24, 1900.

W. W. REID

WHITE, THOMAS (1730-1795), was a magistrate who lived near Whitleysburg, Kent County, DELAWARE. He is important in the history of American Methodism because he gave sanctuary to FRANCIS ASBURY from the fall of 1778 to the spring of 1780, the period in the Revolutionary War when it was not safe for Asbury as an Englishman who would not take the oath of allegiance to travel and preach at large.

White sheltered and defended Asbury at some risk to himself. As a Methodist he was suspected of being at least lukewarm toward the independence of the colonies, and in the spring of 1778 he was arrested and imprisoned for five weeks. Later he was exonerated.

Asbury and others preached in White's home, and in time a Methodist chapel was built on his estate. Also, it was in White's home on April 28, 1779, that Asbury conducted a conference of the preachers on the northern circuits, and at that time they accepted him as their leader.

Asbury held White in high esteem, referring to him

HOME OF JUDGE THOMAS WHITE

as his "dearest friend in America," and adding that White had shown him more "real affection" than "any man I ever met." After the war Asbury referred to White's abode as "my former home."

On learning of White's death, Asbury wrote (May 21, 1795) that the news was "an awful shock." "I have met with nothing like it in the death of any friend on the continent. . . . I have lived days, weeks, and months in his house. . . . He was a friend to the poor and oppressed; he had been a professed Churchman, and was united to the Methodist connection about seventeen or eighteen years. His house and heart were always open. . . . He was an affectionate friend."

In 1810 JESSE LEE referred in his history to Asbury's time in White's home as a period of inactivity. Asbury replied that except for "about two months of retirement, from the direst necessity, it was the most active" part of his life, a period when 1,800 members were won and the foundation laid for the success of Methodism in Delaware.

F. Asbury, *Journal and Letters*. 1958.
E. S. Bucke, *History of American Methodism*. 1964.
Henry C. Conrad, *Samuel White and His Father Judge Thomas White*. Wilmington, Del.: John M. Rogers Press, 1903.
J. Lednum, *Rise of Methodism*. 1859.
M. Simpson, *Cyclopaedia*. 1878.

W. O. HACKETT
ALBEA GODBOLD

WHITE, WILLIAM (1794-?), NEW ZEALAND minister, was ordained in 1822, and arrived from England, via SYDNEY, on May 15, 1823 on the *St. Michael*. Kaeo was fixed upon as the site of the first mission station, and there work was begun under the leadership of SAMUEL LEIGH on June 8, 1823. Later that year, White returned to Sydney hoping to marry, but the lady refused to accompany him to New Zealand, so he came back alone after some six weeks. He left Whangaroa Harbour (on which Kaeo is situated) on Sept. 19, 1825, to go to England, and had not returned when the Wesleydale station was destroyed in 1827.

While in England he married, and returned to New Zealand in January 1830, to resume the Superintendency of the Mission at its new headquarters at Mangungu. He remained there until 1836.

Serious trouble developed between White and his colleagues. Though his sincerity and faithfulness in the early days of the Mission could not be denied, "he suffered from the slow invasion of a worldly spirit, and became increasingly a man of business and affairs. The secular interests of the mission absorbed him until, as one of his brethren said, he became 'a kind of missionary merchant.'" (Laws, *Toil and Adversity*, p. 16). Strong differences with his brethren led to JOHN HOBBS going to TONGA and to JAMES STACK retiring from the mission.

These troubles, as well as certain irregularities of character and administration, led the Sydney authorities of the mission to send NATHANIEL TURNER to New Zealand "to relieve White of his Superintendency of the Mission and to institute a thorough enquiry into the charges against him." (Laws, *First Years*, p. 32.) This enquiry led to the termination of White's employment by the mission, a sad end to a missionary career which had begun with great promise.

White later entered into business in AUCKLAND as a trader and merchant.

C. H. Laws, *First Years at Hokianga, 1827-1836*. Wesley Historical Society, New Zealand, 1945.
——————————. *Toil and Adversity at Whangaroa*. Wesley Historical Society, New Zealand, 1944.   L. R. M. GILMORE

WHITE, WILLIAM (Bishop of the Protestant Episcopal Church in America.) (See COKE-WHITE CORRESPONDENCE.)

WHITE, WOODIE WALTER (1935-   ), American minister, was born in New York City, Aug. 27, 1935 to Woodie W. and Elizabeth (Truitt) White. He graduated from PAINE COLLEGE with the B.A. degree, 1958, as valedictorian. The S.T.B. degree was received from BOSTON SCHOOL OF THEOLOGY in 1961. He served appointments in MASSACHUSETTS during his schooling and was married June 3, 1961 to Kim Tolson.

The DETROIT CONFERENCE ordained Mr. White as deacon, 1961, and elder, 1963. He received the first bi-racial appointment in MICHIGAN as associate minister, East Grand Boulevard Church, DETROIT, and served from 1961-63 and pastor of the same church, 1963-67. For a year, 1967-68, he was the urban missioner for the denomination in Metropolitan Detroit. When The United Methodist Church established the Commission on RELIGION AND RACE in 1968, he became its executive secretary.

Woodie White has been the past president, college chapter, National Association for the Advancement of Colored People; past president, East Citizens for Action (Detroit); past president, Churches on the East Side for Social Action; and member of Interfaith ACTION Council, Inc.; Methodists for Church Renewal; and an organizer of Black Methodists for Church Renewal. In 1968 he received the Urban Award from the Office of Economic Opportunity "for outstanding work with the people of the Ghetto."

Who's Who in The Methodist Church, 1966.
                                        JOHN H. NESS, JR.

WHITEFIELD, GEORGE (1714-1770), was born in Gloucester, the son of an innkeeper, on Dec. 16, 1714. After an imperfect schooling he entered Pembroke College, Oxford, as a servitor (1734), where he became a member of the HOLY CLUB. His early religious concerns came to a crisis early in 1735 when Scougal's *Life of God in the Soul of Man* convinced him of the need for a "new birth," which, after a struggle, he experienced.

GEORGE WHITEFIELD

Later that year Puritan literature brought him to a knowledge of "free grace" and justification "by faith only." He was ordained deacon (June, 1736) and shortly after graduated with a B.A. In 1737 Whitefield began to make his mark in churches and religious societies as a preacher of the new birth. He then worked in GEORGIA (May-September, 1738), where he planned an orphanage and did parochial work as well as preaching before returning to England to collect funds for the orphanage and to obtain ordination as priest (he was received through COUNTESS SELINA HUNTINGDON's interest in January, 1739).

Finding the churches in England closed to him as a result both of his criticism of the clergy and the revelations of "enthusiasm" in his preaching and published *Journal*, Whitefield fell back on preaching to the religious societies and (in Bristol from January, 1739) to field preaching, which became his established custom. He defended his irregularities by claiming that as an Anglican clergyman he needed no further license and was not covered by the Conventicle Act.

He persuaded the Wesleys to join him in field preaching from April 1739, although he saw JOHN WESLEY's main value as one to "confirm those who are awakened" in societies. But in 1739-40 Whitefield's views on grace and predestination became more explicitly Calvinistic, and Wesley's attacks on predestination at this time led to estrangement. For the rest of Whitefield's life there was only occasional cooperation between the two, although they were personally reconciled, and Wesley preached Whitefield's funeral sermon in England. The most violent predestination controversy in England broke out in 1770 in Whitefield's absence and almost at the time of his death.

Whitefield's career as an open-air preacher carried him through the British Isles and also seven times to America. In Wales he was associated with HOWELL HARRIS, and in America with New England revivalists like the Tennents. Whitefield did much to spread and refresh the "Awakening" in America; and he also supported his Georgia orphanage, which he later used to train preachers. Like Wesley, Whitefield had no special plan when he began his evangelistic career. He concentrated largely on preaching tours, though he also worked through the tabernacles which were built for him in London. Unlike Wesley, he did not develop a permanent "connexion" under his own supervision, although some societies and preachers looked to his rather spasmodic oversight, particularly in the west of England; and the tabernacles were organized in CLASSES in the Moravian-Methodist manner.

He was also involved as "Moderator" of Howell Harris' WELSH CALVINISTIC METHODIST Conference, organized from 1743 to cover parts of England as well as Wales with preachers and societies. But Whitefield's real position was recognized when Harris in 1749 formally took over full supervision, and left Whitefield free to "strengthen their hands" as far as his primary preaching activities allowed. He explained to John Wesley that any societies he formed would only be a "Penelope's web" (Letter to J. Wesley, Sept. 1, 1748, in Whitefield's *Works*, ii. 370), so he rejected Wesley's methods for himself and simply preached.

From 1748 he was more closely connected with the Countess of Huntingdon's plan to revive the Church of England, by awakening the existing clergy and obtaining ordination and chapels for new ones as her domestic chaplains. Through her patronage Whitefield increased his access to aristocratic hearers who listened to him at least as a curiosity. Whitefield remained attached, however loosely, to Anglicanism; and the evolution of Lady Huntingdon's connection into a separate body took place some years after his death. In his lifetime the group was essentially an evangelistic umbrella for evangelicals of all kinds, held up by the countess herself.

Whitefield's theology was as much emotional as rational, and his CALVINISM was not rigidly worked out. He began from a concern to emphasize "vital" as against "formal" religion; and theologically to uphold grace, justification by faith, and regeneration against the "salvation of works" with which he charged the currently popular sermons of the late Archbishop Tillotson. This was the root of the theological antagonism he aroused in the Church at large. Wesley himself maintained that Whitefield's primary doctrines were the new birth and justification by faith; though in fact Whitefield did not omit to teach works following justification, and could at times speak strongly of dominion over inward sin. He moved, however—(and notably in conflict with Wesley)—to a more definitely Calvinistic system, emphasizing the comfort of the doctrines of election and final perseverance. He distrusted both Wesley's Arminianism and his perfectionism, which he saw as destructive of grace and goodness, and as relying on works for salvation. Wesley in return accused Whitefield of the crudest predestinarianism, morally intolerable and ethically disastrous. Whitefield was in fact less doctrinaire than controversy made him appear: he frequently begged Wesley not to dispute but to "offer salvation freely by the blood of Jesus"; and this (whether consistently or not) was how he himself preached salvation as if available to all.

In person, Whitefield seems to have been found attractive (despite the much satirized squint). (A. Lyles, *Methodism Mocked*, London, 1960, pp. 127-139.) The defects of his background and education combined with his preaching success to cause him mental conflicts over pride, and made him uncertain in his dealings with the aristocracy. However he was not as obsequious to them as is sometimes alleged. Preaching was almost his sole interest, and he was credited with enormous crowds and devastating effect. His methods were passionate, rhetorical, dramatic, and his sermons extempory and based on little specific preparation. His primary aim was to arouse and convert rather than to consolidate believers. The results are difficult to assess: he mentions large numbers of "inquirers" rather than outright converts; but although he dealt with these by interview and correspondence (the latter giving indefinite and rather generalized advice), the lack of a coherent organization for cultivating their progress meant that others were left to do much of this work. By his own confession and intention, then, Whitefield was an "awakener" and stimulant for the eighteenth-century revival at large; and in this role he provided a certain link between its various branches. His abilities and Wesley's were complementary and in the early days perhaps deliberately so; but theological as well as temperamental differences probably made any systematic cooperation impossible. Worn out with preaching, Whitefield died of asthma at Newburyport, Mass., on Sept. 30, 1770.

L. Tyerman, *George Whitefield*. 1876-77.
A. D. Belden, *George Whitefield*. 1930.
J. Gillies, *George Whitefield*. 1772.

H. RACK

WHITEFIELD HOUSE, a point of interest to American Methodism, is located in the town of Nazareth, Pa., near Allentown and Bethlehem. Through the generosity of WILLIAM SEWARD, his traveling companion, GEORGE WHITEFIELD in April 1740, proposed "to erect a free school for Negro children" and "to take up land and to settle a town for the reception of such English friends whose hearts God shall incline to come and settle there." In May of 1740 Seward negotiated with William Allen of Philadelphia for a tract of 5,000 acres "drained by branches of the Menakasy and Lehietan . . . for 2200 pounds sterling." (See Seward's *Journal of a Voyage from Savannah to Philadelphia*, and *From Philadelphia to England*, 1740.)

According to PETER BÖHLER's *Historical Account of Nazareth*, Whitefield hired newly arrived MORAVIANS from Georgia "to do the woodwork of the [school] building. . . . Indeed, he wanted the Moravians to manage the whole construction . . ." Whitefield named the town Nazareth after the home of Jesus in Galilee.

A quarrel arose between Böhler and Whitefield, partly over theological matters, and Whitefield dismissed his Moravian workmen. Whitefield was unable to continue building, and he returned to England where his financial backer, William Seward, died. Facing a financial crisis, Whitefield sold his Pennsylvania Estate to AUGUSTUS G. SPANGENBERG for the use of the Moravian Brethren. The Moravians completed the building and named it Whitefield House.

The building was never used as a school for Negro children nor for Negro orphans, but was extensively used by the Moravians in their educational work. It housed the Bethlehem girls' boarding school and the Single Sisters Choir during the three and a half years between the middle of 1745 and the end of 1748; a second school for girls from December of 1753 to June of 1756; and a third one between November 1765, and the middle of the nineteenth century. When Bethlehem was too crowded to accommodate the nursery, as was the case during most of the decade between 1749 and 1759, that infant school was also happily quartered in Nazareth's Whitefield House.

In 1746 Whitefield was again on cordial terms with the Moravians and made his one and only visit to the building and land he had once owned. He heartily approved of what the Moravians were doing, and was particularly impressed by the fact that six of the girls in the school were Indians.

In time the house, instead of being used as a school, became a home for retired ministers and missionaries. Today, it is also used for Moravian historical treasures, and the museum part of the House is open to the public. It is said to contain books, paintings, household items of historic interest and some of America's oldest musical instruments.

Mabel Haller, *Early Moravian Education in Pennsylvania.* Nazareth, Pa.: Moravian Historical Society, 1953.

FREDERICK E. MASER

WHITEFIELD'S ORPHAN HOUSE. (See BETHESDA, Whitefield's Orphan House.)

WHITEHEAD, JOHN (1740-1804), was physician to the old Bethlehem Hospital. For a short time he was one of JOHN WESLEY's itinerant preachers, but soon returned to his profession. He joined the Society of Friends but soon went back to Methodism. He attended both John and CHARLES WESLEY during their last illness. On March 9, 1791, he preached John Wesley's funeral sermon in City Road Chapel. Wesley appointed him, with THOMAS COKE and HENRY MOORE, an executor of his will to examine and dispose of his papers and manuscripts. Whitehead was appointed to write the official life of John Wesley, but a dispute arose about the use and possession of Wesley's papers. Thereupon Coke and Moore collaborated in writing a *Life of Wesley* and forestalled the publication of Whitehead's in two volumes, 1793-96. He was interred in Wesley's vault in the graveyard behind City Road Chapel.

JOHN NEWTON

WHITEHOUSE, WILLIAM WHITCOMB (1891-   ), American minister and college president, was born Oct. 28, 1891, in Yorkshire, England, the son of John and Elizabeth (Whitcomb) Whitehouse. Emigrating to the United States in 1913, he was educated at Lebanon (Ohio) University (A.B., 1916), GARRETT (B.D., 1917), LAWRENCE COLLEGE (A.M., 1919), DREW (Th.D., 1922), and NORTHWESTERN (Ph.D., 1927), His academic honors included Phi Beta Kappa and the LL.D., L.H.D., and D.D. degrees. He married Grace May Harrison, June 27, 1917, and they had two children. After her death in 1941, he married Adele Ann Dreyer in 1943.

Admitted on trial in the DETROIT CONFERENCE in 1913, Whitehouse was appointed to Brimley and Mission. He was ordained DEACON in 1915 and ELDER in 1916. Transferring to the WISCONSIN CONFERENCE in 1917, he served Asbury, MILWAUKEE, and then became an army CHAPLAIN. In 1919 he transferred to the MICHIGAN CONFERENCE and was appointed to Parma. There followed two years in school after which all his appointments were to educational institutions: 1922-29, professor of economics, ALBION COLLEGE; 1929-39, dean at Albion; 1939-45, dean at Wayne State University; 1945-60, president of Albion; and 1960-   , president emeritus.

Whitehouse delivered the John Shaffer Foundation Lectures at Northwestern University in 1938, and also lectured at different times at CHICAGO, Ill., Michigan, and

Purdue Universities. In 1958 he was president of the American Association of Colleges. He served on President Eisenhower's Commission on Scientists and Engineers, and in addition held through the years more than twenty other offices and board, commission, and committee memberships relating to educational, governmental, church, business, and community affairs. He was a contributor to professional and educational journals. After retirement in 1960, he continued to live in Albion, Mich.

General Minutes, MEC.
Minutes of the West Michigan Conference, 1971.
Who's Who in America, 1966-67.
Who's Who in The Methodist Church.   ALBEA GODBOLD

WHITELAMB, JOHN (1710-1769), was born near WROOT, in the Isle of Axholme, Lincolnshire, England, the child of very poor parents. Wroot was near Epworth, and Whitelamb was educated largely at the expense of the Wesley family; he helped to prepare SAMUEL WESLEY's *Dissertations on the Book of Job* for the printer. Whitelamb was admitted to Lincoln College, Oxford, in 1731, and became a member of the HOLY CLUB; he did not quite fulfill his early promise, however, and left Oxford without taking a degree; he was accepted for holy orders in 1733. He married MARY WESLEY in January 1734, but she and her first child were buried together on Nov. 1, 1734. Samuel Wesley had resigned the living of Wroot to Whitelamb in 1734, and he remained there as rector for the rest of his life, growing apparently much less certain of his Christian faith. When he died, JOHN WESLEY commented: "Why did he not die forty years ago, when he knew in whom Whitelamb had believed." He was buried on July 29, 1769.

V. H. H. Green, *Young Mr. Wesley.* 1961.
J. Wesley, *Letters,* Vol. V, p. 151, Oct. 4, 1769.

JOHN NEWTON

JOHN WHITELEY

WHITELEY, JOHN (1806-1869), NEW ZEALAND minister and missionary martyr, was born at Kneesall, Nottinghamshire, England, on July 20, 1806, and was brought up in nearby Newark. In 1827, he became a LOCAL PREACHER, and, a little later, was accepted for the ministry. With missionary service in view, he was married to Mary Ann Cooke at South Collington on Sept. 4, 1832, and on Sept. 27, was ordained in Lambeth Chapel. Mr. and Mrs. Whiteley left England by the ship "Caroline" on Oct. 23, 1832, and arrived in New Zealand on May 21, 1833, where they took up their first appointment at Mangungu, on the Hokianga River, North AUCKLAND.

Whiteley quickly learned the Maori language and became familiar with native customs. Two years later he was appointed to a new station at Kawhia, but after only thirteen months, was withdrawn because of "boundary disputes" with the Church Missionary Society. The Whiteleys were transferred to Pakane, near Mangungu, which they renamed Newark. They were able to return early in 1839 to Kawhia, where they served until 1855.

Whiteley's work at Kawhia took him on many hazardous journeys, traveling on foot to visit Maoris in their villages, by canoe up rivers, and over long distances on horseback. He became one of the best preachers in the Maori language and gained the confidence of the people. He acted as magistrate in both Maori and European disputes and his judgments were never questioned. Such was his influence with the Maoris that he was able to persuade the confederation of Waikato tribes to release the slaves taken by them on their war expeditions to Taranaki between 1830 and 1835. He was appointed to New Plymouth to take charge of the work in Taranaki in 1856, where at this time, there was grave threat of trouble between Maoris and Europeans. He traveled tirelessly between the encampments of British soldiers and the Maori villages in the district, and was everywhere received with love and esteem.

It was on one of these journeys that he met his death on Feb. 13, 1869, when the Taranaki Wars were nearly over. He was traveling to Pukearuhe, the most northerly outpost of the Taranaki settlement some thirty miles from New Plymouth, hoping to save the lives of Lieutenant Gascoigne and a few soldiers who were manning the blockhouse there, on which attack by hostile Maoris was imminent. He arrived too late. When the Maoris, flushed with victory, saw an unidentified horseman approaching at dusk, they called on him to stop. This challenge Whiteley ignored, probably in the belief that the Maoris would not molest him, but in their excited state, they fired, first shooting his horse and then killing him.

Whiteley was held in such high esteem that when it was realized that it was he who had been killed, the Maori warriors were overwhelmed with grief and shame. When he heard the news, Chief Wahanui immediately retreated with his men to the King Country, where he spoke the memorable words which virtually ended the fighting between the two peoples: "Here let it end; for the death of Whiteley is more than the death of many men."

Whiteley was buried in the Te Henui Cemetery, New Plymouth. There is a monument to him and to the other victims of the White Cliffs (Pukearuhe) tragedy in the cemetery and also a cairn at the spot where he was killed.

G. G. Carter, *John Whiteley—Missionary Martyr*. Wesley Historical Society, New Zealand, 1952.
W. Morley, *Methodism in New Zealand*. McKee & Co. Wellington, 1900.
B. LAURIE COOPER

WHITEWAY, SOLOMON PARDY (1868-1950), Canadian educator, was born at Musgrave Harbour, Newfoundland. He was educated at the St. John's Methodist College and at Columbia University from which he received the B.S. degree in Education. His teaching career began in 1886; after serving in several smaller Methodist schools, he joined the staff of the Methodist College in St. John's in

1896. When he retired from this post in 1920 he became principal of the Newfoundland Inter-Denominational Normal School, which office he held until 1932.

Throughout his career Whiteway was a member of the Newfoundland Teachers Association. As secretary in 1913-14, he organized the association's participation in tours of the British Isles within the Canadian Hands Across the Seas Movement. He was a member of the Newfoundland Historical Society and secretary of the Newfoundland Nomenclature Board from 1933 to 1950. Moreover, he was an energetic figure on the Methodist College's board and later on the board of Memorial University College. In 1937 he was a delegate at a conference of the Central Advisory Committee on Education in the Maritime Provinces and Newfoundland, held in Halifax.

In his own church he was equally active, as secretary in the late 1930's of the United Church's Board of Evangelism and Social Service, and as archivist for the Newfoundland Conference from 1947 to 1950. He was a member of the Education Council of the United Church in St. John's, Newfoundland and elder in his own congregation, George Street, St. John's.

In 1928 MOUNT ALLISON UNIVERSITY honored him with the LL.D. He refused a cabinet post in Newfoundland and a Canadian senatorship when Confederation took place in 1949.

Whiteway's was a life of service above self, but the quality of his service raised him to a higher place in Newfoundland education than any rewards he might have gained in other aspects of his career. The advancement of education and of his church were the predominant goals of his life. He will never be forgotten by those who came under his influence.

W. F. BUTT

WHITFIELD, GEORGE (1753-1832), Methodist preacher, was stationed in the London Circuit by WESLEY in 1785, and for some years served as his traveling companion as well as BOOK STEWARD. He was named in Wesley's will (1789) as one of a committee to superintend Methodist publishing, but in fact he seems to have exercised a large measure of control both before Wesley's death and (especially) after. At the CONFERENCE of 1804 he was superseded by Robert Lomas, but remained for some time as his assistant. He is to be distinguished from GEORGE WHITEFIELD (1714-1770), to whom he was not related. After a lengthy retirement in London he died Dec. 24, 1832, aged seventy-nine.

FRANK BAKER

WHITING, ETHEL LITITIA (1885-1965), was the central treasurer in INDIA for the WOMAN'S FOREIGN MISSIONARY SOCIETY, 1931-39, and then for the Woman's Division of the Board of Missions of The Methodist Church. Previously she had served eighteen years as principal of the Kanpur (Cawnpore) Girl's High School.

She was born on a farm in Harding, Neb., May 11, 1885, and died at Sherman Oaks, Calif., Nov. 9, 1965. Her college was NEBRASKA WESLEYAN, from which she received a B.A. degree in 1907. In 1926, during a furlough, she received from the same college an M.A. degree in education. A year of study in the Chicago Training School preceded her departure for India in 1912.

Miss Whiting accepted numerous responsibilities and performed them all with precision. For many years she was an ex officio member of the executive board and of the

Interim Committee of the Methodist Church in Southern Asia. At one time or another her responsibilities extended to Pakistan, Burma, and Nepal, and she visited almost every major institution and work center of her church in each of those countries, as well as in India. Her interdenominational connections were numerous and her contributions to them rich and varied. After retirement she served on the staff of the BOARD OF MISSIONS in NEW YORK for two years, with the All-Nations Foundation in LOS ANGELES for three years, and with First Methodist Church in Van Nuys for four years.

Minutes of the Executive Board of the Methodist Church in Southern Asia.   J. WASKOM PICKETT

WHITLA, SIR WILLIAM (1851-1933), Irish physician and author of many medical works, was born at Monaghan, IRELAND. For many years he was Professor of Materia Medica and Therapeutics at Queen's University, BELFAST. His pre-eminence in medicine was recognized by a knighthood and the Presidency of the British Medical Association. He represented Queen's University at Westminster as M.P., 1919-24. He was prominently identified with the Methodist Church in Ireland, and supported the philanthropic work of the city missions. In Belfast, the Whitla Hall of the METHODIST COLLEGE, and the Sir William Whitla Hall of Queen's University, were erected through bequests made by him.

FREDERICK JEFFERY

WHITMORE, BENJAMIN ARTHUR (1892-   ), American publishing agent, banker, and influential layman, was born at Hooper's Island, Md., Feb. 1, 1892, son of Alfred Alexander and Emma Jane (Robinett) Whitmore.

He was educated in the public schools and Hargrove Military Academy, Chatham, Va., 1908-09. FLORIDA SOUTHERN COLLEGE conferred the LL.D. degree upon him in 1935.

He became connected with the Publishing House of the M.E. Church, South, first in its RICHMOND, Va., branch in 1912; later, its manager there, 1920-26; and then in 1926 was elected Publishing Agent of the Church with headquarters at Nashville, Tenn. In 1940 he was elected Publishing Agent of The Methodist Church serving 1940-45, during the important period of reorganization of the former publishing interests of the M.E., M.E. South, and M.P. Churches at and after unification.

From 1946-63 he was vice-president and trust officer of the Third National Bank, NASHVILLE. He was a member of the BOARD OF PUBLICATION (1952-60), The Methodist Church; trustee of the Joint University Library and of SCARRITT COLLEGE. A delegate to several GENERAL and JURISDICTIONAL CONFERENCES, he served for many years as the treasurer of the Southeastern Jurisdiction. He has been prominent in the Nashville Chamber of Commerce.

On Oct. 1, 1913, he was married to Florence Sampson, and their daughter, Ann Robinett is Mrs. William L. Woodruff. After retirement, Mr. Whitmore continued to live in NASHVILLE, Tenn.

Who's Who in The Methodist Church, 1966. J. MARVIN RAST

WHITTIER, CALIFORNIA, U.S.A. The city of Whittier was named for John Greenleaf Whittier, the famous Quaker poet and abolitionist who gave to the CALIFORNIA town

his approval in 1887 for such use of his name. The Society of Friends have always been extremely strong in Whittier.

On March 17, 1888, fifteen Methodists drove their buggies over the dusty streets, or walked through the mustard fields, to assemble in a brick building at Greenleaf and Hadley Streets where they organized the M.E. Church of Whittier.

In the first year there came successively three ministers from Fulton-Wells, G. C. Lewis, F. M. Larkin, and B. F. Wolff, to hold services on Sunday afternoons either in the building at Greenleaf and Hadley, the Friends Academy on East Philadelphia or on the second floor of the Jonathan Bailey School.

Thomas Stalker became first resident pastor in September 1889, and with the Methodist congregation growing, he led a drive for a building. A lot was found at Bailey and Friends Avenue. Here a $2,300 frame building was constructed and paid for. In the early part of 1890 the thirty-seven members proudly gathered for services in the new sanctuary.

In 1904 the 366 members under the leadership of W. A. Betts had the frame building moved away and built a new church which was destined to serve for forty-seven years, until it was replaced by a modern sanctuary in 1952.

Whittier has always been a town of strong Bible classes, and in 1921 the SUNDAY SCHOOL had an enrollment of 1,400 with an average attendance of 700.

The present sanctuary and associated four church buildings were developed from 1952 through 1962, mostly under the ministerial leadership of Russell E. Clay. These are on the same Friends and Bailey Street site that the church has occupied since 1890. Whittier College is only two blocks away.

J. Richard Sneed, whose pastorate began in 1963, led the church to the completion of all indebtedness on Dec. 31, 1967.

The Friends Church, one of the most prestigious in the nation, is a neighbor in the same block. The Quakers and the Methodists through the years have been close friends, and work together amicably in every way. In 1970 the membership of First Church, Whittier, was 2,062, and there is a comparable church staff with three ministers.

General Minutes, UMC, 1970.

WHITWORTH, ABRAHAM, was an Englishman who became an early American Methodist itinerant. He was present at the first conference of American Methodism at ST. GEORGE's in PHILADELPHIA in 1773; he was stationed in Baltimore together with FRANCIS ASBURY, ROBERT STRAWBRIDGE and Joseph Yearbry, and he joined the Conference the following year. He preached with great success along the eastern and western shores of Maryland and in New Jersey where he was instrumental in the conversion of BENJAMIN ABBOTT, a powerful early American Methodist itinerant. Whitworth is mentioned a number of times in Asbury's *Journal.*

He also has the dubious honor of being the first American Methodist itinerant expelled from Methodism, probably for drunkenness. Stevens, the Methodist historian, says, "While on the Kent Circuit he fell by intemperance, and fell apparently to rise no more," During the Revolution he joined the British forces and seems to have died of wounds received in battle. The dates of his birth and death are not known.

J. Lednum, *Rise of Methodism.* 1859.
A. Stevens, *History of the M.E. Church.* 1867.

FREDERICK E. MASER

WHYEL, HARRY (1863-1949), American layman, who in 1941 presented the 179 acres and fifteen buildings of the former Soldier's and Sailor's Orphan School at historic Jumonville, Pa., to the PITTSBURGH CONFERENCE of The Methodist Church for use as a Training Center (see JUMONVILLE TRAINING CENTER). Harry Whyel was a pioneer coal and coke operator in Fayette County, Pa. He was a faithful member of Asbury Methodist Church of Uniontown, Pa. His generous gift made possible the development of "Jumonville" as one of the finest Conference Training Centers of Methodism. In giving the property Whyel said, "I am sure that I will never regret this and will be happy in seeing it develop and grow during the remaining few years that may be allotted to me." He reveled in the development of the property until his death in 1949.

W. G. Smeltzer, *Headwaters of the Ohio.* 1951.

W. GUY SMELTZER

WICHITA, KANSAS, U.S.A. (population 274,448 in 1970), named for the Wichita Indians, was settled in 1868, incorporated in 1870, and chartered as a city in 1886.

Methodism began in Wichita in May, 1870, with the organization of what is now First Church in a room over a livery stable. Two months previously, March 24-28, 1870, the KANSAS CONFERENCE had met in TOPEKA, and in its list of appointments was the notation, "Wichita to be supplied." In 1871 the Wichita charge reported 47 members. In 1872 the Wichita District was formed.

In 1876 a German-speaking congregation was organized in the town. By 1890 there were seven Methodist churches in Wichita with a total of 1,581 members, 920 of them in First Church. Between 1906 and 1942 some ten more churches were organized, one of them, St. Mark's which began in 1910, being a Negro congregation. Ten additional churches were started between 1951 and 1966.

In 1970 The United Methodist Church reported twenty-nine churches in Wichita with a total of 24,781 members, property valued at approximately $13,000,000, and some $2,000,000 raised for all purposes during the year.

First Methodist Church of Wichita—75 Years and Beyond. (Pamphlet). 1945.
General Minutes, MEC, MC, and UMC.   JESSE A. EARL

College Hill Church began Aug. 6, 1907, with a preliminary meeting of forty-five persons in the home of O. J. Taylor. The church was officially organized, Nov. 26, 1907. In December a house under construction on North Chautauqua Street was rented, and the partitions were omitted so as to make one large room which was fitted with 100 chairs. In April 1908, the conference appointed William T. Ward as the first pastor, and on May 1 he received sixty-seven charter members.

In June 1916, a new brick church at 201 North Erie Street was dedicated. At that time the church had 672 members. Later an education building and a temporary structure to be used for the same purpose were added. In 1963 the congregation occupied a new building with a seating capacity of 935 at 2930 East First Street. The sanctuary was dedicated Nov. 26, 1967. College Hill has sent fourteen men into the ministry and six women into full time Christian service.

In 1970 College Hill Church reported 2,474 members, property valued at $1,029,000, and $120,862 raised for all purposes during the year.

General Minutes, UMC.   BETTY KATHRYN TAYLOR

East Heights Church was the first Methodist congregation to be organized in Wichita following the second World War. In October 1945, the conference appointed Basil Johnson to "Oliver Street, Wichita." The next year he reported that the "East Heights Church" had 239 members and property valued at $16,000.

Located in a residential section of Wichita, the East Heights Church grew steadily; the membership exceeded 1,000 by 1952. Johnson continued as pastor for nineteen years. He led in building the chapel and educational unit in 1949 and the sanctuary in 1960.

In 1970 East Heights Church reported 2,312 members, property valued at $1,221,827, and $195,420 raised for all purposes during the year.

General Minutes, MC and UMC.   GEORGE W. RICHARDS

First Church was organized in May, 1870. During the winter of 1870-71, the congregation with W. H. Zellers as pastor, met in the Presbyterian Church. A Methodist edifice was dedicated about Dec. 1, 1872, and it was enlarged about 1878. In 1884 the building was destroyed by fire. The members believed the fire was of incendiary origin because their pastor had fought liquor and vice in the town. By May 1885, a new structure, considered the most beautiful church in the town, was dedicated free of debt. In April 1923, the congregation occupied a new Gothic structure built of artistically arranged limestone. Due to the economic depression, the entire indebtedness of some $150,000 was not paid in full until May, 1942. In recent years several additions have been built.

Within a few years after it was organized First Church became and still is the strongest church in the conference. Its peak membership was 3,786 in 1969. In 1970 the church reported 2,934 members, property valued at $2,598,660, and $364,990 raised for all purposes during the year.

First Methodist Church of Wichita—75 Years and Beyond. 1945.
General Minutes, ME, MC, and UMC.
W. F. Ramsdale, *Sketches Concerning the Wichita Churches.* (Typescript), 1967.   JESSE A. EARL

WICHITA FALLS, TEXAS, U.S.A. (population 94,976 in 1970) was founded in 1882 and became a city in 1889. Organized Methodism came to the area in November 1880, when the NORTH TEXAS CONFERENCE appointed F. O. Miller to the "Wichita Mission." In March 1881, Miller organized what is now First Church with six members. Designated a station in 1889, the church grew to more than 1,000 members by 1915, and in that year a second church, Floral Heights, was organized. The Wichita Falls District was formed in 1915.

In 1921 the WEST TEXAS CONFERENCE (ME) organized a Negro congregation with some twenty-nine members in Wichita Falls. Known as Mount Calvary Church, it became a part of the North Texas Conference in 1970 when the West Texas Conference of the CENTRAL JURISDICTION was merged. In that year Mount Calvary reported 96 members and property valued at $43,000.

In 1970 The United Methodist Church had eleven congregations in Wichita Falls with a total of 8,271 members, property valued at $4,836,763, and $1,062,623 raised for all purposes during the year.

General Minutes, MES, MEC, UMC. ROBBIE H. MCCRORY

First Church was organized in March 1881 by F. O. Miller who in the preceding fall had been appointed to the "Wichita Mission" by the North Texas Conference. The congregation had no building of its own until 1885 when a frame structure costing $300 was erected at Scott and Tenth Streets. Later additions lifted its value to $1,000. A new church was erected at the same location in 1910 when there were 584 members. In 1927 when the church had about 2,700 members it erected an impressive new edifice at a cost of $600,000, incurring a debt of some $137,000. The building was dedicated in 1939.

PAUL E. MARTIN was elected bishop in 1944 while serving as pastor of First Church. Following the second World War the church became widely known for three philanthropists in its membership—JOE J. PERKINS, his wife LOIS C. PERKINS, and J. S. Bridwell. Perkins gave some $10,000,000 to the Southern Methodist School of Theology which now bears his name. Bridwell donated the money for the Bridwell Library of the Perkins School of Theology. Both families also gave liberally to other church institutions and causes.

In 1970 First Church reported 2,052 members, property value at $2,185,094, and $653,767 raised for all purposes during the year.

General Minutes, MES, MC, and UMC.
Minutes of the North Texas Conference.

HOWARD H. HOLLOWELL

LLOYD C. WICKE

WICKE, LLOYD CHRIST (1901-   ), American bishop, was born in Cleveland, Ohio, on May 22, 1901, the son of John and Catherine (Christ) Wicke. He attended BALDWIN-WALLACE COLLEGE, receiving an A.B. degree, 1923, and a D.D., 1941; DREW THEOLOGICAL SEMINARY, B.D. in 1926, and Ph.D., 1938; LYCOMING COLLEGE, and WEST VIRGINIA WESLEYAN, LL.D.; ALLEGHENY COLLEGE, Litt.D. He did postgraduate work at New York, Yale, Columbia, and SYRACUSE Universities, and Union Theological Seminary.

On Sept. 20, 1924, he married Gertrude Allen of Waterville, N. Y. They have two daughters: Shirley Jane (Mrs. F. Robert Shoaf) and Elaine Nalda (Mrs. Bruce S. Cowen).

Bishop Wicke was ordained an ELDER in 1926. His pastorates included East Side Terrace, Paterson, N. J., 1925-26; Lafayette, N. J., 1926-29; Alpine, N. J., 1929-35; Leonia, N. J., 1935-41; Mt. Lebanon, PITTSBURGH, Pa., 1943-48. He was superintendent of the Jersey City District from 1941-43. He was elected bishop in 1948 by the NORTHEASTERN JURISDICTIONAL CONFERENCE and served the Pittsburgh Area, 1948-60; then the NEW YORK Area after 1960.

He was president of the Board of Social and Economic Relations of The Methodist Church; president of the COUNCIL OF BISHOPS, 1964-65; and is a member of the General Board of the WORLD COUNCIL OF CHURCHES.

He also served as president of the World Division of the BOARD OF MISSIONS and Chairman of the Ad Hoc Committee which directed the merger of the E.U.B. Church and The Methodist Church. He is vice-president of the TELEVISION, RADIO AND FILM COMMISSION (TRAFCO).

Bishop Wicke has officially represented American Methodism in ALASKA, South America, MALAYSIA, the Far East, AFRICA, INDIA, Latin America and the PHILIPPINES, and under presidential appointment is a member of the National Citizens' Committee for Community Relations.

Who's Who in America, Vol. 34.
Who's Who in The Methodist Church, 1966.   N. B. H.

WICKE, MYRON FOREST (1907-   ), American minister and church official in the field of higher education, was born at CLEVELAND, Ohio, on Jan. 27, 1907. His parents were John and Katherine (Christ) Wicke. His older brother is Bishop LLOYD C. WICKE.

Myron Wicke received the A.B. degree from BALDWIN-WALLACE, 1930; the A.M. from Western Reserve University, 1934, and a Ph.D. there in 1941. He did postgraduate work in Columbia University, 1932, '33, and '35 and also in Oberlin College in 1935. He married Helen Garfield on Dec. 26, 1937, and they have two sons, Alan and Brian. He joined the TENNESSEE CONFERENCE on trial in 1951 and came into full connection in 1954, having been ordained deacon in 1955 and elder in 1958. He was the dean of Baldwin-Wallace College from 1943-49, and then the director of the Department of Secondary and Higher Education in the BOARD OF EDUCATION of The Methodist Church, Nashville, Tenn., 1949-58. He became associate general secretary, 1961-64, and then general secretary of the Division of Higher Education in 1965. He served for a time as the dean of SOUTHWESTERN UNIVERSITY, Georgetown, Texas, 1958-61, leaving that post to become general secretary, as mentioned above, in NASHVILLE. Dr. Wicke is a trustee of ALASKA METHODIST UNIVERSITY and DILLARD UNIVERSITY. He is the author of *Handbook for Trustees*, 1957; *On Teaching in a Christian*

College, 1959; *The Church-Related College,* 1964; *The Methodist Church and Higher Education,* 1965. He continued in this executive position for the Board of Education in The United Methodist Church after its reorganization in 1968.

Who's Who in The Methodist Church. 1966.   N. B. H.

WIGHTMAN, WILLIAM MAY (1808-1882), American bishop, was born in CHARLESTON, S. C., on Jan. 29, 1808. He graduated from the College of Charleston in 1827 and was licensed to preach the same year. He joined the SOUTH CAROLINA CONFERENCE in 1828 and was sent to the Pee Dee Circuit. Year by year his other appointments were Orangeburg, Charleston, Santee, Camden, and Abbeville.

In 1834 he became financial agent for the newly established RANDOLPH-MACON COLLEGE and served five years in that capacity. He then returned to the pastoral ministry and in 1839 became presiding elder of the Cokesbury District. In 1840 he was made editor of the *Southern Christian Advocate.*

On the organization of the M.E. Church, South—to which he of course adhered—Wightman wrote an editorial in which he urged the Church to establish a mission in CHINA. This so impressed BENJAMIN JENKINS, the printer who set the type for the editorial, that he volunteered to be one of the missionaries. The first GENERAL CONFERENCE (MES) at PETERSBURG, Va., in 1846 organized a Missionary Society and at its first anniversary meeting authorized the China mission, and Jenkins, with CHARLES TAYLOR, M.D., sailed for Shanghai in 1848. Wightman urged through his paper their support and under his leadership the South Carolina Conference became known as "the old missionary conference."

In 1854 Wightman became President of WOFFORD COLLEGE and in 1859 was made Chancellor of Southern University at Greensboro, Ala. He was elected a bishop in 1866. He exercised episcopal supervision over many conferences but made his home at Charleston. He died there on Feb. 15, 1882.

Several of Bishop Wightman's sermons were published in various collections. He was one of the editors of the Standard Hymn Book, and wrote the biography of Bishop WILLIAM CAPERS, who had influenced his decision to enter the ministry.

Flood and Hamilton, *Lives of Methodist Bishops.* 1882.
General Conference *Journal,* MES, 1886.
F. D. Leete, *Methodist Bishops.* 1948.
M. Simpson, *Cyclopaedia.* 1878.   ELMER T. CLARK

WIJESINGHA, CORNELIUS (17?-1865), was the first Asian Wesleyan Methodist minister. Born about the end of the century, he entered the school which W. M. HARVARD, one of the first missionaries, established in Colombo and became a Christian. In 1819 he became an assistant missionary, the first purely Ceylonese minister. He suffered much persecution throughout his forty-six-year ministry but helped lay the foundations of Methodism in CEYLON. He died on June 3, 1865, after speaking at the Jubilee meetings of CEYLON Methodism in Colombo.

W. Moister, *Wesleyan Missionaries.* 1878.   C. J. DAVEY

WILBERFORCE, WILLIAM (1759-1833), famous British evangelical Anglican statesman, was born in Hull, in eastern England, in 1759, the son of a wealthy merchant who had made his fortune in the Baltic and Russian trade. His father died in 1768, and he was brought up in London by relations who had close links with GEORGE WHITEFIELD. He went to St. John's College, Cambridge, 1777-80; he did little there, but in 1780 he was elected M.P. for Hull at the cost of about £8,000, and remained in the House of Commons until 1825. He was converted evangelically in 1785-86 under the influence of Anglican Evangelicals like Isaac Milner and John Newton; from then on he combined politics and religion in a way only equaled among Evangelicals by Lord Shaftesbury. Wilberforce was already known in this way when John Wesley wrote him a letter, dated February 24, 1791, and probably the last letter that Wesley wrote, urging him to combat the slave trade: "Go on in the name of God and in the power of his might till even American slavery (the vilest that ever saw the sun) shall vanish away before it."

Wilberforce regarded himself as having a special divine mission to fight the slave trade abroad, and to improve the moral tone of British society. He saw the abolition of the slave trade as far as Britain was concerned in 1807; the emancipation of slaves in the British Empire was going through Parliament as Wilberforce lay dying. The chief criticism that can be made of him, and that was made of him in his own lifetime, was that despite his enthusiasm for Negro emancipation he remained largely indifferent to the sufferings of the poorer part of the British population itself. He died on July 29, 1833, and was buried in Westminster Abbey as an act of public recognition of his philanthropic character.

F. K. Brown, *Fathers of the Victorians.* London, 1961.
R. Coupland, *Wilberforce, a Narrative.* London, 1923.
D. Newsome, *The Parting of Friends.* London, 1966.
     JOHN KENT

WILBERFORCE UNIVERSITY, the oldest A.M.E. school, is located in Xenia, Ohio. It comprises a four-year accredited liberal arts college and theological school. It was established by the Ohio Annual Conference in 1847, was named Union Seminary and was located near Columbus, Ohio. In 1856 the CINCINNATI CONFERENCE of the M.E. Church opened Wilberforce University at Xenia. Union and Wilberforce were closed at the outbreak of the Civil War (1861). In 1863 Bishop DANIEL A. PAYNE negotiated the purchase of Wilberforce for the A.M.E. CHURCH. Union Seminary near Columbus was discontinued and merged with Wilberforce at Xenia. In 1871 it graduated its first class. In 1887 the Ohio State Legislature established the combined Normal and Industrial Department. The Daniel A. Payne Theological Seminary was established in 1895. In 1899 the Federal Government established a Department of Military Science and Tactics. When in 1947 the State of Ohio withdrew its support from the College of Education and Industrial Arts, Wilberforce organized a College of Education and Business Administration which subsequently (1949) merged with the College of Liberal Arts and Sciences to form a single administrative unit.

Wilberforce is the first institution of higher education in the world founded by Negroes. In 1970 it had 1,066 students and fifty-six teachers. Rembert E. Stokes is President of the college and Charles S. Spivey is Dean of the Seminary.

     GRANT S. SHOCKLEY

WILBRAHAM, MASSACHUSETTS, U.S.A., is located eight miles east of Springfield in western MASSACHUSETTS; it was first settled in 1730. The community is best known as the home of WILBRAHAM ACADEMY. This academy, successor to a school established by a Methodist minister in New Market, N. H. in 1818, became an incorporated body in Massachusetts in 1824; it opened with eight students in September 1825. WILBUR FISK, first principal, served from 1825 until 1831. Originally a co-educational school affiliated with the Methodist Church, the academy became a boys' school in 1912; it is now non-denominational and strictly college preparatory. In a 350-acre rural setting the school occupies nineteen buildings one of which is the 1825 "Old Academy."

Methodist itinerant JESSE LEE preached his first "Massachusetts sermon" in Wilbraham, May 3, 1790. In 1793 a Methodist church was erected; here ASBURY conducted a conference in 1794 and preached in 1795 and 1805. Here also was conducted not only the first official session of the NEW ENGLAND CONFERENCE in 1797, but also the Conference of 1826. This historic building at 450 Main Street, the oldest existing structure in New England raised by Methodists, and the only Methodist-erected edifice still standing in Massachusetts dating from the eighteenth century, was discontinued as a Methodist meetinghouse in 1835.

Methodism continues in Wilbraham through a small segment of the United Church which adheres to the Wesleyan evangelical tradition.

Collier's Encyclopedia, 1966.
Handbook of Private Schools, 1966.
Minutes of the New England Conference.
M. Simpson, *Cyclopaedia.* 1878.   ERNEST R. CASE

WILBRAHAM ACADEMY, Wilbraham, Massachusetts, a secondary school for boys, is the oldest institution of The Methodist Church of autonomous existence and dates back to 1815 when plans were laid for its founding. Among its founders were JOSHUA SOULE and Martin Ruter, the first president. From 1817 until 1823 the school was located at New Market, N. H., and from 1824 to the present at Wilbraham, Mass. WILBUR FISK became president in 1825 and continued until he was elected president of WESLEYAN UNIVERSITY in 1831. While rich in Methodist tradition it has received only limited support from the church during the past few years. The governing board, a self-perpetuating body, has two elected on nomination of the NEW YORK EAST and NEW ENGLAND ANNUAL CONFERENCES.

JOHN O. GROSS

WILBUR, JAMES HARVEY ("Father Wilbur," 1811-1887), American circuit rider, missionary, educator and for two decades, outstanding Indian Agent at Fort Simcoe in WASHINGTON Territory, was born in NEW YORK State on Sept. 11, 1811.

A few months before reaching twenty, he married Lucretia Ann Stephens. Both joined the M.E. Church and in 1842 James became a Methodist minister in the BLACK RIVER CONFERENCE, as a circuit rider in northern New York.

September 1846 saw the Wilburs with a Methodist party bound for the OREGON Territory. They spent nine months sailing around the tip of South America, and thence north to and into the Columbia River as far as Portland.

Wilbur was a huge man in every way. He stood six feet, four inches tall and weighed over 300 pounds, with wide shoulders, powerful muscles and a bull neck, which supported a massive head. His muscled legs and long arms with "ham" fists were his only weapons. He wore a mop of near-black hair and his "hedge-row" eyebrows were above compassionate eyes of understanding, friendliness and promised justice.

He traveled the wild and trackless Oregon Territory on foot, or astride a mule (finding no Indian cayuse able to carry his weight at his demanded pace), teaching, preaching Methodism to red and white indiscriminately, and organizing churches for both.

In 1860 he organized a school at the new Army Post at Fort Simcoe, Washington Territory. He received an appointment as Indian Agent for the Yakima Nation in 1864, and this directly from President Lincoln. This position he held with high honor and great accomplishment until his retirement in 1882. Both Wilbur and his wife continued to teach the children of the Indians and those of the white employees of the Agency that "the Bible and the plow must go hand in hand." He never asked any man to do anything he would not do, but worked beside his pupils to demonstrate his teachings. No man could do as much or as heavy work as Wilbur.

The Indians' love for him inspired the name "Father," a spontaneous work that came naturally, for to the Indians he was a protecting, instructing and providing father. This name became by continued use a lasting monument to him.

"Father" Wilbur penned his final report on his charges and Fort Simcoe on Aug. 15, 1882, attaching thereto his resignation. The aging Wilburs then retired to Walla Walla, Washington Territory. Lucretia died in October 1887. "Father" Wilbur followed in less than a month. The Old Mission in Salem claimed the remains, since this had been their first station upon the Wilburs' arrival in the far West. Their accomplishments can never be confined in any tomb.

H. Dean Guie, *Fort Simcoe.* Published by Fort Simcoe at Mool-Mool Restoration Society. N.d.   ROSCOE SHELLER

WILDMAN, CLYDE EVERETT (1889-1955), American educator, was born March 8, 1889, in Greensburg, Ind. After graduation from the Greensburg High School in 1907 and two years of teaching in the public schools, he enrolled at DEPAUW UNIVERSITY to major in philosophy. While an undergraduate he slept for a year in one of the old college buildings in order to sound an alarm in case the structure caught fire. He graduated in 1913 with Phi Beta Kappa honors and then studied at ILIFF SCHOOL OF THEOLOGY and BOSTON UNIVERSITY SCHOOL OF THEOLOGY, from which latter school he received the S.T.B. in 1916. He was married in 1917, did graduate study in SCOTLAND and SWITZERLAND, became professor of Bible and Religion at CORNELL COLLEGE, Iowa, and in 1924 became the Dean of Cornell College. In 1926 he received a Ph.D. from BOSTON UNIVERSITY and in 1927 a D.D. from Cornell College. Subsequently he received a number of other honorary degrees.

In 1930 he became a professor of Old Testament History and Religion in Boston University School of Theology and in 1936 succeeded President G. BROMLEY OXNAM as President of DePauw University. He was president there for fifteen years, the longest presidency of this institution. Failing health caused him to retire but his health improved and he returned to teaching. He served as visiting professor at SOUTHERN METHODIST, GARRETT SEMINARY, and DICKINSON COLLEGE. He died in Carlisle, Pa., on Nov. 1, 1955.

DePauw Alumnus, December 1955.
Who's Who in America, Vol. 28.   ROBERT S. CHAFEE

WILEY, ALLEN (1789-1848), American preacher, was born in Fredrick County, Va., on Jan. 15, 1789. He joined the M.E. Church in April 1810, was licensed to exhort Sept. 10, 1811, licensed to preach on July 10, 1813, and in 1816 began as a traveling preacher. He traveled for eleven years and then was appointed a PRESIDING ELDER. He served four successive times as a delegate to the GENERAL CONFERENCE.

The first session of the INDIANA CONFERENCE was held in New Albany, Oct. 17, 1832. On the first day of its session Allen Wiley, CALVIN RUTER, and JAMES ARMSTRONG were appointed a committee to consider and report on the propriety of establishing a college or conference seminary. From this effort came Indiana Asbury, later to be known as DEPAUW UNIVERSITY. Allen Wiley superannuated and went with his family to live in Vevay. He died July 23, 1848.

General Conference *Journal*, ME, 1848.
F. C. Holliday, *Allen Wiley*. 1853.
————, *Indiana*. 1873.
Western Christian Advocate, 1845.   ROBERT S. CHAFEE

WILEY, EPHRAIM EMMERSON (1814-1893), American minister and educator, was born in BOSTON, Mass., on Oct. 6, 1814. His family was unable to provide for his education, but a loan from ELIJAH HEDDING, a long-time family friend, enabled him to go to WESLEYAN UNIVERSITY, Middletown, Conn. After his graduation in 1837 he repaid his benefactor completely. In 1839 he became Professor of Ancient Languages at EMORY AND HENRY COLLEGE, Emory, Va. The college was then only three years old. He was elected President of Emory and Henry in 1852 and served that institution for forty years. He also served for five years as President of Martha Washington College, Abingdon, Va.

Wiley was first admitted to the HOLSTON CONFERENCE in 1840. He was called the Conference's most eminent member during his fifty year career. Indicative of the high esteem his colleagues had for him, he was a delegate to several successive GENERAL CONFERENCES, leading his delegation once or twice. He received large votes for the episcopacy several times, but it is believed that he discouraged his friends from considering him for that office.

As a teacher Wiley was remembered by his students as a man who could make the classics serve in teaching the most direct truths of Christianity. As a preacher he was distinguished for his clarity and beauty of style in speaking. Emory and Henry College students had the opportunity of hearing their President preach once or twice a month at the college chapel.

Although a New Englander by birth, he became intensely Southern and supported the South during the Civil War and afterward.

Ephraim Wiley was married twice, first to Elizabeth Eammond, Middletown, Conn., and later to Elizabeth Reeves, Washington County, Tenn. He had three children by this second marriage.

He died March 13, 1893, and is buried in the cemetery on the hillside overlooking the campus of Emory and Henry College.

H. M. DuBose, *History*. 1916.
I. P. Martin, *Holston*. 1945.
Minutes of Holston Conference. 1893.   L. W. PIERCE

WILEY, ISAAC WILLIAM (1825-1884), American bishop, was born in Lewiston, Pa., March 29, 1825, of Protestant Episcopal parents. He was a successful medical practitioner, and early in his practice he felt the call to preach, but when he offered himself to the PITTSBURGH CONFERENCE he was told that there was no room for married men. He continued to serve as physician and local preacher until, in 1850, he was asked to go to China as a medical missionary. He accepted, joined the EAST GENESEE CONFERENCE and with his wife went to China to begin a ministry there, which was limited because of the death of Mrs. Wiley and his own severe illness.

Upon his return in 1854 he was transferred to the NEW JERSEY CONFERENCE, where he made a name for himself as preacher and educator. From 1858 to 1864 he served as Principal of Pennington Seminary (now PENNINGTON SCHOOL). Elected as head of the GENERAL CONFERENCE delegation in 1864, he was appointed by that Conference to be Editor of the *Ladies Repository*, which office he held until 1872, when again he was elected head of the NEWARK CONFERENCE delegation to the General Conference, and was this time elected a bishop.

Bishop Wiley served in the episcopacy for twelve years. On an episcopal visitation to China in 1884, he was taken ill at Foochow and died there Nov. 22, 1884. He was buried in the Mission Cemetery at Foochow.

F. D. Leete, *Methodist Bishops*. 1948.
M. Simpson, *Cyclopaedia*. 1878.   FREDERICK G. HUBACH

WILEY COLLEGE, Marshall, Texas, was founded in 1873 by the FREEDMEN'S AID SOCIETY of the M.E. Church for the education of Negroes. It was named Wiley University for Bishop ISAAC W. WILEY of the M.E. Church. Carnegie Library, one of the first given by Andrew Carnegie, philanthropist, was erected by the labor of faculty and students on the Wiley College campus. A new library and a science building were erected in 1967.

Degrees offered are the B.A. and B.S. The governing board has twenty-five members; it is self-perpetuating. The ownership of the properties is vested with the BOARD OF EDUCATION of the United Methodist Church.

JOHN O. GROSS

WILKES, WILLIAM REID (1902-   ), American bishop of the A.M.E. CHURCH, was born in Putman County, Ga., on April 10, 1902. He was educated at MORRIS BROWN COLLEGE and Turner Theological Seminary, from which schools he received the degrees of A.B. and B.D. in 1928 and 1935 respectively. He later received the D.D. degree from Morris Brown and the LL.D. degree from WILBERFORCE UNIVERSITY. He was ordained DEACON in 1925 and ELDER in 1928. He was pastor of churches in the state of GEORGIA until elected to the episcopacy in 1948 from the pastorate of the Allen Temple Church in ATLANTA,

W. R. WILKES

Ga. He presently resides at CLEVELAND, Ohio and supervises the work of the Third Episcopal Area District, including the states of WEST VIRGINIA, PENNSYLVANIA (Western) and OHIO.

R. R. Wright, *The Bishops*. 1963.   GRANT S. SHOCKLEY

WILKES-BARRE, PENNSYLVANIA, U.S.A., prior to 1770 was so called in honor of John Wilkes and Isaac Barre, two members of the British Parliament who had shown friendliness to the American cause. The name was confirmed when Wilkes-Barre was made a borough in 1806, and when incorporated a city in 1871.

About 1770 settlers from New England erected five forts in the region, one of which was Fort Wyoming, adjoining Wilkes-Barre. This fort appears on maps used by General Sullivan when he camped here with his army on their march against the Indians in 1779. Near here occurred the Wyoming "massacre," July 3 and 4, 1778.

The fact that "Wyoming" had a wide connotation in this section prior to the naming of Wilkes-Barre must be borne in mind when reading the journals of FRANCIS ASBURY and WILLIAM COLBERT, who rarely mentioned Wilkes-Barre even though they may have had that place in mind when mentioning Wyoming. This name to them sometimes meant Wilkes-Barre, and sometimes a circuit or a region. When Wyoming became a circuit it included preaching places in Wilkes-Barre.

Wilkes-Barre's first class leader was Azel Dana. Within the perimeter of Wilkes-Barre the first CLASS LEADER at Hanover was Ashbel Waller who was succeeded by Abram Adams when Waller became a LOCAL PREACHER. Joseph Waller and John How were in the class. Richard Inman at Buttonwood and Comfort Carey and Huldah, his wife, at Careytown, were in this period. Other Wilkes-Barreans mentioned by the journalists were: Putnam, Catlin, Bingham, Satterthwaite, and "mother" Johnson. Their homes were preaching places for Asbury and Colbert as well as other itinerants. So also were the court house and the "meeting house" at Hanover Green, all in greater Wilkes-Barre.

Early in the 1790's Colbert found Wilkes-Barre a hot bed of Deists. However, in 1793 the evangelistic presiding elder, VALENTINE COOK, conducted a revival that brought many into the church here and elsewhere.

"Old Ship Zion," erected in 1800 on Wilkes-Barre's public square, was its first church, supposedly a union project. Misunderstandings having arisen, the Methodists for a time met in the court house. In 1831 they paid $1,000 to the Presbyterians for complete ownership of the building, which they later sold for $600 in 1849. In that year they built Franklin Street, now First, Church. In 1826 GEORGE PECK was appointed to Wyoming circuit. However, Wilkes-Barre soon separated from the circuit with the exception of three other preaching places, retaining Peck as pastor. For a few years Wilkes-Barre fluctuated between membership in the Wyoming circuit and a separate status, the separate status finally prevailing. Wilkes-Barre gave its name to one of the districts of the WYOMING CONFERENCE.

The ONEIDA CONFERENCE met in Wilkes-Barre in 1837, and, since its organization, the Wyoming Conference has met there several times. There were in 1970 six United Methodist churches in this city, with a total membership of 3,186.

A. F. Chaffee, *Wyoming Conference*. 1904.
Minutes of the Wyoming Conference.
L. D. Palmer, *Heroism and Romance*. 1950.

LOUIS D. PALMER

WILKINS, J. ERNEST (1895-1959), American attorney, Assistant Secretary of Labor in the Eisenhower administration, and member and president of the JUDICIAL COUNCIL of The Methodist Church, was born in Farmington, Mo., the son of Henry B. and Susie Olivia (Douthit) Wilkins. His wife was Lucile B. Robinson, whom he married on Nov. 23, 1922. He was educated at the University of Illinois, A.B., 1918; and the University of Chicago Law School, 1921. Lincoln University in MISSOURI gave him the LL.D. in 1941, as did SOUTHWESTERN COLLEGE in KANSAS.

He was a veteran of the first World War, and after that studied law and was a practicing attorney in Cook County (CHICAGO) for thirty-two years. He served a term as president of the Cook County Bar Association. He was elected a member of the GENERAL CONFERENCE of 1944 (TMC) and that Conference elected him to the Commission on WORLD SERVICE AND FINANCE. He was thereafter elected to the Judicial Council in 1948, becoming the first Negro elected to the Council. He was elected for an eight-year term in 1948 and was reelected by the General Conference of 1956 to serve an eight-year term. However, he died before his term was completed. Meanwhile, President Eisenhower appointed him as Assistant Secretary of Labor for International Affairs. He became the second member of his race to hold a sub-cabinet post, and the first to take part officially in cabinet sessions. He was chairman of the United States delegation to the International Labor Organization Conference at GENEVA; was made vice-chairman of the President's Committee on Government Contracts, and of other important committees; and in 1957 the President appointed him a member of the Civil Rights Commission.

For most of his life Wilkins was a member of St. Mark's Methodist Church in Chicago, serving there as Sunday school teacher and trustee. He became the Lay Leader of the LEXINGTON ANNUAL CONFERENCE, and as a member of the Council on World Service and Finance served on its executive committee.

He served as president of the Judicial Council following his election to a second term in 1956. He died rather suddenly on Jan. 19, 1959. On January 21 his body lay in state in Foundry Methodist Church in WASHINGTON, and on January 23 a funeral service was held in the St. Mark's Church in Chicago. He was survived by his wife and three sons. The General Conference of 1960 included a tribute to him in its *Daily Advocate* of May 7, 1960.

Daily Christian Advocate, General Conference, May 7, 1960.
C. T. Howell, *Prominent Personalities.* 1945.   N. B. H.

WILKINSBURG, PENNSYLVANIA, U.S.A. **South Avenue Church** was started about 1831 by Charles A. Holmes and Ezra Hingeley, LOCAL PREACHERS, who regularly walked the sixteen-mile round trip from PITTSBURGH to conduct services. In August 1832 Wilkinsburg became a preaching point on the Braddocksfield Circuit, and for the next eleven years services were held in homes and in a school. In 1843 when there were twenty-four members, a brick church forty by fifty feet, the first church building of any denomination in the town, was erected on Wallace Avenue. Wilkinsburg was incorporated in 1887, and its first burgess, CHARLES W. SMITH, was elected bishop by the 1908 GENERAL CONFERENCE.

In 1892 a new church building was erected on South Avenue. Destroyed by fire in 1907, it was replaced the next year at a cost of $127,000. An education building costing $80,000 was constructed in 1923; it was renovated in 1965 at a cost of $425,000. The church is known for its Young Adult Fellowship of more than 300 which was started over fifty years ago, and for its "Fossils" organization (retired men) which has over 200 members.

In 1970 South Avenue Church reported 1,876 members, property valued at $1,499,742, and $176,446 raised for all purposes during the year.

A Century of Christian Service, A History of South Avenue Church. N.p., n.d.
General Minutes.
Minutes of the Western Pennsylvania Conference.
                                                    ALBEA GODBOLD

WILL, HERMAN, JR. (1915-   ), American church official, was born at Union City, N. J., Sept. 5, 1915, son of Herman and Mamie (Krausser) Will.

He was a student in Crane Junior College, 1932-33, and graduated with the LL.B. degree at Kent College of Law, 1937. He also received the A.B. degree at the University of Chicago, 1947, and engaged in postgraduate study there, 1948-51, and at the AMERICAN UNIVERSITY, Washington, D. C., 1967-69. In 1937 he was admitted to the ILLINOIS bar. He was youth secretary, Methodist Commission on WORLD PEACE, Chicago, 1938-42, and Midwest secretary of the Fellowship of Reconciliation, Chicago, 1942-43. From 1943-46 he was director of the Brethren Castaner Project, PUERTO RICO. He was administrative secretary, Methodist Board of World Peace, Chicago, 1946-60; and since 1960 has been associate general secretary of the Board of Christian SOCIAL CONCERNS, Washington, D. C.

He was youth delegate to the Methodist Uniting Conference, 1939; president, National Council of Methodist Youth, 1939-41; chairman, Youth Study Commission,

1940-42; member GENERAL BOARD OF EDUCATION, 1940-44. He was a lay delegate to the GENERAL CONFERENCE of 1948 and to the NORTH CENTRAL JURISDICTIONAL CONFERENCE of 1960. In 1950 and 1955 he was a member of the Churches and Race study commission, Church Federation Greater Chicago. Since 1963, he has been a denominational representative to the Triennial Assembly of the NATIONAL COUNCIL OF CHURCHES. He has led world peace study tours in Europe, Latin America, and Africa. Since 1948 he has been a member of the board of directors of the National Service Board for Religious Objectors, and since 1945 a member of the National Council of the Fellowship of Reconciliation; also of the American Civil Liberties Union, the American Society of International Law, and the American Society of Christian Ethics.

On Aug. 8, 1942, he was married to Margarita Irie. Their children are Douglas, Donald, Mary, Allan, Debra, and Harold.

Who's Who in The Methodist Church, 1966.
                                                    J. MARVIN RAST

WILLAMETTE UNIVERSITY, Salem, Oregon, was established as Oregon Institute in 1842, with the name changed to the present one in 1853. The school at one time had in addition to its present colleges of liberal arts, music, and law, schools of medicine and theology.

The institution came out of the statesmanlike missionary program begun by JASON LEE in OREGON in 1834. He is said to have preached the first Protestant sermon west of the Rocky Mountains. The college is the oldest on the Pacific slope and the first institution of higher education in Oregon. The charter was granted by the Oregon Territorial Legislature.

Degrees offered are the B.A., B.M. (Music), B.M.E. (Music Education), M.A. in Education, M.Ed., M.M.E. (Music Education), and J.D. (Doctor of Jurisprudence). The governing board has forty-five members: nine are elected by the Oregon Conference, six by the alumni association, the balance by the board.

                                                    JOHN O. GROSS

WILLARD, FRANCES ELIZABETH (1839-1898), American temperance reformer and advocate of woman's suffrage, was born at Churchville, N. Y., Sept. 28, 1839, the daughter of Josiah F. and Mary T. (Hill) Willard. Her parents taught school in New England, studied four years at Oberlin College, and then when Frances was seven, moved to a farm near Janesville, Wis., where she lived for ten years. She was taught by her mother and early became an omnivorous reader. At seventeen she entered Milwaukee Female College and a year later Northwestern Female College, EVANSTON, Ill., where as valedictorian of her class she graduated in 1859. OHIO WESLEYAN UNIVERSITY awarded her the LL.D. degree in 1894. Her family moved to Evanston with her and it became her permanent home.

Not conventionally religious, in her youth she had periods of doubt, but during a siege of typhoid fever she vowed that if she recovered she would be a Christian, and she joined the M.E. Church at twenty-one. Religion to her was largely action; she had a concern to make the world good. The ROCK RIVER CONFERENCE elected her a lay delegate to the 1888 GENERAL CONFERENCE, but that body refused to seat any women as delegates.

If the church of her day had been willing to ordain women, she might have entered the ministry.

Following graduation she set herself a stiff course of reading for the purpose of self-improvement. Influenced by the writings of Charlotte Brontë and Margaret Fuller, she adopted their ideal of independence for women. Briefly she was engaged to but did not marry a young preacher who later became a bishop. Following that experience she returned to her ideal with renewed zeal. She had an ambition to be "widely known, widely helpful and beloved."

Beginning in 1860, she was a successful teacher for most of the next fourteen years, first in country schools and then at Pittsburgh Female College, Genesee Wesleyan Seminary, and Evanston College for Ladies. During that time, spurred by literary ambitions, she wrote articles for papers and magazines, and in 1864 published *Nineteen Beautiful Years,* a biography of her younger sister who had died. There was a two-year tour of Europe with a wealthy woman friend, beginning in 1868. On her return she was asked to deliver a lecture for pay, and the successful venture launched her career as a public speaker. In 1871 she became president of Evanston College for Ladies, the first woman in the world to head a college. In 1874, over her objection, the college was integrated with NORTHWESTERN UNIVERSITY and she was designated as dean of women. Displeased, she resigned, but later she admitted that meshing the two schools was proper.

Other schools immediately offered her attractive positions at good pay, but she hesitated. The temperance movement which was sweeping the country at that time appealed to her idealistic, crusading spirit. Moved by an ambition to make the world good, she saw an opportunity in the temperance crusade. She had a profound trust in woman, and she had not forgotten that as a girl she heard her mother say that prohibition would come when women could vote. She believed the temperance movement would protect the home, lift up the Christian life, and spur people to personal sacrifice.

Turning aside offers in the educational field, she journeyed east to talk to several temperance leaders who impressed her as practical reformers. On the return trip she stopped in PITTSBURGH to see friends who were surprised at her enthusiasm for the temperance crusade. While there she accompanied a group of temperance workers to a saloon where they sang a hymn and called on her to pray. Kneeling on the sawdust floor, she offered her first prayer in public. It was her baptism of fire. She returned to Evanston and within a week was elected president of the Chicago Woman's Christian Temperance Union. Deliberately she gave up professional advancement, economic security, and social position for isolation, poverty, ridicule, and social ostracism.

So complete was her dedication to the temperance movement that for several years she would not take or at least would not ask for a salary, and as a result she sometimes went hungry. Her only income was a little money received from lectures. In time her society provided a salary. But regardless of the sacrifices and the hard work involved, she found happiness in the crusade. Endowed with a remarkable capacity for winning and inspiring followers, she quickly became an outstanding leader in the cause. In 1879 she was elected president of the National Woman's Christian Temperance Union,

and in 1891 president of the World's Woman's Christian Temperance Union. In 1882 she helped to organize the Prohibition Party. As time passed, she persuaded her society, over some opposition, to support woman's suffrage, and she was elected president of the National Council of Women.

The temperance movement gave scope for her oratorical talent, her interest in politics, and her love of travel. In one year she visited all the states and territories. She was welcomed as a temperance speaker in Britain. The greatest orators of the day paid high tribute to her ability as a platform speaker. Her penchant for writing found ample expression in editing the publications of her society and compiling its books. Among her volumes were: *Woman and Temperance,* 1883; *Glimpses of Fifty Years* (autobiography), 1889; and *A Classic Town; The Story of Evanston,* 1892. She was co-editor of *A Woman of the Century,* 1892.

An indefatigable worker, she used up her energies by the time she was a little past fifty. Her mother who had been a great source of inspiration and energy through the years, died in 1892. Soon afterward her own health gave way, and though she made trips and took periods of rest, her old vigor did not return. She died in New York City, Feb. 18, 1898, and after cremation her ashes were interred in her mother's grave in Evanston.

The General Conference that refused to seat Frances Willard as a delegate in 1889, nevertheless adopted a resolution saying she was "an able champion of the rights of women and the cause of total abstinence" and was "recognized as one of the world's greatest leaders." In 1905 the State of ILLINOIS placed her statue in the Rotunda of the Capitol at Washington, and at the dedication Senator Albert J. Beveridge referred to her as "the most beloved character of her time." In 1910 she was elected to the Hall of Fame for Great Americans.

Dictionary of American Biography. Vol. 20.
Anna A. Gordon, *The Beautiful Life of Frances E. Willard.* Chicago: Woman's Temperance Publishing Association. 1898.
Lydia J. Trowbridge, *Frances Willard of Evanston.* Chicago: Willett, Clark and Co., 1938.
Frances E. Willard, *Glimpses of Fifty Years.* Chicago: H. J. Smith and Co., 1889.   ALBEA GODBOLD

WILLERUP, CHRISTIAN EDVARD BALTOR (1815-1886), Scandinavian Methodist pioneer and leader, was born at COPENHAGEN, Denmark, on Oct. 16, 1815. His parents were A. J. Willerup, a customs officer, and his wife, Lovise. He had a good schooling and a solid training in commerce. It is uncertain when he left for America, but the first place at which we can locate him is Strassbourg, Ohio, in 1847, where he had established himself in business. When he came into touch with the Methodist Church is unknown, but he heard a minister by the name of Evans preaching, was converted to God and surrendered to his Savior, and then joined the Church. He became a local preacher, and then in 1850 was asked by the M.E. BOARD OF MISSIONS whether he would be willing to enter into the service of the church as a full-time minister, to go to New York, and to become an assistant to the Swedish minister, O. G. HEDSTROM, who was working hard in the well-known BETHEL SHIP. During those years there was a stream of thousands of Scandinavians to America, and good and pious men were wanted.

CHRISTIAN WILLERUP

Willerup was ordained an elder in the Bethel Ship on Oct. 20, 1850, by Bishop EDMUND S. JANES. Yet he did not stay long at the Bethel Ship. Before Christmas the same year he had to go to the Scandinavian colonists on the prairie in WISCONSIN, and here a revival broke out, and he succeeded greatly as a minister. He built the very first Scandinavian Methodist Church in the world at Cambridge, Wis., in 1852.

After six years' work among the Scandinavians in America, he was asked to go to Norway, where Ole P. Petersen (see NORWAY), a Norwegian-American, had started activities. Petersen had succeeded so well that he could not manage alone, and he therefore asked that Willerup might be sent to Norway as a superintendent. The appointment was made on Feb. 25, 1856, by Bishop THOMAS A. MORRIS.

After two years in Norway, where he built the first Methodist Church in Scandinavia, Willerup was allowed to go to Denmark, and one fine day in July, 1856, he arrived at his native city, Copenhagen. After well over seven years' work there he dedicated the large Jerusalem Church. As early as 1859 he had organized the first Danish congregation. In Copenhagen also his work bore fine fruit.

Gradually the superintendent had obtained the supervision of all Scandinavia. But after a time, as administration increased, he could not stand the work and the tiring travels, and he urgently asked the Board of Missions to release him from his overall responsible task. This was effected in the case of Sweden in 1868, Norway in 1869, and Denmark in 1872.

Willerup returned to America, where for a short time he was in work at Evanston, Illinois, and also attached to the Norwegian-Danish theological college there. Then for a short time he stayed at Fredrikstad in Norway, but his strength was spent. He died in Copenhagen on May 18, 1886. Scandinavian Christianity owes much to Christian Edvard Baltor Willerup.

S. N. Gaarde. *Christian Willerup.* 1915.   NIELS MANN

WILLEY, WAITMAN THOMAS (1811-1900), American layman and one of the founders of the State of WEST VIRGINIA, was born in Monongalia County, (West) Va., Oct. 18, 1811. He graduated from MADISON COLLEGE in 1831 and later received the M.A. degree from both AUGUSTA COLLEGE and Madison College.

In 1833 he was admitted to the bar. He was clerk of the courts for Monongalia County for eleven years, starting in 1841, and was active in the Whig Party. In the VIRGINIA Constitutional Convention of 1861 he opposed secession and withdrew from that body when secession carried.

The Restored Government of Virginia elected him U. S. senator in 1861. As senator, he is credited with having exerted much influence which led to the admission of West Virginia as a state in 1863. After the State of West Virginia was formed, Willey served as senator from the new state from 1863 to 1871.

An active churchman, his influence was felt not only in his home church in Morgantown, W. Va., and in the WEST VIRGINIA CONFERENCE, but also in the Church at large. Although many of his relatives and friends joined the M.P. Church, Willey stayed with the M.E. Church. He used every opportunity to urge greater democracy in his own denomination. At the GENERAL CONFERENCE of 1864 he made an address in support of a proposal to include lay representation. He did much work in support of the 1868 action of the General Conference which resulted in lay representation. In 1872 he was elected the first lay delegate of the West Virginia Conference to the General Conference.

Willey died May 2, 1900.

Charles H. Ambler, *Waitman Thomas Willey, Orator, Churchman, Humanitarian.* Huntington, W. Va.: Standard Printing & Publishing Co., 1954.

Phil Conley, ed., *The West Virginia Encyclopedia.* Charleston: West Virginia Publishing Co., 1929.   LAWRENCE F. SHERWOOD

WILLIAMS, FRANK EARL CRANSTON (1883-1962), American missionary to KOREA and INDIA, was born in New Windsor, Colo., Aug. 4, 1883. He graduated from the UNIVERSITY OF DENVER in 1906, and as a student volunteer set sail with his classmate and bride for Korea that summer.

He was assigned to the newly opened station of Kongju where he remained until 1940, this being the longest continued residence in one area for any member of his mission.

He established a school from which many of Korea's church leaders graduated. In addition to his continued work in the school, he also acted as district superintendent or district missionary, and was known to every church in the area. He was an outstanding leader in the rural church movement. As a pioneer in education he reorganized his school to give a more practical training for rural high school youth.

In 1940 he transferred to Ghaziabad, India Agricultural Institute. In 1945 he was returned to Korea by the U.S. Army to act as agricultural adviser to General John R. Hodge. At the outbreak of the Korean War he returned to mission work and was assigned by the BOARD OF MISSIONS to Nagasaki, JAPAN, to assist in restoring the new junior-senior high school destroyed by the bombing of the second World War. He retired in CALIFORNIA in 1954 and died in SAN DIEGO on June 9, 1962. He was a member of the Korea and Delhi Annual Conferences.

CHARLES A. SAUER

WILLIAMS, FRED (1898-   ), American missionary in the BENGAL (INDIA) CONFERENCE of the Methodist Church in Southern Asia, 1921-44. As director of the Ushagram Educational Colony in Asansol, he was recognized throughout India as a pioneer in introducing educational reforms, especially by encouraging initiative and character development. Government officials and representatives of many churches and missions came to study his work.

Williams was born in Marion, Ind., July 31, 1898. He attended ASBURY COLLEGE, and then KANSAS WESLEYAN at Salina. He earned the A.B. degree in 1920; the M.A. from Teacher's College, Columbia University, in 1927; and there also the doctorate in education, 1938. He first came to India in August, 1921, and in December 1922, his fiancée, Irene Hayes, of Stockton, Kan., arrived, and they were married. He began his work in the Methodist Boys School in Asansol in 1922, and in 1927 succeeded in bringing the boys' and girls' schools together into a coeducational high school. His work stimulated hundreds of teachers and gave to thousands of parents new hope for the future of their children.

After resigning from the BOARD OF MISSIONS in 1944, Dr. Williams served as principal of the Hindman County High School in Kentucky, and then joined the educational service of the Bureau of Indian Affairs in the United States. He served as principal successively in three important schools for American Indian children in ARIZONA and NEW MEXICO.

Irene Hayes Williams died May 23, 1953. On Oct. 27, 1954, Williams married Miss Josephine Lucero.

J. N. Hollister, *Southern Asia.* 1956.   J. WASKOM PICKETT

WILLIAMS, JAMES SAMUEL (1865-1946), American M.P. minister, who served from 1911 to 1941 as the CHAPLAIN to the Mission of the Good Samaritan in ASHEVILLE, N. C., was born near Oak Ridge, N. C., and was educated at OAK RIDGE MILITARY INSTITUTE, WESTERN MARYLAND COLLEGE, and was graduated from WESTMINSTER THEOLOGICAL SEMINARY in 1893. Western Maryland College conferred the D.D. degree upon him in 1922. He served Grace Church, GREENSBORO; Halifax Circuit; First Church, Henderson; and First Church, HIGH POINT, prior to December 1904, when he was assigned to the Asheville Mission, later to become the Merrimon Avenue M.P. Church. In 1911 the Asheville Ministers' Association organized the Mission of the Good Samaritan "to render aid to the health-seekers who were coming to Asheville at the rate of about three thousand a month." Many of these people were tubercular patients. Williams was selected by the Association to serve as the Chaplain at the Mission, and the North Carolina Conference (MP) was asked to assign him to the project. At the height of his work, he was ministering to more than 1,000 patients in the sanitarium, and to many more in homes and hovels. "No one was too poor or too rich to be beyond his reach; Jew, Catholic, Protestant and pagan alike were blessed by his kindly ministry. From the churches, fraternal orders and other sources . . . [he] collected funds to help them in their distress." As a recognition of his ministry, the educa-

tional building of the St. Paul's Methodist Church in Asheville was named the "J. S. Williams Memorial Building." He was buried in Green Hill Cemetery in Greensboro, N. C.

C. W. Bates, "James Samuel Williams," *Memorial Service,* Western North Carolina Conference, 1946.
J. Elwood Carroll, *History of the North Carolina Conference of the Methodist Protestant Church.* Greensboro, 1939.

RALPH HARDEE RIVES

WILLIAMS, NOAH W. (1876-1954), American bishop of the A.M.E. CHURCH, was born in Springfield, Ill., on Dec. 25, 1876. He received his education at WILBERFORCE UNIVERSITY in Ohio, DEPAUW UNIVERSITY in Indiana, and Earlham College also in Indiana. He was converted in 1892 and licensed to preach in 1894. The Illinois Conference (A.M.E.) admitted him in 1899. He held pastorates in ILLINOIS, INDIANA, MISSOURI, TENNESSEE and KENTUCKY. He was elected bishop in 1932, and served in the south, the southwest and the far west of the United States. He retired in 1948 and died in ST. LOUIS, Feb. 12, 1954. He was a commanding and inspiring churchman and episcopal leader.

R. R. Wright, *The Bishops.* 1963.   GRANT S. SHOCKLEY

WILLIAMS, PETER (175?-1823), American Negro sexton of the original JOHN STREET CHURCH, New York City. His parents, natives of Africa, had been brought to America in the slave-trade. Born in the cow-barn back of his owner's house on Beekman Street, Peter often declared what it meant to him to realize the similarity of his birthplace to that of the Saviour.

Converted under Captain THOMAS WEBB's preaching at the Rigging Loft on William Street, Peter became an active member of the Methodist Society led by Webb and PHILIP EMBURY. There Peter met Mary (Molly) Durham, a slave in a family that had come from St. Christopher in the WEST INDIES. They married, as was settled in a joint-relationship of their owners. Peter became sexton of Wesley Chapel on John Street in the early 1770's, serving for many years in that capacity, while Molly kept the small parsonage used by Wesley's preachers as they came and went. Peter and Molly Williams are frequently mentioned in John Street Church Records (Vol. I, "The Old Book").

On June 10, 1783, the trustees of John Street Church "paid Mr. Aymar for his negro Peter—40 pounds." This entry in the records indicates the transaction whereby the trustees protected Peter's Christian dignity and faith by preventing his public auction, and making possible his freedom at their hands when the legal requirements would permit. Mid-December 1785, a formal Paper of Emancipation was enacted at the Court by the trustees, recorded in Lib. 53 of Conveyances, p. 220, of the city's official records. Thus Peter became free.

Skilled under his former master in handling tobacco, Peter established himself in that business, becoming one of the most prosperous of his race in New York City. He aided largely in the financing and building of the first Methodist Church for his people in New York, at Leonard and Church Streets, later known as Zion Church, personally laying the cornerstone. This was a frequent preaching place of FRANCIS ASBURY.

Peter and Molly provided excellent education for their

two children—Peter, Jr., who under the patronage of Bishop Hobart became one of the first ordained Negro clergymen of the Protestant Episcopal Church; Mary (adopted), who kept the accounts and handled all the correspondence of Peter's business. Molly died in 1821, and was buried at Forsyth Street Methodist Church. Her epitaph—"Words cannot express her worth." William Phoebus conducted the service for Peter (1823), John Street Church being crowded to capacity, with many standing in the street. Phoebus said, "Although a black man, he has risen to honor, highly respected, greatly beloved. It was his vital religion that elevated him." In Joseph B. Smith's notable painting of the first church on John Street, Peter may be seen on duty at the door. His portrait is preserved in the archives of the church.

John Street Church *Records*, Vol. I.
S. A. Seaman, *New York.* 1892.
J. B. Wakeley, *Lost Chapters.* 1858.   ARTHUR BRUCE MOSS

WILLIAMS, ROBERT (c1745-1775), was the first traveling Methodist preacher to come to the new world. He came in 1769 and was at work in NEW YORK before the arrival of BOARDMAN and PILMORE, the first two regularly appointed by JOHN WESLEY to serve in America.

Prior to coming to America, Williams served as an itinerant in the Irish Conference from 1766-69. Hearing of the need for assistance in New York, Williams applied to John Wesley for permission to preach in America. Wesley hesitated to give him permission since Williams had been critical of the Anglican clergy and lacked, Wesley thought, a teachable spirit. Wesley finally agreed to let Williams go at his own expense, and on condition that he would work under the direction of Boardman and Pilmore, the official missionaries Wesley had appointed for the colonies. Williams agreed to the conditions and was granted a local preacher's license.

Accounts differ as to where Williams first landed in the new world. Historians like Lee, Stevens, Simpson and others, report that Williams took passage on a boat with Thomas Ashton, an Irish Methodist who paid his way, and that they both landed at New York. The *History of American Methodism* (1964) and others, have Williams traveling with Ashton but landing first at NORFOLK, Va., and then working his way up the coast to New York.

The latter account is based apparently upon a letter written by William H. Dallam of Harford County, Md., on Oct. 29, 1839, to EZEKIEL COOPER. In the letter, which is now in the GARRETT THEOLOGICAL SEMINARY collection of Cooper material, Dallam sets forth some reminiscences about Williams told him by his father. One of these is that Williams' boat was bound for BALTIMORE, but was blown off course by a storm, forcing Williams to land at Norfolk.

At any rate, wherever he first landed, Williams was at work in New York before Richard Boardman arrived. The records of Wesley Chapel (now John Street) indicate that Williams was hard at work there prior to October 1769. A collection of original LOVE FEAST Tickets, now in the Library of DREW UNIVERSITY, Madison, N. J., includes a handwritten ticket signed by Robert Williams and dated Oct. 1, 1769. This is the first known Love Feast Ticket issued in America.

When Boardman arrived in New York in late October 1769, Williams started south. He visited Pilmore in

PHILADELPHIA on November 1, and went on to MARYLAND, where he joined ROBERT STRAWBRIDGE in the work there.

In 1770, Williams' name is listed with Boardman's and Pilmore's in the appointments for America. In 1771 he was stationed at Wesley Chapel in New York. In 1772 he worked with Pilmore in Maryland and VIRGINIA. In June 1773, at the first Conference held in America, Williams was received into the traveling ministry and appointed to PETERSBURG, Va., where he formed the first Circuit in Virginia.

Soon thereafter, Williams met DEVEREUX JARRETT, an Episcopalian clergyman who was sympathetic to the Methodists and who, himself, was of an evangelical spirit. Williams convinced Jarrett "that the Methodists were true members of the Church of England—that their design was to build up and not divide the Church." (*The Life of the Rev. Devereux Jarrett,* Rector of Bath Parish," Baltimore 1806, pp. 107ff).

Jarrett cooperated with Williams and other Methodist preachers in furthering the evangelical movement. Under Jarrett's preaching, the parents of JESSE LEE were converted. Lee always thought of Williams as his spiritual father. Under Williams' guidance also, WILLIAM WATTERS entered the Methodist ministry, the first native born Methodist itinerant. Williams became known as a rousing evangelist with many conversions, even during the Revolutionary War.

In 1774 Williams organized the Brunswick Circuit which extended from Petersburg, Va., into NORTH CAROLINA. Soon thereafter, he married and retired from the traveling ministry. He established a home on the road halfway between Portsmouth and Suffolk. His married life and retirement were brief, for he died on Sept. 26, 1775. Asbury preached his funeral sermon and said of him, in part: "He has been a very useful, laborious man, and the Lord gave him many seals to his ministry. Perhaps no one in America has been an instrument of awakening so many souls, as God has awakened by him."

In addition to his pioneer labors in the colonies, Williams was the first Methodist preacher to publish Wesley's books, tracts and sermons, and to distribute them to the people. He did this without permission from John Wesley in order to meet the needs of people for Christian literature and instruction. His actions came under criticism from Wesley, Asbury and others. Wesley did not like Williams' printing and selling his writings without his permission. Some preachers feared Williams was profiting from the sale of the literature. Wesley reprimanded Williams in a letter, while the Conference of 1773 adopted six rules, two of which read:

4. None of the preachers in America to reprint any of Mr. Wesley's books without his authority (when it can be gotten) and the consent of their brethren.

5. Robert Williams to sell the books he has already printed, but to print no more, unless under the above restrictions.

Williams agreed to stop printing books. However, the need for books, tracts, and sermons which this adventuresome, independent preacher tried to meet, grew as the Methodist movement expanded and after his death the new Church in 1789 established the Methodist BOOK CONCERN.

In addition to being the first publisher of Methodist books in America, Robert Williams has the distinction also of being the first Methodist minister in America to marry, the first to locate, and the first to die.

F. Asbury, *Journal and Letters*. 1958.
W. C. Barclay, *History of Missions*. 1949.
E. S. Bucke, *History of American Methodism*. 1964.
Dictionary of American Biography.
M. Simpson, *Cyclopaedia*. 1878.
W. B. Sprague, *Annals of the Pulpit*. 1861.
A. Stevens, *History of the M.E. Church*. 1864-67.
J. B. Wakeley, *Heroes of Methodism*. 1856.

C. WESLEY CHRISTMAN, JR.

WILLIAMS, ROBERT S. (1856-1932), sixth bishop of the C.M.E. CHURCH, was born on Oct. 27, 1856, in Caddo Parish, La. He attended WILEY and Howard Universities. Bishop Williams joined the C.M.E. Church in 1876 and was ordained DEACON in 1881 and ELDER in 1883. He served churches in TEXAS, WASHINGTON, D. C., SOUTH CAROLINA, and GEORGIA. At the General Conference in 1894, he was elected to the office of bishop. He was a delegate to the third ECUMENICAL METHODIST CONFERENCE in LONDON in 1901, and he also wrote a book of sermons. He served as Senior Bishop for twelve years before his death on Jan. 13, 1932.

Harris and Patterson, *C.M.E. Church*. 1965.
I. Lane, *Autobiography*. 1916.

RALPH G. GAY

WILLIAMS, THOMAS, eighteenth-century British Methodist, was one of Wesley's early assistants, sometimes confused with a preacher of the same name among the CALVINISTIC METHODISTS of South Wales. In the summer of 1747 he became the first Methodist preacher to visit Ireland. He formed a society in DUBLIN and persuaded JOHN WESLEY to pay it a visit. He also pioneered the work in Cork, Limerick, and Londonderry, but later left the connection and obtained Anglican orders.

Wesley Hist. Soc. *Proc.*, i, 106.

JOHN A. VICKERS

WILLIAMS, THOMAS FREDERICK (1876-1948), American preacher, the son of Jacob F. and A. Elizabeth (Bunton) Williams, was born Nov. 5, 1876, at Gentryville, Ind. He was admitted on trial into the INDIANA CONFERENCE in 1900 and transferred to the Northwest Indiana Conference in 1904. He was pastor at Trinity Church, LAFAYETTE, from 1919 to 1948, the longest pastorate in Indiana Methodism. He was a delegate to three General Conferences, two Jurisdictional Conferences and the Uniting Conference. He was President of the Board of Directors of the Indiana Antisaloon League for eighteen years; twenty-two years, president of the Preachers' Aid Society. Loved by young people, he was dean of Battle Ground Epworth League Institute for nine years. Trinity's membership grew from 712 to 1,846 under his inspiring preaching. He was chairman and manager of community fund campaigns. He married Edith Johnson in 1910. They had one son. Williams died at Lafayette, Jan. 14, 1948.

Lafayette *Journal and Courier*, Dec. 5, 1946.
Who's Who in America, 1944-45.

W. D. ARCHIBALD

WILLIAMS, WILLIAM (1717-1791), Welsh Calvinistic Methodist hymnwriter, was born into a Presbyterian family. After hearing HOWELL HARRIS preach in 1738, Williams resolved to devote himself to the ministry, and in 1740 was ordained deacon in the Church of England.

From his mountain curacy he became a leading preacher among the WELSH CALVINISTIC METHODISTS, and at their second "association" in 1743 he agreed to resign his Anglican charge in order to assist DANIEL ROWLANDS. He continued to call himself a minister of the Church of England, but was never priested. His greatest contribution to Welsh religion was in his hymns, stimulated by a challenge issued by Howell Harris. His first book of Welsh hymns, entitled *Alleluia*, was published in 1744, to be followed by many more. His best known is "Arglwydd, arwain trwy'r anialwch," translated into English as "Guide me, O thou great Jehovah." This translation (an adaptation by Williams himself of one by PETER WILLIAMS) first appeared about 1772 as "a favourite hymn sung by Lady Huntingdon's young collegians," and was soon widely adopted. Williams died Jan. 11, 1791 at Pantycelyn, near Llandovery.

Dictionary of National Biography.
John Julian, *Dictionary of Hymnology*, 2nd edition, London, 1907.

FRANK BAKER

WILLIAMS, WILLIAM JONES (1891-1966), South African layman, was born in Newark, N. J., U.S.A., on Sept. 19, 1891 and married Maud Williams on Jan. 8, 1918. He served as a Sergeant-Major in World War I and was administering officer of the Governor-General's War Fund during World War II. He was a most successful Natal businessman, a Rotarian, a founder of the Durban Community Chest and Chairman of the McCord Zulu Hospital. In Methodism he held all local offices and was for many years Chairman of the Board of Governors for EPWORTH HIGH SCHOOL and KEARSNEY COLLEGE. His outstanding service was as Lay General Treasurer of the Methodist Church, an honorary but exacting office which he held for twenty-nine years. In this capacity he helped to establish the Methodist Connexional Office and gave daily attention to the financial affairs of the Church which he placed on a sound basis. He dominated the financial discussions of successive Conferences by his mastery of detail, his sparkle and forthrightness in debate and his obvious dedication to the work. Courageous, clear-sighted and generous, he regarded his service in church, community and commerce as a direct expression of his loyalty to Christ. He died in Durban, Natal, on Dec. 2, 1966.

C. WILKINS

WILLS, JOSEPH NORMAN (1870-1944), American M.P. layman and benefactor, was born on June 15, 1870, in Washington County, N. C. He was the son of RICHARD HENRY and Ann Louisa Norman WILLS and the grandson of WILLIAM H. and Anna Whitaker Wills. Joseph Norman Wills moved as a young boy with his parents to Guilford County, N. C., where, at the age of eleven, he joined Moriah M.P. Church. In October 1889, he became a charter member of the Grace M. P. Church in GREENSBORO, N. C. In 1896 he married Anna Maria Alderman.

Wills became a prominent business leader in Greensboro and a tireless worker in various civic, cultural and religious affairs. For half a century he was one of the most influential laymen in his branch of Methodism. He served as president of the North Carolina Merchant's Association, and from 1896 until 1936 he was a member of every GENERAL CONFERENCE of the M.P. Church. He was also a member of the UNITING CONFERENCE of the Methodist Churches in KANSAS CITY, in April, 1939. He served as

Secretary-Treasurer of the North Carolina Conference Board of Education; Secretary-Treasurer of the Board of Church Extension; Treasurer of the High Point College Building Fund, and later as a trustee of HIGH POINT COLLEGE; and Secretary-Treasurer of the M.P. Publishing House in Greensboro. He was also a trustee of the M.P. Children's Home in High Point and a member of the Board of Missions of the General Conference; of the Commission on Church Union; and the Board of Governors of WESTMINSTER THEOLOGICAL SEMINARY. He made a gift of $100,000 to High Point College at the time of its establishment.

He died on Feb. 3, 1944, and was buried in Greensboro.

J. Elwood Carroll, *History of the North Carolina Annual Conference of the Methodist Protestant Church.* Greensboro, 1939.
The North Carolina Christian Advocate, Feb. 24, 1944.
RALPH HARDEE RIVES

WILLS, RICHARD HENRY (1836-1891), American M.P. minister, was the eldest son of WILLIAM H. and Anna Whitaker WILLS. He was born on Oct. 10, 1836 in Tarboro, N. C., and attended Elba Academy, known also as the HALIFAX MALE ACADEMY, at Brinkleyville, N. C. This school was conducted by his father and JESSE H. PAGE. He was converted at the age of sixteen and his first sermon was preached at Bethesda M.P. Church, at Brinkleyville, about 1855. He served as a local preacher until 1858, when he joined the NORTH CAROLINA CONFERENCE of the M.P. Church. He served the following circuits: Tar River, Albemarle, Haw River, Roanoke, Halifax, Davidson, Winston, Greensboro, Winston Mission and Mocksville. He was president of the North Carolina Conference in 1872-74; 1882-84 and in 1888, and was Secretary of the Conference in 1863-64 and in 1880. He was a member of the GENERAL CONFERENCES of 1866, 1884 and 1888, and of the General Convention of 1877 and the Joint Commission of the Methodist and M.P. bodies at PITTSBURGH, Pa., in 1876. He served as president pro tem of YADKIN COLLEGE in 1883-84. He died on Nov. 5, 1891, and was buried in Green Hill Cemetery in GREENSBORO, N. C.

J. Elwood Carroll, *History of the North Carolina Annual Conference of the Methodist Protestant Church.* Greensboro, 1939.
Journal of the North Carolina Conference, MP.
Olin B. Michael, *Yadkin College, 1856-1924.* Salisbury, 1939.
RALPH HARDEE RIVES

WILLS, W. MILBURN (1917-   ), American businessman and lay leader of the FREE METHODIST CHURCH. He is a member of the John Wesley Church in INDIANAPOLIS and international president of the Light and Life Men's Fellowship. He served as a delegate to the Wabash Conference and is a member of conference committees and is active in the Boy Scouts of America. He is the owner of an important furniture and appliance company of Indianapolis, Ind. He has always been active in home witness crusades. His wife was Deletha A. Mayfield and they were married in 1941. His residence is in Indianapolis.

BYRON S. LAMSON

WILLS, WILLIAM HENRY (1809-1899), American M.P. minister, educator and administrator, was three times President of the NORTH CAROLINA CONFERENCE of the M.P.

Church, and in 1866 was President of the GENERAL CONFERENCE of that denomination. He was born in Tarboro, N. C., on Aug. 4, 1809, and joined WHITAKER'S CHAPEL in 1830. On May 13, 1835, he married Anna Maria Baker Whitaker (Feb. 22, 1817-Feb. 2, 1893), daughter of Cary and Martha Susan Baker Whitaker of Enfield, N. C. They built a permanent home, "Rocky Hill," near Brinkleyville, Halifax County, from which Wills traveled to preach over a wide area of the state, and where his nine children were born and reared. In 1853 Wills became one of the founders of and principal contributors to Bethesda Church which was built at Brinkleyville. As a result of his influence, the Annual Conference met at Bethesda Church in 1862. In 1855 he and JESSE HAYES PAGE, later his son-in-law, opened the HALIFAX MALE ACADEMY at Brinkleyville and shortly afterward the ELBA FEMALE SEMINARY. Wills also served as a trustee of LYNCHBURG COLLEGE during the period of its existence, 1855-61. The D.D. degree was conferred upon him by WESTERN MARYLAND COLLEGE in 1872.

Wills served as Secretary of the North Carolina Conference in 1832, 1833, 1853, 1856, 1857 and as President in 1848, 1849 and 1868. He served the following circuits or stations in the conference: Roanoke, Haw River, Granville, Halifax, Tar River, Greensboro and LaGrange. The Annual Conference of 1878 appointed him Conference Evangelist. He was a delegate to the General Conference of the M.P. Church in 1846, 1850, 1854, 1858, 1862, 1866, 1870, 1877 and 1880. The General Conference of 1866, of which he was president, met in GEORGETOWN, D.C., and during its sessions the members went as a body to call on President Andrew Johnson in the White House. Wills made a short address after which the President spoke.

At a General Convention of the M.P. Church held in Baltimore in May 1877, Wills was a member of a Joint Committee which recommended the adoption of the Basis of Union between the northern and southern branches of the denomination. On May 16, 1877, when the two branches were officially reunited, Wills and his neighbor, L. W. Batchelor from Brinkleyville, were among those who presented voluntary five-minute speeches.

William Henry Wills was said to have been a preacher of "almost pentecostal power" and at a protracted meeting at Double Springs, Guilford County, N. C., a thousand hearers "seemed to have been swayed as by a strong wind." He was well versed in the economy of his church, clearly comprehended its principles, and was a parliamentarian of decided ability.

He died at "Rocky Hill" on June 22, 1889 and was buried at Bethesda Church.

Abridged Compendium of American Genealogy, The.
A. H. Bassett, *Concise History.* 1887.
J. Elwood Carroll, *History of the North Carolina Annual Conference of the Methodist Protestant Church.* Greensboro, 1939.
L. E. Davis, *Democratic Methodism.* 1921.
E. J. Drinkhouse, *History of Methodist Reform,* II, 1899.
J. L. Michaux and A. C. Harris, *Memorial of Reverend William H. Wills, D.D.* N.p., 1889.
Methodist Protestant Church Memorial Collection, North Carolina Wesleyan College, Rocky Mount, N. C.
LULA HUNTER SKILLMAN
RALPH HARDEE RIVES

WILLSON, JAMES McCRORRY (1887-   ), American layman, founder of the Willson lectures at McMURRY

COLLEGE and of other benevolent foundations and long-time delegate to successive General Conferences of the Church, was born at Boonesville, Texas, on Dec. 21, 1887. He was the son of David and Sarah Eugenia (Stange) Willson. He was educated at SOUTHWESTERN UNIVERSITY, Texas, A.B., 1912; and received the LL.D. from TEXAS WESLEYAN COLLEGE, 1947; and the L.H.D. from McMURRAY COLLEGE, 1956. His wife was Mavis Louis Terry whom he married on June 14, 1919, and they had four children.

Mr. Willson began business in a retail lumber yard in 1908 and is presently the owner and operator (with his son) of a large lumber business in TEXAS. He joined the First Methodist Church in Bridgeport, Texas, in 1914, and has been a member of the Floydada, Texas, Church since 1916, serving as steward and trustee almost since that time. He was elected to the GENERAL CONFERENCE of the M.E. Church, South in 1934 and 1938; to the Uniting Conference of 1939, and since that time has served in all successive General Conferences of The Methodist Church and in that of The United Methodist Church. He was the chairman of the Board of Hospitals and Homes of the South Central Jurisdiction, 1949-54; the Texas Association of Methodist Colleges; a member of the National Council of the Boy Scouts of America; trustee of SOUTHERN METHODIST UNIVERSITY, 1930-68, and of McMurry College, 1935-68, and of the WESTERN METHODIST ASSEMBLY. He founded the Willson lectures in 1943 at McMurry College and has always held prominent places in the Church-life of his Jurisdiction. He continues to reside at Floydada, Texas.

Who's Who in The Methodist Church, 1966.   N. B. H.

WILLSON, WILLIAM HOLDEN (1801-1856), American layman, was born in NEW HAMPSHIRE. He came to OREGON as a carpenter with the first reenforcements to the Methodist Mission founded by JASON LEE, arriving May 18, 1837. He learned the fundamentals of the practice of medicine from Dr. Elijah White, and thenceforth was known as "Dr. Willson."

He was sent to Nisqually in Washington by Jason Lee in 1839, in anticipation of the coming of JOHN P. RICHMOND, who arrived there in 1840. On Aug. 16, 1840 Willson was united in marriage to Chloe Aurelia Clark, a Mission teacher from CONNECTICUT, who had come out with the second reenforcement to the Mission on the ship *Lausanne*, and was assigned to teach at Nisqually. This was the first white marriage in the state of Washington, and Richmond officiated.

When the Nisqually Mission was abandoned in 1842, Willson returned to SALEM, and was elected to the board of the Oregon Institute, predecessor of WILLAMETTE UNIVERSITY. Mrs. Willson was the first teacher in the school. Later Willson became secretary of the institution and agent for the sale of the mission property which comprised the entire townsite of Salem.

Willson was one of the secretaries of the Champoeg Meeting, held May 2, 1843. He was one of the managers of the Oregon and California Missionary Society, organized in 1849. He was active in civic and political life of Oregon, once running for congress. He had much to do with the attempt to coin money before and after Oregon became a territory in 1849.

Willson and his wife had three daughters, later prominent citizens of Oregon. They were Frances Aurelia (Mrs.

J. K. Gill); Belle (Mrs. William Wythe); and Katherine (Mrs. William G. Dillingham). A great-grandson, Richard G. Montgomery, became author of several books dealing with the history of Oregon.

Willson died in 1856 and is buried in Salem.

Erle Howell, *Northwest*. 1966.
Pacific Northwest Quarterly, July 1959.   ERLE HOWELL

WILMINGTON, DELAWARE, U.S.A., was founded and located on the west bank of the Delaware River. The city is the location of the world's largest chemical manufacturing companies and their research laboratories.

In 1639 the first Swedish expedition to the new world under the leadership of Peter Minuit, sailed up the Delaware River and into the Christian River to a point then called "The Rocks." Here they established a colony and built Fort Christina. Both the fort and the village surrounding it were named in honor of Queen Christina, the daughter of Gustavus Adolphus, King of SWEDEN. In 1655 the Dutch took Fort Christina ending Swedish rule in Delaware.

The English took control of the colony in 1664 under William Penn. It acquired under his leadership a Quaker character which has never been lost. The area which was to become the City of Wilmington was laid out in 1731.

Methodism traces its origin in Wilmington back to 1766 or 1767 and the coming of Captain THOMAS WEBB. PILMORE in his *Journal* gives a positive date of Nov. 4, 1769 for Captain Webb's second visit. Webb preached his first sermon under some trees near the corner of King and Kent Streets, now 8th and King. John Thelwell, a well-known school teacher, officiated as clerk for the service and led the singing. Subsequently, Thelwell offered his school house as a place of worship. Thelwell was also a bellman, market master and clerk, and was one of the founders of Asbury Church.

Methodism in Wilmington had very humble and precarious beginnings. The first society formed consisted of about fourteen members and was connected with Chester Circuit. ASBURY complained that he could not use the court house, but that the dancing crowd had free access to it at anytime. THOMAS WARE under the date of 1791 tells us of the conditions he faced in the pastorate in Wilmington, "I commenced my labors in Wilmington. This was my first station; but I signed for the backwoods, which were a paradise to me, compared with this suffocating borough infected with mystical miasm, which had a deleterious effect, especially on the youth. They had imbibed this moral poison until it broke out in supercilious contempt of all who were by one class denounced as hirelings and will-worshippers, and by another as free-willers and perfectionists. Our church was surrounded by hundreds of these sons of Beliah, night after night, while there were scarecely fifty worshippers; such was their conduct, that females were afraid to attend our meetings at night; and we had to commence services in time to dismiss the congregation before it was dark." EZEKIEL COOPER was appointed to Wilmington in 1797. He found the church to be in disorder and confusion. "Scarcely any regularity at all, and rather a general anarchy in the affairs of the Society, and a disunity and murmuring, one with another prevails."

In 1789 a lot was purchased at the southeast corner of Walnut and Third Streets and a house of worship was erected fronting Walnut. It was a building about thirty-five feet square with a gallery, and Bishop Asbury dedicated it on Oct. 16, 1789. Asbury wrote concerning it, "Thus far have we come after more than twenty years of labor in this place." This society then consisted of forty-three white and nineteen colored members. The church building was enlarged in 1811 by an addition of twenty feet, and in 1828 there was another addition so that the building thus much enlarged became known as Asbury Church. There was also a small cemetery in connection with the church and in it many of the first members were laid to rest.

Wilmington became a station in 1789 with J. Jessop as pastor, but in 1795 it reverted again to a circuit and alternated between a circuit status and a station until 1806 when JOSHUA WELLS came and it became a permanent station. Growth was slow. In the year 1800, it numbered about 200. In 1805 the black people secured a lot and built a house for separate worship about thirty-five feet square. In 1844 another charge was established which was dedicated on Feb. 23, 1845, known as St. Paul's Church. In 1848, a charge was formed called Union mission, and this in time moved to a more eligible site, and what was known as Union Church was erected under J. D. Curtis. What became known as Scott Church came from the move of a few members from Asbury and Union who had organized a Sabbath school and in time put up a building in 1852.

Grace Church which has long been known as the cathedral church of Wilmington was erected at a cost of over $200,000 on the northwest corner of Ninth and West Streets. In time other churches were started until twenty-seven were reported in 1970 with a total membership of 17,582. Suburban development has given rise to several new parishes—Asbury, Wilmington Manor, Kingswood and Brookside, Aldersgate and more recently Skyline.

Wilmington gave its name to the WILMINGTON CONFERENCE of the M.E. Church which was organized by the authority of the GENERAL CONFERENCE of 1868. This held its first session in Wilmington on March 17, 1869. At the union of Methodism in 1939, the Wilmington Conference became the PENINSULA CONFERENCE, though Wilmington is still the metropolis both of the conference and the state of DELAWARE. The A.M.E. CHURCH and the A.M.E. ZION CHURCH both have had churches in Wilmington for the past 100 years.

Aldersgate Church is the largest church in the Peninsula Conference with a membership of 3,265 in 1970. It is a suburban church which was started by a small group of sixty-five persons in 1948. The Aldersgate Church stands beside Concord Pike, one of the busiest highways in Delaware, and serves a rapidly expanding suburban area. The church is staffed by three ministers, as well as by a Director of Christian Education and a Director of Music.

Aldersgate has become a community center. It operates an accredited kindergarten, employing twelve teachers and accommodating 250 children. It maintains three church services, and two complete church schools every Sunday. The operation of two weekly canteens, one for Junior High and one for Senior High, is part of its youth program. There are three youth choirs. The church is growing at the rate of nearly 300 members per year.

Grace Church is one of the early examples of the architectural shift in America from plain chapels to large and ornate edifices. Certain civil provisions have made

GRACE CHURCH, WILMINGTON, DELAWARE

the State of Delaware advantageous for a great many large business corporations to establish Wilmington as the legal location of their "home offices," so Wilmington has become the center of very considerable wealth. In the middle of the nineteenth century a group of very affluent Methodist laymen incorporated themselves under a Delaware charter and erected Grace Church, commemorating the first 100 years of American Methodism. Newspaper headlines on the day Grace Church was opened, Jan. 23, 1865, called it "the finest Methodist Church in America." Bishop MATTHEW SIMPSON in nearby PHILADELPHIA, refused to appoint a Methodist minister to serve Grace Church after its erection until the trustees, despite their independence as a civil corporation, agreed to execute the Methodist Trust Clause (see DEEDS OF TRUST) as a corollary to their civil charter. Grace Church remains one of the largest and strongest congregations along America's eastern seaboard. In 1970 it reported 1,726 members.

E. C. Hallman, *Garden of Methodism.* 1948.
J. Lednum, *Rise of Methodism.* 1859.
J. Thomas Scharf, *History of Delaware.* L. J. Richards & Co., 1888.
M. Simpson, *Cyclopaedia.* 1878.   WILLIAM O. HACKETT
JAMES R. HUGHES

WILMINGTON CONFERENCE. (See PENINSULA CONFERENCE, and DELAWARE.)

WILMOT, GEORGE WILLIAM (1878-1946), a minister of the Belgian Conference of The Methodist Church, was born in Boulogne, FRANCE, of British parents. He married Edith Rugly and they had three children. He studied for the ministry and became a preacher of the Wesleyan Church in France. During the First World War, he served as interpreter and liaison officer with the French army. He came to BRUSSELS in 1920 to take part in post-war relief work of the newly organized Methodist Mission. He organized the first Methodist congregation in BELGIUM, the Brussels Central Church, and became its pastor, 1922-30, and again from 1933-40. Because of his British nationality, he was sent into exile by the German invasion of 1940. His health broke, and he died in Witney, Oxon, England, in October 1946.

WILLIAM G. THONGER

ALPHEUS W. WILSON

WILSON, ALPHEUS WATERS (1834-1916), American bishop, was born in Baltimore, Md., Feb. 5, 1834, the son of Norval and Cornelia (Howland) Wilson. NORVAL WILSON was a conference leader in his day, an M.E. GENERAL CONFERENCE delegate, 1832-40, and a delegate to the Southern Church General Conference in 1866. Also, he wrote the resolution adopted by the BALTIMORE CONFERENCE (ME) at Staunton, Va., in March, 1861, by which that conference declared itself independent of General Conference authority because of the chapter on slavery placed in the *Discipline* by that body in 1860.

Alpheus Wilson was educated at George Washington University, graduating at eighteen. He studied medicine and later law. RANDOLPH-MACON COLLEGE and VICTORIA UNIVERSITY awarded him the D.D. degree, and the LL.D. was conferred on him by CENTRAL METHODIST COLLEGE and Washington and Lee University. He married Susan B. Lipscomb, March 4, 1857, and they had three sons who died in childhood, and three daughters.

Wilson was admitted on trial in the Baltimore Conference (ME) in 1853, and was ordained DEACON in 1855 and ELDER in 1857. After four years as a junior preacher on different charges, his appointments were: 1857, Warm Springs, Va.; 1858, Blue Sulphur, W. Va.; 1859, supernumerary; 1860-61, Eutaw Street, Baltimore; 1870-72, WASHINGTON, D. C., District (MES); 1873-76, Mount Vernon Place, Washington; 1877, Calvary, Baltimore; and 1878-81, General Missionary Secretary. He was a delegate to the General Conference, 1874-82, and was elected bishop at the 1882 session.

Because Wilson's sympathies were with the South, he would not attend the session of the Baltimore Conference (ME) at Light Street Church, Baltimore, in March, 1862, and which was composed of the minority of preachers who had opposed the action of the majority at Staunton, Va., in March, 1861. The group meeting at Light Street Church declared that the preachers who did not attend had withdrawn, and Wilson and sixty-five others were dropped. Wilson's biographer says the stand he took in 1862 meant the loss of all he possessed. Wilson then began the practice of law in Baltimore and continued at it until five years after the Civil War in order to meet his financial obligations, though he was enrolled as a member of the Baltimore Conference (MES) which convened at Alexandria, Va., in March, 1866. Wilson was carried on the roll as a superannuate the first year and then as supernumerary the next three years.

When Wilson became Missionary Secretary he was soon recognized throughout the connection as an able church leader. Coming on the scene just after the period of Reconstruction, he stirred the Southern Church to action on behalf of missions. He quickly became known as a great preacher; profoundly impressed with his pulpit ability, the preachers in the conferences sat on the edge of their pews when Wilson stood up to preach. Bishop LUTHER B. WILSON (ME), a fellow Baltimorean, declared that A. W. Wilson was the mightiest preacher he personally ever heard. Wilson was a close student of the Bible; during the last thirteen years of his life he read his Greek New Testament through seventy-five times.

Bishop Wilson visited the church's missions in BRAZIL twice and those in the Orient six times, helping to organize the mission in JAPAN on one trip. He was a member of four ECUMENICAL METHODIST CONFERENCES, 1881-1911, delivering important addresses at the first three. In addition to several addresses, he published two books: *The Witnesses to Christ, the Savior of the World*, 1894; and *The Life and Mind of St. Paul*, 1912. In 1924 Bishop W. A. CANDLER edited a volume of Wilson's *Sermons, Lectures, and Addresses.*

After thirty-two years as a bishop, Wilson was superannuated at the 1914 General Conference. He died in Baltimore, Nov. 21, 1916, and was buried there.

General Minutes, ME and MES.
F. D. Leete, *Methodist Bishops.* 1948.
Minutes of the Baltimore Conference, 1917.
General Conference Journal, MES, 1918.
Who Was Who in America, 1897-1942. JESSE A. EARL
ALBEA GODBOLD

WILSON, CLARENCE TRUE (1872-1939), American minister, secretary of the Board of Temperance, Prohibition and Public Morals of the M.E. Church and leader of American Methodism's temperance and prohibition movement for over a generation, was born in Milton, Del., April 24, 1872. His higher education was received at St. John's College, Annapolis, Md., the University of Southern California, and McClay College of Theology. He was ordained DEACON at the age of eighteen, an elder at twenty—the youngest man ever to be so ordained according to *Who's Who in American Methodism* (1916).

Between 1892 and 1905, Wilson served pastorates in various states, and between 1905 and 1910 was pastor of Centenary Methodist Church in PORTLAND, Ore. From 1910 to 1936 he was the general secretary of the Board of Temperance, Prohibition, and Public Morals of the M.E. Church. Under his leadership Methodism waged a great battle to win national prohibition. One of his strategic moves was the building of an impressive office building to house his and other Methodist activities on Capitol Hill, WASHINGTON, D. C., practically in the shadow of the Capitol dome—a building which yet serves as Methodist headquarters in the capital city. Wilson retired at the age of sixty-five to live in Oregon, where he died on Feb. 16, 1939.

The Christian Advocate in its Pacific edition just after his death said: "Clarence True Wilson was one of the most colorful characters produced by modern Methodism . . . Other men of genius will emerge, but the peculiar combination of circumstances which gave him scope for expression will not be duplicated. Dr. Wilson will be especially remembered for his street-corner advocacy of prohibition, for his joint debates with Clarence Darrow and others on the subject, and for the nerve and pertinacity which he displayed in erecting the Methodist Building at Washington."

Christian Advocate, The. Pacific Edition, March 9, 1939. Vol. 88, No. 10, p. 220.
Capitol's *Who's Who for Oregon,* 1936-37. Portland, Oregon: 1936.
C. F. Price, *Who's Who in American Methodism.* 1916.
ROBERT MOULTON GATKE

WILSON, HENRY RAYNOR (1898-   ), is a third-generation Methodist in North INDIA. He was born in Budaun, Dec. 28, 1898. His grandfather was a noncommissioned officer in the army of the East India Company. After retiring he was converted and was baptized by the pioneer missionary, Peachey T. Wilson, whose surname he adopted. A son, baptized at the same time and named Dhappan, was educated in Methodist schools and became a Methodist minister. Henry married Virginia Haqq, a granddaughter of the early convert and first Indian presiding elder, ZAHUR-UL-HAQQ.

Henry Wilson was educated in Parker High School, Moradabad, and in LUCKNOW CHRISTIAN COLLEGE. He joined the North India Conference educational service, and while principal of the Methodist High School in Dwarahat, he was invited to serve also as pastor of the church there. Later he was ordained DEACON and ELDER, but he did not become an Annual Conference member until 1950. From 1931 to 1946, he was principal of the Parker High School at Moradabad, leaving that post to become agent of the LUCKNOW PUBLISHING HOUSE. He was editor of *The Indian Witness,* 1947-50. In 1947 he became the treasurer of the All-India Methodist Provident Fund.

He edited the Hindi-Urdu weekly *Kaukab-i-Hind* (Star of India) for several short periods. He was also editor of a book of daily devotional lessons in Hindustani. In 1951 he returned to Moradabad as district superintendent and gave leadership to more than 20,000 Methodists in that district for six years. He retired and lives in Moradabad. He was delegate to two GENERAL CONFERENCES and was often elected to the CENTRAL CONFERENCE, and the executive board, and to membership on boards of governors of educational and medical institutions.

J. N. Hollister, *Southern Asia.* 1956.
Indian Witness, The.
Journals of North India and Moradabad Annual Conference, 1931-68.
J. WASKOM PICKETT

WILSON, JOHN (1837-1915), British Methodist, was one of those PRIMITIVE METHODIST LOCAL PREACHERS who left a deep mark upon the character of trade unionism in the Northeast, and especially the Durham coal mines. Beginning to work in the pit at the age of twelve, he became general secretary of his union, the Durham Miners' Association; thence he went into local politics as a county councillor and alderman, and for the last twenty-five years of his life he sat as Liberal M.P. for mid-Durham.

E. R. TAYLOR

WILSON, LUTHER BARTON (1856-1928), American bishop, was born at Baltimore, Md., Nov. 14, 1856, the son of Henry M. and Eliza K. (Hollingsworth) Wilson. One of his ancestors was among ROBERT STRAWBRIDGE's first converts and became a member of that preacher's first society.

Wilson was educated at DICKINSON COLLEGE (A.B., 1875; A.M., 1878); and the University of Maryland (M.D., 1877). His honorary degrees were: D.D. in 1892, and LL.D. in 1904 from Dickinson; L.H.D. from SYRACUSE in 1912; and LL.D. from WESLEYAN in 1913. He married Louisa J. Turner, Feb. 17, 1881, and they had two sons and a daughter.

No sooner had Wilson graduated in medicine than he felt called to preach. He joined the BALTIMORE CONFERENCE (ME) in 1878, was ordained DEACON in 1880 and ELDER in 1882. For twenty-six years he was a pastor and presiding elder. He served five charges in or near BALTIMORE, 1878-90. Other appointments were: Wesley, WASHINGTON, 1891-93; Washington District, 1894-99; Foundry, Washington, 1900-02; and West Baltimore District 1903-04. He was a GENERAL CONFERENCE delegate, 1896-1904, leading his delegation and being elected bishop in the latter year. He was the resident bishop in CHATTANOOGA, 1904-08; PHILADELPHIA, 1908-12; and NEW YORK, 1912-28.

Wilson was his denomination'a fraternal delegate to the Methodist Church of CANADA in 1902. In 1895 he was chairman of the committee which called the first convention of the National Anti-Saloon League, and was elected first vice-president of that body in 1901. He was a member of the Church Peace Union, and served as a trustee of AMERICAN UNIVERSITY, Dickinson and MORGAN COLLEGES, and DREW SEMINARY.

Bishop EDWIN H. HUGHES rated Wilson as one of the three greatest "ecclesiastical lawyers" in the history of the M.E. Church. Though he and Bishop ALPHEUS W. WILSON (MES) were not related, they as native Baltimoreans were good friends and they worked for better relations between the two churches. Hughes and others credited L. B. Wilson with making a significant contribution toward the unification of American Methodism.

Though Wilson had been in frail health for several years due to a severe illness contracted while on an episcopal tour in Africa, he undertook the presentation of the episcopal address at the 1928 General Conference. By reason of age he was retired at that conference. He died shortly afterward, June 4, in Baltimore, and was buried there.

General Minutes, ME.
General Conference Journals, ME.
Edwin H. Hughes, *I Was Made a Minister.* Nashville: Abingdon Press, 1943.
F. D. Leete, *Methodist Bishops.* 1948.
National Cyclopedia of American Biography.
Who Was Who in America, 1897-1942.
JESSE A. EARL
ALBEA GODBOLD

WILSON, NORVAL (1802-1876), American minister and Southern church leader, the father of Bishop ALPHEUS W. WILSON, was born at or near Lewisburn, W. Va. His ancestors were of sturdy Scotch-Irish Presbyterian stock. His education was liberal, a broad and deep basis for the subsequent love of letters which marked the whole course of his life. He was student of and an authority on the life and writings of JOHN WESLEY. He could never endure any depreciation of Wesley or Wesley's writings.

Norval Wilson's work as a preacher covered thirty-nine years. This began in the rugged mountains of his own state, but very soon he was transferred to the tide-water counties of the Northern Neck of VIRGINIA, and from there he was sent to BALTIMORE City, Md. He served in various capacities in the BALTIMORE CONFERENCE of the M.E. Church, South. It is said that Norval Wilson, who cast his lot with the Southern Church in 1846, left Baltimore at the outbreak of the war between the States, and managed to take the records of the Old Baltimore Conference back to Virginia with him. He was accused of "stealing the records," by those Baltimoreans who adhered to the North.

The story is that in the attempt to secure the old conference records, the Northern Methodists in Baltimore got a provost guard from the Federal Army then occupying Baltimore to search for them. Wilson, assisted by certain Southern sympathizers, got the records concealed under bales of hay and taken to a ship in the harbor and thence shipped to NORFOLK and from that point they were transported by the old canal along the James River up to Lexington, Va. The Southern Church thus saved the records and they were kept by the Old Baltimore Conference (MES) until that conference was dissolved at union in 1939, when the records were put back in the Lovely Lane Museum in Baltimore.

In 1860, because of failing health, Norval Wilson retired and chose Winchester, Va., as his home. For sixteen years he never ceased working among the churches, as vacancies gave opportunity for Presbyterian, Lutheran, and Reformed congregations to invite him to occupy their pulpits.

Norval Wilson, in his personal appearance, was most striking. He was a man of unbending will and steadfast resolve. However, it was not until one heard him speak that the full measure of his personality could be felt. He was considered, by all who heard him, an excellent preacher—"a man of God." He died Aug. 9, 1876. His son, Bishop Alpheus W. Wilson, survived him many years and was one of the notable bishops in the Southern Church.

J. E. Armstrong, *Old Baltimore Conference*. 1907.

W. W. McINTYRE

WILSON, OLIVER G. (1891-1959), American WESLEYAN METHODIST minister, was born on July 21, 1891 and spent his early years in Minersville, Kan. In 1917 he was ordained by the Kansas Conference (Wesleyan Methodist) and served as pastor in that as well as in the Oklahoma Conference. He was president of the Oklahoma Conference until he was called to Miltonvale Wesleyan College (1929-42) where he served as instructor in theology and Bible, vice-president, and dean of men at various times. In 1943 he was chosen by the denomination to be the Sunday School Secretary and Editor. In 1947 he was named editor of *The Wesleyan Methodist* where he became widely and favorably known for his forceful literary style. He served in this capacity until his death in 1959. Houghton College conferred the D.D. degree on him in 1949. Wilson was in demand as a speaker in camp meetings, conferences of all ages, and filled positions on many boards of the denomination.

GEORGE E. FAILING

WINANS, WILLIAM (1788-1857), pioneer American preacher and leader, was born Nov. 3, 1788, at Chestnut

WILLIAM WINANS

Ridge, Pa. As a youth he moved with his family to Clermont County, Ohio, where in 1807 he had a heart-warming experience. He received license to preach and was admitted on trial into the WESTERN CONFERENCE in October 1808. After one year on the Limestone Circuit in KENTUCKY, he was appointed to Vincennes, Ind. At the session of the Western Conference in 1810, Winans was received in full connection and volunteered to take an appointment in the MISSISSIPPI District. He arrived in Mississippi on Dec. 5, 1810, to begin an outstanding ministry in that state which was destined to last until his death forty-seven years later. At the first session of the MISSISSIPPI CONFERENCE in 1813, he was elected secretary and served ten years in that capacity. He was appointed a missionary to NEW ORLEANS, and while there he bought the lot on which the first Methodist church in that city was built.

After marrying Martha Dubose in 1814, he located for five years, living at Centreville, Miss., in a home he built himself. Three daughters and one son were born of the marriage.

Although Winans had almost no formal education, he became an avid reader and accumulated one of the largest private libraries in the Southwest. He spoke and wrote with freedom, correctness, and force. RANDOLPH-MACON COLLEGE later conferred upon him the D.D. degree.

ELDER's orders were conferred in 1816. After returning to active service in 1820, he served for several years as a presiding elder in addition to those as a pastor. During his active ministry he traveled 140,000 miles.

Winans went to the GENERAL CONFERENCE in Baltimore in 1824, an unknown preacher, and came away well recognized as a powerful church legislator, and well-nigh irresistible in debate. From that year until his death he was a delegate to every General Conference. In 1832, he delivered the Pastoral Address as it was called, to the General Conference. In the years immediately preceding the division of the M.E. Church he was the principal spokesman for the southern group. Bishop McTYEIRE thus describes Winans in the great debate that ensued in 1844:

Dr. Winans (of Mississippi) was the first speaker on the Southern side; a striking figure—tall and raw-boned. The veins of his stringy neck might be seen, swollen with earnestness, for he spoke in Italics and wore no cravat. His limp shirt-collar lay around, his clothes were baggy, and his shoes tied with strings; but his eyes were bloodshot with intensity, and his head a magnificent dome of thought. Exact, logical, forcible, he had become known in the radical controversy of 1824, as unsurpassed in debate. Other elements besides ecclesiastical entered into this question, and he spoke in "the calmness of despair":

"Well, he [Bishop Andrew] was a slave-holder in 1840, exposed to the malediction of the North, and just as unfit for the general superintendency as in January, 1844. . . . What evil had he done by becoming a slave-holder further by marriage, when he was already a slave-holder beyond control?"

When, however, the decision went against the South, Winans was put on the Committee of Nine appointed to draw up the PLAN OF SEPARATION of the Church. He was chairman of the southern group of delegates the next year at the LOUISVILLE CONVENTION of 1845, called for the purpose of organizing the M.E. Church, South. He made the speech at that convention which inspired and stimulated the action that was taken. He called to order the first General Conference of the M.E. Church, South, at PETERSBURG, Va., in 1846. More than any other one man, he was the champion of Southern Methodism.

He died on Aug. 31, 1857, and was buried the following day in the family burial plot in Wilkinson County, Miss.

William Winans, Journals and personal papers.
H. N. McTyeire, *History of Methodism.* 1884.　J. A. LINDSAY

WINCHELL, ALEXANDER (1824-1891), American educator and scientist, whose teachings in regard to evolution caused his dismissal from VANDERBILT UNIVERSITY. He was born on Dec. 31, 1824, in the town of North-East, Dutchess County, N. Y., the son of Horace and Caroline (McAllister) Winchell. He first began to prepare himself for a career in medicine, but eventually graduated from WESLEYAN UNIVERSITY, Middletown, Conn., in 1847, and began an active career in teaching, lecturing and writing.

He taught in the natural history department at Amenia Seminary in 1849; was president of the Masonic University at Selma, Ala. in 1853; chairman of the physics and civil engineering department at the University of Michigan in 1853; and chairman of the geology, zoology, and botany department of the same institution, 1855-73. He became the chancellor of SYRACUSE UNIVERSITY from 1872 to 1874, resigning to teach in the University's department of geology. He then went as professor of geology and zoology to the newly founded VANDERBILT UNIVERSITY, Nashville, Tenn., where he was from 1875 to 1878.

Winchell wrote nearly 250 articles and books, attempting to reconcile the supposed conflict between science and religion. Many critics had objected to evolution because it seemed to be inconsistent with theism. Winchell argued that evolution was rather the best proof of theism; that studies of environment and natural selection were simply attempts to describe God's "instrumental means of accomplishing a certain premeditated result."

Winchell held that matters of science pertained to the intellect, and matters of religion to faith. Faith and intellect were seen as two diverse aspects of man's nature. He believed that the veracity of Scripture was being confirmed by science, archeology, history and ethnology; but he also believed that if Scripture were "utterances of God's truth" they must harmonize with truth in other dimensions.

Many Methodists along with other critics felt such thought might rule out supernatural intervention by relying on a mechanistic interpretation of scientific facts.

Controversy centered upon Winchell's ambiguity in his commitment to natural selection and the genetic descent of man from the anthropoids.

The climax to the problem came in 1878 when the *Northern Christian Advocate* (Syracuse) carried a series of articles on a study by Winchell, "Adamites and Pre-Adamites or a Popular Discussion Concerning the Remote Representatives of the Human Species and their Relations to the Biblical Adam." In this study, Winchell stressed his belief that there was Biblical evidence of pre-Adamites (Romans 5:12-14) and that the black races were pre-Adamite and inferior Adamites. Such thought combined with his belief in derivative evolution eventually effected his expulsion from Vanderbilt University.

Thomas O. Summers, editor of the *Nashville Christian Advocate*, and holder of the chair of systematic theology at Vanderbilt, attacked his fellow professor, as did many other Methodists. Fainally Bishop HOLLAND McTYEIRE, the dominant figure at Vanderbilt, yielded to demands to dismiss Winchell after first requesting Winchell to refuse reappointment, which Winchell declined to do as he claimed he had not been given a chance to defend himself against false charges. He was informed by the University that his chair was abolished for "financial reasons." Winchell was incensed, saying this was a blatant violation of academic freedom. *The Methodist* supported the action of the University with an editorial later published in the *Nashville Christian Advocate*.

Winchell returned to Ann Arbor, Mich., and in 1879 was unanimously recalled to the chair of geology and paleontology at the University of Michigan, where he remained until his death. While at Michigan, he was the chairman of the committee to organize the Geological Society of America, and served as president in 1891. He is credited with having discovered seven new genera and over 300 new species in fossil form.

His best known books are: *Sketches of Creation* (1870), *Geological Chart* (1870), *The Doctrine of Evolution* (1874), *Science and Religion* (1877), *Preadamites* (1880), *Sparks from a Geologist's Hammer* (1881), *World Life* (1883), his textbook, *Geological Studies* (1886), and *Walks and Talks in the Geological Field* (1886).

Robert E. Bystrom, "The Earliest Methodist Response to Evolution, 1870-1880." Northwestern University, 1966.
Dictionary of American Biography.
M. Simpson, *Cyclopaedia.* 1878.　STEPHEN G. COBB

WINCHESTER, VIRGINIA, U.S.A. Just when the first itinerant Methodist preacher visited Winchester is not known. Some claim that RICHARD WRIGHT and WILLIAM WATTERS preached there in the summer of 1772. Wright came to America with FRANCIS ASBURY in September 1771 and returned to England in 1774. It is known that he did preach in PENNSYLVANIA, DELAWARE, and MARYLAND, but there is no record of his work in Virginia. William Watters was the first native American to become a regular itinerant. In 1783 he purchased a farm near McLean, Va., where he lived until his death in 1827. There is good reason to believe that he preached in Winchester as early as 1772. The journal of FREEBORN GARRETTSON clearly states that he preached in Winchester in February 1777.

The leadership and enthusiasm of Francis Asbury played a major part in the establishment and growth of Methodism in Winchester. His first visit to Winchester occurred on June 21, 1783. He was not impressed by the religious climate he found, asserting in his *Journal* of that date that "religion is greatly wanting in these parts. The inhabitants are much divided. . . . They agree in scarcely anything, except it be to sin against God." In all Asbury made twelve visits to Winchester, extending from 1783 to 1809.

On April 6, 1791, John Steed, Samuel Calvert, and Richard Holliday, trustees of the Methodist Church in Winchester, purchased for the congregation a lot on the east side of Cameron Street just south of the Town Run, and by 1793 the first Methodist church in town had been built on that lot. W. G. Russell describes this structure as a large, frame building which stood high and close to the street pavement. He added, "The whole house presents a rude and unsightly appearance, but many a good lesson was taught from the rickety old desk and the rude 'kirk,' and many a one has learned precepts there which have served as stepping stones to a home in heaven."

This first church served the local congregation until 1818, when a new brick church was built at what is now 112 South Cameron Street, a structure which, with many alterations and additions since that date, is known today as the Fairfax Hotel. For thirty-seven years this was to be the sanctuary of Winchester Methodists. Among early Methodist leaders were the brothers Christopher and George Michael Frye, both of whom were lay preachers; and at their home on the northeast corner of Cork and Cameron Streets frequent meetings of the Methodist congregation were held. Another vigorous leader was George Reed (1766-1849), a coppersmith by trade and at one time mayor of the town. Records indicate that the business meetings of the BALTIMORE CONFERENCE for the year 1805 were held in an upper room in his home at the southeast corner of Braddock and Piccadilly Streets. Another of the fathers of Winchester Methodism was James Wall (1767-1852), a carpenter and a local preacher, who in the words of one who knew him, "spent his energies trying to do all the good he could . . . and labored for forty years as a minister of the gospel and was a zealous and good man."

By 1844 the Winchester Methodist Church was able to record some substantial achievements: a SUNDAY SCHOOL of forty-two teachers and 300 scholars; also "a house of worship, which is in good repair; a brick parsonage building purchased in 1840 at a cost of $1,500; a graveyard which has been enclosed with a good fence." (Quarles, p. 40.) The church records of this year also report that there was "a house of worship for our colored people, in good order and free of debt." In 1843 the pastor's salary was $249.70; in 1850 it was $400.

By 1853 a new and larger church was needed and a lot was purchased at the northwest corner of Cameron and Cork Streets. This church was completed and dedicated on May 20, 1855. It was to be called Market Street Church. The old church building was sold to become a female school, sponsored by the church and known as the Valley Female Institute. During the Civil War this building was used almost continuously as a hospital, known as the York Hospital from the name of Sidney P. York, a Methodist preacher who had been the head of the school. After the War the building was purchased by Silas Billings, a Presbyterian minister, who operated there for many years a girls' school known as Fairfax Hall.

The new church had scarcely been completed before a dispute arose among its members over the seating in the church of the young ladies attending the Valley Female Institute. This trivial disagreement caused thirty members of the congregation to withdraw and to organize a separate church. This splinter movement was led by William R. Denny, the father of Bishop COLLINS DENNY. The separatist congregation purchased a lot at the southwest corner of Braddock and Wolfe Streets in October 1855, and in July 1859 the new Braddock Street Church was dedicated.

A more serious division in Winchester came with the coming of the Civil War. The old Baltimore Conference of the M.E. Church had its boundaries cut by the battle lines of the War. The local churches south of the line formed a Conference at ALEXANDRIA, which was later to go into the VIRGINIA CONFERENCE of the M.E. Church, South. As a result of the tensions and strong feelings of the time, many additional members of the Market Street Church moved to the Braddock Street Church, so that by 1865 the membership of the former church had been reduced by two thirds.

Both churches, but especially the Braddock Street Church, suffered severe damages during the War. The Braddock Street Church was used by Union forces as a hospital and for other purposes whenever the Union Army was in possession of the town. As a result, the church had practically to be rebuilt after the War. In 1904 the Federal Government acknowledged a claim for damages done to this church by Union troops, amounting to $2,650. The Market Street Church was also paid the sum of $1,750 by the Federal Government for similar damages.

The two Winchester churches mentioned above have been served by many distinguished ministers. Winchester, sometimes called the "Capital of the Valley" (Shenandoah), has always been a strong preaching point. Among those serving Winchester Circuit as it first was, were JACOB GRUBER (1805); Seely Bunn (1811-12); James Reed (1823-24); and after it became a station, NORVAL WILSON, the father of Bishop A. W. WILSON, served it from 1838-39; JOHN S. MARTIN, 1852-53; and in later years many prominent ministers of the Old Baltimore Conference of the M.E. Church, South.

In 1970 the membership of Braddock Street was 1,808, and that of Market Street was 733, Montague Avenue, 661, and Wesley, 201. These last two churches are comparatively new as compared with older churches.

Winchester has long been the seat of a presiding elder's district. The SHENANDOAH COLLEGE and Shenandoah Conservatory of Music which had been brought to Winchester from Dayton, Va., in 1960, and which had been related to the E.U.B. CHURCH up to that time, became related to The United Methodist Church after the E.U.B.-Methodist Union in 1968.

F. Asbury, *Journal and Letters*. 1958.
Frederick County Deed Books 22, 80.
Garland R. Quarles, *The Churches of Winchester, Virginia*. N.p., n.d.
W. G. Russell, *What I Know About Winchester*. N.p., n.d.
John I. Sloat, *Methodism in Winchester*. N.p., n.d.
General Minutes, UMC, 1970.
H. Smith, *Recollections*. 1848.   GARLAND R. QUARLES

WINDSOR, New South Wales, Australia. In 1815 this was a growing settlement where the Governor had a residence. A class formed by Edward Eagar had been meeting before SAMUEL LEIGH paid his first visit to the township. In 1820 it was divided from Sydney with BENJAMIN CARVOSSO as resident minister. A chapel had been built in 1818 to be replaced by a new church in 1838. The circuit included Castlereagh, Penrith and the Lower Hawkesbury until the Penrith Circuit was formed in 1860, and the Lower Hawkesbury Circuit in 1866. (The latter had been independent of Windsor previously for a short period, 1838-42.) The town of Richmond has always been part of the Windsor Circuit. From descendants of Methodist pioneers in the Hawkesbury River Circuit have come a number of noted ministers of the Australasian Church.

J. Colwell, *Illustrated History*. 1904.
AUSTRALIAN EDITORIAL COMMITTEE

WINFIELD, AUGUSTUS R. (1822-1887), American minister and a leader in ARKANSAS Methodism, was born in Sussex County, Va., Oct. 27, 1822. He studied and practiced law before entering the ministry. He joined the MEMPHIS CONFERENCE (MES), in 1846, but transferred to Arkansas in 1849. His first appointment in Arkansas was Batesville, and his last appointment, except for the editorship of the *Arkansas Methodist*, was the church in LITTLE ROCK which now bears his name. The church was named Winfield Memorial Church in 1888, but since 1946 it has been known simply as the Winfield Methodist Church. It has been for many years one of the great churches of Arkansas Methodism.

Winfield was also pastor of what is now First Church, Little Rock; First Church, Fort Smith, and First Church, Hot Springs and Camden; he was twice PRESIDING ELDER of the Little Rock District, and of the Camden District, and once of the Arkadelphia District. During the War between the States he was CHAPLAIN in the Confederate States Army, and was active in some of Arkansas Methodism's early efforts in the field of education.

He was six times a delegate to the GENERAL CONFERENCE of the M.E. Church, South—1858, 1866, 1870, 1874, 1878, and 1886; in 1858 he was one of the youngest men ever to represent Arkansas Methodism in the General Conference.

He died Dec. 26, 1887, after forty-one years of service in the Methodist ministry. He is buried in Little Rock.

J. A. Anderson, *Arkansas Methodism*. 1935.
H. Jewell, *Arkansas*. 1892.
Kenneth L. Spore, "A History of the First Methodist Church of Camden, Arkansas." Ms.   KENNETH L. SPORE

WINIATA, MAHARAIA (1912-1960), New Zealand Methodist and prominent Maori leader from Tauranga, was trained for the ministry at Trinity College (1937-39), but withdrew before ordination to enter the teaching profession. However, his interest in the Methodist Church did not slacken, and for the rest of his life he held the status of "honorary home missionary." While on the staff of Wesley College, Paerata, he influenced three young Maoris to enter the ministry. Later he became a Maori tutor with the Adult Education Service of the University of AUCKLAND.

In 1952, he was granted a Nuffield Fellowship, which enabled him to visit Great Britain. He gained a Ph.D. of Edinburgh University—the first Maori ever to gain this degree from a British university. His thesis, *The Role of*

the Leader in Maori Society, was published by the University of Edinburgh in 1966. His wide interests led him to visit both the world headquarters of Moral Rearmament at Mackinac Island in the United States, and the People's Republic of CHINA. His death at the early age of forty-eight years robbed the Maoris of a vital and trusted leader.

New Zealand Methodist Conference Minutes, 1960.
L. R. M. GILMORE

WINNIPEG, Manitoba, Canada. **Grace Church.** Methodism reached the Canadian Northwest as early as 1840, but it was not until 1868 that GEORGE YOUNG began Methodist services in a log building in Fort Garry. This settlement, soon to merge with Winnipeg, the capital of the province of Manitoba created in 1870, was at that time a collection of about fifty houses and a few hundred citizens. As a result of Young's vigorous efforts, Wesley Hall was opened in December 1868, and in September 1871, the first Grace Church was put in use. Five years later it was enlarged; and was reopened in 1877.

In 1883, as the city grew in size, a new Grace Church was built, and was dedicated by Young on September 30. By this date, the Grace Church congregation had become the center of Methodism in Winnipeg, in Manitoba, and in the Northwest generally. Through its efforts, Zion, Wesley, McDougall Memorial, Young and Broadway churches were established between 1874 and 1906. Under its auspices, the first regular Methodist conference in the West was held, and from it would come much of the inspiration for the development of Methodism in the western provinces. From its membership, too, would come

WESLEY COLLEGE, WINNIPEG, MANITOBA

the founders of Wesley (UNITED) COLLEGE. In the Church the first significant move towards church union in the west was made. Grace and the other Winnipeg churches learned to deal effectively, too, with the complex challenges presented by the multi-racial society of twentieth-century Winnipeg.

Since 1925, Grace Church has continued as Grace United Church, embodying in its life and tradition the historic strands of Methodism and Presbyterianism in Manitoba.

Grace United Church, Winnipeg, *Seventy-Fifth Anniversary*. Winnipeg, 1943.
Manitoba Free Press, Oct. 15, 1921.   G. S. FRENCH

WINSTON, W. RIPLEY (1847-1918), British Methodist missionary pioneer in BURMA, was born at Preston, England, June 18, 1847, and entered the Wesleyan ministry in 1872. He went to CEYLON in 1876 and began a girls' high school at Point Pedro in 1878, an experience which confirmed his belief in the value of education as a missionary agency. In 1886 Burma was annexed by Britain, and in 1887 he went with J. M. Brown of CALCUTTA to report on missionary possibilities. He remained in Burma, 1887-1904, beginning work first at Mandalay, 1887. Evangelists from Ceylon, trained to work among Buddhists, were introduced as agents, and almost immediately at Mandalay and Pokokku Winston opened girls' boarding schools with effective results. Work has always been slow in Burma, but Winston is noteworthy as beginning work among lepers. Believing that people must be treated as if they had bodies as well as souls, he opened, with sharp criticism from the missionary secretaries, the first ward of the Leper Asylum at Mandalay, 1890. He returned to work in England in 1904 and died Nov. 26, 1918.

W. D. Walker, *Land of the Gold Pagoda*. London, 1940.
W. R. Winston, *Four Years in Burma*. London, 1904.

C. J. DAVEY

WINSTON-SALEM, NORTH CAROLINA, U.S.A., an industrial and manufacturing city is situated in the northwest section of the Carolina Piedmont.

Salem (the old town) was settled by the MORAVIANS from PENNSYLVANIA in 1766. Salem College for young women, established by these people, is one of the oldest institutions for girls in the United States. Old Salem, now being restored, is one of the show places in the Southeast. Following the Civil War, the town of Winston grew up just north of Salem, and in 1913 the two towns were united, thus the name Winston-Salem.

FRANCIS ASBURY came into this general area in the later years of the eighteenth century, preaching at nearby settlements and establishing missions. Love's Chapel, eight miles away at Walkertown, is a flourishing church of his labors. One of the original Methodist congregations of Forsyth County was formed at the home of John Doub a few miles west of Winston-Salem, and is still called Doub's Chapel. The first known congregation within the present limits of the city was called Old Jerusalem Church. From this group grew city-wide Methodism as we know it today. The first large society of Methodists was called Centenary, being formed 100 years after the CHRISTMAS CONFERENCE at BALTIMORE.

There are twenty-three other Methodist churches in the city. Among them are Ardmore, Burkhead, Central Terrace, Green Street, St. Paul's, Wesley Memorial, Mt. Tabor, Trinity, Ogburn Memorial, and Maple Springs, at the gate of Wake Forest College (a Baptist institution). Many Methodist Conferences have been held in the various churches in Winston-Salem, and various bishops and church leaders have spoken from these pulpits, both white and colored. LEE F. TUTTLE, now executive secretary of World Methodism, was formerly superintendent of the Winston-Salem District.

Winston-Salem is the location of the Children's Home, a flourishing Methodist orphanage caring for 400 children. Wake Forest University, a Baptist institution of higher education, is also an important part of Winston-Salem. Winston-Salem College, operated by the state of North Carolina for Negroes, is also located there, to say nothing of a number of other schools of arts and sciences.

Centenary Methodist Church had its beginning in the year 1834 under a mulberry tree where a few people met for worship until they erected the first frame building and called it "Old Jerusalem Church." The little society grew until in the year 1886 a large brick church was erected on Liberty Street near the heart of the growing town. This was named Centenary after the first 100 years of Methodism dating from the Christmas Conference at Baltimore. In 1930 the cornerstone for the present building was laid on West Fifth Street, uniting old Centenary and a younger church called West End. The new structure, cathedral-like in appointments and costing in the range of $2,500,000, is now one of the noteworthy churches in American Methodism. The membership has grown through the years into a congregation of 3,272 in 1970, among whom are some of the leading business and professional men of the growing city.

Centenary Church has given of its resources to every religious, charitable, and humanitarian cause, its annual budget at this writing exceeds $400,000. It was instrumental in establishing Ardmore Church, next in size, as well as a dozen other congregations in and around Winston-Salem. The Children's Home with its 400 orphans in the city is a direct benefaction of Centenary. The Goodwill Industry was brought to the city by the support of this church, now one of the finest in the South. Wake Forest University, a Baptist institution, was relocated in the city by the strong support of Centenary men and women. Salem College, a Moravian institution for young women, has greatly benefitted by Centenary people.

James A. Gray, leading industrialist and official of Centenary Church, donated $2,000,000 to various Methodist colleges in North Carolina, as well as to the state university. ALASKA METHODIST COLLEGE and the International Christian University of JAPAN have received generous gifts from members of this congregation. Centenary's support of missions would make a story in itself, and today the church is represented in various parts of the world by its own missionaries.

A staff of twenty-eight paid workers carries on the services of this congregation. Among the pastors who have served modern Centenary have been GILBERT T. ROWE, CHARLES CLINTON WEAVER (who led in the building of the present gothic structure), G. Ray Jordan, Walter A. Stansbury, Mark Depp, who served sixteen years as pastor, W. KENNETH GOODSON, elected a bishop in 1964 when pastor of Centenary, Charles P. Bowles, and Ernest A. Fitzgerald.

Children's Home, Inc., is an institution founded and operated by the Western North Carolina Conference of The United Methodist Church. At its annual session held in Salisbury, N. C., in 1907, the Conference decided to build such an institution—a Children's Home—and elected a board of trustees. The certificate of corporation was filed in Raleigh, N. C., on June 12, 1908. On Sept. 1, 1909, the Children's Home was formally opened, admitting as the first child an eleven-year-old girl.

According to its charter the Home "shall have for its object the support, care, and training of indigent and orphan children of the white race." In a meeting in Winston-Salem on Oct. 7, 1913, the Board of Trustees amended the by-laws, and the following statement was included: "Destitute children who are deprived of support and protection by death of their parents, or otherwise, not above the age of fourteen years, and who are sound in mind and body may be admitted into the Home by the superintendent with the approval of the committee on admissions." In 1958 the age limitation was removed and any child who has not reached high school graduation may be admitted; and in 1964 the constitution and by-laws were amended by eliminating any reference to race.

The major phase of the work is that carried in the institutional setting. Schooling in grades one through nine is provided by a school located on the Home campus, but operated under the supervision of the Winston-Salem-Forsyth County Schools. Children's Home students in grades ten, eleven, and twelve attend the Richard J. Reynolds High School.

While it has been generally accepted that all young people leave the Home on graduation from high school, the institution feels strongly that its guidance and assistance should extend beyond that time. A growing percentage of the graduates are continuing their training beyond high school. Careful attention is given to planning for this with the young people before their separation from the Home. Persons qualified to guide them are assigned the responsibility for such planning. This applies also to those going immediately into jobs. Financial assistance is given, always with an attempt to develop on the part of the young person a feeling of responsibility and obligation.

There are presently sixteen cottages housing the children. The plant assets are listed at an evaluation of near $5,000,000 and total assets are over $8,000,000.

E. T. Clark, *Western North Carolina*. 1966.
General Minutes.
W. L. Grissom, *North Carolina*. 1905.
Journal of the Western North Carolina Conference.

C. EXCELLE ROZZELLE
M. T. LAMBETH

WISCONSIN, U.S.A, estimated 1967 population 4,188,000 is a north central state which is bounded on the north by Lake Superior and the upper peninsula of MICHIGAN, on the east by Lake Michigan, on the south by ILLINOIS, and on the west by the Mississippi River and MINNESOTA. The first European to visit the Wisconsin area was Jean Nicolet in 1634. French explorers and missionaries followed, and the land became a part of New France. France surrendered the territory to Britain in 1760, and that country ceded it to the United States in 1783, though the British were not completely dislodged until 1815. A part of the Northwest Territory, Wisconsin became a territory in 1836 and was admitted to the Union in 1848.

Known as America's Dairyland, Wisconsin leads in the production of milk and cheese; eighty per cent of its farms are dairy farms. Farm receipts exceed one billion dollars annually. However, the amount added by manufacturing is now over six billion per year. The state produces machinery, food products, transportation equipment, and, since one-half the land is in forests, much pulp and paper. There are forty institutions of higher learning in Wisconsin.

Some Methodist services were held in Wisconsin as early as 1826 by Samuel Ryan, commander at Fort Howard, Green Bay, but the M.E. Church did not officially begin work in the region until 1832. Some civilized Indians had moved from New York state and settled at Green Bay. Consequently the committee on missions in the 1832 General Conference recommended "the extension of the aboriginal missions in the Western and Northwest-

ern frontiers." JOHN CLARK, a delegate from the New York Conference, then offered himself as a missionary to Green Bay and was accepted, and the appointments of his conference for that year read, "John Clark, appointed missionary to Green Bay." Clark arrived at Green Bay on July 21, 1832, soon organized the first Methodist class in Wisconsin, and proceeded to establish missions among the Indians. Within two months he had erected a log building 30 by 24 feet which served as both a church and a school.

Three months after Clark's arrival in Wisconsin, the ILLINOIS CONFERENCE appointed John T. Mitchell to the Galena Mission. From Galena Mitchell extended his work into Platteville and several other points in Wisconsin. In December 1833, Mitchell organized a Methodist society with six members at Platteville and dedicated a meeting-house there.

Immigration in the vicinity of what is now Milwaukee began in the spring of 1835. That fall the Milwaukee and Fox River Missions appeared in the appointments of the Chicago District of the Illinois Conference. In 1836 there were three Wisconsin appointments in the Galena District—Mineral Point, Platteville, and Prairie du Chien Mission—and two in the Chicago District—Milwaukee Station and Green Bay Mission. In 1837 the Milwaukee District was created with seven appointments, while the work in west Wisconsin continued in the Galena District.

In 1840 the ROCK RIVER CONFERENCE was organized to include northern Illinois, Wisconsin and Iowa. The conference met in August, continued the Milwaukee District, and organized a Platteville District with nine charges. The next year the two districts reported 1,491 members.

The 1848 GENERAL CONFERENCE created the WISCONSIN CONFERENCE to include Wisconsin and most of Minnesota. The conference met at Kenosha, Wis., in July, organized four districts, and made appointments to fifty-seven charges with 6,943 members. Also, the conference appointed William H. Sampson as principal of the preparatory department of Lawrence Institute. The school, started in 1847, proved a landmark of progress for Wisconsin Methodism. In 1849 the conference formed a Minnesota Mission District with four charges.

In 1856 both the Minnesota and WEST WISCONSIN CONFERENCES were carved out of the Wisconsin Conference. The MINNESOTA CONFERENCE included the state of Minnesota and northwest Wisconsin, while the southwest part of Wisconsin became the West Wisconsin Conference. In 1855 the Wisconsin Conference had eight districts, 133 charges, and 14,482 white and 185 Indian members. The division of the territory into three conferences in 1856 placed about 1,800 members in the Minnesota Conference, 6,000 in the West Wisconsin Conference, and 8,000 in the Wisconsin Conference.

In 1860 the Northwest Wisconsin Conference was formed by merging part of the West Wisconsin Conference with most of that part of the Minnesota Conference which was in the state of Wisconsin. The part of Wisconsin along Lake Superior was placed in the Detroit Conference for the next eight years. Never large, the Northwest Wisconsin Conference continued for only eight years. It began with two districts, twenty-seven charges, 1,771 members. At its last session in 1867 it reported three districts, thirty-nine charges, and 2,796 members. In 1868 it was absorbed by the West Wisconsin Conference.

There was some foreign language work in Wisconsin

Methodism. At different times both the Wisconsin and West Wisconsin Conferences had a Norwegian District. In 1880 the Norwegian churches became a part of the Northwest Norwegian (later Norwegian-Danish) Conference. The first German churches in Wisconsin were attached to the Chicago German District of the ROCK RIVER CONFERENCE. Later they were in the Northern German Conference. Swedish churches in Wisconsin became a part of the Northwest Swedish Conference.

After the absorption of the Northwest-Wisconsin Conference, the Wisconsin and West Wisconsin Conferences continued intact. In 1961 the name of the Wisconsin Conference was changed to the EAST WISCONSIN CONFERENCE.

From the beginning Methodism grew steadily in Wisconsin. The two conferences reported 23,655 members in 1870, some 41,467 in 1900, and 83,268 in 1939. Other marks of growth were the continued progress of LAWRENCE UNIVERSITY and the establishment of a number of service institutions in the state, such as: the MILWAUKEE Deaconess Home in 1893, the Bellin Memorial Hospital at Green Bay in 1908, Methodist Hospital at Madison, Lakeside Methodist Hospital at Sparta, Morrow Memorial Home for the Aged at Sparta, Schmitt Methodist Home at Richland Center, the Elmore Home for the Aged at Milwaukee which in 1956 was succeeded by Methodist Manor, Incorporated, GOODWILL INDUSTRIES and Northcott Neighborhood House in Milwaukee, four camps for youth, and WESLEY FOUNDATIONS at the state institutions of higher learning.

Since 1944 Wisconsin Methodism has constituted an episcopal area with the bishop's residence in Madison. In 1968 the two Wisconsin Conferences reported six districts, 292 charges, 387 ministers, 134,650 members, property valued at $71,417,136, and some $10,255,136 raised for all purposes during the year.

General Minutes, ME and MC.
Minutes of the Wisconsin Conferences.
P. S. Bennett, *History of Methodism in Wisconsin*. Cincinnati: Cranston & Stowe, 1890.
Elizabeth Wilson, *Methodism in Eastern Wisconsin*. Wisconsin Conference Historical Society, 1938.   ALBEA GODBOLD

WISCONSIN CONFERENCE (ME), was organized at Kenosha, Wis., July 12, 1848 with Bishop THOMAS A. MORRIS presiding. The conference was formed by dividing the ROCK RIVER Conference. At the outset its territory included Wisconsin and most of Minnesota. The conference began with four districts, fifty-seven charges, and 6,943 members. (See WISCONSIN for beginnings of Methodism in the state.)

In 1856 the territory of the Wisconsin Conference was limited to about the eastern half of the state by the formation of both the MINNESOTA and WEST WISCONSIN CONFERENCES and there was little if any change in its boundaries thereafter. The name was changed to the EAST WISCONSIN CONFERENCE at the session held in West Allis, May 25-28, 1961, Bishop RALPH T. ALTON presiding.

From the beginning the Wisconsin Conference was interested in reform. In 1850 it heartily approved a stringent liquor law, and the members pledged themselves against the use of tobacco by precept and example. In 1851 a committee report which mildly condemned SLAVERY did not reach the floor because some opposed conference discussion of the subject. The next year, however, the conference adopted a resolution condemning slavery, protesting the fugitive slave law, and calling for alteration of the *Discipline* so as to prevent slaveholders from becoming members of the church, and also to require those holding slaves to free them if the law allowed. The resolutions against slavery became stronger each year. The conference favored the so-called "new chapter" on slavery which was adopted by the 1860 M.E. GENERAL CONFERENCE. Long afterward the conference journal for 1968 included a long report from its boards of Christian social concerns and social action making strong pronouncements on the subjects of peace and world order, alcohol and the general welfare, and human relations and economic affairs.

The Wisconsin Conference stood for education. Lawrence Institute was established at Appleton in 1847, one year before the conference was organized. At its first session the conference appointed William H. Sampson as principal of the preparatory department at Lawrence. In its 1853 session the conference, after a progress report on Lawrence College, adopted a resolution pledging each minister in charge of a circuit or station to preach or cause to be preached a sermon on education at each principal appointment at least once a year. In 1860 the conference promised to raise money for GARRETT BIBLICAL INSTITUTE. In 1910 Lawrence College was commended, and it was noted that thirty of its 700 students were preparing for the ministry. Garrett, BOSTON, and DREW seminaries were praised, and the report of the conference board of education insisted that more must be done for the denomination's schools for white youths in the mountains and other parts of the South. Also, in 1910 the board asked that an apportionment of $800 be laid on the churches to assist the Methodist pastor at the state university in Madison. Today LAWRENCE UNIVERSITY has an endowment of $21,000,000, a plant valued at $17,000,000, and a student body of 1,300. While no longer the sole property of the conference, the institution is closely related to the church.

Through the years other institutions related to the Wisconsin Conference were developed. In 1893 the Milwaukee Deaconess Home was established in Milwaukee by Methodist women, aided by generous gifts from Mrs. R. P. Elmore. Some 135 deaconesses trained in the home have served as parish workers, visiting nurses, evangelists, and matrons in homes for young and elderly women. The Deaconess Home sponsored the development of the Asbury Girls' Club, the Traveler's Aid of Milwaukee, the Elmore Home for the Aged, Grant Hall for young business women, and Methodist Manor (incorporated in 1956). Some activities of the Deaconess Home have been discontinued as time has passed, but the corporation itself is still intact.

Bellin Memorial Hospital was established at Green Bay in 1908 through the work of two Methodist deaconess nurses who came from CINCINNATI. Title to the hospital was transferred to the conference in 1929, since which time important additions to the institution have been made. In 1919 the Summerfield Church, Milwaukee, helped to establish Goodwill Industries in the state.

In 1968 the East Wisconsin Conference had two additional homes for the aged: Cedar Rest at Janesville, and Evergreen Manor at West Allis. There were two camps: Asbury Acres at Almond, and Camp Byron at Brownsville.

The conference gave almost $140,000 for higher education in 1968, some $20,000 of it going to Garrett Theological Seminary. Also, contributions were made to KENDALL COLLEGE in Chicago and to WILEY COLLEGE, Marshall, Texas. The conference maintains five Wesley Foundations in Wisconsin.

In 1968 the East Wisconsin Conference reported four districts—Fond Du Lac, Green Bay, Janesville, and Milwaukee—164 charges, 244 ministers, 81,478 members, property valued at $50,550,561, and a total raised for all purposes during the year of $7,246,714.

General Minutes, ME and MC.
Minutes of the Wisconsin and East Wisconsin Conferences.
P. S. Bennett, *History of Methodism in Wisconsin.* Cincinnati: Cranston & Stowe, 1890.
Elizabeth Wilson, *Methodism in Eastern Wisconsin.* Wisconsin Conference Historical Society, 1938.   ALBEA GODBOLD

WISCONSIN CONFERENCE (EUB) traced its origin to the time when UNITED BRETHREN missionaries, representing the Wabash Conference, came from ILLINOIS to WISCONSIN as early as 1842. Work progressed so that on May 12, 1857, the GENERAL CONFERENCE of the Church of the United Brethren in Christ, in session at CINCINNATI, Ohio, authorized the formation of the Wisconsin Conference. This organization was effected Sept. 16, 1858, in the Rutland Church in Dane County. Bishop LEWIS DAVIS was the chairman. Thirteen of the fifteen ministers were present. Conference membership was 609. After the first year the membership had increased to 1,447. From 1861 to 1885, the state was divided into two conferences. One part, called the Fox River Mission Conference, was north of a line running from Sheboygan west to the Mississippi River. The territory south of this line was called the Wisconsin Conference. At its highest church membership, the Fox River Conference numbered 639 persons in 1877. In 1885 the two conferences were reunited and the Wisconsin Conference again covered the entire state.

John Lutz, a missionary of the EVANGELICAL ASSOCIATION from the Ohio Conference, came to Wisconsin in 1840. Others followed him. It was not, however, until the General Conference of 1855 that authorization was given for the formation of the Wisconsin Conference. Acting on this decision, the Illinois Conference in session at Freeport, Ill., April 19, 1856, under the chairmanship of Bishop JOHN SEYBERT created the Wisconsin Conference. Twenty-one ministers were assigned to eight missions, seven circuits, and one station with a combined membership of 1,490. The Conference was divided into two districts with two presiding elders. The first regular session of the Wisconsin Conference was held in Zion Church, Helenville, May 6-11, 1857 with Bishop John Seybert presiding. C. A. Schnacke was Secretary. By this time there were twenty-nine ministers with a membership of 2,004. The entire state of Wisconsin has been the geographical boundary of the conference through the years.

Following the union of The EVANGELICAL CHURCH and the Church of the United Brethren in Christ in 1946, the Wisconsin Conference, (EV) and Wisconsin Conference, (UB) united to form the Wisconsin Conference of The E.U.B. Church at Monroe, Wis., May 17, 1951. The German language was used in some churches until 1947, when English became universal. In 1967 there were three districts and three conference superintendents with a membership of 25,951 and a Sunday school enrollment of 17,404.

At the Dallas Uniting Conference, April 1968, the conference became a part of The United Methodist Church. The three Wisconsin Conferences (East Wisconsin and West Wisconsin of the former Methodist Church, and the Wisconsin Conference of The E.U.B. Church) were united Jan. 1, 1970, to form the Wisconsin Conference of The United Methodist Church.

EARL W. REICHERT

WISEMAN, FREDERICK LUKE (1858-1944), son of LUKE H. WISEMAN, was born at York in 1858, and entered the Wesleyan Methodist ministry in 1881, training at DIDSBURY COLLEGE, Manchester. He was best remembered as a robust evangelistic preacher. Most of his lengthy ministry was spent in the service of the HOME MISSIONS DEPARTMENT, of which he was secretary 1913-39, after over twenty years in the BIRMINGHAM Mission. He was elected president of the Wesleyan conference in 1912, of the National Free Church Council in 1914, and of the newly united Methodist Church in 1933. Wiseman was a keen musician, and was chairman of the committee which prepared the Methodist Hymn Book of 1933, in which eleven of his tunes appear. He died Feb. 12, 1944.

FRANK BAKER

LUKE H. WISEMAN

WISEMAN, LUKE HORT (1822-1875), British Methodist, was born at Norwich on Jan. 19, 1822, the son of Samuel Wiseman, an agent of the BRITISH AND FOREIGN BIBLE SOCIETY. He entered the Wesleyan Methodist ministry in 1840 and was trained at RICHMOND Theological COLLEGE, London. He served in many circuits, and in 1868 he was appointed to the Wesleyan Mission House as one of the secretaries of the society. He brought with him a passionate love of the missionary cause which had been fostered by early connection with the Bible Society and the Anti-Slavery Association. He served at the Mission House until 1874; in 1872 he was elected as president of the Wesleyan Methodist Conference. His writings included *Thoughts on Class Meetings and their Improve-*

ment (1854); *Christ in the Wilderness* (1857); *Men of Faith* (1870). He died in London on Feb. 3, 1875.

JOHN KENT

WITHROW, WILLIAM HENRY (1839-1908), Canadian Methodist minister and writer, was born in TORONTO, Aug. 6, 1839. He was educated in Toronto schools and took his undergraduate training at VICTORIA COLLEGE and the University of Toronto. He was ordained by the New Connexion Conference in 1865 and spent five years in its ministry before transferring in 1866 to the Wesleyan Methodist Church.

When the Methodist Church was formed in 1874, he became editor of the *Canadian Methodist Magazine* and of the Sunday school periodicals, a post which he held for thirty-four years. The *Magazine* appeared as a monthly from 1875 to 1906. In its time it was one of Canada's most noteworthy periodicals. In its pages one could always find a balanced mixture of religious information, general comment on events, pen portraits of prominent Methodists, essays, and tolerant reviews. Withrow had a keen interest in literature and archaeology, both of which were well illustrated in the *Magazine*.

As religious editor for the church, Withrow prepared twenty-seven periodicals on a quarterly basis. During his years in office, the circulation rose from 46,000 to 400,000. These publications were characterized by a strong interest in temperance, social reform, and missions, and by the same concern for literary standards as in the *Methodist Magazine*.

Apart from his regular periodical contributions, Withrow published *The Catacombs of Rome* (1874), an important study of the early church; *A Popular History of the Dominion of Canada* (1877), marked by "high patriotism and intelligent piety"; a novel entitled *The King's Messenger* (1879); and *Barbara Heck: A Tale of Early Methodism* (1895).

Despite his heavy editorial responsibilities, Withrow was for many years a CLASS LEADER. In this, as in other activities, he gained the enduring respect and affection of his associates for his kindliness, generosity, and deep interest in others. He was honored in many ways, including the award of a D.D. by Victoria (1882), and a fellowship in the Royal Society of Canada, but undoubtedly he was most delighted with the joys of his work, and his friendships. Withrow died in Toronto, Nov. 12, 1908.

G. H. Cornish, *Cyclopaedia of Methodism in Canada.* 1881, 1903.
C. F. Klinck, ed., *Literary History of Canada.* Toronto: University of Toronto Press, 1965.
Minutes of the Toronto Methodist Conference, 1909.

G. S. FRENCH

WITNESS OF THE SPIRIT is a Christian doctrine traditionally emphasized by Methodist teaching that, by direct experience and practical evidence, God the Holy Spirit enables the Christian to know that he is rightly related to God in Christ. He is assured of his forgiveness and acceptance with God, and consciously enjoys a sense of divine fellowship. His present experience is a foretaste and guarantee of his ultimate destiny.

Natural Bases for Assurance. A sense of assurance and security seem to be essential for wholesome human life. Education and experience develop the natural abilities of man to cope with his environment and thus support his feeling of self-reliance. Various forms of social acceptance and approval give a sense of the meaning and worth of life. But when these or other witnesses to our worth are lacking, life can become intolerable.

Above all, man must have assurance in the ultimate dimension of life, his relationship to God. The happy pagan may accept the natural witnesses noted above as adequate evidence of his acceptance with whatever gods may be. He may give a token of his good will toward God through observing some form of religion. Thus for a time he may have few fears, for he lives in a fool's paradise of ignorance of God and thus of his own true situation.

The Witness of Conscience and the Law. Probably no one can long remain in such a state of pseudosecurity. The inescapable testimony of conscience points to a moral obligation beyond us. Failure to avoid a sense of disapproval from within, especially when reinforced by sanctions of law, inevitably leads to a sense of guilt and fear, i.e., the loss of assurance. The natural witnesses to well-being are inadequate to support a feeling of security. The more clearly man's obligation is seen to be toward his Creator, and the more seriously he undertakes to achieve right relationship to him through obedience to the moral law, the more do guilty fear and remorse destroy his false peace. Strong determination, noble devotion to high ideals and heroic efforts to do the right simply enhance the infinite obligation. Thus man's struggle to secure himself before God issues in defeat, bondage, and despair. Legalism, the attempt to gain assurance through the witness of the law, is probably the greatest single source of insecurity in religion.

The classic account of the struggle of a sincere man to achieve the consciousness of right standing before God through obedience to law is vividly portrayed by Paul in Romans 7. Knowledge of moral responsibility revealed by God's law destroyed his dreaming innocence, convicted him as a sinner, and imposed upon him a holy, but infinite demand which he found impossible to fulfill. Peace was turned into inner conflict, frustration, and defeat. In despair he cried, "Wretched man that I am! Who will deliver me from this body of death?" (vs. 24).

Wesley's Experience. John Wesley, the father of Methodism, tried to follow this path of legalism in the footsteps of men like Paul, Augustine, and Luther. His early life may be described as an intensive search for assurance before God. He was morally upright, at least "not being so bad as other people." He was favorable toward religion and observed its forms, e.g., reading the Bible, attending church and saying his prayers. He became a clergyman, and devoted himself intensively to inward and outward holiness, including sacrificial service to others. Yet all this gave him no "comfort or any assurance of acceptance with God." (*Journal,* May 24, 1738.)

Finally Wesley undertook an arduous mission to America in the hope of "saving his soul" and finding peace with God. This effort also failed. However, on the voyage, he came into contact with some Moravian Christians who manifested the very assurance he lacked. Back in England he was amazed at the "new gospel" of the Moravian, Peter Böhler, that the fruits of faith are "dominion over sin, and constant peace from a sense of forgiveness." (*Ibid.*) He concluded that he had no faith, yet he continued seeking, although "with strange indifference, dulness, and coldness, and unusually frequent lapses into sin." (*Ibid.*)

2583

In the light of this account, the focus of Wesley's famous Aldersgate experience is clearly on the crucial change from the bondage and fear of legalism to the peace and assurance of faith. He wrote,

In the evening I went very unwillingly to a society in Aldersgate street, where one was reading Luther's preface to the Epistle to the Romans. About a quarter before nine, while he was describing the change which God works in the heart through faith in Christ, I felt my heart strangely warmed. I felt I did trust in Christ, Christ alone for my salvation: and *an assurance was given me,* (italics added) that he had taken away *my* sins, even *mine,* and saved *me* from the law of sin and death. (*Ibid.*)

Methodist Emphasis. It is not strange then that Wesley made central in his preaching the assurance of salvation through faith, and held the witness of the Spirit to be a distinguishing doctrine of his movement. Probably no single aspect of the Christian faith has been more distinctively the genius of Methodism. The emphasis in early Methodist preaching on present experience and personal knowledge of God's grace doubtless goes far to explain the enormous popularity of this revival movement. In contrast to the vague, formal worship of the absentee God of Deism, the common people heard gladly the proclamation of the privilege of every believer to realize a personal, vital fellowship with the living God, immanent in the Holy Spirit. Even the doctrine of predestination, which provides some comfort and hope of future salvation through the divine decrees, falls short of the Methodist emphasis on the assurance of forgiveness *now.* (See: PERSEVERANCE, FINAL.)

We turn now to an exposition of the doctrine of the witness of the Spirit. The scriptural statement of it is found in Romans 8:14-16, which is set in significant contrast to the despair of chapter seven. "For all who are led by the Spirit of God are sons of God. For you did not receive the spirit of slavery to fall back into fear, but you have received the spirit of sonship. When we cry, 'Abba! Father!' it is the Spirit himself bearing witness with our spirit that we are the children of God."

Spirit and Holy Spirit. The term "spirit" requires some careful definition. In his sermon on "The Witness of our Own Spirit" (XI), Wesley seems to identify the human spirit with conscience. This he defines broadly as man's consciousness of himself in his present experience and reflection on the past, with the special faculty of evaluating and judging his behavior, motives, and all things as they relate to him. While Wesley's analysis is not complete, his suggestion is important. The dimension of purpose, volition and destiny is surely characteristic of man as a spiritual being. Thus the spirit of man is not some *part* of man, even the highest part, in contrast to some supposed "lower nature," but rather the *total* man in his ultimate and noblest aspects of meaning and relationship.

From this definition it follows that any true witness of the human spirit must be more than an emotional reaction or rational conclusion, for these are partial. Also the human spirit is not an independent faculty. Since man as spirit is concerned with the total meaning of life, especially in regard to his relationship to God, his knowledge is necessarily evoked by that relationship. As the sundial indicates the hour only when it is properly oriented and when the sun shines upon it, so the spirit of man bears witness to his true status only when rightly

related to God, and when the Spirit of God enlightens him (Sermon X, ii, 3-9). Man is the creature of God, and his knowledge of his significance, relationship and destiny is possible only in the light of the revelation of the Creator.

Who or what then is the Spirit of God or the Holy Spirit who witnesses with our spirit? Any adequate answer to this question would require a detailed study of Biblical and other sources. However, for our present purpose, a few suggestions may suffice.

Perhaps the best hint is found in Paul's letter, I Corinthians 2:9-16. Here he suggests that man's own experience as spirit points to the nature of God as Spirit. Man is spiritual because he is able to know himself and realize the divine significance of his life in his supreme relationship to God. Perhaps the term, conscious personal meaning, comes nearest to a description of spirit. Thus we may venture to suggest that God the Spirit is God acting creatively in the consciousness of his own significance. In traditional terms, the Holy Spirit is the transcendent God who is immanent and immediate to human experience. With regard to the historical Christ, the New Testament seems often to identify the Holy Spirit with the risen, living Lord, present with his people.

With these suggested definitions of divine and human spirits in mind, let us summarize by way of a paraphrase of Romans 8:14-16.

(14) All whose lives are humbly and obediently yielded to God as he manifests himself directly to their consciousness are the ones who are vitally and personally related to him, and show by their lives that they belong to him. (15) You, whose lives are so guided and related, have not been dragged back into slavery, the life-orientation of legalism with its inevitable attitude of guilty fear through the bondage of an endless obligation. Rather the total meaning and relationship of your lives is that of those who have been established as free, responsible sons of God (υἱοθεσίας). That glad, lilting cry, "Father!" which rises spontaneously in our consciousness, is the natural expression of a child of God. (16) The entire atmosphere of our lives is expressed in that joyous utterance inspired in us by God himself. God's personal presence, his meaning and purpose for us, his creatures, calls forth a personal identification with him in the total significance and relationship of our lives. Our highest consciousness seems infused with the divine consciousness, which gives us the assurance that we are accepted by God and vitally related to him as a child to his father.

How is the Witness Confirmed? While this consciousness of assurance may seem clear and self-authenticating to the one experiencing it, the question arises, How can one be certain he is not mistaken? We are notoriously inclined to deceive ourselves, accepting favorable witnesses and ignoring contrary evidence. In this regard also the *total* nature of spirit is important. The largest possible perspective provides a criterion which avoids the errors of a partial view. Thus the life of love as the fruit of faith is as surely essential for any true sense of peace with God as a feeling of security or a reasoned conclusion.

Wesley insisted that the inner experience must be corroborated by the outer life of practical ethics. The first he called the direct witness of the Holy Spirit, "an inward impression on the soul, whereby the Spirit of God directly witnesses to my spirit, that I am a child of God." The confirming, indirect witness of the spirit of man "is nearly, if not exactly, the same with the testimony of a good conscience towards God; and is the result of reason, or reflection on what we feel in our own souls. Strictly speaking it is a conclusion drawn partly from the word of God and partly from our own experience." He analyzed a good conscience, "void of offense," as necessarily including a right understanding of God's will, a true knowledge of the self, the agreement of heart and life with the rule of Scripture, and an inward perception of this agreement. We have seen that these elements are characteristics of spirit as defined above.

True, Christian confidence is always to be tested in the light of the objective revelation of the Spirit of God in the life of Christ, conveyed to us both through the record of Scripture and the immediate communication of "the mind of Christ." The believer who receives "the spirit of sonship" will manifest the ethical qualities and behavior which distinguishes a son of God under the criterion of the historical revelation of God the Son. He to whom the Spirit of God gives witness will surely bear "the fruit of the Spirit . . love, joy, peace, patience, kindness, goodness, faithfulness, gentleness, self-control" (Gal. 5:22, 23). No one can remain in the assurance of righteousness while living in knowable unrighteousness.

Is the Witness Essential for Saving Faith? Another question remains to be considered. Is the witness of the Spirit an essential element of saving faith? Is it possible to be in right relation to God in Christ without the conscious realization of our standing?

Wesley was strongly inclined in the early days of his evangelical experience to insist that there can be no true faith in Christ without the clear testimony of the Spirit. During the return voyage from Georgia to England, he analyzed his own need, "I want that faith which none can have without knowing that he hath it." (*Journal*, Feb. 29, 1738.) A faith which is unconscious of the Spirit's witness seemed to him a contradiction in terms. He wrote, ". . . Every Christian believer hath a perceptible testimony of the Spirit, that he is a child of God." Yet a sharper examination of experience led him to conclude that saving faith and the Spirit's witness are not to be so closely identified. In a later letter to his brother Charles, he wrote,

Is justifying faith a sense of pardon? *Negatur* . . . I cannot allow that justifying faith necessarily implies such an explicit assurance of pardon, then every one who has it not, and every one so long as he has it not is under the wrath and curse of God. But this is a supposition contrary to Scripture, as well as to experience . . . How can a sense of our having received pardon be the *condition* of our receiving it? (*Letters*, VI, 660.)

He concluded that the Spirit's gift of assurance is "the ordinary privilege of every Christian believer." However, some live below their privileges. "Possibly some may be in favor with God, and yet go mourning all the day long" due to ignorance or illness. Such may have some degree of peace with God, yet fall short of a "full assurance of faith," which "excludes all doubt and fear." The seasoned view of his old age, gained by long study and experience, was stated in a letter, "The Methodists . . . preach assurance as we always did, as a common privilege of the children of God; but we do not enforce it, under the pain of damnation, denounced on all who do not enjoy it." (Southey, I, 295.)

Conclusion. The doctrine of the witness of the Spirit may be considered a part of the vital heart of the Christian Gospel. Man's redemption from the guilt and power of sin is thus presented, not as some abstract, legal fiction or cosmic transaction, but rather as the personal experience of reconciliation with God and the present acceptance into the fellowship of the family of God. Man's basic need for assurance and security is met by the loving word of God himself, speaking within man's highest consciousness. The realization of God's gift of eternal life is not merely in some future, heavenly existence, but is actually begun here and now. The gracious presence of God makes real in the believer's spirit and life the witness of the Spirit, the "pledge and foretaste (arrabon) of our inheritance." (Eph. 1:14, Weymouth.) Yet the believer is not allowed to presume upon this experience with a false confidence, for he is "saved from the fear, though not from the possibility, of falling away from the grace of God." (*Sermon* I, ii, 4.) (See also ASSURANCE, CHRISTIAN.)

Ernest D. Burton, *Spirit, Soul and Flesh*. Chicago: The University of Chicago Press, 1918.
S. Pfurtner, *Luther and Aquinas on Salvation*. Heidelberg, 1961. English trans. by Quinn, New York, 1964.
W. B. Pope, *Compendium of Christian Theology*. 1880.
H. Wheeler Robinson, *The Christian Experience of the Holy Spirit*. London, 1928.
R. Watson, *Theological Institutes*. 1832.
J. Wesley, *Journal*. 1909-16.
————, *Letters*. 1931.
————, *Standard Sermons*. 1921.
A. S. Yates, *Doctrine of Assurance*. 1952.   ELLIS H. RICHARDS

WITT, WILLIAM UMSTEAD (1875-1961), American minister and worker with the Indians, was born in Medina, Tenn., on Jan. 7, 1875. His parents moved to La Cross, Ark., in 1879 and to Conway in 1893 where he attended HENDRIX COLLEGE, graduating with an A.B. degree. He joined the ARKANSAS CONFERENCE in 1904 but transferred to the OKLAHOMA CONFERENCE in 1906. He was married in 1906 to Maud Edith Southard. He became superintendent of the INDIAN MISSION CONFERENCE in 1925, a post he held until he retired in 1947. He continued to work with the Indian Mission after retirement. He died on July 21, 1961.

Memoir, *Oklahoma Conference Journal*, 1962.
                                    WALTER N. VERNON

WITTENMEYER, ANNIE TURNER (no dates), American reformer and social worker who was the first president of the Woman's Christian Temperance Union, which was organized in Cleveland, Ohio, in 1874. During her leadership the organization was extended to all the states and membership reached 600,000 in 10,000 local unions. The insignia was the wearing of the white ribbon. The reform organizaton grew out of the Women's Crusade against the liquor traffic in the Middle states. In this Mrs. Wittenmeyer had a leading role. She was president of the Woman's Christian Temperance Union from 1874 until 1883, when FRANCES E. WILLARD became president.

Mrs. Wittenmeyer was born in OHIO, grew up in KENTUCKY, moved to Iowa and became the Sanitary Agent of Iowa, an appointment by the legislature. During the later years of the Civil War, she left politics to join church women in the Christian Commission. She had charge of 200 women who opened diet kitchens and prepared food for some 1,800 wounded and sick soldiers. They were cited by General ULYSSES S. GRANT for their outstanding work in alleviating suffering. After the war

Mrs. Wittenmeyer started a home for five hundred orphans of soldiers in the barracks at DAVENPORT, Iowa, which was a gift of Congress.

She then went to Philadelphia and started the Ladies' and Pastors' Union, which was approved by the General Conference (ME) of 1872. These ladies, with their pastors, visited 50,000 needy families and gave religious instruction as well as looking after physical needs.

It was as an outgrowth of this work that Mrs. Wittenmeyer became interested in eradicating the liquor traffic, and joined the Women's national association, of which she became president. She visited many annual conferences speaking on the evils of liquor and urging temperance. She took two petitions to Congress on behalf of prohibition in 1875 and 1878. She wrote two books, *Woman's Work in The Church* and *History of the Woman's Crusade.*

M. Simpson, *Cyclopaedia.* 1878.

WITTON, WILLIAM (1811-1886), Australian pioneer and leader. At the date of his death at Warragul on Sept. 5, 1886, William Witton had long been known and honored throughout the colony as having been one of the truest pioneer leaders of Victorian Methodism, particularly in the Southern districts.

The grandson of Joseph Witton, sometime Chaplain of the Tower of London, he was born in 1811 in the city of LONDON. His father was a merchant engaged in the West India trade and his mother was a daughter of the Rev. Mr. Lambert, a clergyman of the Church of England. Both his parents died during his childhood and he was brought up by an uncle, in whose office he began to work.

As a youth of eighteen he migrated to Hobart and a little later moved to Launceston. There he married into a Methodist family, and in 1834 was converted under the preaching of a Mr. Leach. He became a local preacher, and thereafter spent his life in devoted and outstanding Christian service. In March 1937, he and his wife went to Port Phillip where he found a handful of earnest Methodists. He became their first recognized class leader, and in his house in Lonsdale Street, regular Sunday morning services were held.

He took an active part in all matters relating to the society in the settlement, and in February 1839, with J. W. Dredge, signed the vitally important letter urging upon JOSEPH ORTON, "the appointment of an accredited Wesleyan minister for this township." Joseph Orton himself was appointed temporarily for twelve months before returning to England. During this period with the help of Witton and others, he firmly laid the foundation for future development of the Methodist Society in Victoria.

From MELBOURNE Witton went to Belfast (Port Fairy), where for three years he was employed as a missionary by the District Meeting, the whole of the Western District near the seashore being his station. He was the first Wesleyan to preach in Warrnambool and helped to establish Methodism in Port Fairy and Portland.

As his family increased, and provision had to be made for them, he became a pastoralist (that is, a station holder who raises live stock), purchasing the Hartley Station, some ten miles from Port Fairy. For thirteen years he acted as curate to the Port Fairy congregation. After leaving Hartley he was engaged in business in Port Fairy, Caramut and Kirkstall. Later in life he moved to

Gippsland, and pioneered the cause at Brandy Creek, Longwarry South, Drouin and Warragul. All his days he was a pioneer, blazing trails for the Kingdom. He tramped roads, with staff in hand, preaching where and whenever opportunity was given.

He lived to take part in the Jubilee meeting in the Exhibition Building and died at Warragul in 1886. He saw the little society of seven grow into a church of more than 16,000 members and 100,000 adherents.

AUSTRALIAN EDITORIAL COMMITTEE

WITWER, SAMUEL W. (See JUDICIAL COUNCIL.)

WOFFORD, BENJAMIN (1780-1850), American preacher and philanthropist, was born in Spartanburg County, S. C., on Oct. 19, 1780. He was licensed to preach in 1804, did missionary work in KENTUCKY, served as a local DEACON, and in 1816 entered the SOUTH CAROLINA CONFERENCE. In 1820, at the conference in CHARLESTON, he located. Following his location he devoted himself to farming and later had extensive business dealings in real estate and investments. Throughout his life he maintained an active relation to the church, preaching on occasions, attending CAMP MEETINGS, and giving his time and money to causes of the church.

Wofford was an astute businessman, who by keen conception of economic values and rigid economy accumulated a fortune of $150,000, which was considered enormous in those days. His tendency toward frugality gave him the reputation in his home community of being a miser. One said of him, "He would stop to pick up a stray pin at a time when he could have tendered a check to pay for a ship's cargo of pins." However a Spartanburg Methodist layman who had been asked for a donation to RANDOLPH-MACON COLLEGE is said to have counted on Wofford's reputation for penury and so replied, "I will give as much as brother Wofford." The next day he was informed that he would have to match a gift of $1,000 which Benjamin Wofford had just subscribed.

As Wofford neared the end of his life he sought advice from a number of ministerial friends on how his money could best be used to advance the cause of Methodism. After a conference with H. A. C. Walker, he included in his will a gift of $100,000 for "the establishing and endowing a college for literary, classical, and scientific education, to be located in my native district, Spartanburg, and to be under the control and management of the conference of the Methodist Episcopal Church of my native state, South Carolina." Shortly after making this will, Benjamin Wofford died in Spartanburg, on Dec. 2, 1850. (See WOFFORD COLLEGE.)

Benjamin Wofford Files, Wofford College Library.
D. D. Wallace, *Wofford College.* 1951.

CLARENCE CLIFFORD NORTON

WOFFORD COLLEGE, Spartanburg, South Carolina, was established by the SOUTH CAROLINA CONFERENCE pursuant to a legacy of $100,000 given by BENJAMIN WOFFORD, a local preacher of the M.E. Church, South. In 1850, the legacy represented the largest gift made by an American Methodist for religious or educational purposes. One half of this amount, which had been placed in endowment, was lost after being invested in Confederate bonds during the Civil War.

MAIN BUILDING, WOFFORD COLLEGE,
SPARTANBURG, SOUTH CAROLINA

The college was organized by the Methodist conference of SOUTH CAROLINA in 1853, and the first session began on August 1, 1854. Since that date the college has continued in growth and usefulness as a church-related institution.

Wofford is a college for men, with a strong tradition of emphasis on sound scholarship. The college has a chapter of Phi Beta Kappa, and a large number of students continue in graduate and professional schools after graduation. Ministerial education has always been a strong feature at Wofford, and the majority of the members of the South Carolina Conference are graduates of the college. It offers the B.A. and B.S. degrees. The governing board has twenty-one members: ten ministers and eleven laymen elected to two-year terms by the South CAROLINA ANNUAL CONFERENCE, on nomination of the conference Board of Education.

D. D. Wallace, *Wofford College.* 1951.   JOHN O. GROSS

WOLFF, GEORGE (1736-1828), British Methodist, had the following obituary notice in the *Wesleyan Methodist Magazine* for 1828:

March 8th.—At Balham, in Surrey, George Wolff, Esq., formerly Consul General to the Court of Denmark, in which country he was born, in 1736. For many years he enjoyed the confidence and esteem of Mr. Wesley, of whose Will he was the last surviving executor. He was a man of great humility and ardent piety, and one of the most liberal contributors to the funds of the Methodist charities in London. He died happy in God, at the advanced aged of ninety-two years.

Wolff married the widow of Capt. John Cheesement, of Mile End Green, one of the City Road trustees, whom WESLEY buried in February 1783. Wesley described this lady as "that lovely woman" in a letter to his niece, Sally. Wolff was himself a worshipper at City Road, traveling in his carriage from Balham, a journey as the crow flies of about six miles. Wolff's main claim to fame is, as his obituary notes, being one of Wesley's executors. It was doubtless in this connection that Wesley visited him regularly in the closing years of his life. John Wesley's *Diary* records visits in February, June and December 1783; February, 1784; January, 1786; January, 1787; December, 1789 (with the significant comment, "I then retired to the lovely family at Balham"); January, October, November (the occasion of a christening), and December, 1790; and the last visit, Feb. 23-24, 1791. It was from

Balham that Wesley was taken home to die at City Road. The house at Balham was demolished in 1912, but a photograph is contained in Wesley's published *Journal* (viii).

G. J. Stevenson, *City Road Chapel*, 1872.
J. Wesley, *Journal.* 1909-16.   B. J. N. GALLIERS

WOLLING, JAMES WILLIAM (1850-1928), American preacher and missionary to BRAZIL, was born in CHARLESTON, S. C. on Dec. 27, 1850. Feeling called to preach, he gave up his work to get an education and through the generosity of F. J. Pelzer, he was able to graduate from WOFFORD COLLEGE. After being ordained and serving several churches in SOUTH CAROLINA, he applied for missionary work and was appointed to the Brazilian Mission Conference by Bishop J. C. GRANBERY in 1886.

James Wolling remained in Brazil for twenty years, during which time he held various positions of importance both in Central and in South Brazil Conferences. He was president of the Legal Association, editor for six years of the Methodist weekly, treasurer for seven years of the mission, and was on the first committee of three named to plan for a publishing house (*Imprensa Metodista*), becoming its manager for many years. When JOHN M. LANDER was sent to Juiz de Fóra to found GRANBERY COLLEGE (now INSTITUTO GRANBERY), Wolling went with him to help, as he already knew Portuguese.

In 1896, Wofford College conferred on him the D.D. degree. Wolling was first married in May 1878, to Lidie McDonald Green who went with him to Brazil; but she died of yellow fever in Piracicaba, on December 27, of that same year. On Jan. 3, 1889, he married Lizzie M. Rice, in Union, S. C., by whom he had four children—Marcia, Meredith, William (who died in São Paulo), and James Spencer. Her health also failed in Brazil, so in 1907, they returned definitely to the United States. Here Wolling rejoined the South Carolina Conference in which he worked until superannuation. Mrs. Wolling died in July 1921, and Wolling married Mrs. Fannie Hilton, who survived him.

Wolling had a laborious life, performing many hard tasks in difficult places. He was brave, industrious, and a good and scholarly preacher. He died in Spartanburg County, on March 15, 1928.

J. L. Kennedy, *Metodismo no Brazil.* 1928. D. M. McLEOD

WOMACK, ARTHUR WALTER (1890-1961), twenty-sixth bishop of the C.M.E. CHURCH, was born on July 10, 1890, in Halifax County, Va. He received a B.A. degree from PAINE COLLEGE and a B.D. degree from Howard University in WASHINGTON, D. C. He served churches in Washington, D. C., DETROIT, Mich; ST. LOUIS, Mo.; and INDIANAPOLIS, Ind. At the General Conference in 1950, he was elected to the office of bishop. He presided over the episcopal areas of GEORGIA, MISSISSIPPI, and LOUISIANA. Bishop Womack displayed great interest in foreign missions and made trips to Africa on behalf of his denomination.

Harris and Patterson, *C.M.E. Church.* 1965.
The Mirror, General Conference, C.M.E., 1958.
       RALPH G. GAY

WOMAN'S FOREIGN MISSIONARY SOCIETY (ME). The decade immediately following the close of the War Between the States saw the rise of a new interest in "foreign missions" in the M.E. Church, and the sending of missionary forces to South America, CHINA, and INDIA especially. In earlier decades, Methodist overseas missions—the concern of only a few persons in the church—had been confined to AFRICA where some freed slaves from America had been repatriated to what is now LIBERIA.

These were also years of struggle for "women's rights" in the U.S.A., years when higher education was opening to women, and years when educated women, especially, were entering the professions and taking place in social-religious-educational "movements."

It was in this atmosphere that in 1869 leading women in the M.E. Church began to consider organizing to "extend the Gospel *to women by women*"—somewhat paralleling the general Church's ministry to *men* in lands just opening to missionary efforts.

In 1870 this movement, springing up spontaneously among women of the Church, was formally organized as the "Woman's Foreign Missionary Society of the Methodist Episcopal Church." The first president was Mrs. David Patten, and the first secretary, Mrs. WILLIAM FAIRFIELD WARREN. Through seven decades the Society flourished in membership in missionaries and in funds sent abroad, and in the widening scope of its ministry. As it grew in the concern of Methodist women, "branches" of the Society were established for these areas: New England, New York, Philadelphia, Baltimore, Cincinnati, Northwestern, Des Moines, Minneapolis, Topeka, Pacific, Columbia River. All these "branches"—conducted by women who volunteered their services because of missionary concern—were centers for the recruitment of young women for overseas careers, for education in surrounding churches, and for the securing of funds for missionary support, overseas institutions, etc. It is reported that from 1870 (when receipts were $4,546) through 1939, the total receipts of the W.F.M.S. in all its branches were $61,229,889.

With the unification of the three Methodist Churches to form The Methodist Church in 1940, the Woman's Foreign Missionary Society was one of seven agencies that coalesced to comprise the Woman's Division of Christian Service of the BOARD OF MISSIONS. From 1940 to 1965, the various services and ministries of the W.F.M.S. were kept relatively intact in the Foreign Department of the Woman's Division of Christian Service—though there was constant consultation with the Division of World Missions in order to coordinate plans and prevent overlapping of activities. In 1965 the overseas work of the Woman's Division and that of the Division of World Missions were further consolidated and are now operated under one administrative department for each major field.

On Dec. 31, 1939, the active Woman's Foreign Missionary Society missionaries numbered 498. From the date of organization to 1939, the Society had recruited, trained, and maintained on the fields a grand total of 1,572 women missionaries.

From the beginning, the ministry of the Woman's Missionary Society was intended for women and girls—a ministry to supplement that of male missionaries, a ministry that in many areas could not be given by men because of social custom. In most countries it began with schools for young girls—usually where education for girls and women was unknown or frowned upon. And from these begin-

nings grew high schools and colleges for girls, and in some places co-education. The compassion of the early missionaries led them to give simple medical help, and to teach some methods of sanitation in tribes and villages suffering from the sicknesses brought on by ignorance and lack of cleanliness: and soon there came to American women calls for nurses, women doctors, clinics, and hospitals in needy areas. While in the beginning preaching and the organization of churches were the realm of the male missionaries, "women of light" could not keep from telling the Gospel story where darkness was all around them: so some women missionaries were set aside as evangelists, and led many thousands of women and children to Christ. From this "necessary ministry" there grew the training of choice national women as evangelists, as Bible women, and some few missionary women as pastors. In times and areas where male reinforcements were lacking, some bishops even named W.F.M.S. missionaries as district evangelists or district superintendents. Necessity sometimes overruled the *Book of Discipline!*

India was the first, and for a long time the principal, field to which the W.F.M.S. gave service and personnel. Dr. CLARA SWAIN went out from America in January 1870, the first woman physician sent out by any women's missionary group. ISABELLA THOBURN, with the blessing and support of the same group, went to India to pioneer in education for women. Clara Swain organized a hospital in BAREILLY—first of a group of healing institutions established by the W.F.M.S. Isabella Thoburn began school with a few outcaste girls—and during a lifetime of service saw the development of what is now ISABELLA THOBURN COLLEGE, one of the great educational institutions of all Asia. Through the decades, the work grew in extent and in its influence upon a whole continent.

At the time of Methodist unification in the United States, the W.F.M.S. had missionaries and missionary institutions (hospitals, schools, homes, orphanages) in Africa (Angola, Southern Rhodesia, Portuguese East Africa, Algiers); in Burma; in China (Central, Foochow, West, Hinghwa, Kiangsi, North, and Yenping conferences); in India (Bengal, Bombay, Central Provinces, Gujarat, Hyderabad, Indus River, Lucknow, North India, Northwest India, and South India conferences); in Japan; in Korea; in Malaya; in Sumatra; in the Philippine Islands; in Bulgaria; in Latin America (Mexico, Argentina, Uruguay, and Peru).

References: *Year Book* of the W.F.M.S. (1939) lists all missionaries 1869-1939.

W. W. REID

WOMAN'S FOREIGN MISSIONARY SOCIETY (MP) was organized in PITTSBURGH, Pa., on Feb. 14, 1879, to promote support for the overseas mission program of the METHODIST PROTESTANT CHURCH. At the GENERAL CONFERENCE of 1880 the organization was recognized as a permanent agency of the church. The Society agreed to pay the salary of Miss Harriet G. Brittain, an Episcopalian who, as the first missionary to serve the M.P. Church, opened a school in Yokohama, JAPAN, in October 1880. Three years later, Dr. and Mrs. FREDERICK C. KLEIN, the first M.P. missionaries in the non-Christian world, arrived in Japan and on July 11, 1886, the first Japanese church of the denomination was organized with twelve members. Through the work of the Woman's Foreign Missionary Society and the Board of Foreign Missions of the M.P. Church, Japan had, by 1928, become a well-organized Mission Conference of nineteen charges and nine missions. Nagoya College for men and boys had been founded, as well as a primary and high school for girls, six kindergartens and the Tokyo School for the Blind. The Klein-Coulborn Memorial Church, costing $20,000, was dedicated on June 26, 1927.

The Woman's Foreign Missionary Society began its work in Kalgan, CHINA, when C. S. Heininger accepted the position of missionary under the auspices of the Society on Oct. 5, 1909. Five years later the Society purchased the Kalgan property from the American Board of Foreign Missions for $9,000. This property consisted of three and one-half acres of ground, two dwelling houses, a dispensary, one school each for boys and girls, a chapel and servant's quarters. By joint agreement with the Board of Foreign Missions, the Woman's Foreign Missionary Society accepted the responsibility for all the work of the women and girls at Kalgan. The China Mission Conference was organized on Dec. 12, 1919, with one American minister, one Chinese minister, nine native preachers and delegates. Dr. Roberta Fleagle, the first medical missionary of the M.P. Church, was sent to China by the Society in June 1920. Miss Theresa Frank was in charge of the Society's evangelistic work in China during the 1920's.

The Society worked with the Board of Foreign Missions in the denominational work in INDIA, assisting with the care and instruction of the women and girls and with the medical department.

At the General Conference of 1924, a Constitution for a Union Board of Foreign Missionary Administration aimed toward the unification of missionary organizations was approved. This plan called for the establishment of a board with five members each from the Board of Foreign Missions and the Woman's Foreign Missionary Society, the two executive secretaries of the organizations and the President of the General Conference. In 1928 the Woman's Foreign Missionary Society merged with the Woman's Home Missionary Society and became known as the "Woman's Work of the Methodist Protestant Church." Individual organizations were known as "auxiliaries" or "the ladies aid."

Mrs. E. C. Chandler, *WFMS of the MP.* 1920.
The Methodist Protestant, May 16, 1928.

RALPH HARDEE RIVES

WOMAN'S HOME MISSIONARY SOCIETY. (ME). In response to a growing concern of socially minded groups of Methodist women in all parts of the United States for the welfare of their sisters and young children—especially in the rapidly growing urban areas and among the less privileged people of the nation—the Woman's Home Missionary Society of the M.E. Church came into existence in 1882 in a convention held in Cincinnati, Ohio. The first president was MRS. RUTHERFORD B. HAYES, whose husband had just completed a term as president of the United States; she served for seven years, and large credit for the rapid growth and influence of the Society is due to her planning and devotion to the cause.

The varied needs of women and children in the "old cities" and their slums in the 1880's claimed major attention of these Methodist women. One of their first pioneering efforts was in the establishment of "settlement houses" or "neighborhood houses" that endeavored to give working young women "a home away from home." Wesley Houses

and Bethlehem Centers were but other names for residential houses for working girls and women—often the more poorly-paid workers of their day. While the needs of each community differ—and "houses" and "homes" must vary to meet changing needs, what *all* needed was a community and life where a family atmosphere might be experienced and shared, where recreational facilities would be provided, and where feelings of loneliness in the crowds might be dissipated. The so-called institutional church, endeavoring to minister to the varied needs of women and girls for recreation, worship, and study, grew in part from the Woman's Home Missionary Society's endeavor to meet the needs of these strangers in a strange city.

From such beginnings, in the next half century, Methodist women, led by national W.H.M.S. pioneers, and with the support furnished by thousands of auxiliary societies established in as many local churches and communities, pioneered in many forms of Christian service in the homeland. They developed also a chain of young women's auxiliaries (to the W.H.M.S.), the WESLEYAN SERVICE GUILD, the young people's department, and the junior department. In these small but significant "service arms" of the W.H.M.S., were trained many who today are in places of leadership in The United Methodist Church.

Branching out from initial attention to human needs in the cities, and the Church's attempt to meet them, the W.H.M.S. pioneered in phases of a vast social-service program, forerunner of much that Methodism and other Christian churches are doing in these areas today. It early saw the potentials in ALASKA—and the peculiar needs of the rugged people there: established the Seward General Hospital, the Jesse Lee Home and Orphanage, a hospital in Nome. In CALIFORNIA, ministry to the Chinese included a service to immigrants in SAN FRANCISCO, and a residence hall for Chinese girls in the same city; and a center and home in Los Angeles. Out in Honolulu, the Susannah Wesley Home ministered to women of many nationalities; and in CHICAGO, Marcy Center became a model of service to Jew and Christian alike. Hospitals and dispensaries were established in WASHINGTON, D.C.; JACKSONVILLE, Fla.; BOSTON, Mass. Work among the American Indians—and especially among their long-neglected women—reached into areas assigned to the Navajos, the Yumas, the Poncas. Schools, settlement houses, and clinics ministered to the Mexicans in the U.S. southwest. WOOD JUNIOR COLLEGE and a group of secondary schools served boys as well as girls in the mountain regions of GEORGIA, TENNESSEE, KENTUCKY, and rural MISSISSIPPI. Schools, community centers, and women's and girls' homes were established for work and workers among Negroes in various communities in TEXAS, Mississippi, LOUISIANA, and in the Carolinas; BENNETT COLLEGE, in GREENSBORO, N.C., became a pioneer in the education of Negro young women. And the George O. Robinson School in PUERTO RICO, and the Alma Mathews House in NEW YORK (the latter originally to care for immigrant girls) became models for like institutions established by other agencies.

Esther Halls, Friendship Homes, Mother's Jewels Homes, Neighborhood Houses, and other-named centers for residential care of girls and young working women became nationwide symbols of the Methodist Church's care for its womanhood. That ministry, begun by the Woman's Home Missionary Society, is continued today in The United Methodist Church through the Woman's Division of Christian Service of the BOARD OF MISSIONS.

When, in 1940, the activities of the Woman's Home Missionary Society was merged with other groups in the formation of the Woman's Division of Christian Service, the W.H.M.S. had a total membership of 263,000 women and girls, enrolled in 11,608 units—auxiliaries, young woman's auxiliaries, Wesleyan Service Guilds, young people, and juniors. Each annual conference had an active Conference W.H.M.S. The annual receipts and disbursements for home missionary enterprises through the W.H.M.S. were about $1,250,000.

W. W. REID

WOMAN'S HOME MISSIONARY SOCIETY (MP) was organized at Bridgeton, N. J., at the conclusion of the annual meeting of the WOMAN'S FOREIGN MISSIONARY SOCIETY in 1893. Mrs. S. A. Lipscomb was the first president and national headquarters were located at ADRIAN, Mich., and later at KANSAS CITY, Kan., then at WASHINGTON, D.C., and after 1916 in BALTIMORE, Md. During its early years the organization sponsored missionary projects in the Upper Peninsula of MICHIGAN and in the OKLAHOMA Territory. In 1907 two young women were sent by the Society to the Schauffler Missionary Training School and one of them, Elizabeth Potachnak, later worked for several years among the Slavic people of Baltimore. Miss Constante Field went as a missionary from the Society to the Navajo Indians in 1907. Mrs. M. O. Everett of Washington, D.C., began work the same year among the mountain people of TENNESSEE and KENTUCKY, and as a result the ALVAN DREW SCHOOL at Pine Ridge, Ky., was opened in 1912. Dr. and Mrs. Thomas A. Woodford headed this school for a number of years after 1919. The school had 125 acres and a number of buildings. At one time there were sixty students including eight boarders.

The Woman's Home Missionary Society was incorporated in 1916 with a central committee which, along with the president, had authority to transact business between regular board meetings. In 1922, S. W. Rosenberger, President of the OHIO M.P. Annual CONFERENCE, urged the Society to establish missionary work among the foreign-speaking people in the Ohio Valley, and subsequently Emily Grace Brown worked in that area for four years. Bessie M. Eiss began a mission project at Dillonville, Ohio, in 1927 and within a year had reached 150 children. Other special projects which were supported by the Woman's Home Missionary Society included the Children's Home, founded by Mrs. Minnie Lee Hammer in Denton, N. C., in 1910 and later moved to HIGH POINT; Bethel Tubercular Home, operated by Homer Casto at Weaverville, N. C.; the Pittsburgh Mission, founded in 1925 by Mrs. Jane A. Gordon; and a Business Girl's Home in Baltimore, Md. Mrs. A. G. (Margaret M. Kuhns) Dixon, who in 1908 became the first President of the NORTH CAROLINA Branch of the Woman's Home Missionary Society, became National President in 1909, a position she held for many years.

The Society worked with the Board of Home Missions of the M.P. Church, which was established by the GENERAL CONFERENCE of 1888.

In 1928 the Woman's Home Missionary Society merged with the Woman's Foreign Missionary Society into the United Branch of Missions of the M.P. Church and became known as "The Woman's Work of the Methodist Protestant Church." Mrs. Hammer was elected to serve as the first President. Individual organizations were known as "auxiliaries" or "the Ladies' Aid."

J. Elwood Carroll, *History of the North Carolina Conference of the Methodist Protestant Church.* Greensboro, 1939.
Journal of the North Carolina Conference, MP.
The Methodist Protestant, May 16, 1928.

RALPH HARDEE RIVES

WOMAN'S MISSIONARY RECORDER. A publication of the African Methodist Episcopal Church. (See AFRICAN METHODIST EPISCOPAL CHURCH, Publications.)

WOMELDORF, PAUL D. (1890-　　　), American minister and administrator, was born in Hanover, York County, Pa., Nov. 26, 1890, the son of J. and Vianna Heller Womeldorf.

He attended Pennsylvania State Teachers College, and graduated with the class of 1912. Other schooling was at Pennsylvania State University and the University of Michigan, where he received the A. B. degree in 1919. He later attended ILIFF SCHOOL OF THEOLOGY. SOUTHWESTERN COLLEGE, Winfield, Kan., granted him the D.D. degree in 1944.

He engaged in public school work for a time, serving as principal, Burnham, Pa., 1913-14; superintendent of Port Allegany Schools, 1917-20; then 1918-19 in the Army, A.E.F.; and then the superintendent of city schools, Syracuse, Kan.

He was received on trial in the SOUTHWEST KANSAS CONFERENCE in March 1923, and served the following churches: Centerview, Bethel, Murdock, Bison, Kinsley and Trinity Church in WICHITA; superintendent of the Dodge City District, 1935-39. He was a charter member of the CENTRAL KANSAS CONFERENCE in 1939 and served El Dorado in 1939-40. In 1940 he became executive secretary of the SOUTH CENTRAL JURISDICTIONAL Council and was such until 1960 when he took the retired relationship.

Dr. Womeldorf was elected as delegate to the GENERAL CONFERENCES of 1940, 1944, and 1952; a delegate to the South Central Jurisdictional Conference for 1948 and 1956. He was a member of the General Board of Temperance, 1950-58; a member of the Methodist Rural Fellowship, and president of the Methodist Conference on Christian Education, 1942-43. He resides in Shawnee, Kan.

Journals of the Central Kansas Conference, 1940, 1944, 1948, 1952, 1956, 1960, 1967.
Who's Who in The Methodist Church, 1966.

WILLIAM F. RAMSDALE

WOMEN ITINERANT PREACHERS, British. When SARAH CROSBY approached JOHN WESLEY in 1761 for advice about the 200 people who flocked to her class meeting, he told her to tell them, "The Methodists do not allow of women preachers. . . . But I will just nakedly tell you what is in my heart." (*Letters,* iv, 133, Feb. 14, 1761) In 1771 writing to MARY BOSANQUET and referring to 1 Corinthians 14:34-35, he said that this might admit of exception where there was "an extraordinary call" (*Letters,* v, 257, June 13, 1771). As in other matters where he believed there was a clear call of God, he was ready to lay aside his own prejudices.

The Wesleyan Conference rule of 1803, which only allowed women to preach who had an extraordinary call and then only to female congregations, remained in force until 1910, but Mrs. MARY TAFT preached when an asterisk appeared on her husband's plan. JABEZ BUNTING considered an extraordinary call to be "every fanatic's plea." HUGH BOURNE accepted female itinerants from the early days of PRIMITIVE METHODISM, and more than forty appear before 1844. WILLIAM O'BRYAN's wife was the first among the BIBLE CHRISTIANS, and there were fourteen "Itinerant Females" by the first conference in 1819. In all, seventy-one were accepted between then and 1861. Thirteen more appear between 1890 and 1907.

Wesley Historical Soc. *Proceedings*, xxviii, 89; xxix, 76.

V. E. VINE

WOMEN'S CRUSADE, THE (American), a forerunner of The Woman's Christian Temperance Union, had its beginning in OHIO where women met for prayer, then went to the grog shops, saloons, drugstores, and hotels to pray and to sing and to plead with those engaged in the sale of liquor to desist from the traffic.

These Christian women from many denominations suffered persecution and imprisonment; they had buckets of icy water thrown on them in winter, and were sued by liquor dealers for loss of business. Their worship services on the sidewalks and in the saloons were broken up by rowdies or by singing and dancing girls. But through their consecrated efforts many saloons were closed and the bartenders went into other lines of work. Bishop SIMPSON calls it a "remarkable movement" and states that while it was not directly connected with Methodism, the Methodist women "owing to their greater experience in class meetings and love feasts" were unusually conspicuous in it. It was supplanted in time by the Woman's Christian Temperance Union which had great effect in fighting the liquor traffic.

M. Simpson, *Cyclopaedia*. 1878.

N. B. H.

WOMEN'S FELLOWSHIP (British), began in 1942, when a special committee was set up by the Methodist CONFERENCE to consider problems vital to women. In 1944 the Conference approved the name, recognized an aim and promise and laid down a constitution. The Fellowship is part of the HOME MISSION DEPARTMENT, and is charged with the task of calling women and girls to a Christian womanhood accepting responsibility in the home, the Church, and the State. There is an annually elected President. The Fellowship has organized a mother and a baby home, a home for girls in need of temporary accommodation, especially unmarried girls in the early stages of pregnancy, and a hostel for business and professional girls.

MARGARET STATHAM

WOMEN'S GUILD FELLOWSHIP in New Zealand Methodism was founded to draw together local guilds, which played a valuable part in the life of the church from the earliest days. In the *Law Book* of the NEW ZEALAND Methodist Church the objects were stated thus: "To promote the spiritual and social welfare of its members and of the Church, to assist in the furnishing of the Parsonage and to help in Trust and Circuit enterprises." These objects have been realized. Membership has been open to all women of the church. The usual monthly meetings have assisted the spiritual influence of the church, sometimes to a marked degree.

In each district a district guild fellowship coordinated the work of the individual guilds and gathered isolated guilds into the larger fellowship of the church.

In 1948, the Conference asked the district fellowships to form a New Zealand Methodist Guild Fellowship, and in 1949 the Conference approved the constitution. In its 1960 report, the fellowship reported 6,697 members in 310 guilds, and £20,346 raised for church purposes during the year. The fellowship has always been worthily represented on many nationwide councils and federations outside the strictly church groups. Through the fellowship, the guilds became an important spiritual power in the church. The declared aim has been: "To know Christ and to make Him known."

In May, 1960, its representatives met representatives of the Women's Missionary Auxiliary, when it was decided to form one Women's movement in the church. The unified movement with the title, The New Zealand METHODIST WOMEN'S FELLOWSHIP, was established in 1964.

WILLIAM T. BLIGHT

WOMEN'S MISSIONARY SOCIETY of the M.E. Church, South. (See MISSIONS AND BOARD OF MISSIONS, MES.)

WOMEN'S ORGANIZATIONS, Br. (See METHODIST MISSIONARY SOCIETY and WOMEN'S FELLOWSHIP.)

WOMEN'S SOCIETY OF CHRISTIAN SERVICE, formerly Woman's Society of Christian Service, is the women's organization of The United Methodist Church whose purpose is "to help women grow in the knowledge and experience of God as revealed in Jesus Christ; to challenge them to God's redemptive purpose in the world; to unite them in a Christian Fellowship to make Christ known throughout the world; and to develop a personal responsibility for the whole task of the Church."

This organization is the outreach and ongoing of the missionary work of the M.E. Church, the M.E Church, South, the M.P. Church, and the E.U.B. Church—all now united. The organization has a rich heritage of service, going back to societies organized from 1786 to this present day. In the old JOHN STREET CHURCH, New York, as early as 1768, Methodist women organized to help with the church and parsonage.

With the growth of missionary movement, especially overseas, the WOMAN'S FOREIGN MISSIONARY SOCIETY of the M.E. Church was organized in 1869. In 1873 the Woman's Bible Mission, later the Woman's Foreign Missionary Society of the M.E. Church, South, was organized. Two years later came the organization of the Women's Missionary Association of the Church of the UNITED BRETHREN IN CHRIST, and in 1879 the Woman's Foreign Missionary Society of the M.P. Church.

In 1880 the "home work" of the Church, namely looking after PARSONAGES and local mission work, was entrusted to a separate organization, the WOMAN'S HOME MISSIONARY SOCIETY in the M.E. Church. In 1886 an organization under the same name was created in the M.E. Church, South. It should be said also that in 1884 the Board of Missions of the Evangelical Association ratified the creation of its Woman's Missionary Society. The M.P. Church followed these moves by organizing in 1893 a Woman's Home Missionary Society.

In the M.E. Church, South, in 1910 a Woman's Missionary Council was formed, merging into it all that

Church's missionary interests. The doing away with the separate organizations for home missions caused considerable tension among women in the Southern Church, but better administration called for it. In 1924 the Methodist Protestants united all their missionary interests, and at Methodist union in 1939, all women's organizations of the three churches merged to form the Woman's Division of the Board of Missions. There were to be auxiliary Woman's Societies of Christian Services in annual conferences, districts, and local churches.

A similar merger happened when the EVANGELICAL CHURCH and the United Brethren Church merged in 1946 and they, at that time, put their women's organizations all together in a Women's Society of World Service. In 1964 there was a further reorganization in The Methodist Church and the mission work of the Woman's Division of Christian Service was merged into and with World and National Divisions of the BOARD OF MISSIONS. This was to obviate possible conflict between the Woman's Division (which had an almost world-wide extension of schools, hospitals, and workers), and that of the World Division of the same Board which also had a world-wide outreach and its own special agencies and personnel. While the World Division and the Woman's Division had cooperated in many ways, the merger was to the advantage of all.

In 1968 came the great merger caused by the union of the Churches (E.U.B. and T.M.C.) to form The United Methodist Church. This merger changed the name slightly from Woman's Society to Women's Society of Christian Service. The organization is commonly referred to as "The W.S.C.S."

The work and accomplishments of these women's organizations have been almost miraculous in their support of, planning for, and projecting all sorts of missionary moves at home and abroad, all formerly under the aegis of their respective Churches. Successive Disciplines may be referred to to ascertain the charter regulations, disciplinary guidance, and duties of the W.S.C.S. and its antecedent organizations. These have varied from time to time, and successive GENERAL CONFERENCES may be expected to revise them still further as need seems to call. However, the great forward drive and purpose of the organized women's work in the Church has always been the same— to spread scriptural holiness over all lands and to go into the world for Jesus Christ.

Membership in the combined societies of the United Methodist Church is approximately 1,795,376. The W.S.C.S. has sometimes been called "the largest woman's club in the world." Its membership is open to all women who are members of The United Methodist Church. It functions, as has been said above, in local chapters or societies in the local churches in the districts; in annual conference organizations; and in the jurisdictional groupings in the general Church. Annual conference W.S.C.S. meetings are largely attended and put on helpful programs, and the same can be said of the jurisdictional organizations and their assemblies. The whole organization is under the control of the general Board of Missions, and regulations governing it through that Board are, of course, General Conference enactments.

An enormous literature can be referred to for information in this field. *The History of Methodist Missions*, by Wade Crawford Barclay, will give the most complete account in volumes I and II (which have been published) of early American Methodism; and of the M.E. Church, 1845-1939. A complete bibliography is carried in volume II published by the Board of Missions of The Methodist Church in 1957. There is a thorough treatment of women's work in volume II. (See also MISSIONS AND BOARD OF MISSIONS.)

MRS. JOHN M. PEARSON

WOMEN'S SOCIETY OF WORLD SERVICE (EUB). Among Evangelicals the first such society existed briefly in Immanuel Church, PHILADELPHIA in 1839. Nearly forty years were to elapse before a letter, written by a lady missionary in JAPAN and published in the church papers, was to inspire another effort. A group of women petitioned the BOARD OF MISSIONS in 1878 for permission to organize missionary societies, but as one of them put it, "The wise men said 'no'." Disappointed but undaunted they continued their agitation, and the Board in 1880 approved their request. In 1884 delegates from a number of these societies met in CLEVELAND to draft a petition to General Conference to permit the organization of a denominational Woman's Missionary Society and at the GENERAL CONFERENCE that year, the petition was granted.

"The Sisters' Missionary Society" organized by the women of the OHIO German Conference in 1869, and a similar organization by the women of the CALIFORNIA Conference in 1872 were the beginnings of organized women's missionary activity in the Church of the UNITED BRETHREN IN CHRIST. May 9, 1872 the Miami Branch Association was organized in the Euclid Avenue Church, DAYTON, and the pattern devised was used for other conference branch organizations. General Conference, 1873, gave its approval to the Associations. The following year the Board of Missions heard and approved the plan for a "General Women's Missionary Society," and the General Conference in 1877 formally recognized the "Women's Missionary Association." The successor to the Women's Missionary Association and the Women's Missionary Society in The E.U.B. Church is the Women's Society of World Service.

The purpose of the society shall be to unite all women of The E.U.B. Church in a Christian fellowship to make Christ known throughout the world and to develop a personal responsibility for the whole task of the Church.

The scope of work of the society shall be the needs and interests of women and the concerns and responsibilities of the church in today's world.

The society shall foster spiritual growth, missionary outreach, and Christian service.

LOIS MILLER

WOMEN'S WORK, Br. (See METHODIST MISSIONARY SOCIETY; also WOMEN'S FELLOWSHIP.)

WOOD, AARON (1802-1887), American preacher and administrator, the son of William and Mary (Conn) Wood, was born Oct. 15, 1802, in Pendleton, Va. The family moved to Ohio when he was small. In 1822 he was received on trial in the Ohio Conference. In 1824 he was ordained deacon and appointed to Madison, Ind. In 1826 he was ordained elder and appointed to Bloomington. He sums up his appointments, thus: thirteen years on circuits, fourteen years in station, three teaching and Sabbath preaching, six in chaplaincies and fourteen on districts. He was elected to five General Conferences and a reserve five times. Indiana University conferred on him a D.D. degree. For sixty years he knew the leading men in church and state in Indiana. He married Laura Beauchamp. There were three children. She died in 1835. In 1839 he married Maria Hitt. Seven children blessed their home. In 1885 he retired, having served sixty-three years as an itinerant. He died at Yountsville, Aug. 20, 1887.

J. J. Detzler, *Northwest Indiana Conference.* 1953.
Clarence E. Flynn, ed., *The Indianapolis Area of the Methodist Episcopal Church, 1924-1928: A Record and History.* Indianapolis: Area Council, 1928.
F. C. Holliday, *Indiana.* 1873.   W. D. ARCHIBALD

WOOD, A. HAROLD (1896-   ), Australian preacher, educator and church executive, was born in Geelong, VICTORIA. He was educated in NEW SOUTH WALES at SYDNEY High School and later at Sydney University. He did his theological training in New South Wales; in addition to graduating B.A., he also studied Law at Sydney for two years. His M.A. and B.D. were taken when he was a country minister. Dr. Wood learned to type and take shorthand, and worked as a clerk in a Government Department of Justice, and later as a judge's associate in the quarter-sessions court. This whetted his appetite for the bar, but before he completed his law degree he was asked if he would go to a Sydney suburb which was short of a minister and prepare to offer himself for the ministry at the end of the year.

It was during this time in 1919 that he met his wife, who was a doctor. Immediately after their marriage in 1924 they went to TONGA as missionaries, where they stayed for thirteen years. Dr. Wood was in charge of a boy's school and also trained Tongan boys for the ministry. In Tonga Dr. Wood did the reading and preliminary work for his D.D. degree. However, it was not until 1948 that he finished his thesis and submitted it for examination.

After thirteen years Dr. Wood and his family (his six children were all born in Tonga) returned to Sydney in 1937. He was appointed Principal of the Methodist Ladies College, Hawthorn, Victoria in 1939. When he went to the College in 1939 there were 650 students; when he retired on Dec. 9, 1966, there were 2,200 pupils.

Throughout his career preaching and Christian teaching have been his main concern. In 1952 he was President of the Victorian Conference and during 1957-60 was President-General of the Australian Conference. As General Conference Convenor of Church Union he worked tirelessly for this cause. At the time of his retirement he had a special interest in efforts being made to establish a Sixth Form College within the present College, for Matriculation Students.

After forty-one years in two schools, and five years in Circuit work, he has, since becoming a supernumerary minister, returned to circuit work as the minister of the Deepdene Methodist Church. He states: "I would rather be a minister than follow any other calling."

AUSTRALIAN EDITORIAL COMMITTEE

WOOD, ENOCH (1759-1840), was a noted early potter of Burslem, Staffordshire, England. In 1781 he produced his famous bust of JOHN WESLEY, who gave the artist five separate sittings. It was exhibited at the CONFERENCE in LEEDS, and Wood received commendation, Wesley and others declaring it an excellent likeness. In the first edition Wesley wore his traveling gown, and on ADAM CLARKE's suggestion another was made in full gown. Wood made six different busts of Wesley, and these have been the models for all succeeding artists except the French sculptor Roubiliac. Wood also made busts of Adam Clarke and GEORGE WHITEFIELD. (See also WESLEY POTTERY and BUSTS.)

The Connoisseur, September 1907.
A. D. Cummings, *A Portrait in Pottery.* London: Epworth Press, 1962.
Wesley Historical Society *Proceedings,* June 1907.
          ELMER T. CLARK

WOOD, ENOCH (1804-1888), Canadian Methodist preacher and administrator, promoter of home missions and pioneer of foreign missions in Canadian Methodism, was born Jan. 13, 1804, in Gainsborough, Lincolnshire, England. He was a school-fellow of Thomas Cooper, later a prominent Chartist. He was received on trial in 1826 and ordained immediately so that he might join a group of Wesleyan missionaries bound for the WEST INDIES. Wood was stationed in Montserrat, W. I., where he worked until he was transferred to St. John, New Brunswick, in August 1829.

The next year he was received into full connection, thus beginning a half-century of leadership in British American Methodism. While serving on circuits in the Maritime Provinces, 1829-47, he was an effective preacher and administrator. From 1831 to 1833 he was stationed in the Miramichi area, opening a new church in Chatham and initiating churches at Bathurst and elsewhere. In 1833 he was placed at Fredericton, where his ability in the pulpit and his genial spirit soon attracted numerous hearers.

Since he was especially effective in urban circuits, Wood served in St. John and Fredericton until 1847. From 1843 to 1847 he was chairman of the New Brunswick district. In this position he imparted new vigor to the religious and educational activities of the New Brunswick Wesleyans.

In 1847, at the CANADA CONFERENCE, a long step was taken in Canadian Methodism when Enoch Wood was appointed superintendent of missions. For some years, the Conference had been interested in missions, especially to the Indians, and the Wesleyan Missionary Society had begun a mission in the Northwest. Now, Wood was made responsible for the Canadian missions. He imparted to this enterprise the same energy and imagination he had displayed in New Brunswick. In 1848, he travelled widely and planned an industrial school for the Indian work at Muncey, Upper Canada.

Five years later the Hudson's Bay district was taken over from the Wesleyan Missionary Society and amalgamated with the Indian missions of the Canadian Methodists. This gave Wood administrative responsibility for the missions from coast to coast. At his suggestion, a party led by JOHN RYERSON toured this vast area in 1854. The Canadian Conference now began to conceive of its mission in British North American terms and to appoint outstanding missionaries to the western posts. Among them were GEORGE MCDOUGALL and EGERTON YOUNG, pioneers of the eventual prairie conferences.

Significant as was Enoch Wood's contribution to home missions, his greatest missionary venture was the establishment of a mission to JAPAN in 1873. This bold step marked the beginning of a new epoch in the history of Canadian Methodist missions. He faced firm opposition. Many doubted the wisdom of the venture at a time when so much was needed at home. Many missionaries were existing on inadequate stipends; many Indian tribes were as yet unreached; and there were loud and frequent calls for help from new communities. Nevertheless, in faith and hope Enoch Wood was instrumental in sending to Japan George Cochran, and Davidson MacDonald. They both served with distinction and fruitfulness, justifying the confidence and foresight of the superintendent.

In 1874, the Wesleyan Methodists, the Methodists of the New Connexion, and the Eastern British America Conference united to form the Methodist Church of CANADA. With this union came a consolidation of mission work across Canada, in Newfoundland, Bermuda, and the infant mission in Japan. It was a triumphant conclusion to Wood's dream. In 1874 and 1875, Wood, who had been President of the Canada Conference from 1851 to 1858 was President of the Toronto Conference, a testimony to the affection and respect of his brethren.

The previous year, ALEXANDER SUTHERLAND had been elected assistant secretary of missions. In 1878, Wood resigned in favor of his assistant. He was requested to attend the meetings of the committee and the board as honorary secretary as long as he was able. When the Central Board met in October 1880, a resolution of sympathy was recorded because of the long and painful illness of Enoch Wood, and in gratitude for his faithful service through many years.

Enoch Wood died in Toronto, Jan. 31, 1888 at the age of eighty-four. General Superintendent Williams gave the memorial address at the funeral service, Feb. 5, 1888.

Enoch Wood's life reflected a balance between missionary work and the more settled work of the pastorate. For three years he was a missionary in the West Indies. For the next eighteen years he served the largest centers in New Brunswick. The last thirty years he served in an administrative post as superintendent and later secretary of missions. His story is the account of a vital phase in the growth of Canadian Methodist missions. He was one of the new heroes of the faith who was more honored in his lifetime than after his death.

E. H. Oliver, *His Dominion of Canada*. Toronto: Ryerson, 1932.
T. W. Smith, *Eastern British America*. 1877-90.
Mrs. F. C. Stephenson, *Canadian Methodist Missions*. 1925.
A. Sutherland, *Methodism in Canada*. 1903.

ARTHUR E. KEWLEY

WOOD, THOMAS BOND (1844-1922), missionary from the United States to Latin America, served in ARGENTINA and URUGUAY and was one of the founders of Methodist work in PERU.

He was born on March 18, 1844, at Lafayette, Ind., the son of AARON WOOD, a prominent minister of the NORTHWEST INDIANA CONFERENCE. A brilliant student, he completed studies at Indiana Asbury at nineteen and at twenty had earned the A.B. degree from WESLEYAN UNIVERSITY. After earning the Master's degree at both schools (Indiana Asbury in 1866 and Wesleyan University, 1867), he taught natural science and German for three years at WESLEYAN ACADEMY, WILBRAHAM, Mass. For two years he was president of Valparaiso College, Indiana.

THOMAS B. WOOD

He was received on trial by the NEW ENGLAND CONFERENCE in 1865 and in 1867 transferred to the Northwest Indiana Conference.

Enrolling as a missionary for South America, he was sent to the River Plate region, where he spent a number of years in both Argentina and Uruguay. His first assignment was at ROSARIO, ARGENTINA, where he arrived on May 1, 1870. He began as a minister to the English-speaking community, but within a year had begun services in Spanish. His background in science and education led to the offer of a teaching position at the government university in Rosario. While continuing to work with his churches, he was a professor of astronomy and physics and for a time also served as a United States consul in Rosario.

In Uruguay he established in 1877 *El Evangelisto*, the first evangelical paper in the country, serving as editor until 1888. He was director of a school in Uruguay, 1887-89. Then for two years, 1889-91, he was president of the Buenos Aires Theological Seminary (FACULTAD EVANGELICA DE TEOLOGIA).

"Once a work was started," states EULA K. LONG in writing of him, "Dr. Wood wanted to move on, so he traveled to Lima, Peru, where he followed close there FRANCISCO G. PENZOTTI, whose dramatic imprisonment and release had opened the way for Protestant work." Wood arrived there in 1891 with an appointment as superintendent of the newly formed Western District of the South America Conference which comprised Peru, ECUADOR, and BOLIVIA. Serving in that position four years, he established churches—the first one at Callao—and with the aid of his daughter, Elsie, organized schools.

He visited the United States for the Ecuadorian government from May to July, 1900, and then acted as superintendent of the North Andes Mission, president of the Lima Theological Seminary, and pastor of an English-speaking congregation in LIMA. He had a part in the evangelization of Brazil also, sending there in 1875, João Corrêa, a homeopathic doctor and lay preacher who had been converted under his preaching, and eventually asking Corrêa to move to Brazil and establish a residence and school in Porto Alegre.

Wood spent most of the remainder of his life in and out of Peru. He was briefly in Ecuador in 1900, where he was a founder of normal schools. He was president of the Lima Business College, 1899; president of the Lima Theological Seminary, 1905-13; and director of the Callao mission schools and pastor of the English church in Lima, 1907-13. He retired in 1915.

E.M.B. Jaime in writing about Dr. Wood and his work said, "He was the image of a patriarch; he had the heart of a child, a powerful brain; he was a fearful debater, an orator in Athenian style, an elegant writer and a master in theology."

W. C. Barclay, *History of Methodist Missions.* 1957.
DePauw Alumni Record.
J. J. Detzler, *Northwest Indiana Conference.* 1953.
E. M. B. Jaime, *Metodismo no Rio Grande do Sul.* 1963.

EDWIN H. MAYNARD

WOOD JUNIOR COLLEGE, Mathiston, Mississippi, opened in 1886 as Woodland Seminary, an elementary school at Clarkston, Miss., under the auspices of the WOMEN'S HOME MISSIONARY SOCIETY of the M.E. Church. Initial funds for support came from the FREEDMEN'S AID SOCIETY. Renamed Bennett Academy in 1897, it moved to the present location in 1915 as a secondary school. Junior college instruction began in 1927. The college was given its present name in 1936 to honor its benefactors, Dr. and Mrs. Irving Wood of Omaha, Neb. The governing board has twenty-one members elected by the NORTH MISSISSIPPI CONFERENCE and the Woman's Division of Christian Service of the BOARD OF MISSIONS of The United Methodist Church.

JOHN O. GROSS

WOODFORD, THOMAS REEVES (1871-1945), American M.P. minister and educator, was born in Centreville, Md., on Dec. 6, 1871. In 1894 he sold out his mercantile business and entered WESTERN MARYLAND COLLEGE, where he graduated four years later. For a year he was a student at WESTMINSTER THEOLOGICAL SEMINARY. In 1899 he entered the MARYLAND CONFERENCE of the M.P. CHURCH and on Aug. 7, 1900, he married Mary Elizabeth VanDyke (Sept. 15, 1872—Nov. 9, 1958).

Woodford served pastorates in Belair, Lawsonia, Bethany Church, BALTIMORE (all in MARYLAND) and at Accomac, Va., Stewartstown and Fawn Grove, Pa. While he was agent and publisher for the Board of Publications of the M.P. BOOK CONCERN of Baltimore, he organized the Wilton Heights Church. He was appointed pastor of Grace M.P. Church (now Maynard Avenue Church) in COLUMBUS, OHIO, in 1916. He accepted the position of superintendent of the ALVAN DREW SCHOOL at Pine Ridge, Ky., in 1919 at a forty percent decrease in salary. For the next fifteen years the Woodfords supervised and developed this accredited high school for mountain children, sponsored by the WOMAN'S HOME MISSIONARY SOCIETY of the M.P. Church. Because of ill health, the Woodfords resigned in 1934 and Woodford returned to the Maryland

Conference to serve the First M.P. Church, Wilmington, Del., until 1937. He then superannuated but returned to Pine Ridge to help as he could there for three and one-half years. The Woodfords moved to FLORIDA in 1940, due to their health, and for five years were actively connected with the Goss Memorial Church in ORLANDO. Bishop JAMES H. STRAUGHN said of Woodford: "His preaching was simple and direct, without the slightest affectation of intellectualism or pedantry. He had a simple straight gospel."

The Woodfords were the parents of one daughter and one son. Woodford died on June 21, 1945, and both he and Mrs. Woodford are buried in Centreville, Md.

Journal of the Peninsula Conference, 1946.
The Methodist Protestant, scattered issues.
Pine Ridge Booster, XXII, Summer 1945.
R. B. Stone, "The Story of Alvan Drew School." Ms., 1934.

RALPH HARDEE RIVES
MRS. PAUL A. WILSON

WOODHOUSE GROVE SCHOOL is a "public school" parallel in the north of England to Kingswood School in the south. (See BRADFORD, ENGLAND.)

WOODRING, EDWIN S. (1872-1957), administrator and bishop of the American Evangelical Congregational Church for twenty-two years. He was a leader in perpetuating the form of government of The United Evangelical denomination in the Evangelical Congregational conferences. He was a younger brother to James D. Woodring, an early president of ALBRIGHT COLLEGE at Myerstown, Pa. Graduated from Muhlenberg College, he went to Illinois and studied at the Moody Bible Institute of Chicago. After preaching in the Illinois Conference (UE) for seven years, he came back to eastern Pennsylvania as a pastor and was elected a presiding elder in 1921, and then bishop in 1926. In addition to organizational ability in the conferences, his most noteworthy work was organizing the School of Methods youth conference at Waldheim Park, in Allentown, Pa. This was one of the outstanding youth conferences in its day, using noted speakers from many denominations and attracting hundreds of people annually. Born Feb. 17, 1872 at Wescosville, Lehigh County, Pa., he died Feb. 25, 1957 in Harrisburg, Pa. His body was laid to rest in the West End Cemetery, Allentown, Pa.

ROBERT S. WILSON

WOODRUFF, MAY LEONARD (1862-1948), American missionary leader of the NEWARK CONFERENCE, who gave more than forty years of her life to the organizing and developing of the home missionary work of the entire Church, was born at Sewickly, Pa., on Feb. 4, 1862. Her father was ADNA B. LEONARD, for many years foreign missionary secretary of the M.E. Church, and her brother was Bishop ADNA W. LEONARD. She was the wife of Charles S. Woodruff, and her sons were Clarence Woodruff, a member of the Newark Conference, and C. Rogers Woodruff, an official of the BOARD OF MISSIONS and Church Extension of The Methodist Church, who passed away at a comparatively early age and some years before his mother died. Her daughter, M. Dorothy Woodruff, research librarian of the Board of Missions, will be remembered with great affection by those who used the Library of that Board in the old 150 Fifth Avenue building in New York.

Mrs. Woodruff was described by George G. Vogel as a forward looking leader, who "always advocated the larger and greater things for the tomorrows. She was an advocate of the United Woman's Missionary Societies and for the union of the Churches." She gave great leadership to the women in home mission work in the continental United States. She died at Ocean Grove, N. J., on Feb. 16, 1948.

V. B. Hampton, *Newark Conference*.   N. B. H.

WOODS, DALE A. (1925-   ), American FREE METHODIST, an ordained elder of the East Michigan Conference. He married Betty Ruth McKinney in 1943. On completing his education at Michigan State University at East Lansing, Mich., he became a pastor in the East Michigan Conference of the Free Methodist Church and served as such for fifteen years and then as superintendent for six years. He became editor of the *Church Planning Guide*, the East Michigan Conference magazine, and a frequent contributor to church publications. Since 1967 he has been general director of Evangelistic Outreach. He resides in Warsaw, Ind.

BYRON S. LAMSON

WOODSTOCK, ILLINOIS, U.S.A. Sunset Manor, Inc. was founded and incorporated in 1903 by J. O. Kelsey, a FREE METHODIST minister and named first the Old People's Rest Home. The name was changed to Sunset Manor, Inc. in 1959.

In 1950 new construction provided twenty additional private rooms and baths, and since then twelve apartment units have been constructed. It has a present capacity of sixty and there is a fourteen-bed infirmary, with a registered nurse in charge. Activities include occupational therapy. Religious services are provided by the Free Methodist Church.

Sunset Manor is governed by an independent board. It is a member of the Association of Homes for the Aged, and is an approved Benevolent Institution of the Free Methodist Church.

Assets total $400,000, the annual budget is $125,000. Gifts, annuities and wills make possible consideration of some charity cases. The Manor's purpose is to provide retirement in an evangelical Christian environment where the total needs of the aged are met.

Woodstock Children's Home was founded as Chicago Industrial Home for Children in 1886 in Chicago by T. B. Arnold, publisher for the Free Methodist Church. It was incorporated in 1888 and moved to Woodstock in 1897. The Home cared for orphans and functioned as an adoption agency until in the 1920's when emphasis was changed to provide care for children of broken homes.

In 1957 a high school co-ed cottage was opened. Some college scholarships proved available. In 1966 a "family-type" cottage was established in order to maintain normal family groupings.

It is governed by an independent board, licensed in Illinois by the Department of Children and Family Services, and is a member of the Child Care Association and an approved Benevolent Institution of the Free Methodist Church. Its assets total a quarter of a million dollars. The annual budget is $125,000, one-half coming from contributions. Its purpose is to provide security, understanding, love and protection in an evangelical Christian environment so that its fifty children may become useful citizens.

BYRON S. LAMSON

WOODSWORTH, JAMES (1843-1917), Canadian minister, was born in Toronto, Canada West (Ontario) in 1843, the son of Richard Woodsworth, a Wesleyan local preacher. He studied theology with his district chairman and was ordained in 1868. He married Esther Shaver of Cooksville, near Toronto. There were six children, of whom James Shaver, the eldest, became a Methodist minister and leader of the Co-operative Commonwealth Federation.

After ordination Woodsworth served on several circuits in Ontario; in 1886 he was appointed superintendent of home missions in Manitoba and the Northwest, a post which he held for twenty-nine years. In this interval sixty-eight circuits and one Conference expanded into 650 circuits and three Conferences. Woodsworth's duties involved travel throughout the western provinces by all types of conveyances. During his first four years alone he travelled many thousands of miles.

To staff the growing mission field Woodsworth frequently visited Britain, where he recruited a large number of men who became known as "Woodsworth's Boys." He was a delegate to all GENERAL CONFERENCES between 1886 and 1915 and to the ECUMENICAL METHODIST CONFERENCE of 1891. Not content with territorial expansion, he laid the foundation of religious and social work among the urban immigrant population.

For his great services he was given an honorary degree by VICTORIA UNIVERSITY. Woodsworth's memory lives in the great foothold he established for Methodism in western Canada, a legacy incorporated in The United Church of Canada.

J. Maclean, *Vanguards of Canada*. Toronto: Methodist Missionary Society, 1918.
J. H. Riddell, *Middle West*. 1946.
J. Woodsworth, *Thirty Years in the Canadian North-West*. Toronto: McClelland, 1917.   F. W. ARMSTRONG

WOODSWORTH, JAMES SHAVER (1874-1942), Canadian Methodist minister and political leader, was born near Toronto, on July 29, 1874, to JAMES WOODSWORTH and Esther Josephine Shaver. He was educated at Wesley College (B.A., 1896) and VICTORIA COLLEGE (B.D., 1900), and for one year he studied at Oxford University.

Following in his father's footsteps he became a probationer in 1896. To this task he brought new insights derived from close investigation of social problems, especially in LONDON. He was appalled at what he saw; depressed by the apparent feebleness of English Methodism and made aware of the vast disparity between his own beliefs and practices and those prevalent in British society. Although he accepted ordination in 1900, he became increasingly dubious about his position.

By 1902, Woodsworth was convinced that his growing disbelief in the accepted doctrines of his church disqualified him for the ministry. He attempted to resign in 1902 and again in 1907, but was dissuaded by his brethren who secured his appointment to the All Peoples' Mission, an institution designed to handle the acute social and moral problems of multi-ethnic WINNIPEG. Woodsworth's work in the mission confirmed and strengthened his interest in humanitarian reform.

JAMES S. WOODSWORTH

In part because of Woodsworth's teaching, Manitoba enacted compulsory school attendance legislation and established a system of juvenile courts. In 1909 he published *Strangers Within Our Gates*, a plea for understanding of the European immigrants who were flooding into Winnipeg and the West. In the same year he began to write for a labor newspaper *The Voice*. Increasingly he urged the Methodist Church to take the lead in social reform. The response was greater, however, outside his church than within it. In 1913 he became secretary of the new Social Welfare League, and three years later he became director of the Bureau of Social Research founded by the Prairie Provinces. These posts enabled him to acquaint a wide circle with the immense social stresses confronting a changing Canada.

Unfortunately for Woodsworth, his political opinions were as radical as his views on social questions. When he publicized his pacifist convictions he was forced out of his post, and after a short term as a missionary his brethren willingly accepted the resignation which he had long since proffered on serious theological grounds. Methodism's loss was, however, Canada's gain; as a political reformer Woodsworth continued to symbolize the deepest springs of Christian teaching.

After his resignation, he acquired first-hand knowledge of the worker's world as a Vancouver longshoreman. Spring of 1919 found him in Winnipeg again. His support for the general strike, by which the city was paralyzed, brought arrest for seditious libel, a charge for which he was never tried. It was fitting that in December, 1921, he should win election for Centre Winnipeg to the Canadian House of Commons. His grateful constituents regularly re-elected him until his death.

As an M.P. in the 1920's, Woodsworth fought manfully for humane treatment of the underprivileged and the persecuted. His small group was largely responsible for the introduction of old-age pensions in 1926 and, after

1929, for drawing attention to the desperate plight of the unemployed. When all those concerned to find a radical solution to the depression came together to form the Cooperative Commonwealth Federation in 1932, Woodsworth became its first leader.

From 1932 to 1939, he sought unceasingly and sacrificially to achieve political power and to maintain his crusade against social abuses. The outbreak of war, however, brought his resignation, for he could not join his followers in supporting Canadian participation in it. His political career was effectively at an end. Two years later his frail constitution ceased to function.

J. S. Woodsworth was not so much a socialist as a great Christian, who strove with all his strength to translate and apply the Gospel precept of charity to his own community. As such he was honored by his opponents and his friends, and he left an enduring legacy.

G. MacInnis, *J. S. Woodsworth: A Man to Remember.* Toronto: Macmillan, 1953.
K. W. McNaught, *A Prophet in Politics.* Toronto: University of Toronto Press, 1959.   F. W. ARMSTRONG

WOODVILLE, MISSISSIPPI, U.S.A., in the southwest part of the state, is the site of the oldest Methodist church building in MISSISSIPPI. The congregation was organized about 1810. The present building has been in continuous use as a place of worship since its construction in 1824, and Woodville has been a station appointment since 1835. The MISSISSIPPI ANNUAL CONFERENCE sessions of 1831, 1835, 1843, and 1858 were held there. Plans were made in the 1831 session for setting off part of the Mississippi Conference as the ALABAMA CONFERENCE. ENOCH MARVIN served as pastor in Woodville shortly before his election to the episcopacy. It is the home church of the McGehee family, featured in Stark Young's novel, *So Red the Rose.* Judge EDWARD McGEHEE, charter member of the congregation and well-known church and institutional benefactor, had the first standard gauge railroad in America built into Woodville. This railway is still in use. Also there is the site of the former Woodville Female Academy, later known as Edward McGehee College, a girls' school related to the Methodist Church, serving from 1840-1912. The church and community have been served by many outstanding ministers and laymen.

J. G. Jones, *Mississippi Conference.* 1887. J. A. LINDSEY

WOODWARD, MAX WAKERLEY (1908-   ), British minister, was born in England, Jan. 28, 1908, son of Alfred and Mabel (Wakerley) Woodward. He was educated at HANDSWORTH COLLEGE, BIRMINGHAM, England, 1926-29. On Nov. 3, 1934, he was married to Kathleen May Beaty. Four children were born to this union: Gillian (Mrs. Sidney Porter), John, David and Peter. In 1933 Woodward was admitted into full connection in the British CONFERENCE. For thirteen years (1929-42) he was a missionary to CEYLON, and from 1942 until 1946 served in the British Navy. He served pastorates in Leamington, Finsbury Park, Harrow, and Wesley's Chapel, LONDON from 1946 to 1964. In 1964 he was elected Secretary of the WORLD METHODIST COUNCIL Resident in Great Britain, a responsibility he had carried along with his pastorate on a part-time basis since 1961. He gave full-time service to the Council from 1964-69.

Who's Who in The Methodist Church, 1966. LEE F. TUTTLE

WOOLSEY, THOMAS (1818-1894), Canadian Methodist missionary, was born in Gainsborough, Lincolnshire. He moved to London at an early age and became a member of the CITY ROAD CHAPEL. Before he came to CANADA in 1852, he had been a local preacher for fifteen years. Received on trial in 1853, he was ordained in 1855 and appointed to Fort Edmonton (Alberta).

In 1856 Woolsey re-occupied a mission on Pigeon Lake that had been abandoned by Benjamin Sinclair. About 1860 he began a new mission at Smoking (Smoky) Lake. Two years later the superintendent, GEORGE McDOUGALL, permitted him to move to a new site named Victoria Mission, now Pakan, Alberta.

In 1864, Woolsey left the west for England. On his return he served on various charges in Ontario and Quebec, most of which were Indian missions.

Although he found life in the west difficult, Woosley was a faithful pastor and evangelist. He made use of Evans' syllabic Bible and served as a doctor to the Indians. His devoted spirit and genial personality made a deep and lasting impression. Superannuated in 1885, he lived in Toronto until his death in 1894.

G. M. Hutchinson, *The Roots of the Province.* Telfordville: Alberta Conference, 1955.
J. MacLean, *Vanguards of Canada.* Toronto: Methodist Missionary Society, 1918.   J. E. NIX

WOON, WILLIAM (1804-1858), NEW ZEALAND Methodist minister, was of Cornish birth, and served a lengthy apprenticeship to the printing trade. In 1831 he went to TONGA as a lay agent and there did valuable work translating and printing the Scriptures. Because of ill health he purposed returning to England. However, when the ship called at Hokianga in January 1834, he was persuaded to remain with the New Zealand Mission. For some years (except for a brief term at Kawhia, 1834-35), he was in charge of the Mission Printing Press at Mangungu. Later he was again appointed to Kawhia (1844) and then to South Taranaki (1846-53). Possessed of a fine singing voice, he was affectionately known among the Maoris as "the Organ."

In 1853, he retired to Wanganui, where he resided until his death on Sept. 22, 1858.

C. H. Laws, *First Years at Hokianga.* Wesley Historical Society, New Zealand, 1945.   L. R. M. GILMORE

WOOSLEY, OSCAR VERGUS (1881-1958), American layman and educator, was born in WINSTON-SALEM, N. C., April 10, 1881, the son of John E. and Pauline Sophia (Fishel) Woosley. He was educated at Guilford College, receiving his A.B. degree in 1905.

After college he became a teacher in the public school system of NORTH CAROLINA. In 1917 O. V. Woosley, always a deeply consecrated layman, entered the full-time service of the M.E. Church, South, as superintendent of the WESTERN NORTH CAROLINA CONFERENCE Sunday School Board. His wife was Nell Maxwell, whom he married in 1918.

After directing the Christian education work of the Western North Carolina Conference for more than twelve years, he resigned this position to become superintendent and treasurer of the Children's Home, Winston-Salem, N. C. He continued in this capacity until his retirement in 1954.

Oscar Woosley was a distinctive personality, possessed

of a contagious enthusiasm which he applied to all of his activities. He served his Church as a trustee of both BREVARD COLLEGE and the Methodist Home for the Aged, member of Conference and General Boards of Hospitals and Homes, delegate to the GENERAL CONFERENCE from 1930 to 1952, and member of the 1939 Uniting Conference.

He died Jan. 12, 1958.

WORCESTER, MASSACHUSETTS, U.S.A., located forty miles west of BOSTON on the Blackstone River and Lake Quinsigamond, was settled in 1713. It is known today both as an industrial area with some 700 manufacturing establishments, and as a cultural center with five colleges, two junior colleges, and more than 100 buildings for religious use. Once the home of the inventors Elias Howe and Eli Whitney, and of "the father of rocketry," Robert H. Goddard, here is located the American Antiquarian Society (founded 1812) and the Worcester Art Museum.

On Oct. 15, 1740 GEORGE WHITEFIELD preached in Worcester. ASBURY visited here on several occasions but there is no record of his preaching. The first class was organized by local preacher William Routledge in 1833. From a rented room the group moved to the Town Hall. The following year Emory Washburn was permitted to organize thirteen people into the "Methodist Episcopal Religious Society in the Town of Worcester." GEORGE PICKERING was appointed pastor in 1835; a church was erected in 1837; here the NEW ENGLAND CONFERENCE met in 1841. Destroyed by fire in 1844, a new church facing the Common was built in 1846. By 1876 there were five Methodist churches in Worcester with Grace and Trinity the most influential. Grace Nies Fletcher's book *In My Father's House*, described Worcester Methodism in these years. In 1923 the congregations of Grace and Trinity merged to form Wesley Church, located at the heart of the city in a monumental Gothic edifice.

Today there are six Methodist churches in Worcester: Aldersgate, Covenant, Epworth, Quinsigamond, St. Andrew's and Wesley with an aggregate membership of 3,720 and 1,062 students enrolled in the church schools.

Wesley Church is the largest Methodist church in New England and one of the largest in the NORTHEASTERN JURISDICTION.

As the mother church in the city, it inherits the heritage of a line of forerunners that stretches back to the Church-in-the-Meadows, the first Methodist building in the city. A Francis Asbury window commemorates the visit of the Bishop.

Wesley Church is a well-preserved million dollar structure. The stained glass windows are outstanding in their beauty and perfection. Among them is a Wesley family window; one for the first bishops to INDIA, CHINA, and AFRICA; one for early American Methodists and circuit riders; and windows for prominent women of the Bible and of modern times. The *Te Deum Laudamus* window in the chancel and the rose window over the entrance are in the highest traditions of the stained glass art. Today the church carries on a vigorous ministry in the inner-city as well as to people of the entire area. Religious education, music and the pulpit are the chief avenues of creative ministry. The 1970 report indicated 2,022 members.

General Minutes, UMC, 1970.
Minutes of the New England Conference.
M. Simpson, *Cyclopaedia.* 1878.   ERNEST R. CASE
                                          JAMES R. UHLINGER

WORKMAN, HERBERT BROOK (1862-1951), British Methodist historical scholar and educationalist, was born at Peckham in LONDON in 1862. He was educated at KINGS-WOOD SCHOOL and Owen's College, Manchester, and entered the Wesleyan Methodist ministry in 1885. After serving in various English circuits he went to WEST-MINSTER Teachers' Training COLLEGE, of which he was principal from 1903 to 1930. He was elected president of the Wesleyan Methodist CONFERENCE in 1930; he had given the FERNLEY LECTURE in 1906, taking as his subject *Persecution in the Early Church,* a book which is still in print. He was Cole Lecturer at VANDERBILT UNIVERSITY, Nashville, Tenn., 1916, and temporary professor of Methodist Church history at the University of Chicago in 1927. He was awarded the Litt.D. of London University, and the D.D. (Hon.) of Aberdeen University. His main historical interests lay in the medieval period. He published *The Letters of John Hus* (1904), *The Evolution of the Monastic Ideal* (1913), and a two-volume study of *John Wyclif* (1926). In 1900 he produced *Christian Thought to the Reformation,* a work often used as a textbook by those teaching the history of Christian doctrine. In 1909 he wrote for the *New History of Methodism,* of which he was one of the editors, an introductory chapter entitled "The Place of Methodism in the Catholic Church." This was afterward published separately, and is famous as an attempt to state the place of Methodism in the progress and development of the Catholic Church, over against a school of theologians, more common in 1900 than it is now, who denied that Methodism was essentially a part of the life history of the Catholic Church at all. "In the story of Methodism," he wrote, "only the blind and the irreverent can fail to discern the presence and power of the Master."

Townsend, Workman and Eayrs, *New History.* 1909.

JOHN KENT

WORLD COUNCIL OF CHURCHES, with principal headquarters in GENEVA, SWITZERLAND, is a fellowship of more than 200 churches (communions, denominations) of Protestant, Anglican, Orthodox, and Old Catholic confessions. "They gather for study, witness, service, and the advancement of unity."

The churches in the Council come from more than eighty countries living under many forms of government, and with many varieties of Christian tradition and culture. But their basis of membership in the Council is one and simple: "The World Council of Churches is a fellowship of churches which confess the Lord Jesus Christ as God and Saviour according to the Scriptures, and therefore seek to fulfill together their common calling to the glory of the one God, Father, Son, and Holy Spirit."

The Council affirms that it is not a superchurch since it does not legislate for its members; rather it is the organization through which the churches enter into dialogue with each other about creed, ministry, government, program, and missionary work; helps them seek unity; and unites them in meeting human need and in witnessing to the Lordship of Christ.

The World Council of Churches had its earliest rootage in the international missionary conference in Edinburgh, SCOTLAND, in 1910; and later rootage in the INTERNATIONAL MISSIONARY COUNCIL (founded in 1921), the Faith and Order Movement (1927), and the Life and Work Movement (1925). The work of all three is now in-

corporated in the World Council. The general assemblies of the Council (held every six or seven years) have been: Amsterdam, the Netherlands, 1948; EVANSTON, Illinois, 1954; New Delhi, INDIA, 1961; UPPSALA, Sweden, 1968.

American and British Methodists have been active in leadership in the World Council of Churches since its formation. JOHN R. MOTT, who presided over the Edinburgh Missionary Conference in 1910, was honorary president of the Council when first organized; and presidents of the Council have included Bishop G. BROMLEY OXNAM, Bishop SANTE UBERTO BARBIERI (Argentina), and Dr. CHARLES C. PARLIN. The Council has an American office at 475 Riverside Drive, New York City.

W. W. REID

WORLD FAMILY LIFE COMMITTEE is an outgrowth of the Family Life Conferences in the United States. Bishop HAZEN G. WERNER was appointed by the GENERAL CONFERENCE of 1964 to help develop among the Methodists across the world an awareness of Christian Family Living in which "the Christian family is committed to behavior in keeping with Christian ideals for family relations, community life, and national and world citizenship." (*Discipline,* T.M.C., 1964, Paragraph 1821.)

Regional family life conferences were held in INDIA, KOREA, AFRICA, and other parts of the world. As an outgrowth of these, the First World Methodist Conference on Family Life met in LONDON, Aug. 17, 1966, and this was preceded by a four-day seminar for selected delegates from thirty-six countries. Officers were selected from seven areas of the world, and this group became a committee of the World Methodist Council.

Discipline, TMC, 1964.

FRANCES NALL

WORLD FEDERATION OF METHODIST WOMEN. The idea of the World Federation of Methodist Women came from Asia in the 1920's. In 1923, HELEN KIM, later President of EWHA UNIVERSITY in SEOUL, KOREA, was a student at OHIO WESLEYAN UNIVERSITY, and she had been asked by the Executive Committee of The WOMAN'S FOREIGN MISSIONARY SOCIETY (ME) to speak at DES MOINES, Iowa. Frightened by this assignment, she went to the prayer room before her speech. As she prayed she had a vision of a world fellowship of all Christian women. She entered the sanctuary of the large church, was ushered to the platform, and gave her famous address. "To the Women of the World." "This is the time of times," she said, "when women of the world need to come together into a Women's International Association with its membership including delegates from all kinds of organizations of women in each country." This in 1923, was a revolutionary idea to many American women, but a few, including Mrs. THOMAS NICHOLSON, President of the Woman's Foreign Missionary Society, had the same idea and wondered how it could be implemented.

Four years later, in 1927, the Chinese women were celebrating the tenth anniversary of the China Women's Society, and they too wanted an international fellowship of women. They wrote to their sponsoring organization, The Woman's Missionary Council, saying, "What a work! What a sisterhood it is! The Jubilee in America! The tenth anniversary in China! Americans working in China! China working in Africa, and the women of the whole wide world joining hands to bring in the Kingdom of God. The creation of a world sisterhood begins when the field of service is entered. It is indeed a thrilling story—this cementing of friendship with women and girls of other races and conditions of life, a friendship with women which will last through eternity because it is founded on the love of Jesus Christ." The Woman's Missionary Council took up this challenge and kept in close touch with its conference organizations around the world.

Two years later, the Woman's Foreign Missionary Society acted on the plan of the Korean women and organized its International Department. The women of fourteen countries asked that a separate organization be formed in which each autonomous unit could share equally with all others. On Oct. 26, 1939, the First Assembly of The World Federation of Methodist Women met. Delegates from twenty-seven lands signed the charter and constitution. The basis of membership was: "A fellowship of such organized groups as will accept Jesus Christ as the revelation of God and the Savior of Mankind and will affirm their purpose, 'To Know Him and to Make Him Known.'"

When the three Methodist churches of the United States came together, the World Federation of Methodist Women was recognized by the 1940 GENERAL CONFERENCE as an official organization of The Methodist Church, and the WOMAN'S SOCIETY OF CHRISTIAN SERVICE became a unit of the World Federation.

In 1944, the Second Assembly of The World Federation of Methodist Women re-affirmed the motto with a new wording, "To Know Christ and Make Him Known." The Scripture (Revelation 22:2) was chosen as the special scripture for the new organization, and The Tree of Life, suggested by Lucy Wang of China, became the official symbol of the World Federation.

In 1948, the third Assembly of The World Federation met at Boston, Mass., and a twelve-point program was adopted as the working basis for all units. This program is symbolized by "The Tree of Life" with its twelve fruits "to His Glory": evangelism, medical work, education, literature, children, youth, home and family life, rural projects, economic justice, international friendship, temperance, and world peace.

In 1952 the fourth Assembly gathered at Berkeley, Calif., with delegates from twenty-nine units meeting for a three-day seminar to exchange ideas, program materials, and to deepen their spiritual lives. The assembly voted to ask other Methodist groups, besides those connected with the American Methodist church, to join the World Federation.

In 1956 the new world-wide World Federation of Methodist Women was organized at Lake Junaluska, N. C., and it became known as the First Assembly. At this time a new constitution was signed by forty-one units representing the women of the British tradition, Australasian, and African, both in United States and on the continent bearing the name Africa, in addition to those who were already members of the Federation. This federation became an affiliate of the WORLD METHODIST COUNCIL and set its meeting date three days prior and at the same place as the quinquennial World Methodist Council meeting. Every women's organization whose parent body is a member of the World Methodist Council was eligible for membership in The World Federation of Methodist Women.

In 1961 the World Federation met before the meeting of the World Methodist Council in Oslo, Norway. There were delegates from fifty-two units in forty-seven countries. It was voted to include women from churches united and uniting, if one of their constituting bodies had been Methodist.

In 1966 the Third Assembly of the World Federation was held at Southlands College, near London, England. There were sixty units representing fifty-five countries (Rhodesia with two units, and the United States with five). A leadership training for all women, especially in the developing countries, was launched. Plans included: 1) A representative of the World Federation to become a seminar assistant for in-service training at the Methodist Office for United Nations for at least a year, beginning in the fall of 1966. (Other seminar assistants to be chosen for training later.) 2) Regionals for leadership training to be held in various areas of the world. 3) Representatives from various parts of the world to be chosen as observers at commissions of The United Nations, to be a part of the Churches Commission on International Affairs of the WORLD COUNCIL OF CHURCHES quota. The new officers for 1966-1971 represented four continents, the president from Asia, the vice-president from Africa, the secretary from Australia, and the treasurer from North America. The sixty units are organized into nine areas, each with a President, and four of the areas with vice-presidents who also help implement the program. The World Federation with its sixty units and six million members has became relevant for today's needs, problems, and for tomorrow's possibilities.

FRANCES NALL

WORLD METHODIST CONFERENCES began under the name Ecumenical Methodist Conference in the year 1881. These conferences continued at ten-year intervals through 1931, when, because of World War II, the Seventh Conference was delayed until 1947.

The origin of the Ecumenical Methodist Conference is an interesting historical study in itself. On May 31, 1876, the GENERAL CONFERENCE of the M.E. Church sitting in BALTIMORE, Md., "adopted a preamble and resolutions setting forth grounds on which it appeared desirable that a conference should be called together, representing all the diversified bodies of Methodists which had sprung up throughout the world."

The committee which was appointed by the 1876 General Conference of the M.E. Church corresponded with the different Methodist churches of America. There was such unanimity of opinion that there should be such a conference, that in May 1878 a letter inviting their concurrence was sent to the British Conference of the Wesleyan Methodists. A British committee was appointed to consider the proposal and report to the conference in 1879. A favorable report was made and was adopted by the British Conference in session in BIRMINGHAM, England in August 1879.

As a result of committee activity in all parts of the Methodist world, there assembled in CINCINNATI, Ohio, on May 6, 1880, "such a combined committee of Methodist churches as had never before come together." One of the most interesting aspects of this meeting was the fact that "for the first time since 1844, when the American church was divided, did Bishops of the Methodist Episcopal Church, South, meet at the same board with Bishops of the Methodist Episcopal Church."

With such planning and interest as a background the first Ecumenical Methodist Conference opened on Sept. 7, 1881 at City Road Chapel, LONDON. There were delegates and representatives from twenty-eight different Methodist denominations present.

The Conference lasted for twelve days, hearing many sermons and addresses dealing with general themes of Methodist interests. The organization of the conference was handled by a business committee of twenty persons selected equally from the four divisions of the Methodist world. As in all subsequent conferences, this first one did not seek to legislate for or invade the autonomy of the various churches represented. Instead it sought to deepen the fellowship of Methodist peoples over the barriers of race, nationality, and language.

The Second Ecumenical Methodist Conference met in the Metropolitan M.E. Church, WASHINGTON, D. C., Oct. 7-20, 1891. The program pattern followed was essentially that of the First Conference, except that the organizational structure began to become more evident. The list of officers reveals that there were twenty-five presidents and four secretaries.

The Third Conference was once again held at City Road, London, Sept. 4-17, 1901. The list of presidents was reduced to thirteen with the four secretaries.

The first departure from the "pattern of location" which had been alternating between England and the United States occurred in 1911 when the Fourth Ecumenical Methodist Conference was held in the Metropolitan Methodist Church of TORONTO, CANADA. The dates were Oct. 4-17, 1911. On this occasion the number of presidents was increased to thirty with the usual four secretaries.

The Fifth Conference returned to England in 1921. This time the location was changed from City Road to Central Hall, Westminster, London. The number of presidents was again reduced, this time to twenty-two, with the four secretaries. There was, however, another change in the conference format with the number of days reduced to ten—Sept. 5-16, 1921.

Wesley Memorial Church, ATLANTA, Ga., was the site of the Sixth Conference, Oct. 16-25, 1931. Again the length of the sessions was shortened. There were fifteen presidents with three secretaries and one associate secretary.

The sixteen-year interval between the Sixth and Seventh Ecumenical Conferences necessitated considerable change in organization. Many of the leaders of 1931 were passing off the scene by the time the Conference met in Springfield, Mass., Sept. 24—Oct. 2, 1947. Names of such leaders as Bishop IVAN LEE HOLT, HAROLD ROBERTS, OSCAR T. OLSON, Bishop PAUL N. GARBER, ELMER T. CLARK, Bishop S. L. GREENE, MALDWYN L. EDWARDS, ERIC W. BAKER, Stanley Leyland, W. E. SANGSTER, Wesley Boyd, CHARLES C. PARLIN, EDWIN L. JONES, RALPH W. SOCKMAN, E. BENSON PERKINS, J. B. WEBB, Setareki Tuilovoni, Bishop W. J. WALLS and many others who were to become the mainstays of the Conference, were becoming prominent in its affairs.

Some of the ideas which had strong support in this session were the organization of the WORLD COUNCIL OF CHURCHES, a more effective evangelistic witness, stronger and more frequent contacts between various sections of the Methodist world and a modernized structure in keeping with other World Confessional Organizations.

Looking to these changes, the following report of the Committee on reorganization was presented:

There should be a reorganization of the Ecumenical Methodist Conference, but in order that there may not be too much of a break with the past we propose as officers, to serve until the next Ecumenical Conference: two presidents, two vice-presidents, two secretaries, two treasurers.

Officers elected were:

Chairmen: Bishop Ivan Lee Holt, Wilbert F. Howard
Vice-Chairmen: Bishop Paul N. Garber, A. Victor Murray
Secretaries: Oscar Thomas Olson, Harold Roberts
Treasurers: M. S. Davage, Benjamin Gregory

The Eighth session of the Ecumenical Methodist Conference met in OXFORD, England, Aug. 28—Sept. 7, 1951. It was at this session that the name was changed to World Methodist Council and the Conference continued as the inspirational segment of the Council/Conference sessions. A constitution was adopted and the decision was made to meet at five year intervals. The officers elected were

President: Bishop Ivan Lee Holt
Vice-President: Harold Roberts
The Secretariat: Elmer T. Clark and E. Benson Perkins
Treasurer: Duncan Coomer
Associate Treasurer: Edwin L. Jones

The Ninth World Methodist Council/Conference met at LAKE JUNALUSKA, N. C., U.S.A., Aug. 27—Sept. 12, 1956. The officers elected at this time were: Harold Roberts, President; Bishop Ivan Lee Holt, Past President; Bishop FRED P. CORSON, Oscar T. Olson, Charles C. Parlin, Bishop S. L. Greene, Mrs. OTTILIA DE O. CHAVES, J. B. Webb, James S. Mather, A. HAROLD WOOD, Vice-Presidents; Elmer T. Clark and E. Benson Perkins, Secretaries; Edwin L. Jones and L. A. Ellwood, Treasurers. During this session the World Methodist Council headquarters building at Lake Junaluska was dedicated.

The Tenth World Methodist Council/Conference was held for the first time on the European continent at OSLO, Norway, Aug. 17-25, 1961. In Council sessions, the constitution was revised, and new officers were elected as follows:

President: Bishop Fred P. Corson
Past Presidents: Harold Roberts and Bishop Ivan Lee Holt
Vice-Presidents: Bishop Roy H. Short, Bishop Odd Hagen, Eric W. Baker, J. B. Webb, Bishop Sante Uberto Barbieri, Oscar T. Olson, Frank Hambly, B. M. Chrystall, Charles C. Parlin, Mrs. R. J. Latham, Bishop Herbert Bell Shaw
General Secretaries: Lee F. Tuttle and Max W. Woodward
Secretaries Emeritus: Elmer T. Clark and E. Benson Perkins
Treasurers: Edwin L. Jones and L. A. Ellwood

The Eleventh World Methodist Council/Conference met at Westminster, Central Hall, London, England, Aug. 18-26, 1966. More than 2,000 Council Members, Conference delegates and accredited visitors from more than sixty countries were present. The officers elected were:

President: Bishop Odd Hagen
Past Presidents: Bishop Fred P. Corson, Harold Roberts, Bishop Ivan Lee Holt
Vice-Presidents: Eric Baker, Bernard Chrystall, Carlos T. Gattinoni, Cecil F. Gribble, D. T. Niles, Patrocinio Ocampo, Charles C. Parlin, Bishop Herbert Bell Shaw, Hugh B. Sherlock, Bishop Roy H. Short, J. B. Webb

General Secretaries: Lee F. Tuttle, Max W. Woodward
Secretaries Emeritus: Elmer T. Clark, E. Benson Perkins
Treasurers: Edwin L. Jones, L. A. Ellwood

The most important action was the appointment of a committee with strong powers to recommend and guide restructuring of the Council/Conference so that it would become more fully representative of the entire world. Action in this direction was set in motion so as to become the main work of the Twelfth Council/Conference to be held in DENVER, Colo., U.S.A. in 1971.

During the quadrennium 1966-71 the President, Bishop ODD HAGEN, died, and Charles C. Parlin was elected to fill out his term of office.

Proceedings of the Conferences.   LEE F. TUTTLE

WORLD METHODIST COUNCIL is an association of twenty-one different Methodist denominational groups at work in eighty-six countries of the world. According to its purpose as stated in its constitution, "it does not seek to legislate for them nor to invade their autonomy. Rather it exists to serve them and to give unity to their witness and enterprise."

Although the name World Methodist Council was adopted in 1951, the Council dates from 1881 when the first Ecumenical Methodist Conference met in LONDON, England, with some 400 delegates from thirty Methodist bodies throughout the world in attendance. As the Ecumenical Methodist Conference, this world organization convened at ensuing ten-year intervals, with the exception of the 1941 Conference, which because of World War II was not held until 1947.

The 1947 Conference, which was the seventh such gathering, changed the interval at which the Conferences were held. The eighth Conference met in 1951, and since that time the interval between meetings has been five years. It was at the 1951 Conference in OXFORD, England, that the name was changed from Ecumenical Conference to World Methodist Conference. Organizational changes were also brought about then which made the World Methodist Council similar in form to other world conciliar organizations.

With the name change there came also the setting up of a permanent secretariat with headquarters in both the United States and Great Britain. Two secretaries were elected, but the administration of the council was unified by the selection of only one set of officers. The first officers of the Council were Bishop IVAN LEE HOLT, President; HAROLD ROBERTS, Vice-President; EDWIN L. JONES and L. A. Ellwood, Treasurers; and ELMER T. CLARK and E. BENSON PERKINS, Secretaries.

In 1953 by authority of the World Executive Committee and the Executive Committee of Section XIII, representing The Methodist Church, U.S.A., headquarters in America were established at LAKE JUNALUSKA, N. C., and a handsome stone headquarters building was erected. This building, which contains offices, a library, a reading room and one of the outstanding collections of Wesleyana in the world, was dedicated at the Ninth World Methodist Conference which was held at Lake Junaluska in 1956. Indicating something of the growth of the Council, the headquarters building has twice been enlarged to take care of the expanding work and completing the architectural design.

At the OSLO World Conference in 1961, LEE F. TUTTLE

became the first full-time Secretary of the council, succeeding Elmer T. Clark. At this same Conference MAX W. WOODWARD was elected to succeed E. Benson Perkins, but remained on a part-time basis until 1964. From that time until 1969, he gave full time to the work of the Council. In 1969 Lee F. Tuttle became the single General Secretary with a new title. The office of GENEVA Secretary was created for the administrative officer of the Geneva, Switzerland office.

While the format of the eleven Conferences has changed considerably with an increasingly serious purpose, the Conferences continue to hold tremendous appeal to Methodists from throughout the world. The 1966 Conference in London officially registered 2,090 delegates and Council Members from sixty-four countries of the world, and there were hundreds who attended unofficially.

In 1951 at Oxford an extensive program of publishing was planned including a *Who's Who in Methodism*, an *Album of Methodist History*, an annotated edition of the *Journal and Letters of Francis Asbury*, and an *Encyclopedia of World Methodism*. This program of publication has been duly carried out with the publication of this *Encyclopedia*.

Since 1946 the Council has sponsored a program of ministerial exchanges between Methodist ministers of different countries for both long and short periods. This exchange program has been highly successful and continues to grow rapidly. What started with exchanges between British and American Methodist ministers has now reached out to include GERMANY, SWITZERLAND, SWEDEN, INDIA, NEW ZEALAND, CANADA, and other countries.

Within the past decade an important contribution has been made to Methodist theologians through the OXFORD INSTITUTE OF METHODIST THEOLOGICAL STUDIES, held at four-year intervals at Lincoln College, Oxford, England. On each occasion 100 theologians representing all areas of the world participate by invitation in this enterprise. Three such institutes have been held.

WORLD PARISH is the official periodical of the Council and is published nine times each year under the editorship of the Secretary resident in the United States. Since the new format was adopted in mid-1962, circulation has increased from 1,200 to 7,000 and continues its growth. News of Methodism in all parts of the world makes up the contents of this periodical.

The Council has been actively involved in every phase of the ECUMENICAL MOVEMENT through close consultation and cooperation with the WORLD COUNCIL OF CHURCHES, national and regional councils, as well as being the agency responsible for Methodist observers at the second Vatican Council from 1962 until its conclusion in 1965. At the London World Conference in 1966, for the first time observers were present from the Roman Catholic Church by invitation. The Council also set up a committee to meet with a similar committee representing the Roman Catholic Church to conduct conversations at the world level.

One of the most important and potentially far-reaching decisions of the 1966 Council was the creation of a Committee on Structure and Program to review the past work of the World Methodist Council and to make recommendations to later Executive and Council meetings on expanded structure and procedure.

Proceedings of the Council/Conference.   LEE F. TUTTLE

WORLD MISSIONARY CONFERENCE, Edinburgh. (See ECUMENICITY AND THE METHODIST CHURCH.)

WORLD OUTLOOK, a monthly periodical, is the official organ of the BOARD OF MISSIONS of The United Methodist Church. It began publication under the name of *The Missionary Voice* in January 1911, as the official missionary periodical of the M.E. Church, South. The name was changed to *World Outlook* in May 1932.

In January 1932, a rotogravure picture section appeared, and when the name became *World Outlook* a cover in full color was added, and it became typographically the finest missionary magazine in the world.

The periodical always had two editors, a man and a woman, representing the two sections of the Board of Missions. When the three large Methodist bodies of American Methodism were unified in 1939, *World Outlook* became the official organ of the Board of Missions and Church Extension, although the Woman's Division started another publication, which was originally intended to publish mainly the study materials for the woman's societies. In 1964 *World Outlook* for the first time in its history was placed under the direction of one editor.

In February 1970, *World Outlook* merged with *New*, a publication of the Commission on Ecumenical Mission and Relation of the United Presbyterian Church in the U.S.A., to become *New/World Outlook*. Arthur J. Moore, Jr. is the editor.

ELMER T. CLARK

WORLD PARISH is the publication of the WORLD METHODIST COUNCIL. It is issued monthly and endeavors to publish news of events and happenings in worldwide Methodism. It is edited at the Methodist headquarters in LAKE JUNALUSKA, North Carolina.

N. B. H.

WORLD PEACE, COMMISSION ON, an agency of The Methodist Church, U.S.A., which was formally so named at the time of Methodist Union in 1939. The GENERAL CONFERENCE of the M.E. Church had set up a Committee on World Peace in 1924 for which very limited funds were available. This functioned largely through the staff of the BOARD OF EDUCATION. In 1928 the committee employed an executive secretary, but by 1932 the funds were no longer available for this purpose due to the severe economic depression.

In 1936 the General Conference Commission on World Peace of the M.E. Church was established with a limited budget and staff with its office in CHICAGO. This agency cooperated with other denominations and peace organizations in education concerning international issues and action on important matters of foreign policy. It established a permanent register for Methodist conscientious objectors.

At the time of church union in 1939, the Commission on World Peace became an established agency in The Methodist Church. During the years of World War II it cooperated closely with the COUNCIL OF BISHOPS and many other church agencies in the Crusade for a New World Order. This entailed large meetings across the country, local study of proposals for a United Nations permanent organization, and strong support for U. S. Senate ratification of the U.N. Charter drafted in 1945.

During the years after World War II, an active program of education concerning the United Nations and international organization was conducted, including the program of "seminars" on the U.N. in NEW YORK CITY. An office was established in the Carnegie International Peace Center, which later led to the idea of the Church Center for the United Nations. Prominent in the leadership of the Commission on World Peace over the years were RALPH W. SOCKMAN who served as Chairman for thirty years, ERNEST F. TITTLE, GEORGIA HARKNESS, Bishop G. BROMLEY OXNAM, and the Executive Secretary from 1936 to 1960, CHARLES F. BOSS, JR.

HERMAN WILL

WORLD SERVICE AND FINANCE, COUNCIL ON, of The United Methodist Church is an incorporated body which receives and administers the general funds of the church. The different Churches which have united to form The United Methodist Church have each had commissions and committees on general finance and general budgets, with elected or appointed treasurers to hold in trust and administer their necessary connectional funds.

After union and up until 1952, The Methodist Church had a general Commission on World Service and Finance, a corporation licensed under the laws of ILLINOIS. But the GENERAL CONFERENCE of 1952, following the recommendations of a survey commission which at that time made recommendations with reference to all agencies of the Church, directed that the name of the body should hereafter be the Council on World Service and Finance, and its name was so changed.

The *Discipline* specifies the membership on this powerful Council. Upon it at present are two bishops who are nominated by the COUNCIL OF BISHOPS, and two ministers and two lay persons from each JURISDICTION. There are also seven members at large, at least three of whom are women. These members are not, however, elected by the Jurisdictions, but by the General Conference itself, and no member of the Council not even a bishop, is eligible for membership on, or employment by, any other general agency in the Church—except the Church's Board of TRUSTEES.

The Council prepares and presents the report concerning the church-wide budget and assessments (which are due during each quadrennium) to the General Conference at the beginning of each quadrennium. It must also administer the huge funds which are entrusted to its keeping. The Council works out an equitable schedule of apportionment by which the total World Service budget is distributed and apportioned to the Annual Conferences. The General Conference, as final authority, takes these reports for its "action and determination."

Among the general funds administered by the Council are the World Service Fund, the General Administration Fund, the Episcopal Fund, and certain miscellaneous funds.

The **World Service Fund** represents that part of the general budget of the Church which is administered for the support of the executive agencies of the Church, such as missions, education and the general boards. The **General Administration Fund** provides for the expenses of the sessions of the General Conference, for those of the JUDICIAL COUNCIL, and for such committees and comissions as may be constituted by the General Conference apart from the World Service Boards and Agencies. This

Fund is apportioned on an equitable basis to the Annual Conferences after the General Conference has adopted it. No Annual Conference and no charge or local church is allowed to change or revise their apportionment for the general administration budget.

The **Episcopal Fund** is raised separately from all other funds and is considered a part of the money raised for ministerial support. It provides for the salaries and expenses of effective bishops, for the support of retired bishops, and for that of widows and minor children of deceased bishops. The Council on World Service and Finance recommends to each General Conference the amounts to be fixed as salaries and administrative expense of the effective bishops, and also for the pensions for retired bishops and the widows and minor children of deceased bishops.

Other general funds of The United Methodist Church are the Methodist Investment Fund administered by the National Division of the Board of Missions, and what is called the Temporary General Aid Fund used to supplement the pensions and salaries of the former Central Jurisdictional members. For these regulations *in re* these funds, the current *Discipline* must be referred to.

A Department of RECORDS AND STATISTICS is also administered under this Council, as well as a Convention Bureau and a TRANSPORTATION OFFICE.

In each Annual Conference, there is an Annual Conference Commission on World Service and Finance which has responsibilities within its own Conference for seeing that the general apportionments of World Service of the Church are properly apportioned out; and where an Annual Conference has also a separate budget, as most do, this must also be properly apportioned to the districts and charges. Usually the combined askings from the Council on World Service and those of the Annual Conference Commission on World Service are termed "World Service and Annual Conference Benevolences." Conference Commissions on World Service and Finance, unless they be directed otherwise, have the right to estimate the total amount necessary for the support of the district superintendents and to determine the amount needed for their salaries. Annual Conferences which wish to do so may, however, provide that the support for the respective district superintendents shall be made by the Board of District Stewards in each of the several districts.

Discipline, UMC, 1968.
N. B. Harmon, *Organization*. 1962.   N. B. H.

WORLD'S STUDENT CHRISTIAN FEDERATION. The Student Christian Movement (SCM) comprised the interrelated organizations promoting religious activity among young men and women of the colleges and universities from about the 1850's onward. (Among the organizations were the Young Men's Christian Association, American Intercollegiate Young Men's Christian Association, Interseminary Missionary Alliance, STUDENT VOLUNTEER MOVEMENT, and others.) The SCM was widespread, active not only in Britain and America, but GERMANY, Scandinavia, INDIA, CHINA, and elsewhere.

JOHN R. MOTT, a Methodist layman, did more than any other one person to bring the various SCM's into a world union and fellowship of Christian students under the name of the World's Student Christian Federation (WSCF). Others, such as James B. Reynolds and Luther D. Wishard, greatly helped.

Mott served for two years as an associate in the YMCA's college department, organizing conferences. In 1890 he assumed full responsibility for the work. Dwight L. Moody had impressed Mott with the possibility of a growing Christian unity through large (in conception and understanding) EVANGELISM; and Mott was further influenced while serving as executive secretary of the Student Volunteer Movement (SVM) by its missionary passion and world outreach. He began to think far beyond denominational lines. He became a secretary of the International Committee of the YMCA.

In 1891, at the Amsterdam meeting of the World's Alliance of the YMCA, Mott gave probably his first serious thought to developing a world fellowship of Christian students. He called together some student leaders from different lands to discuss the matter. By 1894 Mott was convinced that the time was ripe for a world-wide union of Christian students. He wanted to retain diversity, allowing for the richness of "particular genius and character" in the developing national SCM's. They were to be linked together in a simple yet effective Federation.

In August 1895, six men met together in Vadstena Castle, SWEDEN, to form the Federation. They represented five Student Movements: the American, the British, the German, the Scandinavian, and "The Student Christian Movement in Mission Lands," the last to include within the Federation all the non-Occidental Student Movements not closely organized at that time. They chose Karl Fries of Sweden to be chairman and John R. Mott as general secretary.

The Federation's purpose was to unite the SCM's of the world to lead students to become disciples of Jesus Christ as only Saviour and God, to quicken their spiritual life, and to enlist them in extending the Kingdom of Christ throughout the whole world. The Federation had no authority except the integrity and vision of its leaders. It could not command, but could suggest and serve. The Federation was evangelistic, influenced by the SVM's watchword, "The evangelization of the world in this generation."

The WSCF sought a unity, at home and abroad, transcending national and denominational lines, but encouraged each national Student Movement to develop along its own distinctive lines and under its own leadership. It emphasized the practical, for along with theological aspects it demanded action and service for the world-wide extension and establishment of the Kingdom of Christ.

The Federation's seventh conference, held in TOKYO in 1907, was the first international conference of any kind, secular or religious, to be held in the East.

The WSCF was influential in bringing into the ecumenical movement the influential Anglo-Catholic element of the Church of England. Also, the conference of the WSCF in Constantinople in 1911 drew the ancient Eastern Churches, for centuries largely isolated from Western Christendom, into touch with the emerging ecumenical movement. In common counsel and fellowship sat members of the Greek Orthodox, Syrian, Armenian, Coptic, Protestant, and Roman Catholic communions. The conference had the blessing of the Ecumenical Patriarch and other leaders of the ancient Eastern Churches. Its aim was to extend the SCM throughout the Near East, and student members of the Eastern Churches were welcomed to the movement. SCM's were organized in many more nations, such as Rumania, Serbia, Bulgaria, Greece, and Russia.

The WSCF suffered during the World Wars, but contributed greatly to European Student Relief, which sought to bring relief to starving fellow students. The WSCF also sought to help displaced persons and refugees. In the early 1920's, the SCM and YMCA fostered the Russian Student Christian Movement in Exile, following the migration or expulsion of at least a million White Russians into Europe.

The Student Movement produced a group of leaders who were to play a great role in the life of the Church. To name only a few, there were: Joseph H. Oldham, Nathan Söderblom, William Temple, John R. Mott, Robert Wilder, W. A. Visser 't Hooft, V. S. Azariah, and many others.

Lay movements, since they are not Churches, are not members of the WORLD COUNCIL OF CHURCHES (WCC). However, the constitution of the WCC provides for a consultative relationship with the WSCF and other lay movements.

David P. Gaines, *The World Council of Churches*. Peterborough, N.H.: Richard R. Smith Co., Inc., 1966.
William Richey Hogg, *Ecumenical Foundations*. New York: Harper and Brothers, 1952.
John R. Mott, *The World's Student Christian Federation*. New York: Association Press, 1947.
Ruth Rouse and Stephen C. Neill (eds.), *A History of the Ecumenical Movement 1517-1948*. Philadelphia: The Westminster Press, 1967.
                                                STEPHEN G. COBB

WORSHIP IN AMERICAN METHODISM, Informal Worship: As may be gathered from the account of worship as it developed in British Methodism, the CLASS MEETINGS, the BANDS, and the LOVE FEASTS gave Methodism a unique type of religious practice, which may be treated under the general head of worship. Their habits and methods of conduct became fixed and will be described below as they were in English Methodism. When JOHN WESLEY was criticized for certain of these practices, he replied, "These are prudential helps, grounded on reason, and experience, in order to apply the general rules given in the scripture to particular experiences" (*Works*, Emory edition, 1850, V., p. 1831). Class meetings especially became a powerful force for self-examination, which led to purification and forgiveness, and heightened the members' sense of duty and responsibility.

In Wesley's *Plain Account of the People Called Methodists* (*Works*, V., pp. 176-194), the reader will find a detailed description of the genesis of these meetings. Obviously, relying on James' exhortation (4:13-16), Wesley wrote:

In order to "confess our faults one to another" and "pray one for another" that we may be healed, we intend,
(1) to meet once a week, at the least.
(2) to come punctually at the hour appointed.
(3) to begin with singing and prayer; to speak each of us in order, freely and plainly, the true state of our souls, with the faults we have committed in thought, word, or deed, and the temptations we have felt since our last meeting.
(4) to desire some person among us (thence called the leader) to speak his own state first, and then to ask the rest, in order, as many and as searching questions as may be, concerning their state, sins, and temptations (*Works*, V., p. 183).

John Wesley, without realizing it, anticipated modern phraseology which has become known as "group therapy." The Wesley plan was to have the men "to meet me every Wednesday evening," and "the women on Sunday . . . that they might receive such particular instructions . . . as might be most needful for them." This has proved to be very wise. He summarized his directions by saying that no extensive rules were needed, except "let nothing spoken in this society be spoken again" (*Works*, V., p. 185). Thus men to men, women to women, they bared their inner feelings one to another, without embarrassment or worry about later gossip and tale-bearing.

The growth effect of these devotional meetings was notable. "They began 'to bear each others' burdens' and naturally to 'care for each other' . . . And 'speaking the truth in love, they grew up into Him in all things, who is the Head, even Chirst'" (*ibid.*, p. 180). So he added, "Many of these soon recovered the ground they had lost. Yea, they rose higher than before, being more watchful than ever, and more meek and lowly, as well as stronger in faith" (*ibid.*, p. 184).

American Methodists followed these British features and continued the Class Meetings, the Bands, and the Love Feasts as has been stated.

FRANCIS ASBURY in his *Journal* (I, p. 131) made this significant observation:

In meeting the Bands, I showed them the impropriety and danger of keeping their thoughts or fears of each other to themselves. This frustrates the design of Bands; produces coolness and jealousies toward each other; and is undoubtedly the policy of Satan.

Thus, what first appeared in English Methodism was continued in America. In addition to regular worship for large numbers, they had a type of confessional worship in small groups. The regular worship services were designed for the public; it aimed at large numbers and got them, and, as Asbury stated, it was aimed "to reach a decision."

But growth in the depth of Christian experience and in the sense of Christian duty was a further need for those who had reached a decision. This objective was carried out in the small meetings. Those who attended had to have a card, as we would now say they were "screened" by the leader. They met, men separately from women, the married separately from the unmarried. No doubt in carrying out these practices the poor preacher had meetings galore, but meetings held in this way must have had powerful influence on helping Methodists grow in the knowledge and grace of the Lord Jesus Christ; or as the Methodists then quaintly stated it, "going on to perfection."

Formal Worship. When John Wesley wrote to COKE, Asbury and the brethren in North America on Sept. 10, 1784, his letter contained this paragraph:

And I have prepared a liturgy little differing from that of the Church of England, (I think, the best constituted national church in the world) which I advise all the traveling preachers to use on the Lord's day, in all the congregations, reading the Litany only on Wednesdays and Fridays, and praying extempore on all other days. I also advise the Elders to administer The Supper of the Lord on every Lord's Day. (*Works*, p. 314)

It is strange that John Wesley, whose formality met so little favor in his missionary term in GEORGIA, and who himself was so informal in his preaching services of the

Methodist Meeting Houses, should have sent such a formal service of worship to the pioneers of the American frontier. It is not surprising that, as Bishop HARMON succinctly pointed out in his book, *The Rites and Ritual of Episcopal Methodism*, the American Methodists did not adopt Wesley's order of service for the Lord's Day nor the reading of the Litany on Wednesday and Friday. The ritual for the Lord's Supper, Baptism, and other occasional offices of the Church, however, were acceptable to the Americans.

That does not mean that there was no order in American worship. On Dec. 1, 1789, a "Council" composed of Coke and Asbury (Coke however was not present), and certain of the ELDERS, met to outline the working rules of the Church. In a manuscript copy of these "Proceedings of Bishop Asbury and Presiding Elders of The Methodist Episcopal Church in Council Assembled" (which is in the GARRETT THEOLOGICAL SEMINARY Library), item one of the purposes of their meeting was, "To render the time and form of public worship, as similar as possible through all their congregations."

Further on, the "proceedings" outline the various measures which should be followed throughout the connection. The second and third of these resolutions deal with worship, to wit:

2. Public worship shall commence at 10:00 o'clock on the Lord's Day, in all places where we have societies and regular preaching, if it be practicable, and if it be not, at 11:00 o'clock.
3. The exercise of public worship on the Lord's Day shall be singing, prayer and reading of the Holy Scriptures, with exhortation or reading a sermon in the absence of a preacher: the officiating person shall be appointed by the Elder, Deacon, or Traveling Preacher for the time being.

The General Conference record of 1792 carries this notation:

Question,   What directions shall be given for the establishment of uniformity in public worship amongst us?

Answer,   1. Let the morning service consist of singing and prayer, the reading of a chapter out of the Old Testament and another out of the New Testament, and preaching.
2. Let the afternoon service consist of singing, prayer, the reading of one chapter out of the Bible and preaching.
3. Let the evening service consist of singing, prayer and preaching.
4. But on the days of administering the Lord's Supper, the two chapters in the morning service may be omitted.
5. Let the Society be met, whenever practicable, on the Sabbath Day. (*Doctrines and Discipline*, (MEC) 1792, pp. 40f)

Such a passage, often in identical wording, was thereafter carried in every issue of the *Doctrines and Discipline*, until 1884.

However, Methodists did not go for uniformity. In the General Conference of 1832 a committee was ordered to "inquire into the forms and customs observed by the several Annual Conferences," and to report later to the Conference. In due time the committee made the following report:

The reading of the Scriptures in the morning and afternoon services, and the public use of the Lord's Prayer is generally

practiced, though not as uniformly as can be wished, and in some instances the sacraments are administered without using our prescribed and excellent forms; but in these things there has been an evident improvement the last four years, and we are confident that a proper attention to this subject in the Annual Conferences will shortly do away with all irregularity, and our public administrations will become uniform, scriptural and edifying. (*Doctrines and Discipline*, 1832)

From time to time frequent references to worship appeared both in the *Journals* of the General Conferences and in the quadrennial issues of the *Discipline*. But progress seemed to be slow. In the General Conference of 1888 the "Committee on Revisals" offered the following resolution:

Whereas various forms of service are being used in different churches of our denomination; and

Whereas such diversity of forms causes much embarrassment at times to strangers conducting services during the absence of the pastor; be it

Resolved that the following "form of service" be adopted by the General Conference, and that the same be printed in the *Discipline*, and be made part of the ritual. (*Journal* of the General Conference of the Methodist Episcopal Church, 1888, p. 125)

Here follows in the General Conference *Journal*, a quite elaborate form of service which form was adopted. However, when the *Discipline* appeared in print, the following editorial corrections had been made to read:

Let the morning service be ordered as far as possible, in the following manner:

1. Singing a hymn from our hymnbook
2. Prayer . . . followed by the Lord's Prayer
3. Readings from Old Testament and New Testament
4. Collection
5. Singing another hymn
6. Preaching
7. Short prayer for blessing on the Word
8. Singing and Doxology
9. Apostolic benediction
   (Par. 43, p. 38) *Discipline*, 1888

In the General Conference of 1892 the subject of orders of worship came up again. Action was then taken providing that the Board of Bishops—"promulgate two orders of service, one taken from the order used in England as adapted from John Wesley's original proposal, the other to be an order the bishops 'judged best,' and that each local church then adopt and follow one or the other." (*Journal* 1892, General Conference Methodist Episcopal Church, p. 215.) Thus, after the lapse of a century, there appeared in the Northern Church, what seems to be the first official reference to John Wesley's "Order for Morning and Evening Prayer." It should be noted, however, that the order taken as a model was not Wesley's original recommendation, but the changes wrought in it by the English Methodists.

However, the movement for liturgical reform was by no means universally acceptable. William McKinley of the MINNESOTA CONFERENCE offered a resolution, which was referred to the Committee on the State of the Church (where in the light of the above it died); namely,

Whereas, simplicity and brevity in religious services are more impressive and helpful than prolixity and tautology; and

Whereas, there are tendencies in many of our churches toward the use of prolix ritualistic forms; and,

Whereas, history shows that as ritualism grows, religion declines; therefore,

Resolved, that this General Conference be requested to adopt such measures as will arrest the growth of ritualism and maintain and perpetuate among us the simplicity and spirituality of our public and social services.

(*Journal,* 1892, p. 311)

The pressures for a better order of service increased in both the Northern and Southern branches of the M.E. Church. The Methodist Protestant wing of the Church continued in a simpler order of worship and made the first considerable elaboration in 1916. Northern and Southern Methodism joined in preparing the Hymnal of 1905. Here the Order of Worship, adopted in 1896, appeared in the first pages of the book. Its interesting feature is that it introduced the confessional movement after the call to worship, invocation, and first hymn.

Bishops THIRKIELD, WELCH, McDOWELL in the Northern Church, and such men as WILBUR FISK TILLET and FITZGERALD PARKER from the South, assumed important leadership in this development. Thirkield published the first Methodist book of "aids" to worship (W. P. Thirkield, *Services and Prayers for Church and Home,* 1918). He did not change the official service as ordered in *The Discipline* and printed in *The Hymnal.* Then he added one noteworthy feature (pp. 199 ff), the Wesley Sunday Service, along with the lectionary, prayers and collects which were part of Wesley's original. This publication was a milestone in Methodism.

The interest in better liturgy developed. Bishop Harmon's book *Rites and Ritual of Episcopal Methodism* (1926) was a further milestone and the first serious historical study of Methodist worship. A growing number of clergymen began to study and read in the history of worship and became more knowledgeable of the theology and form of worship.

The two Churches, joined by The Methodist Protestants, brought out the next hymnal in 1935. In it were two orders of service. The first had the Confession in place of the Creed, provided for a chant, the Creed after the Psalter. The second adhered to the earlier forms. There were two more orders of worship in the back of the volume, one being "adapted" from John Wesley's "Order of Morning and Evening Prayer." It had a better Psalter, and for the first time, a rather limited but very useful collection of prayers, confessions, and collects.

After the union of the three churches, the GENERAL CONFERENCE of 1940 appointed a "Commission on Ritual and Orders of Service" "to draw up richer and wider sources than those available up to the present time." In 1944 it was named the "Commission on Worship," and reappointed in 1948 and 1952. Bishop IVAN LEE HOLT was chairman and able leader of this working body. They prepared and presented to the General Conference of 1944 the *Book of Worship for Church and Home.* This was a remarkable compilation, and a far advance over Bishop Thirkield's trailblazing volume of 1918. The General Conference however did not "adopt" the book, but "authorized" its publication in line with the Commission's recommendation. Even so, it had a wide circulation among the ministers and prepared the way for the next steps.

A feature of the book lay in the elaboration of orders of service. In the early pages it printed three "services for morning worship," three services "for evening worship," and three services each termed "an order of worship for morning and evening." In addition there followed seventeen more "occasional orders for Seasons and Special Days." These services ranged from the simple to the very elaborate, with versicles, litanies, chants. It gave the churches the widest variety of services, and "aid to worship" in the way of responses, confessions, collects, prayers. The wide use of this book prepared the church for the further development which led up to the present.

In 1956, at Bishop Holt's formal retirement, he helped to influence the General Conference to make the Commission on Worship a permanent commission in the Church. This Commission was ordered to revise the Book of Worship and to make a recommendation for a new hymnal, and report four years later.

The Commission brought in a revision of the 1945 Book in 1960, with the recommendation that the study be continued until 1964. Its tentative printed report (commonly called "The Green Book") was recommended for experimental use in the services of worship throughout the Church during the quadrennium. The Green Book was widely used, and many helpful suggestions regarding it were sent to the Commission for consideration. The resultant volume was presented to the General Conference of 1964, and adopted with virtually a unanimous vote. Its main features were as follows:

a. It recommended one order of service, which was printed in two forms, the first in skeleton form, the second elaborated with rubrics, versicles, and sample prayers and collects.

b. The order was revised to conform, at least in part, to the historical usages in the Church Universal. It was built about the five traditional phases of worship—Vision, Confession, Praise, Proclamation of the Word, and Dedication.

c. Prayers were suggested for each worship mood, more congregational participation was enjoined, and more scripture readings suggested, besides the Psalter, an Old Testament lesson, Epistle, and a gospel lection. It provided a new lectionary for this purpose.

d. It had a section devoted to the church year, with suitable aids to worship selected for this purpose. It had also a massive collection of general aids to worship.

e. It worked up a new Psalter, making a new use of the feature of Hebrew poetic parallelism, and added a collection of canticles, new in Methodist usage, and other scriptural readings.

f. The Commission revised the ritual for the sacraments and the other offices of the Church with attention given in part to the liturgies of the Church Universal, and in part to more phraseology.

The Methodist Church (now The United Methodist Church) seems to have accepted the *Book of Worship* with considerable enthusiasm. Its use marks a hesitant change from the traditional ritual of American Methodism. The present work is by no means a radical revision, but it is a step toward bringing Methodist ritual and liturgy into greater conformity with her sister churches. However, in a day of liturgical renewal and experimentation it is hard to predict what direction the movement will take. At least the American Methodists have shown awareness of the ferment going on, and an excellent group of Methodist liturgical scholars promise to keep the Church aware of the developments of the next years.

J. Bishop, *Methodist Worship.* 1950.
Book of Worship for Church and Home, The. Nashville: Methodist Publishing House, 1964.

J. C. Bowmer, *Sacrament.* 1951.

W. F. Dunkle, *Values in the Church Year.* 1959.

F. D. Gealy, *Let Us Break Bread Together.* 1960.

H. G. Hardin, J. D. Quillian, Jr., J. F. White, *The Celebration of the Gospel.* New York: Abingdon Press, 1964.

N. B. Harmon, *Rites and Ritual.* 1926.

A. C. Lovelace and W. C. Rice, *Music and Worship in the Church.* Nashville: Abingdon, 1960.

Methodist Hymnal, The. Nashville: Methodist Publishing House, 1965.

J. E. Rattenbury, *Eucharistic Hymns.* 1948.

Edwin E. Voigt, *Methodist Worship in the Church Universal.* Nashville: Graded Press, 1965.

J. F. White, *Protestant Worship and Church Architecture.* New York: Oxford University Press, 1964.   EDWIN E. VOIGT

WORSHIP, British Methodist. At first, Methodist worship was regarded as complementary to that of the parish churches. WESLEY told the CONFERENCE in 1766, "It presupposes public prayer, like the sermons at the University. Therefore I have over and over advised, Use no *long prayer* either before or after the sermon." (*Minutes of the Methodist Conferences,* London, 1862, p. 59.) The new and distinctive features of eighteenth-century Methodist worship were the hymns, the COVENANT SERVICE, the LOVE FEAST, and the WATCH NIGHT, though each of these was derived rather than newly-created.

Since the Reformation, hymns—apart from those of the New Testament, and the *Veni Creator* in the Ordinal—had disappeared from English service books, though metrical psalms became popular, and Carolines, such as Wither, Herbert, and Ken composed hymns for particular and local occasions. The persecuted Reformation sects had always made hymns a part of their worship, and so did the Dissenters after 1662, not least at the Lord's Supper. Methodist hymnody is therefore an interesting blend of the Catholic and Puritan-pietistic traditions. The Wesleys' vivid and numinous settings of the Gospel and the Scriptures, together with some fine translations of Continental hymns, helped to revitalize worship.

In 1755, Wesley made the Covenant of the Somerset Dissenting clergy, RICHARD and JOSEPH ALLEINE, into a congregational rite. This was, naturally, an occasional office to mark times of particular solemnity. From 1778, it became customary on the first Sunday of the New Year. It was associated with Holy Communion, usually as its climax, though there is one recorded instance of the Sacrament preceding. In its post-1932 form, it is included in the service books of the Church of South India and in the *Book of Worship for Church and Home* of The Methodist Church, U.S.A. (Methodist Publishing House, Nashville, Tennessee, 1964-65.) (See COVENANT SERVICE.)

Love-feast and watch-night services were probably inspired by the Moravian influence, though the former have Puritan antecedents. The love feast sought to revive the primitive agape. Plain cake and water were shared and, afterward, testimonies given, interspersed with hymns. Confined originally to members of bands, then to members of society, love feasts persisted throughout the nineteenth century, as concomitants of Methodist life. They are chiefly of antiquarian interest today, though an attempt was made in the early 1950's to use them as occasions of joint worship of Anglicans and Methodists, in default of intercommunion.

Wesley considered watch nights as tantamount to vigils. Here was undoubtedly an attempt to baptize secular cus-

tom. In the end the services were reserved for New Year's Eve.

Under the Wesleys, Methodism was a Eucharistic revival in an age when there was widespread neglect of the Sacrament of Holy Communion. Not only was Wesley a frequent communicant himself, but he and his brother took their members with them to the parish church communions wherever possible, and when repelled, set up the Table in their own societies. The *Hymns on the Lord's Supper* (1745), paraphrases of an extract from the Caroline, Daniel Brevint, *On the Christian Sacrament and Sacrifice,* contain some devotional language susceptible of interpretation in terms of the Sacrifice of the Mass. They are certainly in the Western tradition in which the Eucharist is primarily a recalling of Calvary, and they are vividly imaginative; but doubtless the Wesleys would distinguish between intense poetry and precise doctrinal formulation.

Wherever the early Methodists needed to plant churches rather than societies, the basis of Sunday worship was the *Book of Common Prayer,* as the custom of the Caribbean and some African districts still bears witness. John Wesley abridged the book in *The Sunday Service of the Methodists in North America* (1784), on what may be termed liberal evangelical principles. This abridgment was prescribed, along with the prayer book, in the PLAN OF PACIFICATION of 1795 as the proper order of worship in the British societies. But although it went into innumerable editions until 1910, it never replaced the prayer book itself in the esteem of British Methodists, many of whom would have agreed with ADAM CLARKE's eulogy that the "genuine original" liturgy of the Church of England is, "next to the Bible, . . . the depository of the pure religion of Christ."

The Mother Church indeed has haunted Methodism throughout its British existence. Some eighteenth-century Anglican customs have persisted to this day, for instance the habit of combining pulpit and reading desk, and conducting the service from one place; the custom of preparing the Communion Table beforehand; and of approaching and leaving the Table in groups. Even when set forms were eschewed the pattern of worship was never Reformed, but a kind of Free Matins or Evensong, which accounts for the fact that the traditional place for the offertory in nonsacramental services is at the point between the readings and prayers and the sermon, tagged on to the "office" in effect, and liturgically meaningless and deplorable.

The Plan of Pacification was so anxious to avoid open rivalry to the Established Church that it virtually jettisoned the morning Communions of the Wesleys' Eucharistic revival by insisting that "the sacrament shall never be administered on those Sundays on which it is administered in the Parish Church." Thus, ironically, the evening Communion came in, and Methodism was made unsafe for the liturgical movement.

Throughout the nineteenth century, the Wesleyans published innumerable service books, all debtors to the *Book of Common Prayer,* which itself continued to be used. In 1874 an attempt was made by the appointment of a conference committee to provide a definitive book. This was also inspired by suspicions of the Anglo-Catholic revival, which caused an anti-prayerbook reaction, so that the committee was charged to remove "all expressions which are susceptible of a sense contrary to the principles of our evangelical Protestantism." Apart from the

Baptismal Office, very little was found to revise, and in approving a new *Book of Public Prayers and Services* in 1882, the Conference did not prohibit the use of any forms previously authorized.

The development of Methodist worship is not however to be wholly understood in the light of service books and Anglican relations. A movement which may be legitimately reckoned among the manifestations of "enthusiasm" will always regard spontaneity as vital to its worship. Extempore prayer had been valued by Wesley, and was the form most congenial to the majority of itinerant preachers and their congregations. In America, contact with the Anglican Church was much slighter than in England, and in any case, the conditions of the frontier necessitated simple revivalistic services. Here the CAMP MEETINGS began, with far-reaching consequences for the home country too.

PRIMITIVE METHODISM was born in the fervent uninhibited prayer of the camp meetings, and the other secessions from 1798 to the 1850's were all inspired by the desire for freedom in worship and government. This did not necessarily imply disregard of the Sacraments. The Primitive Methodists, in particular, treasured their Communion seasons. HUGH BOURNE, fascinated by the parallels between the Passover and the Lord's Supper, was eager for the use of unleavened bread.

All the separated bodies found the need of service books in time, though these were for the Sacraments and occasional offices, not for regular Sunday morning and evening worship. They were provided to be guides, not chains, and never established themselves in the love and devotion of the people.

W. J. TOWNSEND's authorized *Handbook for the Methodist New Connexion* does not contain a Communion Office. The *Bible Christian Book of Services* recommends Communion on the first Sunday of each month; its form is in no sense a liturgy, but rather an explanation of what is being done and its great solemnity. This is also true of the *Book of Services for the Use of the United Methodist Free Churches*, in which the Offertory occurs after the distribution. The Primitive Methodist order consists entirely of prayers and phrases from the Anglican rite, beginning with an edited version of a prayer for the Church Militant, followed by Scripture, Exhortation, Confession, Comfortable Words (but no Sursum Corda or Tersanctus), and a Communion Prayer which adds to an abbreviated Prayer of Consecration a paraphrase of the Prayer of Humble Access. The *United Methodist Book of Services* in 1913 attempts an original order with a definite "movement" of worship, but it never apparently had much vogue. The Baptismal Offices of all the books imply categorically that infants are baptized, not simply dedicated. Again the Primitive Methodist service has most echoes of the prayer book, while the United Methodist book of 1913 is most anxious to guard against any idea of an *opus operatum*.

The *Book of Offices* of the united British Church in 1936 provides for far more congregational participation than the books of the non-Wesleyans had done. It includes an alternative Communion Order, really nonliturgical, but with a Resurrection hymn after the distribution. The book reveals some curious blind spots, and has been much criticized for its seeming lack of a theology of worship. Revision is now contemplated, as in the Anglican Church.

Meanwhile, in all parts of world Methodism there has been greater interest in ordered worship, and in church furnishings. This is due to ecumenical encounter, greater economic affluence, and new educational methods. In some cases ceremonial has entered the sanctuary from the Sunday school. In America printed orders of service are often provided, though the critical eye may sometimes discern an apparent deficiency of Holy Scripture, and a preoccupation more esthetic than theological. In Great Britain *Divine Worship* (1936), a Conference publication, provides various orders of morning and evening, as well as children's services and other offices. Since the Second World War, the Church of Scotland *Book of Common Order* has been much used by leaders of Methodist worship, and its influence upon the 1960 *Report of the Conference Committee on Worship* is marked. The full Communion Service is now used far more often in the English Methodist Church than formerly; morning celebrations are more frequent; and the service is less of an appendix to worship than at one time. The METHODIST SACRAMENTAL FELLOWSHIP, founded just after Union, may be a symptom rather than a cause of this revival. It remains true that for most Methodists the climax, if not the raison d'etre, of worship is the sermon. The principal defect of our usage is the superabundance of the didactic; its great, though often unappropriated and possibly diminishing, assets are its fervor and flexibility. There is no definitive history of Methodist worship. J. C. Bowmer has written on *The Sacrament of the Lord's Supper in Early Methodism* (London, 1951) and *The Lord's Supper in Methodism, 1791-1960* (London, 1961). There are many books on hymns, most notably, J. E. Rattenbury's *The Evangelical Doctrines of Charles Wesley's Hymns* (London, 1941) and *The Eucharistic Hymns of John and Charles Wesley* (London, 1948). The volumes of *Proceedings of the Wesley Historical Society* contain invaluable articles about the various traditions; of particular importance are Wesley F. Swift's studies of the *Sunday Service of the Methodists* (xxix, 12-20; xxxi, 112-18, 133-43). In the *London Quarterly Review* for July, 1923, is T. H. Barratt's famous article on Wesley's practice of Communion. In the same review for July, 1944, is Kenneth Grayston on the Office of Baptism. Other works include Nolan B. Harmon, *Rites and Ritual of Episcopal Methodism* (Publishing House, M.E.C.S., 1926); John Bishop, *Methodist Worship in Relation to Free Church Worship* (London, 1950); H. F. Hall in *Ways of Worship* (London, 1951), pp. 158-68; Horton Davies, *Worship and Theology in England*, from Watts and Wesley to Maurice, (London, 1961), Ch. 8; E. G. Rupp in *The Holy Communion* (London, 1947), Ch. VII; the *Report of the Conference Committee on Worship* (appointed in 1957) was published in 1960.

G. S. WAKEFIELD

WREN, JAMES (1728-1815), of Falls Church, Va., was the great-grandson of Sir Christopher Wren, and James Wren was himself the architect of three VIRGINIA churches of the colonial period—Pohick near Mt. Vernon, Christ Church in Alexandria, and The Falls Church. Although he was a vestryman and church warden (with George Washington and George Mason) of Fairfax Parish of the Anglican Church, he became a leading member of the first Methodist society to be formed in what is now the Virginia suburbs of WASHINGTON, D.C., and gave to the Methodist Church its first church site in what later became ARLINGTON, Va. He was Colonel in the Virginia militia, and at various times Commissioner of Provisional Law, Commissioner of Tax, and Sheriff of Fairfax County. The chapel in the headquarters building of The Methodist Church in Northern Virginia, in ALEXANDRIA, is named in his memory.

Melvin Lee Steadman, Jr., *Falls Church by Fence and Fireside.* Falls Church, Virginia: Falls Church Public Library, publisher, 1964, pp. 471 ff. RAYMOND F. WRENN

WRENSHALL, JOHN (1761-1821), American layman and local preacher, who was instrumental in the founding of Methodism in PITTSBURGH, Pa., in 1796. Born in England, Wrenshall was converted in a Methodist Society there and became a LOCAL PREACHER. He emigrated to PHILADELPHIA in 1794 with his wife and five children. In 1796 he and his brother-in-law—both merchants— opened a second store in Pittsburgh and Wrenshall moved west to manage it. Finding no Methodist services in the town, and the community largely destitute of religion, Wrenshall commenced preaching in October 1796. For the first seven years the Society met under his oversight in the historic "Blockhouse" of old Fort Pitt. Because he had been administering the sacraments, though unauthorized to do so, at the request of Bishop ASBURY he journeyed to a Quarterly Meeting at the Hopewell Meetinghouse on the West Wheeling Circuit where on Sept. 10, 1803 he was ordained DEACON. This was the first Methodist ordination in OHIO.

The wife of President U.S. GRANT, Julia Dent, was a granddaughter of John Wrenshall, Ellen Bray Wrenshall being the wife of Judge Frederick Dent. Wrenshall kept a *Journal* which consists of five small handwritten volumes. Volumes one and two deal with his life in England, and the remainder with his life in America. It deals with both his business and his religious interests.

W. G. Smeltzer, *Headwaters of the Ohio.* 1951.
John Wrenshall "Journal." Western Pennsylvania Conference Commission on Archives and History. W. GUY SMELTZER

WRIDE, THOMAS (17? -1807), British Methodist, entered the ministry in 1768. He was an ingenious mechanic who also dabbled in medicine. His eccentricities and overindulgence in mimicry detracted from his usefulness as a preacher. He was inclined to be officious and obstinate, and on occasions Wesley was obliged to deal bluntly with him. He was, nevertheless, a loyal champion of Methodist usage.

Wesley Historical Society, *Proceedings,* i, 140. J. A. VICKERS

WRIGHT, DUNCAN (1736-1791), Scottish preacher, was born in May, 1736, at Fortingal, Perthshire, and brought up in Edinburgh. Although delicate, he enlisted in the army in 1754 and was converted while serving in Limerick in the winter of 1755-56. The death of a condemned deserter moved him to begin preaching in 1758, and on his discharge in 1764 he was encouraged by Wesley to enter the itinerancy. He traveled with Wesley from 1765 until prevented by failing health. After several English circuits, he was sent to Scotland in 1770, where he preached in Gaelic, especially in Aberdeen, Perth, and Greenock. He took a particular pleasure in helping

younger preachers. He is buried in Wesley's vault at City Road Chapel.

W. F. Swift, *Scotland.* 1947. JOHN A. VICKERS

WRIGHT, GEORGE G. (1820-1896), noted IOWA jurist, was born in Bloomington, Ind. He entered the state college (later Indiana University) in 1835, graduated in 1839, and studied law in the office of his brother, Joseph Albert Wright. In September 1840, he began the practice of law at Keosauqua, in Iowa Territory, where he lived until 1865, when he removed to DES MOINES. On Oct. 19, 1843, he married Hannah Dribble and they had seven children.

Wright became active in Iowa politics soon after settling in Keosauqua. He was prosecuting attorney for Van Buren County from 1846 to 1848, served as state senator in the Second and Third General Assemblies, and was a justice of the Iowa Supreme Court, 1855-70. His decisions as a jurist were of the highest importance to Iowa jurisprudence.

Judge Wright, states Bishop SIMPSON, "united in early life with the M.E. Church and has remained a devoted member, occupying many of its official positions." He discussed "Temperance" at the Methodist State Convention in 1871. A Republican in politics, he served a term in the U.S. Senate (1871-77). He returned to Des Moines in 1877 to practice law with two of his sons, but devoted his attention chiefly to his business interests. From 1881 to 1896 he lectured in the state university law school, which he helped establish in 1865. Judge Wright served as president of the American Bar Association in 1887 and 1888. He died in 1896 in Des Moines, Iowa.

Annals of Iowa, 1900, 1914, 1915, 1924, 1925.
Dictionary of American Methodism.
A. W. Haines, *Makers of Iowa Methodism.* 1900.
Iowa Historical Record, April 1896.
Iowa Journal of History, October 1953.
M. Simpson, *Cyclopaedia.* 1878. MARTIN L. GREER

WRIGHT, MILTON (1828-1917), American bishop of the Church of the UNITED BRETHREN IN CHRIST and father of Wilbur and Orville Wright of aeroplane fame, was born Nov. 17, 1838, in Rush County, Ind., son of Dan, Jr. and Catherine (Reeder) Wright. Endowed with a strong desire to learn, he read everything he could lay his hands on, including anti-slavery literature, until he had advanced far beyond the curriculum offered by the rural schools he attended.

Converted in 1843, at the age of fourteen, he debated between joining the M.E. Church and the Presbyterian Church until 1847, when John Morgan, a minister of the Church of the United Brethren in Christ, persuaded him to become a member of that denomination. He disciplined himself to a rigid program of independent study and took work at Hartsville College, a United Brethren institution, before becoming a public school teacher. In 1850 he took his first steps toward entering the Christian ministry and received an annual conference license from the White River Conference in 1853. In 1856, he was ordained.

After serving as a missionary to OREGON, 1853-57, he taught at Sublimity College, Oregon, when it was opened in 1857, serving as its principal for a time. On Nov. 24, 1859, he married Susan Catherine Koerner in INDIANA. To this union were born the famous inventors, Wilbur and Orville. Milton Wright remained in Indiana, preaching, teaching at Hartsville College, and serving as presiding elder, until he was elected Editor of the *Religious Telescope* in 1869. His forceful, independent spirit and his strong opposition to slavery, alcohol, and secret societies were boldly written across the pages of the publication and played a large part in his election as a bishop in 1877.

The GENERAL CONFERENCE of 1881 did not re-elect him to this high office, largely because of a rising tide of liberalism on the secret societies issue. However, in 1885 he was again elected bishop and assigned to the Pacific Coast, even though he had spent the years 1882-85 publishing an anti-secret society monthly journal, the *Richmond* (Indiana) *Star*. When the General Conference, meeting in York, Pa., in 1889, adopted a revised constitution for the denomination, Bishop Wright and a group of followers withdrew from the body and established the Church of the UNITED BRETHREN IN CHRIST, OLD CONSTITUTION. He served this group, which now has headquarters in Huntingdon, Ind., from 1889 to 1905, when he retired from the office of bishop. He died April 3, 1917 and was buried in the Woodland Cemetery, Dayton, Ohio.

Koontz and Roush, *The Bishops*. 1950. BRUCE C. SOUDERS

WRIGHT, RICHARD (17? - ?), one of the eight official Methodist missionaries sent to America by JOHN WESLEY; he came over with FRANCIS ASBURY in 1771. From the first there was some question about Wright's fitness for the work. After both he and Asbury had preached at ST. GEORGE'S CHURCH, PHILADELPHIA, JOSEPH PILMORE wrote that Asbury's message was "attended with life," while "the people seemed pretty well pleased with" Wright's "*matter*, and as to his *manner*, he will easily improve."

Wright remained in America about three years, and during that time he served in MARYLAND, DELAWARE, VIRGINIA, and NEW YORK CITY, going to the latter place for two short tours of duty. He was present at the first conference in July, 1773. Though a fluent speaker with a pleasing disposition, his ministry seemed to produce divisions that weakened the work. It was said that he became close friends with some people in the societies, thereby arousing jealousies. Also, he accepted material gifts and was sometimes partial in applying the strict discipline required by early Methodism. Asbury said of his work in New York, "He has been spoiled by gifts. He has been pretty strict in the society, but ended all with a general love feast; which I think is undoing all he has done."

Since Wright's work did not improve, the 1774 conference sent him back to England along with RICHARD BOARDMAN and Pilmore who were going at that time. Asbury visited Wright shortly before his departure and "found he had no taste for spiritual subjects." The British Minutes for 1777 list Wright as having desisted from the ministry. Little is known about him after he left the connection.

E. S. Bucke, *History of American Methodism*. 1964.
F. E. Maser, *The Dramatic Story of Early American Methodism*. Nashville: Abingdon Press, 1965.
A. Stevens, *Compendious History*. 1867.   JESSE A. EARL
ALBEA GODBOLD

WRIGHT, RICHARD ROBERT, JR. (1878-1967), American bishop of the A.M.E. CHURCH, was born in Cuthbert, Ga.,

on April 16, 1878. He was educated at Georgia State College where he earned the A.B. degree in 1898. He received the B.D. and A.M. degrees from the University of Chicago in 1901 and 1904, respectively. In 1911 after study at the University of Berlin and Leipzig in Germany, he took the Ph.D. degree at the University of Pennsylvania. He was ordained deacon in 1900 and elder in 1901, served as pastor in ILLINOIS and PENNSYLVANIA, editor of the *Christian Recorder*, business manager of the A.M.E. BOOK CONCERN, and president of WILBERFORCE UNIVERSITY. From this last position he was elected to the episcopacy in 1936. He was the author of several important works in American sociology and A.M.E. history. His book, *The Bishops of the A.M.E. Church*, is an authority in its field and is cited frequently in this *Encyclopedia*. His was a long, busy and eventful life. He died in Lankenau Hospital, Philadelphia, Pa., on Dec. 12, 1967.

Atlanta Journal, Dec. 14, 1967.
Who's Who in America, 1966.
R. R. Wright, Jr., *The Bishops.* 1963. GRANT S. SHOCKLEY

WRINCH, HORACE COOPER (1866-1939), Canadian Methodist medical missionary, was born to Leonard and Elizabeth Wrinch on Jan. 6, 1866, in Essex, England. The family came to Canada in 1880. Horace was educated in Albert Memorial College, Flamingham, England; Albert College, Belleville, Ontario; the faculty of agriculture of Toronto University, from which he graduated as gold medalist in 1888; and Trinity Medical College, Toronto, from which he graduated M.D., C.M. as gold medalist. During university days his thoughts were turned, with encouragement from his fiancée, Alice Breckon, to medical missions overseas, but on graduation no such opening was available. He gladly accepted an appointment to work among the Indians of northern British Columbia.

Following their marriage, Dr. and Mrs. Wrinch left for the West and spent the winter of 1899 in Port Essington, near the mouth of the Skeena. In the summer of 1900 they traveled upriver by Indian canoe to Kispiox where he began his practice. This village was so isolated that, at the time, the mail came only twice a year. After two years at Kispiox, Wrinch moved down river twelve miles to Hazelton and began to build a hospital which, in 1904, admitted its first patients. For many years Hazelton Hospital was a recognized training-school for nurses. Before Dr. Wrinch retired, a fine new fifty-five-bed concrete structure was built and is now known as Wrinch Memorial. Wrinch kept abreast of the advance of medicine with postgraduate courses in New York, Los Angeles, Rochester, Montreal, and Toronto. His surgical skill was recognized across the continent.

He took a deep interest in public affairs, and was one of the few men in Canadian history to have been sought out by both parties at the same time. He was twice elected to the Provincial Legislature, in 1924 and 1928. For three successive years, 1921-24, he was president of the British Columbia Medical Association.

In 1910 he was ordained by the Conference, and as long as he was at Hazelton the hospital was listed as a preaching point. He was man of wide interests and many skills, but he would desire, most of all, to be remembered as a Christian missionary. Prior to an operation he would offer prayer beginning: "A human life is placed in our hands. We must have God's help if we are to do our best. Let us pray."

In 1921 Victoria University, Toronto, conferred the doctorate of divinity on him. He died in Vancouver on October 19, 1939.

A. Barner, *Surgeon of the Skeena* (n.d.).
R. G. Large, *The Skeena: River of Destiny*. Vancouver: Mitchell, 1958.
Mrs. F. C. Stephenson, *Canadian Methodist Missions*. 1925.
W. P. BUNT

PARISH CHURCH, WROOT

WROOT was a Lincolnshire parish near Epworth, in the Isle of Axholme, which SAMUEL WESLEY, JOHN WESLEY's father, received in 1725 and held until 1734, when he resigned it in favor of his son-in-law, JOHN WHITELAMB. Between 1727 and November, 1729, John Wesley often acted as his father's curate in the parish; it was worth about £50 per annum in eighteenth-century money. Wroot today has little about it to mark the influence of the eighteenth-century curates.

JOHN NEWTON

WUNDERLICH, ERHARD (1830-1895), German pioneer leader, emigrated to the United States in 1849. He was converted and joined the Methodists in DAYTON, Ohio. On a visit to his native country in 1850, he bore witness to Christ before his mother and brother and before friends and villagers both of Waltersdorf and of Ruessdorf, the estate of the Wunderlich family. The meetings he held brought about an awakening in Eastern Thuringia. The movement strengthened even under hostilities and persecutions. Contact with the BREMEN Methodist Mission, established in 1851, gave him the support and advice of L. S. JACOBY, who soon visited this new branch of Methodism in Central GERMANY. Wunderlich preached to the societies and visited them on horseback or on foot like the first itinerants on both sides of the Atlantic. At last the persecution of Wunderlich grew so unbearable that even Jacoby advised him to return to America and asked his brother FRIEDRICH WUNDERLICH to continue his work. Erhard left Germany in the fall of 1853, and became a member of the OHIO ANNUAL CONFERENCE in the United States, twice serving as a presiding elder. After 1868 he was a member of the first board of trustees of German Wallace College, BEREA, OHIO. Powerful as a preacher and successful in the cure of souls, he contributed largely to the quick advance of Methodism among German immigrants.

THEOPHIL FUNK

WUNDERLICH, FRIEDRICH (1823-1904), was owner of the Ruessdorf estate in Central GERMANY. In the beginning he did not agree with his brother Erhard's religious enthusiasm, but then he also was converted and became the assistant of his younger brother. When ERHARD WUNDERLICH was forced to leave his native country, Friedrich assumed the responsibilities and hardships of continuing the work in Thuringia. L. S. JACOBY visited it periodically, and his prophecies that religious liberty would come gradually soon proved right. Friedrich, ordained an elder at Bremen in 1865, later called September 15, 1866, the date of the foundation of the Methodist Church in the Grand-dukedom Saxe-Weimar. On that day he and a dozen of his friends were summoned to stop Communion services or to leave the established church. They chose the latter. A movement which had begun with an endeavor to renew the church resulted in founding a free church with a manifold reviving influence on the established churches in Germany. Friedrich Wunderlich was fined several times for his preaching, but he experienced the blessing of God upon his spiritual as well as his temporal work. Erhard and Friedrich Wunderlich proved to be the type of JOHN WESLEY's early itinerant lay preachers revived in nineteenth-century Germany.

THEOPHIL FUNK

FRIEDRICH WUNDERLICH

WUNDERLICH, FRIEDRICH (1896-   ), Methodist bishop and general superintendent of The Methodist Church of East and West GERMANY, was born in Plauen, Saxony, Germany on Jan. 23, 1896, the son of Engelbert and Lydia (Laemmle) Wunderlich. His grandfather was FRIEDRICH WUNDERLICH, a farmer and founder of the Methodist Church in Eastern Germany. He received the Ph.D. from Leipzig University in 1923; D.D. from DEPAUW UNIVERSITY in 1952; and from BIRMINGHAM-SOUTHERN COLLEGE in 1956; and the L.H.D. from BALDWIN-WALLACE COLLEGE in 1963.

On Dec. 6, 1930, he was united in marriage to Maria Straube, and their children are Maria (Mrs. Emanuele Mannarino, who holds an M.D. degree); Friedrich, an

Sc.D.; Gertraud (Mrs. Wolfgang Weber, an M.D.) and Georg, also an M.D.

Friedrich Wunderlich was ordained to the ministry of the M.E. Church in 1924. He was secretary of Christian education in the Methodist Church in Germany, 1924-31; pastor in Hamburg, Germany, 1931-39; professor of theology at the Theological Seminary (Predigerseminar der Methodistenkirke), Frankfurt-am-Main, Germany, 1938-48; president of the same, 1948-53. He was elected bishop of the Methodist Church by the Germany Central Conference and assigned presidential and residential oversight of the Methodist churches of East and West Germany, Frankfurt-am-Main, in 1953.

He has been a member of the Working Fellowship of Christian Churches in Germany since 1949; a member of the Free Church Council, 1938; member of the Committee of Bread for World Protestant German Interchange Aid, 1959; member of the executive committee of the WORLD METHODIST COUNCIL; a delegate to the WORLD COUNCIL OF CHURCHES, held in EVANSTON, in 1954, and New Delhi in 1961. He served with the German Army, 1915-18, and 1940-45.

He is the author of *Methodists Linking Two Continents*, 1960; *Gott Gibt Sein Volk Nicht Auf*, 1960; and *Christus vor Allem*, 1964.

Bishop Wunderlich resides in Frankfurt and from there until he retired in 1964 he continued to supervise Methodist churches in both West and East Germany. His episcopal supervision on both sides of the divided nation was carried on, and his travel east, as well as west, permitted by virtue of his own personal reputation and the trust reposed in him by secular, as well as church, authorities. On the death of Bishop ODD HAGEN, Bishop Wunderlich was recalled to active service and supervised the STOCKHOLM Area until Bishop OLE E. BORGEN was elected Bishop in 1970.

Who's Who in The Methodist Church, 1966.   N. B. H.

WYANDOT INDIAN MISSION

WYANDOT MISSION (sometimes spelled Wyandotte), at Upper Sandusky, OHIO, is sometimes referred to by Methodist historians as the "first systematized missionary work undertaken in the Methodist Episcopal Church." Others claim that the National Missionary Society (now the BOARD OF MISSIONS of The United Methodist Church) was organized in NEW YORK in 1819 as the result of the interest aroused in Methodism by the challenging work accomplished at the Wyandot Mission.

Its beginnings center in the fascinating story of an uneducated Virginian of Negro and Indian blood named JOHN STEWART. Converted in Marietta, Ohio, he joined a Methodist Society and later felt the call of God to preach to the Indians in Northern Ohio. He journeyed, among other places, to Piketown on the Sandusky River where he stopped for a time with a tribe of Delaware Indians. The first night of his arrival the Indians joined in a noisy dance which Stewart feared was in anticipation of killing him. When they stopped dancing, Stewart took his hymnal and began singing hymns. When he ceased one of the Indians said, "Sing more"! Stewart sang more hymns and then, asking for an interpreter, gave them an exhortation. From Piketown, Stewart eventually went northwest until he reached the home of William Walker, Sen., sub-agent of Indian affairs at Upper Sandusky. Walker questioned Stewart closely and then encouraged him in his work. In November 1816 Stewart, having secured an interpreter, began preaching to the Wyandots. Two converted Indian chiefs requested the QUARTERLY CONFERENCE at Urbana to license Stewart to preach, and he was licensed March 1819. In 1821 seven chiefs requested the Annual Conference meeting at Lebanon to organize a Mission School at Upper Sandusky. JAMES B. FINLEY was sent to help Stewart, and in 1822 he built the first Manual Training School in the United States. By 1824, with the assistance of the United States Government, a thirty by forty stone church was built. Revivals broke out and the work quickly spread to other Indian tribes. Four converted chiefs who became especially useful Methodist leaders were: Between-the-Logs, Mononcue, Hicks, and Scuteash. The work continued to prosper among the Wyandots here until they were removed from Ohio into KANSAS. Today the restored stone building at Upper Sandusky is a national Methodist Historic SHRINE.

J. B. Finley, *Life Among the Indians*. 1857.
M. Simpson, *Cyclopaedia*. 1878.   FREDERICK E. MASER

WYLLIE, BERTRAM RUSSELL (1894-   ), Tasmanian and Australian minister, educator, and conference president, was born in Barrington, TASMANIA, on May 9, 1894. He was educated in Tasmania and at the Queen's College University of MELBOURNE where he received the M.A. degree in 1924 and the B.D. from the Melbourne College of Divinity, 1926. In the first World War he saw service in the Fifth Machine Gun Battalion, A.I.F., serving in France, and in the second World War was chaplain in the Royal Australian Air Force, part-time, 1942-45.

He became a candidate for Christian ministry on his discharge from the Army in 1919, and was ordained in 1926. He served as field secretary for the Australian Student Christian Movement in Schools and Universities throughout the Commonwealth 1926-28. From 1929-34, he was at HOBART Methodist Circuit in Tasmania; 1934-39, Hamilton Circuit, Victoria; 1939-43, was at the Wesley Church, Geelong, Victoria; and in 1943 was appointed Master at Wesley College University of Sydney and transferred from Victoria and Tasmania Conference to the NEW SOUTH WALES CONFERENCE. He was elected president of the Conference in 1957 and from 1957-64 was chairman of the Central Sydney Methodist District.

His presidency of Wesley College University of SYDNEY was marked by significant advances in both enrollment of the college and many improvements in student facilities, discipline and morale.

Bertram R. Wyllie has taken a prominent part in ecumenical matters, becoming acting general secretary for two periods and president of the Australian Council of Churches, 1960-65. He was a member of the Central Committee of the WORLD COUNCIL OF CHURCHES in LUCKNOW in 1952 and has traveled extensively over Asia attending conferences on Missions and Interchurch Aid. He is a member of the Council of Newington College and Ravenswood School in Sydney.

Since retirement, he has continued to live in Sydney.

S. G. CLAUGHTON

WYLLIE, MABEL GERTRUDE (1907-   ), wife of BERTRAM RUSSELL WYLLIE, was born on May 8, 1907, ADELAIDE, AUSTRALIA, the daughter of William Herbert Jenkin. She was educated in Melbourne University and received an honours degree of M.A. from Sydney University in 1951. She married B. R. Wyllie in 1933, and they have two sons and one daughter. Mrs. Wyllie has taken a prominent part in women's work, being the president of the Women's Auxiliary Overseas Missions of the NEW SOUTH WALES CONFERENCE for ten years, and has been a member of the General Conference of the Methodist Church in Australia for twelve years. She has been president of the Student Christian Movement, Adelaide University; Methodist representative to the Australian Council of Churches; a member of the executive committee of the Australian Council of Churches; and the founding president of the Australian Church Women, 1962-65. In the WORLD COUNCIL OF CHURCHES, she has been consultant to the Conference of Churches and Missions in the Pacific (Samoa, 1961); a Methodist delegate to the New Delhi Assembly, 1951; and in the World Council of Churches has been a member of the Central Committee attending meetings in Paris, Rochester (New York), Geneva, Nigeria, Crete, and Uppsala. Since 1968, she has been a member of the Committee of the Theological Education Fund of the World Council of Churches attending meetings in England and DENMARK. She has also served as a part-time lecturer in anthropology in Methodist Missionary Training College and later in the All Saints Ecumenical College for Missions. She has served as a full-time lecturer in anthropology at the Australian School of Pacific Administration at Mosman, New South Wales, since 1965. The above school is a school within the Department of Territories of the Commonwealth Government where administration officers and teachers are trained for service in Papua, NEW GUINEA, and for work with the Australian Aboriginals. She with her husband continues to reside in Sydney, Australia.

S. G. CLAUGHTON

WYNN, ALEXANDER MACFARLANE (1827-1906), American pioneer minister, was born on Jan. 20, 1827, though place of birth in NORTH or SOUTH CAROLINA is uncertain, the son of Thomas and Sarah Harriett MacFarlane (there were three sisters with husbands in the SOUTH CAROLINA CONFERENCE). He was orphaned at three weeks, reared by his uncle, Bishop JAMES OSGOOD ANDREW, graduated from EMORY COLLEGE in 1848, and entered the ministry in 1849. He was selected on Oct. 9, 1849 by Bishop ROBERT PAINE to accompany JESSE BORING to CALIFORNIA.

He married Maria, Mrs. Boring's sister. They sailed from NEW ORLEANS to PANAMA, across the Isthmus (where he contracted malaria), and came to SAN FRANCISCO on April 15, 1850.

Wynn organized the first M.E. Church, South, west of TEXAS as Wesley Chapel, San Francisco. He held the first service in the original courthouse. He served other churches in California during the 1850's and was principal of Bascom Institute.

Wynn helped Boring establish the "California Mission" in 1850; the PACIFIC CONFERENCE, 1852. He was conference secretary, 1852-54; and a delegate to the GENERAL CONFERENCE (MES) of 1854. Illness involving a lung hemorrhage necessitated his coming back to GEORGIA.

In Georgia his pastoral record was as follows: ATLANTA and Decatur Circuit, 1849; Athens, 1855; Columbus, 1856; Girard and Colored Charge, 1857; Talbottom, 1858; Eatonton, 1860; SAVANNAH, Trinity and Wesley Chapel, 1862-64, Trinity, 1865. South Georgia: president, Orphanage; Savannah: Isle of Hope and City Mission, 1866; Wesley Church and Mission, 1873-76; Savannah District, 1880; Wesley Monumental, 1886-89; Columbus, Presiding Elder, 1877-79; St. Paul (in Columbus), 1867-70; 1883-84; 1895-97; Rose Hill (in Columbus), 1898; Americus, 1871-72; Thomasville, 1881-82; Macon, First Street, 1885; Waycross, 1893-94; Sandersville, 1899; superannuated, 1900; died Aug. 17, 1906. He was a trustee of Wesleyan Female College.

Pacific Conference Records.
J. C. Simmons, *Pacific Coast.* 1886.   PEARL S. SWEET

WYNN, ROBERT HENRY (1871-1931), American preacher, was born in Waterproof, La., Feb. 23, 1871, and was received on trial in the LOUISIANA CONFERENCE in 1892. He served Parker Memorial, NEW ORLEANS; Algiers; Louisiana Avenue; Homer; Ruston; Minden; and Monroe. In 1911, he was appointed to the Lafayette District, but was called to the presidency of CENTENARY COLLEGE in the summer of 1913, serving that church-related institution for six years. Returning to the pastorate, he served again at Ruston, then was appointed to the Shreveport District. In this period he was instrumental, both in personal finances and leadership, in founding a church in Shreveport bearing the name Wynn Memorial. In 1925 he was appointed to Lake Charles, and in 1929 to Minden for a second time.

The ability and character of Robert H. Wynn were generally recognized by the various honors given. The D.D. degree was conferred upon him in 1913, and four times he was elected to the GENERAL CONFERENCE, once leading the delegation. He served for years on the General Conference BOARD OF EDUCATION.

In 1931, after surgery and apparent improvement, he passed away on December 25, with burial in Minden, La. He was survived by his wife, two daughters and one son.

R. H. Harper, *Louisiana.* 1949.
Journals of the Louisiana Conference, 1892-1932.
KENNETH GLEN RORIE

WYOMING, U.S.A., sometimes called the "Equality State" because it led the way in woman suffrage, is in the northern Rocky Mountain region of the United States. It is bounded by MONTANA on the north, SOUTH DAKOTA and

NEBRASKA on the east, COLORADO and UTAH on the south, and Utah and IDAHO on the west. Rectangular in shape, it has an area of 97,281 square miles, and its population in 1960 was 330,066. A great portion of Wyoming was received from France in the Louisiana Purchase in 1803. The remainder was secured by the annexation of Texas in 1845, by the treaty of 1846 in which Great Britain relinquished claim to the Oregon country, and by the cession of Mexico in 1848.

The first white people to enter Wyoming were trappers, and in 1834 Fort Laramie was built by traders. The Oregon Trail crossed the region. In 1860 the renowned Pony Express was begun. A year later the first telegraph line was erected over the territory. There was trouble with the Indians until 1876 when the army campaigns assured the safety of the region. Laramie and Cheyenne were founded with the coming of the Union Pacific Railway in 1867.

Originally a part of the Dakota Territory, Wyoming was designated as a separate territory in 1868. At the initial session of the territorial legislature in 1869 equal rights were granted to women. In 1870 women began to serve on juries, and Mrs. Esther M. Morris of South Pass was appointed the first female justice of the peace in the world. In 1925 Mrs. Nellie Tayloe Ross became the first woman governor in the United States.

In the early days the cattle industry thrived in Wyoming, partly due to the thick buffalo grass. Before long, however, the ranges were overstocked, and that coupled with a severe winter in 1886-87 caused a depression. With the decline of the cattle industry, sheep raising became important, small farms developed, and more people entered the territory. In 1890 Wyoming became the forty-fourth state in the Union.

Wyoming's industries include wool, lumber, petroleum, and the mining of gold and a limited amount of jade. More recently uranium discoveries have produced considerable income, and the water power of the state has been developed. Tourism has steadily grown. Yellowstone National Park, Grand Teton National Park, Devil's Tower, Jackson Hole National Monument, and eleven national forests attract tourists in great numbers. Sportsmen hunt deer, elk, bear, and birds in Wyoming.

Methodism entered Wyoming in 1834 when JASON LEE passed that way en route to the northwest. However, there is no record that he preached a sermon in the territory. In 1870 Methodism from Colorado came across the border into southern Wyoming; Laramie and Cheyenne became preaching points on the Greeley, Colorado Circuit. Also, Methodist congregations were formed at Rawlins, Rock Springs, Evanston, and Lander.

In 1888 Wyoming became a Mission with DANIEL L. RADER as superintendent. Other preachers in the Mission included O. L. Fisher, J. B. Long, H. L. Wriston, J. W. Linn, H. A. James, and C. R. Laporte. Under pioneer conditions the work developed slowly. N. A. Chamberlain, superintendent 1892-96, was traveling with the pastor at Lander by team and buckboard through the Owl Mountains in early spring when they were caught in a blizzard and nearly perished. The bridge on the Wind River having washed away, the ferryman charged $10 for the crossing. Out of provisions they purchased a dozen eggs from a rancher for $1. Chamberlain then remarked, "One more river to cross and one more dozen eggs to buy and we would bankrupt the missionary society." In 1898 superintendent E. E. Tarbill reported that he had

preached 163 times, traveled 19,000 miles, and had been mistaken for a commercial man, a cattleman, and the advance agent for a theater company. At one place where he was to preach in a saloon, the notice read: "preaching at 7:30, dancing at 9:00, and after the dance, a big poker game."

In 1914 the Wyoming Mission became the Wyoming State Conference, though it did not have and never achieved later the minimum of fifty ministers in full connection required for conference status. The GENERAL CONFERENCE waived the rule for the Wyoming work. In 1957, pursuant to the action of the 1956 WESTERN JURISDICTIONAL CONFERENCE, the WYOMING STATE CONFERENCE and the COLORADO CONFERENCE merged to form the ROCKY MOUNTAIN CONFERENCE. The Wyoming work then became a district in that conference.

In 1968 the statistics for the work in Wyoming were: thirty-three pastoral charges, 13,424 members, and property valued at $6,443,173.

I. H. Beardsley, *Echoes From Peak and Plain.* 1898.
M. Rist, *A Century of Colorado Methodism.* Pamphlet, n.d.
Journals of the Wyoming State and Rocky Mountain Conferences.

HOMER C. CRISMAN

WYOMING CONFERENCE was organized at Carbondale, Pa., July 7, 1852 with Bishop LEVI SCOTT presiding. It was formed by dividing the Oneida Conference. Its territory included northeast PENNSYLVANIA and south central NEW YORK. At the beginning the conference had four districts—Binghamton, New York; Honesdale, Pennsylvania; Owego, New York; and Wyoming, Pennsylvania. There were seventy-four preachers, 113 local preachers, fifty-nine pastoral appointments, and 10,662 members. In 1863 two districts were added—Chenango and Otsego.

The name "Wyoming" is from the Indian word "Waughwaumane" which means "broad valley." The Wyoming valley is four by twenty miles with mountains on either side and the Susquehanna River flowing through it. One Anning Owen escaped the Wyoming Massacre in July, 1778, went to eastern New York where he was in touch with ardent Methodists, and returned to the valley the next year a flaming evangelist. Ten years later Nathaniel B. Mills who was on the Newburg Circuit in New York ranged into the Wyoming valley. He was followed by Joseph Lovell in 1790, and the Wyoming Circuit with 100 members was formed in 1791. In the same year the Otsego Circuit in the New York end of the future Wyoming Conference was organized.

James Campbell from Albany, N. Y., was the first duly appointed preacher on the Wyoming Circuit. In 1792-93 he and WILLIAM COLBERT labored in the region. As time passed preachers were sent into the Wyoming area from the NEW YORK, BALTIMORE, and PHILADELPHIA CONFERENCES before the GENESEE CONFERENCE was organized in 1810 and the ONEIDA CONFERENCE in 1829. Thus when the Wyoming Conference was organized in 1852, it was the successor of five conferences which had perpetuated a name that had stood for an Indian preserve, a circuit, and a district (1845).

Camp meetings flourished within the bounds of the present Wyoming Conference and then ceased. Later some of the sites became centers for youth meetings or conferences. The conference Sky Lake Camp near New Windsor, N. Y. was the location of a camp meeting.

WYOMING SEMINARY, Kingston, Pa., the sole survivor

of four schools started by the conference, is today one of the outstanding preparatory schools in America. The conference has supported the Children's Home, Binghamton, N. Y. for half a century. In 1962 the conference's endowment fund for conference claimants was about $805,000. In recent years the conference has established and is supporting homes for the aged at Binghamton, N. Y., and Elizabeth and Tunkhannock, Pa.

In 1970 the Wyoming Conference had four districts— Binghamton, Oneonta, Scranton, and Wilkes-Barre, 207 ministers, 182 pastoral charges, 84,433 members, and property valued at $49,558,292.

A. F. Chaffee, *Wyoming Conference.* 1904.
Minutes of the Wyoming Conference.
L. D. Palmer, *Heroism and Romance.* 1950.

LOUIS D. PALMER

WYOMING SEMINARY, Kingston, Pennsylvania, was founded in 1844 by the ONEIDA ANNUAL CONFERENCE of the M.E. Church and has operated since that time under its auspices. The school consists of six divisions: college preparatory, secretarial studies, music, summer school, elementary school, and the Payne-Pettebone Nursery and Kindergarten. The governing board has twenty-seven members elected by the Wyoming Annual Conference upon nomination by a committee made up of equal members from the board and the conference.

JOHN O. GROSS

WYOMING STATE CONFERENCE (ME) was organized at Newcastle, Wyo., Sept. 3, 1914 with Bishop EDWIN H. HUGHES presiding. It superseded the Wyoming Mission which had been formed in 1888. When the Mission began it had seven pastoral charges and 329 members (see WYOMING for beginnings of Methodism in the territory). At the outset in 1914 the conference had two districts— Cheyenne and Sheridan, twenty-nine ministers, thirty-one pastoral charges, and 3,248 members.

The conference grew slowly. At unification in 1939 there were thirty-eight charges and 8,072 members. The Woman's Society of Christian Service had over 1,200 members. The conference maintained a Wesley Foundation at the state university in Laramie.

The Wyoming State Conference never achieved the minimum of 50 members in full connection required by the *Discipline* for an annual conference. So in 1956 it requested that it be merged with the Colorado Conference and that the combined body be called the ROCKY MOUNTAIN CONFERENCE. The COLORADO CONFERENCE concurred, the WESTERN JURISDICTIONAL CONFERENCE approved the plan, and the merger was effected in 1957.

In 1968 the Rocky Mountain Conference had in Wyoming 33 appointments, 13,424 members, and property valued at $6,443,173.

General Minutes, ME, TMC.
Journals of the Wyoming State Conference and the Rocky Mountain Conference.

HOMER C. CRISMAN

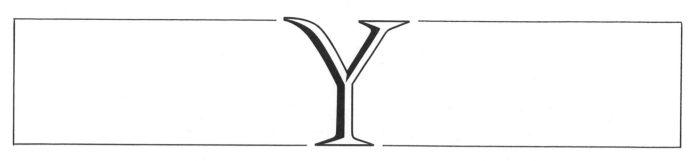

Y

YADKIN COLLEGE, North Carolina, was a training school for ministers of the M.P. Church and other professional men and was operated under the sponsorship of the NORTH CAROLINA CONFERENCE of the M.P. CHURCH. Henry W. Walser (1803-1875), a distinguished state legislator and judge, donated the land for the campus and bore the expense of erecting the first building. He served as chairman of the Board of Trustees until his death. At the Annual Conference of 1852, Walser spoke "in reference to a Seminary of Learning proposed to be located in the County of Davie." A year later the site had been selected in Davidson County eight miles west of Lexington near the Yadkin River. In 1855 the institution was chartered as "Yadkin Institute" by the General Assembly of NORTH CAROLINA, and it was opened in October of the following year. As a preparatory school it made such progress that in 1861 the charter was amended to change the name to "Yadkin College." At this time some eighty students were enrolled, but when the Civil War began sixty of them volunteered for Confederate service, causing classes to be suspended from 1861-67. When Yadkin College reopened, it again operated as a high school until 1873 when it returned to college level work. Women were first admitted to the college in 1878.

The location of Yadkin College was said to be "eminently suitable for health and for study, removed from causes of diversion and from temptation, the sale of ardent spirits within two miles being forbidden by law."

George Hege, a graduate of Trinity College, was the first president of Yadkin Institute, and he was succeeded by others of ability and repute. J. E. Prichard observed in 1927 that "the leading ministers of our denomination in this state for a generation received their instruction" at Yadkin College, as well as "many of our leading laymen."

In 1924, following the rise of consolidated high schools and the opening of HIGH POINT COLLEGE, Yadkin Collegiate Institute closed. The sale of the college property in 1933 brought $100 which was turned over to the local M.P. Church. The Yadkin College Alumni Association was very active for a number of years and was responsible for erecting the old Yadkin College bell on the High Point College campus, and for publishing a history of the college in 1939.

A. H. Bassett, *Concise History*. 1887.
Olin B. Michael, *Yadkin College, 1856-1924: A Historic Sketch.* Salisbury, 1939.
Journal of the North Carolina Conference, MP.

RALPH HARDEE RIVES

YANG, GRACE (Yang Hsi-chen), Chinese Y.W.C.A. secretary and educator, was born in Soochow and studied at Laura Haygood School there. In the United States she attended Mount Holyoke College and Columbia University. She was connected with the student department of the National Committee of the Y.W.C.A. in Shanghai (1919-29), and during that time was a delegate to the meeting of the General Committee of the WORLD STUDENT CHRISTIAN FEDERATION in England in 1924. In 1929 she became principal of McTyeire School for Girls in Shanghai, a position which she held until the school was taken over by the Communists. She was a sister of Y. C. YANG, president of Soochow University. No news could be received about her after the Communist reorganization of the schools.

China Christian Yearbook, 1936-37.   FRANCIS P. JONES

Y. C. YANG

YANG, YUNG-CHING (1891-1956), Chinese educator and diplomat, was born at Wusih, CHINA, on June 26, 1891. He received the B.A. degree at Soochow University in China, the M.A. and the LL.B. degrees from George Washington University, WASHINGTON, D.C. He had honorary degrees from FLORIDA SOUTHERN COLLEGE and Bowdoin College.

Yang was assistant director of the Chinese educational exhibits at the Panama-Pacific International Exposition in 1915, secretary to Wellington Koo, the Chinese ambassador in Washington from 1916 to 1920, advisor to the Chinese delegation at the International Labor Conference in 1919, and attaché and secretary of the Chinese legation at London from 1920 to 1922. He was the secretary of the Chinese delegation at the first assembly of the League of Nations in GENEVA in 1920, secretary of the delegation to the Washington Disarmament Conference, 1921-22, and a member of the Ministry of Foreign Affairs from 1922 to 1927.

In 1926 he was the Chinese consul-general at London, and the following year he was one of the directors of the International Tariff Conference at Peking.

In the United Nations he was a member of the Committee on the Security Council at SAN FRANCISCO in 1945, the Section of Economic and Social Questions at London, and the Economic and Social Council and the Chinese delegation to the Second General Assembly in New York in 1946. He received three decorations from the Chinese Government.

In 1927, Yang became president of Soochow University, the leading institution of the M.E. Church, South in China, and continued in that position until the communists came to power in 1949 when he was virtually placed under house arrest. During this period he was the foremost Methodist layman in China. He delivered a series of lectures at the University of Hawaii, EMORY UNIVERSITY, OHIO WESLEYAN UNIVERSITY, Wellesley College and DUKE UNIVERSITY. He was visiting professor of Chinese civilization at Bowdoin College and Lake Erie College and faculty-visitor under the auspices of the Association of American Colleges.

He was a member of the executive committee of the National Christian Council and the YMCA in China, chairman of the China Christian Educational Association, member of the executive council and chairman of the Board of Christian Education of the Methodist Church in China. He served in three GENERAL CONFERENCES and the UNITING CONFERENCE in 1939. He was the author of a book entitled *China's Religious Heritage,* and contributed to numerous periodicals. He traveled widely not only in his native land and the United States but also in England, FRANCE, BELGIUM, INDIA and CEYLON.

Yang died in Shanghai on March 6, 1956.

China Christian Yearbook.
Who's Who in China.
                                            ELMER T. CLARK

YAP, KIM HAO (1929-   ), first bishop of the autonomous Methodist Church of MALAYSIA and SINGAPORE, was born Feb. 20, 1929, at Port Dickson, Malaysia, the son of Chow-Chong and Yim-Moy (Wong) Yap. A Crusade Scholar, he was educated at BAKER (A.B., 1952) and Boston (S.T.B., 1954) UNIVERSITIES. He married Hee-Choo Koh, Aug. 13, 1955, and they have four children.

In 1953, at the request of the Malaya Conference, Yap was received on trial in the NEW ENGLAND CONFERENCE, ordained DEACON, and immediately transferred back to his home conference. Later (1959-61) he served as supply pastor at East Bridgewater, Mass. Appointments in his own conference were: 1954-56, associate, Wesley Church, Klang, Malaysia; 1957-59, Wesley, Singapore; 1962, Wesley, Kuala Lumpur, Malaysia; and 1964-68, Selango District, Kuala Lumpur.

Yap was a GENERAL CONFERENCE delegate, 1964-68, and served on the COMMISSION ON THE STRUCTURE OF METHODISM OVERSEAS, 1964-68, and on the Structure Committee which arranged for the organization of the autonomous Methodist Church in Malaysia and Singapore. He was elected bishop in 1968, and in that capacity he serves as the spiritual leader of his church, ordains ministers, and, with the aid of an advisory board, appoints the preachers in five annual conferences in West Malaysia, East Malaysia, and Singapore.

Christian Advocate, September 5, 1968.
Who's Who in The Methodist Church.
World Parish, March, 1969.   ALBEA GODBOLD
                                       JESSE A. EARL

YEAKEL, JOSEPH H. (1928-   ), American E.U.B. minister, was born at Mahanoy City, Pa., March 12, 1928.

He spent childhood and youth in Pottsville, Pa., and served with the U.S. Navy in the Pacific theater during World War II. He received degrees from LEBANON VALLEY COLLEGE (A.B. and D.D.) and UNITED THEOLOGICAL SEMINARY (B.D.), and was ordained by the Pennsylvania Conference of the E.U.B. Church, Oct. 8, 1952. Pastorates were served in DAYTON, Ohio; YORK, Pa.; Hagerstown and SILVER SPRING, Md. He was elected assistant secretary of Evangelism, April 29, 1963, and executive secretary April 1, 1965. He is married to Lois Josephine Shank of Waynesboro, Pa., and they are the parents of five children.

Yeakel has served as chairman of the denominational PROGRAM COUNCIL, and on the following boards and committees: General Board of CHRISTIAN EDUCATION, General Board of MISSIONS, Board of PUBLICATION, the Department of Communication, the Department of Stewardship, the adult and children's Councils; the General Church Curriculum Committee, and the Youth Fellowship Executive Committee, and on numerous inter-board and church union committees. He has served on numerous NATIONAL COUNCIL boards and agencies. In September 1967, the Executive Committee of the General Board of EVANGELISM of The Methodist Church and the General Board of Evangelism of the E.U.B. Church appointed him executive secretary of the Division of Leadership Development for both Boards until the formation of The United Methodist Church.

In The United Methodist Church Dr. Yeakel was elected general secretary of the Board of Evangelism in 1968 and holds his membership in the CENTRAL PENNSYLVANIA CONFERENCE.

                                       REUBEN P. JOB

YEAKEL, REUBEN (1827-1904), American Evangelical editor and bishop, was born in Montgomery County, Pa., Aug. 3, 1827, to Carl and Susan Yeakel. His pastoral ministry began in the East Pennsylvania Conference, EVANGELICAL ASSOCIATION, in 1853. His first marriage was to Sarah Schubert in 1855; his second to Mrs. Caroline (Schloser) Klein, widow of John Klein.

In 1859 he was elected corresponding secretary of the missionary society, the first to hold that position. In 1863 he became an editor of Sunday school literature, including *The Sunday School Messenger.* Subsequently, he was made editor of two general church periodicals: *The Evangelical Messenger* in 1871, and assistant editor of *Der Christliche Botschafter* in 1883.

He espoused HOLINESS and became a prominent member of the National Holiness Association, laboring with John Inskip and W. MacDonald. In 1870 he co-founded *The Living Epistle,* the first and only holiness magazine of the denomination.

The bishopric claimed his able executive ability from 1871 to 1879, after which he was principal of Union Biblical Institute, later named EVANGELICAL THEOLOGICAL SEMINARY, until 1883.

His most lasting contribution included these published works: *Jacob Albrecht und seine Mitarbeiter,* 1879, (in English) 1883; *The Church Discipline, Doctrine, and Confession of Faith,* 1899; *The Genius of the Evangelical Church,* 1900; *Geschichte der Evangelischen Gemeinschaft,* Vol. I, 1890, Vol. II, 1895, (in English) 1894 and 1895, respectively; *Bishop Joseph Long,* 1897.

His life ended March 5, 1904 with burial in Cleveland, Ohio.

R. W. Albright, *Evangelical Church*. 1942.
David Koss, "Bishops of the Evangelical Association, United Evangelical and Evangelical Churches." Ms. thesis, Evangelical Theological Seminary, 1959.
R. M. Veh, *Evangelical Bishops*. 1939.   ARTHUR C. CORE

YEAR BOOKS, METHODIST, U.S.A., were annual publications put out for some years by the M.E. Church and (similar ones) by the M.E. Church, South. These contained the general minutes of the conferences of these respective Churches as well as much other material. They usually carried a directory of their Church officers, and sometimes biographical sketches of bishops or of general executives, and quite often a listing of the roll of editors, the roll of bishops from the beginning of the Church, the editors of various official publications, and other information which might prove helpful to the ministry and to the membership of the Church. The Year Book editors endeavored to make these publications interesting by adding unusual information of general interest to Methodists. With the necessity of bringing out larger and larger editions of the *General Minutes* late in the life of the respective Episcopal Methodisms, the Year Books as such ceased to appear. The file of these today is a repository of much useful historic information, bearing on the life of the respective Churches at the time the Year Books were published.

N. B. H.

YONSEI UNIVERSITY, SEOUL, KOREA

YONSEI UNIVERSITY, Seoul, Korea, the largest coeducational Christian university in KOREA, has an enrollment of about 5,000 students of whom 1,000 are women. Originally organized as Chosen Christian College under Methodist-Presbyterian auspices in 1916, it achieved university status in 1946. In 1957 it was united with SEVERANCE UNION MEDICAL COLLEGE, taking its new name, Yonsei, from the initial Chinese characters of the two uniting institutions.

There are ten colleges: Liberal Arts, Commerce, Science and Engineering, Music, Medicine, Nursing, Home Economics, Political Science, Law, and Theology. There are four graduate schools including a business night school, and the United Graduate School of Theology—in which three denominational seminaries (Methodist, Presbyterian, and Anglican) cooperate with the Yonsei Theological College under a grant from the Theological Education Fund (New York), with additional funds from the contributing mission boards. The United Board for Christian Higher Education in Asia has generously supported the university in recent years.

The University Medical Center, including Severance Hospital, occupies a fifteen acre site on the Yonsei campus. The medical science building has facilities for 280 medical students. The five bays of the out-patient clinic can accommodate 1,500 patients daily. Severance Hospital ward building has one of its six floors designated as the Eighth Army Memorial Chest Hospital, donated by the Eighth U.S. Army Armed Forces Assistance to Korea. Rehabilitation specialists operate in two centers: the Church World Service Amputee Rehabilitation Center, and the Crippled Children's Center. The China Medical Board has been of great assistance in making Yonsei Medical Center one of the finest in the far east.

The original college was founded by Horace G. Underwood, pioneer Presbyterian missionary to Korea. Continuous service to the college has been given by his son, Horace H. Underwood, and a grandson, Horace G. Underwood II.

Methodists who have been outstanding in the growth of the university have been Arthur L. Becker, Bliss B. Billings, and Elmer M. Cable. Those in the medical college have been James D. Vanbuskirk, M.D., and Earl W. Anderson, M.D.

Tai-Sun Park, a Methodist, is now president of the university.

CHARLES A. SAUER

YORK, BRANTLEY (1805-1891), American teacher and founder of Union Institute Academy which in time eventuated in DUKE UNIVERSITY, was a Methodist local preacher. He was born in Bush Creek community north of Franklinville, Randolph County, N. C., on Jan. 3, 1805, the son of Eli and Susanna Harden York. One daughter was born from Brantley York's marriage to Fannie Sherwood, and twelve children to his second wife, Mary Wells Linberry.

In 1838 this self-educated teacher of English, classical languages, and mathematics, transformed education at "Brown's Schoolhouse" from a "subscription" school to Union Institute Academy. The academy, located in northwest Randolph County south of High Point, became Trinity College in 1859, was relocated in DURHAM in 1891, and became Duke University in 1925. A historical marker at Trinity, N. C., designates the former site.

Succeeded by his student, BRAXTON CRAVEN, in 1842, Brantley York went to head the North Carolina M.E. Conference school at Clemmonsville. Although blind after 1854, he taught in numerous schools, was a professor at Rutherford College, published four editions of his *Illustrated Grammar* and one of his *Arithmetic*, and preached often.

Brantley York died in Forest City, N. C., on Oct. 7, 1891, and was buried at Rocky Springs Methodist Church, Alexander County, near the site of York Institute which he founded. His *Autobiography* was published in 1910. His son, Bascom A., was an ordained Methodist preacher.

Boyd, ed. *The Autobiography of Brantley York, The John Lawson Monographs* of the Trinity College Historical Society, Volume I, Durham, 1910.
————, "The Rev. Brantley York on Early Days in Randolph County and Union Institute." *Historical Papers* of the Trinity College Historical Society, Series VIII (Durham 1908-1909) pp. 15-34.
York, Bascom A., "Memoirs of Rev. Brantley York, D.D.," *Raleigh Christian Advocate*, Aug. 23, 1893. G. W. BUMGARNER

YORK, England. In the year 1744 the vicar of Birstall in the county of Yorkshire misrepresented something said by the Methodist preacher, JOHN NELSON, and the vicar's version made Nelson guilty of subversion. He was accordingly committed for military service as punishment, and for this purpose was taken to the city of York. Before this, in 1743, JOHN WESLEY himself had passed within a few miles of York on one of his early preaching tours, but he had not gone into the city. But when in 1747 Wesley did make his first recorded entry into York, he found that JOHN NELSON, in the true apostolic tradition, had used his time in detention to preach the gospel, and a small group of Methodists were holding meetings. Already a number of villages around the city contained duly constituted Methodist societies, so that it was to be expected that the city itself should follow suit. And this it did after Wesley's visit in 1747, with a modest initial membership of four persons.

The society's first meeting place was a tiny room in the Bedern. But in spite of prayer and great zeal, the growth of the society was extremely slow: in its first year membership went up from four only to twelve. From this tiny room the Methodists moved to accommodations which carried the curious designation of "the hole in the wall." This place had originally been part of an ancient chapel which had fallen into decay. Part of this chapel had become an alehouse, and this in turn had gone into disrepair and disuse. This was what the Methodists now took over. The old name of the place arose from the fact that there had once been a small connecting door between the old chapel and the splendid York Minster. In this unsalubrious place the Methodists stayed only for a short time, leaving it for a room in Pump Yard, large enough to hold a hundred people. During these early years there had been considerable, and sometimes violent, persecution of the Methodists, but slowly this situation began to change. So in 1759 the little society felt bold enough to face its basic need and build the first Methodist chapel in the city. It was in Peasholme Green and was large enough to hold four or five hundred people. A notable contribution toward the cost of the chapel was provided by the then Dean of York, a college friend of CHARLES WESLEY, who gave no less than one hundred pounds.

From that time the Methodist cause began to gather a certain though restrained momentum. When John Wesley died in 1791 the Methodists had passed through the first stage of their history in the city. They had gained an entry, survived persecution, set up their society, and formed a large circuit around the city, penetrating deep into the countryside. They were poised ready for the coming century, the age of expansion. By 1791 thirty-five village societies were joined with that of York itself to form the York ROUND, and nine of these had built their own chapel. In York the society had 236 members, still with only one chapel, at Peasholme Green. On the occasion of John Wesley's last visit to York, a supper meal brought together the leaders of the York society, and they included Roger Preston, ROBERT SPENCE, William Fowler, RICHARD BURDSALL, and Joseph Agar. These names were among the great ones in early Methodism in this city, and their descendants continued to offer yeoman service in the century that followed Wesley's death.

In January of 1805 the foundation stone of New Street Chapel was laid; and when the building was opened in October, the regular congregation was large enough to fill it, numbering over one thousand. The century of building for the Methodists had begun. Albion Street (in Skeldergate) came in 1816 and St. George's in 1826. And in 1839-40 came the greatest achievement to date—the erection and opening of the Centenary Chapel, which, alone of the four buildings so far named, still stood in 1966. In 1856 Centenary was matched at the other side of the River Ouse (which divides the medieval city) by the building of Wesley Chapel in Priory Street. The elaboration of the premises is illustrated by a comparison between these three buildings. New Street cost about four thousand pounds, Centenary about eight, and Wesley about sixteen. The story of building continued with Melbourne Terrace (1877), Groves (1884), and Southlands (1887); mission rooms came into use in Wilton Street, Layerthorpe, Skeldergate, and Laurence Street. To allay any suspicion that the extent of the building bore no relation to the numbers of people involved, let us look at statements concerning Wesley Chapel and Circuit in the late part of the century. In the circuit the Young Men's Class was commenced on February 22, 1862, with some youths selected from the first class in the Sunday School, none being admitted under fifteen years of age. Twenty years later it was meeting on Sundays at 9:30 A.M. for conversation on biblical and religious subjects, and at 2 P.M. for an address. It now had 403 members, of whom 166 were members of the church, 94 were married, and 300 were registered as total abstainers. A. S. Page, whose father became a member of Wesley Chapel in 1866, and who wrote of the church at its centenary celebration, has stated quite categorically that in the last decade of the nineteenth century "almost every seat in Wesley Chapel (about twelve hundred) was occupied for the ordinary evening service."

As for non-Wesleyan Methodism, PRIMITIVE METHODISM found its way to York in 1819. The society which was formed moved from its first home in a former Calvinistic Baptist chapel (which they took in 1820) to Ebenezer Chapel, their own place, in Little Stonegate. Thence they went in 1864 to a mission hall in Nunnery Lane, and this was followed by the building of their own chapel at Victoria Bar in 1880. After Methodist Union in 1932 the Primitive Methodist Circuit joined with the Wesley Circuit.

In the days of the great Wesleyan Methodist schism in 1849, York Methodism suffered a great setback in membership, largely because one of the leaders of the disturbances was JAMES EVERETT, who lived in York. Although the societies were adversely affected, the erection of new opposition buildings was virtually confined to the chapel at Monk Bar (which styled itself a part of the "Methodist Free Church") and that in Peckitt Street (which belonged to the METHODIST NEW CONNEXION). Not for many years did these societies become once more a part of the parent body.

A second feature in this period was York Methodism's more than average interest in overseas missions. In addition to generous financial support, the York Methodists also supplied missionary workers. WILLIAM WARRENER went to the WEST INDIES, and Thomas Richardson followed him; RICHARD BOARDMAN and JOSEPH PILMORE, pioneers of American Methodism, went out from York; John Hick went to Nova Scotia and Robert Hardy to CEYLON; Thornley Smith and his brother George went to South Africa and Richard Burdsall Lyth to FIJI. And, outstanding even among giants, DAVID HILL gave thirty-two years of unforgettable service to CHINA.

After 1900 York Methodism entered a third phase, one of decline. Wesley Chapel could rely on a congregation of over a thousand every Sunday evening sixty years ago; now it is fortunate to have a hundred. In almost every part of the city the story is a similar one. Where exceptions exist it is because there has been immense housing development (as at Acomb) and the church has had some gain from the vast incoming population. In outward structure York Methodism is substantially what it was in 1900. On the south bank there is still the one Wesley Circuit; on the north bank of the Ouse there are two, Centenary and Clifton. Within the city walls themselves there are still the two vast chapels of Wesley and Centenary, both facing agonizing days of self-questioning about the mission of the Christian Church to the city.

Among the more distinguished ministers who have served Methodism in York are JOHN SCOTT, born at Copmanthorpe in the York Circuit and president of the Wesleyan Methodist Conference in 1843 and 1852. His grandson was JOHN SCOTT LIDGETT, also a president. Four other ministers who served in York at some stage of their career also occupied the chair of the Conference: John Rattenbury, DINSDALE T. YOUNG, Wardle Stafford and HENRY BETT. But of course the people who mattered most to the church were those who gave their whole lives to the service of the one place, the York families themselves. In York Methodism there are certain names which are written into the story of the church there and which occur in successive generations: Agar, Meek, Hill, Rymer, Taylor, Bushell, Shouksmith, Kay, and many others.

WHITFIELD FOY

YORK, PENNSYLVANIA, U.S.A., situated in the southeastern part of the state, was settled in 1749 by German people. During the Revolutionary War, 1777-78, the Continental Congress, driven from PHILADELPHIA, met here. Methodism was early introduced into this part of the country when FREEBORN GARRETTSON in July 1781 preached in the public house near York. Several teamsters were present. A certain James Worley was awakened by the sermon, and was thought by his family and friends to be out of his mind. A physician was sent for who placed him in bed and blistered him, but all his efforts failed to help the patient. The family then sent for Garrettson, who was sixteen miles distant and who explained to him the plan of salvation, and in a little while Worley was converted. This was the introduction of Methodism into the town of York.

In 1782 Jacob Settler bought a lot west of the Codorus, erected a small frame church, and presented it to the society of Methodists. York was made a station in 1818, and a Mission Chapel, which later became Duke Street Church, was built in 1861. In 1870-72 a much larger Duke Street Church was erected.

First Methodist Church in York finished a handsome edifice about thirty-two years ago and that church today has the largest membership of any United Methodist church in the city, with 1,276 members in 1970. There are thirteen other churches within the city limits, with a combined total of 10,372 members (1970). These congregations raised a total of $958,302 for all purposes, and their total property was valued at $7,109,565.

UNITED BRETHREN preachers entered York County several years prior to the formal organization of the denomination in 1800. A conference was held in 1791, seven miles west of the town. It was under the leadership of PHILIP WILLIAM OTTERBEIN and MARTIN BOEHM. The first United Brethren preaching in York was delivered by Martin Boehm prior to 1801 and by CHRISTIAN NEWCOMER in 1802. Although Otterbein had been pastor of the York Reformed Church, 1765-74, he had not yet become associated with those who were to be United Brethren.

That denomination, organized in 1800, was reluctant to organize congregations in cities. It was not until 1840 that the quarterly conference of the York Circuit voted to organize a class in the town. The first Methodist church, west of the Codorus Creek, was purchased for $1,500, since that congregation had relocated. Later the First United Brethren Church organized four additional congregations in York.

EVANGELICAL ASSOCIATION services were begun in York about 1806, when JACOB ALBRIGHT preached at the Courthouse. A congregation was formed which worshipped in that building for more than thirty years. The first church building was erected in 1842. By the time of the union with the United Brethren to form the E.U.B. Church, there were seven Evangelical congregations in the city.

There are eighty-seven United Methodist churches in York County with a combined membership of 29,381 persons (1970). Property for these congregations is valued at $19,879,792.

Asbury Church is one of the oldest and most commanding churches in the CENTRAL PENNSYLVANIA CONFERENCE and the mother church of Methodism in York. The account of Freeborn Garrettson's visit is told above. A Methodist society was formed in York in 1782. Services were conducted in various places until 1791 when three lots, located at Newberry and Philadelphia Streets, were purchased from the Penn Estate for seventeen pounds, ten shillings and a "yearly quit-rent of one Barley Corn on the first day of March in each and every year hereafter, if demanded." The Jacob Sitler who built a log meeting house on the property and presented it to the Methodist society, was not himself a member.

In 1807 FRANCIS ASBURY preached in York to a large congregation. Originally on the Carlisle Circuit, the church became a single station in 1818. Two years later the church was incorporated as the First Methodist Church of York, and in 1824 the church established the first white Sunday school in York.

In 1836 at a cost of $16,000 a new brick church was built at Philadelphia and Beaver Streets, the former building (as is narrated above) being sold in 1840 to the United Brethren in Christ.

In 1873 a new building was erected at a cost of $24,500. Bishop MATTHEW SIMPSON preached at the laying of the cornerstone. Five years later a great revival took place under the evangelist Thomas Harrison. There were four hundred converts.

Asbury Church, as the mother church of Methodism in York, was instrumental in organizing the Duke Street Church in 1861; the Ridge Avenue Church in 1881; the Princess Street Church (later called Epworth) in 1883; the West Street Church in 1888. Epworth and West Street are now united in what is Grace Church.

In 1923 the site of the present building on East Market Street, three blocks east of the Square, was purchased, and three years later the present educational unit was dedicated on May 2.

In 1938 the present Gothic sanctuary was completed at a total cost, including the organ, of $135,000. Foxcroft stone was used in the construction of the building. A stately and graceful spire, known as a French fleche, rises fifty-seven feet above the roof and 110 feet above the ground level, and can be seen from almost any high point in the city. A cross surmounts the fleche.

In 1968 the name of the church was changed to Asbury United Methodist Church. Among the distinguished pastors who have served Asbury was JAMES E. SKILLINGTON, who came in 1943. Dr. Skillington became known over the whole Methodist Church for his ability and knowledge as a parliamentarian in successive GENERAL CONFERENCES.

FREDERICK E. MASER

Otterbein Church is the historic "mother church" of all the former United Brethren churches in York. The congregation was organized Aug. 18, 1840. For eleven years the new church struggled for its life. At the end of this period, however, there were 137 enthusiastic members and the church showed signs of increasing vitality.

The present parsonage was built in 1855, and in 1869 the present two-story brick church structure was erected. One of the first pipe organs in the city of York was installed in 1902. On July 21, 1918, the congregation dedicated a new well equipped educational building at a cost of $52,000.

By 1931 the congregation had increased to 700 members. Growth continued to take place until the present membership numbers approximately 1,000.

Two pastors, JOHN H. NESS, SR. and PAUL E. V. SHANNON, were elected Conference Superintendents. Dr. Ness later became the Executive Secretary of the denominational Board of Pensions; Dr. Shannon was elected a bishop of the E.U.B. Church.

The church has also sent ten men into the ministry and one woman into missionary service. Of these JOHN H. NESS, JR. is serving as Executive Secretary of the Commission on Archives and History of the United Methodist Church, and D. Rayborn Higgins and Paul E. Horn are serving as district superintendents.

A new Christian education building was dedicated in April 1969, at a cost of approximately $300,000, with facilities for children and youth, plus offices and pastors' studies.

For 128 years this congregation was known as the First Church of York. With the formation of the United Methodist Church there were two First Churches in the city. By congregational vote on Sept. 8, 1968, the former First E.U.B. Church became known as the Otterbein United Methodist Church.

General Minutes, 1970.
P. E. Holdcraft, *Pennsylvania Conference.* 1938.
Journal of the Central Pennsylvania Conference.
CALVIN B. HAVERSTOCK, JR.

YOST, WILLIAM (1830-1920), American Evangelical minister, was born Dec. 25, 1830, at Womelsdorf, Pa. He was reared by German parents whose home was the stopping place of EVANGELICAL ASSOCIATION ministers. Bishop JOHN SEYBERT, who was one of these, placed his hand on William's head on one occasion and said, "I have a deep conviction that William will eventually become one of our preachers." Resisting such an impres-

sion, he entered college at the age of twenty, to prepare for a political career. However, broken health intervened and a remarkable conversion and dedication to God's will became a training for a notable ministerial career. As a pastor he served with marked success in the East Pennsylvania Conference of the Evangelical Association (1853-63). During his service as corresponding secretary of the Missionary society (1863-75), the church experienced a rapid expansion of her work in America, Europe, and Japan. From 1863, for forty-four years, Yost was engaged as a general church official.

"The name of William Yost must be written large in the annals of his denomination," said Bishop S. P. SPRENG. "He was an able preacher, unique, original and inimitable in his manner of delivery; thoroughly Biblical and Evangelical." He died in Cleveland, Ohio, May 25, 1920, leaving an aged widow, two sons and three daughters—the eldest, Mrs. Ella Yost Preyer, prominent in the organization of the WOMAN'S MISSIONARY SOCIETY.

Evangelical Herald, Vol. 25, 1920, p. 360.
Evangelical Messenger, Vol. 74, 1920; Vol. 80, 1926.
William Yost, *Reminiscences.* Cleveland, O.: Evangelical Association, 1911.
ROY B. LEEDY

YOUNG, BENJAMIN (dates uncertain), American circuit rider and the first appointed to ILLINOIS, was born in Allegheny County, Pa., the son of an Episcopal father and a Presbyterian mother, and brother of JACOB YOUNG. When he was a child the family moved to KENTUCKY, and there he became a Methodist. He entered the itinerant ministry in 1801, and in October 1803 received appointment as missionary to Illinois from the WESTERN CONFERENCE. Illinois was until 1809 included in INDIANA Territory. A letter of record from Young reports the difficulties he encountered in his attempts to open the land for the gospel. Not only were many of the scattered inhabitants unfriendly, but the Indians had stolen his horse. Nevertheless within one year he had formed five classes and reported sixty-seven members.

Unfortunately he was involved in a Conference trial on charges which today would be regarded as not only minor but unsubstantiated, and was expelled in 1804. His brother, Jacob Young, in his *Autobiography* does not hesitate to label the action quite unjust. Bishop ASBURY himself was apparently uneasy about the Conference action and sought unsuccessfully to reopen the case.

Benjamin Young's later history is obscure. His brother reports that WILLIAM MCKENDREE, who had been instrumental in his expulsion, in later years reclaimed him during a preaching tour in Illinois, "took him into the Church, and, I believe, had his parchments returned." Of this there exists no official record.

FREDERICK A. NORWOOD

YOUNG, DINSDALE THOMAS (1861-1938), British preacher, was the son of a Yorkshire physician. Converted early, he began to preach at fifteen, and in 1879 was accepted as a candidate for the Wesleyan Methodist ministry—the youngest man accepted up to that time. After training at Headingley College, LEEDS, he travelled in four LONDON circuits as well as important provincial centers. A notable ministry at Nicolson Square, Edinburgh, was followed by eight years at Wesley's Chapel, City Road, London. Then he went to make his greatest mark during a twenty-three years' ministry at Westminster Central Hall, London. He was widely known and loved as a preacher beyond the bounds of Methodism, travelling some 10,000 miles a year on preaching and lecturing tours. The hallmarks of his expository and avowedly fundamentalist preaching were simplicity, optimism, and conviction. He was awarded an honorary D.D. by LIVINGSTONE COLLEGE, U.S.A., but his greatest honor was being elected President of the Conference in 1914. He died Jan. 21, 1938, two years after his beloved wife. Young published several books of sermons and addresses, as well as biographies of ROBERT NEWTON, RICHARD ROBERTS, and PETER MACKENZIE. He gave the FERNLEY LECTURE for 1929, on *Popular Preaching*. In 1920 appeared his *Stars of Retrospect: frank chapters of autobiography*.

Harold Murray, *Dinsdale Young, The Preacher*. London: Marshall, Morgan & Scott, 1938.
Dinsdale T. Young, *Stars of Retrospect*. London: Hodder and Stoughton, 1920.   FRANK BAKER

YOUNG, EGERTON RYERSON (1840-1909), Canadian Methodist missionary and writer, was born at Crosby, Upper Canada, on April 7, 1840, the son of William Young and Amanda (Waldron) Young. He was educated at the Toronto Normal School and taught for several years, prior to his ordination in 1867.

In 1868, he was appointed to Norway House (Manitoba), which he reached after a journey of more than two months. Later he opened missions at Nelson River and Berens River. Because of his wife's ill health he gave up his mission in 1876 and turned to fundraising tours in association with THOMAS CROSBY. Subsequently, he served on circuits in Ontario, but in 1888 he was permitted to devote his time to speaking and writing on behalf of Methodist Indian Missions. He died in Bradford, Ontario, in 1909.

Egerton Young was a dauntless soul, who, as pastor and lecturer, greatly strengthened the cause of missions in Canada. His numerous writings, such as *By Canoe and Dog-Train Among the Cree and Salteaux Indians* (1890), *On the Indian Trail* (1897), and *The Apostle of the North* (1899), recreated vividly the triumphs and the miseries of the missionary enterprise.

G. H. Cornish, *Cyclopaedia of Methodism*. 1881, 1903.
J. H. Riddell, *Middle West*. 1946.   F. W. ARMSTRONG

YOUNG, GEORGE (1821-1910), Canadian missionary and writer, was born near Picton (Upper Canada), on Dec. 31, 1821. He was educated in Picton and in 1842 became a probationer in the CANADA CONFERENCE. Ordained in 1846, until 1868 he served on various circuits in the Canadas.

In 1868, in response to an appeal from GEORGE MCDOUGALL, he volunteered for the Western mission. He arrived at Fort Garry in time to witness the stirring events of the first Riel Rebellion. Along with other ministers he was credited with saving the colony from greater disturbances. He was responsible for the establishment of the first Wesleyan congregations in WINNIPEG. He was also the chief promoter of the Manitoba Wesleyan Institute, an academy that functioned from 1873 to 1877.

Young returned briefly to Ontario in 1876 and was elected President of the Toronto Conference in the following year. Two years later he returned to Manitoba as superintendent of missions. When the Manitoba and North-West Conference was organized in 1883 he became its first president. In failing health, he returned to Toronto in 1884. He was able to preach and write until his death in 1910. His work in the west was recalled in *Manitoba Memories*, published in 1897.

George Young was one of those whose contribution to the establishment of Methodism in western CANADA cannot be adequately measured.

G. H. Cornish, *Cyclopaedia of Methodism in Canada*. 1881.
J. Maclean, *Vanguards of Canada*. Toronto: Methodist Missionary Society, 1918.
H. J. Morgan, ed., *The Canadian Men and Women of the Time*. Toronto: Briggs, 1898.   F. W. ARMSTRONG

YOUNG, GEORGE BENJAMIN (?-1949), American bishop of the A.M.E. CHURCH. His birthdate and birthplace in the state of TEXAS are unknown. He was reared on a farm, attended the rural schools of his county, and later was graduated from PAUL QUINN COLLEGE at Waco, Texas. In 1896 he received the B.D. degree from WILBERFORCE UNIVERSITY and was subsequently ordained deacon and elder in his native state. His career in the ministry included a professorship at Paul Quinn College, a presiding eldership and pastorates in Texas. He was elected bishop in 1928, retired in 1948 and died the following year. Bishop Young served the A.M.E. Church with distinction while in Swaziland and RHODESIA, Africa, as well as in the United States.

R. R. Wright, *The Bishops*. 1963.   GRANT S. SHOCKLEY

YOUNG, JACOB (1776-1859), American circuit rider in OHIO, was born March 19, 1776, in Allegheny County, Pa., of an Episcopalian father and a Presbyterian mother. When he was fifteen the family moved west to KENTUCKY, where he grew up, listened to circuiting preachers, and became a Methodist. In 1799 he was appointed exhorter and began his preaching career with an appointment in 1802 to Salt River and Wayne circuits. He was ordained ELDER in 1807.

Almost his entire life was devoted to the itinerant ministry in Kentucky and Ohio, with brief service in TENNESSEE (1806) and MISSISSIPPI (1807-08). In 1812 he was made PRESIDING ELDER of the Ohio District of the OHIO CONFERENCE, and spent the stirring years of the War of 1812 in that capacity. The rest of his life was spent in many appointments in Ohio Methodism. Worn out, he retired in 1856, and died Sept. 16, 1859.

He is best known for his lively *Autobiography of a Pioneer*, written in old age and printed, with editing by D. W. Clark and E. Thomson, by the Western Book Concern in 1857. Done in old age, it is not always reliable in detail; but it represents one of the most valuable and extensive, as well as readable, accounts of Methodism in circuit rider days in the Ohio Valley.

A. Stevens, *History of American Methodism*, IV, 116 ff.
W. W. Sweet, *The Rise of Methodism in the West*. 1920.
J. Young, *Autobiography*. 1857.   FREDERICK A. NORWOOD

YOUNG, ROY LEE (1888-1948), twenty-fourth bishop of the C.M.E. CHURCH, was born on Oct. 2, 1888, at Whynot, Miss. He earned the B.A. degree from PAINE COLLEGE. Bishop Young served as parish minister and presiding elder in MISSISSIPPI, and earned a reputation as a builder of churches and a leading businessman in the church. He was elected to the office of bishop in 1946 but served only two years. He died on March 10, 1948, in NASHVILLE, Tenn.

Harris and Patterson, *C.M.E. Church*. 1965.
The Mirror, General Conference, CME, 1958.   RALPH G. GAY

YOUNG HARRIS COLLEGE, Young Harris, Georgia, was established in 1886 as a mountain school in the northern part of Georgia. Junior college work began in 1912. The institution was named for a benefactor, Judge Young L. G. Harris, of Athens, Georgia. The governing board has forty-two members elected by the trustees and confirmed by the NORTH GEORGIA ANNUAL CONFERENCE.

JOHN O. GROSS

YOUNGER, WILLIAM (1869-1956), was born at Morpeth Northumberland, in 1869. He entered the PRIMITIVE METHODIST ministry in 1894, and served successfully in several English circuits. He gave the HARTLEY LECTURE in 1924, *The International Value of Christian Ethics*. He was president of the last Primitive Methodist Conference, in 1932; he was president of the Conference of the Methodist Church in 1934. He died on Feb. 16, 1956.

JOHN KENT

YOUNGMAN, HENRY (1848-1927), Australian leader, was President of the QUEENSLAND CONFERENCE 1893, 1898 and 1907; President-General of the Methodist Church of Australasia, 1910-13. He gave statesmanlike leadership to the Conference and served in every executive position—Connexional Secretary and Secretary of Property, Loan Fund, and Insurance Committees, Editor Conference Journal and Book Steward. He helped to create the Queensland Conference, directed negotiations for the Union of Methodism in that State, and became its first President.

AUSTRALIAN EDITORIAL COMMITTEE

YOUNGSTOWN, OHIO, U.S.A. (population 140,000 in 1970), first appeared in the OHIO CONFERENCE appointments in 1824 when the circuit reported 777 members. Methodism was introduced in Youngstown by Shadrack Bostwick who had previously served in New England. Refused permission to preach in a log house built by the citizens and occupied by the Presbyterians, Bostwick preached in a barn. He soon formed a small class, and Youngstown became a preaching point successively on the Deerfield, Mahoning, and Youngstown Circuits. ROBERT R. ROBERTS, later bishop, served the circuit in 1806. The Methodists received a deed for a church site in 1814, and a frame structure was soon erected. Remodeled in 1818, it was replaced by a brick church in 1830. In the latter year some fifty "influential and wealthy" members withdrew to form a METHODIST PROTESTANT CHURCH.

In 1842 Youngstown became a station, and Dillon Prosser was appointed to what is now Trinity Church. The church building was remodeled in 1861. Belmont Avenue Church was organized in 1877 and Wilson Avenue in 1883. In the latter year the present Trinity Church was built at a cost of $81,000. The Brown Memorial Church appeared in 1905.

WILBUR E. HAMMAKER, later bishop, was pastor of

Trinity, 1915-36. During his ministry the building was enlarged. SCHUYLER E. GARTH, later bishop, served the church, 1936-44. RUSSELL J. HUMBERT, pastor, 1944-51, became president of DEPAUW UNIVERSITY. H. J. R. Elford has been pastor since 1951.

The Youngstown Community Center is jointly sponsored by the Division of National Missions, Conference Board of Missions, District Missionary Society, and Trinity Church. In 1970 the two mission boards appropriated $10,000 each for the center.

In 1970 The United Methodist Church had seven churches in Youngstown with a total of 4,167 members, property valued at $6,526,420, and $419,184 raised for all purposes during the year.

H. C. Aley, *The Trinity Story*. (Pamphlet), 1957.
General Minutes, MEC, MC, UMC.
M. Simpson, *Cyclopaedia*. 1878.   ALBEA GODBOLD
                                          JESSE A. EARL

YOUTH CLUBS, METHODIST ASSOCIATION OF, was originated in England in 1945 by the Rev. Douglas A. Griffiths and sponsored by the British Methodist Youth Department. It seeks to use the approach to young people through youth clubs as a means of evangelism, education, and service. Recognized as a National Youth Movement, it is supported financially by the Ministry of Education. Its officers are elected annually, with the exception of the secretary, who is a member of the Methodist Youth Department Secretariat and is appointed by Conference.

D. HUBERY

YOUTH DEPARTMENT, METHODIST (British), was set up in 1943 in England, to coordinate the work in British Methodism of the Sunday School and Guild Departments, and to encourage the Youth Club movement within Methodism—later to be known as the Methodist Association of Youth Clubs. The department thus became responsible for the church's program both on Sundays and weekdays for children, young people, and young adults, and for the training of their leaders and teachers. Its policy centers upon churchmanship, education, and evangelism.

A general secretary is appointed by the Conference to superintend the whole work of the department and to organize its schemes of training. Two other secretaries have special responsibility for work among families, young adults, and young people. A fourth is appointed by the council to coordinate the children's work and arrange annual Scripture examinations for Sunday school scholars and teachers. It employs a field staff, usually professionally trained educationalists, who are appointed to districts and circuits in order to interpret policy and lend training programs.

The department controls a Trade Section, which produces Christian educational literature, syllabuses of study, and projects for the various age groups, audio-visual aid material, and a monthly magazine, *Youth*. The Holiday Section arranges bookings for the Wesley Guild Holidays Limited, and organizes regular educational and holiday tours abroad.

New headquarters at Muswell Hill, LONDON, were opened in May 1960, and named "Chester House" as a tribute to the generous services of the department's treasurer, H. Guy Chester. The buildings include a residential hostel for young Methodist workers and students.

The department works closely with the Ministry of Education in the nation's service of youth, and with other Christian educational bodies in the formulation of graded Sunday school lesson notes. It cooperates with the British Council of Churches on all ecumenical matters affecting youth. There is also a liaison with various other organizations, and from this has emerged the Association of Methodist Scouters and the Methodist Federation of Boys' Brigade Officers. The department issues its own certificates and diplomas for those who satisfactorily complete recognized courses of training in leadership among children or young people, and annually arranges Easter and summer schools for its constituency. The statistical returns of 1962 showed that the constituency served includes 560,000 meeting in Sunday departments, 37,500 on weekdays, together with 105,000 Sunday school leaders and teachers and 10,500 leaders of weekday activities. It is estimated that fifty percent of new members received annually into the church come from youth groups served by the Methodist Youth Department.

Youth Department (American, U.M.C.). In the United States work for youth is a department of the BOARD OF EDUCATION. It is known as the Methodist Youth Fellowship in the churches and is composed of youth between the ages of twelve and twenty-one. This includes junior-high youth, ages twelve through fourteen, those enrolled in the seventh, eighth, or ninth grades, known as the Junior High MYF; senior-high youth, ages fifteen through seventeen, known as the Senior MYF; and older youth, post-high-school youth who have not yet assumed adult responsibilities, who are working or in college and are still related to the local church youth program, known as the Older Youth MYF. Each age group has a council of youth officers and adult counselors to carry on all the activities for that age group.

The program of the MYF includes all activities of the youth in a church—Sunday school classes, Sunday evening and weekday meetings for worship, study, and fellowship. In addition, informal interest groups are formed from time to time in such areas as crafts, hobbies, music, nature lore, drama. Scout troops, clubs, and other groups sponsored by the church are a part of the MYF program. In addition, youth are expected to join the adults in the total program of the church, including the regular worship services, special services, and other all-church events.

The Methodist Youth Fellowship carries on an organization and program beyond the local church in subdistricts, districts, and annual conferences, including workshops, summer camps and conferences, and special events. The National Conference of the Methodist Youth Fellowship is the organization on the national level to bring together annually the presidents of annual conference MYF organizations to discuss the youth program, their place in the church, and current issues of vital importance to them.

The central office of the Methodist Youth Fellowship is in the Division of the Local Church of the General Board of Education of The United Methodist Church. Related also to the church's youth ministry is the Department of Youth Publications, Editorial Division in the General Board of Education, and designated staff persons in other boards and agencies. These comprise the Interboard Staff on Youth Work to bring unity and coordination in the total program.

Guidebook for Youth Work in the Church; Handbook for Senior Highs in the Church; Junior Highs and Their MYF; Manual for Workers with Junior Highs; Notebook for Youth Work Beyond the Local Church. (Board of Education, UMC, publications.)

D. S. HUBERY
WALTER N. VERNON

YPRES METHODIST CHURCH (Flemish) is the head of a large Methodist circuit in West Flanders. The origin of the work was the opening in 1920 of the very first postwar relief station in Europe by the M.E. Church, South. A local church was organized in 1923, and a fine chapel and parsonage were erected in 1947 near the famous old Cloth Hall, 13 Beluikstraat. Pastors have been G. Twynham, 1920-21; J. Schyns, 1923-24; F. vanden Wyngaert, 1925-28; A. Mietes, 1929-30; J. van Kesteren, 1931-32; J. Mietes, 1933-37; J. Drubbels, since 1938.

WILLIAM G. THONGER

YUGOSLAVIA (Socialist Federal Republic of Yugoslavia) is located on the Balkan peninsula in southeastern Europe. Yugoslavia was created after World War I and consists of the following six republics: Slovenia, Croatia, Serbia, Bosnia and Herzegovina, Montenegro, and Macedonia. The three official languages of Yugoslavia are Serbo-Croatian, Slovenian, and Macedonian. The population is close to 20,000,000. The capital city is Belgrade, with the other major centers being Zagreb, Lyublyana, Sarayevo, Skopye, and Novi Sad.

No accurate religious census is available but a good estimate would be that about forty per cent of the population belongs to Eastern Orthodoxy (specifically to The Serbian Orthodox Church and The Macedonian Orthodox Church), about thirty percent to the Roman Catholic Church, about ten percent are Muslims, less than one per cent are Protestants and less than one per cent Jewish. The rest of the people are Communists and non-Communist atheists or agnostics. Of the Protestant denominations the largest are the Evangelical (Lutheran), and Reformed (Calvinist) Churches, with Baptists, Methodists, Pentecostals, Free Brethren, and Adventists consisting of tiny minorities, each church having not more than 2,000 members.

Methodism in Yugoslavia. The work of the M.E. Church in the territories of present Yugoslavia, which formerly belonged to the Austro-Hungarian monarchy, was commenced in 1898 when some German members of the Blue Cross Temperance Society in Bachka (a region in northeast Yugoslavia now part of the Autonomous Province of Voyvodina) invited Robert Möller, the Methodist preacher from Vienna, AUSTRIA, to evangelize among them. This led to an invitation to F. H. OTTO MELLE (later bishop of the German Methodist Annual Conference) as one of the first preachers. His work which commenced in 1899 or 1900 was successful despite strong opposition, and definite advances were made among the German colonists in Bachka and later in the other parts of Voyvodina. A number of ministers came from GERMANY, but local men such as John Tessenyi-Jakob were also trained and worked alongside the German pastors. Most of the work was done among the German minority, and some among the Hungarians, but little, if anything was done among the Slavic population.

By 1911 the Austria-Hungary Mission Conference was established, independent of the North German Conference. This conference had its main strength in Bachka where there were some 300 members. Institutional development and membership growth was steady until the outbreak of World War I. World War I apparently took the church by surprise. It did not disrupt the work of the churches, but did check their growth.

When the Kingdom of Serbs, Croats, and Slovenes (later renamed Yugoslavia) was established after World War I, the churches in Voyvodina were incorporated into the newly formed Yugoslavia Mission Conference, to which were added in 1922 churches from Macedonia formerly related to the American Board of Commissioners for Foreign Missions, a Congregational missionary agency from Boston. The Congregationalist missionaries from the United States of America had extended their work from European Turkey and Bulgaria into Macedonia (then still under Turkish control) in 1873. Despite many hardships, approximately ten churches and a Girls' School were founded. These served the Macedonian population. The American Board of Commissioners for Foreign Missions was not able to take proper care of these churches when the Macedonian churches were separated from the headquarters located in Bulgaria as a result of the new political structure. Therefore the Board arranged a transfer of these churches to the Yugoslavia M.E. Mission Conference with cooperation from the Board of Foreign Missions of the M.E. Church in New York. Thus two fairly different groups of churches were united into one Mission Conference, but the merger was successful in every respect.

Some of the opposition experienced by the Macedonian Methodists from members of the Orthodox Churches and local authorities, and similar pressures upon the Voyvodina Methodists from the larger Protestant Churches and local authorities continued but diminished in scope. The church still was not officially recognized by the government but grew in membership until it passed the 1000 mark. The church suffered great financial hardship when appropriations were reduced by more than half of the amount granted, as a result of the depression. Thus the two Girls' Schools in Bitola and Novi Sad had to discontinue their operations in 1929. The other social activities also suffered but were continued. Among the most prominent was an orphanage in Srbobran, a Tuberculosis Sanitarium in Novi Sad, and an Old People's Home in Novi Vrbas. With the exception of the last named all these had to cease operations at the end of World War II as a result of government decrees and the expropriation of property.

During World War II the work of the Church was almost completely disrupted and a large number of members was lost as nearly all the German members fled or were placed in concentration camps. But by 1946 the church started a slow recovery in the face of opposition by the new Communist regime which came to power after the war ended. Small congregations started to function again in about forty localities mainly under the leadership of lay women and to a lesser extent of laymen and the four remaining ministers. The work of the churches was reduced to the strictly religious aspects and obstacles were frequently placed in its course of development. However, membership continued to grow slowly so that it reached a high point near the 3000 mark after it received a boost in membership by the addition of Slovak nationals living in Voyvodina. These had been formerly members of the outlawed Blue Cross Temperance Society. The key figures in this post-war work were George Sebele, Mrs. Paula Mojzes, and Krum Kalajlijev, though the work of others was equally dedicated.

The present Church is permitted to maintain its ties with all agencies of The United Methodist Church as well as with various ecumenical agencies. In recent years, from about 1958 onward, the pressures by the government have been greatly relaxed and church work is carried on with relative freedom of worship. The major Methodist churches are located in Novi Sad (headquarters), Kisach (where the Home for Elderly People is located), Zrenyanin, Pivnitse, Skopye, Prilep, Koleshino, and Strumitsa. The church building in Skopye was seriously damaged by the 1963 earthquake and is being rebuilt with denominational and ecumenical funds from abroad.

The main method of obtaining converts is through personal and mass evangelization and revivals coupled with pastoral care and nurture. The worship is emphatically non-liturgical and informal with the main emphasis on the sermon. The pastors and members are staunchly conservative in theology. The religious and theological training of the membership and clergy is limited by the existing socio-economic conditions. Emphasis is on personal salvation and survival of the church through perpetuation of religious beliefs and personal piety. Despite being a minority church, its main contribution is to provide the opportunity for those dissatisfied with the religious *milieu* of the country to worship in churches more to their liking, and to influence positively many individuals to reform their life and provide an alternative approach to religious living from the one offered by the larger churches. When one considers the continuous opposition and antagonism which has been faced, the conclusion is that their work has been successful.

Festschrift: zur Feier des fünfundzwanzigjährigen Bestehens der Bischöflichen Methodistenkirche im Krg. S.H.S., Novi Sad, 1923.
F. H. Otto Melle (ed.), *Das Walten Gottes im Deutschen Methodismus,* Bremen, 1925(?).
Verhandlungen der Prediger der Bischöflichen Methodistenkirche im Königreiche S.H.S. (Jugoslawien).
Journals of the Annual Missions Conference from 1921 to 1940.
Annual Reports of the Board of Foreign Missions.

PAUL B. MOJZES

YUN, CHANG DUK (1910-   ), the ninth bishop of the Korean Methodist Church, was born in Pyongyang, KOREA, Dec. 8, 1910. His parents were devout Christians and his education was in the Methodist church schools in Pyongyang, graduating from Kwangsyung High in 1931, the Union Methodist Theological Seminary in SEOUL in 1936, and the Theological Department of Kwansei Gakuin College, in Kobe, JAPAN, in 1941.

While in Japan he served as pastor of the Kobe Korean Church. Returning to Korea he served churches in what is now North Korea until the invasion of 1950, when he escaped the communist area, to serve as pastor of First Church of Taegu and as superintendent of the Taegu district.

He was a Crusade Scholar at GARRETT BIBLICAL INSTITUTE in 1954-56, at the same time serving the Korean Methodist Church in CHICAGO.

Returning to Korea he served as district superintendent, of the West Inchon District, as General Secretary of the Board of Evangelism of the Korean Methodist Church, and as pastor of Zion Methodist Church in Seoul.

He was ordained ELDER in 1939, was a delegate to the 1964 GENERAL CONFERENCE meeting in PITTSBURGH, and served four years as chairman of the East Annual Conference.

On Oct. 23, 1970 he was elected by the General Conference of the Korean Methodist Church, meeting in Seoul, on the first ballot as its ninth bishop.

News, November 10, 1970 (Three-page mimeographed Release by United Methodist Information). CHARLES A. SAUER

BARON TCHI HO YUN

YUN, TCHI HO (1864-1945), first Korean to join the M.E. Church, South, was born in Sin-Tchon village, Asan County, South Choong-Chung Province, KOREA, Dec. 26, 1864. His father was a general in the Korean army and one-time Minister of Justice. Yun studied Chinese classics and at the age of seventeen was one of a group of young men selected to study government administration in JAPAN. Here he mastered the Japanese language and began the study of English.

Barely nineteen he was recommended to General Foote, the first U. S. Minister to Korea, as Korean interpreter and they arrived in SEOUL from Japan in June 1883, and were instrumental in aiding ROBERT MACLAY, superintendent of the Methodist mission in Japan, in securing permission for Methodist missionaries to conduct medical and educational work in Korea in 1884. General Foote resigned early in 1885, and Yun went to Shanghai, entered the Anglo-Chinese School of the M.E. Church, South Mission, and was baptized in 1887. After studying at VANDERBILT and EMORY UNIVERSITIES he returned to Shanghai to teach English at his alma mater.

In 1894 as a result of political changes in Korea he was called to accept the position of Vice-Minister of Foreign Affairs. With the rank of baron he occupied many trouble spots for the Korean government and represented Korea at the coronation of the czar at St. Petersburgh.

Upon his return to Korea in 1894, he urged Bishop E. R. HENDRIX and others to establish a Mission of the M.E. Church, South in Korea, and was influential in helping them secure land in both Seoul and Songdo. When the Japanese took control of Korea in 1905 he left government service and organized a boys' school in Songdo. In 1911 Baron Yun and five others, in a gross miscarriage of Japanese justice, were sentenced to six years imprisonment in an alleged plot to assassinate the Governor-General. Four years later he was granted an Imperial pardon and his rights and rank were restored. He became general secretary of the Y.M.C.A. for five years, and was president of that association for many years. He was also active on the boards of various high schools and colleges, as well as in church, cultural and research organizations, so much so that he was often referred to as the most influential Christian in Korea.

Baron Yun spoke five languages and in 1907 in TOKYO he gave an outstanding address to the WORLD STUDENT CHRISTIAN FEDERATION in English, Japanese, and Chinese.

He died in Seoul in 1945.

Y. H. Kim, "A Short Sketch of Dr. T. H. Yun's Life," in *Korea Mission Field,* February 1935.　　　CHARLES A. SAUER

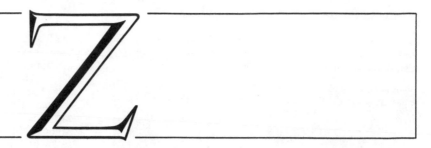

ZAHNISER, ARTHUR DE FRANCE (1865-1935), Free Methodist bishop, was born in Mercer, Pa., on Aug. 26, 1865. He was raised in a strict Presbyterian home. He became a partner in a lumber business, but was converted at age twenty-two, called to preach and joined the Pittsburgh Conference in 1890, where he was pastor and district elder for seventeen years. He was elected general conference evangelist in 1911 and bishop in 1927. In that office he served until death which occurred early in his third term, Aug. 14, 1935. A clear, forceful, logical preacher, he was firm in his convictions and had a great capacity for friendship. His preaching and writing were Christ-centered. He was primarily an evangelist, a "fisher of men," greatly interested in young people. Bishop Zahniser was president of Greenville College Board of Trustees many years.

BYRON S. LAMSON

ZAHNISER, ARTHUR DE FRANCE (1911-   ), an American ordained elder of the Free Methodist Church in the Illinois-Wisconsin Conference. He was born at New Brighton, Pa., and married Audrey Elizabeth Ashe in 1933. Arthur Zahniser was educated at Houghton College, A.B.; Northern Baptist Seminary, B.D.; did post-graduate work at Garrett Biblical Institute and Northern Baptist Seminary. He received the honorary degree of LL.D. from Azusa Pacific College in 1968. He served as pastor in Hornell, N. Y., 1941-45; Melrose Park, Ill., 1946-48; Evanston, Ill., 1948-62. He became executive director of the Evangelical Child Welfare Agency, Chicago, Ill., 1960-61, the director of Public Relations, Children's Home and Sunset Manor Retirement Home, Woodstock, Ill., 1963-66. He has been the general secretary of Higher Education in his Church since 1966. He is also the chairman, Commission on Social Concerns, National Association of Evangelicals, 1950-61; chairman, Council on Social Action, Free Methodist Church of North America, 1969. He resides in Winona Lake, Ind.

BYRON S. LAMSON

ZAHUR-AL-HAQQ (1834- ?), early Moslem convert in India, the first convert in Bareilly, was baptized in June or July, 1859. He was often called the first convert of Methodism in all India. May, June, and July of 1859 brought the first converts in Moradabad and Lucknow, as well as in Bareilly, and four out of five of these were Moslems. Among these Zahur-al-Haqq was outstanding.

Born in a cultured Sunni Moslem family, he early learned Persian and Arabic as well as Urdu and Hindi, and was carefully instructed in the Islamic religion. But he was plagued by doubts, and began to study Hinduism and joined the Parmami sect. Disappointed there, too, he found a job as a teacher in a school in Bareilly. One day he heard the Methodists preaching in the streets. He undertook serious study of Christianity, began attending church services and soon declared his faith and asked for baptism. His wife left him and kept their son from him. His father and other relatives tried diligently and persistently to make him recant. But he persisted, joined the mission school as a teacher, and was successively licensed as an exhorter, then as a local preacher, and finally was ordained as a deacon, and after that an elder. In time he became the first Indian district superintendent. When his Moslem wife refused to return to him, he was married by Christian rites to a Christian. At the age of twenty his Moslem son was converted, and he and two sons by the Christian wife became honored and successful Methodist ministers.

J. WASKOM PICKETT

ZAMBIA. The Republic of Zambia is situated in the heart of the southern half of the continent of Africa. It is fringed by the Portuguese territories of Angola to the west, and Mozambique and Malawi to the east, with Rhodesia to the south, and the Congo and Tanzania to the north. Zambia has no sea coast, and lies entirely at an altitude of between 3,000 and 4,000 feet above sea level. These facts explain why western influence came relatively late to Zambia, and why missionary activity largely preceded any political or trading ventures in the area.

David Livingstone was the great pioneer of Christian activity in this part of Africa, which had been unknown and unexplored until his time. His three great journeys of exploration took place in 1852-57, 1858-64, and 1865-73. His aim was to find a means of easy penetration into the heart of the continent, so that missionaries and traders could follow. After his first tour he declared: "I go back to Africa to try and make an open path for commerce and Christianity." But it was not until after his tragic death at Old Chitambo in 1873, that missionary activity began in earnest.

Methodist work in Zambia began through the efforts of two separate missionary societies representing the Primitive Methodist and the Wesleyan Methodist churches of Britain. The Primitive Methodist Missionary Society had established work in South Africa, and through contact and cooperation with the Paris Evangelical Missionary Society, came to hear of the need for work amongst the subjects of Lewanika of the Barotse in the south and center of Zambia, namely the Balla and the BaTonga. Henry Buckenham led the first party, which arrived in Barotse territory in 1890. Lewanika had just completed a treaty with the British South Africa Company, and was in the throes of misgivings when the party arrived. He was unwilling to give authority for the new work, and at one point the new missionaries were accused of witchcraft! However in 1893 he gave permission for work among the Balla, and sent some of his people to help. Although stations were established at Nkala (1893), Nazhila (1895), Siajoba (1901) and Nambala (1905), the first baptisms among the Balla did not take place until 1906. The fact that the missionaries seemed to have come from Lewanika probably did not predispose the Balla to accept them or their message. Two other centers were opened soon after: Kanchindu (in place of Siajoba) (1907), and Kasenga (1909). The missionaries were more successful in their attempts at educational work and the production of literature in the Ila language. A grammar was published in 1906, and the New Testament in 1914. In 1916 land was purchased at Kafue for a large Training Institute, of which John R. Fell was appointed principal. Here teacher-evangelists were trained for the Wesleyan Methodist Church, the London Missionary Society, and the Primitive Methodist Church.

Meanwhile the Wesleyan METHODIST MISSIONARY SOCIETY had begun work in Zambia. The son of a Lala chief was converted whilst working on a mine in Rhodesia, and was responsible for rousing interest in having a missionary among his own people in Zambia. The first missionary came in 1912, but was invalided home in the following year, being replaced by S. Douglas Gray. Work was established at Chipembi, and spread widely from there, including the first urban work at Lusaka and Broken Hill (now known as Kabwe). A school was later established at Chipembi, which became the country's pioneer in girls' education. When the various branches of British Methodism joined in union in 1932, the work of the two societies in Zambia was united.

The territory today known as Zambia was declared a Crown Colony of the British Empire in 1924, and was then known as Northern Rhodesia. It incorporated the much older Barotse Protectorate, which had been established with Lewanika through the activities of the British South Africa Company. Nineteen hundred twenty-four was a significant moment in the development of Zambia, for the Cooper Mining Companies were coming into production, and African townships were springing up in the north of the territory to house the men from many different tribes drawn there by the opportunity of earning money. African Christians on the Copperbelt gathered together for fellowship and worship, showing little regard for denominational differences. It was not until 1936, however, that missionary activity reached the point of organized cooperation and united activity through a United Mission to the Copperbelt. Methodist staff played an important part in this team, and continued to do so when the churches of the Copperbelt became part of the United Church of Central Africa in Rhodesia (itself a union of the ex-London Missionary Society with Church of Scotland congregations). The African congregations were involved in this from 1945, and the European congregations joined in 1958.

The Methodist Church continued its separate existence in the center and south of the country for another six and a half years. The original mission stations were still centers of activity. Educational work continued to expand with the opening of secondary schools at Chipembi (1948), Kafue (1957) and Njase (1960). Upper primary boarding schools for girls were established at Kasenga, Keembe, Masuku, and Nambala. Teacher training was transferred from Kafue to Livingstone in 1958, when several small colleges were integrated to form a Christian Council College, with a Methodist as its first principal. Primary schools were for a long time supervised by the circuit staffs, but this responsibility came to take a disproportionate part of a minister's time. Two education secretaries were appointed, and a number of African teachers were appointed to replace ministers as managers

of schools. Shortly after Zambia became independent in October 1964, all primary schools were willingly transferred to government management. In large measure this led to the disbandment of the mission stations, which now remain solely as the residences of the ministers responsible for the rural circuits. In some circuits new manses have been erected close to the government administrative centers for the area, for example at Namwala and Sinazongwe.

In January 1965 the Methodist Church became part of the United Church of Zambia, which also includes the earlier United Church of Central Africa in Rhodesia, together with the Church of Barotse, founded by the Paris Evangelical Missionary Society. The problem of ordination was not raised by this union of nonepiscopal churches. All that was necessary was a public recognition that from the time of the United Church's inauguration, there was one "common fellowship within the United Church of Zambia." Colin Morris became the first president, in acknowledgment of the leadership he had given in the country and in the Church, in the struggle for independence. He led the new church for four years before a Zambian president was elected. Doyce Musunsa was the first Synod Clerk, or administrative head of the Church.

The United Church is an autonomous body divided into four presbyteries, which act under the authority of the Synod, the highest court of the Church.

Whilst the aim is for the church to become financially as well as organizationally autonomous, the cost of a full-time minister makes this, as yet, a distant goal.

Every effort is made to recruit Zambian candidates for training for the ministry, and some with nine years' schooling are in training in the United Church Ministerial Training College in the Copperbelt. Missionaries are engaged in pastoral work especially in the English-speaking congregations, as well as occasionally in a specialized capacity. No statistics of church membership or of church officers have been compiled in recent years, but the 1967 edition of the *World Christian Handbook* quoted figures of 648 places of worship and a community of 33,729.

P. Bolink, *Towards Church Union in Zambia*. Franeker T. (Netherlands): Wever Boekhandel, 1968.
S. D. Gray, *Frontiers of the Kingdom in Rhodesia*. London: Cargate, 1923.
K. Kaunda and C. Morris, *Black Government*. Lusaka: U.S.C.L., 1960.
C. Morris, *Church and Challenge in a New Africa*. London: Epworth Press, 1964.
E. G. Nightingale, *Widening Way*. London: Cargate, 1952.
R. I. Rotberg, *Christian Missionaries and the Creation of Northern Rhodesia, 1880-1924*. London: Oxford University Press, Princeton University Press, 1965.
J. V. Taylor and D. Lehmann, *Christians of the Copperbelt*. London: SCM Press, 1961.
World Methodist Council, *Handbook of Information*, 1966-71.
The Zambesi Valley. London: Primitive Methodist Missionary Society, 1860.
D. F. HINSON

ZAPATA, ROLANDO OLIVARES (1911-   ), Mexican church leader, was born in Pachuca Hgo., MEXICO, on July 6, 1911. He took his early training in the Puebla Methodist School. Then studied in Grade School in PANAMA and in the Methodist School in San José, COSTA RICA, where his father was serving as missionary from Mexico. He felt the call to the ministry in 1934, took part of his training at the Union Evangelical Seminary, and finished it through the Conference Course of Study.

He entered the annual conference on trial in 1939,

was ordained deacon in 1941, and elder in 1943 by Bishop ELEAZAR GUERRA. He was pastor of Real del Monte, 1939-42; Pachua, 1943-46; presiding elder of the Northern District, 1947-54. Then he was elected bishop for the period of 1954-58.

Rolando Zapata married Eugenia Reséndiz. They had two children. Rolando, Jr. is at present executive secretary of Cave de Mexico (Audiovisual Evangelical Center). Rolando Zapata was pastor of the Portales Church, 1959-63; Aztecas 1964-67, and is now serving Balderas Church.

GUSTAVO P. VELASCO

ZELLER, ANDREW (1755-1839), American United Brethren preacher and church pioneer, was born in Berks County, Pa., of Swiss ancestry. In 1805 he moved with his family to a farm north of Germantown, Ohio. After his conversion, about 1790, he actively promoted the work of the church. His farmhouse both in PENNSYLVANIA and OHIO became a home for preachers and a place for religious meetings. The first United Brethren congregation west of the Allegheny Mountains was organized in a log meeting house which he built near his Germantown home. He was an active licensed preacher and a member of the first session of the Miami Conference, Church of the UNITED BRETHREN IN CHRIST, in 1810. His dedication and administrative ability were recognized when he was elected to the office of bishop in 1817. He continued in this position until he retired in 1821.

Andrew Zeller married Catherine Forrer in 1779. They had nine children, five daughters and four sons. Reflecting the fact that many preachers stopped at the Zeller home, all his daughters married preachers.

Zeller was an earnest, wholehearted Christian, a plain practical preacher and a man of good judgment in the affairs of the church. He died on May 25, 1839 and was buried in a small graveyard on his farm. In 1865 the body was removed to the Germantown cemetery.

A. W. Drury, *History of the U.B.* 1924.
V. E. Michael, "Gilbert, Zeller, Michael." Ms., 1962.

ROY D. MILLER

ZEUNER, BERNHARD FRIEDRICH WALTHER (1903-   ), German pastor, became a member of Northwest Germany Annual Conference in 1927. Appointment to circuits: London German Methodist Mission, 1927-30; Kiel, 1930-39; Hamburg, 1939-46 and 1957-64. He was appointed as district superintendent of Hamburg District: 1946-57 and a second time in 1964. He was secretary of the Northwest Germany Annual Conference from 1932 to 1946, and has been secretary of the GERMANY CENTRAL CONFERENCE in 1952, 1966, 1968, 1970. He is editor of the German edition of the *Book of Discipline* of The United Methodist Church, 1968. He presently resides in Bramstedt, Germany.

ERNST SOMMER

ZIEGLER, SAMUEL GEORGE (1884-   ), American E.U.B. pastor and General Church officer, was born Oct. 14, 1884, in Hanover, Pa., the son of Daniel and Polly Low Ziegler. He prepared for the ministry in York Collegiate Institute; LEBANON VALLEY COLLEGE (A.B. 1911); and Bonebrake (now UNITED) THEOLOGICAL SEMINARY (B.D. 1914). The honorary D.D. degree was conferred upon him by Lebanon Valley College in 1922. He was

married to Ethel Redding in 1911. Their four children have attained distinction in the fields of medicine, teaching, and social sciences.

Ordained in 1911 by the Pennsylvania Conference, Church of the UNITED BRETHREN IN CHRIST, Ziegler served pastorates as follows: Duncannon, Pa. (1909-11); Wagner-Aley, Ohio (1912-14); BALTIMORE, Md., Otterbein Memorial (1914-17); and Hagerstown, Md., St. Paul's (1917-21). The United Brethren GENERAL CONFERENCE of 1921 elected Dr. Ziegler to the office of General Secretary of the United Brethren Foreign Missionary Society, a position involving extensive traveling throughout the world, and the making of many contacts with Mission Boards and agencies of other denominations. Dr. Ziegler's writings for church periodicals have been extensive. He wrote a number of mission study text books. When the Evangelical and United Brethren denominations merged in 1946, Dr. Ziegler was elected Associate Secretary of the Division of World MISSIONS, a position he served with distinction until his retirement in 1958.

P. E. Holdcraft, *Pennsylvania Conference.* 1938.
Records of the EUB Board of Foreign Missions, 1921-46, 1947-58.
S. G. Ziegler, *Christian Movements in the Orient.* Dayton, O.: Foreign Missionary Society, 1927.
————, *The Fellowship in Action.* Dayton, O.: Foreign Missionary Society, 1931.
————, *God's Will Be Done in World Relations.* Dayton, O.: U.B. Publishing House, 1940.   PAUL E. HOLDCRAFT

ZINSER, JOHN GEORGE (1806-1883), American Evangelical Association pioneer preacher, was born in Wurtenberg, GERMANY, Nov. 28, 1806. His family emigrated to America in 1817 and settled in Pickaway County, Ohio in 1826, where two years later they became members of the EVANGELICAL ASSOCIATION. Zinser joined the Eastern Conference in 1829, and in 1834 began his long and effective career as a pioneer presiding elder. He was a front rank leader in extending the work into western PENNSYLVANIA, OHIO, MICHIGAN, INDIANA, ILLINOIS, WISCONSIN, and IOWA. His Ohio District (1837-43) reached into three states and two territories, requiring a round on horseback of 2,000 miles.

John G. Zinser was a staunch supporter in launching the cause of missions, 1839; publication of the German Bible, 1841; removal and relocating the Evangelical Publishing House in Cleveland, Ohio, 1854; and the founding of the Ebenezer Orphan Home, Tiffin, Ohio, 1866, of which he was the first superintendent.

"His sermons were so profound and intellectually clear," said Bishop REUBEN YEAKEL, "that they made deep impressions. . . . He was a great reader and close thinker, as his editorials while editor of the *Christliche Botschafter*, and many other articles from his pen clearly show. He was probably the last of the chief pioneers of the Evangelical Association, whose heroic labors extended from the East into the far West—who under untold self-denials and hardships, founded and spread the work of God in our church." Death came Oct. 11, 1883 at his home in El Paso, Ill.

Der Christliche Botschafter, 1859.
Evangelical Messenger, 1883.
R. B. Leedy, *Evangelical Church in Ohio.* 1959.
Living Epistle. 1885.
R. Yeakel, *Evangelical Association.* 1894.
Zinser Diaries.   ROY B. LEEDY

COUNT ZINZENDORF

ZINZENDORF, NICOLAUS LUDWIG VON (1700-1760), the leader of the Renewed Church of the United Brethren, was born in Dresden on May 26, 1700. A Lutheran of strong ecumenical leanings, he formed in his youth "The Order of the Mustard Seed," which was to include a bishop, an archbishop, and a cardinal. A layman, he preached every Sunday, and built up a Christian community on his estate at Berthelsdorf. He welcomed the Moravian refugees led by CHRISTIAN DAVID and thus inaugurated the Renewed Church. Zinzendorf became a Moravian bishop and by his generous benefactions saved the Brethren from bankruptcy. He disagreed with JOHN WESLEY, whom he regarded as unsound on justification, and was criticized by him, especially for his "blood and wounds" hymns. Zinzendorf regarded each Church as a Communion, not as the local congregation, but as a *tropus,* or training-ground, within the larger, comprehensive Church, which comprised all Communions. This tropus idea was a valuable contribution to the conception of a world Church. Zinzendorf died at Herrnhut on May 9, 1760.

E. Langton, *History of the Moravian Church.* London, 1956.
C. W. Towlson, *Moravian and Methodist.* 1957.

C. W. TOWLSON

ZION'S ADVOCATE. The earliest United Brethren periodical was the *Zion's Advocate,* sponsored by the Miami Conference, Church of the UNITED BRETHREN IN CHRIST. Sometime about the beginning of September 1829, AARON FARMER, a member of that conference, brought out the first issue. It was an eight-page publication, in English, selling for one dollar per year in advance or one dollar fifty cents if not paid before expiration time. It was issued every two weeks and consisted of a collection of articles taken from various religious publications. It was printed by J. Allen, Office of *Western Annotator,* Salem, Washington County, Ind.

Later that year Aaron Farmer was assigned to Orange Circuit in INDIANA. When the Indiana Conference was formed in 1830, he was listed as a member without appointment. Then in 1831, he was assigned to the Flatrock Circuit. The magazine thus issued by a minister of another conference was discontinued toward the close of volume two.

The magazine failed partly from the inexperience of both the editor and the conference and from lack of subscribers. It was not until 1834 that a successful venture, the *Religious Telescope,* was inaugurated.

J. H. Ness, *History of Publishing.* 1966.
Zion's Advocate, Vol. II, No. 4, Oct. 23, 1830.

JOHN H. NESS, JR.

ZION'S HERALD. From Jan. 9, 1823, until March 16, 1955, *Zion's Herald* enjoyed the reputation of being the oldest Methodist weekly in the world. Never an official paper, it held a position of freedom few church-related papers ever equaled. Its first sponsoring body was called the Society for Giving and Receiving Religious Intelligence, and after several successor groups, it finally came under the auspices of its present owners, the Boston Wesleyan Association, in 1831. There were repeated efforts to merge it with the New York *Christian Advocate* and, indeed for a period of about four years, beginning in 1824, such a combination did appear under the title *The Christian Advocate and Journal and Zion's Herald.* But the New England Methodists had tasted success with their beloved *Herald,* and they called it back. Then, after several sponsoring groups published it, they resumed their regular publication with their newly formed Boston Wesleyan Association.

A series of distinguished editors fired its editorials: ABEL STEVENS made it a lively and lonely supporter of the abolitionist cause from 1841 to 1852. He was followed by ERASTUS O. HAVEN, GILBERT HAVEN, who was later a bishop, Charles Parkhurst, and LEWIS O. HARTMAN, later a bishop. Its editors were always in the thick of things and produced a paper whose unpopularity with "the establishment" was probably its greatest reason for being. It has owed that independence to that amazing group of self-perpetuating Methodist laymen—never more than twenty members—who since 1831 have put the resources of the Boston Wesleyan Association behind this publication.

Housed in the Wesleyan Building at 581 Boylston Street in Boston, *Zion's Herald* still continues to be published as a monthly magazine for New England Methodists. It can be said of it now, what was said of it in 1890 by Frederick Burrill Graves, "New England Methodism is clearly mirrored in the paper; and to know how this branch of our church stands on large or small questions of vital interest to Methodism, no better criteria of judgment can be had than those found in the columns of this paper."

The Centennial of New England Methodism, George A. Crawford, ed. Boston: Crawford, 1891, p. 531.
Files of Zion's Herald.

EMORY S. BUCKE

ZOTTELE, PEDRO (1903-   ), bishop of the LATIN AMERICAN CENTRAL CONFERENCE, Christian educator and journalist, was born in Pisagua, Northern CHILE, South America, on Aug. 31, 1903, the son of Pedro and Eloisa (Clark) Zottele. He was a student at the Iquique English College at Iquique, in 1918; the Theological Seminary at SANTIAGO, Chile, in 1927; became a Bachelor of Theology at the Chicago Divinity School in 1928; and did postgraduate work at the BOSTON UNIVERSITY

PEDRO ZOTTELE

ESCRIVAO A. ZUNGUZE

School of Religious Education, 1932-33, and in the School of Theology, 1940. He married Agnes Elphick on Sept. 12, 1929, and they have one son, Pedro Roberto.

Bishop Zottele taught in the "Iquique English College," 1921-23, and was ordained to the Methodist ministry by Bishop ROBERTO ELPHICK in the Chile Annual Conference in 1936. As pastor he served the Second Methodist Church, Santiago, 1931-41, and the large First Methodist Church in Santiago, 1944-62. He was secretary of Christian Education of his Conference in Santiago, 1924-45, and for several years was also executive secretary of the Board of Social Action of the Chile Annual Conference.

He was elected bishop by the Latin American Central Conference in Buenos Aires in 1962, and assigned to supervise the Area which includes COSTA RICA, PANAMA, PERU, and Chile. He retired in 1969 when the autonomous Methodist Church of Chile was organized under his supervision.

He is the author of *Viviendo en Forma*, 1950; *Lumbre de Vida*, 1951; and was editor of *Mundo Ideal*, 1929.

Who's Who in The Methodist Church, 1966. N. B. H.

ZUNGUZE, ESCRIVÃO ANGLAZE (1914-   ), African bishop for MOZAMBIQUE and one of the first Africans to be elected a bishop in the history of Methodist work in AFRICA. He was born in Morrumbene, Mozambique, on April 14, 1914, the son of Anglaze and Vetilange Zunguze. His parents died when he was small, and he was raised by an uncle, an evangelist. His wife Thelma is a graduate of the Hartzell's Girl School in Chicuque, and they have five children.

He became a Christian in 1928 when attending a revival to which his cousin had invited him. He began his schooling at Chissico Station, Mollumbene, Inhambana, after which he went to the Cambine (Mozambique) Mission where he studied until 1932. There he taught and continued the study of English. He went to Old Umtali (Southern RHODESIA) for secondary work, 1935-38, serving there as a preacher for the juniors. He went on to study theology at the Old Umtali Biblical Institute, 1939-41, and at Carcavelos, PORTUGAL, 1959-60.

Entering the ministry in 1946, he was ordained an elder in 1950, was a delegate to the Africa Central Conference, 1948, '52, and '56; he was elected a delegate to the GENERAL CONFERENCES of 1960 and '64, but was not granted a passport to leave his country for the latter. For several years he was pastor of the large Methodist church at Cambine, one of the largest mission centers in the country. He was elected bishop in 1964.

He is a member of the executive committee of the National Council of Churches in Mozambique. Considered an excellent preacher, as well as a fine singer, he has become well known in Methodist churches in the United States during his periodic visits to that land. His present assignment is Mozambique and SOUTH AFRICA (the area around Johannesburg with Methodist membership of about 19,500). Both of these countries are included in the South East Africa Methodist Conference. He has become well-known in the COUNCIL OF BISHOPS of The United Methodist Church.

N. B. H.

ZÜRICH, Switzerland, is the largest city of the country and has a population of 432,500 (1969) of whom the large majority are Protestants. The place is of great antiquity and early became a Roman station. In 1219 it was declared a free imperial city. In 1351 it joined the Swiss Confederation.

The preaching of Huldrych Zwingli in the cathedral, beginning Jan. 1, 1519, with the continuous explanation of the Gospel according to Matthew, and his statesmanship, made it the center of the German-speaking Swiss Reformation.

The first Methodist to preach in Zürich was Hermann zur Jakobsmühlen, who came there on Oct. 1, 1856. At the first announced service nobody appeared, but very soon the number of hearers increased rapidly up to 400. In 1858 a house, called *Zum Pfauen*, was bought and its dancing hall converted into a church. The first Quarterly Meeting was held on June 4, 1859. Some opposition arose, especially from the state-related Protestant church. But the work progressed and expanded rapidly. Among the successful pioneers was Henri Nuelsen, the father of the later Bishop JOHN L. NUELSEN, who was born in the house *Zum Pfauen.* In the course of the following decades several churches were built in the city and circuits organized in the canton of Zürich.

A special event occurred in 1890 when a first book shop was opened; and in 1892, when a new building for the newly organized publishing house (CHRISTLICHE VEREINSBUCHHANDLUNG) was erected. The book shop was then moved there and printing facilities installed. Later the presiding bishop transferred his office into the same building, which became the administrative center not only of Swiss Methodism but of the whole Central and Southern Europe Central Conference.

In 1911 the deaconess work of the Methodist Church in Germany and Switzerland was divided into three parts. One of the motherhouses was built in Zürich and became Diakonissenhaus Bethanien, and is a hospital and deaconess training center.

More recently, in 1961, a new branch of Methodist life and work was opened. A girls' hostel, belonging to the Zürich First Church, was converted into a hotel which has become well known and is very popular. With its meeting rooms it proves to be a real "Methodist Center," as its name indicates. It is located at Zeltweg 20, in the same building as the pastor's home and office. One of the first conferences held there was the session of the executive committee of the WORLD METHODIST COUNCIL to prepare for the OSLO WORLD METHODIST CONFERENCE. The emblem of the World Methodist Council which then was shown for the first time was designed by Bishop FERDINAND SIGG with the help of two members of the Zürich Methodist churches.

In recent years the five Methodist churches of the city had a membership of about 1,800, fourteen Sunday schools with sixty-five helpers and about 450 children.

Diakonissenhaus Bethanien. On July 8, 1874, during the session of the Annual Conference of the Methodist Church in GERMANY and SWITZERLAND, held in Schaffhausen, Switzerland, four ministers—Carl Weiss, Heinrich Mann, Friedrich Eilers, and Jürgen Wischhusen—decided to found a motherhouse for deaconesses, i.e., for women and girls ready to nurse the sick and the aged and to live a communal life. Outside of a little monthly pocket money, these deaconesses would receive no salary, but the motherhouse was to provide for everything in days of health, sickness, and age. The work began with one deaconess in the apartment of the Methodist minister in FRANKFORT, Germany, Friedrich Eilers. But it grew rapidly, young women coming from different parts of Germany and Switzerland. In 1911 it proved necessary to divide the work into three branches. Motherhouses were established in Hamburg for North Germany, in Frankfort for South Germany, and in Zürich for Switzerland.

In Switzerland, "Bethany" sisters were already at work in St. Gallen and had been since 1885, in Zürich since 1887, in Lausanne since 1890, and in Geneva since 1908. They live in "families" under the leadership of head sisters.

In 1912 a new hospital and motherhouse building was opened in Zürich. At the same time a school of nursing was established, and this obtained the official recognition of the government. The hospital was entirely renovated and modernized in 1965-66, so that today there are 140 beds in two buildings in different medical, surgical, orthopedic, and other branches. Besides these buildings there are two houses for active and retired deaconesses,

a church building or chapel on these grounds, and other buildings.

Other similar houses are in St. Gallen, Gais, Davos, Lucerne, Lausanne, Spiez, Bern, and Geneva, most of these being homes for the aged. The motherhouse (*mutterhaus*) at Zürich is the center of the whole work and the home for 256 deaconesses (1966). About ninety of these work in hospitals belonging to "Bethany"; others work in community hospitals, in homes for the aged, in nurseries, among women prisoners and a few in parishes. Some labor in connection with the Methodist mission in North America.

In the school of nursing, deaconesses and so-called free nurses are trained. This training includes not only medical and nursing knowledge and technique, but also understanding of the Scriptures, church history, psychology of the sick, ethics, etc. The motherhouse is under the supervision of two directors, both ministers of the Methodist Church, who also act as chaplains, and of a head sister. All the deaconesses are members of the Methodist Church. The directors and the head sister share their responsibility with a board of management and a general assembly.

The distinctive signs of the Bethanienschwestern are the white bonnet and a brooch with the triple sign of a cross, an anchor and a heart, symbols for faith, hope, and love. These are the signs under which these deaconesses want to serve their Lord Jesus Christ.

HERMANN SCHAAD

ZWICKAU, Germany, center of the Saxon mining district, was reached by the Methodist revival from Ruessdorf before 1870. The large suburb, Planitz, reported Methodist meetings as early as 1866-67. In 1870 the "Bill for Dissidents" was passed, bringing comparative religious liberty in the Kingdom of Saxony. It became possible to leave the established church and form new societies without long and tedious special petitions. The annual conference now sent a pastor to Zwickau, thus observing the successful Methodist strategy of sending a minister to a town without any members in order to create an urban center for rural and suburban preaching places. After some efforts to perform their evangelistic task within the Lutheran Church, the Methodists founded the Zwickau Circuit of the Methodist Episcopal Church in the Kingdom of Saxony (1871). All Saxon circuits formed in the following half century nominally belonged to this Zwickau Circuit. From here the awakening spread. Since 1873 there has been a candidate for the ministry stationed at Schwarzenberg (Erzgebirge) where the first Methodist chapel in Saxony was built in 1883. Zwickau then became the residence of the presiding elder of the Berlin District; from here Ernst Gebhardt traveled throughout the North and East as superintendent and as gospel singer. There were periods of advance after the consecration of the first church in Zwickau (1885), before and after the building of the new *Friedenskirche* (Peace Church, 1931) and during the serious time in and after the Second World War, including the extension of the Methodist center (district house, home for the aged, a deaconess home). As a center of industry and with its active congregation being the largest Methodist local church in Germany, Zwickau is likely to remain the center of East German Methodism.

THEOPHIL FUNK

WORLD METHODIST HISTORY CHRONOLOGY

1703 John Wesley born

1707 Charles Wesley born

1709 Wesley saved from Epworth rectory fire

1714 Howell Harris born
Wesley entered Charterhouse School, London
George Whitefield born

1720 Wesley entered Christ Church, Oxford

1725 Wesley ordained deacon

1728 Wesley ordained priest

1729 Charles Wesley formed Holy Club at Oxford

1735 Samuel Wesley, rector of Epworth, died
George Whitefield converted
Howell Harris began to evangelize Wales
John and Charles Wesley embarked for Georgia

1736 Wesley formed fellowship societies in Georgia
Charles Wesley returned to England

1737 Wesley published *A Collection of Psalms and Hymns* in Charleston, S.C.

1738 George Whitefield sailed for Georgia
Wesley landed in England from Georgia
Wesley and Peter Böhler formed the Fetter Lane religious society
Charles Wesley converted (21 May)
John Wesley converted (24 May)
Wesley visited Moravians in Germany

1739 Wesley began field-preaching in Bristol
Wesley preached in shell of the New Room, Bristol
Wesley accepted John Cennick as lay preacher at Kingswood
Wesley held first service in the Foundery, London

1741 Wesley accepted Thomas Maxfield as his first "son in the gospel," i.e. full-time itinerant lay preacher

1742 Wesley organized society class at Bristol and issued quarterly tickets to members
Susanna Wesley died at the Foundery, London

1743 First English-Welsh Methodist Association met under chairmanship of George Whitefield
Wesley published *The Nature, Design, and General Rules of the United Societies*

Wesley held first service in West Street Chapel, London, a disused episcopally consecrated Huguenot building which became Wesley's communion center

1744 Wesley called first Methodist Conference, at the Foundery, London

1745 Francis Asbury born

1746 Wesley published first volume of his *Sermons* (others in 1748, 1750, 1760, 1787-8)

1747 Wesley's first visit to Ireland
Thomas Coke born

1748 Opening of reorganized Kingswood School
First Circuit Quarterly Meeting, conducted by William Grimshaw

1749 Charles Wesley married Sarah Gwynne

1751 John Wesley married Mary Vazeille
Wesley's first visit to Scotland

1752 Howell Harris established community at Trevecka, Wales
First Irish Conference, at Limerick
Calendar changed, Old Style Sept. 3 becoming New Style Sept. 14; year no longer ending on March 24
Philip William Otterbein came to America as minister of German Reformed congregation, Lancaster, Pa.

1755 Members of Leeds Conference decided not to separate from the Church of England
Wesley published *Explanatory Notes upon the New Testament*

1756 First regular Methodist fund at national level established—annual collections for Kingswood School
John William Fletcher ordained, assisted Wesley in London Methodism

1759 Methodist chapel opened at Newbiggin-in-Teesdale, England, apparently oldest Methodist chapel in world in continuous use for weekly worship

1760 Philip and Margaret Embury, Paul and Barbara Heck, arrived in New York from County Limerick, Ireland
John Fletcher inducted to living at Madeley, Shropshire

1763 First model trust deed set out in Wesley's "Large" (i.e. consolidated) *Minutes*.

1764? Log hut built for Robert Strawbridge at Sam's Creek, Maryland, for Methodist worship

1765 *Minutes* of British Methodist Con-

ference began annual publication
Laurence Coughland began Methodism in Newfoundland

1766 Deed for building Methodist meeting house in Leesburg, Virginia
New York Methodist society begun by Philip Embury

1767 Captain Thomas Webb consolidated Methodism in New York and Philadelphia

1768 "Methodist" students expelled from St. Edmund Hall, Oxford
Selina, Countess of Huntingdon, opened college at Trevecka, Wales
Wesley Chapel (John Street Church), New York, opened

1769 Hannah Ball began Sunday School at High Wycombe
Richard Boardman and Joseph Pilmore sailed to America as Wesley's authorized itinerant preachers
Old S. George's Chapel, Philadelphia, dedicated

1770 English Conference attacked Calvinism, sparking controversy in which John Fletcher championed Wesley with *Checks to Antinomianism*
George Whitefield died at Newburyport, Massachusetts on his seventh visit to America

1771 Francis Asbury sailed for America
German Evangelical Reformed congregation formed in Baltimore "Old Otterbein Church"

1773 First Methodist Conference in America, in St. George's, Philadelphia
William Watters accepted, first native-born American Methodist itinerant preacher

1774 Lovely Lane Chapel, Baltimore, built
Otterbein became pastor of new "German Evangelical Reformed Church" in Baltimore

1777 Richard Allen converted, a slave who became a bishop and cofounder of the African Methodist Episcopal Church

1778 Wesley began *Arminian Magazine* (became *Methodist Magazine*, 1798-1821, *Wesleyan Methodist Magazine*, 1822-1913, *Magazine of the Wesleyan Methodist Church*, 1914-26, *Methodist Magazine*, 1927-1969, when it was discontinued)
Wesley's Chapel, City Road, London, opened

1779 William Black converted, founder of Methodism in Nova Scotia

1780 Wesley published *A Collection of Hymns for the use of the People called Methodists*

1783 Robert Carr Brackenbury pioneered Methodism in the Channel Islands, whence it spread to France

1784 Wesley's Deed of Declaration secured legal recognition for the annual Conference as the governing body of British Methodism

Wesley ordained Richard Whatcoat and Thomas Vasey as preachers for America; commissioned Thomas Coke to ordain others

Methodist Episcopal Church organized at "Christmas Conference," Baltimore

Francis Asbury ordained by Coke, Otterbein, and probably Whatcoat and Vasey

1785 Strangers' Friend Society formed

First American *Discipline* published in Philadelphia, entitled *Minutes of Several Conversations . . . composing a Form of Discipline*

1786 Thomas Coke landed in West Indies

1787 Cokesbury College opened at Abingdon, Maryland

Free African Society formed in Philadelphia, the beginnings of African Methodist Episcopal Church

1788 Charles Wesley died

1789 Otterbein organized first Annual Conference of his followers

Methodist Book Concern begun in Philadelphia under John Dickins

1790 American Methodists took over British work in Canada

1791 John Wesley died

British Methodism divided into districts

France made a separate circuit of British Methodism

1792 First quadrennial General Conference of American Methodism

James O'Kelly led first major schism in American Methodism, forming Republican Methodist Church, later Christian Church

Methodist Chapel built in Gibraltar

1794 Beginnings of camp meeting movement at Rehoboth, North Carolina

1795 Plan of Pacification settled disputes in British Methodism

1796 Beginnings of Negro group in New York which culminated in the organization of the African Methodist Episcopal Church, Zion

Jacob Albright began preaching with a Methodist Episcopal exhorter's license

1797 Methodist New Connexion established

1800 Wesleyan Methodist missionaries sent to Wales

Camp meetings widely organized as instruments of revival in the United States

Jacob Albright formed three classes among the Germans in Pennsylvania

Philip William Otterbein and Martin Boehm founded The United Brethren in Christ and were elected first bishops

1801 Peter Cartwright, frontier pioneer, converted

1803 Wesleyan Committee of Privileges formed

First conference of Albright's followers held

1806 First Annual Meeting of the Independent Methodists in England

Methodism introduced into South Africa

1807 First English Camp Meeting, on Mow Cop

1808 General Conference adopted what was determined to be the constitution of Methodist Episcopal Church, introducing "restrictive rules" and a delegated General Conference

Jacob Albright died

1809 First *Discipline* and catechism of Albright's followers (*Evangelische Gemeinschaft*) printed

1810 Adam Clarke began *Commentary* on New Testament (3 vols.) and Old Testament (5 vols.)

First Evangelical (and first German) camp meeting held in the United States

1811 William Clowes and Hugh Bourne unite their followers and take the name "Primitive Methodists" in 1812

First ordained Wesleyan missionary to Sierra Leone

1812 First Methodist class meeting and service in Australia

Woodhouse Grove School opened, England

1813 Wesleyan Methodist Missionary Auxiliary Societies formed

Thomas Coke launched mission to Ceylon

Philip William Otterbein ordained Christian Newcomer, who was elected a bishop of The United Brethren in Christ

Philip William Otterbein died

1814 Thomas Coke died, buried in Indian Ocean

1815 First society of Bible Christians formed

Samuel Leigh arrived as first Wesleyan missionary in Australia

First General Conference of United Brethren in Christ formed and first *Discipline* approved

1816 Francis Asbury died

African Methodist Episcopal Church formed, Richard Allen chosen bishop

First General Conference of Evangelical Association convened

Barnabas Shaw went as Wesleyan missionary to South Africa

1817 Methodist mission begun on Indian mainland

First church and first publishing house of Evangelicals built at New Berlin, Pennsylvania

1818 American *Methodist Magazine* began, became *Methodist Magazine and Quarterly Review* in 1830 and *Methodist Quarterly Review* in 1840

1819 First Bible Christian Conference, at Launceston, England

First Primitive Methodist Conference, at Nottingham, England

Missionary societies begun in New York and Philadelphia, Board of Missions claims this date as its origin

1820 Nathan Bangs became editor and general book steward of the Methodist Book Concern, which he reorganized

American Methodist Missionary Society organized

First United Brethren Sunday School held at Croydon, Indiana

African Methodist Episcopal Church, Zion, organized in New York

Wesleyan Methodists began mission to Gambia

1822 Daniel Coker organized Methodist Society for freed slaves en route to Liberia

Samuel Leigh began mission in New Zealand

Walter Lowry began mission in Tonga

1823 *Zion's Herald* began, first Methodist weekly newspaper

Richard Watson began publication of *Theological Institutes* (Vol. 1 of 4)

1824 *Child's Magazine* (later *Kiddies' Magazine*) begun by Wesleyan Methodists in England

African Methodist Episcopal work begun in Haiti and the Dominican Republic

1826 Joseph Rayner Stephens began mission in Sweden

Christian Advocate begun by Nathan Bangs in New York

1827 "Nonconforming Methodists" seceded in Britain, later becoming Protestant Methodists

Child's Magazine begun in America

Alexander McCaine published *The History and Mystery of Methodist Episcopacy*

1829 Primitive Methodists begun mission to the United States

1830 *Methodist Magazine* became *Methodist Quarterly Review*

Randolph-Macon College, Ashland, Virginia, chartered, opened in 1832

Methodist Protestant Church organized in America

1831 Christoph Gottlieb Müller formed

first Methodist circuit in Germany

Wesleyan University, Middletown, Connecticut, chartered and opened with Wilbur Fisk as first president

1832 Mission to Fiji Islands begun

1833 Melville Cox began first American Methodist foreign mission, to Liberia

1834 First Band of Hope begun, in Primitive Methodist School in Preston, England

Samuel Warren opposed Theological Institution in British Methodism

United Brethren Publishing House formed

Religious Telescope begun by United Brethren

1835 First British Methodist weekly newspaper, *The Watchman* (ceased 1884)

Wesleyan Theological Institution opened at Hoxton, London

First Methodist mission in South America begun, to Brazil

Nicholas Snethen published *Lay Representation*

William Nast converted, pioneer of German Methodism

1836 Samuel Warren formed Wesleyan Methodist Association

American Methodists began mission to Argentina and Uruguay

Der Christliche Botschafter begun by Evangelical Association

Emory University, Atlanta, chartered

1838 Thomas Birch Freeman landed at Cape Coast, pioneering missions in West Africa, especially in Ghana

1839 Wesleyan Centenary Celebrations Missions begun in Switzerland

Methodist Episcopal Church acquired Wesleyan Female College, Macon, Georgia, oldest woman's college in the world

1840 Newbury Biblical Institute founded, Newbury, Vermont, first American Methodist seminary, ancestor of Boston University School of Theology (1868)

1842 Didsbury College for theological training opened near Manchester, England

T. B. Freeman began mission in Abeokuta, Western Nigeria

First Methodist Church built in Argentina

1843 Richmond College for theological training opened near London, England

T. B. Freeman began missions in Dahomey and Togo

Orange Scott and others, favoring the abolition of slavery, withdrew from the Methodist Episcopal Church to form the Wesleyan Methodist Church

1844 The Methodist Episcopal Church

divided by the Plan of Separation

1845 Wesley College, Dublin, opened

Methodist Episcopal Church, South, organized at the Louisville Convention of the Southern Conferences

Olaf Gustaf Hedstrom opened Swedish mission in ship "John Wesley" (also known as "Bethel Ship") in New York harbor

1846 First *Fly Sheet* issued, beginning of Wesleyan reform movement in England

First quadrennial General Conference of the Methodist Episcopal Church, South

1847 Judson Dwight Collins established mission in China

United Brethren founded Otterbein College, Westerville, Ohio

1849 Samuel Dunn, James Everett, and William Griffith, expelled from Wesleyan Methodist Church as leaders of the reform movement

Ludwig S. Jacoby established a German Methodist mission in Bremen

1850 Northwestern University, Evanston, Illinois, founded

Ole Peter Petersen appointed as a Local Preacher to Norwegians in Upper Iowa

Johann Conrad Link returned from America to Stuttgart, first preacher of Evangelische Gemeinschaft

1851 Westminster Training College opened

1852 First French Methodist Conference

1853 First British ordained missionaries went to China

London Quarterly Review begun

Ole Peter Petersen was ordained by the Methodist Episcopal Church and assigned to Methodist missions in Norway

1854 *Christian Ambassador*, later *Holborn Review*, begun

1855 Australasian Conference formed

Methodism introduced to Hawaii

United Brethren missionaries to Sierra Leone

Garrett Biblical Institute opened in Evanston, Illinois

1856 American Methodist missions begun in India by Dr. and Mrs. William Butler

William Arthur published *The Tongue of Fire*

1857 The United Methodist Free Church established

Mission to Bulgaria begun

1858 Women's Missionary Auxiliary begun in England

1859 Wesleyan Reform Union formed in England

First Methodist Episcopal society organized in Denmark

1860 Mission to Italy launched from British Methodism

Free Methodist Church formed in United States

1861 *Methodist Recorder* begun in England

United Methodist Free Churches began a mission to Kenya

1864 Methodist New Connexion opened Ranmoor College, Sheffield

1865 Evangelical Mission to Switzerland formed

1866 Methodist Episcopal Church formed Freedmen's Aid Society

Methodist Episcopal Church, South, adopted lay representation in General and Annual Conferences

1867 Drew Theological Seminary opened

Wilberforce University in Wilberforce, Ohio, opened by African Methodist Episcopal Church, first Negro institution for higher education, with Daniel A. Payne, first Negro college president

Missions established in Brazil by Methodist Episcopal Church, South

1868 Headingley College, Leeds, opened

Primitive Methodists opened Theological Institute at Sunderland

Evangelical mission to France

1869 Thomas Bowman Stephenson founded the National Children's Home and Orphange

Methodist Episcopal Church founded the Woman's Foreign Missionary Society

United Brethren Mission to Germany

Boston University incorporated

1870 Colored Methodist Episcopal Church organized (name changed in 1956 to Christian M.E.C.)

Primitive Methodists established a mission in Fernando Po

Methodist preaching began in Austria

1871 First English missionary assigned to Portugal

Union Biblical Seminary opened in Dayton, Ohio

1872 Laymen received into General Conference of the Methodist Episcopal Church

United Methodist Free Churches opened Victoria Park College, Manchester

Southlands Training College for women opened

Trinity Hall, Southport, opened for girls

1873 Mission begun in Mexico

Mission in Japan by both American and Canadian Methodists

Union Biblical Institute founded at Naperville, Illinois

1875 First Methodist service in New Guinea

Vanderbilt University opened

William Burt Pope published *A Compendium of Christian Theology*

Evangelical Mission to Japan

Cape May Commission declared Methodist Episcopal Church and Methodist Episcopal Church, South, were coeval branches of

Methodist Episcopal Church founded in 1784

1876 Methodist Episcopal mission officially recognized as an independent denomination in Sweden

1877 Bishop William Taylor introduced Methodism into Chile and Peru

1878 Laymen accepted into Wesleyan Conference

Matthew Simpson published *Cyclopaedia of Methodism*, its copyright 1876

1879 Bishop James M. Thoburn began Methodist Episcopal work in Burma

1880 An Evangelical young people's society organized in Dayton, Ohio

1881 Handsworth College opened in Birmingham

Hartley College opened in Manchester by Primitive Methodists

Christian Endeavor movement begun by G. E. Clark

First Methodist Ecumenical Conference, London

1882 South African Conference formed

1883 *Joyful News* founded

Irish Christian Advocate founded

1884 Methodist Episcopal Church organized Finland District of Sweden Conference

Methodist Episcopal Church began mission in Korea

1885 Bishop William Taylor began missions in Angola and Congo

Bishop James M. Thoburn began missions in Singapore and Malaysia

1886 Swiss Methodism became Annual Conference of the Methodist Episcopal Church

1887 Army chaplain J. H. Bateson began British Methodist work in Burma

1888 Bishop William Taylor took over work of Congregational Church in Mozambique for the Methodist Episcopal Church

1889 United Brethren mission in China

Epworth League founded in the United States

Church of United Brethren in Christ (Old Constitution) split from parent body

1891 Methodism introduced into Rhodesia

Second Ecumenical Methodist Conference, in Washington, D.C.

1893 Primitive Methodists began missionary work in Eastern Nigeria

1894 The United Evangelical Church divided from The Evangelical Association (reunited in 1922)

1895 The Methodist Episcopal Church, South, began missions in Korea

United Brethren began mission in Japan

1896 Wesley Guild established in Britain

1897 British and American missions in Germany merged

1899 Bishop James M. Thoburn began mission in the Philippines

United Brethren mission begun in Puerto Rico

Methodism established in Cuba by the Methodist Episcopal Church, South

1900 Methodism introduced into Hungary by a German Methodist preacher

Evangelical mission begun in China

A Lay Conference established, parallel to the Annual Conference of ministers, in the Methodist Episcopal Church; women granted "equal laity rights"

1901 Third Ecumenical Methodist Conference, London

United Brethren began missions in Philippines

1902 Methodist mission begun in Borneo

1903 Cliff College, Calver, England, opened to train lay evangelists

1905 Methodism introduced into Panama

Methodist missions begun in Java and Sumatra

United Brethren missions in Germany transferred to the Methodist Episcopal Church

1907 Japan Methodist Church formed the missions of American and Canadian Methodists

United Methodist Church in England formed from the Methodist New Connexion, the Bible Christians, and the United Methodist Free Churches

Canadian United Brethren joined Congregationalists

1908 American Methodist Manifesto on Social Questions prepared (Social Creed of the Churches)

Evangelical Mission begun in Riga, Latvia

Mission to Manchuria begun by the Methodist Episcopal Church, South

1910 New Zealand became Conference independent of Australia

1911 Southern Congo Conference of the African Methodist Episcopal Church established

Bishop Walter R. Lambuth of the Methodist Episcopal Church, South, began work in Central Congo

Fourth Ecumenical Methodist Conference, Toronto

1912 Westminster Central Hall, London, opened

1913 James C. Baker established first Wesley Foundation at Urbana, Illinois

1914 Candler School of Theology founded at Emory University, Atlanta, Georgia

1915 Southern Methodist University opened in Dallas, Texas

1920 Methodist Episcopal Church began work in the Dominican Republic

1921 Wesley House, Cambridge, opened

Baltic and Slavic mission formed from work begun by the Methodist Episcopal Church in Lithuania (1904), Latvia (1912), and Estonia (1921)

Fifth Ecumenical Methodist Conference, London

Red Bird mission work in Kentucky begun

1922 Belgian Mission begun by Methodist Episcopal Church, South

Czechoslovak Mission begun by Methodist Episcopal Church, South

Poland-Danzig Mission begun by Methodist Episcopal Church, South

The Evangelical Church formed from The United Evangelical Church and The Evangelical Association.

1924 James Buchanan Duke endowed Trinity College, Durham, North Carolina, to form Duke University

1925 Canadian Methodist Church joined Congregationalists and Presbyterians to form The United Church of Canada

1927 The Methodist Church of South Africa constituted by Act of Parliament

1929 Methodist Church Union Act passed by British Parliament

1930 Korean Methodist Church formed from the missions of the Methodist Episcopal Church and the Methodist Episcopal Church, South.

Methodist Church of Brazil became autonomous

Methodist Church in Mexico became autonomous

1931 Sixth Ecumenical Methodist Conference, Atlanta, Georgia

1932 The Methodist Church formed by union of the Wesleyan Methodists, the Primitive Methodists and the United Methodists

1939 The Methodist Church formed from the union of the Methodist Episcopal Church, the Methodist Episcopal Church, South, and the Methodist Protestant Church

1940 The French Methodist Conference was united with the Église Réformée de France

1941 The Japanese Methodist Church became part of the new Church of Christ in Japan

1943 Methodist Youth Department formed in England

1944 American Methodist Church launched Crusade for Christ

1945 J. J. Perkins endowed Southern Methodist University School of Theology which became the Perkins School of Theology

1946 Dr. John R. Mott awarded Nobel Peace Prize

Evangelical United Brethren Church formed from union of The Evangelical Church and The Church of the United Brethren in Christ.

Ministerial interchanges initiated by American and British Methodism

1947 Greater London Christian Commando Campaign

Church of South India formed, including 225,000 members from the Methodist Church

Seventh Ecumenical Methodist Conference, Springfield, Massachusetts

International Methodist Historical Society organized

1948 John R. Mott and Bishop G. Bromley Oxnam elected founding bishops of the World Council of Churches

1951 Eighth Ecumenical Methodist Conference, Oxford, organized standing committees and officially adopted name of "World Methodist Council"

1953 Methodist Church in Taiwan organized

1956 Ninth World Methodist Conference, Lake Junaluska, North Carolina

World Federation of Methodist Women formed

1961 Methodist Church of Ghana became autonomous

Tenth World Methodist Conference, Oslo, Norway

1962 Methodist Church of Nigeria became autonomous

Evangelical Methodist Church of Italy became autonomous

1963 Methodist Church of Ceylon became autonomous

1964 Methodist Church of Upper Burma became autonomous

Methodist Church of Indonesia became autonomous

1965 Methodist Church of Lower Burma became autonomous

Methodist Church in Zambia united with two others to form United Church of Zambia

1966 Eleventh World Methodist Conference, London, England

1967 Methodist Church of Sierra Leone became autonomous

Methodist Church of Kenya became autonomous

Methodist Church of the Caribbeans and the Americas became autonomous

1968 In the United States of America The Methodist Church and The Evangelical United Brethren amalgamated to form The United Methodist Church

Methodist Church of Cuba became autonomous

Methodist Church of Malaysia-Singapore became autonomous

Methodist Church of Pakistan became autonomous

1969 Methodist Church of Chile became autonomous

Methodist Church of Argentina became autonomous

Belgian Annual Conference became part of the Protestant Church of Belgium

FRANK BAKER

BISHOPS OF EPISCOPAL METHODIST CHURCHES

AFRICAN METHODIST EPISCOPAL CHURCH

Name	Elected	Date Died or Retired	Name	Elected	Date Died or Retired
Richard Allen	1816	1831	William Sampson Brooks	1920	1931
Morris Brown	1828	1849	William T. Vernon	1920	(Ret.) 1932
Edward Waters	1836	(Ret.) 1844	William A. Fountain	1920	(Ret.) 1952
William P. Quinn	1844	1873	Abraham L. Gaines	1924	1931
Willis Nazrey	1852	1875	Reverdy C. Ransom	1924	(Ret.) 1952
Daniel A. Payne	1852	1893	John A. Gregg	1924	1953
Alexander W. Wayman	1864	1895	Robert A. Grant	1928	1939
Jabez Pitt Campbell	1864	1891	Sherman L. Greene	1928	1967
James A. Shorter	1868	1887	George B. Young	1928	(Ret.) 1948
Thomas M. D. Ward	1868	1894	Monroe H. Davis	1928	(Ret.) 1952
John M. Brown	1868	1893	Noah W. Williams	1932	(Ret.) 1948
Henry M. Turner	1880	1915	David H. Sims	1932	1965
William F. Dickerson	1880	1884	Henry Y. Tookes	1932	1948
Richard H. Cain	1880	1887	Richard R. Wright, Jr.	1936	1967
Richard R. Disney	1884	1891	Edward J. Howard	1936	1941
Wesley J. Gaines	1888	1912	Decatur Ward Nichols	1940	—
Benjamin W. Arnett	1888	1906	George E. Curry	1940	(Ret.) 1946
Benjamin T. Tanner	1888	(Ret.) 1908	Frank M. Reid	1940	1962
Abram Grant	1888	1911	A. Joseph Allen	1940	1956
Benjamin F. Lee	1892	(Ret.) 1924	George W. Baber	1944	1970
Moses B. Salter	1892	(Ret.) 1912	John H. Clayborn	1944	1954
James A. Handy	1892	1911	Lawrence H. Hemingway	1948	1954
William B. Derrick	1896	1913	D. Ormonde Walker	1948	1955
Josiah E. Armstrong	1896	1898	Joseph Gomez	1948	—
James C. Embry	1896	1897	Isaiah H. Bonner	1948	—
Evans Tyree	1900	1921	William R. Wilkes	1948	—
Morris M. Moore	1900	1900	Carey A. Gibbs	1948	—
Charles S. Smith	1900	1922	Howard T. Primm	1952	—
Cornelius T. Shaffer	1900	1919	Frederick D. Jordan	1952	—
Levi J. Coppin	1900	1924	Eugene C. Hatcher	1952	1968
Edward W. Lampton	1908	1910	Francis H. Gow	1956	1968
Henry B. Parks	1908	1936	Ernest L. Hickman	1956	—
Joseph S. Flipper	1908	1944	Samuel R. Higgins	1956	1961
J. Albert Johnson	1908	1928	William H. Ball	1956	—
William H. Heard	1908	1937	Odie L. Sherman	1956	—
John Hurst	1912	1930	John D. Bright	1960	—
William D. Chappelle	1912	1925	George N. Collins	1960	—
Joshua H. Jones	1912	(Ret.) 1932	G. Wayman Blakely	1964	—
James M. Connor	1912	1925	Harold I. Bearden	1964	—
William W. Beckett	1916	1927	Harrison J. Bryant	1964	—
Isaac N. Ross	1916	1927	Hubert N. Robinson	1964	—
William D. Johnson	1920	1936	G. Dewey Robinson	1968	—
Archibald J. Carey	1920	1931	Henry W. Murph	1968	—

AFRICAN METHODIST EPISCOPAL ZION CHURCH

Name	Elected	Date Died or Retired	Name	Elected	Date Died or Retired
James Varick	1821	1827	Peter Ross	1856	1889
Christopher Rush	1828	1872	John Brooks	1864	1874
William Miller	1840	1845	Samson D. Talbot	1864	1872
George Galbraith	1848	1853	John J. Moore	1868	1893
William H. Bishop	1852	1873	Singleton T. Jones	1868	1891
George A. Spywood	1852	1876	Jeremiah W. Loguen	1868	1873
John Tappan	1854	1862	James Walker Hood	1872	1918
Solomon T. Scott	1856	1862	William W. Hillery	1876	1893
James Simmons	1856	1873	Joseph P. Thompson	1876	1894
Joseph J. Clinton	1856	1881	Thomas H. Lomax	1876	1908

Name	Elected	Date Died or Retired	Name	Elected	Date Died or Retired
Cicero R. Harris	1888	1917	William W. Matthews	1928	1962
Charles C. Petty	1888	1900	Frederick M. Jacobs	1928	1931
Alexander Walters	1892	1917	Elijah L. Madison	1936	1946
Isom C. Clinton	1892	1904	William C. Brown	1936	1964
John Holliday	1896	1899	James W. Brown	1936	1941
John B. Small	1896	1915	Walter W. Slade	1944	1963
George Wylie Clinton	1896	1921	Buford F. Gordon	1944	1952
John W. Alstork	1900	1920	Frank W. Alstork	1944	1948
John W. Smith	1904	1910	E. B. Watson	1944	1951
Josiah S. Caldwell	1904	1935	James C. Taylor	1948	1954
Martin R. Franklin	1908	1909	Raymond L. Jones	1948	—
George L. Blackwell	1908	1926	Hampton T. Medford	1948	1964
Andrew J. Warner	1908	1920	Herbert Bell Shaw	1952	—
Linwood W. Kyles	1916	1941	Stephen G. Spottswood	1952	—
Robert B. Bruce	1916	1920	William A. Stewart	1952	—
W. L. Lee	1916	1927	Daniel C. Pope	1952	—
George C. Clement	1916	1934	C. Eubanks Tucker	1956	—
John W. Wood	1920	1940	Joseph Dixon Cauthen	1956	—
Paris A. Wallace	1920	1952	Cecil C. Coleman	1956	1958
Benjamin G. Shaw	1924	1951	Felix S. Anderson	1960	—
Edward D. W. Jones	1924	1935	William M. Smith	1960	—
William J. Walls	1924	1965	S. Dorme Lartey	1960	—
John W. Martin	1924	1955	William A. Hilliard	1960	—
Cameron C. Alleyne	1924	1955	Alfred G. Dunstan	1964	—

CHRISTIAN METHODIST EPISCOPAL CHURCH
(Formerly the Colored Methodist Episcopal Church)

Name	Elected	Date Died or Retired	Name	Elected	Date Died or Retired
Williams H. Miles	1870	1892	James Albert Bray	1934	1944
Richard H. Vanderhurst	1870	1872	John Henry Moore	1934	1951
Joseph A. Beebe	1873	1903	William Yancey Bell	1938	1962
Lucius H. Holsey	1873	1920	Charles Lee Russell	1938	1949
Isaac Lane	1873	1937	Luther Caldwell Stewart	1946	1962
Robert S. Williams	1894	1932	Felix L. Lewis	1946	(Ret.) 1962
Elias Cottrell	1894	1937	Roy Lee Young	1946	1948
Charles Henry Phillips	1902	1948	Bertram W. Doyle	1950	—
Monroe F. Jamison	1910	1918	Arthur Walter Womack	1950	1961
George Washington Stewart	1910	1916	Benjamin Julian Smith	1954	—
Randall Albert Carter	1914	1954	John Claude Allen	1954	—
Nelson Caldwell Cleaves	1914	1930	Elisha P. Murchison	1958	—
Robert Turner Brown	1922	1933	Peter Randolph Shy	1958	—
Joseph C. Martin	1922	1939	Norris Samuel Curry	1962	—
James Arthur Hamlett	1922	1962	Walter Hansel Amos	1962	—
John Wesley McKinney	1922	1946	Henry Clay Bunton	1962	—
Henry Phillips Porter	1934	1962	Joseph A. Johnson	1966	—

EVANGELICAL ASSOCIATION

Name	Elected	Date Died or Retired	Name	Elected	Date Died or Retired
Jacob Albright	1807	1808	Thomas Bowman	1875	1923
John Seybert	1839	1860	S. C. Breyfogel	1891	1934
Joseph Long	1843	1869	William Horn	1891	1917
William W. Orwig	1859	1889	Samuel P. Spreng	1907	1946
John J. Esher	1863	1901	G. Heinmiller	1915	1922
Reuben Yeakel	1871	1904	Lawrence H. Seager	1915	1937
Rudolph Dubs	1875	1915			

THE EVANGELICAL CHURCH

Name	Elected	Date Died or Retired	Name	Elected	Date Died or Retired
S. C. Breyfogel	1922	1934	John S. Stamm	1926	1956
Samuel P. Spreng	1922	1946	Samuel J. Umbreit	1926	1945
Lawrence H. Seager	1922	1937	George E. Epp	1930	—
Matthew T. Maze	1922	1940	Elmer W. Praetorius	1934	1966
John F. Dunlap	1922	1941	Charles H. Stauffacher	1934	1956

UNITED BRETHREN IN CHRIST

Name	Elected	Date Died or Retired	Name	Elected	Date Died or Retired
Philip W. Otterbein	1800	1813	John Dickson	1869	1907
Martin Boehm	1800	1812	Nicholas Castle	1877	1922
Christian Newcomer	1813	1830	Milton Wright	1877 and 1885	1917
Andrew Zeller	1817	1839			
Joseph Hoffman	1821	1856	Ezekiel B. Kephart	1881	1906
Henry Kumler, Sr.	1825	1854	Daniel K. Flickinger	1885	1911
Samuel Hiestand	1833	1838	James W. Hott	1889	1902
William Brown	1833	1868	Job S. Mills	1893	1909
Jacob Erb	1837 and 1849	1883	George M. Mathews	1902	1921
			William M. Weekley	1905	1926
Henry Kumler, Jr.	1841 and 1861	1882	William M. Bell	1905	1933
			Thomas C. Carter	1905	1916
John Coons	1837	1869	Henry H. Fout	1913	1947
John Russel	1845 and 1857	1870	Cyrus J. Kephart	1913	1932
			Alfred T. Howard	1913	1948
Jacob Glossbrenner	1845	1887	William H. Washinger	1917	1928
William Hanby	1845	1880	Arthur R. Clippinger	1921	1958
David Edwards	1849	1876	Arthur B. Statton	1925	1937
Lewis Davis	1853	1890	Grant D. Batdorf	1929	1954
Jacob Markwood	1861	1873	Ira D. Warner	1929	1964
Daniel Shuck	1861	1900	Victor O. Weidler	1938	1950
Jonathan Weaver	1865	1901	Fred L. Dennis	1941	1958
			John B. Showers	1945	1962

THE UNITED EVANGELICAL CHURCH

Name	Elected	Date Died or Retired
Rudolph Dubs	1891	1915
Wesley M. Stanford	1891	1923
C. S. Haman	1891	1916

(From 1891-94, Rudolph Dubs, C. S. Haman, and Wesley M. Stanford served as Bishops, having been elected by the group that afterwards became the United Evangelical Church. During these three years this group called themselves the official Evangelical Association, which was not approved by the courts.)

Name	Elected	Date Died or Retired
H. B. Hartzler	1902	1920
William F. Heil	1902 and 1918	1930
W. H. Fouke	1910	1923
U. F. Swengel	1910	1921
Matthew T. Maze	1918	1940

EVANGELICAL UNITED BRETHREN CHURCH

John S. Stamm (see The Evangelical Church, above)

George E. Epp (see The Evangelical Church, above)

Elmer W. Praetorius (see The Evangelical Church, above)

Charles H. Stauffacher (see The Evangelical Church, above)

Arthur R. Clippinger (see United Brethren Church, above)

Ira D. Warner (see United Brethren Church, above)

Victor O. Weidler (see United Brethren Church, above)

Fred L. Dennis (see United Brethren Church, above)

John B. Showers (see United Brethren Church, above)

Name	Elected	Date Died or Retired
David T. Gregory	1950	1956
Reuben H. Mueller	1954	—
Harold R. Heininger	1954	—
L. L. Baughman	1954	1960
Paul E. V. Shannon	1956	1957
J. Gordon Howard	1957	—
H. W. Kaebnick	1958	—
W. Maynard Sparks	1958	—
Paul M. Herrick	1958	—
Paul W. Milhouse	1960	—
Paul A. Washburn	1968	—

FREE METHODIST CHURCH

General Superintendents	Elected	Date Died or Retired	Name	Elected	Date Died or Retired
Benjamin Titus Roberts	1860	1893	*John Samuel MacGeary	1911	(Ret.) 1915
Edward Payson Hart	1874	(Ret.) 1908	William Henry Clark	1919	1925
George Whitefield Coleman	1886	(Ret.) 1903	David Snethen Warner	1919	(Ret.) 1927
			Arthur DeFrance Zahniser	1927	1935
Bishops			George William Griffith	1927	1936
Burton Rennselaer Jones	1894	(Ret.) 1919	Burton Jones Vincent	1931	1931
Walter Ashbell Sellew	1898	1929	Robert Hopkins Warren	1935	1938
Wilson Thomas Hogue	1903	(Ret.) 1919			
William Pearce	1908	1947	*Missionary Bishop		

Name	Elected	Date Died or Retired	Name	Elected	Date Died or Retired
Leslie Ray Marston	1935	(Ret.) 1964	Myron F. Boyd	1964	—
Mark D. Ormston	1936	(Ret.) 1958	Paul N. Ellis	1964	—
Charles V. Fairbairn	1939	(Ret.) 1961			
J. Paul Taylor	1947	(Ret.) 1964	**Overseas Bishops**		
Walter S. Kendall	1958	—	Kaneo Oda	1946	1962
Edward C. John	1961	—	Takesaburo Uzaki	1962	—

METHODIST EPISCOPAL CHURCH

Name	Consecrated	Date Died or Retired	Name	Consecrated	Date Died or Retired
Thomas Coke	1784	1814	Thomas Benjamin Neely	1904	1925
Francis Asbury	1784	1816	Isaiah Benjamin Scott	1904	1931
Richard Whatcoat	1800	1806	William Fitzjames Oldham	1904	1937
William McKendree	1808	1835	John Edward Robinson	1904	1922
Enoch George	1816	1828	Merriman Colbert Harris	1904	1921
Robert Richford Roberts	1816	1843	William Franklin Anderson	1908	1944
Joshua Soule	1824	1867	John Louis Nuelsen	1908	1946
Elijah Hedding	1824	1852	William Alfred Quayle	1908	1925
James Osgood Andrew	1832	1871	Charles William Smith	1908	1914
John Emory	1832	1835	Wilson Seeley Lewis	1908	1921
Beverly Waugh	1836	1858	Edwin Holt Hughes	1908	1950
Thomas Asbury Morris	1836	1874	Robert McIntyre	1908	1914
Leonidas Lent Hamline	1844	(Ret.) 1852	Frank Milton Bristol	1908	1932
Edmund Storer Janes	1844	1876	Homer Clyde Stuntz	1912	1924
Levi Scott	1852	1882	Theodore Sommers Henderson	1912	1929
Matthew Simpson	1852	1884	William Orville Shepard	1912	1931
Osman Cleander Baker	1852	1871	Naphtali Luccock	1912	1916
Edward Raymond Ames	1852	1879	Francis John McConnell	1912	1953
Francis Burns	1858	1863	Frederick DeLand Leete	1912	1958
Davis Wasgatt Clark	1864	1871	Richard Joseph Cooke	1912	1931
Edward Thomson	1864	1870	Wilbur Patterson Thirkield	1912	1936
Calvin Kingsley	1864	1870	John Wesley Robinson	1912	1947
John Wright Roberts	1866	1875	William Perry Eveland	1912	1916
Thomas Bowman	1872	1914	Herbert Welch	1916	1969
William Logan Harris	1872	1887	Thomas Nicholson	1916	1944
Randolph Sinks Foster	1872	1903	Adna Wright Leonard	1916	1943
Isaac William Wiley	1872	1884	Matthew Simpson Hughes	1916	1920
Stephen Mason Merrill	1872	1905	William Fitzjames Oldham	1916	1937
Edward Gayer Andrews	1872	1907	Charles Bayard Mitchell	1916	1942
Gilbert Haven	1872	1880	Franklin Elmer		
Jesse Truesdell Peck	1872	1883	Ellsworth Hamilton	1916	1918
Henry White Warren	1880	1912	Alexander Priestley Camphor	1916	1919
Cyrus David Foss	1880	1910	Eben Samuel Johnson	1916	1939
John Fletcher Hurst	1880	1903	Francis Wesley Warne	1920	1932
Erastus Otis Haven	1880	1881	John Wesley Robinson	1920	1947
William Xavier Ninde	1884	1901	Lauress John Birney	1920	1937
John Morgan Walden	1884	1914	Frederick Bohn Fisher	1920	(Resigned) 1930
Wilbur Francis Mallalieu	1884	1911	Ernest Lynn Waldorf	1920	1943
Charles Henry Fowler	1884	1908	Charles Edward Locke	1920	1940
William Taylor	1884	1902	Ernest Gladstone Richardson	1920	1947
John Heyl Vincent	1888	1920	Charles Wesley Burns	1920	1938
James Newbury FitzGerald	1888	1907	Anton Bast	1920	1937
Isaac Wilson Joyce	1888	1905	Edgar Blake	1920	1943
John Philip Newman	1888	1899	George Harvey Bickley	1920	1924
Daniel Ayers Goodsell	1888	1909	Frederick Thomas Keeney	1920	1952
James Mills Thoburn	1888	1922	Harry Lester Smith	1920	1951
Charles Cardwell McCabe	1896	1906	Charles Larew Mead	1920	1941
Earl Cranston	1896	1932	Robert Elijah Jones	1920	1960
Joseph Crane Hartzell	1896	1928	Matthew Wesley Clair, Sr.	1920	1943
David Hastings Moore	1900	1915	George Amos Miller	1924	1961
John William Hamilton	1900	1934	Titus Lowe	1924	1959
Edwin Wallace Parker	1900	1901	George Richmond Grose	1924	(Resigned) 1932
Francis Wesley Warne	1900	1932	Brenton Thoburn Badley	1924	1949
Joseph Flintoft Berry	1904	1931	Wallace Elias Brown	1924	1939
Henry Spellmeyer	1904	1910	Raymond J. Wade	1928	1970
William Fraser McDowell	1904	1937	James Chamberlain Baker	1928	1969
James Whitford Bashford	1904	1919	Edwin Ferdinand Lee	1928	1948
William Burt	1904	1936	John Gowdy	1930	1963
Luther Barton Wilson	1904	1928	Chih P'ing Wang	1930	1964

NAME	CONSECRATED	DATE DIED OR RETIRED	NAME	CONSECRATED	DATE DIED OR RETIRED
Jashwant Rao Chitambar	1931	1940	Garfield Bromley Oxnam	1936	1963
Juan E. Gattinoni	1932	1970	Alexander Preston Shaw	1936	1966
Junius Ralph Magee	1932	(Ret.) 1952	John McKendree Springer	1936	1963
Ralph Spaulding Cushman	1932	1960	Roberto Elphick	1936	1961
Jarrell Waskom Pickett	1936	(Ret.) 1956	F. H. Otto Melle	1936	1947
Wilbur Emery Hammaker	1936	1968	Ralph Ansel Ward	1937	1958
Charles Wesley Flint	1936	1964	Chong Oo Kim	1938	1939

METHODIST EPISCOPAL CHURCH, SOUTH

NAME	ELECTED	DATE DIED OR RETIRED	NAME	ELECTED	DATE DIED OR RETIRED
William Capers	1846	1855	John Carlisle Kilgo	1910	1922
Robert Paine	1846	1882	William Belton Murrah	1910	1925
Henry Bidleman Bascom	1850	1850	Walter Russell Lambuth	1910	1921
John Early	1854	1873	Richard Green Waterhouse	1910	1922
Hubbard Hinde Kavanaugh	1854	1884	Edwin DuBose Mouzon	1910	1937
George Foster Pierce	1854	1884	James Henry McCoy	1910	1919
David Seth Doggett	1866	1880	John Monroe Moore	1918	1948
William May Wightman	1866	1882	William Fletcher McMurry	1918	1934
Enoch Mather Marvin	1866	1877	Urban Valentine		
Holland Nimmons McTyeire	1866	1889	Williams Darlington	1918	1954
John Christian Keener	1870	1906	Horace Mellard DuBose	1918	1941
Alpheus Waters Wilson	1882	1916	William Newman Ainsworth	1918	1942
Linus Parker	1882	1885	James Cannon, Jr.	1918	1944
John Cowper Granbery	1882	1907	William Benjamin Beauchamp	1922	1931
Robert Kennon Hargrove	1882	1905	James Edward Dickey	1922	1928
William Wallace Duncan	1886	1908	Samuel Ross Hay	1922	1944
Charles Betts Galloway	1886	1909	Hoyt McWhorter Dobbs	1922	1954
Eugene Russell Hendrix	1886	1927	Hiram Abiff Boaz	1922	1962
Joseph Staunton Key	1886	1920	Arthur James Moore	1930	(Ret.) 1960
Atticus Green Haygood	1890	1896	Paul Bentley Kern	1930	1953
Oscar Penn Fitzgerald	1890	1911	Angie Frank Smith	1930	1962
Warren Akin Candler	1898	1941	Ivan Lee Holt	1938	1967
Henry Clay Morrison	1898	1921	William Walter Peele	1938	1959
Elijah Embree Hoss	1902	1919	Clare Purcell	1938	1964
Alexander Coke Smith	1902	1906	Charles Claude Selecman	1938	1958
John James Tigert, III	1906	1906	John Lloyd Decell	1938	1946
Seth Ward	1906	1909	William Clyde Martin	1938	(Ret.) 1964
James Atkins, Jr.	1906	1923	William Turner Watkins	1938	(Ret.) 1961
Collins Denny	1910	1943			

THE METHODIST CHURCH

NAME	ELECTED	DATE DIED OR RETIRED	NAME	ELECTED	DATE DIED OR RETIRED
John Calvin Broomfield	1939	1950	Willis Jefferson King	1944	(Ret.) 1960
James Henry Straughn	1939	(Ret.) 1948	Arthur Frederick Wesley	1944	(Ret.) 1955
William Alfred Carroll Hughes	1940	1940	John Abdus Subhan	1945	(Ret.) 1964
Lorenzo Houston King	1940	1946	Dionisio Deista Alejandro	1946	(Ret.) 1964
Bruce Richard Baxter	1940	1947	Theodor Arvidson	1946	1964
Shot Kumar Mondol	1941	(Ret.) 1964	Johan Wilhelm Ernst Sommer	1946	1952
Clement Daniel Rockey	1941	(Ret.) 1956	Lloyd Christ Wicke	1948	—
Enrique Carlos Balloch	1941	(Ret.) 1952	John Wesley Lord	1948	—
Z. T. Kaung	1941	1958	John Wesley Edward Bowen	1948	1962
Wen-yuan Chen	1941	1968	Dana Dawson	1948	1964
George Carleton Lacy	1941	1951	Marvin Augustus Franklin	1948	(Ret.) 1964
Fred Pierce Corson	1944	(Ret.) 1968	Roy Hunter Short	1948	—
Walter Earl Ledden	1944	(Ret.) 1960	Richard Campbell Raines	1948	(Ret.) 1968
Lewis Oliver Hartman	1944	1955	Marshall Russell Reed	1948	(Ret.) 1964
Newell Snow Booth	1944	1968	Harry Clifford Northcott	1948	(Ret.) 1960
Schuyler Edward Garth	1944	1947	Hazen G. Werner	1948	(Ret.) 1968
Charles Wesley Brashares	1944	(Ret.) 1964	Glenn Randall Phillips	1948	(Ret.) 1964
Costen Jordan Harrell	1944	(Ret.) 1956	Gerald Hamilton Kennedy	1948	—
Paul Neff Garber	1944	(Ret.) 1968	Donald Harvey Tippett	1948	(Ret.) 1968
William Angie Smith	1944	(Ret.) 1968	José Labarette Valencia	1948	(Ret.) 1968
Paul Elliott Martin	1944	(Ret.) 1968	Sante Uberto Barbieri	1949	(Ret.) 1968
Edward Wendall Kelly	1944	1964			Elected for term
Robert Nathaniel Brooks	1944	1952			

Name	Elected	Date Died or Retired	Name	Elected	Date Died or Retired
Raymond Leroy Archer	1950	1956	William Kenneth Pope	1960	—
Edgar Amos Love	1952	(Ret.) 1964	Paul Vernon Galloway	1960	—
Matthew Walker Clair, Jr.	1952	1968	Aubrey Grey Walton	1960	—
D. Stanley Coors	1952	1960	Kenneth Wilford Copeland	1960	—
Edwin Edgar Voigt	1952	(Ret.) 1964	James Walton Henley	1960	—
Francis Gerald Ensley	1952	—	Walter Clark Gum	1960	(Ret.) 1968
Frederick Buckley Newell	1952	(Ret.) 1960	Paul Hardin, Jr.	1960	—
Henry Bascom Watts	1952	1959	John Owen Smith	1960	—
John W. Branscomb	1952	1959	Everett Walter Palmer	1960	—
Alsie Raymond Grant	1952	1967	Bowman Foster Stockwell	1960	1961
Julio M. Sabanes	1952	1963	Pedro Zottele	1962	(Ret.) 1968
Friedrich Wunderlich	1953	(Ret.) 1968	James Samuel Thomas	1964	—
Odd Arthur Hagen	1953	1970	William McFerrin Stowe	1964	—
Ferdinand Sigg	1954	1965	Robert Marvin Stuart	1964	—
Ralph Edward Dodge	1955	(Ret.) 1968	Dwight Ellsworth Loder	1964	—
Prince Albert Taylor, Jr.	1956	—	Thomas Marion Pryor	1964	—
Eugene Maxwell Frank	1956	—	Francis Emner Kearns	1964	—
Nolan Bailey Harmon	1956	(Ret.) 1964	Lance Webb	1964	—
Bachman G. Hodge	1956	1961	Walter Kenneth Goodson	1964	—
Hobart B. Amstutz	1956	(Ret.) 1968	Edward Julian Pendergrass	1964	—
Mangal Singh	1956	(Ret.) 1968	Homer Ellis Finger, Jr.	1964	—
Gabriel Sundaram	1956	(Ret.) 1968	Earl Gladstone Hunt, Jr	1964	—
Charles Franklin Golden	1960	—	Robert Fielden Lundy	1964	1968
Noah Watson Moore, Jr.	1960	—	Escrivao Zunguze	1964	—
Marquis LaFayette Harris	1960	1966	John Wesley Shungu	1964	—
Ralph Taylor Alton	1960	—	Harry P. Andreassen	1964	—
Edwin Ronald Garrison	1960	(Ret.) 1968	Prabhakar Christopher		
Torney Otto Nall	1960	(Ret.) 1968	Benjamin Balaram	1965	1968
Fred Garrigus Holloway	1960	(Ret.) 1968	Stephen Trowen Nagbe	1965	—
James Kenneth Mathews	1960	—	Alfred Jacob Shaw	1965	—
W. Vernon Middleton	1960	1965	Franz W. Schaefer	1966	—
William Ralph Ward, Jr.	1960	—	L. Scott Allen	1967	—
Oliver Eugene Slater	1960	—	Benjamin I. Guansing	1967	1968

THE UNITED METHODIST CHURCH

Name	Elected	Date Died or Retired	Name	Elected	Date Died or Retired
James A. Armstrong	1968		Abel T. Muzorewa	1968	
D. Frederick Wertz	1968		Joeseph R. Lance	1969	
Roy C. Nichols	1968		R. D. Joshi	1969	
Alsie H. Carleton	1968		Eric A. Mitchell	1969	
William R. Cannon	1968		Federico Jose Pagura	1969	
Cornelio M. Ferrer	1968		Ole E. Borgen	1970	
Paul L. A. Granadosin	1968		Armin Haertel	1970	
John Victor Samuel	1968				

PRESIDENTS OF AMERICAN METHODIST CHURCHES

METHODIST PROTESTANT CHURCH, 1828-1939
General Conference Presidents

Name	Term	Name	Term	Name	Term
Nicholas Snethen	1828-1830	T. B. Graham	1867-	W. S. Hammond	1884-1888
Francis Waters	1830-1834	Francis H. Pierpont	1871-1875	David Jones	1888-1892
Asa Shinn	1838-1842	A. H. Bassett	1875-1877	J. W. Hering	1892-1896
Asa Shinn	1842-1846	J. J. Smith	1877-	J. W. Hering	1896-1900
Francis Waters	1846-1850			D. S. Stephens	1900-1904
Levi R. Reese	1850-1854	*East and South*		F. T. Tagg	1904-1908
John Burns	1854-1858	Francis Waters	1862-1866	T. H. Lewis	1908-1912
William C. Lipscomb	1858-1862	W. H. Wills	1866-	Lyman E. Davis	1912-1916
		J. J. Murray	1867-	Lyman E. Davis	1916-1920
DIVISION OF THE M. P. CHURCH		J. G. Whitfield	1870-1874	T. H. Lewis	1920-1924
North and West		L. W. Bates	1874-1877	T. H. Lewis	1924-1928
George Brown	1858-1860			John C. Broomfield	1928-1932
George Brown	1860-1862	*The Re-united Church*		John C. Broomfield	1932-1936
George Brown	1862-1866	L. W. Bates	1877-1880	James H. Straughn	1936-1939
John Scott	1866-	J. B. McElroy	1880-1884		

PRESIDENTS OF THE WESLEYAN METHODIST CHURCH OF AMERICA

(designated General Superintendents after 1959)

Name	Installed	Date Retired or Died	Name	Elected	Date Died or Retired
Orange Scott	1843	1844	Roy S. Nicholson	1947	1959
Luther Lee	1844	1848	Oliver G. Wilson	1959	1959(2)
Daniel Worth	1848	1852	Rufus D. Reisdorph	1959	1963
Cyrus Prindle	1852	1865	Bernard H. Phaup	1959	1968(3)
Luther Lee	1856	1860	Harold K. Sheets	1959	1968(3)
L. C. Matlack	1860	1864	Virgil A. Mitchell	1963	1968(3)
Luther Lee	1864	1866(1)			
Samuel Salisbury	1867	1871			
Adam Crooks	1871	1875			
Nathan Wardner	1875	1890			
Eber Teter	1899	1927			
T. P. Baker	1927	1927(4)			
E. D. Carpenter	1927	1939			
F. R. Eddy	1939	1947			

(1) Lee resigned and reunited with M.E. Church in 1866.

(2) Wilson died two days following his election, and was replaced by Reisdorph at the same General Conference.

(3) Each of these men served until the merging conference of 1968, which united The Wesleyan Methodist Church and the Pilgrim Holiness Church.

(4) T. P. Baker resigned a few days after his election.

CONFERENCE PRESIDENTS IN GREAT BRITAIN

THE BIBLE CHRISTIANS
Presidents

Year		Year		Year	
1815-27	William O'Bryan	1854	Robert Kent	1881	William B. Reed
1828	William Mason	1855	William Reed	1882	William B. Lark
1829	Andrew Cory	1856	William Courtice	1883	Peter Labdon
1830	Harry Major	1857	James Thorne	1884	Jehu Martin
1831	James Thorne	1858	James Hinks	1885	William Bray
1832	William Reed	1859	John Gammon	1886	Alexander Trengove
1833	Richard Sedwell	1860	Matthew Robins	1887	John H. Batt
1834	William Courtice	1861	Thomas W. Garland	1888	John O. Keen
1835	James Thorne	1862	William Hopper	1889	Mark Brokenshire
1836	Paul Robins	1863	John Brown	1890	William Higman
1837	William Reed	1864	William Luke	1891	Frederick W. Bourne
1838	James Brooks	1865	James Thorne	1892	William Lee
1839	Richard Sedwell	1866	Matthew Robins	1893	James Woolcock
1840	Richard Kinsman	1867	Frederick W. Bourne	1894	Samuel Allin
1841	William Richards	1868	Thomas P. Oliver	1895	John Thorne
1842	James Thorne	1869	Robert Blackmore	1896	Daniel Murley
1843	Paul Robins	1870	William Gilbert	1897	Alexander Trengove
1844	Henry Reed	1871	William James Hocking	1898	William B. Lark
1845	William Reed	1872	William Rowe	1899	Thomas Braund
1846	Matthew Robins	1873	Isaac B. Vanstone	1900	John Luke
1847	James Way	1874	John Tremelling	1901	John Luke
1848	Richard P. Tabb	1875	Frederick W. Bourne	1902	John Dale
1849	Jacob H. Prior	1876	John Gammon	1903	Arthur Hancock
1850	Francis Martin	1877	Thomas C. Penwarden	1904	William R. K. Baulkwill
1851	Richard Kinsman	1878	John C. Honey	1905	Samuel B. Lane
1852	Matthew Robins	1879	Francis John Dymond	1906	John B. Stedeford
1853	James Ching	1880	James Horwill	1907	William B. Lark

IRISH METHODIST CONFERENCE
(Presidents of the Methodist Church in Ireland,
who are *Vice-Presidents* of the British Conference)

Year		Year		Year	
1868	Henry Price	1894	William Nicholas	1920	Henry Shire
1869	James Tobias	1895	Wallace M'Mullen	1921	William H. Smyth
1870	Joseph W. M'Kay	1896	William Crook	1922	James M. Alley
1871	Robinson Scott	1897	James Robertson	1923	James W. Parkhill
1872	William Parker Appelbe	1898	R. Crawford Johnson	1924	William Corrigan
1873	George Vance	1899	Charles H. Crookshank	1925	Edward B. Cullen
1874	Wallace M'Mullen	1900	William Crawford	1926	Robert M. Ker
1875	Gibson M'Millan	1901	John Oliver Park	1927	William H. Smyth
1876	Joseph W. M'Kay	1902	Wesley Guard	1928	Randall C. Phillips
1877	James Tobias	1903	William Nicholas	1929	John C. Robertson
1878	Wallace M'Mullen	1904	Thomas Knox	1930	William Moore
1879	William Guard Price	1905	George Ryles Wedgwood	1931	Frederick E. Harte
1880	William Parker Appelbe	1906	James Robertson	1932	John A. Duke
1881	James Tobias	1907	William Crawford	1933	R. Lee Cole
1882	Oliver M'Cutcheon	1908	James D. Lamont	1934	John A. Walton
1883	William Crook	1909	Joseph W. R. Campbell	1935	Thomas J. Irwin
1884	James Donnelly	1910	John Oliver Park	1936	William H. Massey
1885	Thomas A. M. M'Kee	1911	Wesley Guard	1937	C. Henry Crookshank
1886	Joseph W. M'Kay	1912	George Ryles Wedgwood	1938	Thomas J. Allen
1887	John Donor Powell	1913	Samuel T. Boyd	1939	Alexander McCrea
1888	Wallace M'Mullen	1914	William R. Budd	1940	Hugh M. Watson
1889	William Guard Price	1915	John Olliffe Price	1941	John N. Spence
1890	Oliver M'Cutcheon	1916	Pierce Martin	1942	Beresford S. Lyons
1891	John Woods Ballard	1917	William Maguire	1943	George A. Joynt
1892	William Gorman	1918	Hugh McKeag	1944	William L. Northridge
1893	Wesley Guard	1919	James Kirkwood	1945	Edward Whittaker

Year		Year		Year	
1946	Robert H. Gallagher	1954	Ernest Shaw	1962	James Wisheart
1947	John England	1955	Albert Holland	1963	Frederick E. Hill
1948	W. E. Morley Thompson	1956	Samuel E. McCaffrey	1964	Samuel H. Baxter
1949	John W. Stutt	1957	J. Wesley McKinney	1965	Robert A. Nelson
1950	J. R. Wesley Roddie	1958	Robert J. Good	1966	Samuel J. Johnston
1951	Henry N. Medd	1959	R. Ernest Ker	1967	R. D. Eric Gallagher
1952	John Montgomery	1960	Robert W. McVeigh	1968	Gerald G. Myles
1953	Richard M. L. Waugh	1961	Charles W. Ranson	1969	George E. Good

THE METHODIST CONFERENCE
Presidents

Year		Year		Year	
1932	John Scott Lidgett	1945	Archibald Walter Harrison	1958	Norman Henry Snaith
1933	Frederick Luke Wiseman	1946	Robert Newton Flew	1959	Eric Wilfred Baker
1934	William Younger	1947	William Edward Farndale	1960	Edward Rogers
1935	William Christopher Jackson	1948	Ernest Benson Perkins	1961	Maldwyn Lloyd Edwards
1936	Charles Ensor Walters	1949	Harold Burgoyne Rattenbury	1962	Leslie Davison
1937	Robert Bond	1950	William Edwin Sangster	1963	Frederic Greeves
1938	William Lansdell Wardle	1951	Howard Watkin-Jones	1964	Albert Kingsley Lloyd
1939	Richard Pyke	1952	Colin Augustus Roberts	1965	William Walker Lee
1940	Henry Bett	1953	Donald Oliver Soper	1966	Douglas Weddell Thompson
1941	Walter Henry Armstrong	1954	William Russell Shearer	1967	Irvonwy Morgan
1942	Walter James Noble	1955	Leslie Dixon Weatherhead	1968	Ernest Gordon Rupp
1943	Leslie Frederic Church	1956	Harold Crawford Walters	1969	Brian Stapleton O'Gorman
1944	Wilbert Francis Howard	1957	Harold Roberts	1970	Rupert Eric Davies

THE METHODIST NEW CONNEXION
Presidents

Year		Year		Year	
1797	William Thom	1834	Thomas Waterhouse	1871	Alexander McCurdy
1798	William Thom	1835	William Ford	1872	Joseph H. Robinson
1799	John Grundell	1836	Thomas Scattergood	1873	George Grundy
1800	Stephen Eversfield	1837	Abraham Scott	1874	William B. Wilshaw
1801	William Thom	1838	Joseph Livingston	1875	Henry Piggin
1802	William Thom	1839	Simeon Woodhouse	1876	C. Dewick Ward
1803	William Thom	1840	George Goodall	1877	John Medicraft
1804	William Driver	1841	James Wilson	1878	James Ogden
1805	James Mort	1842	Samuel Hulme	1879	James C. Watts
1806	William Styan	1843	William Cooke	1880	William Cocker
1807	William Brown	1844	John Bakewell	1881	James Stacey
1808	Edward Oakes	1845	William Ford	1882	William Longbottom
1809	George Wall	1846	Thomas Allin	1883	Thomas Rider
1810	Thomas Shore	1847	William Burrows	1884	Thomas D. Crothers
1811	William Thom	1848	James Henshaw	1885	Alexander McCurdy
1812	Joseph Manners	1849	Parkinson T. Gilton	1886	William J. Townsend
1813	William Haslam	1850	William Baggaly	1887	John K. Jackson
1814	George Hendley	1851	Thomas Waterhouse	1888	Thomas T. Rushworth
1815	George Wall	1852	Philip J. Wright	1889	Alfred R. Pearson
1816	William Driver	1853	John Hudston	1890	James Le Huray
1817	Abraham Scott	1854	William Mills	1891	Henry T. Marshall
1818	Thomas Waterhouse	1855	Samuel Hulme	1892	Joseph C. Milburn
1819	Abraham Jackson	1856	Henry Watts	1893	Thomas Scowby
1820	John Harrison	1857	Law Stoney	1894	Michael Bartram
1821	James Mort	1858	John Addyman	1895	George Packer
1822	Thomas Allin	1859	William Cooke	1896	Elisha Holyoake
1823	William Driver	1860	James Stacey	1897	John Innocent
1824	William Haslam	1861	Henry O. Crofts	1898	David Heath
1825	William Styan	1862	Thomas W. Ridley	1899	John E. Radcliffe
1826	Simeon Woodhouse	1863	William Cocker	1900	George S. Hornby
1827	William Shuttleworth	1864	Robert Henshaw	1901	George T. Candlin
1828	William Chapman	1865	William Baggaly	1902	Martin J. Birks
1829	Christopher Atkinson	1866	Samuel Hulme	1903	William Hookins
1830	William R. Wood	1867	John Taylor	1904	Thomas M. Rees
1831	William Salt	1868	Charles Hibbert	1905	Francis H. Robinson
1832	George Wall	1869	William Cooke	1906	Joseph Foster
1833	James Wilson	1870	Thomas Smith	1907	John S. Clemens

THE PRIMITIVE METHODIST CONFERENCE
Presidents

Year		Year		Year	
1820	George Handford	1826	James Bourne	1842	James Bourne
1825	Thomas King	1829	James Bourne	1843	John Garner

Year		Year		Year	
1844	William Clowes	1874	William Rowe	1904	Robert Harrison
1845	William Clowes	1875	Robert Smith	1905	George E. Butt
1846	William Clowes	1876	John Dickenson	1906	George Parkin, M.A., B.D.
1847	John Garner	1877	Thomas Smith	1907	Henry Yooll
1848	Thomas King	1878	Henry Phillips	1908	James Pickett
1849	Stephen Longdin	1879	Thomas Newell	1909	Sir William P. Hartley
1850	John Garner	1880	Colin C. McKechnie	1910	Samuel S. Henshaw
1851	John Garner	1881	Charles Kendall	1911	Edwin Dalton, D.D.
1852	John Garner	1882	Joseph Wood, M.A., D.D.	1912	Thomas Jackson
1853	Joseph Bailey	1883	William Cutts	1913	Joseph Ritson
1854	John Garner	1884	George Lamb	1914	George Bennett
1855	George Tetley	1885	Ralph Fenwick	1915	John Day Thompson
1856	Sampson Turner	1886	John Atkinson	1916	Arthur T. Guttery, D.D.
1857	Thomas Bateman	1887	Thomas Whitehead	1917	J. Tolefree Parr
1858	Sampson Turner	1888	Thomas Whittaker, D.D.	1918	William A. Hammond
1859	William Garner	1889	Joseph Toulson	1919	James Watkin
1860	John Petty	1890	John Hallam	1920	Matthew P. Davison
1861	William Garner	1891	Joseph Ferguson, D.D.	1921	Samuel Horton
1862	William Harland	1892	James Travis	1922	Henry J. Taylor
1863	William Antliff, D.D.	1893	John Stephenson	1923	George Armstrong
1864	James Garner	1894	John Wenn	1924	Joseph T. Barkby
1865	William Antliff, D.D.	1895	John Watson, D.D.	1925	James Lockhart
1866	George Lamb	1896	William Jones	1926	A. Lewis Humphries, M.A.
1867	Thomas Bateman	1897	James Jackson	1927	George Armitage
1868	William Lister	1898	John Smith	1928	John G. Bowran
1869	Philip Pugh	1899	William Goodman	1929	James H. Saxton
1870	Moses Lupton	1900	Joseph Odell	1930	W. Musson Kelley
1871	James Garner	1901	H. Bickerstaffe Kendall, B.A.	1931	Edward McLellan
1872	James Macpherson	1902	Thomas Mitchell, D.D.	1932	William Younger
1873	Samuel Antliff, D.D.	1903	T. Hankey Hunt		

THE UNITED METHODIST CONFERENCE
Presidents

Year		Year		Year	
1907	Edward Boaden	1916	Thomas J. Cox	1925	William Alexander Grist
1908	William J. Townsend	1917	James Wright	1926	Henry James
1909	William B. Lark	1918	John W. Walls	1927	Richard Pyke
1910	Henry T. Chapman	1919	John Moore	1928	Charles Stedeford
1911	George Packer	1920	Henry Smith	1929	R. H. Bowden Shapland
1912	John Luke	1921	William Treffry	1930	Arthur E. J. Cosson
1913	William Redfern	1922	Ernest F. H. Capey	1931	John Ford Reed
1914	George Parker	1923	Charles Pye	1932	William C. Jackson
1915	John B. Stedeford	1924	Joseph Lineham		

UNITED METHODIST FREE CHURCHES
Presidents

Year		Year		Year	
1857	James Everett	1874	Joseph Garside	1891	Matthias T. Myers
1858	Robert Eckett	1875	Joseph Kirsop	1892	John Truscott
1859	John Mann	1876	Thomas M. Booth	1893	Samuel Wright
1860	Thomas Hacking	1877	Anthony Holliday	1894	James Duckworth
1861	Samuel S. Barton	1878	William Boyden	1895	William R. Sunman
1862	William Reed	1879	Thomas W. Townsend	1896	George Turner
1863	John Guttridge	1880	William M. Hunter	1897	Robert Swallow
1864	Joseph Colman	1881	Richard Chew	1898	Ebenezer D. Cornish
1865	William R. Brown	1882	Arthur Hands	1899	James C. Brewitt
1866	Thomas Newton	1883	Henry Thomas Mawson	1900	Frederick Galpin
1867	Richard Chew	1884	Edwin Askew	1901	David Brook
1868	Marmaduke Miller	1885	Alfred Jones	1902	William Redfern
1869	John Mather	1886	Thomas Sherwood	1903	W. H. Cory Harris
1870	John Myers	1887	James S. Balmer	1904	Jabez King
1871	Edward Boaden	1888	Thomas Wakefield	1905	Thomas J. Dickinson
1872	John S. Withington	1889	Ralph Abercrombie	1906	David Irving
1873	John Adcock	1890	Matthias T. Myers	1907	William Barnes

WELSH METHODIST ASSEMBLY
Presidents

Year		Year		Year	
1899	Edward Humphreys	1902	Hugh Hughes	1905	R. Lloyd Jones
1900	Rice Owen	1903	Ishmael Evans	1906	T. Jones-Humphreys
1901	Hugh Jones	1904	Thomas Manuel	1907	Thomas Hughes

Year		Year		Year	
1908	Evan Jones	1929	D. Tecwyn Evans	1949	Robert W. Davies
1909	P. Jones Roberts	1930	E. Berwyn Roberts	1950	David R. Rogers
1910	J. Cadvan Davies	1931	E. Mostyn Jones	1951	Joseph Jenkins
1911	Thomas J. Pritchard	1932	Evan D. Thomas	1952	D. Llewelyn Jones
1912	Richard Morgan	1933	Arthur W. Davies	1953	J. Ellis Williams
1913	Thomas Jones	1934	H. Meirion Davies	1954	John Price
1914	W. Owen Evans	1935	R. Jones Williams	1955	David H. Thomas
1915	Owen Evans	1936	Robert J. Parry	1956	John Hughes
1916	John Felix	1937	E. Tegla Davies	1957	Robert G. Hughes
1917	Evan Isaac	1938	D. Egwys Jones	1958	G. Lloyd Brookes
1918	T. Isfryn Hughes	1939	R. Garrett Roberts	1959	J. Gwyn Jones
1919	Thomas O. Jones	1940	Edward Davies	1960	D. Arthur Morgan
1920	O. Madoc Roberts	1941	Charles Jones	1961	I. Elfyn Ellis
1921	Philip Price	1942	Richard Jones	1962	H. Baldwyn Pugh
1922	A. Colin-Pearce	1943	J. Lloyd Hughes	1963	D. Henriw Mason
1923	R. Mon Hughes	1944	J. Hopkin Morgan	1964	David R. Evans
1924	D. Gwynfryn Jones	1945	Lewis Edwards	1965	O. Prys Davies
1925	Hugh Evans	1946	W. Morris Jones	1966	Rufus Roberts
1926	Thomas Rowlands	1947	T. Gabriel Hughes	1967	Rheinallt L. Jones
1927	Robert W. Jones	1948	J. Roger Jones	1968	Griffith T. Roberts
1928	T. Charles Roberts			1969	Gwilym R. Tilsley

WESLEYAN METHODIST ASSOCIATION
Presidents

Year		Year		Year	
1836	Samuel Warren	1843	John Peters	1850	William Patterson
1837	James Livesey	1844	Enoch Darke	1851	John Peters
1838	James Molineux	1845	James Molineux	1852	Thomas A. Bayley
1839	James Sigston	1846	Robert Eckett	1853	Enoch Darke
1840	David Rowland	1847	Robert Eckett	1854	Anthony Gilbert
1841	Robert Eckett	1848	Henry Breeden	1855	William Dawson
1842	Thomas Townsend	1849	George Smith	1856	Matthew Baxter

THE WESLEYAN METHODIST CONFERENCE
Presidents

Year		Year		Year	
1791	William Thompson	1825	Joseph Entwisle	1859	Samuel D. Waddy
1792	Alexander Mather	1826	Richard Watson	1860	William W. Stamp
1793	John Pawson	1827	John Stephens	1861	John Rattenbury
1794	Thomas Hanby	1828	Jabez Bunting	1862	Charles Prest
1795	Joseph Bradford	1829	James Townley	1863	George Osborn
1796	Thomas Taylor	1830	George Morley	1864	William L. Thornton
1797	Thomas Coke	1831	George Marsden	1865	William Shaw
1798	Joseph Benson	1832	Robert Newton	1866	William Arthur
1799	Samuel Bradburn	1833	Richard Treffry, Sr.	1867	John Bedford
1800	James Wood	1834	Joseph Taylor	1868	Samuel Romilly Hall
1801	John Pawson	1835	Richard Reece	1869	Frederick J. Jobson
1802	Joseph Taylor	1836	Jabez Bunting	1870	John Farrar
1803	Joseph Bradford	1837	Edmund Grindrod	1871	John H. James
1804	Henry Moore	1838	Thomas Jackson	1872	Luke H. Wiseman
1805	Thomas Coke	1839	Theophilus Lessey	1873	George T. Perks
1806	Adam Clarke	1840	Robert Newton	1874	W. Morley Punshon
1807	John Barber	1841	James Dixon	1875	Gervase Smith
1808	James Wood	1842	John Hannah	1876	Alexander M'Aulay
1809	Thomas Taylor	1843	John Scott	1877	William Burt Pope
1810	Joseph Benson	1844	Jabez Bunting	1878	James H. Rigg
1811	Charles Atmore	1845	Jacob Stanley	1879	Benjamin Gregory
1812	Joseph Entwisle	1846	William Atherton	1880	Ebenezer E. Jenkins
1813	Walter Griffith	1847	Samuel Jackson	1881	George Osborn
1814	Adam Clarke	1848	Robert Newton	1882	Charles Garrett
1815	John Barber	1849	Thomas Jackson	1883	Thomas M'Cullagh
1816	Richard Reece	1850	John Beecham	1884	Frederic Greeves
1817	John Gaulter	1851	John Hannah	1885	Richard Roberts
1818	Jonathan Edmondson	1852	John Scott	1886	Robert N. Young
1819	Jonathan Crowther	1853	John Lomas	1887	John Walton
1820	Jabez Bunting	1854	John Farrar	1888	Joseph Bush
1821	George Marsden	1855	Isaac Keeling	1889	Charles H. Kelly
1822	Adam Clarke	1856	Robert Young	1890	William F. Moulton
1823	Henry Moore	1857	Francis A. West	1891	T. Bowman Stephenson
1824	Robert Newton	1858	John Bowers	1892	James H. Rigg

CONFERENCE PRESIDENTS IN GREAT BRITAIN

Year		Year		Year	
1893	Henry J. Pope	1907	John S. Simon	1920	J. T. Wardle Stafford
1894	Walford Green	1908	J. Scott Lidgett	1921	J. Alfred Sharp
1895	David J. Waller	1909	William Perkins	1922	John E. Wakerley
1896	Marshall Randles	1910	John Hornabrook	1923	T. Ferrier Hulme
1897	William L. Watkinson	1911	Henry Haigh	1924	Amos Burnet
1898	Hugh Price Hughes	1912	F. Luke Wiseman	1925	John H. Ritson
1899	Frederic W. Macdonald	1913	Samuel F. Collier	1926	W. Russell Maltby
1900	Thomas Allen	1914	Dinsdale T. Young	1927	W. Hodson Smith
1901	W. Theophilus Davison	1915	R. Waddy Moss	1928	John W. Lightley
1902	John Shaw Banks	1916	John G. Tasker	1929	William F. Lofthouse
1903	Marshall Hartley	1917	Simpson Johnson	1930	Herbert B. Workman
1904	Silvester Whitehead	1918	Samuel Chadwick	1931	C. Ryder Smith
1905	Charles H. Kelly	1919	William T. A. Barber	1932	H. Maldwyn Hughes
1906	Albert Clayton				

WESLEYAN PROTESTANT METHODIST ASSOCIATION
Presidents

Year		Year		Year	
1829	James Sigston	1832	Matthew Johnson	1834	George Slater
1830	Joseph Blythman	1833	James Sigston	1835	George Cookman
1831	George Turton				

METHODIST BISHOPS: THEIR ORDINATION AS DEACONS AND ELDERS

by Roy H. Short

In the tabular compilation below is given the year of each man's elevation to the episcopacy, his name, date of birth, date of death, and the name of the bishop or bishops who ordained him deacon and elder. The table lists all of the bishops of the church from 1784 to 1967, but does not include the bishops elected by The United Methodist Church in 1968 nor those from the former Evangelical United Brethren Church. (This list furnished to answer queries from episcopally ordained men as to their Methodist "succession.")

Year	Name (dates)	D	E
1784	Thomas Coke (1747-1814)	Church of England	Church of England
	Francis Asbury (1745-1816)	Coke	Coke
1800	Richard Whatcoat (1736-1806)	Wesley	Wesley
1808	William McKendree (1757-1835)	Asbury	Asbury
1816	Enoch George (1767-1828)	Asbury	Asbury
	Robert Richford Roberts (1778-1843)	Asbury	Asbury
1824	Joshua Soule (1781-1867)	Whatcoat	Whatcoat
	Elijah Hedding (1780-1852)	Whatcoat	Whatcoat
1832	James Osgood Andrew (1794-1871)	Asbury	McKendree
	John Emory (1789-1835)	Asbury	Asbury
1836	Beverly Waugh (1789-1858)	Asbury	Asbury
	Thomas Asbury Morris (1794-1874)	George	Roberts
1844	Leonidas Lent Hamline (1797-1865)	Andrew	Soule
	Edmund Storer Janes (1807-1876)	Soule & Hedding	Andrew & Hedding
1846	William Capers (1790-1855)	Asbury	McKendree
	Robert Paine (1799-1882)	McKendree	McKendree
1850	Henry Bidleman Bascom (1796-1850)	McKendree	McKendree
1852	Levi Scott (1802-1882)	George	Hedding
	Matthew Simpson (1811-1884)	Andrew	Roberts
	Osman Cleander Baker (1812-1871)	Morris	Soule
	Edward Raymond Ames (1806-1879)	Soule	Roberts
1854	George Foster Pierce (1811-1884)	Andrew	Andrew
	John Early (1786-1873)	Asbury	Asbury
	Hubbard Hinde Kavanaugh (1802-1884)	McKendree	Roberts
1858	Francis Burns (1809-1863)	Janes	Janes
1864	Davis Wasgatt Clark (1812-1871)	Hedding	Waugh
	Edward Thomson (1810-1870)	Andrew	Roberts
	Calvin Kingsley (1812-1870)	Soule	Hamline
1866	William May Wightman (1808-1882)	Soule	Hedding
	Enoch Mather Marvin (1823-1877)	Andrew	Soule
	David Seth Doggett (1810-1880)	Hedding	Hedding
	Holland Nimmons McTyeire (1824-1889)	Paine	Capers
	John Wright Roberts (1812-1875)[1]		
1870	John Christian Keener (1819-1906)	Andrew	Andrew
1872	Thomas Bowman (1817-1914)	Waugh	Waugh
	William Logan Harris (1817-1887)	Soule	Roberts
	Randolph Sinks Foster (1820-1903)	Waugh	Hedding
	Isaac William Wiley (1825-1884)	Janes	Janes
	Stephen Mason Merrill (1825-1905)	Waugh	Morris
	Gilbert Haven (1821-1880)	Janes	Simpson
	Jesse Truesdell Peck (1811-1883)	Hedding	Waugh
	Edward Gayer Andrews (1825-1907)	Janes	Scott
1880	Henry White Warren (1831-1912)	Baker	Ames
	Cyrus David Foss (1834-1910)	Baker	Janes
	John Fletcher Hurst (1834-1903)	Morris	Scott
	Erastus Otis Haven (1820-1881)	Janes	Hedding
1882	Alpheus Waters Wilson (1834-1916)	Scott	Waugh
	Linus Parker (1829-1885)	Paine	Andrew
	John Cowper Granbery (1829-1907)	Paine	Paine
	Robert Kennon Hargrove (1829-1905)	Kavanaugh	Early
1884	William Xavier Ninde (1832-1901)	Ames	Simpson
	John Morgan Walden (1831-1914)	Simpson	Ames

[1] Roberts was elected Missionary Bishop by the Methodist Episcopal Church in 1866.

Wilbur Francis Mallalieu (1828-1911)	D	Scott
	E	Janes
Charles Henry Fowler (1837-1908)	D	Scott
	E	Thomson
William Taylor (1821-1902)	D	Soule
	E	Waugh
1886 William Wallace Duncan (1839-1908)	D	Andrew
	E	Pierce
Charles Betts Galloway (1849-1909)	D	McTyeire
	E	Kavanaugh
Eugene Russell Hendrix (1847-1927)	D	Pierce
	E	McTyeire
Joseph Staunton Key (1829-1920)	D	Paine
	E	Andrew
1888 John Heyl Vincent (1832-1920)	D	Janes
	E	Scott
James Newbury Fitzgerald (1837-1907)	D	Simpson
	E	Baker
Isaac Wilson Joyce (1836-1905)	D	Simpson
	E	Morris
John Philip Newman (1826-1899)	D	Scott
	E	Janes
Daniel Ayres Goodsell (1840-1909)	D	Ames
	E	Baker
James Mills Thoburn (1836-1922)	D	Ames
	E	Ames
1890 Atticus Green Haygood (1839-1896)	D	Pierce
	E	Early
Oscar Penn Fitzgerald (1829-1911)	D	Kavanaugh
	E	Pierce
1896 Charles Cardwell McCabe (1836-1906)	D	Simpson
	E	Morris
Joseph Crane Hartzell (1842-1929)	D	
	E	Scott
Earl Cranston (1840-1932)	D	Janes
	E	Simpson
1898 Warren Akin Candler (1857-1941)	D	Pierce
	E	Keener
Henry Clay Morrison (1842-1921)	D	Doggett
	E	McTyeire
1900 David Hastings Moore (1838-1915)	D	
	E	Ames
John William Hamilton (1845-1934)	D	Kingsley
	E	Scott
Edwin Wallace Parker (1833-1901)	D	Ames
	E	Ames
Francis Wesley Warne (1854-1932)	D	Carman (Canadian Church)
	E	Carman
1902 Alexander Coke Smith (1849-1906)	D	Marvin
	E	Kavanaugh
Elijah Embree Hoss (1849-1919)	D	Kavanaugh
	E	McTyeire
1904 Joseph Flintoft Berry (1856-1931)	D	Ames
	E	Merrill
Henry Spellmeyer (1847-1910)	D	Simpson
	E	Foster
William Fraser McDowell (1858-1937)	D	Bowman
	E	Mallalieu
James Whitford Bashford (1849-1919)	D	
	E	
William Burt (1852-1936)	D	Foss
	E	Warren
Luther Barton Wilson (1856-1928)	D	Andrew
	E	Wiley
Thomas Benjamin Neely (1841-1925)	D	Scott
	E	Thomson
Isaiah Benjamin Scott (1854-1931)	D	Bowman
	E	Harris
William Fitzjames Oldham (1854-1937)	D	
	E	Hurst

John Edward Robinson (1849-1922)	D	Scott
	E	Bowman
Merriman Colbert Harris (1846-1921)	D	Clark
	E	W. L. Harris
1906 John James Tigert III (1856-1906)	D	Doggett
	E	Keener
Seth Ward (1858-1909)	D	Parker
	E	McTyeire
James Atkins (1850-1923)	D	Doggett
	E	Wightman
1908 William Franklin Anderson (1860-1944)	D	Fowler
	E	Mallalieu
John Louis Nuelsen (1867-1946)	D	Newman
	E	
William Alfred Quayle (1860-1925)	D	Walden
	E	Ninde
Charles William Smith (1840-1914)	D	Ames
	E	Janes
Wilson Seeley Lewis (1857-1921)	D	Mallalieu
	E	Merrill
Edwin Holt Hughes (1866-1950)	D	Joyce
	E	Foss
Robert McIntyre (1851-1914)	D	W. L. Harris
	E	Warren
Frank Milton Bristol (1851-1932)	D	Andrews
	E	Wiley
1910 Collins Denny (1854-1943)	D	McTyeire
	E	Wilson
John Carlisle Kilgo (1861-1922)	D	McTyeire
	E	Granbery
William Belton Murrah (1852-1925)	D	Pierce
	E	Paine
Walter Russell Lambuth (1854-1921)	D	Keener
	E	Doggett
Richard Green Waterhouse (1855-1922)	D	McTyeire
	E	Keener
Edwin DuBose Mouzon (1869-1937)	D	O. P. Fitzgerald
	E	Hendrix
James Henry McCoy (1868-1919)	D	Galloway
	E	Duncan
1912 Homer Clyde Stuntz (1858-1924)	D	Warren
	E	Foster
Theodore Sommers Henderson (1868-1929)	D	E. G. Andrews
	E	Fowler
William Orville Shepard (1862-1931)	D	Walden
	E	Foster
Naphtali Luccock (1853-1916)	D	G. Haven
	E	Scott
Francis John McConnell (1871-1953)	D	Newman
	E	Joyce
Frederick DeLand Leete (1866-1958)	D	Hurst
	E	Hurst
Richard Joseph Cooke (1853-1931)	D	Foster
	E	Foster
Wilbur Patterson Thirkield (1854-1936)	D	Wiley
	E	Foster
John Wesley Robinson (1866-1947)	D	Thoburn
	E	Thoburn
William Perry Eveland (1864-1916)	D	Andrews
	E	Newman
1916 Herbert Welch (1862-1969)	D	Foss
	E	Fowler
Thomas Nicholson (1862-1944)	D	Warren
	E	Foss
Adna Wright Leonard (1874-1943)	D	Andrews
	E	Vincent
Matthew Simpson Hughes (1863-1920)	D	Joyce
	E	
Charles Bayard Mitchell (1857-1942)	D	Warren
	E	Merrill
Franklin Elmer Ellsworth Hamilton (1866-1918)	D	Goodsell
	E	Merrill

Name	D	E
Alexander Priestley Camphor (1865-1919)	Joyce	Hartzell
Eben Samuel Johnson (1866-1939)	Ninde	Mallalieu
1918 John Monroe Moore (1867-1948)	C. H. Fowler	Hargrove
William Fletcher McMurry (1864-1934)	Hendrix	Key
Urban Valentine Williams Darlington (1870-1954)	Haygood	Hendrix
Horace Mellard DuBose (1858-1941)	Kavanaugh	Keener
William Newman Ainsworth (1872-1942)	Galloway	Granbery
James Cannon, Jr. (1864-1944)	Wilson	Hendrix
1920 Lauress John Birney (1871-1937)		
Frederick Bohn Fisher (1882-1938)	McCabe	Warne
Ernest Lynn Waldorf (1876-1943)	Mallalieu	Goodsell
Charles Edward Locke (1858-1940)	Harris	Foster
Ernest Gladstone Richardson (1874-1947)	Walden	Hurst
Charles Wesley Burns (1874-1938)	Ninde	Mallalieu
Anton Bast (1867-1937)	Joyce	Newman
Edgar Blake (1869-1943)	Ninde	Warren
George Harvey Bickley (1868-1924)	Walden	Andrews
Frederick Thomas Keeney (1863-1952)	Vincent	Ninde
Harry Lester Smith (1876-1951)	Cranston	Spellmeyer
Charles Larew Mead (1868-1941)	Foss	Fowler
Robert Elijah Jones (1872-1960)	Hurst	Mallalieu
Matthew Wesley Clair, Sr. (1865-1943)	Walden	Andrews
1922 William Benjamin Beauchamp (1869-1931)	Granbery	Fitzgerald
James Edward Dickey (1864-1928)	Haygood	Keener
Samuel Ross Hay (1865-1944)	Key	A. W. Wilson
Hoyt McWhorter Dobbs (1878-1954)	A. W. Wilson	Morrison
Hiram Abiff Boaz (1866-1962)	O. P. Fitzgerald	Hargrove
1924 George Amos Miller (1868-1961)	Foss	J. W. Hamilton
Titus Lowe (1877-1959)	J. N. Fitzgerald	
George Richmond Grose (1869-1953)	Fowler	Newman
Brenton Thoburn Badley (1876-1949)	Warne	Thoburn
Wallace Elias Brown (1868-1939)	Goodsell	Fowler
1928 Raymond J. Wade (1875-1970)	Andrews	Merrill
James Chamberlain Baker (1879-1969)	Andrews	J. W. Hamilton
1930 Edwin Ferdinand Lee (1884-1948)	Lewis	Oldham
John Gowdy (1869-1963)	Cranston	Cranston

Name	D	E
Chih P'ing Wang (1879-1964)		
Arthur James Moore (1888-)	A. W. Wilson	Candler
Paul Bentley Kern (1882-1953)	Hoss	Hoss
Angie Frank Smith (1889-1962)	McCoy	Ainsworth
1931 Jashwant Rao Chitambar (1879-1940)	J. N. Fitzgerald	Warne
1932 Juan E. Gattinoni (1878-1970)	Neely	Bristol
Junius Ralph Magee (1880-1970)	McDowell	Cranston
Ralph Spaulding Cushman (1879-1960)	Goodsell	Warren
1936 Jarrell Waskom Pickett (1890-)	Warne	McDowell
Wilbur Emery Hammaker (1876-1968)	Fitzgerald	Fowler
Charles Wesley Flint (1878-1964)	Hamilton	McDowell
Garfield Bromley Oxnam (1891-1963)	McDowell	Leonard
Alexander Preston Shaw (1879-1966)	Goodsell	Warren
John McKendree Springer (1873-1963)	Hartzell	Hartzell
Roberto Elphick (1873-1961)		Neely
Otto Melle (1875-1947)	Vincent	Vincent
1937 Ralph Ansel Ward (1882-1958)	Warren	Warren
1938 Ivan Lee Holt (1886-1967)	Denny	Hoss
William Walter Peele (1881-1959)	A. W. Wilson	Hoss
Clare Purcell (1884-1964)	Hoss	McCoy
Charles Claude Selecman (1874-1958)	O. P. Fitzgerald	A. W. Wilson
John Lloyd Decell (1887-1946)	Morrison	Denny
William Clyde Martin (1893-)	Mouzon	J. Moore
William Turner Watkins (1895-1961)	Candler	Candler
Chong Oo Kim (1884-1939)	Welch	
1939 James Henry Straughn (1877-)		M. P. Church
John Calvin Broomfield (1872-1950)		M. P. Church
1940 Wm. Alfred Carroll Hughes (1877-1940)		H. W. Warren
Lorenzo Houston King (1878-1946)	Foss	L. B. Wilson
Bruce Richard Baxter (1892-1947)	McDowell	McDowell
1941 Shot Kumar Mondol (1896-)	Fisher	Welch
Clement Daniel Rockey (1889-)	Warne	Warne
Enrique Carlos Balloch (1885-)	Neely	Bristol
Z. T. Kaung (1884-1958)	Atkins	Kilgo
Wen-yuan Chen (1897-1968)		
George Carleton Lacy (1888-1951)	Lewis	Lewis

1944 Fred Pierce Corson (1896-)	D McDowell
	E Wilson
Walter Earl Ledden (1888-)	D Berry
	E Berry
Lewis Oliver Hartman (1876-1955)	D Fowler
	E Cranston
Newell Snow Booth (1903-1968)	D Mead
	E Anderson
Schuyler Edward Garth (1898-1947)	D Nicholson
	E Richardson
Charles Wesley Brashares (1891-)	D Hughes
	E Bristol
Costen Jordan Harrell (1885-1971)	D Hoss
	E Waterhouse
Paul Neff Garber (1899-1972)	D Church of the Brethren
	E Church of the Brethren
William Angie Smith (1894-)	D Dickey
	E Mouzon
Paul Elliott Martin (1897-)	D J. M. Moore
	E Hay
Edward Wendall Kelly (1880-1964)	D McIntyre
	E Thirkield
Robert Nathaniel Brooks (1888-1952)	D Thirkield
	E E. Hughes
Willis Jefferson King (1886-)	D Quayle
	E Hamilton
Arthur Frederick Wesley (1885-)	D McDowell
	E Oldham
1945 John Abdus Subhan (1899-)	D J. W. Robinson
	E Chitambar
1946 Dionisio Deista Alejandro (1893-1972)	D Eveland
	E Stuntz
Theodor Arvidson (1883-1964)	D Cranston
	E Burt
Johan Wilhelm Ernst Sommer (1881-1952)	D Nuelsen
	E Nuelsen
1948 Lloyd Christ Wicke (1901-)	D Wilson
	E Leonard
John Wesley Lord (1902-)	D McConnell
	E Lowe
John Wesley Edward Bowen (1889-1962)	D Leete
	E McDowell
Dana Dawson (1892-1964)	D Mouzon
	E Mouzon
Marvin Augustus Franklin (1894-1972)	D Denny
	E Candler
Roy Hunter Short (1902-)	D Darlington
	E Dickey
Richard Campbell Raines (1898-)	D E. Hughes
	E Anderson
Marshall Russell Reed (1891-1973)	D Leete
	E Henderson
Harry Clifford Northcott (1890-)	D Leete
	E Leete
Hazen G. Werner (1895-)	D Nicholson
	E Nicholson
Glenn Randall Phillips (1894-1970)	D Leonard
	E Leonard
Gerald Hamilton Kennedy (1907-)	D Baker
	E Leete
Donald Harvey Tippett (1896-)	D Mead
	E Waldorf
Jose Labarette Valencia (1898-)	D Leete
	E Lee
1949 Sante Uberto Barbieri (1902-)	D Dobbs
	E J. M. Moore
1950 Raymond Leroy Archer (1887-1970)	D L. B. Wilson
	E L. B. Wilson
1952 Edgar Amos Love (1891-)	D Cranston
	E McDowell

Matthew Wesley Clair, Jr. (1890-1968)	D McDowell
	E McDowell
D. Stanley Coors (1889-1960)	D L. B. Wilson
	E L. B. Wilson
Edwin Edgar Voigt (1892-)	D Bristol
	E Hughes
Francis Gerald Ensley (1907-)	D H. L. Smith
	E McConnell
Frederick Buckley Newell (1890-)	D Wilson
	E Wilson
Henry Bascom Watts (1890-1959)	D McCoy
	E Mouzon
John W. Branscomb (1905-1959)	D J. Moore
	E J. Moore
Alsie Raymond Grant (1897-1967)	D Hughes
	E Hughes
Julio M. Sabanes (1897-1963)	D Oldham
	E Miller
1953 Friedrich Wunderlich (1896-)	D Nuelsen
	E Nuelsen
Odd Arthur Hagen (1905-1970)	D E. H. Hughes
	E Wade
1954 Ferdinand Sigg (1902-1965)	D Nuelsen
	E Nuelsen
1955 Ralph Edward Dodge (1907-)	D
	E
1956 Prince Albert Taylor, Jr. (1907-)	D H. L. Smith
	E Brown
Eugene Maxwell Frank (1907-)	D Brown
	E Mead
Nolan Bailey Harmon (1892-)	D Morrison
	E Morrison
Bachman G. Hodge (1893-1961)	D McMurry
	E McMurry
Hobart B. Amstutz (1896-)	D Nicholson
	E Nicholson
Mangal Singh (1902-)	D Chitambar
	E Badley
Gabriel Sundaram (1900-)	D Warne
	E Warne
1960 Charles Franklin Golden (1912-)	D Keeney
	E Shaw
Noah Watson Moore, Jr. (1902-)	D E. Hughes
	E Richardson
Marquis LaFayette Harris (1907-1966)	D Clair, Sr.
	E Clair, Sr.
Ralph Taylor Alton (1908-)	D Leonard
	E L. Smith
Edwin Ronald Garrison (1897-)	D Leete
	E Locke
Torney Otto Nall (1900-)	D Locke
	E Locke
Fred Garrigus Holloway (1898-)	E Straughn (M.P.)
James Kenneth Mathews (1913-)	D McConnell
	E Badley
W. Vernon Middleton (1902-1965)	D Berry
	E Nicholson
William Ralph Ward, Jr. (1908-)	D Anderson
	E Burns
Oliver Eugene Slater (1906-)	D Boaz
	E Boaz
William Kenneth Pope (1901-)	D Dickey
	E J. Moore
Paul Vernon Galloway (1904-)	D Mouzon
	E Dobbs
Aubrey Grey Walton (1901-)	D Dobbs
	E J. Moore
Kenneth Wilford Copeland (1912-)	E M.P. Church
James Walton Henley (1901-)	D DuBose
	E DuBose

Walter Clark Gum (1897-1969)	D Hendrix	Edward Julian Pendergrass	D John Moore
	E Candler	(1900-)	E Hay
Paul Hardin, Jr. (1903-)	D Mouzon	Homer Ellis Finger, Jr.	D Decell
	E Mouzon	(1916-)	E Decell
John Owen Smith (1902-)	D Mouzon	Earl Gladstone Hunt, Jr.	D Kern
	E Mouzon	(1918-)	E Kern
Everett Walter Palmer	D Richardson	Robert Fielden Lundy	D Kern
(1906-1971)	E Brown	(1920-)	E Kern
Bowman Foster Stockwell	D E. Hughes	Escrivao Zunguze (-)	D Booth
(1899-1961)	E Anderson		E Booth
1962 Pedro Zottele (1903-)	D Miller	John Wesley Shungu	D Booth
	E Gattinoni	(1917-)	E Booth
1964 James Samuel Thomas	D L. H. King	Harry P. Andreassen	D Arvidson
(1919-)	E W. J. King	(1922-)	E Booth
William McFerrin Stowe	D DuBose	1965 Prabhakar Christopher Benjamin	D Pickett
(1913-)	E A. F. Smith	Balaram (1906-1968)	E Pickett
Robert Marvin Stuart	D Burns	Stephen Trowen Nagbe	D W. J. King
(1909-)	E Brown	(1933-1973)	E P. Taylor
Dwight Ellsworth Loder	D Flint	Alfred Jacob Shaw (1906-)	D Rockey
(1914-)	E Flint		E Rockey
Thomas Marion Pryor	D Burns	1966 Franz W. Schaefer (1921-)	D Garber
(1904-)	E Nicholson		E Garber
Francis Emner Kearns	D McDowell	1967 L. Scott Allen (1918-)	D Clair, Sr.
(1905-)	E Welch		E R. E. Jones
Lance Webb (1909-)	D Boaz	Benjamin I. Guansing	D Lee
	E Boaz	(1908-1968)	E Lee
Walter Kenneth Goodson	D Kern		
(1912-)	E Purcell		

TABLE OF
METHODIST CONFERENCES (U. S. A.)

by Albea Godbold

This table lists by states, and by denominations within the states, the annual conferences, provisional annual conferences, mission conferences, and missions (overseas conferences are not included save for one in Canada and those in Cuba and Puerto Rico) of the Methodist Episcopal Church before and after 1844, the Methodist Episcopal Church, South (1845-1939), the Methodist Protestant Church (1828-1939), the Methodist Church (1866-1877), and The Methodist Church (1939-1968). The conferences which continued in The United Methodist Church (1968-   ) are identified, including changes in names and boundaries through June, and in some instances through July 1968.

It should be said that since the M. P. Church was loosely organized, since the action of its General Conference regarding annual conference names, boundaries, dates for mergers and divisions, and the like, was in the last analysis advisory and not binding at the annual conference level, and since the denomination did not print General Minutes to show what actually happened each year in the conferences, it is hardly possible to compile a completely accurate table of its annual conferences. However, it is fair to say that there is documentary evidence for the facts and figures used in this table, and it is believed they are generally reliable.

The reader should remember that while the Methodist Church (1866-1877) was a bona fide ecclesiastical organization and must therefore be recognized as a denomination, it was little more than the northern conferences of the Methodist Protestant Church. For this reason in this table the annual conferences of the Methodist Church (1866-1877) are identified only in connection with the M. P. Church, as indicated in the next paragraph.

To save space and avoid the necessity of listing a large number of annual conferences as belonging to the M. P. Church prior to 1866, showing them again as conferences of the Methodist Church from 1866 to 1877, and then printing them a third time as conferences of the M. P. Church, a code is used in this table. A † sign before the name of a conference means that it was an M. P. conference prior to 1866, an M. C. conference during part or all of the time from 1866 to 1877, and if it continued in existence, was an M. P. conference again after 1877. A ‡ sign before the name of a conference indicates that it was organized or recognized by the M. P. Church during the years 1866 to 1877. A § sign before the name of a conference means that it was organized or recognized by the Methodist Church between 1866 and 1877.

The capital letters in column one and elsewhere in the table stand for the denominations—ME, Methodist Episcopal; MES, Methodist Episcopal, South; MP, Methodist Protestant; MC, Methodist (1866-1877); M, Methodist (1939-1968); and UM, United Methodist.

In column two the conferences in each state are listed alphabetically within each denomination. The arabic numerals preceding the names of the conferences indicate the chronological order of their organization by the denomination in the particular state. If the denomination created two or more conferences in the state in the same year, they are given the same number with letters added, as for example 2a and 2b, or 3a, 3b, and 3c. When the chronological order coincides with the alphabetical order, no numerals are used.

The figures in column three represent the year the annual conference began and the year it disappeared. In this table the beginning date for a conference means the year in which the preachers met with a bishop or other presiding officer and organized the body. In some instances this is not the year in which the General Conference authorized the creation of the conference, nor is it the year in which statistics for the conference first appear in the General Minutes. In instances in which the actual date of organization could not be authoritatively confirmed by the researcher, the date entered in the table is the one given by the best historical authority available.

The dates indicated in this table for the organization of some annual conferences differ from the dates found in their own journals and in the General Minutes. In view of the criteria adopted for the compilation of this table, the differences are both unavoidable and understandable. A number of present day conferences date their beginning from the time of the organization of the first annual conference in their geographical location, regardless of whether or not the conference today bears the same name as the original body. But in this table, every time a conference changes its name or becomes a conference in a new denomination, it is a new conference with a different date of organization. Also, some conferences date their origin from the time of the organization of the mission or mission conference which preceded them, but in this table missions and mission conferences are different entities with their own dates of beginning and conclusion.

Conferences ceased to exist for the following reasons: division into two or more bodies, merger with or absorption by other conferences, mere change of name, the union of denominations, and because the parent church decided to discontinue work in the particular region. The final outcome for each conference up to June 1968 is listed in column six.

Column four gives the location, that is, the territory, of each annual conference when it was organized. Later changes in boundaries are not indicated, except as they may be identified in the data entered in column four in connection with successor conferences which have been created through the years by divisions, mergers, realignments, and changes of name. By noting the chronological order of the creation of annual conferences in a state, the reader may get some idea of conference boundary changes with the passage of time.

For reasons of space, explanations of boundaries as given in column four are condensed. Details are often omitted. For example, if a conference embraces all or the major portion of one state and small segments of several adjoining states, not all of the latter may be named. If possible, the data on the location of each conference are compressed into one line in column four.

Column five shows how each conference was formed. New conferences have continually appeared because of the occupation of new territory by the denomination, because of the division, merger, or change of name of existing conferences, and because of the breakup or union of denominations.

Column six shows what happened to the conferences as time passed. Through the years many well known conference names and others not so well known have disappeared. This happened because the parent denomination had reason to divide, merge, absorb, and even abolish conferences. The division of the church in 1844, the sundering of the M. P. Church in 1866 and its reunion in 1877, unification in 1939, and union in 1968 caused the birth of some new conferences and the demise of many others. On the other hand, a few conferences have continued from the beginning until now with the same name and with part if not all of their original territory. However, as indicated above, every time a continuing conference's denomination changes, the conference itself shows again in this table with a new beginning date, albeit with the same name.

To save space, the word "conference" is used in this table only in those places where it is necessary to distinguish a conference from a mission, a mission conference, or a provisional conference.

When two or more conferences are named in columns five and six, they are *always* separated by commas. The absence of a comma between what may appear to be two conference names denotes a conference with a double title, such as the Missouri and Arkansas Conference ME, or the Arkansas and Louisiana Conference MP.

Asterisks (°) denote Negro annual conferences. Diamond signs (◊) indicate conferences organized by the two Episcopal Methodisms between 1845 and 1939 in territory already included in each other's existing annual conferences at the time of the division in 1844.

Some conferences organized by the M. E. Church in the South immediately following the Civil War included both white and Negro ministers and churches. As time passed, these conferences were divided along racial but not geographical lines. Sometimes the conference retaining the original name was white and sometimes Negro, as indicated in the table.

The names of foreign language conferences—Chinese, Danish, German, Italian, Japanese, Norwegian, Spanish, and Swedish—are printed in this table as they appear in the

General Minutes of the particular denominations, even though in some instances they vary slightly from the names used in the yearly journals of such conferences. Each of these conferences is listed in the table under the state (if any) appearing in its name. If no state is included in the name, the conference is listed under the state in which it had the most churches.

The states in which the various foreign language conferences will be found are as follows: (1) German: California, Illinois, Kansas, Minnesota, New York, Ohio, Texas, and Washington. (2) Swedish: Illinois, Iowa, Minnesota, New York, and Texas. (3) Spanish (Mexican, Latin, and Latin-American): California, Florida, New Mexico, and Texas. (4) Norwegian and Danish: Minnesota and Washington. (5) Oriental: California. (6) Italian: New York.

The phrase "Merged in 1939" appears frequently in column six. It refers of course to the unification of the three branches of Methodism to form The Methodist Church. Generally the M.E., M.E.S., and M.P. conferences totally or partially involved in the 1939 mergers are not named, because the number is too large, and because in many if not in most instances their identity will be clear to the reader anyway. In like manner, when foreign language conferences are absorbed by English-speaking ones, and when Central Jurisdiction conferences are blended with those of other Jurisdictions, usually the bodies involved in the mergers are not named.

Cross references are entered where needed, but there are no duplicate listings of conferences in the table.

Denomination	Conference	Dates	Location	How Formed	Conclusion
			ALABAMA		
ME	1 Alabama	1832-1845	S. Ala., W. Fla. & E. Miss.	Division of Miss.	Superseded by Ala. MES
	3 ◊ Alabama	1867-1939	Ala. & W. Fla.	Superseded ◊ Ala. Miss. Conf.	Merger in 1939
	2 ◊ Ala. Miss. Conf.	1867-1868	Ala. & W. Fla.	◊	Superseded by ◊ Ala.
	4 ° Central Ala.	1876-1939	Ala.	Division of ◊ Ala.	Continued in M
	5 ° Mobile	1900-1907	S. Ala. & W. Fla.	Division of ° Central Ala.	Absorbed by ° Central Ala.
MES	1 Alabama	1846-1863	Ala., W. Fla. & E. Miss.	Superseded Ala. ME	Divided—Mobile & Montgomery
	3a Alabama	1870-1939	S. Ala. & W. Fla.	Partially superseded Mobile & Montgomery	Continued in M
	2a Mobile	1863-1869	W. Ala. & E. Miss.	Division of Ala.	Superseded by Ala., & N. Ala.
	2b Montgomery	1863-1869	E. Ala. & W. Fla.	Division of Ala.	Superseded by Ala., & N. Ala.
	3b North Ala.	1870-1939	N. Ala.	Partially superseded Mobile, Montgomery, & Tenn.	Continued in M
MP	1 Alabama	1829-1939	Ala.	Secession from ME	Merged in 1939
	3 ° Ala. Miss. Conf.	1879-1939	Ala.	Division of Ala.	Merged in 1939
	2 Huntsville	1846-1858	N. Ala. & part of Tenn.	Division of Tenn.	Absorbed by Ala., & Tenn.
M	1a Alabama	1939-1956	S. Ala. & W. Fla.	Superseded Ala. MES, & partially Ala. ME, & MP	Superseded by Ala.-W. Fla.
	2 Ala.-W. Fla.	1957-1968	S. Ala. & W. Fla.	Superseded Ala.	Continued in UM
	1b ° Central Ala.	1939-1968	Ala.	Superseded ° Central Ala. ME	Temporarily continued in UM
	1c North Ala.	1939-1968	N. Ala.	Superseded N. Ala. MES, & partially Ala. ME, & MP	Continued in UM
			ALASKA		
ME	Alaska Mission	1904-1924	Alaska	Organization of new work	Absorbed by Puget Sound
M	Alaska Mission	1939-1960	Alaska	Division of Pacific N.W.[1]	Superseded by Alaska Miss. Conf.

---

[1] See Washington.

Denomi-nation	Conference	Dates	Location	How Formed	Conclusion
	Alaska Mission Conf.	1961-1968	Alaska	Superseded Alaska Mission	Continued in UM

ARIZONA

Denomi-nation	Conference	Dates	Location	How Formed	Conclusion
ME	Ariz. Mission	1880-1919	Arizona	Organization of new work	Absorbed by Sou. Calif.
MES	Arizona	1922-1939	Arizona	Partially superseded Los Angeles	Merged with S. Calif. in 1939

ARKANSAS

Denomi-nation	Conference	Dates	Location	How Formed	Conclusion
ME	Arkansas	1836-1844	Ark. & part of La.	Division of Mo.	Superseded by Ark. MES
	◊Arkansas	1853-1860	Ark., Tex., parts of Mo. & N.M.	Division of ◊Mo.	Merged to form ◊Mo. & Ark.
	◊Arkansas	1873-1920	Ark. & Indian country to west	Division of ◊St. Louis	Absorbed by ◊St. Louis
	°Little Rock	1878-1929	Ark.	Division of ◊Ark.	Merged with °Lincoln² to form °S.W.
	°Southwest	1929-1939	Ark. & Okla.	Merger of °L. Rock & °Lincoln²	Continued in M
MES	1 Arkansas	1845-1913	Ark.	Superseded Ark. ME	Merged with White River to form N. Ark.
	3 Little Rock	1866-1939	S. Ark.	Superseded Ouachita	Continued in M
	5 North Ark.	1914-1939	N. Ark.	Merger of Ark., & White R.	Continued in M
	2 Ouachita	1854-1865	S. Ark.	Division of Ark.	Superseded by Little Rock
	4 White River	1870-1913	N.E. Ark.	Division of Ark.	Merged with Ark. to form N. Ark.
MP	1 Arkansas	1837-1870	Ark., Mo., etc.	Secession from ME	Superseded by Ark. & La.
	6a Arkansas	1884-1939	S. Ark. & La.	Division of Ark. & La.	Merged in 1939
	3 Ark. & La.	1871-1884	S. Ark. & La.	Merger of Ark., & La.	Divided to form Ark., & La.
	7 °Ark. Miss. Conf.	1892-1939	Ark. & La.	Organization of Negro work	Absorbed by °Southwest M
	4a Batesville	1877-1880	N.E. Ark.	Division of N. Ark.	Merged with N. Ark.
	6b Ft. Smith Miss. Conf.	1884-1915	N.W. Ark. & part of Indian Territory	Division of N. Ark.	Merged with Okla. Conf. to form Ft. Smith-Okla. Conf.
	9 Ft. Smith-Okla.	1916-1939	N.W. Ark. & Okla.	Merger of Ft. Smith Mission Conf., & Okla. Conf.	Merged in 1939
	2 N. Ark.	1869-1888	N.E. Ark.	Division of Ark.	Absorbed by Ark.
	8 N.E. Ark.	1900-1908	N.E. Ark. & S.E. Mo.	Division of Ark.	Absorbed by Ark.
	5 Red River Miss. Conf.	1880-1888	S.W. Ark.	Division of Western Ark.	Absorbed by Ark.
	4b Western Ark.	1877-1888	S.W. Ark.	Division of Ark.	Absorbed by Ark.
M	Little Rock	1939-1968	S. Ark.	Superseded L. Rock MES, & in part Mo. ME, & Ark. MP	Continued in UM
	N. Ark.	1939-1968	N. Ark.	Superseded N. Ark. MES, & in part Mo. ME, Ark. MP, & Ft. Smith-Okla. MP	Continued in UM
	°Southwest	1939-1968	Ark. & Okla.	Superseded °Southwest ME, & °Ark. Mission Conf. MP	Temporarily continued in UM

CALIFORNIA

Denomi-nation	Conference	Dates	Location	How Formed	Conclusion
ME	1 California	1851-1939	Calif., Utah & part of N.M.	Division of Ore. & Calif.³	Continued in M
	3 Calif. German Mission	1888-1889	Calif.	Organization of German work	Superseded by Calif. German Mission Conf.
	4 Calif. German Mission Conf.	1890	Calif.	Superseded Calif. Germ. Miss.	Superseded by Calif. German Conf.
	5 Calif. German	1891-1927	Calif.	Superseded Calif. Germ. Miss. Conf.	Absorbed by English-speaking
	7 Chinese Miss.	1904-1907	Calif.	Organization of Chinese work	Absorbed by Pac. Chinese Miss.
	9 Latin Amer. Mission	1920-1939	Calif., Ariz., Nev., etc.	Division of Southern Calif.	Continued in M

² See Oklahoma.   ³ See Oregon.

Denomination	Conference	Dates	Location	How Formed	Conclusion
	8 Pacific Chinese Mission	1907-1939	Western half of U.S.	Superseded Chinese Mission	Superseded by Calif. Oriental Mission M
	6 Pacific Japanese Mission	1900-1939	Pacific Slope & Hawaii	Organization of Japanese work	Superseded by Pac. Japan. Prov. Conf. M
	2 Sou. Calif.	1876-1939	Southern Calif.	Division of Calif.	Continued in M
MES	4 Calif. Oriental Mission	1926-1939	Calif.	Organization of new work	Continued in M
	2 Los Angeles	1870-1921	Sou. Calif., Ariz., etc.	Division of Pacific	Absorbed by Ariz., & Pacific
	1 Pacific	1852-1939	Calif., Ariz., & part of N.M.	Organization of new work	Merged in 1939
	3 Pac. Mexican Mission	1914-1918	Calif., Ariz., etc.	Organization of new work	Merged with part of Mex. Border Mission to form Western Mex. Mission[4]
MP	§California	1866-1880	Calif.	Division of Ore. & Calif.	Superseded by Calif. Miss. Conf.
	Calif. Miss. Conf.	1880-1908	Calif.	Superseded §Calif. Conf.	Dissolved
M	1a California	1939-1948	N. Calif. & part of Nev.	Superseded Calif. ME, & partially Pacific MES	Superseded by Calif.-Nev.
	4 Calif.-Nev.	1949-1968	N. Calif. & part of Nev.	Superseded Calif.	Continued in UM
	1c Calif. Oriental Mission	1939-1944	Western Jurisdiction, except Hawaii	Superseded Calif. Ori. Miss. MES, & Pac. Chin. Miss. ME	Superseded by Calif. Ori. Provisional Conf.
	3 Calif. Oriental Prov. Conf.	1945-1952	Western Juris., except Hawaii	Superseded Calif. Ori. Miss.	Absorbed by English-speaking
	1d Latin Amer. Mission	1939	Western Juris., & part of Mexico	Superseded Latin Amer. Miss. ME, & Pac. Mex. Miss. MES	Superseded by Latin Amer. Prov. Conf.
	2b Latin Amer. Prov. Conf.	1940-1957	Western Juris., & part of Mexico	Superseded Latin Amer. Miss.	Absorbed by English-speaking
	1e Pac. Japan. Prov. Conf.	1939-1964	Western Juris. except Hawaii	Superseded Pacific Japan. Mission ME	Absorbed by English-speaking
	1b Sou. Calif.	1939	Sou. Calif., Ariz., etc.	Superseded Sou. Calif. ME, & Ariz. MES, & Pacific MES in part	Superseded by Sou. Calif.-Ariz.
	2a Sou. Calif.-Arizona	1940-1968	Sou. Calif., Ariz., etc.	Superseded Sou. Calif.	Continued in UM

COLORADO

Denomination	Conference	Dates	Location	How Formed	Conclusion
ME	2 Colorado	1864-1939	Colorado	Superseded Rocky Mountain	Continued in M
	1 Rocky Mountain	1863	Colorado	Division of Kansas	Superseded by Colorado
MES	Denver	1874-1930	Colorado, Mont., & N.M.	Organization of new work	Absorbed by N.M.
M	Colorado	1939-1956	Colorado	Superseded Colo. ME, & partially N.M. MES	Merged to form Rocky Mountain
	Rocky Mountain[5]	1957-1968	Colo., Utah, Wyo., & part of Nev.	Merger of Colo., & Wyo. State	Continued in UM

CONNECTICUT
(See New York and Massachusetts)

DELAWARE

Denomination	Conference	Dates	Location	How Formed	Conclusion
ME	°Delaware[6]	1864-1939	Del., N. J., etc.	Organization of Negro work	Continued in M
	Wilmington	1869-1939	Del., & parts of Md. & Va.	Division of Philadelphia	Superseded by Peninsula M
M	°Delaware	1939-1965	Del., N. J., etc.	Superseded Delaware ME	Absorbed by N.E. Juris. Confs.
	Peninsula	1939-1968	Del. & part of Md.	Superseded Wilmington ME, & in part Baltimore MES, & Md. MP	Continued in UM

FLORIDA

Denomination	Conference	Dates	Location	How Formed	Conclusion
ME	Florida	1845	East & Middle Fla. & part of Georgia	Division of Ga.	Superseded by Fla. MES

---

[4] See Texas. [5] See Utah for Rocky Mountain, 1872-1876. [6] See Ohio for Delaware, 1856-1859.

Denomi- nation	Conference	Dates	Location	How Formed	Conclusion
	°Florida	1873-1939	Florida	Division of °S. Car.	Continued in M
	◇St. John's River	1886-1939	Florida	Division of °Fla.	Merged to form Fla. M
	°S. Fla. Miss.	1905-1920	S. Fla.	Division of °Fla.	Superseded by °S. Fla. Miss. Conf.
	°S. Fla. Miss. Conf.	1921-1924	S. Fla.	Superseded °S. Fla. Mission	Superseded by °S. Fla.
	° S. Fla.	1925-1939	S. Fla.	Superseded °S. Fla. Miss. Conf.	Continued in M
MES	Florida	1846-1939	Fla., except west part, & S. Ga.	Superseded Fla. ME	Continued in M
	Latin Mission	1930-1939	Florida	Division of Florida	Continued in M
MP	Florida	1846-1867	Florida	Organization of new work	Dissolved
	Fla. Miss. Conf.	1889-1939	Florida	Organization of new work	Merged in 1939
M	Florida	1939-1968	Florida	Merger of Fla. MES & St. John's River ME	Continued in UM
	°Florida	1939-1968	North Florida	Superseded °Fla. ME	Temporarily continued in UM
	Latin Mission	1939-1943	Florida	Superseded Latin Miss. MES	Absorbed by Fla.
	°S. Fla.	1939-1952	S. Fla.	Superseded °S. Fla. ME	Absorbed by °Fla.

GEORGIA

Denomi- nation	Conference	Dates	Location	How Formed	Conclusion
ME	6 °Atlanta	1897-1939	North Georgia	Division of °Savannah	Continued in M
	1 Georgia	1788-1794	Georgia	Division of S. Car.	Absorbed by S. Car.
	2 Georgia	1830-1844	Ga. & East & Middle Fla.	Division of S. Car.	Superseded by Ga. MES
	4 ◇Georgia	1868-1939	Georgia	Superseded Ga. Miss. Conf.	Absorbed by N. Ga., & S. Ga. M
	3 ◇Ga. Miss. Conf.	1867	Georgia	◇	Superseded by ◇Georgia
	5 °Savannah	1876-1939	Georgia	Division of ◇Georgia	Continued in M
MES	Georgia	1845-1866	Georgia	Superseded Ga. ME	Divided to form N. Ga., & S. Ga.
	N. Georgia	1866-1939	North Georgia	Division of Georgia	Continued in M
	S. Georgia	1866-1939	South Georgia	Division of Georgia	Continued in M
MP	Georgia	1830-1939	Georgia & East Florida	Secession from ME	Merged in 1939
	°Georgia	1905-1939	Georgia & Florida	Merger of °N. Ga., & °S. Ga. Mission Confs.	Merged in 1939
	°Ga. Miss. Conf.	1878-1891	Georgia & Florida	Organization of Negro work	Divided to form °N. Ga. Miss. Conf., & °S. Ga. Miss. Conf.
	°N. Ga. Miss. Conf.	1892-1904	North Georgia	Division of °Ga. Miss. Conf.	Merged with °S. Ga. Miss. Conf. to form °Ga. Miss. Conf.
	°S. Ga. Miss. Conf.	1892-1904	South Georgia	Division of °Ga. Miss. Conf.	Merged with °N. Ga. Miss. Conf. to form °Ga. Miss. Conf.
M	1a °Atlanta	1939-1952	North Georgia	Superseded °Atlanta ME	Merged with °Savannah to form °Georgia
	2 °Georgia	1952-1968	Georgia	Merger of °Atlanta, & °Savannah	Temporarily continued in UM
	1b N. Georgia	1939-1968	North Georgia	Superseded N. Ga. MES, & in part Ga. ME, & Ga. MP	Continued in UM
	1c °Savannah	1939-1952	South Georgia	Superseded °Savannah ME	Merged with °Atlanta to form °Ga.
	1d S. Georgia	1939-1968	South Georgia	Superseded S. Ga. MES, & in part Ga. ME, & Ga. MP	Continued in UM

HAWAII

Denomi- nation	Conference	Dates	Location	How Formed	Conclusion
ME	Hawaii Mission	1905-1939	Hawaii	Division of Pacific Japanese Mission	Continued in M
M	Hawaii Mission	1939-1967	Hawaii	Superseded Hawaii Mission ME	Absorbed by Sou. Calif.-Ariz.

Denomination	Conference	Dates	Location	How Formed	Conclusion
			IDAHO		
ME	1 Idaho	1884-1923	Parts of Idaho & Ore.	Division of Columbia River	Superseded by Inter-Mountain
	3 Idaho	1928-1939	Parts of Idaho & Ore.	Superseded Inter-Mountain	Continued in M
	2 Inter-Mountain	1924-1927	Parts of Idaho & Ore.	Superseded Idaho	Superseded by Idaho
M	Idaho	1939-1968	Parts of Idaho & Ore.	Superseded Idaho ME	Continued in UM
			ILLINOIS		
ME	5 Central Ill.	1860-1927	Central Ill.	Superseded Peoria	Absorbed by Ill.
	12 Central N.W.	1928-1939	Ill., Ind., Mich., Ohio, & other states in northern U.S.	Merger of Cen. Swed., N. Swed.[7], & Western Swedish confs.	Continued in M
	10 Central Swed.	1894-1927	Illinois, etc.	Division of N.W. Swedish	Merged with N. Swedish,[7] West. Swedish [8] to form Central N.W.
	8 Chicago German	1872-1924	Parts of Ill., Ind., & Wis.	Division of N.W. German	Merged with N.W. German to form Chicago N.W.
	11 Chicago N.W.	1924-1933	Parts of Ill., Ind., Ia., Mich., Wis., & S.Dak.	Merger of Chicago German, & N.W. German	Merged with English-speaking
	1 Illinois	1824-1939	Ill. & Ind.	Realignment of Mo., & Ohio	Continued in M
	9 N.W. Swedish	1877-1893	Ill., Ia., Minn., etc.	Organization of Swedish work	Divided to form Central Swed., Northern Swed.[7] & W. Swed.[8]
	7a N.W. German	1868-1924	Parts of Ill., Ia., Wis., etc.	Superseded Northwestern German	Merged with Chicago German to form Chicago N.W.
	6a Northwestern German	1864-1867	Parts of Ill. & Minn., & Iowa & Wis.	Organization of German work	Superseded by N.W. German
	4 Peoria	1856-1859	North Central Ill.	Division of Ill., & Rock River	Superseded by Central Ill.
	2 Rock River	1840-1939	N. Ill., & Iowa & Wis.	Division of Ill.	Continued in M
	3 Southern Ill.	1851-1939	Southern Ill.	Division of Ill.	Continued in M
	7b Southwest German	1868-1878	Sou. Ill., Kans., Ia. & Mo.	Superseded Southwestern German	Divided to form St. Louis[9] German, & West German[10]
	6b Southwestern German	1864-1867	Sou. Ill., Kans., Ia. & Mo.	Organization of German work	Superseded by Southwest German
MES	◇Illinois	1867-1939	Illinois & Indiana	◇	Merged in 1939
MP	5 Chicago German Miss. Conf.	1898-1904	Ill., Ind., & Mich.	Organization of German work	Absorbed by Indiana
	1 Illinois	1836-1868	Ill., part of Mo., etc.	Division of †Ohio	Superseded by †Ill., & Des Moines Mission Conf.
	6 Illinois	1923-1939	Illinois	Merger of †N. Ill., & †S. Ill.	Merged in 1939
	4 ‡Ill. & Des Moines Miss. Conf.	1870-1877	Parts of Ill., Ia., & Mo.	Merger of Ill., & part of †Ia.	Absorbed by †N. Ill., †Ia., & †Mo.
	2 †North Ill.	1843-1923	North Ill.	Division of Ill.	Merged with †S. Ill. to form Ill.
	3 †South Ill.	1853-1923	South Ill.	Division of Ill.	Merged with †N. Ill. to form Ill.
M	2 Central Ill.	1961-1968	Central Ill.	Superseded Ill.	Continued in UM
	1d Central N.W.	1939-1942	Ill., Minn., Neb., etc.	Superseded Central N.W. ME	Absorbed by English-speaking
	1a Illinois	1939-1960	Central Ill.	Superseded Illinois ME	Superseded by Central Ill.
	1b Rock River	1939-1968	North Ill.	Superseded Rock River ME	Superseded by Northern Ill. UM
	1c Southern Ill.	1939-1968	Southern Ill.	Superseded Southern Ill. ME	Continued in UM
			INDIANA		
ME	Indiana	1832-1939	Ind., & parts of Mich., & Ohio	Division of Ill.	Continued in M

---

[7] See Minnesota.   [8] See Iowa.   [9] See Missouri.   [10] See Kansas.

Denomi-nation	Conference	Dates	Location	How Formed	Conclusion
	North Ind.	1844-1939	North Ind.	Division of Ind.	Continued in M
	Northwest Ind.	1852-1939	Northwestern Ind.	Division of N. Ind.	Continued in M
	Southeastern Ind.	1852-1876	Southeastern Ind.	Division of Ind.	Superseded by Southeast Ind.
	Southeast Ind.	1876-1894	Southeastern Ind.	Superseded Southeastern Ind.	Absorbed by Ind.
MES	◇Indiana	1879-1881	Indiana	Division of ◇Illinois	Absorbed by Louisville [11]
MP	1 †Indiana	1840-1939	Indiana	Division of †Ohio	Merged in 1939
	4 §N. Indiana	1867-1875	North Indiana	Superseded †Wabash	Absorbed by †Indiana
	2 †Wabash	1846-1867	North Indiana	Division of †Indiana	Superseded by §N. Ind.
	3 ‡White Wing Ind.	1859-1877	Indiana	Division of †Ind., & †Wabash	Merged with †Ind.
M	Indiana	1939-1968	Southern Ind.	Superseded Ind. ME	Merged to form S. Ind. UM
	North Indiana	1939-1968	Northeast Indiana	Superseded N.Ind. ME	Continued in UM
	N. W. Indiana	1939-1968	Northwest Indiana	Superseded N.W. Ind. ME	Absorbed by N. Ind. UM

IOWA

Denomi-nation	Conference	Dates	Location	How Formed	Conclusion
ME	4 Des Moines	1864-1931	West Iowa	Merger of Western Iowa & west half of Upper Iowa	Merged with Iowa to form Iowa-Des Moines
	1 Iowa	1844-1931	Iowa	Division of Rock River	Merged with Des Moines to form Iowa-Des Moines
	7 Iowa-Des Moines	1932-1939	South Iowa	Merger of Ia., & Des Moines	Continued in M
	5 N.W. Iowa	1872-1939	N.W. Iowa & Dakota	Division of Des Moines	Continued in M
	2 Upper Iowa	1856-1939	North Iowa	Division of Iowa	Continued in M
	3 Western Iowa	1860-1863	S.W. Iowa	Division of Iowa	Superseded by Des Moines
	6 Western Swedish	1894-1927	Iowa, Kans., Neb., etc.	Division of N.W. Swedish [12]	Merged with Central Swed.,[12] & N. Swed.[13] to form Central N.W.[12]
MP	3 ‡Des Moines Mission Conf.	1868-1870	Iowa	Division of †Iowa	Superseded by ‡Ill. & Des Moines Mission Conf.
	1 †Iowa	1846-1916	Iowa	Division of †North Ill.	Absorbed by Iowa-Mo.
	4 Iowa-Mo.	1916-1939	Iowa & N. Mo.	Merger of †Iowa, & ‡No. Mo.	Merged in 1939
	2 †North Iowa	1858-1875	North Iowa	Division of †Iowa	Absorbed by †Iowa
M	1a Iowa-Des Moines	1939-1958	S. Iowa	Superseded Iowa-Des Moines ME	Superseded by S. Iowa
	2 North Iowa	1949-1968	N. Iowa	Merger of N.W. Ia., & Upper Iowa	Continued in UM
	1b N.W. Iowa	1939-1949	N.W. Iowa	Superseded N.W. Ia. ME	Merged wih Upper Iowa to form N. Iowa
	3 South Iowa	1958-1968	S. Iowa	Superseded Ia.-Des Moines	Continued in UM
	1c Upper Iowa	1939-1948	N. Iowa	Superseded Upper Ia. ME	Merged with N.W. Iowa to form N. Iowa

KANSAS

Denomi-nation	Conference	Dates	Location	How Formed	Conclusion
ME	2 Kansas	1861-1939	Kansas	Division of Kans. & Neb.	Continued in M
	1 Kans. & Neb.	1856-1860	Kansas, Neb., & parts of N.M. & Utah	Division of ◇Missouri	Superseded by Kans., & Neb.
	4 N.W. Kans.	1882-1939	N.W. Kansas	Division of Kansas	Merged with S.W. Kans. to form Central Kansas M
	3 South Kans.	1874-1913	South Kansas	Division of Kansas	Absorbed by Kansas
	5 S.W. Kans.	1882-1939	S.W. Kansas	Division of S. Kansas Superseded in part S.W. German [14]	Merged with N.W. Kans. to form Central Kansas M
	6 West German	1879-1926	Kans., N.W. Mo., Neb., Ia., & Col.		Merged with English-speaking
MES	Kans. Miss. Conf.	1855-1861	Kans., N.M., & Colo.	Division of St. Louis	Dissolved
	Western	1870-1905	Kans., Neb., Ida., Wyo., etc.	Organization of new work	Absorbed by S.W. Mo.

---

[11] See Kentucky.   [12] See Illinois.   [13] See Minnesota.   [14] See Illinois.

MP	‡Kansas	1866-1939	Kansas	Organization of new work	Merged in 1939
	North Kansas	1879-1880	North Kansas	Division of Kansas	Absorbed by Kansas
M	Central Kansas	1939-1968	West Kansas	Merger of N.W. Kans., & S.W. Kans. ME	Continued in UM
	Kansas	1939-1968	East Kansas	Superseded Kansas ME	Continued in UM

KENTUCKY

ME	2 Kentucky	1820-1844	Ky. & parts of Tenn. & Va.	Division of Ohio	Superseded by Ky. MES
	3 ◇Kentucky	1852-1939	Kentucky	◇	Superseded by Ky. M
	4 °Lexington	1869-1939	Ky., Ind., & Ohio	°	Continued in M
	1 Western	1796-1812	Ky., Tenn., etc.	Original conf. in the west	Divided to form Ohio, & Tenn.
MES	Kentucky	1845-1939	Eastern Ky.	Superseded Ky. ME	Continued in M
	Louisville	1846-1939	Central Ky.	Division of Ky.	Continued in M
MP	§Kentucky	1867-1939	Kentucky	Division of Tenn.	Merged in 1939
M	°Lexington	1939-1964	Ky., Ind., & Ohio	Superseded °Lexington ME	Absorbed by N.C. Juris. Confs. & partially by °Tenn.-Ky.
	Kentucky	1939-1968	Eastern Ky.	Superseded Ky. ME, & MES	Continued in UM
	Louisville	1939-1968	Central Ky.	Superseded Louisville MES	Continued in UM

LOUISIANA

ME	2 ◇Gulf Miss.	1893-1896	S. La., & E. Texas	Division of °Louisiana	Superseded by ◇Gulf Miss. Conf.
	3 ◇Gulf Miss. Conf.	1897-1903	S. La., & E. Texas	Superseded ◇Gulf Mission	Superseded by ◇Gulf Conf.
	4 ◇Gulf	1904-1926	La., Miss., & E. Tex.	Superseded ◇Gulf Miss. Conf.	Absorbed by Southern [15]
	1 °Louisiana	1869-1939	Louisiana	Division of °Miss. Miss. Conf.	Continued in M
MES	Louisiana	1847-1939	Louisiana, except east part	Division of Miss.	Continued in M
MP	Louisiana	1846-1870	La. & Tex.	Organization of new work	Superseded by Ark. & La.
	Louisiana	1884-1939	Louisiana	Division of Ark. & La.	Merged in 1939
M	Louisiana	1939-1968	Louisiana	Superseded Louisiana MES	Continued in UM
	°Louisiana	1939-1968	Louisiana	Superseded °Louisiana ME	Temporarily continued in UM

MAINE

ME	2 East Maine	1848-1922	East Maine	Division of Maine	Absorbed by Maine
	1 Maine	1824-1939	Maine & part of N.H.	Division of New England	Continued in M
MP	†Maine	1846-1871	Maine	Organization of new work	Absorbed by †Boston
M	Maine	1939-1968	Maine	Superseded Maine ME	Continued in UM

MARYLAND [16]

ME	Baltimore	1784-1939	Parts of Md., Pa., & Va.	Original conference	Continued in M
	E. Baltimore	1858-1868	N.E. Md., & S. Central Pa.	Division of Baltimore	Absorbed by Baltimore, & Central Pa.
	°Washington	1864-1939	Parts of Md., W.Va., Pa., Va., & D.C.	Organization of Negro work	Continued in M
MES	Baltimore	1866-1939[17]	Md., & part of Va.	Secession from Baltimore ME	Merged in 1939
MP	2 °Baltimore Colored Miss. Conf.	1846-1901	Md., Del., & D.C.	Organization of Negro work	Superseded by °Baltimore-Wash.

---

[15] See Texas.   [16] For Peninsula and Wilmington Conferences, see Delaware.
[17] There was an "Independent" but unofficial Baltimore Conference, MES, 1861-1865.

Denomi-nation	Conference	Dates	Location	How Formed	Conclusion
	3 °Baltimore-Washington	1901-1939	Md., Del., & D.C.	Superseded °Baltimore Col. Miss. Conf.	Merged in 1939 with °Wash.
	1 Maryland	1829-1939	Md., D.C., & part of Va.	Secession from ME	Merged in 1939
M	Baltimore	1939-1968	Parts of Md., Pa., W.Va., & D.C.	Superseded Baltimore ME, & MES, & Md. MP	Continued in UM
	°Washington	1939-1965	Parts of Md., Pa., Va., W.Va., & D.C.	Merger of °Wash. ME, & °Baltimore-Washington MP	Absorbed by N.E. Juris. Confs.

MASSACHUSETTS

Denomi-nation	Conference	Dates	Location	How Formed	Conclusion
ME	New England	1797-1939	New England & part of N.Y.	Original conference	Continued in M
	New England Southern	1881-1939	R.I., & parts of Conn. & Mass.	Superseded Providence[18]	Continued in M
MP	†Boston	1830-1880	Mass., N.H., & R.I.	Secession from ME	Superseded by Boston Miss. Conf.
	Boston Miss. Conf.	1880-1908	Mass., N.H., R.I., & part of Vt.	Superseded †Boston Conf.	Dissolved
M	New England	1939-1968	Massachusetts	Superseded New England ME	Continued in UM
	New England Southern	1939-1968	R.I., & parts of Conn. & Mass.	Superseded New Eng. Sou. ME	Continued in UM

MICHIGAN

Denomi-nation	Conference	Dates	Location	How Formed	Conclusion
ME	2 Detroit	1856-1939	E. Mich., Upper Peninsula, etc.	Division of Michigan	Continued in M
	1 Michigan	1836-1939	Mich. & part of Ohio	Division of Ohio	Continued in M
MP	†Michigan	1854-1939	Michigan	Division of †Ohio	Merged in 1939
	†W. Michigan[22]	1858-1905	W. Mich. & small part of N. Ind.	Division of †Michigan	Absorbed by †Mich.
M	Detroit	1939-1968	E. Mich. & Upper Peninsula	Superseded Detroit ME	Continued in UM
	Michigan	1939-1968	West Michigan	Superseded Michigan ME	Superseded by West Mich. UM

MINNESOTA

Denomi-nation	Conference	Dates	Location	How Formed	Conclusion
ME	1 Minnesota	1856-1939	Minnesota & N.W. Wis.	Division of Wis.	Continued in M
	4 North German	1886-1888	Minn. & North Dakota	Division of N.W. German[19]	Superseded by Northern German
	2 N.W. Norwegian	1880-1884	Minn., Ill., Wis., & Iowa	Organization of Norwegian work	Superseded by Norwegian & Danish
	5 Northern German	1889-1924	Minn. & N. Dak.	Superseded North German	Absorbed by English-speaking
	6a Northern Minn.	1894-1939	Northern Minn.	Division of Minn.	Continued in M
	6b Northern Swed. Miss. Conf.	1894-1899	Minn., Mich., & Wis.	Division of N.W. Swed. Conf.[19]	Superseded by Northern Swed.
	7 Northern Swed.	1900-1927	Minn., Mich., & Wis.	Superseded Northern Swed. Mission Conf.	Merged with Cen. Swed.,[19] West. Swed.[21] to form Central N.W.[19]
	3 Norwegian & Danish[20]	1884-1939	Minn., Ill., Ia., Mich., Wis., etc.	Organization of Norwegian & Danish work	Continued in M
MP	†Minnesoa	1858-1908	Minnesota & Wisconsin	Organization of new work	Dissolved
M	Minnesota	1939-1968	Minnesota	Superseded Minn. ME	Continued in UM
	Northern Minn.	1939-1948	Northern Minn.	Superseded Northern Minn. ME	Absorbed by Minn.
	Norweg. & Danish	1939-1943	U.S. east of Rocky Mts.	Superseded Norweg. & Dan. ME	Absorbed by English-speaking

MISSISSIPPI

Denomi-nation	Conference	Dates	Location	How Formed	Conclusion
ME	1 Mississippi	1813-1844	Miss., La., & Ala.	Division of Tenn.	Superseded by Miss. MES
	3 °Mississippi	1869-1939	Mississippi	Division of °Miss. Mis. Conf.	Continued in M

---

[18] See Rhode Island.   [19] See Illinois.   [20] See Washington for more Norwegian-Danish.   [21] See Iowa.
[22] Unofficially the 1881-1887 printed journals of this conference use the name "West Michigan & North Indiana Conference."

Denomi-nation	Conference	Dates	Location	How Formed	Conclusion
	2 °Miss. Mis. Conf.	1865-1868	Miss., La., & Tex.	°	Partially superseded by °Miss. Conf.
	4 °Upper Miss.	1891-1939	North Miss.	Division of °Miss.	Continued in M
MES	Mississippi	1845-1939	Miss. & part of La.	Superseded Miss. ME	Continued in M
	N. Miss.	1870-1939	North Mississippi	Division of Miss.	Continued in M
MP	Mississippi	1841-1939	Miss., La., & Texas	Organization of new work	Merged in 1939
	North Miss.	1867-1939	North Mississippi	Division of Miss.	Merged in 1939
M	Mississippi	1939-1968	South Miss.	Superseded Miss. MES	Continued in UM
	°Mississippi	1939-1968	South Miss.	Superseded °Miss. ME	Temporarily continued in UM
	North Miss.	1939-1968	North Miss.	Superseded North Miss. MES	Continued in UM
	°Upper Miss.	1939-1968	North Miss.	Superseded °Upper Miss. ME	Temporarily continued in UM

MISSOURI

Denomi-nation	Conference	Dates	Location	How Formed	Conclusion
ME	8 °Central Mo.	1886-1928	Mo. & Kansas	Organization of Negro work	Merged with °Lincoln[23] to form °Central West
	9 °Central West	1929-1939	Mo., Kans., Colo., Ia., & part of Ill.	Merger of °Central Mo., & part of °Lincoln[23]	Continued in M
	1 Missouri	1816-1844	Mo., Ill., Ark., & part of Ind.	Division of Tennessee	Superseded by Mo. MES
	2 ◇Missouri	1848-1851	Mo., Ark., & territory to west	◇	Superseded by ◇Mo. & Ark.
	4 ◇Missouri	1853-1860	Mo. (most), Kans., & Neb.	Division of ◇Mo. & Ark.	Superseded by ◇Mo. & Ark.
	6a ◇Missouri	1869-1939	North Mo. & (later) Ark.	Division of ◇Mo. & Ark.	Merged in 1939
	3 ◇Mo. & Ark.	1852	Mo., Ark., & Tex.	Superseded ◇Missouri	Divided to form ◇Ark., & ◇Mo.
	5 ◇Mo. & Ark.	1861-1868	Mo. & Ark.	Merger of ◇Mo., & ◇Ark.	Divided to form ◇Mo., & ◇St. Louis
	6b ◇St. Louis	1869-1931	S. Mo. & Ark.	Division of ◇Mo. & Ark.	Absorbed by ◇Mo.
	7 St. Louis Ger.	1879-1925	E. Mo., S. Ill., & S.E. Ia.	Partially superseded S.W. German[24]	Absorbed by English-speaking
MES	1 Missouri	1845-1939	Missouri	Superseded Mo. ME	Continued in M
	2 St. Louis	1846-1939	South Missouri	Division of Mo. MES	Continued in M
	4 S.W. Missouri	1874-1939	S.W. Mo.	Superseded West St. Louis	Continued in M
	3 West St. Louis	1870-1873	S.W. Mo.	Division of St. Louis	Superseded by S.W. Mo.
MP	1 †Missouri	1850-1939	Missouri	Organization of new work	Merged in 1939
	3 ‡North Mo.	1867-1916	N.W. Mo.	Division of †Mo.	Merged with †Ia. to form Ia.-Mo.
	2 Platte	1852-1866	N.W. Mo.	Division of †Mo.	Superseded by ‡North Mo.
M	1a °Central West	1939-1966	Mo., S. Ill., Kans., etc.	Superseded °Central West ME	Absorbed by S.C. Juris. Confs.
	1b Missouri	1939-1961	North Missouri	Superseded Mo. MES, & partially Mo. ME, & MP	Merged with St. Louis, & S.W. Mo. to form Mo. E., & Mo. W.
	2a Missouri E.	1961-1968	East Missouri	Merger of St. L. & part of Mo.	Continued in UM
	2b Missouri W.	1961-1968	West Missouri	Merger of S.W. Mo. & part of Mo.	Continued in UM
	1c St. Louis	1939-1961	East Missouri	Superseded St. Louis MES, & partially Mo. ME, & MP	Merged with east half of Mo. to form Missouri E.
	1d S.W. Mo.	1939-1961	S.W. Mo.	Superseded S.W. Mo. MES, & partially Mo. ME, & MP	Merged with west half of Mo. to form Missouri W.

MONTANA

Denomi-nation	Conference	Dates	Location	How Formed	Conclusion
ME	5 Kalispell Mission	1901-1907	Northwest Montana	Division of Montana Conf.	Merged with N. Mont. Mission to form N. Mont. Conf.
	1 Montana	1876-1879	Montana	Partially superseded Rocky Mountain[25]	Superseded by Mont. Mission

[23] See Oklahoma.   [24] See Illinois.   [25] See Utah.

Denomi-nation	Conference	Dates	Location	How Formed	Conclusion
	3 Montana	1887-1923	Montana & part of Idaho	Superseded Montana Mission	Superseded by Mont. State
	2 Mont. Mission	1880-1886	Mont. & parts of Ida. & Wyo.	Superseded Montana Conf.	Superseded by Mont. Conf.
	7 Mont. State	1924-1939	Montana	Merger of Mont., & No. Mont.	Superseded by Montana M
	4 N. Mont. Miss.	1892-1907	N. Montana	Division of Mont. Conf.	Merged with Kalispell Mission to form N. Mont. Conf.
	6 N. Mont. Conf.	1907-1923	N. Montana	Merger of No. Mont. Mission & Kalispell Mission	Merged with Mont. to form Mont. State
MES	Montana	1878-1917	Montana	Division of Denver	Merged with Columbia,[26] & E. Columbia[26] to form Northwest[26]
M	Montana	1939-1968	Montana	Superseded Mont. State ME, & partially Northwest MES	Continued in UM; became Yellowstone in 1969
NEBRASKA					
ME	1 Nebraska	1861-1939	Nebraska	Division of Kans. & Neb.	Continued in M
	3 N. Nebraska	1881-1912	N.E. Nebraska	Division of Nebraska	Absorbed by Nebraska
	5 N.W. Neb.	1892-1924	N.W. Nebraska	Division of West Neb.	Absorbed by Nebraska
	2 West Neb. Miss.	1880-1885	West Nebraska	Division of Nebraska	Superseded by W. Neb. Conf.
	4 West Neb.	1885-1912	West Nebraska	Superseded W. Neb. Mission	Absorbed by Nebraska
MP	†Nebraska	1860-1908	Nebraska	Organization of new work	Dissolved
M	Nebraska	1939-1968	Nebraska	Superseded Nebraska ME	Continued in UM
NEVADA					
ME	Nevada	1865-1884	Nev., Utah, & parts Calif. & N.M.	Division of California	Superseded by Nev. Mission
	Nev. Mission	1884-1917	Nevada	Superseded Nev. Conf.	Absorbed by Calif., & S. Calif.
NEW HAMPSHIRE					
ME	2 New Hampshire	1831-1939	N.H., & parts of Mass. & Vt.	Superseded N.H. & Vt.	Continued in M
	1 N.H. & Vt.	1829-1831	N.H., & parts of Mass. & Vt.	Division of New England	Superseded by New Hamp.
M	New Hampshire	1939-1968	New Hamp. & part of Mass.	Superseded N. Hamp. ME	Continued in UM
NEW JERSEY					
ME	New Jersey	1836-1939	N.J. & parts of N.Y. & Pa.	Division of Philadelphia	Continued in M
	Newark	1857-1939	Northern N.J. & parts of N.Y. & Pa.	Division of New Jersey	Continued in M
MP	†New Jersey	1841-1912	New Jersey	Division of †New York	Merged with Eastern[27]
M	New Jersey	1939-1963	Southern N.J.	Superseded N.J. ME	Superseded by Southern N.J.
	Newark	1939-1963	North. N.J. & parts of N.Y. & Pa.	Superseded Newark ME	Superseded by Northern N.J.
	Northern N.J.	1964-1968	Northern N.J.	Superseded Newark	Continued in UM
	Southern N.J.	1964-1968	Southern N.J.	Superseded New Jersey	Continued in UM
NEW MEXICO					
ME	4 New Mexico	1915-1927	New Mexico, etc.	Merger of N.M. Eng. Miss., & N.M. Spanish Miss. Conf.	Superseded by N. Mexico Mission
	1 New Mexico Miss.	1880-1884	New Mexico	Organization of new work	Divided to form N.M. Eng. Miss., & N.M. Spanish Mission

---

[26] See Oregon.   [27] See New York.

Denomi-nation	Conference	Dates	Location	How Formed	Conclusion
	6 New Mex. Miss.	1928-1939	New Mexico	Superseded N. Mex. Conf.	Superseded by New Mex. M
	2a N.M. Eng. Miss.	1885-1914	New Mex., part of Tex., etc.	Division of N. Mex. Mission	Merged with N.M. Spanish Miss. Conf. to form N. Mex. Conf.
	2b N.M. Spanish Mission	1885-1891	N.M., Ariz., Colo., etc.	Division of N. Mex. Mission	Superseded by N. Mex. Spanish Mission Conf.
	3 N.M. Spanish Mission Conf.	1892-1914	N.M., Ariz., Colo., etc.	Superseded N.M. Span. Miss.	Merged with N. Mex. Eng. Mission to form N. Mex. Conf.
	5 S.W. Spanish Mission	1924-1930	N.M., Ariz., Colo., etc.	Division of N.M. Conf.	Absorbed by Latin American Mission[28]
MES	New Mexico	1890-1939	New Mex. & part of Tex.	Division of Denver	Continued in M
M	New Mexico	1939-1968	New Mex. & part of Tex.	Superseded N.M. Miss. ME, & New Mex. MES	Continued in UM

NEW YORK[29]

Denomi-nation	Conference	Dates	Location	How Formed	Conclusion
ME	5 Black River	1836-1872	Northern N.Y.	Division of Oneida	Superseded by Northern N.Y.
	10 Central N.Y.	1869-1939	Central N.Y.	Merger of part of Oneida, & part of Black River	Continued in M
	6 East Genesee	1848-1872	Western N.Y. & north. Pa.	Division of Genesee	Absorbed by West. N.Y. & Central N.Y.
	9 East German	1868-1939	Pa., N.Y., etc.	Superseded Eastern German	Continued in M
	8 Eastern German	1866-1868	Pa., N.Y., etc.	Organization of German work	Superseded by East German
	14 Eastern Swed.	1901-1939	Maine to New Jersey	Organization of Swedish work	Continued in M
	2 Genesee	1810-1872	Western N.Y., part of Pa., & Lower Canada	Division of N.Y., & Phila.	Superseded by Western N.Y.
	13 Genesee	1876-1939	Western N.Y., & part of Pa.	Superseded Western N.Y.	Continued in M
	15 Italian Miss.	1909-1916	N.Y., N.J., Pa., etc.	Organization of Italian work	Absorbed by English-speaking
	1 New York	1800-1939	Eastern N.Y. & Conn.	Division of New England	Continued in M
	7 N.Y. East	1849-1939	L.I., part of N.Y. City, & part of Conn.	Division of New York	Continued in M
	12 Northern N.Y.	1873-1939	Northern N.Y.	Merger of Black River, & part of Central N.Y.	Continued in M
	3 Oneida	1829-1868	Central N.Y. & part of Pa.	Division of Genesee	Absorbed by Cen. N.Y., & Wyoming
	4 Troy	1833-1939	Northern N.Y. & part of Vt.	Division of New York	Continued in M
	11 Western N.Y.	1872-1875	Western N.Y. & part of Pa.	Merger of Genesee, & part of East Genesee	Superseded by Genesee
MP	3 Champlain	1834-1846	Northern N.Y.	Partially superseded N.Y. & Lower Canada	United With Wesleyan Methodist Church
	7 Eastern	1911-1939	East. N.Y., E. Pa., & Conn.	Merger of †N.Y., & Pa.	Merged in 1939
	2b †Genesee	1830-1908	Western New York	Superseded Rochester	Absorbed by †Onondaga
	2a New York	1830-1853	S.E. New York & Conn.	Secession from ME	Superseded by N.Y. & Vt.
	6 New York	1867-1912	S.E. New York & En. Vt.	Superseded N.Y. & Vt.	Merged with †N.J., & Pa. to form Eastern
	2c N.Y. & Lower Canada	1830-1834	Northern N.Y. & Lower Can.	Secession from ME	Superseded by Champlain
	5 †N.Y. & Vermont	1854-1867	S.E. New York & En. Vt.	Merger of N.Y., & Vt.	Superseded by N.Y.
	4 †Onondaga	1842-1939	Northern New York	Division of †Genesee	Merged in 1939
	1 Rochester	? -1830	Western N.Y.	Secession from ME	Superseded by †Genesee
M	Central N.Y.	1939-1968	Central N.Y.	Superseded Central N.Y. ME	Continued in UM
	East German	1939-1943	Pa., N.Y., etc.	Superseded East German ME	Absorbed by English-speaking
	Eastern Swedish	1939-1941	Maine to New Jersey	Superseded Eastern Swed. ME	Absorbed by English-speaking
	Genesee	1939-1964	Western N.Y.	Superseded Genesee ME	Superseded by Western N.Y.
	New York	1939-1968	E.N.Y., & part of N.Y. City	Superseded N.Y. ME	Continued in UM
	New York East	1939-1964	L.I., part of N.Y. City, & part of Conn.	Superseded N.Y. East ME	Absorbed by New York

[28] See California.   [29] For Wyoming Conference, see Pennsylvania.

Denomination	Conference	Dates	Location	How Formed	Conclusion
	Northern N.Y.	1939-1968	Northern N.Y.	Superseded Northern N.Y. ME	Continued in UM
	Troy	1939-1968	N.E. New York & Vt.	Superseded Troy ME	Continued in UM
	Western N.Y.	1964-1968	Western New York	Superseded Genesee	Continued in UM

NORTH CAROLINA

Denomination	Conference	Dates	Location	How Formed	Conclusion
ME	5 ◇Atlantic Miss. Conf.	1896-1911	Eastern N.C.	Division of ◇Blue Ridge	Merged with ◇Blue Ridge to form ◇Blue Ridge-Atlantic
	4 ◇Blue Ridge	1881-1911	N. Car. & part of S. Car.	Superseded ◇Southern Central	Merged with ◇Atlantic Miss. Conf. to form ◇Blue Ridge-Atlantic
	6 ◇Blue Ridge-Atlantic	1912-1939	N.C. & parts of Va. & S.C.	Merger of ◇Blue Ridge Conf., & ◇Atlantic Mission Conf.	Merged in 1939
	1 North Carolina	1837-1844	Eastern N.C.	Division of Virginia	Superseded by N.C. MES
	2 •North Carolina	1869-1939	North Carolina	Division of ◇Va. & N.C. Mission Conf.[30]	Continued in M
	3 ◇Southern Central	1879-1880	North Carolina	Merger of parts of ◇Holston[31] ME, & •N.C. ME	Superseded by ◇Blue Ridge
MES	North Carolina	1845-1939	Eastern N. Car.	Superseded N. Car. ME	Continued in M
	Western N.C.	1890-1939	Western N. Car.	Division of N.C., & Holston[31]	Continued in M
MP	5 Allegheny	1877-1879	Western N. Car.	Superseded §Western N.C.	Absorbed by Western N.C.
	6a Deep River	1878-1891	North Carolina	MC Remnant that did not merge in 1877 or later	Dissolved
	4a §East N.C.	1875-1877	Eastern N.C.	Division of N. Carolina	Absorbed by N. Carolina
	1 North Carolina	1828-1939	North Carolina	Secession from ME	Merged in 1939
	2 §North Carolina	1866-1875	North Carolina	Division of N. Carolina	Divided to form §E.N.C., & §W.N.C.
	3 §•N.Car. Colored Miss. Conf.	1871- ?	North Carolina	Organization of Negro work	Dissolved
	4b §Western N.C.	1875-1877	Western N.C.	Division of §North Car.	Superseded by Allegheny
	6b Western N.C.	1878-1880	Western N.C.	Division of North Car.	Absorbed by North Carolina
M	1a North Carolina	1939-1968	Eastern N.C.	Superseded N. Car. MES	Continued in UM
	1b •North Carolina	1939-1964	North Carolina & Va.	Superseded •N. Car. ME	Superseded by •N. Car.-Va.
	2 •N.C.-Virginia	1964-1968	N. Car. & Va. (except S.W. part)	Superseded •N. Car.	Absorbed by S.E. Juris. Confs.
	1c Western N.C.	1939-1968	Western N.C.	Superseded W.N.C. MES, & partially ◇Blue Ridge-Atlantic ME	Continued in UM

NORTH DAKOTA

Denomination	Conference	Dates	Location	How Formed	Conclusion
ME	N. Dak. Miss.	1884-1885	North Dakota	Division of Minnesota	Superseded by N. Dak. Conf.
	North Dakota	1886-1939	North Dakota	Superseded N. Dak. Miss.	Continued in M
M	North Dakota	1939-1968	North Dakota	Superseded N. Dak. ME	Continued in UM

OHIO

Denomination	Conference	Dates	Location	How Formed	Conclusion
ME	6 Central German	1864-1933	Ohio, W.Va., Ind., Ky., Tenn., & W. Pa.	Organization of German work	Absorbed by English-speaking
	5 Central Ohio	1860-1913	Northwestern Ohio	Superseded Delaware (Ohio)	Merged with Cincinnati to form West Ohio
	3 Cincinnati	1852-1913	Southwest Ohio	Division of Cinn. & Ky.	Merged with Central Ohio to form West Ohio
	4 Delaware	1856-1860	Northwest Ohio	Division of North Ohio	Superseded by Central Ohio
	7 East Ohio	1876-1911	East Ohio	Division of Erie, & Pittsburgh	Merged with North Ohio to form N.E. Ohio
	2 North Ohio	1840-1912	North Ohio	Division of Michigan	Merged with E. Ohio to form N.E. Ohio

---

[30] See Virginia.   [31] See Tennessee.

Denomi-nation	Conference	Dates	Location	How Formed	Conclusion
	8 Northeast O.	1912-1939	Northeast Ohio	Merger of E. Ohio, & N. Ohio	Continued in M
	1 Ohio	1812-1939	Ohio & E. Ky.	Division of Western[32]	Continued in M
	9 West Ohio	1913-1927	West Ohio	Merger of Central Ohio, & Cincinnati	Absorbed by Ohio
MP	2 †Muskingum	1851-1918	Eastern Ohio	Division of †Pittsburgh	Absorbed by Ohio
	1 †Ohio	1829-1939	Ohio & Indiana	Secession from ME	Merged in 1939
M	Northeast Ohio	1939-1968	Northeast Ohio	Superseded Northeast O. ME	Merged to form Ohio East UM
	Ohio	1939-1968	South and West Ohio	Superseded Ohio ME	Merged to form Ohio West UM

OKLAHOMA

Denomi-nation	Conference	Dates	Location	How Formed	Conclusion
ME	8 ◊E. Okla. Miss.	1906-1911	East Oklahoma	Superseded Indian Terr. Mission	Absorbed by ◊Okla.
	2 Indian Mission	1880-1889	Oklahoma	◊	Superseded by Indian Miss. Conf.
	1 Indian Miss. Conf.	1844	Oklahoma, Kans., & Neb.	Organization of new work	Superseded by Indian Miss. Conf. MES
	3 ◊Indian Miss. Conf.	1889-1892	Indian Territory & Okla.	Superseded Indian Mission	Superseded by ◊Okla. Conf.
	7 ◊Ind. Ter. Miss.	1904-1905	Indian Territory	Division of ◊Okla. Conf.	Superseded by ◊E. Okla. Miss.
	6 *Lincoln	1903-1928	Okla., Kans., Neb., & Western Mo.	Superseded *Okaneb	Partially merged with *Little Rock to form *Southwest[33]
	5 *Okaneb	1902	Okla., Kans., Neb., & Western Mo.	Merger of parts of Okla., & Central Mo.	Superseded by *Lincoln
	4 ◊Oklahoma	1892-1939	Oklahoma	Superseded ◊Ind. Miss. Conf.	Superseded by E. Okla., & W. Okla. M
MES	3a East Okla.	1911-1929	East Oklahoma	Division of Okla.	Superseded by Okla.
	1 Indian Miss. Conf.	1845-1905	Okla. & Kans.	Superseded Indian Miss. Conf. ME	Superseded by Okla.
	4 Indian Miss.	1918-1939	East Oklahoma	Division of E. Okla. Conf.	Continued in M
	2 Oklahoma	1906-1910	Oklahoma	Superseded Ind. Miss. Conf.	Divided to form E. Okla., & W. Okla.
	5 Oklahoma	1930-1939	Oklahoma	Merger of E. Okla. & W. Okla.	Superseded by E. Okla., & W. Okla. M
	3b West Okla.	1911-1929	West Oklahoma	Division of Oklahoma	Superseded by Oklahoma
MP	2a Chickasaw Mission Conf.	1896-1908	Two Indian Reservations in Okla. Territory	Organization of Indian work	Absorbed by Okla. Conf.
	4 Choctaw Miss. Conf.	1904-1908	Indian Territory	Organization of Indian work	Absorbed by Okla. Conf.
	1 Indian Miss. Conf.	1887-1908	Indian Territory	Organization of Indian work	Absorbed by Okla. Conf.
	2b Okla. Miss. Conf.	1896-1904	Oklahoma Territory	Division of Ft. Smith Miss.[34]	Superseded by Okla. Conf.
	5 Oklahoma	1904-1916	Oklahoma Territory	Superseded Okla. Miss. Conf.	Superseded by Ft. Smith-Okla.[34]
	3 S.W. Okla. Miss. Conf.	1900-1908	S.W. Okla. Territory	Organization of Indian work	Absorbed by Okla. Conf.
M	1a East Okla.	1939-1953	East Okla.	Superseded E. Okla. MES, & partially Okla. ME	Merged with W. Okla. to form Okla.
	3 Indian Miss.	1939-1968	Oklahoma	Superseded Indian Miss. MES	Continued in UM
	4 Oklahoma	1954-1968	Oklahoma	Merger of E. Okla., & W. Okla.	Continued in UM
	2a West Okla.	1939-1953	West Oklahoma	Superseded W. Okla. MES, & partially Okla. ME	Merged with E. Okla. to form Okla.

OREGON

Denomi-nation	Conference	Dates	Location	How Formed	Conclusion
ME	3 E. Ore. & Wash.	1873-1876	Washington and E. Ore.	Division of Oregon	Superseded by Columbia River[35]

---

[32] See Kentucky.   [33] See Arkansas.   [34] See Arkansas.   [35] See Washington.

Denomination	Conference	Dates	Location	How Formed	Conclusion
	2 Oregon	1852-1939	Oregon and Washington	Division of Oregon & Calif.	Continued in M
	1 Ore. & Calif. Miss. Conf.	1849-1851	Ore., Calif., & N. Mex.	Organization of new work	Divided to form Calif., & Ore. Confs.
MES	Columbia	1866-1917	Ore., Wash., & part of Calif.	Division of Pacific[36]	Merged with E. Columbia, & Mont. to form Northwest
	E. Columbia	1890-1917	E. Ore. & Wash.	Division of Columbia	Merged with Columbia, & Mont. to form Northwest
	Northwest	1918-1939	Ore., Wash., Ida., & Mont.	Merger of Columbia, E. Columbia, & Montana	Merged in 1939
MP	§Oregon	1866-1880	Oregon & Washington	Division of Ore. & Calif.	Superseded by Ore. Mission
	Ore. & Calif.	1850-1866	Oregon & California	Organization of new work	Divided to form §Calif., & §Ore.
	Oregon Miss. Conf.	1880-1892	Oregon and Washington	Superseded §Ore. Conf.	Absorbed by Washington
	Oregon Miss. Conf.	1896-1908	Oregon	Division of Washington	Dissolved
M	Oregon	1939-1968	Oregon	Superseded Ore. ME, & partially Northwest MES	Continued in UM

PENNSYLVANIA

Denomination	Conference	Dates	Location	How Formed	Conclusion
ME	5 Central Pa.	1869-1939	Central Pennsylvania	Division of Phila., & E. Balt.[37]	Continued in M
	3 Erie	1836-1939	N.W. Pa., N.E. Ohio, & W.N.Y.	Division of Pittsburgh	Continued in M
	1 Philadelphia	1788-1939	Parts of Pa., N.Y., N.J. & Del.	Original Conference	Continued in M
	2 Pittsburgh	1824-1939	Western Pa.	Division of Ohio, & Baltimore	Continued in M
	4 Wyoming	1852-1939	N.E. Pa. & S. Central N.Y.	Division of Oneida[38]	Continued in M
MP	1 Pennsylvania	1829-1911	Eastern Pa., etc.	Secession from ME	Merged with †N.Y., & †N.J. to form Eastern
	4 §Pennsylvania	1866-1875	Eastern Pa.	Division of Pa.	Merged with †New York
	3 Philadelphia	1846-1850	Pa. east of Susquehanna R.	Division of Maryland	Absorbed by Maryland
	2 †Pittsburgh	1833-1939	W. Pa., E. Ohio, & W. Va.	Division of †Ohio	Merged in 1939
M	1e Central Pa.	1939-1968	Central Pa.	Superseded Central Pa. ME	Continued in UM
	1c Erie	1939-1961	N.W. Pa. & Western N.Y.	Superseded Erie ME, & partially Pittsburgh MP	Merged with Pittsburgh to form Western Pa.
	1a Philadelphia	1939-1968	Southeast Pa.	Superseded Philadelphia ME, & partially Eastern MP	Continued in UM
	1b Pittsburgh	1939-1961	Western Pa.	Superseded Pittsburgh ME, & partially Pittsburgh MP	Merged with Erie to form Western Pa.
	2 Western Pa.	1962-1968	Western Pa.	Merger of Erie, & Pittsburgh	Continued in UM
	1d Wyoming	1939-1968	N.E. Pa. & S. Central N.Y.	Superseded Wyoming ME	Continued in UM

RHODE ISLAND

Denomination	Conference	Dates	Location	How Formed	Conclusion
ME	Providence	1841-1880	R.I., & parts of Conn. & Mass.	Division of New England	Superseded by N. Eng. Southern[39]

SOUTH CAROLINA

Denomination	Conference	Dates	Location	How Formed	Conclusion
ME	South Carolina	1787-1844	S.C. & Ga., & part of N.C.	Division of Virginia	Superseded by S. Car. MES
	°S.C. Miss. Conf.	1866-1868	S.C. & Florida	°	Superseded by °S. Car.
	°South Car.	1869-1939	S.C. & Florida	Superseded °S. C. Miss. Conf.	Continued in M
MES	South Carolina	1845-1939	South Carolina	Superseded S. Car. ME	Continued in M
	Upper S. Car.	1915-1939	Upper South Carolina	Division of S. Car.	Continued in M
MP	2 °Charleston Colored Mis. Conf.	1888-1924	South Carolina	Organization of Negro work	Superseded by °S. Car. Colored Mission Conf.
	1 South Carolina	1839-1939	South Carolina	Division of Georgia	Merged in 1939

---

[36] See California.   [37] See Maryland.   [38] See New York.   [39] See Massachusetts.

Denomi-nation	Conference	Dates	Location	How Formed	Conclusion
	3 °S.C. Colored Mission Conf.	1924-1939	South Carolina	Superseded °Charleston Colored Mission Conf.	Merged in 1939
M	South Carolina	1939-1968	Lower half of S. Carolina	Superseded S. Car. MES	Continued in UM
	°South Carolina	1939-1968	South Carolina	Superseded °S.C. ME, & °S.C. Colored Mission Conf. MP	Temporarily continued in UM
	Upper S. Car.	1939-1948	Upper S. Carolina	Superseded Upper S.C. MES	Absorbed by S. Carolina

SOUTH DAKOTA

Denomi-nation	Conference	Dates	Location	How Formed	Conclusion
ME	1a Black Hills Mission	1880-1891	West S. Dakota & parts of Wyo. & Montana	Organization of new work	Superseded by Black Hills Mission Conf.
	5 Black Hills Mission	1901-1913	West S. Dakota & parts of Wyo. & Montana	Superseded Black Hills Conf.	Absorbed by Dakota Conf.
	3a Black Hills Mission Conf.	1892-1895	West S. Dakota & parts of Wyo. & Montana	Superseded Black Hills Miss.	Superseded by Black Hills Conf.
	4a Black Hills Conf.	1896-1900	West S. Dakota & parts of Wyo. & Montana	Superseded Black Hills Mission Conf.	Superseded by Black Hills Miss.
	1b Dakota Miss.	1880-1885	East S. Dakota	Organization of new work	Superseded by Dakota Conf.
	2 Dakota	1885-1892	East S. Dakota	Superseded Dakota Mission	Superseded by S. Dakota
	4b Dakota	1896-1939	East S. Dakota	Superseded S. Dakota	Continued in M
	3b South Dakota	1892-1895	East S. Dakota	Superseded Dakota	Superseded by Dakota
M	Dakota	1939-1952	South Dakota	Superseded Dakota ME	Superseded by South Dakota
	South Dakota	1953-1968	South Dakota	Superseded Dakota	Continued in UM

TENNESSEE

Denomi-nation	Conference	Dates	Location	How Formed	Conclusion
ME	7 ◇Central Tenn.	1877-1939	Central Tennessee	Division of °Tennessee	Merged in 1939
	8 °East Tenn.	1880-1939	East Tennessee	Division of ◇Holston	Continued in M
	2 Holston	1824-1844	E. Tenn., S.W. Va., Western N.C. & N.E. S. Car.	Division of Tennessee	Superseded by Holston MES
	4 ◇Holston	1865-1939	E. Tenn. & Western N.C.	◇	Merged in 1939
	3 Memphis	1840-1844	W. Tenn., W. Ky., & N. Miss.	Division of Tennessee	Superseded by Memphis MES
	1 Tennessee	1812-1844	Tenn., Ill., Miss., W. Ky. & N. Ala.	Division of Western	Superseded by Tenn. MES
	5 °Tenn. Mission Conf.	1866-1868	Middle & West Tenn.	°	Superseded by °Tenn. Conf.
	6 °Tennessee	1869-1939	Middle & West Tenn.	Superseded °Tenn. Miss. Conf.	Continued in M
MES	Holston	1845-1939	E. Tenn., S.W. Va., & West. N.C.	Superseded Holston ME	Continued in M
	Memphis	1845-1939	W. Tenn., W. Ky. & No. Miss.	Superseded Memphis ME	Continued in M
	Tennessee	1845-1939	Middle Tenn. & N. Ala.	Superseded Tennessee ME	Continued in M
MP	4 ‡Holston	1870-1874	E. Tenn. & S.W. Va.	Division of N.C., & Va.	Absorbed by Va.
	2 Huntsville	1846-1858	North Alabama	Division of Tenn.	Absorbed by Tenn., & Ala.
	6 °Spring Creek Colored Miss. Conf.	1884-1920	West Tennessee	Organization of Negro work	Dissolved
	1 Tennessee	1829-1939	Tennessee	Secession from ME	Merged in 1939
	5 §Tenn. & N.Ga.	1871-1875	Tennessee & N. Ga.	Organization of new work	Dissolved
	3 West Tenn.	1851-1888	W. Tenn. & part of Ky.	Division of Tenn.	Absorbed by Tenn.
M	°E. Tenn.	1939-1964	E. Tenn. & parts of Ky., Va., & W. Va.	Superseded °E. Tenn. ME	Merged with °Tenn., & part of °Lexington[40] to form °Tenn.-Ky.
	Holston	1939-1968	E. Tenn. & S.W. Va.	Superseded Holston ME & MES	Continued in UM
	Memphis	1939-1968	W. Tenn. & W. Ky.	Superseded Memphis MES	Continued in UM
	Tennessee	1939-1968	Middle Tenn.	Superseded Tenn. MES, & partially Cen. Tenn., ME, & Tenn. MP	Continued in UM

[40] See Kentucky.

Denomi-nation	Conference	Dates	Location	How Formed	Conclusion
	°Tennessee	1939-1964	Middle & W. Tenn.	Superseded °Tenn. ME	Merged with °E. Tenn., & part of °Lexington [40] to form °Tenn-Ky.
	°Tenn.-Ky.	1964-1968	Tenn., Ky., & part of Va.	Superseded °Tenn., °E. Tenn., & partially °Lexington	Absorbed by S.E. Juris. Confs.

TEXAS

Denomi-nation	Conference	Dates	Location	How Formed	Conclusion
ME	5 ◇Austin	1877-1911	Texas	Division of °West Texas	Absorbed in part by ◇Gulf,[41] & Okla.; superseded in part by Southern Swedish Mission Conf.
	2a Eastern Tex.	1845	Eastern Texas	Division of Texas	Superseded by Eastern Tex. MES
	7 ◇Southern	1925-1939	Parts of Tex. & La., & Miss.	Superseded ◇Southern German	Merged in 1939
	5a ◇Sou. German	1874-1924	Texas	Organization of German work	Superseded by ◇Southern
	6 ◇Sou. Swed. Miss. Conf.	1912-1926	Texas	Partially superseded ◇Austin	Absorbed by ◇Southern
	1 Texas	1840-1843	Texas, except N.E. part	Division of Mississippi	Divided to form Eastern Texas, and Western Texas
	3 °Texas Miss. Conf.	1867-1868	Texas	Division of °Miss. Miss. Conf.	Superseded by °Texas
	4 °Texas	1869-1939	Texas	Superseded °Texas Miss. Conf.	Continued in M
	5b °West Texas	1874-1939	West Texas	Division of °Texas	Continued in M
	2b Western Texas	1845	West Texas	Division of Texas	Superseded by Texas MES
MES	12 Central Tex.	1910-1939	Central Texas	Division of Northwest Tex.	Continued in M
	3 East Texas	1847-1901	East Texas	Superseded Eastern Tex.	Absorbed by Texas
	1 Eastern Texas	1846-1847	East Texas	Superseded Eastern Tex. ME	Superseded by East Texas
	9b German Miss. Conf.	1874-1917	Texas & Louisiana	Organization of German work	Superseded by S.W. Texas
	10 Mex. Border	1885-1914	S.W. & W. Texas & part of Mexico	Division of West Texas	Merged with N.W. Mex. Miss. Conf. to form Mex. Border Conf.
	14 Mex. Border Conf.	1914-1918	Texas west of Pecos River, N. Mex., & part of Mexico	Partial merger of Mex. B. Miss. Conf. & N.W. Mex. Miss. Conf.	Merged with Pacif. Mex. Miss.[42] to form Western Mex. Miss.
	9a North Texas	1874-1939	N.E. Texas	Superseded Trinity	Continued in M
	11 N.W. Mex. Miss. Conf.	1891-1914	Southwestern U.S. & part of Mexico	Organization of Mexican work	Partially merged with Mex. B. Miss. Conf. to form Mex. Border Conf.
	6 N.W. Texas	1866-1939	N.W. Texas	Merger of parts of Texas, & Rio Grande	Continued in M
	4 Rio Grande Miss. Conf.	1859-1863	West, S.W., & part of N.W. Texas	Division of Texas	Superseded by Rio Grande Conf.
	5 Rio Grande	1864-1865	West, S.W., & part of N.W. Texas	Superseded Rio Grande Miss. Conf.	Superseded by West Texas
	15a S.W. Texas	1918	Texas	Superseded German Miss. Conf.	Absorbed by English-speaking District in West Texas Conf.
	2 Texas	1846-1939	Texas west of Trinity River	Superseded Western Tex. ME	Continued in M
	13 Tex. Mex. Miss.	1914-1929	Texas east of Pecos River	Partially superseded Mex. Border Miss. Conf.	Superseded by Tex. Mex. Conf.
	16a Tex. Mex. Conf.	1930-1938	Texas east of Pecos River	Superseded Tex. Mex. Miss.	Merged with Western Mex. to form S.W. Mex. M
	8 Trinity	1867-1873	N.E. Texas	Division of East Texas	Superseded by North Texas
	7 West Texas	1866-1939	S.W. Texas	Superseded Rio Grande	Superseded by S.W. Tex. M

[41] See Louisiana.   [42] See California.

Denomi-nation	Conference	Dates	Location	How Formed	Conclusion
	15b Western Mex. Mission	1918-1929	Tex. west of Pecos R., N.M., Ariz., Calif., etc.	Merger of Mex. Border Conf., & Pacific Mex. Mission[42]	Superseded by Western Mex. Conf.
	16b Western Mex.	1930-1938	Tex. west of Pecos R., N.M., Ariz., Calif., etc.	Superseded Western Mex. Mission	Merged with Tex. Mex. to form S.W. Mex. M
MP	3 Central Tex.	1870-1912	North Central Texas	Division of Texas	Absorbed by Texas
	2a Colorado	1860-1880	Texas west of Brazos River	Division of Texas	Superseded by Colorado Texas
	4 Colorado Tex	1880-1912	Texas west of Brazos River	Superseded Colorado	Superseded by Colo. Tex. Gulf
	8 °Colo. Texas Colored Miss. Conf.	1878-1939	West Texas	Organization of Negro work	Merged in 1939
	7 Colo. Tex. Gulf	1912-1916	South & S.W. Tex.	Superseded Colo. Tex., Texas Gulf Miss. Conf. & S.W. Tex. Miss. Conf.	Absorbed by Texas
	6 °Dallas Colored Miss. Conf.	1896-1908	N.E. Texas	Organization of Negro work	Dissolved
	2b McCaine	1860-1883	East Central Texas	Division of Texas	Absorbed by Central Tex., & Tex.
	5a N.W. Tex. Miss. Conf.	1892-1916	Northwest Texas	Division of Texas	Absorbed by Texas
	5b S.W. Tex. Miss. Conf.	1892-1912	Southwest Texas	Division of Colorado Texas	Merged with Colo. Tex., & Tex. Gulf Miss. Conf. to form Colo. Tex. Gulf
	1 Texas	1848-1939	Texas	Division of Louisiana	Merged in 1939
	5c Tex. Gulf Miss. Conf.	1892-1912	South Texas	Division of Texas	Merged with Colo. Tex., & S.W. Tex. Miss. Conf. to form Colo. Tex. Gulf
	9 Texhoma Miss. Conf.	1931-1936	N.W. Tex. & W. Okla.	Division of Tex., & Ft. Smith-Okla.[43]	Absorbed by Ft. Smith-Okla.[43]
M	1a Central Tex.	1939-1968	Central Texas	Superseded Cen. Tex. MES, & in part ◊South-ern ME, & Tex. MP	Continued in UM
	1b North Texas	1939-1968	Northeast Texas	Superseded N. Tex. MES, & in part ◊Southern ME, & Tex. MP	Continued in UM
	1c N.W. Texas	1939-1968	Northwest Texas	Superseded N.W. Tex. MES	Continued in UM
	2 Rio Grande	1948-1968	Texas & New Mexico	Superseded S. W. Mexican	Continued in UM
	1d S.W. Mex.	1939-1947	Texas & New Mexico	Merger of S.W. Span. Miss.[44] ME; & Tex. Mex. Con., & W. Mex. Con. MES	Superseded by Rio Grande
	1e S.W. Texas	1939-1968	Southwest Texas	Superseded West Tex. MES	Continued in UM
	1f Texas	1939-1968	Southeast Texas	Superseded Texas MES	Continued in UM
	1g °Texas	1939-1968	East Texas	Superseded °Texas ME	Temporarily continued in UM
	1h °West Texas	1939-1968	West Texas	Superseded °West Texas ME	Temporarily continued in UM

UTAH

Denomi-nation	Conference	Dates	Location	How Formed	Conclusion
ME	Rocky Mountain[45]	1872-1876	Utah, Ida., Mont., & part of Wyo.	Organization of new work	Divided to form Ont., & Utah
	Utah	1877-1879	Utah	Division of Rocky Moun-tain	Superseded by Utah Mis-sion
	Utah Mission	1880-1939	Utah & part of Nev.	Superseded Utah Conf.	Continued in M
M	Utah Mission	1939-1948	Utah & part of Nev.	Superseded Utah Miss. ME	Absorbed by Colorado

VERMONT

Denomi-nation	Conference	Dates	Location	How Formed	Conclusion
ME	Vermont	1844-1939	Eastern Vermont	Division of New Hamp-shire	Continued in M
MP	Vermont	1830-1853	Vermont	Secession from ME	Merged to form N.Y., & Vt.
M	Vermont	1939-1940	Eastern & Northern Vt.	Superseded Vermont ME	Absorbed by Troy

[43] See Arkansas.   [44] See New Mexico.   [45] See Colorado for Rocky Mountain, 1863, & 1957-1968.

VIRGINIA

ME	1 Virginia	1785-1844	Virginia & eastern N.C.	Original conference	Superseded by Virginia MES
	3 ◊Virginia	1869-1906	Virginia	Division of ◊Va. & N.C. Mission Conf.	Absorbed by Baltimore, ◊Holston & W. Va.
	2 ◊Va. & N. C.	1867-1868	Virginia & N.C.	◊	Divided to form ◊Va., & *N.C.
MES	Virginia	1845-1939	Virginia	Superseded Virginia ME	Continued in M
MP	E. Va.	1829-1834	Virginia east of Allegheny Mts.	Secession from ME	Superseded by Virginia
	Virginia	1834-1877	Virginia east of Allegheny Mts.	Superseded E. Va.	Partially absorbed by Md., & N.C.
	Virginia[46]	1877-1939	S.W. Va. & E. Tenn.	Merger of parts of N.C., & Va. (1834-77)	Merged in 1939
M	Virginia	1939-1968	Virginia	Superseded Va. MES, & partially Baltimore ME & MES	Continued in UM

WASHINGTON

ME	1 Columbia River	1876-1928	E. Ore., E. Wash., & W. Ida.	Superseded E. Ore. & Wash.	Superseded by Pacific N.W.
	3a N. Pacific German Miss.	1888-1891	Wash., Ore., Ida., & Mont.	Division of Oregon	Superseded by N. Pacific German Miss. Conf.
	4a N. Pac. German Miss. Conf.	1892-1904	Wash., Ore., Ida., & Mont.	Superseded N. Pac. German Miss.	Superseded by Pacific Ger. Conf.
	3b N.W. Norweg.-Danish Miss.	1888-1891	Wash., Ore., & Ida.	Organization of Norwegian-Danish work	Superseded by Western Norweg.-Danish Mission
	6 Pacific German	1905-1928	Wash., Ore., Ida., & Mont.	Superseded N. Pacific German Miss. Conf.	Absorbed by English-speaking
	8 Pacific N.W.	1929-1939	Wash., part of Ida., & Alaska	Merger of Columbia River, & Puget Sound	Continued in M
	7 Pacif. Swed. Miss. Conf.	1908-1928	All states west of Rocky Mts.	Organization of Swed. work	Absorbed by English-speaking
	2 Puget Sound	1884-1928	West Wash.	Division of Oregon	Superseded by Pacific N.W.
	4b W. Norweg.-Dan. Miss.	1892-1895	Wash., Ore., Ida., Mont., Calif. & Utah	Superseded Northwestern Norweg.-Dan. Miss.	Superseded by Western Norweg.-Dan. Conf.
	5 W. Norweg.-Danish	1896-1939	Wash., Ore., Ida., Mont., Calif. & Utah	Superseded Western Norweg.-Danish Miss.	Absorbed by English-speaking
MP	2 Washington	1896-1924	Washington	Division of Wash. & Ore.	Superseded by Wash. Miss. Conf.
	3 Wash. Miss. Conf.	1924-1939	Washington	Superseded Wash. Conf.	Merged in 1939
	1 Wash. & Ore.	1892-1896	Washington & Oregon	Organization of new work	Divided to form Wash. Conf., & Ore. Miss. Conf.
M	Pacific N.W.	1939-1968	Washington & part of Idaho	Superseded Pacif. N.W. ME, & partially Northwest MES [47]	Continued in UM

WEST VIRGINIA

ME	2 West Va.	1865-1939	West Virginia & small part of Md.	Superseded Western Va.	Continued in M
	1 Western Va.	1848-1864	West Virginia	Division of Pittsburgh	Superseded by W. Va.
MES	◊Western Va.	1850-1939	West Virginia & small part of Ky.	Division of Kentucky	Merged in 1939
MP	‡West Va.	1870-1939	West Virginia	Superseded †Western Va.	Merged in 1939
	†Western Va.	1854-1870	Western part of Va.	Division of †Pittsburgh	Superseded by ‡West Va.
M	West Virginia	1939-1968	West Virginia	Superseded Western Va. MES, & West Va. ME, & MP	Continued in UM

---

[46] Unofficially circa 1925 the printed journals of this conference use the name "Virginia-Tennessee Conference."
[47] See Oregon.

WISCONSIN

ME	3 N.W. Wis.	1860-1867	Northwest Wis.	Merger of parts of Minn., & West Wis.	Absorbed by West Wis.
	2 West Wis.	1856-1939	S.W. Wis.	Division of Wis.	Continued in M
	1 Wisconsin	1848-1939	Wis. & Minn. (most)	Division of Rock River	Continued in M
MP	†Wisconsin	1850-1871	Wisconsin	Division of Minn.	Merged with †N. Ill.
M	2 E. Wis.	1961-1968	E. Wis.	Superseded Wis.	Continued in UM
	1b West Wis.	1939-1968	West Wis.	Superseded W. Wis. ME	Continued in UM
	1a Wisconsin	1939-1960	E. Wis.	Superseded Wis. ME	Superseded by E. Wis.

WYOMING

ME	Wyoming Miss.	1888-1913	Wyoming	Organization of new work	Superseded by Wyoming State
	Wyoming State	1914-1939	Wyoming	Superseded Wyoming Mission	Continued in M
M	Wyoming State	1939-1956	Wyoming	Superseded Wyo. State ME	Merged with Colo. to form Rocky Mountain

CANADA, CUBA, AND PUERTO RICO

ME	Canada	1824-1828	Upper Canada	Division of Genesee	Formed Meth. Ch. of Canada
MES	Cuban Mission	1904-1923	Cuba	Organization of Cuban work	Superseded by Cuba Conf.
	Cuba	1923-1939	Cuba	Superseded Cuban Mission	Continued in M
M	Cuba	1939-1964	Cuba	Superseded Cuba MES	Formed Autonomous Meth. Ch.
ME	Puerto Rico Mission	1902-1912	Puerto Rico & nearby Islands	Organization of new work	Superseded by P.R. Miss. Conf.
	Puerto Rico Miss. Conf.	1913-1939	Puerto Rico & nearby Islands	Superseded Puerto Rico Miss.	Superseded by P.R. Provisional Conf. M
M	Puerto Rico Prov. Conf.	1940-1968	Puerto Rico & nearby Islands	Superseded Puerto Rico Miss. Conf. ME	Continued in UM, becoming Puerto Rico in 1969

TABLE OF E.U.B. CONFERENCES

By John H. Ness, Jr.

This table lists by states, and by denominations within the states, the annual conferences of the Evangelical Association (1807-1922), The United Evangelical Church (1894-1922), The Evangelical Church (1922-1946), Church of the United Brethren in Christ (1800-1946), and The Evangelical United Brethren Church (1946-1968). There is no attempt to differentiate between a mission conference and a regular conference.

The capital letters used in the table stand for:

EUB—Evangelical United Brethren Church
UB—United Brethren in Christ
Ev. Assn. (EA)—Evangelical Association
Ev. Ch. (EC)—Evangelical Church
UE—United Evangelical Church

(U)—former United Brethren conference in Evangelical United Brethren Church
(E)—former Evangelical Church conference in Evangelical United Brethren Church
(United)—former United Evangelical conference in The Evangelical Church
UM—United Methodist Church

Since merger plans have been completed for most of the former E.U.B. annual conferences, this table has been extended beyond 1968 to show the conclusion of the conferences in The United Methodist Church.

Introductory material preceding the Table of Methodist Conferences furnishes further explanatory details for this table as well.

Denomination	Conference	Dates	Location	How Formed	Conclusion
			ARIZONA (See California)		
			ARKANSAS (See Missouri)		
			CALIFORNIA		
UB	California	1861-1946	California	Missionary effort from east	Continued in EUB
EV. ASSN.	2 California	1884-1922	California	Division of Pacific	Continued in EC
	1 Pacific	1875-1884	California and Oregon	Missionary effort	Divided—Calif., & Ore.
EV. CH.	California	1922-1946	California	Superseded California EA	Continued in EUB
EUB	California (E)	1946-1951	California	Superseded California EC	Merged with Calif. (U)
	California (U)	1946-1951	California	Superseded California UB	Merged with Calif. (E)
	California	1951-1968	California	Merger of Calif. (E), & (U)	Continued in UM
UM	California	1968-1969	California	Superseded Calif. EUB	Merged with Calif.-Nev., & S. Calif.-Ariz. (Meth.)
			CANADA		
UB	Ontario	1856-1906	Province of Ontario	Missionary work	United with Congregationalists of Canada
EV. ASSN.	Canada	1864-1922	Province of Ontario	Division of New York[1]	Continued in EC
EV. CH.	Canada	1922-1946	Province of Ontario	Superseded Canada EA	Continued in EUB
	Northwest Canada	1927-1946	Western Canada	Missionaries from Canada Con.	Continued in EUB
EUB	Canada	1946-1967	Ontario	Superseded Canada EC	Merged with United Church of Canada
	Northwest Canada	1946-1968	Western Canada	Superseded N.W. Canada EC	Continued in UM
UM	Northwest Canada	1968-	Western Canada	Superseded N.W. Canada EUB	Continues
			COLORADO		
UB	Colorado	1872-1929	Colorado & Wyoming	Missionary work of Board Missions	Merged with New Mexico[2] to form Colo.-N.M.
	Colorado-New Mexico	1929-1946	Colo., N.M., & Wyoming	Merger of Colo., & N.M.	Continued in EUB
EV. ASSN.	Colorado	1920-1922	Colorado	Realignment of Kan., & Neb.	Continued in EC
EV. CH.	Colorado	1922-1946	Colorado	Superseded Colo. EA	Continued in EUB

---

[1] See New York. [2] See New Mexico.

Denomination	Conference	Dates	Location	How Formed	Conclusion
EUB	Colorado	1946-1951	Colorado	Superseded Colo. EC	Merged with Colo.-N.M. to form Rocky Mt.
	Colorado-N.M.	1946-1951	Colo., N.M., & Wyoming	Superseded Colo.-N.M. UB	Merged with Colorado to form Rocky Mt.
	Rocky Mountain	1951-1968	N.M., Colo., & Wyoming	Merger of Colo., & Colo.-N.M.	Continued in UM
UM	Rocky Mountain	1968-1969	N.M., Colo., & Wyoming	Superseded Rocky Mt. EUB	Merged with N.M., & Rocky Mt. (Meth.)

FLORIDA

Denomination	Conference	Dates	Location	How Formed	Conclusion
UB	2 Florida	1917-1946	S.W. Florida & S. Georgia	Superseded Ga.-Fla.	Continued in EUB
	1 Ga.-Fla.	1913-1917	S.W. Fla. & S. Georgia	Superseded Georgia	Superseded by Florida UB
EUB	Florida	1946-1968	Southern Florida	Superseded Florida UB	Continued in UM
UM	Florida	1968	Southern Florida	Superseded Florida EUB	Merged with Florida Confs. (Meth.)

GEORGIA

Denomination	Conference	Dates	Location	How Formed	Conclusion
UB	Georgia	1902-1913	S.W. Fla. & S. Georgia	Organized independently	Superseded by Ga.-Fla. UB

IDAHO (See Oregon and Washington)

ILLINOIS

Denomination	Conference	Dates	Location	How Formed	Conclusion
UB	3 Cen. Illinois	1865-1901	Central Illinois	Division of Illinois	Merged with Rock River to form Northern Illinois
	1 Illinois	1845-1905	West central Illinois	Division of Wabash[3]	Merged with N. Ill.
	6 Illinois	1918-1946	Illinois	Union of N.Ill., & Lower Wabash[4]	Continued in EUB
	5 Northern Ill.	1901-1918	Northern Illinois	Merger of C. Ill., & Rock River	Merged with Lower Wabash[4]
	2 Rock River	1853-1901	Northern Illinois	Division of Ill.	Merged with Central Ill. to form N. Ill.
	4 Southern Ill.	1871-1889	Southern Illinois	Board of Missions work	Merged with Lower Wabash[4]
EV. ASSN.	Illinois	1844-1922	Illinois	Division of Ohio[5]	Continued in EC
UE	Illinois	1894-1922	Illinois	Formed by church split	Continued in EC
EV. CH.	Illinois	1922-1946	Illinois	Superseded Illinois EA	Continued in EUB
	Illinois (United)	1922-1927	Illinois	Superseded Illinois UE	Merged with Illinois
EUB	Illinois (E)	1946-1953	Illinois	Superseded Illinois EC	Merged with Illinois (U)
	Illinois (U)	1946-1953	Illinois	Superseded Illinois UB	Merged with Illinois (E)
	Illinois	1953-1968	Illinois	Merger of Ill. (E), & (U)	Continued in UM
UM	Illinois	1968	Illinois	Superseded Illinois EUB	Merged with N. Ill., C. Ill., & Southern Ill. (Meth.)

INDIANA

Denomination	Conference	Dates	Location	How Formed	Conclusion
UB	1 Indiana	1830-1946	Southern Indiana	Division of Miami[5]	Continued in EUB
	6 Indiana German	1861-1865	Indiana and Illinois	German work in Northwest	Merged with Ohio German[5] & respective English Conferences
	5a Lower Wabash	1858-1918	Southern Ill. & S.W. Ind.	Division of Wabash	Merged with N. Ill.[7]
	3 St. Joseph	1845-1946	Ind. north of White River Conf.	Division of Wabash	Continued in EUB
	5b Upper Wabash	1858-1909	N.W. Ind. & N.E. Ill.	Division of Wabash	Divided into N. Ill.,[7] St. Joseph, & White River
	2 Wabash	1835-1858	W. Ind. & E. Ill.	Division of Indiana	Divided into Lower Wabash, & Upper Wabash
	4 White River	1847-1946	Central Indiana	Division of Indiana	Continued in EUB
EV. ASSN.	Indiana	1852-1922	Indiana	Division of Ohio,[6] & Ill.[7]	Continued in EC
	Southern Ind.	1875-1893	Southern Ind.—German work	Realignment of work in Sou. Ind., S. Ohio, Ky., & S. Ill.	Merged with Indiana
EV. CH.	Indiana	1922-1946	Indiana	Superseded Ind. EA	Continued in EUB
EUB	1a Indiana (E)	1946-1951	Indiana	Superseded Ind. EC	Merged with White River, Ind. (U), & St. Joseph

---

[3] See Indiana.   [4] See Indiana.   [5] See Ohio.   [6] See Ohio.   [7] See Illinois.

Denomination	Conference	Dates	Location	How Formed	Conclusion
	1b Indiana (U)	1946-1951	Southern Indiana	Superseded Ind. UB	Merged with Ind. (E), White River, & St. Joseph
	2a Ind. North	1951-1968	Northern Indiana	Merger of St. Joseph, White River, & Ind. (E)	Continued in UM
	2b Ind. South	1951-1968	Southern Indiana	Merger of Ind. (U), White River, & Ind. (E)	Continued in UM
	1c St. Joseph	1946-1951	Northern Indiana	Superseded St. Joseph UB	Merged with Ind. (E), & White River
	1d White River	1946-1951	Central Indiana	Superseded White River UB	Merged with Ind. (E), Ind. (U), & St. Joseph
UM	Indiana North	1968-1969	Northern Indiana	Superseded Ind. North EUB	Merged with three Meth. Confs. and realigned to become N. Ind., & S. Ind.
	Indiana South	1968-1969	Southern Indiana	Superseded Ind. South EUB	

IOWA

Denomination	Conference	Dates	Location	How Formed	Conclusion
UB	2 Des Moines	1853-1861	Central and western Iowa	Division of Iowa	Divided into East and West Des Moines
	5 Des Moines	1889-1909	Western Iowa	Superseded W. Des Moines	Merged with Iowa
	3a E. Des Moines	1861-1889	East central Iowa	Division of Des Moines	Merged with Iowa
	1 Iowa	1845-1946	Eastern Iowa until 1909; then statewide	Division of Wabash[8]	Continued in EUB
	4 North Iowa	1862-1874	Northern Iowa	Division of Iowa	Merged with Iowa
	3b W. Des Moines	1861-1889	Western Iowa	Division of Des Moines	Superseded by Des Moines
EV. ASSN.	2 Des Moines	1875-1912	Western Iowa	Division of Iowa	Merged with Iowa
	1 Iowa	1860-1922	Eastern Iowa	Division of Illinois[9]	Continued in EC
UE	Des Moines	1894-1922	Southern Iowa	Formed by church division	Continued in EC
	Northwestern	1899-1922	N. Iowa, Minn., N.D., & S.D.	Division of Des Moines	Continued in EC
EV. CH.	Des Moines	1922-1927	South Iowa	Superseded Des Moines UE	Merged with Iowa
	Iowa	1922-1946	Iowa	Superseded Iowa EA	Continued in EUB
	Northwestern	1922-1923	N. Iowa, Minn., N.D., & S.D.	Superseded Northwestern UE	Merged with Des Moines, & Iowa
EUB	Iowa (E)	1946-1951	Iowa	Superseded Iowa EC	Merged with Iowa (U)
	Iowa (U)	1946-1951	Iowa	Superseded Iowa UB	Merged with Iowa (E)
	Iowa	1951-1968	Iowa	Merger of Iowa (E), & (U)	Continued in UM
UM	Iowa	1968-1969	Iowa	Superseded Iowa EUB	United with N. Iowa, & S. Iowa (Meth.) to form Iowa

KANSAS

Denomination	Conference	Dates	Location	How Formed	Conclusion
UB	4 Ark. Valley	1881-1905	S.W. Kansas	Division of Osage	Superseded by S.W. Kansas
	1 Kansas	1857-1901	Kan. state line until 1869; then N.E. Kan.	Division of Missouri[10]	Superseded by N.E. Kansas
	11 Kansas	1914-1946	Kansas	Merger of Neosho, N.Kan., & S.W. Kansas	Continued in EUB
	5 Neosho	1885-1914	S.E. Kansas	Superseded Osage	Merged with S.W. Kan., & N. Kan.
	10 North Kansas	1909-1914	Northern Kansas	Merger of N.E. Kan., & N.W. Kan.	Merged with S.W. Kan., & Neosho
	8 Northeast Kan.	1901-1909	N.E. Kansas	Superseded Kansas	Merged with N.W. Kan. to become North Kansas
	6 Northwest Kan.	1889-1909	Western Kansas	Superseded W. Kansas	Merged with N.E. Kan. to become North Kansas
	2 Osage	1869-1885	Kansas south of 38th parallel & Mo. south of Mo. River	Division of Kansas	Superseded by Neosho
	7 Southwest Kan.	1893-1897	Southwest Kansas	Division of Ark. Valley	Merged with Ark. Valley
	9 Southwest Kan.	1905-1914	Southwest Kansas	Superseded Ark. Valley	Merged with N. Kan., & Neosho
	3 West Kansas	1879-1889	Western Kansas	Division of Kansas	Superseded by N. W. Kansas

---

[8] See Indiana.   [9] See Illinois.   [10] See Missouri.

Denomi-nation	Conference	Dates	Location	How Formed	Conclusion
EV. ASSN.	Kansas	1864-1922	Kansas	Division of Iowa	Continued in EC
UE	Kansas	1902-1922	Kansas and Oklahoma	Division of Platte River	Merged with Kansas EA
EV. CH.	Kansas	1922-1946	Kansas and Oklahoma	Merger of Kan. UE, & Kan. EA	Continued in EUB
EUB	Kansas (E)	1946-1956	Kansas	Superseded Kansas EC	Merged with Kansas (U)
	Kansas (U)	1946-1956	Kansas	Superseded Kansas UB	Merged with Kansas (E)
	Kansas	1956-1968	Kansas	Merger of Kan. (E), & (U)	Continued in UM
UM	Kansas	1968	Kansas	Superseded Kansas EUB	Merged with Kansas East, & Kansas West (Meth.)

KENTUCKY

Denomi-nation	Conference	Dates	Location	How Formed	Conclusion
UB	Ky. Mission Conf.	1857-1921	Cumberland area	Separated from Indiana[11]	Merged with Tennessee[12]
EUB	Kentucky	1955-1968	Cumberland & Red Bird Mission Districts	Memorial to Gen. Conf.	Continued in UM
UM	Kentucky	1968	Cumberland & Red Bird areas	Superseded Kentucky EUB	Western portion merged with Louisville (Meth.); Red Bird Conf. formed by remainder

LOUISIANA

Denomi-nation	Conference	Dates	Location	How Formed	Conclusion
UB	Louisiana	1901-1921	Louisiana	Immigration from the north	Merged with Missouri[13]

MAINE (See Massachusetts and Pennsylvania)

MARYLAND

Denomi-nation	Conference	Dates	Location	How Formed	Conclusion
UB	Hagerstown	1829-1830	Md., Va., Pa.	Change of name from Original	Divided into Va.,[14] & Pa.[15]
	Maryland	1887-1901	Baltimore & W. Md. not included in Pa. Conf.	Division of Virginia[14]	Merged with Pa.[15]
	Original	1800-1828	Md., Va., Pa.	Organization of denomination	Name changed to Hagers-town

MASSACHUSETTS

Denomi-nation	Conference	Dates	Location	How Formed	Conclusion
UB	Massachusetts	1862-1864	Massachusetts	Missionary effort of Sandusky Conf.	Dissolved
EV. ASSN.	New England	1896-1922	New England states	Detached from E. Pa.[15]	Continued in EC
EV. CH.	New England	1922-1946	New England states	Superseded New England EA	Continued in EUB
EUB	New England	1946-1957	New England states	Superseded New England EC	Merged with E. Pa. (E)[15], & Atlantic[16] to form Northeastern[15]

MICHIGAN

Denomi-nation	Conference	Dates	Location	How Formed	Conclusion
UB	Michigan	1853-1869	Southern Mich. & Northern Ohio	Missionary work of Sandusky	Merged with N. Ohio[17]
	Michigan	1869-1946	Southern Mich.	Superseded N. Mich. 1869	Continued in EUB
	North Michigan	1862-1869	Central Michigan	Division of Mich.	Name changed to Mich. 1869
	North Michigan	1881-1897	Northern Michigan	Superseded Saginaw	Merged with Mich.
	Saginaw	1877-1881	Northern Michigan	Division of Mich.	Name change to N. Mich.
EV. ASSN.	Michigan	1864-1922	Central & south Michigan	Division of Ohio[18]	Continued in EC
EV. CH.	Michigan	1922-1946	Central & south Michigan	Superseded Michigan EA	Continued in EUB
EUB	Michigan (E)	1946-1951	Central & south Michigan	Superseded Michigan EC	Merged with Mich. (U)
	Michigan (U)	1946-1951	Central & south Michigan	Superseded Michigan UB	Merged with Mich. (E)
	Michigan	1951-1968	Central & south Michigan	Merger of Mich. (E), & (U)	Continued in UM
UM	Michigan	1968-1969	Michigan	Superseded Michigan EUB	Merged with Detroit, & W. Mich. (Meth.)

MINNESOTA

Denomi-nation	Conference	Dates	Location	How Formed	Conclusion
UB	Minnesota	1857-1946	Minnesota	Missionary effort of Board of Missions	Continued in EUB
EV. ASSN.	Minnesota	1868-1922	Minnesota	Division of Wisconsin[19]	Continued in EC

[11] See Indiana.   [12] See Tennessee.   [13] See Missouri.   [14] See Virginia.   [15] See Pennsylvania.
[16] See New York.   [17] See Ohio.   [18] See Ohio.   [19] See Wisconsin.

Denomination	Conference	Dates	Location	How Formed	Conclusion
EV. CH.	Minnesota	1922-1946	Minnesota	Superseded Minn. EA	Continued in EUB
EUB	Minnesota (E)	1946-1951	Minnesota	Superseded Minn. EC	Merged with Minn. (U)
	Minnesota (U)	1946-1951	Minnesota	Superseded Minn. UB	Merged with Minn. (E)
	Minnesota	1951-1968	Minnesota	Merger of Minn. (E), & (U)	Continued in UM
UM	Minnesota	1968-1969	Minnesota	Superseded Minnesota EUB	Merged with Minn. (Meth.)

MISSOURI

Denomination	Conference	Dates	Location	How Formed	Conclusion
UB	1 Missouri	1854-1946	Missouri north of Mo. River; entire state of Mo. & N. Ark. after 1897; also La. after 1921	Missionary efforts from east	Continued in EUB
	3 S. Missouri	1885-1897	Southern Mo. & North Ark.	Superseded Southwestern Mo.	Merged with Missouri
	2 Southwestern Missouri	1881-1885	Southern Mo. & North Ark.	Division of Osage[20]	Superseded by S. Mo.
EUB	Missouri	1946-1968	Missouri, Ark., & Louisiana	Superseded Missouri UB	Continued in UM
UM	Missouri	1968	Missouri, Ark., & Louisiana	Superseded Missouri EUB	Merged with Mo. East, Mo. West, Little Rock, & Louisiana (Meth.)

MONTANA

Denomination	Conference	Dates	Location	How Formed	Conclusion
UB	Montana	1911-1946	Montana and western N.D.	Missionary effort from east	Continued in EUB
EV. CH.	Montana	1927-1946	Montana	Division of Nebraska[21]	Continued in EUB
EUB	Montana (E)	1946-1948	Montana	Superseded Montana EC	Merged with Montana (U)
	Montana (U)	1946-1948	Montana	Superseded Montana UB	Merged with Montana (E)
	Montana	1948-1968	Montana	Merger of Montana (E), & (U)	Continued in UM
UM	Montana	1968-1969	Montana	Superseded Montana EUB	Most of conf. left denomination; remainder united with Montana (Meth.) to form Yellowstone Conf.

NEBRASKA

Denomination	Conference	Dates	Location	How Formed	Conclusion
UB	2a East Nebraska	1878-1913	Eastern Nebraska	Division of Nebraska	Merged with N. & W. Neb. into Nebraska
	3 Elkhorn	1882-1885	Northern Nebraska	Division of W. Neb.	Merged with Dakota
	4 Elkhorn-Dakota	1885-1901	Northern Neb. & S.D.	Merger of Dakota[22] & Elkhorn	Superseded by N. Neb.
	1 Nebraska	1873-1878	Nebraska	Division of W. Des Moines[23] & Kansas[24]	Divided into E., & W. Neb.
	6 Nebraska	1913-1946	Nebraska and S.D.	Merger of E., W., & N. Neb.	Continued in EUB
	5 North Nebraska	1901-1913	N.E. Neb. and S.D.	Superseded Elkhorn-Dakota	Merged with E., & W. Neb. into Neb.
	2b West Nebraska	1878-1913	Western Nebraska	Division of Nebraska	Merged with E., & N. Neb. into Nebraska
EV. ASSN.	Nebraska	1879-1922	Eastern Nebraska	Division of Iowa[23]	Merged with Platte R. UE
	Platte River	1881-1912	Western Nebraska	Division of Nebraska	Merged with Nebraska
UE	Platte River	1894-1922	Nebraska and Montana	Formed by church division	Merged with Neb. EA
EV. CH.	Nebraska	1922-1946	Nebraska	Merger of Platte R. UE, & Nebraska EA	Continued in EUB
EUB	Nebraska (E)	1946-1951	Nebraska	Superseded Nebraska EC	Merged with Neb. (U)
	Nebraska (U)	1946-1951	Nebraska	Superseded Nebraska UB	Merged with Neb. (E)
	Nebraska	1951-1968	Nebraska	Merger of Neb. (E), & (U)	Continued in UM
UM	Nebraska	1968-1969	Nebraska	Superseded Nebraska EUB	Merged with Neb. (Meth.)

NEW MEXICO

Denomination	Conference	Dates	Location	How Formed	Conclusion
UB	New Mexico	1913-1928	New Mexico	Missionary work among Spanish-speaking people	Merged with Colorado to form Colo.-New Mexico[25]

---

[20] See Kansas. [21] See Nebraska. [22] See South Dakota. [23] See Iowa. [24] See Kansas. [25] See Colorado.

Denomi- nation	Conference	Dates	Location	How Formed	Conclusion

NEW JERSEY (See New York and Pennsylvania)

NEW YORK

Denomi- nation	Conference	Dates	Location	How Formed	Conclusion
UB	Erie	1861-1946	Western N.Y. and counties in Pa. east of Allegheny R. & north of Allegheny Conf.	Realignment of N.W. corner of Pa. & new territory in N.Y.	Continued in EUB
EV. ASSN.	2 Atlantic	1875-1922	Urban centers in eastern N.Y., N.J., east Pa., & Baltimore, Md.	Organized German work along Atlantic seaboard	Continued in EC
	1 New York	1849-1922	Western N.Y. and upper Canada (Canada dropped in 1864)	Division of East Pa.[26]	Continued in EC
EV. CH.	Atlantic	1922-1946	N.Y. City, Baltimore, Phil., & N.J.	Superseded Atlantic EA	Continued in EUB
EUB	New York	1922-1946	Western New York	Superseded New York EA	Continued in EUB
	Atlantic	1946-1957	N.Y. City, Baltimore, Phil., & N.J.	Superseded Atlantic EC	Merged with E.Pa. (E),[26] and New England[27]
	Erie	1946-1968	Western N.Y., counties in Pa. east of Allegheny R. & north of Allegheny Conf.	Superseded Erie UB	Continued in UM
UM	New York	1946-1968	Western New York	Superseded New York EC	Continued in UM
	Erie	1968-	Western N.Y., counties in Pa. east of Allegheny R. & north of Allegheny Conf.	Superseded Erie EUB	Continuing at present
	New York	1968	Western New York	Superseded New York EUB	Merged with Western N.Y. & Central N.Y. (Meth.)

NORTH DAKOTA

Denomi- nation	Conference	Dates	Location	How Formed	Conclusion
EV. ASSN.	North Dakota	1920-1922	North Dakota	Division of Dakota[28]	Continued in EC
EV. CH.	North Dakota	1922-1946	North Dakota	Superseded North Dak. EA	Continued in EUB
EUB	North Dakota	1946-1951	North Dakota	Superseded North Dakota EC	Merged with S.D.[28]

OHIO

Denomi- nation	Conference	Dates	Location	How Formed	Conclusion
UB	6 Auglaize	1857-1901	W. Central Ohio & E. Central Ind.	Superseded Maumee	Merged with Sandusky, & North Ohio
	9 Central Ohio	1878-1901	South central Ohio	Division of Scioto	Merged with Scioto to become S.E. Ohio
	10 East Ohio	1886-1946	Northeast Ohio	Merger of Muskingum & Western Reserve	Continued in EUB
	5a Maumee	1853-1857	E. Central Ind. & W. Central Ohio	Division of Miami	Superseded by Auglaize
	1 Miami	1810-1946	Southwest Ohio	Westward expansion	Continued in EUB
	2 Muskingum	1818-1886	East central Ohio	Division of Miami	Merged with Western Reserve to become East Ohio
	8 North Ohio	1862-1901	N.W. Ohio, N.E. Ind., S. Mich.	Realignment of Mich.,[29] St. Joseph,[30] & Sandusky	Merged with Sandusky, and Auglaize
	5b Ohio German	1853-1930	Ohio, Ind., Ill.	Organization of German Churches	Merged with English-speaking conferences
	4 Sandusky	1834-1946	N.W. Ohio & adjacent counties in Ind. and Mich.	Westward expansion	Continued in EUB
	3 Scioto	1825-1901	Southeast Ohio	Division of Miami	Merged with Central Ohio to become S.E. Ohio
	11 Southeast Ohio	1901-1946	Southeast Ohio	Merger of C. Ohio, & Scioto	Continued in EUB
	7 Western Reserve	1861-1886	West of Erie Conf. in Pa. & N.W. Ohio counties	Division of Erie[31]	Merged with Muskingum to become East Ohio
EV. ASSN.	Ohio	1839-1922	Ohio, Ind., Ill., Wis., & Mich.	Division of Western[32]	Continued in EC

---

[26] See Pennsylvania.   [27] See Massachusetts.   [28] See South Dakota.   [29] See Michigan.   [30] See Indiana.
[31] See New York.   [32] See Pennsylvania.

Denomi-nation	Conference	Dates	Location	How Formed	Conclusion
UE	Ohio	1892-1922	Ohio	Formed by church split	Continued in EC
EV. CH.	Ohio	1922-1946	Ohio	Merger of Ohio EA, & Ohio UE	Continued in EUB
EUB	Ohio (United)	1922-1923	Ohio (former UE)	Superseded Ohio UE	Merger with Ohio
	1a East Ohio	1946-1951	Northeast Ohio	Superseded East Ohio UB	Merged with part of Ohio
	1b Miami	1946-1951	Southwest Ohio	Superseded Miami UB	Merged with part of Ohio
	1c Ohio	1946-1951	Ohio	Superseded Ohio EC	Merged with East Ohio, S.E. Ohio, Sandusky, & Miami
	2a Ohio East	1951-1968	Northeast Ohio	Superseded E. Ohio UB	Continued in UM
	2b Ohio Miami	1951-1968	Southwest Ohio	Superseded Miami UB	Continued in UM
	2c Ohio Sandusky	1951-1968	Northwest Ohio	Superseded Sandusky UB	Continued in UM
	2d Ohio South-east	1951-1968	Southeast Ohio	Superseded S.E. Ohio UB	Continued in UM
	1d Sandusky	1946-1951	Northwest Ohio	Superseded Sandusky UB	Merged with part of Ohio to form Ohio Sandusky
	1e Southeast Ohio	1946-1951	Southeast Ohio	Superseded S.E. Ohio UB	Merged with part of Ohio to form Ohio Southeast
UM	Ohio East	1968-1970	Northeast Ohio	Superseded Ohio East EUB	Merging with Northeast Ohio, & Ohio (Meth.) to form East Ohio, & West Ohio effective June 1970
	Ohio Miami	1968-1970	Southwest Ohio	Superseded Miami EUB	
	Ohio Sandusky	1968-1970	Northwest Ohio	Superseded Ohio Sandusky EUB	
	Ohio Southeast	1968-1970	Southeast Ohio	Superseded Ohio South-east EUB	

OKLAHOMA

Denomi-nation	Conference	Dates	Location	How Formed	Conclusion
UB	Oklahoma	1898-1946	Oklahoma	Division of Ark. Valley[33]	Continued in EUB
EUB	Oklahoma	1946-1956	Oklahoma	Superseded Oklahoma UB	Merged with Texas[34] to form Okla.-Texas
	Oklahoma-Texas	1956-1968	Oklahoma and Texas	Merger of Okla., & Texas[34]	Continued in UM
UM	Oklahoma-Texas	1968	Oklahoma and Texas	Superseded Okla.-Texas EUB	Merged with Okla. (Meth.), with Texas churches going into appropriate confs.

OREGON

Denomi-nation	Conference	Dates	Location	How Formed	Conclusion
UB	Oregon	1855-1946	Ore., & Wash. territory west of Cascade range; after 1925 all of Wash. & Idaho	Formed by missionaries from east	Continued in EUB
EV. ASSN.	Oregon	1884-1922	Oregon	Division of Pacific[35]	Continued in EC
	Oregon (U)	1891-1894	Oregon and Wash.	Formed by church division	Continued in UE
UE	Oregon	1893-1922	Oregon and Wash.	Superseded Oregon (U)	Continued in EC
EV. CH.	Oregon	1922-1935	Oregon	Superseded Oregon EA	Merged with Washington[36]
	Oregon (U)	1922-1923	Oregon and Washington	Superseded Oregon UE	Merged with Oregon
	Oregon-Wash.	1935-1946	Oregon and Washington	Merger of Oregon, & Washington	Continued in EUB
EUB	Oregon	1946-1955	Oregon and coastal Wash.	Superseded Oregon UB	Merged with Oregon-Wash.
	Oregon-Wash.	1946-1955	Oregon and Washington	Superseded Oregon-Wash. EC	Merged with Oregon to form Pacific Northwest
	Pacific N.W.	1955-1968	Oregon and Washington	Merger of Ore., & Ore.-Wash.	Continued in UM (more than half of churches split to form the Ev. Church of North America)
UM	Pacific N.W.	1968-	Oregon and Washington	Superseded Pacific N.W. EUB	Will merge into Pacific N.W., Oregon, & Idaho (Meth.); no exact date set

PENNSYLVANIA

Denomi-nation	Conference	Dates	Location	How Formed	Conclusion
UB	2 Allegheny	1839-1946	Western Pennsylvania	Division of Pennsylvania	Continued in EUB
	6 East German	1869-1877	German work east of Allegheny Mts. in Md. and Pa.	Division of E. Pa.	Superseded by Eastern 1877

[33] See Kansas.   [34] See Texas.   [35] See California.   [36] See Washington.

Denomination	Conference	Dates	Location	How Formed	Conclusion
	9 East German	1885-1897	German work east of Allegheny Mts. to Atlantic Ocean	Superseded Eastern German	Superseded by Eastern 1897
	3a East Penna.	1846-1901	English work east of Susquehanna River	Division of Pennsylvania	Merged with Eastern 1901 to form Eastern Pa.
	12 East Penna.	1905-1946	English work east of Susquehanna River	Superseded Eastern Pa.	Continued in EUB
	7 Eastern	1877-1881	German work east of Allegheny Mts. to Atlantic Ocean	Superseded East German 1877	Superseded by Eastern German
	10 Eastern	1897-1901	German work east of Allegheny Mts. to Atlantic Ocean	Superseded East German 1897	Merged with E.Pa. to form Eastern Pa.
	8 Eastern German	1881-1885	German work east of Allegheny Mts. to Atlantic Ocean	Superseded Eastern	Superseded by East German
	11 Eastern Penna.	1901-1905	Included all work east of Susquehanna River	Merger of Eastern, & East Pennsylvania	Superseded by East Pa.
	5 Erie	1853-1861	N.E. Ohio, Crawford, Erie, Warren, & part of Mercer counties, Pa.	Division of Muskingum[37] & part of territory allotted to Allegheny	Superseded by Western Reserve[37]
	1 Pennsylvania	1830-1846	Pennsylvania & Frederick Co. Md.	Division of Original[38]	Superseded by East Pa., & West Pa.
	4 Pennsylvania	1850-1946	Pa. west of Susquehanna & east of Juniata River; added Md. Conf. territory in 1901	Superseded W. Pa.	Continued in EUB
	3b West Penna.	1846-1850	West of Susquehanna & east of Juniata River	Division of Pennsylvania	Superseded by Pa. 1850
EV. ASSN.	6 Central Pa.	1859-1894	West of east branch of Susquehanna River in Md. & Pa., & east of Allegheny Mts.	Superseded West Pa.	Continued in UE
	4 East Penna.	1840-1922	N.Y., and Pa. east of Susquehanna River	Superseded Eastern	Continued in UE
	2a Eastern	1827-1839	Pa. east of Susquehanna River, N. Y., and upper Canada	Division of Original	Superseded by East Pa., and West Pa.
	7 Erie	1876-1922	German work in N.E. Ohio, western Pa., & two churches in N. Y.	Organization of German work	Absorbed by Ohio,[39] Pittsburgh, & New York[40]
	1 Original	1807-1827	Pa., Md., N. Y., & Ohio	Organization of church	Superseded by Eastern, & Western
	5 Pittsburgh	1852-1893	Pa. west of Allegheny Mts.	Realignment of W. Pa., & Ohio[39]	Continued in UE
	2b Western	1827-1839	All land west of Allegheny Mts.	Division of Original	Superseded by Ohio, & W.Pa.
	3 West Penna.	1839-1859	All of Pa. west of Susquehanna R., Carroll & Wash. Co., Md., & Shenandoah Valley, Va.	Realignment of Eastern, & Western	Superseded by Central Pa.
UE	Central Pa.	1894-1922	West of east branch of Susquehanna R. in Md. and Pa.	Superseded Central Pa. EA in church split	Continued in EC
	East Penna.	1894-1922	East of Susquehanna River	Superseded E. Pa. EA in church split	Continued in EC
	Pittsburgh	1893-1922	West of Allegheny Mountains	By church split; superseded Pittsburgh EA	Continued in EC
EV. CH.	East Penna.	1922-1946	East of Susquehanna R. in Pa.	Superseded E. Pa. EA	Continued in EUB
	East Penna. (United)	1922-1929	UE work east of Susquehanna R. in Pa.	Superseded E. Pa. UE	Merged with E.Pa.
	Pittsburgh	1922-1946	West of Allegheny Mts. in Pa.	Merger of Pittsburgh UE, & Pittsburgh EA	Continued in EUB

[37] See Ohio.   [38] See Maryland.   [39] See Ohio.   [40] See New York.

Denomination	Conference	Dates	Location	How Formed	Conclusion
EUB	1a Allegheny	1946-1951	West of Juniata R. & south of Erie Conf. territory UB	Superseded Allegheny UB	Superseded by Western Pa.
	1b Central Penna.	1946-1954	Ev. work west of Susquehanna R. east of Allegheny Mts. into Md. and Pa.	Superseded C. Pa. EC	Superseded by Susquehanna
	1c East Penna. (E)	1946-1957	Evangelical work east of Susquehanna River	Superseded E. Pa. EC	Superseded by Northeastern
	1d East Penna. (U)	1946-1957	UB work east of Susquehanna R.	Superseded E. Pa. UB	Superseded by E. Penna.
	3a East Penna.	1957-1963	UB work in Pa. east of Susquehanna R.	Superseded E. Pa. (U)	Superseded by Eastern
	4 Eastern	1963-1968	All work east of Susquehanna R.	Merger of E. Pa., & Northeastern	Continued in UM
	3b Northeastern	1957-1963	Evangelical work east of Susquehanna R. in Pa., New Eng., N.J., and N.Y. City	Merger of New England,[41] Atlantic,[42] & E. Pa. (E)	Superseded by Eastern
	1e Pennsylvania	1946-1964	UB work west of Susquehanna R. & east of Juniata R. in Md. & Pa.	Superseded Penna. UB	Superseded by Susquehanna
	1f Pittsburgh	1946-1951	West of Allegheny Mts. in Pa.	Superseded Pittsburgh EC	Superseded by Western Pa.
	5 Susquehanna	1964-1968	All work in Md., & Pa. west of Susquehanna and east of Juniata Rivers or its equiv.	Merger of C. Pa., & Pa.	Continued in UM
	2 Western Pa.	1951-1968	All work west of Allegheny Mts. in Pa.	Merger of Allegheny, & Pittsburgh	Continued in UM
UM	Eastern	1968-1970	New Eng. states, N.J., & eastern Pa.	Superseded Eastern EUB	Merging with N.E. Juris. Confs. partly in 1968 & remainder in 1969
	Susquehanna	1968-1970	Md. and Central Pa.	Superseded Susquehanna EUB	Merge with C.Pa. & Baltimore (Meth.) 1969
	Western Pa.	1968-1970	Western Pa.	Superseded Western Pa. EUB	Merge with C.Pa., & W. Pa. (Meth.) 1969

RHODE ISLAND (See Massachusetts and Pennsylvania)

SOUTH DAKOTA

Denomination	Conference	Dates	Location	How Formed	Conclusion
UB	Dakota	1871-1885	Western Iowa & S. Dakota	Division of W. Des Moines[43]	United with Elkhorn[44]
EV. ASSN.	Dakota	1884-1920	North and South Dakota	Division of Minnesota[45]	Divided into N.D., & S.D.
	South Dakota	1920-1922	South Dakota	Division of Dakota	Continued in EC
EV. CH.	South Dakota	1922-1946	South Dakota	Superseded S.D. EA	Continued in EUB
EUB	Dakota	1951-1968	South Dakota & North Dakota	Merger of N.D., & S.D.	Continued in UM
	South Dakota	1946-1951	South Dakota	Superseded S.D. EC	Merged with N.D.
UM	Dakota	1968-1969	North & South Dakota	Superseded Dakota EUB	Mreged with North Dakota, & South Dakota (Meth.)

TENNESSEE

Denomination	Conference	Dates	Location	How Formed	Conclusion
UB	2a Chicamauga	1896-1913	Work among Negroes in Tenn. & states to south	Missionary work among Negroes in south	Dissolved
	2b East Tenn.	1896-1918	Tenn. east of Cumberland Mts.	Division of Tenn.	Merged with W.Tenn.
	1 Tennessee	1866-1896	Bounded by Cumberland & Paint Rock Mts.; later all of state east of Nashville	Missionary effort of Va.	Divided into Tenn. River, & East Tenn.
	4 Tennessee	1918-1946	Tenn. east of Nashville; added Ky. work 1921	Merger of W. Tenn., & E. Tenn.	Continued in EUB
	2c Tenn. River	1896-1897	Tenn. west of Cumberland Mts.	Division of Tennessee	Superseded by W. Tenn.

---

[41] See Massachusetts. [42] See New York. [43] See Iowa. [44] See Nebraska. [45] See Minnesota.

Denomination	Conference	Dates	Location	How Formed	Conclusion
	3 West Tenn.	1897-1918	Tenn. west of Cumberland Mts.	Superseded Tenn. River	Merged with E. Tenn.
EUB	Tennessee	1846-1968	Entire state east of Nashville; and Ky. until 1955.	Superseded Tenn. UB	Continued in UM
UM	Tennessee	1968-1969	Tennessee	Superseded Tenn. EUB	Merged with Tenn., Holston (Meth.)

TEXAS

Denomination	Conference	Dates	Location	How Formed	Conclusion
UB	North Texas	1908-1913	N.W. Texas, Okla. Panhandle, & New Mexico	Missionary effort from east	Abosrbed by Oklahoma[46]
EV. ASSN.	Texas	1887-1922	Texas	Missionary effort	Continued in EC
EV. CH.	Texas	1922-1946	Texas	Superseded Texas EA	Continued in EUB
EUB	Texas	1946-1956	Texas	Superseded Texas EC	Merged with Okla.-Texas[46]

VIRGINIA

Denomination	Conference	Dates	Location	How Formed	Conclusion
UB	Virginia	1830-1946	Shenandoah Valley, W.Va., & W. Md. (W.Va. withdrew 1857 & Md. 1887)	Division of Original[47]	Continued in EUB
EUB	Virginia	1946-1968	Shenandoah Valley & eastern and panhandle section of W.Va.	Superseded Virginia UB	Continued in UM
UM	Virginia	1968-1970	Shenandoah Valley & eastern and panhandle section of W.Va.	Superseded Virginia EUB	Merge with Baltimore, W. Va., & Va. (Meth.)

WASHINGTON

Denomination	Conference	Dates	Location	How Formed	Conclusion
UB	1 Cascade	1865-1873	Washington territory north & east of Cascade Range	Division of Oregon[48]	Superseded by Walla Walla
	3 Columbia River	1893-1925	Oregon & Wash. east of Cascade Mts. & Idaho	Superseded Walla Walla	Merged with Oregon[48]
	2 Walla Walla	1873-1893	Oregon & Wash. east of Cascade Mts., & Idaho Terr.	Superseded Cascade	Superseded by Columbia R.
EV. ASSN.	Washington	1896-1922	Washington	Division of Oregon[48]	Continued in EC
EV. CH.	Washington	1922-1925	Washington	Superseded Wash. EA	Merged with Oregon[48]

WEST VIRGINIA

Denomination	Conference	Dates	Location	How Formed	Conclusion
UB	Parkersburg	1858-1897	W.Va. west of Allegheny Mts. & Western Md.	Division of Virginia[49]	Superseded by W.Va.
	West Virginia	1897-1946	W.Va. west of Allegheny Mts. & Western Md.	Superseded Parkersburg UB	Continued in EUB
EUB	West Virginia	1946-1968	W.Va. west of Allegheny Mts. & Western Md.	Superseded W.Va. UB	Continued in UM
UM	West Virginia	1968-1969	W.Va. west of Allegheny Mts. & Western Md.	Superseded W.Va. EUB	Merged with W.Va. (Meth.)

WISCONSIN

Denomination	Conference	Dates	Location	How Formed	Conclusion
UB	Fox River	1861-1885	Northern Wisconsin	Division of Wisconsin	United with Wisconsin
	Wisconsin	1858-1946	Entire state after 1885	Division of Rock River[50]	Continued in EUB
EV. ASSN.	Wisconsin	1856-1922	Wisconsin	Division of Illinois[50]	Continued in EC
EV. CH.	Wisconsin	1922-1946	Wisconsin	Superseded Wisconsin EA	Continued in EUB
EUB	Wisconsin (E)	1946-1951	Wisconsin	Superseded Wisconsin EC	United with Wisconsin (E)
	Wisconsin (U)	1946-1951	Wisconsin	Superseded Wisconsin UB	United with Wisconsin (U)
	Wisconsin	1951-1968	Wisconsin	Merger of Wisconsin (E), & (U)	Continued in UM
UM	Wisconsin	1968-1970	Wisconsin	Superseded Wisconsin EUB	United with East Wis., & West Wis. (Meth.) to form Wisconsin 1970

WYOMING (See Colorado)

---

[46] See Oklahoma.   [47] See Maryland.   [48] See Oregon.   [49] See Virginia.   [50] See Illinois.

STATISTICAL SUMMARY
OF EDUCATIONAL INSTITUTIONS

related to The United Methodist Church (1970-1971)

Institution	Faculty	Enrollment
Universities		
American University (Washington, D. C.)	472	8,909
Boston University (Boston, Mass.)	1,700	17,800
Duke University (Durham, N. C.)	1,037	6,977
Emory University (Atlanta, Ga.)	815	5,277
Northwestern University (Evanston, Ill.)	2,327	16,259
Southern Methodist University (Dallas, Tex.)	642	8,363
Syracuse University (Syracuse, N. Y.)	1,428	12,657
University of Denver (Denver, Colo.)	527	7,623
Total—Universities	8,948	83,865
Schools of Theology		
Boston University School of Theology (Boston, Mass.)	31	440
Drew University School of Theology (Madison, N J.)	25	159
Duke University, The Divinity School (Durham, N. C.)	30	290
Emory University, Candler School of Theology (Atlanta, Ga.)	31	479
Evangelical Theological Seminary (Naperville, Ill.)	16	122
Gammon Theological Seminary[1] (Atlanta, Ga.)	14	69
Garrett Theological Seminary (Evanston, Ill.)	40	415
Iliff School of Theology (Denver, Colo.)	16	183
Methodist Theological School in Ohio (Delaware, Ohio)	21	174
Perkins School of Theology, Southern Methodist University (Dallas, Tex.)	28	370
Saint Paul School of Theology Methodist (Kansas City, Mo.)	25	213
School of Theology at Claremont (Claremont, Calif.)	35	353
United Theological Seminary (Dayton, Ohio)	23	236
Wesley Theological Seminary (Washington, D. C.)	24	262
Total—Schools of Theology	359	3,765

[1] Gammon is part of Interdenominational Theological Center. Statistics shown are for Gammon only.

Institution	Faculty	Enrollment
Senior Colleges		
Adrian College (Adrian, Mich.)	92	1,529
Alaska Methodist University (Anchorage, Alaska)	67	571
Albion College (Albion, Mich.)	123	1,858
Albright College (Reading, Pa.)	93	1,211
Allegheny College (Meadville, Pa.)	120	1,610
Athens College (Athens, Ala.)	55	1,171
Baker University (Baldwin City, Kan.)	70	884
Baldwin-Wallace College (Berea, Ohio)	155	2,697
Bennett College (Greensboro, N. C.)	74	656
Bethune-Cookman College (Daytona Beach, Fla.)	59	1,239
Birmingham-Southern College (Birmingham, Ala.)	89	1,044
Centenary College of Louisiana (Shreveport, La.)	92	947
Central Methodist College (Fayette, Mo.)	65	907
Claflin College (Orangeburg, S. C.)	42	701
Clark College (Atlanta, Ga.)	103	1,024
Columbia College (Columbia, S. C.)	59	878
Cornell College (Mount Vernon, Iowa)	86	1,003
Dakota Wesleyan University (Mitchell, S. D.)	44	758
DePauw University (Greencastle, Ind.)	163	2,419
Dickinson College (Carlisle, Pa.)	107	1,585
Dillard University[2] (New Orleans, La.)	95	915
Drew University (Madison, N. J.)	123	1,493
Emory and Henry College (Emory, Va.)	56	831
Florida Southern College (Lakeland, Fla.)	90	1,442
Greensboro College (Greensboro, N. C.)	52	661

Institution	Faculty	Enrollment
Hamline University (St. Paul, Minn.)	85	1,261
Hawaii Loa College (Kaneohe, Hawaii)	14	94
Hendrix College (Conway, Ark.)	49	947
High Point College (High Point, N. C.)	62	1,111
Huntingdon College (Montgomery, Ala.)	53	812
Huston-Tillotson College[2] (Austin, Tex.)	42	701
Illinois Wesleyan University (Bloomington, Ill.)	131	1,650
Indiana Central College (Indianapolis, Ind.)	67	1,599
Iowa Wesleyan College (Mount Pleasant, Iowa)	55	834
Kansas Wesleyan (Salina, Kan.)	40	722
Kentucky Wesleyan College (Owensboro, Ky.)	62	818
LaGrange College (LaGrange, Ga.)	42	634
Lambuth College (Jackson, Tenn.)	62	819
Lawrence University (Appleton, Wis.)	133	1,371
Lebanon Valley College (Annville, Pa.)	69	976
Lycoming College (Williamsport, Pa.)	97	1,480
MacMurray College (Jacksonville, Ill.)	71	930
McKendree College (Lebanon, Ill.)	35	532
McMurry College (Abilene, Tex.)	85	1,501
Methodist College (Fayetteville, N. C.)	54	936
Millsaps College (Jackson, Miss.)	69	937
Morningside College (Sioux City, Iowa)	74	1,317
Mount Union College (Alliance, Ohio)	95	1,256
Nebraska Wesleyan University (Lincoln, Nebr.)	99	1,278
North Carolina Wesleyan College (Rocky Mount, N.C.)	46	648
North Central College (Naperville, Ill.)	64	826
Ohio Northern University (Ada, Ohio)	163	2,228
Ohio Wesleyan University (Delaware, Ohio)	172	2,461
Oklahoma City University (Oklahoma City, Okla.)	131	3,622

[2] Also related to the United Church of Christ.

Institution	Faculty	Enrollment
Otterbein College (Westerville, Ohio)	98	1,430
Paine College[3] (Augusta, Ga.)	62	680
Pfeiffer College (Misenheimer, N. C.)	65	814
Philander Smith College (Little Rock, Ark.)	46	635
Randolph-Macon College (Ashland, Va.)	67	845
Randolph-Macon Woman's College (Lynchburg, Va.)	86	813
Rocky Mountain College[4] (Billings, Mont.)	45	558
Rust College (Holly Springs, Miss.)	49	573
Scarritt College (Nashville, Tenn.)	20	169
Simpson College (Indianola, Iowa)	72	907
Southwestern College (Winfield, Kan.)	47	710
Southwestern University (Georgetown, Tex.)	65	882
Tennessee Wesleyan College (Athens, Tenn.)	47	699
Texas Wesleyan College (Fort Worth, Tex.)	72	1,416
Union College (Barbourville, Ky.)	58	849
United States International University (San Diego, Calif.)	No Report	
University of Evansville (Evansville, Ind.)	167	3,819
University of Puget Sound (Tacoma, Wash.)	155	3,099
University of the Pacific (Stockton, Calif.)	343	3,843
Virginia Wesleyan College (Norfolk, Va.)	31	474
Wesleyan College (Macon, Ga.)	53	515
West Virginia Wesleyan College (Buckhannon, W. Va.)	108	1,771
Western Maryland College (Westminster, Md.)	95	1,092
Westmar College (LeMars, Iowa)	65	1,201
Westminster College[4] (Salt Lake City, Utah)	38	798
Wiley College (Marshall, Tex.)	44	460
Willamette University (Salem, Oregon)	129	1,610
Wofford College (Spartanburg, S. C.)	63	1,007
Total—Senior Colleges	6,585	96,004

[3] Also related to the C.M.E. Church.

[4] Also related to the United Church of Christ and to the United Presbyterian Church in the U.S.A.

STATISTICAL SUMMARY OF EDUCATIONAL INSTITUTIONS

Institution	Faculty	Enrollment
Junior Colleges		
Andrew College (Cuthbert, Ga.)	19	361
Brevard College (Brevard, N. C.)	45	663
Centenary College for Women (Hackettstown, N. J.)	70	688
Ferrum Junior College (Ferrum, Va.)	52	1,067
Green Mountain College (Poultney, Vt.)	47	715
Hiwassee College (Madisonville, Tenn.)	32	627
Kendall College (Evanston, Ill.)	59	1,156
Lindsey Wilson College (Columbia, Ky.)	34	515
Lon Morris College (Jacksonville, Tex.)	20	407
Louisburg College (Louisburg, N. C.)	48	806
Martin College (Pulaski, Tenn.)	23	330
Morristown College (Morristown, Tenn.)	12	159
Oxford College of Emory University (Oxford, Ga.)	32	464
Reinhardt College (Waleska, Ga.)	19	392
Shenandoah College (Winchester, Va.)	32	422
Spartanburg Junior College (Spartanburg, S. C.)	36	798
Sue Bennett College (London, Ky.)	19	268
Wesley College (Dover, Del.)	46	805
Wood Junior College (Mathiston, Miss.)	17	206
Young Harris College (Young Harris, Ga.)	22	370
Total—Junior Colleges	**684**	**11,219**
Secondary Schools		
Allen High School (Asheville, N. C.)	10	64

Institution	Faculty	Enrollment
Beverly Boarding School (Beverly, Ky.)	22	322
Boylan-Haven-Mather Academy (Camden, S. C.)	17	97
Harwood School (Albuquerque, N. M.)	12	61
Hillcrest Christian College (Medicine Hat, Alberta, Canada)	5	27
Holding Institute (Laredo, Tex.)	19	191
Kents Hill School (Kents Hill, Maine)	28	296
Lydia Patterson Institute (El Paso, Tex.)	28	536
McCurdy School (Santa Cruz, N. M.)	38	432
Navajo Methodist Mission School (Farmington, N. M.)	36	180
Pennington School (Pennington, N. J.)	22	254
Randolph-Macon Academy (Front Royal, Va.)	24	264
Robinson School (San Juan, Puerto Rico)	37	475
Tilton School (Tilton, N. H.)	30	280
Vashti School (Thomasville, Ga.)	12	85
Wyoming Seminary (Kingston, Pa.)	64	698
Total—Secondary Schools	**404**	**4,262**
Other Schools		
Meharry Medical College (Nashville, Tenn.)	159	487
Port Arthur College (Port Arthur, Tex.)	14	304
Sager-Brown School (Baldwin, La.)	24	163
Shenandoah Conservatory of Music (Winchester, Va.)	24	233
Total—Other Schools	**221**	**1,187**
GRAND TOTALS	**17,201**	**200,302**

PRESIDENTS
OF EDUCATIONAL INSTITUTIONS, U. S. A.

(This listing is incomplete, but additional information was not available to the compiler, and the material given will be helpful.)

Institution	President	Tenure
Adrian College Adrian, Michigan 49221	Asa Mahan	1859-1864
	John McEldowney	1865-1867
	Asa Mahan	1867-1871
	G. B. McElroy	1873-1880
	A. H. Lowrie, Acting	1871-1873
	M. B. Taylor, Acting	1880-1882
	D. S. Stephens	1882-1888
	J. F. McCulloch	1888-1893
	D. C. Thomas	1893-1898
	David Jones	1898-1902
	T. H. Lewis	1902-1904
	B. W. Anthony	1904-1915
	A. F. Hess	1915-1917
	G. H. Miller, Acting	1917-1918
	Harlan L. Feeman	1918-1940
	Samuel J. Harrison	1940-1951
	Edmund Babbitt, Acting	1951-1954
	John H. Dawson	1954-
Alaska Methodist University Anchorage, Alaska 99504	Frederick P. McGinnis	1959-1970
	William E. Davis, Acting	1970-
Albion College Albion, Michigan 49224	Charles Franklin Stockwell	1843-1846
	Clark Titus Hinman	1846-1853
	Ira Mayhew	1853-1854
	Thomas Henry Sinex	1854-1864
	George B. Jocelyn	1864-1869
	J. LaGrange McKown	1869-1870
	John McEldowney	1869-1870
	William B. Silber	1870-1871
	George B. Jocelyn	1871-1877
	Lewis Ransom Fiske	1877-1897
	John Paul Ashley	1897-1901
	Samuel Dickie	1901-1921
	John Wesley Laird	1921-1924
	Frederick S. Goodrich	1924-
	John L. Seaton	1924-1945
	William W. Whitehouse	1945-1960
	Louis William Norris	1960-1970
	Bernard T. Lomas	1970-
Albright College Reading, Pennsylvania		
Central Pennsylvania College Myerstown, Pa.	Aaron E. Cobble	1887-1902
Albright College Myerstown, Pa.	James D. Woodring	1902-1908
	Clellan A. Bowman, Acting	1908-1909
	John F. Dunlap	1909-1915
	Levi C. Hunt	1915-1923
	Clellan A. Bowman	1923-1928
Schuylkill College Reading, Pa.	Warren F. Teel	1923-1928

Institution	President	Tenure
Albright College Reading, Pa.	Warren F. Teel	1928-1932
	John Warren Klein, Acting	1932-1933
	John Warren Klein	1933-1938
	Harry V. Masters	1938-1965
	Arthur LeRoy Schultz	1965-
Allegheny College Meadville, Pennsylvania 19604	Timothy Alden	1815-1831
	Martin Ruter	1833-1837
	Homer J. Clark	1837-1847
	John Barker	1847-1860
	George Loomis	1860-1874
	Lucius H. Bugbee	1875-1882
	David H. Wheeler	1883-1888
	Wilbur G. Williams	1888-1889
	David H. Wheeler	1889-1893
	William H. Crawford	1893-1920
	Frederick Whitlo Hixson	1920-1924
	James Beebe	1926-1930
	William P. Tolley	1931-1942
	John R. Schultz	1942-1947
	Louis T. Benezet	1948-1955
	Lawrence L. Pelletier	1955-
Allen High School Asheville, North Carolina 28801	Alsie B. Dole	1887-1920
	Edith Mitchell	1920-1921
	Louisa A. Bell	1921-1937
	Carmen Lowry	1938-1941
	Julia Titus	1941-1945
	Claire Lennon	1945-1957
	Ruth M. Walther	1957-
The American University Washington, D. C.	John Fletcher Hurst	1891-1902
	Charles Cardwell McCabe	1902-1906
	Wilbur Leroy Davidson	1906-1907
	Franklin E. Hamilton	1907-1916
	John William Hamilton	1916-1922
	Lucius Charles Clark	1922-1932
	Edwin Holt Hughes	1932-1933
	Joseph M. Gray	1933-1940
	Edward William Engel	1940-1941
	Paul Franklin Douglass	1941-1951
	James Jacob Robbins	1951-1952
	Hurst Robins Anderson	1952-1968
	George Howard Williams	1968-
Andrew College Cuthbert, Georgia	John H. Grant, Pro tem	1854-
	Augustus A. Allen	1855-
	Weyman H. Potter	1855-1857
	Oliver P. Anthony	1857-1859
	James D. Wade	1863-1865
	C. C. Andrews	
	A. L. Hamilton	1865-1871
	Abner Flewellyn	1871-1875
	John Boynkin MaGehee	1871-
	A. L. Hamilton	187(6 or 7)-1881
	Howard W. Key	1881-1891
	P. S. Twitty	1891-1895
	Homer Bush	1895-1906
	J. W. Malone	1906-1918
	Frank G. Branch	1918-1929
	S. C. Oliff	1929-1951
	Albert W. Ray	1951-1955
	George W. Gambill	1956-

Institution	President	Tenure
Athens College	R. H. Rivers	1843-1849
Athens, Alabama	Benjamin H. Hubbard	1849-1852
35611	Smith W. Moore	1852-1853
	Isham R. Finley	1853-1855
	George E. Naff	1855-1858
	Mrs. J. Hamilton Childs	1858-1867
	James M. Wright	1867-1873
	James K. Armstrong	1873-1877
	C. L. Smith	1877-1883
	William A. Rogers	1883-1884
	Mrs. E. L. Thach	1884-
	M. G. Williams	1885-1892
	Howard Key	1892-1893
	V. O. Hawkins	1893-1895
	Z. A. Parker	1895-1898
	H. W. Browder	1898-1900
	H. G. Davis	1900-1902
	E. M. Glenn	1902-1904
	Mary Norman Moore	1904-1916
	B. B. Glasgow	1916-1925
	Mary Moore McCoy	1925-1930
	R. Naylor	1930-1949
	Perry B. James	1949-1959
	Virgil B. McCain	1959-1966
	Guy E. Snavely	1966-
	Frank N. Philpot	1966-
	Luther L. Gobbel	
	Sidney E. Sandridge	
Baker University	Werter Renick Davis	1858-1862
Baldwin City,	George Washington Paddock	1862-1864
Kansas 66006	Leonard Leidy Hartman	1864-1865
	John Wesley Locke	1865-1866
	John Wesley Horner	1866-1867
	Elial Jay Rice	1867-1868
	John Alexander Simpson	1869-
	Patterson McNutt	1870-1871
	Robert Latimore Harford	1871-1873
	Samuel S. Weatherby	1873-1874
	Joseph J. Denison	1874-1879
	William Henry Sweet	1879-1886
	Hillary Asbury Gobin	1886-1890
	William Alfred Quayle	1890-1894
	Lemuel Herbert Murlin	1894-1911
	Wilbur Nesbitt Mason	1911-1917
	Samuel Alexander Lough	1917-1921
	Osmon Grant Markham	1921-1922
	Wallace Bruce Fleming	1922-1936
	Nelson Paxson Horn	1936-1956
	William John Scarborough	1956-1966
	James Edward Doty	1966-

Institution	President	Tenure
Baldwin-Wallace College		
Berea, Ohio 44017		
Baldwin Institute	Holden Dwight	1846-
	Alfred Holbrook	1847-
	Lorenzo Warner	1847-1848
	William L. Harris	1848-1851
	Owen T. Reeves	1851-
	Gershom M. Barber	1851-1853
	Alexander Nelson	1853-1855
Baldwin University	John Wheeler	1855-1870
	William D. Godman	1870-1875
	Aaron Schuyler	1875-1885
	William Kepler	1885-1886
	Joseph E. Stubbs	1886-1894
	Millard F. Warner	1894-1899
	R. M. Freshwater	1899-1902
	G. A. Reeder	1902-1905
	George B. Rogers	1905-1907
	George F. Collier	1907-1909
	Robert L. Waggoner	1909-1911
	G. A. Reeder	1911-1913

Institution	President	Tenure
German Wallace College	William Nast	1865-1894
	Karl Riemenschneider	1894-1908
	Edwin Havighorst	1908-1910
	Arthur L. Breslich	1910-1913
Baldwin-Wallace College	Arthur L. Breslich	1913-1918
	Albert B. Storms	1918-1933
	Delo C. Grover	1933-1934
	Louis C. Wright	1934-1948
	Albert Riemenschneider	1948-1949
	John L. Knight	1949-1954
	Harry J. Smith	1954-1955
	Alfred B. Bonds, Jr.	1956-
Bennett College	W. J. Parkinson	1873-1875
Greensboro, N. C.	Edward O. Thayer	1875-1881
27420	W. F. Steele	1881-1889
	C. N. Grandison	1889-1892
	J. D. Chavis	1892-1905
	Silas A. Peeler	1905-1913
	James E. Wallace	1913-1916
	Frank Trigg	1917-1926
	David D. Jones	1926-1955
	Willa B. Player	1955-1966
	Isaac H. Miller, Jr.	1966-
Bethune-Cookman College	Mary McLeod Bethune	1904-1942
	James A. Colston	1942-1946
Daytona Beach,	Mary McLeod Bethune	1946-1947
Florida 32015	Richard Vernon Moore	1947-
Beverly Boarding School	Donald Scott	
Beverly, Ky. 40913		

Birmingham-
Southern College
Birmingham,
Alabama 35204

Institution	President	Tenure
Southern University	W. M. Wightman	1858-1867
	Edward Wadsworth	1867-1870
	Allen Skeen Andrews	1870-1875
	Luther M. Smith	1875-1879
	Josiah Lewis	1879-1881
	F. M. Peterson	1881-1883
	Allen S. Andrews	1883-1894
	John O. Keener	1894-1899
	S. M. Hosmer	1899-1910
	Andrew Sledd	1910-1914
	Charles A. Rush	1914-1917
	C. C. Daniel	1917-1918
Birmingham College	Z. A. Parker	1898-1899
	E. M. Glenn	1899-1902
	John S. Robertson	1902-1903
	Anson West	1903-1904
	John R. Turner	1904-1906
	James H. McCoy	1906-1910
	John D. Simpson	1910-1916
	Thornwell Haynes	1916-1917
	E. L. Colebeck, Acting	1917-1918
Birmingham-Southern	C. C. Daniel	1918-1921
	Guy E. Snavely	1921-1938
	Raymond R. Paty	1938-1942
	George R. Stuart, Acting	1942-1955
	Guy E. Snavely, Chancellor	1955-1957
	Henry King Stanford	1957-1962
	Howard M. Phillips	1963-1968
	Robert F. Henry	1968-1969
	Charles D. Hounshell	1969-1972
	Ralph M. Tanner	1972-

Boston University
Boston,
Massachusetts

Institution	President	Tenure
Newbury Biblical Institute (1839-1846) Newbury, Vermont		
General Biblical Institute Concord, New Hampshire	Elijah Hedding	1847-1866
Boston University	William Fairfield Warren	1867-1903
	William Edwards Huntington	1904-1911
	Lemuel Herbert Murlin	1911-1925
	Daniel Lash Marsh	1926-1951
	Harold Claude Case	1951-1967
	Arland Frederick Christ-Janer	1967-
Boylan-Haven-Mather Academy Camden, South Carolina 29020	Barbara Boultinghouse	
Brevard College Brevard, North Carolina		
Owl Hollow (or Happy Home) Academy	Robert Laban Abernethy	1853-1858
Rutherford Academy	Robert Laban Abernethy	1858-1861
Rutherford Seminary	Robert Laban Abernethy	1861-1870
Rutherford College	Robert Laban Abernethy	1870-1894
	William E. Abernethy	1894-1899
	Charles Clinton Weaver	1900-1903
	Alonzo Carlton Reynolds	1903-1905
	Joseph Henry West	1905-
	Loy Durant Thompson	1905-1907
	William Walter Peele	1907-1909
	Irving Bascom McKay	1909-1911
	Melvin Taliafero Hinshaw	1911-1925
	William Foster Starnes	1925-1927
	Edgar Park Billups	1927-1931
	Lucius Stacy Weaver	1932-1933
Weaverville College	James Americus Reagan, M.D.	1872-1875
	James S. Kennedy	1875-1878
	W. C. McCarthy	1878-1880
	Elbert Mitchell Goolsby	1880-1883
	Daniel Atkins	1883-1887
	S. R. Trawick	1887-1888
	J. Frank Austin	1888-1889
	Marion A. Yost	1889-1898
	George F. Kirby	1898-1901
	James M. Robeson	1901-1905
	Logan Berge Abernethy	1905-1908
	Marion A. Yost	1908-1909
	Olin Sandeford Dean	1909-1912
Weaver College (same as above school)	W. A. Newell	1912-1916
	John Rutland	1916-1917
	Eugene Blake	1917-1919
	David S. Hogg	1919-1920
	Andrew Martin Norton	1920-1923
	Carl Hoyt Trowbridge	1923-1934
Brevard Institute	Fitch Taylor	1895-1903
	E. E. Bishop	1903-1907
	C. H. Trowbridge	1907-1923
	Oliver Hamilton Orr	1923-1927
	James Fielding Winton	1927-1932
	Daisy Ritter	1932-1933
Brevard College	Eugene Jarvis Coltrane	1934-1950
	George Brinkmann Ehlhardt	1950-1951

Institution	President	Tenure
	Jesse Joel Stevenson	1951-1952
	Robert H. Stamey	1952-1957
	Emmett Kennedy McLarty	1957-1968
	Robert A. Davis	1969-
Centenary College of Louisiana Shreveport, Louisiana		
College of Louisiana Jackson, La.	Jeremiah Chamberlain	1825-1828
	H. H. Gird	1829-1834
	James Shannon	1835-1840
	William D. Lacy	1840-1843
Centenary College Brandon Springs, Miss.	T. C. Thornton	1841-1844
	William Winans	1844-
Centenary College of Louisiana Jackson, La.	D. O. Shattuck	1846-1848
	A. B. Longstreet	1848-1849
	R. H. Rivers	1849-1854
	B. M. Drake	1854-
	Dr. Thweatt	1854-1859
	John C. Miller	1859-1865
	William H. Watkins	1865-1870
	C. G. Andrews	1870-1882
	D. M. Rush	1883-1885
	T. A. S. Adams	1885-1887
	George H. Wiley	1887-1888
	W. L. C. Hunnicutt	1888-1894
	C. W. Carter	1894-1898
	I. W. Cooper	1898-1902
	Henry B. Carré	1902-1903
	C. C. Miller	1903-1908
Centenary College of Louisiana Shreveport, La.	William L. Weber	1908-1910
	Felix R. Hill	1910-1913
	Robert H. Wynn	1913-1918
	R. W. Bourne	1919-1920
	R. E. Smith	1920-1921
	George S. Sexton	1921-1932
	W. Angie Smith	1932-1933
	Pierce Cline	1933-1943
	Joe J. Mickle	1945-1964
	Jack S. Wilkes	1964-
	John Horton Allen	
Centenary College for Women Hackettstown, New Jersey 07840	George H. Whitney	1869-1895
	Wilbert P. Ferguson	1895-1900
	Charles Wesley McCormick	1900-1902
	Eugene Allen Noble	1902-1908
	Jonathan Magie Meeker	1908-1917
	Robert Johns Trevorrow	1940-1943
	Hurst Robins Anderson	1943-1948
	Edward W. Seay	1948-
Central Methodist College Fayette, Missouri 65248	Nathan Scarritt	1857-1858
	A. A. Morrison	1858-1860
	C. W. Pritchett	1860-
	W. A. Anderson	1860-1861
	(closed 1861-1868)	
	W. A. Smith	1868-1870
	F. X. Forster	1870-
	J. C. Wills	1870-1878
	E. R. Hendrix	1878-1886
	O. H. P. Corprew	1886-1888
	J. D. Hammond	1888-1896
	Tyson S. Dines	1896-1897
	E. B. Craighead	1897-1901
	T. Berry Smith, Acting	1901-1903
	James C. Morris	1903-1907
	William A. Webb	1907-1913
	Paul H. Linn	1913-1924
	E. P. Puckett	1924-
	W. F. McMurry	1924-1930
	Robert H. Ruff	1930-1942
	Harry S. DeVore	1942-1947

Institution	President	Tenure
	E. P. Puckett, Acting	1947-1950
	Ralph L. Woodward	1950-1971
	Harold P. Hamilton	1971-
Claflin College Orangeburg, S. C. 29115	Alonzo Webster	1869-1874
	Edward Cooke	1874-1883
	L. M. Dunton	1884-1913
	Joseph Benjamin Randolph	1914-1945
	John Jarvis Seabrook	1945-1955
	H. V. Manning	1956-
Clark College Atlanta, Georgia 30314	E. O. Thayer	1883-
	W. H. Hickman	1889-1893
	D. C. John	1893-1896
	Silas E. Idleman	1910-1912
	M. S. Davage	1924-1941
	James P. Brawley	1941-1964
	Vivian Henderson	1967-
Columbia College Columbia, South Carolina 29203	Whiteford D. Smith	1859-1860
	William Martin	1860-1861
	Henry M. Mood	1861-1865
	Samuel B. Jones	1873-1876
	J. L. Jones	1876-1881
	Osgood A. Darby	1881-1890
	Samuel B. Jones	1890-1894
	John A. Rice	1894-1900
	William W. Daniel	1900-1916
	Griffith T. Pugh	1916-1920
	J. Caldwell Guilds	1920-1948
	Walter K. Greene	1948-1950
	R. Wright Spears	1951-
Cornell College Mount Vernon, Iowa 52314	Richard W. Keeler	1857-1859
	Samuel M. Fellows	1853-1863
	William Fletcher King	1863-1908
	Harlan Updegraff	-1927
	Herbert J. Burgstahler	1928-1938
	John Benjamin Magee	1939-1943
	Russell D. Cole	1943-1961
	Arland F. Christ-Janer	1961-1967
	Samuel E. Stumpf	1967-
Dakota Wesleyan University Mitchell, South Dakota 57301	William Brush	1885-1891
	Charles O. Merica	1892-1893
	William I. Graham	1893-1903
	Thomas Nicholson	1903-1908
	Samuel F. Kerfoot	1908-1912
	William Grant Seaman	1912-1916
	William D. Schermerhorn	1917-1922
	Edward Delor Kohlstedt	1922-1927
	Earl Alan Roadman	1927-1936
	Leon H. Sweetland	1936-1937
	Joseph H. Edge	1937-1946
	Samuel M. Hilburn	1946-1951
	Matthew D. Smith	1952-1958
	Jack J. Early	1958-
	Robert R. Huddleston	
	Robert H. Wagner, Acting	
Black Hills College	John Hancher	1890-1897
	Elmer B. Limer	1897-1900
DePauw University Greencastle, Indiana 46135	Cyrus Nutt	1837-1839
	Matthew Simpson	1839-1848
	William C. Larrabee	1848-1849
	Lucien W. Berry	1849-1854
	Daniel Curry	1854-1857
	Cyrus Nutt	1857-1858
	Thomas Bowman	1858-1872
	Reuben Andrus	1872-1875
	Alexander Martin	1875-1889
	J. P. D. John	1889-1895
	Hillary Asbury Gobin	1895-1903
	Edwin Holt Hughes	1903-1909

Institution	President	Tenure
	Francis John McConnell	1909-1912
	George Richmond Grose	1912-1924
	Henry Boyer Longden	1924-1925
	Lemuel Herbert Murlin	1925-1928
	G. Bromley Oxnam	1928-1936
	Clyde Everett Wildman (Emeritus—1951-55)	1936-1955
	Russell Jay Humbert	1951-1962
	William Edward Kerstetter	1963-
Dickinson College Carlisle, Pennsylvania 17013	Charles Nisbet	1785-1804
	Robert Davidson	1804-1809
	Jeremiah Atwater	1809-1815
	John McKnight	1815-1816
	John Mitchell Mason	1821-1824
	William Neill	1824-1829
	Samuel Blanchard How	1830-1832
	John Price Durbin	1834-1845
	Robert Emory	1845-1848
	Jesse Truesdell Peck	1848-1852
	Charles Collins	1852-1860
	Herman Merrills Johnson	1860-1868
	Robert Laurenson Dashiell	1868-1872
	James Andrew McCauley	1872-1888
	George Edward Reed	1889-1911
	Eugene Allen Noble	1911-1914
	James Henry Morgan	1914-1928
	Mervin Grant Filler	1928-1931
	James Henry Morgan	1931-1932
	Karl Tinsley Waugh	1931-1933
	James Henry Morgan	1933-1934
	Fred Pierce Corson	1934-1944
	Cornelius William Prettyman	1944-1946
	William Wilcox Edel	1946-1959
	Gilbert Malcolm	1959-1961
	Howard Lane Rubendall	1961-
Dillard University New Orleans, Louisiana 70122	William Stuart Nelson	1936-1941
	A. W. Dent	1941-1970
	Broadus N. Butler	1970-
Drew University Madison, New Jersey 07940	John McClintock	1867-1870
	Ralph Sinks Foster	1870-1873
	John Fletcher Hurst	1873-1880
	Henry Anson Buttz	1880-1912
	Ezra Squier Tipple	1912-1928
	Arlo Ayres Brown	1929-1948
	Fred G. Holloway	1948-1960
	Robert F. Oxnam	1960-
Duke University Durham, North Carolina		
Brown's Schoolhouse	Brantley York	1838-1839
Union Institute	Brantley York	1839-1842
	Braxton Craven	1842-1851
Normal College	Braxton Craven	1851-1859
Trinity College	Braxton Craven	1859-1882
	Marquis L. Wood	1883-1884
	John Franklin Crowell	1887-1894
	John Carlisle Kilgo	1894-1910
	William Preston Few	1910-1924
Duke University	William Preston Few	1924-1940
	Robert Lee Flowers	1941-1948
	Arthur Hollis Edens	1949-1960
	Julian Deryl Hart	1960-1963
	Douglas M. Knight	1963-1969
	Terry Sanford	1969-
Emory University Atlanta, Georgia		
Emory College	Ignatius Alonzo Few	1837-1840

Institution	President	Tenure
	Augustus Baldwin Longstreet	1840-1848
	George Foster Pierce	1848-1854
	Alexander Means	1854-1855
	James R. Thomas	1855-1867
	Luther M. Smith	1868-1871
	Osborn L. Smith	1871-1875
	Atticus G. Haygood	1875-1884
	Isaac Stiles Hopkins	1884-1888
	Warren Akin Candler	1888-1898
	Charles E. Dowman	1898-1902
	James Edward Dickey	1902-1915
Emory University	Harvey W. Cox	1920-1942
	Goodrich C. White	1942-1957
	S. Walter Martin	1957-1962
	Sanford S. Atwood	1963-
Emory and Henry College Emory, Virginia 24327	Charles Collins	1838-1852
	E. E. Wiley	1852-1879
	John L. Buchanan	1879-1880
	David Sullins	1880-1885
	E. E. Hoss	1885-
	Thomas W. Jordan	1885-1888
	Major R. W. Jones	1888-1889
	James Atkins	1889-1893
	R. G. Waterhouse	1893-1910
	C. C. Weaver	1910-1920
	J. Stewart French	1920-1922
	James Noah Hillman	1922-1941
	Foye G. Gibson	1941-1956
	Earl G. Hunt	1956-1964
	William C. Finch	1965-1970
	C. Glen Mingledorff	1970-
Evangelical Theological Seminary Naperville, Illinois	J. J. Esher	1875-1877
Union Biblical Institute	J. J. Esher	1875-1877
	Reuben Yeakel	1877-1883
	C. A. Paeth	1883-1886
	H. J. Kiekhoefer	1886-1888
	S. L. Umbach	1888-1908
	S. J. Gamertsfelder	1908-1909
Evangelical Theological Seminary	S. J. Gamertsfelder	1909-1919
	G. B. Kimmel	1919-1939
	Harold R. Heininger	1939-1955
	Paul H. Eller	1955-1967
	Wayne K. Clymer	1967-
Ferrum Junior College Ferrum, Virginia 24088	Benjamin M. Beckman	1913-1934
	John A. Carter	1934-1935
	James Archer Chapman	1935-1944
	Luther J. Derby	1944-1948
	Nathaniel H. Davis	1948-1952
	Stanley E. Emrich	1952-1954
	C. Ralph Arthur	1954-1970
	Joseph T. Hart	1971-
Florida Southern College Lakeland, Florida 33802		
Florida Conference College Leesburg	Joshua Hollingsworth	1886-1888
	W. W. Seals	1888-1889
	Theophilus W. Moore	1889-1891
	Henry E. Partridge	1891-1892
	Wightman F. Melton	1892-1895
	James T. Nolen	1895-1897
	Thomas G. Lang	1897-1902
Florida Seminary Sutherland	Shade W. Walker	1902-1907
Southern College Southerland	John P. Hilburn	1907-1912
	Walter L. Clifton	1912-1914
	Rhenus H. Alderman	1914-1925

Institution	President	Tenure
Florida Southern College Lakeland	Ludd M. Spivey	1925-1957
	Charles T. Thrift, Jr.	1957-
Gammon Theological Seminary Atlanta, Georgia	Uriah Cleary	1870-1883
	W. P. Thirkield	1883-1899
	L. G. Adkinson	1901-1906
	J. W. E. Bowen	1906-1911
	Silas E. Idleman	1911-1914
	Phillip Watters	1914-1925
	George C. Trevor	1925-1928
	Franklin H. Clopp	1928-1932
	Willis J. King	1932-1944
	John W. Haywood	1944-1948
	Harry V. Richardson	1948-1959
	Master J. Wynn	1959-1967
	John F. Norwood	1967-1968
	Major J. Jones	1968-
Garrett Theological Seminary Evanston, Illinois	John Dempster	1853-1863
	Matthew Simpson	1863-1865
	William X. Ninde	1878-1884
	Henry B. Ridgeway	1884-1885
	Charles J. Little	1895-1911
	Charles M. Stuart	1912-1924
	Frederick C. Eiselen	1924-1932
	Horace G. Smith	1932-1953
	Dwight E. Loder	1955-1964
	Orville H. McKay	1965-
	Merlyn W. Northfelt	
Chicago Training School (united with Garrett 1934)	Lucy Rider Meyer	1885-1917
	Josiah Sheley Meyer	1885-1917
	Louis F. W. Lesemann	1918-1934
Green Mountain College Poultney, Vermont	Jesse P. Bogue	1935-
	B. W. Hartley	1939-
	Howard C. Ackley	1946-1958
	Raymond A. Withey	1958-
Greensboro College Greensboro, North Carolina 27402		
Davenport College	H. M. Mood	1858-1862
	R. N. Price	1862-1863
	A. G. Stacy	1863-1864
	G. H. Round	1864-1865
	J. R. Griffith	1865-1867
	Samuel Lander	1867-1870
	W. M. Robey	1870-1877

(college destroyed by fire in 1877; building partially rebuilt and used as high school in 1881 for 20 years)

	C. M. Pickens	1899-1901
	R. C. Craven	1901-1903
	Charles C. Weaver	1903-1910
	J. B. Craven	1910-1921
	Clifford Lee Hornaday	1922-1926
	W. A. Jenkins	1926-1933
Greensboro College	Solomon Lea	1846-1847
	Albert Micajah Shipp	1847-1850
	Charles Force Deems	1850-1854
	Turner Myrick Jones	1854-1890
	Benjamin Franklin Dixon	1890-1893
	Frank Lewis Reid	1893-1894
	Dred Peacock	1894-1902
	Mrs. Lucy Henderson Owen Robertson	1902-1913
	Samuel Bryant Turrentine	1913-1935
	Luther Lafayette Gobbel	1935-1952
	Harold Horton Hutson	1952-1964
	Joseph Ralph Jolly David G. Mobberley	1964-

Institution	President	Tenure
Hamline University St. Paul, Minnesota 55101	Jabez Brooks	1854-1857
	Benjamin Crary	1857-1861
	Jabez Brooks	1861-1869
	David Clarke John	1880-1883
	George Henry Bridgmen	1883-1912
	Samuel Fletcher Kerfoot	1912-1927
	Alfred Franklin Hughes	1927-1932
	Henry Leslie Osborn	1932-1933
	Charles Nelson Pace	1934-1948
	Hurst Robins Anderson	1948-1952
	Walter Castella Coffey	1952-1953
	Paul Henry Giddens	1953-1968
	Richard P. Bailey	1968-
Harwood School Albuquerque, New Mexico 87102	Mary Lou Moore, Supt.	
Hawaii Loa College Kaneohe, Hawaii	Chandler W. Rowe	1965-
Hendrix College Conway, Arkansas		
Galloway Woman's College	S. H. Babcock	1889-1892
	John H. Dye	1892-1897
	C. C. Gooden	1897-1907
	J. M. Williams	1907-1931
	John H. Reynolds	1931-1933
Henderson-Brown College	G. C. Jones	1890-1897
	Cadesman Pope	1897-1899
	J. H. Hinemon	1904-1911
	George H. Crowell	1911-1915
	J. M. Workman	1915-1927
	G. L. Hornaday	1927-1928
	James W. Workman	1928-1929
Hendrix College	Isham L. Burrow	1884-1887
	A. C. Millar	1887-1902
	Stonewall Anderson	1902-1910
	A. C. Millar	1910-1913
	John H. Reynolds	1913-1945
	Matt L. Ellis	1945-1958
	Marshall T. Steel	1958-
	Roy B. Shilling, Jr.	
High Point College High Point, North Carolina 27262	R. M. Andrews	1924-1930
	Gideon I. Humphreys	1930-1949
	Dennis H. Cooke	1949-1959
	Wendell M. Patton, Jr.	1959-
Hillcrest Christian College Medicine Hat, Alberta, Canada	Floyd S. Magsig	1941-1954
	Jacob B. Keller	1954-1959
	Alvin W. Maetche	1959-1969
	Gerhard W. Epp	1969-
Hiwassee College Madisonville, Tennessee 37354	Ebenezer Doak	1849-1854
	J. H. Brunner	1854-1860
	J. H. Brunner	1865-1868
	J. H. Brunner	1872-1883
	Hale Snow Hamilton	1884-1884
	J. H. Brunner	1884-1891
	J. H. Brunner	1892-1894
	Sidney Gilbreath	1894-1899
	J. E. Lowry	1899-1908
	Eugene Blake	1914-1924
	Joel Martin Reedy	1924-1930
	Jefferson Monroe Colston	1930-1936
	Thomas A. Frick	1936-1942
	Donald Rudy Youell	1942-1955
	H. N. Barker	1955-
Holding Institute Laredo, Texas 78040	Maurice C. Daily, Supt.	
Huntingdon College Montgomery, Alabama 36106	A. A. Lipscomb	1856-1859
	G. W. F. Price	1859-1863
	Jesse Wood	1863-1864

Institution	President	Tenure
	C. D. Elliott	1864-1865
	G. W. F. Price	1865-1872
	H. D. Moore	1872-1875
	E. L. Loveless	1875-1876
	John Massey	1876-1909
	W. E. Martin	1909-1915
	M. W. Swartz	1915-1922
	W. D. Agnew	1922-1938
	Hubert Searcy	1938-1967
	Allen K. Jackson	1968-
Huston-Tillotson College Austin, Texas 78702		
Sam Houston College	Stanley E. Grannum	
	Robert F. Harrington	
Huston-Tillotson College	Matthew Davage	1952-1955
	J. J. Seabrook	1955-1965
	John T. King	1965-
Iliff School of Theology Denver, Colorado	Harris Franklin Rall	1910-1914
	James Albert Beebe	1914-1918
	Edwin Wesley Dunleavy	1918-1924
	Elmer Guy Cutshall	1924-1931
	Charles E. Schofield	1935-1942
	Harris T. Morris	1943-1946
	Edward R. Bartlett	1947-1951
	Harold Ford Carr	1953-1961
	Lowell B. Swan	1962-
	Jameson Jones	
Illinois Wesleyan University Bloomington, Illinois 61701	W. Goodfellow	1850-1857
	O. S. Munsell	1857-
	W. H. H. Adams	1882-
	W. H. Wilder	1888-1898
	William J. Davidson	1923-1932
	W. H. McPherson	1933-1936
	Wiley G. Brooks	1937-
	William E. Shaw	1945-1947
	Merrill J. Holmes	1947-
	Lloyd M. Bertholf	1958-1968
	Robert S. Eckley	1968-
Iowa Wesleyan College Mount Pleasant, Iowa 52641		
Mount Pleasant Collegiate Institute	Aristides Joel Huestis	1842-1849
	Joseph McDowell	1849-1850
	Alexander Nelson	1850-1851
	James Marshall McDonald	1852-1853
	James Harlan	1853-1855
Iowa Wesleyan University	Lucien W. Berry	1855-1857
	Charles Elliott	1858-1861
	George Bemis Jocelyn	1861-1862
	Charles Elliott	1863-1866
	Charles Avery Holmes	1866-1869
	John Wheeler	1870-1875
	Wesley J. Spaulding	1876-1884
	John Thomas McFarland	1884-1891
	Charles Lewis Stafford	1891-1899
	Francis Durbin Blakeslee	1899-1900
	John William Hancher	1901-1908
	Edwin Allison Schell	1908-1910
Mount Pleasant German College	Rudolph Havighorst	1873-1874
	Heinrich Lahrman	1874-1875
	Henry Schutz	1875-1877
	George F. W. Willey	1877-1878
	Friedrich Wilhelm Balcke	1878-1885
	John Schlagenhauf	1885-1891
	George A. Mulfinger	1891-1893
	Friedrich Munz	1893-1897
	E. E. Schuette	1897-1898

Institution	President	Tenure
	Edwin Stanton Havighorst	1898-1908
	Henry G. Leist	1908-1909
Iowa Wesleyan College	Edwin Allison Schell	1910-1918
	Ulysses Simpson Smith	1919-1927
	James Ephraim Coons	1928-1935
	Harry DeWitt Henry	1935-1938
	Stanley Barnum Niles	1938-1949
	John Raymond Chadwick	1950-1961
	John Wayne Henderson	1962-1965
	Franklin Hamlin Littell	1965-
	Louis A. Haselmayer	
Indiana Central College Indianapolis, Indiana	J. T. Roberts	1905-1908
	Lewis D. Bonebrake	1909-1915
	Irby J. Good	1915-1944
	I. Lynd Esch	1945-1970
	Gene E. Sease	1970-
Kansas Wesleyan University Salina, Kansas 67401	William F. Swahlen	1886-1887
	Aaron Schuyler	1887-1894
	Edward W. Mueller	1894-1896
	George J. Hagerty	1896-1899
	Milton E. Phillips	1900-1902
	Thomas W. Roach	1903-1908
	Robert P. Smith	1908-1915
	John F. Harmon	1915-1918
	Larkin Bruce Bowers	1919-1937
	E. K. Morrow	1938-1946
	Herbert Jackson Root	1946-1950
	A. Stanley Trickett	1950-1954
	D. Arthur Zook	1955-
	Paul W. Renich	
Kendall College Evanston, Illinois 60204		
Swedish M. E. Theological Seminary	N. O. Westergreen	1870-1872
	C. A. Viren	1872-1875
	William Henschen	1875-1883
	Albert Ericson	1883-1909
	C. G. Wallenius	1909-1918
	F. A. Lundberg	1918-1924
Wesley Academy and Theological Seminary	C. G. Wallenius	1924-1931
	John W. Swenson	1931-1934
Kendall College	T. Otmann Firing	1934-1954
	Wesley M. Westerberg	1954-
Kents Hill School Kents Hill, Maine 04349	Donald M. Jacobs	
Kentucky Wesleyan College Owensboro, Kentucky 42301	Charles Taylor	1866-1870
	A. G. Murphy (Acting)	1869-1870
	Benjamin Arbogast	1870-1873
	John Darby	1873-1875
	Thomas J. Dodd	1875-1876
	William H. Anderson	1876-1879
	David W. Batson	1879-1883
	David W. Batson	1884-1893
	Alexander Redd	1883-1884
	Benjamin T. Spencer	1893-1895
	Eugene H. Pearce	1895-1900
	Executive Duties Administered by the Faculty	1900-1901
	John L. Weber	1901-1906
	Henry K. Taylor	1906-1909
	John J. Tigert	1909-1911
	James L. Clark	1911-1919
	William B. Campbell	1919-1924
	U. V. W. Darlington	1924-1925
	David C. Hull	1925-1928

Institution	President	Tenure
	Walter V. Cropper (Acting)	1928-1929
	Clarence M. Dannelly	1928-1932
	Reginald V. Bennett	1932-1937
	Paul S. Powell	1937-1950
	John F. Baggett	1950-1951
	Oscar W. Lever	1951-1959
	Harold P. Hamilton	1959-1970
	William James	1972-
LaGrange College LaGrange, Georgia	Thomas Stanley	1831-1834
	John Clark	1834-1843
	Joseph Montgomery	1843-1857
	W. C. Conner	1857-1858
	William Jeremiah Sasnett	1858-1859
	William C. Harris	1859-1860
	Gadwell J. Pearce	1860-1863
	J. M. Armstrong	1863-1866
	Ichabod F. Cox	1866-1869
	Morgan Callaway	1869-1871
	Edmund Pendleton Burch	1871-1872
	James T. Johnson	1872-1875
	J. R. Mason	1875-1881
	John W. Heidt	1881-1885
	Rufus W. Smith	1885-1915
	Daisy Davies	1915-1920
	William E. Thompson	1920-1938
	Hubert T. Quillian	1938-1948
	Waights G. Henry, Jr.	1948-
Lambuth College Jackson, Tennessee		
Memphis Conference Female Institute	Lorenza Lea	1843-1850
	Benjamin H. Hubbard	1850-1853
	Amos W. Jones	1853-1878
	A. B. Jones	1878-1880
	Amos W. Jones	1880-1892
	Mrs. A. W. Jones, Acting	1891-1892
	Howard W. Key	1892-1897
	A. B. Jones	1897-1911
	S. A. Steel	1911-1913
	H. G. Hawkins	1913-1917
	E. R. Naylor	1917-1920
	J. W. Blackard	1920-1924
Lambuth College	Richard E. Womack	1924-1952
	Luther Lafayette Gobbel	1952-1962
	James Sampson Wilder, Jr.	1962-
Lawrence University Appleton, Wisconsin 54911	William Harkness	1849-1853
	Edward Cooke	1853-1859
	R. Z. Mason	1859-1865
	G. M. Steele	1865-1879
	E. D. Huntley	1879-1883
	B. P. Raymond	1883-1889
	C. W. Gallagher	1889-1893
	Samuel Plantz	1894-1924
	Henry M. Wriston	1925-1937
	Thomas N. Barrows	1937-1943
	N. M. Pusey	1944-1953
	Douglas M. Knight	1954-1963
	Curtis W. Tarr	1963-1968
	Thomas Stevenson Smith	1969-
Lebanon Valley College Annville, Pennsylvania	Thomas R. Vickroy	1866-1871
	Lucian H. Hammond	1871-1876
	David D. DeLong	1876-1877
	Edmund S. Lorenz	1887-1889
	Cyrus J. Kephart	1889-1890
	E. Benjamin Bierman	1890-1897
	Hervin U. Roop	1897-1906
	Abram P. Funkhouser	1906-1907
	Lawrence W. Keister	1907-1912
	George D. Gossard	1912-1932
	Clyde A. Lynch	1932-1950
	Frederic K. Miller	1950-1967

Institution	President	Tenure
	Allan W. Mund	1967-1968
	Frederick P. Sample	1968-
Lindsey Wilson College Columbia, Kentucky 42728	John B. Horton	
Alexander Collegiate Institute	Isaac Alexander	1875-1890
	G. J. Nunn	1890-1896
	E. R. Williams	1896-1904
	W. K. Strother	1904-1909
	F. E. Butler	1909-1912
	M. L. Lefler	1912-1914
	W. K. Strother	1915-1918
	R. G. Boger	1918-1923
Lon Morris College	G. F. Winfield	1923-1928
	E. M. Stanton	1928-1932
	Herman T. Morgan	1932-1935
	Cecil E. Peeples	1935-
Louisburg College Louisburg, North Carolina 27549	James P. Nelson	1857-1858
	J. J. Avirett	1858-1859
	Columbus Andrews	1859-1861
	James Southgate	1862-1865
	Turner M. Jones	1866-1869
	William Royall	1872-1874
	F. L. Reid	1877-
	S. G. Bagley	1889-
	J. A. Green	1894-1896
	Matthew Davis	1897-1906
	Mrs. Mary Davis Allen	1906-1917
	Franklin S. Love	1917-1920
	L. S. Massey	1920-1922
	Arthur W. Mohn	1922-1929
	Clark C. Alexander	1929-1931
	Armour David Wilcox	1931-1937
	D. E. Earnhardt	1937-1939
	Walter Patton	1939-1947
	Samuel M. Holton	1947-1955
	Cecil W. Robbins	1955-
Lycoming College Williamsport, Pennsylvania		
Williamsport Dickinson Seminary	Thomas H. Bowman	1848-1858
	John H. Dashiel	1858-1860
	Thomas Mitchell	1860-1869
	Wilson L. Spottswood	1869-1874
	Edward J. Gray	1874-1905
	William P. Eveland	1905-1912
	Benjamin C. Conner	1912-1921
	John W. Long	1921-1929
Williamsport Dickinson Seminary and Junior College	John W. Long	1929-1948
Lycoming College	D. Frederick Wertz	1955-1964
	Harold H. Hutson	1964-
Lydia Patterson Institute El Paso, Texas 79940	Noe E. Gonzales	
MacMurray College Jacksonville, Illinois 62650		
Illinois Conference Female Academy (1846)	James F. Jacquess	1848-1855

Institution	President	Tenure
Illinois Conference Female College (1851)	Reuben Andrus	1855-1856
	Asa S. McCoy	1856-1858
	Charles Adams	1858-1863
Illinois Female College	Charles Adams	1863-1868
	William H. DeMotte	1868-1875
	William F. Short	1875-1893
	Joseph R. Harker	1893-1899
Illinois Women's College	Joseph R. Harker	1899-1925
	Clarence P. McClelland	1925-1930
MacMurray College for Women	Clarence P. McClelland	1930-1952
MacMurray College	Louis W. Norris	1952-1960
	Gordon E. Michalson	1960-1968
	John J. Wittich, Jr.	1968-
Martin College Pulaski, Tennessee	William K. Jones	1870-1874
	R. H. Rivers	1874-1879
	William K. Jones	1879-1884
	Joseph L. Armstrong	1884-1885
	Ida E. Hood	1885-1890
	R. M. Saunders	1890-1893
	Alice Foxworthy	1894-
	Judith Steele	1895-
	S. M. Barker	1896-1898
	D. W. Dodson	1898-
	L. L. Vann	1899-
	B. E. Atkins	1900-1901
	B. F. Haynes	1902-1904
	Mrs. J. H. Jennings	1907-
	W. T. Wynn	1908-1918
	George A. Morgan	1919-1930
	Sinclair Daniel	1930-1937
	K. L. Rudolph	1937-1941
	J. H. Swann	1941-
	R. B. Stone	1942-
	Paul B. Kern	1943-1944
	E. H. Elam	1944-1950
	Joseph D. Quillian, Jr.	1950-1954
	J. Fort Fowler	1954-1960
	W. C. Westenberger	1961-1970
	Thomas E. Gray	1971-
McCurdy School Espanola, New Mexico 87532	Dale E. Robinson, Supt.	
McKendree College Lebanon, Illinois 62254		
Lebanon Seminary	Edward Raymond Ames	1828-1833
McKendree College	Peter Akers	1833-1836
	John Dew	1836-1838
	John Wesley Merrill	1838-1841
	James C. Finley	1841-1845
	Peter Akers	1845-1846
	Erastus Wentworth	1846-1850
	Anson W. Cummings	1850-1852
	Peter Akers	1852-1857
	Werner Davis, Acting	1857-1858
	Nelson E. Cobleigh	1858-1863
	Robert Allyn	1863-1874
	John W. Locke	1874-1878
	Ross Clark Houghton	1878-1879
	Daniel W. Phillips	1879-1883
	William Fletcher Swahlen	1883-1886
	Edward A. Whitwam	1886-1887
	Isaiah Villars	1887-1889
	A. G. Jepson	1889-1890
	Thomas Hanson Herdman	1890-1893
	Morris Lincoln Barr	1893-1894

Institution	President	Tenure
	McKendree H. Chamberlain	1894-1908
	John F. Harmon	1908-1915
	James Dolley	1915-
	Huber William Hurt	1915-1917
	Edwin Percy Baker	1917-1919
	George McCammon	1919-1923
	Edwin Percy Baker	1923-
	Clark R. Yost	1923-1945
	Carl C. Bracy	1945-1949
	Lewis B. Van Winkle	1949-
	Russell Grow	1950-1957
	Webb B. Garrison	1957-1960
	W. N. Grandy	1960-
	Max P. Allen	1960-1964
	Edwin Edgar Voigt	1964-1968
	Eric N. Rackham	1968-
McMurry College Abilene, Texas	J. W. Hunt	1923-1934
	O. P. Clark	1934-
	C. Q. Smith	1934-1935
	Thomas Watson Brabham	1935-1938
	Frank L. Turner	1938-1942
	Harold G. Cooke	1942-1958
	Gordon R. Bennett	1958-1970
	Thomas K. Kim	1970-
Meharry Medical College Nashville, Tenn.	G. W. Hubbard	1915-1921
	John W. Mullowney	1921-1938
	Edward L. Turner	1938-1944
	M. Don Clawson	1945-1950
	Robert Lambert	1950-1952
	Harold D. West	1952-1966
	Robert Anderson	1966-1968
	Lloyd C. Elam	1968-
Methodist College Fayetteville, North Carolina	L. Stacey Weaver	1956-
Methodist Theological School in Ohio Delaware, Ohio	John W. Dickhaut	1959-
Morristown College Morristown, Tennessee 37814	Judson S. Hill	1889-1931
	E. C. Paustian	1931-1936
	John W. Haywood	1937-1944
	M. W. Boyd	1944-1952
	Henry Dickason	1953-1957
	Leonard Haynes, Jr.	1957-1959
	Elmer P. Gibson	1959-1969
	J. Otis Erwin	1969-1972
	Raymon E. White	1972-
Mount Union College Alliance, Ohio 44601	Orville Nelson Hartshorn	1846-1887
	Tamerlane Pliny Marsh	1888-1898
	Albert Birdsall Riker	1898-1908
	William Henry McMaster	1908-1938
	Charles Burgess Ketcham	1938-1953
	Carl Cluster Bracy	1954-1967
	Ronald G. Weber	1967-
Navajo Methodist Mission School Farmington, New Mexico 87401	Rodney E. Roberts	
Nebraska Wesleyan University Lincoln, Nebraska	C. F. Creighton	1888-1893
	Isaac Crook	1893-1896
	D. W. C. Huntington	1898-1908
	W. J. Davidson	1908-1910
	Clark A. Fulmer	1911-1917
	I. B. Schreckengast	1917-1932
	E. Guy Cutshall	1932-1937
	Harry L. Upperman	1938-
	B. F. Schwartz	1938-1946

Institution	President	Tenure
	John L. Knight	1946-1947
	Carl O. Bracy	1949-1954
	A. Leland Forrest	1954-1957
	Vance D. Rogers	1957-
North Carolina Wesleyan College Rocky Mount, North Carolina 27802	Thomas A. Collins	1959-
North Central College Naperville, Illinois		
Plainfield College	Augustine A. Smith	1861-1864
North-Western College	Augustine A. Smith	1864-1883
	Henry H. Rassweiler	1883-1888
	Herman J. Kiekhoefer	1889-1910
	Lawrence H. Seager	1911-1916
	Edward E. Rall	1916-1926
North Central College	Edward E. Rall	1926-1946
	C. Harve Geiger	1946-1960
	Arlo L. Schilling	1960-
Northwestern University Evanston, Illinois 60201		
Evanston College for Ladies	Frances E. Willard	1871-
Northwestern University	Clark Titus Hinman	1853-1854
	Henry Sanborn Noyes	1854-1856
	Randolph Sinks Foster	1856-1860
	Henry Sanborn Noyes	1860-1867
	David Hilton Wheeler	1867-1869
	Erastus Otis Haven	1869-1872
	Charles Henry Fowler	1872-1876
	Oliver Marcy	1876-1881
	Joseph Cummings	1881-1890
	Henry Wade Rogers	1890-1900
	Daniel Bonbright	1900-1902
	Edmund J. James	1902-1904
	Thomas F. Holgate	1904-1906
	Abram W. Harris	1906-1916
	Thomas F. Holgate	1916-1919
	Lynn Harold Hough	1919-1920
	Walter Dill Scott	1920-1939
	Franklyn Bliss Snyder	1939-1949
	James Roscoe Miller	1949-1970
	Robert H. Strotz	1970-
Ohio Northern University Ada, Ohio 45810	Albert E. Smith	1905-1929
	Robert Williams	1929-1943
	Robert O. McClure	1943-1949
	F. B. McIntosh	1949-1965
	Samuel L. Meyer	1965-
Ohio Wesleyan University Delaware, Ohio 43015	Edward Thomson	1844-1860
	Frederick Merrick	1860-1873
	L. D. McCabe, Acting	1873-1876
	C. H. Payne	1876-1888
	James W. Bashford	1889-1904
	Herbert Welch	1905-1916
	John Washington Hoffman	1916-1928
	Edmund Davison Soper	1928-1938
	Edward L. Rice, Acting	1938-1939
	Herbert J. Burgstahler	1939-1947
	Clarence Ficken, Acting	1947-1948
	Arthur S. Fleming	1948-1958
	George W. Burns, Acting	1958-1959
	David L. Lockmiller	1959-1961
	Elden T. Smith	1961-
	Thomas E. Wenzlau	

Institution	President	Tenure
Oklahoma City University Oklahoma City, Oklahoma 73106		
Texas Wesleyan College (1881)	Percival M. White	1884-1885
	A. A. Johnson	1885-1889
Fort Worth University (1889)	A. A. Johnson	1889-1890
	W. I. Graham	1890-1891
	Oscar L. Fisher	1891-1903
	George McAdam	1903-1905
	William Fielder	1905-1911
Epworth University (1904)	R. B. McSwain	1904-
	S. C. Jones, Acting	1904-
	George Henry Bradford	1906-1910
	William Fielder	1913-1914
	Edward Hislop	1914-1918
	E. G. Green	1916-1918
Oklahoma City College (1919)	E. G. Green	1919-1923
	E. M. Antrim	1923-1934
	Walter Scott Athearn	1934-
	A. G. Williamson	1934-1941
	C. Q. Smith	1941-1957
	C. Q. Smith, Chancellor	1957-1960
	Jack Stauffer Wilkes	1957-1963
	Dolphus Whitten, Jr., Acting	1963-1964
	John F. Olson	1964-
	Dolphus Whitten, Jr.	
Otterbein College Westerville, Ohio		
Otterbein University	William R. Griffith	1847-1849
	William Davis	1849-1850
	Lewis Davis	1850-1857
	Ralph M. Walker, Acting	1857-1858
	Alexander Owen	1858-1860
	Lewis Davis	1860-1871
	Daniel Eberly	1871-1872
	Henry A. Thompson	1872-1886
	Henry Garst	1886-1889
	C. A. Bowersox	1889-1891
	Thomas J. Sanders	1891-1901
	George Scott	1901-1904
	Lewis Bookwalter	1904-1909
	Walter G. Clippinger	1909-1917
Otterbein College	Walter G. Clippinger	1917-1939
	J. Ruskin Howe	1939-1945
	Royal F. Martin	1945-
	J. Gordon Howard	1945-1957
	Floyd J. Vance	1957-1958
	Lynn W. Turner	1958-1971
	Thomas Jefferson Kerr IV	1971-
Paine College Augusta, Georgia 30901	Morgan Calloway	1882-1884
	George W. Walker	1884-1911
	John D. Hammond	1911-1915
	D. E. Atkins	1915-1917
	Albert Deems Betts	1917-1923
	Ray L. Tomlin	1923-1929
	E. C. Peters	1929-1956
	E. Clayton Calhoun	1958-
	Lucius H. Pitts	
Pennington School Pennington, New Jersey 08534	Edward Cook	1840-1847
	Stephen M. Vail	1847-1849
	J. Townley Crane	1849-1858
	Isaac W. Wiley	1858-1863
	Daniel Clark Knowles	1863-1867
	Thomas O'Hanlon	1867-1872
	J. A. Dilks	1872-1876
	Thomas O'Hanlon	1876-1902
	James W. Marshall	1902-1905
	Frank Moore	1905-1908

Institution	President	Tenure
	J. Morgan Read	1908-1910
	Frank McDaniel	1910-1920
	Francis Harvey Green	1921-1943
	Joseph Wentworth Seay	1943-1945
	Francis Harvey Green	1945-1946
	J. Rolland Crompton	1946-1951
	Ira S. Pimm	1951-1958
	Charles R. Smyth	1958-
	Nelson M. Hoffman, Jr.	
Perkins School of Theology Dallas, Texas 75222	Joseph D. Quillian, Jr., Dean	
Pfeiffer College Misenheimer, North Carolina 28109		
Oberlin Home and School	Emily C. Prudden	1885-1903
Ebenezer Mitchell Industrial Home and School	Lizzie Kennedy	1903-1913
Ebenezer Mitchell School	Mrs. A. B. Gowell	1913-1927
	Carolyn Young	1927-1933
Ebenezer Mitchell Junior College	W. S. Sharp	1933-1943
Pfeiffer Junior College	Chi M. Waggoner	1944-1953
Pfeiffer College	J. Lem Stokes	1953-1968
	Jack J. Early	1969-1970
	D. D. Holt, Interim	1970-1971
	Douglas R. Sasser	1971-
Philander Smith College Little Rock, Arkansas (George R. Smith College merged with Philander Smith in 1933)	Thomas Mason	1877-1896
	James Monroe Cox	1896-1924
	George Collins Taylor	1924-1936
	Marquis Lafayette Harris	1936-1960
	Roosevelt David Crockett	1961-1964
	Ernest T. Dixon	1965-
	Walter R. Hazzard, Sr.	
Port Arthur College Port Arthur, Texas 77641	Carl Vaughn	
	W. D. Mauldin	
	W. M. Monroe	
Randolph-Macon Academy Front Royal, Virginia 22630	B. W. Bond	1892-1897
	W. W. Smith	1897-1899
	Charles L. Melton	1899-1933
	John C. Boggs	1933-1965
	Robert P. Parker	1965-1969
	Arvin S. Williams	1969-
Randolph-Macon College Ashland, Virginia 23005	Martin P. Parks, Acting	1832-1834
	Stephen Olin	1834-1836
	Landon C. Garland	1836-1846
	William A. Smith	1846-1866
	Thomas C. Johnson	1866-1868
	James A. Duncan	1868-1877
	W. W. Bennett	1877-1886
	Waugh Smith	1886-1897
	John A. Kern	1897-1899
	W. G. Starr	1899-1902
	Robert Emory Blackwell	1902-1938
	Samuel Claiborne Hatcher, Acting	1938-1939
	Earl Moreland	1939-1967
	Luther W. White, III	1967-
Randolph-Macon Woman's College Lynchburg, Virginia 24504	William Waugh Smith	1893-1912
	William Alexander Webb	1913-1919
	Dice Robins Anderson	1920-1931
	Theodore Henley Jack	1933-1952
	William F. Quillian, Jr.	1952-

Institution	President	Tenure
Reinhardt College	J. T. Linn	1884-1886
Waleska, Georgia	O. C. Simmons	1886-1887
30183	C. M. Ledbetter	1887-1888
	Hubert M. Smith	1888-1889
	R. F. Eakes	1890-1891
	C. E. Pattillo	1891-1894
	E. A. Cole	1894-1895
	Richard W. Rogers	1895-1901
	Ramsey C. Sharp	1901-1916
	E. P. Clark	1916-1918
	T. M. Sullivan	1918-1922
	Ramsey C. Sharp	1922-1927
	W. M. Bratton	1927-1944
	J. R. Burgess, Jr.	1944-
Robinson School	Hannah Hegeman	1902-1910
Santurce, Puerto	J. C. Murray	1911-1918
Rico	Mrs. J. C. Murray	1918-1931
	Alzena Dickinson	1932-1933
	Mary Anderson	1934-1937
	Mrs. Estelle Searles Howard	1937-1944
	Verr Zeliff	1944-1950
	Helen Aldrich	1950-1957
	John E. Shappell	1957-1967
	William N. Wright, Acting	1967-1968
	John E. Shappell	1968-
Rocky Mountain	William D. Copeland	1947-1951
College	Herbert W. Hines	1951-1958
Billings, Montana	Philip M. Widenhouse	1958-1966
59102	Lawrence F. Small	1966-
Rust College	A. C. McDonald	1866-1876
Holly Springs,	A. W. Hooper	1876-1885
Mississippi 36835	Charles E. Libby	1885-1897
	W. W. Foster, Jr.	1897-1909
	James T. Dockings	1909-1915
	George Evans	1915-1920
	M. S. Davage	1920-1924
	L. M. McCoy	1924-1957
	E. A. Smith	1957-1967
	W. A. McMillan	1967-
Sager-Brown School	Rosie Ann Cobb, Supt.	
Baldwin, Louisiana		
70514		
Saint Paul School of	Don W. Holter	1958-1971
Theology Methodist	William K. McElvaney	1971-
Kansas City,		
Missouri 64127		
Scarritt College		
Nashville, Tennessee		
37203		
Scarritt Bible &	Maria Layng Gibson	1892-1918
Training School		
Kansas City,		
Missouri		
Scarritt College	Edmund Francis Cook	1919-1921
Nashville	Jesse Lee Cuninggim	1921-1943
	Hugh Clark Stuntz	1943-1956
	Foye Goodner Gibson	1956-1959
	D. Dillon Holt	1959-1970
	Gerald Harry Anderson	1970-
School of Theology	Ernest Cadman Colwell	1957-1968
at Claremont	Gordon Elliott Michalson	1968-
Claremont,		
California 01711		
Shenandoah College	Robert P. Parker	
Winchester, Virginia		
22601		

Institution	President	Tenure
Simpson College	S. M. Vernon	1866-1868
Indianola, Iowa	Alexander Burns	1868-1878
50125	Thomas S. Berry	1878-1880
	Edwin L. Parks	1880-1887
	William A. Hamilton	1887-1889
	Edmund M. Holmes	1889-1893
	Fletcher Brown	1893-1898
	Joseph B. Harris	1898-1899
	Charles E. Shelton	1899-1911
	Francis L. Strickland	1911-1915
	James W. Campbell	1917-1920
	John L. Hillman	1920-1936
	Earl E. Harper	1936-1938
	John L. Gross	1938-1942
	Edwin E. Voigt	1942-1953
	William E. Kerstetter	1953-1963
	Ralph C. John	1963-1972
	Richard B. Lancaster	1972-
Southern Methodist		
University		
Dallas, Texas 75222		
North Texas	G. C. Parks	1870-
Female College	W. I. Cowles	
	James Reed Cole	1876-1880
	J. C. Parham	1880-1881
	E. D. Pitts	1881-1883
	J. M. Onions	1883-1886
	Mrs. Lucy Ann Kidd-Key	1888-1916
	Edwin Kidd	1917-1919
Kidd-Key College	Edwin Kidd	1919-1923
and Music		
Conservatory		
Kidd-Key College	E. A. Spurlock	1923-1928
	Edwin Kidd	1928-1935
Southern Meth-	Robert Stewart Hyer	1911-1920
odist University	Hiram A. Boaz	1920-1922
	Charles C. Selecman	1923-1938
	Umphrey Lee	1938-1954
	Willis M. Tate	1954-
Southwestern	John E. Earp	1886-1890
College	Milton E. Phillips	1890-1894
Winfield, Kansas	Chester A. Place	1895-1899
67156	Fred C. Demorest	1900-1903
	George F. Cook	1903-1905
	Frank E. Mossman	1905-1918
	Albert E. Kirk	1919-1928
	Ezra T. Franklin	1928-1931
	Frank E. Mossman	1931-1942
	Charles E. Schofield	1942-1944
	Mearl P. Culver	1945-1949
	Alvin W. Murray	1949-1953
	C. Orville Strohl	1954-1972
	Donald B. Ruthenberg	1972-
Southwestern		
University		
Georgetown, Texas		
Rutersville	Chauncey Richardson	1840-1845
College	William Halsey	1845-1856
McKenzie College	J. W. P. McKenzie	1841-1869
Wesleyan College	Lester Janes	1844-1846
	Foster Blades	1846-1847
Soule University	J. M. Follansbee	1856
	William Halsey	1856-1860
	G. W. Carter	1860-1861
	William Halscy	1861-1864
	J. W. Follansbee	1864-1868
	Francis Asbury Mood	1868-1872
Southwestern	Francis Asbury Mood	1873-1884
University	J. W. Heidt	1885-1889

Institution	President	Tenure
	J. W. McLean	1889-1897
	Robert S. Hyer	1898-1911
	C. W. Bishop	1911-1922
	Paul W. Horn	1922-1924
	James S. Barcus	1924-1928
	King Vivion	1928-1935
	John William Bergin	1935-1942
	J. N. R. Score	1941-1949
	William Finch	1949-1961
	Durwood Fleming	1961-
Spartanburg Junior College Spartanburg, South Carolina 29301	David English Camak	1911-1923
	Rembert Bennett Burgess	1923-1962
	Henry Lester Kingman	1963-1970
	James S. Barrett	1970-
Sue Bennett College London, Kentucky 40741	Miss Oscie Sanders	1950-
	Earl F. Hays	1967-
Syracuse University Syracuse, New York 13210	Alexander Winchell	1872-1874
	Erastus O. Haven	1874-1881
	Charles N. Sims	1881-1894
	James Roscoe Day	1894-1922
	Charles W. Flint	1922-1937
	William Pratt Graham	1937-1942
	William Pearson Tolley	1942-1969
	John E. Corbally, Jr.	1969-1971
Tennessee Wesleyan College Athens, Tennessee	Erastus Rowley	1857-1866
	Percival C. Wilson	1866-1867
	Nelson E. Cobleigh	1867-1872
	James A. Dean	1872-1875
	John J. Manker	1875-
	John F. Spence	1875-1893
	Isaac W. Joyce	1891-1896
	John H. Race	1897-1913
	Fred W. Hixon	1914-1920
	Arlo Ayres Brown	1921-1925
	James Lindsay Robb	1925-1950
	LeRoy Albert Martin	1950-1959
	Ralph Wilson Mohney	1959-1965
	Charles C. Turner, Jr.	1966-
Texas Wesleyan College Fort Worth, Texas 76105		
Polytechnic College	J. W. Adkisson	1891-1894
	W. F. Floyd	1894-1899
	R. B. McSwain	1899-1900
	G. J. Nunn	1900-1902
	Hiram A. Boaz	1902-1911
	Frank P. Culver	1912
	Richard A. Hearon	1912-1913
	Hiram A. Boaz	1913-1914
Texas Woman's College	Hiram A. Boaz	1914-1918
	J. D. Young	1918
	Henry E. Stout	1919-1931
	Tom W. Brabham	1931-1934
Texas Wesleyan College	Tom W. Brabham	1934-1935
	Law Sone	1935-1968
	William M. Pearce	1968-
Tilton School Tilton, New Hampshire	William D. Cass	1845-1846
	Richard S. Rust	1846-1851
	John C. Clarke	1850-1851
	James E. Latimer	1851-1854
	Calvin S. Harrington	1854-1860
	Ralza M. Manly	1860-1862
	Henry Lummis	1862-1864
	Lorenzo D. Barrows	1864-1870
	John B. Robinson	1871-1877
	Lorenzo D. Barrows	1877

Institution	President	Tenure
	Silas E. Quimby	1878-1885
	Daniel C. Knowles	1885-1891
	Jesse M. Durrell	1891-1896
	George L. Plimpton	1896-1929
	Thomas W. Watkins	1929-1934
	James E. Coons	1935-1951
	J. Rolland Crompton	1951-1957
	J. Gordon Jeffries, Acting	1957-1958
	Herbert B. Moore	1958-1965
	Robert E. Butler	1965-
	Joseph H. Chadbourne, Jr.	
Union College Barbourville, Kentucky 40906	Abraham H. Harritt	1879-1882
	Thomas Clay Poynter	1882-1884
	Hartford P. Grider	1884-1886
	George H. Dains	1886-1888
	Daniel Stevenson	1888-1897
	James P. Faulkner	1897-1905
	James W. Easley	1905-1910
	James D. Black	1910-1912
	Percy L. Ports	1912-1914
	Emery R. Overley	1914-1915
	Ezra T. Franklin	1915-1928
	John Owen Gross	1929-1938
	Conway Boatman	1938-1959
	Mahlon A. Miller	1959-
United States International University San Diego, California 92106	William C. Rust	
United Theological Seminary Dayton, Ohio		
Union Biblical Seminary Dayton, Ohio	Lewis Davis	1871-1885
	George A. Funkhouser	1885-1907
	J. P. Landis	1907-1909
Bonebrake Theological Seminary Dayton, Ohio	J. P. Landis	1909-1910
	J. P. Landis	1910-1921
	A. T. Howard	1921-1929
	J. H. Harris	1929-1933
	A. T. Howard, Acting	1933-1935
	A. T. Howard	1935-1938
	Walter N. Roberts	1938-1954
Schuylkill Seminary and School of Theology Reading, Pa.	Charles B. Bowman	1901-1910
	S. C. Breyfogel	1910-1927
Evangelical School of Theology Reading, Pa.	S. C. Breyfogel	1927-1934
	John S. Stamm	1934-1941
	J. Arthur Heck	1941-1954
United Theological Seminary Dayton, Ohio	Walter N. Roberts	1954-1965
	John R. Knecht	1965-
University of Chattanooga Chattanooga, Tennessee	Edward S. Lewis	1886-1889
	John F. Spence	1889-1893
	Isaac W. Joyce	1893-1896
	John H. Race	1897-1913
	Fred W. Hixson	1914-1920
	Arlo A. Brown	1921-1929
	Alexander Guerry	1929-1938
	Archie M. Palmer	1938-1942
(John H. Race Foundation)	David A. Lockmiller	1942-1959
	LeRoy A. Martin	1959-1966
	William H. Masterson	1966-
University of Denver Denver, Colorado	George S. Phillips	1864
	Orville A. Willard, Acting	1865
	George S. Richardson	1865-1866
	Bethuel Thomas Vincent	1866-1867

Institution	President	Tenure
	P. D. Barnhart	1867
	Miss Sarah F. Morgan	1868
	David H. Moore	1880-1889
	Ammi Bradford Hyde	1889-1890
	William Fraser McDowell	1890-1899
	Henry Augustus Buchtel	1899-1920
	Wilbur D. Engle	1920-1922
	Heber Reece Harper	1922-1927
	Wilbur D. Engle, Acting	1927-1928
	Frederick M. Hunter	1928-1935
	David Shaw Duncan	1935-1941
	Caleb F. Gates, Jr.	1941-1943
	Ben Mark Cherrington	1943-1946
	Caleb F. Gates, Jr.	1946-1947
	James F. Price, Acting	1947-1948
	James F. Price	1948
	Alfred C. Nelson	1948-1949
	Albert C. Jacobs	1949-1953
	Levette J. Davidson, Acting	1953
	Chester M. Alter	1953-1967
	Wilbur C. Miller, Acting	1966-1967
	Maurice B. Mitchell	1967-

University of
Evansville
Evansville, Indiana
47704

Institution	President	Tenure
Moores Hill Male and Female Collegiate Institute	Samuel Rogers Adams	1856-1862
	William O. Pierce	1862-1864
	Thomas Harrison	1864-1870
	John H. Martin	1870-1872
	Francis A. Hester	1872-1876
	John P. D. John	1876-1879
	John P. D. John	1880-1882
	John H. Doddridge	1882-1887
	Louis D. Adkinson	1882-1887
Moores Hill College	George P. Jenkins	1887-1890
	John H. Martin	1890-1897
	Charles W. Lewis	1897-1903
	John H. Martin	1903-1904
	Frank C. English	1904-1908
	William S. Bovard	1908-1909
	Harry Andrews King	1909-1915
	Andrew J. Bigney, Acting	1915-1916
	Alfred F. Hughes	1916-1919
Evansville College	Alfred F. Hughes	1919-1927
	Earl E. Harper	1927-1936
	Charles E. Torbet, Acting	1936
	F. Marion Smith	1936-1940
	Lincoln B. Hale	1940-1954
	Dean Long, Acting	1954-1955
	Melvin W. Hyde	1955-1967
University of Evansville	Wallace B. Graves	1967-

University of the
Pacific
Stockton, California
95204

	President	Tenure
	E. Bannister	1851-1854
	M. C. Briggs	1854-1856
	J. W. Maclay	1856-1857
	A. S. Gibbons	1857-1860
	E. Bannister	1860-1867
	T. H. Sinex	1867-1872
	A. S. Gibbons	1872-1877
	C. C. Stratton	1877-1887
	A. C. Hirst	1887-1892
	Isaac Crook	1892-1893
	W. C. Sawyer	1893-1894
	F. F. Jewell	1894-1896
	Eli McClish	1896-1906
	M. S. Cross, Acting	1906-1907
	W. W. Guth	1908-1913
	John L. Seaton	1914-1918
	Tully C. Knoles	1919-1948

Institution	President	Tenure
	Robert E. Burns	1948-1971
	Allister W. McCrone, Acting	1971-

University of Puget
Sound
Tacoma,
Washington

(The following academies are considered to be precursors of
the University of Puget Sound:

1. Puget Sound Wesleyan Institute, Olympia, Wash., 1856-1876
2. Olympia Union Academy, Olympia, Wash., 1876-1879
3. Olympia Collegiate Institute, Olympia, Wash., 1883-1894.)

	President	Tenure
	D. W. Tyler	1888-1890
	Fletcher B. Cherington	1890-1892
	Crawford R. Thoburn	1892-1898
	Wilmot Whitfield	1899-1902
	Charles O. Boyer	1902-1903
	Edwin M. Randall, Jr.	1903-1904
	Joseph E. Williams	1904-1907
	Lee L. Benbow	1907-1909
	Julius C. Zeller	1909-1913
	Edward H. Todd	1913-1942
	R. Franklin Thompson	1942-

Institution	President	Tenure
Vashti School Thomasville, Georgia 31792	Annie Heath	1901-1907
	E. E. Bishop	1907-1919
	Charlotte Dye	1919-1933
	Daisy Ritter	1933-1939
	Mary Floyd	1939-1945
	Gladice Bower	1945-1954
	Woodward Adams	1954-1960
	Dorothy Marie Watson	1960-1966
	John H. Rogers	1966-

Vermont College
Montpelier, Vermont
05602

Institution	President	Tenure
Newbury Seminary	Charles Adams	1833-1839
	Osman C. Baker	1839-1844
	Clark T. Hinman	1844-1846
	Harvey Colcord Wood	1846-1847
	Francis Southack Hoyt	1847-1848
	Joseph Elijah King	1848-1854
	Henry Sanborn Noyes	1854-1855
	Charles Wesley Cushing	1855-1858
	Fenner E. King	1858-1862
	George Crosby Smith	1862-1866
	Silas Quimby	1866-1867
	Simeon E. Chester	1867-1869
Montpelier Seminary	Charles Wesley Wilder	1869-1872
	J. C. Watson Coxe	1872-1874
	Lorenzo White	1874-1877
	Julius B. Southworth	1877-1881
	Elwell Alexander Bishop	1881-1893
	Edgar M. Smith	1893-1898
	William N. Newton	1898-1901
	Walter Rice Davenport	1901-1903
	Frank W. Howe, Acting	1903-1904
	Elwell Alexander Bishop	1904-1913
	John Wood Hatch	1913-1931
	Charles Cleveland Chayer	1931-1935
	Arthur Wentworth Hewitt	1935-1936
Vermont College	Arthur Wentworth Hewitt	1936-1938
	John H. Kingsley	1938-1949
	Ralph E. Noble	1949-1966
	William L. Irvine	1966-

Institution	President	Tenure
Virginia Wesleyan College Norfolk, Virginia 23502	Joseph Shackford Johnston	1965
	Lambuth McGeehee Clarke	1966-

Institution	President	Tenure
Wesley College	J. M. Williams	1873-1878
Dover, Delaware	Robert H. Skinner	1878-1884
19901	W. L. Gooding	1884-1898
	Vaughn S. Collins	1898-1901
	E. L. Cross	1901-1911
	Henry G. Budd	1911-1926
	Clarence A. Short	1926-1932
	(College closed 1932-1941)	
	Arthur J. Jackson	1941-1943
	O. A. Bartley	1943-1951
	J. Paul Slaybaugh	1951-1960
	Robert H. Parker	1960-
Wesley Theological Seminary Washington, D. C.		
Westminster Theological Seminary	Thomas Hamilton Lewis	1882-1886
	James Thomas Ward	1886-1896
	Hugh Latimer Elderdice	1897-1932
	Fred Garrigus Holloway	1932-1935
	Charles Edward Forlines	1935-1943
	Lester Allen Welliver	1943-1955
Wesley Theological Seminary	Norman Leibman Trott	1955-1967
	John Lowden Knight, Jr.	1967-
Wesleyan College	George Foster Pierce	1838-1840
Macon, Georgia	William H. Ellison	1841-1851
	Edward Myers	1851-1854
	Osborne Smith	1854-1859
	John M. Bonnell	1859-1871
	Edward H. Myers	1871-1874
	William C. Bass	1874-1894
	Edgar H. Rowe	1894-1896
	John D. Hammond	1896-1898
	James William Roberts	1898-1903
	DuPont Guerry	1903-1909
	William N. Ainsworth	1909-1912
	Charles R. Jenkins	1912-1920
	William F. Quillian	1920-1931
	Dice R. Anderson	1931-1941
	Arthur J. Moore	1941-1942
	Nenien Cotesworth McPherson	1942-1946
	Silas Johnson	1946-1951
	William F. Quillian	1952-1953
	B. Joseph Martin	1953-1960
	W. Earl Strickland	1960-
West Virginia	Bennett W. Hutchinson	1890-1898
Wesleyan College	Frank B. Trotter, Acting	1898
Buckhannon, West	Simon L. Boyers	1898-1900
Virginia 26201	John Wier	1900-1907
	Carl G. Doney	1907-1913
	Thomas W. Haught, Acting	1913-1914
	Wallace B. Fleming	1915-1922
	Thomas W. Haught, Acting	1922-1923
	Elmer Guy Cutshaw	1924-1925
	Thomas W. Haught, Acting	1925-1926
	Homer E. Wark	1926-1931
	Roy McCuskey	1931-1941
	Wallace B. Fleming, Acting	1941-1942
	Joseph Warren Broyles	1942-1945
	Arthur Allen Schoolcraft	1945-1946
	William John Scarborough	1946-1956
	Arthur Allen Schoolcraft	1956-1957
	Stanley Hubert Martin	1957-
Western Maryland	James Thomas Ward	1867-1886
College	Thomas Hamilton Lewis	1886-1920
Westminster,	Albert Norman Ward	1920-1935
Maryland 21157	Fred Garrigus Holloway	1935-1947
	Lowell Skinner Ensor	1947-
Westmar College Le Mars, Iowa 51031		

Institution	President	Tenure
Lane University	Soloman Weaver	1865-
LeCompton,	N. B. Bartlett	
Kansas	C. M. Brooke	-1903
Gould College	A. W. Bishop	1881-
Harlan, Kansas	V. M. Noble	
	Peter Wagner	-1890
Campbell Normal	J. H. Miller	1882-1888
University	E. J. Hoenshel	1888-1896
Holton, Kansas	B. F. Kizer	1896-1902
Kansas City	D. S. Stephens	1896-
University	F. W. May	1924-
Kansas City,	W. O. Jones	1931-
Kansas		
Campbell College		1903-1913
(Merged with Kansas City University, 1913)		
York College	J. George	1890-1894
	W. S. Reese	1894-1897
	William E. Schell	1897-1913
	M. O. McLaughlin	1913-1919
	Hervin U. Roop	1919-1921
	W. O. Jones	1921-1924
	E. W. Emery	1924-1928
	J. R. Overmiller	1928-1938
	D. E. Weidler	1938-1948
	Walter E. Bachman	1948-1953
	A. V. Howland	1953-1956
Western Union	Herman H. Thoren	1900-1906
College	Charles C. Poling	1906-1908
	David E. Thomas	1908-1911
	Charles A. Mock	1911-1930
	David O. Kime	1932-1948
Westmar College	David O. Kime	1948-1956
Le Mars, Iowa	Harry H. Kalas	1956-1968
	Laurence C. Smith	1968-
Westminster College	John M. Coyner	1875-1885
Salt Lake City,	J. F. Millspaugh	1885-1890
Utah 84105	Charles S. Richardson	1890-1891
	Robert J. Caskey	1891-1896
	John Eaton	1896-1902
	George Bailey	1902-1906
	Robert M. Stevenson	1906-1912
	Herbert W. Reherd	1913-1939
	Robert D. Steele	1939-1952
	B. C. J. Wheatlake	1952
	J. Richard Palmer	1952-1956
	Frank E. Duddy, Jr.	1956-1963
	W. Fred Arbogast	1963-1967
	Manford A. Shaw	1968-
Wiley College	W. H. Davis	-1883
Marshall, Texas	George Whitaker	1889-1891
75670	P. A. Cool	1892-1893
	I. B. Scott	1894-1895
	Matthew W. Dogan	1896-1941
	E. C. McLeod	1942-1947
	J. S. Scott	1948-1959
	Thomas W. Cole	1960
Willamette	Francis S. Hoyt	1853-1860
University	Thomas Milton Gatch	1860-1865
Salem, Oregon	Joseph Henry Wythe	1865-1867
97301	Luther T. Woodward	1867-1868
	Nelson Rounds	1868-1870
	Thomas Milton Gatch	1870-1879
	Charles E. Lambert	1879-1880
	Thomas Van Scoy	1880-1891
	George Whitaker	1891-1893
	Willis C. Hawley	1893-1902
	John Coleman	1902-1907
	Fletcher Homan	1907-1914

Institution	President	Tenure
	George H. Alden, Acting	1914-1915
	Carl Gregg Doney	1915-1934
	Bruce Richard Baxter	1934-1941
	Carl Sumner Knopf	1941-1942
	George Herbert Smith	1942-1969
	Roger Jay Fritz	1969-
Wofford College Spartanburg, South Carolina	William May Wightman	1853-1859
	Albert Micajah Shipp	1859-1875
	James Henry Carlisle	1875-1902
	Henry Nelson Snyder	1902-1942
	Arthur Mason DuPre, Acting	1920-1921
	Walter Kirkland Greene	1942-1951
	Clarence Clifford Norton	1951-1952
	Francis Pendleton Gaines, Jr.	1952-1957
	Philip Stanhope Covington, Acting	1957-1958
	Charles Franklin Marsh	1958-1968
	Paul Hardin, III	1968-

Institution	President	Tenure
Wood Junior College Mathiston, Mississippi 39752	E. W. Seay	
	C. M. Waggoner	-1945
	W. D. Olsen	
	Charles T. Morgan	1948-1957
	Felix Sutphin	1958-
Young Harris College Young Harris, Georgia 30582	C. C. Spence	1891-1894
	W. F. Robinson	1894-1899
	J. W. Boyd, Acting	1899-
	Joseph Astor Sharp	1899-1916
	George King	1917
	John L. Hall	1918-1922
	Joseph Astor Sharp	1922-1930
	Mrs. Joseph Astor Sharp	1930
	T. J. Lance	1930-1942
	J. Worth Sharp	1942-1947
	W. L. Downs	1947-1950
	Charles R. Clegg	1950-1963
	Robert P. Andress, Acting	1963-1964
	Raymond A. Cook	1964-1966
	Douglas Reid Sasser	1966-1971

HOSPITALS AND HOMES

THE UNITED METHODIST CHURCH

(These institutions when described individually will be found under the city where they are located.)

Location	Institution	Capacity (Beds)
Alabama (Birmingham)	Carraway Methodist Hospital	419
Alaska (Nome)	Maynard-McDougall Memorial Hospital	30
Alaska (Seward)	Wesleyan Hospital for Chronic Diseases	33
Arizona (Phoenix)	Good Samaritan Hospital	600
Arkansas (Paragould)	Community Methodist Hospital	92
California (Arcadia)	Methodist Hospital of Southern California	300
California (Oakland)	California-Nevada Methodist Homes	

The following Hospital is under supervision of above corporation:

Location	Institution	Capacity (Beds)
(Madera)	Dearborn Community Hospital	40
District of Columbia (Washington)	Sibley Memorial Hospital	346
Florida (Jacksonville)	United Methodist Hospital	164
Georgia (Atlanta)	Crawford W. Long Memorial Hospital	432
Georgia (Atlanta)	Emory University Hospital	335
Georgia (Savannah)	Candler General Hospital	301
Illinois (Alton)	Alton Memorial Hospital	212
Illinois (Chicago)	Bethany Home and Hospital of The Methodist Church	
(Chicago)	Bethany Methodist Hospital	195
(Chicago)	Chicago Wesley Memorial Hospital	650
Illinois (Peoria)	The Methodist Hospital of Central Illinois	554
Indiana (Fort Wayne)	Parkview Memorial Hospital	526
Indiana (Gary)	The Methodist Hospital of Gary, Inc.	350
Indiana (Indianapolis)	Methodist Hospital of Indiana, Inc.	1,020
Iowa (Cedar Rapids)	St. Luke's Methodist Hospital	432
Iowa (Des Moines)	Iowa Methodist Hospital	541
Iowa (Sioux City)	St. Luke's Medical Center	320
Kansas (Dodge City)	The Trinity Methodist Hospital Association	90
Kansas (Hayes)	Hadley Regional Medical Center	130
Kansas (Hutchinson)	Grace Hospital and School of Nursing, Inc.	149
Kansas (Kansas City)	Bethany Hospital	296
Kansas (Salina)	Asbury Hospital	163
Kansas (Wichita)	Wesley Medical Center	670
Kentucky (Beverly)	Doctors Clinic	100
Kentucky (Beverly)	Red Bird Mission Hospital	31
Kentucky (Henderson)	Community Methodist Hospital	170
Kentucky (Lexington)	Good Samaritan Hospital	226
Kentucky (Louisville)	Methodist-Evangelical Hospital, Inc.	300
Kentucky (Pikeville)	The Methodist Hospital of Kentucky, Inc.	193
Louisiana (New Orleans)	Flint-Goodridge Hospital of Dillard University	135
(New Orleans)	Methodist Hospital	134

Location	Institution	Capacity (Beds)
Louisiana (West Monroe)	Glenwood Hospital	179
Massachusetts (Boston)	New England Deaconess Hospital	360
Michigan (Kalamazoo)	Bronson Methodist Hospital	435
Minnesota (Rochester)	Rochester Methodist Hospital	585
Minnesota (St. Louis Park)	Methodist Hospital	354
Mississippi (Hattiesburg)	Methodist Hospital	197
Missouri (Joplin)	Freeman Hospital	127
Missouri (St. Joseph)	Methodist Hospital and Medical Center	415
Missouri (St. Louis)	Barnes Hospital	1,124
Missouri (Springfield)	Lester E. Cox Medical Center	535
Montana (Billings)	Billings Deaconess Hospital	202
Montana (Bozeman)	Bozeman Deaconess Hospital	104
Montana (Great Falls)	Montana Deaconess Hospital	360
Nebraska (Lincoln)	Bryan Memorial Hospital	305
Nebraska (Omaha)	Nebraska Methodist Hospital	327
Nebraska (Scottsbluff)	West Nebraska General Hospital	112
New Mexico (Albuquerque)	Bataan Memorial Methodist Hospital	232
New Mexico (Espanola)	Espanola Community Hospital	70
New York (Brooklyn)	Methodist Hospital of Brooklyn	467
North Carolina (Durham)	Duke University Medical Center	754
North Dakota (Kenmare)	Kenmare Deaconess Hospital	36
Ohio (Cincinnati)	Bethesda Hospital and Deaconess Association	

The following Hospital is under supervision of above corporation:

Location	Institution	Capacity (Beds)
Ohio (Cincinnati)	Bethesda Hospital	352
Ohio (Cincinnati)	The Christ Hospital	679
Ohio (Cleveland)	St Luke's Hospital Association	486
Ohio (Columbus)	Riverside Methodist Hospital	508
Ohio (Toledo)	The Flower Hospital	189
Oregon (Milwaukie)	Willamette Methodist Hospital, Inc.	120
Pennsylvania (Philadelphia)	Methodist Hospital	249
South Dakota (Mitchell)	Methodist Hospital	100
Tennessee (Memphis)	Methodist Hospital	780
Tennessee (Nashville)	Hubbard Hospital of Meharry Medical College	227
Tennessee (Oak Ridge)	The Oak Ridge Hospital of The Methodist Church, Inc.	227
Texas (Baytown)	San Jacinto Methodist Hospital	75
Texas (Dallas)	Methodist Hospital of Dallas	406
Texas (El Paso)	Newark United Methodist Hospital and Houchen Community Center	25
Texas (Fort Worth)	Harris Hospital	510
Texas (Houston)	Methodist Hospital, Inc.	1,030
Texas (Lubbock)	Methodist Hospital	390
Texas (San Antonio)	Southwest Texas Methodist Hospital	196

Location	Institution	Capacity (Beds)
Texas (Weslaco)	Knapp Memorial Methodist Hospital	100
Washington(Richland)	Kadlec Methodist Hospital	107
Washington (Spokane)	Deaconess Hospital	300
Washington (Wenatchee)	Central Washington Deaconess Hospital	99
West Va. (Clarksburg)	Union Protestant Hospital	146
Wisconsin (Green Bay)	Bellin Memorial Hospital	226
Wisconsin (Madison)	Methodist Hospital	212
Wisconsin (Rice Lake)	Lakeside Methodist Hospital	57

HOMES FOR THE AGED

Location	Institution	Capacity (Beds)
Alabama (Birmingham)	Methodist Home for the Aging	

The following two homes are under supervision of above corporation:

Location	Institution	Capacity (Beds)
Alabama (Birmingham)	Fair Haven	210
Alabama (Birmingham)	Wesley Manor	100
Arkansas (Fort Smith)	Methodist Nursing Home	88
California (Burbank)	Pacific Homes	88
California (Los Angeles)	Pacific Homes	

The following seven homes and seven nursing facilities are under supervision of above corporation:

Location	Institution	Capacity (Beds)
Phoenix (Arizona)	Desert Crest Retirement Residence	195
Phoenix (Arizona)	Crestview Convalescent Hospital	66
(Chula Vista)	Fredericka Manor	485
(Chula Vista)	Fredericka Convalescent Hospital	165
(Claremont)	Claremont Manor	325
(Claremont)	Claremont Convalescent Hospital	53
(La Jolla)	Casa de Manana	255
(La Jolla)	La Jolla Convalescent Hospital	39
(Los Angeles)	Kingsley Manor	435
(Los Angeles)	Kingsley Convalescent Hospital	60
(Los Angeles)	Sparr Convalescent Hospital and Home	78
(San Diego)	Wesley Palms	370
Kaneohe, Oahu (Hawaii)	Pohai Nani Retirement Residence	283
Kaneohe, Oahu (Hawaii)	Kahanoala Convalescent Hospital	40
California (Oakland)	Beulah Home, Inc.	130
California (Oakland)	California-Nevada Methodist Homes	

The following three homes are under supervision of above corporation:

Location	Institution	Capacity (Beds)
(Oakland)	Lake Park	336
(Oakland)	Prather Methodist Memorial Home	28
(Pacific Grove)	Forest Hill Manor	144
California (Pasadena)	Robincroft	134
Colorado (Boulder)	Frasier Meadows Manor	225
Connecticut (Shelton)	The United Methodist Convalescent Homes of Connecticut, Inc.	90
Connecticut (West Haven)	Methodist Church Home of the Connecticut Central District	36
Delaware (Wilmington)	Peninsula United Methodist Homes and Hospitals, Inc.	

The following two homes are under supervision of above corporation:

Location	Institution	Capacity (Beds)
(Seaford)	Methodist Manor House	216
(Wilmington)	The Methodist Country House	250
(Washington, D. C.)	The Methodist Home of the District of Columbia	92
Florida (Bradenton)	Asbury Towers	160

Location	Institution	Capacity (Beds)
Florida (Jacksonville)	Jacksonville Methodist Home, Inc. (Wesley Manor)	255
Florida (Miami)	Biscayne Methodist Home, Inc.	85
Florida (St. Petersburg)	Sunny Shores Villas	247
Georgia (Americus)	Magnolia Manor	398
Georgia (Atlanta)	Wesley Homes, Inc.	362
Illinois (Chicago)	Bethany Home and Hospital	

The following two homes are under supervision of above corporation:

Location	Institution	Capacity (Beds)
(Chicago)	Bethany Methodist Home	415
(Morton Grove)	Bethany Terrace	252
Illinois (Chicago)	Methodist Old People Home Corporation	

The following two homes are under supervision of above corporation:

Location	Institution	Capacity (Beds)
(Chicago)	The Methodist Home	160
(Evanston)	The Georgian	245
Illinois (Lawrenceville)	The Methodist Home of Southern Illinois Conference	243
Illinois (Pontiac)	Evenglow Lodge	194
Illinois (Quincy)	Sunset Home of The United Methodist Church	144
Illinois (Rockford)	Wesley Willows, A Methodist Retirement Home	139
Indiana (Frankfort)	Northwest Indiana Methodist Home, Inc.	

The following two homes are under supervision of above corporation:

Location	Institution	Capacity (Beds)
(Frankfort)	Wesley Manor	175
(Greencastle)	Asbury Towers	61
Indiana (Franklin)	The Franklin United Methodist Home	356
Indiana (New Carlisle)	The Haven Hubbard Home of The United Methodist Church	136
Indiana (Warren)	The Methodist Memorial Home for the Aged	593
Iowa (Cedar Falls)	Western Home	260
Iowa (Cedar Rapids)	Meth-Wick Manor, Inc.	207
Iowa (Des Moines)	South Iowa Methodist Homes, Inc.	

The following three homes under supervision of above corporation:

Location	Institution	Capacity (Beds)
(Atlantic)	Heritage House	100
(Des Moines)	Wesleyan Acres	128
(Washington)	Halcyon House	25
Iowa (Fort Dodge)	Friendship Haven, Inc.	685
Iowa (Storm Lake)	Methodist Manor	130
Kansas (Hutchinson)	Wesley Towers	185
Kansas (Newton)	Friendly Acres	150
Kansas (Topeka)	Methodist Home for the Aged	271
Kentucky (Franklin)	Lewis Memorial Home	13
Kentucky (Louisville)	Wesley Manor	104
Louisiana (New Orleans)	Lafon Protestant Home	89
Maine (Rockland)	Methodist Conference Home, Inc.	60
Maryland (Baltimore)	N. M. Carroll Home for Aged	31
Maryland (Baltimore)	The Wesley Home, Inc.	226
Maryland (Gaithersburg)	Asbury Methodist Home, Inc.	175
Massachusetts (Concord)	New England Deaconess Association	178

The following two homes are under supervision of above corporation:

Location	Institution	Capacity (Beds)
(Concord)	Rivercrest Nursing Home	
(Magnolia)	Shore Cliff Rest Home	
Michigan (Ann Arbor)	Retirement Homes of the Detroit Annual Conference	

Location	Institution	Capacity (Beds)
The following two homes are under supervision of above corporation:		
(Chelsea)	Chelsea United Methodist Home	235
(Detroit)	Boulevard Temple United Methodist Home	121
Michigan (Grand Rapids)	M. J. Clark Memorial Home	338
Minnesota (Fairmont)	Lakeview United Methodist Home	110
Minnesota (Minneapolis)	Walker Methodist Residence and Nursing Home, Inc.	505
Minnesota (Montevideo)	Montevideo Methodist Home, Inc. (Brookside Manor)	85
Minnesota (Winona)	Paul Watkins Memorial Methodist Home	115
Mississippi (Biloxi)	Seashore Manor	122
Mississippi (Tupelo)	North Mississippi Home for the Aging, Inc. (Traceway Manor)	100
Missouri (Marionville)	The Ozarks Methodist Manor	120
Montana (Bozeman)	Hillcrest Retirement Home	120
Nebraska (Benkelman)	Sarah Ann Hester Memorial Home	84
Nebraska (Blair)	Crowell Memorial Home	115
Nebraska (Holdrege)	Methodist Memorial Homes, Inc.	115
New Jersey (Collingswood)	United Methodist Home	85
New Jersey (Ocean Grove)	Methodist Homes of New Jersey	
The following three homes are under supervision of above corporation:		
(Branchville)	Methodist Manor	76
(Ocean Grove)	Wesley Manor	120
(Ocean Grove)	Methodist Home	230
New Mexico (Carlsbad)	Landsun Methodist Manor	60
New York (Binghamton)	Elizabeth Church Manor	—
New York (Bronx)	Methodist Church Home for the Aged	90
New York (Brooklyn)	Bethany Methodist Home of Brooklyn, Inc.	29
New York (Brooklyn)	Brooklyn Methodist Church Home	110
New York (Herkimer)	Folts Home	133
New York (Ossining)	Bethel Methodist Home	120
New York (Rochester)	Rochester Methodist Home	135
New York (Williamsville)	Niagara Frontier Methodist Home, Inc. (Beechwood)	158
North Carolina (Asheville)	Brooks-Howell Home	92
North Carolina (Charlotte)	The Methodist Home	231
North Carolina (Charlotte)	Wesley Nursing Center	276
North Carolina (Durham)	The Methodist Retirement Homes, Inc.	200
Ohio (Cincinnati)	Bethesda Hospital and Deaconess Association	
The following home is under supervision of above corporation:		
(Cincinnati)	Bethesda Home for the Aged	213
Ohio (Cincinnati)	The Methodist Home on College Hill	360
Ohio (Columbus)	Wesley Glen	14
Ohio (Elyria)	United Methodist Home	354
Ohio (Lebanon)	The Otterbein Home	170
Ohio (Sebring)	The Cope United Methodist Home (Copeland Oaks)	150
Ohio (Sylvania)	Crestview of Ohio, Inc.	465

Location	Institution	Capacity (Beds)
The following two facilities are under supervision of above corporation:		
(Sylvania)	Crestview Club Apartments	
(Sylvania)	Lake Park Hospital and Nursing Care Center	
Oklahoma (Clinton)	The Methodist Home of Clinton, Inc.	30
Oklahoma (Enid)	The Methodist Home of Enid, Inc.	68
Oklahoma (Tulsa)	Oklahoma Methodist Home for the Aged, Inc.	185
Oregon (Medford)	Rogue Valley Manor	330
Oregon (Portland)	Rose Villa, Inc.	300
Oregon (Portland)	Willamette View Manor, Inc.	391
Oregon (Salem)	The United Methodist Home	83
Pennsylvania (Cornwall)	Cornwall Manor of The United Methodist Church	295
Pennsylvania (Lewisburg)	Evangelical Home	133
Pennsylvania (Meadville)	The Methodist Home for the Aged	90
Pennsylvania (Mechanicsburg)	Retirement Homes of Central Pennsylvania	
The following two homes are under supervision of above corporation:		
(Mechanicsburg)	Bethany Village United Methodist Home for the Aged, Inc.	143
(Tyrone)	Epworth Manor	118
Pennsylvania (Narrowsburg, N.Y.)	Murray-Tufts-Garrett Manor	23
Pennsylvania (Philadelphia)	Evangelical Manor	87
Pennsylvania (Philadelphia)	Philadelphia United Methodist Home for the Aged	250
Pennsylvania (Pittsburgh)	The Methodist Home	215
Pennsylvania (Quincy)	Quincy United Methodist Home for Children and Aging	276
Pennsylvania (Scranton)	Scranton Home	16
Pennsylvania (Tunkhannock)	Tunkhannock Methodist Manor	35
South Carolina (Orangeburg)	The Methodist Home	200
South Dakota (Gettysburg)	Oahe Manor, Inc.	59
South Dakota (Mitchell)	Wesley Acres, Inc.	124
South Dakota (Watertown)	Jenkins Methodist Home, Inc.	77
Tennessee (Hermitage)	McKendree Manor	108
Tennessee (Maryville)	Holston Methodist Homes for the Retired	
The following two facilities under supervision of above corporation:		
(Maryville)	Asbury Acres Retirement Home	102
(Maryville)	Asbury Acres Health Center	58
Texas (Abilene)	Sears Memorial Methodist Center	35
Texas (Dallas)	C. C. Young Memorial Home	172
Texas (Galveston)	Moody House, Inc.	
The following two homes are under supervision of above corporation:		
(Bryan)	Crestview, Inc.	84
(Galveston)	Moody House	317
Texas (Georgetown)	Wesleyan Homes, Inc.	158
Texas (Hereford)	King's Manor	47

Location	Institution	Capacity (Beds)
Texas (Kerrville)	Hilltop Village, Inc.	150
Texas (La Porte)	Happy Harbor Methodist Home	128
Texas (Lockhart)	Golden Age Home	82
Texas (San Antonio)	Morningside Manor, Inc.	260
Texas (Weslaco)	Wesley Manor, Inc.	285
Virginia (Richmond)	Virginia Methodist Homes, Inc.	

The following six homes are under supervision of above corporation:

Location	Institution	Capacity (Beds)
(Alexandria)	Hermitage in Northern Virginia	300
(Norfolk)	Lydia H. Roper Home	27
(Onancock)	The Hermitage on the Eastern Shore	100
(Richmond)	Hermitage-Westwood	260
(Richmond)	Snyder Memorial Home	40
(Roanoke)	The Methodist Home in Roanoke	100
Washington (Des Moines)	Wesley Gardens Corporation (Wesley Gardens, Wesley Terrace and Wesley Cottages)	550
Washington (Seattle)	Bayview Manor	230
Washington (Spokane)	Rockwood Manor	—
West Virginia (Bluefield)	Glenwood Park Methodist Home	50
Wisconsin (Richland Center)	Schmitt Methodist Home	75
Wisconsin (Sparta)	Methodist Morrow Memorial Home for the Aged	95
Wisconsin (West Allis)	East Wisconsin Methodist Homes	

The following three homes under supervision of above corporation:

Location	Institution	Capacity (Beds)
(Janesville)	Cedar Crest	115
(Oshkosh)	Evergreen Manor	140
(West Allis)	Methodist Manor	205

FACILITIES FOR RETIRED MINISTERS

Location	Institution	Capacity (Beds)
Alabama (Birmingham)	Superannuate Homes	119
Alabama (Andalusia)	Board of Pensions and Claimants Homes	55
California (Rowland Heights)	Colonel R. M. Baker Home for Retired Ministers	46
Florida (Lakeland)	Preacher's Relief Fund	61
Georgia (St. Simons Island)	Epworth by the Sea	—
Louisiana (Shreveport)	Retired Ministers' Homes Board, Inc.	27
South Carolina (Columbia)	Retired Ministers' Homes	10
Texas (Stephenville)	Homes for Retired Ministers of the Central Texas Conference	50
Virginia (Fredericksburg)	Home Corporation of Virginia Conference	27

AGENCIES FOR CHILDREN AND YOUTH

Location	Institution	Capacity (Beds)
Alabama (Selma)	Methodist Children's Home	100
Alaska (Anchorage)	The Jesse Lee Home	40
Arkansas (Little Rock)	Methodist Children's Home of Arkansas, Inc.	112
California (Gardena)	Spanish American Institute	34
California (La Verne)	David and Margaret Home for Children, Inc.	51
California (Oakland)	Fred Finch Children's Home, Inc.	38
Florida (Enterprise)	The Florida Methodist Children's Home, Inc.	108

Location	Institution	Capacity (Beds)
Georgia (Atlanta)	Southeastern Methodist Agency for the Retarded, Inc.	*
Georgia (Cedartown)	The Ethel Harpst Home for Children and the Youth, Inc.	70
Georgia (Cedartown)	Sarah D. Murphy Home, Inc.	35
Georgia (Decatur)	The Methodist Children's Home	130
Georgia (Macon)	Methodist Home of South Georgia Conference	90
Illinois (Chicago)	Lake Bluff/Chicago Homes for Children	
Illinois (Chicago)	Methodist Youth Services, Inc.	25
Illinois (Mt. Vernon)	United Methodist Children's Home of the Southern Illinois Conference	39
Illinois (Normal)	The Baby Fold	23
Illinois (Quincy)	Chaddock Boys School	52
Illinois (Rockford)	Rosecrance Memorial Homes for Children	32
Illinois (Urbana)	Cunningham Children's Home	52
Indiana (Goshen)	Bashor Home of The United Methodist Church Inc.	24
Indiana (Lebanon)	Indiana United Methodist Children's Home, Inc.	135
Iowa (Dubuque)	Hillcrest Services to Children and Youth	24
Kansas (Newton)	Methodist Youthville, Inc.	61
Kentucky (Frakes)	Henderson Settlement, Inc.	20
Kentucky (Versailles)	Methodist Home of Kentucky	88
Louisiana (Houma)	MacDonnell Methodist Center	40
Louisiana (New Orleans)	The Methodist Home Hospital	70
Louisiana (Ruston)	Louisiana Methodist Children's Home	84
Maryland (Baltimore)	Board of Child Care	60
Michigan (Detroit)	Methodist Children's Home Society	63
Mississippi (Amory)	North Mississippi Methodist Agency for the Retarded, Inc.	*
Mississippi (Jackson)	The Methodist Children's Home	102
Missouri (Kansas City)	Spofford Home	28
Missouri (St. Louis)	Methodist Children's Home of Missouri	36
Missouri (Webster Groves)	Epworth School for Girls	34
Montana (Helena)	Inter-Mountain Deaconess Home for Children	40
Nebraska (York)	Epworth Village	36
New York (Binghamton)	Children's Home of Wyoming Conference	35
New York (Brooklyn)	Bethany Deaconess Society	—
New York (Dobbs Ferry)	St. Christopher's School	70
New York (Williamsville)	Gateway (Methodist Home for Children)	54
North Carolina (Raleigh)	Methodist Home for Children	150
North Carolina (Winston-Salem)	The Children's Home, Inc.	270
Ohio (Berea)	United Methodist Children's Home	38
Ohio (Cincinnati)	Emmanuel Community Center	*

* (No residential care)

Location	Institution	Capacity (Beds)
Ohio (Flat Rock)	Flat Rock Children's Home of The United Methodist Church	48
Ohio (Worthington)	The Methodist's Children's Home	50
Oklahoma (Gore)	Boys' Ranch of The United Methodist Church of Oklahoma	40
Oklahoma (Tahlequah)	Oklahoma Methodist Homes	

The following two homes are supervised by above corporation:

Location	Institution	Capacity (Beds)
(Tahlequah)	Oklahoma Methodist Home	120
(Tulsa)	Frances E. Willard Home	34
Pennsylvania (Allison Park)	Zoar Home for Mothers and Babies	62
Pennsylvania (Mechanicsburg)	Methodist Home for Children	54
Pennsylvania (Oakmont)	Elizabeth A. Bradley Children's Home	23
Pennsylvania (Philadelphia)	Methodist Home for Children	54
Pennsylvania (Pittsburgh)	Robert Boyd Ward Home for Children	44
Pennsylvania (Quincy)	Quincy United Methodist Home for Children and Aging	80
Pennsylvania (Sheffield)	Ruth M. Smith Children's Home	26
South Carolina (Columbia)	Epworth Children's Home	182
Tennessee (Greeneville)	Holston Methodist Home, Inc.	44
Texas (San Antonio)	Methodist Mission Home of Texas	120
Texas (Waco)	Methodist Home	359
Virginia (Richmond)	Virginia Methodist Children's Home	176
Washington (Everett)	Deaconess Children's Home	28
West Virginia (Beckley)	Beckley Child Care Center	26
West Virginia (Burlington)	Burlington United Methodist Home	40
Wisconsin (Madison)	Methodist Children's Services of Wisconsin, Inc.	40

RESIDENCES

Location	Institution	Capacity (Beds)
Alabama (Birmingham)	Eva Comer Cooperation Home	74
California (Hollywood)	Frances De Pauw International House	75
California (San Francisco)	Gum Moon Residence Hall	41
California (San Francisco)	Mary Elizabeth Inn	90
Indiana (Indianapolis)	Lucille Raines Residence	70

Location	Institution	Capacity (Beds)
Iowa (Des Moines)	Iowa National Esther Hall	142
Iowa (Sioux City)	Shesler Hall	34
Louisiana (Shreveport)	Business Girls' Inn	50
Maryland (Baltimore)	Business Girls' Lodge	64
Michigan (Grand Rapids)	Esther Hall	31
Minnesota (St. Paul)	Emma Norton Residence	66
New York (New York)	Alma Mathews House	50
Ohio (Columbus)	McKelvey Hall	24
Ohio (Toledo)	Flower Esther Hall	31
Pennsylvania (Philadelphia)	Esther Hall	16
Pennsylvania (Pittsburgh)	Methodist Residence for Young Women	27
Rhode Island (Providence)	Providence Deaconess Home	17
South Carolina (Columbia)	Killingsworth Home	24
Utah (Ogden)	Esther Hall	21
Virginia (Richmond)	Wilson Inn	80

UNDER CONSTRUCTION (1972)

Location	Institution
Alabama (Birmingham)	The Methodist Hospital, Inc.
California (Oakland)	California-Nevada Methodist Homes

The following hospital is under supervision of above corporation

Location	Institution
(Madera)	Madera Community Hospital
California (Sacramento)	Methodist Hospital of Sacramento
Georgia (Atlanta)	Asbury Hills, Inc.
Massachusetts (Concord)	New England Deaconess Association

The following home is under supervision of above corporation:

Location	Institution
(Northampton)	Rockridge Home
New York (Binghamton)	Chenango Manor
New York (Huntington, Long Island)	Methodist Retirement Community
New York (Saratoga Springs)	Saratoga Retirement Center, Inc., and Wesley Nursing Home, Inc.
Pennsylvania (Lewisburg)	United Methodist Nursing Home, Inc.
Rhode Island (East Providence)	The United Methodist Retirement Center
South Carolina (Greenwood)	Greenwood Methodist Home
Tennessee (Maryville)	Holston Methodist Homes for the Retired

The following home is under supervision of above corporation:

Location	Institution
Virginia (Wytheville)	Birdmont Manor Nursing Home

BOOK STEWARDS, BOOK AGENTS, EDITORS, AND PUBLISHING AGENTS

Here follows the list of those who have served as Book Stewards, Book Agents, Editors, and Publishing Agents of American Methodism, and the years of their election:

THE METHODIST EPISCOPAL CHURCH

1789	John Dickins	Philadelphia
1799	Ezekiel Cooper	Philadelphia
1804	Ezekiel Cooper, John Wilson	New York
1808	John Wilson, Daniel Hitt	New York
1812	Daniel Hitt, Thomas Ware	New York
1816	Joshua Soule (Bishop, 1824), Thomas Mason	New York
1820	Nathan Bangs, Thomas Mason	New York
	Martin Ruter	Cincinnati
1824	Nathan Bangs, John Emory	New York
	Martin Ruter	Cincinnati
1828	John Emory (Bishop, 1832), Beverly Waugh	New York
	Charles Holiday	Cincinnati
1832	Beverly Waugh (Bishop, 1836) Thomas Mason	New York
	Charles Holiday, J. F. Wright	Cincinnati
1836	Thomas Mason (Resigned, 1840) George Lane	
	P. P. Sanford (Elected by Book Committee, 1841)	New York
	J. F. Wright	Cincinnati
1840	George Lane, P. P. Sanford	New York
	Leroy Swormstedt	Cincinnati
1844	George Lane, C. B. Tippett	New York
	Leroy Swormstedt, J. T. Mitchell	Cincinnati
1848	George Lane, Levi Scott (Bishop, 1852)	New York
	Leroy Swormstedt, J. H. Power	Cincinnati
1852	Thomas Carlton, Zebulon Phillips	New York
	Leroy Swormstedt, Adam Poe	Cincinnati
1856	Thomas Carlton, James Porter	New York
	Leroy Swormstedt, Adam Poe	Cincinnati
1860	Thomas Carlton, Zebulon Phillips	New York
	Adam Poe, Luke Hitchcock	Cincinnati
1864	Thomas Carlton, Zebulon Phillips	New York
	Adam Poe, Luke Hitchcock	Cincinnati
1868	Thomas Carlton, John Lanahan	New York
	Luke Hitchcock, John M. Walden	Cincinnati
1872	Reuben Nelson, John M. Phillips	New York
	Luke Hitchcock, John M. Walden	Cincinnati
1876	Reuben Nelson, John M. Phillips	New York
	Luke Hitchcock, John M. Walden	Cincinnati
1879	Sandford Hunt (Elected by Book Committee on death of Reuben Nelson)	New York
1880	John M. Phillips, Sandford Hunt	New York
	J. M. Walden (Bishop, 1884), W. P. Stowe	Cincinnati
1884	John M. Phillips, Sandford Hunt	New York
	Earl Cranston (Bishop, 1896), William P. Stowe	Cincinnati
1888	John M. Phillips, Sandford Hunt	New York
	Earl Cranston, W. P. Stowe	Cincinnati
1889	Homer Eaton (Elected by Book Committee on death of J. M. Phillips)	New York
1892	Sandford Hunt, Homer Eaton	New York
	Earl Cranston, Lewis Curts	Cincinnati
1894	Homer Eaton, George P. Mains	New York
	Lewis Curts, Henry C. Jennings	Cincinnati

1900	Homer Eaton, George P. Mains	New York
	H. C. Jennings, Samuel H. Pye	Cincinnati
1904	Homer Eaton, George P. Mains	New York
	H. C. Jennings, Edwin R. Graham	Cincinnati
1908	Homer Eaton, George P. Mains	New York
	H. C. Jennings, E. R. Graham	Cincinnati
1912	Homer Eaton, George P. Mains	New York
	Henry C. Jennings	Cincinnati
	Edwin R. Graham	Chicago
1913	(On the death of Homer Eaton, the Book Committee elected H. C. Jennings as General Agent, and John H. Race, Agent at Cincinnati)	
1916	Henry C. Jennings, General Agent	Chicago
	Edwin R. Graham	New York
	John H. Race	Cincinnati
1920	Edwin R. Graham	New York
	John H. Race	Cincinnati
	Robert H. Hughes	Chicago
1921	On the death of Edwin R. Graham, the Book Committee made the following arrangement: John H. Race, Robert Hughes, Agents; H. C. Jennings, George P. Mains, Agents Emeritus	
1924	John H. Race	New York
	George C. Douglass	Cincinnati
	O. Grant Markham	Chicago
	George P. Mains, Emeritus	
1928	John H. Race	New York
	George C. Douglass	Cincinnati
	O. Grant Markham	Chicago
	George P. Mains, Emeritus (D., 1930)	
1932	John H. Race	New York
	George C. Douglass	Cincinnati
	O. Grant Markham	Chicago
1936	O. Grant Markham	New York
	George C. Douglass	Cincinnati
	Fred D. Stone	Chicago
	John H. Race, Emeritus	

EDITORS OF THE *METHODIST REVIEW*:

1818-32	The Book Agents (Not published in 1829)
1832-36	Nathan Bangs
1836-40	Samuel Luckey
1840-48	George Peck
1848-56	John McClintock
1856-84	Daniel D. Whedon
1884-88	Daniel Curry
1888-92	James W. Mendenhall
1892-96	William V. Kelley (Elected by the Book Committee)
1896-20	William V. Kelley
1920-30	George Elliot
1931	(6 months), Editorial Committee.

The Review was discontinued at this time. A little later, John W. Langdale, then the Book Editor, began the publication of *Religion In Life* (which see).

BOOK EDITORS, M. E. CHURCH

For many years the Book Agents filled this position. Then up to 1904 the Editor of *The Methodist Review*.

1904-12	Richard J. Cooke (Bishop 1912)
1912-28	David G. Downey
1928-40	John W. Langdale

EDITORS OF CHURCH SCHOOL PUBLICATIONS:

1844-56	Daniel P. Kidder
1856-68	Daniel Wise
1868-88	John H. Vincent (Bishop in 1888)
1888-00	Jesse L. Hurlbut
1900-04	Thomas B. Neely (Bishop in 1904)
1904-14	John T. McFarland
1914-29	Henry H. Meyer
1929-	Lucius H. Bugbee

EDITORS OF *THE CHRISTIAN ADVOCATE*:
(New York City)

1826-28	Barber Badger
1828-32	Nathan Bangs
1832-34	J. P. Durbin
1834-36	Nathan Bangs
1836-40	Samuel Luckey
1840-48	Thomas E. Bond
1848-52	George Peck
1852-56	Thomas E. Bond
1856-60	Abel Stevens
1860-64	Edward Thomson (Bishop in 1864)
1864-76	Daniel Curry
1876-80	C. H. Fowler (Elected Missionary Secretary in 1880 and Bishop in 1884)
1880-12	J. M. Buckley
1912-15	George P. Eckman (Resigned in 1915)
1915-16	J. R. Joy (Elected by Book Committee)
1916-	J. R. Joy
1938-40	Harold Paul Sloan

Pittsburgh Christian Advocate:

Feb. 1, 1834-June 30, 1836	Charles Elliott
June 30, 1836-Aug. 11, 1836	Charles Cooke
1836-40	William Hunter
1840-44	Charles Cooke
1844-52	William Hunter
1852-56	Homer J. Clark
1856-60	Isaac N. Baird
1860-72	S. H. Nesbit
1872-76	William Hunter
1876-84	Alfred Wheeler
1884-08	Charles W. Smith (Bishop in 1908)
1908-28	John J. Wallace
1928-32	Ralph B. Urmy (Note: Combined with *The Christian Advocate*, January 1, 1932)

The Christian Advocate—Western Edition (Cincinnati).

1834-36	Thomas A. Morris (Bishop in 1836)
1836-48	Charles Elliott
1848-52	Matthew Simpson (Elected Bishop in 1852)
1852-56	Charles Elliott
1856-64	Calvin Kingsley (Bishop in 1864)
1864-68	John Morrison Reid
1868-72	Stephen M. Merrill (Bishop in 1872)
1872-84	Francis S. Hoyt
1884-89	Jeremiah H. Bayliss
1889-92	David H. Moore (Elected by Book Committee)
1892-00	David H. Moore (Bishop in 1900)
1900-16	Levi Gilbert
1916-32	Ernest C. Wareing
1932-	Orien W. Fifer

Der Christliche Apologete (Cincinnati).

1839-92	William Nast
1892-18	Albert J. Nast (Resigned in 1918)
1918-20	August J. Bucher (Elected by Book Committee)
1920-	August J. Bucher

The Christian Advocate—California Edition (San Francisco).

1851-56	S. D. Simonds
1856-68	Eleazer Thomas
1868-80	H. C. Benson

1880-94	B. F. Crary
1894-00	W. S. Matthew
1900-13	F. D. Bovard
1913-16	F. M. Larkin (Elected by Book Committee)
1916-24	F. M. Larkin
1924-32	E. P. Dennett
1932-	E. L. Mills

The Christian Advocate—Northwestern Edition (Chicago).

1852-56	James V. Watson
1856-68	Thomas M. Eddy
1868-72	John M. Reid
1872-01	Arthur Edwards
1901-08	D. D. Thompson (Elected by Book Committee in 1901)
1908-12	Charles M. Stuart (Elected by Book Committee in 1909)
1912-24	Elbert Robb Zaring
1924-32	Dan B. Brummitt (Note: Combined with the *Central Edition* by the General Conference of 1932.)

The Christian Advocate—Central Edition
(Kansas City, Missouri).

1852-54	W. D. R. Trotter
1854-56	J. L. Conklin
1856-60	Joseph Brooks
1860-64	Charles Elliott
1864-72	Benjamin F. Crary
1872-91	Benjamin St. James Fry
1891-92	Samuel Williams (Elected by the Book Committee)
1892-00	Jesse Bowman Young
1900-32	Claudius B. Spencer (Editor of the authorized *Rocky Mountain Christian Advocate*, 1896-1900, when it was merged with *The Central Christian Advocate*).
1932-	Dan B. Brummitt (Note: Combined with the *Northwestern Edition* by the General Conference of 1932).

The Christian Advocate—Pacific Edition (Portland, Oregon).

1855-64	Thomas H. Pearne
1864-68	H. C. Benson
1868-76	Isaac Dillon
1876-80	J. H. Acton
1880-88	H. K. Hines
1888-92	W. S. Harrington
1892-04	A. N. Fisher
1904-11	D. L. Rader
1911-12	R. H. Hughes (Elected by Book Committee)
1912-20	R. H. Hughes
1920-32	Edward Laird Mills (Note: Combined with the *California Edition* by the General Conference of 1932).

The Christian Advocate—Southwestern Edition
(New Orleans, Louisiana).

The New Orleans Christian Advocate was edited and published by John P. Newman from January 6, 1866, to November 29, 1869.

1873-76	Joseph C. Hartzell (Private enterprise. Adopted by General Conference in 1876).
1876	Hiram R. Revels (Elected, but resigned).
1876-82	Joseph C. Hartzell (Elected by Book Committee. Elected Missionary Bishop for Africa, 1896).
1882-84	Lewis P. Cushman (Elected by Book Committee).
1884-88	Marshall W. Taylor
1888-92	A. E. P. Albert
1892-96	E. W. S. Hammond
1896-04	Isaiah B. Scott (Missionary Bishop for Africa, 1904).
1904-20	Robert E. Jones (Bishop in 1926).
1920-31	L. H. King
1931-32	A. P. Shaw

The Epworth Herald (*Chicago, Illinois*).

1890-04	Joseph F. Berry (Bishop in 1904)
1904-12	Stephen J. Herben
1912-24	Dan B. Brummitt
1924-	W. E. J. Gratz

The Christian Advocate—Southern Edition
(*Athens, Tennessee*).

1892-04	R. J. Cooke (Elected Book Editor in 1904 and Bishop in 1912).
1904-16	J. J. Manker
1916-32	J. M. Melear (Note: Discontinued by the General Conference of 1932).

THE METHODIST EPISCOPAL CHURCH, SOUTH.
(Organized in 1846).

Book Agents:

1846-50	John Early (Elected bishop in 1854)
1854	Stevenson and Owen
1858	J. B. McFerrin
1866-70-74	A. H. Redford
1878-82-86	J. B. McFerrin (Died in 1887)
1887	J. D. Barbee (by Book Committee, July)
1890-94-98	J. D. Barbee, Senior Agent
	D. M. Smith, Assistant Agent
1902	R. J. Bigham, Senior Agent
	D. M. Smith, Assistant Agent
1903	D. M. Smith, Senior Agent
	A. J. Lamar, Assistant Agent (by Book Committee, July).

Publishing Agents: (as the name became in 1906)

1906-10	
1914-18	D. M. Smith
	A. J. Lamar
1922-26	A. J. Lamar
	J. W. Barton (resigned, September, 1926)
	D. M. Smith, Emeritus (Book Committee)
	B. A. Whitmore elected by Book Committee to succeed J. W. Barton
1930	A. J. Lamar
	B. A. Whitmore
	D. M. Smith, Emeritus
1934	B. A. Whitmore
	Alfred F. Smith
1938	B. A. Whitmore
	Alfred F. Smith
(1940 Unification)	

Editors of *The Christian Advocate* (in the South before the division of the Methodist Episcopal Church)

Western Methodist

1834	Lewis Garrett and John N. Maffitt

Southwestern Christian Advocate

1836	Thomas Stringfield
1840	Charles A. Davis
1844	J. B. McFerrin

(In the M. E. Church, South)
Nashville Christian Advocate

1846-50-54	J. B. McFerrin

Christian Advocate

1858	H. N. McTyeire (Elected bishop in 1866)
1866-70-74	Thomas O. Summers
1878-82-86	O. P. Fitzgerald (Elected bishop in 1890)
1890-94-98	E. E. Hoss (Elected bishop in 1902)
1902-06	G. B. Winton
1910-14-22	Thomas N. Ivey (Died May 15, 1923)
1923	Alfred E. Smith (Book Committee, June)
1926	Alfred E. Smith
1930	Alfred E. Smith
1934	W. P. King
1938	W. P. King
(1940 Unification)	

Editors of the *Quarterly Review*

1832-36-40-44	Same as Book Editor
1846	H. B. Bascom
1850	William H. Anderson, who declined.
1850-54	D. S. Doggett
1858	T. O. Summers

(In 1862 the publication of the *Review* was suspended, and, except for a brief period when an arrangement was made with Bledsoe's *Southern Review*, the Church was without an official *Review*)

1878	J. W. Hinton (Committee)
1879	T. O. Summers (Committee)
1882	J. W. Hinton

(Since 1886 the Editor of the *Quarterly Review* has also been the Book Editor, see below.)

BOOK EDITORS

1882-86-90	W. P. Harrison
1894-	
1898-1902	J. J. Tigert (Elected Bishop in 1906)
1906-10-14	Gross Alexander (Died September 6, 1915)
1915	H. M. Du Bose (Book Committee, October; elected Bishop in 1918).
1918	F. M. Thomas (Died May 9, 1921)
1921	G. T. Rowe (Committee, June).
1922-26	G. T. Rowe (Resigned June, 1928)
1928-30	W. P. King (Book Committee, July)
1930-34	W. P. King—By The General Conference
1934-38	Alfred F. Smith—By The General Conference
1938	Alfred F. Smith—By The General Conference

SUNDAY SCHOOL EDITORS

1870-74	A. G. Haygood (Elected Bishop in 1890)
1878	
1886-90	W. G. E. Cunnyngham
1894	W. D. Kirkland (Died, 1896)
1896	James Atkins (Committee, June)
1898-1902	James Atkins (Elected Bishop in 1906)
1906-10-14	
1918-22-26	E. B. Chappell
1930-34-38	C. A. Bowen

THE METHODIST CHURCH—1940-1968
Editor, *Christian Advocate*:

1940	Roy L. Smith
1952	T. Otto Nall (Elected Bishop in 1960)
1956	Leland Case
1960	Ewing T. Wayland (Editorial Director)

Together/Christian Advocate

1964	Richard C. Underwood (Editor, *Together*)
	James M. Wall (Editor, *Christian Advocate*)

Sunday School Editors

1940	Lucius Bugbee, C. A. Bowen
1944	C. A. Bowen
1948	H. C. Bullock

Book Editors

1940-56	Nolan B. Harmon (Elected Bishop in 1956)
1956-	Emory S. Bucke

Publishing Agents

1940-48	B. A. Whitmore, Fred D. Stone
1948-52	Fred D. Stone, Lovick Pierce
1952-	Lovick Pierce became Publisher of The Methodist Church in general reorganization of Church agencies taking place then.

MEMBERSHIP STATISTICS

METHODIST DENOMINATIONS CURRENTLY IN THE U.S.A., 1775-1965

		1775	1800	1825	1850	1875	1900	1925	1950	1965
Methodist Episcopal	(1784)*	3,148	64,894	341,144	799,431	1,580,559	2,584,863	4,711,994		
Methodist Episcopal, South	(1844)				621,135	712,765	1,470,520	2,478,623		
Methodist Protestant	(1830)				62,305	64,319	184,097	186,275		
The Methodist Church	(1939)								8,942,647	10,304,184
African Methodist Episcopal	(1816)			N.A.**	N.A.	200,000	641,727	650,000	886,735	1,166,301
African Methodist Episcopal Zion	(1821)				N.A.	225,000	528,461	490,000	530,116	770,000
Christian Methodist Episcopal	(1870)					67,888	198,628	366,315	381,000	444,493
Free Methodist	(1860)					6,000	26,353	34,751	50,033	58,164
Wesleyan Methodist	(1843)					20,000	17,202	21,000	33,796	59,622
Union American Methodist Episcopal	(1850)						15,000	18,812	9,369	27,560
Reformed Methodist Union Episcopal	(1885)						N.A.	2,126	1,025	16,000
Congregational Methodist	(1852)					N.A.	13,000	21,000	11,189	14,274
Primitive Methodist	(1829)					2,800	6,470	9,986	12,000	12,805
Reformed Zion Union Apostolic	(1869)					N.A.	2,346	10,000	12,000	12,000
Evangelical Methodist	(1946)								N.A.	8,041
Congregational Methodist of U.S.A.	(1852)					N.A.	319	1,256	5,857	7,500
African Union First Colored Methodist Protestant	(1886)					N.A.	3,437	3,750	2,504	5,000
Southern Methodist Church	(1939)								6,327	4,025
Holiness Methodist (N. Dakota)	(1911)							N.A.	650	1,000
Independent African Methodist Episcopal	(1907)							N.A.	1,000	N.A.
People's Methodist	(1939)								N.A.	1,000
Fundamental Methodist	(1942)								332	650
New Congregational Methodist	(1881)						4,000	1,256	1,149	518
Holiness Methodist (Lumber River N. C.)	(1900)						N.A.	N.A.	662	360
Reformed New Congregational Methodist	(1916)							N.A.	336	N.A.
Apostolic Methodist	(1932)								31	100
Cumberland Methodist	(1950)								60	65
United Wesleyan Methodist	(1905)							N.A.	N.A.	N.A.

* Date in parentheses indicates the year of organization of the denomination.
** N.A.—Data Not Available

Sources: General Minutes of The Methodist Episcopal Church: General Minutes of The Methodist Episcopal Church, South; General Minutes of The Methodist Protestant Church; General Minutes of The Methodist Church; The Methodist Almanac; The Year Book of American Churches; The Handbook of Denominations in the United States.

MEMBERSHIP, WORLD METHODISM

AFRICA

Algeria and Tunisia	274	Fernando Po	600
Angola	14,250	Gambia	1,244
Botswana	4,437	Ghana—	
Burundi	4,548	A.M.E.	3,000
Congo	67,000	A.M.E. Zion	6,560
Dahomey & Togo	47,000	C.M.E.	1,160

Methodist Church in Ghana	69,260
Ivory Coast	18,000
Kenya, Methodist Church	11,876
Liberia—	
A.M.E.	2,000
A.M.E. Zion	3,000
Methodist Church in Liberia	21,000
Mozambique—	
United Methodist	6,723
Free Methodist Church of North America	5,385
Wesleyan Methodist Mission	2,500
Nigeria—	
A.M.E.	30,000
A.M.E. Zion	2,500
Methodist Church in Nigeria	54,332
Rhodesia—	
A.M.E.	6,000
Free Methodist Church of North America	1,286
Methodist Church, U.K.	28,014
United Methodist Church	14,920
Rwanda—	
Free Methodist Church of North America	1,929
Sierra Leone—	
A.M.E.	200
American Wesleyan Mission	642
Methodist Church	23,232
West African Methodist Church	12,219
South Africa—	
A.M.E.	41,509
Free Methodist Church of North America	866
Methodist Church, South Africa	730,000
Methodist Church, S. E. Conference	1,000
Southwest Africa—	
A.M.E.	3,389
Methodist Church	1,589
Spanish Equatorial Africa, Methodist Church	300
Swaziland, Methodist Church of South Africa	2,349
United Arab Republic—	
Free Methodist	4,250
Zambia—	
A.M.E.	750
United Church of Zambia—part formerly Methodist	23,702
	1,274,795

ASIA

Burma—	
Methodist Church, UMC	1,526
Methodist Church, UK	6,429
Ceylon	13,278
China, Republic of (last available figures)	250,000
Hong Kong—	
Church of Christ in China	21,000
Free Methodist Church	1,190
Methodist Church, UMC	1,315
Methodist Church, UK	150
India—	
Free Methodist Church	569
Methodist Church in Southern Asia	155,819
Wesleyan	278
Church of South India—part formerly Methodist	413,299
Church of North India	800,000
Indonesia—	
Methodist Church (Sumatra)	16,303
Japan—	
United Church of Christ—part formerly Methodist	204,000
Okinawa	1,378
Korea, Methodist Church	84,152
Malaysia—Singapore, Methodist Church	40,000
Pakistan—Methodist Church	17,942
Philippines—	
Free Methodist Church	425

Evangelical	30,000
Methodist Church	73,159
United Church of Christ in the Philippines—part formerly Methodist	142,405
Taiwan—	
Free Methodist	1,448
Methodist Church	2,985
Wesleyan Methodist	25
	2,279,075

AUSTRALASIA AND PACIFIC ISLANDS

Australasia, Methodist Church	482,000
Wesleyan Methodist	250
Fiji Islands	38,200
New Guinea, Papua and Solomon Islands	11,768
New Zealand	46,000
West Samoa	6,140
Tonga, Free Wesleyan Methodist	8,100
	590,458

EUROPE

Austria, Methodist Church	771
Belgium, Methodist Church	1,336
Bulgaria, Methodist Church	632
Czechoslovakia, Evangelical Methodist Church	3,000
Denmark, Methodist Church	3,536
Finland, Methodist Church	1,230
France, Methodist Church	1,200
Germany	65,000
Great Britain—	
Independent Methodist Churches	7,500
The Methodist Church	701,306
Wesleyan Reform Union	5,576
Ireland, Methodist Church	32,904
Italy, Methodist Church	3,669
Norway, Methodist Church	8,251
Poland	18,734
Portugal—	
Evangelical Methodist Church of	650
Sweden, Methodist Church	10,905
Switzerland, Methodist Church	11,147
U.S.S.R., Estonian Methodist	750
Wales	13,000
Yugoslavia, Methodist	2,000
	893,097

NORTH AND LATIN AMERICA

Bahamas	3,171
Barbados	14,613
British Honduras	1,801
Canada—	
Free Methodist	4,752
United Church of Canada (part formerly Methodist)	1,000,000
Costa Rica—	
Methodist Church, UMC	1,000
Methodist Church, Caribbean	2,399
Cuba—	
Methodist Church of Cuba	10,000
Dominican Republic—	
A.M.E.	500
Free Methodist Church	1,479
Guatemala—	
Primitive Methodist	1,800
Haiti—	
Free Methodist Church	160
Methodist Church	2,728

Honduras—
Methodist Church	2,326
Wesleyan Methodist Mission	105

Jamaica—
A.M.E.	520
Methodist Church, Caribbean	20,106
Wesleyan Methodist Mission	800

Leeward and Windward Islands—
Methodist Church, Caribbean	14,301

Mexico—
Free Methodist Church	615
Methodist Church	25,807

Netherlands Antilles (Curacao)—
Methodist Missionary Society	1,338

Panama and Canal Zone—
Methodist Church	491

Puerto Rico—
American Wesleyan Mission	475
Methodist Church	10,500

Trinidad and Tobago—
A.M.E.	400
Methodist Church	14,613

United States—
A.M.E.	1,250,000
A.M.E. Zion	1,100,000
African Union First Colored Methodist Protestant Church, Inc.	5,000
Bible Protestant Church	2,500
C.M.E.	466,718
Congregational Methodist	14,274
Congregational	7,500
Evangelical Methodist Church	8,728
Free Methodist Church of North America	135,096

Holiness Methodist Church	1,000
The United Methodist Church	10,623,026
Primitive Methodist Church, U.S.A.	11,945
Reformed Methodist Union Episcopal Church	16,198
Reformed Zion Union Apostolic Church	16,000
Southern Methodist Church	4,025
Union American Methodist Episcopal Church	27,560
The Wesleyan Church	85,000
	14,911,370

South America

Argentina	7,338
Bolivia	1,386

Brazil—
Free Methodist Church	1,334
Methodist Church	57,756

Chile—
Pentecostal Church (offshoot of Methodist Church)	400,000
Methodist Church	4,900

Columbia—
Wesleyan Methodist	387

Guyana—
A.M.E.	230
Methodist Church	5,428

Paraguay—
Free Methodist	124

Peru—
Methodist Church	1,439
Uruguay	1,768
	482,090
GRAND TOTAL	20,430,885

1796 ANNUAL CONFERENCES – METHODIST EPISCOPAL CHURCH

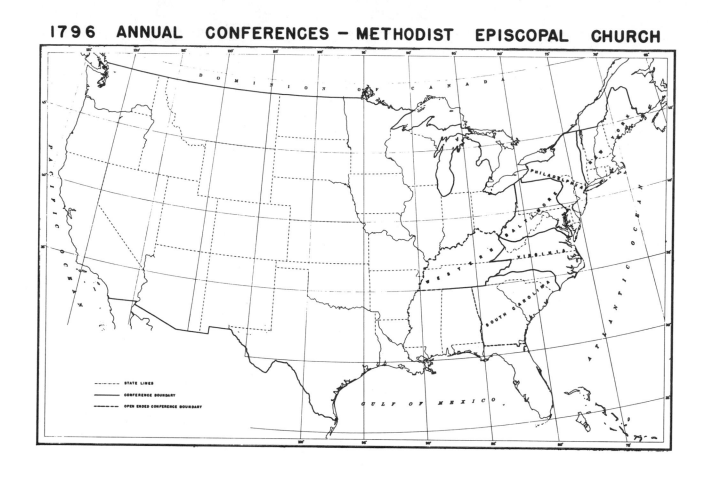

1828 ANNUAL CONFERENCES – METHODIST EPISCOPAL CHURCH

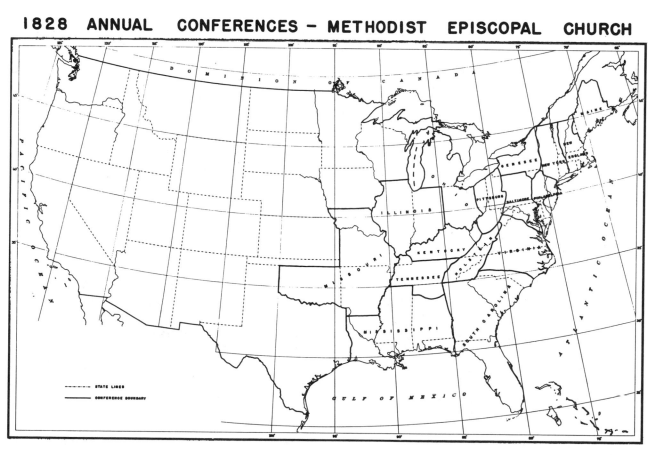

1844 ANNUAL CONFERENCES - METHODIST EPISCOPAL CHURCH

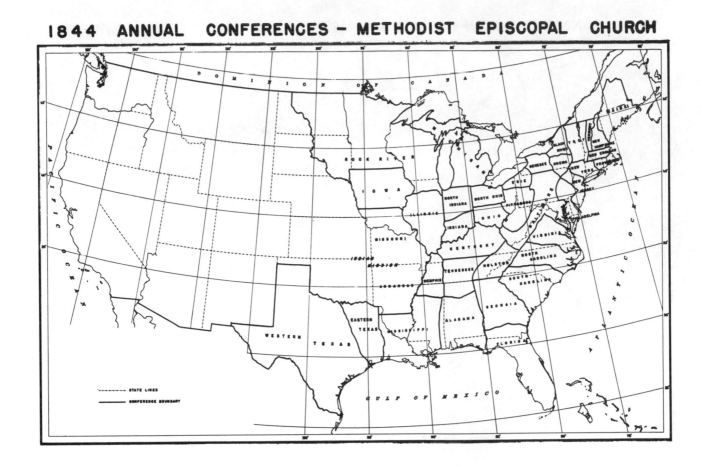

1848 ANNUAL CONFERENCES - METHODIST EPISCOPAL CHURCH

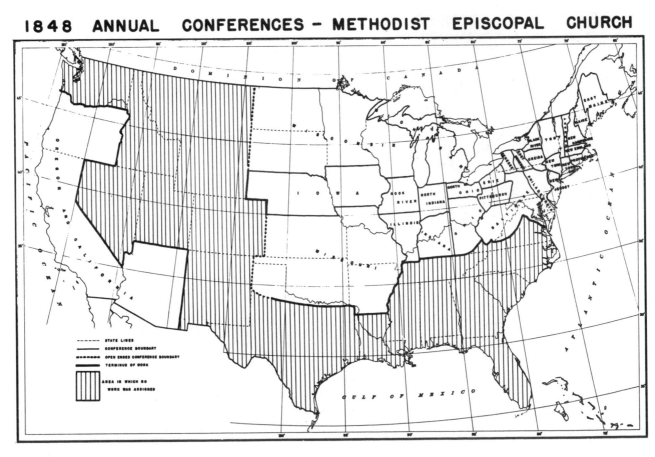

1868 ANNUAL CONFERENCES — METHODIST EPISCOPAL CHURCH

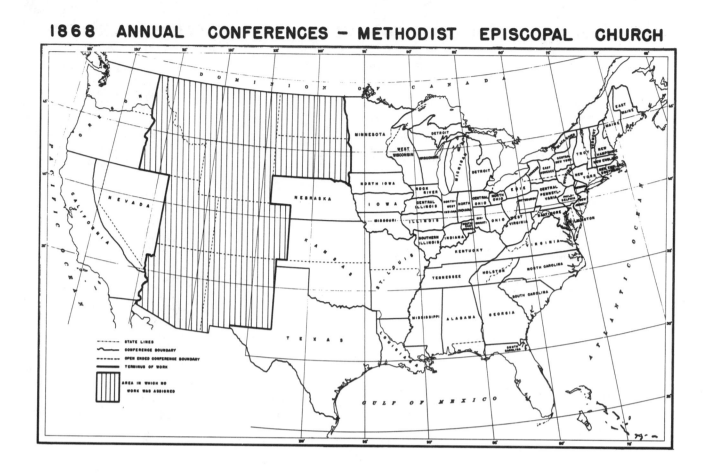

1904 ANNUAL CONFERENCES — METHODIST EPISCOPAL CHURCH

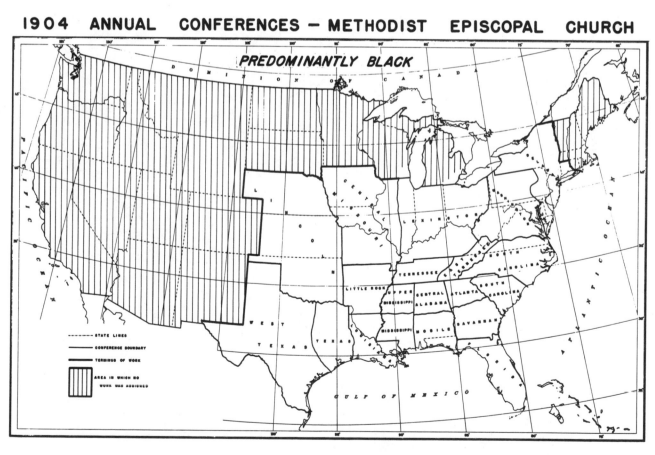

2717

1904 ANNUAL CONFERENCES – METHODIST EPISCOPAL CHURCH

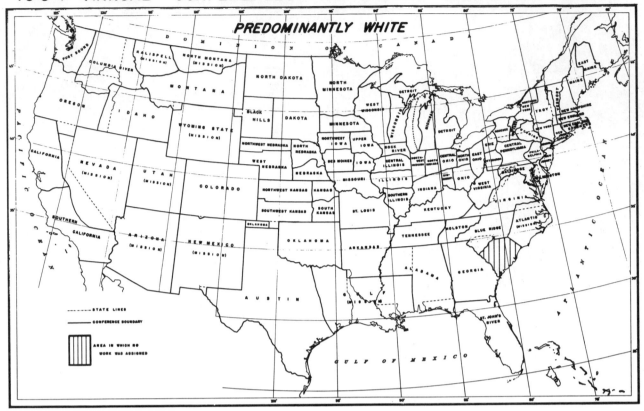

1846 ANNUAL CONFERENCES—METHODIST EPISCOPAL CHURCH SOUTH

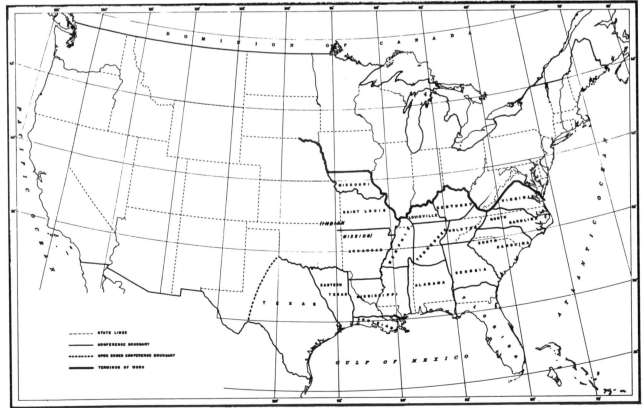

1866 ANNUAL CONFERENCES—METHODIST EPISCOPAL CHURCH SOUTH

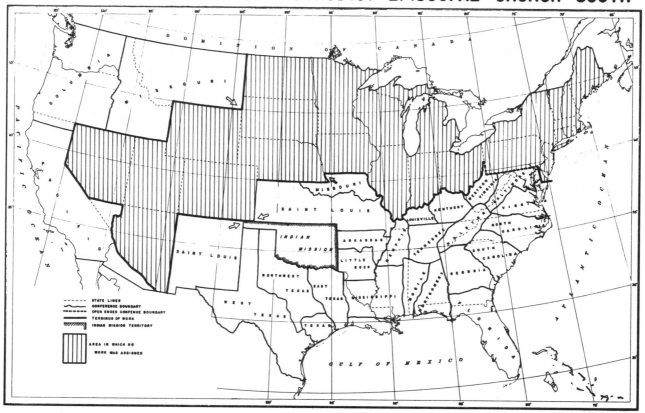

1923 ANNUAL CONFERENCES—METHODIST EPISCOPAL CHURCH SOUTH

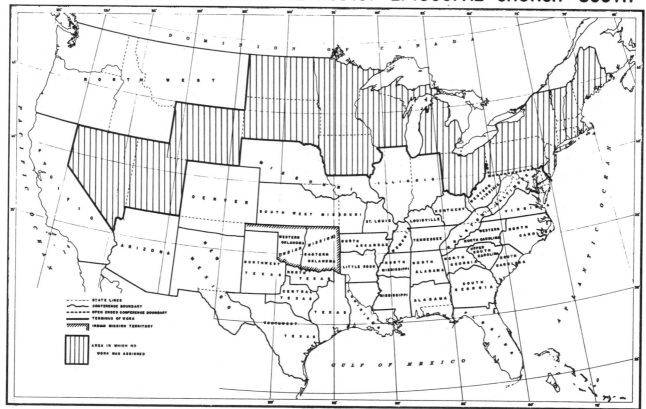

1956 ANNUAL CONFERENCES - THE METHODIST CHURCH

NOT INCLUDING CENTRAL JURISDICTION

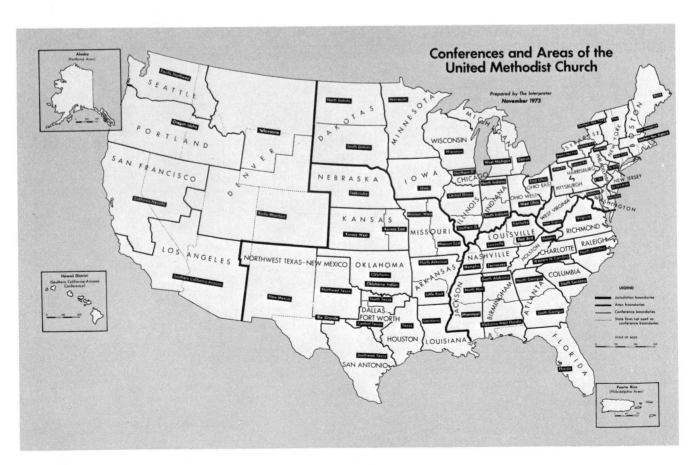

Conferences and Areas of the
United Methodist Church

Prepared by The Interpreter
November 1973

BIBLIOGRAPHY

In a monumental undertaking such as this *Encyclopedia* a multitude of authorities have been consulted, some of them many times over. To most of the articles one or two printed sources of further information are appended, some works appearing many times. Those which have been used in five or more articles are here listed in the alphabetical order of their authors or (for anonymous or serial works) titles. For these select works full bibliographical data are supplied in this listing only, and after the individual articles only short titles appear. This not only saves much duplication of details of little interest to many people, but brings together one of the most comprehensive bibliographies of world Methodism ever published, which we believe will be of great service to librarians and scholars. To render this of even greater value, we have appended a rearrangement of these short titles under subject headings, so that the reader can discover at a glance the major works upon many broad Methodist topics. This arrangement by subjects moves from reference works to twenty-four distinct categories both topical and topographical, arranged in alphabetical order, several of them subdivided. These major categories and their subdivisions are listed below.

Our thanks are due to Mr. Gordon Duncan of the Abingdon Press for much bibliographical research in connection with this feature, ably supported by the secretarial labors of Mrs. Evelyn Sutton of Lake Junaluska, and especially of Mrs. Louise Queen, who also coordinated the bibliographical entries in the articles themselves with this bibliography.

FRANK BAKER

SUBJECT BIBLIOGRAPHY

I. REFERENCE WORKS

A. GENERAL (abbreviations to be used are in parentheses)

American Universities and Colleges. 1968. (AUC)
Dictionary of American Biography. (DAB)
Dictionary of National Biography. (DNB)
Who's Who in America. (Who's Who (U.S.))
Who's Who in Great Britain. (Who's Who (G.B.))

B. METHODIST

Batten, J. M. *Outline and Bibliographical Guide.* 1954.

Beckerlegge, O. A. *United Methodist Ministers and Their Circuits*. 1968.

Clark and Stafford. *Who's Who in Methodism*. 1952.

Cornish, G. H. *Cyclopaedia of Methodism in Canada*. 1881, 1903.

Hall's Circuits and Ministers. 1913, 1925.

Hill, W. *Alphabetical Arrangement*. 1819.

Howell, C. T. *Prominent Personalities*. 1945.

Little, B. B. *Methodist Union Catalog*. 1967.

Martin and Sheldon. *Ministers and Probationers*. 1964.

Osborn, G. *Outlines of Wesleyan Bibliography*. 1869.

Price, C. F. *Who's Who in American Methodism*. 1916.

Register of Circuit Plans. 1960.

Simpson, M. *Cyclopaedia*. 1878.

Tindall, E. H. *Wesleyan Methodist Atlas*. 1871.

Who's Who in The Methodist Church. 1966.

Who's Who in Methodism. 1933.

Williams, E. L. *Biographical Directory of Negro Ministers*. 1966.

World Methodist Council Handbook. 1966.

Wright, R. R. *Centennial Encyclopaedia* (AME). 1916, 1948.

C. METHODIST SERIALS

The A.M.E. Church Review. 1884- .

Arminian Magazine. 1778-97; continued as *Methodist Magazine*, etc. to 1970.

Batsel, J. D. *Union List of Methodist Serials*. 1968, 1970.

Christliche Apologete. 1839-1941.

Christliche Botschafter. 1836-1946.

Evangelical Messenger. 1848-1946.

London Quarterly Review. 1853- .

The Methodist Church (USA.) *Daily Christian Advocate* (Gen. Conf.)

———————————— *Daily Christian Advocate* (Juris. Conf.)

———————————— *Doctrines and Discipline*. 1939-68.

———————————— *Journal of the General Conf*. 1940-68.

———————————— *Jurisdictional Conf. Journals*. 1940-68.

———————————— *General Minutes*. 1940-68.

M. E. Church. *Daily Christian Advocate* (Gen. Conf.)

———————————— *Journal of General Conf*. 1796-1936.

———————————— *Minutes of the Annual Confs*. 1773-1939.

M. E. Church, South. *Daily Christian Advocate* (Gen. Conf.)

———————————— *Doctrines and Discipline*. 1846-1938.

———————————— *Journal of the General Conf*. 1846-1938.

———————————— *Minutes of the Annual Confs*. 1845-1940.

Methodist History. 1962- .

The Methodist Magazine (N.Y.) 1818-1932.

The Methodist Protestant. 1834-1940.

M.P. Church. *Constitution and Discipline*. 1830-1938.

———————————— *Journal of the General Conf*.

Methodist Recorder. 1839-1929.

Minutes of the Methodist Conferences (G.B.) 1744- .

Minutes of the Methodist Conferences in Ireland. 1752-1819.

Missionary Seer (AMEZ). 1900- .

Mutual Rights. 1824-34.

Nashville *Christian Advocate*. 1832-1940.

New York *Christian Advocate*. 1826-1940.

Primitive Methodist Journal. 1892- .

Proceedings of the World Methodist Conference. 1881-1966.

Proceedings of the Wesley Historical Society. 1898- .

Quarterly Review of the M.E. Church, South. 1847-1930.

Religion in Life. 1932- .

Southern Christian Advocate. 1837-1940.

Telescope Messenger. 1947-63.

United Meth. Church (USA). *Daily Christian Advocate* (Gen. Conf.)

———————————— *Daily Christian Advocate* (Juris. Conf.)

———————————— *Doctrines and Discipline*. 1968.

———————————— *Journal of the General Conf*. 1968, 1970.

———————————— *Jurisdictional Conf. Journals*. 1968.

———————————— *General Minutes*. 1968-70.

The Wesleyan Methodist. 1843- .

II. AFRICA

Bartels, F. L. *Ghana Methodism*. 1965.

Calhoun, E. C. *Congo Quest*. 1961.

Findlay and Holdsworth, *Wesleyan Meth. Miss. Soc*., Vol. IV, 1922.

Fox, W. *Wesleyan Missions* (Western Africa). 1851.

Garrett, A. E. F. *South African Methodism*. 1965.

Hewson, L. A. *South Africa*. 1950.

Holden, W. C. *South Africa*. 1877.

James, H. I. *Rhodesia*. 1935.

King, W. J. *Liberia*. n.d.

Mears, W. G. A. *Baralong Mission*. 1969.

———————— *Great Namaqualand*. 1969.

Oduyoye, M. *Yorubaland*. 1969.

Reid, A. J. *Congo Drumbeat*. 1964.

Sadler, C. *William Shaw*. 1967.

Shaw, B. *South Africa*.

Taylor, W. *Darkest Africa*. 1898.

———————— *South Africa*. 1867.

Whiteside, J. *South Africa*. 1906.

III. ASIA

Badley, B. H. *Indian Missionary Directory*. 1876, 1881.

Badley, B. T. *Southern Asia*. 1931.

Baker, R. T. *China*. 1947.

Bashford, J. W. *China*. 1916.

———————— *China and Methodism*. 1906.

Burton, J. W. *Call of the Pacific*. 1912.

Butler, W. *Boston to Bareilly*. 1885.

Deats, R. L. *Philippines*. 1964.

Dimmitt, M. A. *Isabella Thoburn College*. 1963.

Fifty Years of Light (Korea). 1938.

Findlay and Holdsworth, *Wesleyan Meth. Miss. Soc*. Vol. V, 1924.

Ford, E. L. *Educational Work in China*. 1938.

Harper, M. H. *India*. 1936.

Harris, M. C. *Japan*. 1907.

Harvard, W. M. *Ceylon and India*. 1823.

Hedley, J. *North China* (MNC). 1907.

Hollister, J. N. *Southern Asia*. 1956.

Lacy, W. N. *China*. 1948.

Maclay, R. S. *Life Among the Chinese.* 1861.
Means, N. T. *Malaysia.* n.d.
Mudge, J. *Handbook of India.* 1877.
Noble, M. W. *Korea.* 1933.
Paik, G. L. *Korea.* 1929.
Pickett, J. W. *India.* 1933.
Price, F. B. *India.* 1907.
Ryang, J. S. *Korea.* 1930.
Scott, J. E. *Southern Asia.* 1906.
Taylor, W. *India.* 1875.
———— *Ten Years in India.* 1882.
Thoburn, J. M. *India and Malaysia.* 1892.
Thomson, E. *Oriental Missions.* 1871.

IV. AUSTRALASIA

Benson, C. I. *Victorian Methodism.* 1935.
Blamires and Smith. *Wes. Meth. Church in Victoria.* 1886.
Burton, J. W. *Call of the Pacific.* 1912.
Burton and Deane. *Fiji.* 1936.
Colwell, J. *Century in the Pacific.* 1914.
———— *Illustrated History.* 1904.
———— *New South Wales.* 1904.
Danks, B. *South Seas.* 1909.
Dingle, R. S. C. *Queensland.* 1947.
Guy and Potter. *Prim. Meth. in New Zealand.* 1893.
Lawry, W. *Friendly and Feejee Islands.* 1850.
Morley, W. *New Zealand.* 1900.
Tippett, A. R. *Fiji.* 1954.
Williams, W. J. *New Zealand.* 1922.

V. BIOGRAPHIES

A. Collective

Atmore, C. *Methodist Memorial.* 1801, 1871.
Blews, R. R. *Master Workmen.* 1939.
Carroll, J. *Case and His Cotemporaries.* 1867-77.
Coles, G. *Heroines.* 1857.
Crookshank, C. H. *Women of Irish Methodism.* 1882.
Duncan, W. B. *South Carolina Conference.* 1901.
Espino, J. *Perfiles.* 1963.
Fitzgerald, O. P. *Centenary Cameos.* 1885.
Fitzgerald and Galloway. *Eminent Methodists.* 1897.
Flood and Hamilton. *Lives of Methodist Bishops.* 1882.
Gallagher, R. H. *Pioneer Preachers* (Irish). 1965.
Gorrie, P. D. *Lives of Ministers.* 1852.
Haines, A. W. *Makers of Iowa Methodism.* 1900.
Hedges, J. W. *Crowned Victors.* 1878.
Herod, G. *Biographical Sketches.* 1855.
Holt, Ivan Lee. *Missouri Bishops.* 1953.
Huestis, G. O. *Wesleyan Missionaries in Eastern British America.* 1872.
Jackson, T. *Lives of Early Methodist Preachers.* 1837-38.
Joy, J. R. *Teachers of Drew.* 1942.
Koontz and Roush. *The Bishops.* 1950.
Lafferty, J. J. *Sketches of Virginia Conference.* 1880 and other eds.
Lawson, W. D. *Wesleyan Local Preachers.* 1874.
Leete, F. D. *Methodist Bishops.* 1948.
M'Clintock, Jr. *Sketches.* 1854.
Moister, W. *Wesleyan Missionaries.* 1878.
Morrow, T. M. *Early Methodist Women.* 1967.
Pettigrew, M. C. *Miles to Johnson.* 1970.
Sandford, P. P. *Memoirs.* 1843.
Seamands, J. T. *Pioneers.* 1967.
Sherman, D. *Sketches.* 1860.
Stevens, A. *Women of Methodism.* 1866.

Stevenson, G. J. *Methodist Worthies.* 1884-86.
Summers, T. O. *Biographical Sketches.* 1858.
Sweet, W. W. *Men of Zeal.* 1935.
Taft, Z. *Biographical Sketches.* 1825.
Thompson, H. A. *Our Bishops.* 1889.
Tyerman, L. *Oxford Methodists.* 1873.
Veh, R. M. *Evangelical Bishops.* 1939.
Weekley and Fout. *Our Heroes.* 1908-11.
Wesley and His Successors. 1891.
Wheeler, M. S. *WFMS of the ME Church.* 1881.
Wise, D. *Sketches.* 1886.
Wright, R. R. *Bishops* (AME). 1963.
Wunderlich, F. *Methodists Linking Two Continents.* 1960.

B. Individual

Abbott, Benjamin. Ffirth, J. ed. *Benjamin Abbott.* 1805.
Albright, Jacob. Miller, G. *Jakob Albrecht und Georg Miller.* 1834.
———— Miller, G. (trans. Epp). *Jacob Albright.* 1959.
———— Yeakel, R. *Jacob Albright.* 1883.
Allen, Richard. Allen, R. *Life Experience.* 1833.
———— Baxter, D. M. *Richard Allen.* 1923.
———— Wesley, C. H. *Richard Allen.* 1935.
Andrew, James Osgood. Smith, G. G. *Life and Letters.* 1882.
Arthur, William. Stephenson, T. B. *William Arthur.* 1907.
Asbury, Francis. Asbury, Francis, *Extract from the Journal of.* 1792.
———— Asbury, Francis, *Extract from the Journal of.* 1802.
———— Asbury, Francis. *Journal.* 1821.
———— Clark et al. eds. *Journal and Letters.* 1958.
———— Asbury, Herbert. *Methodist Saint.* 1927.
———— Carroll, H. K. *Francis Asbury.* 1923.
———— Larrabee, W. C. *Asbury and His Colaborers.* 1868.
———— Rudolph, L. C. *Francis Asbury.* 1966.
———— Smith, G. G. *Life and Labors.* 1896.
———— Strickland, W. P. *Pioneer Bishop.* 1858.
———— Tipple, E. S. *Francis Asbury.* 1916.
Averell, Adam. Stewart and Revington. *Memoir.* 1843.

Balcke, F. W. Haselmayer, L. A. *Life Memories.* 1963.
Ball, Hannah. Cole, J. *Hannah Ball.* 1796.
———— McQuaid, I. D. *Hannah Ball.* 1964.
Bangs, Nathan. Stevens, A. *Life and Times.* 1863.
Beggs, Stephen R. Beggs, S. R. *Early History.* 1868.
Benson, Joseph. Macdonald, J. *Memoirs.* 1822.
———— Treffry, R. *Memoirs.* 1840.
Black, William. Maclean, J. *Apostle of Methodism.* 1907.
———— Richey, M. *Memoir.* 1839.
Boardman, Richard. Lockwood, J. P. *Western Pioneers.* 1881.
Boehm, Henry. *Reminiscences.* 1875.
Bohler, Peter. Lockwood, J. P. *Peter Bohler.* 1868.
Bourne, Hugh. Antliff, W. *Life.* 1872.

——————— Walford, J. *Hugh Bourne*. 1855, 1856.

——————— Wilkinson, J. T. *Hugh Bourne*. 1952.

Brackenbury, R. C. Smith, Mrs. R. *Raithby Hall*. 1859.

Bradburn, Samuel. Blanshard, T. W. *Life*. 1870.

——————— Bradburn, E. W. *Memoirs*. 1816.

Bramwell, William. Sigston, J. *Memoir*. 1820.

Breeden, Henry. *Striking Incidents*. 1878.

Brown, George. *Autobiography*. 1908.

Brunson, Alfred. *Western Pioneer*. 1872, 1879.

Bunting, Jabez. Bunting, T. P. *Life*. 1887.

——————— Kent, J. *Jabez Bunting*. 1955.

Burdsall, R. *Memoirs*. 1797.

Butler, William. Butler, C. *William Butler*. 1902.

——————— *Land of the Veda*. 1871.

Candler, Warren A. Pierce, A. M. *Warren Akin Candler*. 1948.

Cannon, James. Dabney, V. *Dry Messiah*. 1949.

Capers, William. Wightman, W. M. *Life*. 1858.

Cartwright, Peter. *Autobiography*. 1856.

——————— *Fifty Years*. 1871.

Casson, Hodgson. Gregory, B. *Humorous Revivalist*. 1897.

Cennick, John. Cennick, J. *Life*. 1745.

Chivington, John M. Craig, R. S. *Fighting Parson*. 1959.

Clarke, Adam. Clarke, J. B. B. *Adam Clarke*. 1833.

——————— Etheridge, J. W. *Life*. 1858.

——————— Everett, J. *Adam Clarke*. 1843, 1849.

Clowes, William. *Journals*. 1844.

——————— Garner, W. *Life*. 1868.

——————— Wilkinson, J. T. *William Clowes*. 1951.

Coke, Thomas. Candler, W. A. *Life*. 1923.

——————— *Extracts of the Journals*. 1793.

——————— *Extracts of the Journals*. 1816.

——————— Crowther, J. *Life*. 1815.

——————— Davey, C. J. *Thomas Coke*. 1947.

——————— Drew, S. *Life*. 1818.

——————— Etheridge, J. W. *Life*. 1860.

——————— Vickers, J. A. *Thomas Coke*. 1969.

Cooper, Ezekiel. Phoebus, G. A. *Beams of Light*. 1887.

Coppin, L. J. *Unwritten History*. 1919.

Cox, Melville B. *Remains*. 1840.

——————— Guptill and Clark. *Melville B. Cox*. 1932.

Dawson, William. Everett, J. *William Dawson*. 1844.

Dickey, Sarah A. Griffith, H. *Dauntless in Mississippi*. 1965.

Dickins, John. Cooper, E. *Funeral Discourse*. 1799.

Dickinson, Peard. *Memoirs*. 1803.

Dixon, James. *Methodism in America*. 1849.

Dow, Lorenzo. *Dealings of God*. 1853.

——————— *Cosmopolite*. 1814.

Draper, D. J. Symons, J. C. *Daniel James Draper*. 1870.

Drew, Samuel. Drew, J. H. *Life*. 1835.

Dunn, Samuel. Harris, T. R. *Samuel Dunn*. 1963.

Dyer, John L. *Autobiography*. 1890.

Early, Jordan W. Early, S. J. *Life and Labors*. 1894.

Edwards, David. Davis, L. *Life*. 1883.

Emory, John. Emory, R. *Life*. 1841.

Entwisle, Joseph. Entwisle, Jr., J. *Joseph Entwisle*. 1848.

Everett, James. Chew, R. *James Everett*. 1875.

Finley, James B. *Autobiography*. 1853.

——————— *Life Among the Indians*. 1857.

——————— *Memorials of Prison Life*. 1850.

——————— *Sketches of Western Methodism*. 1857.

Fisher, F. B. Fisher, W. H. *Frederick Bohn Fisher*. 1944.

Fisk, Wilbur. Holdich, J. *Life*. 1842.

——————— Prentice, G. *Wilbur Fisk*. 1890.

Fitzgerald, O. P. *Fifty Years*. 1903.

——————— *Sunset Views*. 1900.

Fletcher, John. Benson, J. *John William de la Flechere*. 1804.

——————— Lawton, G. *Shropshire Saint*. 1960.

——————— Tyerman, L. *Wesley's Designated Successor*. 1882.

Fletcher, Mary. Moore, H. *Mrs. Mary Fletcher*.

Flickinger, D. K. Flickinger, D. K. *Fifty-five Years*. 1907.

Fowler, Henry Hartley. Fowler, E. H. *Henry Hartley Fowler*. 1912.

Freeman, Thomas B. Birtwhistle, A. *Thomas Birch Freeman*.

——————— *Journals*. 1844.

Garrettson, Freeborn. Bangs, N. *Life*. 1829.

——————— *Experience and Travels*. 1791.

Gatch, Philip. M'Lean, J. *Sketch*. 1854.

George, Enoch. Fry, B. S. *Life*. 1852.

Glendinning, William. *Life*. 1795.

Glossbrenner. Drury, A. W. *Glossbrenner*. 1889.

Green, Anson. *Life and Times*. 1877.

Gregory, Benjamin. Gregory, J. R. *Benjamin Gregory*. 1903.

Gilbert, Nathaniel. Thompson, E. W. *Nathaniel Gilbert*. 1961.

Glide, Lizzie H. McPheeters, J. C. *Life Story*. 1936.

Griffith, William. Chew, R. *William Griffith*. 1885.

Harris, Howell. Hughes, H. J. *Howell Harris*. 1892.

——————— Nuttall, G. F. *Howel Harris*, 1965.

——————— Roberts, G. T. *Howell Harris*. 1951.

Hart, Virgil C. Hart, E. I. *Virgil C. Hart*. 1917.

Haven, Gilbert. Daniels, W. H. *Gilbert Haven*. 1880.

——————— Prentice, G. *Life*. 1883.

Hayes, Lucy Webb. Davis, Mrs. J. *Lucy Webb Hayes*. 1890.

Hayes, Thomas. *Recollections*. 1902.

Haygood, Atticus G. Mann, H. W. *Atticus Greene Haygood*. 1965.

Haygood, Laura Askew. Brown, O. E. *Life and Letters*. 1904.

Heck, Barbara. Withrow, W. H. *Barbara Heck*. 1895.

Hedding, Elijah. Clark, D. W. *Life and Times*. 1855.

Hedström, O. G. Lawson, E. B. *Olof Gustaf Hedström*. 1945.

Hendrix, Eugene R. Holt, Ivan Lee. *Eugene Russell Hendrix*. 1950.

Hick, Samuel. Everett, J. *Village Blacksmith*. 1879.

Hill, David. Rattenbury, H. B. *David Hill*. 1949.

Holsey, L. H. Cade, J. B. *Holsey*. 1964.

——————— *Autobiography*. 1898.

Hughes, Edwin Holt. *I Was Made a Minister.* 1943.

Hughes, Hugh Price. Hughes, D. P. *Hugh Price Hughes.* 1904.

Hunt, John. Birtwhistle, A. *John Hunt.* 1954.

Huntingdon, Countess of. Seymour, A. C. H. *Countess of Huntingdon.* 1839.

———————————— New, A. H. *Coronet and the Cross.* 1857.

Hurst, John Fletcher. Osborn, A. *John Fletcher Hurst.* 1905.

Hutton, James. Benham, D. *Memoirs.* 1856.

Ingham, Benjamin. Thompson, R. W. *Benjamin Ingham.* 1958.

Isaac, Daniel. Everett, J. *Polemic Divine.* 1839.

Jackson, Thomas. *Recollections.* 1873.

———————————— Rupp, E. G. *Thomas Jackson.* 1954.

Jacoby, Ludwig S. Mann, H. *Ludwig S. Jakoby.* 1892.

Jarratt, Devereux. *Life.* 1806.

Jobson, F. J. Gregory, B. *Life.* 1884.

Keeble, S. E. Edwards, M. L. *S. E. Keeble.* 1949.

Kephart, Ezekiel B. John, L. F. *Life.* 1907.

Kilham, Alexander. Blackwell, J. *Life.* 1838.

———————————— Grundell, and Hall. *Life.* 1799.

Kim, Helen. Potts, J. M. *Grace Sufficient.* 1964.

Lane, Isaac. *Autobiography.* 1916.

———————————— Savage, H. C. *Life and Times.* 1958.

Lanktree, Matthew. Lanktree, M. *Biographical Narrative.* 1836.

Lee, Daniel. Lee and Frost. *Ten Years in Oregon.* 1844.

Lee, Jason. Brosnan, C. J. *Jason Lee.* 1932.

Lee, Jesse. Lee, L. M. *Life and Times.* 1848.

———————————— Thrift, M. *Memoir.* 1823.

Lee, John. Lee, Jesse. *Short Account.* 1805.

Lidgett, J. Scott. Davies, R. E. *John Scott Lidgett.* 1957.

———————————— *My Guided Life.* 1936.

McConnell, Francis J. *Autobiography.* 1952.

M'Kendree, William. Paine, Robert. *Life and Times.* 1869.

Mackenzie, Peter. Dawson, J. *Life and Labours.* 1896.

———————————— Young, D. T. *Peter Mackenzie.* 1904.

McTyeire, H. N. Tigert, J. J. *Holland Nimmons McTyeire.* 1955.

Marvin, Enoch M. Finney, T. M. *Life and Labors.* 1880.

———————————— M'Anally, D. R. *Life and Labors.* 1878.

Maxwell, Darcy, Lady. Atherton, W. *Life of Lady Maxwell.* 1863.

Moore, John M. *Life and I.* 1948.

Mortimer, Elizabeth. Bulmer, A. *Memoirs.* 1859.

Mott, John R. Mathews, B. *John R. Mott.* 1934.

Moulton, James Hope. Moulton, H. K. *James Hope Moulton.* 1919.

Nast, William. Wittke, C. *William Nast.* 1960.

Newcomer, Christian. Hough, S. S. *Christian Newcomer.* 1941.

———————————— *Journal.* 1834.

Newton, Robert. Jackson, T. *Life.* 1855.

North, Frank Mason. Lacy, C. *Frank Mason North.* 1967.

O'Bryan, William. *Narrative of Travels.* 1836.

———————————— Thorne, S. L. *William O'Bryan.* 1878.

Oglethorpe. Church, L. F. *Oglethorpe.* 1932.

O'Kelly, James. MacClenny, W. E. *Life.* 1910.

Olin, Stephen. *Life and Letters.* 1853.

Otterbein, Philip W. Core, A. C. *Otterbein.* 1968.

———————————— Drury, A. W. *Otterbein.* 1884.

———————————— Milhouse, P. W. *Otterbein.* 1968.

Ouseley, Gideon. Arthur, W. *Life.* 1876.

Payne, Daniel. *Recollections.* 1888.

Peake, Arthur Samuel. Wilkinson, J. T. *Arthur Samuel Peake.* 1958.

Perkins, E. Benson. *Autobiography.* 1964.

Petersen, O. P. Hardy, Aage. *O. P. Petersen.* 1953.

Phillips, C. H. *Autobiography.* 1932.

Pierce, George Foster. Smith, G. G. *George Foster Pierce.* 1888.

Pierce, William H. Hicks, J. P. *William Henry Pierce.* 1933.

Piggott, Henry James. Piggott and Durley. *Henry James Piggott.* 1921.

Pilmore, Joseph. Lockwood, J. P. *Western Pioneers.* 1881.

———————————— Maser and Maag. *Journal of Joseph Pilmore.* 1969.

Pitezel, John H. *Lights and Shades.* 1883.

Pollard, Samuel. Kendall, R. E. *Samuel Pollard.* 1949.

Price, Joseph Charles. Walls, W. J. *Joseph Charles Price.* 1943.

Punshon, William Morley. Macdonald, F. W. *William Morley Punshon.* 1887.

Reed, William. Thorne, J. *William Reed.* 1869.

Reeves, Hannah. Brown, G. *Lady Preacher.* 1870.

Reeves, William. Corderoy, E. *Father Reeves.* 1882.

Richardson, Charles. Coulson, J. E. *Charles Richardson.* 1867.

Richardson, James. Webster, T. *James Richardson.* 1876.

Rigg, James Harrison. Telford, J. *James Harrison Rigg.* 1909.

Roberts, Benjamin T. Roberts, B. H. *Benjamin Titus Roberts.* 1900.

Roberts, Robert R. Elliott, C. *Robert R. Roberts.* 1844.

———————————— Fry, B. S. *Robert R. Roberts.* 1856.

———————————— Tippy, W. M. *Robert Richford Roberts.* 1958.

Rogers, Hester Ann. Coke, T. *Mrs. H. A. Rogers (Funeral Sermon).* 1795.

———————————— *Experience.* 1793.

———————————— *Spiritual Letters.* 1796.

Russell, T. *Record of Events.* 1869.

Ruter, Martin. Smith, E. A. *Martin Ruter.* 1915.

Ryerson, Egerton. *My Life.* 1883.

———————————— Sissons, C. B. *Egerton Ryerson.* 1937, 1947.

Sangster, W. E. Sangster, P. E. *Doctor Sangster.* 1962.

Scott, George. Westin, G. *George Scott.* 1928, 1929.

Scott, John. *Recollections*. 1898.
Scott, Orange. Matlack, L. C. *Orange Scott*. 1848.
Seybert, John. Neitz, S. *Johannes Seybert*. 1862.
——————— Spreng, S. P. *John Seybert*. 1888.
Shaw, William. Sadler, Celia. *William Shaw*. 1967.
——————— *Story of My Mission*. 1872.
Shepard, Cyrus. Mudge, Z. A. *Cyrus Shepard*. 1848.
Simons, G. A. Marshall, L. A. *American Pioneer in Russia*. 1928.
Simpson, Matthew. Clark, R. D. *Matthew Simpson*. 1956.
——————— Crooks, G. R. *Matthew Simpson*. 1890.
——————— Wood, E. M. *Matthew Simpson*. 1909.
Smith, David. Smith, D. *David Smith*. 1881.
Smith, Henry. *Recollections*. 1848.
Snethen, Nicholas. Feeman, H. L. *Asbury's Silver Trumpet*. 1950.
Soule, Joshua. DuBose, H. M. *Joshua Soule*. 1911.
Spence, Robert. Burdekin, R. *Robert Spence*. 1840.
Stateler, L. B. Stanley, E. J. *L. B. Stateler*. 1907.
Stephens, Joseph R. Holyoake, G. J. *Joseph Rayner Stephens*. 1881.
Stevens, Abel. *Sketches*. 1851.
Stevenson, William. Vernon, W. N. *William Stevenson*. 1964.
Stewart, John. *Highways and Hedges*. 1872.
Stewart, John. Finley, J. B. *Life Among the Indians*. 1857.
Straughn, James H. Stephenson, F. W. *James H. Straughn*. 1967.
Summers, T. O. Fitzgerald, O. P. *Dr. Summers*. 1885.
Sung, John. Lyall, L. T. *John Sung*. 1954.
Swain, Clara A. *Glimpse of India*. 1909.
——————— Hoskins, Mrs. R. *Clara A. Swain*. 1912.
——————— Wilson, D. C. *Clara Swain*. 1968.

Taft, Mary Barritt. *Memoirs*. 1827.
Tatham, Thomas. Dunn, S. *Thomas Tatham*. 1847.
Taylor, William. *Story of My Life*. 1895.
Thoburn, Isabella. Thoburn, J. M. *Isabella Thoburn*. 1903.
Thoburn, James Mills. Oldham, W. F. *Thoburn*. 1918.
——————— *My Missionary Apprenticeship*. 1884.
Thorne, James. Bourne, F. W. *James Thorne*. 1895.
——————— Thorne, John. *James Thorne*. 1873.
Thorne, Samuel Thomas. Ruddle, T. *Samuel Thomas Thorne*. 1893.
Told, Silas. *Life*. 1786.
Travis, Joseph. *Autobiography*. 1856.
Treffry, Richard, Jr. Treffry, R., Sr. *Memoirs*. 1838.

Van Orsdel, W. W. Lind, R. W. *"Brother Van."* 1961.

Walker, Jesse. Pennewell, A. M. *Jesse Walker*. 1958.
Wallbridge, Elizabeth. Richmond, L. *Elizabeth Wallbridge*.
Walsh, Thomas. Morgan, J. *Thomas Walsh*. 1762.
Ware, Thomas. *Sketches*. 1839.
Warne, Francis W. Badley, B. T. *Warne of India*. 1932.
Watson, Richard. Jackson, T. *Richard Watson*. 1834.

Watters, William. Watters, D. A. *William Watters*. 1898.
——————— *Short Account*. 1806.
Weaver, Jonathan. Thompson, H. A. *Jonathan Weaver*. 1901.
Webb, Thomas. Pritchard, J. *Captain Webb*. 1797.
Weekley, William M. *Twenty Years*. 1924.
Whatcoat, Richard. Phoebus, W. *Richard Whatcoat*. 1828.
——————— Fry, B. S. *Richard Whatcoat*. 1852.
——————— Bradley, S. B. *Richard Whatcoat*. 1936.
Whitefield, George. Belden, A. D. *George Whitefield*. 1930.
——————— Dallimore, A. A. *George Whitefield*. 1970.
——————— Gillies, J. *George Whitefield*. 1772.
——————— Henry, S. C. *George Whitefield*. 1957.
——————— Philip, R. *George Whitefield*. 1837.
——————— Tyerman, L. *George Whitefield*. 1876.
——————— *Journals*. 1960.
Wiley, Allen. Holliday, F. C. *Allen Wiley*. 1853.
Willerup, Christian. Gaarde, S. N. *Chr. Willerup*. 1915.

Yost, William. *Reminiscences*. 1911.
Young, Egerton R. *By Canoe and Dog Train*. 1890.
Young, Jacob. *Autobiography*. 1857.

Zinzendorf, Count. Lewis, A. J. *Zinzendorf*. 1962.
——————— Weinlick, J. R. *Count Zinzendorf*. 1956.

VI. BRITISH ISLES (See also XXIII, D, "Eighteenth Century Methodism in the British Isles")

A. GENERAL

Baker, F. *Charge to Keep*. 1947.
Brash, W. B. *Methodism*. 1928.
Cumbers, F. *Book Room*. 1956.
Currie, R. *Methodism Divided*. 1968.
Davey, C. J. *Methodist Story*. 1955.
Davies, R. E. *Methodism*. 1963.
——————— *Methodists and Unity*. 1962.
Davies and Rupp. *Meth. Church in Great Britain*, Vol. I, 1965.
Dimond, S. G. *Psychology of Methodism*. 1932.
Dolbey, G. W. *Architectural Expression*. 1964.
Edwards, M. L. *After Wesley*. 1935.
——————— *Methodism and England*. 1943.
——————— *This Methodism*. 1939.
Harrison, A. W. *Separation from the Church of England*. 1945.
Kissack, R. *Church or No Church*. 1964.
Nightingale, J. *Portraiture*. 1807.
Redfern, W. *Modern Developments*. 1906.
Townsend, Workman and Eayrs. *New History*. 1909.
Urwin, E. C. *Significance of 1849*. 1949.
Wakefield, G. S. *Methodist Devotion*. 1966.
Warner, W. J. *Industrial Revolution*. 1930.
Wearmouth, R. F. *Social and Political Influence*. 1957.
——————— *Trade Unions*. 1959.
——————— *Struggle of the Working Classes*. 1954.
——————— *Working-Class Movements*. 1937.

Wood, A. S. *Inextinguishable Blaze*. 1960.

B. CHANNEL ISLES

Guiton, Francois, *Iles de la Manche*. 1846.
Hargreaves, J. R. *Channel Islands*. 1884.
Lelievre, M. *Iles de la Manche*. 1885.
Moore, R. D. *Channel Islands*. 1952.

C. ENGLAND

Allen, R. *Methodism in Preston*. 1866.
Baker, F. *Methodist Pilgrim in England*. 1951.
Bolitho, H. *North Hill Circuit*. 1947.
Braithwaite, M. *Bishop Auckland Circuit*. 1885.
Caine, C. *Crewe Circuit*. 1883.
Chick, E. *Methodism in Exeter*. 1907.
Cocking, T. *Methodism in Grantham*. 1836.
Court, L. H. *Dartmoor Saints*. 1927.
Dickons, J. N. *Kirkgate Chapel, Bradford*. 1903.
Dyson, J. B. *Leek Circuit*. 1853.
————— *Congleton Circuit*. 1856.
————— *Isle of Wight*. 1865.
Eayrs, G. *Wesley and Kingswood*. 1911.
Hall. J. *West Bromwich*. 1886.
Harwood, G. H. *Nottingham*. 1872.
Hayman, J. G. *North Devon*. 1871.
Hocken, J. *Grimsby Circuit*. 1839.
Larkin, W. *City of Norwich*. 1825.
Lester, G. *Grimsby Methodism*. 1890.
Lyth, J. *Methodism in York*. 1885.
Mallinson, J. *Huddersfield, Holmfirth, etc.* 1898.
Martin, J. H. *Wesley's London Chapels*. 1946.
Moore, B. *Burnley and East Lancashire*. 1899.
Phillips, W. *Shropshire*. 1896.
Robinson, J. R. *Dewsbury and Birstal*. 1900.
Rockledge, J. *Easingwold Circuit*. 1872.
Seed, T. A. *Norfolk Street Chapel and Sheffield*. 1907.
Shaw, T. *Cornish Methodism*. 1967.
Sheldon, W. C. *Birmingham*. 1903.
Simon, J. S. *Dorset*. 1870.
Smith, B. *Macclesfield*. 1875.
Smith, H. *Portsmouth*. 1895.
Stamp, W. W. *Bradford*. 1841.
————— *Orphan-House of Wesley*. 1863.
Stevenson, G. J. *City Road Chapel*. 1872.
Symons, W. *West Somerset*. 1898.
Taylor, J. *Apostles of Fylde*. 1885.
Tuck, S. *Frome*. 1814.
Ward, J. *Thirsk Circuit*. 1860.
————— *Bingley*. 1863.
Watmough, A. *City of Lincoln*. 1829.
Woodward, M. W. *Wesley's Chapel*. 1966.
Woolcock, J. *Isle of Wight*. 1897.

D. INDEPENDENT METHODIST CHURCH

Mounfield, A. *Independent Methodism*. 1905.
Vickers, J. *Independent Methodism*. 1920.

E. IRELAND

Cole, R. L. *Methodism in Dublin*. 1932.
————— *Methodism in Ireland*. 1960.
Crook, W. *Ireland and American Methodism*. 1866.
Crookshank, C. H. *Methodism in Ireland*. 1885-88.
Gallagher, R. H. *Pioneer Preachers* (Irish). 1965.
Haire, R. *Wesley's Visits to Ireland*. 1947.
Jeffery, F. *Irish Methodism*. 1964.
Jones, J. W. *Belfast*. 1893.
McCrea, A. *Irish Methodism*. 1931.
Minutes of Meth. Conferences in Ireland. 1864.

F. THE METHODIST CHURCH

Anglican-Methodist Unity. The Scheme. 1968.
Currie, R. *Methodism Divided*. 1968.

Harrison, A. W. et al. *Methodist Church*. 1932.
Spencer and Finch. *Constitutional Practice*. 1951.

G. PRIMITIVE METHODIST CHURCH

Bourne, H. *Primitive Methodists*. 1823.
Clowes, W. *Journals*. 1844.
Farndale, W. E. *Secret of Mow Cop*. 1950.
Herod, G. *Biographical Sketches*. 1855.
Kendall, H. B. *Primitive Methodist Church*. 1905.
————— *Origin and History* (PMC). 1905-06.
Patterson, W. M. *Northern Primitive Methodism*. 1909.
Petty, J. *Primitive Methodist Connexion*. 1860.
Probert, J. C. C. *Primitive Methodism in Cornwall*. 1966.
Ritson, J. *Primitive Methodism*. 1909.
Russell, T. *Record of Events*. 1869.
Walford, J. *Hugh Bourne*. 1855-56.
Wilkinson, J. T. *Hugh Bourne*. 1952.
————— *William Clowes*. 1951.

H. SCOTLAND

Atherton, W. *Life of Lady Maxwell*. 1863.
Swift, W. F. *Scotland*. 1947.
Thomson, D. P. *Lady Glenorchy*. 1967.

I. UNITED METHODIST CHURCH

Askew, E. *Free Methodist Manual*. 1899.
Baxter, M. *U. M. Free Churches*. 1865.
Beckerlegge, O. A. *Free Methodism in Cornwall*. 1960.
————— *U. M. Ministers and Their Circuits*. 1968.
————— *U. M. Churches*. 1957.
Bourne, F. W. *Bible Christians*. 1905.
Centenary of the Methodist New Connexion. 1897.
Eayrs, G. *United Methodist Church*. 1913.
Handbook of the Methodist New Connexion. 1875.
Hulme, S. *Jubilee*. 1848.
Jubilee Memorial of Bible Christian Connexion. 1866.
Pyke, R. *Early Bible Christians*. 1941.
————— *Golden Chain*. 1915.
Shaw, T. *Bible Christians*. 1965.
Smith, H. et al. *United Methodist Church*. 1933.
Sunman, W. R. *Free Methodism in Newcastle-on-Tyne*. 1902.
Thorne, J. *Bible Christian Connexion*. 1865.
Townsend, W. J. *Methodist New Connexion*. 1899.
————— *Methodist Union*. 1906.
Urwin, E. C. *Significance of 1849*. 1949.
Woolcock, J. *Isle of Wight*. 1897.

J. WALES

Bennett, R. *Howell Harris*. 1962.
Beynon, T. *Harris, Reformer and Soldier*. 1958.
————— *Harris's Visits to London*. 1960.
————— *Harris's Visits to Pembrokeshire*. 1966.
Jenkins, D. E. *Calvinistic Methodist Holy Orders*. 1911.
Jones, M. H. *Trevecka Letters*. 1934.
Jones, T. W. *Brecon Circuit*. 1888.
Roberts, G. M. *Selected Trevecka Letters* (1742-1747). 1956.
————— *Selected Trevecka Letters* (1747-1794). 1962.
Williams, A. H. *Welsh Wesleyan Methodism*. 1935.
Williams. W. *Welsh Calvinistic Methodism*. 1884.
Young, D. *Wales and the Borders*. 1893.

K. WESLEYAN METHODIST CHURCH (See also *Wesleys and Their Times*)

Crowther, J. *Methodist Manual*. 1810.
———— *Portraiture of Methodism*. 1811.
Findlay, G. G. *Wesleyan Methodist Miss. Soc.* 1913.
Findlay and Holdsworth, *Wesleyan Methodist Miss. Soc.* 1921-24.
Gregory, B. *Side Lights*. 1898.
Jackson, T. *Centenary of Wesleyan Methodism*. 1839.
Jessop, W. *Rossendale*. 1880.
Jobson, F. J. *Chapel and School Architecture*. 1850.
Kent, J. H. *Age of Disunity*. 1966.
Laycock, J. W. *Methodist Heroes*. 1909.
Moister, W. *Wesleyan Missions*. 1871.
———— *Wesleyan Missionaries*. 1878.
Peirce, W. *Ecclesiastical Principles*. 1873.
Pocock, W. W. *Southern Counties of England*. 1885.
Rosser, J. *Isle of Man*. 1849.
Simon, J. S. *Methodist Law and Discipline*. 1897.
Smith, G. *Wesleyan Methodism*. 1857-61.
Stevenson, G. J. *Methodist Hymn-Book and Its Associations*. 1869.
Walker, J. U. *Halifax*. 1836.
Wansbrough, C. E. *Handbook and Index*. 1890.
Warren and Stephens. *Chronicles*. 1827.
Wynne-Jones, T. *Brecon Circuit*. 1888.

L. WESLEYAN REFORM UNION

Jones, W. H. *Wesleyan Reform Union*. 1952.
Origin and History of the Wesleyan Reform Union. 1896.

VII. CANADA

Carroll, J. *Case and His Cotemporaries*. 1867-77.
Centennial of Canadian Methodism. 1891.
Champion, T. E. *Churches of Toronto*. 1899.
Cornish, G. H. *Cyclopaedia of Methodism in Canada*. 1881, 1903.
French, G. S. *Parsons and Politics*. 1962.
Grant, J. W. *Canadian Church Union*. 1967.
Hopper, Mrs. R. P. *Primitive Methodism in Canada*. 1904.
Huestis, G. O. *Wesleyan Missionaries in Eastern British America*. 1872.
Johnson, D. W. *Eastern British America*. 1924.
Pidgeon, G. C. *United Church of Canada*. 1950.
Pierce, L. A. *Chronicle of a Century*. 1929.
Playter, G. F. *Canada*. 1862.
Riddell, J. H. *Middle West*. 1946.
Robson, E. *British Columbia*. 1905.
Ryerson, E. *Canadian Methodism*. 1882.
Sanderson, J. E. *First Century in Canada*. 1908-10.
Sigsworth, J. W. *Free Methodist Church in Canada*. 1960.
Silcox, C. E. *Church Union in Canada*. 1933.
Sissons, C. B. *Victoria University*. 1952.
Smith, T. W. *Eastern British America*. 1877.
Stephenson, Mrs. F. C. *Canadian Methodist Missions*. 1925.
Sutherland, A. *Methodism in Canada*. 1903.
Webster, T. *M. E. Church in Canada*. 1870.
Young, E. R. *By Canoe and Dog Train*. 1890.

VIII. CARIBBEAN

Adams, H. *West Indies*. 1908.
Ching, D. S. *For Ever Beginning* (Jamaica). 1960.
Coke, T. *West Indies*. 1808-11.

Duncan, P. *Jamaica*. 1849.
Findlay and Holdsworth. *Wesleyan Meth. Miss. Soc.* Vol. 2, 1921.
Foster, H. B. *Wesleyan Methodism in Jamaica*. 1881.
Horsford, J. *West Indies*. 1856.
Lawrence and Dorsett. *Caribbean Conquest*. 1947.
Mitchel, P. D. *Cuba Calling*. 1949.
Neblett, S. A. *Methodism in Cuba*. 1966.
Pilkington, F. *Daybreak in Jamaica*. 1950.
Samuel, P. *Jamaica and Honduras*. 1850.
Walker, F. D. *West Indies*. n.d.
Watson, R. *West Indies*. 1817.

IX. ECUMENICAL MOVEMENT

Anglican-Methodist Unity. The Scheme. 1968.
Currie, R. *Methodism Divided*. 1968.
Grant, J. W. *Canadian Church Union*. 1967.
Harrison, A. W. *Evangelical Revival*. 1942.
Holt, Ivan Lee. *Methodists of the World*. 1950.
Hunter, F. *John Wesley*. 1968.
Minear, P. S. *Nature of the Unity*. 1958.
Minus, P. M. *Methodism's Destiny*. 1969.
Oecumenical Methodist Conference. *Proceedings*. 1881-1947.
Rack, H. D. *Future of Wesley's Methodism*. 1965.
Silcox, C. E. *Church Union in Canada*. 1933.
Ward, M. *Pilgrim Church* (Church of South India). 1953.
Williams, C. W. *Wesley's Theology Today*. 1960.
World Methodist Conference. *Proceedings*. 1951-71.

X. EDUCATION

A. GENERAL POLICY AND HISTORY

Albright and Leedy. *Religious Education in the Evangelical Church*. 1932.
Baker, J. C. *First Wesley Foundation*. 1960.
Berry, J. F. *Epworth League*. 1893.
Body, A. H. *Wesley and Education*. 1936.
Brown, A. A. *Religious Education*. 1923.
Brummitt, D. B. *Epworth League*. 1906.
Cummings, A. W. *Early School of Methodism*. 1886.
Duvall, S. M. *M. E. Church and Education*. 1928.
Ford, E. L. *Educational Work in China*. 1938.
Godbold, A. *Church College*. 1944.
Hancher, J. W. *Educational Jubilee*. 1918.
Mathews, H. F. *Methodism and Education*. 1949.
Prince, J. W. *Wesley on Religious Education*. 1926.
Pritchard, F. C. *Secondary Education*. 1949.
Schisler, J. Q. *Christian Education in Local Churches*. 1969.
Tewsbury, D. G. *Founding of American Colleges*. 1932.
Wicke, M. F. *University Senate*. 1956.
———— *Higher Education*. 1965.

B. HISTORY OF SELECTED INSTITUTIONS

Adrian. Feeman et al. *Story of a Noble Devotion*. 1945.
Boston. Cameron, R. M. *Boston Univ. School of Theology*. 1968.
———— Speare, E. R. *Boston University*. 1957.
Cokesbury. Coke and Asbury. *Address for the Support of Cokesbury College*. 1787.
DePauw. Sweet, W. W. *Indiana Asbury-DePauw University*. 1937.
Dickinson. Morgan, J. H. *Dickinson College*. 1933.
Drew. Sitterly, C. F. *Drew Univ*. 1938.
Drew. Joy, J. R. *Teachers of Drew*. 1942.
———— Tipple, E. S. *Drew Theological Seminary*. 1917.

Emory. English, T. H. *Emory University*. 1966.
———— Bullock, H. M. *Emory University*. 1936.
Kingswood. Hastling et al. *Kingswood School*. 1898.
———————— Ives, A. G. *Kingswood School*. 1970.
Meharry. Roman, C. V. *Meharry Medical College*. 1934.
Northwestern. Ward, E. F. *Northwestern University*. 1924.
Ohio. Hubbart, H. C. *Ohio Wesleyan*. 1943.
Otterbein. Bartlett, W. W. *Otterbein College*. 1934.
Pacific. Hunt, R. D. *College of the Pacific*. 1951.
Randolph-Macon. Irby, R. *Randolph-Macon College*. 1899.
Richmond. Cumbers, F. H. *Richmond College*. 1944.
Scarritt. Gibson and Haskin. *Scarritt*. 1928.
Syracuse. Galpin, W. F. *Syracuse University*. 1952, 1960.
Thoburn. Dimmitt, M. A. *Isabella Thoburn College*. 1963.
Trinity. Chaffin, N. C. *Trinity College*. 1950.
Vanderbilt. Mims, E. *Vanderbilt University*. 1946.
———— Thompson, B. *Vanderbilt Divinity School*. 1958.
Victoria. Sissons, C. B. *Victoria University*. 1952.
Wesleyan. Price, C. F. *Wesleyan's First Century*. 1932.
Westminster. Pritchard, F. C. *Westminster College*. 1951.
Willamette. Gatke, R. M. *Willamette University*. 1943.
Wofford. Wallace, D. D. *Wofford College*. 1951.

C. Sunday Schools

Arnett, B. W. *Colored Sunday Schools*. 1896.
Bowen, C. A. *Child and Church*. 1960.
Brown, E. *Trained Teachers*. 1966.
Brown, M. C. *Sunday-School Movements*. 1901.
Cope, H. F. *Evolution of the Sunday School*. 1911.
Gilbert, S. *Lesson System*. 1879.
Knox, A. W. *Infant Sunday School*. 1870.
Lankard, F. G. *Sunday School Curriculum*. 1927.
Sangster, P. E. *Pity My Simplicity*. 1964.
Wardle, A. G. *Sunday School Movement*. 1918.

XI. EUROPE

Erikson, J. M. *Metodismen i Sverige*. 1895.
Findlay & Holdsworth. *Wesleyan Meth. Miss. Soc.* Vol. IV. 1922.
Garber, P. N. *Continental Europe*. 1949.
Grob, R. E. *Bischöfliche Methodistenkirche in der Schweiz*. 1931.
Haagensen, A. *Den Norsk-Danske Methodismes*. 1894.
Hagen, Odd. *Methodism in Northern Europe*. 1961.
Hurtig, K. J. *Methodismen i Finland*. 1925.
Hurtig and Hurtig. *Helsingfors Svenska Metodist-församling*.
Julen, J. *Metodistkyrkan i Sverige*. 1923.
Kissack, R. *Methodists in Italy*. 1960.
Mann, H. *Ludwig S. Jakoby*. 1892.
Marshall, L. A. *American Pioneer in Russia*. 1928.
Melle, F. H. O. *Das Walten Gottes*. 1925.
Nuelsen, J. L. *Methodismus in Deutschland*. n.d.
———— *Methodistenkirche in der Schweiz*. 1932.
Peter, L. *Bischoflichen Methodistenkirchen in der Schweiz*. 1893.
Roux, T. *Methodisme en France*. 1940.
Thorkildsen, J. *Norske Metodistkirkes Historie*. 1926.
Wunderlich, F. *Methodists Linking Two Continents*. 1960.

XII. HYMNOLOGY

A. Hymnological Studies

Baker, F. *Charles Wesley's Verse*. 1964.
Benson, L. F. *English Hymn*. 1962.
Bett, H. *Hymns of Methodism*. 1913, 1920, 1945.
Crawford, B. F. *Theological Trends*. 1939.
Creamer, D. *Methodist Hymnology*. 1848.
Findlay, G. H. *Christ's Standard Bearer*. 1956.
Flew, R. N. *Hymns of Charles Wesley*. 1953.
Gregory, A. S. *Praises with Understanding*. 1936.
Hodges and Allchin. *Rapture of Praise*. 1966.
Lightwood, J. T. *Music of the Methodist Hymn-book*. 1955.
McCutchan, R. G. *Our Hymnody*. 1937.
Manning, B. L. *Hymns of Wesley and Watts*. 1942.
Nuelsen, J. L. *Wesley und das deustche Kirchenlied*. 1938.
Nutter, C. S. *Hymn Studies*. 1884.
Nutter and Tillett. *Hymns and Hymn Writers*. 1911.
Price, C. F. *Music and Hymnody*. 1911.
Rattenbury, J. E. *Eucharistic Hymns*. 1948.
———————— *Evangelical Doctrine*. 1941.
Stevenson, G. J. *Methodist Hymn-Book and Its Associations*. 1869.
———————— *Methodist Hymn Book Illustrated*. 1883.
Stevenson, R. M. *Protestant Church Music*. 1953.
Telford, J. *Methodist Hymn-Book*. 1906.
———— *New Methodist Hymn-Book Illustrated*. 1934.
Tillett, W. F. *Our Hymns and Their Authors*. 1889.

B. Hymn Books and Tune Books

Collection of Hymns of the Evangelical Association. 1835.
Collection of Hymns for People Called Methodists. 1780, 1830, 1876.
Collection of Hymns of the United Brethren. 1835.
Collection of Hymns. 1847, and others.
Collection of Hymns . . . M. E. 1821, and others.
Collection of Psalms and Hymns. 1737, 1964.
Evangelical Hymn and Tune Book. 1889.
Evangelical Hymnal. 1921.
Geistliche Saitenspiel. 1817.
Geistliche Viole. 1818.
Hymnal of The E.U.B. Church. 1957.
Hymnal of the UEC. 1897.
Hymn Book of the A.M.E. Church. 1873.
Hymn-Book of the EA. 1882.
Hymn Book of the Methodist Church (MP). 1858.
Hymn Book of the M. P. Church. 1856.
Hymns for the Sanctuary. 1874.
Hymns and Songs. 1969.
Hymns for the M. E. Church. 1850.
Hymns for the M. E. Church, with Tunes. 1857.
Lute of Zion. 1853, 1856.
Methodist Harmonist. 1825.
Methodist Pocket Hymn-Book. 1813.
New Evangelical Hynmbook. 1867.
New Hymn and Tune Book (A.M.E.Z.) 1888.
Otterbein Hymnal. 1890.
Pocket Hymn Book. 1785.
Revivalist. 1869.
Sacred Choral. 1854.
Sacred Harmony. 1848.
Selection of Hymns. 1813.
Voice of Praise. 1876.
Wesley Hymn Book. 1959.

XIII. LATIN AMERICA

Arms, G. F. *Missions in South America.* 1921.
Butler, J. W. *ME Church in Mexico.* 1918.
Butler, W. *Mexico.* 1892.
Drees, A. M. C. *Mexico.* 1915.
Jaime, E. M. B. *Metodismo no Rio Grande do Sul.* 1963.
Kennedy, J. L. *Metodismo no Brasil.* 1928.
Mendoza, V. *Iglesia Metodista de Mexico.* 1948.
Methodist Church in Bolivia. 1962.
Miller, G. A. *Panama-Costa Rica.* 1936.
Souvenir of the M. E. Church in Mexico. 1924.
Tallon, A. G. *Rio de la Plata.* 1936.

XIV. MINISTRY (including Deaconesses)

Bancroft, J. M. *Deaconesses in Europe.* 1889.
Bangs, N. *Original Church of Christ.* 1837.
——————— *Vindication of Methodist Episcopacy.* 1820.
Coke, T. *Sermon . . . at Ordination of . . . Francis Asbury.* 1785.
——————— *Four Discourses on the Duties of a Minister.* 1820.
Cooke, R. J. *Historic Episcopate.* 1896.
Davis, J. A. *Episcopacy.* 1902.
Emory, J. *Defence of Our Fathers.* 1827.
Golder, C. *Geschichte der Weiblichen Diakonie.* 1901.
Jenkins, D. E. *Calvinistic Methodist Holy Orders.* 1911.
Lawson, A. B. *John Wesley.* 1963.
Lee, E. M. *Deaconesses.* 1963.
M'Caine, A. *Defense of the Truth.* 1829.
——————— *History and Mystery of Meth. Episcopacy.* 1827.
McCulloh, Gerald O. *Ministry.* 1960.
Meyer, L. R. *Deaconesses.* 1889.
Moede, G. F. *Office of Bishop.* 1964.
Neely, T. B. *Bishops and the Supervisional System.* 1912.
——————— *Evolution of Episcopacy.* 1888.
Nuelsen, J. L. *Ordination im Methodismus.* 1935.
Thoburn, J. M. *Deaconess.* 1893.
Thompson, E. W. *Wesley: Apostolic Man.* 1957.
Wheeler, H. *Deaconesses.* 1889.

XV. MISSIONS

A. GENERAL

Arms. G. F. *Missions in South America.* 1921.
Bangs, N. *History of Missions.* 1832.
Barclay, W. C. *History of Missions.* 1949-50, 1957.
Berry, L. L. *Century of Missions* (A.M.E.) 1942.
Butler, J. W. *M.E. Church in Mexico.* 1918.
Caldwell, M. B. *Shawnee Mission.* 1839.
Cannon, J. *Southern Meth. Missions.* 1926.
Danks, B. *South Seas.* 1909.
Drees, A. M. C. *Mexico.* 1915.
Eller, P. H. *Evangelical Missions.* 1942.
Findlay, G. G. *Wesleyan Meth. Miss. Soc.* 1913.
Findlay and Holdsworth. *Wesleyan Meth. Miss. Soc.* 1921-24.
Finley, J. B. *Wyandott Mission.* 1840.
Goode, W. H. *Outposts of Zion.* 1863.
John, I. G. *Hand Book of Missions.* 1893.
Lamson, B. S. *Free Meth. Missions.* 1951.
Miller, G. A. *Panama-Costa Rica.* 1936.
Moister, W. *Wesleyan Missions.* 1869.
——————— *Hand Book of Missions.* 1883.
——————— *Wesleyan Missionaries.* 1878.
Neely, T. B. *Foreign Missions.* 1923.
Ogburn, T. J. *Foreign Missions* (M.P.) 1906.
Platt, W. *Methodism and the Republic.* 1908.

Project Handbook: Overseas Missions. 1969.
Project Handbook: Home Fields. 1967.
Reid, J. M. *Missions.* 1895-96.
Schmidt, M. *Der junge Wesley.* 1955.
Stephenson, Mrs. F. C. *Canadian Methodist Missions.* 1925.
Strickland, W. P. *Missions.* 1850.
Thomson, E. *Oriental Missions.* 1871.
Wasson, A. W. *Missionary Expansion.* 1948.
Wilson, A. W. *Missions.* 1882.

B. WOMEN'S WORK

Baker, F. J. *WFMS of the ME Church.* 1895.
Brummitt, S. W. *WHMS of the ME Church.* 1930.
Butler, Mrs. F. A. *WFMS, MES.* 1912.
Chandler, Mrs. E. C. *WFMS of the MP.* 1920.
Daggett, Mrs. L. H. *Missionary Societies.* 1879.
Gracey, Mrs. J. T. *Medical Work.* 1881.
Haskin, S. E. *Women and Missions.* 1920.
Howell, M. K. *Women and the Kingdom.* 1928.
Isham, M. *Valorous Ventures.* 1936.
Meeker, R. E. *WHMS of the ME Church.* 1969.
Miller, Mrs. M. A. *WFMS of the MP Church.* 1896.
Reber, A. E. *WSWS of the EUB Church.* 1969.
Tatum, N. D. *Crown of Service.* 1960.
Tomkinson, Mrs. T. L. *WHMS of the ME Church.* 1903.
Wheeler, M. S. *WFMS of the ME Church.* 1881.

XVI. POLITY

Askew, E. *Free Methodist Manual.* 1899.
Baker, O. C. *Administration of the Discipline.* 1855, 1860, 1873-84.
Bangs, N. *Reformer Reformed.* 1818.
Bascom, H. B. *Brief Appeal.* 1848.
Breyfogel, S. C. *Evangelical Assoc.* 1888.
Buckley, J. M. *Constitutional and Parliamentary History.* 1912.
Denny, Collins. *Manual of the Discipline.* 1931.
Drury, A. W. *Disciplines* (U.B.). 1895
Elliott, C. *Great Secession.* 1855.
Emory, J. *Defence of Our Fathers.* 1827.
Emory, R. *History of the Discipline.* 1844.
Graves, J. R. *Great Iron Wheel.* 1855.
Handbook of the Methodist New Connexion. 1875.
Harmon, N. B. *Organization.* 1948, 1953, 1962.
Harris, C. R. *Historical Catechism.* 1916.
Hedding, E. *Administration of Discipline.* 1842.
Jennings, S. K. *Exposition of the Late Controversy.* 1831.
Jones, E. D. W. *Catechism* (AMEZ). 1934.
Kendall, H. B. *Primitive Methodist Church.* 1905.
Kephart, E. B. *Manual of Church Discipline* (U.B.) 1895.
Kilgore, C. F. *James O'Kelly Schism.* 1963.
Kissack, R. *Church or No Church?* 1964.
Leiffer, M. H. *Role of District Supt.* 1960.
M'Caine, A. *Defense of the Truth.* 1829.
——————— *History and Mystery of Meth. Episcopacy.* 1827.
MacVey, W. P. *Genius of Methodism.* 1903.
McTyeire, H. N. *Manual of the Discipline.* 1870.
M. E. Church. *Doctrines and Discipline.* 1785-1939.
——————— *General Conference Journals.* 1792-1939.
M. E. Church, South. *Doctrines and Discipline.* 1846-1939.
——————— *General Conference Journals.* 1846-1939.
M. P. Church. *Constitution and Discipline.* 1830-1939.

———— *General Conference Journals.* 1834-1939.
Moore, J. M. *Belief and Action.* 1946.
Morris, T. A. *Church Polity.* 1860.
Neely, T. B. *Bishops and the Supervisional System.* 1912.
———— *Evolution of Episcopacy.* 1888.
———— *Governing Conference.* 1892.
Norwood, F. A. *Church Membership.* 1958.
Norwood, J. N. *Schism in the M.E. Church.* 1923.
Peirce, W. *Ecclesiastical Principles.* 1854.
Perkins, E. B. *Preaching Houses and the Law.* 1952.
Peterson, P. A. *Revisions of the Discipline.* 1889.
Rigg, J. H. *Comparative View of Church Organizations.* 1897.
Sherman, D. *Revisions of Discipline.* 1874, 1877, 1890.
Simon, J. S. *Methodist Law and Discipline.* 1897.
Snethen, N. *Essays on Lay Representation.* 1835.
Spencer and Finch. *Constitutional Practice.* 1951.
Sutton, R. *Church Property Case.* 1851.
Tigert, J. J. *Constitutional History.* 1894.
———— *Making of Methodism.* 1898.
Townsend, W. J. *Methodist New Connexion.* 1899.
Turner, H. M. *Genius and Theory.* 1885.
Wansbrough, C. E. *Handbook and Index.* 1890.
Warren and Stephens. *Chronicles.* 1827.
Wasson, A. W. *Missionary Expansion.* 1948.
Worley, H. W. *Central Conference.* 1940.

XVII. PREACHING

Doughty, W. L. *John Wesley, Preacher.* 1955.
Methodist Preacher. 1859.
Peck, G. M. E. *Pulpit.* 1854.
Smithson, W. T. *Methodist Pulpit South.* 1859.
Sprague, W. B. *Annals of the Pulpit.* 1861.
Stevens, A. *Essays on Preaching.* 1855.
Whitefield, G. *Select Sermons.* 1958.
———— *Sermons on Important Subjects.* 1836.
Willson, S. W. *Methodist Preacher.* 1830.

XVIII. PUBLISHING

Archibald, F. A. *Methodism and Literature.* 1883.
Batten, J. M. *Outline and Bibliographical Guide.* 1954.
Centennial of the Book Concern. 1890.
Cumbers, F. *Book Room.* 1956.
Herbert, T. W. *John Wesley.* 1940.
Jennings, H. C. *Book Concern.* 1924.
Lanahan, J. *Era of Frauds.* 1896.
Ness, J. H. *History of Publishing* (EUB). 1966.
Pilkington, J. P. *Methodist Publishing House.* 1968.
Shepherd, T. B. *Methodism and Literature.* 1940.
Shuey, W. A. *U.B. Publishing House* 1892.
Whitlock, W. F. *Book Concerns.* 1903.

XIX. SLAVERY AND EARLY BLACK METHODISM

Bascom, H. B. *Methodism and Slavery.* 1845.
Brookes, I. L. *Defense of Southern Slavery.* 1851.
Harris, W. L. *Constitutional Powers.* 1860.
Harrison, W. P. *Gospel Among the Slaves.* 1893.
Haygood, A. G. *Brother in Black.* 1881.
Mathews, D. G. *Slavery and Methodism.* 1965.
Matlack, L. C. *Antislavery Struggle.* 1881.
———— *History of Slavery.* 1849.
McCarter, J. M. *Border Methodism.* 1858.
McTyeire, H. N. *Duties of Christian Masters.* 1859.
Morrow, R. E. *Northern Methodism.* 1956.
Norwood, J. N. *Schism in the M.E. Church.* 1923.
Peck, G. *Slavery and the Episcopacy.* 1845.
Peck, J. K. *Stevens Answered.* 1859.
Shaw, J. B. F. *The Negro.* 1954.

Stevens, A. *An Appeal.* 1859.
Swaney, C. B. *Episcopal Methodism and Slavery.* 1926.
Sweet, W. W. *M.E. Church and the Civil War.* 1912.
Whedon, D. *Letter to Stevens.* 1859.

XX. SOCIAL CONCERNS

Bebb, E. D. *Wesley.* 1950.
Bready, J. W. *England: Before and After Wesley.* 1938.
Cameron, R. W. *Methodism and Society.* 1961.
Edwards, M. L. *After Wesley.* 1935.
———— *Methodism and England.* 1943.
———— *Wesley and the Eighteenth Century.* 1933.
Harkness, G. *Social Thought and Action.* 1964.
Muelder, W. G. *Methodism and Society.* 1961.
Schilling, S. P. *Methodism and Society.* 1960.
Sherwin, O. *John Wesley.* 1961.
Smith, T. *Revivalism and Social Reform.* 1957.
Stotts and Deats. *Methodism and Society.* 1962.
Taylor, E. R. *Methodism and Politics.* 1935.
Urwin and Wollen. *John Wesley.* 1937.
Ward, A. D. *Social Creed.* 1965.
Warner, W. J. *Wesleyan Movement.* 1930.
Wearmouth, R. F. *Social and Political Influence.* 1957.
———— *Trade Unions.* 1959.
———— *Working-Class Movements.* 1937.
———— *Struggle of the Working Classes.* 1954.
Wheeler, H. *Temperance Reformation.* 1882.

XXI. THEOLOGY

Baker, E. W. *Faith of a Methodist.* 1958.
Bangs, N. *Errors of Hopkinsianism.* 1815.
———— *Doctrine of Predestination.* 1817.
———— *Original Church of Christ.* 1837.
Bett, H. *Spirit of Methodism.* 1937.
Boland, J. M. *Problem of Methodism.* 1889.
Burtner and Chiles. *Compend of Wesley's Theology.* 1954.
Cannon, W. R. *Theology of John Wesley.* 1946.
Cell, G. C. *Rediscovery of John Wesley.* 1935.
Chiles, R. E. *Theological Transition.* 1965.
Clarke, A. *Holy Bible.* 1810-25.
Coke, T. *Commentary on the Holy Bible.* 1812.
———— *Sermon on the Godhead of Christ.* 1785.
Comfort, S. *Exposition of the Articles of Religion.* 1847.
Conant, N. C. *Present Day Methodism.* 1949.
Coward, S. L. C. *Entire Sanctification.* 1901.
Cox, L. G. *Wesley's Concept of Perfection.* 1964.
Crawford, B. F. *Theological Trends.* 1939.
Ffirth, J. *Truth Vindicated.* 1794, 1810, 1814.
Fisk, W. *Calvinistic Controversy.* 1837.
Flew, R. N. *Idea of Perfection.* 1934.
———— *Nature of the Church.* 1952.
Hildebrandt, F. *Christianity.* 1956.
———— *Luther to Wesley.* 1951.
Hodgson, F. *System of New Divinity.* 1839.
Jimeson, A. A. *Twenty-five Articles.* 1853.
Kirkpatrick, D. *Doctrine of the Church.* 1964.
Lerch, D. *Heil und Heiligung bei John Wesley.* 1941.
Lindstrom, H. *Wesley and Sanctification.* 1946.
MacVey, W. P. *Genius of Methodism.* 1903.
McConnell, F. J. *Essentials of Methodism.* 1916.
Merritt, T. *Perseverance of the Saints.* 1807.
Moore, J. M. *Belief and Action.* 1946.
Mudge, J. *Growth in Holiness.* 1895.
Nagler, A. W. *Pietism and Methodism.* 1918.

Neely, T. B. *Doctrinal Standards.* 1918.
Outler, A. C. *John Wesley.* 1964.
Parris, J. R. *Wesley's Doctrine of the Sacraments.* 1963.
Peters, J. L. *Christian Perfection.* 1956.
Phoebus, W. *Doctrine and Order of the Evangelical Church.* 1817.
Pope, W. B. *Compendium of Christian Theology.* 1880.
Rall, H. F. *Modern Premillennialism.* 1920.
Rattenbury, J. E. *Evangelical Doctrine.* 1941.
Sangster, W. E. *Path to Perfection.* 1943.
Schwab, R. K. *Christian Perfection in the Evangelical Association.* 1922.
Searles, J. E. *Holiness Revival.* 1887.
Shinn, A. *Plan of Salvation.* 1813.
Smith, T. L. *Story of the Nazarenes.* 1962.
Spicer, T. *Sin to Sanctification.* 1857.
Spörri, T. *Das wesentliche methodischer Theologie.* 1954.
Spreng, S. P. *What Evangelicals Believe.* 1929.
Starkey, L. M. *Work of the Holy Spirit.* 1962.
Steele, D. *Defense of Christian Perfection.* 1896.
Strawson, W. *Methodist Theology.* 1969.
Thompson, E. W. *Doctrine of the Church.* 1939.
———————— *Wesley: Apostolic Man.* 1957.
Turner, G. A. *More Excellent Way.* 1951.
Watson, R. *Theological Institutes.* 1823-26.
Wheeler, H. *Articles of Religion.* 1908.
Williams, C. W. *Wesley's Theology Today.* 1960.
Wilson, G. W. *Methodist Theology.* 1904.
Yates, A. S. *Doctrine of Assurance.* 1952.

XXII. UNITED STATES OF AMERICA

A. GENERAL (see also world geographical areas, Missions, separate denominations)

Bascom, H. B. *Brief Appeal.* 1848.
Bucke, E. S. *History of American Methodism.* 1964.
Buckley, J. M. *History of Methodists.* 1896.
Chiles, R. E. *Theological Transition.* 1965.
Clark, E. T. *Small Sects.* 1937, 1949.
Crook, W. *Ireland and American Methodism.* 1866.
Elliott, C. *Great Secession.* 1855.
Emory, J. *Defence of Our Fathers.* 1827.
Emory, R. *History of the Discipline.* 1857.
Faulkner, J. A. *The Methodists,* 1903.
Graves, J. R. *Great Iron Wheel.* 1855.
Jobson, F. J. *American Methodism.* 1857.
Jones, G. H. *Guidebook.* 1966.
Lednum, J. *Rise of Methodism.* 1859.
Lee, Jesse. *Short History.* 1810.
Moore, H. H. *The Republic.* 1891.
Neely, T. B. *American Methodism.* 1915.
Origin of American Methodism. 1916.
Price, C. F. *Who's Who.* 1916.
Shaw, J. B. F. *The Negro.* 1954.
Simpson, M. *Hundred Years.* 1876.
Smith, T. *Revivalism and Social Reform.* 1957.
Stevens, A. *Centenary.* 1865.
———————— *Memorials of the Introduction.* 1848.
———————— *Memorials of Early Progress.* 1852.
Sweet, W. W. *Methodism in American History.* 1933.
———————— *Methodists.* 1946.
Tigert, J. J. *Constitutional History.* 1894.
Wakeley, J. B. *Heroes of Methodism.* 1856.
———————— *Lost Chapters.* 1858.

B. AFRICAN METHODIST EPISCOPAL CHURCH

Adams, E. A. *Yearbook and Historical Guide.* 1959.

Berry, L. L. *Century of Missions* (AME). 1942.
Davis, J. A. *Episcopacy.* 1902.
Gaines, W. J. *African Methodism.* 1890.
Handy, J. A. *AME History.* 1901.
Jenifer, J. T. *Centennial Retrospect* (AME). 1916.
Payne, D. A. *History* (AME). 1891.
Ransom, R. C. *Preface* (AME). 1950.
Ridgel, A. L. *African Methodism.* 1896.
Singleton, G. A. *African Methodism.* 1952.
Smith, C. S. *History* (AME). 1922.
Tanner, B. T. *Apology.* 1867.
———————— *Outline of History.* 1884.
Turner, H. M. *Genius and Theory.* 1885.
Wright, R. R. *Bishops* (AME). 1963.
———————— *Centennial Encyclopaedia.* 1916, 1948.

C. AFRICAN METHODIST EPISCOPAL ZION CHURCH

Bradley, D. H. *AMEZ Church.* 1956.
Harris, C. R. *Historical Catechism.* 1916.
Hood, J. W. *One Hundred Years.* 1895.
Jones, E. D. W. *Catechism* (AMEZ). 1934.
Moore, J. J. *History* (AMEZ). 1884.
Rush, C. *Short Account* (AMEZ). 1843.
Spurgeon, F. C. *Handbook* (AMEZ). 1952-56.

D. CHRISTIAN METHODIST EPISCOPAL CHURCH

Harris and Craig. *C.M.E. Church.* 1949.
Pettigrew, M. C. *Miles to Johnson.* 1970.
Phillips, C. H. *History* (CME). 1898, 1925.

E. THE EVANGELICAL UNITED BRETHREN CHURCH

Albright, R. W. *Evangelical Church.* 1942.
Berger, D. *History of UB.* 1897.
Bowman, T. *Evangelical Association.* 1894.
Breyfogel, S. C. *Evangelical Assoc.* 1888.
Core, A. C. *Otterbein.* 1968.
Drury, A. W. *History of the U.B.* 1924.
———————— *Glossbrenner.* 1889.
———————— *Otterbein.* 1884.
Eberly, Albright and Brane. *History of the U.B. Church.* 1911.
Eller, P. H. *Evangelical Missions.* 1942.
———————— *These E.U.B.* 1950, 1957.
Gibble, P. B. *East Pennsylvania Conference* (UB). 1951.
Holdcraft, P. E. *Pennsylvania Conference* (UB). 1938.
Hough, S. S. *Christian Newcomer.* 1941.
Kephart, E. B. *Manual of Church Discipline* (UB). 1895.
Koontz and Roush. *The Bishops.* 1950.
Lawrence, J. *History of the U.B.* 1860.
Leedy, R. B. *Evangelical Church in Ohio.* 1959.
Milhouse, P. W. *Otterbein.* 1968.
Miller G. *Jakob Albrecht und Georg Miller.* 1834.
———————— (trans. Epp). *Jacob Albright.* 1959.
Neitz, S. *Johannes Seybert.* 1862.
Ness, J. H. *History of Publishing* (EUB). 1966.
Newcomer, C. *Journal.* 1834.
Orwig, W. W. *Evangelical Association.* 1858.
Reber, A. E. *WSWS of the U.B. Church.* 1969.
Schwab, R. K. *Christian Perfection in the Evangelical Association.* 1922.
Shortess and Gramley. *Central Pennsylvania Conference* (EC). 1940.
Shuey, W. A. *U.B. Publishing House.* 1892.
Spayth and Hanby. *History of U. B. Church.* 1851.
Spreng, S. P. *Evangelical Association.* 1913.
———————— *John Seybert.* 1888.
———————— *What Evangelicals Believe.* 1929.
Stapleton, A. *Evangelical Association.* 1896.

——————— *Flashlights.* 1908.
——————— *Jacob Albright.* 1917.
Thompson, H. A. *Our Bishops.* 1889.
Veh, R. M. *Evangelical Bishops.* 1939.
Weekley and Fout. *Our Heroes.* 1908, 1911.
Yeakel, R. *Jacob Albright.* 1883.
——————— *Evangelical Association.* 1894, 1895.

F. FREE METHODIST CHURCH

Blews, R. R. *Master Workmen.* 1939, 1960.
Bowen, E. *Free Methodist Church.* 1871.
Hogue, W. T. *Free Methodist Church.* 1915.
Lamson, B. S. *Free Methodist Missions.* 1951.
——————— *Venture!* 1960.
Marston, L. R. *From Age to Age.* 1960.
M'Geary, J. S. *Free Methodist Church.* 1908.
Roberts, B. T. *Why Another Sect?* 1879.

G. THE METHODIST CHURCH

Armstrong, C. A. *North Dakota.* 1960.
Baumhofer, E. F. *Trails in Minnesota.* 1966.
Brooks, W. E. *Florida Methodism.* 1965.
Bugbee, L. E. *Wyoming Conference.* 1952.
Cameron, R. M. *Methodism and Society.* 1961.
Carter, C. T. *Tennessee Conference.* 1948.
Clark, E. T. *Western North Carolina.* 1966.
Clark and Stafford. *Who's Who.* 1952.
Clegg and Oden. *Oklahoma.* 1968.
Curl, R. F. *Southwest Texas.* 1951.
Detzler, J. J. *Northwest Indiana Conference.* 1953.
Evers, J. C. *Southern Illinois Conference.* 1964.
Gallaher, R. A. *Methodism in Iowa.* 1944.
Garber, P. N. *Methodists Are One People.* 1939.
Graham, J. H. *Mississippi Circuit Riders.* 1967.
Hallman, E. C. *Garden of Methodism.* 1948.
Hampton, V. B. *Newark Conference.* 1957.
Harkness, G. *Social Thought and Action.* 1964.
Harmon, N. B. *Organization.* 1948, 1953, 1962.
Harper, R. H. *Louisiana.* 1949.
Haymes, J. O. *Northwest Texas Conference.* 1962.
Heller, H. L. *Indiana Conference.* 1956.
Holter, D. W. *Fire on the Prairie.* 1969.
Howell, E. *Northwest.* 1966.
Jackman, E. E. *Nebraska.* 1954.
Jenkins, W. M. *Steps Along the Way.* 1967.
Jervey, E. D. *Southern California and Arizona.* 1960.
Lazenby, M. E. *Alabama and West Florida.* 1960.
Lee, E. M. *Deaconesses.* 1963.
Loofbourow, L. L. *In Search of God's Gold.* 1950.
——————— *Steeples Among the Sage.* 1964.
Macmillan, M. B. *Michigan.* 1967.
Martin, I. P. *Holston.* 1945.
McElreath, W. *Methodist Union in the Courts.* 1946.
Mills, E. L. *Plains, Peaks and Pioneers.* 1947.
Moore, J. M. *Long Road to Union.* 1943.
Muelder, W. G. *Methodism and Society.* 1961.
Nail, O. W. *Southwest Texas Conference.* 1958.
——————— *Texas Methodism.* 1961.
Norwood, F. A. *North Indiana Conference.* 1957.
Pace, C. N. *Minnesota.* 1952.
Pierce, A. M. *Georgia.* 1956.
Project Handbook: Overseas Missions. 1969.
Project Handbook: Home Fields. 1967.
Schilling, S. P. *Methodism and Society.* 1960.
Smeltzer, W. G. *Headwaters of the Ohio.* 1951.
Smith, M. D. *South Dakota.* 1965.
Stanger, F. B. *New Jersey.* 1961.
Stotts and Deats. *Methodism and Society.* 1962.
Straughn, J. H. *Inside Methodist Union.* 1958.
Sweet, W. M. *Virginia.* 1955.

Tucker, F. C. *Missouri.* 1966.
Vernon, W. N. *North Texas.* 1967.
Versteeg, J. M. *Ohio Area.* 1962.
Ward, A. D. *Social Creed.* 1965.
Weldon, J. W. *Century of Progress.* 1946.
Yarnes, T. D. *Oregon.* 1958.

H. METHODIST EPISCOPAL CHURCH (see also General (A))

Allen, Ray. *Genesee Conference.* 1911.
——————— *East Genesee Conference.* 1908.
Allen and Pilsbury. *Methodism in Maine.* 1887.
Andersen, A. W. *Salt of the Earth.* 1962.
Anthony, C. V. *Fifty Years* (California Conf.) 1901.
Archibald, F. A. *Methodism and Literature.* 1883.
Armstrong, J. E. *Old Baltimore Conference.* 1907.
Atkinson, J. *Wesleyan Movement in America.* 1896.
——————— *Centennial History.* 1884.
——————— *Memorials in New Jersey.* 1860.
Atwood, A. *Conquerors.* 1907.
Atwood, A. *Glimpses on Puget Sound.* 1903.
Baker, F. J. *WFMS of the ME Church.* 1898.
Bangs, N. *History of the M.E. Church.* 1838-41.
——————— *History of Missions.* 1832.
——————— *Original Church of Christ.* 1837.
——————— *Present State.* 1850.
——————— *Reformer Reformed.* 1818.
Barker, J. M. *Ohio Methodism.* 1898.
Beardsley, I. H. *Echoes from Peak and Plain* (Colorado). 1898.
Bennett and Lawson. *Wisconsin.* 1890.
Bennett, W. W. *Virginia.* 1871.
Bibbins, R. M. *How Methodism Came.* 1945.
Breihan, B. C. *Südlich-Deutschen Konferenz.* 1922.
Brill, H. E. *Oklahoma.* 1939.
Brummitt, S. W. *WHMS of the ME Church.* 1930.
Buckley, J. M. *Constitutional and Parliamentary History.* 1912.
Caldwell, M. B. *Shawnee Mission.* 1839.
Chaffee, A. F. *Wyoming Conference.* 1904.
Cliffe, A. W. *Our Methodist Heritage.* 1957.
Cole and Baketel. *New Hampshire Conference.* 1929.
Cooke, R. J. *History of the Ritual.* 1900.
Crook, W. *Ireland and American Methodism.* 1866.
Curts, L. *General Conferences.* 1900.
DePuy, W. H. *Centennial Year-Book.* 1883.
Diffendorfer, R. E. *World Service.* 1923.
Doctrines and Discipline. 1785-1939.
Douglass, P. F. *German Methodism.* 1939.
Eggleston, C. F. *Philadelphia Conference.* 1937.
Elliott, C. *South-Western Methodism.* 1868.
Extracts of Letters. 1805.
Fellows, S. N. *Upper Iowa Conference.* 1907.
Ffirth, J. *Truth Vindicated.* 1814.
Finley, J. B. *Sketches of Western Methodism.* 1854.
——————— *Wyandott Mission.* 1840.
Fradenburgh, J. N. *Erie Conference.* 1907.
Golder, C. *Zentral Deutschen Konferenz.* 1907.
Gracey, Mrs. J. T. *Medical Work.* 1881.
Graham, H. *Troy Conference.* 1908.
Gregg, S. *Erie Conference.* 1865, 1873.
Hammond, E. J. *M.E. Church in Georgia.* 1935.
Harmon, N. B. *Rites and Ritual.* 1926.
Harwood, T. *New Mexico.* 1908, 1910.
Henke, E. W. *Nordwest Deutsche Konferenz.* 1913.
Herbert, Barton and Ward. *Southwest Kansas Conference.* 1932.
Herrick and Sweet. *North Indiana Conference.* 1917.

Hines, H. K. *Pacific Northwest.* 1899.
Hobart, C. *Minnesota.* 1887.
Holliday, F. C. *Indiana.* 1873.
Isham, M. *Valorous Ventures.* 1936.
Jennings, S. K. *Exposition of the Late Controversy.* 1831.
Kilgore, C. F. *James O'Kelly Schism.* 1963.
Kriege, O. E. *West Deutschen Konferenz.* 1906.
Leaton, J. *Illinois.* 1883.
Liljegren, N. M. *Svenska Metodismen: Amerika.* 1895.
Loeppert, A. J. *Chicago Deutschen Konferenz.* 1921.
M'Anally, D. R. *Missouri.* 1881.
M'Caine, A. *History and Mystery of Meth. Episcopacy.* 1827.
Magaret, E. C. *St. Louis Deutschen Konferenz.* 1904.
Marquette, D. *Nebraska.* 1904.
Matlack, L. C. *Antislavery Struggle.* 1881.
Meeker, R. E. *WHMS of the ME Church.* 1969.
Merkel, H. M. *Utah.* 1938.
Miller, A. *German Methodist Preachers.* 1859.
———— *German Missions.* 1843.
Miller, R. C. *New England Southern Conference.* 1898.
Miller, W. H. *Nördlichen Deutschen Konferenz.* 1903.
Mitchell, B. *Northwest Iowa Conference.* 1904.
Moede, G. F. *Office of Bishop.* 1964.
Mood, F. A. *Charleston.* 1856.
Morrow, R. E. *Northern Methodism.* 1956.
Mudge, J. *New England Conference.* 1910.
Muller, H. *Ost-Deutschen Konferenz.* 1916.
Neely, T. B. *Bishops and the Supervisional System.* 1912.
———— *Evolution of Episcopacy.* 1888.
———— *Foreign Missions.* 1923.
———— *Governing Conference.* 1892.
Palmer, L. D. *Heroism and Romance.* 1950.
Payton, J. S. *Our Fathers Have Told Us.* 1938.
Peck, G. *Old Genesee Conference.* 1860.
Phoebus, G. A. *Beams of Light.* 1887.
Pilcher, E. H. *Michigan.* 1878.
Pilkington, J. P. *Methodist Publishing House.* 1968.
Randall, D. B. *Maine Conference.* 1893.
Redford, A. H. *Western Cavaliers.* 1876.
Reid, J. M. *Missions.* 1895-96.
Robinson, J. B. *Rock River Conference.* 1908.
Scott, Orange. *Address to General Conf.* 1836.
Seaman, S. A. *New York.* 1892.
Sherman, David. *Revisions of the Discipline.* 1874.
Snethen, N. *Essays on Lay Representation.* 1835.
Stevens, A. *Compendious History.* 1867.
———— *History of the M.E. Church.* 1864-67.
———— *Supplementary History.* 1899.
Strickland, W. P. *Missions.* 1850.
Sutton, R. *Church Property Case.* 1851.
Sweet, W. H. *Northwest Kansas.* 1920.
Sweet, W. W. *Indiana.* 1916.
———— *M.E. Church and the Civil War.* 1912.
———— *Methodists.* 1946.
Tees, F. H. *Beginnings of Methodism.* 1940.
———— *Methodist Origins.* 1948.
Tomkinson, Mrs. T. L. *WHMS of the ME Church.* 1903.
Waring, E. H. *Iowa Conference.* 1910.
Wheeler, M. S. *WFMS of the ME Church.* 1881.
Whitlock, E. D. *Central Ohio Conference.* 1914.
Wilson, E. *Eastern Wisconsin.* 1938.
Worley, H. W. *Central Conference.* 1940.

I. METHODIST EPISCOPAL CHURCH, SOUTH

Alexander, G. *History of MES.* 1894.
Anderson, J. A. *Arkansas Methodism.* 1935.
Arnold, W. E. *Kentucky.* 1935-36.
Babcock and Bryce. *Oklahoma.* 1937.
Betts, A. D. *South Carolina.* 1952.
Butler, Mrs. F. A. *WFMS, MES.* 1912.
Cain, J. B. *Mississippi Conference.* 1939.
Cannon, J. *Southern Methodist Missions.* 1926.
Chreitzberg, A. M. *Methodism in the Carolinas.* 1897.
Deems, C. F. *Annals.* 1856, 1857, 1858.
Doctrines and Discipline. 1846-1939.
DuBose, H. M. *History.* 1916.
Farish, H. D. *Circuit Rider Dismounts.* 1938.
Gray, M. L. *Missouri Methodism.* 1907.
Grissom, W. L. *North Carolina.* 1905.
Harmon, N. B. *Rites and Ritual.* 1926.
Haskin, S. E. *Women and Missions.* 1920.
History of the Organization of the MES. 1845.
Howell, M. K. *Women and the Kingdom.* 1928.
Jewell, H. *Arkansas.* 1892.
John, I. G. *Hand Book of Missions.* 1893.
Jones, J. G. *Mississippi Conference.* 1908.
Jones, W. B. *Mississippi Conference.* 1951.
Lindsey, J. A. *Mississippi Conference.* 1964.
M'Ferrin, J. B. *Tennessee.* 1869-73.
McTyeire, H. N. *Manual of the Discipline.* 1870.
Miller, G. R. *North Mississippi.* 1966.
Moede, G. F. *Office of Bishop.* 1964.
Moore, M. H. *North Carolina and Virginia.* 1884.
Nail, O. W. *Texas Centennial Yearbook.* 1934.
Neely, T. B. *Evolution of Episcopacy.* 1888.
Peterson, P. A. *Revisions of the Discipline.* 1889.
Phelan, M. *Texas.* 1924.
———— *Expansion in Texas.* 1937.
Pilkington, J. P. *Methodist Publishing House.* 1968.
Price, R. N. *Holston.* 1903-13.
Redford, A. H. *Organization of MES.* 1871.
———— *Kentucky.* 1868-70.
Shipp, A. M. *South Carolina.* 1883.
Simmons, J. C. *Pacific Coast.* 1886.
Skelton, D. E. *Lexington Conference.* 1950.
Smith, G. G. *Georgia.* 1913.
———— *Georgia and Florida.* 1877.
Stanley, E. J. *Montana.* 1884.
Summers, T. O. *Commentary on the Ritual.* 1873.
Sutton, R. *Church Property Case.* 1851.
Tatum, N. D. *Crown of Service.* 1960.
Thrall, H. S. *Texas.* 1872.
Thrift, C. T. *Florida.* 1944.
West, A. *Alabama.* 1893.
Wilson, A. W. *Missions.* 1882.

J. METHODIST PROTESTANT CHURCH

Barnes, I. A. *MP in West Virginia.* 1926.
Bassett, A. H. *Concise History.* 1877.
Chandler, Mrs. E. C. *WFMS of the MP.* 1920.
Colhouer, T. H. *Sketches of the Founders.* 1880.
Davis, L. E. *Democratic Methodism.* 1921.
Drinkhouse, E. J. *History of Methodist Reform.* 1899.
Hamrick, W. L. *Mississippi Conference (MP).* 1957.
Jennings, S. K. *Exposition of the Late Controversy.* 1831.
Lewis, T. H. *Centennial Anniversary.* 1928.
———— *Maryland Conference (MP).* 1879.
M'Caine, A. *History and Mystery of Methodist Episcopacy.* 1827.
Miller, Mrs. M. A. *WFMS of the MP Church.* 1896.

Ogburn, T. J. *Foreign Missions* (MP). 1906.
Paris, J. *History* (MP). 1849.
Snethen, N. *Essays on Lay Representation.* 1835.
Williams, J. R. *History.* 1843.

K. UNITED METHODIST CHURCH (U.S.A.)

Washburn, P. A. *United Methodist Primer.* 1969.
Gealy, Lovelace and Young. *Companion to the Hymnal.* 1970.

L. WESLEYAN CHURCH

Jennings, A. T. *History.* 1902.
Matlack, L. C. *Antislavery Struggle.* 1881.
———— *History of Slavery.* 1849.
McLeister, I. F. *Wesleyan Methodist Church of America.* 1959.
Scott, Orange. *Address to General Conference.* 1836.

M. OTHER METHODIST CHURCHES

Acornley, J. H. *Primitive Methodist Church.* 1909.
Clark, E. T. *Small Sects.* 1937, 1949.
Corbett, L. *Southern Methodist Church.* 1956.
Hanna, J. C. *Centennial Services* [Union Am. ME Church]. 1889.
Kilgore, C. F. *James O'Kelly Schism.* 1963.
MacClenny, W. E. *James O'Kelly.* 1910.
McDaniel, S. C. *Congregational Methodist Church.* 1881.
Russell, D. J. *African Union MP Church.* 1920.
Smith, T. L. *Story of the Nazarenes.* 1962.
Williams, D. J. *Welsh Calvinistic Methodism.* 1937.

XXIII. WESLEYS AND THEIR TIMES

A. THE WESLEY FAMILY

Baker, F. *Charles Wesley.* 1948.
———— *John Wesley.* 1970.
Bebb, E. D. *Wesley.* 1950.
Body, A. H. *Wesley and Education.* 1936.
Brailsford, M. R. *Tale of Two Brothers.* 1954.
Butler, D. *Wesley and Whitefield.* 1898.
Cannon, W. R. *Theology of John Wesley.* 1946.
Cell, G. C. *Rediscovery of John Wesley.* 1935.
Clark, E. T. *What Happened at Aldersgate.* 1938.
Clarke, A. *Memoirs of the Wesley Family.* 1836.
Clarke, E. *Susanna Wesley.* 1886.
Coke and Moore. *John Wesley.* 1792.
Collier, F. W. *John Wesley.* 1928.
Cox, L. G. *Wesley's Concept of Perfection.* 1964.
Deschner, J. W. *Wesley's Christology.* 1960.
Doughty, W. L. *John Wesley, Preacher.* 1955.
Edwards, M. L. *Astonishing Youth.* 1959.
———— *Family Circle.* 1949.
———— *Sons to Samuel.* 1961.
Flint, C. W. *Charles Wesley.* 1957.
Gill, F. C. *Charles Wesley.* 1964.
———— *John Wesley.* 1962.
Green, J. B. *John Wesley and William Law.* 1945.
Green, R. *John Wesley.* 1905.
Green, V. H. H. *John Wesley.* 1964.
———— *Young Mr. Wesley.* 1961.
Haddal, I. *John Wesley.* 1961.
Hampson, J. *John Wesley.* 1791.
Harmon, R. L. *Susanna Wesley.* 1968.
Harrison, G. E. *Son to Susanna.* 1937.
Higgins, P. L. *John Wesley.* 1960.
Hildebrandt, F. *Christianity according to the Wesleys.* 1956.
Hill, A. W. *John Wesley.* 1958.
Hunter, F. *John Wesley.* 1968.

Jackson, T. *Charles Wesley.* 1841.
Jeffery, T. R. *John Wesley.* 1960.
Jones, D. M. *Charles Wesley.* 1919.
Kirk, J. *Mother of the Wesleys.* 1864.
Lawson, A. B. *John Wesley.* 1963.
Lawton, G. *John Wesley.* 1962.
Lee, U. *John Wesley.* 1936.
———— *Lord's Horseman.* 1928.
Leger, J. A. *La Jeunesse de Wesley.* 1910.
———— *Wesley's Last Love.* 1910.
Lelievre, M. *John Wesley.* 1868.
Lindstrom, H. *Wesley and Sanctification.* 1946.
McConnell, F. J. *John Wesley.* 1961.
Monk, R. C. *John Wesley.* 1966.
Moore, H. *John Wesley.* 1824-25.
Newton, J. A. *Susanna Wesley.* 1968.
Parris, J. R. *Wesley's Doctrine of the Sacraments.* 1963.
Piette, M. *Wesley in the Evolution of Protestantism.* 1937.
Petri, L. *John Wesley.* 1928.
Prince, J. W. *Wesley on Religious Education.* 1926.
Rattenbury, J. E. *Conversion of the Wesleys.* 1938.
———— *Wesley's Legacy.* 1928.
Rigg, J. H. *Living Wesley.* 1874.
Routley, E. *Musical Wesleys.* 1968.
Schmidt, M. *John Wesley.* 1953, 1966.
———— *Der junge Wesley.* 1955.
Sherwin, O. *John Wesley.* 1961.
Simon, J. S. *John Wesley.* 1925.
———— *Wesley, Last Phase.* 1934.
———— *Wesley, Master-Builder.* 1927.
———— *Wesley and the Methodist Societies.* 1923.
———— *Wesley and the Religious Societies.* 1921.
Southey, R. *Wesley.* 1820.
Sparrow Simpson, W. J. *Wesley and the Church of England.* 1934.
Starkey, L. M. *Work of the Holy Spirit.* 1962.
Stevenson, G. J. *Wesley Family.* 1876.
Telford, J. *Charles Wesley.* 1886.
———— *John Wesley.* 1886.
———— *Sayings and Portraits of Charles Wesley.* 1927.
———— *Sayings and Portraits of John Wesley.* 1924.
Thompson, E. W. *Wesley: Apostolic Man.* 1957.
———— *Wesley at Charterhouse.* 1938.
Todd, J. M. *John Wesley.* 1958.
Tyerman, L. *John Wesley.* 1870-71.
———— *Samuel Wesley.* 1866.
Vulliamy, C. E. *John Wesley.* 1931.
Watson, R. *John Wesley.* 1831.
———— *Observations.* 1820.
Wedgwood, J. *John Wesley.* 1870.
Whitehead, J. *John Wesley.* 1793, 1796.
Williams, C. *Wesley's Theology Today.* 1960.
Wood, A. S. *Burning Heart.* 1967.

B. THE WESLEYS' WRITINGS

Baker, F. *Union Catalogue of the Works of John and Charles Wesley.* 1966.
Burtner and Chiles. *Compend of Wesley's Theology.* 1954.
Creamer, D. *Methodist Hymnology.* 1848.
Findlay, G. H. *Christ's Standard Bearer.* 1956.
Flew, R. N. *Hymns of Charles Wesley.* 1953.
Green, R. *Works of John and Charles Wesley.* 1896.
Herbert, T. W. *John Wesley.* 1940.

Lightwood, J. T. *Samuel Wesley, Musician.* 1937.
Outler, A. C. *John Wesley.* 1964.
Rattenbury, J. E. *Eucharistic Hymns.* 1948.
Wesley, C. *Journal.* 1849; *Early Journal.* 1909.
——————— *Representative Verse.* 1962.
Wesley, J. *Collection of Hymns.* 1780.
——————— *Collection of Psalms and Hymns.* 1737.
——————— *Explanatory Notes upon the New Testament.* 1755.
——————— *Journal.* 1909-16.
——————— *Letters.* 1931.
——————— *Selections from Notes.* 1955.
——————— *Standard Sermons.* 1921.
——————— *Sunday Service.* 1784.
——————— *Works* (ed. T. Jackson). 1829-31.
Wesley, J. and C. *Poetical Works.* 1868-72.

C. THE WESLEYS' CONTEMPORARIES

Atherton, W. *Life of Lady Maxwell.* 1863.
Atmore, C. *Methodist Memorial.* 1801, 1871.
Baker, E. W. *Herald of the Evangelical Revival* (William Law). 1948.
Baker, F. *John Cennick: Handlist of His Writings.* 1958.
——————— *William Grimshaw.* 1963.
Belden, A. D. *George Whitefield.* 1930.
Benson, J. *John William de la Flechere.* 1804.
Beynon, T. *Harris, Reformer and Soldier.* 1958.
——————— *Harris's Visits to London.* 1960.
——————— *Harris's Visits to Pembrokeshire.* 1966.
Blanshard, T. W. *Samuel Bradburn.* 1816.
Bulmer, A. *Elizabeth Mortimer.* 1859.
Burdsall, R. *Memoirs.* 1797.
Cennick, J. *Life.* 1745.
Church, L. F. *Oglethorpe.* 1932.
Coke, T. *Mrs. H. A. Rogers* (Funeral Sermon). 1795.
Cole, J. *Hannah Ball.* 1796.
Dallimore, A. A. *George Whitefield.* 1970.
Davies, G. C. B. *Early Cornish Evangelicals.* 1951.
Dickinson, P. *Memoirs.* 1803.
Gillies, J. *George Whitefield.* 1772.
Henry, S. C. *George Whitefield.* 1957.
Hughes, H. J. *Howell Harris.* 1892.
Jackson, T. *Lives of Early Methodist Preachers.* 1837-38.
Lawton, G. *Shropshire Saint* (Fletcher of Madeley). 1960.
Lewis, A. J. *Zinzendorf.* 1962.
Lockwood, J. P. *Peter Böhler.* 1868.
McQuaid, I. D. *Hannah Ball.* 1964.
Moore, H. *Mrs. Mary Fletcher.* n.d.
Morgan, J. *Thomas Walsh.* 1762.
Morrow, T. M. *Early Methodist Women.* 1967.
New, A. H. *Coronet and the Cross.* 1857.
Nuttall, G. F. *Howel Harris.* 1965.
Philip, R. *George Whitefield.* 1837.
Pritchard, J. *Capt. Webb.* 1797.
Reynolds, J. S. *Evangelicals at Oxford.* 1953.
Roberts, G. T. *Howell Harris.* 1951.
Rogers, H. A. *Experience.* 1793.
——————— *Spiritual Letters.* 1796.
Sandford, P. P. *Memoirs.* 1843.
Seymour, A. C. H. *Countess of Huntingdon.* 1839, 1840.
Smith, Mrs. R. *Raithby Hall.* 1859.
Stevens, A. *Women of Methodism.* 1866.
Taft, Z. *Biographical Sketches.* 1825.
Telford, J. *Wesley's Veterans.* 1909-14.
Thompson, R. W. *Benjamin Ingham.* 1958.
Told, S. *Life.* 1786.
Towlson, C. W. *Moravian and Methodist.* 1957.
Tyerman, L. *George Whitefield.* 1876-77.

——————— *Oxford Methodists.* 1873.
——————— *Wesley's Designated Successor* (John Fletcher). 1882.
Vickers, J. A. *Thomas Coke.* 1969.
Whitefield, G. *Journals.* 1960.
——————— *Select Sermons.* 1958.
——————— *Sermons on Important Subjects.* 1836.
——————— *Works.* 1771-72.
Wood, A. S. *Thomas Haweis.* 1957.

D. EIGHTEENTH CENTURY METHODISM IN BRITISH ISLES

Baker, F. *John Wesley.* 1970.
——————— *Society of Friends and Early Methodism.* 1949.
Barr, J. H. *Early Methodists Under Persecution.* 1916.
Bett, H. *Spirit of Methodism.* 1937.
Bowmer, J. C. *Lord's Supper.* 1951.
Bready, J. W. *England: Before and After Wesley.* 1938.
Bretherton, F. F. *Early Methodism in Chester.* 1903.
Carter, H. *Methodist Heritage.* 1951.
Church, L. F. *Early Methodist People.* 1948.
——————— *More About the Early Methodist People.* 1949.
Dimond, S. G. *Methodist Revival.* 1926.
Doughty, W. L. *Wesley: His Conferences and Preachers.* 1944.
Edwards, M. L. *Wesley and the Eighteenth Century.* 1955.
Everett, J. *Wesleyan Methodism in Sheffield.* 1823.
——————— *Wesleyan Methodism in Manchester.* 1827.
Fitchett, W. H. *Wesley and His Century.* 1906.
Gill, F. C. *Romantic Movement.* 1937.
Lyles, A. M. *Methodism Mocked.* 1960.
Laycock, J. W. *Methodist Heroes.* 1909.
Myles, W. *Chronological History.* 1799.
North, E. M. *Methodist Philanthropy.* 1914.
Pawlyn, J. S. *Bristol Methodism.* 1877.
Pearce, J. *Wesleys in Cornwall.* 1964.
Roberts, G. M. *Selected Trevecka Letters (1742-1747).* 1956.
——————— *Selected Trevecka Letters (1747-1749).* 1962.
Sangster, P. E. *Pity My Simplicity.* 1964.
Shepherd, T. B. *Methodism and Literature.* 1940.
Stamp, W. W. *Orphan-House of Wesley.* 1863.
Stevenson, G. J. *City Road Chapel.* 1872.
Sugden, E. H. *Wesley's London.* 1932.
Swallow, J. A. *Methodism.* 1895.
Telford, J. *Wesley's Chapel and Home.* 1906.
Thompson,, W. H. *Hull Methodism.* 1895.
Wearmouth, R. F. *Methodism and the Common People.* 1945.
Whiteley, J. H. *Wesley's England.* 1938.
Wilson, D. D. *Many Waters Cannot Quench.* 1969.

XXIV. WORLD METHODISM

Anderson, W. K. *Methodism.* 1947.
Baker, F. *Charge to Keep.* 1947.
Clark, E. T. *Album of Methodist History.* 1952.
Clark, J. O. A. *Wesley Memorial Volume.* 1881.
Daniels, W. H. *Illustrated History.* 1887.
Ecumenical Methodist Conference. *Proceedings.* 1881 etc.
Gregory, J. R. *History of Methodism.* 1911.
Holt, I. L. *Methodists of the World.* 1950.
Holt and Clark. *World Methodist Movement.* 1956.

Hurst, J. F. *History of Methodism.* 1901-04.
Hyde, A. B. *Story of Methodism.* 1889.
Lee, J. W. *Illustrated History.* 1900.
Luccock and Hutchinson. *Story of Methodism.* 1926.
M'Tyeire, H. N. *History of Methodism.* 1924.
Minus, P. M. *Methodism's Destiny.* 1969.
Nuelsen, Mann and Sommer. *Kurzgefasste Geschichte des Methodismus.* 1920.
Simpson, M. *Cyclopaedia.* 1878.
Stevens, A. *History of the Religious Movement.* 1858-61.
Townsend, Workman and Eayrs. *New History.* 1909.
World Methodist Council *Handbook.* 1966.

XXV. WORSHIP

Baker, F. *Love-Feast.* 1957.
Bible Christian Church Book of Services. 1903.
Billington, R. J. *Liturgical Movement.* 1969.
Bishop, J. *Methodist Worship.* 1950.

Bowmer, J. C. *Lord's Supper.* 1961.
Cooke, R. J. *History of the Ritual.* 1900.
Dearing, T. *Wesleyan and Tractarian Worship.* 1966.
Dunkle, W. F. *Values in the Church Year.* 1959.
Garber, P. N. *Methodist Meeting House.* 1941.
Gealy, F. D. *Let Us Break Bread Together.* 1960.
Gorham, B. W. *Camp Meeting Manual.* 1853.
Harmon, N. B. *Rites and Ritual.* 1926.
Hildebrandt, F. *I Offered Christ.* 1967.
Johnson, C. A. *Frontier Camp Meeting.* 1955.
Micklem, N. *Christian Worship.* 1936.
Parris, J. R. *Wesley's Doctrine of Sacraments.* 1963.
Rattenbury, J. E. *Eucharistic Hymns.* 1948.
——————— *Holy Communion.* 1958.
——————— *Vital Elements.* 1936.
Summers, T. O. *Commentary on the Ritual.* 1873.
Tripp, D. H. *Renewal of the Covenant.* 1969.
United Methodist Church (Br.) *Book of Services.* 1913.
Wesley, J. *Sunday Service.* 1784.

GENERAL BIBLIOGRAPHY

Acornley, John Holmes. *A History of the Primitive Methodist Church in the United States of America from its origin and the landing of the first missionaries in 1829 to the present time.* Fall River, Mass.: B. R. Acornley, 1909.

Adams, E. A., ed. *Yearbook and Historical Guide to the African Methodist Episcopal Church.* Columbia, S.C.: Bureau of Research and Survey, A.M.E. Church, 1959.

Adams, Henry. *Methodism in the West Indies.* London: Robert Culley, 1908.

The A.M.E. Church Review, published at Philadelphia, 1884-

Albright, Isaiah H. See Eberly, Albright and Brane. *History of the UB Church.* 1911.

Albright, Raymond W. *A History of the Evangelical Church.* Harrisburg, Pa.: Evangelical Press, 1942.

Albright, Raymond W., and Leedy, Roy B. *A Story of Religious Education in the Evangelical Church, 1832-1932.* Cleveland, O.: Evangelical Press, 1932.

Alexander, Gross. *A History of the Methodist Church, South, in the United States.* New York: Christian Literature Co.; Nashville: Smith & Lamar, 1894.

Allchin, Arthur MacDonald. See Hodges and Allchin. *Rapture of Praise.* 1966.

Allen, R. *History of Methodism in Preston.* Preston: Toulmin, 1866.

Allen, Ray. *A Century of the Genesee Annual Conference of the Methodist Episcopal Church, 1810-1910.* Rochester, N.Y.: the author, 1911.

——————— *History of the East Genesee Annual Conference of the Methodist Episcopal Church.* Rochester, N.Y.: the author, 1908.

Allen, Richard. *The Life Experience and Gospel Labors. . . Written by Himself.* Philadelphia: Martin & Boden, 1833. Reprint, Nashville: Abingdon Press, 1960.

Allen, Stephen, and Pilsbury, W. H. *History of Methodism in Maine, 1793-1886.* Augusta, Me.: Charles E. Nash, 1887.

American Universities and Colleges. 10th ed., ed. Otis A. Singletary. Washington, D. C.: American Council on Education, 1968.

Andersen, Arlow W. *The Salt of the Earth: A History of Norwegian-Danish Methodism in America.* N.p.: Norwegian-Danish Methodist Historical Society, 1962.

Anderson, James A. *Centennial History of Arkansas Methodism: A History of the Methodist Episcopal Church, South, in the State of Arkansas, 1815-1935.* N.p., 1935.

Anderson, William Ketcham, ed. *Methodism.* Nashville: Methodist Publishing House, 1947.

Anglican-Methodist Unity. Report of the Anglican-Methodist Unity Commission. Part 2. *The Scheme.* London: S.P.C.K. and The Epworth Press, 1968.

Anthony, C. V. *Fifty Years of Methodism: A History of the Methodist Episcopal Church Within the Bounds of the California Annual Conference from 1847 to 1897.* San Francisco: Methodist Book Concern, 1901.

Antliff, William. *The Life of the Venerable Hugh Bourne.* London: George Lamb, 1872; rev. Colin C. McKechnie, 1892.

Archibald, F. A., ed. *Methodism and Literature: A Series of Articles from Several Writers on the Literary Enterprise and Achievements of the Methodist Episcopal Church.* Cincinnati: Walden & Stowe; New York: Phillips & Hunt, 1883.

Arminian Magazine, published in London, 1778-97; continued as *Methodist Magazine,* 1798-1821; continued as *Wesleyan Methodist Magazine,* 1822-1913; continued as *Magazine of the Wesleyan Methodist Church,* 1914-26; continued as *Methodist Magazine,* 1927-70.

Arms, Goodsil F. *History of the William Taylor Self-Supporting Missions in South America.* New York: Methodist Book Concern, 1921.

Armstrong, C. A., ed. *History of the Methodist Church in North Dakota and Dakota Territory.* N.p.: North Dakota Conference Historical Society, 1960.

Armstrong, James Edward. *History of the Old Baltimore Conference from the Planting of Methodism in 1773 to the Division of the Conference in 1857.* Baltimore: the author, 1907.

Arnett, Benjamin W. *Colored Sunday Schools.* Nashville: A.M.E. Sunday School Union, 1896.

Arnold, William Erastus. *A History of Methodism in Kentucky.* 2 vols. Louisville, Ky.: Herald Press, 1935, 1936.

Arthur, William. *The Life of Gideon Ouseley.* London: Wesleyan Conference Office, 1876.

Asbury, Francis. *An Extract from the Journal of Francis Asbury. . . From August 7, 1771, to Dec. 29, 1778.* Philadelphia: John Dickins, 1792. *An Extract . . . From Jan. 1st, 1779, to Sep. 3d, 1780.* Philadelphia: Ezekiel Cooper, 1802.

——————— *The Journal of the Rev. Francis Asbury. . . From August 7, 1771, to December 7, 1815.* 3 vols. New York: N. Bangs & T. Mason, 1821.

——————— *The Journal and Letters of Francis Asbury,* ed. Elmer T. Clark, J. Manning Potts, and Jacob S. Payton. 3 vols. Nashville: Abingdon Press, 1958.

——————— See Coke and Asbury. *Address for Support of Cokesbury College.* 1787.

Asbury, Herbert. *A Methodist Saint: The Life of Bishop Asbury.* New York: Alfred A. Knopf, 1927.

Askew, Edwin, ed. *Free Methodist Manual; Comprising a Statement of the Origin, Doctrines, and Constitution of the United Methodist Free Churches; with Alphabetical Arrangements of Ministers and Circuits . . . from 1836 to 1898.* London: Andrew Crombie, 1899.

Atherton, W. *Life of Darcy, Lady Maxwell.* London: Mason, 1863.

Atkinson, John. *The Beginnings of the Wesleyan Movement in America and the Establishment Therein of Methodism.* New York: Hunt & Eaton; Cincinnati: Cranston & Curts, 1896.

——————. *Centennial History of American Methodism, inclusive of its ecclesiastical organization in 1784 and its subsequent development under the superintendency of Francis Asbury. With Sketches of the Character and History of all the Preachers known to have been Members of The Christmas Conference; also, an appendix, showing the Numerical Position of the Methodist Episcopal Church as compared with other leading Evangelical Denominations in the Cities of the United States; and the Condition of the Educational Work of the Church.* New York: Phillips & Hunt; Cincinnati: Cranston & Stowe, 1884.

——————. *Memorials of Methodism in New Jersey.* Philadelphia: Perkinpine & Higgins, 1860.

Atmore, Charles. *The Methodist Memorial: Being an Impartial Sketch of the Lives and Characters of the Preachers Who Have Departed This Life Since the Commencement of the Work of God Among the People Called Methodists, Late in Connection with the Rev. John Wesley, Deceased. Drawn from the most authentic sources, and disposed in Alphabetical Order. Introduced with a brief Account of the State of Religion from the Earliest Ages, and a Concise History of Methodism.* Bristol: Richard Edwards, 1801. New ed., *With an Original Memoir of the Author, and Notices of some of his Contemporaries;* London: Hamilton, Adams, & Co., 1871.

Atwood, Albert. *The Conquerors: Historical Sketches of the American Settlement of the Oregon Country, Embracing Facts in the Life and Work of Rev. Jason Lee, the Pioneer and Founder of American Institutions on the Western Coast of North America.* Cincinnati: Jennings & Graham, 1907.

——————. *Glimpses in Pioneer Life on Puget Sound.* Seattle, Wash.: n.p., 1903.

Babcock, Sidney Henry, and Bryce, John Young. *History of Methodism in Oklahoma: Story of the Indian Mission Annual Conference of the Methodist Episcopal Church, South.* N.p., 1937.

Badley, Brenton Hamline. *Indian Missionary Directory and Memorial Volume.* Lucknow: Methodist Episcopal Church Press, 1876; rev. ed., 1881.

Badley, Brenton Thoburn. *Visions and Victories in Hindustan: A Story of the Mission Stations of the Methodist Episcopal Church in Southern Asia.* Diamond Jubilee Edition. Madras: Methodist Publishing House, 1931.

——————. *Warne of India: The Life-story of Bishop Francis Wesley Warne.* Madras: Publishing House, 1932.

Baker, Eric Wilfred. *The Faith of a Methodist.* London: Epworth Press; Nashville: Abingdon Press, 1958.

——————. *A Herald of the Evangelical Revival: A Critical Inquiry into the Relation of William Law to John Wesley and the Beginnings of Methodism.* London: Epworth Press, 1948.

Baker, Frances J. *The Story of the Woman's Foreign Missionary Society of the Methodist Episcopal Church, 1869-1895.* Cincinnati: Cranston & Curts, 1896; rev. ed., 1898.

Baker, Frank. *A Charge to Keep: An Introduction to the People Called Methodists.* London: Epworth Press, 1947. 2nd ed., 1954.

——————. *Charles Wesley, as Revealed by His Letters.* London: Epworth Press, 1948.

——————. *Charles Wesley's Verse, An Introduction.* London: Epworth Press, 1964.

——————. *John Cennick (1718-55): A Handlist of His Writings.* London: Wesley Historical Society, 1958.

——————. *John Wesley and the Church of England.* London: Epworth Press; Nashville: Abingdon Press, 1970.

——————. *Methodism and the Love-Feast.* London: Epworth Press, 1957.

——————. *The Methodist Pilgrim in England.* London: Epworth Press, 1951.

——————. *The Relations Between the Society of Friends and Early Methodism.* London: the author, 1949.

——————. *Representative Verse of Charles Wesley.* London: Epworth Press, 1962.

——————, comp. *A Union Catalogue of the Works of John and Charles Wesley.* Durham: Divinity School, Duke Univ., 1966.

——————. *William Grimshaw, 1708-1763.* London: Epworth Press, 1963.

Baker, James C. *The First Wesley Foundation.* Nashville: the author, 1960.

Baker, Osmon Cleander. *A Guide-Book in the Administration of the Discipline of the Methodist Episcopal Church.* New York: Carlton & Phillips, 1855. Rev. ed., 1860. Rev. eds. by William L. Harris, 1873-84.

Baker, Richard Terrill. *Ten Thousand Years, The Story of Methodism's First Century in China.* New York: Board of Missions and Church Extension, 1947.

Baketel, Oliver S. See Cole and Baketel. *New Hampshire Conference.* 1929.

Bancroft, Jane M. *Deaconesses in Europe and Their Lessons for America.* New York: Hunt & Eaton, 1889.

Bangs, Nathan. *An Authentic History of the Missions under the Care of the Missionary Society of the Methodist Episcopal Church.* New York: Emory & Waugh, 1832.

——————. *The Errors of Hopkinsianism Detected and Refuted in Six Letters to the Rev. S. Williston.* New York: Printed for the author by John C. Totten, 1815.

——————. *An Examination of the Doctrine of Predestination as Contained in a Sermon.* New York: the author, 1817.

——————. *A History of the Methodist Episcopal Church.* New York: vols. 1-3, T. Mason & G. Lane, 1838-40; vol. 4, G. Lane & P. P. Sandford, 1841. 12th ed. rev., 1860.

——————. *The Life of the Rev. Freeborn Garrettson: Compiled from His Printed and Manuscript Journals, and Other Authentic Documents.* New York: J. Emory & B. Waugh, 1829.

——————. *An Original Church of Christ: Or, a Scriptural Vindication of the Orders and Powers of the Ministry of the Methodist Episcopal Church.* New York: Mason & Lane, 1837.

——————. *The Present State, Prospects, and Responsibilities of the Methodist Episcopal Church with an Appendix of Ecclesiastical Statistics.* New York: Lane & Scott, 1850.

——————. *The Reformer Reformed: Or, Errors of Hopkinsianism, Being an Examination of Williston's "Vindication of Some of the Most Essential Doctrines of the Reformation."* New York: John C. Totten, 1818.

——————. *Vindication of Methodist Episcopacy.* New York: Bangs & Mason, 1820.

Barber, B. Aquila. See Harrison, et al. *Methodist Church.* 1932.

Barclay, Wade Crawford. *History of Methodist Missions.* 3 vols. Part One, "Early American Methodism, 1769-1844": Vol. I, "Missionary Motivation and Expansion"; Vol. II, "To Reform the Nation." Part Two, "Methodist Episcopal Church, 1845-1939": Vol. III, "Widening Horizons, 1845-95." New York: Board of Missions, The Methodist Church, 1949, 1950, 1957.

Barker, John Marshall. *History of Ohio Methodism.* Cincinnati: Curts & Jennings, 1898.

Barnes, Isaac A. *The Methodist Protestant Church in West Virginia.* Baltimore: Stockton Press, 1926.

Barr, Josiah Henry. *Early Methodists Under Persecution.* New York: Methodist Book Concern, 1916.

Bartels, Francis Lodowic. *The Roots of Ghana Methodism.* Cambridge University Press, 1965.

Bartlett, Willard W. *Education for Humanity: The Story of Otterbein College.* Westerville, O.: Otterbein College, 1934.

Barton, W. B. See Herbert, Barton and Ward. *Southwest Kansas Conference.* 1932.

Bascom, Henry B. *A Brief Appeal to Public Opinion, in a Series of Exceptions to the Course and Action of the Methodist Episcopal Church, from 1844 to 1848, Affecting the Rights and Interests of the Methodist Episcopal Church, South.* Louisville, Ky.: John Early, agent, M.E. Church, South, 1848.

——————. *Methodism and Slavery: With Other Matters in Controversy between the North and South; Being a Review of the Manifesto of the Majority, in Reply to the Protest of the Minority, of the Late General Conference of the Methodist E. Church, in the Case of Bishop Andrew.* Frankfort, Ky.: Hodges, Todd and Pruett, printers, 1845.

Bashford, James W. *China, An Interpretation.* New York: Abingdon Press, 1916. Rev. ed., 1919.

——————. *China and Methodism.* Cincinnati: Jennings & Graham, 1906.

Bassett, Ancel H. *A Concise History of the Methodist Protestant Church.* Pittsburgh: James Robison, 1877. Rev. eds., 1882, 1887.

Batsel, John David. *Union List of Methodist Serials, Second Checking Edition.* Published by Methodist Librarians' Fellowship and Assoc. of Methodist Historical Societies, 1968. *First Supplement,* published by Methodist Librarians' Fellowship and Commission on Archives and History, 1970.

Batten, J. Minton. *An Outline and Bibliographical Guide for the Study of the History of the Methodist Publishing House.* Nashville: Personnel and Public Relations Division, The Methodist Publishing House, 1954.

Baumhofer, Earl F., ed. *Methodist Trails in Minnesota.* N.p.: Historical Society, Minnesota Methodist Conference, 1966.

Baxter, Daniel Minort. *Bishop Richard Allen and His Spirit.* Philadelphia: A.M.E. Book Concern, 1923.

Baxter, Matthew. *Methodism: Memorials of the United Methodist Free Churches, With Recollections of the Rev. Robert Eckett and Some of His Contemporaries.* London: W. Reed, 1865.

Beardsley, Isaac Haight. *Echoes from Peak and Plain; or, Tales of Life, War, Travel, and Colorado Methodism.* Cincinnati: Curts & Jennings, 1898.

Bebb, Evelyn Douglas. *Wesley: A Man with a Concern.* London: Epworth Press, 1950.

Beckerlegge, Oliver Aveyard. *Free Methodism in Cornwall.* Truro, Cornwall: Cornish Methodist Historical Association, 1960.

——————. *The United Methodist Free Churches: A Study in Freedom.* London: Epworth Press, 1957.

——————. *United Methodist Ministers and Their Circuits.* London: Epworth Press, 1968.

Beggs, Stephen R. *Pages from the Early History of the West and North-West: Embracing Reminiscences and Incidents of Settlement and Growth, and Sketches of the Material and Religious Progress of the States of Ohio, Indiana, Illinois, and Missouri, with Especial Reference to the History of Methodism.* Cincinnati: n.p., 1868.

Belden, Albert David. *George Whitefield—the Awakener: A Modern Study of the Evangelical Revival.* London: S. Low, Marston & Co., 1930. 2nd ed., rev.; London: Rockliff Publishing Corp., 1953.

Benham, Daniel. *Memoirs of James Hutton: Comprising the Annals of His Life, and Connection with the United Brethren.* London: Hamilton, Adams, & Co., 1856.

Bennett, P. S., and Lawson, James. *History of Methodism in Wisconsin.* N.p.: the authors, 1890.

Bennett, Richard. *The Early Life of Howell Harris.* Tr. Gomer Morgan Roberts. London: Banner of Truth Trust, 1962.

Bennett, William Wallace. *Memorials of Methodism in Virginia, from Its Introduction into the State, in the Year 1772, to the Year 1829.* Richmond, Va.: the author, 1871.

Benson, Clarence Irving, ed. *A Century of Victorian Methodism.* Melbourne: Spectator Publishing Co., 1935.

Benson, Joseph. *The Life of the Rev. John William de la Flechère.* London: R. Lomas, 1804. 2nd ed. enl., 1805.

Benson, Louis F. *The English Hymn: Its Development and Use in Worship.* New York: George H. Doran Company, 1915; reprinted Richmond: John Knox Press, 1962.

Berger, Daniel. *History of the Church of the United Brethren in Christ.* Dayton, O.: United Brethren Publishing House, 1897.

Berry, Joseph F. *Four Wonderful Years, A Sketch of the Origin, Growth, and Working Plans of the Epworth League.* New York: Hunt & Eaton, 1893.

Berry, Lewellyn Longfellow. *A Century of Missions of the African Methodist Episcopal Church, 1840-1940.* New York: Missionary Department, A.M.E. Church, 1942.

Bett, Henry. *The Hymns of Methodism.* London: Charles H. Kelly, 1913; enl. 1920; rev. and greatly enl., 1945.

——————. *The Spirit of Methodism.* London: Epworth Press, 1937.

Betts, Albert Deems. *History of South Carolina Methodism.* Columbia, S. C.: Advocate Press, 1952.

Beynon, Tom, ed. and tr. *Howell Harris, Reformer and Soldier (1714-1773).* Caernarvon, Wales: Calvinistic Methdist Bookroom, 1958.

——————. *Howell Harris's Visits to London.* Aberystwyth, Wales: the editor, 1960.

——————. *Howell Harris's Visits to Pembrokeshire.* Aberystwyth, Wales: the editor, 1960.

Bibbins, Ruthella Mory. *How Methodism Came: The Beginnings of Methodism in England and America.* Baltimore: The American Methodist Historical Society of the Baltimore Annual Conference, 1945.

[Bible Christian Church] *Book of Services for the Use of the Bible Christian Church.* New ed. London: Bible Christian Book Room, 1903.

Billington, Raymond John. *The Liturgical Movement and Methodism.* London: Epworth Press, 1969.

Birtwhistle, Allen. *In His Armour: The Life of John Hunt of Fiji.* London: Cargate Press, 1954.

——————. *Thomas Birch Freeman.* London: Cargate Press, 1950.

Bishop, John. *Methodist Worship.* London: Epworth Press, 1950.

Blackwell, John. *Life of the Rev. Alexander Kilham.* London: R. Groombridge, 1838.

Blamires, W. L., and Smith, John B. *The Early Story of the Wesleyan Methodist Church in Victoria.* Melbourne: Wesleyan Book Depot, 1886.

Blanshard, Thomas W. *The Life of Samuel Bradburn, The Methodist Demosthenes.* London: Elliot Stock, 1870.

Blews, Richard Rutherford. *Master Workmen: Biographies of All the Deceased Bishops of the Free Methodist Church.* Winona Lake, Ind.: Light & Life Press, 1939. Centennial ed., enl., 1960.

Body, Alfred Harris. *John Wesley and Education.* London: Epworth Press, 1936.

Boehm, Henry. *Reminiscences, Historical and Biographical, of Sixty-four Years in the Ministry.* Ed. Joseph B. Wakeley. New York: Carlton & Porter, 1865. Reissued, with additions by Wakeley et al., as *The Patriarch of One Hundred Years;* New York: Nelson & Phillips, 1875.

Boland, J. M. *The Problem of Methodism: Being a Review of the Residue Theory of Regeneration and the Second Change Theory of Sanctification and the Philosophy of*

Christian Perfection. Nashville: Printed for the author by the Publishing House of the M. E. Church, South, 1889.

Bolitho, H. *Truly Rural: History of North Hill Circuit.* Leeds: Whitehead, 1947.

Bourne, Frederick William. *The Bible Christians: Their Origin and History, 1815-1900.* London: Bible Christian Book Room, 1905.

———————————. *Centenary Life of James Thorne.* London: Bible Christian Book Room, 1895.

Bourne, Hugh. *History of the Primitive Methodists.* Bemersley: Primitive Methodist Connexion, 1823. 2nd ed., 1835.

Bowen, Cawthon Asbury. *Child and Church; a History of Methodist Church-School Curriculum.* Nashville: Abingdon Press, 1960.

Bowen, Elias. *History of the Origin of the Free Methodist Church.* Rochester, N. Y.: B. T. Roberts, 1871.

Bowman, Thomas. *Historical Review of the Disturbance in the Evangelical Association.* Cleveland, O.: Thomas & Mattill, 1894.

Bowmer, John Coates. *The Lord's Supper in Methodism, 1791-1960.* London: Epworth Press, 1961.

———————————. *The Sacrament of the Lord's Supper in Early Methodism.* Westminster (London): Dacre Press, 1951.

Bradburn, Eliza Weaver, ed. *Memoirs of the Late Rev. Samuel Bradburn: Consisting principally of A Narrative of his Early Life, written by himself; and Extracts from a Journal, which he kept upwards of Forty Years.* London: Richard Edwards, 1816. *To which is added, a selection from his manuscripts.*

Bradley, Sidney Benjamin. *The Life of Bishop Richard Whatcoat.* N.p.: the author, 1936.

Bradley, David Henry. *A History of the A.M.E. Zion Church, 1796-1872.* Bedford, Pa.: the author, 1956. Vol. II, *1872-1968.* Bedford, Pa.: the author, 1970.

Brailsford, Mabel Richmond. *A Tale of Two Brothers: John and Charles Wesley.* London: Rupert Hart-Davis, 1954.

Braithwaite, M. *History of Methodism in Bishop Auckland Circuit.* Bp. Auckland: the author, 1885.

Brane, C. I. B. See Eberly, Albright and Brane. *History of the UB Church,* 1911.

Brash, William Bardsley. *Methodism.* London: Methuen & Co., 1928.

Bready, John Wesley. *England: Before and After Wesley: The Evangelical Revival and Social Reform.* London: Hodder & Stoughton, 1938.

Breeden, Henry. *Striking Incidents of Saving Grace Recorded by the Rev. H. Breeden, United Methodist Free Church Minister.* 1878.

Breihan, B. C., et al. *Kurze Geschichte der Südlich-Deutschen Konferenz.* N.p.: the conference, 1922.

Bretherton, Francis Fletcher. *Early Methodism In and Around Chester, 1749-1812.* Chester, Cheshire: the author, 1903.

Breyfogel, S. C. *Landmarks of the Evangelical Association, 1800-1887.* Reading, Pa.: Eagle Book Print, 1888.

Brill, Henry Elmore. *Story of the Methodist Episcopal Church in Oklahoma.* Oklahoma City University Press, 1939.

[Brookes, Iveson L.]. *A Defense of Southern Slavery Against the Attacks of Henry Clay and Alexander Campbell.* Hamburg, S. C.: Robinson and Carlisle, 1851.

Brooks, William Erle. *History Highlights of Florida Methodism.* N.p.: Florida Conference Historical Society, 1965.

Brosnan, Cornelius J. *Jason Lee, Prophet of the New Oregon.* New York: Macmillan Co., 1932.

Brown, Arlo Ayres. *A History of Religious Education in Recent Times.* New York: Abingdon Press, 1923.

Brown, Elmore. *The Struggle for Trained Teachers: The Story of John W. Shackford's Early Efforts to Provide Trained Teachers in the Church.* Nashville: Board of Education, 1966.

Brown, George. *George Brown: Pioneer, Missionary and Explorer: An Autobiography.* London: Hodder & Stoughton, 1908.

———————————. *The Lady Preacher; or, The Life and Labors of Mrs. Hannah Reeves.* Philadelphia: Daughaday & Becker, 1870.

———————————. *Recollections of Itinerant Life.* Cincinnati: R. W. Carroll & Co., 1866.

Brown, Marianna C. *Sunday-School Movements in America.* New York: Fleming H. Revell Co., 1901.

Brown, Oswald Eugene and Anna Muse. *Life and Letters of Laura Askew Haygood.* Nashville: Publishing House of the M.E. Church, South, 1904.

Brummitt, Dan B. *Epworth League Methods.* Cincinnati: Jennings & Graham, 1906.

Brummitt, Stella Wyatt. *Looking Backward, Thinking Forward, The Jubilee History of The Woman's Home Missionary Society of The Methodist Episcopal Church.* Cincinnati: Woman's Home Missionary Society, 1930.

Brunson, Alfred. *A Western Pioneer: or, Incidents of the Life and Times of Rev. Alfred Brunson, A.M. D.D., Embracing a Period of Over Seventy Years.* 2 vols. Cincinnati: Hitchcock & Walden, 1872, 1879.

Bryce, John Young. See Babcock and Bryce. *Oklahoma.* 1937.

Bucke, Emory Stevens, et al., eds. *The History of American Methodism.* 3 vols. Nashville: Abingdon Press, 1964.

Buckley, James Monroe. *Constitutional and Parliamentary History of the Methodist Episcopal Church.* New York: Eaton & Mains, 1912.

———————————. *A History of Methodists in the United States.* American Church History Series, Vol. V. New York: Christian Literature Co., 1896. Reissued in 2 vols., ill., under title *A History of Methodism . . . ,* 1897.

Bugbee, Leroy E. *He Holds the Stars in His Hands: The Centennial History of the Wyoming Annual Conference of the Methodist Church.* N.p.: the conference, 1952.

Bullock, Henry M. *A History of Emory University.* Nashville: Parthenon Press, 1936.

Bulmer, Agnes. *Memoirs of Mrs. Elizabeth Mortimer.* London: Mason, 1836.

Bunting, Thomas Percival. *The Life of Jabez Bunting, D.D., with Notices of Contemporary Persons and Events.* Vol. I; London: Longman, Brown, Green, Longmans & Roberts, 1859. Complete ed., finished by G. Stringer Rowe; London: T. Woolmer, 1887.

Burdekin, Richard. *Memoir of the Life and Character of Mr. Robert Spence of York.* York: the author, 1827. 2nd ed., enl., *with notices of the early introduction of Methodism into York,* 1840.

Burdsall, Richard. *Memoirs of the Life of Richard Burdsall . . . written by himself.* York: the author, 1797. 2nd ed., corr., enl., and improved; York: R. & J. Richardson, 1811. 3rd ed., corr., enl., and improved, with preface and appendix by John Burdsall; Thetford: J. Rogers, 1823.

Burtner, Robert W., and Chiles, Robert E., eds. *A Compend of Wesley's Theology.* Nashville: Abingdon Press, 1954.

Burton, John Wear. *The Call of the Pacific.* 1914.

———————————, and Deane, Wallace. *A Hundred Years in Fiji.* London: Epworth Press, 1936.

Butler, Clementina. *William Butler: The Founder of Two Missions of the Methodist Episcopal Church.* New York: Eaton & Mains, 1902.

Butler, Dugald. *John Wesley and George Whitefield in Scotland; or, The Influence of the Oxford Methodists on Scottish Religion.* Edinburgh: William Blackwood & Sons, 1898.

Butler, Mrs. F. A. (Sarah Frances Stringfield). *History of the Woman's Foreign Missionary Society, M. E. Church, South.* Nashville: Publishing House of the M.E. Church, South, 1904. Rev. ed., 1912.

Butler, John Wesley. *History of the Methodist Episcopal Church in Mexico: Personal Reminiscences, Present Conditions and Future Outlook.* New York: Methodist Book Concern, 1918.

Butler, William. *From Boston to Bareilly and Back.* New York: Phillips & Hunt, 1885.

——————. *The Land of the Veda: Being Personal Reminiscences of India; Its People, Castes, Thugs, and Fakirs; Its Religions, Mythology, Principal Monuments, Palaces, and Mausoleums: Together with the Incidents of the Great Sepoy Rebellion.* New York: Carlton & Lanahan, 1871.
——————. *Mexico in Transition from the Power of Political Romanism to Civil and Religious Liberty.* 2nd ed., rev.; New York: Hunt & Eaton, 1892.

Cade, John Brother. *Holsey—The Incomparable.* New York: Pageant Press, 1964.

Cain, John Buford. *Methodism in the Mississippi Conference, 1846-1870.* Jackson, Miss.: Hawkins Foundation, 1939.

Caine, Caesar. *History of Wesleyan Methodism in the Crewe Circuit.* Crewe: Hinchcliff, 1883.

Caldwell, Martha B., comp. *Annals of Shawnee Methodist Mission and Indian Manual Labor School.* Topeka: Kansas State Historical Society, 1939.

Calhoun, E. Clayton. *Of Men Who Ventured Much and Far: The Congo Quest of Dr. Gilbert and Bishop Lambuth.* Atlanta: Institute Press, 1961.

Cameron, Richard Morgan. *Boston University School of Theology, 1839-1968.* Boston: Boston University School of Theology, 1968.

——————. *Methodism and Society in Historical Perspective.* ("Methodism and Society," vol. I.) Nashville: Abingdon Press, 1961.

Candler, Warren Akin. *Life of Thomas Coke.* Nashville: Publishing House, M.E. Church, South, 1923.

Cannon, James, III. *History of Southern Methodist Missions.* Nashville: Cokesbury Press, 1926.

Cannon, William Ragsdale. *The Theology of John Wesley.* Nashville: Abingdon-Cokesbury Press, 1946.

Cargo, Ruth E. See Feeman, Cargo and Hay. *Story of a Noble Devotion.* 1945.

Carroll, Henry King. *Francis Asbury in the Making of American Methodism.* New York: Methodist Book Concern, 1923.

Carroll, John. *Case and His Cotemporaries; or, The Canadian Itinerants' Memorial: Constituting a Biographical History of Methodism in Canada, from its Introduction into the Province, till the Death of the Rev. Wm. Case in 1855.* 5 vols. Toronto: Wesleyan Printing Establishment (or Conference Office), 1867-77.

Carter, Cullen T. *History of the Tennessee Conference.* Nashville: the author, 1948.

Carter, Henry. *The Methodist Heritage.* London: Epworth Press; Nashville: Abingdon-Cokesbury Press, 1951.

Cell, George Croft. *The Rediscovery of John Wesley.* New York: Henry Holt & Co., 1935.

Cennick, John. *The Life of Mr. J. Cennick.* 2nd ed.; Bristol: the author, 1745. The first ed. was in print by March 1744, but no copy is extant.

The Centenary of the Methodist New Connexion, 1797-1897.

Centennial of Canadian Methodism. Toronto: William Briggs, 1891.

Centennial of the Methodist Book Concern and Dedication of the New Publishing and Mission Building of the Methodist Church. New York: Hunt & Eaton, 1890.

Chaffee, A. F. *History of the Wyoming Conference of the Methodist Episcopal Church.* New York: Eaton & Mains, 1904.

Chaffin, Nora Campbell. *Trinity College, 1839-1892.* (later Duke University) Durham, N. C.: Duke University Press, 1950.

Champion, Thomas Edward. *The Methodist Churches of Toronto: A History of the Methodist Denomination and its Churches in York and Toronto, with Biographical Sketches of many of the Clergy and Laity.* Toronto: G. M. Rose & Sons Co., 1899.

Chandler, Mrs. E. C. (Rosalia Porter). *History of the Woman's Foreign Missionary Society of the Methodist Protestant Church, 1879-1919.* Pittsburgh: Headquarters, W.F.M.S., 1920.

Chew, Richard. *James Everett: A Biography.* London: Hodder & Stoughton, 1875.

——————. *William Griffith: Memorials and Letters.* London: Andrew Crombie, 1885.

Chick, E. *History of Methodism in Exeter and the Neighbourhood from the year 1739 until 1907.* Exeter: Drayton, 1907.

Chiles, Robert Eugene. *Theological Transition in American Methodism: 1790-1935.* Nashville: Abingdon Press, 1965.

——————. See Burtner and Chiles. *Compend of Wesley's Theology.* 1954.

Ching, Donald S., et al. *For Ever Beginning: Two Hundred Years of Methodism in the Western Area.* Kingston, Jamaica: Literature Dept. of the Methodist Church (Jamaica District), 1960.

Chreitzberg, A. M. *Early Methodism in the Carolinas.* Nashville: Publishing House of the M. E. Church, South, 1897.

Christliche Apologete, Cincinnati, M. E. Church for the German Language Conferences, 1839-1941.

Christliche Botschafter, published at New Berlin, Pa., Cleveland, O., and Harrisburg, Pa., 1836-1946.

Church, Leslie F. *The Early Methodist People.* London: Epworth Press, 1948.

——————. *More About the Early Methodist People.* London: Epworth Press, 1949.

——————. *Oglethorpe: A Study of Philanthropy in England and Georgia.* London: Epworth Press, 1932.

Clark, Davis Wasgatt. *Life and Times of Rev. Elijah Hedding, D.D., Late Senior Bishop of the Methodist Episcopal Church.* New York: Carlton & Phillips, 1855.

Clark, Elmer Talmage. *An Album of Methodist History.* Nashville: Abingdon-Cokesbury Press, 1952.

——————. *Methodism in Western North Carolina.* N.p.: Western North Carolina Conference, The Methodist Church, 1966.

——————. *The Small Sects in America.* Nashville: Cokesbury Press, 1937. Rev. ed., Abingdon-Cokesbury Press, 1949.

——————. *What Happened at Aldersgate.* Nashville: Methodist Publishing House, 1938.

Clark, Elmer T., and Stafford, T. A., eds. *Who's Who in Methodism.* Chicago: A. N. Marquis Co., 1952.

——————. See Guptill and Clark. *Melville B. Cox.* 1932.

——————. See Holt and Clark. *World Methodist Movement.* 1956.

Clark, J. O. A., ed. *The Wesley Memorial Volume.* New York: Phillips & Hunt; Cincinnati: Walden & Stowe. J. W. Burke & Co., Macon, Ga.; J. B. McFerrin, Agent, Nashville, Tenn.; L. D. Dameron & Co., St. Louis, Mo., 1880.

Clark, Robert Donald. *The Life of Matthew Simpson.* New York: Macmillan Co., 1956.

Clarke, Adam. *The Holy Bible . . . , With a Commentary and Critical Notes.* London: Joseph Butterworth, 1810-25. American ed., 6 vols.; New York: Bangs & Mason, 1823-25.

——————. *Memoirs of the Wesley Family; Collected Principally from Original Documents.* London: J. Kershaw, 1823. 2nd ed., rev., cor., and considerably enl.; London: T. Tegg & Son, 1836.

Clarke, Eliza. *Susanna Wesley.* London: W. H. Allen & Co., 1886.

Clarke, J. B. B. *An Account of the Infancy, Religious and Literary Life of Adam Clarke.* 3 vols. London: T. S. Clarke, 1833.

Clegg, Leland and Oden, William B. *Oklahoma Methodism in the Twentieth Century.* N.p.: Oklahoma Conference, The Methodist Church, 1968.

Cliffe, Albert W. *The Glory of Our Methodist Heritage.* N.p., 1957.

Clowes, William. *The Journals of William Clowes, a Primitive*

Methodist Preacher . . . 1810 to 1838. London: John Hallam & Thomas Holliday, 1844.

Cocking, Thomas. *The History of Wesleyan Methodism in Grantham and Its Vicinity.* London: Simpkin, Marshall, 1836.

Coke, Thomas. *Commentary on the Holy Bible.* Old Testament, London: 1801-3; New Testament, New York: by Daniel Hitt, for the Methodist Connexion in the United States, 1812.

——————. *Four Discourses on the Duties of a Minister of the Gospel.* London: Printed for G. Whitfield, 1798. New York: Bangs & Mason, 1820.

——————. *Extracts of the Journals of the Rev. Dr. Coke's Five Visits to America.* London: printed by G. Paramore, sold by G. Whitfield, 1793.

——————. *Extracts of the Journals of the Late Rev. Thomas Coke, LL.D.; Comprising Several Visits to North-America and the West-Indies; His Tour Through a Part of Ireland, and His Nearly Finished Voyage to Bombay in the East-Indies: To Which Is Prefixed, A Life of the Doctor.* Dublin: printed for the Methodist Book-Room by R. Napper, 1816.

——————. *A Funeral Sermon on the Death of Mrs. H. A. Rogers; With an Appendix Written by Her Husband.* Birmingham: J. Belcher, 1795.

——————. *A History of the West Indies, Containing the Natural, Civil, and Ecclesiastical History of Each Island: With an Account of the Missions Instituted in Those Islands, from the Commencement of Their Civilization; But More Especially of the Missions Which Have Been Established in That Archipelago by the Society Late in Connexion with the Rev. John Wesley.* 3 vols. Liverpool and London: the author, 1808-11.

——————. *Sermon on the Godhead of Christ.* London: J. Paramore, 1785.

——————. *The Substance of a Sermon Preached at Baltimore . . . at the Ordination of the Rev. Francis Asbury to the Office of Superintendent.* London: J. Paramore, 1785.

Coke, Thomas, and Asbury, Francis. *An Address to the Annual Subscribers for the Support of Cokesbury College, and to the Members of the Methodist Society. To Which are Added, the Rules and Regulations of the College.* New York: printed by W. Ross, 1787.

Coke, Thomas, and Moore, Henry. *The Life of the Rev. John Wesley, A.M., Including an Account of the Great Revival of Religion, in Europe and America, of which He was the First and Chief Instrument.* London: printed by Paramore, sold by G. Whitfield, 1792. First American ed., Philadelphia: printed by P. Hall, sold by J. Dickins, 1793.

Cole, Joseph, ed. *Memoirs of Miss Hannah Ball, of High Wycombe.* York: (printed for her sister), 1796. Rev. and enl. by John Parker; London: John Mason, 1839.

Cole, Otis, and Baketel, Oliver S., eds. *History of the New Hampshire Conference of the Methodist Episcopal Church.* N.p.: the conference, 1929.

Cole, Richard Lee. *A History of Methodism in Dublin.* Dublin, 1932.

——————. *History of Methodism in Ireland* (1860-1960). (Vol. 4, continuing Crookshank's *History.*) Belfast: Irish Methodist Publishing Co., 1960.

Coles, George. *Heroines of Methodism; or, Pen and Ink Sketches of the Mothers and Daughters of the Church.* New York: Carlton & Porter, 1857.

Colhouer, Thomas Henry. *Sketches of the Founders of the Methodist Protestant Church.* Pittsburgh: M. P. Book Concern, 1880.

A Collection of Hymns for Public, Social, and Domestic Worship. Charleston: by John Early, for the M. E. Church, South, 1847. Numerous other eds.

A Collection of Hymns Selected from Various Authors for Use of the Evangelical Association. New Berlin, Pa., 1835.

A Collection of Hymns for the Use of the Methodist Episcopal Church, Principally from the Collection of the Rev. John Wesley. New York: by N. Bangs & T. Mason, for the M. E. Church; Abraham Paul, printer, 1821. Numerous other eds.

Collection of Hymns for the Use of the People Called Methodists. London: J. Paramore, 1780; with a supplement, 1830; with a supplement, making 1,026 hymns, 1876.

A Collection of Psalms and Hymns. Charles-Town, 1737. A facsimile with additional material issued as John Wesley's First Hymn-Book, by Frank Baker and George Walton Williams, 1964.

Collier, Frank Wilbur. *John Wesley Among the Scientists.* New York: Abingdon Press, 1928.

Colwell, James, ed. *A Century in the Pacific.* London: Charles H. Kelly, 1914.

——————. *The Illustrated History of Methodism.* Sydney: William Brooks & Co., 1904.

——————. *Methodism in New South Wales.* Sydney: William Brooks & Co., 1904.

Comfort, Silas. *An Exposition of the Articles of Religion of the Methodist Episcopal Church.* New York: the author, 1847.

Conant, Newton C. *Present Day Methodism and the Bible.* Camden, N. J.: Bible Protestant Press, 1949.

Constitution and Discipline of the Methodist Protestant Church. First ed., 1830; then usually published following the General Conference. Last ed. 1938.

Cooke, Richard Joseph. *The Historic Episcopate, A Study of Anglican Claims and Methodist Orders.* New York: Eaton & Mains; Cincinnati: Jennings & Pye, 1896.

——————. *History of the Ritual of the Methodist Episcopal Church.* Cincinnati: Jennings & Pye, 1900.

Cooper, Ezekiel. *A Funeral Discourse, on the Death of That Eminent Man the Late Reverend John Dickins.* Philadelphia: printed by H. Maxwell for Asbury Dickins, 1799.

Cope, Henry Frederick. *The Evolution of the Sunday School.* Boston: Pilgrim Press, 1911.

Coppin, L. J. *Unwritten History.* Philadelphia: A.M.E. Book Concern, 1919.

Corbett, Lynn. *What, Why, How?—History, Organization, and Doctrinal Belief of the Southern Methodist Church.* Greenville, S. C.: Foundry Press, 1956.

Corderoy, Edward. *Father Reeves, the Methodist Class-Leader; a Brief Account of Mr. William Reeves, Thirty-four Years a Class Leader in the Wesleyan Methodist Society, Lambeth.* London: Hamilton, Adams & Co., 1853.

Core, Arthur C. *Philip William Otterbein: Pastor, Ecumenist.* Dayton, O.: Board of Publication, E.U.B. Church, 1968.

Cornish, George H. *Cyclopaedia of Methodism in Canada.* 2 vols. Toronto: Methodist Book & Publishing House, 1881, 1903.

Coulson, John E. *The Peasant Preacher: Memorials of Mr. Charles Richardson.* London: Hamilton, Adams & Co., 1867.

Court, Lewis Henry. *Some Dartmoor Saints and Shrines: Studies in Experimental Religion Among the Homely Folk.* London: Morgan & Scott, 1927.

Coward, S. L. C., ed. *Entire Sanctification from 1739 to 1901.* Louisville: Pentecostal Herald, 1901.

Cox, Leo George. *John Wesley's Concept of Perfection.* Kansas City, Mo.: Beacon Hill Press, 1964.

Cox, Melville B. *Remains of . . . With a Memoir.* Boston: Light & Horton, 1835; rev. ed., naming Gershom F. Cox as author of memoir, New York: T. Mason & G. Lane, 1840.

Craig, Maxie Harris. See Harris and Craig. *CME Church.* 1949.

Craig, Reginald S. *The Fighting Parson, the Biography of Colonel John M. Chivington.* Los Angeles: the author, 1959.

Crawford, Benjamin Franklin. *Theological Trends in Methodist Hymnody.* Carnegie, Pa.: Carnegie Church Press, 1939.

Creamer, David. *Methodist Hymnology; Comprehending*

Notices of the Poetical Works of John and Charles Wesley. New York: the author, 1848.

Crook, William. *Ireland and the Centenary of American Methodism.* London: Hamilton, Adams & Co., 1866.

Crooks, George Richard. *The Life of Bishop Matthew Simpson of the Methodist Episcopal Church.* New York: Harper & Bros., 1890.

Crookshank, Charles Henry. *History of Methodism in Ireland.* 3 vols. Belfast: R. S. Allen, Son & Allen, 1885-88. Vol. 4 by R. L. Cole; Belfast: Irish Methodist Publishing Co., 1960.

——————————. *Memorable Women of Irish Methodism in the Last Century.* London: Wesleyan Methodist Book-Room, 1882.

Crowther, Jonathan. *The Life of the Rev. Thomas Coke.* Leeds: Alexander Cumming, 1815.

——————————. *The Methodist Manual; or, A Short History of the Wesleyan Methodists.* Halifax (Yorkshire): J. Walker, 1810.

——————————. *A True and Complete Portraiture of Methodism.* London: Richard Edwards, 1811. 2nd ed., enl., omitting "True and Complete," 1815.

Cumbers, Frank Henry. *The Book Room: The Story of the Methodist Publishing House and Epworth Press.* London: Epworth Press, 1956.

——————————. *Richmond College, 1843-1943.* London: Epworth Press, 1944.

Cummings, Anson W. *The Early Schools of Methodism.* New York: Phillips & Hunt, 1886.

Curl, R. F. *Southwest Texas Methodism.* N.p.: Inter-Board Council, Southwest Texas Conference, The Methodist Church, 1951.

Currie, Robert. *Methodism Divided: A Study in the Sociology of Ecumenicalism.* London: Faber & Faber, 1968.

Curtis, Lewis, ed. *The General Conferences of the Methodist Episcopal Church from 1792 to 1896.* Cincinnati: Curts & Jennings; New York: Eaton & Mains, 1900.

Dabney, Virginius. *Dry Messiah: The Life of Bishop Cannon.* New York: Alfred A. Knopf, 1949.

Daggett, Mrs. L. H., ed. *Historical Sketches of Woman's Missionary Societies in America and England.* Boston: the author, 1879.

Daily Christian Advocate, published daily during sessions of General Conference of the M. E. Church, M. E. Church, South, The Methodist Church, and The United Methodist Church. Also published daily during the quadrennial sessions of the Jurisdictional Conferences.

Dallimore, Arnold A. *George Whitefield: The Life and Times of the Great Evangelist of the Eighteenth-Century Revival.* Vol. 1. London: Banner of Truth Trust, 1970.

Daniels, William Haven. *The Illustrated History of Methodism in Great Britain and America, from the Days of the Wesleys to the Present Time.* New York: Methodist Book Concern, 1879. Abridged ed., *A Short History of "The People Called Methodists,"* London: Hodder & Stoughton, 1882. New ed. rev. and brought down to the year 1887, New York: Phillips & Hunt, 1887.

——————————. *Memorials of Gilbert Haven.* Boston: B. B. Russell & Co., 1880.

Danks, B. *Methodist Missions in the South Seas, 1821-1909.* Sydney, N.S.W.: Methodist Missionary Society of Australasia, 1909.

Davey, Cyril J. *The Man Who Wanted the World: The Story of Thomas Coke.* London: Methodist Missionary Society, 1947.

——————————. *The Methodist Story.* London: Epworth Press, 1955.

Davies, E. Tegla. See Harrison et al. *Methodist Church.* 1932.

Davies, G. C. B. *The Early Cornish Evangelicals, 1735-60; A Study of Walker of Truro and Others.* London: S.P.C.K., 1957.

Davies, Rupert E. ed. *John Scott Lidgett: A Symposium.* London: Epworth Press, 1957.

——————————. *Methodism.* Harmondsworth, Middlesex: Penguin Books, 1963.

——————————. *Methodists and Unity.* London: A. R. Mowbray & Co., 1962.

Davies, Rupert E., and Rupp, E. Gordon, eds. *A History of the Methodist Church in Great Britain.* Vol. 1. London: Epworth Press, 1965.

Davis, James A. *The History of Episcopacy, Prelatic and Moderate.* Nashville: A.M.E. Church Sunday School Union, 1902.

Davis, Mrs. John. *Lucy Webb Hayes: A Memorial Sketch.* Cincinnati: Woman's Home Missionary Society, 1890.

Davis, Lewis. *The Life of Rev. David Edwards, D.D.* Dayton, O.: United Brethren Publishing House, 1883.

Davis, Lyman Edwyn. *Democratic Methodism in America: A Topical Survey of the Methodist Protestant Church.* New York: Fleming H. Revell Co., 1921.

Dawson, Joseph. *Peter Mackenzie: His Life and Labours.* London: Charles H. Kelly, 1896.

Dearing, Trevor. *Wesleyan and Tractarian Worship.* London: Epworth Press and Society for Promoting Christian Knowledge, 1966.

Deats, Paul, Jr. See Stotts and Deats, *Methodism and Society.* 1962.

Deats, Richard L. *The Story of Methodism in the Philippines.* Manila: National Council of Churches in the Philippines, 1964.

Deems, Charles F., ed. *Annals of Southern Methodism for 1855.* New York: J. A. Gray's Fire-Proof Printing Office, 1856. Ed. *for 1856,* Nashville: Stevenson & Owen, 1857. Ed. *for 1857,* Nashville: J. B. M'Ferrin, 1858.

Denny, Collins, ed. *A Manual of the Discipline of the Methodist Episcopal Church, South, including the Decisions of the College of Bishops.* Nashville: Publishing House of the M. E. Church, South, 1931.

De Puy, William Harrison, ed. *The Methodist Centennial Year-Book for 1884, the One Hundredth Year of the Separate Organization of American Methodism.* New York: Phillips & Hunt, 1883.

Deschner, John W. *Wesley's Christology.* Dallas, Tex.: Southern Methodist University Press, 1960.

Detzler, Jack J. *The History of the Northwest Indiana Conference of the Methodist Church, 1852-1951.* N.p.: the conference, 1953.

Dickinson, Peard. *Memoirs.* Ed. Joseph Benson. London: George Whitfield, 1803.

Dickons, J. Norton. *Kirkgate Chapel, Bradford, and Its Associations with Methodism.* Bradford: the author, 1903.

Diffendorfer, Ralph E., ed. *The World Service of the Methodist Episcopal Church.* Chicago: Council of Boards of Benevolence, M. E. Church, 1923.

Dimmitt, Marjorie A. *Isabella Thoburn College: A Record from Its Beginnings to Its Diamond Jubilee, 1961.* Cincinnati: World Outlook Press, 1963.

Dimond, Sydney George. *The Psychology of Methodism.* London: Epworth Press, 1932.

——————————. *The Psychology of the Methodist Revival: An Empirical & Descriptive Study.* London: Oxford University Press, 1926.

Dingle, R. S. C., ed. *Annals of Achievement: A Review of Queensland Methodism, 1847-1947.* Brisbane: Queensland Book Depot, 1947.

Dixon, James. *Methodism in America: With the Personal Narrative of the Author, During a Tour Through a Part of the United States and Canada.* London: the author, 1849. Abridged ed., *Personal Narrative of a Tour,* etc.; New York: Lane & Scott, 1849.

Dixon, James Main. See Lee, J. W. et al. *Illustrated History.* 1900.

Doctrines and Discipline of The Methodist Church, first ed.

1939; beginning in 1940 published quadrennially following the General Conference.

Doctrines and Discipline of the Methodist Episcopal Church, published annually 1785-92; then 1796, 1798, 1800, 1801, 1804, 1805. Beginning in 1808 published quadrennially following the General Conference. Last ed. 1936.

Doctrines and Discipline of the Methodist Episcopal Church, South, first ed. 1846 and then published quadrennially following the General Conference. Last ed. 1938.

Doctrines and Discipline of The United Methodist Church, 1968.

Dolbey, George W. *The Architectural Expression of Methodism: The First Hundred Years.* London: Epworth Press, 1964.

Dorsett, Cyril. See Lawrence and Dorsett. *Caribbean Conquest.* 1947.

Doughty, William Lamplough. *John Wesley: His Conferences and His Preachers.* London: Epworth Press, 1944.

——————. *John Wesley, Preacher.* London: Epworth Press, 1955.

Douglass, Paul F. *The Story of German Methodism.* New York: Methodist Book Concern, 1939.

Dow, Lorenzo. *The Dealings of God, Man and the Devil; as Exemplified in the Life, Experience, and Travels of Lorenzo Dow, in a Period of Over Half a Century, together with his Polemic and Miscellaneous Writings, Complete. To which is added The Vicissitudes of Life, by Peggy Dow.* New York: Lamport, Blakeman, and Law, 1853.

——————. *History of Cosmopolite; or the Four Volumes of Lorenzo's Journal . . . from Childhood, to near his Fortieth Year.* New York: John C. Totten, 1814.

Drees, Ada M. C., ed. *Thirteen Years in Mexico* (from Letters of Charles W. Drees). New York: Abingdon Press, 1915.

Drew, Jacob Halls. *The Life, Character, and Literary Labours of Samuel Drew.* New York: Harper & Brothers, 1835.

Drew, Samuel. *The Life of the Rev. Thomas Coke, LL.D., Including in Detail His Various Travels and Extraordinary Missionary Exertions, in England, Ireland, America, and the West-Indies: With an Account of his Death, on the 3d of May, 1814, While on a Missionary Voyage to the Island of Ceylon, in the East-Indies. Interspersed with Numerous Reflections; and Concluding with an Abstract of His Writings and Character.* New York: J. Soule & T. Mason, 1818; London: Thomas Cordeux, 1817.

Drinkhouse, Edward J. *History of Methodist Reform, Synoptical of General Methodism 1703 to 1898; With Special and Comprehensive Reference to Its Most Salient Exhibition in the History of the Methodist Protestant Church.* 2 vols. Baltimore and Pittsburgh: Board of Publication of the Methodist Protestant Church, 1899.

Drury, Augustus W., ed. and trans. *The Disciplines of the United Brethren in Christ, 1814-1841.* Dayton, O.: United Brethren Publishing House, 1895.

——————. *History of the Church of the United Brethren in Christ.* Dayton, O.: Otterbein Press, 1924. Rev. ed., 1931.

——————. *Life of Bishop J. J. Glossbrenner, D.D.* Dayton, O.: United Brethren Publishing House, 1889.

——————. *The Life of Rev. Philip William Otterbein.* Dayton, O.: United Brethren Publishing House, 1884.

——————, ed. and trans. *The Minutes of the Annual and General Conferences of the Church of the United Brethren in Christ, 1800-1818.* Dayton, O.: United Brethren Publishing House, 1897.

Du Bose, Horace M. *A History of Methodism.* Vol. 2 of McTyeire's *History of Methodism,* covering 1884-1916. Nashville: Publishing House of the M. E. Church, South, 1916.

——————. *Life of Joshua Soule.* ("Methodist Founders' Series.") Nashville: Publishing House of the M. E. Church, South, 1911.

Duncan, Peter. *A Narrative of the Wesleyan Mission to Jamaica.* London: Partridge & Oakey, 1849.

Duncan, Watson B., ed. *Twentieth Century Sketches of the South Carolina Conference, M. E. Church, South.* Columbia, S. C.: State Co., 1901. 2nd ed., 1914. 3rd ed.; E. O. Watson, ed., *Builders;* Columbia, S. C.; Southern Christian Advocate, 1932. 4th ed.; George K. Way and Clarence E. Peele, eds., *Methodist Ministers in South Carolina;* 1942: 5th ed.; George K. Way, ed.; Columbia, S. C.: South Carolina Methodist Advocate, 1952. 6th ed.; Adlai C. Holler, ed.; 1961.

Dunkle, William F., Jr. *Values in the Church Year for Evangelical Protestantism.* Nashville: Abingdon Press, 1959.

Dunn, Samuel. *Memoirs of Mr. Thomas Tatham and of Wesleyan Methodism in Nottingham.* London: Tegg, 1847.

Durley, T. See Piggott and Durley. *Henry James Piggott.* 1921.

Duvall, Sylvanus Milne. *The Methodist Episcopal Church and Education up to 1869.* New York: Teachers College, Columbia University, 1928.

Dyer, John L. *The Snow-Shoe Itinerant. An Autobiography of the Rev. John L. Dyer, Familiarly Known as "Father Dyer" of the Colorado Conference, Methodist Episcopal Church.* Cincinnati: Cranston & Stowe, 1890.

Dyson, John B. *A Brief History of Rise and Progress of Wesleyan Methodism in the Leek Circuit; with Biographical Sketches of Several Eminent Characters.* Leek: printed by Edward Hallowes, sold by J. Mason, 1853.

——————. *The History of Wesleyan Methodism in the Congleton Circuit.* London: J. Mason, 1856.

——————. *Methodism in the Isle of Wight: Its Origin and Progress Down to the Present Times.* Ventnor, I.W.: George M. Burt, 1865.

Early, Sarah J. W. *Life and Labors of Rev. Jordan W. Early.* Nashville: A.M.E. Church Sunday School Union, 1894.

Eayrs, George. *A Short History of the United Methodist Church.* London: Henry Hooks, 1913.

——————. *Wesley and Kingswood and Its Free Churches.* Bristol: J. W. Arrowsmith, 1911.

——————. See Townsend, Workman and Eayrs. *New History.* 1909.

Eberly, Daniel; Albright, Isaiah H., and Brane, C. I. B. *Landmark History of the United Brethren Church.* Reading, Pa.: Behney & Bright, 1911.

Edwards, Maldwyn Lloyd. *After Wesley: A Study of the Social and Political Influence of Methodism in the Middle Period (1791-1849).* London: Epworth Press, 1935.

——————. *The Astonishing Youth: A Study of John Wesley as Men Saw Him.* London: Epworth Press, 1959.

——————. *Family Circle: A Study of the Epworth Household in Relation to John and Charles Wesley.* London: Epworth Press, 1949.

——————. *John Wesley and the Eighteenth Century: A Study of His Social and Political Influence.* London: G. Allen & Unwin, 1933. Rev. ed., London: Epworth Press, 1955.

——————. *Methodism and England: A Study of Methodism in Its Social and Political Aspects During the Period 1850-1932.* London: Epworth Press, 1943.

——————. *S. E. Keeble, Pioneer and Prophet.* London: Epworth Press, 1949.

——————. *Sons to Samuel.* London: Epworth Press, 1961.

——————. *This Methodism: Eight Studies.* London: Epworth Press, 1939.

Eggleston, Charles F., ed. *Pioneering in Penn's Woods: Philadelphia Methodist Episcopal Annual Conference Through One Hundred Fifty Years.* N.p.: Philadelphia Conference Tract Society, 1937.

Eller, Paul Himmel. *History of Evangelical Missions.* Harrisburg, Pa.: Evangelical Press, 1942.

——————. *These Evangelical United Brethren.* Dayton, O.: Otterbein Press, 1950. Rev. ed., 1957.

Elliott, Charles. *History of the Great Secession from the Methodist Episcopal Church in the Year 1845, Eventuating in the Organization of the New Church, Entitled the "Methodist Episcopal Church, South."* Cincinnati: Swormstedt & Poe, for the M. E. Church, 1855.

——————. *The Life of the Rev. Robert R. Roberts.* Cincinnati: J. F. Wright & L. Swormstedt, 1844.

——————. *South-Western Methodism: A History of the M. E. Church in the South-West, from 1844 to 1864; Comprising the Martyrdom of Bewley and Others, Persecutions of the M. E. Church, and Its Reorganization, etc.* Ed. and rev. by Leroy M. Vernon. Cincinnati: the editor, 1868.

Emory, John. *A Defence of "Our Fathers," and of the Original Organization of the Methodist Episcopal Church, Against the Rev. Alexander M'Caine, and Others; With Historical and Critical Notices of Early American Methodism.* New York: N. Bangs & J. Emory, 1827.

Emory, Robert. *History of the Discipline of the Methodist Episcopal Church.* New York: G. Lane & P. P. Sandford, 1844. 5th ed., rev. by W. P. Strickland; New York: Carlton & Porter, 1857.

——————. *The Life of the Rev. John Emory, D.D., One of the Bishops of the Methodist Episcopal Church. By his eldest son. With an Appendix.* New York: G. Lane, 1841.

English, Thomas H. *Emory University, 1915-1965: A Semicentennial History.* Atlanta: Emory University, 1966.

Entwisle, Joseph, Jr. *Memoir of the Rev. Joseph Entwisle.* Bristol: N. Lomax, 1848.

Erb, Jacob, and Rhinehart, William, eds. *A Collection of Hymns, for the Use of the United Brethren in Christ, Taken from the Most Approved Authors, and Adapted to Public and Private Worship.* Circleville, O., 1835.

Erikson, Jakob Maximilian. *Metodismen i Sverige.* Stockholm: K. J. Bohlins Förlag, 1895.

Espino, Jose, *Perfiles.* El Paso, Tex.: n.p., 1963.

Etheridge, John Wesley. *The Life of the Rev. Adam Clarke.* London: John Mason, 1858.

——————. *The Life of the Rev. Thomas Coke, D.C.L.* London: John Mason, 1860.

The Evangelical Hymnal. Cleveland, O.: Publishing House of the Evangelical Association, 1921.

Evangelical Hymn and Tune Book. Cleveland, O.: Publishing House of the Evangelical Association, 1889. Rev. eds., 1906, 1914.

Evangelical Messenger, published at New Berlin, Pa. and then Cleveland, O. and Harrisburg, Pa., 1848-1946. Superseded by *Telescope-Messenger.*

Everett, James. *Adam Clarke Portrayed.* 2 vols. London: Hamilton, Adams, & Co., 1843, 1849.

——————. *Historical Sketches of Wesleyan Methodism in Sheffield and Its Vicinity.* Sheffield: James Montgomery, 1823.

——————. *Memoirs of the Life, Character, and Ministry of William Dawson, Late of Barnbow, near Leeds.* London: Hamilton, Adams, & Co., 1842.

——————. *The Polemic Divine; or, Memoirs of the Life, Writings, and Opinions of the Rev. Daniel Isaac.* London: Hamilton, Adams, & Co., 1839; 2nd ed., 1851; 3rd ed., 1867.

——————. *The Village Blacksmith . . . Memoir of Samuel Hick, Late of Micklefield, Yorkshire.* London: Hamilton, Adams, & Co., 2nd ed., 1831.

——————. *Wesleyan Methodism in Manchester and Its Vicinity.* Manchester: Executors of S. Russell, 1827.

Evers, Joseph Calvin. *The History of the Southern Illinois Conference, The Methodist Church.* Bloomington, Ill.: Southern Illinois Conference Historical Society, 1964.

Extracts of Letters Containing Some Account of the Work of God Since the Year 1800. Written by the Preachers and Members of the Methodist Episcopal Church, to Their Bishops. New York: published by E. Cooper and J. Wilson, for the Methodist Connection in the United States, 1805.

Farish, Hunter Dickinson. *The Circuit Rider Dismounts: A Social History of Southern Methodism, 1865-1900.* Richmond, Va.: Dietz Press, 1938.

Farndale, William Edward. *The Secret of Mow Cop: A New Appraisal of the Origins of Primitive Methodism.* London: Epworth Press, 1950.

Faulkner, John Alfred. *The Methodists.* New York: The Baker & Taylor Co., 1903.

Feeman, Harlan L. *Francis Asbury's Silver Trumpet.* Daytona Beach, Fla.: the author, 1950.

Feeman, Harlan L.; Cargo, Ruth E., and Hay, Fanny A. *The Story of a Noble Devotion.* Adrian, Mich.: Adrian College Press, 1945.

Fellows, Stephen Norris. *History of the Upper Iowa Conference of the Methodist Episcopal Church, 1856-1906.* N.p.: Semi-Centennial Commission of the conference, 1907.

Ffirth, John, comp. *The Experience and Gospel Labors of the Rev. Benjamin Abbott, To Which Is Annexed a Narrative of His Life and Death.* New York: Cooper & Wilson, 1805.

——————. *Truth Vindicated; or, A Scriptural Essay, Wherein the Vulgar and Frivolous Cavils, Commonly Urged Against the Methodist Episcopal Church, Are Briefly Considered in a Letter to a Friend.* Burlington, N. J.: Neale, 1794. 2nd ed., rev.; New York: Daniel Hitt, 1810. 3rd ed., 1814.

Fifty Years of Light: Prepared by Missionaries of the Woman's Foreign Missionary Society of the Methodist Episcopal Church in Commemoration of the Completion of Fifty Years of Work in Korea. Seoul, Korea: Woman's Foreign Missionary Society of the M. E. Church, 1938.

Finch, Edwin. See Spencer and Finch. *Constitutional Practice.* 1951.

Findlay, George G. and Mary Grace. *Wesley's World Parish: A Sketch of the Hundred Years' Work of the Wesleyan Methodist Missionary Society.* London: Hodder & Stoughton; Charles H. Kelly, 1913.

Findlay, George Gillanders, and Holdsworth, William West. *The History of the Wesleyan Methodist Missionary Society.* 5 vols. London: Epworth Press, 1921-24.

Findlay, George Hugo. *Christ's Standard Bearer: A Study of the Hymns of Charles Wesley.* London: Epworth Press, 1956.

Finley, James B. *Autobiography of Rev. James B. Finley; or Pioneer Life in the West.* Ed. W. P. Strickland. Cincinnati: Methodist Book Concern, 1853.

——————. *History of the Wyandott Mission at Upper Sandusky, Ohio, Under the Direction of the Methodist Episcopal Church.* Cincinnati: Wright & Swormstedt, 1840.

——————. *Life Among the Indians.* Cincinnati: Swormstedt & Poe, 1857.

——————. *Memorials of Prison Life.* Ed. B. F. Tefft. Cincinnati: Swormstedt & Poe, 1850.

——————. *Sketches of Western Methodism: Biographical, Historical, and Miscellaneous, Illustrative of Pioneer Life.* Cincinnati: the author, 1854.

Finney, Thomas Monroe. *The Life and Labors of Enoch Mather Marvin.* St. Louis, Mo.: James H. Chambers, 1880.

Fisher, Welthy Honsinger. *Frederick Bohn Fisher: World Citizen.* New York: Macmillan Co., 1944.

Fisk, Wilbur. *The Calvinistic Controversy.* New York: Mason and Lane, 1837.

Fitchett, William Henry. *Wesley and His Century: A Study in Spiritual Forces.* London: Smith, Elder & Co., 1906.

Fitzgerald, Oscar Penn. *Centenary Cameos, 1784-1884.* Nashville: Southern Methodist Publishing House, 1885.

——————. *Dr. Summers: A Life-Study.* Nashville: Southern Methodist Publishing House, 1885.

——————————. *Fifty Years: Observations—Opinions —Experiences.* Nashville: Publishing House of the M. E. Church, South, 1903.

——————————. *Sunset Views, in Three Parts.* Nashville: Publishing House of the M. E. Church, South, 1900.

——————————, and Galloway, Charles Betts. *Eminent Methodists: Twelve Booklets in One Book.* Nashville: O. P. Fitzgerald, 1897.

Flew, Robert Newton. *The Hymns of Charles Wesley: A Study of Their Structure.* London: Epworth Press, 1953.

——————————. *The Idea of Perfection in Christian Theology.* London: Oxford University Press, 1934.

——————————. *The Nature of the Church.* New York: Harper & Brothers, 1952.

Flickinger, D. K. *Fifty-five Years of Active Ministerial Life.* Dayton, O.: United Brethren Publishing House, 1907.

Flint, Charles Wesley. *Charles Wesley and His Colleagues.* Washington, D. C.: Public Affairs Press, 1957.

Flood, Theodore L., and Hamilton, John W., eds. *Lives of Methodist Bishops.* New York: Phillips and Hunt, 1882.

Ford, Eddy Lucius. *The History of the Educational Work of the Methodist Episcopal Church in China, A Study of Its Development and Present Trends.* Foochow, China: Christian Herald Mission Press, 1938.

Foster, Henry Blaine. *Rise and Progress of Wesleyan-Methodism in Jamaica.* London: Wesleyan Conference Office, 1881.

Fout, Henry H. See Weekley and Fout. *Our Heroes.* 1908-11.

Fowler, Edith Henrietta. *The Life of Henry Hartley Fowler, First Viscount Wolverhampton, G.C.S.I.* By his daughter. London: Hutchinson & Co., 1912.

Fox, William. *A Brief History of The Wesleyan Missions on The Western Coast of Africa: Including Biographical Sketches of all the Missionaries who have Died in that Important Field of Labour.* London: the author, 1851.

Fradenburgh, Jason Nelson. *History of Erie Conference.* 2 vols. N.p.: the author, 1907.

Freeman, Thomas Birch. *Journals of Various Visits to the Kingdoms of Ashanti, Aku, and Dahomi in Western Africa.* London, 1844. Facsimile, with intro. by Harrison M. Wright; London: Frank Cass & Co., 1968.

French, Goldwin S. *Parsons and Politics.* Toronto: Ryerson Press, 1962.

Frost, J. H. See Lee and Frost. *Ten Years in Oregon.* 1844.

Fry, Benjamin St. James. *The Life of Rev. Enoch George.* New York: Carlton & Phillips, 1852.

——————————. *The Life of Rev. Richard Whatcoat.* New York: Carlton & Phillips, 1852.

——————————. *The Life of Robert R. Roberts.* New York: Carlton & Phillips, 1856.

Gaarde, S. N. *Chr. Willerup, den første Danske praest i Methodistkirken.* Vejle, Denmark: Kristelig Bogforenings Forlag, 1915.

Gaines, Wesley J. *African Methodism in the South.* Atlanta: Franklin Publishing House, 1890.

Gallagher, Robert Henry. *Pioneer Preachers of Irish Methodism.* Belfast: Wesley Historical Society, Irish Branch, 1965.

Gallaher, Ruth A. *A Century of Methodism in Iowa.* Mount Vernon, Ia.: Inter-Conference Commission on the Iowa Centennial of Methodism, 1944.

Galloway, Charles Betts. See Fitzgerald and Galloway. *Eminent Methodists.* 1897.

Galpin, William Freeman. *Syracuse University.* 2 vols. Syracuse, N.Y.: Syracuse University Press, 1952, 1960.

Garber, Paul Neff. *The Methodists Are One People.* Nashville: Cokesbury Press, 1939.

——————————. *The Methodists of Continental Europe.* New York: Board of Missions, The Methodist Church, 1949.

——————————. *The Methodist Meeting House.* New York: Board of Missions and Church Extension, The Methodist Church, 1941.

Garner, William. *The Life of the Rev. and Venerable William Clowes.* New ed., London: Wm. Lister, 1868.

Garrett, A. E. F., ed. *South African Methodism: Her Missionary Witness.* Cape Town: Methodist Publishing House, 1965.

Garrettson, Freeborn. *The Experience and Travels of Mr. Freeborn Garrettson.* Philadelphia: John Dickins, 1791.

Gatke, Robert Moulton. *Chronicles of Willamette, the Pioneer University of the West.* Portland, Ore.: Binfords & Mort, 1943.

Gealy, Fred D. *Let Us Break Bread Together.* Nashville: Abingdon Press, 1960.

——————————; Lovelace, Austin C., and Young, Carlton R. *Companion to the Hymnal: A Handbook to the 1964 Methodist Hymnal.* Nashville: Abingdon Press, 1970.

Geistliche Saitenspiel oder eine Sammlung auserlesener, erbaulicher, geistreicher Lieder, zum Gebrauch aller Gottliebenden Seelen, insonderheit für die Gemeinen der Evangelischen Gemeinschaft. New Berlin, Pa.: Miller & Niebel, 1817.

Geistliche Viole, oder eine kleine Sammlung alter und never Geistreicher Lieder. New Berlin, Pa.: Miller & Niebel, 1818.

General Minutes of the Annual Conferences of The United Methodist Church, 1968-70.

Gibble, Phares Brubaker. *History of the East Pennsylvania Conference of the Church of the United Brethren in Christ.* Harrisburg, Pa.: the conference, 1951.

Gibson, Maria Layng, and Haskin, Sara Estelle. *Memories of Scarritt.* Nashville: Cokesbury Press, 1928.

Gilbert, Simeon. *The Lesson System.* New York: Phillips & Hunt, 1879.

Gill, Frederick Cyril. *Charles Wesley: The First Methodist.* London: Epworth Press; Nashville: Abingdon Press, 1964.

——————————. *In the Steps of John Wesley.* London: Lutterworth Press, 1962.

——————————. *The Romantic Movement and Methodism: A Study of English Romanticism and the Evangelical Revival.* London: Epworth Press, 1937.

Gillies, John. *Memoirs of the Life of the Reverend George Whitefield, M.A.* London: Edward & Charles Dilly, 1772. 2nd ed., rev. Aaron C. Seymour; Dublin, n.p., 1811. With 27 sermons and other writings; New-Haven, Conn.: Whitmore & Buckingham and H. Mansfield, 1834.

Glendinning, William. *The Life of William Glendinning, Preacher of the Gospel. Written by Himself.* Philadelphia: the author, 1795.

Godbold, Albea. *The Church College of the Old South.* Durham: Duke University Press, 1944.

Golder, Christian. *Die Geschichte der Weiblichen Diakonie.* Cincinnati, 1901. Eng. trans., *History of the Deaconess Movement.* Cincinnati: Jennings & Pye, 1903.

——————————, et al. *Geschichte der Zentral Deutschen Konferenz; Einschliesslich der Anfangsgeschichte des deutschen Methodismus.* Cincinnati: the conference, 1907.

Goode, William H. *Outposts of Zion, with Limnings of Mission Life.* Cincinnati: Poe & Hitchcock, 1863.

Gorham, Barlow Weed. *Camp Meeting Manual, a Practical Book for the Camp Ground; in two Parts.* Binghamton, N. Y.: Binghamton District Ministerial Association, 1853.

Gorrie, Peter Douglass. *The Lives of Eminent Methodist Ministers; Containing Biographical Sketches, Incidents, Anecdotes, Records of Travel, Reflections, etc.* Auburn, N. Y.: Derby & Miller, 1852.

Gracey, Mrs. J. T. *Medical Work of the Woman's Foreign Missionary Society, Methodist Episcopal Church.* Dansville, N. Y.: n.p., 1881.

Graham, Henry. *History of the Troy Conference of the Methodist Episcopal Church.* Albany, N. Y.: n.p., 1908.

Graham, John H. *Mississippi Circuit Riders, 1865-1965.* Nashville: Parthenon Press, 1967.

Gramley, A. D. See Shortess and Gramley. *Central Pennsylvania Conference* (EC). 1940.

Grant, John Webster. *The Canadian Experience of Church Union.* Ecumenical Studies in History, No. 8. Richmond, Va.: John Knox Press, 1967.

Graves, James Robinson. *The Great Iron Wheel; or, Republicanism Backwards and Christianity Reversed. In a Series of Letters Addressed to J. Soule, Senior Bishop of the M. E. Church, South.* Nashville: Graves & Marks, 1855.

Gray, Marcus Lemon. *The Centennial Volume of Missouri Methodism: Methodist Episcopal Church, South.* N.p., 1907.

Green, Anson. *The Life and Times of the Rev. Anson Green, D.D., Written by Himself, at the Request of the Toronto Conference.* Toronto: Methodist Book Room, 1877.

Green, John Brazier. *John Wesley and William Law.* London: Epworth Press, 1945.

Green, Richard. *John Wesley, Evangelist.* London: Religious Tract Society, 1905.

——————. *Anti-Methodist Publications Issued During the Eighteenth Century.* London: for the author by C. H. Kelly, 1902.

——————. *The Works of John and Charles Wesley: A Bibliography.* London: for the author by C. H. Kelly, 1896. 2nd ed., enl., 1906.

Green, Vivian Hubert Howard. *John Wesley.* London: Thomas Nelson & Sons, 1964.

——————. *The Young Mr. Wesley: A Study of John Wesley and Oxford.* London: Edward Arnold, 1961.

Gregg, Samuel. *The History of Methodism Within the Bounds of the Erie Annual Conference of the Methodist Episcopal Church.* 2 vols. N.p.: the author, 1865, 1873.

Gregory, Arthur Stephen. *Praises with Understanding; Illustrated from the Words and Music of the Methodist Hymn-Book.* London: Epworth Press, 1936.

Gregory, Benjamin. *The Life of Frederick James Jobson.* London: T. Woolmer, 1884.

——————. *Hodgson Casson, the Humorous Revivalist.* London: Charles H. Kelly, 1897.

——————. *Side Lights on the Conflicts of Methodism During the Second Quarter of the Nineteenth Century, 1827-1852; Taken chiefly from the Notes of the late Rev. Joseph Fowler of the Debates in the Wesleyan Conference; A Centenary Contribution to the Constitutional History of Methodism. With a Biographical Sketch.* London: Cassell & Co., 1898.

Gregory, John Robinson, ed. *Benjamin Gregory: Autobiographical Recollections . . . with Memorials of His Later Life.* London: Hodder & Stoughton, 1903.

——————. *A History of Methodism, Chiefly for the Use of Students.* 2 vols. London: Charles H. Kelly, 1911.

Griffith, Helen. *Dauntless in Mississippi: the Life of Sarah A. Dickey, 1838-1904.* South Hadley, Mass.: the author, 1965.

Grissom, William Lee. *History of Methodism in North Carolina, from 1772 to the Present Time.* Nashville: Publishing House of the M.E. Church, South, 1905.

Grob, R. Ernst. *Die Bischöfliche Methodistenkirche in der Schweiz.* Zurich: Christliche Vereinsbuchhandlung, 1931.

Grundell, John, and Hall, Robert. *The Life of Mr. Alexander Kilham.* Nottingham: C. Sutton, 1799.

Guiton, François. *Histoire du Methodisme Wesleyan dans les Iles de la Manche.* London: John Mason, 1846.

Guptill, Roger S., and Clark, Elmer T. *Though Thousands Fall: The Story of Melville B. Cox.* Nashville: Cokesbury Press, 1932.

Guy, J., and Potter, W. S. *Fifty Years of Primitive Methodism in New Zealand.* Wellington: Primitive Methodist Book Depot, 1893.

Haagensen, Andrew. *Den Norsk-Danske Methodismes Historie: Paa begge Sider Havet.* Chicago: Norsk-Danske Boghandels Officin, 1894.

Haddal, Ingvar. *John Wesley: A Biography.* London: Epworth Press, 1961.

Hagen, Odd. *Preludes to Methodism in Northern Europe.* Oslo: Norsk Forlagsselskap, 1961.

Haines, Aaron W. *The Makers of Iowa Methodism: A Twentieth-Century Memorial of the Pioneers.* Cincinnati: the author, 1900.

Haire, Robert. *Wesley's One-and-Twenty Visits to Ireland.* London: Epworth Press, 1947.

Hall, James. *Methodism in West Bromwich from 1742 to 1885.* 1886.

Hall, Joseph. *Hall's Circuits and Ministers.* An Alphabetical List of the Circuits in Great Britain, with the names of the ministers stationed in each circuit, together with the appointments to Departments and other Offices, from 1765 to 1912. Rev. and enl. ed., by T. Galland Hartley; London: The Methodist Publishing House, 1914. Supplement for 1913-23, ed. T. G. Hartley; London: Methodist Publishing House, 1925.

Hall, Robert. See Grundell and Hall. *Alexander Kilham.* 1799.

Hallman, Ernest Clifton. *The Garden of Methodism.* N.p.: Peninsula Annual Conference, The Methodist Church, 1948.

Hamilton, John W. See Flood and Hamilton. *Lives of Methodist Bishops.* 1882.

Hammond, Edmund Jordan. *The Methodist Episcopal Church in Georgia.* N.p., 1935.

Hampson, John, Jr. *Memoirs of the late Rev. John Wesley, A.M., with a review of his life and writings, and a History of Methodism, from its commencement in 1729, to the present time.* 3 vols. Sunderland: the author, 1791.

Hampton, Vernon Boyce. *Newark Conference Centennial History, 1857-1957: A Hundred Years of Methodism.* N.p.: Historical Society, Newark Annual Conference, The Methodist Church, 1957.

Hamrick, William Lee. *The Mississippi Conference of the Methodist Protestant Church.* Jackson, Miss.: Hawkins Foundation, 1957.

Hanby, William. See Spayth and Hanby. *History of the UB Church.* 1851.

Hancher, John W. *The Educational Jubilee.* Cincinnati: Methodist Book Concern, 1918.

Handbook of the Methodist New Connexion, 1875.

Handy, James A. *Scraps of African Methodist Episcopal History.* Philadelphia: A.M.E. Book Concern, 1901.

Hanna, John C., ed. *The Centennial Services of Asbury Methodist Episcopal Church.* Wilmington, Del.: n.p., 1889. [Information on the formation of the Union American Methodist Episcopal Church.]

Hardy, Aage. *O. P. Petersen, Metodistkirkens grunnlegger i Norge.* Oslo: Norsk Forlagsselskap, 1953.

Hargreaves, John Richard. *Methodism in the Channel Islands: Its Introduction and Growth.* Jersey: Centenary Committee, 1884.

Harkness, Georgia. *The Methodist Church in Social Thought and Action.* Nashville: Abingdon Press, 1964.

Harmon, Nolan Bailey. *The Organization of the Methodist Church: Historic Development and Present Working Structure.* Nashville: Abingdon-Cokesbury Press, 1948. Rev. eds., 1953, 1962.

——————. *The Rites and Ritual of Episcopal Methodism: With Particular Reference to the Rituals of the Methodist Episcopal Church and the Methodist Episcopal Church, South, Respectively.* Nashville: Publishing House of the M. E. Church, South, 1926.

Harmon, Rebecca Lamar. *Susanna, Mother of the Wesleys.* Nashville: Abingdon Press, 1968.

Harper, Marvin Henry. *The Methodist Episcopal Church in India; a Study of Ecclesiastical Organization and Administration.* Lucknow: Lucknow Publishing House, 1936.

Harper, Robert Henry. *Louisiana Methodism.* Washington, D. C.: Kaufmann Press, 1949.

Harris, C. R. *Zion's Historical Catechism*. Charlotte, N. C.: A.M.E. Zion Publishing House, 1916.

Harris, Merriman C. *Christianity in Japan*. New York: Eaton & Mains, 1907.

Harris, Thomas Roberts. *Samuel Dunn, Reformer, 1798-1882*. Redruth, Cornwall: Cornish Methodist Historical Association, 1963.

Harris, William L. *The Constitutional Powers of the General Conference, with a Special Application to the Subject of Slaveholding*. Cincinnati: Methodist Book Concern, 1860.

Harris, Eula Wallace, and Craig, Maxie Harris. *Colored Methodist Episcopal Church Through the Years*. Jackson, Tenn.: C.M.E. Church Publishing House, 1949. Rev. ed. by E. W. Harris and Naomi Ruth Patterson, *Christian Methodist . . .* , 1965.

Harrison, Archibald W. *The Evangelical Review and Christian Reunion*. London: Epworth Press, 1942.

——————————. *The Separation of Methodism from the Church of England*. London: Epworth Press, 1945.

——————————; Barber, B. Aquila; Hornby, George G.; Davies, E. Tegla. *The Methodist Church: Its Origin, Divisions, and Reunion*. London: Methodist Publishing House, 1932.

Harrison, G. Elsie (Grace Elizabeth Simon). *Son to Susanna: The Private Life of John Wesley*. London: I. Nicholson & Watson, 1937.

Harrison, W. P., ed. *The Gospel Among the Slaves. A Short Account of Missionary Operations Among the African Slaves of the Southern States*. Nashville: Publishing House of the M. E. Church, South, 1893.

Hart, E. I. *Virgil C. Hart: Missionary Statesman, Founder of American and Canadian Missions in Central and West China*. N.p.: the author, 1917.

Harvard, William Martin. *A Narrative of the Establishment and Progress of the Mission to Ceylon and India, Founded by the Late Rev. Thomas Coke*. London: the author, 1823.

Harwood, George H. *The History of Wesleyan Methodism in Nottingham and Its Vicinity*. Nottingham: W. Bunny, 1859. New and enl. ed., J. Ellis, 1872.

Harwood, Thomas. *History of New Mexico Spanish and English Missions of the Methodist Episcopal Church from 1850 to 1910*. 2 vols. Albuquerque. N. M.: El Abogado Press, 1908, 1910.

Haselmayer, Louis A., ed. *The Life Memories and Day Book of Friedrich Wilhelm Balcke, 1847-1926*. N.p.: the author, 1963.

Haskin, Sara Estelle. *Women and Missions in the Methodist Episcopal Church, South*. Nashville: Publishing House of the M. E. Church, South, 1920.

——————————. See Gibson and Haskin. *Scarritt*. 1928.

Hastling, Arthur Henry Law; Willis, Walter Addington, and Workman, Walter Percy. *The History of Kingswood School; Together with Registers of Kingswood School and Woodhouse Grove School, and a List of Masters*. London: Charles H. Kelly, 1898.

Hawkins, John Russell. See Wright and Hawkins. *Centennial Encyclopedia*. 1916.

Hay, Fanny A. See Feeman, Cargo and Hay. *Story of a Noble Devotion*. 1945.

Hayes, Thomas. *Recollections of Sixty-three Years of Methodist Life*. London: the author, 1902.

Haygood, Atticus G. *Our Brother in Black*. Nashville: Southern Methodist Publishing House, 1881.

Hayman, John Gould. *History of Methodism in North Devon*. London: Conference Office, 1871. New and enl. ed., 1898.

Haymes, Joseph Oscar. *History of the Northwest Texas Conference, The Methodist Church; First 50 Years, 1910-1960*. N.p.: Northwest Texas Conference Historical Society, 1962.

Hedding, Elijah. *A Discourse on the Administration of Discipline*. New York: G. Lane & P. P. Sanford, 1842.

Hedges, John W. *Crowned Victors: The Memoirs of Over Four Hundred Methodist Preachers*. Baltimore: Methodist Episcopal Book Depository, 1878.

Hedley, John. *Our Mission in North China, being a Short Record of Methodist New Connexion Missionary Work*. London: the author, 1907.

Heller, Herbert Lynn. *Indiana Conference of the Methodist Church, 1832-1956*. N.p.: Historical Society, Indiana Conference, 1956.

Henke, E. W., et al. *Nordwest Deutsche Konferenz der Bischöflichen Methodistenkirche*. N.p.: the conference, 1913.

Henry, Stuart Clark. *George Whitefield: Wayfaring Witness*. Nashville: Abingdon Press, 1957.

Herbert, P. C.; Barton, W. B., and Ward, William T., eds. *History of the Southwest Kansas Conference of the Methodist Episcopal Church*. N.p.: the conference, 1932.

Herbert, Thomas Walter. *John Wesley as Editor and Author*. Princeton University Press, 1940.

Herod, George. *Biographical Sketches of Some of Those Preachers Whose Labours Contributed to the Origination and Early Extension of the Primitive Methodist Connexion*. London: Thomas King, 1855.

Herrick, Horace N., and Sweet, William Warren. *A History of the North Indiana Conference of the Methodist Episcopal Church*. Indianapolis: W. K. Stewart Co., 1917. Vol. 2 by Frederick A. Norwood, *History of the North Indiana Conference, 1917-1956*; n.p.: Conference Hisorical Society, 1957.

Hewson, Leslie A. *An Introduction to South African Methodists*. N.p.: the author, 1950.

Hicks, J. P., ed. *From Potlatch to Pulpit: Being the Autobiography of the Rev. William Henry Pierce, Native Missionary to the Indian Tribes of the Northwest Coast of British Columbia*. Vancouver, B.C.: Vancouver Bindery Limited, 1933.

Higgins, Paul Lambourne. *John Wesley: Spiritual Witness*. Minneapolis, Minn.: T. S. Denison & Co., 1960.

Hildebrandt, Franz. *Christianity According to the Wesleys*. London: Epworth Press, 1956.

——————————. *From Luther to Wesley*. London: Lutterworth Press, 1951.

——————————. *I Offered Christ: A Protestant Study of the Mass*. London: Epworth Press, 1967.

Hill, Alfred Wesley. *John Wesley Among the Physicians: A Study of Eighteenth-Century Medicine*. London: Epworth Press, 1958.

Hill, William, ed. *An Alphabetical Arrangement of All the Wesleyan Methodist Preachers, and Missionaries*. Bradford, Yorkshire: T. Inkersley, 1819. Many later eds.; latest by J. Henry Martin and J. Bernard Sheldon, eds., *Ministers and Probationers of the Methodist Church*; London: Methodist Publishing House, 1964.

Hines, Harvey K. *Missionary History of the Pacific Northwest, Containing the Wonderful Story of Jason Lee, with Sketches of Many of His Co-Laborers, All Illustrating Life on the Plains and in the Mountains in Pioneer Days*. Portland, Ore.: the author, 1899.

History of the Organization of the Methodist Episcopal Church, South: Comprehending all the Official Proceedings of the General Conference; the Southern Annual Conferences, and the General Convention; with such other matters as are necessary to a right understanding of the case. Nashville: Compiled and Published by the Editors and Publishers of the *South-Western Christian Advocate*, for the M. E. Church, South. By order of the Louisville Convention. William Cameron, printer, 1845.

Hobart, Chauncey. *History of Methodism in Minnesota*. N.p.: Minnesota Annual Conference, M. E. Church, 1887.

Hocken, Joshua. *A Brief History of Wesleyan Methodism in the Grimsby Circuit; including references to Horncastle, Boston, etc*. London: J. Mason, 1839.

Hodges, Herbert Arthur, and Allchin, Arthur MacDonald. Introduction to *A Rapture of Praise: Hymns of John and Charles Wesley*. London: Hodder & Stoughton, 1966.

Hodgson, Francis. *An Examination of the System of New Divinity.* New York: Mason & Lane, 1839.

Hogue, Wilson Thomas. *History of the Free Methodist Church of North America.* 2 vols. Chicago: Free Methodist Publishing House, 1915. 3rd ed., 1938.

Holdcraft, Paul Ellsworth. *History of the Pennsylvania Conference of the Church of the United Brethren in Christ.* York, Pa.: the conference, 1938.

Holden, William Clifford. *A Brief History of Methodism, and of Methodist Missions in South Africa.* London: the author, 1877.

Holdich, Joseph. *The Life of Willbur Fisk, D.D., First President of the Wesleyan University.* New York: Harper & Bros., 1842.

Holdsworth, William West. See Findlay and Holdsworth. *Wesleyan Meth. Miss. Soc.* 1921-24.

Holliday, Fernando Cortes. *Indiana Methodism: Being an Account of the Introduction, Progress, and Present Position of Methodism in the State; and Also a History of the Literary Institutions Under the Care of the Church, with Sketches of the Principal Methodist Educators in the State.* Cincinnati: Hitchcock & Walden, 1873.

——————————. *Life and Times of Rev. Allen Wiley, A.M., Containing Sketches of Early Methodist Preachers in Indiana, and Notices of the Introduction and Progress of Methodism in the State; also, Including His Original Letters, entitled, "A Help to the Performance of Ministerial Duties."* Cincinnati: Swormstedt & Poe, 1853.

Hollister, John N. *The Centenary of the Methodist Church in Southern Asia.* Lucknow Publishing House of The Methodist Church, 1956.

Holsey, L. H. *Autobiography, Sermons, Addresses, and Essays.* Atlanta: Franklin Printing & Publishing Co., 1898.

Holt, Ivan Lee. *Eugene Russell Hendrix, Servant of the Kingdom.* Nashville: the author, 1950.

——————————. *The Methodists of the World.* New York: Board of Missions and Church Extension, The Methodist Church, 1950.

——————————. *The Missouri Bishops.* Nashville: the author, 1953.

——————————, and Clark, Elmer T. *The World Methodist Movement.* Nashville: Upper Room, 1956.

Holter, Don W. *Fire on the Prairie: Methodism in the History of Kansas.* N.p.: Editorial Board of the Kansas Methodist History, 1969.

Holyoake, George Jacob. *The Life of Joseph Rayner Stephens, Preacher and Political Orator.* London: Williams and Norgate, 1881.

Hood, James Walker. *One Hundred Years of the African Methodist Episcopal Zion Church.* New York: A.M.E. Zion Book Concern, 1895.

Hooper, W. S., ed. *Fifty Years as a Presiding Elder* (Peter Cartwright). Cincinnati: Hitchcock and Walden, 1871.

Hopper, Mrs. R. P. (Jane Agar). *Old-Time Primitive Methodism in Canada (1829-1884).* Toronto: William Briggs, 1904.

Hornby, George G. See Harrison et al. *Methodist Church.* 1932.

Horsford, John. *A Voice from the West Indies.* London: Alexander Heylin, 1856.

Hoskins, Mrs. Robert. *Clara A. Swain, M.D.: First Medical Missionary to the Women of the Orient.* Boston: Woman's Foreign Missionary Society, M. E. Church, 1912.

Hough, Samuel S., ed. *Christian Newcomer, His Life, Journal and Achievements.* Dayton, O.: Board of Administration, Church of the United Brethren in Christ, 1941.

Howell, Clinton Talmage, ed. *Prominent Personalities in American Methodism.* Birmingham, Ala.: the editor, 1945.

Howell, Erle. *Methodism in the Northwest.* Des Moines, Wash.: Historical Society, Pacific Northwest Annual Conference, 1966.

Howell, Mabel Katharine. *Women and the Kingdom: Fifty Years of Kingdom Building by the Women of the Meth-*

odist Episcopal Church, South, 1878-1928. Nashville: Cokesbury Press, 1928.

Hubbart, Henry Clyde. *Ohio Wesleyan's First Hundred Years.* Delaware, O.: Ohio Wesleyan University, 1943.

Huestis, George Oxley. *Memorials of Wesleyan Missionaries and Ministers, who have Died Within the Bounds of the Conference of Eastern British America, Since the Introduction of Methodism into these Colonies.* N.p.: the author, 1872.

Hughes, Dorothea Price. *The Life of Hugh Price Hughes.* By his daughter. London: Hodder & Stoughton, 1904.

Hughes, Edwin Holt. *I Was Made a Minister: An Autobiography.* New York and Nashville: Abingdon-Cokesbury Press, 1943.

Hughes, Hugh J. *Life of Howell Harris, the Welsh Reformer.* Newport, Mon.: William Jones, 1892.

Hulme, Samuel, ed. *The Jubilee of the Methodist New Connexion: Being a Grateful Memorial of the Origin, Government, and History of the Denomination.* London: John Bakewell, 1848.

Hunt, Rockwell D. *History of the College of the Pacific. 1851-1951.* Stockton, Calif.: College of the Pacific, 1951.

Hunter, Frederick. *John Wesley and the Coming Comprehensive Church.* London: Epworth Press, 1968.

Hurst, John Fletcher, ed. *The History of Methodism.* Vols. i-iii, "British Methodism"; London: Charles H. Kelly, 1901. Vols. iv-vi, "American Methodism"; New York: Eaton & Mains, 1903. Vol. vii, "World-wide Methodism," 1904.

Hurtig, Karl Jakob. *Metodismen i Finland: Dess fyrtioarige historia i korta drag technad av.* Helsingfors: Metodistkyrkans Svenska Bokförlag, 1925.

——————————, and Hurtig, Mansfield. *Helsingfors Svenska Metodistförsamling, 1884-1934.*

Hutchinson, Paul. See Luccock and Hutchinson. *Story of Methodism.* 1926.

Hyde, Ammi Bradford. *The Story of Methodism . . . Giving an Account of Its Various Influences and Institutions of To-Day.* Greenfield, Mass.: Willey & Johns, Publishers, 1887. Rev. ed., 1889.

The Hymnal of The Evangelical United Brethren Church. Dayton, O.: Board of Publication, 1957.

Hymnal of the United Evangelical Church. Harrisburg, Pa.: Publishing House of the United Evangelical Church, 1897.

The Hymn Book of the African Methodist Episcopal Church; being a Collection of Hymns, Sacred Songs and Chants, designed to supercede all others hitherto made use of in that Church. Selected from Various Authors. Compiled by H. M. Turner, 1873.

Hymn-Book of the Evangelical Association. Cleveland, O.: Publishing House, 1882.

Hymn Book of the Methodist Church. Compiled by Authority of the Convention of 1858. 18th ed. Springfield, O.: A. H. Bassett, Publishing Agent, 1870. A publication of the Methodist Protestant Church in the West.

Hymn Book of the Methodist Protestant Church. 18th ed. Baltimore: Published by the President and Directors, Book Concern, M. P. Church, 1856.

Hymns and Songs: A Supplement to the Methodist Hymn Book. London: Methodist Publishing House, 1969.

Hymns for the Use of the Methodist Episcopal Church. Rev. ed., New York: Lane & Scott, 1850.

Hymns for the Use of the Methodist Episcopal Church, with Tunes for Congregational Worship. New York: Carlton & Porter, 1857.

Irby, Richard. *History of Randolph-Macon College, Virginia: The Oldest Incorporated Methodist College in America.* Richmond: Whittet & Shepperson, 1899.

Isham, Mary. *Valorous Ventures. A Record of Sixty and Six Years of the Woman's Foreign Missionary Society, Methodist Episcopal Church.* Boston: Woman's Foreign Missionary Society, M. E. Church, 1936.

Ives, A. G. *Kingswood School in Wesley's Day and Since.* London: Epworth Press, 1970.

Jackman, Everett E. *The Nebraska Methodist Story.* N.p.: Nebraska Conference Methodist Historical Society, 1954.

Jackson, Thomas. *The Centenary of Wesleyan Methodism: A Brief Sketch of the Rise, Progress, and Present State of The Wesleyan-Methodist Societies Throughout the World.* London: John Mason, 1839.

——————. *The Life of the Rev. Charles Wesley, M.A.* 2 vols. London: John Mason, 1841. Abridged ed., *Memoirs of the Rev. Charles Wesley,* 1848.

——————. *The Life of the Rev. Robert Newton.* London: John Mason, 1855.

——————, ed. *The Lives of Early Methodist Preachers. Chiefly Written by Themselves.* 3 vols.; London: John Mason, 1837-38. 2nd ed., 2 vols., 1846. 3rd ed., with introductory essay and 4 additional lives; 6 vols.; London: Wesleyan Conference Office, 1865-66. 4th ed., 1871-72. 5th ed., Wesleyan-Methodist Book-Room, 1878. Annotated by John Telford under title *Wesley's Veterans;* vols. 1-2; London: Robert Culley, 1909; vols. 3-7; London: Charles H. Kelly, 1912-14.

——————. *Memoirs of the Life and Writings of the Rev. Richard Watson, Late Secretary to the Wesleyan Missionary Society.* New York: Waugh & Mason, 1834.

——————. *Recollections of My Own Life and Times.* London: Wesleyan Conference Office, 1873.

Jaime, Eduardo Menna Barreto. *História do Metodismo no Rio Grande do Sul.* Porto Alegre: Empresa Grafica Moderna, 1963.

James, Henry I. *Missions in Rhodesia under the Methodist Episcopal Church, 1898-1934.* Rhodesia: the author, 1935.

Jarratt, Devereux. *The Life of the Reverend Devereux Jarratt, Rector of Bath Parish, Dinwiddie County, Virginia. Written by Himself, in a Series of Letters Addressed to the Reverend John Coleman, one of the ministers of the Protestant Episcopal Church, in Maryland.* Baltimore: printed by Warner & Hanna, 1806.

Jeffery, Frederick. *Irish Methodism: An Historical Account of Its Traditions, Theology and Influence.* Belfast: Epworth House, 1964.

Jeffery, Thomas Reed. *John Wesley's Religious Quest.* New York: Vantage Press, 1960.

Jenifer, John T. *Centennial Retrospect History of the African Methodist Episcopal Church.* Nashville: A.M.E. Sunday School Union, 1916.

Jenkins, David Erwyd. *Calvinistic Methodist Holy Orders.* Caernarvon, Wales: D. O'Brien Owen, 1911.

Jenkins, Warren Marion. *Steps Along the Way: The Origin and Development of the South Carolina Conference of the Central Jurisdiction of the Methodist Church.* Columbia, S. C.: Socamead Press, 1967.

Jennings, Arthur T. *History of American Wesleyan Methodism.* Syracuse, N.Y.: Wesleyan Methodist Publishing Association, 1902.

Jennings, H. C. *The Methodist Book Concern: A Romance of History.* New York & Cincinnati: Methodist Book Concern, 1924.

Jennings, Samuel Kennedy. *An Exposition of the Late Controversy in the Methodist Episcopal Church; of the True Objects of the Parties Concerned Therein, and of the Proceedings by which Reformers were Expelled, in Baltimore, Cincinnati, and Other Places; or, A Review of the Methodist Magazine and Quarterly Review, on Petitions and Memorials.* Baltimore: John J. Harrod, 1831.

Jervey, Edward Drewry. *History of Methodism in Southern California and Arizona.* N.p.: Historical Society, Southern California-Arizona Conference, The Methodist Church, 1960.

Jessop, William. *An Account of Methodism in Rossendale and The Neighbourhood.* Manchester: Tubbs, Brook, and Chrystal, 1880.

Jewell, Horace. *History of Methodism in Arkansas.* N.p., 1892.

Jimeson, A. A. *Notes on the Twenty-five Articles.* Cincinnati: Applegate and Company, 1853.

Jobson, Frederick James. *America and American Methodism.* London: J. S. Virtue, 1857.

——————. *Chapel and School Architecture, As Appropriate to the Buildings of Noncomformists, Particularly to Those of the Wesleyan Methodists. With Practical Directions for the Erection of Chapels and School-Houses.* London: Hamilton, Adams, & Co., 1850.

John, I. G. *Hand Book of Methodist Missions.* Nashville: Publishing House of the M. E. Church, South, 1893.

John, Lewis F. *Life of Ezekiel Boring Kephart.* Dayton, O.: United Brethren Publishing House, 1907.

Johnson, Charles Albert. *The Frontier Camp Meeting, Religion's Harvest Time.* Dallas, Tex.: Southern Methodist University Press, 1955.

Johnson, D. W. *History of Methodism in Eastern British America.* Sackville, N.B.: Tribune Printing Co., 1924.

Jones, Dora M. *Charles Wesley: A Study.* Skeffington & Son, 1919.

Jones, E. D. W. *Comprehensive Catechism of the A.M.E. Zion Church and Other Things You Should Know.* Washington, D. C.: n.p., 1934.

Jones, George H. *The Methodist Tourist Guidebook.* Nashville: Tidings, 1966.

Jones, J. W. *Belfast Methodism, 1756-1893.* Belfast: Adams, 1893.

Jones, John Griffing. *A Complete History of Methodism as Connected with the Mississippi Conference of the Methodist Episcopal Church, South.* Vol. 1, *1799-1817;* n.p.: the author, 1887. Vol. 2, *1817-45,* with two chapters by T. L. Mellen; 1908. Vol. 3 by John Buford Cain, *Methodism in the Mississippi Conference, 1846-1870;* Jackson, Miss.: Hawkins Foundation, 1939. Vol. 4 by William Burwell Jones, *1870-1894;* 1951. Vol. 5 by J. Allen Lindsey, *1894-1919;* 1964. Facsimile reprint of vols. 1-2 in one vol., with intro. and indexes by E. Russ Williams, Jr.; Baton Rouge, La.: Claitor's Book Store, 1966.

Jones, M. H., ed. *The Trevecka Letters.* Caernarvon, Wales: Calvinistic Methodist Book-Room, 1934.

Jones, William Burwell. *Methodism in the Mississippi Conference, 1870-1894.* Jackson, Miss.: Hawkins Foundation, 1951. See John Griffing Jones.

Jones, William Henry. *History of the Wesleyan Reform Union.* London: Epworth Press, 1952.

Journal of the General Conference of The Methodist Church, published quadrennially 1940-1968. The *Journal of the Uniting Conference* was published in 1939.

Journal of the General Conference of the Methodist Episcopal Church, published following each General Conference, 1796-1936.

Journal of the General Conference of the Methodist Episcopal Church, South, published quadrennially following each General Conference, 1846-1938.

Journal of the General Conference of the Methodist Protestant Church, published following the General Conference, 1830-1936.

Joy, James Richard, ed. *The Teachers of Drew, 1867-1942.* Madison, N. J.: Drew University, 1942.

A Jubilee Memorial of Incidents in the Rise and Progress of the Bible Christian Connexion. 2nd ed. 1866.

Julén, Jonatan. *Metodistkyrkan i Sverige.* Stockholm: N.B.A., 1923.

Jurisdictional Conference *Journals* were published quadrennially for the several Jurisdictions in The Methodist Church—Central, North Central, Northeastern, South Central, Southeastern, Western—1940-68.

Kendall, Holliday Bickerstaffe. *Handbook of Primitive Methodist Church Principles and Polity.* London: Edwin Dalton, 1905.

——————. *The Origin and History of the*

Primitive Methodist Church. London: Robert Bryant, [1905]. Completed in 2 vols., London: Edwin Dalton, [1906].

Kendall, R. Elliott. *Beyond the Clouds: the Story of Samuel Pollard of South-West China.* 1st ed., 1949; 2nd ed., London: Cargate Press, 1954.

Kennedy, James L. *Cincoenta Annos de Methodismo no Brasil.* São Paulo: Imprensa Methodista, 1928.

Kent, John Henry Somerset. *The Age of Disunity.* London: Epworth Press, 1966.

————————. *Jabez Bunting, the Last Wesleyan: A Study in the Methodist Ministry After the Death of John Wesley.* London: Epworth Press, 1955.

Kephart, Ezekiel B. *A Manual of Church Discipline of the United Brethren in Christ.* Dayton, O.: United Brethren Publishing House, 1895.

Kilgore, Charles Franklin. *The James O'Kelly Schism in the Methodist Episcopal Church.* Mexico, D.F.: Casa Unida de Publicaciones, 1963.

Kim, Helen. *Grace Sufficient.* Ed. J. Manning Potts. Nashville: Upper Room, 1964.

King, Willis J. *History of the Methodist Church Mission in Liberia.* N.p., n.d.

Kirk, John. *The Mother of the Wesleys: A Biography.* London: Henry James Tresidder, 1864.

Kirkpatrick, Dow, ed. *The Doctrine of the Church.* Nashville: Abingdon Press, 1964.

Kissack, Reginald. *Church or No Church? A Study of the Development of the Concept of Church in British Methodism.* London: Epworth Press, 1964.

————————. *Methodists in Italy.* London: Cargate Press, 1960.

Knox, Alice W. and Charles E. *The Infant Sunday School.* New York: Carlton & Porter, 1870.

Koontz, Paul Rodes, and Roush, Walter Edwin. *The Bishops, Church of the United Brethren in Christ.* 2 vols. Dayton, O.: Otterbein Press, 1950.

Kriege, Otto E., et al. *Souvenir der West Deutschen Konferenz der Bischöflichen Methodistenkirche.* N.p.: the conference, 1906.

Lacy, Creighton. *Frank Mason North.* Nashville: Abingdon Press, 1967.

Lacy, Walter N. *A Hundred Years of China Methodism.* Nashville: Abingdon-Cokesbury Press, 1948.

Lafferty, John James. *Sketches of the Virginia Conference, Methodist Episcopal Church, South.* Richmond, Va.: Christian Advocate Office, 1880. Enl. ed., 1890. Twentieth Century Ed., 1901.

Lamson, Byron Samuel. *Lights in the World: Free Methodist Missions at Work.* Winona Lake, Ind.: Light & Life Press, 1951.

————————. *Venture! The Frontiers of Free Methodism.* Winona Lake, Ind.: Light & Life Press, 1960.

Lanahan, John. *The Era of Frauds in the Methodist Book Concern at New York.* Baltimore: Methodist Book Depository, 1896.

Lane, Isaac. *Autobiography of Bishop Isaac Lane, L.L.D., With a Short History of the C.M.E. Church in America and of Methodism.* Nashville: the author, 1916.

Lankard, Frank Glenn. *A History of the American Sunday School Curriculum.* New York and Cincinnati: Abingdon Press, 1927.

Lanktree, Matthew. *A Biographical Narrative of Matthew Lanktree, Wesleyan Minister: Embracing a Period of Upwards of Forty Years; Comprising Numerous Characteristic Sketches of Cotemporaries, and Historical Notices of the Rise, Progress, and Influence of Methodism in Various Parts of Ireland.* Belfast: James Wilson, 1836.

Larkin, W. *A Concise History of the First Establishment of Wesleyan Methodism in the City of Norwich, in the year 1754.* Norwich: Matchett, 1825.

Larrabee, William C. *Asbury and His Colaborers.* Ed. D. W.

Clark. 2 vols. Cincinnati: Hitchcock & Walden; New York: Carlton & Lanahan, 1868.

Lawrence, George E., and Dorsett, Cyril. *Caribbean Conquest: the Story of Dr. Coke and Methodism in the West Indies.* London: Cargate Press, 1947.

Lawrence, John. *The History of the Church of the United Brethren in Christ.* 2 vols. Dayton, O.: United Brethren Printing Establishment, 1860, 1861. Rev. ed., 1868.

Lawry, Walter. *Friendly and Feejee Islands: A Missionary Visit to Various Stations in the South Seas, in the Year 1842.* Ed. Elijah Hoole. London: Charles Gilpin, 1850.

Lawson, Albert Brown. *John Wesley and the Christian Ministry: The Sources and Development of His Opinions and Practice.* London: Society for Promoting Christian Knowledge, 1963.

Lawson, Evald Benjamin. *Olof Gustaf Hedström, Pioneer Leader of Swedish Methodism.* East Orange, N. J.: Upsala College, 1945.

Lawson, James. See Bennett and Lawson. *Wisconsin.* 1890.

Lawson, William D. *Wesleyan Local Preachers.* Newcastle-upon-Tyne: the author, 1874.

Lawton, George. *John Wesley's English: A Study of His Literary Style.* London: George Allen & Unwin, 1962.

————————. *Shropshire Saint: A Study in the Ministry and Spirituality of Fletcher of Madeley.* London: Epworth Press, 1960.

Laycock, J. W., ed. *Methodist Heroes in the Great Haworth Round, 1734 to 1784.* Keighley: Wadsworth & Co., 1909.

Lazenby, Marion Elias. *History of Methodism in Alabama and West Florida.* N.p.: North Alabama Conference, Alabama-West Florida Conference, The Methodist Church, 1960.

Leaton, James. *History of Methodism in Illinois, from 1793 to 1832.* Rushville, Ill.: the author, 1883.

Lednum, John. *A History of the Rise of Methodism in America. Containing Sketches of Methodist Itinerant Preachers, from 1736 to 1785, Numbering One Hundred and Sixty or Seventy. Also, A Short Account of Many Hundreds of the First Race of Lay Members, Male and Female, from New York to South Carolina. Together with an Account of Many of the First Societies and Chapels.* Philadelphia: the author, 1859.

Lee, Daniel, and Frost, J. H. *Ten Years in Oregon.* New York: the authors, 1844.

Lee, Elizabeth Meredith. *As Among the Methodists: Deaconesses Yesterday, Today, and Tomorrow.* Cincinnati: Woman's Division of Christian Service, Board of Missions, The Methodist Church, 1963.

Lee, James W.; Luccock, Naphtali; Dixon, James Main. *The Illustrated History of Methodism: The Story of the Origin and Progress of the Methodist Church, from its Foundation by John Wesley to the Present Day.* St. Louis, Mo.: The Methodist Magazine Publishing Co., 1900.

Lee, Jesse. *A Short Account of the Life and Death of the Rev. John Lee, a Methodist Minister in the United States of America.* Baltimore: printed by John West Butler, 1805.

————————. *A Short History of the Methodists in the United States of America; Beginning in 1766, and Continued till 1809. To which is Prefixed, A Brief Account of Their Rise in England, in the Year 1729, etc.* Baltimore: printed by Magill and Clime, 1810. Reprint, Nashville: Cokesbury Press, 1925.

Lee, Leroy M. *The Life and Times of the Rev. Jesse Lee.* Louisville, Ky.: John Early, 1848.

Lee, Umphrey. *John Wesley and Modern Religion.* Nashville: Cokesbury Press, 1936.

————————. *The Lord's Horseman.* New York: Century Co., 1928. Reissued, with appendices, Nashville: Abingdon Press, 1954.

Leedy, Roy B. *The Evangelical Church in Ohio, Being a History of the Ohio Conference and Merged Conferences of the Evangelical Church in Ohio, Now the Evangelical United Brethren Church, 1816-1951.* N.p.: Ohio Conference, Evangelical United Brethren Church, 1959.

——————. See Albright and Leedy. *Religious Education in the Evangelical Church*. 1932.

Leete, Frederick D. *Methodist Bishops*. Nashville: the author, 1948.

Léger, J. Augustin. *John Wesley's Last Love*. London: J. M. Dent & Sons, 1910.

——————. *La Jeunesse de Wesley*. Paris: Librairie Hachette, 1910.

Leiffer, Murray Howard. *The Role of the District Superintendent in The Methodist Church*. Evanston, Ill.: Bureau of Social and Religious Research, Garrett Biblical Institute, 1960.

Lelièvre, Matthieu. *Histoire du Méthodisme dans les Iles de la Manche*. Paris: Librairie Evangelique; London: Theophilus Woolmer, 1885.

——————. *John Wesley, sa vie et son oeuvre*. Paris: Librairie Evangelique, 1868. Tr. A. J. French, *John Wesley, His Life and His Work*; London: Wesleyan Conference Office, 1871. 3rd ed., rev. and enl.; Paris: Librairie Evangelique, 1891; tr. J. W. Lelièvre; London: Charles H. Kelly, 1900.

Lerch, David. *Heil und Heiligung bei John Wesley*. Zurich: Christliche Vereinsbuchhandlung, 1941.

Lester, George. *Grimsby Methodism (1743-1889), and the Wesleys in Lincolnshire*. London: Conference Office, 1890.

Lewis, Arthur James. *Zinzendorf, the Ecumenical Pioneer: A Study in the Moravian Contribution to Christian Mission and Unity*. London: Student Christian Movement Press, 1962.

Lewis, Thomas Hamilton. *Centennial Anniversary of the Methodist Protestant Church, 1828-1928*, N.p.: General Conference, M. P. Church, 1928.

——————, ed. *Historical Record of the Maryland Annual Conference of the Methodist Protestant Church*. N.p.: the editor, 1879. Rev. eds., 1903, 1918, 1928, 1939.

——————. See Murray and Lewis. *Maryland Conference* (MP). 1882.

Lidgett, J. Scott. *My Guided Life*. London: Methuen, 1936.

Lightwood, James T. *The Music of the Methodist Hymn-book*. London: Epworth Press, 1935. Rev. ed., Francis B. Westbrook, 1955.

——————. *Samuel Wesley, Musician: the Story of His Life*. London: Epworth Press, 1937.

Liljegren, Nils M., et al. *Svenska Metodismen i Amerika*. Chicago: Svenska M. E. Bokhandes-Föreningens Förlag, 1895.

Lind, Robert W. *From the Ground Up: the Story of "Brother Van," Montana Pioneer Minister, 1848-1919*. N.p.: the author, 1961.

Lindsey, J. Allen. *Methodism in the Mississippi Conference, 1894-1919*. Jackson, Miss.: Hawkins Foundations, 1964. See John Griffing Jones.

Lindström, Harald. *Wesley and Sanctification*. Tr. H. S. Harvey. Stockholm: Nya Bokförlags Aktiebolaget; London: Epworth Press, 1946.

Little, Brooks Bivens, ed. *Methodist Union Catalog of History, Biography, Disciplines, and Hymnals*. Lake Junaluska, N. C.: Association of Methodist Historical Societies, 1967.

Lockwood, John P. *Memorials of the Life of Peter Bohler, Bishop of the Church of the United Brethren*. London: Wesleyan Conference Office, 1868.

——————. *The Western Pioneers; or, Memorials of the Lives and Labours of the Rev. Richard Boardman and the Rev. Joseph Pilmoor, the First Preachers Appointed by John Wesley to Labour in North America*. London: Wesleyan Conference Office, 1881.

Loeppert, Adam J. *Jubiläumsbote der Chicago Deutschen Konferenz*. Chicago: the conference, 1921.

London Quarterly Review, London, 1853-58; continued as *London Review*, 1858-62; continued as *London Quarterly Review*, 1862-1968; continued as *Church Quarterly*, 1968- .

Loofbourow, Leon L. *In Search of God's Gold: A Story of Continued Christian Pioneering in California*. San Francisco: Historical Society, California-Nevada Annual Conference, The Methodist Church, 1950.

——————. *Steeples Among the Sage: A Centennial Story of Nevada's Churches*. N.p.: Historical Society, California-Nevada Annual Conference, The Methodist Church, 1964.

Lorenz, Edmund S., ed. *The Otterbein Hymnal*. Dayton, O.: United Brethren Publishing House, 1890.

——————, and Lanthurn, W. H., eds. *Hymns for the Sanctuary and Social Worship*. Dayton, O.: United Brethren Publishing House, 1874.

Lovelace, Austin C. See Gealy et. al. *Companion to the Hymnal*. 1970.

Luccock, Halford E., and Hutchinson, Paul. *The Story of Methodism*. New York: Methodist Book Concern, 1926. Rev. and supplemented by Robert W. Goodloe. Nashville: Abingdon-Cokesbury Press, 1949.

Luccock, Naphtali. See J. W. Lee, et al. *Illustrated History*. 1900.

The Lute of Zion: a Collection of Sacred Music Designed for the Use of the Methodist Episcopal Church. Eds. I. B. Woodbury and H. Mattison. New York: Carlton & Phillips, 1853. *The New Lute of Zion*, ed. I. B. Woodbury. New York: Carlton & Porter, 1856.

Lyall, Leslie T. *John Sung*. London: China Inland Mission, 1954.

Lyles, Albert Marion. *Methodism Mocked: The Satiric Reaction to Methodism in the Eighteenth Century*. London: Epworth Press, 1960.

Lyth, John. *Glimpses of Early Methodism in York, and the Surrounding District*. York: W. Sessions, 1885.

M'Anally, David Rice. *History of Methodism in Missouri; From the Date of Its Introduction, in 1806, Down to the Present Day; with an Appendix, Containing Full and Accurate Statistical Information*. Vol. I. St. Louis, Mo.: Advocate Publishing House, 1881.

——————. *The Life and Labors of Rev. E. M. Marvin*. St. Louis, Mo.: Advocate Publishing House, 1878.

M'Caine, Alexander. *A Defence of the Truth, as Set Forth in the "History and Mystery of Methodist Episcopacy," Being a Reply to John Emory's "Defence of Our Fathers."* Baltimore: Richard Matchett, 1829.

——————. *The History and Mystery of Methodist Episcopacy, or, A Glance at "The Institutions of the Church, as We Received Them from Our Fathers."* Baltimore: Richard J. Matchett, 1827.

McCarter, J. Mayland. *Border Methodism and Border Slavery, Being a Statement and Review of the Action of the Philadelphia Annual Conference Concerning Slavery, at Its Late Sessions at Easton, Pennsylvania*. Philadelphia: Collins, 1858.

MacClenny, Wilbur E. *The Life of Rev. James O'Kelly and the Early History of the Christian Church in the South*. Raleigh, N. C.: n.p., 1910.

M'Clintock, John, ed. *Sketches of Eminent Methodist Ministers*. New York: Carlton & Phillips, 1854.

McConnell, Francis John. *By the Way: An Autobiography*. New York: Abingdon-Cokesbury Press, 1952.

——————. *The Essentials of Methodism*. New York: Methodist Book Concern, 1916.

——————. *John Wesley*. New York: Abingdon Press, 1939. Reissued, 1961.

McCrea, Alexander, ed. *Irish Methodism in the Twentieth Century: A Symposium*. Belfast: Irish Methodist Publishing Co., 1931.

McCulloh, Gerald O., ed. *The Ministry in the Methodist Heritage*. Nashville: Board of Education, The Methodist Church, 1960.

McCutchan, Robert Guy. *Our Hymnody: A Manual of the Methodist Hymnal*. New York: Methodist Book Concern, 1937.

McDaniel, S. C. *The Origin and Early History of the Congregational Methodist Church*. Atlanta: Jas. P. Harrison & Co., 1881.

McElreath, Walter. *Methodist Union in the Courts*. Nashville: Abingdon-Cokesbury Press, 1946.

M'Ferrin, John B. *History of Methodism in Tennessee*. 3 vols. Nashville: Southern Methodist Publishing House, 1869-73.

M'Geary, John Samuel. *The Free Methodist Church: A Brief Outline History of Its Origin and Development*. Chicago: W. B. Rose, 1908. 4th ed., 1917.

M'Lean, John. *Sketch of Rev. Philip Gatch*. Cincinnati: Swormstedt & Poe, 1854.

M'Leister, Ira Ford. *History of the Wesleyan Methodist Church of America*. Syracuse, N. Y.: Wesleyan Methodist Publishing Association, 1934. 3rd ed., rev. by Roy Stephen Nicholson; Marion, Ind.: Wesley Press, 1959.

McPheeters, Julian C. *The Life Story of Lizzie H. Glide*. San Francisco: the author, 1936.

McQuaid, Ina DeBord. *Miss Hannah Ball: A Lady of High Wycombe*. New York: Vantage Press, 1964.

McTyeire, Holland Nimmons. *A History of Methodism: Comprising a View of the Rise of this Revival of Spiritual Religion in the First Half of the Eighteenth Century, and of the Principal Agents by whom it was Promoted in Europe and America: with some account of the Doctrine and Polity of Episcopal Methodism in the United States, and the Means and Manner of its Extension down to A.D. 1884*. Nashville: Southern Methodist Publishing House, 1884.

——————————. *A Manual of the Discipline of the Methodist Episcopal Church, South; Including the Decisions of the College of Bishops and Rules of Order Applicable to Ecclesiastical Courts and Conferences*. Nashville: Southern Methodist Publishing House, 1870. 13th ed., rev. by Robert K. Hargrove, 1899. 17th ed., rev. & enl. by Collins Denny, 1920. 19th ed., 1931.

MacVey, William Pitt. *The Genius of Methodism: A Sociological Interpretation*. Cincinnati: Jennings & Pye, 1903.

Maag, Howard T. See Maser and Maag. *Journal of Joseph Pilmore*. 1969.

Macdonald, Frederic William. *The Life of William Morley Punshon, LL.D.* London: Hodder & Stoughton, 1887.

Macdonald, James. *Memoirs of the Rev. Joseph Benson*. London: T. Blanshard, 1822.

Maclay, Robert Samuel. *Life Among the Chinese: With Characteristic Sketches and Incidents of Missionary Operations and Prospects in China*. New York: Carlton & Porter, 1861.

Maclean, John. *William Black: The Apostle of Methodism in the Maritime Provinces of Canada*. Halifax, N.S.: Methodist Book Room, 1907.

Macmillan, Margaret Burnham. *The Methodist Church in Michigan: The Nineteenth Century*. Grand Rapids, Mich.: Michigan Area Methodist Historical Society, 1967.

Magaret, Ernst Carl, et al. *Jubiläumsbuch der St. Louis Deutschen Konferenz*. N.p.: the conference, 1904.

Mallinson, Joel. *History of Methodism in Huddersfield, Holmfirth, and Denby Dale*. London: Charles H. Kelly, 1898.

Mann, Harold Wilson. *Atticus Greene Haygood, Methodist Bishop, Editor, and Educator*. Athens, Ga.: University of Georgia Press, 1965.

Mann, Heinrich. *Ludwig S. Jakoby: . . . Sein Leben und Werken*. Bremen: Verlag des Traktathauses, 1892.

Mann, Theophil. See Nuelsen, Mann and Sommer. *Kurzgefasste Geschichte des Methodismus*. 1920.

Manning, Bernard Lord. *The Hymns of Wesley and Watts*. London: Epworth Press, 1942.

Marquette, David. *A History of Nebraska Methodism, First Half-Century, 1854-1904*. N.p., 1904.

Marshall, Leslie A. *The Romance of a Tract and Its Sequel: The Story of an American Pioneer in Russia and the Baltic States*. Riga, Latvia: Jubilee Fund Commission, Baltic and Slavic Mission Conference, M. E. Church, 1928.

Marston, Leslie Ray. *From Age to Age a Living Witness: A Historical Interpretation of Free Methodism's First Century*. Winona Lake, Ind.: Light & Life Press, 1960.

Martin, Isaac Patton. *Methodism in Holston*. Knoxville, Tenn.: Methodist Historical Society, Holston Conference, 1945.

Martin, James Henry. *John Wesley's London Chapels*. London: Epworth Press, 1946.

——————————. *Ministers and Probationers of the Methodist Church; Formerly Wesleyan, Primitive and United Methodist, With Their Appointments in Chronological and Alphabetical Order; Also Lists of the Presidents, Vice-Presidents and the Secretaries of the Several Conferences, Together with an Alphabetical List of Deceased Ministers*. 25th ed., rev. to Sep. 1, 1957. London: Methodist Publishing House, 1957.

Maser, Frederick E., and Maag, Howard T., eds. *The Journal of Joseph Pilmore, Methodist Itinerant, For the Years August 1, 1769 to January 2, 1774; with a Biographical Sketch of Joseph Pilmore by Dr. Frank B. Stanger*. Philadelphia: Historical Society, Philadelphia Annual Conference, United Methodist Church, 1969.

Mathews, Basil Joseph. *John R. Mott, World Citizen*. New York & London: Harper & Bros., 1934.

Mathews, Donald G. *Slavery and Methodism, a Chapter in American Morality, 1780-1845*. Princeton University Press. 1965.

Mathews, Horace Frederick. *Methodism and the Education of the People, 1791-1851*. London: Epworth Press, 1949.

Matlack, Lucius C. *The Antislavery Struggle and Triumph in the Methodist Episcopal Church*. New York: Phillips & Hunt, 1881.

——————————. *The History of American Slavery and Methodism, from 1780 to 1849: and History of the Wesleyan Methodist Connection of America; in Two Parts, With an Appendix*. New York: n.p., 1849.

——————————. *The Life of Rev. Orange Scott: Compiled from his personal narrative, correspondence, and other authentic sources of information*. New York: C. Prindle & L. C. Matlack, 1848.

Means, Nathalie Toms. *Malaysia Mosaic, a Story of Fifty Years of Methodism*. Singapore: Methodist Book Room, n.d.

Mears, Walter G. A. *Wesleyan Baralong Mission in Trans-Orangia, 1821-1884*. Rondebosch, South Africa: the author, 1969.

——————————. *Wesleyan Missionaries in Great Namaqualand, 1820-1867*. Rondebosch, South Africa: the author, 1969.

Meeker, Ruth Esther. *Six Decades of Service, 1880-1940: A History of the Woman's Home Missionary Society of the Methodist Episcopal Church*. N.p.: Continuing Corporation of the Woman's Home Missionary Society, M. E. Church, 1969.

Melle, F. H. Otto, ed. *Das Walten Gottes im deutschen Methodismus*. Bremen: Kommissionsverlag des Traktathauses, 1925.

Mendoza, Vicente, ed. *Libro Conmemorativo de las Bodas de Diamante de la Iglesia Metodista de Mexico, 1873-1948*. Mexico, D.F.: Imprenta Nueva Educacion (Metodista), 1948.

Merkel, Henry Martin. *History of Methodism in Utah*. N.p., 1938.

Merritt, Timothy. *An Essay on the Perseverance of the Saints*. Portland, Ore.: printed by J. M'Kown, 1807.

The Methodist Church in Bolivia. N.p.: Historical Society of the Methodist Church in Bolivia, 1962.

The Methodist Harmonist. New York: N. Bangs & J. Emory, 1825.

Methodist History, quarterly, published by the Association of Methodist Historical Societies, 1962-68; continued by Commission on Archives and History, United Methodist Church, 1968-

Methodist Magazine (London), see *Arminian Magazine*.

The Methodist Magazine. Published in New York by the Methodist Episcopal Church, monthly, 1818-28; as *The Methodist Magazine and Quarterly Review*, 1830-41; as *The Methodist Quarterly Review*, 1841-85; as *The Methodist Review*, 1885-1932; replaced by *Religion in Life*, 1932- , published in Nashville by Abingdon Press.

The Methodist Pocket Hymn-Book; revised and improved: Designed as a Constant Companion for the Pious of all Denominations. Collected from Various Authors. 40th ed. New York: D. Hitt and T. Ware, 1813. With this is bound *A Selection of Hymns from Various Authors,* designed as a supplement to *The Methodist Pocket Hymn-Book,* compiled under the direction of Bishop Asbury, and Published by Order of the General Conference. 6th ed. New York: D. Hitt and T. Ware, 1813. Popularly known as the "Double Hymnbook."

The Methodist Preacher; Containing Twenty-Eight Sermons, on Doctrinal and Practical Subjects. By Bishop Hedding, Dr. Fisk, Dr. Bangs, Dr. Durbin, and Other Ministers of the Methodist Episcopal Church. New York: C. M. Saxton, 1859.

The Methodist Protestant. Published at Baltimore by the M. P. Church, 1834-1929. Merged with *Methodist Recorder* to become *Methodist Protestant-Recorder,* 1929-40. Ceased publication in 1940.

Methodist Quarterly Review (MES), see *Quarterly Review of the M. E. Church, South.*

Methodist Recorder. Methodist Protestant Church. First published Zanesville, O., then Springfield, O.; moved to Pittsburgh 1871. Published first as *Western Recorder,* 1839-54; as *Western Methodist Protestant,* 1855-66; as *Methodist Recorder,* 1866-1929. See *Methodist Protestant* for later years.

Methodist Review, see *The Methodist Magazine.*

Methodist Year Book. New York: Methodist Book Concern, 1833-1933. Title varies: *The Methodist Almanac,* 1834-79; *The Methodist Year Book,* 1880-1933.

Meyer, Lucy Rider. *Deaconesses, Biblical, Early Church, European, American, with the Story of the Chicago Training School . . . and the Chicago Deaconess Home.* Chicago: Message Pub. Co., 1889.

Micklem, Nathaniel, ed. *Christian Worship: Studies in Its History and Meaning by Members of Mansfield College.* New York: Oxford University Press, 1936.

Milhouse, Paul W. *Phillip William Otterbein: Pioneer Pastor to Germans in America.* Nashville: Upper Room, 1968.

Miller, Adam, ed. *Experience of German Methodist Preachers.* Mount Pleasant, Ia.: the auther, 1859.

—————. *Origin and Progress of the German Missions in the Methodist Episcopal Church.* Cincinnati: J. F. Wright & L. Swormstedt, 1843.

Miller, Gene Ramsey. *A History of North Mississippi Methodism, 1820-1900.* Nashville: the author, 1966.

Miller, George. *Kurze Beschreibung der würkenden Gnade Gottes bey dem erleuchteten evangelischen Prediger Jacob Albrecht.* Reading, Pa.: the author, 1811. English trans. George Edward Epp, *Jacob Albright;* Dayton, O.: Historical Society of the Evangelical United Brethren Church, 1959.

—————. *Leben, Erfahrung und Amtsführung zweyer evangelischer Prediger, Jakob Albrecht und Georg Miller.* New Berlin, Pa.: the author, 1834.

Miller, George A. *Twenty Years After: The Panama-Costa Rica Project of the California Conference Epworth League of the Methodist Episcopal Church.* N.p.: the author, 1936.

Miller, Mrs. M. A. *History of the Woman's Foreign Missionary Society of the Methodist Protestant Church.* Pittsburgh: Woman's Foreign Missionary Society, 1896.

Miller, Renetts C., ed. *Souvenir History of the New England Southern Conference.* Nantasket, Mass.: the editor, 1898.

Miller, W. H. *Wegweiser der Nördlichen Deutschen Konferenz der Bischöflichen Methodistenkirche.* N.p.: the conference, 1903.

Mills, Edward Laird. *Plains, Peaks and Pioneers: Eighty Years of Methodism in Montana.* Portland, Ore.: Binfords & Mort, 1947.

Mims, Edwin. *History of Vanderbilt University.* Nashville: Vanderbilt University Press, 1946.

Minear, Paul S., ed. *The Nature of the Unity We Seek.* St. Louis: Bethany Press, 1958.

Minus, Paul M., Jr., ed. *Methodism's Destiny in an Ecumenical Age.* Nashville: Abingdon Press, 1969.

Minutes of the Annual Conferences of The Methodist Church, published annually; 1940-47 the *Minutes* were published in two sections—Spring Conferences and Fall Conferences; 1948-68 these were combined and published as *The General Minutes of the Annual Conferences of The Methodist Church.*

Minutes of the Annual Conferences of the Methodist Episcopal Church were published annually, 1773-1939. From 1878 through 1939 the *Minutes* were published in two sections —Spring Conferences and Fall Conferences. Several collected editions of the earlier years have been published.

Minutes of the Annual Conferences of the Methodist Episcopal Church, South, published annually from 1845; from 1923-24 through 1939-40 published as *The General Minutes and Yearbook of the M. E. Church, South.*

Minutes of the Methodist Conferences, from the first, held in London, by the late Rev. John Wesley, A.M. in the year 1744. Best edition, collected in composite volumes, and then annual volumes, beginning Vol. I, London: Mason, at the Wesleyan Conference Office, 1862, which includes the minutes from 1744-1798, including Wesley's "Large Minutes" arranged in parallel columns.

Minutes of the Methodist Conferences in Ireland. Dublin: Religious & General Book Co., 1864. Vol. I, 1752-1819.

Missionary Seer, official monthly missionary periodical, published by A.M.E. Zion Church at Washington, D. C., 1904-

Mitchel, Paul Denny. *Cuba Calling: A Golden Anniversary Volume.* Buenos Aires: Imprenta Metodista, 1949.

Mitchell, Bennett. *History of the Northwest Iowa Conference, 1872-1903.* Sioux City, Ia.: Perkins Bros. Co., 1904.

Moede, Gerald F. *The Office of Bishop in Methodism: Its History and Development.* Zurich, Switzerland: Publishing House of the Methodist Church; Nashville: Abingdon Press, 1964.

Moister, William. *Conversations on the Rise, Progress, and Present State of Wesleyan Missions in Various Parts of the World.* London: Hamilton, Adams & Co., 1869. 3rd & rev. ed., *A History of Wesleyan Missions,* London: Elliot Stock, 1871.

—————. *A Hand Book of Wesleyan Missions, Briefly Describing Their Rise and Present State in Various Parts of the World.* London: the author, 1883.

—————. *Heralds of Salvation; Being Brief Memorial Sketches of Wesleyan Missionaries Who Have Died in the Work Since the Commencement of the Enterprise.* London: Wesleyan Conference Office, 1878.

Monk, Robert Clarence. *John Wesley: His Puritan Heritage.* Nashville: Abingdon Press, 1966.

Mood, Francis Asbury. *Methodism in Charleston: A Narrative of the Chief Events Relating to the Rise and Progress of the Methodist Episcopal Church in Charleston, S. C., with Brief Notices of the Early Ministers Who Labored in That City.* Ed. Thomas O. Summers; Nashville: E. Stevenson & J. E. Evans, 1856.

Moore, Benjamin. *History of Wesleyan Methodism in Burnley and East Lancashire.* Burnley: Gazette Printing Works, 1899.

Moore, Henry. *The Life of the Rev. John Wesley, A.M. . . , in Which are Included the Life of His Brother, the Rev. Charles Wesley, A.M. . . ; and Memoirs of Their Family.* 2 vols. London: Printed for John Kershaw; New York: N. Bangs & J. Emory, 1824-25.

—————. *The Life of Mrs. Mary Fletcher, Consort and Relict of the Rev. John Fletcher. . . Compiled from Her*

Journal and Other Authentic Documents. London: Conference Office, 1818.

—————. See Coke and Moore. *John Wesley.* 1792.

Moore, Homer H. *The Republic, To Methodism, Dr.* Cincinnati: Cranston & Stowe; New York: Hunt & Eaton, 1891.

Moore, John Jamison. *History of the A.M.E. Zion Church in America.* York, Pa.: Teachers Journal Office, 1884.

Moore, John Monroe. *Life and I; or, Sketches and Comments.* Nashville: the author, 1948.

—————. *The Long Road to Methodist Union.* Nashville: Abingdon-Cokesbury Press, 1943.

—————. *Methodism in Belief and Action.* Nashville: Abingdon-Cokesbury Press, 1946.

Moore, Matthew Henry. *Sketches of the Pioneers of Methodism in North Carolina and Virginia.* Nashville: Southern Methodist Publishing House, 1884.

Moore, Richard Douglas. *Methodism in the Channel Islands.* London: Epworth Press, 1952.

Morgan, James. *The Life and Death of Mr. Thomas Walsh.* London: H. Cock, 1762.

Morgan, James Henry. *Dickinson College: The History of One Hundred and Fifty Years, 1783-1933.* Carlisle, Pa.: Dickinson College, 1933.

Morley, William. *History of Methodism in New Zealand.* Wellington: McKee & Co., 1900.

Morris, T. A. *A Discourse on Methodist Church Polity.* Cincinnati: Swormstedt & Poe, 1860.

Morrow, Ralph Ernest. *Northern Methodism and Reconstruction.* East Lansing: Michigan State University Press, 1956.

Morrow, Thomas M. *Early Methodist Women.* London: Epworth Press, 1967.

Moulton, Harold Keeling. *James Hope Moulton, 1863-1917.* N.p., 1919. Reissued, London: Epworth Press, 1963.

Mounfield, Arthur. *A Short History of Independent Methodism.* Warrington: Independent Methodist Bookroom, 1905.

Mudge, James. *Growth in Holiness Toward Perfection.* New York: Hunt & Eaton, 1895.

—————. *Handbook of Methodism, Prepared For and Dedicated to The Methodist Church of India.* Lucknow: American Methodist Mission Press, 1877.

—————. *History of the New England Conference of the Methodist Episcopal Church, 1796-1910.* Boston: the conference, 1910.

Mudge, Zachariah Atwell. *The Missionary Teacher: A Memoir of Cyrus Shepard, Embracing a Brief Sketch of the Early History of the Oregon Mission.* New York: Carlton & Porter, 1848.

Muelder, Walter G. *Methodism and Society in the Twentieth Century.* ("Methodism and Society," vol ii). Nashville: Abingdon Press, 1961.

Müller, Henry, et al. *Geschichte der Ost-Deutschen Konferenz.* New York: the conference, 1916.

Murray, Joshua Thomas, and Lewis, Thomas Hamilton. *History of the Maryland Annual Conference of the Methodist Protestant Church.* Baltimore: W. J. C. Dulany, 1882. Reprinted in T. H. Lewis, ed., *Historical Record of the Maryland Annual Conference,* 4th & 5th eds.

Mutual Rights of Ministers and Members of the Methodist Episcopal Church, 1824-28; as *Mutual Rights and Christian Intelligencer,* 1828-30. In 1830 it became a publication of the Methodist Protestant Church, and was published as *The Mutual Rights and Methodist Protestant,* 1831-34. See *The Methodist Protestant* for later years.

Myles, William. *A Chronological History of the People Called Methodists.* Liverpool: printed for the author by J. Nuttall, 1799. 4th ed., considerably enl., London: printed at the Conference Office, by Thomas Cordeux, agent, 1813.

Nagler, Arthur Wilford. *Pietism and Methodism; or, The Significance of German Pietism in the Origin and Early Development of Methodism.* Nashville: Publishing House, M. E. Church, South; Smith & Lamar, Agents, 1918.

Nail, Olin W. *The First Hundred Years of the Southwest Texas Conference of The Methodist Church, 1858-1958.* San Antonio, Tex.: the conference, 1958.

—————, ed. *History of Texas Methodism, 1900-1960.* Austin, Tex.: Capital Printing Co., 1961.

—————, et al., eds. *Texas Methodist Centennial Yearbook, 1834-1934.* Elgin, Tex.; Olin W. Nail, 1934.

Nashville *Christian Advocate,* published by the M. E. Church, South, began in 1832 as *South-Western Christian Advocate;* became property of the M. E. Church, South in 1845; continued until 1940.

Neblett, Sterling Augustus. *Methodism in Cuba: The First Thirteen Years.* Macon, Ga.: Wesleyan College, 1966.

Neely, Thomas Benjamin. *American Methodism: Its Divisions and Unification.* New York: Fleming H. Revell Co., 1915.

—————. *The Bishops and the Supervisional System of the Methodist Episcopal Church.* Cincinnati: Jennings & Graham, 1912.

—————. *Doctrinal Standards of Methodism.* New York: Fleming H. Revell Co., 1918.

—————. *The Evolution of Episcopacy and Organic Methodism.* New York: Phillips & Hunt, 1888.

—————. *A History of the Origin and Development of the Governing Conference in Methodism, and Especially of the General Conference of the Methodist Episcopal Church.* Cincinnati: Cranston & Stowe, 1892.

—————. *The Methodist Episcopal Church and Its Foreign Missions.* New York: Methodist Book Concern, 1923.

Neitz, Solomon. *Das Leben und Wirken des seligen Johannes Seybert.* Cleveland, O.: Charles Hammer, 1862.

Ness, John H., Jr. *One Hundred Fifty Years: A History of Publishing in the Evangelical United Brethren Church.* Dayton, O.: Board of Publication of the Evangelical United Brethren Church, 1966.

New, Alfred Henry. *The Coronet and the Cross; or, Memorials of the Right Hon. Selina, Countess of Huntingdon.* London: Partridge & Co., 1857.

Newcomer, Christian. *Life and Journal of the Rev'd Christian Newcomer.* Transcribed, corrected and translated by John Hildt. Hagerstown, Md.: n.p., 1834.

The New Evangelical Hymnbook. Cleveland, O.: Publishing House of the Evangelical Association, 1867.

New Hymn and Tune Book: An Offering of Praise for the Use of the African M. E. Zion Church of America. 1888.

Newton, John Anthony. *Susanna Wesley and the Puritan Tradition in Methodism.* London: Epworth Press, 1968.

New York *Christian Advocate,* official paper of the Methodist Episcopal Church, first published as the *Christian Advocate and Journal,* beginning in 1826. Published as *Christian Advocate and Journal and Zion's Herald,* Aug. 1828 to Aug. 1833. Published as *Christian Advocate,* 1866-1940.

Nightingale, Joseph. *A Portraiture of Methodism.* London: Longman, Hurst, Rees, & Orme, 1807.

Noble, Mattie Wilcox, ed. *Victorious Lives of Early Christians in Korea.* Seoul: Christian Literature Society of Korea, 1927. Eng. tr., 1933.

North, Eric McCoy. *Early Methodist Philanthropy.* New York: Methodist Book Concern, 1914.

Norwood, Frederick Abbott. *Church Membership in the Methodist Tradition.* Nashville: Methodist Publishing House, 1958.

—————. *History of the North Indiana Conference, 1917-1956.* Winona Lake, Ind.: Light & Life Press, 1957. See Herrick and Sweet, *North Indiana Conference.* 1917.

Norwood, John Nelson. *The Schism in the Methodist Episcopal Church, 1844: A Study of Slavery and Ecclesiastical Politics.* Alfred, N.Y.: Alfred University, 1923.

Nuelsen, John Louis. *Der Methodismus in Deutschland nach dem Krieg.* Bremen: Buchhandlung und Verlag des Traktathauses, n.d.

—————. *Die Methodistenkirche in religiösen*

Leben der Schweiz. Zurich: Christliche Vereinsbuchhand-lung, 1932.

——————. *Die Ordination im Methodismus.* Bremen: Verlagshaus der Methodistenkirche, 1935.

——————. *John Wesley und das deutsche Kirchen-lied.* Bremen: Ankerverlag, 1938.

——————. Mann, Theophil; Sommer, J. J. *Kurzge-fasste Geschichte des Methodismus von seinen Anfängen bis zur Gegenwart.* Bremen: Traktathaus, 1920. Rev. ed., 1929.

Nuttall, Geoffrey F. *Howel Harris, 1714-1773: The Last En-thusiast.* Cardiff: University of Wales Press, 1965.

Nutter, Charles S. *Hymn Studies: An Illustrated and Anno-tated Edition of the Hymnal of the Methodist Episcopal Church.* New York: Phillips & Hunt, 1884.

——————, and Tillett, Wilbur Fisk. *The Hymns and Hymn Writers of the Church: An Annotated Edition of The Methodist Hymnal.* New York: Eaton & Mains; Cin-cinnati; Jennings & Graham; Nashville: Smith & Lamar, 1911.

O'Bryan, William. *A Narrative of Travels in the United States of America, With Some Account of American Manners.* Shebbear, Devonshire: Samuel Thorne, 1836.

Oden, William B. See Clegg and Oden. *Oklahoma.* 1968.

Oduyoye, Modupe. *The Planting of Christianity in Yoruba-land, 1842-1888.* Ibadan, Nigeria: Daystar Press, 1969.

Ogburn, T. J. *Foreign Missions of the Methodist Protestant Church.* Baltimore: Board of Publication, Methodist Prot-estant Church, 1906.

Oldham, William F. *Thoburn—Called of God.* New York: Methodist Book Concern, 1918.

Olin, Stephen. *The Life and Letters of Stephen Olin, D.D., LL. D., Late President of the Wesleyan University.* 2 vols. New York: Harper & Bros., 1853.

Origin of American Methodism. Report of the Joint Commis-sion representing the Methodist Episcopal Church, the Methodist Episcopal Church, South, and the Methodist Protestant Church. Chicago: Methodist Book Concern, 1916.

Origin and History of the Wesleyan Reform Union; With a Brief Summary of Methodist Secessions. Sheffield: Wes-leyan Reform Union Book Room, 1896.

Orwig, William W. *Geschichte der Evangelischen Gemein-schaft.* Cleveland, O.: Charles Hammer, 1857. English trans., *History of the Evangelical Association,* 1858.

Osborn, Albert. *John Fletcher Hurst: A Biography.* New York: Eaton & Mains, 1905.

Osborn, George. *Outlines of Wesleyan Bibliography.* London: Wesleyan Conference Office, 1869.

Outler, Albert Cook, ed. *John Wesley.* ("A Library of Prot-estant Thought" series). New York: Oxford University Press, 1964.

Pace, Charles Nelson, ed. *Our Fathers Built: A Century of Minnesota Methodism.* N.p.: Historical Society, Minne-sota Methodist Conference, 1952.

Paik, L. George. *The History of Protestant Missions in Korea, 1832-1910.* Pyengyang: Union Christian College Press, 1929.

Paine, Robert. *Life and Times of William M'Kendree, Bishop of the Methodist Episcopal Church.* 2 vols. Nashville: Southern Methodist Publishing House, 1869.

Palmer, Louis DeForest. *Heroism and Romance: Early Meth-odism in Northeastern Pennsylvania.* Stroudsburg, Pa.: the author, 1950.

Paris, John. *History of the Methodist Protestant Church: Giv-ing a General View of the Causes and Events that Led to the Organization of That Church; and a More Par-ticular Account of Transactions in North Carolina, Never Before Published.* With an Appendix. Baltimore: printed by Sherwood & Co., 1849.

Parris, John R. *John Wesley's Doctrine of the Sacraments.* Lon-don: Epworth Press, 1963.

Patterson, W. M. *Northern Primitive Methodism.* London: E. Dalton, 1909.

Pawlyn, John S. *Bristol Methodism in John Wesley's Day, with Monographs of the Early Methodist Preachers.* Bristol: W. C. Hemmons, 1877.

Payne, Daniel Alexander. *A History of the African Methodist Episcopal Church.* Ed. C. S. Smith. Nashville: Publishing House of the A.M.E. Sunday-School Union, 1891.

——————. *Recollections of Seventy Years.* Com-piled by Sarah C. B. Scarborough, ed. C. S. Smith. Nash-ville: Publishing House of the A.M.E. Sunday School Union, 1888. Facsimile reprint, New York: Arno Press, 1968.

Payton, Jacob Simpson. *Our Fathers Have Told Us: The Story of the Founding of Methodism in Western Pennsylvania.* Cincinnati: Ruter Press, 1938.

Pearce, John, ed. *The Wesleys in Cornwall: Extracts from the Journals of John and Charles Wesley and John Nelson.* Truro, Cornwall: D. Bradford Barton, 1964.

Peck, George. *Early Methodism Within the Bounds of the Old Genesee Conference from 1788 to 1828.* New York: Carlton & Porter, 1860.

——————, ed. *The Methodist Episcopal Pulpit: A Collec-tion of Original Sermons from Living Ministers of the M. E. Church,* Davis W. Clark, Coll. and reviser. New York: Carlton & Phillips, 1854.

——————. *Slavery and the Episcopacy: Being an Exami-nation of Dr. Bascom's Review . . . in the Case of Bishop Andrew.* New York: Lane & Tippett, 1845.

Peck, J. K. *Stevens Answered in His Appeal to the Methodist Episcopal Church.* Montrose, Pa.: "Republican" Steam Power Press, 1859.

Peirce, William. *The Ecclesiastical Principles and Polity of the Wesleyan Methodists.* London: Hamilton, Adams, & Co., 1854. 3rd ed., rev. by Frederick J. Jobson; London: Wes-leyan Conference Office, 1873.

Pennewell, Almer Mitchell. *A Voice in the Wilderness: Jesse Walker.* Niles, Ill.: n.p., 1958.

Perkins, E. Benson. *Methodist Preaching Houses and the Law.* London: Epworth Press, 1952.

——————. *So Appointed: An Autobiography.* Lon-don: Epworth Press, 1964.

Peter, L. *Geschichte der bischöflichen Methodistenkirchen in der Schweiz.* Zurich: Christliche Verlagsbuchhandlung, 1893.

Peters, John L. *Christian Perfection and American Methodism.* Nashville: Abingdon Press, 1956.

Peterson, Peter Archibald. *History of the Revisions of the Discipline of the Methodist Episcopal Church, South.* Nashville: Publishing House of the M. E. Church, South, 1889.

Petri, Laura. *John Wesley.* Uppsala, Sweden: Lindblad, 1928.

Pettigrew, M. C. *From Miles to Johnson.* Memphis, Tenn.: C.M.E. Church Publishing House, 1970.

Petty, John. *The History of the Primitive Methodist Connexion.* London: Richard Davies, 1860. New ed., rev. and enl. by James MacPherson; London: John Dickenson, 1880.

Phelan, Macum. *A History of Early Methodism in Texas, 1817-1866.* Nashville: Cokesbury Press, 1924.

——————. *A History of the Expansion of Methodism in Texas, 1867-1902.* Dallas, Tex.: Mathis, Van Nort & Co., 1937.

Philip, Robert. *The Life and Times of the Reverend George Whitefield, M.A.* London: George Virtue, 1837.

Phillips, Charles Henry. *From the Farm to the Bishopric: An Autobiography.* Nashville: the author, 1932.

——————. *The History of the Colored Methodist Episcopal Church in America.* Jackson, Tenn.: Publishing House C.M.E. Church, 1898. 3rd ed., enl., 1925.

Phillips, William. *Early Methodism in Shropshire.* Shrewsbury: W. G. Napier, 1896.

Phoebus, George Alfred. *Beams of Light on Early Methodism in America. Chiefly Drawn from the Diary, Letters, Manuscripts, Documents, and Original Tracts of the Rev. Ezekiel Cooper.* New York: Phillips & Hunt, 1887.

Phoebus, William. *An Essay on the Doctrine and Order of the Evangelical Church of America.* New York: printed for the author by Abraham Paul, 1817.

——————. *Memoirs of the Rev. Richard Whatcoat, Late Bishop of the Methodist Episcopal Church.* New York: Joseph Allen, 1828.

Pickett, J. Waskom. *Christian Mass Movements in India.* Cincinnati: The Abingdon Press, 1933.

Pidgeon, George C. *The United Church of Canada: The Story of the Union.* Toronto: Ryerson Press, 1950.

Pierce, Alfred M. *Giant Against the Sky: The Life of Bishop Warren Akin Candler.* New York: Abingdon-Cokesbury Press, 1948.

——————. *A History of Methodism in Georgia, February 5, 1736—June 24, 1955.* N.p.: North Georgia Conference Historical Society, 1956.

Pierce, Lorne A. *The Chronicle of a Century.* Toronto: United Church Publishing House, 1929.

Piette, Maximin. *La reaction Wesleyenne dans l'evolution protestante.* Brussels: La Lecture au foyer, 1925. Tr. J. B. Howard, *John Wesley in the Evolution of Protestantism;* London and New York: Sheed & Ward, 1937.

Piggott, T. C., and Durley, T. *Life and Letters of Henry James Piggott, B.A., of Rome.* London: Epworth Press, 1921.

Pilcher, Elijah H. *Protestantism in Michigan: Being a Special History of the Methodist Episcopal Church and Incidentally of Other Denominations.* Detroit, Mich.: R. D. S. Tyler & Co., 1878.

Pilkington, Frederick. *Daybreak in Jamaica.* London: Epworth Press, 1950.

Pilkington, James Penn. *The Methodist Publishing House: A History.* Vol. I. Nashville: Abingdon Press, 1968.

Pilsbury, W. H. See Allen and Pilsbury. *Methodism in Maine.* 1887.

Pitezel, John H. *Lights and Shades of Missionary Life: Containing Travels, Sketches, Incidents, and Missionary Efforts, during Nine Years Spent in the Region of Lake Superior.* Cincinnati: the author, 1859. New ed., Walden & Stowe, 1883.

Platt, Ward, ed. *Methodism and the Republic, A View of the Home Field, Present Conditions, Needs and Possibilities.* Philadelphia: Board of Home Missions, M. E. Church, 1908.

Playter, George F. *The History of Methodism in Canada: with an Account of the Rise and Progress of the Work of God Among the Canadian Indian Tribes, and Occasional Notices of the Civil Affairs of the Province.* Toronto: Anson Green for the author, 1862.

A Pocket Hymn Book, Designed as a Constant Companion for the Pious, comp. by Robert Spence of York, England. 4th ed. York: printed for and sold by R. Spence; and sold also by T. Scollick; London: 1785.

Pocock, William Wilmer. *A Sketch of the History of Wesleyan-Methodism in Some of the Southern Counties of England.* London: Wesleyan-Methodist Book-Room, 1885.

Pope, William Burt. *A Compendium of Christian Theology.* 3 vols. London: Wesleyan-Methodist Book-Room, 1880.

Potter, W. S. See Guy and Potter. *Primitive Methodism in New Zealand.* 1893.

Prentice, George. *The Life of Gilbert Haven.* New York: Phillips & Hunt, 1883.

——————. *Wilbur Fisk.* Boston: Houghton, Mifflin & Co., 1890.

Price, Carl F. *The Music and Hymnody of The Methodist Hymnal.* New York: Eaton & Mains, 1911.

——————. *Wesleyan's First Century.* Middletown, Conn.: Wesleyan University, 1932.

——————. *Who's Who in American Methodism.* New York: E. B. Treat & Co., 1916.

Price, Frederick B., ed. *India Mission Jubilee of the Methodist Episcopal Church in Southern Asia.* Calcutta: Methodist Publishing House, 1907.

Price, Richard Nye. *Holston Methodism; From Its Origin to the Present Time.* 5 vols. Nashville: Publishing House of the M. E. Church, South, 1903-13.

Primitive Methodist Journal, monthly, published by the Primitive Methodist Church at Shenandoah, Pa. 1892- .

Prince, John Wesley. *Wesley on Religious Education.* New York: Methodist Book Concern, 1926.

Pritchard, Frank Cyril. *Methodist Secondary Education.* London: Epworth Press, 1949.

——————. *The Story of Westminster College, 1851-1915.* London: Epworth Press, 1951.

Pritchard, John. *Sermon Occasioned by the Death of the Late Capt. Webb; and Preached at Portland-Chapel, Bristol . . . at the Time of His Interment.* Bristol: printed and sold by R. Edwards, 1797.

Proceedings of the Ecumenical Methodist Conference . . . 1881. London: Wesleyan Conference Office, 1881. Published at ten-year intervals, following each conference, 1891, 1901, 1911, 1921, 1931, 1947. Name changed to *World Methodist Conference* in 1951 and held quinquennially, with *Proceedings* published 1951, 1956, 1961, 1966, 1971.

Project Handbook: Overseas Missions. Cincinnati: Board of Missions, United Methodist Church, 1969.

Project Handbook: Section of Home Fields. Cincinnati: Board of Missions, The Methodist Church, 1967.

Pyke, Richard. *The Early Bible Christians.* London: Epworth Press, 1941.

——————. *The Golden Chain.* The Story of the Bible Christian Methodists from the formation of the First Society in 1815 to the Union of the Denomination in 1907 with the Methodist New Connexion and the United Methodist Free Churches in Forming the United Methodist Church. London: Henry Hooks, 1915.

Quarterly Review of the M. E. Church, South. Published under this title 1847-61, 1879-86; 1889-94; also published as *Southern Methodist Review,* 1887-88; as *The Methodist Review,* 1895-1903 and 1906-8; as *The Methodist Quarterly Review,* 1903-6, 1908-30. Discontinued in 1930.

Rack, Henry D. *The Future of John Wesley's Methodism.* (Ecumenical Studies in History, No. 2). Richmond, Va.: John Knox Press, 1965.

Rall, Harris Franklin. *Modern Premillennialism and the Christian Hope.* New York: Abingdon Press, 1920.

Randall, Daniel Boody. *A Statistical History of the Maine Conference of the M. E. Church from 1793 to 1893.* Portland, Me.: Lakeside Press, 1893.

Ransom, Reverdy C. *Preface to the History of the A.M.E. Church.* Nashville: A.M.E. Sunday School Union, 1950.

Rattenbury, Harold B. *David Hill, Friend of China.* London: Epworth Press, 1949.

Rattenbury, John Ernest. *The Conversion of the Wesleys.* London: Epworth Press, 1938.

——————. *The Eucharistic Hymns of John and Charles Wesley.* London: Epworth Press, 1948.

——————. *The Evangelical Doctrines of Charles Wesley's Hymns.* London: Epworth Press, 1941.

——————. *Thoughts on Holy Communion.* London: Epworth Press, 1958.

——————. *Vital Elements in Public Worship.* London: Epworth Press, 1936.

——————. *Wesley's Legacy to the World: Six Studies in the Permanent Values of the Evangelical Revival.* London: Epworth Press, 1928.

Reber, Audrie E. *Women United for Mission: A History of the Women's Society of World Service of the Evangelical United Brethren Church.* Cincinnati: Board of Missions, United Methodist Church, 1969.

Redfern, William. *Modern Developments in Methodism.* London: National Council of Evangelical Free Churches, 1906.

Redford, Albert H. *The History of Methodism in Kentucky.* 3 vols. Nashville: Southern Methodist Publishing House, 1868-70.

——————. *History of the Organization of the Methodist Episcopal Church, South.* Nashville: the author, 1871.

——————. *Western Cavaliers: Embracing the History of the Methodist Episcopal Church in Kentucky from 1832 to 1844.* Nashville: Southern Methodist Publishing House, 1876.

Register of Methodist Circuit Plans, 1777-1860, Society of Cirplanologists. Manchester: A. Whipp, 1960.

Reid, Alexander J. *Congo Drumbeat: History of the First Half Century in the Establishment of the Methodist Church Among the Atetela of Central Congo.* New York: World Outlook Press, 1964.

Reid, John Morrison. *Missions and Missionary Society of the Methodist Episcopal Church.* 2 vols. New York: Phillips & Hunt, 1879. Rev. and extended by John Talbot Gracey; 3 vols.; New York: Hunt & Eaton, 1895-96.

Religion in Life, see *Methodist Magazine* (New York).

Religious Telescope, published at Circleville and Dayton, O., 1834-1946. See *Telescope Messenger.*

Revington, George. See Stewart and Revington. *Adam Averell.* 1843.

The Revivalist: A Collection of Choice Revival Hymns and Tunes, ed. Joseph Hillman. Rev. and Enl. ed., Troy, N. Y.: the editor, 1869.

Reynolds, J. S. *The Evangelicals at Oxford, 1735-1781: A Record of an Unchronicled Movement.* Oxford: Basil Blackwell, 1953.

Rhinehart, William. See Erb and Rhinehart. *Collection of Hymns . . . UB.* 1835.

Richey, Mathew. *A Memoir of the Late Rev. William Black, Wesleyan Minister, Halifax, N. S., Including an Account of the Rise and Progress of Methodism in Nova Scotia; Characteristic Notices of Several Individuals; with Copious Extracts from the Unpublished Correspondence of the Rev. John Wesley, Rev. Dr. Coke, Rev. Freeborn Garrettson, etc.* Halifax, N.S.: William Cunnabell, 1839.

Richmond, Legh. *The Dairyman's Daughter* (Elizabeth Wallbridge). London: Warne, ?

Riddell, John Henry. *Methodism in the Middle West.* Toronto: Ryerson Press, 1946.

Ridgel, Alfred Lee. *Africa and African Methodism.* Atlanta: Franklin Publishing Co., 1896.

Rigg, James Harrison. *A Comparative View of Church Organizations, Primitive and Protestant. With a Supplement on Methodist Secessions and Methodist Union.* 3rd edn., rev. and enl., London: Kelly, 1897.

——————. *The Living Wesley.* London: Wesleyan Conference Office, 1874. Rev. eds., 1891, 1905.

Ritson, Joseph. *The Romance of Primitive Methodism.* London: Edwin Dalton, 1909.

Roberts, Benjamin Titus. *Why Another Sect? Containing a Review of Articles by Bishop Simpson and Others on the Free Methodist Church.* Rochester, N. Y.: Earnest Christian Publishing House, 1879.

Roberts, Benson Howard. *Benjamin Titus Roberts, Late General Superintendent of the Free Methodist Church.* North Chili, N. Y.: Earnest Christian Office, 1900.

Roberts, Gomer Morgan, ed. *Selected Trevecka Letters.* Vol. 1, *1742-47;* Vol. 2, *1747-94.* Caernarvon, Wales: Calvinistic Methodist Bookroom, 1957, 1962.

Roberts, Griffith T. *Howell Harris.* London: Epworth Press, 1951.

Robinson, John Bunyan. *History of Rock River Conference.* DeLand, Fla.: n.p., 1908.

Robinson, John Ryley. *Notes on Early Methodism in Dewsbury, Birstal, and Neighbourhood.* Batley: J. Fearnsides & Sons, 1900.

Robson, Ebenezer. *How Methodism Came to British Columbia.* Toronto: Methodist Book & Publishing House, 1905.

Rockledge, J. *Memoirs of Early Methodism in Easingwold Circuit.* 1872.

Rogers, Hester Ann. *The Experience of Mrs. H. A. Rogers, Written by Herself.* London: G. Paramore, 1793.

——————. *Spiritual Letters, Written before and after Her Marriage.* Bristol: R. Edwards, 1796.

Roman, Charles Victor. *Meharry Medical College: A History.* Nashville: Sunday School Publishing Board of the National Baptist Convention, Inc., 1934.

Rosser, James. *The History of Wesleyan Methodism in the Isle of Man.* Douglas, I. M.: the author, 1849.

Roush, Walter Edwin. See Koontz and Roush. *The Bishops.* 1950.

Routley, Erik. *The Musical Wesleys.* London: Herbert Jenkins, 1968.

Roux, Theophile. *Le Methodisme en France: Pour servir a l'Histoire religieuse d'hier et d'avant-hier.* Paris: Librairie Protestante, 1940.

Ruddle, Thomas. *Samuel Thomas Thorne, Missionary to Yunnan.* London: Bible Christian Missionary Committee, 1893.

Rudolph, Lavere Christian. *Francis Asbury.* Nashville: Abingdon Press, 1966.

Rupp, E. Gordon. *Thomas Jackson: Methodist Patriarch.* London: Epworth Press, 1954.

——————. See Davies and Rupp. *Methodist Church in Great Britain.* 1965.

Rush, Christopher. *A Short Account of the Rise and Progress of the African Methodist Episcopal Church in America.* New York: the author, 1843.

Russell, Daniel James. *History of the African Union Methodist Protestant Church.* Philadelphia: Union Star Book & Job Printing & Publishing House, 1920.

Russell, Thomas. *Record of Events in Primitive Methodism.* London: William Lister, 1869.

Ryang, Ju Sam, ed. *Southern Methodism in Korea: Thirtieth Anniversary.* Seoul: Board of Missions, Korea Annual Conference, Methodist Episcopal Church, South, 1930.

Ryerson, Egerton. *Canadian Methodism: Its Epochs and Characteristics.* Toronto: William Briggs, 1882.

——————. *The Story of My Life.* Ed. J. George Hodgins. Toronto: William Briggs, 1883.

The Sacred Choral: Choice Collection of Sacred Music, ed. S. Wakefield. Cincinnati: Swormstedt & Poe, 1854.

Sacred Harmony. New York: Lane & Tippett, 1848.

Sadler, Celia, ed. *Never a Young Man. Extracts from the Letters and Journals of the Rev. William Shaw.* Cape Town, 1967.

Samuel, Peter. *The Wesleyan-Methodist Missions in Jamaica and Honduras Delineated.* London: Partridge & Oakey, 1850.

Sandford, Peter P. *Memoirs of Mr. Wesley's Missionaries to America.* New York: G. Lane & P. P. Sandford, 1843.

Sanderson, J. E. *The First Century of Methodism in Canada.* 2 vols. Toronto: William Briggs, 1908, 1910.

Sangster, Paul Edwin. *Doctor Sangster.* London: Epworth Press, 1962.

——————. *Pity My Simplicity: The Evangelical Revival and the Religious Education of Children, 1739-1800.* London: Epworth Press, 1964.

Sangster, William Edwin. *The Path to Perfection: An Examination and Restatement of John Wesley's Doctrine of Christian Perfection.* London: Hodder & Stoughton, 1943.

Savage, Horace C. *Life and Times of Bishop Isaac Lane.* Nashville: National Publication Co., 1958.

Schilling, S. Paul. *Methodism and Society in Theological Perspective.* ("Methodism and Society," vol. iii). Nashville: Abingdon Press, 1960.

Schisler, John Q. *Christian Education in Local Methodist Churches.* Nashville: Abingdon Press, 1969.

Schmidt, Martin. *Der junge Wesley als Heidenmissionar und Missionstheologe.* Gütersloh: C. Bertelsmann, 1955. Tr.

L. A. Fletcher, *The Young Wesley: Missionary and Theologian of Missions;* London: Epworth Press, 1958.

——————. *John Wesley.* 2 vols. Zurich: Gotthelf-Verlag, 1953, 1966. Vol. 1, tr. Norman P. Goldhawk, *John Wesley: A Theological Biography;* London: Epworth Press; Nashville: Abingdon Press, 1962.

Schwab, Ralph K. *The History of the Doctrine of Christian Perfection in the Evangelical Association.* Menasha, Wis.: George Banta Publishing Co., 1922.

Scott, Jefferson Ellsworth. *History of Fifty Years: Comprising the Origin, Establishment, Progress and Expansion of the Methodist Episcopal Church in Southern Asia.* Madras, India: Methodist Episcopal Press, 1906.

Scott, John. *Recollections of Fifty Years in the Ministry.* Pittsburgh, Baltimore: Methodist Protestant Board of Publication, 1898.

Scott, Orange. *Address to the General Conference of the Methodist Episcopal Church.* New York: H. R. Piercy, printer, 1836.

Seaman, Samuel Augustus. *Annals of New York Methodism; Being a History of the Methodist Episcopal Church in the City of New York from A.D. 1766 to A.D. 1890.* New York: Hunt & Eaton, 1892.

Seamands, John T. *Pioneers of the Younger Churches.* Nashville: Abingdon Press, 1967.

Searles, J. E. *History of the Present Holiness Revival.* Boston: McDonald & Gill, 1887.

Seed, Thomas Alexander. *Norfolk Street Wesleyan Chapel, Sheffield; Being a History of This Famous Sanctuary together with . . . History of Methodism in the Town and Neighbourhood.* London: Jarrold & Sons, 1907.

Seymour, Aaron Crossley Hobart. *The Life and Times of Selina, Countess of Huntingdon.* 2 vols. London: William Edward Painter, 1839, 1840.

Shaw, Barnabas, *Memorials of South Africa.* New York: G. Lane & P. P. Sandford, 1841.

Shaw, James Beverly F. *The Negro in the History of Methodism.* Nashville: the author, 1954.

Shaw, Thomas. *The Bible Christians, 1815-1907.* London: Epworth Press, 1965.

——————. *A History of Cornish Methodism.* Truro, Cornwall: D. Bradford Barton, 1967.

Shaw, William. *The Story of My Mission Among the Native Tribes of South Eastern Africa.* London: Wesleyan Mission House, 1872.

Sheldon, W. C. *Early Methodism in Birmingham.* Birmingham: Buckler & Webb, 1903.

Shepherd, Thomas Boswell. *Methodism and the Literature of the Eighteenth Century.* London: Epworth Press, 1940.

Sherman, David. *History of the Revisions of the Discipline of the Methodist Episcopal Church.* New York: Nelson & Phillips, 1874. Rev. eds., 1877, 1890.

——————. *Sketches of New England Divines.* New York: Carlton & Porter, 1860.

Sherwin, Oscar. *John Wesley, Friend of the People.* New York: Twayne Publishers, Inc., 1961.

Shinn, Asa. *Essay on the Plan of Salvation.* Baltimore: Neal, Wills, and Cole, 1813.

Shipp, Albert M. *The History of Methodism in South Carolina.* Nashville: Southern Methodist Publishing House, 1883. Rev. ed., 1884.

Shortess, John David, and Gramley, A. D. *History of the Central Pennsylvania Conference of the Evangelical Church, 1839-1939.* N.p.: the conference, 1940.

Shuey, William A. *Manual of the United Brethren Publishing House: Historical and Descriptive.* Dayton, O.: United Brethren Publishing House, 1892.

Sigston, James. *A Memoir of the Life and Ministry of Mr. Wm. Bramwell.* London: James Nichols, 1820.

Sigsworth, John Wilkins. *The Battle Was the Lord's: A History of the Free Methodist Church in Canada.* Oshawa, Ont.: Sage Publishers, 1960.

Silcox, Claris Edwin. *Church Union in Canada.* New York: Institute of Social and Religious Research, 1933.

Simmons, J. C. *The History of Southern Methodism on the Pacific Coast.* Nashville: Southern Methodist Publishing House, 1886.

Simon, John Smith. *John Wesley and the Advance of Methodism.* London: Epworth Press, 1925.

——————. *John Wesley, The Last Phase.* London: Epworth Press, 1934.

——————. *John Wesley, the Master-Builder.* London: Epworth Press, 1927.

——————. *John Wesley and the Methodist Societies.* London: Epworth Press, 1923.

——————. *John Wesley and the Religious Societies.* London: Epworth Press, 1921.

——————. *Methodism in Dorset.* Weymouth, Dorsetshire: James Sherren, 1870.

——————. *A Summary of Methodist Law and Discipline.* London: Charles H. Kelly, 1897.

Simpson, Matthew, ed. *Cyclopaedia of Methodism. Embracing Sketches of Its Rise, Progress, and Present Condition, with Biographical Notices and Numerous Illustrations.* Philadelphia: Everts & Stewart, 1878. 5th rev. ed., 1882.

——————. *A Hundred Years of Methodism.* New York: Nelson & Phillips, 1876.

Singleton, George A. *The Romance of African Methodism.* New York: Exposition Press, 1952.

Sissons, Charles Bruce. *Egerton Ryerson: His Life and Letters.* 2 vols. Toronto: Clarke, Irwin & Co., 1937, 1947.

——————. *A History of Victoria University.* University of Toronto Press, 1952.

Sitterly, Charles Fremont. *The Building of Drew University.* New York: Methodist Book Concern, 1938.

Skelton, David E. *History of Lexington Conference.* N.p., 1950.

Smeltzer, Wallace Guy. *Methodism on the Headwaters of the Ohio: The History of the Pittsburgh Conference of The Methodist Church.* Nashville: the author, 1951.

Smith, Benjamin. *Methodism in Macclesfield.* London: Conference Office, 1875.

Smith, Charles Spencer. *A History of the African Methodist Episcopal Church. Being a Volume Supplemental to a History of the African Methodist Episcopal Church, by Daniel Alexander Payne . . . Chronicling the Principal Events in the Advance of the African Methodist Episcopal Church from 1856 to 1922.* Philadelphia: Book Concern of the A.M.E. Church, 1922.

Smith, David. *The Biography of Rev. David Smith, of the A.M.E. Church.* Xenia, Ohio: Xenia Gazette Office, 1881.

Smith, Ernest Ashton. *Martin Ruter.* New York, Cincinnati: Methodist Book Concern, 1915.

Smith, George. *History of Wesleyan Methodism.* 3 vols. London: Longman, Brown, Green, Longmans & Roberts, 1857-61.

Smith, George Gilman. *The History of Georgia Methodism from 1786 to 1866.* Atlanta, Ga.: A. B. Caldwell, 1913.

——————. *The History of Methodism in Georgia and Florida, from 1785 to 1865.* Macon, Ga.: Jno. W. Burke & Co., 1877.

——————. *Life and Labors of Francis Asbury.* Nashville: Publishing House, M. E. Church, South, 1896.

——————. *The Life and Letters of James Osgood Andrew.* Nashville: Southern Methodist Pub. House, 1882.

——————. *The Life and Times of George Foster Pierce, Bishop of the Methodist Episcopal Church, South, with His Sketch of Lovick Pierce, His Father.* Sparta, Ga.: Hancock Pub. Co., 1888.

Smith, Henry (b. 1769). *Recollections and Reflections of an Old Itinerant.* A series of letters originally published in the *Christian Advocate and Journal,* and the *Western Christian Advocate,* ed. George Peck. New York: Lane & Tippett, 1848.

Smith, Henry (b. 1857). *Wesleyan Methodism in Portsmouth.* London: Charles H. Kelly, 1894.

_____; Swallow, John E.; Treffry, William. *The Story of the United Methodist Church*. London: Henry Hooks, 1933.

Smith, John B. See Blamires and Smith. *Wes. Meth. Church in Victoria*. 1886.

Smith, Matthew D., et al. *Circuit Riders of the Middle Border: A History of Methodism in South Dakota*. N.p.: South Dakota Conference, The Methodist Church, 1965.

Smith, Mary Ann (Clarke). *Raithby Hall: or, Memorial Sketches of Robert Carr Brackenbury of Lincolnshire*. London: Wertheim, Macintosh & Hunt, 1859.

Smith, Timothy. *Revivalism and Social Reform in Mid-Nineteenth-Century America*. Nashville: Abingdon Press, 1957.

Smith, Timothy L. *Called unto Holiness: The Story of the Nazarenes, the Formative Years*. Kansas City, Mo.: Nazarene Publishing House, 1962.

Smith, T. Watson. *History of the Methodist Church within the Territories Embraced in the Late Conference of Eastern British America*. 2 vols. Halifax, N. S.: Methodist Book Room, 1877, 1890.

Smithson, William T., comp. *The Methodist Pulpit South*. 3rd ed. Washington, D. C.: the author, 1859.

Snethen, Nicholas. *Essays on Lay Representation and Church Government, Collected from the Wesleyan Repository, The Mutual Rights, and the Mutual Rights & Christian Intelligencer, from 1820 to 1829 inclusive, and now published in a chronological order, with an introduction by the Rev. Nicholas Snethen*. Baltimore: John J. Harrod, 1835.

Sommer, J. J. See Nuelsen, Mann and Sommer. *Kurzgefasste Geschichte des Methodismus*. 1920.

Southern Christian Advocate, began publication in Charleston, S. C., 1837; became property of M. E. Church, South, 1845-1940. Continued as *South Carolina Methodist Advocate*.

Southern Methodist Review, see *Quarterly Review of the M. E. Church, South*.

Southey, Robert. *The Life of Wesley; and the Rise and Progress of Methodism*. 2 vols. London: Longman, Hurst, Rees, Orme, and Brown, 1820. 3rd ed., with notes by the late Samuel Taylor Coleridge, Esq., and remarks on the life and character of John Wesley, by the late Alexander Knox, ed. by Charles Cuthbert Southey, 1846. Ed. by Maurice H. Fitzgerald, 2 vols., London: Oxford University Press, 1925.

South-Western Christian Advocate, see *Nashville Christian Advocate*.

Souvenir Book of the Golden Anniversary or Jubilee of the Methodist Episcopal Church in Mexico, 1873-1923. Mexico, D.F.: Casa Unida de Publicaciones, 1924.

Sparrow Simpson, William John. *John Wesley and the Church of England*. London: Society for Promoting Christian Knowledge, 1934.

Spayth, Henry G., and Hanby, William. *History of the Church of the United Brethren in Christ*. Circleville, O.: Conference Office of the United Brethren in Christ, 1851.

Speare, E. Ray. *Interesting Happenings in Boston University's History, 1839 to 1951*. Boston: Boston University Press, 1957.

Spencer, Harold, and Finch, Edwin, eds. *The Constitutional Practice and Discipline of the Methodist Church: Prepared by Order of the Methodist Conference*. London: Methodist Publishing House, 1951. 4th ed., rev. by J. Bernard Sheldon, 1964.

Spicer, Tobias. *The Way from Sin to Sanctification, Holiness, and Heaven*. 4th ed., New York: Carlton & Porter, 1857.

Sporri, Theophil. *Das wesentliche methodischer Theologie*. Zurich: Christliche Vereinsbuchhandlung, 1954.

Sprague, William B., ed. *Annals of the American Methodist Pulpit; or, Commemorative Notices of Distinguished American Clergymen of the Methodist Denomination, from Its Commencement to the Close of the Year Eighteen Hundred and Fifty-five with an Historical Introduction*. New York: Robert Carter & Bros., 1861.

Spreng, Samuel P. *A History of the Evangelical Association*. Cleveland, O.: Publishing House of the Evangelical Association, 1913. Rev. ed., *A History of the Evangelical Church*; Harrisburg, Pa.: Board of Publication of the Evangelical Church, 1927.

_____. *The Life and Labors of John Seybert*. Cleveland, O.: Lauer & Mattill, 1888.

_____. *What Evangelicals Believe*. Cleveland, O.: Publishing House of the Evangelical Church, 1929.

Spurgeon, F. Claude, ed. *A.M.E. Zion Handbook*. Washington, D.C., 1952-56.

Stafford, T. A. See Clark and Stafford. *Who's Who in Methodism*. 1952.

Stamp, William Wood. *Historical Notices of Wesleyan Methodism in Bradford and Its Vicinity*. London: Mason, Bradford, Henry Wardman, 1841.

_____. *The Orphan-House of Wesley; with Notices of Early Methodism in Newcastle-upon-Tyne and Its Vicinity*. London: John Mason, 1863.

Stanger, Frank Bateman, ed. *The Methodist Trail in New Jersey: One Hundred and Twenty-five Years of Methodism in the New Jersey Annual Conference, 1836-1961*. N.p.: New Jersey Annual Conference, The Methodist Church, 1961.

Stanley, Edwin James. *Minutes of the Seventh Session of the Montana Annual Conference . . . 1884; Together with a Brief History of the M. E. Church, South, in Montana from 1864 to 1884*. N.p.: the conference, 1884.

_____. *Life of Rev. L. B. Stateler*. Nashville: Publishing House of the M. E. Church, South, 1907; rev. ed., 1916.

Stapleton, Ammon. *Annals of the Evangelical Association of North America and History of the United Evangelical Church*. Harrisburg, Pa.: Publishing House of the United Evangelical Church, 1896. Rev. ed., 1900.

_____. *Flashlights on Evangelical History . . . ; Also Evangelical Daughters of Song*. York, Pa.: the author, 1908.

_____. *A Wonderful Story of Old Time Evangelical Evangelism, Being a Simple Account of the Life and Times of the Rev. Jacob Albright*. Harrisburg, Pa.: Publishing House of the United Evangelical Church, 1917.

Starkey, Lycurgus Monroe, Jr. *The Work of the Holy Spirit: A Study in Wesleyan Theology*. Nashville: Abingdon Press, 1962.

Steele, Daniel. *A Defense of Christian Perfection*. New York: Hunt & Eaton, 1896.

Stephens, John. See Warren and Stephens. *Chronicles*. 1827.

Stephenson, Frank W. *For Such a Time: Bishop James H. Straughn*. N.p.: the author, 1967.

Stephenson, Mrs. Frederick C. (Annie D.). *One Hundred Years of Canadian Methodist Missions, 1824-1924*. 2 vols. Toronto: Missionary Society of the Methodist Church, 1925.

Stephenson, T. Bowman. *William Arthur: A Brief Biography*. London: Charles H. Kelly, 1907.

Stevens, Abel. *An Appeal to the Methodist Episcopal Church Concerning What Its Next General Conference Should Do on the Question of Slavery*. New York: the author, 1859.

_____. *The Centenary of American Methodism: A Sketch of Its History, Theology, Practical System, and Success*. New York: Carlton & Porter, 1865.

_____. *A Compendious History of American Methodism*. New York: Carlton & Porter, 1867.

_____. *Essays on the Preaching Required by the Times, and the Best Methods of Obtaining It*. New York: Carlton & Phillips, 1855.

_____. *History of the Methodist Episcopal Church in the United States of America*. 4 vols. New York: Carlton & Porter, 1864-67.

_____. *The History of the Religious Movement of the*

Eighteenth Century Called Methodism, Considered in Its Different Denominational Forms, and Its Relations to British and American Protestantism. 3 vols. New York: Carlton & Porter; London: Alexander Heylin, 1858-61.

——————. *Life and Times of Nathan Bangs, D.D.* New York: Carlton & Porter, 1863.

——————. *Memorials of the Early Progress of Methodism in the Eastern States: Comprising Biographical Notices of Its Preachers, Sketches of Its Primitive Churches, and Reminiscences of Its Early Struggles and Successes.* Boston: C. H. Peirce & Co., 1852.

——————. *Memorials of the Introduction of Methodism into the Eastern States: Comprising Biographical Notices of Its Early Preachers, Sketches of Its First Churches, and Reminiscences of Its Early Struggles and Successes.* Boston: Charles H. Peirce, 1848.

——————. *Sketches from the Study of A Superannuated Itinerant.* Boston: Charles H. Peirce, 1851.

——————. *Supplementary History of American Methodism: A Continuation of the Author's Abridged History of American Methodism.* New York: Eaton & Mains, 1899.

——————. *The Women of Methodism: Its Three Foundresses, Susanna Wesley, the Countess of Huntingdon, and Barbara Heck; with Sketches of Their Female Associates and Successors in the Early History of the Denomination.* New York: Carlton & Porter, 1866.

Stevenson, George John. *City Road Chapel, London, and Its Associations, Historical, Biographical, and Memorial.* London: the author, 1872.

——————. *Memorials of the Wesley Family.* London: S. W. Partridge & Co.; New York: Nelson & Phillips, 1876.

——————. *The Methodist Hymn Book, Illustrated with Biography, History, Incident, and Anecdote.* London: S .W. Partridge & Co., 1883.

——————. *The Methodist Hymn-Book and Its Associations.* London: Hamilton, Adams & Co., 1869.

——————. *Methodist Worthies: Characteristic Sketches of Methodist Preachers of the Several Denominations, with Historical Sketch of Each Connexion.* 6 vols. London: Thomas C. Jack, 1884-86.

Stevenson, Robert M. *Patterns of Protestant Church Music.* Durham, N. C.: Duke University Press, 1953.

Stewart, Alexander, and Revington, George. *Memoir of the Life and Labours of the Rev. Adam Averell, for Nearly Thirty Years President of the Primitive Wesleyan Methodist Conference.* Dublin: Methodist Book-Room, 1843.

Stewart, John. *Highways and Hedges; or, Fifty Years of Western Methodism.* Cincinnati: Hitchcock & Walden, 1872.

Stotts, Herbert E., and Deats, Paul, Jr. *Methodism and Society: Guidelines for Strategy.* ("Methodism and Society," vol. iv). Nashville: Abingdon Press, 1962.

Straughn, James Henry. *Inside Methodist Union.* Nashville: Methodist Publishing House, 1958.

Strawson, William. *Methodist Theology, 1850-1950.* London: Epworth Press, 1969.

Strickland, William Peter, ed. *Autobiography of Rev. James B. Finley; or, Pioneer Life in the West.* Cincinnati: Methodist Book Concern, 1853.

——————, ed. *Autobiography of Peter Cartwright, the Backwoods Preacher.* New York: Methodist Book Concern, 1856.

——————. *History of the Missions of the Methodist Episcopal Church.* Cincinnati: Swormstedt & Power, 1850.

——————. *The Pioneer Bishop; or, The Life and Times of Francis Asbury.* New York: Carlton & Porter, 1858.

Sugden, Edward Holdsworth. *John Wesley's London: Scenes of Methodist and Worldwide Interest, with Their Historical Associations.* London: Epworth Press, 1932.

Summers, Thomas O., ed. *Biographical Sketches of Eminent Itinerant Ministers . . . Within the Bounds of the Methodist Episcopal Church, South.* Nashville: E. Stevenson & F. A. Owen, 1858.

——————. *Commentary on the Ritual of the Methodist Episcopal Church, South.* Nashville: A. H. Redford, Agent, 1873.

——————, ed. *Duties of Christian Masters,* by Holland N. M'Tyeire. Nashville: Southern Methodist Publishing House, 1859.

Sunman, W. R. *The History of Free Methodism in and About Newcastle-on-Tyne.* Newcastle: A. Dickson, 1902.

Sutherland, Alexander. *Methodism in Canada: Its Work and Its Story; Being the Thirty-third Fernley Lecture Delivered in Penzance, 31st July 1903.* London: Charles H. Kelly, 1903.

Sutton, R. *The Methodist Church Property Case.* New York: Lane & Scott, 1851.

Swain, Clara R. *A Glimpse of India, Being a Collection of Extracts from the Letters of Dr. Clara A. Swain, First Medical Missionary to India of the Woman's Foreign Missionary Society of the Methodist Episcopal Church in America,* edited anonymously. New York: James Pott & Co., 1909.

Swallow, J. Albert. *Methodism in the Light of the English Literature of the Last Century.* Erlanger: A. Deichert, 1895.

Swallow, John E. See Smith et al. *United Methodist Church.* 1933.

Swaney, Charles Baumer. *Episcopal Methodism and Slavery; With Sidelights on Ecclesiastical Politics.* Boston: Richard G. Badger, 1926.

Sweet, William Henry. *A History of Methodism in Northwest Kansas.* Salina, Kans.: Kansas Wesleyan University, 1920.

Sweet, William Warren. *Circuit-Rider Days in Indiana.* Indianapolis: W. K. Stewart Co., 1916.

——————. *Indiana Asbury-DePauw University, 1837-1937: A Hundred Years of Higher Education in the Middle West.* New York: Abingdon Press, 1937.

——————. *Men of Zeal: The Romance of American Methodist Beginnings.* New York: Abingdon Press, 1935.

——————. *Methodism in American History.* New York: Methodist Book Concern, 1933. Rev. ed., Nashville: Abingdon Press, 1954.

——————. *The Methodist Episcopal Church and the Civil War.* Cincinnati: Methodist Book Concern, 1912.

——————, ed. *The Methodists: A Collection of Source Materials.* Vol. IV of "Religion on the American Frontier, 1783-1840." University of Chicago Press, 1946.

——————. *Virginia Methodism: A History.* N.p.: Virginia Conference Historical Society, 1955.

——————. See Herrick and Sweet. *North Indiana Conference.* 1917.

Swift, Wesley F. *Methodism in Scotland: The First Hundred Years.* London: Epworth Press, 1947.

Symons, John C. *Life of the Rev. Daniel James Draper.* London: Hodder & Stoughton, 1870.

Symons, W. *Early Methodism in West Somerset and the Lorna Doone Country.* London: Charles H. Kelly, 1898.

Taft, Mary Barritt. *Memoirs.* Ripon, Yorkshire: the author, 1827; 2nd ed., York, 1828.

Taft, Zechariah. *Biographical Sketches of the Lives and Public Ministry of Various Holy Women.* 2 vols. London: the author, 1825, 1828.

Tallon, Alberto G. *Historia del Metodismo en el Rio de la Plata.* Buenos Aires: Imprenta Metodista, 1936.

Tanner, Benjamin T. *An Apology for African Methodism.* Baltimore: n.p., 1867.

——————. *An Outline of Our History and Government for African Methodist Churchmen.* Philadelphia: Grant, Faires & Rodgers, 1884.

Tatum, Noreen Dunn. *A Crown of Service: A Story of Woman's Work in the Methodist Episcopal Church, South, from*

1878-1940. Cincinnati: Board of Missions, Woman's Division of Christian Service, 1960.

Taylor, Ernest Richard. *Methodism and Politics, 1791-1851.* Cambridge University Press, 1935.

Taylor, John. *The Apostles of Fylde Methodism.* London: T. Woolmer, 1885.

Taylor, William. *Christian Adventures in South Africa.* London: Jackson, Walford, & Hodder, 1867.

————. *The Flaming Torch in Darkest Africa.* New York: Eaton & Mains, 1898.

————. *Four Years' Campaign in India.* London: Hodder & Stoughton, 1875.

————. *Story of My Life, An Account of What I Have Thought and Said and Done in My Ministry of More Than Fifty-three Years in Christian Lands and Among the Heathen, Written by Myself.* New York: Eaton & Mains, 1895; Rev. ed., 1896.

————. *Ten Years of Self-Supporting Missions in India.* New York: the author, 1882.

Tees, Francis Harrison. *The Beginnings of Methodism in England and in America.* Nashville: Parthenon Press, 1940.

————. *Methodist Origins.* Nashville: Parthenon Press, 1948.

Tefft, B. F. See Finley, J. B. *Memorials of Prison Life.* 1850.

Telescope Messenger, first published at Circleville and Dayton, O. as *Religious Telescope,* 1834-1946; merged with *Evangelical Messenger* and published at Harrisburg, Pa., 1947-63.

Telford, John. *The Life of the Rev. Charles Wesley, M.A.* London: Religious Tract Society, 1886. Rev. & enl. ed., London: Wesleyan Methodist Book Room, 1900.

————. *The Life of James Harrison Rigg, D.D., 1821-1909.* By his son-in-law. London: Robert Culley, 1909.

————. *The Life of John Wesley.* London: Hodder & Stoughton, 1886. Rev. & enl. ed., London: Wesleyan Methodist Book Room, 1899.

————. *The Methodist Hymn-Book Illustrated.* London: Charles H. Kelly, 1906. 2nd ed., rev. 1909. 4th ed., 1924.

————. *The New Methodist Hymn-Book Illustrated in History and Experience.* London: Epworth Press, 1934.

————, ed. *Sayings and Portraits of Charles Wesley with Family Portraits, Historic Scenes, and Additional Portraits of John Wesley.* London: Epworth Press, 1927.

————, ed. *Sayings and Portraits of John Wesley.* London: Epworth Press, 1924.

————. *Wesley's Chapel and Wesley's House.* London: Charles H. Kelly, 1906. Rev. ed., 1926.

————. *Wesley's Veterans.* See Jackson. *Lives of Early Methodist Preachers.* 1837-38.

Tewksbury, Donald G. *The Founding of American Colleges and Universities Before the Civil War, with Particular Reference to the Religious Influences Bearing Upon the College Movement.* New York: Columbia University, 1932.

Thoburn, James M. *The Deaconess and Her Vocation.* New York: Hunt & Eaton, 1893.

————. *India and Malaysia.* New York: Hunt & Eaton, 1892.

————. *Life of Isabella Thoburn.* Cincinnati: Jennings & Pye, 1903.

————. *My Missionary Apprenticeship.* New York: Phillips & Hunt, 1884.

Thompson, Bard. *Vanderbilt Divinity School: A History.* Nashville: Vanderbilt University, 1958.

Thompson, Edgar W. *The Methodist Doctrine of the Church.* London: Epworth Press, 1939.

————. *Nathaniel Gilbert: Lawyer and Evangelist.* London: Epworth Press, 1961.

————. *Wesley: Apostolic Man.* London: Epworth Press, 1957.

————. *Wesley at Charterhouse.* London: Epworth Press, 1938.

Thompson, H. A. *Biography of Jonathan Weaver, D.D.* Dayton O.: United Brethren Publishing House, 1901.

————. *Our Bishops.* Chicago: Elder Publishing Co., 1889. Rev. ed., Dayton, O.: United Brethren Publishing House, 1903. 3rd ed., 1906.

Thompson, Richard Walker. *Benjamin Ingham and the Inghamites.* Kendal, Westmorland: the author, 1958.

Thompson, W. H. *Early Chapters in Hull Methodism, 1746-1800.* London: Charles H. Kelly, 1895.

Thomson, D. P. *Lady Glenorchy and Her Churches.* Crieff, Scotland: Research Unit, 1967.

Thomson, Edward. *Our Oriental Missions.* Vol. I, *India and China.* Vol. II, *China and Bulgaria.* Cincinnati: Hitchcock & Walden, 1871.

Thorkildsen, Johan. *Den Norske Metodistkirkes Historie.* Oslo: Norsk Forlagsselskab, 1926.

Thorne, James. *Memoir of William Reed, Bible Christian Minister.* Shebbear, Devonshire: Bible Christian Book Committee, 1869.

————, et al. *A Jubilee Memorial of Incidents in the Rise and Progress of the Bible Christian Connexion.* Shebbear, Devonshire: Bible Christian Book Committee, 1865.

Thorne, John. *James Thorne of Shebbear: A Memoir.* London: Bible Christian Bookroom, 1873.

Thorne, Samuel Ley. *William O'Bryan, Founder of the Bible Christians.* Bradford, 1878.

Thrall, Homer S. *History of Methodism in Texas.* Houston, Tex.: E. H. Cushing, 1872.

Thrift, Charles Tinsley, Jr. *The Trail of the Florida Circuit Rider: An Introduction to the Rise of Methodism in Middle and East Florida.* Lakeland, Fla.: Florida Southern College Press, 1944.

Thrift, Minton. *Memoir of the Rev. Jesse Lee; With Extracts from His Journals.* New York: N. Bangs & T. Mason, 1823.

Tigert, John J. *A Constitutional History of American Episcopal Methodism.* Nashville: Publishing House of the M. E. Church, South, 1894. Rev. ed., 1904. 6th ed., 1916.

————. *The Making of Methodism: Studies in the Genesis of Institutions.* Nashville: Publishing House of the M. E. Church, South, 1898.

Tigert, John James, IV. *Bishop Holland Nimmons McTyeire, Ecclesiastical and Educational Architect.* Nashville: Vanderbilt University Press, 1955.

Tillett, Wilbur Fisk. *Our Hymns and Their Authors: An Annotated Edition of the Hymn Book of the Methodist Episcopal Church, South.* Nashville: Publishing House of the M. E. Church, South, 1889.

————. See Nutter and Tillett. *Hymns and Hymn Writers.* 1911.

Tindall, Edwin H. *The Wesleyan Methodist Atlas of England and Wales, containing fifteen plates, carefully designed and arranged by . . .* London: Wesleyan Conference Office, n.d. [1871].

Tippett, Alan R. *The Christian: Fiji, 1835-1867.* London: Methodist Missionary Society, 1954.

Tipple, Ezra Squier, ed. *Drew Theological Seminary, 1867-1917: A Review of the First Half Century.* New York: Methodist Book Concern, 1917.

————. *Francis Asbury, the Prophet of the Long Road.* New York: Methodist Book Concern, 1916.

Tippy, Worth M. *Frontier Bishop: The Life and Times of Robert Richford Roberts.* Nashville: Abingdon Press, 1958.

Todd, John Murray. *John Wesley and the Catholic Church.* London: Hodder & Stoughton, 1958.

Told, Silas. *An Account of the Life and Dealings of God with Silas Told.* Ed. Samuel Smith. London: Gilbert & Plummer, 1786. Abridgment by John Wesley, *The Life of Mr. Silas Told;* London: Paramore, 1790; recent reprint, London: Epworth Press, 1954.

Tomkinson, Mrs. T. L. *Twenty Years' History of the Woman's Home Missionary Society of the Methodist Episcopal Church, 1880-1900.* Cincinnati: Woman's Home Missionary Society, M. E. Church, 1903.

Towlson, Clifford W. *Moravian and Methodist.* London: Epworth Press, 1957.

Townsend, William John. *The Handbook of the Methodist New Connexion.* London, 1899.

——————. *The Story of Methodist Union.* London: Milner & Co., 1906.

——————; Workman, H. B.; and Eayrs, George, eds. *A New History of Methodism.* 2 vols. London: Hodder & Stoughton, 1909.

Travis, Joseph. *Autobiography of the Rev. Joseph Travis, A.M., a Member of the Memphis Annual Conference. Embracing a Succinct History of the Methodist Episcopal Church, South; Particularly in part of Western Virginia, the Carolinas, Georgia, Alabama, and Mississippi. With Short Memoirs of Several Local Preachers, and an Address to His Friends.* Ed. Thomas O. Summers. Nashville: E. Stevenson & J. E. Evans, 1856.

Treffry, Richard. *Memoirs of the Rev. Joseph Benson.* London: John Mason, 1840.

Treffry, Richard, Sen. *Memoirs of the Rev. Richard Treffry, Jun.* London: John Mason, 1838.

Treffry, William. See Smith et al. *United Methodist Church.* 1933.

Tripp, David H. *The Renewal of the Covenant in the Methodist Tradition.* London: Epworth Press, 1969.

Tuck, Stephen. *Wesleyan Methodism in Frome, Somersetshire.* Frome: the author, 1814.

Tucker, Frank C. *The Methodist Church in Missouri, 1798-1939.* N.p.: Joint Committee of the Historical Societies of the Missouri East and the Missouri West Annual Conferences, 1966.

Turner, George Allen. *The More Excellent Way: The Scriptural Basis of the Wesleyan Message.* Winona Lake, Ind.: Light & Life Press, 1952. Rev. ed., *The Vision Which Transforms: Is Christian Perfection Scriptural?* Kansas City, Mo.: Beacon Hill Press, 1964.

Turner, Henry McNeal. *The Genius and Theory of Methodist Polity, or the Machinery of Methodism.* Philadelphia: Publication Department, A.M.E. Church, 1885.

Tyerman, Luke. *The Life of the Rev. George Whitefield.* 2 vols. London: Hodder & Stoughton, 1876, 1877.

——————. *The Life and Times of the Rev. John Wesley, M.A., Founder of the Methodists.* 3 vols. London: Hodder & Stoughton, 1870-71.

——————. *The Oxford Methodists: Memoirs of the Rev. Messrs. Clayton, Ingham, Gambold, Hervey, and Broughton, with Biographical Notices of Others.* London: Hodder & Stoughton, 1873.

——————. *The Life and Times of the Rev. Samuel Wesley, M.A., Rector of Epworth, and Father of the Revs. John and Charles Wesley, the Founders of the Methodists.* London: Simpkin, Marshall & Co., 1866.

——————. *Wesley's Designated Successor: The Life, Letters, and Literary Labours of the Rev. John William Fletcher, Vicar of Madeley, Shropshire.* London: Hodder & Stoughton, 1882.

United Methodist Church (British). *Book of Services,* 1913.

Urwin, Evelyn Clifford. *The Significance of 1849: Methodism's Greatest Upheaval.* London: Epworth Press, 1949.

——————, and Wollen, Douglas. *John Wesley, Christian Citizen: Selections from His Social Teaching.* London: Epworth Press, 1937.

Veh, Raymond M. *Thumbnail Sketches of Evangelical Bishops.* Harrisburg, Pa.: Evangelical Publishing House, 1939.

Vernon, Walter N. *Methodism Moves Across North Texas.* Dallas, Tex.: Historical Society, North Texas Conference, The Methodist Church, 1967.

——————. *William Stevenson, Riding Preacher.* N.p.: Annual Conference Historical Societies in Texas, 1964.

Versteeg, John M., ed. *Methodism: Ohio Area (1812-1962).* N.p.: Ohio Area Sesquicentennial Committee, 1962.

Vickers, James. *History of Independent Methodism: Sketches of Worthies, Origins of Circuits, Expositions of Principles and Polity.* Bolton: Independent Methodist Bookroom, 1920.

Vickers, John A. *Thomas Coke: Apostle of Methodism.* London: Epworth Press, 1969.

The Voice of Praise; a Collection of Hymns for the Use of the Methodist Church. Compiled and published by Authority of the General Conference. 9th ed. Pittsburgh: Jas. Robison, Publishing Agent, 1876. A publication of the Methodist Protestant Church in the West.

Vulliamy, Colwyn Edward. *John Wesley.* London: Geoffrey Bles, 1931.

Wakefield, Gordon Stevens. *Methodist Devotion: The Spiritual Life in the Methodist Tradition, 1791-1945.* London: Epworth Press, 1966.

Wakeley, Joseph Beaumont. *The Heroes of Methodism: Containing Sketches of Eminent Methodist Ministers and Characteristic Anecdotes of Their Personal History.* New York: Carlton & Phillips, 1856.

——————. *Lost Chapters Recovered from the Early History of American Methodism.* New York: the author, 1858.

Walford, John. *Memoirs of the Life and Labours of the Late Venerable Hugh Bourne.* 2 vols. London: Thomas King, 1855, 1856.

Walker, Frank Deaville. *The Call of the West Indies.* London: Methodist Missionary Society.

Walker, J. U. *A History of Wesleyan Methodism in Halifax, and Its Vicinity.* Halifax, Yorkshire: Hartley & Walker, 1836.

Wallace, David Duncan. *History of Wofford College, 1854-1949.* Nashville: Vanderbilt University Press, 1951.

Walls, William Jacob. *Joseph Charles Price, Educator and Race Leader.* N.p.: the author, 1943.

Wansbrough, Charles E. *Handbook and Index to the Minutes of the Conference.* London: Wesleyan Methodist Book-Room, 1890.

Ward, Alfred Dudley. *The Social Creed of the Methodist Church.* Nashville: Abingdon Press, 1961. Rev. ed., 1965.

Ward, Estelle Frances. *The Story of Northwestern University.* New York: Dodd, Mead & Co., 1924.

Ward, John. *Historical Sketches of the Rise and Progress of Methodism in Bingley, with Brief Notices of Other Places in the Circuit.* Bingley: John Harrison & Son, 1863.

——————. *Methodism in the Thirsk Circuit.* Thirsk: David Peat, 1860.

Ward, Marcus. *The Pilgrim Church: An Account of the First Five Years in the Life of the Church of South India.* London: Epworth Press, 1953.

Ward, William T. See Herbert, Barton and Ward. *Southwest Kansas Conference.* 1932.

Wardle, Addie Grace. *History of the Sunday School Movement in the Methodist Episcopal Church.* New York: Methodist Book Concern, 1918.

Ware, Thomas. *Sketches of the Life and Travels of Rev. Thomas Ware.* New York: Mason & Lane, 1839.

Waring, Edmund H. *History of the Iowa Annual Conference of the Methodist Episcopal Church.* N.p., 1910.

Warner, Wellman J. *The Wesleyan Movement in the Industrial Revolution.* London: Longmans, Green & Co., 1930.

Warren, Samuel, and Stephens, John. *Chronicles of Wesleyan Methodism.* 2 vols. London: John Stephens, 1827.

Washburn, Paul Arthur. *United Methodist Primer.* Nashville: Tidings, 1969.

Wasson, Alfred W. *The Influence of Missionary Expansion upon Methodist Organization.* New York: Commission on Central Conferences, The Methodist Church, 1948.

Watmough, Abraham. *History of Methodism in the Neighbourhood and City of Lincoln.* London: J. Mason, 1829.

Watson, Richard. *A Defence of the Wesleyan Methodist Missions in the West Indies.* London: Thomas Cordeux, 1817.

——————. *The Life of the Rev. John Wesley, A.M., Sometime Fellow of Lincoln College, Oxford, and Founder of the Methodist Societies.* London: John Mason, 1831.

——————. *Observations on Southey's "Life of Wesley:" Being a Defence of the Character, Labours, and Opinions, of Mr. Wesley, Against the Misrepresentations of That Publication.* London: Printed by T. Cordeux, sold by T. Blanchard, 1820.

——————. *Theological Institutes; or, A View of the Evidences, Doctrines, Morals, and Institutions of Christianity.* 4 vols. London: John Kershaw, 1823-26.

Watters, Dennis Alonzo. *First American Itinerant of Methodism, William Watters.* Cincinnati: Curts & Jennings, 1898.

Watters, William. *A Short Account of the Christian Experience and Ministereal Labours of William Watters, Drawn up by Himself.* Alexandria, Va.: S. Snowden, 1806.

Wearmouth, Robert F. *Methodism and the Common People of the Eighteenth Century.* London: Epworth Press, 1945.

——————. *Methodism and the Struggle of the Working Classes, 1850-1900.* Leicester (England): Edgar Backus, 1954.

——————. *Methodism and the Trade Unions.* London: Epworth Press, 1959.

——————. *Methodism and the Working-Class Movements of England, 1800-1850.* London: Epworth Press, 1937. 2nd ed., 1947.

——————. *The Social and Political Influence of Methodism in the Twentieth Century.* London: Epworth Press, 1957.

——————. *Some Working-Class Movements of the Nineteenth Century.* London: Epworth Press, 1949.

Webster, Thomas. *History of the Methodist Episcopal Church in Canada.* Hamilton, Ont.: Canada Christian Advocate Office, 1870.

——————. *Life of Rev. James Richardson, a Bishop of the Methodist Episcopal Church in Canada.* Toronto: J. B. Magurn, Publisher, 1876.

Wedgwood, Julia. *John Wesley and the Evangelical Reaction of the Eighteenth Century.* London: Macmillan & Co., 1870.

Weekley, William M. *Twenty Years on Horseback.* Dayton, O.: United Brethren Publishing House, 1907. 2nd ed., Dayton, Va.: n.p., 1924.

——————, and Fout, Henry H. *Our Heroes.* 2 vols. Dayton, O.: United Brethren Publishing House, 1908, 1911.

Weinlick, John Rudolf. *Count Zinzendorf.* Nashville: Abingdon Press, 1956.

Weldon, Johncy Wood, ed. *Century of Progress, 1846-1946.* Hopkinsville, Ky.: Historical Society, Louisville Annual Conference, The Methodist Church, 1946.

Wesley, Charles. *The Journal of the Rev. Charles Wesley, M.A.* Ed. Thomas Jackson. 2 vols. London: John Mason, 1849. *The Early Journal, 1736-1739,* only, ed. John Telford; London: Robert Culley, 1909.

Wesley, Charles H. *Richard Allen, Apostle of Freedom.* Washington, D. C.: Associated Publishers, Inc., 1935.

Wesley, John, ed. *A Collection of Hymns, For the Use of the People Called Methodists.* London: J. Paramore, 1780.

——————, ed. *A Collection of Psalms and Hymns.* Charles-Town (Charleston, S. C.): Printed by Lewis Timothy, 1737. Rev. eds., London, 1738, 1741, etc. Reprint of first ed. with preface by George Osborne; London: T. Woolmer, 1882. Facsimile in Frank Baker and George Walton Williams, eds., *John Wesley's First Hymn-Book;* Charleston, S. C.: Dalcho Historical Society; London: Wesley Historical Society, 1946.

——————. *Explanatory Notes upon the New Testament.* London: William Bowyer, 1755. American ed.; 3 vols.; Philadelphia: John Dickins, 1791. Recent reprint; London: Epworth Press, 1952.

——————. *The Journal of the Rev. John Wesley, A.M.* Ed. Nehemiah Curnock. Standard Ed. 8 vols. London: Robert Culley (vols. 2-8, Charles H. Kelly), 1909-16.

——————. *The Letters of the Rev. John Wesley, A.M.* Ed. John Telford. Standard Ed. 8 vols. London: Epworth Press, 1931.

——————. *Selections from John Wesley's 'Notes on the New Testament'; Systematically Arranged, with Explanatory Comments.* Ed. John Lawson. London: Epworth Press, 1955.

——————, ed. *The Sunday Service of the Methodists in North America; With Other Occasional Services.* London: n.p., 1784. Rev. ed., omitting "in North America," 1786.

——————. *Wesley's Standard Sermons.* Ed. Edward H. Sugden. 2 vols. London: Epworth Press, 1921.

——————. *The Works of the Rev. John Wesley, A.M.* 32 vols. Bristol: W. Pine, 1771-74. 3rd ed.: 14 vols.; ed. Thomas Jackson; London: John Mason, 1829-31. 4th ed., 1840-42. American ed.; 7 vols.; ed. John Emory; New York: J. Emory & B. Waugh, 1831. Recent reproduction of an 1872 reprint of Jackson 4th ed.; 14 vols.; Grand Rapids, Mich.: Zondervan Publishing House, 1958-59.

——————, and Charles. *The Poetical Works of John and Charles Wesley.* Ed. George Osborn. 13 vols. London: Wesleyan-Methodist Conference Office, 1868-72.

Wesley and His Successors. London: Charles H. Kelly, 1891.

Wesley Historical Society. *Proceedings of. . . .* Burnley and London, 1898- (biennial volumes). *General Index* to Vols. 1-30 published separately.

Wesley Hymn Book. Ed. Franz Hildebrandt. London: A. Weekes & Co., 1959.

The Wesleyan Methodist. Published by the Wesleyan Methodist Church, first at Syracuse, N. Y.; moved to Marion, Ind. 1957. 1843-

Wesleyan Methodist Magazine, see *Arminian Magazine.*

West, Anson. *A History of Methodism in Alabama.* N.p.: the author, 1893.

Western Recorder, see *Methodist Recorder.*

Westin, Gunnar. *George Scott och hans verksamhet i Sverige.* 2 vols. Stockholm: Svenska Kyrkans Diakonistyrelses Bokförlag, 1928, 1929.

Whedon, Daniel. *Letter to Rev. Dr. Stevens, on the Subject of His Late Appeal to the Methodist Episcopal Church.* New York: C. A. Alvord, 1839.

Wheeler, Henry. *Deaconesses, Ancient and Modern.* New York: Hunt & Eaton, 1889.

——————. *History and Exposition of the Twenty-five Articles of Religion of the Methodist Episcopal Church.* New York: Eaton & Mains, 1908.

——————. *Methodism and the Temperance Reformation.* Cincinnati: Walden & Stowe, 1882.

Wheeler, Mary Sparkes. *First Decade of the Woman's Foreign Missionary Society of the Methodist Episcopal Church, With Sketches of its Missionaries.* New York: Phillips & Hunt, 1881.

Whitefield, George. *Journals.* 7 vols. London: James Hutton, 1738-41. *A Short Account of God's Dealings with the Reverend Mr. George Whitefield,* 1740. *A Further Account of God's Dealings with the Reverend Mr. George Whitefield;* London: [the author], 1747. Combined ed., *The Two First Parts of His Life, with His Journals, Revised, Corrected, and Abridged;* London: [the author], 1756. Ed. William Wale, with 1756 omissions restored in brackets; London: Henry J. Drane, 1905; facsimile, Gainesville, Fla.: Scholar's Facsimiles & Reprints, 1969. Ed. Iain Murray, as in 1905 ed., with newly discovered additional journal; London: Banner of Truth Trust, 1960.

——————. *Select Sermons.* London: Banner of Truth Trust, 1958.

——————. *Sermons on Important Subjects; with a Memoir of the Author,* by Samuel Drew, A.M., *and a Dissertation on his Character, Preaching, etc.* by the Rev. Joseph Smith. London: Thomas Tegg & Son, 1836.

———————. *Works.* 6 vols. London: Edward & Charles Dilly, 1771-72.

Whitehead, John. *The Life of the Rev. John Wesley, M.A., Some time Fellow of Lincoln College, Oxford. Collected from his private papers and printed works; and written at the request of his executors. To which is prefixed, some account of his ancestors and relations; with the life of the Rev. Charles Wesley, M.A., collected from his private journal, and never before published. The whole forming a History of Methodism, in which the Principles and Economy of the Methodists are unfolded.* 2 vols. London: printed by Stephen Couchman, sold by Knight & Son, 1793, 1796.

Whiteley, John Harold. *Wesley's England: A Survey of XVIIIth Century Social and Cultural Conditions.* London: Epworth Press, 1938.

Whiteside, J. *History of the Wesleyan Methodist Church of South Africa.* London: Elliot Stock, 1906.

Whitlock, Elias D., et al. *History of the Central Ohio Conference of the Methodist Episcopal Church.* N.p., 1914.

Whitlock, William Francis. *The Story of the Book Concerns.* Cincinnati: Jennings & Pye, 1903.

Who's Who in Methodism, 1933. An Encyclopaedia of the Personnel and Departments, Ministerial and Lay, in the United Church of Methodism. London: Methodist Times and Leader, 1933.

Who's Who in the Methodist Church. Nashville: Abingdon Press, 1966.

Wicke, Myron F. *The Methodist Church and Higher Education, 1939-64.* Nashville: Board of Education, The Methodist Church, 1965.

———————. *A Brief History of the University Senate of The Methodist Church.* Nashville: Board of Education, The Methodist Church, 1956.

Wightman, William May. *Life of William Capers, D.D., One of the Bishops of the Methodist Episcopal Church, South; Including an Autobiography.* Nashville: J. B. M'Ferrin, Agent, 1858.

Wilkinson, John T., ed. *Arthur Samuel Peake, 1865-1929.* London: Epworth Press, 1958.

———————. *Hugh Bourne, 1772-1852.* London: Epworth Press, 1952.

———————. *William Clowes, 1780-1851.* London: Epworth Press, 1951.

Williams, A. H. *Welsh Wesleyan Methodism, 1800-1858: Its Origins, Growth and Secessions.* Bangor, Wales: Cyhoeddwyd Can Lyfrfa'r Methodistiaid, 1935.

Williams, Colin W. *John Wesley's Theology Today.* Nashville: Abingdon Press; London: Epworth Press, 1960.

Williams, Daniel Jenkins. *One Hundred Years of Welsh Calvinistic Methodism in America.* Philadelphia: Westminster Press, 1937.

Williams, Ethel L. *Biographical Directory of Negro Ministers.* New York: Scarecrow Press, 1966.

Williams, James R. *History of the Methodist Protestant Church.* Baltimore: Book Committee, M. P. Church, 1843.

Williams, *Welsh Calvinistic Methodism,* 1884.

Williams, William James. *Centenary Sketches of New Zealand Methodism.* Christchurch: Lyttelton Times Co., 1922.

Willis, Walter A. See Hastling, Willis and Workman. *Kingswood School.* 1898.

Willson, Shipley Well, ed. *The Methodist Preacher.* Boston: John Putnam, 1830.

Wilson, Alpheus W. *Missions of the Methodist Episcopal Church, South.* Nashville: Southern Methodist Publishing House, 1882.

Wilson, David Dunn. *Many Waters Cannot Quench: A Study of the Sufferings of Eighteenth-Century Methodism and Their Significance for John Wesley and the First Methodists.* London: Epworth Press, 1969.

Wilson, Dorothy Clarke. *Palace of Healing: The Story of Dr. Clara Swain, First Woman Missionary Doctor, and the Hospital She Founded.* New York: McGraw-Hill Book Co., 1968.

Wilson, Elizabeth. *Methodism in Eastern Wisconsin. Section One, From the Arrival of the First Missionary in 1832, to the First Publication of the Wisconsin Conference Minutes in 1850.* Milwaukee: Wisconsin Conference Historical Society, M. E. Church, 1938.

Wilson, George W. *Methodist Theology vs. Methodist Theologians.* Cincinnati: Jennings & Pye, 1904.

Wise, Daniel. *Sketches and Anecdotes of American Methodists of "The Days That Are No More."* New York: Phillips & Hunt; Cincinnati: Cranston & Stowe, 1883.

Withrow, William Henry. *Barbara Heck: A Tale of Early Methodism.* Cincinnati: Cranston & Curts, 1895.

Wittke, Carl. *William Nast, Patriarch of German Methodism.* Detroit: Wayne State University Press, 1960.

Wollen, Douglas. Urwin and Wollen. *John Wesley.* 1937.

Wood. Arthur Skevington. *The Burning Heart: John Wesley, Evangelist.* Exeter, Devonshire: Paternoster Press, 1967.

———————. *The Inextinguishable Blaze: Spiritual Renewal and Advance in the Eighteenth Century.* London: Paternoster Press, 1960.

———————. *Thomas Haweis, 1734-1820.* London: S.P.C.K., 1957.

Wood, Ezra Morgan. *The Peerless Orator: The Rev. Matthew Simpson, Bishop of the Methodist Episcopal Church.* N.p.: the author, 1908.

Woodward, Max Wakerley. *One at London: Some Account of Mr. Wesley's Chapel and London House.* London: Epworth Press, 1966.

Woolcock, James. *A History of the Bible Christian Churches on the Isle of Wight.* Newport, I.W.: F. Lee, 1897.

Workman, H. B. See Townsend, Workman and Eayrs. *New History.* 1909.

Workman, Walter Percy. See Hastling, Willis and Workman. *Kingswood School,* 1898.

World Methodist Conference. See *Proceedings of the Ecumenical Methodist Conference.*

World Methodist Council. *Handbook of Information.* Lake Junaluska, N. C., 1966.

Worley, Harry Wescott. *The Central Conference of the Methodist Episcopal Church: A Study in Ecclesiastical Adaptation, or A Contribution of the Mission Field to the Development of Church Organization.* Foochow, China: Christian Herald Mission Press, 1940.

Wright, Richard Robert, Jr. *The Bishops of the African Methodist Episcopal Church.* Nashville: A.M.E. Sunday School Union, 1963.

———————, and Hawkins, John Russell, eds. *Centennial Encyclopaedia of the African Methodist Episcopal Church.* Philadelphia: Book Concern of the A.M.E. Church, 1916. 2nd ed., *The Encyclopaedia,* etc., 1948.

Wunderlich, Friedrich. *Methodists Linking Two Continents.* Nashville: Methodist Publishing House, 1960.

Wynne-Jones, T. *Wesleyan Methodism in the Brecon Circuit; And Introduction of English & Welsh Methodism into the Principality: A Historical and Biographical Sketch from 1750 to 1888.* Brecon, Wales: Edwin Poole, 1888.

Yarnes, Thomas D. *A History of Oregon Methodism.* N.p.: Oregon Methodist Conference Historical Society, 1958.

Yates, Arthur Stanley. *The Doctrine of Assurance; with Special Reference to John Wesley.* London: Epworth Press, 1952.

Yeakel (Jäckel), Reuben. *Geschichte der Evangelischen Gemeinschaft.* 2 vols. Cleveland, O.: Publishing House of the Evangelical Association, 1890, 1895. English trans., *History of the Evangelical Association,* 1894, 1895.

———————. *Jakob Albrecht und seine Mitarbeiter.* Cleveland, O.: W. F. Schneider, 1879. Eng. trans., *Jacob Albright and His Co-Laborers;* Cleveland, O.: Publishing House of the Evangelical Association, 1883.

Yost, William. *Erinnerungen.* Cleveland, O.: Evangelical Association, 1911. Eng. trans., *Reminiscences,* 1911.

Young, Carlton R. See Gealy et al. *Companion to the Hymnal.* 1970.

Young, David. *The Origin and History of Methodism in Wales and the Borders.* London: Charles H. Kelly, 1893.

Young, Dinsdale T. *Peter Mackenzie as I Knew Him.* London: Hodder & Stoughton, 1904.

Young, Egerton Ryerson. *By Canoe and Dog-Train Among the Cree and Salteaux Indians.* London: Charles H. Kelly, 1890.

Young, Jacob. *Autobiography of a Pioneer: or, The Nativity, Experience, Travels, and Ministerial Labors of Rev. Jacob Young, with Incidents, Observations, and Reflections.* Cincinnati: L. Swormstedt & A. Poe, 1857.

INDEX

Disosway, Israel, 2239
dispensaries, 690
dissenters, 576, 1444
Dissinger, Moses, 690
district, 690
District Conferences, 558, 692
District Meeting, 1630
District of Columbia, 100, 691, 2459, 2520
district steward, 2249
district superintendent, 497, 690, 1969, 2239, 2284, 2346, 2347
district trustees, 2371
Divinity of Christ, 693
divorce, 792, 796, 924, 1520, 2193
Dixon, Arminius Gray, 695
Dixon, Dora, 411
Dixon, Ernest Thomas, Jr., 695
Dixon, James, 695
Dixon, James Main, 696
Dixon, John Henry Willis, 696
Dixon, Margaret M. Kuhns, 696, 1577
Dixon, Myles Coupland, 1416
Doak, Rufus, 105
Doak, Samuel, 46
Doane, Nehemiah, 696, 2080
Dobbs, Hoyt McWhorter, 697
Dobbs, Samuel Candler, 1999
Dobby, Eleanor, 697
Dobes, Joseph, 619, 697
Dobson, Hugh Wesley, 697
doctrinal standards, 168, 427, 693, 698, 950, 1149
doctrine, 489, 576, 761, 797, 822, 877, 973, 1024, 1303, 2003, 2366, 2583
Dodd, James Best, 703
Dodd, Thomas John, 703
Dodge, Eleanor, 2436
Dodge, Ella J., 123
Dodge, Ralph Edward, 703
Dodge City, Kan., 704
Dodson, Mary Irene, 2106
Doering, Karl E., 1061
Doescher, Arthur H., 704
Doggert, David Seth, 705
Doherty, Robert R., 705
Dold, Jane, 190
Dollarhide, Edna, 407
Dolliver, Jonathan Prentiss, 706
Dollner, Harald, 656
Dominican Evangelical Church, 706
Dominican Republic, 87, 706, 879, 1056, 1415, 1636, 2533
Donoghue, Catherine, 2365
Donaldson, Moselle Mar, 338
Donaldson, Thomas, 816
Doney, Carl Gregg, 708
Donly, John, 1417
Donly, Rosa, 1417
Donnan, William Hanover, 1498
Donnati, Mateo, 707
Donnelly, Walter Edward, 708
Donohugh, Emma, 709
Donohugh, Thomas S., 708, 1426
Dorchester, Daniel, 2229
Dorchester, Jean, 1069
Dorey, George, 402
Dorion, Thomas A., 1513
Dorman, Edna, 1406
Dorough, Millie, 1906
Dorsey, Daniel, 436
Dorsey, Dennis B., 709, 915, 1578
Dorsey, Eliza, 1504
Doty, Anne, 689

Doub, Peter, 709, 1038, 1120
Doub, Valentine, 1320
Doucette, Kathleen, 2289
Dougherty, George, 710
Dougherty Manual Labor School, S. C., 2208
Doughty, Benjamin B., 237
Doughty, Clara C., 1012
Doughty, Maurine, 2125
Doughty, Rachel, 182
Douglas, Briley, 1657
Douglas, George, 710, 2397
Douglas, John, 2382
Douglass, Celia, 1846
Douglass, Rose D., 69
Douglass, Thomas Logan, 383, 710
Douthit, Susie Olivia, 2563
Dove, James, 711
Dover, N. H., 711
Dow, Lorenzo, 382, 384, 512, 711, 1066, 1339, 1456, 1703, 1951, 1953, 2024
Dowd, Lenora A., 1245
Dowdell, Mrs. E. C., 179
Dowds, Lucretia, 1306
Downer, Pierce, 712
Downers Grove, Ill., 712
Downes, Charles, 712, 1686
Downes, John, 712, 2498, 2515
Downey, David George, 712
Downey, J. R., 713, 2334
Downey, Calif., 713
Downs, Ellen, 2034
Downs, Jane Baldwin, 2349
Downs, John, 638
Doxology, 713
Doyle, Bertram Wilbur, 714
Doyle, Rotha Dorun, 1822
Draher, Minnie, 506
Drake, Benjamin M., 714, 1643, 1730
Drake, Ethelbert, 2433, 2434
Drake, Grace, 1354
Drake, Laura Stevenson, 2098
Draper, Daniel J., 715, 1544, 2423, 2469
Dravo, John Fleming, 716
Dream, Emily H., 2256
Dredge, James, 2423
Drees, Charles W., 132, 716, 1963
Dreisbach, John, 716, 803, 1755
Dreisbach, Martin, 716, 970
Drescher, Mildred G., 717
dress, 717, 1408
Drew, Daniel, 718, 719
Drew, Laura, 2549
Drew, Samuel, 719
Drew Seminary for Women, 751, 1741
Drew University, 202, 718, 719, 2530
Drew Univ. Theological School, 433, 720, 922, 1725
Drewry, William Francis, 2433
Dreyer, Adele Ann, 2555
Dribble, Hannah, 2610
Driffield, William, 1926
Drinkhouse, Edward Jacob, 720
Driver, LaRose, 1384
Dromgoole, Edward, 720, 874
Dropiowski, Hania Maria, 2453
Dropiowski, Peter Z. W., 721, 1928
Drummond, James, 721
Drury, Augustus Waldo, 721
Drury, Marion Richardson, 722
Drury, Philo, 707
Dryden, Miriam Byrd, 415
Dryer, Ardalissa, 1612
Duarte, Glaucia W., 2437

Dublin, Ireland, 722
Du Bose, Horace Mellard, 723
Dubose, Martha, 2575
Dubrovin, Sergei, 204
Dubs, C. Newton, 476, 723
Dubs, Rudolph, 724, 2394
Dudley, Hannah, 841
Dudley, Mary Anne, 1650
Duer, James, 381
Dugmore, Henry Hare, 724
Duke, James, 1498
Duke, James Buchanan, 725
Duke, Washington, 725, 734, 1771
Duke, William, 725
Duke Endowment, 725
Duke University, 602, 725, 726, 734, 750, 839, 1768, 1771, 2530
Duke Univ. Divinity School, 727
Duluth, Minn., 727
Duncan, Hugh, 2432
Duncan, James A., 727
Duncan, Lydia, 281
Duncan, Mary M. Faris, 418
Duncan, William Wallace, 728
Duncan Chapel, Va., 826
Dunedin, N. Z., 728
Dunham, Darius, 729
Dunholme Theological College, N. Z., 179, 899
Dunkle, William Frederick, Jr., 729
Dunlap, David R., 455, 456
Dunlap, E. Dale, 2520
Dunlap, John Francis, 730
Dunn, Bessie, 243
Dunn, Charles S. H., 730
Dunn, Harriet, 1386
Dunn, Mary Alice, 1201
Dunn, Mary McCarthy, 94
Dunn, Samuel, 333, 730, 859, 2142, 2508, 2526, 2527
Dunnavant, Martha Virginia, 1011
Dunstan, Alfred Gilbert, 731
Dunton, Lewis Marion, 731, 2209
Dunwell, Joseph R., 731, 1001
Dunwoody, Samuel, 731, 2101
DuPre, Arthur Mason, 731
Dupree, Eula, 1974
Durbin, John A., 682
Durbin, John Price, 732, 1076
Durbin, Mary, 1157
Durbin, William, 816
Durdis, George R., 204
Duren, William Larkin, 733
Durfee, Lillian, 2368
Durham, Emily, 1675
Durham, Molly, 2567
Durham, Plato Tracy, 733
Durham, N. C., 734
Durst, Margaret, 1518
Dusenberry, Elizabeth, 2430
Dustin, Caleb, 512
Duttenhoffer, Julia Marie, 584
Duvall, Richard P., 1372
Dwane, James, 2203
Dwarahath, India, 96
Dyar, Phoebe Martha, 1166
Dycus, Effie, 1341
Dyer, Alice Marie, 2236
Dyer, John L., 134, 544, 734, 827, 2093
Dyer, N. M., 1904
Dymond, Francis John, 735, 1932
Dyson, Martin, 2083, 2425

Eagan, Ellen, 171
Eagles, J. Ernest, 2531
Eagon, Sampson, 2241
Eakle, Sarah, 1925
Eammons, Elizabeth, 2562
Early, John, 736, 1724, 1984
Early, Jordan Winston, 736, 1729
East Alabama College, 2097
East Asia Christian Conference, 736
East Baltimore Conf., 209, 437
East Columbia Conf., 1657, 1784, 1820, 2458
East Des Moines Conf. (UB), 963, 1232
Easter, John, 738, 1892
Eastern Conf. (EA), 970, 1634, 2287; (EUB), 738; (MP), 1737, 2217; (UB), 965
Eastern Pennsylvania Conf., 2069
Eastern Swedish Conf., 739, 1736, 2295
East Florida Seminary, 857
East Genesee Conf., 436, 922, 1736
East German Conf. (ME), 737, 922, 1736
East German Conf. (UB), 961
East Greenwich Academy, R. I., 751, 1721, 1958, 2009
East Maine Conf., 737, 919, 921, 1506, 1507
East Maine Conf. Seminary, 737
Eastman, C. R., 513
East Nebraska Conf. (UB), 966, 984
East North Carolina Conf. (MP), 1769
East Ohio Conf. (UB), 1802; (ME), 737, 786, 1777, 1779, 1799, 1922; (UM), 1779
East Oklahoma Conf. (MES), 1806
East Oklahoma Mission (ME), 1806
East Orange, N. J., 737
East Oregon and Washington Conf., 1820, 1844, 2458
East Pennsylvania Conf. (EA), 971; (UB), 959, 961, 962, 965, 984, 2287
East Tennessee Conf. (ME), 1145, 2325; (UB), 966, 2325
East Tennessee Female Institute, 1475
East Texas Conf. (ME), 1778, 2329; (MES), 738
East Wisconsin Conf., 2581
Eatherton, James, 1431
Eaton, John, 2530
Eayrs, Essay, 739
Ebbert, Isabel B., 1169
Ebenezer Academy, Va., 162, 739, 2433
Ebenezer Manual Labor School, Ill., 72
Ebenezer Mitchell Industrial School, N. C., 1893
Eberhart, Lila Maude, 1154
Ebert, Philip, 464
Ebright, Donald F., 740
Eby, C. S., 1260
Eby, Edwin S., 1901
Ecaussines D'Eghien, Belgium, 740
Eccles, Robert S., 2520
ecclesiastical code, 923

McFarlane, Sarah Harriett, 2614
McFarlin, Robert, 1763
McFate, Alta E., 1531
McFerrin, James, 1487
McFerrin, John Berry, 644, 1487
McFerrin, Myra Anderson, 2260
McGary, Hugh, 817
McGee, Adelaide Frances, 2484
McGee, Emma O., 1282
McGee, Frances, 711
McGee John and William, 382
MacGeary, John Samuel, 1488
McGehee, Edward, 1488, 1727, 2597
McGovern, George Stanley, 1489
McGrew, George Harrison, 2288
McIan, Robert Ronald, 2515
McIntire, Zora Belle, 1161
McIntosh, Alice, 2264
McIntosh, Mabel Ida, 581
McIntosh, Patsy, 260
McIntosh, William, 1210, 1211
McIntyre, Carl, 1851
McIntyre, Robert, 1489
McKay, Kate, 1872
McKay, Orville Herbert, 1489
McKay, William John, 1489
McKean, Franklin, 134, 1904
McKean, James, 1257
McKechnie, Colin Campbell, 1490
McKendree, William, 369, 574, 780, 1490, 1805, 1980, 2284
McKendree Chapel, 1491, 1646, 2150
McKendree College, 72, 614, 1491
McKenna, David L., 1491
McKenny, Samuel, 2461
McKenry, Lydia, 2342
McKenzie, John W. P., 1492
MacKenzie, Peter, 1492
Mackenzie College, Brazil, 379
McKenzie College, Texas, 1492, 1778, 2220
McKinley, Harriet, 1003
McKinley, William, 408, 826, 1492, 1562, 2463
McKinney, Betty Ruth, 2596
McKinney, John Wesley, 1492
MacKinnon, Sallie Lou, 1493
McKinnon, Susie, 1610
McKnight, E. B., 1928
McKnight, George, 1493, 1768
McKnight, W. P., 596
McKown, Burr H., 183
McLain, John, 619
McLain, Peter, 1263
McLarty, Alexander, 1607
McLaughlin, David, 2245
McLaughlin, E. T., 1108
McLaughlin, John Russell, 1493
McLaughlin, Susan E., 852
McLaughlin, William Patterson, 1493
Maclay, Charles, 1494
Maclay, Robert S., 475, 1350, 1494, 1635
Maclay College of Theology, Calif., 1494, 2108
McLean, Frances, 1489
McLean, James, 1307
McLean, John (1775-61), 930, 1494
Maclean, John (1851-28), 1495

McLean, John H., 1495, 2438
McLellan, Margaret, 1607
McLenahan, William, 851
McLeod, Asabella, 2176
M'Leod, D. C., 1211
MacLeod, Earle H., 608
McLeod, Samuel, 260
McLoughlin, John, 1407, 2410
M'Mackin, Martha, 1478
McMahan, Samuel D., 135, 1495, 2328
McMahan Chapel, 1495, 2150, 2328, 2331
McMain, P. P., 864
McMichael, Jack, 794
McMillan, Carrie, 348
McMillan, Ethel, 1496
MacMillan, Kirkpatrick, 2087
M'Mullen, James, 1002, 1496
McMullen, Wallace, 1496
McMurdy, R. M., 2024
McMurray, Grace Eleanor, 314
MacMurray, James E., 1496
McMurray, Ruth, 337
MacMurray College, 1496, 1786
McMurry, William Fletcher, 1496
McMurry College, 46, 1496
McNabb, G. Y., 271
McNamar, John, 1803
MacNaughton, Norman, 1497
McNeely, Laura, 2482
McNeil, Amy, 370
Macon, Nathaniel, 1984
Macon, Ga., 1497
McPheeters, Julian C., 1498, 2090
McPherson, Harry W., 1498
McPherson, Laura A., 1380
McQuigg, James, 1499
McRaeny, Kate L., 70
MacRossie, Allan, 1499
McSwain, Mary, 2026
McSwean, Nancy, 612
McSween, John, 856
M'Timkulu, D. G. S., 87
McTyeire, Amelia, 2343
McTyeire, Holland N., 488, 1499, 2411
McTyeire Home and School, China, 1101
McVeigh, Eliza Whiteman, 1319
McVittie, Dorothy Eloise, 1353
McWherter, Adelaide, 633
McWright, A., 1185
Macy, Victor, W., 1500
Madan, Martin, 1500
Maddock, John, 1417
Maddy, Ruth, 1014
Madeira, 1089
Madhya Pradesh Conf., 1500
Madison, James, 1436
Madison, Wisc., 1501
Madison College, Miss., 1642, 2131
Madison College, Pa., 937, 1473, 1501, 1579, 1922
Madsdatter, Birthe, 483
Mael, Edra, 1125
Maffitt, J. N., 918
Magaret, Ernst Carl, 1501
Magata, David, 1502
magazines, 1502; see also Periodicals
Magee, J. C., 429
Magee, Junius Ralph, 608, 1503
Magic Methodists, 603, 672, 863, 1504
Magor, Louise Eugenia, 2348

Magruder, Susan Priscilla Hawkins, 715
Mahabane, Ezekiel Egbert, 1504
Mahabane, Zaccheus Richard, 1504
Mahaffie, Frances Marie, 1698
Mahan, Asa, 1140
Mahator, Samuel, 1204
Mahin, Milton, 1504
Mahon, Robert Henry, 1505
Mahoney, Obadiah, 1921
Mahurin, Mary K., 2036
Mahy, William, 577, 802, 871
Main, Idabelle Lewis, 1505
Maine, 737, 1325, 1505-7, 1654, 1935, 1989, 2065
Maine Camp Meetings, 1506
Maine Conf. (ME), 737, 915, 1506, 1507, 1721; (MP) 936
Maine Wesleyan Seminary, 1324, 1506, 1507, 2359
Mair, George, 756
Maitland, Australia, 1507
Maize, Michael, 993
Major, John, 991
Makowska, Zofja, 2303
Malaysia, 126, 1205, 1221, 1470, 1507, 1635, 1810, 2096, 2161, 2454, 2618
Malaysia and Singapore, Methodist Church of, 1509
Malaysia Mission Conf., 1509
Malden, Mass., 1509
Maldini, Ida, 2198
Malin, Doris, 1032
Mallalieu, Willard Francis, 1509
Mallan, Walter, 2245
Mallilieu University, Neb., 1707
Mallinson, William, 1509
Mallinson Trust, 1510
Maltby, William Russell, 1510
Malvern, Ark., 1510
Manchester, Ark., 1510
Manchester, Conn., 1510
Manchester, England, 1511
Manchester, N. H., 1512
Manefield, Albert George, 1513
Manget, Fred P., 1517
Mangungu, N. Z., 1513
Manhattan, Kan., 1513
Manila, Philippines, 1514
Manley, John, 1514, 1874
Manley, Robert, 1517
Manley's Chapel, 1514, 1874
Manluff, John G., 652
Mann, Ernst, 1917, 2297
Mann, Horace, 430, 1019
Mann, James and John, 279, 386, 1737
Mann, Johann, 1231
Manning, Charles, 1515
Mansell, Henry, 1467, 1515, 2288
Mansfield, Ralph, 1515
Mansfield Female College, La., 1457, 1777
Manska, Irena, 250
Manso, Juana, 1515
Mantripp, Joseph Closs, 1516
Manual Labor School, Ga., 1516
Maori King Movement, 1516
Maoris, 481, 1743, 2486
Marchant, George, 329
Marchinton, Philip, 1057
Mariah, Henrietta, 1235
Marietta, Ga., 1516
Marietta, Ohio, 1517
Marion, Ohio, 1517

Marion College, Ind., 2524
Markey, M. Belle, 1518
Markham, Edwin, 1518
Markham, Thomas, 1415
Markham, W. H., 2074
Marksman, Peter, 1383, 1518
Markwood, Jacob, 1518
Marlatt, Earl, 549
Marlatt, Washington, 1513, 1519
Marrett, William, 1695
marriage, 796, 912, 1519, 1998, 2025, 2193; of ministers, 1521
Marriott, William, 1521, 2530
Marrs, Mary Elizabeth, 2187
Marsden, Mrs. John E., 884
Marsden, Joseph H., 1441
Marsden, Samuel, 1418
Marsh, Charles Frank, 1521
Marsh, Daniel L., 1522
Marsh, Edward, 1717
Marsh, Freeman, 533
Marsh, Madeleine Elizabeth, 677
Marsh, Rose, 1871
Marshall, Charles Kimball, 1522
Marshall, Romey P., 1817
Marshall, Thomas Joseph, 622
Marshall, William, 1522
Marshall Scholarships, 1523
Marston, David, 1655
Marston, Leslie Ray, 1523
Martha's Vineyard Camp Meeting Assoc., 1523
Martin, Charlotte, 2505
Martin, Erma, 1106
Martin, Even W., 513
Martin, George W., 1845
Martin, Glenn L., 1313
Martin, Ida L., 2181
Martin, Irene, 1187
Martin, Isaac Patton, 1524
Martin, John R., 319
Martin, John S., 210, 1524
Martin, John Thomas, 1524, 1526, 1946
Martin, Joseph C., 1524
Martin, Laura A., 602
Martin, Margaret Kerr, 455
Martin, Paul Elliott, 1525
Martin, Samuel, 2205
Martin, William Clyde, 547, 1525
Martin College, 1526
Martindale, William J., 1526
Martins, Alcina, 1254
Martins, Nair G., 2437
Marvin, Enoch Mather, 1526, 2070
Marvin, John E., 1604
Marvin, Marcia, 418
Marvin College, 436, 2074
Maryland, 111, 204, 260, 291, 464, 533, 612, 816, 863, 874, 892, 927, 1023, 1050, 1054, 1185, 1317, 1320, 1432, 1462, 1528, 1529, 1670, 1830, 1877, 2040, 2156, 2188, 2261, 2359, 2541, 2545, 2546
Maryland Conf. (MP), 650, 1529, 1877, 2433, 2445, 2459; (UB), 963, 964, 965
Marylebone, London, 1445
Maryville German Institute, 374
Maser, Frederick Ernest, 1530, 2068
Mashaba, Ndevu, 1683
Mashaba, Robert, 1530

Showers, John Balmer, 2148
Showers, Justina Lorenz, 2148
Shreveport, La., 2149
Shrewsbury, William J., 2150
Shrines, Landmarks, and Sites, 2150
Shuck, Daniel, 2150
Shuey, William J., 2151, 2153
Shuler, Robert P., 2151
Shultz, Elsie, 2121
Shultz, W. M., 1018
Shumaker, Edward S., 2153
Shumaker, Jacob, 1459
Shumaker, James L., 2146
Shumate, W. D., 1343
Shungu, John Wesley, 568, 2152, 2489
Shupp, Helen May, 755
Shuttleworth, J. K., 2279
Shy, Peter Randolph, 2152
Sia Sek-ong, 2126
Siberts, S. W., 825
Sierra Leone, 59, 197, 428, 836, 960, 1016, 1087, 1313, 1574, 2001, 2152, 2156, 2177, 2444, 2455, 2524
Sigg, Ferdinand, 2154
Sigston, James, 1957
Sillers, Caroline, 774
Silva, Alfredo Henrique da, 1939, 2154
Silva, Evodia C., 1392
Silva, F. S. de, 441
Silva, G. Denzil de, 441
Silva, Joao P. Daronch da, 2155
Silva, Juvenal Ernesto da, 2155
Silva, Lydia W. da, 2437
Silva, Oswaldo Dias da, 2156
Silveira, Guaracy, 2156
Silver, Mabel Irene, 2156
Silvera, Aurelio, 610
Silvera, Teresa, 1392
Silver Spring, Md., 2156
Simenton, Minnie, 1159
Simeon, Charles, 806
Simerson, Sarah Ellen, 1010
Simester, Elsie, 899
Simon, Grace Elizabeth, 1084
Simon, Lottye B., 2132
Simonds, Joseph Henry, 2157
Simmons, Florence, 2010
Simmons, James, 2157
Simmons, John C., 2157
Simmons, Laura Maria, 2261
Simmons, Ned, 1936
Simms, James, 2229
Simon, John Smith, 2157
Simons, George Albert, 759, 843, 2057, 2157
Simpson College, 667, 850, 2160
Simpson, David, 2158
Simpson, Edward R., 1264
Simpson, Elizabeth, 724
Simpson, Hannah, 1032
Simpson, James, 2158
Simpson, John Dixon, 2159
Simpson, John Fisher, 2159
Simpson, Lula Mae, 2381
Simpson, Matthew, 134, 640, 663, 1897, 2159
Simpson, Robert, 2221
Simpson, Thomas H., 1939
Simpson, William, 1814, 2160
Sims, David Henry, 2160
Sims, James, 1198
Sims, Mary T., 2472
sin, 1875
Sinclair, Benjamin, 2244, 2598
Sinclair, Effie, 302
Sinclair, Elijah, 857
Sinclair, W. A., 1834

Singapore, 101, 443, 1470, 1474, 1507, 1635, 1810, 2161
Singh, Ashoke B., 2162
Singh, J. C. Bhan, 233
Singh, Lilavati, 2162
Singh, Mangal, 2162
Singh, Masih Charan, 2163
Singh, Satyavati, 478
singing, 967
Sioux Falls, S. D., 2163
Sioux Indian Mission, 2164
Sipple, Marian and Waitman, 227
Sipprell, Wilford James, 2164
Sisk, Henry Clay, 1633
Sites, Nathan, 2165
sites, 2150
Sitler, Jacob, 2621
Skagge, Eva, 1483
Skelton, Eliza, 2493
Skevington, John, 2165
Skillington, James Edgar, 688, 2165
Slade, Edmond B., 2165
Slade, John, 857, 2166
Slason, James L., 1396
Slater, Josiah, 2201
Slater, Oliver Eugene, 2166
slavery, 790, 876, 912, 914, 915, 930, 958, 1571, 2167, 2171, 2323, 2384, 2434, 2500, 2523
Sledd, Andrew, 405, 2172
Sleeper, Jacob, 304, 1076, 2172
Slicer, Henry, 2172
Sloan, David, 247
Sloan, Harold Paul, 2173
Sloane, Israel, 2173
Slocum, William Esler, 1817
Sloss, Nell Virginia, 309
Slutz, Frank Durward, 2173
Slutz, Leonard Doering, 2173
Sluyter, Eunice, 2174
Smales, Gideon, 2174
Small, John Bryan, 2174
Small, Sam, 1992
Smart, A. B., 2531
Smart, James S., 2175
Smart, Wyatt Aiken, 898, 2175
Smedly, Narcissus, 1012
Smetham, James, 2175
Smiley, Velma Grace, 541
Smith, Alexander Coke, 2176
Smith, Alfred Franklin, 2176
Smith, Alicia, 1387
Smith, Alma Pauline, 354
Smith, Amelia, 2056
Smith, Angie Frank, 2176
Smith, Anna, 1983
Smith, Anna B., 2011
Smith, Anna Churchill, 2177
Smith, Belle C., 343
Smith, Benjamin Julian, 2177
Smith, Bessie Archer, 1392
Smith, Bethavery, 2437
Smith, Boje, 656
Smith, Carlotta Grace, 1833
Smith, Charles Ryder, 2177
Smith, Charles Spencer, 2177
Smith, Charles William, 2178, 2564
Smith, Chester A., 2178
Smith, Claude L., 1200
Smith, David Morton, 2178
Smith, E. McLeod, 2091
Smith, E. Thursfield, 2530
Smith, Earl M., 2179
Smith, Earnest Andrew, 2179
Smith, Edward, 606, 834, 2179
Smith, Edwin, William, 2180
Smith, Eleanor M., 1540

Smith, Elizabeth, 906, 1014
Smith, Elmeda, 730
Smith, Emily, 2020
Smith, Epie Duncan, 1926
Smith, Ethel Christian, 511
Smith, Eugene Lewis, 2180
Smith, Eugenia, 244
Smith, Eula Ethel, 1877
Smith, F. Porter, 598
Smith, Ferdinand, 1652
Smith, Franklyn G., 2221
Smith, George, 1046, 1318, 2180
Smith, George Gilman, 2180
Smith, Gervase, 2181
Smith, Gladys, 262
Smith, Harriet, 1332
Smith, Harry Lester, 2181
Smith, Henry, 2181
Smith, Henry A., 1460
Smith, Henry Weston, 642, 2181
Smith, Horace Greeley, 2182
Smith, Isaac, 546, 2182
Smith, J. A., 805
Smith, J. Hal, 2177
Smith, J. W., 2400
Smith, James, 917
Smith, Jedediah Strong, 372, 642, 1719, 2088, 2183, 2405
Smith, John, 1998, 2183
Smith, John Bryan, 1001
Smith, John L., 2183
Smith, John M., 1680
Smith, John Owen, 2183
Smith, Joseph, 731
Smith, Josephine, 2122
Smith, Legrand B., 2184
Smith, Leonora, 2096
Smith, Lucien, 805
Smith, Lucius C., 470
Smith, Lucy G., 2399
Smith, Lula, 2127
Smith, Margaret Frances, 2359
Smith, Marion Lofton, 2184
Smith, Martha Eloise, 645
Smith, Mary A., 825
Smith, Mary Ann Akle, 1254
Smith, Matthew Dinsdale, 2184
Smith, Merlin G., 2185
Smith, Mildred, 1842
Smith, Ola, 861
Smith, Philander, 391, 2185
Smith, Rachel, 1003
Smith, Richard, 816
Smith, Rockwell Carter, 2185
Smith, Rodney ("Gipsy"), 380, 2185
Smith, Roy L., 2186
Smith, Ruth, 429, 1183
Smith, Sarah Elizabeth, 1196
Smith, Sylvester, 2128
Smith, Thomas Watson, 2186
Smith, Thornley, 2620
Smith, Wilbur Kirkwood, 2186
Smith, William, 532
Smith, William Andrews, 2187
Smith, William Angie, 2187, 2432
Smith, William Milton, 2188
Smith, William Waugh, 1472, 2433
Smithies, John, 2189, 2539
Smith Island, 2188
smoking, 797
smuggling, 2189
Smyth, Tobias, 887
Smyth, William Henry, 2189
Smythe, Hannah B., 2020
Snader, William, 816
Snaith, Norman Henry, 2189

Snavely, Guy Everett, 2190
Snavely, H. R., 1402
Snead, John H., 2190
Snead College, Ala., 2190
Sneath, Richard, 381
Snelling, Joseph, 1699
Snethen, Nicholas, 495, 643, 1529, 1578, 2190, 2419
Snider, Susie, 1330
Snook, Delilah S., 886
Snow, Elizabeth M., 299
Snow Creek Church, 2191
Snowden, Rita Frances, 2911
Snowfields, London, 1445
Snyder, Alice C., 1442
Snyder, Elizabeth, 1718
Snyder, Henry Nelson, 2191
Snyder, Samuel S., 2191
Snyder, Thorton A., 1009
social concerns (Br.), 483, 2192; (Can.) 397; (N.Z.) 1746
Social Concerns, Board of Christian, 584, 790, 1565, 1572, 1594, 2171, 2192
Social Creed, 792, 926, 1562, 1565, 2193
society, 509, 520, 2194, 2249, 2525
Society for the Propagation of the Gospel in Foreign Parts, 2195
Society of Friends, 1969
Sockman, Ralph Washington, 1739, 2195
Soete, Hans, 204
Soledade, Anna de, 1017
Solomon, Abraham, 2195
Solomon, Halina, 2132
Solomon Islands, 340, 1833, 2196, 2393
Someillan, Enrique Benito, 610, 2196
Someillan, H. B., 1392
Someren, Van, 1070
Sommer, C. Ernst, 2196
Sommer, J. W. Ernst, 2196
Sommers, Louisa, 1112
Sone, Law, 2331
Soochow University, China, 2618
Soong, Charles Jones, 416, 456, 465, 2197
Soong, T. V., 416
Soothill, William Edward, 477, 2197
Soper, Donald, 2198
Soper, Edmund Davison, 2198
Soremekun, Joseph, 1756
sortilege, 2116, 2198
Sosa, Adam F., 2198
Soto, Asensi Miguel, 2199
Soule, Agnes Louisa, 2126
Soule, Joshua, 574, 914, 1458, 1572, 2199
Soulesbury Institute, Ark., 136
Soule University, Texas, 1662, 2220
South, Margaret E., 2451
South Africa, 43, 64, 94, 124, 125, 190, 312, 332, 360, 376, 518, 578, 599, 678, 724, 748, 755, 784, 818, 879, 907, 1072, 1101, 1139, 1247, 1306, 1316, 1321, 1333, 1340, 1354, 1432, 1455, 1502, 1504, 1530, 1534, 1542, 1636, 1653, 1671, 1673, 1794, 1856, 1889, 2018, 2078, 2111, 2133, 2135, 2136, 2200,

Uzaki, Kogoro, 2406
Uzaki, Takesaburo, 2407

Vail, Lucy Ann, 1975
Vaktaren, 437
Valdosta, Ga., 2408
Valencia, Jose Labarrete, 2408
Valens, Jessie Walker, 125
Valentine, Eliza, 1319
Valenzuela, Raimundo A., 473, 2408
Valley Stream, N. Y., 2409
Valton, John, 2409
Van Anda, J. A., 1644
Vance, Anne Edgeworth, 1950
Vance, Robert B., 409
Van Cott, Margaret Newton, 2409
Van Courtland, Pierre, 2409
Vancouver, Wash., 2410
Vancura, Vaclav, 619, 2410
Vanderberg, Martha, 1429
Vanderbilt, Cornelius, 648, 2411
Vanderbilt University, 749, 900, 931, 932, 1113, 1500, 1777, 1819, 2410, 2576
Vanderhorst, Richard H., 488, 2412
Vandervies, Maria, 1388
Vanderwood, Ralph, 805
Van Deusen, Henry R., 1286, 2410
Vanduzar, J. E. A., 2412
Vandyke, Edward Howard, 2412
Van Dyke, Mary Elizabeth, 2595
Van Erden, Eva, 110
Van Groningen, Annie J. M., 2412
Vann, Beulah Jackson, 2181
Van Ness, Sarah, 47
Van Orsdel, William W., 478, 1095, 1108, 1195, 1644, 1656, 1817, 2413
Van Pelt, Benjamin, 1144, 2414
Vanpelt, John F., 455
Van Pelt, Peter, 1739, 2239, 2414
Vanstone, Thomas Grills, 1932, 2414
Van Valin, Clyde E., 2414
Vanvelzer, Edith, 708
Vargas, E. B., 805
Varick, James, 2055, 2414
Vary, Jessie A., 143
Vasey, Thomas, 495, 529, 604, 1200, 1556, 1989, 2415
Vashti Industrial Institute, 484, 992, 2211
Vasquez, Remigio, 133
Vatican Council, 745, 1566, 1608
Vaugh, W. H., 2438
Vaughn, Rissie, 1155
Vaught, Mary Emma, 1255
Vazeille, Mary, 1280, 1887, 2415, 2512
Veh, Raymond M., 2416
Velasco Urda Epigmenio, 1597, 2416
Venezuela, 1882, 2416
Venn, Henry, 541, 806, 2417
Verback, Harriet, 1793
Vermillion, S. D., 2417
Vermont, 1037, 1997, 2417, 2418, 2419
Vermont Christian Messenger, 2419
Vermont College, 1737, 2418
Vermont Conf. (ME), 918,

Vermont Conf. (ME)—*cont'd*
1723, 2369, 2418, 2419; (MP) 2418
Verney, Mary, 2353
Vernon, M. Leroy, 802, 1240, 2419
Vernon, Walter N., Jr., 2419
Vernon, William Tecumseh, 2420
Vernor, F. Dudleigh, 670
Verona Female College, Miss., 1777
Versailles, Ind., 2420
Vertue, George, 2515
Vestal, Laura, 1950
Vevers, William, 2420
Vianna, Persides Leal, 537
Vick, Amanda Maria, 1522
Vick, Newit, 1522, 1642, 2421, 2422
Vickers, George, 937
Vickery, Ebenezer, 2475
Vickroy, Thomas Rees, 1404, 2022
Vicksburg, Miss., 2421
Victoria, Canada, 2422
Victoria and Tasmania Conf., 2423
Victoria Park College, 1087, 1512, 2332, 2423
Victoria University, 310, 391, 402, 2397, 2426, 2515
Villanueva, Juan, 1858
Villard, Eliza, 1105
Vilvorde, Belgium, 2429
Vincent, Bethuel T., 434
Vincent, Burton Jones, 2429
Vincent, George E., 460
Vincent, John Heyl, 460, 783, 1561, 2429
Vineland, N. J., 2430
Viney, Richard, 2430
Virgin, Charles, 830
virgin birth, 694
Virgin Islands, 1415
Virginia, 85, 110, 138, 330, 627, 739, 774, 826, 839, 875, 1144, 1280, 1331, 1413, 1472, 1473, 1749, 1760, 1846, 1892, 1938, 1984, 2018, 2027, 2139, 2146, 2231, 2241, 2430, 2432; (UB) 957, 960, 2432
Virginia and North Carolina Mission Conf., 1772, 1768
Virginia City, Mont., 2432
Virginia Conf., (EUB) 2434; (ME) 922, 1768, 1980; (MES-TMC) 138, 209, 912, 1720, 1768, 1771, 2431, 2432; (MP) 939, 2432; (UB) 957, 960, 2287, 2537
Virginia Methodist Advocate, 211, 2434
Virginia Wesleyan College, 2433, 2435
Visick, Ada May, 2455
visiting, pastoral, 1868
Voegelein, Frederick William, 2435
Vogel, Carl E., 166
Vogt, A. Erwin, 2436
Voice of Missions, 2436
Voigt, Edwin Edgar, 2436
Voigt, Mary, 1887
Volino, M. L., 2086
Voller, Ellwood A., 2437
Voorheis, Janet Ruth, 1491
Vordenbaumen, Frederick, 994, 2437
vote by orders, 909, 1400

Voz Missionaria, 781 2437
Vredenburg, Hackaliah, 1367, 1784
Vrindaban, India, 2437
Vurlod, Aleixo, 1228
Vurlod, Luiza, 2093, 2384

Waag, Lilly, 106
Wabash Conf. (MP), 936, 1216; (UB) 958, 959, 1198, 1217
Waco, Texas, 2438
Waddell, G. H., 547
Waddy, Richard, 2438
Waddy, Samuel Dousland, 2438
Wade, Alexander Luark, 2439
Wade, Cyrus Ulysses, 2439
Wade, Dorethea, 1852
Wade, Lucy, 2026
Wade, Mabel, 1183
Wade, Maria J., 1463
Wade, Raymond J., 2057, 2439
Wade, Thomas Smith, 2440
Wadham, Alvira, 1862
Wadsworth, Cornelia Evelyn, 261
Wadsworth, Julian S., 1511
Wagener, David, 1381
Wagner, Ellasue Canter, 2440
Wagner, Philip, 1935
Wagnsson, Gustaf, 843
Wahl, Priscilla Marie, 2234
Waikouaiti, N. Z., 2440
Waima, N. Z., 2440
Wainman, Fannie, 2259
Waingaroa, N. Z., 2441
Wainright, Samuel H., 2352, 2441
Wakefield, Mary Louise, 2225
Wakeley, Joseph Beaumont, 2441
Wakeman, Caroline A., 1478
Wakerley, Mabel, 2597
Walden, Amy Patton, 1077
Walden, John Morgan, 1963, 2441
Walden University, 1543
Walden Seminary, Ark., 1899
Waldo, Emma, 2549
Waldorf, Ernest Lynn, 2442
Waldron, Amanda, 2623
Waldron, Ann M., 1907
Waldron, Jessie, 1263
Wales, Florence Ruth, 1851
Wales, 178, 236, 346, 452, 632, 813, 816, 1080, 1170, 1274, 1277, 2052, 2290, 2442, 2487, 2569
Walker, Alan, 2444
Walker, Corilla, 274
Walker, Courtney M., 1407
Walker, Dougal O. B., 2444
Walker, Emma Clement, 522
Walker, F. T., 539
Walker, Fannie, 511
Walker, George Williams, 1004, 2444
Walker, Harriet, 1153, 2450
Walker, Hay C., 1226
Walker, Helen, 2111
Walker, Jesse, 135, 466, 467, 1197, 1211, 1644, 1726, 1780, 1882, 2069, 2115, 2445
Walker, Margaret, 1484
Walker, Melissa E., 1812
Walker, Robert, 816
Walker, Samuel, 2445
Walker, Thomas, 1717, 1781
Walker, William, 2252
Wall, James, 2577
Wall, Jessie Marion, 1482

Wallace, Benson, 1213
Wallace, Bertha Elizabeth, 2184
Wallace, Jennie, 1322
Wallace College, 994
Wallahan, Hester, 2240
Wallbridge, Elizabeth, 2445
Waller, Alvan, 1820, 2080, 2445
Waller, Ashbel, 2563
Walline, Emily, 1345
Wallis, James, 2309, 2441, 2446
Walls, William Jacob, 2446
Walser, Henry W., 2617
Walsh, Thomas, 2446
Walter, John, 2446
Walters, Harold Crawford, 2447
Walters, Orville Selkirk, 2447
Waltham, Mass., 2447
Walton, Allie, 812
Walton, Annie, 1382
Walton, Aubrey Grey, 2448
Walton, John, 2201
Walton, Viola, 2448
Walz, John, 973
Wang, Chih Ping, 2448
Wang, Lucy, 2448
Wannamaker, Harriet, 1071
war, 790, 948, 969, 2193
war damage (Br.), 2448
war damage claim (MES), 1588
Ward, Albert Norman, 2387, 2449
Ward, Alfred Dudley, 2449
Ward, Allen T., 595
Ward, Charles B., 232, 1222, 1469
Ward, Ernest F., 1206, 2449
Ward, George S., 350
Ward, Harry Frederick, 794, 2449
Ward, James Thomas, 1422, 2450, 2545
Ward, Mary, 1422
Ward, Phillip, 468
Ward, Ralph Ansel, 2450
Ward, Robert, 1013, 1746, 2451
Ward, Seth, 2451
Ward, Thomas, 2452
Ward, Valentine, 2111, 2452
Ward, Walter William, 2452
Ward, William Ralph, Jr., 2452
Ward, William Taylor, 232, 1222
Ward, Zella B., 2349
Wardle, Emma J., 104
Wardle, William Lansdell, 2453
Ware, Anne Bacon, 1948
Ware, Marie, 1406
Ware, Thomas, 492, 574, 593, 2453, 2571
Warfield, Mrs. Alexander, 816
Warfield, Gaither P., 608, 721, 2453
Waring, Edmund H., 2454
Warne, B. Allen, 317
Warne, Francis Wesley, 1538, 2454
Warne, Frank W., 1635, 2096
Warne Baby Fold, 224
Warner, Ariel Nathaniel, 2455
Warner, David Snethen, 2455
Warner, Ira David, 2455
Warner, Mary Priscilla, 234
Warren, Elizabeth, 1062
Warren, George, 59, 2153, 2455
Warren, Henry White, 660, 1196, 2455